WEBSTER'S NEW WORLD® INTERNATIONAL SPANISH DICTIONARY

English/Spanish
Spanish/English

Second Edition

WEBSTER'S NEW WORLD® DICCIONARIO INTERNACIONAL ESPAÑOL

Inglés/Español
Español/Inglés

Segunda Edición

WEBSTER'S NEW WORLD® DICCIONARIO INTERNACIONAL ESPAÑOL

Inglés/Español
Español/Inglés
Segunda Edición

Roger Steiner,
Director

WILEY

Wiley Publishing, Inc.

WEBSTER'S NEW WORLD® INTERNATIONAL SPANISH DICTIONARY

English/Spanish
Spanish/English
Second Edition

Roger Steiner,
Editor in Chief

WILEY
Wiley Publishing, Inc.

Published by Wiley, Hoboken, NJ

For general information on our other products and services or to obtain technical support please contact our Customer Care Department within the U.S. at 800-762-2974, outside the U.S. at 317-572-3993 or fax 317-572-4002.

Wiley also publishes its books in a variety of electronic formats. Some content that appears in print may not be available in electronic books.
ISBN: 0-7645-7643-7
Library of Congress Catalog Card Number: 97-072124

Page layout and typesetting by Innodata Corporation, Brooklyn, New York
Manufactured in the United States of America

10 9 8 7 6 5 4 3

Editorial Staff — Cuerpo Editorial

Table of Contents — Tabla de Materias

Prefacio

Este diccionario ha sido concebido con la esperanza de que contribuya a una mayor entendimiento entre dos pueblos. Esta necesidad de entenderse el pueblo hispanohablante con el anglohablante se remonta a la época de la Armada Invencible, hace más de cuatrocientos años, con la aparicíon del primer diccionario bilingüe español-inglés. Ese diccionario antiguo sirvió de puente entre dos lenguas y culturas, y este nuevo diccionario fue compilado con el propósito de construir ese mismo puente entre ambas culturas.

Esta segunda edición aparece casi veinticinco años después de la primera edición que fue publicada a principios de 1973. Los objetivos permanecen iguales como los espresados antes en el prefacio de la primera edición:

1) Conservar la esencia del idioma e interpretar sus transformaciones debido a los cambios del lenguaje;

2) Demostrar eficazmente la función gramatical y el uso sintáctico de los vocablos;

3) Reflejar con exactitud el lenguaje del momento histórico.

En este diccionario se reflejan los cambios del lenguaje. En nuestre época muchos y grandes cambios han ocurrido en el mundo, cambios que han dado origen a muchas palabras y acepciones nuevas, como también nuevas ideas. La aceleración de los sucesos, el surgimiento de nuevos conceptos de vida, el acrecentamiento de nuevos intereses, la invención de nuevos dispositivos y el descubrimiento de nuevas relaciones han injertado en el inglés y el español millares de nuevas palabras y de significados nuevos. Este volumen ofrece neologismos que son productos de un lenguaje en constante evolución. Se encontrarán, sin lugar a dudas, palabras de gran importancia en todos los ramos del conocimiento humano y en las actividades e intereses humanos, sean ya términos técnicos de la ordenadora o palabras tales como 'videojuego' y 'madre de alquiler'.

Éste es un diccionario completo. Por ejemplo, aquí hay una serie de palabras cabezas de artículo:

creation
creationism
creative
creatively
creativeness
creativity
creator
creatural

No todos los diccionarios *monolingües* completos contienen la secuencia precedente de entradas. Sin embargo, este diccionario las tiene a pesar de ser un diccionario *bilingüe* y que por lo tanto nos provee con una entrada en ambos idiomas. La comprensibilidad del mismo es evidente al incluir locuciones, expresiones, frases hechas y frases idiomáticas en cada entrada. Por ejemplo, hay docenas de éstas bajo el vocablo **mano** en la sección español-inglés y bajo el vocablo **hand** en la sección inglés-español. Hay cien de éstas bajo el vocablo **take** y se ha sido dedicado una página completa a esta entrada. Las palabras de su traducción al español reciben el mismo tratamiento generoso en la sección español-inglés cuando ellas son entradas. En un diccionario la inclusión de vulgaridades y obscenidades lo hace más comprensible. Éstas le permitan al usuario comprender ciertos pasajes de novelas y películas actuales. Previene al lector de ciertos usos de las palabras, por ejemplo: **concha.** Normalmente significa la parte dura del cuerpo de un molusco; a veces significa el órgano sexual femenino. Si la palabra es dicha, oída o escrita, el lector o el hablante lo encontrará en este diccionario. Los indicadores 'despectivo' (despec.) o 'derogatory' (derog.) señalan las pullas que insultan las minorías étnicas. Algunas usuarios encontrarán de su agrado: "Si no lo encuentra en ninguna parte, búsquelo en el *Diccionario Internacional Simon and Schuster.*"

Este diccionario es un diccionario internacional con respeto a su tratamiento de la lengua inglesa y la lengua castellana. En su parte inglesa, el diccionario incluye variantes del inglés canadiense, australiano, irlandés, escocés, británico y americano. Aquí incluimos algunas diferencias entre el inglés británico y el inglés americano:

1) *ortografía*, ej.: **jewelry** americano y **jewellerey** británico.

2) *pronunciación*, ej.: **stop.** La vocal americano es "ah" [ɑ] y la vocal británica es "aw" [ɔ].

3) *significado*, ej.: bloody tiene un significado literal en EEUU, pero puede ser un vulgarismo pejorativo en Inglaterra.

4) *regionalismos*, ej.: **johnnycake** es un americanismo. En Inglaterra, **circus** puede significar una plaza donde convergen varias calles.

Este diccionario le brinda al usuario estadounidense una cobertura completa del inglés americano en contraste con los diccionarios que sólo contienen inglés británico.

En cuanto al español, este diccionario ofrece más que el castellano para ofrecer variedades regionales de España, los americanismos de América Central y de Sudamérica y los regionalismos de cada país. Hay veintiún indicadores para identificar estos regionalismos. Por ejemplo, en el Perú **remoler** puede significar "exasperar" y en Chile puede significar "salir a divertirse."

La completísima cobertura ofrecida por el *Diccionario Internacional Simon and Schuster* es una contribución al entendimiento entre gentes de distantes partes del mundo. Este diccionario ofrece la oportunidad de comprender y usar dos lenguas con la esperanza de contribuir a la paz universal entre todas las naciones de la tierra.

—Roger J. Steiner
Director
Segunda Edición

Foreword

This dictionary was conceived with the hope that it would contribute to a greater understanding between two peoples. The Spanish-speaking and the English-speaking peoples have had a need to understand each other since the time of the Spanish Armada four hundred years ago when the first Spanish and English bilingual dictionary appeared. That old dictionary served as a bridge between two languages and cultures, and this new dictionary was compiled with the purpose of building that same bridge between Anglo-Saxon and Hispanic cultures.

This second edition appears almost twenty-five years after the appearance of the first edition at the beginning of 1973, but the objective remains the same as those stated in the foreword to the first edition:

1. To preserve the essence of the languages along with the novelties due to language change;
2. To show as well as explain grammatical function and syntactic use;
3. To reflect the language of the historical moment.

This dictionary reflects language change. In our time great changes have taken place in the world and those changes have brought into existence many new words and meanings, and many new ideas. The acceleration of events, the rise of new concepts of living and the spread of new interests, the invention of new devices, and the discovery of new relationships have brought into English and Spanish thousands of new words and meanings. This dictionary will provide these neologisms, the product of language change. Here are found words of unquestionable importance today in all branches of human knowledge and human activity and interest, whether they are computer terms or words such as "downsizing" and "glass ceiling."

This dictionary is a complete dictionary. For example, here is a sequence of headwords:

creation
creationism
creative
creatively
creativeness
creativity
creator
creatural

Not all large unabridged *monolingual* dictionaries contain the preceding sequence of entries but this dictionary does, even though it is a *bilingual* dictionary and must provide an entry in both languages. The comprehensiveness of this dictionary is also apparent in its inclusion of locutions, expressions, set phrases, and idioms as run-on entries. For example, there are dozens of these under **hand** on the English/Spanish side and dozens more under **mano** on the Spanish/English side. There are a hundred of them under the entry **take,** which occupies a full page. Its Spanish translations are reversed to the Spanish/English side where they also receive the generous treatment of abundant run-ons. The dictionary is all the more complete because of the inclusion of vulgarisms and obscenities. These allow the user to comprehend certain passages of current novels and films. They provide the user with warning, for example in the entry **pussy,** which can be translated by a word for "cat" but also can be translated by an obscene word for the female sexual organ. If the lexeme is said, heard, or written, the reader or speaker will find it in this dictionary. Even ethnic slurs and insults are included—with the appropriate warning label: "despectivo" (despec.) or "derogatory" (derog.). As some users find to their satisfaction: "If you can't find it anywhere else, look in the *Simon & Schuster's International Dictionary.*"

This dictionary is an international dictionary in respect to its treatment of the English language and the Spanish language. For English, the dictionary includes varieties of Canadian, Australian, Irish, Scottish, British, and American English. Here are some differences between British English and American English:

1. *spelling,* ex.: American **jewelry** and British **jewellery**.
2. *pronunciation,* ex.: **stop** The American vowel is "ah" [ɑ] and the British vowel is "aw" [ɔ].
3. *meaning,* ex.: **bloody** has a literal meaning in America but in Britain it can be a slang, pejorative word.
4. *regionalisms,* ex.: **johnnycake** is an Americanism and **circus** is a Britishism when it means a plaza where several streets converge.

This dictionary gives the American user complete coverage of American English in contrast to bilingual dictionaries that contain only British English.

For Spanish, this dictionary goes beyond castellano (the basic prestige dialect of the Spanish-speaking world) to add the regional varieties of Spain, the *americanismos* of Central and South America and the national regionalisms. There are twenty-one labels that identify these national regionalisms. For example, in Peru **remoler** can mean "to exasperate" and in Chile it can mean "to live it up, to go out on the town."

The complete coverage shown in *the Simon and Schuster's International Dictionary* is a contribution to understanding among different peoples of the world. This dictionary offers the opportunity to understand and to use two languages with the hope of contributing to universal peace among the nations of the world.

—Roger Steiner
Editor-in-Chief
Second Edition

Guide to the Use of This Dictionary

Vocabulary, encyclopedic terms, symbols and initials are treated under separate entries, all listed alphabetically.

The entry word is printed in large bold face type; grammatical labels, abbreviated, in italics; equivalents, meanings and definitions are in roman type, idiomatic expressions in small bold face, and examples in italics.

The different equivalents and uses of the entry word are separated by numbers, akin meanings by semicolons, and synonyms by commas. The grammatical functions are separated by a period and hyphen. When these functions can be rendered by the same translation the labels are grouped, separated by a comma.

Capitals are used only in the case of proper nouns. Should a term apply to both, a substantive and a proper noun, each is indicated with its corresponding initial and a period.

In examples and expressions the entry word is represented by its initial and a period, in order to avoid repeating it within the entry.

Abbreviations indicating field, specialty, origin and idiomatic application of the entry word are in parenthesis and precede the translation. Should they refer instead to a rendered equivalent, abbreviations appear after the translation of said equivalent.

Irregular verbs in the Spanish-English part are followed by a number in parenthesis. This refers the reader to the corresponding conjugation in the Table of Irregular Verbs.

Normas para el Uso de Este Diccionario

El caudal léxico, los términos enciclopédicos, símbolos y siglas aparecen en artículos separados, todos por orden alfabético.

El vocablo que inicia el artículo está impreso en letra negra; los rótulos gramaticales en cursiva y abreviados; los equivalentes, significados y definiciones en letra redonda, los ejemplos en cursiva, y las expresiones idiomáticas en negritas.

Los números separan los diferentes usos y equivalentes del vocablo. El punto y coma separa los significados afines, y la coma los sinónimos. Las funciones gramaticales van separadas por guión y punto. Si dichas funciones de un vocablo pueden ser vertidas al otro idioma por una misma traducción, los rótulos gramaticales van agrupados, separados por coma.

Usamos mayúscula sólo en caso de nombres propios. De aplicar el vocablo a un nombre común y también a uno propio, se indica cada cual con su inicial correspondiente y punto. En las expresiones idiomáticas y los ejemplos el vocablo se representa por su letra inicial y punto, a fin de evitar repetirlo dentro del artículo.

Las abreviaturas de campo, materias, origen y uso idiomático del vocablo van entre paréntesis antes de la traducción. Al referirse a los sentidos consignados, dichas abreviaturas van immediatamente después de la traducción.

En la parte Español-Inglés cada verbo irregular va seguido de un número entre paréntesis. Dicha cifra remite al lector a la conjugación correspondiente en la Tabla de Verbos Irregulares.

PART I

English-Spanish

PARTE I

Inglés-Español

Guía Para la Pronunciación Inglesa

Nota

Las pronunciaciones en inglés que indicamos en este diccionario son las más generalizadas hoy en día en el mundo de habla inglesa, principalmente en los Estados Unidos y la Gran Bretaña. No pretendemos abarcar la gama de matices regionales, pero en ciertos casos hemos señalado varias modalidades cuando éstas son de uso frecuente.

Utilizamos el sistema de transcripción fonética que emplea los símbolos del Alfabeto Fonético Internacional (IPA). No siendo éste un tratado de fonética, hemos adoptado ciertas normas de simplificación por considerarlas prácticas para el lector de un diccionario general bilingüe. Más adelante en este prefacio damos los símbolos de dicho alfabeto que empleamos.

Normas que rigen la transcripción fonética

1. LA PRONUNCIACIÓN figurada va entre corchetes, inmediatamente después del vocablo.

Aparece en primer término la pronunciación norteamericana y, de existir, sus variantes separadas por una coma. Le sigue la pronunciación británica precedida por una B mayúscula. Ejemplo:

dance [dæns, B dɑns]
err [ɜr, ɛr, B ɜ]

De no aparecer la B que antecede a la pronunciación británica, se entiende que el vocablo se pronuncia igualmente en el inglés norteamericano y el británico.

LOS TÉRMINOS COMPUESTOS no llevan transcripción fonética si sus elementos separados aparecen en el cuerpo del diccionario. Así, por ejemplo, la pronunciación de *patent leather* deberá buscarse, alfabéticamente, bajo el vocablo *patent* y el vocablo *leather.*

LOS VOCABLOS EXTRANJEROS de uso frecuente en el habla inglesa van transcritos en su pronunciación adaptada al inglés y no siempre coincide con la original de sus respectivos idiomas.

EN CASOS DE VOCABLOS HOMÓGRAFOS QUE TAMBIÉN SON HOMÓFONOS sólo se indica la pronunciación del que alfabéticamente aparece primero. Ejemplo:

dab [dæb] *s.* 1. golpe . . . (etc.)
dab, *s.* (ichth.) . . . (etc.)

2. EL ACENTO principal del vocablo va indicado con una virgulilla en el ángulo superior antes de la sílaba que se acentúa; el acento secundario con otra en el ángulo inferior de la misma. Ejemplo:

dustpan ['dʌstˌpæn]

3. LOS GUIONES se emplean para evitar repeticiones, en substitución de:

a) elementos que coinciden en varias pronunciaciones de un mismo vocablo. Ejemplo:

contradict [ˌkɑntrə'dɪkt, B ˌkɔn-]

b) elementos que coinciden en various vocablos consecutivos. Ejemplo:

contradict [ˌkɑntrə'dɪkt, B ˌkɔn-]
contradictable [-'dɪktəbəl]
contradiction [-'dɪkʃən]
contradictor [-'dɪktər, B -tə]

4. LA PRONUNCIACIÓN BRITÁNICA con frecuencia omite el sonido de la *r* — aunque nunca antes de una vocal o entre vocales, desde luego. A fin de señalar esa omisión de la letra *r* antes de la consonante que inicia una sílaba acentuada, el guión va precedido por el acento, sea principal o secundario. Ejemplo:

farfamed ['fɑr'feɪmd, B 'fɑ'-]
fatherland ['fɑðərˌlænd, B 'fɑðəˌ-]

Debe recordarse que aun cuando un determinado tipo de pronunciación aparezca adjudicado al inglés británico, de ningún modo significa ello su exclusión del inglés norteamericano, sino que dentro de esa denominación dicho tipo de pronunciación resulta marginal.

Más adelante damos ejemplos de algunas diferencias entre la pronunciación norteamericana y la británica.

SÍMBOLOS FONÉTICOS Y LOS SONIDOS QUE REPRESENTAN

VOCALES Y DIPTONGOS

Símbolo:	*Descripción:*	*Ejemplo:*
[i]	como la *i* en *misa*	beet [bit]
[ɪ]	como la *i* en *afirmar*	bit [bɪt]
[eɪ]	como *ei* en *seis*	bait [beɪt]
[ɛ]	como la *e* en *perro*	bet [bɛt]
[æ]	sonido intermedio entre la *a* en *caso* y la *e* en *perro*	bat [bæt]
[ʌ]	sonido intermedio entre la *o* y la *e*, parecido al de la *o* en la palabra francesa *homme*	but [bʌt]
[ə]	sonido intermedio entre la *e* y la *o*, parecido al de la *e* en el artículo definido francés *le*	ago [əgoʊ]
[ɜr]	sonido parecido a *eu* en la palabra francesa *leur* (se omite la *r* en el inglés británico)	bird [bɜrd, B bɜd]
[ər]	versión corta del sonido norteamericano [ɜr] en sílabas átonas	pepper ['pɛpər, B -ə]
[u]	sonido de la *u* en *uno*, prolongado	boot [but]
[ʊ]	sonido de la *u* en *curro*, acortado	book [bʊk]
[oʊ]	sonido de la *o* en *sola* seguido de la *u* de *curro*	boat [boʊt]
[ɔ]	sonido de la *o* en *por*, prolongado	bought [bɔt]
[ɑ]	soniido de la en *bajo*, prolongado	balm [bɑlm]
[aɪ]	como *ai* en *baile*	bite [baɪt]
[aʊ]	como *au* en *causa*	bout [baʊt]
[ɔɪ]	como *oi* en *soy*	boil [bɔɪl]
[ɪə]	como *ia* en *mía*	beer [bɪr, B bɪə]
[ɛə]	como *ea* en *fea*	bare [bɛr, B bɛə]
[ʊə]	como *uo* en *búho*	boor [bɔr, B bɔə]
[ɔə]	como *oa* en *roa*	bore [bɔr, B bɔə]
[eɪə]	como *ie* en *reyes*	payer ['peɪər, B -ə]
[aɪə]	como *aie* en *aire*	buyer ['baɪər, B -ə]
[ɔɪə]	como *oie* en *oye*	employer [ɪm'plɔɪər, B -ə]
[aʊə]	como *aue* en *fraude*	bower ['baʊər, B -ə]
[oʊə]	como *ó-u-e* en *incólume*	blower ['bloʊər, B -ə]

CONSONANTES

Símbolo:	*Descripción:*	*Ejemplo:*
[b]	como la *b* en *ambos* (aspirada)	be [bi]
[k]	como la *c* en *caso* (aspirada)	cold [koʊld]
[d]	como la *d* en *conde* (aspirada)	deed [did]
[f]	como la *f* en el español	fee [fi]
[g]	como la *g* en *goma* (aspirada)	game [geɪm]
[h]	como la *j* en *jerga,* pero mucho más suave	heed [hid]
[l]	como la *l* en el español	leaf [lif]
[m]	como la *m* en el español	me [mi]
[n]	como la *n* en *nota*	need [ni]
[p]	como la *p* en *pan* (aspirada)	pea [pi]
[r]	(la *r* norteamericana es un sonido semivocal que se articula elevando la lengua hacia la bóveda palatina) (la *r* británica, prevocálica o intervocálica, es un sonido fricativo parecido a la *r* en *pero*)	around [ə'raʊnd]
[s]	como la *s* en el español	see [si]
[t]	como la *t* en *tos* (aspirada)	tea [ti]
[v]	*v* fuerte y definida como en la palabra francesa *avec*	veal [vil]

Símbolo:	*Descripción:*	*Ejemplo:*
[w]	como *hu* en *hueco*	wine [waɪn]
[z]	como la *s* en *mismo*, per más sonora y vibrada	zeal [zil]
[ð]	como la *d* en *hada*	then [ðɛn]
[θ]	como la *c* en *dice* y la *z* en *zapato* en la pronunciación castiza española	theme [θ im]
[ʒ]	como la *ll* en *llegar* y la *y* en *ayer* en la pronunciación típica argentina	measure 'mɛʒər, B -ə]
[dʒ]	como el sonido anterior, pero mucho más fuerte y con un vestigio de *ch*	jeep [dʒip]
[ʃ]	sonido parecido al que hacemos al callar a alguien, como la *ch* en la palabra francesa *chez*	sheet [ʃit]
[tʃ]	como la *ch* en *mucho*	chest [tʃɛst]
[j]	como la *y* en *yo* y la *i* en *ionosfera*	yield [jild]
[hw]	como *ju* en *juerga*, pero mucho más suave	wheel [hwil]
[ŋ]	como la *n* en *tengo*	sing [siŋ]

A continuación, ejemplos de algunas diferencias entre la pronunciación norteamericana y la británica.

Pronunciación Norteamericana	*Pronunciación Británica*	*Ejemplo*
[æ]	[ɑ]	ask [æsk, B ɑsk]
[æ]	[ɑ]	dance [dæns, B dɑns]
[ɑ]	[ɔ]	not [nɑt, B nɔt]
[ɑ]	[ɔ]	common ['kɑmən, B 'kɔm-]
[ɑ]	[ɔ]	response [rɪs'pɑns, B -'pɔns]
[ɛr]	[ɑ]	clerk [klɛrk, B klɑk]
[ɑ]	[ɔ]	want [wɑnt, B wɔnt]
[u]	[ju]	due [du, B dju]
[ər]	[ə]	letter ['lɛtər, B -tə]
[ɜr]	[ɜ]	thirty ['θɜrtɪ, B 'θɜtɪ]
[ɜ]	[ʌ]	burrow ['bɜroʊ, B 'bʌroʊ]
[ɔr]	[ɔ]	course [kɔrs, B kɔs]
[ɔr]	[ɔ]	more [mɔr, B mɔ]
[ɔr]	[ɔ]	cork [kɔrk, B kɔk]
[aɪr]	[aɪə]	fire [faɪr, B faɪə]
[ˌ-tɛrɪ]	[-trɪ]	secretary ['sɛkrəˌtɛrɪ, B -trɪ]
[sk]	[ʃ]	schedule ['skɛdʒʊl-əl, B 'ʃɛdjul]
[i]	[ɛ]	leisure ['liʒər, B 'lɛʒə]

Elementos de la Gramática Inglesa

Nota

Las indicaciones que damos a continuación tienen el propósito de ayudar al lector a compenetrarse con las frases y oraciones que encontrará en el cuerpo de este diccionario. En modo alguno constituye esta sección un tratado completo de gramática inglesa.

EL SUSTANTIVO

El género

El género de los sustantivos en inglés puede ser determinado por:

a) UN SUFIJO (principalmente para indicar el femenino), por ej. *actor-actress* (actor-actriz), *hero-heroine* (héroe-heroína); aunque el cambio es por lo general del masculino al femenino, ocurre lo contrario en ciertas palabras, por ej. *bride-bridegroom* (novia-novio — desposados), *widow-widower* (viuda-viudo).

b) UN PREFIJO (para indicar el sexo de un sustantivo de género epiceno), por ej. *he-bear — she-bear* (oso-osa), *male-child — female-child* (niño-niña).

En ciertos casos se emplean palabras diferentes para designar la contraparte femenina o masculina, por ej. *boy-girl* (muchacho-muchacha), *man-woman* (hombre-mujer), *uncle-aunt* (tío-tía).

El plural

1. El plural regular se forma añadiendo una *s* al singular, por ej. *girl-girls* (muchacha-s), *boy-boys* (muchacho-s), *horse-horses* (caballo-s).

2. Los sustantivos que terminan en *s, sh, ch, x, z* reciben *es* en el plural, por ej. *gas-gases* (gas-es), *brush-brushes* (cepillo-s, brocha-s), *church-churches* (iglesia-s), *box-boxes* (caja-s), *topaz-topazes* (topacio-s).

3. Algunos sustantivos que terminan en *o* también reciben *es* en el plural, por ej. *hero-heroes* (héroe-s), *volcano-volcanoes* (volcán-volcanes); otros reciben sólo *s*, por ej. *bamboo-bamboos* (bambú-es), *halo-halos* (nimbo-s).

4. Los sustantivos que terminan en *y* precedida de una consonante forman el plural cambiando dicha *y* por *ies*, por ej. *city-cities* (ciudad-es), *lady-ladies* (señora-s).

5. Muchos sustantivos que terminan en *f* o en *fe* cambian a *ve* en el plural, por ej. *leaf-leaves* (hoja-s), *knife-knives* (cuchillo-s); otros, que terminan igualmente en *f* o en *fe*, no sufren alteración, por ej. *chief-chiefs* (jefe-s), *roof-roofs* (techo-s, tejado-s).

6. Algunos sustantivos forman el plural mediante un cambio de vocal interna, por ej. *man-men* (hombre-s), *woman-women* (mujer-es), *tooth-teeth* (diente-s), *foot-feet* (pie-s). Ortográficamente cambia también la consonante final de estos casos: *mouse-mice* (ratón-ratones), *louse-lice* (piojo-s).

7. Tres sustantivos reciben *en* o *ren* en el plural: *ox-oxen* (buey-es), *child-children* (niño-s), *brother-brethren* (cofrade-s, hermano-s — de una congregación o cofradía; en el caso de "hermano consanguíneo" se usa el plural regular, *brothers*).

8. Algunos sustantivos de cantidad quedan inalterados en el plural, por ej. *ten head of cattle* (diez cabezas de ganado), *two dozen eggs* (dos docenas de huevos).

9. Ciertos sustantivos de origen extranjero han retenido su plural original, por ej. *analysis-analyses* (análisis), *basis-bases* (base-s), *oasis-oases* (oasis), *phenomenon-phenomena* (fenomeno-s), *memorandum-memoranda* (memorándum-s); en ciertos casos se admite también el plural regular, como en los dos últimos: *memorandums, phenomenons.*

10. En sustantivos compuestos se añade la terminación del plural de la palabra principal, por ej. *father-in-law — fathers-in-law* (suegro-s). Sin embargo, cuando el primer elemento es *man* o *woman,* ambas partes del sustantivo compuesto sufren alteración, por ej. *woman-driver — women-drivers* (conductora-s — de vehículos), *man-servant — men-servants* (criado-s, sirviente-s).

11. Hay sustantivos que carecen de singular, por ej. *clothes* (ropa-s), *goods* (mercancía-s), *trousers* (pantalones), *scissors* (tijera-s).

12. La palabra *news* (noticia-s), aunque en su forma es un plural, toma el verbo en singular, por ej. *the news is good* (la-s noticia-s es-son buena-s). Igual sucede con *mews* (caballeriza-s), *measles* (sarampión-sarampiones) y *mumps* (paperas).

13. Algunos sustantivos no alteran su forma en el plural, por ej. *deer* (venado-s), *sheep* (oveja-s), *aircraft* (aeronave-s).

EL ARTÍCULO

El artículo definido

1. Este artículo se usa con menos frecuencia en inglés que en español. Debe omitirse en estos casos:

a) Después de un sustantivo en plural cuando se usa en sentido general, por ej. *lions are fierce* (los leones son feroces), *people began to understand* (la gente empezó a comprender).

b) En palabras usadas en sentido general, por ej. *man cannot live by bread alone* (no sólo de pan vive el hombre), *truth is eternal* (la verdad es eterna).

c) En los nombres de las profesiones, artes y ciencias, por ej. *journalism is an interesting career* (el periodismo es una carrera interesante).

d) En los nombres de idiomas, estaciones del año, títulos de rango o profesión, designación de parentesco, por ej. *Italian is not taught here* (aquí no se enseña el italiano), *spring was late this year* (la primavera llegó tarde este año), *President Lincoln* (el presidente —), *Doctor Foster* (el doctor —), *Sergeant Smith* (el sargento —), *Aunt Mary* (la tía María).

e) En nombres propios calificados por un adjetivo, por ej. *poor John lost his watch* (el pobre Juan perdió su reloj).

f) En ciertas expresiones de tiempo y ocasión, por ej. *they arrived at four o'clock* (llegaron a las cuatro), *lunch is at one o'clock* (el almuerzo se sirve a la una), *last week* (la semana pasada), *next year* (el próximo año).

g) En ciertos sustantivos usados en sentido general cuando se piensa más bien en sus funciones que en sus características, por ej. *school begins in September* (la escuela empieza en septiembre), *they went to church* (fueron a la iglesia); pero sí se dice *the school was painted* (pintaron la escuela), *the church is far from here* (la iglesia está lejos de aquí).

2. Además de su función determinativa, el artículo definido se usa en estos casos:

a) Antes de números ordinales en títulos, por ej. *Henry the Eighth* (Enrique VIII), *Pius the Twelfth* (Pío XII).

b) Con función de adverbio indicando grado o cantidad, por ej. *the more he eats the thinner he becomes* (cuanto más come más flaco se pone).

El artículo indefinido

Este artículo se usa con más frecuencia en inglés que en español. Se usa *a* antes de consonante y *an* antes de vocal o *h* muda, excepto en las palabras que empiezan por *u* o *eu,* por ej. *a university* (una universidad), *a European* (un europeo).

Aparte de su función particularizante, se usa:

a) En sustantivos que designan nacionalidad, origen, rango, ocupación, religión, etc., por ej. *he is a Frenchman* (es francés), *he is a Moslem* (es musulmán), *she wants to be an actress* (quiere ser actriz).

b) Antes de sustantivos en aposición, por ej. *his father, a surgeon of great renown . . .* (su padre, cirujano de gran fama . . .).

c) Antes de palabras como *other* (otro-a), *certain* (cierto-a), *half* (medio-a); después de las palabras *such* (tal), *what* (qué), cuando van seguidas de sustantivos en singular; en las palabras *hundred* (cien), *thousand* (mil), etc. cuando van seguidas de sustantivos en plural, por ej. *I bought another hat* (compré otro sombrero), *I called a certain friend of yours* (llamé a cierto amigo tuyo), *she brought a half kilo of sugar* (trajo medio kilo de azúcar), *he had such a shock that he was speechless* (se pegó tal susto que enmudeció), *what a pretty girl!* (¡qué chica tan bonita!), *a hundred pounds* (cien libras), *a thousand pages* (mil páginas).

d) Después de *as* (de, en calidad de, como) al hablarse de una persona o cosa representativa de su clase, por ej. *he is well known as a pacifist* (es bien conocido como pacifista), *at times he works as a postman* (a veces trabaja de cartero).

e) Después de *with* y *without* (con, sin) cuando la singularidad del siguiente sustantivo no es de importancia, por ej. *a street without a name* (una calle sin nombre).

EL ADJETIVO

Generalidades

1. El adjetivo es invariable y siempre se antepone al sustantivo. Entre las pocas excepciones a esta regla se encuentran frases hechas como: *the heir apparent* (el heredero forzoso), *from time immemorial* (de tiempos inmemoriales).

2. El adjetivo en inglés generalmente va seguido de un sustantivo o del pronombre *one-s* (un-unos), por ej. *an old man* (un viejo), *she had a red hat and two blue ones* (tenía un sombrero rojo y dos azules).

3. Ciertos adjetivos y participios pasados precedidos del artículo definido se comportan como sustantivos en plural y por lo tanto no necesitan ir seguidos de otra palabra, por ej. *the rich, the wounded, the poor, the English, the French* (los ricos, los heridos, los pobres, los ingleses, los franceses).

Los adjetivos posesivos

my (mi-s), *your* (tu-s), *his* (su-s — de él), *her* (su-s — de ella), *its* (su-s — neutro), *our* (nuestro-s, nuestra-s), *your* (vuestro-s, vuestra-s; tuyo-s, tuya-s), *their* (su-s — de ellos, de ellas).

1. El género y el número de los adjetivos posesivos en inglés varían de acuerdo con el poseedor y no con el objeto poseído, por ej. *he lost his glove-s* (perdió su-s guante-s), *she came with her cousin-s* (ella vino con su-s primo-s).

2. En ciertos casos, especialmente al referirse a partes del cuerpo humano, en inglés se usa el adjetivo posesivo cuando en español se usa el artículo definido, por ej. *he had his hair cut* (se cortó el pelo), *she raised her hand* (levantó la mano).

3. *Whose,* forma posesiva del pronombre *who* (quien), se usa también como adjetivo posesivo, por ej. *this is the girl whose dog I found last night* (esta es la chica cuyo perro encontré anoche).

Los adjetivos interrogativos

1. En inglés hay dos adjetivos interrogativos, *what* y *which* (qué).

a) *What* se usa cuando la posibilidad de elegir no es restringida, por ej. *what peoples conquered Spain after the Romans?* (¿qué pueblos conquistaron a España después de los romanos?), *what books did you buy?* (¿qué libros compraste?).

b) *Which* se usa cuando la posibilidad de elegir es restringida, por ej. *which American president was a bachelor?* (¿qué presidente norteamericano era soltero?), *which poem of Whitman's do you like best?* (¿qué poesía de Whitman te gusta más?).

c) En algunos casos *what* y *which* pueden usarse indistintamente, por ej. *what bus goes to Miami? which bus goes to Miami?* (¿qué autobús va a Miami?).

2. *Whose,* forma posesiva del pronombre *who* (quién), se usa también como adjetivo interrogativo, por ej. *whose suitcase is this?* (¿de quién es esta maleta?).

La comparación de los adjetivos

1. Los adjetivos de una sílaba y aquéllos de dos sílabas de las que la segunda va acentuada añaden *-er* y *-est* para formar el comparativo y el superlativo respectivamente, por ej. *tall, taller, tallest* (alto-a); *polite, politer, politest* (cortés). Excepción: *real, more real, most real* (real, verdadero).

2. Los adjetivos de dos sílabas, de las que la primera lleva el acento, así como los de más de dos sílabas, usan *more* y *most* para formar el comparativo y el superlativo respectivamente, por ej. *vivid, more vidid, most vivid* (vívido-a); *beautiful, more beautiful, most beautiful* (bello-a). Excepción: los adjetivos que terminan en *y,* por ej. *pretty, prettier, prettiest* (bonito-a); *happy, happier, happiest* (feliz).

3. Ciertos adjetivos tienen comparativos y superlativos irregulares, por ej. *bad, worse, worst* (malo-a); *good, better, best* (bueno-a); *much, more, most* (mucho-a).

4. La conjunción inglesa *than* corresponde a las españolas *que* y *de* en la construcción de las formas comparativas, por ej. *I am taller than you* (soy más alto que tú); *she spent more than twenty dollars* (gastó más de veinte dólares).

EL ADVERBIO

1. En inglés los adverbios de modo se forman:

a) Añadiendo *-ly* al adjetivo, por ej. *weak, weakly* (débil, débilmente); *marvelous, marvelously* (maravilloso, maravillosamente).

b) Usando el adjetivo mismo, por ej. *he runs very fast* (corre velozmente), *she went straight home* (se fue directamente a casa).

2. Los adverbios de tiempo (*soon, always, etc.* —pronto, siempre, etc.), los de lugar (*here, outside, etc.* —aquí, afuera, etc.) y los de cantidad (*almost, very, etc.* —casi, muy, etc.) tienen formas muy diversas y deben aprenderse individualmente.

3. Le comparación de los adverbios se forma de la misma manera que la de los adjetivos.

EL PRONOMBRE

Los pronombres personales

sujeto:	*complemento:*
I (yo)	*me*
you (tú)	*you*
he (él)	*him*
she (ella)	*her*
it (ello)	*it*
we (nosotros-as)	*us*
you (vosotros-as)	*you*
they (ellos-as)	*them*

1. *I* (yo) siempre se escribe con mayúscula.

2. El pronombre como sujeto de la oración no puede omitirse en inglés a menos que haya dos o más verbos regidos por el mismo pronombre en la oración, por ej. *she opened the box* (abrió la caja); *she opened the box and took out a ring* (abrió la caja y sacó un anillo).

3. El pronombre de sujeto siempre precede al verbo, excepto:

a) en preguntas, por ej. *is he English?* (¿es inglés?);

b) después de expresiones negativas que encabezan la oración, por ej. *not only did he recognize me, but he embraced me as well* (no sólo me reconoció sino que también me abrazó), *never have I seen such a boring picture* (nunca he visto una película tan aburrida).

4. *We, you, they* e *it* a menudo se traducen en español por el pronombre impersonal SE, por ej. *it is said that he was mad* (se dice que estaba loco), *they have built a new school* (se ha construido una nueva escuela).

5. *It* se usa en construcciones impersonales cuando en español se omite el pronombre, por ej. *it seems that he is innocent*

(parece que es inocente), *it is easy to do* (es fácil de hacer), *it is raining, snowing, etc.* (está lloviendo, nevando, etc.).

It se usa también en preguntas y respuestas como *who is it?* (¿quién es?), *it is me, it is us* (soy yo, somos nosotros). Nótese que en el habla corriente en inglés se usa el pronombre de complemento en estos casos.

Los pronombres reflexivos

singular	*plural*
myself: I	*ourselves:* we
yourself: you	*yourselves:* you
himself: he	*themselves:* they
herself: she	
itself: it	
oneself: one	

El pronombre reflexivo tiene dos usos en inglés:

a) Con verbos transitivos cuya acción recae en el sujeto, por ej. *he hurt himself* (se lastimó), *they expressed themselves very well* (se expresaron muy bien).

b) Para dar énfasis a la acción expresada por un verbo, por ej. *I painted it myself* (lo pinté yo mismo), *she herself put it there* (ella misma lo puso ahí).

Ciertos verbos que son reflexivos en español no lo son en inglés, por ej. *he is shaving* (se está afeitando), *get dressed* (vístete).

Los pronombres relativos

Sujeto:	*Complemento:*	*Forma posesiva:*	
who (que) personas	*who-m* (quien-es)	*whose*	(cuyo-a, cuyos-as)
which (que) animales, objetos	*which* (que)	*whose*	
that (que) personas, animales, objetos	*that* (quien-es, que)	*whose*	
what (lo que)			

El relativo usado como complemento generalmente se omite en el inglés hablado, por ej. *the man (that) you met last night is my brother* (el hombre que conociste anoche es mi hermano).

Si el relativo va acompañado de una preposición, ésta suele pasar al final de la oración y puede entonces omitirse el pronombre, por ej. *the friend from whom I heard the news* . . . o *the friend I heard the news from* (el amigo que me comunicó la noticia . . .).

Los pronombres demostrativos

this (éste, ésta, esto)
these (éstos, éstas)
that (ése, ésa, eso; aquél, aquélla, aquello)
those (ésos, ésas; aquéllos, aquéllas)

Se añade la palabra auxiliar *one-s* cuando los pronombres se refieren al sujeto expresado en la oración precedente, por ej. *that wine is too sweet, I prefer this one* (ese vino es muy dulce, prefiero éste); *those colors seem brighter than these ones* (aquellos colores parecen más vivos que éstos).

Las formas sin *one-s* se usan cuando el sujeto queda expresado en la misma oración, por ej. *this is her hat* (éste es su sombrero), *these are her children* (aquéllos son sus hijos).

Los pronombres posesivos

mine (mío-s, mía-s; el mío, la mía; los míos, las mías)
yours (tuyo-s, tuya-s; el tuyo, la tuya; los tuyos, las tuyas)
his, hers, its (suyo-s, suya-s; el suyo, la suya; los suyos, las suyas)
ours (nuestro-s, nuestra-s; el nuestro, la nuestra; los nuestros, las nuestras)
yours (vucstro-s, vucstra-s; cl vucstro, la vuestra; los vuestros, las vuestras)
theirs (suyo-s, suya-s; el suyo, la suya; los suyos, las suyas)

El género y el número de los pronombres posesivos ingleses varían de acuerdo al poseedor y no a la cosa poseída, por ej. *that house is his* (esa casa es suya — de él); *those books are hers* (esos libros son suyos — de ella).

Los pronombres interrogativos

Sujeto:	*Complemento:*	*Forma posesiva:*
who? (quién)	*who(m)*?	*whose*?
which? (cuál)	*which*?	*whose*?
what? (qué)	*what*?	

La forma de complemento *whom* se usa rara vez en el inglés hablado; se prefiere *who.*

LA PREPOSICIÓN

Las preposiciones inglesas se pueden trasladar al final de la oración en casos en que acompañan a pronombres o adjetivos interrogativos y pronombres relativos, por ej. *what newspaper did you subscribe to? to what newspaper did you subscribe?* (¿a qué periódico te suscribiste?); *we couldn't recognize the man (who-m) she was talking to; we couldn't recognize the man to whom she was talking* (no pudimos reconocer al hombre con quien ella hablaba). El pronombre relativo se puede omitir en esos casos (excepto *what*).

LOS VERBOS

1. El verbo inglés conserva, en todos los tiempos, la misma forma para todas las personas del singular y el plural, a excepción de:

a) La tercera persona singular del tiempo presente (salvo en los verbos defectivos).

b) El singular del presente del verbo *to be* (ser, estar).

2. Hay dos clases de verbos en inglés, regulares e irregulares. Regulares son aquéllos que forman el pretérito indefinido y el participio pasado añadiendo *-ed* o *-d* al infinitivo, por ej. *open, opened; love, loved.* Se llaman verbos irregulares los que forman el pretérito indefinido y/o el participio pasado de estas maneras:

a) Con una terminación distinta a las mencionadas, por ej. *bend, bent, bent.*

b) Cambiando la radical, por ej. *sing, sang, sung.*

c) Conservando la misma forma para el presente, pretérito indefinido y participio pasado, por ej. *cut, cut, cut.*

3. El verbo inglés tiene cuatro modos: INFINITIVO, INDICATIVO, SUBJUNTIVO e IMPERATIVO.

a) El INFINITIVO tiene las siguientes formas: INFINITIVO, GERUNDIO, PARTICIPIO PRESENTE y PARTICIPIO PASADO.

N.B. El gerundio (*gerund*) y el participio presente (*present participle*) son idénticos en forma pero cumplen distintas funciones. La forma llamada *gerund* es equivalente a un sustantivo y corresponde en español al infinitivo y no al gerundio, por ej. *he likes walking* (le gusta caminar); *working here is a pleasure* (trabajar aquí es un placer). La forma llamada *present participle,* en cambio, corresponde al gerundio del español, por ej. *he is sleeping* (está durmiendo).

b) El INDICATIVO tiene los siguientes tiempos principales: PRESENTE, PRETÉRITO INDEFINIDO, FUTURO (que se forma usando los auxiliares *shall* y *will*) y POTENCIAL (que se forma usando los auxiliares *should y would*).

c) El SUBJUNTIVO de los verbos ingleses (salvo los defectivos) tiene las mismas formas del indicativo, excepto la tercera persona singular del presente, que no lleva *s* final, por ej. *I suggest that he return tomorrow* (sugiero que él vuelva mañana).

El verbo *to be* (ser, estar) es el único que tiene formas propias para el subjuntivo. Se usa la forma *be* para todas las personas del presente; se usa la forma *were* para todas las personas del pretérito, por ej. *we insist that the message be delivered* (insistimos en que se entregue el mensaje); *if I were younger* . . . (si yo fuera más joven . . .).

El uso del subjuntivo es muy restringido en inglés.

d) El IMPERATIVO tiene sólo una persona, la segunda (singular y plural), cuya forma es la misma del infinitivo sin la partícula *to,* por ej. *close the door* (cierra, cierre, cerrad, cierren la puerta).

4. Los verbos auxiliares y defectivos, llamados *modal verbs* en inglés, son los siguientes:

a) *to be:* se usa para formar la voz pasiva.

b) *to have:* se usa para formar los tiempos compuestos de otros verbos y en diversas formas idiomáticas.

c) *to do:* se usa en las formas negativa, interrogativa y enfática de otros verbos.

d) *shall y will:* se usan para formar el futuro de otros verbos y también en ciertas construcciones como, por ej. *shall I let him in?* (¿lo dejo entrar? ¿estás de acuerdo en dejarlo entrar?); *I will not do it* (me niego a hacerlo).

e) *should y would:* se usan para formar el condicional de otros verbos y en construcciones como, por ej. *would you help me, please?* (¿me ayuda-s-n, por favor? ¿quiere-s-n ayudarme, por favor?); *you should not say that* (no debería-s-n decir eso).

f) *can* (en el presente) y *could* (en el pretérito y el condicional): se usan para expresar capacidad, habilidad, posibilidad o permiso, por ej. *my father can-could speak four languages* (mi padre sabe-sabía hablar cuatro idiomas); *we can-could send it to you tomorrow* (podemospodríamos mandártelo mañana); *you can go tonight* (puedes — tienes licencia para — ir esta noche); *he said I could go tonight* (dijo que yo podía — que tengo licencia para — ir esta noche).

g) *may* y *might:* se usan para indicar posibilidad o permiso, por ej. *she may-might be ill* (puede estar enferma); *you may use my bicycle* (puedes — te permito — usar mi bicicleta); *he said I might use his bicycle* (me dijo que podía usar su bicicleta).

h) *must:* se usa para expresar obligación, necesidad o suposición, por ej. *one must obey the law* (hay que acatar la ley); *I must call my lawyer* (tengo que llama a mi abogado); *he must be crazy* (debe estar loco).

i) *ought:* se usa para expresar obligación moral o que algo es recomendable o aconsejable (generalmente intercambiable con *should*), por ej. *you ought to visit your parents* (deberías visitar a tus padres).

Shall, should, will, would, can, could, may, might y *must* se construyen seguidos del infinitivo sin la partícula *to,* mientras que *ought* siempre require la partícula. Ninguno de ellos lleva *s* en la tercera persona ni se puede conjugar en tiempo futuro. No tienen formas de infinitivo, subjuntivo ni imperativo.

5. La voz pasiva se forma usando el verbo *to be* como auxiliar con el participio pasado del verbo principal, por ej. *it is eaten raw* (se come crudo); *he was elected president* (lo eligieron presidente).

La interrogación

Para las formas interrogativas se usa el verbo auxiliar *to do,* anteponiéndolo al sujeto, por ej. *does he like beer?* (¿le gusta la cerveza? — a él); *why did you call me?* (¿por qué me llamaste?).

No se usa *to do* en interrogaciones, sino que simplemente se antepone el verbo al sujeto:

a) Cuando se efectúa la interrogación mediante otro verbo auxiliar, por ej. *has he gone out?* (¿ha salido? — él); *will they arrive late?* (¿llegarán tarde?); *are you sure?* (¿estás seguro?).

b) Cuando los pronombres interrogativos *who, what y which (one)* actúan como sujeto, por ej. *who saw him?* (¿quién lo vio? — a él); *what happened to you?* (¿qué te pasó?); *which (one) comes first?* (¿cuál viene primero?).

La negación

En oraciones negativas la palabra *not* se pone detrás del verbo y se emplean los auxiliares de acuerdo con las reglas que rigen para la interrogación, por ej. *we are not French* (no somos franceses); *he will not come* (no vendrá — él); *I did not see you yesterday* (no te vi ayer), excepto en la forma negativa del imperativo de *to be,* que requiere el uso del auxiliar *do,* por ej. *don't (do not) be silly* (no seas tonto); *don't (do not) be afraid* (no tengas miedo).

N.B. Cuando *have* se usa como verbo principal, las formas interrogativa y negativa con frecuencia se construyen con el auxiliar *to do,* por ej. *do you have a cigarette?* (¿tienes un cigarrillo?); *did you have breakfast already?* (¿ya tomaste el desayuno?); *we didn't have time to do it* (no tuvimos tiempo de hacerlo).

Al usarse el auxiliar *can,* la palabra *not* se puede juntar al verbo, por ej. *you cannot leave so early* (no puedes irte tan temprano).

En el inglés familiar se contrae *not* con el uso de un apóstrofe y se une al verbo, por ej. *we aren't French; he won't come; I didn't see you yesterday.*

La forma interrogativa en negaciones

Cuando se usa la forma completa de *not,* el orden de las palabras es: verbo sujeto *not,* por ej. *did he not give you the news?* (¿no te dio la noticia?); *can she not return tomorrow?* (¿no puede volver mañana? — ella). Al usar la contracción *n't,* ésta queda unida al verbo, por ej. *didn't he give you . . .? can't she return . . .?*

Abreviaturas Usadas en Este Diccionario

Parte I: Inglés-Español

a.	adjetivo
(a.a.)	aire acondicionado
abrev.	abreviatura; abreviado
(acús.)	acústica
adv.	adverbio
(aer.)	aeronáutica
(aeroesp.)	aeroespacial
(agr.)	agricultura
(Am.)	América; americanismo
(anat.)	anatomía
(anglo-ind.)	uso anglo-indio
(ant.)	antiguo; uso anticuado
(antrop.)	antropologiá
apl.	aplícase
apr.	aproximadamente
(Arg.)	Argentina
(arit.)	aritmética
(arm.)	armadura; armas
(arq.)	arquitectura
(arqueol.)	arqueologiá
art.	artículo
(arte)	bellas artes
(artil.)	artillería
(astr.)	astronomía
(astrol.)	astrología
(astronáut.)	astronáutica
(Aust.)	Australia
(aut.)	automovilismo
aux.	auxiliar
(avia.)	aviación
(bact.)	bacteriología
(bibl.)	bíblico
(biol.)	biología
(bioquím.)	bioquímica
(Bol.)	Bolivia
(bot.)	botánica
(Can.)	Canadá
(Car.)	región del Caribe
(carp.)	carpintería
(cart.)	cartografía
(cer.)	cerámica
(cient.)	científico
(cine.)	cinematografía
(cir.)	cirugía
(Col.)	Colombia
(com.)	comercio; comercial
comp.	comparativo
(comput.)	computadora
conj.	conjunción
(const.)	construcción
contr.	contracción
(cost.)	costura
(C. Rica)	Costa Rica
(crim.)	criminología
(crist.)	cristalografía
(Cuba)	Cuba
(cul.)	culinario; cocina
(Chile)	Chile
defec.	defectivo
(dep.)	deportes
(der.)	derecho; leyes
(despec.)	despectivo
(dial.)	dialecto
(dib.)	dibujo
díc.	dícese
dim.	diminutivo
(dipl.)	diplomacia
E.	este
(ecol.)	ecología
(econ.)	economía
(Ecuad.)	Ecuador
(educ.)	educación
ej.	ejemplo
(elec.)	electricidad; eléctrico
(electrón.)	electrónica
(embr.)	embriología
(enc.)	encuadernación
(ento.)	entomología
(e.p.)	economía política
(equit.)	equitación
(esc.)	escultura
(Esco.)	Escocia
(esgr.)	esgrima
(Esp.)	España
esp.	especialmente
(etnol.)	etnología
(E.U.)	Estados Unidos
(eufem.)	eufemismo
f.	femenino
(fam.)	familiar
(farm.)	farmacia
(f.c.)	ferrocarril
(fig.)	figurado; figurativamente
(filat.)	filatelia
(Filip.)	Filipinas
(filol.)	filología
(filos.)	filosofía
(fin.)	finanzas
(fís.)	física
(fisiol.)	fisiología
(fon.)	fonética
(for.)	forense
(fort.)	fortificación
(fotgmt.)	fotogrametría
(foto.)	fotografía
(fr.)	francés
(fund.)	fundición
(G.B.)	Gran Bretaña
gen.	generalmente
gén.	género
(geof.)	geofísica
(geog.)	geografía
(geol.)	geología
(geom.)	geometría
ger.	gerundio
(gram.)	gramática
(Guat.)	Guatemala
(heb.)	hebreo
(her.)	heráldica
(hidr.)	hidráulica
(hist.)	historia; histórico
(Hond.)	Honduras
(hor.)	horticultura
(hum.)	humorístico
(ict.)	ictiología
imper.	imperativo
impers.	impersonal
(impr.)	imprenta
(ind.)	industria
indef.	indefinido
indic.	indicativo
inf.	infinitivo
(ing.)	ingeniería
(Ingl.)	Inglaterra
(inter.)	internacional
interj.	interjección
invar.	invariable
(Irl.)	Irlanda
(irón.)	irónico
irr	irregular
(jer.)	jerga
(joy.)	joyería
(lab.)	laboratorio
(lat.)	latin
(ling.)	lingüística
(lit.)	literatura; literario
(litog.)	litografía
(lóg.)	lógica
m.	masculino
(maq.)	maquinaria
(mar.)	maritimo
(mat.)	matemáticas
(mec.)	mecánica
(med.)	medicina
(metal.)	metalurgia
(meteor.)	meteorología
(Méx.)	México
(mil.)	militar
(min.)	mineralogía; minería
(mitol.)	mitología
(mot.)	motores
(mús.)	música
N.	norte
(N.A.)	Norteamérica
(nav.)	navegación
(neol.)	neologismo
(Nic.)	Nicaragua
(numis.)	numismática
O.	oest
(ocean.)	oceanografía
(odont.)	odontología
(oft.)	oftalmología
(ópt.)	óptica
(orn.)	ornitología
(pal.)	paleontología
(Pan.)	Panamá
(Par.)	Paraguay
pers.	personal; persona
(Perú)	Perú
p. ext.	por extensión
(pint.)	pintura
pl.	plural
(poét.)	poético
(pol.)	política
pos.	posesivo
p.p.	participio pasado
p. pr.	participio presente
pr.	principalmente
prep.	preposición
pres.	presente
pret.	pretérito
(P. Rico)	Puerto Rico
pron.	pronombre
(psic.)	psicología
(quím.)	química
(rad.)	radio
ref.	referencia; referente
refl.	reflexivo
(reg.)	regional
rel.	relativo
(relig.)	religión
(Rep. Dom.)	República Dominicana
(ret.)	retórica; uso retórico
S.	sur
s.	sustantivo
(S.A.)	Sudamérica
(Salv.)	El Salvador
(señal)	señal
simb.	simbolo
sing.	singular
(sociol.)	sociología
subj.	subjuntivo
super.	superlativo
t.	también
(taur.)	tauromaquia
(teat.)	teatro
(tec.)	tecnología
(tej.)	tejeduría
(tele.)	telefonía; radiotelefonía
(teleg.)	telegrafía; radiotelegrafía
(ten.)	teneduría de libros
(teo.)	teología
(tip.)	tipografía
(TM)	marca de fábrica
(top.)	topografía
(trig.)	trigonometría
(t.v.)	televisión
u.	uso
ú.	úsase
u. refl.	usado reflexivamente
(Urug.)	Uruguay
v.	verbo
var.	variante
(Ven.)	Venezuela
(vet.)	veterinaria
v.i.	verbo intransitivo
v.r.	verbo reflexivo
v.t.	verbo transitivo
(vulg.)	vulgarismo
(zool.)	zoología

A

A [eɪ] *s.* 1. a, primera letra del alfabeto inglés. 2. el primero, lo mejor (en su clase). 3. (mús.) la. 4. **from A to Z,** del primero al último, de pe a pa, de cabo a rabo.

a [eɪ, ə] *art. indef.* 1. un, una, ej., *a factory,* una fábrica; cuando precede a una palabra que empieza por vocal o h muda se transforma en *an,* ej., *an ass,* un asno, *an hour,* una hora. Se pospone a los adjetivos *many, such, what* y a los adjetivos precedidos de *as, how, so, too,* ej., *such a man,* semejante hombre, *too old a man,* un hombre demasiado viejo. 2. (con el sentido de *in*) a, por, el, la, ej., *twice a week,* dos veces por semana, *ten cents a dozen,* a diez centavos la docena. 3. mismo, ej., *three of a kind,* tres del mismo tipo. 4. un tal, un cierto, ej., *a Mr. Smith was looking for you,* un tal Sr. Smith le estaba buscando a Ud. 5. **not a one,** ni uno, ni siquiera uno. —*prep.* 1. se usa como prefijo representando *at, in, on, to, towards* o *into,* o indicando modo o condición, ej., *abed,* en cama, *afoot,* a pie, *ashore,* en tierra, a tierra, *aside,* aparte, a un lado, *asunder,* en dos. 2. (reg.) se usa a veces antes del p.pr. para indicar modo o continuidad de la acción, ej., *he goes a-hunting,* se va de caza.

a. *abrev. de* 1. **adjective,** adjetivo. 2. **about,** alrededor de. 3. **answer,** contestación.

A. *abrev. de* 1. **America, American,** América, norteamericano. 2. **angstrom unit,** unidad angstrom.

AA *abrev. de* 1. **antiaircraft,** antiaéreo. 2. **Automobile Association,** Asociación Automovilística. 3. **Alcoholics Anonymous,** Alcohólicos Anónimos, A.A.

AAA *abrev. de* 1. **American Automobile Association,** Asociación Norteamericana Automovilística. 2. **Amateur Athletic Association,** Asociación de Atletismo Amateur.

A.A.A.L. *abrev. de* **American Academy of Arts and Letters,** Academia Norteamericana de Artes y Letras.

AAM *abrev. de* **air-to-air missile,** proyectil del aire al aire, cohete aire-aire.

aardvark ['ɑrdˌvɑrk, B 'ɑdˌvɑk] *s.* (zool.) cerdo hormiguero.

aardwolf [-ˌwʊlf] *s.* (especie de) hiena sudafricana.

Aaronic [æ'rɑnɪk, ɛ-, B ɛə'rɔn-] *a.* 1. (bíbl.) aarónico, aaronita. 2. (relig.) del clero menor de los mormones.

AAUP *abrev. de* **American Association of University Professors.**

A.B. *abrev. de* **Artium Baccalaureus** (Lat.) **Bachelor of Arts.**

aba [ə'bɑ, 'ɑbə] *s.* 1. tela de pelo de camello. 2. túnica árabe.

A.B.A. *abrev. de* **American Bar Association,** Asociación Norteamericana de Abogados; **Amateur Boxing Association,** Asociación de Boxeo Amateur.

abaca [ˌæbə'kɑ] *s.* (bot.) abacá, plátano de las Islas Filipinas; cáñamo de Manila.

aback [ə'bæk] *adv.* 1. por sorpresa, desprevenidamente, de improviso. 2. (ant.) atrás. 3. **to lay flat a.,** (mar.) poner (las velas) en facha; **to take a.,** desconcertar.

abacus ['æbəkəs] *s.* ábaco (aparato para contar y calcular); (arq.) ábaco (tablero que corona el capitel de una columna).

abaft [ə'bæft, B ə'bɑft] *adv.* (mar.) a popa, en popa, hacia la popa, atrás; **to go a.,** ir hacia la popa. —*prep.* detrás de.

abalone [ˌæbə'loʊnɪ] *s.* (zool.) abalone, oreja marina, oreja de San Pedro.

abandon [ə'bændən] *v.t.* abandonar; dejar, desamparar, desertar; desistir, renunciar; evacuar; repudiar; **a. oneself to,** entregarse a; **abandon ship!** ¡evacuar el barco! ¡todos a los botes! —*s.* desenfreno, desbordamiento; **to dance with wild abandon** bailar desenfrenadamente.

abandoned [-dənd] *a.* 1. abandonado, desamparado; desierto, deshabitado. 2. entregado a los vicios, perdido.

abandonee [əˌbændə'ni] *s.* (der.) asegurador que retiene el buque naufragado y salvado después de haber pagado la indemnización.

abandonment [ə'bændənmənt] *s.* 1. abandono, desamparo; deserción. 2. entrega (de sí mismo), arrebato. 3. (der., com.) cesión, dejación (de bienes).

abase [ə'beɪs] *v.t.* rebajar, humillar, degradar, abatir; envilecer.

abasement [-mənt] *s.* humillación, degradación; envilecimiento.

abash [ə'bæʃ] *v.t.* avergonzar, confundir, desconcertar.

abashment [-mənt] *s.* vergüenza, confusión, desconcierto.

abatable [ə'beɪtəbəl] *a.* (der.) abolible.

abate [ə'beɪt] *v.t.* 1. disminuir, aminorar, mitigar; reducir, debilitar. 2. terminar, hacer cesar; eliminar, omitir. 3. descontar, deducir, rebajar, ej., *to a. part of the price,* rebajar parte del precio. 4. (der.) abolir, anular. —*v.i.* disminuir, aminorar, amainar; debilitarse, ceder, ej., *the disease is abating,* la enfermedad está cediendo.

abatement [-mənt] *s.* 1. disminución; mitigación. 2. descuento, rebaja. 3. (der.) abolición, cesación.

abatis ['æbəˌti, 'æbətəs] *s.* (fort.) tala, abatida, barricada de alambre de púas.

abattoir ['æbəˌtwɑr, B -ˌtwɑ] *s.* matadero de reses.

abaxial [æ'bæksɪəl] *a.* (biol.) abaxial; (mec.) extraaxial.

abb [æb] *s.* urdimbre, lana en borra.

abbacy ['æbəsɪ] *s.* abadía (oficio o jurisdicción de un abad).

abbatial [ə'beɪʃəl] *a.* abadengo, abacial.

abbé ['æbeɪ] *s.* abate.

abbess ['æbəs] *s.* abadesa.

abbey ['æbɪ] *s.* (*pl.* **abbeys**) abadía (iglesia o monasterio regido por un abad o abadesa); **the A.,** (G.B.) la Abadía de Westminster.

abbot ['æbət] *s.* abad.

abbotship [-ˌʃɪp] *s.* abadía (dignidad y oficio de abad).

abbreviate [ə'brivɪˌeɪt] *v.t.* abreviar, resumir, reducir, compendiar, condensar; (mat.) simplificar.

abbreviation [əˌbrivɪ'eɪʃən] *s.* (*short form*) abreviatura; (*shortening*) abreviación.

ABC *abrev. de* **American Broadcasting Company,** Compañía Norteamericana de Radiodifusión.

ABC [ˌeɪˌbi'si] *s.* 1. el abecé *m;* 2. (*pl.*) **ABC's** abecedario.

abdicate ['æbdɪˌkeɪt] *v.t., v.i.* abdicar, renunciar, dimitir; (der.) desconocer, no reconocer por suyo.

abdication [ˌæbdɪ'keɪʃən] *s.* abdicación, renuncia, dimisión.

abdomen ['æbdəmən, æb'doʊmən] *s.* abdomen, vientre.

abdominal [æb'dɑmənəl, B -'dɔm-] *a.* abdominal.

abdominous [-ənəs] *a.* panzudo, abultado de vientre.

abduce [æb'dus, B -'djus] *v.t.* (fisiol., anat.) abducir (miembro o parte del cuerpo).

abducent [-ənt] *a.* (fisiol., anat.) abductor (músculo o nervio, que realiza una abducción).

abduct [æb'dʌkt] *v.t.* 1. secuestrar, raptar, llevarse por fuerza o por medio de fraude. 2. (fisiol., anat.) abducir (miembro o parte del cuerpo).

abduction [-'dʌkʃən] *s.* 1. rapto, secuestro. 2. (fisiol., anat., lóg.) abducción.

abductor [-tər, B -tə] *s.* 1. raptor. 2. (fisiol., anat.) (músculo) abductor.

abeam [ə'bim] *adv.* (mar.) por el través, en ángulo recto con la quilla.

abecedarian [ˌeɪbisi'dɛrɪən, B -'dɛər-] *s.* 1. el que está aprendiendo el abecedario, novicio, novato. 2. maestro que enseña las primeras letras. —*a.* 1. elemental; rudimentario. 2. alfabético, ordenado alfabéticamente.

abed [ə'bɛd] *adv.* acostado, en cama.

Abel ['eɪbəl] *s.* (bíbl.) Abel.

abele [ə'bil] *s.* (bot.) abelo, chopo blanco, álamo.

abelian group [ə'biljən-] (mat.) grupo abeliano o conmutativo.

abelmosk ['eɪbəlˌmɑsk, B -ˌmɔsk] *s.* (bot.) abelmosco, ambarcillo, ambarina.

Aberdonian [ˌæbər'doʊnɪən, B -bə'-] *a.* de Aberdeen. —*s.* habitante de Aberdeen, ciudad de Escocia.

aberrance [ə'bɛrəns] **aberrancy** [-ənsɪ] *s.* aberración; anormalidad, anomalía.

aberrant [-ənt] *a.* 1. aberrante, descaminado, extraviado. 2. anormal, anómalo. 3. (anat., zool.) atípico. 4. (ópt.) aberrante.

aberration [ˌæbə'reɪʃən] *s.* 1. aberración, extravío, desliz. 2. deficiencia intelectual. 3. (fisiol.) aberración; ser u órgano aberrante. 4. (astr.) aberración (desvío aparente de los astros). 5. (ópt.) aberración (falta de coincidencia de los rayos luminosos).

abet [ə'bɛt] *v.t.* (*pret., p.p.* ABETTED; *p.pr.* ABETTING) instigar, incitar, inducir; apoyar a (delito o delincuente); **to aid and a.,** ayudar y encubrir.

abetment [-mənt] *s.* instigación; apoyo.

abettor [-ər, B -ə] *s.* instigador, fautor.

abeyance [ə'beɪəns] *s.* suspensión, expectativa, espera; **in a.,** en suspenso; latente; en reserva; **lands in a.,** bienes mostrencos (sin dueño conocido); **inheritance in a.,** herencia yacente.
abeyant [-ənt] *a.* en suspenso; expectante.
abhor [əb'hɔr, æb-, B əb'hɔ] *v.t.* aborrecer, detestar, abominar, repudiar.
abhorrence [-əns, -'hɑr-, B -'hɔrəns] *s.* aborrecimiento, odio, aversión, execración; abominación.
abhorrent [-ənt] *a.* detestable, aborrecible; abominable.
abidance [ə'baɪdəns] *s.* 1. (con *in*) permanencia. 2. (con *by*) respeto (de), adhesión (a) (reglas, prescripciones, etc.).
abide [ə'baɪd] *v.i.* (*pret., p.p.* ABODE [ə'boʊd] o ABIDED; *p.pr.* ABIDING) 1. permanecer, continuar; morar, habitar. 2. **a. by,** guiarse por, seguir o cumplir con, respetar (regla, condición, etc.). —*v.t.* 1. soportar, tolerar. 2. sostener, resistir. 3. esperar, aguardar. 4. esperar (a uno), ej., *nothing good abides me in this affair,* no me espera nada bueno en este asunto. 5. aceptar, resignarse.
abiding [-ɪŋ] *a.* constante, duradero; obediente.
abietineous [ˌæbɪə'tɪnɪəs] *a.* (bot.) abietáceo.
ability [ə'bɪlətɪ] *s.* habilidad, facultad; capacidad, aptitud, inteligencia, alcance, talento, ingenio; **to the best of one's a.,** lo mejor que uno pueda.
abiogenesis [ˌeɪˌbaɪoʊ'dʒɛnəsəs] *s.* (biol.) abiogénesis, generación espontánea.
abiogenetic [-dʒə'nɛtɪk] *a.* (biol.) abiogenético.
abiotic [-'ɑtɪk, B -'ɔt-] *a.* (biol.) abiótico.
abject ['æbˌdʒɛkt, æb'dʒɛkt, B 'æbˌdʒɛkt] *a.* abyecto, despreciable, vil; **in abject poverty,** en la mayor miseria.
abjection [æb'dʒɛkʃən] **abjectness** ['æbˌdʒɛktnəs, æb'dʒɛkt-, B 'æbˌdʒɛkt-] *s.* abyección, envilecimiento, bajeza.
abjuration [ˌæbdʒə'reɪʃən] *s.* abjuración.
abjure [æb'dʒʊr, B -'dʒʊə] *v.t.* abjurar, renunciar o retractarse solemnemente; repudiar.
ablactation [ˌæblæk'teɪʃən] *s.* (med.) ablactación.
ablate [ə'bleɪt] *v.t.* extirpar por corte, desgastar por erosión. —*v.i.* ser extirpado o removido por corte o erosión.
ablation [æ'bleɪʃən] *s.* 1. (med.) ablación, extirpación. 2. (geol.) desgaste (de una roca o glaciar por la acción del agua o por el deshielo).
ablative ['æblətɪv] *s., a.* (gram.) ablativo.
ablative absolute (gram. lat.) ablativo absoluto.
ablaut ['æbˌlaʊt] *s.* (filol.) apofonía.
ablaze [ə'bleɪz] *adv.* en llamas, ardiendo. —*a.* 1. encendido, llameante. 2. (fig.) inflamado, ardiente. 3. (fig.) brillante, radiante.
able ['eɪbəl] *a.* capaz, hábil, competente; con capacidad legal o intelectual; **to be a.,** poder, ser capaz (de), tener poder (para), estar capacitado (para).
able, *s.* palabra del código de comunicaciones para la letra *a.*
able-bodied [-'bɑdɪd, B -'bɔd-] *a.* fuerte y sano.
able-bodied seaman, able seaman, (mar.) marinero experimentado y práctico; marinero matriculado.
ablegate ['æbləgət] *s.* ablegado, nuncio.
ablepharia [ˌæblə'fɛrɪə] *s.* (med.) ablefaria.
ablepsia [-'blɛpsɪə] **ablepsy** [-sɪ] *s.* (med.) ablepsia, ceguera.
abloom [ə'blum] *a., adv.* en flor, floreciente.
abluent ['æbluənt] *a.* (med.) abluente, detersivo, detergente. —*s.* substancia abluente.
ablush [ə'blʌʃ] *a.* sonrojado, ruborizado.
ablution [ə'bluʃən] *s.* 1. (*ú. gen. en pl.*) ablución (ceremonia de purificar por medio del agua, según el rito de algunas religiones). 2. ablución (líquido usado para la purificación).
ably ['eɪblɪ] *adv.* hábilmente, competentemente.
ABM *abrev. de* **anti-ballistic missile,** proyectil antibalístico.
abnegate ['æbnɪˌgeɪt] *v.t.* 1. renunciar, privarse de. 2. negar, abjurar, renunciar, rechazar.
abnegation [ˌæbnɪ'geɪʃən] *s.* 1. abnegacion, renunciación, sacrificio. 2. negación, abjuración, rechazo.
abnormal [æb'nɔrməl, B -ˌnɔməl] *a.* anormal, irregular, deforme, anómalo.
abnormality [ˌæbnɔr'mælətɪ, B -nɔ'-] *s.* anormalidad, irregularidad, deformidad, anomalía.
abnormal psychology, psicología patológica, psicología clínica.
aboard [ə'bɔrd, B ə'bɔd] *adv.* a bordo; **all a.!** ¡pasajeros a bordo!; **to go a.,** embarcarse, ir a bordo; **to take a.,** embarcar, llevar a bordo. —*prep.* a bordo de.
abode [ə'boʊd] *s.* domicilio, habitación, residencia, morada; **to make** (o **take up**) **one's a.,** establecer o fijar domicilio, domiciliarse; **welcome to my humble abode!** ¡ (hum.) bienvenido a mi humilde morada!
abode, *pret., p.p. de* **abide.**
abolish [ə'bɑlɪʃ, B -'bɔl-] *v.t.* abolir, suprimir, anular, revocar.
abolition [ˌæbə'lɪʃən] *s.* abolición; (hist.) la abolición de la esclavitud.
abolitionism [-əˌnɪzəm] *s.* (hist.) abolicionismo, política en favor de la abolición de la esclavitud.
abolitionist [-ənəst] *s.* abolicionista (partidario de la abolición de alguna cosa, esp. de la esclavitud).
abomasum [ˌæboʊ'meɪsəm] *s.* (*pl.* ABOMASA [-sə]) (zool.) abomaso, cuajar, cuarto estómago (de un rumiante).
A-bomb ['eɪˌbɑm, B -ˌbɔm] *s.* bomba atómica, bomba A.
abominable [ə'bɑmənəbəl, B ə'bɔm-] *a.* abominable, execrable, detestable.
abominably [-blɪ] *adv.* abominablemente.
abominate [-əˌneɪt] *v.t.* abominar, execrar, detestar, aborrecer.
abomination [əˌbɑmə'neɪʃən, B -ˌbɔm-] *s.* abominación.
aboral [æ'bɔrəl] *a.* (med.) aboral.
aborally [-əlɪ] *adv.* (med.) de manera aboral.
aboriginal [ˌæbə'rɪdʒənəl] *a.* aborigen, originario, primitivo. —*s.* aborigen, nativo, indígena.
aborigines [-əˌniz] *s. pl.* aborígenes, moradores: plantas y animales propios de una región.
aborning [ə'bɔrnɪŋ, B ə'bɔnɪŋ] *a., adv.* mientras nace, naciente.
abort [ə'bɔrt, B ə'bɔt] *v.i., v.t.* abortar, parir prematuramente; (biol.) abortar, atrofiarse; (med.) abortar; (fig.) malograrse, frustrarse.
abortion [ə'bɔrʃən, B ə'bɔʃən] *s.* 1. aborto, malparto; **to have an a.,** hacerse un aborto; **to perform an a.,** practicar un aborto. 2. (fig.) aborto, fracaso, fiasco.
abortionist [-əst] *s.* abortador, abortista.
abortive [ə'bɔrtɪv, B ə'bɔt-] *a.* abortivo, fracasado, frustrado, infructuoso; (biol.) rudimentario, atrofiado.
abortively [-lɪ] *adv.* prematuramente.
abound [ə'baʊnd] *v.i.* abundar; **a. in,** abundar en; ej., *a stream abounding in fish,* un arroyo rico en peces.
abounding [-ɪŋ] *a.* abundante, rico, cuantioso.
about [ə'baʊt] *prep.* 1. alrededor de, cerca de, hacia. 2. tocante a, respecto a, sobre. 3. a eso de, ej., *a. six o'clock,* a eso de las seis. 4. por, ej., *a. town,* por la ciudad. 5. **look a. you!** ¡tenga Ud. cuidado!; **to beat a. the bush,** andarse por las ramas; **to send (one) a. one's business,** enviar (a uno) a paseo; **what are you a.?** ¿qué estás tramando?; **what are you thinking a.?** ¿en qué piensa Ud.? —*adv.* casi, poco más o menos; alrededor, por ahí, aquí y allá, en contorno; ocupado en; a punto de; alternadamente; en dirección opuesta; en torno; **a. face! a. turn!** (mil.) ¡media vuelta!; **all a.,** por todas partes; **to be a.,** estar a mano; **to be a. to (do),** estar a punto de (hacer); **to be out and a.,** reanudar sus actividades normales (después de un periodo de inactividad); **to be up and a.,** estar levantado (de la cama); **to bring a.,** ocasionar. —*a.* en movimiento, de un lado para otro.
about-face [-'feɪs] *s.* 1. media vuelta. 2. cambio de opinión o conducta, cambio de partido.
above [ə'bʌv] *adv.* 1. (más) arriba, encima, en lo alto, ej., *as stated a.,* como se expresa arriba, *the stars a.,* las estrellas en el firmamento. 2. más arriba, más allá, ej., *they found the boat three miles a.,* encontraron el bote tres millas más arriba (del río). 3. más, ej., *twenty and above,* veinte y más. —*prep.* 1. encima de, sobre; superior a, más que, más de; más allá de, ej., *a. all,* sobre todo, *a. criticism,* por encima de toda crítica, *a. one's strength,* más allá de las fuerzas de uno; *ten degrees a. zero,* diez grados sobre cero. 2. **a. and beyond,** mucho más allá de, ej., *a. and beyond his responsibility,* mucho más allá de su responsabilidad. —*s.* 1. lo alto; el cielo, ej., *manna from a.,* maná del cielo. 2. (más) alta autoridad, ej., *these orders come from a.,* estas órdenes vienen de una autoridad superior. —*a.* dicho, susodicho, antedicho; superior, precedente.
aboveboard [-ˌbɔrd, B -'bɔd] *a.* franco, honesto, sin engaño; sin tapujos. —*adv.* abiertamente.
above-mentioned [-'mɛntʃənd, B -'mɛnʃənd] *a.* antes mencionado, arriba citado, susodicho.
abracadabra [ˌæbrəkə'dæbrə] *s.* abracadabra, jerigonza, galimatías.
abradant [ə'breɪdənt] *a., s.* abrasivo.
abrade [ə'breɪd] *v.t.* raer, gastar, escoriar.
Abraham ['eɪbrəˌhæm] *s.* (bíbl.) Abrahán.
abranchial [eɪ'bræŋkɪəl] **abranchiate** [-ət] *a.* (zool.) abranquio.
abrasion [ə'breɪʒən] *s.* abrasión, desgaste, erosión.
abrasive [-sɪv, -zɪv, B -sɪv] *a., s.* abrasivo, raspante.
abreact [ˌæbrɪ'ækt] *v.t.* (psic.) liberar (una emoción o complejo reprimido) por medio de palabras.
abreaction [-'ækʃən] *s.* (psic.) abreacción, liberación de una emoción o complejo reprimido.
abreast [ə'brɛst] *adv.* lado a lado; a nivel, parejo, al mismo paso; en una línea, ej., *five a.,* cinco en una línea; **to be** (o **to keep**) **a. of** (o **with**), correr parejo con; estar al tanto de, estar al corriente de.
abridge [ə'brɪdʒ] *v.t.* 1. abreviar, acortar, compendiar, condensar. 2. (mat.) reducir.
abridged [ə'brɪdʒd] *a.* abreviado, compendiado, condensado.
abridged edition, edición abreviada.
abridgment, abridgement [ə'brɪdʒmənt] *s.* abreviación, contracción; resumen, compendio, epítome; limitación (de derechos, etc.).

abroach [əˈbroʊtʃ] *a.* espitado, con grifo (tonel, cuba, etc.).
abroad [əˈbrɔd] *adv.* fuera del país; en el extranjero, en todas partes o direcciones; **there is a rumor a.,** corre la voz; **to go a.,** ir al extranjero; **to get a.,** propalarse, trascender (un secreto; información, etc.).
abrogate [ˈæbrəˌgeɪt] *v.t.* abrogar, revocar, anular.
abrogation [ˌæbrəˈgeɪʃən] *s.* abrogación, abolición.
abrupt [əˈbrʌpt] *a.* 1. abrupto, escarpado, quebrado, áspero. 2. abrupto, brusco; repentino. 3. (bot.) truncado.
abruption [əˈbrʌpʃən] *s.* ruptura; (med.) abrupción, fractura.
abruptly [əˈbrʌptlɪ] *adv.* abruptamente, bruscamente, ásperamente.
abruptness [-nəs] *s.* brusquedad, rudeza, aspereza.
ABS *abrev. de* **antilock braking system** ABS *m.* sistema de frenos antibloqueo.
abscess [ˈæbˌsɛs] *s.* (med.) absceso, apostema.
abscise [æbˈsaɪz] *v.t.* cortar por abscisión o escisión. —*v.i.* separarse por abscisión o escisión.
abscissa [æbˈsɪsə] *s.* (*pl.* ABSCISSAS O ABSCISSAE [-i]) (geom.) abscisa.
abcission [-ˈsɪʒən] *s.* abscisión, separación.
abscond [æbˈskɑnd, B -ˈskɔnd] *v.i.* ocultarse, esconderse; fugarse, marcharse; amadrigarse (los animales); **to abscond with** alzarse con.
absconder [-ər, B -ə] *s.* fugitivo, prófugo; (der.) contumaz.
absence [ˈæbsəns] *s.* ausencia; falta; ensimismamiento, arrobo; **a. makes the heart grow fonder** la ausencia es al amor lo que al fuego el aire; **a. of mind,** distracción; **in the a. of,** a falta de; **leave of a.,** permiso, licencia temporal.
absent [-sɛnt] *a.* 1. ausente. 2. distraído, abstraído. —*v.t.* [æbˈsɛnt] **a. oneself,** no presentarse; ausentarse; retirarse, mantenerse aparte.
absentee [ˌæbsənˈti] *s.* ausente (persona que se ausenta), esp. propietario que vive fuera de su propiedad.
absentee ballot, absentee vote, voto en ausencia, voto por correspondencia o por poder.
absenteeism [-ˌɪzəm] *s.* ausentismo, absentismo.
absentee landlord, absentista, dueño que no habita su propiedad inmueble.
absent-minded [ˌæbsəntˈmaɪndəd] *a.* distraído.
absent without leave, (mil.) ausente sin permiso, ausente sin licencia.
absinthe, absinth [ˈæbˌsɪnθ] *s.* ajenjo (bebida aderezada con esencia de ajenjo).
absolute [ˈæbsəˌlut] *a.* 1. absoluto, total. 2. puro, libre de mezclas (alcohol, etc.). 3. absoluto, autocrático (monarca, etc.). 4. (gram.) absoluto, de uso intransitivo. 5. (gram.) (puesto) en aposición (frase, adjetivo, pronombre posesivo). 6. (fís.) absoluto. 7. (filos.) **the A.,** lo absoluto, el noúmeno.
absolute ceiling, (aer.) techo absoluto o teórico.
absolutely [-li] *adv.* absolutamente; **a. not,** absolutamente.
absolute monarchy, monarquía absoluta.
absoluteness [-nəs, ˌæbsəˈlut-, B ˈæbseˌlut-] *s.* carácter absoluto, terminante o categórico.
absolute pitch, (mús.) sonido absoluto; oído absoluto.
absolute scale, (fís.) escala de temperatura Kelvin o absoluta.
absolute temperature, (fís.) temperatura absoluta.
absolute value, (mat.) módulo, valor absoluto.
absolute zero, (fís.) cero absoluto.
absolution [ˌæbsəˈluʃən] *s.* absolución, perdón.
absolutism [ˈæbsəˌlutˌɪzəm] *s.* absolutismo, autocracia.
absolutist [-əst] *s.* absolutista, autócrata.
absolve [əbˈzɑlv, -ˈsɑlv, B -ˈzɔlv, -ˈsɔlv] *v.t.* 1. absolver (de pecado, etc.), dispensar, eximir (de obligación, etc.). 2. absolver, exculpar, exonerar.
absorb [əbˈsɔrb, -ˈzɔrb, B -ˈsɔb, -ˈzɔb] *v.t.* 1. absorber, embeber, empapar. 2. (fig.) absorber, asimilar profundamente (estudio, método, etc.). 3. (fig.) absorber, embelesar (la atención, el pensamiento, etc.); **to be absorbed in,** estar absorto o enfrascado en. 4. amortiguar una deuda, cubrir el costo de (una operación financiera, capitalización, etc.).
absorbed [-ˈsɔrbd, -ˈzɔrbd, B -ˈsɔbd, -ˈzɔbd] *a.* (fig.) absorto; abstraído, enfrascado.
absorbency [-bənsɪ] *s.* (quím., fís., med.) absorbencia.
absorbent [-bənt] *a., s.* absorbente.
absorbent cotton, algodón absorbente, algodón hidrófilo.
absorbing [-bɪŋ] *a.* (fig.) cautivante, absorbente.
absorption [əbˈsɔrpʃən, -ˈzɔrp-, B -ˈsɔp-, -ˈzɔp-] *s.* 1. (fís., quím., med.) absorción, absorbencia. 2. (mec.) amortiguamiento. 3. (fig.) abstracción, ensimismamiento. 4. **a. dynamometer,** dinamómetro friccional; **a. spectrum,** (fís.) espectro de absorción; **a. tube,** (lab.) tubo de absorción; **a. wavemeter,** (rad.) ondámetro de absorción.
absorptive [-tɪv] *a.* absorbente.
absorptivity [ˌæbsɔrpˈtɪvətɪ, -zɔrp-, B -sɔp-, -zɔp-] *s.* absorbencia.
abstain [əbˈsteɪn] *v.i.* (con *from*) abstenerse (de votar, participar, etc.); privarse (de gusto o placer).
abstainer [-ər, B -ə] *s.* 1. abstemio, persona sobria. 2. el que se asbtiene de votar o participar en una elección o actividad.
abstemious [æbˈstimɪəs] *a.* abstemio, abstinente, frugal.
abstention [əbˈstɛntʃən, B -ˈstɛnʃən] *s.* abstención, abstinencia.
absterge [æbˈstɔrdʒ, B əbˈstɛdʒ] *v.t.* limpiar, lavar, enjugar; (med.) abstergar, deterger.
abstergent [-ənt] *a., s.* (med.) abstergente, detersivo.
abstinence [ˈæbstənəns] **abstinency** [-ɪ] *s.* abstinencia, continencia.
abstinent [-nənt] *a.* abstinente; abstemio.
abstract [ˈæbˌstrækt, æbˈstrækt] *a.* abstracto. —*s.* 1. extracto, resumen, sumario, cuadro. 2. condición o carácter abstracto; idea abstracta. 3. **in the a.,** en astracto. — [æbˈstrækt, ˈæbˌstrækt] *v.t.* 1. separar, quitar. 2. abstraer. 3. resumir, compendiar, epitomar. 4. sustraer.
abstract art, arte abstracto o no figurativo.
abstracted [-əd] *a.* 1. abstraído, absorto; distraído, ensimismado. 2. compendiado, resumido.
abstract expressionism, (arte) expresionismo abstracto.
abstraction [æbˈstrækʃən] *s.* 1. abstracción, separación. 2. idea o concepto abstracto. 3. abstracción, ensimismamiento. 4. abstracción, carácter abstracto (de algo). 5. sustracción. 6. (fig.) **Platonic abstraction,** éxtasis, visión mística.
abstractionism [-ˌɪzəm] *s.* arte abstracto, expresión abstracta (en las artes).
abstrict [æbˈstrɪkt] *v.t.* (bot.) cercenar (un filamento esporógeno).
abstriction [-ˈstrɪkʃən] *s.* (bot.) abstricción.
abstruse [əbˈstrus, æb-] *a.* abstruso, recóndito, obscuro.
abstruseness [-nəs] *s.* incomprensibilidad, ininteligibilidad.
absurd [əbˈsɜrd, -ˈzɜrd, B -ˈsɜd] *a.* absurdo; **don't be absurd!,** ¡no seas ridículo!
absurdity [-ətɪ] *s.* 1. absurdo, irracionalidad. 2. absurdo, disparate.
abulia [eɪˈbulɪə, ə-] *s.* (psic.) abulia, carencia de voluntad.
abulic [-lɪk] *a.* (psic.) abúlico.
abundance [əˈbʌndəns] *s.* abundancia, caudal, plenitud.
abundant [-dənt] *a.* abundante, copioso.
abuse [əˈbjuz] *v.t.* 1. abusar de (confianza, autoridad, poder, etc.). 2. denostar, injuriar, insultar. 3. maltratar; violar, ultrajar. — [əˈbjus] *s.* 1. abuso, mal uso. 2. denuesto, injuria, insulto. 3. maltrato; ultraje, violación.
abusive [əˈbjusɪv, -zɪv, B -sɪv] *a* 1. abusivo. 2. insultante, injurioso, ofensivo.
abusiveness [-nəs] *s.* carácter abusivo; comportamiento abusivo o injurioso.
abut [əˈbʌt] *v.i.* (*pret., p.p.* ABUTTED; *p.pr.* ABUTTING) 1. (con *upon*) lindar, confinar (con), estar contiguo (a). 2. (con *on* o *against*) terminar (en); (con *on*) descansar, apoyar (sobre).
abutilon [əˈbjutəlˌɑn, B -ən] *s.* (bot.) abutilón.
abutment [əˈbʌtmənt] *s.* 1. linde, confín, lindero. 2. (arq.) estribo, macho. 3. (carp.) empalme.
abuttal [-əl] *s.* (*ú. gen. en pl.*) linde, límite, confín.
abutter [-ər, B -ə] *s.* (der.) colindante, propietario del terreno colindante.
abutting [-ɪŋ] *a.* colindante, confinante, limítrofe.
abysm [əˈbɪzəm] *s.* (poét.) *var. de* **abyss.**
abysmal [əˈbɪzməl] *a.* abismal; insondable, profundo, ej., *a. ignorance,* ignorancia supina.
abyss [əˈbɪs] *s.* 1. abismo, sima. 2. profundidad, precipicio. 3. abismo, báratro, infierno.
abyssal [-əl] *a.* abismal, insondable, profundo.
Abyssinian [ˌæbəˈsɪnɪən] *s., a.* natural de Abisinia, etíope.
A/C, a/c, *abrev. de* **account,** cuenta (cta.).
Ac *símb. de* **actinium,** actinio (Ac).
A.C. *abrev. de* 1. **alternating current,** corriente alterna. 2. **ante Cristum (before Christ),** antes de Jesucristo (a. de J.C.). 3. **Athletic Club,** club atlético.
acacia [əˈkeɪʃə] *s.* 1. (bot.) acacia. 2. goma arábiga.
Academe [ˈækəˌdim] *s.* 1. (hist. griega) Academia. 2. (E.U.) el ámbito universitario.
academic [ˌækəˈdɛmɪk] *a.* 1. académico. 2. relativo a las humanidades. 3. culto, instruido. 4. convencional, formal. 5. teórico, especulativo; **of purely a. interest,** de interés puramente intelectual.
academic freedom, libertad de enseñanza; libertad de cátedra.
academician [ˌækədəˈmɪʃən, əˌkæd-, B əˌkæd-] *s.* 1. académico. 2. miembro de una academia.
academic year, año académico o lectivo.
academy [əˈkædəmɪ] *s.* academia.
Academy Award ceremony, ceremonia de la entrega de los Oscars.
academy of art, escuela de bellas artes.
academy of music, conservatorio.
Acadia [əˈkeɪdɪə] *s.* Acadia, antigua colonia francesa en el Canadá.
Acadian [-ən] *a.* 1. natural de Acadia. 2. (geol.) acadiano.

acajou ['ækəʒu] *s.* (bot.) acajú, anacardo, caoba del Brasil; nuez o castaña del acajú.
acaleph ['ækəˌlɛf] *s.* (zool.) acalefo.
acanthaceous [ˌækən'θeɪʃəs] *a.* (bot.) acantáceo.
acanthite [ə'kænˌθaɪt] *s.* (geol.) acantita (mineral de plata).
acanthocephalan [əˌkænθə'sɛfələn] *a.* (zool.) acantocéfalo. —*s.* gusano acantocéfalo.
acanthoid [ə'kænˌθɔɪd] *a.* (bot.) acanatoide, espinoso.
acanthopterygian [ˌækənˌθɑptə'rɪdʒɪən, B -ˌθɔp-] *a.* (zool.) acantopterigio. —*s.* acantóptero.
acanthous [ə'kænθəs] *a.* (bot.) acantoide, espinoso.
acanthus [ə'kænθəs] *s.* 1. (bot.) acanto, hierba gigante. 2. (arq.) acanto (ornamento que imita las hojas de acanto).
a cappella [ˌɑkə'pɛlə] (mús.) coro al unísono, generalmente sin acompañamiento instrumental.
acariasis [ˌækə'raɪəsəs] *s.* (med.) acariasis o acaridiasis.
acarid ['ækərəd] *s.* (zool.) acárido, ácaro.
acaroid ['ækəˌrɔɪd] *a.* acaroideo; (bot., med.) acaroide.
acarpelous, acarpellous [eɪ'kɑrpələs, B -'kɑpə-] *a.* (bot.) acarpelado.
acarpous [-pəs] *a.* (bot.) acarpo, acárpico.
acarus ['ækərəs] *s.* (*pl.* ACARI [-ˌraɪ]) (zool.) ácaro, arador.
acatalectic [ˌeɪˌkætəl'ɛktɪk, B ˌæ-] *a.*, *s.* (poét.) acataléctico, acatalecto (verso).
acatalepsy [-'kætəlˌɛpsɪ] *s.* (filos.) acatalepsia.
acaudal [eɪ'kɔdəl, B ə-] *a.* (bot.) acaudado, sin cola; (zool., med.) acáudeo.
acaulescent [ˌeɪkɔ'lɛsənt, B ˌæ-] **acauline** [eɪ'kɔˌlaɪn, ə-] **acaulous** [-ləs] *a.* (bot.) acaule, sin tallo aparente.
acc. *abrev. de* 1. **acusative,** acusativo (acus.). 2. **acceleration,** aceleración. 3. **account,** cuenta.
accede [æk'sid] *v.i.* 1. (con *to*) acceder, asentir, consentir. 2. (con *to*) llegar a (un oficio o dignidad), subir, ascender a (trono, etc.).
accelerant [ˌæk'sɛlərənt] *s.* acelerador; (quím.) catalizador, acelerante.
accelerate [ɪk'sɛləˌreɪt, æk-, B ək-] *v.t.* acelerar, apresurar. —*v.i.* apresurarse, darse prisa.
acceleration [-ˌsɛlə'reɪʃən] *s.* aceleración, aceleramiento.
acceleration of gravity, (fís.) aceleración de la gravedad.
accelerator [-'sɛləˌreɪtər, B -ə] *s.* 1. (aut.) acelerador. 2. (fisiol.) músculo acelerador; nervio acelerador. 3. (quím.) catalizador. 4. (fís.) acelerador de partículas.
accelerometer [-ˌsɛlə'rɑmətər, B ək-'rɔmətə] *s.* (fís.) acelerómetro.
accent ['ækˌsɛnt] *s.* 1. acento (con que se realza una sílaba). 2. acento ortográfico. 3. acento, dejo (característico de una nación, región, idioma, etc.); **to have** (o **to speak with**) **an a.,** hablar con dejo extranjero (un idioma). 4. énfasis. 5. (mús.) acento (énfasis sobre una nota o marca que lo indica). —*v.t.* acentuar, recalcar.
accent mark, tilde.
accentual [æk'sɛntʃuəl, B -'sɛntjuəl] *a.* relativo al acento en música, ortografía, oratoria, etc.
accentuate [æk'sɛntʃʊˌeɪt] *v.t.* acentuar, intensificar.
accentuation [ækˌsɛntʃʊ'eɪʃən, B -tjʊ-] *s.* acentuación.
accentuator [æk'sɛntʃʊˌeɪtər, B -tə] *s.* (rad.) circuito acentuador.

accept [ɪk'sɛpt, æk-, B ək-] *v.t.* aceptar, admitir, acoger, recibir; aprobar; (com.) aceptar (letra de cambio, etc.).
acceptability [-ˌsɛptə'bɪlətɪ] *s.* aceptabilidad, admisibilidad.
acceptable [-'sɛptəbəl] *a.* aceptable, admisible.
acceptance [-təns] *s.* 1. aceptación, admisión, aprobación, acogida. 2. (com.) aceptación (de letra, condiciones, etc.). 3. **to ask (one's) a. of (something),** rogar (a alguien) que acepte (algo); **to find a.,** tener buena acogida.
acceptation [ˌækˌsɛp'teɪʃən] *s.* 1. aceptación, aprobación, acogida. 2. acepción, sentido, significado (de una palabra).
accepted [ɪk'sɛptəd, æk-, B ək-] *a.* aceptado, de uso general, admitido.
access ['ækˌsɛs] *s.* 1. acceso, entrada, paso, lugar o manera de entrada. 2. permiso para entrar, entrada. 3. (med.) acceso, arrebato, ataque. 4. **easy of a.,** de fácil acceso. —*v.t.* (comput) obtener acceso a, entrar a.
accessibility [ækˌsɛsə'bɪlətɪ, ɪk- B ək-] *s.* accesibilidad, asequibilidad.
accessible [-'sɛsəbəl] *a.* 1. accesible, asequible (objeto o lugar). 2. (con *to*) accesible, susceptible (a influencia, lisonjas, etc.). 3. comprensible.
accession [-'sɛʃən] *s.* 1. accesión, acceso. 2. ascensión, ascenso (al trono, dignidad, etc.). 3. accesión, asentimiento, consentimiento. 4. (der.) accesión. —*v.t.* ingresar, catalogar (en orden de adquisicion).
accessorial [ˌæksə'sɔrɪəl] *a.* accesorio, suplementario.
accessory [ɪk'sɛsərɪ, æk-, B ək-] *a.* 1. accesorio, secundario, adicional. 2. (con *to*) participante, asociado (en crimen, etc.). —*s.* 1. accesorio, aditamento. 2. (*pl.*) pertenencias, dependencias. 3. (der.) cómplice.
accessory after the fact, (der.) cómplice, encubridor, copartícipe.
accessory before the fact, (der.) cómplice instigador, inductor de un delito.
accidence ['æksədəns] *s.* (gram.) estudio de accidentes, inflexiones (de las palabras).
accident ['æksədənt] *s.* 1. accidente, casualidad. 2. desgracia. 3. (gram.) accidente, inflexión. 4. (lóg.) accidente (cualidad o característica no esencial). 5. (geog.) desigualdad (del terreno). 6. **by a.,** accidentalmente, por casualidad; **traffic a.,** accidente de circulación o tránsito.
accidental [ˌæksə'dɛntəl] *a.* accidental, casual, contingente. —*s.* 1. circunstancia o suceso accidental. 2. (mús.) accidente. 3. (*pl.*) (pint.) efectos accidentales.
accidentally [-ɪ] *adv.* accidentalmente.
accident insurance, seguro contra accidentes.
accident-prone ['æksədəntproʊn] *a.* propenso a sufrir accidentes.
accipiter [æk'sɪpətər, B -ə] *s.* (orn.) accípitre.
acclaim [ə'kleɪm] *v.t.* 1. aclamar, aplaudir. 2. proclamar. —*v.i.* vitorear. —*s.* aclamación, ovación.
acclamation [ˌæklə'meɪʃən] *s.* aclamación, voto unánime; **by a.,** por aclamación.
acclamatory [ə'klæməˌtɔrɪ, B -tərɪ] *a.* aclamatorio.
acclimate [ə'klaɪmət, 'ækləˌmeɪt, B ə'klaɪmɪt] *v.t.* aclimatar, acondicionar.
acclimation [ˌækˌlaɪ'meɪʃən] *s.* aclimatación.
acclimatize [ə'klaɪməˌtaɪz] *v.t.* aclimatar.
acclivity [ə'klɪvətɪ] *s.* cuesta ascendente, subida
accolade ['ækəˌleɪd] *s.* 1. acolada, espaldarazo, homenaje; crítica elogiosa, aplauso. 2. (mús.) corchete. 3. (arq.) moldura de conopio. —*v.t.* armar caballero.

accommodate [ə'kɑməˌdeɪt, B -'kɔm-] *v.t.* 1. (con *to*) acomodar, adaptar, amoldar, ajustar (a). 2. reconciliar (personas); arreglar (diferencias, disputas, etc.). 3. (con *with*) acomodar, proveer, surtir (de). 4. acomodar, alojar, hospedar, albergar; dar cabida a. 5. complacer, hacer un favor a. —*v.i.* (con *to*) acomodarse, adaptarse (a).
accommodating [-ɪŋ] *a.* servicial, acomodaticio, complaciente.
accommodation [əˌkɑmə'deɪʃən, B -ˌkɔm-] *s.* 1. adaptación, ajuste. 2. acomodamiento, arreglo. 3. favor, servicio; préstamo. 4. (*pl.*) facilidades, comodidades. 5. alojamiento, hospedaje. 6. reconciliación, convenio, avenencia.
accommodation ladder, (mar.) escala de popa, escala de portalón (al costado de un buque).
accompaniment [ə'kʌmpənɪmənt] *s.* acompañamiento, accesorio, complemento; (mús.) acompañamiento.
accompanist [-nəst] *s.* (mús.) acompañante.
accompany [ə'kʌmpənɪ] *v.t.* acompañar, escoltar, conducir. —*v.i.* (mús.) tocar el acompañamiento.
accomplice [ə'kɑmpləs, -'kʌm-, B -'kɔm-, -'kʌm-] *s.* cómplice.
accomplish [-plɪʃ] *v.t.* 1. efectuar, realizar, llevar a cabo, consumar, lograr. 2. perfeccionar, adiestrar, ejercitar, instruir.
accomplished [-plɪʃt] *a.* 1. realizado, ejecutado. 2. consumado, perfecto, acabado, ej., *an a. mathematician,* un matemático consumado; **an accomplished musician,** un músico de mucho talento. 3. instruido, versado, culto.
accomplishment [-plɪʃmənt] *s.* 1. consumación, realización, logro, perfección. 2. talento, habilidad.
accord [ə'kɔrd, B ə'kɔd] *v.t.* 1. acordar, conciliar, armonizar. 2. otorgar, conceder; imponer a. —*v.i.* acordar, concordar, avenirse, armonizar. —*s.* 1. acuerdo, convenio; (der.) convenio, arreglo. 2. acuerdo, conformidad, concierto, armonía. 3. **in a. with,** de acuerdo con; **of one's own a.,** espontáneamente; **to be in a. with** (*information, a report*) coincidir con, concordar con.
accordance [-əns] *s.* 1. conformidad, acuerdo, concordancia, correspondencia. 2. concesión, otorgamiento. 3. **in a. with,** de acuerdo con.
accordant [-ənt] *a.* acorde, conforme, consonante (con).
according [-ɪŋ] *adv.* conforme; **a. to,** según, conforme a, con arreglo a.
accordingly [-li] *adv.* 1. en conformidad, como corresponde, en la debida forma. 2. por consiguiente, en consecuencia.
accordion [ə'kɔrdɪən, B -'kɔd-] *s.* acordeón. —*a.* doblado; plegadizo.
accordionist [-ənəst] *s.* acordionista.
accost [ə'kɔst] *v.t.* abordar, dirigirse a; trabar conversación con; incomodar; faltar al respeto (a una mujer).
accouchement [ə'kuʃˌmɑnt, B -ˌmɑŋ] *s.* parto, alumbramiento.
accoucheur [ˌæˌku'ʃɜr, B -'ʃɜ] *s.* comadrón, partero.
account [ə'kaʊnt] *s.* 1. (ten., com.) cuenta. 2. cuenta, razón; declaración, informe. 3. narración, cuento, relación, descripción. 4. mérito, valor; aprecio, consideración, estimación; importancia, dignidad. 5. ventaja, provecho. 6. **by all accounts,** según el decir general, en todo respecto; **in a. with,** en cuenta con; **of a.,** de cuenta, de importancia, de nota; **of no a.,** insignificante, de poca monta (gente, etc.); **on a.,** a

cuenta; **on a. of,** a causa de, a favor de; **on no a.,** de ninguna manera; **on one's a.,** por amor de uno; **on one's own a.,** por su propia cuenta; **to bring to a.,** pedir cuentas a; **to buy on a.,** comprar a crédito o a plazos; **to call to a.,** pedir cuentas a; **to close an a. (with),** cerrar la cuenta (con); **to give a. of,** dar cuenta de, dar razón de; **to give a good a. of oneself,** hacer buena impresión, portarse bien; **to keep a. of,** llevar cuenta de; **to keep accounts,** llevar cuentas; **to leave out of a.,** no tomar en cuenta, hacer caso omiso de; **to lose a. of,** perder la cuenta de; **to make little a. (of),** no hacer mucho caso (de); **to one's a.,** a favor de uno; **to open a. with,** abrir cuenta con; **to settle an a.,** saldar o pagar una cuenta; **to square** o **settle accounts with (someone),** saldar la cuenta con (alguien); (fig.) ajustar cuentas con (alguien); **to take a. of,** tomar en cuenta; advertir, observar; **to take into a.,** tomar en cuenta, considerar; **to turn to a.,** sacar provecho de. —*v.t.* 1. dar cuenta o razón de. 2. considerar, juzgar, tener por. —*v.i.* (con **for**) dar razón (de); responder (por); explicar.

accountable [-əbəl] *a.* 1. (con *for* o *to*) responsable (de o ante). 2. explicable.

accountancy [-ənsɪ] *s.* contaduría, contabilidad.

accountant [ə'kaʊntənt] *s.* contador, contable.

account book, (ten.) libro de cuentas.

account executive, funcionario responsable del manejo de la cuenta de un cliente (esp. en agencias publicitarias).

accounting [-ɪŋ] *s.* 1. contabilidad. 2. rendición de cuentas.

account payable, (ten.) cuenta por pagar.

account receivable, (ten.) cuenta por cobrar.

accouter, accoutre [ə'kutər, B -ə] *v.t.* ataviar, aviar, equipar; (ant., mil.) armar.

accouterment, accoutrement [-mənt, -trəmənt] *s.* (*ú gen. en pl.*) avío, atavío, equipaje, apresto, vestidura; (mil.) pertrechos, equipos.

Accra [ə'krɑ] *s.* Accra, capital de Ghana.

accredit [ə'krɛdət] *v.t.* 1. acreditar, dar crédito a, reconocer. 2. acreditar, dar credenciales a (embajador, etc.).

accreditation [əˌkrɛdə'teɪʃən] *s.* acreditación, autorización, identificación.

accrete [ə'krit] *v.i., v.t.* (bot., fisiol.) acrecentar, aumentar.

accretion [ə'kriʃən] *s.* acrecentamiento, acreción; (med.) acrementación; (der.) acrecencia.

accretive [ə'kritɪv] *a.* acrecentador; (bot.) acrementicio.

accrue [ə'kru] *v.i.* 1. acrecentar, aumentar, acumular (suma, capital, etc.). 2. resultar. 3. acumularse.

accrued interest [ə'krud-] (fin.) interés devengado o acumulado.

acct. *abrev. de* **account,** cuenta.

acculturate [ə'kʌltʃəˌreɪt] *v.t., v.i.* (antrop.) transformar(se) por asimilación cultural.

acculturation [əˌkʌltʃə'reɪʃən] *s.* (antrop.) aculturación, asimilación cultural (entre grupos sociales o pueblos).

accumulate [ə'kjumjəˌleɪt] *v.t.* acumular, amontonar, atesorar. —*v.i.* acumularse, amontonarse.

accumulation [əˌkjumjə'leɪʃən] *s.* acumulación, amontonamiento, hacinamiento.

accumulative [ə'kjumjələtɪv] *a.* acumulativo.

accumulator [-ˌleɪtər, B -ə] *s.* acumulador, amontonador; (elec. G.B.) acumulador; (hidr.) condensador.

accuracy ['ækjərəsɪ] *s.* exactitud, precisión, esmero.

accurate [-rət] *a.* exacto, preciso; (*aim, blow*) certero; (*translation*) exacto, fiel; **usually a.** generalmente acierta.

accurately [-lɪ] *adv.* exactamente, con precisión.

accursed [ə'kɜrst, -'kɜrsəd, B -'kɜsɪd] *a.* maldito, maldecido; detestable.

accusable [ə'kjuzəbəl] *a.* acusable.

accusation [ˌækjə'zeɪʃən] *s.* acusación, cargo, imputación.

accusative [ə'kjuzətɪv] *s.* (gram.) acusativo. —*a.* 1. (gram.) acusativo. 2. acusatorio.

accusatorial procedure [əˌkjuzə'tɔrɪəl-] (der.) procedimiento o juicio legal (en el cual el acusador y el juez no son la misma persona; opuesto a inquisitorial).

accusatory [ə'kjuzəˌtɔrɪ, B -tərɪ] *a.* acusatorio.

accuse [ə'kjuz] *v.t.* acusar.

accused [ə'kjuzd] *a.* acusado, inculpado; **the a.,** el acusado; los acusados; **they were accused of** los acusaron de.

accuser [ə'kjuzər, B -zə] *s.* acusador.

accustom [ə'kʌstəm] *v.t.* acostumbrar, habituar.

accustomed [-təmd] *a.* 1. acostumbrado, avezado. 2. usual, habitual.

AC/DC ['eɪsi'disi] *s. abrev. de* **alternating current/direct current** corriente alterna/corriente continua. —*a.* **he's AC/DC** es bisexual.

ace [eɪs] *s.* 1. as (de naipes, dados o dominó). 2. (fig.) as (persona que sobresale de manera notable en un ejercicio o profesión). 3. (tenis) servicio que no se puede devolver; (golf) hoyo hecho en un solo golpe. 4. **a. in the hole** (fam.), as de reserva (cualquier hecho, plan o argumento importante que se reserva para el momento oportuno). —*v.t.* 1. marcar (un tanto) de un golpe; (golf) jugar (un hoyo) de un golpe. 2. **a. out,** (fam.) recibir la calificación más alta (en examen o prueba). —*a.* primerísimo, excelente (en calidad), sobresaliente.

acephalous [eɪ'sɛfələs, B ə-] *a.* (zool., bot.) acéfalo (sin cabeza); (fig.) acéfalo (sin jefe o director).

acerate ['æsəˌreɪt] **acerated** [-əd] *a.* (bot.) acerado, puntiagudo.

acerb [ə'sɜrb, B -'sɜb] *a.* 1. acerbo, amargo. 2. (fig.) acerbo, cruel.

acerbate ['æsərˌbeɪt, B -səˌbeɪt] *v.t.* agriar, exasperar, irritar, exacerbar.

acerbity [ə'sɜrbətɪ, B -'sɜbɪtɪ] *s.* 1. acerbidad, acritud, aspereza. 2. (fig.) aspereza.

acerose ['æsəˌroʊs] **acerous** [-rəs] *a.* (bot.) acerado, aciculado.

acescent [ə'sɛsənt] *a.* acescente; acídulo.

acetaldehyde [ˌæsə'tældəˌhaɪd] *s.* (quím.) acetaldehido.

acetamide [ə'sɛtəˌmaɪd] *s.* (quím.) acetamida.

acetanilide [ˌæsə'tænəlˌaɪd] **acetanilid** [-əd] *s.* (quím.) acetanilida.

acetate ['æsəˌteɪt] *s.* (quím.) acetato.

acetate of copper, (quím.) cardenillo, verdegrís.

acetic [ə'sitɪk] *a.* (quím.) acético; ácido acético.

acetification [əˌsɛtəfɪ'keɪʃən] *s.* (quím.) acetificación.

acetify [ə'sɛtəˌfaɪ] *v.t.* (quím.) acetificar.

acetimeter [ˌæsə'tɪmətər, B -ə] **acetometer** [-'tɑm-, B -'tɔm-] *s.* (quím.) acetímetro.

acetone ['æsəˌtoʊn] *s.* (quím.) acetona.

acetonuria [ˌæsəˌtoʊ'nurɪə, B -'njʊr-] *s.* (med.) acetonuria.

acetophenetidin [-fə'nɛtədən] *s.* (quím.) acetofenetidina.

acetose ['æsəˌtoʊs] **acetous** [ə'sɛtəs] *a.* (quím.) acetoso, acedo.

acetyl [ə'sitəl, 'æsət-, B 'æsɪt-] *s.* (quím.) acetilo.

acetylene [ə'sɛtəlɪn] *s.* acetileno.

acetylene torch, *s.* soplete oxiacetilénico.

Achaean [ə'kiən] *a., s.* aqueo, natural de Acaya (antigua Grecia).

Achates [ə'keɪtiz] *s.* (mitol.) Acates, compañero de Eneas; (fig.) acates, amigo fiel.

ache [eɪk] *v.i.* 1. doler, ej., *my feet a.,* me duelen los pies. 2. tener ansia, ansiar, ej., *he ached to see her,* él tenía ansias de verla. —*s.* 1. dolor persistente; desconsuelo, aflicción. 2. (bot.) apio silvestre.

achene [ə'kin] *s.* (bot.) aquenio.

achenial [ə'kinɪəl] *a.* (bot.) aquénico.

Acheron ['ækəˌrɑn, B -ˌrɔn] *s.* (mitol.) Aquerón, Aqueronte, río de los infiernos.

achievable [ə'tʃivəbəl] *a.* factible, hacedero, ejecutable.

achieve [ə'tʃiv] *v.t.* 1. llevar a cabo, ejecutar, realizar. 2. alcanzar, lograr, obtener. —*v.i.* alcanzar éxito.

achievement [-mənt] *s.* 1. ejecución, realización. 2. obra, realización. 3. logro, proeza, hazaña.

achievement test, prueba o test vocacional (Am.).

Achilles [ə'kɪliz] *s.* (mitol.) Aquiles, héroe de *La Ilíada.*

Achilles' heel, (fig.) talón de Aquiles.

Achilles' tendon, (anat.) aquiles, tendón aquíleo.

aching ['eɪkɪŋ] *a.* doliente; afligido.

achlamydeous [ˌæklə'mɪdɪəs] *a.* (bot.) aclámide.

achlorhydria [ˌeɪˌklɔr'haɪdrɪə, B -ˌklɔ'-] *s.* (med.) aclorhidria.

achondrite [-'kɑnˌdraɪt, B -'kɔn-] *s.* (geol.) acondrito.

achondroplasia [-ˌkɑndrə'pleɪʒə, B -ˌkɔn-zɪə] *s.* (med.) acondroplasia, acondroplastia

achromatic [ˌækrə'mætɪk] *a.* 1. (ópt.) acromático (que refleja la luz sin descomponerla en sus colores constituyentes). 2. (bot.) acromático, incoloro. 3. (mús.) diatónico, sin accidentes de modulación.

achromatic lens, (fís.) lente acromático.

achromatin [eɪ'kroʊmətən, B ə-] *s.* (biol.) acromatina.

achromatism [-ˌtɪzəm] *s.* 1. (ópt., bot.) acromatismo. 2. (mús.) sistema diatónico.

achromatize [-ˌtaɪz] *v.t.* (ópt.) acromatizar.

achromatous [-təs] *a.* (med.) acrómico.

achromic [eɪ'kroʊmɪk, B ə-] **achromous** [-əs] *a.* acrómico, incoloro.

acicula [ə'sɪkjələ] *s.* (*pl.* ACICULAE [-ˌli]) (bot.) acícula; (anat.) acículo.

acicular [-lər, B -lə] *a.* (bot.) acicular, aciforme.

acid ['æsəd] *a.* ácido, acedo. —*s.* 1. ácido. 2. (jer.) LSD, droga alucinante.

acidanthera [ˌæsə'dænθərə] *s.* (bot.) acidanter.

acid cell, (elec.) acumulador ácido de plomo.

acid-fast ['æsəd'fæst, B -'fɑst] *a.* (bact.) a prueba de ácidos (bacteria, etc.).

acid head, el que toma LSD con exceso.

acidic [ə'sɪdɪk] *a.* ácido; (quím.) acidógeno.

acidification [əˌsɪdəfə'keɪʃən] *s.* (quím.) acidificación.

acidifier [ə'sɪdəˌfaɪər, B -ˌfaɪə] *s.* (quím.) (substancia) acidificante.

acidify [-ˌfaɪ] *v.t.* (*pret., p.p.* ACIDIFIED; *p.pr.* ACIDIFYING) 1. acidificar, acedar, agriar. 2. (quím.) acidificar.

acidimeter [ˌæsə'dɪmətər, B -ə] *s.* (fís.) acidímetro.

acidity [ə'sɪdətɪ] *s.* acidez, acedía.

acidly ['æsədlɪ] *adv.* (fig.) ácidamente, ásperamente.
acidophile [ə'sɪdəˌfaɪl] **acidophil** [-ˌfɪl] *s.* substancia, tejido, u organismos acidófilos.
acidophilus milk, lactobacilina.
acidosis [ˌæsə'doʊsəs] *s.* (med.) acidosis.
acid-proof ['æsədˌpruf] *a.* a prueba de ácidos.
acid rain *s.* lluvia ácida.
acid-resistant [-rɪ'zɪstənt] *a.* antiácido, resistente al ácido.
acid salt, sal ácida, oxisal.
acid test, (fig.) prueba decisiva, prueba de fuego.
acidulate [ə'sɪdʒəˌleɪt, B -djʊ-] *v.t.* acidular, avinagrar.
acidulent [-lənt] **acidulous** [-ləs] *a.* 1. acídulo. 2. (fig.) avinagrado, agriado.
acierate ['æsɪəˌreɪt] *v.t.* acerar, convertir en acero (el hierro).
aciform ['æsəˌfɔrm, B -ˌfɔm] *a.* aciforme, con forma de aguja.
aciniform [ə'sɪnəˌfɔrm, B -ˌfɔm] *a.* (bot.) aciniforme.
acinose ['æsənoʊs] **acinous** [-əs] *a.* (bot.) acinoso.
acinus ['æsənəs] *s.* (*pl.* ACINI [-ˌnaɪ]) (anat., bot.) ácino.
ack-ack ['ækˌæk] *s.* cañon o fuego antiaéreo; artillería antiaérea.
acknowledge [ɪk'nɑlɪdʒ, æk- B -'nɔl-] *v.t.* 1. reconocer, aceptar, admitir, confesar. 2. acusar (recibo), confirmar; agradecer. 3. (der.) certificar, testificar.
acknowledged [-ɪdʒd] *a.* generalmente reconocido o aceptado.
acknowledgment, acknowledgement [-ɪdʒmənt] *s.* 1. reconocimiento. 2. admisión, aceptación. 3. confirmación; acuse (de recibo). 4. agradecimiento. 5. (der.) certificación.
aclastic [ə'klæstɪk] *a.* (ópt.) aclástico.
acle ['æklɪ] *s.* (bot.) acle.
aclinic [ˌeɪ'klɪnɪk, B ə-] *a.* (fís.) aclínico.
aclinic line, (fís.) línea aclínica.
acme ['ækmɪ] *s.* colmo, cima, cumbre; apogeo; **a. thread,** (méc.) rosca de 29.
acne ['æknɪ] *s.* (med.) acné.
acock [ə'kak, B ə'kɔk] *adv.* ladeado, puesto al sesgo (sombrero, etc.).
acology [ə'kɑlədʒɪ, B ə'kɔl-] *s.* (med.) acología.
acolyte ['ækəˌlaɪt] *s.* 1. acólito, monaguillo. 2. (fig.) acólito, satélite, acompañante.
aconite ['ækəˌnaɪt] **aconitum** [ˌækə'naɪtəm] *s.* 1. (bot.) acónito, napelo, anapelo, pardal. 2. (farm.) aconitina.
acorn ['eɪˌkɔrn, B -ˌkɔn] *s.* (bot.) bellota.
acorn barnacle, (zool.) bellota de mar, percebe.
acorn tube, (rad.) válvula bellota.
acotyledon [eɪˌkɑtə'lɪdən, B æˌkɔt-] *s.* (bot.) acotiledón, acotiledónea.
acotyledonous [-əs] *a.* (bot.) acotiledóneo.
acoustic [ə'kustɪk] **acoustical** [-stɪkəl] *a.* acústico.
acoustical tile, ladrillo antisonoro.
acoustic compliance, (rad.) capacitancia acústica.
acoustic current meter, (hidr.) molinete acústico.
acoustic feedback, (rad.) realimentación, retroalimentación o regeneración acústica.
acoustician [ˌæˌku'stɪʃən, B ə-] *s.* experto en acústica.
acoustics [ə'kustɪks] *s. pl.* 1. (fís.) acústica. 2. (t. **acoustic**) propiedades acústicas (de una sala o recinto).
acoustic treatment, tratamiento antisonoro, medidas acústicas.

acquaint [ə'kweɪnt] *v.t.* (con *of* o *with*) informar, familiarizar (con), enterar (de); **a. oneself with,** ponerse al corriente de; **to be acquainted,** conocerse (uno a otro); **to be acquainted with,** conocer, estar al corriente de.
acquaintance [-əns] *s.* 1. (con *with*) conocimiento (de). 2. conocido, conocimiento (persona). 3. relaciones, trato. 4. **to make someone's a.,** trabar conocimiento con alguien, ser presentado a alguien.
acquaintanceship [-ˌʃɪp] *s.* relaciones, trato.
acquest [ə'kwɛst] *s.* (der.) adquisición, cosa adquirida.
acquiesce [ˌækwɪ'ɛs] *v.i.* asentir, consentir; aceptar, acceder (a), conformarse (con).
acquiescence [-əns] *s.* asentimiento, consentimiento, asenso, conformidad, aquiescencia; resignación.
acquiescent [-ənt] *a.* acomodadizo, consentidor, condescendiente.
acquirable [ə'kwaɪrəbəl] *a.* obtenible, asequible.
acquire [ə'kwaɪr, B -'kwaɪə] *v.t.* adquirir, conseguir, obtener.
acquired immune-deficiency syndrome (AIDS) síndromé de inmunidad deficiente adquirida (SIDA).
acquired trick, (bridge) baza ganada.
acquirement [-mənt] *s.* 1. adquisición. 2. (*ú. pr. en pl.*) conocimientos, habilidades.
acquisition [ˌækwə'zɪʃən] *s.* 1. adquisición. 2. (astronáut.) procedimiento de ubicación de un satélite, proyectil o cápsula espacial.
acquisitive [ə'kwɪzətɪv] *a.* codicioso, ávido.
acquisitiveness [-nəs] *s.* codicia, avidez.
acquit [ə'kwɪt] *v.t.* (*pret., p.p.* ACQUITTED; *p.pr.* ACQUITTING) 1. absolver, exculpar, exonerar. 2. **a. oneself,** desempeñarse (bien o mal); (con *of*) desempeñar (sudeber, obligación, cometido, etc.).
acquittal [-əl] *s.* absolución, descargo.
acquittance [-əns] *s.* pago; recibo, finiquito.
acratia [ə'kreɪʃə] *s.* (med.) acracia.
acre ['eɪkər, B -kə] *s.* 1. acre (medida de superficie). 2. (*pl.*) finca, terrenos; **God's a.** camposanto.
acreage [-kərɪdʒ] *s.* superficie *f* medida en acres.
acrid ['ækrəd] *a.* 1. acre, áspero, picante, corrosivo. 2. (fig.) acre, mordaz.
acridity [æ'krɪdətɪ, ə-] **acridness** ['ækrədnəs] *s.* acritud, acrimonia.
acriflavine [ˌækrə'fleɪˌvin] *s.* (farm.) acriflavina.
acrimonious [-'moʊnɪəs] *a.* acre, áspero, cáustico, mordaz, acrimonioso.
acrimony ['ækrəˌmoʊnɪ] *s.* acrimonia, acritud, aspereza (de genio).
acrobat ['ækrəˌbæt] *s.* acróbata, volatinero, saltimbanqui.
acrobatic [ˌækrə'bætɪk] *a.* acrobático.
acrobatics [-ɪks] *s. pl.* acrobacia.
acrobystitis [ˌækroʊbɪs'taɪtəs] *s.* (med.) acrobistitis.
acrocarpous [-'kɑrpəs, B 'kɑpəs] *a.* (bot.) acrocarpo, acrocarpal, acrocarpio.
acrodont ['ækrəˌdɑnt, B -ˌdɔnt] *a.* (zool.) acrodonte, acrodonto. —*s.* (zool.) acrodonte.
acrodrome [-ˌdroʊm] *a.* (bot.) acródromo.
acrogenous [ə'krɑdʒənəs, B ə'krɔdʒ-] **acrogenic** [ˌækrə'dʒɛnɪk] *a.* (bot.) acrógeno.
acrolein [ə'kroʊlɪən] *s.* (quím.) acroleína.
acromegaly [ˌækroʊ'mɛgəlɪ] *s.* (med.) acromegalia.
acrometer ['ækroʊˌmitər, B -ə] *s.* (med.) oleómetro, acrómetro.

acromial [ə'kroʊmɪəl] *a.* (anat.) acromial, acromiano.
acromion [-ən] *s.* (anat.) acromio.
acronical, acronycal [ə'krɑnəkəl, B ə'krɔn-] *a.* (astr.) acrónico.
acronym ['ækrəˌnɪm] *s.* sigla (palabra formada con las letras o sílabas iniciales de un nombre compuesto).
acropetal [ə'krɑpətəl, B ə'krɔp-] *a.* (bot.) acropétalo.
acrophobia [ˌækrə'foʊbɪə] *s.* acrofobia, vértigo de las alturas.
acropolis [ə'krɑpələs, B ə'krɔp-] *s.* acrópolis, ciudadela (esp. la de Atenas).
acrospire ['ækrəˌspaɪr, B -ˌspaɪə] *s.* (bot.) acrospiro.
acrospore [-ˌspɔr, B -ˌspɔ] *s.* (biol.) acróspora.
across [ə'krɔs] *adv.* 1. a través; al otro lado, allende; al través, transversalmente; horizontalmente. 2. (elec.) en paralelo. 3. **to come a.,** cruzar la calle; llegar, ser recibido (ej., mensaje radiofónico); **to get a.,** (fam.) explicar, hacer entender o aceptar; **to go a.,** ir al otro lado; **to put a.,** hacer entender. —*prep.* a través de, al través de, por; al otro lado de; **a. the street** (o **way**), enfrente; **to come a.,** encontrarse (accidentalmente) con; tropezar con; **to go a.,** atravesar, cruzar.
across-the-board [-ðə'bɔrd, B -'bɔd] *a.* 1. que comprende toda clase de categorías, general. 2. de apuesta combinada (en carreras de caballo, jai-alai, etc.).
acrostic [ə'krɔstɪk] *s., a.* acróstico.
acrostolium [ˌækrə'stoʊlɪəm] *s.* (*pl.* ACROSTOLIA [-lɪə]) (mar.) acrostolio.
acroterium [-'tɪrɪəm] *s.* (*pl.* ACROTERIA [-ɪə]) (arq.) acrotera, acroteria.
acrotism ['ækrəˌtɪzəm] *s.* (med.) acrotismo.
acrylate ['ækrəˌleɪt] *s.* (quím.) acrilicato.
acrylic [ə'krɪlɪk] *a.* (quím.) acrílico.
acrylic acid, (quím.) ácido acrílico.
acrylic fiber, (tej.) fibra acrílica.
act [ækt] *s.* 1. hecho, acción, acto. 2. acta, protocolo, minuta. 3. (teat.) acto. 4. número (de circo o variedades). 5. (der.) ley, decreto. 6. **to be in the a. of (doing),** disponerse a (hacer); estar ocupado con (hacer); **to catch in the a.,** coger con las manos en la masa; **to pass an a.,** aprobar una ley; **to put on an a.,** fingir, simular. —*v.i.* 1. actuar, obrar, ej., *a. with foresight,* obrar con previsión. 2. actuar, desempeñarse (en el teatro). 3. fingir, aparentar. 4. actuar, portarse, conducirse. 5. funcionar, servir (para algo). 6. surtir efecto. 7. **a. as,** actuar como, actuar en lugar de; **a. for,** representar a; **a. on,** guiarse por; **a. on** o **a. upon,** actuar sobre (ej., una solución química); influir, obrar sobre; **a. openly,** actuar a cara descubierta; **a. out,** representar (escena, papel), expresar (impulsos reprimidos o inconscientes) en conducta sin inhibiciones (esp. durante investigación psicoanalítica); **a. up,** portarse mal; alardear; **a. up to,** portarse de acuerdo a, obrar en conformidad con. —*v.t.* 1. hacer, desempeñar, ejecutar (un papel). 2. (teat.) representar, hacer el papel de. 3. comportarse apropiadamente, ej., *act your age!* ¡pórtate de acuerdo a tu edad! ¡no seas chiquilín! (Am.).
actin ['æktən] *s.* (fisiol.) actina.
acting ['æktɪŋ] *s.* (teat.) actuación, interpretación; **to go into acting,** ser actor. —*a.* en funciones, en ejercicio; interino, suplente; de servicio.
acting mayor, alcalde interino.
actinia [æk'tɪnɪə] *s.* (zool.) actinia.
actinic [æk'tɪnɪk] *a.* (fís., quím.) actínico.
actinic ray, (fís., quím.) rayo actínico.

actinide series ['æktə,naɪd-] (quím.) actínidos.
actiniform [æk'tɪnə,fɔrm, B -,fɔm] *a.* (zool.) actinimorfo, actiniforme.
actinium [æk'tɪnɪəm] *s.* actinio (elemento).
actinoelectricity [,æktɪnoʊ,lɛk'trɪsətɪ] *s.* (fotgmt.) actinoelectricidad.
actinograph [æk'tɪnə,græf, B -,grɑf] *s.* (ópt., foto.) actinógrafo, actinómetro.
actinoid ['æktə,nɔɪd] *a.* actinoide, radiado, dispuesto en forma de rayos.
actinolite [æk'tɪnəl,aɪt] *s.* (min.) actinota, actinolita (anfíbol).
actinometer [,æktə'nɑmətər, B -'nɔmɪtə] *s.* (fís., meteor.) actinómetro.
actinometry [-trɪ] *s.* (fís., meteor.) actinometría.
actinomorphic [,æktənoʊ'mɔrfɪk, B -'mɔfɪk] **actinomorphous** [-fəs] *a.* (biol.) actinomorfo, radiado.
actinomorphy ['æktənoʊ,mɔr,fi, B -,mɔ,-] *s.* (biol.) actinomorfia, actinomorfismo.
actinomyces [,æktənoʊ'maɪ,siz] *s. pl.* (*sing.* ACTINOMYCES) (bact.) actinomices.
actinomycete [-,sit] *s.* (bact.) actinomiceto.
actinomycin [-'maɪsən] *s.* (med.) actinomicina.
actinomycosis [-,mɪ'koʊsəs] *s.* (vet.) actinomicosis.
actinon ['æktə,nɑn, B -,nɔn] *s.* (quím.) actinón.
actinotherapy [,æktənoʊ'θɛrəpɪ] *s.* (med.) actinoterapia.
actinozoans [-,noʊ'zoʊən] *s. pl.* (zool.) actinozoos.
action ['ækʃən] *s.* 1. acción. 2. actividad, movimiento, operación. 3. acto, hecho, obra. 4. influencia, efecto. 5. (*pl.*) actos, conducta. 6. acción de guerra, batalla. 7. (teat.) acción, trama, argumento. 8. (der.) demanda, proceso, litigio. 9. (mec.) mecanismo; golpe. 10. **to bring an a.,** entablar juicio; **to bring into a.,** poner en movimiento; **to put out of a.,** inutilizar; **to take a.,** tomar medidas.
actionable [-əbəl] *a.* (der.) procesable, justiciable.
action-packed, lleno de acción.
action painting, (arte) escuela de pintura no figurativa caracterizada por técnicas de improvisación para lograr un efecto de espontaneidad total.
action stations, (mil.) puestos de combate.
activate ['æktə,veɪt] *v.t.* activar; ionizar, radioactivar; (quím.) activar.
activated carbon [-əd-] (quím.) carbón activado.
activation [,æktə'veɪʃən] *s.* (fís., quím.) activación.
active ['æktɪv] *a.* 1. activo, en movimiento. 2. vigente (ley). 3. enérgico. 4. (gram.) activa (voz del verbo). 5. (póker) en juego (para ganar la apuesta). 6. (com.) productivo, que devenga interés. 7. (mil.) en servicio activo.
active current, (elec.) corriente activa o vatada.
active power, (elec.) potencia activa o efectiva.
active service, (mil.) servicio activo.
active verb, (gram.) verbo activo, verbo transitivo.
activism ['æktɪ,vɪzəm] *s.* (pol.) activismo.
activist [-vəst] *a., s.* activista.
activity [æk'tɪvətɪ] *s.* actividad, diligencia; (*pl.*) actividades, ocupaciones.
act of faith, acto de fe.
act of God, hecho de fuerza mayor; obra de Dios.
act of grace, act of mercy, obra de misericordia o clemencia.
act of treason, (der.) traición.
act of war, acto bélico, acto de guerra.
actomyosin [,æktə'maɪəsən] *s.* (biol.) actomiosina.
acton ['æktən] *s.* (arm.) gambax, gambosina.
actor ['æktər, B -tə] *s.* 1. (teat.) actor, cómico. 2. participante, integrante. 3. (der.) demandante.
actress [-trəs] *s.* actriz.
actual ['æktʃʊəl] *a.* 1. actual, presente. 2. real, efectivo, verdadero.
actuality [,æktʃʊ'ælətɪ] *s.* 1. realidad. 2. (*pl.*) condiciones.
actualization [,æktʃʊələ'zeɪʃən] *s.* actualización, realización.
actualize ['æktʃʊə,laɪz] *v.t.* realizar; describir vívidamente.
actually [-lɪ] *adv.* en efecto, en realidad; efectivamente.
actuary ['æktʃʊ,ɛrɪ, B -tjʊərɪ] *s.* (fin.) actuario de seguros (experto en el cálculo de primas, anualidades, etc.).
actuate ['æktʃʊ,eɪt, B -tjʊ-] *v.t.* 1. activar, impulsar, estimular. 2. poner en acción, hacer funcionar, accionar (una máquina, mecanismo, etc.).
actuator [-ər, B -ə] *s.* (mec.) actuador, actuante.
acuity [ə'kjuətɪ] *s.* acuidad, agudeza.
aculeate [ə'kjulɪət] *a.* (zool.) acúleo, aculado; (bot.) aculeolado.
aculeus [ə'kjulɪəs] *s.* (zool.) acúleo, aguijón; (bot.) aculéolo, espina.
acumen [ə'kjumən] *s.* cacumen, perspicacia, agudeza.
acupuncture [,ækjʊ'pʌŋktʃər, B -tʃə] *s.* (med.) acupuntura.
acute [ə'kjut] *a.* 1. agudo. 2. (med.) agudo (enfermedad). 3. (mús.) agudo (sonido, nota). 4. (geom.) agudo (díc. de un ángulo menor de 90); acutángulo (díc. de un triángulo formado por ángulos agudos). 5. (gram.) agudo (acento, sílaba, etc.). 6. agudo, sutil, sagaz. 7. sensible, impresionable. 8. crítico, grave. 9. agudo, severo (dolor).
acute accent, (gram.) acento agudo.
acute angle, (geom.) ángulo agudo.
acutely [-lɪ] *adv.* agudamente.
acyclic [eɪ'saɪklɪk, B æ'sɪ-] *a.* (elec.) unipolar, acíclico.
acyl ['æsəl] *s.* (quím.) acilo.
ad [æd] *s.* (fam.) anuncio.
A.D. *abrev. de* **Anno Domini, in the year of our Lord,** Año de Cristo (A.C.), Era Cristiana.
adage ['ædɪdʒ] *s.* adagio, refrán, proverbio.
adagio [ə'dɑdʒoʊ, B -ɪoʊ] *adv.* (mús.) lentamente, en forma suave y grácil. *—s.* 1. (mús.) adagio, aire lento. 2. parte lenta de un *pas de deux* en ballet.
Adam ['ædəm] *s.* 1. Adán. 2. **not know (someone) from A.,** no conocer en absoluto (a alguien). 3. **the old A.** la inclinación al pecado.
Adam-and-Eve [,ædəmən'iv] *s.* (bot.) variedad de orquídeas.
adamant ['ædəmənt, -,mɑnt, B -mənt] *a.* obstinado, inflexible, inquebrantable; duro, diamantino.
adamantine [,ædə'mæn,tin, B -,taɪn] *a.* (min.) diamantino; inquebrantable, irrompible.
Adam's ale, A.'s wine['ædəmz-] (fam.) agua.
Adam's apple, nuez de la garganta, nuez de Adán.
Adam's-needle [-'nidəl] *s.* (bot.) yuca, mandioca.
adapt [ə'dæpt] *v.t.* 1. adaptar, acomodar, ajustar. 2. (teat.) adaptar, refundir. 3. **a. oneself (to o for),** adaptarse (a o para).
adaptability [ə,dæptə'bɪlətɪ] *s.* adaptabilidad, flexibilidad.
adaptable [ə'dæptəbəl] *a.* adaptable, acomodable, ajustable.
adaptation [,ædæp'teɪʃən] *s.* 1. adaptación. 2. (biol., fisiol., antrop.) adaptación. 3. (teat., cinem.) adaptación, refundición.
adapter [ə'dæptər, B -tə] *s.* 1. adaptador. 2. (quím.) alargadera.
adaxial [æ'dæksɪəl] *a.* (bot.) adaxial.
ADC *abrev. de* **aide-de-camp,** edecán, ayudante de campo.
add [æd] *v.t.* 1. añadir, agregar, juntar, sumar. 2. **a. in,** incluir; **a. insult to injury,** añadir ofensa al daño; **a. up,** sumar. *—v.i.* 1. juntarse, sumarse. **2. a. to,** aumentar, incrementar; agravar; **a. up,** (fam.) tener sentido; **it adds up to,** asciende a, (todo esto) resulta en; (todo esto) quiere decir.
adda ['ædə] *s.* (zool.) escinco.
addax ['æd,æks] *s.* (zool.) adax, antílope africano.
addend ['æd,ɛnd, ə'dɛnd] *s.* (mat.) sumando.
addendum [ə'dɛndəm] *s.* (*pl.* ADDENDA [-də]) adición, apéndice, suplemento (a un libro, etc.); (mec.) cabeza.
adder ['ædər, B -ə] *s.* víbora; serpiente, culebra.
adder's-tongue ['ædərz,tʌŋ, B 'ædəz-] (bot.) lengua de sierpe.
addible ['ædəbəl] *a.* que se puede agregar o sumar, añadible.
addict [ə'dɪkt] *v.t.* 1. dedicar, entregar, acostumbrar (a una práctica, vicio, etc.). 2. enviciar. 3. **a. oneself to,** entregarse a, enviciarse en o con. *—s.* ['ædɪkt] adicto, partidario; enviciado.
addicted [-əd] *a.* enviciado, adicto; **to be a.** to, estar enviciado con; abandonarse a, darse a; ser aficionado a, tener interés apasionado por.
addiction [ə'dɪkʃən] *s.* 1. enviciamiento. 2. afición.
adding machine, máquina sumadora.
Addis Ababa ['ædəs'æbəbə, -'ɑb-] *s.* Addis Abeba, capital de Etiopía.
Addison's disease['ædəsənz-] (med.) enfermedad de Addison.
additament [ə'dɪtəmənt] *s.* aditamento, añadidura.
addition [ə'dɪʃən] *s.* 1. adición, añadidura. 2. suma. 3. **in a.,** por añadidura, además; **in a. to,** además de, a más de.
additional [-əl] *a.* adicional.
additionally [-əlɪ] *adv.* adicionalmente, por añadidura.
additive ['ædətɪv] *a.* aditivo. *—s.* aditivo.
addle ['ædəl] *a.* 1. huero, podrido. 2. vano, vacío; confuso, tonto. *—v.t., v.i.* enhuerar(se), podrir(se); volver(se) chocho.
addlebrained [-,breɪnd] **addleheaded** [-,hɛdəd] *a.* confuso, tonto, chocho.
address [ə'drɛs] *v.t.* 1. dirigir. 2. dirigirse a. 3. dirigir la palabra a. 4. poner las señas a, dirigir (una carta, etc.). 5. (com.) consignar. 6. (golf) aprestarse para golpear (la pelota). 7. **a. oneself to,** dirigirse a (persona o personas); emprender (una tarea). *—* [ə'drɛs, 'æd,rɛs, B ə-] *s.* 1. señas, dirección (en cartas, etc.). 2. discurso, alocución. 3. destreza, habilidad. 4. trato, porte. 5. tono, gracia. 6. (*pl.*) atenciones, galanteos. 7. (golf) postura (del jugador para golpear la pelota). 8. **ease of a.,** soltura, desenvoltura (en hablar, cantar, etc.); **to deliver an a.,** pronunciar un discurso; **to pay one's addresses to,** galantear, cortejar.
addressee [,æd,rɛs'i, ə,drɛs-, B ,æd-] *s.* destinatario; (com.) consignatario.
addresser [ə'drɛsər, B -ə] *s.* remitente; exponente.
addressor, *var. de* **addresser.**
adduce [ə'dus, B ə'djus] *v.t.* aducir, alegar; citar.
adducent [-ənt] *a.* (anat.) aductor.
adduct [ə'dʌkt] *v.t.* (anat.) acercar (un miembro u órgano) al eje del cuerpo.

adduction [ə'dʌkʃən] *s.* 1. alegato. 2. (anat.) aducción.
adductor [-tər, B -tə] *s.* (anat.) aductor, músculo aductor.
adenectomy [ˌædən'ɛktəmɪ] *s.* (med.) adenectomía.
adenine [ædənˌin] *s.* (bioquím.) adenina.
adenitis [ˌædə'naɪtəs] *s.* (med.) adenitis.
adenocarcinoma [ˌædənˌoʊˌkɑrsən'oʊmə, B -ˌkɑs-] *s.* (med.) adenocarcinoma.
adenoid ['ædənˌɔɪd] *a.* (anat.) adenoideo. —*s.* (*pl.*) vegetaciones (adenoideas).
adenoidal [ˌædən'ɔɪdəl] *a.* (anat.) adenoideo.
adenology [-'ɑlədʒɪ, B -'ɔl-] *s.* (med.) adenologia.
adenoma [-'oʊmə] *s.* (*pl.* ADENOMATA [-mətə] o ADENOMAS) (med.) adenoma.
adenopathy [-'ɑpəθɪ, B -'ɔp-] *s.* (med.) adenopatía.
adenose ['ædənˌoʊs] *a.* adenoso, glandular.
adenosine [ə'dɛnəˌsin] *s.* (bioquím.) adenosina.
Adephaga [ə'dɛfəgə] *s. pl.* (ento.) adéfagos.
adephagia [ˌædə'feɪdʒɪə] *s.* (med.) adefagia.
adept [ə'dɛpt] *a.* experto, versado (en). ['ædˌɛpt] *s.* experto, perito; adepto.
adequacy ['ædɪkwəsɪ] *s.* suficiencia.
adequate [-kwət] *a.* adecuado, suficiente; idóneo.
adequately [-lɪ] *adv.* adecuadamente.
adermin [eɪ'dɜrmən, B -'dɜm-] *s.* adermina, piridoxina, vitamina B.
adf *abrev. de* **automatic direction finder,** radiocompás automático.
adhere [æd'hɪr, əd-, B -'hɪə] *v.i.* adherirse, unirse, pegarse.
adherence [-əns, B -rəns] *s.* adherencia (de cosas); adhesión, apego, fidelidad (a ideas, personas, etc.).
adherent [-ənt, B -rənt] *a.* 1. adhesivo, pegajoso. 2. adherente; partidario (de). —*s.* adherente, partidario, seguidor.
adhesion [-'hiʒən] *s.* adhesión, adherencia; (med., fis.) adherencia.
adhesive [-'hisɪv, -'hiz-] *a.* adhesivo, adherente, pegadizo. —*s.* sustancia adhesiva.
adhesive tape, cinta adhesiva, tafetán adhesivo; (med.) esparadrapo.
adhibit [æd'hɪbət] *v.t.* dejar entrar, admitir; aplicar, administrar; unir, agregar.
ad hoc [æd'hɑk, B -'hɔk] *adj.* ad hoc, a propósito para el caso. —*adv.* según van surgiendo.
adiabatic [ˌædɪə'bætɪk] *a.* (fís.) adiabático.
adiaphoresis [ˌædɪˌæfə'risəs] *s.* (med.) adiaforesis.
adiathermancy [ˌædɪə'θɜrmənsɪ, B -'θɜmən-] *s.* (fís.) adiatermancia.
adieu [ə'du, B ə'dju] *interj.* adiós. —*s.* (*pl.* ADIEUS, ADIEUX) adiós, despedida; **to bid a.,** decir adiós; **to take one's a.,** despedirse.
ad infinitum [ˌædˌɪnfə'naɪtəm] sin fin, sin límite.
ad interim [æd'ɪntərəm] entre tanto, mientras tanto.
adipose ['ædəˌpoʊs] *a.* adiposo, grasiento.
adipose tissue, (anat.) tejido adiposo.
adiposity [ˌædə'pɑsətɪ, B -'pɔs-] *s.* adiposidad, obesidad.
adit ['ædət] *s.* bajada, acceso, entrada inclinada (a una mina), bocamina.
adiz. *abrev. de* **air defense identification zone,** zona de identificación para fines de defensa antiaérea.
adj. *abrev. de* **adjective,** adjetivo (adj.).
adjacency [ə'dʒeɪsənsɪ] *s.* adyacencia, contigüidad, proximidad, vecindad.
adjacent [-ənt] *a.* adyacente, contiguo.
adjectival [ˌædʒɪk'taɪval] *a.* (gram.) adjetival.
adjective ['ædʒɪktɪv] *s.* (gram.) adjetivo. —*a.* 1. (gram.) adjetivo, adjetival. 2. dependiente, secundario.
adjoin [ə'dʒɔɪn] *v.t.* 1. juntar, unir, asociar, agregar (cosa), añadir (observación, etc.). 2. estar contiguo a, lindar con. —*v.i.* colindar.
adjoining [-ɪŋ] *a.* colindante, contiguo, adyacente.
adjourn [ə'dʒɜrn, B ə'dʒɜn] *v.t.* suspender, levantar, aplazar, clausurar o diferir (una sesión, juicio, etc.); trasladar (una sesión). —*v.i.* 1. levantar y aplazar la sesión, terminarse la sesión. 2. trasladarse, pasar (esp. de un cuarto a otro).
adjournment [-mənt] *s.* 1. suspensión, aplazamiento, clausura. 2. traslación.
adjudge [ə'dʒʌdʒ] *v.t.* 1. fallar, juzgar, decidir (jurídicamente). 2. decretar. 3. adjudicar.
adjudicate [ə'dʒudɪˌkeɪt] *v.t.* fallar, juzgar; declarar. —*v.i.* ejercer las funciones de juez.
adjudication [əˌdʒudɪ'keɪʃən] *s.* fallo, sentencia.
adjunct ['ædʒˌʌŋkt] *s.* 1. adjunto, aditamento, accesorio. 2. adjunto, ayudante. 3. (gram.) adjunto, atributo. —*a.* adjunto, contiguo; auxiliar, subordinado.
adjunction [æ'dʒʌŋkʃən] *s.* adición, añadidura.
adjuration [ˌædʒə'reɪʃən] *s.* 1. juramento solemne. 2. conjuro, ruego.
adjure [ə'dʒʊr, B ə'dʒʊə] *v.t.* 1. ordenar o mandar bajo juramento solemne. 2. conjurar, implorar, suplicar.
adjust [ə'dʒʌst] *v.t.* 1. ajustar, arreglar, componer. 2. ajustar, adaptar, amoldar. 3. ajustar, corregir. 4. conciliar. 5. liquidar, ajustar (reclamaciones).
adjustable [-əbəl] *a.* ajustable, adaptable; **a. resistor,** (rad.) resistencia graduable, resistor ajustable.
adjuster [-ər, B -ə] *s.* ajustador; (mec.) regulador; (seguros) liquidador, ajustador (de reclamaciones).
adjusting [-ɪŋ] *s.* (mec.) ajustaje, regulación; (rad.) corrección.
adjustment [-mənt] *s.* ajuste, acomodamiento, arreglo; corrección, aliño; liquidación, ajuste.
adjutancy ['ædʒətənsɪ] *s.* (mil.) ayudantía.
adjutant [-tənt] *s.* (mil.) ayudante, asistente.
adjutant bird, (orn.) marabú, grulla de la India.
adjutant general, (*pl.* ADJUTANTS GENERAL) ayudante general.
adjuvant [-vənt] *s., a.* ayudante, adyuvante, auxiliar, adjutor.
Adlerian [æd'lɪrɪən] *a.* (psic.) adleriano, relativo a la teoría de Adler.
ad lib, ad-lib [ˌæd'lɪb] *s.* (fam.) improvisación de un actor, locutor u orador. —*v.i., v.t.* (*pret. p.p.* AD-LIBBED; *p.pr.* ADLIBBING) (jer.) meter morcilla, improvisar.
Adm. *abrev. de* **Admiral,** Almirante.
adman ['ædˌmæn] *s.* (fam.) publicitario, publicista; creador de anuncios.
admeasure [æd'mɛʒər, B -ʒə] *v.t.* repartir, prorratear.
admeasurement [-mənt] *s.* repartición, prorrateo.
admin. *abrev. de* **administration, administrator;** administración, administrador.
adminicle [æd'mɪnəkəl] *s.* 1. adminículo, ayuda, auxilio. 2. (der.) prueba corroborativa.
administer [əd'mɪnəstər, B -stə] *v.t.* 1. administrar, manejar. 2. administrar (sacramento, remedio); suministrar. 3. formular (preguntas, etc.). 4. **a. an oath (to),** tomar juramento (a). —*v.i.* 1. administrar, actuar como administrador. 2. a. to, atender a, remediar (necesidades), ayudar, cuidar de (una persona); contribuir a.
administrable [-strəbəl] *a.* administrable, manejable.
administrant [-strənt] *a., s.* administrador.
administrate [-ˌstreɪt] *v.t. var. de* administer.
administration [-ˌmɪnə'streɪʃən] *s.* 1. administración, manejo. 2. dirección, administración, gobierno; **the A.,** (E.U.) el Gobierno (de la nación). 3. administración (de sacramentos o medicamentos); toma (de juramento).
administrative [-'mɪnəˌstreɪtɪv, -strət-] *a.* administrativo.
administrator [-ˌstreɪtər, B -tə] *s.* 1. administrador; gobernante. 2. (der.) albacea, administrador, tenedor de bienes.
admirable ['ædmərəbəl] *a.* admirable.
admirably [-əblɪ] *adv.* admirablemente.
admiral ['ædmərəl] *s.* 1. almirante. 2. (ento.) nínfalo (mariposa).
admiral of the fleet, almirante supremo.
admiralship [-ˌʃɪp] *s.* almirantazgo, dignidad de almirante.
admiralty [-tɪ] *s.* almirantazgo; Ministerio de Marina.
admiration [ˌædmə'reɪʃən] *s.* admiración.
admire [əd'maɪr, B -'maɪə] *v.t.* 1. admirar. 2. (fam.) expresar admiración por.
admirer [-ər, B -rə] *s.* 1. admirador. 2. cortejador, enamorado. 3. aficionado (al arte, música, etc.).
admiring [-ɪŋ] *a.* admirador, admirativo.
admissibility [ədˌmɪsə'bɪlətɪ] *s.* admisibilidad.
admissible [-ˌmɪsəbəl] *a.* admisible, aceptable, permitido.
admission [-'mɪʃən] *s.* 1. admisión, recepción. 2. acceso, entrada; precio de entrada. 3. admisión, reconocimiento. 4. concesión. 5. (eng.) admisión, aspiración. 6. **a. cam,** leva de admisión; **a. stroke,** carrera de admisión, tiempo de aspiración; **a. valve,** válvula de admisión o de aspiración o de toma.
admissive [-'mɪsɪv] *a.* concesivo, que implica admisión.
admit [əd'mɪt] *v.t.* (*pret., p.p.* ADMITTED; *p.pr.* ADMITTING) 1. admitir, dar entrada a (persona). 2. admitir, permitir. 3. admitir, reconocer, confesar, conceder. —*v.i.* 1. (con *to*) dar entrada (a un lugar). 2. (con *to*) reconocer, confesar (a). 3. (con *of*) dejar lugar o margen (a duda, mejora, etc.).
admittance [-əns] *s.* 1. admisión, acceso. entrada; **no a.,** se prohibe la entrada. 2. (elec.) admitancia.
admix [æd'mɪks] *v.t.* mezclar, agregar.
admixture [-tʃər, B -tʃə] *s.* 1. mezcla, mixtura. 2. (const.) agregado en polvo, aditivo; compuesto impermeabilizador. 3. (quím.) agregado coloidal. 4. (esp. fig.) añadido, ingrediente (agregado).
admonish [æd'mɑnɪʃ, B əd'mɔn-] *v.t.* 1. amonestar, reprender. 2. advertir, prevenir.
admonishment [-mənt] *s.* amonestación, admonición, advertencia, exhortación, parénesis.
admonition [ˌædmə'nɪʃən] *s.* admonición, amonestación, advertencia.
admonitor [æd'mɑnetər, B -'mɔnɪtə] *s.* admonitor.
admonitory [-ˌtɔrɪ, B -tərɪ] *a.* admonitivo, exhortativo.
adnate ['ædˌneɪt] *a.* (bot., zool.) adnato.
ad nauseam [æd'nɔzɪəm] hasta la saciedad, incansablemente.

adnexa [-'nɛksə] *s. pl.* (anat.) anexos, partes asociadas.
adnexal [-səl] *a.* anexo.
ado [ə'du] *s.* 1. alharaca, bulla. 2. trabajo, dificultad. 3. **much a. about nothing,** mucho ruido y pocas nueces; **with much a.,** con mucha dificultad, a duras penas; **without more a.,** sin más discusión.
adobe [ə'doʊbɪ] *s.* 1. adobe, (barro o arcilla de) ladrillo cocido al sol. 2. construcción o casa de adobe.
adolescence [ˌædəl'ɛsəns] *s.* adolescencia.
adolescent [-'ɛsənt] *s., a.* adolescente.
Adonai [ædə'naɪ] *s.* (heb.) Adonaí, título de reverencia dado a Dios.
Adonis [ə'dɑnəs, B ə'doʊn-] *s.* 1. (mitol.) Adonis. 2. (fig.) adonis, joven hermoso. 3. (bot.) adonis, ojo de perdiz. 4. (ento.) variedad de mariposa.
adopt [ə'dɑpt, B ə'dɔpt] *v.t.* 1. adoptar, prohijar. 2. adoptar, aceptar; asumir.
adoptable [-əbəl] *a.* adoptable.
adopter [-ər, B -ə] *s.* adoptador, adoptante.
adoption [ə'dɑpʃən, B ə'dɔp-] *s.* adopción; **I'm a New Yorker by a.,** New York es mi ciudad adoptiva.
adoptionism [-ˌɪzəm] *s.* (teo.) adopcionismo.
adoptive [ə'dɑptɪv, B ə'dɔp-] *a.* adoptivo.
adorable [ə'dɔrəbəl] *a.* adorable; (fam.) encantador.
adoration [ˌædə'reɪʃən] *s.* adoración; idolatría.
adore [ə'dɔr, B ə'dɔ] *v.t.* 1. adorar; glorificar; idolatrar. 2. encantarse, ej., *I adore apples* me encantan las manzanas.
adorer [-ər, B -rə] *s.* amante, enamorado ferviente.
adoringly [-ɪŋlɪ, B -rɪŋ-] *adv.* con adoración.
adorn [ə'dɔrn, B ə'dɔn] *v.t.* adornar, ornamentar, ataviar, engalanar, aderezar.
adornment [-mənt] *s.* adorno, ornamento, atavío, aderezo.
adrenal [ə'drinəl] *a., s.* (anat.) adrenal, suprarrenal.
adrenal gland, (anat.) glándula adrenal o suprarrenal.
adrenalin [ə'drɛnələn] *s.* (med.) adrenalina.
adrenergic [ˌædrə'nɜrdʒɪk, B -'nɜdʒ-] *a.* (med.) adrenérgico.
adrenocortical [əˌdrinoʊ'kɔrtɪkəl, B -'kɔt-] *a.* (med.) adrenocortical.
Adriatic [ˌeɪdrɪ'ætɪk] *a.* adriático. —*s.* Adriático, mar Adriático.
adrift [ə'drɪft] *adv., a.* 1. (mar.) al garete, a la deriva. 2. (fig.) abandonado, desorientado, a la ventura. 3. **to come a.,** desatarse; **to turn a.,** abandonar a la deriva.
adroit [ə'drɔɪt] *a.* 1. diestro, hábil. 2. listo, mañoso.
adroitly [-lɪ] *adv.* 1. diestramente, hábilmente. 2. mañosamente, astutamente.
adroitness [-nəs] *s.* 1. destreza, habilidad. 2. maña, astucia.
adscititious ['ædsə'tɪʃəs] *a.* adventicio; adicional, suplementario.
adscript ['ædˌskrɪpt] *a.* escrito después.
adsorb [æd'sɔrb -'zɔrb, B -'sɔb] *v.t.* adsorber.
adsorbent [-ənt] *a.* adsorbente.
adsorber [-ər, B -ə] *s.* adsorbedor.
adsorption [-'sɔrpʃən, -'zɔrp-, B -'sɔp-] *s.* adsorción.
adularia [ˌædʒə'lɛrɪə B ˌædjʊ-] *s.* (min.) adularia.
adulate ['ædʒəˌleɪt B 'ædjʊ-] *v.t.* adular, lisonjear.
adulation [ˌædʒə'leɪʃən, B ˌædjʊ-] *s.* adulación, lisonja.
adulator ['ædʒəˌleɪtər, B -tə] *s.* adulador.
adulatory [-ləˌtɔrɪ, B -ˌleɪtərɪ] *a.* adulador, lisonjero, halagador.
adult [ə'dʌlt, 'ædˌʌlt] *a.* adulto, maduro. —*s.* persona mayor; **adults only,** sólo para adultos.
adulterant [ə'dʌltərənt] *a.* adulterante, adulterador (sustancia). —*s.* sustancia adulterante.
adulterate [-ˌreɪt] *v.t.* adulterar, falsificar, viciar. —*a.* [ə'dʌltərət] adulterino, adulterado, viciado, falso, espurio.
adulteration [əˌdʌltə'reɪʃən] *s.* 1. adulteración, falsificación, corrupción. 2. producto adulterado.
adulterer [ə'dʌltərər, B -ə] *s.* adúltero.
adulteress [-tərəs] *s.* adúltera.
adulterine [-ˌraɪn, -ˌrin] *a.* adulterino, espurio.
adulterous [-rəs] *a.* adúltero.
adultery [-rɪ] *s.* adulterio.
adulthood [ə'dʌltˌhʊd] *s.* edad adulta.
adumbrate ['ædəmˌbreɪt, ə'dʌm-, B 'æd-] *v.t.* 1. (pint.) adumbrar, sombrear. 2. bosquejar, esquiciar. 3. (fig.) presagiar, dar indicios de. 4. (fig.) obscurecer, deslustrar.
adumbration [ˌædəm'breɪʃən] *s.* 1. (pint.) adumbración, sombreado. 2. trazo, esbozo, bosquejo, esquicio. 3. (fig.) indicio, presagio. 4. (fig.) obscurecimiento.
adunc [ə'dʌŋk] **aduncous** [-əs] *a.* adunco, corvo, encorvado.
adust [ə'dʌst] *s.* 1. requemado, tostado. 2. (fig.) adusto, melancólico, sombrío.
adv. *abrev. de* **adverb,** adverbio (adv.).
ad valorem [ˌædvə'lɔrəm] (com.) ad valórem, por avalúo, por evaluación.
advance [əd'væns, B -'vɑns] *v.t.* 1. adelantar, avanzar. 2. adelantar, acelerar, fomentar, mejorar. 3. promover, ascender (en rango, puesto, etc.). 4. anticipar, adelantar (dinero, paga, etc.). 5. adelantar (reloj, hora, fecha, etc.). 6. proponer (plan, ideas, etc.), exponer, ofrecer (opinión, teoría, etc.), formular (derecho, reclamo, etc.). 7. aumentar (precio, alquiler, etc.). —*v.i.* 1. adelantarse, avanzar, progresar; ir acercándose (a). 2. avanzar (esp. tropas). 3. elevarse, aumentarse. —*s.* 1. progreso, movimiento hacia adelante; avance (esp. de tropas). 2. progreso, adelanto, mejora. 3. anticipo, adelanto (de dinero, paga, etc.). 4. aumento, alza (de precios, etc.). 5. (*pl.*) propuestas, sugerencias, insinuaciones, tanteos; obsequios o requerimientos de amor. 6. **in a.,** por adelantado; de antemano; por anticipado, anticipadamente; **to make advances,** hacer requerimientos de amor. —*a.* adelantado, anticipado, previo.
advance copy, ejemplar que se envía antes de la aparición oficial de un libro.
advanced [-'vænst, B -'vɑnst] *a.* 1. avanzado, progresista (idea, estudios, etc.). 2. adelantado, desarrollado. 3. maduro (edad). 4. **a. in years,** entrado en años.
advanced standing, reconocimiento de estudios universitarios realizados en otra institución.
advanced studies, estudios superiores.
advance guard, (mil.) avanzada.
advancement [-mənt] *s.* 1. adelanto, progreso. 2. mejora, ascenso. 3. anticipo, adelanto.
advancer [-ər, B -ə] *s.* promotor, impulsor.
advance sheet, (impr.) capilla.
advantage [əd'væntɪdʒ, B -'vɑnt-] *s.* 1. ventaja, superioridad, delantera. 2. ventaja, provecho, beneficio, ganancia. 3. facilidad, comodidad, conveniencia. 4. (tenis) ventaja (después del empate en un juego). 5. **to a.,** ventajosamente, con provecho; **to gain (an) a. over,** sacar ventaja a; **to have the a. (of),** tener o llevar la ventaja (de); **to one's a.,** con ventaja o provecho propio; **to take a. (of),** aprovecharse, valerse (de); engañar, embaucar. —*v.t.* favorecer, beneficiar, ayudar.
advantaged [-tɪdʒd] *a.* privilegiado.
advantageous [ˌædˌvæn'teɪdʒəs, B -vən-] *a.* ventajoso, provechoso, beneficioso, conveniente.
advantageousness [-nəs] *s.* ventaja, provecho, beneficio.
advection [æd'vɛkʃən] *s.* (meteor.) advección.
Advent ['ædˌvɛnt, B -vənt] *s.* 1. (relig.) Adviento. 2. **a.,** advenimiento, llegada.
Adventism [-ˌɪzəm] *s.* (relig.) adventismo.
Adventist [-əst] *s., a.* (relig.) adventista.
adventitia [ˌædvən'tɪʃə] *s.* (anat.) adventicia.
adventitious [-'tɪʃəs] *a.* 1. adventicio, extraño. 2. (biol., bot.) adventicio, accidental.
adventive [æd'vɛntɪv] *a.* (biol., bot.) adventicio, accidental.
adventure [əd'vɛntʃər, B -tʃə] *s.* 1. aventura; lance. 2. suerte, fortuna, riesgo. —*v.i.* 1. arriesgarse, correr riesgos, osar. 2. atreverse, aventurarse. —*v.t.* aventurar, arriesgar.
adventurer [-ər, B -rə] *s.* aventurero.
adventuresome [-səm] *a.* aventurado; aventurero, audaz.
adventuress [-əs, B -rɪs] *s.* aventurera.
adventurism [-ˌɪzəm, B -ˌrɪz-] *s.* afán aventurero; improvisación o experimentación temeraria (esp. en política o asuntos exteriores o en desafío de normas establecidas).
adventurous [-əs, B -rəs] *a.* aventurado, arriesgado, audaz, temerario.
adventurously [-lɪ] *adv.* aventuradamente, arriesgadamente.
adverb ['ædˌvɜrb, B -ˌvɜb] *s.* (gram.) adverbio.
adverbial [æd'vɜrbɪəl, B -'vɜb-] *a.* (gram.) adverbial.
adversary ['ædvərˌsɛrɪ, B -vəˌ-] *s.* adversario, contrario, enemigo; **the A.,** el diablo, Satanás. —*a.* adverso, contrario, opuesto, enemigo.
adversative [əd'vɜrsətɪv, B -'vɜs-] *a.* (gram.) adversativo. —*s.* palabra o proposición adversativa.
adverse [æd'vɜrs, 'ædvɜrs, B -ˌvɜs] *a.* 1. adverso, opuesto. 2. adverso, contrario, desfavorable, antagónico.
adversely [-lɪ] *adv.* adversamente, desfavorablemente.
adverseness [-nəs] *s.* oposición, contrariedad, resistencia.
adversity [æd'vɜrsətɪ, B əd'vɜs-] *s.* adversidad, desgracia, calamidad, infortunio.
advert [æd'vɜrt, B -'vɜt] *v.i.* (ú. con *to*) 1. advertir, fijarse (en). 2. referirse, aludir (a).
advertence [-əns] **advertency** [-ənsɪ] *s.* advertencia, aviso; atención, cuidado.
advertent [-ənt] *a.* atento, cuidadoso.
advertise ['ædvərˌtaɪz, B -vəˌ-] *v.t.* 1. anunciar, publicar, divulgar, propagar. 2. informar, notificar, avisar, advertir. —*v.i.* poner un aviso, anunciar; **a. for,** buscar mediante anuncios (en periódicos).
advertisement [ˌædvər'taɪzmənt, əd'vɜrtəz-, B əd'vɜtɪs-] *s.* anuncio, aviso; publicidad, propaganda.
advertiser ['ædvərˌtaɪzər, B -vəˌtaɪzə] *s.* anunciante, anunciador.
advertising [-ɪŋ] *s.* propaganda, publicidad. —*a.* publicitario, de publicidad.
advertising agency, agencia de publicidad, agencia publicitaria.
advice [əd'vaɪs] *s.* 1. consejo. 2. (com.) aviso, noticia, informe; parecer. 3. opinión, parecer. 4. **letter of a.,** notificación (de una letra de cambio); **to give a.,** dar consejos; **to take a.,** seguir consejos.

advisability [-ˌvaɪzə'bɪlətɪ] *s.* conveniencia.
advisable [-'vaɪzəbəl] *a.* aconsejable, conveniente.
advise [əd'vaɪz] *v.t.* 1. aconsejar, dar consejo a, recomendar. 2. avisar, informar, notificar. 3. advertir. —*v.i.* dar consejo, orientar.
advised [-'vaɪzd] *a.* deliberado, premeditado; **to keep a.**, tener al corriente.
advisement [-'vaɪzmənt] *s.* 1. deliberación; consideración, reflexión; **to take something under a.** considerar algo. 2. consejo, orientación.
adviser, advisor [-ər, B -ə] *s.* consejero, asesor, consultor; **financial a.**, asesor financiero.
advisory [-ərɪ] *a.* 1. consultor, consultivo, asesor, ej., *a. board,* cuerpo consultivo, junta consultiva; **in an a. capacity,** en calidad de asesor. 2. avisador, notificativo (señal, etc.).
advocacy ['ædvəkəsɪ] *s.* (con *of*) defensa, amparo, apoyo, promoción (de una causa, etc.).
advocate [-kət, -ˌkeɪt] *s.* 1. abogado, letrado. 2. (fig.) abogado, defensor. —*v.t.* [-ˌkeɪt] abogar por, defender, amparar, apoyar.
advowson [əd'vaʊzən] *s.* (relig.) patronato, derecho de colación.
advt. *abrev. de* **advertisement,** anuncio.
adynamia [ˌædə'neɪmɪə] *s.* (med.) adinamia.
adynamic [ˌeɪˌdaɪ'næmɪk, B ˌædaɪ-] *a.* (med.) adinámico, débil.
adytum ['ædətəm] *s.* (*pl.* ADYTA [-tə]) ádito.
adz, adze [ædz] *s.* azuela. —*v.t.* azolar, desbastar con la azuela.
AEC *abrev. de* **Atomic Energy Commission,** Comisión de Energía Atómica (C E A).
aëdes [eɪ'idiz] *s. pl.* (ento.) (mosquitos) aedes.
aedile ['iˌdaɪl] *s.* edil (oficial romano).
aedileship [-ʃɪp] *s.* edilidad.
Aegean [ɪ'dʒiən] *s.* 1. mar Egeo. 2. Islas del Egeo. —*a.* egeo.
aegis ['idʒəs] *s.* 1. (mitol.) égida. 2. (fig.) égida, escudo, protección.
Aegisthus [ɪ'dʒɪsθəs] *s.* (mitol.) Egisto, primo de Agamenón.
Aeneas [ɪ'niəs, B 'iniæs] *s.* (mitol.) Eneas, héroe troyano.
Aeneid [ɪ'niəd, B 'inɪɪd] *s.* Eneida, poema épico de Virgilio.
Aeneolithic [eɪˌinɪoʊ'lɪθɪk] *a.* (pal.) eneolítico.
Aeolian [i'oʊlɪən] *a., s.* 1. eolio, natural de Eólida (colonia de la Grecia antigua). 2. eólico (dialecto). 3. (geog., geol.) eólico.
aeolian harp, arpa eolia o eólica.
Aeolic [i'ɑlɪk, B i'ɔl-] *a.* 1. eolio, natural de Eólida. 2. eólico. —*s.* eólico (dialecto).
aeolipile [i'ɑləˌpaɪl, B i'ɔlɪ-] *s.* eolípida.
Aeolis ['iələs] *s.* la Eólida, antigua región de Asia Menor.
Aeolus ['iələs] *s.* 1. (mitol.) Eolo, dios de los vientos. 2. Eolo, rey de Tesalia.
aeon, eon ['iˌən, 'iɑn, B 'iən] *s.* (geol.) eón, evo.
aeonian [i'oʊnɪən] *a.* (geol.) inconmensurable, perpetuo (tiempo).
aequoreal [i'kwɔrɪəl] *a.* (raro, poét.) ecuóreo, perteneciente al mar.
aerate ['ɛrˌeɪt, B 'ɛər-] *v.t.* 1. airear, ventilar, orear. 2. oxigenar (la sangre); gasear (un líquido.)
aerated [-əd] *a.* 1. (med.) aireado. 2. gaseoso.
aeration [ˌɛr'eɪʃən, B ˌɛər-] *s.* 1. ventilación, aireación, oreo. 2. (med.) aeración (de la sangre o de un líquido).
aerator ['ɛrˌeɪtər, B 'ɛərˌeɪtə] *s.* sifón; aeróforo; aparato fumigador.
aerial ['ɛrɪəl, B 'ɛər-] *a.* 1. aéreo, de aire. 2. elevado. 3. (fig.) etéreo, sutil, vaporoso. 4. atmosférico. 5. (bot.) aéreo, aerófito. —*s.* (elec.) antena.
aerial cableway, cablecarril, cablevía, vía de cable, andarivel.
aerialist [-əst] *s.* volatinero, equilibrista que trabaja en la cuerda floja.
aerial ladder, escalera plegable y extensible (equipo de bomberos).
aerial mapping, aerofotogrametría.
aerial photography, aerofotografía.
aerie [ɛrɪ, B 'ɛərɪ] *s.* 1. aguilera; nido de águilas y de aves de rapiña. 2. nidada de aguiluchos; (fig.) morada en la cumbre, refugio en la cima.
aeriferous [ɛ'rɪfərəs] *a.* aerífero.
aerification [ˌɛrəfə'keɪʃən, B ˌɛər-] *s.* 1. aerificación. 2. aireación.
aeriform ['ɛrəˌfɔrm, B 'ɛərɪˌfɔm] *a.* aeriforme; gaseoso.
aerify [-ˌfaɪ] *v.t.* (*pret,. p.p.* AERIFIED; *p.pr.* AERIFYING) 1. (fís., quím.) aerificar. 2. airear, ventilar.
aerily [-lɪ] *adv.* de manera aérea o etérea.
aeroballistics [ˌɛroʊbə'lɪstɪks, B ˌɛər-] *s. pl.* (*sing. o pl. en const.*) aerobalística.
aerobatics [-'bætɪks] *s.* acrobacia, acrobacia aérea; maniobras de exhibición de aviones en vuelo.
aerobe [ɛrˌoʊb, B 'ɛər-] *s.* (biol.) aerobio.
aerobic [ˌɛ'roʊbɪk, B ˌɛə-] *a.* (biol.) aeróbico.
aerobiology [ˌɛroʊbaɪ'ɑlədʒɪ, B ˌɛər-oʊ-'ɔl-] *s.* aerobiología.
aerobiosis [-'oʊsəs] *s.* (biol.) aerobiosis.
aerocartography ['ɛrəkɑr'tɑgrəfɪ, B -ˌɛərəkɑ'tɔg-] *s.* cartografía aérea.
aerodrome ['ɛrəˌdroʊm, B 'ɛərə-] *s.* (G.B.) aeródromo, aeropuerto.
aerodynamic [ˌɛroʊdaɪ'næmɪk, B ˌɛəroʊ-] *a.* aerodinámico.
aerodynamics [-ɪks] *s. pl.* (*sing. en const.*) aerodinámica.
aerodyne ['ɛrəˌdaɪn, B 'ɛə-] *s.* (aer.) aerodino, vehículo aéreo más pesado que el aire.
aeroembolism [ˌɛroʊ'ɛmbəˌlɪzəm, B ˌɛəroʊ-] *s.* (med.) aeroembolismo.
aerogenic [-dʒɛnɪk] *a.* aerógeno.
aerogram, aerogramme ['ɛrəˌgræm, B 'ɛərə-] *s.* 1. aerograma; radiograma. 2. carta aérea.
aerographer [ˌɛ'rɑgrəfər, B ɛə'rɔg-fə] *s.* meteorologista naval.
aerography [-fɪ] *s.* aerografía.
aerolite ['ɛrəˌlaɪt, B 'ɛərə-] **aerolith** [-ˌlɪθ] *s.* (astr.) aerolito, meteorito.
aerolitic [ˌɛrə'lɪtɪk, B ˌɛərə-] *a.* aerolítico.
aerological [-'lɑdʒɪkel, B -'lɔdʒ-] *a.* aerológico.
aerology [ɛ'rɑlədʒɪ, B ɛə'rɔl-] *s.* 1. aerología. 2. meteorología.
aeromancy ['æroʊˌmænsɪ, B 'ɛəroʊ-] *s.* aeromancia, adivinación supersticiosa por las señales e impresiones del aire.
aeromantic [ˌɛrə'mæntɪk, B ˌɛərə-] *a., s.* aeromántico.
aeromarine [ˌɛroʊmə'rin, B ˌɛərə-] *a.* aeromarítimo.
aeromechanic [-mɪ'kænɪk] *s.* mecánico de aviación.
aeromechanics [-ɪks] *s. pl.* (*sing. en const.*) aeromecánica.
aeromedicine [-'mɛdəsən] *s.* (biol.) aeromedicina.
aerometer [ɛ'rɑmətɛr, B ɛə'rɔmɪtə] *s.* aerómetro.
aerometry [-trɪ] *s.* aerometría.
aeromotor ['ɛrəˌmoʊtər, B 'ɛər-tə] *s.* aeromotor.
aeronaut [-'nɔt] *s.* aeronauta.
aeronautic [ˌɛrə'nɔtɪk, B ˌɛərə-] **aeronautical** [-ɪkəl] *a.* aeronáutico.
aeronautics [-ɪks] *s. pl.* (*sing. en const.*) aeronáutica.
aeroneurosis [-oʊnʊ'roʊsəs, B -njʊ-] *s.* (med.) aeroneurosis.
aeropause ['ɛroʊˌpɔz, B 'ɛəroʊ-] *s.* (meteor.) nivel en que la atmósfera se torna enrarecida.
aerophobia [ˌɛrə'foʊbɪə, B ˌɛərə-] *s.* (med.) aerofobia.
aerophobic [-bɪk] *a.* aerófobo.
aerophone ['ɛrəˌfoʊn, B 'ɛərə-] *s.* aerófono.
aerophore [-, fɔr, B -ˌfɔ] *s.* (geol.) aerófora.
aerophotogrammetry [ˌɛrəˌfoʊtə'græmətrɪ, B ˌɛərə-] *s.* aerofotogrametría.
aerophotography [ˌɛroʊfə'tɑgrəfɪ, B ɛər-'tɔg-] *s.* fotografía aérea, aerofotografía.
aeroplane ['ɛrəˌpleɪn, B 'ɛərə-] *s.* aeroplano, avión.
aeroscope [-ˌskoʊp] *s.* aeroscopio.
aerosol [-ˌsɑl, B -ˌsɔl] *s.* (quím.) aerosol.
aerosol bomb, bomba de aerosol, envase cuyo contenido es descargado en forma de rocío.
aerosolize [-ˌaɪz] *v.t.* dispersar (partículas sólidas o líquidas) en un gas.
aerospace [-oʊˌspeɪs] *s.* el espacio. —*a.* aeroespacial.
aerosphere [-ˌsfɪr, B -ˌsfɪə] *s.* aerosfera.
aerostat [-ˌstæt] *s.* aeróstato, globo aerostático, globo dirigible.
aerostatic [ˌɛroʊ'stætɪk, B ˌɛərə-] *a.* aerostático.
aerostatics [-ɪks] *s. pl.* (*sing. en const.*) aerostática.
aerostation [-'steɪʃən] *s.* aerostación.
aerosurveying [-'sɛrˌveɪɪŋ, B 'sɛˌ-] *s.* aerofotogrametría, fotogrametría aérea.
aerotherapeutics [-ˌθɛrə'pjutɪks] **aerotherapy** [-'θɛrəpɪ] *s.* (med.) aeroterapia.
aerothermodynamics [-ˌθɜrmədaɪ'næmɪks, B -ˌθɜmə-] *s. pl.* (*sing. en const.*) (fís.) aerotermodinámica.
aerugo [ɪ'rugoʊ] *s.* cardenillo, moho (del cobre).
aery ['ɛrɪ, 'eɪrɪ, B 'ɛərɪ] *a.* aéreo, etéreo.
Aeschylean [ˌɛskə'liən, B ˌis-] *a.* (característico) de Esquilo.
Aeschylus ['ɛskələs, B 'is-] *s.* Esquilo, poeta griego.
Aesculapian [ˌɛskjə'leɪpɪən, B ˌis-] *a.* de Esculapio; médico, medicinal.
Aesculapius [-ɪəs] *s.* (mitol.) Esculapio, dios romano de la medicina.
Aesop ['iˌsɑp, -səp, B -ˌsɔp] *s.* Esopo, fabulista griego.
Aesopian [i'soʊpɪən] **Aesopic** [i'sɑpɪk, B i'sɔp-] *a.* esópico, relativo a o característico de Esopo.
aesthesia [ɛs'θiʒə] *s.* estesia, sensibilidad.
aesthete ['ɛsˌθit, B 'is-] *s.* esteta.
aesthetic [ɛs'θɛtɪk, B is-] *a.* estético.
aesthetics [-'θɛtɪks] *s. pl.* (*sing. en const.*) estética.
aestival ['ɛstəvəl, B is'taɪvel] *a.* estival, estivo.
aestivate ['ɛstəˌveɪt, B 'istɪ-] *v.i.* (zool.) veranear, pasar el estío en estado de letargo.
aestivation [ˌɛstə'veɪʃən, B ˌistɪ-] *s.* 1. (zool.) veraneo. 2. (bot.) estivación, prefloración.
Aetna ['ɛtnə] *s.* Etna, volcán en Italia. **A.F.** *abrev. de* 1. **air force,** fuerza aérea. 2. **audio-frequency,** audiofrecuencia.
afar [ə'fɑr, B ə'fɑ] *adv.* lejos, distante; **from a.,** de lejos, desde lejos.
AFC *abrev. de* **automatic frequency control,** control de frecuencia automática.
affability [ˌæfə'bɪlətɪ] *s.* afabilidad, amabilidad.

affable ['æfəbəl] *a.* afable, amable, cortés, atento.
affair [ə'fɛr, B ə'fɛə] *s.* 1. asunto, negocio, ej., *that is my a.,* ése es asunto mío. 2. lance, acontecimiento, ej., *a. of honor,* lance de honor, *a social a.,* un acontecimiento social. 3. aventura (amorosa). 4. (*pl.*) negocios. 5. caso, ej., *the Hamilton a.,* el caso Hamilton. 6. (fam.) cosa, ej., *his car is a gorgeous a.,* su carro es una cosa magnífica. 7. amorío, relaciones amorosas. 8. **state of affairs,** situación, estado de cosas.
affair of state, cuestión de gabinete, asunto de estado.
affect ['æˌfɛkt] *s.* (psic.) sentimiento, emoción, anhelo (como factores determinantes del pensamiento y la conducta).
affect [ə'fɛkt] *v.t.* 1. gustar de, lucir (artículos de vestir). 2. afectar, fingir, aparentar, presumir. 3. asumir.
affect, *v.t.* 1. afectar, atacar (un órgano, parte del cuerpo, etc.). 2. afectar, producir alteración; influir en, impresionar; conmover.
affectation [ˌæfˌɛk'teɪʃən] *s.* afectación; **to be completely without a.,** ser nada afectado.
affected [ə'fɛktəd] *a.* 1. afectado, amanerado. 2. afectado, fingido. 3. (t. con *towards*) afecto, inclinado (a algo). 4. (con *with*) afectado (por), aquejado (de). 5. conmovido, emocionado.
affectedly [-lɪ] *adv.* afectadamente, con afectación.
affecting [-tɪŋ] *a.* conmovedor, emocionante, patético.
affectingly [-lɪ] *adv.* patéticamente, en forma conmovedora.
affection [ə'fɛkʃən] *s.* 1. afecto, cariño, querencia. 2. afección, afición, inclinación. 3. afección, impresión, afecto. 4. afección, dolencia, enfermedad.
affectionate [-ət] *a.* afectuoso, cariñoso; **to be a. toward someone,** ser cariñoso con alguien; **your a. daughter, Mary,** (*at the end of a letter*) tu hija que te quiere, María.
affective [ə'fɛktɪv] *a.* afectivo, emocional.
afferent ['æfərənt] *a.* (biol.) aferente, que trae.
affiance [ə'faɪəns] *s.* palabra o compromiso matrimonial. —*v.t.* prometer en matrimonio.
affiant [-ənt] *s.* (der.) deponente, declarante.
affidavit [ˌæfə'deɪvət] *s.* (der.) declaración jurada (escrita), atestiguamiento o atestiguación (escritas), afidávit.
affiliate [ə'fɪlɪˌeɪt] *v.t.* 1. afiliar, asociar. 2. (der.) imputar la paternidad de un hijo ilegítimo. —*v.i.* asociarse, afiliarse, unirse. —*s.* socio, asociado, compañía afiliada.
affiliation [əˌfɪlɪ'eɪʃən] *s.* afiliación, asociación, unión.
affine [ə'faɪn] *a.* (mat., geom.) afine, afín.
affined [ə'faɪnd] *a.* afín, conexo, relacionado.
affinity [ə'fɪnətɪ] *s.* 1. afinidad; analogía, semejanza. 2. atracción. 3. (biol., quím.) afinidad.
affirm [ə'fɛrm, B ə'fɛm] *v.t.* 1. afirmar, asegurar, aseverar, sostener. 2. confirmar, ratificar. —*v.i.* declarar formalmente, dar testimomonio, testificar.
affirmable [-əbəl] *a.* que se puede afirmar.
affirmance [-əns] *s.* afirmación; ratificación, confirmación.
affirmant [-ənt] *s.* afirmador, afirmante; (der.) declarante.
affirmation [ˌæfər'məɪʃən, B ˌæfə'-] *s.* 1. afirmación, aserto, aserción. 2. (der.) declaración solemne (no jurada).
affirmative [ə'fɜrmətɪv, B ə'fɜmə-] *a.* afirmativo. —*s.* aserción; afirmativa; **in the a.,** afirmativamente.
affirmative action, discriminación positiva, acción afirmativa (*determinada a favorecer a las minorías*).
affirmer [-mər, B -mə] *s.* afirmante, el que afirma.
affix [ə'fɪks] *v.t.* 1. adherir (sello), pegar. 2. añadir, agregar (firma, posdata). 3. aplicar, fijar (multa, etc.), atribuir (culpa). — ['æfˌɪks] *s.* 1. (gram.) afijo. 2. añadidura.
afflatus [ə'fleɪtəs] *s.* aflato, inspiración (divina o poética).
afflict [ə'flɪkt] *v.t.* afligir, acongojar; **to be afflicted with,** sufrir de, padecer de, estar aquejado de.
affliction [ə'flɪkʃən] *s.* 1. aflicción, dolor moral, pena; calamidad. 2. achaque, mal, enfermedad.
afflictive [ə'flɪktɪv] *a.* aflictivo, penoso; gravoso, molesto.
affluence ['æfˌluəns] *s.* 1. afluencia, aflujo. 2. abundancia, opulencia, riqueza.
affluent [-ənt] *s.* afluente, tributario (de un río). —*a.* 1. afluente, abundante, copioso. 2. opulento, rico.
afflux ['æfˌlʌks] *s.* 1. afluencia, aflujo, flujo. 2. (med.) fluxión, acumulación de humores.
afford [ə'fɔrd, B ə'fɔd] *v.t.* 1. dar, proporcionar, suplir, proveer de. 2. permitirse, darse el lujo de, tener medios (o recursos) para; afrontar, ej., *I cannot a. such expenses,* no puedo afrontar semejantes gastos.
afforest [æ'fɔrəst, -'fɑr-, B -'fɔr-] *v.t.* poblar de árboles.
afforestation [æˌfɔrə'steɪʃən, -ˌfɑr-, B -ˌfɔr-] *s.* repoblación forestal, forestación.
affranchise [æ'frænˌtʃaɪz, ə-] *v.t.* manumitir.
affray [ə'freɪ] *s.* refriega, riña, pendencia.
affreightment [ə'freɪtmənt] *s.* fletamiento (de un buque).
affricate ['æfrɪkət] *s.* (fon.) africada.
affrication [ˌæfrə'keɪʃən] *s.* (fon.) africación.
affront [ə'frʌnt] *v.t.* 1. afrentar, insultar, ultrajar. 2. confrontar, arrostrar. —*s.* afrenta, insulto, ultraje, agravio.
affusion [æ'fjuʒən, ə-] *s.* 1. infusión (en el bautismo). 2. (med.) afusión.
Afghan ['æfˌgæn, -gən] *a.* afgano, del Afganistán. —*s.* 1. afgano, natural o idioma del Afganistán. 2. a., manta o cubrecama de estambre; alfombra de estambre.
Afghanistan [æf'gænəˌstæn] *s.* Afganistán.
aficionado [əˌfɪsiə'nɑdoʊ, əˌfisiə-] *s.* aficionado.
afield [ə'fild] *adv.* 1. en o por el campo. 2. al campo. 3. fuera, afuera. 4. fuera de camino, fuera de la ruta (acostumbrada); (fig.) fuera del tema o argumento. 5. **far a.,** afuera, lejos, a distancia.
afire [ə'faɪr, B ə'faɪə] *a.* ardiendo, incendiado.
aflame [ə'fleim] *a.* en llamas; (fig.) inflamado.
AFL-CIO *abrev. de* **American Federation of Labor and Congress of Industrial Organizations,** Federación Norteamericana de Trabajo y Congreso de Organizaciones Industriales.
afloat [ə'floʊt] *adv.* 1. a flote, flotando. 2. a bordo. 3. (fig.) a flote, solvente, sin deudas, sin dificultades. 4. en circulación, corriente. 5. sin rumbo. 6. inundado, con agua (cubierta de un barco). 7. **to be a.,** estar a flote; correr, circular, ej., *a rumor is a.,* corre o circula un rumor.
aflutter [ə'flʌtər, B -tə] *a.* 1. revoloteando. 2. nervioso, agitado, excitado.
afoot [ə'fʊt] *adv.* 1. a pie. 2. levantado (después de enfermedad). 3. preparándose, en preparación; en vías de realizarse.
afore [ə'fɔr, B ə'fɔ] *prep.* 1. (mar.) delante de. 2. (ant.) antes de. —*adv.* antes, anticipadamente.
aforegoing [-ˌgoʊɪŋ] *a.* (ant.) precedente.
aforehand [-ˌhænd] *adv.* (pr. dial.) de antemano, con preparación.
aforementioned [-ˌmɛntʃənd, B -ˌmɛnʃənd] *a.* susodicho, sobredicho, referido.
aforesaid [-ˌsɛd] *a.* antedicho.
aforethought [-ˌθɔt] *a.* premeditado; **with malice a.,** con premeditación. —*s.* premeditación, deliberación.
aforetime [-ˌtaɪm] *adv.* (ant.) en otro tiempo, en tiempo pasado, antiguamente.
a fortiori [ˌɑˌfɔrtɪ'ɔrɪ, B 'eɪˌfɔtɪ'ɔraɪ] con más razón, con mayor apremio.
afoul [ə'faʊl] *adv., a.* en colisión, enredado; **to run a. of,** enredarse con.
afraid [ə'freɪd] *a.* asustado, intimidado, atemorizado; **I am a. (that),** (fam.) me temo (que); **to be a.,** estar asustado; **to be a. of,** tener miedo de (o a).
afreet ['æfˌrit, ə'frit] *s.* demonio, espíritu maligno (en la mitología árabe).
afresh [ə'frɛʃ] *adv.* de nuevo, otra vez, nuevamente.
Africa ['æfrɪkə] *s.* África.
African [-kən] *a.* africano. —*s.* africano.
African-American, *a.* afroamericano. —*s.* afroamericano (*negro norteamericano*).
Africander, *var. de* **Afrikander.**
Africanist [-kənəst] *s.* africanista.
African rue, (bot.) alargama, alármega, alhámega, alharma.
Afrikaans [ˌæfrɪ'kɑns, -'kɑnz, B -'kɑns] *s.* afrikaans (dialecto holandés hablado en Sudáfrica).
Afrikander [-'kændər, B -də] *s.* afrikaner, sudafricano blanco (esp. de ascendencia holandesa).
Afrikaner [-'kɑnər, B -nə] *var. de.* **afrikander.**
afro ['æfroʊ] *a.* (jer., E.U.) perteneciente al atuendo y la cultura del negro americano contemporáneo que se identifica con lo africano.
Afro-American [ˌæfroʊə'mɛrəkən] *a.* afroamericano. —*s.* afroamericano (*negro norteame ricano*).
Afro-Cuban [-'kjubən] *a.* afrocubano (estilo en música y literatura).
aft [æft, B ɑft] *adv.* (mar.) a popa, en popa; **fore and aft,** de proa a popa.
after ['æftər, B 'ɑftə] *prep.* 1. detrás de (algo o alguien); después de, al cabo de (cierto tiempo); tras. 2. según, de acuerdo a, conforme a, con arreglo a, a la manera de. 3. por. 4. **a. all,** después de todo, a pesar de todo; **a. a few days,** unos días más tarde, pasados algunos días; **a. an hour,** al cabo de una hora; **a. much trouble,** tras mucha dificultad; **(a picture) a. Rubens,** (un cuadro) a la manera de Rubens; **a. you,** ¡pase Ud.! ¡Ud. primero!; **a. one's own heart,** al gusto de uno; **day a. day,** día tras día; **day a. tomorrow,** pasado mañana; **named a.,** llamado como; llamado en honor a, ej., *named a. his father,* llamado como su padre, *named America a. Americo Vespucci,* llamada América en honor a Américo Vespucio; **one a. the other,** uno tras otro; **to be a.,** estar en busca de, interesarse por; perseguir; **to take a.,** asemejarse a, parecerse a. —*adv.* después; atrás; **before and a.,** antes y después; **look before and a.,** mire adelante y atrás; **soon** o **shortly a.,** poco después. —*a.* 1. siguiente, próximo, subsiguiente. 2. (mar.) de popa. 3. **the day a.,** el día siguiente. —*conj.* después (de) que.
afterbay [-ˌbeɪ] *s.* (hidr.) cámara de salida.
afterbirth [-ˌbɜrθ, B -ˌbɜθ] *s.* (med.) secundinas, placenta.

afterbrain [-ˌbreɪn] *s.* cerebro posterior.
afterburner [-ˌbɜrnər, B -ˌbɜnə] *s.* (aer.) quemador auxiliar, dispositivo de postcombustión.
afterburning [-nɪŋ] *s.* combustión retardada.
aftercare [-ˌkɛr, B -ˌkɛə] *s.* (med.) terapia de la convalecencia, asistencia postoperatoria.
afterclap [-ˌklæp] *s.* revés sorpresivo, percance inesperado (que resulta de un asunto considerado ya como terminado).
aftercrop [-ˌkrɑp, B -ˌkrɔp] *s.* segunda cosecha.
afterdamp [-ˌdæmp] *s.* (min.) mofeta.
afterdeck [-ˌdɛk] *s.* (mar.) cubierta de popa.
after-dinner [-'dɪnər, B -'dɪnə] *a.* de sobremesa.
aftereffect ['æftərəˌfɛkt] *s.* 1. efecto posterior o subsiguiente. 2. (med.) efecto secundario (que aparece después de aplacado el primer efecto).
afterglow [-ˌgloʊ] *s.* resplandor crepuscular.
aftergrass [-ˌgræs, B -ˌgrɑs] *s.* segunda hierba, segunda cosecha de heno.
after-hours ['æftər'aʊrz, B 'ɑftər'aʊəz] *a.* fuera de hora, a deshora, tarde.
afterimage [-ˌɪmɪdʒ] *s.* (psic.) imagen consecutiva, imagen accidental.
afterlife ['æftərˌlaɪf, B 'ɑftəˌ-] *s.* 1. vida futura, después de la muerte. 2. parte subsiguiente de la vida.
aftermath [-ˌmæθ] *s.* 1. segunda siega. 2. (fig.) secuela, resultados, consecuencias, ej., *the a. of war,* las consecuencias desastrosas de la guerra.
aftermost [-ˌmoʊst] *a.* (mar.) inmediato a la popa, popel; posterior, trasero.
afternoon [ˌæftər'nun, B ˌɑftə'-] *s.* (primeras horas de la) tarde; **at five o' clock in the a.,** a las cinco de la tarde; **every Sunday a.,** todos los domingos por lo tarde; **good afternoon!,** ¡buenas tardes!, ¡buenas! (fam.); **to take the afternoon off** tomar la tarde libre. —*a.* de la tarde.
afternoon nap, siesta.
afternoon tea, (G.B.) té *m.* de las cinco (*merienda*).
afterpains ['æftərˌpeɪnʒ, B 'ɑftəˌ-] *s. pl.* (med.) entuertos, dolores posteriores al parto.
afterpiece [-ˌpis] *s.* (teat.) sainete, entremés.
after-shave lotion, loción para después de afeitarse *or* del afeitado.
aftertaste [-ˌteɪst] *s.* dejo, gustillo, resabio.
afterthought [-ˌθɔt] *s.* idea tardía o posterior, ocurrencia nueva.
aftertime [-ˌtaɪm] *s.* tiempo venidero, porvenir, futuro.
afterward [-wərd, B -wed] **afterwards** [-wərdz, B -wədz] *adv.* después, en seguida, más tarde, en lo venidero; **long a.,** mucho tiempo después.
afterworld [-ˌwɜrld, B -ˌwɜld] *s.* (fig.) el otro mundo; el más allá.
AG *abrev. de* 1. **Attorney General,** Procurador (o Fiscal) General. 2. **Adjutant General,** Ayudante General.
again [ə'gɛn, ə'geɪn] *adv.* 1. otra vez, de nuevo, nuevamente, más. 2. además, por otra parte, luego. 3. **a. and a., time and a.,** una y otra vez, repetidas veces; **as much a.,** otro tanto más; **never a.,** nunca más; **now and a.,** de vez en cuando.
against [ə'gɛnst, ə'geɪnst] *prep.* 1. contra; en contra de. 2. frente a, enfrente de; junto a, contiguo a. 3. para, para el caso de. 4. en contraste con, comparado con. 5. por, ej., *the rate of exchange was 100 pesos a. one dollar,* el tipo de cambio fue 100 pesos por un dólar. 6. **a. his coming,** (en preparación) para su llegada, para cuando llegue; **a. the grain,** (lit. y fig.) a contrapelo; (**to work, run, talk**) **a. time,** (trabajar) apremiado por el tiempo; (correr) contra reloj; (hablar) para pasar el tiempo; **as a.,** comparado con, en contraste con; **to have (something, nothing) a. it,** tener (algo) en contra; no tener (nada) en contra; **to run (up) a.,** tropezar con.
agalloch [ə'gæləka] *s.* (bot.) agáloco, palo de áloe.
agama ['ægəmə] *s.* (zool.) especie de lagarto europeo de colores variables.
Agamemnon [ˌægə'mɛmˌnɑn, B -nən] *s.* (mitol.) Agamenón, rey de Micenas.
agamete [ˌeɪgə'mit, eɪ'gæmˌɪt] *s.* (biol.) agameto.
agamic [eɪ'gæmɪk] *a.* (biol.) agámico, asexual; (bot.) ágamo.
agamogenesis [ˌeɪˌgæmə'dʒɛnəsəs ˌægəmoʊ-] *s.* (biol.) agamogénesis.
agamospermy [-'spɜrmɪ, B -'spɜmɪ] *s.* (biol.) agamospermia.
agamous ['ægəməs] *a.* (bot.) ágamo, criptógamo.
Aganippe [ˌægə'nɪpɪ] *s.* (mitol.) Aganipe, ninfa de la fuente consagrada a las musas.
agapanthus [ˌægə'pænθəs] *s.* (bot.) agapanto, estrella de mar.
agape [ə'geɪp] *adv.* boquiabierto.
agape [ɑ'gɑˌpeɪ, 'ɑgə-, B 'ægəpi] *s.* 1. ágape, fiesta de caridad (de los primeros cristianos). 2. amor desinteresado, amor fraternal, amor espiritual.
agar-agar [ˌɑgˌɑr'ɑgˌɑr, B 'eɪgɑr'eɪgɑ] *s.* (bact., farm.) agar-agar.
agaric ['ægərɪk, ə'gærɪk] *s.* (bot.) agárico, garzo.
agaricin [ə'gærəsən] *s.* (farm.) agaricina.
agasp [ə'gæsp, B ə'gɑsp] *a.* jadeante; sin aliento.
agate ['ægət] *s* 1. (min.) ágata. 2. (impr.) tipo ágata ($5^1/_2$— puntos). 3. canica, bolita (de ágata).
agate line, (impr.) línea ágata.
agateware [-ˌwɛr, B -ˌwɛə] *s.* loza o ferretería jaspeadas (para imitar el ágata).
agave [ə'gɑvɪ, B ə'geɪvɪ] *s.* (bot.) agave, pita, maguey.
agaveworm [-ˌwɜrm, B -ˌwɜm] *s.* (zool.) tecol.
agaze [ə'geɪz] *adv.* mirando fijamente.
age [eɪdʒ] *s.* 1. edad. 2. edad, era, época; **atomic a.,** era atómica; **down through the ages,** a través de los tiempos; **the A. of Aquarius,** el siglo de Acuario; **the Elizabethan A.,** la era isabelina. 3. vejez, ancianidad. 4. mayoría de edad. 5. (*pl.*) (fam.) siglos, muchísimo tiempo, ej., *I haven't seen him for ages,* hace siglos que no lo veo. 6. **golden a.,** edad de oro, siglo de oro; **of a.,** mayor de edad; **over a.,** demasiado viejo; **to come of a.,** llegar a la mayoría de edad; **under a.,** menor de edad. —*v.i.* 1. envejecer (se). 2. madurar, sazonarse. —*v.t.* 1. envejecer. 2. madurar, sazonar.
aged ['eɪdʒəd] *a.* 1. envejecido, viejo, anciano, cargado de años. 2. [eɪdʒd] de la edad de, ej., *a. forty four,* de la edad de cuarenta y cuatro años. 3. maduro, sazonado.
age group, agrupamiento por edades, grupo etario.
age-harden *v.i.* (metal.) endurecerse por envejecimiento.
ageless ['eɪdʒləs] *a.* 1. siempre joven. 2. eterno, sempiterno.
agelong [-ˌlɔŋ] *a.* eterno, de siempre.
agency ['eɪdʒənsɪ] *s.* 1. agencia; (*of the government*) ministerio; (*of the U.N.*) organismo; **employment a.,** oficina de empleo. 2. medio, acción. 3. **by the a. of,** por medio de; **free a.,** libre albedrío.
agenda [ə'dʒɛndə] *s.* agenda, orden del día, programa.
agenesia [ˌædʒə'niʒə, B -zɪə] **agenesis** [eɪ'dʒɛnəsəs] *s.* agenesia.
agent ['eɪdʒənt] *s.* 1. agente, gestor, comisionado, representante. 2. agente, causa, factor. 3. (quím.) agente. 4. (der.) mandatario, apoderado. 5. **every man is a free a.,** todo hombre tiene su libre albedrío.
agential [eɪ'dʒɛntʃəl, B -'dʒɛnʃəl] *a.* de agente.
agent officer, (mil.) oficial pagador.
agent provocateur [ˌɑʒˌɑnproʊˌvɑkə'tɛr, 'eɪdʒənt-, B 'æʒɑŋ-ˌvɔkə'tɜ] agente *m.* provocador, agitador, enemigo insospechado que se infiltra en un grupo para instigar a cometer actos ilegales.
age of consent, (der.) edad en que el consentimiento propio cobra validez (esp. en caso de seducción).
age of discretion, (der.) edad de madurez legal (cuando la ley imputa al menor responsabilidad por sus actos).
Age of Reason, período caracterizado por el predominio de la razón.
age-old [eɪ'dʒoʊld] *a.* secular; antiquísimo.
ageratum [ˌædʒə'reɪtəm, B ə'dʒɛrə-] *s.* (bot.) agérato; eupatorio.
ageusia [ə'gjuziə] *s.* (med.) ageusia.
agglomerate [ə'glɑməˌreɪt, B ə'glɔm-] *v.t., v.i.* aglomerar(se), amontonar(se). —*s.* conglomerado, conjunto, masa, montón. —*a.* aglomerado.
agglomeration [əˌglɑmə'reɪʃən, B əˌglɔm-] *s.* aglomeración, amontonamiento.
agglutinant [ə'glutənənt] *s., a.* aglutinante.
agglutinate [-ˌeɪt] *v.t., v.i.* aglutinar(se), conglutinar(se). —*a.* (filol.) aglutinante.
agglutination [əˌglutən'eɪʃən] *s.* 1. aglutinación, conglutinación. 2. (filol.) aglutinación.
agglutinative [ə'glutənˌeɪtɪv, B -ətɪv] *a.* 1. aglutinante, adhesivo. 2. (filol.) (lenguas) aglutinantes.
agglutinin [-ənən] *s.* (bioquím.) aglutinina.
aggradation [ˌægrə'deɪʃən] *s.* (geol.) agradación.
aggrandize [ə'grænˌdaɪz, 'ægrən-] *v.t.* 1. agrandar. 2. (fig.) engrandecer, ensalzar, exaltar; exagerar.
aggrandizement [ə'grændɪzmənt] *s.* engrandecimiento, exaltación.
aggrandizer [-ˌdaɪzər, B -zə] *s.* engrandecedor, ensalzador.
aggravate ['ægrəˌveɪt] *v.t.* 1. agravar, empeorar. 2. irritar, exasperar, molestar.
aggravating [-ɪŋ] *a.* 1. agravante. 2. irritante, exasperante.
aggravation [ˌægrə'veɪʃən] *s.* agravación; (fam.) irritación, provocación.
aggregate ['ægrɪˌgeɪt] *v.t.* 1. agregar, juntar, unir. 2. sumar, totalizar. —*a.* [-gət] agregado, unido, junto; colectivo. —*s.* [-gət] agregado, colección, conjunto, totalidad; **in the a.,** colectivamente, en conjunto.
aggregation [ˌægrɪ'geɪʃən] *s.* agregado, conjunto, colección.
aggress [ə'grɛs] *v.i.* (raro) lanzar un ataque, agredir, acometer.
aggression [ə'grɛʃən] *s.* agresión, acometida, asalto.
aggressive [ə'grɛsɪv] *a* 1. agresivo. 2. emprendedor, enérgico, ej., *an a. merchant,* un comerciante emprendedor.
aggressively [-lɪ] *adv.* agresivamente.
aggressiveness [-nəs] *s.* agresividad, acometividad.

aggressor [-ər, B -ə] *s.* agresor, provocador.
aggrieve [ə'griv] *v.t.* (*ú. gen. en pasivo*) 1. apenar, apesadumbrar. 2. afligir, gravar, dañar.
aghast [ə'gæst, B ə'gɑst] *a.* espantado, horrorizado, estupefacto.
agile ['ædʒəl, B -aɪl] *a.* ágil, ligero, expedito.
agility [ə'dʒɪlətɪ] *s.* agilidad, soltura, ligereza.
agio ['ædʒ,oʊ, B 'eɪdʒɪ,oʊ] *s.* (com.) agio.
agiotage [,æʒə'tɑʒ, ,ædʒə-, B 'ædʒətɪdʒ] *s.* (com.) agiotaje; tráfico de divisas.
agitate ['ædʒə,teɪt] *v.t.* 1. agitar, mover. 2. agitar, inquietar, perturbar, alborotar. 3. discutir, debatir. *—v.i.* promover agitación, excitar la opinión pública.
agitation [,ædʒə'teɪʃən] *s.* agitación; perturbación, conmoción.
agitato [,ædʒə'tɑtoʊ] *a.* (mús.) vivo, agitado.
agitator ['ædʒə,teɪtər, B -tə] *s.* 1. agitador, instigador, incitador, perturbador. 2. (quím.) agitador.
agitprop ['ædʒət,prɑp, B -,prɔp] *s.* (pol.) agitación y propaganda.
agleam [ə'glim] *a.* (poét.) brillante, fulgoroso.
aglet ['æglət] *s.* 1. herrete. 2. (bot.) amento.
aglow [ə'gloʊ] *a.* fulgurante, incandescente; (fig. con *with*) radiante (de).
agnail ['æg,neɪl] *s.* uñero; padrastro.
agnate [-,neɪt] *s.* (der.) agnado.
agnation [æg'neɪʃən] *s.* agnación; parentesco.
agnomen [æg'noʊmən] *s.* (*pl.* AGNOMINA [-'nɑmənə, B -'nɔm-]) agnomento, sobrenombre.
agnosia [æg'noʊʒɪə] *s.* (med.) agnosia.
agnostic [-'nɑstɪk, B -'nɔs-] *s., a.* agnóstico.
agnosticism [-tə,sɪzəm] *s.* agnosticismo.
agnus castus ['ægnəs'kæstəs] (bot.) agnocasto.
Agnus Dei [,ægnʊs'deɪ,i, -'di,aɪ] agnusdéi.
ago [a'goʊ] *adv.* hace, ha; **a good while a.,** hace ya bastante tiempo; **five years a.,** hace cinco años; **how long a.?** ¿cuánto tiempo hace?; **long a.,** hace mucho tiempo.
agog [ə'gɑg, B ə'gɔg] *a.* 1. ansioso, anhelante. 2. curioso. *—adv.* ansiosamente; con curiosidad, con vivo interés; **to leave a.,** dejar intrigado.
à go-go [ɑ'goʊ,goʊ] *a.* (jer.) de un modo alegre y espontáneo (baile, música, modas).
agon ['ɑg,ɑn, -,oʊn] *s.* competencia artística o atlética en la Grecia antigua.
agonal ['ægənəl] *a.* agónico, agonizante.
agonic [eɪ'gɑnɪk, B -'gɔn-] *a.* (geom.) ágono.
agonist ['ægənəst] *s.* 1. agonista, luchador. 2. (anat.) músculo agonista.
agonistic [,ægə'nɪstɪk] **agonistical** [-ɪkəl] *a.* (hist.) agonístico, agonal.
agonize ['ægə,naɪz] *v.i.* 1. atormentarse, sufrir angustias, agonizar. 2. luchar desesperadamente. *—v.t.* atormentar, angustiar.
agonized [-,naɪzd] *a.* desesperado, atormentado.
agonizing [-ɪŋ] *a.* angustioso, agonizante; doloroso.
agonizingly [-,naɪzɪŋlɪ] *adv.* agonizadamente.
agony ['ægənɪ] *s.* 1. agonía (del moribundo). 2. (fig.) agonía, angustia, zozobra, aflicción extrema. 3. paroxismo.
agony column, sección del periódico donde se solicita información acerca de una persona desaparecida.
agora ['ægərə] *s.* (*pl.* AGORAE [-ri]) (hist.) ágora; plaza pública.
agoraphobia [,ægərə'foʊbɪə] *s.* (med.) agorafobia.
agouti [ə'gutɪ] *s.* (zool.) agutí, acutí.
agraffe, agrafe [ə'græf] *s.* broche, grapa; gancho ornamental.
agranulocyte [eɪ'grænjəloʊ,saɪt] *s.* (biol.) agranulocito.
agranulocytosis [,eɪ,grænjəloʊ,saɪ'toʊsəs] *s.* (med.) agranulocitosis.
agraphia [eɪ'græfɪə] *s.* (med.) agrafia.
agrarian [ə'grɛrɪən] *a.* agrario; perteneciente a la agricultura.
agrarianism [-ə,nɪzəm] *s.* agrarismo, movimiento o doctrina en pro de la reforma agraria.
agree [ə'gri] *v.i.* 1. (con *to*) consentir, acceder (a). 2. (con *with*) estar de acuerdo (con); ponerse de acuerdo, concordar (con). 3. convenir, quedar (en). 4. avenirse, entenderse. 5. concordar (con), corresponder (a), ej., *the signatures do not a.,* las firmas no concuerdan. 6. (con *with*) convenir, sentar bien (a). 7. (con *on*) convenir (en). 8. (gram.) concordar. *—v.t.* concurrir o convenir en (opinión, hacer algo, etc.).
agreeable [ə'griəbəl] *a.* 1. concorde, conforme; adaptable, compatible. 2. ameno, complaciente.
agreeablenes [-nəs] *s.* 1. amenidad, afabilidad. 2. (con *to*) conformidad (con).
agreed [ə'grid] *a.* convenido, acordado, aprobado.
agreement [ə'grimənt] *s.* 1. acuerdo, convenio, pacto, tratado. 2. conformidad, concordancia. 3. (gram.) concordancia. 4. **by mutual a.,** de común acuerdo; **in a. (with),** de acuerdo (con); **to reach an a.,** llegar a un acuerdo.
agrestic [ə'grɛstɪk] *a.* agreste, campestre, rústico.
agribusiness ['ægrɪ,bɪznəs] *s.* industria agropecuaria, comercio en productos agrícolas.
agricultural [,ægrɪ'kʌltʃərəl] *a.* agrícola, agrario, de la agricultura; de lalabranza.
agricultural engineer, ingeniero agrónomo.
agiculture ['ægrɪ,kʌltʃər, B -tʃə] *s.* 1. agricultura. 2. agronomía.
agriculturist [,ægrɪ'kʌltʃərəst] **agriculturalist** [-rələst] *s.* 1. agricultor, agrícola, labrador. 2. agrónomo.
agrimony ['ægrə,moʊnɪ, B -mənɪ] *s.* (bot.) agrimonia.
agriology [,ægrɪ'ɑlədʒɪ, B -'ɔl-] *s.* estudio de las costumbres de tribus primitivas.
Agrippa [ə'grɪpə] *s.* Agripa, general romano que venció a Antonio y Cleopatra.
Agrippina [,ægrɪ'paɪnə, B -'pi-] *s.* Agripina, madre de Nerón.
agrologic [,ægrə'lɑdʒɪk, B -'lɔdʒ-] *a.* agrológico.
agrologist [ə'grɑlədʒəst, B -'grɔl-] *s.* experto en agrología.
agrology [-dʒɪ] *s.* agrología, ciencia que estudia la producción agrícola.
agronomist [ə'grɑnəməst, B ə'grɔn-] *s.* agrónomo.
agronomy [-mɪ] *s.* agronomía.
agrostology [,ægrə'stɑlədʒɪ, B -'stɔl-] *s.* agrostología, el estudio de las hierbas.
aground [ə'graʊnd] *adv.* 1. (mar.) encallado, varado. 2. (estacionado) en tierra; **to run a.,** (mar.) encallar; (fig.) fracasar.
ague ['eɪgju] *s.* 1. (med.) fiebre palúdica, fiebre intermitente. 2. calofrío, escalofrío.
aguish ['eɪgjuɪʃ] *a.* 1. palúdico. 2. trémulo, tembloroso.
ah [ɑ] *interj.* ¡ah! ¡ay!
a-h (elec.) *abrev. de* **ampere-hour,** amperiohora, amperhora (Ah).
aha [ɑ'hɑ] *interj.* ¡ajá!
ahead [ə'hɛd] *adv.* 1. adelante, más allá, delante; de frente. 2. (mar.) por la proa, avante. 3. **go a.!** ¡adelante!; **to be a.,** ir a la cabeza, estar adelante; **to get a.,** adelantarse, ganar la delantera, progresar; tener éxito; **to go a.,** adelantar, proseguir, continuar; **to set the clock** (o **watch**) **a.,** adelantar el reloj. *—a.* inmediato, (que está) adelante.
ahead of, *prep.* 1. delante de; antes de. 2. en exceso de; arriba de, por encima de.
ahem! [ə'hɛm, B m'm] *interj.* (empleada para ganar tiempo o llamar la atención).
ahoy! [ə'hɔɪ] *interj.* (mar.) ¡ahó! ¡ha! ¡ah!; **ship a.!** ¡ah del barco!
ahull [ə'hʌl] *adv.* (mar.) a palo seco.
A.I. *abrev. de* **artificial intelligence,** inteligencia artificial; **artificial insemination,** inseminación artificial; **Amnesty International,** Amnistía Internacional.
A.I.A. *abrev. de* **American Institute of Architects,** Instituto Norteamericano de Arquitectos.
aid [eɪd] *v.t.* ayudar, auxiliar, asistir. *—s.* 1. ayuda, asistencia, auxilio, socorro. 2. asistente, ayudante. 3. instrumento o medio auxiliar. 4. **in a. of,** para ayudar, en pro de; **first a.,** primeros auxilios.
AID *abrev. de* **Agency for International Development,** Agencia para el Desarrollo International (AID).
aide [eɪd] *s.* ayudante (esp. militar o naval).
aide-de-camp [,eɪddɪ'kæmp, B -də'kɑŋ] *s.* (mil.) edecán, ayudante de campo.
aidman ['eɪd,mæn] *s.* (mil.) sanitario.
AIDS [eɪdz] *s.* (med.) SIDA *m.* (síndrome de inmunodeficiencia adquirida).
aiglet ['eɪglət] *var. de* **aglet.**
aigrette [eɪ'grɛt, 'eɪgrət] *s* 1. cresta, penacho. 2. (orn.) garceta.
aiguille [eɪ'gwil, -'gwi] *s.* 1. pico, picacho, roca en forma de aguja (esp. en los Alpes). 2. barrena para roca.
aiguillette [,eɪgwə'lɛt] *s.* (mil.) (*gen. pl.*) agujetas, cordones, entorchados (del uniforme).
ail [eɪl] *v.t.* afligir, aquejar, doler, molestar; **what ails him?** ¿qué le molesta a ése? ¿qué le pasa? *—v.i.* sufrir, estar enfermo o indispuesto.
ailanthus [eɪ'lænθəs] *s.* (bot.) ailanto, árbol del cielo, barniz del Japón.
aileron ['eɪlə,rɑn, B -, rɔn] *s.* alerón (del avión o de una casa).
ailing ['eɪlɪŋ] *a.* enfermizo, achacoso.
ailment [-mənt] *s.* 1. dolencia, enfermedad. 2. indisposición, malestar.
aim [eɪm] *v.t.* (*ú.* con *at*) 1. apuntar, asestar (arma a). 2. dirigir, lanzar (golpe, etc. a). 3. (fig.) dirigir (observación, crítica, etc. contra). *—v.i.* aspirar, pretender, proponerse; **a. at,** ancañonar; **a. high,** ambicionar mucho. *—s.* 1. apunte, puntería. 2. tiro (de un arma), alcance, ej., *its a. is accurate up to 200 meters,* su tiro (de un arma) es preciso hasta 200 metros. 3. fin, finalidad, objeto, propósito. 4. **to miss one's a.,** errar el tiro; **to take a. at** apuntar a; **to take accurate a.,** afinar la puntería.
aimless ['eɪmləs] *a.* sin objeto, sin propósito, a la deriva.
ain't [eɪnt] (substandard) or (hum.) *contr. de* **am not, is not** o **are not.** El uso de la contracción **ain't** refleja un nivel de lenguaje pobre e inculto.
air [ɛr, B ɛə] *s.* 1. aire. 2. (mús.) aire, tonada. 3. aire, aspecto, apariencia, porte, ademanes. 4. (*pl.*) aires, vanidad, engreimiento. 5. (filat.) sello aéreo, estampilla aérea. 6. (poét.) aura, céfiro. 7. **airs and graces,** aires, afectación; **(to send; to travel) by a.,** (enviar) por avión; (viajar) en avión; **fresh a.,** aire fresco; **foul a.,** aire viciado; **in the open a.,** al raso, al aire libre; **is in the a.,** queda en el aire, queda en suspenso, está sin decidir; se rumorea; **on the a.,** en el aire, transmitiendo (radio, televisión); **to give a. to (one's feelings, opinion, etc.),** dar expresión a (los sentimientos, opinión, etc. de uno); **to give**

oneself airs, darse aires; **to give someone the a.,** (jer.) despedir a alguien (del empleo); desairar a alguien; **to go on the a.,** (rad., t.v.) empezar a trasmitir; **to put on airs,** (jer.) darse muchos aires, darse ínfulas; **to tread on a.,** bañarse en agua de rosas; **up in the a.,** incierto, no resuelto; perplejo, desorientado. —*v.t.* 1. airear, ventilar, orear, poner al aire. 2. (fig.) ventilar, divulgar. —*v.i.* ventilarse.
air attaché, (dip.) agregado de aviación.
air attack, ataque aéreo.
air bag *s.* (aut.) bolsa de aire.
air base, (mil.) base aérea, centro de operaciones y entrenamiento de la aviación.
air battle, combate aéreo.
air beacon, faro aéreo.
air-bladder [-ˌblædər, B -də] *s.* vejiga natatoria (de los peces).
air blast, (mec.) chorro de aire.
airborne [-ˌbɔrn, B -ˌbɔn] *a.* 1. aerotransportado; transportado por aire. 2. en el aire, volando.
air brake, freno neumático; (aer.) freno aerodinámico.
air breaker, (elec.) disyuntor en aire.
airbrush [-ˌbrʌʃ] *s.* aerógrafo.
airburst [-ˌbɜrst, B -ˌbɜst] *s.* (mil.) explosión en el aire (de una bomba, granada, etc.).
airbus ['ɛrbʌs] *s.* aerobús *m.*; **a. service** puente *m.* aéreo.
air casing, cámara aisladora.
air castle, quimera, castillo en el aire.
air cell, (orn.) saco aéreo (de aves).
air chamber, cámara de aire.
air cleaner, filtro de aire.
air coach, avión comercial para pasajeros de clase económica.
air cock, llave de admisión (o de escape) de aire.
air command, (E.U., aer., mil.) comando aéreo.
air compressor, compresor de aire.
air condenser, condensador de aire por enfriamiento.
air-condition [-kən'dɪʃən] *v.t.* acondicionar el aire, proveer de aire acondicionado.
air-conditioned [-ənd] *a.* con aire acondicionado.
air conditioner [-ənər, B -ənə] *s.* aparato para acondicionar el aire, acondicionador del aire.
air conditioning [-ənɪŋ] (instalación de) acondicionamiento del aire.
air-cool ['ɛr'kul, B 'ɛə'-] *v.t.* refrigerar o enfriar por aire.
air-cooled [-'kuld] *a.* refrigerado por aire, enfriado por aire.
air-cooled transformer ['ɛr'kuld, B 'ɛə'-] (elec.) transformador enfriado por aire.
air-cooling [-'kulɪŋ] *s.* refrigeración por aire.
air-core transformer [-'kɔr-, B -'kɔ-] (elec.) transformador sin núcleo magnético.
Air Corps, (mil.) cuerpo de aviación.
air corridor, corredor aéreo, pasillo aéreo (ruta aérea establecida por convenio internacional).
air cover, (mil.) protección aérea (de tropas, trenes, etc.).
aircraft [-ˌkræft, B -ˌkrɑft] *s.* (*pl.* AIRCRAFT) vehículo(s) aéreo(s), aeronave(s).
aircraft carrier, (mil., mar.) portaaviones.
aircraftman [-mən] **aircraftsman** [-ˌkræfts-, B -ˌkrɑfts-] *s.* (pr. G.B.) suboficial (en la Fuerza Aérea).
aircrew [-ˌkru] *s.* tripulación del avión.
air cushion, 1. cojín neumático. 2. amortiguador de aire.
air defense, defensa antiaerea.
air drill, taladro de aire comprimido, perforadora neumática.
airdrome [-ˌdroʊm] *s.* (G.B.) aeródromo, aeropuerto.
airdrop [-ˌdrɑp, B -ˌdrɔp] *s.* (aer.) suministro (de carga o de personal) por medio de paracaídas.
air-dry [-'draɪ] *a.* completamente seco, deshumedecido.
air-duct [-ˌdʌkt] *s.* tubo de ventilación.
airedale ['ɛrˌdeɪl, B 'ɛəˌ-] *s.* perro foxterrier.
air express, (aer.) expreso aéreo; carga de expreso aéreo.
airfield ['ɛrˌfild, B 'ɛəˌ-] *s.* campo de aviación, campo de aterrizaje.
air fleet, flota aérea.
airflow [-ˌfloʊ] *s.* (aer.) régimen del aire; corriente de aire.
airfoil [-ˌfɔɪl] *s.* (aer.) superficie de sustentación; plano aerodinámico.
air force, (mil.) fuerza aérea.
airframe [-ˌfreɪm] *s.* (aer.) armazón de una nave aérea, célula.
airfreight [-'freɪt] *s.* carga aérea, flete por avión. —*v.t.* aerotransportar.
airfreighter [-ər, B -ə] *s.* avión de carga.
air freshener, ambientador *m.*, desodorante *m.* ambiental.
air furnace, horno de tiro natural.
air gap, (elec.) entrehierro, intervalo de aire.
air gauge, manómetro de aire, calibrador neumático.
airglow [-ˌgloʊ] *s.* resplandor atmosférico (causado por radiación solar); incandescencia del aire (explosión nuclear).
air gun, 1. pistola de aire (comprimido). 2. pistolete para pintar, pulverizador de aire comprimido, aerógrafo.
air hammer, (mec.) martillo neumático o de aire.
air hole [-ˌhoʊl] 1. respiradero. 2. (aer.) bolsa de aire, vacío, bache.
air hostess, azafata, aeromoza, camarera de avión de pasajeros.
airily ['ɛrəlɪ, B 'ɛər-] *adv.* ligeramente, frívolamente.
airiness [-ɪnəs] *s.* 1. frescura. 2. ligereza, insubstancialidad. 3. afectación, pretensión.
airing [-ɪŋ] *s.* 1. ventilación, oreo. 2. paseo (para tomar el aire). 3. (fig.) ventilación (de quejas, etc.).
air intake, (aer., aut.) toma o entrada de aire.
air lane, ruta aérea.
airless ['ɛrləs, B 'ɛələs] *a.* falto de ventilación, sofocante; sin brisa.
air letter, carta aérea.
airlift ['ɛrˌlɪft, B 'ɛə,-] *s.* (mil.) puente aéreo. —*v.t.* aerotransportar, transportar por el aire.
air line, 1. línea recta. 2. tubería neumática.
airline [-ˌlaɪn] *s.* línea aérea, aerolínea, compañía de aviación.
airliner [-ˌlaɪnər, B -nə] *s.* avión de línea comercial.
air lock, esclusa de aire, esclusa neumática, antecámara de compresión; burbuja de aire que impide el paso de un líquido (en una cañería, un tubo, etc.).
airmail [-'meɪl, -ˌmeɪl] *s.* correo aéreo, vía aérea. —*a.* aéreo (carta, envío, etc.), aeropostal (servicio, etc.) —*v.t.* enviar por correo aéreo.
air-mail stamp, sello aéreo.
airman [-mən] *s.* 1. aviador. 2. (mil.) soldado de la Fuerza Aérea.
airmanship [-ˌʃɪp] *s.* habilidad para pilotear aviones.
air map, aeromapa, carta elaborada por aerofotos.
Air Marshal, (G.B.) mariscal (en la Real Fuerza Aérea, equivalente a teniente general).
air mass, (meteor.) masa de aire.
air mattress, colchón de aire, colchón neumático.
air-minded [-'maɪndəd] *a.* adicto a la aviación, interesado en aviones.
airometer [ɛr'ɑmətər, B ɛər'ɔmɪtə] *s.* (avia.) contador de aire, anemómetro.
air photography, aerofotografía.
air-pipe [-ˌpaɪp] *s.* tubo de ventilación.
air piracy, aeropiratería.
air pistol, pistola de aire.
airplane [-ˌpleɪn] *s.* aeroplano, avión.
airplane carrier, portaaviones.
air pocket, bache o bolsa de aire; depresión.
airport [-ˌpɔrt, B -ˌpɔt] *s.* aeropuerto.
air power, (mil.) potencia aérea, poder aéreo.
air pressure, presión del aire; presión neumática.
airproof [-ˌpruf] *a.* hermético.
air pump, bomba de vacío; bomba compresora de aire; elevador de agua por aire; (aut.) bomba para neumáticos; bomba neumática, bomba de aire comprimido.
air raid, ataque aéreo.
air-raid alarm [-ˌreɪd-] *aviso o señal de ataque aéreo.*
air-raid drill, ejercicio antiaéreo.
air-raid shelter, refugio antiaéreo.
air-raid warden, encargado de la defensa civil en un área de una ciudad.
air-raid warning, alarma de incursión aérea.
air rifle, escopeta de aire comprimido.
air right, derecho aéreo, derecho de paso.
air route, ruta aérea.
air sac, (orn.) bolsa de aire (en el cuerpo de las aves).
airscrew [-ˌskru] *s.* (G.B.) hélice del avión.
air shaft, (min.) pozo de ventilación o de aire; caja de ventilación, tiro ventilador, tragante, chimenea de aire.
airship [-ˌʃɪp] *s.* aeronave.
airsick [-ˌsɪk] *a.* mareado, atacado de mal de altura (esp. en viajes aéreos).
airsickness [-nəs] *s.* mareo (en viaje aéreo).
airspace [-ˌspeɪs] *s.* espacio aéreo (de una nación o territorio).
air speed, (aer.) velocidad propia, velocidad relativa en el espacio con respecto a la velocidad en tierra.
air-spray [-ˌspreɪ] *s.* pulverizador a presión.
air-spraying [-ɪŋ] *s.* fumigación aérea.
airstream [-ˌstrim] *s.* corriente de aire.
air strike, ataque aéreo.
airstrip [-ˌstrɪp] *s.* pista de aterrizaje y despegue.
air supremacy, dominio del aire (esp. militar).
air survey, levantamiento aéreo de planos.
air tempering, (metal.) atemperación del aire.
airtight [-'taɪt] *a.* hermético, herméticamente cerrado.
air-to-air ['ɛrtə'ɛr, B 'ɛətə'ɛə] *a.* de un avión a otro (estando ambos en vuelo).
air-to-ground [-'graʊnd] **air-to-surface** [-'sɜrfəs, B -'sɜfəs] *a.* de la acción o comunicación de una aeronave en vuelo con la tierra.
air traffic, tránsito aéreo.
air trap, 1. tubo en U, válvula de inodoro. 2. (aer.) bolsa de aire.
air umbrella, (G.B.) fuerza aérea protectora (de tropas, etc. terrestres).
air valve, válvula de aire, ventosa, respiradero.
air vent, respiradero, aspirador de aire, ventosa.
air vesicle, (anat.) vesícula aérea.
airwar ['ɛrˌwɔr, B 'ɛəˌwɔ] *s.* guerra aérea.
airwave [-ˌweɪv] *s.* 1. (*gen. pl.*) (rad., t.v.) onda aérea. 2. (rad.) canal de transmisión (de una frecuencia establecida).
airway [-ˌweɪ] *s.* 1. aerovía, vía aérea. 2. línea aérea, compañía de aviación. 3. (anat.) vía respiratoria. 4. (min.) galería de ventilación. 5. (rad.)

canal de transmisión (de una frecuencia establecida).
air well, pozo de ventilación, pozo de aire.
airworthy [-ˌwɜrðɪ, B -ˌwɜðɪ] *a.* (aer.) en condiciones de volar.
airy [ˈɛrɪ, B ˈɛərɪ] *a.* 1. aéreo, de la atmósfera. 2. bien ventilado, fresco; ventoso. 3. (fig.) aéreo, etéreo. 4. ligero, insubstancial. 5. frívolo, ligero, fútil. 6. airoso, vivaz, gracioso, delicado. 7. afectado, pretensioso.
aisle [aɪl] *s.* 1. pasillo, pasadizo (en iglesia, teatro, cine, etc.); **to be rolling in the aisles** (fig.) estar muerto de risa. 2. (arq.) nave lateral, ala.
aisle seat, asiento al lado del pasillo.
ait [eɪt] *s.* (G.B.) isleta, isla pequeña en un río o lago.
aitch [eɪtʃ] *s.* (letra) hache; **to drop one's aitches,** no pronunciar las haches, hablar incorrectamente (el idioma inglés).
aitchbone [ˈeɪtʃˌboʊn] *s.* 1. hueso de la cadera (de vacunos). 2. carne de cadera.
ajar [əˈdʒɑr, B əˈdʒɑ] *a.* 1. entreabierto, entornado. 2. discorde, en desacuerdo (con).
Ajax [ˈeɪˌdʒæks] *s.* (mitol.) Áyax, guerrero troyano.
AKC *abrev. de* **American Kennel Club,** Club Norteamericano de Dueños de Perros.
akimbo [əˈkɪmboʊ] *a., adv.* en jarra, en asas; **with arms a.,** con los brazos en jarra.
akin [əˈkɪn] *a.* 1. consanguíneo, emparentado. 2. semejante, parecido.
Akkadian [əˈkeɪdɪən] *s., a.* acadio, perteneciente a, o nativo de Acadia.
akvavit [ˈɑkwəˌvit, ˈɑkvɑ-] *var. de* **aquavit.**
Al *símb. de* **aluminum,** aluminio (Al).
Ala. *abrev. de* **Alabama,** Alabama (E.U.).
Alabama [ˌæləˈbæmə] *s.* Alabama, estado de los E.U.
Alabamian [ˌæləˈbæmiən] *a.* natural o residente de Alabama, perteneciente al Estado de Alabama.
alabandite [ˌæləˈbænˌdaɪt] *s.* (min.) alabandina.
alabaster [ˈæləˌbæstər, B -ˌbɑstə] *s., a.* alabastro.
alabastrine [ˌæləˈbæstrən, B -ˈbɑs-] *a.* alabastrino.
à la carte [ˌæləˈkɑrt, ˌɑl-, B ˌɑlɑˈkɑt] (fr.) a la carta, según la lista (de comidas).
alack [əˈlæk] **alack-a-day, alackaday** [-əˌdeɪ] *interj.* (ant.) ¡ay de mí! ¡qué pena! ¡qué lástima!
alacrity [əˈlækrətɪ] *s.* alacridad, presteza.
Aladdin [əˈlædən] *s.* (lit.) Aladino.
Aladdin's lamp, la lámpara de Aladino.
à la king [ˌæləˈkɪŋ, ˌɑlə-, B ˌɑlɑ-] (cocina) con salsa de crema, hongos y pimientos.
alalia [əˈleɪlɪə] *s.* (med.) alalia.
á la mode [ˌæləˈmoʊd, ɑl-, B ˌɑlɑ-] (fr.) 1. a la moda. 2. servido con helado (postre). 3. estofado con verdura picada.
alamode [ˌæləˈmoʊd, ˌɑl-] *s.* tela fina de seda.
alanine [ˈæləˌnin, B -ˌnaɪn] *s.* (quím.) alanina.
alar [ˈeɪlər, B -lə] *a.* 1. del ala. 2. aliforme. 3. (anat.) axilar.
Alaric [ˈælərɪk] *s.* (hist.) Alarico, rey visigodo.
alarm [əˈlɑrm, B -ˈlɑm] *v.t.* 1. alarmar, dar alarma. 2. (fig.) alarmar, asustar, inquietar, perturbar. —*s.* 1. alarma; rebato. 2. (fig.) alarma, sobresalto. 3. timbre de alarma (en el reloj despertador). 4. **to give** (o **to sound) the a.,** dar la alarma, tocar a rebato.
alarm bell, campana de rebato o de alarma.
alarm clock, (reloj) despertador.
alarming [əˈlɑrmɪŋ, B əˈlɑmɪŋ] *a.* alarmante, inquietante, turbador.
alarmingly [-lɪ] *adv.* de manera alarmante.
alarmist [-əst] *s.* alarmista.
alarm-post [-ˌpoʊst] *s.* atalaya, puesto de aviso.
alarm valve, válvula de alarma, válvula de seguridad.
alarum [əˈlærəm, B əˈlɛər-, əˈlɑr-] *s.* (ant.) *var. de* **alarm.**
alary [ˈeɪlərɪ] *a.* 1. del ala. 2. aliforme.
alas [əˈlæs] *interj.* ¡ay! ¡ay de mi! ¡qué pena! ¡qué lástima!
Alaska [əˈlæskə] *s.* Alaska, estado de los E.U.
Alaskan malamute [əˈlæskən-] (zool.) malamute de Alaska.
alate [ˈeɪˌleɪt] **alated** [-əd] *a.* alado, con alas.
alb [ælb] *s.* (igl.) alba (que se ponen los sacerdotes para celebrar la misa).
albacore [ˈælbəˌkɔr, B -ˌkɔ] *s.* (ict.) albacora, bonito.
Albania [ælˈbeɪnɪə, ɔl-] *s.* Albania.
Albanian [-ən] *a.* albanés. —*s.* 1. albanés, natural de Albania. 2. (idioma) albanés.
albatross [ˈælbəˌtrɔs, -ˌtrɑs, B -ˌtrɔs] *s.* 1. (orn.) albatros. 2. (fig.) (*burden*) pena, sufrimiento.
albedo [ælˈbidoʊ] *s.* (fís., astr.) albedo.
albeit [ælˈbiɪt, ɔl-, B ɔl-] *conj., adv.* aunque, bien que, no obstante, si bien.
Albertus Magnus [ælˈbɜrtəsˈmægnəs, B -ˈbɜt-] (hist.) Alberto Magno, teólogo y filósofo alemán, preceptor de Tomás de Aquino.
albescent [ælˈbɛsənt] *a.* blanquecino.
Albigensian [ˌælbəˈdʒɛntʃən, B -ˈdʒɛnsɪən] *a.* (relig.) albigense, relativo a la herejía albigense.
albinism [ˈælbəˌnɪzəm, ælˈbaɪ-, B ˈælbɪ-] *s.* (med.) albinismo, falta de pigmentación de la piel.
albino [ælˈbaɪnoʊ, B -ˈbi-] *s.* albino.
Albion [ˈælbɪən] *s.* (poét.) Albión, nombre poético de Inglaterra.
albite [ˈælˌbaɪt] *s.* (min.) albita.
album [ˈælbəm] *s.* álbum.
albumen [ælˈbjumən, B ˈælˌbjʊ-] *s.* 1. (bioquím.) albúmina. 2. (bot.) albumen (materia nutritiva que rodea la semilla en muchas plantas).
albumin [ælˈbjumən, B ˈælˌbjʊ-] *s.* (bioquím.) albúmina.
albuminoid [-məˌnɔɪd, B ælˈbju-] *a.* (bioquím.) albuminoideo. —*s.* albuminoide, proteína.
albuminous [-nəs] *a.* (bioquím.) albuminado, albuminoso.
albuminuria [ælˌbjuməˈnʊrɪə, B -ˈnjʊr-] *s.* (med.) albuminaria.
albuminuric [-ik] *a.* (med.) albuminúrico.
albumose [ˈælbjəˌmoʊs, -ˌmoʊz] *s.* (bioquím., bot.) albumosa.
alburnum [ælˌbɜrnəm, B -ˈbɜnəm] *s.* (bot.) alburno, albura.
Alcaeus [ælˈsiəs] *s.* (hist.) Alceo, poeta lírico griego.
alcaic [ælˈkeɪɪk] *a.* (poét.) alcaico (verso).
alcaide, alcayde [ælˈkaɪdɪ, B -ˈkeɪd] *s.* (hist.) alcaide (el que tenía a su cargo la guardia de una fortaleza).
Alcatraz [ˈælkəˌtræz] *s.* (E.U.) Alcatraz, isla en la bahía de San Francisco, antiguamente ocupada por una prisión federal.
Alcestis [ælˈsɛstɪs] *s.* (mitol.) Alcestes, esposa del rey Admeto de Tesalia.
alchemic [ælˈkɛmɪk] **alchemical** [-ɪkəl] *a.* alquímico.
alchemist [ˈælkəməst] *s.* alquimista.
alchemy [-mɪ] *s.* 1. alquimia, crisopeya. 2. (fig.) proceso alquímico, transmutación mágica; poder de atracción humana.
Alcibiades [ˌælsəˈbaɪəˌdiz] *s.* (hist.) Alcibíades, general y político ateniense.
Alcmene [ælkˈminɪ] *s.* (mitol.) Alcmena, madre de Hércules.
alcohol [ˈælkəˌhɔl] *s.* 1. alcohol. 2. bebida alcohólica.
alcoholate [-lət, B -ˌleɪt] *s.* (quím., farm.) alcoholato.
alcoholic [ˌælkəˈhɔlɪk, -ˈhɑl-, B -ˈhɔl-] *a.* alcohólico. —*s.* bebedor alcoholizado.
Alcoholics Anonymous, Alcohólicos Anónimos.
alcoholism [ˈælkəˌhɔˌlɪzəm] *s.* alcoholismo.
alcoholization [ˌælkəˌhɔləˈzeɪʃən, B -laɪ-] *s.* alcoholización, saturación con alcohol.
alcoholize [ˈælkəˌhɔˌlaɪz] *v.t.* 1. alcoholizar, tratar o saturar con alcohol. 2. convertir en alcohol.
alcoholometer [ˌælkəˌhɔˈlɑmətər, B -ˈlɔmɪtə] *s.* (fís.) alcoholímetro.
alcove [ˈælˌkoʊv] *s.* 1. nicho; gabinete. 2. glorieta, cenador.
Alcuin [ˈælkwən] *s.* Alcuino, sabio y teólogo inglés consejero de Carlomagno.
Alcyone [ælˈsaɪəni, -nɪ] *s.* 1. (mitol.) Alcione. 2. (astr.) Alcione, Alción.
aldehyde [ˈældəˌhaɪd] *s.* (quím.) aldehído.
alder [ˈɔldər, B -də] *s.* (bot.) aliso.
alder buckthorn, a. dogwood, (bot.) arraclán.
alderman [ˈɔldərmən, B -dəmən] *s.* concejal, regidor.
aldermanic [ˌɔldərˈmænɪk, B -dəˈ-] *a.* perteneciente al regidor.
Aldine [ˈɔlˌdaɪn, -ˌdin] *a.* (tip.) aldino (edición, caracteres, etc.).
aldol [ˈælˌdɔl, -ˌdoʊl, B -ˌdɔl] *s.* (quím.) aldol.
aldose [-ˌdoʊs, -ˌdoʊz] *s.* (quím.) aldosa.
ale [eɪl] *s.* (tipo de) cerveza espesa y amarga.
aleatory [ˈeɪlɪəˌtɔrɪ, B -tərɪ] *a.* 1. (der.) aleatorio. 2. de suerte, de riesgo, imprevisto, de azar.
alee [əˈli] *adv.* (mar.) a sotavento, al abrigo del viento.
alegar [ˈæləgər, B -gə] *s.* cerveza agria, vinagre de cerveza.
alehouse [ˈeɪlˌhaʊs] *s.* cervecería, taberna.
Alemannic [ˌæləˈmænɪk] *s.* (filol.) alemán, grupo de dialectos alemanes.
alembic [əˈlɛmbɪk] *s.* alambique.
Alencon [əˈlɛnsən, -ˌsɑn, B -ˌsɔn] *s.* Alenzón, ciudad de Francia famosa por la elaboración de encajes finos.
aleph [ˈɑlɛf] *s.* álef, primera letra del alfabeto hebreo.
aleph-null [-ˈnʌl] *s.* (mat.) alef cero.
Aleppo evil [əˈlɛpoʊ-] enfermedad de furúnculos (forúnculos).
Aleppo pine, (bot.) pino carrasco, pino carrasqueño, pincarrasco.
alert [əˈlɜrt, B əˈlɜt] *a.* 1. alerta, cuidadoso, vigilante. 2. prevenido. 3. activo, ágil, vivo, despierto. —*s.* 1. (mil.) alarma. 2. aviso de ataque aéreo; estado de alarma (contra ataque). 3. **on the a.,** alerta, sobre aviso, en guardia. —*v.t.* alertar, poner sobre aviso.
alertness [-nəs] *s.* 1. cuidado, vigilancia. 2. agilidad. 3. viveza, agudeza (mental).
alette [əˈlɛt, æ-] *s.* (arq.) alero.
aleurone [ˈæljəˌroʊn, B əˈljʊrən, -ˌroʊn] *s.* (bot., bioquím.) aleurona.
Aleut [əˈlut, B ˈælɪˌut] *s.* aleuta.
Aleutian [əˈluʃən] *s.* aleuta, habitante de las islas Aleutianas.
Aleutian Islands, Islas Aleutianas, archipiélago que remata la península de Alaska.
alewife [ˈeɪlˌwaɪf] *s.* (*pl.,* ALEWIVES [-ˌwaɪvz]) 1. cervecera, tabernera. 2. (ict.) pez norteamericano parecido al sábalo o arenque.

alexander [ˌælɪg'zændər, B -'zɑndə] *s.* cóctel helado hecho con crema de cacao, crema de leche y ginebra o aguardiente.
Alexander the Great, (hist.) Alejandro Magno.
Alexandria [ˌælɪg'zændrɪə, B -'zɑn-] *s.* Alejandría, ciudad de Egipto.
Alexandrian [-ən] *a.* 1. alejandrino, relativo a Alejandría o la cultura helénica que allí floreció. 2. (hist.) relativo a Alejandro Magno.
alexandrine [-drən, B -'zænˌdraɪn] *s.* (poét.) alejandrino (verso).
alexia [ə'lɛksɪə] *s.* (med.) alexia.
alexin [ə'lɛksən] *s.* (bioquím.) alexina.
alexipharmic [əˌlɛksə'fɑrmɪk, B -'fɑmɪk] *s., a.* (med.) alexifármaco, contraveneno.
Alfa ['ælfə] *s.* 1. palabra usada en el código de comunicaciones para la letra *a.* 2. (bot.) esparto.
alfalfa [æl'fælfə] *s.* (bot.) alfalfa, mielga común.
al fine [ɑl'finɛ] (mús.) hasta el fin.
alforja [æl'fɔrhə, B -'fɔhə] *s.* (O. de E.U). alforja, talega o bolsa de la montura.
alfresco [æl'frɛskoʊ] *a., adv.* al aire libre.
alga ['ælgə] *s.* (*pl.* ALGAE [-ˌdʒi]) (bot.) alga.
algebra ['ældʒəbrə] *s.* álgebra.
algebraic [ˌældʒə'breɪɪk] **algebraical** [-əkəl] *a.* algebraico, algébrico.
algebraic number, (mat.) número algebraico.
algebraic sum, (mat.) suma algebraica (en la que se tienen en cuenta los signos de las variable).
algebraist ['ældʒəˌbreɪəst, B ˌæl-'breɪ-] *s.* algebrista, algébrico.
Algeria [ˌæ'dʒɪrɪə, B -'dʒɪər-] *s.* Argelia.
Algerian [-ɪən] **Algerine** [ˌældʒə'rin] *s., a.* argelino, natural de Argel o Argelia.
algerienne [ælˌdʒɪrɪ'ɛn, B -ˌdʒɪər-] *s.* tejido a rayas de colores vivos.
algid ['ældʒəd] *a.* álgido, muy frío, glacial.
algidity [æl'dʒɪdətɪ] *s.* algidez, frialdad glacial.
Algiers [æl'dʒɪrz, B -'dʒɪəz] *s.* Argel, capital de Argelia.
algin [ˌældʒən] *s.* (quím.) algina.
algoid ['ælgɔɪd] *a.* (bot.) algáceo.
algolagnia [ˌælgoʊ'lægnɪə] *s.* (med.) algolagnia.
algology [ˌæl'gɑlədʒɪ, B -'gɔl-] *s.* algología, ficología, estudio de las algas.
Algonkian [æl'gɑŋkɪən, B -'gɔn-] **Algonquian** [-'gɑnkwɪən, -'gɑŋ-, B -'gɔŋ-] *a., s.* (E.U.) algonquino, relativo a la tribu de indios del mismo nombre.
Algonquin [-kwɪn] *var. de* **Algonkian.**
algophobia [ˌælgə'foʊbɪə] *s.* (med.) algofobia, temor morboso al dolor.
algor ['ælgɔr, B -gɔ] *s.* (med.) algidez.
algorism ['ælgəˌrɪzəm] **algorithm** [-ˌrɪðəm] *s.* (mat.) algoritmia, algoritmo.
Alhambraic [ˌælˌhæm'breɪɪk] **Alhambresque** [-'brɛsk] *a.* del Alhambra, al estilo alhambreño, del palacio moro de Granada.
alias ['eɪlɪəs, B -æs] *s.* (*pl.* ALIASES) alias, nombre supuesto, seudónimo o apodo.
alibi ['æləˌbaɪ] *s.* 1. coartada. 2. (fam., E.U.) excusa, pretexto. *—v.i.* presentar una excusa. *—v.t.* disculpar (a alguien) con una coartada.
alible ['æləbəl] *a.* alible, alimenticio, nutritivo.
alice blue ['ælɪs-] azul pálido.
Alice in Wonderland [-ɪn'wʌndərˌlænd, B -dəˌ-] (lit.) Alicia en el país de las maravillas.
alidade ['æləˌdeɪd] *s.* (fís., astr.) alidada.
alien ['eɪlɪən, -jən] *a.* 1. ajeno, extraño; extranjero. 2. (con *from*) distinto (a, de), diferente (de). 3. (con *to*) ajeno (a). 4. (con *to*) contrario, hostil (a). *—s.* forastero, extranjero; (*science fiction*) extraterrestre, alienígena. *—v.t.* 1. (poét.) apartar, enemistar. 2. (der.) alienar, enajenar, traspasar.

alienability [ˌeɪljənə'bɪlətɪ, -lɪə-] *s.* (der.) carácter enajenable (de una propiedad).
alienable ['eɪljənəbəl, -lɪə-] *a.* (der.) alienable, enajenable, traspasable.
alienate [-ˌneɪt] *v.t.* 1. (con *from*) apartar, alejar, enajenar (de), enemistar (con). 2. quitar, robar (el afecto, etc.). 3. (der.) alienar, enajenar, traspasar.
alienation [ˌeɪlɪə'neɪʃən, ˌeɪljə-] *s.* 1. enajenación, extrañeza, desavenencia. 2. alienación, enajenación mental. 3. (der.) alienación, traspaso.
alienee [-'ni] *s.* (der.) aquél a quien pasa la propiedad (de una cosa).
alienism ['eɪlɪəˌnɪzəm, 'eɪljə-] *s.* 1. (med.) alienismo. 2. (der.) extranjería (de una persona en un país).
alienist [-nəst] *s.* (med.) alienista.
alienor [ˌeɪlɪə'nɔr, ˌeɪljə-, B -'nɔ] *s.* (der.) enajenador, enajenante.
aliform ['æləˌfɔrm, B -ˌfɔm] *a.* aliforme.
alight [ə'laɪt] *v.i.* (*pret., p.p.* ALIGHTED o *t.* ALIT [ə'lɪt] *p.pr.* ALIGHTING), descender, bajar, apearse; posarse (aves, etc.); (aer.) aterrizar, amarar. *—a.* 1. iluminado. 2. encendido, ardiendo, en llamas, ej., *the house is a. with flames,* la casa está en llamas.
align [ə'laɪn] *v.t.* alinear, poner en línea. *—v.i.* 1. alinearse. 2. unirse a otros en una causa o partido.
alignment [-mənt] *s.* alineación, alineamiento; (rad.) sincronización, alineación; **to be out of a.,** (aut.) no estar alineado.
alike [ə'laɪk] *adv.* igualmente, de la misma manera; en común; a la par. *—a.* semejante, similar, parecido; **to look a.,** parecerse.
aliment ['æləmənt] *s.* alimento, nutrimiento; (fig.) sustento (espiritual, etc.). [-ˌmɛnt] *v.t.* alimentar, dar alimento a.
alimental [ˌælə'mɛntəl] *a.* alimenticio, nutritivo.
alimentary [-ərɪ] *a.* 1. alimental, alimenticio. 2. alimentario.
alimentary canal, (anat.) conducto alimenticio, tubo digestivo.
alimentation [ˌæləmən'teɪʃən] *s.* alimentación.
alimony ['æləˌmoʊnɪ, B -ɪmənɪ] *s.* (der.) asistencias de divorcio o separación, pensión.
aline [ə'laɪn] **alinement** [-mənt] *var. de* **align, alignment.**
aliped ['æləpɛd] *a., s.* (zool.) alípedo, quiróptero.
aliphatic [ˌælə'fætɪk] *a.* (quím.) alifático, graso.
aliquant ['æləkwənt] *a.* (mat.) alicuanta (parte).
aliquot ['æləˌkwɑt, B -ˌkwɔt] *s., a.* (mat.) alícuota.
aliunde [ˌeɪˌlɪ'ʌndi, ˌɑl-] *a.* (der.) de otra parte, de fuente extrínseca.
alive [ə'laɪv] *a.* 1. vivo, viviente, con vida. 2. en vigencia; en uso, funcionando. 3. activo, enérgico, animado. 4. (con *to*) consciente (de posibilidades, ideas, etc.), atento (a) (peligro, etc.); que aprecia (situaciones, etc.). 5. (con *with*) lleno (de), poblado (de, con), pululante (de). 6. **look a.!** ¡apúrate! ¡muévete!; **the greatest man a.,** el hombre más grande de nuestra época; **to come a.,** cobrar vida; **to keep a.,** hacer perdurar o sobrevivir; sobrevivir, lograr sobrevivir.
alizarin [ə'lɪzərən] *s.* (quím.) alizarina.
alkahest ['ælkəˌhɛst] *s.* alcaesto, alcaest, solvente universal buscado por los alquimistas.
alkalescence [ˌælkə'lɛsəns] *s.* (quím.) alcalescencia.
alkalescent [-ənt] *a.* (quím.) alcalescente, alcalino.

alkali ['ælkəˌlaɪ] *s.* (*pl.* ALKALIES O ALKALIS) (quím.) álcali.
alkalimeter [ˌælkə'lɪmətər, B -ə] *s.* (quím.) alcalímetro.
alkaline ['ælkələn, -ˌlaɪn, B -ˌlaɪn] *a.* (quím.) alcalino.
alkaline earth, tierra alcalina.
alkalinize [-ləˌnaɪz] *v.t.* (quím.) alcalizar.
alkali reserve, (bioquím.) reserva alcalina.
alkalization [ˌælkəlɪ'zeɪʃən] *s.* (quím.) alcalización.
alkalize ['ælkəˌlaiz] *v.t.* (quím.) alcalizar.
alkaloid [-ˌlɔɪd] (quím.) *s.* alcaloide. *—a.* alcaloideo.
alkaloidal [ˌælkə'lɔɪdəl] *a.* (quím.) alcaloideo.
alkalosis [-'loʊsəs] *s.* (med.) alcalosis.
alkanet ['ælkəˌnɛt] *s.* (bot.) 1. pie de paloma, palomilla, onoquiles. 2. ancusa, ancusa de tintes.
Alka-Seltzer (TM) ['ælkə'sɛltzər] *s.* alka-seltzer.
all [ɔl] *a.* 1. todo, ej., *a. day,* todo el día, *a. his life,* toda su vida; (*con el s. en pl.*) todos, ej., *a. the others,* todos los demás. 2. **a. that kind of crap,** (vulg.) y demás porquerías, y así sucesivamente; **a. this and heaven too,** el oro y el moro; **of a. (days, nights, people, things,** etc.), (expresa sorpresa, reprobación o desagrado) de todos (los días, las noches, las personas, etc.) tenía que ser (éste, él, ella, etc.); entre todas (las cosas) tenía que ser (ésta, etc.), ej., *he was elected chairman, of a. people,* de todas las personas tenía que ser él quien fuera elegido presidente, *this night of a. nights!* ¡entre todas las noches tenía que ser ésta!; **of a. things!** ¡imagínate! *—adv.* 1. todo, del todo, completamente, enteramente. 2. (dep.) por cada bando, por bando. 3. **a. along,** siempre, durante todo el tiempo; constantemente, desde el principio; **a. along the line,** de cabo a rabo, de pe a pa; **a. at once, a. of a sudden,** de repente, de golpe; **a. in,** exhausto, agotado; **a. of,** no menos de (un kilómetro, etc.); **a. out,** a más no poder; **a. over,** por todas partes, en toda la superficie o extensión; en todo el cuerpo; concluido, terminado (una relación amorosa, etc.); típicamente, característicamente, ej., *that is me a. over,* eso es típicamente mío, esa acción me pinta de cuerpo entero; **a. right,** muy bien; apropiado, satisfactorio; **a. set,** listo, dispuesto; **a. the better,** tanto mejor, menos mal; **a. the same,** a pesar de todo, sin embargo; **a. the way,** (fam.) sin reserva alguna, completamente; hasta el fin; **a. the worse,** tanto peor; **a. there,** (fam.) en su juicio, en sus cabales; **a. too soon,** demasiado pronto; **a. wet,** (fam.) equivocado, falso, incorrecto; **to be a. the same (to),** ser indiferente (para), dar lo mismo (a). *—pron.* 1. todo, totalidad. 2. todo lo que tiene (uno), todos los bienes (de uno), ej., *he lost his a.,* perdió todo lo que tenía. 3. todos, todo el mundo. 4. **a. aboard,** todos a bordo; **a. but,** casi; **a.** o **in a.,** en conjunto, contando todo, con todo; **a. of it,** todo, todo eso; **a. of us,** todos nosotros; **a. told,** con todo, considerado todo; **a. very fine (but), a. very well (but),** todo eso está muy bien (pero); **at a.,** del todo; siquiera algo, siquiera alguno, ej., *if you have any idea at a.,* si tienes siquiera alguna idea; (en frases verbales) ej., *if you will come at a.,* es decir, si llegas a venir; (en negaciones) en (lo) absoluto, ej., *I have no idea at a.,* no tengo ninguna idea en absoluto; **above a.,** sobre todo, ante todo; **after a.,** después de todo, al fin y al cabo; **and a.,** y demás, y otras cosas por el estilo, etc.; **for a.,** en lo que, ej., *for a. I care,* en lo que a mí me toca . . . ; a despecho de, a pesar

de; ej., *for a. his knowledge, he is a stupid man,* a pesar de saber tanto, es un hombre estúpido; **for a. I know,** que yo sepa; **for good and a.,** para siempre; **it's a. one,** es igual, da lo mismo; **not at a.,** (en respuesta a agradecimiento) de nada, por nada, no hay de qué; **one and a., a. and sundry,** todos y cada uno; individual y colectivamente; **once and for a.,** de una vez por todas; **that is a. there is to it,** eso es todo, no hay más que hablar, sanseacabó.

Allah ['ælə, ɑ'lɑ, B 'ælə, 'ɑlɑ] *s.* (islam.) Alá.

all-American [ˌɔlə'mɛrəkən] *a.* 1. típicamente norteamericano. 2. (dep., E.U.) escogido como el mejor de todas las regiones de los Estados Unidos para jugar en un seleccionado.

allantoic [ˌælən'toʊɪk] *a.* (med.) alantoico.

allantois [ə'læntoʊəs] *s.* (*pl.* ALLANTOIDES [ˌælən'toʊəˌdiz]) (med.) alantoides, membrana alantoica.

all-around [ˌɔlə'raʊnd] *a.* 1. de aptitudes variadas. 2. de uso variado, de utilidad general, versátil. 3. completo, ej., *an all-around failure,* un fracaso completo.

allay [ə'leɪ] *v.t., v.i.* aliviar (se), aquietar(se), calmar(se), apaciguar(se), mitigar(se), moderar(se).

all-clear [ɔl'klɪr] *s.* señal de que ha pasado el peligro (esp. de ataque aéreo).

all-comprehensive ['ɔlˌkɑmprɪ'hɛnsɪv, B -ˌkɔm-] *a.* que comprende la totalidad.

all-conquering [-'kɑŋkərɪŋ, B -'kɔŋ-] *a.* irresistible, que todo lo vence.

all-consuming [-kən'sumɪŋ, B -'sju-] *a.* consumidor, devastador.

all-day ['ɔl'deɪ] *a.* que dura todo el día.

allegation [ˌælɪ'geɪʃən] *s.* 1. alegación. 2. (der.) alegato. 3. argumento, excusa, algo que se aduce sin pruebas para corroborarlo.

allege [ə'lɛdʒ] *v.t.* 1. alegar, afirmar. 2. sostener, pretender.

alleged [ə'lɛdʒd, ə'lɛdʒəd, B ə'lɛdʒd] *a.* alegado, afirmado; supuesto, pretendido.

alleger [ə'lɛdʒər, B -ə] *s.* alegador, afirmante.

allegiance [ə'lidʒəns] *s.* lealtad, fidelidad.

allegoric [ˌælə'gɔrɪk] **allegorical** [-ɪkəl] *a.* alegórico.

allegorically [-ikəlɪ] *adv.* alegóricamente.

allegorist ['æləˌgɔrəst, B -gɔrɪst] *s.* autor de alegorías.

allegorize [-ˌaɪz, -gəraɪz, B -ˌaɪz] *v.t.* alegorizar, interpretar alegóricamente.

allegory [-ˌgɔrɪ, B -gərɪ] *s.* alegoría.

allegretto [ˌælə'grɛtoʊ, ɑl-, B ˌælɪ-] *a., adv., s.* (*pl.* ALLEGRETTOS) (mús.) alegreto.

allegro [ə'lɛgroʊ, ə'leɪ-] *a., adv., s.* (*pl.* ALLEGROS) (mús.) alegro.

allele [ə'lil] *s.* (biol.) alelo.

allelomorph [ə'lɛləˌmɔrf, B ə'li-mɔf] *s.* (biol.) alelomorfo.

allelomorphic [əˌlɛlə'mɔrfɪk, B əˌli'mɔf-] *a.* (biol.) alelomórfico.

allelujah, alleluia [ˌælə'lujə] *s. interj.* ¡aleluya!

allemande [ˌælə'mænd, B 'ælmɑnd] *s.* (mús.) alemanda.

all-embracing ['ɔlɪm'breɪsɪŋ] *a.* que lo abarca todo, exhaustivo, global.

allergen ['ælərdʒən, B -ədʒən] *s.* (med.) alergeno, alergina.

allergic [ə'lɜrdʒɪk, B ə'lɜdʒɪk] *a.* (med.) alérgico.

allergist ['ælərdʒəst, B -ədʒəst] *s.* especialista en alergias, alergista.

allergy ['ælərdʒɪ, B -ədʒɪ] *s.* (med.) alergia.

alleviate [ə'liviˌeɪt] *v.t.* aliviar, aligerar, mitigar.

alleviation [əˌlivɪ'eɪʃən] *s.* alivio, aligeramiento, mitigación.

alleviative [ə'liviˌeɪtɪv, B -ətɪv] *s.* paliativo, calmante.

alley ['ælɪ] *s.* 1. callejón, callejuela; pasillo, pasadizo. 2. **it's up (my, your) a.,** es algo que conozco (conoces) muy bien.

alley cat, 1. gato callejero, corriente. 2. (jer.) persona sexualmente promiscua.

alleyway [-ˌweɪ] *s.* callejuela o pasadizo estrecho (entre dos edificios).

all-fired ['ɔl'faɪrd, B -ˌfaɪəd] *a.* (jer., E.U.) extremo, excesivo. —*adv.* en extremo, excesivamente.

All Fools' Day, día de engañabobos (el primero de abril).

all-fours [-'fɔrz, B -'fɔz] *s. pl.* 1. extremidades (del hombre o un animal) 2. **on a.-f.,** en cuatro patas, a gatas.

all hail, *interj.* (ant.) ¡salud! ¡bienvenido!

Allhallows [ˌɔl'hæloʊz] *s.* día de Todos los Santos (primero de noviembre).

allheal ['ɔlˌhil] *s.* (bot.) valeriana.

alliaceous ['ælɪ'eɪʃəs] *a.* (bot.) aliáceo.

alliance [ə'laɪəns] *s.* 1. alianza, unión, liga. 2. enlace. 3. afinidad, relación.

allied [ə'laɪd, 'æˌlaɪd] *a.* 1. aliado, confederado. 2. (dic. de cosas o conceptos abstractos) relacionado, conexo, afín.

Allies ['ælˌaɪz, ə'laɪz] *s. pl.* (los) Aliados en las guerras mundiales.

alligator ['æləˌgeɪtər, B -ə] *s.* 1. (zool.) caimán, lagarto de Indias. 2. cocodrilo, cuero de cocodrilo o caimán. 3. rastra; bote que puede moverse sobre el terreno.

alligator clips, (elec.) pinzas de conexión instantánea, pinzas de cocodrilo.

alligator pear, (bot.) aguacate, palta.

alligator shear, (mec.) cizalla de palanca.

alligator wrench, (mec.) llave dentada o de mordaza.

all-important ['ɔlɪm'pɔrtənt, B -'pɔtənt] *a.* de suma importancia.

all-in ['ɔlˌɪn] *a.* 1. incluido todo, con todos los medios. 2. (fam.) **to be a.,** estar molido, estar hecho polvo.

all-inclusive [-ɪn'klusɪv] *a.* exhaustivo. global.

alliterate [ə'lɪtəˌreɪt] *v.t., v.i.* formar aliteración; ordenar (palabras, rimas, etc.) en aliteraciones.

alliteration [əˌlɪtə'reɪʃən] *s.* (poét.) aliteración.

alliterative [ə'lɪtəˌreɪtɪv, -rət-] *a.* aliterado.

all-knowing [ˌɔl'noʊɪŋ] *a.* omnisciente.

all-night ['ɔl'naɪt] *a.* (*party, vigil, journey*) que dura toda la noche; (*store, restaurant, cafe*) que está abierto toda la noche.

allocate ['æləˌkeɪt] *v.t.* distribuir, repartir, asignar.

allocation [ˌælə'keɪʃən] *s.* 1. distribución, repartición, reparto, asignación. 2. cuota, asignación, partida.

allocution [ˌælə'kjuʃən] *s.* alocución, discurso, arenga.

allod ['ælɑd, B 'ælɔd] *var. de* **allodium.**

allodial [ə'loʊdɪəl] *a.* (der.) alodial.

allodial property, (der.) bienes alodiales.

allodium [-əm] *s.* (der.) alodio.

allogamy [ə'lɑgəmɪ, B -'lɔg-] *s.* (bot.) alogamia.

allomerism [ə'lɑməˌrɪzəm, B ə'lɔm-] *s.* alomerismo.

allometric [ˌælə'mɛtrɪk] *a.* (bot.) alométrico.

allometry [ə'lɑmətrɪ, B ə'lɔm-] *s.* (bot.) alometría.

allomorph ['æləˌmɔrf, B -ˌmɔf] *s.* (min., quim., gram.) alomorfo.

allomorphism [-ˌɪzəm] *s.* (min., quím.) alomorfismo.

allonym ['æləˌnɪm] *s.* alónimo, nombre asumido (de otra persona por un autor).

allopath ['æləˌpæθ] *s.* (med.) alópata.

allopathic [ˌælə'pæθɪk] *a.* (med.) alopático (método, tratamiento, etc.).

allopathy [ə'lɑpəθɪ, B ə'lɔp-] *s.* (med.) alopatía.

allopatric [ˌælə'pætrɪk] *a.* (bot.) alopátrico.

allophane ['æləˌfeɪn] *s.* (min.) alófana.

allophone ['æləˌfoʊn] *s.* (fon.) alófono, forma variante de un fonema.

all-or-none [ˌɔlər'nʌn, B ˌɔlə'-] *a.* absoluta o ninguna (efectividad, reacción, etc.).

allot [ə'lɑt, B ə'lɔt] *v.t.* (*pret., p.p.* ALLOTTED; *p.pr.* ALLOTTING) distribuir, repartir, asignar, destinar.

allotment [-mənt] *s.* 1. asignación, distribución. 2. lote, porción, asignación, cupo, cuota.

allotrope ['æləˌtroʊp] *s.* (quím.) forma alotrópica.

allotropic [ˌælə'trɑpɪk, B -'trɔp-] *a.* (quím.) alotrópico.

allotropism [ə'lɑtrəˌpɪzəm, B ə'lɔt-] **allotropy** [-pɪ] *s.* (quím.) alotropía.

allottee [əˌlɑt'i, B əˌlɔt'i] *s.* suscriptor, beneficiario de una asignación.

all-out ['ɔl'aʊt] *a.* (fam.) extremo (esfuerzo, etc.); con toda energía, resuelto.

allover [-ˌoʊvər, B -və] *a.* de diseño repetido en toda su extensión (tela o superficie).

allow [ə'laʊ] *v.t.* 1. asignar (suma, pensión, etc.), dar (tiempo). 2. dejar, permitir, conceder. 3. admitir, reconocer. 4. descontar, deducir (rebaja, porcentaje, etc.). 5. permitir la presencia o entrada de (personas, animales, etc.), ej., *no dogs allowed,* no se permiten perros. 6. **a. (two pounds, a gallon, etc.) for,** calcular o considerar (dos libras, un galón, etc.) para; **a. me,** (como fórmula de cortesía) ¡permítame!; **a. oneself,** permitirse, darse el placer de. —*v.i.* **a. for,** tener en cuenta.

allowable [-əbəl] *a.* admisible, permisible, tolerable.

allowance [-əns] *s.* 1. permiso, autorización. 2. concesión, indulgencia. 3. tolerancia (en peso, tamaño, etc.). 4. asignación, pensión, mesada; (E.U.) estipendio (para niños). 5. (com.) descuento, rebaja. 6. (dep.) ventaja (dada a un competidor). 7. **to make a. for,** tener en cuenta, tomar en consideración; **to make allowances,** ser indulgente. —*v.t.* 1. asignar una mesada o ración a. 2. poner a dieta, adietar.

alloy [ə'lɔɪ, 'ælɔɪ, B ə'lɔɪ] *v.t.* 1. alear, ligar, mezclar (los metales). 2. (fig.) adulterar, deteriorar; templar, moderar. ['ælˌɔɪ, ə'lɔɪ] *s.* 1. ley, quilate del oro, ley de la plata. 2. aleación, amalgama, liga, mezcla.

alloy steel, acero de liga, acero de aleación.

all-powerful ['ɔl'paʊrfəl, B -'paʊəfəl] *a.* todopoderoso, omnipotente.

all-purpose [-'pɜrpəs, B -'pɜpəs] *a.* de uso múltiple, para usos variados, de utilidad general.

all right, 1. satisfactorio, apropiado; correcto, no errado. 2. sin daño, ileso. 3. si, de acuerdo; indudablemente, sin duda.

all-right, *a.* 1. digno de confianza. 2. bueno, excelente.

all-round [-'raʊnd] *var. de* **all-around.**

All Saints' Day, día de Todos los Santos (primero de noviembre).

allseed [-ˌsid] *s.* planta que produce muchas semillas.

all-seeing [-'siɪŋ] *a.* que todo lo ye.

All Souls' Day, día de los Difuntos, día de los fieles Difuntos; día de los Muertos (Am.). (dos de noviembre).

allspice [-ˌspaɪs] *s.* 1. (bot.) pimienta malagueta, pimienta de Jamaica. 2. (cocina) pimienta inglesa.
all-star [-'stɑr, B -'stɑ] *a.* formado (exclusivamente) por ases o primeras figuras, ej., *an a.-s. football team,* un equipo formado (exclusivamente) por ases del fútbol, *an a.-s. cast,* un elenco formado (exclusivamente) por estrellas (del teatro, cine, etc.).
all-time [-'taɪm] *a.* (experimentado) hasta el presente, record, ej., *an all-time low,* el (punto, nivel, etc.) más bajo hasta el presente.
allude [ə'lud] *v.i.* (con *to*) aludir (a), referirse.
allure [ə'lʊr, B ə'ljʊə] *v.t.* fascinar, tentar, atraer, seducir. *—s.* fascinación, encanto, tentación, atracción, seducción.
alluring [-ɪŋ, B -rɪŋ] *a.* atractivo, atrayente, seductor, tentador, fascinante.
allusion [ə'luʒən] *s.* alusión, indirecta.
allusive [ə'lusɪv, -zɪv, B -sɪv] *a.* alusivo.
allusive arms, (her.) armas parlantes.
alluvial [ə'luvɪəl] *a.* aluvial, de aluvión.
alluvial cone, alluvial fan, abanico aluvial.
alluvial tin, estaño de acarreo (casiterita).
alluvion [-ən] *s.* 1. aluvión, avenida. 2. inundación.
alluvium [-əm] *s.* terreno aluvial.
all-wave ['ɔl'weɪv] *a.* (rad.) de toda onda.
all-weather [-'wɛðər, B -ə] *a.* de todo tiempo; para todas las estaciones.
ally [ə'laɪ, 'æl,aɪ] *v.t.* (*pret., p.p.* ALLIED; p.pr. ALLYING) (con *to* o *with*) unir; confederar, coligar, hacer alianza (con); **a. oneself (with),** aliarse (con). *—v.i.* aliarse, confederarse. *—s.* ['æl,aɪ, ə'laɪ] aliado, confederado.
allyl ['æləl] *s.* (quím.) alilo.
allylene ['ælәlin] *s.* (quím.) alileno.
almagest ['ælmə,dʒɛst] *s.* (astr.) almagesto.
alma mater [ˌælmə'mɑtər, B -ə] *s.* la universidad donde uno se ha recibido.
almanac ['ɔlmə,næk, 'æl- B'ɔl-] *s.* almanaque, calendario.
almandine ['ælmən,din] **almandite** [-ˌdaɪt] *s.* (min.) almandina, granate almandino.
almightiness [ɔl'maɪtɪnəs] *s.* omnipotencia.
almighty [ɔl'maɪtɪ] *a.* omnipotente, todopoderoso; **an a. bore** (jer.) un plomazo; **God A.!** (*interj.*) ¡santo cielo!, ¡Virgen Santísima!; **the A.,** el Todopoderoso.
almique [ælmə'ki] *s.* (zool.) almiquí, aire, pequeño mamífero de Cuba.
almond ['ɑmənd, 'æm-, 'æl-, B 'ɑm-] *s.* 1. almendra. 2. (bot.) almendro, almendrera, allozo.
almond-eyed [-ˌaɪd] *a.* de ojos almendrados.
almond paste, (cocina) pasta de almendras.
almond-shaped [-ˌʃeɪpt] *a.* almendrado.
almond tree, almendro, almendrera, allozo.
almoner ['ælmənər, 'ɑm-, B -ə] *s.* 1. limosnero. 2. (G.B.) asistente médico-social (en un hospital).
almonry [-ənrɪ] *s.* sitio donde se reparten limosnas.
almost ['ɔl,moʊst] *adv.* casi, por poco.
alms [ɑmz, ɑlmz, B ɑmz] *s.* (*pl.* ALMS) limosna, caridad; **to give a.,** dar limosna.
alms box, alms chest, cepillo o alcancía para las limosnas.
almsgiver ['ɑms,gɪvər, B -ə] *s.* limosnero (el que da limosna).
almsgiving [-ɪŋ] *s.* caridad, beneficencia.
almshouse [-ˌhaʊs] *s.* hospicio, casa de beneficencia, asilo de pobres.
almsman [-mən] *s.* mendigo, pordiosero.
almswoman [-ˌwʊmən] *s.* mendiga, pordiosera.
almucantar [ˌælmju'kæntər, B -ə] *s.* (astr.) almicantarat, almicantarada.
alnico ['ælnɪ,koʊ] *s.* (metal.) álnico (aleación de aluminio, níquel y cobre).
alod ['ælɑd, B -ɔd] **alodium** [ə'loʊdɪəm] *vars. de* **allodium.**
aloe ['æloʊ] *s.* (bot.) áloe, lináloe, acíbar, zabila.
aloeswood ['æloʊz,wʊd] *s.* (bot.) palo de áloe, agáloco.
aloft [ə'lɔft] *adv.* 1. arriba, en alto. 2. en el aire; en vuelo. 3. (mar.) arriba, en la arboladura. 4. (aer.) en vuelo.
aloha [ə'loʊə, ɑ'loʊ,hɑ] *s.* (Hawaiano) bienvenido, saludos, adiós.
aloin ['æloʊɪn] *s.* (quím.) aloína.
alone [ə'loʊn] *a.* 1. solo, solitario. 2. único. 3. **let a.,** sin hablar de; mucho menos; **to leave** (o **to let**) **a.,** dejar en paz, no molestar; no tocar; **to stand a.,** ser único. *—adv.* sólo, solamente.
along [ə'lɔŋ] *prep.* 1. por, ej., *I was going a. the street,* iba por la calle. 2. a lo largo de, ej., *a. the road,* a lo largo del camino. 3. paralelamente a, paralelo a, ej., *sailing a. the coast,* navegando paralelamente a la costa, *path a. the road,* pista paralela al camino. 4. en el curso de. 5. en conformidad con, ej., *investigation a. established principles,* investigación en conformidad con principios establecidos. 6. en movimiento, hacia adelante. *—adv.* 1. a lo largo. 2. adelante. 3. junto con. 4. conmigo, consigo, ej., *come a. with me,* venga usted conmigo. 5. **a. with,** conjuntamente con; **all a.,** desde el principio; **get a. with you!** (G.B. vulg.) ¡no me vengas con eso!; **move a.!** ¡apárte(n)se!; ¡muéva(n)se de aquí!; **to carry a.,** llevar consigo; **to get a.,** (fam.) poder arreglárselas; **to get a. with (someone),** llevarse (bien) con (alguien); **to go a. with,** acompañar; (jer.) aprobar o aceptar (una idea, sugerencia, etc.).
alongshore [-'ʃɔr, B -'ʃɔ] *adv.* a lo largo de la costa; a la orilla; **to come a.,** atracar, acercarse a la costa.
alongside [-ˌsaɪd] *adv.* 1. a lo largo, al lado. 2. (mar.) al costado, borda con borda. 3. **to bring a.,**abarloar; **to come a.,** acostarse, abarloarse, atracar al costado (de otro barco). *—prep.* 1. a lo largo de, junto a. 2. (mar.) al costado de.
aloof [ə'luf] *adv.* 1. lejos, aparte. 2. (mar.) (más allá) a barlovento. 3. **to keep** o **stand a. (from),** mantenerse apartado (de), no intervenir (en). *—a.* reservado, distante.
aloofness [-nəs] *s.* retraimiento, indiferencia, alejamiento.
alopecia [ˌælə'piʃə, B -sɪə] *s.* (med.) alopecia, calvicie.
aloud [ə'laʊd] *adv.* 1. en voz alta. 2. con voz fuerte.
alouette [ˌælu'ɛtə] *s.* (fr.) 1. alondra. 2. canción infantil que se canta en grupo.
alow [ə'loʊ] *adv.* (mar.) abajo.
aloysia [ˌælə'ɪʃə, B -'ɪsɪə] *s.* (bot.) luisa, hierba luisa, reina luisa.
alp [ælp] *s.* montaña elevada; **the Alps,** los Alpes.
alpaca [æl'pækə] *s.* 1. alpaca, mamífero natural de Sudamérica. 2. piel de dicho animal. 3. tejido fuerte de algodón y lana que se usa para forrar atuendos invernales.
alpenglow ['ælpən,gloʊ] *s.* resplandor rojizo que se ve en las cumbres de las montañas antes de caer o salir el sol.
alpenhorn [-ˌhɔrn, B -ˌhɔn] *s.* cuerno alpino de potente sonoridad (de madera, usado por los montañeses suizos).
alpenstock [-ˌstɑk, B -ˌstɔk] *s.* bastón puntiagudo (de los alpinistas).
alpestrine [æl'pɛstrən] *a.* alpestre, alpino.
alpha ['ælfə] *s.* 1. alfa, primera letra del alfabeto griego. 2. Alfa, la estrella más importante de una constelación.
alpha and omega, (fig.) alfa y omega, el principio y el fin, lo más importante de un asunto.
alphabet ['ælfə,bɛt, -bət] *s.* alfabeto, abecedario; (fig.) rudimentos de (una ciencia, una disciplina).
alphabetic [ˌælfə'bɛtɪk] **alphabetical** [-ɪkəl] *a.* alfabético.
alphabetize ['ælfəbə,taɪz] *v.t.* 1. alfabetizar, ordenar alfabéticamente. 2. proveer de un alfabeto.
alpha iron, (metal.) hierro alfa.
alphameric [ˌælfə'mɛrɪk] **alphanumeric** [-nu-, B -nju-] *a.* que imprime o usa letras y números (máquinas de contabilidad o computadoras).
alpha particle, (fís.) partícula alfa.
alpha ray, (fís.) rayo alfa.
alpha rhythm, (med.) ritmo alfa, una de las ondas más comunes en un encefalograma.
Alphonsine Tables [ˌæl'fɑnsən-, B -'fɔn-] (astr.) Tablas Alfonsinas.
alphos ['ælfɑs, B -fɔs] *s.* (med.) albarazo, albarraz.
alpine ['æl,paɪn] *a.* alpino. *—s.* (bot.) planta nativa de las regiones boreales o alpinas.
alpine currant, (bot.) calderilla.
alpinism ['ælpə,nɪzəm] *s.* alpinismo.
alpinist [-nəst] *s.* alpinista.
alpist ['ælpəst] *s.* (bot.) alpiste.
alquifou [ˌælkɪ'fu] *s.* (quím.) alquifol.
already [ɔl'rɛdɪ] *adv.* ya, desde entonces, antes de ahora.
Alsace [æl'sæs, -'seɪs, B 'ælsæs] *s.* Alsacia.
Alsace Lorraine [-lə'reɪn, -lɔ-] Alsacia Lorena.
Alsatian [æl'seɪʃən] *a.* alsaciano, de Alsacia. *—s.* 1. alsaciano. 2. (zool.) perro lobo.
alsike clover ['ɔl,sæk-, -ˌsaɪk-] (bot.) trébol híbrido, trébol de Suecia, trébol de los pantanos.
also ['ɔlsoʊ] *adv.* también, igualmente, asimismo, además.
also-ran [-ˌræn] *s.* 1. perdedor (en carreras). 2. (fam.) fracasado.
Altaic [æl'teɪɪk] *a.* altaico, perteneciente a la familia lingüística del mismo nombre.
altar ['ɔltər, B -tə] *s.* 1. altar, ara. 2. **A.,** (astr.) Ara. 3. **to lead to the a.,** conducir al altar, casarse con.
altar boy, (rel.) acólito, monaguillo.
altar call, (rel.) exhortación de los pastores protestantes a los devotos.
altar cloth, (relig.) mantel del altar, sabanilla, palia.
altar of repose, (relig.) altar lateral (en una iglesia católica) donde se guarda la hostia consagrada desde el Jueves al Viernes Santo.
altar piece, retablo.
altar rail, comulgatorio, reja que separa el altar de los fieles.
altar stone, (relig.) ara (losa de piedra que contiene reliquias de mártires y que forma parte del altar católico).
altazimuth [æl'tæzəməθ] *s.* (astr.) altacimut.
alter ['ɔltər, B -tə] *v.t.* 1. alterar, cambiar, modificar, transformar. 2. (E.U.) castrar. 3. **to a. course,** (mar.) cambiar de rumbo. *—v.i.* alterarse, cambiar(se), transformarse.
alterability [ˌɔltərə'bɪlətɪ] *s.* alterabilidad.
alterable ['ɔltərəbəl] *a.* alterable, mudable.
alteration [ˌɔltə'reɪʃən] *s.* alteración, modificación, cambio, mudanza, arreglo (de un vestido, etc.).

alterative ['ɔltəˌreɪtɪv, -rət] *s., a.* (med.) alterante.
altercate ['ɔltərˌkeɪt, B -təˌ-] *v.i.* altercar, disputar.
altercation [ˌɔltər'keɪʃən, B -tə'-] *s.* altercado, discusión acalorada, disputa.
alter ego [ˌɔltə'rigoʊ] 1. (psic.) álter ego, el otro yo. 2. amigo de confianza.
altern [ɔl'tɜrn, B -'tɜn] *a.* (ant.) alterno.
alternant [-ənt] *a.* alternante, alterno.
alternate ['ɔltərnət, 'æl- B ɔl'tɜnɪt] *a.* 1. alterno. 2. (bot., geom.) alterno 3. **on a. days** un día si y otro no. —*s.* 1. substituto, suplente. — [-ˌneɪt, B 'ɔltəˌ-] *v.t.* alternar, variar. —v.i. alternar, turnar(se).
alternate angles, (geom.) ángulos alternos.
alternately [-lɪ] *adv.* alternativamente, por turno.
alternating ['ɔltərˌneɪtɪŋ, B -təˌ-] *a.* alternante, alterno, alternativo.
alternating current, (elec.) corriente alterna.
alternating pull, (mec.) tracción alternada.
alternating stress, (mec.) esfuerzo alternante.
alternation [ˌɔltər'neɪʃən, ˌæl-, B -tə'-] *s.* alternancia, alternación, turno.
alternation of generations, (biol.) alternancia de generaciones.
alternative [ɔl'tɜrnətɪv, æl-, B -'tɜnət-] *s.* alternativa. —*a.* 1. alternativo. 2. (gram., lóg.) disyuntivo. 3. otro, ej., *an a. method* otro método.
alternative conjunction, (gram.) conjunción disyuntiva.
alternator ['ɔltərˌneɪtər, B 'æltəˌ-tə] *s.* (elec.) alternador.
althaea, althea [æl'θiə] *s.* (bot.) malvavisco, alter.
althorn ['æltˌhɔrn, B -ˌhɔn] *s.* (mús.) tuba tenor.
although, altho [ɔl'ðoʊ] *conj.* aunque, a pesar de que, bien que, si bien.
altigraph ['æltəˌgræf, B -ˌgrɑf] *s.* altímetro, registrador, aneroide registrador.
altimeter [æl'tɪmətər, B 'æltɪmitə] *s.* (aer.) altímetro.
altimetry [æl'tɪmətrɪ] *s.* altimetría.
altiplano [ˌæltɪ'plɑnoʊ] *s.* altiplano, altiplanicie, meseta.
altitude ['æltəˌtud, B -ˌtjud] *s.* altitud, altura, elevación.
altitude sickness, (med.) mal de altura, mal de las montañas, mareo de la cordillera.
alto ['æltoʊ] *s.* (mús.) 1. contralto. 2. cualquier instrumento de registro intermedio.
altocumulus [-'kjumjələs] *s.* (meteor.) altocúmulo.
altogether [ˌɔltə'gɛðər, B -ə] *adv.* 1. enteramente, del todo, por completo. 2. en conjunto, en totalidad, en suma. **—in the a.,** (fam.) completamente desnudo, en cueros.
alto-relievo ['æltoʊrɪlivoʊ] *s.* alto relieve.
altostratus [-'streɪtəs, -'stræt-, B -'streɪt-, -'strɑt-] *s.* (meteor.) altoestrato.
altruism ['æltrʊˌɪzəm] *s.* altruismo, amor al prójimo.
altruist [-əst] *a., s.* altruista.
altruistic [ˌæltrʊ'ɪstɪk] *a.* altruista.
alula ['æljələ] *s.* (*pl.* ALULAE [-ˌli, -ˌlaɪ]) (ento.) álula.
alum ['æləm] *s.* (quím.) alumbre.
alumel [ə'luməl, B ə'ljum-] *s.* (metal.) aleación de níquel y aluminio.
alumina [ə'lumənə, B ə'lju-] *s.* (quím.) alúmina.
aluminate [-nət] *s.* (quím.) aluminato.
aluminic [ˌæljə'mɪnɪk] *a.* alumínico.
aluminiferous [əˌlumə'nɪfərəs, B əˌlju-] *a.* aluminífero.
aluminite [ə'luməˌnaɪt, B ə'lju-] *s.* (min.) aluminita.
aluminium [ˌæljə'mɪnɪəm] *s.* (pr. G.B.) *var. de* **aluminum.**
aluminize [ə'luməˌnaɪz, B ə'lju-] *v.t.* aluminizar, revestir o tratar con aluminio.
aluminothermic welding [əˌlumənoʊ'θɜrmɪk, B əˌlju-'θɜmɪk] soldadura por aluminotermia.
aluminothermy [ə'lumənoʊˌθɜrmɪ, B ə'lju-ˌθɜmɪ] *s.* (quím.) aluminotermia.
aluminous [ə'lumənəs, B ə'lju-] *a.* aluminoso.
aluminum [ə'lumənəm, B ə'lju-] *s.* aluminio.
aluminum brass, latón de aluminio.
aluminum foil, hoja o lámina de aluminio.
aluminum oxide, (quím.) óxido de aluminio, alúmina.
aluminum paint, pintura alumínica.
aluminum powder, aluminio en polvo.
alumna [ə'lʌmnə] *s.* (*pl.* ALUMNAE [-ni]) exalumna (de una universidad o escuela).
alumnus [ə'lʌmnəs] *s.* (*pl.* ALUMNI [-ˌnaɪ]) exalumno (de una universidad o escuela).
alum rock, (min.) piedra alumbre.
alumstone ['æləm'stoʊn] *s.* (min.) aluminita, alunita.
alunite ['æljəˌnaɪt] *s.* (min.) alunita.
alveolar [ˌæl'viələr, B -lə] *a.* (anat., gram., fon.) alveolar.
alveolar arch, (anat.) arco alveolar.
alveolate [-lət] *a.* alveolado.
alveolus [æl'viələs] *s.* (*pl.* ALVEOLI [-ˌlaɪ]) (anat., zool.) alvéolo.
alvine ['ælvɪn, B -ˌvaɪn] *a.* (med.) alvino.
always ['ɔlwɪz, -wəz, -ˌweɪz] *adv.* siempre, para siempre.
alyssum [ə'lɪsəm, B 'ælɪs-] *s.* (bot.) 1. especie de alhelí (planta brasícea). 2. alhelicillo.
Alzheimer's disease ['ɔltshaɪmərz] *s.* enfermedad de Alzheimer, mal de Alzheimer.
am, (*primera pers. sing. del pres. de indic. de* to be) soy, estoy.
Am. *abrev. de* **American, American,** (E.U.) Norteamérica, Norteamericano.
Am *símb. de* **americium,** americio (Am).
A.M. *abrev. de 1.* **ante meridiem,** antes del mediodía. 2. **Master of Arts,** Maestro en Humanidades. 3. **amplitude modulation,** (rad.) amplitud modulada.
AMA *abrev. de* **American Medical Association,** Asociación Norteamericana de Médicos.
amadou ['æmədu] *s.* yesca.
amah ['ɑmə] *s.* ama de cría, ama de leche (en la India y el Extremo Oriente).
amain [ə'meɪn] *adv.* (poét.) vigorosamente, vehementemente; con prisa.
amalgam [ə'mælgəm] *s.* 1. (quím.) amalgama, aleación. 2. (fig.) amalgama, mezcla.
amalgamate [-gəˌmeɪt] *v.t., v.i.* amalgamar(se); mezclar(se), unir(se).
amalgamation [əˌmælgə'meɪʃən] *s.* 1. (quím.) amalgamación, aleación. 2. fusión (de compañías comerciales, etc.).
amalgamation process, mezcla de metales por amalgamación.
amandin ['æməndən, ə'mæn-] *s.* (bioquím.) amandina.
amandine ['ɑmənˌdin, 'æm-, B ə'mænˌdaɪn] *a.* almendrado.
amanita [ˌæmə'naɪtə, -'nitə] *s.* (bot.) amanita.
amanuensis [əˌmænjʊ'ɛnsəs] *s.* (*pl.* AMANUENSES [-siz]) 1. amanuense, escribano. 2. (hum.) secretario.
amaranth ['æməˌrænθ] *s.* 1. (bot.) amaranto, borlones. 2. (color) púrpura oscuro. 3. (poét.) flor inmarcesible (imaginaria), imperecedera.
amaranthine [ˌæmə'rænθən, B -ˌθaɪn] *a.* 1. (bot.) amarantáceo. 2. purpúreo, purpurino. 3. (poét.) inmarcesible, imperecedero.
amaryllidaceous [ˌæməˌrɪlə'deɪʃəs] *a.* (bot.) amarilídeo.
amaryllis [-'rɪləs] *s.* (bot.) amarilis.
amass [ə'mæs] *v.t.* acumular, amontonar, juntar.
amassment [-mənt] *s.* acumulación, montón, cúmulo.
amateur ['æməˌtɜr, -ətər, B -tə, -ˌtjʊə] *s.* 1. aficionado. 2. (dep.) amateur.
amateurish [ˌæmə'tɜrɪʃ, B -'tjʊr-] *a.* superficial; a manera de aficionado; torpe.
amative ['æmətɪv] *a.* amatorio, amativo.
amatol ['æməˌtɔl] *s.* (quím.) amatol.
amatorial [ˌæmə'tɔrɪəl] **amatorious** [-ɪəs] **amatory** ['æməˌtɔrɪ, B -tərɪ] *a.* amatorio, amoroso.
amaurosis [ˌæmɔ'roʊsəs] *s.* (med.) amaurosis.
amaze [ə'meɪz] *v.t.* dejar maravillado, asombrar. —*s.* sorpresa, asombro.
amazement [-mənt] *s.* asombro, sorpresa, estupefacción.
amazing [-ɪŋ] *a.* asombroso, maravilloso.
amazingly [-lɪ] *adv.* asombrosamente.
Amazon ['æməˌzɑn, B -əzən] *s.* 1. Amazonas. 2. amazona. 3. (fig.) amazona, marimacho.
Amazonian [ˌæmə'zoʊnɪən] *a.* 1. amazónico, del río Amazonas. 2. amazónico (característico de las amazonas).
amazonite ['æməzəˌnaɪt] *s.* (min.) amazonita.
ambages ['æmbɪdʒəz] *s. pl.* (ant.) ambages, rodeos de palabras, circunloquios.
ambassador [æm'bæsədər, B -də] *s.* embajador; enviado.
ambassador-at-large [-dərət'lɑrdʒ, B -'lɑdʒ] *s.* enviado especial, embajador viajero.
ambassador extraordinary, embajador enviado para una misión extraordinaria.
ambassadorial [æmˌbæsə'dɔrɪəl] *a.* de(l) embajador.
ambassador plenipotentiary, embajador plenipotenciario, autorizado para negociar y firmar tratados.
ambassadorship [-'bæsədərˌʃɪp, B -dəˌ-] *s.* embajada, cargo de embajador.
ambassadress [-drəs] *s.* embajadora; (fam.) esposa de embajador.
amber ['æmbər, B -bə] *s.* ámbar, cárabe, succino. —*a.* ambarino; del color del ámbar.
amberfish [-ˌfɪʃ] *s.* (ict.) casabe.
ambergris [-ˌgrɪs, -ˌgris] *s.* ámbar gris.
amber seed, (bot.) semilla de abelmosco.
ambiance, *var. de* **ambience.**
ambidexter [ˌæmbɪ'dɛkstər, B -stə] *a., var. de* **ambidextrous.** —*s.* hipócrita, persona de dos caras.
ambidextrous [-strəs] *a.* 1. ambidextro. 2. falso, hipócrita, doble.
ambience ['æmbɪəns] *s.* ambiente.
ambient [-ənt] *a.* ambiente, circundante.
ambiguity [ˌæmbə'gjuətɪ] *s.* ambigüedad, anfibología, palabra o frase ambigua.
ambiguous [æm'bɪgjʊəs] *a.* ambiguo, vago, impreciso, indefinido, anfibológico.
ambiguousness [-nəs] *s.* ambigüedad, vaguedad, incertidumbre.
ambit ['æmbət] *s.* ámbito, circuito, contorno.
ambition [æm'bɪʃən] *s.* ambición, aspiración. —*v.t.* ambicionar, aspirar.
ambitious [-əs] *a.* ambicioso, codicioso; (E.U.) emprendedor.

ambitiously [-lɪ] *adv.* ambiciosamente.
ambitiousness [-nəs] *s.* ambición, afán.
ambivalence [æm'bɪvələns] *s.* ambivalencia.
ambivalent [-lənt] *s.* ambivalente.
ambiversion [ˌæmbɪ'vɜrʒən, -ʃən, B -'vɜʒən, -ʃən] *s.* (psic.) ambiversión.
amble ['æmbəl] *v.i.* 1. amblar. 2. ambular, andar con pasos cómodos. —*s.* 1. ambladura. 2. paso cómodo.
ambler [-blər. B -blə] *s.* amblador.
amblygonite [æm'blɪgəˌnaɪt] *s.* (min.) ambligonita.
amblyopia [ˌæmblɪ'oupɪə] *s.* (med.) ambliopía.
ambo ['æmbou] *s.* ambón, púlpito (en las antiguas iglesias cristianas).
amboceptor ['æmbouˌsɛptər, B -tə] *s.* (fisiol.) amboceptor.
ambrosia [æm'brouʒə, B -zɪə] *s.* 1. ambrosía (manjar de los dioses). 2. (fig.) ambrosía (cosa deleitable al paladar y espíritu). 3. (bot.) ambrosía.
ambrosial [-əl] *a.* (fig.) delicioso, deleitable; celestial, divino.
Ambrosian [-ən] *a.* ambrosiano, de San Ambrosio (cantos).
ambry ['æmbrɪ] *s.* armario, despensa, alacena.
ambsace ['eɪmˌzeɪs] *s.* 1. ambos ases (la tirada más baja de los dados). 2. (fig.) poca cosa, insignificancia. 3. mala suerte, infortunio.
ambulacral [ˌæmbjə'lækrəl] *a.* (zool.) ambulacral.
ambulacrum [-rəm] *s.* (*pl.* AMBULACRA [-rə]) (zool.) ambulacro.
ambulance ['əmbjələns] *s.* ambulancia (vehículo para transportar enfermos).
ambulance chaser, (jer.) abogado que no repara en medios para conseguir clientes; picapleitos, tinterillo.
ambulance driver, conductor de ambulancia, ambulanciero.
ambulant [-lənt] *a.* 1. ambulante. 2. (med.) ambulante (lesión, enfermedad); ambulatorio (tratamiento o enfermedad).
ambulate [-ˌleɪt] *v.i.* ambular, deambular, andar, pasear.
ambulation [ˌæmbjə'leɪʃən] *s.* paseo.
ambulatory ['æmbjʊləˌtɔrɪ, B -lətərɪ] *s.* 1. ambulante, variable, mudable. 2. (med.) ambulatorio. —*s. pl.* (arq.) deambulatorio, galería o claustro para pasearse.
ambuscade ['æmbəˌskeɪd, B ˌæmbəs'keɪd] *var. de* **ambush.**
ambush ['æmˌbʊʃ] *v.t.* emboscar, acechar, poner celada a. —*v.i.* emboscarse. —*s.* emboscada, celada, trampa; **to fall into an a.,** caer en una emboscada; **to lay an a.,** tender una emboscada; **to lie in a.,** estar emboscado.
ameba, ameban, *vars. de* **amoeba, amoeban.**
amebiasis [ˌæmɪ'baɪəses] *s.* (med.) amibiasis.
amebic dysentery [əmibɪk-] (med.) disentería amibiana.
ameer, amir, *vars. de* **emir.**
ameliorate [ə'miljəˌreɪt] *v.t., v.i.* mejorar.
amelioration [əˌmiljə'reɪʃən] *s.* mejora, mejoramiento, mejoría, alivio.
amen ['eɪ'mɛn, 'ɑ-] *adv., s.* amén; **to say a.** to (fam.), sancionar, aprobar; terminar un asunto. —*interj.* amén, así sea, ojalá sea así.
amenability [əˌminə'bɪlətə, əˌmɛn-, B əˌmin-] *s.* receptibilidad, acuerdo, docilidad.
amenable [ə'minəbəl, ə'mɛn-, B ə'min-] *a.* 1. receptivo. 2. sujeto a juicio o examen. 3. tratable; dócil. 4. (con *to*) dispuesto a aceptar (razones, razonamiento, etc.).
amen corner, rincón donde concurren los fieles más devotos (en iglesias protestantes).
amend [ə'mɛnd] *v.t.* enmendar, corregir, recitificar. —*v.i.* reformarse, enmendarse.
amendable [-əbəl] *a.* enmendable, corregible, reformable.
amendment [-mənt] *s.* 1. enmienda, rectificación, corrección. 2. (der.) enmienda (de una ley).
amends [ə'mɛndz] *s. pl.* indemnización, reparación, satsifacción, compensación; **to make a. (for),** compensar, dar cumplida satisfacción (por).
amenity [ə'mɛnətɪ, ə'min-] *s.* 1. amenidad, afabilidad. 2. cosa amena, comodidad 3. (*pl.*) modales agradables o atractivos.
amenorrhoea, amenorrhea [eɪˌmɛnə'riə] *s.* (med.) amenorrea.
ament ['æmənt, 'eɪ-] *s.* (bot.) amento, candelilla.
amentaceous [ˌæmən'teɪʃəs, ˌeɪ-] *a.* (bot.) amentáceo.
amentia [əɪ'mɛntʃə, B ə'mɛnʃə] *s.* amencia, trastorno mental, imbecilidad.
amentiferous [ˌæmən'tɪfərəs, ˌeɪ-] *a.* (bot.) amentifloro.
Amer. *abrev. de* **America, American,** (E.U.) Norteamérica, norteamericano.
amerce [ə'mɜrs, B ə'mɜs] 1. (der.) multar. 2. penar, castigar.
amercement [-mənt] *s.* (der.) multa.
amerciable [-sɪəbəl] *a.* (der.) sujeto a multa.
America [ə'mɛrəkə] *s.* 1. América (el continente). 2. (fig.) los Estados Unidos, Norteamérica, América. 3. **the Americas** América, el continente americano.
American [-kən] *a., s.* americano; (E.U.) norteamericano, estadounidense.
Americana [əˌmɛrə'kænə, -'kɑnə] *s. pl.* (E.U.) colección de documentos, objetos, etc. (literarios, históricos, etnológicos, etc.) relativos a los Estados Unidos.
American beauty, (bot.) especie de rosa grande encarnada.
American cheese, (E.U.) queso tipo Cheddar.
American eagle, águila americana (escudo de armas de los E.U.).
American English *s.* inglés americano.
Americanese [ə'mɛrəkəˌniz, -ˌnis] *s.* manera de hablar o argot propio de los Estados Unidos.
American Federation of Labor, Confederación Norteamericana del Trabajo.
American Indian *a.* amerindio, de los indios americanos. —*s.* indio americano, amerindio.
Americanism [-kəˌnɪzəm] *s.* americanismo; (*custom*) costumbre norteamericana.
Americanist [-nəst] *s.* 1. americanista, estudiante de algún aspecto de la cultura de las Américas o de Estados Unidos. 2. simpatizante de los Estados Unidos o de su política.
American ivy, (bot.) enredadera de Virginia.
Americanize [-ˌnaɪz] *v.t., v.i.* norteamericanizar(se).
American Legion, organización de veteranos de las fuerzas armadas de los E.U.
American plan, habitación con pensión completa.
American sable (bot.) marta cebellina americana.
American saddle horse, caballo de silla criado en Kentucky.
American trotter, (tipo de) caballo ligero americano de trote y paso.
Americium [ˌæmə'rɪsɪəm, -'rɪʃ-] *s.* (quím.) americio.
Amerind ['æməˌrɪnd] *s.* amerindio, indio americano.
Amerindian [ˌæmə'rɪndɪən] **Amerindic** [-dɪk] *a.* amerindio.
ametabolic [ˌeɪˌmɛtə'bɑlɪk, B -'bɔl-] *a.* (fisiol.) ametábolo.
ametabolism [ˌeɪmə'tæbəˌlɪzəm] *s.* (fisiol.) ametabolia.
amethyst ['æməθəst] *s.* (min.) amatista.
ametropia [ˌæmə'troupɪə] *s.* (med.) ametropía.
ametropic [-pɪk] *a.* (med.) ametrópico.
Amharic [æm'hærɪk] *s., a.* amhárico, idioma de Etiopía.
amiability [ˌeɪmɪə'bɪlətɪ] *s.* amabilidad.
amiable ['eɪmɪəbəl] *a.* amable, afable, amistoso.
amianthus [ˌæmɪ'ænθəs] *s.* (min.) amianto.
amicability [ˌæmɪkə'bɪlətɪ] *s.* cordialidad, disposición amistosa.
amicable ['æmɪkəbəl] *a.* amigable, amistoso.
amicableness [-nəs] *s.* cordialidad, disposición amistosa.
amice ['æməs] *s.* (relig.) amito.
amicronucleate [ˌeɪˌmaɪkrou'nuklɪət, B -'nju-] *a.* (biol.) sin micronúcleo.
amicus curiae [əˌmikəs'kjʊrɪˌaɪ] (der.) persona invitada a dar su opinion en un asunto en el cual no es parte interesada.
amid [ə'mɪd] *prep.* 1. entre, en medio de, rodeado por. 2. en el curso de, durante.
amide ['æmˌaɪd] *s.* (quím.) amida.
amidol ['æməˌdɔl] *s.* (quím.) amidol.
amidships [ə'mɪdˌʃɪps] *adv.* (mar.) en medio del buque.
amidst [ə'mɪdst] *var. de* **amid.**
amine [ə'min, 'æmən, B 'æmaɪn] *s.* (quím.) amina.
aminic [ə'minɪk, ə'mɪn-] *a.* (quím.) amínico.
amino acid [ə'minou-] (quím.) aminoácido.
amir, *var. de* **emir.**
Amish ['amɪʃ] amish; **the A.** los amish.
amiss [ə'mɪs] *adv.* mal, impropiamente, fuera de lugar; erradamente; **to take a.,** tomar a mal. —*a.* impropio, errado; malo, inoportuno, inconveniente.
amitosis [ˌæmɪ'tousəs] *s.* (biol.) amitosis.
amity ['æmətɪ] *s.* amistad, concordia (esp. entre naciones).
Amman [ə'mɑn] *s.* Amán, capital de Jordania.
ammeter ['æmˌitər, B -ɪtə] *s.* (elec.) amperímetro.
ammine ['æmˌin, -ən] *s.* (quím.) amina.
ammo ['æmou] *s.* (fam.) *abrev. de* **ammunition,** munición.
Ammon ['æmən] *s.* 1. (mitol.) Amón, deidad egipcia. 2. antiguo reino de los amonitas (hoy Jordania).
ammonal [-əl] *s.* amonal.
ammonia [ə'mounjə] *s.* (quím.) 1. amoníaco. 2. agua amoniacal.
ammoniacal [ˌæmə'naɪəkəl] **ammoniac** [ə'mounɪˌæk] *a.* (quím.) amoniacal, amoniáceo, amónico; amoníaco.
ammonia gas, (quím.) gas amoníaco.
ammonia water, (quím.) agua amoniacal.
ammonification [əˌmounəfə'keɪʃən] *s.* 1. impreganción con amoníaco. 2. transformación en amoníaco o substancia amoniacal.
ammonite ['æməˌnaɪt] *s.* 1. (pal.) amonita, amonites (molusco fósil). 2. (quím.) amonita. 3. abono. 4. amonita, antiguo habitante de Jordania.
ammonium [ə'mounɪəm] *s.* (quím.) amonio.
ammonium chloride, (quím.) cloruro de amonio.
ammonium hydroxide, (quím.) hidróxido de amonio, agua amoniacal.
ammonium nitrate, nitrato amónico o de amonio.
ammonium sulphate, sulfato amónico o de amonio; (geol.) mascagnita.

ammonoid ['æmə,nɔɪd] *s.* (pal.) amonita.
ammophilous [ə'mɑfələs, B ə'mɔf-] *a.* (zool.) amófilo, que vive en la arena.
ammunition [,æmjə'nɪʃən] *s.* 1. munición, municiones. 2. argumentos, ej., *his remarks provided a. for his opponents* sus comentarios dieron argumentos a sus contrincantes. —*v.t.* (mil.) proporcionar municiones, pertrechar.
ammunition belt, banda de cartuchos.
ammunition dump, depósito de municiones.
amnesia [æm'niʒə, B -zjə] *s.* (med., psic.) amnesia.
amnesiac [-zɪ,æk] **amnesic** [-zɪk] *a.* amnésico.
amnesty ['æmnəstɪ] *s.* amnistía, indulto. —*v.t.* indultar.
amnion ['æmnɪ,ɑn, -ən, B -ɔn] *s.* (*pl.* AMNIONS o AMNIA [-nɪə]) (zool.) amnios.
amniotic [,æmnɪ'ɑtɪk, B -'ɔt-] *a.* (anat.) amniótico.
amniotic fluid, (fisiol.) agua del amnios.
amoeba [ə'mibə] *s.* (*pl.* AMOEBAS o AMOEBAE [-bi]) ameba, amiba.
amoebaen verse [,æmə'biən-] (poét.) verso amebeo.
amoeban [ə'mibən] *a.* (zool.) amibiano.
amoebiasis, *var. de.* **amebiasis.**
amoebic [-bɪk] *a.* (zool.) amíbico.
amoebic dysentery, (med.) disentería amibiana.
amoebocyte [ə'mibə,saɪt] *s.* (biol.) amibocito.
amoeboid [-,bɔɪd] *a.* amiboideo.
amok, *var. de* **amuck.**
amole [ə'moʊlɪ] *s.* (bot.) amole.
amomum [ə'moʊməm] *s.* (bot.) amomo.
among [ə'mʌŋ] **amongst** [ə'mʌŋst, -'mʌŋst] *prep.* 1. entre, mezclado con, en medio de. 2. entre (todos). ej., *they ate a whole loaf a. themselves,* se comieron un pan entero entre ellos.
amontillado [ə,mɑntə'lɑdoʊ, B ə,mɔn-] *s.* (vino) amontillado.
amoral [eɪ'mɔrəl, æ-] *a.* amoral, sin moralidad; ni moral ni inmoral.
amoralism [-ə,lɪzəm] *s.* (filos.) amoralismo.
amorality [,eɪmə'rælətɪ, ,æ-] *s.* amoralidad.
amorino [,ɑmɔ'rinoʊ] *s.* (arte) querubín.
amorist ['æmərəst] *s.* 1. amante, galán. 2. escritor romántico.
amorous [-rəs] *a.* 1. amoroso, enamoradizo. 2. (con *of*) enamorado (de). 3. de amor. 4. tierno, cariñoso.
amorousness [-nəs] *s.* naturaleza o propensión amorosa.
amorpha [ə'mɔrfə, B ə'mɔfə] *s.* (bot.) amorfa.
amorphism [-,fɪzəm] *s.* amorfia.
amorphous [-fəs] *a.* amorfo, informe.
amort [ə'mɔrt, B ə'mɔt] *a.* (poét.) exánime.
amortization [,æmɔrtə'zeɪʃən, ə,mɔrt-, B ə,mɔt-, ,æmɔt-] *s.* amortización.
amortize ['æmər,taɪz, ə'mɔr-, B ə'mɔ,taɪz] *v.t.* amortizar.
amount [ə'maʊnt] *v.i.* (con *to*) 1. importar, sumar, ascender a, llegar a. 2. significar, venir a ser, ser igual a, ej., *his negligence almost amounts to a crime,* su negligencia es casi (igual a) un crimen. —*s.* importe, monto; cantidad.
amour [ə'mʊr, æ-, B ə'mʊə, æ-] *s.* amorío, amor, intriga de amor.
amp [æmp] *s.* 1. (elec.) amperio. 2. (electrón.) amplificador.
ampelideous [,æmpə'lɪdɪəs] *a.* (bot.) ampelídeo.
ampelite ['æmpə,laɪt] *s.* (min.) ampelita.
ampelography [,æmpə'lɑgrəfɪ, B -'lɔg-] *s.* ampelografía.
ampelopsis [,æmpə'lɑpsəs, B -'lɔp-] *s.* (bot.) ampelopsis.
amperage ['æmpərɪdʒ, -,pɪr-] *s.* (elec.) amperaje.
ampere ['æmp,pɪr, B -pɛə] *s.* (elec.) amperio.
ampere-hour [-'aʊr, B -,pɛər'aʊə] *s.* (elec.) amperio-hora.
amperemeter [-,mitər, B -tə] *s.* amperímetro.
ampere-turn [-'tɜrn, B -'tɜn] *s.* (elec.) amperio-espira, amperio-vuelta.
ampersand ['æmpər,sænd, B -pə,-] *s.* el signo & (que significa *and,* y).
amphetamine [æm'fɛtə,min, -mən] *s.* (farm.) anfetamina.
amphiarthrosis [,æmfɪɑr'θroʊsəs, B -ɑ'-] *s.* (anat.) anfiartrosis.
amphibian [,æ'fɪbɪən] *a.* anfibio. —*s.* 1. (biol., zool.) anfibio. 2. avión anfibio; vehículo anfibio.
amphibiotic [,æmfɪbaɪ'ɑtɪk, B -'ɔt-] *a.* (ento.) anfibiótico.
amphibious [æm'fɪbɪəs] *a.* 1. (zool., bot.) anfibio. 2. (mil.) anfibio, que puede maniobrar en tierra y agua.
amphibole ['æmfə,boʊl] *s.* (min.) anfíbol.
amphibolite [æm'fɪbə,laɪt] *s.* (min.) anfibolita.
amphibology [,æmfə'bɑlədʒɪ, B -'bɔl-] *s.* anfibología, doble sentido, ambigüedad.
amphibrach ['æmfə,bræk] *s.* (poét.) anfíbraco.
amphictyony [æm'fɪktiənɪ] *s.* (hist.) anfictionía (confederacion de las antiguas ciudades griegas).
amphidiploid [,æmfɪ'dɪp, lɔɪd] *a.* (biol.) anfidiploide.
amphigamous [æm'fɪgəməs] *a.* (bot.) anfígamo.
amphigory ['æmfə,gɔrɪ, B -fɪgərɪ] *s.* composición literaria sin sentido.
amphimacer [æm'fɪməsər, B -sə] *s.* (poét.) anfímacro.
amphimictic [,æmfɪ'mɪktɪk] *a.* (biol.) anfimíctico.
amphimixis [-'mɪksəs] *s.* (biol.) anfimixis, reproducción sexual.
amphineura [-'njʊrə] *s. pl.* (zool.) anfineuros.
amphineurous [-rəs] *a.* (zool.) anfineuro.
Amphion [æm'faɪən] *s.* (mitol.) Anfión, príncipe tebano.
amphioxus [,æmfɪ'ɑksəs, B -'ɔk-] *s.* (zool.) anfioxo.
amphipod ['æmfɪ,pɑd, B -,pɔd] *s.* (zool.) anfípodo.
amphiprostyle [,æmfɪ'proʊ,staɪl] *s.* (arq.) anfipróstilo.
amphisbaena [,æmfəs'binə] *s.* (zool.) anfisbena.
amphiscians [æm'fɪʃɪənz] *s. pl.* (geog.) anfiscios, habitantes de la zona tórrida.
amphistylar [,æmfɪ'staɪlər, B -lə] *a.* (arq.) con columnas a ambos lados.
amphitheater, amphitheatre [,æmfə,θiətər, -,θɪ-, B -tə] *s.* anfiteatro.
Amphitrite [,æmfə'traɪtɪ, B 'æmfɪ,traɪtɪ] *s.* (mitol.) Anfitrite, hija de Océano y esposa de Poseidón.
amphitropous [æm'fɪtrəpəs] *a.* (bot.) anfítropo.
Amphitryon [-trɪən] *s.* (mitol.) Anfitrión, rey de Tirinto, famoso por la esplendidez de sus banquetes.
amphora ['æmfərə] *s.* ánfora.
amphoteric [,æmfə'terɪk] *a.* (quím.) anfótero, que puede reaccionar como ácido o como base.
amp-hr *abrev. de* **ampere-hour,** amperiohora, amperhora (ah).
ample ['æmpəl] *a.* 1. amplio, extenso, espacioso, ej., *a. space,* espacio amplio. 2. abundante, copioso, ej., *a. resources,* abundantes recursos. 3. adecuado.
ampleness [-nəs] *s.* 1. gran extensión, anchura. 2. abundancia.
amplexicaul [æm'plɛksɪ,kɔl] *a.* (bot.) amplexicaulo (díc. de órganos que abrazan el tallo).
amplification [,æmpləfə'keɪʃən] *s.* 1. amplificación, ampliación. 2. (der.) prórroga. 3. (electrón.) amplificación.
amplifier ['æmplə,faɪər B -ə] *s.* 1. amplificador, ampliador. 2. (fís.) amplificador (válvula o aparato).
amplify [-,faɪ] *v.t., v.i.* amplificar, ampliar; (fís.) amplificar.
amplitude [-,tud, B -,tjud] *s.* 1. amplitud, extensión. 2. abundancia. 3. (fís., rad., astr.) amplitud.
amplitude compass, (naveg.) brújula de azimut.
amplitude meter, (ing.) vibrómetro.
amplitude modulation, (rad.) modulación de amplitud.
amply ['æmplɪ] *adv.* ampliamente, abundantemente, holgadamente, con creces.
ampoule ['æmpul] **ampul** [-pjul] **ampule** [-pjul] *s.* (farm.) ampolla, ampolleta (de inyecciones).
ampulla [æm'pʊlə, -'pʌlə, B -'pʊlə] *s.* (*pl.* AMPULLAE [-i]) 1. ampolla (para vino, ungüentos, etc. esp. la usada por los antiguos romanos). 2. (anat.) ampolla.
amputate ['æmpjə,teɪt] *v.t.* amputar.
amputation [,æmpjə'teɪʃən] *s.* amputación, ablación.
amputee [-'ti] *s.* persona que ha sufrido una amputación.
Amsterdam ['æmstər,dæm, B -stə,-] *s.* Amsterdam, capital de Holanda.
Amtrak ['æm,træk] *s.* Ferrocarriles de los EEUU.
amu *abrev. de* **atomic mass unit,** unidad de peso atómico.
amuck [ə'mʌk] *s.* amok, locura homicida. —*adv.* furiosamente, frenéticamente; **to run a.,** estar atacado de locura homicida, correr destruyendo todo lo que se encuentra, atacar a ciegas, a troche y moche. —*a.* frenético.
amulet ['æmjələt] *s.* amuleto, dije, talismán.
amuse [ə'mjuz] *v.t.* entretener, distraer, divertir; **a. oneself,** divertirse, recrearse, distraerse.
amusement [-mənt] *s.* 1. diversión, distracción. 2. diversión. 3. recreo, pasatiempo.
amusement park, parque de atracciones o de diversiones.
amusing [-ɪŋ] *a.* divertido, entretenido, gracioso; **to be a.,** tener gracia, ser divertido.
amygdala [ə'mɪgdələ] *s.* (*pl.* AMYGDALAE [-li]) (anat.) amígdala.
amygdalaceae [ə,mɪgdə'leɪsɪ,i] *s. pl.* (bot.) amigdaláceas.
amygdalin [ə'mɪgdələn] *s.* (quím.) amigdalina.
amygdaline [-lɪn, -laɪn] *a.* amigdalino.
amygdaloid [-,lɔɪd] *s.* (min.) roca amigdaloide. —*a.* 1. (min.) amigdaloide. 2. amigdaleo.
amyl ['æməl] *s.* (quím.) amilo.
amylaceous ['æmə'leɪʃəs] *a.* (bot.) amiláceo.
amyl alcohol, (quím.) alcohol amílico.
amylase ['æmə,leɪs] *s.* (quím., bioquím.) amilasa.
amylene [-,lin] *s.* (quím.) amileno.
amylic [ə'mɪlɪk] *a.* (quím.) amílico.
amyloid ['æmə,lɔɪd] *a.* (quím.) amiloideo.
amyloidosis [,æmə,lɔɪ'doʊsəs] *s.* (med.) amiloidosis, amilosis.
amylolysis [,æmə'lɑləsəs, B -'lɔl-] *s.* (quím.) amilólisis.
amylolytic [-loʊ'lɪtɪk] *a.* (quím.) amilolítico.
amylopsin [-'lɑpsən, B -'lɔp-] *s.* (bioquím.) amilopsina.

amylum ['æmələm] *s.* (quím.) amilón, almidón.
amyotonia [ˌeɪˌmaɪə'toʊnɪə] *s.* (med.) amiotonía.
an [ən, æn] *art. indef.* un, uno, una (es el mismo art. indef. *a* al que se le añade una *n* cuando antecede a una palabra que comienza con vocal o *h* muda, no a las que comienzan con *u* o *h* aspirada, ej., *an apple,* una manzana, *an hour,* una hora; *a unicorn,* un unicornio, *a horse,* un caballo).
ana ['ænə, B 'ɑnə] *s.* 1. colección de anécdotas y fotografías de una persona o lugar notable. 2. anecdotario. —*adv.* (farm.) ana, por partes iguales.
Anabaptism [ˌænə'bæpˌtɪzəm] *s.* (relig.) anabaptismo.
Anabaptist [-təst] *s., a.* (relig.) anabaptista.
anabatic [-'bætɪk] *a.* (meteor.) ascendente.
anabiosis [-baɪ'oʊsəs] *s.* (biol.) anabiosis.
anabolic [-'bɑlɪk, B -'bɔl-] *a.* (med.) anabólico.
anabolic steroid *s.* esteroide anabólico.
anabolism [ə'næbəˌlɪzəm] *s.* (med.) anabolismo.
anabolite [-'laɪt] *s.* (biol.) anabolina.
anacardiaceous [ˌænəˌkɑrdɪ'eɪʃəs, B -'kɑd-] *a.* (bot.) anacardiáceo.
anacardic [-'kɑrdɪk, B -'kɑd-] *a.* (quím.) anacárdico.
anacardium [-ɪəm] *s.* (bot.) anacardio.
anachronism [ə'nækrəˌnɪzəm] *s.* anacronismo.
anachronistic [əˌnækrə'nɪstɪk] *a.* anacrónico.
anaclastic [ˌænə'klæstɪk] *a.* (fís.) anaclástico.
anaclisis [-'klaisəs] *s.* anaclisis, dependencia psicológica.
anacoluthon [-kə'luˌθɑn, B -ˌθɔn] *s.* (*pl.* ANACOLUTHA [-'luθə] o ANACOLUTHONS) (gram.) anacoluto.
anaconda [ˌænə'kɑndə, B -'kɔn-] *s.* (zool.) anaconda.
Anacreon [ə'nækrɪən] *s.* Anacreonte, poeta lírico griego.
Anacreontic [əˌnækrɪ'ɑntɪk, B -'ɔn-] *a.* 1. anacreóntico. 2. jovial y festivo. —*s.* anacreóntica.
anacrusis [ˌænə'krusəs] *s.* (poét.) anacrusis.
anaculture ['ænəˌkʌltʃər, B -tʃə] *s.* (bact.) anacultivo.
anadem ['ænəˌdɛm] *s.* (poét.) anadema, guirnalda.
anadiplosis [ˌænədə'ploʊsəs] *s.* (ret.) anadiplosis.
anadromous [ə'nædrəməs] *a.* (zool.) anadromo.
anaemia, anaemic, *vars. de* **anemia, anemic.**
anaerobe ['ænəˌroʊb, ə'nɛrˌoʊb] *s.* (bot., biol.) anaerobio, anaerobionte.
anaerobic [ˌænə'roʊbɪk, B -ˌɛə'roʊb-] *a.* (bot., biol.) anaerobio.
anaesthesia, anaesthetic, *vars. de* **anesthesia, anesthetic.**
anaglyph ['ænəˌglɪf] *s.* 1. (arqueol.) anáglifo (obra tallada al bajo relieve). 2. (foto.) anaglifo (fotografía estereoscópica).
anaglyphical [ˌænə'glɪfɪkəl] *a.* (arq.) anaglífico.
anagnorisis [æˌnæg'nɔrəsəs] *s.* (poét.) anagnórisis.
anagoge ['ænəˌgoʊdʒɪ] *s.* anagogía, interpretación mística de una palabra o texto.
anagogical ['ænə'gɑdʒɪkəl, B -'gɔdʒ-] *a.* anagógico; místico, espiritual.
anagogy, *var. de* **anagoge.**
anagram ['ænəˌgræm] *s.* anagrama.
anagrammatic [ˌænəgrə'mætɪkəl] *a.* anagramático.
anagrammatism [-'græməˌtɪzəm] *s.* anagramatismo, arte de formar anagramas.
anal ['eɪnəl] *a.* (anat., psic.) anal.
anal character, (psic.) carácter anal.
analcime [ə'nælˌsim -ˌsaɪm] *s.* (min.) analcima.
analects ['ænəlˌɛkts] *s. pl.* analectas, selecciones o extractos de una obra literaria o grupo de obras.
analemma [ˌænəl'ɛmə] *s.* (astr.) analema.
analepsis [-'ɛpsəs] *s.* (*pl.* ANALEPSES [-ˌsiz]) (med.) analepsia.
analeptic [-'ɛptɪk] *s., a.* (med.) analéptico.
anal-expulsive [ˌeɪnəlɪks'pʌlsɪv] *a.* (psic.) (carácter) expulsivo anal.
analgen [æn'ældʒən] *s.* (farm., quím.) analgeno.
analgesia [ˌænəl'dʒiʒə, B -næl'dʒizɪə] *s.* (med.) analgesia.
analgesic [-'dʒizɪk, -sɪk] *a., s.* analgésico.
analog computer ['ænəlˌɔg-] *s.* computadora analógica, ordenador analógico.
analogical [ˌænəl'ɑdʒɪkəl, B -'ɔdʒ-] *a.* analógico, análogo.
analogism [ə'næləˌdʒɪzəm] *s.* (lóg.) analogismo.
analogize [-ˌdʒaɪz] *v.t.* explicar por analogía.
analogous [-gəs] *a.* análogo, semejante, paralelo, parecido.
analogue, analog ['ænəlˌɔg] *s.* 1. palabra o cosa análoga. 2. (zool., bot.) órgano análogo.
analogy [ə'nælədʒɪ] *s.* 1. analogía, semejanza, correlación, afinidad. 2. (filol., lóg.) analogía.
analphabetic [ˌænˌælfə'bɛtɪk] *a.* 1. analfabético; contrario al orden alfabético. 2. analfabeto.
anal stage, (psic.) etapa anal (en el desarrollo de la personalidad).
analysand [ə'næləˌsænd] *s.* persona que se somete al psicoanálisis.
analyse, analyser, *vars. de* **analyze, analyzer.**
analysis [ə'næləsəs] *s.* (*pl.* ANALYSES [-ˌsiz]) 1. análisis. 2. (quím.) análisis, separación de una substancia en sus componentes. 3. (mat.) análisis, metodología del cálculo y el álgebra. 4. psicoanálisis.
analyst ['ænələst] *s.* 1. analizador, analista. 2. psicoanalista.
analytic [ænəl'ɪtɪk] **analytical** [-ɪkəl] *a.* (lóg., gram., mat.) analítico.
analytic geometry, geometría analítica.
analytics [-ɪks] *s. pl.* (*sing. en const.*) (lóg.) analítica.
analyzable [-'aɪzəbəl] *a.* analizable.
analyzation [-ə'zeɪʃən] *s.* análisis.
analyze, (pr. G.B.) **analyse** ['ænəlˌaɪz] *v.t.* 1. analizar, hacer análisis de. 2. (lóg., mat., quím.) analizar. 3. psicoanalizar.
analyzer [-ər, B -ə] *s.* analizador.
anamnesis [ˌænˌæm'nisəs] *s.* (*pl.* ANAMNESES [-ˌsiz]) 1. anamnesis, reminiscencia. 2. (med.) antecedentes o historia clínica de una enfermedad o de un paciente.
anamnestic [-'nɛstɪk] *a.* anamnéstico.
anamniote [æ'næmnɪˌoʊt] *s.* (zool.) anamniota.
anamorphic [ˌænə'mɔrfɪk, B -'mɔfɪk] *a.* (ópt.) anamórfico.
anamorphosis [-fəsəs] *s.* (zool., bot.) anamorfosis.
anandrous [æn'ændrəs] *a.* (bot.) anandriario.
anapaest, anapest ['ænəˌpɛst] *s.* (poét.) anapesto.
anapestic [ˌænə'pɛstɪk] *a.* (poét.) anapéstico.
anaphase ['ænəˌfeɪz] *s.* (biol.) anafase.
anaphora [ə'næfərə] *s.* (ret.) anáfora.
anaphoric [ˌænə'fɔrɪk] **anaphorical** [-ɪkəl] *a.* (ret.) anafórico.
anaphrodisia [ˌænˌæfrə'dɪʒə, B -'dɪzɪə] *s.* anafrodisia, ausencia o disminución del deseo sexual.
anaphrodisiac [-'dɪzɪˌæk] *a., s.* (med.) anafrodisíaco.
anaphylaxis [ˌænəfə'læksəs] *s.* (med.) anafilaxis.
anaplasty ['ænəˌplæstɪ] *s.* (med.) anaplastia.
anaptyxis [ˌænæp'tɪksəs] *s.* (fon.) anaptixis.
anarch ['æn, ɑrk, B -ˌɑk] *s.* caudillo anarquista.
anarchic [æn'ɑrkɪk, B -'ɑkɪk] **anarchical** [-ɪkəl] *a.* anárquico.
anarchism ['ænərˌkɪzəm, B 'ænəˌ-] *s.* (pol.) anarquismo.
anarchist [-kəst] *s., a.* anarquista.
anarchistic [ˌænər'kɪstɪk, B ænə'-] *a.* anarquista.
anarcho-syndicalism [æˌnɑrkoʊ'sɪndɪkəˌlɪzəm, B ˌænəkoʊ-] *s.* (pol.) anarcosindicalismo.
anarcho-syndicalist [-ləst] *s.* anarcosindicalista.
anarchy ['ænərkɪ, B 'ænəkɪ] *s.* anarquía; desorden.
anarthria [æ'nɑrθrɪə, B -'nɑθrɪə] *s.* anartria, pérdida del habla.
anasarca [ˌænə'sɑrkə, B -'sɑkə] *s.* (med.) anasarca.
anastatic [-'stætɪk] *a.* (impr.) anastático, en relieve (impresión con troqueles de acero).
anastigmat [æ'næstɪgˌmæt] *s.* (ópt.) lente anastigmático.
anastigmatic [ˌænəˌstɪg'mætɪk] *a.* (ópt.) anastigmático.
anastomose [ə'næstəˌmoʊz, -ˌmoʊs] *v.i.* (anat., bot.) anastomizarse, anastomarse.
anastomosis [əˌnæstə'moʊsəs] *s.* (*pl.* ANASTOMOSES [-ˌsiz]) (anat., bot.) anastomosis.
anastomotic [-'mɑtɪk, B -'mɔt-] *s., a.* (anat., bot.) anastomótico.
anastrophe [ə'næstrəfɪ] *s.* (ret.) anástrofe.
anatase ['ænəˌteɪs, -ˌteɪz] *s.* (min.) anatasa.
anathema [ə'næθəmə] *s.* (*pl.* ANATHEMAS) 1. (relig.) anatema. 2. anatema, cosa execrable. 3. persona odiada.
anathematization [əˌnæθəmətə'zeɪʃən] *s.* imposición del anatema, excomunión.
anathematize ['ənæθəməˌtaɪz] *v.t.* anatematizar, excomunicar.
Anatolian [ˌænə'toʊlɪən] *s.* 1. nativo o habitante de la Anatolia (nombre antiguo del Asia Menor). 2. lengua (antigua) de Anatolia. —*a.* de Anatolia.
anatomic [ˌænə'tɑmɪk, B -'tɔm-] **anatomical** [-ɪkəl] *a.* anatómico.
anatomist [ə'nætəməst] *s.* anatomista, anatómico, anatómica.
anatomize [-ˌmaɪz] *v.t.* 1. anatomizar, disecar. 2. (fig.) analizar minuciosamente.
anatomy [-mɪ] *s.* 1. anatomía. 2. (fam.) esqueleto, momia. 3. anatomía, cuerpo humano. 4. análisis, disección.
anatoxin [ænə'tɑksən, B -'tɔk-] *s.* (med.) anatoxina.
anatropous [ə'nætrəpəs] *a.* (bot.) anátropo (óvulo vegetal).
Anaxagoras [ˌænæk'sægərəs] *s.* (hist.) Anaxágoras, filósofo griego.
Anaximenes [ˌænæk'sɪməniz] *s.* Anaxímenes, preceptor de Alejandro Magno.
anbury ['ænbərɪ] *s.* (vet.) tumor blando, furúnculo (en los caballos).
ANC *abrev. de.* **African National Congress** Congresso Nacional Africano; **the ANC** el CNA.
ancestor ['ænˌsɛstər, B -tə] *s.* antepasado; **ancestors** antepasados, ascendientes, abuelos.

ancestral [æn'sɛstrəl] *a.* ancestral, atávico.
ancestry ['æn,sɛstrɪ] *s.* 1. ascendencia. 2. **of noble a.** de noble linaje. 3. **to trace one's a.** hacerse el árbol genealógico.
anchor ['æŋkər, B -kə] *s.* 1. ancla, áncora. 2. (fig.) soporte, fuente de esperanza. 3. **at a.**, anclado, al ancla; **to cast** o **to drop a.**, echar anclas, dar fondo; **to drag a.**, arrastrar el ancla; **to ride at a.**, estar al ancla o fondeado; **to stock the a.**, encepar el ancla; **to weigh a.**, levar anclas. —*v.i.* anclar, ancorar, echar anclas. —*v.t.* ancorar; fijar, asegurar; (fig.) sujetar.
anchorage ['æŋkərɪdʒ] *s.* (mar.) 1. anclaje. 2. ancladero, anclaje, fondeadero. 3. (fig.) base segura, soporte firme.
anchor back, galga del ancla.
anchor beam, (mar.) serviola.
anchor bill, pico del ancla.
anchor buoy, (mar.) boya de anclaje, muerto de amarre.
anchor crown, diamante del ancla.
anchoress ['æŋkərəs] *s.* anacoreta (*f.*), ermitaña.
anchoret [-,rɛt] *s.* anacoreta (*m.*), ermitaño.
anchor fluke, oreja del ancla.
anchor ground, (mar.) fondeadero.
anchorite [-,raɪt] *s.* anacoreta (*m.*), ermitaño.
anchor lining, (mar.) varadero del ancla.
anchor palm, oreja del ancla.
anchorman ['ækərmæn] *s.* 1. (t.v.) anunciador, locutor, presentador. 2. (dep.) última persona.
anchor ring, arganeo, argolla del ancla.
anchor shank, caña del ancla.
anchor stock, cepo del ancla.
anchorwoman ['ænkərwʊmən] *s.* 1. (t.v.) anunciadora, locutora, presentadora; 2. (dep.) última persona.
anchovy ['æn,tʃoʊvɪ, -tʃəvɪ] *s.* (ict.) anchoa, anchova, haleche, boquerón.
anchylose, anachylosis, *vars. de* **ankylose, ankylosis.**
ancient ['eɪnʃənt, -tʃənt, B -ʃənt] *a.* antiguo, vetusto. —*s.* anciano; **the ancients,** los antiguos, la antigüedad.
ancient history, 1. historia antigua. 2. (fam.) cosa o asunto viejo, pasado de moda.
ancilla [æn'sɪlə] *s.* (*pl.* ANCILLAS) asistente, ayudante, ayudanta.
ancillary ['ænsə,lɛrɪ, B æn'sɪlərɪ] *a.* subordinado, dependiente, auxiliar.
ancipital [æn'sɪpətəl] *a.* (bot.) ancipital.
ancon ['æŋ,kɑn, B -kən] *s.* (arq.) ancón.
and [ənd, ænd, ən] *conj.* y o e; **a. so forth, a. so on,** etcétera, y así sucesivamente; **a. so,** entonces; **ifs and ands,** dimes y diretes; **nice a. warm,** agradablemente tibio; **try a. (come),** (fam.) trata de (venir), procura (venir).
Andalusian [,ændə'luʒən, B -'luzjən] *a.* andaluz, de Andalucía. —*s.* andaluz, andaluza.
andalusite [-'lu,saɪt] *s.* (min.) andalucita.
andante [ɑn'dɑn,teɪ, B æn'dæntɪ] *adv., a., s.* (mús.) andante.
andantino [,ɑn,dɑn'tinoʊ, B ,ændæn-] *adv., a., s.* (mús.) andantino.
Andean ['ændiən, æn'diən] *a.* andino, de los Andes.
Andes ['ændiz] *s.* (*pl.*) Andes.
andesite ['ændə,zaɪt] *s.* (min.) andesita.
andesitic [,ændə'zɪtɪk] *a.* (min.) andesítico.
andiron ['æn,daɪərn, B -,daɪən] *s.* morillo, soporte de hierro que sostiene los leños en la chimenea.
and/or ['ænd'ɔr] *conj.* y/o.
Andorran [æn'dɔrən] *a., s.* andorrano, natural de Andorra.
andradite ['ædrɑd,ait, 'ændrəd-] *s.* (min.) andradita.
Androcles ['ændrə,kliz] *s.* Androcles, esclavo de la leyenda romana.
androecium [æn'drisɪəm] *s.* (*pl.* ANDROECIA [-sɪə]) (bot.) androceo.
androgen ['ændrədʒən] *s.* (biol.) andrógeno (hormona masculina).
androgenic [,ændrə'dʒɛnɪk] *a.* (biol.) andrógeno.
androgynous [æn'drɑdʒənəs, B -'drɔdʒ-] *a.* (bot., zool.) andrógino.
androgyny [-dʒənɪ] *s.* (bot., zool.) androginia.
android ['ændrɔɪd] *s.* androide, robot.
Andromache [æn'drɑməkɪ, B -'drɔm-] *s.* (mitol.) Andrómaca, esposa de Héctor.
Andromeda [-ədə] *s.* (mitol., astr.) Andrómeda.
Andronicus [,ændrə'naɪkəs, æn'drɑnɪkəs, B -'drɔn-] *s.* (hist.) Andrónico.
androphagous [æn'drɑfəgəs, B -'drɔf-] *a.* andrófago, antropófago, caníbal.
androphobia [,ændrə'foʊbɪə] *s.* (med.) androfobia.
androphore ['ændrə,fɔr, B -,fɔ] *s.* (bot.) andróforo.
androsterone [æn'drɑstə,roʊn, B -'drɔs-] *s.* (bioguím.) androsterona.
anecdotage ['ænɪk,doʊtɪdʒ] *s.* anecdotario, libro o conjunto de anécdotas.
anecdotal [,ænɪk'doʊtəl] *a.* anecdótico.
anecdote ['ænɪk,doʊt] *s.* anécdota, relato, cuento.
anecdotic [,ænɪk'dɑtɪk, B -'dɔt-] **anecdotical** [-'doʊtəl] *a.* anecdótico.
anechoic [,ænɪ'koʊɪk] *a.* a prueba de ecos, sordo.
anechoic chamber, (acús.) cámara sorda.
anele [ə'nil] *v.t.* (ant.) olear, administrar la extremaunción.
anelectric [,ænə'lɛktrɪk] *a.* (fís.) aneléctrico.
anemia [ə'nimɪə] *s.* (med.) anemia.
anemic [-mɪk] *a.* (med.) anémico.
anemograph [ə'nɛmə,græf, B -,grɑf] *s.* (meteor.) anemógrafo, anemoscopio.
anemographic [æ,nɛmə'græfɪk] *a.* (meteor.) anemográfico.
anemography [,ænə'mɑgrəfɪ, B -'mɔg-] *s.* (meteor.) anemografía.
anemometer [-'mɑmətər, B -'mɔmətə] *s.* (meteor.) anemómetro.
anemometry [-ətrɪ] *s.* (meteor.) anemometría.
anemone [ə'nɛmənɪ] *s.* 1. (bot.) anémona, anémone. 2. (zool.) anémone de mar.
anemophilous [,ænə'mɑfələs, B -'mɔf-] *a.* (bot.) anemófilo.
anemophily [-lɪ] *s.* (bot.) anemofilia.
anemoscope [ə'nɛmə,skoʊp] *s.* (meteor.) anemoscopio.
anent [ə'nɛnt] *prep.* (ant.) tocante a, concerniente a, acerca de, respecto a.
aneroid ['ænə,rɔɪd] *a.* (fís.) aneroide.
aneroid barometer, barómetro aneroide (sin mercurio o fluido).
anesthesia [,ænəs'θiʒə, B -'θizjə] *s.* (med.) anestesia.
anesthesiologist [-,θizɪ'ɑlədʒəst, B -'ɔl-] *s.* (med.) anestesiador, anestesista; especialista en anestesiología.
anesthesiology [-dʒɪ] *s.* (med.) anestesiología.
anesthetic [-'θɛtɪk] *a., s.* anestésico, anestético.
anesthetist [ə'nɛsθətəst, B ə'nis-] *s.* anestesista.
anesthetize [-'taɪz] *v.t.* anestesiar.
anestrous [æn'ɛstrəs] *a.* (vet.) 1. sin estro. 2. de quietud entre estros (período).
anestrus [-trəs] *s.* (vet.) período de quietud (sexual) entre dos estros.
aneurysm, aneurism ['ænjə,rɪzəm] *s.* (med.) aneurisma.
aneurysmal [,ænjə'rɪzməl] *a.* (med.) aneurismal.
anew [ə'nu, B ə'nju] *adv.* de nuevo, nuevamente, otra vez; en forma diferente.
anfractuosity [æn,frækt∫ʊ'ɑsətɪ, B -'ɔs-] *s.* 1. anfractuosidad, sinuosidad. 2. (anat.) anfractuosidad, canal o pasaje sinuoso.
anfractuous [-t∫ʊəs] *a.* anfractuoso, sinuoso, tortuoso.
angary ['æŋgərɪ] *s.* (der.) derecho de un país beligerante a embargar, usar o destruir la propiedad de neutrales en caso de necesidad.
angel ['eɪndʒəl] *s.* 1. ángel. 2. (G.B.) antigua moneda de oro. 3. (jer.) patrocinador (de producciones teatrales, etc.).
angel cake, (cocina) bizcochuelo blanco y ligero de clara de huevo, azúcar y harina.
angelfish [-,fɪʃ] *s.* (ict.) ángel de mar, angelote, angelito.
angel food *var. de* **angel cake.**
angel food cake *var. de* **angel cake.**
angelic [æn'dʒɛlɪk] **angelical** [-ɪkəl] *a.* angélico, angelical; **to make a.** o **become a.,** angelizar.
angelica [-ɪkə] *s.* (bot.) angélica.
angelically [-lɪ] *adv.* angelicalmente.
angelin ['ændʒəlɪn] *s.* (bot.) pangelín, angelín.
angel of death, ángel exterminador.
angelus [-ləs] *s.* (relig.) ángelus.
angel water, (farm.) agua angélica.
anger ['æŋgər, B -gə] *s.* 1. ira, cólera, enfado. 2. (dial. G.B.) (med.) inflamación (de una llaga, úlcera, etc.). 3. **a fit of a.,** un acceso de cólera. —*v.t.* encolerizar, enfurecer, enfadar, enojar. —*v.i.* encolerizarse, enfurecerse.
Angevin ['ændʒəvən] *a.* (hist.) angevino, de la casa de Anjou.
angina [æn'dʒaɪnə] *s.* (med.) angina.
angina pectoris [-'pɛktərəs] (med.) angina de pecho.
angiocholitis [,ændʒɪəkə'laɪtəs] *s.* (med.) angiocolitis.
angioclast ['ændʒɪə,klæst] *s.* (med.) angioclasto.
angiography [,ændʒɪ'ɑgrəfɪ, B -'ɔg-] *s.* (anat.) angiografía.
angiology [-'ɑlədʒɪ, B -'ɔl-] *s.* (anat.) angiología.
angioma [-'oʊmə] *s.* (*pl.* ANGIOMATA [-mətə] o ANGIOMAS) (med.) angioma, tumor.
angiosperm ['ændʒɪə,spɜrm, B -,spɜm] *s.* (bot.) angiosperma.
angle ['æŋgəl] *v.i.* 1. pescar con caña. 2. (con *for*) intrigar para conseguir, tratar de conseguir artificiosamente.
angle, *s.* 1. ángulo, esquina, codo. 2. (geom.) ángulo. 3. (hierro en) ángulo. 4. (fig.) ángulo, punto de vista, aspecto. 5. (jer.) plan tortuoso y mal intencionado para conseguir algo. 6. **at an a.,** en ángulo; **at right angles,** en ángulo recto. —*v.t.* 1. doblar o mover en ángulo. 2. presentar (noticias, reporte) con prejuicio o desde un solo punto de vista. —*v.i.* doblar o moverse en ángulo.
angle bar, (f.c.) eclisa de ángulo, eclisa cantonera, barra angular, brida angular.
angle brace, (const.) cuadral, riostra angular, esquinal.
angled ['æŋgəld] *a.* (*ú. pr. en compuestos*) angular, ej., *three-a.,* triangular, *right-a.,* rectangular.
angledozer ['æŋgəl,doʊzər, B -zə] *s.* (const.) hoja de empuje angular.
angle iron, hierro angular, ángulo, escuadra de hierro.

angle meter, (top.) clinómetro; goniómetro.
angle of attack, (aer.) ángulo de ataque (ángulo agudo entre la dirección del viento y las alas).
angle of deflection, ángulo de desviación, ángulo de desvío.
angle of incidence, (fís.) ángulo de incidencia.
angle of lag, (elec.) ángulo de retraso, ángulo de atraso.
angle of lead, (elec.) ángulo de avance.
angle of reflection, (fís.) ángulo de reflexión.
angle of refraction, (fís.) ángulo de refracción.
angle of view, (foto.) ángulo visual.
angler ['æŋglər, B -glə] *s.* 1. pescador de caña. 2. (jer.) persona que usa trucos para conseguir algo. 3. (ict.) pejesapo, alacrán marino, pescador.
angle rafter, (arq.) lima tesa.
anglesite ['æŋgəl,saɪt] *s.* (min.) anglesita.
angle vise, tornillo ajustable, cárcel o morsa de ángulo.
angleworm [-,wɜrm, B -,wɜːn] *s.* lombriz de tierra.
Anglia ['ænglɪə] *s.* Anglia, nombre latino de Inglaterra.
Anglian [-ən] *a., s.* anglo, inglés.
Anglican [-kən] *s., a.* (relig.) anglicano.
Anglicanism [-kə,nɪzəm] *s.* (relig.) anglicanismo.
Anglicism ['æŋglə,sɪzəm] *s.* 1. (filol.) anglicismo. 2. carácter típicamente inglés. 3. anglomanía.
Anglicist [-səst] *s.* especialista en lingüística inglesa.
Anglicize [-,saɪz] *v.t.* 1. hacer adoptar costumbres inglesas. 2. adaptar al inglés (palabras de otro idioma).
angling ['æŋglɪŋ] *s.* pesca con caña.
Anglo-American [,æŋgloʊə'mɛrəkən] *a., s.* angloamericano.
Anglo-Catholic [-'kæθəlɪk] *a., s.* anglocatólico.
Anglo-Indian [-'ɪndɪən] *s., a.* angloindio.
Anglomania [-'meɪnɪə] *s.* anglomanía.
Anglomaniac [-ɪæk] *s.* anglómano.
Anglo-Norman [-'nɔrmən, B -'nɔmən] *a., s.* anglonormando.
Anglophile ['æŋglə,faɪl] *s.* anglófilo.
Anglophobe [-,foʊb] *s.* anglófobo.
Anglophobia [,æŋglə'foʊbɪə] *s.* anglofobia.
Anglophobic [-'foʊbɪk] *a.* anglófobo.
Anglo-Saxon [-gloʊ'sæksən] *s., a.* anglosajón.
angora [æŋ'gɔrə] *s.* tejido de lana de angora.
Angora cat, gato de Angora.
Angora goat, cabra de Angora.
angostura bark [,æŋgə'stʊrə-, B -'stjʊrə] corteza de angostura (de sabor amargo, usada como tónico y febrífugo).
angrily ['æŋgrəlɪ] *adv.* airadamente, con cólera, con enfado.
angry ['æŋgrɪ] *a.* 1. airado, enojado, enfadado, colérico, enfurecido. 2. (fig., poét.) amenazador, iracundo (cielo, horizonte, etc.). 3. (med.) inflamado. 4. **to be a. at** o **about (something),** estar enojado por (algo); **to be a. with (someone),** estar enojado con (alguien); **to get a.,** emperrar.
angst [æŋkst] *s.* (psic.) ansiedad, angustia, zozobra, desasosiego.
angstrom ['æŋstrəm] *s.* (fís.) angstrom (unidad de longitud de un cienmillonésimo de centímetro).
anguiliform [æŋ'gwɪlə,fɔrm, B -,fɔm] *a.* (zool.) anguiliforme.
anguish ['æŋgwɪʃ] *s.* angustia, tormento, aflicción. —*v.i., v.t.* atormentar(se), torturar(se), causar angustia.
anguished [-gwɪʃt] *a.* angustiado, atormentado, afligido, acongojado.
angular ['æŋgjələr, B -lə] *a.* 1. angular. 2. anguloso. 3. (fig.) esquinado. 4. flaco y estirado (persona).
angularity [,æŋgjə'lærətɪ] *s.* angularidad; angulosidad; (*pl.*) esquinas, aristas, recodos.
angular momentum, (fís.) momento angular.
angular parallax, (ópt.) paralaje angular, ángulo paraláctico.
angular speed, a. velocity, (fís.) velocidad angular.
angulate ['æŋgjələt, -,leɪt] *a.* angulado. —*v.t.* doblar en ángulo.
angulation [,æŋgjə'leɪʃən] *s.* formación de ángulos; escuadración.
anhydride [æn'haɪ,draɪd] *s.* (quím.) anhídrido.
anhydrite [-,draɪt] *s.* (min.) anhidrita.
anhydrosis [,ænhaɪ'droʊsəs, ,ænhɪ-] *s.* (med.) anhidrosis.
anhydrous [æn'haɪdrəs] *a.* (quím.) anhidro.
anhydrous lime, (quím.) cal anhidra.
anil ['ænəl] *s.* (bot.) añil.
anile ['æ,naɪl, 'eɪ-] *a.* vieja, caduca, chocha.
aniline ['ænələn] *s.* (quím.) anilina.
aniline dye, tinte o color de anilina.
animadversion [,ænə,mæd'vɜrʒən, -məd-, B -'vɜʃən] *s.* animadversión; censura, amonestación.
animadvert [-'vɜrt, B -'vɜt] *v.i.* (ú. con *on*) censurar, reprochar, amonestar.
animal ['ænəməl] *s.* animal; **¡you a.!,** ¡animal! ¡bestia! —*a.* 1. animal, ej., *a. kingdom,* reino animal. 2. animal, carnal, sensual, ej., *a. appetites,* apetitos animales.
animalcular [,ænə'mælkjələr, B -le] *a.* (zool.) de animálculos.
animalcule [-'mæl,kjul] *s.* (zool.) animálculo.
animal husbandry, ganadería, cría de animales de granja.
animalism ['ænəmə,lɪzəm] *s.* 1. animalismo. 2. carnalidad, sensualidad. 3. doctrina que sostiene que lo animal predomina en el hombre.
animalist [-ləst] *s.* 1. animalista, pintor o escultor de animales. 2. libertino.
animality [,ænə'mælətɪ] *s.* 1. animalidad. 2. reino animal.
animalization [,ænəmələ'zeɪʃən] *s.* animalización.
animalize ['ænəmə,laɪz] *v.t.* animalizar.
animal kingdom, el reino animal.
animal magnetism, 1. magnetismo animal. 2. hipnotismo, mesmerismo. 3. sensualismo. 4. (ciencia cristiana) error o ilusión del materialismo.
animal power, fuerza de tracción animal, fuerza de sangre.
animal rights, derechos de los animales.
animal spirits, vivacidad, ardor, exuberancia vital.
animate ['ænə,meɪt] *v.t.* 1. animar, dar vida a, vivificar, avivar. 2. animar, alentar. 3. animar (dibujos); producir en película de dibujos animados, filmar en dibujos animados. — [-mət] *a.* viviente, animado.
animated [-əd] *a.* 1. animado, vivo, alegre. 2. animado, a cuerda (juguete, muñeca, etc.). 3. animado, que se mueve.
animated cartoon, (película de) dibujos animados.
animating [-ɪŋ] *a.* animador, animante, vivificante.
animation [,ænə'meɪʃən] *s.* 1. animación. 2. producción de películas de dibujos animados.
animator ['ænə,meɪtər, B -tə] *s.* 1. animador. 2. productor de dibujos animados.
animé ['ænəmeɪ, -mi] *s.* (bot.) anime; goma copal.
animism [-,mɪzəm] *s.* (filos., psic.) animismo.
animist [-məst] *s.* (filos., psic.) animista.
animistic [,ænə'mɪstɪk] *a.* (filos., psic.) animístico.
animosity [-'mɑsətɪ, B -'mɔs-] *s.* animosidad, aversión, ojeriza, rencor.
animus ['ænəməs] *s.* 1. ánimo, disposición, intención. 2. animosidad, aversión, rencor.
anion ['æn,aɪən] *s.* (elec.) anión, ion negativo.
anise ['ænəs] *s.* (bot.) anís.
aniseed [-,sid] *s.* semilla de anís.
aniseikonia [,æn,aɪ,saɪ'koʊnɪə] *s.* (med.) aniseiconía.
anisette [,ænə'sɛt, -'zɛt, B -'zɛt] *s.* anisado, licor de anís.
anisogamous [,ænaɪ'sɑgəməs, B -'sɔg-] **anisogamic** [-sə'gæmɪk] *a.* (biol.) caracterizado por anisogamia.
anisogamy [-əmɪ] *s.* (biol.) anisogamia.
anisomerous [-'sɑmərəs, B -'sɔm-] *a.* (zool.) anisómero.
anisometric [-sə'mɛtrɪk] *a.* (bot., min., geom.) anisométrico.
anisometropia [,æn,aɪsəmə'troʊpɪə] *s.* (fisiol.) anisometropía.
anisopetalous [-sə'pɛtələs] *a.* (bot.) anisopétalo.
anisophyllous [-'fɪləs] *a.* (bot.) anisófilo.
anisotropic [-'trɑpɪk, B -'trɔp-] *a.* (fís.) anisótropo, anisotrópico.
anisotropy [-'sɑtrəpɪ, B -'sɔt-] **anisotropism** [-,pɪzəm] *s.* 1. (min., fís.) anisotropía. 2. (bot.) anisotropismo.
Ankara ['æŋkərə, 'ɑŋ-, B 'æŋ-] *s.* Angora, capital de Turquía.
ankerite ['æŋkə,raɪt] *s.* (min.) ankerita.
ankh [æŋk] *s.* cruz egipcia, usada contemporáneamente por los hippies como símbolo de vida.
ankle ['æŋkəl] *s.* tobillo.
anklebone [-,boʊn] *s.* hueso del tobillo.
ankle-length sock [-,lɛŋkθ-] media corta.
ankle strap, tirita tobillera.
ankle support, (dep.) tobillera.
anklet ['æŋklət] *s.* 1. ajorca, brazalete para el tobillo. 2. calcetín corto.
ankylose ['æŋkɪ,loʊs] *v.t., v.i.* (med.) anquilosar(se).
ankylosis [,æŋkɪ'loʊsəs] (med.) anquilosis.
anlage ['ɑn,lɑgə] *s.* fundamento, principio.
anna ['ɑnə, B 'ænə] *s.* ana (antigua moneda de la India, Pakistán y Birmania).
annalist ['ænələst] *s.* analista, cronista.
annalistic [,ænə'lɪstɪk] *a.* analístico, de una crónica o reportaje.
annals ['ænəlz] *s. pl.* anales, crónicas.
Annam [æ'næm, 'æn,æm] *s.* Anam, región de Vietnam.
Annamese [ænə'miz, -'mis, B -'miz] *s.* (*pl.* ANNAMESE) 1. anamita. 2. antiguo nombre del idioma vietnamita.
annates ['æneɪts] *s. pl.* (relig.) anata.
annatto [ə'nɑtoʊ, B ə'næt-] *s.* (*pl.* ANNATTOS) 1. (bot.) achiote, onoto, bija (árbol). 2. bijol (semilla y colorante).
anneal [ə'nil] *v.t.* 1. recocer, templar (cristal, metales). 2. (fig.) endurecer, fortalecer.
annealing [-ɪŋ] *s.* temple, recocido, recocción.
annelid ['ænələd] *s., a.* (zool.) anélido.
annex [ə'nɛks] *v.t.* anexar, anexionar (país, ciudad, etc.); añadir, agregar. — ['æn,ɛks, -ɪks] *s.* 1. anexo, apéndice (a un documento, etc.). 2. pabellón, ala complementaria (de un edificio).
annexation [,æn,ɛk'seɪʃən] *s.* anexión, adición, unión.

annexationist [-əst] *s.* anexionista.
annihilate [ə'naɪəˌleɪt] *v.t.* aniquilar, destruir. —*v.i.* (fís.) aniquilarse (un positrón y un electrón, por ejemplo).
annihilation [əˌnaɪə'leɪʃən] *s.* 1. aniquilación, aniquilamiento, destrucción total. 2. (fís.) aniquilación de materia.
annihilator [ə'naɪəˌleɪtər, B -tə] *s.* aniquilador.
anniversary [ˌænə'vɜrsərɪ, B -'vɜs-] *s.* aniversario. —*a.* de aniversario.
annonaceous [ˌænə'neɪʃəs] *a.* (bot.) anonáceo.
annotate ['ænəˌteɪt] *v.t.* anotar, comentar (obra literaria, tema, etc.). —*v.i.* hacer anotaciones, poner notas.
annotation [ˌænə'teɪʃən] *s.* anotación, nota, comentario.
annotator ['ænəˌteɪtər, B -tə] *s.* anotador, comentador.
announce [ə'naʊns] *v.t.* anunciar, proclamar, declarar. —*v.i.* 1. ser locutor (de estación de radio, televisión etc.). 2. postular a (gobernador, director etc.). 3. anunciar.
announcement [-mənt] *s.* anuncio, notificación, aviso; declaración.
announcer [-sər, B -sə] *s.* 1. anunciador, anunciadora. 2. locutor o locutora (de radio o televisión).
annoy [ə'nɔɪ] *v.t.* molestar, fastidiar, incomodar. —*v.i.* ser molesto o fastidioso. —*s.* (ant.) molestia, fastidio.
annoyance [-əns] *s.* molestia, fastidio, engorro; disgusto, incomodidad.
annoying [-ɪŋ] *a.* molesto, enojoso, fastidioso, importuno, irritante; **how a.!,** ¡qué rabia! ¡qué bestia!
annoyingly [-lɪ] *adv.* molestamente, importunamente.
annual ['ænjʊəl, -jəl] *a.* anual. —*s.* 1. (bot.) planta anual. 2. publicación anual, anuario.
annual bluegrass, (bot.) coracán.
annually [-ɪ] *adv.* anualmente, cada año.
annuitant [ə'nuətənt, B -'nju-] *s.* rentista, censualista.
annuity [-tɪ] *s.* anualidad, renta o pensión anual.
annuity bond, (fin.) bono perpetuo, bono sin vencimiento.
annuity certain, (der.) anualidad incondicional.
annuity payable, (der.) anualidad pasiva.
annul [ə'nʌl] *v.t.* anular, invalidar, cancelar, abolir.
annular ['ænjələr, B -jʊlə] *a.* anular.
annular eclipse, (astr.) eclipse anular.
annular ligament, (anat.) ligamento anular.
annulate [-lət, -ˌleɪt] **annulated** [-ˌleɪtəd] *a.* 1. anuloso. 2. (zool.) anillado.
annulet [-lət] *s.* 1. sortijilla, anillejo. 2. (arq.) ánulo, anillo. 3. (her.) anulete.
annulment [ə'nʌlmənt] *s.* anulación (esp. del matrimonio); rescisión, derogación, revocación.
annulose ['ænjəˌloʊs] *a.* anuloso, anillado.
annulus [-ləs] *s.* 1. (bot., zool., astr.) anillo. 2. (geom.) corona circular.
annum ['ænəm] *s.* (lat.) año.
annunciate [ə'nʌnsɪˌeɪt, -ʃɪ-] *v.t.* anunciar, proclamar, intimar.
annunciation [əˌnʌnsɪ'eɪʃən] *s.* 1. anunciación. 2. **A.,** (relig.) Anunciación (25 de marzo).
annunciator [ə'nʌnsɪˌeɪtər, -ʃɪ-, B -tə] *s.* (elec.) indicador, anunciador, cuadro indicador.
Anobiidae [ˌænə'baɪədi] *s. pl.* (ento.) anóbidos.
anode ['ænˌoʊd] *s.* (fís.) ánodo.
anodic [æn'ɑdɪk, B -'ɔd-] *a.* (fís.) anódico.
anodize ['ænəˌdaɪz] *v.t.* anodizar, revestir (un metal) de una capa (de otro metal); hacer una galvanoplastia.
anodyne [-ˌdaɪn] *a.* (med.) anodino. —*s.* 1. anodino, calmante (del dolor). 2. (fig.) anodino, insubstancial, insípido, sin gracia.
anoint [ə'nɔɪnt] *v.t.* 1. untar, ungir. 2. (relig.) ungir.
anointment [-mənt] *s.* unción, ungimiento, consagración.
anoli, anole [ə'noʊlɪ] *s.* (zool.) anolis.
anomalism [ə'nɑməˌlɪzəm, B ə'nɔm-] *s.* 1. anomalía, irregularidad. 2. (astr.) anomalía.
anomalistic [əˌnɑmə'lɪstɪk, B əˌnɔm-] *a.* 1. anomalístico, irregular. 2. (astr.) anomalístico.
anomalistic year, (astr.) año anomalístico.
anomalous [ə'nɑmələs, B ə'nɔm-] *a.* anómalo, irregular.
anomaly [-lɪ] *s.* 1. anomalía, irregularidad. 2. (astr.) anomalía.
anomie, anomy ['ænəmɪ] *s.* 1. destrucción de las estructuras de una sociedad. 2. sentimiento de alienación resultante de dicha situación.
anomuran [ˌænə'mjʊrən] *a., s.* (zool.) anomuro.
anon [ə'nɑn B ə'nɔn] *adv.* 1. luego, otra vez. 2. (ant.) **ever and a.,** de cuando en cuando.
anonym ['ænəˌnɪm] *s.* anónimo; seudónimo.
anonymity [ˌænə'nɪmətɪ] *s.* carácter o estado anónimo.
anonymous [ə'nɑnəməs, B ə'nɔn-] *a.* anónimo.
anonymously [-lɪ] *adv.* anónimamente.
anopheles [ə'nɑfəˌliz, B ə'nɔf-] *s.* (ento.) (mosquito) anófeles.
anoplotherium [ˌænəˌploʊ'θɪrɪəm, B əˌnɔp-] *s.* (pal.) anoploterio.
anopluriform [ˌænə'plʊrəˌfɔrm, B -ˌfɔm] *a.* (zool.) anopluro.
anorak ['ænəˌræk] *s.* chaqueta de los esquimales con capucha de tela o piel.
anorexia [ˌænə'rɛksɪə] *s.* (med.) anorexia.
anorthite [ə'nɔrˌθaɪt, B ə'nɔˌ-] *s.* (min.) anortita.
anosmia [æ'nɑzmɪə, B -'nɔs-] *s.* (med.) anosmia.
another [ə'nʌðər, B ðə] *a.* otro, distinto, diferente; **a. one,** uno más; **a. time,** otra vez. —*s.* otro; otro más, uno más; **one a.,** uno a otro, unos a otros.
anoxemia [ˌænˌɑk'simɪə, B ˌænək-] *s.* (med.) anoxemia.
ansate ['ænˌseɪt] *a.* que tiene asas.
anserine ['ænsəˌraɪn] *a.* 1. (zool.) ansarino. 2. (fig.) tonto, necio, estúpido.
answer ['ænsər, B 'ɑnsə] *s.* 1. respuesta, contestación. 2. (con *to*) solución (a un problema, misterio, etc.). 3. explicación. 4. (der.) réplica, contestación (a la demanda). 5. (mús.) respuesta. 6. **to know all the answers,** saberlo todo. —*v.t.* 1. responder, contestar. 2. corresponder a, convenir a, satisfacer (propósito, demanda, necesidad, etc.). 3. resolver, solucionar. 4. refutar, replicar a. 5. (der.) responder, contestar, replicar. 6. **a. the door,** contestar el timbre de la puerta; **a. the helm,** obedecer al timón (díc. de un barco, etc.). —*v.i.* 1. dar contestación, contestar. 2. (con *for*) responder (por), garantizar; responder (de acto, crimen, etc.). 3. (con *to*) corresponder (a); responder (a). 4. **a. back,** replicar con impertinencia; **a. to the name of (Smith,** etc.), responder al nombre de (Smith, etc.), tener por nombre, llamarse.
answerable [-ərəbəl] *a.* 1. responsable, ej. *I am a.,* soy responsable, yo respondo. 2. contestable, refutable. 3. (con *to*) equivalente, correspondiente.
answering machine, contestador automático.
answering service, servicio de contestación automático.
ant [ænt] *s.* (ento.) hormiga; **to have ants in one's pants,** (jer.) tener avispas en el culo.
anta ['æntə] *s.* 1. (zool.) anta, danta, tapir. 2. (arq.) anta.
ANTA *abrev. de* **American National Theatre and Academy,** (E.U.) Asociación Nacional de Teatro.
antacid ['ænt'æsəd] *s., a.* (med., quím.) antiácido.
antagonism [æn'tægəˌnɪzəm] *s.* antagonismo, oposición, hostilidad, rivalidad, contienda.
antagonist [-nəst] *s.* 1. antagonista, contrario, adversario, rival. 2. (anat.) (músculo) antagonista.
antagonistic [ænˌtægə'nɪstɪk] *a.* antagónico, contrario, opuesto, hostil.
antagonize [æn'tægəˌnaɪz] *v.t.* enemistar, enajenar, provocar la hostilidad de.
antalkaline [ænt'ælkəˌlaɪn] *a.* antialcalino.
Antarctic [ænt'ɑrktɪk, -'ɑrt-, B -'ɑk-] *a.* antártico, del sur, austral.
Antarctica [-ə] *s.* Antártida.
Antarctic Circle, (geog.) círculo polar antártico.
Antarctic Ocean, Océano Antártico.
ant bear, (zool.) oso hormiguero.
ant cow, (ento.) pulgón afidio.
ante ['æntɪ] *s.* 1. (póker) apuesta inicial (que se hace antes de ver la mano). 2. (fam.) precio, pago (esp. adelantado). 3. **to put up the a.,** poner la apuesta inicial; pagar (esp. por adelantado), entregar o depositar su parte o el dinero; **to raise the a.,** (fig.) subir el precio, aumentar el costo, poner condiciones más duras. —*v.t.* (*pret., p.p.* ANTED ['æntɪd] *p.pr.* ANTEING ['æntɪɪŋ]) 1. apostar. 2. (fam.) pagar, hacer su contribución a (esp. por adelantado).
ant-eater ['æntˌitər B -tə] *s.* (zool.) oso hormiguero, tamanduá.
ante-bellum [ˌæntɪ'bɛləm] *a.* (hist. E.U.) perteneciente al período anterior a la guerra civil.
antecede [ˌæntə'sid] *v.t., v.i.* anteceder, ir delante, preceder.
antecedence [-əns] *s.* antecedencia, precedencia, prioridad.
antecedent [-ənt] *s., a.* (gram., lóg., mat.) antecedente.
antecessor [ˌæntɪ'sɛsər, B -sə] *s.* antecesor, predecesor.
antechamber ['æntɪˌtʃeɪmbər, B -bə] *s.* antecámara, antesala.
antechoir [-ˌkwaɪr, B -ˌkwaɪə] *s.* (arq.) antecoro.
antedate [-ˌdeɪt] *v.t.* 1. adelantar, poner fecha anterior a. 2. preceder (en el tiempo), ser anterior a. —*s.* antedata, fecha anterior (a la que debiera tener un documento).
antediluvian [ˌæntɪdə'luvɪən] *a.* 1. antediluviano, anterior al Diluvio. 2. (fam.) antediluviano, antiquísimo, anticuado, viejísimo. —*s.* (fam.) persona de costumbres muy a la antigua.
antefix ['æntɪˌfɪks] *s.* (arq.) antefija, antefijo.
antelope ['æntəlˌoʊp] *s.* (zool.) antílope.
antemeridian [ˌæntɪmə'rɪdɪən] *a.* antemeridiano.
ante meridiem [-ɪəm] *adv.* en la mañana, antes del medio día.
ante mortem [ˌæntɪ'mɔrtəm, B -'mɔt-] *adv.* antes de morir.
antemundane [-'mʌnˌdeɪn] *a.* antemundano, anterior al mundo.
antenatal [-'neɪtəl] *a.* antenatal, prenatal.
antenna [æn'tɛnə] *s.* 1. (fís., rad.) (*pl. gen.* ANTENNAS) antena. 2. (zool.) (*pl.* ANTENNAE [-ni]) antena.

antenna array, (rad.) antena direccional.

antenna connection, (rad.) toma o contacto de antena.

antenna reflector, (rad.) antena de reflexión o de inversión.

antennule [-'tɛnjul] *s.* (zool.) anténula.

antenuptial [ˌæntɪ'nʌpʃəl] *a.* prenupcial, anterior a las nupcias.

antependium [-'pɛndɪəm] *s.* (*pl.* ANTEPENDIUMS O ANTEPENDIA [-dɪə]) (relig.) antependio, frontal, paramento (de la mesa del altar o del púlpito).

antepenult [-'piˌnʌlt, -pɪ'nʌlt] *s.* (gram.) sílaba antepenúltima (de una palabra).

antepenultimate [-pɪ'nʌltəmət] *a.* antepenúltimo, inmediatamente anterior al último. —*s.* cosa o parte antepenúltima.

anterior [æn'tɪrɪər, B -'tɪərɪə] *a.* anterior, precedente.

anteriority [ˌæntɪrɪ'ɔrətɪ, B -tɪərɪ-] *s.* anterioridad, antelación, prioridad.

anteroom ['æntɪˌrum -ˌrʊm] *s.* antesala, antecámara, sala de espera, recibimiento.

ant fly, hormiga alada (que se usa como carnada para pescar).

anthelion [ænt'hiljən, B æn'θil-] *s.* (*pl.* ANTHELIA [-jə] O ANTHELIONS) (meteor.) antelia.

anthelmintic [ˌæntˌhɛl'mɪntɪk, ˌænˌθɛl-] *s., a.* (med.) antihelmíntico.

anthem ['ænθəm] *s.* himno (nacional, etc.); (rel.) antífona, cántico.

anthemion [æn'θimɪən] *s.* (*pl.* ANTHEMIA [-mɪə]) (arq., pint.) antemio.

anther ['ænθər, B -θə] *s.* (bot.) antera, borlilla.

anther dust, (bot.) polen.

antheridium [ˌænθə'rɪdɪəm] *s.* (*pl.* ANTHERIDIA [-ɪə]) (bot.) anteridio, anteridia.

antherozoid ['ænθərəˌzɔɪd] *s.* (bot.) anterozoide.

anthesis [æn'θisəs] *s.* (bot.) antesis, florescencia.

anthill ['æntˌhɪl] *s.* hormiguero (en forma de montículo).

anthocyanin [ˌænθə'saɪənən] *s.* (bioquím.) antocianina.

anthodium [æn'θoʊdɪəm] *s.* (*pl.* ANTHODIA [-dɪə]) (bot.) antodio.

anthological [ˌænθə'lɑdʒɪkəl, -'lɔdʒ-] *a.* antológico.

anthologist [æn'θɑlədʒəst, B -'θɔl-] *s.* antólogo, compilador de antologías.

anthologize [-ˌdʒaɪz] *v.t.* recopilar en una antología.

anthology [-dʒɪ] *s.* antología, florilegio.

Anthony ['ænθənɪ, -tə-] *s.* (hist., relig.) Antón, Antonio.

anthophagous [æn'θɑfəgəs, B -'θɔf-] *a.* (zool.) antófago, que come flores.

anthophagy [-ədʒɪ] *s.* antofagia.

anthophyte ['ænθəˌfaɪt] *s.* (bot.) antófita.

Anthozoa [ˌænθə'zoʊə] *s. pl.* (zool.) antozoos, antozoarios, coralarios.

anthozoan [-'zoʊən] *s., a.* (zool.) antozoario.

anthracene ['ænθrəˌsin] *s.* (quím.) antraceno, antracina.

anthracite [-ˌsaɪt] *s.* (min.) antracita, carbón fósil.

anthracitic [ˌænθrə'sɪtɪk] *a.* (min.) antracítico.

anthracnose [æn'θrækˌnoʊs] *s.* (agr.) antracnosis.

anthracosis [ˌænθrə'koʊsəs] *s.* (med.) antracosis.

anthraquinone [ˌænθrəkwɪn'oʊn, -'kwɪnˌoʊn] *s.* (quím.) antraquinona.

anthrax ['ænˌθræks] *s.* (med.) ántrax, tumor inflamatorio.

anthropic [æn'θrɑpɪk, B -'θrɔp-] *a.* antrópico, relativo al hombre, esp. en paleontología o antropología.

anthropocentric [ˌænθrəpə'sɛntrɪk] *a.* (filos.) antropocéntrico.

anthropocentricity [-sɛn'trɪsətɪ] *s.* (filos.) antropocentrismo.

anthropocentrism [-'sɛnˌtrɪzəm] *s.* (filos.) antropocentrismo.

anthropogenesis [-'dʒɛnəsəs] *var. de* anthropogeny.

anthropogenic [-'dʒɛnɪk] *a.* (biol.) antropógeno.

anthropogeny [-'pɑdʒənɪ, B -'pɔ-] *s.* (biol.) antropogenia.

anthropography [-'pɑgrəfɪ, B -'pɔg-] *s.* antropografía.

anthropoid ['ænθrəˌpɔɪd] *a.* antropomorfo, antropoide. —*s.* (mono) antropoideo, antropoide.

anthropolatry [ˌænθrə'pɑlətrɪ, B -'pɔl-] *s.* antropolatría.

anthropolite [æn'θrɔpəˌlaɪt] **anthropolith** [-ˌlɪθ] *s.* (geol.) antropolito, fósil humano.

anthropological [ˌænθrəpə'lɑdʒɪkəl, B -'lɔdʒ-] *a.* antropológico.

anthropologist [-'pɑlədʒəst, B -'pɔl-] *s.* antropólogo.

anthropology [-dʒɪ] *s.* antropología.

anthropometric [ˌænθrəpə'mɛtrɪk] **anthropometrical** [-rɪkəl] *a.* antropométrico.

anthropometry [-'pɑmətrɪ, B -'pɔm-] *s.* antropometría, estudio de las dimensiones del cuerpo humano.

anthropomorphic [ˌænθrəpə'mɔrfɪk, B -'mɔfɪk] *a.* antropomórfico.

anthropomorphism [-ˌfɪzəm] *s.* antropomorfismo.

anthropomorphous [-fəs] *a.* antropomorfo.

anthropopathism [ˌænθrə'pɑpəˌθɪzəm, B -'pɔp-] *s.* (psic.) antropopatismo, antropopatía.

anthropophagous [-'pɑfəgəs, B -'pɔf-] *a.* antropófago, caníbal.

anthropophagy [-ədʒɪ] *s.* antropofagia, canibalismo.

Anthropopithecus [ˌænθrəˌpoʊpə'θikəs] *s.* (zool., pal.) (*pl.* ANTHROPOPITHECI [-'θisaɪ]) antropopiteco.

anthroposophy [-'pɑsəfɪ, B -'pɔs-] *s.* (filos.) antroposofía.

anti [ˌænˌtaɪ, 'æntɪ] *prep.* opuesto a, contrario a, ej. *he has always been a. social legislation,* él siempre ha sido contrario a la legislación social.

antiabortion ['æntɪə'bɔrʃən] *a.* antiabortista.

antiabortionist ['æntɪə'bɔrʃənɪst] *s.* antiabortista.

antiaesthetic ['ɛs'θɛtɪk, B -is-] *a.* antiestético.

antiaircraft [-'ɛrˌkræft, B -'ɛəˌkrɑft] *a.* antiaéreo (díc. de armas de defensa contra ataque aéreo).

antiaircraft gun, cañón antiaéreo, ametralladora antiaérea.

antialcoholism [-'ælkəˌhɔˌlɪzəm] *s.* antialcoholismo.

antiallergenic [ˌæntɪ'ælɛr'dʒɛnɪk] *a.* antialérgico.

anti-American [-ə'mɛrəkən] *a., s.* antinorteamericano, antiyanqui.

antiapoplectic [-ˌæpə'plɛktɪk] *a.* (med.) antiapoplético.

antiarin ['æntɪˌɑrən, -ərɪn] *s.* (quím.) antiarina.

antiarthritic [-ɑr'θrɪtɪk, B -ɑ'-] *a., s.* (med.) antiartrítico.

antiasthmatic [-ˌæz'mætɪk] *a.* (med.) antiasmático.

antibacchius [-'bækɪəs] *s.* (poét.) antibaquio.

antibacterial [-bæk'tɪrɪəl] *a.* (bact.) antibacteriano.

antiballistic missile ['æntɪbə'lɪstɪk] mísil antibalístico, antimisil.

antibiosis [-baɪ'oʊsəs] *s.* (biol.) antibiosis.

antibiotic [-'ɑtɪk, B -'ɔt-] *s., a.* (farm.) antibiótico.

antibody ['æntɪˌbɑdɪ, B -ˌbɔdɪ] *s.* 1. (med.) anticuerpo. 2. (fís.) cuerpo compuesto de antimateria.

antic ['æntɪk] *a.* bufonesco, retozón. —*s.* (*ú. gen. en pl.*) travesuras, bufonadas, payasadas.

anticatalyst [-'kætələst] *s.* (quím.) anticatalizador, substancia que retarda una reacción.

anticatarrhal [-kə'tɑrəl] *a.* (med.) anticatarral.

anticathode [-'kæθˌoʊd] *s.* (fís., electrón.) anticátodo.

anti-Catholic [-'kæθəlɪk] *a.* anticatólico.

antichlor ['æntɪˌklɔr, B -ˌklɔ] *s.* (quím.) anticloro.

anticholinergic [ˌæntɪˌkoʊlə'nɜrdʒɪk, B -'nɜdʒ-] *a., s.* (fisiol.) anticolinérgico.

antichresis [-'krisəs] *s.* (*pl.* ANTICHRESES [-iz]) (der.) anticresis.

antichretic [-'kritɪk] *a.* (der.) anticrético.

antichrist ['antɪˌkraɪst] *s.* 1. anticristo. **2. A.,** (teol.) el Anticristo.

antichristian [ˌæntɪ'krɪstʃən, B -tjən] *a.* anticristiano.

antichristianism [-ˌɪzəm] *s.* anticristianismo.

anticipant [æn'tɪsəpənt] *a.* (ú. con *of*) (que está) a la expectativa (de).

anticipate [-ˌpeɪt] *v.t.* 1. prever, esperar; considerar con anticipación. 2. anticipar, acelerar. 3. anticipar, adelantar (un pago, etc.), cumplir anticipadamente con (una obligación, etc.). 4. contar anticipadamente con. 5. anticiparse a (deseos de uno, etc.). 6. impedir, prevenir.

anticipation [ænˌtɪsə'peɪʃən] *s.* 1. anticipación, previsión. 2. expectación, esperanza. 3. prevención. 4. (mús.) anticipación. 5. (com.) descuento (por pago adelantado). 6. **in a.,** anticipadamente, de antemano, ej., *thanking you in a.,* (como fórmula comercial en cartas) agradeciéndoles de antemano.

anticipatory [æn'tɪsəpəˌtɔrɪ, B -ˌpeɪtərɪ] *a.* anticipador, previsor.

anticlerical [ˌantɪ'klɛrəkəl] *a.* anticlerical.

anticlimax [-'klaɪˌmæks] *s.* anticlímax, desengaño.

anticlinal [-'klaɪnəl] *a.* (geol.) anticlinal.

anticlinorium [-klaɪ'nɔrɪəm] *s.* (*pl.* ANTICLINORIA [-ɪə]) (geol.) anticlinorio.

anticoagulant [-koʊ'ægjələnt] *s.* (med.) (substancia) anticoagulante.

anticommunist [-'kɑmjənəst, B -'kɔm-] *a., s.* anticomunista.

anticonformist [-kən'fɔrməst, B -'fɔm-] *a., s.* anticonformista, no conformista.

anticyclone [-'saɪˌkloʊn] *s.* (meteor.) anticiclón.

antidemocratic [-ˌdɛmə'krætɪk] *a.* antidemocrático.

antidepressant ['æntɪdɪ'prɛsənt] *a.* & *s.* antidepresivo.

antidotal [ˌæntɪ'doʊtəl] *a.* que sirve de antídoto (substancia).

antidote ['æntɪˌdoʊt] *s.* antídoto, contraveneno; (fig.) contrarrestante.

anti-dumping ['æntɪ'dʌmpɪn] *a.* anti-dumping.

antiemetic [ˌæntɪɪ'mɛtɪk] *a., s.* (med.) antiemético.

antienzyme [-'ɛnˌzaɪm] *s.* (fisiol.) antienzima.

antifebrile [ˌæntɪ'fɛbrəl, B -'fiˌbraɪl] *a.* (med.) antifebril.
antifeminism ['æntɪ'fɛmɪnɪzəm] *s.* antifeminismo.
antifeminist ['æntɪ'fɛmɪnɪst] *a.* & *s.* antifeminista.
antifreeze ['æntɪˌfriz] *s.* anticongelante.
antifriction [ˌæntɪ'frɪkʃən] *s.* antifricción, contrafricción.
antifriction metal, metal antifricción.
antigen ['æntɪdʒən] *s.* (med.) antígeno.
antiglare [ˌæntɪ'glɛr, B -'glɛə] *a.* antideslumbrante, que protege contra el brillo excesivo (del sol, etc.).
antiglare shield, pantalla o cristal antideslumbrante.
Antigone [æn'tɪgənɪ] *s.* (mitol.) Antígona, hija de Edipo, prototipo del amor filial.
Antigonus [-ənəs] *s.* (hist.) Antígono, rey de Judea.
antigovernment [ˌæntɪ'gʌvərnmənt, B -'gʌvən-] **antigovernmental** [-ˌgʌvn'mɛntəl] *a.* antigubernamental, enemigo de los gobiernos constituidos.
Antigua [æn'tigə] *s.* Antigua.
antihelix [ˌæntɪ'hilɪks] *s.* (*pl.* ANTIHELICES [-'hɛlɪˌsiz] o ANTIHELIXES [-'hilɪksəz]) (anat.) antihélix.
antihero [-'hiroʊ, -'hɪroʊ] *s.* antihéroe.
antihistamine [-'hɪstəˌmin, -mən] *a.* & *s.* (med.) antihistamínico.
antihydropic [-haɪ'drɑpɪk, B -'drɔp-] *a.* (med.) antihidrópico.
antihygienic [-ˌhaɪdʒɪ'ɛnɪk, B -'dʒinɪk] *a.* antihigiénico.
anti-imperialism [-ɪm'pɪrɪəˌlɪzəm] *s.* antiimperialismo.
anti-imperialistic [-ɪmˌpɪrɪə'lɪstɪk] *a.* antiimperialista.
anti-inflationary [-ɪn'fleɪʃə'nɛrɪ, B -ʃənərɪ] *a.* antiinflacionista.
anti-Jewish [-'dʒuɪʃ] *a.* antisemita.
antiknock [-'nɑk, B -'nɔk] *a., s.* (combustible) antidetonante.
Antillean [æn'tɪlɪən] *a., s.* antillano, de las Antillas.
Antilles [-'tɪliz] *s.* las Antillas.
antilock ['æntɪ'lak] *a.* antibloque.
antilock brakes, frenos antibloque.
antilogarithm [ˌæntɪ'lɔgəˌrɪðəm, -'lɑg-, B -'lɔg-] *s.* (mat.) antilogaritmo.
antilogy [æn'tɪlədʒɪ] *s.* (lóg.) antilogía.
antimacassar [ˌæntɪmə'kæsər, B -ə] *s.* antimacasar; funda para proteger sillas; cubierta para proteger muebles.
antimagnetic [-mæg'nɛtɪk] *a.* antimagnético.
antimalarial [-mə'lɛrɪəl] (med.) *a.* antimalárico, antipalúdico.
antimatter ['antɪˌmætər, B -ə] *s.* (fís.) antimateria.
antimere ['æntɪmɪr, B -mɪə] *s.* (zool.) antímero.
antimilitarism [ˌæntɪ'mɪlətəˌrɪzəm] *s.* antimilitarismo.
antimilitarist [-rəst] *a.* antimilitarista.
antimissile missile [-'mɪsəl-] proyectil antibalístico.
antimonarchical [-mə'nɑrkɪkəl, B -'nɑk-] *a.* antimonárquico.
antimonial [ˌæntə'moʊnɪəl] *a.* (quím.) antimonial. —*s.* preparación antimonial.
antimonic [-'mɑnɪk, B -'mɔn-] *a.* (quím.) antimónico.
antimonious [-'moʊnɪəs] *a.* (quím.) antimonioso.
antimonite ['æntəməˌnaɪt] *s.* (quím.) antimonito.
antimony ['æntəˌmoʊnɪ B 'æntɪmənɪ] *s.* (quím.) antimonio.
antimony white, trióxido de antimonio.
antinephritic [ˌæntɪnɪ'frɪtɪk] *a.* (med.) antinefrítico.
antineuralgic [-nʊ'rældʒɪk, B -njʊ-] *a.* antineurálgico.
antineutron [-'nuˌtrɑn, B -'njuˌtrɔn] *s.* (fís.) antineutrón.
antinode ['æntɪˌnoʊd] *s.* (fís., rad.) antinodo.
antinomianism [ˌæntɪ'noʊmɪəˌnɪzəm] *s.* antinomianismo, creencia en que la fe por sí sola asegura la salvación.
antinomy [æn'tɪnəmɪ] *s.* (lóg.) antinomia.
antinucleon [ˌæntɪ'nuklɪˌɑn, B -'njuklɪˌɔn] *s.* (fís.) antinúcleo.
Antioch ['æntɪˌɑk, B -ˌɔk] *s.* Antioquía, capital de la antigua Siria.
Antiochian [ˌæntɪ'oʊkɪən] *a., s.* antioqueño.
antioxidant [-'ɑksədənt, B -'ɔk-] *a., s.* (quím.) (substancia) antioxidante.
antipapist [-'peɪpəst] *a., s.* antipapista, que no reconoce la soberanía del papa.
antiparticle [-'pɑrtɪkəl, B -'pɑt-] *s.* (fís.) antipartícula.
antipasto [-'pæsˌtoʊ, -'pɑs-] *s.* entremés.
antipathetic [-pə'θɛtɪk] **antipathetical** [-ɪkəl] *a.* (con *to*) opuesto (a), averso (a); antagónico.
antipathy [æn'tɪpəθɪ] *s.* antipatía, aversión, antagonismo.
antipersonnel [-ˌpərsən'ɛl, B -ˌpɜs-] *a.* (mil.) antipersonal, contrapersonal (ataque, mina, carga, etc.).
antiperspirant [-'pərspərənt, B -'pɜs-] *a., s.* desodorante.
antiphlogistic [-flə'dʒɪstɪk] *s., a.* (med.) antiflogístico.
antiphon ['æntəfən, -ˌfɑn, B -fən, -ˌfɔn] *s.* (mús., relig.) antífona.
antiphonal [æn'tɪfənəl] *s., a.* (mús., relig.) (libro) antifonal.
antiphonary [-ˌnɛrɪ, B -nərɪ] *a., s.* (mus., relig.) antifonario, antifonal.
antiphrasis [æn'tɪfrəsəs] *s.* (ret.) (*pl.* ANTIPHRASES [-ˌsiz]) antífrasis.
antipodal [-'tɪpədəl] *a.* 1. antípoda. 2. diametralmente opuesto.
antipode ['æntəˌpoʊd] *s.* (*pl.* ANTIPODES [æn'tɪpəˌdiz]) 1. antípoda. 2. lo opuesto, lo contrario.
antipollution ['æntɪpə'luʃən] *a.* contra la contaminación (del aire, agua).
antipope ['æntɪˌpoʊp] *s.* antipapa.
antipoverty program [ˌæntɪ'pɑvərtɪ-, B -'pɔvətɪ-] *s.* (E.U.) proyecto del gobierno para erradicar la pobreza.
antiproton [-'proʊˌtɑn B -ˌtɔn] *s.* (fís.) antiprotón.
antipyretic [-paɪ'rɛtɪk] *s.* (med.) antipirético.
antipyrine [-'paɪˌrin, B -'paɪərɪn] *s.* (farm.) antipirina.
antiquarian [ˌæntɪ'kwɛrɪən, B -'kwɛər-] *s.* anticuario. —*a.* de cosas viejas, ej., *an a. bookshop,* una tienda de libros viejos o antiguos.
antiquary ['æntəˌkwɛrɪ, B -kwərɪ] *s.* anticuario.
antiquate [-ˌkweɪt] *v.t.* anticuar, dar aspecto de antiguo (a objeto o mueble).
antiquated [-əd] *a.* anticuado, en desuso, fuera de moda.
antique [æn'tik] *a.* 1. antiguo. 2. histórico. —*s.* 1. objeto antiguo, reliquia de arte antiguo. 2. (impr.) tipo antiguo. 3. **the antique,** estilo antiguo. —*v.t.* dar apariencia de antigüedad a muebles u objetos.
antique dealer, anticuario.
antique shop, tienda de antigüedades.
antiquity [æn'tɪkwətɪ] *s.* 1. antigüedad, mundo antiguo, tiempos antiguos. 2. (*pl.*) antigüedad (objeto o reliquia del arte antiguo).
antirabic [ˌæntɪ'reɪbɪk] *a.* (med.) antirrábico.
antirationalism [-'ræʃənəˌlɪzəm] *s.* antirracionalismo.
antireligious [-rɪ'lɪdʒəs] *a.* antirreligioso.
antirevolutionary [-rɛvə'luʃəˌnɛrɪ, B -nərɪ] *a., s.* antirrevolucionario.
antirrhinum [-'raɪnəm] *s.* (bot.) antirrino; dragón, becerra.
antiscian [æn'tɪʃən] *a.* (geog.) antiscio, anteco.
antiscorbutic [ˌæntɪskɔr'bjutɪk, B -skɔ'-] *a., s.* (med.) antiescorbútico.
anti-Semite [-'sɛmˌaɪt, B -'sim-] *s.* antisemita.
anti-Semitic [-sə'mɪtɪk] *a.* antisemítico, antisemita.
anti-Semitism [-'sɛməˌtɪzəm] *s.* antisemitismo.
antisepsis [-'sɛpsəs] *s.* (med.) antisepsia.
antiseptic [-sɛptɪk] *a.* & *s.* (med.) antiséptico.
antiserum [-'sɪrəm] *s.* (med) antisuero.
antislavery [-'sleɪvərɪ] *a.* antiesclavista, opuesto a la esclavitud. —*s.* oposición a la esclavitud.
antisocial [-'soʊʃəl] *a.* 1. antisocial, perjudicial a la sociedad. 2. adverso a la compañía de otros; misantrópico.
antispasmodic [-spæz'mɑdɪk, B -'mɔd-] *s., a.* (med.) antiespasmódico.
antistatic ['æntɪ'stætɪk] *a.* antiestático.
Antisthenes [æn'tɪsθəˌniz] *s.* (hist.) Antístenes, filósofo griego, fundador de la escuela cínica.
antistrophe [æn'tɪstrəfɪ] *s.* (poét.) antistrofa.
antisubmarine [ˌæntɪ'sʌbməˌrin] *a.* (mil.) antisubmarino, (de defensa) contra submarinos.
antitank [-'tæŋk] *a.* (mil.) antitanque (cañón, proyectil, mina, etc.).
antiterrorism ['æntɪ'tɛrərɪsm] *s.* antiterrorismo.
anti-tetanus [-'tɛtənəs] **antitetanic** [-tə'tænɪk] *a.* (med.) antitetánico.
antitheft device ['æntɪ'θɛft] *s.* dispositivo antirrobo, sistema antirrobo.
antitheism [-'θiˌɪzəm] *s.* (filos.) antiteísmo.
antithesis [æn'tɪθəsəs] *s.* (*pl.* ANTITHESES [-ˌsiz]) (lóg., ret.) antítesis, contraposición, contraste.
antithetic [ˌæntə'θɛtɪk] ANTITHETICAL [-ɪkəl] *a.* antitético; opuesto, contrario.
antitoxic [-'tɑksɪk, B -'tɔk-] *a.* (med.) antitóxico.
antitoxin [-sən] *s.* (med.) antitoxina.
antitrade winds ['æntɪ'treɪd-] (mar.) vientos antialisios.
antitragus [æn'tɪtrəgəs] *s.* (anat.) antitrago.
antitrust [ˌæntɪ'trʌst] *a.* contra los monopolios, antimonopolio (legislación, leyes).
antitussive [-'tʌsɪv] *a.* (med.) antitusivo.
antitype ['æntɪˌtaɪp] *s.* 1. antitipo, prototipo, tipo modelo. 2. anti-tipo, prototipo completamente opuesto a un original.
antitypical [ˌæntɪ'tɪpɪkəl] *a.* antitípico, no característico.
antivenereal [-və'nɪrɪəl, B -'nɪər-] *a.* (med.) antivenéreo, que combate las afecciones venéreas.
antivenin [-'vɛnən] *s.* antiveneno, contraveneno.
antiviral [-'vaɪrəl] *a.* (med.) antiviral, antivirulento.

antivirus [-rəs] *s.* (med.) antivirus.

anti-war [ˌæntɪ'wɔr, B -'wɔ] *a.* opuesto a la guerra, antibelicista.

antler ['æntlər, B -lə] *s.* asta, cornamenta, cuerno (del ciervo).

antlered [-lərd, B -ləd] *a.* armado de astas (ciervo).

antlerite ['æntləˌraɪt] *s.* (geol.) antlerita, sulfato de cobre nativo.

ant lion, (zool.) hormiga león.

Antonine ['æntəˌnaɪn] *a.* antoniniano. *—s. pl.* Antoninos, emperadores romanos.

antoninianus [ˌæntəˌnɪnɪ'eɪnəs] *s.* (*pl.* ANTONINIANI [-ˌnaɪ]) (numis.) antoniniano.

antonomasia [ˌæntənoʊ'meɪʒə, B -zɪə] *s.* (ret.) antonomasia.

antonomastic [-'mæstɪk] **antonomastical** [-ɪkəl] *a.* (ret.) antonomástico.

antonym ['æntəˌnɪm] *s.* (gram.) antónimo.

antonymous [æn'tɑnəməs, B -tɔn-] *a.* (gram.) antónimo.

antrum ['æntrəm] *s.* (*pl.* ANTRA [-trə]) (anat.) seno o cavidad.

Antwerp ['æntˌwɜrp, B -ˌwɜp] *s.* Amberes, provincia y ciudad de Bélgica.

Anura [ə'nʊrə, B ə'njʊrə] *s.* (*pl.*) (zool.) anuros.

anuresis [ˌænjʊ'risəs] *s.* (*pl.* ANURESES [-siz]) (med.) anuresis.

anuretic [-'rɛtɪk] *a.* (med.) anurético.

anuria [ə'nʊrɪə, B ə'njur-] *s.* (med.) anuria.

anuric [-ɪk] *a.* (med.) anúrico.

anurous [↓əs] *a.* (zool.) anuro.

anus ['eɪnəs] *s.* (anat.) ano.

anvil ['ænvəl] *s.* 1. yunque, ayunque, bigornia. 2. (anat.) yunque (huesecillo del oído). 3. **on the a.,** (fig.) sobre el tapete; en preparación.

anvil vise, (mec.) yunque de tornillo.

anxiety [æŋ'zaɪətɪ] *s.* 1. ansia, angustia, ansiedad. 2. anhelo, afán.

anxiety neurosis, (psic.) neurosis de angustia, neurosis de ansiedad.

anxious ['æŋkʃəs, 'æŋʃəs] *a.* 1. ansioso, inquieto, perturbado. 2. anheloso, deseoso, ej., *a. to please,* deseoso de agradar.

anxiousness [-nəs] *s.* ansiedad, inquietud.

any ['ɛnɪ] *a.* 1. cualquier, cualquiera; to do, ej., *a. doubt you may have,* cualquier duda que puedas tener, *a. money you may find is yours,* el dinero que puedas encontrar es tuyo, *a. woman will know that,* cualquier mujer sabrá eso. 2. algún, alguno, alguna, ej., *if you have a. doubt,* si tienes alguna duda, *is there a. proof?* ¿hay prueba alguna?; (*en negación o con prep. privativa; alternativamente*) ningún, ninguno, ninguna, ej., *I haven't a. idea,* no tengo idea alguna, o ninguna idea, *I don't see a. difference,* no veo diferencia alguna, o ninguna diferencia, *without a. difficulty,* sin dificultad alguna, o ninguna dificultad. 3. *en sentido partitivo gen. no se traduce,* ej., *have you a. money?* ¿tiene Ud. dinero? 4. **at a. cost,** a toda costa; **at a. rate,** de todas maneras, de todos modos; **at a. time,** a cualquier hora, cuando quiera; **in a. case,** en todo caso, de todos modos. *—adv.* 1. algo, en alguna forma, de modo alguno, ej., *is it a. better now?* ¿está algo mejor ahora? 2. *gen. no se traduce en frases negativas e interrogativas cuando sólo refuerza el sentido de otro adv. subsiguiente,* ej., *could you do it a. better?* ¿podrías hacerlo mejor? *I can't go a. sooner,* no puedo ir más temprano. 3. *(puesta al final de frases negativas)* en absoluto, en nada, ej., *this won't help me a.,* esto no me ayudará en nada. 4. **a. farther,** más lejos, **a. longer,** más tiempo, todavía; **a. more,** más; aún; **not . . . a. longer, not . . . a. more,** ya no, no . . . más, ej., *I can not tolerate it a. longer,* no puedo tolerarlo más, ya no puedo tolerarlo; *he does not love me a. more,* él no me quiere más, él ya no me quiere; *I'm not a. the wiser,* no sé más (que antes). *—pron.* cualquiera; ninguno, ninguna, ej., *if a. of them can tell you,* si cualquiera de ellos puede decirte, *I would not touch a. of those,* yo no tocaría ninguno de ésos, *we have no weapons and no hope of ever receiving a.,* no tenemos armas ni esperanzas de recibir ninguna; **if a.,** si las hay, ej., *the difficulties, if a., will be solved,* las dificultades, si las hay, serán resueltas.

anybody [-ˌbɑdɪ, -ˌbʌdɪ, B -ˌbɔdɪ] *pron.* alguno, alguna, alguien; cualquiera, quienquiera; todo el mundo; (*después de negación*) ninguno, nadie, ej., *two or three anybodies,* dos o tres personas cualquiera (sin importancia), *is a. at home?* ¿hay alguien en casa? *a. can do it,* cualquiera (todo el mundo) puede hacerlo, *hardly a. wants it,* casi nadie lo desea.

anyhow [-ˌhaʊ] *adv.* de cualquier modo, en cualquier forma, como quiera que sea, en cualquier caso.

anymore [ˌɛnɪ'mɔr, B -'mɔ] *adv.* (*ú. en negaciones*) nunca más, no más, ya no.

anyone [ɛnɪˌwʌn, -wən] *var. de* **anybody.**

anyplace [-ˌpleɪs] *adv.* en cualquier parte, dondequiera; a cualquier parte.

anything [-'θɪŋ] *pron.* algo, alguna cosa, cualquier cosa; todo, todo lo que, ej., *a. at all,* cualquier cosa (que sea), *a. else,* cualquier otra cosa, *a. else?* ¿alguna otra cosa? *a. you like,* todo lo que le guste, *have you a. to do now?* ¿tiene Ud. algo que hacer ahora? *—adv.* en lo mínimo, en (lo) absoluto; **a. like,** (fam.) (siquiera) un poco, ej., *if she is a. like pretty,* si ella es (siquiera) un poco bonita.

anything but, en lo absoluto, en ningún respecto; **to be a. b.,** ser todo menos, no ser . . . ni con mucho, ej., *she is a. b. pretty,* ella es todo menos bonita; ella no es bonita, ni con mucho.

anyway [-ˌweɪ] *adv.* 1. de cualquier modo, en cualquier forma. 2. de todos modos, en todo caso.

anywhere [-ˌhwɛr, -ˌwɛr, B -ˌwɛə, -ˌhwɛə] *adv.* en cualquier parte, dondequiera. *—s.* cualquier parte, todas partes.

anywise [-ˌwaɪz] *adv.* de cualquier modo, en cualquier forma.

a/o *abrev. de* **account of,** cuenta (cta.) de.

Aonian [eɪ'oʊnɪən] *a.* (hist.) aonio, beocio.

aorist ['eɪərəst, 'ɛər-] *s.* (gram. griega) aoristo.

aorta [eɪ'ɔrtə, B -ɔtə] *s.* (anat.) aorta.

aortal [-əl] **aortic** [-ɪk] *a.* aórtico, de la aorta.

AP *abrev. de* **Associated Press,** Prensa Asociada (AP).

apace [ə'peɪs] *adv.* de prisa, rápidamente, con presteza, con prontitud.

apache [ə'pæʃ] *s.* bandido, salteador; (ant.) hombre de los barrios bajos de París.

Apache [ə'pætʃɪ] *s.* (*pl.* APACHES O APACHE) apache (indio norteamericano).

apanage, *var. de* **appanage.**

apart [ə'pɑrt, B ə'pɑt] *adv.* aparte; separadamente, independientemente; a un lado, a distancia; **a. from,** aparte de; con la excepción de; **joking a.,** bromas aparte; **to come a.,** desunirse, desprenderse; **to fall a.,** desbaratarse, (fig.) destruirse a sí mismo; **to take a.,** desarmar; **to set a.,** apartar, reservar, destinar; **to stand a.,** mantenerse apartado; distinguirse; **to tear a.,** deshacer, despedazar; **to tell a.,** distinguir, diferenciar. *—a.* aparte, separado.

apartheid [ə'pɑrˌteɪt, -ˌtaɪt, B ə'pɑtˌheɪt] *s.* apartheid, separación de las razas (esp. en Sudáfrica).

apartment [ə'pɑrtment, B ə'pɑt-] *s.* apartamento, apartamiento, departamento, piso.

apartment building, edificio de departamentos (Am.), edificio de pisos.

apartment hotel, apartotel.

apathetic [æpə'θɛtɪk] *a.* apático, indolente, impasible, indiferente.

apathy ['æpəθɪ] *s.* apatía, indolencia, impasibilidad de ánimo, dejadez.

apatite ['æpəˌtaɪt] *s.* (min.) apatita.

ape [eɪp] *s.* 1. mono, simio, antropoide. 2. (fig.) imitador, persona que imita o remeda; mona (fam.). 3. (fam.) persona ruda o torpe. 4. **to play the a.,** hacerse el gracioso. *—v.t.* imitar, remedar.

apeak [əˌpik] *adv.* (mar.) a pique, verticalmente.

Apelles [ə'pɛliz] *s.* Apeles, pintor griego de la antigüedad.

ape-man ['eɪpˌmæn] *s.* hombre mono; forma primitiva del hombre.

Apennines ['æpəˌnaɪnz] *s.* (*pl.*) Apeninos (montes).

apepsy [ə'pɛpsɪ] *s.* (med.) apepsia, falta de digestión.

aperient [ə'pɪrɪənt, B ə'pɪər-] *s., a.* (farm.) laxante.

aperiodic [ˌeɪˌpɪrɪ'ɑdɪk, B -ˌpɪərɪ'ɔd-] *a.* (fís.) aperiódico.

apéritif [ɑˌpɛrə'tif] *s.* aperitivo.

aperitive [ə'pɛrətɪv] *s., a.* aperitivo.

aperture ['æpərˌtʃʊr, -tʃər, B -ˌtjʊə, -tʃə] *s.* abertura, orificio; paso; rendija; (ópt., fot.) abertura de diafragma.

apery ['eɪpərɪ] *s.* monería, monada.

apetalous [eɪ'pɛtələs] *a.* (bot.) apétalo, sin pétalos.

apex ['eɪˌpɛks] *s.* (*pl.* APEXES [-əz] O APICES ['eɪpəˌsiz, 'æ-]) 1. ápice, cima, cúspide. 2. (fig.) ápice, punto culminante. 3. punta, vértice. 4. (anat., hist., astr.) ápex.

aphaeresis [ə'fɛrəsəs B æ'fɪər-] *s.* (gram.) aféresis.

aphagia [ə'feɪdʒɪə] *s.* (med.) afagia, imposibilidad de deglutir.

aphanipterous [ˌæfə'nɪptərəs] *a.* (ento.) afaníptero (dícese de los insectos que carecen de alas).

aphanite ['æfəˌnaɪt] *s.* (min.) afanita.

aphanitic [ˌæfə'nɪtɪk] *a.* (min.) afanítico.

aphasia [ə'feɪʒə, B ə'feɪzjə] *s.* (med.) afasia.

aphelion [æ'filjən] *s.* (*pl.* APHELIA [-jə]) (astr.) afelio.

aphesis ['æfəsəs] *s.* (gram.) aféresis.

aphid ['eɪfəd, 'æf-] *s.* (ento.) áfido, pulgón.

aphis [-əs] *s.* (*pl.* APHIDES [-fəˌdiz]) (ento.) áfido.

aphlogistic [ˌæflə'dʒɪstɪk] *a.* (quím.) aflogístico.

aphonia [eɪ'foʊnɪə, B æ-] *s.* afonía.

aphonic [-'fɑnɪk, B -'fɔn-] *a.* afónico, mudo, sin voz; (fon.) mudo.

aphorism ['æfəˌrɪzəm] *s.* aforismo.

aphoristic [ˌæfə'rɪstɪk] *a.* aforístico.

aphotic [eɪ'foʊtɪk, B æ-] *a.* afótico, desprovisto de luz.

aphrodisiac [ˌæfrə'dɪzɪæk] *a., s.* afrodisíaco.

Aphrodite [-'daɪtɪ] *s.* (mitol.) Afrodita, nombre griego de Venus.

aphthous ['æfθəs] *a.* (med.) aftoso, de la fiebre que ataca a las reses.

aphthous fever, (vet.) fiebre aftosa.

aphyllous [eɪ'fɪləs, B ə-] *a.* (bot.) áfilo.

apian ['eɪpɪən] *a.* (ento.) apiario.

apiarist ['eɪpɪərəst] *s.* colmenero, apicultor.

apiary [-ˌɛrɪ, B -ərɪ] *s.* colmenar, abejar.

apical ['æpɪkəl, 'eɪp-] *a.* 1. cimero, que está en la cumbre. 2. (fon.) apical.

apiculture [ˈeɪpɪˌkʌltʃər, B -tʃə] *s.* apicultura.
apiculturist [ˌeɪpɪˈkʌltʃərəst] *s.* apicultor.
apiculus [əˈpɪkjələs] *s.* (*pl.* APICULI [-laɪ]) (bot.) apículo.
apiece [əˈpis] *adv.* a cada uno, por cada uno, para cada uno, ej., *five dollars a.*, cinco dólares para (por) cada uno.
apiology [ˌeɪpɪˈɑlədʒɪ, B -ˈɔl-] *s.* estudio de las abejas.
apish [ˈeɪpɪʃ] *a.* 1. simiesco, monesco, símico. 2. imitador, remedador. 3. (fig.) tonto, necio.
apishness [-nəs] *s.* monería, monada; imitación burlesca, gesto frívolo.
apivorous [eɪˈpɪvərəs] *a.* (ento.) apívoro, que come abejas.
aplacental [ˌeɪpləˈsɛntəl, B ˌæp-] *a.* (zool.) aplacentario.
aplanatic [ˌæpləˈnætɪk] *a.* (ópt.) aplanático, aplanético.
aplenty [əˈplɛntɪ] *a., adv.* mucho, en abundancia.
aplitic [æpˈlɪtɪk] *a.* (geol.) aplítico.
aplomb [əˈplɑm, B əˈplɔm] *s.* aplomo, ecuanimidad, sangre fría.
apnea, apnoea [ˈæpnɪə, æpˈniə] *s.* (med.) apnea.
APO *abrev. de* **Army Post Office,** oficina de correos en un puesto militar.
apocalypse [əˈpɑkəˌlɪps, B əˈpɔk-] *s.* 1. **A.,** (teo.) Apocalipsis. 2. revelación profética.
apocalyptic [əˌpɑkəˈlɪptɪk, B əˌpɔk-] **apocalyptical** [-tɪkəl] *a.* apocalíptico.
apocarpous [ˌæpəˈkɑrpəs, B -ˈkɑp-] *a.* (bot.) apocárpico.
apocatastasis [ˌæpəkəˈtæstəsəs] *s.* 1. (med.) restablecimiento de la salud. 2. (filos.) apocatástasis.
apochromatic [ˌæpəkroʊˈmætɪk] *a.* (ópt.) apocromático.
apocopate [əˈpɑkəˌpeɪt, B əˈpɔk-] *v.t.* (gram.) apocopar.
apocope [-pɪ] *s.* (gram.) apócope.
apocrisiary [ˌæpəˈkrɪʒɪˌɛrɪ, B -ˈkrɪsɪərɪ] *s.* (hist.) apocrisiario, embajador en el imperio griego.
Apocrypha [əˈpɑkrəfə, B əˈpɔk-] *s. pl.* (*sing. o pl. en const.*) libros apócrifos.
apocryphal [-fəl] *a.* apócrifo, supuesto, de dudosa autenticidad.
apocynaceous [əˌpɑsəˈneɪʃəs, B əˌpɔs-] *a.* (bot.) apocináceo.
apodal [ˈæpədəl] *a.* (zool.) ápodo.
apodictic [ˌæpəˈdɪktɪk] *a.* apodíctico, evidente.
apodosis [əˈpɑdəsəs, B əˈpɔd-] *s.* (*pl.* APODOSES [-dəsiz]) (gram.) apódosis.
apogamy [əˈpɑgəmɪ, B əˈpɔg-] *s.* (bot.) apogamia.
apogean [ˌæpəˈdʒiən] *a.* (astr.) apogeico.
apogean tides, mareas muertas o de apogeo.
apogee [ˈæpədʒi] *s.* 1. (astr.) apogeo. 2. (fig.) apogeo, súmmum (de la grandeza o perfección); cúspide, cima.
apograph [ˈæpəˌgræf, B -ˌgrɑf] *s.* apógrafo, copia, transcripción (de un escrito original).
apolitical [ˌeɪpəˈlɪtɪkəl, B ˌæ-] *a.* 1. apolítico. 2. sin significado político.
apolitically [-ɪ] *adv.* de modo apolítico.
Apollinarian [əˌpɑləˈnɛrɪən, B əˌpɔləˈnɛər-] *a., s.* (relig.) apolinarista.
Apollinarianism [-ˌɪzəm] *s.* (relig.) apolinarismo.
Apolline [əˈpɑlən, -laɪn, B əˈpɔl-] *a.* (poét.) apolíneo, de gran belleza.
Apollo [əˈpɑloʊ, B əˈpɔloʊ] *s.* 1. (mitol.) Apolo, dios del sol, la música, la poesía, la medicina y las artes. 2. joven hermoso.
Apollodorus [əˌpɑləˈdɔrəs B əˌpɔl-] *s.* Apolodoro (de Damasco), arquitecto griego que trabajó en el Foro de Trajano en Roma.
Apollonian [ˌæpəˈloʊnɪən] *a.* 1. apolíneo. 2. armonioso, moderado, equilibrado.
apologetic [əˌpɑləˈdʒɛtɪk, B əˌpɔl-] *a.* 1. apologético. 2. lleno de excusas o disculpas.
apologia [ˌæpəˈloʊdʒɪə] *s.* apología, discurso en defensa de alguien o de algo.
apologist [əˈpɑlədʒəst, B əˈpɔl-] *s.* apologista.
apologize [-ˌdʒaɪz] *v.i.* disculparse, excusarse, pedir disculpas o perdón; **a. for,** disculparse por de; **a. to,** disculparse con, pedir disculpas a.
apologue [ˈæpəˌlɔg, -ˌlɑg, B -ˌlɔg] *s.* apólogo.
apology [əˈpɑlədʒɪ, B əˈpɔl-] *s.* (*pl.* APOLOGIES) 1. disculpa, excusa, justificación. 2. apología, discurso de defensa o excusa. 3. substituto o expediente inadecuado.
apomixis [ˌæpəˈmɪksəs] *s.* (biol.) apomixis.
apomorphine [-ˈmɔrˌfin, B -ˈmɔˌ-] *s.* (med.) apomorfina.
aponeurosis [-nʊˈroʊsəs, B -njʊ-] *s.* (anat.) aponeurosis.
aponeurotic [-ˈrɑtɪk, B -ˈrɔt-] *a.* (anat.) aponeurótico.
aponeurotome [-ˈnʊrəˌtoʊm, B -ˈnjʊ-] *s.* (med.) aponeurótomo.
apoop [əˈpup] *adv.* (mar.) en o hacia la popa.
apophasis [əˈpɑfəsəs, B əˈpɔf-] *s.* (ret.) insinuación por pretendida omisión.
apophony [əˈpɑfənɪ, B əˈpɔf-] *s.* (fon.)apofonía.
apophthegm *var.* de **apothegm.**
apophyge [əˈpɑfədʒɪ, B əˈpɔf-] *s.* (arq.) apófige, imoscapo.
apophyllite [ˌæpəˈfɪlˌaɪt] *s.* (min.) apofilita.
apophysis [əˈpɑfəsəs, B əˈpɔf-] *s.* (*pl.* APOPHYSES [-ˌsɪz]) (anat.) apófisis.
apoplectic [ˌæpəˈplɛktɪk] *a.* apoplético.
apoplexy [ˈæpəˌplɛksɪ] *s.* (med.) apoplejía.
aport [əˈpɔrt, B əˈpɔt] *adv.* (mar.) a babor.
aposematic [ˌæpəsɪˈmætɪk] *a.* (zool.) conspicuo, llamativo, preventivo (coloración o estructuración de ciertos animales).
aposiopesis [ˌæpəˌsaɪəˈpisəs] *s.* (ret.) aposiópesis.
apostasy [əˈpɑstəsɪ, B əˈpɔs-] *s.* apostasía, abandono (de la fe religiosa o de un partido político).
apostate [-ˌteɪt, -tət] *s.* apóstata. —*a.* de apostasía.
apostatize [əˈpɑstəˌtaɪz, B əˈpɔs-] *v.i.* apostatar, renegar.
apostematous [ˌæpəˈstɛmətəs] *a.* (med.) apostemoso.
aposteme [ˈæpəˌstɛm] *s.* (med.) apostema, absceso.
a posteriori [ˌɑpoʊˌstɪrɪˈɔrɪ, ˌeɪpɑs-, B ˈeɪpɒsˌtɛrɪˈɔraɪ] (filos.) a posteriori; del efecto a la causa.
apostle [əˈpɑsəl, B əˈpɔs-] *s.* apóstol.
Apostle of the Gentiles, apóstol de los gentiles (San Pablo).
Apostles' Creed, Credo de los Apóstoles.
apostolate [əˈpɑstəˌleɪt, -lət, B əˈpɔs-] *s.* apostolado.
apostolic [ˌæpəˈstɑlɪk, B -ˈstɔl-] *a.* apostólico.
apostolic father, (hist.) padre apostólico (de los siglos I y II).
Apostolic See, Sede Apostólica.
apostrophe [əˈpɑstrəfɪ, B əˈpɔs-] *s.* 1. (ret.) apóstrofe. 2. (gram.) apóstrofo.
apostrophic [æpəˈstrɑfɪk, B -ˈstrɔf-] *a.* del apóstrofe, apóstrofo.
apostrophize [əˈpɑstrəˌfaɪz, B əˈpɔs-] *v.t.* apostrofar.
apothecaries' measure [əˈpɑθəˌkɛriz-, B əˈpɔθɪkər-] *s.* sistema norteamericano de medidas para líquidos, usado esp. por los farmacéuticos.
apothecaries' weight, sistema inglés de medidas de peso, usado en G.B. y E.U. por los boticarios.
apothecary [-ˌkɛrɪ, B -kərɪ] *s.* 1. boticario, farmacéutico. 2. farmacia, botica, droguería (Am.).
apothecium [ˌæpəˈθiʃɪəm] *s.* (*pl.* APOTHECIA [-ʃɪə]) (bot.) apotecio.
apothegm [ˈæpəˌθɛm] *s.* apotegma, sentencia breve e ingeniosa.
apothem [ˈæpəˌθɛm] *s.* (geom.) apotema.
apotheosis [əˌpɑθɪˈoʊsəs, ˌæpəˈθiə-, B əˌpɔθɪˈoʊ-] *s.* apoteosis, deificación, glorificación, ensalzamiento.
apotheosize [ˌæpəˈθiəˌsaɪz, əˈpɑθɪə-, B əˈpɔθ-] *v.t.* glorificar, exaltar.
apozem [ˈæpəˌzɛm] *s.* (farm.) apócema, apócima.
Appalachian [ˌæpəˈleɪtʃən, -ˈlæ-, B -ˈleɪtʃɪ-] *s.* apalache.
Appalachian Mountains, Montes Apalaches o Alleghenys (E.U.).
appall, appal [əˈpɔl] *v.t.* pasmar, asombrar, consternar.
appalling [-ɪŋ] *a.* pasmoso; que causa consternación.
appanage [ˈæpənɪdʒ] *s.* 1. (hist.) infantado (territorio para la manutención de uno de los infantes reales). 2. (der.) herencia. 3. dependencia, pertenencia.
apparatus [ˌæpəˈrætəs, -ˈreɪt-, B -ˈreɪt-] *s.* (*pl.* APPARATUS O APPARATUSES [-əz]) 1. aparato, (conjunto de) instrumento(s). 2. (fig.) aparato, mecanismo (del estado, etc.). 3. (fisiol.) aparato (digestivo, respiratorio, etc.). 4. aparejo; conjunto de normas y materiales (para hacer una prueba psicológica, etc.).
apparel [əˈpærəl] *s.* 1. ropa, vestido, traje. 2. (mar.) aparejo. —*v.t.* 1. vestir, trajear. 2. ataviar, adornar. 3. (mar.) aparejar, equipar.
apparent [əˈpærənt, əˈpɛr-] *a.* aparente, patente, manifiesto.
apparent horizon, (geog.) horizonte sensible.
apparently [-lɪ] *adv.* aparentemente; por lo visto, manifiestamente.
apparition [ˌæpəˈrɪʃən] *s.* aparición, visión, fantasma, espectro.
appeal [əˈpil] *v.t.* apelar de (la sentencia). —*v.i.* (ú. con *to*) 1. apelar (a). 2. recurrir, acudir, suplicar (a). 3. atraer, interesar (a), gustar (a), llamar la atención (de). 4. **to appeal for,** solicitar. —*s.* 1. (der.) apelación. 2. petición, súplica; recurso, instancia. 3. atracción, encanto. 4. **without appeal,** inapelable.
appealer [-ər, B -ə] *s.* (der.) apelante.
appeal for annulment (der.) recurso de nulidad.
appeal for habeas corpus, (der.) recurso de habeas corpus.
appealing [-ɪŋ] *a.* 1. implorante, suplicante, ej., *a. look,* mirada suplicante. 2. conmovedor, ej., *a. sermon,* sermón conmovedor. 3. atrayente, apetecible, ej., *a. colors,* colores atractivos.
appear [əˈpɪr, B əˈpɪə] *v.i.* 1. aparecer, asomarse, manifestarse, estar a la vista. 2. parecer. 3. aparecer, publicarse, editarse. 4. (der.) comparecer, presentarse, responder.
appearance [-əns, B -rəns] *s.* 1. apariencia, aspecto. 2. aparición, publicación, debut. 3. (*gen. pl.*) apariencias, bien parecer. 4. (der.) comparecencia (ante el tribunal o el juez). 5. **appearances are deceitful,** las apariencias engañan; **first a.,** debut (de un actor); **for**

appearances, **for appearances' sake,** por el bien parecer; **to all a.,** a todas luces; **to keep up appearances,** salvar las apariencias; **to put in an a.,** aparecer, hacer acto de presencia.
appease [ə'piz] *v.t.* 1. apaciguar, aplacar, reconciliar, aquietar. 2. conciliar, apaciguar (por medio de concesiones políticas, económicas, etc.).
appeasement [-mənt] *s.* apaciguamiento, pacificación.
appeaser [-ər, B -ə] *s.* apaciguador, pacificador, reconciliador.
appellant [ə'pɛlənt] *s.* (der.) apelante.
appellate [-lət] *a.* (der.) de apelación (tribunal, jurisdicción, etc.).
appellation [ˌæpə'leɪʃən] *s.* denominación, título.
appellative [ə'pɛlətɪv] *s.* 1. (gram.) apelativo, nombre apelativo. 2. nombre, título. —*a.* (gram.) apelativo.
appellee [ˌæpə'li] *s.* (der.) apelado, demandado.
append [ə'pɛnd] *v.t.* 1. añadir, agregar, anexar. 2. poner, fijar (sello, firma, etc.).
appendage [-ɪdʒ] *s.* 1. dependencia, accesorio, pertenencia. 2. (bot., zool.) apéndice.
appendant [-ənt] *a.* 1. asociado, acompañante, concomitante. 2. anexo (a). 3. (der.) accesorio. —*s.* 1. herencia o derecho accesorios. 2. dependencia. 3. apéndice.
appendectomy [ˌæpən'dɛktəmɪ] *s.* (med.) apendectomía, apendicectomía.
appendicitis [əˌpɛndə'saɪtəs] *s.* (med.) apendicitis.
appendicle [ə'pɛndɪkəl] *s.* (bot.) apendículo, pequeño apéndice.
appendicular [ˌæpən'dɪkjələr, B -lə] *a.* (anat., zool.) apendicular.
appendix [ə'pɛndɪks] *s.* (*pl.* APPENDIXES [-əz] o APPENDICES [-dəˌsiz]) 1. apéndice, suplemento (a un libro, documento, etc.). 2. (anat.) apéndice, esp. apéndice vermicular o vermiforme. 3. (bot., zool.) apéndice. 4. accesorio; dependencia.
apperceive [ˌæpər'siv, B -pə'-] *v.t.* (psic.) captar, apercibir, asimilar (nuevas ideas, etc.).
apperception [-'sɛpʃən] *s.* (psic.) apercepción.
apperceptive [-'sɛptɪv] *a.* (psic.) aperceptivo.
appertain [-'teɪn] *v.i.* (ú. con *to*) 1. pertenecer (como propiedad, parte, etc.) (a). 2. corresponder (como atributo, etc.) (a), relacionarse (con).
appetence ['æpətəns] **appetency** [-ənsɪ] *s.* 1. apetencia, apetito, anhelo. 2. propensión natural. 3. (quím.) afinidad (entre substancias, etc.).
appetent [-ənt] *a.* (ú. esp. fig.) ávido, codicioso.
appetite ['æpəˌtaɪt] *s.* apetito; **lack of a.,** inapetencia; **to whet the a.,** abrir o despertar el apetito.
appetitive [-ˌtaɪtɪv, æ'pɛtətɪv] *a.* apetitoso, apetitivo.
appetizer ['æpəˌtaizər, B -zə] *s.* aperitivo.
appetizing [-zɪŋ] *a.* apetitoso, apetitivo, gustoso, sabroso.
Appian Way ['æpɪən-] Vía Apia (en Roma).
appl. *abrev. de* **applied,** aplicado, aplícase (a).
applaud [ə'plɔd] *v.t.* aplaudir; elogiar, alabar. —*v.i.* dar palmadas; hacer elogios.
applause [ə'plɔz] *s.* aplauso, aclamación; aprobación.
apple ['æpəl] *s.* 1. (bot.) manzano (árbol). 2. manzana (fruta). 3. **a. of the eye,** pupila; **a. of one's eye,** (fig.) niña de los ojos, pedazo del alma.
apple butter, mermelada de manzana condimentada con especias aromáticas.
apple-cart [-ˌkɑrt, B -ˌkɑt] *s.* carretilla del vendedor de manzanas; **to upset a person's a.-c.,** (fig.) malograr los planes de una persona.
apple fritter, buñuelo de manzana.
applejack [-ˌdʒæk] *s.* (E.U.) aguardiente de manzana.
apple mint, (bot.) mastranzo, mentastro.
apple of discord, manzana de la discordia.
apple orchard, manzanar.
apple pie, pastel de manzana.
apple-pie [-'paɪ] *a.* 1. (fam.) excelente, perfecto; **in a. order,** en perfecto orden.
apple-polisher [-ˌpɑlɪʃər, B -ˌpɔlɪʃə] *s.* (fam.) sobón, adulón, chupamedias (Am.).
applesauce [-ˌsɔs] *s.* 1. compota de manzana. 2. (jer.) adulación, halago insincero. 3. (jer.) disparate, tontería, insensatez.
apple tree, (bot.) manzano.
appliance [ə'plaɪəns] *s.* 1. aplicación. 2. instrumento, dispositivo. 3. artefacto, aparato (eléctrico, casero, etc.).
applicability [ˌæplɪkə'bɪlətɪ] *s.* 1. campo de aplicación, aptitud, utilidad. 2. pertinencia.
applicable ['æplɪkəbəl, ə'plɪk-] *a.* 1. aplicable. 2. (con *to*) pertinente (a), apropiado (para).
applicant ['æplɪkənt] *s.* 1. solicitante, aspirante, candidato. 2. (der.) demandante.
application [ˌæplə'keɪʃən] *s.* 1. aplicación, uso, modo de emplearse. 2. esmero, dedicación. 3. solicitud de empleo, etc. 4. formulario que debe llenar el solicitante. 5. **to make an a.,** formular una solicitud (en persona o por escrito).
application blank, application form, solicitud, cédula en blanco.
applicator ['æpləˌkeɪtər, B -tə] *s.* aplicador, brocha o dispositivo para hacer una aplicación (de medicamento, pintura, etc.).
applied [ə'plaɪd] *a.* 1. aplicado, ej., *a. science,* ciencia aplicada. 2. adaptado, utilizado. 3. **a. for,** pedido, solicitado.
applied mathematics, matemáticas aplicadas, matemáticas mixtas.
appliqué [ˌæplə'keɪ, B æ'plikeɪ] *s.* aplicación, sobrepuesto; ornamento aplicado a una superficie (tela, etc.).
apply [ə'plaɪ] *v.t.* (*pret., p.p.* APPLIED; *p.pr.* APPLYING) 1. aplicar (pintura; remedio; reglas, palabra, conocimiento; frenos). 2. **a. oneself to,** aplicarse a, dedicarse a, darse a (tarea, etc.). —*v.i.* 1. ser pertinente, corresponder. 2. ajustarse, encajarse. 3. aplicarse, afanarse. 4. **a. for, a. to,** solicitar (puesto, empleo), pedir (ayuda, etc.).
appoggiatura [əˌpɑdʒə'tʊrə, B əˌpɔdʒ-] *s.* (mús.) apoyatura.
appoint [ə'pɔɪnt] *v.t.* 1. nombrar, designar, ej., *a. him governor,* designarlo o nombrarlo gobernador. 2. fijar, establecer, decretar. 3. (*ú. gen. en p.p.*) equipar, surtir; amueblar, ej., *well appointed,* bien amueblado. 4. (der.) disponer de, asignar (propriedad o bienes).
appointee [əˌpɔɪn'ti, ˌæpɔɪn-] *s.* 1. electo, persona designada. 2. (der.) beneficiario.
appointive [ə'pɔɪntɪv] *a.* electivo; elector.
appointment [-mənt] *s.* 1. nombramiento, designación. 2. oficio, puesto, empleo. 3. cita, compromiso; **by a.,** cita previa. 4. (*pl.*) equipo; mobiliario. 5. (der.) disposición, asignación. 6. **to break an a.,** romper un compromiso, faltar a una cita; **to keep an a.,** cumplir con un compromiso, acudir a una cita.
apportion [ə'pɔrʃən, B ə'pɔʃən] *v.t.* distribuir, repartir, ratear, asignar.
apportionment [-mənt] *s.* distribución, reparto, prorrateo, esp. de los cuerpos legislativos en E.U. o de los impuestos, basados en la población.
appose [æ'poʊz] *v.t.* yuxtaponer, añadir.
apposite ['æpəzət] *a.* apropiado, propio, oportuno, a propósito.
apposition [ˌæpə'zɪʃən] *s.* 1. (gram.) aposición. 2. añadidura, adición. 3. yuxtaposición.
appositive [ə'pɑzətɪv, B ə'pɔz-] *a.* (gram.) apositico, en aposición.
appraisal [ə'preɪzəl] **appraisement** [-mənt] *s.* 1. evaluación, valoración, tasación (esp. la de una autoridad). 2. apreciación, estimación.
appraise [ə'preɪz] *v.t.* evaluar, valorar, tasar.
appraiser [-ər, B -ə] *s.* tasador, evaluador.
appreciable [ə'priʃəbəl] *a.* 1. apreciable, estimable. 2. apreciable, considerable, notable.
appreciate [-ʃɪˌeɪt] *v.t.* 1. apreciar, reconocer (importancia, esfuerzo, etc.). 2. apreciar, estimar. 3. agradecer. 4. aumentar el valor o precio de. —*v.i.* subir de precio o valor.
appreciation [əˌpriʃɪ'eɪʃən] *s.* 1. apreciación, valoración. 2. apreciación, aprecio, reconocimiento. 3. agradecimiento. 4. aumento (de precio o valor). 5. crítica (de obra de arte, libro, película, etc.).
appreciative [ə'priʃɪˌeɪtɪv, B -ʃjətɪv] *a.* 1. apreciador, estimatorio. 2. reconocido, agradecido.
apprehend [ˌæprɪ'hɛnd] *v.t.* 1. aprehender, prender, arrestar, detener. 2. comprender, entender, aprehender, percibir. 3. temer, recelar. —*v.i.* aprehender, comprender.
apprehensible [-'hɛnsəbəl] *a.* aprehensible, comprensible.
apprehension [-'hɛntʃən, B -ʃən] *s.* 1. aprensión, temor, recelo. 2. aprehensión, captura, arresto, detención. 3. percepción, comprensión, reconocimiento.
apprehensive [-'hɛnsɪv] *a.* 1. aprensivo, receloso, tímido. 2. capaz de aprehender, discernidor, penetrante, perspicaz.
apprehensiveness [-nəs] *s.* aprensión, recelo, temor.
apprentice [ə'prɛntəs] *s.* aprendiz; novicio, principiante. —*v.t.* poner de aprendiz.
apprenticeship [-ʃɪp] *s.* aprendizaje, noviciado.
apprise, apprize [ə'praɪz] *v.t.* 1. (con *of*) dar parte a. 2. apreciar, valorar.
approach [ə'proʊtʃ] *v.t.* 1. acercarse a. 2. aproximarse a, parecerse a. 3. abordar, hacer propuestas a. —*v.i.* acercarse; esp. (golf) golpear la pelota para que caiga en el césped cerca del hoyo. —*s.* 1. acercamiento, aproximación. 2. vía de entrada, paso, acceso. 3. (mil.) (*pl.*) aproches. 4. propuesta, tentativa. 5. (con *to*) enfoque, planteamiento (de un problema, asunto, etc.). 6. (golf) golpe de aproximación.
approachability [əˌproʊtʃə'bɪlətɪ] *s.* accesibilidad.
approachable [ə'proʊtʃəbəl] *a.* accesible, de fácil acceso; tratable.
approach light, (avia.) farol de acercamiento, luz de aproximación o de acceso.
approbate ['æprəˌbeɪt] *v.t.* (E.U.)aprobar aprobar formalmente, sancionar.
approbation [ˌæprə'beɪʃən] *s.* aprobación, beneplácito; encomio; sanción.
approbatory ['æprəbəˌtɔrɪ, B -ˌbeɪtərɪ] *a.* aprobatorio.
appropriable [ə'proʊprɪəbəl] *a.* apropiable.
appropriate [ə'proʊprɪət] *a.* apropiado, apto, adecuado, propio, oportuno; a propósito. —[-ˌeɪt] *v.t.* 1. apropiarse de. 2. adueñarse de, posesionarse de (cosa ajena), ej., *he appropriated my pen,* él se adueño de mi pluma. 3. destinar, asignar, consignar (dinero, etc.).
appropriation [əˌproʊprɪ'eɪʃən] *s.* 1. apropiación. 2. asignación, consignación.
appropriator [ə'proʊprɪˌeɪtər, B -tə] *s.* apropiador.

approvable [ə'pruvəbəl] *a.* digno de aprobación, encomiable.
approval [-vəl] *s.* aprobación, beneplácito, consentimiento; **on a.,** a prueba; (com.) previa aceptación.
approve [ə'pruv] *v.t.* aprobar, sancionar, ratificar. —*v.i.* dar su aprobación; **a. of,** aprobar, dar por bueno.
approvingly [-ɪŋlɪ] *adv.* con aprobación.
approx. *abrev. de* **approximate,** aproximado; **approximately,** aproximadamente.
approximate [ə'prɑksəmət, B ə'prɔk-] *a.* 1. aproximado, aproximativo. 2. próximo, cercano. — [-ˌmeɪt] *v.t., v.i.* aproximar(se); acercar(se).
approximately [-lɪ] *adv.* aproximadamente.
approximation [əˌprɑksə'meɪʃən, B əˌprɔk-] *s.* 1. aproximación. 2. (mat.) aproximación, cálculo, suma o número aproximados.
approximatively [ə'prɑksəˌmeɪtɪvlɪ, B ə'prɔksəmə-] *adv.* aproximadamente, aproximativamente.
appurtenace [ə'pɜrtənəns, B ə'pɜt-] *s.* 1. adjunto, aditamiento. 2. (*pl.*) pertenencias, accesorios. 3. (*pl.*) (der.) anexidades.
appurtenant [-nənt] *a.* 1. accesorio, auxiliar. 2. (der.) anexo (derecho, servidumbre o cosa). —*s.* (der.) anexidad.
Apr. *abrev. de* **April,** abril.
apraxia [eɪ'præksɪə] *s.* (med.) apraxia.
apricot ['æprəˌkɑt, 'eɪ-, B 'eɪprɪˌkɔt] *s.* albaricoque, damasco; albaricoquero (árbol), damasco.
April ['eɪprəl] *s.* abril, cuarto mes del año.
April fool, inocenton, víctima de las bromas que se gastan el primero de abril (como en el día de inocentes).
April Fool's Day, día de los inocentes (el primer día de abril).
a priori [ˌɑprɪ'ɔrɪ, ˌæ-, B 'eɪpraɪ'ɔraɪ] a priori, de la causa al efecto.
apriorism [-'ɔrˌɪzəm] *s.* (filos.) apriorismo.
aprioristic [eɪˌpraɪə'rɪstɪk] *a.* (filos.) apriorístico.
apriority [ˌeɪpraɪ'ɔrətɪ] *s.* (filos.) calidad de a priori.
apron ['eɪprən, -pərn, B -prən] *s.* 1. delantal; mandil (de un obrero, etc.). 2. (teat.) proscenio. 3. guarnición (debajo de la repisa de una ventana). 4. (aer.) faja de estacionamiento (para aviones delante del hangar), explanada. 5. (mec.) mandil, placa delantal. 6. (aut.) zócalo, delantal. 7. (geol.) cono aluvial. 8. (const. mar.) albitana, contrabranque, contrarroda. 9. **to be tied to the a. strings,** (fig.) estar dominado por (madre, esposa, etc.).
apropos [ˌæprə'pou, 'æprəˌpou] *adv.* a propósito; oportunamente. —*a.* oportuno, pertinente.
apropos of, *prep.* respecto a, por lo que concierne a, tocante a.
apse [æps] *s.* 1. ábside (parte posterior abovedada de un templo). 2. (astr.) ápside, ábside.
apse aisle, (arq.) deambulatorio.
apsis ['æpsəs] *s.* (*pl.* APSIDES [-səˌdiz, B æp'saɪ-]) (astr.) ápside.
apsychia [æp'sɪkɪə] *s.* (med.) apsiquia.
apt [æpt] *a.* 1. apto, capaz, listo. 2. apto, apropiado. 3. propenso, inclinado, dispuesto, ej., *children are a. to be noisy,* los niños son por naturaleza bulliciosos; *difficulties are a. to occur,* probablemente habrá dificultades.
apt. *abrev. de* **apartment,** piso, departamento, apartamiento (Am.).
apterous ['æptərəs] *s.* (zool., bot.) áptero.
apteryx [-rɪks] *s.* (zool.) aptérix, kiwi.
aptitude ['æptəˌtud, B -ˌtjud] *s.* aptitud.
aptitude test, prueba de aptitud.
aptyalism [æp'taɪəˌlɪzəm] *s.* (med.) aptialismo, aptialia, carencia o falta de saliva.
Apuleius [ˌæpjə'liəs] *s.* (hist.) Apuleyo, escritor satírico de la antigua Roma.
Apulia [ə'pjuljə] *s.* Apulia, La Pulla, región de Italia.
Apus ['eɪpəs] *s.* (astr.) (constelación) Ave.
apyretic [ˌeɪpaɪ'rɛtɪk, B ˌæ-] *a.* (med.) apirético.
apyrexy [eɪ'paɪˌrɛksɪ] *s.* (med.) apirexia.
apyrous [ˌeɪ'paɪrəs, B ˌæ'paɪər-] *a.* (quím.) incombustible.
aqua ['ækwə, 'ɑk-, B 'æk-] *s.* (*pl.* AQUAE [-wi] o AQUAS) (quím.) líquido, solución acuosa.
aquacade [-ˌkeɪd] *s.* espectáculo acuático.
aquafortis [ˌækwə'fɔrtəs, B -'fɔt-] *s.* (farm.) agua fuerte, ácido nítrico.
aqualung ['ækwəˌlʌŋ] *s.* aparato de respiración que usan los buzos.
aquamarine [ˌækwəmə'rin] *s.* 1. aguamarina. 2. color de aguamarina.
aquanaut ['ækwəˌnɔt] *s.* acuanauta; buzo, buceador.
aquaplane [-ˌpleɪn] *s.* acuaplano, hidropatín.
aqua pura [ˌækwə'pjʊrə] (quím.) agua destilada.
aqua regia [-'ridʒɪə] (farm.) agua regia, ácido nítrico.
aquarelle [-'rɛl] *s.* (pint.) acuarela.
aquarium [ə'kwɛrɪəm, B ə'kwɛər-] *s.* (*pl.* AQUARIUMS o AQUARIA [-ɪə]) acuario, pecera.
Aquarius [-ɪəs] *s.* (astr., astrol.) Acuario.
aquatic [ə'kwɑtɪk, ə'kwæt-, B ə'kwɔt-] *a.* acuático. —*s.* 1. planta o animal acuático. 2. (*pl.*) deportes acuáticos.
aquatint ['ækwəˌtɪnt] *s.* (impr.) acuatinta, aguatinta.
aqua tofana [-tə'fɑnə] agua tofana, veneno muy activo.
aquavit ['ɑkwəˌvit, B 'æk-] *s.* aguardiente escandinavo hecho con centeno.
aqua vitae [ˌækwə'vaɪtɪ] alcohol; aguardiente.
aqueduct ['ækwəˌdʌkt] *s.* acueducto, conducto de agua.
aqueous ['eɪkwrəs, 'æk-] *a.* acuoso, ácueo.
aqueous humor, (med.) humor acuoso.
aquiculture ['ækwɪˌkʌltʃər, B -tʃə] *s.* acuicultura, método para cultivar plantas.
aquifer ['ækwəfɜr] *s.* (geol.) capa freática.
aquiferous [æ'kwɪfərəs] *a.* (geol.) acuífero.
aquifoliaceous [ˌækwɪˌfoulɪ'eɪʃəs] *a.* (bot.) aquifoliáceo.
aquiline ['ækwəˌlaɪn, -lən] *a.* aquilino, aguileño.
Aquinas, Saint Thomas[ə'kwaɪnəs-] Santo Tomás de Aquino.
Aquitaine [ˌækwə'teɪn] *s.* (hist.) Aquitania (provincia del Imperio Romano en la cuenca del Garona en Francia).
Aquitainian [-nɪən] *a.* aquitano, aquitánico. —*s.* 1. aquitano, natural de Aquitania. 2. (geol.) aquitaniense.
Ar *simb. de* **argon,** argón (A).
a.r. *abrev. de.* **account receivable,** cuenta a cobrar.
ar. *abrev. de* **arrival,** llegada.
Arab ['ærəb] *a.* árabe, arábigo. —*s.* árabe.
arabesque [ˌærə'bɛsk] *s.* 1. (arte) arabesco. 2. figura plástica en ballet.
Arabia [ə'reɪbɪə] *s.* Arabia.
Arabian [-bɪən] *s., a.* árabe, de Arabia. —*s.* árabe, natural de un país árabe.
Arabian Desert, Desierto Arábigo.
Arabian jasmine, (bot.) gemela, diamela, sampaguita.
Arabian Nights, Las mil y una noches.
Arabian Sea, Mar. Arábigo.
Arabic ['ærəbɪk] *s.* árabe, idioma árabe. —*a.* árabe, arábigo.
Arabic numerals, números arábigos.
Arabist [-bəst] *s.* arabista; el que cultiva el idioma y la literatura árabes.
Arabization [ˌærəbə'zeɪʃən] *s.* arabización.
arable ['ærəbəl] *a.* arable, cultivable. —*s.* tierra cultivable.
Arab League, Liga de Naciones Arabes.
Araby ['ærəbɪ] *s.* (ant. poét.) Arabia.
araceous [ə'reɪʃəs] *a.* (bot.) aráceo.
Arachne [ə'ræknɪ] *s.* (mitol.) Aracne, mujer de Lidia que osó retar a la diosa Atenea.
arachnid [-nəd] *s.* (zool.) arácnido.
arachnoid [-ˌnɔɪd] *a.* aracnoideo. —*s.* aracnoides.
arachnology [ˌæræk'nɑlədʒɪ, B -'nɔl-] —*s.* aracnología.
araeostyle [ə'riəˌstaɪl] *s.* (arq.) areóstilo.
Aragon ['ærəˌgɑn, B -gən] *s.* Aragón (provincia de España).
Aragonese ['ærəgəˌniz, -ˌnis] *a.* aragonés. —*s.* (*pl.* ARAGONESE) aragonés.
aragonite [ə'rægəˌnaɪt] *s.* (min.) aragonita, aragonito.
aralia [ə'reɪlɪə] *s.* (bot.) bibona.
araliaceous [əˌreɪlɪ'eɪʃəs] *a.* (bot.) araliáceo.
Aramaean [ˌærə'miən] *a., s.* arameo; de la antigua Siria.
Aramaic [-'meɪɪk] *s.* arameo, idioma arameo.
araneid [ə'reɪnɪəd] *s.* (zool.) araña, arácnido.
arapaima [ˌærə'paɪmə] *s.* (ict.) arapaima.
araroba [ˌærə'roubə] *s.* 1. (bot.) araroba, arariba. 2. polvo de araroba.
Araucan [ə'raʊkən, B ə'rɔ-] *a., s.* araucano; idioma de los araucanos; tribu india de Chile y Argentina.
Araucanian [əˌraʊ'kɑnɪən, B ˌærɔ'keɪn-] *a., s.* araucano.
araucaria [ˌærˌɔ'kærɪə, B -'kɛər-] *s.* (bot.) araucaria.
Arawak ['ærəˌwɑk] *s.* arahuaco, arauaco, miembro de una antigua tribu de indios que ocupó las Antillas y emigró hasta el Paraguay.
arbalest ['ɑrbələst, B 'ɑb-] *s.* ballesta.
arbalester [-ˌlɛstər, B -tə] *s.* ballestero.
arbiter ['ɑrbətər, B 'ɑbɪtə] *s.* árbitro, arbitrador; **a. of fashions,** árbitro de la moda; **a. of his fate,** artífice de su destino.
arbitrage ['ɑrbəˌtrɑʒ, B ˌɑbɪ'trɑʒ, 'ɑbɪtrɪdʒ] *s.* arbitraje.
arbitral ['ɑrbətrəl, B 'ɑb-] *a.* arbitral.
arbitrarily [ˌɑrbə'trɛrəlr, B 'ɑbɪtrərɪlɪ] *adv.* arbitrariamente.
arbitrariness ['ɑrbəˌtrɛrɪnəs, B 'ɑbɪtrər-] *s.* arbitrariedad.
arbitrary [-ˌtrɛrɪ, B -trərɪ] *a.* arbitrario.
arbitrate [-ˌtreɪt] *v.t.* 1. arbitrar. 2. someter a arbitrio. 3. determinar, decidir.
arbitration [ˌɑrbə'treɪʃən, B ˌɑbɪ-] *s.* arbitraje.
arbitrator ['ɑrbəˌtreɪtər, B 'ɑbɪ-tə] *s.* arbitrador, árbitro.
arbor (pr. G.B.) **arbour** ['ɑrbər, B 'ɑbə] *s.* glorieta, cenador, emparrado, enramada.
arbor, *s.* 1. (mec.) árbol, eje, eje o husillo (de una rueda); portaherramientas. 2. (const.) viga principal. 3. (bot.) (ant.) árbol.
arboraceous [ˌɑrbə'reɪʃəs, B ˌɑbə-] *a.* arbóreo.
Arbor Day (E.U.) día del árbol (día de fines de abril o principios de mayo, designado para plantar árboles).

arboreal [ɑr'bɔrɪəl, B ɑ'-] *a.* 1. arbóreo. 2. (bot., zool.) arborícola.
arboreous [-ɪəs] *a.* 1. arbolado. 2. (bot.) arborescente. 3. (bot., zool.) arborícola.
arborescent [ˌɑrbə'rɛsənt, B ˌɑbə-] *a.* arborescente.
arboretum [-'ritəm] *s.* (*pl.* ARBORETUMS o ARBORETA [-'ritə]) *s.* 1. jardín botánico. 2. vivero.
arboriculture ['ɑrbərəˌkʌltʃər, B 'ɑbə-tʃə] *s.* arboricultura, cultivo de los árboles.
arboriculturist [ˌɑrbə-'kʌl-rəst, B ˌɑbə-] *s.* arboricultor.
arborization [-'zeɪʃən] *s.* (min., anat., quím.) arborización.
arborvitae [ˌɑrbər'vaɪtɪ, B ɑbə'-] *s.* 1. (bot.) árbol de la vida, tuya. 2. (anat.) árbol de la vida.
arbutus [ɑr'bjutəs, B ɑ'-] *s.* (bot.) 1. madroño, aborio. 2. epigea rastrera.
arc [ɑrk, B ɑk] *s.* arco; (astr., geom.) arco; (elec.) arco (voltaico). —*v.i.* (elec.) formar un arco (voltaico).
A R C *abrev. de* **American Red Cross,** Cruz Roja Norteamericana.
arcade [ɑr'keɪd, B ɑ'-] *s.* 1. (arq.) arcada, conjunto o serie de arcos. 2. galería.
arcaded [-əd] *a.* (arq.) formado por arcos; decorado con arcos o arcadas.
Arcadia [-ɪə] *s.* Arcadia, región montañosa de la antigua Grecia, símbolo del idilio pastoril.
Arcadian [-ɪən] *a.* 1. árcade, arcadio, arcádico. 2. (fig.) arcádico, idílico, campestre. —*s.* 1. árcade, natural de la Arcadia. 2. idioma arcádico. 3. persona de costumbres sencillas.
arcane [ɑr'keɪn, B ɑ'-] *a.* arcano, secreto, misterioso.
arcanum [-'keɪnəm] *s.* (*pl.* ARCANA [-nə]) arcano, misterio, secreto; (filos.) piedra filosofal.
arcature ['ɑrkətʃʊr, B 'ɑkətʃə] *s.* (arq.) arcatura.
arch. *abrev. de* 1. **archaic,** arcaico, antiguo. 2. **archipelago,** archipiélago. 3. **architect,** arquitecto. 4. **architecture,** arquitectura.
arch [ɑrtʃ, B ɑtʃ] *s.* (arq.) arco. —*a.* 1. insigne, de primer orden. 2. principal. 3. socarrón, pícaro, astuto. —*v.t.* 1. cubrir con un arco o arcos. 2. dar forma de arco a, enarcar; arquear (las cejas, espalda, etc.). —*v.i.* 1. tomar forma de arco. 2. seguir una línea o trayectoria curva.
archaelogical [ˌɑrkɪə'lɑdʒɪkəl, B ˌɑkɪə'-lɔdʒ-] *a.* arqueológico.
archaelogist [-kɪ'ɑlədʒəst, B -'ɔl-] *s.* arqueólogo.
archaeology [-dʒɪ] *s.* arqueología.
archaeopteryx [-'ɑptərɪks, B -'ɔp-] *s.* (pal.) arqueópterix.
archaic [ɑr'keɪɪk, B ɑ'-] *a.* arcaico, anticuado.
archaism ['ɑrkiˌɪzəm, -keɪ-, B 'ɑkeɪ-] *s.* arcaísmo.
archaist [-əst] *s.* arcaísta, persona que con frecuencia emplea arcaísmos.
archaize [-ˌaɪz] *v.i.* usar arcaísmos. —*v.t.* dar carácter de antigua a (una lengua mediante el empleo de arcaísmos).
archangel ['ɑrkˌeɪndʒəl, B 'ɑk-] *s.* 1. arcángel. 2. (bot.) arcangélica, angélica.
archangelic [ˌɑrkæn'dʒɛlɪk, B ˌɑk-] *a.* arcangélico, arcangelical.
archanthropine [ɑr'kænθrəˌpaɪn, B ɑ'-] *s.* hombre primitivo.
archbishop ['ɑrtʃˌbɪʃəp, B 'ɑtʃ-] *s.* arzobispo.
archbishopric [-əprɪk] *s.* arzobispado.
arch dam, (const.) presa en arco o de arco simple, presabóveda.
archdeacon [-'dikən] *s.* arcediano, arcedíacono, archidiácono.
archdeaconate [-kənət] **archdeaconry** [-kənrɪ] *s.* arcedianato.
archdiocesan [-daɪ'ɑsəsən, B -'ɔs-] *a.* archidiocesano, arquidiocesano.
archdiocese [-'daɪəsəs] *s.* archidiócesis, arquidiócesis, diócesis arzobispal.
archducal [-'dukəl, B -'djuk-] *a.* archiducal.
archduchess [-'dʌtʃəs] *s.* archiduquesa.
archduchy [-'dʌtʃɪ] *s.* archiducado.
archduke [-'duk, B -'djuk] *s.* archiduque.
arched [ɑrtʃt, B ɑtʃt] *a.* arqueado, enarcado, encorvado.
archegonium [ˌɑrkɪ'goʊnɪəm, B ˌɑkɪ-] *s.* (*pl.* ARCHEGONIA [-ɪə]) (bot.) arquegonio.
Archelaus [ˌɑrkɪ'leɪəs, B ˌɑkɪ-] *s.* Arquelao, rey legendario de Esparta.
archenemy [ɑrtʃ'ɛnəmɪ, B 'ɑtʃ-] *s.* archienemigo, enemigo principal; **A.,** Satanás, el enemigo malo.
archenteron [ɑr'kɛntəˌrɑn, B ɑ'-ˌrɔn] *s.* (anat.) arquéntero.
archeological, archeologist, archeology, *vars. de* **archaeological, archaeologist, archaeology.**
Archeozoic [ˌɑrkɪə'zoʊɪk, B ˌɑkɪ-] *s.* (geol.) era arquezoica. —*a.* (geol.) arqueozoico.
archer ['ɑrtʃər, B 'ɑtʃə] *s.* 1. arquero. 2. **A.,** (astr.) Sagitario.
archery [-ərɪ] *s.* 1. tiro de arco; habilidad en el tiro de arco. 2. ballestería, arcos (en conjunto). 3. (cuerpo de) arqueros.
archespore ['ɑrkɪˌspɔr, B 'ɑkɪˌspɔ] *s.* (bot.) arquesporio.
archetypal [ˌɑrkɪ'taɪpəl, B ˌɑkɪ-] *a.* arquetípico, prototípico.
archetype ['ɑrkɪˌtaɪp, B 'ɑkɪ-] *s.* arquetipo, prototipo.
archetypical [ˌɑrkɪ'tɪpɪkəl, B ˌɑkɪ-] *a.* arquetípico, prototípico.
archfiend [ɑrtʃ'find, B 'ɑtʃ-] *s.* el enemigo mayor; (fig.) Satanás.
archiblast ['ɑrkəˌblæst, B 'ɑkɪˌblɑst] *s.* (biol.) arquiblasto.
archicarp ['ɑrkɪˌkɑrp, B 'ɑkɪˌkɑp] *s.* (bot.) arquicarpo.
archidiaconal [ˌɑrkɪdaɪ'ækənəl, B ˌɑkɪ-] *a.* de arcediano o archidiácono.
archiepiscopal [-ə'pɪskəpəl] *a.* arquiepiscopal, arzobispal.
archiepiscopate [-pət, -ˌpeɪt] *s.* arzobispado.
archil ['ɑrtʃəl, 'ɑrkəl, B 'ɑtʃɪl, 'ɑkɪl] *s.* 1. (bot.) orchilla, orcella. 2. orcina, orchilla, materia colorante.
Archilochus [ɑr'kɪləkəs, B ɑ'-] *s.* Arquíloco, poeta satírico griego.
archimandrite [ˌɑrkə'mænˌdraɪt, B ˌɑkɪ-] *s.* (relig.) archimandrita.
Archimedean [-'midɪən, -mɪ'diən] *a.* de Arquímedes.
Archimedes [ˌɑrkɪ'midiz, B ˌɑkɪ-] *s.* Arquímedes, ilustre matemático y físico de la antigüedad.
Archimedes principle, (fís.) principio de Arquímedes.
Archimedes' screw, rosca o tornillo de Arquímedes (que se usa para elevar agua para regadíos).
archipelagic [ˌɑrkəpə'lædʒɪk, B ˌɑkɪ-] *a.* de(l) archipiélago.
archipelago [-'pɛləˌgoʊ] *s.* archipiélago.
archiplasm ['ɑrkəˌplæzəm, B 'ɑkɪ-] *s.* (biol.) arquiplasma.
architect ['ɑrkəˌtɛkt, B 'ɑkɪ-] *s.* arquitecto.
architectonic [ˌɑrkətɛk'tɑnɪk, B 'ɑkɪ-'tɔn-] *a.* arquitectónico.
architectural [-'tɛktʃərəl] *a.* arquitectural, arquitectónico.
architecture ['ɑrkəˌtɛktʃər, B 'ɑkɪ-tʃə] *s.* arquitectura.
architrave ['ɑrkəˌtreɪv, B 'ɑkɪ-] *s.* (arq.) arquitrabe.
archival [ɑr'kaɪvəl, B ɑ'-] *a.* de archivos, de archivar.
archive ['ɑrˌkaɪv, B 'ɑˌ-] *s.* archivo.
archivist ['ɑrkəvəst, -ˌkaɪ-, B 'ɑkɪ-] *s.* archivero, archivista.
archivolt ['ɑrkəˌvoʊlt, B 'ɑkɪ-] *s.* (arq.) archivolta.
archly ['ɑrtʃlɪ, B 'ɑtʃ-] *adv.* sutilmente, taimadamente, socarronamente, astutamente.
archness [-nəs] *s.* socarronería, astucia, picardía.
arch of heaven, (poét.) bóveda celeste.
archon ['ɑrˌkɑn, -kən, B 'ɑkən] *s.* 1. (hist.) arconte. 2. p. ext. gobernador, presidente.
archpriest ['ɑrtʃ'prist, B 'ɑtʃ-] *s.* (relig.) arcipreste.
archway [-ˌweɪ] *s.* corredor o pasaje abovedado; arco sobre un pasaje o arcada.
arciform ['ɑrsəˌfɔrm, B 'ɑsɪˌfɔm] *a.* curvado, arqueado, de forma de arco.
arc lamp, (elec.) lámpara de arco, arco voltaico.
arctic ['ɑrktɪk, 'ɑrtɪk, B 'ɑk-] *a.* 1. ártico, polar, septentrional. 2. (fig.) frígido. —*s.* 1. polo norte, regiones polares septentrionales. 2. chanclo impermeable (que se lleva sobre el calzado).
Arctic Circle, (geog.) Círculo Polar Ártico.
Arctic fox, (zool.) zorra ártica, isatis, zorro azul.
Arctic Ocean, Océano Glacial Ártico.
Arcturus [ɑrk'tʊrəs, B ɑk'tjʊər-] *s.* (astr.) Arturo.
arcuate ['ɑrkjʊət, -ˌeɪt, B 'ɑk-] *a.* arqueado, curvo, curvado.
arc welding, soldadura por arco, soldadura de arco.
ardeb ['ɑrˌdɛb, B 'ɑˌ-] *s.* medida de capacidad que se usa en Egipto.
Ardeidae [ɑr'diəˌdi, B ɑ'-] *s. pl.* (orn.) ardeidos.
ardency ['ɑrdənsɪ, B 'ɑd-] *s.* ardor, vehemencia.
Ardennes [ɑr'dɛn, B ɑ'-] *s.* (*pl.*) Ardenas, región de Francia.
ardent ['ɑrdənt, B 'ɑd-] *a.* 1. ardiente. 2. (fig.) ardiente, ferviente, fervoroso.
ardently [-lɪ] *adv.* ardientemente, fervorosamente, apasionadamente.
ardent spirits, licores espirituosos, aguardientes.
ardor, (pr. G.B.) **ardour** ['ɑrdər, B 'ɑdə] *s.* 1. ardor, calor ardiente. 2. (fig.) ardor, pasión.
arduous ['ɑrdʒʊəs, B 'ɑdʒ-] *a.* 1. arduo, escarpado. 2. arduo, difícil, trabajoso.
are [ɑr, B ɑ] *segunda pers. sing. y pl. del v.* **to be.**
are [ɛr, ɑr, B ɑ] *s.* área (medida de superficie que equivale a cien metros cuadrados).
area ['ɛrɪə B 'ɛər-] *s.* 1. área, terreno. 2. superficie, extensión, espacio. 3. región, zona. 4. campo, terreno (de actividades, operaciones, etc.).
area code, (E.U.) (tele.) prefijo local, código de la zona, código territorial.
areaway [-ˌweɪ] *s.* patio estrecho de entrada al nivel del sótano.
areca [ə'rikə, 'ærɪkə] *s.* (bot.) areca.
arena [ə'rinə] *s.* 1. arena, liza, ruedo, estadio. 2. campo, terreno (de interés, desacuerdo, etc.).
arenaceous [ˌærə'neɪʃəs] *a.* arenisco, arenoso.
arenation [-'neɪʃən] *s.* (med.) arenación.
arenicolous [ˌærə'nɪkələs] *a., s.* (zool., bot.) arenícola.
aren't [ɑrnt, 'ɑrənt, B ɑnt] *contr. de* **are not.**
areola [ə'riələ] *s.* (*pl.* AREOLAE [-li] o AREOLAS) (med., anat., bot.) aréola.

areolar [-lər, B -lə] *a.* (cient.) areolar.
areometer [ˌærɪ'ɑmətər, B -'ɔmɪtə] *s.* (fís.) areómetro, pesalicores.
Areopagite [ˌærɪ'ɑpəˌdʒaɪt, B -'ɔpəˌgaɪt] *s.* (hist.) areopagita.
Areopagus [-'ɑpəgəs, B -'ɔp-] *s.* (hist.) Areópago, tribunal de la antigua Atenas.
arête [ə'reɪt] *s.* arista, cresta peñascosa (de una montaña).
Arethusa [ˌærə'θuzə, B -'θju-] *s.* 1. (mitol.) Aretusa. 2. **a.,** (bot.) aretúsea.
argal ['ɑrgəl, B 'ɑgəl] *s.* (quím.) argol.
argali ['ɑrgəlɪ, B 'ɑgə-] *s.* (*pl.* ARGALI O ARGALIS) (zool.) argalí, carnero salvaje de Asia.
argan tree ['ɑrgən-, B 'ɑgən-] (bot.) erguen, argán.
argent ['ɑrdʒənt, B 'adʒənt] *s.* 1. (her.) argén, plata. 2. (fig.) blancura. 3. (ant.) plata. —*a.* (ant.) de plata; argénteo, blanquecino; brillante.
argentiferous [ˌɑrdʒən'tɪfərəs, B ɑˌ-] *a.* (min.) argentífero.
Argentina [ˌɑrdʒən'tinə, B ˌɑdʒən-] *s.* la Argentina.
argentine ['ɑrdʒənˌtaɪn, -ˌtɪn, B ɑdʒən-] *a.* argentino, argénteo. —*s.* metal blanco plateado; argentina.
Argentine [-ˌtaɪn, -ˌtin] *a.* argentino, natural de la Argentina. —*s.* argentino; **the A.,** la Argentina.
Argentinean, Argentinian [ˌɑr-'tɪnɪən, B ˌɑdʒən-] *a.* argentino, natural de la Argentina.
argentite ['ɑrdʒənˌtaɪt, B 'ɑdʒən-] *s.* (min.) argentita, argirosa.
argentous [ɑr'dʒɛntəs, B ɑ'-] *a.* (quím.) argentoso.
argil ['ɑrdʒəl, B 'ɑdʒəl] *s.* arcilla, argila.
argilaceus [ˌɑrdʒə'leɪʃəs, B ˌɑdʒɪ-] *a.* arcilloso.
argillite ['ɑrdʒəˌlaɪt, B 'ɑdʒɪ-] *s.* (min.) argilita.
arginine [-ˌnin] *s.* (quím.) arginina.
Argive ['ɑrˌdʒaɪv, -ˌgaɪv, B 'ɑˌgaɪv] *a., s.* argivo, natural de Argos o de la Argólida; griego.
Argo ['ɑrgoʊ, B 'ɑgoʊ] *s.* 1. (mitol.) Argos. 2. (astr.) Navío, Navío Argos.
argol ['ɑrgəl, B 'ɑgəl] *s.* ácido tártrico que se deposita en los toneles de vino.
Argolis ['ɑrgələs, B 'ɑg-] *s.* Argólida, región de la Grecia antigua.
argon ['ɑrˌgɑn, B 'ɑˌgɔn] *s.* (quím.) argo, argón.
argonaut ['ɑrgəˌnɔt, B 'ɑgə-] *s.* 1. **A.,** (mitol.) argonauta. 2. aventurero. 3. (zool.) argonauta, náutilo, marinero.
Argo Navis ['ɑrgoʊ'neɪvɪs, B 'ɑgoʊ-] (astr.) Navío Argos.
argosy ['ɑrgəsɪ, B 'ɑgə-] *s.* 1. (hist.) bajel o buque mercante grande (esp. con cargamento valioso). 2. flota de bajeles. 3. (fig.) mina, fuente rica (de conocimientos, etc.).
argot ['ɑrgət, -goʊ, B 'ɑgoʊ] *s.* jerga, jerigonza, germanía; vocabulario propio de una profesión.
arguable ['ɑrgjʊəbəl, B 'ɑgjʊ-] *a.* discutible, disputable.
argue ['ɑrgju, B 'ɑgju] *v.i.* 1. argüir, argumentar, razonar. 2. disputar. —*v.t.* 1. indicar, demostrar, ser prueba de. 2. debatir, discutir. 3. argüir, sostener, afirmar (que). 4. **a. (someone) into,** persuadir (a alguien) a; **a. it away,** (*ú. esp. negativamente*) eliminar (dificultad, acusación, etc.) con razonamiento; **a. (someone) out of,** disuadir (a alguien) de.
arguer [-ər, B -ə] *s.* argumentador, discutidor.
argufy ['ɑrgjəˌfaɪ, B 'ɑgju-] *v.t., v.i.* (fam.) argüir pertinazmente, esp. sobre algo insignificante.
argument [-mənt] *s.* 1. argumento, razonamiento. 2. discusión, disputa. 3. argumento, resumen.
argumentation [ˌɑr-mən'teɪʃən, B ˌɑgjʊ-] *s.* argumentación, raciocinio; debate.
argumentative [-'mɛntətɪv] *a.* 1. argumentativo; sujeto a controversia. 2. argumentador, disputador.
argumentum [-'mɛntəm] *s.* (*pl.* [-'məntə]) (filos.) argumento, prueba.
Argus ['ɑrgəs, B 'ɑgəs] *s.* 1. (mitol.) Argos. 2. (fig.) argos, vigilante, observador incansable.
Argus-eyed [-ˌaɪd] *a.* de ojos de lince, de vista de lince.
argyle ['ɑrˌgaɪl, B ɑˌ-] *a., s.* 1. dibujo en forma de rombos a colores. 2. (*pl.*) calcetines o medias con este dibujo.
argyrodite [ɑr'dʒɪrəˌdaɪt, B ɑ'-] *s.* (min.) argirodita.
argyrol ['ɑrdʒəˌroʊl, B 'ɑdʒɪ-] *s.* (farm.) argirol.
arhat ['ɑrhət, B'ɑhət] *s.* arhat (monje budista que ha llegado al nirvana).
aria ['ɑrɪə] *s.* (mús.) aria.
Ariadne [ˌærɪ'ædnɪ] *s.* (mitol.) Ariadna, la que dio a Teseo el hilo con que pudo salir del Laberinto.
arian ['ærɪən, 'ɛr-, B 'ɛər-] *var. de* **aryan.**
Arian *a., s.* (relig.) arriano.
Arianism [-ˌɪzəm] *s.* (relig.) arrianismo.
ariboflavinosis [eɪˌraɪbəˌfleɪvə'noʊsəs] *s.* (med.) arriboflavinosis.
arid ['ærəd] *a.* árido.
aridity [ə'rɪdətɪ] *s.* aridez.
Aries ['ærɪˌiz, B 'ɛərˌiz] *s.* (astr., astrol.) Aries.
arietinous [ˌærɪ'ɛtənəs] *a.* arietino, semejante a la cabeza del carnero.
arietta [ˌɑrɪ'ɛtə, B ˌær-] *s.* (mús.) arieta, aria corta.
aright [ə'raɪt] *adv.* rectamente; correctamente; **to set a.,** corregir, rectificar.
aril ['ærəl] *s.* (bot.) arilo.
arise [ə'raɪz] *v.i.* (*pret.* AROSE [ə'roʊz] *p.p.* ARISEN [ə'rɪzən] *p.pr.* ARISING [ə'raɪzɪŋ]) 1. levantarse. 2. presentarse, surgir. 3. (con *from*) proceder, resultar (de), originarse (en). 4. subir; ascender, elevarse. 5. resucitar. 6. **if the need arises,** si fuera necesario; 7. **should the question a.,** si se plantea la cuestión.
arista [ə'rɪstə] *s.* (*pl.* ARISTAE [-ti, -taɪ]) (bot.) arista.
aristocracy [ˌærə'stɑkrəsɪ, B -'stɔk-] *s.* aristócracia.
aristocrat [ə'rɪstəˌkræt, 'ærə-] *s.* aristócrata.
aristocratic [əˌrɪstə'krætɪk, ˌærɪs-] *a.* aristocrático.
Aristophanes [ˌærə'stɑfəˌniz, B -'stɔf-] *s.* Aristófanes, comediógrafo griego.
Aristotelian [ˌærɪstə'tiljən] *a., s.* aristotélico.
Aristotelianism [-ˌɪzəm] *s.* (filos.) aristotelismo.
Aristotelian logic, lógica aristotélica.
Aristotle ['ærəˌstɑtəl, B -ˌstɔt-] *s.* Aristóteles, filósofo griego.
Aristotle's lantern, (zool.) linterna de Aristóteles.
arithmetic [ə'rɪθmətɪk] *s.* aritmética. — [ˌærɪθ-'mɛtɪk] *a.* aritmético.
arithmetical [ˌærɪθ'mɛtɪkəl] *a.* aritmético.
arithmetician [əˌrɪθmə'tɪʃən] *s.* aritmético, experto en aritmética.
arithmetic progression, (mat.) progresión aritmética.
arithmometer [ˌærɪθ'mɑmətər, B -'mɔmɪtə] *s.* (mat.) aritmómetro.
Arius [ə'raɪəs, B 'ɛərɪəs] *s.* Arrio, sacerdote de Alejandría, fundador del arrianismo.
Ariz. *abrev. de* **Arizona,** Arizona (E.U.).
Arizona [ˌærə'zoʊnə] *s.* Arizona, estado de los E.U.
ark [ɑrk, B ɑk] *s.* (bíbl.) 1. arca, barcaza. 2. arca, caja, cofre.
Ark. *abrev. de* **Arkansas,** Arkansas (E.U.).
Arkansas ['ɑrkənˌsɔ, B 'ɑkən-] *s.* Arkansas, estado de los E.U.
ark of the covenant, arca de la Alianza (que contenía las tablas de los diez mandamientos).
arm [ɑrm, B ɑm] *s.* 1. (anat.) brazo. 2. manga (de vestidos). 3. brazo (del sillón, de la balanza; de mar, etc.). 4. brazo, pata delantera (de un animal). 5. (fig.) brazo, mano, autoridad, poder, (de la ley, etc.). 6. **a. of a lever,** (mec.) brazo de palanca; **at arm's reach,** al alcance del brazo; **at arm's length,** a prudente distancia; **(infant) in arms,** (niño) de pecho; **secular a.,** brazo secular, autoridad de los tribunales seculares; **to be the right a. of,** (fig.) ser el brazo derecho de; **with open arms,** (fig.) con los brazos abiertos.
arm, *s.* (*ú. gen. en pl.*) arma, armamento; **call to arms,** rebato; **in arms,** en armas, armado; **small arms,** armas de fuego de pequeño calibre; **to arms! ¡a las armas!; to bear arms,** portar armas, servir como soldado; **to carry arms,** ir armado; **to lay down arms,** rendir las armas, cesar las hostilidades; **to present arms,** (mil.) presentar armas; **to rise up in arms,** alzarse en armas; **to take up arms,** (pr. fig.) tomar las armas. —*v.t.* 1. armar. 2. acorazar, blindar. —*v.i.* armarse; **a. for war,** armar en guerra.
armada [ɑr'mɑdə, -'meɪdə, B ɑ'-] *s.* armada, flota; **the Spanish A.,** la Armada Invencible.
armadillo [ˌɑrmə'dɪloʊ, B ˌɑmə-] *s.* (zool.) armadillo.
Armageddon [ˌɑrmə'gɛdən, B ˌɑmə-] *s.* (bíbl.) Armagedón; (fig.) la guerra final, el apocalipsis.
armament ['ɑrməmənt, B 'ɑmə-] *s.* 1. armamento. 2. preparación bélica. 3. potencia ofensiva o militar.
armamentarium [ˌɑrməˌmɛn'tɛrɪəm, B ˌɑm-] *s.* (*pl.* ARMAMENTARIA [-ɪə]) armamentárium o armamentario (equipo, utensilios, libros y métodos usados en una empresa o campo de actividad).
armament race, carrera armamentista; competencia de habilitación bélica entre las naciones.
armature ['ɑrmətʃər, B -tʃə] *s.* 1. armadura. 2. (fís.) armadura (de una dinamo, en la botella de Leiden, etc.).
armature band, (elec.) bandaje o zuncho del inducido.
armature bore, (elec.) diámetro del hueco para el inducido.
armature leakage, (elec.) dispersión en el inducido.
armature winding, (elec.) devanado o arrollamiento del inducido.
armband ['ɑrmbænd] *s.* brazalete, brazal.
armchair ['ɑrmˌtʃɛr, B 'ɑmˌtʃɛə] *s.* sillón, silla de brazos, butaca. —*a.* 1. teórico, de café, ej., *a. strategist,* estratega de café. 2. imaginario, ej., *a. explorer,* explorador imaginario (que no se mueve de su casa).
armed forces [ɑrmd-, B ɑmd-] fuerzas armadas de una nación.
armed holdup, piñatería.
armed robbery, robo a mano armada.
Armenian [ɑr'minɪən, B ɑ'-] *a., s.* armenio.
Armenian bole, bol arménico, rúbrica lemnia.
Armenian stone, carbonato azul de cobre, lapislázuli.

armful ['ɑrm,fʊl, B 'ɑm-] *s.* brazado, brazada; (fig.) persona que se abraza cariñosamente con los brazos.
armhole [-,hoʊl] *s.* (cost.) sisa.
armiger ['ɑrmɪdʒər, B 'ɑmɪdʒɛ] *s.* hidalgo (con derecho a llevar armas heráldicas); armígero, escudero que porta las armas.
armillary sphere ['ɑrmə,lɛrɪ-, ɑr'mɪlərɪ-, B ɑ'-] (hist., astr.) esfera armilar.
arm-in-arm ['ɑrmən'ɑrm, B 'ɑm-'ɑm] *adv.* del brazo; (fig.) (actuar) de acuerdo, en conjunto.
Arminian [ɑr'mɪnɪən B ɑ'-] *s., a.* (teo.) arminiano, seguidor de la doctrina de Arminio; propio de esta doctrina.
Arminius [-ɪəs] *s.* Arminio (Jacobo), teólogo protestante, fundador de la secta de los arminianos.
armistice ['ɑrməstəs, B 'ɑm-] *s.* armisticio, tregua.
armlet ['ɑrmlət, B 'ɑm-] *s.* 1. brazalete, brazal. 2. pequeño brazo de mar o de río.
armload [-,loʊd] *s.* brazado, brazada.
armlock ['ɑrmlɑk] *s.* llave, ej., *to get someone in an armlock,* hacerle una llave a alguien.
armoire ['ɑrmər, B ɑm'wɑ] *s.* armario, guardarropa.
armor, (pr. G.B.) **armour** ['ɑrmər, B 'ɑmə] *s.* 1. armadura. 2. coraza, blindaje. 3. (mil.) vehículos blindados. 4. (her.) arma, blasón. —*v.t.* blindar, acorazar.
armor-bearer [-,bɛrər, B -,bɛərə] *s.* armígero, escudero.
armor-clad [-,klæd] *a.* acorazado, blindado. —*s.* acorazado, buque blindado.
armored car, (mil.) carro blindado.
armored column, (mil.) columna blindada.
armorer [-mərər, B -rə] *s.* armero (que fabrica, cuida o repara armas).
armorial [ɑr'mɔrɪəl, B ɑ'-] *a.* heráldico.
armorial bearings, (her.) escudo de armas, blasón.
armoric [ɑr'mɔrɪk, B ɑ'-] **armorican** [-ən] *a.* de Armórica, provincia de Francia (hoy la Bretaña). —*s.* natural de Armórica, bretón.
armor-piercing ['ɑrmər,pɪrsɪŋ, B 'ɑmə,pɪəs-] *a.* (mil.) perforante.
armor plate, plancha de blindaje, coraza.
armory ['ɑrmərɪ, B 'ɑm-] *s.* 1. armería, fábrica de armas, depósito de armas, arsenal. 2. armas, armamento. 3. (her.) armería.
armpit ['ɑrm,pɪt, B 'ɑm-] *s.* (anat.) sobaco, axila.
armrest [-,rɛst] *s.* apoyabrazos, brazo (de un sillón).
arms race, carrera de armamentos, carrera armamentista
arm twisting, presión; **after a bit of a.,** presionándolo un poco.
arm wrestling: very good at a., muy bueno echando pulsos, muy bueno pulseando.
army ['ɑrmɪ, B 'ɑmɪ] *s.* 1. ejército. 2. (fig.) multitud, muchedumbre, legión.
army ant, (ento.) hormiga devastadora (de África.)
army brat, (fam.) hijo de un oficial o soldado nacido y criado en un puesto militar.
army chaplain, capellán castrense.
army corps, (mil.) cuerpo de ejército.
army post, puesto militar.
army register, escalafón.
army surplus, excedentes del ejército, desechos militares.
arnica ['ɑrnɪkə, B 'ɑnɪ-] *s.* 1. (bot.) árnica. 2. (farm.) (tintura de) árnica.
aroid ['ær,ɔɪd, 'ɛr-] *a.* (bot.) aroideo.
aroma [ə'roʊmə] *s.* aroma, fragancia.
aromatic [,ærə'mætɪk] *a.* aromático. —*s.* planta, droga o medicina aromática.
aromatization [ə,roʊmətə'zeɪʃən] *s.* aromatización.
arose [ə'roʊz] *pret. de* **arise.**
around [ə'raʊnd] *adv.* 1. alrededor, en derredor, a la redonda, en torno. 2. a la vuelta, en la dirección contraria. 3. cerca, aproximadamente. 4. **the other way a.,** al contrario, al revés; **the year a.,** por todo el año; **to come a.,** visitar, venir de visita; volver en sí; (fig.) aceptar una idea u opinión antes rechazada; **to get a.,** viajar, desplazarse, moverse; divulgarse (noticia, rumor); **to get a. to,** llegar a hacer o atender algo; **to have been a.,** (fam.) haber corrido mundo, tener experiencia. —*prep.* alrededor de; cerca de; a la vuelta de; **all a. the country,** por todo el país.
around-the-clock, *adv.* continuamente; todo el día; las veinticuatro horas del día.
arousal [ə'raʊzəl] *s.* despertar, excitación (esp. sexual).
arouse [ə'raʊz] *v.t.* despertar; animar, excitar, incitar; **a. to (the necessity, expediency,** etc.), incitar a (la necesidad, conveniencia, etc.). —*v.i.* despertarse.
arpeggio [ɑr'pɛdʒɪ,oʊ, B ɑ'-] *s.* (mús.) arpegio.
arpent ['ɑrpənt, B 'ɑpənt] *s.* arpenta (vieja medida agraria francesa).
arquebus ['ɑrkwɪbəs, B 'ɑkwɪ-] **arquebusier** [,ɑr-'sɪr B ,ɑk-'sɪə] *vars. de* **harquebus, harquebusier.**
arrack ['ærək] *s.* arrac, raque; licor anisado que esp. se bebe en el Oriente Medio.
arraign [ə'reɪn] *v.t.* (der.) citar, emplazar, hacer comparecer ante un tribunal; acusar, procesar. —*s.* emplazamiento.
arraignment [-mənt] *s.* emplazamiento; acusación, proceso.
arrange [ə'reɪndʒ] *v.t.* 1. arreglar, disponer, ordenar; (*an interview*) concertar. 2. (mús.) arreglar, adaptar (una composición para voces o instrumentos). —*v.i.* 1. (con *with*) convenir llegar a un acuerdo (con). 2. (con *for*) tomar medidas o hacer arreglos para, disponer.
arrangement [-mənt] *s.* 1. arreglo, disposición. 2. (*pl.*) planes, medidas. 3. arreglo, convenio, avenencia. 4. (mús.) arreglo, adaptación (de una composición).
arranger [-ər, B -ə] *s.* el que arregla, dispone o prepara algo; (mús.) experto que transcribe o compone una instrumentación.
arrant ['ærənt] *a.* 1. notorio, consumado, redomado; **a. nonsense,** suma idiotez. 2. descarado.
arrantly [-lɪ] *adv.* abominablemente, vergonzosamente, redomadamente.
arras ['ærəs] *s.* (*pl.* ARRAS) 1. tapicería de Arrás. 2. tapiz, colgadura.
array [ə'reɪ] *v.t.* 1. (mil.) colocar o disponer en orden de batalla, ordenar, formar (las tropas). 2. vestir, adornar, ataviar. 3. (fig.) revestir. 4. (der.) elegir (jurado). —*s.* 1. (mil.) orden (del campo de batalla), formación. 2. orden, arreglo. 3. conjunto, serie, colección. 4. vestido, atavío (rico y lujoso). 5. (mat.) ordenación, matriz.
arrear [ə'rɪr, B ə'rɪə] *s.* (*pl.*) deudas, atrasos; **in arrears,** atrasado, endeudado.
arrearage [ə'rɪrɪdʒ, B ə'rɪər-] *s.* 1. atrasos, deudas. 2. atraso, demora (en pagos).
arrest [ə'rɛst] *s.* 1. arresto, detención. 2. paro, interrupción, suspensión. 3. **under a.,** detenido, arrestado. —*v.t.* 1. arrestar, detener, capturar. 2. detener, atajar, impedir movimiento o progreso de (motor, enfermedad, etc.). 3. cautivar, atraer (atención, admiración).
arrester, arrestor [-ər, B -ə] *s.* aprehensor; el que arresta, detiene o aprehende.
arresting [-ɪŋ] *a.* cautivador, llamativo, impresionante.
arrhizal [ə'raɪzəl] *a.* (bot.) arrizo, sin raíces.
arrhythmia [ə'rɪðmɪə] *s.* (med.) arritmia (esp. de los latidos cardíacos).
arrhythmic [-mɪk] **arrhythmical** [-əl] *a.* (med.) arrítmico.
arrière pensée ['ærɪ,ɛrpɑn'seɪ, B 'ærɪɛə,-] (fr.) reserva mental, motivo recóndito.
arris ['ærəs] *s.* (arq.) arista, esquina, canto, borde afilado (esp. en las molduras).
arrival [ə'raɪvəl] *s.* 1. llegada, arribo. 2. (el que ha) llegado, ej., *we have a new a.,* tenemos un recién llegado.
arrive [ə'raɪv] *v.i.* 1. (con *at, in, upon*) llegar, arribar (a un lugar). 2. (con *at*) llegar, alcanzar (un objetivo, etc.), ej., *a. at a conclusion,* llegar a una conclusión. 3. llegar, venir (el tiempo, el momento, etc.). 4. alcanzar éxito. 5. (ant.) avenir, suceder.
arrivé [,ærɪ'veɪ] *s.* advenedizo, persona que ha alcanzado su meta de éxito, esp. sin merecerlo.
arriviste [-'vist] *s.* arrivista, advenedizo.
arrogance ['ærəgəns] *s.* arrogancia, altivez, soberbia, presunción.
arrogant [-gənt] *a.* arrogante, altivo, soberbio.
arrogantly [-lɪ] *adv.* arrogantemente, altivamente.
arrogate ['ærə,geɪt] *v.t.* 1. arrogarse, atribuirse, apropiarse (facultades, derechos, etc.). 2. (con *to*) arrogar, atribuir (a otro indebida o injustamente).
arrogation [,ærə'geɪʃən] *s.* (der.) arrogación.
arrondisement [ə'rɑndəsmənt, B ə'rɔn-] *s.* (fr.) barrio, distrito, condado.
arrow ['æroʊ] *s.* flecha, saeta.
arrowhead [-,hɛd] *s.* 1. punta de saeta o flecha. 2. (bot.) saetilla, flecha de agua, sagitaria.
arrowroot [-,rut] *s.* (bot.) 1. maranta. 2. arrurruz.
arrowwood [-,wʊd] *s.* (bot.) (variedad de) viburno, cachanilla.
arrowy [-ɪ] *a.* como una flecha; rápido, veloz, penetrante.
arse [ɑrs, B ɑs] *s.* (G.B., vulg.) nalgas, culo, trasero.
arsenal ['ɑrsənəl, B 'ɑs-] *s.* arsenal; (fig.) arsenal, caudal.
arsenate ['ɑrsənət, -,neɪt, B 'ɑsə-] *s.* (quím.) arseniato.
arsenic ['ɑrsənɪk, B 'ɑs-] *s.* (quím.) arsénico. — [ɑr'sɛnɪk, B ɑ'-] *a.* arsénico.
arsenic acid, (quím.) ácido arsénico.
arsenical [ɑr'sɛnɪkəl, B ɑ'-] *a.* arsenical. —*s.* compuesto arsenical.
arsenide ['ɑrsən,aɪd, B 'ɑs-] *s.* (quím.) arsénido, arseniuro.
arsenious [ɑr'siniəs B ɑ'-] *a.* (quím.) arsenioso.
arsenite ['ɑrsən,aɪt, B 'ɑs-] *s.* (quím.) arsenito.
arsenopyrite [,ɑrsənoʊ'paɪ,raɪt, B ,ɑs-] *s.* (min.) pirita arsenical.
arsine [ɑr'sin, B ɑ'-] *s.* (quím.) arsina, arsenamina.
arsis ['ɑrsəs, B 'ɑs-] *s.* (poét., mús.) arsis, sílaba acentuada.
arson ['ɑrsən, B 'ɑsən] *s.* incendio premeditado, delito de incendiar.
arsonist [-əst] *s.* incendiario, pirómano.
arsphenamine [ɑrs'fɛnə,min, B ɑs-] *s.* (farm.) arsenofenilamina.
art [ɑrt, ərt, B ɑt, ət] *segunda pers. sing. ant. del v.* **to be.**
art [ɑrt, B ɑt] *s.* 1. arte (esp. pintura escultura, música, etc.). 2. habilidad, arte. 3. (*pr. pl.*) letras, humanidades. 4. estratagema, artificio, maña. —*a.* 1. artístico. 2. de arte.

Artaxerxes [ˌɑrtəˈzɛrkˌsiz, B ˌɑtəˈzɛk-] *s.* (hist.) Artajerjes, rey de Persia.
art dealer, marchante de arte.
artel [ɑrˈtɛl, B ɑˈ-] *s.* artel, asociación de trabajadores independientes (que realizaban trabajos colectivos en Rusia, en el siglo XIX, repartiendo los beneficios.)
Artemis [ˈɑrtəməs B ˈɑt-] *s.* (mitol.) Artemisa, diosa griega de la caza.
artemisia [ˌɑrtəˈmɪʒɪə, -ˈmɪz-, B ˌɑtəˈmɪz-] *s.* (bot.) artemisa.
arterial [ɑrˈtɪrɪəl, B ɑˈ-] *a.* 1. (med.) arterial. 2. pertinente al tránsito urbano.
arterialization [ɑrˌtɪrɪələˈzeɪʃən, B ɑˌ-] *s.* (med.) arterialización.
arterialize [ɑrˈtɪrɪəˌlaɪz, B ɑˈ-] *v.t.* (med.) arterializar.
arterial tension, (med.) tensión o presión arterial.
arteriole [-ɪˌoʊl] *s.* arteriola, pequeña arteria.
arteriosclerosis [ɑrˌtɪrɪoʊskləˈroʊsəs, B ɑˌ-] *s.* (med.) arteriosclerosis, arterioesclerosis.
arteriosclerotic [-ˈrɑtɪk, B -ˈrɔt-] *a.* (med.) arteriosclerótico, arterioesclerótico.
arteriovenous [-ˈvinəs] *a.* (med.) arteriovenoso.
arteritis [ˌɑrtəˈraɪtəs B ˌɑt-] *s.* (med.) arteritis.
artery [ˈɑrtərɪ, B ˈɑt-] *s.* 1. (anat.) arteria. 2. (fig.) arteria, vía importante (en una ciudad).
artesian well [ɑrˈtiʒən-, B ɑˈtizjən] pozo artesiano.
artful [ˈɑrtfəl, B ˈɑt-] *a.* 1. diestro, habilidoso. 2. astuto, artificioso.
artfully [-ɪ] *adv.* 1. astutamente, ladinamente. 2. artificiosamente, con artificio. 3. con arte, diestramente.
artfulness [-nəs] *s.* 1. astucia. 2. artificio, ingenio. 3. habilidad, destreza.
art gallery, 1. museo de arte, pinacoteca. 2. (*shop*) galería de arte.
arthralgia [ɑrˈθrældʒə, B ɑˈ-] *s.* (med.) artralgia, artroneuralgia.
arthralgic [-dʒɪk] *a.* (med.) artrálgico.
arthritic [ɑrˈθrɪtɪk, B ɑˈ-] *a., s.* (med.) artrítico.
arthritis [-ˈθraɪtəs] *s.* (med.) artritis.
arthrology [ɑrˈθrɑlədʒɪ, B ɑˈθrɔl-] *s.* (anat.) artrología.
arthromere [ˈɑrθrəˌmɪr, B ˈɑθrəˌmɪə] *s.* (zool.) artrómero.
arthropod [ˈɑrθrəˌpɑd, B ˈɑθrəˌpɔd] *s.* (zool.) artrópodo.
arthropodal [ɑrˈθrɑpədəl, B ɑˈθrɔp-] **arthropodous** [-dəs] *a.* (zool.) artrópodo, articulado.
arthrosis [ɑrˈθroʊsəs, B ɑˈ-] *s.* (anat.) artrosia, articulación.
arthrospore [ˈɑrθrəˌspɔr, B ˈɑθrəˌspɔə] *s.* (bot.) artrósporo.
arthrosporic [ˌɑrθrəˈspɔrɪk, B ˌɑθrə-] **arthrosporous** [-əs] *a.* (bot.) artrospóreo.
Arthurian [ɑrˈθʊrɪən, B ɑˈθjʊər-] *a.* (G.B. hist.) del rey Arturo, arturiano, artúrico.
artichoke [ˈɑrtəˌtʃoʊk, B ˈɑtə-] *s.* (bot.) alcachofa, alcaucil.
article [ˈɑrtɪkəl, B ˈɑt-] *s.* 1. artículo, escrito. 2. artículo, cláusula (en un documento, contrato, ley, etc.). 3. artículo, objeto, pieza; mercancía. 4. (gram.) artículo. —*v.t.* exponer o formular en artículos.
articular [ɑrˈtɪkjələr, B ɑˈ-lə] *a.* articular.
articulate [-lət] *a.* 1. articulado. 2. capaz de hablar. 3. inteligible, claro. 4. (zool.) articulado. [-ˌleɪt] *v.t.* 1. articular, anunciar claramente (palabras, etc.). 2. articular, unir con articulaciones. 3. expresar claramente (emoción, sentimiento, etc.). —*v.i.* articular, enunciar claramente.
articulated joint, articulación, unión articulada; unión de rótula, cardán.
articulately [-lətlɪ] *adv.* articuladamente; inteligiblemente.
articulation [ɑrˌtɪkjəˈleɪʃən, B ɑˌ-] *s.* (anat., zool., bot., fon.) articulación.
articulator [-ˈtɪkjəˌleɪtər, B -ə] *s.* 1. pronunciador. 2. organo articulador. 3. odontógrafo (aparato para medir los dientes).
articulatory [-ˈtɪkjələˌtɔrɪ, B -lətərɪ] *a.* (anat., gram.) articulatorio.
artifact [ˈɑrtəˌfækt, B ˈɑt-] *s.* artefacto.
artifice [-fəs] *s.* 1. artificio, estratagema, ardid. 2. artificio, aparato o expediente ingenioso. 3. ingeniosidad, habilidad.
artificer [ɑrˈtɪfəsər, B ɑˈ-sə] *s.* 1. artesano. 2. (fig.) (con *of*) artífice, inventor, autor (de).
artificial [ˌɑrtəˈfɪʃəl, B ˌɑtə-] *a.* 1. artificial, fabricado. 2. artificioso, contranatural, afectado. 3. (bot.) cultivado. 4. artificioso, astuto, ladino.
artificial flowers, flores de trapo.
artificial insemination, inseminación artificial.
artificial intelligence, inteligencia artificial.
artificial leg, pierna ortopédica.
artificiality [-fɪʃɪˈælətɪ] *s.* artificialidad, arte, afectación.
artificially [-ˈfɪʃəlɪ] *adv.* artificialmente.
artificialness [-nəs] *s.* artificialidad, arte, afectación.
artificial respiration, respiración artificial.
artificial tooth, diente postizo.
artillerist [ɑrˈtɪlərəst, B ɑˈ-] *s.* artillero.
artillery [-ərɪ] *s.* 1. artillería. 2. (jer.) revólver, pistola.
artilleryman [-mən] *s.* artillero.
artily [ˈɑrtəlɪ, B ˈɑt-] *adv.* pseudoartísticamente, con pretensión artística.
artiness [-ɪnəs] *s.* carácter pseudoartístico.
artiodactyl [ˌɑrtɪoʊˈdæktəl, B ˌɑt-] *s.* (zool.) artiodáctilo.
artisan [ˈɑrtəzən, B ˌɑtɪˈzæn] *s.* artesano, artífice.
artist [ˈɑrtəst, B ˈɑt-] *s.* 1. artista (que se dedica a alguna de las bellas artes). 2. (fig.) maestro en su oficio o vocación, ej., *she's an a. in the kitchen,* es una cocinera superior.
artiste [ɑrˈtist, B ɑˈ-] *s.* (hum.) artista (profesional del canto, baile, etc.).
artistic [-ˈtɪstɪk] *a.* artístico.
artistry [ˈɑrtəstrɪ, B ˈɑt-] *s.* arte, habilidad artística.
artist's proof, (impr.) primera prueba (de un grabado).
artless [-ləs] *a.* 1. sin arte; tosco, inculto. 2. natural, ingenuo; sencillo.
artlessness [-nəs] *s.* candidez, ingenuidad, naturalidad.
art nouveau [-ˌnuˈvoʊ] *s.* Art Nouveau (estilo de arte, decoración y arquitectura ca. 1900, caracterizado por diseño sinuoso y ondulante).
art paper, papel cuché.
arts and crafts, artesanía fina, artes y oficios.
arts and crafts fair, feria de artesanía.
art school, escuela de Bellas Artes.
art student, estudiante de Bellas Artes.
artsy-craftsy [-sɪˈkræftsɪ, B -ˈkrɑft-] *a.* que pretende ser artístico o novedoso.
art work, (impr.) ilustraciones que acompañan al texto, material gráfico.
arty [ˈɑrtɪ, B ˈɑtɪ] *a.* (fam.) ostentosamente artístico, pseudoartístico.
arum [ˈærəm, B ˈɛər-] *s.* (bot.) aro, yaro, jaro; (especie de) serpentaria, cala.
arum lily, (bot.) aro de Etiopía, alcatraz, cala.
arundinaceous [əˌrʌndəˈneɪʃəs] *a.* (bot.) arundíneo.
Aryan [ˈærɪən, ˈɛr-, B ˈɛər-, ˈɑr-] *a., s.* (antrop.) ario.
arytenoid [ˌærəˈtiˌnɔɪd, əˈrɪtən-, B ˌærɪˈti-] *a.* (anat.) aritenoideo. —*s.* (anat.) aritenoide.
as [æz, əz] *conj.* 1. como, ej., *do as you wish,* haga como quiera, *heavy as lead,* pesado como el plomo. 2. tal como, al igual que, ej., *even as you and I,* tal como tú y yo. 3. cuando, al (*seguido de un inf.*), ej., *he closed the door as he went out,* cerró la puerta al salir. 4. aunque; por . . . (adjetivo) . . . que sea, ej., *rich as he is,* por rico que sea; *small as it is, it's mine,* aunque sea chico, es mío. 5. como, para, ej., *he so arranged matters, as to suit everyone,* él arregló las cosas para satisfacer a todos. 6. **as against,** comparado con; **as from,** a partir de; **as for,** en cuanto a, por lo que respecta a; **as if,** como si; **as if to,** como para; **as is, as it is,** tal como está; **as it seems,** según parece, por lo visto; **as it were,** por decirlo así; **as of, as on,** en la fecha de; **as per,** (com.) según; **as regards,** en cuanto a, en lo tocante a; **as though,** como si; **as to,** en cuanto a, en lo tocante a; **as yet,** hasta ahora, todavía, aún; **as you please,** como usted desee; **so as to (do),** para, a fin de, con el objeto de (hacer). —*adv.* 1. (tal) como, ej., *big cities, as New York, Paris, London,* etc., grandes ciudades, tales como Nueva York, París, Londres, etc. 2. **as best he can,** como mejor pueda; **as far as I am concerned,** en cuanto a mí me toca; **as far as I know,** que yo sepa; **as good as,** prácticamente, ej., *it's as good as new,* es prácticamente nuevo; **as long as,** ya que; **as many as,** tantos como; **as much as,** tanto como, nada menos que; **as soon as,** tan pronto como; **as the case may be,** según sea el caso; **as well,** también; **as well as,** así como, (así) como también; **such as,** tal como. —*pron. rel.* 1. (después de *same* o *such*) que, como, ej., *I had the same difficulties as you,* tuve las mismas dificultades que usted, *such cities as New York,* (tales) ciudades como Nueva York. 2. como (es), ej., *he is Russian, as is evident from his accent,* él es ruso, como es evidente por su acento. —*prep.* 1. como, ej., *he works as an engineer,* trabaja como ingeniero. 2. por, ej., *as a rule,* por regla general.
as [æs] *s.* (*pl.* ASSES [-iz, -əz]) (numis.) as, moneda de la antigua Roma.
As *símb. de* **arsenio,** arsénico (As).
AS *abrev. de* **Anglo-Saxon,** anglosajón.
asafetida, asafoetida [ˌæsəˈfɪtədə, -ˈfɛt-] *s.* (bot., med.) asafétida, goma que se usa como antiespasmódico.
asarabacca [ˌæsərəˈbækə] *s.* (bot.) asarabácara, ásaro, oreja de fraile.
asbestine [æsˈbɛstɪn] *a.* asbestino, incombustible.
asbestos [æsˈbɛstəs, æz-] *s.* asbesto.
asbestos cement, fibrocemento, cemento amianto.
asbestos fiber, fibra de amianto.
asbestosis [ˌæsˌbɛsˈtoʊsəs, ˌæz-] *s.* (med.) asbestosis.
asbestos rock, roca asbestina.
ASCAP *abrev. de* **American Society of Composers, Authors and Publishers,** Sociedad Norteamericana de Compositores, Autores y Editores.
ascariasis [ˌæskəˈraɪəsəs] *s.* (med.) ascariasis.
ascarid [ˈæskərəd] *s.* (zool.) ascáride; lombriz intestinal.
ascend [əˈsɛnd] *v.i.* 1. ascender, subir. 2. elevarse. 3. remontarse. —*v.t.* subir (la escalera, una cuesta, etc.), remontar, escalar; ascender al (trono).

ascendable, ascendible [-əbəl] *a.* escalable, que se puede subir, accesible.
ascendance, ascendence [-əns] *var. de* ascendancy.
ascendancy, ascendency [-ɪ] *s.* influjo creciente, dominio, predominio, ascendiente.
ascendant, ascendent [-ənt] *s.* 1. dominación, dominio, predominio. 2. ascendiente, antepasado. 3. (astrol.) ascendente. 4. **in the a.,** ganando en fama, fortuna, influencia; (astrol.) predominante. —*a.* 1. ascendiente. 2. predominante. 3. (bot.) erguido (tallo, inflorescencia, etc.).
ascender [-ər, B -ə] *s.* (impr.) 1. trazo alto, cabeza, rasgo ascendente, cola. 2. letra larga, letra con trazo alto.
ascension [əˈsɛntʃən, B əˈsɛnʃən] *s.* ascensión; **the A.** (relig.) la Ascensión.
ascensional [-əl] *a.* ascensional, que asciende.
ascensive [əˈsɛnʃɪv] *a.* ascendiente, tendiente a subir, progresivo.
ascent [əˈsɛnt] *s.* 1. ascensión, subida. 2. cuesta, subida, pendiente. 3. ascenso, promoción, progreso.
ascertain [ˌæsərˈteɪn, B ˌæsəˈ-] *v.t.* averiguar, indagar, cerciorarse de.
ascertainable [-əbəl] *a.* averiguable.
ascertainment [-mənt] *s.* averiguación, comprobación.
ascetic [əˈsɛtɪk] *a.* ascético. —*s.* asceta.
asceticism [-əˌsɪzəm] *s.* ascetismo, disciplina rigurosa.
ascian [ˈæʃɪən] *s.* (geog.) ascio, habitante de la zona tórrida.
ascidian [əˈsɪdɪən] *s.* (zool.) ascidia; tunicado.
ascites [əˈsaɪtiz] *s.* (med.) ascitis.
ascitic [əˈsɪtɪk] *a.* (med.) ascítico.
asclepiad [əˈsklipɪəd] *s.* (bot.) asclepiadea.
asclepiadaceous [əˌsklipɪəˈdeɪʃəs] *a.* (bot.) asclepiadeo, asclepiadáceo.
Asclepiadean [æsˌklipɪəˈdiən] *s.* (poét.) verso asclepiadeo.
Asclepius [əˈsklipɪəs] *s.* (mitol.) Asclepio, dios griego de la medicina, llamado Esculapio por los romanos.
ascocarp [ˈæskəˌkɑrp, B -ˌkɑp] *s.* (bot.) fruto ascocarpo (de ciertos hongos).
ascogonium [ˌæskəˈgoʊnɪəm] *s.* (*pl.* ASCOGONIA [-nɪə]) (bot.) ascogonio.
ascomycetous [ˌæskoʊˌmaɪˈsitəs] *a.* (bot.) ascomiceto.
ascorbic acid [əˈskɔrbɪk-, B əsˈkɔbɪk] *s.* (quím.) ácido ascórbico, vitamina C.
ascospore [ˈæskəˌspɔr, B -ˌspɔ] *s.* (bot.) ascospora.
ascot [ˈæskət, -ˌkɑt, B -kət] *s.* corbata a la inglesa; chalina.
ascribable [əˈskraɪbəbəl] *a.* atribuible, imputable.
ascribe [əˈskraɪb] *v.t.* atribuir, achacar, imputar, adscribir.
ascription [əˈskrɪpʃən] *s.* atribución, adscripción.
ascus [ˈæskəs] *s.* (*pl.* ASCI [ˈæsaɪ]) (bot.) asca, teca.
aseismatic [ˌeɪsaɪzˈmætɪk] *a.* resistente a terremotos.
aseity [əˈsiətɪ] *s.* (filos.) aseidad.
asepsis [eɪˈsɛpsəs, ə-, B æ-] *s.* (med.) asepsia.
aseptic [-ˈsɛptɪk] *a.* aséptico; (fig.) seco, parco.
asexual [eɪˈsɛkʃʊəl, B æ-] *a. asexual, asexuado.*
asexualization [-ˌsɛkʃʊələˈzeɪʃən, B -laɪ-] *s.* asexualización, castración.
ash [æʃ] *s.* 1. (*gen. ú. en pl.*) ceniza; (fig.) cenizas, restos mortales; **to lay to ashes;** reducir a cenizas (en una guerra). 2. (bot.) fresno.
ashamed [əˈʃeɪmd] *a.* avergonzado; **to be a. (to do),** tener vergüenza (de hacer); **to be a. (of, for)** estar avergonzado (de); **to feel a.,** darse vergüenza; **you ought to be a. of yourself,** debiera darte vergüenza.
ashamedly [-ədlɪ] *adv.* con vergüenza.
ash-blond [ˈæʃˈblɑnd] *a.* rubio ceniza. —*s.* rubia ceniza.
ash can, 1. basurero, cubo o lata de basura. 2. (jer.) carga de profundidad (contra submarinos).
ashcan, Ashcan [ˈæʃˌkæn] *a.* de crudo realismo (díc. del estilo literario o artístico que representa la vida de la ciudad en sus aspectos más humanos).
ash colored, de color ceniza.
ashen [-ən] *a.* 1. ceniciento, gris; pálido. 2. fresnal, de madera de fresno.
ashen-faced [ˈæʃənˈfeɪst] *a.* lívido.
Ashkenazi [ˌæʃkəˈnæzɪ, B -ˈnɑzɪ] *s.* (*pl.* ASHKENAZIM [-əm]) askenazi (judío del centro y norte de Europa).
ashlar [ˈæʃlər, B -lə] *s.* 1. sillar, piedra cuadrada, piedra picada. 2. (const.) sillería.
ashlar masonry, albañilería de piedra labrada, albañilería de hilera, cantería.
ashler, *var. de* **ashlar.**
ashore [əˈʃɔr, B əˈʃɔ] *a., adv.* (mar.) en tierra, a tierra, en o hacia la costa; **to go a.,** bajar a tierra, desembarcar; **to run a.,** varar, encallar.
ash pan, cenicero, cajón de ceniza (en estufa, hogar, etc.).
ashpit [ˈæʃˌpɪt] *s.* cenicero, foso de cenizas, cenizal, zanja cenicera.
ash tray, cenicero.
Ash Wednesday, (relig.) miércoles de ceniza.
ashy [ˈæʃɪ] *a.* 1. cenizoso. 2. (fig.) ceniciento, intensamente pálido.
Asia [ˈeɪʒə, ˈeɪʃə] *s.* Asia.
Asia Minor, Asia Menor.
Asian [ˈeɪʒən, -ʃən] **Asiatic** [ˌeɪʒɪˈætɪk, ˌeɪʃɪ-] *a., s.* asiático.
Asiatic cholera, (med.) cólera asiático.
Asiatic crowfoot, (bot.) francesilla, marimoña.
Asiatic flu, (med.) gripe asiática.
Asiatic ox, (zool.) cebú.
aside [əˈsaɪd] *adv.* 1. al lado, a un lado; aparte, ej., *jesting a.,* bromas aparte. 2. **to cast (o throw) a.,** echar a un lado; **to lay a.,** apartar; **to set a.,** anular, desechar (fallo, decisión, veredicto); **to step a.,** hacerse a un lado; **to take a.,** llevar aparte. —*s.* 1. (teat.) aparte. 2. digresión.
aside from, *prep.* 1. además de, aparte de. 2. excepto, fuera de.
asinine [ˈæsənˌaɪn] *a.* estúpido, necio; tonto.
ask [æsk, B ɑsk] *v.t.* 1. preguntar. 2. formular (una pregunta). 3. pedir, solicitar. 4. invitar; convidar. 5. **a. (someone) for (something),** pedir (algo) a (alguien); **a. someone something,** preguntar algo a alguien; **a. (someone) a favor, a. a favor of (someone),** pedir un favor a (alguien); **a. someone to (do something),** pedir a alguien que (haga algo). —*v.i.* formular preguntas, averiguar; **a. after, for** o **about,** preguntar por; **a. for,** pedir; requerir, necesitar; **a. for it,** (fam.) provocar líos, tenerlo merecido, buscarse molestias; **a. for trouble,** buscar problemas; **to be had for the asking,** basta pedirlo para conseguirlo gratis.
askance [əˈskæns] **askant** [əˈskænt] *adv.* 1. de reojo, oblicuamente, de soslayo. 2. (p. ext.) con desdén, sospecha o desconfianza; **look a. at,** mirar con sospecha o desconfianza.
askew [əˈskju] *a.* oblicuo, torcido. —*adv.* oblicuamente, torcidamente; **to look a.,** no mirar de frente, mirar de soslayo, mirar con desdén.
asking price, precio inicial.
aslant [əˈslænt, B əˈslɑnt] *adv.* oblicuamente, sesgadamente, al sesgo. —*prep.* a través de.
asleep [əˈslip] *a.* 1. dormido. 2. (fig.) adormecido, entumido (pie, etc.). 3. adormecido (en potencia, facultad, habilidad, etc.). 4. (eufem.) muerto. 5. **to be fast a.,** estar profundamente dormido. —*adv.* durmiendo; **to fall a.,** quedarse dormido.
aslope [əˈsloʊp] *a.* oblicuo, inclinado, al sesgo. —*adv.* diagonalmente, en declive o pendiente.
ASM *abrev. de* **air-to-surface missile,** proyectil del aire a tierra, cohete aire-suelo.
Asmodeus [ˌæzməˈdiəs, B æsˈmoʊdjəs] *s.* (bíbl.) Asmodeo, espíritu del mal.
asocial [eɪˈsoʊʃəl] *a.* 1. solitario, retraído. 2. egoísta, indiferente a los demás.
asp [æsp] *s.* 1. (zool.) áspid. 2. (poét.) serpiente venenosa. 3. (bot.) *var. de* **aspen.**
asparagin(e) [əˈspærəˌdʒin] *s.* (quím.) asparagina.
asparagus [əˈspærəgəs] *s.* (bot.) espárrago.
asparagus fern, esparraguera.
aspartic acid [əˈspɑrtɪk-, B əˈspɑt-] (quím.) ácido aspártico o asparagínico.
ASPCA (E.U.) *abrev. de* **American Society for the Prevention of Cruelty to Animals,** Sociedad Protectora de Animales.
aspect [ˈæsˌpɛkt] *s.* 1. aspecto, apariencia. 2. (gram.) aspecto, forma de realidad (de los verbos). 3. (astrol.) aspecto (situación respectiva entre dos planetas o astros).
aspect ratio, (t.v.) proporción dimensional (de la imagen).
aspen [ˈæspən] *s.* (bot.) álamo temblón. —*a.* 1. de álamo. 2. (fig.) tembloroso, tremulante.
asperges [əˈspɜrdʒiz, B əˈspɜdʒiz] *s.* (relig.) asperges, hisopo.
aspergillosis [ˌæspərdʒɪlˈoʊsəs, B -pədʒɪl-] *s.* (med.) aspergilosis.
aspergillum [-ˈdʒɪləm] *s.* (*pl.* ASPERGILLA [-ˈdʒɪlə]) (relig.) aspersorio, hisopo.
asperity [æˈspɛrətɪ, ə-] *s.* aspereza.
asperse [əˈspɜrs, B əˈspɜs] *v.t.* 1. calumniar, difamar. 2. rociar, asperjar, hisopear.
aspersion [əˈspɜrʒən, B əˈspɜʃən] *s.* 1. calumnia, difamación. 2. aspersión, rociadura.
asphalt [ˈæsˌfɔlt, B -ˌfælt] *s.* asfalto. —*v.t.* asfaltar, revestir de asfalto.
asphaltic [æsˈfɔltɪk, B -ˈfæl-] *a.* asfáltico.
asphaltite [ˈæsˌfɔlˌtaɪt, B -ˌfæl-] *s.* (min.) asfaltita.
aspherical [eɪˈsfɪrɪkəl, -ˈsfɛr-] *a.* (ópt.) de forma esférica imperfecta.
asphodel [ˈæsfəˌdɛl] *s.* (bot.) asfódelo, gamón.
asphyxia [æsˈfɪksɪə] *s.* asfixia.
asphyxiate [-ˌeɪt] *v.t.* asfixiar, sofocar. —*v.i.* asfixiarse.
asphyxiation [-ˌfɪksɪˈeɪʃən] *s.* asfixia, sofocación.
aspic [ˈæspɪk] *s.* 1. (cocina) gelatina de caldo o tomate. 2. (bot.) espliego.
aspidistra [ˌæspəˈdɪstrə] *s.* (bot.) aspidistra.
aspirant [ˈæspərənt, əˈspaɪ-] *a.* aspirante. —*s.* aspirante, pretendiente, candidato.
aspirate [ˈæspəˌreɪt] *v.t.* 1. (fon.) aspirar (la h). 2. (med.) aspirar, extraer por succión.
aspiration [ˌæspəˈreɪʃən] *s.* 1. aspiración, aliento. 2. (fig.) aspiración, ambición, pretensión. 3. (fon.) aspiración.
aspirator [ˈæspəˌreɪtər, B -tə] *s.* (med.) aspirador.
aspiratory [əˈspaɪrəˌtɔrɪ, B -tərɪ] *a.* aspiratorio, de aspiración.
aspire [əˈspaɪr, B -ə] *v.i.* 1. (con *to* o *after*) aspirar (a), ambicionar, anhelar. 2. (fig., ant.) elevarse, subir.

aspirer [-ər, B -rə] *s.* aspirante, pretendiente.

aspirin ['æspərən] *s.* (farm.) aspirina.

asquint [ə'skwɪnt] *adv.*, *a.* de reojo, de soslayo, de través.

ass [æs] *s.* 1. asno; burro, jumento. 2. (fig.) [B ɑs] asno (persona torpe o necia). 3. **he made an a. of himself** (fam.) quedó como un imbécil, quedó en ridículo; **to make an a. of** (fam.) abochornar a alguien en público.

ass [æs, B ɑs] *s.* (vulg.) culo, nalgas, trasero.

assagai ['æsə,gaɪ] *s.* 1. (bot., zool.) azagaya. 2. especie de lanza o jabalina de Sur Africa. —*v.t.* herir o atravesar con dicha lanza.

assai [ɑ'saɪ] *s.* 1. (bot.) asahí. 2. [ɑs'saɪ] (mús.) muy, mucho.

assail [ə'seɪl] *v.t.* asaltar, atacar, acometer; **a. with,** abrumar (con preguntas, etc.).

assailable [-əbəl] *a.* capaz de ser asaltado, expugnable.

assailant [-ənt] *s.* asaltante, asaltador, agresor.

assailer [-ər, B -ə] *s.* asaltante, agresor.

Assamese [,æsə'miz] *s.* (*pl.* ASSAMESE) habitante y lengua de Asam, estado de la India.

assassin [ə'sæsən] *s.* asesino.

assassinate [-,eɪt] *v.t.* asesinar, matar alevosamente.

assassination [ə,sæsən'eɪʃən] *s.* asesinato.

assassin bug, (ento.) reduvio.

assault [ə'sɔlt] *s.* 1. asalto, ataque, agresión. 2. (esgr.) asalto. 3. **a. and battery,** (der.) asalto y agresión, maltrato de palabra y obra; **indecent a.,** (der.) atentado sexual; **to take by a.,** tomar por asalto. —*v.t.* **asaltar, atacar.**

assault craft, barcaza de asalto.

assaulter [-ər, B -ə] *s.* asaltante, agresor.

assault rifle, rifle de asalto.

assault wave, (mil.) ola de asalto.

assay ['æs,eɪ, ə'seɪ] *s.* 1. ensaye, ensayo (examen de la calidad de los metales). 2. muestra de ensaye. —*v.t.* ensayar (metales o aleación).

assayer [-ər, B -ə] *s.* (metal.) ensayador, aquilatador.

assemblage [ə'sɛmblɪdʒ] *s.* 1. asamblea. 2. conjunto, colección (de cosas). 3. (mec.) montaje, empalme. 4. (arte) collaje.

assemble [-bəl] *v.t.* 1. congregar, reunir, convocar; juntar. 2. (mec.) montar, armar, ensamblar (una máquina, etc.). —*v.i.* juntarse, congregarse.

assembler [-blər, B -blə] *s.* montador; coordinador.

assembly [-blɪ] *s.* 1. asamblea, congregación, reunión, junta. 2. (mec.) montaje; armadura. 3. (mil.) toque de llamada.

assembly hall, salón de sesiones, salón de actos.

assembly line, línea de montaje, cadena de montaje, cadena de ensamblaj.

assemblyman [-mən] *s.* asambleísta (esp. en la legislatura de los Estados Unidos).

assembly plant, planta de montaje, fábrica de montaje.

assembly room, sala de actos, sala de fiestas.

assent [ə'sɛnt] *s.* 1. asentimiento, consentimiento, aquiescencia, aprobación. 2. sanción, ej., *royal a.,* sanción oficial (del soberano a las leyes aprobadas por el parlamento). —*v.t.* (con *to*) asentir, consentir, convenir.

assentation [,æsən'teɪʃən] *s.* consentimiento (esp. adulador e insincero).

assert [ə'sɜrt, B ə'sɜt] *v.t.* 1. aseverar, afirmar. 2. hacer valer, sostener, ej., *a. a claim,* sostener un derecho a. 3. **a. oneself,** imponerse, infundir respeto.

assertion [ə'sɜrʃən, B ə'sɜʃən] *s.* aserción, afirmación, declaración positiva.

assertive [ə'sɜrtɪv, B ə'sɜtɪv] *a.* 1. afirmativo. 2. confiado; agresivo. 3. dogmático.

assertiveness [-nəs] *s.* agresividad, dogmatismo.

assertory [ə'sɜrtərɪ, B ə'sɜt-] *a.* afirmativo, declaratorio.

assess [ə'sɛs] *v.t.* 1. (con *at*) valorar, avalorar, valuar, tasar, estimar (en). 2. acotar (impuestos, contribución, etc.). 3. poner impuesto a, gravar; multar. 4. fijar, determinar (daños, monto de reparaciones, etc.).

assessment [-mənt] *s.* 1. avaluación, avalúo, tasación. 2. tasa, gravamen, contribución.

assessor [-ər, B -ə] *s.* asesor; tasador.

asset ['æs,ɛt] *s.* 1. posesión, propiedad. 2. (*pl.*) (der.) bienes. 3. (*pl.*) (com.) activo, partidas del activo. 4. (fig.) ventaja; persona muy útil. 5. (*pl.*) (com.) **active a.,** activo corriente; **fixed a.,** activo fijo; **intangible a.,** activo intangible o social; **personal a.,** bienes personales; **real a.,** bienes raíces.

asseverate [ə'sɛvə,reɪt] *v.t.* aseverar, asegurar, afirmar.

asseveration [ə,sɛvə'reɪʃən] *s.* aseveración, afirmación.

asshole ['æs,hoʊ] *s.* (vulg.) ojete, ano; **to be an a.,** ser un idiota.

assibilate [ə'sɪbə,leɪt] *v.t.* (fon.) asibilar.

assibilation [ə,sɪbə'leɪʃən] *s.* (fon.) asibilación.

assiduity [,æsə'duətɪ B -djuetɪ] *s.* asiduidad, aplicación infatigable.

assiduous [ə'sɪdʒʊəs] *a.* asiduo, perseverante.

assiduously [-lɪ] *adv.* asiduamente.

assiduousness [-nəs] *s.* asiduidad, perseverancia.

assign [ə'saɪn] *v.t.* 1. asignar, señalar; destinar. 2. designar, nombrar (para puesto, tarea, etc.). 3. atribuir (razón, causa, etc.). 4. (der.) transferir, traspasar. —*s.* cesionario, beneficiario.

assignable [-əbəl] *a.* asignable, transferible, negociable.

assignat ['æsɪg,næt, B ,æsɪn'jɑ] *s.* (hist.) asignado (papel moneda en el gobierno revolucionario de Francia).

assignation [,æsɪg'neɪʃən] *s.* 1. asignación. 2. atribución. 3. cita (con una prostituta). 4. (der.) transferencia, cesión, traspaso.

assignee [ə,saɪ'ni, ,æsɪ-] *s.* 1. (der.) apoderado, poderhabiente. 2. cesionario, beneficiario (de una asignación o transferencia).

assigner *var. de* **assignor.**

assignment [ə'saɪnmənt] *s.* 1. asignación. 2. tarea, deber, encargo; puesto. 3. (der.) cesión; escritura de cesión. 4. (der.) traspaso, transferencia.

assignor [-ər, B -ə] *s.* (der.) cedente, transferidor.

assimilability [ə,sɪmələ'bɪlətɪ] *s.* asimilabilidad.

assimilable [ə'sɪmələbəl] *a.* asimilable, absorbible.

assimilate [-,leɪt] *v.t.* 1. (con *to* o *with*) asimilar, hacer similar; asemejar, comparar. 2. asimilar, apropiarse de (ideas, conocimientos, etc.). —*v.i.* asimilarse, absorberse, integrarse.

assimilation [ə,sɪmə'leɪʃən] *s.* asimilación; (med., fon.) asimilación; (sociol., antrop.) integración cultural.

assimilative [ə'sɪmə,leɪtɪv] *a.* asimilativo.

assimilatory [-lə,tɔrɪ, B -lətərɪ] *a.* asimilativo.

assist [ə'sɪst] *v.i.* 1. asistir, prestar ayuda. 2. (con *at*) presenciar; (con *in*) tomar parte (en). —*v.t.* asistir, auxiliar, socorrer, apoyar. —*s.* 1. ayuda, auxilio. 2. (dep.) pase.

assistance [-əns] *s.* asistencia, ayuda, auxilio, socorro, apoyo.

assistant [-ənt] *s.* asistente, ayudante, auxiliar. —*a.* ayudante, auxiliar, sub-, ej., *a. manager,* sub-gerente, *a. professor,* profesor auxiliar, ayudante de cátedra.

assistant director, ayudante de dirección.

assistantship [-ʃɪp] *s.* (E.U.) beca a cambio de un trabajo de asistente en una universidad.

assize [ə'saɪz] *s.* (G.B.) sesión periódica de los jueces de las audiencias superiores (para ver y fallar causas en cada condado).

ass-kisser ['æs,kɪsər, B 'ɑs-ə] *s.* (vulg.) lameculos, adulador.

assn. *abrev. de* **association,** asociación.

associate [ə'soʊʃɪ,eɪt] *v.t.* 1. asociar, juntar. 2. **a. oneself with,** plegarse a (una causa), tomar parte en (asunto). —*v.i.* 1. asociarse, unirse (en negocios o amistad). 2. (con *with*) tener trato, tratar(se) (con). — [-ət, -eɪt] *s.* 1. socio, miembro. 2. compañero; cómplice. —*a.* asociado; aliado; adjunto, ej., *a. company,* compañía asociada.

Associated Press, Prensa Asociada (servicio de noticias).

associate professor, profesor adjunto.

association [ə,soʊsɪ'eɪʃən] *s.* 1. asociación, unión, alianza. 2. asociación, sociedad, organización.

association football, (pr. G.B.) fútbol, balompié.

association of ideas, (psic.) asociación de ideas.

associative [ə'soʊʃɪ,eɪtɪv, B -ətɪv] *a.* asociativo.

assoil [ə'sɔɪl] *v.t.* (ant.) absolver, expiar.

assonance ['æsənəns] *s.* (fon., poét.) asonancia.

assonant [-nənt] *a.*, *s.* (fon., poét.) asonante.

assort [ə'sɔrt, B ə'sɔt] *v.t.* clasificar, ordenar, arreglar.

assorted [-əd] *a.* 1. surtido, mixto, ej. *a. chocolates,* chocolates surtidos. 2. apareado, clasificado.

assorter [-ər, B -ə] *s.* clasificador.

assortment [-mənt] *s.* 1. clasificación. 2. surtido, colección variada.

asst. *abrev. de* **assistant,** ayudante.

assuage [ə'sweɪdʒ] *v.t.* mitigar, calmar, aliviar, aplacar, aminorar.

assuagement [-mənt] *s.* mitigación, aplacamiento.

assuasive [ə'sweɪsɪv, -zɪv] *a.* mitigante, calmante, lenitivo.

assumable [ə'suməbəl, ə'sjum-] *a.* presumible.

assume [ə'sum, ə'sjum] *v.t.* 1. asumir (tarea, obligación, presidencia, papel, etc.). 2. tomar, adoptar (aspecto, proporciones, etc.). 3. arrogar, usurpar. 4. fingir, simular. 5. presumir, suponer, dar por sentado. 6. (der.) encargarse de; **a. to oneself (right,** etc.), arrogarse (derecho, etc.).

assumed [ə'sumd, ə'sjumd] *a.* 1. supuesto, presunto. 2. fingido, ficticio. 3. usurpado.

assumed name, nombre supuesto o falso.

assuming [ə'sumɪŋ, ə'sjum-] *a.* pretensioso, presuntuoso, arrogante.

assumpsit [ə'sʌmpsət] *s.* (der.) proceso por incumplimiento de contrato; contrato sin sellar.

assumption [ə'sʌmpʃən] *s.* 1. suposición, hipótesis, conjetura. 2. usurpación, arrogación. 3. (mat.) premisa. 4. asunción.

Assumptionist [-əst] *a.*, *s.* (relig.) asuncionista.

assumptive [ə'sʌmptɪv] *a.* 1. supuesto, presunto. 2. presuntuoso, pretensioso, arrogante.

assurance [ə'ʃʊrəns] *s.* 1. promesa, compromiso, garantía. 2. aseveración, afirmación. 3. seguridad, certidumbre. 4. aplomo, serenidad. 5. (pr. G.B.) seguro, aseguración, ej., *life a.,* seguro de vida.

assure [ə'ʃʊr, B ə'ʃʊə] *v.t.* asegurar, afirmar; **a. of,** dar seguridad o prueba de (lealtad, etc.).

assured [ə'ʃʊrd, B ə'ʃʊəd] *a.* 1. seguro, cierto. 2. seguro de sí mismo, confiado. 3. asegurado (contra incendio, etc.).

assuredly [ə'ʃʊrədlɪ] *adv.* 1. seguramente, ciertamente. 2. decididamente, sin vacilación.
assuredness [-nəs] *s.* certeza, firmeza, decisión.
assurer [ə'sʊrər, B -ə] *s.* asegurador.
Assyrian [ə'sɪrɪən] *a., s.* asirio, de Asiria.
Assyriology [əˌsɪrɪ'ɑlədʒɪ, B -'ɔl-] *s.* asiriología, estudio de las civilizaciones antiguas de Asiria.
astarboard [ə'stɑrbərd, B ə'stɑbəd] *adv.* (mar.) por el lado de estribor.
astatic [eɪ'stætɪk] *a.* astático, inestable, inseguro; (fís.) astático.
astatic needles, (fís.) agujas astáticas (situadas de tal manera que no están afectadas por el magnetismo de la tierra).
astatic system, (fís., mec.) sistema astático.
astatine ['æstəˌtin] *s.* (quím.) astatinio.
aster ['æstər, B -tə] *s.* (bot.) aster, reina Margarita.
asteria [æ'stɪrɪə] *s.* (min.) asteria, variedad de zafiro.
asterisk ['æstəˌrɪsk] *s.* asterisco. *—v.t.* marcar con asterisco.
asterism [-ˌrɪzəm] *s.* (astr., min.) asterismo.
astern [ə'stɜrn, B ə'stɜn] *adv.* (mar.) 1. a popa. 2. detrás de la nave. 3. hacia atrás. 4. **a. of,** detrás de (la nave); **hard a.** ¡marcha atrás a toda máquina!
asternal [eɪ'stɜrnəl, B ə'stɜn-] *a.* (anat.) 1. asternal (costilla). 2. sin esternón.
asteroid ['æstəˌrɔɪd] *a.* asteroide, en forma de estrella. *—s.* 1. (astr.) asteroide. 2. (zool.) asteria, estrella de mar.
Asteroidea [ˌæstə'rɔɪdɪə] *s. pl.* (zool.) asteroideos.
asteroidean [-dɪən] *a.* (zool.) asteroideo.
asthenia [æs'θinɪə] *s.* (med.) astenia.
asthenic [-'θɛnɪk] *a., s.* (med.) asténico.
asthma ['æzmə, B 'æs-] *s.* asma.
asthmatic [æz'mætɪk, B æs-] *s., a.* asmático.
astigmatic [ˌæstɪg'mætɪk] *a.* (ópt.) astigmático.
astigmatism [ə'stɪgməˌtɪzəm] *s.* (med., ópt.) astigmatismo.
astigmometer [ˌæstɪg'mɑmətər, B -'mɔmɪtə] *s.* (med., ópt.) astigmómetro.
astir [ə'stɜr, B ə'stɜ] *a.* 1. activo, en movimiento, en actividad. 2. fuera de la cama, levantado.
astomatous [eɪ'stɑmətəs, -'stoʊ-, B -'stɔm-] *a.* (biol.) ástomo.
astonish [ə'stɑnɪʃ, B ə'stɔn-] *v.t.* asombrar, pasmar, sorprender.
astonishing [-ɪŋ] *a.* asombroso, pasmoso, sorprendente.
astonishingly [-lɪ] *adv.* asombrosamente.
astonishment [-mənt] *s.* asombro, pasmo, sorpresa.
astound [ə'staʊnd] *v.t.* pasmar, consternar, asombrar.
astounding [-ɪŋ] *a.* sorprendente, asombroso.
astoundingly [-lɪ] *adv.* asombrosamente.
astraddle [ə'strædəl] *adv.* a horcajadas.
astragal ['æstrəgəl] *s.* (arq., arm.) astrágalo.
astragalus [ə'strægələs] *s.* (*pl.* ASTRAGALI [-ˌlaɪ]) 1. (anat.) astrágalo. 2. (bot.) tragacanto.
astragalus, *var. de* **astragal.**
astrakhan ['æstrəkən, B ˌæstrə'kæn] *s.* astracán (piel o tela).
astral ['æstrəl] *a.* 1. astral, de los astros. 2. (bot.) asterea (planta). 3. (teosofía) astral (cuerpo, espíritu, etc.).
astral body, (astr.) cuerpo astral.
astral lamp, lámpara astral (que no proyecta sombra sobre la mesa).
astray [ə'streɪ] *adv.* fuera del camino, por mal camino; en error; **to go a.,** errar el camino; errar el blanco (tiro, proyectil); perderse, extraviarse; **to lead a.,** descaminar, descarriar; (fig.) despistar, desviar. *—a.* descaminado, desviado, equivocado, errado.
astrict [ə'strɪkt] *v.t.* astringir, constreñir, restringir, confinar (esp. por reglas morales o legales).
astrictive [-ɪv] *s., a.* (med.) astringente, constringente.
astrictiveness [-nəs] *s.* (med.) astringencia.
astride [ə'straɪd] *adv.* a horcajadas; **a. of the road,** a través del camino, bloqueando el camino. *—prep.* a horcajadas sobre; a través de. *—a.* atravesado.
astringency [ə'strɪndʒənsɪ] *s.* astringencia; (fig.) austeridad.
astringent [-dʒənt] *a.* 1. (med.) astringente, astrictivo. 2. (fig.) austero, severo. *—s.* (med.) astringente.
astrionics [ˌæstrɪ'ɑnɪks, B -'ɔn-] *s.* electrónica empleada en la astronavegación.
astrobiology [ˌæstroʊˌbaɪ'ɑlədʒɪ, B -'ɔl-] *s.* astrobiología.
astrocyte ['æstrəˌsaɪt] *s.* (biol.) astrocito.
astrodome [-ˌdoʊm] *s.* 1. domo o cúpula transparente; lugar de observación en un avión. 2. **A.,** estadio cerrado con domo transparente.
astrodynamics [ˌæstroʊˌdaɪ'næmɪks] *s.* (*sing. en constr.*) (fís.) astrodinámica, dinámica espacial.
astrogate ['æstrəˌgeɪt] *v.t., v.i.* navegar en el espacio interplanetario.
astrogation [ˌæstrə'geɪʃən] *s.* navegación espacial o interplanetaria.
astrogator ['æstrəˌgeɪtər, B -tə] *s.* piloto espacial.
astrogeology [ˌæstrədʒɪ'ɑlədʒɪ, B -'ɔl-] *s.* astrogeología, estudio de la estructura y composición de los planetas y demás cuerpos del sistema solar.
astrograph [-ˌgræf, B -grɑf] *s.* astrógrafo, instrumento fotográfico usado en la navegación espacial.
astrolabe [-ˌleɪb] *s.* (astr.) astrolabio.
astrologer [ə'strɑlədʒər, B ə'strɔlədʒə] *s.* astrólogo, astróloga.
astrology [ə'strɑlədʒɪ, B ə'strɔl-] *s.* astrología.
astronaut ['æstrəˌnɔt] *s.* astronauta, cosmonauta, piloto espacial.
astronautics [ˌæstrə'nɔtɪks] *s., pl.* (*sing. en const.*) 1. astronáutica (ciencia de la construcción y navegación de astronaves o naves espaciales). 2. navegación espacial e interplanetaria.
astronavigation [ˌæstroʊˌnævə'geɪʃən] *s.* navegación espacial.
astronomer [ə'strɑnəmər, B ə'strɔnəmə] *s.* astrónomo.
astronomic [ˌæstrə'nɑmɪk, B -'nɔm-] **astronomical** [-ɪkəl] *a.* 1. astronómico, de la astronomía. 2. (fig.) astronómico, enorme (cantidad, cifra, etc.).
astronomically [-əlɪ] *adv.* astronómicamente.
astronomical unit, unidad astronómica de distancia (distancia Tierra-Sol).
astronomy [ə'strɑnəmɪ, B ə'strɔn-] *s.* astronomía.
astrophotography [ˌæstroʊfə'tɑgrəfɪ, B -'tɔg-] *s.* astrofotografía, fotografía de los astros (tomada desde una nave espacial.)
astrophotometry [-'tɑmətrɪ, B -'tɔm-] *s.* astrofotometría.
astrophysicist [ˌæstrə'fɪzəsəst] *s.* astrofísico.
astrophysics [-'fɪzɪks] *s. pl.* (*sing. en const.*) astrofísica, rama de la astronomía que estudia las propiedades físicas de los cuerpos celestes.
astrosphere ['æstrəˌsfɪr, B -ˌsfɪə] *s.* (biol.) astrosfera.
Asturian [æs'tʊrɪən, B -'tjʊr-] *a.* asturiano, de Asturias, región de España.
astute [ə'stut, B ə'stjut] *a.* astuto, sagaz, agudo.
astutely [-lɪ] *adv.* astutamente, con astucia.
astuteness [-nəs] *s.* astucia, agudeza.
astylar [əɪ'staɪlər, B -lə] *a.* (arq.) sin columnas o pilastras.
asunder [ə'sʌndər, B -də] *adv.* en partes, en dos, a pedazos; **to tear a.,** despedazar. *—a.* aparte, separado, lejano.
asylum [ə'saɪləm] *s.* 1. asilo, lugar de refugio. 2. asilo, protección, amparo. 3. asilo; casa de beneficencia; hospicio.
asymmetric [ˌeɪsə'mɛtrɪk, B ˌæ-] **asymmetrical** [-əl] *a.* asimétrico.
asymmetry [eɪ'sɪmətrɪ, B æ-] *s.* asimetría, falta de simetría.
asymptomatic [ˌeɪˌsɪmptə'mætɪk, B ə-] *a.* (med.) asintomático.
asymptote ['æsəmˌtoʊt] *s.* (mat.) asíntota, asíntote, asímptota.
asymptotic [ˌæsəm'tɑtɪk, B -'tɔt-] **asymptotical** [-əl] *a.* (mat.) asintótico.
asynchronism [eɪ'sɪŋkrəˌnɪzəm] *s.* asincronismo.
asynchronous [eɪ'sɪŋkrənəs] *a.* asincrónico, sin concordancia temporal, sin cronología.
asyndetic [ˌæsən'dɛtɪk] *a.* (ret.) asindético, sin conjunciones.
asyndeton [ə'sɪndəˌtɑn, B -tən] *s.* (ret.) asíndeton.
asystole [eɪ'sɪstəlɪ] *s.* (med.) asistolia.
at [æt, ət] *prep.* a; en. 1. antepuesta a un sustantivo que indica lugar, expresa el sitio o su proximidad, ej., *at school,* en la escuela, *he arrived at the airport,* él llegó al aeropuerto, *a man is at the door,* hay un hombre a la puerta. 2. antepuesta a una palabra que indica tiempo, expresa la coincidencia de ese momento con la acción, ej., *she came at nine o'clock,* ella vino a las nueve en punto. 3. antepuesta a un superlativo expresa el estado de la cosa, ej., *at most,* a lo sumo, cuando más, en el mejor de los casos, *at least,* por lo menos, cuando menos, *at best* (*worst*), en el mejor (peor) de los casos. 4. puede expresar también la condición o estado particular del sujeto, ej., *at home,* en casa, *at play,* en el juego, jugando, *at work,* en el trabajo, trabajando, *I am at your command,* estoy a su disposición, *we are at peace,* estamos en paz. 5. usada con algunos verbos indica la dirección de la acción, ej., *to aim at,* apuntar; (fig.) aspirar a, proponerse, *to rush at,* acometer, abalanzarse sobre, *to shoot at,* disparar a, tirar a. 6. **at a distance,** a lo lejos; **at all,** en modo alguno; (*con negativo*) de ningún modo, de ninguna manera, en lo absoluto; **at a loss,** indeciso, perplejo; **at a pinch, at a push,** en aprietos; **at ease,** tranquilo; cómodo; (mil.) descansen; **at first,** al principio, inicialmente; **at hand,** a mano; **at last,** por último, por fin; **at once,** al instante, inmediatamente; **at random,** al azar; **at sea,** en el mar, navegando; (fig.) turbado, incierto, perplejo; **at that,** así, sin más; todavía, más aún, para colmo, ej., *he lost an arm, and the right arm at that,* perdió un brazo y para colmo el derecho; **to be at,** estar ocupado en, ocuparse de, dedicarse a.
atabal ['ætəbəl] *s.* atabal, tambor árabe.
atacamite [ˌætə'kæmˌaɪt] *s.* (min.) atacamita.
ataractic [ˌætə'ræktɪk] **ataraxic** [-'ræksɪk] *s.* droga tranquilizadora. *—a.* tranquilizante, que causa ataraxia.

atavism ['ætə,vɪzəm] *s.* (biol.) 1. atavismo. 2. persona que presenta atavismo; fenómeno atávico.
atavistic [,ætə'vɪstɪk] *a.* (biol.) atávico.
ataxia [ə'tæksɪə] *s.* (med.) ataxia.
ataxic [-sɪk] *a., s.* (med.) atáxico.
ataxite [-,saɪt] *s.* (min.) ataxito.
ATC *abrev. de* **Air Traffic Control,** control de tráfico aéreo.
ate [eit] *pret. de* **eat.**
atelier [,ætəl'jeɪ, B 'ætəlɪ,eɪ] *s.* atelier, taller, estudio (de un artista).
a tempo [ɑ'tɛm,poʊ] (mús.) a ritmo, de nuevo a ritmo normal.
Athamas ['æθə,mæs] *s.* (mitol.) Atamas, rey de Beocia.
athanasia [,æθə'neɪʒɪə] *s.* inmortalidad.
Athanasian Creed [,æθə'neɪʒən, B -ʃən] (relig.) credo de Atanasio.
athanasy [ə'θænəsɪ] *s.* inmortalidad.
athanor furnace ['æθə,nɔr-, B -,nɔ] hornillo de atenor.
atheism ['eɪθɪ,ɪzəm] *s.* ateísmo.
atheist [-əst] *s.* ateo.
atheistic [,eɪθɪ'ɪstɪk] **atheistical** [-tɪkəl] *a.* ateísta, ateístico.
Athena [ə'θɪnə] *s.* (mitol.) Atena, Atenea, diosa griega de la sabiduría.
athenaeum, atheneum [,æθə'niəm] *s.* ateneo, asociación literaria o cultural; lugar de reunión o sede cultural.
Athene [ə'θini] *var. de* **Athena.**
Athenian [ə'θiniən] *a., s.* ateniense.
Athens ['æθənz] *s.* Atenas, capital de Grecia.
atherine ['æθəraɪn, -ən] *s.* (ict.) pejerrey.
athermanous [æ'θɜrmənəs, B -'θɜmə-] *a.* (fís.) atérmano.
atheroma [,æθə'roʊmə] *s.* (med.) ateroma, quiste sebáceo.
atheromasia [,æθərə'meɪʒə] *s.* (med.) ateromasia.
atheromatosis [,æθə,roʊmə'toʊsəs] *s.* (med.) ateromatosis, aterosis.
atheromatous [-'rɑmətəs, B -'rɔm-] *a.* (med.) ateromatoso.
atherosclerosis [-roʊsklə'roʊsəs] *s.* (med.) aterosclerosis.
athirst [ə'θɜrst, B ə'θɜst] *a.* sediento; (con *for*) ávido (por).
athlete ['æθ,lit] *s.* atleta.
athlete's foot, (med.) pie de atleta, tiña podal, tricotifosis de los pies.
athletic [æθ'lɛtɪk] *a.* atlético, fuerte, robusto.
athletics [-ɪks] *s. pl.* (*sing. o pl. en const.*) ejercicios atléticos; atletismo.
athletic supporter (*wearing apparel*), suspensorios, suspensorio, suspensor.
at home [ət'hoʊm] recepción, recibo de visitantes (durante ciertas horas prefijadas).
athrepsia [ə'θrɛpsɪə] *s.* (med.) atrepsia, atrofia o marasmo infantil.
athwart [ə'θwɔrt, B ə'θwɔt] *adv.* oblicuamente, de través, para frustrar, en oposicion, en contra. —*prep.* a través de; en oposición a, contra.
atilt [ə'tɪlt] *a., adv.* inclinado; **to ride a.,** montar a caballo con la lanza en ristre.
Atlantean [,æt,læn'tiən, ət'læntɪ-] *a.* 1. como Atlas, de Atlas; fuerte. 2. perteneciente a la Atlántida.
atlantes [ət'læntiz] (arq.) *pl. de* **atlas.**
Atlantic [ət'læntɪk] *a.* 1. atlántico, del Atlántico. 2. (mitol.) del titán Atlas.
Atlantic Charter, (pol.) Carta del Atlántico.
Atlantic Ocean, Océano Atlántico.
Atlantic puffin, (orn.) frailecillo.
Atlantis [ət'læntɪs] *s.* (mitol.) Atlántida.
atlas ['ætləs] *s.* 1. atlas (colección de mapas). 2. (anat.) atlas, primera vértebra del cuello. 3. (mitol.) **A.,** Atlas. 4. (arq.) atlante, estatua de hombre que soporta un arquitrabe.
Atlas Mountains, cordillera Atlas, en el noroeste africano.
ATM *abrev. de* **Automated Teller Machine,** cajero automático.
atmology [æt'mɑlədʒɪ, B -'mɔl-] *s.* (fís.) atmología.
atmometer [æt'mɑmɪtər, B -'mɔm-ə] *s.* atmómetro, vaporímetro.
atmosphere ['ætmə,sfɪər, B -,sfɪə] *s.* 1. (meteor.) atmósfera. 2. (fig.) ambiente, atmósfera (social, de una novela, etc.), ej., *this restaurant has no a.,* este restaurante no tiene ambiente. 3. (fís.) atmósfera (unidad de presión del aire). 4. **corrosive a.,** atmósfera corrosiva; **rarified a.,** atmósfera rarificada.
atmospheric [,ætmə'sfɪrɪk, -'sfɛr-, B -'sfɛr-] *a.* (meteor., fís., mec.) atmosférico; **a. pressure,** presión atmosférica; **a. disturbances,** interferencias o perturbaciones atmosféricas.
atmospherics [-ɪks] *s. pl.* (rad., t.v.) atmosférica, estática, perturbaciones atmosféricas.
at. no. *abrev. de* **atomic number,** número atómico.
atoll ['æ,tɔl, -,tɑl, B -,tɔl] *s.* (geog.) atolón.
atom ['ætəm] *s.* (quím., fís.) átomo; **hot a.,** átomo con máxima energía interna; **parent a.,** átomo padre; **there's not an a. of truth in it,** eso no tiene ni pizca de verdad; **to split the a.** dividir el átomo.
atom bomb, *var. de* **atomic bomb.**
atomedics [,ætə'mɛdɪks] *s.* atomedicina, medicina atómica (aplicación de las ciencias electrónica y atómica a la medicina).
atomic [ə'tɑmɪk, B ə'tɔm-] *a.* 1. atómico. 2. (fig.) diminuto, muy pequeño.
atomic age, era atómica.
atomic bomb, bomba atómica.
atomic cocktail, (med.) cóctel atómico (medicación contra algunas formas del cáncer, administrada por vía oral).
atomic dust, polvo radioactivo.
atomic energy, energía atómica.
atomic hydrogen welding, soldadura con soplete de hidrógeno atómico.
atomicity [,ætə'mɪsətɪ] *s.* (quím., fís.) atomicidad.
atomic mass, masa atómica.
atomic mass unit, (fís.) unidad de masa atómica.
atomic number, (quím.) número atómico.
atomic pile, (fís.) pila atómica.
atomic reactor, reactor atómico.
atomics [ə'tɑmɪks, B ə'tɔm-] *s., pl.* (*sing. en const.*) (fís.) ciencia de los átomos (esp. cuando trata de la energía atómica).
atomic theory, teoría atómica.
atomic weapon, arma atómica.
atomic weight, (quím., fís.) peso atómico.
atomism ['ætə,mɪzəm] *s.* (filos.) atomismo.
atomist [-məst] *s.* (filos.) atomista.
atomistic [,ætə'mɪstɪk] *a.* 1. atomístico. 2. (fig.) fragmentado (sociedad, etc.).
atomize ['ætə,maɪz] *v.t.* atomizar, pulverizar.
atomizer [-ər, B -ə] *s.* pulverizador (de líquidos, perfumes, medicamentos para inhalaciones, etc.), vaporizador.
atom smasher, acelerador de partículas atómicas.
atomy ['ætəmɪ] *s.* (ant.) 1. átomo, partícula. 2. pigmeo.
atonal [eɪ'toʊnəl, æ-, B æ-] *a.* (mús.) atonal.
atonality [,eɪtə'nælətɪ, B ,æ-] *s.* (mús.) atonalidad.
atone [ə'toʊn] *v.t.* expiar, reparar (un crimen o culpa). —*v.i.* (con *for*) expiar, dar reparación (por), compensar (por).
atonement [-mənt] *s.* expiación; reparación, compensación, satisfacción; redención.
atonic [eɪ'tɑnɪk, B æ'tɔn-] *a.* 1. (med.) atónico, débil. 2. (gram.) átono. —*s.* (gram.) vocal, sílaba o partícula átonas.
atony ['ætənɪ] *s.* (med.) atonía.
atop [ə'tɑp, B ə'tɔp] *prep.* encima de, en la cumbre de. —*adv.* encima, en la cumbre.
atrabiliary [,ætrə'bɪlɪərɪ] *a.* (anat., med.) atrabiliario, atrabilioso.
atrabilious [,ætrə'bɪljəs] *a.* atrabilioso, atrabiliario, desabrido, destemplado, melancólico, morboso.
atrabiliousness [-nəs] atrabilis, desabrimiento, mal humor, acrimonia.
Atreus ['eɪ,trus, -trɪəs] *s.* (mitol.) Atreo, rey de Micenas.
atrial ['eɪtrɪəl] *a.* del atrio.
atrioventricular [,eɪtrɪoʊ,vɛn'trɪkjələr, B -lə] *a.* (anat.) atrioventricular.
atrip [ə'trɪp] *a.* (mar.) levada, levantada (ancla).
atrium ['eɪtrɪəm, B 'ɑ-] *s.* (*pl.* ATRIA [-ə]) 1. (arq.) atrio, patio interior. 2. (anat.) atrio, cavidad, cámara (esp. del corazón).
atrocious [ə'troʊʃəs] *a.* atroz; malísimo, abominable.
atrociously [-lɪ] *adv.* atrozmente.
atrocity [ə'trɑsətɪ, B -'trɔs-] *s.* atrocidad.
atrophic [ə'trɑfɪk, æ-, B æ'trɔf-] *a.* atrófico.
atrophied ['ætrəfid] *a.* atrofiado.
atrophy [-fɪ] *s.* (med., biol.) atrofia. —*v.i.* atrofiarse, sufrir atrofia. —*v.t.* atrofiar, producir atrofia en.
atropine ['ætrə,pin, -pən] *s.* (quím.) atropina.
atropism [-,pɪzəm] *s.* (med.) atropismo, envenenamiento por atropina.
att. *abrev. de* **attorney,** abogado.
attabal, *var. de* **atabal.**
attaboy ['ætəbɔɪ] *interj.* ¡bravo! ¡arriba!
attach [ə'tætʃ] *v.t.* 1. atar, ligar, unir, juntar. 2. unir, vincular (por lazos de amistad, afecto, etc.); aficionar, apegar. 3. agregar, adjuntar. 4. atribuir (importancia, etc.). 5. (der.) embargar, incautarse de, secuestrar. —*v.i.* 1. (con *to*) acompañar, unirse (a). 2. corresponder (culpa, etc. a alguien).
attachable [-əbəl] *a.* 1. (der.) sujeto a embargo o incautación, embargable; secuestrable. 2. que se puede unir o fijar.
attaché [,ætə'ʃeɪ, B ə'tæ,ʃeɪ] *s.* (dip.) agregado (de embajada o legación).
attaché case [ə'tæʃɪ-, ,ætə'ʃeɪ-] *s.* cartera, portafolio, maletín.
attached [ə'tætʃt] *a.* (con *to*) 1. aficionado (a), encariñado (con), apegado (a). 2. anexo, adjunto (a carta, documento, etc.). 3. (zool.) fijo (a superficie, etc.).
attachment [ə'tætʃmənt] *s.* 1. fijación, unión. 2. apego, afecto, adhesión, fidelidad. 3. (fig.) lazo, vínculo. 4. (der.) embargo. 5. (mec.) aditamento, accesorio eléctrico.
attack [ə'tæk] *v.t.* 1. atacar, acometer, asaltar, embestir. 2. (fig.) acometer, abordar (una tarea, un problema, etc.). 3. (quím.) atacar. —*v.i.* ir al ataque. —*s.* 1. ataque, asalto, acometida, embestida. 2. dolencia súbita.
attagirl ['ætəgʌrl] *interj.* ¡arriba! ¡vamos!
attain [ə'teɪn] *v.t.* 1. alcanzar, llegar a. 2. lograr, conseguir. —*v.i.* (con *to*) llegar, arribar, alcanzar (a).
attainability [ə,teɪnə'bɪlətɪ] *s.* asequibilidad; posibilidad de realización.

attainable [əˈteɪnəbəl] *a.* alcanzable, realizable; asequible.

attainder [əˈteɪndər, B -də] *s.* (der.) muerte civil, proscripción.

attainment [əˈteɪnmənt] *s.* 1. logro, consecución, realización. 2. (*pl.*) prendas, habilidades.

attaint [əˈteɪnt] (ant.) *v.t.* acusar; corromper, infectar; afectar (una enfermedad). —*s.* mancha, mácula, baldón, desgracia.

attar [ˈætər, -ˌtɑr, B -tə] *s.* aceite esencial o esencia de attar (rosas).

attempt [əˈtɛmpt] *v.t.* intentar, procurar, probar, ensayar. —*s.* 1. intento, prueba, tentativa. 2. ataque, asalto.

attend [əˈtɛnd] *v.t.* 1. atender, cuidar, asistir (a alguien). 2. concurrir a, asistir a (espectáculo, reunión, escuela, etc.). 3. acompañar, escoltar. 4. (**well** etc.) **attended,** (bien, etc.) concurrido (espectáculo, reunión). —*v.i.* 1. (con *to*) atender (a), prestar atención (a). 2. (gen. con *on* o *upon*) atender (a), servir.

attendance [-əns] *s.* 1. atención, servicio, asistencia. 2. asistencia, concurrencia, presencia. 3. séquito. 4. **to be in a.,** estar de servicio, estar de turno; servir obsequiosamente.

attendant [-ənt] *a.* 1. concomitante (circunstancia, etc.). 2. asistente, concurrente (público, etc.). —*s.* 1. ayudante, asistente; acompañante. 2. concurrente.

attention [əˈtɛntʃən, B əˈtɛnʃən] *s.* 1. atención, cuidado, miramiento, esmero. 2. cuidado, ojo; (mil.) ¡atención! 3. (*pl.*) atenciones, cortesías; cortejo. 4. **¡A.!** ¡cuidado! ¡ojo!; **to attract** (o **to call**) **one's a.,** llamar o atraer la atención de uno; **to come to a.,** (mil.) cuadrarse; **to come to one's a.,** hacérsele presente a uno; **to give** (o **to pay**) **a.** (**to**), atender (a), prestar atención (a); **to pay one's attentions** (**to**), hacer la corte (a); **to stand at a.,** (mil.) estar en posición de firmes.

attentive [əˈtɛntɪv] *a.* atento.

attentively [-lɪ] *adv.* atentamente.

attentiveness [-nəs] *s.* atención.

attenuant [əˈtɛnjʊənt] *a., s.* (med.) diluente.

attenuate [əˈtɛnjʊˌeɪt] *v.t.* 1. atenuar. 2. atenuar, debilitar, aminorar, disminuir. 3. enrarecer, reducir. —*v.i.* 1. atenuarse, disminuir(se). — [-ət] *a.* 1. atenuado, disminuido, aminorado. 2. (bot.) asaetada, lanceolada (hoja).

attenuation [əˌtɛnjʊˈeɪʃən] *s.* atenuación, amortiguamiento; **corona a.,** atenuación de efecto de corona; **attenuator a.,** atenuación de amortiguador; **crosstalk a.,** atenuación diafónica; **operative a.,** atenuación efectiva; **spherical-earth a.,** atenuación por la redondez de la tierra.

attenuator [əˈtɛnjʊˌeɪtər, B -ə] *s.* 1. (elec.) atenuador. 2. (mec.) amortiguador. 3. **calibrated a.,** atenuador calibrado; **waveguide a.,** atenuador de microondas; **potential a.,** atenuador de voltaje.

attest [əˈtɛst] *v.t.* 1. atestiguar, deponer, afirmar, dar fe de. 2. testificar, certificar. 3. juramentar. —*v.i.* (gen con *to*) dar testimonio (de), testificar.

attestant [-ənt] *s.* testigo, deponente, certificador.

attestation [ˌæˌtɛsˈteɪʃən] *s.* atestación, testimonio.

Attic [ˈætɪk] *a.* 1. ático, natural del Ática o de Atenas. 2. ático (díc. del estilo artístico o literario simple, puro y refinado). —*s.* 1. ático, ateniense. 2. (dialecto) ático.

attic, *s.* 1. desván, guardilla, buhardilla. 2. (arq.) ático.

Attica [ˈætɪkə] *s.* Ática, región de Grecia.

attic column, (arq.) columna ática, columna de base cuadrada.

Atticism [ˈætəˌsɪzəm] *s.* aticismo, clasicismo.

Atticist [-səst] *s.* aticista, clasicista.

Attic salt, A. wit, sal ática.

Attila [ˈætələ] *s.* (hist.) Atila, rey de los hunos.

attire [əˈtaɪr, B əˈtaɪə] *v.t.* vestir, ataviar. —*s.* 1. vestido, traje, atavió. 2. astas de ciervo o venado.

attitude [ˈætəˌtud, B -ˌtjud] *s.* 1. actitud, postura. 2. actitud, disposición, ej., *a. of mind,* actitud mental, modo de pensar. 3. **to strike an a.,** asumir una actitud estudiada. 4. (aer.) posición. 5. **a. jet,** (astronáut.) tobera de maniobra o posición; **a. control,** piloto automático.

attitudinize [ˌætəˈtudənˌaɪz, B -ˈtjud-] *v.i.* asumir una actitud afectada; pavonearse.

attorn [əˈtɜrn, B əˈtɜn] *v.t., v.i.* (der.) transferir, traspasar; reconocer legalmente un nuevo dueño.

attorney [əˈtɜrnɪ, B əˈtɜnɪ] *s.* (der.) abogado; procurador, agente legal; apoderado.

attorney at law, abogado, procurador judicial.

attorney general, (der.) procurador general, fiscal general; (E.U.) ministro de justicia, que actúa como abogado de la nación; (G.B.) fiscal de la Corona.

attorneyship [-ˌʃɪp] *s.* procuraduría, oficio de procurador; fiscalía.

attract [əˈtrækt] *v.t.* 1. atraer, traer hacia sí. 2. atraer, captar (voluntad, favor). 3. llamar, atraer (la atención). —*v.i.* ejercer atracción.

attractable [-əbəl] *a.* que puede ser atraído, atraíble.

attraction [əˈtrækʃən] *s.* 1. atracción. 2. atractivo. 3. (fís.) atracción (fuerza por la cual se atraen recíprocamente las diversas partes de un todo). 4. **cohesive a.,** atracción de cohesión; **electrostatic a.,** atracción electrostática; **interionic a.,** atracción inter-iónica.

attractive [əˈtræktɪv] *a.* atractivo, atrayente, agradable.

attractively [-lɪ] *adv.* en forma atractiva, de modo atractivo, atrayentemente.

attractiveness [-nəs] *s.* atracción, cualidades atractivas.

attributable [əˈtrɪbjətəbəl] *a.* atribuible, imputable, achacable.

attribute [əˈtrɪbjət] *v.t.* atribuir, asignar, achacar, imputar.

attribute [ˈætrəˌbjut] *s.* 1. atributo, cualidad, propiedad, característica. 2. (gram.) atributo.

attribution [ˌætrəˈbjuʃən] *s.* 1. atribución. 2. atributo, cualidad.

attributive [əˈtrɪbjətɪv] *a.* (gram., lóg.) atributivo. —*s.* (gram.) atributo.

attrite [əˈtraɪt] **attrited** [-əd] *a.* 1. frotado, desgastado por la fricción, rozado. 2. (relig.) atrito.

attrition [əˈtrɪʃən] *s.* 1. frotación, fricción, rozadura. 2. desgaste; agotamiento. 3. (relig.) atrición.

attune [əˈtun, B -ˈtjun] *v.t.* armonizar, poner a tono, afinar.

atty. *abrev. de* **attorney,** abogado.

Atty. Gen. *abrev. de* **Attorney General,** procurador general, fiscal.

atwitter [əˈtwɪtər] *a.* (hum.) **she was all a.,** estaba que no cabía en sí de la excitación.

at. wt. *abrev. de* **atomic weight,** peso atomico.

atypical [eɪˈtɪpɪkəl] *a.* atípico.

Au *símb. de* **aurum,** oro (Au).

A.U. *abrev. de* **angstrom unit,** unidad angstrom.

aubade [oʊˈbɑd] *s.* (mús.) alborada.

auburn [ˈɔbərn, B -bən] *s., a.* castaño rojizo.

auction [ˈɔkʃən] *s.* subasta, almoneda, remate; **to sell** (o **to put up**) **at, by** o **to a.,** subasta, poner en pública subasta. —*v.t.* subastar, vender en pública subasta, rematar.

auction bridge, bridge-remate.

auctioneer [ˌɔkʃəˈnɪr, B -ˈnɪə] *s.* subastador, martillero, rematista. —*v.t.* subastar, vender en pública subasta, rematar. —*v.i.* rematar, subastar.

auction room, sala de subastas.

audacious [ɔˈdeɪʃəs] *a.* 1. audaz, atrevido. 2. (despec.) descarado.

audaciously [-lɪ] *adv.* audazmente, osadamente; con descaro.

audaciousness [-nəs] *s.* 1. audacia, arrojo. 2. osadía, desenfado.

audacity [ɔˈdæsətɪ] *s.* 1. audacia, osadía, atrevimiento. 2. acto audaz. 3. (despec.) descaro, ej., **he had the a. to say** tuvo el descaro de decir.

audibility [ˌɔdəˈbɪlətɪ] *s.* audibilidad.

audible [ˈɔdəbəl] *a.* audible, perceptible.

audibly [-blɪ] *adv.* en forma audible, de modo audible.

audience [ˈɔdɪəns] *s.* 1. audiencia. 2. auditorio, oyentes (en conjunto), público. 3. audición, entrevista.

audile [ˈɔˌdaɪl] *a.* auditivo. —*s.* (psic.) persona auditiva, persona de memoria auditiva; tipo auditivo.

audio [ˈɔdɪˌoʊ] *a.* 1. de frecuencia audible; de(l) sonido. 2. rel. a frecuencias de onda de sonido audible entre 20 y 20.000 hertzios. —*s.* (rad., t.v.) transmisión del sonido.

audio cassette [ˈɔdɪoʊkəˈsat] *s.* cassette, cassete.

audio frequency [-ˈfrikwənsɪ] *s.* (rad.) audiofrecuencia (frecuencia comprendida entre los 20 y 20.000 hertzios).

audiogram [-əˌgræm] *s.* (med.) audiograma.

audiometer [ˌɔdɪˈɑmətər, B -ˈɔmɪtə] *s.* (fís., rad.) audiómetro, fonómetro, sonómetro.

audiophile [ˈɔdɪəˌfaɪl] *s.* aficionado a las reproducciones musicales (esp. las de alta fidelidad), audiófilo.

audio-visual [ˌɔdɪoʊˈvɪʒʊəl] *a.* audio-visual.

audio-visual aids, materiales auditivos y gráficos (libros, filmes, discos, etc.) que se usan conjuntamente en una clase o sesión instructiva.

audiotape [ˈɔdɪoʊˈteɪp] *s.* cinta de cassette. —*v.t.* grabar en cassette.

audiphone [ˈɔdəˌfoʊn] *s.* (fís., rad.) audífono.

audit [ˈɔdət] *s.* (com.) examen o intervención de cuentas; verificación contable. —*v.t.* examinar, revisar, verificar (cuenta, balance, etc.).

audition [ɔˈdɪʃən] *s.* 1. audición, facultad de oír. 2. audición (sesión de prueba de un artista). —*v.t.* dar audición a, escuchar, probar a (cantante, actor, etc.) —*v.i.* actuar en una audición de prueba.

auditive [ˈɔdətɪv] *a.* auditivo.

auditor [-ətər, B -ə] *s.* 1. oyente. 2. (com., ten.) auditor, verificador de cuentas, interventor. 3. alumno oyente, alumno libre.

auditorium [ˌɔdəˈtɔrɪəm] *s.* auditorio, salón de actos, sala de conferencias, aula, anfiteatro.

auditory [ˈɔdəˌtɔrɪ, B -tərɪ] *s., a.* auditorio, auditivo.

auditory nerve, (anat.) nervio auditivo.

Audubon's caracara [ˈɔdəbənzkærəˈkærə, -kəˈrɑ] (orn.) caricari.

auf wiedersehen [aʊfˈvidərˌzeɪn, B -dəˌ-] (alemán) adiós, hasta la vista, hasta luego.

Aug. *abrev. de* **August,** agosto.

Augean [ɔˈdʒiən] *a.* de Augías; p. ext. sucísimo; corrupto.

Augean Stables, (mitol.) los establos de Augías.

auger [ˈɔgər, B -gə] *s.* (carp.) barrena; taladro, berbiquí; sonda.

auger bit, broca salomónica.

aught [ɔt, ɑt, B ɔt] *s.* 1. alguna cosa; (acompañado de una negación) nada. 2. (mat.) cifra, cantidad. —*adv.* en modo alguno, en lo absoluto, de ninguna manera.
augite ['ɔˌdʒaɪt] *s.* (min.) augita.
augment [ɔg'mɛnt] *v.t.* 1. aumentar, acrecentar, incrementar. 2. (filol.) añadir (una vocal inicial) o alargar (la vocal inicial) para denotar el pretérito (en los verbos griegos y sánscritos). —*v.i.* crecer, aumentar(se).
augmentable [-əbəl] *a.* aumentable, acrecentable.
augmentation [ˌɔgmənt'teɪʃən] *s.* aumento, acrecentamiento.
augmentative [ɔg'mɛntətɪv] *a.* 1. aumentador. 2. (gram.) aumentativo (sufijo o palabra). —*s.* (sufijo o palabra) aumentativo.
augmented [-'mɛntəd] *a.* (mús.) aumentada (sexta, séptima, etc.).
augmenter [-ər, B -ə] *s.* (aer.) aumentador (de un motor a reacción), incrementador.
au gratin [oʊ'grɑtən, B -'grætɛŋ] *a.* (cocina) gratinado, cubierto de queso y salsa espesa y horneado.
augur ['ɔgər, B -gə] *s.* (hist.) augur; p. ext. adivino. —*v.t.* augurar, predecir, anunciar, pronosticar; **the events a. no good,** los acontecimientos no nos prometen nada bueno.
augury ['ɔgjerɪ] *s.* augurio, agüero, presagio.
August ['ɔgəst] *s.* agosto.
august [ɔ'gʌst] *a.* augusto, majestuoso, venerable.
Augustan [ɔ'gʌstən] *a.* 1. (hist. rom.) augustal, de Augusto. 2. (del período) neoclásico (de las artes y literatura inglesas).
Augustinian [ˌɔgə'stɪnɪən] *a., s.* (relig.) agustiniano, agustino.
Augustinianism [-ɪəˌnɪzəm] *s.* (relig.) agustinianismo.
Augustus [ɔ'gʌstəs] *s.* (hist.) Augusto, primer emperador romano.
au jus [oʊ'ʒus, -'dʒus] *a.* (cocina) al jugo.
auk [ɔk] *s.* (orn.) alca.
auklet ['ɔklət] *s.* (orn.) alca pequeña, de las costas del Océano Pacífico.
au lait [oʊ'lɑɪ] (fr.) con leche.
auld lang syne [ˌoʊldˌlæŋ'zaɪn, B 'ɔld'saɪn] (esco.) antaño, tiempos pasados.
aulic ['ɔlɪk] *a.* áulico, cortesano, palaciego.
au naturel [ˌoʊˌnætə'rɛl] (fr.) al natural.
aunt [ænt, ɑnt, B ɑnt] *s.* tía.
auntie ['ænti] *s.* (fam.) tía, tiíta.
aura ['ɔrə] *s.* 1. emanación, exhalación (de las flores, etc.). 2. (fig.) efluvio, atmósfera particular (que rodea a una persona). 3. (med.) aura (epiléptica o histérica).
aural ['ɔrəl] *a.* auricular, auditivo.
Aurantiaceae [əˌræntɪ'eɪsɪˌi] *s., pl.* (bot.) auranciáceas, dicotiledóneas de hoja perenne.
aureate ['ɔrɪət] *a.* 1. áureo; resplandeciente. 2. afectado, ampuloso, rimbombante (estilo, etc.).
Aurelius, Marcus [ɔ'riljəs'mɑrkəs, B -'mɑkəs] *s.* (hist.) Marco Aurelio, filósofo, escritor y emperador de Roma.
aureole ['ɔrɪˌoʊl] **aureola** [ɔ'riələ] *s.* 1. aureola, gloria, corona. 2. (meteor.) aureola, halo (círculo luminoso que rodea al sol cuando se le ve a través de la niebla).
aureomycin [ˌɔrɪoʊ'maɪsɪn] *s.* (med.) aureomicina.
au revoir [ˌoʊrəv'wɑr, B -'wɑ] (fr.) adiós, hasta la vista, hasta luego.
auric ['ɔrɪk] *a.* (quim.) áurico, de oro.
auricle ['ɔrɪkəl] *s.* (anat., zool., bot.) aurícula.
auricula [ɔ'rɪkjələ] *s.* (*pl.* AURICULAE [-ˌli, -laɪ] o AURICULAS) 1. (bot.) aurícula, oreja de oso. 2. (anat.) aurícula (del corazón).
auricular [-lər, B -lə] *a.* 1. auricular, del oído. 2. auricular, secreto, ej., *a. confession,* confesión auricular. 3. (anat., zool., bot.) de la aurícula.
auriculate [-lət] *a.* 1. (bot.) auriculado. 2. en forma de oreja.
auriculoventricular [ɔˌrɪkjəloʊˌvɛn'trɪkjələr, B -lə] *a.* (anat.) auriculoventricular, atrioventricular.
auriferous [ɔ'rɪfərəs] *a.* aurífero, que contiene oro.
Aurignacian [ˌɔrɪ'neɪʃən, B -rɪg-] *a.* (arqueol.) aurignacense, auriñacense, del período o cultura del paleolítico superior.
aurist ['ɔrɪst] *s.* (med.) aurista, otólogo.
aurochs ['aʊˌrɑks, 'ɔ- B 'ɔˌrɔks] *s.* (zool.) bisonte europeo.
aurora [ə'rɔrə, ɔ-] *s.* 1. aurora (claridad que precede a la salida del sol). 2. (fig.) aurora, alba, amanecer.
aurora australis, aurora austral.
aurora borealis, aurora boreal.
aurous ['ɔrəs] *a.* áureo.
aurum ['ɔrəm, 'aʊr-] *s.* (quim.) oro.
auscultate ['ɔskəlˌteɪt] *v.t., v.i.* (med.) auscultar.
auscultation [ˌɔskəl'teɪʃən] *s.* (med.) auscultación.
auscultatory [ɔ'skʌltəˌtɔrɪ, B -tərɪ] *a.* (med.) auscultatorio.
auspice ['ɔspəs] *s.* 1. auspicio, agüero. 2. (*pl.*) auspicios, protección, favor, ej., *under the auspices of the king,* con los auspicios del rey.
auspicious [ɔ'spɪʃəs] *a.* de buen agüero, favorable, propicio; afortunado.
Aussie ['ɔsɪ, B 'ɔzɪ] *s.* (fam.) australiano.
austenite ['ɔstəˌnaɪt] *s.* (metal.) austenita.
Auster ['ɔstər, B -tə] *s.* ábrego, viento del sur.
austere [ɔ'stɪr, B ɔ'stɪə] *a.* austero, rígido, severo, estricto; sin adornos; grave, sombrío.
austerity [ɔ'stɛrətɪ] *s.* austeridad, severidad.
austerity program, programa de austeridad.
Austin Friars ['ɔstən-] frailes agustinos.
austral ['ɔstrəl] *a.* 1. austral. 2. **A.,** australiano.
Australia [ɔ'streɪljə, ɑ-, B ɔ-] *s.* Australia.
Australian [-jən] *s., a.* australiano, de Australia.
Australian pea, (bot.) caraconno.
Austria ['ɔstrɪə, 'ɑs-, B 'ɔs-] *s.* Austria.
Austrian [-trɪən] *a., s.* austríaco.
Austrian pine, (bot.) pino cascalbo.
Austroasiatic ['ɔstroʊˌeɪʒɪ'ætɪk, 'ɑs-, B 'ɔs-ʃɪ'æt-] *a.* austroasiático (de un grupo de idiomas, entre ellos el vietnamita).
Austro-Hungarian [-ˌhʌŋ'gɛrɪən, B 'gɛər-] *a.* austrohúngaro.
autacoid ['ɔtəˌkɔɪd] *s.* (fisiol.) autacoide (hormonal).
autarchic, autarchical, autarchy, *vars. de* **autarkic, autarkical, autarky.**
autarkic [ɔ'tɑrkɪk, B ɔ'tɑkɪk] **autarkical** [-kɪkəl] *a.* autárquico, absolutamente soberano.
autarky ['ɔˌtɑrkɪ, B 'ɔˌtɑkɪ] *s.* (e.p.) autarquía, independencia económica.
autecology [ˌɔtɪ'kɑlədʒɪ, B -'kɔl-] *s.* autecología.
authentic [ə'θɛntɪk, ɔ-, B ɔ-] *a.* auténtico, legítimo, genuino, fidedigno. —*s.* (hist.) **Authentics,** auténticas (de Justiniano).
authenticate [-ɪˌkeɪt] *v.t.* autenticar, autorizar.
authentication [əˌθɛntɪ'keɪʃən, ɔ-, B ɔ-] *s.* autenticación.
authenticity [ˌɔˌθɛn'tɪsətɪ, -θən-] *s.* autenticidad.
authentic mode, (mús.) modo auténtico.
author ['ɔθər, B -θə] *s.* autor; creador.
authoress [-θərəs] *s.* autora.
authoritarian [ɔˌθɑrə'tɛrɪən, ə-, -ˌθɔr-, B ɔˌθɔrɪ'tɛər-] *a., s.* autoritario.
authoritarianism [-əˌnɪzəm] *s.* autoritarismo.
authoritative [ə'θɑrəˌteɪtɪv, ɔ-, -'θɔr-, B ɔ'θɔrɪtət-, ə-] *a.* 1. autoritario. 2. autorizado. 3. dictatorial, perentorio.
authority [-ətɪ] *s.* 1. autoridad, poder legítimo. 2. (*gen. en. pl.*) autoridades (escolares, estatales, públicas, etc.). 3. autoridad, experto (en alguna materia). 4. autoridad, jurisdicción. 5. autoridad, autorización, facultad. 6. autoridad, mando. 7. autoridad, texto que se cita en apoyo de lo que se dice, ej., *I have it on good a.,* lo sé de buena tinta.
authorization [ˌɔθərə'zeɪʃən, B -raɪ-] *s.* autorización, sanción, legalización.
authorize ['ɔθəˌraɪz] *v.t.* autorizar, facultar, aprobar, justificar, legalizar.
authorized [-ˌraɪzd] *a.* autorizado, reglamentario.
Authorized Version, versión autorizada (de la Biblia).
author's copy, ejemplar del autor (de su propio libro).
authorship ['ɔθərˌʃɪp, B 'ɔθəˌ-] *s.* 1. profesión de autor. 2. paternidad literaria, origen (de una obra literaria).
author's royalties, derechos de autor.
autism ['ɔˌtɪzəm] *s.* (psic.) autismo, abstracción.
auto ['ɔtoʊ, 'ɑt-, B 'ɔt-] *s.* auto, automóvil.
autoantibody [ˌɔtoʊ'æntɪˌbɑdɪ, B -ˌbɔdɪ] *s.* (med.) autoanticuerpo.
autobahn ['ɔtoʊˌbɑn, 'aʊt-] *s.* (alemán) autopista.
autobiographer [ˌɔtəbaɪ'ɑgrəfər, -bɪ-, B -'ɔg-fə] *s.* autobiógrafo.
autobiographical [-baɪə'græfɪkəl] **autobiographic** [-ɪk] *a.* autobiográfico.
autobiography [-baɪ'ɑgrəfɪ, -bɪ-, B -'ɔg-] *s.* autobiografía.
autoblast [-ˌblæst, B -ˌblɑst] *s.* autoblasto.
autobus ['ɔtoʊˌbʌs] *s.* autobús.
autocade [-ˌkeɪd] *s.* desfile de automóviles.
autocar [-ˌkɑr, B -ˌkɑ] *s.* automóvil grande de turismo.
autocatalysis [ˌɔtoʊkə'tæləsəs] *s.* (quim.) autocatálisis.
autochrome ['ɔtəˌkroʊm] *s.* (foto.) autocromo, emulsión fotográfica.
autochthon [ɔ'tɑkθən, B ɔ'tɔk-] *s.* (*pl.* AUTOCHTHONS O AUTOCHTHONES [-θəˌniz]) autóctono.
autochthonous [-θənəs] *a.* autóctono.
autochthony [-nɪ] *s.* autoctonía.
autoclastic [ˌɔtoʊ'klæstɪk] *a.* (geol.) autoclástico.
autoclave ['ɔtoʊˌkleɪv] *s.* autoclave, marmita hermética. —*v.t.* esterilizar en autoclave.
autocollimation [ˌɔtoʊˌkɑlə'meɪʃən, B -ˌkɔl-] *s.* (avia., cart.) autocolimación.
autocracy [ɔ'tɑkrəsɪ, B ɔ'tɔk-] *s.* (pol.) autocracia.
autocrat ['ɔtəˌkræt] *s.* autócrata.
autocratic [ˌɔtə'krætɪk] **autocratical** [-ɪkəl] *a.* autocrático.
autodidact [ˌɔtoʊ'daɪˌdækt] *s.* autodidacto.
autodidactic [-ˌdaɪ'dæktɪk] *a.* autodidacto (persona); autodidáctico (método, libro, etc.).
autodynamic [-daɪ'næmɪk] *a.* autodinámico.
autodyne ['ɔtəˌdaɪn] *s.* (electrón.) autodino.
autoejection [ˌɔtoʊɪ'dʒɛkʃən] *s.* (arm.) autoeyección.
autoeroticism [-'rɑtəˌsɪzəm, B -'rɔt-] **autoerotism** [-'ɛrəˌtɪzəm] *s.* autoerotismo, masturbación.
autogamous [ɔ'tɑgəməs, B ɔ'tɔg-] *a.* (bot.) autógamo.

autogamy [-mɪ] *s.* (bot.) autogamia, autofecundación.
autogenesis [ˌɔtoʊˈdʒɛnəsəs] *s.* autogénesis, generación espontánea; (biol., med.) abiogénesis.
autogenous [ɔˈtɑdʒənəs, B -ˈtɔdʒ-] *a.* autógeno; **a. welding,** soldadura autógena.
autogiro *var. de* **autogyro.**
autograph [ˈɔtəˌgræf, B -grɑf] *s.* autógrafo. —*v.t.* 1. escribir a mano, firmar. 2. autografiar.
autograph hunter, cazador de autógrafos.
autographic [ˌɔtəˈgræfɪk] *a.* 1. autógrafo. 2. autográfico (procedimiento, aparato, etc.).
autography [ɔˈtɑgrəfɪ, B ɔˈtɔg-] *s.* autografía, colección de autógrafos.
autogyro [ˌɔtoʊˈdʒaɪroʊ, B -ˈdʒaɪər-] *s.* (aer.) autogiro.
autohypnosis [-hɪpˈnoʊsəs] *s.* autohipnosis.
autoignition [-ɪgˈnɪʃən] *s.* combustión espontánea.
autoinduction [-ɪnˈdʌkʃən] *s.* (elec.) autoinducción.
autoinfection [-ɪnˈfɛkʃən] *s.* (med.) autoinfección.
autoinoculation [-ɪnˌɑkjəˈleɪʃən, B -ˌɔk-] *s.* (med.) autoinoculación.
autointoxication [-ɪnˌtɑksəˈkeɪʃən, B -ˌtɔk-] *s.* (med.) autointoxicación.
autoionization [-ˌaɪənəˈzeɪʃən, B -naɪ-] *s.* (quím.) autoionización.
autoloading [-ˈloʊdɪŋ] *a.* semiautomático (fusil, etc.).
autologous [ɔˈtɑləgəs, B ɔˈtɔ-] *a.* derivado de sí mismo.
Autolycus [ɔˈtɑləkəs, B ɔˈtɔl-] *s.* (mitol.) Autólico, hijo de Hermes y abuelo de Ulises.
autolysate [ɔˈtɑləˌseɪt, -ˌzeɪt, B ɔˈtɔlə-ˌ-seɪt] *s.* (biol.) autolisado.
autolysin [-sən] *s.* (med.) autolisina.
autolysis [-səs] *s.* (quím.) autólisis.
automat [ˈɔtəˌmæt] *s.* cafetería (donde máquinas automáticas despachan la comida).
automata [ɔˈtɑmətə] *pl. de* **automaton.**
automate [ˈɔtəˌmeɪt] *v.t.* 1. operar por automatización. 2. automatizar, convertir (fábrica, oficina, etc.) en una instalación de funcionamiento controlado por computadoras.
automated teller *s.* (*in a bank*) cajero automático.
automatic [ˌɔtəˈmætɪk] *a.* automático. —*s.* pistola automática.
automatic clutch, embrague automático.
automatic data processing, elaboración automática de información.
automatic direction finder, radiocompás automático.
automatic flush tank, sifón de limpieza automática, tanque de lavado automático, sifón de descarga automática.
automatic pilot, (aer.) piloto automático.
automatic rifle, fusil ametrallador.
automatic tensioning, autotensado; **a. t. device,** autotensor.
automatic transmission, (aut.) transmisión automática.
automation [ˌɔtəˈmeɪʃən] *s.* (ind.) automatización, automación, uso de computadoras u ordenadores.
automatism [ɔˈtɑməˌtɪzəm, B -tɔm-] *s.* (filos., fisiol., psic.) automatismo.
automatize [-ˌtaɪz] *v.t.* automatizar, volver automático.
automaton [-ətən, -ˌtɑn, B -ən] *s.* (*pl.* AUTOMATA [-ətə] o AUTOMATONS) autómata, robot.
automobile [ˌɔtəmoʊˈbil, ˈɔt-, bil, ˌɔtəˈmoʊ-] *s.* automóvil. —*a.* automóvil, automotor.
automobile accident, accidente de auto, accidente de coche.
automobile show, exhibición de automóviles.
automobilist [-əst] *s.* automovilista.
automotive [ˌɔtəˈmoʊtɪv] *a.* automotor, automotriz.
automotive engineering, ingeniería de automoción.
autonomic [-ˈnɑmɪk, B -ˈnɔm-] *a.* (fisiol., anat.) autónomo (reflejo, sistema nervioso, etc.).
autonomist [ɔˈtɑnəməst, B ɔˈtɔn-] *a.* autonomista.
autonomous [-məs] *a.* autónomo, que goza de autonomía; autonómico.
autonomy [-mɪ] *s.* autonomía, independencia (esp. política).
autophyte [ˈɔtəˌfaɪt] *s.* (bot.) autófito.
autopilot [ˈɔtoʊˌpaɪlət] *s.* (aer.) piloto automático.
autoplastic [ˌɔtoʊˈplæstɪk] *a.* (bot., med.) autoplástico.
autoplasty [ˈɔtoʊˌplæstɪ] *s.* (med.) autoplastia.
autopsy [ˈɔˌtɑpsɪ, ˈɔtəp-, B ˈɔtəp-, ˈɔˌtɔp-] *s.* (med.) autopsia, necropsia.
autosomal [ˌɔtəˈsoʊməl] *a.* (biol.) de un autosoma.
autosome [ˈɔtəˌsoʊm] *s.* (biol.) autosoma, cromosoma.
autostability [ˈɔtoʊstəˈbɪlɪtɪ] *s.* (mec.) autoestabilidad, estabilidad inherente (de un mecanismo, cuerpo, etc.).
autosuggestion [ˌɔtoʊsəgˈdʒɛstʃən, -səˈdʒɛs-, -ˈdʒɛʃtʃən] *s.* autosugestión.
autosynchronous [-ˈsɪŋkrənəs] *a.* autosíncrono.
autoteller [ˈɔtoʊˌtɛlər] *s.* (*in a bank*) cajero automático.
autotomic [ˌɔtəˈtɑmɪk, B -ˈtɔm-] *a.* (biol.) caracterizado por la autotomía.
autotomy [ɔˈtɑtəmɪ, B ɔˈtɔt-] *s.* (biol.) autotomía, autodivisión.
autotoxemia [ˈɔtoʊtɑkˈsimɪə, B -tɔk-] *s.* (med.) autotoxemia, autointoxicación.
autotoxicosis [-ˌtɑksəˈkoʊsəs, B -ˌtɔk-] *s.* (med.) autotoxicosis, autointoxicación.
autotoxin [ˌɔtəˈtɑksən, B -ˈtɔk-] *s.* (med.) autotoxina.
autotransformer [ˌɔtoʊtrænsˈfɔrmər, B -ˈfɔmə] *s.* (elec.) compensador, autotransformador.
autotrophic [ˌɔtəˈtrɑfɪk, -ˈtroʊ-, B -ˈtrɔf-] *a.* (bot., bact.) autotrófico.
autotrophy [ɔˈtɑtrəfɪ, B ɔˈtɔ-] *s.* (bot., bact.) autotrofia.
autotruck [ˈɔtoʊˌtrʌk] *s.* autocamión.
autotype [ˈɔtəˌtaɪp] *s.* 1. facsímil, facsímile, copia o imitación perfecta. 2. (foto.) autotipia.
autumn [ˈɔtəm] *s.* otoño; *(of life)* otoño; **in the a. of life,** otoñal.
autumnal [ɔˈtʌmnəl] *a.* otoñal, autumnal, de otoño.
autumnal equinox, equinoccio de otoño.
autumn crocus, (bot.) azafrán, azafrán croco, cólquico.
autunite [oʊˈtʌnˌaɪt, B ˈɔtən-] *s.* (min.) autunita.
Auvergne [oʊˈvɛrn, -ˈvɜrn, B -, vɛən, -ˈvɜn] *s.* Auvernia, región de Francia.
auxesis [ɔgˈzisəs, ɔkˈsi-] *s.* (biol.) auxesia, crecimiento.
auxetic [-ˈzɛtɪk, -ˈsɛt-] *a.* (biol.) auxético.
auxiliary [ɔgˈzɪljərɪ, -ˈzɪlə-] *a.* auxiliar, subsidiario, asistente, adicional, complementario. —*s.* 1. asistente, ayudante, auxiliar. 2. (gram.) verbo auxiliar. 3. (*pl.*) tropas auxiliares.
auximone [ˈɔksəˌmoʊn] *s.* (bot.) auximón, substancias que estimulan el crecimiento de las plantas.
av. *abrev. de* **avenue,** avenida (Ave., Av., Avda.).
avail [əˈveɪl] *v.t.* beneficiar, ayudar; **a. oneself of,** aprovecharse de, valerse de. —*v.i.* valer, servir, ser útil. —*s.* 1. uso, utilidad, provecho, beneficio, ventaja. **2. of a.,** de provecho; **of no a.,** fútil, de ningún efecto; **to (u of) little a.,** de poca utilidad, de poco beneficio; **to no a.,** en vano.
availability [əˌveɪləˈbɪlətɪ] *s.* disponibilidad.
available [əˈveɪləbəl] *a.* 1. disponible. 2. obtenible, asequible, a mano. 3. útil, aprovechable. 4. (der.) válido (alegato, acusación, etc.).
availableness [-nəs] *s.* disponibilidad.
avalanche [ˈævəˌlæntʃ, B -, lanʃ] *s.* 1. alud. 2. (fig.) alud, torrente (de palabras, cartas, etc.). —*v.i.* derrumbarse, precipitarse. —*v.t.* abrumar, inundar.
avant-garde [ˌɑvˌɑntˈgɑrd, B ˈævɑŋˈgɑd] *s.* vanguardia (esp. de artistas, movimiento artístico, literario, etc.).
avant-gardism [-, ɪzəm] *s.* vanguardismo.
avant-gardist [-əst] *s.* vanguardista.
avarice [ˌævərəs] *s.* avaricia, codicia.
avaricious [ˌævəˈrɪʃəs] *a.* avaro, avaricioso, avariento.
avast [əˈvæst, B əˈvast] *interj.* (mar.) ¡forte! ¡cesen! ¡basta!
avatar [ˈævəˌtɑr, B ˌævəˈtɑ] *s.* (mitol.) avatar (de una deidad hindú); encarnación.
avaunt [əˈvɔnt, əˈvɑnt, B əˈvɔnt] *adv.* (ant.) ¡fuera! ¡largo de aquí!
avdp. *abrev. de* **avoirdupois,** sistema de pesas utilizado en E.U. y G.B.
ave. *abrev. de* **avenue,** avenida (Ave., Av., Avda.).
Ave Maria [ˌɑveɪməˈriə] avemaría (oración).
avenge [əˈvɛndʒ] *v.t.*, *v.i.* vengar, vengarse de, vindicar.
avenger [-ər, B -ə] *s.* vengador.
avens [ˈævənz] *s.* (*pl.* AVENS) (bot.) gariofilea, clavel silvestre.
aventail [ˈævənˌteɪl] *s.* pieza del cuello en una armadura.
aventurine [əˈvɛntʃəˌrin, -rən] *s.* 1. (min.) venturina. 2. venturina artificial.
avenue [ˈævəˌnu, B -ˌnju] *s.* 1. avenida. 2. (pr. G.B.) alameda. 3. (gen. fig.) vía, ruta.
aver [əˈvɜr, B əˈvɜ] *v.t.* 1. afirmar, declarar. 2. (der.) verificar.
average [ˈævərɪdʒ] *s.* 1. promedio, término medio. 2. (mar.) avería. 3. **on an o the a.,** por término medio. —*a.* medio, mediano, de término medio; ordinario, corriente, común. —*v.t.* 1. alcanzar, pasar o hacer en promedio. 2. calcular el término medio. 3. prorratear. —*v.i.* alcanzar un promedio (de), ser de un promedio.
average agreement, acuerdo de averías, convenio sobre cargos de estadía.
average bond, fianza por indemnización de averías.
averment [əˈvɜrmənt, B əˈvɜmənt] *s.* 1. afirmación, aseveración. 2. (der.) verificación.
Averroism [əˈvɛroʊˌɪzəm, ˌævəˈroʊ-] *s.* (filos.) averroísmo, doctrina de Averroes basada en Aristóteles.
Averroist [-əst] *s.* (filos.) averroísta.
averse [əˈvɜrs, B əˈvɜs] *a.* 1. adverso, contrario, opuesto, remiso, ej., *a. to war,* contrario a la guerra. 2. (bot.) apartado o separado del tallo.
aversion [əˈvɜrʒən, -ʃən, B əˈvɜʃən] *s.* aversión, antipatía, repugnancia, animadversión, ojeriza.
avert [əˈvɜrt, B əˈvɜt] *v.t.* 1. desviar, apartar (mirada, pensamientos, etc.). 2. prevenir (peligro, catástrofe, etc.).

avian ['eɪvɪən] *a.* característico de las aves.
avianize [-əˌnaɪz] *v.t.* modificar o atenuar (ej., un virus) por cultivo repetido en un embrión de pollo en desarrollo.
aviarist [-ərəst] *s.* pajarero (persona que cría pájaros); avicultor.
aviary [-ˌɛrɪ, B -ərɪ] *s.* pajarera, aviario.
aviation [ˌeɪvɪ'eɪʃən, ˌæv-] *s.* aviación.
aviator ['eɪvɪˌeɪtər, 'æv-, B 'eɪvɪ-tə] *s.* aviador, piloto de avión.
aviatrix [ˌeɪvɪ'eɪtrɪks, ˌæv-, B ˌeɪ-] *s.* aviadora, mujer piloto.
aviculture ['eɪvəˌkʌltʃər, 'æv-, B -tʃə] *s.* avicultura, cría de aves.
aviculturist [ˌeɪvə'kʌltʃərəst, ˌæv-, B ˌeɪ-] *s.* avicultor.
avid ['ævəd] *a.* ávido, ansioso, codicioso.
avidity [ə'vɪdətɪ, æ-] *s.* 1. avidez, codicia. 2. (quím.) fuerza (de un ácido o de una base). 3. afinidad (de los átomos).
avifauna [ˌeɪvə'fɔnə, ˌæv-, B ˌeɪ-] *s.* (zool.) las aves, o las clases de aves de una región (en conjunto).
avigation [ˌævə'geɪʃən] *s.* avigación, navegación aérea.
Avignon [ˌævinˌjoʊn, B -'vɪn-] *s.* Aviñón, ciudad de Francia.
avionics [ˌeɪvɪ'ɑnɪks, ˌæv-, B -'ɔn-] *s., pl.* electrónica de la aviación.
avirulent [eɪ'vɪrələnt] *a.* (med.) avirulento, no virulento.
avitaminosis [ˌeɪˌvaɪtəmə'noʊsəs, B ˌæˌvɪt-] *s.* (med.) avitaminosis.
avocado [ˌævə'kɑdoʊ, ˌɑv-, B ˌæv-] *s.* aguacate, palta.
avocation [ˌævə'keɪʃən, 'ævəˌkeɪ-, B ˌævoʊ'keɪ-] *s.* 1. ocupación menor, pasatiempo. 2. diversión, distracción.
avocet, avoset ['ævəˌset] *s.* (zool.) avoceta.
avoid [ə'vɔɪd] *v.t.* 1. evitar, eludir. 2. huir de, evitar a (alguien). 3. abstenerse de, evitar (hacer). 4. (der.) invalidar, anular, dejar sin efecto.
avoidable [-əbəl] *a.* evitable, eludible, revocable, anulable.
avoidance [-əns] *s.* 1. evitación, prevención. 2. abstinencia (de hacer algo). 3. (der.) anulación, invalidación.
avoidance play, (bridge) juego de evasión.
avoirdupois [ˌævərdə'pɔɪz, B -ədə-] *s.* 1. sistema de pesas utilizado en G.B. y E.U. 2. (fam.) peso, gordura.
avouch [ə'vaʊtʃ] *v.t.* 1. afirmar, declarar, sostener. 2. garantizar, responder de. 3. reconocer, confesar.
avow [ə'vaʊ] *v.t.* 1. declarar, manifestar. 2. reconocer, admitir, confesar.
avowal [-əl] *s.* declaración, confesión, reconocimiento, admisión.
avowed [ə'vaʊd] *a.* reconocido, declarado, admitido.
avulsion [ə'vʌlʃən] *s.* (med., der.) avulsión, separación o extracción súbita y violenta.
avuncular [ə'vʌŋkjələr, B -lə] *a.* avuncular, de tío, como tío.
await [ə'weɪt] *v.t., v.i.* esperar, aguardar.
awake [ə'weɪk] *a.* despierto, alerta. —*v.i.* (*pret.* AWOKE [ə'woʊk] o AWAKED [ə'weɪkt] *p.p.* AWAKED o AWOKE; *p.pr.* AWAKING) 1. despertar(se). 2. (fig.) cobrar vida, cobrar fuerza. 3. (con *to*) (fig.) darse cuenta (de), cobrar consciencia (de). —*v.t.* (lit. y fig.) despertar>.
awaken [ə'weɪkən] *v.t., v.i. var. de* **awake.**
awakening [-ənɪŋ] *s.* despertar, despertamiento.
award [ə'wɔrd, B ə'wɔd] *v.t.* 1. conceder, asignar, conferir (premio, honores, etc.). 2. (der.) adjudicar; otorgar (indemnización, etc.). —*s.* 1. premio; honor (que se confiere), condecoración. 2. (der.) fallo, decisión judicial; laudo; adjudicación.
aware [ə'wɛr, B ə'wɛə] *a.* consciente, enterado, sabedor, informado; **to be a. of** (o **that**), tener conciencia o estar enterado de; **to become a. of,** darse cuenta, percatarse de.
awareness [-nəs] *s.* conciencia, conocimiento.
awash [ə'wɔʃ, ə'wɑʃ, B ə'wɔʃ] *a., adv.* 1. a flor de agua; lavado por las olas o la marea. 2. inundado. 3. a flote, flotante (en el agua), a merced de las olas.
away [ə'weɪ] *adv.* 1. lejos, a lo lejos, a distancia, ej., *a. from the house,* lejos de la casa, *far a.,* muy lejos, *from a.,* desde lejos, *three miles a.,* a tres millas de distancia. 2. constantemente, continuamente, sin cesar; con ahínco, ej., *to work a.,* trabajar sin cesar o con ahínco. 3. enseguida, inmediatamente, ej., *fire a.!* ¡abra(n) fuego! 4. **a. with the king!** ¡abajo el rey! ¡muera el rey!; **a. with you,** ¡váyase Ud. de aquí!; **dying a.,** desvaneciéndose, apagándose, muriéndose (sonido, entusiasmo, etc.); **to be a.,** estar ausente, estar fuera; **to do a. with,** matar; terminar con, deshacerse de, prescindir de; **to get a.,** escapar; **to get a. with,** hacer con impunidad; salir airoso; (jer.) escapar con (algo robado); **to give a.,** regalar; deshacerse de; delatar, revelar; **to go a.,** irse, marcharse; **to make a. with,** destruir, matar; alzarse con; **to put a.,** (fam.) encerrar (en una prisión o manicomio); (jer.) comer mucho; **to take a.,** quitar; **to wither a.,** irse marchitando. —*a.* 1. ausente. 2. distante, lejano, alejado. 3. (dep.) (de) fuera de casa, visitante; (béisbol) (puesto) fuera de juego.
awe [ɔ] *s.* 1. temor reverente, admiración temerosa. 2. (ant.) pavor, espanto. 3. **to fill with a .,** llenar de admiración; asustar; **to hold** (o **keep**) **in a.,** mantener asustado, tener sujeto o sometido por el temor; **to stand in a. of,** temer a, admirar a. —*v.t.* infundir temor reverente, imponer respeto a.
aweary [ə'wɪrɪ, B ə'wɪərɪ] *a.* (poét.) cansado, fatigado.
aweather [ə'wɛðər, B -ə] *adv.* (mar.) a barlovento.
aweigh [ə'weɪ] *a.* (mar.) pendiente, a plomo (díc. del ancla).
awe-inspiring ['ɔɪnˌspaɪrɪŋ] *a.* impresionante, imponente.
aweless ['ɔləs] *a.* irreverente; falto de temor.
awesome ['ɔsəm] *a.* pavoroso, pasmoso, imponente.
awestricken ['ɔˌstrɪkən] **awestruck** ['ɔˌstrʌk] *a.* anonadado, despavorido, pasmado.
awful ['ɔfəl] *a.* 1. pasmoso, impresionante, respetable. 2. horrible, atroz. 3. (fam.) feísimo, pésimo, detestable, atroz; muy grande, enorme, tremendo, ej, *a. manners,* modales detestables, *an a. lot,* muchísimo, *he took an a. chance,* corrió un riesgo enorme, *it's an a. picture,* es una película atroz.
awfully ['ɔfəlɪ, 'ɔflɪ] *adv.* 1. pasmosamente, pavorosamente. 2. detestablemente, atrozmente. 3. (fam.) muy; excesivamente, ej., *it's a. good,* es muy bueno.
awhile [ə'hwaɪl, ə'waɪl] *adv.* por un rato.
awhirl [ə'hwɜrl, ə'wɜrl, B ə'wɜl, ə'hwɜl] *adv.* en rotación; en giro, en torbellino.
awkward ['ɔkwərd, B -wəd] *a.* 1. desmañado, torpe, poco diestro. 2. desgarbado, sin gracia. 3. desproporcionado, difícil de manejar, inconveniente. 4. embarazoso, desagradable. 5. delicado, difícil (situación, etc.).
awkward age, edad difícil, adolescencia.
awkwardly [-lɪ] *adv.* torpemente; desgarbadamente; embarazosamente; inconvenientemente.
awkwardness [-nəs] *s.* torpeza; falta de garbo; ineptitud; carácter embarazoso, incomodidad; índole delicada (de una situación, etc.).
awl [ɔl] *s.* lezna; punzón.
awl-shaped ['ɔlˌʃeɪpt] *a.* (bot.) aleznado.
awn [ɔn] *s.* (bot.) arista; cañamiza.
awning ['ɔnɪŋ, 'ɑn-, B 'ɔ-] *s.* toldo, cubierta de lona, marquesina; (mar.) toldilla.
awoke [ə'woʊk] *pret. y p.p. de* **awake.**
AWOL ['eɪˌwɔl, ˌeɪˌdʌbəljʊˌoʊ'ɛl] *adv., a.* (mil.) ausente sin licencia (*abrev. de* **Absent Without Official Leave,** ausente sin permiso oficial).
awry [ə'raɪ] *a.* sesgado, torcido, oblicuo. —*adv.* de soslayo, oblicuamente, torcidamente; erradamente, incorrectamente; **to go, run** o **tread a.,** (fig.) abandonar el camino recto, pecar; **to look a.,** (lit. y fig.) mirar de soslayo.
ax, axe [æks] *s.* (*pl.* AXES ['æksəz]) hacha, segur; **to get the ax,** (jer.) ser despedido o echado (de empleo o colegio); **to have an ax to grind,** (fam.) tener una obsesión, tener una queja y porfiar en reiterarla. —*v.t.* podar o cortar con hacha, matar con hacha; (fig.) recortar, reducir (gastos, personal, etc.).
axenic [eɪ'zɛnɪk, -'zi-] *a.* (biol.) áxeno.
axes *s. pl.* ['ækˌsiz] de **axis,** o ['æksəz] de **ax (e).**
axial ['æksɪəl] *a.* axil, axial, perteneciente al eje.
axial-flow turbine, turbina axial.
axial skeleton, (anat.) esqueleto axil, armazón axial.
axil ['æksəl, -ˌsɪl] *s.* (bot.) axila.
axile [-ˌsaɪl] *a.* (bot.) axilar, axial.
axilla [æk'sɪlə] *s.* (*pl.* AXILLAE [-i, -ˌaɪ]) axila, sobaco.
axillar [æk'sɪlər, B -a] *s.* (orn.) pluma axilar (en el ala de una ave).
axillary ['æksəˌlɛrɪ, B æk'sɪlərɪ] *a.* (anat., zool., bot.) axilar, de la axila, del sobaco.
axinite ['æksəˌnaɪt] *s.* (min.) axinita.
axiological [ˌæksɪə'lɑdʒɪkəl, B -'lɔdʒ-] *a.* (filos.) axiológico.
axiology [-'ɑlədʒɪ, B -'ɔl-] *s.* (filos.) axiología.
axiom ['æksɪəm] *s.* axioma, postulado.
axiomatic [ˌæksɪə'mætɪk] *a.* axiomático, incontrovertible, evidente.
axis ['æksəs] *s.* (*pl.* AXES [-, siz]) 1. eje, ej., *the earth's a.,* el eje terrestre. 2. (anat.) axis (la segunda vértebra del cuello). 3. (bot.) eje (del fruto, inflorescencia, etc.). 4. (ópt.) eje. 5. (min.) eje (de los cristales). 6. (pol.) eje, alianza, esp. **the A.,** el Eje (de las naciones fascistas de la Segunda Guerra Mundial). 7. (arte) eje (línea imaginaria a la cual se refieren las diferentes partes de un diseño). 8. (mec.) eje, árbol. 9. **anticlinal a.,** (geol.) eje anticlinal; **centroidal a.,** eje baricéntrico; **alignment a.,** eje de alineación; **a. of elevation,** eje de levantamiento; **rotation a.,** eje de rotación; **crystalline a.,** eje de simetría.
axite [-ˌsaɪt] *s.* (anat.) axón, axona.
axle ['æksəl] *s.* eje, árbol; **pony-truck a.,** (f.c.) eje de bisel; **drum a.,** eje del tambor; **leading a.,** eje frontal; **floating a.,** eje desplazable; **steering a.,** (auto.) eje de dirección; (*on each side of a differential*) semieje.
axle box, (mec.) caja del eje, buje.
axle generator, (f.c.) generador impulsado por el eje.
axletree [-ˌtri] *s.* (mec.) eje de carretón, eje de ruedas de carruaje.
axolotl ['æksəˌlɑtəl, B -ˌlɔt-] *s.* (zool.) ajolote.

axon ['æk,sɑn, B -, sɔn] **axone** [-,soʊn] *s.* (anat.) axón, neuroeje.
axonometer [,æksə'nɑmətər, B -'nɒmɪtə] *s.* axonómetro.
axonometric projection[,æksənoʊ'mɛtrɪk-] (dib.) proyección axonométrica.
axstone ['æk,stoʊn] *s.* (min.) piedra de hacha.
ay [aɪ] *interj.* ay; **ay me!** ¡ay de mí!
ayah ['aɪə, 'ɑjə] *s.* aya, doncella o sirvienta en la India.
ayatollah ['aɪə'toʊlə] *s.* ayatolah, imam.
aye [aɪ] *adv.* sí. —*s.* (*pl.* AYES) voto afirmativo; **the ayes have it,** los votos afirmativos han logrado mayoría.
aye [eɪ] *adv.* (ant., dial.) siempre, para siempre; (poét.) **for aye,** por siempre jamás.

aye-aye ['aɪ,aɪ] *s.* (zool.) ayeaye.
Aymara [,aɪmə'rɑ] *s.* aimara, aimará (tribu india de América del Sur, su pueblo y su idioma).
Aymaran [-'rɑn] *a.* aimara, aimará.
azalea [ə'zeɪljə] *s.* (bot.) azalea.
azarole ['æzə,roʊl] *s.* (bot.) acerola.
azedarach [ə'zɛdə,ræk] *s.* (bot.) acederaque.
azide ['æz,aɪd, 'eɪ,zaɪd] *s.* (quím.) azida.
azimuth ['æzəməθ] *s.* (astr.) acimut, azimut.
azine ['æz,in, 'eɪ,zin] *s.* (quím.) azina.
azoic [eɪ'zoʊɪk, ə-, B ə-, æ-] *a.* (geol., quím.) azoico.
azole ['æz,oʊl, 'eɪ,zoʊl, B 'æz-] *s.* (quím.) azol.
azonal [eɪ'zoʊnəl, B æ-] *a.* (geol.) azonal.
Azores [ə'zɔrs] *s.* (*pl.*) islas Azores.

azote ['æz,oʊt, ə'zoʊt] *s.* (quím.) **ázoe,** nitrógeno.
azotemia [,æzə'timɪə] *s.* (med., vet.) azotemia, uremia.
azoth ['æz,ɔθ] *s.* (alquimia) azoth, mercurio.
azotic [æ'zoʊtɪk, B ə'zɔt-] *a.* (quím.) azoico.
azoturia [,æzə'tʊrɪə, B -'tjʊr-] *s.* (med.) azoturia, azouria.
Aztec ['æz,tɛk] *s., a.* azteca.
azure ['æʒər, B -ə] *s.* 1. azul celeste. 2. (her.) azur. —*a.* azul celeste, azur.
azurite [-ə,raɪt] *s.* (min.) azurita, malaquita azul.
azygous, azygos ['æzɪgəs] (anat.) *a.* ácigo, ácigos, impar. —*s.* ácigos, vena ácigos.

B

B [bi] *s.* 1. b, segunda letra del alfabeto inglés. 2. (mús.) si.
B. *abrev. de* 1. **British.** 2. **Bishop,** alfil (en ajedrez). 3. **Bacillus,** bacilo.
b. *abrev. de* 1. **base,** base. 2. **bay,** bahía. 3. **book,** libro. 4. **born,** nacido. 5. **brother,** hermano.
Ba *símb. de* **barium,** bario (Ba).
B.A. *abrev. de* **1. Bachelor of Arts,** Licenciado en Artes. 2. **British Academy,** Academia Británica. 3. **Buenos Aires,** Buenos Aires.
baa [bæ, bɑ] *s.* be, ba (onomatopeya del balido del carnero, el cordero o la oveja). —*v.i.* 1. balar, dar balidos (la oveja, el cordero o el carnero). 2. imitar el balido de la oveja.
Baal [beɪl, 'beɪəl] *s.* (*pl.* BAALS O BAALIM ['beɪləm, -əˌlɪm]) Baal (divinidad semítica).
Baalism ['beɪlˌɪzəm, 'beɪəl-] *s.* culto de Baal.
Baalite [-ˌaɪt] *s.* baalita, adorador de Baal.
baba ['bɑbə] *s.* clase de pastel, bizcocho.
baba au rhum ['bɑˌbɑoʊ'rʌm] *s.* saboyana, pastel almibarado rociado con ron.
babacoote [ˌbæbə'kutɪ, B -'koʊtoʊ] *s.* (zool.) babacoto (simio de Madagascar).
Babbitt ['bæbət] *s.* (E.U.) (fig., despec.) burgués conformista (aferrado a las normas éticas y sociales de su clase o grupo).
Babbitt metal, metal babbit, metal antifricción; antimonio, metal blanco.
babble ['bæbəl] *v.i.* 1. balbucir, balbucear. 2. barbotar, barbullar (un niño, un idiota, etc.). 3. parlotear, chacharear. 4. (fig.) murmurar, susurrar (arroyo). —*v.t.* 1. decir barbullando, barbotar, barbullar (palabras). 2. revelar, descubrir indiscretamente (secreto, etc.). —*s.* 1. barboteo. 2. cháchara, parloteo. 3. (fig.) susurro, murmullo (de un arroyo).
babbler ['bæblər, B -lə] *s.* charlatán, parlanchín.
babbling [-lɪŋ] *s.* charlatanería, cháchara. —*a.* charlatán, murmurador.
Babcock test ['bæbˌkɑk-, B -ˌkɔk-] *s.* prueba de Babcock (para determinar la cantidad de grasa en la leche).
babe [beɪb] *s.* 1. criatura, criaturita, infante, nene. 2. niño, cándido, inocente. 3. (jer.) mujer, mujychacha (esp. la sexualmente atractiva).
babe in arms, niño de pecho.
babe in the woods, (fig.) novato, persona inexperta e inocente.
Babel ['beɪbəl, 'bæb-, B 'beɪb-] *s.* 1. (bíbl.) Babel. 2. **b.** (fig.) babel, lugar de confusión; algarabía, caos.
Babinski reflex [bə'bɪnskɪ-] *s.* reflejo de Babinski (reflejo en la planta del pie).
babirusa, babiroussa, babirussa [ˌbæbə'rusə, B ˌbɑbɪ-] *s.* (zool.) babirusa.
Babism ['bɑbɪzəm] *s.* (relig.) babismo.
baboon [bæ'bun, B bə-] *s.* (zool.) babuino, mandril.
baboosh [bə'buʃ, bɑ-]**babouche** *s.* babucha, pantufla.
babu ['bɑbu] *s.* caballero hindú; señor (forma respetuosa de dirigirse a una persona).
babul [bə'bul] *s.* (bot.) (variedad de) acacia del África del Norte.
babushka [bə'bʊʃkə] *s.* pañolón para la cabeza.
baby ['beɪbɪ] *s.* 1. bebé, nene, pequeñuelo, criatura, crío. 2. (fig.) persona pueril. 3. el menor, el más joven (de un grupo). 4. (fam.) chica, mujer, amiga. 5. (fig.) creación o idea propia favorita de uno mismo. 6. (jer.) tipo, hombre. 7. **to hold** (o **to carry**) **the b.,** cargar con una responsabilidad (no deseada). —*a.* 1. de bebé, para bebés. 2. infantil, pueril. 3. menor (de su clase), (de tamaño) chico. —*v.t.* mimar, tratar como a un niño.
baby beef, 1. carne tierna de res. 2. carne de ternera.
baby blue, azul pálido, celeste.
baby boom, boom de la natalidad.
baby boomer ['bumər] , persona nacida durante los veinte años después de la segunda guerra mundial.
baby boy, nene, niño.
baby buggy, carriola; (E.U.) cochecito de bebé.
baby carriage, cochecito de bebé.
baby face, cara de niño, facciones infantiles.
baby farm, guardería infantil, centro para cuidar bebés.
baby farming, guardería infantil, como negocio (tenido en poca estima).
baby girl, nena, niña.
baby grand, piano de media cola.
babyhood ['beɪbɪˌhʊd] *s.* primera infancia.
babyish [-ɪʃ] *a.* infantil, aniñado.
babylike [-ˌlaɪk] *a.* de bebé, como un bebé.
Babylon ['bæbələn, -ˌlɑn, B -lən] *s.* 1. (hist.) Babilonia. 2. (fig.) ciudad grande e inmoral. 3. (fig., E.U.) la patria americana (como símbolo de opresión y abuso, entre los negros que luchan por sus derechos civiles).
Babylonian [ˌbæbə'loʊnjən] *a.* 1. babilónico, de Babilonia. 2. (fig.) babilónico, caótico; fastuoso. —*s.* babilonio, natural de Babilonia.
babylonical [-'lɑnɪkəl, B -'lɔn-] *a.* tumultuoso, caótico.
baby-sit ['beɪbɪˌsɪt] *v.i.* 1. (fam.) cuidar niños durante la ausencia de sus padres. 2. (fig.) quedar al cuidado de un asunto.
baby sitter [-ər, B -ə] *s.* cuidaniños, niñera, persona (gen. remunerada) que cuida niños durante algunas horas en ausencia de sus padres.
baby talk, balbuceo infantil.
baby tooth, diente de leche.
bacca ['bækə] *s.* (*pl.* BACCAE ['bækˌsi]) (bot.) baya, grano, simiente (ej., del cafeto).
baccalaureate [ˌbækə'lɔrɪət] *s.* bachillerato.
baccalaureate degree, licenciatura.
baccarat [ˌbɑkə'rɑ, ˌbæk-, B 'bækəˌrɑ] *s.* 1. bacará, juego de naipes. 2. Baccarat, cristal fino fabricado en Francia.
baccate ['bækˌeɪt] *a.* (bot.) 1. abayado, parecido a una baya. 2. que produce bayas.
Bacchae ['bækˌi, -ˌaɪ] *s. pl.* (mitol.) bacantes; sacerdotisas que rendían culto al dios Baco.
bacchanal [-ənəl, 'bækə'næl, B 'bækənəl] *a.* bacanal. —*s.* bacanal, orgía.
Bacchanalia [ˌbækə'neɪljə] *s. pl.* bacanales, bacanal.
bacchanalian [-jən] *a.* bacanal. —*s.* 1. devoto de Baco; bacante. 2. juerguista ebrio, borracho.
bacchant [bə'kænt, -'kɑnt, B 'bækənt] *s.* (*pl.* BACCHANTS or BACCHANTES [bə'kæntiz, -'kɑnt-, B -'kænt-]) sacerdote de Baco; (fig.) hombre disoluto o borracho, parrandero.
bacchante [bə'kæntɪ, -'kɑntɪ, B -'kæntɪ, -'kænt] *s.* bacante, ménade, sacerdotisa de Baco; (fig.) bacante, mujer ebria y disoluta.
bacchic ['bækɪk] *a.* báquico.
Bacchus ['bækəs] *s.* (mitol.) Baco.
bacciferous [bæk'sɪfərəs] *a.* (bot.) bacífero.
baccivorous [-'sɪvərəs] *a.* bacívoro (que se alimenta de bayas).
bach [bætʃ] *s.* (fam.) *abrev. de* **bachelor.** —*v.i.* (fam.) vivir como soltero.
bachelor ['bætʃələr, B -lə] *s.* 1. célibe, soltero. 2. bachiller. 3. (hist.) doncel.
bachelorhood [-ˌhʊd] *s.* soltería, celibato, condición de soltero.
Bachelor of Arts, Licenciado en Letras.
Bachelor of Science, Licenciado en Ciencias.
bachelor's button, (bot.) aciano, azulejo, cabezuela; margarita.
bacillar [bə'sɪlər, B -lə] **bacillary** ['bæsəˌlɛrɪ, bə'sɪlərɪ] *a.* (med., min.) bacilar.
bacilliform [bə'sɪləˌfɔrm, B -ˌfɔm] *a.* baciliforme.
bacillus [bə'sɪləs] *s.* (*pl.* BACILLI [-ˌaɪ, -ˌi]) (bact.) bacilo, bacteria.
bacitracin [ˌbæsə'treɪsən] *s.* (farm.) bacitracina (antibiótico).
back [bæk] *s.* 1. espalda; columna vertebral, espinazo. 2. lomo (de cuadrúpedos). 3. parte posterior o trasera. 4. respaldo, espaldar (de una silla, etc.). 5. dorso (de la mano), reverso (de la moneda), lomo (de un libro, etc.), envés, revés. 6. final, últimas páginas (de un libro, etc.). 7. (dep.) zaguero, defensa. 8. **at the b.,** al fondo; **at the b. of,** detrás de; b. **to b.,** espalda con espalda; **behind one's b.,** por detrás, a espaldas de uno; **in b. of,** detrás de; **to be on one's b.** estar postrado, estar boca arriba; guardar cama; **to break one's b.,** agobiar, agotar a uno; esforzarse al máximo; **to break the b. of,** terminar la parte más difícil de (tarea, trabajo, etc.), solucionar la parte más difícil de (problema); **to get off (someone's) b.,** (jer.) (*ú. gen. en imper.*) dejar de fastidiar (a alguien), ej., *get off my b.!* !deja de fastidiarme!; **to have at the b. of one's mind,** tener presente; **to have** (o **carry**) **on one's b.,** llevar a cuestas o en hombros; **to have (someone) on one's b.,** tener (a alguien) encima; **to know like the b. of one's hand,** conocer como la palma de la mano; **to turn one's b. upon,** volver las espaldas a, desdeñar, abandonar; **with one's b. to the wall,** acosado, entre la espada y la pared. —*a.* 1. posterior, trasero, de atrás. 2. dorsal. 3. anterior, pasado; atrasado. 4. de vuelta. 5. apartado, lejano. 6. contrario (movimiento, corriente, etc.). 7. (mec.) de retroceso, de regreso, de atrás. 8. **to take a b. seat,** (fig.) conformarse con una posición inferior,

rebajarse. —*adv.* 1. atrás, detrás. 2. otra vez, de nuevo. 3. de vuelta, de regreso. 4. **b. and forth,** de atrás para adelante, de un lado a otro; **b. in the old days,** allá en los tiempos viejos; **b. of,** detrás de; **to answer b.,** replicar, rebatir; **to be b.,** estar de vuelta, de regreso; **to beat b.,** rechazar; **to come b.,** regresar, volver; **to give b.,** devolver; **to go b.,** regresar; **to go b. and forth,** ir y venir; **to go b. on** (o **upon**), faltar a (una promesa, etc.); **to hold b.,** retener; **to keep b.,** mantenerse alejado; quedar atrás; tener a raya; **to put b.,** poner en su sitio; devolver; **to send b.,** hacer volver (a alguien); devolver; **to step b.,** dar un paso atrás; **years b.,** años atrás. —*v.t.* 1. (t. con *up*) apoyar, respaldar; sostener. 2. (t. con *up*) endosar, justificar con pruebas. 3. financiar, costear (empresa); respaldar (moneda). 4. (t. con *up*) hacer retroceder, dar marcha atrás. 5. (gen. con *up*) cubrir, revestir. 6. servir de fondo, estar detrás de. 7. **b. water,** (mar.) ciar. —*v.i.* 1. (t. con *up* u *off*) moverse hacia atrás, retroceder, dar marcha atrás. 2. (gen. con *on, onto o against*) ir o ponerse de espaldas (a). 3. **b. and fill,** (mar.) zigzaguear; (fig.) titubear, vacilar; **b. away,** alejarse retrocediendo; **b. down,** ceder, echarse atrás, dar paso atrás; **b. out (of),** retirarse (de); dejar de cumplir.

back, *s.* cuba poco profunda (usada en las cervecerías y tenerías).

backache [ˈbækˌeɪk] *s.* dolor de espalda.

back alley, callejón posterior de una manzana.

backasswards [ˌbækˈæswərdz, B -ˈɑswədz] *adv.* (vulg.) al revés, desordenadamente, confusamente.

backband [ˈbækˌbænd] *s.* lomera (de libro).

back-bencher [-ˈbɛntʃər, B -tʃə] *s.* (pol. G.B.) diputado novel (de menor prestigio o experiencia).

backbite [ˈbækˌbaɪt] *v.t., v.i.* calumniar, murmurar, hablar mal del ausente.

backbiter [-ər, B -ə] *s.* calumniador, murmurador, detractor.

backboard [-ˌbɔrd, B -ˌbɔd] *s.* espaldar, tabla de respaldo o refuerzo.

backbone [-ˈboʊn] *s.* 1. espina dorsal, columna vertebral, espinazo. 2. (fig.) firmeza moral, determinación. 3. lomo (de un libro).

back-break [-ˌbreɪk] *s.* (min.) fractura fuera de la línea de barrenos.

backbreaking [-ɪŋ] *a.* agobiador, agotador.

backcloth [-ˌklɔθ] *s.* (teat.) telón de fondo.

back court, (dep.) parte posterior de una cancha de juego.

backcross [ˈbækˌkrɔs] *v.t.* cruzar (un híbrido de primera generación) con uno de sus padres.

back door, puerta posterior, puerta excusada, puerta falsa.

backdoor [-ˌdɔr, B -ˈdɔ] *a.* (fig.) clandestino, secreto; **b. lover,** amante secreto.

backdown [-ˌdaʊn] *s.* (fam.) retractación, palinodia, cesión. [ˌbækˈdaʊn] *v.t.* retractarse.

backdrop [-ˌdrɑp, B -ˌdrɔp] *s.* 1. (teat.) telón de fondo. 2. (fig.) fondo, último término, lontananza.

backer [ˈbækər, B -ə] *s.* 1. favorecedor, partidario. 2. patrocinador, financiador. 3. apostador.

backfall [-ˌfɔl] *s.* caída de espaldas.

backfield [-ˌfild] *s.* (fútbol) 1. terreno detrás de la línea delantera. 2. defensas, zagueros.

backfire [-ˌfaɪr, B -ˌfaɪə] *s.* 1. contracandela (quema que se hace para evitar que se extienda un incendio). 2. medida o acción defensiva. 3. (aut.) petardeo. —*v.i.* 1. producir una contracandela. 2. petardear. 3. (fig.) salir el tiro por la culata.

back-formation [-fɔrˌmeɪʃən, B -fɔˌ-] *s.* (gram.) formación regresiva.

backgammon [ˈbækˌgæmən] *s.* juego de chaquete; **b. board,** tablas reales.

background [ˈbækˌgraʊnd] *s.* 1. fondo (de un cuadro o vista), trasfondo; lontananza. 2. medio, ambiente; acompañamiento. 3. información básica, datos esenciales, fundamento. 4. antecedentes; experiencia, conocimientos (de una persona). 5. (fig.) segundo término, segundo plano; oscuridad. 6. (rad.) ruido de fondo.

background music, (teat., rad., t.v.) música de fondo.

backhand [-ˌhænd] *s.* 1. (dep.) revés. 2. escritura inclinada a la izquierda. —*a.* (dep.) de revés, dado con el revés de la mano.

backhanded [-əd] *a.* 1. (hecho o dado) con el revés de la mano. 2. inclinado a la izquierda (escritura). 3. indirecto, tortuoso, ambiguo.

backhoe [-ˌhoʊ] *s.* retroexcavadora.

backhouse [-ˌhaʊs] *s.* excusado, letrina o retrete (al fondo de la casa o en el traspatio).

backing [ˈbækɪŋ] *s.* 1. ayuda, respaldo, garantía. 2. refuerzo, forro, respaldar.

backlash [-ˌlæʃ] *s.* 1. retroceso, resaca (de las olas). 2. (fig.) reacción violenta. 3. (mec.) contragolpe, marcha muerta, culateo, punto muerto; juego entre dientes (engranaje). 4. (elec.) corriente inversa de rejilla.

backless [-ləs] *a.* sin espalda.

back-light [-ˌlaɪt] *s.* iluminación de fondo. —*v.t.* iluminar desde el fondo.

back-lighted [-ˌlaɪtəd] *a.* (foto.) a contraluz.

backlog [-ˌlɔg, -ˌlɑg, B -ˌlɔg] *s.* 1. acumulación (de pedidos, trabajo, etc.); reserva. 2. leño trasero de soporte (en una hoguera o chimenea). —*v.t., v.i.* acumular(se) (pedidos o reservas); amontonar(se).

back matter, apéndice, glosario, índice (al final de un libro).

back number, 1. número atrasado (de una publicación). 2. (fam.) cosa pasada de moda, persona de costumbres anticuadas.

back-packing [-ˌpækɪŋ] *s.* (min.) relleno, acuñamiento, calzamiento (de socavones, túneles, etc).

back pay, salario o sueldo atrasado.

backpedal [bækˌpɛdəl] *v.i.* pedalear hacia atrás.

backpiece [-ˌpis] **backplate** [-ˌpleɪt] *s.* (arm.) espaldarón (armadura que protege la espalda).

back porch, terraza posterior de la casa.

back rent, alquiler vencido o atrasado.

backrest [-ˌrɛst] *s.* espaldar, respaldo (de un asiento).

backroad [-ˌroʊd] *s.* camino vecinal, posterior al principal o lejos de la carretera que comunica una comarca.

backsaw [-ˌsɔ] *s.* sierra de trasdós, sierra de lomo.

backscatter [-ˌskætər, B -ə] **backscattering** [-ərɪŋ] *s.* (fís.) retrodispersión.

back seat, asiento posterior o trasero (de un vehículo); **take a b.s.,** ocupar una posición inferior o secundaria.

backset [-ˌsɛt] *s.* contratiempo, revés; contracorriente.

backshop [-ˌʃɑp, B -ˌʃɔp] *s.* 1. trastienda. 2. pequeña tiendecita alejada del centro de una población.

backside [ˈbækˈsaɪd] *s.* 1. parte posterior. 2. (fam.) trasero, nalgas, culo.

back sight, alza, retrovisual (de la mira de armas de fuego).

backslap [-ˌslæp] *v.t.* (fig.) tratar con excesiva buena voluntad. —*v.i.* mostrar excesiva cordialidad o compañerismo.

backslapper [-ər, B -ə] *s.* (fig.) persona excesivamente efusiva o cordial.

backslapping [-ɪŋ] *s.* espaldarazos, palmaditas en la espalda; (fig.) muestra de excesiva efusividad.

backslide [-ˌslaɪd] *v.i.* recaer, reincidir; volverse negligente, descuidar(se), resbalar; (fig.) descarriarse, volver a errar o pecar.

backspacer [-ˌspeɪsər, B -ə] *s.* tecla de retroceso (en máquina de escribir).

backspin [-ˌspɪn] *s.* rotación hacia atrás, efecto de retroceso (de la bola de billar, pelota de golf o tenis, etc.).

backstage [ˈbækˈsteɪdʒ] *a.* 1. (teat.) de las bambalinas, los camerinos o camarines. 2. (fig.) privado, reservado, confidencial. —*adv.* (teat.) entre bastidores, detrás del escenario, en los camerinos. —*s.* (teat.) bambalinas; camerinos.

back stairs, escalera de servicio.

backstairs [-ˌstɛrz, B -ˈstɛəz] **backstair** [-ˌstɛr, B -ˈstɛə] *a.* (fig.) secreto, clandestino, solapado.

backstay [-ˌsteɪ] *s.* 1. (mar.) amarre; burda. 2. soporte, refuerzo posterior.

backstitch [-ˌstɪtʃ] (cost.) *s.* pespunte, punto atrás. —*v.t., v.i.* pespuntar, pespuntear.

backstop [-ˌstɑp, B -ˌstɔp] *s.* 1. (dep.) red o valla para detener la pelota. 2. (béisbol) receptor, zaguero. 3. tope de retención.

backstrap [-ˌstræp] *s.* lomera (de la guarnición de caballerías).

back street, calle posterior; pequeña arteria urbana poco transitada.

backstretch [-ˌstrɛtʃ] *s.* pista opuesta a la recta final (en carreras de caballos).

backstroke [ˈbækˌstroʊk] *s.* 1. brazada de espaldas (en natación). 2. (golpe de) revés (en tenis). 3. (mot.) carrera de retroceso. 4. golpe devuelto.

backswept [-ˌswɛpt] *a.* inclinado hacia atrás; (aer.) en flecha (alas).

backsword [-ˌsɔrd, B -ˌsɔd] *s.* 1. sable. 2. alfanje.

back talk, réplica insolente, respuesta insolente, respuesta impertinente.

back to back, consecutivo.

backtrack [-ˌtræk] *v.i.* 1. desandar, retroceder. 2. retirarse, abandonar una posición o disputa.

backup [-ˌʌp] *s.* 1. soporte, apoyo. 2. acumulación de trabajo atrasado. 3. substituto.

backward [ˈbækwərd, B -wəd] *adv.* hacia atrás; en orden o dirección contraria; al revés; decayendo, empeorándose; **to know (something) b.,** saber al dedillo (algo); **to move b.,** retroceder; cejar, desistir; **to read b.,** leer al revés, leer de la derecha a la izquierda. —*a.* 1. (dirigido) hacia atrás, ej., *a b. glance,* una mirada dirigida hacia atrás; (fig.) una mirada al pasado; **b. motion,** retroceso, movimiento hacia atrás. 2. tardo, retardado, ej., *a b. child,* un niño retardado. 3. atrasado, subdesarrollado, ej., *a b. country,* un país subdesarrollado.

backwardness [-nəs] *s.* 1. estado retardado, falta de desarrollo, atraso. 2. torpeza.

backwards [ˈbækwərdz, B -wərd] *adv. var. de* **backward.**

backwash [-ˌwɔʃ, -ˌwɑʃ, B -ˌwɔʃ] *s.* 1. contracorriente, resaca. 2. (fig.) consecuencias.

backwater [-ˌwɔtər, -ˌwɑt-, B -ˌwɔtə] *s.* 1. rebalsa, agua de rechazo, agua estancada (a causa de una contracorriente, marea o represa). 2. (fig.) lugar apartado o atrasado, rincón tranquilo.

backwoods [ˈbækˈwʊdz, -ˌwʊdz, B -ˈwʊdz] *s. pl.* (*sing. o pl. en const.*) 1. región remota y silvestre. 2. (fig.) lugar poco desarrollado. —*a.* poco refinado, tosco, rústico.

backwoodsman [-mən] *s.* montañés, persona que vive en el monte o en región remota.
backyard ['bæk'jɑrd, B -'jɑd] *s.* patio posterior, corral; **in one's own b.,** en las propias puertas de uno.
bacon ['beɪkən] *s.* tocino, tocineta; **to bring home the b.,** (fam.) traer el sustento a la casa o la familia.
Baconian [beɪ'koʊnɪən] *a.* baconiano, baconista (filosofía, pensamiento, etc. relativos a Francis Bacon). —*s.* baconista.
Baconianism [-ˌɪzəm] *s.* baconismo.
bacteremia [ˌbæktə'rimɪə] *s.* (med.) bacteremia.
bacterial [-ɪəl] *a.* bactérico, bacteriano.
bactericidal [bækˌtɪrə'saɪdəl, B -ˌtɪərɪ-] *a.* bactericida.
bactericide [-'tɪrəˌsaɪd, B -'tɪərɪ-] *s.* (suero) bactericida.
bacterin ['bæktərən] *s.* (med.) bacterina.
bacteriologic [bækˌtɪrɪə'lɑdʒɪk, B -ˌtɪərɪə-'lɔdʒ-] **bacteriological** [-əl] *a.* bacteriológico.
bacteriologist [-ɪ'ɑlədʒəst, B -'ɔl-] *s.* bacteriólogo.
bacteriology [-dʒɪ] *s.* bacteriología.
bacteriolysis [-'ɑləsɪs, B -'ɔl-] *s.* bacteriólisis (descomposición de las bacterias).
bacteriophage [-'tɪrɪəˌfeɪdʒ, B -'tɪərɪə-] *s.* bacteriofago (agente destructor de las bacterias).
bacterioscopy [-ˌtɪrɪ'ɑskəpɪ, B -ˌtɪərɪ'ɔs-] *s.* bacterioscopía.
bacteriostasis [-ɪə'steɪsəs] *s.* bacteriostasis.
bacteriostatic [-'stætɪk] *a.* bacteriostático.
bacterium [bæk'tɪrɪəm, B -'tɪər-] *s.* (*pl.* BACTERIA [-ɪə]) bacteria, microbio.
bacterize ['bæktəˌraɪz] *v.t.* (med.) bacterizar, inocular con bacterias.
Bactrian ['bæktrɪən] *a., s.* bactriano, natural de la Bactriana, antiguo país del Asia.
baculiform ['bækjələˌfɔrm, bæ'kjulə-, B -ˌfɔm] *a.* baculiforme, en forma de bastón.
bad [bæd] *a.* (WORSE [wɜrs, B wɜs]; WORST [wɜrst, B wɜst]) 1. malo, inferior, deficiente (calidad, condición, libro, trabajo, etc.). 2. malo, desfavorable (impresión, renombre, etc.). 3. descompuesto (comida, carne, fruta, etc.). 4. malo, depravado (personal, libro, etc.). 5. impropio (palabra, expresión, etc.). 6. malo, desagradable (sabor, olor, etc.). 7. malo, abatido, indispuesto, enfermo. 8. malo, dañino, nocivo (clima, etc.). 9. intenso, severo (frío, invierno, resfrío, etc.). 10. grave, serio, desastroso (accidente, incendio, error, etc.). 11. malo, incorrecto, erróneo, equivocado (ortografía, suposición, etc.). 12. falso (moneda). 13. **a b. one,** (fam.) mal tipo, mal sujeto; **from b. to worse,** de mal en peor; **in a b. sense,** en mal sentido, en un sentido desfavorable o adverso; **to be b. for,** ser malo para, hacer daño a; **to go b.,** echarse a perder; descomponerse; **to look b.,** tener mala cara; **(that's) too b.!** ¡(es) una lástima! —*adv.* mal. —*s.* mal, desgracia; **to take the b. with the good,** aceptar lo bueno y lo malo.
bad blood, mala sangre, animosidad, encono.
bad check, cheque sin fondos.
bad company o **bad friends,** malos lados.
bad debt, (com.) deuda irrecuperable; **b. debts,** deudas incobrables.
badderlocks ['bædərˌlɑks, B -əˌlɔks] *s.* (bot.) especie de alga marina comestible.
bade [bæd, beɪd] *pret. de* **bid.**
bad egg, (fam.) mal sujeto, mal tipo.
bad form, mal gusto; malacrianza, malos modales.
badge [bædʒ] *s.* distintivo, insignia, divisa, placa; (fig.) señal, símbolo. —*v.t.* otorgar una insignia o distintivo.
badger ['bædʒər, B -ə] *s.* 1. (zool.) tejón. 2. **B.,** (fam. E.U.) natural de Wisconsin. —*v.t.* fastidiar, molestar, importunar.
badinage [ˌbædən'ɑʒ, 'bæd-ɪdʒ, B 'bæd-ɑʒ] *s.* chacota, broma, burla, chiste.
badlands ['bædˌlændz] *s. pl.* tierras de baldío (formaciones sedimentarias de rocas blandas y de escasa vegetación); comarca yerma.
bad-looking [-'lʊkɪŋ] *a.* feo, mal parecido.
bad lot, (fam.) mal sujeto, mal tipo.
badly ['bædlɪ] *adv.* (WORSE; WORST) 1. mal, sin éxito, defectuosamente, incorrectamente. 2. malvadamente, cruelmente; peligrosamente. 3. muchísimo, con urgencia, ej., *to want a thing b.,* desear muchísimo una cosa; *I need it b.,* lo necesito con urgencia.
badminton ['bædˌmɪntən] *s.* badminton, juego del volante.
badness ['bædnəs] *s.* maldad; mala calidad, mal estado.
bad-tempered [-'tɛmpərd, B -pəd] *a.* de mal genio, de carácter irascible.
Baedeker ['beɪdɪkər, B -kə] *s.* guía de viajeros (de la serie publicada por Karl Baedeker o en general).
baffle ['bæfəl] *v.t.* 1. desconcertar, deslumbrar, confundir. 2. frustrar. —*s.* 1. deflector, desviador. 2. (rad.) pantalla acústica.
bafflement [-mənt] *s.* deslumbramiento, confusión, desconcierto.
baffle plate, reductor de velocidad, chicana, placa deflectora.
baffling ['bæflɪŋ] *a.* desconcertante.
bag [bæg] *s.* 1. bolsa; saco, costal; cartera, bolso; maleta, maletín, valija. 2. vejiga; ubre (de la vaca); bolsa (bajo los ojos). 3. caza, total de lo cazado o pescado (por una persona); presa, botín. 4. (jer.) mujer o muchacha desaliñada; vieja fea. 5. talega de medida determinada. 6. **b. and baggage,** (con) todo lo suyo, (con) todos sus efectos (díc. esp. al ser despedido o echado alguien); **b. of bones,** costal de huesos (díc. de persona o animal muy flaco); **the whole b. of tricks,** todos los detalles; todo, todo el conjunto; **to be in the b.,** estar seguro o asegurado (triunfo, premio, etc.); **to be left holding the b.,** cargar con el muerto; **to let the cat out of the b.,** divulgar un secreto (esp. involuntariamente); **to pack up b. and baggage,** liar bártulos, liar el hato. —*v.t.* 1. abultar, hacer un bulto. 2. ensacar, entalegar. 3. capturar; cazar, cobrar (una pieza de caza). 4. coger, apoderarse de; (jer.) hurtar, robar. —*v.i.* hincharse, abultarse.
bagasse [bə'gæs] *s.* bagazo, orujo (de la uva).
bagatelle [ˌbægə'tɛl] *s.* 1. bagatela, fruslería. 2. billar romano. 3. (mús.) composición corta, gen. para piano.
bagel ['beɪgəl] *s.* (cocina) rosca de pan.
bagful ['bægˌfʊl] *s.* (*pl.* BAGFULS O BAGSFUL) contenido de un saco o bolsa; (fig.) gran cantidad (de algo).
baggage ['bægɪdʒ] *s.* 1. equipaje, maletas. 2. (mil.) bagaje, los efectos y tiendas de un ejército.
baggage car, (f.c.) furgón, vagón de equipajes.
baggagemaster [-ˌmæstər, B -ˌmɑstə] *s.* jefe de equipajes.
baggage room, sala o depósito de equipaje.
baggy ['bægɪ] *a.* (BAGGIER; BAGGIEST) abolsado, holgado, flojo, bombacho; **b. trousers,** pantalones abombados por el uso.
Baghdad, Bagdad ['bægˌdæd, bæg'dæd] *s.* Bagdad, capital de Iraq.
bag lady, (jer.) repartidora de un botín o ganancias, cobradora de chantajistas.
bagman ['bægmən] *s.* 1. (G.B) agente, vendedor viajero. 2. (jer.) repartidor de un botín o ganancias (esp. ilícitas); cobrador de chantajistas.
bag net , nasa, red.
bagnio ['bænjoʊ, B 'bɑn-] *s.* (*pl.* BAGNIOS) 1. burdel, lupanar. 2. baño (esp. en Italia y Turquía). 3. (ant.) prisión para esclavos (en el Oriente).
bagpipe ['bægˌpaɪp] *s.* (mús.) gaita.
bagpiper ['ər, B -ə] *s.* gaitero.
B. Agr. *abrev. de* **Bachelor of Agriculture,** Ingeniero Agrónomo.
baguette [bæ'gɛt] *s.* 1. (arq.) astrágalo pequeño, tondino. 2. (joy.) piedra rectangular.
bag woman, (jer.) repartidora de un botín o ganancias, cobradora de chantajistas.
bah [bɑ, bæ, B bɑ] *interj.* ¡bah!
Bahai [bɑ'hɑˌi, -'haɪ, B bə'hiə] *s.* 1. Bahai, religión que se originó en el Irán. 2. creyente del bahaísmo.
Bahaism [-ˌɪzəm] *s.* bahaísmo, behaísmo.
Bahamas [bə'hɑməz -'heɪ-, B -'hɑ-] *s. pl.* (Archipiélago de) las Bahamas, Islas Lucayas.
bail [beɪl] *s.* 1. (der.) fianza, caución. 2. fiador. 3. soporte de toldo en forma de arco, aro; asa, agarradero (de cubo, etc.). 4. sujeta papel (en máquina de escribir). 5. (G.B.) barra de división (entre los compartimientos de un establo). 6. (criquet) una de las estacas que se colocan sobre los palitroques. 7. (ant.) cubo para achicar el agua. 8. **on b.,** bajo fianza; **to admit to b.,** libertar bajo fianza; **to forfeit b.,** perder la fianza (por incumplimiento); **to jump b.,** escapar, fugarse (mientras está uno bajo fianza); **to stand b. for (someone),** salir fiador (de alguien). —*v.t.* 1. dar fianza o caución por (alguien). 2. depositar, consignar. 3. libertar bajo fianza. 4. zunchar con aros o fajas. 5. (mar.) achicar (el agua). 6. **b. out,** dar fianza por, salir fiador de (un detenido); (fam.) sacar de apuros a (alguien); achicar el agua de (un bote, etc.). —*v.i.* 1. achicar agua. 2. **b. out,** saltar en paracaídas (de un avión).
bailee [beɪ'li] *s.* (der.) depositario, comodatario.
bailer ['beɪlər, B -ə] *s.* depositante, fiador.
bailey ['beɪlɪ] *s.* (hist., fort.) 1. muralla y el espacio que ésta encierra. 2. **Old B.,** tribunal de lo criminal en Londres.
bailie ['beɪlɪ] *s.* (pr. dial.) magistrado inferior; (esco.) concejal.
bailiff ['beɪlɪf] *s.* 1.alguacil, corchete. 2. (pr. G.B.) administrador (de una finca, hacienda, etc.).
bailiwick [-ɪˌwɪk] *s.* alguacilazgo; competencia, jurisdicción; **to be in the b. of (someone),** ser de la competencia de (alguien).
bailment [-mənt] *s.* (der.) depósito, entrega (en calidad de depósito o fianza para procurar la libertad de alguien).
bailsman ['beɪlzmən] *s.* (der.) fiador.
bain-marie [ˌbænmə'rɪ] *s.* (fr., cocina) baño de María.
bairn [bɛrn, B bɛən] *s.* (esco.) niño.
bait [beɪt] *s.* 1. cebo, carnada. 2. (fig.) carnada, añagaza. 3. **to take** (o **swallow**) **the b.,** (fig.) tragar el anzuelo. —*v.t.* 1. poner cebo a, ej., *b. the hook* (*o trap*), poner cebo al anzuelo (o a la trampa). 2. azuzar. 3. (fig.) picar, provocar, atormentar.
baize [beɪz] *s.* bayeta; **green b.,** tapete verde que cubre las mesas de juego.
bake [beɪk] *v.t.* cocer, hornear (pan, ladrillos, etc.); asar al horno. —*v.i.* cocerse, asarse, endurecerse. —*s.* cocción al horno, calcinar.
baked beans, judías en salsa de tomate.
baked potatoes, patatas al horno.
Bakelite ['beɪkəˌlaɪt] *s.* (quím.) baquelita.
baker ['beɪkər, B -ə] *s.* 1. panadero, hornero, tahonero. 2. (orn.) hornero. 3. b.'s, panadería. 4. hornilla portátil.

baker's dozen, trece, docena de fraile.
bakery [-ərɪ] *s.* (*pl.* BAKERIES) pandería, tahona; pastelería.
baking dish, funete para el horno.
baking powder, polvo de hornear, levadura química.
baking soda, bicarbonato de sosa.
baklava [ˌbɑkləˈvɑ] *s.* pastel de nueces y miel oriundo del Oriente Medio.
baksheesh, bakshish [ˈbækˌʃɪʃ] *s.* propina, limosna (en los países árabes).
balaenid [bəˈlinəd] *s.* (zool.) cetáceo, balénido.
balalaika [ˌbæləˈlaɪkə] *s.* (mús.) balalaica.
balance [ˈbæləns] *s.* 1. balanza (para pesar). 2. equilibrio. 3. contrapeso. 4. resto, saldo. 5. (com.) balance. 6. (com.) saldo. 7. volante de reloj. 8. **to lose one's b.,** perder el equilibrio, faltarle a uno los pies; **to strike a b.,** lograr un equilibrio razonable. —*v.t.* balancear, poner en equlibrio; equilbrar, ej., *b. the budget,* equilibrar el presupuesto. —*v.i.* 1. equilibrarse. 2. (com.) saldarse.
balanced [-ənst] *a.* 1. equilibrado, mesurado (opinión, mezcla). 2. simétrico, parejo, equilibrado. 3. compensado o balanceado (régimen alimenticio).
balance due, (com.) saldo deudor.
balance in hand, (com.) saldo disponible.
balance of payments, (econ. pol.) balanza de pagos.
balance of power, (pol.) equilibrio de poder (entre las naciones).
balance of trade, (com.) balanza de comercio (entre naciones o entidades).
balancer [ˈbælənsər, B -sə] *s.* 1. equilibrista. 2. (ento.) balancín. 3. fiel de balanza. 4. pesador. 5. (mec.) balancín.
balance sheet, (com.) hoja de balance, balance, balance general.
balance wheel, volante compensador; rueda compensadora; (reloj) volante, rueda catalina.
balas [ˈbæləs] *s.* (min.) balaje, rubí, espinela.
balata [ˈbəˈlɑtə, ˈbælətə] *s.* (bot.) balatá.
balbriggan [bælˈbrɪgən] *s.* género de punto de lana o algodón (empleado para ropa interior, medias, etc.).
balcony [ˈbælkənɪ] *s.* 1. balcón. 2. (teat.) galería.
bald [bɔld] *a.* calvo, pelado, morondo. 2. franco, directo, ej., *b. statement,* declaración franca, sin reserva.
baldachin, baldaquin [ˈbɔldəkən, ˈbæl-, B ˈbɔl-] *s.* 1. (hist.) baldaquín, tela de seda y oro, 2. baldaquín, baldaquino. 3. (arq.) dosel, baldaquín.
bald eagle, 1. (orn.) águila calva. 2. ave heráldica de los Estados Unidos de América.
balderdash [ˈbɔldərˌdæʃ, B -dəˌ-] *s.* disparate, tontería.
baldhead [ˈbɔldˌhɛd] *s.* 1. calvo, calva. 2. (orn.) pato lavanco.
bald-headed [-əd] *a.* calvo.
baldness [-nəs] *s.* calvicie.
baldpate [-ˌpeɪt] *s.* 1. la calva. 2. (orn.) pato lavanco.
baldpated [-əd] *a.* tonsurado, rapado, calvo.
baldric [ˈbɔldrɪk] *s.* tahalí; cinturón donde se cuelga un objeto como la espada, la corneta, la cantimplora.
bald spot, región rala o calva (en la cabellera, en un sembrado, en tejido aterciopelado).
Baldwin [ˈbɔldwən] *s.* 1. variedad de manzana americana. 2. famosa marca de pianos de concierto.
bale [beɪl] *s.* 1. (ant.) mal, desgracia. 2. (poét.) pena, dolor, pesar, miseria.
bale [beɪl] *s.* bala, fardo, atado (de mercancías), ej., *a b. of cotton,* una bala de algodón. —*v.t.* embalar, empaquetar.
Balearic [ˌbælɪˈɛrɪk, B -ˈær-] *a.* baleárico, balearic, balear.
Balearic Islands, islas Baleares, las Baleares.
baleen [bəˈlin] *s.* ballena; lámina córnea en la mandíbula superior de la ballena.
balefire [ˈbeɪlˌfaɪr, B -ˌfaɪə] *s.* 1. hoguera, fogata, fuego de señales. 2. (ant.) pira funeraria.
baleful [-fəl] *a.* malsano, maléfico, pernicioso; ominoso, funesto.
balefully [-ɪ] *adv.* ominosamente, funestamente.
balefulness [-nəs] *s.* maleficencia, influencia malsana.
baler [ˈbeɪlər, B -ə] *s.* embalador, empaquetador.
Balinese [ˌbɑlɪˈniz, bæl-, B ˌbɑ-] *a.* balinés —*s.* (*pl.* BALINESE) balines, natural de Bali.
balk [bɔk] *s.* 1. viga; madero. 2. lomo de tierra. 3. obstáculo, impedimento; desengaño. 4. (dep.) tentativa inconclusa (de saltar, arrojar, etc.). 5. (billar) cuadro; ancla. —*v.t.* 1. impedir, desbaratar; frustrar; desengañar. 2. eludir (tema, tarea, etc.), perder (oportunidad, turno, etc.). 3. (ant.) amontonar, apilar. —*v.i.* 1. detenerse, plantarse, repropiarse (caballo). 2. (con *at*) negarse, resistir, oponerse (a), repudiar.
Balkan [ˈbɔlkən] *a.* balcánico, de los Balcanes.
balkanize [-ˌaɪz] *v.t.* dividir en estados pequeños y hostiles (como los Estados Balcanicos a principios de este siglo).
Balkans [-kənz] *s.* (*pl.*) Balcanes.
balk line, (billar) 1. línea de saque. 2. línea de cuadro (paralela a uno de los lados) 3. carambola al cuadro.
ball [bɔl] *s.* 1. bola, pelota. 2. (juego de) pelota, esp. béisbol. 3. globo; **b. of the eye,** globo del ojo. 4. bala, proyectil. 5. yema (del dedo). 6. (*pl.* vulg.) testículos. 7. **on the b.,** (jer.) alerta, atento; competente, capaz; **to have a b.,** (jer.) divertirse, pasarla bien; **to keep the b. rolling,** hacer su parte; no dejar decaer (conversación, etc.); **to play b. (with),** cumplir su cometido (con), cooperar (con), obrar en armonía (con). —*v.t.* formar una bola de (algo), dar forma de bola a (algo); **to b. up (something),** (fam.) embrollar, confundir (algo); **to be all balled up,** estar hecho un lío; **to b. (someone),** (vulg.) echarse un polvo con (*alguien*).
ball, *s.* baile, sarao; fiesta social.
ballad [ˈbæləd] *s.* 1. balada, trova, romance. 2. (mús.) canción romántica.
ballade [bəˈlɑd, B bæ-] *s.* (poét., mús.) balada.
balladeer [ˌbæləˈdɪr, B -ˈdɪə] *s.* trovador, el que canta baladas; romancero.
ballad monger, coplero, populachero; poetastro.
balladry [ˈbælədədrɪ] *s.* el arte de componer o ejecutar baladas.
ball-and-socket joint [ˌbɔlənˈsɑkət-, B -ˈsɔk-] (mec.) articulación de rótula, articulación esférica; articulación universal.
ballast [ˈbæləst] *s.* 1. (mar.) lastre. 2. lastre, madurez, juicio. 3. (f.c.) balasto. 4. cascajo, grava (en hormigón). 5. **in b.,** en lastre. —*v.t.* 1. lastrar, echar lastre al (navío). 2. balastar, afirmar.
ballasting [-ɪŋ] *s.* 1. balasto, tender el balasto. 2. (mar.) lastre.
ball bearing, cojinete de bolas o de municiones, rodamiento; municionero (Ven.).
ball cock, (mcc.) llave de bola, grifo de bola.
ballerina [ˌbæləˈrinə] *s.* bailarina (de ballet), ballerina.
ballet [ˈbæˌleɪ bæˈleɪ, B ˈbæleɪ, -lɪ] *s.* 1. ballet, baile clásico. 2. (música de) ballet. 3. cuerpo y compañía de ballet.
ballet dancer, bailarín, bailarina (de ballet).
balletomane [bæˈlɛtəˌmeɪn, B ˈbælɪtoʊ-] *s.* aficionado al ballet.
ball float, flotador de bola.
ball game, juego de pelota.
ball governor, (máq.) regulador de bolas.
ball inclinometer, (avia.) inclinómetro de bola.
ballista [bəˈlɪstə] *s.* (*pl.* BALLISTAE [-ˌti]) (arm., hist.) ballesta; balista.
ballistic [bəˈlɪstɪk] *a.* balístico.
ballistic missile, misil balístico.
ballistics [-tɪks] *s.* balística.
ballistic wave, onda balística.
ballistocardiogram [bəˌlɪstoʊˈkɑrdɪəˌgræm, B -ˈkɑd-] *s.* balistocardiograma.
ballistocardiography [-ˌkɑrdɪˈɑgrəfɪ, B -ˌkɑdɪˈɔg-] *s.* balistocardiografía.
ball of fire, (fam.) persona vivaz y diligente.
ballonet [ˌbæləˈneɪ, -ˈnɛt] *s.* (aer.) globo compensador (en un dirigible).
balloon [bəˈlun] *s.* 1. globo, globo aerostático. 2. (quím.) balón. —*v.t.* inflar, distender. —*v.i.* inflarse como un globo; (fig.) extenderse o aumentarse rápidamente.
balloon barrage, barrera de globos, barrera antiaérea de globos cautivos.
ballooning [-ɪŋ] *s.* aerostación, aterrizaje brusco.
balloonist [-əst] *s.* aeronauta (que maneja o dirige un globo), aérostata.
balloon sail, (mar.) foque balón.
balloon tire, neumático balón, neumático de baja presión.
balloon vine, (bot.) farolillo.
ballot [ˈbælət] *s.* 1. balota, bolilla para votar. 2. cédula electoral, boleta, papeleta para votar. 3. votación. 4. total de votos. 5. derecho de votar, sufragio. 6. voto. —*v.i.* votar, balotar, decidir por voto.
ballotade [ˌbæləˈteɪd] *s.* (equit.) balotada.
ballot box, urna electoral.
balloter [ˈbælətər, B -ə] *s.* elector, votante.
ballottement [bəˈlɑtmənt, B -ˈlɔt-] *s.* (med.) peloteo (uterino o renal).
ballpark [ˈbɔlpark] *s.* estadio de beísbol, parque de beísbol; **in the b.,** (fig.) al alcance.
ballpark estimate, cálculo aproximado.
ballpark figure, cifra aproximada.
ballplayer [ˈbɔlˌpleɪər, B -ə] *s.* pelotero, jugador de pelota, beisbolista.
ball-point pen [-ˌpɔɪnt-] bolígrafo, pluma esferográfica; birome (Arg.); punto bola (Bol.); esfero (Col.).
ballroom [ˈbɔlˌrum, -ˌrʊm] *s.* salón de baile.
ballroom dancing, baile de salón.
ball valve, válvula de bola.
ballyhoo [ˈbælɪˌhu] *s.* bombo, publicidad con bombo y platillos; alharaca. —*v.t.* dar exagerada publicidad a, anunciar con bombo.
ballyrag [ˈbælɪˌræg] *var. de* **bullyrag.**
balm [bɑm] *s.* 1. bálsamo. 2. (bot.) melisa, cidronela, toronjil. 3. (fig.) bálsamo, consuelo.
balminess [ˈbɑmɪnəs] *s.* 1. fragancia, aroma. 2. suavidad. 3. (jer.) locura.
balm of Gilead, (bot.) abeto balsámico; bálsamo de Judea o de la Meca.
balmoral [bælˈmɔrəl, -ˈmɑr-, B -ˈmɔr-] *s.* 1. falda de lana (prendida y recogida que deja ver la enagua). 2. bota con cintas. 3. gorro escocés redondo y plano.
balmy [ˈbɑmɪ] *a.* 1. balsámico. 2. suave, suavizante, refrescante. 3. aromático, fragante. 4. (jer.) loco, mentecato.
balneology [ˌbælnɪˈɑlədʒɪ, B -ˈɔl-] *s.* (med.) balneología.

balneotherapy [-nɪə'θɛrəpɪ] *s.* balneoterapia.
baloney [bə'lounɪ] *s.* 1. (fam.) salchicha de Bolonia. 2. (jer.) (*nonsense*) chorradas, disparates; (*lies*) cuentos de camino.
balsa ['bɔlsə] *s.* 1. (bot.) balsa. 2. balsa, armadía.
balsam ['bɔlsəm] *s.* 1. bálsamo, ungüento. 2. (bot.) balsamina. 3. (fig.) bálsamo, consuelo, lenitivo.
balsam apple, (bot.) momórdiga, balsamina.
balsam fir, (bot.) abeto balsámico.
balsamic [bɔl'sæmɪk] *a.* balsámico.
balsam of Peru, bálsamo del Perú.
balsam poplar, (bot.) álamo balsámico.
Balt [bɔlt] *a., s.* báltico, balto.
Baltic ['bɔltɪk] *a.* báltico.
Baltic Sea, mar Báltico.
Baltic States, Países Bálticos.
baltimore oriole ['bɔltəˌmɔr-] (orn.) oropéndola norteamericana.
Baluchi [bə'lutʃɪ] *s.* 1. natural del Beluchistán, balucho. 2. beluqui, idioma de los baluches.
baluster ['bæləstər, B -stə] *s.* (arq.) balaustre.
balustrade [-ˌstreɪd, B ˌbælə'streɪd] *s.* balaustrada, barandilla, baranda.
bambino [bæm'binou, bɑm-] *s.* niño.
bamboo [bæm'bu] *s.* (bot.) bambú.
Bamboo Curtain, (pol.) cortina de bambú, (fig.) la China.
bamboozle [bæm'buzəl] *v.t.* (fam.) soflamar, engañar, burlar, embaucar.
bamboozler [-'buzlər, B -lə] *s.* embaucador, timador.
ban [bæn] *v.t.* proscribir, prohibir. —*s.* 1. prohibición, proscripción (por la ley o la autoridad). 2. desaprobación, execración pública. 3. (relig.) excomunión, interdicto; maldición. 4. (hist.) bando, proclamación, llamado a las armas (dirigido a los vasallos).
banal [bə'nɑl, -'næl, 'beɪnəl, B bə'nɑl] *a.* banal, trivial, insignificante, trillado.
banality [bə'nælətɪ] *s.* banalidad, trivialidad.
banana [bə'nænə, B -'nɑnə] *s.* (bot.) plátano, banano, guineo; **to go bananas,** (jer.) chiflarse.
banana fish, (ict.) macabí, lisa francesa.
banana oil, (quím.) acetato de alcohol amílico.
banana peel, cáscara de plátano, piel de plátano.
banana plug, (elec.) clavija tipo banana.
banana republic, (fig., pol.) república bananera.
banana split, (E.U.) postre hecho con plátano, helado, sirope y nueces picadas.
banana tree, plátano, banano.
banat, banate [bə'nɑt, 'bɑnˌɑt] *s.* territorio gobernado por el Ban (antiguo título dado a un gobernador regional en ciertos países de Europa).
band [bænd] *s.* 1. banda, faja, cinta. 2. lista, franja. 3. (fig.) traba, vínculo. 4. aro, zuncho, fleje; abrazadera (del fusil); anillo (de cigarro); liga de goma. 5. (enc.) piolín; nervio. 6. haz (de luz, etc.); (rad.) banda (de frecuencias); (gramófono) banda (de grabación). —*v.t.* 1. atar, fajar, vendar. 2. franjar, franjear, marcar o decorar con bandas.
band, *s.* 1. banda (de guerrilleros, asaltantes, ladrones); cuadrilla, partida. 2. (mús.) banda (esp. militar), charanga; orquesta, orquestina (de jazz, de baile). —*v.i.* (gen. con *together*) agruparse, apiñarse; unirse, asociarse, confederarse. —*v.t.* agrupar, apiñar; asociar, reunir, confederar.
bandage ['bændɪdʒ] *s.* vendaje, venda. —*v.t.* vendar, fajar.
Band-Aid ['bændˌeɪd] *s.* (marca de fábrica) tirita.
bandanna, bandana [bæn'dænə, B -'dɑnə, -'dænə] *s.* pañuelo o bufanda grande de colores.
bandbox ['bændˌbɑks, B -'bɔks] *s.* sombrerera, caja de sombreros.
band break, freno de cinta.
band conveyor, transportador de banda sin fin.
bandeau [bæn'dou, B 'bændou] *s.* (*pl.* BANDEAUX [-'douz, B 'bændouz]) 1. cinta para sujetar el pelo. 2. sostén, portasenos.
banderole, banderol ['bændəˌroul] *s.* banderola, pendón, gallardete.
bandit ['bændət] *s.* bandido, bandolero, proscrito.
banditry [-ətrɪ] *s.* bandolerismo, bandidaje.
band leader, director de una orquesta popular, banda, etc.
bandmaster ['bændˌmæstər, B -ˌmɑstə] *s.* (mús.) director de una banda, esp. de circo o militar.
bandog ['bænˌdɔg] *s.* perro de guarda (que se tiene encadenado).
bandoleer, bandolier [ˌbændə'lɪr, B -'lɪə] *s.* bandolera, cartuchera, canana.
bandoline ['bændəˌlin] *s.* bandolina, fijador para el pelo.
bandonion [bæn'dounɪən] *s.* (mús.) bandoneón.
bandore ['bænˌdɔr, B -ˌdɔ] *s.* (mús.) bandurria.
band pass filter, (rad.) filtro de banda.
band saw, sierra sinfín, sierra cinta, aserradora de banda, sierra cordón.
band shell, (mús.) plataforma con concha acústica (para orquesta).
bandsman ['bændzmən, 'bænz-] *s.* miembro de una banda u orquesta.
band spread, (rad.) ensanche de banda.
bandstand ['bændˌstænd] *s.* quiosco de música.
bandwagon [-ˌwægən] *s.* 1. carro de la banda, carro de la música (en un desfile, esp. de un circo). 2. (fig., fam.) carro (imaginario) de caudillos políticos; causa triunfante. 3. **to get on the b.,** unirse a los ganadores, hacer suya una causa triunfante.
bandwidth ['bændˌwɪdθ, -ˌwɪtθ] *s.* (rad.) anchura de banda, ancho de faja.
bandy ['bændɪ] *v.t.* intercambiar, pasar o golpear de un lado a otro; **to have one's name bandied about,** tener uno su nombre en boca de todos. —*a.* curvado; **b.-legged,** patizambo, estevado.
bane [beɪn] *s.* 1. (*ú. en palabras compuestas*) veneno, ponzoña, ej., *ratsbane,* veneno para ratas. 2. (fig.) (causa de) ruina o aflicción, ej., *drink was his b.,* la bebida fue la causa de su ruina.
baneberry ['beɪnˌbɛrɪ] *s.* (bot.) hierba de San Cristóbal.
baneful [-fəl] *a.* venenoso, mortífero; funesto.
banewort [-ˌwɜrt, B -ˌwɜt] *s.* (bot.) 1. belladona. 2. (G.B.) flámula. 3. planta venenosa.
bang [bæŋ] *v.t.* 1. chocar, golpear. 2. golpear ruidosamente, golpear con violencia. 3. cerrar de golpe. 4. (vulg.) violar sexualmente. 5. recortar (el pelo) en flequillo. 6. **b. the door,** dar un portazo; **b. up,** estropear, arruinar. —*v.i.* 1. (pr. con *against*) chocar (contra). 2. detonar, dar estampido. 3. precipitarse. 4. **b. away,** seguir disparando esporádicamente, tirar a voluntad. —*s.* 1. detonación, estampido. 2. golpe resonante, impacto fuerte, puñetazo. 3. energía, vigor, brío. 4. (*pl.*) cerquillo, flequillo (de pelo). 5. **to get a b. out of,** (jer.) gozar con (algo). —*interj.* ¡zas! —*adv.* (fam.) precisamente, directamente; **b. in the middle of (the street),** en plena (calle, etc.); **to go b.,** detonar, explotar.
bang, *var. de* **bhang.**
Bangkok ['bæŋˌkɑk, bæŋ'kɑk, B bæŋ'kɔk] *s.* 1. Bangkok, capital de Tailandia. 2. sombrero de paja de Bangkok.
Bangladesh [ˌbæŋglə'dɛʃ] *s.* la nación bengalí, Bangladesh.
bangle ['bæŋgəl] *s.* ajorca, esclava, brazalete sin cierre.
Bang's disease [bæŋz-] (vet.) enfermedad de Bang.
bangtail ['bæŋˌteɪl] *s.* 1. (jer.) caballo de carrera. 2. caballo salvaje, caballo cimarrón (Am.).
banish ['bænɪʃ] *v.t.* 1. desterrar, deportar, expulsar, proscribir. 2. disipar (sospechas, temores, etc.).
banishment [-mənt] *s.* deportación, destierro, proscripción.
banister ['bænəstər, B -stə] *s.* 1. balaustre. 2. (*gen. pl.*) balaustrada, baranda. 3. pasamano, barandal.
banjo ['bænˌdʒou] *s.* (mús.) banjo.
banjoist [-əst] *s.* músico que toca el banjo.
bank [bæŋk] *s.* 1. banco, establecimiento de crédito. 2. banca (en juegos de azar), p. ext. banquero. 3. depósito de reservas (de algo), banco. 4. **to break the b.,** hacer saltar la banca (en juegos de azar). —*v.i.* 1. ser banquero. 2. (gen. con *in*) tener depósitos o cuenta (en un banco). 3. tener la banca (en juegos de azar). 4. **b. on** (o **upon**), contar con, confiar mucho en (algo). —*v.t.* depositar (dinero en un banco).
bank [bæŋk] *s.* 1. ribera, margen, orilla (de un río, lago, etc.). 2. banco, bajo, bajío (en el mar). 3. montículo, caballón (de tierra); terraplén, bancal. 4. montón (de nubes); masa (de niebla). 5. talud, escarpa. 6. peralto (de una pista, vía férrea, etc.); inclinación lateral, ladeo (de un avión en vuelo). 7. (min.) boca del pozo. 8. (billar) banda (de la mesa). 9. **on the banks of,** a orillas de. —*v.t.* 1. amontonar, apilar. 2. peraltar (una pista, vía, etc.); inclinar, ladear (un avión). 3. (t. con *up*) cubrir, amontonar. 4. formar hileras de, poner en filas. 5. (billar) jugar (la bola) sobre la banda. —*v.i.* 1. (ú. gen. con *up*) amontonarse, apilarse. 2. inclinarse, ladearse (pista, avión).
bank, *s.* 1. banco (en galeras). 2. fila, hilera (de objetos), ej., *b. of oars,* hilera de remos (en una galera). 3. subtítulo (en periódico). 4. (elec.) grupo, fila (de transformadores), batería (de lámparas). 5. (avia.) inclinación transversal, lateral. 6. **b. of keys,** teclado (de un órgano, máquina de escribir).
bankable ['bæŋkəbəl] *a.* que puede ser depositado en un banco; descontable, negociable.
bank acceptance, (com.) giro contra un banco que lo acepta.
bank account, cuenta bancaria, cuenta corriente.
bank-and-turn indicator, (avia.) inclinómetro, indicador de virajes.
bankbook [-ˌbʊk] *s.* libreta de banco (del depositante).
bank discount, descuento bancario.
bank draft, (com.) letra bancaria, giro de un banco contra otro.
banker ['bæŋkər, B -kə] *s.* 1. banquero, propietario o gerente de un banco. 2. banquero, el que tiene la banca (en un juego). 3. banca, juego de azar.
bank holiday, día feriado para el ramo bancario.
banking [-kɪŋ] *s.* 1. banca, comercio del banco o de los banqueros. 2. (avia.) inclinación lateral, escoramiento.
banking house, institución bancaria, casa bancaria.
bank note, billete bancario, billete de banco.
bank of issue, banco emisor, banco de emisión.
bank paper, efectos o valores bancarios, papel moneda.
bank rate, tasa de descuento bancario, tipo bancario.

bankroll ['bæŋkˌroʊl] *s.* (fig.) fondos, caudal. —*v.t.* financiar, suscribir.
bankrupt ['bæŋkrʌpt, -krəpt] *s.* quebrado, insolvente. —*v.t.* llevar a la quiebra, empobrecer, arruinar. —*a.* 1. quebrado, insolvente. 2. de quiebras (ley, etc.). 3. fracasado, arruinado (carrera, vida, político, etc.). 4. **to go b.,** declararse en quiebra.
bankruptcy [-sɪ, -krəpsɪ] *s.* 1. bancarrota, insolvencia, quiebra. 2. (fig.) quiebra, fracaso total, descrédito.
bankruptcy proceedings, concurso de acreedores, pleito de acreedores.
bank statement, estado de cuentas.
bank vault, bóveda de seguridad (en un banco).
banner ['bænər, B -ə] *s.* bandera, pendón, estandarte; **b. head-line** o **b. head,** titular a toda plana, titular a toda página (de un periódico). —*a.* excelente, sobresaliente.
bannered [-ərd, B -əd] *a.* abanderado, embanderado.
banneret ['bænərət, ˌbænə'rɛt] *s.* 1. bandereta, banderín. 2. caballero abanderado.
bannerol ['bænəˌroʊl] *var. de* **banderole.**
bannock ['bænək] *s.* 1. (esco., dial.) (especie de) pan ázimo. 2. (Nueva Ingl.) pan de maíz, tortilla de maíz.
banns, bans [bænz] *s. pl.* amonestaciones, bandos; **to publish** (o **to put up**) **the b.,** correr las amonestaciones; **to forbid the b.,** (fig., hum.) prohibir las bodas, no dar consentimiento al matrimonio.
banquet ['bæŋkwət, 'bæn-, B 'bæŋ-] *s.* banquete. —*v.t., v.i.* banquetear, invitar o ser invitado a banquetes.
banquette [bæŋ'kɛt] *s.* 1. (fort.) banqueta. 2. acera, vereda (Am.). 3. asiento tapizado.
banshee ['bænˌʃi, B bæn'ʃi] *s.* (Irl., Esco.) fantasma, espíritu (cuyos gemidos presagian muerte en una casa).
bantam ['bæntəm] *s.* 1. gallo Bantam (enano y pendenciero). 2. persona pequeña y pendenciera. —*a.* 1. diminuto, pequeño. 2. pendenciero.
bantamweight [-ˌweɪt] *s.* (boxeo) peso gallo.
banter ['bæntər, B -ə] *v.t.* burlarse de, tomar el pelo a. —*v.i.* hablar en forma humorística o burlona, burlar, chancear. —*s.* burla, chanza.
banterer [-ərər, B -ərə] *s.* bromista.
ban-the-bomb ['bænðə'bɑm, B -'bɔm] *a.* contra la bomba atómica, en pro de la proscripción de la bomba atómica, por el desarme nuclear (movimiento, manifestación, etc.).
bantling ['bæntlɪŋ] *s.* chicuelo, rapaz.
Bantu ['bænˌtu, 'bɑn-] *a., s.,* bantú; perteneciente a una tribu africana.
banyan, banian ['bænjən] *s.* 1. baniano, comerciante hindú. 2. túnica o casaca corta (usadas en la India). 3. (bot.) higuera de Bengala, baniano.
banyan day, (mar.) día en que no se sirve carne.
banyan hospital, hospital para animales.
banzai ['bɑn'zaɪ] *s.* vítor japonés.
banzai attack, (mil.) ataque suicida (practicado por los soldados japoneses).
baobab ['baʊˌbæb, B 'beɪoʊ-] *s.* (bot.) baobab.
baptism ['bæpˌtɪzəm] *s.* 1. (relig.) bautismo, bautizo. 2. (fig.) bautismo, iniciación.
baptismal [bæp'tɪzməl] *a.* bautismal, de bautismo.
baptism of fire, bautismo de fuego, primer combate.
baptist ['bæptəst] *s., a.* (relig.) bautista, baptista.
baptistery ['bæptəstrɪ, B -tɪstərɪ] **baptistry** [-təstrɪ] *s.* bautisterio, baptisterio; pila bautismal.
baptize [bæp'taɪz, 'bæpˌtaɪz, B bæp'taɪz] *v.t.* 1. bautizar. 2. (fig.) bautizar, apodar. 3. (fig.) purificar, elevar. 4. (fig.) iniciar. —*v.i.* administrar el sacramento del bautismo.
bar [bɑr, B bɑ] *s.* 1. barra. 2. valla, barrera; (fig.) impedimento, obstáculo. 3. barra, banco, bajío (de arena, etc.). 4. barra, barandilla (que separa a los jueces del público en un tribunal); jurado, tribunal. 5. (*pl.*) rejas, ej., *behind bars,* entre rejas. 6. (con *the*) abogacía; cuerpo de abogados. 7. bar, cantina; mostrador (en el bar); **to tend b.,** despachar bebidas en el bar. 8. franja, banda, cinta (de luz, color, etc.). 9. (mil.) galón. 10. (mús.) barra (entre compases); compás. 11. (mec.) palanca, alzaprima; tranca. 12. (her.) barra. 13. (metal.) barra, lingote. 14. to **be called** (o **admitted**) **to the b.,** recibirse de abogado; **to put behind bars,** poner entre rejas, encarcelar. —*v.t.* (*pret., p.p.* BARRED; *p.pr.* BARRING) 1. trancar, atrancar (puerta, ventana, etc.). 2. enrejar (ventana). 3. obstruir, impedir (paso, avance, etc.). 4. prohibir. 5. desechar, no tomar en cuenta. 6. rayar, gayar. 7. (mús.) dividir con barras (pentagrama). 8. **b. from,** excluir de; prevenir, impedir que; **b. in,** encerrar en, confinar en; **b. out,** cerrar la puerta a, excluir.
bar, *prep.* excepto, salvo; **b. none,** sin excepción.
bar, (quím.) bario, medida internacional de presión.
Barabbas [bə'ræbəs] *s.* (bíbl.) Barrabás.
barb [bɑrb, B bɑb] *s.* 1. púa; lengüeta (de anzuelo, flecha, etc.). 2. barbilla (del pez). 3. barba (de la pluma). 4. (fig.) observación aguda o irónica. 5. (zool.) caballo berberisco; paloma berberisca. —*v.t.* armar con lenguetas o púas.
Barbados [bɑr'beɪdˌoʊz, B bɑ'-] *s.* isla de Barbados.
barbarian [bɑr'bɛrɪən, B bɑ'bɛər-] *s.* bárbaro. —*a.* bárbaro, barbárico.
barbaric [bɑr'bærɪk, B bɑ'-] *a.* barbárico, bárbaro.
barbarism ['bɑrbəˌrɪzəm, B 'bɑb-] *s.* 1. barbaridad, inhumanidad. 2. (gram.) barbarismo.
barbarity [bɑr'bærətɪ, B bɑ'-] *s.* 1. barbarie, barbarismo. 2. barbaridad, atrocidad.
barbarize ['bɑrbəˌraɪz, B 'bɑb-] *v.t., v.i.* barbarizar; corromper.
Barbarossa [ˌbɑrbə'rɑsə, -'roʊsə, B -'rɔsə] *s.* Barbarroja.
barbarous ['bɑrbərəs, B 'bɑb-] *a.* 1. bárbaro, cruel, inhumano. 2. (hist.) bárbaro, extranjero.
Barbary ['bɑrbərɪ, B 'bɑb-] *s.* Berbería, región de África del Norte.
Barbary ape, (zool.) mono de Berbería, macaco.
barbate ['bɑrˌbeɪt, B 'bɑˌ-] *a.* (bot., zool.) barbado; (bot.) aristado.
barbecue ['bɑrbəˌkju, B 'bɑbɪ-] *s.* 1. barbacoa, banquete al aire libre (en que se sirve carne asada a la parrilla). 2. parrillada, carne asada a la parrilla; pachamanca (S.A). —*v.t.* 1. asar a la parrilla. 2. cocinar en salsa picante. 3. asar un animal entero.
barbecue sauce, salsa para barbacoa.
barbed [bɑrbd, B bɑbd] *a.* barbado, armado de púas; (fig.) cortante, mordaz, ej., *b. words,* palabras mordaces, hirientes.
barbed wire, alambre de púas.
barbel ['bɑrbəl, B 'bɑbəl] *s.* 1. barbilla (que crece en la mandíbula de ciertos peces). 2. (ict.) barbo, comiza. 3. (vet.) tolano (enfermedad de las encías).
barbell ['bɑrˌbɛl, B 'bɑˌ-] *s.* barra con pesas (de gimnasio).
barbellate ['bɑrbəˌleɪt, B 'bɑbə-] *a.* (bot., zool.) barbelulado, de pelos cortos y duros.
barber ['bɑrbər, B 'bɑbə] *s.* barbero, peluquero. —*v.t.* atender como barbero. —*v.i.* ser barbero.
barberry ['bɑrˌbɛrɪ, B 'bɑbərɪ] *s.* 1. (bot.) bérbero, agracejo, aguavilla, palo de rosa. 2. bérbero, agracejina (fruto).
barbershop ['bɑrbərˌʃɑp, B 'bɑbəˌʃɔp] *s.* barbería, peluquería (de hombres).
barbershop quartet, cuarteto vocal armónico (que canta canciones sentimentales).
barber's itch, (med.) herpes o tiña tonsorial.
barber's pole, percha de barbero (pintada en espiral en rojo y blanco).
barbet ['bɑrbət, B 'bɑbət] *s.* (orn.) barbudo, ave tropical.
barbette [bɑr'bɛt, B bɑ'-] *s.* 1. (fort.) barbeta. 2. (mar.) blindaje de cañón.
barbican ['bɑrbɪkən, B 'bɑbɪ-] *s.* (fort.) barbacana.
barbicel ['bɑrbəˌsɛl, B 'bɑbə-] *s.* (zool.) barbicela, cilio.
barbital ['bɑrbəˌtɔl, B 'bɑbɪ-] **barbitone** [-ˌtoʊn] *s.* (quím.) barbital.
barbiturate [bɑr'bɪtʃərət, -ˌreɪt B bɑ'-tjʊər-] *s.* (quím.) barbiturato.
barbituric [ˌbɑrbə'tʊrɪk, B ˌbɑbɪ'tjʊər-] *a.* (farm.) barbitúrico.
barbituric acid, ácido barbitúrico.
barbule ['bɑrˌbjul, B 'bɑˌ-] *s.* (orn.) bárbula.
barcarole, barcarolle ['bɑrkəˌroʊl, B 'bɑkə-] *s.* (mús.) barcarola.
bar code, (electrón.) código barrado, código de barras.
bard [bɑrd, B bɑd] *s.* bardo, poeta, vate.
bard, barde [bɑrd, B bɑd] *s.* barda, armadura de caballo. —*v.t.* guarnecer con barda (caballo).
bare [bɛr, B bɛə] *a.* 1. desnudo, pelado, descubierto. 2. sin muebles, vacío (cuarto, habitación, choza, pared, etc.); sin aislamiento, desnudo (alambre); sin pintura, sin revestir. 3. (con *of*) desprovisto (de). 4. mero, puro, solo. 5. escaso, mínimo. 6. (bridge) solo, ej., *a b. king,* un rey solo. 7. **to lay b.,** poner al descubierto, revelar. —*v.t.* 1. desnudar. 2. (fig.) descubrir, revelar.
bare-assed [ˌbɛr'æst, B ˌbɛər'ɑst] *a.* (jer.) en cueros, desnudo; con el trasero al aire.
bareback ['bɛrˌbæk, B 'bɛəˌ-] **barebacked** [-'bækt] *a., adv.* montado a pelo; sin silla.
bareboned [-ˌboʊnd] *a.* flaco, descarnado, huesudo.
barefaced [-'feɪst] *a.* 1. de cara descubierta. 2. imberbe. 3. (fig.) descarado, desvergonzado, audaz (mentiroso).
barefacedly [-'feɪsədlɪ, -'feɪstlɪ] *adv.* descaradamente.
barefoot [-ˌfʊt] *a., adv.* descalzo, con los pies desnudos.
barège [bə'rɛʒ] *s.* (tej.) barés, tela fina de seda o algodón.
bare-handed ['bɛr'hændəd B 'bɛə'-] *adv., a.* 1. sin guantes. 2. sin (usar) herramientas o armas, desarmado. 3. con las manos vacías.
bareheaded [-'hɛdəd] *a., adv.* con la cabeza descubierta, sin sombrero.
bare-knuckle ['bɛr'nʌkəl] *a. & adv.* sin guantes, a puño limpio.
barelegged [-'lɛgd, -'lɛgəd] *a.* con las piernas descubiertas, en pernetas.
barely ['bɛrlɪ, B 'bɛəlɪ] *adv.* 1. apenas. 2. pobremente, escasamente, meramente.
barenecked ['bɛr'nɛkt, B 'bɛə'-] *a.* escotado, con el cuello descubierto.
bareness [-nəs] *s.* 1. desnudez. 2. (fig.) pobreza, deficiencia.
barfly ['bɑrˌflaɪ, B 'bɑˌ-] *s.* (fam., E.U.) persona que frecuenta los bares y clubes nocturnos.
bargain ['bɑrgən, B 'bɑgɪn] *s.* 1. convenio, pacto, trato de compraventa. 2. negocio, ej., *bad b.,* mal negocio. 3. ganga, chiripa. 4. **at a b.**

price, baratísimo, con gran rebaja; **into the b.,** como adehala, además de lo pactado; de añadidura; **to make a b.,** hacer un trato, convenir; **to make the best of a bad b.,** no amilanarse en la desventura; **to strike a b.,** cerrar un trato, concluir un negocio. —*v.t.* 1. regatear. 2. pactar, concertar, negociar. 3. **b. away,** malvender, malbaratar; **they hadn't bargained for . . .** no habían tenido en cuenta, no habían contado con, no contaban con. . . .

bargain basement, sótano de una tienda donde se venden artículos a precios reducidos.

bargain counter, puesto para la venta de saldos, baratillo.

bargain day, día de gangas.

bargain driver, regateador, regatón.

bargain hunter, buscador de gangas, cazador de gangas.

bargain hunting, busca de gangas; **to go b.** ir en basca de gangas, ir de rebajas.

bargaining [-ɪŋ] *s.* 1. regateo. 2. pacto, trato.

bargain sale, ocasiones, venta de saldos, venta a precios rebajados, realización, liquidación.

barge [bɑrdʒ, B bɑdʒ] *s.* 1. barcaza, gabarra, alijador, lanchón. 2. (mar.) bote del jefe de escuadra. 3. embarcación de recreo; casa flotante. —*v.t.* transportar por barcaza. —*v.i.* (fam.) moverse pesadamente; **b. in,** irrumpir, entrar intempestivamente; **b. in on,** entrar (a ver) sin tocar a la puerta; **b. into,** entrometerse en (una conversación); irrumpir en (un cuarto).

bargeboard ['bɑrdʒˌbɔrd, B 'bɑdʒˌbɔd] *s.* (arq.) alero, guardamalleta.

bargee [bɑr'dʒi, B bɑ'-] *s.* (G.B.) barquero.

bargeman ['bɑrdʒmən, B 'bɑdʒ-] *s.* barquero, lanchero.

bargemaster [-ˌmæstər, B -ˌmɑstə] *s.* patrón de barcaza.

barge pole, botador; **I would not touch it with a b. pole,** no me metería en ese asunto por nada del mundo.

bar hop, 1. persona que anda de taberna en taberna sin detenerse en ninguna. 2. botones o mensajero que trabaja en un bar.

baric ['bærɪk] *a.* 1. (quím.) bárico. 2. barométrico.

barilla [bə'riljə, bə'rɪlə] *s.* (bot., quím.) barrilla.

bar iron, hierro en barras.

barite ['bɛrˌaɪt, B 'bɛər-] *s.* (quím.) baritina.

baritone ['bærəˌtoʊn, 'bɛr-, B 'bær-] *s.* (mús.) barítono.

barium ['bærɪəm, 'bɛr-, B 'bɛər-] *s.* (quím.) bario.

barium sulfate, (quím.) sulfato de bario.

bark [bɑrk, B bɑk] *s.* 1. ladrido. 2. corteza. 3. barca, barco. 4. estampido (de armas de fuego); tos fuerte. 5. **its b. is worse than its bite,** perro que ladra no muerde. —*v.i.* 1. ladrar. 2. (fig.) ladrar, regañar. 3. **b. up the wrong tree,** (fam.) equivocarse de objetivo (en crítica, denuncia, etc.). —*v.t.* 1. (pr. con *out*) vociferar, gritar (órdenes, injurias, etc.). 2. curtir, teñir. 3. descortezar, raspar, despellejar.

bark beetle, escarabajo horadador que ataca la corteza de los árboles.

barkeeper ['bɑrˌkipər, B 'bɑˌ-ə] *s.* tabernero, cantinero.

barkentine ['bɑrkənˌtin, B 'bɑkən-] *s.* (mar.) bergantín.

barker ['bɑrkər, B 'bɑkə] *s.* 1. descortezador. 2. vociferador, gritón, pregonero (en una feria, etc.). 3. pistola; cañón.

bark grafting, injerto de corona o coronilla.

barky ['bɑrkɪ, B 'bɑkɪ] *a.* de apariencia de corteza; cortezudo.

barley ['bɑrlɪ, B 'bɑlɪ] *s.* (bot.) cebada.

barley bread, pan de cebada.

barley broth, 1. sopa de cebada. 2. calducho.

barley corn, grano de cebada.

barley sugar, alfeñique (dulce en barras retorcidas); azúcar candi (en granos).

barley water, hordiate, bebida de cebada, usada esp. para el tratamiento de la diarrea de infantes.

barm [bɑrm, B bɑm] *s.* 1. (G.B.) levadura. 2. giste.

bar magnet, barra imantada.

barmaid ['bɑrˌmeɪd, B 'bɑˌ-] *s.* moza de bar, moza de taberna, camarera, cantinera.

barman [-mən] *s.* camarero o mozo de bar, cantinero, barman.

Barmecidal [ˌbɑrmə'saɪdəl, B ˌbɑmɪ-] **Barmecide** ['bɑrməˌsaɪd, B 'bɑmɪ-] *a.* ilusorio, imaginario, festín, fantástico.

bar mitzvah [bɑr'mɪtsvə, B bɑ'-] *s.* bar mitzvah (muchacho judío de 13 años que asume responsabilidades religiosas; ceremonia en la sinagoga en que se consagra a un muchacho de 13 años).

barmy ['bɑrmɪ, B 'bɑmɪ] *a.* 1. espumoso. 2. (fam.) excéntrico, chiflado, tonto.

barn [bɑrn, B bɑn] *s.* 1. granero, pajar, troche. 2. establo, cuadra, corral; cochera. 3. (fís.) barnio, barn, medida usada para expresar la sección transversal nuclear.

barnacle ['bɑrnəkəl, B 'bɑnə-] *s.* 1. (zool.) percebe, bálano, balano. 2. (fig.) persona o cosa pegajosa, que se adhiere con tenacidad.

barnacle goose, (orn.) bernicla, pato marino.

barn dance, baile campesino (donde se baila música folclórica, en un granero).

barn owl, (orn.) lechuza bodeguera, lechuzón de campanario.

barnstorm ['bɑrnˌstɔrm, B 'bɑnˌstɔm] *v.i.* 1. viajar por pueblos pequeños ofreciendo obras teatrales, conferencias, o pronunciando discursos políticos. 2. aparecer en ferias y festivales de provincias piloteando un avión de acrobacias. 3. hacer una campana electoral por el campo.

barnstormer [-ər, B -ə] *s.* actor ambulante, cómico de la legua.

barnyard [-ˌjɑrd, B -ˌjɑd] *s.* corral o patio de granja.

barnyard fowl, aves de corral.

barogram ['bærəˌgræm] *s.* (meteor.) barograma.

barograph [-ˌgræf, B -ˌgrɑf] *s.* barógrafo, barómetro registrador automático.

barometer [bə'rɑmətər, B -'rɔmɪtə] *s.* barómetro.

barometric [ˌbærə'mɛtrɪk] **barometrical** [-əl] *a.* (meteor.) barométrico; **barometric altimeter,** altímetro barométrico.

barometric gradient, (meteor.) pendiente o gradiente barométrica (entre dos estaciones); inclinación de una superficie isobárica.

barometric pressure, (meteor.) presión barométrica.

barometry [bə'rɑmətrɪ, B -'rɔm-] *s.* barometría.

baron ['bærən, 'bɛr-, B 'bær-] *s.* 1. barón. 2. (fig.) magnate, barón (de industria, comercio, etc.).

baronage [-ənɪdʒ] *s.* 1. baronía. 2. barones (en conjunto).

baroness [-ənəs] *s.* baronesa.

baronet [-ənət, -əˌnɛt] *s.* baronet (dignidad hereditaria u honoraria en Ingl.).

baronetcy [-sɪ] *s.* dignidad o rango de baronet.

barong [bə'rɔŋ, -'rɑŋ, B -'rɔŋ] *s.* cuchillo de hoja ancha que usaban los moros de Filipinas.

baronial [bə'roʊnɪəl] *a.* 1. señorial, noble. 2. de barón.

baron of beef, solomillo doble.

barony ['bærənɪ, 'bɛr-, B 'bær-] *s.* 1. baronía. 2. finca extensa.

baroque [bə'roʊk, B bə'rɔk] *a.* 1. (arq.) barroco. 2. irregular (díc. esp. de perlas). 3. grotesco, de mal gusto, recargado. —*s.* (época o estilo) barroco.

baroscope ['bærəˌskoʊp] *s.* baroscopio, baróscopo.

barothermograph [ˌbærə'θɜrməˌgræf, B -'θɜməˌgrɑf] *s.* barotermógrafo.

barouche [bə'ruʃ] *s.* birlocho, carruaje ligero y sin cubierta.

barque, barquentine, *vars. de* **bark, barentine.**

barracan ['bærəkæn] *s.* barragán; tela o abrigo impermeable.

barrack ['bærək, 'bɛr-, B 'bær-] *s.* 1. (mil.) (*gen. pl.*) cuartel. 2. (*gen. pl.*) barracón, barracas. —*v.t.* acuartelar.

barrack, (Aust., G.B.) *v.t.* abuchear, hostilizar (a un jugador o equipo de fútbol, criquet, etc.). —*v.i.* dar grita, abuchear.

barracoon [ˌbærə'kun] *s.* barracón.

barracuda [ˌbærə'kudə, ˌbɛr-, B ˌbær-] *s.* (ict.) barracuda, baracuda.

barrage [bə'rɑʒ, -'rɑdʒ, B 'bærɑʒ] *s.* 1. presa, azud. 2. barrera de fuego. 3. andanada (de preguntas, palabras, etc.). 4. (bridge) partido decisivo. —*v.t.* dirigir una barrera de fuego contra.

barrage balloon, (mil.) globo de barrera, globo de protección (contra bombardeos aéreos).

barranca [bə'ræŋkə] *s.* barranco, barranca.

barrator ['bærətər, 'bɛr-, B 'bærətə] *s.* (der.) culpable de baratería; picapleitos, pleitista.

barratry [-trɪ] *s.* 1. (der.) baratería. 2. (der., mar.) baratería de patrón o de capitán. 3. (der.) pleito vejaminoso, incitación persistente al litigio.

barred [bɑrd, B bɑd] *a.* 1. listado, rayado, gayado. 2. (her.) barrado. 3. atrancado, asegurado (puerta, etc.).

barrel ['bærəl, 'bɛr-, B 'bær-] *s.* 1. barril, barrica, tonel. 2. (medida variable del) contenido de un tonel. 3. cañon (de fusil, pluma, etc.); tambor (de reloj); fuste, caño (de bisagra); tambor, cilindro (de torno). 4. **to be over a b.,** (jer.) estar con el agua al cuello (gen. por deudas); estar bajo la férula (de otro). 5. gran cantidad (de algo); **a b. of fun,** muy divertido. —*v.t.* (*pret., p.p.* BARRELED O BARRELLED; *p.pr.* BARRELING O BARRELLING) embarrilar, entonelar. —*v.i.* (fam.) correr a gran velocidad (esp. vehículos).

barrelful [-ˌfʊl] *s.* (*pl.* BARRELFULS O BARRELSFUL) barrilada; (con *of*) contenido de un barril lleno.

barrelhouse [-ˌhaʊs] *s.* 1. (jer., E.U.) taberna de mala reputación. 2. estilo de jazz originario de este tipo de tabernas de Nueva Orleans.

barrel organ, organillo.

barrel roll, (avia.) barrena horizontal, rizo-tonel; vuelta alrededor del eje longitudinal del avión.

barrel vault, (arq.) bóveda cilíndrica, bóveda de cañon.

barren ['bærən, 'bɛr-, B 'bær-] *a.* 1. estéril, infecundo. 2. yermo, árido. 3. infructuoso, improductivo, vano. 4. (con *of*) desprovisto, falto (de). 5. insensible; deslucido, aburrido. —*s.* yermo, tierra yerma.

Barren Grounds, B. Lands, tundras o planicies sin árboles del Norte del Canadá.

barrette [bɑ'rɛt, bə-] *s.* hebilla o broche para sujetar el cabello.

barricade ['bærəˌkeɪd, 'bɛr-, B ˌbærɪ'keɪd] *s.* 1. barricada. 2. (fig.) barrera, obstáculo. —*v.t.* obstruir o cerrar con barricada.

barrier ['bærɪər, 'bɛr-, B 'bærɪə] *s.* 1. barrera, parapeto, valla. 2. barrera de hielo (en la antártida). 3. (fig.) barrera, impedimento, obstáculo. 4. (carrera de caballos) portal de salida.
barrier lights, (avia.) luces de barrera; barrera de luz de proyectores.
barrier line, línea demarcadora.
barrier reef, arrecife de coral (paralelo a la costa pero separado de ella por una albufera).
barring ['bɑrɪŋ] *prep.* salvo, exceptuando, ej., *b. accident,* salvo accidente.
barring engine, (avia.) servomotor para el arranque.
barrister ['bærəstər, 'bɛr-, B 'bʉrɪstə] *s.* (G.B.) abogado (autorizado a defender casos en las cortes superiores).
barroom ['bɑrˌrum, -ˌrʊm, B 'bɑˌ-] *s.* cantina, bar.
barrow ['bæroʊ, 'bɛr-, B 'bær-] *s.* 1. (sólo en nombres geográficos) montículo. 2. túmulo. 3. angarillas, parihuelas. 4. carretilla. 5. cerdo castrado.
barstool ['bɑrˌstul, B 'bɑˌ-] *s.* banqueta alta de bar.
bartender [-ˌtɛndər, B -də] *s.* camarero o mozo de bar, cantinero, barman.
barter ['bɑrtər, B 'bɑtə] *v.t.* trocar, cambalachear, cambiar. —*v.i.* traficar, comerciar trocando, hacer baratas. —*s.* trueque, barata.
barterer [-ərər, B -ərə] *s.* baratador, trocador, traficante.
bartizan ['bɑrtəzən, ˌbɑrtə'zæn, B 'bɑtɪˌzæn] *s.* (fort.) atalaya, garita.
barycenter ['bærəˌsɛntər, B -tə] *s.* (fís.) baricentro, centro de gravedad.
baryon ['bærɪˌɑn, 'bɛr- B 'bærɪˌɔn] *s.* grupo de partículas sub-atómicas.
barysphere ['bærəˌsfɪr, B -ˌsfɪə] *s.* (geol.) barisfera.
baryta [bə'raɪtə] *s.* (quím.) barita.
barytic [-'rɪtɪk] *a.* (quím.) barítico.
basal ['beɪsəl] *a.* fundamental, básico; de base.
basal metabolism, (biol.) metabolismo basal.
basalt [bə'sɔlt, 'beɪˌsɔlt, B 'bæsɔlt] *s.* (min.) basalto.
basaltic [bə'sɔltɪk] *a.* basáltico.
bascule ['bæskjul] *s.* báscula, balancín.
bascule bridge, puente levadizo o basculante.
base [beɪs] *s.* 1. base, fundamento, apoyo, fondo. 2. (geom.) base. 3. (arq.) basa, base. 4. (anat., bot., zool.) base. 5. (quím.) base (substancia que con un ácido forma una sal). 6. (mar., mil., avia.) base (de operaciones, submarinos, etc.). 7. (béisbol) base, barrera. 8. **off b.,** equivocado; de improviso; desprevenido; **to catch someone off b.,** (jer.) pillar o agarrar a alguien prevenido; **to get to first b.,** (jer.) vencer el primer obstáculo, lograr el primer éxito. —*a.* de base. —*v.t.* (con *on, upon*) basar (en, sobre), apoyar (en), fundamentar (en).
base, *a.* 1. deshonesto, ruin, vil, villano, rastrero. 2. (mús., ant.) bajo, grave. 3. (filol.) bajo (latín, etc.). 4. (metal.) bajo, común, de baja ley.
baseball ['beɪsˌbɔl] *s.* (dep.) 1. béisbol. 2. pelota de béisbol. —*a.* beisbolístico.
baseball game, partido de beisbol.
baseball player, beisbolero, beisbolista.
baseboard [-ˌbɔrd, B ˌbɔd] *s.* zócalo, friso inferior (de la pared).
baseborn [-'bɔrn, B -'bɔn] *a.* 1. bastardo, ilegítimo. 2. plebeyo, bajo, de humilde cuna.
base burner, estufa de fuego continuo, horno de alimentación automática.
base court, patio exterior (de un castillo); patio posterior (de una granja).
base hit, (béisbol) batazo con que el bateador gana la primera base sin beneficio de un error del oponente.
Basel ['bɑzəl] *s.* Basilea, ciudad de Suiza.
baseless ['beɪsləs] *a.* infundado, sin base, sin fundamento, ej., *b. accusation,* acusación infundada.
base level, nivel de base (de un río en su desembocadura).
base line, 1. línea básica o de base. 2. (béisbol) área entre bases (dentro de la que debe mantenerse un jugador). 3. (tenis) línea de saque, línea de fondo. 4. (mil.) línea demarcadora, línea de referencia.
baseman [-mən] *s.* (béisbol) jugador cuyo puesto es una de las tres bases.
basement ['beɪsmənt] *s.* sótano, pieza subterránea, basamento.
base metal, metal base; (fig.) el dinero.
baseness ['beɪsnəs] *s.* vileza, bajeza, ruindad.
basenji [bə'sɛndʒɪ] *s.* perro africano que se caracteriza por emitir un sonido suave en vez de ladrar.
base pay, salario o paga básicos (sin pagos adicionales o bonificaciones).
base runner, (béisbol) corredor de bases.
bash [bæʃ] *s.* (fam. pr. G.B.) 1. golpe, porrazo. 2. intento, tentativa, ej., *to have a b. at,* intentar, hacer una tentativa de, probar, ensayar. 3. (jer.) fiesta o reunión sumamente alegre y ruidosa. —*v.t.* (fam.) golpear fuertemente, asestar un golpe fuerte a; (con *in*) romper con un golpe (de porra, objeto pesado, etc.). —*v.i.* estrellarse, romperse.
bashaw [bə'ʃɔ] *s.* 1. *var. de* **pasha.** 2. (fam.) persona importante.
bashful ['bæʃfəl] *a.* tímido, vergonzoso, ruboroso.
bashfully [-ɪ] *adv.* tímidamente.
bashfulness [-nəs] *s.* timidez, vergüenza.
basic ['beɪsɪk] *a.* 1. básico, fundamental, ej., *b. fact,* hecho básico. 2. de base. 3. (quím.) básico, que contiene una base, de reacción alcalina. 4. (geol.) básico.
basically [-əlɪ] *adv.* básicamente, fundamentalmente, esencialmente.
Basic English, inglés básico, inglés simplificado.
basicity [beɪ'sɪsətɪ] *s.* (quím.) basicidad.
basidial [bə'sɪdɪəl] *a.* (bot.) basidial.
basidiomycete [bəˌsɪdɪoʊ'maɪˌsit, -ˌmaɪ'sit] *s.* (bot.) basidiomiceto.
basidiospore [bə'sɪdɪoʊˌspɔr, B -ˌspɔ] *s.* (bot.) basidióspora.
basidium [bə'sɪdɪəm] *s.* (*pl.* BASIDIA [-ɪə]) (bot.) basidio.
basify ['beɪsəˌfaɪ] *v.t.* (*pret., p.p.* BASIFIED; *p.pr.* BASIFYING) (quím.) basificar.
basil ['bæzəl, 'beɪs-, B 'bæz-] *s.* (bot.) albahaca.
basilar ['bæsələr, B -lə] **basilary** [-ˌlɛrɪ, B -lərɪ] *a.* (anat.) basilar.
Basilian [bə'zɪlɪən -'sɪl-] *a., s.* (relig.) basilio.
basilica [bə'sɪlɪkə, -'zɪl-] *s.* 1. (hist.) basílica, casa real. 2. (hist. romana) basílica (edificio para reuniones públicas). 3. basílica (iglesia católica romana que goza de ciertos privilegios).
basilic vein [bə'sɪlɪk-] (med.) vena basílica.
basilisk ['bæsəˌlɪsk, B 'bæz-] *s.* 1. basilisco (animal fabuloso). 2. (zool.) basilisco, lagarto de América. 3. (arm.) basilisco (cañón).
basin ['beɪsən] *s.* 1. vasija, bacía, jofaina, palangana, tazón. 2. pila. 3. cuenca (de un río, lago, etc.), ej., *the Amazon b.,* la cuenca del Amazonas. 4. depresión, hoya (en el fondo del mar). 5. dique, dársena.
basinet [ˌbæsə'nɛt] *s.* (arm.) bacinete.
basipetal [beɪ'sɪpətəl] *a.* (bot.) basípeto.
basis ['beɪsəs] *s.* (*pl.* BASES [-ˌsiz]) base, fundamento; **on the b. of,** a base de, en base a.
bask [bæsk, B bɑsk] *v.i.* 1. tomar el sol, asolearse; calentarse (a la lumbre del hogar). 2. (fig.) (con *in*) complacerse (en).
basket ['bæskət, B 'bɑs-] *s.* 1. cesta, canasta, cestón, capacho. 2. (aer.) barquilla, góndola; **the pick of the b.,** la flor de la canela. —*v.t.* encestar, encanastar (lo comprado, botellas, etc.); echar en la canasta (papel, desperdicios).
basketball [-ˌbɔl] *a.* basquetbolista. —*s.* (*game*) baloncesto, básquetbol, básquet; (*ball*) pelota de básquetbol, balón de baloncesto, básquet.
basketball player, jugador de baloncesto, basquetbolero, basquetbolista.
basket chair, sillón de mimbre (con respaldar y brazos de una sola pieza).
basket fern, (bot.) 1. helecho macho. 2. variedad de helecho tropical.
basketful [-ˌfʊl] *s.* cesdata, canastada.
basket-handle arch [-ˌhændəl-] (arq.) arco carpanel, arco zarpanel.
basket hilt, empuñadura con taza (de espada o florete).
basketry ['bæskətrɪ, B 'bɑs-] *s.* cestería; labor de cestería.
basket weave, tejido esterilla; ligamento radiado.
basketwork [-ˌwɜrk, B -ˌwɜk] *s.* cestería; labor de cestería.
Basle [bɑl] *s.* Basilea, ciudad de Suiza.
bas mitzvah [bɑs'mɪtsvə] 1. muchacha judía de 13 años que asume responsabilidades religiosas. 2. ceremonia en la sinagoga en que se consagra a dicha muchacha.
basophil ['beɪsəˌfɪl] **basophile** [-ˌfaɪl] *a.* (biol.) basófilo. —*s.* (biol.) basófilo.
basophilia [ˌbeɪsə'fɪlɪə] *s.* (med.) basofilia.
basophilic [-lɪk] **basophilous** [beɪ'sɑfələs, B -'sɔf-] *a.* (biol.) basófilo.
Basque [bæsk] *a., s.* 1. vasco, vascongado. 2. vascuence, vasco (lengua de los vascos).
basque, *s.* jubón, chaquetilla ajustada de mujer.
Basque Country, el País Vasco.
Basque Provinces, las tres provincias Vascongadas, al N. de España.
basquine [bæ'skin] *s.* basquiña; saya o falda interior.
bas-relief, bass-relief [ˌbɑrɪ'lif, B 'bæsrɪˌlif, 'bɑrɪ-] *s.* bajo relieve, bajorrelieve.
bass [bæs] *s.* 1. (zool.) perca, lobina, róbalo. 2. (bot.) tilo americano.
bass [beɪs] *a.* (mús.) bajo. —*s.* 1. (mús.) bajo, grave. 2. (mús.) contrabajo.
bassarisk ['bæsəˌrɪsk] *s.* (zool.) basáride.
bass-baritone ['beɪs'bærəˌtoʊn] *s.* (mús.) bajo (voz y cantante).
bass clef, (mús.) clave de fa.
bass drum, (mús.) bombo.
basset ['bæsət] *s.* (zool.) perro basset, perro de caza parecido al pachón. —*v.i.* (geol., min.) aflorar, campear.
basset horn, (mús.) clarinete tenor en fa.
bass fiddle, (mús.) contrabajo (esp. en una orquesta de jazz).
bass horn, (mús.) tuba.
bassinet [ˌbæsə'nɛt] *s.* cuna de mimbre sin pedestal.
bassist ['beɪsəst] *s.* músico que toca instrumentos de registro bajo.
basso ['bæsoʊ] *s.* (mús.) bajo (esp. el que canta en la ópera).
bassoon [bə'sun] *s.* (mús.) fagot, bajón.
bassoonist [-əst] *s.* (mús.) fagotista, bajonista.

basso profundo [ˌbæsoʊprəˈfʌndoʊ, ˌbɑs-, -ˈfʊn-] (mús.) bajo profundo (cantante o voz).

bass saxhorn, b. tuba, (mús.) bombardón.

bass viol, (mús.) contrabajo, violón, violoncelo.

basswood [ˈbæsˌwʊd] *s.* 1. (bot.) tilo americano. 2. tulipanero.

bast [bæst] *s.* 1. (bot.) floema. 2. líber. 3. cuerda, estera, etc., hecha de líber.

bastard [ˈbæstərd, B -təd, ˈbɑs-] *s.* 1. bastardo, hijo ilegítimo. 2. objeto espurio o falso. 3. (jer.) bribón, sinvergüenza; **you b.!,** ¡cabrón! —*a.* 1. bastardo, ilegítimo. 2. bastardo, espurio, falso, adulterado. 3. (*mixed*) híbrido. 4. (impr.) bastardo.

bastardize [-ˌaɪz] *v.t.* 1. declarar bastardo. 2. bastardear, viciar.

bastard title, (impr.) portadilla, anteportada.

bastardy [-ɪ] *s.* 1. ilegitimidad. 2. procreación de hijos bastardos.

baste [beɪst] *v.t.* 1. hilvanar, bastear. 2. lardear, enlardar. 3. (fam.) apalear.

Bastille [bæsˈtil] *s.* La Bastilla.

bastinade [ˌbæstəˈneɪd, -ˈnɑd] **bastinado** [-ˈneɪdoʊ, -ˈnɑd-] *s.* bastonazo, bastonada; paliza. —*v.t.* apalear, dar una paliza a bastonazos.

basting [ˈbeɪstɪŋ] *s.* 1. hilván. 2. acción de hilvanar. 3. pringue (que se usa para bañar la carne mientras se asa). 4. paliza.

bastion [ˈbæstʃən, B -tɪən] *s.* bastión, baluarte.

bastioned [-tʃənd, B -tɪənd] *a.* bastionado, fortificado.

Basuto [bəˈsutoʊ] *s.* basuto, indígena de Basutolandia.

bat [bæt] *s.* 1. maza, palo, garrote. 2. golpe, porrazo. 3. (dep.) bate (usado en el béisbol y el criquet). 4. (dep.) bateador; turno al bate, ej., *at b.,* al bate; (fig.) en acción. 5. algodón batanado, algodón en rama. 6. tejoleta; ladrillo crudo (secado al aire). 7. (G.B.) velocidad. 8. (fam.) juerga, jarana, parranda. 9. **(right) off the b.,** sin demora, al instante, en el acto; **to go to b. for (someone),** acudir a la ayuda o defensa de (alguien). —*v.t.* (*pret., p.p.* BATTED; *p.pr.* BATTING) batear, dar o pegar con un bate o palo; **b. around** (o **back and forth**), pelotear sobre, discutir mucho (asunto, tema, plan, etc.). —*v.i.* 1. (béisbol) batear, tomar su turno al bate. 2. (gen. con *around*) vagar.

bat [bæt] *s.* (zool.) murciélago; **blind as a b.,** más ciego que un topo; **to have bats in the belfry** (jer.), estar más loco que una cabra.

bat [bæt] *v.t.* pestañear, guiñar (el ojo); **not to b. an eye** (o **eyelid**), no mover pestaña, no pestañear; quedar indiferente; **without batting an eyelid,** permanecer imperturbable.

Bataan [bəˈtæn, -ˈtɑn] *s.* Bataán, península de las Filipinas, escena de la victoria japonesa sobre las fuerzas filipino-estadounidenses, durante la II Guerra Mundial.

Batavian [bəˈteɪvɪən] *a., s.* bátavo, de Batavia, antiguo nombre de Jakarta.

batch [bætʃ] *s.* 1. cochura, hornada. 2. tanda, lote. 3. rimero, cúmulo (de cosas), grupo (de personas), lío, fajo (de papeles). 4. (fam.) diminutivo de **bachelor,** soltero. 5. (comput.) lote.

batch distillation, (quím.) destilación intermitente.

batch mixer, (const.) hormigonera, mezclador por lotes.

batch processing, (comput.) procesamiento por lotes, tratamiento por lotes.

bate [beɪt] *v.t.* 1. disminuir, moderar, suspender, reprimir, contener, ej., *with bated breath,* con ansiedad, con aliento entrecortado, conteniendo el aliento. 2. reducir, deducir. —*v.i.* **aletear** (el halcón).

bate [beɪt] *s.* baño alcalino (que se usa en las tenerías para ablandar los cueros y pieles).

bateau [bæˈtoʊ] *s.* (*pl.* BATEAUX [-ˈtoʊz]) barco de fondo chato (que se usa para navegar en los ríos del Can. y E.U.).

batfish [ˈbætˌfɪʃ] *s.* (ict.) rubio volador; pastinaca.

batfowl [-ˌfaʊl] *v.t.* cazar pájaros por la noche (atrayéndolos a una red por medio de la luz).

bath [bæθ, B bɑθ] *s.* (*pl.* BATHS, [bæðz, B bɑðz]) 1. baño. 2. cuarto de baño. 3. (quím.) baño, solución.

bathe [beɪð] *v.t.* 1. bañar. 2. bañar, lavar, ej., *b. the eyes,* lavarse los ojos, *eyes bathed in tears,* ojos bañados en lágrimas. 3. bañar, mojar, empapar, humedecer. —*v.i.* bañarse, tomar un baño; **to go bathing,** ir a bañarse (a la playa, piscina, etc.).

bather [ˈbeɪðər, B -ə] *s.* bañador, bañista.

bathetic [bəˈθɛtɪk] *a.* que pasa de lo sublime a lo ridículo o vulgar (díc. esp. del estilo).

bathhouse [ˈbæθˌhaʊs, B ˈbɑθ-] *s.* casa de baños; vestidor, caseta en la playa.

bathing beauty [ˈbeɪðɪŋ-] *s.* bañista joven y atractiva que se exhibe en la playa o la piscina.

bathing cap, gorra de baño.

bathing resort, balneario.

bathing suit, traje o vestido de baño, bañador.

bathing trunks, calzón de baño.

bath mat, alfombrilla de baño.

batholith [ˈbæθəˌlɪθ] *s.* (geol.) batolito.

bathometer [bəˈθɑmətər, B -ˈθɔmətə] *s. var. de* **bathymeter.**

bathos [ˈbeɪˌθɑs, B -ˌθɔs] *s.* 1. caída de lo sublime a lo ridículo. 2. trivialidad. 3. sensiblería, lástima fingida, efecto patético forzado.

bathrobe [ˈbæθˌroʊb, B ˈbɑθ-] *s.* bata de baño, albornoz.

bathroom [-ˌrum, -ˌrʊm] *s.* baño, cuarto de baño.

bathroom fixtures, aparatos sanitarios, grifería sanitaria, artefactos de baño.

bathroom scale, balanza de baño.

Bathsheba [bæθˈʃibə, ˈbæθʃɪbə] *s.* (bíbl.) Betsabé, esposa de David, madre de Salomón.

bath towel, toalla de baño.

bathtub [ˈbæθˌtʌb, B ˈbɑθ-] *s.* bañera, baño, bañadera, tina.

bathyal [ˈbæθɪəl] *a.* (ocean.) batial, relativo a las profundidades del mar situadas entre 180 y 3.700 metros.

bathymeter [bəˈθɪmətər, B -tə] *s.* (ocean.) batímetro, instrumento para medir las profundidades del mar por medio de ondas acústicas registradas en un marcador de banda.

bathymetry [-trɪ] *s.* (ocean.) batimetría, ciencia que trata de la medida del fondo del mar con el fin de determinar su topografía.

bathyscaphe [ˈbæθɪˌskæf, -ˌskeɪf] *s.* (ocean.) batíscafo, vehículo instrumentado autodirigido que se usa en las exploraciones submarinas.

bathysphere [-ˌsfɪr, B -ˌsfɪə] *s.* (ocean.) batiesfera, cámara esférica instrumentada y habitable que se arría a grandes profundidades con el propósito de observar y estudiar el fondo del mar.

batik [bəˈtik, ˈbætɪk, B ˈbæt-] *s.* (tej.) batik, método javanés para teñir telas en colores variados.

batiste [bəˈtist, bæ-] *s.* (tej.) batista, holán; tejido fino de algodón.

batman [ˈbætmən] *s.* (G.B., mil.) ordenanza.

baton [bəˈtɑn, bæ-, B ˈbætən, -tɔn] *s.* 1. bastón de mando. 2. vara (de policía o del tambor mayor). 3. (mús.) batuta (del director de orquesta). 4. (dep.) posta (en carreras de relevo).

batrachian [bəˈtreɪkɪən] *a., s.* (zool.) batracio.

bats [bæts] *a.* (jer.) loco, chalado, chiflado.

batsman [ˈbætsmən] *s.* (dep.) bateador (en béisbol y criquet).

batt [bæt] *s.* algodón o lana en lámina.

battalion [bəˈtæljən] *s.* (mil.) batallón; (*pl.*) fuerzas; tropas.

batten [ˈbætən] *v.i.* 1. engordar, ponerse gordo. 2. (con *on*) comer glotonamente, alimentarse (de). 3. (fig.) (con *in*) deleitarse (en). 4. (fig.) medrar, prosperar. —*v.t.* cebar, engordar. —*s.* tabla o listón para cubrir pisos o cerrar accesos; **to b. down the hatches,** (mar.) asegurar las escotillas (con listones).

batter [ˈbætər, B -ə] *s.* 1. pasta, batido, mezcla pastelera. 2. (dep.) bateador. —*v.t.* 1. golpear, apalear, batir. 2. desmenuzar, romper; demoler, derribar.

battered [ˈbætərd] *a.* (*baby, child, wife*) maltratado, golpeado; (*reputation*) maltrecho; (*hat*) estropeado: (*car*) abollado; (*bruised*) magullado.

battering ram [-ərɪŋ] (mil.) ariete.

battery [ˈbætərɪ] *s.* (*pl.* BATTERIES) 1. (mil.) batería. 2. (elec.) batería (eléctrica), pila (eléctrica), batería (de acumuladores, de pilas), grupo de acumuladores eléctricos. 3. grupo, serie (de maquinaria, aparatos, etc.). 4. (der.) agresión. 5. (béisbol) pareja de lanzador y recibidor.

battery booster, (elec., hidr.) batería de lanzamiento.

battery cell, (elec.) elemento de batería, pila.

battery charger, (elec.) cargador de acumuladores.

battery gauge, (elec., aut.) voltímetro de acumulador.

battery filler, (elec., aut.) electrólito.

battery ignition, (elec.) (sistema de) encendido por acumulador.

battery tester, (elec.) densímetro.

batting [ˈbætɪŋ] *s.* 1. guata, algodón en hoja (empleado para hacer colchas, cobertores, etc.). 2. (béisbol) bateo.

batting average, promedio de bateo.

batting order, orden de bateo.

battle [ˈbætəl] *s.* 1. batalla. 2. lucha, combate, pelea. 3. **b. cry,** grito de combate; **line of b.,** frente de batalla; **pitched b.,** batalla campal; **soldier's b.,** batalla ganada por el valor; **to do b.,** librar batalla; **to give b.,** atacar, pasar al ataque; **to join b.,** trabar batalla; **to offer b.,** presentar batalla; **to refuse b.,** eludir la batalla. —*v.i.* batallar; (con *with* o *against*) luchar (con o contra). —*v.t.* combatir.

battle array, orden de batalla.

battle-ax [-ˌæks] *s.* 1. hacha de armas. 2. (jer.) vieja fornida y gruñona.

battle cruiser, (mar.) crucero, crucero de combate.

battle cry, grito de guerra; (fig.) lema.

battledore [-ˌdɔr, B -ˌdɔ] *s.* 1. pala (del panadero); paleta. 2. pala (en el juego del volante); raqueta; **b. and shuttlecock,** (juego del) volante.

battle fatigue, neurosis de guerra, fatiga de combate.

battlefield [-ˌfild] **battleground** [-ˌgraʊnd] *s.* campo de batalla.

battle front, frente de batalla.

battlement [-mənt] *s.* (fort., ant.) almena (en los muros de las antiguas fortalezas); (*pl.*) almenaje.

battle-piece [-ˌpis] *s.* (pint.) escena de batalla.

battle royal, 1. lucha de todos contra todos. 2. riña promiscua, sarracina; disputa acalorada; pelotera.

battle-scarred [-ˌskɑrd, B -ˌskɑd] *a.* que muestra cicatrices causadas por una batalla; (fig.) que muestra los efectos de una crisis moral.

battleship [-ˌʃɪp] *s.* acorazado, buque de guerra.
battleship gray, gris plomo.
battle station, (mar.) puesto de combate.
battology [bəˈtɑlədʒɪ, B -ˈtɔl-] *s.* (ret.) batología.
battue [bæˈtu, -ˈtju] *s.* 1. (caza) batida. 2. matanza colectiva.
batty [ˈbætɪ] *a.* (fam.) tonto, chiflado, excéntrico.
batwing [ˈbætˌwɪŋ] *a.* como el ala del murciélago (mangas de blusa, etc.).
bauble [ˈbɔbəl, ˈbɑb-, B ˈbɔb-] *s.* 1. chuchería, fruslería, futesa. 2. juguete. 3. cetro de cintas y cascabeles (como el del bufón o rey del carnaval).
bauxite [ˈbɔkˌsaɪt] *s.* (min.) bauxita.
Bavarian [bəˈvɛrɪən, B -ˈvɛər-] *s.* 1. bávaro, natural de Baviera, región de Alemania. 2. dialecto bávaro.
bawbee [ˈbɔbi, B bɔˈbi] *s.* (esco.) medio penique.
bawd [bɔd] *s.* 1. celestina, alcahueta. 2. regente de un burdel.
bawdiness [ˈbɔdɪnəs] *s.* obscenidad.
bawdy [-ɪ] *a.* obsceno, concupiscente.
bawdy house, burdel, lupanar, casa de citas.
bawl [bɔl] *v.i.* 1. (con *at*) gritar a voz en cuello. 2. llorar a gritos. —*v.t.* pregonar, decir gritando, gritar, vocear; **b. (someone) out,** regañar a, echar una reprimenda a (alguien).
bay [beɪ] *s.* bahía, ensenada, ancón, rada.
bay [beɪ] *s.* 1. (arq.) intercolumnio, entrepaño, vano. 2. mirador, ventana saliente. 3. (jer.) panza, barriga. 4. compartimiento, ej., *bomb b.,* (mil., aer.) compartimiento de las bombas.
bay [beɪ] *s.* 1. aprieto, acorralamiento. 2. ladrido, aullido. 3. **at b.,** a raya, acorralado; **to hold at b.,** mantener a raya. —*v.t.* 1. ladrar a, aullar a. 2. acorralar. —*v.i.* ladrar, aullar; **b. at the moon,** ladrar a la luna.
bay [beɪ] *s.* 1. (bot.) laurel. 2. (fig.) corona de laurel, triunfos, fama.
bay [beɪ] *s., a.* bayo (caballo); color bayo.
bayadere [ˈbaɪəˌdɪr, -ˌdɛr, B -ˌdɪə] *s.* 1. bayadera, bailarina hindú. 2. tela a rayas de colores.
bayberry [ˈbeɪˌbɛrɪ] (bot.) *s.* 1. baya del laurel. 2. (E.U.) árbol de la cera; baya del árbol de la cera. 3. baya del arrayán brabántico.
bay leaf, hoja (seca) de laurel (para cocinar).
Bay of Biscay, golfo de Vizcaya, golfo de Gascuña (en el mar Cantábrico).
bayonet [ˈbeɪənət, -ˌnɛt, B -nɪt] *s.* bayoneta. —*v.t.* (*pret., p.p.* BAYONETED O BAYONETTED; *p.pr.* BAYONETING O BAYONETTING) herir con bayoneta, bayonetear. —*v.i.* luchar con bayoneta; **to fix b.,** calar o armar la bayoneta.
bayonet coupling, (mec.) acoplador de tipo bayoneta.
bayonet lock, (mec.) cierre de bayoneta.
bayonet socket, 1. (arm.) cubo de bayoneta. 2. (elec.) enchufe de bayoneta, portalámparas de bayoneta.
Bayonne [beɪˈoʊn, bɑˈjɔn] *s.* Bayona, ciudad del sudoeste de Francia.
bayou [ˈbaɪoʊ, -u, -ˌjoʊ, -ˌju] *s.* brazo pantanoso de un río; canalizo (en el S.O. de E.U.).
bay rum, ron de laurel, ron de malagueta; agua aromática de dicha planta, producto para el tocador.
Bay State, nombre dado al estado de Massachusetts (E.U.).
bay tree, laurel.
bay window, 1. mirador, ventana sobresaliente. 2. (jer.) persona de barriga prominente.
baywood [ˈbeɪˌwʊd] *s.* caoba tosca del golfo de Campeche, Méx.
bazaar [bəˈzɑr, B -ˈzɑ] *s.* 1. bazar. 2. feria, quermese, tómbola (con fines caritativos).
bazooka [bəˈzukə] *s.* bazuka, lanzacohetes antitanque.
B.B.A. *abrev. de* **Bachelor of Business Administration,** Licenciado en Administración Comercial.
B battery , (quím.) batería de placas, batería anódica.
BBC *abrev. de* **British Broadcasting Corporation,** Corporación Radiodifusora Británica.
BB gun [ˈbiˈbi-] arma que dispara balas de pequeño calibre.
BC *abrev. de* 1. **Before Christ,** antes de Jesucristo (*a. de J.C.*). 2. **British Columbia,** Columbia Británica.
BCG vaccine , vacuna anti-tuberculosa.
B.CHE. *abrev. de* **Bachelor of Chemical Engineering,** Licenciado en Ingeniería Química.
B complex [ˈbi-] (med.) grupo o complejo de vitaminas B.
B.D. *abrev. de* **Bachelor of Divinity,** Licenciado en Teología.
bdellium [ˈdɛlɪəm] *s.* bedelio, resina aromática parecida a la mirra.
be [bi] *v.i.* (*pret.* WAS [wɑz, wɔz, wəz, B wɔz, wəz]; *p.p.* BEEN [bɪn, bin]) 1. ser, ej., *to be or not to be,* ser o no ser, *he is young,* es joven, *she is a teacher,* ella es maestra. 2. estar, ej., *he is at school,* está en la escuela, *she will be here tomorrow,* estará aquí mañana, *he is writing,* está escribiendo. 3. tener, ej., *I'm hungry,* tengo hambre, *I'm cold,* tengo frío, *you're right,* tiene Ud. razón, *he is six years old,* tiene seis años. 4. haber, ej., *there's a big house on the corner,* hay una casa grande en la esquina, *there are two cats on the roof,* hay dos gatos en la azotea, *there was a cup on the table,* había una taza en la mesa, *I'm sorry I was late,* siento haber llegado tarde. 5. hacer, ej., *it's hot,* hace calor, *it's sunny,* hace sol. 6. ocuparse, dedicarse, ej., *what would you like to be?* ¿a qué le gustaría dedicarse? 7. encontrarse, hallarse, ej., *they are here,* se encuentran aquí. 8. (*seguido de un inf.*) deber, ej., *I am to inform you,* debo informarle. 9. (*seguido de* **to be** *y un p.p.*) ser de; poder; haber de, ej., *it is to be regretted,* es de lamentar, *the book is not to be found anywhere,* no se puede encontrar el libro en ninguna parte, *they are to be shot at dawn,* han de ser fusilados al amanecer. 10. existir, vivir, ej., *Napoleon is no more,* Napoleón ya no existe. 11. **be about (to do),** estar por (hacer), estar a punto de (hacer); **to be had** o **taken,** (jer.) ser engañado, burlado, estafado; **be for,** abogar por, estar con; **be in,** estar (en casa, oficina, etc.), haber llegado, ej., *Is Mr. Smith in?* ¿Está el Sr. Smith? *Mr. Smith is not in yet,* el Sr. Smith no ha llegado todavía; **be off,** irse, marcharse; ser inexacto, ej., *his figures were way off,* sus cálculos eran muy inexactos; **be out,** haber salido, ej., *I'm sorry, Mr. Smith is out,* lo siento, el Sr. Smith ha salido; **be quiet!** ¡ cállate!; **be that as it may,** sea como fuere; **be up to,** estar a la altura de, ser capaz de; proponerse, andar en, estar urdiendo; incumbir, tocar a; **for the time being,** por lo pronto, por el momento; **maybe,** posible; **might-have-beens,** posibilidades del pasado, oportunidades perdidas; **to have been around;** haber corrido mucho mundo; **would-be,** presunto, supuesto, pretendido.
Be *símb. de* **beryllium,** berilio (Be).
B.E. *abrev. de* 1. **Bachelor of Education,** Licenciado en Pedagogía. 2. **Bachelor of Engineering,** Licenciado en Ingeniería.
BEA *abrev. de* **British European Airways,** Aerolíneas Europeas Británicas.
beach [bitʃ] *s.* playa, ribera (de mar o río). —*v.t., v.i.* varar, poner en seco; hacer encallar; impeler o arrastrar a la playa.
beachcomb [ˈbitʃˌkoʊm] *v.i.* raquear, andar o ir al raque; (fig.) vaguear, vagabundear, vivir sin preocupaciones. —*v.t.* registrar (un área) raqueando.
beachcomber [-ər, B -ə] *s.* raquero; vago, vagabundo (en puertos, playas, costas).
beachcombing [-ɪŋ] *s.* 1. raque. 2. andar al raque; (fig.) vagabundear por la playa.
beachfront [ˈbitʃfrʌnt] *s.* zona frente a la playa.
beachfront property, inmueble frente a la playa.
beach grass, (bot.) barrón.
beachhead [ˈbitʃˌhɛd] *s.* (mil.) cabeza de playa.
beach robe, albornoz, bata de playa.
beach umbrella, sombrilla o parasol de playa.
beach wagon, (E.U.) camioneta.
beachy [-ɪ] *a.* pedregoso.
beacon [ˈbikən] *s.* 1. baliza, almenara, fanal, faro. 2. (fig.) faro, guía. 3. (t. **radio b.**) radiofaro. —*v.t.* 1. proveer de faro, poner faro en. 2. iluminar; (fig.) guiar. —*v.i.* brillar.
bead [bid] *s.* 1. cuenta, abalorio, bolita perforada (de un collar); mostacilla. 2. (*pl.*) rosario, sarta de cuentas. 3. gota, burbuja, ej., *a b. of sweat,* una gota de sudor. 4. punto (de fusil). 5. (arq.) moldura, listón. 6. (carp.) reborde. 7. (aut.) talón de cubierta (de la llanta). 8. (quím.) botón, glóbulo. 9. (elec.) perla aisladora. 10. **to draw a b. on,** tomar puntería; **to say** (**tell** o **count**) **one's beads,** rezar el rosario. —*v.t.* 1. adornar con cuentas o abalorios. 2. ensartar. —*v.i.* formarse en gotas.
beading [ˈbidɪŋ] *s.* (arq.) moldura, reborde; astrágalo.
beadle [ˈbidəl] *s.* pertiguero (en la iglesia), alguacil, ministril, bedel.
beadledom [-dəm] *s.* (fig.) burocracia torpe (que se sujeta escrupulosamente a la rutina).
beadroll [ˈbidˌroʊl] *s.* 1. (relig.) lista de personas (por cuyas almas se reza); martirologio. 2. rosario.
bead tree, (bot.) acederaque, cinamomo, agríon, rosariera.
beadwork [ˈbidˌwɜrk, B -ˌwɜk] *s.* ornamento de abalorios; (carp.) reborde, moldura.
beady [-ɪ] *a.* adornado con abalorios; que tiene apariencia de gotas brillantes; **b. eyed,** que tiene ojos pequeños y como cuentas.
beady-eyed [ˈbidiˈaid] *a.* de o con ojos redondos y brillantes.
beagle [ˈbigəl] *s.* (perro) pachón, especie de sabueso pequeño.
beak [bik] *s.* 1. pico (de un ave). 2. nariz; nariz corva. 3. rostro, espolón (de antiguas galeras). 4. (fam., G.B.) magistrado.
beaker [ˈbikər, B -ə] *s.* 1. bocal o jarra con pico. 2. (quím., farm.) cubeta, vaso de laboratorio.
beakhead [ˈbikˌhɛd] *s.* (mar.) beque.
be-all [ˈbiˌɔl] *s.* parte esencial, lo esencial, el todo; **be-all and end-all,** toda la finalidad (de una empresa, etc.).
beam [bim] *s.* 1. viga, tablón, madero. 2. barra de hierro; cama del arado; astil de la balanza. 3. haz, rayo (de luz, de calor, o de esperanza). 4. (mar.) manga, ancho máximo de un barco; través. 5. (rad.) rayo, haz. 6. (máq.) balancín. 7. **on the b.,** (mar.) por el través; **on the lee b.,** (mar.) por el través de sotavento; **to be on the b.,** (aer.) estar siguiendo el haz (del radiofaro); estar sobre la pista, estar bien informado, correcto o alerta; (fig.) estar actuando acertadamente, estar funcionando bien. —*v.t.* emitir;

(rad.) emitir en forma dirigida, dirigir, ej., *programs beamed to Latin America,* programas dirigidos hacia la América Latina. —*v.i.* 1. brillar. 2. rebosar de alegría.

beam and scales, peso de cruz, balanza de cruz.

beam antenna, (rad.) antena direccional.

beam compass, compás deslizante o de vara.

beam-ends ['bim,ɛndz] *s. pl.* (mar.) los extremos de los baos de un barco; **on the b.-e.,** (mar.) empeñado (díc. de un barco escorado y que no puede adrizarse); **to be on one's b.-e.,** estar limpio, no tener más dinero.

beaming ['bimɪŋ] beamish [-ɪʃ] *a.* 1. brillante, radiante. 2. (fig.) radiante, rebosante de alegría.

beam load, carga transversal, carga de flexión.

beamy [-ɪ] *a.* 1. radiante, brillante. 2. (mar.) de manga considerable, excesivamente ancho (navío). 3. (poét.) macizo, fuerte, grande.

bean [bin] *s.* 1. haba, habichuela, judía, alubia, frijol. 2. judía verde. 3. haba, grano, semilla (de café, cacao, etc.). 4. (jer.) moneda, plata, céntimo; ej., *I haven't a b.,* no tengo un céntimo. 5. (jer.) coco, cabeza. 6. **full of beans,** (fam.) mentiroso, equivocado; persona llena de entusiasmo y energía; **beans,** cantidad insignificante, ej., *she doesn't know beans about politics,* ella no sabe nada de política; **spill the beans,** (fam.) revelar un secreto, por accidente o imprudencia; **old b.,** viejo, viejo amigo.

bean bag, saquito de frijoles con que juegan los niños.

bean curd, queso de soja.

beanery ['binərɪ] *s.* restaurant barato y malo.

beanie ['binɪ] *s.* casquete (gorro) pequeño que usan los niños varones.

bean pole, 1. rodrigón para habas. 2. persona larguirucha.

bean sprout, brote de soja, soja germinada.

beanstalk [-,stɔk] *s.* el tallo principal del frijol.

bean tree, (bot.) catalpa.

bear [bɛr, B bɛə] *v.t.* (*pret.* BORE; *p.p.* BORNE o BORN; *p.pr.* BEARING) 1. llevar, cargar, portar. 2. conducir, acompañar, llevar. 3. llevar, tener, ostentar. 4. sentir, abrigar, guardar, profesar (amor, odio, etc.). 5. dar, prestar. 6. mantener, sostener. 7. soportar, cargarse con. 8. tolerar, aguantar, sufrir. 9. permitir, admitir. 10. dar a luz, parir; (cuando se refiere al hombre o a mamíferos el *p.p.* es BORN, ej., *born in 1901,* nacido en 1901, *born of,* nacido de, pero se usa BORNE con referencia a la madre, ej., *she has borne a child,* ha dado a luz un niño). 11. producir; rendir (frutos), devengar (interés). 12. **b. a grudge,** guardar rencor; **b. a hand,** echar una mano, ayudar; **b. a part in,** compartir; **b. arms,** portar armas, servir como soldado; **b. away,** llevarse, ganar (premio, la palma, etc.); **b. down,** abrumar; **b. in mind,** recordar, tener presente, tener en cuenta; **b. off,** llevarse, ganar (premio); **b. one-self (well, badly,** etc.), comportarse (bien, mal, etc.); **b. out,** probar, confirmar; **b. up,** sostener, soportar, ayudar; **b. witness,** dar testimonio, atestiguar; **to be borne away,** ser arrebatado (por fuerzas externas o impulsos del ánimo). —*v.i.* 1. dirigirse, encaminarse. 2. moverse, pasar (en cierta dirección). 3. ejercer presión, pesar. 4. producir, rendir (bien, mal). 5. soportar peso, resistir. 6. **b. away,** (mar.) desatracar; cambiar el rumbo; **b. down,** abatirse (ave, etc.), caer encima; (mar.) recalar (sobre); navegar con el viento; **b. down on** (o **upon**), atacar, caer sobre; marchar hacia; recaer, pesar sobre, afligir; **b. hard on,** oprimir; **b. off,** (mar.) alejarse (barco); **b. on** (o **upon**), referirse a, relacionarse con, atañer a; **b. up,** cobrar ánimo, no amilanarse; (mar.) tomar rumbo a sotavento; **b. up against,** resistir, luchar contra; **b. up for,** (mar.) cambiar rumbo para; **b. with,** tener paciencia, ser indulgente con, soportar pacientemente; **to bring to b.,** aplicar, ejercer.

bear [bɛr, B bɛə] *s.* 1. (zool.) oso. 2. hombre tosco y rudo. 3. (fin.) bajista.

bearable ['bɛrəbəl] *a.* sufrible, soportable, tolerable.

bearbaiter [-ər, B -ə] *s.* azuzador.

bearbaiting ['bɛr,beɪtɪŋ, B 'bɛə-] *s.* deporte que consiste en azuzar perros contra un oso.

bearberry [-,bɛrɪ] *s.* (bot.) gayuba, uvaduz, aguavilla.

bear cat 1. (zool.) panda, mamífero parecido al oso, que vive en el Himalaya. 2. (fig.) persona agresiva o pendenciera.

beard [bɪrd, B bɪəd] *s.* 1. barba. 2. (bot.) arista (de espiga). 3. lengüeta (de flecha); barba (de pluma). —*v.t.* 1. agarrar por la barba, tirar por la barba 2. subirse a las barbas de, hacer frente a, desafiar.

bearded ['bɪrdəd, B 'bɪəd-] *a.* 1. barbado, barbudo; que tiene barbas o aristas; armado con lengüetas. 2. (astr.) barbato (cometa).

bearded eagle, b. vulture, (orn.) águila barbuda.

beardless [-ləs] *a.* imberbe, barbilampiño.

bearer ['bɛrər, B 'bɛərə] *s.* 1. portador 2. árbol fructífero. 3. (com.) portador (de cheque, etc.). 4. (mil.) camillero.

bear garden, lugar donde se tienen osos para diversión del público.

bear grass, (bot.) especie de yuca del N.O. de los Estados Unidos.

bearing ['bɛrɪŋ, B 'bɛər-] *s.* 1. presencia, porte, aire, modales, ej., *his military b. is excellent,* su porte militar es excelente. 2. producción, fructificación; gestación. 3. (her.) carga, figura (en un escudo de armas). 4. relación, conexión, fuerza, valor (de una expresión), ej., *that has no b. on the matter,* eso no tiene relación con el asunto. 5. (arq.) apoyo, apuntalamiento. 6. (mec.) cojinete, chumacera, apoyo, asiento, soporte, descanso, muñonera, manga del eje. 7. (mar.) orientación, marcación, rumbo; situación, demora; línea de flotación. 8. (top.) ángulo formado en el punto de observación entre el meridiano magnético y el objeto. 9. (rad., mar.) marcación; (avia.) rumbo. 10. **to get** (o **find**) **one's bearings,** orientarse; **to lose one's bearings,** desorientarse; aturdirse; **to take a b.,** (mar., top.) determinar un rumbo; **to take bearings,** (mar.) determinar la posición (del barco).

bearing pressure, (const.) presión de apoyo; (maq.) presión sobre la chumacera.

bearing rein, engallador, parte del arnés que mantiene erguida la cabeza del caballo.

bearish ['bɛrɪʃ, B 'bɛər-] *a.* 1. osuno. 2. (fig.) rudo, áspero. 3. con tendencia a la baja (en la bolsa de valores).

bear's-breech ['bɛrz,britʃ, B 'bɛəz-] *s.* (bot.) acanto, branca ursina.

bearskin ['bɛr,skɪn, B 'bɛə,-] *s.* piel de oso; alfombra de piel de oso.

beast [bist] *s.* 1. bestia, bruto, res, cuadrúpedo. 2. bruto, bestia, hombre brutal. 3. **b. of burden,** bestia de carga; **b. of prey,** animal de rapiña; **the b.,** la bestia, naturaleza animal (del hombre).

beastliness ['bistlɪnəs] *a.* bestialidad, brutalidad.

beastly [-lɪ] *a.* 1. bestial, animal. 2. bestial, brutal; (fam.) detestable, abominable. —*adv.* (fam.) muy, atrozmente, excesivamente; **it is b. cold,** hace un frío atroz.

beat [bit] *v.t.* (*pret.* BEAT; *p.p.* BEATEN ['bitən] o BEAT; *p.pr.* BEATING) 1. golpear, apalear, aporrear, azotar. 2. batir (metal; las alas; huevos, crema, etc.). 3. batir, derrotar, vencer. 4. sobrepasar, adelantar. 5. recorrer (ronda, etc.), pisar. 6. sacudir (alfombra, etc.). 7. (caza) batir (el monte), dar una batida a. 8. (mús.) llevar (el compás); tocar (el tambor). 9. **b. a path,** abrir un sendero; **b. a retreat,** batirse en retirada; **b. back,** repeler, hacer retroceder; **b. black and blue,** moler a golpes; **b. down,** superar, vencer (resistencia); lograr rebajar (regateando precio); **b. it,** (jer.) largarse, marcharse, darse el bote; **b. off,** rechazar (ataque, etc.); **b. one's brains,** devanarse los sesos; **b. the breast,** golpearse el pecho (en arrepentimiento); **b. the rap,** (jer.) quedar absuelto (de un cargo ante un tribunal); evadir la pena; **b. time,** marcar el compás; **b. to death,** matar a golpes; **b. (one) to it,** cogerle (a uno) la delantera; **beat someone to something,** pisarle algo a alguien; **b. up,** batir (huevos, crema, etc.); moler a palos; **it beats me (how he did it,** etc.), no me explico (cómo lo ha hecho, etc.). —*v.i.* 1. latir, pulsar, palpitar. 2. batir. 3. (mar.) voltejear, dar bordadas. 4. avanzar laboriosamente. 5. **b. about,** (mar.) voltejear, dar bordadas; ir buscando (en todas partes); **b. about the bush,** andar con rodeos; **b. against,** estrellarse contra; **b. down on,** batir (rayos del sol, etc.) sobre, chocar en; **b. (up) on,** golpetear sobre (ej., la lluvia sobre las ventanas, techo, etc.); **b. to windward,** (mar.) navegar de bolina. —*s.* 1. golpe, latido, pulsación. 2. (mús.) compás, ritmo, tiempo. 3. (elec.) batimiento. 4. noticia exclusiva (en periódico). 5. ronda, ej., *watchman's b.,* ronda del guardián. 6. (jer.) bohemio asocial y amoral. 7. **off one's b.,** (fig.) fuera de la competencia de uno; **off the b., off b.,** fuera de ritmo; fuera del camino trillado, desacostumbrado, fuera de lo regular. —*a.* fatigado, agotado, exhausto; **the b. generation,** la generación perdida o desorientada (de la década del 1950 en E.U.).

beaten ['bitən] *a.* 1. trillado, pisado (pista, sendero). 2. batido, martillado (metal). 3. agotado, exhausto. 4. batido, vencido.

beater [-ər, B -ə] *s.* 1. batidor, sacudidor; pisón, maza. 2. (caza) batidor.

beat frequency, (rad.) frecuencia heterodina, frecuencia de pulsación.

beatific [,biə'tɪfɪk] *a.* 1. (rel.) beatífico. 2. beatífico, feliz, benigno (sonrisa, cara, etc.).

beatification [bi,ætəfə'keɪʃən] *s.* (rel.) beatificación.

beating ['bitɪŋ] *s.* 1. paliza, zurra. 2. pulsación, latido (del corazón, etc.). 3. (mar.) navegación de bolina. 4. **b. of wings,** aleteo; **b. up,** pateadura; **to take a b.,** recibir una paliza; sufrir una derrota.

beatitude [bi'ætə,tud, B -,tjud] *s.* beatitud, bienaventuranza, la bienaventuranza eterna; prosperidad, felicidad.

beatnik ['bitnɪk] *s.* beatnik (bohemio, joven rebelde de la segunda postguerra que protestaba contra los valores convencionales de la sociedad).

beat-up ['bit'ʌp] *a.* (jer.) desgastado, estragado, vencido.

beau [boʊ] *s.* (*pl.* BEAUX o BEAUS [boʊz]) 1. petimetre, hombre elegante. 2. admirador, enamorado.

Beaufort scale ['boʊfərt-, B -fət-] (fís.) escala de Beaufort.

beau geste [boʊ'ʒɛst] gesto noble, gesto bello.

beau ideal [-,aɪ'dil] el bello modelo, el tipo ideal.

beau monde [-'mɑnd, B -'mɔnd] mundo elegante, gran mundo.

beauteous ['bjutɪəs] *a.* (poét.) bello, hermoso.

beautician [bju'tɪʃən] *s.* cosmetólogo, cosmetóloga.
beautician's school, academia de peluquería.
beautification [ˌbjutəfə'keɪʃən] *s.* embellecimiento.
beautifier ['bjutəˌfaɪər, B -ˌfaɪə] *s.* embellecedor.
beautiful [-fəl] *a.* bello, hermoso. —*s.* **the b.,** lo bello.
beautiful people, los escogidos de una secta o grupo social o étnico.
beautify [-ˌfaɪ] *v.t.* (*pret., p.p.* BEAUTIFIED; *p.pr.* BEAUTIFYING) embellecer, hermosear, arreglar, adornar. —*v.i.* embellecerse, arreglarse, adornarse, maquillarse.
beauty ['bjutɪ] *s., a.* 1. belleza, hermosura. 2. beldad, belleza, mujer hermosa. 3. (fig.) hermosura, belleza, ejemplar perfecto o magnífico, ej., *here's a b.!* ¡es una belleza! ¡he aquí un ejemplar perfecto! *the fish we caught were beauties,* los peces que cogimos eran una hermosura (o eran magníficos ejemplares). 4. **b. is but skin deep,** las apariencias engañan.
beauty contest, concurso de belleza.
beauty parlor, b. salon, b. shop, salón de belleza, peluquería.
beauty queen, reina de un concurso de belleza.
beauty sleep, primer sueño (antes de medianoche); cualquier siesta que restablece el ánimo.
beauty spot, 1. lunar postizo. 2. lunar o mancha de la piel.
beaux-arts [boʊ'zɑr, B -'zɑ] *s. pl.* (fr.) bellas artes.
beaver ['bivər, B -ə] *s.* 1. (zool.) castor. 2. piel de castor. 3. (paño hecho del pelo de) castor. 4. (arm.) barbote, barberol, visera.
beaverboard [-ˌbɔrd, B -ˌbɔd] *s.* cartón de fibra para paredes y tabiques.
bebop ['biˌbɑp, B -ˌbɔp] *s.* estilo de jazz que se caracteriza por ritmos rápidos y sincopados.
becalm [bɪ'kɑm] *v.t.* 1. calmar, serenar. 2. (mar.) encalmar, dejar (un velero) inmóvil la falta de viento.
became [-'keɪm] *pret. de* **become.**
because [bɪ'kɔz] *conj.* porque, ya que, pues; **b. of,** por causa de, a causa de, debido a, por motivo de.
beccafico [ˌbɛkə'fikoʊ] *s.* (orn.) becafigo, papafigo, picafigo.
bechamel [ˌbeɪʃə'mɛl] *s.* salsa bechamel, besamel, o bechamela (crema a base de leche y harina).
bechance [bɪ't ʃæns, B -'t ʃɑns] *v.i.* (ant.) acontecer, acaecer.
beche-de-mer [ˌbeɪʃdə'mɛr, B ˌbɛʃdə'mɛə] *s.* 1. (zool.) pepino de mar. 2. lengua franca de Melanesia.
beck [bɛk] *s.* gesto, ademán, seña de llamada; **to be at someone's b. and call,** estar a la entera disposición de alguien, servir a alguien con sumo esmero.
becket ['bɛkət] *s.* (mar.) estorbo, vinatera.
beckon ['bɛkən] *v.t.* 1. hacer señas, llamar con o por señas. 2. tentar, atraer.
becloud [bɪ'klaʊd] *v.t.* nublar, anublar; obscurecer.
become [bɪ'kʌm] *v.i.* (*pret.* BECAME; *p.p.* BECOME; *p.pr.* BECOMING) 1. llegar a existir, nacer, adquirir identidad. 2. volverse, tornarse, hacerse, ponerse. 3. convertirse en (presidente, héroe, etc.); (*seguido de un p.p.*) llegar a (ser), resultar, ej., *at last he became obsessed with the idea,* al fin la idea llegó a obsesionarlo. 4. seguido de un *a.* o *p.p.* se traduce a veces por un solo verbo que indica el cambio que corresponde, ej., *b. angry,* enojarse, enfadarse, *b. dirty,* ensuciarse, *b. fat,* engordar, *b. old,* envejecer. 5. (gen. con *of*) acontecer a, hacerse de, ser de, ej., *What has b. of him?* ¿Qué ha sido de él? *What will b. of us?* ¿Qué será de nosotros? *What became of my friend?* ¿Qué fue de mi amigo? —*v.t.* 1. sentar bien a, venir bien a. 2. convenir a, ser propio o digno de, corresponder a.
becoming [-ɪŋ] *a.* 1. que sienta bien, decoroso, ej., *a b. dress,* un vestido que sienta bien. 2. propio o digno (de), apropiado, ej., *his behavior is b. to a ruler,* su comportamiento es propio o digno de un gobernante.
becomingly [-lɪ] *adv.* correctamente, decorosamente, apropriadamente.
Becquerel ray [bɛ'krɛl-] *s.* (fís.) rayo de Becquerel.
bed [bɛd] *s.* 1. cama, lecho. 2. lecho, cauce, fondo (de ríos, etc.). 3. cuadro, era (de flores, etc.). 4. base, fundamento. 5. (geol.) lecho, estrato. 6. (const.) capa, cama, tendel (de mortero, yeso, etc.). 7. (ing.) firme (de carreteras, vías férreas, etc.). 8. (mec.) bancada. 9. **flower b.,** macizo de flores; **to get up on the wrong side of the bed,** (fig.) levantarse con el pie izquierdo; **to go to b.,** acostarse; **to lie in the b. one has made,** (fig.) recoger los frutos de lo que se ha sembrado; **to make the b.,** hacer la cama; **to stay in b.,** quedarse en cama; **to take to one's b.,** caer en cama. —*v.t.* (*pret., p.p.* BEDDED; *p.pr.* BEDDING) 1. (t. con *down*) acostar; dar cama a, alojar. 2. poner en cama, llevar a la cama; encamar. 3. encajar, asentar. 4. plantar en cuadros (en el jardín). 5. amasar (tierra) en lomos o cuadros. —*v.i.* 1. (gen. con *down*) acostarse; alojarse (por la noche). 2. (con *with*) alojarse (con); acostarse, dormir, tener relaciones sexuales (con). 3. asentarse, depositarse (en capas). 4. (mec.) amoldarse, estar a ras de.
bed and board, techo y sustento; (der.) mesa y lecho, relaciones conyugales.
bed and breakfast, cama con desayuno, alojamiento y desayuno.
bedaub [bɪ'dɔb] *v.t.* 1. embadurnar, manchar, ensuciar, mancillar. 2. recargar con adornos.
bedazzle [bɪ'dæzəl] *v.t.* 1. deslumbrar, encandilar, ofuscar. 2. (fig.) deslumbrar, impresionar hondamente; encantar, hechizar.
bedbug ['bɛdˌbʌg] *s.* (ento.) chinche.
bedchamber [-ˌt ʃeɪmbər, B -bə] *s.* dormitorio, alcoba, recámara (Méx.).
bedclothes [-ˌkloʊðz] *s. pl.* ropa de cama.
bedcover [-ˌkʌvər, B -ə] *s.* cubrecama; edredón.
bedding [-ɪŋ] *s.* 1. ropa de cama. 2. cama de paja (para las caballerías). 3. (geol.) capa, estratificación.
bedeck [bɪ'dɛk] *v.t.* adornar, acicalar, aderezar.
bedevil [-'dɛvəl] *v.t.* 1. endemoniar, endiablar, hechizar. 2. confundir. 3. desesperar, acosar.
bedew [-'du, B -'dju] *v.t.* rociar, humedecer.
bedfast ['bɛdˌfæst, B -ˌfɑst] *a.* postrado, recluido en cama.
bedfellow [-ˌfɛloʊ] *s.* 1. compañero de cama. 2. (fig.) aliado, asociado. 3. **strange bedfellows,** alianza de personas incompatibles, afinidad inesperada.
bedgown [-ˌgaʊn] *s.* (G.B.) camisa de noche (de mujer), camisón.
bedim [bɪ'dɪm] *v.t.* oscurecer; amortiguar (la luz); ofuscar.
bedizen [-'daɪzən] *v.t.* (ant.) emperejilar, adornar profusamente o con mal gusto.
bed jacket, chambra, chaquetilla ligera que complementa el camisón de dormir; mañanita (Am.).
bedlam ['bɛdləm] *s.* 1. batahola, bulla, jaleo, olla de grillos. 2. manicomio, casa de locos.
bedlamite [-ˌaɪt] *s.* orate, lunático, loco.
bed linen, ropa de cama.
bed of roses, (fig.) lecho de rosas; sinecura.
Bedouin ['bɛdʊɪn] *s.* beduino, nómada.
bedpan ['bɛdˌpæn] *s.* 1. silleta, bacín plano, orinal (utilizado por enfermos que guardan cama). 2. calentador de cama.
bedplate [-ˌpleɪt] *s.* (mec.) plancha de fondo o de asiento, placa de base, bancaza.
bedpost [-ˌpoʊst] *s.* pilar de cama; (fig.) **between you and me and the b.,** muy confidencialmente.
bedraggle [bɪ'drægəl] *v.t.* mojar, embarrar, enlodar, ensuciar, manchar (la ropa, arrastrándola).
bedraggled [-əld] *a.* 1. sucio, manchado (como si hubiera sido arrastrado por el suelo). 2. destartalado.
bedrail ['bɛdˌreɪl] *s.* barandilla de la cama (de un niño o enfermo).
bedrid [-ˌrɪd] **bedridden** [-ən] *a.* postrado en cama (por enfermedad o invalidez); extenuado, decrépito.
bedrock [-ˌrɑk, B -ˌrɔk] *s.* 1. lecho o cama de roca. 2. (fig.) base o fundamento sólidos. 3. (fig.) punto o nivel más bajos.
bedroll [-ˌroʊl] *s.* paquete-cama, lecho portátil.
bedroom [-ˌrum, -ˌrʊm] *s.* dormitorio, cuarto de dormir, alcoba, recámara.
bedroom farce, comedia sicalíptica.
bedroom suite, juego de dormitorio; departamento con dormitorio en un hotel.
bedsheet ['bɛdʃit] *s.* sábana.
bedside ['bɛdˌsaɪd] *s.* lado de la cama, cabecera (esp. de un enfermo). —*a.* algo práctico para el enfermo (mesita, timbre, etc.).
bedside manner, (fig.) trato atento y gentil (esp. del médico con el enfermo).
bedside table, velador, mesilla de noche.
bedsore [-ˌsɔr B -ˌsɔ] *s.* úlcera por decúbito (causada por la prolongada permanencia en el lecho).
bedspread [-ˌsprɛd] *s.* sobrecama, cubrecama, cobertor, colcha.
bedspring [-ˌsprɪŋ] *s.* bastidor de resortes (de cama o catre).
bedstead [-ˌstɛd] *s.* armadura de la cama.
bedstraw [-ˌstrɔ] *s.* 1. (bot.) galio, cuajaleche. 2. paja para jergón.
bedtime [-ˌtaɪm] *s.* hora de acostarse, hora de dormir.
bedtime story 1. cuento que se dice a los niños al acostarlos. 2. (fig.) mentira, cuento que nadie cree.
bedwetting ['bɛdˌwɛtɪ˺] *s.* eneuresis nocturna.
bee [bi] *s.* 1. (ento.) abeja. 2. (fig.) trabajador laborioso. 3. (E.U.) reunión, tertulia. 4. concurso, competencia, ej., *spelling b.,* concurso de deletreo. 5. manía, chifladura. 6. **to have a b. in one's bonnet,** estar un poco chiflado, tener ideas absurdas o fantásticas; **busy as a b.,** ocupadísimo, embebido en el trabajo.
bee [bi] *s.* (mar.) aleta del bauprés.
beebread ['biˌbrɛd] *s.* hámago, ámago, polen almacenado por las abejas.
beech [bit ʃ] *s.* (bot.) haya.
beechen ['bit ʃən] *a.* hecho (de madera) de haya.
beechnut [-ˌnʌt] *s.* (bot.) hayuco, fayuco, nuez del haya.
beechwood [-ˌwʊd] *s.* madera de haya.
beef [bif] *s.* 1. carne de res. 2. res vacuna, ganado vacuno engordado. 3. (fig., fam.) fuerza muscular, músculo sólido. 4. (jer.) (*pl.*) (*beefs*) queja, lamento. —*v.i.* (jer.) quejarse. —*v.t.* (gen. con *up*) fortalecer.
beef cattle, ganado vacuno para carne.

beefeater ['bif,itər, B -tə] *s.* 1. (G.B.) alabardero, soldado o guardia (esp. de la Torre de Londres). 2. persona gruesa.
beefed up, *a.* reforzado, mejorado.
bee fly, (ento.) abejorro.
beefsteak ['bif,steɪk] *s.* bistec, biftec.
beef tea, jugo de carne cocida (para personas delicadas); consomé, caldo concentrado de carne de res.
beef-wood [-,wʊd] *s.* (bot.) casuarina, balatá.
beefy [-ɪ] *a.* rollizo, metido en carnes; fuerte, musculoso.
bee glue, cera aleda.
beehive ['bi,haɪv] *s.* colmena.
beekeeper [-,kipər, B -ə] *s.* apicultor.
beekeeping [-,kipɪŋ] *s.* apicultura, cría de abejas.
beeline [-,laɪn] *s.* línea recta; **to make a b. for,** ir en línea recta hacia.
Beelzebub [bi'ɛlzɪ,bʌb] *s.* (bíbl.) Belcebú.
bee martin, (orn.) tirano.
been [bɪn, bin] *p.p. de* **be.**
beep [bip] *s.* 1. sonido corto y agudo de una bocina. 2. señal electrónica repetida en clave. *—v.t.* emitir dicho sonido.
beer [bɪr, B bɪə] *s.* 1. cerveza. 2. bebida gaseosa hecha de raíces (jengibre, etc.).
beer and skittles, bebida y juego; diversión.
beer garden, cervecería o taberna al aire libre.
beery ['bɪrɪ, B 'bɪərɪ] *a.* 1. provocado por la cerveza (sentimentalismo, afección, canto, etc.). 2. que huele a cerveza (cantina, cuarto, etc.).
beestings ['bistɪŋz] *s. pl.* calostro, primera leche de la hembra.
beeswax ['biz,wæks] *s.* cera de abejas. *—v.t.* encerar.
beeswing [-,wɪŋ] *s.* flor o nata de vino añejo.
beet [bit] *s.* (bot.) remolacha, betarraga.
beetle ['bitəl] *s.* (ento.) escarabajo, coleóptero; **blind as a b.,** ciego como un topo.
beetle ['bitəl] *s.* 1. martillo de madera, mazo, maza, pisón. 2. mano de mortero, majador de almirez. 3. (tej.) batán. 4. **three-man b.,** pisón pesado (que requiere tres hombres para alzarlo). *—v.t.* golpear con pisón, aplastar, apretar (tierra, etc.). *—v.i.* sobresalir, proyectarse. *—a.* proyectado, prominente.
beetle-browed [-,braʊd] *a.* cejijunto, ceñudo, adusto.
beetlehead [-,hɛd] *s.* estúpido, tonto, necio.
bee tree 1. tronco hueco de árbol (en el que las abejas hacen sus colmenas). 2. (bot.) tilo americano.
beetroot ['bit,rut] *s.* (raíz de) remolacha, betarraga.
beet sugar, azúcar de remolacha.
bee wolf, (zool.) larva del escarabajo (que infesta las colmenas de abejas).
befall [bɪ'fɔl] *v.i.* suceder, acontecer, sobrevenir. *—v.t.* acontecer a.
befell [-'fɛl] *pret. de* **befall.**
befit [bɪ'fɪt] *v.t.* convenir a, venir bien a, ser conveniente a o para; ser propio de.
befitting [-ɪŋ] *a.* conveniente, propio, **digno.**
befog [bɪ'fɔg] *v.t.* 1. obscurecer, envolver en niebla. 2. confundir, desconcertar.
befool [-'ful] *v.t.* engañar, embaucar.
before [bɪ'fɔr, B -'fɔ] *adv.* 1. delante, adelante, al frente, ej., *to go* (*run,* etc.) *b.,* ir (correr, etc.) adelante o al frente. 2. antes, anteriormente, previamente, ya, ej., *all that went b.,* todo lo que pasó antes; *I told you b.,* ya te lo dije, *long b.,* mucho tiempo antes, hace mucho tiempo. *—prep.* 1. frente a, delante de, ante. 2. anterior a, antes de. 3. **b. Christ,** antes de Cristo; **b. God,** ante Dios; **b. the mast,** (mar.) a proa del mástil; como marinero. *—conj.* primero, antes de, antes que, antes de que, ej., *he would die b. lying,* moriría antes que mentir, *I'll call you b. I start,* lo llamaré antes de salir; *let me know b. he comes,* avísame antes de que llegue. **— b. long,** dentro de poco.
beforehand [-,hænd] *adv.* de antemano, previamente, con anticipación, ya, ej., *I knew it b.,* ya lo sabía.
beforetime [-,taɪm] *adv.* (ant.) en otro tiempo, tiempo atrás.
befoul [bɪ'faʊl] *v.t.* 1. ensuciar, embadurnar. 2. desbaratar. 3. enredar.
befriend [-'frɛnd] *v.t.* favorecer, ayudar, proteger, ofrecer amistad.
befuddle [-'fʌdəl] *v.t.* confundir, dejar perplejo, aturdir.
beg [bɛg] *v.t.* (*pret., p.p.* BEGGED; *p.pr.* BEGGING) implorar, suplicar, rogar, pedir; **b. the question,** dar por sentado lo que queda por probar; **b. (someone) to (do),** suplicar o pedir (a alguien) que (haga); **I b. your pardon,** ¡excúseme! ¡dispénseme! perdone ¿qué dijo Ud.? *—v.i.* 1. mendigar, pedir limosna, pordiosear. 2. (con *for*) pedir, solicitar, suplicar. 3. (*said of a dog*) ponerse en dos patas (*el perro*). 4. **b. off,** excusarse.
began [bɪ'gæn] *pret. de* **begin.**
beget [-'gɛt] *v.t.* (*pret.* BEGOT *p.p.* BEGOTTEN; *p.pr.* BEGETTING) 1. engendrar. 2. (fig.) engendrar, provocar, causar.
beggar ['bɛgər, B -ə] *s.* 1. mendigo, pordiosero. 2. indigente. 3. **beggars cannot be choosers,** a caballo regalado no se le mira el colmillo.
beggarly [-lɪ] *a.* mísero, mezquino, pobre, miserable.
beggar's-lice ['bɛgərz,laɪs, B -gəz-] **beggar-lice** ['bɛgər-, B -gə,-] *s. pl.* (*sing. o pl. en const.*) (bot.) cadillo; la frutilla espinosa del cadillo (que se adhiere a la ropa).
beggarweed ['bɛgər,wid, B -gə,-] *s.* (bot.) cuscuta.
beggary ['bɛgərɪ] *s.* 1. mendicidad. 2. los mendigos (en conjunto), pobretería. 3. miseria, pobreza absoluta.
begin [bɪ'gɪn] *v.t.* (*pret.* BEGAN [-'gæn]; *p.p.* BEGUN [-'gʌn] *p.pr.* BEGINNING) comenzar, empezar, iniciar; **not b. to,** ni con mucho, ej., *you do not b. to meet the qualifications,* usted no alcanza ni con mucho a llenar los requisitos. *—v.i.* empezar, comenzar, principiarse, iniciarse; **b. at,** comenzar en; **b. with,** empezar con, tomar (considerar) primero; **to b. with,** para empezar en primer lugar, ej., *to b. with, he's too small,* en primer lugar, él es demasiado pequeño.
beginner [-ər, B -ə] *s.* 1. aprendiz, principiante, novicio, novato. 2. originador, iniciador.
beginning [-ɪŋ] *s.* 1. comienzo, principio, origen; iniciación, albor(es). 2. causa primera. 3. **b. with,** a partir de; **from b. to end,** del principio al fin, de cabo a rabo; **the b. of the end,** el principio del fin.
begird [bɪ'gərd, B -'gɜd] *v.t.* 1. atar, ceñir con un cinturón. 2. cercar, rodear.
begone [bɪ'gɔn, -'gɑn, B -'gɔn] *interj.* (*imper.*) ¡fuera! ¡vete de aquí!
begonia [bɪ'goʊnjə] *s.* (bot.) begonia.
begrime [bɪ'graɪm] *v.t.* tiznar, enmugrecer, ensuciar, emporcar.
begrudge [-'grʌdʒ] *v.t.* escatimar; dar o tomar de mala gana.
begrudgingly [-ɪŋlɪ] *adv.* de mala gana, a regañadientes, ej., *he gave the money b.,* dio el dinero de mala gana.
beguile [bɪ'gaɪl] *v.t.* engañar, seducir, ilusionar, encantar (con falsas promesas).
beguine [bɪ'gin] *s.* baile originario de las Antillas francesas.
begum ['bigəm, B 'beɪ-] *s.* begum, begún, princesa o dama musulmana de alto rango.
begun [bɪ'gʌn] *p.p. de* **begin.**
behalf [bɪ'hæf, B -'hɑf] *s.* beneficio, interés, favor; **in (on) b. of,** por, a favor de, en pro de; en nombre de, de parte de; **to act on someone's b.,** actuar en nombre de alguien.
behave [bɪ'heɪv] *v.i.* 1. comportarse, portarse, conducirse. 2. portarse bien. 3. (fig.) funcionar, trabajar (bien, mal, etc.; díc. de máquinas). 4. **b. towards,** tratar (bien, mal, etc.). *—v.r.* 1. comportarse, portarse, conducirse. 2. portarse, bien; **b. yourself!** ¡pórtate bien!
behavior, (pr. G.B.) **behaviour** [-jər, B -jə] *s.* comportamiento, conducta; reacción; funcionamiento; **to be on one's best b.,** portarse lo mejor posible.
behaviorism [bɪ'heɪvjə,rɪzəm] *s.* (psic.) behaviorismo.
behaviorist [-rəst] *s.* partidario de la teoría del behaviorismo.
behead [bɪ'hɛd] *v.t.* decapitar, descabezar.
beheld [-'hɛld] *pret., p.p. de* **behold.**
behemoth [bɪ'himəθ, B -'mɔθ] *s.* 1. (bíbl.) behemot, bestia colosal. 2. monstruo, gigante.
behest [bɪ'hɛst] *s.* orden (*f.*), mandato; **at the b. of,** a instancias de.
behind [bɪ'haɪnd] *adv.* 1. detrás, atrás, hacia atrás. 2. atrasado, en retardo, a la zaga. 3. **from b.,** por detrás; **to fall b.,** quedarse atrás; **to fall b. with (payments, rent,** etc.), atrasarse con (pagos, alquiler, etc.); **to stay b.,** quedarse, detenerse. *—prep.* detrás de, tras, tras de; **b. one's back,** a espaldas de uno, en ausencia de uno; **b. schedule, b. time,** tarde, atrasado; **b. the eight ball,** (jer.) en apuros; **b. the scenes,** entre bastidores; **b. the times,** atrasado (de noticias); **to put b. one,** poner de lado, dejar fuera de consideración. *—s.* trasero, nalgas, tafanario, posaderas.
behindhand [-,hænd] *adv.* tardíamente, con atraso. *—a.* retrasado, tardío; atrasado.
behold [bɪ'hoʊld] *v.t.* (*pret.* BEHELD; *p.p.* BEHELD o (ant.) BEHOLDEN) 1. mirar, avistar. 2. contemplar. *—interj.* ¡mirad! ¡he aquí!
beholden [bɪ'hoʊldən] *a.* obligado (por gratitud).
beholder [-ər, B -ə] *s.* (ant., poét.) espectador.
behoof [bɪ'huf] *s.* ventaja, provecho, utilidad.
behoove [-'huv] **behove** [-'hoʊv] *v.t.* (*impers.*) convenir a, corresponder a, competer a, tocar, incumbir. *—v.i.* (*impers.*) ser propio; ser menester.
beige [beɪʒ] *a.* de color beige, amarillento.
being ['biɪŋ] *p.pr. de* **to be; for the time b.,** por el momento. *—conj.* ya que, puesto que. *—s.* 1. ser, ente, criatura. 2. existencia, vida. 3. **in b.,** existente; **the Supreme B.,** el Ser Supremo, Dios.
Beirut [beɪ'rut] *s.* Beirut, capital del Líbano.
bejesus [bɪ'dʒizəs] *s.* **the b.,** (jer.) entrañas (apl. a personas); **to knock (beat, hit, kick) the b. out of (someone),** descalabrar a (alguien), romperle la crisma a (alguien).
bejewel [bɪ'dʒuəl] *v.t.* enjoyar, alhajar, adornar con joyas.
bel [bɛl] *s.* (fís.) belio.
belabor, belabour [bɪ'leɪbər, B -ə] *v.t.* espaciarse en, elaborar (un tema, argumento, etc.).
belated [bɪ'leɪtəd] *a.* atrasado, tardío, demorado (Am.).
belatedly [-lɪ] *adv.* tarde, con atraso, tardíamente.
belay [bɪ'leɪ] *v.t.* amarrar (una cuerda alrededor de una cabilla); cercar, bloquear. *—v.i.* (mar.) (*ú. gen. en imper.*) ¡párese! ¡basta! ¡deténgase!

—*s.* (alpinismo) saliente de roca (del cual puede sujetarse una soga), agarradero.

belaying pin, (mar.) cabilla de maniobra.

belch [bɛltʃ] *v.i.* 1. eructar, regoldar. 2. salir con fuerza (humo, llamas, etc.). —*v.t.* vomitar, arrojar (lavas o llamas un volcán; fuego un cañón; blasfemias o injurias una persona). —*s.* eructo, regüeldo.

beldam, beldame ['bɛldəm] *s.* vieja bruja, tarasca.

beleaguer [bɪ'ligər, B -ə] *v.t.* 1. sitiar, cercar, bloquear. 2. (fig.) acosar, molestar, importunar.

belemnite ['bɛləm,naɪt] *s.* (pal.) belemnita.

belfry ['bɛlfrɪ] *s.* campanario.

Belgian ['bɛldʒən] *a.* belga. —*s.* 1. belga, oriundo o ciudadano de Bélgica. 2. caballo de tiro fuerte y pesado.

Belgian hare, *s.* especie de conejo pequeño.

Belgian sheepdog, perro pastor belga.

Belgium [-dʒəm] *s.* Bélgica.

Belgrade ['bɛl,greɪd] *s.* Belgrado, capital de Yugoslavia.

Belial ['biliəl] *s.* Belial, Luzbel, el diablo, Satanás; espíritu del mal; ángel caído; **man of B.,** hombre réprobo, malvado.

belie [bɪ'laɪ] *v.t.* 1. desmentir, contradecir. 2. falsear, representar falsamente. 3. frustrar, defraudar (esperanza).

belief [bɪ'lif] *s.* 1. creencia, credo, religión. 2. crédito, ej., *claims unworthy of b.,* pretensiones indignas de crédito. 3. fe, confianza. 4. convencimiento, opinión, parecer.

believable [-'livəbəl] *a.* creíble.

believe [bɪ'liv] *v.i.* 1. creer, tener fe. 2. creer, opinar. 3. **b. in,** creer en; tener fe en, confiar en; ser partidario de; **to make b.,** aparentar, fingir. —*v.t.* 1. creer, creer en. 2. tener por.

Believe It or Not, Aunque Ud. No Lo Crea (de Ripley).

believer [-ər, B -ə] *s.* creyente, fiel.

belike [bɪ'laɪk] *adv.* (ant.) quizás, tal vez, probablemente.

belittle [bɪ'lɪtəl] *v.t.* 1. empequeñecer, reducir. 2. menospreciar, desestimar.

Belize [bə'liz] *s.* Belice, capital de Honduras Británica.

bell [bɛl] *s.* 1. campana. 2. timbre, campanilla. 3. esquila, cencerro. 4. campanada, toque de campana. 5. (bot.) corola (de una flor). 6. (mús.) pabellón (de los instrumentos de viento). 7. (mús.) (*pl.*) carillón. 8. (mar.) media hora (de guardia). 9. **b., book and candle,** (fórmula de) anatema; **passing b.,** campana que dobla a muerto; **sound as a b.,** en perfecta salud; sin defecto (plan, argumento, etc.); **that (it) rings a b.,** (jer.) eso me recuerda, eso me hace recordar, eso me trae a la memoria una cosa; **to ring the b.,** tocar la campana (el timbre, la campanilla); llevarse el premio; **with bells on,** (jer.) en vestido de gala; con muchísimo gusto; con creces, de sobra. —*v.t.* 1. poner esquila o cascabel a (un animal). 2. tocar el timbre. 3. cubrir con campana de cristal. 4. **to b. the cat,** (fig.) ponerle el cascabel al gato. —*v.i.* 1. tocar el timbre. 2. (gen. con *out*) acampanarse, hincharse. 3. formarse o crecer en corola (flor, etc.). — **diving b.,** (mar.) campana de buzo; **fog b.,** (mar.) campana de niebla; **rescue b.,** (mar.) campana de salvamento submarino.

bell [bɛl] *s.* bramido, rugido. —*v.i.* bramar, berrear (como el venado en celo).

belladonna [,bɛlə'dɑnə, B -'dɔnə] *s.* (bot., farm.) belladona.

belladonna lily, (bot.) amarilis.

bellbird ['bɛl,bɜrd, B -,bɜd] *s.* (orn.) campanero; tordo norteamericano.

bell-bottomed [-,bɑtəmd, B -,bɔt-] *a.* acampanado (díc. del pantalón como el de los marineros).

bellboy [-,bɔɪ] *s.* botones, paje de hotel.

bell buoy, (mar.) boya de campana, boya sonora.

belle [bɛl] *s.* beldad, belleza, joven bella y muy asediada por admiradores.

belles-lettres ['bɛl'lɛtrə] *s.* bellas letras, literatura.

bellflower ['bɛl,flauər, B -ə] *s.* 1. (bot.) campánula, farolillo, adenófora. 2. campanilla.

bell gable, espadaña (armadura de pozo o campanario).

bell-glass [-,glæs, B -,glɑs] *s.* fanal, campana de cristal (de laboratorio, para cubrir cultivos, etc.).

bellhop [-,hɑp, B -,hɔp] *s.* (fam. E.U.) *var. de* **bellboy.**

bellicose ['bɛlɪ,koʊs] *a.* belicoso.

bellicosity [,bɛlɪ'kɑsɪtɪ, B -'kɔs-] *s.* belicosidad.

bellied ['bɛlid] *a.* barrigón, panzudo, ventrudo.

belligerence [bə'lɪdʒərəns] *s.* belicosidad, beligerancia.

belligerent [-ərənt] *a.* beligerante, agresivo, belicoso. —*s.* nación participante en una guerra.

bell jar, *var. de* **bell glass.**

bellman ['bɛlmən] *s. var. de* **bellboy.**

bell metal, bronce campanil, metal campanil, aleación campanil.

bellmouthed [-,maʊðd, -,maʊθt] *a.* acampanado, abocinado, abocardado.

bellow ['bɛloʊ] *v.i., v.t.* bramar, gritar, vociferar. —*s.* bramido, grito.

bellows ['bɛloʊz] *s. pl.* (*sing. o pl. const.*) 1. fuelle, barquín. 2. fuelle (de una máquina fotográfica, etc.). 3. **rubber b.,** fuelle de goma; **balance b.,** (ing.) fuelle equilibrador; **metallic b.,** fuelle metálico.

bell pepper, pimiento dulce.

bell ringer, 1. campanero. 2. (fam.) éxito rotundo.

bell-shaped ['bɛl,ʃeɪpt] *a.* acampanado.

bell tent, tienda cónica de campaña; pabellón circular.

bell tower, campanario.

bell trap, (const.) trampa de campana, sifón de campana (en instalación sanitaria).

bellwether [-,wɛðər, B -ə] *s.* la bestia que encabeza la recua o el rebaño; (fig.) líder, cabecilla.

bellwort [-,wɜrt B -,wɜt] *s.* (bot.) campánula.

belly ['bɛlɪ] *s.* 1. vientre, barriga, panza. 2. estómago. 3. vientre, útero. 4. (fig.) apetito, glotonería. 5. vientre, cavidad. 6. vientre, barriga, panza (de vasijas, etc.). 7. (mar.) bolso (de una vela). 8. (impr.) levantamiento (de la forma). 9. (const.) barriga (de pared). —*v.t.* (*pret., p.p.* BELLIED; *p.pr.* BELLYING) inflar, hinchar. —*v.i.* 1. inflarse, hincharse. 2. (const.) pandear, combarse.

bellyache [-,eɪk] *s.* dolor de vientre; cólico. —*v.i.* (jer.) quejarse, lamentarse.

bellyband [-,bænd] *s.* 1. cincha (que asegura la silla); barriguera (de las caballerías). 2. ventrera.

belly button, (fam.) ombligo.

belly dance, danza del vientre.

belly dancer, bailarina de danzas sensuales del Oriente Medio.

bellyful [-,fʊl] *s.* (fam.) panzada, hartazgo; **to get a b. of,** darse una panzada de.

belly laugh, carcajada, risotada; **to give a b. l.,** soltar una carcajada o risotada.

belong [bɪ'lɔŋ] *v.i.* 1. pertenecer, atañer, corresponder, tocar. 2. (con *to*) pertenecer a, ser de (su propiedad). 3. ser de, deber estar, ej., *this old chair belongs in the kitchen,* esta silla vieja debe estar en la cocina; *with his talents he belongs in the academy,* con sus aptitudes él debería estar en la academia. 4. estar en su medio, ser aceptado (en un grupo, sociedad, etc.).

belonging [-ɪŋ] *s.* (*gen. pl.*) pertenencias, bienes, efectos personales.

Belorussian [,bɛloʊ'rʌʃən] *s.* 1. nativo o habitante de Bielorrusia. 2. (idioma) bielorruso.

beloved [bɪ'lʌvd, -'lʌvəd] *a.* amado, querido, caro. —*s.* persona amada.

below [bɪ'loʊ] *adv.* 1. abajo, debajo, hacia abajo. 2. en la tierra. 3. en el infierno. 4. río abajo. 5. **to go b.,** (mar.) bajar (desde la cubierta). —*prep.* 1. bajo, debajo de; por debajo de. 2. inferior a. 3. indigno de. 4. **b. cost,** (com.) bajo costo; **b. one's breath,** entre dientes, en voz baja; **b. zero,** bajo cero.

Belshazzar [bɛl'ʃæzər, B -ə] *s.* (bíbl.) Baltasar.

belt [bɛlt] *s.* 1. cinturón, cinto. 2. cinta, banda, correa, faja. 3. (bot., zool., geog., meteor.) zona, región. 4. **to hit below the b.,** (dep., fig.) golpear bajo; **to pull one's b. in,** (jer.) prepararse para hacer frente a tiempos difíciles, alistarse para una tarea ardua; **to tighten one's b.,** ajustarse el cinturón, ceñirse, estrecharse; **under one's b.,** en el estómago de uno; en poder de uno. —*v.t.* 1. ceñir. 2. liar, zunchar. 3. rodear, cercar. 4. azotar, zurrar. 5. golpear, asestar un golpe a. 6. (gen con *out*) cantar en voz chillona. 7. (mec.) poner correa a (máquina). —*v.i.* pasar con violencia o a todo correr; **b. up,** (jer., G.B.) callarse la boca; **safety b.,** (aut., avia.) cinturón de seguridad.

belt [bɛlt] *s.* 1. golpe. 2. (jer.) emoción viva, conmoción.

belt conveyor, (mec.) correa transportadora, transportadora de banda, transportador de cinta sin fin.

belt course, (arq.) cordón, bocel.

belt highway, carretera de circunvalación, ronda de circunvalación, periférico.

belting ['bɛltɪŋ] *s.* 1. material para correas o cinturones. 2. correaje, correas de transmisión. 3. tunda, zurra.

belt line 1. (f.c.) línea de circunvalación. 2. cordón de emergencia (de bomberos).

beltway ['bɛltweɪ] *s.* carretera de circunvalación, ronda de circunvalación, periférico.

beluga *s.* (ict.) beluga, esturión blanco.

belvedere ['bɛlvə,dɪr, B -,dɪə] *s.* 1. belvedere, mirador, terraza. 2. cigarro puro, habano fino.

BEM *abrev. de* **British Empire Medal,** Medalla del Imperio Británico.

bema ['bimə] *s.* 1. (*pl.* BEMATA [-mətə]) (hist., arq.) bema (plataforma del altar en los templos de la antigua Grecia). 2. tabernáculo.

bemean [bɪ'min] *v.t.* **b. oneself,** rebajarse, humillarse, degradarse.

bemire [-'maɪr, B -'maɪə] *v.t.* enfangar, enlodar, encenagar.

bemoan [-'moʊn] *v.t.* lamentar, plañir, gemir por.

bemock [-'mɑk, B -'mɔk] *v.t.* (ant.) mofarse de, burlarse de.

bemuse [bɪ'mjuz] *v.t.* causar estupefacción, pasmar, dejar perplejo.

bemused [-'mjuzd] *a.* absorto, pensativo, meditabundo.

bench [bɛntʃ] *s.* 1. banco, banca, banqueta. 2. (der.) corte (de justicia), tribunal; asiento de los jueces. 3. (der.) judicatura, cuerpo de jueces. 4. (G.B.) escaño (en el parlamento). 5. travesaño, asiento (en un bote). 6. mesa de trabajo. 7. concurso canino; plataforma de exhibición (para perros). 8. (geog., geol.) banqueta, escalón. 9. antepecho (en una mina). 10. (dep.) banca (de los jugadores de reserva o en descanso). 11. **to be on the b.,** ser juez u obispo; **to be raised to the b.,** ser nombrado juez u obispo. —*v.t.* 1. proveer de bancos o bancas. 2. sentar en un banco. 3. exhibir (perros) en un concurso canino. 4. (dep.) hacer descansar o expulsar del campo (a un jugador).

bencher [ˈbɛntʃər, B -ə] *s.* 1. el que se sienta o trabaja en un banco. 2. (der., G.B.) decano de un colegio de abogados. 3. el que frecuenta las tabernas.

bench mark, (top.) hito, marca fija; (fig.) punto de referencia, parámetro.

benchmark test, (comput.) prueba de referencia, patrón de referencia.

bench show, exposición canina.

bench warmer, (dep.) jugador de reemplazo (que calienta el banco esperando entrar en acción).

bench warrant, (der.) auto de detención expedido por un juez o tribunal.

bend [bɛnd] *s.* 1. curva, vuelta, recodo (de un río, camino, etc.). 2. inclinación. 3. combadura, curvatura. 4. (*pl.*) aeroembolismo, aeroembolia, parálisis de los buzos, apoplejía por cambios bruscos de presión. 5. (her.) barra o banda (diagonales). 6. (mar.) nudo. 7. **to go around the b.,** (jer., G.B.) privarse de juicio, volverse loco. —*v.t.* (*pret., p.p.* BENT; *p.pr.* BENDING) 1. doblar, inclinar, torcer. 2. combar, encorvar. 3. arquear, enarcar; doblar (las rodillas); inclinar (la cabeza). 4. aplicar, emplear (voluntad, energías), encauzar, dirigir (esfuerzos). 5. dirigir (pasos, ojos). 6. hacer inclinar, someter. 7. (*ú. en voz pasiva*) resolver, tomar determinación. 8. (mar.) ayustar (cabos); envergar (velas); entalingar (cable al ancla). 9. **b. one's efforts to,** encaminar o dirigir sus esfuerzos a; **b. someone's will,** hacer cambiar de parecer a alguien, doblegar la voluntad de alguien. —*v.i.* 1. encorvarse, torcerse. 2. doblegarse, inclinarse, someterse. 3. tener inclinación, tender. 4. (con *to*) aplicarse, entregarse (al trabajo, etc.). 5. **b. down** (u **over**), inclinarse; **b. to the oars,** curvarse sobre los remos; **bend someone's ear,** fastidiar a alguien hablando con exceso.

Ben Day process [ˈbɛnˈdeɪ-] (impr.) procedimiento bendei, para fotograbados.

bender [ˈbɛndər, B -də] *s.* 1. dobladora, curvadora, instrumento para doblar. 2. (jer., G.B.) medio chelín. 3. (jer.) borrachera, juma, turca. 4. **on a b.,** (jer.) jaraneando, emborrachándose.

bending [-dɪŋ] *s.* flexión, comba, cimbreo; (mec.) flexión; **b. coefficient,** coeficiente de flexión; **b. moment,** (mec.) momento de flexión, momento flector; **b. point,** punto de flexión; **b. strength,** resistencia a la flexión; **b. stress,** esfuerzo de flexión.

beneath [bɪˈniθ] *adv.* abajo, debajo. —*prep.* debajo de, por debajo de, inferior a, indigno de; (que) no es digno ni de, ej., *he is b. contempt,* no es digno ni siquiera de desprecio.

benedicite [ˌbɛnəˈdɪsətɪ, B -ˈdaɪ-] *s.* (relig.) benedícite.

benedict [ˈbɛnəˌdɪkt] **benedick** [-ˌdɪk] *s.* recién casado (esp. si ha sido soltero mucho tiempo).

Benedictine [ˌbɛnəˈdɪktən, -ˌtin] *s.* 1. (relig.) benedictino. 2. [-ˌtin] licor benedictino.

benediction [ˌbɛnəˈdɪkʃən] *s.* bendición, gracia.

benefaction [-ˈfækʃən, ˈbɛnəˌfæk-] *s.* 1. acto de beneficencia. 2. beneficio, favor, merced.

benefactor [ˈbɛnəˌfæktər, B -tə] *s.* bienhechor, benefactor.

benefactress [-trəs] *s.* bienhechora, benefactora.

benefic [bəˈnɛfɪk] *a.* benéfico.

benefice [ˈbɛnəfəs] *s.* (relig.) beneficio, prebendas, emolumentos (que recibe un eclesiástico). —*v.t.* conferir prebendas a (un eclesiástico).

beneficence [bəˈnɛfəsəns] *s.* 1. beneficencia, caridad. 2. acto de beneficencia.

beneficent [-sənt] *a.* benéfico, caritativo.

beneficial [ˌbɛnəˈfɪʃəl] *a.* beneficioso, provechoso, útil, productivo.

beneficiary [-ˈfɪʃɪˌɛrɪ, B -ərɪ] *s.* beneficiario, beneficiado.

benefit [ˈbɛnəˌfɪt] *s.* 1. beneficio, ventaja, provecho; ganancia (esp. pecunaria). 2. prestación, beneficio (de seguro social a enfermos, ancianos, etc.). 3. ayuda, esp. en: **without b. of,** sin la ayuda de. 4. (teat.) (función de) beneficio. 5. **for the b. of,** en pro de, a favor de; por el bien de, en consideración a; **to give (one) the b. of the doubt,** suponer inocencia antes que culpabilidad; **without the b. of clergy,** sin sanción de la iglesia (díc. de parejas no casadas). —*v.t.* beneficiar, aprovechar a. —*v.i.* (gen. con *by* o *from*) beneficiarse, disfrutar, sacar utilidades o provecho (de).

benefit performance, funcion benéfica.

benevolence [bəˈnɛvələns] *s.* 1. benevolencia, buena voluntad. 2. caridad; dádiva.

benevolent [-lənt] *a.* benévolo, caritativo, bondadoso.

Bengalese [ˌbɛŋgəˈliz] *a.* bengalí. —*s.* bengalí, natural de Bengala.

Bengali [bɛnˈgɔlɪ, bɛŋ-] *s.* 1. bengalí, natural de Bengala. 2. (lenguaje) bengalí. 3. (orn.) bengalí. —*a.* bengalí, de Bengala.

bengaline [ˈbɛŋgəˌlin] *s.* (tej.) bengalina.

Bengal light [ˈbɛŋgɔl-] luz de Bengala.

bengal tiger, tigre de bengala, tigre real.

benighted [bɪˈnaɪtəd] *a.* anochecido, sorprendido por la noche; sumido en la obscuridad; (fig.) sumido en la ignorancia.

benign [bɪˈnaɪn] *a.* 1. benigno, afable, bondadoso. 2. favorable, propicio. 3. (med.) benigno, ej., *b. tumor,* tumor benigno.

benignant [bɪˈnɪgnənt] *a.* 1. benigno, afable, bondadoso. 2. beneficioso, favorable.

benignity [-nətɪ] *s.* benignidad; bondad, buena voluntad.

benison [ˈbɛnəsən, -zən] *s.* bendición.

benjamin [ˈbɛndʒəmən] *s.* 1. (quím.) benjuí. 2. (bot.) aro. 3. (bot.) balsamina, flor de china, belén.

Benjamin, *s.* (fig.) benjamín (el hijo más pequeño y querido).

benne [ˈbɛnɪ] *s.* semilla de sésamo o ajonjolí.

bent [bɛnt] *a.* 1. curvado, doblado, torcido. 2. (ú. con *on*) inclinado (a), propenso (a), dispuesto o resuelto (a). —*s.* 1. tendencia, disposición, propensión, inclinación, afición. 2. capacidad. 3. (ing.) caballete, castillete, pilón, armadura. 4. curvatura, encorvadura. 5. páramo; puna; matorral. 6. (bot.) agrostida, agrostis. 7. **to follow one's b.,** obrar de acuerdo a sus inclinaciones; **to the top of one's b.,** cuanto quiera uno, hasta la saciedad.

Benthamism [ˈbɛnθəˌmɪzəm] *s.* (filos.) bentamismo.

benthos [ˈbɛnˌθɑs, B -ˌθɔs] *s.* (biol.) bentos, conjunto de organismos que viven en las profundidades de las aguas.

bentonite [ˈbɛntənˌaɪt] *s.* (geol.) bentonita.

benumb [bɪˈnʌm] *v.t.* entumecer, entorpecer; aterir, pasmar (de frío).

benzaldehyde [bɛnˈzældəˌhaɪd] *s.* (quím.) aldehido benzoico, benzaldehido.

benzedrine [ˈbɛnzəˌdrin] *s.* (quím., med.) bencedrina.

benzene [ˈbɛnˌzin, ˌbɛnˈzin] *s.* (quím.) benceno.

benzene ring, (quím.) núcleo bencénico.

benzidine [ˈbɛnzəˌdin] *s.* (quím.) bencidina.

benzine [ˈbɛnˌzin, ˌbɛnˈzin] *s.* (quím.) bencina.

benzoate [ˈbɛnzoʊˌeɪt] *s.* (quím.) benzoato.

benzocaine [-zəˌkeɪn] *s.* (med.) benzocaína.

benzoic [bɛnˈzoʊɪk] *a.* (quím.) benzoico.

benzoin [ˈbɛnzoʊɪn, -ˌzɔɪn] *s.* 1. (quím.) benzoína. 2. (quím., bot.) benjuí.

benzol [ˈbɛnˌzɔl, -ˌzoʊl] *s.* (quím.) benzol, benceno.

benzophenone [ˌbɛnzoʊfiˈnoʊn] *s.* (quím.) benzofenona.

benzyl [ˈbɛnˌzil, -zəl] *s.* (quím.) bencilo.

bequeath [bɪˈkwiθ, -ˈkwið] *v.t.* 1. legar, donar o dejar en testamento. 2. (fig.) legar (un ejemplo, una obra, etc. a la posteridad).

bequest [-ˈkwɛst] *s.* legado, donación.

berate [bɪˈreɪt] *v.t.* regañar, reñir, reprender con vehemencia, zaherir.

Berber [ˈbɜrbər, B ˈbɜbə] *a.* berberisco, bereber, natural de Berbería. —*s.* bereber, berberisco.

berberine [ˈbɜrbəˌrin, B ˈbɜbə-] *s.* (quím.) berberina.

bereave [bɪˈriv] *v.t.* (*pret., p.p.* BEREAVED o BEREFT [-ˈrɛft]; *p.pr.* BEREAVING). 1. (con *of*) privar (de bienes espirituales, esperanza, etc.). 2. desolar, afligir (esp. por la muerte de un ser querido).

bereaved [-ˈrivd] *a.* desolado, acongojado, (la viuda, los huérfanos, los sobrevivientes del fallecido).

bereavement [-ˈrivmənt] *s.* congoja, aflicción, desconsuelo; desgracia, luto, duelo.

bereft [bɪˈrɛft] *a.* (con *of*) privado (de); desnudo (de), ej., *b. of happiness,* privado de felicidad.

beret [bəˈreɪ, B ˈbɛrˌeɪ] *s.* boina, gorra francesa o vizcaína.

berg [bɜrg, B bɜg] *s.* 1. iceberg, banquisa, témpano de hielo. 2. (S. África) montaña.

bergamot [ˈbɜrgəˌmɑt, B ˈbɜgəˌmɔt] *s.* 1. (bot.) bergamoto (árbol). 2. bergamota (fruto). 3. (bot.) (variedad de) menta o hierba buena.

berhyme, berime [bɪˈraɪm] *v.t.* rimar, poner en verso; escribir en verso.

beribboned [-ˈrɪbənd] *a.* 1. encintado, adornado, engalanado con cintas. 2. oficial o militar que ostenta sus condecoraciones.

beriberi [ˈbɛrɪˈbɛrɪ] *s.* (med.) beriberi.

berkelium [ˈbɜrklɪəm, B ˈbɜk-] *s.* (quím.) berkelio.

Bering Sea [ˈbɛrɪŋ-] mar de Bering.

Berks *abrev. de* **Berkshire,** Berkshire (condado en G.B.); cadena de montañas en E.U.

Berlin [bərˈlɪn, B bəˈ-, ˈbɜlɪn] *s.* 1. antigua capital de Alemania, actualmente dividida y constituida, en su sector oriental, en capital de la República Democrática Alemana. 2. b., berlina (coche).

Berliner [bərˈlɪnər, B bəˈlɪnə] *s.* berlinés.

berm, berme [bɜrm, B bɜm] *s.* (fort.) berma.

Bermuda [bərˈmjudə, B bəˈ-] *s.* las islas Bermudas.

Bermuda onion, (bot.) cebolla grande y morada.

Bermuda rig, (mar.) aparejo de Bermuda (formado por una vela triangular y un mástil con el ápice inclinado).

Bermuda shorts, bermudas (pantalones cortes).

Bermuda Triangle, triángalo de las Bermudas.

Bern [bɜrn, bɛrn, B bɜn, bɛən] *s.* Berna, capital de Suiza.

Bernardine ['bɜrnər͵dɪn, -͵din, B 'bɜnə͵-] *a., s.* bernardino, monje de esta orden o congregación.
Bernese [bər'niz, B bə'-] *a.* bernés. —*s.* bernés, bernesa; de Berna.
berretta [bə'rɛtə] *s.* (relig.) birreta, solideo rojo de los cardenales.
berried ['bɛrid] *a.* 1. que produce bayas. 2. que tiene huevas (díc. de langostas y cangrejos).
berry ['bɛrɪ] *s.* 1. baya, fruta pequeña. 2. semilla, grano, haba (de café, etc.). 3. huevo, huevecillo (de langosta o peces). —*v.i.* 1. producir bayas, llenarse de bayas. 2. recoger o buscar bayas; coger fresas, moras, etc.
berserk [bər'sɜrk, -'zɜrk, B bə'sɜk] *a.* furioso, frenético, enloquecido. —*adv.* con furia, en estado frenético; **to go b.,** enloquecerse; excederse. —*s.* (t. **berserker**) (hist.) feroz guerrero escandinavo que era considerado invulnerable.
berth [bɜrθ, B bɜθ] *s.* 1. (mar.) amarradero, anclaje. 2. (mar.) espacio para bornear. 3. litera, cama (en un barco o coche de ferrocarril); camarote. 4. sitio, puesto; acomodación, acomodo, empleo. 5. **to give (a) wide b. to,** evitar, mantenerse apartado de (alguien o algo), no ir cerca de. —*v.t.* 1. (mar.) amarrar, atracar. 2. acomodar. —*v.i.* (mar.) atracar.
bertha ['bɜrθə, B 'bɜθə] *s.* berta, cuello ancho de encaje (en vestido de escote bajo).
bertillonage ['bɜrtələ͵nɑdʒ, B 'bɜtɪ-] *s.* sistema de identificación individual, anterior al de las huellas digitales.
beryl ['bɛrəl] *s.* (min.) berilo.
beryllium [bə'rɪlɪəm] *s.* (quím.) berilio, glucinio.
beseech [bɪ'sitʃ] *v.t.* (*pret., p.p.* BESOUGHT [-'sɔt] o BESEECHED; *p.pr.* BESEECHING) suplicar, implorar, instar.
beseecher [-ər, B -ə] *s.* suplicante.
beseeching [-ɪŋ] *a.* suplicante.
beseem [bɪ'sim] *v.t., v.i.* (ant.) convenir, parecer bien, sentar bien.
beset [bɪ'sɛt] *v.t.* (*pret., p.p.* BESET; *p.pr.* BESETTING) 1. sitiar, rodear. 2. acosar, hostigar, perseguir, molestar. 3. (con *with, ú. gen. en voz pasiva*) engastar (con), ej., *a crown b. with diamonds,* una corona engastada con diamantes. 4. (con *with, ú. gen. en voz pasiva*) plagar (de), llenar (de), ej., *a house b. with rats,* una casa plagada de ratas, *a task b. with difficulties,* una tarea llena de dificultades. 5. ocupar, bloquear (una carretera, vía, etc.).
besetting [-ɪŋ] *a.* habitual, constante, dominante (vicio, etc.).
beside [bɪ'saɪd] *prep.* 1. junto a, cerca de, al lado de. 2. lejos de, fuera de. 3. además de. 4. junto con; comparado con. 5. **b. oneself,** fuera de sí; **b. the point,** (que) no viene al caso.
besides [-'saɪdz] *adv.* además, también, ej., *we need these and others b.,* necesitamos éstos y otros también. —*prep.* 1. además de, ej., *others must help b. him,* otros deben ayudar además de él. 2. (*en negaciones o interrogaciones*) excepto, fuera de.
besiege [bɪ'sidʒ] *v.t.* sitiar; asediar, acosar.
besieger [-ər, B -ə] *s.* sitiador, asediador.
besmear [bɪ'smɪr, B -'smɪə] *v.t.* salpicar, ensuciar; embadurnar.
besmirch [-'smɜrtʃ, B -'smɜtʃ] *v.t.* ensuciar, manchar; (fig.) deshonrar, mancillar.
besom ['bizəm] *s.* 1. escoba (esp. un manojo de ramas que se usa para barrer). 2. (bot.) retama blanca.
besot [bɪ'sɑt, B -'sɔt] *v.t.* (*pret., p.p.* BESOTTED; *p.pr.* BESOTTING) infatuar, atontar, embrutecer.
besought [-'sɔt] *pret., p.p. de* **beseech.**
bespatter [-'spætər, B -tə] *v.t.* 1. salpicar, manchar (con agua, lodo o suciedad). 2. (fig.) difamar, desacreditar.
bespeak [bɪ'spik] *v.t.* (*pret.* BESPOKE [-'spoʊk]; *p.p.* BESPOKEN [-ən]; *p.pr.* BESPEAKING) 1. ordenar, alquilar, reservar. 2. demostrar, indicar, revelar. 3. indicar, presagiar, advertir. 4. dirigir la palabra a, hablar a.
bespectacled [-'spɛktəkəld] *a.* con anteojos, con gafas, con lentes.
bespoke [-'spoʊk] *pret., p.p. de* **bespeak.**
bespread [-'sprɛd] *v.t.* (ant.) cubrir, esparcir, tender sobre.
besprinkle [-'sprɪŋkəl] *v.t.* rociar, salpicar; esparcir.
Bessarabia [͵bɛsə'reɪbɪə] *s.* Besarabia, región entre la Unión Soviética y Rumania.
Bessemer converter['bɛsəmər-, B -ə-] (metal.) convertidor Béssemer.
Bessemer process, (metal.) procedimiento to Béssemer (para la elaboración del acero).
Bessemer steel, (metal.) acero Béssemer.
best [bɛst] (*super. de* **good**) *a.* superior, óptimo; mayor; **b. wishes, Charles,** un abrazo, Carlos; muchos recuerdos, Carlos; saludos, Carlos; **the b. part,** la mayor parte, casi todo, lo mejor; **to put one's b. foot forward,** tratar de causar buena impresión. —(*super. de* **well**) *adv.* mejor, más oportunamente, en la mejor forma posible; **had b.,** sería mejor que, debería. —*s.* el mejor, los mejores; **all the b.,** mis mejores votos, felicidades, buena suerte; **at b.,** en el mejor de los casos, a lo más; **(he did it) for the b.,** (lo hizo) con la mejor intención; **one's b.** o **one's Sunday b.,** las mejores ropas, las galas domingueras de uno; **second b.,** el mejor después del primero; **to be at one's b.,** lucirse, estar en su elemento; **to do one's b.,** hacer todo lo posible; **to have the b. of it,** tener ventaja, ir ganando (discusión, pelea, pleito, etc.); **to make the b. of,** salir lo mejor posible de, contentarse con; **to the b. of (one's abilities, power,** etc.), en la medida de (sus posibilidades, capacidad, etc.).
best-before date, (com.) fecha de consumo preferente.
bestead [bɪ'stɛd] (ant.) *a.* colocado, situado. —*v.t.* servir, ayudar, asistir.
best girl, (fam.) novia, amiga preferida.
bestial ['bɛstʃəl, B -tjəl] *a.* 1. bestial, brutal. 2. bestial, animal (instintos apetitos, etc.).
bestiality [͵bɛstʃɪ'ælətɪ, B -tɪ-] *s.* bestialidad, brutalidad; contacto carnal entre persona y animal.
bestialize ['bɛstʃə͵laɪz, B -tjə-] *v.t.* bestializar, embrutecer.
bestiary [-tʃɪ͵ɛrɪ, B -tɪərɪ] *s.* bestiario (libro o colección de estampas de animales y sus peculiaridades).
bestir [bɪ'stɜr, B -'stɜ] *v.t.* mover, remover, agitar, menear, incitar.
best man, padrino de boda.
bestow [bɪ'stoʊ] *v.t.* 1. (gen. con *on* o *upon*) conferir, otorgar, conceder; donar a, agraciar. 2. usar, emplear, aplicar.
bestraddle [-'strædəl] *v.t.* montar a horcajadas.
bestrew [-'stru] *v.t.* rociar, esparcir.
bestride [bɪ'straɪd] *v.t.* 1. montar a horcajadas. 2. (fig.) alzarse sobre, encumbrarse sobre, dominar. 3. cruzar un tranco.
best seller, (*book*) bestseller, éxito de librería; (*product*) superventas, gran éxito de venta.
bet [bɛt] *s.* apuesta, postura. —*v.t.* (*pret., p.p.* BET o BETTED; *p.pr.* BETTING) 1. apostar, poner (cierta suma). 2. apostar con (alguien). 3. **b. one's boots,** estar completamente seguro. —*v.i.* apostar; **b. on,** apostar por (caballo, etc.); **you b.!** (fam.) ¡sin duda! ¡por supuesto!
beta ['beɪtə, B 'bitə] *s.* 1. beta, segunda letra del alfabeto griego. 2. (fís.) rayo o partícula beta.
betaine ['bitə͵in] *s.* (quím.) betaína.
betake [bɪ'teɪk] *v.t.* **b. oneself,** trasladarse, dirigirse.
beta particle, (fís.) partícula beta.
beta ray, (fís.) rayo beta.
betatron ['beɪtə͵trɑn, B 'bitə͵trɔn] *s.* (fís.) betatrón.
betel ['bitəl] *s.* (bot.) betel, areca.
Betelgeuse ['bɛtəl͵dʒuz, B ͵bitəl'ʒɜz] *s.* (astr.) Betelgeuze.
betel nut, (bot.) nuez de betel.
betel palm, (bot.) areca.
bête noire [͵beɪtnə'wɑr, B -'nwɑ] *s.* (fr.) persona o cosa detestable.
bethel ['bɛθəl] *s.* 1. iglesia o capilla para marineros. 2. (G.B.) capilla de no-conformistas.
bethink [bɪ'θɪŋk] *v.t.* (ant.) **b. oneself,** reflexionar, pensar bien; **b. oneself (to do something),** metérsele a uno en la cabeza (hacer algo).
Bethlehem ['bɛθlɪ͵hɛm, -lɪəm] *s.* Belén.
Bethlehemite [-aɪt] *s.* betlemita, natural de Belén.
betide [bɪ'taɪd] *v.i., v.t.* (*defectivo, ú. sólo en tercera pers. del pres. de subj.*) suceder (a), acontecer (a); **whate'er b.,** suceda lo que suceda.
betimes [-'taɪmz] *adv.* con tiempo, oportunamente, temprano, a buena hora.
betoken [-'toʊkən] *v.t.* 1. indicar, presagiar, anunciar. 2. demostrar, evidenciar, revelar.
betony ['bɛtənɪ] *s.* (bot.) betónica.
betray [bɪ'treɪ] *v.t.* 1. traicionar, delatar, denunciar. 2. revelar, descubrir, ej., *his words betrayed his ignorance,* sus palabras revelaban su ignorancia. 3. engañar, abandonar.
betrayal [-əl] *s.* 1. traición; engaño, seducción, abandono (de una mujer). 2. revelación, delación, denuncia.
betrayer [-ər, B -ə] *s.* traidor, delator; seductor.
betroth [bɪ'trɑθ, -'trɔθ, B -'troʊð] *v.t.* prometer en matrimonio; **to be betrothed,** desposarse.
betrothal [-əl] *s.* compromiso, fiesta de compromiso.
betrothed [-'trɔθt, B -'troʊðd] *s.* prometido, novio; prometida, novia.
better ['bɛtər, B -ə] (*comp. de* **good**) *a.* mejor; mayor; preferible; superior; **b. half,** cara mitad, media naranja, esposa o esposo; **b. part,** la mayor parte, casi todo; **the b. part of,** más de la mitad de. —*v.t.* mejorar, aumentar, sobrepasar, exceder, aventajar; **b. oneself,** mejorar su posición, adelantar, progresar. —(*comp. de* **well**) *adv.* mejor, en forma superior, en mayor grado; **all the b.,** tanto mejor; **b. and b.,** cada vez mejor; **b. late than never,** más vale tarde que nunca;**b. off,** más rico, más acomodado; en mejores condiciones, en mejor posición; **b. than** (seguido de un número) más de, sobre; **had b.,** sería mejor que, sería más prudente, más vale que, ej., *we had b. go,* más vale que nos vayamos; **no b. than,** no (valer) más que; **so much the b.,** tanto mejor; **the sooner the b.,** cuanto antes mejor; **to get b.,** mejorar (un enfermo); **to go one b.,** mejorar la oferta, prometer más; **to grow b.,** mejorarse (situación, cosa, etc.); **to know b.,** no ser tan tonto (como para creer, aceptar o hacer algo); **to like b.,** gustar más a uno, preferir; **to think b. of,** cambiar de idea. —*s.* 1. (*gen. pl.*) superior, persona de más rango. 2. algo mejor. 3. **for the b.,** para mejorar; **to get the b. of,**

superar, vencer; **to have the b. of,** salir airoso de (una discusión, etc.).
better, *var. de* **bettor.**
betterment [-mənt] *s.* 1. mejora, mejoría, mejoramiento; aumento, adelanto, perfeccionamiento. 2. (der.) mejora (de una propiedad para que rinda más).
bettor ['bɛtər, B -ə] *s.* apostador.
betulaceous [ˌbɛtʃʊ'leɪʃəs, B -tjʊ-] *a.* (bot.) betuláceo.
between [bɪ'twin] *prep.* entre; **b. the devil and the deep blue sea,** entre la espada y la pared, sin escapatoria; **b. you and me, b. ourselves,** entre nosotros, en confianza. —*adv.* de por medio, entre los dos; **far b.,** a grandes intervalos; **in b.,** mientras tanto; en medio; **to come b.,** interponerse; **to stand b.,** mediar, interceder; servir como protección.
between decks, (mar.) entrecubiertas, entrepuentes; entre cubiertas.
betweentimes [-ˌtaɪmz] **betweenwhiles** [-ˌhwaɪlz, -ˌwaɪlz] *adv.* a ratos, a intervalos.
betwixt [bɪ'twɪkst] *prep., adv.* (ant., poét.) entre; **b. and between,** a medias, ni lo uno ni lo otro.
bev *abrev. de* **billion electron volts,** gigaelectronvoltio (GeV).
bevatron ['bɛvəˌtrɑn, B -ˌtrɔn] *s.* (fis.) bevatrón.
bevel ['bɛvəl] (mec.) *s.* 1. bisel, chaflán, falseo. 2. falsa escuadra. 3. (impr.) bisel, pestaña, faceta. —*v.t.* (*pret., p.p.* BEVELED O BEVELLED; *p.pr.* BEVELING O BEVELLING) biselar, chaflanar, achaflanar. —*v.i.* inclinarse. —*a.* biselado, chaflanado, achaflanado.
bevel cut, corte a bisel, corte a inglete.
beveled [-əld] *a.* biselado, achaflanado, falseado.
bevel edge, canto biselado, bisel.
beveler [-ələr, B -lə] *s.* biselador; (grab.) máquina biseladora.
bevel gage, (mec.) falsa escuadra.
bevel gear, (mec.) engranaje cónico o en bisel.
beveling [-lɪŋ] *a.* achaflanado, biselado; **b. machine,** biseladora.
bevel joint, (mec.) ensambladura a bisel, junta a inglete.
bevel pinion, piñón cónico, piñón angular.
bevel plane, (mec.) cepillo de achaflanar.
bevel square, (mec.) falsa escuadra, escuadra plegable.
bevel washer, (mec.) arandela ahusada o achaflanada.
bevel wheel, (mec.) rueda cónica.
beverage ['bɛvərɪdʒ] *s.* bebida, brebaje.
bevy ['bɛvɪ] *s.* bandada (de aves), manada (de corzos, ciervos, etc.); grupo, junta, corro (de mujeres).
bewail [bɪ'weɪl] *v.t.* lamentar, llorar, deplorar. —*v.i.* plañir, lamentar.
beware [-'wɛr, B -'wɛə] *v.i.* (ú. con *of, lest, how*) estar en guardia (contra), estar alerta, precaverse (de algún riesgo o peligro); **b.!** ¡cuidado! ¡ojo! —*v.t.* cuidarse de (algo); guardarse (de).
bewilder [bɪ'wɪldər, B -də] *v.t.* confundir, azorar, aturrullar, dejar perplejo.
bewildered [-dərd] *a.* perplejo, confundido; enredado.
bewildering [-ɪŋ] *a.* azarante.
bewilderment [-dərmənt, B -dəmənt] *s.* perplejidad, azoramiento, aturdimiento, estupefacción.
bewitch [bɪ'wɪtʃ] *v.t.* 1. embrujar, hechizar. 2. encantar, fascinar.
bewitching [-ɪŋ] *a.* fascinante, encantador, cautivante, hechicero.
bewitchment [-mənt] *s.* 1. hechizo, embrujo, encanto. 2. encantamiento, conjuro, hechicería.
bey [beɪ] *s.* (hist.) bey, gobernador turco.
beyond [bɪ'ɑnd -'jɑnd, B -'jɔnd, -'ɔnd] *adv.* más allá, más lejos; allende, al otro lado; **let us go b.,** vayamos más lejos. —*prep.* allende, más allá de, al otro lado de, fuera de, además de; después de; superior a; **b. dispute,** incontestable; **b. doubt,** fuera de duda, sin lugar a duda; **b. help,** sin remedio; **b. measure,** desmesuradamente, sobremanera; **b. one's reach,** fuera del alcance de uno; **b. question,** indiscutible; **b. the frontier,** al otro lado de la frontera; **b. the grave,** más allá de la tumba; **b. the sea,** allende al mar; **it's b. me,** no lo comprendo, no lo entiendo; **she is living b. her means,** ella gasta más de lo que tiene. —*s.* **the b.,** el futuro, lo desconocido, el más allá.
bezant ['bɛzənt] *s.* 1. besante (antigua moneda bizantina). 2. (arq.) disco chato (utilizado en ornamentación). 3. (her.) besante, roel, disco en el escudo.
bezel ['bɛzəl] *s.* bisel, chaflán, faceta; cristal cortado en bisel; engaste.
bezique [bə'zik] *s.* besigue, un juego de naipes.
bezoar [biˌzɔr, B -ˌzɔ] *s.* bezoar, bezar; masa en el intestino de ciertos rumiantes a la que antiguamente se atribuían poderes curativos.
bf *abrev. de* **boldface,** (impr.) negrilla, negrita.
B.F.A. *abrev. de* **Bachelor of Fine Arts,** Licenciado en Bellas Artes.
B-girl ['biˌgɜrl, B -ˌgɜl] *s.* (jer.) tanguista, gancho, muchacha o cantinera que sirve de atracción en una taberna.
bhakti ['bʌktɪ] *s.* (relig.) bhakti.
bhang [bæŋ] *s.* 1. cáñamo de la India. 2. mariguana, hachís.
bhp *abrev. de* **brake horsepower,** potencia al freno, caballo de fuerza al freno.
bi, *prefijo* dos, doble.
Bi *simb. de* **bismuth,** bismuto (Bi).
biangular [baɪ'æŋgjələr, B -gjʊlə] *a.* biangular.
biannual [ˌbaɪ'ænjuəl] *a.* semestral, semianual.
biarticulate [-ɑr'tɪkjələt, B -ɑ'-] *a.* (zool.) biarticulado.
bias ['baɪəs] *s.* 1. propensión, inclinación, predilección. 2. prejuicio, ej., *it's wrong to judge him with such b.,* no es justo juzgarlo con tanto prejuicio. 3. (cost.) sesgo, ej., *I want the skirt cut on the b.,* quiero la falda cortada al sesgo. 4. (elec.) polarización negativa de la grilla (de un tubo electrónico). —*a.* sesgado. —*v.t.* (*pret., p.p.* BIASED O BIASSED; *p.pr.* BIASING O BIASSING) 1. sesgar, soslayar. 2. prejuzgar. 3. influir, predisponer, ej., *her opinions have been biased by her friends,* sus opiniones han sido influenciadas por sus amigos. —*adv.* (cost.) diagonalmente, sesgadamente.
bias chase, (imp.) rama sesgada.
biascope ['baɪəˌskoʊp] *s.* *(ópt.) biascopio, variedad primitiva del estereoscopio.*
biased, biassed [-əst] *a.* parcial, con prejuicio, prejuiciado.
bias resistor, (rad.) resistencia de polarización negativa.
biatomic [ˌbaɪə'tɑmɪk, B -'tɔm-] *a.* (quím.) biatómico.
biauricular [ˌbaɪɔ'rɪkjələr, B -lə] **biauriculate** [-lət] *a.* (med.) biauricular.
biaxal [baɪ'æksɪəl] *a.* biaxial.
bib [bɪb] *s.* 1. babador, babero. 2. pechera (del delantal). 3. (ict.) faneca. 4. **best b. and tucker,** (fam.) las mejores ropas. —*v.t., v.i.* (ant.) (*pret., p.p.* BIBBED; *p.pr.* BIBBING) beber, sorber.
bibasic [baɪ'beɪsɪk] *a.* (quím.) bibásico.
bibb [bɪb] *s.* 1. llave, grifo, espita. 2. (bot.) **b. lettuce,** especie de lechuga.
bibber ['bɪbər, B -ə] *s.* (ant.) bebedor.
bibcock ['bɪbˌkɑk, B -ˌkɔk] *s.* grifo, caño, espita.
bibelot [ˌbɪb'loʊ, ˌbib-] *s.* 1. dije, chuchería, bibelot. 2. objeto en miniatura.
Bible ['baɪbəl] *s.* (la) Biblia; (fig.) biblia, autoridad suprema (libro, persona, etc.).
Bible Belt, (E.U.) región al sur y oeste central donde prevalecen las creencias religiosas de los fundamentalistas protestantes.
Bible paper, papel Biblia, papel de imprimir delgado y resistente.
Biblical ['bɪblɪkəl] *a.* bíblico.
biblicist ['bɪbləsəst] *s.* 1. experto en la Biblia. 2. persona que interpreta la Biblia literalmente.
bibliofilm ['bɪblɪoʊˌfɪlm] *s.* película micrográfica de un libro.
bibliographer [ˌbɪblɪ'ɑgrəfər, B -'ɔg-fə] *s.* bibliógrafo.
bibliographic [-ə'græfɪk] **bibliographical** [-əl] *a.* bibliográfico.
bibliography [ˌbɪblɪ'ɑgrəfɪ, B -'ɔg-] *s.* bibliografía.
bibliolatry [-'ɑlətrɪ, B -'ɔl-] *s.* 1. bibliolatría, interpretacíon de la Biblia al pie de la letra. 2. bibliolatría, adoración por los libros.
bibliomania [ˌbɪblɪə'meɪnɪə] *s.* bibliomanía, afán excesivo por poseer y comprar libros.
bibliomaniac [-ˌæk] *s., a.* bibliómano.
bibliopegy [ˌbɪblɪ'ɑpədʒɪ, B -'ɔp-] *s.* arte de la encuadernación (de libros).
bibliophile ['bɪblɪəˌfaɪl] *s.* bibliófilo.
bibliopole [-ˌpoʊl] *s.* bibliopola, librero (esp. el que vende libros raros o curiosos).
bibliotheca [ˌbɪblɪə'θikə] *s.* 1. biblioteca. 2. catálogo de libros.
bibliotics [ˌbɪblɪ'ɑtɪks, B -'ɔt-] *s. pl.* (*sing. en const.*) bibliología, examen de documentos para determinar su autenticidad u origen.
biborate of soda [baɪ'bɔreɪt-] *s.* bórax, borato de sosa hidratado.
bibulous ['bɪbjələs] *a.* 1. poroso, esponjoso; bíbulo, absorbente. 2. bebedor, borrachín.
bicameral [baɪ'kæmərəl] *a.* (pol.) bicameral.
bicapsular [-'kæpsələr, B -lə] *a.* (bot.) bicapsular (fruto).
bicarbonate [baɪ'kɑrbəˌneɪt, B -'kɑbənɪt] *s.* (quím.) bicarbonato.
bicarbonate of soda, bicarbonato de soda o de sosa.
bice [baɪs] *s.* (pint.) verde o azul malaquita.
bicentenary [ˌbaɪsɛn'tɛnərɪ, -'sɛntənˌɛrɪ, B -sɛn'tinərɪ] *a., s.* bicentenario.
bicentennial [-sɛn'tɛnɪəl] *a., s.* bicentenario.
bicentric [-'sɛntrɪk] *a.* de dos centros.
bicephalous [-'sɛfələs] *a.* bicéfalo, bicípite, de dos cabezas.
biceps ['baɪˌsɛps] *s.* (anat.) bíceps.
bichloride [baɪ'klɔrˌaɪd] *s.* (quím.) bicloruro.
bichloride of mercury, (quím.) bicloruro de mercurio.
bichromate [-'kroʊˌmeɪt] *s.* (quím.) bicromato. —*v.t.* (quím.) tratar o combinar con un bicromato.
bichromate cell, (elec.) pila de bicromato.
bichrome ['baɪˌkroʊm] *a.* (pint., tej.) bicromático, bicolor.
bicipital [baɪ'sɪpətəl] *a.* (anat.) bicípide (músculo).
bicker ['bɪkər, B -ə] *v.i.* 1. altercar, disputar, porfiar, discutir por una insignificancia. 2. (poét.) flamear, brillar (una llama). —*s.* 1. altercado, disputa, porfía, pelea, pendencia. 2. (esco.) tazón de madera (para gachas, puches o licor).

bickerer [-ər, B -ərə] *s.* pleitista, pendenciero.
bicolor, [cf1](pr. G.B.) [cf3]bicolour [ˈbaɪˌkʌlər, B -ə] **bicolored,** (pr. G.B.) **bicoloured** [-ərd, B -əd] *a.* bicolor, bicromático.
biconcave [ˌbaɪkɑnˈkeɪv, -ˈkɑnˌkeɪv, B -ˈkɔn-] *a.* (geom.) bicóncavo.
biconvex [-kɑnˈvɛks, -ˈkɑnˌvɛks, B -ˈkɔn-] *a.* (geom.) biconvexo.
bicorn [ˈbaɪˌkɔrn, B -ˌkɔn] **bicornuate** [baɪˈkɔrnjʊət, B -ˈkɔnjʊ-] *a.* 1. bicorno, que tiene dos cuernos. 2. en forma de media luna.
bicuspid [baɪˈkʌspəd] *a.* bicúspide; (anat.) bicúspide; (bot.) bicuspidado. —*s.* (odont.) bicúspide.
bicuspidate [-pəˌdeɪt] *a.* (bot.) bicuspidado; (anat.) bicúspide.
bicycle [ˈbaɪˌsɪkəl, B ˈbaɪsɪk-] *s.* bicicleta. —*v.i.* ir en bicicleta, montar bicicleta.
bicyclic [baɪˈsaɪklɪk, -ˈsɪk-] **bicyclical** [-lɪkəl] *a.* de dos ciclos; (bot., quím., fis.) bicíclico.
bicyclist [ˈbaɪˌsaɪkləst, B -sɪklɪst] *s.* ciclista.
bicycle lock, cadena antirrobo.
bid [bɪd] *v.t.* (*pret.* BADE [bæd] o BID; *p.p.* BIDDEN [ˈbɪdən] o BID; *p.pr.* BIDDING) 1. pedir, mandar, ordenar. 2. expresar (deseo, saludo), dar (la bienvenida), decir (adiós). 3. invitar, convidar. 4. (*pret., p.p.* BID) licitar, pujar, ofrecer; (bridge) declarar, rematar. 5. **b. defiance,** desafiar; **b. farewell (to),** despedirse (de), decir adiós (a); **b. welcome,** dar la bienvenida a, saludar. —*v.i.* hacer una oferta o postura; (bridge) hacer una declaración; **b. fair (to do),** prometer, dar indicios de; mostrarse dispuesto a (hacer). —*s.* 1. licitación. 2. postura, oferta, propuesta. 3. ruego, súplica. 4. invitación. 5. (naipes, esp. bridge) declaración. 6. **to make a b. for,** (fig.) hacer un esfuerzo para conseguir (premio, triunfo, favor, etc.).
biddable [ˈbɪdəbəl] *a.* 1. (bridge) declarable. 2. dócil, obediente.
bidder [-ər, B -ə] *s.* postor, licitador (en una subasta o almoneda); (bridge) declarante; **the highest b.,** el mejor postor.
bidding [-ɪŋ] *s.* 1. licitación, remate, puja. 2. puja (cantidad ofrecida). 3. orden (*f.*), mandato; llamada, llamamiento; invitación. 4. (bridge) licitación, remate. 5. **to do the b. of,** obedecer a la orden de, cumplir el mandato de.
biddy [ˈbɪdɪ] *s.* 1. (fam.) gallina, pollo. 2. (jer.) criada respondona. 3. vieja chismosa.
bide [baɪd] *v.i.* (*pret.* BODE [boʊd]; *p.p.* BIDED; *p.pr.* BIDING) (ant.) estarse, quedarse, permanecer. —*v.t.* 1. esperar. 2. (ant.) resistir, aguantar. 3. **b. one's time,** esperar su oportunidad; aguaitar la laucha (Chile).
bidentate [baɪˈdɛnˌteɪt] *s.* bidentado, bidente.
bidet [bɪˈdeɪ, B ˈbideɪ] *s.* (fr.) bidé, recipiente de aseo personal.
biennial [baɪˈɛnɪəl] *a.* bienal. —*s.* 1. bienal (exposición, concurso, etc.). 2. (bot.) planta bienal.
biennium [-ɪəm] *s.* (*pl.* BIENNIA [-ɪə]) bienio.
bier [bɪr, B bɪə] *s.* féretro; catafalco; andas funerarias.
bifacial [baɪˈfeɪʃəl] *a.* 1. bifronte, de dos frentes o caras. 2. (bot.) bifacial (hoja).
bifarious [-ˈfɛrɪəs, B -ˈfɛər-] *a.* (bot.) bifario.
biff [bɪf] *s.* (fam.) golpe, bofetada, bofetón. —*v.t.* (fam.) golpear, abofetear.
biffin [ˈbɪfɪn] *s.* (G.B.) manzana de cáscara roja de sabor agridulce; postre que se confecciona con dicha manzana.
bifid [ˈbaɪˌfɪd] *a.* (bot.) bífido.
bifilar [baɪˈfaɪlər, B -lə] *a.* bifilar, formado o soportado por dos hilos (usado especialmente en suspensiones bifilares); **b. micrometer,** micrómetro bifilar.
biflex [ˈbaɪˌflɛks] *a.* doblado en dos direcciones opuestas y alternadamente cóncavo y convexo.
biflorate [baɪˈflɔˌreɪt] **biflorous** [-rəs] *a.* (bot.) bifloro.
bifocal [baɪˈfoʊkəl] *a.* bifocal. —*s. pl.* anteojos bifocales.
bifoliate [-ˈfoʊlɪət] *a.* (bot.) bifoliado.
biforate [-ˈfɔˌreɪt] *a.* (biol.) que tiene dos aberturas o perforaciones.
biform [ˈbaɪˌfɔrm, B -ˌfɔm] **biformed** [-ˌfɔrmd, B -ˌfɔmd] *a.* (poét.) biforme.
bifront [-ˌfrʌnt] **bifrontal** [baɪˈfrʌntəl] *a.* bifronte.
bifurcate [ˈbaɪfərˌkeɪt, B -fəˌ-] *v.t., v.i.* bifurcar, bifurcarse, dividir (se) en dos. — [-ˈfɜrkət, B -fəˌkeɪt] *a.* bifurcado.
bifurcation [ˌbaɪfərˈkeɪʃən, B -fəˈ-] *s.* bifurcación.
big [bɪg] *a.* (BIGGER; BIGGEST) 1. grande; extenso. 2. fuerte (tormenta, voz, etc.). 3. cargado, lleno. 4. importante, imponente. 5. en gran escala (negocio, comercio, gobierno, etc.). 6. (fam.) magnánimo, noble. 7. **b. sounding,** altisonante; **b. with child,** embarazada (mujer); **to get** (o **to grow**) **too b. for one's breeches,** (fam.) volverse presuntuoso, fanfarronear, darse aires; **to look** (o **to talk**) **b.,** darse aires, fanfarronear, tomar postura jactanciosa; **to make it b.,** (jer.) tener éxito. —*adv.* 1. pomposamente, pretenciosamente. 2. con gran éxito, excelentemente.
bigamist [ˈbɪgəməst] *s.* bígamo.
bigamous [-əməs] *a.* bígamo.
bigamy [-əmɪ] *s.* (der.) bigamia.
big band, orquesta grande de jazz (esp. entre 1930 y 1950).
big-bang theory [ˈbɪgˈbæŋ-] teoría del big bang, teoría de la gran explosión.
Big Bear, (astr.) Osa Mayor.
big-bellied [-ˌbɛlid] *a.* barrigona, embarazada (mujer), preñada (animal).
Big Ben[-ˈbɛn] campana en el reloj del parlamento de Londres; dicho reloj.
Big Bertha, cañon de largo alcance (usado por Alemania en la primera guerra mundial).
big board, (fam.) mercado de valores de Nueva York.
big-boned [ˈbɪgˈboʊnd] *a.* huesudo.
big boy, (jer.) persona importante o influyente.
big brother, 1. hermano mayor. 2. hermano a otro, persona que protege o ampara a un delincuente o a un muchacho desamparado. 3. **B. B.,** personaje omnipresente que todo lo ve; brazo omnipotente del gobierno (el término se originó en la novela *1984* de George Orwell).
big business, (las) empresas grandes, (los) grandes intereses (colectivamente); el gran capital, el mundo de las altas finanzas; **to be b.** ser un gran negocio.
big cheese, (jer.) pez gordo.
big daddy, (jer.) señorón, peje gordo.
Big Dipper, (astro.) Carro Mayor, Osa Mayor.
big-eared [-ˈɪrd, B -ˈɪəd] *a.* orejudo.
bigeminal [baɪˈdʒɛmɪnəl] *a.* (med.) bigémino, bigeminado.
bigeminate [-ˌneɪt] *a.* bigeminado.
bigeminy [-ˈdʒɛmənɪ] *s.* (med.) bigeminia, bigeminismo.
big end, (ing.) cabeza de biela.
bigeneric [ˌbaɪdʒəˈnɛrɪk] *a.* híbrido, derivado de dos géneros diferentes.
big finger, dedo pulgar.
big game, 1. caza mayor (animales). 2. (fig.) objetivo importante.
biggie [-ɪ] *var. de* **bigwig.**
biggin [ˈbɪgən] *s.* gorro de niño, capucha, capirote, gorro de dormir; (hist., G.B.) toca de los abogados; (ant.) gorro de dormir.
biggish [ˈbɪgɪʃ] *a.* bastante grande, grandecito.
bighead [-ˌhɛd] *s.* 1. (vet.) enfermedad caracterizada por hinchazón de la cabeza. 2. (fig.) humos, vanidad, presunción, altivez.
bigheaded [-əd] *a.* engreído, ufano.
bighearted [-ˌhɑrtəd, B -ˌhɑtɪd] *a.* generoso, bondadoso, cordial.
bigheartedly [-lɪ] *adv.* generosamente, bondadosamente.
bighorn [-ˌhɔrn, B -ˌhɔn] *s.* (zool.) carnero cimarrón de cuernos grandes, oriundo de las Montañas Rocosas de E.U.
big house, (jer.) la cárcel.
bight [baɪt] *s.* 1. (mar.) vuelta, lazo (en un cable, soga, cadena, etc.). 2. recodo (de una cordillera o río). 3. (mar.) caleta, ensenada, seno (en la costa). —*v.t.* 1. enlazar. 2. sujetar o inmovilizar con lazos. 3. hacer un lazo en (soga, cable, cadena, etc.).
big-league [ˈbɪgˈlig] *s.* 1. (dep., E.U.) liga mayor (en el béisbol profesional), división superior (en otros deportes). 2. (fig.) liga mayor, círculo influyente (en los negocios, etc.).
big leaguer [-ər, B -ə] (dep., E.U.) jugador de una liga mayor.
big lie, the, 1. exagerada falsificación de los hechos, que se adorna y se repite para hacerla creíble. 2. técnica de propaganda política que utiliza este método.
big mouth, (jer.) bocón, persona que habla mucho; chismoso; delator.
big-mouthed [ˈbɪgˈmaʊðd] *s., a.* 1. bocudo, bocón. 2. (fig.) bocón, picudo, hablador.
big name, (fam.) persona célebre.
bigness [-nəs] *s.* grandeza; (fig.) grandeza; altisonancia, pomposidad (de palabras, afirmaciones, etc.).
big noise, (jer.) pez gordo, hombre de fuste.
bignonia [bɪgˈnoʊnɪə] *s.* (bot.) bignonia.
bigot [ˈbɪgət] *s.* fanático, persona intolerante o guiada por prejuicios.
bigoted [-əd] *a.* fanático, intolerante.
bigotry [-rɪ] *s.* fanatismo, intolerancia.
big shot, (jer.) pez o peje gordo, hombre de fuste, personaje importante.
big stick, alarde de fuerza, poder de coacción.
big stink, 1. (jer.) queja larga y enérgica. 2. escándalo.
big talk, 1. (jer.) baladronadas, bravatas. 2. lenguaje altisonante.
big-time [ˈbɪgˌtaɪm] *a.* influyente, de campanillas.
big time, 1. (teat.) circuito de variedades bien remunerado. 2. lo selecto, lo más distinguido, lo mejor. 3. gran éxito. 4. **to have a b. t.,** divertirse de lo lindo.
big toe, dedo gordo del pie.
big top, 1. tienda o carpa mayor del circo. 2. (fam.) el circo.
big tree, (bot.) abeto gigante, secoya.
bigwig [-ˌwɪg] *s.* (fam.) señor de campanillas, hombre de fuste.
big words, 1. (jer.) palabras jactanciosas. 2. disputa acalorada, palabras mayores.
bihourly [baɪˈaʊrlɪ, B -ˈaʊəlɪ] *a.* que se repite cada dos horas.
bijou [ˈbiˌʒu] *s.* (fr.) (*pl.* BIJOUX [-ˌʒuz]) dije, joya.
bijouterie [bɪˈʒutəˌri] *s.* bisutería.
bijugate [ˈbaɪdʒəˌgeɪt] **bijugous** [-gəs] *a.* (bot.) biyugado (dícese de la hoja pinada).
bike [baɪk] *s. abrev. fam. de* **bicycle,** bici, bicicleta.
bikini [bəˈkinɪ] *s.* bikini (traje de baño minúsculo).

bilabial [baɪˈleɪbɪəl] (filo., fon.) *a.* bilabial. —*s.* consonante bilabial.
bilabiate [-bɪət] *a.* (bot.) bilabiado (corola o cáliz).
bilander [ˈbɪləndər, ˈbaɪ-, B -də] *s.* (mar.) balandra.
bilateral [baɪˈlætərəl] *a.* bilateral.
bilaterally [-ɪ] *adv.* bilateralmente.
bilberry [ˈbɪlˌbɛrɪ, B -bərɪ] *s.* (bot.) arándano.
bilbo [ˈbɪlˌboʊ] *s.* 1. (*pl.*) barras o lingotes de hierro con grillos. 2. (ant.) espada o estoque de Bilbao.
bile [baɪl] *s.* 1. (med.) bilis. 2. (fam.) ira, cólera, mal humor.
bile duct, (anat.) conducto biliar.
bilge [bɪldʒ] *s.* 1. (mar.) pantoque. 2. (mar.) sentina; suciedad acumulada en la sentina. 3. (fig.) sandez, tontería.
bilged [bɪldʒd] *a.* (mar.) varado, desfondado (un barco).
bilge pump, (mar.) bomba de carena, bomba de sentina.
bilge water, (mar.) agua de sentina, agua cuaderna.
bilge ways, (mar.) anguilas.
bilharziasis [ˌbɪlhɑrˈzaɪəsɪs, B -hɑˈ-] *s.* (med.) bilharziasis, bilharziosis, esquistosomiasis.
biliary [ˈbɪlɪˌɛrɪ, B -jərɪ] *a.* (med.) biliar, de la bilis.
bilinear [baɪˈlɪnɪər, B -ɪə] *a.* (mat.) bilineal.
bilingual [-ˈlɪŋgwəl] *a.* bilingüe.
bilingual dictionary, diccionario bilingüe.
bilingualism [-ˌɪzəm] *s.* bilingüismo.
bilious [ˈbɪljəs] *a.* 1. (med.) bilioso. 2. (fig.) colérico, malhumorado. 3. de mal semblante, pálido.
biliousness [-nəs] *s.* biliosidad, cólera, mal humor.
bilirubin [ˌbɪləˈrubən] *s.* (bioquím.) bilirrubina.
biliteral [baɪˈlɪtərəl] *a.* bilítero, de dos letras; (letra) que remite a dos consonantes (como en ciertas lenguas semitas).
biliverdin [ˌbɪləˈvɜrdən, B -ˈvɜd-] *s.* (bioquím.) biliverdina.
bilk [bɪlk] *v.t.* 1. rehuir el pago a (los acreedores), estafar. 2. engañar, defraudar, frustrar. 3. evadir, burlar. —*s.* tramposo, estafador.
bill [bɪl] *s.* 1. documento, escrito. 2. cartel, letrero; volante. 3. (E.U.) billete (de banco). 4. cuenta (en restaurante, etc.). 5. (com.) factura. 6. (com.) giro, letra. 7. lista. 8. (der.) minuta, declaración. 9. proyecto (de ley). 10. (teat.) programa. 11. **to fill the b.,** ser adecuado, llenar los requisitos; **to foot the b.,** pagar la cuenta; cargar con los gastos. —*v.t.* 1. registrar en una minuta, poner en una lista. 2. facturar, cargar en cuenta a. 3. anunciar (en cartel, letrero o programa).
bill, *s.* 1. pico (de ave). 2. hocico. 3. (mar.) uña (del ancla). —*v.i.* acariciarse (las aves con el pico); (fig.) acariciar, mimar; **b. and coo,** arrullarse, acariciarse y decirse ternezas (los enamorados).
bill, *s,* (mil., hist.) alabarda, pica con cuchilla corva.
billabong [ˈbɪləˌbɔŋ] *s.* (Aust.) 1. brazo de río que no desemboca sino que termina en un punto ciego. 2. arroyo seco. 3. rebalsa.
billboard [ˈbɪlˌbɔrd, B -ˌbɔd] *s.* 1. cartelera, valla anunciadora. 2. (mar.) varadero de ancla.
billed [bɪld] *a.* picudo, que tiene pico.
biller [ˈbɪlər, B -ə] *s.* facturador; facturadora (máquina).
billet [ˈbɪlət] *s.* 1. (mil.) boleta, orden de alojamiento; alojamiento. 2. (jer.) situación, empleo. 3. (ant.) billete, esquela, carta breve. —*v.t.* (mil.) 1. dar orden de acantonar tropas. 2. alojar.
billet, *s.* 1. leño, zoquete. 2. (metal) lingote (pequeño), tocho. 3. (arq.) billete. 4. (her.) cartela.
billet-doux [ˌbɪleɪˈdu] *s.* (*pl.* BILLETS-DOUX [-ˈduz]) esquela o carta amorosa.
billfold [ˈbɪlˌfoʊld] *s.* (E.U.) billetero, cartera de bolsillo.
billhead [-ˌhɛd] *s.* (com.) encabezamiento o membrete de factura.
billhook [-ˌhʊk] *s.* (agr.) hocino, podadera.
billiard [ˈbɪljərd, B -jəd] *s.* carambola. —*a.* de billar (bola, mesa, etc.).
billiard ball, bola de billar.
billiard cloth, paño de billar.
billiard hall, b. parlor, b. room, b. saloon, salón de billar.
billiard pocket, tronera de billar.
billiards [-jərdz, B -jədz] *s. pl.* billar, el deporte en sí.
billiard table, mesa de billar.
billing [ˈbɪlɪŋ] *s.* (teat., cinem.) jerarquía de importancia en un elenco o compañía, ej., *top billing,* estrellato.
billing machine, facturadora.
billingsgate [ˈbɪlɪŋzˌgeɪt, B -gɪt] *s.* (G.B.) lenguaje soez.
billion [ˈbɪljən] *s.* (G.B.) billón, (E.U.) mil millones.
billionaire [ˌbɪljəˈnɛr, ˈbɪl-ˌnɛr, B ˌbɪlˈnɛə] *a., s.* billonario.
billionth [ˈbɪljənθ] *a., s.* billonésimo.
billman [ˈbɪlmən] *s.* 1. segador, que maneja la hoz. 2. cartelero, que pega carteles en paredes o postes.
bill of appeal, (der.) demanda de apelación, escrito de apelación.
bill of attainder, (der.) escrito de proscripción y confiscación.
bill of costs, (der.) pliego de costos.
bill of credit, (com.) carta de crédito.
bill of exchange, (com.) letra de cambio.
bill of fare, menú, minuta, lista de platos; (fig.) programa.
bill of goods, guía de mercancías; **to sell (someone) a b. of g.,** (fam.) persuadir (a alguien) con engaños para que acepte, crea o haga algo.
bill of health, carta o patente de sanidad; **a clean b. of h.,** (fig.) buenos informes, recomendacíon.
bill of lading, (com.) (nav.) conocimiento de embarque; (f.c.) carta de porte.
bill of materials, lista de materiales o de piezas.
bill of particulars, (der.) declaración, exposición de hechos.
bill of privilege, (G.B.) petición de un par para ser juzgado o interpelado por otros pares.
Bill of Rights, carta o declaración de derechos (las diez primeras enmiendas a la constitución de los Estados Unidos).
bill of sale, (com.) contrato de compra y venta.
billon [ˈbɪlən] *s.* (min.) vellón.
billow [ˈbɪloʊ] *s.* ola, oleada. —*v.i.* 1. ondular, alzarse y rodar (como las olas). 2. (gen. con *out*) abultarse (como el velamen en el viento), hincharse.
billowy [-ɪ] *a.* ondulante.
billposter [ˈbɪlˌpoʊstər, B -tə] **billsticker** [-ˌstɪkər, B -ə] *s.* cartelero, que pega carteles en paredes o postes.
billy [ˈbɪlɪ] *s.* 1. vara, porra (esp. de policía). 2. (Aust.) bote de lata (para cocinar al aire libre).
billy club, vara, porra.
billycock [-ˌkɑk, B -ˌkɔk] *s.* (G.B.) sombrero hongo.
billy goat, macho cabrío.
bilobate [baɪˈloʊˌbeɪt] *a.* bilobulado, bilobado, de dos lóbulos.
bilocation [ˌbaɪloʊˈkeɪʃən] *s.* bilocación, presencia de una misma persona en dos lugares.
bilocular [-ˈlɑkjələr, B -ˈlɔkjʊlə] **biloculate** [-lət] *a.* (bot.) bilocular.
biltong [ˈbɪlˌtɔŋ] *s.* cecina, tasajo, chalona (Am.), charqui (Am.).
bimanal [ˈbɪmənəl, B baɪˈmeɪnəl] **bimanous** [baɪˈmeɪnəs, B ˈbɪmənəs] *a.* bímano.
bimanual [-ˈmænjʊəl] *a.* bimanual.
bimbo [ˈbɪmboʊ] *s.* 1. (fam.) (despec.) joven bonita y tonta. 2. (fam.) (ant.) memo, imbécil.
bimester [-ˈmɛstər, B -tə] *s.* bimestre, período de dos meses.
bimestrial [-trɪəl] *a.* bimestral, cada dos meses.
bimetallic [ˌbaɪməˈtælɪk] *a.* 1. (quím.) bimetálico. 2. (fin.) bimetálico. 3. **b. plates,** (litog.) planchas (fotolitográficas) bimetálicas.
bimetallism [-ˈmɛtəlˌɪzəm] *s.* (fin.) bimetalismo, uso del oro y la plata como patrón.
bimetallist [-əst] *a., s.* (fin.) bimetalista.
bimillenary [-ˈmɪləˌnɛrɪ, B -nərɪ] *s.* 1. período de dos mil años. 2. segundo milenio. —*a.* que se repite cada dos mil años.
bimillennium [-mɪˈlɛnɪəm] *s.* segundo milenio.
bimolecular [-məˈlɛkjələr, B -lə] *a.* (quím.) bimolecular.
bimonthly [-ˈmʌnθlɪ] *a.* 1. bimestral. 2. bimensual. —*s.* publicación bimensual. —*adv.* bimestralmente.
bimorphemic [-mɔrˈfimɪk, B -mɔˈ-] *a.* (gram.) bimorfémico.
bimotored [-ˈmoʊtərd, B -təd] *a.* de dos motores, bimotor.
bin [bɪn] *s.* cajón, arcón, recipiente (para guardar cosas o echar basura); **looney b.,** (jer.) manicomio.
binary [ˈbaɪnərɪ] *a.* 1. binario, doble, de dos partes. 2. (quím.) binario. 3. (mat.) binario, con base dos. —*s. entidad que tiene dos partes.*
binary code, (comput.) código binario.
binary fission, reproducción asexual (en animales).
binary star, (astr.) estrella binaria.
binate [-ˌneɪt] *a.* (bot.) binado.
binaural [baɪˈnɔrəl] *a.* (med.) biauricular, binaural.
bind [baɪnd] *v.t.* (*pret., p.p.* BOUND [baʊnd]; *p.pr.* BINDING) 1. atar, liar, amarrar. 2. (fig.) enlazar, ligar, juntar, unir. 3. (gen. con *up*) ceñir, vendar. 4. obligar, comprometer, constreñir. 5. apretar (díc. de prendas). 6. encuadernar, empastar (libros). 7. ribetear (alfombra, etc.). 8. escriturar, contratar. 9. confirmar, ratificar (pacto, convenio, etc.). 10. estreñir. 11. (quím.) trabar, fijar. 12. (der.) compeler, obligar. 13. (seguros) efectuar (póliza, seguro). 14. **b. oneself,** (fig.) atarse las manos; **b. over,** (der.) poner bajo fianza; obligar. —*v.i.* 1. endurecerse, trabarse. 2. atascarse. 3. tener fuerza obligatoria; ser obligatorio. —*s.* 1. lazo, enlace. 2. (jer.) apuro, aprieto, lío, ej., *what a b.,* ¡qué lío!. 3. **in a b.,** (jer.) en calzas prietas.
binder [ˈbaɪndər, B -də] *s.* 1. atador. 2. faja, ligadura. 3. encuadernador, empastador (Am.). 4. (agr.) atadora, agavilladora. 5. (quím.) substancia aglutinante, materia adherente. 6. (arq.) traviesa, ligazón. 7. sobretripa, capa interior (de cigarros). 8. tablas (con tornillos) para sujetar (hojas sueltas, revistas, etc.). 9. recibo (de un pago a cuenta del precio de un inmueble). 10. (seguros) documento provisional de seguro.
bindery [-dərɪ] *s.* taller de encuadernación.
binding [-dɪŋ] *s.* 1. encuadernación. 2. (cost.) guarnición, ribete, tira. 3. atadura, ligadura, faja; ligazón, ligamento. —*a.* obligatorio; (der.) valedero, obligatorio.

binding bandage, (med.) vendaje o apósito contentivo.
binding energy, (fís., quím.) energía de descarga, la cantidad de energía descargada durante la formación de un átomo o molécula de partículas alfa, protones, etc., a costa de la masa total.
binding post, (elec.) borne, poste de conexión, sujetahílo.
bindweed ['baɪnd,wid] *s.* (bot.) correhuela, enredadera.
bine [baɪn] *s.* (bot.) tallo trepador, sarmiento, vástago flexible (de la vid, del lúpulo, etc.).
Binet test [bɪ'neɪ-] (psic.) test de Binet que consiste en preguntas, problemas y actividades manuales.
binge [bɪndʒ] *s.* (fam.) parranda, ej., *to go on a b.,* ir de parranda.
bingo ['bɪŋgoʊ] *s.* bingo (juego semejante a la lotería).
binnacle ['bɪnəkəl] *s.* (mar.) bitácora.
binocle ['bɪnəkəl] *s.* 1. gemelos, binóculo. 2. cierto juego de naipes.
binocular [baɪ'nɑkjələr, bə-, B -'nɔkjʊlə] *a.* binocular.
binoculars [-lərz, B -ləz] *s. pl.* binóculo, prismáticos, gemelos.
binomial [baɪ'noʊmiəl] *s.* 1. (mat.) binomio. 2. (biol.) binario. —*a.* 1. (mat.) binomio. 2. (biol.) binario, binomial, binominal.
binomial system, (biol.) sistema binario, sistema que asigna un nombre doble latinizado a cada planta o animal; el primero indica su género y el segundo su especie.
binomial theorem, teorema binomio (indica la forma general de cualquier potencia de un binomio algebraico).
binuclear [-'nuklɪər, B -'nju-ə] **binucleate** [-ət] *a.* (biol.) binuclear, binucleado.
bioassay [,baɪoʊ'æs,eɪ, -ə'seɪ] *s.* (bioquím.) bioensayo. —*v.t.* probar por medio de un bioensayo.
bioastronautics [-,æstrə'nɔtɪks] *s.* bioastronáutica, ciencia que estudia las reacciones de seres vivientes en el ambiente espacial (durante un viaje espacial).
biocatalyst [-'kætələst] *s.* (quím., med.) biocatalizador.
biocenology [-sɪ'nɑlədʒi, B -'nɔl-] *s.* (biol.) estudio de la biocenosis.
biocenosis [-sɪ'noʊsəs] *s.* mancomunidad de plantas y animales integrados a un ambiente.
biochemical [-'kɛmɪkəl] *a.* bioquímico.
biochemist [-əst] *s.* bioquímico.
biochemistry [,baɪoʊ'kɛməstrɪ] *s.* bioquímica.
biocide ['baɪə,saɪd] *s.* agente usado para erradicar pestes; insecticida.
bioclimatology [,baɪoʊ,klaɪmə'tɑlədʒɪ, B -'tɔl-] *s.* bioclimatología.
biodegradable [-dɪ'greɪdəbəl] *a.* biodegradable, que se descompone naturalmente.
biodegrade [,baɪodɪ'greɪd] *v.i.* biodegradarse.
biodynamics [-daɪ'næmɪks] *s.* (*sing. en const.*) biodinámica.
bioecology [-ɪ'kɑlədʒɪ, B -'kɔl-] *s.* bioecología.
bioelectricity [-ɪ,lɛk'trɪsətɪ] *s.* bioelectricidad, electricidad producida por organismos y células vivientes.
biogenesis [,baɪoʊ'dʒenəsɪs] *s.* (biol.) biogénesis.
biogenetic [-dʒə'nɛtɪk] *a.* biogenético.
biogenic [-'dʒɛnɪk] *a.* (biol.) biógeno.
biogeny [baɪ'ɑdʒənɪ, B -'ɔdʒ-] *var. de* biogénesis.
biogeochemical cycle [,baɪoʊ,dʒioʊ'kɛməkəl-] ciclo biogeoquímico.
biogeography [-dʒɪ'ɑgrəfɪ, B -'ɔg-] *s.* (biol.) biogeografía.
biographer [baɪ'ɑgrəfər, B -'ɔg-fə] *s.* biógrafo.
biographic [,baɪə'græfɪk] **biographical** [-əl] *a.* biográfico.
biography [baɪ'ɑgrəfɪ, bɪ-, B -'ɔg-] *s.* biografía.
biologic [,baɪa'lɑdʒɪk, B -'lɔdʒ-] **biological** [-ɪkəl] *a.* biológico.
biological clock, mecanismo biológico que controla las funciones periódicas en los animales.
biologically [-ɪkəlɪ] *adv.* biológicamente.
biological warfare, guerra biológica, guerra bacteriológica.
biologist [baɪ'ɑlədʒəst, B -'ɔl-] *s.* biólogo.
biology [baɪ'ɑlədʒɪ, B -'ɔl-] *s.* 1. biología. 2. biota, flora y fauna (de una región).
biolysis [-səs] *s.* biolisis, destrucción de la vida, por bacterias o microorganismos.
biomass ['baɪoʊ,mæs] *s.* (biol.) biomasa, cantidad de materia viviente (en determinada área).
biomechanics [,baɪoʊmə'kænɪks] *s. pl.* (*sing. en const.*) biomecánica.
biomedicine [-'mɛdəsən, B -'mɛdsɪn] *s.* biomedicina.
biometrics [-'mɛtrɪks] *s. pl.* (*sing. en const.*) estadística de datos biológicos.
biometry [baɪ'ɑmətrɪ, B -'ɔm-] *s.* biometría.
bionomic [,baɪə'nɑmɪk, B -'nɔm-] **bionomical** [-ɪkəl] *a.* bionómico, relativo a la bionomía o ecología.
bionomics [-ɪks] *s.* (biol., econ.) bionomía, la unión de dos disciplinas, biología y economía, para estudiar la relación entre los organismos y su ambiente.
biontic [baɪ'ɑntɪk, B -'ɔnt-] *a.* (biol.) bióntico.
biophysics [,baɪoʊ'fɪzɪks] *s. pl.* (*sing. en const.*) biofísica.
bioplasm ['baɪoʊ,plæzəm] *s.* (biol.) bioplasma, protoplasma.
biopsy [-,ɑpsɪ, B -,ɔp-] *s.* (med.) biopsia.
biopsychology [,baɪoʊ,saɪ'kɑlədʒi, B -'kɔl-] *s.* biopsicología.
bioscope ['baɪə,skoʊp] *s.* proyector cinematográfico antiguo, ca. 1900.
biosociology [,baɪoʊ,soʊsɪ'ɑlədʒi, B -'ɔl-] *s.* biosociología.
biosphere ['baɪə,sfɪr, B -,sfɪə] *s.* (biol.) biosfera, las partes habitables de la Tierra y su atmósfera.
biostatics [,baɪoʊ'stætɪks] *s. pl.* (*sing. en const.*) biostática.
biosynthesis [-'sɪnθəsəs] *s.* biosíntesis.
biota [baɪ'oʊtə] *s.* biota, flora y fauna (de una región).
biotherapy [,baɪoʊ'θɛrəpɪ] *s.* bioterapia.
biotic [baɪ'ɑtɪk, B -'ɔt-] *a.* biótico, relativo a las ciencias biológicas.
biotic potential, potencial biótico, capacidad biótica (en seres vivientes de una región, de un tipo determinado de suelo, etc.).
biotite ['baɪə,taɪt] *s.* (min.) biotita, mica negra.
biotype [-,taɪp] *s.* (biol.) biotipo.
biparous ['bɪpərəs] *a.* (biol.) bíparo.
bipartisan [baɪ'pɑrtəzən, B -,pɑtɪ'zæn] *a.* de ambos partidos (políticos), bipartidario.
bipartite [-'pɑr,taɪt, B -'pɑ,-] *a.* 1. bipartido, bífido, partido en dos. 2. bilateral (contrato, tratado, etc.).
bipartition [,baɪ,pɑr'tɪʃən, B -,pɑ'-] *s.* bipartición.
biped ['baɪ,pɛd] *a., s.* bípedo.
bipetalous [baɪ'pɛtələs] *a.* (bot.) bipétalo.
bipinnate [-'pɪn,eɪt] *a.* (bot.) bipinado.
biplane ['baɪ,pleɪn] *s.* (aer.) biplano.
bipod [-,pɑd, B -,pɔd] *s.* bípode, soporte de dos pies.
bipolar [baɪ'poʊlər, B -lə] *a.* bipolar, de dos polos; de dos opiniones contradictorias.
bipropellant [-prə'pɛlənt] *s.* (astronáut.) bipropulsante, combustible compuesto de dos ingredientes.
biquadrate [-'kwɑdrət, -,reɪt, B -'kwɔd-] *s.* (mat.) cuarta potencia, cuadrado del cuadrado.
biracial [-'reɪʃəl] *a.* de dos razas.
biradial [-'reɪdɪəl] *a.* de simetría bilateral y radial.
birch [bɜrtʃ, B bɜtʃ] *s.* 1. (bot.) abedul. 2. férula, palmeta, palmatoria (del maestro de escuela). —*v.t.* fustigar, varear.
birchbark ['bɜrtʃ,bɑrk, B 'bɜtʃ,bɑk] *s.* canoa hecha de corteza de abedul.
Bircher ['bɜrtʃər, B 'bɜtʃə] *s.* (E.U.) miembro o simpatizante de la *John Birch Society,* organización ultraconservadora anticomunista.
bird [bɜrd, B bɜd] *s.* 1. pájaro, **ave. 2.** (fam.) sujeto, tío, tipo (raro). 3. (jer., G.B.) muchacha. 4. **a b. in hand is worth two in the bush,** más vale pájaro en mano que ciento volando; **b. of ill omen,** pájaro de mal agüero; **birds of a feather flock together,** Dios los cría y ellos se juntan; **(strictly) for the birds,** (sólo) para los bobos, para los papanatas; **to kill two birds with one stone,** matar dos pájaros de un tiro. —*v.i.* 1. buscar nidos (de pájaros). 2. observar pájaros (en su propio ambiente).
birdbath ['bɜrd,bæθ, B 'bɜd,bɑθ] *s.* alberquilla o pila de baño para pájaros.
birdbrain [-,breɪn] *s.* (jer.) estúpido, mentecato.
birdcage [-,keɪdʒ] *s.* jaula de pájaros.
birdcall [-,kɔl] *s.* 1. voz del ave (cuando llama a otra de su especie). 2. (caza) reclamo, añagaza.
bird colonel, (jer., E.U.) coronel del ejército.
bird dog, perro de presa (adiestrado para cazar aves).
bird fancier, pajarero (el que cría o vende pájaros), el que tiene por pasatiempo criar pájaros exóticos.
bird feeder, comedero para pájaros.
birdhouse [-,haʊs] *s.* pajarera, aviario; jaula de pájaros.
birdie [-ɪ] *s.* 1. pajarito. 2. (golf) marca de un golpe menos del par.
birdlime [-,laɪm] *s.* liga, ajonje, hisca. —*v.t.* cazar con liga.
bird louse, (ento.) piojillo.
birdman [-mən] *s.* 1. pajarero; ornitólogo. 2. (fam.) aviador.
bird of paradise, 1. ave del paraíso, pájaro del sol. 2. flor de vistosos colores que tiene forma de ave.
bird of passage, 1. ave de paso, pájaro migratorio. 2. (fam.) ave de paso (dicho de una persona).
bird of peace, la paloma como símbolo de la paz.
bird of prey, ave de rapiña, ave de presa.
bird pepper, (bot.) guindilla, guindillo de Indias, pimiento de cerecilla.
birdseed [-,sid] *s.* alpiste; alimento de pájaros.
bird's-eye ['bɜrdz,aɪ, B 'bɜdz-] *s.* 1. (bot.) primavera, prímula. 2. (tej.) diseño moteado; tela de diseño moteado. 3. ojo de perdiz (defecto en madera).
bird's-eye view, a vista de pájaro.
bird shot, perdigones.
bird watcher, observador de pájaros (aficionado que observa e identifica pájaros silvestres).
birectangular [,baɪrɛk'tæŋgjələr, B -gjʊ-lə] *a.* (mat.) birrectángulo.

birefringence [-rɪ'frɪndʒəns] *s.* (fís.) birrefringencia, doble refracción.
bireme ['baɪˌrim] *s.* (mar.) birreme.
biretta [bɪ'rɛtə] *s.* (relig.) birreta, birrete.
birl [bɜrl, B bɜl] *v.t., v.i.* girar, dar vueltas (a); pararse sobre un tronco flotante y hacerlo rodar. —*s.* zumbido, susurro.
birr [bɜr, B bɜ] *s.* 1. fuerza (como la del viento), ímpetu, energía, vigor. 2. zumbido.
birth [bɜrθ, B bɜθ] *s.* 1. nacimiento. 2. parto, alumbramiento. 3. (fig.) nacimiento, origen, principio. 4. (fig.) nacimiento, descendencia, linaje. 5. **by b.,** de nacimiento; **(a person) of b.,** (una persona) bien nacida; **to give b. to,** dar a luz, parir.
birth certificate, partida de nacimiento.
birth control, control de la natalidad.
birth control pill, píldora anticonceptiva.
birthday ['bɜrθˌdeɪ, B 'bɜθ-] *s.* 1. día natal, día de nacimiento. 2. cumpleaños, fecha de nacimiento. 3. **b. suit,** la propia piel, ej., *in one's b. suit,* en cueros, sin ropa.
birthmark [-ˌmɑrk, B -ˌmɑk] *s.* marca de nacimiento (ej., un lunar).
birth pill, píldora anticonceptiva.
birthplace [-ˌpleɪs] *s.* lugar de nacimiento; suelo natal.
birthrate [-ˌreɪt] *s.* 1. natalidad. 2. índice de natalidad.
birthright [-ˌraɪt] *s.* derechos de nacimiento; derecho de primogenitura.
birthstone [-ˌstoʊn] *s.* piedra preciosa popularmente considerada como símbolo del mes en que uno ha nacido.
birthwort [-ˌwɜrt, B -ˌwɜt] *s.* (bot.) aristoloquia larga o macho.
bis [bɪs] *adv.* (ú. esp. en mús.) bis; repítase.
Bisayan [bə'saɪən] *s.* bisayo, natural de las Bisayas (Islas Filipinas).
Biscay ['bɪsˌkeɪ, -kɪ] *s.* Vizcaya.
Biscayan [bɪs'keɪən] *a., s.* vizcaíno.
biscuit ['bɪskət] *s.* 1. (G.B.) bizcocho, galleta. 2. (E.U.) bollo. 3. (cerám.) bizcocho (objeto de loza o porcelana antes de recibir barniz o esmalte). 4 color amarillento.
bisect ['baɪˌsɛkt, baɪ'sɛkt] *v.t.* 1. (geom.) bisecar. 2. cortar o dividir en dos partes. 3. empalmar (dos caminos).
bisection [baɪ'sɛkʃən] *s.* 1. (geom.) bisección. 2. división en dos partes.
bisector ['baɪˌsɛktər, B baɪ'sɛktə] *s.* (geom.) bisector, bisectriz.
bisexual [baɪ'sɛkʃʊəl, B -'sɛksjʊəl] *a.* bisexual; hermafrodita.
bishop ['bɪʃəp] *s.* 1. obispo; prelado. 2. (ajedrez) alfil, arfil.
bishopric [-rɪk] *s.* obispado, episcopado; diócesis.
bishop's cape, capa consistorial, capa magna.
bishop's weed, (bot.) biznaga, gingidio; ameos, ami.
bismuth ['bɪzməθ] *s.* bismuto.
bismutite ['bɪzməˌtaɪt] *s.* (min.) bismutita.
bison ['baɪsən, 'baɪz-, B 'baɪs-] *s.* (*pl.* BISON) (zool.) bisonte.
bisque [bɪsk] *s.* 1. sopa de mariscos o verdura en crema. 2. helado que contiene nueces o almendras picadas. 3. (cerám.) porcelana sin vidriar.
bissextile [bɪ'sɛkstəl, B -ˌtaɪl] *a.* bisiesto. —*s.* año bisiesto.
bister ['bɪstər, B -tə] *s.* (pint.) bistre (color castaño oscuro preparado con hollín).
bistort ['bɪsˌtɔrt, B -ˌtɔt] *s.* (bot.) bistorta.
bistoury ['bɪstərɪ] *s.* (cir.) bisturí.
bistro ['bɪsˌtroʊ, 'bis-] *s.* (fr.) 1. pequeña cantina o bar. 2. club nocturno.
bisulcate [baɪ'sʌlˌkeɪt] *a.* (zool.) bisulco.
bisulfate [-ˌfeɪt] *s.* (quím.) bisulfato.
bisulfide [-ˌfaɪd] *s.* (quím.) bisulfuro.
bisyllabic [ˌbaɪsɪ'læbɪk] *a.* bisílabo, bisilábico.
bisymmetrical [-'mɛtrɪkəl] *a.* (bot.) doblemente simétrico.
bit [bɪt] *s.* 1. pedacito, trocito, pizca, ápice. 2. bocado (de comida). 3. ratito. 4. bocado, embocadura (del freno de las caballerías). 5. broca, mecha, barrena (del taladro). 6. mordiente, borde cortante (de una herramienta). 7. paletón (de la llave). 8. (teat., cine.) papel corto o secundario. 9. **a b.,** algo, un poquito, ej., *I'm a b. angry,* estoy algo enojado;**a good b.,** una buena cantidad, bastante; **b. by b.,** poco a poco, parte por parte; **b. player** (o **actor**), partiquino; **every b. as (stubborn,** etc.) **as,** exactamente tan (terco, etc.) como; **not a b.,** en lo más mínimo, en lo absoluto; **to blow to bits,** hacer trizas; **to do one's b.,** poner (o hacer) de su parte; **to give (someone) a b. of one's mind,** decirle (a alguien) cuántas son cinco; **to take the b. between one's teeth,** rebelarse, independizarse, seguir su propio camino. —*v.t.* (*pret., p.p.* BITTED; *p.pr.* BITTING) poner el bocado en la boca del (caballo), enfrenar; refrenar, contener.
bit, *pret., p.p. de* **bite.**
bit brace, (mec.) berbiquí.
bitch [bɪtʃ] *s.* 1. perra. 2. (vulg.) zorra, ramera. 3. (jer.) tarea o cosa desagradable. 4. (jer.) queja. —*v.i.* (jer.) quejarse, lamentarse. —*v.t.* (jer.) 1. averiar, estropear, chapucear. 2. quejarse de.
bitchy [bɪtʃɪ] *a.* (fig.) malintencionado, malhumorado.
bite [baɪt] *v.t.* (*pret.* BIT [bɪt]; *p.p.* BITTEN ['bɪtən]; *p.pr.* BITING) 1. morder. 2. picar, punzar (díc. de insectos, serpientes o aves). 3. picar, quemar, resquemar, ej., *mustard bites my tongue,* la mostaza me quema la boca. 4. penetrar, hundir en (díc. de un arma afilada). 5. corroer (metales). 6. (mar.) morder, agarrar (díc. del ancla). 7. engañar, defraudar. 8. **b. one's lips,** morderse los labios (para contener indignación, ira, etc.); **b. the dust,** (fig.) morder el polvo; **bitten with,** poseído de (una manía, entusiasmo, etc.). —*v.i.* 1. morder. 2. cortar, penetrar (herramienta, arma). 3. picar, morder el anzuelo (pez y fig.). 4. prender, hacer presa. —*s.* 1. mordedura, dentellada; picadura (de insecto, serpiente o ave). 2. bocado, mordisco. 3. (fam.) alimento; bocado, refrigerio, ej., *to take a b.,* tomar un bocado. 4. resquemo (de ciertos alimentos y bebidas); fuerza cortante (del viento). 5. (mec.) asimiento, cogedura. 6. (impr.) mordido, mordedura (del ácido en una lámina de metal). 7. (impr.) lardón, fraile (blanco que queda en la impresión). 8. **put the b. on (someone),** (fig.) pedir dinero prestado a alguien.
bitewing ['baɪtˌwɪŋ] *s.* (odont.) película de rayos-x que muestra simultáneamente las coronas de los dientes superiores e inferiores.
biting ['baɪtɪŋ] *a.* 1. penetrante; picante. 2. (fig.) mordaz, sarcástico, cáustico.
bit part, (teat.) papel secundario.
bitstock ['bɪtˌstɑk, B -ˌstɔk] *s.* manubrio de taladro, berbiquí.
bitt [bɪt] *s.* (mar.) bita, abitón. —*v.t.* abitar (un cable).
bitten ['bɪtən] *p.p. de* **bite.**
bitter ['bɪtər, B -ə] *a.* 1. amargo. 2. (fig.) amargo, desagradable, penoso; cruel (decepción, etc.). 3. (fig.) amargo, disgustado, áspero; punzante, mordaz. 4. enconado, encarnizado (enemigo, lucha, etc.). 5. severo, intenso, agudo (frío, dolor, etc.). —*s.* 1. amargura, momento amargo (de la vida). 2. (*pl.*) amargo, bitter, licor amargo. 3. (G.B.) cerveza amarga.
bitter almond, almendra amarga.
bitter apple, (bot.) coloquíntida.
bitter cassava, (bot.) mandioca, yuca agria, yuca amarga, yuca brava.
bitter end, (mar.) última vuelta del cable del ancla (que queda en la bita); **to the b.e.,** (fig.) hasta el extremo, hasta las últimas consecuencias; hasta vencer o morir.
bitterling ['bɪtərlɪŋ, B -əlɪŋ] *s.* (ict.) bermejuela.
bitterly ['bɪtərlɪ, B -əlɪ] *adv.* amargamente, rencorosamente; **to weep b.,** llorar a lágrima viva.
bittern ['bɪtərn, B -ən] *s.* 1. (orn.) avetoro. 2. agua madre.
bitterness ['bɪtərnəs, B -ənəs] *s.* 1. amargura, amargor. 2. (fig.) amargura, encono, rencor. 3. (fig.) amargura, pena. 4. severidad. 5. encarnizamiento.
bitter principle, (quím.) extracto amargo (de plantas).
bitterroot [-ˌrut] *s.* (bot.) variedad de verdolaga (de las Montañas Rocosas de E.U.).
bitter rot, (bot.) podredumbre amarga.
bitters ['bɪtərz, B -əz] *s.* gotas amargas, condimento de cocina y de bar.
bittersweet [-ərˌswɪt, B -əˌ-] *a.* 1. dulce y amargo a la vez, agridulce. 2. medio amargo (chocolate). —*s.* (bot.) dulcamara; evónimo americano.
bitterwood [-ˌwʊd] *s.* (bot.) cuasia amarga.
bittock ['bɪtək] *s.* (esco.) un poco, un poquito.
bitty ['bɪtɪ] *a.* incoherente, inconexo; desigual, fragmentado.
bitumen [bə'tumən, B -' tju-] *s.* bitumen, betún natural.
bituminize [-ˌaɪz] *v.t.* bituminizar.
bituminous [-əs] *a.* bituminoso.
bituminous coal, carbón bituminoso, carbón blando.
bivalence [baɪ'veɪləns] *s.* (quím.) bivalencia.
bivalent [-lənt] *a.* (quím., biol.) bivalente.
bivalve ['baɪˌvælv] *a.* (zool.) bivalvo. —*s.* (zool.) bivalvo, molusco bivalvo.
bivouac ['bɪvˌwæk] *s.* (mil.) vivac, vivaque. —*v.i.* (*pret., p.p.* BIVOUACKED; *p.pr.* BIVOUACKING) (mil.) vivaquear, acampar, pasar la noche al raso.
biweekly [baɪ'wiklɪ] *a.* 1. quincenal, cada dos semanas. 2. bisemanal, dos veces por semana. —*s.* publicación quincenal. —*adv.* quincenalmente.
bixaceous [bɪk'seɪʃəs] *a.* (bot.) bixáceo, bixíneo.
biyearly [baɪ'jɪrlɪ, B -'jɜlɪ] *a.* semestral, (que sucede u ocurre) dos veces al año (uso incorrecto pero ya generalizado).
bizarre [bə'zɑr, B -'zɑ] *a.* raro, extravagante, excéntrico, grotesco (estilo, moda, idea, etc.).
bizone ['baɪˌzoʊn] *s.* dos zonas combinadas.
B.J. *abrev. de* **Bachelor of Journalism,** Licenciado en Periodismo.
Bk *símb. de* **berkelium,** berkelio (Bk).
B.L. *abrev. de* 1.**Bachelor of Law,** Licenciado en Derecho. 2.**Bachelor of Literature,** Licenciado en Literatura.
B/L *abrev. de* **bill of lading,** conocimiento de embarque.
blab [blæb] *v.t.* (*pret., p.p.* BLABBED; *p.pr.* BLABBING) (gen. con *out*) revelar indiscretamente (secretos, etc.). —*v.i.* parlotear indiscretamente, chismear. —*s.* 1. chismoso. 2. habladuría, chisme.
blabber ['blæbər, B -ə] *v.t., v.i.* barbotar, charlar, parlotear, cotorrear. —*s.* 1. parloteo, cotorreo, cháchara. 2. chismoso, hablador, bocaza.

blabbermouth [-ˌmaʊθ] *s.* hablador, cuentista, chismoso.

black [blæk] *a.* 1. negro. 2. negro, obscuro, obscurecido (cielo, noche, etc.). 3. (fig.) negro, sombrío, tenebroso, lúgubre. 4. siniestro, malvado; infame, atroz. 5. amoratado (ojo, por efecto de un golpe). 6. **b. mark,** marca negra (de descrédito). —*s.* 1. (color) negro. 2. luto, vestido negro. 3. obscuridad. 4. **B.** o **b.** negro, persona de raza negra. 5. **in the b.,** (com.) con ganancia. —*v.t.* 1. ennegrecer; embetunar (zapatos). 2. amoratar (el ojo de alguien, golpeándolo). 3. **b. out,** apagar las luces (como defensa antiaérea); obscurecer (las ventanas, ciudad, etc.); suprimir, eliminar (artículo, etc. mediante la censura). —*v.i.* **b. out,** (aer.) cegarse momentáneamente; perder el conocimiento, desmayarse.

black amber, azabache.

blackamoor [ˈblækəˌmʊr, B -ˌmʊə] *s.* negro (esp. africano).

black-and-blue [-ənˈblu] *a.* amoratado, lívido, cárdeno.

Black and Tan, policía reclutado en Inglaterra para servir en Irlanda en 1919-21, contra la rebelión de los irlandeses.

black and white, escritura; **in b. a. w.,** en blanco y negro, por escrito.

black art, magia negra, nigromancia.

blackball [-ˌbɔl] *s.* bola negra (utilizada para votar en contra, esp. para expulsar de una asociación, etc.); balota secreta. —*v.t.* votar en contra de (alguien); dar bola negra a (alguien); (fig.) boicotear.

black bear, (zool.) 1. oso negro, baribal. 2. oso tibetano.

blackbeetle [-ˌbitəl] *s.* (ento., pr. G.B.) cucaracha.

black belt, 1. (E.U.) región habitada principalmente por negros. 2. cinturón o banda de color negro que se otorga a los maestros de karate o judo.

blackberry [-ˌbɛrɪ, B -bɛrɪ] *s.* 1. (bot.) zarzamora, morera, mora. 2. mora (fruto).

black bile, (med.) atrabilis.

blackbird [-ˌbɜrd, B -ˌbɜd] *s.* (orn.) mirlo.

blackboard [-ˌbɔrd, B -ˌbɔd] *s.* pizarra, pizarrón.

blackbody [-ˌbɑdɪ, B -ˌbɔdɪ] *s.* (fís.) antirradiante, cuerpo negro que absorbe radiación completamente.

black book, 1. (libro que contiene) listas negras. 2. (fam., E.U.) librito donde se apuntan los nombres y teléfonos de amigas fáciles. 3. **to be in one's b. book,** estar en desgracia (con uno); haber perdido el favor (de uno).

black box, 1. (elec.) caja negra. 2. (aer.) registrador de vuelo.

black bread, pan moreno.

blackcap [-ˌkæp] *s.* 1. (G.B.) gorra negra (que se ponían los jueces al pronunciar una sentencia de muerte). 2. (orn.) paro carbonero. 3. (bot.) frambuesa negra. 4. (bot.) espadaña.

black currant, (bot.) casis.

blackdamp [-ˌdæmp] *s.* (min.) mofeta.

Black Death, (hist.) peste negra (del siglo XIV), peste bubónica.

black diamond, 1. (*pl.*) carbón. 2. carbonado; diamante negro. 3. hematita negra.

blacken [ˈblækən] *v.t.* 1. ennegrecer, obscurecer, atezar, teñir de negro. 2. (fig.) denigrar, (fama, reputación, etc.).

black eye, 1. ojo amoratado, ojo morado, ojo a la funerala. 2. defecto o falta grave. 3. mala fama.

black-eyed[-ˈaɪd] *a.* ojinegro, de ojos negros.

black-eyed pea, (bot.) frijol de carete, carita.

black-eyed Susan [-ˈsuzən] (bot.) margarita amarilla.

blackface [-ˌfeɪs] *s.* 1. (teat.) maquillaje negro. 2. actor maquillado como negro. 3. (tip.) tipo de negritas. —*a.* 1. carinegro, moreno. 2. impreso en negritas.

blackfellow [-ˌfɛloʊ] *s.* aborigen (en Australia).

blackfish [-ˌfɪʃ] *s.* 1. (ict.) calderón. 2. (zool.) ballena delfínida.

black flag, bandera negra (de los piratas).

blackfly [-ˌflaɪ] *s.* (ento.) jején.

Blackfoot [-ˌfʊt] *s.* (*pl.* BLACKFEET [-ˌfit]) pies negros (pieles rojas de Alberta, Can., y Montana, E.U.).

Black Forest, Selva Negra (en Alemania).

Black Friar, fraile negro (apodo de los dominicos).

blackguard [ˈblægərd, B -gɑd] *s.* sinvergüenza, tunante, pillastre, bribón. —*v.t.* insultar, denostar.

blackguardly [-lɪ] *a.* bribón, desvergonzado.

black-haired [ˈblækˈhɛrd, B -ˈhɛəd] *a.* pelinegro.

black hand, mano negra, sociedad secreta de chantajistas.

blackhead [-ˌhɛd] *s.* 1. comedón, espinilla, grano (Am.), barro. 2. (orn.) pato marino de cabeza negra. 3. (vet.) enterohepatitis (de los pavos).

blackheart [-ˌhɑrt, B -ˌhɑt] *s.* (bot.) cereza, guinda.

black-hearted [-ˈhɑrtəd, B -ˈhɑtəd] *a.* malvado, perverso.

black hole, (astr.) agujero negro.

black humor, (lit.) humor negro, humor morboso o macabro.

blacking [ˈblækɪŋ] *s.* betún (para limpiar calzado).

blackish [-ɪʃ] *a.* negruzco, que tira a negro.

blackjack [-ˌdʒæk] *s.* 1. (naipes) veintiuna. 2. (E.U.) cachiporra. 3. bandera de pirata. 4. (bot.) roble pequeño de corteza negra. 5. (min.) blenda, sulfuro de zinc. 6. (mec.) martillo de chapista. —*v.t.* golpear con cachiporra; obligar con amenazas.

black lead, (min.) grafito, plombagina.

blackleg [-ˌlɛg] *s.* 1. (vet.) morriña negra, carbunco sintomático. 2. (bot.) enfermedad de la col. 3. (fam.) estafador, tahur, jugador deshonesto. 4. (G.B.) rompe-huelgas, esquirol.

black letter, (tip.) letra gótica; negrita.

black liberation, movimiento político que lucha por obtener la liberación económica y social de los negros en los E.U.

black light, luz negra, luz infrarroja o ultravioleta.

blacklist [-ˌlɪst] *s.* lista negra (lista donde figuran los nombres de personas consideradas indeseables o sospechosas por parte de un gobierno, una organización, etc.). —*v.t.* poner (a alguien) en lista negra.

black magic, magia negra, brujería, nigromancia.

blackmail [-ˌmeɪl] *s.* chantaje. —*v.t.* chantajear, amenazar.

blackmailer [-ər, B -ə] *a.* chantajista.

Black Maria, 1. (fam.) coche celular, camión de policía (en que se transporta a los detenidos). 2. (fam., mil.) granada humeante (que produce una gran cantidad de humo al estallar).

black mark, marca o mancha negra, estigma.

black market, mercado negro.

black-market [-ˈmɑrkɪt, B -ˈmɑ-] *v.t.* vender en el mercado negro. —*v.i.* comerciar u operar en el mercado negro.

black marketeer, tratante en el mercado negro, estraperlista (Esp.).

black martin, (orn.) vencejo, oncejo.

black mass, misa negra, parodia blasfema de la misa que hacen los adoradores de Satanás.

black measles, (med.) sarampión negro, sarampión hemorrágico.

black mica, (min.) mica negra, biotita.

Black Monk, monje benedictino (apodo).

Black Muslims, (E.U.) organización de negros que profesan la religión mahometana y que abogan por la separación entre negros y blancos, Musulmanes Negros.

blackness [ˈblæknəs] *s.* 1. negrura, color negro (de algo o alguien). 2. obscuridad.

black nightshade, (bot.) solano, hierba mora.

black oak, (bot.) roble americano (de corteza y follaje oscuro).

blackout [-ˌaʊt] *s.* 1. apagón, obscurecimiento total (de una ciudad). 2. supresión, suspensión (esp. temporal). 3. privación de sentido, desmayo. 4. (aer.) velo negro. 5. (teat.) apagamiento (de las luces).

Black Panther, (E.U.) Pantera Negra, miembro del partido político radical de los negros y su organización de defensa, designada por el mismo nombre.

black pepper, pimienta negra.

blackpoll [-ˌpoʊl] *s.* (orn.) cerrojillo.

black poplar, (bot.) chopo.

Black Power, (E.U.) Poder Negro, movimiento entre los negros para alcanzar la igualdad social y económica por medio del poder político de la comunidad negra.

black race, la raza negra.

black rot, (bot.) especie de gangrena (causada por hongos).

Black Sea, el mar Negro.

black sheep, (fig.) oveja negra (de una familia o grupo respetable).

Blackshirt [-ˌʃɜrt, B -ˌʃɜt] *s.* Camisa Negra, fascista.

blacksmith [-ˌsmɪθ] *s.* herrero, herrador, forjador.

blacksmith welding, soldadura de forja a mano, soldadura a la forja, soldadura a la calda.

blacksnake [-ˌsneɪk] *s.* 1. (zool.) culebra negra. 2. látigo de cuero trenzado.

black spruce, (bot.) abeto negro.

black-tailed deer [-ˌteɪld-] (zool.) venado americano de cola negra.

black tea, té negro, té que se deja marchitar y fermentar antes de secarse.

blackthorn [-ˌθɔrn, B -ˌθɔn] *s.* (bot.) endrino, ciruelo silvestre, andrino, asarero, acacia bastarda.

black tie 1. corbata negra de lazo. 2. traje de etiqueta de hombre, **smoking.**

blacktop [-ˌtɑp, B -ˌtɔp] *s.* superficie bituminosa (para caminos); alquitranado. —*v.t.* cubrir con superficie bituminosa.

black vomit, (med.) vómito negro.

black vulture, (orn.) urubú.

black walnut, (bot.) nogal negro; cedro negro.

blackwater [-ˌwɔtər, -ˌwɑt-, B -ˌwɔtə] *s.* (med.) sangre en la orina; **b. fever,** malaria, paludismo.

black whale, (zool.) cachalote.

black widow, (ento.) viuda negra (araña).

bladder [ˈblædər, B -ə] *s.* 1. (anat.) vejiga, vesícula. 2. bolsa, saco, ampolla.

bladder green, verdevejiga.

bladder kelp, (bot.) variedad de alga.

bladdernose [-ˌnoʊz] *s.* (zool.) especie de foca.

bladder senna, (bot.) espantalobos.

bladder wrack, (bot.) alga negra común.

blade [bleɪd] *s.* 1. hoja, cuchilla, pala, paleta, aspa, álabe. 2. hoja (de hélice, navaja, espada, cuchillo). 3. cuchilla (del patín). 4. álabe (de la turbina). 5. pala (del remo). 6. aspa (de molino). 7. (fig.) espada; espadachín. 8. (anat.) omóplato, paletilla. 9. (bot.) hoja, brizna.

blague [blæg] *s.* (fr.) broma pesada, engaño jocoso.

blah [blɑ] *s.* pamplina, monada; **to get the blahs,** sentirse desazonado, sin ganas de hacer nada.

blain [bleɪn] *s.* llaga, ampolla.

blamable, blameable ['bleɪməbəl] *a.* culpable, censurable.

blame [bleɪm] *s.* 1. culpa. 2. censura. 3. **to bear the b. (for),** tener la culpa (por); **to put the b. on,** echar la culpa a. —*v.t.* 1. culpar; responsabilizar. 2. censurar, reprochar. 3. **to be to b. (for),** tener la culpa (por), ser culpable (de); **b. (something) on (someone),** culpar (a alguien) por (algo).

blamed [bleɪmd] *a., adv.* (fam.) maldito (expletivo ligero).

blameless ['bleɪmləs] *a.* intachable, inocente, libre de culpa.

blameworthy [-ˌwɜrðɪ, B -ˌwɜðɪ] *a.* censurable, culpable.

blanch [blæntʃ, B blɑntʃ] *v.t.* 1. blanquear; descolorar. 2. (bot.) descolorar (las plantas) protegiéndolas del sol. 3. (cocina) blanquear mondando (almendras, etc.). 4. blanquear (metales). —*v.i.* palidecer, ponerse pálido. —*a.* (her.) de plata, plateado.

blancmange [blə'mɑndʒ, B -ˌmɑnʒ] *s.* (cocina) manjar blanco.

bland [blænd] *a.* 1. blando, suave, dulce. 2. suave, imperturbable. 3. insípido, insulso.

blandish ['blændɪʃ] *v.t.* lisonjear, halagar, engatusar. —*v.i.* valerse de lisonjas.

blandishment [-mənt] *s.* lisonja, halago, zalamería.

blank [blæŋk] *a.* 1. en blanco (documento, escrito, cheque, etc.). 2. vago, sin expresión (cara, mirada). 3. vacío; sin labrar; llano, liso (muralla, pared); sin adornos. 4. monótono; sin perspectivas. 5. confuso, desconcertado. 6. rotundo, terminante, ej., *a b. refusal,* una negativa rotunda. 7. **to leave b.,** dejar en blanco. —*s.* 1. blanco (en formulario, papel). 2. formulario. 3. blanco, laguna. 4. raya (que sustituye una palabra). 5. centro del blanco (de tiro). 6. disco en blanco (para ser grabado); llave ciega; cospel, tejo (para acuñar monedas). 7. cartucho de fogueo, cartucho sin bala; **b. round,** bala de fogueo, bala de salva. 8. vacío, ej., *a b. stare,* mirada vacía. 9. **his mind (memory) is a b.,** tiene la mente en blanco (sin recuerdos); **to draw a b.,** obtener resultados nulos. —*v.t.* 1. (gen. con *out*) tachar, borrar (palabra, línea, etc. en un escrito); suprimir, anular. 2. (con *off*) tapar, cerrar (tubo, túnel, etc.). 3. estampar, cortar a troquel. 4. sustituir con puntos suspensivos (palabra que no se quiere escribir). 5. (dep.) anular (a un jugador, equipo), impedir que anote tantos. —*v.i.* (ú. con *out*) ofuscarse, desvanecerse.

blank cartridge, (mil.) cartucho de fogueo, cartucho sin bala.

blank check, 1. cheque en blanco. 2. (fig.) carta blanca, vía libre en un asunto.

blank endorsement, (com.) endoso en blanco, endoso al portador.

blank flange, brida ciega.

blanket ['blæŋkət] *s.* 1. manta, frazada (Am.), cubre. 2. (fig.) manto. 3. **to throw a wet b. on,** echar un jarro de agua fría a; aguar (la fiesta, etc.). —*v.t.* 1. arropar, cobijar (con manta); cubrir. 2. acallar, ahogar (un escándalo). 3. (rad.) suprimir, obstruir (una transmisión). 4. (mar.) quitarle el viento (una embarcación a otra). —*a.* general, universal.

blanket insurance, seguro general.

blanket mortgage, hipoteca colectiva, hipoteca general.

blankety-blank ['blæŋkətɪ'blæŋk] *a., adv.* (jer.) maldito (eufemismo por algo ofensivo que no se quiera decir a las claras).

blanking press ['blæŋkɪŋ-] (metal.) prensa punzonadora.

blank key, llave ciega.

blank page, (impr.) guarda; página en blanco.

blank tire, neumático sin pestaña; **b.t. wheel,** llanta de neumático sin pestaña.

blank verse, verso libre, suelto o blanco.

blare [blɛr, B blɛə] *v.t.* 1. sonar a toda fuerza, emitir (sonido) estrepitosamente. 2. proclamar ruidosamente. —*v.i.* resonar, sonar con estruendo. —*s.* 1. sonido estridente (esp. de una trompeta); fragor, estruendo. 2. brillo deslumbrante, resplandor.

blarney ['blɑrnɪ, B 'blɑnɪ] *s.* zalamería, lisonja. —*v.t.* lisonjear, engatusar.

Blarney stone, piedra del castillo de Blarney en Irlanda, de la cual se dice que concede elocuencia y simpatía al que la besa.

blasé [blɑ'zeɪ] *a.* (fr.) hastiado, aburrido, indiferente.

blaspheme [blæs'fim] *v.i.* blasfemar; **b. against,** blasfemar contra. —*v.t.* vilipendiar, denigrar.

blasphemous ['blæsfəməs] *a.* blasfemo.

blasphemy [-mɪ] *s.* blasfemia, vilipendio.

blast [blæst, B blɑst] *s.* 1. ráfaga, ventolera, chorro, descarga. 2. soplo (de un fuelle o soplete). 3. trompetazo. 4. carga de un barreno; voladura (de roca, etc.); explosión. 5. (jer.) jarana, alboroto. 6. (fig.) explosión, estallido, arranque (de ira). 7. (hidr.) agujero de entrada de una bomba. 8. **full b.,** a toda máquina. —*v.i.* 1. detonar explosivos. 2. (gen. con *away*) seguir disparando (con arma de fuego); atacar a alguien, criticar, denostar. 3. (con *off*) despegar (cohete, cápsula espacial, etc.); (fam.) salir disparado, partir apresuradamente. —*v.t.* 1. hacer volar, reventar; demoler, destrozar. 2. (jer.) maldecir, execrar. 3. **b. (it)!** ¡maldito sea!; **b. open,** abrir con explosivos.

blasted ['blæstəd, B 'blɑst-] *a.* 1. marchito, ajado. 2. maldito.

blastema [blæ'stimə] *s.* (biol.) blastema.

blast engine, máquina sopladora.

blast furnace, alto horno.

blast-hole ['blæstˌhoul, B 'blɑst-] *s.* barreno (en roca, obra de fábrica); hornillo (en mina).

blasting ['blæstɪŋ, B 'blɑst-] *s.* 1. (min., mil.) voladura, estallido. 2. (rad.) sobrecarga.

blasting cap, cápsula explosiva o detonante, fulminante detonador.

blasting charge, carga explosiva o de barreno.

blastocele ['blæstəˌsil] *s.* (biol.) blastocele.

blastocyst [-ˌsɪst] *s.* (biol.) blastocisto.

blastoderm [-ˌdɜrm, B -ˌdɜm] *s.* (biol.) blastodermo.

blastodermatic [ˌblæstəˌdɜr'mætɪk, B -dɜ'-] **blastodermic** [-'dɜrmɪk, B -'dɜm-] *a.* blastodérmico.

blastodisc ['blæstəˌdɪsk] *s.* (biol.) blastodisco.

blast-off ['blæstˌɔf, B 'blɑst-] *s.* despegue (ej., de un cohete).

blastogenesis [ˌblæstə'dʒɛnəsəs] *s.* (biol.) blastogénesis.

blastomere ['blæstəˌmɪr, B -ˌmɪə] *s.* (biol.) blastómera.

blastomycete [ˌblæstə'maɪˌsit] *s.* (bot.) blastomiceto.

blastopore ['blæstəˌpɔr, B -ˌpɔ] *s.* (biol.) blastóporo.

blastosphere [-ˌsfɪr, B -ˌsfɪə] *s.* (biol.) blastosfera.

blastula ['blæstʃələ, B 'blɑs-] *s.* (biol.) blástula.

blast wave, (fís.) onda de choque (de una explosión nuclear).

blat [blæt] *v.i.* 1. balar, mugir. 2. hablar en voz ronca. 3. hablar sin consideración, parlotear. —*v.t.* decir sin consideración o atolondradamente.

blatancy ['bleɪtənsɪ] *s.* vocinglería, alarde ofensivo.

blatant [-ənt] *s.* 1. vocinglero, chillón. 2. flagrante, evidente, ej., *b. lie,* mentira flagrante.

blather ['blæðər, B -ə] **blether** ['blɛð-] *s.* 1. charlatanería. 2. bulla, conmoción. —*v.i.* charlotear disparatadamente.

blatherskite [-ˌskaɪt] *s.* (fam.) charlatán, parlanchín; fanfarrón.

blaze [bleɪz] *s.* 1. fuego vivo, llamarada; hoguera; incendio. 2. arranque (de pasión, ira, rabia, etc.). 3. esplendor, brillo (de joyas, etc.). 4. mancha blanca, estrella (en la frente de un caballo o buey). 5. marca en la corteza de un árbol (para señalar el camino). 6. **go to blazes!** ¡váyase al diablo!**in a b.,** en llamas; **like blazes,** como un rayo, velozmente; de ninguna manera; **what the blazes!** ¡qué diablos! —*v.i.* 1. arder, llamear. 2. resplandecer, brillar. 3. **b. away,** disparar continuamente, seguir disparando (con arma de fuego); seguir arengando; trabajar con entusiasmo (en algo); **blazing indiscretion,** indiscreción ingenua o flagrante. —*v.t.* 1. proclamar (en forma llamativa), difundir, esparcir, publicar. 2. marcar (senda), abrir (camino). 3. **b. a trail** (o **path**), abrir una senda; (fig.) marcar el camino.

blazer ['bleɪzər, B -ə] *s.* 1. chaqueta de lana ligera. 2. (fam., G.B.) mentira flagrante.

blazing [-ɪŋ] *a.* 1. llameante. 2. deslumbrante. 3. (fig.) rabioso, airado. 4. (fig. G.B.) tremendo, enorme.

blazon ['bleɪzən] *s.* 1. (her.) blasón, escudo de armas. 2. ostentación, jactancia. —*v.t.* 1. blasonar. 2. adornar, decorar. 3. (fig.) proclamar; ostentar, jactarse.

blazoner [-ər, B -ə] *s.* blasonador.

blazonry [-rɪ] *s.* 1. (her.) blasón. 2. exhibición deslumbrante.

bldg. *abrev. de* **building,** edificio; construcción.

bleach [blitʃ] *v.t.* blanquear, descolorar (al sol o por procedimientos químicos), aclarar (el pelo). —*v.i.* blanquear; palidecer. —*s.* 1. blanqueo. 2. blancura.

bleacher ['blitʃər, B -ə] *s.* 1. blanqueador. 2. (*pl.*) gradería, gradas o tendido de sol (de un estadio).

bleaching powder, polvo de blanquear.

bleak [blik] *a.* 1. desierto, desolado, yermo. 2. frío, cortante. 3. (fig.) desolado; monótono, triste, sombrío, ej., *b. outlook,* perspectiva sombría. —*s.* (ict.) albur, breca; pez cuyas escamas se emplean para fabricar perlas artificiales.

bleakness ['bliknəs] *s.* desolación; monotonía.

blear [blɪr, B blɪə] *v.t.* nublar, empañar, enturbiar (la visión, el entendimiento). —*a.* turbio (visión), empañado.

bleary ['blɪrɪ, B 'blɪərɪ] *a.* 1. nublado, turbio (ojos, visión). 2. indistinto, confuso (contorno, vista, etc.). 3. cansadísimo, agotado.

bleary-eyed [-ˌaɪd] *a.* lagrimoso, legañoso, pitarroso, con los ojos hinchados, con la vista nublada.

bleat [blit] *v.i.* 1. balar (carnero, cabra, etc.). 2. (fam., despec.) gemir, plañir, lamentarse. —*v.t.* decir entre plañidos. —*s.* 1. balido (de carnero, cabra, etc.). 2. (fam., despec.) gemido, plañido, lamento.
bleb [blɛb] *s.* ampolla, vejiga (en la piel); burbuja (en el agua); glóbulo de aire (en cristal o vidrio).
bleed [blid] *v.i.* (*pret., p.p.* BLED [blɛd]; *p.pr.* BLEEDING) 1. sangrar, perder sangre. 2. derramar sangre (esp. en campo de batalla, etc.). 3. (fig.) pagar mucho, derrochar dinero; ser víctima de extorsión. 4. (bot.) exudar (una planta), llorar (la vid). 5. (impr.) ensancharse, hacer sangre. 6. (tintorería) vetearse (un paño teñido). 7. **b. to death,** desangrarse, morir desangrado; **(one's) heart bleeds (for),** el corazón (de uno) sangra de dolor, siente gran pena (por). —*v.t.* 1. sangrar, sacar sangre a. 2. (jer.) desplumar, sacar dinero a otro. 3. (bot.) sangrar, resinar (planta, árbol). 4. (mec.) sangrar (ej., un tanque de aceite); desinflar (una llanta, etc.). 5. (impr.) imprimir a sangre o sin margen (ilustración, grabado, etc.). 6. **b. (someone) white,** desangrar; (fig.) arrancar el último centavo a (alguien). —*s.* (impr.) borde impreso, corte. —*a.* (impr.) sin margen, a sangre, volado.
bleeder ['blidər, B -ə] *s.* 1. purgador, drenador, sangrador. 2. (med.) hemótico. 3. (mec.) purgador. 4. abusador, explotador, (G.B.) persona indeseable.
bleeder drain, (mec.) válvula de purga.
bleeder port, lumbrera de purga.
bleeder resistance, (rad.) resistencia derivadora, resistencia de compensación.
bleeder resistor, (rad.) resistencia de drenaje.
bleeding [-ɪŋ] *s.* 1. sangría, sangradura, purga, drenaje. 2. flujo de sangre. 3. (mec.) purga. 4. (rad.) drenaje.
bleeding heart, 1. (bot.) dicentra. 2. (E.U., hist.) mote despectivo que daba el senador McCarthy a los acusados por él de ser subversivos, durante las investigaciones de su comité ante el Congreso.
blemish ['blɛmɪʃ] *v.t.* manchar, mancillar; empañar, desdorar. —*s.* mancha, tacha, mancilla, imperfección; **without b.,** intachable, inmaculado.
blench [blɛntʃ] *v.i.* cejar, vacilar, acobardarse, hacer un quite.
blend [blɛnd] *v.t.* (*pret., p.p.* BLENDED O BLENT [blɛnt]; *p.pr.* BLENDING) mezclar (tés, tabacos, perfumes; opiniones, ideas, etc.); combinar, matizar (colores); armonizar (estilos, etc.). —*v.i.* mezclarse; combinarse, armonizar. —*s.* mezcla, mixtura; combinación.
blende [blɛnd] *s.* (min.) blenda.
blender ['blɛndər, B -ə] *s.* licuadora, mezcladora.
blending [-ɪŋ] 1. combinación, mezcla. 2. fusión armoniosa o compatible.
blennorrhea [ˌblɛnə'riə] *s.* (med.) blenorrea.
blenny ['blɛnɪ] *s.* (ict.) blenia, baboso.
blepharitis [ˌblɛfə'raɪtəs] *s.* (med.) blefaritis.
blesbok ['blɛsˌbɑk, B -ˌbɔk] **blesbuck** [-ˌbʌk] *s.* (zool.) antílope de Sudáfrica.
bless [blɛs] *v.t.* (*pret., p.p.* BLESSED O BLEST [blɛst]; *p.pr.* BLESSING). 1. bendecir. 2. consagrar. 3. alabar, exaltar, glorificar. 4. proteger, guardar. 5. **b. me! b. you! b. my soul!** ¡válgame Dios!; **b. oneself,** santiguarse; **God b. him!** ¡que Dios lo bendiga!; **God b. you!** ¡salud! (expresión de cortesía cuando alguien estornuda).
blessed ['blɛsəd] *a.* 1. bendito. 2. santo. 3. bienaventurado, afortunado; dichoso, feliz. 4. (eufem.) maldito, miserable. 5. (irón.) dichoso. 6. **not to know a b. thing about,** no saber maldita cosa de; **to be b. with,** ser el afortunado poseedor de.
blessed event, acontecimiento feliz (refiriéndose al nacimiento de un niño o al recién nacido).
blessedness [-nəs] *s.* beatitud, bienaventuranza, gloria; santidad; felicidad.
Blessed Virgin, (relig.) Santísima Virgen.
blessing [-ɪŋ] *s.* 1. bendición, gracia, protección. 2. felicidad, satisfacción, buena suerte. 3. aprobación, consentimiento, apoyo. 4. **a b. in disguise,** no hay mal que por bien no venga. 5. **blessings on . . .!** ¡bien haya(n) . . .!
blest [blɛst] *pret., p.p. de* **bless.** —*var. de* **blessed.**
blew [blu] *pret. de* **blow.**
blight [blaɪt] *s.* 1. (agr.) plaga, enfermedad (de plantas); roya, tizón. 2. plaga, infortunio, desgracia. —*v.t.* 1. agostar, marchitar. 2. malograr, frustrar, arruinar (esperanza, perspectiva, etc.). —*v.i.* atizonarse; agostarse, marchitarse.
blimey ['blaɪmɪ] *interj.* (G.B.) ¡caramba! (sorpresa, asombro).
blimp [blɪmp] *s.* 1. pequeño dirigible flexible. 2. **Colonel B.,** (G.B.) personaje reaccionario patriotero (creado por David Low).
blind [blaɪnd] *a.* 1. ciego. 2. (fig.) ciego, cegado, obcecado; insensato. 3. invisible, oculto. 4. a ciegas. 5. ilegible, incompleto (dirección en cartas). 6. (fam.) borracho. barracho. 7. **b. as a bat,** ciego como un topo; **b. in one eye,** tuerto; **b. man,** ciego; **b. side,** lado vulnerable; **b. with** ciego de (ira, pasión, etc.); **the b.,** los ciegos; **to turn a b. eye (to),** hacer la vista gorda; pretender no ver (algo). —*s.* 1. celosía, persiana, cortina de enrollar, cortina de tiro (para ventanas). 2. (fig.) pretexto, subterfugio; pantalla. 3. anteojera. 4. (caza) escondite, escondrijo. 5. (mil.) blinda. 6. (jer., G.B.) holgorio. 7. **to act as a b. for,** servir de pantalla a. —*v.t.* 1. cegar. 2. deslumbrar. 3. (fig.) cegar, obcecar, ofuscar. 4. (const.) cegar, macizar. 5. (mil.) blindar. 6. **b. oneself to,** (fig.) rehusar percatarse (de algo).
blindage ['blaɪndɪdʒ] *s.* (mil.) blindaje.
blind alley, callejón sin salida.
blind date, (fam.) cita entre dos personas de distinto sexo que no se conocen; persona citada de esta manera.
blind door, puerta falsa.
blinder ['blaɪndər, B -ə] *s.* anteojera (del caballo y fig.).
blind flying, (avia.) vuelo sin visibilidad, vuelo ciego, vuelo por instrumentos.
blindfold [-ˌfoʊld] *v.t.* 1. vendar los ojos a. 2. (fig.) despistar, ofuscar. —*a.* con los ojos vendados; a ciegas; ofuscado. —*s.* venda (en los ojos).
blind gut, (anat.) intestino ciego.
blind hookey, (naipes) (cierto) juego de azar.
blinding [-ɪŋ] *a.* deslumbrador, deslumbrante, encandilante; cegador.
blind landing, (avia.) aterrizaje a ciegas.
blindly [-lɪ] *adv.* ciegamente, a ciegas.
blindman's buff [-ˌmænz'bʌf] (juego de) la gallinita ciega.
blindness [-nəs] *s.* ceguera, ceguedad (física, intelectual o moral).
blind spot, 1. (anat.) punto ciego (de la retina). 2. (fig.) punto débil (el que por prejuicio o falta de conocimientos se tiene sobre un tema). 3. (rad.) lugar ciego (donde no se captan bien las ondas). 4. (avia.) ángulo muerto.
blind stitch, (cost.) puntada invisible.
blindstory [-ˌstɔrɪ] *s.* (arq.) piso sin ventanas.
blind tiger, (jer.) pequeña taberna clandestina abierta a deshoras.
blind window, (arq.) ventana falsa o figurada.
blindworm [-ˌwɜrm, B -ˌwɜm] *s.* (zool.) lución.
blini ['blɪnɪ] *s. pl.* (cocina) pequeños panqueques que se sirven con caviar y crema ácida.
blink [blɪŋk] *v.i.* 1. parpadear, pestañear. 2. centellear, brillar en forma intermitente. 3. entornar los ojos. 4. (gen. con *at*) pasar por alto, no hacer caso (de); tolerar. 5. (con *at*) mirar con sorpresa. 6. **blinking lights,** luces intermitentes. —*v.t.* 1. guiñar (el ojo). 2. (gen. con *away*) contener las làgrimas parpadeando. 3. evadir, eludir (esp. un hecho, la verdad, etc.). 4. **b. an eye,** hacer la vista gorda. —*s.* 1. guiño, pestañeo, parpadeo. 2. centelleo, destello. 3. blancura en el horizonte (debido al reflejo de hielo en el mar). 4. **on the b.,** (fam.) estropeado, en malas condiciones, que funciona mal (máquinas, etc.); indispuesto (persona).
blinkard ['blɪŋkərd, B -əd] *s.* 1. persona que parpadea constantemente. 2. (fig.) persona obtusa.
blinker [-ər, B -ə] *s.* 1. baliza intermitente, faro intermitente. 2. (avia., nav.) baliza de haz intermitente. 3. (mil). proyector de destellos. 4 (jer.) ojo. 5. anteojera (parte del arnés de ciertas caballerías). 6. (aut.) intermitente.
blinking [-ɪŋ] *a.* (jer., eufem.) maldito.
blintze ['blɪntsə] **blintz** [blɪnts] *s.* (cocina) panqueque relleno (gen. con queso).
blip [blɪp] *s.* 1. (rad.) cresta de eco; 2. (*on radar screen*) señal luminosa. 3. (*sound*) bip, pitidito. 4. (*interruption*) corte del sonido. 5. (fig.) accidente, problema pasajero.
bliss [blɪs] *s.* arrobamiento, felicidad, dicha.
blissful ['blɪsfəl] *a.* dichoso, arrobado.
blister ['blɪstər, B -ə] *s.* 1. ampolla, vejiga acuosa (en la piel). 2. burbuja (en metal, esmalte, etc.). 3. (med.) vejigatorio. 4. (bot.) verruga. 5. (mar.) cámara de aire (dentro del casco del buque de guerra que sirve de protección contra torpedos). 6. (aer.) cabina del piloto o del artillero. —*v.t.* 1. ampollar, levantar ampollas. 2. criticar o reprender acerbamente. —*v.i.* formarse ampollas o burbujas en (pintura, esmalte, etc.).
blister beetle, (ento.) pilme, abadejo.
blister gas, gas vesicante.
blister rust, (bot.) roya de los pinos.
B. Lit. *abrev. de* **Bachelor of Literature,** Licenciado en Letras.
blithe [blaɪθ, blaɪð, B blaɪð] *a.* 1. alegre, animado. 2. descuidado, despreocupado.
blithering ['blɪðərɪŋ] *a.* (fam.) que habla sin freno ni sentido; **b. idiot,** idiota charlatán; **b. fool,** tonto de capirote.
blithesome ['blaɪθsəm, 'blaɪð-, B 'blaɪð-] *a.* alegre, animado, jovial.
blitz [blɪts] *s. abrev. de* **blitzkrieg.** —*v.t.* devastar (esp. por bombardeo intenso).
blitzkrieg ['blɪtsˌkrig] *s.* (mil.) guerra relámpago. —*v.t.* (fam.) vencer con guerra relámpago, atacar con bombardeo aéreo.
blizzard ['blɪzərd, B -əd] *s.* ventisca, tempestad de nieve.
bloat [bloʊt] *v.t.* 1. hinchar, inflar. 2. (fig.) envanecer. 3. ahumar, curar (arenques). —*v.i.* hincharse, abotagarse. —*s.* 1. (vet.) empastamiento, empastado, hinchazón (esp. del ganado vacuno y caballar). 2. (fam.) borracho.
bloated ['bloʊtəd] *a.* 1. hinchado abultado, abotagado, grueso (cuerpo, etc.). 2. crecido, inflado. 3. ahumado y salado (pescado).
bloater [-ər, B -ə] *s.* arenque ahumado.
blob [blɑb, B blɔb] *s.* gota; glóbulo; borujo, burujo, bulto pequeño (de color, pasta, engrudo, etc.). —*v.t.* salpicar, embadurnar.

bloc [blɑk, B blɔk] *s.* (pol.) (de grupos o partidos), ej., *farm b.,* bloque agrario.

block [blɑk, B blɔk] *v.t.* 1. bloquear, atajar, obstruir. 2. cegar, cerrar. 3. conformar (sombrero). 4. calzar (rueda). 5. (carp.) reforzar (un ángulo). 6. (fin.) bloquear, congelar (fondos, pagos, etc.). 7. (pol.) obstruir (una moción, etc.). 8. (med.) bloquear, anestesiar. 9. (dep.) parar, detener (pelota, jugada). 10. **b. in** (o **out**), delinear, esbozar; **b. the way,** cerrar el paso; **b. up,** cegar, taponar; confinar, encerrar; (bridge) bloquear. —*s.* 1. bloque (de piedra), troza, zoquete, taco (de madera). 2. tajo (para partir carne o sobre el cual se cortaba la cabeza a los condenados). 3. horma de sombrero. 4. adoquín, tarugo. 5. cubo (de madera, piedra, plástico) para construcciones infantiles. 6. (mec.) bloque (de cilindros). 7. plataforma (para subastas). 8. cepo (de yunque). 9. taco (de calendario); taco de papel (para apuntes). 10. manzana, cuadra (Am.) (de casas); calle de una manzana. 11. grupo, conjunto. 12. polea, garrucha; (mar.) motón. 13. (mec.) almohadillo (del freno). 14. (impr.) base, piso, zócalo, taco (en que se montan los grabados); plancha, clisé, grabado. 15. obstrucción, estorbo. 16. (med.) bloqueo (arterial, etc.). 17. (dep.) bloqueo (de un jugador o jugada). 18. (f.c.) tramo. 19. (elec.) placa, bloque (de fusible). 20. bruto, zoquete, tonto. 21. (jer.) coco, cabeza. 22. **a chip off the old b.,** de tal palo, tal astilla; **to go to the b.,** ir al cadalso; **to put on the b.,** poner en subasta pública.

blockade [blɑ'keɪd, B blɔ-] *s.* 1. bloqueo, asedio, sitio. 2. obstrucción. 3. **paper b.,** bloqueo declarado que no se ha puesto en práctica; **to raise the b.,** levantar el bloqueo; **to run the b.,** burlar o forzar el bloqueo, romper el bloqueo. —*v.t.* 1. bloquear, asediar, sitiar. 2. obstruir.

blockade-runner [-ˌrʌnər, B -ə] *s.* forzador de bloqueo.

blockage ['blɑkɪdʒ, B 'blɔk-] *s.* obstrucción, atracamiento; bloqueo.

block and tackle, aparejo de poleas.

block anesthesia, (med.) anestesia de bloque, anestesia regional.

block brake, (mec.) freno de almohadillas.

blockbuster [-ˌbʌstər, B -ə] *s.* 1. (mil.) bomba de demolición. 2. cualquier cosa de efecto devastador e impresionante.

blockbusting [-ɪŋ] *a.* que tiene un efecto impresionante. —*s.* la práctica de vender o alquilar casas a negros en un barrio habitado exclusivamente por blancos, con el propósito de depreciar las propiedades y especular.

blockhead [-ˌhɛd] *s.* zopenco, zoquete, estúpido, mostrenco.

blockhouse [-ˌhaʊs] *s.* (fort.) blocao, fortín.

blocking [-ɪŋ] *s.* 1. (carp.) entramado, encribado, entibado. 2. (f.c., rad.) bloqueo. 3. (const.) endentado, adaraja.

blockish [-ɪʃ] *a.* estúpido, bruto.

block letter 1. mayúscula, letra de molde. 2. (tip.) tipo de letra grande y acentuada.

block plane, (carp.) cepillo de contrafibra.

block printing, impresión hecha con bloques de madera.

block signal, (f.c.) señal de bloque o de tramo.

block system, 1. (f.c.) sistema de señales por tramos de vía, sistema de bloque. 2. (agr.) irrigación por cuadros rebordeados.

block tin, estaño de comercio, estaño en lingotes.

blocky[-ɪ] *a.* 1. macizo, grueso; fornido. 2. aterronado; fraccionado, variado.

bloke[bloʊk] *s.* (fam. G.B.) tipo, fulano, sujeto cualquiera.

blond[blɑnd, B blɔnd] *a.* (*fem.* BLONDE) rubio, blondo. —*s.* (hombre) rubio; (mujer) rubia.

blond lace, blonda, blondina, encaje de seda.

blood[blʌd] *s.* 1. sangre. 2. jugo, zumo, vida. 3. derrame de sangre, asesinato. 4. temperamento, carácter, (mal) genio. 5. sangre, linaje, alcurnia. 6. petimetre, joven elegante; lechuguino. 7. **his b. is up,** está con ánimo de pelea; **his b. ran cold,** se le heló la sangre; **in cold b.,** a sangre fría; **one's own flesh and b.,** carne de su carne, de la propia sangre; **to have in one's b.,** llevar en la sangre; **to make one's b. boil,** hacer hervir la sangre a uno; **to run in the b.,** llevarse en la sangre; **to stir up bad b.,** fomentar animosidad; **to sweat b.,** sudar la gota gorda, sudar tinta; **whole b.,** sangre pura, pura raza, por parte de padre y madre; **with b. and iron,** a sangre y fuego. —*v.t.* 1. manchar con sangre. 2. (caza) encarnar (al perro). 3. dar experiencia a, acostumbrar.

blood bank, (med.) banco de sangre.

bloodbath ['blʌdˌbæθ, B -ˌbɑθ] *s.* (fig.) carnicería, matanza.

blood brother, hermano de sangre.

blood cell, célula de la sangre.

blood clot, (med.) coágulo de sangre, coágulo sanguíneo.

blood count, (med.) recuento globular, recuento sanguíneo.

bloodcurdling [-ˌkɜrdlɪŋ, B -ˌkɜd-] *a.* espeluznante, horripilante.

blood donor, (med.) donante de sangre.

blooded [-əd] *a.* 1. de pura sangre, de la mejor casta. 2. (*ú. en voces compuestas*) de sangre, ej., *blue-b.,* de sangre azul, aristocrático, *cold b.,* de sangre fría; cruel.

blood feud, enemistad entre familias o clanes.

blood group, (med.) grupo sanguíneo.

bloodguilty [-ˌgɪltɪ] *a.* culpable de derramamiento de sangre, culpable de homicidio.

blood heat, (fisiol.) calor de la sangre, temperatura del cuerpo (humano).

bloodhound [-ˌhaʊnd] *s.* 1. sabueso. 2. (fam.) sabueso, policía.

bloodily [-əlɪ] *a.* sangrientamente, cruentamente, encarnizadamente.

bloodiness [-ɪnəs] *s.* sanguinolencia, ensangrentamiento; crueldad.

blooding ['blʌdɪŋ] *s.* (caza) encarna.

bloodless [-ləs] *a.* 1. exangüe, desangrado. 2. incruento. 3. desanimado. 4. insensible.

bloodletting [-ˌlɛtɪŋ] *s.* sangría, flebotomía.

bloodline [-ˌlaɪn] *s.* ascendientes directos en linaje; casta, familia (esp. de animales).

bloodmobile [-moʊˌbil] *s.* equipo móvil para extracción de sangre de donadores.

blood money, dinero obtenido a costa de la vida ajena.

blood orange, naranja sanguínea, naranja de jugo veteada de rojo.

blood plasma, (med.) plasma sanguíneo.

blood platelet, (anat.) plaqueta de la sangre.

blood poisoning, (med.) envenenamiento de la sangre.

blood pressure, (fisiol.) presión sanguínea, tensión arterial.

blood pudding, morcilla, salchicha de sangre.

blood-red [-'rɛd] *a.* de color rojo sangre.

blood relation, pariente consanguíneo.

blood relationship, consaguinidad.

blood relative, *var. de* **blood relation.**

bloodroot [-ˌrut] *s.* (bot.) sanguinaria.

blood royal, familia real.

blood sausage, morcilla, salchicha de sangre.

blood serum, (anat.) suero sanguíneo.

bloodshed [-ˌʃɛd] *s.* derramamiento de sangre; matanza.

bloodshot [-ˌʃɑt, B -ˌʃɔt] *a.* ensangrentado, infiamado; inyectado de sangre (ojos, etc.).

blood sport, deporte que requiere derramamiento de sangre, como la tauromaquia, la pelea de gallos.

bloodstain [-ˌsteɪn] *s.* mancha de sangre.

bloodstone [-ˌstoʊn] *s.* (min.) restañasangre, heliotropo, albín, hematites.

bloodstream [-ˌstrim] *s.* corriente sanguínea, flujo de sangre.

bloodsucker [-ˌsʌkər, B -ə] *s.* 1. sanguijuela. 2. (fig.) sanguijuela; gorrista.

blood test, análisis de sangre.

bloodthirsty [-ˌθɜrstɪ, B -ˌθɜstɪ] *a.* sanguinario.

blood transfusion, (med.) transfusión de sangre.

blood type, (med.) grupo o tipo sanguíneo.

blood vessel, (anat.) vaso sanguíneo (como una arteria, vena o tubo capilar).

bloodwort [-ˌwɜrt, B -ˌwɜt] *s.* (bot.) 1. romaza. 2. centaura menor. 3. (planta) hemodorácea.

bloody ['blʌdɪ] *a.* 1. sangriento, sanguinolento, ensangrentado. 2. sanguinario. 3. sangriento, encarnizado, cruento (batalla, lucha, etc.). 4. (fam. G.B.) maldito, mísero, infame; **shut the b. door!** ¡cierra la puerta, coño! —*adv.* (vulg. G.B.) muy. —*v.t.* ensangrentar, herir, ej., **it's b. useless** no sirve para un carajo. —*interj.* **b. murder!** (jer.) ¡demonios! ¡maldita sea!

bloody mary, cóctel de vodka y jugo de tomate.

bloom [blum] *s.* 1. flor. 2. florescencia, florecimiento. 3. frescura, lozanía. 4. vello, pelusilla (que cubre ciertos frutos y hojas). 5. aroma (del vino, etc.). 6. (metal.) lupia, changote, zamarra, lingote. 7. (geol.) eflorescencia. 8. (t.v.) florescencia de imagen, expansión excesiva de la imagen. 9. **b. of youth,** flor de la edad; **in b.,** florido, en flor; **to take the b. off (something),** (fig.) quitar la frescura a (algo). —*v.i.* 1. florecer. 2. (fig.) florecer. —*v.t.* prestar frescura o brillo a.

bloomers ['blumərz, B -əz] *s. pl.* (ant.) calzón bombacho, bombacho (de mujer).

bloomery [-ərɪ] *s.* (metal.) horno y forja de lingotes.

blooming [-ɪŋ] *a.* 1. floreciente, lozano. 2. (jer., eufem., pr. G.B.) maldito.

blooming mill, (metal.) laminador preliminar de tochos, desbastador de grueso o de tochos.

bloomy [-ɪ] *a.* 1. floreciente, florido. 2. velloso, cubierto de pelusilla (fruto o planta).

blooper ['blupər, B -ə] *s.* 1. (*clumsey mistake*) (fam.) metida de pata, metedura de pata, pifia, plancha. 2. (béisbol) voleo alto y tendido.

blossom ['blɑsəm, B 'blɔs-] *s.* 1. flor. 2. brote, capullo, pimpollo. 3. florescencia, floración. 4. **in b.,** en cierne, en flor. —*v.i.* 1. florecer, echar flor, brotar. 2. (fig.) desarrollarse, prosperar.

blot [blɑt, B blɔt] *s.* 1. borrón, mancha, tacha. 2. tachadura. 3. (en ciertos juegos) peón en posición arriesgada. —*v.t.* (*pret., p.p.* BLOTTED; *p.pr.* BLOTTING) 1. manchar, ensuciar, empañar. 2. obscurecer, eclipsar. 3. secar (con papel secante o con arena). 4. **b. one's record,** manchar su hoja de servicios; **b. out,** rayar, tachar, borrar (lo escrito); destruir, aniquilar; (fig.) empañar, hacer olvidar. —*v.i.* correrse (la tinta), emborronarse (el papel).

blotch [blɑtʃ, B blɔtʃ] *s.* 1. mancha, borrón. 2. (med.) roncha, erupción. —*v.t.* llenar de manchas o ronchas.

blotchy ['blɑtʃɪ, B 'blɔtʃɪ] *a.* lleno de manchones o de ronchas.

blotter ['blɑtər, B 'blɔtə] *s.* 1. (papel) secante, teleta. 2. cuaderno de borrador.

blotting paper, papel secante.
blotto [-oʊ] *a.* (jer.) completamente borracho, mamado.
blouse [blaʊs, B blaʊz] *s.* blusa.
blow [bloʊ] *v.i.* (*pret.* BLEW [blu]; *p.p.* BLOWN [bloʊn]; *p.pr.* BLOWING). 1. soplar, correr (viento, aire); soplar (una persona). 2. silbar (pito); sonar (trompeta, órgano, etc.). 3. jadear, resollar. 4. soplar, resoplar (ballena), bufar (caballo, toro). 5. (fig.) rabiar. 6. hincharse, esponjarse (por fermentación). 7. (fam.) alardear, fanfarronear. 8. volar, flotar, pasar (en el aire arrastrado por el viento). 9. reventar (llanta, mosqueta, etc.). 10. quemarse, fundirse (fusible). 11. resquebrar, resquebrajar (cemento). 12. (jer.) irse, largarse. 13. **b. hot and cold,** estar entre sí y no, cambiar de humor a cada rato; **b. in,** (fam.) llegar inesperadamente; **b. off,** escaparse (vapor); evacuar vapor (caldera, locomotora, etc.); **b. off about,** quejarse de; **b. on** (o **upon**), denunciar, desacreditar; **b. open,** abrirse (a causa del viento); **b. out,** apagarse, ser extinguido (por el viento); reventar (un neumático); saltar, fundirse (fusible); **b. over,** pasar sin efecto, ser olvidado; **b. shut,** cerrarse de golpe (a causa del viento); **b. up,** estallar, explosionar; reventar (de cólera), encolerizarse; inflarse, hincharse; aumentar en intensidad (viento). —*v.t.* 1. soplar sobre (fuego, etc.); soplar (un pito, etc.). 2. echar, expeler (aire, humo, etc.); sonarse (las narices). 3. inflar; soplar (vidrio). 4. tocar (instrumento de viento). 5. soplar, llevar, arrastrar (algo el viento). 6. volar, hacer estallar o saltar. 7. reventar, romper. 8. depositar huevos o larvas en (carne, etc., díc. de insectos). 9. (*ú. esp. en p.p.*) dejar sin aliento, desalentar. 10. quemar (fusible). 11. (con *to*) convidar (a), regalar (con). 12. (fam.) malgastar, despilfarrar, destrozar. 13. (fam.) maldecir. 14. (jer.) fallar, perder (juego, oportunidad). 15. (jer.) irse de, huir de (ciudad, la casa). 16. (vulg.) chupar, mamar *(estimular el pene oralmente)*. 17. **b. away,** soplar, disipar soplando; llevarse (el viento); **b. down,** derribar, echar por tierra (algo, el viento); **b. in,** (metal.) poner a funcionar (alto horno); **b. off,** soplar, arrojar de (soplando); **b. off steam,** (fig.) desahogarse; **b. one's own trumpet,** (fig.) alabarse a sí mismo, ponderarse; **b. one's top (cork, roof),** (jer.) salir uno de sus casillas, perder la paciencia, montar en cólera; **b. out,** apagar (soplando); quemar (un fusible); (metal.) apagar (alto horno); **b. out one's brains,** saltarse la tapa de los sesos, pegarse un tirol; **b. the gaff,** revelar el secreto; **b. the lid off,** poner al descubierto; **b. up,** inflar; volar, hacer saltar, (foto.) ampliar. —*s.* 1. soplo, soplido; resoplido. 2. ventarrón, ventolera. 3. toque; bocinazo, trompetazo. 4. fanfarronada. 5. (jer.) fanfarrón.
blow [bloʊ] *s.* 1. golpe, porrazo. 2. golpe, contratiempo, desastre, desgracia. 3. **at one b., at a single b.,** de un golpe, de un solo golpe, de una vez; **b. on the face, b. with the hand,** bofetada; **b. with the fist,** puñetazo; **to come to blows,** llegar a las manos; **to strike a b. for (against),** ayudar (oponerse) a; **b. with a club,** porrazo.
blow-by-blow ['bloʊbaɪ'bloʊ] *a.* (fam.) con pelos y señales.
blower [-ər, B -ə] *s.* 1. soplador, soplete. 2. aventador, ventilador, fuelle. 3. (fam.) fanfarrón. 4. persona, máquina o animal que resopla. 5. (mec.) compresor; **b. section,** sección del compresor. 6. (jer., G.B.) teléfono.
blowfish [-ˌfɪʃ] *s.* (ict.) pez globo.
blowfly [-ˌflaɪ] *s.* (ento.) mosca azul, moscarda, moscón.
blowgun [-ˌgʌn] *s.* cerbatana, bodoquera.
blowhard [-ˌhɑrd, B -hɑd] *s.* valentón, fanfarrón.
blowhole [-ˌhoʊl] *s.* 1. respiradero. 2. (metal.) sopladura. 3. (zool.) espiráculo de los cetáceos. 4. agujero en el hielo (respiradero de ballenas y focas).
blowing [-ɪŋ] *s.* 1. soplido, soplo, sopladura. 2. silbido (del viento).
blowjob [-ˌdʒɑb, B -ˌdʒɔb] *s.* (vulg., E.U.) chupada, mamada.
blowlamp [-ˌlæmp] *s.* soplete, lámpara de soldar, lámpara de plomero.
blown [bloʊn] *p.p. de* **blow.** —*a.* 1. abierto, en flor, en florescencia, ej., *a full-b. rose,* una rosa en plena florescencia. 2. hinchado, lleno de gas (como el que ha comido demasiado). 3. jadeante, agotado, desalentado.
blown glass, vidrio soplado.
blowoff [ˌbloʊˌɔf] *s.* 1. descarga, escape, fuga, explosión. 2. (fam.) fanfarrón. 3. **b. valve,** válvula de escape.
blowout [-ˌaʊt] *s.* 1. (auto., avia.) reventón, explosión. 2. (elec.) fundirse un fusible. 3. (jer.) comilona, festín, gran función.
blow patch, parche para neumático.
blowpipe [-ˌpaɪp] *s.* 1. soplete, tobera. 2. caña de vidriero. 3. cerbatana, bodoquera.
blowtorch [-ˌtɔrtʃ, B -ˌtɔtʃ] *s.* soplete, lámpara de soldar, lámpara de plomero.
blowtube [-ˌtub, B -ˌtjub] *s.* 1. tobera, soplete. 2. caña de vidriero, bodoquera.
blowup [-ˌʌp] *s.* 1. explosión. 2. (fig.) estallido de ira. 3. (foto.) ampliación.
blowy [-ɪ] *a.* ligero, ventoso.
blowzy ['blaʊzɪ] **blowzed** [blaʊzd] *a.* desaliñado, desmelenado; coloradote.
blub [blʌb] *v.i* (fam.) echar a llorar, deshacerse en lágrimas.
blubber ['blʌbər, B -ə] *s.* 1. grasa de ballena. 2. grasa (en el cuerpo). 3. llanto ruidoso. —*v.i.* romper a llorar, llorar a lágrima viva. —*v.t.* expresar con llanto, decir llorando.
blubber lip, bezo, labio grueso.
blubbery [-ərɪ] *a.* 1. gelatinoso (como la grasa de ballena); grasoso. 2. hinchado, protuberante.
blucher ['blutʃər, B -tʃə] *s.* borceguí; botina, media bota.
bludgeon ['blʌdʒən] *s.* cachiporra. —*v.t.* 1. aporrear, apalear. 2. (fig.) forzar, intimidar.
blue [blu] *a.* 1. azul. 2. triste, melancólico, desanimado. 3. lívido, amoratado (esp. a causa del frío o de un golpe). 4. **b. funk,** (fam.) estado de depresión emocional; **b. murder** (interj.) demonios!; **true b.,** fiel, leal; legítimo. —*s.* 1. (color) azul. 2. azulete, añil (para el lavado de la ropa). 3. (fam.) autoridad, policía. 4. **out of the b.,** como llovido, inesperadamente; **the b.,** el cielo; el mar. —*v.t.* (*pret., p.p.* BLUED [blud]; *p.pr.* BLUING O BLUEING) 1. azular, añilar. 2. pavonar (el hierro o el acero). 3. (fam.) malgastar, despilfarrar. —*v.i.* amoratarse, ponerse lívido.
blue baby, (med.) niño que padece de cianosis congénita.
blue balls, (vulg., E.U.) persona atacada de enfermedad venérea.
bluebeard ['bluˌbɪrd, B -ˌbɪəd] *s.* (fig.) barba azul.
bluebell [-ˌbɛl] *s.* (bot.) campánula.
blueberry [-ˌbɛrɪ, B -bərɪ] *s.* (bot.) (variedad de) arándano, vaccinio.
bluebird [-ˌbɜrd, B -ˌbɜd] *s.* 1. (orn.) azulejo. 2. (fig.) pájaro azul de la felicidad.
blue blood, sangre azul, aristocracia; persona de linaje noble, aristócrata.
bluebonnet [-ˌbɑnət, B -ˌbɔn-] *s.* 1. gorra azul escocesa de lana. 2. (fig.) escocés. 3. (bot.) azulejo, aciano mayor; lupino.
blue book, 1. libro azul, anuario de la alta sociedad y personas de relieve. 2. (E.U.) libreta para exámenes universitarios. 3. (G.B.) conjunto de documentos diplomáticos o parlamentarios.
bluebottle [-ˌbɑtəl, B -ˌbɔt-] *s.* 1. (bot.) liebrecilla, aldiza, azulejo. 2. (ento.) moscarda, moscón azul.
blue cheese, queso azul, queso de gusanos (queso tipo Roquefort).
blue chip, 1. ficha de póker de alto valor. 2. (fin.) acciones selectas (apreciadas por su estabilidad en la Bolsa).
blue chip securities, fianzas fiables.
bluecoat [-ˌkoʊt] *s.* 1. (fam.) policía uniformado. 2. (hist., E.U.) soldado del Norte en la guerra civil.
blue-collar [-ˌkɑler, B -ˌkɔlə] *a.* de la clase obrera que se desempeña en fábricas y en trabajos manuales.
Blue Cross, (E.U.) sistema de seguro médico.
blue devils, 1. melancolía, depresión. 2. (jer.) delírium trémens, delirio producido por el abuso del alcohol.
blue-eyed [-'aɪd] *a.* 1. de ojos azules, ojizarco, ojigarzo. 2. (fig., fam.) favorito, predilecto, mimado. 3. (jer.) inocente, crédulo.
bluefish [-ˌfɪʃ] *s.* (ict.) (especie de) pez azulado y plateado; pomátomo.
blue flag, (bot.) lirio azul.
blue grass, género de hierba sedosa y azulada, típica de una región del estado de Kentucky en E.U.
blue gum, (bot.) eucalipto de Australia.
blueing, blueish, *vars. de* **bluing, bluish.**
bluejack [-ˌdʒæk] *s.* 1. (quím.) vitriolo azul, sulfato de cobre. 2. (bot.) (variedad de) roble.
bluejacket [-ˌdʒækət] *s.* marinero uniformado; (E.U., G.B.) miembro del cuerpo de la Marina.
blue jay, (orn.) gayo.
blue jeans, (*pl.*)pantalones vaqueros, jeans, tejanos.
blue joke, chiste de color subido; cuento sicalíptico.
blue law, 1. ley de los puritanos (de Nueva Inglaterra). 2. estatuto que reglamenta el trabajo, el comercio y las diversiones en los domingos.
blue lead, 1. (min.) galena. 2. plomo azul (pigmento).
blue Monday, (fig.) lunes triste (por ser el día en que hay que reanudar la lucha cotidiana, después de la fiesta o el descanso dominguero).
blue moon, lapso largo; **once in a b.m.,** muy de tarde en tarde, de higos a brevas.
Blue Nile, Nilo azul (que en confluencia con el Nilo blanco pasa por Egipto y desemboca en el Mediterráneo).
bluenose [-ˌnoʊz] *s.* 1. (fam.) persona puritana o pretensiosa. 2. **B.,** nativo de Nueva Escocia.
blue pencil, lápiz negro (en la censura).
blue-pencil [-'pɛnsəl] *v.t.* corregir (un escrito) con lápiz azul; censurar, suprimir, tachar con lápiz negro.
blue peter, (mar.) bandera de despedida.
bluepoint [-ˌpɔɪnt] *s.* (E.U.) ostra pequeña que se da en el estrecho de Long Island en Nueva York.
blue point, tipo de gato siamés.
blueprint [-ˌprɪnt] *s.* 1. copia azul, fotocalco azul, cianocopia, copia heliográfica. 2. (fig.) programa detallado de acción (para movilización, organización de una empresa, etc.); anteproyecto. —*v.t.* copiar en cianotipo, fotocalcar.
blue ribbon, 1. galardón máximo (en una exhibición o un concurso). 2. (G.B.) cinta azul de la Orden de la Jarretera.

blue-ribbon [-ˈrɪbən] *a.* perito en una materia; experto especialmente capacitado.
blue-ribbon jury, jurado especial para juicios importantes.
blues [bluz] *s.* 1. estilo de jazz, de matiz melancólico, derivado de las canciones de los negros del sur de E.U. 2. (gen. **the b.**) melancolía, nostalgia, morriña, ej. *I've got the b.,* tengo tristeza. 3. (E.U.) uniforme azul de la Marina.
blue-sky law [ˈbluˈskaɪ-] (E.U.) ley reguladora del comercio bursátil.
bluestocking [-ˌstɑkɪŋ, B -ˌstɔk-] *s.* (G.B., ant.) mujer literata o pedante, marisabidilla.
bluestone [-ˌstoʊn] *s.* 1. (quím.) vitriolo azul, sulfato de cobre. 2. (min.) azurita, malaquita azul.
blue streak, 1. rayo, relámpago. 2. tarabilla. 3. **to talk a b. s.,** soltar la tarabilla, hablar por los codos.
bluet [ˈbluət] *s.* (bot.) azulejo, aciano.
blue titmouse, (orn.) holleco, herrerillo, trepatroncos.
blue vitriol, (quím.) vitriolo azul, caparrosa azul, sulfato de cobre.
blueweed [-ˌwid] *s.* (bot.) viperina.
blue wildebeest [-ˈwɪldəˌbist] (zool.) ñu azul.
bluff [blʌf] *s.* 1. farallón, escarpadura, barranca, risco. 2. engaño con simulación, baladronada, fanfarronada, bluff. 3. fanfarrón. 4. **to call someone's b.,** desenmascarar a un farsante. —*a.* escarpado, enhiesto. —*v.t.* 1. engañar simulando (recursos o medios); blufear (en juego de naipes). 2. hacer creer (en) mediante falsas apariencias; hacer aceptar o desistir simulando fuerza. —*v.i.* aparentar, simular, baladronear.
bluffer [ˈblʌfər, B -ə] *s.* fanfarrón, baladrón.
bluing [ˈbluɪŋ] *s.* azulete, añil (para la ropa blanca).
bluish [-ɪʃ] *a.* azulado, azulino.
blunder [ˈblʌndər, B -ə] *s.* error craso, desacierto, disparate, patochada. —*v.i.* 1. andar a tropezones, moverse torpemente. 2. equivocarse, desbarrar. 3. **b. upon,** tropezar con, dar de chiripa con (algo). —*v.t.* 1. descolgarse con, expresar desatinadamente. 2. manejar mal, arruinar (negocio, etc.); meter la pata.
blunderbuss [-ˌbʌs] *s.* 1. trabuco, escopeta corta de boca ancha. 2. desmañado, desatinado.
blunderer [-dərər, B -dərə] *s.* desatinado.
blunt [blʌnt] *a.* 1. rudo, brusco, contundente, directo. 2. boto, romo, obtuso, desafilado, despuntado (instrumento, arma). 3. obtuso, lerdo, tardo. —*v.t.* 1. embotar, enromar, desafilar. 2. adormecer, mitigar.
bluntly [ˈblʌntlɪ] *adv.* bruscamente, contundentemente.
bluntness [-nəs] *s.* 1. falta de filo o punta (en arma blanca o instrumento). 2. brusquedad, aspereza.
blur [blɜr, B blɜ] *s.* borrón, mancha. —*v.t.* (*pret., p.p.* BLURRED; *p.pr.* BLURRING) hacer borroso o indistinto; empañar, velar, borrar (la visibilidad, etc.). —*v.i.* ponerse borroso o confuso.
blurb [blɜrb, B blɜb] *s.* 1. (fam.) bombo, propaganda o noticia encomiástica (de un autor o producto). 2. (E.U.) subtítulo periodístico.
blurred [blɜrd, B blɜd] *a.* borroso, confuso.
blurry [ˈblɜrɪ] *a.* borroso, indistinto (perfil, fotografía, etc.); manchado, empañado.
blurt [blɜrt, B blɜt] *v.t.* (ú. gen. con *out*) decir o soltar abruptamente, hablar sin tino.
blush [blʌʃ] *v.i.* 1. sonrojarse, ruborizarse, abochornarse. 2. sentir vergüenza. 3. florecer. 4. **b. at,** avergonzarse de, ponerse como un tomate. —*s.* 1. rubor, sonrojo, bochorno. 2. color rosado. 3. vistazo, ojeada. 4. **at first b.,** a primer vistazo.
blushing [ˈblʌʃɪŋ] *a.* ruborizado. —*s.* rubor, sonrojo, erubescencia.
bluster [ˈblʌstər, B -tə] *v.i.* 1. soplar (el viento) con ráfagas violentas. 2. fanfarronear, bravear. —*v.t.* proferir con cólera. —*s.* 1. ráfaga violenta (de viento). 2. bravata. 3. ruido, tumulto.
blvd. *abrev. de* **boulevard,** avenida, bulevar.
B.M. *abrev. de* **Bachelor of Medicine,** Licenciado en Medicina.
B-movie [ˈbiˈmuvi] *s.* película de serie B, película de bajo presupuesto.
B. Mus. *abrev. de* **Bachelor of Music,** Licenciado en Música.
BO *abrev. de* **body odor,** mal olor (del cuerpo).
boa [ˈboʊə] *s.* 1. (zool.) boa (*f.*). 2. boa (*m.*) (prenda de pieles o plumas que usan las mujeres).
BOAC *abrev. de* **British Overseas Airways Corporation,** Aerolíneas Internacionales Británicas.
boar [bɔr, B bɔ] *s.* 1. (zool.) **wild b.,** jabalí, jabalina. 2. verraco, cerdo padre.
board [bɔrd, B bɔd] *s.* 1. tabla, tablero, tablilla. 2. mesa; comida, pensión. 3. tribunal; consejo, junta. 4. (mar.) bordo. 5. (mar.) bordada. 6. (*pl.*) tablas, escenario. 7. (elec.) tablero, cuadro (de instrumentos, mando, etc.). 8. (bridge) (el) muerto. 9. (enc.) cartón (de tapa), tapa. 10. **above b.,** franco, sincero, correcto; **b. and lodging,** cuarto y comida; **free on b.,** (com.) libre de gastos a bordo; **on b.,** a bordo; **to be on the boards,** (fig.) ser actor o actriz; **to go by the b.,** caerse (un mástil, etc.) por el costado del buque; (fig.) fracasar, frustrarse, echarse a perder; **to sweep the b.,** ganar o llevarse todos los premios (en una competencia). —*v.t.* 1. subir a bordo de (un tren, buque, avión, etc.). 2. (mar.) abordar, tomar al abordaje. 3. enmaderar, entarimar; (con *up*) entablar. 4. hospedar; tomar en pupilaje. —*v.i.* (gen. con *with*) vivir en pensión o alojarse con.
boarder [ˈbɔrdər, B ˈbɔdə] *s.* 1. pensionista, huésped. 2. (mar.) abordador.
board foot, pie de tabla, pie cuadrado de tabla (unidad de medida que equivale a una tabla de un pie cuadrado de una pulgada de espesor).
boarding [-ɪŋ] *s.* 1. tablazón, entablado, tabique de tablas. 2. (mar.) abordaje.
boardinghouse [-ˌhaʊs] *s.* casa de huéspedes, pensión, pupilaje.
boarding pass, tarjeta de embarque.
boarding pike, (mar.) botavante.
boarding school, internado, escuela de internos.
board meeting, reunión de directorio.
board of directors, (com.) junta directiva, directorio.
board of education, junta de educación, consejo de educación.
board of health, junta de sanidad, consejo de sanidad.
board of trade, (E.U.) junta de comercio; **B. T.** (G.B.) ministerio de comercio.
board of trustees, junta directiva, junta de síndicos.
board room, 1. (com.) sala de sesiones (de la junta directiva). 2. salón de la bolsa, sala de compra y venta (en la bolsa de valores).
board wages, alojamiento y comida en pago de servicios.
boardwalk [ˈbɔrdˌwɔk, B ˈbɔd-] *s.* paseo entablado (en las playas).
boardhound [ˈbɔrˌhaʊnd, B ˈbɔˌ-] *s.* (zool.) dogo alemán, perro jabalinero.
boarish [ˈbɔrɪʃ] *a.* fiero, cruel (como el jabalí); lascivo.
boast [boʊst] *v.i.* alardear, vanagloriarse, jactarse, ufanarse; **it's nothing to b. of,** no es cosa para jactarse. —*v.t.* jactarse de, ostentar. —*s.* jactancia, alarde, vanagloria.
boastful [ˌboʊstfəl] *a.* jactancioso, alardoso.
boat [boʊt] *s.* 1. bote, barca, chalupa, lancha, esquife; barco, buque, nave, navío, bajel, embarcación. 2. salsera; taza (en forma de bote). 3. (quím.) gamella, artesa. 4. **gravy b.,** salsera; **to be in the same b.,** correr la misma suerte, pasar los mismos apuros (que otra persona); **to burn one's boats,** quemar las naves; **to have an oar in everyone's b.,** ser muy entremetido; **to miss the b.,** perderse una oportunidad, no aprovechar una ocasión; quedarse en Babia. —*v.i.* viajar en bote, dar un paseo en bote.
boatbill [ˈboʊtˌbɪl] *s.* (orn.) garza caracolera, garza de pico cuchara.
boat deck, (mar.) cubierta de botes o lanchas.
boater [-ər, B -ə] *s.* 1. botero. 2. sombrero de paja, rígido y plano.
boat hook, (mar.) bichero.
boathouse [-ˌhaʊs] *s.* cobertizo de lanchas, caseta de botes.
boat hull, 1. (mar.) casco del barco, buque, etc. 2. (avia.) casco de hidroavión.
boating [-ɪŋ] *s.* paseo en bote.
boatload [-ˌloʊd] *s.* barcada.
boatman [-mən] *s.* 1. barquero, botero. 2. el que alquila o posee un barco.
boatneck [-ˌnɛk] *s.* escote ancho y redondo.
boat-race [-ˌreɪs] *s.* regata.
boatswain [ˈboʊsən] *s.* (mar.) contramaestre.
boatswain's chair, (mar.) balso, guindola.
boatswain's mate, (mar.) segundo contramaestre.
boat train, barco trasbordador de trenes, tren de empalme con un barco.
bob [bɑb, B bɔb] *s.* 1. breve movimiento o sacudida, meneo (verticales); reverencia (esp. la que hace una niña); ej., *b. of the head,* sacudida de la cabeza. 2. peso o plomo (que cuelga de una cuerda, vara, etc.). 3. cola cortada del caballo; corte de pelo muy corto (de niño o de mujer). 4. trineo articulado; especie de patín. 5. (pesca) corcho, flotador. 6. (fam. G.B.) (*pl.* **bob**) chelín. 7. (dial.) ramo de flores, ramillete. 8. (const.) peso de la plomada. —*v.t.* (*pret., p.p.* BOBBED; *p.pr.* BOBBING) 1. dar un golpe ligero a; tocar (la puerta). 2. mover, sacudir, menear (de arriba abajo). 3. cortar (el pelo) muy corto. —*v.i.* 1. hacer reverencia, saludar. 2. (con *up*) surgir, presentarse súbitamente. 3. pescar con carnada. 4. **b. for (apples, cherries,** etc.), tratar de coger con la boca (manzanas, cerezas, etc., colgadas en el aire o que flotan en el agua); **b. up and down,** subir y bajar con sacudidas rápidas, fluctuar rápidamente; **b. up like a cork,** (fig.) recuperarse fácilmente (después de una derrota, etc.).
bobber [ˈbɑbər, B ˈbɔbə] *s.* corcho o flotador de la caña de pescar.
bobbery [-ərɪ] *s.* toletole, alboroto.
bobbin [ˈbɑbən, B ˈbɔb-] *s.* 1. carrete, bobina, canilla (de máquina de coser). 2. (cost.) bolillo (para hacer encajes). 3. cuerda o cordoncillo delgado.
bobbin bit, (carp.) broca para hacer agujeros profundos.
bobbinet [ˌbɑbəˈnɛt, B ˈbɔbɪnɛt] *s.* encaje o bordado de algodón hecho a máquina (que imita el encaje de bolillos).
bobbin lace, encaje de bolillos.
bobble [ˈbɑbəl, B ˈbɔb-] *v.i.* 1. moverse, sacudirse. 2. equivocarse, fallar. —*v.t.* estropear, malograr. —*s.* falla, falta, error.

bobby ['bɑbɪ, B 'bɔbɪ] *s.* (fam. G.B.) policía, guardia.
bobby pin, horquilla, pasador.
bobby socks, bobby sox, calcetines cortos, tobilleras.
bobby-soxer [-ˌsɑksər, B -ˌsɔksə] *s.* (fam.) jovencita adolescente, mocita.
bobcat ['bɑbˌkæt, B 'bɔb-] *s.* (zool., E.U.) lince o gato montés.
bobolink ['bɑbəˌlɪŋk, B 'bɔb-] *s.* (orn.) chambergo, charlatán.
bob skate, patín con dos cuchillas o soportes paralelos.
bobsled [-ˌslɛd]ƀσƀšλəɩ̰ ɥ [-ˌsleɪ] *s.* (dep.) trineo de carreras, con eje direccional.
bobstay [-ˌsteɪ] *s.* (mar.) barbiquejo.
bobtail [-ˌteɪl] *s.* rabo o cola cortada; perro o caballo con el rabo cortado. —*a.* 1. rabón, de rabo cortado. 2. (fig.) abreviado, cortado; deficiente. —*v.t.* cortar o cercenar la cola o el rabo de (un animal); cortar.
bobwhite [-'hwaɪt, -'waɪt] *s.* (orn., E.U.) perdiz, codorniz.
boccie ['bɑtʃɪ, B 'bɔtʃɪ] *s.* juego de bochas.
Boche [bɔʃ] *s., a.* (jer. despec.) boche, alemán, tudesco.
bock [bɑk, B bɔk] *s.* (t. **bock beer**) cerveza fuerte y oscura, cerveza de marzo.
bock beer, cerveza de marzo.
bode [boʊd] *v.t., v.i.* presagiar, predecir, pronosticar, agorar; **b. ill,** ser de mal agüero.
bodice ['bɑdəs, B 'bɔd-] *s.* corpiño, jubón, almilla sin mangas; (ant.) corsé.
bodied ['bɑdid, B 'bɔd-] *a.* (*ú. en palabras compuestas*) de cuerpo, ej., *able-b.,* de cuerpo sano, robusto.
bodiless [-ɪləs] *a.* incorpóreo, inmaterial.
bodily [-əlɪ] *a.* corporal, material, corpóreo. —*adv.* 1. corporalmente, en persona. 2. enteramente, en conjunto.
bodily fear, temor al daño físico.
boding ['boʊdɪŋ] *s.* presentimiento, agüero, presagio. —*a.* ominoso, presagioso.
bodkin ['bɑdkɪn, B 'bɔd-] *s.* 1. punzón (para hacer ojales). 2. espadilla, rascador, rascamoño, pasador. 3. aguja de jareta. 4. (impr.) punzón o punta. 5. daga, estilete.
body ['bɑdɪ, B 'bɔdɪ] *s.* 1. cuerpo. 2. cuerpo, cadáver. 3. cuerpo, tronco, parte principal; nave (de iglesia); casco (de buque); cuerpo (de avión); tronco (de árbol); carrocería (de automóvil). 4. persona, individuo; (fam. y dial.) uno (refiriéndose a sí mismo). 5. (jer. E.U.) mujer sexualmente atractiva. 6. (der.) persona (natural). 7. cuerpo, gremio, corporación, comunidad, sociedad, liga. 8. mayoría. 9. cuerpo, agregado, conjunto. 10. (mil.) fuerza (de soldados); grueso (de un ejército). 11. cuerpo, colección (de leyes o preceptos). 12. cuerpo, masa. 13. cuerpo, consistencia; sustancia, espesor. 14. (impr.) árbol (del tipo); cuerpo, calibre, grado (de la letra de imprenta). 15. **a b. of troops,** (mil.) un destacamento, una fuerza; **a b. of water,** una extensión de agua; **heavenly b.,** cuerpo celeste; **in a b.,** todos juntos, colectivamente, en masa; **to keep b. and soul together,** vivir de milagro, subsistir, quedar vivo. —*v.t.* (*pret., p.p.* BODIED; *p.pr.* BODYING) 1. encarnar, dar cuerpo a. 2. (gen. con *forth*) representar (una idea, etc.).
body-builder [-ˌbɪldər, B -də] *s.* 1. fabricante de carrocerías (de vehículos). 2. alimento nutritivo. 3. aparato para desarrollar la musculatura. 4. levantador de pesas.
body corporate, (der.) persona jurídica.
bodyguard [-ˌgɑrd, B -ˌgɑd] *s.* guardaespaldas, escolta, guardia personal.
body-line [-ˌlaɪn] *a.* (criquet, tenis) dirigido contra el cuerpo (del bateador o del otro jugador).
body politic, entidad política, poderes (de una nación).
body section, (avia.) sección del fuselaje.
body snatcher, ladrón de cadáveres.
body tank, (avia.) depósito de fuselaje.
body varnish, (avia.) laca de apomazar.
boehm flute [beɪm-] (mús.) flauta travesera.
boehmite ['beɪmˌaɪt] *s.* (min.) boehmita.
Boeotian [bɪ'oʊʃən, B -ʃjən] *a.* 1. beocio, de Beocia (comarca griega). 2. (fig.) beocio, torpe, grosero. —*s.* natural de Beocia, beocio.
Boer [bɔr, bʊr, B 'boʊə] *s.* bóer, sudafricano descendiente de los pobladores holandeses. —*a.* perteneciente a los bóers.
boffo ['bɑfoʊ, B 'bɔfoʊ] *s.* (jer.) persona muy popular o exitosa.
Bofors gun ['boʊfərz-, B -əz-] cañón automático antiaéreo.
bog [bɑg, bɔg, B bɔg] *s.* tremedal, pantano, marisma, ciénaga. —*v.t., v.i.* empantanar(se), hundir(se) en una ciénaga; **b. down** o **to get bogged down,** (fig.) empantanar(se), atascar(se).
bog asphodel, (bot.) abama.
bogey ['bʊgɪ, 'boʊ-, B 'boʊ-] *s.* 1. demonio, duende, espantajo; (fig.) espectro, fantasma. 2. (golf) número de golpes con que un jugador promedio debe hacer cada hoyo.
bogeyman [-ˌmæn] *s.* coco, cuco, fantasma (para asustar a los niños).
boggle ['bɑgəl, B 'bɔg-] *v.i.* 1. sobresaltarse, sobrecogerse, intimidarse. 2. recular, cejar, vacilar (por escrúpulos, miedo, indecisión, etc.). —*v.t.* hacer una patochada. —*s.* sobresalto; reculada; desatino, disparate. —*var. de* **bogle.**
boggy ['bɑgɪ, 'bɔgɪ, B 'bɔgɪ] *a.* pantanoso, cenagoso.
bogie ['boʊgɪ] *s.* 1. (G.B., f.c.) carro de plataforma, carro plano. 2. (G.B., f.c.) bogui, carretilla (que soporta la parte delantera de la locomotora). —*var. de* **bogey.**
bogle ['boʊgəl] *s.* (dial. G.B.) fantasma, duende, espectro.
Bogota [ˌboʊgə'tɑ, B ˌbɔ-] *s.* Bogotá, capital de Colombia.
bogtrotter ['bɑgˌtrɑtər, B 'bɔgˌtrɔtə] *s.* 1. (despec.) irlandés. 2. (orn.) lechuza de los campos, lechuzón de los pajonales.
bogus ['boʊgəs] *a.* falso, postizo, espurio.
bogy, *s.* (*pl.* BOGIES) *var. de* **bogie** o **bogey.**
bohea [boʊ'hi] *s.* té negro de la China.
Bohemia [boʊ'himɪə] *s.* 1. Bohemia. 2. bohemia (los gitanos en conjunto o grupo de personas que llevan vida bohemia).
Bohemian [-ɪən] *s., a.* 1. bohemio, vagabundo, gitano. 2. bohemio, artista, poeta. 3. persona de costumbres libres y vida irregular. 4. natural e idioma de Bohemia.
boil [bɔɪl] *v.i.* 1. hervir, bullir, cocer. 2. (fig.) hervir, excitarse, acalorarse. 3. **blood boils,** hierve la sangre; **b. away,** consumirse, evaporarse (líquido) ;**b. down (to),** quedar reducido (a); **b. over,** rebosarse, derramarse (al hervir); **to keep the pot boiling,** ganarse el sustento. —*v.t.* cocer (alimentos); meter en agua hirviente, hervir (ropa, instrumentos quirúrgicos, etc.); hacer hervir; **b. down,** reducir por cocción o evaporación, convertir en vapor; (fig.) reducir, condenar, acortar; **boiled shirt,** (fam.) camisa con el frente almidonado. —*s.* 1. ebullición, hervor. 2. (med.) furúnculo, divieso, golondrino, ganglio infartado. 3. **at a b.** u **on the b.,** hirviendo; **to bring to a b.,** calentar hasta que hierva; **to come to a b.,** alzar o levantar el hervor, comenzar a hervir; **to a b.,** hasta que rompa a hervir.
boiler ['bɔɪlər, B -ə] *s.* 1. hervidor, paila, cazo, caldero. 2. caldera (a vapor).
boiler hatch, escotilla de caldera.
boilerhouse [-ˌhaʊs] *s.* casa de calderas.
boilermaker [-ˌmeɪkər, B -ə] *s.* 1. calderero, calderista. 2. mezcla de whiski y cerveza.
boiler plate, plancha de caldera, chapa de caldera.
boiler room, sala o cuarto de calderas.
boiler shell, casco o cuerpo de caldera.
boiler tube, tubo de caldera.
boiling [-ɪŋ] *a.* hirviente. —*s.* hervor, ebullición.
boiling point, punto de ebullición, temperatura de ebullición.
boisterous ['bɔɪstərəs] *a.* 1. ruidoso, estrepitoso. 2. alborotado, tumultuoso, turbulento (muchedumbre, etc.). 3. bullicioso, exuberante (persona, manera de hablar, etc.). 4. furioso, violento, borrascoso, tempestuoso (mar, viento, etc.).
bold [boʊld] *a.* 1. valiente, intrépido. 2. arrojado, atrevido, imprudente. 3. osado, temerario. 4. fresco, descarado. 5. vigoroso, libre, audaz (imaginación, dibujo, descripción, etc.). 6. escarpado, empinado, ej., *b. shore,* acantilado, costa escarpada. 7. conspicuo, destacado, pronunciado, marcado, bien delineado o definido, ej., *b. features,* facciones marcadas. 8. (impr.) destacado. —*s.* (impr.) (tipo de) negrita(s) o negrilla(s).
boldface ['boʊldˌfeɪs] *s.* (impr.) negrita(s), negrilla(s); **in b.,** (impreso) en negritas o negrillas.
bold-faced [-ˌfeɪst] *a.* 1. atrevido, descarado, descocado. 2. (impr.) en negritas.
boldness [-nəs] *s.* arrojo, intrepidez, valentía, osadía, audacia, descaro.
bold type, (tip.) negrilla, negrita.
bole [boʊl] *s.* 1. tronco de árbol. 2. (variedad de) tierra arcillosa fina. 3. (esco.) abertura sin vidrio (en la pared de una casa); hornacina, alacena, armario empotrado (en la pared).
bolero [bə'lɛroʊ, B -'lɛər-] *s.* 1. bolero, chaquetilla corta. 2. (mús.) bolero, danza y ritmo de origen español.
bolide ['boʊlaɪd] *s.* (meteor.) bólido, meteoro.
Bolivarian [ˌboʊlɪ'vɛrɪən, B -'vɛər-] *a.* bolivariano, perteneciente al Libertador, sus conceptos e imagen.
Bolivia [bə'lɪvɪə] *s.* Bolivia.
Bolivian [-ɪən] *a., s.* boliviano.
boll [boʊl] *s.* cápsula, vaina (de una planta, esp. del algodón o el lino).
bollard ['bɑlərd, B 'bɔləd] *s.* (mar.) bolardo, noray.
bollix ['bɑlɪks, B 'bɔl-] *v.t.* desordenar, estropear, averiar.
boll weevil, 1. (ento.) gorgojo del algodón. 2. esquirol, obrero rompehuelgas.
boll worm, gusano del maiz y el algodón.
bolo ['boʊloʊ] *s.* bolo (cuchillo grande que se usa en Filipinas).
Bologna [bə'loʊnjə] *s.* Bolonia, ciudad de Italia.
bologna [bə'loʊnɪ, B -njə] *s. abrev. de* **b. sausage,** salchicha de Bolonia.
Bolognese [ˌboʊlə'niz] *a., s.* (*pl.* BOLOGNESE) boloñés.
bolometer [bə'lɑmətər, B -'lɔmɪtə] *s.* (fís.) bolómetro.
boloney [bə'loʊnɪ] *s.* 1. salchicha de Bolonia. 2. (jer. E.U.) (*nonsense*) chorradas, disparates; (*lies*) cuentos de camino.
Bolshevik ['boʊlʃəˌvɪk, 'bɑl-, B 'bɔl-] *s.* (*pl.* BOLSHEVIKS O BOLSHEVIKI [-ɪ]) bolchevique.
Bolshevism [-ˌvɪzəm] *s.* bolchevismo, bolchequismo.

Bolshevist [-vəst] *a.* bolchevista, bolchevique, bolcheviquista. —*s.* bolchevique.
bolshie, bolshy ['boʊlʃɪ, B 'bɔlʃɪ] *s.* (jer.) bolchevique, comunista.
bolson ['boʊlsən] *s.* (esp. S.O. de E.U.) valle ancho y árido.
bolster ['boʊlstər, B -stə] *s.* 1. travesero, travesaño. 2. (arq.) can, cartela; collarín (del capitel jónico). 3. (const.) solera, soporte, sostén, refuerzo. 4. (mec.) cojín. 5. (mar.) almohada. —*v.t.* (gen. con *up*) sostener, apoyar; reforzar, auxiliar.
bolt [boʊlt] *s.* 1. flecha, saeta (corta y pesada de la ballesta). 2. rayo, centella, relámpago. 3. sobresalto, salto brusco. 4. desbocamiento (de un caballo). 5. huida, fuga. 6. tornillo, perno. 7. rollo (de tela); rollo (de papel). 8. pestillo (de la cerradura). 9. cerrojo, cerrojillo, pestillo, falleba (en puertas o ventanas). 10. cerrojo (del fusil). 11. madero cachizo; madero barcal corto. 12. **b. from the blue,** (fig.) golpe inesperado, desgracia repentina; suceso inopinado; **to shoot one's b.,** hacer uno todo cuanto pueda, agotársele el ingenio a uno. —*v.t.* 1. acerrojar, cerrar con pestillo, echar el cerrojo. 2. empernar, fijar o asegurar con pernos, tornillos o clavijas. 3. hacer saltar, hacer salir (liebre de su guarida). 4. (con *out*) decir intempestivamente, soltar abruptamente, decir de sopetón o a boca de jarro (palabra, la verdad, etc.). 5. engullir, tragar sin masticar (la comida). 6. (pol., E.U.) abandonar, negar apoyo a (partido, candidato, etc.). 7. **b. in, b. out,** encerrar; dejar fuera, excluir, cerrar la puerta a. —*v.i.* 1. moverse rápidamente, hacer un movimiento brusco. 2. desbocarse, dispararse (caballo). 3. (t. con *away, from, off, out,* etc.) dispararse, largarse, huir, salir disparado. 4. (pol., E.U.) irse, retirar su apoyo. 5. **b. up o upright,** erguirse de golpe. —*adv.* en posición erguida; **b. upright,** enhiesto, derecho y rígido. —*v.t.* cernir, tamizar (harina, etc.).
bolt clevis, (mec.) pasador.
bolter [boʊltər, B -ə] *s.* 1. caballo que suele desbocarse. 2. disidente, renegado (político). 3. cedazo, criba, tamiz.
bolthead [-ˌhɛd] *s.* cabeza de tornillo o perno.
boltrope [-ˌroʊp] *s.* (mar.) relinga.
bolus ['boʊləs] *s.* (farm.) bolo, píldora grande.
bomb [bɑm, B bɔm] *s.* 1. bomba. 2. (fig.) sorpresa, acontecimiento inesperado. 3. bomba gamma. 4. (jer., E.U., fútbol) pase largo de una sola jugada. 5. (jer.) fracaso, fiasco. —*v.t.* bombardear; **b. out,** obligar a salir de un recinto por bombardeo. —*v.i.* 1. bombardear. 2. (jer.) (gen. con *out*) ser o resultar un fracaso.
bombard ['bɑmˌbɑrd, B 'bɔmˌbɑd] *s.* bombarda (cañón antiguo de gran calibre). — [bɑm'bɑrd, bəm-, B bɔm'bɑd] *v.t.* 1. (mil.) bombardear. 2. (fig.) asediar, importunar (con preguntas, peticiones, etc.). 3. (fís.) bombardear, someter (un cuerpo) al bombardeo de partículas eléctricas o rayos.
bombardier [ˌbɑmbə'dɪr, B ˌbɔm-'dɪə] *s.* 1. bombardero (en avión). 2. (G.B.) cabo de artillería.
bombardment [bɑm'bɑrdmənt, bəm-, B bɔm'bɑd-] *s.* bombardeo.
bombardon [bɑm-ən, B bɔm-] *s.* (mús.) 1. bombarda (antiguo instrumento de viento). 2. bombardón, helicón; tuba bajo o contrabajo. 3. bombarda (del órgano).
bombasine, *var. de* **bombazine.**
bombast ['bɑmˌbæst B 'bɔm-] *s.* expresión, discurso o escrito rimbombante o ampuloso.
bombastic [bɑm'bæstɪk, B bɔm-] *a.* bombástico, ampuloso, rimbombante, pomposo, altisonante.
bombazine ['bɑmbə'zin, B 'bɔm-ˌzin] *s.* bombasí, fustán; tela de algodón.
bomb bay, (avia., mil.) compartimiento de bombas.
bomb crater, embudo, cráter, hoyo hecho por una bomba.
bomb disposal, neutralización de bombas fallidas.
bombe [bɑm, B bɔm] *s.* (fr.) postre helado.
bombed [bɑmd, B bɔmd] *a.* (jer.) borracho.
bomber ['bɑmər, B 'bɔmə] *s.* (mil.) bombardero; avión de bombardeo.
bombinate ['bɑmbəˌneɪt, B 'bɔm-] *v.i.* zumbar; susurrar, murmurar; hablar monótonamente.
bombination [ˌbɑmbə'neɪʃən, B ˌbɔm-] *s.* zumbido, susurro.
bombing ['bɑmɪŋ, B 'bɔm-] *s.* bombardeo.
bombproof [-ˌpruf] *a.* (mil.) a prueba de bombas.
bomb rack, (avia.) portabombas.
bomb release, (aer.) lanzabombas.
bombshell [-ˌʃɛl] *s.* 1. (mil.) bomba; granada. 2. (fig.) zambombazo, gran sorpresa, acontecimiento inesperado. 3. (jer.) mujer sexualmente atractiva.
bomb shelter, refugio contra bombardeos.
bombsight [-ˌsaɪt] *s.* (aer., mil.) visor de bombardeo.
bomb-site [-'saɪt] *s.* (avia., mil.) objetivo.
bomb squad, brigada antiexplosivos, brigada de explosivos.
bombycid ['bɑmbəsɪd, B 'bɔm-] *s.* (zool.) bombícido.
bona fide ['boʊnəˌfaɪd, B -'faɪdɪ] de buena fe; auténtico, genuino.
bonanza [bə'nænzə] *s.* 1. mina, valiosa veta mineral. 2. (fig.) mina, negocio lucrativo.
Bonapartist ['boʊnəˌpɑrtəst, B -ˌpɑt-] *a., s.* bonapartista, partidario de Napoleón y su dinastía.
bonbon ['bɑnˌbɑn, B 'bɔnbɔn] *s.* bombón, confite.
bonbonnière [ˌbɑnbə'nɪr, B ˌbɔn-'nɪə] *s.* (fr.) bombonera, fuente o cofre de confites.
bond [bɑnd, B bɔnd] *s.* 1. lazo, atadura, enlace, vínculo. 2. yugo, traba. 3. (*pl.*) cadenas, cautiverio, ej., *the bonds of love,* las cadenas del amor. 4. (fig.) nexo, lazo. 5. obligación, contrato. 6. (fuerza de) cohesión, liga, unión; sustancia adhesiva. 7. (com., fin.) bono, título; título de renta fija. 8. fianza, caución, garantía. 9. (const.) aparejo, trabazón. 10. (quím.) grado de afinidad, enlace. 11. (f.c.) ligazón. 12. **in b.,** afianzado, en depósito bajo fianza; en almacén aduanero; **to take out of b.,** despachar en la aduana (pagando los derechos). —*v.t.* 1. hipotecar (bienes); poner (una mercancía) en depósito afianzado. 2. garantizar, afianzar (un empleado, etc.). 3. ligar, trabar. —*v.i.* trabarse, unirse, pegarse.
bondage ['bɑndɪdʒ, B 'bɔnd-] *s.* cautiverio, esclavitud, servidumbre.
bonded [-əd] *a.* en depósito; en garantía; depositado bajo fianza; hipotecado.
bonded warehouse, almacén afianzado, depósito de artículos bajo fianza.
bonded whiskey, (E.U.) whiski curado al menos durante cuatro años en almacén afianzado por la autoridad estatal.
bondholder [-ˌhoʊldər, B -də] *s.* (com.) obligacionista, tenedor de bonos.
bond issue, (fin.) emisión de bonos.
bondmaid [-ˌmeɪd] *s.* esclava, sierva.
bondman [-mən] *s.* siervo feudal; esclavo.
bond paper, papel bond, papel de hilo.
bond servant, esclavo, esclava.
bondsman ['bɑndzmən, B 'bɔndz-] *s.* fiador, garante.
bondstone ['bɑndˌstoʊn, B 'bɔnd-] *s.* (const.) perpiaño.
bondwoman [-ˌwʊmən] *s.* esclava, sierva.
bone [boʊn] *s.* 1. hueso; espina (de pez). 2. semilla, hueso (de fruta). 3. barba de ballena; ballena (en corsé). 4. (*pl.*) cuerpo, esqueleto, ej., *my old bones,* mi pobre cuerpo (esp. cansado o agotado). 5. (*pl.*) huesos, restos mortales. 6. (*pl.*) especie de castañuelas. 7. (*pl.*) dados. 8. **bred in the b.,** muy arraigado, inextirpable (costumbre, vicio, etc.); **skin and** b., piel y hueso, muy delgado; **to feel in one's bones,** estar seguro (o convencido) de (algo); **to have a b. to pick with someone,** tener una discusión o disputa con alguien; to **make no bones of** (o **about**), no andarse con rodeos; **to the b.,** (congelado) hasta los huesos. —*v.t.* 1. deshuesar; quitar las espinas a (un pescado). 2. emballenar, poner ballenas a (un corsé). 3. (ing.) nivelar, alinear, tomar el nivel de. 4. (jer. G.B.) ratear, hurtar. —*v.i.* **to b. up on (something),** estudiar duro; aprender, repasar (tema o asignatura).
bone ash, (metal.) cendra, cendrada.
bone black, carbón animal.
bone china, porcelana translúcida.
boned [boʊnd] *a.* 1. sin huesos, deshuesado (fruta o carne); sin espinas (pescado). 2. de osamenta (grande, pequeña, etc.), ej. **big-boned,** de osamenta recia.
bone-dry ['boʊn'draɪ] *a.* 1. completamente seco. 2. sediento, deshidratado.
bonefish [-ˌfɪʃ] *s.* (ict.) macabí, lisa francesa.
bonehead [-ˌhɛd] *s.* (fam.) estúpido, tonto.
boneheaded, (fam.) estúpido.
bone lace, encaje de bolillos.
boneless [-ləs] *a.* 1. sin huesos, deshuesado (fruta o carne); sin espinas (pescado). 2. (fig.) débil, sin fuerza (de carácter, etc.).
bone meal, harina de huesos (fertilizante).
bone of contention, manzana de la discordia, materia de desavenencia.
boner ['boʊnər, B -ə] *s.* (fam.) patochada, disparate, error (ridículo y estúpido); **to pull a b.,** meter la pata.
bones [boʊnz] *s. pl.* (jer.) flaco, persona muy delgada.
boneset ['boʊnˌsɛt] *s.* (bot.) eupatorio, consuelda.
bonfire ['bɑnˌfaɪr, B 'bɔnˌfaɪə] *s.* fogata, hoguera.
bong [bɑŋ, B bɔŋ] *s.* tan, talán. —*v.i., v.t.* tocar, sonar, tañer, repicar, campanillear.
bongo ['bɑŋgoʊ, B 'bɔŋ-] *s.* (*pl.* BONGOS o BONGOES) (mús.) bongó.
bonheur [bə'nɜr, B -'nɜ] *s.* (fr.) felicidad, dicha.
bonhomie, bonhommie [ˌbɑnə'mi, B 'bɔnɔmi] *s.* bonhomía, afabilidad.
boniface ['bɑnəfəs, B 'bɔnɪfeɪs] *s.* hostelero, mesonero.
boniness ['boʊnɪnəs] *s.* cualidad de óseo o huesudo.
bonito [bə'nitoʊ] *s.* (*pl.* BONITOS o BONITO) (ict.) bonito, especie de atún.
bon mot ['boʊn'moʊ] (fr.) (*pl.* BONS MOTS) donaire, agudeza, ocurrencia.
Bonn [bɑn, B bɔn] *s.* Bonn, capital de Alemania Occidental.
bonne [bɔn] *s.* (fr.) ama, niñera; criada.
bonne femme ['bɔn'fɛm] (fr.) cocina sencilla, casera.
bonnet ['bɑnət, B 'bɔn-] *s.* 1. gorro, gorra. 2. toca, sombrero de mujer. 3. (mec.) sombrerete, casquete (de válvula). 4. (aut., G.B.) capota, cubierta (del motor). 5. (mar.) boneta. 6. sombrerete (de horno, chimenea). 7. (fort.) bonete. 8. (zool.) bonete. —*v.t.* cubrir con una gorra.

bonnet nut, tuerca ciega.

bonny ['bɑnɪ, B 'bɔnɪ] *a.* 1. lindo, bonito. 2. plácido, grato, agradable, gentil. 3. saludable, regordete.

bonnyclabber [-ˌklæbər, B -ə] *s.* cuajo, leche cuajada.

bontebok ['bɑntəˌbɑk, B 'bɔntɪˌbɔk] *s.* (zool.) antílope sudafricano.

bon ton['bɑn'tɑn, B 'bɔn'tɔn] *s.* (fr.) buen tono, buena educación; el gran mundo, la alta sociedad.

bonus ['boʊnəs] *s.* bonificación, adehala; prima, dividendo.

bon vivant [ˌbɑnvi'vɑnt, B ˌbɔn-] (fr.) persona que disfruta de la buena vida.

bon voyage [-vɔɪ'ɑʒ, -vwaɪ-] (fr.) ¡buen viaje! ¡feliz viaje!

bony ['boʊnɪ] *s.* 1. óseo; huesudo. 2. descarnado. 3. espinoso (pez).

bonze [bɑnz, B bɔnz] *s.* bonzo (sacerdote budista).

bonzer ['bɑnzər, B 'bɔn-] *a.* (jer., Aust.) excelente, muy bueno.

boo [bu] *s.* abucheo, rechifla. *—interj.* bú (exclamación para asustar a los niños y para expresar descontento o desaprobación); **can't say b.,** no dice ni chus ni mus; **can't say b. to a goose,** es sumamente tímido. *—v.t., v.i.* abuchear.

boob [bub] *s.* (jer.) 1. bobo, papanatas. 2. persona inocentona y crédula. *—v.i.* (G.B.) cometer un error estúpido.

boo-boo ['buˌbu] *s.* 1. (dial.) magulladura, contusión o lastimadura. 2. (jer.) disparate, patochada.

boobs [bubz] *s. pl.* (jer.) busto, pecho, senos.

booby ['bubɪ] *s.* 1. tonto, bobalicón. 2. (jer.) (*pl.*) pechos de muchacha.

booby hatch, (fam.) manicomio; (jer. E.U.) prisión, cárcel.

booby prize, premio dado al peor concurrente; premio de consolación.

booby trap, 1. trampa. 2. zancadilla; situación que sorprende. 3. (mil.) trampa explosiva.

booby-trap bomb, bomba cazabobos, bomba trampa.

boodle ['budəl] *s.* 1. (fam.) cuadrilla, partida. 2. soborno. 3. botín; ganancias ilícitas. 4. moneda falsa. 5. **kit and b.,** todo, totalidad.

boogie ['bʊgɪ, 'bugɪ] *s.* (jer., despec.) negro.

boogie-woogie [ˌbʊgɪ'wʊgɪ, B 'bu-'wu-] *s.* estilo de jazz esp. para piano caracterizado por repetición rítmica en las notas bajas.

boo-hoo [ˌbu'hu] *v.i.* llorar ruidosamente.

book [bʊk] *s.* 1. libro. 2. libro, tomo, volumen. 3. (teat.) libreto. 4. talonario (de cheques); atado (de madejas de seda). 5. registro de apuestas; total de apuestas (en una carrera). 6. (bridge) seis primeras bazas (hechas por el declarante). 7. (*pl.*) libros (de cuentas). 8. **by the b.,** según las reglas, correctamente; **in one's b.,** según opinión de uno; **one for the books,** hazaña o hecho memorable (digno de ser registrado en los libros); **on the books,** registrado, anotado (esp. en una lista de miembros, asociados, etc.); **the B.,** la Biblia; **to be able to read someone like a b.,** leer los pensamientos de alguien como un libro abierto; **to be in one's bad (good) books,** estar en malas (buenas) relaciones con uno; **to keep books,** (com.) llevar libros; **to know like a b.,** conocer a fondo; **to speak like a b.,** hablar con mucha formalidad; **to suit one's b.,** resultar conveniente, convenir a alguien; **to throw the b. at (someone),** tratar (a alguien) con todo el rigor de la ley; reprender severamente (a alguien); **without b.,** de memoria. *—v.t.* 1. reservar, hacer reservación de (cuarto en hotel, asiento en teatro, tren, avión, etc.). 2. contratar (artista, actor). 3. asentar, registrar en un libro. 4. formular cargos contra, acusar formalmente a alguien (díc. esp. de la policía). 5. **to be booked up,** estar agotado o vendido (díc. de entradas); tener compromisos, ej., *the theater is b. up for the whole month,* las entradas para el teatro están vendidas (o agotadas) para todo el mes; *I'm b. up for the week,* tengo compromisos para toda la semana.

bookbinder ['bʊkˌbaɪndər, B -ə] *s.* encuadernador de libros.

bookbinding [-ɪŋ] *s.* encuadernación.

bookcase [-ˌkeɪs] *s.* armario, estante (para libros); estantería.

book club, club del libro (organización que vende libros, gen. a precios reducidos a miembros que han convenido en comprar una mínima cantidad anual).

bookend [-ˌɛnd] *s.* sujetalibros, apoyalibros.

bookie ['bʊkɪ] *s.* (jer.) corredor de apuestas (en las carreras de caballos).

booking [-ɪŋ] *s.* 1. reservación (de pasaje, cuarto en hotel, etc.). 2. compromiso (de un artista, actor, etc.).

booking clerk, vendedor de billetes (de viaje o de teatro).

booking office, despacho de pasajes, oficina de reservaciones de billetes de viaje y entradas de espectáculos.

bookish [-ɪʃ] *a.* 1. estudioso, aficionado a los libros; versado en libros. 2. pedante, teórico.

book jacket, forro, cubierta de libro.

bookkeeper [-ˌkipər, B -ə] *s.* tenedor de libros, contable.

bookkeeping [-ɪŋ] *s.* teneduría de libros, contabilidad.

book learning, mera teoría, sabiduría teórica (sin conocimiento de la vida).

booklet [-lət] *s.* folleto, opúsculo.

booklover [-ˌlʌvər, B -ə] *s.* bibliófilo.

bookmaker [-ˌmeɪkər, B -ə] *s.* 1. impresor, encuadernador o diseñador de libros. 2. corredor de apuestas, apostador de profesión (en las carreras de caballos).

bookmark [-ˌmɑrk, B -ˌmɑk] *s.* marcador de libro.

book-match [-ˌmætʃ] *v.t.* producir simetría perfecta de las vetas (ej., en dos hojas de madera para chapear).

bookmobile [-moʊˌbil] *s.* biblioteca ambulante, bibliobús; librería ambulante.

book of account, libro de contabilidad, libro de cuentas.

book of books, el libro de los libros, la Biblia.

Book of Common Prayer, libro de oraciones de la Iglesia Anglicana.

Book of Mormon, texto sagrado de la Iglesia Mormona.

book of reference, libro de consulta.

bookplate [-ˌpleɪt] *s.* 1. ex libris. 2. placa grabada para impresión de libros.

book review, reseña de libros recién publicados.

bookseller [-ˌsɛlər, B -ə] *s.* librero, vendedor de libros.

bookshelf [-ˌʃɛlf] *s.* estantería, repisa para libros.

bookshop [-ˌʃɑp, B -ˌʃɔp] *s.* librería.

bookstack [-ˌstæk] *s.* montón o pila de libros.

bookstall [-ˌstɔl] *s.* 1. puesto de libros (en la calle). 2. (pr. G.B.) puesto de periódicos.

bookstand [-ˌstænd] *s.* 1. puesto de libros. 2. atril.

bookstore [-ˌstɔr, B -ˌstɔ] *s.* librería, almacén de libros.

book value, (com.) valor escriturado de una propiedad o de acciones de una sociedad; valor contable.

bookworm [-ˌwɜrm, B -ˌwɜm] *s.* 1. gusano, polilla que roe los libros. 2. (fig.) ratón de biblioteca.

boom [bum] *s.* 1. (mar.) botavara (de la vela); botalón, tangón. 2. aguilón, pescante (de grúa). 3. barrera de maderos, cadena de cables (en la boca de un puerto). 4. cadena de troncos flotantes (para mantener juntos los demás). *—v.t.* (mar.) 1. (con *out*) extender la vela sobre el botalón. 2. obstruir (río o boca de un puerto) con una barrera flotante.

boom [bum] *v.i.* 1. retumbar, tronar, hacer estampido. 2. mugir, bramar. 3. estar en auge, medrar (economía, mercado, comercio, etc.); gozar de prosperidad repentina, desarrollarse rápidamente (ciudad, industria, etc.). *—v.t.* 1. hacer retumbar, decir en voz resonante. 2. incrementar, fomentar en forma rápida, dar impulso repentino a (comercio, industria, etc.). *—s.* 1. retumbo, estampido, ruido profundo y resonante; trueno (de un cañón, etc.). 2. mugido, bramido. 3. auge o prosperidad repentina, incremento o desarrollo rápido.

boomerang ['bumәˌræŋ] *s.* 1. bumerang (arma australiana en forma de arco, que regresa al que la arroja). 2. (fig.) acto o proceder cuyas consecuencias recaen sobre su autor. *—v.i.* ser contraproducente, (fig.) salir por la culata.

boom hoist, elevador del aguilón, izador del botalón.

booming [-ɪŋ] *a.* 1. resonante (voz); retumbante (cañón, etc.). 2. floreciente.

boomlet [-lət] *s.* (mar.) botalón pequeño; botavara o aguilón pequeños.

boom town, pueblo o ciudad que se está desarrollando rápidamente y disfruta de bonanza.

boon [bun] *s.* 1. beneficio, bendición, dicha. 2. dádiva, don; favor, merced. *—a.* 1. alegre, jovial. 2. (poét.) bondadoso, benigno (díc. esp. de la naturaleza).

boon companion, compañero constante.

boondocks ['bunˌdɑks, B -ˌdɔks] *s. pl.* 1. **the b.,** (jer.) monte, región selvática, selva. 2. (jer.) región olvidada, los quintos infiernos.

boondoggle [-ˌdɔgəl, -ˌdɑg-, B -ˌdɔg-] *s.* 1. trenzado de cuero; artículos de cuero o mimbre trenzados. 2. (fig.) ocupación trivial, trabajo inútil. *—v.i.* (fig.) trabajar inútilmente, perder tiempo en ocupación trivial.

boondoggler [-ˌdɔglər, -ˌdɑg-, B -ˌdɔglə] *s.* persona que realiza trabajo inútil, pero remunerativo.

boonie ['bunɪ] *s.* (jer. mil.) la gorra de dril típica del soldado norteamericano en la guerra de Vietnam.

boor [bʊr, B bʊә] *s.* 1. campesino, rústico. 2. patán, palurdo, grosero.

boorish ['bʊrɪʃ, B 'bʊәr-] *a.* 1. rústico. 2. patán, grosero, tosco.

boost [bust] *v.t.* 1. levantar, alzar, empujar hacia arriba. 2. fomentar, incrementar. 3. (fig.) elevar, levantar (la moral, coraje, etc.). 4. alabar, loar; promover, propagar (artículo, fama, etc.). 5. aumentar, sobrealimentar (en fuerza, presión, etc.). 6. (elec.) elevar (el voltaje). *—s.* 1. empuje, impulso, ayuda. 2. (tec.) incremento, aumento; refuerzo.

booster ['bustər, B -tә] *s.* 1. impulsador, fomentador. 2. (med.) inyección de refuerzo (esp. dosis suplementaria de un agente inmunizador para aumentar su efecto). 3. (elec.) elevador de potencial, elevador de tensión; rectificador reforzador; sobretensor. 4. (rad.) amplificador de antena; amplificador intermedio, repetidor; 5. (aero., astronáut.) sección propulsadora en proyectiles guiados. 6. (mil.) detonador auxiliar; multiplicador.

booster battery, (elec.) batería auxiliar, batería elevadora de tensión.

booster cable, cable de arranque.

booster pump, bomba reforzadora, bomba sobrealimentadora.

booster shot, (med.) inyección de refuerzo.

booster station, (rad.) repetidor.

boostershot transformer, (elec.) transformador elevador de tensión.

boot [but] *s.* 1. bota, botín. 2. calceta, bota de tortura. 3. cubierta o envoltura (ej., la que se usa para cubrir parte de la pata y casco del caballo); mandil o cubierta de cuero (en la parte delantera de los carruajes para protección de las piernas). 4. (pr. G.B.) maletera, portaequipajes (de un automóvil). 5. puntapié; despedida brusca. 6. (E.U.) recluta de marina (en entrenamiento inicial). 7. **b. and saddle,** (mil.) botasilla; **the b. is on the other leg,** es justamente el otro que tiene la responsabilidad; **like old boots,** (fam.) estupendamente; **to be in the boots of,** estar en el pellejo de; **to die in one's boots,** morir con las botas puestas; **to get the b.,** ser despedido del empleo; **to lick someone's boots,** lamer los zapatos a; **to wipe one's boots on (someone),** tratar con la punta del pie a, maltratar a (alguien); **you can bet your boots,** puedes apostar cualquier cosa, puedes estar absolutamente seguro. *—v.t.* 1. calzar. 2. dar puntapiés a. 3. (esp. con *out*) sacar a puntapiés; despedir, echar fuera (de empleo, etc.). 4. **to b.,** además, para colmos, por añadidura.

bootblack ['butˌblæk] *s.* limpiabotas, lustrabotas.

boot camp, (mil.) campamento de entrenamiento de reclutas de la infantería de marina y la marina de guerra.

boot disk, (comput.) disco de arranque.

booted ['butəd] *a.* calzado con botas.

bootee, bootie [-i] *s.* botita de lana para bebés.

Boötes [boʊ'oʊtiz] *s.* (astr.) Boyero, constelación del hemisferio norte.

booth [buθ, B buð] *s.* 1. casilla, garita, barraca. 2. cabina (telefónica, de votación). 3. puesto, quiosco (en feria, mercado, etc.).

boot hook, tirabotas.

bootjack ['butˌdʒæk] *s.* sacabotas.

bootlace [-ˌleɪs] *s.* (G.B.) cordón del zapato.

bootleg [-ˌlɛg] *s.* 1. caña (de una bota). 2. (E.U.) licor falsificado o de contrabando. *—v.t., v.i.* (*pret., p.p.* BOOTLEGGED; *p.pr.* BOOTLEGGING) manufacturar, transportar o vender (licores) ilegalmente; producir, distribuir o vender (algo) ilícitamente o sin permiso; contrabandear (productos extranjeros). *—a.* ilícito; de contrabando.

bootlegger [-ˌlɛgər, B -ə] *s.* contrabandista de licores.

bootless [-ləs] *a.* inútil, sin provecho, infructuoso.

bootlick [-ˌlɪk] *v.t., v.i.* (E.U.) adular, lisonjear, ser zalamero; comportarse de manera servil.

bootlicker [-ər, B -ə] *s.* quitamotas, lamesuelas, adulón; persona servil.

boots [buts] *s.* (G.B.) sirviente, esp. limpiabotas de hotel.

bootstrap ['butˌstræp] *s.* 1. oreja o tirante de bota para ayudar a calzarla. 2. **by one's (own) bootstraps,** por esfuerzo propio, sin ayuda ajena; **a boostrap operation,** realizado por esfuerzo propio, sin ayuda de otros.

boot tree, horma de zapato o de bota.

booty ['butɪ] *s.* 1. botín, presa, despojo. 2. ganancia, ventaja, recompensa, premio.

booze [buz] *s.* (jer.) licor, alcohol; borrachera. *—v.i., v.t.* (jer.) beber mucho alcohol.

boozed [buzd] *a.* achispado, borracho.

boozer ['buzər, B -ə] *s.* borrachín, bebedor.

bop [bɑp, B bɔp] *v.t.* (*pret., p.p.* BOPPED; *p.pr.,* BOPPING) (fam.) golpear, pegar, asestar un golpe a. *—s.* golpe.

bop, *s. abrev. de* **bebop.**

bo-peep [boʊ'pip] *s.* juego que consiste en esconderse y aparecer luego súbitamente frente a un niño; **to play b.,** evadirse, emplear evasivas (políticos, argumentistas, etc.); no dar la cara.

bora ['bɔrə] *s.* viento del norte frío y fuerte que azota el mar Adriático.

boracic [bə'ræsɪk] *a.* (quím.) bórico.

boracic acid, ácido bórico.

boracite ['bɔrəˌsaɪt] *s.* (min.) boracita.

borage ['bɔrɪdʒ] *s.* (bot.) borraja.

boraginaceous [bəˌrædʒə'neɪʃəs] *a.* (bot.) borragináceo, borragíneo.

borane ['bɔrˌɑn, B -ˌɔn] *s.* (quím.) borano.

borate ['bɔrˌeɪt] *s.* (quím.) borato.

borated [-əd] *a.* (quím.) boratado.

borax ['bɔrˌæks, -əks, B -æks] *s.* (quím.) bórax.

borazon ['bɔrəˌzɑn, B -ˌzɔn] *s.* (quím.) borazón.

Bordeaux [bɔr'doʊ, B bɔ'-] *s.* 1. Burdeos, región de Francia. 2. burdeos (vino producido en la región de este nombre).

bordello [bɔr'dɛloʊ, B bɔ'-] *s.* burdel.

border ['bɔrdər, B 'bɔdə] *s.* 1. orilla, borde, margen. 2. frontera, límite, confín. 3. orla, guarnición, ribete, franja, dobladillo. 4. borde angosto plantado de flores (en un jardín). 5. **the B.,** (E.U.) frontera entre E.U. y México; (G.B.) frontera (o región fronteriza) entre Ingl. y Esco. *—v.t.* 1. lindar; confinar, limitar. 2. rodear, bordear. 3. orlar, ribetear, guarnecer. *—v.i.* **b. on,** lindar con; (fig.) rayar en, lindar en, ej., *his argument borders on the ridiculous,* su argumento raya en lo ridículo, *b. on madness,* lindar en la locura.

borderland [-ˌlænd] *s.* 1. comarca o zona fronteriza. 2. (fig.) estado transitorio, condición intermedia (ej., entre la vigilia y el sueño).

border line, 1. límite, línea de demarcación, frontera. 2. línea indefinida entre dos cualidades o condiciones.

borderline [-ˌlaɪn] *a.* 1. limítrofe. 2. incierto, dudoso, indeterminado; en el límite.

borderline case, 1. caso entre lo normal y lo anormal. 2. (G.B.) tipo medio loco.

border patrol, patrulla de fronteras.

bordure ['bɔrdʒər, B 'bɔdjʊə] *s.* (her.) bordura.

bore [bɔr, B bɔ] *v.t.* 1. taladrar, barrenar, horadar, perforar. 2. (fam.) cansar, aburrir, fastidiar, ej., *the book bored me,* el libro me aburrió. 3. **b. one's way (through),** avanzar gradualmente (por), abrirse paso (entre), ej., *he bored his way through the crowd,* se abrió paso entre la multitud; **to be (o get) bored stiff,** aburrirse como una ostra. *—v.i.* abrirse paso, avanzar. *—s.* 1. taladro, barreno. 2. diámetro interior (de un tubo, etc.). 3. ánima, alma (del cañón de un fusil, pistola, etc.); calibre (de un arma de fuego). 4. subida de la marea, marea poderosa, oleada (en estuarios). 5. (fam.) majadero, pelmazo, latoso, pesado. 6. fastidio, lata.

bore [bɔr, B bɔ] *pret. de* **bear.**

boreal ['bɔrɪəl] *a.* boreal, septentrional.

Boreas [-ɪəs, B -ɪæs] *s.* 1. bóreas (viento norte). 2. (mitol.) Bóreas, dios del viento norte.

boredom ['bɔrdəm, B 'bɔd-] *s.* hastío, aburrimiento, tedio.

borer ['bɔrər, B -ə] *s.* 1. barrena, taladro, broca, trépano. 2. perforador, taladrador. 3. (ant.) barrenillo, taladrilla, gorgojo.

boresome [-səm, B 'bɔsəm] *a.* aburridor, cansador, tedioso.

boric ['bɔrɪk] *a.* (quím.) bórico.

boric acid, (quím.) ácido bórico.

boride [-aɪd] *s.* (quím.) boruro.

boring ['bɔrɪŋ] *s.* 1. horadación, perforación; sondeo. 2. (*pl.*) partículas que se desprenden al taladrar o barrenar. *—a.* fastidioso, aburrido, latoso.

boring and turning machine, (mec.) máquina torno-barreno.

born [bɔrn, B bɔn] *a.* 1. nacido. 2. (*ú. esp. en palabras compuestas*) de nacimiento, ej., *Spanish-b.,* español de nacimiento. 3. nato, innato. 4. **a b. fool,** un tonto de capirote; **a b. liar,** un mentiroso nato; **born-again,** ferviente partidario de; **born-again Christian,** cristiano convertido a una secta evangélica; **b. under a lucky star,** nacido con buena estrella; **b. with a silver spoon in (his, her) mouth,** destinado (a) a la riqueza desde su nacimiento; **first-b.,** primogénito; **in all my b. days,** en toda mi vida; **to be b.,** nacer.

borne [bɔrn, B bɔn] *p.p.* de **bear.**

borneol ['bɔrnɪˌɔl, B 'bɔnɪ-] *s.* (quím.) borneol, alcanfor de Borneo.

bornite [-ˌnaɪt] *s.* (min.) bornita.

boron ['bɔrˌɑn, B 'bɔrˌɔn] *s.* (quím.) boro.

boron carbide, (quím.) carburo de boro.

boron trioxide, (quím.) anhídrido bórico.

borosilicate [ˌbɔroʊ'sɪlɪkət, -ˌkeɪt] *s.* (quím.) borosilicato.

borough ['bɜroʊ, 'bʌr-, B 'bʌrə] *s.* 1. villa; municipio; ayuntamiento. 2. (E.U.) distrito electoral de Nueva York. 3. (G.B.) pueblo con representación parlamentaria; pueblo con corporación y privilegios conferidos por cédula real.

borrow ['bɑroʊ, B 'bɔr-] *v.t.* 1. pedir prestado, tomar prestado. 2. apropiarse de, ej., *b. an idea,* apropiarse de una idea (ajena). 3. (mat.) tomar prestado (un número mayor en la resta). 4. **b. trouble,** buscarse molestias sin razón. *—v.i.* tomar a préstamo; tomar préstamos.

borrower [-ər, B -ə] *s.* 1. prestatario. 2. sablista, gorrón.

borrowing [-ɪŋ] *s.* 1. préstamo recibido. 2. adopción (de costumbre, cultura, palabra, etc.).

borsch, borscht [bɔrʃ, bɔrʃt, B bɔʃ] *s.* (cocina) borsch, sopa rusa de remolacha y otras verduras.

borstal ['bɔrstəl, B 'bɔs-] *s.* (G.B.) establecimiento correccional para jóvenes delincuentes.

bort [bɔrt, B bɔt] *s.* diamante negro de poco valor, gen. aprovechado en usos industriales.

borzoi ['bɔrˌzɔɪ, B 'bɔˌ-] *s.* barzoi (galgo ruso).

boscage, boskage ['bɑskɪdʒ, B 'bɔs-] *s.* boscaje, soto, espesura.

bosh [bɑʃ, B bɔʃ] *s.* 1. etalaje (de altos hornos). 2. (fam.) tontería, necedad.

bosk [bɑsk, B bɔsk] **bosket** ['bɑskət, B 'bɔsk-] *s.* espesura, matorral; bosquecillo.

bosky [-ɪ] *a.* 1. arbolado, frondoso. 2. (poét.) nemoroso, ej., *b. shadows,* sombras nemorosas.

bos'n, bo's'n ['boʊsən] *vars. de* **boatswain.**

Bosnian ['bɑznɪən, B 'bɔz-] *a., s.* bosnio, bosníaco, de Bosnia.

bosom ['bʊzəm, 'buz-, B 'bʊz-] *s.* 1. seno, pecho. 2. (fig.) seno, regazo, intimidad, ej., *the b. of the earth,* las entrañas de la tierra. 3. (fig.) corazón. 4. pechera de camisa. *—a.* íntimo, querido; **b. friend,** amigo del alma. *—v.t.* 1. abrazar. 2. guardar, esconder, ocultar.

bosomed [-əmd] *a.* (*ú. en compuestos*) de pechos (voluminosos).

bosomy [-əmɪ] *a.* de pecho voluminoso; (fig.) pechugona.

Bosphorus ['bɑsfərəs, B 'bɔs-] **Bosporus** [-pər-] *s.* estrecho del Bósforo.

boss [bɔs] *s.* 1. jefe; amo; patrón, capataz. 2. (E.U.) cacique político. —*v.t.* dirigir, supervisar, mandar, dominar; **b. the show,** (jer.) ser el jefe. —*a.* principal, maestro.

boss [bɑs, bɔs, B bɔs] *s.* 1. protuberancia. 2. clave o tachón de adorno (como en el centro de un escudo), bollón, bollo de relieve. 3. (arq.) pinjante. 4. (mec.) lomo, parte mayor del eje o árbol. —*v.t.* decorar, tachonar.

boss-eyed ['bɑs,aɪd, 'bɔs-, B 'bɔs-] *a.* (jer.) bizco, bisojo, ojituerto.

bossiness [-ɪnəs] *s.* carácter mandón, naturaleza autoritaria.

bossism [-,ɪzəm] *s.* (pol.) autoritarismo, caciquismo.

bossy [-ɪ] *a.* 1. mandón, dominante. 2. decorado de relieve; tachonado.

boston ['bɔstən] *s.* 1. **B.,** ciudad de E.U. 2. boston, juego de cartas.

Boston bag, maletín, cartera, valija para documentos, libros, etc., cerrada por dos agarraderas.

Boston cream pie, torta rellena con crema de huevo y vainilla.

Boston ivy, hiedra trepadora.

Boston terrier, perro pequeño de hocico chato.

bosun, bo'sun ['boʊsən] *vars. de* **boatswain.**

bot [bɑt, B bɔt] *s.* rezno, larva de moscardón; **the botts,** enfermedad del caballo causada por reznos.

botanical [bə'tænɪkəl] *a.* botánico.

botanical garden, *s.* jardín botánico.

botanist ['bɑtənəst, B 'bɔt-] *s.* botanista, botánico.

botanize [-,aɪz] *v.i.* herborizar. —*v.t.* explorar con fines botánicos.

botany ['bɑtənɪ, B 'bɔt-] *s.* 1. botánica. 2. flora, vida vegetal (de una región).

botch [bɑtʃ, B bɔtʃ] *s.* 1. chambonada, chapucería. 2. baturrillo, batiborrillo, mescolanza. 3. llaga inflamada. —*v.t.* 1. remendar toscamente; frangollar, chapucear. 2. (con *it*) cometer una torpeza, meter la pata.

botcher ['bɑtʃər, B 'bɔtʃə] *s.* torpe, chapucero, chambón, zarramplín.

botchy [-ɪ] *a.* chapucero, defectuoso.

botfly ['bɑt,flaɪ, B 'bɔt-] *s.* (ento.) moscardón, estro.

both [boʊθ] *a.* ambos, los dos, entreambos; **to have it b. ways,** sacar provecho de uno u otro modo, salir airoso de todos modos; argüir en forma contradictoria. —*pron.* ambos, los dos, uno y otro; **b. of them,** ellos dos, los dos; **b. of us,** nosotros dos. —*conj.* **b. . . . and,** tanto . . . como; . . . así como; . . . y . . . a la vez, ej., *b. good and cheap,* bueno y barato a la vez, *b. North and South,* tanto el norte como el sur.

bother ['bɑðər, B 'bɔðə] *v.t.* 1. incomodar, molestar. 2. preocupar, inquietar. —*v.i.* molestarse, preocuparse; **b. about, b. with,** preocuparse de; hacer caso de, prestar atención a, ocuparse de. —*s.* molestia, incomodidad, inconveniente, disturbio; perturbación, preocupación.

bothersome [-səm] *a.* molesto, fastidioso, incómodo.

botonée, botonnée [,bɑtən'eɪ, B 'bɔtə,ner] *a.* (her.) recruzada (cruz).

Bo tree ['boʊ-] árbol sagrado del Budismo.

botryoidal [,bɑtrɪ'ɔɪdəl, B ,bɔ-] **botryoid** ['bɑtrɪ,ɔɪd, B 'bɔ-] *a.* (min.) botricido, arracimado.

bottle ['bɑtəl, B 'bɔt-] *s.* botella, frasco; **brought up on the b.,** criado con biberón; **over a b.,** (discutir, hablar, etc.) mientras se bebe; **the b.,** (fig.) la bebida, el beber, la botella; **to hit the b.,** (jer.) tomar (bebidas alcohólicas) excesiva o frecuentemente. —*v.t.* embotellar, enfrascar; **b. up,** reprimir, contener, ej., *he bottled up his anger,* contuvo su ira.

bottle cap, chapa; **game of tossing bottle caps,** chapas.

bottled [-əld] *a.* 1. envasado, embotellado. 2. (fam. G.B.) ajumado, bebido, borracho.

bottle-fed ['bɑtəl,fɛd, B 'bɔt-] *a.* amamantado con biberón.

bottle-feeding [-,fidɪŋ] *s.* lactancia artificial.

bottle gourd, (bot.) güira, calabaza vinatera, cogorda.

bottleholder [-,hoʊldər, B -də] *s.* 1. estante de botellas. 2. ayudante (de un boxeador).

bottleneck [-,nɛk] *s.* 1. embotellamiento (de tráfico, etc.). 2. atolladero, atascadero. 3. (fig.) atascadero, obstáculo, dificultad. —*a.* estrecho, angosto. —*v.t.* paralizar, frustrar. —*v.i.* 1. atascarse, paralizarse. 2. volver estrecho, angostarse.

bottle-nose [-,noʊz] *s.* 1. nariz hinchada (por la excesiva bebida). 2. (zool.) delfín de nariz en forma de botella.

bottle party, reunión social a la que cada invitado lleva una botella de licor.

bottler ['bɑtlər, B 'bɔtlə] *s.* embotellador.

bottle-washer ['bɑtəl,wɔʃər, -,wɑ-, B 'bɔt-,wɔʃə] *s.* (G.B.) factótum, criado de todo servicio.

bottom ['bɑtəm, B 'bɔt-] *s.* 1. fondo (de una caja, botella, etc.). 2. parte, plano o superficie inferior. 3. fondo (de un lago, mar, río, etc.). 4. (*pl.*) tierra baja, hondonada. 5. extremo, fin; punto más bajo; pie (de un muro, cerro, de la página, etc.). 6. último lugar. 7. base, fundamento. 8. asiento (de una silla). 9. trasero, nalgas. 10. (*pl.*) pantalón (esp. de pijama). 11. (mar.) carena, fondo, fondos (del buque). 12. (mar.) nave, buque. 13. **at b.,** en el fondo, en realidad, ej., *at b. he is honest,* en el fondo es honrado; **b. up,** boca abajo; **bottoms up!** ¡salud! (brindis que incita a beber de un tirón); **from the b. of one's heart,** sinceramente, profundamente; **from the b. up,** desde el principio, completamente; **to be at the b. of,** ser la causa de, ser responsable por; **to get to the b. of (a case),** llegar al fondo de (un asunto); **to send to the b.,** echar a fondo, echar a pique, hundir; **to touch b.,** (lit. y fig.) tocar fondo. —*a.* 1. último. 2. del fondo. 3. (el) más bajo, (la) más baja (precio, parte, etc.). 4. fundamental, básico. 5. **to bet one's b. dollar,** apostar hasta el último centavo. —*v.t.* 1. poner fondo a (una silla, olla, etc.). 2. basar, fundamentar (un argumento, etc.). 3. bajar al fondo de (mar, océano, etc.). 4. (fig.) llegar al fondo de (un asunto).

bottom dead center, (ing.) punto muerto inferior.

bottom drawer, (G.B.) último cajón del armario (donde las novias guardan su ajuar); **a b. d. affair,** asunto que se olvida o posterga.

bottom end, (mec.) pie de la biela.

bottoming [-ɪŋ] *s.* capa de fundación (de una carretera).

bottoming tap, macho cilíndrico.

bottomless [-ləs] *a.* insondable, sin fondo.

bottommost [-,moʊst] *a.* 1. (lo) más bajo, ínfimo; último; lo más profundo u hondo. 2. (lo) más básico.

bottom round, landrecilla, peceto, bistec de lomo.

bottomry [-rɪ] *s.* (com., mar.) préstamo o contrato a la gruesa, préstamo sobre casco y quilla. —*v.t.* pignorar, dar en prenda (un barco) en contrato a la gruesa.

botulin ['bɑtjələn, B 'bɔtjʊ-] *s.* (med.) botulina.

botulinal [,bɑtʃə'laɪnəl, B ,bɔtjʊ-] *a.* de la botulina, causado por la botulina.

botulism ['bɑtʃə,lɪzəm, B 'bɔtjʊ-] *s.* (med.) botulismo.

bouclé, boucle [bu'kleɪ] *a.* (tej.) rizado (hebra, tela, etc.).

boudoir ['bud,wɑr, B -,wɑ] *s.* tocador, camarín, saloncito íntimo de señora.

bouffant [bu'fɑnt] *a.* esponjado (peinado); abultado (vestido de falda ancha).

bouffe [buf] *a.* (mús.) bufo, cómico.

bougainvillaea, bougainvillea [,bugən'vɪljə] *s.* (bot.) buganvilla.

bough [baʊ] *s.* (bot.) rama, cepo (de un árbol).

bought [bɔt] *pret. y p.p. de* **buy.** —*a.* comprado hecho (traje, ropa).

bougie ['bu,ʒi] *s.* 1. bujía, vela de cera. 2. (med.) candelilla, sonda. 3. (med.) supositorio.

bouillabaisse [,bujə'beɪs, ,buljə-] *s.* (fr.) bullabesa, sopa muy sazonada, con varias clases de pescado.

bouillon ['bu,jɑn, 'bʊl-, B 'bu,jɔŋ] *s.* caldo, consomé.

bouillon cube, cubito de caldo concentrado.

boulder ['boʊldər, B -də] *s.* pedrón rodado; piedra grande.

bouldery [-dərɪ] *a.* pedregoso.

boule, *var. de* **buhl.**

boulevard ['bʊlə,vɑrd, B 'bulvɑ, -lɪvɑd] *s.* avenida, rambla, paseo, bulevar.

boulevardier [,bul,vɑrd'jeɪ, bʊlə,vɑr'dɪr, B -vɑ'dɪə] *s.* frecuentador de los bulevares; p. ext. hombre de mundo, hombre sociable y elegante.

boulter ['boʊltər, B -tə] *s.* palangre (cordel del cual penden ramales con anzuelos).

bounce [baʊns] *v.i.* 1. rebotar. 2. brincar, dar saltos. 3. irrumpir, ej., *b. into a room,* irrumpir en un cuarto. 4. (pr. G.B.) jactarse, alardear, fanfarronear. 5. ser devuelto o rechazado (cheque sin fondos). 6. **b. back,** (fig.) recuperar la fuerza, reaccionar; **b. back on,** (fig.) repercutir adversamente en. —*v.t.* 1. hacer rebotar, ej., *b. a ball,* hacer rebotar una pelota. 2. (fam. E.U.) echar, arrojar; despedir, poner de patitas en la calle. —*s.* 1. salto, brinco. 2. rebote. 3. vigor, brío. 4. jactancia, fanfarronada. 5. (fam. E.U.) despedida violenta.

bouncer ['baʊnsər, B -sə] *s.* 1. apagabroncas (que echa a la calle los ebrios o alborotadores de un bar). 2. ejemplar gigante. 3. mentira grande. 4. (G.B.) fanfarrón, valentón; mentiroso.

bouncing [-sɪŋ] *a. rollizo, robusto, fuerte.*

bouncing-pin [-,pɪn] *s.* (mec.) aguja indicadora.

bouncy [-sɪ] *a.* 1. boyante, campante, alegre, exuberante. 2. elástico. 3. accidentado, desigual (camino).

bound [baʊnd] *a.* (con *for*) destinado (a), dirigido (a), con rumbo (a), con destino (a); **where are you b. for?** ¿a dónde se dirige usted? ¿para dónde va usted?

bound, *s.* 1. (*ú. gen. en pl.*) límite, confín, lindero, término, frontera. 2. (*pl.*) coto, dominio, territorio o región (dentro de ciertos límites). 3. **beyond the bounds of reason,** más allá de los límites de la razón; **out of bounds,** (dep.) fuera de la cancha; sin límite, descontrolado; **to put bounds to,** restringir, controlar; **within bounds,** a raya, dentro de los límites. —*v.t.* 1. deslindar, marcar los límites de. 2. confinar, bordear, rodear. 3. **to be bounded by,** limitar con (otro país), lindar con (terreno, finca, etc.).

bound, *pret. y p.p. de* **bind.** —*a.* 1. atado, ligado, amarrado; confinado, limitado. 2. destinado, inevitable, seguro, ej., **she's b. to be late,** es seguro que ella llegará tarde, *it's b. to happen,* sucederá inevitablemente o seguramente. 3. obligado (legal o moralmente). 4. encuadernado (revista o libro). 5. (fam., E.U.) resuelto, decidido, ej., *I am b. to do it,* estoy resuelto a hacerlo. 6. **b. up in,** dedicado a, absorto o enfrascado en; **b. up with,** ligado a, con los mismos intereses que. —*v.i.* saltar, brincar; rebotar. —*s.* 1. salto, brinco. 2. bote, rebote. 3. **by leaps and bounds,** con gran rapidez, a saltos gigantes.

boundary ['baʊndrɪ, -dərɪ] *s.* término, límite, linde, lindero, frontera, confín.

boundary stone, mojón, hito.

bounded ['baʊndəd] *a.* limitado, circunscrito.

bounden [-dən] *a.* (ant.) obligado (por lealtad, favor, etc.).

bounder [-dər, B -də] *s.* (pr. G.B., fam.) persona vulgar.

bound forms, (gram.) formas inseparables (afijos y radicales).

boundless [-dləs] *a.* ilimitado, sin límites ni fronteras; infinito, vasto.

bounteous ['baʊntɪəs] *a.* 1. generoso, liberal, dadivoso. 2. amplio, abundante.

bountied ['baʊntid] *a.* 1. beneficiado, favorecido (con una donación, dádiva, etc.). 2. remunerado o remunerable con una concesión o subsidio.

bountiful [-ɪfəl] *a.* 1. dadivoso, generoso. 2. abundante, copioso.

bounty ['baʊntɪ] *s.* 1. liberalidad, munificencia, generosidad. 2. merced, gracia; dádiva, regalo. 3. subvención, subsidio. 4. (G.B.) premio de enganche, gratificación (que se da a soldados y marineros cuando se alistan).

bouquet [boʊ'keɪ, bu-] *s.* 1. ramo de flores, ramillete. 2. aroma, nariz (del vino, etc.).

bourbon ['bʊrbən, B 'bʊəbən] *s.* 1. **B.,** Borbón, miembro de la familia de los Borbones. 2. político de espíritu anacrónico; (esp. E.U.) miembro conservador del partido demócrata.

bourbon whisky ['bɜr-, B 'bɜbən] (E.U.) whiski de maíz o de maíz y centeno (elaborado en el condado de Bourbon, Kentucky).

bourdon [bʊrdən, B 'bʊəd-] *s.* (mús.) bordón; roncón de gaita; registro de bordón (en órgano o armonio).

Bourdon gage, (meteor.) manómetro de Bourdon.

bourg [bʊrg, B bʊəg] *s.* (hist.) burgo; villa.

bourgeois ['bʊrʒˌwɑ, B 'bʊəʒ-] *s.* (*pl.* BOURGEOIS) burgués. —*a.* 1. burgués, de la clase media. 2. aburguesado.

bourgeoisie [ˌbʊrʒˌwɑ'zi, B ˌbʊəʒ-] *s.* burguesía, clase media.

bourn, bourne [bɔrn, bʊrn, B bʊən] *s.* 1. arroyo, riachuelo. 2. (ant.) límite, confines; meta, destino; **b. of time and place,** confines del tiempo y del espacio.

bourrée [bʊ'reɪ, B 'bʊreɪ] *s.* (mús.) bourrée (baile francés del siglo XVII).

bourse [bʊrs, B bʊəs] *s.* (com.) bolsa, lonja, mercado de valores.

bouse [baʊz] *v.t., v.i.* (mar.) arriar o halar con una jarcia.

boustrophedon [ˌbustrə'fidən, B ˌbaʊ-] *s.* bustrófedon, escritura trazada de derecha a izquierda con el siguiente renglón de izquierda a derecha, imitando los surcos del arado.

bout [baʊt] *s.* 1. tanda, turno (de trabajo o ejercicio). 2. ataque (de enfermedad). 3. encuentro; asalto (de esgrima o boxeo). 4. **drinking b.,** juerga.

boutique [bʊ'tik] *s.* tienda pequeña o departamento en una tienda mayor, donde se venden artículos de moda, gen. caros.

boutonniere [ˌbutən'ɪr, -'ɛr, B -'jɛə] *s.* flor (que se lleva) en el ojal de la solapa.

bouzouki [bu'zukɪ] *s.* busuqui, instrumento griego parecido a la mandolina, que acompaña canciones y bailes folklóricos.

bovid ['boʊvɪd] *a., s.* (zool.) bóvido.

Bovidae [-i] *s. pl.* (zool.) bóvidos.

bovine ['boʊˌvaɪn] *a.* 1. bovino, vacuno, bueyuno, boyuno. 2. (fig.) bovino (carácter); paciente, calmoso, sufrido, lerdo. —*s.* res, animal bovino.

bow [baʊ] *s.* venia, reverencia, saludo; **to make a b.,** hacer una reverencia; **to make one's b.,** (fig.) presentarse o despedirse (haciendo una venia al público, audiencia, etc.); abandonar la escena, irse. —*v.i.* 1. (con *to*) ceder (a), someterse (a), conformarse (con). 2. (con *to* o *before*) inclinarse, hacer reverencia (delante de). 3. (con *to*) saludar con una venia, inclinar la cabeza (hacia). 4. **bowing acquaintance,** relación superficial (entre personas); conocimiento superficial; **b. out,** retirarse, separarse, salir (de un negocio, asunto, etc.). —*v.t.* 1. inclinar (la cabeza), doblar (la rodilla), encorvar (el cuerpo). 2. someter (la voluntad de otro). 3. indicar (conformidad) con una venia. 4. **b. down,** doblegar, agobiar, ej., *bowed down with years of work,* doblegado por años de trabajo, *bowed down by cares,* agobiado por las penas.

bow [boʊ] *s.* 1. arco, curva. 2. arco iris. 3. arco (arma). 4. (mús.) arco (de violín u otro instrumento de cuerdas). 5. arquero. 6. lazo, moño. 7. **to have several** (o **many**) **strings to one's b.,** tener más de un recurso. —*v.t.* curvar, doblar (en forma de arco). —*v.i.* curvarse, doblarse.

bow [baʊ] *s.* 1. proa (de barco o avión). 2. boga de proa, proel. 3. **on the b.,** (mar.) por la amura.

Bow bells ['boʊˌbɛlz] (G.B.) las campanas de la iglesia de *St. Mary-le-Bow* (en Londres); **within the sound of B. bells,** en el mismo corazón de Londres.

bow compass ['boʊ-] compás de bomba, compás pequeño de resorte, bigotera.

bowdlerize ['boʊdləˌraɪz, B 'baʊd-] *v.t.* expurgar, mutilar o recortar (un escrito).

bowel ['baʊəl] *s.* intestino, tripas; (*pl.*) entrañas; (fig.) entrañas (lo más oculto o profundo), ej., *the bowels of the earth,* las entrañas de la tierra, en lo más profundo. —*v.t.* destripar; desentrañar.

bowel movement, evacuación, deposición intestinal.

bower ['baʊər, B -ə] *s.* 1. emparrado, cenador. 2. (poét.) morada campestre; tocador, saloncito de señora. 3. (mar.) ancla de proa, ancla de leva. 4. violinista, músico que toca un instrumento de arco. —*v.t.* emparrar, enramar; encerrar.

bowerbird [-ˌbɜrd, B -ˌbɜd] *s.* (orn.) (variedad australiana del) ave del Paraíso.

bowery ['baʊərɪ] *a.* frondoso, emparrado. —*s.* 1. (hist.) plantación o hacienda (de los colonos holandeses en E.U.). 2. **B.,** una calle en Nueva York frecuentada por vagabundos.

bowfin ['boʊˌfɪn] *s.* (ict.) amia, lamia (de los Grandes Lagos y del Misisipí).

bowfront [-ˌfrʌnt] *a.* (arq.) de frente convexo (armario, cómoda, etc.); con ventana arqueada (casa, edificio).

bowie knife ['buɪˌnaɪf, B 'boʊɪ-] cuchillo de caza (de hoja larga y fuerte).

bowing ['baʊɪŋ] *s.* reverencia; deferencia; **with much b. and scraping,** con mucha ceremonia y adulación.

bowing ['boʊɪŋ] *s.* (mús.) técnica del arco (de un instrumento de cuerdas).

bowknot ['boʊˌnɑt, B -ˌnɔt] *s.* lazo corredizo.

bowl [boʊl] *s.* 1. tazón, escudilla, cuenco; bol, ponchera. 2. palangana, jofaina. 3. tabaquera (de la pipa); paleta (de la cuchara); taza (del inodoro). 4. cuenco, concavidad. 5. (geog.) cuenca. 6. construcción en forma cóncava, esp. estadio (de deportes).

bowl [boʊl] *s.* 1. bolo, bocha, rulo, bola (en el juego de bolos). 2. (*pl.*) bolos. 3. boleo, tiro de bola (en el juego de bolos). —*v.i.* 1. bolear, lanzar la bola; jugar a los bolos o bochas. 2. (esp. con *along*) rodar rápidamente (vehículo, etc.). —*v.t.* 1. lanzar (la bola, en el juego de bolos). 2. marcar (tantos en el juego de bolos). 3. **b. off** o **down,** tumbar, derribar; **b. out,** (criquet) poner fuera de juego (al bateador); **b. over,** (fig.) arrollar, aturdir, sorprender.

bowleg ['boʊˌlɛg] *s.* pierna arqueada, corva o estevada.

bow-legged [-ˌlɛgd, -ˌlɛgəd] *a.* patizambo, estevado.

bowler ['boʊlər, B -ə] *s.* jugador de bolos; **b. hat,** bombín, sombrero de hongo.

bowline ['boʊˌlaɪn] *s.* (mar.) bolina, as de guía; **on a b.,** de bolina.

bowling alley ['boʊlɪŋ-] *s.* bolera, boliche.

bowling green, *s.* bolera en el césped.

bowls [boʊlz] *s.* bolos, bochas.

bowl-type tilting mixer ['boʊlˌtaɪp-] (maq.) mezcladora basculante del tipo de tazón, hormigonera.

bowman ['boʊmən] *s.* arquero, flechero.

bowman ['baʊ-] *s.* proel, boga de proa, remero.

bow pen ['boʊ-] (dib.) compás con tiralíneas.

bow pencil ['boʊ-] (dib.) compás con lápiz.

bow saw ['boʊ-] (mec.) sierra de arco, segueta.

bowshot ['boʊˌʃɑt, B -ˌʃɔt] *s.* 1. tiro de flecha. 2. alcance de un tiro lanzado por arco.

bowsprit ['baʊˌsprɪt, B 'boʊ-] *s.* (mar.) bauprés.

bowstring ['boʊˌstrɪŋ] *s.* cuerda de arco. —*v.t.* estrangular con una cuerda.

bowstring beam, (const.) viga de cuerda y arco.

bow tie ['boʊ-] corbatín, corbata de lazo, pajarita.

bow window ['boʊ-] ventana saliente arqueada; mirador.

bowwow ['baʊ'waʊ] *s.* (fam.) 1. guau-guau, perro, perrito. 2. alboroto, protesta, clamor. —*v.t.* ladrar.

bowwow theory, *s.* (filol.) teoría de la onomatopeya.

bowyer ['boʊjər, B -jə] *s.* fabricante de arcos (arma); arquero.

box [bɑks, B bɔks] *s.* 1. caja, cajón; estuche; cofre, arca. 2. casilla, compartimiento; apartado, casilla (de correo). 3. caja, arca (de dinero). 4. cama (de una carreta o carro). 5. palco (de teatro). 6. casilla de establo (para caballos). 7. pescante (en que se sienta el conductor de coches). 8. caseta, garita. 9. bofetón, bofetada, manotón, puñetazo. 10. (bot.) boj (arbusto que se usa para setos y bordes en los jardines). 11. (mec.) caja de chumacera. 12. (impr.) cajetín, compartimiento (de la caja tipográfica); recuadro, cuadro, encuadrado (en periódicos). 13 (béisbol) puesto del lanzador o del bateador. 14. (dep.) boxeo. 15. **in the wrong b.,** en posición embarazosa, en difícil situación; **to put in the b.,** guardar, ahorrar (dinero). —*v.t.* 1. encajonar, colocar o meter en cajón (es). 2. (mar.) virar (el barco) en redondo. 3. dar de manotadas, dar un puñetazo. 4. (impr.) recuadrar, encerrar. 5. **b. (someone's) ears,** dar una manotada a (alguien); **b. in** (o **up**), encajonar; **b. the compass,** (mar.) cuartear la aguja, recitar en orden correcto los rumbos de la rosa náutica; (fig.) dar vuelta completa, volver a su posición original (en discusión,

política, etc.). —*v.i.* boxear; **b. off,** (mar.) caer a sotavento (buque).
box and pin, (mec.) macho y hembra.
box camera, (foto.) cámara rígida, cámara de cajón.
boxcar ['bɑksˌkɑr, B 'bɔksˌkɑ] *s.* (f. c.) furgón, vagón cubierto de carga, vagón cerrado.
boxer [-ər, B -ə] *s.* 1. boxeador, púgil. 2. (zool.) especie de perro oriundo de Alemania. 3. embalador. 4. **B.,** (hist.) miembro de una antigua sociedad patriótica de la China llamada los Bóxers.
boxfish [-ˌfɪʃ] *s.* (ict.) cofre.
box girder, (const.) viga tubular, viga de alma doble o de caja.
boxhaul [-ˌhɔl] *v.t.* (mar.) virar en redondo, girar, abroquelar.
boxing [-ɪŋ] *s.* 1. boxeo, pugilato. 2. embalaje, empaque, encajonamiento. 3. material para embalar. 4. (carp.) marco de puerta o de ventana. 5. (mar.) escarpe.
Boxing Day, (G.B.) primer día laborable después de Navidad (en el que se dan propinas a los carteros, sirvientes, etc.).
boxing gloves, guantes de boxeo (de cuero y acolchados).
box kite, cometa celular, cometa en forma de caja.
boxlike [-ˌlaɪk] *a.* semejante a una caja.
box lunch, almuerzo preparado que se lleva (a la escuela, a un picnic) en una caja o envase.
box nut, (mec.) tuerca ciega.
box office, 1. taquilla, boletería (Am.) (en los teatros y cines). 2. atracción taquillera o de taquilla, ej., *he's very good b. o.,* él es una gran atracción taquillera.
box-office success, éxito de taquilla, éxito taquillero.
box saw, sierra de arco, sierra de contornear.
box score, (dep.) cuadro sumario de resultados (de un partido, en un diario).
box seat, (teat.) asiento de palco; (fig.) posición favorable.
box spring, colchón de muelles o resortes.
boxthorn [-ˌθɔrn, B -ˌθɔn] *s.* (bot.) arto, cambronera.
box wagon, (G.B.) furgón, vagón de carga, vagón cerrado.
boxwood [-ˌwʊd] *s.* 1. (bot.) boj. 2. madera de boj.
box wrench, llave de cubo, llave de casquillo estriado.
boxy [-ɪ] *a.* 1. semejante a una caja, como una caja. 2. angular, de corte angular o cuadrado.
boy [bɔɪ] *s.* 1. muchacho, chico, niño. 2. hijo, ej., *my b. goes to school next year,* mi hijo irá al colegio el año próximo. 3. (despec.) portero, ascensorista, mensajero, sirviente (esp. tratándose de personas de color). 4. (fam.) (esp. en vocativo) hombre; **old b.,** viejo.
boycott ['bɔɪˌkɑt, B -kət] *s.* boicoteo, boicot. —*v.t.* boicotear.
boyfriend [-ˌfrɛnd] *s.* novio, galán, enamorado; amigo.
boyhood [-ˌhʊd] *s.* niñez, pubertad (del varón).
boyish [-ɪʃ] *a.* amuchachado, juvenil (ref. a varones).
boy scout, niño explorador.
boysenberry ['bɔɪzənˌbɛrɪ, 'bɔɪs-] *s.* (hort., E.U.) especie de mora grande y oscura.
bozo ['boʊzoʊ] *s.* (jer.) sujeto, tipo, tío.
Br. *abrev. de* **British,** británico.
Br *símb. de* **bromine,** bromo (Br).
B.R. *abrev. de* **British Railways,** Ferrocarriles Británicos.
bra [brɑ] *abrev. de* **brassiere,** sostén (prenda interior femenina).
Brabant [brə'bænt] *s.* 1. Brabante. 2. b., (tej.) bramante.
brabble ['bræbəl] *v.t.* (dial.) reñir, disputar; armar camorra. —*s.* discusión, riña, disputa.
brace [breɪs] *s.* 1. abrazadera, grapa, laña. 2. riostra, tirante, tensor. 3. (*pl.* G.B.) tirantes (de pantalón). 4. (med.) braguero. 5. (mús.) corchete. 6. (mar.) braza, cabo para fijar las vergas. 7. (carp.) berbiquí, taladro. 8. (const.) puntal, codal, tornapunta. 9. (tip.) llave, corchete. 10. par, ej., *a b. of dogs,* un par de perros. —*v.t.* 1. arriostrar, acodalar, apuntalar. 2. ligar, asegurar, reforzar. 3. vigorizar, refrescar; animar, fortalecer, preparar (para recibir mala noticia, golpe, etc.). 4. (mar.) bracear (vergas). 5. **b. aback,** (mar.) bracear en facha; **b. about,** (mar.) cambiar (vela); **b. oneself,** cobrar ánimo, prepararse; **b. round,** (mar.) bracear (vergas) en cruz; **b. up,** fortalecer, animar, vigorizar; (mar.) poner en viento (vela). —*v.i.* (ú. con *up*) tomar o cobrar ánimo, alentarse, fortalecerse.
brace and bit, (carp.) berbiquí y barrena.
bracelet ['breɪslət] *s.* 1. brazalete, pulsera, ajorca. 2. (*pl.*) (irón.) esposas.
bracer ['breɪsər, ʙ-sə] *s.* 1. bebida estimulante; tónico fortificante. 2. brazal (del esgrimidor o del arquero).
bracero [brə'sɛroʊ, ʙ-'sɛər-] *s.* peón mexicano que emigra a los E.U. para trabajar en las cosechas.
brachial ['brækɪəl, B 'breɪkɪ-] *a.* braquial.
brachiate [-ˌeɪt] *a.* (bot.) braquiado.
brachiopod ['brækɪəˌpɑd, B -ˌpɔd] *s.* (zool.) braquiópodo.
Brachiopoda [ˌbrækɪ'ɑpədə, B -'ɔp-] *s. pl.* (zool.) braquiópodos.
brachycephalic [-sɪ'fælɪk, B -kɛ'fæl-] *a.* (antrop.) braquicefálico, braquicéfalo.
brachycranial [-'kreɪnɪəl] **brachycranic** [-nɪk] *a.* (antrop.) braquicranio.
brachydactylous [-'dæktələs] *a.* (zool.) braquidactilo.
brachydactyly [-lɪ] *s.* (zool.) braquidactilia.
brachypterous [bræ'kɪptərəs] *a.* (ento.) braquióptero.
brachyura [ˌbrækɪ'jʊrə] *s. pl.* (zool.) braquiuros.
brachyuran [-rən] *s.* (zool.) braquiuro.
bracing ['breɪsɪŋ] *a.* 1. fortificante, tónico, tonificante, vigorizante. 2. arriostramiento, riostras. 3. ademado, entibación, apuntalamiento, acodalamiento.
bracken ['brækən] *s.* 1. (bot.) helecho. 2. helechal.
bracket ['brækət] *s.* 1. puntal, repisa, mérsula, cartela; brazo de lámpara adosado a una pared o columna. 2. (*pl.*) corchetes o paréntesis angulares. 3. clase, grupo, categoría. 4. (mil.) tiro de horquilla. —*v.t.* 1. poner entre paréntesis. 2. apuntalar, mensular. 3. clasificar; agrupar, juntar, poner en la misma categoría. 4. (mil.) horquillar (el blanco).
brackish ['brækɪʃ] *a.* 1. salino, salobre. 2. de sabor desagradable, nauseabundo.
bract [brækt] *s.* (bot.) bráctea.
bracteal ['bræktɪəl] *a.* (bot.) bracteal.
bracteole [-tɪˌoʊl] **bractlet** ['bræktlɪt] *s.* (bot.) bractéola.
brad [bræd] *s.* puntilla, agujuela, hita, clavito.
bradawl ['brædˌɔl] *s.* lezna, lesna, punzón (para hacer huecos para clavos, tornillos, etc.).
bradycardia [ˌbrædɪ'kɑrdɪə, B -'kɑd-] *s.* (med.) bradicardia.
bradypepsy ['brædɪˌpɛpsɪ] *s.* (med.) bradipepsia.
Bradypus ['brædɪpəs] *s.* (zool.) bradipo.
brae [breɪ] *s.* (dial., esco.) falda, cuesta, valle.
brag [bræg] *v.i.* jactarse, fanfarronear, blasonar. —*v.t.* hacer alarde de, dárselas de.
braggadocio [ˌbrægə'doʊʃɪˌoʊ, B -'doʊt-ʃɪ-] *s.* 1. fanfarrón, bravucón, jactancioso. 2. bravata, ronca, fanfarronada, jactancia.
braggart ['brægərt, B -ət, -ɑt] *s.* jactancioso, bravucón, fanfarrón.
Brahman ['brɑmən] *s.* 1. brahmán, miembro de la casta hindú a la que pertenecen los sacerdotes. 2. ['breɪmən, 'brɑm-] raza de ganado, derivada del cebú.
Brahmanic [brɑ'mænɪk] **Brahmanical** [-əl] *a.* brahmánico.
Brahmanism ['brɑmənˌɪzəm] *s.* brahmanismo.
Brahmin ['brɑmən] *s.* 1. brahmán, bracmán. 2. persona culta; (irón.) intelectual pretencioso.
Brahminical [brɑ'mɪnɪkəl] *a.* propio de la persona culta o del intelectual pretencioso.
braid [breɪd] *v.t.* 1. trenzar, entrelazar. 2. trencillar, galonear. —*s.* 1. trenza. 2. trencilla, galón, cinta.
brail [breɪl] *s.* (mar.) briol, cargadera, candaliza (para cargar las velas). —*v.t.* (mar.) cargar (las velas).
Braille [breɪl] *s.* Braille (escritura en relieve para uso de los ciegos).
Braillewriter ['breɪlˌraɪtər, B -ə] *s.* máquina para escribir en el sistema Braille.
brain [breɪn] *s.* 1. (anat.) cerebro. 2. (*pl.*) sesos. 3. (fig.) (*sing. o pl.*) cerebro, intelecto, inteligencia; juicio. 4. **to blow one's brains out,** saltarse la tapa de los sesos; **to cudgel** (o **rack**) **one's brains,** devanarse los sesos; **to have (something) on the b.,** tener metido (algo) entre ceja y ceja, estar obsesionado con (algo); **to pick someone's brains,** hurgar para averiguar las ideas de alguien; **to turn someone's brains,** quitar el juicio a alguien. —*v.t.* romper la cabeza, romper la crisma a (alguien).
braincase ['breɪnˌkeɪs] *s.* (anat.) caja del cráneo, caja craneal.
brain cell, (anat.) neurona cerebral.
brainchild [-ˌtʃaɪld] *s.* idea, invento, parto del ingenio.
brain dead, clínicamente muerto.
brain drain, fuga de cerebros, éxodo de técnicos (pérdida de profesionales o personas educadas que sufre un país cuando éstas emigran en busca de mejores oportunidades).
brain fever, (med) fiebre cerebral.
braininess [-ɪnəs] *s.* inteligencia, ingenio.
brainless [-ləs] *a.* insensato, desatinado, tonto, irracional, estúpido.
brainpan [-ˌpæn] *s.* (anat.) cráneo, sesera.
brainpower [-ˌpaʊər, B -ə] *s.* capacidad intelectual.
brainsick [-ˌsɪk] *a.* enajenado; loco.
brainstorm [-ˌstɔrm, B -ˌstɔm] *s.* frenesí, acceso de locura; (fig.) idea genial, inspiración súbita. —*v.i.* devanarse los sesos.
brainstorming ['breɪnstɔrmɪŋ] *s.* brainstorming.
brainstorming session, sesión de brainstorming.
brain trust, grupo de expertos (esp. el que aconseja a un gobierno).
brain tumor, (med.) tumor cerebral.
brainwash [-ˌwɔʃ, -ˌwɑʃ, B -ˌwɔʃ] *v.t.* (fig.) lavar el cerebro (gen. a prisioneros de guerra o a gente excesivamente crédula o dócil).
brainwashing [-ɪŋ] *s.* (fig.) lavado del cerebro; mentira que por argucia o repetición llega a creerse.

brain wave, 1. onda cerebral (flujo de corriente cerebral debido a la fluctuación rítmica de voltaje entre sus partes). 2. idea luminosa, idea genial, inspiración súbita.
brain work, trabajo u ocupación intelectual.
brainy ['breɪnɪ] *a.* (BRAINIER; BRAINIEST) (fam.) sesudo, inteligente, despierto.
braise [breɪz] *v.t.* (cocina) dorar o ablandar a fuego moderado en cazuela tapada.
brake [breɪk] *s.* 1. (bot.) (especie de) helecho. 2. maleza, zarzal, jaral, matorral.
brake [breɪk] *s.* 1. (agr.) agramadera. 2. (mec.) plegadora de palastro, dobladora de chapas, pestañadora.
brake [breɪk] *s.* freno (de ferrocarril, automóvil, carro, etc.); (fig.) freno, control. —*v.t.* frenar. —*v.i.* 1. poner o aplicar los frenos. 2. trabajar de guardafrenos.
brake band, (aut.) cinta de freno, mordaza de freno.
brake blocks, almohadillas de freno, zapatas.
brake booster, reforzador de freno, amplificador de enfrenamiento.
brake dog, (mec.) trinquete o fiador de freno.
brake drum, (aut.) tambor de freno.
brake lining, (aut.) forro, guarnición de freno.
brakeman ['breɪkmən] *s.* (f.c.) guardafrenos.
brake shoe, zapata de freno, patín de freno.
braking [-ɪŋ] *s.* frenada, frenaje.
braky [-ɪ] *a.* jaroso, matoso, espinoso.
bramble ['bræmbəl] *s.* (bot.) zarza, cambrón.
brambleberry [-ˌbɛrɪ] *s.* zarzamora.
brambling [-blɪŋ] *s.* (orn.) pinzón.
bran [bræn] *s.* salvado, afrecho, bren.
branch [bræntʃ, B brantʃ] *s.* 1. rama (de árbol, familia); rama, ramo (de una ciencia, arte, industria, técnica, etc.). 2. bifurcación, ramal (de una vía férrea, un camino, etc.). 3. brazo, tributario (de un río, delta, ría, etc.). 4. brazo (de un candelabro, cornamenta, etc.). 5. (com.) sección, división; agencia, sucursal, dependencia. 6. (elec.) derivación. 7. (S. y Centro de E.U.) riachuelo, arroyuelo. —*v.i.* 1. ramificarse, echar ramas. 2. divergir, bifurcarse, dividirse en ramas o ramales, ej., *the road branches to the right,* el camino se bifurca a la derecha. 3. **b. from,** derivarse de; **b. off,** bifurcarse; **b. out,** ramificarse; (fig.) ampliar las actividades (de uno), hacer algo en mayor escala; **b. out into,** añadir (nuevo ramo) a sus actividades.
branchia ['bræŋkɪə] *s.* (*pl.* BRANCHIAE [-kɪˌi]) (zool.) branquia, agalla (de pez, crustáceo, etc.).
branchial [-kɪəl] *a.* (zool.) branquial.
branchiate [-kɪət] *a.* (zool.) branquífero.
branchiferous [ˌbræŋ'kɪfərəs] *a.* (zool.) branquífero.
branchiopod ['bræŋkɪəˌpad, B -ˌpɔd] *s.* (zool.) branquiópodo.
branchlet ['bræntʃlət, B 'brantʃ-] *s.* ramita (gen. terminal).
branch line, 1. (f.c.) ramal. 2. (elec.) línea derivada.
branch office, sucursal.
brand [brænd] *s.* 1. tizón. 2. (fig.) tizón, estigma; ignominia. 3. hierro de marcar; hierro, marca. 4. marca de fábrica; tipo, clase, ej., *a b. of flour,* una clase de harina. 5. (poét.) espada; antorcha. —*v.t.* 1. marcar, herrar (con hierro candente). 2. marcar, poner marca de fábrica en. 3. (fig.) estigmatizar, marcar. 4. (fig.) grabar (en la memoria, el ánimo). 5. (con *as*) motejar (de), apodar.
branding ['brændɪŋ] *s.* herradero, hierra (Am.).
branding iron, calimba o carimba; hierro con que se marca a las reses.
brandish ['brændɪʃ] *v.t.* blandir, blandear, sacudir, agitar. —*s.* (esgrima) floreo, molinete.
brandling ['brændlɪŋ] *s.* (zool.) (especie de) gusano amarillento (usado como cebo en la pesca).
brand name, marca registrada (de un producto).
brand-new [bræ'nu, 'brænd-, B -'nju] *a.* flamante, enteramente nuevo.
brandy ['brændɪ] *s.* coñac, aguardiente de uva. —*v.t.* (*pret., p.p.* BRANDIED; *p.pr.* BRANDYING) mezclar o sazonar con coñac, dar sabor de coñac a; conservar en coñac.
brannigan ['brænɪgən] *s.* 1. holgorio, parranda. 2. pendencia, riña.
brant [brænt] *s.* (zool.) ganso silvestre, oca silvestre.
brash [bræʃ] *a.* 1. impetuoso, temerario. 2. desatinado, indiscreto. 3. descarado, insolente. 4. frágil, quebradizo. —*s.* desecho, montón (de escombros, etc.).
brasier, *var. de* **brazier.**
brasiletto [ˌbrasɪ'lɛtoʊ] *s.* (bot.) brasil, brasilete.
Brasilia [brə'zɪljə, -'zil-] *s.* Brasilia, capital del Brasil.
brasque [bræsk, B brask] *s.* (metal.) brasca.
brass [bræs, B bras] *s.* 1. latón, azófar. 2. cobre, utensilio de cocina. 3. ornamento de latón. 4. color bronce. 5. (fig.) descaro, desvergüenza, impertinencia. 6. (mec.) bronce, casquillo de bronce (de cojinete). 7. (jer. G.B.) plata, dinero. 8. **the b.** (o **brasses**), cobres, metales, instrumentos metálicos de viento; **the b.,** (jer., mil.) el alto mando, los espadones; **to get down to b. tacks,** entrar en materia, ir al grano.
brassard [brə'sard, B 'bræsad] **brassart** [-'sart, B -sat] *s.* 1. brazal, guardabrazo (de la armadura). 2. brazal (distintivo que se lleva al brazo).
brass band, (mús.) charanga; banda (militar); murga.
brassbound ['bræsˌbaʊnd, B 'bras-] *a.* provisto de bordes de latón.
brasses [-əz] *s. pl.* (mec.) bronces, casquillos o cojinetes de bronce.
brass hat, (jer., mil.) oficial de estado mayor; espadón.
brassie ['bræsɪ, B 'brasɪ] *s.* palo de golf con cabeza plana de latón.
brassière [brə'zɪr, B 'bræsɪə] *s.* sostén, portasenos (prenda interior femenina).
brassiness ['bræsɪnəs, B 'bras-] *s.* 1. comportamiento descarado, desfachatez. 2. aspecto de metal barato. 3. estridor.
brass knuckles, *s.* (*pl.*) manopla, nudilleras de metal.
brass-plated [-'pleɪtəd] *a.* bronceado, latonado.
brass rubbing, (arte) calco de plancha sepulcral de latón.
brass shop, latonería, hojalatería.
brassware [-ˌwɛr, B -ˌwɛə] *s.* latonería, obra u objeto de latón (cobre).
brass winds, (mús.) cobres (instrumentos metálicos de viento).
brasswork [-ˌwɜrk, B -ˌwɜk] *s.* obra(s) de latón, objetos de cobre.
brassy [-ɪ] *a.* 1. de latón, adornado con latón. 2. bronceado. 3. descarado, desvergonzado. 4. (mús.) estridente, metálico (sonido).
brat [bræt] *s.* (despec.) rapaz, mocoso, rapazuelo, malcriado.
brattice ['brætəs] *s.* 1. (min.) tabique de ventilación; ademe. 2. (fort. ant.) apuntalamiento temporal o galería construida en un trabajo avanzado. —*v.t.* tabicar; ademar.
brattle ['brætəl] (esco.) *s.* traqueteo, matraqueo. —*v.i.* traquetear, matraquear.
bravado [brə'vadoʊ] *s.* (*pl.* BRAVADOES, BRAVADOS) bravata, alarde, jactancia, baladronada.
brave [breɪv] *a.* bravo, valiente, esforzado; gallardo, garboso. —*s.* 1. valiente. 2. guerrero indio de N. A. 3. (ant.) bravata, reto, desafío; fanfarrón, bravucón. —*v.t.* 1. encarar, afrontar, arrostrar. 2. (ant.) desafiar, retar. 3. **b. it out,** encarar (sospecha, acusación, etc.) de modo desafiante.
bravery ['breɪvərɪ] *s.* 1. valentía, intrepidez, valor. 2. atavío, pompa, ostentación, boato.
bravissimo [bra'visɪˌmoʊ] *a., interj.* excelente, óptimo.
bravo ['bravˌoʊ] *interj.* ¡bravo! ¡bien hecho! —*s.* malhechor, matón.
bravura [brə'vʊrə, -'vjʊr-, B -'vʊər-] *s.* 1. (mús.) bravura. 2. arrojo, brío.
braw [brɔ] *a.* (esco.) garboso, elegantemente vestido; espléndido, hermoso.
brawl [brɔl] *v.i.* alborotar, armar camorra, disputar con ruido, trapisondear. —*s.* alboroto, disputa, camorra, riña, pendencia, altercado.
brawler ['brɔlər, B -ə] *s.* alborotador, camorrista, pendenciero.
brawn [brɔn] *s.* 1. músculo (esp. del brazo y la pierna). 2. fuerza muscular. 3. (G.B.) carne de verraco.
brawny ['brɔnɪ] *a.* musculoso, membrudo, fuerte.
braws [brɔz] *s. pl.* (esco.) ropa fina, vestido de gala.
braxy ['bræksɪ] *s.* fiebre carbuncular del ganado lanar; res lanar atacada de este mal. —*a.* atacada de dicha fiebre.
bray [breɪ] *s.* rebuzno, roznido; ruido bronco. —*v.i.* rebuznar. —*v.t.* 1. decir en voz ronca. 2. majar, triturar.
brayer ['breɪər, B -ə] *s.* (impr.) rodillo de mano (para distribuir la tinta); moleta.
braze [breɪz] *v.t.* 1. broncear, adornar con bronce o latón. 2. soldar con latón, soldar en fuerte.
brazen ['breɪzən] *a.* 1. bronceado, hecho de bronce o latón. 2. bronco. 3. descarado, desvergonzado. —*v.t.* (con *out* o *through*) afrontar descaradamente, sostener con desfachatez.
brazenfaced [-ˌfeɪst] *a.* descarado, descocado, desvergonzado.
brazenness [-nəs] *s.* descaro, desfachatez, descoco, taquería.
brazer ['breɪzər, B -ə] *s.* soldador (hombre); máquina soldadora.
brazier ['breɪʒər, B -zjə] *s.* 1. latonero, broncista, calderero. 2. brasero, rejuela.
brazil [brə'zɪl] *s.* 1. palo brasil. 2. tinte rojizo (obtenido del palo brasil).
Brazil, *s.* el Brasil.
brazilein [-ɪən] *s.* (quím.) brasileína.
Brazilian [-jən] *a., s.* brasileño.
Brazilian rosewood, (bot.) palisandro.
brazilin ['bræzəlɪn] *s.* (quím.) brasilina.
Brazil nut, nuez del Brasil, nuez de Pará, castaña del Marañón.
Brazil nut tree, (bot.) juvia, almendrón.
brazilwood [brə'zɪlˌwʊd] *s.* palo de Brasil, palo brasil, brasilete.
brazing ['breɪzɪŋ] *s.* soldadura fuerte.
brazing metal, latón de soldar, soldadura de latón.
Brazzaville ['bræzəˌvɪl, 'braˌvɪl] Brazzaville, capital de la república del Congo.
breach [britʃ] *s.* 1. rotura, ruptura, rompimiento (de relaciones, entre amigos, etc.). 2. infracción, quebrantamiento, contravención, violación (de una ley, obligación, contrato, etc.). 3. brecha,

abertura (en muro, fortificación, etc.). 4. desgarramiento, desgarrón (de la piel, en tela, etc.). 5. (mar.) rompimiento (de las olas). 6. salto de una ballena (fuera del agua). 7. **clean b.,** (mar.) desarbolo completo (por las olas); **to stand in the b.,** (lit. y fig.) llevar el peso de la batalla. —*v.t.* 1. abrir una brecha en. 2. violar, quebrantar (la ley, un contrato, etc.). —*v.i.* saltar fuera del agua (la ballena).

breach of contract, (der.) violación o incumplimiento de contrato.

breach of faith, abuso de confianza, falta de lealtad o fidelidad.

breach of promise, incumplimiento de la palabra, esp. de casamiento.

breach of the peace, (der.) perturbación del orden público.

bread [brɛd] *s.* 1. pan. 2. (relig.) pan bendito. 3. (jer.) dinero, guita. 4. **b. buttered on both sides,** prosperidad fácil; **on b. and water,** a pan y agua; **ship's b.,** (mar.) galleta dura; **to break b.,** tomar alimento; unirse en la Cena del Señor; **to break b. with,** comer con; **to cast one's b. upon the waters,** hacer el bien sin mirar a quien; **to earn one's b.,** ganarse la vida; **to know which side one's b. is buttered,** saber lo que a uno le conviene; **to take the b. out of one's mouth,** quitarle a uno el pan de la boca, dejar a uno sin sustento (por competencia o rivalidad). —*v.t.* empanar.

bread and butter, 1. pan con mantequilla. 2. (fam.) pan de cada día, subsistencia. 3. **to earn one's bread and butter,** ganarse el pan o la vida.

bread-and-butter ['brɛdən'bʌtər, B -ə] *a.* 1. práctico; prosaico, corriente, de uso general. 2. (pr. G.B.) juvenil, adolescente.

bread-and-butter letter, carta de agradecimiento por la hospitalidad recibida.

breadbasket ['brɛdˌbæskət, B -ˌbɑs-] *s.* 1. panera, cesto para el pan. 2. (fig.) granero (de un país). 3. (fam.) estómago, panza.

bread crumbs, migajas; (cocina) pan rallado.

breadfruit [-ˌfrut] *s.* 1. (bot.) árbol del pan. 2. fruto del árbol del pan.

breadline [-ˌlaɪn] *s.* (E.U.) cola de desocupados (que esperan para recibir alimentos que se distribuyen gratis).

breadstuff [-ˌstʌf] *s.* 1. cereales, granos, harina. 2. pan.

breadth [brɛdθ, brɛtθ] *s.* 1. ancho, anchura. 2. extensión, espacio, envergadura. 3. (fig.) largueza, liberalidad, tolerancia. 4. (cost.) paño, ancho de tela. 5. **to a hair's b.,** exactamente.

breadthways ['brɛdθˌweɪz, 'brɛtθ-] **breadthwise** [-ˌwaɪz] *adv.* a lo ancho.

breadwinner ['brɛdˌwɪnər, B -ə] *s.* 1. sostén de la familia. 2. medios de subsistencia.

break [breɪk] *v.t.* (*pret.* BROKE [broʊk]; *p.p.* BROKEN ['broʊkən]; *p.pr.* BREAKING) 1. romper, quebrar. 2. partir, dividir; truncar, descompletar, desaparear (un juego completo). 3. cambiar (un billete). 4. cortar, interrumpir (viaje, circuito eléctrico, etc.). 5. romper, infringir, violar, quebrantar (ley, contrato, promesa), faltar a (la palabra, juramento). 6. quebrar, batir (una marca deportiva). 7. quebrar (resistencia, voluntad, etc.). 8. domar, amansar; disciplinar. 9. agotar, abatir; arruinar. 10. invalidar (un testimonio). 11. resolver (caso, misterio, etc.), descifrar (clave, código). 12. amortiguar (golpe, caída, etc.), quebrantar, moderar (fuerza, velocidad, etc.). 13. refutar (coartada). 14. comunicar, divulgar, dar (noticia). 15. doblar el cañón de (un fusil, revólver); articular (ala de un avión). 16. degradar (soldado). 17. **b. a lance with,** batirse con, oponerse a, argüir contra; **b. a trail,** abrir una senda; **b. asunder,** dividir en dos (partes); desunir; **b. camp,** levantar el campo; **b. cover,** salir de un escondite; **b. down,** quebrar la resistencia o espíritu de; refutar (coartada); detallar, pormenorizar, analizar; **b. ground,** abrir la tierra; (fig.) comenzar una empresa; abrir camino; **b. in,** forzar (puerta, etc.); **b. jail,** escaparse de la prisión; **b. off,** romper, separar, desgajar; cortar, interrumpir, suspender (discusión, comunicación, etc.); **b. one's back,** (fig.) romperse el lomo de trabajos; **b. one's fast,** romper uno el ayuno; **b. one's health,** quebrantar la salud de uno; **b. one's neck,** desnucar(se); romperse el alma; **b. oneself of a habit,** librarse de un hábito; **b. open,** abrir por la fuerza, forzar; (mar.) descargar, sacar de la bodega; desplegar (bandera); (mar.) aflojar (el ancla, antes de levarla); **b. ranks,** (mil.) romper filas; **b. ship,** (mar.) desertar (un marinero); **b. the back of,** deslomar; quitar la fuerza a (movimiento, epidemia, etc.); **b. the bank,** hacer saltar la banca (en juego de azar); **b. the ice,** (fig.) romper el hielo; abrir camino (siendo primero en hacer algo); **b. to pieces,** despedazar, destrozar; **b. up,** dividir, desmenuzar; roturar (la tierra); disolver (una manifestación, reunión, etc.); dispersar (a manifestantes, una muchedumbre, etc.); terminar (asociación), acabar con (matrimonio; actividades ilícitas); quebrantar, apesadumbrar; **b. wind,** pear ventosear. —*v.i.* 1. romperse, quebrarse. 2. separar(se) (púgiles, compañeros de baile, etc.). 3. dispersarse (tropas, muchedumbre, nubes, etc.). 4. romper (las olas). 5. quebrar, ceder. 6. quebrantarse (salud), debilitarse, abatirse. 7. estallar (tormenta, etc.). 8. cortarse, sufrir interrupción. 9. brotar. 10. romper, apuntar, rayar (el día, el alba). 11. reventarse (absceso, etc.). 12. subir a la superficie (peces). 13. divulgarse, revelarse (noticia, escándalo, etc.). 14. mudar, cambiar (la voz; el tiempo). 15. bajar, sufrir una baja (precios, valor de acciones). 16. cambiar de línea, desviarse (pelota). 17. echarse a correr, arrancar (caballo de carrera, perro de caza). 18. plegarse (cama); doblarse (cañón del fusil, revólver). 19. **b. apart,** desunirse, separarse; **b. away,** escaparse; **b. away from,** romper con, abandonar (caudillo; tradición, costumbre, etc.); **b. down,** descomponerse, desbaratarse, estropearse; fallar; perder la resistencia o el ánimo; quedar agotado; **b. even,** no ganar ni perder, quedar iguales; **b. for,** lanzarse o dar una arrancada hacia; hacer una pausa para (almorzar, comer, tomar una cerveza, etc.); **b. forth,** brotar; salir de repente; **b. free,** desatarse, escaparse; **b. from,** desprenderse, separarse; **b. in,** entrar por fuerza en (casa, tienda, etc.); irrumpir; interrumpir; **breaking and entering,** (der.) escalo, escalamiento; **b. into,** escalar, entrar por la fuerza en (casa, tienda, etc.); romper a, echarse a, empezar a; romper en, prorrumpir en (llanto, sonrisa, etc.); irrumpir en (un cuarto, etc.); estallar en (revuelta, etc.); **b. loose,** desatarse, soltarse; (fig.) desencadenarse, desatarse (tormenta, etc.); **b. off,** dejar de hablar, interrumpirse; separarse, desprenderse; **b. out,** estallar (guerra, revolución, etc.; epidemia; risa, etc.); brotar (granos en la piel, sarampión, etc.); **b. out of,** salir de, escaparse de (cárcel, etc.); **b. through,** abrirse paso por (una multitud, etc.); **b. up,** levantarse (sesión, reunión, etc.); dispersarse, disolverse (muchedumbre); separarse (esposos, socios, etc.); **b. with,** romper con (amigo, novia, etc.; tradición, costumbres, etc.); **one's heart breaks,** se le rompe el corazón a uno. —*s.* 1. rotura, rompimiento, ruptura. 2. abertura, grieta, raja. 3. vacío, claro, hueco. 4. pausa, descanso, intervalo. 5. cambio (del tiempo; en tratamiento, actitud; del tema), cambio abrupto. 6. comienzo, principio. 7. arrancada, salida, corrida. 8. huida, fuga, escape (de la cárcel, etc.). 9. gallo, nota falsa. 10. (mús.) pasaje improvisado (en jazz). 11. (poét.) cesura. 12. (geol.) falla, hendedura. 13. (elec.) interrupción, distancia de interrupción; abertura (en circuito). 14. (com.) baja (de precio o valores). 15. (impr.) salto, blanco (en texto). 16. (dep.) desviación, cambio de dirección (de la pelota). 17. (boxeo) separación (de los púgiles). 18. (billar) corrida, serie (de carambolas). 19. (fam.) coyuntura feliz, oportunidad, suerte, chiripa. 20. **an even b.,** oportunidad igual; **bad b.,** mala suerte; desatino, gazapo; **b. of day,** alba, amanecer; **to give (someone) a b.,** dar una oportunidad (a alguien).

breakable ['breɪkəbəl] *a.* quebradizo, frágil, rompible.

breakage [-ɪdʒ] *s.* 1. fractura, rotura, rompimiento, destrozo. 2. objetos quebrados; indemnización por cosas quebradas (en tránsito).

breakaway [-əˌweɪ] *s.* ruptura, rompimiento (con un grupo o tradición).

breakax, breakaxe [-ˌæks] *s.* quebracho, quiebrahacha.

breakbone fever [-ˌboʊn-] (med.) dengue.

break dancer, balarín de break.

break dancing, break.

breakdown [-ˌdaʊn] *s.* 1. avería, falla (de máquina, mecanismo, aparato, etc.), interrupción, paralización (de servicio, organización, etc.). 2. fracaso, malogro (de empresa, negociaciones, conferencia, etc.). 3. colapso (de fuerzas, nervios, etc.), ej., *nervous b.,* colapso nervioso. 4. detalle, análisis; clasificación. 5. (quím.) descomposición, desintegración.

breakdown torque, (ing.) momento máximo de torsión.

breaker [-ər, B -ə] *s.* 1. rompedor, quebrador; infractor. 2. cachón, oleada; rompiente. 3. (elec.) interruptor automático, disyuntor. 4. (min.) quebrantador, quebradora. 5. (mar.) barrica, barril pequeño.

breaker arm, (aut.) brazo de ruptura, palanca ruptora.

breaker strip, tira de tela (en los neumáticos).

break-even point [breɪk'ivən] *s.* punto de equilibrio, punto de indiferencia, umbral de rentabilidad.

breakfast ['brɛkfəst] *s.* desayuno. —*v.i.* desayunarse.

breakfast cereals o **breakfast food,** cereales para el desayuno.

breakfront cabinet ['breɪkˌfrʌnt-] bargueño alto.

breaking [-ɪŋ] *s.* fractura, desgaje, rompimiento, interrupción.

breaking point, punto límite, extremo, colmo; (fís.) punto de ruptura.

break lathe, (maq.) torno de bancada partida.

breakneck [-ˌnɛk] *a.* 1. peligroso, arriesgado. 2. vertiginoso, pasmoso, ej., *b. road,* camino peligroso, *b. speed,* velocidad vertiginosa o pasmosa.

breakout [-ˌaʊt] *s.* (mil.) salida.

breakthrough [-ˌθru] *s.* 1. (mil.) brecha, ruptura; penetración. 2. punto de penetración. 3. (fig.) adelanto o descubrimiento (importante).

breakup [-ˌʌp] *s.* 1. separación, dispersión, disolución. 2. desintegración; colapso.

breakwater [-ˌwɔtər, -ˌwɑt-, B -ˌwɔtə] *s.* rompeolas, escollera, malecón.

bream [brim] *s.* (ict.) brema, pez de agua dulce. —*v.t.* (mar.) flamear, chamuscar, limpiar (fondo del barco).
breast [brɛst] *s.* 1. pecho, seno. 2. pecho, mama, teta (de las hembras de los mamíferos). 3. pechuga (de ave). 4. peto (de armadura). 5. (fig.) pecho, corazón. 6. reja (de un arado). 7. **to beat one's b.,** (lit. y fig.) darse golpes de pecho; **to make a clean b. of,** confesar, reconocer con franqueza; **to make a clean b. of it,** confesarlo todo. —*v.t.* 1. enfrentar(se), afrontar, arrostrar. 2. luchar contra (las olas, etc.); subir laboriosamente (pendiente, colina, etc.).
breastbone ['brɛstˌboʊn] *s.* (anat.) esternón.
breast drill, taladro o berbiquí de pecho, berbiquí de herrero.
breast fast, breast line, (mar.) amarra del través, codera, rejera de través.
breast-fed [-ˌfɛd] *a.* criado de pecho, amamantado por la madre.
breast-feed [-ˌfid] *v.t.* amamantar, dar el pecho a un infante.
breast-feeding [-ˌfidɪŋ] *s.* lactancia materna, lactancia natural.
breast harness, petral, collera del arnés de las caballerías.
breastpin [-ˌpɪn] *s.* broche, prendedor de corbata.
breastplate [-ˌpleɪt] *s.* 1. peto (de armadura). 2. (rel. judía) vestidura del sumo sacerdote. 3. (zool.) concha inferior (de las tortugas).
breastrail [-ˌreɪl] *s.* (arq.) antepecho.
breaststroke [-ˌstroʊk] *s.* (dep.) brazada de pecho (en natación).
breastsummer [-ˌsʌmər, B 'brɛsəmə] *s.* (arq., carp.) solera.
breastwork [-ˌwɜrk, B -ˌwɜk] *s.* 1. (fort.) parapeto, pretil, antepecho. 2. (mar.) propao.
breath [brɛθ] *s.* 1. aliento, respiración. 2. hálito. 3. soplo (de aire, viento, etc.). 4. exhalación, emanación, aliento. 5. (fig.) ánima, vida. 6. (fig.) respiro, pausa. 7. susurro, murmullo. 8. (fig.) sombra, vestigio (de sospecha, escándalo, etc.). 9. (fig.) instante, momento. 10. **below one's b.,** en voz baja, en un susurro; **b. of life,** la vida misma; **in a b.,** de un tirón, en un instante; **in one and the same b.,** de un resuello, al mismo tiempo; **it's (just) wasted b.,** es hablar de más; **out of b.,** sin aliento, falto de aliento; **short of b.,** corto de resuello; **to catch one's b.,** contener el aliento; recobrar el aliento; **to gasp for b.,** jadear; **to hold one's b.,** contener el aliento; **to take one's b. away,** dejar sin resuello; dejar pasmado; **to waste b.,** hablar inútilmente.
breathable ['briðəbəl] *a.* respirable.
Breathalyzer ['brɛθəlaɪzər] *s.* alcoholímetro.
breathe [brið] *v.i.* 1. respirar, alentar. 2. (fig.) respirar, vivir. 3. soplar suavemente. 4. **b. again, easily** o **freely,** respirar, resollar, cobrar aliento; (fig.) sosegarse, tranquilizarse; **b. down one's neck,** pisarle a uno los talones. —*v.t.* 1. respirar, aspirar. 2. (con *in, into*) inspirar, infundir (en). 3. expresar, decir; revelar; susurrar. 4. dar un respiro a, descansar. 5. **b. in,** aspirar; b. **life into,** (fig.) avivar, resucitar; **b. one's last breath,** dar el último suspiro, expirar; **b. out,** exhalar, espirar; **not to b. a word,** no decir palabra, no revelar nada en absoluto.
breathed [brɛθt] *a.* (fonét.) muda, aspirada.
breather ['brɪðər, B -ə] *s.* 1. respirador, respiradero. 2. (fig.) respiro, tregua, pausa, descanso corto. 3. ejercicio fuerte (que quita el aliento). 4. **to take a b.,** tomar un respiro, hacer una pausa.
breathing [-ɪŋ] *s.* 1. respiración. 2. (fig.) respiro, pausa. 3. instante, momento. 4. (gram. griega) espíritu. —*a.* (fig.) vivo, palpitante.
breathing line, (a. a.) nivel de respiración (5 pies del piso).
breathing space, b. spell, b. time, respiro, pausa de descanso; tregua.
breathless ['brɛθləs] *a.* 1. falto de aliento, sofocado, jadeante. 2. (fig.) sin resuello, sin aliento, pasmado, estupefacto. 3. exánime. 4. intenso, extremo. 5. sofocante, mal ventilado.
breath sweetener, mascadijo.
breath-taking [-ˌteɪkɪŋ] *a.* 1. soberbio, grandioso. 2. asombroso, pasmoso.
breath test *s.* prueba del alcohol, prueba del alcoholímetro. —*v.t.* someter a la prueba del alcoholímetro.
breccia ['brɛtʃɪə] *s.* (geol.) brecha.
brecciate ['brɛtʃɪˌeɪt] *v.t.* (geol.) formar (roca) en brecha.
brecciation [ˌbrɛtʃɪ'eɪʃən] *s.* (geol.) brechación.
bred [brɛd] *pret. y p.p. de* **breed.**
bree [bri] *s.* (esco.) caldo; licor.
breech [britʃ] *s.* 1. trasero, posaderas, nalgas. 2. recámara, culata (de un arma de fuego). 3. (mec.) rabera, rabo (de motón). —*v.t.* (ant.) poner calzones a (niño); poner recámara a un arma.
breechblock ['britʃˌblɑk, B -ˌblɔk] *s.* bloque de cierre (de un cañon de recámara), obturador.
breechcloth [-ˌklɔθ] **breechclout** [-ˌklaʊt] *s.* taparrabo, culero.
breeches ['brɪtʃəz] *s. pl.* calzones, pantalones; **to wear the b.,** (fig.) llevar los pantalones; **too big for one's b.,** sacar los pies del plato, echárselas de lo que no se es en realidad.
breeches buoy, (mar.) boya de salvamento (que pasa sobre un andarivel); salvavidas.
breeching ['britʃɪŋ, B 'brɪtʃ-] *s.* 1. retranca, grupera (del arnés). 2. (arm., mar.) braguero.
breechloader ['britʃ'loʊdər, B -ə] *s.* arma de retrocarga.
breech-loading [-'loʊdɪŋ] *a.* de retrocarga (arma).
breech plug, (mec.) obturador.
breed [brid] *v.t.* (*pret., p.p.* BRED [brɛd] *p.pr.* BREEDING) 1. procrear, engendrar. 2. criar (ganado, peces, etc.). 3. (fig.) engendrar, producir (violencia, odio, etc.). 4. criar, educar (a los hijos), ej., *well bred,* bien educado. —*v.i.* 1. criarse, procrearse, multiplicarse. 2. estar encinta o preñada. —*s.* 1. raza, casta. 2. progenie, prole. 3. clase, especie.
breeder ['bridər, B -ə] *s.* 1. criador (de animales). 2. semental, reproductor (animal).
breeder reactor, (fís.) reactor reproductor, generador.
breeding [-ɪŋ] *s.* 1. cría, crianza, reproducción. 2. crianza, educación, modales, urbanidad, ej., *bad b.,* mala crianza.
breeding place, (lit. y fig.) criadero.
breeze [briz] *s.* 1. brisa, aura. 2. (fam.) cosa fácil. 3. cisco de carbón de leña. 4. (ento.) tábano. —*v.i.* **b. in,** entrar o llegar alegre y vivazmente; ganar fácilmente; **b. to,** lograr (triunfo) en forma fácil; **b. through,** pasar (examen, etc.) con facilidad; leer o repasar superficialmente.
breezeway ['brizˌweɪ] *s.* pasaje abierto y techado (entre dos edificios, etc.).
breezy [-ɪ] *a.* 1. airoso (tiempo, sitio). 2. (fig.) animado, vivo, jovial.
bregma ['brɛgmə] *s.* (*pl.* BREGMATA [-mətə]) (anat.) bregma.
bremsstrahlung ['brɛmˌʃtrɑləŋ] *s.* (rad.) radiación de frenado.
brent [brɛnt] *a.* (esco.) alto, sin arrugas (díc. de la frente). —*s. var. de* **brant.**
brethren ['brɛðrən] *s.* (*pl. de* **brother**) hermanos (de una hermandad o confraternidad).
Breton ['brɛtən] *s., a.* bretón, de Bretaña.
breve [briv] *s.* 1. (mús.) breve. 2. (fon.) signo (que se pone sobre ciertas vocales para indicar su brevedad).
brevet [brə'vɛt, B 'brɛvɪt] *s.* (mil.) graduación honoraria (que otorga un grado superior al correspondiente al sueldo). —*v.t.* (*pret., p.p.* BREVETTED OBREVETED; *p.pr.* BREVETTING OBREVETING) (mil.) conferir grado honorario.
breviary ['brivjərɪ] *s.* (relig.) breviario.
brevier [brə'vɪr, B -'vɪə] *s.* (tip.) breviario, tipo de ocho puntos.
brevipennate [ˌbrɛvɪ'pɛnˌeɪt] *a.* (orn.) brevipenne, corredor.
brevity ['brɛvətɪ] *s.* brevedad, concisión.
brew [bru] *v.t.* 1. fabricar (cerveza); cocer (una tisana). 2. tramar, urdir, maquinar. —*v.i.* 1. elaborar cerveza. 2. formarse, prepararse; amenazar, ej., una tormenta. —*s.* 1. infusión, licor mezclado, bebida cocida (tisana, etc.). 2. preparación de cerveza. 3. calderada de cerveza. 4. cocción, mezcla.
brewage ['bruɪdʒ] *s.* brebaje, infusión, licor mezclado, bebida cocida.
brewer [-ər, B -ə] *s.* cervecero.
brewer's yeast [-ərz-, B -əz-] levadura de cerveza, cerevisina.
brewery [-ərɪ] *s.* cervecería, fábrica de cerveza.
briar ['braɪər, B -ə] *s.* 1. *var. de* **brier.** 2. pipa hecha de la raíz del brezo blanco.
bribe [braɪb] *s.* soborno, cohecho. —*v.t., v.i.* sobornar.
briber ['braɪbər, B -ə] *s.* sobornador, cohechador.
bribery [-ərɪ] *s.* soborno.
bric-a-brac ['brɪkəˌbræk] *s.* curiosidades, antigüedades; chucherías ornamentales.
brick [brɪk] *s.* 1. ladrillo. 2. lingote (de oro). 3. (fam.) indiscreción, ej., *to drop a b.,* cometer una indiscreción. —*a.* de ladrillo. —*v.t.* enladrillar, pavimentar; (gen. con *up*) tapar con ladrillos.
brickbat ['brɪkˌbæt] *s.* 1. pedazo de ladrillo. 2. (fig.) palabra hiriente, insulto.
brickkiln [-ˌkɪln, -ˌkɪl] *s.* horno de cocer ladrillos.
bricklayer [-ˌleɪər, B -ə] *s.* enladrillador, albañil.
bricklaying [-ˌleɪɪŋ] *s.* albañilería.
brickle [-əl] *a.* (dial.) frágil, quebradizo, deleznable.
brickmaker [-ˌmeɪkər, B -ə] *s.* ladrillero.
brickmason [-'meɪsən] *s.* ladrillador, albañil.
brick-on-edge partition ['brɪkɔn'ɛdʒ-, -ɑn-, B -ɔn-] (const.) tabique de panderete.
brick red, (de color) rojo ladrillo.
brick veneer, revestimiento de ladrillos.
brickwork [-ˌwɜrk, B -ˌwɜk] *s.* enladrillado, albañilería; enladrilladura (de suelos).
brickyard [-ˌjɑrd B -ˌjɑd] *s.* almacén o fábrica de ladrillos.
bridal ['braɪdəl] *s.* boda. —*a.* nupcial, de la boda, de la novia.
bridal bed, tálamo.
bridal gown, traje de novia.
bridal party, invitados a la boda.
bridal suite, suite nupcial.
bridal song, epitalamio.
bridal wreath, (bot.) espirea.
bride [braɪd] *s.* novia, desposada; **the b. and groom,** los novios.
bridegroom ['braɪdˌgrum, -ˌgrʊm] *s.* novio, desposado.
bridesmaid ['braɪdzˌmeɪd] *s.* dama de honor (de la novia); **always the b.,** siempre la segundona.

bridewell ['braɪdˌwɛl, -wəl] *s.* (G.B.) cárcel, prisión; casa de corrección.
bridge [brɪdʒ] *s.* 1. puente. 2. (mar.) puente (de mando). 3. (anat.) caballete (de la nariz). 4. puente o caballete (del violín); puente dental. 5. bridge (juego de naipes). 6. (billar) violín, apoyo (para el taco). 7. **don't cross your bridges before you come to them,** no adelantes los acontecimientos; **golden b.,** (fig.) puente de plata (para el enemigo que huye); **in b.,** (elec.) en paralelo; **much water has flowed under the b. since then,** mucho ha llovido desde entonces. —*v.t.* tender un puente sobre; **b. a gap,** (fig.) llenar un vacío o claro.
bridgeboard ['brɪdʒˌbɔrd, B -ˌbɔd] *s.* (carp.) gualdera, larguero de escalera.
bridgehead [-ˌhɛd] *s.* (mil.) cabeza o cabecera de puente.
bridge loan, préstamo puente, crédito puente.
Bridge of Sighs, (hist.) Puente de los Suspiros en Venecia.
bridgework [-ˌwɜrk, B -ˌwɜk] *s.* construcción de puente; puente dental.
bridging [-ɪŋ] *s.* (arq.) puntales de refuerzo.
bridle ['braɪdəl] *s.* 1. brida. 2. (fig.) freno, restricción. 3. (anat.) frenillo. 4. (mar.) poa, pata de ganso. 5. (mec.) tirante. 6. (elec., f.c.) retenida. —*v.t.* 1. embridar. 2. guiar o enfrenar (el caballo) con la brida. 3. (mar.) afrenillar (los remos).
bridle guy, (elec.) retenida diagonal o de cruceta.
bridle joint, (carp.) ensambladura a horquilla.
bridle path, sendero para caballos, camino de herradura.
bridle rod, (f.c.) tirante de agujas, barra de chucho.
bridlewise ['braɪdəlˌwaɪz] *a.* entrenado (caballo).
bridoon [brɪ'dun] *s.* (mil.) bridón, filete.
brief [brif] *a.* 1. breve, corto. 2. conciso, lacónico, sucinto. —*s.* 1. (relig.) breve, buleto. 2. (der.) alegato, escrito, memorial, informe. 3. sumario, resumen. 4. (aer. mil.) instrucciones (a la tripulación de un avión de guerra). 5. (*pl.*) calzoncillos muy cortos, trusa. 6. **in b.,** en una palabra, en resumen; **to hold a b. for,** abogar por, defender a. —*v.t.* 1. resumir, compendiar. 2. (G.B.) instruir, dar instrucciones a, contratar (un abogado). 3. dar instrucciones breves, aleccionar.
briefcase ['brifˌkeɪs] *s.* cartera, portafolio, portapapeles, maletín.
briefing [-ɪŋ] *s.* instrucciones, información (para cumplir un trabajo o misión).
briefless [-ləs] *a.* carente de procesos, carente de clientela (abogado).
briefly [-lɪ] *adv.* brevemente, concisamente, en resumen, en una palabra; por corto tiempo.
briefness [-nəs] *s.* brevedad, concisión.
brier ['braɪər, B -ə] *s.* (bot.) 1. brezo. 2. zarza, rosal silvestre.
brierroot [-ˌrut] **brierwood** [-ˌwʊd] *s.* 1. madera de las raíces del brezo. 2. pipa hecha de esta madera.
briery [-ərɪ] *a.* zarzoso, espinoso.
brig [brɪg] *s.* 1. (mar.) bergantín. 2. (jer.) calabozo, cárcel militar.
Brig. *abrev. de* **Brigadier,** general de brigada.
brigade [brɪ'geɪd] *s.* (mil.) brigada. —*v.t.* unir en brigada, formar una brigada de (regimientos, etc.).
brigadier [ˌbrɪgə'dɪr, B -'dɪə] *s.* (mil.) general de brigada.
brigand ['brɪgənd] *s.* bandolero, bandido.
brigandage [-ɪdʒ] *s.* bandolerismo, bandidaje.
brigandine ['brɪgənˌdin] *s.* brigantina, cota de malla.
brigantine [-ˌtin, B -ˌtaɪn] *s.* (mar.) bergantín, goleta.
Briggsian logarithm ['brɪgzɪən-] (mat.) logaritmo común.
bright [braɪt] *a.* 1. brillante, claro. 2. (fig.) brillante (porvenir), luminoso (idea), radiante (belleza). 3. subido (color). 4. despierto, listo, inteligente. 5. vivo, alegre. —*adv.* brillantemente; **to shine b.,** brillar.
brighten ['braɪtən] *v.t.* 1. aclarar, iluminar, abrillantar. 2. (fig.) iluminar, alegrar, avivar. —*v.i.* aclarar(se), despejarse (cielo), iluminarse (el rostro de satisfacción, alegría).
bright-eyed ['brɑɪtɑɪd] *a.* de ojos vivos.
bright idea, ocurrencia.
brightly [-lɪ] *adv.* 1. brillantemente. 2. lúcidamente, claramente. 3. vivazmente.
brightness [-nəs] *s.* 1. brillantez, esplendor. 2. inteligencia, sagacidad, viveza. 3. luminosidad, intensidad luminosa.
Bright's disease ['braɪts-] (med.) mal de Bright, albuminuria, nefritis.
brightwork ['braɪtˌwɜrk, B -ˌwɜk] *s.* partes metálicas lustrosas (como las de un automóvil o del puente de un navío).
brill [brɪl] *s.* (ict.) rodaballo.
brilliance ['brɪljəns] *s.* (lit. y fig.) brillo, brillantez.
brilliancy [-jənsɪ] *s.* brillo, brillantez.
brilliant [-jənt] *a.* 1. brillante, refulgente. 2. (fig.) brillante, talentoso, espléndido, admirable. —*s.* 1. brillante, diamante brillante. 2. (tip.) cuerpo pequeño de cuatro puntos o tres y medio.
brilliantine [-jənˌtin] *s.* 1. brillantina (para el cabello). 2. brillantina, percalina de lustre.
Brill's disease ['brɪlz-] (med.) enfermedad de Brill, forma atenuada de tifus exantemático.
brim [brɪm] *s.* 1. borde, margen, canto (de un precipicio, cráter, etc.), labio, borde, filo (de una vasija). 2. ala (de sombrero). —*v.t.* llenar hasta el borde. —*v.i.* 1. estar de bote en bote. 2. llenarse, rebosar. 3. **b. over,** rebosar, desbordarse; **to be brimming with,** estar rebosante de.
brimful ['brɪm'fʊl] *a.* lleno (hasta el borde), repleto, pletórico.
brimmer [-ər, B -ə] *s.* copa o vaso lleno.
brimming [-ɪŋ] *a.* 1. lleno hasta el borde. 2. (fig.) rebosante (de entusiasmo o alegría).
brimstone [-ˌstoʊn] *s.* (nombre antiguo del) azufre.
brindle ['brɪndəl] *a.* leonado, mosqueado, moteado, remendado. —*s.* animal mosqueado.
brindled [-dəld] *a.* leonado, mosqueado, moteado, remendado.
brindled gnu, (zool.) ñu azul (antílope de Africa del Sur).
brine [braɪn] *s.* 1. salmuera, agua salobre. 2. mar, agua del mar. 3. (quím.) solución salina. 4. (poét.) lágrimas. —*v.t.* poner en salmuera.
Brinell hardness [brɪ'nɛl-] grado de dureza de los metales (medido con la máquina de Brinell).
bring [brɪŋ] *v.t.* (*pret., p.p.* BROUGHT [brɔt]; *p.pr.* BRINGING) 1. traer, traer consigo. 2. conducir, hacer llegar; hacer venir. 3. producir, rendir. 4. inducir, persuadir. 5. resultar en, producir, acarrear. 6. **b. about,** causar, originar; (mar.) hacer virar (buque); **b. around,** reanimar, resucitar; convencer; (mar.) hacer virar (buque); **b. away,** llevarse; **b. back,** devolver; recordar, hacer memoria; **b. down,** traer hacia abajo, bajar (precios, etc.); tumbar, abatir; **b. down the house,** traer abajo el teatro (con aplausos); **b. forth,** procrear, parir, dar a luz; producir (frutos, etc.); **b. forward,** poner de manifiesto, poner sobre el tapete, presentar (un argumento); (ten.) llevar (un saldo); **b. home the bacon,** (fam.) ganar el pan; tener éxito, obtener resultados; **b. home to,** convencer (de algo), dar a entender claramente, demostrar de modo concluyente; **b. in,** introducir (una moda); presentar (una cuenta); servir (una comida); dar, pronunciar (un veredicto, fallo); hacer pasar (a una persona a la sala); producir (ganancia, etc.); **b. into,** comprometer (a una persona en un asunto); **b. into play,** poner en juego; **b. into the world,** dar a luz, traer al mundo; **b. near,** acercar, arrimar; **b. off,** rescatar; llevar (una empresa) al éxito; lograr hacer; **b. on,** conducir a; causar, traer, tener (consecuencias); **b. oneself to,** resignarse a; **b. out,** poner en escena; presentar en sociedad (muchacha); emitir, lanzar, publicar; hacer resaltar, sacar a relucir (buenas cualidades, etc.); **b. to pass,** efectuar, realizar; **b. round,** reanimar, resucitar; curar; persuadir, convertir; **b. suit,** entablar un pleito; **b. support,** prestar apoyo; **b. to,** reanimar, hacer volver en sí; parar, detener; (mar.) ponerse a la capa; **b. to bear,** aplicar (influencia, conocimiento, etc.); asestar, dirigir, apuntar; **b. to book,** llamar a capítulo, pedir cuentas a; **b. to light,** revelar, descubrir; **b. to mind,** rememorar, hacer recordar; **b. to ruin,** arruinar; **b. to task,** reprender; **b. to terms,** obligar a aceptar condiciones; **b. together,** reunir; confrontar, reconciliar; **b. up,** criar, educar; sacar a colación, hacer mención de; parar; vomitar; **b. up the rear,** (mil.) cubrir la retaguardia; cerrar la marcha; **b. upon oneself,** atraerse, buscarse (desgracia, infortunio); **brought forward,** (ten.) suma y sigue, viene (de la página anterior).
brinish ['braɪnɪʃ] *s.* salobre, salino, salado.
brink [brɪŋk] *s.* borde, margen; **on the b. of,** al borde de; a punto de.
brinkmanship ['brɪŋkmənˌʃɪp] *s.* (pol.) práctica de llevar las cosas muy cerca de la línea fronteriza de peligro o al borde de una guerra.
briny [braɪnɪ] *a.* salobre, salino; **the b.,** (jer.) el mar.
brio ['briˌoʊ] *s.* (mús.) brío, vivacidad.
brioche [brɪ'oʊʃ, -'ɔʃ, B 'briɔʃ] *s.* brioche (pan de huevo y mantequilla).
briolette [ˌbriə'lɛt] *s.* diamante cortado en forma de huevo o de pera.
briquette [brɪ'kɛt] *s.* briqueta, comprimido de carbon.
brisance [brɪ'zɑns] *s.* potencia rompedora (de explosivos).
brisk [brɪsk] *a.* 1. vivo, activo, lleno de vida. 2. enérgico, rápido, avispado. 3. vivo, fresco (aire). 4. vigorizante, tonificante (bebida). —*v.t.* (gen. con *up*) animar, avivar, acelerar. —*v.i.* (con *up*) avivarse.
brisket ['brɪskət] *s.* 1. pecho (de un animal). 2. carne cortada del pecho de un animal.
bristle ['brɪsəl] *s.* cerda, pelusa. —*v.i.* 1. erizarse, ponerse tieso, ponerse de punta (pelos, plumas o púas de animales). 2. montar en cólera; encresparse. 3. **b. with,** estar erizado de (miedo, rabia, etc.). —*v.t.* 1. erizar, encrespar (cabello, plumaje, etc.). 2. proveer de cerdas, poner cerdas a.
bristletail [-ˌteɪl] *s.* (ento.) lepisma.
bristly ['brɪslɪ] *a.* cerdoso; erizado.
bristol board ['brɪstəl-] *s.* bristol (especie de cartulina para dibujo).
brit [brɪt] *s.* 1. arenque joven. 2. crustáceos diminutos (que sirven de alimento a las ballenas).
Brit. *abrev. de* **Britain, British,** Gran Bretaña, británico.
Britain ['brɪtən] *s. abrev. de* **Great Britain,** Gran Bretaña.
britannia metal [brɪ'tænjə-] britannia, metal inglés.

Britannic [-ɪk] *a.* británico.
Briticism ['brɪtəˌsɪzəm] *s.* anglicismo, palabra o frase peculiar de la Gran Bretaña.
British ['brɪtɪʃ] *a.* británico. —*s.* 1. bretón, céltico (de los antiguos britanos). 2. inglés británico. 3. **the B.,** los británicos, el pueblo de G. B.
British Columbia, la Colombia Británica, Columbia Británica (provincia del Canadá).
British Commonwealth of Nations, Comunidad Británica de Naciones.
British Empire, Imperio Británico.
Britisher [-ər, B -ə] *s.* inglés, súbdito británico.
British Guiana, Guayana Británica, antiguo protectorado británico en el N. de Sudamérica, hoy Guyana, parte de la comunidad británica de naciones independientes.
British Isles, Islas Británicas.
British standard candle, bujía internacional.
Briton ['brɪtən] *s.* britano.
Brittany ['brɪtənɪ] *s.* Bretaña, región de Francia.
brittle ['brɪtəl] *a.* 1. quebradizo, frágil. 2. (fig.) frágil, débil, inseguro. 3. susceptible, irritable (persona, personalidad, etc.).
broach [broʊtʃ] *s.* 1. asador, espetón (para asar). 2. espita. 3. pincho, punzón, lezna. 4. (carp.) broca, mecha; escariador. 5. broche, prendedor. —*v.t.* 1. espitar (tonel, barril, etc.), sacar (un líquido del barril). 2. escariar (un agujero). 3. abrir por primera vez (negocio, mina, etc.); publicar por primera vez; introducir (un tópico en la conversación).
broad [brɔd] *a.* 1. ancho; amplio, extenso, espacioso, vasto. 2. claro, obvio, explícito. 3. pleno (luz del día), ej., *in b. daylight,* en pleno día. 4. amplio, generalizado (sentido), general (término). 5. liberal comprensivo, tolerante. 6. marcado, pronunciado (acento, tono, etc.). 7. vulgar, indelicado, libre, atrevido (cuento, relato, etc.). 8. principal, esencial. 9. (fon.) abierto. 10. **b. hint,** insinuación evidente. —*s.* 1. (G.B.) (*ú. gen. en pl.*) extension ancha del río. 2. parte ancha (ej., de la mano). 3. (jer.) mujer (despectivamente). —*adv.* en forma general; plenamente, completamente.
broadax ['brɔdˌæks] *s.* hacha de armas; segur.
broad bean, (bot.) haba cochinera.
broad-blown [-'bloʊn] *a.* en plena florescencia, completamente florecido.
broadbrim [-ˌbrɪm] *s.* 1. sombrero de ala ancha. 2. (apodo que se le da a un) cuáquero.
broadcast ['brɔdˌkæst, B -ˌkɑst] *v.t.* (*pret., p.p.* BROADCAST OBROADCASTED; *p.pr.* BROADCASTING) 1. (rad., t.v.) radiar, transmitir, difundir, emitir (programa, etc.). 2. (agr.) sembrar al voleo. —*v.i.* **to b. live** (t.v.) transmitir en directo. —*s.* 1. (rad.) radiodifusión, trasmisión, emisión. 2. (agr.) siembra al voleo. —*a.* 1. difundido, esparcido, diseminado. 2. radiodifundido.
broadcaster [-ər, B -ə] *s.* (rad., t.v.) locutor radiodifusor; (fig.) entidad o compañía radiodifusora.
broadcasting [-ɪŋ] *s.* 1. (rad., t.v.) transmisión, emisión. 2. (agr.) siembra al voleo. —*a.* emisor, de radiodifusión.
broadcloth ['brɔdˌklɔθ] *s.* 1. velarte (paño fino de lana). 2. tela de seda o algodón de textura firme y suave.
broaden ['brɔdən] *v.t., v.i.* ensanchar(se), dilatar(se), ampliar(se).
broad gauge, (f.c.) trocha ancha.
broad-gauged [-'geɪdʒd] *a.* (f.c.) de vía ancha.
broad jump, (dep.) salto largo o de longitud.
broadleaf [-ˌlif] *s.* tabaco de hoja ancha que se utiliza en la elaboración de cigarros puros. —*a.* de hoja ancha.
broadloom [-ˌlum] *a.* tejido en telar ancho; tejido en un solo color.
broadly [-lɪ] *adv.* 1. ampliamente; claramente. 2. liberalmente. 3. en general, generalmente.
broad-minded [-'maɪndəd] *a.* comprensivo, tolerante; magnánimo.
broad-shouldered [-'ʃoʊldərd, B -dəd] *a.* ancho de espaldas.
broadside [-ˌsaɪd] *s.* 1. (mar.) costado (de un buque). 2. andanada, descarga (de artillería del costado de un barco). 3. (fig.) andanada, sarta (de insultos, improperios, etc.). 4. (imp.) pliego suelto. 5. **b. on,** (mar.) dando el costado. —*adv.* 1. (mar.) dando el costado. 2. al azar. —*a.* de costado.
broad-spectrum [-'spɛktrəm] *a.* (med.) de amplia efectividad (ej., antibiótico).
broadsword [-ˌsɔrd, B -ˌsɔd] *s.* espadón, chafarote, espada ancha de dos filos.
broadtail [-ˌteɪl] *s.* 1. (zool.) caracul. 2. piel de (nonato de) caracul.
Broadway ['brɔdˌweɪ] *s.* 1. calle famosa de Nueva York, centro de teatros y variedades. 2. la farándula neoyorquina. 3. el teatro comercial de Nueva York.
Brobdingnagian [ˌbrɑbdɪŋ'nægɪən, B 'brɔb-] *a.* gigantesco, enorme.
brocade [broʊ'keɪd] *s.* (tej.) brocado. —*v.t.* decorar con brocado.
brocatelle [ˌbrɑkə'tɛl, B ˌbrɔk-] *s.* 1. (tej.) brocatel. 2. mármol veteado en colores.
broccoli ['brɑkəlɪ, B 'brɔk-] *s.* (bot.) brécol, bróculi, brócoli.
brochette [broʊ'ʃɛt] *s.* asador, espeto, broqueta, brocheta (para asar a la parrilla).
brochure [broʊ'ʃʊr, B 'broʊʃjʊə] *s.* folleto.
brock [brɑk, B brɔk] *s.* (zool.) tejón.
brocket ['brɑkət, B 'brɔk-] *s.* gamo de dos años.
brogan ['broʊgən] *s.* zapato tosco.
brogue [broʊg] *s.* 1. zapato tosco y claveteado. 2. zapato estilo Oxford. 3. acento o pronunciación regional (apl. esp. al acento irlandés).
broil [brɔɪl] *v.t.* 1. asar sobre las ascuas, asar a la parrilla. 2. (fig.) asar, tosta. 3. alborotar. —*v.i.* 1. asarse, dorarse. 2. (fig.) asarse, padecer calor. 3. armar camorra, pelearse, querellarse. —*s.* 1. carbonada, carne asada a la parrilla. 2. riña, pleito, alboroto, pendencia.
broiler ['brɔɪlər, B -ə] *s.* 1. parrilla, rejilla de horno. 2. pollo tierno (para asarse a la parrilla). 3. día muy caluroso.
broiling [-ɪŋ] *a.* sumamente cálido, tórrido.
broke [broʊk] *pret. y p.p. ant. de* **to break.** —*a.* (fam.) pelado, tronado, sin un real, en bancarrota.
broken ['broʊkən] *p.p. de* **to break.** —*a.* 1. roto; fracturado, quebrado. 2. violado (juramento, promesa). 3. interrumpido, inquieto (sueño). 4. decaído, deshecho, quebrantado, decrépito, débil, ej., *b. health,* salud quebrantada. 5. contrito, amilanado, angustiado. 6. irregular, áspero (terreno). 7. domado (potro, etc.). 8. separado, suelto. 9. incierto, cambiadizo. 10. imperfecto, chapurreado, mal pronunciado, ej., *b. Spanish,* castellano chapurreado. 11. (com.) arruinado, en quiebra, en bancarrota.
broken-down [-'daʊn] *a.* 1. decrépito, agotado (persona). 2. roto, descompuesto (cosa).
brokenhearted [-'hɑrtəd, B -'hɑt-] *a.* acongojado, traspasado de dolor.
broken line, (geom.) línea quebrada.
broken wind, (vet.) huélfago.
broken-winded [-'wɪndəd] *a.* falto de resuello, jadeante.
broker ['broʊkər, B -kə] *s.* 1. (com.) corredor, cambista. 2. agente, comisionista; intermediario (en negocios). 3. (G.B.) el que compra y vende de segunda mano.
brokerage [-kərɪdʒ] *s.* (com.) corretaje, correduría.
bromal ['broʊməl] *s.* (quím.) bromal.
bromate ['broʊˌmeɪt] *s.* (quím.) bromato. —*v.t.* tratar o combinar con un bromato.
bromegrass ['broʊmˌgræs, B -ˌgrɑs] *s.* (bot.) bromo; lanco.
bromeliaceous [broʊˌmilɪ'eɪʃəs] *a.* (bot.) bromeliáceo.
bromeliad [-'milɪˌæd] *s.* (bot.) bromelia, bromeliácea.
bromhydric [ˌbroʊm'haɪdrɪk] *a.* (quím.) bromhídrico.
bromic ['broʊmɪk] *a.* (quím.) brómico.
bromide ['broʊˌmaɪd] *s.* 1. (quím.) bromuro. 2. (fam.) persona aburrida.
bromidic [broʊ'mɪdɪk] *a.* pesado, aburrido, falto de interés.
bromine ['broʊˌmin] *s.* (quím.) bromo.
bromize [-ˌmaɪz] *v.t.* (med.) tratar con bromo.
bronc [brɑŋk, B brɔŋk] *var. de* **bronco.**
bronchia ['brɑŋkɪə, B 'brɔŋ-] *s. pl.* (anat.) bronquios.
bronchial [-kɪəl] *a.* (anat.) bronquial.
bronchial tube, (anat.) bronquio, bronquíolo.
bronchiectasis [ˌbrɑŋkɪ'ɛktəsɪs B ˌbrɔŋ-] *s.* (med.) bronquiectasia.
bronchiole ['brɑŋkɪˌoʊl, B 'brɔŋ-] *s.* (anat.) bronquíolo.
bronchitic [brɑn'kɪtɪk, B brɔŋ-] *a.* bronquítico.
bronchitis [-'kaɪtəs] *s.* (med.) bronquitis.
broncho, *var. de* **bronco.**
bronchopneumonia [ˌbrɑŋkoʊnʊ'moʊnɪə, B ˌbrɔŋ-njʊ-] *s.* (med.) bronconeumonía.
bronchorrhea [ˌbrɑŋkə'riə, B ˌbrɔŋ-] *s.* (med.) broncorrea.
bronchoscope ['brɑŋkəˌskoʊp, B 'brɔŋ-] *s.* (med.) broncoscopio.
bronchoscopy [brɑn'kɑskəpɪ, B 'brɔŋkəˌskoʊ-] *s.* (med.) broncoscopia.
bronchotomy [brɑn'kɑtəmɪ, B brɔŋ'kɔt-] *s.* (cir.) traqueotomía, broncotomía.
bronchus ['brɑŋkəs, B 'brɔŋ-] *s.* (*pl.* BRONCHI [-ˌkaɪ]) (anat.) bronquio.
bronco ['brɑŋˌkoʊ, B 'brɔŋ-] *s.* (O. de E.U.) potro bronco, potro cerril.
broncobuster [-ˌbʌstər, B -tə] *s.* (O. de E.U.) domador de potros broncos; vaquero.
brontosaurus [ˌbrɑntə'sɔrəs, B ˌbrɔn-] *s.* (zool.) brontosaurio.
Bronx cheer [brɑŋks-, B brɔŋks-] (fam. E.U.) trompetilla (Méx., Antilles), ruido explosivo insultante o insolente hecho con labios o lengua.
bronze [brɑnz, B brɔnz] *s.* 1. bronce. 2. (estatua, busto, etc. de) bronce. 3. color bronce. —*v.t.* broncear. —*a.* de bronce; de color de bronce, bronceado.
Bronze Age, (hist.) Edad de Bronce.
bronzing ['brɑnziŋ, B 'brɔnz-] *s.* bronceado.
broo [bru] *s.* (Esco., N. de Ingl., Irl.) caldo; jugo, zumo; agua, líquido.
brooch [broʊtʃ, brutʃ, B broʊtʃ] *s.* broche, prendedor, alfiler de adorno.
brood [brud] *s.* 1. camada, nidada, pollada, cría. 2. progenie, prole. 3. raza, casta, ralea; clase, especie. —*v.t.* empollar, incubar. —*v.i.* 1. (gen. con *on* u *over*) meditar, cavilar, rumiar (amarga o tristemente). 2. (con *over* u *on*) cernerse (sobre).
brooder ['brudər, B -ə] *s.* 1. (*hen*) clueca. 2. (*enclosure*) incubadora. 3. (*thinker*) rumiador.

brood hen, gallina clueca.
brood mare, yegua de cría.
brooding [ɪŋ] *a.* *(thinking)* cavilación.
broody [-ɪ] *a.* 1. contemplativo, caviloso, triste. 2. clueca (gallina).
brook [brʊk] *s.* arroyo, arroyuelo. —*v.t.* tolerar, soportar, aguantar.
brooklet ['brʊklət] *s.* arroyuelo.
Brooklynite ['brʊklən,aɪt] *s.* residente de Brooklyn, sección de la ciudad de Nueva York.
broom [brum] *s.* 1. escoba. 2. (bot.) hiniesta, retama. —*v.t.* barrer.
broomcorn ['brum,kɔrn, B -,kɔn] *s.* (bot.) millo de escoba, variedad de sorgo.
broomrape [-,reɪp] *s.* (bot.) orobanca, hierba tora.
broomstick [-,stɪk] *s.* palo de escoba.
bros. *abrev. de* **brothers,** hermanos (hnos.).
broth [brɔθ] *s.* caldo.
brothel ['brɑθəl, 'brɔθ-, B 'brɔθ-] *s.* burdel, lupanar.
brother ['brʌðər, B -ə] *s.* 1. hermano. 2. (jer., *ú. en vocativo*) compadre, amigo. 3. hermano, camarada; personas que se identifican con un grupo, esp. racial o de clase económica baja. —*v.t.* 1. hermanar. 2. llamar hermano.
brotherhood [-,hʊd] *s.* 1. hermanazgo, hermandad. 2. hermandad, cofradía, congregación.
brother-in-law ['brʌðərɪ,lɔ] *s.* *(husband of one's sister or brother of one's wife or husband)* cuñado, hermano político; *(husband of one's wife's or husband's sister)* concuñado.
brotherliness ['brʌðərlɪnəs, B -əlɪ-] *s.* fraternidad, confraternidad.
brotherly [-lɪ] *a.* fraterno, fraternal.
brotulid ['brɑtʃʊlɪd, B -brɔ-] *s.* (ict.) brótula.
brougham ['bruəm, 'broʊəm, B 'bru-] *s.* berlina; automóvil tipo berlina.
brought [brɔt] *pret., p.p. de* **bring.**
brouhaha [bru'hɑ,hɑ] *s.* alboroto, tumulto; furor, frenesí.
brow [braʊ] *s.* 1. ceja. 2. ceja, cresta (del monte). 3. frente. 4. (t. fig.) rostro, cara, semblante, aspecto. 5. **to knit one's brows,** fruncir las cejas.
browbeat ['braʊ,bit] *v.t.* 1. amedrentar, amilanar, acobardar. 2. (con *into*) obligar, constreñir.
brown [braʊn] *a.* pardo, castaño; moreno; tostado (por el sol). —*s.* color castaño pardo. —*v.t., v.i.* 1. tostar(se); broncear(se). 2. (cocina) dorar. 3. **to be browned off,** (jer. G.B.) estar harto, estar hasta la coronilla.
brown betty, budín de manzana y pan desmigado.
brown bread, pan moreno; borona o pan de centeno.
brown coal, lignito, carbón fósil.
Brownian movement, B. motion['braʊnɪən-] (fís.) movimiento browniano (de las partículas microscópicas en suspensión en líquidos o gases).
brownie [-ɪ] *s.* 1. bizcocho pequeño de chocolate y nueces. 2. niña guía exploradora. 3. duendecillo benévolo.
Browning automatic rifle [-ɪŋ-] rifle o fusil automático Browning.
brownish [-ɪʃ] *a.* pardusco castaño.
brown nose, *s.* (vulg.) lameculos, lamehuevos. —*v.t.* (vulg.) lamer el culo a, lamer los huevos a. —*v.i.* lamer culos, lamer huevos.
brownout [-,aʊt] *s.* (E.U.) apagón parcial.
brown paper, papel de estraza.
Brown Power, (E.U.) Poder Mestizo, consigna de los Chicanos (mexicanos-americanos), que expresa la necesidad de adquirir fuerza política y defender sus derechos ciudadanos.
brown rat, (zool.) rata de alcantarilla.
brown rice, arroz no pulimentado, arroz integral.
brownshirt [-,ʃɜrt, B -,ʃɜt] *s.* Camisa Parda (miembro del partido nazi alemán).
brownstone [-,stoʊn] *s.* 1. piedra arenisca de color pardo rojizo (usada en construcción). 2. *(house)* casa de piedra arenisca, casa de piedra rojiza.
brown study, ensimismamiento, pensamiento profundo.
brown sugar, azúcar rubia, azúcar morena o terciada.
browse [braʊz] *v.t.* 1. pacer, ramonear, comer (ramas, pimpollos o renuevos). 2. hojear (un libro). —*v.i.* curiosear (en una biblioteca, librería o tienda).
brucellosis [,brusə'loʊsəs] *s.* (med.) brucelosis.
brucine ['bru,sin] *s.* (farm.) brucina.
Bruges [bruʒ] *s.* Brujas, ciudad de Bélgica.
bruin ['bruən] *s.* (personificación del) oso.
bruise [bruz] *v.t.* 1. magullar, golpear. 2. machucar, abollar. 3. majar. 4. (fig.) herir (los sentimientos, el ánimo, etc.). —*v.i.* 1. infligir magulladuras. 2. machucarse (fruta, tomates, etc.). 3. (fig.) sentirse herido. —*s.* 1. magulladura, contusión, cardenal. 2. abolladura. 3. (fig.) ofensa, dardo.
bruiser ['bruzər, B -zə] *s.* púgil, boxeador profesional; (jer.) matón.
bruit [brut] *v.t.* rumorear, divulgar, esparcir (noticias).
Brumaire[bru'mɛr, B -'mɛə] *s.* (hist.) brumario (segundo mes del calendario de la Revolución Francesa).
brumal ['bruməl] *a.* invernal, brumal, brumoso.
brumby ['brʌmbɪ] *s.* (Aust.) caballo bronco.
brume [brum] *s.* (poét.) bruma, niebla, neblina.
brummagem ['brʌmədʒəm] *a.* charro, baladí. —*s.* charrada, oropel.
brunch [brʌntʃ] *s.* combinación de desayuno y almuerzo.
brunet (*m.*), **brunette** (*f.*) [bru'nɛt] *s.* moreno; morena. —*a.* moreno, trigueño; morena, trigueña, morocha.
brunt [brʌnt] *s.* fuerza, impacto (de un golpe); choque (en un ataque); **to bear the b. of,** llevar el peso de, soportar lo más arduo de (un combate, tarea, etc.).
brush [brʌʃ] *s.* 1. cepillo, escobilla. 2. brocha, pincel. 3. cola peluda (de zorro, ardilla, tejón, etc.). 4. penacho de cerdas o plumillas (en sombrero). 5. toque, roce. 6. (elec.) escobilla. 7. matorral, breñal. 8. **to give (someone) the b.,** (jer.) desairar a, no hacer caso de (alguien). —*v.t.* 1. cepillar, escobillar, limpiar con cepillo. 2. frotar, restregar. 3. rozar, rasar. 4. pintar con brocha. 5. **b. aside,** (fig.) ignorar, dejar de lado (objeción, protesta); **b. away,** remover con el cepillo, cepillar; **b. off,** limpiar o remover con el cepillo; (fig.) desatender, desairar (a alguien); **b. over,** pintar ligeramente; **b. up,** pulir, acicalar; (fig.) retocar, repasar. —*v.i.* 1. (gen. con *by, along, through,* etc.) mover (se) o pasar rápidamente. 2. (con *against*) rozar (con). 3. **b. up on,** renovar, repasar, refrescar (uno) sus conocimientos de (un idioma, matemáticas, historia, etc.).
brush discharge, (elec.) descarga radiante.
brush fire, incendio de matorrales.
brush lag, (elec.) retraso de la escobilla.
brush lead, avance de la escobilla.
brush-off ['brʌʃ,ɔf] *s.* (jer.) despedida brusca, desaire.
brushwood [-,wʊd] *s.* 1. matorral, breñal, zarzal, maleza. 2. broza, ramojo, despojo de ramas secas.
brushwork [-,wɜrk, B -,wɜk] *s.* (pint.) manejo del pincel; estilo de pincelada.
brushy ['brʌʃɪ] *a.* 1. peludo, velludo, hirsuto, cerdoso. 2. zarzoso, matoso, cubierto de matojos.
brush yoke, (elec.) puente portaescobilla.
brusque, brusk [brʌsk, B brʊsk] *a.* brusco, rudo; abrupto.
brusquely ['brʌsklɪ, B 'brʊsk-] *a.* bruscamente, rudamente; abruptamente.
brusqueness [-nəs] *s.* brusquedad, rudeza.
brusquerie [,brʌskə'ri] (fr.) *var. de* **brusqueness.**
Brussels ['brʌsəlz] *s.* Bruselas, capital de Bélgica.
Brussels lace, encaje de Bruselas.
Brussels sprouts, *s. pl.* bretones, col de Bruselas.
brut [brut] *a.* seco (champán y otros vinos).
brutal ['brutəl] *a.* brutal, bestial, cruel, salvaje.
brutality [bru'tælətɪ] *s.* brutalidad; barbaridad, salvajada.
brutalization [,brutələ'zeɪʃən, B -laɪ-] *s.* embrutecimiento.
brutalize ['brutəl,aɪz] *v.t.* 1. embrutecer. 2. tratar brutalmente. —*v.i.* embrutecerse, bestializarse.
brutally [-ɪ] *adv.* brutalmente.
brute [brut] *a.* bruto; brutal. —*s.* bruto, bestia, animal.
brute force, fuerza bruta.
brutish ['brutɪʃ] *a.* brutal, bestial; tosco, grosero.
Brutus ['brutəs] *s.* (hist.) Bruto, uno de los conspiradores que asesinaron a Julio César.
bryology [braɪ'ɑlədʒɪ, B -,ɔl-] *s.* briología.
bryony ['braɪənɪ] *s.* (bot.) brionia, nueza, anorza.
bryophyte [-,faɪt] *s.* (bot.) briofita.
bryozoan [,braɪə'zoʊən] *a., s.* (zool.) briozoario.
Brython ['brɪθ,ɑn, -ən, B -,ɔn] *s.* britano; galés de habla céltica.
B.S. *abrev. de* **Bachelor of Science,** Licenciado en Ciencias.
B.T.U. *abrev. de* **British Thermal Unit,** unidad de calor británica.
bub [bʌb] **bubby** ['bʌbɪ] *s.* (fam.) hermanito; amiguito; chicuelo.
bubal, bubale ['bjubəl] **bubalis** [-bələs] *s.* (zool.) búbal.
bubble ['bʌbəl] *s.* 1. burbuja, borbollo, ampolla; **to blow bubbles** hacer pompas. 2. bagatela; ilusión, sueño, quimera. 3. burbujeo, borbolleo. 4. **to prick the b.,** desengañar, desilusionar. —*v.i.* 1. burbujear, borbollar, bullir. 2. eructar (un nene). 3. **b. over (with),** rebosar (de), desbordar; **b. with,** reventar de (risa, ira, etc.). —*v.t.* 1. hacer bullir. 2. decir o pronunciar efusivamente.
bubble and squeak, (G.B.) plato de carne, patatas y col fritas.
bubble bath, baño de espuma, baño de burbujas.
bubble chamber, (fís.) cámara de burbujas.
bubble gum, chicle de globo, chicle de bomba, chicle de burbuja.
bubble point, punto de burbujeo, punto de ebullición.
bubbler ['bʌblər, B -lə] *s.* (reg.) surtidor de agua potable.
bubble sextant, sextante de burbuja.
bubble-top ['bʌbəltɑp] *s.* cúpula transparente y a prueba de balas, que se instala en los automóviles de los mandatarios.
bubbling [-lɪŋ] *a.* burbujeante, efervescente; (fig.) efusivo.
bubbly [-lɪ] *s.* (fam., hum.) champaña. —*a.* burbujeante, espumoso, efervescente.
bubo ['bjuboʊ] *s.* (*pl.* BUBOES [-boʊz]) (med.) bubón, búa, buba.

bubonic [bju'bɑnɪk, b-'bɔn-] *a.* bubónico.
bubonic plague, (med.) peste bubónica.
buccal ['bʌkəl] *a.* bucal, de la boca.
buccaneer [ˌbʌkə'nɪr, B -'nɪə] *s.* bucanero, filibustero, pirata.
Bucephalus [bju'sɛfələs] *s.* Bucéfalo, el caballo de Alejandro Magno.
Bucharest [ˌbjukə'rɛst] *s.* Bucarest, capital de Rumania.
buck [bʌk] *s.* 1. macho cabrío, gamo; buco o cabrón. 2. macho (del venado, antílope, ciervo, liebre o conejo). 3. caballerete, pisaverde, petimetre. 4. (fam. E.U.) joven indio. 5. corcovo, brinco (del caballo). 6. (fútbol, E.U.) carga (contra la línea defensiva contraria). 7. **to pass the b. to,** cargarle la responsabilidad a (otro). —*v.t.* 1. arrojar (el caballo al jinete) por el testuz. 2. (fam. E.U.) resistir tenazmente, oponerse. 3. (fútbol, E.U.) cargar (la línea de defensa). —*v.i.* 1. corcovear, saltar violentamente (caballo, mulo). 2. moverse a sacudidas (máquina, automóvil, etc.). 3. esforzarse, empeñarse (en adquirir o conseguir algo). 4. **b. up,** (jer.) animarse; apresurarse. —*a.* 1. macho. 2. raso, sin rango, ej., *b. private,* soldado raso.
buck, *s.* 1. (E.U.) banquillo de aserrar o cepillar madera. 2. caballete, potro (de gimnasia). 3. (jer., E.U.) dólar.
buck and wing, (ant.) zapateado de los negros norteamericanos.
buckaroo, buckeroo [ˌbʌkə'ru] *s.* (O. de E.U., Can.) domador de potros, vaquero, amansador.
buckbean ['bʌkˌbin] *s.* (bot.) trébol de pantano.
buckboard [-ˌbɔrd, B -ˌbɔd] *s.* calesa de cuatro ruedas grandes sin muelles.
bucker ['bʌkər, B -ə] *s.* 1. contraestampa, sufridera, contramartillo. 2. leñador; trozador.
bucket ['bʌkət] *s.* 1. cubo, cubeta, balde. 2. cangilón (de noria, draga, excavadora, etc.). 3. **to kick the b.,** (fam.) estirar la pata. —*v.t.* 1. sacar o transportar (agua, etc.) en cubos. 2. (G.B.) cabalgar (un caballo) duramente. —*v.i.* 1. darse prisa, apresurarse, precipitarse. 2. moverse a sacudidas. 3. (jer.) morir.
bucket dredge, draga de escalera, de rosario, de cangilones o de arcaduces.
bucket seat, asiento envolvente (de los autos deportivos).
bucket shop, (com.) oficina de corretaje deshonesto (que especula con acciones, mercancías, etc.).
buckeye [-ˌaɪ] *s.* 1. (bot.) (variedad de) castaño de Indias. 2. (fam. E.U.) (apodo de) nativo de Ohio.
buck fever, (fam. E.U.) nerviosidad del cazador novicio (al avistar la caza); p. ext., ansiedad de enamorado.
bucking ['bʌkɪŋ] *s.* (elec.) oposición de circuitos.
bucking bar, sufridera, contraestampa.
Buckingham Palace['bʌkɪŋəm-] palacio de Buckingham, residencia oficial del monarca británico.
buckhound ['bʌkˌhaʊnd] *s.* galgo escocés.
buckish [-ɪʃ] *a.* 1. elegantón, engalanado. 2. impetuoso, vivaz.
buckle ['bʌkəl] *s.* 1. hebilla. 2. curva, comba, pandeo. —*v.t.* (*pret., p.p.* BUCKLED; *p.pr.* BUCKLING) 1. (gen. con *up, on*) abrochar, sujetar con hebilla; ceñirse (la espada). 2. corvar, abombar, encorvar. —*v.i.* 1. pandear, encorvarse, abombarse, combarse, acombarse. 2. doblarse (las rodillas). 3. **b. down** (o **down to**), aplicarse, dedicarse con empeño al (trabajo, tarea, etc.).
buckler [-lər, B -lə] *s.* 1. escudo, broquel, adarga, rodela. 2. (fig.) escudo, amparo, defensa. —*v.t.* escudar, defender, proteger.
buckling [-lɪŋ] *s.* pandeo, flexión lateral.
bucko ['bʌkoʊ] *s.* rufián, fanfarrón.
buck passer, el que pasa la responsabilidad o culpa propia a otro.
buck private, (E.U.) soldado raso.
buckram ['bʌkrəm] *s.* (tej.) bucarán, bocací. —*v.t.* 1. engomar, almidonar, entiesar. 2. reforzar con bocací. —*a.* 1. hecho de bucarán. 2. tieso, rígido, formal.
bucksaw ['bʌkˌsɔ] *s.* sierra de bastidor, sierra de ballesta, sierra con armazón.
buckshot [-ˌʃɑt, B -ˌʃɔt] *s.* (caza) posta, perdigón zorrero.
buckskin [-ˌskɪn] *s.* 1. (piel de) ante; cuero flexible. 2. (*pl.*) calzones (de piel) de ante. 3. bayo encerado (caballo). 4. (hist. E.U.) soldado de la guerra revolucionaria.
buckthorn [-ˌθɔrn, B -ˌθɔn] *s.* (bot.) cambrón, palo bañón, aladierna, espino cerval.
bucktooth [-'tuθ] *s.* diente saliente.
buckwheat [-ˌhwit, -ˌwit] *s.* (bot.) trigo sarraceno, alforjón.
buckwheat cake, panqué hecho con harina de trigo sarraceno.
bucolic [bju'kɑlɪk, B -'kɔl-] *a.* bucólico, pastoril. —*s.* 1. (poét.) poema pastoral, égloga. 2. (irón.) rústico, campesino.
bucranium [bjʊ'kreɪnɪəm] *s.* (*pl.* BUCRANIA [-nɪə]) (arq.) bucráneo.
bud [bʌd] *s.* 1. brote, cogollo, botón. 2. (bot., zool.) yema. 3. jovencito, jovenzuelo. 4. (fam.) amigo, compadre. 5. **to nip in the b.,** destruir en germen, sofocar en su origen, cortar en flor. —*v.i.* (*pret., p.p.* BUDDED; *p.pr.* BUDDING) 1. brotar, abotonar, echar botones. 2. (fig.) florecer, prometer (negocio, empresa, etc.). —*v.t.* 1. echar (hojas, etc., los botones de las plantas). 2. injertar (yema de una planta en otra).
Budapest ['budəˌpɛst, 'bju-] *s.* Budapest, capital de Hungría.
Buddha ['budə, B 'bʊdə] *s.* Buda, filósofo hindú, fundador del budismo.
Buddhism [-ˌdɪzəm] *s.* budismo.
Buddhist [-dəst] *s., a.* budista.
buddle ['bʌdəl] *s.* (min.) lavadero, artesa, gamella.
buddleia ['bʌdlɪə] *s.* (bot.) budleya, mariposa.
buddy ['bʌdɪ] *s.* (fam., E.U.) camarada, compañero, compinche.
budge [bʌdʒ] *v.i.* moverse, menearse, bullirse. —*v.t.* mover, bullir. —*s.* piel de cordero curtida, con la que se solía guarnecer las togas de los académicos.
budgerigar ['bʌdʒərɪˌgɑr, B -ˌgɑ] *s.* (zool.) periquito australiano.
budget ['bʌdʒət] *s.* 1. presupuesto. 2. acumulación; surtido. —*v.t.* 1. presupuestar. 2. incluir en el presupuesto. —*v.i.* hacer un presupuesto. —*a.* de costo reducido, económico.
budgetary [-əˌtɛrɪ, B -tərɪ] *a.* presupuestario, presupuestal.
budgie ['bʌdʒɪ] *s. abrev. de* **budgerigar.**
Buenos Aires ['bweɪnəs'ɛriz, B -'aɪər-] *s.* Buenos Aires, capital de Argentina.
buff [bʌf] *s.* 1. piel de búfalo, buey o ante. 2. (fam.) entusiasta, aficionado (de la ópera, el jazz, etc.). 3. (fam.) piel humana, ej., *in the b.,* desnudo, en cueros. 4. color amarillo, color de ante. 5. rueda pulidora. 6. (dial.) bofetada; golpe. —*a.* de color de ante. —*v.t.* pulir, pulimentar, alisar con ante o rueda pulidora.
buffalo ['bʌfəˌloʊ] *s.* (zool.) búfalo. —*v.t.* (fam. E.U.) engañar; confundir.
buffalo grass, (bot.) variedad de hierba pequeña (muy común en las praderas en que vive el búfalo).
buffalo robe, piel de búfalo (o de bisonte).
buffer ['bʌfər, B -ə] *s.* 1. parachoques, amortiguador (de choques). 2. (f.c.) tope. 3. pulidor, rueda o máquina pulidora.
buffer amplifier, (rad.) amplificador separador.
buffer state, estado tapón, estado o país que sirve de valla entre dos naciones rivales.
buffet ['bʌfət] *s.* bofetada, bofetón; (fig.) embate, golpe (de la fortuna, de la suerte). —*v.t.* abofetear, dar golpes a. —*v.i.* golpear, luchar; abrirse paso luchando o a golpes.
buffet [bə'feɪ, B 'bʊfeɪ] *s.* 1. ambigú, comida, refrescos (en una reunión social, etc.). 2. bufet, salón o mesa de refrescos y comidas. 3. (pr. G.B.) cantina, bar (en estaciones de f.c., etc.). 4. reunión en que los invitados se sirven a sí mismos. 5. aparador, copero, alacena.
buffet car, (f.c.) vagón donde se sirven refrigerios.
buffing wheel, (mec.) rueda pulidora.
buffoon [bə'fun] *s.* bufón, payaso, juglar.
buffoonery [-ərɪ] *s.* bufonadas, payasadas, conducta irresponsable.
bug [bʌg] *s.* 1. insecto, bicho, sabandija. 2. chinche. 3. (fam.) microbio, bacteria. 4. (jer.) falla, defecto (en un aparato o máquina). 5. (fam.) aficionado, entusiasta. 6. (jer.) micrófono, grabadora o dictáfono oculto (para escuchar conversación clandestinamente). —*v.t.* (*pret., p.p.* BUGGED; *p.pr.* BUGGING) 1. (jer.) ocultar grabadora, micrófono o dictáfono en (casa, cuarto, etc.) para escuchar clandestinamente. 2. (jer.) molestar, fastidiar, enojar. 3. (jer.) confundir, dejar perplejo.
bugaboo ['bʌgəˌbu] *s.* coco, fantasma, espantajo, espectro.
bugbear ['bʌgˌbɛr, B -ˌbɛə] *s.* coco, espantajo, fantasma, duende, espectro.
bug-eyed [-ˌaɪd] *a.* (jer.) de ojos saltones.
bugger ['bʌgər, B -ə] *s.* 1. sodomita. 2. bribón. 3. (hum.) sujeto, tipo, individuo. —*v.t.* 1. (vulg.) practicar sodomía con. 2. (jer.) agotar, extenuar.
buggery [-ərɪ] *s.* (jer.) sodomía.
buggy ['bʌgɪ] *a.* 1. lleno de chinches o de insectors. 2. (jer.) loco, destornillado, bobo.
buggy, *s.* 1. coche ligero de un solo caballo. 2. cochecito para niño.
bughouse ['bʌˌhaʊs] *s.* (fam., E.U.) manicomio.
bugle ['bjugəl] *s.* 1. corneta, clarín; corneta o trompa de caza. 2. (mús.) bugle. 3. (bot.) planta rastrera de la familia de la menta, de flores azules. 4. abalorio tubular, cañutillo (para adornar vestidos). —*v.i., v.t.* tocar la corneta.
bugle call, toque de corneta.
bugler [-glər, B -glə] *s.* (mil.) corneta (*m.*).
bugleweed [-gəlˌwid] *s.* (bot.) consuelda media.
bugloss ['bjuˌglɑs, -ˌglɔs, B -ˌglɔs] *s.* (bot.) buglosa, hierba melera.
bugout ['bʌgˌaʊt] *s.* 1. (mil., jer.) retirada apresurada (gen. desobedeciendo órdenes). 2. (jer.) persona que abandona su obligación.
bugs [bʌgz] *a.* (jer.) loco.
buhl [bul] *s.* (carp.) taracea, marquetería. —*a.* taraceado.
bulh saw, sierra de calar, serrezuela.
buhrstone, burrstone ['bɜrˌstoʊn, B 'bɜˌ-] *s.* (min.) asperón (usado para piedras de molino).
build [bɪld] *v.t.* (*pret., p.p.* BUILT [bɪlt]; *p.pr.* BUILDING) 1. construir; erigir, edificar; fabricar. 2. formar, hacer. 3. establecer, basar, fundamentar, ej., *b. an argument on facts,* basar un argumento sobre hechos. 4. **b. up,** construir edificios en, ocupar con construcciones (terreno, solar); formar, desarrollar (ej., un sistema); establecer (ej., reputación), dar publicidad a; construir gradualmente (ej., un imperio). —*v.i.* 1. ser constructor,

construir. 2. construirse, estar en construcción. 3. (fig.) formarse, tomar cuerpo. 4. **b. on** (o **upon**), basarse en; contar con, confiar en, fiarse de (promesas, esperanzas, etc.); **b. up,** intensificarse; aumentarse. —*s.* estructura; forma, figura (esp. del cuerpo).

builder ['bɪldər, B -də] *s.* constructor; arquitecto, maestro de obras.

builder's hoist, (const.) montacarga de una obra en construcción.

building [-dɪŋ] *s.* edificio, casa, construción.

building line, línea de edificación, línea municipal.

building lot, solar, terreno raso.

buildup ['bɪldˌʌp] *s.* 1. acumulación progresiva (de fuerzas, tropas, etc.). 2. propaganda preliminar, publicidad.

built-in ['bɪlt'ɪn] *a.* 1. empotrado. 2. inamovible, incorporado; (fig.) inherente.

built-up ['bɪlt'ʌp] *a.* 1. ensamblado, compuesto, conglomerado. 2. poblado, desarrollado (región, ciudad, terreno).

bulb [bʌlb] *s.* 1. (bot.) bulbo; tubérculo. 2. (anat.) bulbo, abultamiento. 3. (elec.) bombilla, foco. 4. (fís.) cubeta (de termómetro, barómetro, etc.). —*v.i.* hincharse, abultarse.

bulbil ['bʌlbəl, -ˌbɪl] *s.* (bot.) bulbillo.

bulbous [-bəs] *a.* bulboso.

bulbul ['bʊlˌbʊl] *s.* 1. (zool.) bulbul, (especie de) ruiseñor persa. 2. cantor, poeta.

Bulgar ['bʌlˌgɑr, 'bʊl-, B 'bʌlˌgɑ] *s.* búlgaro.

Bulgaria[bʌl'gɛrɪə] *s.* Bulgaria.

Bulgarian [bʌl'gærɪən, bʊl-, -'gɛr-, B bʌl'gɛərɪən] *s.* 1. búlgaro, natural de Bulgaria. 2. (idioma) búlgaro. —*a.* búlgaro.

bulge [bʌldʒ] *s.* 1. pandeo, comba; saliente, protuberancia, bulto. 2. (mar.) sentina, pantoque (de la nave); fondo (de un tonel). —*v.i.* 1. pandearse, combarse. 2. hincharse; sobresalir; abultarse, estar abultado, ej., *her pocket is bulging,* su bolsillo está abultado. —*v.t.* hinchar, abultar.

bulging ['bʌldʒɪŋ] *a.* 1. hinchado, abultado. 2. reventón; saltón (ojo), prominente. —*s.* combadura, bombeo, pandeo.

bulgy [-ɪ] *a.* protuberante; abultado.

bulimia [bju'lɪmɪə] *s.* (med.) bulimia; apetito insaciable.

bulk [bʌlk] *s.* 1. magnitud, volumen, tamaño, ej., *to increase in b.,* aumentar en tamaño. 2. bulto, masa, agregado. 3. mole; gran talla, cuerpo pesado. 4. la mayor parte, la parte mayor, ej., *the b. of an estate,* la parte mayor de una propiedad. 5. cargamento, carga. 6. **in b.,** a granel, suelto; **to load in b.,** cargar a granel (granos, etc.). —*v.i.* 1. hincharse, dilatarse; aumentar (bulto, forma, apariencia). 2. ser de peso, cobrar importancia o celebridad, ej., *his fame bulks large,* su fama cobra mucha importancia. —*v.t.* 1. hinchar. 2. rellenar. 3. (gen. con *up*) amontonar, apilar (ej., mercancías, cabello, etc.).

bulkhead ['bʌlkˌhɛd] *s.* 1. (mar.) mamparo. 2. tabique, mamparo (de compartimientos estancos). 3. escotillón, muro de contención en la ribera. 4. (const.) sotechado, altillo.

bulkhead dam, (hidr.) presa insumergible o de retención; dique sin derrame o de cierre.

bulkiness [-ɪnəs] *s.* volumen, corpulencia, bulto.

bulky [-kɪ] *a.* 1. voluminoso, abultado, corpulento, macizo. 2. pesado, difícil de manejar.

bull [bʊl] *s.* 1. toro; macho (de bovinos y de ciertos animales de gran tamaño). 2. (fig.) toro (hombre robusto). 3. (com.) alcista (en la bolsa). 4. (jer.) policía, detective. 5. **B.,** (astron.) Tauro (constelación). 6. **b. in a china shop,** persona burda en situación delicada; **to take the b. by the horns,** coger al toro por los cuernos, enfrentarse decididamente a algo. —*a.* 1. macho. 2. grande (dentro de su género). 3. (com.) ascendente, en alza (mercado de valores). —*v.t.* 1. (com.) jugar al alza en (el mercado de valores); provocar el alza de (valores). 2. forzar. —*v.i.* 1. avanzar a fuerza bruta. 2. (com.) aumentar de precio (valores).

bull, *s.* (jer. EU.) 1. cháchara, parloteo, chorradas. 2. disparate, mentira. 3. **to shoot the b.,** parlotear, chacharear, decir chorradas. —*v.i.* parlotear, chacharear, cotorrear.

bulla ['bʊlə] *s.* 1. bula, sello de plomo (de documentos papales). 2. (anat.) protuberancia ósea. 3. (med.) ampolla, vejiguilla cutánea (que contiene humor seroso).

bullbat ['bʊlˌbæt] *s.* (orn.) (especie de) chotacabras.

bull dike, (jer.) lesbiana que adopta modales y atuendo masculinos.

bulldog [-ˌdɔg] *s.* 1. buldog, perro dogo, perro de presa. 2. revólver de calibre grande y cañón corto. 3. (fam. G.B.) alguacil, policía; ayudante del censor universitario. —*a.* tenaz, obstinado. —*v.t.* (E.U.) derribar un novillo (cogiéndolo por los cuernos y doblándole el pescuezo).

bulldoze [-doʊz] *v.t.* 1. nivelar, limpiar (*el terreno*) con empujadora niveladora. 2. (fam. E.U.) intimidar, obligar, forzar. 3. abrirse (paso) como una niveladora.

bulldozer [-ˌdoʊzər, B -zə] *s.* 1. rasador, rasadora, tractor nivelador, topadora. 2. (metal.) dobladora de ángulos. 3. (jer., E.U.) valentón, rufián.

bullet ['bʊlət] *s.* bala (de arma pequeña).

bulletin ['bʊlətən] *s.* 1. boletín, publicación periódica. 2. anuncio, comunicado, boletín (de interés público).

bulletin board, tablero de anuncios, tablón de anuncios.

bulletproof ['bʊlət'pruf] *a.* a prueba de bala.

bull fiddle, (mús.) contrabajo (instrumento).

bullfight ['bʊlˌfaɪt] *s.* corrida de toros.

bullfighter [-ər, B -ə] *s.* torero, diestro, matador; (*pl.*) gente de coleta.

bullfighting [-ɪŋ] *s.* tauromaquia, toreo, toros.

bullfinch ['bʊlˌfɪntʃ] *s.* 1. (orn.) pinzón real, piñonero.

bullfrog [-ˌfrɔg, -ˌfrɑg, B -ˌfrɔg] *s.* (zool.) rana toro, rana mugidora o bramadora.

bull gear, (mec.) engranaje de giro; engranaje principal.

bullhead [-ˌhɛd] *s.* (ict.) siluro, barbo, bagre.

bullheaded [-'hɛdəd] *a.* terco, testarudo, obstinado, de cabeza dura.

bullhorn [-ˌhɔrn, B -ˌhɔn] *s.* megáfono, altoparlante portátil.

bullion ['bʊljən] *s.* 1. oro o plata en barras o lingotes. 2. (cost.) encaje u orla hecha con hilo dorado o plateado; entorchado (en uniformes).

bullish ['bʊlɪʃ] *a.* 1. semejante al toro; testarudo. 2. (com.) en alza (mercado de valores).

bull mastiff, (zool.) mastín inglés.

bullnecked [-'nɛkt] *a.* de cuello corto y robusto, como el toro.

bullock ['bʊlək] *s.* (zool.) buey, toro castrado.

bullpen [-ˌpɛn] *s.* 1. toril, redil para toros. 2. (fam.) barraca. 3. prevención de policía, celda común de una comisaría. 4. (béisbol) descansadero de los lanzadores de reserva (donde esperan su turno).

bullpoint [-ˌpɔɪnt] *s.* punta rompedora, rompedora de mano; barreta de punta, punterola.

bull ring, plaza de toros; arena, ruedo (de la plaza de toros).

bull session, (jer. E.U.) discusión larga sobre un tema (esp. entre estudiantes y músicos).

bull's-eye [-ˌzaɪ] *s.* 1. lente abombada, lente de linterna. 2. (linterna de) ojo de buey. 3. centro del blanco; (mil.) diana. 4. tiro acertado (que da en el centro del blanco); (fig.) acierto, éxito completo. 5. (arq.) ojo de buey, ventana o apertura circulares. 6. (mar.) cristal de portilla; lumbrera de cubierta. 7. (mar.) guardacabo.

bullshit, bull-shit [-ˌʃɪt] *s.* (vulg.)1. sandeces; **b.!,** ¡qué coño! 2. mentira, insinceridad, exageración. —*v.t.* engañar; **don't b. me!** ¡no me vengas con sandeces! —*v.i.* decir sandeces.

bullshitter [-ˌʃɪtər] *s.* (vulg.) farolero.

bullterrier[-'tɛrɪər, B -ɪə] *s.* (zool.) bulterrier.

bull tongue, (agr.) arado de una sola cuchilla.

bull wheel, rueda de giro, rueda impulsora; malacate para herramientas.

bullwhip [-ˌhwɪp, -ˌwɪp] *s.* látigo largo de cuero, zurriago.

bully [ˌbʊlɪ] *s.* pendenciero, abusador. —*a.* (fam.) excelente, de lo mejor, de primera clase. —*v.t.* (*pret., p.p.* BULLIED; *p. pr.* BULLYING) intimidar, amedrentar. —*v.i.* bravear, fanfarronear.

bully beef, carne de vaca en conserva.

bullyrag [-ˌræg] *v.t.* molestar, fastidiar, atormentar, intimidar.

bully tree, (bot.) balata, ácana.

bulrush ['bʊlˌrʌʃ] *s.* (bot.) junco, enea.

bulwark [-wərk, 'bʌl-, B 'bʊlwək] *s.* 1. (fort.) baluarte, bastión. 2. (fig.) baluarte, defensor o defensa poderosa. 3. rompeolas. 4. (mar.) malecón. —*v.t.* fortificar con baluartes; proteger, defender.

bulwark stay, (mar.) barraganete.

bum [bʌm] *s.* (jer.) 1. vagabundo, vago, holgazán; pobre diablo; borrachín. 2. gorrón, sableador. —*v.i.* (*pret., p.p.* BUMMED; *p.pr.* BUMMING) (jer.) 1. (gen. con *around*) zanganear, vagabundear. 2. gorrear, vivir de gorra, vivir a expensas de otro(s), ej., *he bums from others all the time,* siempre vive de gorra. —*v.t.* (jer.) obtener (algo) de gorra o de sablazos.

bum *a.* 1. inferior, de mala calidad. 2. falso, malo; estropeado.

bum, *s.* (dial., pr. G.B.) zumbido, susurro. —*v.i.* canturrear, tararear, zumbar, susurrar.

bumbailiff [ˌbʌm'beɪləf] *s.* (G.B., despec.) alguacil, corchete.

bumble['bʌmbəl] *v.i.* 1. fallar, errar. 2. hablar ineptamente; (con *through*) pronunciar (discurso, etc.) a tropezones. 3. andar a tropezones. 4. zumbar (insectos). 5. menearse retumbando (coche, etc.).

bumblebee [-ˌbi] *s.* (ento.) abejorro, abejón.

bumbling ['bʌmblɪŋ] *a.* inepto, incapaz; torpe; chapucero.

bumboat [-ˌboʊt] *s.* (mar.) bote cantina (para venta de víveres a los barcos en los puertos).

bumf [bʌmf] *s.* (jer. G.B.) 1. papeleo. 2. papel higiénico.

bummer ['bʌmər, B -ə] *s.* (jer.) gorrero, sableador, holgazán, pillo. —*a.* (jer.) desagradable, de mala calidad.

bump [bʌmp] *v.t.* golpear, darse contra; **b. off,** (jer.) matar, despachar. —*v.i.* 1. (gen. con *into* o *against*) chocar (contra); tropezar (con); encontrarse (con oposición, resistencia, etc.). 2. correr o pasar traqueteando (carro, etc.). 3. **b. into,** darse de cara con (persona). —*s.* 1. choque, golpe, porrazo, topetón, encontrón, tumbo. 2. protuberancia, chichón.

bumper ['bʌmpər, B -pə] *s.* 1. amortiguador de golpes, defensa, parachoques (de automóvil, etc.). 2. taza o vaso colmado. —*a.* excelente, desusadamente grande, abundante, ej., *b. crop,* abundante cosecha.

bumping post [-pɪŋ-] (f.c.) poste de guarda, tope de vía.
bumpkin ['bʌmpkən] *s.* 1. patán, palurdo, campesino, payo. 2. (mar.) pescante de la amura del trinquete.
bumptious ['bʌmpʃəs] *a.* envanecido, engreído, presuntuoso, pomposo, ostentoso.
bumpy ['bʌmpɪ] *a.* 1. desigual, con irregularidades, baches o protuberancias (camino, carretera, etc.). 2. agitado (por el aire) como el vuelo de un avión.
bum's rush, the b.'s r., (jer.) 1. expulsión a viva fuerza (de alguien de un cuarto o local público). 2. trato descortés (empleado para deshacerse de alguien). 3. **to give (someone) the b.'s r.,** deshacerse de alguien en forma descortés.
bum steer, (jer.) información falsa; recomendación equivocada.
bun [bʌn] *s.* 1. bollo, pan o panecillo. 2 moño (del pelo).
Buna ['bunə, 'bjunə] *s.* (quím.) buna, caucho artificial.
bunch [bʌntʃ] *s.* racimo, ristra (de cebollas, etc.); puñado; montón; haz, mazo, manojo, atado; montón (de cosas, personas, órdenes, etc.); grupo, conjunto; (fam.) cuadrilla, banda. —*v.t.* agrupar, juntar, amontonar. —*v.i.* arracimarse, juntarse.
buncher ['bʌntʃər, B -tʃə] *s.* (rad.) resonador agrupador.
bunchy ['bʌntʃɪ] *a.* racimoso, arracimado, apelotonado.
bunco ['bʌŋkoʊ] *s.* 1. (jer.) estafa. 2. banca (en juegos de mesa).
buncombe ['bʌŋkəm] *s.* (fam.) discurso altisonante; palabras insinceras.
bund [bʊnd, bʌnd] *s.* 1. confederación o liga. 2. **B.,** organización germano-norte-americana pro nazi que surgió en 1930.
bundle ['bʌndəl] *s.* 1. haz, atado, mazo, manojo. 2. montón, lío, envoltorio. 3. paquete, fardo, bulto. 4. (jer.) suma de dinero (esp. grande). 5. manojo (de nervios), ej., *she's a b. of nerves,* está hecha un manojo de nervios. —*v.t.* liar, atar, enfardelar, empaquetar; **b. off** o **away,** despedir de prisa, sin ceremonia, despedir a cajas destempladas. —*v.i.* **b. up,** arropar bien.
bundling [-ɪŋ] *s.* (E.U.) práctica de cortejarse o pelar la pava abrigados en cama, sin desnudarse (antigua costumbre de Nueva Inglaterra en tiempo frío).
bung [bʌŋ] *v.t.* 1. taponar, atarugar; obstruir, atorar. 2. (jer.) arrojar, lanzar. 3. (con *up*) magullar, machacar. 4. **bunged up,** atorado, obstruido; hinchado (ojo). —*s.* tapón, tarugo, bitoque.
bungalow ['bʌŋgə,loʊ] *s.* pequeña casa particular; casita playera o campestre.
bunghole ['bʌŋ,hoʊl] *s.* piquera; boca de tonel, canillero.
bungle ['bʌŋgəl] *v.t.* chapucear, estropear, frangollar. —*v.i.* equivocarse, obrar con torpeza. —*s.* chabacanería, chapucería.
bungler [-glər, B -glə] *s.* chapucero, chambón, zarramplín.
bungling ['bʌŋglɪŋ] *a.* chapucero; desmañado. —*s.* desmaña.
bunion ['bʌnjən] *s.* juanete, hueso saliente del pie.
bunk [bʌŋk] *s.* 1. litera, tarima para dormir. 2. (fam.) palabrería, faramalla, baladronada. —*v.i.* dormir en litera; acostarse, habitar temporalmente; ej., *I b. with a friend,* paro en casa de un amigo.
bunk bed, cama camerote.
bunker ['bʌŋkər, B -kə] *s.* 1. (mar.) carbonera, pañol de carbón. 2. (golf) hoya de arena; obstáculo (de un montón de tierra, zanja, arbusto, etc.). 3. (mil.) casamata (gen. subterránea); refugio a prueba de bombas. —*v.i.* (mar.) hacer carbón. —*v.t.* 1. (mar.) almacenar en pañol. 2. hacer caer (la pelota) en un obstáculo (con golpe mal ejecutado).
bunkhouse ['bʌŋk,haʊs] *s.* barraca, barracón (para alojar a obreros, soldados, etc.).
bunko ['bʌŋkoʊ] *var. de* **bunco.**
bunkum [-kəm] *var. de* **buncombe.**
bunny ['bʌnɪ] *s.* gazapo, conejillo.
Bunsen burner ['bʌnsən-] lámpara o mechero de Bunsen.
bunt [bʌnt] *v.t.* 1. topetar, topetear, topar, con cuernos; dar empellones, empellar. 2. (béisbol) golpear ligeramente la pelota para que ruede muy poco. —*s.* 1. empellón, topetazo. 2. (béisbol) golpecito muy suave. 3. (agr.) añublo, tizón (de los cereales). 4. (mar.) barriga, seno (de una vela o una red).
bunting ['bʌntɪŋ] *s.* 1. lanilla, estameña (usada para banderas y colgaduras). 2. banderas (de adorno). 3. (orn.) fringilino, pinzón (pajarillo de vivo color).
buntline [-,laɪn] *s.* (mar.) briol.
buoy ['buɪ, bɔɪ, B bɔɪ] *s.* (mar.) boya, baliza. —*v.t.* 1. aboyar, poner boyas, abalizar. 2. (con *up*) hacer flotar, mantener a flote; (fig.) sostener, animar, dar valor. —*v.i.* boyar, flotar.
buoyancy [-ənsɪ] *s.* 1. flotabilidad. 2. (fís.) flotación. 3. (aer.) fuerza ascensional. 4. (fig.) elasticidad, vigor, vivacidad (del ánimo).
buoyant [-ənt] *a.* 1. boyante. 2. (fig.) animado, vigoroso.
buprestid [bju'prɛstəd] *s.* (ento.) bupréstido, revientabuey.
bur, *var. de* **burr.**
Burberry ['bɜrbərɪ, -,bɛrɪ, B 'bɜbərɪ] *s.* (tela) impermeable.
burble ['bɜrbəl, B 'bɜb-] *v.i.* 1. burbujear; (fig.) hervir (de rabia, de gozo, etc.). 2. parlotear, farfullar. —*s.* burbuja, ampolla; burbujeo.
burbot ['bɜrbət, B 'bɜb-] *s.* (ict.) pez zoárcido, lota.
burden ['bɜrdən, B 'bɜd-] *s.* 1. carga, peso. 2. (fig.) carga, obligación, gravamen, preocupación; peso (de responsabilidad, etc.). 3. carga, cargamento, ej., *beast of b.,* animal de carga. 4. (mar.) arqueo, porte, cabida (de un barco). 5. esencia, parte principal (de una idea o tema). —*v.t.* 1. cargar. 2. (fig.) cargar, gravar, oprimir; agobiar, ej., *burdened with pain,* agobiado de dolor.
burden of proof, (der.) peso o carga de la prueba, obligación de probar.
burdensome [-səm] *a.* gravoso, pesado, oneroso, opresivo.
burdock ['bɜr,dɑk B 'bɜ,dɔk] *s.* (bot.) bardana, lampazo, lapa.
bureau ['bjʊroʊ] *s.* (*pl.* BUREAUS o BUREAUX [-oʊz]) 1. (E.U.) cómoda, tocador. 2. escritorio. 3. oficina, despacho, negociado; (E.U.) agencia del gobierno.
bureaucracy [bjʊ'rɑkrəsɪ, B -'rɔk-] *s.* burocracia.
bureaucrat ['bjʊrə,kræt] *s.* burócrata.
bureaucratic [,bjʊrə'krætɪk] *a.* burocrático.
burette, buret [bjʊ'rɛt] *s.* (quím.) bureta, probeta.
burg [bɜrg, B bɜg] *s.* 1. burgo, villa; ciudadela medieval. 2. (fam.) aldea, ciudad, pueblo.
burgee [,bɜr'dʒi, B 'bɜ,dʒi] *s.* (mar.) bandera del armador; banderola (de señales).
burgeon ['bɜrdʒən, B 'bɜdʒ-] *s.* (bot.) brote, botón, yema, capullo. —*v.i.* 1. brotar; germinar, retoñar. 2. (fig.) crecer, ramificarse, florecer.
burger ['bɜrgər, B 'bɜgə] *s. var. de* **hamburger,** emparedado de carne picada.
burgess ['bɜrdʒəs, B 'bɜdʒɪs] *s.* 1. (G.B.) burgués, ciudadano libre. 2. (G.B.) representante de un distrito, ciudad o universidad en el parlamento. 3. (hist., E.U.) representante de Maryland y Virginia (en la cámara baja de la legislatura colonial).
burgh [bɜrg, B bɜg] *s.* villa, distrito (esp. en Esco.).
burgher ['bɜrgər, B 'bɜgə] *s.* 1. ciudadano, vecino de un distrito o ciudad. 2. pequeño comerciante; burgués.
burglar [-lər, B -lə] *s.* ladrón, escalador nocturno.
burglar alarm, alarma contra robo, alarma contra ladrones.
burglarious [,bɜr'glɛrɪəs, B ,bɜ'glɛər-] *a.* 1. para robar, (con intención) de robo. 2. de ladrón.
burglarize ['bɜrglə,raɪz, B 'bɜg-] *v.t.* robar (una casa, tienda, etc. esp. de noche).
burglarproof [-lər,pruf, B -lə,-] *a.* a prueba de robo.
burglary [-glərɪ] *s.* robo con allanamiento de morada; ratería.
burgle [-gəl] *v.t.* robar con allanamiento (de una casa, tienda, etc., esp. de noche).
burgomaster [-gə,mæstər, B -,mɑstə] *s.* burgomaestre, alcalde (esp. en los Países Bajos, Alemania, Austria y Suiza).
burgonet [-gə,nɛt] *s.* (arm.) borgoñota, celada.
burgoo ['bɜr,gu, B 'bɜ,gu] *s.* gachas, sopa espesa; guiso de carne y legumbres.
burgrave [-,greɪv] *s.* (hist.) burgrave, señor de un castillo o una fortaleza.
Burgundian [bər'gʌndɪən, B bə'-] *a., s.* borgoñón, borgoñés.
Burgundy ['bɜrgəndɪ, B 'bɜg-] *s.* Borgoña, región de Francia. 2. vino de borgoña. 3. color vino tinto.
burial ['bɛrɪəl] *s.* entierro, sepultura.
burial ground, cementerio, camposanto.
burier [-ər, B -ə] *s.* enterrador, sepulturero.
burin ['bjʊrən] *s.* buril, cincel.
burl [bɜrl, B bɜl] *s.* 1. mota, borra, nudo (en un hilo o tela). 2. (E.U.) nudo (en madera). —*v.t.* desborrar, desmotar; despinzar (telas y paños).
burlap ['bɜr,læp, B 'bɜ,-] *s.* arpillera, harpillera, rázago.
burled [bɜrld, B bɜld] *a.* nudoso (díc. de maderas).
burlesque [bər'lɛsk, B bə'-] *s.* 1. imitación, parodia, farsa, caricatura. 2. (E.U.) bataclán, espectáculo de variedades picarescas. —*a.* imitativo, paródico, caricaturesco. —*v.t.* imitar, parodiar, caricaturizar (en forma burlesca).
burley ['bɜrlɪ, B 'bɜlɪ] *s.* (E.U.) tabaco de hojas delgadas y color claro, cultivado en Kentucky.
burly [-lɪ] *a.* 1. corpulento, fornido, musculoso. 2. espontáneo, jovial.
Burma ['bɜrmə, B 'bɜmə] *s.* Birmania.
Burmese [,bɜr'miz, -'mis, B ,bɜ'miz] *s.* 1. birmano, nativo de Birmania. 2. birmano (lenguaje). —*a.* birmano.
burn [bɜrn, B bɜn] *v.i.* (*pret., p.p.* BURNED [bɜrnd, B bɜnd] o BURNT [bɜrnt, B bɜnt]; *p.pr.* BURNING) 1. quemarse; arder. 2. estar encendido, (lámpara, gas, etc.). 3. arder (de cierto modo), ej., *b. blue,* arder con llama azul, *b. low,* arder con llama baja. 4. quemarse, asarse (de calor); abrasarse (plantas, cosecha, etc.). 5. quemar, abrasar. 6. (fig., ú. con *with*) arder, consumirse (de deseo, ira, pasión, curiosidad, etc.). 7. estar impaciente. 8. morir en la hoguera; (jer.) morir en la silla eléctrica. 9. quemar (díc. en juego de

niños al estar a punto de hallar el objeto oculto). 10. **b. down,** ser consumido por el fuego, quemarse por completo; **b. out,** quemarse, fundirse (fusible, bombilla); apagarse, extinguirse (el fuego); (fig.) agotarse, gastarse; **b. up,** enfurecerse. —*v.t.* 1. quemar, incendiar, abrasar. 2. endurecer al fuego; cocer (ladrillo, cal), calcinar (minerales). 3. quemar en la hoguera. 4. soldar, fundir (metales). 5. (med.) cauterizar. 6. disipar, desperdiciar (dinero). 7. (jer.) irritar, enfurecer. 8. (jer.) engañar, embaucar. 9. **b. down,** destruir por fuego, reducir a cenizas; **b. in** (o **into**), marcar a fuego; (fig.) inculcar en, grabar en; **b. one's ships,** (fig.) quemar las naves; **b. out,** quemar el interior de (una casa, etc.), consumir el contenido de (algo); **b. the candle at both ends,** vivir de prisa; **b. the midnight oil,** (fig.) quemarse las pestañas o cejas; **b. up,** destruir por fuego; (fig.) agotar, consumir; (fig., jer.) indignar, irritar, enfurecer; **b. water,** arponear salmón a la luz de antorchas. —*s.* 1. quemadura. 2. quemado (en el monte). 3. arrancada, impulso (de los cohetes de una nave espacial). 4. (jer.) irritación, ira, cólera.

burner ['bɜrnər, B 'bɜnə] *s.* 1. quemador. 2. mechero (de una lámpara de gas, etc.).

burnet [bər'nɛt, B 'bɜnɪt] *s.* (bot.) pimpinela.

burning ['bɜrnɪŋ, B 'bɜn-] *s.* 1. quema, quemazón, ardor. 2. quemadura. 3. combustión. 4. (cerám.) cocción. —*a.* abrasador, ardiente, vehemente (discusión, etc.); candente, ej., *a b. question,* una cuestión candente.

burning glass, (fís.) espejo ustorio.

burning scent, (caza) rastro fuerte.

burning shame, vergüenza inaudita.

burnish [-ɪʃ] *s.* brillo, lustre, bruñido. —*v.t.* lustrar, bruñir, dar brillo a (esp. cuando se usa pulimento o pasta); pulir, pulimentar. —*v.i.* tomar brillo o lustre.

burnisher [-ər, B -ə] *s.* bruñidor, pulidor.

burnoose, burnous [bər'nus, B bə'-] *s.* albornoz.

burnsides ['bɜrnˌsaɪdz B 'bɜn-] *s.* estilo de barba con patillas y bigote, con la barbilla afeitada.

burnt [bɜrnt, B bɜnt] *pret., p.p. de* **burn.** —*a.* quemado, abrasado, cocido, escaldado.

burnt almond, almendra garrapiñada.

burnt-out ['bɜrnt'aʊt, B 'bɜnt-] *a.* 1. apagado, extinto, ej., *b.-o. volcano,* volcán extinto o apagado. 2. completamente abrasado, consumido (por el fuego); (fig.) consumido, fundido (por vicisitudes o libertinaje).

burnt sienna, (pint.) siena rojizo.

burnt umber, (pint.) ocre oscuro.

burp [bɜrp, B bɜp] *s.* eructo, regüeldo. —*v.i.* eructar. —*v.t.* ayudar (a un nene) a eructar (dándole golpecitos en la espalda).

burp gun, (jer.) pistola automática.

burr [bɜr, B bɜ] *s.* 1. (gen. **bur**) erizo, carda, zurrón espinoso. 2. (gen. **bur**) erizo, cardencha, mata espinosa. 3. nudo (en la madera), protuberancia (en los árboles). 4. virola, arandela (que se coloca al extremo de un perno o en el de un remache antes de estamparlo). 5. aspereza, rebaba (esp. en el borde de algún hueco, hecho con taladro, barrena, etc.). 6. disco nebuloso alrededor de la luna. 7. zumbido. 8. taladro, fresa de dentista. 9. piedra para rueda de molino; piedra de afilar. 10. (fon.) pronunciación gutural de las erres. —*v.i.* 1. hablar pronunciando las erres guturalmente. 2. zumbar. —*v.t.* quitar la rebaba a (bordes, etc.).

burr chisel, cortafrío quitarrebabas.

burro ['bɜroʊ, 'bʊr-] *s.* burro, asno, pollino.

burrow ['bɜroʊ, B 'bʌroʊ] *s.* 1. madriguera, conejera, vivar. 2. escondrijo, refugio, retiro. —*v.t.* excavar (un hueco, una madriguera, etc.), minar, horadar. —*v.i.* 1. amadrigarse, vivir en una madriguera. 2. esconderse. 3. (fig., ú. con *into, through,* etc.) ahondar, investigar (en, entre, etc.).

burry ['bɜrɪ] *a.* 1. erizado, espinoso, punzante. 2. ronca y gutural (voz, pronunciación, etc.).

bursa ['bɜrsə, B 'bɜsə] *s.* (anat., zool.) saco, cavidad, bolsa.

bursar ['bɜrsər, -ˌsɑr, B 'bɜsə] *s.* tesorero (esp. el de una universidad u orden religiosa).

bursary [-sərɪ] *s.* tesorería (de una universidad o convento).

burse [bɜrs, B bɜs] *s.* bolsa de seda o brocado en la cual se lleva al altar el corporal doblado.

bursiform ['bɜrsəˌfɔrm, B 'bɜsə-] *a.* (bot., zool.) bursiforme.

bursitis [bər'saɪtəs, B bə'-] *s.* (med.) bursitis.

burst [bɜrst, B bɜst] *v.i.* (*pret. p.p.* BURST OBURSTED; *p.pr.* BURSTING) reventar (se), estallar, explotar (bomba, pólvora, globo, ampolla, etc.), romperse (dique, cable, cuerda, etc.), abrirse (brote); **b. in,** irrumpir; interrumpir; **b. into,** irrumpir en (cuarto, etc.); estallar en (llamas); desatarse en (lágrimas, imprecaciones, etc.); **b. open,** abrirse violentamente, abrirse con un estallido (puerta, ventana, etc.); **b. out,** prorrumpir, exclamar; romper a, echar a, ej., *b. out crying,* romper a llorar; *b. out laughing,* carcajear; *b. out in tears,* desatarse en lágrimas; **b. upon,** irrumpir en, invadir (territorio enemigo, soledad, etc.); **b. with,** reventar de (comida, risa, etc.); rebosar de (emoción o sentimientos). —*v.t.* 1. reventar. 2. romper, quebrar. 3. **b. in (door),** forzar, derribar (puerta); **b. one's sides laughing,** desternillarse de risa. —*s.* 1. estallido, explosión, reventón. 2. rotura. 3. (mil.) andanada, ráfaga (de tiros). 4. **b. of energy,** derroche repentino de energías; **b. of laughter,** estallido de risa, carcajada; **b. of speed,** arranque de velocidad.

bursted ['bɜrstəd, B 'bɜst-] *a.* (jer.) reventado (gen. **busted**).

burstwort [-ˌwɜrt, B -ˌwɜt] *s.* (bot.) quebrantapiedras, milgranos.

burton ['bɜrtən, B 'bɜt-] *s.* (G.B.) (especie de) cerveza fuerte. 2. (mar.) palanquín, estrellera.

burweed ['bɜrˌwid, B 'bɜˌ-] *s.* (bot.) (plantas como) bardana, lampazo, cadillo (cuyos frutos se agarran a los vestidos).

bury ['bɛrɪ] *v.t.* (*pret. p.p.* BURIED; *p.pr.* BURYING) 1. enterrar, inhumar, sepultar. 2. enterrar, esconder, ocultar. 3. **b. in,** sumergir, absorber, ej., *buried in his thoughts,* absorto en sus pensamientos; **b. the hatchet,** enterrar el hacha (de la guerra), renunciar a una lucha; echar pelillos a la mar; hacer las paces.

burying beetle, (ento.) enterrador.

burying ground, burying place, camposanto, cementerio.

bus [bʌs] *s.* (*pl.* BUSES OBUSSES) 1. ómnibus, autobús; colectivo (S.A.). 2. (elec.) barra colectora. —*v.i.* (*pret., p.p.* BUSED; *p.pr.* BUSING) 1. viajar en ómnibus. 2. trabajar como ayudante de camarero. —*v.t.* 1. transportar en ómnibus. 2. (E.U.) transportar (escolares) diariamente a otro distrito para evitar la segregación de razas y minorías pobres.

bus boy, ayudante de camarero (en un restaurante).

busby ['bʌzbɪ] *s.* chacó o morrión de piel (de los húsares).

bush [bʊʃ] *s.* 1. arbusto, mata, maleza. 2. matorral, breña; (Aust., África) área cubierta de chaparrales. 3. rabo peludo. 4. (mec.) forro, casquillo, cojinete, camisa, buje. 5. (ant.) rama de hiedra (que colgaba antiguamente en la puerta de las tabernas). 6. **to beat about the b.,** andar con rodeos. —*v.t.* 1. separar, lindar, proteger con arbustos; poblar de arbustos o matas. 2. (mec.) forrar, revestir, encasquillar.

bush baby, (zool, África) galago.

bush bean, (bot.) frijol enano.

bush beard, (jer.) barba enmarañada.

bushed [bʊʃt] *a.* 1. cubierto de malezas o arbustos. 2. (jer.) cansado, exhausto. 3. (Aust.) perdido; desorientado, perplejo.

bushel ['bʊʃəl] *s.* 1. medida de áridos (E.U. 35,23 litros; G.B. 36,35). 2. recipiente que la contiene. 3. (fig.) montón, sinnúmero, tonelada.

bushel, *v.t.* (*pret., p.p.* BUSHELED OBUSHELLED; *p.pr.* BUSHELING OBUSHELLING) (cost.) remendar, arreglar (vestido, ropa, etc.).

bushhammer ['bʊʃˌhæmər, B -ə] *s.* martellina, escoda.

Bushido [ˌbuʃɪ'doʊ] *s.* bushido (antiguo código caballeresco del Japón).

bushing ['bʊʃɪŋ] *s.* 1. (mec.) forro, manguito, casquillo, cojinete, camisa, boquilla; buje. 2. (elec.) manguito aislador, boquilla.

bush league, (jer., béisbol) liga menor.

bush leaguer, (jer., béisbol) jugador de segunda clase.

Bushman [-mən] *s.* 1. bosquimán. 2. b., montaraz; (Aust.) colonizador del interior; rústico.

bushmaster [-ˌmæstər, B -ˌmɑstə] *s.* (zool.) laquesida, laquesis, serpiente venenosa.

bush pilot, piloto de avión fletado (que vuela por regiones remotas fuera de las rutas regulares).

bushranger [-ˌreɪndʒər, B -dʒə] *s.* 1. habitante de una zona boscosa, montaraz. 2. (Aust.) salteador de caminos (que se esconde en el bosque).

bushtit [-ˌtɪt] *s.* (orn.) paro (del O. de E.U.).

bushwhack [-ˌhwæk, -ˌwæk] *v.i.* 1. abrir camino en la maleza (esp. talando arbustos y ramaje); halar un bote agarrándose de los arbustos de la orilla. 2. vivir o esconderse en los bosques; guerrillear o atacar desde la maleza. —*v.t.* emboscar.

bushwhacker [-ər, B -ə] *s.* 1. guerrillero, montonero (E.U., esp. de los confederados en la Guerra de Secesión). 2. (Aust.) leñador.

bushy ['bʊʃɪ] *a.* espeso, tupido, ej., *b. hedge,* seto tupido, *b. eyebrows,* cejas tupidas.

busily ['bɪzəlɪ] *adv.* diligentemente, solícitamente, atareadamente.

business ['bɪznəs] *s.* 1. ocupacion, profesión, especialidad. 2. tarea, deber. 3. incumbencia, asunto propio, ej., *that is his* (*my, your,* etc.) *b.,* eso es cosa suya (mía, tuya, etc.), (*that is*) *none of my* (*your,* etc.) *b.,* (eso) no es de mi (tu, etc.) incumbencia, no me (te, etc.) incumbe, no es asunto mío (tuyo, etc.). 4. asunto (esp. difícil), problema; (despec.) cosa, asunto, lío, ej., *a strange b.,* un asunto raro, *what a b.!* ¡qué cosa tan difícil! ¡qué lío! 5. comercio, negocio, empresa (comercial). 6. movimiento, negocios, compras y ventas, ej., *b. increased,* aumentaron las ventas, mejoraron los negocios, *he's doing a great b.,* está haciendo un excelente negocio. 7. **the b.,** (jer.) paliza dura; muerte. 8. **b. as usual,** todo sigue igual (a pesar de las circunstancias); **b. of the day,** tarea, orden del día; **good b.!** ¡bien hecho!; **on b.,** por negocios; en capacidad oficial; **to be sick of the whole b.,** estar harto de todo el asunto, estar hasta la coronilla de la cosa; **to give one the b.,** (jer.) propinarle a uno una paliza dura; matar, despachar, liquidar a uno; **to have no b. to,** no tener derecho a, no tener por qué, ej., *he has no b. to be here,* no tiene por qué estar aquí; **to make it one's b.,** asumir, encargarse de, proponerse; **to mean b.,** hablar o actuar en serio; **to mind one's own b.,** ocuparse de sus propios asuntos y no meterse en los ajenos; **to send (someone) about his (her) b.,** enviar a paseo.

business college, escuela de comercio.

business connections, relaciones de negocio.

business deal, trato comercial.

business dinner, cena de negocios.

business district, barrio comercial.

business hours, horas de oficina, horas hábiles.

business law, derecho empresarial.

businesslike [-ˌlaɪk] *a.* sistemático, eficiente, práctico, rápido, bien ordenado.

businessman [-ˌmæn] *s.* hombre de negocios; comerciante, negociante.

business suit, terno de calle, traje civil (de color y corte discretos).

businesswoman [-ˌwʊmən] *s.* mujer de negocios; mujer de empresa.

busk [bʌsk] *s.* ballena del corsé.

busker ['bʌskər, B -kə] *s.* (G.B.) saltimbanqui; músico ambulante.

buskin [-kɪn] *s.* 1. borceguí; bota alta. 2. coturno. 3. (fig.) tragedia, género trágico, vena trágica.

bus line, ruta, línea o compañía de autobuses.

busman ['bʌsmən] *s.* conductor de ómnibus.

busman's holiday, día de fiesta en el que se trabaja como en día hábil.

buss [bʌs] *s.* (dial.) (ant.) beso, beso sonado. —*v.t., v.i.* (dial.) (ant.) besar.

bust [bʌst] *s.* 1. (anat.) busto; pecho de mujer. 2. (arte) busto, escultura.

bust, *s.* 1. juerga, parranda, ej., *to go on a b.,* ir de juerga, andar de parranda. 2. quiebra; chasco; fracaso. 3. (jer.) golpe, puñetazo. —*a.* quebrado, en bancarrota, ej., *to go b.,* quebrar, ir a la quiebra. —*v.t.* 1. estallar, reventar. 2. llevar a la quiebra. 3. amansar, domeñar (potro, etc.). 4. degradar, despojar de grado. 5. (jer.) dar un puñetazo a, golpear (con el puño). 6. (jer.) forzar (una caja fuerte, la entrada de una casa) para robar. 7. (E.U., fam.) arrestar. 8. **b. a gut,** utilizar toda la fuerza posible (para cumplir con un deber determinado). —*v.i.* 1. reventarse (de risa). 2. fracasar; quebrar, ir a la quiebra. 3. (naipes) pasarse.

bustard ['bʌstərd, B 'bʌstəd] *s.* (zool.) avutarda; sisón.

buster ['bʌstər, B -tə] *s.* 1. niño robusto. 2. (fam.) tipo, tío; (en vocativo) compadre. 3. (forma abrev. de **broncobuster**) domador de potros cerriles. 4. destructor, rompedor; **trust b.,** el que disuelve un trust. 5. grave caída. 6. cosa extraordinaria, maravilla. 7. (Aust.) viento fuerte.

bustle ['bʌsəl] *v.i.* 1. apresurarse, ir o venir apresuradamente. 2. (gen. con *about*) trabajar con ahínco. 3. (con *with*) bullir (con), abundar (en). —*s.* 1. alboroto, bullicio. 2. polisón, almohadilla (que usaban las mujeres antiguamente para abultar las faldas por detrás).

bust out, escaparse de la cárcel o el colegio.

bust-up ['bʌstˌʌp] *s.* 1. disolución, rompimiento; fin. 2. gran ceremonia, reunión social muy concurrida. 3. (G.B.) riña, pelea.

busway ['bʌsˌweɪ] *s.* (elec.) conducto para barras colectoras, canal de barras colectoras.

busy ['bɪzɪ] *a.* 1. ocupado, ej., *I'm b. now,* estoy ocupado ahora, *the line is b.,* la línea (telefónica) está ocupada. 2. atareado; activo, laborioso. 3. oficioso, entremetido. 4. bullicioso, movido. 5. recargado, inquietante (ej., diseño). 6. **b. as bee,** ocupadísimo; **to be b. at,** estar ocupado en; **to get b.,** poner manos a la obra. —*v.t.* (*pret., p.p.* BUSIED; *p.pr.* BUSYING) mantener ocupado, tener ocupado (a alguien); **b. oneself,** mantenerse ocupado, atarearse. —*v.i.* atarearse.

busybody [-ˌbɑdɪ, B -ˌbɔdɪ] *s.* entremetido, chismoso.

busyness [-nəs] *s.* actividad, diligencia, aplicación.

busy signal, (tele.) señal de ocupado.

but [bʌt] *conj.* 1. pero, mas, ej., *poor b. proud,* pobre, pero digno. 2. sino, al contrario, antes bien, ej., *it's not made of wood b. of leather,* no es de madera, sino de cuero. 3. (después de negaciones) (de) que, ej., *there's no doubt b. Germany has lost the war,* no hay duda de que Alemania ha perdido la guerra. 4. al menos, ej., *I can b. try it,* al menos puedo intentarlo. 5. menos que, ej., *I cannot b. do my duty,* no puedo menos que cumplir con mi deber. 6. sin que, sin que . . . no, ej., *it never rains b. it pours,* llover sobre mojado; (fig.) sobre miel, buñuelos. 7. **all b.,** casi, ej., *he was so nervous that he all b. wrecked the machine,* estaba tan nervioso que casi rompió la máquina; **b. for,** a no ser por; **b. then,** pero por otra parte; **last b. one,** penúltimo. —*adv.* sólo, solamente, no más que, ej., *she is b. a child,* ella no es más que una criatura, es sólo una criatura. —*prep.* salvo, excepto, ej., *they are all wrong but him,* todos están equivocados excepto él. —*s.* pero, objeción, ej., *there are no buts about it,* no hay peros que valgan.

butadiene [ˌbjutə'daɪˌin] *s.* (quím.) butadieno.

butane ['bjuˌteɪn] *s.* (quím.) butano.

butanol [-tənˌɔl] *s.* (quím.) butanol.

butch [bʊtʃ] *a.* 1. rudo, varonil. 2. ref. a corte de pelo al cepillo. —*s.* 1. hombre o muchacho rudo. 2. **B.,** nombre familiar de hombre o muchacho. 3. (jer.) lesbiana que hace el papel de hombre.

butcher ['bʊtʃər, B -ə] *s.* 1. carnicero (oficio). 2. hombre sanguinario. 3. chapucero. 4. **b.'s,** carnicería (tienda); **the b., the baker, the candlestick-maker,** toda clase de personas, cualquier ciudadano. —*v.t.* 1. matar (reses). 2. asesinar sanguinariamente. 3. (fig.) chapucear, estropear, ej., *he butchered the part,* destrozó el papel (actor, en una obra de teatro, etc.).

butcher-bird [-ˌbərd, B -ˌbəd] *s.* (orn.) alcaudón, galdón, (pájaro) verdugo, desollador.

butcher's broom, (bot.) rusco, brusco, jusbarba.

butcher's shop, carnicería (tienda).

butchery ['bʊtʃərɪ] *s.* 1. oficio de carnicero. 2. (fig.) carnicería, matanza. 3. matadero. 4. (fig.) estropeo, chapucería.

butene ['bjuˌtin] *s.* (quím.) buteno, butileno.

buteonine [bju'tiəˌnaɪn] *a., s.* (orn.) buteonina (ave).

butler ['bʌtlər, B -lə] *s.* mayordomo, despensero.

butler's pantry, cuarto de servicio de mesa (entre el comedor y la cocina).

butomaceous [ˌbjutə'meɪʃəs] *a.* (bot.) butomáceo, butomeo.

butt [bʌt] *s.* 1. mango, cabo, extremo más ancho; mocho (de un instrumento o utensilio). 2. culata (de fusil o revólver). 3. tocón (de un árbol). 4. colilla o punta (de cigarro o cigarrillo). 5. blanco; (fig.) blanco de burlas, bromas, insultos. 6. parabalas (detrás del blanco en el campo de tiro). 7. topetazo; empujón, embestida. 8. pipa, barrica, tonel. 9. bisagra. —*v.t.* 1. topetar, topar; embestir, lanzarse contra (esp. de cabeza). 2. empalmar, juntar a tope. —*v.i.* dar topetadas; **b. against** o **upon,** colindar o empalmar con; **b. in,** (fig.) entremeterse.

butte [bjut] *s.* (E.U.) otero, terromontero, montecillo aislado.

butt-end ['bʌt'ɛnd] *s.* remanente; mocho, tope.

butter ['bʌtər, B -ə] *s.* 1. mantequilla, manteca de vaca. 2. mantequilla (vegetal), pasta, ej., *peanut b.,* mantequilla de maní, *apple b.,* pasta de manzana. 3. (fig., fam.) zalamería, lisonjas. 4. **to look as though b. would not melt in one's mouth,** hacerse la mosquita muerta. —*v.t.* untar con mantequilla; **b. up,** (fig., fam.) lisonjear, adular.

butter bean, habichuela verde, judía, alubia, frijol; (S. de E.U.) haba.

buttercup [-ˌkʌp] *s.* (bot.) ranúnculo, botón de oro, hierba belida.

butterfat [-ˌfæt] *s.* grasa de la leche.

butterfingers [-ˌfɪŋgərz, B -gəz] *s. pl.* (*sing. o pl. en const.*) descuidado, torpe de manos (que deja caer las cosas).

butterfish [-ˌfɪʃ] *s.* (ict.) pampanito; blenio.

butterfly [-ˌflaɪ] *s.* 1. (ento.) mariposa. 2. (fig.) calavera, persona veleidosa. 3. (*pl.*) (fam.) mareo, náuseas.

butterfly bush, (bot.) mariposa, budleya.

butterfly fish, (ict.) budión; mariposa.

butterfly swimming stroke, estilo mariposa.

butterfly valve, (mec.) válvula de mariposa, válvula pivotada, válvula de estrangulación.

butterfly weed, (bot.) vencetósigo; seda vegetal.

butteris ['bʌtərəs] *s.* pujavante, instrumento que usa el herrero para rebajar el casco a las caballerías.

buttermilk [-ərˌmɪlk, B -əˌ-] *s.* suero de la leche, leche cortada; leche de manteca.

butternut [-ˌnʌt] *s.* 1. nuez de Cuba. 2. (bot.) nogal ceniciento. 3. (fam.) soldado confederado; partidario de los confederados (durante la Guerra Civil de E.U.).

butterscotch [-ˌskɑtʃ, B -ˌskɔtʃ] *s.* caramelo (hecho de azúcar y mantequilla). —*a.* de (sabor) caramelo.

buttery ['bʌtərɪ] *a.* 1. mantecoso. 2. (fam.) lisonjero, adulador, zalamero. —*s.* 1. despensa, bodega. 2. (G.B.) (en algunas universidades) lugar donde se venden refrescos a los estudiantes.

butt gage, (carp.) gramil para bisagras.

butt hinge, bisagra plana.

butt joint, junta de cubrejunta, empalme o junta de tope, empate de tope (en pilotes).

buttock ['bʌtək] *s.* 1. (*u. gen. en pl.*) nalga, trasero. 2. anca (de animales), grupa (del caballo). 3. (mar.) cucharro de popa, anca.

button ['bʌtən] *s.* 1. botón. 2. botón (de flor), capullo. 3. tirador (de puerta), perilla (ej., del timbre). 4. glóbulo de metal (que queda después de soldar). 5. tope o botón (en la punta del florete). 6. (jer. boxeo) punta de la barbilla. 7. **a b. short,** (fam.) de mentalidad pobre, mentecato; **on the b.,** (jer.) perfecto, correcto, acertado; exactamente, puntualmente; **to take by the b.,** detener para conversar. —*v.t.* 1. abotonar. 2. poner botones en. 3. **b. up one's lip,** (jer.) callarse la boca. —*v.i.* abotonarse; **b. up,** (jer.) callarse.

buttonhole [-ˌhoʊl] *s.* 1. ojal, presilla de botón. 2. flor (que se lleva) en el ojal de la solapa. 3. (fam. G.B.) boca pequeña. —*v.t.* 1. hacer ojales o presillas en; bordar con punto de ojal. 2. (fig.) detener y retener a alguien para conversar.

buttonhole stitch, (cost.) punto de ojal.

buttonhook [-ˌhʊk] *s.* abotonador, abrochador.

buttons ['bʌtənz] *s. pl.* (pr. G.B.) botones, paje de librea, lacayo.

buttress ['bʌtrəs] *s.* 1. (arq.) contrafuerte, estribo, machón, botarel. 2. puntal, apoyo, refuerzo, sostén. 3. (geog.) estribación, estribo (de un

cerro o montaña). —*v.t.* apuntalar, sostener, apoyar.
buttress thread, (mec.) rosca trapezoidal.
butt shaft, flecha sin punta, flecha roma (usada en el deporte de tiro de arco).
buttstock [-ˌstɑk, B -ˌstɔk] *s.* culata (de arma de fuego).
butt weld, soldadura a tope.
butyl ['bjutəl] *s.* (quím.) butilo.
butylene [-ˌin] *s.* (quím.) butileno.
butyraceous [ˌbjutə'reɪʃəs] *a.* butiráceo, mantecoso.
butyral ['bjutəˌræl] *s.* (quím.) butiral.
butyrate [-ˌreɪt] *s.* (quím.) butirato.
butyric acid [bju'tɪrɪk] (quím.) ácido butírico.
butyrin ['bjutərən] *s.* (quím.) butirina.
butyrometer [ˌbjutə'rɑmətər, B -'rɔmɪtə] *s.* butirómetro, medidor de la grasa de leche.
buxaceous [bʌk'seɪʃəs] *a.* (bot.) buxáceo.
buxom ['bʌksəm] *s.* persona rolliza o de proporciones voluminosas.
buy [baɪ] *v.t.* (*pret., p.p.* BOUGHT [bɔt]; *p.pr.*BUYING) 1. comprar. 2. (jer.) creer en (algo), aceptar (algo) como cierto. 3. **b. off,** dar dinero (a alguien) para librarse de él; (bridge) rescatar (un contrato); **b. out,** comprar la parte de (un socio, etc.); **b. over,** sobornar; **b. up,** acaparar; **I'll b. it,** (fam.) me doy por vencido, no lo sé (en respuesta a una pregunta o acertijo). —*v.i.* hacer compras; **b. into,** comprar acciones en (una compañía, etc.). —*s.* 1. compra. 2. ganga, buena compra.
buyer ['baɪər, B -ə] *s.* comprador; agente comprador.
buyers' market, (econ.) mercado abundante en mercancías a bajo precio.
buzz [bʌz] *s.* 1. zumbido. 2. susurro; cuchicheo. 3. rumor. 4. (jer.) llamada (telefónica). 5. (jer.) beso. —*v.i.* 1. zumbar. 2. susurrar, cuchichear. 3. llenarse de murmullos (un local, lugar, etc.). 4. **b. about,** ajetrearse; **b. off,** (jer.) largarse. —*v.t.* 1. murmurar al oído. 2. llamar o señalar con timbre o zumbador. 3. volar (un avión) muy cerca de (tropas, muchedumbre, etc.). 4. (dial. G.B.) apurar hasta la última gota (botella de vino, etc.).
buzzard ['bʌzərd, B -əd] *s.* 1. (orn.) buitre, milano, busardo, gallinazo, aura, alfaneque. 2. (fig.) buitre (persona vil).
buzz bomb, (mil.) bomba voladora.
buzzer ['bʌzər, B -ə] *s.* zumbador; timbre eléctrico.
buzzing [-ɪŋ] *s.* zumbido (en los oídos, etc.). —*a.* zumbador.
buzz planer, (maq.) juntera, cepilladora rotatoria de eje vertical.
buzz saw, sierra circular.
buzz word, palabra de moda.
B.W.I. 1. *abrev. de* **British West Indies,** Indias Occidentales Británicas. 2. **b.w.i., bee wee,** (fam.) unidad monetaria de dichas islas.
by [baɪ] *prep.* 1. (indicando tiempo o duración) por, de, ej., *by day,* por el día, de día, *by night,* por la noche, de noche, *by the hour,* por hora. 2. (indicando agente, instrumento o causa) por, a, ej., *by fire,* por el fuego, a fuego, *by machine,* a máquina, *by order of,* por orden de, *done by him,* hecho por él. 3. (indicando lugar o dirección) por, junto a, cerca de; hacia, ej., *by land and sea,* por tierra y por mar, *by the sea,* junto al mar, cerca del mar, *North by West,* hacia el Noroeste. 4. (indicando modo, medida o cantidad) por, a, ej., *by lamplight,* a la luz de la lámpara, *by chance,* por casualidad, *by nature,* por naturaleza, *by hundreds,* por centenares, *by a yard,* por una yarda, *little by little,* poco a poco. 5. (indicando límite de tiempo) para, ej., *by six o'clock,* para las seis, *by then,* para entonces, *by tomorrow,* (para) mañana. 6. (indicando origen) de, ej., *English by blood,* de sangre inglesa, *he had three children by his first wife,* tuvo tres hijos de su primera esposa. 7. (mat.) por; entre, ej., *multiply six by two,* multiplicar seis por dos; *divide six by two,* dividir seis entre dos. 8. **by all means,** de todos modos; **by appearances,** por las apariencias; **by degrees,** gradualmente; **by far,** con mucho; **by God!** ¡por Dios!; **by heart,** de memoria; **by itself,** por sí solo, de por sí; **by means of,** mediante; **by no means,** de ningún modo; **by now,** ahora, a esta hora, ya; **by oneself,** solo, de por sí; **by rail,** por ferrocarril; **by rights,** de justicia; **by the by,** de paso, a propósito; **by the dozen,** por docenas; **by the light of,** (lit. y fig.) a la luz de; **by the rules,** según las reglas; **by the way,** de paso, a propósito, entre paréntesis, incidentalmente; **by this time,** a esta hora; **by train,** en tren; **day by day,** día por día, día tras día; **to be known by the name of,** ser conocido por el nombre de; **to begin** (o **end**) **by (doing),** empezar (o terminar) con (hacer); **to go by,** guiarse por, regirse por; **to know by name,** conocer de nombre; **to stand by (someone),** ser fiel a, ayudar, defender, estar de parte de (alguien); **what do you mean by that?** ¿qué quiere decir Ud. con eso? —*adv.* 1. cerca, al lado. 2. aparte, a un lado. 3. **by and by,** poco a poco; **by and large,** de una manera general, en conjunto; **close by,** por aquí (allí) cerca; **to go by,** pasar (de largo); **to put by,** poner a un lado; poner aparte, ahorrar; **to stop by,** hacer una visita.
by-and-by [ˌbaɪən'baɪ] *s.* ocasión futura; con el tiempo, a la larga.
by-by, bye-bye ['baɪ'baɪ] *s.* (fam.) hasta luego, adiós.
bye [baɪ] *s.* 1. (dep.) condición del jugador (o equipo) que pasa a la siguiente rueda sin tener que jugar. 2. (golf) hoyo(s) que se queda(n) sin jugar al terminar el partido. 3. (criquet) tanto marcado cuando no se golpea la pelota lanzada.
by-election, bye-election ['baɪəˌlɛkʃən] *s.* (G.B.) eleccion complementaria (de diputado).
Byelorussian [ˌbjɛlə'rʌʃən] *a., s.* bielorruso, ruso blanco.
bygone ['baɪˌgɔn, -ˌgɑn, B -ˌgɔn] *a.* pasado, de otro tiempo, antiguo. —*s.* algo pasado u olvidado; (*pl.*) el pasado, las ofensas pasadas; **let bygones be bygones,** lo pasado, olvidado (o pasado); echar pelillos a la mar.
by-law, bye-law [-ˌlɔ] *s.* estatuto; regla, reglamento interno (de un club, una empresa pública o privada).
by-line [-ˌlaɪn] *s.* nombre del autor (que encabeza un artículo o crónica).
byname [-ˌneɪm] *s.* apodo, sobrenombre.
bypass [-ˌpæs, B -ˌpɑs] *s.* 1. vía de circunvalación. 2. (mec.) paso, desvío, derivación, tubo de paso, desagüe secundario. 3. (elec.) derivación. —*v.t.* 1. evitar, pasar de lado. 2. (fig.) pasar por alto. 3. desviar.
bypath [-ˌpæθ, B -ˌpɑθ] *s.* desvío, camino privado; (lit. y fig.) camino apartado, senda.
byplay [-ˌpleɪ] *s.* aparte (en una conversación); (teat.) escena muda, juego escénico.
by-product [-ˌprɑdəkt, B -ˌprɔd-] *s.* producto secundario, subproducto, residuo, derivado; (fig.) secuela, consecuencia.
byre [baɪr, B 'baɪə] *s.* establo (de vacas).
byroad ['baɪˌroʊd] *s.* camino apartado; atajo, andurrial.
Byronic [baɪ'rɑnɪk, B -'rɔn-] *a.* byroniano, característico de lord Byron.
byssus ['bɪsəs] *s.* 1. (zool.) biso. 2. (hist.) biso (tela fina).
bystander ['baɪˌstændər, B -də] *s.* circunstante, espectador.
bystreet [-ˌstrit] *s.* callejuela, calle desviada.
byway [-ˌweɪ] *s.* desvío, camino apartado.
byword [-ˌwɜrd, B -ˌwɜd] *s.* 1. proverbio, refrán. 2. prototipo (gen. de algo malo), ej., *a b. for iniquity,* el prototipo de la iniquidad. 3. objeto de escarnio. 4. sobrenombre (esp. de desprecio). 5. palabra o expresión favorita (de alguien).
Byzantine ['bɪzənˌtin, bə'zæn-, B bɪ'zænˌtaɪn] *a.* bizantino (arte, pintura, arquitectura, etc.). —*s.* bizantino, natural de Bizancio.
Byzantium [bɪ'zænʃɪəm, B -tɪəm] *s.* Bizancio.

C

C [si] *s.* 1. c, tercera letra del alfabeto inglés. 2. (mús.) do. 3. (jer.) cien dólares, billete de cien dólares. 4. (jer.) cocaína.
C. *abrev. de 1.* **cent,** céntimo, centavo (ctvo.). 2. **century,** siglo.
C *símb. de* **carbón,** carbono (C).
c. *abrev. de* **centigrade,** centígrado (C).
ca. *abrev. de* **circa,** alrededor de (época).
C.A. *abrev. de* **Central America,** Centro-américa.
Ca *símb. de* **calcium,** calcio (Ca).
Caaba, *var. de* **Kaaba.**
cab [kæb] *s.* 1. taxi, taxímetro, auto de alquiler. 2. caseta o cabina (del maquinista o fogonero en la locomotora; del conductor en el camión y la grúa). 3. cabriolé.
cabal [kə'bæl] *s.* 1. cábala, intriga, trato secreto. 2. camarilla, junta de intrigantes, facción, bandería. —*v.i.* (*pret., p.p.* CABALLED; *p.pr.* CABALLING) integrar una facción, formar una camarilla; maquinar.
cabala ['kæbələ, B kə'bɑlə] *s.* (hist.) cábala (interpretación mística de las Escrituras); adivinación, doctrina esotérica, ocultismo.
cabalist [-ləst] *s.* cabalista.
cabalistic [ˌkæbə'lɪstɪk] *a.* cabalístico, oculto, misterioso.
cabaret [ˌkæbə'reɪ] *s.* cabaret, café cantante, centro nocturno.
cabbage ['kæbɪdʒ] *s.* 1. (bot.) col, repollo. 2. yema de palmito. 3. (jer.) billetes de banco, dinero de papel. —*v.i.* formar una cabeza como la del repollo, repollar.
cabbage butterfly, mariposa de la col.
cabbage palm, (bot.) palmito.
cabby, cabbie ['kæbɪ] *s.* (fam.) chófer, chofer (Am.), taxista.
cabdriver ['kæbˌdraɪvər, B -ə] *s.* taxista, cochero.
caber ['kɑbər, B 'keɪbə] *s.* tronco de pino que se lanza en un deporte escocés.
cabin ['kæbən] *s.* 1. cabaña, choza. 2. (mar.) camarote, cámara. 3. cabina (de avión, camión, etc.). —*v.i.* vivir en una cabaña; habitar un camarote.
cabin boy, (mar.) camarero de a bordo; grumete.
cabin class, (mar.) pasaje de segunda clase.
cabin cruiser, pequeño yate de motor con camarote.
cabinet ['kæbənət] *s.* 1. armario, cómoda. 2. vitrina, escaparate. 3. gabinete, consejo de ministros. —*a.* 1. de gabinete, ministerial. 2. de ebanistería (madera).
cabinet council, consejo de ministros.
cabinet crisis, crisis ministerial.
cabinetmaker [-ˌmeɪkər, B -ə] *s.* 1. ebanista. 2. (irón. G.B.) presidente designado del consejo de ministros.
cabinetwork [-ˌwɜrk, B -ˌwɜk] *s.* ebanistería, marquetería.
cable ['keɪbəl] *s.* 1. cable, maroma. 2. cablegrama, cable. 3. (mar.) cable, calabrote; cable de cadena. 4. (elec.) cable eléctrico; cable submarino. —*v.t.* 1. cablegrafiar, enviar (un telegrama) por cable. 2. amarrar con cable. 3. (mar.) corchar.
cable address, direccíon cablegráfica.
cable car, 1. vagón funicular; coche aéreo, telecabina (de teleférico). 2. tranvía tirado por cable.
cablecast ['keɪblkæst] *s.* emisión de televisión por cable. —*v.t.* emitir por cable.
cable chain, (mar.) cable de cadena.
cablegram [-ˌgræm] *s.* cablegrama.
cable-laid [-'leɪd] *a.* acalabrotado, corchado (cable, cuerda).
cable railway, funicular.
cablese ['keɪbəˌliz, -ˌlis] *s.* (jer.) lenguaje cablegráfico, en clave o muy abreviado.
cable ship, buque cablero (el que tiende el cable submarino).
cable stitch, punto de trenza, ochos, trenzas.
cablet ['keɪblət] *s.* (mar.) calabrote de menos de diez pulgadas de circunferencia, estacha.
cable tape, (elec.) cinta aisladora.
cable television, televisión por cable, televisión.
cableway ['keɪbəlˌweɪ] *s.* cable transportador, teleférico, funicular aéro.
cabman ['kæbmən] *s.* cochero, taxista.
cabob [kə'bɑb, B -'bɔb] *s.* trocito de carne sazonado y asado en espetones.
cabochon ['kæbəˌʃɑn, B -ˌʃɔn] *s.* (joy.) cabujón, piedra preciosa, pulida sin tallar.
caboodle [kə'budəl] *s.* (jer.) montón, cantidad, conjunto; **the whole c.,** todo el conjunto, el montón entero (cosas); toda la banda (personas).
caboose [kə'bus] *s.* **1.** (f.c., E.U.) furgón de cola. 2. (mar.) cocina, fogón (en la cubierta del barco).
cabotage ['kæbəˌtɑʒ] *s.* (mar.) cabotaje.
cabretta [kə'brɛtə] *s.* piel cabritilla.
cabrilla [kə'brijə, B -'brɪlə] *s.* (ict.) cabrilla.
cabriole ['kæbrɪˌoʊl] *s.* 1. cabriola, voltereta, salto ligero. 2. pata curvada y ornamentada (de muebles antiguos).
cabriolet [ˌkæbrɪə'leɪ] *s.* 1. automóvil descapotable. 2. cabriolé, especie de birlocho.
cabstand ['kæbˌstænd] *s.* estación o parada de taxis.
cacao [kə'kaʊ, -'keɪoʊ, B -'kɑoʊ] *s.* (bot.) cacao (árbol o semilla).
cachalot ['kæʃəˌlɑt, -ˌloʊ, B -ˌlɔt] *s.* (zool.) cachalote.
cache [kæʃ] *s.* 1. escondrijo, escondite, hueco. 2. provisiones escondidas; reserva secreta (de armas, municiones, dinero, etc.). —*v.t.* ocultar o guardar en un escondrijo.
cachectic [kæ'kɛktɪk] *a.* (med.) caquéctico.
cachet [kæ'ʃeɪ, B 'kæʃeɪ] *s.* 1. sello distintivo, sello aprobatorio. 2. carácter o cualidad peculiar; prestigio, marca de distinción. 3. (farm.) cápsula. 4. (filat.) sello conmemorativo.
cachexia [kæ'kɛksɪə] *s.* (med.) caquexia.
cachinnate ['kækəˌneɪt] *v.i.* reír de buena gana.
cachinnation [ˌkækə'neɪʃən] *s.* carcajada, risa desenfrenada.
cachou [kæ'ʃu, 'kæʃu] *s.* 1. cato, cachú, materia aromática extraída de árboles orientales. 2. pastilla de cachú (para perfumar el aliento).
cacique [kə'sik] *s.* 1. cacique (jefe indio). 2. cacique, jefe político (de un grupo, comunidad, etc.). 3. (orn.) oropéndola tropical, cacique.
caciquism [-ˌɪzəm] *s.* caciquismo.
cackle ['kækəl] *s.* 1. cacareo, cloqueo. 2. risa entrecortada o temblorosa, risa senil. 3. cháchara. —*v.i.* 1. cacarear, cloquear. 2. reír como los ancianos. 3. chacharear, parlotear.
cacochymia [ˌkækoʊ'kɪmɪə] **cacochymy** ['kækoʊˌkɪmɪ] *s.* (med.) cacoquimia.
cacodyl ['kækəˌdɪl, B -ˌdaɪl] *s.* (quím.) cacodilo.
cacodylic [ˌkækə'dɪlɪk] *s.* (quím.) cacodílico.
cacoethes [ˌkækoʊ'iθiz] *s.* manía, deseo insaciable (de hacer algo).
cacogenesis [ˌkækə'dʒɛnəsəs] *s.* (med.) cacogénesis.
cacogenics [-'dʒɛnɪks] *s. pl.* (*sing. en const.*) 1. (biol.) estudio de la cacogenesia. 2. (med.) cacogénica.
cacography [kæ'kɑgrəfɪ, B -'kɔg-] *s.* cacografía, mala ortografía.
cacomistle ['kækəˌmɪsəl] *s.* (zool.) basáride.
cacophonous [kæ'kɑfənəs, B -'kɔf-] *a.* cacofónico.
cacophony [-ənɪ] *s.* 1. (fon.) cacofonía, vicio del lenguaje. 2. (mús.) discordancia.
cactaceous [kæk'teɪʃəs] *a.* (bot.) cactáceo, cácteo.
cactus ['kæktəs] *s.* (*pl.* CACTI [-taɪ]) (bot.) cacto.
cacuminal [kæ'kjumənəl] *a.* (fon.) cacuminal.
cad [kæd] *s.* sinvergüenza, pillo.
cadastral [kə'dæstrəl] *a.* (top.) catastral.
cadastre [-tər, B -tə] *s.* (top.) catastro.
cadaver [kə'dævər, B -'deɪvə] *s.* cadáver.
cadaveric [-'dævərɪk] *a.* (med., fisiol.) cadavérico.
cadaverous [-ərəs] *a.* cadavérico, pálido, ojeroso, macilento.
caddie ['kædɪ] *s.* 1. (golf) ayudante (que lleva los palos del jugador), portador de palos. 2. carrito (para transportar objetos).
caddis ['kædəs] *s.* hilado de estambre; cinta de estambre.
caddis fly, (ento.) frigánea, frígano.
caddish ['kædɪʃ] *a.* propio de un pillo.
caddisworm ['kædəsˌwɜrm, B -ˌwɜm] *s.* (ento.) larva del frígano.
caddy ['kædɪ] *s.* cajita, lata o bote pequeño (esp. para guardar té).
caddy *var. de* **caddie.**
cade [keɪd] *a.* criado sin madre (díc. de un animal). —*s.* (bot.) cada, enebro.
cadence [ˌkeɪdəns] *s.* 1. cadencia, ritmo, modulación. 2. (mús.) cadencia. 3. (mil.) marcha al paso.
cadent [-ənt] *a.* cadencioso.
cadenza [kə'dɛnzə] *s.* (mús.) cadencia.
cadet [kə'dɛt] *s.* 1. (mil.) cadete. 2. hijo o hermano menor. 3. (jer.) alcahuete.
cadge [kædʒ] *v.i.* vivir de gorra, gorrear. —*v.t.* pedir, mendigar.
cadger ['kædʒər, B -ə] *s.* sablista, gorrón.
cadi ['kɑdɪ, 'keɪ-] *s.* cadí, juez (en los países musulmanes).
Cadmean [kæd'miən] *a.* cadmeo (relativo a una victoria lograda a costa del propio vencedor).

cadmium ['kædmɪəm] *s.* (quím.) cadmio.
cadre ['kædrɪ, B 'kɑdə] *s.* 1. cuadro, armazón. 2. (mil.) cuadro, conjunto de jefes.
caduceus [kə'dusɪəs, B -'dju-] *s.* caduceo, la varilla alada de Hermes y Mercurio, símbolo del comercio y la medicina.
caducity [kə'dusətɪ, B -'dju-] *s.* 1. caduquez, transitoriedad. 2. senilidad, vejez. 3. (der.) caducidad.
caducous [-'dukəs, B -'dju-] *a.* 1. caduco, perecedero, transitorio. 2. (bot.) caducífloro.
caecal, caecum, *vars. de* **cecal, cecum.**
Caelum ['siləm] *s.* (astr.) Buril (constelación austral).
Caesar ['sizər, B -zə] *s.* 1. César (título dado a los emperadores romanos). 2. dictador, autócrata.
Caesarea [ˌsizə'riə] *s.* Cesarea, antigua ciudad de Palestina, ahora centro de interés turístico en Israel.
Caesarean, Caesarian, *vars. de* **Cesarean, Cesarian.**
Caesarism ['sizəˌrɪzəm] *s.* cesarismo, autocracia, dictadura.
caesium, *var. de* **cesium.**
caespitose ['sɛspəˌtoʊs] *a.* (bot.) cespitoso.
caesura [sɪ'ʒʊrə, B -'zjʊərə] *s.* (*pl.* CAESURAS o CAESURAE [-ri]) cesura, corte o pausa en un verso.
C.A.F. *abrev. de* **cost and freight,** costo y flete (C y F).
café, cafe [kæ'feɪ, kə-, B 'kæfeɪ, -fɪ] *s.* 1. café, cafetería, restaurante. 2. club nocturno.
café au lait [-oʊ'leɪ] (fr.) café con leche.
café chantant [-'ʃɑnˌtɑn, B -ˌtɑŋ] (fr.) café cantante.
café society, (E.U.) la sociedad ociosa y elegante que frecuentaba lugares de moda durante los años 30.
cafeteria [kæfə'tɪrɪə, B -'tɪər-] *s.* restaurante autoservicio, self-service; *in a school or hospital)* cafeteria, cantina.
caffeine [kæ'fin, 'kæfɪən, B 'kæˌfin] *s.* cafeína.
caftan [kæf'tæn] *s.* caftán (túnica larga y suelta que se usa en los países árabes).
cage [keɪdʒ] *s.* 1. jaula. 2. (dep.) meta, portería, arco (en hockey); canasta, cesto (en baloncesto). —*v.t.* 1. enjaular. 2. (dep.) encestar (la pelota).
cageling ['keɪdʒlɪŋ] *s.* pájaro enjaulado.
cagey, cagy [-ɪ] *a.* (fam.) evasivo, cauteloso, astuto.
cageyness, caginess [-nəs] *s.* (fam.) cautela, astucia.
cahier [kɑ'jeɪ] *s.* (fr.) 1. cuaderno. 2. memorándum, informe.
cahoots [kə'huts] *s.* (fam.) sociedad, confabulación; **to be in c. with,** estar confabulado con.
Caiaphas ['keɪəfəs, B 'kaɪəfæs] *s.* (bíbl.) Caifás.
caiman, *var. de* **cayman.**
Cain [keɪn] *s.* Cáin; (fig.) asesino, fratricida; **to raise C.,** armar un escándalo.
caïque [kɑ'ik] *s.* (mar.) caique.
cairn [kɛrn, B kɛən] *s.* montón de piedras para señal o hito.
cairngorm ['kærnˌgɔrm, 'kɛrn-, B 'kɛənˌ-gɔm] *s.* (min.) cuarzo ahumado.
Cairn terrier, terrier pequeño de Escocia.
Cairo ['kaɪroʊ] *s.* El Cairo, capital de la República Árabe Unida (Egipto).
caisson ['keɪˌsɑn, -sən, B kə'sun] *s.* 1. (mil.) cajón, furgón de municiones. 2. (ing.) cajón hidráulico (para trabajar bajo el agua). 3. (mar.) artesón, compuerta flotante.
caisson disease, (med.) aeroembolia, parálisis de los buzos.
caitiff ['keɪtəf] *s., a.* (poét., ant.) vil, miserable; cobarde.
cajeput ['kædʒəpət, -ˌpʊt] *s.* (bot.) cayeputi, árbol de la India.
cajole [kə'dʒoʊl] *v.t.* engatusar, halagar, lisonjear; **c. someone into (doing something),** persuadir a alguien con lisonjas para que (haga algo); **c. (something) out of someone,** conseguir (algo) de alguien mediante lisonjas.
cajolery [-ərɪ] *s.* engatusamiento, lisonja, camelo.
cake [keɪk] *s.* 1. pastel, torta, bizcocho, bollo. 2. pan (de jabón, cera, etc.). 3. capa, costra. 4. **a piece of c.,** (fam.) una delicia; algo fácil; una ganga; **it takes the c.,** (fam.) es el colmo; **you cannot have your cake and eat it too,** no se puede oír misa y andar en la procesión. —*v.i.* incrustrarse, coagularse, cuajarse, aterronarse.
cakewalk ['keɪkˌwɔk] *s.* (E.U.) baile de origen negro.
Cal. *abrev. de* **California,** California (E.U.).
calaba balsam [kə'lɑbə-] *s.* bálsamo de calaba, bálsamo de María.
Calabar bean [ˌkælə'bɑr-, B -'bɑ-] semilla de Calabar (venenosa, usada por brujos africanos).
calabash ['kæləˌbæʃ] *s.* 1. (bot.) calabacera, calabaza. 2. calabaza (el fruto, seco y vacío que se utiliza como vasija o estuche). 3. (mús.) güiro.
calabash tree, (bot.) calabacero, totumo, güira (Am.).
calaboose ['kæləˌbus] *s.* (fam.) chirona, calabozo, cárcel; cana (Am.).
Calabrian [kə'leɪbrɪən, -'lɑb-, B -'læb-] *a., s.* calabrés.
calabur tree ['kæləˌbʊr-, B -ˌbʊə] (bot.) carraspero, capulí (Am.).
caladium [kə'leɪdɪəm] *s.* (bot.) caladio, papagayo.
calamanco [ˌkælə'mæŋkoʊ] *s.* (tej.) calamaco.
calamary ['kæləˌmɛrɪ B -mərɪ] **calamar** [-ˌmɑr, B -ˌmɑ] *s.* (zool.) calamar, chipirón.
calamine ['kæləˌmaɪn] *s.* (min.) calamina.
calamint ['kæləˌmɪnt] *s.* (bot.) calamento, calaminta.
calamistrum [ˌkælə'mɪstrəm] *s.* (*pl.* CALAMISTRA [-trə]) (arqueol.) calamistro.
calamite ['kæləˌmaɪt] *s.* (pal.) planta calamitea.
calamitous [kə'læmətəs] *a.* calamitoso, desastroso.
calamity [kə'læmətɪ] *s.* calamidad, desastre, desgracia.
calamondin [ˌkælə'mɑndən, B -'mɔn-] *s.* (bot.) calamondín, fruto cítrico de Filipinas.
calamus ['kæləməs] *s.* 1. (bot.) ácoro. 2. cálanis, cálamo aromático (raíz). 3. (zool.) cálamo, cañón de pluma.
calander [kə'lændər, B -də] *s.* (orn.) calandria, gulloría.
calando [kɑ'lɑndoʊ] *a.* (mús.) de ritmo y sonoridad decrecientes.
calash [kə'læʃ] *s.* 1. calesa, carretela. 2. capota o cubierta (de calesa). 3. antigua capota o bonete femenino.
calathos ['kæləˌθɑs, B -ˌθɔs] **calathus** [-θəs] *s.* (*pl.* CALATHI [-ˌθaɪ, -ˌθi]) (arqueol.) cálato.
calcaneal [kæl'keɪnɪəl] *a.* (anat.) calcáneo (hueso).
calcaneum [-nɪəm] *s.* (anat.) calcáneo, calcañar.
calcar ['kælˌkɑr, B -ˌkɑ] *s.* (*pl.* CALCARIA [kæl'kɛrɪə]) 1. (bot.) parte calcariforme. 2. (orn.) calcar.
calcareous [kæl'kɛrɪəs, B -'kɛər-] *a.* calcáreo, calizo.
calceiform ['kælsɪəˌfɔrm, B -ˌfɔm] *a.* (bot.) calceiforme.
calceolaria [ˌkælsɪə'lɛrɪə, B -'lɛərɪə] *s.* (bot.) calceolaria.
calceolate ['kælsɪəˌleɪt] *a.* calceiforme, formado como una zapatilla (como ciertas orquídeas).
Calchas ['kælkəs] *s.* (mitol.) Calcas, profeta y sabio griego.
calcic ['kælsɪk] *a.* (quím.) cálcico.
calciferous [kæl'sɪfərəs] *a.* calcífero.
calcification [ˌkælsəfə'keɪʃən] *s.* 1. calcificación, petrificación. 2. estructura calcificada.
calcifuge ['kælsəˌfjudʒ] *s.* (bot.) planta calcífuga.
calcify ['kælsəˌfaɪ] *v.t., v.i.* (*pret., p.p.* CALCIFIED; *p.pr.* CALCIFYING) calcificar (se); petrificar(se).
calcimeter [kæl'sɪmətər, B -tə] *s.* calcímetro.
calcimine ['kælsəˌmaɪn] *s.* jalbegue, lechada, pintura al agua. —*v.t.* enjalbegar, blanquear, dar lechada.
calcination [ˌkælsə'neɪʃən] *s.* calcinación, calcinamiento.
calcine [kæl'saɪn, B 'kælˌsaɪn] *v.t., v.i.* calcinar(se).
calcite ['kælˌsaɪt] *s.* (min.) calcita.
calcium ['kælsɪəm] *s.* (quím.) calcio.
calcium carbide, (quím.) carburo de calcio.
calcium carbonate, (quím.) carbonato de calcio o de cal.
calcium chloride, (quím.) cloruro cálcico o de calcio.
calcium hydroxite, (quím.) hidrato de calcio, hidróxido de cal.
calcium light, luz de calcio.
calcium phospate, (quím.) fosfato cálcico.
calc-sinter ['kælkˌsɪntər, B -tə] *s.* concreción calcárea (como la de estalactitas).
calcspar [-ˌspɑr, B -ˌspɑ] *s.* (min.) calcita, espato calizo.
calc-tufa [-ˌtufə B -ˌtjufə] **calc-tuff** [-ˌtʌf] *s.* toba calcárea.
calculable ['kælkjələbəl] *a.* calculable.
calculate ['kælkjəˌleɪt] *v.t.* 1. calcular, computar. 2. (fam. E.U.) creer, considerar, suponer. 3. **(to be) calculated to (do),** (estar) proyectado, designado o aprestado para (hacer). —*v.i.* 1. hacer cálculos. 2. **c. on,** contar con, fiarse de.
calculated [-əd] *a.* 1. calculado. 2. proyectado, planeado (para cumplir un propósito o función). 3. deliberado, intencional.
calculated bearing, (avia., top.) rumbo calculado.
calculating [-ɪŋ] *a.* 1. calculador. 2. prudente; interesado, egoísta.
calculating machine, máquina calculadora, calculadora.
calculation [ˌkælkjə'leɪʃən] *s.* 1. cálculo, cómputo. 2. prudencia, cuidado. 3. astucia, artificio.
calculator ['kæl-ˌleɪtər, B -tə] *s.* 1. calculador. 2. libro de cálculos. 3. máquina calculadora.
calculous ['kælkjələs] *a.* (med.) calculoso.
calculus [-ləs] *s.* (*pl.* CALCULI [-ˌlaɪ, -ˌli]) 1. med. cálculo, piedra. 2. (mat.) cálculo, ej., *differential c.,* cálculo diferencial, *integral c.,* cálculo integral.
Calcutta [kæl'kʌtə] *s.* Calcuta, ciudad de la India.
caldron ['kɔldrən] *s.* caldera, calderón.
calèche [kə'lɛʃ] *s.* calesa.
Caledonian [ˌkælə'doʊnɪən] *a., s.* caledonio (escocés).
calefacient [-'feɪʃənt] *a.* calefaciente. —*s.* (farm.) remedio calefaciente.
calefaction [-'fækʃən] *s.* calefacción, calentamiento.

calendar ['kæləndər, B -də] *s.* 1. calendario, almanaque. 2. orden del día; lista, horario. 3. (der.(tabla o lista (de causas). 4. santoral, lista de santos y mártires. 5. (G.B.) anuario o catálogo (de una universidad). —*v.t.* anotar o registrar en un calendario.
calendar day, día civil.
calendar year, año civil.
calender ['kæləndər, B -də] *s.* (mec.) calandria, máquina para satinar papel. —*v.t.* calandrar, satinar.
calends ['kæləndz] *s. pl.* (*sing. o pl. en const.*) calendas, primer día de cada mes en la antigua Roma.
calendula [kə'lɛndʒələ, B -djʊ-] *s.* (bot.) caléndula, maravilla.
calenture ['kælən,tʃʊr, B -,tjʊə] *s.* (med.) calentura.
calf [kæf, B kɑf] *s.* (*pl.* CALVES [kævz, B kɑvz]) 1. ternero, becerro; cría (de los bovinos y otros mamíferos grandes como el elefante, el hipopótamo, etc.). 2. piel o cuero de becerro. 3. (fam.) joven, tontuelo. 4. masa pequeña de hielo (desprendida de un ventisquero o témpano). 5. (anat.) pantorrilla. 6. **golden c.,** becerro de oro; **in** (o **with**) **c.,** preñada (vaca); **to kill the fatted c.,** preparar una fiesta de bienvenida; **to slip her c.,** abortar (vaca).
calf bone, (anat.) peroné.
calf love, amor pueril, enamoramiento de muchacho.
calfskin ['kæf,skɪn, B 'kɑf-] *s.* (piel de) becerro, becerrillo, piel de ternero.
calf wheel, malacate para tuberías; torno para herramientas.
Caliban ['kælə,bæn] *s.* Calibán, personaje grotesco de *La Tempestad,* obra de Shakespeare.
caliber, calibre ['kæləbər, B -bə] *s.* 1. calibre (de un proyectil, arma de fuego o tubo). 2. (fig.) calibre, capacidad, aptitud. 3. (fig.) calibre, importancia, calidad.
calibrate ['kælə,breɪt] *v.t.* 1. calibrar. 2. graduar, marcar los grados.
calibration [,kælə'breɪʃən] *s.* 1. calibración. 2. marca (de grado).
calices ['keɪlə,siz, 'kæl-] *pl. de* **calix.**
calicle, *var. de* **calycle.**
calico ['kælɪ,koʊ] *s.* 1. calicó; percal, cotonada, indiana. 2. (G.B.) tela de algodón blanca. 3. animal manchado con pintas. —*a.* 1. (hecho) de calicó, de percal. 2. manchado (animal).
calico bass, (ict.) variedad de róbalo.
calico bush, (bot.) calmia.
calico printing, (tej.) (proceso de) estampado en telas de algodón (esp. en calicó o indiana).
calif, califate, *vars. de* **caliph, caliphate.**
Calif. *abrev. de* **California,** California (E.U.).
California [,kælə'fɔrnjə, B -'fɔnjə] *s.* California, estado de los E.U.
Californian [,kælə'fɔrnjən, B -'fɔnjən] *a., s.* californiano.
California poppy [-njə-] *s.* (bot.) amapola de California, copa de oro.
californium [-nɪəm] *s.* (quím.) californio.
caliginous [kə'lɪdʒənəs] *a.* caliginoso, oscuro, nebuloso.
Caligula [kə'lɪgjələ] *s.* Calígula, emperador romano.
calipash ['kælə,pæʃ] *s.* sustancia gelatinosa y verde que tiene la tortuga bajo el carapacho (apreciada como manjar exquisito).
calipee [-,pi] *var. de* **calipash.**
caliper ['kæləpər, B -pə] *s.* calibrador. —*v.t.* calibrar.
caliper compass, calibrador, compás de calibres.
caliper gauge, calibrador fijo de espesor.
caliper square, escuadra ajustable; pie de rey.
caliph ['keɪləf, 'kæl-] *s.* califa, título de los príncipes sarracenos.
caliphate [-,eɪt, -ət] *s.* califato, jurisdicción del califa.
calisaya bark [,kælə'seɪə-] (farm.) calisaya, quina amarilla.
calisthenics, callisthenics [,kæləs'θɛnɪks] *s. pl.* (*sing. en const.*) calistenia.
calix ['keɪlɪks, 'kæl-] *s.* (*pl.* CALICES [-ə,siz]) 1. copa; (relig.) cáliz. 2. (bot.) *var. de* **calyx.**
calk, calker, *vars. de* **caulk, caulker.**
calk [kɔk] *s.* ramplón (para herradura). —*vt.* 1. poner ramplones en (la herradura). 2. herir con un ramplón. 3. calafatear.
call [kɔl] *v.i.* 1. dar voces; llamar; gritar. 2. hacer una visita, ir (o venir) a visitar. 3. hacer una llamada (telefónica). 4. reclamarse (las aves). 5. (mar.) hacer escala. 6. (bridge) declarar, licitar. 7. **c. after,** llamar a; **c. again,** venir otra vez (de visita o buscando a alguien); **c. at,** hacer una visita a, pasar por (la casa, oficina, etc. de alguien); (mar.) tocar en, hacer escala en (un puerto); **c. back,** volver a llamar (por teléfono); **c. for,** requerir, necesitar, ej., *this letter calls for a quick reply,* esta carta necesita una respuesta inmediata; pedir, demandar; ir (o venir) a buscar o recoger (a alguien); **c. on,** invocar, apelar a; visitar (a alguien); **c. out,** exclamar, soltar un grito; **c. to,** llamar, dar una voz a (uno); **c. upon,** dirigir una llamada a. —*v.t.* 1. llamar. 2. enunciar, proclamar (en alta voz). 3. convocar, llamar; (der.) emplazar. 4. llamar (por teléfono), telefonear. 5. ordenar, proclamar (huelga, pausa, descanso, etc.). 6. despertar, llamar. 7. reclamar (a aves). 8. considerar, juzgar. 9. (con *on*) censurar, responsabilizar, ej., *we could c. him on that,* podríamos censurarlo o responsabilizarlo por eso. 10. (com.) demandar el reembolso de (ej., un préstamo). 11. (bridge) invitar a jugar (cierto palo o naipe). 12. (póquer) pedir (a otro jugador) que exponga su mano (igualando su apuesta). 13. (dep.) suspender, dar por terminado (ej., un partido de béisbol). 14. **c. aside,** llamar aparte; **c. away,** llamar (a uno que está haciendo algo); **c. back,** regresar; volver a llamar (por teléfono); **c. down,** (fam. E.U.) regañar, reconvenir; **c. forth,** provocar, producir, originar; **c. in,** hacer entrar; llamar para consulta (a un médico, experto, etc.); (econ.) retirar de circulación (moneda); (com.) demandar el pago de (deuda, préstamo, etc.); **c. in question,** poner en tela de juicio; **c. into being,** crear; **c. into play,** (fig.) hacer entrar en juego; **c. it a day,** dar por terminadas las labores del día; **c. off,** hacer que dejen de molestar; terminar, suspender (investigación); dar por anulado (cita, conferencia, etc.); aplazar, dar por terminado (un juego); **c. one's own,** llamar suyo, disponer de, poseer; **c. oneself,** llamarse, titularse; **c. out,** llamar, pedir que salga; hacer entrar en acción (a guardias, bomberos, etc.), hacer uso de (ej., tropas para ayudar a las autoridades civiles); desafiar, retar (a duelo); llamar a la huelga (a obreros); **c. (somebody) names,** insultar (a alguien); **c. to account,** reprender, reprobar; **c. to mind,** evocar, traer a la memoria; **c. to order,** llamar al orden (al abrir la sesión); **c. to the bar,** recibir de abogado; **c. to the colors,** llamar al servicio militar; **c. together,** convocar, reunir; **c. up,** evocar, imaginar; llamar por teléfono; convocar (para servicio militar); **to be called (up) on,** corresponderle a (uno), tener la obligación de. —*s.* 1. llamada, llamado, exclamación. 2. llamado, llamamiento; invitación, instancia. 3. llamada telefónica. 4. visita (corta). 5. (mar., aer.) escala. 6. vocación (religiosa o profesional). 7. ululeo (de ciertas aves). 8. reclamo (para llamar a las aves). 9. toque (de corneta, tambor). 10. motivo, porqué, ej., *there's no c. for rejoicing,* no hay por qué (o no hay motivo para) regocijarse. 11. demanda, pedido; exigencia. 12. (bolsa) opción de compra. 13. (bridge) licitación, declaración. 14. **a close c.,** peligro que se evade por un tris; **on c.,** a la mano; (com.) a vista, a la demanda; **to pay a c.,** hacer una visita; **within c.,** al alcance de la voz.
calla ['kælə] *s.* (bot.) cala.
callable ['kɔləbəl] *a.* (com.) pagadero a la demanda.
calla lily, (bot.) cala, aro de Etiopía, lirio de agua.
call bell, timbre de llamada.
callboard ['kɔl,bɔrd, B -,bɔd] *s.* tablilla (de noticias, listas, etc.).
callboy [-,bɔɪ] *s.* 1. (teat.) traspunte. 2. paje, botones.
call-down [-,daʊn] *s.* (fam. E.U.) regaño, reprensión.
caller ['kɔlər, B - e] *s.* visita, visitante; llamador.
call girl, prostituta (que se puede citar por teléfono).
call house, casa de citas.
Callicrates [kə'lɪkrə,tiz] *s.* Calícrates, arquitecto y escultor griego.
calligrapher [kə'lɪgrəfər, B -fə] *s.* 1. calígrafo. 2. copiante, copista.
calligraphic [,kælə'græfɪk] *a.* caligráfico.
calligraphy [kə'lɪgrəfɪ] *s.* 1. caligrafía. 2. letra, escritura (de una persona).
calling ['kɔlɪŋ] *s.* 1. llamado, llamamiento. 2. vocación, ocupación, profesión. 3. celo (esp. de la gata).
calling card, tarjeta de visita.
calliope [kə'laɪəpɪ] *s.* 1. órgano de vapor (que se usaba en circos, ferias, barcos, etc.). 2. **C.,** (mitol.) Calíope, musa de la poesía épica.
calliopsis [,kælɪ'ɑpsəs, B -'ɔp-] *s.* (bot.) coreópsida.
callipers, *var. de* **calipers.**
callipygian [,kælə'pɪdʒɪən] *a.* bien proporcionado(da) de caderas.
Callisthenes [kə'lɪsθə,niz] *s.* Calístenes, cronista de Alejandro Magno.
Callisto [kə'lɪstoʊ] *s.* (astr., mitol.) Calisto.
call letters, (rad.) letras de identificación de una estación transmisora.
call loan, (com.) préstamo que deberá pagarse al presentarse la solicitud de reembolso.
call money, (com.) dinero prestado, pagadero al presentarse la solicitud de reembolso.
call number, cifra de clasificación (de un libro en una biblioteca).
call of the wild, atracción por la vida bucólica o silvestre.
callose ['kæl,oʊs] *s.* (bot.) calosa.
callosity [kæ'lɑsətɪ, kə-, B -'lɔs-] *s.* 1. callosidad. 2. (fig.) dureza, insensibilidad.
callous ['kæləs] *a.* 1. calloso, encallecido. 2. (fig.) duro, insensible.
callow ['kæloʊ] *a.* 1. implume. 2. (fig.) inexperto.
call rate, (com.) tipo de interés aplicado a préstamos a la vista.
call slip, papeleta de comprobante al portador.
call to arms, (mil.) llamada a las armas.
call-up ['kɔl,ʌp] *s.* (mil.) llamamiento al servicio activo.
callus ['kæləs] *s.* (med., bot.) callo.
calm [kɑm] *s.* 1. calma; quietud, serenidad, tranquilidad. 2. **dead c.,** (mar.) calma chicha, calma muerta. —*a.* calmado, quieto, tranquilo, sereno. —*v.t.* calmar. —*v.i.* calmarse, abonanzarse, apaciguarse, aplacarse (el viento, el genio, etc.); **c. down,** recobrar la calma, serenarse.

calmative [-ətɪv, 'kælm-] *a., s.* sedante, calmante.
calmness ['kɑmnəs] *s.* calma, tranquilidad.
calomel ['kæləməl, -ˌmɛl] *s.* (farm.) calomel, calomelanos.
caloric [kə'lɔrɪk] *s.* 1. calórico. —*a.* 1. referente al calor, térmico. 2. de calorías.
caloricity [ˌkælə'rɪsətɪ] *s.* (fisiol.) caloricidad.
calorie ['kælərɪ] *s.* (fís., quím.) caloría.
calorific [ˌkælə'rɪfɪk] *a.* calorífico.
calorification [kəˌlɔrəfɪ'keɪʃən] *s.* (fisiol.) calorificación.
calorimeter [ˌkælə'rɪmətər, B -tə] *s.* (fís.) calorímetro.
calorimetric [-rə'mɛtrɪk] *a.* (fís.) calorimétrico.
calorimetry [-'rɪmətrɪ] *s.* (fís.) calorimetría.
calory *var. de* **calorie.**
calotte [kə'lɑt, B -'lɔt] *s.* solideo; casquete de los eclesiásticos.
caloyer [kə'lɔɪər, 'kæləjər, B 'kæˌlɔɪə] *s.* caloguero, monje de la iglesia ortodoxa griega.
calpac, calpack ['kælˌpæk] *s.* bonete, gorro grande de zalea (usado por turcos y armenios).
caltrop ['kæltrəp] č ʎɿɥʳɑþ [-θrəp] *s.* 1. (bot.) abrojo, tríbulo. 2. (mil.) abrojo.
calumba [kə'lʌmbə] *s.* (bot.) colombo.
calumet ['kæljəˌmɛt, -mət] *s.* pipa ceremonial (de los indios norteamericanos), pipa de la paz.
calumniate [kə'lʌmnɪˌeɪt] *v.t.* calumniar, difamar.
calumniator [-ər, B -ə] *s.* calumniador.
calumniatory [-nɪəˌtɔrɪ, B -ətərɪ] *a.* calumnioso, difamatorio.
calumnious [-nɪəs] *a.* calumnioso.
calumny ['kæləmnɪ] *s.* calumnia, difamación.
calvados [ˌkælvə'dɔs, B 'kælvəˌdɔs] *s.* aguardiente de manzana.
Calvary ['kælvərɪ] *s.* 1. (bíbl.) Calvario, Vía Crucis. 2. (fig.) calvario (serie de adversidades).
calve [kæv, B kɑv] *v.i.* 1. parir la vaca. 2. separarse de un témpano (díc. de una masa de hielo).
calves, *pl. de* **calf.**
Calvin ['kælvən] *s.* Calvino, reformador religioso francés.
Calvinism [-ˌɪzəm] *s.* calvinismo.
Calvinist [-əst] *s., a.* calvinista.
calx [kælks] *s.* (*pl.* CALXES ['kælˌsiz] o CALCES) (quím.) escorias (de minerales o metales calcinados).
calyces, *pl. de* **calyx.**
calycine ['keɪləˌsaɪn, B 'kælə-] **calycinal** [kə'lɪsənəl] *a.* (bot.) calicino, calicinal.
calycle ['keɪlɪkəl, B 'kæl-] *s.* (bot., zool.) calículo.
calycular [kə'lɪkjələr, B -lə] *a.* (bot.) calicular.
calyculus [-ləs] *s.* (*pl.* CALYCULI [-ˌlaɪ, -ˌli]) (bot., anat., zool.) calículo.
calypso [kə'lɪpsoʊ] *s.* 1. (mús.) calipso, balada improvisada, típica de Trinidad. 2. (bot.) tipo de orquídea. 3. (mitol.) **C.,** Calipso.
calyx ['keɪlɪks, 'kæl-] *s.* (*pl.* CALYXES [-əˌsiz] o CALYCES [-əˌsiz]) 1. (bot., anat.) cáliz. 2. (mec.) corona dentada.
cam [kæm] *s.* (mec.) leva, levador, cama.
camaraderie [ˌkæmə'rædərɪ, ˌkɑmə'rɑd-, B ˌkæm-] *s.* camaradería, compañerismo.
camarilla [ˌkæmə'rɪlə] *s.* 1. camarilla; cábala, cuerpo de consejeros extraoficiales. 2. cámara pequeña.
camber ['kæmbər, B -bə] *s.* 1. comba, combadura. 2. curvatura, peralte, torsión, alabeo (de viga, cubierta, camino, etc.). 3. (aut.) inclinación (de ruedas delanteras). —*v.t., v.i.* combar(se), arquear(se).
cambist ['kæmbəst] *s.* (com.) cambista, banquero especialista en cambiar divisas.
cambium ['kæmbɪəm] *s.* (*pl.* CAMBIUMS O CAMBIA [-bɪə]) (bot.) cámbium, cambio.
Cambodia [kæm'boʊdɪə] *s.* Camboya.
Cambodian [-ɪən] *s.* 1. camboyano, natural de Camboya. 2. khmer, camboyano (lengua).
Cambrian ['kæmbrɪən] *s.* 1. cambriano. 2. (geol.) cámbrico, cambriano. —*a.* cámbrico, cambriano (perteneciente a Gales).
cambric ['keɪmbrɪk] *s.* (tej.) cambray, batista, holanda.
came [keɪm] *s.* engarce de plomo (en vidrieras). —*pret. de* **come.**
camel ['kæməl] *s.* 1. (zool.) camello. 2. (mar.) camello, dique flotante (esp. para poner a flote embarcaciones sumergidas).
cameleer [ˌkæmə'lɪr, B -'lɪə] *s.* camellero.
camel grass, (bot.) esquenanto, junco oloroso.
camellia [kə'miljə] *s.* (bot.) camelia.
camelopard [kə'mɛləˌpɑrd, B 'kæmɪləˌpɑd] *s.* 1. (zool.) camello pardal, jirafa. 2. (astr.) Camaleopardo (constelación).
camel's hair, pelo o lana de camello.
Camembert ['kæməmˌbɛr, B -ˌbɛə] *s.* Camembert (queso).
cameo ['kæmɪˌoʊ] *s.* (*pl.* CAMEOS) camafeo.
camera ['kæmərə] *s.* 1. (foto.) cámara de fotografiar; cámara oscura. 2. (der.) cámara del juez. 3. cámara apostólica. 4. **in c.,** (der.) en la cámara del juez; en privado.
cameralism [-ˌlɪzəm] *s.* (econ.) cameralismo (escuela económica).
camera lucida [-'lusədə] (ópt.) cámara lúcida, cámara clara.
cameraman [-ˌmæn, -mən] *s.* (cinem., t.v.) camarógrafo.
camera obscura [-əb'skjʊrə] (ópt.) cámara oscura.
camera stand, trípode o sostén para apoyar la cámara.
camion ['kæmɪən] *s.* (aut., mil.) camión.
camise [kə'miz, -'mis] *s.* camisa o túnica amplia y larga.
camisole ['kæməˌsoʊl] *s.* camisola, cubrecorsé, fustán (Am.).
camlet ['kæmlət] *s.* (tej.) camelote, rico tejido oriental que antiguamente se hacía con lana de camello.
camomile ['kæməˌmaɪl] *s.* (bot.) camomila, manzanilla.
Camorrist [kə'mɔrəst] *s.* "camorrista", miembro de la "Camorra" (antigua organización criminal napolitana).
camouflage ['kæməˌflɑʒ] *s.* 1. (mil.) camuflaje, enmascaramiento. 2. simulación, engaño, fingimiento. —*v.t.* 1. (mil.) camuflar, enmascarar. 2. fingir, simular, ocultar.
camp [kæmp] *s.* 1. campo (ej., de concentración); campamento. 2. (mil.) campamento. 3. (fig.) vida de cuartel, vida militar. 4. (fig.) campo, partido, grupo (de intereses o ideas comunes). —*v.i.* 1. acampar(se). 2. **c. out,** vivir en tiendas de campaña (en excursión, etc.). —*v.t.* acampar (tropas); acomodar.
camp [kæmp] *s.* 1. banalidad, superficialidad; afectación frívola. 2. cultura y manerismos de la juventud norteamericana que adopta lo más cursi del arte y la moda del período entre las dos guerras mundiales. 3. (G.B.) afeminado, amanerado.
campaign [kæm'peɪn] *s.* campaña (militar, de publicidad, política, de ventas, etc.). —*v.i.* 1. hacer una campaña (militar, de publicidad, etc.); hacer campaña (para). 2. servir en campaña.
campaign button, prendedor publicitario que llevan los partidarios de un candidato político durante la campaña electoral.
campaigner [-ər, B -ə] *s.* 1. luchador; partidario militante. 2. propagandista. 3. **old c.,** veterano.
campaign ribbon, (mil.) cinta de condecoración por servicio en campaña.
campaniform [kæm'pænəˌfɔrm, B -ˌfɔm] *a.* campaniforme.
campanile [ˌkæmpə'nilɪ] *s.* (arq.) campanario.
campanology [-'nɑlədʒɪ, B -'nɔl-] *s.* 1. campanología (arte de fundir y de tañer campanas). 2. estudio de las campanas.
campanula [kæm'pænjələ, B kəm-] *s.* (bot.) campánula, farolillo.
campanulaceous [-ˌpænjə'leɪʃəs] *a.* (bot.) campanuláceo.
campanulate [-'pænjələt, -ˌleɪt] *a.* (bot.) campanulado.
camp chair, silla plegadiza, silla de tijera.
camper ['kæmpər, B -pə] *s.* 1. excursionista que acampa en una tienda de campaña, acampador. 2. vehículo de remolque para acampar.
campestral [kæm'pɛstrəl] *a.* campestre, silvestre.
campfire ['kæmpˌfaɪr, B -ˌfaɪə] *s.* hoguera de campamento; reunión de tropas, niños exploradores, etc., alrededor de una hoguera.
camp follower, 1. vivandero. 2. persona no combatiente que acompaña a un ejército, esp. prostituta. 3. adherente, partidario.
campground [-ˌgraʊnd] *s.* campo o terreno (usado para campamento o reunión de feligreses, escolares, etc.); acampada.
camphine, camphene ['kæmˌfin] *s.* (quím.) canfeno.
camphor ['kæmfər, B -fə] *s.* (quím.) alcanfor.
camphorate ['kæmfəˌreɪt] *v.t.* alcanforar.
camphorated oil [-əd-] (farm.) aceite alcanforado.
camphor ball, bola de alcanfor (contra la polilla).
camphoric [kæm'fɔrɪk] *a.* (quím.) canfórico.
camphor ice, (farm.) cerato de alcanfor.
camphor tree, (bot.) alcanforero, alcanfor.
camp hospital, (mil.) hospital de sangre.
camping [-ɪŋ] *s.* acampada.
campion ['kæmpɪən] *s.* (bot.) colleja.
camp meeting, (E.U.) reunión religiosa que se celebra al aire libre.
camporee [ˌkæmpə'ri] *s.* asamblea de niños exploradores.
campsite ['kæmpˌsaɪt] *s.* lugar de campamento.
campstool [-ˌstul] *s.* silla plegadiza, silla portátil, silla de tijera.
campus ['kæmpəs] *s.* campus, ciudad universitaria; terrenos de una escuela, colegio o universidad; **to live on c.,** vivir en el campus, vivir dentro del recinto universitario.
campy ['kæmpɪ] *a.* (jer.) afectado, extravagante, frívolo (en modales, arte, moda).
camshaft ['kæmˌʃæft, B -ˌʃɑft] *s.* (mec.) árbol de levas.
can [kæn, kən] *v. aux. defectivo* (pret. y condicional COULD; CARECE DE INFINITIVO Y PARTICIPIOS, QUE SE SUPLEN CON *to be, able to*) 1. poder (hacer algo), ej., *I will do what I c.,* haré lo que pueda. 2. saber (hacer algo), ej., *he cannot read,* no sabe leer. 3. (fam.) poder, tener permiso para, ej., *you c. go,* puede usted irse.
can [kæn] *s.* 1. vaso, vasija. 2. bote de lata, lata. 3. (jer.) chirona, cárcel. 4. (jer. mil.) carga de profundidad. 5. (jer. mil.) destructor. 6. (jer.) retrete. 7. (jer.) nalgas. —*v.t.* (*pret., p.p.* CANNED; *p.pr.* CANNING) 1. enlatar, envasar. 2. (jer.) expulsar de la escuela; despedir (de empleo).

3. grabar (en disco o cinta), ej., *canned music,* música grabada. 4. (jer.) **c. it!** ¡basta! ¡ni una palabra más!
Can. *abrev. de* **Canada, Canadian,** el Canadá, canadiense.
Cana ['keɪnə] *s.* (bíbl.) Caná.
Canaan [-nən] *s.* (bíbl.) Canaán; (fig.) tierra de promisión.
Canaanite [-ˌaɪt] *a., s.* (bíbl.) cananeo.
Canada ['kænədə] *s.* (el) Canadá.
Canada balsam, bálsamo del Canadá.
Canada goose, (zool.) ganso silvestre de Norteamérica.
Canada thistle, (bot.) cardo negro.
Canadian [kə'neɪdɪən] *a., s.* canadiense.
canaille [kə'neɪl, -'naɪ] *s.* canalla, gentuza, chusma.
canal [kə'næl] *s.* 1. canal. 2. acequia, zanja (de irrigación). 3. (anat., zool.) conducto, canal, meato. 4. (arq.) estría, media caña.
canalboat [-ˌboʊt] *s.* barcaza de transporte (para servicio en canales fluviales).
canaliculus [ˌkænə'lɪkjələs] *s.* (*pl.* CANALICULI [-ˌlaɪ, -ˌli]) (anat., zool.) canalículo.
canalization [kəˌnælə'zeɪʃən, B ˌkænəlaɪ-] *s.* canalización; (med.) canalización.
canalize [kə'nælˌaɪz, B 'kænəl-] *v.t.* 1. canalizar. 2. (fig.) encauzar, canalizar (esfuerzos, emociones, etc.). *—v.i.* correr por un canal, desembocar en un canal.
canal lock, esclusa.
canal rays, (fís.) rayos canales.
Canal Zone, Zona del Canal (Panamá).
canapé ['kænəˌpeɪ] *s.* (cocina) canapé, bocadillo, aperitivo.
canard [kə'nɑrd, B kæ'nɑd] *s.* patraña, filfa, bola, noticia falsa.
Canarian [kə'nɛrɪən, B -'nɛər-] *a., s.* canario, canariense.
canary [kə'nɛrɪ, B -'nɛərɪ] *s.* 1. (orn.) canario. 2. color canario. 3. vino de las Islas Canarias. 4. (jer.) soplón.
canary grass, (bot.) alpiste (hierba).
Canary Islands, (Islas) Canarias.
canary seed, alpiste (semilla).
canasta [kə'næstə] *s.* (naipes) canasta.
Canberra ['kænˌbɛrə, B -bərə] *s.* Canberra, capital de Australia.
can buoy, (mar.) boya de tambor, boyatonel, boya cilíndrica.
cancan ['kænˌkæn] *s.* cancán, baile de origen parisiense.
cancel ['kænsəl] *v.t.* (*pret., p.p.* CANCELLED; *p.pr.* CANCELLING) 1. suprimir, eliminar, tachar. 2. cancelar, rescindir, revocar. 3. invalidar, anular. 4. neutralizar, inutilizar. 5. aniquilar, destruir. 6. (gen. con *out*) contrabalancear, compensar. 7. sellar, inutilizar (sellos de correo, timbres). 8. (mat.) eliminar (coeficientes en una ecuación). 9. (mús.) suprimir (alteración de una nota). *—v.i.* (gen. con *out*) compensarse, eliminarse mutuamente. *—s.* cancelación.
canceler [-ər, B -ə] *s.* anulador; matasellos.
cancellation [ˌkænsə'leɪʃən] *s.* 1. cancelación, anulación. 2. obliteración, marca de inutilización.
cancellous ['kænsələs] *a.* (anat.) canceloso.
cancer ['kænsər, B -sə] *s.* 1. (med.) cáncer, tumor maligno. 2. **C.,** (astr.) Cáncer.
cancerous [-sərəs] *a.* (med.) canceroso.
cancroid ['kæŋˌkrɔɪd] *a.* 1. (med.) cancroideo, semejante al cáncer. 2. (zool.) parecido al cangrejo.
candelabrum [ˌkændə'lɑbrəm, -'læb-] *s.* (*pl.* CANDELABRA [-rə] o CANDELABRUMS) candelabro, candelero de varios brazos.
candent ['kændənt] *a.* (ant.) candente, incandescente.
candescence [kæn'dɛsəns] *s.* candencia, incandescencia.
candescent [-'dɛsənt] *a.* candente, incandescente, resplandeciente, deslumbrante.
candid ['kændəd] *a.* 1. imparcial, justo. 2. franco, sincero. 3. cándido, sencillo. 4. espontáneo (fotografía, entrevista). 5. (ant.) blanco; puro, inocente.
candidacy ['kændədəsɪ] *s.* candidatura.
candidate ['kændəˌdeɪt, -dət] *s.* 1. candidato, pretendiente. 2. graduando (en una universidad).
candidature [-dədəˌtʃʊr, -tʃər, B -tʃə] *s.* candidatura.
candid camera, 1. (foto.) cámara pequeña (con que se puede tomar instantáneas sin llamar la atención). 2. (fig.) cámara indiscreta.
candidly ['kændədlɪ] *adv.* candidamente, candorosamente, ingenuamente.
candied ['kændid] *a.* confitado, azucarado, acaramelado, almibarado.
candle ['kændəl] *s.* 1. vela, bujía, candela. 2. (fís.) bujía, unidad luminosa. 3. **not hold a c. to,** no llegarle a la suela del zapato a (uno); **the game is not worth the c.,** el resultado no justifica el costo o la molestia; **to burn the c. at both ends,** vivir de prisa. *—v.t.* examinar al trasluz (huevos, etc.).
candleberry [-ˌbɛrɪ] *s.* (bot.) árbol de la cera.
candleholder [-'hoʊldər, B -ə] *s.* candelero.
candlelight [-ˌlaɪt] *s.* 1. luz de vela; luz suave (artificial). 2. atardecer, crepúsculo. 3. (fig.) a media luz (ambiente romántico).
candlemaker [-ˌmeɪkər, B -ə] *s.* candelero, velero (el que hace o vende cirios).
Candlemas [-məs] *s.* (relig.) Candelaria.
candlepin [-ˌpɪn] *s.* bolo ahusado (que se usa en ciertos juegos de bolos).
candlepower [-ˌpaʊər, B -ə] *s.* (fís.) bujía.
candlestick [-ˌstɪk] *s.* candelero, palmatoria.
candlewick [-ˌwɪk] *s.* 1. pabilo (de la vela). 2. (bot.) espadaña.
candlewood [-ˌwʊd] *s.* 1. pino u otro árbol resinoso. 2. cuelmo, tea.
candor, (pr. G.B.) **candour** ['kændər, B -də] *s.* 1. candor, sencillez; sinceridad, franqueza. 3. imparcialidad, equidad. 3. (ant.) limpieza; pureza, blancura; benevolencia.
candy ['kændɪ] *s.* 1. caramelo, azúcar cristalizada. 2. (E.U.) confite, bombón, dulce, confitura. *—v.t.* (*pret., p.p.* CANDIED; *p.pr.* CANDYING) 1. confitar, acaramelar, almibarar, garapiñar. 2. (fig.) endulzar, almibarar. *—v.i.* acaramelarse.
candy apple, manzana acaramelada.
candy bar, golosina en barra.
candy floss, (G.B.) dulce de hilos de almíbar.
candytuft [-ˌtʌft] *s.* (bot.) carraspique.
cane [keɪn] *s.* 1. caña. 2. caña de azúcar, caña. 3. bastón, báculo, cayado. 4. palo, vara. 5. bejuco (usado para tejer cestos, asientos para sillas, etc.). 6. tallo (de ciertos frutos pequeños como el de la frambuesa). *—v.t.* 1. apalear. 2. tejer (cestos, asientos, etc.) de bejuco.
canebrake ['keɪnˌbreɪk] *s.* cañaveral, matorral de cañas.
canephora [kə'nɛfərə] *s.* (*pl.* CANEPHORAE [-ˌri]) (hist., arq.) canéfora, doncella que llevaba flores en ciertas fiestas paganas de Grecia.
caner ['keɪnər, B -ə] *s.* costero, canastero (que trabaja con mimbre o bejuco).
canescent [kə'nɛsənt] *a.* (bot.) blanquecino.
cane seat, asiento de rejilla.
cane sugar, azúcar de caña.
cangue [kæŋ] *s.* canga; cepo que se usaba en la antigua China como instrumento de tortura.
Canícula [kə'nɪkjələ] *s.* (astr.) Canícula, Sirio.
canicular [-lər, B -lə] *a.* canicular.
canine ['keɪˌnaɪn] *a.* 1. canino, perruno. 2. (zool.) canino, ej., *c. tooth,* diente canino. *—s.* 1. colmillo, (diente) canino. 2. can. 3. (mil.) **c. corps,** destacamento habilitado de perros rastreadores.
caning ['kæniŋ] *s.* castigo con palmeta.
Canis Major ['keɪnəs-] (astr.) Can Mayor.
Canis Minor, (astr.) Can Menor.
canister ['kænəstər, B -stə] *s.* bote, cajita, lata pequeña (para guardar té, café, etc.); caja.
canister shot, (mil.) bote de metralla.
canker ['kæŋkər, B -kə] *s.* 1. (bot.) cancro (úlcera de los árboles, plantas y frutos). 2. (fig.) influencia maligna. 3. llaga gangrenosa; cáncrum (pequeña úlcera en la boca). *—v.t., v.i.* gangrenar(se); corromper(se).
cankerous [-kərəs] *a.* gangrenoso, corrosivo.
canker rash, (med.) escarlatina.
canker sore, (med.) pequeña ulceración dolorosa (esp. en labios y boca).
cankerworm [-kərˌwɜrm, B -kəˌwɜm] *s.* (zool.) especie de oruga (que ataca plantas y frutos).
canna ['kænə] *s.* (bot.) planta canácea; cañacoro.
cannabin ['kænəbən] *s.* (quím.) canabina.
cannabinaceous [ˌkænəbə'neɪʃəs] *a.* (bot.) canabíneo.
cannabis ['kænəbəs] *s.* (bot.) cáñamo, cáñamo de la India (del que se derivan el hachís y la mariguana).
cannaceous [kə'neɪʃəs] *a.* (bot.) canáceo.
canned [kænd] *a.* 1. envasado, en lata, ej., *c. goods,* alimentos enlatados. 2. grabado, conservado en grabación (en disco o cinta), ej., *c. music,* música grabada. 3. (fig., jer.) trillado, estereotipado. 4. (jer.) ajumado, borracho. 5. (jer.) despedido (de un empleo).
canned heat, combustible enlatado, práctico para calentar comida al aire libre.
cannel coal ['kænəl-] carbón mate, carbón de bujía.
cannelon ['kænəlˌɑn, B -ˌɔn] *s.* (cocina) canelón.
canner ['kænər, B -ə] *s.* envasador, enlatador (de alimentos).
cannery [-ərɪ] *s.* fábrica de conservas.
cannibal ['kænəbəl] *a., s.* caníbal, antropófago.
cannibalism [-ˌɪzəm] *s.* canibalismo, antropofagia.
cannibalistic [ˌkænəbə'lɪstɪk] *a.* caníbal, del canibalismo.
cannibalize ['kænəbəˌlaɪz] *v.t.* 1. desarmar una máquina o motor dañado para utilizar sus piezas servibles en otro aparato. 2. despojar; adjudicarse de personal y equipo para habilitar otra unidad u oficina.
cannikin ['kænɪkən] *s.* 1. latita, vaso pequeño. 2. (dial.) cubo (de madera).
cannily ['kænəlɪ] *adv.* astutamente.
canniness [-ɪnəs] *s.* astucia, sutileza.
canning ['kænɪŋ] *s.* elaboración de conservas.
cannon ['kænən] *s.* 1. cañón, pieza de artillería. 2. cañón (pieza del bocado del caballo). 3. (billar, G.B.) carambola. *—v.t.* cañonear.
cannonade [ˌkænə'neɪd] *s.* cañoneo. *—v.t.* cañonear. *—v.i.* bombardear.
cannonball ['kænənˌbɔl] *s.* 1. bala de cañón. 2. (tenis) servicio fuerte. 3. (fam.) tren rápido. *—v.i.* pasar a gran velocidad.
cannon bone, canilla, caña.
cannoneer [ˌkænə'nɪr, B -'nɪə] *s.* artillero, cañonero.

cannon fodder, carne de cañón.
cannonry ['kænənrɪ] *s.* fuego de artillería.
cannon shot, 1. cañonazo, tiro de cañón. 2. bala(s) de cañón. 3. alcance de un cañón.
cannot ['kænɑt, kə'nɑt, B 'kænɔt] *contr. de* **can not.**
cannula ['kænjələ] *s.* (*pl.* CANNULAE [-ˌli]) (med.) cánula, tubo, sonda.
cannular [-lər, B -lə] *a.* canular, tubular.
canny ['kænɪ] *a.* 1. prudente, cauto, previsor. 2. astuto, sagaz, sutil. 3. bellaco, socarrón. 4. económico, frugal. 5. (esco.) quieto, confortable; afortunado; cuidadoso. 6. (dial. G.B.) agradable, placentero.
canoe [kə'nu] *s.* canoa, piragua. *—v.i.* remar, pasear o viajar en canoa.
canoeist [-əst] *s.* canoero, piragüero.
canon ['kænən] *s.* 1. canon, regla o dogma. 2. (relig.) canon (parte de la misa). 3. canon (catálogo de los libros auténticos de las Sagradas Escrituras). 4. catálogo, lista, rol. 5. canónigo. 6. canon, criterio, precepto, regla, ej., *canons of art,* reglas del arte. 7. (mús.) canon (composición a contrapunto). 8. (tip.) canon, gran canon (grado de letra de imprenta).
cañon ['kænjən] *var. de* **canyon.**
canoness ['kænənəs] *s.* (relig.) canonesa.
canonical [kə'nɑnɪkəl, B -'nɔn-] *a.* 1. canónico (conforme a los cánones). 2. canonical, del canónigo.
canonical hour, (relig.) hora canónica.
canonicals [-kəlz] *s. pl.* hábitos o vestimentas eclesiásticas (prescritas por el canon).
canonist ['kænənəst] *s.* canonista, especialista en derecho canónico.
canonization [ˌkænənə'zeɪʃən, B -ənaɪ-] *s.* canonización.
canonize ['kænəˌnaɪz] *v.t.* 1. (relig.) canonizar. 2. (fig.) canonizar, aprobar.
canon law, (relig.) derecho canónico.
canonry ['kænənrɪ] *s.* canonjía, prebenda.
can opener, abrelatas, abridor de latas.
Canopic jar, C. vase[kə'noʊpɪk-] (arqueol.) canope.
canopied ['kænəpid] *a.* endoselado.
canopus [kə'noʊpəs] *s.* 1. (arqueol.) canope. 2. (astr.) **C.,** Canopo.
canopy ['kænəpɪ] *s.* 1. pabellón (de cama). 2. dosel, palio, baldaquín, pabellón (de trono, altar, etc.). 3. (fig., poét.) pabellón, bóveda (del cielo, follaje, etc.). 4. (arq.) doselete. 5. (elec.) escudete, escudo. 6. casquete (del paracaídas). 7. (aer.) cubierta corrediza (de la cabina). *—t.v.* cubrir con un pabellón, endoselar.
canorous [kə'nɔrəs] *a.* (poét.) canoro, melodioso, armónico, musical.
canst [kænst, kənst] (ant.) *segunda pers. sing. del pres. del indic. de* **can.**
can't [kænt, B kɑnt] *contr. de* **cannot.**
cant [kænt] *s.* 1. canturreo, tono afectado; gemido, quejido. 2. jerigonza, germanía, caló. 3. jerga, lenguaje peculiar (de una ciencia, profesión, etc.). 4. hipocresía, gazmoñería, mojigatería. 5. canto, chaflán. bisel. 6. cara oblicua, plano inclinado. 7. pendiente, sesgo, inclinación. *—v.i.* 1. salmodiar, hablar en tono plañidero o canturreado (ej., un mendigo); mendigar, solicitar. 2. hablar en jerga. 3. hablar hipócritamente. 4. inclinarse. 5. (mar.) escorar (el barco). *—v.t.* 1. chaflanar, biselar. 2. poner al sesgo, inclinar; ladear. *—a.* 1. sesgado. 2. chaflanado, biselado. 3. (dial. G.B.) lozano, vigoroso, brioso.
cantabile [kɑn'tɑbəˌleɪ, B kæn'tɑbɪlɪ] (mús.) *a.* cantable. *—s.* cantábile.
Cantabrian [kæn'teɪbrɪən] *a.* cantábrico, cántabro. *—s.* cántabro, cántabra.
Cantabrigian [ˌkæntə'brɪdʒɪən] *a.* de Cambridge; de la Universidad de Cambridge.
cantaloupe ['kæntəˌloʊp, B -ˌlup] *s.* (bot.) cantalupo (*con pulpa anaranjada*).
cantankerous [kæn'tæŋkərəs, kən-] *a.* avinagrado, pendenciero, reñidor.
cantata [kən'tɑtə] *s.* (mús.) cantata.
canteen [kæn'tin] *s.* 1. cantina, tienda en un puesto militar. 2. cantimplora.
canter ['kæntər, B -tə] *s.* (equit.) medio galope. *—v.t., v.i.* andar (el caballo) a paso largo y sentado.
Canterburian [ˌkæntər'bjʊrɪən, B -tə'-] *a., s.* canturiense.
Canterbury ['kæntərˌbɛrɪ, B -təbərɪ] *s.* Cantórbery.
Canterbury bell, (bot.) farolillo, adenófora.
cant frame, (mar.) cuaderna revirada.
cantharides [kæn'θærəˌdiz] *s.* (farm.) polvo de cantárida.
cantharis ['kænθərəs] *s.* (*pl.* CANTHARIDES [kæn'θærəˌdiz]) (ento.) cantárida.
cant hook, gafa de palanca, arpeo, palanca de gancho.
canthus ['kænθəs] *s.* (anat.) ángulo o rabillo del ojo.
canticle ['kæntɪkəl] *s.* cántico, canto, himno (esp. religioso).
Canticles [-kəlz] *s. pl.* (bíbl.) cánticos; Cantar de los Cantares.
cantilever ['kæntəˌlivər, -ˌlɛv-, B -ˌlivə] *s.* ménsula, viga voladiza; cantilever.
cantilever arm, (ing.) brazo volado.
cantilever bridge, puente volado o voladizo.
cantilever span, (ing.) tramo volado.
cantilever spring, (ing.) ballesta cantilever.
cantilever wing, (aer.) ala en cantilever.
cantillate ['kæntəˌleɪt] *v.t.* entonar, recitar un texto litúrgico; improvisar (canto, música en sinagogas e iglesias).
cantina [kæn'tinə] *s.* (S.O. de E.U.) taberna.
cantle ['kæntəl] *s.* 1. trozo, pedazo, fragmento. 2. (equit.) arzón, fuste de la silla.
canto ['kæntoʊ] *s.* (*pl.* CANTOS) canto, parte de un poema épico.
canton ['kæntən, -ˌtɑn, B -ˌtɔn, -tən] *s.* 1. cantón, distrito (en Suiza). 2. rectángulo de una bandera (en la esquina superior próxima al asta). 3. (her.) cantón. *—v.t.* 1. [-tən, -ˌtɑn, B -ˌtɔn] dividir en partes o cantones. 2. [kæn'toʊn, -'tɑn, B kən'tun] (mil.) acantonar, acuartelar (tropas).
cantonal ['kæntənəl, kæn'tɑn-, B 'kæntən-] *a.* cantonal.
Canton crepe ['kænˌtɑn-, B kæn'tɔn-] (tej.) crepé de seda.
cantoned ['kæntənd, -ˌtɑnd, B kæn'tɔnd] *a.* (her.) cantonado.
Cantonese [ˌkæntə'niz] *a.* cantonés. *—s.* cantonés (nativo o dialecto de Cantón).
Canton flannel, (tej.) muletón.
cantonment [kæn'toʊnmənt, -'tɑn-, B -'tun-] *s.* 1. (mil.) acuartelamiento, acantonamiento (de tropas). 2. (mil.) barracas temporales. 3. puesto militar, fuerte (en la India).
cantor ['kæntər, B -tɔ] *s.* 1. chantre. 2. solista (que canta música litúrgica en una sinagoga).
cant timber, (mar.) cuaderna revirada.
cantus ['kæntəs] *s.* (*pl.* CANTUS ['kæntəs, -ˌtus]) (mús.) melodía, esp. la parte principal de una composición polifónica.
cantus firmus [-'fɪrməs, -'fɜr-, B -'fɪəməs] (mús.) 1. canto llano o firme. 2. tema melódico, esp. de contrapunto.
canty ['kæntɪ] *a.* (dial. G.B.) alegre, jovial, festivo.
Canuck, Canuk [kə'nʌk] *s.* (despec.) canadiense; canadiense de ascendencia francesa, francocanadiense.
canvas ['kænvəs] *s.* 1. lona, cañamazo, tela de cáñamo. 2. velamen; vela (de lona). 3. toldo, tienda; grupo de tiendas de campaña. 4. (fig.) circo; vida del circo. 5. (pint.) lienzo, pintura, cuadro. 6. **on the c.,** derribado, en la lona; (fig.) al borde de la derrota; **under c.,** bajo tienda(s); con las velas desplegadas.
canvasback [-ˌbæk] *s.* (zool.) pato marino norteamericano.
canvass ['kænvəs] *s.* 1. escrutinio, examen minucioso. 2. solicitación de votos, subscripciones, opiniones, etc. *—v.t.* 1. escudriñar, examinar (los votos, en una elección). 2. solicitar (votos, fondos, opiniones, etc.) en recorrido por un barrio o distrito.
canvasser [-ər, B -ə] *s.* 1. solicitante (de votos, fondos, etc.). 2. escrutador (de votos). 3. vendedor ambulante.
canyon ['kænjən] *s.* cañón, desfiladero, garganta.
canzonet [ˌkænzə'nɛt] *s.* 1. (mús.) cancioneta. 2. canción graciosa.
caoutchouc [kaʊ'tʃuk, -'tʃʊk, B 'kaʊˌtʃʊk, -ˌtʃuk] *s.* caucho.
cap [kæp] *s.* 1. gorro, gorra. 2. toca; bonete, birrete. 3. casco, casquete, ej., *steel c.,* casco de acero. 4. cápsula, fulminante. 5. capa (de hielo, azúcar, etc.). 6. capa de reencauche (de un neumático). 7. tapa, chapa (de botella), casquete (de tubo). 8. puntera (de zapato). 9. (mar.) tamborete (para sujetar a un palo otro sobrepuesto). 10. (bot.) sombrerete (de hongo). 11. **(with) c. in hand,** humildemente; **to put on one's thinking c.,** reflexionar, pensar; **to set one's cap for,** proponerse conquistar como novio a; **if (o when) the c. fits, wear it,** aplícate el cuento, si te sientes ofendido date por aludido. *—v.t.* 1. cubrir. 2. rematar, coronar. 3. sobrepasar, superar, exceder. 4. **c. a story,** contar una historia mejor (que la anterior).
capability [ˌkeɪpə'bɪlətɪ] *s.* capacidad, idoneidad, aptitud; **has capabilities,** tiene capacidad (en potencia, no desarrollada).
capable ['keɪpəbəl] *a.* 1. (con *of*) capaz (de). 2. hábil, competente; inteligente, capaz, talentoso. 3. (con *of*) susceptible (de), ej., *c. of several interpretations,* susceptible de varias interpretaciones.
capacious [kə'peɪʃəs] *a.* capaz, ancho, espacioso.
capacitance [kə'pæsətəns] *s.* (elec.) capacitancia.
capacitate [-ˌteɪt] *v.t.* capacitar, habilitar; calificar, acreditar.
capacitor [-tər, B -tə] *s.* (elec.) condensador.
capacity [kə'pæsətɪ] *s.* 1. capacidad, cabida, contenido. 2. capacidad, habilidad, aptitud, talento. 3. capacidad, rendimiento; rendimiento máximo. 4. calidad, carácter, condición. 5. (der.) capacidad, aptitud legal. 6. (elec.) capacidad. 7. **filled to c.,** lleno hasta el tope; lleno por completo; **in the c. of,** en calidad de.
capacity house, lleno (teatro, sala, estadio).
cap and bells, gorro con campanillas (símbolo del payaso).
cap and gown, birrete y toga (atuendo del académico).
cap-a-pie [ˌkæpə'pi] *adv.* de pies a cabeza, de punta en blanco, ej., *armed c.,* armado de pies a cabeza.
caparison [kə'pærəsən] *s.* 1. caparazón, gualdrapa. 2. jaez. *—v.t.* 1. enjaezar (un caballo). 2. vestir suntuosamente.

cape [keɪp] *s.* 1. capa, mantón. 2. esclavina, manteleta. 3. (geog.) cabo, promontorio, punta de tierra.

Cape doctor, viento fuerte del África del Sur.

Cape Horn, Cabo de Hornos.

capelin ['kæpələn] *s.* (ict.) capelán.

capeline ['kæpə,lin, -lɪn] *s.* (hist., arm., med.) capellina, capelina.

Capella [kə'pɛlə] *s.* (astr.) Cabra.

Cape of Good Hope, Cabo de Buena Esperanza.

caper ['keɪpər, B -ə] *s.* 1. (bot.) alcaparra. 2. cabriola, salto, brinco. 3. **to cut capers,** dar cabriolas, cabriolar; hacer travesuras; andar de parranda. —*v.i.* cabriolar, triscar, brincar.

capercaillie [,kæpər'keɪljɪ, B -pə'-] **capercailzie** [-zɪ, -jɪ] *s.* (orn.) urogallo, gallo silvestre.

capeskin ['keɪp,skɪn] *s.* piel de cabra, para guantes.

Cape Verde ['keɪp'vɜrd, B -'vɜd] islas de Cabo Verde.

capework [-,wɜrk, B -,wɜk] *s.* juego del torero con el capote de lidia.

capful ['kæp,fʊl] *s.* el contenido de la tapa de un frasco (gen. de medicina).

capias ['keɪpɪəs, B -æs] *s.* (der.) orden de arresto.

capillaceous [,kæpə'leɪʃəs] *a.* (bot.) capiláceo, capilar.

capillarity [-'lærətɪ] *s.* capilaridad; (fís.) capilaridad, atracción capilar.

capillary ['kæpə,lɛrɪ, B kə'pɪlərɪ] *a.* capilar. —*s.* (anat.) vaso capilar.

capillary attraction, (fís.) fuerza capilar, atracción capilar.

capillary tube, (anat.) tubo capilar.

capital ['kæpətəl] *s.* 1. capital (de país o provincia). 2. mayúscula. 3. (com.) capital social, caudal de un negocio. 4. (arq.) capitel de columna. 5. **to make c. out of,** sacar partido de. —*a.* 1. capital (pena, sentencia). 2. (castigable) con pena de muerte, ej., *c. crime* o *c. offense,* crimen punible con pena capital. 3. capital (error, idea, etc.); sumo, primerísimo, ej., *of c. importance,* de suma importancia.

capital account, (ten.) cuenta de capital, cuenta patrimonial.

capital area, capitalidad.

capital assets, *pl.* (ten.) activo fijo, activo permanente, bienes de capital, bienes de equipo.

capital expenditure, (ten.) gasto o inversión de capital.

capital gains, (ten.) ganancia de capital, utilidades de capital.

capital goods, (com.) bienes raíces, elementos utilizados en la producción.

capitalism [-,ɪzəm] *s.* capitalismo.

capitalist [-əst] *s.* capitalista.

capitalization [,kæpətələ'zeɪʃən, B -laɪ-] *s.* 1. capitalización. 2. empleo de letras mayúsculas.

capitalize ['kæpətəl,aɪz, B kə'pɪt-] *v.t.* 1. capitalizar. 2. proveer de capital. 3. escribir con mayúscula(s). —*v.i.* 1. acumular capital. 2. (con *on*) aprovechar (de), sacar provecho (de).

capital letter, letra mayúscula.

capital loss, (fin.) merma del capital.

capital punishment, (der.) pena capital, pena de muerte.

capital stock, (ten., com.) capital social, capital en acciones.

capitate ['kæpə,teɪt] *a.* (bot.) capitado.

capitation [,kæpə'teɪʃən] *s.* capitación.

capitol ['kæpətəl] *s.* capitolio, edificio majestuoso y elevado.

Capitol Hill, sede del Congreso de los Estados Unidos de América.

Capitoline [-,aɪn, B kə'pɪtə,laɪn] *a.* capitolino (monte).

capitular [kə'pɪtʃələr, B -'pɪtjʊlə] *s., a.* capitular.

capitulary [-,lɛrɪ, B -lərɪ] *s.* 1. capitular, miembro de un capítulo. 2. ordenanza (eclesiástica); (*pl.*) colección de ordenanzas.

capitulate [-,leɪt] *v.i.* capitular.

capitulation [-,pɪtʃə'leɪʃən, B -,pɪtjʊ-] *s.* 1. capitulación, rendición. 2. recapitulación, resumen.

capitulum [-'pɪtʃələm] *s.* (*pl.* CAPITULA [-lə]) (bot.) capítula, capullo.

capnomancy ['kæpnoʊ,mænsɪ] *s.* capnomancia, predicción supersticiosa hecha por medio del humo.

cap nut, tuerca tapa o ciega.

capo ['keɪpoʊ] *abrev. de* **capotasto.**

capon ['keɪ,pɑn, B -pən] *s.* capón, pollo castrado.

caponize ['keɪpə,naɪz] *v.t.* castrar, capar (pollos).

caporal ['kæpərəl, ,kæpə'ræl, B -'rɑl] *s.* (especie de) tabaco áspero.

capotasto [,kɑpoʊ'tɑstoʊ] *s.* (*pl.* CAPOTASTI [-'tɑstɪ] o CAPOTASTOS) (mús.) cejilla, cejuela, ceja (en guitarra y laúd).

capote [kə'poʊt] *s.* capote o capa (con capucha).

Cappadocia [,kæpə'doʊʃə, B -'doʊsjə] *s.* Capadocia, antiguo país de Asia Menor.

cappa magna ['kæpə'mægnə] (relig.) capa magna, capa consistorial.

capparidaceous [,kæpərɪ'deɪʃəs] *a.* (bot.) caparidáceo, caparídeo.

capper ['kæpər, B -ə] *s.* 1. máquina coronadora. 2. (jer. E.U.) señuelo (ej., de un tahúr o jugador).

cap pistol, pistola de juguete o fulminante.

capreolate ['kæprɪə,leɪt] *a.* (bot.) capreolado.

capric acid ['kæprɪk-] (quím.) ácido cáprico.

capriccio [kə'pri,tʃoʊ, B -'prɪtʃɪ,oʊ] *s.* capricho; (mús.) capricho.

capriccioso [-,prɪtʃɪ'oʊsoʊ, B -zoʊ] *a.* (mús.) a capricho, según la fantasía del intérprete.

caprice [kə'pris] *s.* capricho, veleidad, extravagancia; (mús.) capricho.

capricious [-'prɪʃəs] *a.* caprichoso, caprichudo, antojadizo.

capriciously [-lɪ] *adv.* caprichosamente, caprichudamente.

Capricorn ['kæprɪ,kɔrn, B -,kɔn] *s.* (astr.) Capricornio.

capricorn beetle, (ento.) capricornio.

caprificate ['kæprəfə,keɪt] *v.t.* cabrahigar.

caprifig [-,fɪg] *s.* (bot.) cabrahigo, higuera silvestre, higuera de Egipto.

caprifoliaceous [,kæprə,foʊlɪ'eɪʃəs] *a.* (bot.) caprifoliáceo.

capriole ['kæprɪ,oʊl] *s.* cabriola, brinco. —*v.i.* cabriolar, dar cabriolas.

cap rock, (min.) rocas de cubierta.

caproic acid [kə'proʊɪk-] (quím.) ácido caproico.

caprylic acid [-'prɪlɪk-] (quím.) ácido caprílico.

caps [kæps] *s.* (fam., tip.) letras mayúsculas.

capsaicine [kæp'seɪəsən] *s.* (quím.) capsaicina.

cap screw, tornillo de cabeza, tornillo de casquete cuadrado.

Capsian ['kæpsɪən] *a.* del período paleolítico superior del N. de África.

capsicum ['kæpsɪkəm] *s.* (bot.) pimiento, ají (Am.); guindilla.

capsize ['kæp,saɪz, B kæp'saɪz] *v.t.* volcar, voltear. —*v.i.* (mar.) zozobrar dando la vuelta, irse a la banda.

capstan ['kæpstən] *s.* (mar.) cabrestante, argüe; **to rig the c.,** guarnir el cabrestante.

capstan bar, (mar.) barra del cabrestante, manuella.

capstan lathe, (mec.) torno revólver.

capstone [-,stoʊn] *s.* 1. (arq.) albardilla, coronamiento. 2. (fig.) coronamiento.

capsular ['kæpsələr, B -sjʊlə] *a.* capsular.

capsulate [-,leɪt] **capsulated** [-əd] *a.* encerrado en una cápsula.

capsule ['kæpsəl, -,sul, B -,sjul] *s.* 1. (anat., bot., quím., zool.) cápsula. 2. (farm.) cápsula. 3. resumen corto, escrito o discurso conciso. 4. cápsula (de astronave). —*a.* muy corto, muy condensado.

Capt. *abrev. de* **Captain,** capitán (Cap.).

captain ['kæptən] *s.* capitán.

captaincy [-sɪ] *s.* capitanía.

captain general, (hist., mil.) capitán general.

captainship [-,ʃɪp] *s.* capitanía.

caption ['kæpʃən] *s.* 1. encabezamiento; título, titular; epígrafe. 2. leyenda; (cinem.) subtítulo. —*v.t.* encabezar, poner título a.

captioned account [-ʃənd-] (ten.) cuenta del epígrafe.

captious ['kæpʃəs] *a.* 1. criticón, reparón. 2. capcioso, falaz, insidioso.

captivate ['kæptə,veɪt] *v.t.* cautivar, fascinar, encantar.

captivation [,kæptə'veɪʃən] *s.* fascinación, encanto.

captivator ['kæptə,veɪtər, B -ə] *s.* fascinador, cautivador.

captive ['kæptɪv] *a.* 1. cautivo, preso, prisionero. 2. (fig.) cautivado, fascinado. 3. **to hold c.,** tener en cautiverio; **to take c.,** tomar preso. —*s.* cautivo, prisionero.

captive audience, personas forzadas a ver o escuchar algo en contra de su voluntad.

captive balloon, (aer.) globo cautivo.

captivity [kæp'tɪvətɪ] *s.* cautiverio, cautividad, prisión.

captor ['kæptər, -,tɔr, B -tə, -tɔ] *s.* apresador, aprehensor, capturador.

capture [-tʃər, B -tʃə] *s.* 1. captura, apresamiento. 2. toma (de una ciudad, plaza, etc.). 3. presa, cosa capturada, esp. nave apresada. 4. (ajedrez, damas) toma (de una pieza). —*v.t.* 1. capturar, hacer prisionero, tomar preso. 2. tomar (una ciudad, plaza, etc.); apresar (una nave). 3. ganar (un premio, etc.). 4. cautivar (la atención, imaginación, etc.). 5. (ajedrez, damas) tomar, comer (una pieza). 6. (bridge) capturar.

capuche [kə'putʃ, B -'puʃ] *s.* capucha, capucho, caperuza.

capuchin ['kæpjəʃən, -tʃən] *s.* 1. capuchino (monje). 2. capuchón, capotillo con capucha. 3. (zool.) capuchino. 4. (orn.) capuchino, paloma capuchina.

Capulet ['kæpjələt, B -jʊ,lɛt] *s.* Capuleto, nombre de la familia de Julieta en la obra de Shakespeare *Romeo y Julieta.*

capybara [,kæpɪ'bærə, B -'bɑrə] *s.* (zool.) capibara, carpincho (Am.).

car [kɑr, B kɑ] *s.* 1. automóvil, coche, carro. 2. coche (de ferrocarril o de tranvía). 3. caja o jaula (de ascensor). 4. (aer.) barquilla (de globo aerostático o de dirigible). 5. (poét.) carroza.

carabao [,kærə'baʊ] *s.* (*pl.* CARABAOS) (zool.) carabao.

carabid ['kærəbɪd] *s.* (ento.) carábido, coleóptero.

carabineer [,kærəbə'nɪr, B -'nɪə] *s.* carabinero.

carabinier, *var. de* **carabineer.**

caracara [ˌkærəˈkærə, B ˌkɑrəˈkɑrə] *s.* (orn.) caracará.

Caracas [kəˈrækəs] *s.* Caracas, capital de Venezuela.

caracole [ˈkærəˌkoʊl] *s.* 1. (equit.) caracol, vuelta o torno del caballo. 2. escalera de caracol. —*v.i.* (*pret., p.p.* CARACOLED O CARACOLLED; *p.pr.* CARACOLING O CARACOLLING) caracolear, hacer caracolas (el caballo).

caracul [ˈkærəkəl] *s.* piel del caracul, astracán.

carafe [kəˈræf, -ˈrɑf] *s.* garrafa.

carambola [ˌkærəmˈboʊlə] *s.* 1. (bot.) carambolo (árbol). 2. carambola (fruto).

caramel [ˈkærəməl, ˈkɑrməl, B ˈkærəmɛl] *s.* 1. caramelo. 2. azúcar quemado. 3. confite o pastilla de leche y azúcar.

caramelize [-ˌaɪz] *v.t., v.i.* caramelizar(se), acaramelar.

carangid [kəˈrændʒəd] *a., s.* (ict.) carángido.

carapace [ˈkærəˌpeɪs] *s.* (zool.) carapacho, concha, coraza.

carat [ˈkærət] *s.* quilate.

caravan [ˈkærəˌvæn] *s.* 1. caravana. 2. carricoche. 3. casa rodante, carreta de gitanos.

caravansary [ˌkærəˈvænsərɪ] *s.* caravanera; patio-posada donde pernoctan las caravanas.

caravel, caravelle [ˈkærəˌvɛl] *s.* (mar.) carabela.

caraway [ˈkærəˌweɪ] *s.* 1. (bot.) alcaravea (planta). 2. carvi, alcaravea (simiente).

carbamate [ˈkɑrbəˌmeɪt, B ˈkɑbə-] *s.* (quím.) carbamato.

carbamic acid [kɑrˈbæmɪk, B kɑˈ-] (quím.) ácido carbámico.

carbarn [ˈkɑrˌbɑrn, B ˈkɑˌbɑn] *s.* cochera o cobertizo para tranvías y autobuses; usina (Am.).

carbazole [ˈkɑrbəˌzoʊl, B ˈkɑbə-] *s.* (quím.) carbazol.

carbide [ˈkɑrˌbaɪd, B ˈkɑˌ-] *s.* (quím.) carburo.

carbine [ˈkɑrˌbaɪn, -ˌbin, B ˈkɑˌbaɪn] *s.* carabina.

carbineer [ˌkɑrbəˈnɪr, B ˌkɑbɪˈnɪə] *s.* carabinero.

carbinol [ˈkɑrbəˌnɔl, B ˈkɑbɪ-] *s.* (quím.) carbinol.

carbodynamite [ˌkɑrboʊˈdaɪnəˌmaɪt, B ˌkɑboʊ-] *s.* carbodinamita.

carbohydrate [-ˈhaɪˌdreɪt, -drət] *s.* (quím.) carbohidrato, hidrato de carbono.

carbolated [ˈkɑrbəˌleɪtəd, B ˈkɑbə-] *a.* mezclado con ácido fénico o carbólico.

carbolic acid [kɑrˈbɑlɪk-, B kɑˈbɔl-] (quím.) ácido carbólico o fénico.

carbolineum [ˌkɑrbəˈlɪnɪəm, B ˌkɑboʊ-] *s.* (quím.) carbolíneo.

carbolize [ˈkɑrbəˌlaɪz, B ˈkɑbə-] *v.t.* (quím.) mezclar o tratar con ácido carbólico o fénico.

carboloy [-ˌlɔɪ] *s.* (quím.) aleación de tungsteno, carbono y cobalto.

car bomb, coche bomba.

carbon [ˈkɑrbən, B ˈkɑbən] *s.* 1. (quím.) carbono. 2. (elec.) carbón (de una pila voltaica o lámpara de arco). 3. papel carbón; copia hecha con papel carbón. 4. (aut.) carbón (que se deposita sobre el émbolo).

carbonaceous [ˌkɑrbəˈneɪʃəs, B ˌkɑbə-] *a.* carbónico, carbonoso.

carbonado [-ˈneɪdoʊ] *s.* (*pl.* CARBONADOES O CARBONADOS) 1. carbonado, diamante negro. 2. carbonada (pieza de carne o pescado asado a la parrilla). —*v.t.* (ant.) tajar, picar.

carbon arc, arco entre electrodos de carbón, arco carbónico.

carbonate [ˈkɑrbəˌneɪt, -nət, B ˈkɑbə-] *s.* (quím.) carbonato. —*v.t.* [-ˌneɪt] 1. carbonatar, convertir en carbonato. 2. cargar de ácido carbónico (agua, etc.).

carbonated water [-ˌneɪtəd-] agua gaseosa.

carbonation [ˌkɑrbəˈneɪʃən, B kɑbə-] *s.* carbonatación.

carbon copy, copia (hecha) con papel carbón; **to be the c. of someone** (or **something**) ser un calco de alguien (o algo).

carbon cycle, ciclo del carbono.

carbon dating, datación por C-14.

carbon diamond, carbonado, diamante negro.

carbon dioxide, (quím.) bióxido de carbono, anhídrido carbónico.

carbonic [kɑrˈbɑnɪk, B kɑˈbɔn-] *a.* (quím.) carbónico.

carbonic acid, (quím.) ácido carbónico.

carbonic-acid gas [-ˌæsɪd-] (quím.) dióxido de carbono, anhídrido carbónico.

carboniferous [ˌkɑrbəˈnɪfərəs, B ˌkɑbə-] *a.* carbonífero. —*s.* (geol.) (período) carbonífero, carbónico.

carbonium [kɑrˈboʊnɪəm, B kɑˈ-] *s.* (fís.) carbonio.

carbonization [ˌkɑrbənəˈzeɪʃən, B ˌkɑbə-naɪ-] *s.* carbonización.

carbonize [ˈkɑrbəˌnaɪz, B ˈkɑb-] *v.t.* carbonizar.

carbon monoxide, (quím.) monóxido de carbono.

carbonous [-nəs] *a.* 1. carbonoso. 2. quebradizo y de color obscuro.

carbon paper, papel carbón, papel de calco, papel carbónico.

carbon process, (foto.) procedimiento al carbón.

carbonyl [ˈkɑrbəˌnɪl, B ˈkɑbə-] *s.* (quím.) carbonilo.

carborundum [ˌkɑrbəˈrʌndəm, B ˌkɑbə-] *s.* carborundo.

carborundum paper, lija de carborundo.

carboxyl [kɑrˈbɑksəl, B kɑˈbɔk-] *s.* (quím.) carboxilo.

carboxylase [-səˌleɪs, -ˌleɪz] *s.* (biol.) carboxilasa (enzima).

carboxylic [ˌkɑrbɑkˈsɪlɪk, B ˌkɑbɔk-] *a.* (quím.) carboxílico.

carboy [ˈkɑrˌbɔɪ, B ˈkɑˌ-] *s.* damajuana, garrafón, bombona.

carbuncle [ˈkɑrˌbʌŋkəl, B ˈkɑˌ-] *s.* 1. carbúnculo, rubí. 2. (med.) carbunclo, carbunco, furúnculo, forúnculo. 3. (vet.) carbunclo, carbunco, ántrax.

carburant [ˈkɑrbərənt, B ˈkɑbjʊ-] *s.* carburante.

carburet [ˈkɑrbəˌreɪt, B ˈkɑbjʊˌrɛt] *s.* (quím. ant.) carburo. —*v.t.* (*pret., p.p.* CARBURETED O CARBURETTED; *p.pr.* CARBURETING O CARBURETTING), carburar, combinar con carbono.

carburetant [-ənt] *s.* carburante, agente carburador.

carburetion [ˌkɑrbəˈreɪʃən, B ˌkɑbjʊˈrɛʃən] *s.* carburación.

carburetor, carburettor [ˈkɑrbəˌreɪtər, B ˈkɑbjʊˌrɛtə] *s.* carburador.

carburization [ˌkɑrbərəˈzeɪʃən, B ˌkɑbjʊraɪ-] *s.* carburación.

carburize [ˈkɑrbəˌraɪz, B ˈkɑbjʊ-] *v.t.* (quím.) carburar.

carcajou [ˈkɑrkəˌdʒu, -ˌʒu, B ˈkɑkə-] *s.* (zool.) especie de tejón o de glotón de América; lince del Canadá.

carcanet [ˈkɑrkənət, B ˈkɑkəˌnɛt] *s.* (ant.) cadena, collar o cinta para adornar el cabello (gen. de oro y con piedras preciosas).

carcase, *s.* (G.B.) *var. de* **carcass.**

carcass [ˈkɑrkəs, B ˈkɑkəs] *s.* 1. cadáver (de animal), (despec.) cadáver humano. 2. res o ave muerta. 3. (despec.) cuerpo humano. 4. esqueleto (de navío, edificio, etc.). 5. (aut.) carcasa (de un neumático). 6. (mil.) granada incendiaria. 7. **to save one's c.,** (fam.) salvar el pellejo, salvar la vida.

carcinogen [kɑrˈsɪnədʒən, B kɑˈ-] *s.* (med.) carcinógeno.

carcinogenic [ˈkɑrsənəˈdʒɛnɪk] *a.* cancerígeno, carcinogénico.

carcinoma [ˌkɑrsəˈnoʊmə, B ˌkɑs-] *s.* (*pl.* CARCINOMAS O CARCINOMATA [-tə]) (med.) carcinoma, tumor maligno.

carcinomatosis [-ˌnoʊməˈtoʊsəs] *s.* (med.) carcinomatosis.

car coat, abrigo corto, propio para automovilistas.

card [kɑrd, B kɑd] *s.* 1. naipe, carta (de la baraja). 2. (*pl.*) juego de naipes o cartas, ej., *to play cards,* jugar a los naipes. 3. (fig.) carta, recurso. 4. tarjeta (postal, de visita o de invitación). 5. programa. 6. menú; lista de vinos. 7. (forma abrev. de *compass c.*) rosa náutica, rosa de los vientos. 8. (fam.) tipo gracioso. 9. **c. up one's sleeve,** plan secreto, recurso en reserva; **Christmas c.,** tarjeta de Navidad; **house of cards,** (fig.) castillo de naipes; **in the cards,** posible, probable, esperado; **pack of cards,** baraja (de naipes); **safe c.,** plan seguro; **queer c.,** tipo raro (persona); **to make a c.,** hacer una baza con una carta; **to put one's cards on the table,** poner las cartas sobre la mesa; **to show one's cards,** (fig.) mostrar sus cartas; enseñar el juego; **to cut the cards,** estar al mando; **visiting c.,** tarjeta de visita; **wedding c.,** participación de boda. —*v.t.* 1. poner (nombre, signo, etc.) en tarjeta. 2. proveer con tarjeta. 3. registrar en tarjeta. 4. (dep.) marcar (puntaje) en tarjeta, anotar (el marcador) en tarjeta.

card, *s.* carda. —*v.t.* cardar.

cardamom [ˈkɑrdəməm, B ˈkɑd-] *s.* (bot.) cardamomo.

Cardan joint [ˈkɑrdæn-, B ˈkɑd-] (aut.) cardán, junta cardánica, articulación cardán.

cardboard [ˈkɑrdˌbɔrd, B ˈkɑdˌbɔd] *s.* cartulina, cartón delgado; cartón grueso.

cardboard binding, encuadernación de cartón o en pasta.

cardboard box, caja de cartón.

card-carrying member [-ˌkærɪɪŋ-] miembro de carnet, miembro con carnet, partidario confirmado.

carder [-ər, B -ə] *s.* (tej.) 1. cardador (oficio). 2. carda, máquina de cardar.

card game, juego de cartas o naipes; partida de cartas.

cardholder [-ˌhoʊldər, B -ə] *s.* 1. titular (de tarjeta de crédito); miembro registrado (de un partido político, asociación, etc.). 2. sujetapapeles (en máquina de escribir).

cardiac [ˈkɑrdɪˌæk, B ˈkɑdɪ-] *a.* (med.) cardíaco, cardiaco. —*s.* 1. remedio para el corazón. 2. cardíaco, cardiaco, enfermo del corazón.

cardialgia [ˌkɑrdɪˈældʒɪə, B ˌkɑd-] *s.* (med.) cardialgia.

cardigan [ˈkɑrdɪgən, B ˈkɑd-] *s.* chaqueta de lana tejida; albornoz corto.

cardinal [ˈkɑrdənəl, B ˈkɑd-] *s.* 1. (relig.) cardenal, purpurado. 2. número cardinal. 3. capa corta con capucha (para mujer). 4. (orn.) cardenal. —*a.* fundamental, principal.

cardinalate [-ˌeɪt] *s.* (relig.) cardenalato, capelo; **the c.,** los cardenales (en conjunto).

cardinal flower, (bot.) lobelia escarlata.

cardinal number, número cardinal.

cardinal points, los puntos cardinales.

cardinal sins, los pecados capitales.

cardinal virtues, (filos.) las cuatro virtudes cardinales.

card index, fichero, registro de tarjetas.
carding ['kɑrdɪŋ, B 'kɑd-] *s.* 1. cardadura. 2. lana cardada.
cardiogram ['kɑrdɪəˌgræm, B 'kɑd-] *s.* (med.) cardiograma.
cardiograph [-ˌgræf] *s.* cardiógrafo.
cardiography [ˌkɑrdɪ'ɑgrəfɪ, B ˌkɑdɪ'ɔg-] *s.* cardiografía.
cardiologist [-'ɑlədʒəst, B -'ɔl-] *s.* cardiólogo.
cardiology [-dʒɪ] *s.* cardiología.
cardiomegaly [-oʊ'mɛgəlɪ] *s.* (med.) ensanchamiento anormal del corazón.
cardiovascular [-'væskjələr, B -lə] *a.* (anat.) cardiovascular.
carditis [kɑr'daɪtəs, B kɑ'-] *s.* (med.) carditis.
cardoon [kɑr'dun, B kɑ'-] *s.* (bot.) cardo, cardo de Castilla, cardón.
cardsharp ['kɑrdˌʃɑrp, B 'kɑdˌʃɑp] **cardsharper** [-ərˌ B -ə] *s.* fullero, tahúr.
card table, mesa de juego.
card trick, truco de naipes.
care [kɛr, B kɛə] *s.* 1. cuidado, solicitud. 2. atención, cautela, detenimiento. 3. preocupación, ansiedad, inquietud. 4. cargo, custodia, protección. 5. **in c. of,** a cargo de; **to have a c., to take c.,** tener cuidado; **to take c. not to (offend,** etc.), guardarse de (ofender, etc.); **to take c. of,** cuidar, tener a su cuidado; **to take c. of oneself,** cuidarse a sí mismo, acicalarse; mantenerse por esfuerzo propio. —*v.i.* 1. inquietarse, preocuparse. 2. importarle a uno, ej., *I don't c.,* no me importa. 3. (con *about*) ser importante para uno, ej., *I c. very much about music,* la música es muy importante para mí. 4. (con *about*) interesarse (por). 5. (con *for*) cuidar (a un anciano, inválido, etc.). 6. (con *for*) sentir afecto (por), tener cariño (por). 7. (con *for*) gustarle a uno, ej., *I don't c. for his impetuosity,* no me gusta su impetuosidad. 8. **c. to (do),** tener ganas de (hacer); **I don't c. if I do,** no me disgustaría hacerlo.
CARE, (E.U.) *abrev. de* **Cooperative for American Remittances Everywhere,** organizacíon que envía ropas, alimentos, libros, etc., a personas necesitadas en otros países.
careen [kə'rin] *v.t.* 1. (mar.) carenar, despalmar (una nave). 2. (mar.) dar de quilla. 3. volcar, inclinar. —*v.i.* 1. volcarse, inclinarse. 2. tambalearse. —*s.* (ant.) carena, carenadura.
careenage [-ɪdʒ] *s.* (mar.) 1. carenaje, carenadura, carena. 2. carenero. 3. costo del carenaje.
career [kə'rɪr, B -'rɪə] *s.* 1. carrera, avance rápido, ímpetu. 2. carrera, curso (de la vida). 3. carrera, paso, curso (de los astros, etc.). 4. carrera, profesión. 5. **in full c.,** en plena carrera. —*a.* de carrera (ej., un diplomático). —*v.i.* correr a carrera tendida; correr alocadamente.
careerism [-'rɪrˌɪzəm, B -'rɪər-] *s.* afán desmedido por lograr éxito en una profesión.
careerist [-əst] *s.* ambicioso, arribista.
carefree ['kɛrˌfri, B 'kɛəˌ-] *a.* despreocupado, libre de cuidado; alegre.
careful [-fəl] *a.* 1. cuidadoso; cauteloso, meticuloso, prudente; esmerado. 2. **to be c.,** tener cuidado.
carefully [-ɪ] *adv.* cuidadosamente, cautelosamente, meticulosamente; esmeradamente.
carefulness [-nəs] *s.* cuidado, cautela; esmero.
careless ['kɛrləs, B 'kɛəlɪs] *a.* 1. descuidado, negligente. 2. indiferente; desconsiderado. 3. alegre, despreocupado.
carelessly [-lɪ] *adv.* descuidadamente, negligentemente; sin esmero.
carelessness [-nəs] *s.* descuido, negligencia; indiferencia.
caress [kə'rɛs] *s.* caricia, cariño, mimo. —*v.t.* (*pret., p.p.* CARESSED; *p.pr.* CARESSING) 1. acariciar, hacer caricias, mimar. 2. (fig.) acariciar, halagar.
caresser [-ər, B -ə] *s.* acariciador.
caret ['kærət] *s.* (impr.) signo de intercalación (que usan los escritores y correctores de pruebas).
caretaker ['kɛrˌteɪkər, B 'kɛəˌ-ə] *s.* celador, guardián, cuidador, vigilante. —*a.* interino, provisional (administración o funcionario).
caretaker government, gobierno interino.
careworn [-ˌwɔrn, B -ˌwɔn] *a.* lleno de ansiedad, agobiado, cargado de inquietudes.
carfare ['kɑrˌfɛr, B 'kɑˌfɛə] *s.* 1. valor del pasaje (en ómnibus, tranvía, etc.). 2. (fam.) cambio, menudo, sencillo (Amer.).
cargo ['kɑrgoʊ, B 'kɑgoʊ] *s.* (*pl.* CARGOES O CARGOS) carga, flete, cargamento (de un buque, avión, etc.).
cargo boat, buque carguero, barco de carga.
cargo boom, aguilón de buque.
cargo dead-weight tonnage, (mar.) porte efectivo, tonelaje de carga, carga neta.
carhop ['kɑrˌhɑp, B 'kɑˌhɔp] *s.* camarero que sirve comida o bebidas a los parroquianos en sus automóviles.
Carib ['kærəb] **Cariban** [-əbən, kə'ribən] *s.* caribe.
Caribbean [ˌkærə'biən, kə'rɪbɪ-] *s.* caribe. —*a.* caribe; antillano.
Caribbean Sea, Mar Caribe, Mar de las Antillas.
caribou ['kærəˌbu] *s.* (zool.) caribú.
caricature ['kærɪkəˌtʃʊr, B ˌkærɪ-'tjʊə] caricatura. —*v.t.* 1. caricaturizar, hacer caricaturas. 2. ridiculizar.
caricaturist [-ˌtʃʊrəst, B -'tjʊərɪst] *s.* caricaturista.
caries ['kæriz, 'kɛr-, B 'kɛərɪiz] *s.* (*pl.* CARIES) (med.) caries, cariadura.
carillon ['kærəˌlɑn, kə'rɪljən, B 'kærɪljən] *s.* 1. (mús.) carillón. 2. toque de carillón. 3. registro de carillón (en el órgano). —*v.i.* (*pret., p.p.* CARILLONED; *p.pr.* CARILLONING) tocar el carillón.
carillonneur [ˌkærəlɑ'nɜr, kəˌrɪljə-, B -'nɜ] *s.* campanero mayor.
carina [kə'raɪnə] *s.* (anat., bot., zool.) carina.
carinate ['kærəˌneɪt, -nət] *a.* (zool., bot.) carinado, aquillado.
Carioca [ˌkærɪ'oʊkə] *s.* 1. carioca (nativo de Río de Janeiro). 2. baile y música característicos del Brasil.
cariole ['kærɪˌoʊl] *s.* 1. carruaje ligero de un solo caballo. 2. tipo de trineo canadiense. 3. carriola.
carious ['kærɪəs, 'kɛr-, B 'kɛər-] *a.* cariado (hueso).
caritative ['kærəˌteɪtɪv] *a.* caritativo.
carjacking ['kɑrˌdʒækɪŋ] *s.* secuestro de un coche.
cark [kɑrk, B kɑk] *s.* inquietud, preocupación. —*v.t.* inquietar, preocupar. —*v.i.* inquietarse, preocuparse.
carking ['kɑrkɪŋ, B 'kɑk-] *a.* oneroso, gravoso, penoso.
carl [kɑrl, B kɑl] *s.* 1. (esco.) patán, palurdo. 2. (ant.) villano, hombre vulgar.
carline thistle ['kɑrlən-, B 'kɑlɪn-] (bot.) angélica carlina, cardo ajonjero, aljonje, ajonje.
carling [-ɪŋ] *s.* (mar.) galeota, entremiche.
Carlism ['kɑrlˌɪzəm, B 'kɑl-] *s.* (pol.) carlismo.
Carlist [-əst] *a.* (pol.) carlista.
carload ['kɑrˌloʊd, B 'kɑˌ-] *s.* carga de carro, vagonada, furgonada, carretada.
Carlovingian [ˌkɑrlə'vɪndʒɪən, B ˌkɑl-] *var. de* **Carolingian.**
carmagnole ['kɑrmənˌjoʊl, B 'kɑmən-] *s.* (hist.) carmañola (chaqueta o canción popular del tiempo de la Revolución Francesa).
carman ['kɑrmən, B 'kɑmən] *s.* empleado de tranvía; carretero.
Carmelite ['kɑrməˌlaɪt, B 'kɑmə-] *s.* 1. (relig.) carmelita. 2. tela fina de lana.
carminative [kɑr'mɪnətɪv, B 'kɑmɪ-] *a., s.* (med.) carminativo (medicamento).
carmine ['kɑrmən, B 'kɑˌmaɪn] *s.* carmín carmesí (tinte y color).
carminite [-məˌnaɪt] *s.* (min.) carminita.
carnage ['kɑrnɪdʒ, B 'kɑnɪdʒ] *s.* carnicería, gran mortandad, matanza.
carnal ['kɑrnəl, B 'kɑn-] *a.* 1. carnal; corporal. 2. carnal, sexual, lascivo, sensual, lujurioso.
carnality [kɑr'nælətɪ, B kɑ'-] *s.* carnalidad, lascivia, lujuria, sensualidad, concupiscencia.
carnal knowledge, (der.) ayuntamiento carnal, coito, cópula.
carnallite ['kɑrnəlˌaɪt, B 'kɑn-] *s.* (min.) carnalita.
carnation [kɑr'neɪʃən, B kɑ'-] *s.* (bot.) clavel doble, clavel reventón. —*a.* encarnado.
carnauba [kɑr'nɔbə, B kɑ'-] *s.* (bot.) carnauba, palmera de Brasil.
carnelian [kɑr'niljən, B kə'-] *s.* (min.) carniola, cornalina.
carnification [ˌkɑrnəfɪ'keɪʃən, B ˌkɑnɪ-] *s.* (med.) carnificación.
carnify ['kɑrnəˌfaɪ, B 'kɑn-] *v.t.* (pret., *p.p.* CARNIFIED, *p.pr.* CARNIFYING) (med.) carnificarse.
carnival ['kɑrnəvəl, B 'kɑnɪ-] *s.* 1. carnaval, carnestolendas. 2. parque de atracciones, feria; circo viajero 3. festín; orgía.
carnivore ['kɑrnəˌvɔr, B 'kɑnəˌvɔ] *s.* 1. (zool.) carnívoro. 2. (bot.) planta insectívora (que se alimenta de insectos).
carnivorous [kɑr'nɪvərəs, B kɑ'-] *a.* 1. (zool.) carnívoro, carnicero. 2. (bot.) insectívoro.
carnose ['kɑrˌnoʊs, B 'kɑˌ-] *a.* carnoso, carnudo; (bot.) carnoso.
carnosine ['kɑrnəˌsin, -sən, B 'kɑnə-] *s.* (quím.) carnosina.
carnosity [kɑr'nɑsətɪ, B kɑ'nɔs-] *s.* carnosidad.
carnotite ['kɑrnəˌtaɪt, B 'kɑn-] *s.* (min.) carnotita.
carny ['kɑrnɪ, B 'kɑnɪ] *s.* (G.B., jer.) 1. feria, espectáculo de atracciones; circo viajero. 2. artista de circo (viajero).
carob ['kærəb] *s.* (bot.) algarrobo, ervilla, arveja.
caroche [kə'roʊtʃ, -'roʊʃ] *s.* (ant.) carroza.
carol ['kærəl] *s.* 1. canción de Navidad, villancico. 2. canto alegre y piadoso. —*v.i.* (*pret., p.p.* CAROLED O CAROLLED; *p. pr.* CAROLING O CAROLLING) 1. cantar alegremente. 2. ir cantando villancicos de Navidad. —*v.t.* alabar, glorificar.
Caroline ['kærəˌlaɪn, -lən] *a.* 1. carolingio. 2. carolino (de Carlos I o II de Inglaterra).
Caroline Islands, Islas Carolinas.
Carolingian [ˌkærə'lɪndʒɪən] *a., s.* carolingio, carlovingio.
Carolinian [-'lɪnjən] *a., s.* carolinense, natural de Carolina.
carom ['kærəm] *s.* 1. (billar) carambola. 2. rebote (esp. en ángulo). —*v.i.* 1. hacer carambola, carambolear. 2. rebotar.
carotene ['kærəˌtin] *s.* (bioquím.) caroteno, carotina.
carotid [kə'rɑtəd, B -'rɔt-] *s.* (anat.) carótida. —*a.* carótida (arteria).

carotid gland, (anat.) glándula carotídea.
carousal [kəˈraʊzəl] *s.* jarana, juerga, parranda; francachela.
carouse [kəˈraʊz] *s.* 1. francachela, jarana, juerga, parranda. 2. (ant.) brindis. —*v.i.* correr una juerga, jaranear.
carousel [ˈkærəˈsɛl] *s.* (*merry-go-round*) caballitos, carrusel, tiovivo; (*for baggage in an airport*) cinta transportadora, correa transportadora; (*in a slide projector*) carrete de diapositivas.
carouser [-ər, B -ə] *s.* jaranero, bebedor.
carp [ˈkɑrp, B kɑp] *s.* (*pl.* CARP o CARPS) (ict.) carpa. —*v.i.* quejarse, censurar, criticar.
carpal [ˈkɑrpəl, B ˈkɑpəl] *a.* (anat., zool.) carpiano. —*s.* hueso carpiano, hueso del carpo o de la muñeca.
Carpathian Mountains [kɑrˈpeɪθɪən, B kɑˈ-] *s.* (*pl.*) Cárpatos.
carpel [ˈkɑrpəl, B ˈkɑpəl] *s.* (bot.) carpelo.
carpellate [-pəˌleɪt, -lət] *a.* (bot.) carpelado.
carpenter [ˈkɑrpəntər, B ˈkɑpəntə] *s.* carpintero. —*v.t.*, *v.i.* carpintear.
carpenter bee, (ento.) carpintero, abeja carpintera.
carpenter's horse, (carp.) caballete, burro.
carpentry [-pəntrɪ] *s.* carpintería.
carpet [ˈkɑrpət, B ˈkɑpɪt] *s.* alfombra, tapete, tapiz; **on the c.,** sobre el tapete, en discusión; **to call** o **have (someone) on the c.,** (fam.) reprender, llamar a capítulo (a alguien). —*v.t.* alfombrar, tapizar.
carpetbag [-ˌbæg] *s.* maleta, morral (esp. de alfombra).
carpetbagger [-ər, B -ə] *s.* 1. (hist., E.U.) explotador, aventurero (norteño que iba al Sur después de la Guerra de Secesión). 2. candidato político (ajeno al distrito).
carpetbeater [-ˌbitər, B -ə] *s.* sacudidor de alfombras.
carpet bed, cuadro de jardín con macizos.
carpet beetle, (ento.) polilla de alfombras.
carpeting [ˈkɑrpətɪŋ, B ˈkɑpət-] *s.* 1. material para alfombras. 2. alfombrado.
carpet knight, (despec.) soldado de gabinete.
carpet slipper, zapatilla casera de fieltro.
carpet sweeper, escoba automática para barrer la alfombra.
carpetweed [-ˌwid] *s.* (bot.) especie de hierba mala de N.A.
carpi, *pl. de* **carpus.**
carping [ˈkɑrpɪŋ, B ˈkɑp-] *a.* capcioso, criticón, mordaz.
carpology [kɑrˈpɑlədʒɪ, B kɑˈpɔl-] *s.* (bot.) carpología, rama de la botánica que estudia los frutos.
car pool, convenio entre dueños de automóviles particulares para transportar pasajeros.
carpophagous [-ˈpɑfəgəs, B -ˈpɔf-] *a.* (bot.) carpófago, que come fruta.
carpophore [ˈkɑrpəˌfɔr, B ˈkɑpəˌfɔ] *s.* (bot.) carpóforo.
carport [ˈkɑrˌpɔrt, B ˈkɑˌpɔt] *s.* cobertizo para automóviles, cochera abierta por los lados.
carpospore [ˈkɑrpəˌspɔr, B ˈkɑpəˌspɔ] *s.* (bot.) carpóspora.
carpus [ˈkɑrpəs, B ˈkɑpəs] *s.* (*pl.* CARPI [-ˌpaɪ]) (anat.) carpo, huesos que forman la muñeca.
carrack [ˈkærək] *s.* (hist.) carraca, galeón.
carrageen, carragheen [ˈkærəˌgin] *s.* (bot.) carragahen, musgo de Irlanda.
carrefour [ˌkærəˈfʊr, B -ˈfʊə] *s.* 1. encrucijada. 2. plaza, plazuela.
carrel [ˈkærəl] *s.* recinto o gabinete de estudio, próximo a una biblioteca.
carriage [ˈkærɪdʒ] *s.* 1. coche, carro, carruaje. 2. (G.B.) carruaje de tren, vagón. 3. porte, transporte, conducción, acarreo. 4. porte, costo de transporte. 5. porte (del cuerpo, de la cabeza, etc.). 6. manejo, administración (de una empresa). 7. (mec.) carrito, carro (de una máquina de escribir, etc.); carro corredizo (de un torno). 8. (mil.) cureña (de un cañón).
carriage free, (com.) porte franco.
carriage trade, (fam.) clientela adinerada.
carrick bend [ˈkærɪk-] (mar.) nudo al derecho.
carrick bitts, (mar.) bitas que sostienen el molinete.
carrier [ˈkærɪər, B -ə] *s.* 1. mensajero, mandadero. 2. cargador, portador, transportador. 3. compañía de transportes, empresa porteadora. 4. portaequipajes. 5. (med.) portador (de una enfermedad contagiosa). 6. (quím.) agente (catalítico). 7. (elec., rad.) onda portadora. 8. (mec.) conductor, portador. 9. (mar.) (*forma abrev. de* **aircraft c.**) portaaviones.
carrier pigeon, paloma mensajera.
carrier spectrum, (elec.) espectro de frecuencias portadoras.
carrier wave, (elec., rad.) onda portadora.
carriole, *var. de* **cariole.**
carrion [ˈkærɪən] *s.* 1. carroña. 2. (fig.) inmundicia, suciedad.
carrion crow, (orn.) corneja, cuervo negro, zopilote.
carronade [ˌkærəˈneɪd] *s.* (hist.) carronada, cañón corto y grueso.
carrot [ˈkærət] *s.* zanahoria; **c. top,** (fam.) pelirrojo.
carroty [-ɪ] *a.* de color zanahoria; pelirrojo.
carrousel [ˌkærəˈsɛl, -ɛl, B -ruˈzɛl] *s. var. de* **carousel.**
carry [ˈkærɪ] *v.t.* (*pret.*, *p.p.* CARRIED; *p.pr.* CARRYING) 1. llevar, transportar. 2. conducir, llevar, ej., *a canal carries water,* un canal lleva agua, *wire carries electricity, sound,* etc., el alambre conduce la electricidad, el sonido, etc. 3. llevar consigo, tener (encima). 4. portar (armas, estandarte, etc.). 5. tener (en una lista, planilla, etc.). 6. incluir, comprender, contener. 7. traer consigo, acarrear (ej., un castigo). 8. producir (interés, cosecha, etc.). 9. sostener, alimentar (pasto al ganado). 10. soportar (peso; columnas, un arco, domo, etc.). 11. tener en existencia. 12. ganar (premio, elecciones); ganar las elecciones en (un distrito, etc.) 13. aprobar (proyecto, ley, etc.); lograr la aprobación de (un proyecto, proposición, etc.); ser aprobado en (senado, consejo, etc.). 14. capturar (una plaza, ciudad, etc.). 15. extender, llevar más allá. 16. impulsar, mover. 17. (mat., ten.) llevar (suma, saldo); (ten.) transferir (ej., cuenta al libro mayor). 18. (mar.) llevar puesto (velamen, velas). 19. (caza) rastrear, seguir (la pista, díc. del perro). 20. (golf) cubrir (distancia de un solo golpe); salvar (un obstáculo). 21. **c. about,** llevar de un lado a otro; llevar a todas partes; **c. a heavy load,** (jer.) estar borracho; **c. along,** llevar consigo; **c. arms,** llevar armas; **c. a torch for,** estar enamorado de; abogar por, ser partidario de; **c. authority,** estar revestido de autoridad (gestos, voz, etc.); **c. away,** llevarse; (fig.) entusiasmar; arrebatar, hacer perder el sentido o la calma; **c. back,** devolver; **c. (one) back,** (fig.) hacer recordar (a uno); **c. coals to Newcastle,** llevar hierro a Vizcaya, llevar leña al monte; **c. conviction,** tener fuerza convincente (declaración, argumento, etc.); **c. forward,** (ten.) llevar (saldo); **c. his child,** llevar su hijo en las entrañas; **c. insurance,** tener (póliza de) seguro, estar asegurado; **c. (war, fight) into,** llevar o extender (guerra, lucha) a; **c. into effect,** llevar a la práctica, realizar; **c. it off well,** salir bien del asunto; **c. news,** llevar noticias; **c. a tune,** poder vocalizar una melodía; **c. off,** llevarse (premio); llevar a la tumba, matar (díc. de una enfermedad, dolencia, etc.); **c. off to prison,** llevar a la cárcel; **c. on** llevar adelante; sostener (conversación, correspondencia); asumir el manejo o dirección de (un negocio); **c. one's liquor (well),** ser buen bebedor; **c. oneself,** portarse, comportarse; **c. out,** llevar a cabo, realizar, llevar a la práctica; cumplir con; **c. over,** reservar, guardar (mercancías); convencer o ganarse a una persona; (ten.) llevar (saldo); diferir, traspasar (pérdida, parte no utilizada de un préstamo, etc.); **c. (one's) point,** lograr que prevalezca (su) punto de vista, comprobar (su) argumento; **c. the day,** triunfar, salir airoso; **c. through,** ayudar a superar (dificultades); completar, llevar hasta su término; **c. (things) too far,** forzar la nota, excederse; **c. weight,** llevar lastre (caballo de carrera); (fig.) ser de peso; tener influencia; **c. with one,** guardar en la memoria, conservar (la memoria de algo). —*v.i.* 1. llegar, tener alcance (proyectil); propagarse (voz, sonido), ej., *sound will c. well over water,* el sonido se extiende bien sobre la superficie del agua. 2. progresar, llegar lejos, ej., *the arrow will not c. against the wind,* la flecha no llegará lejos contra el viento. 3. tener efecto, hacer impresión (entre lectores, oyentes, público) (díc. de una obra). 4. (caza) no perder el rastro (perro). 5. llevarse, poder ser llevado (fácil o difícilmente). 6. ser aprobado (proyecto, ley, etc.). 7. **c. on,** continuar, seguir (haciendo) como antes; comportarse escandalosamente; **c. on with (someone),** tener relaciones amorosas con (alguien); **c. on with (something),** seguir adelante con (algo), ej., *c. on with your work,* siga adelante con su trabajo; **c. over,** durar, perdurar; **to fetch and c. (for),** trabajar servilmente (para), ser el esclavo (de).
carryall [-ˌɔl] *s.* **1. bolsa grande, maletín.** 2. coche ligero de un solo caballo. 3. camioneta que todo lo transporta.
carrying capacity, (elec.) capacidad de corriente o de conducción.
carrying charge [-ɪŋ-] 1. gabela. 2. recargo (sobre el precio de mercancías vendidas a plazos).
carry-on bag, carry-on luggage, equipaje de mano.
carry-over [-ˌoʊvər, B -ə] *s.* 1. remanente, sobrante. 2. (ten.) saldo anterior, suma traspasada (de la página anterior).
carsickness [ˈkɑrˌsɪknəs, B ˈkɑˌ-] *s.* mareo, malestar producido por viaje en auto o tren.
cart [kɑrt, B kɑt] *s.* carreta, carretón; **to put the c. before the horse,** empezar la casa por el tejado; confundir los valores. —*v.t.* llevar, acarrear, transportar.
cartage [ˈkɑrtɪdʒ, B ˈkɑt-] *s.* 1. carretaje, acarreo, conducción, transporte. 2. costo del carretaje o transporte.
carte [kɑrt, B kɑt] *s.* 1. carta, lista, menú. 2. (esgr.) cuarta (posición). 3. **a la c.,** a la carta, fuera del menú del día.
carte blanche[ˈkɑrtˈblɑnʃ, B ˈkɑt-] carta blanca, poderes a discreción.
cartel [kɑrˈtɛl, B kɑˈ-] *s.* 1. monopolio; convenio de industriales para controlar precios y normas. 2. cartel, documento en que se estipulan condiciones entre enemigos, esp. en el canje de prisioneros.
Cartesian [kɑrˈtiʒən, B kɑˈtizjən] *s.* (filos.) cartesiano, partidario de Descartes. —*a.* relativo a las teorías cartesianas.
Cartesianism [-ˌɪzəm] *s.* (filos.) cartesianismo.

Carthage ['kɑrθɪdʒ, B 'kɑθɪdʒ] *s.* Cartago.
Carthaginian [ˌkɑrθə'dʒɪnɪən, B ˌkɑθə-] *a., s.* cartaginés, cartaginense.
Carthusian [kɑr'θuʒən, B kɑ'θjuzjən] *s., a.* cartujo (monje).
cartilage ['kɑrtəlɪdʒ, B 'kɑt-] *s.* (biol.) cartílago, ternilla.
cartilaginous [ˌkɑrtə'lædʒənəs, B ˌkɑtɪ-] *a.* cartilaginoso.
cartload ['kɑrtˌloʊd, B 'kɑt-] *s.* carretada; **by cartloads,** a carretadas.
cartogram ['kɑrtə, græm, B 'kɑtə-] *s.* cartograma, mapa de diagramas de estadísticas geográficas.
cartographer [kɑr'tɑgrəfər, B kɑ'tɔgrəfə] *s.* cartógrafo.
cartographic [ˌkɑrtə'græfɪk, B ˌkɑtə-]
cartographical [-əl] *a.* cartográfico.
cartography [kɑr'tɑgrəfɪ, B kɑ'tɔg-] *s.* cartografía, arte y oficio de diseñar y elaborar mapas.
cartomancy ['kɑrtəˌmænsɪ, B 'kɑtə-] *s.* cartomancia, adivinación del futuro por medio de los naipes.
carton ['kɑrtən, B 'kɑt-] *s.* 1. caja (de cartón). 2. envase de un conjunto de objetos o piezas. 3. centro del blanco (de tiro).
cartoon [kɑr'tun, B kɑ'-] *s.* 1. dibujo cómico, caricatura. 2. (*comic strip*) tira cómica. 3. (cinem.) dibujo animado. 4. (arte) cartón.
cartoonist [-əst] *s.* caricaturista, humorista, dibujante de chistes.
cartouche, cartouch [kɑr'tuʃ, B kɑ'-] *s.* 1. (mil.) cartucho. 2. (arq.) cartela, modillón, pequeño ornamento (esp. en los capiteles jónicos). 3. figura oval (de jeroglíficos que representa el nombre de un faraón). 4. (pirotecnia) cartucho.
cartridge ['kɑrtrɪdʒ, B 'kɑt-] *s.* 1. cartucho. 2. pastilla (fonocaptora). 3. (foto.) cartucho (para rollo de película). 4. **blank c.,** cartucho sin bala.
cartridge belt, canana, cartuchera.
cartridge clip, cargador de cartuchos, peine de balas.
cartulary ['kɑrtʃəˌlɛrɪ, B 'kɑtʃʊlərɪ] *s.* (der., hist.) cartulario (registro de cédulas, títulos y privilegios, esp. de un monasterio).
cartwheel ['kɑrtˌhwil, -ˌwil, B 'kɑt-] *s.* 1. rueda de carreta. 2. voltereta lateral. 3. (fam. E.U.) moneda grande, dólar. 4. **to turn cartwheels,** dar saltos mortales (de alegría o excitación).
caruncle ['kærˌʌŋkəl, kə'rʌŋ-] *s.* (anat., bot., zool.) carúncula, carnosidad.
carunculate [kə'rʌŋkjələt] **carunculated** [-ˌleɪtəd] *a.* carunculado.
carvacrol ['kɑrvəˌkrɔl, B 'kɑvə-] *s.* (farm.) carvacrol (antiséptico).
carve [kɑrv, B kɑv] *v.t.* 1. tallar, entallar, cincelar, esculpir. 2. trinchar (la carne, el asado, el pavo, etc.). 3. **c. into,** convertir (material) en (figura, ornamento, diseño) tallado; **c. out,** separar (parte de algo); (fig.) adueñarse de (parte de un territorio, país, etc.) esp. por las armas; **c. out of, in** o **on,** tallar o esculpir en (algún material). —*v.i.* 1. trinchar la carne. 2. trabajar como tallador, ser tallador.
carvel ['kɑrvəl, -ˌvɛl, B 'kɑvəl] *var. de* **caravel, caravelle.**
carvel-built [-ˌbɪlt] *a.* (mar.) construido a tope.
carvel-joint [-ˌdʒɔɪnt] *s.* (mar.) junta a tope.
carven ['kɑrvən, B 'kɑvən] *a.* (poét.) tallado, esculpido.
carving [-vɪŋ] *s.* escultura, talla, entalladura.
carving knife, trinchante, cuchillo de trinchar.
car wash, túnel de lavado, tren de lavado, lavado automático.
caryatid [ˌkærɪ'ætəd] *s.* (*pl.* CARYATIDS O CARYATIDES [-əˌdiz]) (arq.) cariátide.
caryophyllaceous [ˌkærɪoʊfə'leɪʃəs] *a.* (bot.) cariofilácea.
caryopsis [-'ɑpsəs, B -'ɔp-] *s.* (bot.) cariópside.
casaba [kə'sɑbə] *s.* melón de Indias, melón de la China.
casbah ['kæzˌbɑ, 'kɑz-] *s.* casba, antiguo barrio y alcazaba musulmana en las poblaciones norafricanas.
cascade [kæ'skeɪd] *s.* cascada, salto (de agua); cascada (de encaje, brocado, etc.). —*v.i.* caer o colgar en cascadas. —*v.t.* 1. verter o echar en cascadas. 2. (elec.) conectar en cascada.
cascade aerator, (a.a.) aereador de escalones o de cascada.
cascara [kæ'skærə, B -'skɑrə] *s.* (bot.) (arbusto de California cuya corteza es la) cáscara sagrada.
cascara sagrada [-sə'grɑdə] (farm.) cáscara sagrada.
cascarilla [ˌkæskə'rɪlə] *s.* 1. (bot.) cascarillo. 2. (farm.) cascarilla.
case [keɪs] *s.* 1. caso. 2. condición, estado, situación (de cosas). 3. caso clínico, paciente, enfermo. 4. argumento, tesis, punto de vista. 5. (fam.) tipo raro, persona extravagante. 6. (gram.) caso. 7. (der.) causa, proceso, pleito, acción. 8. **c. in point,** caso en cuestión, caso pertinente; **in any c.,** en todo caso, de todas maneras; **in c.,** caso que, en caso (de) que, si acaso; **in c. of,** en caso de; **in no c.,** de ninguna manera; **in such a c., in that c.,** en tal caso; **in the c. of,** en cuanto a, respecto a, cuando lo de; **it's not a c. of,** no se trata de, no es el caso de que; **it is not the c.,** no es cierto esto, no es ése el caso; **leading c.,** (der.) causa determinante; **to bring a c. against,** poner (o meter) pleito a; **to make out one's c.,** demostrar su tesis, establecer su punto de vista; **in c. of (fire, theft,** etc.), en caso de (fuego, robo, etc.).
case, *s.* 1. caja, estuche; cajón (para embalar); forro, cubierta; funda, vaina; caja (de reloj). 2. (mec.) caja, camisa, forro, manguito. 3. (carp.) bastidor, marco (de puerta o ventana). 4. (tip.) caja de imprenta; **lower c.,** caja baja (de minúsculas); **upper c.,** caja alta (de mayúsculas). —*v.t.* 1. embalar, encajonar; enfundar, envainar; poner en una caja o estuche. 2. (con *with*) envolver (en), revestir (de). 3. (jer.) inspeccionar, obtener información sobre espiar (una casa, tienda, etc.) en que se intenta robar.
casease ['keɪsɪ, eɪs] *s.* (bioquím.) caseasa.
caseate [-ˌeɪt] *v.i.* (med.) caseificarse.
caseation [ˌkeɪsɪ'eɪʃən] *s.* (med.) caseificación.
case bay, (const.) conjunto de vigas y viguetas de un tramo del edificio.
caseharden ['keɪsˌhɑrdən, B -'hɑd-] *v.t.* 1. (metal.) cementar, carburizar, templar, endurecer por fuera. 2. (fig.) volver insensible.
casehardened [-ənd] *a.* insensible, empedernido, endurecido; apático, indiferente.
case history, antecedentes (de una persona); (med.) hoja clínica, historia clínica.
casein ['keɪˌsin, B 'keɪsiɪn] *s.* (quím.) caseína.
caseinogen [ˌkeɪsɪ'ɪnədʒən, keɪ'sin-] *s.* (bioquím.) caseinógeno.
case knife, cuchillo provisto de vaina; cuchillo de mesa.
case law, (der.) jurisprudencia, precedentes.
case load, número de casos (atendidos por un médico, asistente social etc.).
casemate ['keɪsˌmeɪt] *s.* (fort., mil., mar.) casamata.
casement [-mənt] *s.* 1. bastidor, hoja batiente. 2. ventana a bisagra, ventana batiente.
caseous ['keɪsɪəs] *a.* caseoso, como el queso.
casern, caserne [kə'zɜrn, B -'zɜn] *s.* (mil.) cuartel.
case shot, (mil.) bote de metralla.
case study, estudio de un individuo o grupo, esp. como modelo de incidencias médicas, psicológicas o sociales.
casework ['keɪsˌwɜrk, B -ˌwɜk] *s.* (sociol.) trabajo de asistencia social individualizada, estudio de rehabilitación (de personas o familias inadaptadas).
caseworker ['keɪs'wɜrkər] *s.* asistente social.
cash [kæʃ] *s.* (*sing., pl.*) 1. dinero efectivo, al contado. 2. (com.) pago al contado. 3. **for c.,** al contado; **to be out of c.,** estar sin dinero; **to convert into c.,** convertir en efectivo; **to pay c.,** pagar al contado. —*v.t.* cobrar en efectivo, cambiar por efectivo, ej., *to c. a check,* cambiar o cobrar un cheque; **c. in, c. in one's chips,** abandonar una empresa; (jer.) morir; **c. in on,** sacar provecho de, aprovecharse de (algo, gen. gracias a una información exclusiva o confidencial).
cash account, (ten.) cuenta de caja.
cash and carry, *s.* almacén de venta al por mayor (pagar al contado y acarrear uno mismo). —*a.* (*business*) de venta al por mayor.
cashbook ['kæʃˌbʊk] *s.* (ten.) libro de caja.
cashbox [-ˌbɑks, B -ˌbɔks] *s.* caja.
cash discount, descuento por pago al contado.
cashew ['kæʃu, kə'ʃu, B kæ-] *s.* 1. (bot.) anacardo, pajuil (Am.). 2. almendra anacardo, nuez de acajú.
cash flow, flujo de caja, cash-flow.
cash flow problem, problema de liquidez.
cashier [kæ'ʃɪr, B kə'ʃɪə] *s.* cajero. —*v.t.* 1. destituir, echar, despedir; (mil.) dar de baja. 2. descartar, eliminar.
cashier's check, (fin.) cheque de caja, cheque propio, cheque de la gerencia (a cargo del mismo banco).
cashmere ['kæʒˌmɪr, 'kæʃ-, B kæʃ'mɪə] *s.* (tej.) 1. lana fina de cabra. 2. cachemira, casimir. 3. chal o tela de lana fina.
cash on delivery, (com.) entrega contra pago.
cash on hand, efectivo en caja.
cashoo [kə'ʃu] *s.* (bot., farm.) cato, cachú, catecú.
cash payment, pago al contado.
cash prize, premio en efectivo.
cash register, caja registradora.
cash value, valor efectivo.
casing ['keɪsɪŋ] *s.* 1. funda, cubierta, envoltura, estuche. 2. revoque de una pared. 3. marco (de puerta o ventana). 4. tripa (de salchicha). 5. (anat.) envoltura. 6. (bot.) película (de las gramíneas). 7. (cost.) jareta. 8. (aut.) cubierta de neumático.
casino [kə'sinoʊ] *s.* 1. casino, casa de juego. 2. (naipes) casino.
cask [kæsk, B kɑsk] *s.* barril, tonel, pipa, cuba, casco. —*v.t.* entonelar, meter en toneles, envasar.
casket ['kæskət, B 'kɑs-] *s.* 1. cofrecito, cajita, estuche. 2. (*coffin*) ataúd. —*v.t.* poner en un cofrecito.
Caspian ['kæspɪən] *a., s.* Caspio.
Caspian Sea, Mar Caspio.
casque [kæsk] *s.* (hist.) casco, yelmo, capacete, almete, morrión.
cassaba, *var. de* **casaba.**
Cassandra [kə'sændrə] *s.* 1. (mitol.) Casandra. 2. (fig.) Casandra, profeta o profetisa de mal agüero.

cassation [kæ'seɪʃən] *s.* (der.) casación, revocación, anulación.
cassava [kə'sɑvə] *s.* (bot.) mandioca, yuca.
casserole ['kæsəˌroʊl] *s.* (cocina) 1. cacerola. 2. plato de carnes y verdura al horno.
cassette [kə'sɛt] *s.* 1. (foto.) chasis (para placa o película plana); cartucho (para rollo de película). 2. cassette, cassete (cartucho de cinta magnetofónica); **on c.,** en cassette, grabado.
cassette deck, platina, pletina.
cassette player, pasacintas, cassette (Esp.), pasacassettes (Arg.), tocacassettes (Chile).
cassette recorder, grabadora, grabador (de cassettes), cassette (Esp.).
cassia ['kæʃə, B 'kæsɪə] *s.* **1. (bot.) casia.** 2. canela de la China.
cassimere ['kæzəˌmɪr, B 'kæsɪˌmɪə] *s.* (tej.) casimir.
cassino, *var. de* **casino** (naipes).
Cassiopeia [ˌkæsɪə'piə] *s.* (mitol., astr.) Casiopea.
cassis [kæ'si] *s.* 1. (bot.) casis. 2. licor del grosellero negro.
cassiterite [kə'sɪtəˌraɪt] *s.* (min.) casiterita.
Cassius ['kæʃəs, B 'kæsɪəs] *s.* Casio, líder de la conspiración contra Julio César.
cassock ['kæsək] *s.* sotana, balandrán.
cassowary ['kæsəˌwɛrɪ, B -ˌwɛərɪ] *s.* (orn.) casuario.
cast [kæst, B kɑst] *v.t.* (*pret., p.p.* CAST; *p.pr.* CASTING) 1. lanzar, tirar (dados, red o anzuelo para pescar); echar (voto, balota, suertes; anclas; ojeada, mirada). 2. soltar, perder (herradura el caballo); mudar de (piel o plumaje). 3. calcular, ej., *c. (a column of) figures,* sumar (una columna de) números. 4. formar, moldear; vaciar (estatua, etc.), fundir (hierro, metal, balas, estatuas, etc.). 5. (impr.) estereotipar. 6. (der.) decidir contra. 7. (teat.) repartir (papeles); darle un papel a (actor). 8. combar, alabear (una viga, etc.). 9. **c. a horoscope,** hacer un horóscopo; **c. a (brilliant, faint,** etc.) **light on,** iluminar con una luz (brillante, tenue, etc.); **c. a shadow on,** echar una sombra sobre; (fig.) ensombrecer; **c. ashore,** varar, echar a la playa; **c. aside,** desechar (ropa, etc.); **c. a spell on,** hechizar, encantar; **c. away,** tirar, abandonar; arrojar (náufragos a una isla, etc.); **c. blame upon,** tachar de culpable; **c. calf,** abortar (la vaca); **c. doubt upon,** poner en duda; **c. down,** abatir, derribar; bajar (los ojos); descorazonar; **c. into prison,** enviar a la cárcel; **c. light on,** (fig.) verter luz sobre, esclarecer; **c. loose,** soltar; (mar.) desamarrar (un bote); **c. off,** soltar, desatar, desamarrar (un bote); desechar (vestido, prenda, etc.); abandonar (disimulo, moderación, etc.); (impr.) calcular el espacio para (material, composición, etc.); **c. on,** echarse (vestido, etc.) de prisa; empezar (un tejido); **c. one's cares upon,** hacer partícipe de sus preocupaciones; **c. out,** echar fuera, arrojar; **c. out devils,** exorcizar demonios; **c. the blame on,** echar la culpa a, imputar; **c. the lead,** (mar.) sondar o sondear, echar el escandallo; **c. your bread upon the water,** haz bien y no mires a quien; **the die is c.,** (fig.) la suerte está echada; **to be c. away,** zozobrar (embarcación), naufragar (personas); **to be c. down,** estar abatido. —*v.i.* 1. tirar el anzuelo, pescar con caña. 2. sumar, hacer adiciones. 3. combarse, alabearse (madera, viga, etc.). 4. moldearse, fundirse (metal, etc.). 5. **c. about,** buscar por todas partes; (mar.) virar (el barco); **c. about for,** tratar de encontrar (una solución, ayuda, medios, etc.); **c. loose,** (mar.) desamarrar; **c. off,** terminar una vuelta (de tejido); (mar.) desamarrar, partir; **c. on,** empezar una hilera (de tejido). —*s.* 1. lanzamiento (de una red, del anzuelo), tirada (de dados). 2. molde, moldura, forma. 3. pieza fundida. 4. aspecto, aire, semblante; clase, tipo. 5. tinte, matiz. 6. enyesadura, vendaje enyesado. 7. pellejo (de reptil que lo ha mudado). 8. (teat.) reparto. 9. alcance de tiro (de un arma arrojadiza). 10. anzuelo con sedal (de una caña de pescar). 11. **c. in the eye,** ligera bizquera, ojo gacho.
castable ['kæstəbəl, B 'kɑst-] *s.* compuesto para moldear, concreto refractario.
Castalides [kə'stælɪˌdiz] *s. pl.* (mitol.) Castálidas, las musas.
castanet [ˌkæstə'nɛt] *s.* (mús.) castañuela, castañeta, palillos.
castaway ['kæstəˌweɪ, B 'kɑst-] *s., a.* 1. náufrago. 2. abandonado. 3. réprobo, proscrito.
caste [kæst, B kɑst] *s.* 1. casta. 2. sistema (social) de castas. 3. **to lose c.,** descender en la escala social; desprestigiarse.
castellan ['kæstələn] *s.* castellano, gobernador de un castillo.
castellated [-ˌleɪtəd] *a.* 1. almenado. 2. como un castillo. 3. con castillos (distrito, región, etc.). 4. (her.) castillado.
caster ['kæstər, B 'kɑstə] *s.* 1. fundidor, vaciador, moldeador. 2. (impr.) fundidora, máquina fundidora (de tipos). 3. ruedecilla de mueble o máquina portátil. 4. vinagrera, angarillas.
castigate ['kæstəˌgeɪt] *v.t.* castigar; reprobar o criticar severamente.
castigation [ˌkæstə'geɪʃən] *s.* castigo.
castigator ['kæstəˌgeɪtər, B -ə] *s.* castigador.
Castile [kæs'til] *s.* Castilla.
Castile soap, jabón de Castilla.
Castilian [kæ'stɪljən] *s., a.* castellano.
casting ['kæstɪŋ, B 'kɑst-] *s.* 1. fundición, vaciado; hierro fundido. 2. (teat.) reparto, distribución (de papeles). 3. pellejo (que ha mudado un reptil); pluma o plumas (perdidas por un pájaro); excremento (de un animal).
casting shop, fundición, taller de fundición.
casting vote, voto decisivo.
cast iron, hierro fundido.
cast-iron [-'aɪərn, B -'aɪən] *a.* 1. de hierro fundido. 2. (fig.) de hierro, fuerte, resistente (ej., estómago). 3. (fig.) férreo (determinación, voluntad, etc.). 4. (fig.) firme, irrefutable (coartada); irrebatible (caso), inalterable (frase idiomática).
castle ['kæsəl, B 'kɑsəl] *s.* 1. castillo. 2. (ajedrez) torre, roque. —*v.t., v.i.* (ajedrez) enrocar (al rey).
castled [-əld] *a.* 1. almenado. 2. con castillos, fortificado (región, etc.).
castle nut, tuerca almenada o entallada.
castles in Spain, (G.B., fig.) castillos en el aire.
castles in the air, (fig.) castillos en el aire; **to build castles in the air,** hacer castillos en el aire.
cast net, casting net, esparavel, atarraya.
castoff ['kæstˌɔf, B 'kɑst-] *a.* desechado, de desecho, ej., *c. clothing,* ropa vieja. —*s.* 1. desecho. 2. ropa de desecho. 3. (impr.) cálculo de espacio, cálculo tipográfico, cálculo de la composición.
cast off, *v.t.* 1. desechar, descartar, tirar; abandonar. 2. mudar (el plumaje). 3. (mar.) soltar amarras, levar el ancla.
castor ['kæstər, B 'kɑstə] *s.* 1. castóreo. 2. (sombrero de) castor. 3. (zool.) castor.
Castor, *s.* (mitol., astr.) Cástor (una de las dos estrellas principales de la constelación de los Gemelos).
Castor and Pollux, *s. pl.* 1. (astr.) Astillejos. 2. (mitol.) Cástor y Pólux.
castor bean, 1. (bot.) ricino. 2. semilla del ricino.
castor oil, aceite de ricino, palmacristi.
castor-oil plant ['kæstərˌɔɪl- B 'kɑs-] (bot.) ricino, higuera del infierno, higuereta, querva.
castrametation [ˌkæstrəmə'teɪʃən] *s.* (mil.) castrametación.
castrate ['kæsˌtreɪt, B kæ'streɪt] *v.t.* 1. castrar, capar, emascular. 2. expurgar (un libro).
castration [kæ'streɪʃən] *s.* 1. castración, castra, capadura, emasculación. 2. expurgación (de un libro).
Castroism ['kæstroʊˌɪzəm] *s.* Castrismo, interpretación e implementación de teorías políticas por Fidel Castro.
cast steel, acero fundido, acero moldeado o colado.
casual ['kæʒʊəl, B -jʊəl] *a.* 1. casual, accidental, fortuito. 2. ocasional, eventual. 3. indiferente, desprendido. 4. informal. 5. improvisado, impensado.
casually [-ɪ] *adv.* casualmente, indiferentemente, informalmente.
casualty ['kæʒəltɪ, B -jʊəl-] *s.* 1. accidente, desgracia, desastre. 2. contingencia. 3. víctima (de un accidente). 4. (mil.) baja.
casual wear, ropa informal y cómoda.
casuarina [ˌkæʒʊə'rinə] *s.* (bot.) casuarina.
casuist ['kæʒʊəst, B 'kæzjʊ-] *s.* casuista, versado en casuística.
casuistic [ˌkæʒʊ'ɪstɪk, B ˌkæzjʊ-] *a.* casuístico; sofístico.
casuistry ['kæʒʊəstrɪ, B 'kæzjʊɪ-] *s.* casuística, casuismo.
casus belli [ˌkɑsəs'bɛlˌi, ˌkeɪsəs'bɛlˌaɪ] *s.* motivo de guerra.
cat [kæt] *s.* 1. (zool.) gato. 2. (zool.) felino. 3. mujer desalmada. 4. (mar.) gata, aparejo del ancla (para izarla hasta la serviola). 5. (forma abrev. de **cat-o'-nine-tails)** azote (de nueve ramales). 6. (ict.) bagre. 7. (jer.) aficionado al jazz. 8. **curiosity killed the c.,** la curiosidad mató al gato; **c.-and-dog life,** vida de continuas peleas; **to have no room to swing a c.,** no caber ni un alfiler; **the cat's meow (pajamas, whiskers),** (jer.) persona (cosa, plan) excelente o notable; **to be like c. and dog,** andar como perro y gato; **to bell the c.,** poner el cascabel al gato; **to let the c. out of the bag,** (fig.) revelar un secreto; **to rain cats and dogs,** llover a cántaros; **to see which way the c. jumps,** ver qué giro toma un asunto; **while the c. is away, the mice play,** mientras los gatos duermen, los ratones bailan. —*v.t.* 1. fustigar, azotar con látigo. 2. (mar.) elevar el ancla hasta la serviola.
CAT *s.* **(computerized axial tomography)** TAC.
CAT scanner, escáner TAC.
catabolic ['kætə'bɑlɪk, B -'bɔl-] *a.* (med.) catabólico.
catachresis [ˌkætə'krisəs] *s.* (*pl.* CATACHRESES [-ˌsiz]) (ret.) catacresis.
cataclysm ['kætəˌklɪzəm] *s.* cataclismo.
cataclysmic [kætə'klɪzmɪk] **cataclysmal** [-'klɪzməl] *a.* catastrófico, desastroso.
catacomb ['kætəˌkoʊm, B -ˌkum] *s.* catacumba.
catadioptric [ˌkætəˌdaɪ'ɑptrɪk, B -ɔp-] *a.* (ópt.) catadióptrico.
catadromous [kə'tædrəməs] *a.* (ict.) catádromo.
catafalque ['kætəˌfælk, -ˌfɔlk, B -ˌfælk] *s.* catafalco.
Catalan ['kætələn, -ˌæn] *s., a.* catalán.
catalase ['kætəlˌeɪs] *s.* (quím.) catalasa.
catalectic verse [ˌkætəl'ɛktɪk-] (poét.) verso cataléctico.
catalepsy ['kætəlˌɛpsɪ] *s.* (med.) catalepsia.

cataleptic [ˌkætəl'ɛptɪk] *a.* cataléptico.
catalog, catalogue ['kætəlˌɔg, -ˌɑg, B -ˌɔg] *s.* catálogo. —*v.t.* catalogar.
cataloger, cataloguer [-ər, B -ə] *s.* catalogador.
Catalonia [ˌkætəl'oʊnjə] *s.* Cataluña.
Catalonian [-njən] *a., s.* catalán.
catalpa [kə'tælpə, -'tɔl-, B -'tæl-] *s.* (bot.) catalpa.
catalysis [kə'tæləsəs] *s.* (quím.) catálisis.
catalyst ['kætələst] *s.* (quím.) catalizador.
catalytic [ˌkætəl'ɪtɪk] *a.* catalítico, catalizador.
catalytic cracker, desintegrador catalítico (de petróleos).
catalytic converter, catalizador.
catalyze ['kætəlˌaɪz] *v.t.* catalizar, producir catálisis.
catamaran [ˌkætəmə'ræn] *s.* 1. (mar.) catamarán. 2. bote de casco doble. 3. persona pendenciera.
catamenia [ˌkætə'minɪə] *s.* (fisiol.) catamenia, menstruación.
catamenial [-nɪəl] *a.* catamenial.
catamite ['kætəˌmaɪt] *s.* bardaje, catamito, sodomita.
catamount ['kætəˌmaʊnt] *s.* (zool.) 1. gato montés. 2. lince, puma (Am.).
catamountain [ˌkætə'maʊntən] *s.* (zool.) leopardo, pantera.
cat and mouse, (fig.) **to play c.,** jugar al gato y al ratón.
cataphoresis [ˌkætəfə'risəs] *s.* (med., quím.) cataforesis.
cataplasia [-'pleɪʒə] *s.* (biol.) cataplasia.
cataplasm ['kætəˌplæzəm] *s.* (med.) cataplasma.
catapult ['kætəˌpʌlt, -ˌpult, B -ˌpʌlt] *s.* 1. (hist.) catapulta. 2. honda, tiragomas, tirador. 3. (aer.) catapulta. —*v.t.* catapultar, disparar, lanzar.
cataract ['kætəˌrækt] *s.* 1. catarata, salto grande de agua. 2. aguacero, inundación. 3. (med.) catarata, telilla opaca sobre la niña del ojo. 4. (mec.) catarata.
catarrh [kə'tɑr, B -'tɑ] *s.* (med.) catarro.
catarrhal [-'tɑrəl] *a.* catarral.
catastasis [kə'tæstəsəs] *s.* (ant., teat.) catástasis.
catastrophe [kə'tæstrəfɪ] *s.* 1. catástrofe, cataclismo, calamidad. 2. catástrofe, desenlace (de un drama).
catastrophic [ˌkætə'strɑfɪk, B -'strɔf-] *a.* catastrófico.
catatonia [-'toʊnɪə] *s.* (med.) catatonía.
catbird ['kætˌbɜrd, B -ˌbɜd] *s.* (orn.) tordo americano (cuyo reclamo es parecido al maullido del gato).
catboat [-ˌboʊt] *s.* (mar.) laúd.
catbrier [-ˌbraɪər, B -ə] (bot.) (especie de) zarzaparrilla.
cat burglar, ladrón que escala paredes.
catcall [-ˌkɔl] *s.* rechifla, silbatina, siseo. —*v.i., v.t.* rechiflar, silbar, sisear.
catch [kætʃ] *v.t.* (*pret., p.p.* CAUGHT [kɔt] *p.pr.* CATCHING) 1. atrapar, capturar. 2. coger, agarrar; adueñarse de. 3. engancharse (camisa, manga, etc. en algo); 4. (con *in, at*) coger (con), pillar, pescar, sorprender (en). 5. contraer, coger (una enfermedad). 6. contagiarse de (entusiasmo, atmósfera, etc.). 7. adquirir (acento, hábito, etc.). 8. atraer, cautivar (atención, mirada, etc.). 9. tomar, alcanzar (tren, avión, etc.). 10. entender, captar (idea, palabras, lo dicho, etc.). 11. captar, reproducir (ej., una escena en una fotografía o cuadro). 12. pegar, darle (a uno) (en); asestar (golpe) (a uno), ej., *he caught him on the chin,* le pegó o le dio en la barbilla. 13. recibir (golpe, bala, etc.; rayos del sol, fuerza del viento, etc.), ej., *the blow caught him in the stomach,* recibió el golpe en el estómago, *the plane caught the full force of the wind,* el avión recibió toda la fuerza del viento. 14. **c. a glimpse of,** vislumbrar; **c. a likeness,** reproducir (semblante, etc.) fielmente (en pintura o fotografía); **c. fire,** prender (fuego); **c. hold of,** asirse de, agarrarse de; **c. it,** ganarse una zurra o reprimenda; **c. one's breath,** recobrar el aliento; **c. one's eye,** atraer la atención de uno; **c. one's fancy,** antojársele a uno; **c. oneself,** contenerse; darse cuenta, ej., *he was on the point of blurting out the truth but caught himself in time,* estaba a punto de revelar la verdad pero se contuvo a tiempo, *he caught himself staring at her,* se dio cuenta de que estaba mirándola fijamente; **c. sight of,** avistar, echar la vista encima; **c. up,** adquirir (hábito, acento, etc.); agarrar, arrebatar; alcanzar, ponerse al día (en el trabajo, etc.); interrumpir (al que habla). —*v.i.* 1. prender fuego. 2. (con *on*) engancharse, prender (en). 3. (con *in*) quedar cogido, aprisionado o enredado (en). 4. (jer.) comprender. 5. **c. at,** (tratar de) asir o agarrar; **c. on,** comprender, caer en la cuenta; volverse popular (canción, moda, etc.); **c. up with,** alcanzar (a alguien); ponerse al día en (el trabajo, estudio, etc.). —*s.* 1. cogida (de la pelota). 2. pesca; botín, presa. 3. retén, pestillo; lengüeta (de una trampa). 4. impedimento, dificultad (esp. ocultos). 5. engañifa, trampa. 6. buen partido (dic. de un novio rico, etc.).
catchall ['kætʃˌɔl] *s.* armario, caja o cesto para guardar una variedad de cosas.
catch-as-catch-can ['kætʃəzˌkætʃ'kæn] *a.* al azar, improvisadamente, como quiera. —*s.* estilo de lucha libre.
catch basin, sumidero, pocillo, cisterna de desagüe.
catch bolt, picaporte.
catch drain, cuneta o tubo de desagüe.
catcher ['kætʃər, B -ə] *s.* 1. el que agarra o recoge. 2. (dep.) catcher o receptor en béisbol.
catchfly [-ˌflaɪ] *s.* (bot.) pegamoscas.
catching [-ɪŋ] *a.* 1. contagioso, infeccioso. 2. pegadizo, fascinante (canción, hábito, etc.).
catchment [-mənt] *s.* 1. captación, estancación (del agua). 2. estanque.
catchment area, c. basin, cuenca de captación, cuenca colectora.
catchpenny [-ˌpɛnɪ] *a.* 1. trapacero. 2. barato, de pacotilla.
catch phrase, frase o consigna publicitaria que atrae la atención.
catch pit, sumidero.
catchpole, catchpoll [-ˌpoʊl] *s.* alguacil, funcionario menor.
catchup, *var. de* **catsup.**
catchword ['kætʃˌwɜrd, B -ˌwɜd] *s.* 1. lema, mote, divisa. 2. (impr.) llamada, reclamo. 3. (teat.) pie, apunte.
catchy [-ɪ] *a.* (CATCHIER; CATCHIEST) 1. agradable, fascinante, pegadizo, ej., *a c. tune,* una tonada pegadiza. 2. capcioso, tramposo, engañoso, ej., *a c. question,* una pregunta engañosa o capciosa.
cat distemper, (vet.) enteritis felina.
cate [keɪt] *s.* (ant.) (*gen. en pl.*) viandas delicadas y finas.
catechesis [ˌkætə'kisəs] *s.* (*pl.* CATECHESES [-ˌsiz]) catequesis.
catechism ['kætəˌkɪzəm] *s.* catecismo.
catechist [-ˌkɪst, -kəst] *s.* catequista.
catechistic [ˌkætə'kɪstɪk] *a.* catequístico.
catechization [-kə'zeɪʃən, B -kaɪ-] *s.* 1. catequización. 2. examen, interrogatorio.
catechize ['kætəˌkaɪz] *v.t., v.i.* 1. catequizar. 2. examinar, interrogar.
catechizer [-ər, B -ə] *s.* catequizador, catequizante.
catechu ['kætəˌtʃu] *s.* cato, cachú, catecú, (substancia astringente).
catechumen [ˌkætə'kjumən] *s.* (relig.) catecúmeno, catecúmena.
catechumenate [-ˌeɪt] *s.* catecumenado.
categorical [ˌkætə'gɔrɪkəl, -'gɑr-, B -'gɔr-] *a.* categórico, absoluto, rotundo, explícito.
categorical imperative, (filos.) imperativo categórico.
categorically [-ɪ] *adv.* categóricamente.
categorization [ˌkætɪgərə'zeɪʃən] *s.* categorización, clasificación.
categorize ['kætɪgəˌraɪz] *v.t.* categorizar, clasificar por categorías.
category ['kætəˌgɔrɪ, B -gərɪ] *s.* categoría, clase, división.
catena [kə'tinə] *s.* (*pl.* CATENAE [-ni] o CATENAS) cadena, serie.
catenary ['kætəˌnɛrɪ, B kə'tinərɪ] (mat.) *a.* (curva) catenaria. —*s.* curva catenaria.
catenate ['kætəˌneɪt] *v.t.* concadenar, encadenar, enlazar.
catenation [ˌkætə'neɪʃən] *s.* concatenación, encadenamiento.
catenulate [kə'tɛnjələt] *a.* catenular.
cater ['keɪtər, B -ə] *v.i.* 1. (con *for*) proveer, abastecer, surtir (de víveres gen. para banquetes y fiestas). 2. (con *to*) complacer (a una persona, gustos etc.).
catercorner [ˌkætɪ'kɔrnər, B -'kɔnə] **catercornered** ['kætɪˌkɔrnərd, B -ˌkɔnəd] *a.* esquinado, atravesado, cruzado, oblicuo, sesgado. —*adv.* oblicuamente, en diagonal.
caterer ['keɪtərər, B -ərə] *s.* proveedor, abastecedor (esp. para recepciones, banquetes y fiestas en clubes o casas particulares).
catering [-ərɪŋ] *s.* arte u oficio de proveer banquetes a domicilio.
caterpillar ['kætərˌpɪlər, B -əˌpɪlə] *s.* 1. (ento.) oruga. 2. tractor de orugas, tractor de carriles.
caterpillar tread, rodado tipo oruga.
caterwaul ['kætərˌwɔl, 'kætəˌ-] *v.i.* chillar, maullar (el gato). —*s.* marramao, maullido.
catfacing ['kætˌfeɪsɪŋ] *s.* (agr.) desfiguración (de las frutas a causa de plagas).
catfall [-ˌfɔl] *s.* (mar.) cable o cadena del ancla.
catfish [-ˌfɪʃ] *s.* (ict.) siluro, barbo, bagre (Am.).
catgut [-ˌgʌt] *s.* catgut, cuerda de tripa de gato (para suturas quirúrgicas, raquetas de tenis e instrumentos musicales).
catharsis [kə'θɑrsəs, B -'θɑsɪs] *s.* 1. (med.) catarsis, purga. 2. catarsis, purificación (de sentimientos, sensaciones o gusto).
cathartic [-tɪk] *a.* catártico. —*s.* (med.) purgante.
Cathay [kə'θeɪ, kæ-] *s.* (ant.) Catay, nombre dado a la China por los autores medievales.
cathead ['kætˌhɛd] *s.* 1. (mar.) serviola, pescante, gaviete. 2. (min.) cabrestante pequeño. 3. torno, carretel; manguito de refuerzo.
cathect [kə'θɛkt] *v.t.* infundir ímpetu libidinoso en (alguien).
cathedra [kə'θidrə] *s.* (relig., educ.) cátedra; episcopado y profesorado.
cathedral [-drəl] *s.* iglesia catedral. —*a.* catedral, catedralicio.
catherine wheel ['kæθərən-] 1. rueda catalina. 2. girándula, rueda giratoria (de fuegos artificiales). 3. voltereta lateral sobre las manos.
catheter ['kæθətər, B -ə] *s.* (med.) catéter, sonda.

catheterize [-əˌraɪz] *v.t.* (med.) cateterizar.
cathetometer [ˌkæθə'tɑmətər, B -'tɔmɪtə] *s.* (fís.) catetómetro.
cathexis [kə'θɛksəs] *s.*(psic.) catexis.
cathode ['kæθˌoʊd] *s.* (fís., quím.) cátodo.
cathode ray, (fís.) rayo catódico.
cathode-ray tube [-ˌreɪ-] tubo de rayos catódicos, válvula catódica.
cathodic [kæ'θɑdɪk, B -'θɔd-] *a.* catódico.
catholic ['kæθəlɪk] *a.* 1. católico, universal, general. 2. liberal, tolerante. 3. **C.,** (relig.) católico. —*s.* **C.,** católico, católico romano.
Catholicism [kə'θɑləˌsɪzəm, B -'θɔl-] *s.* 1. catolicismo. 2. catolicismo romano.
catholicity [ˌkæθə'lɪsətɪ] *s.* 1. catolicidad, catolicismo. 2. liberalidad, tolerancia. 3. catolicidad, aceptación general, universalidad.
catholicize [kə'θɑləˌsaɪz, B -'θɔl-] *v.t.* catolizar, hacer católico.
catholicon [-ˌkɑn, B -ˌkɔn] *s.* catolicón, panacea.
cathouse ['kætˌhaʊs] *s.* (jer.) burdel.
Catiline ['kætəlˌaɪn] *s.* (hist.) Catilina, político romano, enemigo de Cicerón.
cation ['kætˌaɪən] *s.* (fís., quím.) catión.
cationic [ˌkætaɪ'ɑnɪk, B -'ɔn-] *a.* (quím.) catiónico.
catkin ['kætkən] *s.* (bot.) amento, candelilla (inflorescencia colgante del sauce o del avellano).
catlike [-ˌlaɪk] *a.* 1. gatuno. 2. suave, silencioso, cauteloso, furtivo, ej., *c. tread,* modo de caminar cauteloso.
catmint [-ˌmɪnt] *s.* (bot.) nébeda; hierba gatera.
cat nap [-ˌnæp] *s.* sueño corto, siesta corta.
catnip [-ˌnɪp] *s.* (bot.) calamento, nébeda, hierba gatera.
Cato ['keɪtoʊ] *s.* (hist.) Catón, cónsul romano.
Catonian [keɪ'toʊnɪən] *a.* catoniano, severo.
cat-o'-nine-tails [ˌkætə'naɪnˌteɪlz] *s.* azote o látigo de nueve ramales.
catoptric [kə'tɑptrɪk, B -'tɔp-] *a.* (fís., ópt.) catóptrico.
catoprics [-trɪks] *s. pl.* (*sing. en const.*) catóptrica.
cat rig, (mar.) aparejo de cúter, aparejo de tartana.
cat's cradle, cunita (juego de los niños).
cat's-eye ['kætsˌaɪ] *s.* (min.) ojo de gato, gema o cristal que se asemeja a un ojo de gato.
cat's paw [-ˌpɔ] *s.* 1. (fig.) instrumento (persona utilizada o aprovechada por otra). 2. (mar.) brisa ligera, ventolina. 3. (mar.) nudo de boca de lobo, ahorcaperro.
catsup ['kɛtʃəp, 'kætʃəp, 'kætsəp] *s.* (cocina) salsa de tomate (sazonada con vinagre, azúcar y especias).
cat's whisker, 1. (rad.) punta detectora, buscador. 2. (G.B., fam.) persona graciosa o muy solicitada (*ú. gen. en pl.*); **you're the c. w.,** eres estupendo.
cat tackle, (mar.) aparejo de gata.
cattail ['kætˌteɪl] *s.* (bot.) 1. espadaña, enea, anea. 2. amento.
cattalo ['kætəlˌoʊ] *s.* (*pl.* CATTALOES o CATTALOS) (zool.) bisonte híbrido (cruce con ganado doméstico).
cat thyme, (bot.) maro, almaro.
cattily ['kætəlɪ] *adv.* maliciosamente.
cattiness [-ɪnəs] *s.* disposición maliciosa, propensión a la malicia.
cattle ['kætəl] *s.* ganado; ganado vacuno.
cattle bell, esquilón.
cattle car, carro ganadero, vagón jaula.
cattle crossing, indicación de carretera que advierte la presencia de ganado; (señal) ganado.
cattle guard, guardaanimales, guardaganado, guardavaca.
cattleman [-mən] *s.* ganadero.
cattle pass, (f.c.) alcantarilla o paso para ganado.
cattle prod, aguijón eléctrico para arrear al ganado.
cattle raising, ganadería.
cattle ranch, rancho, granja de ganado, hacienda o estancia ganadera (Am.).
cattle-rustler [-ˌrʌslər, B -lə] *s.* abigeo, ladrón de ganado, cuatrero.
cattle show, exposición ganadera.
catty ['kætɪ] *a.* 1. gatuno, felino. 2. (fig.) malicioso, chismoso. —*s.* medida de peso en el Asia.
catty-cornered [-ˌkɔrnərd, B -ˌkɔnəd] *var. de* **cater-cornered.**
Catullus [kə'tʌləs] *s.* Cátulo, poeta latino, amante de Lesbia.
catwalk ['kætˌwɔk] *s.* andén o pasadizo angosto (en f.c., tramoya de teatro, etc.).
Caucasian [kɔ'keɪʒən, B -'keɪzjən] *s., a.* caucasiano, caucásico, caucáseo.
Caucasus ['kɔkəsəs] *s.* 1. Caucasia (región). 2. Cáucaso (montañas).
caucus ['kɔkəs] *s.* 1. junta de los dirigentes (de un partido político esp. para designar candidatos). 2. (G.B.) comité político (en una localidad). —*v.i.* reunir una junta política.
caudal ['kɔdəl] *a.* (anat., zool.) caudal.
caudal anesthesia, (med.) anestesia caudal.
caudate [-ˌdeɪt] *a.* (bot., zool., astr.) caudado, caudato.
caudex [-ˌdɛks] *s.* (*pl.* CAUDICES [-dəˌsiz] o CAUDEXES) (bot.) caudex, tallo, tronco.
caudillo [kaʊ'ðijoʊ, -'ðiljoʊ] *s.* caudillo, líder (esp. militar).
Caudine Forks ['kɔˌdin'fɔrks, B -ˌdaɪn'-fɔks] (hist.) Horcas Caudinas.
caudle ['kɔdəl] *s.* bebida hecha con vino tibio y especias que se da a los enfermos.
caught [kɔt] *pret. y p.p. de* **catch.**
caul [kɔl] *s.* (med.) 1. omento, epiplón, redaño. 2. amnios (membrana que envuelve el feto).
cauldron ['kɔldrən] *var. de* **caldron.**
caulescent [kɔ'lɛsənt] *a.* (bot.) caulescente.
caulicle ['kɔlɪkəl] *s.* (bot.) rejo, tallo rudimentario.
cauliflower ['kɔlɪˌflaʊər, 'kɑl-, B 'kɔl-ə] *s.* (bot.) coliflor.
cauliflower ear, oreja deformada (como la de los boxeadores).
cauline ['kɔˌlaɪn] *a.* (bot.) caulino, caulinar, caulífero.
caulk [kɔk] *v.t.* 1. (mar.) calafatear, recalcar, acollar (buques). 2. rellenar, tapar (grietas).
caulker ['kɔkər, B -ə] *s.* calafate, calafateador, recalcador.
caulking [-ɪŋ] *s.* (mar.) calafateo, retaque, recalcadura.
caulking chisel, (mar.) afolador, calafate, estopero, cincel de calafatear, escoplo de calafatear, acollador.
causal ['kɔzəl] *a.* 1. causal, de causas. 2. causativo. 3. (gram.) causal.
causality [kɔ'zælətɪ] *s.* causalidad.
causation [-'zeɪʃən] *s.* 1. proceso causativo. 2. causalidad.
causative ['kɔzətɪv] *a.* causante, causativo.
cause [kɔz] *s.* 1. causa, motivo, razón; origen, principio. 2. causante, autor. 3. (der.) causa, proceso. 4. **to make common c. with,** hacer causa común con; **to plead a c.,** defender una causa; **to show c.,** (der.) presentar motivos justificantes. —*v.t.* 1. causar, motivar (algo). 2. mover, hacer (a alguien hacer algo).
cause célèbre [ˌkoʊzseɪ'lɛbrə, B ˌkɔz-sə'lɛb] *s.* 1. (fr., der.) caso jurídico, que produce sensación pública. 2. episodio controversial o escandaloso.
causeless ['kɔzləs] *a.* sin causa, sin motivo; infundado, sin razón.
causerie [ˌkoʊzə'ri, B 'koʊzərɪ] *s.* 1. charla. 2. artículo corto, escrito en tono familiar.
causeway ['kɔzˌweɪ] *s.* 1. calzada elevada (sobre terreno pantanoso, etc.), arrecife, camino empedrado. 2. carretera.
caustic ['kɔstɪk] *a.* 1. (quím.) cáustico. 2. (fig.) cáustico, mordaz. —*s.* 1. (quím.) cáustico, substancia cáustica. 2. (fís., mat.) cáustica.
causticity [kɔ'stɪsətɪ] *s.* causticidad, mordacidad.
caustic lime, cal cáustica o viva.
caustic potash, (quím.) potasa cáustica.
caustic soda, (quím.) soda cáustica.
cauterization [ˌkɔtərə'zeɪʃən B -raɪ-] *s.* cauterización.
cauterize ['kɔtəˌraɪz] *v.t.* cauterizar.
cautery [-rɪ] *s.* 1. cauterización, cauterio. 2. cauterio (instrumento).
caution ['kɔʃən] *s.* 1. cautela, cuidado, precaución. 2. advertencia, amonestación, aviso; **caution** (señal) cuidado. —*v.t.* 1. advertir, prevenir de (un riesgo o peligro). 2. amonestar, advertir.
cautionary [-ˌɛrɪ, B -ərɪ] *a.* amonestador, avisador; preventivo.
cautious ['kɔʃəs] *a.* cauto, cauteloso, precavido, prevenido, prudente.
cautiously [-lɪ] *adv.* cautamente, cautelosamente, prudentemente.
cavalcade [ˌkævəl'keɪd, 'kæv-ˌkeɪd, B ˌkæv-'keɪd] *s.* cabalgata, desfile.
cavalier [ˌkævə'lɪr, B -'lɪə] *s.* 1. caballero, jinete, soldado de caballería. 2. galán, escolta (de una dama). —*a.* 1. alegre, desenvuelto. 2. altivo, arrogante.
Cavalier, *s.* (G.B., hist.) partidario de Carlos I.
cavalla [kə'vælə] *s.* (*pl.* CAVALLA o CAVALLAS) (ict.) caballa, pez común en los mares de España.
cavalry ['kævəlrɪ] *s.* caballería.
cavalry charge, carga de caballería.
cavalryman [-mən] *s.* soldado de caballería.
cavatina [ˌkævə'tinə] *s.* (mús.) cavatina.
cave [keɪv] *s.* cueva, caverna, gruta. —*v.t.* excavar, ahuecar, hacer un hueco. —*v.i.* (con *in*) 1. caerse, hundirse, derrumbarse. 2. rendirse, ceder, darse por vencido.
caveat ['keɪvɪˌæt, 'kæv-] *s.* 1. (der.) notificación de suspender el procedimiento. 2. advertencia, amonestación.
cave dweller, cavernícola, hombre de las cavernas, troglodita.
cave-in ['keɪvˌɪn] *s.* derrumbe, hundimiento.
cave-man [-ˌmæn] *s.* 1. cavernícola (esp. en la Edad de Piedra). 2. hombre rudo.
cavendish ['kævəndɪʃ] *s.* tableta de tabaco (de hojas ablandadas y endulzadas).
cave painting, pintura rupestre; arte prehistórico.
cavern ['kævərn, B -ən] *s.* caverna, antro, cueva. —*v.t.* colocar en una cueva.
cavernous [-əs] *a.* cavernoso (obscuridad, profundidad, boca, ojos, etc.).
cavesson ['kævəsən] *s.* (equit.) cabezón, cabezón de serreta.
cavetto [kə'vɛtoʊ] *s.* (arq.) caveto, esgucio, antequino, canaleto, mediacaña.
caviar, caviare ['kævɪˌɑr, ˌkævɪ'ɑr, B 'kævɪˌɑ] *s.* caviar; **c. to the general,** cosa demasiado buena para ser apreciada por cualquiera.
cavicorn ['kævəˌkɔrn, B -ˌkɔn] *a.* (zool.) cavicornio.
cavil ['kævəl] *s.* observación, trivial, quisquilla, objeción capciosa, cavilación. —*v.i.* (*pret., p.p.* CAVILED o CAVILLED; *p.pr.* CAVILING o CAVILLING) (con *at* o *about*) poner reparos capciosos

(a), hacer observaciones quisquillosas (sobre), criticar capciosamente. —*v.t.* poner reparos a.
caviling, cavilling [-ɪŋ] *a.* quisquilloso, criticón.
cavitation [ˌkævəˈteɪʃən] *s.* 1. (med.) cavitación, formación de cavidades o cavernas (ej., en el pulmón). 2. (fís.) cavitación.
cavity [ˈkævətɪ] *s.* cavidad, espacio hueco, oquedad; caries (de dientes).
cavort [kəˈvɔrt, B -ˈvɔt] *v.i.* 1. dar o hacer cabriolas; retozar, juguetear. 2. divertirse.
cavy [ˈkeɪvɪ] *s.* (zool.) conejillo de Indias, agutí, cobayo, cuy, acure (Am.).
caw [kɔ] *v.i.* graznar, (cuervos, grajos). —*s.* graznido.
cay [ki, keɪ] *s.* cayo, islote.
Cayenne [kaɪˈɛn, keɪ-, B keɪ-] *s.* Cayena, capital de la Guayana Francesa.
cayenne pepper [-ˈɛn-, B ˈkeɪɛn-] 1. pimienta del ají de Cayena.
cayman [kəɪˈmæn, B ˈkeɪmən] *s.* (zool.) caimán.
Cb *simb. de* **columbium,** colombio.
C battery, (rad.) batería de rejilla.
CBC *abrev. de* **Canadian Broadcasting Corporation,** Corporación Radiodifusora del Canadá.
C.B.D. *abrev. de* **cash before delivery,** pago antes de entrega.
CBE *abrev. de* **Commander of the Order of the British Empire,** Comendador de la Orden del Imperio Británico.
CBS *abrev. de* **Columbia Broadcasting System,** Red Radiodifusora de Columbia.
cc. *abrev. de* **cubic centimeter,** centímetro cúbico (c.c.).
C clef, (mús.) clave de do.
Cd *simb. de* **cadmium,** cadmio (Cd).
CD *abrev. de* 1. **Civil Defense,** Defensa Civil. 2. **Corps Diplomatique,** Cuerpo Diplomático. 3. **Compact Disc, compact disk,** CD. 4. **Certificate of Deposit,** (fin.) certificado de depósito.
CDD *abrev. de* **certificate of disability for discharge,** certificado de inutilidad total.
Ce *símb. de* **cerium,** cerio (Ce).
C.E. *abrev. de* 1. **Chemical Engineer,** Ingeniero Químico. 2. **Civil Engineer,** Ingeniero Civil.
cearin [ˈsiərɪn] *s.* (med.) cearina.
cease [sis] *v.i.* 1. cesar, acabarse, terminar(se), pararse. 2. (con *from*) desistir de, dejar de. —*v.t.* acabar, terminar, suspender; **c. fire!** (mil.) ¡alto el fuego!; **c. firing,** suspender el fuego. —*s.* cese (sólo se emplea en **without c.,** incesantemente).
cease-fire [ˈsisˈfaɪər, B -ə] *s.* 1. (mil.) suspensión del fuego, cese de fuego. 2. tregua.
ceaseless [-ləs] *a. incesante, perpetuo, perenne.*
cecal [ˈsikəl] *a.* (anat.) cecal.
Cecilia [səˈsiljə, B -ˈsɪl-] *s.* (relig.) Cecilia (santa), patrona de la música.
cecum [ˈsikəm] *s.* (*pl.* SECA [-kə]) (anat.) intestino ciego.
CED *abrev. de* **Committee of Economic Development,** Comisión de Desarrollo Económico.
cedar [ˈsidər, B -ə] *s.* (bot.) cedro.
cedar chest, arca o cofre de cedro.
cedar of Lebanon, (bot.) cedro del Líbano.
cede [sid] *v.t.* 1. ceder, transferir, traspasar, entregar. 2. (bridge) ceder, conceder (una baza).
cedilla [sɪˈdɪlə] *s.* cedilla (acento gráfico).
cedrium [ˈsidrɪəm] *s.* (quím.) cedria.
ceiba tree [ˈseɪbə-] (bot.) ceiba.
ceil [sil] *v.t.* 1. revestir, forrar (un barco de madera). 2. cubrir o revestir con un cielo raso (el techo).
ceiling [ˈsilɪŋ] *s.* 1. cielo raso, techo (interior). 2. tope, máximo, límite (fijado para precios, salarios, jornales, alquileres, etc.). 3. (aer.) techo, límite de visibilidad; altura máxima (que puede alcanzar un vehículo aéreo). 4. (mar.) entabladura interior. 5. **to hit the c.,** (jer.) encolerizarse, enojarse.
ceiling price, (com.) precio de tope, precio máximo.
celadon green [ˈsɛləˌdɑn-, B -ˌdɔn-] verdeceledón.
celandine [ˈsɛlənˌdaɪn] *s.* (bot.) celidonia, hirundinaria, golondrinera.
Celebes [ˈsɛləˌbiz, B sɛˈli-] *s.* Célebes, islas y península (antiguo nombre de Sulawesi).
celebrant [ˈsɛləbrənt] *s.* celebrante, sacerdote (esp. el que oficia la misa).
celebrate [ˈsɛləˌbreɪt] *v.t.* 1. celebrar, oficiar (misa, ceremonia). 2. celebrar, exaltar, alabar. 3. celebrar, conmemorar, solemnizar, festejar (día, aniversario, etc.). —*v.i.* 1. oficiar (el sacerdote). 2. celebrar, festejar, tener festejos.
celebrated [-əd] *a.* célebre, famoso, distinguido, notorio.
celebration [ˌsɛləˈbreɪʃən] *s.* 1. celebración. 2. fiesta, festejo.
celebrator [ˈsɛləˌbreɪtər, B -ə] *s.* celebrante, parrandista.
celebrity [səˈlɛbrətɪ] *s.* 1. celebridad, renombre, fama. 2. celebridad, persona célebre.
celeriac [səˈlɛrɪˌæk] *s.* (bot.) variedad de apio.
celerity [səˈlɛrətɪ] *s.* celeridad, rapidez, velocidad.
celery [ˈsɛlərɪ] *s.* (bot.) apio.
celesta [səˈlɛstə] *s.* (mús.) celesta, celeste.
celestial [səˈlɛstʃəl, B -tjəl] *a.* 1. celestial, celeste, del espacio. 2. (fig.) celestial, deleitoso, divino. —*s.* chino.
celestial body, cuerpo celeste, astro.
Celestial Empire, Celeste Imperio (dic. de la antigua China).
celestial globe, (astr.) globo celeste.
celestial guidance, guía telemétrica de un navío espacial que se basa en las posiciones de los astros.
celestial horizon, (astr.) horizonte racional.
celestial mechanics, mecánica celestial, astronomía gravitacional.
celestial navigation, navegación astronómica.
celestite [ˈsɛləsˌtaɪt, səˈlɛs-] *s.* (min.) celestina.
celiac [ˈsilɪˌæk] *a.* (anat.) celíaco, de la cavidad abdominal.
celiac disease, (med.) enfermedad celíaca, infantilismo intestinal.
celibacy [ˈsɛləbəsɪ] *s.* celibato, soltería.
celibate [-bət] *s., a.* célibe, soltero.
cell [sɛl] *s.* 1. celda (en un convento, una cárcel, etc.). 2. célula, cavidad (en minerales, organismos, etc.). 3. (biol.) célula (gen. microscópica). 4. celdilla (de panal de abejas). 5. (zool.) ventosa (del pulpo). 6. (elec.) célula (fotoeléctrica, etc.). 7. (elec.) elemento, par (en pila, acumulador, etc.). 8. célula (de un partido o movimiento político). 9. (rel. hist.) dependencia (de un convento o monasterio).
cellar [ˈsɛlər, B -ə] *s.* 1. sótano. 2. bodega, ej., *wine c.,* bodega de vinos, cava.
cellarage [-ərɪdʒ] *s.* 1. bodega, sótano, sitio para almacenar. 2. almacenaje en una bodega.
cellarer [-ərər, B -ərə] *s.* cillerero, el que suministra vinos y víveres en un monasterio.
cellarette, cellaret [ˌsɛləˈrɛt] *s.* estante o aparador para botellas (de vino y licor).
cellist [ˈtʃɛləst] *s.* (mús.) violoncelista.
cell membrane, (biol.) membrana plasmática; (biol.) pared de una célula.
cello [ˈtʃɛloʊ] *s.* (mús.) violoncelo.
celloidin [səˈlɔɪdən] *s.* (quím.) celoidina.
cellophane [ˈsɛləˌfeɪn] *s.* celofán.
cellular [ˈsɛljələr, B -lə] *a.* celular; (*telephone*) celular.
cellulase [-ˌleɪs] *s.* (bioquím.) celulosa.
cellule [ˈsɛljul] *s.* (anat.) celulilla, celdilla.
cellulitis [ˌsɛljəˈlaɪtəs] *s.* (med.) celulitis.
celluloid [ˈsɛljəˌlɔɪd] *s.* celuloide.
cellulose [-ˌloʊs] *s.* (quím.) celulosa.
cellulose acetate, (quím.) acetocelulosa, acetato de celulosa.
cellulose nitrate, (quím.) nitrocelulosa.
celom [ˈsiləm] *var. de* **coelom.**
Celsius [ˈsɛlsɪəs] *s.* Celsio, centígrado.
Celt [sɛlt, kɛlt] *s.* 1. celta. 2. **c.** [sɛlt] hacha o cincel prehistórico.
Celtiberian [ˌsɛltəˈbɪrɪən, ˌkɛlt-, B -ˈbɪər-] *a.* celtíbero, celtibérico.
Celtic [ˈsɛltɪk, ˈkɛlt-] *a.* céltico (pueblo o idioma). —*s.* celta (idioma).
Celticism [-əˌsɪzəm] *s.* celtismo, afición por la cultura celta.
cembalo [ˈtʃɛmbəˌloʊ] *s.* (mús.) cémbalo, clavecín.
cement [sɪˈmɛnt] *s.* 1. cemento. 2. (fig.) cemento, vínculo. —*v.t.* 1. cimentar, cubrir con cemento. 2. (fig.) cimentar, unir, conglutinar; consolidar, fortalecer, estrechar (amistad, relaciones etc.). 3. (metal.) cementar (hierro). —*v.i.* pegarse, unirse, consolidarse.
cementation [ˌsiˌmɛnˈteɪʃən] *s.* 1. cimentación. 2. (fig.) consolidación, fortalecimiento. 3. (metal.) cementación (de hierro).
cement block, bloque de hormigón.
cement-bound macadam [sɪˈmɛntˌbaʊnd-] macadán enlechado o ligado con cemento.
cement gun, canon de cemento, canon lanzacemento; lanzamortero; cementadora.
cementite [-ˌaɪt] *s.* (metal.) cementita.
cement mixer, (const.) dosificador de cemento.
cement rock, roca calcárea.
cementum [sɪˈmɛntəm] *s.* (anat.) cemento (de los dientes de los mamíferos).
cemetery [ˈsɛməˌtɛrɪ B -ɪtrɪ] *s.* cementerio, camposanto, necrópolis.
Cenacle [ˈsɛnəkəl] *s.* (bíbl.) Cenáculo (donde tuvo lugar la Última Cena).
cenobite [ˈsɛnəˌbaɪt, B ˈsinə-] *s.* (relig.) cenobita.
cenobitic [ˌsɛnəˈbɪtɪk, B ˌsinə-] **cenobitical** [-əl] *a.* cenobítico, perteneciente a una comunidad religiosa.
cenogenesis [ˌsinəˈdʒɛnəsəs] *s.* (biol.) cenogénesis.
cenogenetic [-dʒəˈnɛtɪk] *a.* (biol.) cenogenético.
cenotaph [ˈsɛnəˌtæf, B -ˌtɑf] *s.* cenotafio, tumba vacía, erigida a la memoria de un personaje sepultado en otra parte.
cenote [sɪˈnoʊtɪ] *s.* cenote, pozo de agua.
Cenozoic [ˌsinəˈzoʊɪk, ˌsɛnə-] *a., s.* (geol.) cenozoico.
cense [sɛns] *v.t.* incensar, perfumar con incienso, turibular.
censer [ˈsɛnsər, B -ə] *s.* incensario, turíbulo.
censor [ˈsɛnsər, B -ə] *s.* 1. censor (de películas cinematográficas, libros, correspondencia, etc.). 2. censor, criticón. —*v.t.* censurar, someter a la censura.
censorial [sɛnˈsɔrɪəl] *a.* censorio.
censorious [-ɪəs] *a.* censurador, criticón, reprobador.
censorship [ˈsɛnsərˌʃɪp, B -səˌ-] *s.* censura.
censurable [ˈsɛntʃərəbəl, B ˈsɛnʃər-] *a.* censurable, reprensible.
censure [ˈsɛntʃər, B ˈsɛnʃə] *s.* censura, crítica, reprobación. —*v.t.* censurar, criticar, reprobar.

census ['sɛnsəs] *s.* censo, empadronamiento, registro general de ciudadanos; **to take a c.,** empadronar, levantar el censo. —*v.t.* empadronar, levantar el censo.
census taker, empadronador, enumerador censal.
cent [sɛnt] *s.* centavo.
cent. *abrev. de* **centigrade,** centigrado.
centaur ['sɛn,tɔr, B -,tɔ] *s.* 1. centauro (monstruo mitad hombre y mitad caballo). 2. **C.,** (astr.) Centauro.
centaurea [sɛn'tɔrɪə] *s.* (bot.) centaura.
centenarian [,sɛntən'ɛrɪən, B -'ɛər-] *s., a.* centenario.
centenary [sɛn'tɛnərɪ, 'sɛntən,ɛrɪ, B sɛn'-tinərɪ] *a.* centenario, de cien años. —*s.* centuria, centenario.
centennial [sɛn'tɛnɪəl] *a.* centenario. —*s.* centenario, fiesta centenaria.
center (pr. G.B.) **centre** ['sɛntər, B -ə] *s.* 1. centro. 2. (geom., fís., mil., pol., dep., fig.) centro. 3. (anat.) centro (nervioso, cerebral, gustativo, etc.). 4. punta (de torno). 5. núcleo, alma (de cable). 6. (arq.) cimbra (de arco). 7. **dead c.,** punto muerto (en un pistón, péndola, etc.); **railroad c.,** centro ferroviario; **storm c.,** centro de tormenta; **the motor c., (anat.) centro motor.** —*v.t.* 1. centrar. 2. centralizar; concentrar. 3. (dep.) centrar (la pelota). —*v.i.* (gen. con *in, on, at, round, about*) centrarse, concentrarse (en, alrededor de).
center bit, (ing.) barrena de guía, mecha centradora.
centerboard [-,bɔrd, B -,bɔd] *s.* (mar.) orza de deriva.
center distance, (maq.) distancia entre ejes.
center drill, broca de centrar, mecha centradora.
center field, (béisbol) jardín central.
center forward, (dep.) delantero centro, centro delantero.
center gage, calibre de centro; plantilla o escantillón para puntas.
center half, (fútbol) centromedio.
centering ['sɛntərɪŋ] *s.* 1. centraje, centrado. 2. (arq.) cimbra. —*a.* centrador.
center of attraction, 1. (fig.) centro de interés. 2. (ast.) centro de atracción.
center of gravity, (fís.) centro de gravedad.
center of mass, (fís.) centro de masa, centro de inercia.
centerpiece ['sɛntər,pis, B -tə,-] *s.* centro de mesa (adorno).
center punch, (mec.) granete, punzón de marcar, aguja para marcar, punzón de centrar.
center stage, centro de escenario; (fig.) **to be in c.,** estar en primer plano.
center tap, (electrón.) derivación central.
centesimal [sɛn'tɛsəməl] *a.* centesimal. —*s.* centésimo.
centiare ['sɛntɪ,ɛr, B -,ɛə] *s.* centiárea.
centibar [-tə,bɑr, B -,bɑ] *s.* centibara (medida).
centigrade [-tə,greɪd] *a.* centígrado, de cien grados.
centigram [-,græm] *s.* centigramo.
centiliter (pr. G.B.) **centilitre**[-,litər, B -ə] *s.* centilitro.
centime ['sɑn,tim] (fr.) céntimo.
centimeter ['sɛntə,mitər, B -ə] *s.* centímetro.
centimeter-gram-second [-'græm'sɛkənd] *a.* cegesimal, centímetro-gramo-segundo.
centipede ['sɛntə,pid] *s.* (ento.) ciempiés, centípedo, escolopendra.
centner ['sɛntnər, B -nə] *s.* quintal métrico (medida europea).
cento ['sɛn,toʊ] *s.* (*pl.* SCENTONES [sɛn'toʊniz]) 1. centón, manta de retazos a colores. 2. centón, colección de fragmentos literarios.
central ['sɛntrəl] *a.* 1. central, céntrico, del centro. 2. central, principal, dominante. 3. (anat., fisiol.) central (díc. de parte del sistema nervioso). —*s.* 1. central telefónica. 2. operador (en central telefónica); telefonista.
Central America, América Central, Centroamérica.
Central American, *simb.a., s.* centroamericano.
central heating, calefacción central.
Central Intelligence Agency, (E.U.) Agencia Central de Inteligencia (CIA).
centralism [-,ɪzəm] *s.* (pol.) centralismo.
centralist [-əst] *s., a.* centralista.
centrality [sɛn'trælətɪ] *s.* posición central, ubicación céntrica.
centralization [,sɛntrələ'zeɪʃən, B -laɪ-] *s.* centralización.
centralize ['sɛntrə,laɪz] *v.t.* centralizar.
Central Powers, potencias centrales, imperios centrales (que pelearon contra los Aliados en la primera guerra mundial).
Central Standard Time, (E.U.) hora central (que corresponde al sexto huso horario al oeste de Greenwich).
centric ['sɛntrɪk] *a.* céntrico, central.
centricity [sɛn'trɪsətɪ] *s.* posición céntrica.
centrifugal [sɛn'trɪfjəgəl, -'trɪfɪgəl, B -'trɪfjʊ-] *a.* 1. centrífugo. 2. (fisiol.) centrífugo, eferente. —*s.* centrífuga, centrifugadora.
centrifugal force, (fís.) fuerza centrífuga.
centrifuge ['sɛntrə,fjudʒ] *s.* centrífuga, centrifugadora. —*v.t.* centrifugar.
centriole ['sɛntrɪ,oʊl] *s.* (biol.) 1. centríolo. 2. centrosoma.
centripetal [sɛn'trɪpətəl] *a.* 1. centrípeto. 2. (fisiol.) centrípeto, aferente.
centripetal force, (fís.) fuerza centrípeta.
centrist ['sɛntrəst] *s.* (pol.) centrista.
centrobaric [,sɛntrə'bærɪk] *a.* (mec.) centrobárico.
centroid ['sɛn,trɔɪd] *s.* centroide, centro de masa, centro de gravedad.
centroidal [sɛn'trɔɪdəl] *a.* centroidal.
centroidal axis, (ing.) eje baricéntrico.
centrosome ['sɛntrə,soʊm] *s.* (biol.) centrosoma.
centrosphere [-,sfɪr, B -,sfɪə] *s.* 1. (geol.) núcleo central (de la tierra). 2. (biol.) centrosfera.
centrum ['sɛntrəm] *s.* 1. (biol.) centro espinal. 2. (geol.) epicentro (de un terremoto).
centuple ['sɛntʊpəl, sɛn'tu-, B 'sɛntjʊ-] *a.* céntuplo, centuplicado, cien veces mayor. —*v.t.* centuplicar.
centuplicate [sɛn'tuplə,keɪt, B -'tjʊ-] *v.t.* centuplicar. — [-,keɪt, -kət] *a., s.* céntuplo.
centurial [sɛn'tʊrɪəl, B -'tjʊər-] *a.* 1. (hist.) de la centuria. 2. secular.
centurion [-ɪən] *s.* (hist.) centurión, jefe de una centuria.
century ['sɛntʃərɪ, B -tʃʊrɪ] *s.* 1. siglo, centuria. 2. (hist.) centuria.
century plant, (bot.) agave, pita, maguey.
cephalad ['sɛfə,læd] *adv.* (anat.) hacia la cabeza.
cephalalgia [,sɛfə'lældʒə] *s.* (med.) cefalalgia.
cephalic [sə'fælɪk, B kɛ-] *a.* (anat.) cefálico.
cephalin ['sɛfələn] *s.* (bioquím.) cefalina.
cephalitis [,sɛfə'laɪtəs] *s.* cefalitis.
cephalization [-lə'zeɪʃən] *s.* (zool.) cefalización.
Cephalochorda [-'kɔrdə, B -'kɔdə] **Cephalochordata** [-kɔr'deɪtə, B -kɔ'-] *s.* (*pl.*) (zool.) cefalocordados.
cephalopod ['sɛfələ,pɑd, B -,pɔd] *s., a.* (zool.) cefalópodo.
cephalothorax [,sɛfələ'θɔr,æks] *s.* (zool.) cefalotórax.
cephalous ['sɛfələs] *a.* (zool.) que tiene cabeza.
Cepheid ['sifiəd] *s.* (astr.) Cefeida, estrella doble de luz variable.
Cepheus ['si,fjus] *s.* 1. (astr.) Cefeo, constelación boreal. 2. (mitol.) Cefeo, padre de Andrómeda.
ceraceous [sə'reɪʃəs] *a.* ceroso.
ceramal [sə'ræməl] *s.* (metal.) cermet.
ceramic [sə'ræmɪk] *a.* cerámico.
ceramics [-ɪks] *s. pl.* (*sing. en const.*) cerámica, alfarería; (objeto de) cerámica.
ceramist [-əst, 'sɛrəm-] **ceramicist** [sə'ræməsəst] *s.* ceramista.
cerastes [sə'ræstiz] *s.* (zool.) cerasta, ceraste, cerastas, cerastes.
cerate ['sɪr,eɪt, B 'sɪərɪt] *s.* (farm.) cerato.
ceratoid ['sɛrə,tɔɪd] *a.* hecho de cuerno, córneo.
Cerberean [sər'bɪrɪən, B sə'bɪər-] *a.* parecido al Cancerbero o relativo a él.
Cerberus ['sərbərəs, B 'sɜbə-] *s.* (astr., mitol.) Cerbero.
cere [sɪr, B sɪə] *s.* (orn.) cera, membrana cérea (de la nariz de ciertas aves). —*v.t.* envolver (un cadáver en mortaja encerada).
cereal ['sɪrɪəl, B 'sɪər-] *s., a.* cereal.
cerebellum [,sɛrə'bɛləm] *s.* (anat.) cerebelo.
cerebral [sə'ribrəl, 'sɛrə-, B 'sɛrɪ-] *a.* 1. cerebral, del cerebro. 2. (fig.) cerebral, intelectualmente refinado, reflexivo.
cerebral cortex, (anat.) corteza cerebral.
cerebral palsy, (med.) parálisis cerebral, diplejía espástica.
cerebrate ['sɛrə,breɪt] *v.i.* raciocinar, pensar, reflexionar.
cerebration [,sɛrə'breɪʃən] *s.* cerebración, pensamiento.
cerebroside ['sɛrəbroʊ,saɪd] *s.* (quím.) cerebrósida.
cerebrospinal [sə,ribroʊ'spaɪnəl, ,sɛrə-] *a.* cerebroespinal.
cerebrospinal meningitis, (med.) meningitis cerebroespinal, fiebre cerebroespinal.
cerebrum [sə'ribrəm, 'sɛrə-, B 'sɛrɪ-] *s.* (anat.) cerebro.
cerecloth ['sɪr,klɔθ, B 'sɪə,-] *s.* 1. hule. 2. paño encerado que se usaba antiguamente para amortajar.
cerement [-mənt] *s.* (*ú. gen. en pl.*) mortaja (gen. encerada).
ceremonial [,sɛrə'moʊnɪəl] *a.* ceremonial. —*s.* ceremonial, rito, ritual.
ceremonious [-əs] *a.* ceremonioso.
ceremoniously [-lɪ] *adv.* ceremoniosamente.
ceremony ['sɛrə,moʊnɪ, B -mənɪ] *s.* ceremonia; *to stand upon c.,* hacer ceremonias, guardar las distancias.
Ceres ['sɪr,iz, B 'sɪər-] *s.* 1. (mitol.) Ceres, diosa latina de la agricultura. 2. (astr.) Ceres.
cereus ['sɪrɪəs, B 'sɪər-] *s.* (bot.) candelabro, pitahaya.
ceria ['sɪrɪə, B 'sɪər-] *s.* (quím.) bióxido de cerio.
ceric [-ɪk] *a.* (quím.) cérico, de cerio, que contiene cerio.
cerise [sə'ris, -'riz] *s., a.* color cereza.
cerium ['sɪrɪəm, B 'sɪər-] *s.* (quím.) cerio.
cerium metals, (quím.) céridos.
cermet ['sər,mɛt, B 'sɜ,-] *s.* (metal.) cermet.
cernuous ['sərnjʊəs, B 'sɜn-] *a.* (bot.) inclinado.
cero ['sɛroʊ, 'sɪroʊ] *s.* (*pl.* SCERO O CEROS) (ict.) caballa o sierra.
ceroplastics [,sɪrə'plæstɪks, B ,sɪərə-] *s. pl.* (*sing. en const.*) ceroplástica.

cerotic acid [sɪ'roʊtɪk, -'rɑt-, B -'rɔt-] ácido cerótico.

cert. *abrev. de* **certificate,** certificado.

certain ['sɜrtən, B 'sɜt-] *a.* 1. cierto, seguro, fijo; indudable, inevitable. 2. cierto, verdadero. 3. cierto, alguno. 4. **a c.,** cierto, un tal; **for c.,** por cierto; **to be c. of,** estar cierto o seguro de; **dead c.,** completamente seguro; ser inevitable que (haga), deber de (hacer) ej., *it is c. to rain tomorrow,* sin duda lloverá mañana; **to make c. of,** asegurarse de; **to a c. degree,** hasta cierto punto.

certainly [-lɪ] *adv.* 1. ciertamenta, indudablemente. 2. (fam.) con mucho gusto.

certainty [-tɪ] *s.* 1. certeza, certidumbre. 2. cosa segura, hecho patente. 3. **with c.,** a ciencia cierta.

certifiable ['sɜrtəˌfaɪəbəl, B 'sɜtɪ-] *a.* 1. certificable. 2. (G.B.) demente.

certificate [sər'tɪfɪkət, B sə'-] *s.* 1. certificado, constancia, atestado, testimonio, fe, partida; diploma; título. 2. (fin.) bono, obligación. —[-əˌkeɪt] *v.t.* proveer de certificado; dar certificado a.

certificate of baptism, fe de bautismo, partida de bautismo.

certificate of death, partida de defunción.

certificate of deposit, certificado de depósito.

certificate of marriage, partida de matrimonio, certificado de matrimonio.

certificate of origin, (com.) certificado de origen.

certification [ˌsɜrtəfə'keɪʃən, B ˌsɜt-] *s.* certificación, atestado, constancia.

certified ['sɜrtəˌfaɪd, B 'sɜt-] *a.* certificado, garantizado.

certified check, (E.U.) cheque certificado, cheque aprobado.

certified mail, correo certificado o registrado.

certified public accountant, (E.U.) contador público titulado (C.P.A.).

certify ['sɜrtəˌfaɪ, B 'sɜtɪ-] *v.t.* (*pret., p.p.* CERTIFIED; *p.pr.* CERTIFYING) 1. certificar, atestiguar, dar or dejar constancia de; **this is to c. that,** por la presente certifico que, doy fe de que; **to c. that,** declarar que. 2. (fin., E.U.) garantizar (un cheque). 3. (G.B.) declarar alienado.

certiorari [ˌsɜrʃɪə'rɛrɪ, -'rɑrɪ, B ˌsɜtɪɔ'rɛəraɪ] *s.* (der.) auto de avocación (con que un tribunal superior solicita la causa pendiente en un tribunal inferior).

certitude ['sɜrtəˌtud, B 'sɜtɪˌtjud] *s.* certidumbre, certeza.

cerulean [sə'rulɪən] *a.* cerúleo. —*s.* color cerúleo, azul oscuro.

cerumen [sə'rumən, B -mɛn] *s.* cerumen, cerilla (de los oídos).

ceruse [sə'rus, 'sɪrˌus, B 'sɪər-] *s.* (quím.) cerusa, albayalde.

cerussite [sə'rʌsˌaɪt, 'sɛrəˌsaɪt, B 'sɪərə-] *s.* (min.) cerusita.

Cervantine [sər'vænˌtaɪn, B sə'-] *a.* cervantino, cervantesco.

Cervantist [-təst] *a., s.* cervantista.

cervical ['sɜrvɪkəl, B sə'vaɪkəl] *a.* (anat.) cervical, cérvico, de la cerviz.

cervicitis [ˌsɜrvə'saɪtəs, B ˌsɜv-] *s.* (med.) cervicitis.

cervine ['sɜrˌvaɪn, B 'sɜˌ-] *a.* (zool.) cervuno, cervino.

cervix ['sɜrvɪks, B 'sɜvɪks] *s.* (*pl.* SCERVICES [-vəˌsiz sər'vaɪsiz, B sə'-] ♀ℂ♂△?♂ℂ⅄) (anat., zool.) 1. cerviz, nuca, parte posterior del cuello. 2. cerviz, cuello del útero.

cesarean, cesarian [sɪ'zɛrɪən, B -'zɛər-] *s.* (med.) operación cesárea. —*a.* cesáreo.

cesium ['sizɪəm] *s.* (quím.) cesio.

cespitose ['sɛspəˌtoʊs] *a.* (bot.) cespitoso, de césped.

cessation [sɛ'seɪʃən] *s.* cese, cesación; suspensión, paro.

cession ['sɛʃən] *s.* cesión, traspaso.

cessionary [-əˌnɛrɪ, B -ənərɪ] *s.* (*pl.* SCESSIONARIES) (der.) cesionario.

cesspool ['sɛsˌpul] *s.* 1. letrina, pozo negro, sumidero de desagüe. 2. (fig.) lugar inmundo, centro de corrupción.

cestode ['sɛsˌtoʊd] *s., a.* (zool.) cestodo. —*a.* cestoide.

cestus ['sɛstəs] *s.* (*pl.* SCESTI [-ˌtaɪ]) (hist.) cesto (armadura para las manos de los púgiles romanos); ceñidor, cinturón.

cesura, cesural, *simb.var. de* **caesura, caesural.**

Cetacea [sɪ'teɪʃə] *s. pl.* (zool.) cetáceos.

cetacean [-ʃən] *a., s.* (zool.) cetáceo.

cetaceous [-ʃəs] *a.* cetáceo.

cetane ['siˌteɪn] *s.* (quím.) cetano.

cetane rating, (quím) índice de cetano.

cetin ['sitən] *s.* (quím.) cetina.

cetrarin [sə'trɛrən] *s.* (quím.) cetrarina.

Cetus ['sitəs] *s.* (astr.) Ballena.

cetyl ['sitəl] *s.* (quím.) cetilo.

Ceylon [sə'lɑn, B -'lɔn] *s.* Ceilán.

Ceylonese [ˌseɪlə'nɪz, -si-] *s., a.* ceilanés, cingalés.

Cf *simb. de* **californium,** californio (Cf).

C.F. *abrev. de* **cost and freight,** costo y flete (C y F).

Cfm *abrev. de* **cubic feet per minute,** pies cúbicos por minuto.

Cfs *abrev. de* **cubic feet per second,** pies cúbicos por segundo.

cg., cgm. *abrev. de* **centigram,** centigramo (cg.).

cgs. *abrev. de* **centimeter-gram-second,** centímetro-gramo-segundo.

Chablis ['ʃæbˌli, ʃæ'bli, B 'ʃæbli] *s.* (fr.) chablis, tipo de vino blanco.

cha-cha ['tʃɑˌtʃɑ] *s.* (mús.) cha-cha-chá (baile).

chacma ['tʃækmə] *s.* (zool.) chacma, variedad de mandril o papión.

chaconne [ʃɑ'kɔn, B ʃə-] *s.* (mús.) chacona.

Chad [tʃæd] *s.* Chad.

chaetognath ['kitˌɑgˌnæθ, B -ˌɔg-] *s.* (zool.) quetognato.

chafe [tʃeɪf] *v.t.* 1. frotar, ej., *c. one's hands,* frotarse las manos (para calentarlas). 2. raspar, rozar, excoriar, ej., *c. one's skin,* excoriarse la piel. 3. irritar, exacerbar, enfadar. —*v.i.* 1. irritarse, exacerbarse, enfadarse. 2. rozarse, frotarse, excoriarse. —*s.* 1. irritación, exacerbación, enfado, cólera. 2. excoriación.

chafer ['tʃeɪfər, B -ə] *s.* (ento.) abejorro.

chaff [tʃæf, B tʃɑf] *s.* 1. barcia, ahechaduras. 2. paja desmenuzada (para forraje). 3. broza, desperdicios. 4. (fig.) broza, cosa inútil, cosa trivial. 5. fisga, chanza, zumba, vaya. 6. (bot.) bráctea (de algunas flores). 7. **caught with c.,** engañado fácilmente; **to separate the c. from the grain,** (fig.) separar la cizaña del buen grano. —*v.t.* fisgar(se) de, chancearse de, zumbar (a), zumbarse de.

chaffer ['tʃæfər, B -ə] *s.* regateo; comercio, negocio. —*v.i.* 1. (G.B.) charlar, andar en dimes y diretes. 2. (ant.) negociar; regatear. —*v.t.* comprar o vender; traficar, intercambiar, trocar, cambalachear; **c. away,** dar por una bicoca, vender regalado.

chaffinch ['tʃæfɪntʃ] *s.* (zool.) pinzón, pinchón.

chaffy ['tʃæfɪ, B 'tʃɑfɪ] *a.* 1. cubierto de barcia, brozoso. 2. (fig.) trivial, sin valor. 3. de chanza, chancero, burlón.

chafing dish ['tʃeɪfɪŋ-] escalfeta, escalfador, braserillo calentador (para la mesa).

chagrin [ʃə'grɪn, B 'ʃægrɪn] *s.* mortificación, sofocón, disgusto, desazón. —*v.t.* mortificar, enfadar.

chain [tʃeɪn] *s.* 1. cadena. 2. (fig.) (*pl.*) cadenas, trabas, grillos. 3. (fig.) cadena, encadenación, serie, ej., *c. of mountains,* cadena de montañas, cordillera, *c. of events,* cadena de acontecimientos. 4. (top.) cadena de agrimensor (de 100 eslabones). 5. (*pl.*) opresión; esclavitud. 6. tiendas (restaurantes, teatros, etc.) pertenecientes a una misma empresa. 7. **in chains,** encadenado. —*v.t.* encadenar, aherrojar.

chain belt, (mec.) correa de cadena, cadena de transmisión, correa articulada.

chain block, garrucha diferencial de cadena, aparejo de cadena; polea diferencial, montacarga de cadena.

chain cable, (mar.) cadena de ancla.

chain conveyor, (mec.) transportador a cadena, cadena transportadora.

chain coupling, (f.c.) cadena de enganche (entre los vagones como protección adicional).

chain drive, (mec.) accionamiento por cadena, transmisión de cadena.

chain gang, cadena, cuerda o cuadrilla de presidiarios (que ejecutan trabajos forzados).

chain gear, (mec.) rueda de cadena, transmisión por rueda y cadena.

chain letter, carta de una cadena de la buena suerte que multiplica cada destinatario.

chain lightning, relámpagos o relampagueo en zig-zag.

chain mail, cota de mallas.

chainman ['tʃeɪnmən] *s.* cadenero, portacadena (agrimensor).

chain of mountains, cadena de montañas, cordillera.

chain pulley, (mec.) polea o rueda de cadena, rueda dentada.

chain pump, (mec.) bomba de cadena, noria.

chain-react ['tʃeɪnrɪ'ækt] *v.i.* (fís., quím.) experimentar reacción en cadena (materia fisionable).

chain reaction, (fís., quím.) reacción en cadena.

chain reactor, (fís., quím.) *s.* pila de reacción en cadena.

chain riveting, (mec.) remachado paralelo o de cadena.

chain saw, sierra de cadena.

chain shot, (hist., mil.) bala encadenada, balas enramadas.

chain-smoker [-ˌsmoʊkər, B -ə] *s.* fumador empedernido (que enciende un cigarrillo tras otro).

chain stitch, (cost.) punto de cadeneta.

chain store, tienda de una serie (perteneciente a una misma empresa).

chain tongs, *s. pl.* llave o tenaza de cadena.

chain wheel, rueda dentada para cadena.

chain work, (tej.) cadeneta.

chair [tʃɛr, B tʃɛə] *s.* 1. silla. 2. sillón de la presidencia; (fig.) presidencia; presidente (de una junta, asamblea, etc.) ej., *who has the c. this year?* ¿quién es presidente este año? 3. cátedra (de profesor de universidad). 4. silla de manos. 5. (f.c.) cojinete (para riel de doble hongo). 6. forma abrev. de **electric c.,** silla eléctrica. 7. **to address the c.,** dirigirse al presidente; **to leave the c.,** levantar la sesión; **to take a c.,** sentarse, tomar asiento; **to take the c.,** asumir la presidencia, abrir la sesión. 8. (*of a committee or university department*) presidente, presidenta. —*v.t.* 1. asentar. 2. instalar en oficio (a un presidente, una autoridad, etc.). 3. presidir (una junta, asamblea, etc.). 4. (G.B.) llevar en triunfo en una silla.

chair car, (f.c.) coche-salón.
chair lift, telesilla (para los esquiadores).
chairman ['tʃɛrmən, B 'tʃɛəmən] *s.* 1. presidente (de una junta directiva, conferencia, grupo de funcionarios, etc.). 2. silletero, portador (de la silla de manos). —*v.t.* (*pret., p.p.* CHAIRMANED o CHAIRMANNED; *p.pr.* CHAIRMANING o CHAIRMANNING) presidir (una junta, asamblea, reunión, etc.).
chairmanship [-ʃɪp] *s.* presidencia (de una junta, etc.).
chairperson ['tʃɛr,pɜrsən] *s.* presidente, presidenta.
chair rail, guardasilla (moldura que protege la pared de los respaldos de las sillas).
chairwoman [-,wʊmən] *s.* presidenta.
chaise [ʃeɪz] *s.* 1. silla volante, calesín, carruaje ligero de dos ruedas. 2. silla de posta.
chaise longue ['ʃeɪz,lɔŋ] meridiana (sofá de cabecera para recostarse).
chalaza [kə'leɪzə] *s.* (zool., bot.) chalaza.
chalcanthite [kæl'kæn,θaɪt] *s.* (min.) calcantita, sulfato de cobre nativo.
chalcedony [kæl'sɛdənɪ] *s.* (min.) calcedonia.
chalcid [kælsəd] *a., s.* (ento.) calcídido, (insecto).
chalcocite ['kælkə,saɪt] *s.* (min.) calcosita, calcosina.
chalcographic [,kælkə'græfɪk] *a.* calcográfico.
chalcography [kæl'kɑgrəfɪ, B -'kɔg-] *s.* calcografía, grabado en metales.
chalcopyrite [,kælkə'paɪr,aɪt] *s.* (min.) calcopirita, pirita de cobre.
Chaldaic [kæl'deɪɪk] *a.* caldeo, caldaico, natural de Caldea.
Chaldea [kæl'diə] *s.* (hist.) Caldea.
Chaldean [-ən] *s.* 1. caldeo, natural de Caldea. 2. mago, astrólogo, adivino. —*a.* caldeo.
chaldron ['tʃɔldrən] *s.* (G.B.) antigua medida de sólidos en grano.
chalet [ʃæ'leɪ, B 'ʃæleɪ] *s.* chalé, chalet.
chalice ['tʃæləs] *s.* (relig., bot.) cáliz.
chalk [tʃɔk] *s.* 1. creta; greda. 2. tiza (para escribir en la pizarra). 3. (G.B.) punto, tanto (en juegos). —*v.t.* 1. marcar con tiza; escribir o apuntar con tiza. 2. (billar) empolvar con tiza (taco), dar de tiza a, entizar (Am.). 3. **c. out,** esbozar, hacer un esquema de (un plan, etc.); **c. up,** apuntar, ej., *c. up the score,* apuntar los tantos (en el juego), *c. it up* (*to my account*), apúntelo (en mi cuenta); atribuir; anotarse, acreditarse (ganancias, triunfos, etc.). —*v.i.* volverse gredoso.
chalkstone ['tʃɔk,stoʊn] *s.* (med.) tofo, nodo, tumor (que se forma en los huesos).
chalky [-ɪ] *a.* (CHALKIER; CHALKIEST) cretáceo, gredoso.
challenge ['tʃæləndʒ] *s.* 1. reto, desafío. 2. (der.) recusación, objeción, tacha. 3. (mil.) quién vive. 4. (dep.) reto. —*v.t.* 1. retar, desafiar. 2. poner en tela de juicio; (E.U.) impugnar (un voto). 3. requerir, exigir, demandar (explicación, prioridad, etc.); poner a prueba (habilidad, valor, etc.). 4. estimular, excitar (interés, imaginación, etc.) 5. (der.) recusar, poner reparos a (un testigo, jurado). 6. (mil.) dar el quién vive. 7. (dep.) retar (a un concurso).
challenger [-ər, B -ə] *s.* retador, desafiador; demandante.
challenging [-ɪŋ] *a.* 1. desafiador, provocador (gesto, manera, etc.). 2. provocativo, fascinante (sonrisa, personalidad, etc.). 3. intrigante, excitante (problema, hipótesis, etc.).
challis ['ʃælɪ, B -ɪs] *s.* (tej.) chalí.
chalone ['kæl,oʊn] *s.* (med.) calona.
chalybeate [kə'lɪbɪət] *a.* calibeado (manantial, aguas minerales, etc.). —*s.* medicina calibeada o ferruginosa.
chamade [ʃə'mɑd] *s.* (ant., mil.) llamada.
chamber ['tʃeɪmbər, B -bə] *s.* 1. cuarto, cámara, esp. aposento, alcoba, dormitorio. 2. cámara (del cuerpo legislativo, judicial, etc.). 3. (*pl.*) despacho (del juez). 4. recámara, cámara (de las armas de fuego). —*a.* de cámara, ej., *c. music,* música de cámara. —*v.t.* 1. poner o alojar en un cuarto. 2. servir de cuarto para.
chamberlain [-lən] *s.* 1. chambelán, gentilhombre de cámara. 2. (relig.) camarlengo. 3. tesorero.
chambermaid [-,meɪd] *s.* camarera, doncella, sirvienta; recamarera (Mex.).
chamber of commerce, cámara de comercio.
chamber of deputies, Cámara de Diputados.
chamber orchestra, (mús.) orquesta de cámara.
chamber pot, orinal, bacín, vaso de noche.
chamber working, (min.) labor de anchurón y pilar, minería de pilares y salones.
chambray ['ʃæm,breɪ] *s.* (tej.) cambray.
chameleon [kə'miljən] *s.* 1. (zool.) camaleón. 2. (fig.) camaleón, persona inconstante.
chamfer ['tʃæmfər, B -fə] *s.* 1. chaflán, bisel. 2. (arq.) estría. —*v.t.* 1. biselar, chaflanar. 2. (arq.) estriar, acanalar (columna).
chamois ['ʃæmi, B -wɑ] *s.* (*pl.* CHAMOIS o CHAMOIX) 1. (zool.) gamuza (especie de) antílope pequeño. 2. (piel de la) gamuza.
chamomile ['kæmə,maɪl, -,mil] *var. de* **camomile.**
champ [tʃæmp] *s.* (fam.) campeón. —*v.t., v.i.* tascar (hierba, forraje, el freno); mordisquear, mascar, masticar con fuerza; **c. at the bit,** (fig.) tascar el freno, impacientarse.
champac ['tʃæm,pæk, 'tʃʌm,pʌk] *s.* (bot.) campacán.
Champagne [ʃæm'peɪn] *s.* 1. Champaña, región de Francia. 2. **c.,** champaña, vino champán.
champaign [ʃæm'peɪn, B 'tʃæmpeɪn] *s.* campiña, campo abierto, pradera, llanura. —*a.* abierto o llano.
champerty ['tʃæmpərtɪ, B -pətɪ] *s.* (der.) ayuda ilegal a un litigante a cambio del reparto de los bienes.
champignon [ʃæm'pɪnjən, B tʃæm-] *s.* (bot., fr.) champiñón, hongo, seta.
champion ['tʃæmpɪən] *s.* 1. campeón. 2. (fig.) campeón, adalid, defensor, paladín. 3. (dep.) campeón, ganador, vencedor. —*v.t.* defender, abogar por, proteger. —*a.* supremo, sin par, sin rival.
champion lode, (min.) filón principal.
championship [-,ʃɪp] *s.* campeonato.
chance [tʃæns, B tʃɑns] *s.* 1. fortuna, suerte. 2. azar, casualidad. 3. oportunidad, ocasión. 4. posibilidad; (esp. en pl.) probabilidad, ej., *chances are that,* la probabilidad es que. 5. riesgo, contingencia. 6. billete de lotería. 7. **by c.,** por casualidad; **on the c. (of, that),** con la esperanza (de, que); **there is no c.,** no hay esperanzas; **to give (someone) a c.,** dar una oportunidad (a alguien); **to stand a c.,** tener una posibilidad; **to take chances,** correr riesgos, confiar en la suerte; **to take one's c.,** correr el albur, aventurarse, arriesgarse. —*v.t.* (*pret., p.p.* CHANCED; *p.pr.* CHANCING) arriesgar, correr el riesgo de; probar. —*v.i.* suceder, acontecer, acaecer; **c. to (do, be, have)** hacer, estar, tener) por casualidad, ej., *I chanced to be there,* por casualidad estaba allí, *he chanced to look up,* por casualidad levantó la mirada; **c. upon,** encontrar, encontrarse con (por casualidad), tropezarse con. —*a.* casual, accidental, fortuito.
chancel ['tʃænsəl, B 'tʃɑn-] *s.* presbiterio, antealtar.
chancellery [-ərɪ] *s.* cancillería.
chancellor ['tʃænsələr, B 'tʃɑnsələ] *s.* canciller.
Chancellor of the Exchequer, (G.B.) Ministro de Hacienda.
chance-medley [-,mɛdlɪ] *s.* (der.) delito (esp. homicidio) accidental.
chancery ['tʃænsərɪ, B 'tʃɑns-] *s.* 1. cancillería. 2. (der., G.B.) división de la Corte Suprema de Justicia que preside el Lord Canciller; (E.U.) juzgado. 3. (oficina de) registros públicos. 4. (dep.) llave que toma la cabeza (en lucha libre). 5. **in c.,** con la cabeza aprisionada (en la lucha); en litigio; en situación apurada, en apuros.
chancre ['ʃæŋkər, B -kə] *s.* (med.) chancro, esp. chancro duro.
chancroid [-,krɔɪd] *s.* (med.) chancroide, chancro blando.
chancy ['tʃænsɪ, B 'tʃɑnsɪ] *a.* 1. arriesgado, riesgoso, peligroso. 2. (esco.) de buen agüero, de buena suerte.
chandelier [,ʃændə'lɪr, B -'lɪə] *s.* araña de luces, candelabro colgante.
chandelle [ʃæn'dɛl, ʃɑn-] *s.* (aer.) maniobra de subida lateral (en la cual el avión se eleva a consecuencia de la fuerza cinética al hacer un viraje brusco).
chandler ['tʃændlər, B 'tʃɑndlə] *s.* 1. cerero, velero, el que hace o vende cirios o velas. 2. tendero, abacero, pulpero (Am.). 3. (t. **ship c.**) comerciante de efectos navales.
chandlery [-lərɪ] *s.* 1. cerería; tienda de abastos. 2. mercancías, abarrotes (Am.).
change [tʃeɪndʒ] *v.t.* 1. cambiar, alterar, mudar; modificar, transformar; convertir; reemplazar, substituir, trocar. 2. **c. clothes,** cambiar de ropa; **c. color,** mudar de color, demudarse; ruborizarse; palidecer; **c. countenance,** mudar de color o expresión (demostrando sorpresa, miedo, etc.); **c. front,** cambiar de bando, tomar una nueva posición (en argumento, disputa, etc.); **c. hands,** cambiar de manos, pasar a otro dueño; **c. money,** cambiar dinero; **c. one's condition,** mejorar; casarse; **c. one's mind,** cambiar de opinión; **c. one's tune** o **note,** (fig.) cambiar de tono; **c. step,** cambiar de paso; **c. trains, boats,** etc., cambiar de tren, barco, etc. —*v.i.* 1. cambiar, mudar; transformarse, reformarse, corregirse. 2. **c. off,** turnarse con otro (en hacer algo), alternarse (en actos diferentes, en tocar instrumentos o entre acción y descanso). —*s.* 1. cambio, alteración, sustitución, mutación, mudanza. 2. novedad, variedad. 3. muda (de ropa). 4. vuelta o vuelto (de dinero); suelto, moneda suelta. 5. (G.B.) bolsa (de cambio). 6. (G.B.) (*gen. pl.*) serie de tañidos (de las campanas). 7. **for a c.,** para variar; **on C.,** (G.B.) (empleado o trabajando) en la Bolsa; **to get no c. out of,** no obtener la cooperación de, no lograr ningún progreso con (una persona); **to keep the c.,** quedarse con la vuelta; **to ring the changes,** (fig.) agotar todas las formas posibles (de hacer o colocar una cosa).
changeable ['tʃeɪndʒəbəl] *a.* 1. alterable, cambiable, mudable. 2. variable, cambiadizo, inconstante. 3. tornasolado.
changeful [-fəl] *a.* veleidoso, inconstante, variable.
changeless [-ləs] *a.* inmutable, constante.
changeling [-lɪŋ] *s.* 1. criatura suplantada (subrepticiamente por otra). 2. renegado, traidor. 3. (ant.) imbécil.

change of heart, cambio de intenciones, cambio de parecer.
change of life, edad crítica, menopausia.
change of venue, (der.) traslado de jurisdicción, cambio de tribunal (en un proceso).
changeover [-ˌouvər, B -və] *s.* alteración (de un sistema), cambio (de situación, opinión, etc.).
change-over switch, (elec.) conmutador, permutador, llave conmutadora.
changer [-ər, B -ə] *s.* 1. aparato cambiador, esp. cambiadiscos. 2. (ant.) cambista.
channel ['tʃænəl] *s.* 1. canal. 2. cauce, álveo, lecho, madre (de un río). 3. caño, canalizo (de un puerto). 4. (fig.) canal, conducto. 5. (const.) (t. **c. bar**) viga canal, viga U. 6. (mec.) ranura, garganta, cajera, acanaladura. 7. (comput., t.v.) canal, cadena. *—v.t.* (*pret., p.p.* CHANNELED o CHANNELLED; *p.pr.* CHANNELING o CHANNELLING) 1. acanalar, estriar, ranurar. 2. canalizar, encauzar, conducir (por).
channel iron, hierro de canal, hierro en U.
Channel Islands, Islas Anglonormandas, Islas del Canal.
channelization [ˌtʃænələ'zeɪʃən, B -laɪ-] *s.* canalización, encauzamiento.
channelize ['tʃænəlˌaɪz] *v.t.* canalizar, encauzar.
chanson [ʃɑn'sɔn, B 'ʃænsən] *s.* (mús., fr.) canción, canto, cuplet.
chanson de geste [-də'ʒɛst, B -'dʒɛst] (fr.) cantar de gesta, poema épico.
chant [tʃænt, B tʃɑnt] *v.t.* cantar (esp. salmos; alabanzas, loas, etc.). *—v.i.* cantar o recitar monótonamente, salomar. *—s.* 1. canto, cantar; salmo, cántico, cantinela. 2. canturía, saloma, salmodia.
chanter ['tʃæntər, B 'tʃɑntə] *s.* 1. cantor, corista. 2. chantre (de la iglesia). 3. puntero (de la gaita). 4. (G.B.) tratante deshonesto de caballos.
chanterelle [ˌʃæntə'rəl, B ˌtʃæntə-] *s.* (bot.) hongo comestible amarillo de olor agradable.
chanteuse [ʃɑn'tʌz, ʃæn'tuz, B -'tɜz] *s.* (fr.) cantante, canzonetista, cupletista.
chantey ['ʃæntɪ, 'tʃæn-, B 'tʃɑn-] *s.* (mar.) saloma.
chanticleer [ˌtʃæntə'klɪr, 'tʃæn-ˌklɪr, B ˌtʃæn-'klɪə] *s.* gallo.
chantry ['tʃæntrɪ, B 'tʃɑn-] *s.* (relig.) 1. capellanía. 2. sacerdotes cantores de misas especiales; capilla o altar de capellanía; capellanes.
chanty, *s. var. de* **chantey.**
chaos ['keɪˌɑs, B -ˌɔs] *s.* caos, confusión, desorden.
chaotic [keɪ'ɑtɪk, B -'ɔt-] *a.* caótico, confuso, desordenado.
chap [tʃæp] *s.* 1. (fam.) mozo, joven, sujeto. 2. (*pl. en const.*) chaparreras, zahones, zamarros (de cuero).
chap [tʃæp] *v.t., v.i* (*pret., p.p.* CHAPPED; *p.pr.* CHAPPING) hender, rajar, agrietarse, cuartearse (la piel); resquebrajar(se). *—s.* grieta, rajadura, hendidura.
chaparral [ˌtʃæpə'ræl, ˌʃæp-] *s.* chaparral; matorral de arbustos espinosos.
chaparral cock, (orn.) correcaminos, barranquera, caminera común.
chapbook ['tʃæpˌbuk] *s.* (ant.) librito de versos, cuentos, ensayos, etc. (que vendían los buhoneros).
chape [tʃeɪp] *s.* adorno de metal (en la vaina o funda de una espada o daga); contera, regatón.
chapel ['tʃæpəl] *s.* 1. capilla, santuario. 2. servicio religioso (en los colegios o universidades). 3. (G.B.) iglesia no anglicana (esp. de no-conformistas). 4. (ant.) imprenta.
chapel of ease, iglesia anglicana subordinada (para comodidad de los que viven aislados), capilla sufragánea.
chapelmaster [-ˌmæstər, B -ˌmɑstə] *s.* maestro de capilla.
chaperon, chaperone ['ʃæpəˌroun] *s.* chaperona, dueña, dama de compañía, acompañante de señoritas. *—v.t.* acompañar (a una señorita a fiesta, viaje, lugar público, etc.).
chaperonage [-ɪdʒ] *s.* vigilancia (de la acompañante de señoritas).
chapfallen ['tʃæpˌfɔlən, 'tʃɑp-, B 'tʃæp-] *a.* carilargo, cariacontecido, alicaído, desanimado.
chapiter ['tʃæpətər, B -tə] *s.* (arq.) capitel.
chaplain ['tʃæplən] *s.* 1. capellán (sacerdote a cargo de una capilla). 2. capellán castrense.
chaplet ['tʃæplət] *s.* 1. guirnalda o corona de flores; diadema (de oro, piedras preciosas, etc.). 2. cinco décadas del rosario. 3. (fig.) rosario, sarta, serie. 4. (arq.) moldura (esp. astrágalo) ornamentada.
chaplinesque [ˌtʃæplə'nɛsk] chaplinesco, relativo al personaje tragicómico creado en los principios del cine por el actor Charlie Chaplin.
chapman ['tʃæpmən] *s.* 1. (G.B.) buhonero, vendedor ambulante. 2. (ant.) comerciante.
chapped [tʃæpt] *a.* cuarteado (ej., piel, mano, etc.).
chappy ['tʃæpɪ] *a.* (CHAPPIER; CHAPPIEST) cuarteado (ej., piel, mano, etc.).
chaps [tʃæps, ʃæps] *s. pl.* chaparreras, zahonas.
chapter ['tʃæptər, B -tə] *s.* 1. capítulo (de un libro, tratado, etc.). 2. (relig.) capítulo (de los canónigos de una iglesia o los miembros de una orden religiosa). 3. organización local (de una confraternidad o sociedad). 4. **c. and verse,** referencia completa, información exacta; con (todos sus) pelos y señales; **to the end of the c.,** hasta el fin, para siempre. *—v.t.* dividir u ordenar en capítulos (un libro, etc.).
chapter 11 bankruptcy, reorganización del negocio bajo la ley de quiebras.
chapter house, 1. sala capitular. 2. edificio de una sociedad o confraternidad.
char [tʃɑr, B tʃɑ] *v.t., v.i.* (*pret., p.p.* CHARRED; *p.pr.* CHARRING) carbonizar(se), quemar; socarrar(se), chamuscar(se). *—s.* carbón de leña.
char [tʃɑr, B tʃɑ] *s.* (ict.) trucha de escamas pequeñas.
char [tʃɑr, B tʃɑ] (pr. G.B.) *s.* 1. (*forma abrev. de* **charwoman**) criada por horas o días. 2. faena, tarea doméstica, trabajo rutinario. *—v.i.* (*pret., p.p.* CHARRED; *p.pr.* CHARRING) trabajar como criada por horas o días.
charabanc ['ʃærəˌbæŋ] *s.* (G. B.) charabán, autobús de turismo.
character ['kærɪktər, B -tə] *s.* 1. carácter, temperamento (de una persona, raza, etc.). 2. carácter, índole, característica. 3.marca, distintivo. 4. carácter, signo (de escritura); tipo, carácter (de imprenta); escritura, letra, caligrafía (de una persona). 5. carácter, entereza, firmeza. 6. tipo original, cómico o curioso. 7. (teat., lit.) personaje. 8. **c. reference,** recomendación o testimonio de solvencia moral; **c. role,** (teat.) papel para actor o actriz que representa un personaje de edad; **in c.,** típico de, ej., *what she did was quite in c.,* lo que hizo fue muy típico de ella; **out of c.,** inusitado (en), desusado (en), (ej., *his actions are out of c.,* su actuación es inusitada en él.
characteristic [ˌkærɪktə'rɪstɪk] *a.* característico, distintivo, propio, típico, peculiar. *—s.* característica, cualidad, propiedad.
characterization [-tərə'zeɪʃən, B -raɪ-] *s.* caracterización, representación.
characterize ['kærɪktəˌraɪz] *v.t.* caracterizar.
character witness, persona que da testimonio de la solvencia moral de otra.
charade [ʃə'reɪd, B -'rɑd] *s.* charada, acertijo.
charcoal ['tʃɑrˌkoul, B 'tʃɑˌ-] *s.* 1. carbón de leña, carbón de palo. 2. (dib.) carboncillo; dibujo al carbón.
charcoal burner, aparato para cocinar al carbón.
charcoal drawing, dibujo al carbón o carboncillo.
charcoal furnace, horno de hacer carbón.
chard [tʃɑrd, B tʃɑd] *s.* (bot.) acelga.
chare [tʃɛr, tʃɛə] *var. de* **char,** trabajo ocasional, gen. doméstico.
charge [tʃɑrdʒ, B tʃɑdʒ] *v.t.* (*pret., p.p.* CHARGED; *p.pr.* CHARGING) 1. cargar (un arma de fuego); cargar, recargar (una batería, un acumulador); cargar, alimentar (un horno); llenar (el aire con vapor, olores, etc., el agua con un ácido, etc.). 2. exhortar, instruir; mandar (hacer algo). 3. (mil.) cargar, atacar. 4. (com., ten.) debitar, cargar, ej., *c. it to my account,* cárguelo a mi cuenta. 5. **c. with,** encargar (tarea, trabajo, etc.); acusar de, hacer cargos contra. *—v.i.* 1. ir a la carga o al ataque; embestir. 2. cobrar (tal precio). *—s.* 1. carga, peso (lit. y fig.). 2. carga (de acumulador, horno, arma de fuego). 3. tarea, deber, responsabilidad, obligación. 4. mando, dirección. 5. (mil.) carga, ataque. 6. acusación, alegato. 7. encargo, orden; exhortación, instrucciones (de juez, obispo, etc.). 8. pupilo, protegido, persona a cargo de otra. 9. gasto, costo; honorario. 10. cargo, cuidado, custodia. 11. (com.) cargo. 12. (elec.) carga. 13. **in c. of,** a cargo de (alguien o algo), encargado de; **to return to the c.,** volver al ataque, reanudar (discusión, faena, etc.); **to take c.,** asumir el mando (de puesto, situación); **to take c. of,** encargarse de, hacerse cargo de.
chargeable ['tʃɑrdʒəbəl, B 'tʃɑdʒ-] *a.* acusable, imputable; que se puede cargar a cuenta.
charge account, cuenta abierta, cuenta de crédito.
charge-a-plate [-əˌpleɪt] *s.* tarjeta de crédito (enchapada en metal).
charged [tʃɑrdʒd, B tʃɑdʒd] *a.* 1. (fís.) cargado (cuerpo, partícula, sistema). 2. intenso, apasionado. 3. **the atmosphere is c.,** la atmósfera está cargada (fig. y lit.).
chargé d'affaires [ˌʃɑrˌʒeɪdə'fɛr, B 'ʃɑˌ-'fɛə] encargado de negocios (de legación o embajada).
charger ['tʃɑrdʒər, B 'tʃɑdʒə] *s.* 1. (engen. y mec.) cargador. 2. (elec.) cargador de acumuladores (o baterías). 3. peine de balas. 4. (mil.) corcel, caballo de batalla.
charging [-ɪŋ] *a.* furioso, esp. animal; **a c. bull,** un toro que embiste.
charging rate, (elec.) régimen de carga, corriente de carga (de un acumulador).
charging voltage, tensión de carga.
charily ['tʃɛrəlɪ, 'tʃær-, B 'tʃɛər-] *adv.* cautelosamente, cuidadosamente.
chariness [-ɪnəs] *s.* cautela; frugalidad.
chariot ['tʃærɪət] *s.* 1. carroza. 2. (hist.) cuadriga, carro romano (de guerra y dep.).
charioteer [ˌtʃærɪə'tɪr, B -'tɪə] *s.* 1. (hist., poét.) cuadriguero, auriga. 2. C., (astr.) Auriga.
charisma [kə'rɪzmə] **charism** ['kærˌɪzəm] *s.* (*pl.*) CHARISMATA [kə'rɪzmətə] o CHARISMS) 1. don de gentes, duende; liderazgo, poder de captación; **to have c.,** tener duende. 2. (teo.) carisma.
charismatic [ˌkærəz'mætɪk] *a.* carismático.
charitable ['tʃærətəbəl] *a.* 1. caritativo, benéfico. 2. benévolo, tolerante.

charitableness [-nəs] *s.* caridad, beneficencia.
charitably [-blɪ] *adv.* 1. caritativamente. 2. con tolerancia.
charity ['tʃærətɪ] *s.* 1. caridad, bondad, benevolencia (de juicio, opinión, etc.). 2. caridad, obra o instituto de caridad, institución de beneficencia. 3. tolerancia. 4. caridad, limosna, acto de beneficencia. 5. **c. begins at home,** la caridad (bien entendida) comienza por casa.
charity performance, función benéfica.
charivari [ˌʃrvə'ri, ʃəˌrɪv-, B 'ʃɑrɪ'vɑrɪ] *s.* cencerrada; ruidosa serenata nupcial que se da a los viudos que se vuelven a casar.
charlatan ['ʃɑrlətən, B 'ʃɑlə-] *s.* charlatán; curandero; embaucador.
charlatanism [-ˌɪzəm] **charlatanry** [-rɪ] *s.* charlatanismo, charlatanería.
Charlemagne ['ʃɑrləˌmeɪn, B 'ʃɑlə'meɪn] *s.* Carlomagno, rey de los francos.
Charles's Wain ['tʃɑrlzəz'weɪn, B 'tʃɑl-] (astr.) Osa Mayor.
Charleston ['tʃɑrlstən, B 'tʃɑl-] *s.* tipo de baile popular en la segunda década del siglo, charlestón.
charley horse ['tʃɑrlɪ-, B 'tʃɑlɪ-] (fam. E.U.) calambre; inflamación muscular.
Charlie [-lɪ] *s.* 1. palabra en el código de comunicaciones para la letra **c.** 2. soldado del Viet Cong. 3. (jer., E.U.) nombre usado por los negros para referirse a los blancos.
charlock ['tʃɑrˌlɑk, -lək, B 'tʃɑlɔk] *s.* (bot.) (variedad de) mostaza silvestre.
charlotte russe ['ʃɑrlət'rus, B 'ʃɑlət-] carlota rusa, postre de torta y crema, relleno de gelatina o fruta.
charm [tʃɑrm, B tʃɑm] *s.* 1. gracia, atractivo. 2. encanto, hechizo. 3. amuleto, dije. 4. **like a c.,** como por magia, perfectamente; **to have a lot of c.,** tener mucho ángel; **to have c.,** tener duende. —*v.t.* encantar, hechizar, cautivar, atraer, deleitar. —*v.i.* practicar hechicería; ejercer fascinación.
charmer ['tʃɑrmər, B 'tʃɑmə] *s.* 1. encantador, mago, ej., *snake c.,* encantador de serpientes. 2. mujer encantadora; persona fascinante.
charming [-ɪŋ] *a.* encantador, fascinante, seductor.
charmingly [-lɪ] *adv.* encantadoramente, seductoramente.
charnel ['tʃɑrnəl, B 'tʃɑn-] *s.* 1. osario, carnero. 2. (ant.) cementerio. —*a.* sepulcral.
charnel house, (ant.) osario, sepultura.
charpoy ['tʃɑrˌpɔɪ, B 'tʃɑˌ-] *s.* (angloind.) cama.
chart [tʃɑrt, B tʃɑt] *s.* 1. mapa; carta de navegar; mapa hidrográfico. 2. gráfica, diagrama; hoja de papel graduado. 3. esquema, cuadro, tabla. —*v.t.* 1. cartografiar, trazar (mapas). 2. planear, proyectar (curso, estrategia, etc.). 3. **c. a course,** (mar.) trazar un derrotero.
chartaceous [kɑr'teɪʃəs, B kɑ'-] *a.* 1. (hecho) de papel. 2. (bot.) cartáceo.
charter ['tʃɑrtər, B 'tʃɑtə] *s.* 1. carta, cédula, título; carta constitucional, ej., *the U. N. C.,* la Carta de las Naciones Unidas. 2. permiso legal (para constituir una compañía, universidad, etc.). 3. privilegio, exención, inmunidad. 4. alquiler (de un buque, avión, etc.). —*v.t.* 1. otorgar o constituir por carta. 2. fletar (navío, avión); alquilar (un vehículo).
chartered accountant [-ərd-, B -əd-] (G.B.) contador público, perito mercantil.
charter flight, vuelo charter.
charterhouse [-ərˌhaʊs, B -əˌ-] *s.* cartuja.
charter member, socio fundador.
charter party, (mar.) contrato de fletamento, carta de partida.
chart house, (mar.) caseta de derrota (donde se tienen los mapas e instrumentos de navegación de un buque).
chartist ['tʃɑrtəst, B 'tʃɑt-] *s.* 1. cartógrafo. 2. experto en la bolsa de valores.
chartless [-ləs] *a.* sin rumbo, desorientado.
chartographer [kɑr'tɑgrəfər, B kɑ'tɔgrəfə] *s.* cartógrafo.
chartography [-fɪ] *s.* cartografía.
chartometer [tʃɑr'tɑmətər, B tʃɑ'tɔmɪtə] *s.* cartómetro.
chartreuse [ʃɑr'truz, -'trus, B ʃɑ'trɜz] *s.* 1. licor preparado por los cartujos. 2. color verde pálido.
chart room, *var. de* **chart house.**
chartulary, *var. de* **cartulary.**
charwoman ['tʃɑrˌwʊmən, B 'tʃɑˌ-] *s.* criada por día u hora.
chary ['tʃærɪ, 'tʃɛrɪ, B 'tʃɛərɪ] *a.* 1. cuidadoso, cauteloso. 2. (con *of*) frugal, parco, celoso, ej., *c. of praise,* parco en los elogios. 3. receloso, desconfiado (de).
chase [tʃeɪs] *s.* 1. persecución. 2. (con *the*) caza, cacería, montería. 3. **in c. of,** a la caza de; **to give c. (to),** dar caza (a). —*v.t.* 1. perseguir, acosar, dar caza a. 2. **c. from** (o **out of**), expulsar, echar (fuera de); **c. off** (o **away**), ahuyentar; **go c. yourself!** (jer.) ¡vete! ¡lárgate! —*v.i.* 1. (con *about, around,* etc.) correr de aquí para allá. 2. **c. after,** dar caza a, ir en persecución de.
chase, *s.* 1. ranura, muesca. 2. ánima (del cañón); caña (del cañón antiguo). 3. acanaladura (en pared para tubos, etc.). 4. (print.) marco, rama. —*v.t.* 1. repujar, grabar en relieve, cincelar (metal). 2. engastar (una joya, etc. con perlas, diamantes, etc.). 3. ranurar, acanalar. 4. (mec.) roscar, filetear (tornillo).
chaser ['tʃeɪsər, B -ə] *s.* 1. cazador; perseguidor. 2. (mar.) cañón de proa o de popa (para la caza del enemigo). 3. cazasubmarinos. 4. (fam.) bebida ligera que se toma después de beber un licor fuerte. 5. (mec.) fileteadora, herramienta para filetear (tornillos). 6. cincelador, buril. 7. (joy.) engastador.
chasing [-ɪŋ] *s.* 1. caza, persecución. 2. (joy.) engaste, cinceladura.
chasing lathe, (maq., mec.) torno para roscar, torno de filetear.
chasing tool, (mec.) herramienta de filetear, fileteadora.
chasm ['kæzəm] *s.* 1. abismo, precipicio, sima, grieta; ruptura; vacío. 2. (fig.) abismo, diferencia abismal (entre opiniones, intereses, etc.).
chassé [ʃæ'seɪ, B 'ʃæseɪ] *s.* paso de (baile parecido al) patinaje. —*v.i.* ejecutar el paso de patinaje.
chasseur [ʃæ'sɜr, B -'sɜ] *s.* 1. cazador. 2. (mil.) cazador. 3. portero de librea.
chassis ['ʃæsɪ, 'tʃæsɪ, B 'ʃæ-] *s.* 1. chasis, armazón (de un automóvil). 2. chasis, armazón, base, bastidor, marco. 3. (jer.) figura, cuerpo (de una mujer).
chaste [tʃeɪst] *a.* 1. casto, continente, púdico. 2. puro, sencillo (ornamento, líneas de un diseño, estilo, gusto, etc.).
chastely ['tʃeɪstlɪ] *adv.* castamente, púdicamente.
chasten ['tʃeɪsən] *v.t.* 1. castigar, disciplinar, enmendar. 2. depurar, purificar (de vicios, defectos).
chasteness ['tʃeɪstnəs] *s.* castidad, pureza, continencia.
chastening ['tʃeɪsənɪŋ] *s.* castigo, medida disciplinaria.
chaste tree, (bot.) agnocasto, sauzgatillo, incienso japonés, pimiento silvestre.
chastise [tʃæs'taɪz] *v.t.* castigar; reformar, corregir.
chastisement [-mənt, B 'tʃæstɪz-] *s.* castigo, corrección.
chastiser [tʃæs'taɪzər, B -zə] *s.* castigador.
chastity ['tʃæstətɪ] *s.* 1. castidad, continencia. 2. castidad, pureza (del estilo, lenguaje, etc.).
chastity belt, (hist.) cinturón de castidad.
chasuble ['tʃæzjʊbəl] *s.* (rel.) casulla.
chat [tʃæt] *v.i.* (*pret., p.p.* CHATTED; *p.pr.* CHATTING) charlar. —*s.* 1. charla. 2. (orn.) culiblanco; charla.
château [ʃæ'toʊ, B 'ʃætoʊ] *s.* (*pl.* CHATEAUS, CHATEAUX) 1. (hist., fr.) castillo feudal. 2. residencia lujosa en una región rural.
chatelaine ['ʃætəlˌeɪn] *s.* 1. dueña y señora de un castillo o una residencia grande y opulenta. 2. cadena ornamental que se lleva a la cintura para colgar las llaves. 3. adorno que lleva la mujer en la solapa de la chaqueta.
chatoyance [ʃə'tɔɪəns] **chatoyancy** [-ɪ] *s.* brillo tornasolado.
chatoyant [-ənt] *a.* de un brillo tornasolado (de joyas y sedas).
chat show, (G.B.) (Am.: **talk show**) programa de entrevistas.
chattel ['tʃætəl] *s.* 1. (der.) bien mueble. 2. esclavo, vasallo.
chattel mortgage, (der.) hipoteca prendaria, crédito mobiliario.
chatter ['tʃætər, B -ə] *v.i.* 1. charlar, cotorrear, parlotear. 2. chacharear, hablar por los codos. 3. castañetear, rechinar (los dientes). 4. traquetear (ciertas herramientas y máquinas). —*s.* charla, cháchara, habladuría.
chatterbox [-ˌbɑks, B -ˌbɔks] *s.* charlador, hablador, parlanchín.
chatterer [-ərər, B -ərə] *s.* 1. parlanchín. 2. (orn.) picotero.
chatter mark, resquebrajaduras, grietas (que dejan en la superficie de la pieza labrada ciertas herramientas neumáticas).
chattily [-əlɪ] *adv.* locuazmente; en tono ligero.
chattiness [-ɪnəs] *s.* locuacidad, garrulidad.
chatty [-ɪ] *a.* parlanchín, gárrulo.
chauffeur ['ʃoʊfər, ʃoʊ'fɜr, B 'ʃoʊfə] *s.* chófer, chofer (Am.), conductor de automóvil. —*v.t.* 1. llevar en automóvil (a alguien). 2. conducir (un automóvil como chófer).
chaulmoogra [tʃɔl'mugrə] *s.* (bot.) chaulmugra.
chaulmoogra oil, aceite o manteca de chaulmugra (antiguamente usado como remedio en enfermedades cutáneas).
chauvinism ['ʃoʊvəˌnɪzəm] *s.* patriotería, chauvinismo.
chauvinist [-nəst] *s.* chauvinista, patriotero.
chaw [tʃɔ] (dial.) *v.t., v.i.* mascar. —*s.* mascada, bocado.
chay [tʃeɪ, tʃaɪ] *s.* (bot.) (raíz de) una planta de Indonesia que produce un tinte rojo.
chayote [tʃɑ'joʊtɪ] *s.* (bot.) cayote, chayote.
cheap [tʃip] *a.* 1. barato. 2. fácil (triunfo, etc.). 3. de pacotilla, vulgar, común. 4. vil, despreciable. 5. barato, a bajo interés (préstamo, etc.). 6. **dirt c.,** baratísimo, regalado; **to feel c.,** sentirse inferior o rebajado. —*adv.* barato, ej., *to get it c.,* conseguirlo barato.
cheapen ['tʃipən] *v.t., v.i.* abaratar(se), depreciar(se); vulgarizar(se).
cheap-jack [-ˌdʒæk] *s.* 1. trafagón. 2. buhonero.
cheaply [-lɪ] *adv.* barato, a bajo precio.
cheapness [-nəs] *s.* 1. baratura. 2. mezquindad, pobreza. 3. vulgaridad.

cheapskate [-ˌskeɪt] *s.* (jer.) tacaño, mezquino, cicatero.
cheat [tʃit] *s.* 1. tramposo, timador. 2. trampa, timo, engaño. —*v.t.* engañar, timar; **c. (someone) out of (something),** defraudar o estafar (a alguien). —*v.i.* 1. practicar fraude o engaño. 2. hacer trampas (en el juego).
cheater ['tʃitər, B -ə] *s.* tramposo, estafador, embustero, defraudador.
check [tʃɛk] *s.* 1. freno, control. 2. comprobación, verificación, fiscalización, inspección. 3. talón, contramarca, contraseña. 4. cuenta (de restaurante). 5. ficha (de juego). 6. cuadro (en telas, etc.); tela de cuadros. 7. (com.) cheque; ficha (Am.). 8. (mec.) freno; tope, retén. 9. (mil.) interrupción súbita (de un avance), ligero revés. 10. (ajedrez) jaque. 11. **to keep in c.,** tener en jaque, tener refrenado, tener a raya, contener (al enemigo, competidor, etc.). —*v.t.* 1. detener, parar, frenar. 2. impedir, obstaculizar. 3. refrenar, contener, contrarrestar. 4. (ajedrez) dar jaque al (rey). 5. (con *with*) cotejar, confrontar. 6. comprobar, verificar, inspeccionar, fiscalizar, registrar. 7. marcar, contramarcar, poner contraseña a. 8. depositar o tomar en depósito (ropa, equipaje, etc.). 9. consignar (baúl, paquete, etc.) para el despacho. 10. cuadricular; dividir o marcar en cuadros o cuadrados. 11. **c. off,** marcar o contar uno por uno; descartar, eliminar; **c. out,** (mandar) verificar; llevar prestado (libros de una biblioteca); retirar (fondos de una cuenta bancaria); **c. through,** hacer pasar por un control; expedir; **c. up,** verificar, comprobar. —*v.i.* 1. detenerse, pararse. 2. corresponder, estar conforme. 3. dar jaque. 4. (aer.) facturar, chequear el equipaje. 5. **c. in at, c. into,** registrarse en (un hotel); **c. on,** verificar; inspeccionar, controlar; **c. out,** pagar la cuenta y partir (en un hotel); **c. up on,** comprobar (algo); controlar, estar tras de (alguien).
check analysis, análisis de comprobación, contra-ensayo.
checkbook ['tʃɛkˌbʊk] *s.* talonario de cheques.
check girl, encargada de la guardarropía (en teatros, restaurantes, etc.).
checker [-ər, B -ə] *s.* 1. cuadro (en telas); diseño a cuadros. 2. ficha (en el juego de damas). 3. comprobador, verificador. —*v.t.* escaquear, formar escaques o cuadros.
checkerberry [-ˌbɛrɪ] *s.* (bot.) gaultería y su baya.
checkerboard [-ˌbɔrd, B -ˌbɔd] *s.* tablero (de damas o ajedrez).
checkered [-ərd, B -əd] *a.* 1. escaqueado; a cuadros (diseño, tela, etc.). 2. (fig.) variado, diversificado, ej., *c. career,* vida variada, vida con altibajos. 3. (her.) ajedrezado, jaquelado.
checkers ['tʃɛkərz, B -əz] *s. pl.* (*sing. en const.*) juego de damas.
check-in ['tʃɛkɪn] *s.* registro: (aer.) facturación de equipajes.
check-in counter o **check-in desk,** (*at a hotel*) recepción; (aer.) mostrador de facturación.
checking account [-ɪŋ-] cuenta de cheques.
check-in time, hora de facturación.
check list, lista de verificación.
check mark, marca, contraseña.
checkmate [-ˌmeɪt] *s.* (ajedrez) jaque mate. —*v.t.* 1. dar (jaque) mate. 2. (fig.) frustrar, anular, vencer, derrotar.
check nut, tuerca de seguridad o de sujeción.
checkoff [-ˌɔf] *s.* rebaja de las cuotas sindicales hecha por los patrones.
checkout ['tʃɛkaʊt] *s.* inspección, verificación; (*cashier*) caja.
checkout counter, caja (*de supermercado*).
checkout time, hora de salida (*de un hotel*).
checkpoint [-ˌpɔɪnt] *s.* punto de control, punto de inspección (de vehículos); punto de referencia (en navegación).
checkrein [-ˌreɪn] *s.* engallador, gamarra (del arnés de las caballerías).
checkroom [-ˌrum, -ˌrʊm] *s.* guardarropa, consigna, depósito de equipajes.
check template, plantilla de prueba.
check test, contraprueba.
checkup [-ʌp] *s.* examen, revisión; examen médico general; (Amer.) chequeo (médico).
Cheddar ['tʃɛdər, B -ə] *s.* queso (de) Cheddar.
cheek [tʃik] *s.* 1. mejilla, carrillo, cachete. 2. (*insolence*) tupé, descaro, frescura, desfachatez. 3. (*pl.*) quijada (de tenazas, pinzas, etc.). 4. bracillo (del freno del caballo). 5. (arq.) jamba. 6. (*pl.*) (mar.) cacholas. 7. **c. by jowl,** cara a cara, en estrecha intimidad, lado a lado; **to have the c. to,** tener la desfachatez o frescura de (decir o hacer algo). —*v.t.* tratar con descaro.
cheekbone ['tʃikˌboʊn] *s.* (anat.) pómulo, malar, hueso malar.
cheekily[-əlɪ] *adv.* descaradamente, con impertinencia.
cheekiness [-ɪnəs] *s.* desfachatez, impertinencia.
cheekpiece [-ˌpis] *s.* quijera (de la cabezada del caballo, parte de su arnés).
cheek pouch, (zool.) abazón (de roedores y monos).
cheek strap, *var. de* **cheekpiece.**
cheeky ['tʃikɪ] *a.* (fam.) descarado, fresco.
cheep [tʃip] *v.t.* piar, chirriar (las aves pequeñas). —*s.* piada, pipío, chirrido.
cheer [tʃɪr, B tʃɪə] *s.* 1. humor, genio, estado de ánimo. 2. ánimo, alegría, regocijo. 3. aplauso, vítor. 4. **cheers!** ¡salud! (como brindis familiar); **to be of good c.,** sentirse animoso; **to make good c.,** comer opíparamente. —*v.t.* 1. consolar, alentar; animar, alegrar, regocijar. 2. aplaudir, vitorear. —*v.i.* (gen. con *up*) reanimarse; regocijarse; **c. up!** ¡ánimo! ¡valor!
cheerful ['tʃɪrfəl, B 'tʃɪəfəl] *a.* 1. alegre, animado, jovial. 2. alentador, grato, placentero.
cheerfully [-ɪ] *adv.* alegremente, con júbilo; de buena gana.
cheerfulness [-nəs] *s.* alegría, jovialidad, buen humor.
cheerily ['tʃɪrəlɪ, B 'tʃɪər-] *adv.* animadamente, de buena gana; alegremente.
cheeriness [-ɪnəs] *s.* alegría, animación, jovialidad.
cheerio [ˌtʃɪrɪ'oʊ, B 'tʃɪərɪ-] *interj.* (fam. pr. G.B.) 1. adiós, chao (Am.). 2. salud (como brindis).
cheerleader ['tʃɪrˌlidər, B 'tʃɪə-ə] *s.* líder que dirige y alienta los vítores de un grupo de partidarios de un equipo.
cheerless [-ləs] *a.* triste, melancólico; inhospitalario (región, zona, cuarto, etc.).
cheery [-ɪ] *a.* alegre, animado, jovial.
cheese [tʃiz] *s.* 1. queso. 2. (jer.) persona importante; **he's the big c. now,** ahora él es el más importante.
cheeseboard ['tʃizbɔrd] *s.* plato de quesos, tabla de quesos.
cheeseburger ['tʃizˌbərgər, B -ˌbɜgə] *s.* (cul.) hamburguesa con queso.
cheesecake [-ˌkeɪk] *s.* 1. quesadilla, tarta de queso. 2. (fam.) fotografía de bellezas femeninas, esp. semidesnudas. 3. curvas o encantos (femeninos).
cheesecloth [-ˌklɔθ] *s.* estopilla o tela ordinaria.
cheese mite, (ento.) ácaro, gusano del queso.
cheeseparing [-ˌpɛrɪŋ, B -ˌpɛər-] *a.* mezquino, tacaño. —*s.* 1. cosa sin valor. 2. tacañería, cicatería.
cheese rennet, (cocina) cuajaleche.
cheesy [-ɪ] *a.* 1. caseoso, como el queso. 2. (fam., E.U.) barato, de pacotilla, vulgar.
cheetah ['tʃitə] *s.* (zool.) (especie de) leopardo.
chef [ʃɛf] *s.* cocinero, jefe de cocina.
chef d'oeuvre [ʃeɪ'dərvrə, B -'dɜvrə] *s.* (*pl.* CHEFS D'OEUVRE) obra maestra.
chela ['kilə] *s.* (*pl.* CHELAE [-li]) (zool.) quela (de los crustáceos); quelícero (de los arácnidos).
chela ['tʃeɪlə] *s.* discípulo, novicio (en el budismo).
chelate ['kiˌleɪt] *a.* (zool.) quelado (crustáceo o arácnido). —*s.* (quím.) quelato.
chelicera [kɪ'lɪsərə] *s.* (zool.) (*pl.* CHELICERAE [-ˌri]) quelícero.
chelidonate ['kɛlədənˌeɪt] *s.* (quím.) celidonato.
chelonian [kɪ'loʊnɪən] *a., s.* (zool.) quelonio.
chemic ['kɛmɪk] *a.* (ant.) alquímico, químico.
chemical ['kɛmɪkəl] *a.* químico. —*s.* producto químico.
chemically [-ɪ] *adv.* químicamente.
chemical engineering, ingeniería química o industrial.
chemical gaging, (hidr.) aforo químico o por disolución de sal o por titulación.
chemical proportioner, dosificador de productos químicos.
chemical warfare, guerra química.
chemical weathering, (geol.) descomposición química.
chemiluminescence [ˌkɛmɪˌlumə'nɛsəns] *s.* fosforescencia química.
chemise [ʃə'miz] *s.* 1. camisa (interior de mujer). 2. vestido de mujer sin entallar.
chemism ['kɛmˌɪzəm] *s.* afinidad o actividad química.
chemist ['kɛməst] *s.* químico; farmacéutico; **c.'s,** botica, farmacia.
chemistry [-əstrɪ] *s.* química.
chemosmosis [ˌkɛmɑs'moʊsəs, B -ɔs-] *s.* (med.) ósmosis química.
chemotaxis [-oʊ'tæksəs] *s.* (biol.) quimiotaxis, quimiotactismo.
chemotherapy [-'θɛrəpɪ] *s.* quimioterapia, quimioterapéutica.
chemotropism [kə'mɑtrəˌpɪzəm, B -'mɔ-] *s.* (biol.) quimiotropismo.
chenille [ʃə'nil] *s.* (tej.) felpilla.
chenopod ['kinəˌpɑd, 'kɛn-, B -ˌpɔd] *s.* (bot.) quenopodio, pata de ganso.
cheque, (pr. G.B.) *var. de* **check.**
chequer, chequerboard, *var. de* **checker, checkerboard.**
cherish ['tʃɛrɪʃ] *v.t.* 1. apreciar, estimar, halagar, regalar. 2. (fig.) acariciar, abrigar, alimentar (esperanza, idea, recuerdo, etc.).
Cherokee ['tʃɛrəˌki, ˌtʃɛrə'ki] *s.* cheroquí, pueblo, idioma y miembro de esta tribu de indios norteamericanos.
Cherokee rose, (bot.) especie de rosa blanca trepadora.
cheroot [ʃə'rut] *s.* cigarro puro con ambos extremos cortados.
cherry ['tʃɛrɪ] *s.* 1. (bot.) cerezo. 2. cereza. 3. color cereza. 4. (jer.) himen; (fig.) virginidad.
cherry brandy, aguardiente de cereza.
cherry laurel, (bot.) lauroceraso, laurel cerezo, laurel real.
cherry orchard, cerezal.
cherry pepper, cerecilla, guindilla, pimiento picante; chile.

cherry picker, (const.) grua alzacarros.
cherry red, color cereza, rojo cereza.
cherrystone ['tʃɛrɪˌstoʊn] *s.* 1. (zool.) tipo de almeja. 2. hueso de cereza. 3. (fig.) bicoca.
chert [tʃɜrt, B tʃɜt] *s.* (min.) variedad de cuarzo.
cherub ['tʃɛrəb] *s.* (*pl.* CHERUBS O CHERUBIM [-əˌbɪm]) querubín.
cherubic [tʃə'rubɪk] *a.* querúbico.
chervil ['tʃɜrvəl, B 'tʃɜvɪl] *s.* (bot.) perifollo, cerafolio.
chess [tʃɛs] *s.* 1. ajedrez. 2. (bot.) bromo. 3. (ing.) tabla de piso (en puente de pontones).
chessboard ['tʃɛsˌbɔrd, B -ˌbɔd] *s.* tablero de ajedrez.
chessman [-ˌmæn, -mən] *s.* pieza de ajedrez, trebejo.
chess player, jugador de ajedrez, ajedrecista.
chess set, ajedrez (conjunto de las piezas y el tablero).
chest [tʃɛst] *s.* 1. arca, cofre, cajón, baúl, caja. 2. (anat.) pecho; tórax. 3. tesoro, caja (de una institución). 4. **to get something off one's c.,** (fam.) desahogar(se), decir cuatro verdades; **to have something on one's c.,** quedarse con una queja o querella guardada.
chest cavity, (anat.) cavidad torácica.
chesterfield ['tʃɛstərˌfild, B -təˌ-] *s.* 1. abrigo o sobretodo elegante con cuello de terciopelo. 2. sofá grande.
chestnut ['tʃɛsˌnʌt] *s.* 1. (bot.) castaño. 2. castaña. 3. color castaño. 4. zaino (caballo color castaño). 5. callosidad (en la pata del caballo). 6. (fam.) cuento o chiste gastados. 7. **to pull someone's chestnuts out of the fire,** sacarle las castañas del fuego a alguien. —*a.* castaño, marrón.
chest of drawers, cómoda, buró.
chesty ['tʃɛstɪ] *a.* (fam.) 1. de pecho grande. 2. arrogante, engreído.
cheval-de-frise [ʃəˌvældə'friz] *s.* (mil.) caballo de frisa.
cheval glass [ʃə'væl-] espejo móvil de cuerpo entero, psiquis.
chevalier [ˌʃɛvə'lɪr, B -'lɪə] *s.* (fr.) 1. caballero galante. 2. [ʃə'vælˌjeɪ] miembro de una distinguida orden de Francia.
cheviot ['ʃɛvɪət, B 'tʃɛv-] *s.* 1. (tej.) cheviot, lana de Escocia. 2. **C.,** (zool.) cordero de Escocia.
chevron ['ʃɛvrən] *s.* 1. (her.) cheurón, cabrío. 2. (arq.) cabrío. 3. (mil.) sardineta, galón.
chevrotain ['ʃɛvrəˌteɪn] *s.* (zool.) especie de almizclero pequeño.
chevy ['tʃɛvɪ] (dial.) *v.t., v.i., var. de* **chiv(v)y.**
chew [tʃu] *v.t.* masticar, mascar; **c. out,** (jer.) reprender, reconvenir severamente (a alguien); **c. the fat,** (jer.) parlotear, chacharear, chismorrear; **c. the rag,** (jer.) parlotear, chacharear; refunfuñar; **c. one's ear off,** dar lata, conversar larga y tediosamente. —*v.i.* 1. mascar tabaco. 2. (con *upon, over*) meditar (sobre). —*s.* 1. mascadura, masticación. 2. mascada (de tabaco).
chewing gum, goma de mascar, chicle.
chewink [tʃɪ'wɪŋk] *s.* (orn.) (especie de) pinzón americano.
Cheyenne [ʃaɪ'æn, -'ɛn] *s.* (E.U.) una de las grandes tribus de indios norteamericanos.
Chianti [ki'ɑntɪ, -'æn- B kɪ'æn-] *s.* quianti, vino italiano.
chiaroscuro [kɪˌɑrə'skʊroʊ, B -'skʊər-] *s.* (pint.) claroscuro, contraste de luz y sombra.
chiasma [kaɪ'æzmə] *s.* (*pl.* CHIASMATA [-tə] o chiasmas) (anat.) quiasma, decusación (de las cintillas ópticas).
chiastolite [kaɪ'æstəˌlaɪt] *s.* (geol.) quiastolita (andalusita).
chibcha ['tʃɪbˌtʃɑ] *s.* chibcha, tribu ya extinta de indios de Colombia, de avanzada cultura.
chibouk, chibouque [tʃə'buk] *s.* chibuquí, pipa turca.
chic [ʃik] *a.* chic, elegante, fino. —*s.* chic, buen tono, elegancia.
chicane [ʃɪ'keɪn, tʃɪ-] *s.* 1. tramoya, trampa, argucia, chicana (Am.). 2. (bridge) falta de triunfos (en una mano). —*a.* sin triunfos (mano o jugador de naipes). —*v.t., v.i.,* emplear engaños, prevaricar, trampear, embrollar.
chicanery [-ərɪ] *s.* trampa legal, trapacería, embrollo, empleo de engaños.
Chicano [ʃɪ'kɑno] *s.* (E.U.) mexicano-americano.
chichi ['ʃiʃi, 'tʃitʃi, B 'ʃiʃi] *a.* 1. vistoso, ostentoso. 2. excesivamente refinado; afeminado.
chick [tʃɪk] *s.* 1. polluelo. 2. pollito, niño. 3. (jer.) jovencita, muchacha bonita.
chickadee ['tʃɪkəˌdi] *s.* (orn.) paro carbonero, oriundo de E.U.
chickaree ['tʃɪkəˌri] *s.* (zool.) ardilla norteamericana.
chicken ['tʃɪkən] *s.* 1. pollo, polluelo. 2. jovencita, ej., *she's no c.,* ella (ya) no es una jovencita. 3. cobarde. 4. **their chickens are coming home to roost,** están pagando las consecuencias; **to count one's chickens before they are hatched,** vender la piel del oso antes de cazarlo; esperar demasiado de un proyecto; **to go to bed with the chickens,** acostarse muy temprano. —*v.i.* **c. out,** (jer.) retirarse por miedo (de un plan, tarea, empresa), acobardarse.
chicken colonel, (jer. mil.) coronel (distinguido del teniente coronel por la insignia de un águila que los soldados llaman despectivamente *chicken* "pollo").
chicken coop, gallinero.
chicken feed, 1. alimento para pollos. 2. (jer.) bagatela; poco dinero.
chicken hawk, (orn.) halcón gallinero.
chicken-hearted [-ˌhɑrtəd, B -ˌhɑt-] *a.* cobarde, asustadizo, medroso, pusilánime.
chicken pox, (med.) varicela, viruela(s) loca(s).
chicken shit, (jer., vulg.) 1. tareas tontas y menudas que manda hacer cualquier autoridad severa. 2. mentiras insignificantes, banalidades.
chicken wire, tela metálica (para cercar gallineros).
chick-pea ['tʃɪkˌpi] *s.* (bot.) garbanzo.
chickweed [-ˌwid] *s.* (bot.) álsine; pamplina, pamplina de canarios.
chicle ['tʃɪkəl] *s.* chicle, gomorresina.
chicory ['tʃɪkərɪ] *s.* (bot.) achicoria.
chide ['tʃaɪd] *v.t., v.i.* (*pret.,* CHID [tʃɪd] O CHIDED ['tʃaɪdəd] *p.p.* CHID O CHIDDEN ['tʃɪdən]) regañar, reprender, increpar.
chiding ['tʃaɪdɪŋ] *s.* regaño, reprimenda, increpación. —*a.* regañón, increpante.
chidingly [-lɪ] *adv.* en tono de reprimenda.
chief [tʃif] *s.* 1. jefe, adalid, caudillo, cacique. 2. jefe (de tribu o clan). 3. (mil.) jefe; **commander in c.,** comandante en jefe. 4. jefe principal de una entidad comercial u oficina. —*a.* principal, primero.
chief executive, (E.U.) primer mandatario, el presidente de la nación.
chief justice, presidente de un tribunal (de justicia); (E.U.) presidente de la Corte Suprema.
chiefly ['tʃiflɪ] *adv.* principalmente, especialmente, mayormente.
chief of staff, (mil.) jefe del estado mayor.
chief of state, jefe de estado; primer mandatario, presidente.
chieftain [-tən] *s.* cacique, jefe (de una tribu); caudillo, capitán, cabecilla.
chiffchaff ['tʃɪfˌtʃæf] *s.* (orn.) (especie de) curruca pequeña.
chiffon [ʃɪ'fɑn, 'ʃɪfˌɑn, B -ˌɔn] *s.* (tej.) chifón, gasa, velo.
chiffonier [ˌʃɪfə'nɪr, B -'nɪə] *s.* cómoda alta con espejo.
chigger ['tʃɪgər, 'dʒɪg-, B 'tʃɪgə] *var. de* chigoe.
chignon ['ʃinˌjɑn, B -ˌjɔŋ] *s.* moño (pelo largo anudado a la nuca).
chigoe ['tʃɪgoʊ] *s.* (ento.) nigua, pique.
chilblain ['tʃɪlˌbleɪn] *s.* (med.) sabañón.
child [tʃaɪld] *s.* (*pl.* CHILDREN ['tʃɪldrən]) 1. niño, niña; criatura. 2. hijo, hija. 3. (fig.) producto, ej., *a c. of his imagination,* un producto de su imaginación. 4. **c.'s play,** juego de niños, tarea fácil; cosa insignificante; **c. wife,** esposa muy joven; **children should be seen and not heard,** los niños hablan cuando las gallinas mean; **with c.,** embarazada, encinta.
child abuse, (*battering*) malos tratos a la infancia, maltrato de los hijos, abuso infantil; (*sexual*) abusos deshonestos a un niño, abusos deshonestos a una niña, abuso sexual infantil.
childbearing ['tʃaɪldˌbɛrɪŋ, B -ˌbɛər-] *s.* maternidad. —*adj.* capacitado para (o relacionado con) la maternidad, ej., *the childbearing years,* los años de fertilidad (de una mujer).
childbed [-ˌbɛd] *s.* sobreparto; **in c.,** de parto.
childbed fever, (med.) fiebre puerperal.
childbirth [-ˌbɜrθ, B -ˌbɜθ] *s.* parto, alumbramiento.
child care, puericultura.
child care center, guardería infantil, jardín de la infancia, creche.
Childermas ['tʃɪldərməs, B -dəmæs] *s.* (ant.) día de los inocentes (28 de diciembre).
childhood ['tʃaɪldˌhʊd] *s.* niñez; infancia; **from early c.,** desde muy niño; **second c.,** segunda infancia; chochez.
childish [-ɪʃ] *a.* pueril, aniñado, infantil.
childishly [-lɪ] *adv.* puerilmente.
childishness [-nəs] *s.* puerilidad, niñería.
child labor, trabajo infantil, trabajo de menores.
childless [-ləs] *a.* sin hijos, yerma.
childlike [-ˌlaɪk] *a.* 1. como un niño, de (un) niño, infantil, ej., *he has c. features,* tiene rasgos de niño, tiene rasgos infantiles. 2. inocente, candoroso, ingenuo.
child molester, persona que somete a un niño a abusos deshonestos.
child prodigy, niño prodigio.
childproof ['tʃaɪldpruf] *a.* a prueba de niños.
child psychology, psicología infantil.
children ['tʃɪldrən] *s. pl. de* **child.**
children's home, casa cuna, casa de beneficencia.
Chile ['tʃɪlɪ] *s.* Chile.
Chilean [-ən] *a., s.* chileno.
chili, chile ['tʃɪlɪ] *s.* (bot.) chile, ají; guindilla.
chiliad ['kɪlɪˌæd] *s.* mil, millar; mil años, milenio.
chiliasm [-ˌæzəm] *s.* (relig.) milenarismo, doctrina del milenio.
chiliast [-ˌæst] *s.* milenario, creyente en el milenarismo.
chill [tʃɪl] *s.* 1. frío, frialdad. 2. tiritón, escalofrío. 3. (fig.) frialdad, frigidez (de modales, en el trato, etc.). 4. (fig.) enfriamiento, depresión; pasmo. 5. **chills and fever,** fiebre intermitente; **to cast a c. over,** enfriar, deprimir; **to catch a c.,** tomar frío; **to take the c. off the water** (o **wine**), entibiar o templar el agua (o vino). —*a.* 1. frío, desapacible. 2. (fig.) frío, frígido. 3. (fig.) deprimente. —*v.t.* 1. enfriar, refrigerar, ej., *chilled wine,* vino refrigerado, frío. 2. (fig.) deprimir, desanimar, desalentar. 3. (metal.) enfriar,

acerar, templar. —*v.i.* 1. enfriarse. 2. tiritar, estremecerse de frío; tener escalofríos. 3. (metal.) enfriarse, acerarse.

chiller ['tʃɪlər, B -ə] *s.* 1. estremecedor, espeluznante. 2. (a.a.) enfriador.

chilli, *var. de* **chile, chili.**

chillily ['tʃɪləlɪ] *adv.* fríamente, frígidamente.

chilly ['tʃɪlɪ] *a.* (CHILLIER; CHILLIEST) 1. frío. 2. friolento, friolero; escalofriado. 3. (fig.) frígido, frío (de modales). 4. (fig.) pasmoso, medroso. —*adv.* fríamente.

chimaera [kaɪ'mɪrə, kə-, B -'mɪərə] 1. *var. de* **chimera.** 2. (ict.) quimera, pez de los holocéfalos.

chime [tʃaɪm] *s.* 1. carillón, campanas. 2. timbre, campana, campanilla (en una puerta, etc.). 3. campaneo, repique (de campanas). 4. son, sonsonete, melodía. 5. (fig.) armonía, concordancia. —*v.i.* 1. tañer las campanas; repicar, repiquetear. 2. sonar (el timbre, una campanilla, etc.). 3. llamar (las campanas a misa, etc.). 4. (fig.) (con *with*) armonizar, concordar (con). 5. **c. in,** hacer oír su voz, aportar su opinión, terciar (en conversación, discusión, etc.); hacer coro. —*v.t.* 1. tocar (campanas). 2. dar (la hora) con campanadas. 3. repetir monótonamente.

chime [tʃaɪm] *s.* cabo de barril, remate de cuba o tina.

chime clock, reloj de música, péndola de carillón.

chimera [kaɪ'mɪrə, kə-, B -'mɪərə] *s.* 1. quimera, ilusión. 2. (mitol.) monstruo fabuloso; espectro.

chimere [ʃə'mɪr, tʃə-, B -'mɪə] *s.* (relig.) sobrepelliz (de obispo).

chimeric [kaɪ'mɛrɪk, -'mɪr-, kə-, B kaɪ'mɛr-] **chimerical** [-əl] *a.* quimérico, visionario, imaginario; fantástico.

chimerically [-əlɪ] *adv.* quiméricamente, imaginariamente.

chimney ['tʃɪmnɪ] *s.* 1. chimenea; cañón, humero de chimenea. 2. tubo de vidrio de una lámpara. 3. chimenea o respiradero natural (de volcán, etc.). 4. (montañismo) chimenea, grieta o abertura estrecha (por la que se escala una pared escarpada). 5. (ant.) chimenea, hogar. 6. **to smoke like a c.,** fumar demasiado.

chimney-piece [-ˌpis] *s.* repisa de chimenea.

chimney pot, mitra, remate o sombrerete de chimenea; guardavientos.

chimney swallow, (orn.) golondrina común.

chimney sweep, deshollinador, limpiachimeneas.

chimp [tʃɪmp] *s.* (fam.) chimpancé.

chimpanzee [ˌtʃɪmˌpæn'zi, -'pænzi, B tʃɪmpən'zi] *s.* (zool.) chimpancé.

chin [tʃɪn] *s.* mentón, barbilla, barba; **to keep one's c. up,** (fig.) no desanimarse; **up to the c., c. deep,** (fig.) hasta el cuello, hasta las cachas (en deudas, dificultades, etc.). —*v.t.* (*pret., p.p.* CHINNED; *p.pr.* CHINNING) 1. apretar o sostener con la barbilla (violín). 2. (gimnasia) tocar con la barbilla (la barra al hacer flexiones con el brazo); **c. oneself,** hacer flexiones en la barra tocándola con la barbilla. —*v.i.* (jer.) parlotear, chacharear.

china ['tʃaɪnə] *s.* 1. porcelana china; vajilla; objeto de porcelana. 2. **C.,** la China. —*a.* chino, de la China.

China aster, (bot.) reina margarita, extraña.

chinaberry [-ˌbɛrɪ] *s.* (bot.) 1. jaboncillo. 2. acederaque, paraíso, lila de la China, cinamomo, rosariera.

china closet, chinero, mueble o vitrina donde se guarda la vajilla fina.

Chinaman [-mən] *s.* (despec.) chino.

chinaroot [-ˌrut] *s.* (bot.) china, lampatán.

China rose, (bot.) rosa de la China, tulipán, tulipán rojo.

China sea, el mar de la China.

Chinatown [-ˌtaʊn] *s.* barrio chino.

China tree, (bot.) 1. jaboncillo. 2. acederaque, árbol del paraíso, lila de la China, panjí, agriaz.

chinaware [-ˌwɛr, B -ˌwɛə] *s.* (objetos de) china o porcelana, vajilla de porcelana.

chinch [tʃɪntʃ] *s.* (ento.) chinche; insecto que ataca los granos y cereales, especie de gorgojo.

chincilla [tʃɪn'tʃɪlə] *s.* 1. (zool.) chinchilla. 2. piel de chinchilla. 3. (tej.) paño grueso de lana.

chin-chin ['tʃɪn'tʃɪn] *interj.* ¡salud! (como brindis).

chine [tʃaɪn] *s.* 1. espinazo; lomo. 2. (top.) cumbre, cerro.

Chinese [tʃaɪ'niz, -'nis, B -'niz] *a.* chino, de la China. —*s.* (*pl.* CHINESE) chino (natural e idioma de la China).

Chinese anise, (bot.) badián, badiana.

Chinese checkers, damas chinas.

Chinese fan palm, (bot.) latania.

Chinese gooseberry, (bot.) carambola.

Chinese lantern, 1. linterna china, farolillo de papel. 2. (bot.) alquequenje.

Chinese puzzle, rompecabezas, problema difícil.

Chinese red, rojo escarlata.

Chinese wall, la muralla china.

chink [tʃɪŋk] *s.* 1. grieta, hendidura, rajadura, abertura. 2. tintín, sonido metálico. 3. **C.,** (despec.) chino. 4. (jer.) blanca, plata, dinero. —*v.i., v.t.* 1. retiñir, tintinear (copas, monedas, etc.). 2. hacer tintinear. 3. calafatear; rellenar, tapar (grietas, etc.).

chino ['tʃinoʊ, 'ʃi-] *s.* 1. tela fuerte de algodón que se usa para ropas de trabajo, uniformes, etc. 2. (*pl.*) pantalones informales (de hombre).

chinoiserie [ˌʃɪnˌwɑzə'ri, -'wɑzərɪ] *s.* estilo chinesco en arte; objeto o decoración de estilo chinesco (esp. en el *art nouveau* de a principios del siglo).

Chinook [ʃə'nʊk, tʃə-, B tʃɪ-] *s.* 1. miembro e idioma de una numerosa tribu de indios norteamericanos. 2. viento cálido del O. de los E.U.

chinquapin ['tʃɪŋkəˌpɪn] *s.* (bot.) chincapino, castaño enano y su fruto.

chin strap, barboquejo, carrillera.

chintz [tʃɪnts] *s.* (tej.) calicó lustroso, zaraza.

chintzy ['tʃɪntsɪ] *a.* 1. decorado con quimón o zaraza. 2. llamativo, chillón, chabacano.

chiolite ['kaɪəˌlaɪt] *s.* (min.) quiolita, chiolita.

chip [tʃɪp] *s.* 1. brizna, astilla; (*pl.*) ripio, cascajo. 2. hojuela, ej., *potato chips,* hojuelas de patata frita. 3. ficha, tanto (en juegos de azar). 4. (*pl.*) patatas fritas. 5. desportilladura. 6. (*pl.*) (jer.) moneda suelta, dinero. 7. (comput.) microplaquita. 8. **a. c. off the old block,** de tal palo tal astilla; **fish and chips,** pescado y patatas fritos; **the chips are down,** (jer.) la suerte está echada; **to be in the chips,** (jer.) estar rico, tener plata; **to cash in one's chips,** (fam.) estar listo a irse, morir; **to have a c. on one's shoulder,** (fam.) propensión a buscar camorra, guardar rencor, estar resentido. —*v.t.* (*pret., p.p.* CHIPPED; *p.pr.,* CHIPPING) 1. astillar, picar; tajar con cincel. 2. (esp. con *off* o *from*) desportillar, descantillar. 3. (jer. G.B.) embromar (a), chancear con, tomar el pelo a. —*v.i.* 1. (esp. con *off*) desportillarse, descantillarse. 2. **c. in,** (jer.) contribuir (su parte de los gastos, etc.); aportar su opinión (en conversación, discusión, etc.).

chip ax, hachuela, azuela.

chipmunk ['tʃɪpˌmʌŋk] *s.* (zool.) ardilla listada.

Chippendale ['tʃɪpənˌdeɪl] *a.* estilo de muebles finos ingleses del siglo XVIII.

chipper ['tʃɪpər, B -ə] *s.* 1. martillo cincelador, descantilladora, picadora. 2. cincelador (operario). —*a.* (fam. E.U.) vivo, alegre, jovial.

chipping hammer [-ɪŋ] cincelador, martillo-cincel, martillo burilador; rebabadora.

chippy, chippie ['tʃɪpɪ] *s.* (jer.) mujer ligera, mujer fácil.

chippy ['tʃɪpɪ] *a.* 1. (jer., G.B.) seco, sin interés. 2. que siente náuseas (de borrachera, etc.). 3. (Can., jer.) irritable, pendenciero.

chip shot, (golf) golpe corto (para colocar la pelota cerca del hoyo).

chirk [tʃɜrk, B tʃɜk] *a.* (fam.) alegre, jovial. —*v.t., v.i.* (con *up*) alegrar(se), avivar(se).

chirographer [kaɪ'rɑgrəfər, B -'rɔgrəfə] *s.* calígrafo, escribano, escribiente; quirógrafo.

chirographic [ˌkaɪrə'græfɪk] **chirographical** [-ɪkəl] *a.* caligráfico, quirografario.

chirography [kaɪ'rɑgrəfɪ, B -'rɔg-] *s.* caligrafía, quirografía.

chiromancer ['kaɪrəˌmænsər, B -sə] *s.* quiromántico.

chiromancy [-sɪ] *s.* quiromancia, adivinación por las líneas de las manos.

chiropodist [kə'rɑpədəst, ʃə- B -rɔp-] *s.* quiropodista, pedicuro, callista.

chiropody [-ədɪ] *s.* quiropodia.

chiropractic [ˌkaɪrə'præktɪk] *s.* (med.) quiropráctica.

chiropractor ['kaɪrəˌpræktər, B -tə] *s.* quiropractor, quiropráctico.

chiropter [kaɪ'rɑptər, B -'rɔptə] *s.* (zool.) quiróptero.

Chiroptera [-tərə] *s. pl.* (zool.) quirópteros.

chiropterous [-tərəs] *a.* (zool.) quiróptero.

chirp [tʃɜrp, B tʃɜp] *v.t., v.i.* chirriar, gorjear, pipiar, piar (pájaros); chicharrear (la cigarra). —*s.* chirrido, gorjeo; canto.

chirpy ['tʃɜrpɪ, B 'tʃɜpɪ] *a.* vivaz, alegre, animado.

chirr [tʃɜr, B tʃɜ] *v.i.* chirriar (como el saltamonte). —*s.* chirrido.

chirrup ['tʃɜrəp, 'tʃɪr-, B 'tʃɪr-] *v.i., v.t.* chirriar (repetidamente); gorjear, trinar. —*s.* gorjeo, trino.

chisel ['tʃɪzəl] *s.* 1. escoplo, formón (para labrar madera); cincel, puntero, uñeta (para labrar piedra); buril, cincel, gradiño (del escultor); cortadera, cortadora, cortafrío, trancha (para labrar metales); cortador de ladrillos. 2. (fam.) engaño, fraude. —*v.t.* (*prep., p.p.* CHISELED O CHISELLED; *p.pr.* CHISELING O CHISELLING) 1. escoplear, cincelar, burilar; esculpir. 2. (fam.) engañar, embaucar; obtener con fraude. —*v.i.* 1. emplear el buril, trabajar con el cincel. 2. (fam.) emplear medios dudosos; practicar engaños, cometer fraude. 3. **c. in,** (fam.) entrometerse, introducirse con miras de obtener beneficios.

chiseled, chiselled [-əld] *a.* 1. cincelado, burilado. 2. (bien) marcado (rasgo, facción).

chiseler [-ələr, B -lə] *s.* 1. el que escoplea. 2. (fam.) engañador, oportunista.

chit [tʃɪt] *s.* (G.B.) 1. chiquillo, niño pequeño. 2. vale, nota, billete, cuenta (que se debe por bebida, etc.). 3. jovencita, jovenzuela, ej., *a c. of a girl,* (despec.) jovenzuela delgaducha.

chitchat ['tʃɪtˌtʃæt] *s.* cháchara, charla, palique, parloteo.

chitin ['kaɪtən] *s.* (zool.) quitina.

chitlings, chitlins ['tʃɪtlənz] *var. de* **chitterlings.**

chiton ['kaɪtən, -ˌtɑn, B -tɔn] *s.* 1. (zool.) quitón, chitón. 2. (hist.) quitón, túnica, prenda de vestir griega.

chitterlings ['tʃɪtlənz, B 'tʃɪtəlɪŋz] *s. pl.* menudencias, intestinos del cerdo o la res, fritos o cocidos.

chivalric [ʃə'vælrɪk, B 'ʃɪvəlrɪk] *var. de* chivalrous.
chivalrous ['ʃɪvəlrəs] *a.* 1. caballeroso, caballeresco, cortés, atento. 2. quijotesco.
chivalrously [-lɪ] *adv.* caballerosamente.
chivalrousness [-nəs] *s.* caballerosidad, cortesía.
chivalry ['ʃɪvəlrɪ] *s.* 1. caballerosidad, hidalguía. 2. caballeros (en conjunto). 3. (ant.) caballería.
chive [tʃaɪv] *s.* (bot.) cebollino, cebollana; ajo moruno.
chivy, chivvy ['tʃɪvɪ] *v.t.* (*pret., p.p.* CHIVIED, CHIVVIED; *p.pr.* CHIVYING, CHIVVYING) 1. perseguir, cazar. 2. acosar, molestar, fastidiar. —*s.* caza, persecución.
chlamydospore [klə'mɪdəˌspɔr, B -ˌspɔ] *s.* (bot.) clamidóspora.
chlamys ['klæməs, 'kleɪ-] *s.* (hist. griega) clámide, capa corta y ligera usada por los griegos, más tarde adoptada por los romanos.
chloral ['klɔrəl] *s.* (quím.) cloral.
chloral hydrate, (quím.) hidrato de cloral (como anestésico).
chloramination [ˌklɔrəmə'neɪʃən] *s.* (quím.) cloraminación.
chloramine [-əˌmin] *s.* (farm., quím.) cloramina.
chlorate [-ˌeɪt, -ɪt] *s.* (quím.) clorato.
chloric [-ɪk] *a.* (quím.) clórico.
chloric acid, (quím.) ácido clórico.
chloride [-ˌaɪd] *s.* (quím.) cloruro, sal del ácido clorhídrico.
chloride of lime, cloruro de cal.
chlorimeter, *s.* clorómetro, clorímetro.
chlorinate ['klɔrəˌneɪt] *v.t.* tratar con cloro, clorinar, clorar (esp. el agua para desinfectarla).
chlorination [ˌklɔrə'neɪʃən] *s.* desinfección con cloro; clorinación.
chlorine ['klɔrˌin] *s.* (quím.) cloro.
chlorite [-ˌaɪt] *s.* 1. (min.) clorita. 2. (quím.) clorito.
chloritic [klə'rɪtɪk] *a.* (min.) clorítico.
chlorobenzene [ˌklɔrə'bɛnˌzin] *s.* (quím.) clorobenceno.
chloroform ['klɔrəˌfɔrm, B -ˌfɔm] *s.* (quím.) cloroformo. —*v.t.* anestesiar con cloroformo.
chlorohydrin [ˌklɔrə'haɪdrən] *s.* (quím.) clorhidrina.
chloromycetin [-ˌmaɪ'sitən] *s.* (farm.) cloromicetina.
chlorophyll, chlorophyl ['klɔrəˌfɪl] *s.* (farm.) clorofila.
chlorophyllose [ˌklɔrə'fɪlˌoʊs] **chlorophyllous** [-əs] *a.* (bot.) clorofílico.
chloropicrin [-'pɪkrən] *s.* (quím.) cloropicrina.
chloroplast ['klɔrəˌplæst] *s.* (bot.) cloroplasto, cloroplastio.
chlorosis [klə'roʊsəs] *s.* 1. (med.) clorosis, morbo virgíneo, enfermedad verde. 2. (bot.) clorosis, ocrosis.
chlorotic [-'rɑtɪk, B -'rɔt-] *a.* (med., bot.) clorótico.
chlorous ['klɔrəs] *a.* (quím.) cloroso.
chlortetracycline [ˌklɔrˌtɛtrə'saɪˌklin, B ˌklɔˌ-] *s.* (farm.) clorotetraciclina.
choana ['koʊənə] *s.* (anat.) (*pl.* CHOANAE [-ˌni]) coana.
chock [tʃɑk, B tʃɔk] *s.* 1. calzo, calza, calce, cuña, alza; (mar.) tojino. 2. (mar.) cornamusa. —*v.t.* calzar, apear, afianzar; acuñar, fijar con cuñas. —*adv.* (lleno) hasta el tope, hasta el máximo, por completo.
chock-a-block ['tʃɑkəˌblɑk, B 'tʃɔkəˌblɔk] *a.* 1. (mar.) a besar. 2. apretado, apiñado, atestado.
chock-full [-'fʊl] *a.* colmado, rebosante, de bote en bote, repleto.
chocoholic ['tʃɔkə'hɔlɪk] *s.* persona que le gustaba demasiado el chocolate.
chocolate ['tʃɑklət, 'tʃɔk-, -ələt, B 'tʃɔk-] *s.* chocolate. —*a.* de chocolate; achocolatado, de color chocolate.
chocolate chip, pedacito de chocolate.
chocolate-chip cookie, galleta con pedacitos de chocolate.
chocolate soldier, soldado de chocolate, soldado de opereta, soldado de escritorio que nunca ve el campo de batalla.
chocolate tree, (bot.) (árbol del) cacao.
Choctaw ['tʃɑkˌtɔ, B 'tʃɔk-] *s.* 1. chacta, tribu de indios norteamericanos, sus miembros y su lenguaje. 2. (fam., fig.) lenguaje o habla ininteligible.
choice [tʃɔɪs] *s.* 1. selección, elección. 2. opción, alternativa. 3. preferencia, cosa escogida, persona preferida. 4. variedad, surtido (de objetos entre los que se puede escoger). 5. (con *of*) flor y nata, lo más selecto, lo mejor (de). 6. **to have no c.,** no tener alternativa; **to make a c.,** escoger, elegir; **to take one's c.,** decidirse (entre posibilidades); **by c.,** por votación. —*a.* escogido, selecto, florido, granado, (de calidad) superior, ej., *c. apples,* manzanas escogidas o superiores.
choir [kwaɪr, B 'kwaɪə] *s.* 1. (mús., rel.) coro. 2. (arq.) coro (de iglesia o catedral). 3. cuerpo de baile.
choirboy ['kwaɪrˌbɔɪ, B 'kwaɪə-] *s.* niño cantor; niño que canta en el coro de una iglesia.
choir loft, (galería del) coro.
choirmaster [-ˌmæstər, B -ˌmɑstə] *s.* director de coro.
choke [tʃoʊk] *v.t.* 1. estrangular, sofocar, asfixiar (persona o animal). 2. ahogar, apagar (fuego). 3. (t. con *up*) obturar, atorar, atascar, obstruir (un tubo, conducto, etc.). 4. (fig., pr. con *off, back, down*) sofocar (sentimientos), reprimir, disimular con dificultad (emociones), contener (risa). 5. taponar (cartucho, carga de pólvora en cañón, etc.). 6. (aut.) estrangular, obturar (carburador). 7. **c. down,** tragar o pasar (comida) con esfuerzo. —*v.i.* 1. sofocarse, asfixiarse. 2. atragantarse. 3. (t. con *up*) atorarse, atascarse. 4. **c. on,** atragantarse con. —*s.* 1. sofocamiento, ahogo. 2. atoramiento, obstrucción. 3. (aut.) regulador de aire, estrangulador, obturador.
chokeberry ['tʃoʊkˌbɛrɪ] *s.* (bot.) amelanquier.
chokecherry [-ˌtʃɛrɪ] *s.* (bot.) cerezo silvestre norteamericano.
choke coil, (rad.) bobina de choque, bobina de reducción.
chokedamp [-ˌdæmp] *s.* mofeta, aire irrespirable (en minas).
choker [-ər, B -ə] *s.* 1. estrangulador. 2. (fam.) cuello, alzacuello (de los clérigos). 3. bufanda ancha. 4. collar pegado al cuello.
choke valve, (auto.) válvula estranguladora, mariposa del cebador.
choky ['tʃoʊkɪ] *a.* asfixiante, sofocante.
cholagogue ['kɑləˌgɑg, B 'kɔləˌgɔg] *a., s.* (med.) colagogo.
cholate ['koʊˌleɪt] *s.* (quím.) colato.
cholecystectomy [ˌkoʊləˌsɪs'tɛktəmɪ, ˌkɑl-, B ˌkɔl-] *s.* (med.) colecistectomía.
cholecystitis [-'taɪtəs] *s.* (med.) colecistitis.
choler ['kɑlər, 'koʊl-, B 'kɔlə] *s.* 1. (med., ant.) bilis. 2. (poét., ant.) ira, cólera, iracundia, enojo; irascibilidad.
cholera ['kɑlərə, B 'kɔl-] *s.* (med., vet.) cólera.
cholera infantum [-ɪn'fæntəm] (med.) cólera infantil, gastroenteritis coleriforme de los niños.
cholera morbus [-'mɔrbəs, B -'mɔbəs] (med.) cólera morbo, cólera asiático.
choleric ['kɑlərɪk, kə'lɛr-, B 'kɔlər-] *a.* colérico, irascible.
cholerine ['kɑlərən, B 'kɔləraɪn] *s.* (med.) colerina, colerín.
cholesterin [kə'lɛstərən] *s.* (med.) colesterina.
cholesterol [kə'lɛstəˌrɔl, -ˌroʊl, B -ˌrɔl] *s.* (quím.) colesterol.
cholic acid ['koʊlɪk-, 'kɑl-, B 'kɔl-] ácido cólico.
cholinesterase [ˌkoʊlə'nɛstəˌreɪs, ˌkɑl-, B ˌkɔl-] *s.* (biol.) colinesterasa.
cholla ['tʃoʊjə] *s.* (bot.) cholla.
chondriome ['kɑndrɪˌoʊm, B 'kɔn-] *s.* (biol.) condrioma.
chondriosome [-drɪəˌsoʊm] *s.* (biol.) condriosoma, mitocondría.
chondrite ['kɑnˌdraɪt, B 'kɔn-] *s.* (astr., geol.) condrito.
chondrocranium [ˌkɑndroʊ'kreɪnɪəm, B ˌkɔn-] *s.* (anat.) **condrocráneo.**
chondrology [kɑn'drɑlədʒɪ, B kɔn'drɔl-] *s.* (anat.) condrología.
chondroma [-'droʊmə] *s.* (*pl.* CHONDROMAS O CHONDROMATA [-tə]) (med.) condroma.
chondrule ['kɑnˌdrul, B 'kɔn-] *s.* (astr., geol.) cóndrulo.
choose [tʃuz] *v.t.* (*pret.* CHOSE [tʃoʊz]; *p.p.* CHOSEN ['tʃoʊzən]; *p.pr.* CHOOSING) 1. escoger, elegir, seleccionar. 2. decidir por, optar por. 3. **there's nothing to c. between them,** no hay (mucha) diferencia entre ellos, son prácticamente iguales. —*v.i.* 1. escoger, hacer una selección. 2. preferir, gustarle (a uno). 3. **c. to (do),** optar por (hacer); **to pick and c.,** ser quisquilloso, ser muy exigente.
chooser ['tʃuzər, B -ə] *s.* escogedor, quien escoge; **beggars cannot be choosers,** a caballo regalado no se le mira el colmillo.
choosy, choosey [-ɪ] *a.* (fam.) exigente, melindroso, quisquilloso.
chop [tʃɑp, B tʃɔp] *v.t.* (*pret., p.p.* CHOPPED; *p.pr.* CHOPPING) 1. cortar, tajar. 2. (con *off, down*) recortar, tranchar. 3. (gen. con *up*) picar (carne); desmenuzar. 4. (fig.) (con *down*) reducir, disminuir (influencia, poder, etc.). 5. (tenis, golf) dar un golpe seco y tajante a (la pelota). —*v.i.* (gen. con *at*) hacer cortes (en); **c. in,** intervenir (en una conversación, discusión, etc.). —*s.* 1. corte, tajo. 2. tajada, rebanada. 3. (cocina) chuleta. 4. aguas agitadas (del mar, lago, etc.).
chop [tʃɑp, B tʃɔp] *v.i.* (con *round, about*) cambiar de dirección, virar (esp. el viento o un barco); **c. and change,** vacilar; ser inconstance. —*v.t.* **c. logic,** pararse en quisquillas, argüir falazmente.
chop-chop ['tʃɑp'tʃɑp, B 'tʃɔp'tʃɔp] *adv., interj.* (jer.) presto, pronto.
chophouse [-ˌhaʊs] *s.* restaurante donde se sirven principalmente chuletas, bifteks y otras carnes.
chopine [tʃoʊ'pin, 'tʃɑpən, B 'tʃɔp-] *s.* chapín (chanclo de corcho usado por las mujeres).
chopper ['tʃɑpər, B 'tʃɔpə] *s.* 1 tajador. 2. hachuela; cuchilla de carnicero. 3. (rad.) interruptor rotatorio. 4. (jer.) helicóptero.
chopping bit [-ɪŋ-] (mec.) barrena picadora.
chopping block, tajo de cocina, tajadero, picador.
chopping board, tajadera.
chopping knife, cuchilla, tajadera.
choppy [-ɪ] *a.* 1. rajado, hendido. 2. picado, agitado (mar.). 3. variable (viento). 4. (fig.) discontinuo, inconexo, incoherente.
chops [tʃɑps, B tʃɔps] *s. pl.* mentón, quijada, mandíbula; papada; **to lick one's chops,** relamerse, regodearse por anticipado.

chopsticks ['tʃɑp,stɪks, B 'tʃɔp-] *s. pl.* palillo chino (para comer).
chop-suey [,tʃɑp'suɪ, B ,tʃɔp-] *s.* plato chino a base de carne, pollo y verduras picadas.
choragus [kə'reɪgəs] *s.* (hist.) corago, director de coro griego.
choral ['kɔrəl] *a., s.* (mús.) coral.
chorale [kə'ræl, B kɔ'rɑl] *s.* (mús.) coral.
choral music, música para coro.
choral society, orfeón.
chord [kɔrd, B kɔd] *s.* 1. cuerda (de un arpa, etc.). 2. (fig.) fibra, cuerda sensible, ej., *to touch the right c.,* tocar la cuerda sensible. 3. (anat.) cuerda, cordón, tendón, ej., *vocal c.,* cuerda vocal. 4. (geom.) cuerda. 5. (mús.) acorde. 6. (aer.) cuerda (de un perfil). 7. **to strike a c.,** hacer recordar o evocar a uno.
chordate ['kɔrdət, -,deɪt, B 'kɔ,-] *a., s.* (zool.) cordado.
chore [tʃɔr, B tʃɔ] *s.* faena, tarea doméstica; trabajo rutinario, quehacer.
chorea [kə'riə] *s.* (med.) corea, baile o mal de San Vito.
choreic [-'riɪk] *a.* (med., poét.) coreico.
choreograph ['kɔrɪə,græf, B -,grɑf] *v.t.* hacer la coreografía de. *—v.i.* trabajar como coreógrafo.
choreographer [,kɔrɪ'ɑgrəfər, B -'ɔgrəfə] *s.* coreógrafo.
choreographic [-ə'græfɪk] *a.* coreográfico.
choreography [-'ɑgrəfɪ, B -'ɔg-] *s.* coreografía.
choriamb ['kɔrɪ,æm, -,æmb] *s.* (*pl.* CHORIAMBS) (poét.) coriambo.
choriambic [,kɔrɪ'æmbɪk] *a.* (poét.) coriámbico.
choric ['kɔrɪk] *a.* coral; al estilo del coro griego.
chorine ['kɔrin] *s.* (teat., jer.) corista.
chorion ['kɔrɪ,ɑn, B -,ɔn] *s.* (anat., zool.) corión.
chorister ['kɔrəstər, B -stə] *s.* director de un coro.
C-horizon, (geol.) horizonte-C.
chorographer [kə'rɑgrəfər, B -'rɔgrəfə] *s.* (geog.) corógrafo.
chorography [-rəfɪ] *s.* (geog.) corografía.
choroid ['kɔr,ɔɪd] (anat.) *a.* coroideo. *—s.* coroides, membrana coroides.
chortle ['tʃɔrtəl, B 'tʃɔt-] *v.i.* reír entre dientes, cloquear. *—s.* risa ahogada, risita alegre.
chorus ['kɔrəs] *v.t., v.i.* cantar o hablar a coro; decir al unísono. *—s.* 1. coro. 2. estribillo, refrán. 3. **in c.,** a coro; al unísono.
chorus girl, (teat.) corista, tanguista.
chose [tʃouz] *pret. de* **choose.**
chose [ʃouz] *s.* (der.) cualquier objeto de propiedad personal.
chosen ['tʃouzən] *p.p. de* **choose.** *—a.* escogido, señalado; **the c. people,** el pueblo escogido, el pueblo de Dios (los judíos).
chough [tʃʌf] *s.* (orn.) chova, chova pinariega, grajo de pico amarillo.
chow [tʃau] *s.* 1. (jer.) comida, vituallas, provisiones, alimentos. 2. perro de raza china muy lanudo.
chow-chow ['tʃau,tʃau] *s.* mezcla de encurtidos picados, en salsa de mostaza.
chowder ['tʃaudər, B -də] *s.* (E.U., cocina) sopa o guisado a base de pescado, almejas u otros mariscos.
chowline [-,laɪn] *s.* (fam.) fila de personas (gen. en un campamento militar) esperando que les sirvan comida.
chow mein [-'meɪn] (cocina china) guisado de carne, pollo, etc. con verduras chinas, servido sobre fideos fritos.
chow time, (jer.) hora de comer.
chrestomathy [krɛs'tɑməθɪ, B -'tɔm-] *s.* crestomatía, antología, florilegio.
chrism ['krɪzəm] *s.* (relig.) crisma, aceite consagrado.
chrismatory ['krɪzmə,tɔrɪ, B -mətərɪ] *s.* (relig.) crismera.
chrisom ['krɪzəm] *s.* (relig.) ropaje blanco de bautizo.
Christ [kraɪst] *s.* Cristo, Jesucristo; **the C.-child,** el niño Jesús.
christcross['krɪs,krɔs] *s.* cristus (señal de la cruz antiguamente puesta al principio del abecedario).
christen ['krɪsən] *v.t.* 1. bautizar. 2. bautizar, dar nombre a. 3. (fam.) bautizar, estrenar (barco, edificio, etc.).
Christendom [-dəm] *s.* cristiandad, cristianismo.
christening [-ɪŋ] *s.* bautismo, bautizo. *—a.* bautismal.
Christian ['krɪstʃən, B -tjən] *a.* cristiano. *—s.* 1. cristiano, persona cristiana. 2. (dial.) ser humano.
Christian Brothers, Hermanos de la Doctrina Cristiana.
Christian Era, era de Cristo, era cristiana.
christiania [,krɪstʃɪ'ænɪə, B -tɪ'ɑnjə] *s.* (esquí) media vuelta (ejecutada para detenerse o cambiar de dirección en carrera).
Christianity [-'ænətɪ] *s.* cristiandad.
Christianize ['krɪstʃə,naɪz, B -tjə-] *v.t.* cristianizar.
Christian name, nombre de pila.
Christian Science, Ciencia Cristiana, sistema de enseñanza religiosa.
Christless ['kraɪstləs] *a.* no cristiano, infiel, herético.
Christlike [-,laɪk] *a.* propio de Cristo, parecido a Cristo.
Christmas ['krɪsməs] *s.* (Pascua de) Navidad; **Merry C.!** ¡Feliz Navidad! ¡Felices Pascuas!
Christmas card, aleluya navideña, tarjeta de felicitación por Navidades.
Christmas carol, villancico, cántico de Navidad.
Christmas Day, día de Navidad, 25 de diciembre.
Christmas Eve, Nochebuena, víspera de Navidad (24 de diciembre).
Christmas gift o **present,** regalo de Navidad, regalo Navideño.
Christmas rose, (bot.) eléboro negro.
Christmastide [-,taɪd] *s.* Pascuas, festividades de Navidad y de Año Nuevo (de vísperas de Navidad hasta Año Nuevo o Reyes).
Christmas tree, árbol de Navidad.
Christological [,krɪstə'lɑdʒɪkəl, B -'lɔdʒ-] *a.* cristológico.
Christology [krɪs'tɑlədʒɪ, B -'tɔl-] *s.* (relig.) cristología.
Christ's-thorn ['kraɪsts,θɔrn, B -,θɔn] *s.* (bot.) espina santa, cambrones.
chroma ['kroumə] *s.* pureza o intensidad del color.
chromate ['krou,meɪt, B -mɪt] *s.* (quím.) cromato.
chromatic [krou'mætɪk] *a.* 1. (mús., ópt.) cromático. 2. (impr.) policromo, ej., *c. printing,* impression policroma. *—s.* (mús.) cromático, semitono cromático.
chromatic aberration, (ópt.) aberración cromática.
chromaticism [-'mætə,sɪzəm] *s.* (mús.) cromatismo.
chromaticity [,kroumə'tɪsətɪ] *s.* (ópt.) cromatismo.
chromatics [krou'mætɪks] *s. pl.* (*sing. en const.*) cromática, ciencia del colorido.
chromatic scale, (mús.) escala cromática.
chromatid ['kroumətəd] *s.* (biol.) cromátide.
chromatin [-tən] *s.* (biol.) cromatina.
chromatism [-,tɪzəm] *s.* 1. cromatismo. 2. (bot.) decoloración de las hojas de plantas usualmente verdes.
chromatology [,kroumə'tɑlədʒɪ, B -'tɔl-] *s.* cromatología, estudio de los colores.
chromatolysis [-'tɑləsəs, B -'tɔl -] *s.* (med.) cromatólisis.
chromatolytic [krou,mætə'lɪtɪk] *a.* (med.) cromatolítico.
chromatophore [-'mætə,fɔr, B 'kroumətə,fɔ] *s.* (biol.) cromatóforo.
chrome [kroum] *s.* 1. cromo. 2. pigmento de cromo. *—a.* de cromo, ej., *c. green* (*red, yellow*), verde (rojo, amarillo) de cromo. *—v.t.* cromar.
chrome alum, alumbre crómico.
chromeplate ['kroum,pleɪt] *v.t.* cromar.
chromic [-ɪk] *a.* crómico, de cromo.
chromic iron, (metal.) cromita.
chromite [-,aɪt] *s.* (min.) cromita.
chromium [-ɪəm] *s.* (quím.) cromo.
chromium-plated [-,pleɪtəd] *a.* cromado.
chromium steel, chrome steel, acero cromado, acero al cromo, acerocromo.
chromo ['kroumou] *s. forma abrev. de* **chromolithograph,** cromolitografía.
chromogen ['kroumədʒən] *s.* bacteria cromógena.
chromogenic [,kroumə'dʒɛnɪk] *a.* cromógeno.
chromolithograph [-'lɪθə,græf, B -,grɑf] *s.* cromolitografía. *—v.t.* cromolitografiar.
chromolithographer [-lɪθ'ɑgrəfər, B -'ɔgrəfə] *s.* cromolitógrafo.
chromolithography [-fɪ] *s.* cromolitografía (arte).
chromomere ['kroumə,mɪr, B -,mɪə] *s.* (biol.) cromómero.
chromonema [,kroumə'nimə] *s.* (*pl.* CHROMONEMATA [-tə]) (biol.) cromonema.
chromophil ['kroumə,fɪl] *a.* (biol.) cromófilo.
chromophore [-,fɔr, B -,fɔ] *s.* (quím.) cromóforo.
chromoplasm [-,plæzəm] *s.* (biol.) cromoplasma, cromatoplasma.
chromoplast [-,plæst] *s.* (biol.) cromoplasto, cromoplástida.
chromoprotein [,kroumə'prou,tin, -'proutɪən] *s.* (biol.) cromoproteína.
chromosome ['kroumə,soum] *s.* (biol.) cromosoma.
chromosphere [-,sfɪr, B -,sfɪə] *s.* (astr.) cromosfera.
chromotypography [,kroumə,taɪ'pɑgrəfɪ, B -'pɔg-] *s.* (imp.) cromotipografía.
chromous ['krouməs] *a.* (quím.) cromoso.
chron. *abrev. de* 1. **chronological,** cronológico. 2. **chronology,** cronología.
Chron. *abrev. de* **Chronicles,** Crónicas.
chronaxie ['krou,næksɪ] *s.* (med.) cronaxia.
chronic ['krɑnɪk, B 'krɔn-] *a.* 1. crónico. 2. inveterado, arraigado.
chronically [-əlɪ] *adv.* crónicamente.
chronicity [krɑ'nɪsətɪ, B krɔ-] *s.* cronicidad.
chronicle ['krɑnɪkəl, B 'krɔn-] *s.* crónica (historia). *—v.t.* relatar, narrar, contar, escribir la crónica de (eventos, etc.).
chronicler [-klər, B -klə] *s.* cronista, historiador.
Chronicles [-kəlz] *s. pl.* (bíbl.) Crónicas (dos libros del Antiguo Testamento).

chronograph ['krɑnəˌgræf, 'kroʊnə-, B 'krɔnəˌgrɑf] *s.* cronógrafo (aparato para medir tiempos sumamente pequeños).
chronologic [ˌkrɑnə'lɑdʒɪk, B ˌkrɔnə'-lɔdʒ-] **chronological** [-ɪkəl] *a.* cronológico.
chronologically [-ɪkəlɪ] *adv.* cronológicamente.
chronologist [krə'nɑlədʒəst, B -'nɔl-] *s.* cronologista.
chronology [-dʒɪ] *s.* cronología.
chronometer [-'nɑmətər, B -'nɔmɪtə] *s.* cronómetro, reloj de precisión para usos especializados.
chronometry [-trɪ] *s.* cronometría, cálculo científico del tiempo.
chronoscope ['krɑnəˌskoʊp, B 'krɔn-] *s.* (fís.) cronoscopio.
Chronotron [-ˌtrɑn, B -ˌtrɔn] *s.* (marca de fábrica) dispositivo para medir espacios de tiempo extremadamente cortos, comparándolos con pulsaciones eléctricas.
chrysalid ['krɪsələd] *var. de* **chrysalis.**
chrysalis [-ləs] *s.* (*pl.* CHRYSALIDES [krə'sæləˌdiz]) (ento.) crisálida, ninfa.
chrysanthemum [krɪ'sænθəməm] *s.* (bot.) crisantemo.
chrysarobin [ˌkrisə'roʊbən] *s.* (farm.) crisarobina.
chryselephantine [ˌkrɪsɛlə'fæntin, B -taɪn] *a.* criselefantino (recamado de oro y marfil, como ciertas estatuas griegas).
chrysene ['krɪˌsin] *s.* criseno.
chrysoberyl ['krɪsəˌbɛrəl] *s.* (min.) crisoberilo.
chrysolite [-ˌlaɪt] *s.* (min.) crisólito, esp. crisólito oriental.
chrysoprase [-ˌpreɪz] *s.* (min.) crisoprasa.
chrysotile [-ˌtaɪl] *s.* (min.) crisotilo.
chthonian ['θoʊnɪən] *a.* (mitol.) relativo al mundo de los muertos, sus dioses y espíritus.
chub [tʃʌb] *s.* (ict.) cacho, galleguito.
chubby ['tʃʌbɪ] *a.* regordete, gordinflón, rechoncho.
chubby-cheeked [-'tʃikt] *a.* mofletudo, cariancho.
chuck [tʃʌk] *v.t.* 1. sopapear, hacer la mamola a (uno). 2. tirar, echar. 3. (mec.) sujetar en el portaherramientas. 4. desperdiciar, perder (oportunidad, etc.). —*s.* 1. mamola, sopapo; golpe seco. 2. (med.) portabroca, portamecha, boquilla (de un torno, máquina-herramienta, etc.); portaherramienta, mandril. 3. (fam., O. de E.U.) comida, alimento. 4. biftec de la parte del lomo y cuello de la vaca.
chuck-a-luck ['tʃʌkəˌlʌk] *s.* juego en el cual los jugadores apuestan al tiro de tres dados.
chucker-out ['tʃʌkər'aʊt] *s.* (*pl.* CHUCKERS-OUT) (G.B.) apagabroncas.
chuck-full [-'fʊl] *var. de* **chock-full.**
chuckhole ['tʃʌkˌhoʊl] *s.* bache, hendidura u obstáculo natural en un camino; badén.
chuckle ['tʃʌkəl] *v.i.* 1. reírse entre dientes; (con *over*) sentir júbilo (por), recrearse (con). 2. cloquear (la gallina). —*s.* risa ahogada, risita.
chucklehead [-ˌhɛd] *s.* tonto, bobo, cabezota.
chuck plate, (maq.) portaplato, brida para plato, portamandril.
chuck wagon, (E.U.) carreta de provisiones (de los pioneros, vaqueros, peones, etc.).
chuck-will's-widow [ˌtʃʌkˌwɪlz'wɪdoʊ] *s.* (orn.) chotacabras americana.
chuck wrench, (mec.) llave para mandril.
chuff [tʃʌf] *s.* patán, rústico, palurdo.
chuffy ['tʃʌfɪ] *a.* (dial.) rechoncho, regordete.
chug [tʃʌg] *s.* resoplido, ruido corto y explosivo (como de locomotora al arrancar); traqueteo. —*v.i.* (fam.) traquetear.
chug-a-lug ['tʃʌgəˌlʌg] *v.t., v.i.* (jer.) beber de un trago, o sorbiendo rápidamente.
chukka boot ['tʃʌkə-] *s.* zapato deportivo estilo mediabota, hasta el tobillo y entizado.
chukker, chukkar ['tʃʌkər, B -ə] *s.* (juego de polo) período (de juego).
chum [tʃʌm] *s.* 1. compinche, camarada. 2. compañero de cuarto o de estudios. —*v.i.* ser buen camarada; compartir cuarto (con otro); **c. up with,** trabar amistad con, compartir cuarto o estudios con.
chum [tʃʌm] *s.* cebo, carnada (de pescado picado o desperdicios que se echan al agua).
chummy ['tʃʌmɪ] *s.* sociable, amistoso.
chump [tʃʌmp] *s.* 1. tronco, trozo de madera grueso; tarugo. 2. (fam., G.B.) coco, cabeza. 3. (fam.) tonto, bobalicón. 4. extremidad gruesa.
chunk [tʃʌŋk] *s.* 1. pedazo grueso y corto, trozo (de algo). 2. cantidad grande, porción o parte substancial. 3. (fam., E.U.) cuadrúpedo fornido (esp. un caballo).
chunky ['tʃʌŋkɪ] *a.* (fam.) corto y rechoncho; grueso, abundante en carnes.
church [tʃɜrtʃ, B tʃɜtʃ] *s.* 1. iglesia, templo. 2. iglesia, congregación de los fieles. 3. **the C.,** la Iglesia; el clero. 4. misa, servicio, culto, ej., *after c.,* después de la misa (o del servicio). 5. **poor as a c. mouse,** más pobre que una rata; **to go to c.,** ir a la iglesia, oír misa.
church calendar, santoral.
churchgoer ['tʃɜrtʃˌgoʊər, B 'tʃɜtʃ-ə] *s.* fiel, devoto (que asiste regularmente a la iglesia).
churchgoing [-ɪŋ] *a.* devoto, religioso.
church key, (jer.) abridor de latas o botellas de cerveza.
churchless [-ləs] *a.* sin afiliación religiosa.
churchly [-lɪ] *a.* 1. eclesiástico; de la iglesia. 2. religioso, devoto.
churchman [-mən] *s.* 1. miembro de la iglesia, feligrés (de una parroquia). 2. sacerdote.
church militant, iglesia militante.
church music, música sacra, música eclesiástica.
Church of Christ, Scientist, *var. de* **Christian Science,** iglesia de la ciencia cristiana.
Church of England, iglesia anglicana.
Church of Jesus Christ of Latter-day Saints, iglesia de los mormones.
church register, registro parroquial.
church supplies, *s. pl.* artículos del culto.
churchwarden [-ˌwɔrdən, B -ˌwɔd-] *s.* 1. mayordomo (de una cofradía), fabriquero. 2. (fam. G.B.) pipa larga de barro.
churchwoman [-ˌwʊmən] *s.* feligresa (de una parroquia).
churchyard [-ˌjɑrd, B -ˌjɑd] *s.* patio de la iglesia; (usado a menudo como) cementerio.
churl [tʃɜrl, B tʃɜl] *s.* 1. rústico, palurdo. 2. grosero, patán. 3. tacaño, miserable.
churlish ['tʃɜrlɪʃ, B 'tʃɜl-] *a.* rústico; grosero; recalcitrante, intratable.
churn [tʃɜrn, B tʃɜn] *s.* 1. mantequera (en que se fabrica la mantequilla). 2. agitación, batido. —*v.t.* 1. agitar, revolver, remover. 2. batir (manteca). 3. (fig.) (t. con *out*) producir en profusión (ideas, etc.). —*v.i.* 1. hacer mantequilla (en la mantequera). 2. agitarse, revolverse.
churr [tʃɜr, B tʃɜ] *s.* zumbido sordo (como el de la perdiz). —*v.i.* emitir dicho sonido.
churrigueresque [ˌtʃʊrɪgə'rɛsk] *a.* (arq.) churrigueresco; del estilo que reúne elementos góticos, platerescos y barrocos.
chute [ʃut] *s.* 1. canaleja, conducto, sumidero (por donde baja el agua). 2. salto de agua. 3. tobogán (al borde de piscinas para deslizarse; chorrera (para niños); de la calle al sótano en almacenes para transportar mercancía con rapidez). 4. *forma abrev. de* **parachute,** paracaídas.
chutney ['tʃʌtnɪ] *s.* condimento de la India a base de frutas, pimiento, cebolla, mostaza y vinagre.
chutzpah, chutzpa ['hʊtspə] *s.* (fam.) desfachatez, atrevimiento, desenfado.
chylaceous [kaɪ'leɪʃəs] *a.* (biol.) quiloso.
chyle [kaɪl] *s.* (biol.) quilo.
chylification [ˌkaɪləfə'keɪʃən] *s.* (fisiol.) quilificación.
chylous ['kaɪləs] *a.* quiloso.
chyme [kaɪm] *s.* (biol.) quimo.
chymification [ˌkaɪməfə'keɪʃən] *s.* (fisiol.) quimificación.
chymotrypsin [-'trɪpsən] *s.* (biol.) quimotripsina.
CIA *abrev. de* **Central Intelligence Agency,** Agencia Central de Inteligencia.
ciao [tʃaʊ] *interj.* (ital.) chao, expresión informal de saludo y despedida.
ciborium [sə'bɔrɪəm] *s.* (*pl.* CIBORIA [-ɪə]) 1. (arq.) ciborio, dosel del altar. 2. (relig.) copón, sagrario.
cicada [sə'keɪdə, -'kɑdə] *s.* (ento.) cigarra.
cicala [-'kɑlə] *var. de* **cicada.**
cicatricial [ˌsɪkə'trɪʃəl] *a.* (med.) cicatrizal.
cicatricle ['sɪkəˌtrɪkəl, B sɪ'kætrɪk-] **cicatricule** [-ˌtrɪkjʊl, B sɪ'kætrɪk-] *s.* (bot., zool.) cicatrícula.
cicatrix ['sɪkəˌtrɪks] *s.* (*pl.* CICATRICES [ˌsɪkə't-raɪsiz]) cicatriz.
cicatrization [ˌsɪkətrɪ'zeɪʃən] *s.* cicatrización.
cicatrize ['sɪkəˌtraɪz] *v.t., v.i.* cicatrizar.
cicely ['sɪsəlɪ] *s.* (bot.) perifollo oloroso.
Cicero ['sɪsərˌoʊ] *s.* Cicerón, estadista, orador y filósofo romano.
cicerone [ˌsɪsə'roʊnɪ, ˌtʃɪtʃə-] *s.* (*pl.* CICERONI [-nɪ] o CICERONES) cicerone, guía; acompañante de turistas.
Ciceronian [ˌsɪsə'roʊnɪən] *a.* ciceroniano. —*s.* admirador de Cicerón.
cicisbeo [ˌtʃɪtʃəz'beɪoʊ] *s.* chichisbeo, amante (de una mujer casada).
Cid [sɪd] *s.* el Cid Campeador.
CID *abrev. de* **Criminal Investigation Department,** Departamento de Investigación Criminal.
cider ['saɪdər, B -ə] *s.* sidra; bebida hecha de manzana; **hard c.,** sidra fermentada; **sweet c.,** el jugo de la fruta sin fermentar.
cider press, lagar para extraer el jugo de las manzanas.
CIF *abrev. de* **cost, insurance and freight,** costo, seguro y flete (CIF).
cigar [sɪ'gɑr, B -'gɑ] *s.* cigarro, puro.
cigar band, anillo de cigarro.
cigar case, cigarrera, petaca para portar puros.
cigarette [ˌsɪgə'rɛt, 'sɪgəˌrɛt, B ˌsɪgə'rɛt] *s.* cigarrillo, pitillo.
cigarette case, pitillera.
cigarette holder, boquilla.
cigarette lighter, encendedor, mechero automático; chofeta.
cigarillo [ˌsɪgə'rɪloʊ] *s.* pequeño puro o tabaquito, casi tan corto y delgado como un cigarrillo.
cigar store, cigarrería, tabaquería, estanquillo.
cilia ['sɪlɪə] *s. pl.* 1. cilios; pestañas. 2. (zool., bot.) cilios.
ciliary ['sɪlɪˌɛrɪ, B -ərɪ] *a.* (anat.) ciliar.
ciliate [-ət, -ˌeɪt] **ciliated** [-ˌeɪtəd] *a.* (zool., bot.) ciliado. —*s.* (zool.) ciliado.
cilice ['sɪlɪs] *s.* cilicio.
cilium [ˌsɪlɪəm] *s. sing. de* **cilia.**
cimarron ['sɪməˌroʊn] *s.* cimarrón; cerril, salvaje.
Cimbri ['sɪmbri] *s. pl.* (hist.) cimbros; antigua raza germánica que los romanos vencieron.

cimex ['saɪmeks] *s.* (*pl.* CIMICES ['sɪmə,siz]) (ento.) chinche común.
Cimmerian [sə'mɪrɪən, B -'mɪər-] *s.* cimerio. —*a.* (fig.) lúgubre, tenebroso.
cinch [sɪntʃ] *s.* (E.U.) 1. cincha (de la silla o albarda). 2. (fig.) control, dominio. 3. (fam.) cosa segura, certidumbre; cosa fácil. —*v.t.* (E.U.) 1. cinchar. 2. (fig.) controlar, acorralar, dominar. 3. asegurar, hacer seguro (victoria, nombramiento, elección, etc.).
cinchona [sɪŋ'koʊnə] *s.* 1. (bot.) chinchona, cascarillo, cascarillero, quino. 2. quinina.
cinchona bark, (farm.) quina, corteza del cascarillo.
cinchonine ['sɪŋkə,nin] *s.* (quím.) cascarillina.
cinchonism [-,nɪzəm] *s.* (med.) quinismo.
cincture ['sɪŋktʃər, B -tʃə] *s.* 1. cinto, ceñidor, cincho. 2. (fig.) cinturón. —*v.t.* ceñir; rodear, cercar.
cinder ['sɪndər, B -də] *s.* 1. escarbillo, carbonilla; (*pl.*) cenizas, pavesas. 2. escoria volcánica.
cinder block, ladrillo de cenizas, bloque de concreto de cenizas (para cimientos, etc.).
Cinderella [,sɪndə'rɛlə] *s.* la Cenicienta.
cinder track, (dep.) pista de cenizas (para carreras).
cinéaste [,sineɪ'æst, sɪni,æst] *s.* (fr.) cineasta; realizador de películas.
cinema ['sɪnəmə] *s.* cine, cinematógrafo; **the c.,** el cine, la cinematografía.
cinemascope [-,skoʊp] *s.* cinemascopio; el cine proyectado en pantalla gigantesca y ligeramente curvada.
cinematic [,sɪnə'mætɪk] *a.* (fís.) cinemático.
cinematograph [-ə,græf, B -,grɑf] *s.* cinematógrafo.
cinematographer [-mə'tɑgrəfər, B -'tɔgrəfə] *s.* (G.B.) camarógrafo u operador (de cine).
cinematographic [-,mætə'græfɪk] *a.* cinematográfico.
cinematography [-mə'tɑgrəfɪ, B -'tɔg-] *s.* cinematografía.
cinéma vérité [,sineɪ,mɑveɪrɪ'teɪ] (fr.) cine vérité; la escuela del realismo en el cine.
cineole ['sɪnɪ,oʊl] *s.* (quím.) cineol.
Cinerama [,sɪnə'rɑmə] *s.* cinerama; procedimiento de filmar y exhibir películas para dar un efecto tridimensional muy realista.
cineraria [-'rɛrɪə, B -'rɛər-] *s.* (bot.) cineraria.
cinerarium [-ɪəm] *s.* (*pl.* CINERARIA [-ɪə]) nicho para la urna cineraria.
cinerary ['sɪnə,rɛrɪ, B -rərɪ] *a.* cinerario, ej., *c. urn,* urna cineraria.
cinerator [-,reɪtər, B -ə] *s.* incinerador, crematorio, horno crematorio.
cinereous [sə'nɪrɪəs, B -'nɪər-] *a.* 1. cinéreo, ceniciento (díc. esp. del plumaje de las aves). 2. cenizoso.
cingulate ['sɪŋgjələt] *a.* (zool.) provisto de cíngulos; (med.) marcado con cíngulos.
cingulum [-ləm] *s.* (*pl.* CINGULA [-lə]) 1. (zool., med.) cíngulo. 2. cíngulo que ciñe el alba (atuendo eclesiástico).
cinnabar ['sɪnə,bɑr, B -,bɑ] *s.* (min.) cinabrio.
cinnamic [sə'næmɪk] *a.* (quím.) cinámico.
cinnamon ['sɪnəmən] *s.* 1. (bot.) canelo. 2. canela. —*a.* de color canela.
cinque [sɪŋk] *s.* cinco (en dados o cartas).
cinquecento [,tʃɪŋkwɪ'tʃentoʊ] *s.* el siglo XVI en el arte y la literatura italianos.
cinquefoil ['sɪŋk,fɔɪl] *s.* 1. (bot.) cincoenrama, quinquefolio. 2. (arq.) rosetón o diseño circular de cinco arcos.
CIO *abrev. de* **Congress of Industrial Organizations,** Congreso de Organizaciones Industriales.
cion ['saɪən] *var. de* **scion.**
cipher ['saɪfr, B -fə] *s.* 1. cifra, número. 2. (mat.) cero. 3. (fig.) nulidad, cero (persona). 4. cifra, código, clave. 5. cifra, monograma. —*v.i.* (mat.) usar cifras; escribir en cifras. —*v.t.* 1. cifrar (con clave). 2. calcular, computar.
cipher message, mensaje en clave.
cipolin ['sɪpəlɪn] *s.* 1. variedad de cebolla. 2. mármol cipolino.
circa ['sɜrkə, B 'sɜkə] *prep.* alrededor de, cerca de (cierta fecha).
Circassian [sər'kæʃən, B sə'kæsɪ-] *a., s.* circasiano, de la Circasia, región del Cáucaso.
Circe ['sɜrsi, B 'sɜsɪ] *s.* (mitol.) Circe (personaje de *La Odisea*).
circinate ['sɜrsən, eɪt, B 'sɜs-] *a.* (bot.) circinado.
circle ['sɜrkəl, B 'sɜkəl] *s.* 1. (geom.) circulo. 2. círculo, circunferencia, ruedo, anillo. 3. círculo, rueda, corro, grupo (de personas). 4. ciclo, período. 5. (log.) círculo, ej., *vicious c.,* círculo vicioso. 6. (fig.) esfera, área (de influencia, acción, etc.) 7. (teat.) hemiciclo de palcos. 8. **high circles,** (fig.) altas esferas (sociales); **to come full c.,** cumplir un ciclo completo, terminar en el punto de partida; **to square the c.,** hallar la cuadratura del círculo, pretender lo imposible. —*v.t.* 1. circundar, rodear. 2. girar alrededor de. 3. dar la vuelta a. —*v.i.* 1. circular, dar vueltas. 2. girar.
circle marker, (avia.) círculo de aterrizaje.
circlet [-klət] *s.* 1. círculo pequeño; anillo, collar, brazalete, corona. 2. (her.) rodete.
circuit ['sɜrkət, B 'sɜkɪt] *s.* 1. circuito, contorno. 2. circuito, área, ámbito. 3. gira, viaje. 4. rodeo, camino indirecto. 5. cadena (de teatros, cines, etc.). 6. (der.) circuito (que recorre un juez), distrito, jurisdicción (de un juez). 7. (elec.) circuito; **short c.,** corto circuito. —*v.t.* rodear por, contornear. —*v.i.* (gen. con *about*) dar vueltas (alrededor de un sitio, etc.).
circuitation [,sɜrkjʊə'teɪʃən, B sɜ,-] *s.* (elec.) circulación.
circuit board, placa base.
circuit breaker, (elec.) cortacircuitos, interruptor automático.
circuit court, tribunal de circuito, juzgado de circuito.
circuitous [sər'kjuətəs, B sə'-] *a.* tortuoso, sinuoso, indirecto (camino, ruta, etc.).
circuit rider, (E.U.) predicador viajero.
circuitry ['sɜrkətrɪ, B 'sɜkɪ-] *s.* (elec.) sistema de circuitos.
circular [-kjələr, B -lə] *a.* 1. circular; redondo. 2. tortuoso, indirecto. —*s.* circular, carta circular.
circularity [,sɜrkjə'lærətɪ, B ,sɜkjʊ-] *s.* 1. circularidad, redondez. 2. (fig.) tortuosidad (de argumento, razonamiento, etc.).
circularize ['sɜrkjələ,raɪz, B 'sɜkjʊ-] *v.t.* enviar (cartas) circulares a; anunciar por circulares; dar forma circular a.
circular measure, (geom.) medida en radianes.
circular mil, milipulgada circular; milésimo circular, mil circular.
circular pitch, (mec.) paso circunferencial.
circular sailing, navegación ortodrómica.
circular saw, sierra giratoria.
circulate ['sɜrkjə,leɪt, B 'sɜkjʊ-] *v.i.* 1. circular (sangre, noticias, moneda, libros, etc.). 2. circular, mezclarse (entre gentes). —*v.t.* hacer circular; propagar, divulgar, diseminar, hacer correr (rumor, noticia, etc.).
circulating capital [-ɪŋ-] (e.p.) capital en circulación, capital circulante.
circulating decimal, (mat.) decimal periódico.
circulating medium, medio circulante, moneda corriente.
circulation [,sɜrkjə'leɪʃən, B ,sɜkjʊ-] *s.* 1. circulación (de la sangre, la savia, etc.). 2. circulación (de monedas, periódicos, etc.). 3. diseminación, divulgación (de noticias, etc.). 4. circulación, tirada (de periódicos, revistas, etc.).
circulator ['sɜrkjə,leɪtər, B 'sɜkjʊ-] *s.* 1. divulgador (de noticias, rumores, etc.). 2. distribuidor (de periódicos, revistas, etc.).
circulatory [-lə,tɔrɪ, B ,sɜkjʊ'leɪtərɪ] *a.* circulatorio, circulante, circular.
circumambiency [,sɜrkəm'æmbɪənsɪ, B ,sɜkəm-] *s.* medio ambiente.
circumambient [-ənt] *a.* circundante (aire, ruido, etc.), circumambiente.
circumambulate [-bjə,leɪt] *v.t., v.i.* andar alrededor de (un lugar); deambular, vagar; andarse por las ramas.
circumcise ['sɜrkəm,saɪz, B 'sɜkəm-] *v.t.* circuncidar, retajar.
circumcision [,sɜrkəm'sɪʒən, B ,sɜkəm-] *s.* circuncisión; **C.,** (relig.) fiesta de la Circuncisión de Cristo (el 1 de enero).
circumference [sər'kʌmfərəns, B sə'-] *s.* circunferencia, perímetro, periferia, contorno.
circumferential [-,kʌmfə'rɛntʃəl, B -'rɛnʃəl] *a.* circunferencial, periférico.
circumflex ['sɜrkəm,flɛks, B sɜkəm-] *s.* acento circunflejo; (impr.) capucha. —*a.* circunflejo (acento); (anat.) circunflejo (nervio, vena, músculo). —*v.t.* poner acento circunflejo sobre (una vocal).
circumfluence [,sɜr'kʌmflʊəns, B ,sɜ'-] *s.* derrame circular.
circumfluent [-ənt] *a.* circundante, circunfluente.
circumfuse [,sɜrkəm'fjuz, B ,sɜkəm-] *v.t.* derramar (líquido) en derredor de (objeto); circundar (objeto) con (líquido).
circumlocution [-loʊ'kjuʃən] *s.* circunlocución, circunloquio, verbosidad.
circumlunar [-'lunər, B -nə] *a.* circunlunar, que rodea a la luna.
circumnavigate [-'nævə,geɪt] *v.t.* circunnavegar (esp. el globo).
circumnavigation [-,nævə'geɪʃən] *s.* circunnavegación.
circumnavigator [-'nævə,geɪtər, B -ə] *s.* circunnavegante.
circumpolar [-'poʊlər, B -lə] *a.* (astr., geog.) circumpolar.
circumscribe ['sɜrkəm,skraɪb, ˎsɜrkəm-'skraɪb, B 'sɜkəm,skraɪb, ˎsɜkəm-'skraɪb] *v.t.* 1. circunscribir, circunferir, restringir, limitar. 2. demarcar, delinear. 3. (geom.) circunscribir.
circumscript ['sɜrkəm,skrɪpt, B 'sɜkəm-] *a.* circunscrito, restringido, limitado.
circumscription [,sɜrkəm'skrɪpʃən, B ,sɜkəm-] *a.* 1. circunscripción, restricción, limitación. 2. circunscripción, división administrativa. 3. inscripción, leyenda circular (en moneda, etc.).
circumspect ['sɜrkəm,spɛkt, B 'sɜkəm-] *a.* circunspecto, discreto, prudente, cauteloso.
circumspection [,sɜrkəm'spɛkʃən, B ,sɜkəm-] *s.* circunspección, discreción, prudencia, cautela.
circumstance ['sɜrkəm,stæns, B 'sɜkəm-stəns] *s.* 1. circunstancia; incidente, acontecimiento; (*pl.*) circunstancias, condición (esp. económica de alguien). 2. detalle (en una narración, etc.). 3. ceremonia, aparato. 4. **in easy**

circumstances, acomodado; **in** (o **under**) **the circumstances,** bajo o debido a las circunstancias; **under no circumstances,** bajo ninguna circunstancia, de ninguna manera, en ningún caso; **without c.,** sin ceremonia.
circumstantial [ˌsɜrkəm'stæntʃəl, B ˌsɜkəm'stænʃəl] *a.* 1. circunstancial, ej., *c. evidence,* prueba(s) circunstancial(es) o indiciaria(s), prueba(s) de indicios. 2. circunstanciado, minucioso (relato, informe, etc.).
circumstantially [-ɪ] *adv.* circunstancialmente.
circumstantiate [-tʃɪˌeɪt, B -'stænʃɪ-] *v.t.* respaldar con pruebas circunstanciales.
circumvallate [-'vælˌeɪt] *v.t.* circunvalar. *—a.* cercado, rodeado.
circumvallation [-ˌvæ'leɪʃən] *s.* circunvalación.
circumvent [-'vɛnt] *v.t.* 1. circunvenir (la ley, propósitos, etc.). 2. rodear, circundar, evitar. 3. enredar, embaucar, entrampar.
circumvolution [-və'luʃən] *s.* circunvolución; vuelta, rodeo.
circumvolve [-'vɑlv, B -'vɔlv] *v.t., v.i.* revolver, voltear, dar vueltas (a).
circus ['sɜrkəs, B 'sɜkəs] *s.* 1. circo, arena, ruedo. 2. el circo (espectáculo). 3. (G.B.) plaza circular, ej., *Piccadilly Circus* (en Londres). 4. (fam.) suceso, persona, circunstancia ruidosa o jocosa.
cirque [sɜrk, B sɜk] *s.* 1. (poét.) arena; circo, anfiteatro natural. 2. (geol.) depresión o excavación natural causada en un cerro por erosión glacial.
cirrate ['sɪrˌeɪt, B 'sɪər-] *a.* cirroso.
cirrhosis [sə'roʊsəs] *s.* (med.) cirrosis.
cirrhotic [-'rɑtɪk, B -'rɔt-] *a.* (med.) cirrótico.
cirriped ['sɪrəˌpɛd] **cirripede** [-ˌpid] *s.* (zool.) cirrípedo.
cirripedial [ˌsɪrə'pidrəl] *a.* (zool.) cirrípedo.
cirrocumulus [ˌsɪroʊ'kjumjələs] *s.* (meteor.) cirrocúmulo.
cirrose ['sɪrˌoʊs, B 'sɪər-] *a.* cirroso.
cirrostratus [ˌsɪroʊ'streɪtəs, B -'strɑtəs] *s.* (meteor.) cirrostrato.
cirrous ['sɪrəs] *var. de* **cirrose.**
cirrus ['sɪrəs] *s.* (*pl.* CIRRI [-ˌaɪ]) 1. (bot.) cirro, zarcillo. 2. (zool.) cirro, tentáculo filiforme. 3. (meteor.) cirros.
CIS *abrev. de* **Community of Independent States,** CEI (Comunidad de Estados Independientes).
cisalpine [sɪs'ælpaɪn] *a.* cisalpino; aquende los Alpes.
cisandine [-'ænˌdin, B -ˌdaɪn] *a.* cisandino; aquende los Andes.
cisatlantic [-ət'læntɪk] *a.* cisatlántico; aquende el Atlántico.
cisco ['sɪskoʊ] (ict.) arenque de lago.
cislunar [sɪs'lunər, B -nə] *a.* (astr.) situado entre la tierra y la luna.
cismontane [-'mɑnteɪn, B -'mɔn-] *a.* cismontano; aquende los montes.
cissoid ['sɪsɔɪd] *s.* (geom.) cisoide.
cist [sɪst] *s.* (arqueol.) cista, arquilla; sepulcro.
cistaceous [sɪs'teɪʃəs] *a.* (bot.) cistáceo.
Cistercian [sɪs'tɜrʃən, B -'tɜʃən] *s., a.* (relig.) cisterciense.
cistern ['sɪstərn, B -tən] *s.* 1. cisterna, aljibe, tanque (esp. de agua). 2. (anat.) cisterna.
cistus ['sɪstəs] *s.* (bot.) cisto, jara, estepa.
citadel ['sɪtədəl] *s.* (fort.) ciudadela.
citation [saɪ'teɪʃən] *s.* 1. citación 2. (mil.) mención (esp. honorífica). 3. (der.) citación, emplazamiento.
citatory ['saɪtəˌtɔrɪ, B -tərɪ] *a.* (der.) citatorio (mandamiento, poder, etc.).
cite [saɪt] *v.t.* 1. citar, referirse a, dar como ejemplo, mencionar. 2. (der.) citar, emplazar. 3. (mil.) mencionar (en despachos).
cithara ['sɪθərə] *s.* 1. (hist.) (especie de) lira griega. 2. (mús.) cítara.
cither ['sɪθər, B -ə] *var. de* **cithern.**
citify ['sɪtɪˌfaɪ] *v.t.* (*pret., p.p.* CITIFIED; *p.pr.* CITIFYING) acostumbrar a la vida urbana, urbanizar (a alguien).
citizen ['sɪtəzən] *s.* ciudadano; (*of a town or city*) habitante, vecino.
citizen of the world, 1. cosmopolita. 2. ciudadano del mundo.
citizenry [-rɪ] *s.* (*pl.* CITIZENRIES) ciudadanía, (los) ciudadanos (en conjunto).
citizen's arrest, detención llevada a cabo por un ciudadano común.
citizenship [-ˌʃɪp] *s.* ciudadanía; nacionalidad.
citizenship papers, certificado de ciudadanía (que se otorga al ciudadano naturalizado al nacionalizarse en el país de su elección).
citrate ['sɪˌtreɪt, 'saɪ-] *s.* (quím.) citrato.
citric ['sɪtrɪk] *a.* cítrico; de frutas cítricas como el limón, la naranja y la toronja.
citric acid, (quím.) ácido cítrico.
citrine [-ˌtraɪn, -trɪn] *a.* citrino, cetrino. — [-ˌtrin] *s.* (min.) citrino.
citron ['sɪtrən] *s.* 1. (bot.) cidro. 2. cidra. 3. cidrada (cáscara de fruta cítrica, confitada).
citronella [ˌsɪtrə'nɛlə] *s.* 1. (bot.) citronela, limoncillo. 2. (quím.) aceite y esencia de citronela.
citron melon, sandía blanca (que se usa principalmente en conserva confitada).
citrus ['sɪtrəs] *a., s.* (*pl.* CITRUS O CITRUSES) (bot.) 1. cualquier planta o fruto del género cítrico. 2. cidra.
cittern ['sɪtərn, B -ən] *s.* (mús.) especie de mandolina plana.
city ['sɪtɪ] *s.* ciudad; población, urbe, municipio.
city council, concejo municipal.
city editor, 1. (E.U.) redactor de noticias locales. 2. (G.B.) redactor de noticias financieras y bancarias.
city hall, 1. ayuntamiento, municipalidad. 2. gobierno municipal; (despec.) burocracia municipal.
city manager, administrador municipal.
City of Brotherly Love, (E.U.) ciudad del amor fraternal (la ciudad de Filadelfia).
city plan, plan orgánico municipal.
city planning, planificación municipal, urbanización.
cityscape ['sɪtɪˌskeɪp] *s.* paisaje urbano, vista de la ciudad.
city slicker, (despec.) nombre despectivo que dan los campesinos al capitalino o habitante de gran ciudad.
city-state [-'steɪt] *s.* ciudad-estado.
civet ['sɪvət] *s.* (zool., quím.) civeto, algalia.
civet cat, (zool.) civeta, gato de algalia.
civic ['sɪvɪk] *a.* cívico; ciudadano.
civics ['sɪvɪks] *s. pl.* (*sing. en const.*) educación cívica.
civil ['sɪvəl] *a.* 1. civil, ciudadano, comunal. 2. cortés, atento, civil, urbano. 3. civil (no militar). 4. civil, laico, seglar (no eclesiástico), ej., *c. marriage,* matrimonio civil. 5. (der.) civil (no criminal).
civil death, (der.) muerte civil (privación de los derechos civiles a un ciudadano en castigo por traición u otro delito grave).
civil defense, (organización de) defensa civil (esp. contra bombardeos aéreos).
civil disobedience, resistencia pasiva (contra un gobierno o una ley).
civil engineer, ingeniero civil.
civil engineering, ingeniería civil.
civilian [sə'vɪljən] *s.* civil, paisano. *—a.* civil (no militar).
civilian clothes, traje de paisano.
civility [sə'vɪlətɪ] *s.* civilidad, urbanidad, cortesía.
civilizable ['sɪvəˌlaɪzəbəl] *a.* civilizable.
civilization [ˌsɪvələ'zeɪʃən, B -laɪ-] *s.* civilización.
civilize ['sɪvəˌlaɪz] *v.t.* civilizar, educar. *—v.i.* civilizarse.
civilized [-ˌlaɪzd] *a.* civilizado.
civil law, derecho civil, derecho común.
civil liberties, libertades ciudadanas que la ley y las costumbres garantizan al individuo.
civil list, (G.B.) presupuesto de gastos de la casa real, autorizado por el Parlamento.
civilly ['sɪvəlɪ] *adv.* 1. civilmente, cortésmente, con urbanidad. 2. (der.) civilmente.
civil marriage, matrimonio por lo civil.
civil procedure, (der.) enjuiciamiento civil.
civil rights, 1. derechos civiles, garantías constitucionales. 2. movimiento en pro de los derechos civiles de un grupo minoritario, esp. a favor de los negros en E.U.
civil servant, funcionario público, empleado del estado.
civil service, (ramo civil de la) administración pública.
civil war, guerra civil.
civil year, año civil.
civvies ['sɪviz] *s. pl.* (fam., mil.) traje de paisano, ropas civiles (de un soldado franco).
C.J. *abrev. de* **Chief Justice,** presidente del Tribunal Supremo (E.U.).
cl. *abrev. de* **centiliter,** centilitro (cl.).
Cl *símb. de* **chlorine,** cloro (Cl).
clabber ['klæbər, B -ə] *v.i.* cuajarse (la leche). *—s.* cuajo, leche agria cuajada.
clack [klæk] *s.* 1. ruido o golpe corto; triquitraque. 2. parloteo, cháchara. 3. castañeteo. *—v.i.* 1. parlotear, chacharear. 2. castañear. 3. cloquear (gallina).
clack valve, (hidr.) válvula de charnela, chapaleta.
clad [klæd] *v.t.* revestir (un metal con otro). *—pret. y p.p. de* **clothe.**
cladding ['klædɪŋ] *s.* (elec., mec.) revestimiento metálico.
cladocera [klə'dɑsərə, B -'dɔs-] *s. pl.* (zool.) cladóceros.
cladode ['klædˌoʊd] **cladophyll** [-əˌfɪl] *s.* (bot.) cladodio.
claim [kleɪm] *v.t.* 1. reclamar, demandar, exigir, ej., *c. one's attention,* reclamar la atención de uno, *c. the prize,* reclamar el premio. 2. afirmar, alegar, sostener, mantener, ej., *he claimed to be the owner,* afirmó ser el dueño, *he claims that these figures are incorrect,* él sostiene que estas cifras son incorrectas. *—s.* 1. reclamación. 2. demanda, reclamo, exigencia; derecho, título (a algo), ej., *to assert one's c. to (vote,* etc.), hacer valer el derecho de uno al (voto, etc.), *to have a c. against,* tener motivo para reclamar contra. 3. denuncio (de una mina). 4. **to jump a c.,** apropiarse de una mina ya denunciada por otro.
claimable ['kleɪməbəl] *a.* reclamable.
claim agent, *s.* agente de reclamación.
claimant [-mənt] *s.* 1. (der.) reclamante, demandante, demandador. 2. pretendiente (al trono, etc.). 3. denunciante (de una mina).
claim check, *s.* comprobante.
clairvoyance [klɛr'vɔɪəns, klær-, B klɛə'-] *s.* clarividencia.
clairvoyant [-ənt] *a., s.* clarividente.

clam [klæm] *s.* 1. (zool.) almeja. 2. (fig.) chiticalla, arca cerrada. —*v.i.* recoger almejas (esp. cavando); **c. up,** (jer.) negarse a hablar, negarse a revelar algo.
clam, *var. de* **clamp.**
clamant ['kleɪmənt] *a.* 1. clamante, insistente. 2. urgente, apremiante.
clambake ['klæm͵beɪk] *s.* 1. merienda campestre (esp. en la playa, donde se cuecen almejas sobre piedras muy calientes). 2. reunión bulliciosa, mitin (político).
clamber ['klæmbər, B -bə] *v.i.* trepar a gatas, encaramarse, gatear.
clammily ['klæməlɪ] *adv.* de modo viscoso o húmedo.
clammy [-ɪ] *a.* 1. húmedo y frío. 2. viscoso, pegajoso.
clamor, (pr. G.B.) **clamour** ['klæmər, B -ə] *s.* 1. algarada, algarabía, vocerío. 2. clamoreo, clamor. 3. estruendo, fragor. —*v.i.* 1. gritar, vociferar. 2. (esp. con *for* o *against*) clamar, clamorear (por, contra).
clamorous [-ərəs] *a.* 1. clamoroso, bullicioso, tumultuoso. 2. vociferante.
clamp [klæmp] *s.* 1. abrazadera, grapa, laña. 2. tornillo de presión, tornillo de ajuste. 3. (mar.) durmiente, contradurmiente. 4. montón (de patatas cubiertas de tierra y paja, ladrillos para hornear, basura en jardines, etc.). —*v.t.* sujetar, afianzar con abrazadera, engrapar, lañar. —*v.i.* **c. down,** (jer.) ponerse severo, apretar las clavijas a.
clamp coupling, acoplamiento de abrazadera o de compresión.
clamp holder, sujetagrapa.
clamshell ['klæm͵ʃɛl] *s.* 1. concha de almeja. 2. cucharón de almeja, cucharón de doble pala.
clamshell bucket, cucharón de almeja, cucharón de mordazas.
clamshell dredge, draga de cucharón, draga a balde.
clan [klæn] *s.* 1. clan.
clandestine [klæn'dɛstən] *a.* clandestino, secreto, furtivo, subrepticio.
clandestinely [-lɪ] *adv.* clandestinamente.
clandestinity [͵klændəs'tɪnətɪ] *s.* clandestinidad.
clang [klæŋ] *s.* estruendo, estrépito, sonido metálico (de armas, campanas, trompetas, etc.); campanada; retumbo. —*v.t., v.i.* (hacer) sonar o retumbar (armas, trompetas, etc.).
clangor, (pr. G.B.) **clangour** ['klæŋər, -gər, B -ə, -gə] *s.* estruendo o retumbo continuo; estrépito; clangor.
clangorous [-ərəs, -gərəs] *a.* estruendoso, retumbante, estrepitoso.
clank [klæŋk] *s.* resonancia o ruido metálicos, chacoloteo (choque de metales, cadenas, etc.). —*v.t.* hacer chacolotear o resonar (metales, cadenas, etc.). —*v.i.* chacolotear, resonar.
clannish ['klænɪʃ] *a.* leal a su familia, grupo, etc.; unido, exclusivista.
clansman ['klænzmən] *s.* miembro de un clan.
clap [klæp] *s.* 1. ruido seco, estampido. 2. palmada, palmoteo, aplauso. 3. (jer., vulg.) gonorrea. 4. **c. of thunder,** trueno. —*v.t.* (*pret., p.p.* CLAPPED O CLAPT; *p.pr.* CLAPPING) 1. aplaudir. 2. batir, cerrar de golpe, golpear. 3. dar una palmada a, ej., *c.* (*someone*) *on the back,* dar una palmada a (alguien) en el hombro. 4. poner, meter o aplicar vigorosamente. 5. **c. eyes on,** poner ojos en, divisar; **c. in prison,** arrojar a la cárcel; **c. spurs to horse,** espolear al caballo. —*v.i.* aplaudir, dar palmadas, palmotear; **to c. shut,** cerrarse de golpe.
clapboard ['klæbərd, B 'klæp͵bɔd] *s.* tabla de chilla, tingladillo. —*v.t.* tinglar, cubrir con tablas de chilla.
clapboard house, casa hecha de tablillas.
clapper ['klæpər, B -ə] *s.* 1. palmoteador. 2. badajo (de campana). 3. carraca, matraca. 4. (mec.) chapaleta, válvula de bomba. 5. tarabilla, cítola. 6. tableta, tejoleta. 6. (jer.) lengua (de un charlatán). 7. castañuela.
claptrap ['klæp͵træp] *s.* 1. artificio para alcanzar populachería. 2. faramalla, música celestial.
claque [klæk] *s.* (teat.) claque, alabarderos, aplaudidores de oficio.
Clare [klɛr, B klɛə] *s.* (relig.) clarisa (monja).
clarence ['klærəns] *s.* carruaje, clarens.
clarendon [-əndən] *s.* (impr.) letra negrita de varios tamaños.
claret ['klærət] *s.* 1. clarete; vino tinto claro. 2. (jer.) sangre.
clarificant [klæ'rɪfəkənt] *s.* (quím.) clarificador.
clarification [͵klærəfɪ'keɪʃən] *s.* clarificación, esclarecimiento.
clarify ['klærə͵faɪ] *v.t.* (*pret., p.p.* CLARIFIED; *p.pr.* CLARIFYING) clarificar, aclarar, poner en claro, esclarecer. —*v.i.* clarificarse, aclararse.
clarinet [͵klærə'nɛt] *s.* (mús.) clarinete.
clarinetist, clarinettist [-əst] *s.* clarinetista, clarinete.
clarion ['klærɪən] *s.* 1. (mús.) clarín (instrumento y registro de órgano). 2. clarinada. —*a.* fuerte y claro, estentóreo, sonoro.
clarionet [͵klærɪə'nɛt] *s. var. de* **clarinet.**
clarity ['klærətɪ] *s.* claridad.
clarkia ['klɑrkɪə, B 'klɑkjə] *s.* (bot.) variedad de vellorita o primavera.
clary ['klɛrɪ, B 'klɛərɪ] *s.* (bot.) amaro, esclarea, bácara.
clash [klæʃ] *v.i.* 1. chocar, entrechocarse, encontrarse. 2. discordar, estar en conflicto. —*v.t.* batir, golpear, hacer chocar. —*s.* 1. choque, colisión, encontronazo. 2. estruendo, fragor (de colisión, de armas que entrechocan, de campanas tañidas a la vez). 3. choque, encuentro, contienda. 4. conflicto, discordia (de opiniones, personalidades, etc.).
clasp [klæsp, B klɑsp] *s.* 1. broche, hebilla, corchete, grapa, abrazadera, presilla. 2. apretón (de manos). —*v.t.* 1. abrochar, encorchetar; enganchar. 2. agarrar. 3. estrechar, apretar (la mano). 4. abrazar.
clasp knife, navaja; navaja de muelle.
class [klæs, B klɑs] *s.* 1. clase. 2. condición, categoría, grado. 3. orden, linaje, género. 4. (E.U.) promoción (de alumnos). 5. elegancia, distinción, (alta) calidad. 6. honores (en universidad), ej., *to take* (*first, second*) *c.,* ganar honores (de primera, segunda categoría, en exámenes). 7. **no c.,** (jer.) muy inferior. —*a.* de calidad, de clase (Am.). —*v.t.* clasificar, calificar, ordenar.
class-conscious ['klæs͵kɑntʃəs, B 'klɑs-͵kɔnʃəs] *a.* que tiene conciencia de su clase social.
class-consciousness [-nəs] *s.* conciencia de clase social.
class distinction, diferencia entre clases.
classic ['klæsɪk] *a.* 1. clásico (arte, estilo, etc.). 2. típico (ejemplo, etc.). —*s.* 1. clásico, autor clásico, obra clásica (díc. de las letras o de la cultura griega y latina). 2. ejemplo típico.
classical [-ɪkəl] *a.* clásico.
classicalist [-əst] *s.* clasicista.
classically [-ɪ] *adv.* clásicamente.
classical music, música clásica.
classical scholar, erudito en lenguas clásicas.
classicism ['klæsə͵sɪzəm] *s.* clasicismo.
classicist [-sɪst] *s.* clasicista.
classicize [-͵saɪz] *v.t., v.i.* hacer clásico; imitar el estilo clásico.
classics ['klæsɪks] *s. pl.* estudios clásicos (griegos y latinos).
classifiable ['klæsə͵faɪəbəl] *a.* clasificable; calificable.
classification [͵klæsəfɪ'keɪʃən] *a.* clasificación.
classificatory ['klæsəfəkə͵tɔrɪ, B ͵klæs-'keɪtərɪ] *a.* clasificador.
classified ['klæsə͵faɪd] *a.* 1. clasificado. 2. (E.U.) secreto, reservado (documento, información, etc.).
classified advertisement, anuncio or aviso clasificado, anuncio breve, anuncio por palabras.
classifier [-͵faɪər, B -͵faɪə] *a.* clasificador.
classify [-͵faɪ] *v.t.* (*pret., p.p.* CLASSIFIED; *p.pr.* CLASSIFYING) clasificar, graduar, ordenar.
classis ['klæsəs] *s.* (*pl.* CLASSES [-͵iz]) junta directiva en ciertas iglesias reformadas.
class list, (educ.) lista de alumnos clasificados por nota.
classmate ['klæs͵meɪt, B 'klɑs-] *s.* compañero de clase, condiscípulo; (E.U.) compañero de promoción.
classroom [-͵rum, -͵rum] *s.* clase, aula, sala de clases.
class struggle, lucha de clases.
classy [-ɪ] *a.* (CLASSIER; CLASSIEST) (jer.) de alta calidad, superior, excelente, elegante.
clastic ['klæstɪk] *a.* 1. (geol.) clástico. 2. compuesto de fragmentos.
clathrate ['klæθ͵reɪt] *a.* (biol.) claturelino.
clatter ['klætər, B -ə] *v.i.* 1. chacolotear, chapalear, matraquear. 2. parlotear, paliquear, charlar. —*s.* 1. chacoloteo, chapaleo, matraqueo. 2. conmoción, alboroto, ruido, estruendo. 3. parloteo, gritería.
claudication [͵klɔdə'keɪʃən] *s.* claudicación, cojera.
clause [klɔz] *s.* 1. (der.) cláusula, artículo, condición, estipulación, inciso. 2. (gram.) oración, cláusula, frase.
claustral ['klɔstrəl] *a.* claustral, monástico.
claustrophobia [͵klɔstrə'foubɪə] *s.* claustrofobia.
clavate ['kleɪ͵veɪt] *a.* (bot., zool.) claviforme.
clavichord ['klævə͵kɔrd, B -͵kɔd] *s.* (mús.) clavicordio.
clavicle ['klævəkəl] *s.* (anat.) clavícula.
clavicorn ['klævə͵kɔrn, B -͵kɔn] *a.* (ento.) clavicornio, clavicorne.
clavicular [klæ'vɪkjələr, B -lə] *a.* (anat.) clavicular.
claviculate [-lət] *a.* (zool.) claviculado.
clavier [klə'vɪr, 'kleɪvɪər, B 'klævɪə] *s.* (mús.) 1. teclado. 2. [B klə'vɪə] clavicordio.
claviform ['klævə͵fɔrm, B -͵fɔm] *a.* (bot., zool.) claviforme.
claw [klɔ] *s.* 1. garra, garfa, tenaza, uña; pinza (de cangrejo, langosta, etc.). 2. oreja (de martillo). 3. (mec.) gancho, garfio, uña, diente. 4. (despec.) garra, mano. 5. arañazo. 6. (bot.) peciolo. 7. **to cut the claws of,** (fig.) cortar las uñas de, desarmar a (alguien). —*v.t., v.i.* 1. arañar, desgarrar, rasgar; arpar, gafar, rascar. 2. (mar.) barloventear, navegar de bolina.
claw bar, barra sacaclavos, sacaclavos de horquilla, desclavador, pata de cabra.
claw clutch, (mec.) embrague de garra.
claw coupling, (mec.) acoplamiento dentado, acoplamiento de garras.

claw hammer, 1. martillo de orejas. 2. (fam.) casaca, frac.
claw hatchet, hachuela de uña o de oreja.
clay [kleɪ] *s.* 1. arcilla, greda. 2. p. ext. barro, lodo, tierra. 3. (fig.) limo de la tierra, materia (del cuerpo humano). 4. pipa (hecha) de arcilla (para fumar). —*v.t.* engredar, filtrar en barro.
claybank ['kleɪˌbæŋk] *s.* caballo de color amarillento.
clayey ['kleɪɪ] *a.* arcilloso, gredoso.
clay ironstone, (min.) mineral de hierro arcilloso, arcilla ferruginosa.
clayish [-ɪʃ] *a.* arcilloso.
claymore [-ˌmɔr, B -ˌmɔ] *s.* claymor (espada escocesa de dos filos).
clay pan, capa de arcilla compacta.
clay pigeon, pichón de barro; platillo (para hacer blanco en el aire).
clay pipe, 1. tubería de arcilla, tubería de barro. 2. pipa de arcilla, pipa de tierra (para fumar).
clay pit, gredal, mina de arcilla.
clay stone, piedra arcillosa.
clean [klin] *a.* 1. limpio, aseado; puro, inocente, honesto. 2. puro (solución química, mercurio, etc.; placer, satisfacción, etc.); puro, limpio (piedra preciosa; estilo, conciencia, etc.). 3. despejado, desembarazado, sin malezas (campo, terreno, etc.). 4. claro, nítido. 5. parejo, liso, alisado (canto, borde, etc.). 6. bien proporcionado, de formas finas, de líneas elegantes, ej., *a c. ship,* una nave de líneas elegantes. 7. en blanco (papel, hoja). 8. libre, exento, ej., *c. timber,* madera libre o exenta de nudos. 9. libre de radiactividad. 10. apropiado, decente (chiste, cuento, etc.). 11. completo, radical (cambio, rompimiento, etc.). 12. (dep.) diestro, hábil (jugada, etc.). 13. (bíbl.) sano, limpio de impurezas (carne de animal). 14. (jer.) no armado, sin arma (oculta en el cuerpo). 15. (jer.) pelado, sin dinero. 16. **c. as a whistle,** limpio como una patena; **to come c.,** confesarlo todo; **to make a c. sweep,** limpiar radicalmente, hacer borrón y cuenta nueva. —*adv.* completamente, por completo, totalmente, enteramente. —*v.t.* 1. limpiar, asear, aderezar. 2. despojar; vaciar. 3. depurar (oro, aire, etc.). 4. dejar limpio (plato). 5. abrir, limpiar (un pollo, pescado, etc.). 6. (jer., gen. con *out*) pelar, dejar pelado (a jugador). 7. **c. oneself,** limpiarse, asearse; **c. out,** dejar vacío; eliminar, expulsar, expeler; agotar (mercaderías el público); **c. up,** ganarse (una fortuna, etc.); dejar (completamente) limpio, limpiar a fondo; erradicar, extirpar (vicio, monopolio, etc.), eliminar; acabar con. —*v.i.* **c. house,** (fig.) poner en orden; (gen. con *up*) hacer la limpieza; **c. up,** asearse; ganar mucho dinero; **c. up after (someone),** limpiar las cosas sucias dejadas por (alguien).
clean bill of health, patente limpia de sanidad; (fig.) aprobación incondicional.
clean-cut ['klin'kʌt] *a.* perfilado nítidamente; bien definido; claro; de aspecto sano (joven, etc.), limpio.
cleaner [-ər, B -ə] *s.* 1. tintorero, lavandero. 2. limpiador, quitamanchas. 3. **to be taken to the cleaners,** (jer.) quedarse pelado (a causa de engaño, estafa, compromiso).
cleanhanded [-'hændəd] *a.* de manos limpias, probo, intachable, honrado.
cleaning [-ɪŋ] *s.* limpieza, aseo, limpiadura.
cleaning fluid, líquido quitamanchas.
cleaning rag, trapo o paño para limpiar.
cleaning woman, dentrodera.
clean-limbed [-'lɪmd] *a.* bien proporcionado, de miembros bien formados.
cleanliness ['klɛnlɪnəs] *s.* aseo, limpieza, pulcritud.
cleanly [-lɪ] *a.* (CLEANLIER; CLEANLIEST) limpio (por hábito), aseado, pulcro. — ['klin-] *adv.* limpiamente, nítidamente.
cleanness ['klinnəs] *s.* limpieza, aseo.
cleanse [klɛnz] *v.t.* limpiar; depurar, purificar, purgar, expurgar, liberar (de); (bíbl.) curar (al leproso, etc.).
cleanser ['klɛnzər, B -ə] *s.* limpiador, purificador; evacuante, purgante.
clean-shaven ['klin'ʃeɪvən] *a.* bien afeitado.
cleanup [-ˌʌp] *s.* 1. limpieza, limpiadura. 2. erradicación, eliminación. 3. (jer.) ganancia grande.
clear [klɪr, B klɪə] *a.* 1. claro (luz, día, cielo, color, sonido, texto, palabra, argumento, etc.). 2. diáfano, lúcido, transparente. 3. (con *of*) libre (de penas, cuidados, deudas, obstáculos, etc.). 4. completo, entero, ej., *a c. four meters,* cuatro metros completos. 5. con *on*) convencido, seguro, cierto. 6. abierto, libre, despejado, descampado (terreno, camino, etc.). 7. (com.) neto, líquido, sin pérdida ni reducción. 8. claro, evidente, patente. 9. (der.) seguro, limpio (ej., título). 10. **c. as mud,** completamente oscuro o incomprensible (explicación, teoría, etc.); **c. of,** libre de; **the coast is c.,** no hay moros en la costa. —*adv.* 1. claro, claramente, con claridad. 2. enteramente, completamente. 3. aparte, sin tocar. 4. **to speak loud and c.,** hablar fuerte y claramente; **to stand c.,** estar aparte, mantenerse aparte; **to steer c. (of),** evitar. —*v.t.* 1. aclarar, clarificar; limpiar, depurar. 2. absolver, exonerar (de culpa, sospecha, etc.). 3. limpiar, remover (obstáculos, estorbo, etc.). 4. despejar (camino, sala, etc.), desembarazar, desatorar (vía, conducto, etc.), limpiar, rozar, desbrozar (terreno); desenredar (cable, cordón, etc.). 5. desocupar, evacuar (cuarto, etc.). 6. salvar (obstáculo), pasar por encima de, saltar; evitar, pasar de lado. 7. ganar o sacar (cierta suma) en neto. 8. (com.) saldar, liquidar (cuenta, deuda); satisfacer (hipoteca). 9. (com.) realizar, rematar (saldos de mercaderías). 10. pasar, aprobar (artículo para publicación, proposición, cheque, etc.). 11. pasar, compensar (cheque por banco); pasar por (aduana, legislatura, comité, etc.); despachar (*mercancías en la aduana*). 12. (mar.) franquear (una embarcación). 13. (aer.) dar permiso a, autorizar (avión para que aterrice, despegue, etc.). 14. (bridge) establecer (un palo). 15. **c. away,** limpiar, despejar; quitar (obstáculo, la mesa); **c. (someone) for (confidential work, etc.),** aprobar (a alguien) para participar en (trabajo confidencial, etc.); **c. land,** desmontar, preparar (terreno) para el cultivo; **c. (an equation) of fractions,** quitar los denominadores (de una ecuación); **c. off,** librarse de, desembarazarse de, liquidar (obligación, deuda, etc.); **c. one's mind (of strange ideas, etc.),** quitarse uno de la cabeza (ideas raras, etc.); **c. one's name,** dejar uno su reputación; **c. one's throat,** aclarar la voz, carraspear; **c. out,** limpiar, vaciar, desocupar; **c. out of,** echar de, desalojar de; **c. out of the way,** quitar del medio, eliminar; **c. the air,** renovar el aire; (fig.) despejar sospechas, aclarar malentendidos; **c. the decks for action,** despejar las cubiertas, alistar el buque para el combate, hacer zafarrancho de combate; **c. the table,** levantar (o alzar) la mesa; **c. the way,** abrir camino; **c. through,** pasar por, despachar en (la aduana); **c. up,** aclarar, esclarecer, dilucidar; arreglar, poner en orden. —*v.i.* 1. aclararse, volverse limpio (agua, etc.). 2. (fig.) serenarse, calmarse (ej., expresión); volverse (más) claro (perspectivas, situación, etc.). 3. derretirse (la nieve); disiparse (la muchedumbre); desaparecer (síntoma). 4. venderse (mercadería). 5. (com.) pasar por banco (ej., un cheque). 6. (mar.) ganar franquía (una embarcación). 7. **c. away,** disiparse, disolverse (niebla, humo, etc.); largarse, marcharse; **c. off,** disolverse, derretirse; (imper.) ¡largo de aquí!; **c. out,** irse, marcharse (de un lugar); **c. through,** pasar por (la aduana); ser aprobado por (comité, autoridades, etc.); **c. up,** despejarse (el cielo, el tiempo); serenarse el tiempo. —*s.* claro, espacio libre; **in the c.,** libre de sospecha; a salvo, fuera de peligro; en (texto) claro; medido por dentro.
clearance ['klɪrəns, B 'klɪər-] *s.* 1. despejo, evacuación; desmonte. 2. compensación (de cheques). 3. permiso, autorización. 4. aprobación, habilitación (para un trabajo confidencial, etc.). 5. realización, liquidación (de saldos de mercaderías). 6. despacho aduanero, franquía (de una embarcación); certificado de franquía. 7. luz, espacio libre (entre dos cuerpos). 8. (mot.) juego, espacio muerto; (f.c.) paso libre, sección libre; (aut.) despejo, luz.
clearance papers, certificación del pago de derechos de aduana.
clearance point, (f.c.) punto de gálibo, punto de cartabón.
clearance ring, anillo de desgaste (en bombas).
clearance sale, venta de realización, liquidación.
clear-cut ['klɪr'kʌt, B 'klɪə'-] *a.* bien definido, bien delineado; claro, inequívoco.
clear-eyed [-'aɪd, B -'raɪd] *a.* discernidor, perspicaz, penetrante.
clear-headed [-'hɛdəd, B 'klɪə'-] *a.* racional, inteligente, perspicaz.
clearing ['klɪrɪŋ, B 'klɪər-] *s.* 1. claro (en un bosque). 2. desmonte, desbroce, roza. 3. compensación (bancaria de cheques, cuentas, etc.).
clearing house, 1. banco de liquidación, oficina de compensación. 2. centro distribuidor (esp. de información).
clearly ['klɪrlɪ, B 'klɪəlɪ] *adv.* claramente; evidentemente, sin duda; llanamente; abiertamente.
clearness [-nəs] *s.* claridad, perspicacia.
clear-sighted [-'saɪtəd] *a.* (fig.) perspicaz, discernidor.
clearstarch [-'stɑrtʃ, B -'stɑtʃ] *v.i., v.t.* almidonar (con una mezcla ligera de almidón, sin añil).
clear track, vía libre.
cleat [klit] *s.* 1. cuña, calza, calce. 2. (mar.) cornamusa; tojino. 3. (carp.) listón, travesero, abrazadera. —*v.t.* 1. calzar, acuñar, poner calce a. 2. enlistonar, entablillar.
cleat insulator, presilla aislante, mordaza aisladora, abrazadera-aislador.
cleavable ['klivəbəl] *a.* hendible.
cleavage [-vɪdʒ] *s.* 1. hendedura, resquebrajadura, división. 2. espacio entre los senos de una mujer. 3. (fig.) división, separación, desunión. 4. (quím.) desdoblamiento, descomposición. 5. (biol.) segmentación. 6. (geol.) clivaje.
cleave [kliv] *v.i.* (*pret., p.p.* CLEAVED O CLOVE [kloʊv] O CLAVE [kleɪv]; *p.pr.* CLEAVING) pegarse, adherirse, unirse; ser leal.
cleave [kliv] *v.t.* (*pret.* CLEFT [klɛft] CLEAVED O CLOVE [kloʊv]; *p.p.* CLEFT, CLEAVED O CLOVEN ['kloʊvən]; *p.pr.* CLEAVING). 1. hender (las aguas un barco, el aire una flecha o avión; las nubes el sol, etc.); abrir (un sendero, camino, etc.); penetrar, abrirse paso; rajar. 2. (fig.) partir, dividir, separar (en grupos, etc.); partir (el corazón). 3. **c. asunder,** partir en dos. —*v.i.* henderse, rajarse, partirse.

cleaver ['klivər, B -və] *s.* 1. cuchilla de carnicero. 2. hendedor, partidor. 3. hacha, destral.
cleavers [-vərz, B -vəz] *s. pl.* (*sing. en const.*) (bot.) presera, amor de hortelano, cuajaleche.
cleek [klik] *s.* (golf) maza de palo largo con cabeza de hierro larga y estrecha.
clef [klɛf] *s.* (mús.) clave (símbolo que antecede las notas en el pentagrama).
cleft [klɛft] (*pret. y p.p. de* CLEAVE) *a.* 1. hendido, rajado, agrietado, partido. 2. (bot.) hendido (ej., una hoja en forma lobulada). —*s.* hendidura, raja, grieta, fisura.
cleft palate, (med.) fisura palatina o del paladar.
cleistogamic [ˌklaɪstə'gæmɪk] **cleistogamous** [klaɪ'stɑgəməs, B -'stɔg-] *a.* (bot.) cleistógamo.
clematis ['klɛmətɪs, klə'mætəs, B 'klɛmət-] *s.* (bot.) clemátide.
clemency ['klɛmənsɪ] *s.* clemencia, piedad, indulgencia, misericordia.
clement [-ənt] *a.* clemente, benigno, indulgente, misericordioso.
clench [klɛntʃ] *v.t.* 1. agarrar firmemente; cerrar, apretar (puño, dientes). 2. remachar, redoblar (la punta de un clavo ya introducido). —*s.* agarro, apretadura.
Cleopatra [ˌkliə'pætrə] *s.* (hist.) Cleopatra, reina de Egipto.
clepsydra ['klɛpsɪdrə] *s.* (*pl.* CLEPSYDRAE [-ˌdri] o CLEPSYDRAS) clepsidra, reloj de agua.
cleptomania, *var. de* **kleptomania.**
clerestory, clearstory ['klɪrˌstɔrɪ, B 'klɪəstərɪ] *s.* (arq.) 1. triforio. 2. galería.
clergy ['klɜrdʒɪ, B 'klɜdʒɪ] *s.* clero, clerecía.
clergyman [-mən] *s.* clérigo, sacerdote, cura; pastor (protestante).
cleric ['klɛrɪk] *s.* clérigo. —*a.* clerical.
clerical [-ɪkəl] *a.* 1. clerical; eclesiástico. 2. de oficina, del personal, ej., *c. error,* error de oficina (cometido por un empleado), *c. duties,* deberes del personal. —*s.* 1. clérigo. 2. (*pl.*) (fam.) traje de clérigo, atuendo de sacerdote.
clerical collar, alzacuello (de los clérigos).
clericalism [-ˌɪzəm] *s.* clericalismo.
clericalist [-əst] *s.* clerical.
clerical work, trabajo de oficina.
clerihew ['klɛrɪˌhju] *s.* verso cómico (en gen. de cuatro líneas).
clerisy ['klɛrəsɪ] *s.* (la) intelectualidad, conjunto de los literatos y eruditos.
clerk [klɜrk, B klɑk] *s.* 1. oficinista, empleado de oficina; secretario. 2. dependiente, empleado de tienda, vendedor. 3. escribano; escribiente, amanuense. 4. clérigo. —*v.i.* trabajar como empleado oficinista.
clerkship ['klɜrkʃɪp, B 'klɑk-] *s.* condición de empleado; puesto de empleado; (der.) escribanía.
clever ['klɛvər, B -ə] *a.* 1. hábil, diestro, listo, mañoso. 2. avisado, inteligente; ingenioso.
cleverly [-lɪ] *adv.* 1. hábilmente, ingeniosamente. 2. inteligentemente.
cleverness [-nəs] *s.* 1. habilidad, destreza, maña. 2. inteligencia, ingenio.
clevis ['klɛvəs] *s.* abrazadera, horquilla, grillete.
clevis bolt, pasador roscado de chaveta.
clew [klu] *s.* 1. ovillo, bola (de hilo o cordel). 2. (gen. **clue**) indicio, pista (que puede dar la solución de un problema o misterio). 3. (mar.) puño de escota; bolina de coy. —*v.t.* (*pret., p.p.* CLEWED o CLUED; *p.pr.* CLEWING, CLUEING o CLUING) 1. enrollar, ovillar, hacer una bola u ovillo. 2. indicar, apuntar, dar una pista. 3. (con *up* o *down*) (mar.) cargar (una vela).
clew line, (mar.) chafaldete.
cliché [klɪ'ʃeɪ, B 'kliʃeɪ] *s.* 1. (impr.) cliché, clisé, grabado. 2. (fig.) frase gastada.
click [klɪk] *s.* 1. golpecito, ruido ligero. 2. piñoneo (de armas de fuego). 3. chasquido (de la lengua). 4. (fon.) clic (sonido producido por succión bucal). 5. tecleo (de la máquina de escribir). —*v.t.* 1. dar un golpecito a algo. 2. chascar (la lengua). 3. **c. one's heels,** chocar los talones (al cuadrarse). —*v.i.* 1. piñonear (armas de fuego). 2. salir bien, tener éxito. 3. hacer tictac. 4. entenderse o llevarse bien (con otra persona).
click beetle, (ento.) escarabajo de resorte.
client ['klaɪənt] *s.* cliente, parroquiano; cliente (de un abogado u otro profesional).
clientele [ˌklaɪən'tɛl, ˌkliˌɑn-, B -'teɪl] *s.* clientela, parroquianos (en conjunto).
cliff [klɪf] *s.* risco, farallón, peñasco, despeñadero.
cliff dweller, 1. morador de los barrancos, antiguo indio norteamericano que habitaba en cuevas de barrancos rocosos. 2. (jer.) inquilino de un gran edificio de departamentos.
cliff-hanger ['klɪfˌhæŋər, B -ə] *s.* 1. melodrama o aventuras en serie (cuyos episodios terminan en circunstancias críticas). 2. competencia tan reñida que su desenlace es incierto hasta el final.
climacteric [klaɪ'mæktərɪk, ˌklaɪˌmæk'tɛr-] *a.* climatérico, crítico. —*s.* 1. crisis. 2. (med.) período crítico; menopausia, climaterio.
climactic [klaɪ'mæktɪk] *a.* culminante, decisivo; supremo.
climate ['klaɪmət] *s.* clima.
climatic [klaɪ'mætɪk] *a.* climático, del clima.
climatological [ˌklaɪmətəl'ɑdʒɪkəl, B -'ɔdʒ-] *a.* climatológico.
climatology [-'tɑlədʒɪ, B -'tɔl-] *s.* climatología, tratado de los climas.
climax ['klaɪˌmæks] *s.* 1. (ret., teat., med., lit.) clímax. 2. clímax, punto culminante, culminación. —*v.t., v.i.* culminar, llevar o llegar a la culminación.
climb [klaɪm] *v.i.* 1. escalar, ascender, subir, trepar. 2. ascender lentamente (sol, aeroplano, etc.), elevarse (social, moral o intelectualmente). 3. **to c. down,** bajar; (fig.) volverse atrás, desistir; **to c. up,** empinar. —*v.t.* subir, escalar, trepar. —*s.* 1. subidero, trepador (de cerros, escaleras, árboles, etc.). 2. escalada, escalamiento, trepa. 3. ascenso, subida.
climber ['klaɪmər, B -mə] *s.* 1. trepador, escalador. 2. arribista. 3. trepadera, garfio de trepa. 4. (orn.) trepador. 5. (bot.) trepadora, enredadera.
climb indicator, (aer.) indicador de régimen ascensional, ascensómetro.
climbing angle, (avia.) ángulo de ascenso, ángulo ascensional.
climbing irons, trepadoras, garfios de trepar, arpeos de pie.
climbing plant, planta trepadora, enredadera.
climbing rope, cuerda de trepar, cuerda de nudos.
climbing speed, (aer.) velocidad de subida, velocidad ascensional, velocidad de toma de altura.
clime [klaɪm] *s.* (poét.) clima; región.
clinch [klɪntʃ] *v.t.* 1. remachar, roblar (la punta de un clavo). 2. agarrar firmemente, fijar, afianzar, abrazar; apretar (puño, dientes). 3. concluir, finiquitar (tratado, venta, etc.), decidir (disputa), terminar con (asunto), confirmar (sospechas). 4. ganarse (título, puesto, etc.). 5. (mar.) atar (soga) con medio nudo. —*v.i.* 1. (boxeo) luchar cuerpo a cuerpo. 2. acapizarse. 3. (jer.) abrazarse (enamorados). —*s.* 1. remache; abrazadera. 2. (mar.) medio nudo. 3. conclusión, finiquito, término (de un tratado, argumento, venta, etc.). 4. (boxeo) forcejeo, lucha cuerpo a cuerpo. 5. (jer.) abrazo apasionado.
clincher ['klɪntʃər, B -tʃə] *s.* 1. rebotador, remachador. 2. clavo remachado. 3. argumento o hecho decisivo. 4. (aut.) neumático de talón.
clinching [-tʃɪŋ] *s.* remachado o robladura; (mar.) solapadura.
cling [klɪŋ] *v.i.* (*pret., p.p.* CLUNG [klʌŋ]; *p.pr.* CLINGING) 1. asirse, agarrarse, adherirse, pegarse. 2. (fig.) pegarse, aficionarse, mantenerse fiel (a un amigo, hábito, idea, etc.); persistir (en la memoria). 3. **c. together,** quedarse unidos o abrazados.
clingstone ['klɪŋˌstoʊn] *s.* fruto con carne pegada al hueso, esp. pavía, albérchigo, peladillo, violeto.
ClingWrap (TM) ['klɪŋˌwræp] *s.* film transparente.
clinic ['klɪnɪk] *s.* clínica, consultorio, dispensario.
clinical [-ɪkəl] *a.* 1. clínico. 2. analítico, desapasionado.
clinical chart, hoja clínica, gráfica individual de un enfermo.
clinical thermometer, termómetro clínico.
clinician [klɪ'nɪʃən] *s.* médico clínico.
clink [klɪŋk] *v.i.* retiñir, tintinear (vaso, objetos metálicos, etc. al chocarse). —*v.t.* hacer tintinear. —*s.* 1. tañido, tintineo, tintín. 2. (jer.) cárcel, celda, prisión. 3. **in the c.,** (jer.) en la cárcel.
clinker ['klɪŋkər, B -kə] *s.* 1. ladrillo vítreo; ladrillo refractario. 2. escoria. —*v.t.* escorificar, convertir en escoria.
clinker-built [-ˌbɪlt] *a.* (mar.) de tingladillo.
clinkstone ['klɪŋkˌstoʊn] *s.* (min.) piedra sonora, perlita, fonolita.
clinometer [klaɪ'nɑmətər, B -'nɔmɪtə] *s.* clinómetro.
clinquant ['klɪŋkənt] *s.* (ant.) oropel. —*a.* resplandeciente con oropel.
clip [klɪp] *s.* 1. grapa, pinza, sujetador (de papeles), sujetapapeles; abrazadera; (f.c.) presilla, planchuela (de rieles). 2. prendedor, broche. 3. cargador (de cartuchos). —*v.t.* (*pret., p.p.* CLIPPED; [klɪpt]; *p.pr.* CLIPPING) 1. agarrar, prender. 2. ceñir. 3. juntar con grapa.
clip [klɪp] *v.t.* (*pret., p.p.* CLIPPED; *p.pr.* CLIPPING) 1. cortar con tijeras, tijeretear; esquilar, trasquilar (ovejas, lana, etc.); cercenar; podar, mondar (ramos, hojas, seto vivo, etc.); recortar (artículos del periódico, cupones, etc.). 2. recortar, acortar. 3. acortar (palabras omitiendo letras o sílabas), omitir (letras). 4. (jer.) pegar, golpear. 5. (jer.) estafar (cobrando precios exorbitantes). 6. **c. one's wings,** (fig.) cortarle las alas a uno. —*v.i.* 1. hacer cortes o recortes. 2. ir o pasar con rapidez. —*s.* 1. tijeretada, tijeretazo; talla, recorte; esquileo, trasquila (de lana). 2. cortaúñas. 3. golpe seco. 4. paso rápido.
clipboard ['klɪpˌbɔrd, B -ˌbɔd] *s.* tablilla con sujetapapeles.
clip joint, (jer.) tugurio, restaurante o cabaret que cobra precios exorbitantes.
clipper [-ər, B -ə] *s.* 1. máquina cortadora de pelo; cortauñas. 2. cortador, trasquilador. 3. caballo muy rápido. 4. (mar., aer.) clíper, navío o avión rápidos.
clipping [-ɪŋ] *s.* 1. recorte (de un periódico). 2. (*pl.*) recortes.
clipsheet [-ˌʃit] *s.* (impr.) pliego de periódico impreso sólo por un lado (para facilitar el recorte y la reimpresión).
clique [klik, klɪk, B klik] *s.* pandilla, camarilla.
cliquish ['klikɪʃ, 'klɪk-, B 'klik-] *a.* camarillesco, exclusivista.
clitellum [klə'tɛləm] *s.* (*pl.* CLITELLA [-lə]) (zool.) clitelo.

clitoral ['klɪtərəl, 'klaɪt-] **clitoric** [klaɪ'tɔrɪk, klə-] *a.* (anat.) clitorídeo.
clitoris ['klɪtərəs, 'klaɪt-] *s.* (anat.) clítoris.
cloaca [kloʊ'eɪkə] *s.* (*pl.* CLOACAE [-ˌki, -ˌsi]) 1. cloaca, alcantarilla. 2. retrete. 3. (zool.) cloaca.
cloak [kloʊk] *s.* 1. capa, manto. 2. (fig.) cubierta, manto (de nieve, etc.). 3. (fig.) capa, manto, pretexto, excusa, ej., *under the c. of,* so capa de, con el pretexto de. —*v.t.* 1. encapar. 2. cubrir, esconder, disfrazar, disimular. —*v.i.* encaparse.
cloak-and-dagger ['kloʊkən'dægər, B -ə] *a.* de capa y espada, de espías y misterios (novela, drama).
cloakroom [-ˌrum, -ˌrʊm] *s.* guardarropa, ropería.
clobber ['klɑbər, B 'klɔbə] *v.t.* (jer.) 1. golpear sin piedad, zurrar. 2. vencer o derrotar abrumadoramente.
clobber ['klɑbər, B 'klɔbə] *s.* (jer., GB.) 1. ropa. 2. equipo.
clochard [klɔ'ʃɑr, B -'ʃɑ] *s.* (fr.) vagabundo.
cloche [kloʊʃ] *s.* 1. sombrero de mujer de forma acampanada. 2. campana para proteger plantas.
clock [klɑk, B klɔk] *s.* 1. reloj (que no es de pulsera o bolsillo). 2. cronómetro (para tomar el tiempo en carreras). 3. bordado, cuadrado (en las medias). 4. **to set the c. back,** (fig.) volver el reloj atrás. —*v.t.* 1. tomar el tiempo de, cronometrar (una carrera, un competidor, etc.). 2. registrar, ej., *c. in* (*out*) registrar la entrada (la salida) de (empleados en una oficina, obreros en una fábrica, etc.).
clock dial, c. face, esfera (del reloj), cuadrante.
clock meter, (elec.) contador de reloj.
clock watcher, empleado que mira mucho el reloj (esperando la hora de irse).
clockwise ['klɑkˌwaɪz, B 'klɔk-] *a., adv.* en el sentido de las manecillas del reloj.
clockwork [-ˌwɜrk, B -ˌwɜk] *s.* mecanismo de relojería; **like c.,** como un reloj, con precisión.
clod [klɑd, B klɔd] *s.* 1. terrón, gleba. 2. zoquete, simplón.
cloddish ['klɑdɪʃ, B 'klɔd-] *a.* pesado, insensible, torpe, rústico.
cloddy [-ɪ] *a.* 1. terregoso. 2. fornido y bajo, robusto (animal, esp. perro).
clodhopper [-ˌhɑpər, B -ˌhɔpə] *s.* 1. patán, rústico. 2. zapato basto, zueco.
clodpate ['klɑdˌpeɪt, B 'klɔd-] **clodpoll, clodpole** [-ˌpoʊl] *s.* simplón, mentecato, zoquete.
clog [klɑg, B klɔg] *s.* 1. traba. 2. (fig.) traba, obstáculo, impedimento. 3. zueco, chanclo. —*v.t.* (*pret., p.p.* CLOGGED; *p. pr.* CLOGGING) 1. trabar (un animal). 2. (fig.) trabar, obstaculizar, echar trabas a. 3. atascar, atorar, obstruir. —*v.i.* 1. atascarse, atorarse. 2. coagularse, espesarse. 3. bailar el zapateado.
clog dance, zapateado.
clogging ['klɑgɪŋ, B 'klɔg-] *s.* 1. atoramiento, atascamiento, atasco. 2. coagulación.
cloisonné [ˌklɔɪzən'eɪ, B ˌklwɑzə'neɪ] *s.* esmalte tabicado.
cloister ['klɔɪstər, B -stə] *s.* 1. claustro, convento, monasterio. 2. la clausura, la reclusión monástica. 3. (arq.) claustro. —*v.t.* 1. enclaustrar, encerrar, recluir. 2. (arq.) rodear con claustros.
cloistered [-stərd, B -stəd] *a.* 1. enclaustrado. 2. (fig.) recluido, solitario.
cloistral [-strəl] *a.* claustral.
clonal ['kloʊnəl] *a.* (biol.) de un clon, de una clona.
clone [kloʊn] (biol.) *s.* clona, clon. —*v.t.* reproducir agámicamente, reproducir asexualmente.
clonic ['kloʊnɪk, 'klɑn-, B 'klɔn-] *a.* (fisiol.) clónico.
clonism ['kloʊˌnɪzəm, 'klɑn-, B 'klɔn-] *s.* (fisiol.) clonismo.
clonus ['kloʊnəs] *s.* (fisiol.) clonus, clono.
close [kloʊz] *v.t.* 1. cerrar (puerta, ventana, ojos, boca, puño, cajón, casa, cuenta, etc.); cerrar, bloquear (una calle, un conducto, el paso, etc.); cerrar, clausurar (negocio, ciclo escolar, etc.). 2. tapar, obstruir (la vista, etc.). 3. concluir, terminar, finalizar (acto, representación, sesión, etc.). 4. cerrar, concluir, finiquitar (trato, negocio, etc.). 5. llenar, tapar (grietas, etc.). 6. juntar. 7. recorrer, cubrir (cierta distancia); acortar (distancia). 8. **c. down,** cerrar definitivamente, clausurar; **c. in,** encerrar, rodear, cercar; **c. one's days,** terminar sus días, morir; **c. one's eyes upon,** cerrar sus ojos ante, pasar por alto; **c. out,** excluir; liquidar (mercadería), vender; saldar (una cuenta); **c. ranks,** cerrar filas; **c. up,** llenar, rellenar; cerrar definitivamente; **c. up shop,** cerrar el negocio; cesar toda actividad. —*v.i.* 1. cerrarse. 2. terminar, concluirse. 3. (gen. con *with*) terminar diciendo. 4. acercarse, acortar distancias. 5. disminuirse (distancia). 6. (mil.) cerrar filas. 7. **c. down,** clausurarse, cerrarse definitivamente; **c. in,** acercarse rodeando; ir acortándose (días); **c. in on,** rodear, cercar (al enemigo); apoderarse de; **c. up,** cerrarse, clausurarse (negocio); quedar callado, rehusarse a hablar; **c. upon** (o **on**), agarrar, asir. —*s.* 1. fin, terminación, conclusión. 2. (mús.) coda. 3. **at the c. of day,** a la caída de la tarde. — [kloʊs] *a.* 1. cerrado. 2. estrecho, limitado, restringido. 3. pesado, sofocante (aire), mal ventilado (cuarto). 4. cerrado, denso, compacto, tupido, ej., *c. texture,* tejido tupido; apretado, ej., *c. writing,* letras apretadas. 5. prohibido, limitado, de veda. 6. secreto, ocultado, escondido. 7. callado, reservado. 8. cercano, próximo, inmediato, ej., *c. proximity,* proximidad inmediata. 9. íntimo, estrecho (amigo, relaciones, etc.). 10. exacto, preciso (razonamiento, argumentación, etc.), fiel (traducción, etc.). 11. estricto, riguroso (vigilancia, custodia, etc.). 12. detenido, profundo (estudio, conocimiento, etc.), asiduo (estudiante, etc.), minucioso (observador; copia; interrogatorio). 13. completo, total, ej., *this will need your c. attention,* esto requiere toda su atención (o su atención completa). 14. ajustado, ceñido, ej., *a close-fitting gown,* un vestido ajustado. 15. reñido (final, carrera, votación, etc.). 16. tacaño, mezquino. 17. (fon.) cerrada (vocal). 18. (com.) escaso (dinero). 19. (ajedrez) cerrado (juego, apertura). 20. **at c. quarters,** de cerca, cuerpo a cuerpo; **at c. range,** de cerca; a quemarropa, a boca de jarro; **so close,** tan acá. —*adv.* cerca, proximo a; **c. by,** cerca, en las cercanías; **c. to,** cerca de, próximo a; poco antes de, faltando poco para, ej., *c. to a hundred,* casi (o muy cerca de) cien, *c. to midnight,* poco antes de medianoche.
close call [kloʊs-] (fam.) salvación milagrosa; **to have a c. c.,** salvarse de milagro, escapar por un pelo.
close column, (mil.) columna cerrada.
close combat, combate cuerpo a cuerpo, combate a corta distancia.
close corporation, (com.) compañía propietaria.
close coupling, (elec.) acoplamiento estrecho o cerrado.
close-cropped ['kloʊsˌkrɑpt, B -ˌkrɔpt] *a.* trasquilimocho, pelado al rape.
closed [kloʊzd] *a.* 1. cerrado; clausurado. 2. concluido, terminado. 3. exclusivo, reservado. 4. vedada (temporada). 5. (fon.) cerrada (vocal).
closed chapter, asunto concluido.
closed circuit, (elec.) circuito cerrado (de televisión).
closed-circuit battery [-'sɜrkət-, B -'sɜkət-] (elec.) pila de circuito cerrado.
closed-circuit television, televisión en circuito cerrado.
closed-door ['dɔr-, B -'dɔ] *a.* a puerta cerrada.
closed-end ['kloʊzd'ɛnd] *a.* (com.) de capital limitado (compañía).
closedown ['kloʊzˌdaʊn] *s.* 1. caída (de la noche). 2. cierre (de fábrica, operaciones, etc.). 3. (rad., G.B.) fin de la transmisión, cierre de la transmisión.
closed sea, (der. intern.) mar enteramente jurisdiccional.
closed season, veda.
closed session, sesión a puerta cerrada.
closed shop, taller exclusivo, taller agremiado.
closefisted ['kloʊs'fɪstəd] *a.* tacaño, manicorto, agarrado, miserable.
close-fitting [-'fɪtɪŋ] *a.* ajustado, ceñido, estrecho (vestido, jubón, etc.).
close formation, (mil.) formación cerrada, columna cerrada.
close-grained [-'greɪnd] *a.* de grano fino o cerrado, tupido, compacto.
close-hauled [-'hɔld] *a.* (mar.) de bolina, ciñendo el viento.
close-lipped [-'lɪpt] *a.* taciturno, callado, reservado.
closely ['kloʊslɪ] *adv.* 1. cerca, de cerca; próximo; contiguamente. 2. estrechamente. 3. densamente (construido, poblado, etc.); apretadamente (escrito, impreso); (impr.) en forma compacta. 4. atentamente. 5. exactamente, fielmente; minuciosamente.
closemouthed [-'maʊðd] *a.* discreto, reservado, callado.
closeness [-nəs] *s.* 1. cercanía, proximidad; contigüidad. 2. densidad; estrechez, falta de ventilación. 3. exactitud, fidelidad (a un texto, etc.).
close order, (mil.) formación cerrada.
closeout ['kloʊzˌaʊt] *s.* (com.) liquidación (de existencias).
close quarters [kloʊs-] habitación estrecha, lugar estrecho.
closer ['kloʊzər, B -zə] *s.* 1. cerrador. 2. (arq.) remate. 3. pieza final (de un programa).
close range, corto alcance, corta distancia.
close-range ['kloʊs'reɪndʒ] *a.* a corta distancia (ataque, combate); a corto alcance (fuego).
close-range fighting, (mil.) lucha cuerpo a cuerpo.
close resemblance, gran semejanza, gran parecido.
close score, (mús.) partitura corta (para música vocal, con las voces femeninas juntadas en un pentagrama y las masculinas en otro).
close shave, 1. afeitada a ras (de piel). 2. (jer.) escape por un pelo, escape por un tris.
close study, aplicación.
closet ['klɑzət, B 'klɔ-] *s.* 1. cuarto pequeño; gabinete, clóset (Am.), placard (Am.). 2. armario empotrado, alacena. 3. retrete, excusado. 3. **to come out of the c.,** (jer.) anunciarse públicamente, darse a conocer; declararse abiertamente homosexual. —*v.t.* encerrar en un gabinete; **to be closeted with,** estar en consulta a puerta cerrada con (alguien).
closet, *a.* 1. privado (juramento, declaración, etc.). 2. de salón, teorético (político, estratega, filósofo, etc.). 3. (*gay*) tapado, encubierto, de closet.
closet drama, drama para la lectura (y no para representación), teatro leído.

closet gay, gay de tapada.
close time, veda (para cazar o pescar).
closet strategist, estratega de salón.
close-up ['kloʊsˌʌp] *s.* 1. (foto., cinem.) toma o vista de primer plano. 2. vista de cerca, escrutinio.
close vowel, (gram.) vocal cerrada.
close-woven ['kloʊs'woʊvən] *a.* estrechamente tejido, tupido, acipado.
closing price, (com.) precio de cierre, último precio (de la bolsa).
closure ['kloʊʒər, B -ʒə] *s.* 1. cierre, clausura, fin, conclusión. 2. limitación del (tiempo del) debate (en el parlamento). —*v.t.* limitar el debate (en el parlamento).
clot [klɑt, B klɔt] *s.* 1. coágulo; grumo. 2. conglomerado, grupo. 3. (fam.) zoquete, tonto. —*v.i.* (*pret., p.p.* CLOTTED; *p.pr.* CLOTTING) coagularse, cuajarse; engrumecerse, aburujarse. —*v.t.* coagular; aburujar.
cloth [klɔθ, klɑθ, B klɔθ] *s.* 1. paño, tela, género, lienzo. 2. mantel; paño, trapo. 3. traje talar, vestido clerical; **the c.,** el clero. 4. (enc.) tela. 5. **to cut the coat according to the c.,** ajustar los gastos a los ingresos; **to lay the c.,** poner la mesa.
clothbound ['klɔθˌbaʊnd, 'klɑθ-, B 'klɔθ-] *a.* encuadernado en tela.
clothe [kloʊð] *v.t.* (*pret., p.p.* CLOTHED [kloʊðd] o CLAD [klæd]; *p.pr.* CLOTHING) 1. vestir, arropar, cubrir. 2. investir, ej., *clothed with dignity,* investido de dignidad. 3. (fig.) envolver, ej., *her face was clothed in smiles,* su cara estaba envuelta en sonrisas. 4. (fig.) vestir, dar expresión a, ej., *c. ideas in words,* vestir ideas con palabras.
clothes [kloʊz, kloʊðz] *s. pl.* ropa, vestimenta, vestuario, indumentaria.
clothes basket, cesto para ropa.
clothesbrush ['kloʊzˌbrʌʃ, 'kloʊðz-] *s.* cepillo de ropa.
clothes closet, armario ropero.
clothes hanger, percha, perchero; colgador de ropa.
clotheshorse [-ˌhɔrs, B -ˌhɔs] *s.* 1. secarropa de travesaños. 2. (fig.) persona que presta excesiva atención a su atuendo y aliño personal.
clothesline [-ˌlaɪn] *s.* tendedero, tendalero, cuerda.
clothes moth, polilla de la ropa.
clothespin [-ˌpɪn] *s.* ganchito o pinza para tender ropa.
clothespress [-ˌprɛs] *s.* guardarropa, armario.
clothes tree, percha, perchero (de pie).
cloth filter, filtro de paño.
clothier ['kloʊðjər, B -ðɪə] *s.* ropero, pañero; el que vende ropa hecha.
clothing ['kloʊðɪŋ] *s.* 1. ropa, vestimenta, atuendo, ropaje. 2. (fig.) ropa, cobertura, cubierta.
cloth joint, bisagra de tela.
cloth yard, yarda de 36 pulgadas.
cloture ['kloʊtʃər, B -tʃə] *s.* limitación (del tiempo) del debate (en el parlamento). —*v.t.* limitar el debate (en el parlamento).
cloud [klaʊd] *s.* 1. nube. 2. nube, sombra (en piedras preciosas, líquidos, etc.). 3. nube, grupo (de pájaros, insectos, flechas, jinetes, etc.); multitud, sinnúmero. 4. nube, chal de lana ligera. 5. **in the clouds,** místico, irreal, imaginario (díc. de cosas); en las nubes, abstraído, distraído (díc. de personas); **on c. seven,** (jer.) sumamente feliz, completamente satisfecho; **under a c.,** triste, preocupado, deprimido; desacreditado, caído en desgracia, bajo sospecha; **under the c. of night,** protegido por la obscuridad de la noche. —*v.i.* (esp. con *up* o *over*) (lit. y fig.) 1. anublarse, nublarse. 2. tomar la forma de una nube. —*v.t.* (lit. y fig.) anublar, nublar, empañar, enturbiar, obscurecer.
cloudberry ['klaʊdˌbɛrɪ] *s.* (bot.) especie de frambueso.
cloudburst [-ˌbɜrst, B -ˌbɜst] *s.* aguacero, chaparrón, manga de agua.
cloud-capped ['klaʊdˌkæpt] *a.* coronado de nubes, envuelto en nubes.
cloud chamber, (fís.) cámara de niebla, cámara anublada.
cloudily [-əlɪ] *adv.* nebulosamente, indistintamente, obscuramente.
cloudiness [-ɪnəs] *s.* nebulosidad, nubosidad.
cloudland [-ˌlænd] *s.* (fig.) las nubes, mundo imaginario.
cloudless [-ləs] *a.* despejado, sin nubes, claro.
cloudlet [-lət] *s.* nube pequeña.
cloud point, (ópt.) punto de oscuridad.
cloud seeding, bombardeo de las nubes con hielo seco para producir lluvia.
cloudy ['klaʊdɪ] *a.* (CLOUDIER; CLOUDIEST) 1. nublado, nubloso, encapotado. 2. nebuloso, falto de lucidez, oscuro, sombrío. 3. nublado, turbio.
clough [klʌf] *s.* garganta, desfiladero.
clout [klaʊt] *s.* 1. paño, trapo. 2. chapa de hierro (para proteger la suela del zapato). 3. bofetada, golpe de mano. 4. (fam.) poder o influencia, esp. política. 5. blanco de paño (para tirar con arco). —*v.t.* 1. abofetear, golpear con fuerza. 2. remendar con parche, parchar.
clove [kloʊv] *pret. de* **cleave.**
clove [kloʊv] *s.* 1. (bot.) clavero. 2. clavo de especia. 3. diente (de ajo, chalote, etc.).
clove hitch, (mar.) ballestrinque.
cloven ['kloʊvən] *p.p. de* **cleave.** —*a.* hendido, rajado.
cloven-foot, cloven-footed [-'fʊtəd] *a.* 1. patihendido. 2. (fig.) diabólico, satánico, perverso, maligno.
cloven hoof, pata hendida; **to show the c. h.,** enseñar la oreja (o la pata), sacar el rabo, ponerse en evidencia.
clove pink, (bot.) clavel doble, clavel reventón.
clover ['kloʊvər, B -və] *s.* (bot.) trébol; **to be** (o **live**) **in c.,** vivir en la abundancia.
cloverleaf [-ˌlif] *s.* cruce de trébol (en las intersecciones de carreteras).
clown [klaʊn] *s.* payaso, bufón, gracioso, hazmerreír, mimo. —*v.i.* hacerse el gracioso, bufonear.
clownish ['klaʊnɪʃ] *a.* bufón, bufonesco, chocarrero.
clownishness [-nəs] *s.* disposición bufonesca; bufonería, payasada.
cloy [klɔɪ] *v.t.* saciar, hartar, hastiar, empalagar (a alguien de comida, placeres, etc.). —*v.i.* empalagar, causar hastío (comida, placeres, etc.).
club [klʌb] *s.* 1. porra, cachiporra, maza, garrote. 2. palo (de golf o hockey). 3. (naipes) (palo que corresponde al de bastos en la baraja española); (*pl.*) (palo de) tréboles. 4. club, círculo, asociación, peña. —*v.t.* (*pret., p.p.* CLUBBED; *p.pr.* CLUBBING) 1. aporrear; golpear (con la culata de un arma). 2. unir, agrupar, juntar. 3. contribuir (ideas, dinero) para un fin común. 4. (pr. mil. G.B.) desbaratar (un batallón, etc.). 5. (t. con *down*) (mar.) garrear (el ancla). —*v.i.* (gen. con *together*) reunirse, juntarse, agruparse; (con *with*) asociarse (con), aliarse (con).
clubbable, clubable ['klʌbəbəl] *a.* elegible como socio (de un club, asociación, etc.).
clubby ['klʌbɪ] *a.* 1. sociable, amigable. 2. exclusivista, hostil a los que no son miembros de un club o asociación.
club car, (f.c.) coche salon (con sillas movibles, escritorio, revistas, etc.).
club chair, butaca grande tapizada y cómoda.
clubfoot ['klʌb'fʊt] *s.* pie deforme.
clubhaul [-ˌhɔl] *v.t.* (mar.) virar por avante (el barco) fondeando el ancla de sotavento.
clubhouse [-ˌhaʊs] *s.* 1. casino, club. 2. cuarto de vestir (de un equipo atlético).
club-law [-'lɔ] *s.* la ley del más fuerte.
clubman [-mən, -ˌmæn] **clubwoman** [-'wʊmən] *s.* clubista, miembro de un club, adicto a la vida social.
club moss, (bot.) licopodio.
clubroom ['klʌbˌrum, -ˌrʊm] *s.* sala de reunión de un club.
club sandwich, emparedado gigante.
club soda, agua de seltz.
club steak, bistec pequeño.
cluck [klʌk] *s.* 1. cloqueo. 2. (jer.) simplón, bobalicón. —*v.i.* 1. cloquear. 2. chascar (con la lengua).
clue [klu] *s.* indicio, pista, (que puede dar la solución de un problema o misterio); **not to have a c.,** ignorar por completo, no tener la menor idea. —*v.t.* 1. dar una pista o indicio. 2. (fam.) (gen. con *in*) proveer (a alguien) con la información necesaria.
clue, *var. de* **clew.**
clueless ['kluləs] *a.* (fam., G.B.) desorientado; ignorante, estúpido.
clumber ['klʌmbər, B -bə] *s.* perro de aguas (del distrito de Clumber, Ingl.).
clump [klʌmp] *s.* 1. grupo (de árboles o arbustos), montón, masa; terrón. 2. pisada fuerte, andar pesado. —*v.i.* 1. pisar fuertemente, caminar torpemente. 2. amontonarse, amasarse. —*v.t.* amontonar, amasar.
clumsily ['klʌmzəlɪ] *adv.* torpemente, desmañadamente, sin discreción ni arte.
clumsiness [-zɪnəs] *s.* torpeza, desmaña.
clumsy ['klʌmzɪ] *a.* (CLUMSIER; CLUMSIEST) 1. torpe, desmañado. 2. desatinado. 3. chabacano, mal hecho, incómodo.
clung [klʌŋ] *pret., y p.p. de* **cling.**
clunk [klʌŋk] *s.* 1. sonido metálico sordo. 2. (fam.) golpe fuerte (físico o moral). 3. (jer.) persona tonta o estúpida.
clunker ['klʌŋkər, B -ə] *s.* (jer.) cacharro.
clupeid ['klupiəd] *s.* (ict.) clupeido.
cluster ['klʌstər, B -tə] *s.* racimo, ramo, ramillete; hato, manada, caterva (de ganado); enjambre (de abejas); multitud (de personas, de cosas); grupo. —*v.t.* agrupar, apiñar, amontonar. —*v.i.* arracimarse; amontonarse; **c. around,** apiñarse o reunirse en torno a.
cluster bomb, bomba de dispersión, bomba de racimo.
clustered column ['klʌstərd-, B -təd-] (arq.) haz de columnas, columnas agrupadas.
cluster pine, (bot.) pino rodeno, pinastro, pino marítimo.
clutch [klʌtʃ] *v.t.* asir, agarrar, empuñar fuertemente; embragar. —*v.i.* **c. at,** tratar de agarrar o de empuñar. —*s.* 1. garra (de ave, de fiera); (*pl.*) (despec.) garras, mano; (fig.) garras, poder. 2. agarro, asimiento. 3. nidada. 4. (mec.) embrague. 5. **to fall into the clutches** of, caer en las garras de; **to let** (o **throw**) **in the c.,** embragar, soltar el pedal de embrague.
clutch bag, pequeño bolso de mujer sin asas.
clutch bearing, (aut.) cojinete de desembrague.
clutter ['klʌtər, B -ə] *v.t.* (gen. con *up*) llenar desordenadamente, obstruir. —*v.i.* correr con ruido, correr atropelladamente, atropellarse. —*s.* 1. montón o masa confusa. 2. confusión, baraúnda, batahola, desorden.

Clydesdale ['klaɪdzˌdeɪl] *s.* (especie de) caballo percherón.
clypeus ['klɪpɪəs] *s.* (*pl.* CLYPEI [-ɪˌaɪ]) (ento.) clípeo.
clyster ['klɪstər, B -tə] *s.* (med.) clister, lavativa, enema. —*v.t.* aplicar un clister.
Clytemnestra [ˌklaɪtəm'nɛstrə] *s.* (mitol.) Clitemnestra, esposa de Agamenón, madre de Electra y Orestes.
cm. *abrev. de* **centimeter,** centímetro (cm.).
Cm *símb. de* **curium,** curio (Cm).
Cmdr. *abrev. de* **Commander,** comandante.
CN *abrev. de* **credit note,** nota de crédito.
c/o *abrev. de* **care of,** a cargo de (c/o).
Co *símb. de* **cobalt,** cobalto (Co).
Co. *símb. de* 1. **company,** compañía (Cía.). 2. **county,** condado.
CO *símb. de* 1. **commanding officer,** comandante, jefe. 2. **conscientious objector,** el que por razones de conciencia rehúsa cumplir con el servicio militar.
coacervate [koʊ'æsərˌveɪt, B -'æsəˌ-] *s.* (quím.) coacervado.
coacervation [-ˌæsər'veɪʃən, B -ˌæsə'-] *s.* (quím.) coacervación.
coach [koʊtʃ] *s.* 1. coche, carruaje, carroza. 2. (f.c.) vagón, coche ordinario de viajeros. 3. asiento de segunda clase (tren, avión, etc.). 4. maestro particular; (dep.) entrenador. —*v.t.* preparar (a un estudiante); entrenar (a un equipo deportivo, etc.). —*v.i.* viajar en coche.
coach box, pescante (del cochero).
coach dog, perro dálmata.
coacher ['koʊtʃər, B -ə] *s.* entrenador.
coach house, cochera (garaje).
coaching ['koʊtʃɪŋ] *s.* 1. instrucción (esp. particular); preparación (para un examen, etc.). 2. (dep.) entrenamiento.
coachman ['koʊtʃmən] *s.* cochero, auriga (poét.).
coachwhip [-ˌhwɪp, -ˌwɪp] *s.* látigo, manopla.
coact [koʊ'ækt] *v.i.* actuar conjuntamente, obrar de concierto, cooperar.
coaction [-'ækʃən] *s.* coacción; acción concertada.
coactive [-'æktɪv] *a.* coactivo; cooperante.
coadjutant [-'ædʒətənt] *a.* coadyuvante, auxiliar.
coadjutor [koʊ'ædʒətər, ˎkoʊə'dʒutər, B koʊ'ædʒʊtə] *s.* 1. coadjutor, ayudante. 2. (relig.) coadjutor.
coadunate [-'ædʒənət, -ˌneɪt] *a.* (fisiol., bot.) coadunado, unido.
coadunation [-ˌædʒə'neɪʃən] *s.* (fisiol., bot.) coadunación.
coagent [ˌkoʊ'eɪdʒənt] *s.* coagente, cooperador.
coagulability [koʊˌægjələ'bɪlətɪ] *s.* coagulabilidad.
coagulable [-'ægjələbəl] *a.* coagulable.
coagulant [-lənt] *s.* coagulante.
coagulase [-ˌleɪs] *s.* (quím.) coagulasa.
coagulate [koʊ'ægjələt, -ˌleɪt] *a.* coagulado. — [-ˌleɪt] *v.t.* coagular, cuajar. —*v.i.* coagularse, cuajarse.
coagulating bath [-ˌleɪtɪŋ-] (quím.) baño de precipitación, baño de coagulación.
coagulation [-ˌægjə'leɪʃən] *s.* coagulación; coágulo; cuajamiento.
coagulator [-'ægjəˌleɪtər, B -tə] *a.* (quím.) coagulante.
coagulum [-'ægjələm] *s.* (*pl.* COAGULA [-lə]) coágulo, masa o substancia coagulada.
coal [koʊl] *s.* carbón, hulla; carbón de piedra, carbón mineral, antracita; brasa; **to blow the coals,** avivar la llama (de una pasión, etc.); **to call, haul** o **drag over the coals,** reprender severamente; **to carry coals to Newcastle,** llevar hierro a Vizcaya. —*v.t.* 1. proveer de carbón (un barco, etc.). 2. carbonear. —*v.i.* proveerse de carbón (barco, etc.).
coalbin ['koʊlˌbɪn] *s.* carbonera, arcón carbonero.
coal black, completamente negro, negro como el carbón.
coal bunker, carbonera, arcón carbonero.
coal car, vagón carbonero.
coal dust, cisco o polvo de carbón.
coaler ['koʊlər, B -lə] *s.* tren o barco carbonero.
coalesce [ˌkoʊə'lɛs] *v.i.* conglutinarse, juntarse, aliarse, unirse, soldarse.
coalescence [-əns] *s.* coalescencia, conglutinación, coalición, unificación, unión (de partidos políticos, etc.).
coalescent [-ənt] *a.* coalescente.
coalfield ['koʊlˌfild] *s.* 1. yacimiento de carbón. 2. (*gen. pl.*) minas de carbón.
coal gas, gas de hulla o de carbón.
coaling ['koʊlɪŋ] *s.* toma de carbón (de buques).
coaling station, estación carbonera.
coalition [ˌkoʊə'lɪʃən] *s.* coalición, confederación, liga, alianza; unión, fusión.
coalitionist [-əst] *s.* coalicionista.
coal measures, (geol.) formación carbonífera, rocas carboníferas.
coal mine, mina de carbón.
coal oil, aceite de carbón, nafta, kerosén.
coalpit ['koʊlˌpɪt] *s.* mina de carbón, carbonera.
coal scuttle, cubo para carbón.
coal tar, alquitrán mineral o de hulla; **c. t. pitch,** brea de hulla.
coaming ['koʊmɪŋ] *s.* (mar.) brazola (de escotilla).
coaptation [koʊˌæp'teɪʃən] *s.* (cir.) coaptación.
coarse [kɔrs, B kɔs] *a.* 1. grueso (arena, grava; serrucho, criba, etc.); burdo, basto, ordinario, grosero (paño, lana, etc.); áspero (cutis, piel). 2. tosco, crudo, ordinario, común. 3. rudo, vulgar, soez, grosero (vocabulario). 4. agudo, estridente, desapacible (voz, sonido).
coarse file, (mec.) lima de desbastar.
coarse-grained ['kɔrs'greɪnd, B 'kɔs-] *a.* de grano grueso; (fig.) crudo, sin delicadeza.
coarse grinding, (mec.) esmerilado basto.
coarsely [-lɪ] *adv.* toscamente, groseramente.
coarsen ['kɔrsən, B 'kɔs-] *v.t.* engrosar, engruesar, hacer grueso; vulgarizar. —*v.i.* volverse grueso, burdo o vulgar.
coarseness ['kɔrsnəs, B 'kɔs-] *s.* aspereza; tosquedad, vulgaridad, ordinariez.
coarse sieve, (quím.) criba ordinaria.
coast [koʊst] *s.* 1. costa, litoral. 2. (E.U., Can.) deslizadero (para trineo, tobogán, etc.); deslizamiento. 3. **the c. is clear,** no hay moros en la costa. —*v.i.* 1. costear, navegar a lo largo de la costa. 2. deslizarse (en un trineo, tobogán, etc.); correr cuesta abajo (en bicicleta sin pedalear), correr por inercia, marchar por gravedad, correr sin motor. —*v.t.* (mar.) costear.
coastal ['koʊstəl] *a.* costanero, costero, costeño.
coast artillery, (mil.) artillería de costa.
coaster ['koʊstər, B -tə] *s.* 1. barco de cabotaje. 2. mesita rodante (para servir bebidas). 3. portavasos.
coaster brake, freno de rueda libre.
coast guard, guardacostas, servicio costanero; resguardo marítimo.
coastguardsman [-ˌgɑrdzmən, B -ˌgɑdz-] **coastguardman** [-ˌgɑrdmən, B -ˌgɑd-] *s.* guardacostas.
coastland [-ˌlænd] *s.* litoral, costa.
coastline [-ˌlaɪn] *s.* línea costera, costa, litoral.
coastward [-wərd, B -wəd] *a.* dirigido hacia la costa. —*adv.* hacia la costa.
coastwards [-wərdz, B -wədz] *adv.* hacia la costa.
coastwise [-ˌwaɪz] *a.* de cabotaje, a lo largo de la costa, costanero. —*adv.* a lo largo de la costa.
coat [koʊt] *s.* 1. americana, chaqueta, saco (Am.); abrigo, gabán, sobretodo. 2. (fig.) capa, manto, cubierta. 3. piel, pelo, pelaje, lana (de un animal). 4. capa, mano (de pintura, etc.). 5. **to dust one's c.,** sacudirle las pulgas a uno, apalear a uno; **to turn one's c.,** (fig.) volver (la) casaca, cambiar de partido; **to wear the king's c.,** servir al rey (como soldado). —*v.t.* 1. vestir con chaqueta. 2. dar una capa o mano de pintura a; cubrir, tapar, revestir.
coated ['koʊtəd] *a.* 1. cubierto, revestido, bañado. 2. saburroso (la lengua). 3. impregnado (tela, etc.). 4. (impr.) estucado, cuché (papel).
coatee [koʊ'ti, 'koʊti] *s.* chaquetilla, casaquilla.
coat hanger, colgador, percherо.
coati [koʊ'ɑtɪ, ˎkoʊə'ti] **coatimundi** [koʊ'ɑtɪ'mʌndɪ] *s.* (zool.) coatí.
coating ['koʊtɪŋ] *s.* 1. revestimiento, capa, mano (de pintura, etc.). 2. (sastrería) tela para confeccionar abrigos.
coat of arms, escudo de armas.
coat of mail, cota de malla.
coat room, guardarropa.
coattail [-ˌteɪl] *s.* 1. faldón. 2. (*pl.*) faldones, faldillas (de un frac). 3. **on the coattails of,** a raíz de cierto suceso; **to ride on someone's coattails,** aprovecharse del éxito de otra persona.
coauthor [koʊ'ɔθər, B -θə] *s.* coautor, colaborador. —*v.t.* escribir conjuntamente.
coax [koʊks] *v.t.* 1. engatusar, instar. 2. (con *into, to*) persuadir o inducir con halagos (a hacer algo); (con *out of*) conseguir o sacar (de alguien) con halagos. 3. lograr o conseguir con paciencia, ej., *c. a fire to light,* conseguir con paciencia que se prenda el fuego.
coaxial [koʊ'æksɪəl] *a.* (mat.) coaxil, coaxial.
coaxial cable, cable coaxial.
coaxing ['koʊksɪŋ] *s.* engatusamiento; ruego.
cob [kɑb, B kɔb] *s.* 1. mazorca del maíz. 2. jaca fornida. 3. cisne macho. 4. (G.B.) mezcla de arcilla y paja (para construir paredes).
cobalt ['koʊˌbɔlt, B koʊ'bɔlt] *s.* (quím.) cobalto.
cobalt blue, (pigmento de) azul de cobalto.
cobalt bomb, bomba de cobalto.
cobalt glass, vidrio de cobalto.
cobalt green, (quím.) verde de cobalto, verde de Rinmann.
cobaltic [koʊ'bɔltɪk] *a.* (quím.) cobáltico.
cobaltic oxide, (quím.) óxido cobáltico.
cobaltite ['koʊbɔlˌtaɪt] **cobaltine** [-ˌtin] *s.* (min.) cobaltina.
cobber ['kɑbər, B 'kɔbə] *s.* (jer., Aust.) camarada, compañero.
cobble ['kɑbəl, B 'kɔb-] *s.* 1. canto rodado, adoquín, guijarro, guija (para pavimentar). 2. (*pl.*) (pr. G.B.) carbones del tamaño de guijarros. —*v.t.* 1. pavimentar con guijarros, empedrar con adoquines. 2. (pr. G.B.) remendar (esp. el calzado).
cobbler ['kɑblər, B 'kɔblə] *s.* 1. (zapatero) remendón. 2. bebida helada compuesta de vino y frutas. 3. (E.U.) un pastel de frutas.
cobblestone ['kɑbəlˌstoʊn, B 'kɔb-] *s.* adoquín, canto rodado, guijarro (para empedrar o pavimentar).
cob coal, hulla en pedazos redondos.

cobelligerent [ˌkoʊbəˈlɪdʒərənt] *s.* cobeligerante.
cobia [ˈkoʊbɪə] *s.* (ict.) pez de mares tropicales o subtropicales.
coble [ˈkoʊbəl] *s.* (G.B.) barca pesquera de fondo chato.
cobnut [ˈkɑbˌnʌt, B ˈkɔb-] *s.* (bot.) avellana.
cobra [ˈkoʊbrə] *s.* (zool.) cobra, culebra de anteojos o de capuchón.
cobweb [ˈkɑbˌwɛb, B ˈkɔb-] *s.* 1. telaraña. 2. (fig.) red, tejido, ardid, embrollo, tramoya. 3. (fig.) telaraña, cosa sutil. 4. **to blow away the cobwebs,** orearse, ponerse listo.
cobwebbed [-ˌwɛbd] **cobwebby** [-ˌwɛbɪ] *a.* telarañoso, cubierto de telarañas.
coca [ˈkoʊkə] *s.* (bot.) coca; cuca, hayo (Am.).
Coca-Cola (TM) [ˈkoʊkəˈkoʊlə] *s.* Coca-Cola.
cocain, cocaine [koʊˈkeɪn, ˈkoʊˌkeɪn, B kəˈkeɪn] *s.* (quím.) cocaína.
cocainism [koʊˈkeɪnˌɪzəm] *s.* (med.) cocainomanía, cocainismo.
cocainization [-ˌkeɪnəˈzeɪʃən, B -naɪ-] *s.* cocainización.
cocainize [koʊˈkeɪnˌaɪz] *v.t.* tratar o anestesiar con cocaína.
coccid [ˈkɑksəd, B ˈkɔk-] *s.* (ento.) cóccido.
coccidioidomycosis [kɑkˌsɪdɪˌɔɪdoʊˌmaɪˈkoʊsəs, B kɔk-] *s.* (med.) coccidioidosis, coccidioidomicosis.
coccidiosis [-ˌsɪdɪˈoʊsəs] *s.* (med.) coccidiosis.
cocciferous [kɑkˈsɪfərəs, B kɔk-] *a.* (bot.) que produce bayas.
coccus [ˈkɑkəs, B ˈkɔk-] *s.* (*pl.* COCCI [-ˌsaɪ]) (bact.) coco, bacteria cocácea.
coccygeal [kɑkˈsɪdʒɪəl, B kɔk-] *a.* (anat.) coccígeo.
coccyx [ˈkɑksɪks, B ˈkɔk-] *s.* (anat.) cóccix, coxis.
Cochin China [ˈkoʊtʃənˈtʃaɪnə] 1. antiguo nombre del sur de Vietnam. 2. cochinchina (gallina).
cochineal [ˈkɑtʃəˌnil, ˈkoʊtʃ-, B ˈkɔtʃ-] *s.* 1. (ento.) cochinilla. 2. cochinilla (tinte).
cochineal insect, (ento.) cochinilla.
cochlea [ˈkɑklɪə, B ˈkɔk-] *s.* (anat.) cóclea, caracol (del oído interno).
cochlear [-lɪər, B -ə] *a.* (anat.) coclear.
cock [kɑk, B kɔk] *s.* 1. gallo. 2. macho (de ave), ej., *c. robin,* macho del petirrojo, *c. sparrow,* gorrión macho. 3. veleta, giraldilla. 4. campeón; galán; jefe, líder, amo. 5. (en vocativo) (fam. G.B.) compadre, jefe, amigo. 6. llave, grifo, espita; robinete, llave de cierre. 7. gatillo, martillo (de armas de fuego). 8. montoncillo (de paja, heno, estiércol, etc.). 9. fiel, aguja (de balanza); estilo, gnomon (de reloj solar). 10. inclinación, sesgo (del sombrero, de la cabeza, etc.). 11. (jer. G.B.) necedad, estupidez. 12. (vulg.) pene. 13. **at full c.,** amartillado (arma de fuego); **at half c.,** casi amartillado (arma de fuego); **c. of the walk,** gallito del lugar, amo del cotarro; **that c. won't fight,** ese asunto no marchará, ese proyecto (plan, pedido, etc.) no dará resultados; **to go off at half c., to go off half cocked,** actuar precipitadamente. —*v.i.* 1. (con *up*) levantarse, erguirse, enderezarse. 2. contonearse, pavonearse, engreírse, gallear. —*v.t.* 1. montar, amartillar (un arma de fuego). 2. enderezar, levantar. 3. hacinar, amontonar (paja, heno, estiércol, etc.). 4. **c. one's eye (at),** echar un vistazo (a); **c. one's hat,** poner el sombrero al sesgo; **c. the ears,** aguzar el oído.
cockade [kɑˈkeɪd, B kɔ-] *s.* escarapela, cucarda, roseta (en el sombrero).
cock-a-doodle-doo [ˈkɑkəˌdudəlˈdu, B ˈkɔk-] *s.* quiquiriquí.
cock-a-hoop [ˌkɑkəˈhup, B ˌkɔk-] *a.* alegre, jubiloso, triunfante. —*adv.* jubilosamente, triunfalmente.
Cockaigne [kɑˈkeɪn, B kɔ-] *s.* país imaginario de vida cómoda y lujosa.
cock-a-leekie [ˌkɑkɪˈlikɪ, B ˌkɔkɪ-] *s.* (esco.) sopa de pollo y puerro o cebolleta.
cockalorum [-əˈlɔrəm] *s.* gallito, persona pequeña y pendenciera.
cockamamie [ˈkɑkəˌmeɪmɪ, B ˈkɔk-] *a.* (jer.) absurdo, quijotesco; de inferior calidad.
cock-and-bull story [ˈkɑkənˈbʊl-, B ˈkɔk-] patraña, cuento increíble, exageración.
cockateel, cockatiel [ˌkɑkəˈtil, B ˌkɔk-] *s.* (orn.) variedad de cacatúa con cabeza amarilla.
cockatoo [ˈkɑkəˌtu, B ˌkɔkəˈtu] *s.* (orn.) cacatúa.
cockatrice [ˈkɑkətrəs, -ˌtraɪs, B ˈkɔk-] *s.* (mitol.) basilisco.
cockboat [-ˌboʊt] *s.* (mar.) chalupa, barca, barquilla.
cockchafer [-ˌtʃeɪfər, B -fə] *s.* (ento.) abejorro.
cockcrow [-ˌkroʊ] *s.* (fig.) alba, amanecer, aurora; **at c.,** al cantar el gallo, al despuntar el alba.
cocked hat [ˈkɑkt-, B ˈkɔkt-] sombrero de tres picos, tricornio, sombrero de tres candiles; **to knock into a c. h.,** arruinar, destruir (algo) completamente.
cocker [ˈkɑkər, B ˈkɔkə] *v.t.* acariciar, mimar, consentir (a niños, enfermos, etc.). —*s.* gallero, el que cría y cuida gallos de lidia.
cockerel [ˈkɑkərəl, B ˈkɔk-] *s.* pollo, gallo joven.
cocker spaniel, perro cócker.
cockeyed [ˈkɑkˌaɪd, B ˈkɔk-] *a.* 1. bizco. 2. torcido, sesgado. 3. (fam.) loco, insano; disparatado, equivocado, falso. 4. (fam.) extravagante, excéntrico; confuso, caótico. 5. (jer.) ajumado, borracho; tonto, absurdo.
cockfight [-ˌfaɪt] **cockfighting** [-ɪŋ] *s.* pelea de gallos.
cockhorse [ˈkɑkˌhɔrs, B ˈkɔkˌhɔs] *adv.* a horcajadas. —*s.* caballito mecedor.
cockiness [ˈkɑkɪnəs, B ˈkɔk-] *s.* engreimiento, impertinencia.
cocking lever [-ɪŋ-] (arm.) palanca de armar.
cockish [-ɪʃ] *a.* (fam.) engreído, hinchado.
cockle [ˈkɑkəl, B ˈkɔk-] *s.* 1. (bot.) neguilla, candileja; cizaña. 2. carbón, tizón, tizoncillo. 3. (zool.) berberecho. 4. barqueta. 5. **cockles of the heart,** (fig.) las entretelas del corazón.
cockle, *v.t., v.i.* arrugar(se), ampollar(se). —*s.* arruga, pliegue.
cocklebur, cockleburr [-ˌbɜr, B -ˌbɜ] *s.* 1. (bot.) ajonjera, cardo ajonjero. 2. erizo (de plantas).
cockleshell [-ˌʃɛl] *s.* 1. concha o valva de coquina. 2. cascarón de nuez, barqueta.
cockloft [ˈkɑkˌlɔft, B ˈkɔk-] *s.* desván, gatero, zaquizamí.
cockney [ˈkɑknɪ, B ˈkɔk-] *s.* 1. nativo londinense (esp. de clase popular). 2. acento vulgar londinense. —*a.* londinense (esp. de las clases populares).
cockpit [ˈkɑkˌpɪt, B ˈkɔk-] *s.* 1. gallera, reñidero (de gallos), cancha (Am.). 2. (mar.) parte baja de popa (esp. de un yate). 3. (aer.) cabina del piloto. 4. (fig.) arena, palestra. — **c. cowling,** (avia.) carenaje de la cabina.
cockroach [-ˌroʊtʃ] *s.* (ento.) cucaracha, corredera, blata.
cockscomb, coxcomb [ˈkɑksˌkoʊm, B ˈkɔks-] 1. cresta (de gallo); gorro de bufón. 2. (bot.) cresta de gallo, amaranto. 3. moco de pavo (Am.).
cockshut [ˈkɑkˌʃʌt, B ˈkɔk-] *s.* (dial. G.B.) crepúsculo (vespertino).
cockspur [-ˌspɜr, B -ˌspɜ] *s.* 1. espolón o navaja de gallo. 2. quemador de gas (en forma de espolón de gallo).
cocksure [-ˈʃʊr, B -ˈʃʊə] *a.* 1. demasiado seguro, muy confiado, engreído, creído. 2. segurísimo, perfectamente seguro.
cocksy [-sɪ] *var. de* **cocky.**
cocktail [-ˌteɪl] *s.* 1. coctel, aperitivo. 2. caballo rabón; caballo de raza impura. —*a.* de coctel.
cocktail party, coctel (reunión o fiesta).
cocktail shaker, coctelera.
cocky [ˈkɑkɪ, B ˈkɔkɪ] *a.* (COCKIER; COCKIEST) presumido, engreído, petulante, arrogante.
coco [ˈkoʊkoʊ] *s.* (*pl.* COCOS) 1. (bot.) coco, cocotero (árbol). 2. coco (fruto).
cocoa [ˈkoʊkoʊ] *s.* 1. (bot.) cacao. 2. (bebida de) cacao.
cocoa bean, grano de cacao.
cocoa butter, manteca de cacao.
cocondensation [koʊˌkɑnˌdɛnˈseɪʃən, B -ˌkɔn-] *s.* (ind.) condensación heterogénea.
coconut [ˈkoʊkəˌnʌt, -nət] *s.* (bot.) coco (fruto).
coconut fiber, bonote.
coconut oil, manteca de coco, aceite de coco.
coconut palm, coconut tree, (bot.) cocotero.
cocoon [kəˈkun] *s.* capullo (del gusano de seda y de otros insectos).
cocotte [koʊˈkɑt, B -ˈkɔt] *s.* (fr.) mujer de vida fácil, ramera elegante.
cod [kɑd, B kɔd] *s.* bacalao, abadejo, curadillo.
C.O.D. *abrev. de* **collect on delivery,** —*adv.* contra reembolso. —*s.* pago contra entrega.
coda [ˈkoʊdə] *s.* (mús.) coda; pasaje que finaliza una composición.
coddle [ˈkɑdəl, B ˈkɔd-] *v.t.* 1. mimar, consentir; cuidar demasiado (a sí mismo o a otros). 2. cocer a fuego lento (huevos, frutas, etc.).
code [koʊd] *s.* 1. (der.) código, compilación de leyes. 2. (teleg., mil.) código, cifra, clave. —*v.t.* cifrar, componer en clave o cifra.
codeclination [ˌkoʊˌdɛkləˈneɪʃən] *s.* (astr.) complemento de la declinación, distancia polar.
codefendant [-dɪˈfɛndənt] *s.* (der.) codemandado, coencausado; coacusado.
codeine [ˈkoʊˌdin, -dɪən, B -ˌdin] *s.* (quím.) codeína.
Code Napoleon, código napoleónico de derechos ciudadanos.
code word, palabra en clave, cifra.
codex [ˈkoʊˌdɛks] *s.* (*pl.* CODICES [ˈkoʊdəˈsiz]) códice.
codfish [ˈkɑdˌfɪʃ, B ˈkɔd-] *s.* bacalao, abadejo.
codfisher [-ər] *s.* (mar.) bacaladero *(barco).*
codger [ˈkɑdʒər, B ˈkɔdʒə] *s.* (fam.) tipo raro, excéntrico (esp. viejo).
codicil [ˈkɑdəsəl, -ˌsɪl, B ˈkɔd-] *s.* (der.) codicilo.
codicillary [ˌkɑdəˈsɪlərɪ, B ˌkɔdɪ-] *a.* (der.) codicilar.
codification [ˌkɑdəfəˈkeɪʃən, ˌkoʊd-, B ˌkɔd-] *s.* (der.) codificación.
codifier [ˈkɑdəˌfaɪər, ˈkoʊd-, B ˈkɔdɪˌfaɪə] *s.* codificador.
codify [-ˌfaɪ] *v.t.* (*pret., p.p.* CODIFIED; *p.pr.* CODIFYING) 1. poner en cifra o clave. 2. codificar. 3. sistematizar, clasificar, compilar.
codlin [ˈkɑdlən, B ˈkɔd-] *var. de* **codling** (manzana).
codling [ˈkɑdlɪŋ, B ˈkɔd-] *s.* 1. bacalao pequeño. 2. (ict.) brótola.
codling, *s.* manzana verde; (variedad de) manzana inglesa de forma alargada.

codling moth, gusano de la manzana.
cod-liver oil ['kɑd,lɪvər-, B 'kɔd-ə] aceite de hígado de bacalao.
coed, co-ed ['koʊ,ɛd] *s.* (fam., E.U.) alumna de un plantel coeducacional. —*a.* 1. coeducacional. 2. de alumnas (baile, etc.).
coeducation [,koʊ,ɛdʒə'keɪʃən] *s.* coeducación, educación para alumnos de ambos sexos.
coeducational [-əl] *s.* coeducacional.
coefficient [,koʊə'fɪʃənt] *s.* (mat.) coeficiente.
coelacanth ['silə,kænθ] *s.* (ict.) celacanto.
Coelenterata [sɪ,lɛntə'reɪtə] *s. pl.* (zool.) celenterios, celenterados.
coelenterate [sɪ'lɛntə,reɪt, -rət] *a., s.* (zool.) celenterado.
coeliac ['silɪ,æk] *a.* (anat.) celíaco.
coelom ['siləm] *s.* (anat., zool.) celoma.
coenesthesis [,sinɪs'θisəs] **coenesthesia** [-'θiʒə, B -'θiziə] *s.* (fisiol., psic.) cenestesia.
coenobite, coenobitic, *var. de* **cenobite, cenobitic.**
coenzyme [koʊ'ɛn,zaɪm] *s.* (quím.) coenzima.
coequal [koʊ'ikwəl] *a.* recíproco, mutuamente igual.
coequality [,koʊi'kwɑlətɪ, B -'kwɔl-] *s.* igualdad recíproca.
coerce [koʊ'ɜrs, B -'ɜs] *v.t.* 1. coercer, contener, reprimir, refrenar, restringir. 2. forzar, obligar, constreñir.
coercible [-əbəl] *a.* coercible.
coercion [-'ɜrʃən, -ʒən, B -'ɜʃən] *s.* coerción, coacción.
coercive [-'ɜrsɪv, B -'ɜsɪv] *a.* coercitivo; coactivo, obligatorio.
coessential [,koʊɪ'sɛntʃəl, B -'sɛnʃəl] *a.* coesencial.
coetaneous [,koʊə'teɪnɪəs] *a.* coetáneo.
coeternal [-ɪ'tɜrnəl, B -'tɜn-] *a.* coeterno.
coeternity [-'tɜrnətɪ, B -'tɜn-] *s.* coeternidad.
coeval [koʊ'ivəl] *s., a.* coevo, coetáneo, contemporaneo.
coexecutor [,koʊɪg'zɛkjətər, B -ə] *s.* 1. coejecutor. 2. (der.) albacea mancomunado, coalbacea.
coexist [,koʊɪg'zɪst] *v.i.* coexistir.
coexistence [-əns] *s.* coexistencia, existencia simultánea.
coexistent [-ənt] *a.* coexistente.
coextensive [,koʊɪk'stɛnsɪv] *a.* coextenso.
coffee ['kɔfɪ, 'kɑfɪ, B 'kɔfɪ] *s.* 1. café, cafeto; **c. with milk,** café con leche. 2. grano de café 3. café (bebida).
coffee bean, grano de café.
coffee break, descanso para tomar café (en oficinas, etc.).
coffee cake, bizcocho con fruta seca, plum cake.
coffee cup, taza de café.
coffee grounds, poso o borras del café.
coffeehouse [-,haʊs] *s.* café (establecimiento).
coffee klatsch, reunión informal donde se sirven refrescos o café.
coffee maker, máquina de café, cafetera.
coffee mill, molinillo de café.
coffee plantation, cafetal.
coffeepot [-,pɑt, B -,pɔt] *s.* cafetera.
coffee shop, café (establecimiento), pequeño restaurante, cafetería (Am.).
coffee spoon, cucharilla de café.
coffee table, mesita baja, mesa de centro.
coffee-table book, libro ilustrado de gran formato.
coffee tree, (bot.) cafeto.
coffer ['kɔfər, 'kɑf-, B 'kɔfə] *s.* 1. cofre, arca, caja (de caudales, valores, etc.). 2. (*pl.*) tesorería, fondos. 3. (ing., hidr.) caja-dique, encajonado. 4. (arq.) artesón. —*v.t.* 1. atesorar. 2. (arq.) artesonar.
cofferdam [-,dæm] (ing., hidr.) ataguía, cajadique.
coffin ['kɔfən, 'kɑf-, B 'kɔf-] *s.* 1. ataúd, féretro, caja (mortuoria), cajón (Am.). 2. casco (de las caballerías). —*v.t.* meter en un ataúd; (fig.) encerrar, ocultar.
coffin bone, (zool.) falange tercera (en el casco de las caballerías), bolillo.
coffin nail, (jer.) cigarrillo (clavo de ataúd, literalmente, por ser nocivo a la salud).
coffle ['kɔfəl, 'kɑf-, B 'kɔf-] *s.* (ant.) cáfila, caravana de esclavos o bestias.
C. of S. *abrev. de* **chief of staff,** jefe del estado mayor.
cog [kɑg, B kɔg] *s.* 1. (mec.) diente (de una rueda); cama, leva. 2. (carp.) espiga; lengüeta. 3. (fig.) elemento, factor, pieza (individuo que desempeña un papel secundario en una organización). —*v.t.* (*pret., p.p.* COGGED; *p.pr.* COGGING) 1. puntear o poner dientes a (una rueda). 2. (carp.) ensamblar con espigas. 3. **to c. a die,** cargar un dado. —*v.i.* hacer trampa.
cogency ['koʊdʒənsɪ] *s.* fuerza, eficacia (del argumento, de los motivos, etc.).
cogent ['koʊdʒənt] *a.* convincente, persuasivo, poderoso, eficaz.
cogged [kɑgd, B kɔgd] *a.* dentado, engranado; **c. dice,** dados cargados.
cogitate ['kɑdʒə,teɪt, B 'kɔdʒɪ-] *v.t.* reflexionar, ponderar, pensar, meditar; (filos.) cogitar. —*v.i.* sumirse en meditación.
cogitation [,kɑdʒə'teɪʃən, B ,kɔdʒɪ-] *s.* reflexión, meditación; (filos.) cogitación.
cogitative ['kɑdʒə,teɪtɪv, B 'kɔdʒɪ-] *a.* pensativo, reflexivo, meditativo; (filos.) cogitativo.
cognac ['koʊn,jæk, 'kɑn-, B 'kɔn-] *s.* coñac.
cognate ['kɑg,neɪt, B 'kɔg-] *a.* **cognado,** consanguíneo, pariente; afín, semejante, análogo; (der.) cognático, cognaticio. —*s.* cognado, cognada.
cognatic ['kɑg,nætɪk, B kɔg'næt-] *a.* cognaticio.
cognation [kɑg'neɪʃən, B kɔg-] *s.* (ú. esp. en filol.) cognación; origen común.
cognition [-'nɪʃən] *s.* 1. cognición, conocimiento, entendimiento. 2. percepción, sensación, noción.
cognitive ['kɑgnətɪv, B 'kɔg-] *a.* cognoscitivo.
cognizable ['kɑgnəzəbəl, kɑg'naɪ-, B 'kɔg-nɪ-] *a.* 1. cognoscible, conocible. 2. (der.) conocible, justiciable (causa).
cognizance ['kɑgnəzəns, B 'kɔg-] *s.* 1. conocimiento; comprensión, percepción. 2. control, dominio. 3. (der.) conocimiento (de una causa); competencia, jurisdicción. 4. (hist.) divisa, emblema, distintivo (de un caballero armado y su comitiva). 5. **to be beyond one's c.,** ir fuera de la competencia de uno; **to have c. of,** tener conocimiento de; **to take c. of,** tomar conocimiento de; considerar debidamente.
cognizant [-zənt] *a.* (ú. con *of*) conocedor (de); sabedor, informado (de).
cognize ['kɑg,naɪz, kɑg'naɪz, B kɔg'naɪz] *v.t.* (filos.) conocer, saber.
cognomen [kɑg'noʊmən, B kɔg-] *s.* (*pl.* COGNOMENS o COGNOMINA [-'nɑmənə, B -'nɔm-]) 1. apodo, sobrenombre. 2. apellido; nombre. 3. (hist.) último de los tres nombres que llevaban los romanos; cognomento.
cognoscente ['koʊnjoʊ'ʃɛnteɪ, B ,kɔn-tɪ] *s.* (*pl.* COGNOSCENTI [-'ʃɛnti]) conocedor (de las artes, etc.).
cognoscible [kɑg'nɑsəbəl, B kɔg'nɔs-] *a.* cognoscible, conocible.
cognovit [kɑg'noʊvɪt, B kɔg-] *s.* (der.) admisión de sentencia (por parte del demandado).
cogon [koʊ'goʊn] *s.* (bot.) cogón, cisca, carrizo.
cog railway, (f.c.) ferrocarril de cremallera, riel dentado.
cogwheel ['kɑg,hwil, -,wil, B 'kɔg-] *s.* rueda dentada.
cohabit [koʊ'hæbət] *v.i.* cohabitar.
cohabitant [-ənt] *s.* convecino, co-habitante.
cohabitation [,koʊ,hæbə'teɪʃən] *s.* cohabitación.
coheir ['koʊ'ɛr, B -'ɛə] *s.* coheredero.
coheiress [-'ɛrəs, B -'ɛərɪs] *s.* coheredera.
cohere [koʊ'hɪr, B -'hɪə] *v.i.* 1. adherirse entre sí, pegarse, unirse. 2. tener coherencia, estar bien enlazados o ligados (argumentos, estilos, etc.). 3. mostrar unidad; cooperar.
coherence [koʊ'hɪrəns, B -'hɪər-] *s.* coherencia, cohesión, enlace, consistencia.
coherency [-ənsɪ] *var. de* **coherence.**
coherent [-ənt] *a.* coherente, consistente.
coherently [-əntlɪ] *adv.* coherentemente.
coherer [koʊ'hɪrər, B -'hɪərə] *s.* (rad.) cohesor.
cohesion [koʊ'hiʒən] *s.* cohesión, adhesión, unión, enlace; (fís.) cohesión.
cohesive [koʊ'hisɪv] *a.* cohesivo, coherente; adherente.
cohibit [koʊ'hɪbət] *v.t.* cohibir, restringir.
cohobate ['koʊhoʊ,beɪt] *v.t.* (quím.) cohobar.
cohobation [,koʊhoʊ'beɪʃən] *s.* (quím.) cohobación.
cohort ['koʊ,hɔrt, B -,hɔt] *s.* 1. banda (de guerreros); grupo, cohorte (de personas). 2. (*pl.*) secuaces, compañeros.
cohune [kə'hun] *s.* (bot.) corojo, mantequero, palma centroamericana.
coif [kɔɪf, kwɑf, B kɔɪf] *s.* 1. cofia, toca, gorro, papalina. 2. (hist.) gorro de tela (que usaban los soldados debajo del casco). 3. tocado, peinado.
coiffeur [kwɑ'fɜr, B -'fɜ] *s.* (fr.) peluquero, peinador.
coiffeuse [kwɑ'fʊz] *s.* (fr.) peluquera, peinadora.
coiffure [kwɑ'fjʊr, B -'fjʊə] *s.* tocado, peinado. —*v.t.* peinar (de cierto modo).
coign [kɔɪn] *s.* (ant.) esquina o ángulo saliente, cuña; **c. of vantage,** posición ventajosa.
coil [kɔɪl] *s.* 1. rollo. 2. espiral, serpentín. 3. vuelta, aduja, rosca (de cable, etc.). 4. rizo (de cabellos), bucle. 5. (elec.) bobina, carrete. 6. (ant., poét.) desorden, baraúnda; **this mortal coil,** el tumulto de la vida. —*v.t.* enrollar; (mar.) adujar (cable); enroscar. —*v.i.* andar en círculos, serpentear, enrollarse, enroscarse; **to c. up,** hacerse un ovillo.
coil clutch, embrague espiral.
coil condenser, (mec.) condensador refrigerante en espiral.
coil cooler, (mec.) refrigerante en serpentín.
coil spring, resorte espiral.
coin [kɔɪn] *s.* moneda, (com.) dinero, numerario; **to pay one in his own c.,** pagar a uno con la misma moneda. —*v.t.* 1. acuñar (moneda); amonedar (metal). 2. (fig.) acuñar, forjar, crear (palabra, frase, epigrama, etc.). 3. convertir en dinero, sacar dinero de. 4. **to c. money,** amasar fortuna.
coinage ['kɔɪnɪdʒ] *s.* 1. acuñación; moneda, monedaje. 2. sistema monetario. 3. invención; palabra o frase acuñada.
coincide [,koʊɪn'saɪd] *v.i.* coincidir (en tiempo o espacio), concurrir; coincidir, convenir (en opinión).
coincidence [koʊ'ɪnsədəns] *s.* coincidencia; casualidad.

coincident [-sədənt] *a.* coincidente; (con *with*) acorde (con).
coincidental [koʊˌɪnsə'dɛntəl] *a.* 1. coincidente. 2. casual, fortuito.
coincidentally [-'dɛntəlɪ] **coincidently** [-'dɛntlɪ] *adv.* coincidentalmente, al mismo tiempo.
coiner ['kɔɪnər, B -ə] *s.* 1. acuñador. 2. (pr. G.B.) falsificador, monedero falso. 3. inventor (de palabra nueva, etc.).
coinheritance [ˌkoʊɪn'hɛrətəns] *s.* herencia en común.
coinheritor [-'hɛrətər, B -tə] *s.* coheredero.
coinstantaneous [koʊˌɪnstən'teɪnɪəs] *a.* simultáneo, que ocurre al mismo momento.
coinsurance [ˌkoʊən'ʃʊrəns, B -ɪn'ʃʊər-] *s.* (com.) coseguro, seguro copartícipe.
Cointreau ['kwɑnˌtroʊ, kwɑn'troʊ] *s.* clase de licor; Cointreau, marca registrada de un licor francés.
coir [kɔɪr, B 'kɔɪə] *s.* bonete; fibra de la corteza del coco usada para hacer soga, etc.
coition [koʊ'ɪʃən] **coitus** ['koʊətəs] *s.* coito, cópula, concúbito.
coke [koʊk] *s.* 1. coque, cok. 2. (jer.) cocaína. —*v.t.*, *v.i.* convertir(se) en coque, coquizar.
Coke (TM), Coca-Cola (refresco).
coke oven, horno de coque.
cokernut ['koʊkərˌnʌt, B koʊkəˌ-] *s.* (fam.) coco.
col [kɑl, B kɔl] *s.* desfiladero, puerto (entre montañas); depresión (en la cresta de una cordillera).
Col. *abrev. de* 1. **Colombia,** Colombia. 2. **Colonel,** Coronel. 3. **Colorado,** Colorado. 4. **Colossians,** Colosenses (Nuevo Testamento).
cola ['koʊlə] *pl. de* **colon.**
cola ['koʊlə] *s.* 1. (bot.) cola. 2. bebida carbonatada que contiene extracto de cola.
colander ['kʌləndər, 'kɑl-, B 'kʌləndə] *s.* colador, coladera, escurridor. —*v.t.* colar, pasar por una coladera.
colatitude [koʊ'lætəˌtud, B -ˌtjud] *s.* (astr.) colatitud, complemento de latitud.
colcannon [kɑl'kænən, B kɔl-] *s.* plato irlandés a base de patatas y verduras cocidas.
colchicine ['kɑltʃəˌsin, 'kɑlkə-, B 'kɔlkɪˌ-saɪn] *s.* (farm.) colquicina.
colchicum ['kɑltʃɪkəm, 'kɑlkɪ , B 'kɔl-] *s.* 1. (bot.) cólquico. 2. tintura de cólquico.
colcothar ['kɑlkəθər, B 'kɔlkəθə] *s.* (quím.) colcótar.
cold [koʊld] *a.* 1. frío; helado. 2. (fig.) frío, indiferente, impasible, insensible. 3. (fig.) frío, frígido. 4. depresivo, desalentador. 5. pasado, sin interés (ej., noticias). 6. débil (rastro, pista). 7. lejos de la verdad, lejos del objeto buscado. 8. indefenso, desamparado. 9. impersonal (ej., estadísticas). 10. muerto. 11. (jer. ú. gen. con *out*) inconsciente, ej., *he knocked the fellow out c.*, puso inconsciente al tipo de un (solo) golpe; *he passed out c.*, perdió totalmente el conocimiento. 12. (pint.) que tira a gris pálido. 13. **in c. blood,** a sangre fría; **to be c.,** tener frío (personal), hacer frío (tiempo); **to have someone c.,** (jer.) tener a alguien a su merced; **to throw c. water on,** echar un jarro de agua fría a (plan, entusiasmo, etc.); desalentar. —*adv.* 1. de repente, en seco, ej., *he was stopped c.*, lo pararon en seco. 2. de plano, llanamente, ej., *he was turned down c.*, lo rechazaron de plano. 3. perfectamente, ej., *I knew the answers c.*, sabía las respuestas perfectamente (o al dedillo). 4. **to blow hot and c.,** vacilar, cambiar sucesivamente de parecer. —*s.* frío; **c. in the head,** resfrío, resfriado, catarro; **to catch c.,** resfriarse, constiparse, acatarrarse; **to leave out in the c.,** dejarle (a uno) en la estacada, abandonar (a uno) a su suerte.
cold area, (fís.) área sin actividad.
cold-blooded ['koʊld'blʌdəd] *a.* 1. cruel, despiadado, desalmado. 2. insensible, impasible. 3. (zool.) de sangre fría. 4. friolento, friolero.
cold-bloodedly [-lɪ] *adv.* a sangre fría; impasivamente.
cold-bloodedness [-nəs] *s.* sangre fría.
cold chisel, cortafrío, cortahierro, cortafierro (Am.).
cold cream, crema para el cutis.
cold cuts, fiambres variados.
cold-drawn ['koʊld'drɔn] *a.* (metal.) estirado en frío.
cold duck, vino tinto gaseado.
cold feet, (fam.) temor, miedo, acobardamiento; **to get c. f.,** acobardarse, echarse atrás.
cold fish, (jer.) tipo aburrido, persona desabrida.
cold forging, (metal.) forjado en frío, troquelado al frío.
cold frame, cajonera para proteger plantas nuevas (en jardines).
cold front, (meteor.) frente frío.
cold-hearted ['koʊld'hɑrtəd, B -'hɑt-] *a.* frío de corazón, insensible, indiferente, impasible.
cold-heartedness [-nəs] *s.* frialdad, indiferencia.
coldish ['koʊldɪʃ] *a.* bastante frío, fresco.
cold laboratory, (fís.) laboratorio para sustancias inactivas.
cold light, luz fría.
coldly ['koʊldlɪ] *adv.* fríamente, con frialdad o indiferencia.
cold meat 1. carne fría, fiambre, fiambres. 2. (jer.) cadáver, cadáveres.
cold moulding, (ind.) moldeado en frío.
coldness ['koʊldnəs] *s.* 1. frío, temperatura fría. 2. (fig.) frialdad, frigidez. 3. (fig.) frialdad, indiferencia, despego, esquivez.
cold pack, (med.) compresa fría.
cold-press ['koʊld'prɛs] *v.t.* prensar o exprimir en frío. —*s.* prensa de satinar en frío.
cold riveting, (metal.) remachado en frío.
cold-rolled ['koʊld'roʊld] *a.* (metal.) laminado en frío.
cold saw, (metal.) sierra de cortar en frío.
cold-setting [-'sɛtɪŋ] *s.* (ing.) fraguado en frío, endurecimiento en frío.
cold-short ['koʊldˌʃɔrt, B -ˌʃɔt] *a.* (metal.) quebradizo al frío (hierro, etc.).
cold shoulder, (fam.) frialdad, indiferencia; desaire, desatención; **to give one the c. s.,** tratar a uno con frialdad.
cold snap, racha repentina de tiempo frío.
cold sore, (med.). herpe labial, granitos herpéticos, afta.
cold spell, ola de frío.
cold steel, armas blancas.
cold storage, 1. conservación en frigorífico. 2. (fig.) carpetazo, postergación indefinida; **to put into c. s.,** dar carpetazo a, postergar indefinidamente.
cold sweat, sudor frío; (med.) escalofrío.
cold turkey, (jer.) síndrome de abstinencia; **he went c.,** estuvo con el síndrome de abstencia, estuvo con el mono; **to quit** *(something)* **c.,** abandonar algo total y repentinamente, cortar en seco con, parar en seco con.
cold war, (pol.) guerra fría.
cold wave, 1. (meteor.) ola de frío. 2. ondulación permanente en frío (del pelo).
cole [koʊl] *s.* (bot.) col, berza, esp. colza.
colectomy [kə'lɛktəmɪ] *s.* (cir.) colectomía.
colegatee [ˌkoʊlɛgə'ti] *s.* (der.) colegatario, legatario con otro.
Coleoptera [ˌkoʊlɪ'ɑptərə, ˌkɑlɪ-, B ˌkɔlɪ'ɔp-] *s. pl.* (ento.) coleópteros.
coleopterous [-tərəs] *a.* (ento.) coleóptero.
coleorhiza [ˌkoʊlɪə'raɪzə, ˌkɑlɪə-, B ˌkɔlɪə-] *s.* (bot.) coleorriza.
coleslaw ['koʊlˌslɔ] *s.* (E.U.) ensalada de col fresca picada en briznas.
colessor [koʊ'lɛsər, B -ə] *s.* coarrendador.
coleus ['koʊlɪəs] *s.* (bot.) coleo.
colewort ['koʊlˌwɜrt, B -ˌwɜt] *s.* (bot.) col rizada, berza verde.
colic ['kɑlɪk, B 'kɔlɪk] *s., a.* (med.) cólico, relativo al colon o a un cólico.
colicky ['kɑləkɪ, B 'kɔl-] *a.* que tiende a producir cólicos.
coliseum [ˌkɑlə'siəm, B ˌkɔlɪ'sɪəm] *s.* coliseo, anfiteatro.
colitis [koʊ'laɪtəs, B kɔ-] *s.* (med.) colitis.
coitus interruptus['koʊətəs'ɪntəˌrʌptəs] *s.* coito interrupto.
collaborate [kə'læbəˌreɪt] *v.i.* colaborar.
collaboration [kəˌlæbə'reɪʃən] *s.* colaboración.
collaborationism [-ˌɪzəm] *s.* política de colaboración.
collaborationist [-əst] *s.* (derog.) colaboracionista.
collaborator [kə'læbəˌreɪtər, B -ə] *s.* colaborador (en una obra, trabajo, etc.); colaboracionista (que coopera con el enemigo).
collage [kə'lɑʒ, B 'kɔlɑʒ] *s.* (arte) collage, montaje (de fotografías, recortes, etc. que forman un conjunto armonioso o sugestivo).
collagen ['kɑlədʒən, B 'kɔl-] *s.* (bioquím.) colágena.
collapse [kə'læps] *v.i.* 1. desplomarse, derrumbarse, caerse. 2. hundirse, venirse abajo. 3. (fig.) desintegrarse, disolverse; fracasar. 4. (med.) postrarse, sufrir un colapso. 5. plegarse, doblarse. —*v.t.* 1. derrumbar. 2. plegar. —*s.* 1. desplome, derrumbe; hundimiento. 2. (fig.) fracaso, ruina. 3. (med.) colapso, postración.
collapsible [kə'læpsəbəl] *a.* plegadizo, plegable; **c. boat,** canoa plegadiza; **c. hat,** chistera plegable.
collar ['kɑlər, B 'kɔlə] *s.* 1. cuello (del vestido, camisa, etc.). 2. collar (de perro); collera (de caballo). 3. captura, arresto. 4. (mec.) collar, cuello, collarín, virola, anillo, aro. 5. (G.B.) carne o pescado enrollado. 6. **to slip the c.,** escaparse, desenredarse. —*v.t.* 1. agarrar del cuello. 2. coger, capturar. 3. ceñir con collar, poner collar o cuello. 4. (fam.) apropiarse de (algo), hurtar. 5. (G.B. enrollar (un trozo de carne).
collar beam, (arq.) entrecinta.
collar bearing, (mec.) cojinete de apoyo radial.
collarbone [-ˌboʊn] *s.* (anat.) clavícula.
collard ['kɑlərd, B 'kɔləd] *s.* (bot.) variedad de col rizada, berza.
collaret, collarette [ˌkɑlə'rɛt, B ˌkɔlə-] *s.* cuello de encaje o piel, collarín.
collar plate, (const. naval) placa de cierre; arandela.
collate [kə'leɪt, 'kɑlˌeɪt, B kɔ'leɪt] *v.t.* 1. colacionar, cotejar, comparar, compulsar, confrontar. 2. (relig.) colar un beneficio a (un sacerdote). 3. (impr.) colacionar (páginas impresas).
collateral [kə'lætərəl] *a.* colateral; paralelo, simultáneo, accesorio. —*s.* 1. colateral (pariente). 2. (com.) (garantía) colateral, resguardo.
collaterally [-ərəlɪ] *adv.* colateralmente, subsidiariamente.
collation [kə'leɪʃən, kɑ-, B kɔ-] *s.* 1. colación, cotejo, comparación. 2. colación, refrigerio.

collator [kə'leɪtər, 'kɑl,eɪt-, B kɔ'leɪtə] *s.* colador; cotejador.
colleague ['kɑl,ig, B 'kɔl-] *s.* colega, compañero.
collect [kə'lɛkt] *v.t.* 1. juntar, reunir, acopiar, congregar. 2. coleccionar (sellos postales, pinturas, etc.). 3. colectar, recaudar (impuestos, arbitrios, etc.). 4. cobrar (pasajes, cheque, letra, una suma, etc.). 5. inferir, deducir. 6. (fam.) recoger (a alguien o algo). 7. ordenar, concentrar (pensamientos), recobrar (ánimo, energías, etc.). 8. **c. oneself,** recobrarse, reponerse; serenarse. —*v.i.* 1. reunirse. 2. juntarse, acumularse. 3. ser coleccionista (de sellos postales, pinturas, etc.). 4. **c. on delivery,** cobrar al entregar, pagadero al destino. — ['kɑlɛkt, B 'kɔl-] *s.* (relig.) colecta (oración).
collectable, collectible [kə'lɛktəbəl] *a.* cobrable; (*for collectors*) coleccionable.
collect call, (tele.) conferencia a cobro revertido.
collected [kə'lɛktəd] *a.* 1. reunido, juntado. 2. sosegado, calmado, sereno, tranquilizado. 3. completo, ej., *c. works,* obras completas (de un autor).
collection [kə'lɛkʃən] *s.* 1. colección. 2. acumulación (de agua, polvo, etc.). 3. colección, serie. 4. compilación, recopilación. 5. cobranza, cobro. 6. recaudación (de impuestos). 7. colecta. 8. (*pl.*) (G.B.) examen final (en una universidad).
collection agency, agencia de cobro.
collection of poetry, poemario.
collective [kə'lɛktɪv] *a.* colectivo, congregado. —*s.* colectividad.
collective bargaining, negociación colectiva, trato colectivo (entre patronos y sindicatos obreros).
collective farm, granja colectiva.
collectively [kə'lɛktɪvlɪ] *adv.* colectivamente, en masa.
collective noun, (gram.) nombre colectivo.
collective security, seguridad colectiva (de una asociación de naciones).
colectivism [kə'lɛktɪ,vɪzəm] *s.* (pol., sociol.) colectivismo.
collectivist [-tɪvəst] *a., s.* colectivista.
collectivistic [kə,lɛktɪ'vɪstɪk] *a.* colectivista.
collectivity [,kɑlɛk'tɪvətɪ, B ,kɔl-] *s.* colectividad.
collectivization [kə,lɛktɪvə'zeɪʃən, B -vaɪ-] *s.* colectivización.
collectivize [kə'lɛktɪ,vaɪz] *v.t.* colectivizar.
collector [kə'lɛktər, B -tə] *s.* 1. colector, cobrador, recaudador. 2. coleccionista (de sellos postales, pinturas, etc.). 3. (elec.) colector, toma de corriente.
collectorate [-tərət] **collectorship** [-tər,ʃɪp, B -tə,ʃɪp] *s.* colecturía.
colleen ['kɑl,in, kə'lin, B 'kɔl-, kɔ'lin] *s.* (Irl.) niña, muchacha.
college ['kɑlɪdʒ, B 'kɔl-] *s.* 1. colegio (corporación o edificio). 2. universidad; facultad universitaria; (G.B.) colegio autónomo universitario. 3. colegio, corporación (de abogados, médicos, etc.). 4. compañía, asociación. 5. (E.U.) escuela, curso (esp. vocacional), ej., *teachers c.,* escuela normal, *war c.,* escuela militar.
College of Cardinals, (relig.) Colegio de Cardenales.
college pudding, (G.B.) pequeño budín (para una persona).
collegial [kə'lidʒɪəl] *a.* colegial; (E.U.) universitario.
collegian [kə'lidʒɪən] *s.* estudiante universitario; estudiante graduado (de un colegio o universidad).
collegiate [-dʒɪət] *a.* 1. colegiado. 2. colegial. 3. (E.U.) universitario.
collegiate church, colegiata, iglesia colegial.
collegium [kə'lidʒɪəm] *s.* cuerpo colegiado (esp. de una junta administrativa en la Unión Soviética).
collembolan [kə'lɛmbələn] *s.* (ento.) colémbolo.
collenchyma [kə'lɛŋkəmə] *s.* (bot.) colénquima.
collet ['kɑlət, B 'kɔlɪt] *s.* 1. (mec.) collar, boquilla. 2. (joy.) engaste.
collide [kə'laɪd] *v.i.* chocar, embestir, estrellarse; estar en conflicto; **c. with,** chocar con, estrellarse contra.
collie ['kɑlɪ, B 'kɔlɪ] *s.* collie, perro de pastor escocés.
collier ['kɑljər, B 'kɔlɪə] *s.* 1. minero de carbón. 2. carbonero (que hace carbón de leña). 3. barco carbonero; marinero en un barco carbonero.
colliery [-jərɪ] *s.* mina de carbón, carbonera.
collieshangie ['kɑlɪ,ʃæŋɪ, B 'kɔlɪ-] *s.* (esco.) riña, camorra.
colligate ['kɑlə,geɪt, B 'kɔl-] *v.t.* 1. coligar, unir, juntar. 2. (lóg.) conectar, enlazar, ligar (esp. hechos aislados).
colligation [,kɑlə'geɪʃən, B ,kɔl-] *s.* coligación, unión.
collimate ['kɑlə,meɪt, B 'kɔl-] *v.t.* 1. ajustar la visual (de un telescopio). 2. (ópt.) hacer paralelos, alinear (rayos de luz).
collimation [,kɑlə'meɪʃən, B ,kɔl-] *s.* (ópt., astr.) colimación.
collimator ['kɑlə,meɪtər, B 'kɔlɪ,meɪtə] *s.* (ópt.) colimador.
collinear [kə'lɪnɪər, B kɔ'lɪnjə] *a.* colineal, en la misma línea recta.
Collins ['kɑlənz, B 'kɔl-] *s.* bebida helada compuesta de ginebra, azúcar y limón.
collision [kə'lɪʒən] *s.* 1. colisión, choque, impacto (entre trenes, autos, etc.). 2. (fig.) colisión, pugna, oposición, antagonismo (de ideas, intereses, etc.). 3. **to come into c. with,** chocar con.
collocate ['kɑlə,keɪt, B 'kɔl-] *v.t.* colocar, disponer, situar.
collocation [,kɑlə'keɪʃən, B ,kɔl-] *s.* colocación, disposición, arreglo.
collocutor [kə'lɑkjətər, B kə'lɔkjʊtə] *s.* interlocutor, colocutor.
collodion [kə'loʊdɪən] *s.* (quím.) colodión.
collogue [kə'loʊg] *v.i.* 1. hablar confidencialmente. 2. (dial.) conspirar, confabular.
colloid ['kɑl,ɔɪd, B 'kɔl-] *s.* (quím.) coloide. —*a.* (quím.) coloidal, coloideo, gelatinoso.
colloidal [kə'lɔɪdəl] *a.* (quím.) coloidal, coloideo.
collop ['kɑləp, B 'kɔl-] *s.* pedacito, bocado o tajada (esp. de carne).
colloquial [kə'loʊkwɪəl] *a.* familiar, dialogal (lenguaje).
colloquialism [-,ɪzəm] *s.* expresión familiar o corriente, palabra o estilo familiar.
colloquy ['kɑləkwɪ, B -kɔl-] *s.* coloquio, conversación, plática, diálogo.
collotype ['kɑlə,taɪp, B 'kɔl-] *s.* (impr.) colotipia.
collude [kə'lud] *v.i.* coludir, confabularse, conspirar.
collusion [kə'luʒən] *s.* confabulación, colusión, connivencia.
collusive [kə'lusɪv] *a.* colusorio.
collyrium [kə'lɪrɪəm] *s.* (*pl.* COLLYRIA [-ɪə] o COLLYRIUMS) (farm.) colirio.
collywobbles ['kɑlɪ,wɑbəlz, B 'kɔlɪ,wɔb-] *s. pl.* (fam.) 1. borborigmo. 2. dolor de vientre.
Colo. *abrev. de* **Colorado,** Colorado (E.U.).
colobus ['kɑləbəs, B 'kɔl-] *s.* (zool.) colobo.
colocynth ['kɑlə,sɪnθ, B 'kɔl-] *s.* (bot.) coloquíntida.
cologne [kə'loʊn] *s.* colonia, agua de Colonia.
cologne spirit, (quím.) alcohol rectificado.
Colombia [kə'lʌmbrɪə, B -'lɔm-] *s.* Colombia.
Colombian [-bɪən] *s., a.* colombiano.
Colombo [kə'lʌmboʊ] *s.* Colombo, capital de Ceylán.
colon ['koʊlən] *s.* 1. (anat.) colon. 2. (*pl.* COLONS) dos puntos (signo de puntuación). 3. [kə'loʊn] colono, terrateniente de un territorio colonial. 4. [kə'loʊn] colón, unidad monetaria de Costa Rica.
colonel ['kɜrnəl, B 'kɜnəl] *s.* (mil.) coronel.
Colonel Blimp, (G.B.) personaje reaccionario y militarista creado por el dibujante británico David Low.
colonelcy [-sɪ] **colonelship** [-,ʃɪp] *s.* coronelía, coronelato (Am.).
colonial [kə'loʊnjəl] *a.* colonial. —*s.* colono.
colonialism [-,ɪzəm] *s.* régimen colonial; colonialismo, política colonizadora.
colonialist [-əst] *s.* colonialista, partidario del colonialismo.
colonic [kə'lɑnɪk, B koʊ'lɔn-] *a.* (anat.) colónico.
colonist ['kɑlənəst, B 'kɔl-] *s.* colonizador, colono.
colonization [,kɑlənə'zeɪʃən, B ,kɔlənaɪ-] *s.* colonización.
colonize ['kɑlə,naɪz, B 'kɔl-] *v.t.* 1. colonizar, poblar, establecerse en (una región). 2. (pol., E.U.) llevar votantes fraudulentamente a (un distrito electoral). 3. (jer.) infiltrar (con agentes, etc.). —*v.i.* (con *in*) establecerse (en), establecer colonias (en).
colonizer [-ər, B -ə] *s.* colonizador.
colonnade [,kɑlə'neɪd, B ,kɔlə-] *s.* cocolumnata, peristilo.
colony ['kɑlənɪ, B 'kɔl-] *s.* (*pl.* COLONIES) colonia; (biol., bact.) colonia.
colophon ['kɑləfən, B 'kɔləfən] *s.* (tip.) 1. colofón, pie de imprenta. 2. sello editorial.
colophony ['kɑlə,foʊnɪ, B kə'lɔfənɪ] *s.* colofonia (resina).
color, (pr. G.B.) **colour** ['kʌlər, B -ə] *s.* 1. color. 2. color, colorante, tinte. 3. color (de la cara), buen color. 4. (*pl.*) colores, distintivo, divisa, insignia, enseña. 5. (*pl.*) colores (de la bandera), bandera; estandarte; servicio militar. 6. color, luz, apariencia, aspecto. 7. (fig.) color, pretexto. 8. (mús., pint.) color, colorido. 9. (fig.) color, colorido, matiz, carácter. 10. **off c.,** descolorido; indispuesto, desazonado; colorado, verde, libre (cuento, chiste, etc.); **to call to the colors,** llamar al servicio militar; **to change c.,** mudar o cambiar de color (sonrojarse o palidecer); **to get one's colors,** (pr. G.B.) ser incluido en el equipo (deportivo); **to hoist the colors,** enarbolar la bandera; **to join the colors,** alistarse; **to lend c. to,** dar visos de verosimilitud a; **to loose c.,** palidecer, tornarse pálido; **to paint in bright** (o **dark**) **colors,** (fig.) pintarlo muy bien (o negro); **to put false colors upon,** presentar bajo una luz (o color) falsa; **to sail under false colors,** (fig.) ser hipócrita o impostor; **to see (someone, something) in its true colors,** darse cuenta del verdadero carácter de (alguien, algo); **to serve with the colors,** sentar plaza, servir de soldado; **to show one's colors,** mostrar su carácter verdadero; **with flying colors,** con banderas desplegadas; triunfalmente, con todo éxito; **with the colors,** en filas, en servicio

militar. —*v.t.* 1. colorar, pintar; teñir. 2. (fig.) colorear, colorar, embellecer, exagerar. 3. paliar, disculpar (una mentira, etc.). 4. afectar, influir en. —*v.i.* sonrojarse, ruborizarse, ponerse colorado.

colorable, (pr. G.B.) **colourable** ['kʌlərəbəl] *a.* 1. que puede ser colorado o coloreado. 2. aparente, especioso; engañoso. 3. falsificado, fingido, pretendido.

Colorado [ˌkɑlə'rædoʊ, -'rɑd-, B ˌkɔl-] *s.* Colorado, estado de los E.U.

Colorado beetle, (ento.) (especie de) escarabajo (que destruye las plantas de patatas).

colorant ['kʌlərənt] *s.* colorante.

coloration, (pr. G.B.) **colouration** [ˌkʌlə'reɪʃən] *s.* 1. coloración. 2. colorido.

coloratura [ˌkʌlərə'tʊrə, B ˌkɔl-'tʊərə] *s.* (mús.) coloratura; floreos y cadencias de la soprano.

color bar, color line, (fig.) barrera (de prejuicio y situación entre personas de distintas razas).

color bearer, abanderado, portaestandarte.

color-blind ['kʌlərˌblaɪnd, B 'kʌləˌ-] *a.* daltoniano, acromatópsico (que no distingue los colores).

color-blindness [-nəs] *s.* daltonismo.

colorcast [-ˌkæst, B -ˌkɑst] *s.* (t.v.) transmisión en colores. —*v.t., v.i.* transmitir un programa de televisión en colores.

color chart, carta, muestrario o guía de colores.

color coding, codificación con colores.

colored, (pr. G.B.) **coloured** ['kʌlərd, B -əd] *s.* 1. colorado, coloreado; pintado, teñido. 2. (ant.) de color (personas). 3. lleno de colorido (relato, etc.). 4. parcial, exagerado, desfigurado, distorsionado (noticias, etc.).

colorfast [-ˌfæst, B -ˌfɑst] *a.* de color(es) sólido(s), de color(es) estable(s), de color(es) fijo(s).

color filter, filtro para fotografía en colores; (impr.) filtro cromofotográfico.

color film, película en colores.

colorful, (pr. G.B.) **colourful** ['kʌlərfəl, B 'kʌləfəl] *a.* 1. lleno de colorido. 2. pintoresco, vívido, brillante. 3. (fig.) policromo (ej., fantasía, imaginación, etc.).

color guard, (mil.) escolta de la bandera.

colorific [ˌkʌlə'rɪfɪk, B ˌkɔl-] *a.* (fís.) colorífico, colorativo.

colorimeter [-'rɪmətər, B -ə] *s.* colorímetro.

colorimetry [-'rɪmətrɪ] *s.* colorimetría.

coloring, (pr. G.B.) **colouring** ['kʌlərɪŋ] *s.* 1. coloración. 2. colorante, color, tinte. 3. colorido, color natural, tez. 4. (fig.) colorido.

coloring book, libro de colorear, libro para colorear.

colorist, (pr. G.B.) **colourist** [-ərəst] *s.* (arte) colorista.

colorize ['kʌləraɪz] *v.t.* (cine.) hacer la versión en color de.

colorless, (pr. G.B.) **colourless** [-ərləs, B -əlɪs] *a.* 1. incoloro, descolorido. 2. pálido. 3. (fig.) apagado, indiferente; aburrido.

color photography, fotografía en color.

color rinse, enjuague de color.

color salute, (mil.) saludo con la bandera.

color scheme, combinación de colores.

color screen, (impr.) filtro cromofotográfico.

color television, televisión en color; (*set*) televisor en color.

colossal [kə'lɑsəl, B -'lɔs-] *a.* colosal, descomunal.

colosseum [ˌkɑlə'siəm B ˌkɔlə-] *s.* coliseo.

Colossian [kə'lɑʃən, B -'lɔʃ-] *a., s.* colosense.

colossus [kə'lɑsəs, B -'lɔs-] *s.* (*pl.* COLOSSI [-ˌaɪ] o COLOSSUSES) coloso, estatua gigantesca; **C.,** Coloso (de Rodas).

colostomy [kə'lɑstəmɪ, B -'lɔs-] *s.* (cir.) colostomía.

colostrum [kə'lɑstrəm, B -'lɔs-] *s.* calostro, leche secretada por las glándulas mamarias después del parto.

colour, colourable, (pr. G.B.) *vars. de* color, colorable.

colporteur ['kɑlˌpɔrtər, B 'kɔlˌpɔtə] *s.* repartidor de folletos (esp. religiosos).

colt [koʊlt] *s.* 1. potro. 2. mozuelo, mozalbete inexperto. 3. (mar.) azote, látigo de soga. 4. (astr.) **C.,** Caballo Menor. 5. **C.,** pistola o revólver de marca Colt.

colter, (G.B.) **coulter** ['koʊltər, B -ə] *s.* cuchilla (fijada delante de la reja del arado).

coltish ['koʊltɪʃ] *a.* juguetón, retozón.

coltsfoot ['koʊltsˌfʊt] *s.* (*pl.* COLTSFOOTS) (bot.) fárfara, tusílago, uña de caballo.

colubrid ['kɑljəbrəd, B 'kɔl-] *s., a.* (zool.) colúbrido.

colubrine [-ˌbraɪn] *a.* 1. colubrino, culebrino, astuto. 2. colúbrido.

columbarium [ˌkɑləm'bɛriəm, B ˌkɔləm-'bɛər-] *s.* (*pl.* COLUMBARIA [-ɪə]) (hist.) columbario; edificio con nichos para urnas funerarias.

columbary ['kɑləmˌbɛrɪ B 'kɔləmbərɪ] *s.* palomar.

Columbia [kə'lʌmbɪə] *s.* (poét.) Columbia (los Estados Unidos de América).

Columbian [-bɪən] *a.* 1. colombino; relativo a Cristóbal Colón. 2. de los Estados Unidos de América.

columbine ['kɑləmˌbaɪn, B 'kɔl-] *s.* (bot.) aguileña, pajarilla; flor que parece una paloma. —*a.* columbino.

columbite [kə'lʌmˌbaɪt] *s.* (min.) columbita.

columbium [kə'lʌmbɪəm] *s.* (quím.) columbio.

Columbus [kə'lʌmbəs] *s.* Colón (Cristóbal Colón).

Columbus Day, Día de la Raza (12 de octubre).

columella [ˌkɑljə'mɛlə B ˌkɔljʊ-] *s.* (*pl.* COLUMELLAE [-'mɛlˌi]) 1. (bot., zool.) columela. 2. eje central, columnilla.

column ['kɑləm, B 'kɔləm] *s.* 1. columna; pilar; soporte. 2. (mil.) columna de efectivos.

columnar [kə'lʌmnər, B -nə] *a.* columnar, columnario.

columned ['kɑləmd, B 'kɔl-] *a.* dotado de columnas, con columnas.

columniation [kəˌlʌmnɪ'eɪʃən] *s.* (arq.) columnata.

columnist ['kɑləmnəst, -əməst, B 'kɔl-] *s.* columnista, articulista (encargado de una sección especial de un periódico).

column still, (quím.) destilador en columna.

colure [kə'lʊr, 'koʊlʊr, B kə'ljʊə] *s.* (astr.) coluro.

colza ['kɑlzə, B 'kɔl-] *s.* (bot.) colza.

coma ['koʊmə] *s.* 1. (med.) coma. 2. estupor, letargo, sopor.

coma ['koʊmə] *s.* (*pl.* COMAE ['koʊmi]) 1. (astr.) cola o cabellera (de un cometa). 2. (bot., zool.) coma. 3. (ópt.) aberración de coma.

Coma Berenices [-ˌbɛrə'naɪˌsiz] (astr.) cabellera de Berenice.

comaker ['koʊˌmeɪkər, B -ə] *s.* (com.) fiador, garante.

Comanche [kə'mæntʃɪ] *a., s.* comanche (raza azteca de indios norteamericanos).

comate ['koʊˌmeɪt] *s.* compañero, camarada. —*a.* peloso, peludo, cabelludo, velloso.

comatose ['koʊməˌtoʊs, 'kɑm-, B 'koʊ-] *a.* (med.) comatoso.

comatula [kə'mætʃələ] **comatulid** [-ələd] *s.* (*pl.* COMATULAE [-əˌli, -əˌlaɪ]) (zool.) comátula.

comb [koʊm] *s.* 1. peine. 2. peine, carda. 3. almohaza. 4. (elec.) peine. 5. cresta (de ave, esp. de gallo); cresta (de ola o montaña). 6. panal (de abejas). —*v.t.* 1. peinar. 2. cardar 3. almohazar (caballería, etc.). 4. (t. con *out*) registrar, escudriñar, ej., *c. the town,* registrar (toda) la ciudad. 5. **c. out,** desenredar, desenmarañar; eliminar. —*v.i.* encresparse (las olas).

combat ['kɑmˌbæt, B 'kɔmbət] *s.* combate, batalla, lucha. — [kəm'bæt, 'kɑmˌbæt, B 'kɔmbət, 'kʌm-] *v.t.* (*pret., p.p.* COMBATTED; *p.pr.* COMBATING) combatir, luchar contra, oponerse a. —*v.i.* combatir, luchar, pelear, contender.

combatant [kəm'bætənt, 'kɑmbət-, B 'kɔmbət-] *s.* combatiente.

combat duty, (mil.) servicio de combate, servicio en el frente.

combat fatigue, (mil., med.) fatiga de combate.

combative [kəm'bætɪv, B 'kɔmbət-] *a.* combativo, belicoso.

combativeness [-nəs] *s.* combatividad.

combat team, (mil.) agrupación mixta de combate.

combat-worthy ['kɑmˌbætˌwɜrðɪ, B 'kɔmbətˌwɜðɪ] *a.* apto para el combate.

combe [kum] *s.* (G.B.) valle estrecho, desfiladero.

comber ['koʊmər, B -mə] *s.* 1. peinador, cardador. 2. ola encrespada.

combinable [kəm'baɪnəbəl] *a.* combinable.

combination [ˌkɑmbə'neɪʃən, B ˌkɔm-] *s.* 1. combinación; unión, mezcla. 2. combinación (prenda interior femenina). 3. (mat., quím.) combinación.

combination fuse, espoleta de doble efecto.

combination last, horma de zapato de talón más estrecho que el que corresponde al de su empeine o pala.

combination lock, cerradura de combinación.

combinative ['kɑmbəˌneɪtɪv, kəm'baɪnət-, B 'kɔmbɪnət-] *a.* combinador, combinatorio.

combine [kəm'baɪn] *v.t.* combinar; unir, aunar. —*v.i.* 1. combinarse. 2. unirse, cooperar, mancomunarse, aunarse. — ['kɑmˌbaɪn, B 'kɔm-] *s.* 1. combinación, unión, asociación (de personas); monopolio. 2. (agr.) segadora trilladora.

combined [-'baɪnd] *a.* compuesto; juntos; unidos.

combined power output, (ing.) potencia total.

combing ['koʊmɪŋ] *s.* 1. peinada, cardadura. 2. (*pl.*) peinadura (cabellos que se arrancan con el peine).

combining form [kəm'baɪnɪŋ-] (gram.) elemento de compuestos.

combo ['kɑmboʊ, B 'kɔm-] *s.* (jer.) 1. combinación. 2. pequeña orquesta de jazz o de música bailable.

comb perforation, (filat.) dentado de peine.

combust [kəm'bʌst] *v.t.* quemar. —*a.* (astrol.) díc. del planeta o estrella tan cercana al sol que se oscurece.

combustibility [-ˌbʌstə'bɪlətɪ] *s.* combustibilidad.

combustible [-'bʌstəbəl] *a.* 1. combustible. 2. excitable, impetuoso. —*s.* combustible.

combustion [-tʃən] *s.* combustión; tumulto, alboroto.

combustion chamber, (maq.) cámara de combustión.

combustion engine, motor de combustión.

combustor [-tər, B -tə] *s.* cámara de combustión (de una turbina de gas o motor de reacción a chorro).

comdr. *abrev. de* **commander,** comandante.

comdt. *abrev. de* **commandant,** comandante.

come [kʌm] *v.i.* (*pret.* CAME [keɪm] *p.p.* COME; *p.pr.* COMING) 1. venir. 2. llegar, ej., *I came to know her,* llegué a conocerla. 3. recorrer, ej., *I have c. three miles,* he recorrido tres millas, *we have c. a long way,* hemos llegado lejos. 4. progresar, desarrollarse, ej., *our plans were coming along splendidly,* nuestros planes progresaban (o se desarrollaban) espléndidamente. 5. costar, ej., *fine cars c. high,* los carros buenos cuestan mucho. 6. (vulg.) tener un orgasmo, venirse, acabar (Am.), correrse. 7. resultar (fácil, cierto, natural, caro, etc.). 8. **come!** ¡vamos! ¡venga! ¡ven!; ¡vaya! (Esp.), ej., *c., you can't mean it!* ¡vaya! no puede Ud. hablar en serio; **c. about,** suceder, acaecer; (mar.) virar (viento, barco); **c. across,** encontrarse con, dar con, toparse con; (jer.) cumplir, entregar, cumplir con, pagar o entregar dinero; **c. after,** venir detrás de; seguir, venir después; venir en busca de; **c. again,** venir otra vez, volver; (*en imper.*) (fam.) ¡repítalo! ¿cómo dijo?; **c. along,** progresar; acompañar, ir con (alguien); (*en imper.*) ¡vamos! ¡apresúrate!; **c. and go,** ir y venir; llegar e irse; **c. apart,** separarse, desunirse; partirse (en dos); **c. apart at the seams,** (jer.) reventar, reventarse (de cólera, etc.); **c. around (o round),** volver en sí; restablecerse (de enfermedad); cambiar de direccíon; virar (el barco); ceder (en su opinión); hacer una visita casual, visitar en forma casual; **c. around (o round) to (point of view,** etc.), convencerse y aceptar (punto de vista, etc.); **c. asunder,** deshacerse; **c. at,** encontrar, tropezar con, descubrir; abalanzarse sobre, atacar; **c. away,** irse retirarse; desprenderse; **c. back,** volver; volver a la mente; (fam.) recobrarse, rehabilitarse; replicar; desquitarse; **c. before,** llegar antes; anteponerse, venir antes de; comparecer ante (juez, etc.); **c. between,** interponerse, ponerse entre (madre e hijo, etc.); interferir (entre); **c. by,** venir por (tren, etc.); obtener, conseguir; **c. clean,** desembuchar, confesar todo; **c. down,** bajar, caer; demolerse, desplomarse; llegar por tradición, ser transmitido; venir a menos, decaer; **c. down on (o upon),** caer encima; reprochar, regañar, reñir; **c. down to,** llegar a descender hasta; **c. down with,** caer enfermo con; **c. easy to,** costar poco esfuerzo a; tener aptitud para; **c. for,** venir por, venir a buscar; **c. forth,** aparecer, hacer su aparición; **c. forward,** responder a la llamada, presentarse; **c. home to,** darse cuenta de, convencerse de; **c. in,** entrar; llegar (en carrera), ej., *c. in second,* llegar segundo, llegar en segundo lugar; estar, ej., *where does the joke c. in?* ¿dónde está el chiste?; ganar, sacar, *where do I c. in?* ¿qué ganaré yo con esto? ¿qué voy a sacar yo de esto?; (*en imper.*) ¡entre! ¡adelante!; **c. in for,** recibir (castigo, etc.); recibir su parte de, corresponder a uno (cierta suma); heredar; **c. in handy** (o **useful**), resultar útil; **c. into,** entrar en; adueñarse de; recibir (herencia), heredar; **c. into one's own,** (fig.) ser reconocido, hacer valer sus méritos; entrar en su propio terreno; **c. into play,** entrar en juego; **c. into sight,** divisarse; **c. into style,** ponerse de moda; **c. into the world,** venir al mundo, nacer; **c. into trouble,** meterse en aprietos; **c. near,** acercarse; faltar poco para, ej., *he came near winning the race,* le faltó poco para ganar la carrera; **c. next,** seguir, venir después (de); **c. of,** venir de, descender de, proceder de (buena familia, etc.); **c. of age,** llegar a la mayoría de edad; **c. off,** soltarse, desatarse, caer; salir (bien, mal; ganador, perdedor, etc.); suceder, resultar; tener éxito, salir bien; **c. off it!** ¡no me vengas con eso!; **c. on,** avanzar, seguir avanzando; progresar, mejorar; salir a escena; (*en imper.*) ¡vamos! ¡venga!; **c. one's way,** caerle a uno por casualidad; **c. out,** salir; revelarse, descubrirse, salir a luz; publicarse; debutar, ser presentado (en sociedad); pronunciarse; declararse en huelga; salir, quitarse (mancha, etc.); **c. (well o badly) out of,** salir (bien o mal) parado de; **c. out with,** salir con, publicar (noticias); revelar, anunciar; salirse con, saltar con (una observación, sugerencia, idea, etc.), soltar (una maldición, etc.); **c. over,** venir (de lejos), ej., *she came over from Los Angeles to see me,* vino desde Los Ángeles para verme; cambiar de opinión, dejarse convencer o persuadir; pasar, ej., *I don't know what has c. over him, why he is so angry,* no sé qué le pasó, porqué está tan enojado; **c. over to,** pasarse a (otro bando, etc.); **c. short of,** no llegar a, quedar debajo de, ej., *it came short of my expectations,* no llegó a (o está lejos de) lo que yo esperaba; **c. through,** salir (bien) de, soportar (prueba, experiencia, etc.); (jer.) cumplir, pagar; tener éxito, cumplirse; **c. to,** llegar a, llegar hasta, ej., *when we c. to the next house,* cuando lleguemos a la casa siguiente, *we c. now to the problem of,* ahora llegamos al problema de, *the skirt came to her knees,* la falda le llegaba hasta las rodillas; volver en sí, ocurrir a, pasar a, ej., *no harm will c. to you,* no sufrirás ningún daño; heredar; sumar, ascender a; (mar.) orzar; (mar.) detenerse (barco); **c. to a head,** madurar, definirse; **c. to an end,** llegar a su fin; **c. to a point,** rematar en punta; **c. to blows,** llegar a golpes; **c. together,** reunirse, juntarse; **c. to grief,** fracasar, salir mal parado; **c. to grips with,** afrontar, atacar, habérselas con; **c. to hand,** llegar a la mano (de uno), ser recibida (carta, etc.); **c. to harm,** dañarse, lastimarse; **c. to life,** volver en sí, reanimarse; (fig.) cobrar vida; **c. to life again,** renacer; **c. to light,** salir a la luz; **c. to mind,** ocurrirse, venir a la memoria; **c. to nothing,** fracasar, reducirse a nada; **c. to oneself,** volver en sí; recobrar la calma; **c. to one's senses,** recobrar la razón; **c. to pass,** suceder, ocurrir; **c. to stay,** quedarse para siempre; ser permanente; **c. to terms,** llegar a un acuerdo, convenirse; **c. to that,** en cuanto a eso; **c. to the point,** ir al grano; **c. true,** resultar, realizarse; **c. under,** clasificarse en, venir bajo (letra, capítulo, etc.); estar sometido a (influencia); **c. undone** (o **unstuck**), deshacerse, desatarse; **c. up,** subir; surgir, presentarse (problema, etc.); brotar, salir (hierba, etc.); ponerse de moda; (G.B.) ingresar en la universidad; (*en imper.*) ¡arre! **c. up to,** alcanzar, estar a la altura de, satisfacer; abordar, acercarse a; **c. up with,** dar alcance a (uno); dar (una idea, etc.); **c. upon,** caer encima, atacar por sorpresa, embestir; dar con, encontrarse con; **c. what may,** venga lo que venga; **easy c., easy go,** los dineros del sacristán cantando vienen y cantando van; **how c.?** ¿cómo es eso? ¿por qué? ¿cómo es posible?; **it comes to this,** en resumen, en suma; **to c.,** más, todavía, ej., *we are well supplied for years to c.,* estamos bien abastecidos para (muchos) años más; del futuro, del porvenir, ej., *the shape of things to c.,* el aspecto de las cosas del futuro o del porvenir, *two years c. Christmas,* la próxima Navidad hará dos años.

come-and-go ['kʌmənd'goʊ] *s.* vaivén.

comeback ['kʌm,bæk] *s.* 1. réplica. 2. retorno (esp. a posición de fama, etc.). 3. (fam.) rehabilitación.

comedian [kə'midɪən] *s.* 1. comediante, cómico. 2. hombre chistoso.

comedienne [-,midɪ'ɛn] *s.* (fr.) comedianta, cómica; actriz de género chico.

comedo ['kɑmə,doʊ, B 'kɔm-] *s.* (*pl.* COMEDOS o COMEDONES [,kɑmə'doʊniz, B ,kɔm-]) (med.) comedón, espinilla (en la piel).

comedown ['kʌm,daʊn] *s.* desilusión, revés; pérdida de dignidad o rango, descenso en fortuna; humillación.

comedy ['kɑmədɪ, B 'kɔm-] *s.* 1. (teat.) comedia. 2. ficción, fingimiento.

comedy of intrigue, (teat.) comedia de misterio o intriga.

comedy of manners, (teat.) comedia frívola de costumbres modernas.

comedy of situation, (teat.) comedia de enredo.

come-hither [,kʌm'hɪðər, B -ə] *a.* seductor, sugestivo.

comeliness ['kʌmlɪnəs] *s.* gracia, donaire.

comely [-lɪ] *a.* gracioso, bonito; bien parecido.

come-on ['kʌm,ɑn, -,ɔn, B -,ɔn] *s.* aliciente, señuelo, añagaza (artificio para atraer con engaño).

comer ['kʌmər, B -ə] *s.* 1. el que llega, el llegado, ej., *first c.,* el que llega primero, el primer llegado. 2. interesado, ej., *open to all comers,* abierto para todos los interesados, *all comers are welcome,* todos los que vengan serán bienvenidos. 3. (fig.) promesa, hombre que llegará lejos.

comestible [kə'mɛstəbəl] *a.* comestible. —*s.* (*gen. pl.*) víveres, comestibles.

comet ['kɑmət, B 'kɔmɪt] *s.* (astr.) cometa.

cometary [-ə,tɛrɪ, B -ɪtərɪ] *a.* (astr.) cometario.

comeuppance [kə'mʌpəns] *s.* (fam. E.U.) merecido; reprimenda merecida, castigo justo; **he got his c.,** llevó su merecido.

comfit ['kʌmfət, 'kɑm-, B 'kʌm-, 'kɔm-] *s.* confite, dulce.

comfort ['kʌmfərt, B -fət] *s.* 1. comodidad. 2. consuelo, solaz, alivio. 3. bienestar, confort; (*pl.*) comodidades físicas. —*v.t.* consolar, confortar, alentar, ayudar.

comfortable ['kʌmftəbəl, -fərtəbəl, B -fət-] *a.* 1. confortable, cómodo. 2. confortador, agradable. 3. sosegado, tranquilo. 4. de medios adecuados, holgado.

comfortableness [-nəs] *s.* comodidad, bienestar.

comfortably [-blɪ] *adv.* confortablemente, cómodamente.

comforter ['kʌmfərtər, B -fətə] *s.* 1. confortador, consolador. 2. **the C.,** (bíbl., teo.) el Espíritu Santo. 3. (E.U.) cobertor, colcha. 4. bufanda de lana. 5. (G.B.) chupete, chupón (para los niños) (Am.).

comfortless [-ləs] *a.* 1. sin comodidades. 2. desconsolado, triste, desolado, inconsolable.

comfort-loving [-'lʌvɪŋ] *a.* comodón.

comfort station, lugar de descanso; retrete, lavatorio; excusado público.

comfrey ['kʌmfrɪ] *s.* (bot.) consuelda, sínfito.

comfy ['kʌmfɪ] *a.* (fam.) confortable, cómodo.

comic ['kɑmɪk, B 'kɔm-] *a.* cómico, divertido, gracioso. —*s.* 1. cómico, comediante. 2. (*pl.*) tiras cómicas (de los periódicos).

comical [-ɪkəl] *a.* cómico, gracioso, burlesco, bufo.

comically [-kəlɪ] *adv.* cómicamente, graciosamente, burlescamente.

comic book, revista de tiras cómicas, muñequitos.

comic opera, ópera bufa, ópera cómica.

comic relief, hecho inesperado que rompe la tensión de una situación seria o difícil.

comic strip, tira cómica (en los periódicos).

coming ['kʌmɪŋ] *a.* 1. venidero, próximo. 2. con mucho futuro, de gran porvenir (ej., un abogado joven). 3. **he had it c. to him,** no podía esperar otra cosa, lo ha merecido. —*s.* llegada; advenimiento.

coming-out [-'aʊt] *s.* (*pl.* COMINGS-OUT) debut, presentación (en sociedad).
coming-out party, baile de debutantes.
Comintern ['kɑmən,tɜrn, B 'kɔmɪn,tɜn] *s.* Comintern, comité ejecutivo de la Tercera Internacional.
comitia [kə'mɪʃɪə] *s. pl.* (hist. romana) comicios.
comity ['kɑmətɪ, B 'kɔm-] *s.* cortesía, urbanidad; **c. of nations,** (der. intern.) cortesía entre naciones (al reconocer en sus propios territorios las decisiones y los actos legislativos, administrativos o judiciales de otros estados).
comma ['kɑmə, B 'kɔmə] *s.* 1. (gram.) coma. 2. (mús.) coma, ligera diferencia entre tonos enarmónicos como el sol sostenido y el la bemol.
comma bacillus, (biol.) bacilo coma que produce el cólera.
command [kə'mænd, B -'mɑnd] *v.t.* 1. ordenar, mandar, dictar, imponer, regir. 2. poseer, disponer de (medios, riqueza, habilidad, etc.). 3. demandar, exigir (ej., honorario alto). 4. merecer (simpatía, compasión, respeto, etc.). 5. dominar, contener (ira, pasión, etc.). 6. (mil.) comandar (tropas, etc.). 7. (mil.) dominar (posición). 8. **yours to c.,** a sus órdenes. —*v.i.* 1. mandar, dar orden. 2. imperar, gobernar. 3. tener el mando, ser comandante. —*s.* 1. mando, orden, mandato, mandamiento, ordenanza. 2. autoridad, mando, dirección, cargo, gobierno. 3. dominio (de un idioma); dominio, control (del terreno, de un desfiladero, del aire, del mar, de una situación, etc.). 4. alcance, disposición, recursos. 5. (mil.) mando, comando. 6. (mil.) comandancia. 7. **at one's c.,** a la disposición de uno; **great c. of language,** elocuencia; **in c. of,** (mil.) al mando de; **to have c. of oneself,** saber dominarse, tener dominio de sí mismo; **to take c.,** asumir o tomar el mando; **under (the) c. of,** bajo el mando de; **word of c.,** (mil) voz de mando.
commandant ['kɑmən,dænt, -,dɑnt, B ,kɔmən'dænt] *s.* (mil.) comandante (de una plaza, fuerte, ejército, etc.).
commandeer [,kɑməndɪər, B ,kɔmən'dɪə] *v.t.* 1. requisar. 2. reclutar por la fuerza. 3. confiscar, adueñarse de.
commander [kə'mændər, B -'mɑndə] *s.* 1. comandante; jefe. 2. capitán de fragata. 3. comendador (de una orden de caballeros). 4. (const.) pisón, machota.
commander in chief, comandante en jefe, jefe supremo.
commandery [-ərɪ] *s.* comandancia; encomienda, dignidad de comendador.
commanding [kə'mændɪŋ, B kə'mɑnd-] *a.* 1. dominante, imperante. 2. imponente, impresionante, convincente. 3. (mil.) autorizado.
commanding officer, (mil.) comandante en jefe.
commandment [-mənt] *s.* mandamiento, mandato, precepto; **the Ten Commandments,** los diez mandamientos, el decálogo.
commando [kə'mændoʊ, B kə'mɑn-] *s.* (*pl.* COMMANDOS O COMMANDOES) comando (soldados o tropas especialmente adiestrados para efectuar misiones muy peligrosas).
command performance, función dada por disposición del rey, el presidente, o a petición del público; función de gran realce.
command post, (mil.) puesto de mando.
commeasurable [kə'mɛʒərəbəl] *a.* conmensurable.
commedia dell'arte [kə,meɪdɪədɛl'ɑrtɪ, -,mɛd-, B -'ɑtɪ] *s.* (teat.) tipo de comedia desarrollado en Italia en el siglo XVI, comedia del arte, comedia de capricho.
comme il faut [,kʌm,il'foʊ, B ,kɔm-] (fr.) correcto, como debe ser.
commemorate [kə'mɛmə,reɪt] *v.t.* conmemorar, celebrar.
commemoration [-,mɛmə'reɪʃən] *s.* conmemoración, celebración.
commemorative [-'mɛmərətɪv, -,reɪt-] *a.* conmemorativo. —*s.* (filat.) sello conmemorativo.
commence [kə'mɛns] *v.t.* comenzar, empezar, iniciar. —*v.i.* 1. tener comienzo, empezar, principiarse; ponerse (a hacer algo). 2. (G.B.) optar a un grado universitario.
commencement [-mənt] *s.* 1. principio, comienzo; inauguración. 2. día de graduación; ceremonia de graduación (en las universidades y colegios secundarios).
commend [kə'mɛnd] *v.t.* 1. encomendar, encargar. 2. recomendar. 3. ensalzar, alabar, loar.
commendable [-əbəl] *a.* recomendable, loable, meritorio, plausible.
commendably [-blɪ] *adv.* loablemente, meritoriamente.
commendam [kə'mɛndəm] *s.* (relig.) beneficio provisional (concedido hasta el nombramiento de un titular).
commendation [,kɑmən'deɪʃən, B ,kɔmɛn-] *s.* 1. recomendación. 2. encomio, alabanza.
commendatory [kə'mɛndə,tɔrɪ, B kɔ-tərɪ] *a.* 1. laudatorio; recomendatorio, comendatorio. 2. (relig.) comendaticio.
commensal [kə'mɛnsəl] *s.* comensal, compañero de mesa; (biol.) comensal.
commensalism [-sə,lɪzəm] *s.* 1. (biol.) asociado. 2. comensalía.
commensurability [kə,mɛnsərə'bɪlətɪ, -,mɛntʃ-, B -,mɛnʃ-] *s.* conmensurabilidad.
commensurable [kə'mɛnsərəbəl, -'mɛntʃ-, B -,mɛnʃ-] *a.* 1. (mat.) conmensurable. 2. proporcionado.
commensurate [-ərət] *a.* 1. (con *with*) de medida igual (a), coextenso (con). 2. (con *to* o *with*) en proporción (con), proporcionado (a); igual (a).
commensurately [-lɪ] *adv.* proporcionadamente.
comment ['kɑm,ɛnt, B 'kɔm-] *s.* comentario, comento, glosa; explicación; observación, exposición. —*v.i.* hacer observaciones o críticas; juzgar; **c. on** (o **upon**), comentar, escribir comentarios. —*v.t.* comentar; hacer comentarios sobre (un asunto o evento); glosar, explicar.
commentary [-ən,tɛrɪ, B -tərɪ] *s.* comentario, glosa; observación; (*pl.*) comentarios.
commentate [-,teɪt] *v.t.* dar un comentario sobre; narrar (un evento deportivo, una ceremonia, etc. en la radio). —*v.i.* actuar como comentador o comentarista.
commentator [-ər, B -ə] *s.* 1. comentarista, glosador. 2. comentador; locutor, narrador, comentarista (de radio o televisión).
commerce ['kɑmərs, B 'kɔməs] *s.* 1. comercio, negocio, tráfico. 2. comercio, trato, comunicación. 3. comercio, ayuntamiento (carnal). 4. comercio (un juego de naipes). — ['kɑm-, kə'mɜrs, B -'mɜs] *v.i.* (ant.) (gen. con *with*) comunicarse, tratar(se) (con).
commercial [kə'mɜrʃəl, B -'mɜʃəl] *a.* comercial, mercantil. —*s.* (rad., t.v.) anuncio comercial, aviso de propaganda, propaganda comercial.
commercial art, arte comercial o publicitario.
commercial code, clave comercial para enviar mensajes por cable a costo mínimo.
commercialism [-,ɪzəm] *s.* comercialismo, mercantilismo.
commercialization [kə,mɜrʃələ'zeɪʃən, B -,mɜʃəlaɪ-] *s.* comercialización.
commercialize [-'mɜrʃə,laɪz, B -'mɜʃə-] *v.t.* 1. comerciar (un producto). 2. comercializar, mercantilizar. 3. (fig.) desmeritar, rebajar el valor artístico o moral de alguien o algo.
commercial law, (der.) código mercantil.
commercially [-lɪ] *adv.* comercialmente, mercantilmente.
commercial paper, efecto, documento, instrumentos o valores negociables.
commercial traveler, agente viajero.
commie ['kɑmɪ, B 'kɔmɪ] *s.* (despec.) rojo, comunista.
comminate ['kɑmə,neɪt, B 'kɔm-] *v.t.* conminar, anatematizar.
commination [,kɑmə'neɪʃən, B ,kɔm-] *s.* conminación, amenaza.
comminatory ['kɑmənə,tɔrɪ, kə'mɪn-, B 'kɔmɪnətərɪ] *a.* conminatorio.
commingle [kə'mɪŋgəl, B kɔ-] *v.t., v.i.* mezclar(se); unir(se), compenetrar(se), barajar(se); hacer mezcla.
comminute ['kɑmə,nut, B 'kɔmɪ,njut] *v.t.* triturar, pulverizar, moler; desmenuzar; fraccionar (una propiedad).
comminuted fracture, (med.) fractura conminuta.
comminution [,kɑmə'nuʃən, B ,kɔmɪ'nju-] *s.* trituración, pulverización, fracturación; fraccionamiento, división.
commiserable [kə'mɪzərəbəl] *a.* doliente, lastimoso.
commiserate [-,reɪt] *v.t.* compadecer, apiadarse de, compadecerse. —*v.i.* (ú. con *with*) tener lástima o compasión (de).
commiseration [-,mɪzə'reɪʃən] *s.* conmiseración, compasión, piedad.
commiserative [-'mɪzə,reɪtɪv] *a.* compasivo.
commissar ['kɑmə'sɑr, B ,kɔmɪ'sɑ] *s.* comisario (en la Unión Soviética, llamado *ministro* desde el 1946).
commissarial [,kɑmə'sɛrɪəl, B ,kɔmɪ'sɛər-] *a.* de comisario.
commissariat [-ət] *s.* 1. comisariato (en la Unión Soviética, hoy ministerio). 2. (mil.) comisaría general, intendencia.
commissary ['kɑmə,sɛrɪ, B 'kɔmɪsərɪ] *s.* 1. comisario, delegado. 2. (mil.) cooperativa militar, economato. 3. comestibles.
commission [kə'mɪʃən] 1. comisión, encargo. 2. cometido, encargo, misión, encomienda. 3. comisión, delegación, comité; junta (municipal). 4. comisión, perpetración (de un delito, crimen, etc.). 5. (mil.) patente, nombramiento; grado (de oficial). 6. (com.) comisión (que cobra un agente por servicios prestados o mercancías vendidas). 7. **on c.,** (com.) a base de comisión; como comisionista; **out of c.,** fuera del servicio; inservible, descompuesto, desarreglado; **to put out of c.,** jubilar, retirar del servicio; inutilizar, arruinar; (fam.) poner fuera de combate, acabar con. —*v.t.* 1. comisionar, delegar. 2. encargar, autorizar, apoderar, capacitar, facultar 3. mandar hacer, encargar (un trabajo). 4. (mar.) poner en servicio activo (un navío); (mil.) nombrar, diputar (a un oficial); (mar.) nombrar comandante o capitán.
commissionaire [kə,mɪʃə'nɛr, B -'nɛə] *s.* (pr. G.B.) portero uniformado (en teatros, cines, tiendas); mensajero.
commissioned officer, oficial (de las fuerzas armadas); teniente en el ejército, alférez en la marina de guerra, cuando son nombrados por escrito.
commissioner [kə'mɪʃənər, B -nə] *s.* comisionado, comisario; (E.U.) miembro de la junta municipal.

commission merchant, (com.) comisionista.
commissure ['kɑmə,ʃʊr, B 'kɔmɪ,sjʊə] *s.* (anat.) comisura.
commit [kə'mɪt] *v.t.* (*pret., p.p.* COMMITTED; *p.pr.* COMMITTING) 1. cometer (error, crimen, etc.). 2. encomendar, confiar, cometer. 3. consignar, depositar, entregar. 4. someter, presentar (un proyecto a un comité legislativo). 5. confinar, recluir (en prisión, manicomio, etc.). 6. registrar, consignar (ideas, hechos, etc.). 7. comprometer; obligar. 8. condenar, enjuiciar. 9. **c. oneself,** comprometerse; **c. to memory,** aprender de memoria; **c. to writing,** poner por escrito.
commitment [-mənt] *s.* 1. compromiso, obligación, cometido. 2. comisión, encargo. 3. confinamiento, reclusión (en prisión, manicomio, etc.). 4. sometimiento, presentación (de un proyecto a un comité legislativo).
committable [-əbəl] *a.* perpetrable.
committal [-əl] *s.* 1. confinamiento (en prisión, manicomio, etc.), reclusión. 2. comprometimiento. 3. entierro.
committee [kə'mɪtɪ] *s.* comité, comisión, junta.
committeeman [-mən] *s.* 1. miembro de comité, comisionado. 2. (pol.) jefe regional de partido.
committee of the whole, comisión de la totalidad de los miembros de una asamblea reunidos en junta con carácter puramente deliberativo.
committee of ways and means, (E.U.) comisión de arbitrios.
commix [kə'mɪks, kɑ-, B kɔ-] *v.t., v.i.* mezclar(se), unir(se).
commixture [-tʃər, B -tʃə] *s.* mezcla; mezcladura, conmistión.
commode [kə'moʊd] *s.* 1. cómoda. 2. sillaretrete, sillico. 3. palanganero movible.
commodious [-ɪəs] *a.* cómodo, espacioso, holgado, amplio.
commodiously [-lɪ] *adv.* cómodamente, holgadamente, ampliamente.
commodiousness [-nəs] *s.* comodidad, holgura, espaciosidad.
commodity [kə'mɑdətɪ, B kə'mɔd-] *s.* 1. mercancía, mercadería; producto, género. 2. (ant. y der.) comodidad, conveniencia, utilidad.
commodore ['kɑmə,dɔr, B 'kɔmə,dɔ] *s.* 1. comodoro. 2. capitán de escuadra. 3. presidente (de un club náutico).
common ['kɑmən, B 'kɔm-] *a.* 1. común, corriente, familiar; ordinario, vulgar. 2. elemental (cortesía, honradez, etc.). 3. (mat.) común (número). 4. (gram.) común (género, nombre, etc.). —*s.* 1. pasto o terreno comunal, ejido. 2. (*pl.,* G.B.) (el) pueblo, (el) vulgo; comunes (en el parlamento); Cámara de los Comunes. 3. (*pl.*) refectorio (esp. en colegio); víveres, provisiones; ración diaria. 4. (der.) derecho conjunto, derecho de usufructo conjunto. 5. **in c.,** en común, igualmente; mancomunadamente; compartido; **in c. with,** del mismo modo que, al igual que; **out of the c.,** insólito, raro, extraño.
commonable [-əbəl] *a.* común, comunal (animales, tierras, pastos).
commonage [-ɪdʒ] *s.* 1. terreno comunal. 2. estado llano, estado común; derecho de pasto.
commonalty ['kɑmənəltɪ, B 'kɔm-] **commonality** [,kɑmə'nælətɪ, B ,kɔm-] *s.* 1. (el) vulgo, (el) pueblo; estado llano, estado común. 2. corporación. 3. comunidad, grupo, conjunto.
common carrier, empresa de transporte público.
common cold, (med.) resfriado común.
common council, ayuntamiento, concejo, municipalidad.
common councilman, concejal.
common crier, pregonero.
common denominator, (mat.) común denominador.
commoner ['kɑmənər, B 'kɔmənə] *s.* 1. plebeyo. 2. (G.B.) miembro de la Cámara de los Comunes. 3. (G.B.) estudiante que no ha conseguido una beca. 4. comunero.
Common Era, era vulgar o común, era cristiana, era de Cristo.
common fraction, (mat.) fracción o quebrado común.
common ground, tema, asunto o materia de interés mutuo.
common knowledge, información o hecho conocido por muchos; conocimiento general.
common herd, el vulgo, el común de las gentes.
common law, (der.) derecho consuetudinario; derecho tácito, no legislado.
common-law marriage ['kɑmən,lɔ-, B 'kɔm-] (der.) casamiento por mero acuerdo y cohabitación; matrimonio consensual, concubinato.
common logarithm, (mat.) logaritmo común u ordinario.
commonly ['kɑmənlɪ, B 'kɔm-] *adv.* comúnmente, usualmente.
common man, 1. hombre promedio. 2. (fig., E.U.) héroe no loado (en la literatura que surgió a raíz de la Depresión).
common market, 1. mercado común, asociación de países formada con objeto de establecer una estrecha relación comercial, esp. a través de concesiones aduanales. 2. **C.M.,** Mercado Común Europeo.
common measure, 1. (mús.) tiempo de 4/4 (t. **common time**). 2. (mat.) medida común.
common noun, (gram.) apelativo, nombre común o genérico.
common nuisance, molestia pública, estorbo público.
commonplace ['kɑmən,pleɪs, B 'kɔm-] *s.* lugar común; dicho trillado, trivialidad. —*a.* común, vulgar, trivial.
commonplace book, libro de acontecimientos memorables, de notas personales; minuta.
common pleas, (der.) pleitos, causas o acciones civiles; **C.P.,** tribunal de primera instancia para acciones civiles.
common prayer, liturgia de la Iglesia Anglicana.
common room, sala o cuarto de descanso (para los miembros de una comunidad o una facultad).
Commons ['kɑmənz, B 'kɔm-] *s. pl.* G.B. la cámara baja; (miembros de) la Cámara de los Comunes.
common school, escuela de primera enseñanza, escuela primaria.
common sense, sentido común.
common soldier, soldado raso.
common speech, lenguaje corriente, consuetudinario.
common steel, (metal.) acero al carbono.
common stock, (com.) acciones ordinarias.
common touch, habilidad de conmover y comunicarse con el pueblo.
commonweal ['kɑmən,wil, B 'kɔm-] *s.* 1. bienestar público. 2. (ant.) comunidad (de naciones).
commonwealth [-,wɛlθ] *s.* 1. comunidad (de naciones); mancomunidad, estado libre asociado. 2. cosa pública, república. 3. asociación o grupo en que los integrantes se reparten las utilidades.
common year, año común (no bisiesto).
commotion [kə'moʊʃən] *s.* conmoción, disturbio, tumulto, agitación, alteración, escándalo.
commove [kə'muv] *v.t.* 1. conmover, perturbar, turbar, agitar, revolver. 2. excitar, incitar.
communal [kə'mjunəl, 'kɑmjənəl, B 'kɔm-, kə'mjun-] *a.* comunal, público, de la comunidad.
communalism [-,ɪzəm] *s.* (pol.) organización social en forma comunal, sistema confederativo de comunes.
communalize [-,aɪz] *v.t.* hacer comunal.
Communard [,kɑmjʊ'nɑrd, B ,kɔmjʊ'nɑd] *s.* (fr.) comunero, participante en las comunas de París (1871).
commune [kə'mjun] *v.i.* 1. (con *with*) comunicarse, conversar (con), platicar. 2. (relig.) comulgar, recibir la comunión.
commune ['kɑm,jun, kə'mjun, B 'kɔmjun] *s.* 1. comunidad, pueblo. 2. pueblo común; estado llano. 3. (hist.) municipio, corporación municipal. 4. **the C.,** (pol., hist.) comuna (esp. la de París). 5. (E.U.) vivienda colectiva, habitada por varias familias de *hippies.*
communicability [kə,mjunɪkə'bɪlətɪ] *s.* comunicabilidad.
communicable [-'mjunɪkəbəl] *a.* comunicable.
communicant [-kənt] *s.* 1. (relig.) comulgante. 2. comunicante, informador.
communicate [kə'mjunə,keɪt] *v.t.* 1. comunicar, participar, dar parte de. 2. transmitir, comunicar, pegar (una enfermedad). —*v.i.* 1. comunicarse, tener comunicación (por correo, señas, etc.). 2. comunicarse (entre sí) (cuartos, etc.). 3. (relig.) comulgar.
communication [-,mjunə'keɪʃən] *s.* 1. comunicación; transmisión. 2. comunicado, mensaje, parte. 3. paso, acceso, entrada. 4. (*pl.*) sistema de comunicaciones (teléfono, telégrafo, etc.); comunicaciones, vías de comunicación (de una nación como prensa, radio, t.v., etc.).
communications satellite, (aeroesp.) satélite de communicaciones.
communicative [kə'mjunə,keɪtɪv, -nɪkətɪv] *a.* comunicativo, expansivo.
communicativeness [-nəs] *s.* comunicatividad.
communicatory [-kə,tɔrɪ, B -kətərɪ] *a.* comunicatorio.
communion [kə'mjunjən] *s.* 1. comunión, contacto, comunicación. 2. comunión, participación (en algo). 3. (relig.) comunión, eucaristía.
communion-cup [-'kʌp] *s.* cáliz.
communion rail, comulgatorio.
communiqué [kə'mjunə,keɪ, -,mjunə'keɪ, B -'mjunɪ,keɪ] *s.* (fr.) comunicado, boletín oficial.
communism ['kɑmjə,nɪzəm, B 'kɔm-] *s.* (pol.) comunismo.
communist [-nəst] *s., a.* comunista.
communistic [,kɑmjə'nɪstɪk, B ,kɔm-] *a.* 1. comunal. 2. comunista.
Communist International, Internacional Comunista.
Comunist Manifesto, el Manifiesto Comunista proclamado en 1848, escrito por Karl Marx y Friedrich Engels.
Communist Party, partido comunista.
communitarian [kə,mjunə'tɛrɪən, B -'tɛər-] *a., s.* partidario de pequeñas cooperativas.
community [kə'mjunətɪ] *s.* comunidad; **the c.,** el público, la colectividad, la sociedad.
community center, centro social (de una población, un barrio o distrito).
community chest, fondo de caridad (para beneficio de la comunidad).
community college, (E.U.) colegio que comprende dos años de universidad, y es mantenido en parte por la comunidad a la cual sirve.

community property, (der.) comunidad de bienes; bien común; bienes comunales.
communization [ˌkɑmjənəˈzeɪʃən, B ˌkɔmjʊnaɪ-] *s.* comunización.
communize [ˈkɑmjəˌnaɪz, B ˈkɔm-] *v.t.* comunizar, hacer común; confiscar, someter a administración comunista; hacer comunista.
commutability [kəˌmjutəˈbɪlətɪ] *s.* conmutabilidad.
commutable [-ˈmjutəbəl] *a.* conmutable.
commutate [ˈkɑmjəˌteɪt, B ˈkɔmjʊ-] *v.t.* (elec.) conmutar, cambiar la dirección de una corriente eléctrica.
commutation [ˌkɑmjəˈteɪʃən, B ˌkɔm-] *s.* 1. conmutación, permuta, cambio, trueque. 2. (elec.) conmutación o cambio (de corriente). 3. (der.) conmutación (de pena). 4. (E.U.) viajes cotidianos (con billete de abono).
commutation ticket, billete de abono.
commutative [ˈkɑmjəˌteɪtɪv, kəˈmjutət, B kəˈmjutət-, ˈkɔm-ˌteɪt-] *a.* conmutativo; (mat.) conmutativo, de propiedad conmutativa.
commutator [ˈkɑmjəˌteɪtər, B ˈkɔm-ə] *s.* (elec.) conmutador, colector.
commutator bar, (elec.) segmento colector, cuña del colector, delga.
commutator segment, (elec.) segmento colector.
commute [kəˈmjut] *v.t.* 1. conmutar, trocar, cambiar. 2. conmutar, reducir (una pena); (elec., com.) conmutar. 3. (E.U.) abonarse, viajar diariamente (con billete de abono).
commuter [-ər, B -ə] *s.* viajero abonado (esp. para los viajes diarios al trabajo).
comose [ˈkoʊˌmoʊs] *a.* (bot.) cabelludo.
compact [kəmˈpækt, kɑm-, ˈkɑmˌpækt, B kəmˈpækt] *a.* 1. compacto, denso; apretado. 2. (con *of*) compuesto, hecho (de). 3. sólido, firme (cuerpo). 4. breve, conciso (estilo, frase, etc.). — [ˈkɑmˌpækt, kɔm-] *s.* 1. estuche de polvos, estuche de afeites, polvera de bolsillo. 2. carro o coche compacto, automóvil de tamaño mediano. —*v.t.* 1. consolidar. 2. apretar, comprimir; condensar. 3. componer.
compact [ˈkɑmˌpækt, B ˈkɔm-] *s.* pacto, convenio, acuerdo, trato; **general c.,** común acuerdo.
compact disc (o **compact disk**), disco compacto, compact-disc, disco digital.
compact disk player, reproductor de compact-disc.
compacted [-əd] *a.* firme, apretado, consolidado.
compaction [kəmˈpækʃən] *s.* 1. compresión. 2. solidificación, trabamiento.
compactly [-ˈpæktlɪ] *adv.* sólidamente, densamente, apretadamente.
compactness [-ˈpæktnəs] *s.* 1. densidad, solidez. 2. tamaño reducido, estrechez, exactitud (de masa).
companion [kəmˈpænjən] *s.* 1. compañero, camarada; socio, asociado, consocio. 2. (fig.) compañero, ej., *this volume is a c. to the other,* este volumen es compañero del otro. 3. acompañante, dama de compañia. 4. caballero (de una orden), ej., *C. of the Bath,* Caballero de la Orden del Baño. 5. (mar.) tambucho (de la escalera de cámara); escalera de cámara.
companionable [-əbəl] *a.* sociable, afable.
companionably [-əblɪ] *adv.* afablemente, agradablemente, socialmente.
companion-at-arms [-ətˈɑrmz, B -ˈɑmz] *s.* compañero de armas.
companionate [-ət] *a.* entre compañeros, de compañerismo.
companionate marriage, forma de matrimonio en la que, no habiendo progenie, los contrayentes pueden divorciarse sin gravamen.
companion hatch, (mar.) cubierta de escotilla.
companion ladder, (mar.) escalera de toldilla.
companionship [-ˌʃɪp] *s.* compañerismo, camaradería; asociación, unión, compañía.
companionway [-ˌweɪ] *s.* escalera de cámara o cabina.
company [ˈkʌmpənɪ] *s.* 1. compañía. 2. huésped(es), invitado(s), ej., *we have c. for dinner,* tenemos huésped(es) o invitado(s) para la comida. 3. visitante, visita, ej., *don't disturb me when I have c.,* no me molesten cuando tengo visita (o un visitante). 4. compañero; acompañante. 5. (com.) compañía, sociedad, empresa. 6. (mil., teat.) compañía. 7. (mar.) tripulación. 8. **to bear (someone) c.,** acompañar (a alguien); **to keep c.,** asociarse con; cortejar, galantear; recibir galanteos, ser cortejada; **to keep (someone) c.,** acompañar (a alguien); **to part c. (with),** separarse (de), desunirse.
company man, empleado que se identifica completamente con la compañía y no con los otros empleados.
company manners, buenos modales asumidos sólo ante extraños.
company store, tienda propia de una compañía (donde el empleado compra a crédito respaldado por su sueldo).
company union, gremio o sindicato interno, controlado por los patronos.
company wife, esposa abnegada de un empleado que es excesivamente obsequioso con sus patronos.
comparable [ˈkɑmpərəbəl, B ˈkɔm-] *a.* comparable, cotejable.
comparably [-blɪ] *adv.* comparablemente.
comparative [kəmˈpærətɪv] *a.* 1. comparativo. 2. relativo, ej., *in c. comfort,* en relativa comodidad; poco menos (que), ej., *he's a c. stranger,* es poco menos que un extraño. 3. (gram.) comparativo. 4. comparado (derecho, literatura, anatomía, etc.). —*s. (gram.) grado comparativo.*
comparative literature, literatura comparada.
comparatively [-lɪ] *adv.* comparativamente, relativamente.
comparative science, (biol.) ciencia de observación.
comparative statement, (com., ten.) cuadro comparado.
comparator [kəmˈpærətər, ˈkɑmpəˌreɪt-, B kəmˈpærətə] *s.* (fís., elec.) comparador.
compare [kəmˈpɛr, B -ˈpɛə] *v.t.* 1. comparar, cotejar, equiparar, confrontar, comprobar. 2. (gram.) formar el grado (comparativo o superlativo) de (un adjetivo). 3. **c. notes,** comparar datos e informes, cambiar impresiones; **(is) not to be compared to,** no se puede comparar con, no puede ser comparado con. —*v.i.* (con *with*) poderse comparar (con), ser comparable (con, a), ser igual (a); **c. favorably** o **well with,** no ser inferior a, no ser menos que. —*s.* comparación; **beyond, without** o **past c.,** sin par, sin igual, sin rival, incomparable.
comparison [-ˈpærəsən] *s.* 1. comparación, confrontación, cotejo, equiparación. 2. semejanza, identidad. 3. (gram.) comparación. 4. **beyond c.,** sin comparación; **degrees of c.,** (gram.) grados de comparación; **in c. with,** comparado con, frente a; **to bear no c. (with),** no poder comparse (con).
comparison shopper, empleado de una tienda que visita los establecimientos de competidores para comparar precios y mercancía.
compart [kəmˈpɑrt, B -ˈpɑt] *v.t.* dividir en partes; dividir de acuerdo con un plano.
compartment [-mənt] *s.* compartimiento. 2. división, sección, sector, departamento. 3. (mar.) compartimiento (de un navío).
compartmentalize [-ˌpɑrtˈmɛntəlˌaɪz, B -ˌpɑt-] *v.t.* dividir en compartimientos, separar en categorías.
compass [ˈkʌmpəs, ˈkɑm-, B ˈkʌm-] *s.* 1. círculo, circunferencia, circuito. 2. espacio, recinto, ámbito; extensión, alcance. 3. (mús.) cuerda; extensión (de la voz o de un instrumento). 4. **(compasses** o **pair of compasses)** compás (para trazar círculos, etc.). 5. (mar.) compás, brújula, aguja. 6. **to box the c.,** (mar.) cuartear la aguja; (fig.) dar vuelta completa, volver al punto de partida, volver a su posición original (en discusión, política, etc.). —*v.t.* 1. circundar, rodear; cercar, sitiar. 2. dar la vuelta a. 3. urdir, tramar, maquinar. 4. conseguir, lograr, alcanzar. 5. concebir, comprender.
compassable [-pəsəbəl] *a.* asequible.
compass bearing, rumbo, marcación; (aer.) orientación magnética, marcación magnética.
compass card, rosa náutica, rosa de los vientos.
compass course, rumbo de brújula.
compass deviation, desvío o error de la brújula.
compassion [kəmˈpæʃən] *s.* compasión, conmiseración, lástima, piedad; **to move to c.,** conmover, inspirar compasión.
compassionable [-əbəl] *a.* digno de compasión.
compassionate [-ət] *a.* compasivo, misericordioso. — [-ˌeɪt] *v.t.* compadecer, compadecerse de.
compassionately [-lɪ] *adv.* compasivamente.
compass needle, (aer.) aguja de la brújula.
compass point, (mar.) cuarta.
compass saw, serrucho de calar o de punta, sierra de contornear, segueta.
compass survey, (top.) levantamiento con la brújula.
compass timber, madera curvada.
compatibility [kəmˌpætəˈbɪlətɪ] *s.* compatibilidad.
compatible [-ˈpætəbəl] *a.* compatible.
compatriot [kəmˈpeɪtrɪət, -ˌɑt, B -ˈpætrɪət] *s.* compatriota, paisano, conterráneo.
compeer [ˈkɑmˌpɪr, kəmˈpɪr, B kɔmˈpɪə] *s.* 1. igual, par. 2. compañero, camarada, compadre.
compel [kəmˈpɛl] *v.t.* (*pret., p.p.* COMPELLED; *p.pr.* COMPELLING) compeler, constreñir, forzar, obligar; exigir, imponer.
compellation [ˌkɑmpəˈleɪʃən, B ˌkɔm-] *s.* tratamiento (que se da a una persona), nombre.
compelling [kəmˈpɛlɪŋ] *a.* apremiante, obligatorio, preciso, urgente.
compend [ˈkɑmˌpɛnd, B ˈkɔm-] *var. de* **compendium.**
compendious [kəmˈpɛndɪəs] *a.* compendioso, resumido, sumario.
compendiously [-lɪ] *adv.* compendiosamente.
compendiousness [-nəs] *s.* concisión, brevedad.
compendium [-dɪəm] *s.* (*pl.* COMPENDIUMS o COMPENDIA [-dɪə]) compendio, resumen, sumario, sinopsis, extracto.
compensable [kəmˈpɛnsəbəl] *a.* compensable.
compensate [ˈkɑmpənˌseɪt, -ˌpɛn-, B -kɔm-] *v.t.* 1. compensar; indemnizar; recompensar, remunerar. 2. (mec.) compensar. —*v.i.* (con *for*) compensar, equivaler, igualar.
compensating balance [-ɪŋ-] volante compensador (de reloj).
compensating tab, (avia., ing.) aleta compensadora, superficie de compensación; compensador, equilibrador.
compensation [ˌkɑmpənˈseɪʃən, -ˌpɛn-, B ˌkɔm-] *s.* 1. compensación; indemnización, reparación, desagravio; remuneración, recompensa. 2. (biol., med., psic.) compensación.

compensation bridge, (quím.) aparato de compensación.
compensation pendulum, (fís.) péndulo de compensación.
compensative ['kɑmpən͵seɪtɪv, -͵pɛn-, kəm'pɛnsət-, B kəm'pɛn-, 'kɔmpɛnseɪt-] *a.* compensativo, compensatorio, equivalente.
compensator ['kɑmpən͵seɪtər, -͵pɛn-, B 'kɔm-ə] *s.* compensador; (elec., ópt.) compensador.
compensatory [kəm'pɛnsə͵tɔrɪ, B -tərɪ] *a.* compensatorio, compensativo, equivalente.
compensatory damages, (der.) indemnización por daños o perjuicio.
compensatory leads, (elec.) conductores de compensación.
compete [kəm'pit] *v.i.* competir, contender, rivalizar, concursar, desafiar; **to c. for,** opositar a.
competence ['kɑmpətəns, B 'kɔm-] **competency** [-ənsɪ] *s.* 1. competencia, capacidad, aptitud. 2. suficiencia (de medios de vida); subsistencia. 3. (der.) competencia, capacidad (del juez, etc.).
competent [-ənt] *a.* 1. competente, capaz, apto, calificado; adecuado. 2. (con *to*) propio (de), pertinente (a). 3. (der.) competente (juez, etc.).
competently [-lɪ] *adv.* competentemente.
competition [͵kɑmpə'tɪʃən, B ͵kɔm-] *s.* 1. competencia, competición, rivalidad. 2. competencia, certamen, concurso. 3. (com.) competencia.
competitive [kəm'pɛtətɪv] *a.* 1. de competencia (deportes, espíritu); de libre competencia (mercado); selectivo (examen, concurso). 2. competitivo (precios).
competitor [-tər, B -tə] *s.* competidor, rival.
compilation [͵kɑmpə'leɪʃən, B ͵kɔm-] compilación, recopilación, recolección.
compile [kəm'paɪl] *v.t.* compilar, recopilar.
compiler [-ər, B -ə] *s.* compilador, recopilador.
complacence [kəm'pleɪsəns] **complacency** [-ənsɪ] *s.* complacencia; satisfacción o contento de sí mismo.
complacent [-ənt] *a.* complaciente; complacido, satisfecho de sí mismo.
complain [kəm'pleɪn] *v.i.* 1. quejarse, lamentarse. 2. (der.) querellarse, demandar, hacer una denuncia, entablar demanda. 3. **c. of** (o **about**), quejarse (de).
complainant [-ənt] *s.* (der.) demandante, demandador, querellante, litigante.
complainingly [-ɪŋlɪ] *adv.* en tono quejoso, de modo quejoso.
complaint [-'pleɪnt] *s.* 1. queja, lamento. 2. mal, enfermedad. 3. (der.) denuncia; demanda; queja, querella, agravio. 4. **to lodge a c.,** entablar una demanda; iniciar una querella; hacer una reclamación.
complaisance [kəm'pleɪsəns, -'pleɪz-, B -'pleɪz-] *s.* afabilidad, cortesía, deferencia.
complaisant [-ənt] *a.* afable, cortés, complaciente, deferente.
complaisantly [-lɪ] *adv.* afablemente; con deferencia.
complect [kəm'plɛkt] *v.t.* entretejer, enlazar.
complected [kəm'plɛktəd] *a.* 1. (fam.) de tez, ej., *dark c.,* de tez morena. 2. enlazado, entretejido.
complement ['kɑmpləmənt, B 'kɔm-] *s.* 1. complemento; accesorio. 2. (gram., biol., geom., mat.) complemento. 3. dotación, tripulación (esp. de un barco). [-͵mɛnt] *v.t.* complementar, completar.
complemental [͵kɑmplə'mɛntəl, B ͵kɔm-] *a.* de complemento, complementario, suplementario.
complementary [-'mɛntərɪ] *a.* complementario (ángulo, colores, arcos, etc.).
complementary angle, ángulo complementario, cualquiera de los dos ángulos que juntos forman un ángulo de 90.
complementary colors, (arte, quím.) colores complementarios.
complement fixation, (bact.) fijación del complemento.
complete [kəm'plit] *a.* 1. completo, entero, cabal, íntegro. 2. acabado, consumado, perfecto. —*v.t.* completar, acabar, concluir, terminar.
completely [-lɪ] *adv.* completamente, íntegramente.
completeness [-nəs] *s.* entereza, integridad.
completion [-'pliʃən] *s.* terminación, consumación, cumplimiento, fin.
completive [-'plitɪv] *a.* completivo.
complex [kɑm'plɛks, kəm-, 'kɑm͵plɛks, B 'kɔm-] *a.* complejo, complicado, intrincado; múltiple, compuesto. ['kɑm͵plɛks, B 'kɔm-] *s.* 1. complejo, conjunto. 2. (psic.) complejo, obsesión.
complex fraction, (mat.) quebrado compuesto, fracción compuesta.
complexion [kəm'plɛkʃən] *s.* 1. tez, cutis; color (de la piel). 2. (fig.) naturaleza, aspecto, carácter.
complexional [-əl] *a.* complexional, temperamental.
complexioned [-ʃənd] *a.* de tal o cual matiz o tez.
complexity [kəm'plɛksətɪ, kɑm-, B kəm-, kɔm-] *s.* (*pl.* COMPLEXITIES) complejidad, complexidad.
complex number, (mat.) número complejo.
complex sentence, (gram.) oración compuesta.
compliance [kəm'plaɪəns] *s.* 1. sumisión, docilidad; condescendencia, acatamiento. 2. (rad.) elasticidad. 3. **in c. with,** de acuerdo con, accediendo a.
compliancy [-ənsɪ] *var. de* **compliance.**
compliant [-ənt] *a.* dócil, obediente, sumiso, condescendiente.
compliantly [-lɪ] *adv.* dócilmente, sumisamente, obedientemente.
complicacy ['kɑmplɪkəsɪ, B 'kɔm-] *s.* 1. complejidad. 2. complicación, enredo, embrollo.
complicate ['kɑmplə͵keɪt, B 'kɔm-] *v.t.* complicar, enredar, hacer complicado o difícil. —*v.i.* complicarse. [-plɪkət] *a.* complicado, complejo.
complicated [-əd] *a.* complicado, complejo; enmarañado, enredado.
complication [͵kɑmplə'keɪʃən, B ͵kɔm-] *s.* 1. complicación. 2. (med.) complicación, enfermedad que agrava otra afección.
complicity [kəm'plɪsətɪ] *s.* complicidad (en un delito, etc.).
complier [-'plaɪər, B -ə] *s.* consentidor.
compliment ['kɑmpləmənt, B 'kɔm-] *s.* 1. cumplido, cumplimiento; lisonja, requiebro, galantería, fineza; piropo (fam.). 2. (*pl.*) saludos, recuerdos. 3. **to make** (o **pay**) **a c.,** hacer un cumplido o cumplimiento; **to pay** (o **send**) **one's compliments,** enviar uno sus saludos. —[-mɛnt] *v.t.* cumplimentar, felicitar; lisonjear, requebrar, galantear, piropear (fam.).
complimentary [͵kɑmplə'mɛntərɪ, B ͵kɔm-] *a.* 1. halagador, elogioso (crítica, observación, referencia, etc.). 2. de cortesía, gratuito (billete, ejemplar, etc.).
complimentary close, fórmula de despedida que en una carta precede a la firma.
compline ['kɑmplən, -͵plaɪn, B 'kɔm-] *s.* (relig.) completas (*pl.*).
complot ['kɑm͵plɑt B 'kɔm͵plɔt] *s.* complot, conspiración, trama, conjuración.
complot [kɑm'plɑt, kəm-, B kɔm'plɔt] *v.t., v.i.* complotar, conspirar, tramar.
comply [kəm'plaɪ] (*pret., p.p.* COMPLIED; *p.pr.* COMPLYING) *v.i.* cumplir, obedecer, conformarse, acomodarse; **c. with,** cumplir con, acatar, observar (orden, reglamento, etc.); obrar de acuerdo con.
compo ['kɑmpoʊ, B 'kɔm-] *s.* 1. compuesto, mezcla (metálica, etc.). 2. cemento, estuco.
component [kəm'poʊnənt] *s.* 1. componente, constituyente, ingrediente. 2. (fís.) componente. —*a.* componente, constituyente.
comport [kəm'pɔrt, B -'pɔt] *v.i.* **c. with,** concordar con, ir bien con, sentar bien a. —*v.t.* **c. oneself,** comportarse, portarse, conducirse.
comportment [-mənt] *s.* comportamiento, conducta.
compose [kəm'poʊz] *v.t.* 1. componer, formar, construir. 2. redactar, escribir. 3. (mús., lit., impr.) componer. 4. arreglar, ordenar. 5. componer, arreglar (diferencias, disputa, etc.). 6. calmar, sosegar, aquietar. 7. **c. oneself,** dominarse, calmarse, sosegarse, tranquilizarse. —*v.i.* componer; hacer una composición (musical); ser compositor.
composed [-'poʊzd] *a.* sereno, de porte y modales tranquilos.
composedly [-'poʊzədlɪ] *adv.* serenamente, sosegadamente, con aplomo.
composedness [-nəs] *s.* serenidad, calma, sosiego, aplomo.
composer [-'poʊzər, B -zə] *s.* (mús.) compositor.
composing frame, c. stand [-zɪŋ-] (impr.) chibalete.
composing rule, (impr.) filete, regleta.
composing stick, (impr.) componedor.
Compositae [kəm'pɑzɪ͵ti, B -'pɔz-] *s. pl.* (bot.) compuestas.
composite [kɑm'pɑzət, kəm-, B 'kɔmpəzɪt] *a.* 1. compuesto, mixto. 2. (bot., arq.) compuesto. 3. (mar.) de madera con armazón metálica (navío). —*s.* 1. compuesto. 2. (astronáut.) cohete o proyectil que tiene más de una etapa en tránsito. 3. (arq.) orden compuesto. 4. (bot.) compuesta (planta).
composite column, (arq.) columna compuesta de varios elementos en orden clásico.
composite number, (mat.) número compuesto.
composite order, (arq.) orden compuesto de elementos clásicos.
composite photograph, fotografía compuesta, fotografía de superposición.
composition [͵kɑmpə'zɪʃən, B ͵kɔm-] *s.* 1. composición; formación, construcción. 2. compuesto, mezcla; substancia artificial. 3. ensayo, ejercicio (de colegial). 4. (mús., lit., pint., gram., impr.) composición.
compositive [kəm'pɑzətɪv, B -'pɔz-] *a.* (gram.) compositivo.
compositor [kəm'pɑzətər, B -'pɔzɪtə] *s.* (impr.) cajista.
compost ['kɑm͵poʊst, B 'kɔm͵pɔst] *s.* 1. compuesto, mezcla. 2. (agr.) abono, estiércol, mantillo. —*v.t.* abonar, estercolar (la tierra); convertir en abono.
composure [kəm'poʊʒər, B -ʒə] *s.* compostura, serenidad, tranquilidad, calma.
compote ['kɑm͵poʊt, B 'kɔm͵pɔt] *s.* 1. compota, dulce de almíbar. 2. compotera.
compound [kɑm'paʊnd, kəm-, 'kɑm͵paʊnd, B kəm'paʊnd, kɔm-] *v.t.* 1. componer, combinar, mezclar. 2. componer, arreglar, ajustar (disputa, pleito, etc.). 3. incrementar, agravar (error, problema, etc.). 4. (com.) componer (intereses). 5. **to compound a felony,** no

procesar, encubrir (un crimen, etc.) por dinero (u otros motivos personales). —*v.i.* 1. combinarse, amalgamarse. 2. (con *with*) componerse (con acreedores, etc.), ponerse de acuerdo (con), transigir (con), arreglarse. — ['kɑm,paʊnd, B 'kɔm-] *a.* compuesto, mezclado; (zool., bot., gram.) compuesto. —*s.* 1. compuesto, mezcla, mixtura; preparación. 2. (gram.) palabra compuesta. 3. recinto que contiene un número de residencias y oficinas separadas del resto de la comunidad.

compound circuit, (elec.) circuito compuesto de uno cerrado conectado con uno abierto, circuito combinado.

compounder [kɑm'paʊndər, kəm-, B kəm-ə, kɔm-] *s.* mezclador; componedor, mediador.

compound eye, (ento.) ojo compuesto.

compound fraction, (mat.) quebrado compuesto, fracción compuesta.

compound fracture, (med.) fractura complicada o abierta.

compound interest, (com.) interés compuesto.

compound leaf, (bot.) hoja compuesta.

compound magnet, (fís.) imán laminado.

compound mill, (quím.) molino de mezcla.

compound microscope, (ópt.) microscopio compuesto, con dos juegos de lentes.

compound number, (mat.) número complejo o denominado.

compound pendulum, (fís.) péndulo compuesto.

compound sentence, (gram.) oración compuesta.

compound steel, acero de aleación.

compound winding, (elec.) devanado mixto.

comprador [,kɑmprə'dɔr, B ,kɔm-'dɔ] *s.* jefe del personal nativo (en una casa de negocios extranjera en la antigua China).

comprehend [,kɑmprɪ'hɛnd, B ,kɔm-] *v.t.* 1. comprender, entender, concebir. 2. contener, abarcar, incluir.

comprehensibility [-,hɛnsə'bɪlətɪ] *s.* comprensibilidad.

comprehensible [-'hɛnsəbəl] *a.* comprensible, inteligible.

comprehension [-'hɛnʃən] *s.* 1. comprensión, entendimiento, inteligencia. 2. comprensión, envergadura.

comprenhensive [-sɪv] *a.* 1. comprensivo. 2. amplio, completo, de gran extensión.

comprenhensively [-lɪ] *adv.* comprensivamente.

comprehensiveness [-nəs] *s.* 1. comprensión, entendimiento. 2. gran extensión, envergadura, alcance.

compress [kɔm'prɛs] *v.t.* comprimir, apretar, estrechar; (fig.) condensar, abreviar, resumir, reducir. — ['kɑm,prɛs, B 'kɔm-] *s.* 1. (med.) compresa, cabezal. 2. prensa de embalar (algodón, etc.).

compressed [-'prɛst] *a.* comprimido.

compressed air, aire comprimido, aire compreso.

compressed air-brake, (ing.) freno neumático.

compressed air-tunnel, (aer.) túnel aerodinámico.

compressibility [-,prɛsə'bɪlətɪ] *s.* compresibilidad.

compressible [-'prɛsəbəl] *a.* compresible, comprimible.

compression [kəm'prɛʃən] *s.* compresión; condensación.

compression chamber, cámara de compresión.

compression ignition, encendido por compresión.

compression piston-ring, (mot.) segmento de compresión.

compression ratio, (ing.) índice o relación de compresión, compresoproporción.

compression stroke, (ing.) carrera de compresión, golpe o tiempo de compresión.

compressive [kəm'prɛsɪv] *a.* compresivo.

compressor [-'prɛsər, B -ə] *s.* compresor.

comprise [kəm'praɪz] *v.t.* comprender, contener, incluir, abarcar, abrazar; constar de; encerrar.

compromise ['kɑmprə,maɪz, B 'kɔm-] *s.* concesión, componenda, arreglo, acomodo, avenencia. —*v.t.* 1. arreglar, acomodar, componer (disputa, etc.). 2. comprometer (la reputación, etc.). —*v.i.* transigir, avenirse, someterse a un compromiso.

compromiser [-ər, B -ə] *s.* 1. el que arregla o compone. 2. comprometedor.

compromising [-ɪŋ] *a.* 1. comprometedor. 2. transigente.

comptometer [kɑmp'tɑmətər, B kɔmp'tɔmɪtə] *s.* contómetro; (máquina) calculadora (nombre de fábrica).

comptroller [kən'troʊlər, B -lə] *s.* 1. jefe de contaduría, contador mayor. 2. contralor, interventor. 3. senescal, mayordomo.

comptrollership [-,ʃɪp] *s.* contraloría, veeduría.

compulsion [kəm'pʌlʃən] *s.* compulsión, apremio, coacción.

compulsive [-sɪv] *a.* compulsivo, apremiante, coercitivo.

compulsively [-lɪ] *adv.* compulsivamente, apremiantemente.

compulsiveness [-nəs] *s.* carácter compulsivo.

compulsorily [-'pʌlsərɪlɪ] *adv.* obligatoriamente; compulsivamente.

compulsory [-sərɪ] *a.* obligatorio; compulsivo.

compunction [kəm'pʌŋkʃən] *s.* 1. compunción, contrición, remordimiento. 2. escrúpulo, ej., *without c.,* sin escrúpulo.

compunctious [-ʃəs] *a.* compungido, contrito.

compurgation [,kɑmpər'geɪʃən, B ,kɔmpə'-] *s.* (der.) compurgación, purgación jurídica.

compurgator ['kɑmpər,geɪtər, B 'kɔmpə,-ə] *s.* compurgador.

computable [kəm'pjutəbəl] *a.* computable, calculable.

computation [,kɑmpjʊ'teɪʃən, B ,kɔm-] *s.* computación, cómputo, cálculo.

compute [kəm'pjut] *s.* cómputo, computación. —*v.t.* computar, calcular.

computer [-ər, B -ə] *s.* ordenador. computadora.

computer-aided [kəm'pjutər'eɪdəd] *a.* asistido por ordenador.

computer-assisted [kəm'pjutərə'sɪstəd] *a.* asistido por ordenador.

computer chip, microplaquita.

computer dating service, agencia matrimonial por ordenador.

computer game, videojuego.

computer-generated [kəm'pjutər'dʒɛnəreɪtəd] *a.* realizado por ordenador.

computer graphics, grafismo por computadora.

computerize [-ə,raɪz] *v.t.* computarizar, computerizar; (*an office*) instalar ordenadores en.

computerized [-ə,raɪzd] *a.* computadorizado.

computer language, lenguaje de ordenador, lenguaje de programación, lenguaje de máquina.

computer literacy, capacidad de operar con un ordenador.

computer program, programa de ordenador.

computer programming, programación de ordenadores.

computer science, informática.

computer virus, virus de ordenadores.

computing [kəm'pjutɪŋ] *s.* informática.

comrade ['kɑm,ræd, -rəd, B 'kɔmrɪd, 'kʌm-] *s.* 1. camarada, compañero. 2. camarada (comunista).

comrade in arms, compañero de armas, conmilitón.

comradery [-rɪ] *s.* camaradería, compañerismo.

comradeship [-,ʃɪp] *s.* camaradería, compañerismo.

comstockery ['kɑm,stɑkərɪ, B 'kʌm,stɔk-] *s.* (E.U.) mojigatería, remilgo; censura exagerada de la literatura y otras artes.

Comtism ['kɑm,tɪzəm, B 'kɔn-] *s.* la filosofía de Augusto Comte, positivismo.

con ['kɑn, B kɔn] *v.t.* (*pret., p.p.* CONNED; *p.pr.* CONNING) 1. examinar, estudiar. 2. memorizar, aprender de memoria. 3. (E.U.) estafar, timar. 4. **c. into,** persuadir engañosamente; **c. out of,** sacar con trucos, timar. —*s.* 1. contra, opinión contraria; **pros and cons,** los pros y los contras. 2. (jer.) presidiario.

Conakry ['kɑnə,kri, B 'kɔn-] *s.* Conakry, capital de Guinea.

conation [koʊ'neɪʃən] *s.* (psic.) conación, voluntad, esfuerzo; cualquier impulso mental.

conative ['koʊnətɪv, -,neɪt-, B 'koʊnət-] *a.* (psic.) conativo.

conatus [koʊ'neɪtəs] *s.* (*pl.* CONATUS) (psic.) conato.

concatenate [kɑn'kætə,neɪt, kən-, B kɔn-, kən-] *v.t.* concatenar, concadenar, eslabonar. — [-nət, B -,neɪt] *a.* concatenado, eslabonado.

concatenation [-,kætə'neɪʃən] *s.* concatenación, encadenamiento, eslabonamiento, sucesión, serie.

concave ['kɑn,keɪv, B 'kɔn-] *a.* cóncavo. —*s.* cóncavo, concavidad.

concavity [kɑn'kævətɪ, B kɔn-] *s.* concavidad.

concavo-concave [kɑn'keɪvoʊ'kɑn,keɪv, B kɔn-'kɔn-] *a.* cóncavo por ambos lados, bicóncavo.

concavo-convex [-kɑn'vɛks, B -,kɔn-] *a.* concavoconvexo, cóncavo por un lado y convexo por el otro.

conceal [kən'sil] *v.t.* ocultar, esconder, encubrir, disimular.

concealment [-mənt] *s.* 1. ocultación, escondimiento. 2. disimulo, encubrimiento. 3. escondrijo, escondite.

concede [kən'sid] *v.t.* 1. conceder, otorgar, consentir. 2. admitir, reconocer. —*v.i.* ceder, hacer una concesión.

conceit [kən'sit] *s.* 1. orgullo, presunción, engreimiento, vanidad. 2. noción, concepto. 3. idea fantástica, dicho ingenioso, capricho.

conceited [-əd] *a.* vanidoso, presumido, engreído, presuntuoso.

conceitedly [-lɪ] *adv.* vanamente, engreídamente.

conceitedness [-nəs] *s.* presunción, engreimiento, vanidad.

conceivability [kən,sivə'bɪlətɪ] *s.* calidad de concebible.

conceivable [-'sivəbəl] *a.* concebible, imaginable.

conceivably [-blɪ] *adv.* de un modo imaginable o plausible.

conceive [kən'siv] *v.t.* 1. concebir, comprender, imaginar, idear, formarse idea de (algo). 2. concebir (una pasión, un prejuicio, etc.). 3. concebir, engendrar (una criatura). 4. opinar, pensar. 5. (*ú. gen. en voz pasiva*) formular, expresar. —*v.i.* 1. concebir, quedar preñada. 2. (con *of*) conceptuar, imaginar.

concelebrate [kən'sɛlə,breɪt] *v.i.* (relig.) concelebrar.

concenter [kən'sɛntər, B -ə] *v.t., v.i.* concentrar(se), centrar(se), convergir.

concentrate ['kɑnsən,treɪt, -,sɛn-, B 'kɔn-] *v.t.* concentrar. —*v.i.* concentrarse, reconcentrarse; **c. on,** concentrarse en. —*s.* (quím.) concentrado (de un líquido, una substancia, etc.).

concentration [ˌkɑnsənˈtreɪʃən, -ˌsɛn-, B ˈkɔn-] *s.* concentración, recogimiento; abstracción.
concentration camp, campo de concentración.
concentrator [ˈkɑnsənˌtreɪtər, -ˌsɛn-, B ˈkɔn-ə] *s.* concentrador, máquina de concentración.
concentric [kənˈsɛntrɪk, B kɔn-] *a.* concéntrico.
concentrically [-əlɪ] *adv.* concéntricamente.
concentricity [ˌkɑnˌsɛnˈtrɪsətɪ, B ˌkɔn-] *s.* concentricidad.
concept [ˈkɑnˌsɛpt, B ˈkɔn-] *s.* concepto, noción, idea.
conceptacle [kənˈsɛptɪkəl] *s.* (bot.) conceptáculo.
conception [kənˈsɛpʃən] *s.* 1. concepción (de una criatura o de una idea). 2. concepto; entendimiento, comprensión.
conceptional [-əl] *a.* concepcional.
conceptive [kənˈsɛptɪv] *a.* conceptivo.
conceptual [-tʃʊəl, kɑn-, B kən-tjʊəl] *a.* conceptual.
conceptualism [-ˌɪzəm] *s.* (filos.) conceptualismo.
conceptualist [-əst] *s.* conceptualista.
conceptualize [-ˈsɛptʃʊəlˌaɪz, B -tjʊ-] *v.t.* conceptuar, formar conceptos de una cosa. —*v.i.* formar conceptos, ideas o teorías.
concern [kənˈsɜrn, B -ˈsɜn] *v.t.* 1. importar, interesar, atañer, concernir, afectar, incumbir. 2. tratar de, ej., *this book concerns the origins of life,* este libro trata de los orígenes de la vida. 3. estar relacionado con, relacionarse con, ej., *our failure concerned the lack of supplies,* nuestro fracaso estaba relacionado con la falta de abastecimientos. 4. preocupar, tener preocupado, inquietar, ej., *his lack of interest concerns me,* su falta de interés me preocupa. 5. **as concerns,** respecto de; **as far as he is concerned,** en cuanto le toca a él; **c. oneself with, in** o **about (something),** ocuparse de, interesarse en (algo); **to be concerned in,** tener parte en, tener interés en. —*s.* 1. negocio, asunto, cosa, ej., *meddling in my concerns,* entremetiéndose en mis asuntos. 2. interés, incumbencia. 3. relación, conexión, ej., *it has no c. with,* no tiene relación o conexión con. 4. inquietud, ansiedad, preocupación, ej., *he asked with deep c.,* preguntó con gran ansiedad. 5. empresa, negocio, firma comercial. 6. **it's no c. of mine,** no me incumbe, no es cosa mía; **of c.,** de interés, de importancia; **of what c. is it to you?** ¿qué más le da a Ud.?
concerned [-ˈsɜrnd, B -ˈsɜnd] *a.* interesado; preocupado, ansioso, ej., *with a c. expression,* con aire preocupado, *I'm c. to hear,* estoy preocupado de saber, *I'm c. at the news,* estoy preocupado por las noticias, *I'm c. about his health,* estoy preocupado por su salud.
concerning [-ˈsɜrnɪŋ, B -ˈsɜnɪŋ] *prep.* concerniente a, respecto de o a, tocante a, acerca de; en cuanto a.
concernment [-mənt] *s.* 1. asunto, interés, concernencia. 2. importancia. 3. ansiedad, cuidado, pena.
concert [kənˈsɜrt, B -ˈsɜt] *v.t.* concertar, acordar, ajustar, componer. —*v.i.* (gen. con *with*) obrar en concierto (con). — [ˈkɑnsərt, B ˈkɔnsət] *s.* 1. convenio, acuerdo. 2. (mús.) concierto.
concerted [-ˈsɜrtəd, B -ˈsɜtəd] *a.* 1. concertado, arreglado. 2. unido, combinado (esfuerzos, etc.).
concert grand [ˈkɑnsərt-, B ˈkɔnsət-] piano de cola mayor (que se usa en las salas de conciertos).
concertina [ˌkɑnsərˈtinə, B ˌkɔnsəˈ-] *s.* 1. (mús.) concertina. 2. (mil.) alambrada plegable.
concertino [ˌkɑntʃərˈtinoʊ, B ˌkɔntʃəˈ-] *s.* (mús.) 1. concertino, instrumentos de solo (en un concierto grosso). 2. concierto breve.
concertize [ˈkɑnsərˌtaɪz, B ˈkɔnsəˌ-] *v.i* dar conciertos (solista o grupo) esp. en giras.
concertmaster [-sərtˌmæstər, B -sətˌ-mɑstə] *s.* (mús.) concertino, primer violín, violinista principal de una orquesta, que actúa como ayudante del director.
concerto [kənˈtʃɛrtoʊ, B -ˈtʃɜtoʊ] *s.* (*pl.* CONCERTI [-tɪ] o CONCERTOS) (mús.) concierto (el acto que se presenta, y la composición que interpreta un solista acompañado de orquesta).
concert pitch, (mús.) diapasón de concierto.
concession [kənˈsɛʃən] *s.* concesión; privilegio.
concessionaire [-ˌsɛʃəˈnɛr, B -ˈnɛə] *s.* concesionario.
concessionary [-ˈsɛʃəˌnɛrɪ, B -nərɪ] *a.* de(l) concesionario.
concessive [kənˈsɛsɪv] *a.* concesivo, concedente; (gram.) concesivo.
conch [kɑŋk, kɑntʃ, B kɔŋk, kɔntʃ] *s.* 1. caracola. 2. concha de caracol. 3. trompa de caracol. 4. (fam.) natural, habitante o deambulante de pequeña isla tropical.
concha [ˈkɑŋkə, B ˈkɔŋkə] *s.* (*pl.* CONCHAE [-ˌki]) (anat.) concha (del oído); (arq.) concha.
conchiferous [kɑŋˈkɪfərəs, B kɔŋ-] *a.* (zool., geol.) conchífero.
conchiolin [-ˈkaɪələn] *s.* (min.) conquiolina.
conchoid [ˈkɑŋˌkɔɪd, B ˈkɔŋ-] *s.* (geom.) concoide.
conchoidal [kɑŋˈkɔɪdəl, B kɔŋ-] *a.* concoidal, concoideo.
conchologist [-ˈkɑlədʒəst, B -ˈkɔl-] *s.* conquiliólogo, conquiliólogo.
conchology [-dʒɪ] *s.* (zool.) conquiliología.
conchy [ˈkɑntʃɪ, B ˈkɔn-] *s. forma abrev. de* **conscientious objector,** objetor (de la guerra), pacifista por conciencia.
concierge [ˌkɔnˈsjɛrʒ, B -sɪˈɛəʒ] *s.* conserje, portero (esp. en Francia).
conciergerie [-ərɪ] *s.* conserjería, portería.
conciliar [kənˈsɪlɪər, B -ə] *a.* (relig.) conciliar.
conciliate [-ˌeɪt] *v.t.* 1. conciliar, propiciar, pacificar. 2. conciliar, conformar, reconciliar (proposiciones, opiniones, etc.).
conciliation [-ˌsɪlɪˈeɪʃən] *s.* conciliación; reconciliación.
conciliative [-ˈsɪlɪˌeɪtɪv, B -ətɪv] *a.* conciliativo.
conciliator [-ər, B -ə] *s.* conciliador, mediador.
conciliatory [-ˈsɪljəˌtɔrɪ, B -tərɪ] *a.* conciliatorio.
concise [kənˈsaɪs] *a.* conciso, sucinto, breve, corto.
concisely [-lɪ] *adv.* concisamente.
conciseness [-nəs] *s.* concisión, brevedad.
concision [kənˈsɪʒən] *s.* 1. concisión, brevedad. 2. (bíbl.) circuncisión; mutilación.
conclave [ˈkɑnˌkleɪv, B ˈkɔn-] *s.* conciliábulo, cónclave, congreso, junta; (relig.) cónclave.
conclavist [-əst] *s.* (relig.) conclavista.
conclude [kənˈklud] *v.t.* 1. concluir, acabar, terminar, finalizar. 2. concluir, inferir, deducir, sacar en limpio. 3. concluir, decidir, resolver. —*v.i.* concluirse; inferir.
conclusion [-ˈkluʒən] *s.* 1. conclusión, terminación, fin, término, final. 2. conclusión, deducción, inferencia. 3. conclusión, decisión, resolución. 4. (lóg.) conclusión. 5. **in c.,** en conclusión, en suma, por último.
conclusive [-sɪv] *a.* conclusivo, decisivo, concluyente, convincente.
conclusively [-lɪ] *adv.* concluyentemente, finalmente.
concoct [kənˈkɑkt, kɑn-, B kənˈkɔkt] *v.t.* 1. confeccionar, mezclar (sopa, bebida, etc.). 2. (fig.) fabricar, fraguar, urdir, tramar (historias, mentiras, etc.).
concoction [-ˈkɑkʃən, B -ˈkɔk-] *s.* 1. mezcolanza, mezcla, mixtura. 2. (fig.) fabricación, maquinación, trama.
concomitance [kənˈkɑmətəns, B -ˈkɔm-] *s.* concomitancia.
concomitant [-ənt] *a.* concomitante. —*s.* circunstancia o cosa concomitante; acompañamiento; **to be a c. of,** concomitar.
concord [ˈkɑnˌkɔrd, ˈkɑŋ-, B ˈkɔŋkɔd, ˈkɔn-] *s.* 1. concordia, acuerdo, armonía. 2. (mús.) concordancia, consonancia. 3. (gram.) concordancia.
concordance [kənˈkɔrdəns, kɑn-, B kənˈkɔd-] *s.* 1. concordancia, acuerdo, conformidad, armonía. 2. concordancias (índice alfabético de los temas y nombres principales contenidos en un libro).
concordant [-ənt] *a.* 1. concordante, concorde. 2. (mús.) consonante, armonioso.
concordantly [-lɪ] *adv.* concordemente.
concordat [kənˈkɔrˌdæt, B -ˈkɔˌ-] *s.* (relig.) concordato.
concourse [ˈkɑnˌkɔrs, ˈkɑŋ-, B ˈkɔŋˌkɔs, ˈkɔn-] *s.* 1. concurso, confluencia; concurrencia (de gentes). 2. confluencia (de caminos, ríos, etc.). 3. (f.c.) sala de espera, vestíbulo abierto (en estaciones). 4. calle ancha, bulevar.
concrescence [kənˈkrɛsəns] *s.* (biol) concrescencia.
concrete [kɑnˈkrit, ˈkɑnˌkrit, B ˈkɔn-] *a.* 1. concreto, unido, sólido. 2. concreto, preciso, efectivo, real (opuesto a ideal o abstracto). 3. concreto, particular, específico (opuesto a general). 4. de hormigón o concreto (Am.); para cemento u hormigón. —*s.* 1. concreto, concreción, conglomerado. 2. (const.) hormigón, concreto (Am.). — [B kənˈkrit] *v.t.* 1. conglomerar, conglutinar, solidificar (en una masa). 2. hacer o cubrir con hormigón. —*v.i.* solidificarse, endurecerse.
concrete block, bloque de hormigón, bloque de concreto (Am.).
concrete-block machine [-ˌblɑk-, B -ˌblɔk-] máquina fabricadora de bloques de hormigón, prensa para bloques de hormigón.
concrete lift, (const.) hormigonada.
concrete mixer, mezcladora, hormigonera.
concrete nail, clavo para hormigón, clavo para concreto (Am.).
concrete steel, hormigón armado.
concreting [kənˈkritɪŋ] (const.) hormigonaje, hormigonado.
concretion [kɑnˈkriʃən, kən-, B kən-] *s.* concreción; (med., geol.) cálculo.
concretionary [-ˌɛrɪ, B -ərɪ] *a.* (miner.) concrecionario.
concretize [ˈkɑnkrəˌtaɪz, B ˈkɔn-] *v.t.* concretar, precisar.
concubinage [kɑnˈkjubənɪdʒ, kən-, B kɔn-, kən-] *s.* concubinato, amancebamiento.
concubine [ˈkɑnkjəˌbaɪn, B ˈkɔn-] *s.* concubina, manceba, barragana.
concupiscence [kɑnˈkjupəsəns, B kən-] *s.* concupiscencia, lujuria, lascivia.
concupiscent [-sənt] *a.* concupiscente, libidinoso, lascivo.
concur [kənˈkɛr, kɑn-, B -ˈkɛ] *v.i.* (*pret., p.p.* CONCURRED; *p.pr.* CONCURRING) 1. concurrir, convenir, concordar, asentir. 2. coincidir, ocurrir

simultáneamente. 3. colaborar, cooperar, unirse, juntarse.
concurrence [-əns, -'kʌrəns, B -'kʌrəns] *s.* 1. concurrencia, coincidencia. 2. acuerdo; cooperación. 3. (geom.) concurrencia, punto de intersección. 4. (der.) concurrencia.
concurrent [-ənt] *a.* concurrente, coincidente. —*s.* circunstancia concurrente.
concurrently [-lɪ] *adv.* concurrentemente.
concurrent resolution, resolución conjunta (aprobada por las dos cámaras legislativas pero que carece de la fuerza de la ley).
concuss [kən'kʌs] *v.t.* (fig.) sacudir, agitar, conmover, intimidar, perturbar.
concussion [-'kʌʃən] *s.* 1. concusión, sacudimiento, sacudida; golpe, choque. 2. (med.) concusión.
concussion-fuse [-ˌfjuz] *s.* (mil.) espoleta de percusión (en granadas, etc.).
concussion of the brain, (med.) conmoción cerebral.
condemn [kən'dɛm] *v.t.* 1. condenar, censurar, desaprobar, reprobar. 2. condenar, sentenciar. 3. confiscar (contrabando, etc.). 4. **c. to death,** condenar a muerte.
condemnable [-əbəl, -nəbəl] *a.* condenable, censurable.
condemnation [ˌkɑnˌdɛm'neɪʃən, -dəm-, B ˌkɔn-] *s.* condenación; condena.
condemnatory [kən'dɛmnəˌtɔrɪ, B -tərɪ] *a.* condenatorio.
condensability [kənˌdɛnsə'bɪlətɪ] *s.* condensabilidad.
condensable [-'dɛnsəbəl] *a.* condensable.
condensate ['kɑndənˌseɪt, kən'dɛn-, B 'kɔndɛn-] *s.* (fís., quím.) condensado.
condensation [ˌkɑnˌdɛn'seɪʃən, - dən-, B ˌkɔn-] *s.* 1. condensación. 2. versión condensada (de un libro, etc.).
condensative [kən'dɛnsətɪv] *a.* condensativo.
condense [kən'dɛns] *v.t., v.i.* (lit., fig.) condensar(se), comprimir(se), espesar (se); abreviar.
condensed milk [-'dɛnst-] leche condensada.
condenser [-'dɛnsər, B -sə] *s.* (mec., elec., ópt.) condensador.
condensing coil [-sɪŋ-] serpentín refrigerante.
condescend [ˌkɑndɪ'sɛnd, B ˌkɔn-] *v.i.* dignarse, condescender.
condescendence [-ˌsɛndəns] *s.* condescendencia.
condescending [-dɪŋ] *a.* condescendiente.
condescendingly [-lɪ] *adv.* condescendientemente; con aire de superioridad.
condescension [-'sɛntʃən, B -'sɛnʃən] *s.* condescendencia, aire de superioridad.
condign [kən'daɪn, 'kɑnˌdaɪn, B kən'daɪn] *a.* condigno, adecuado, merecido (castigo o censura).
condiment ['kɑndəmənt, B 'kɔn-] *s.* condimento, aderezo, aliño.
condition [kən'dɪʃən] *s.* 1. condición, estado. 2. condición, estipulación. 3. (*pl.*) circunstancias, condiciones. 4. condición, categoría, linaje. 5. (gram.) cláusula condicional. 6. (lóg.) condición. 7. **in c.,** en buenas condiciones; **on c. that,** a condición de que, con tal que; **under existing conditions,** bajo las condiciones imperantes; **would not do it under any c.,** no lo haría de ninguna manera. —*v.t.* 1. condicionar, estipular. 2. acondicionar (el aire); preparar (atletas, caballos de carrera). 3. (ind.) humidificar (fibras, hilos, textiles, etc.). 4. (psic.) condicionar.
conditional [-əl] *a.* 1. condicional. 2. (gram.) condicional. 3. **to be c. on,** depender de. —*s.* (gram.) palabra, cláusula, conjunción o modo condicional.
conditionality [-ˌdɪʃə'nælətɪ] *s.* carácter condicional; limitación.
conditionally [kən'dɪʃənəlɪ] *adv.* condicionalmente.
conditioned [kən'dɪʃənd] *a.* 1. condicionado, acondicionado. 2. condicional.
conditioned reflex, (psic.) reflejo condicionado.
conditioner [-ənər, B -nə] *s.* acondicionador.
conditioning [-ənɪŋ] *s.* (a) condicionamiento.
condole [kən'doʊl] *v.i.* condolerse, compadecerse, dar el pésame.
condolence [-'doʊləns, 'kɑndə-, B kən'doʊ-] *s.* condolencia, pésame; (*pl.*) declaración formal de condolencia a los familiares de un fallecido.
condom ['kɑndəm, B 'kɔndɔm] *s.* condón, preservativo.
condominium [ˌkɑndə'mɪnɪəm, B 'kɔndə-] *s.* condominio, conjunto residencial.
condonation [ˌkɑndoʊ'neɪʃən, -də-, B ˌkɔn-] *s.* condonación, perdón.
condone [kən'doʊn] *v.t.* condonar, perdonar; tolerar.
condor ['kɑndər, -ˌdɔr, B 'kɔndɔ] *s.* (orn.) cóndor.
condottiere [ˌkɑndə'tjɛrɪ, B ˌkɔndə'tjɛərɪ] *s.* (italiano) (*pl.* CONDOTTIERI) condotiero, soldado mercenario.
conduce [kən'dus, B -'djus] *v.i.* (con *to*) conducir a; contribuir.
conducive [-'dusɪv, B -'djusɪv] *a.* (con *to*) conducente (a), favorable (a), propicio (a).
conduct ['kɑndʌkt, B 'kɔn-] *s.* 1. conducta, comportamiento, proceder; **good c.,** buena conducta. 2. conducción, dirección, manejo, gestión. — [kən'dʌkt] *v.t.* 1. conducir, guiar, dirigir, llevar. 2. dirigir, manejar, administrar (negocio, etc.). 3. (mús.) dirigir (orquesta, coro, concierto, etc.). 4. (mil.) comandar (ejército, tropas, etc.). 5. (fís.) conducir (electricidad, calor, etc.). 6. **c. oneself,** comportarse, conducirse. —*v.i.* 1. (con *to*) conducir a (díc. de un camino, vía, etc.). 2. actuar como director (de orquesta, coro, etc.). 3. (fís.) ser (buen) conductor (de electricidad, calor, etc.).
conductance [kən'dʌktəns] *s.* (elec.) conductancia, potencia conductora.
conducted tour [-təd-] gira con guía, gira guiada (de una ciudad, etc.).
conductibility [-ˌdʌktə'bɪlətɪ] *s.* (fís.) conductibilidad.
conductible [-'dʌktəbəl] *a.* conductible.
conduction [kən'dʌkʃən] *s.* conducción, transmisión.
conduction anesthesia, (med.) anestesia regional, anestesia de bloque.
conductivity [ˌkɑnˌdʌk'tɪvətɪ, kən-, B ˌkɔn-] *s.* conductividad.
conductor [kən'dʌktər, B -tə] *s.* 1. conductor, guía (*m.*) 2. (fís.) conductor. 3. (mús.) director (de orquesta, coro, etc.). 4. (f.c., tranvía) recogedor de billetes, cobrador, revisor, conductor (Am.). 5. canalón, caño de bajada (en una casa). 6. pararrayos.
conductress [-trəs] *s.* conductora; directora; cobradora (en trenes, autobuses, etc.).
conduit ['kɑnˌduət, -ˌdwɪt, B 'kɔndɪt] *s.* 1. conducto, caño, encañado, surtidero, arcaduz. 2. (elec.) tubo, conducto portacables, conducto celular, canal de cables.
conduplicate [kɑn'duplɪkət, B kɔn'dju-] *a.* (bot.) conduplicado.
condyle ['kɑnˌdaɪl, -dəl, B 'kɔn-] *s.* (anat.) cóndilo.
condyloid [-dəˌlɔɪd] *a.* (anat.) condiloideo.
condyloma [ˌkɑndə'loʊmə, B ˌkɔn-] *s.* (med.) condiloma.
cone [koʊn] *s.* 1. (geom., geol.) cono. 2. (bot.) cono, piña. 3. cono, cucurucho, barquillo (de helados, etc.). —*v.t.* dar forma cónica a, ahusar.
cone bearing, (mec.) cojinete de cono.
cone-bearing ['koʊn'bɛrɪŋ, B -'bɛər-] *a.* (bot.) conífero.
cone brake, freno de cono.
cone clutch, (aut.) embrague cónico.
cone frustum, (geom.) cono truncado.
cone gear, (mec.) engranaje cónico.
cone of silence, (rad., aer.) cono de silencio.
cone pulley, polea escalonada o de cono.
cone-shaped [-ˌʃeɪpt] *a.* cónico, coniforme.
Conestoga [ˌkɑnəˌstoʊgə, B ˌkɔn-] *s.* (E.U., hist.) carromato de carga (usado para transporte en las llanuras del Oeste).
coney ['koʊnɪ] *var. de* **cony.**
confab [kən'fæb, 'kɑnˌfæb, B 'kɔnˌfæb] *v.i.* (*pret., p.p.* CONFABBED ; *p.pr.* CONFABBING) *abrev. fam. de* **confabulate,** confabular.
confabulate [kən'fæbjəˌleɪt] *v.i.* confabular, platicar, charlar.
confabulation [-ˌfæbjə'leɪʃən] *s.* plática, charla; confabulación.
confarreation [kɑnˌfærɪ'eɪʃən, B kɔn-] *s.* (hist.) confarreación, rito matrimonial entre los patricios romanos.
confect [kən'fɛkt] *v.t.* confeccionar, preparar; confitar.
confection [kən'fɛkʃən] *s.* 1. confección, hechura, preparación. 2. confección, mixtura, composición. 3. confitura, dulce, conserva; bombón. 4. (farm.) confección.
confectionary [-ʃəˌnɛrɪ, B -ʃənərɪ] *a.* confitado, confeccionado. —*s.* 1. confitería. 2. confitura, dulces, confites.
confectioner [-ʃənər, B -ə] *s.* confitero, repostero, dulcero.
confectioner's sugar, azúcar glas, azúcar glasé, azúcar en polvo.
confectionery [-ʃəˌnɛrɪ, B -ʃənərɪ] *s.* 1. confitura, dulces, confites. 2. confitería, repostería.
confederacy [kən'fɛdərəsɪ] *s.* 1. confederación, liga, alianza, coalición. 2. C., (E.U., hist.) Confederación.
confederate [-'fɛdərət] *a.* confederado, aliado. —*s.* cómplice, compinche, aliado. — [-reɪt] *v.t., v.i.* confederar(se).
confederation [kənˌfɛdə'reɪʃən] *s.* confederación.
confederative [-'fɛdərətɪv, -əˌreɪtɪv] *a.* confederativo, federativo.
confer [kən'fɜr, B -'fɜ] *v.t.* (*pret., p.p.* CONFERRED ; *p.pr.* CONFERRING) conferir, otorgar. —*v.i.* conferenciar, conferir, tratar, consultar.
conferee [ˌkɑnfə'ri, B ˌkɔn-] *s.* 1. participante en una conferencia, miembro de una conferencia. 2. conferido, beneficiario, recipiente.
conference ['kɑnfərəns, B 'kɔn-] *s.* 1. conferencia; consulta; junta; deliberación; entrevista. 2. conferimiento, otorgamiento.
conferential [ˌkɑnfə'rɛntʃəl, B ˌkɔnfə'rɛnʃəl] *a.* propio de la conferencia.
conferment [kən'fɜrmənt, B -'fɜm-] *s.* conferimiento, otorgamiento.
conferva [kən'fɜrvə, B -'fɜvə] *s.* (*pl.* CONFERVAE [-ˌvi] o CONFERVAS) (bot.) conferva.
confess [kən'fɛs] *v.t.* 1. confesar, reconocer. 2. (relig.) confesar. —*v.i.* 1. hacer una confesión. 2. confesarse; oír confesión.
confessedly [-ədlɪ] *adv.* reconocidamente, manifiestamente, por confesión propia.
confession [kən'fɛʃən] *s.* 1. confesión, reconocimiento (de un hecho, delito, etc.). 2. (relig.) confesión, credo. 3. **to hear confession,** (relig.) oír confesión.

confessional [-əl] *s.* (relig.) 1. confesonario. 2. confesión. —*a.* confesional.

confessor [kən'fɛsər, B -ə] *s.* 1. confesor, confesante. 2. penitente. 3. (relig.) confesor.

confetti [kən'fɛtɪ] *s. pl.* confeti, pedacitos de papel de colores, que se arrojan en los días de carnaval.

confidant ['kɑnfəˌdænt, -ˌdɑnt, B ˌkɔnfɪ'dænt] *s.* confidente.

confidante [-ˌdænt, -ˌdɑnt, B -ˌdænt] *s.* confidente.

confide [kən'faɪd] *v.t.* confiar (negocio, secreto, etc.). —*v.i.* 1. (con *in*) fiarse (de), confiar (en). 2. demostrar confianza; decir confidencias a.

confidence ['kɑnfədəns, B 'kɔn-] *s.* 1. confianza (en alguien o algo). 2. fe, confianza, esperanza. 3. seguridad. 4. confidencia, comunicación reservada. 5. **in c.,** en confianza, en secreto; **in one's c.,** en su confianza de uno; **to place one's c. in,** depositar uno su confianza en.

confidence game, c. trick, fraude, embaucamiento (en que el timador se aprovecha de la confianza del otro).

confidence man, timador, estafador (que se aprovecha de la confianza del otro).

confident [-dənt] *a.* confiado, cierto, seguro; **to be c.,** confiarse. —*s.* confidente.

confidential [ˌkɑnfə'dɛnʃəl, B ˌkɔnfɪ'dɛnʃəl] *a.* 1. confidencial, reservado, secreto (asunto, carácter, etc.). 2. de confianza (empleado, etc.); íntimo (amigo, gesto).

confidentially [-əlɪ] *a.* confidencialmente, en confianza, en secreto.

confidently ['kɑnfədəntlɪ, B 'kɔn-] *adv.* confiadamente.

confiding [kən'faɪdɪŋ] *a.* confiado, crédulo.

configurate [kən'fɪgjəˌreɪt] *v.t.* configurar.

configuration [-ˌfɪgjə'reɪʃən] *s.* configuración, figura; (astr., psic.) configuración.

configurative [-'fɪgjəˌreɪtɪv, B -rətɪv] *a.* configurativo.

configure [-'fɪgjər, B -'fɪgə] *v.t.* configurar, dar forma y figura a (una cosa).

confine ['kɑnˌfaɪn, B 'kɔn-] *s.* (*gen. pl.*) confín, frontera, límite, término. — [kən'faɪn] *v.t.* 1. confinar, recluir; (fig.) aprisionar. 2. limitar, restringir. 3. **c. oneself (to),** limitarse (a); **to be confined,** guardar cama; estar de parto. —*v.i.* lindar, estar contiguos (países, fincas, etc.).

confinement [kən'faɪnmənt] *s.* 1. prisión, encierro; reclusión, confinamiento. 2. restricción, limitación, límite. 3. parto, sobreparto.

confirm [-'fɜrm, B -'fɜm] *v.t.* 1. confirmar, corroborar, ratificar. 2. (relig.) confirmar.

confirmation [ˌkɑnfər'meɪʃən, B ˌkɔnfə'-] *s.* 1. confirmación, ratificación, corroboración. 2. (relig.) confirmación.

confirmative [kən'fɜrmətɪv, B -'fɜm-] *s.* confirmativo.

confirmatively [-tɪvlɪ] *adv.* confirmativamente.

confirmatory [-ˌtɔrɪ, B -tərɪ] *a.* confirmatorio.

confirmed [-'fɜrmd, B -'fɜmd] *a.* 1. confirmado. 2. inveterado, habitual (mentiroso, fumador, etc.); crónica (enfermedad).

confiscable [kən'fɪskəbəl, B kɔn-] *a.* confiscable.

confiscate ['kɑnfəˌskeɪt, B 'kɔn-] *v.t.* confiscar, comisar, decomisar.

confiscation [ˌkɑnfə'skeɪʃən, B ˌkɔn-] *s.* confiscación, comiso, decomiso.

confiscator ['kɑnfəˌskeɪtər, B 'kɔn-ə] *s.* confiscador.

confiscatory [kən'fɪskəˌtɔrɪ, B -kətərɪ] *a.* confiscatorio, que confisca, de confiscación.

confiteor [kən'fitɪər, B -'fɪtɪɔ] *s.* (relig.) confiteor (el "yo pecador").

confiture ['kɑnfɪˌtʃʊr, B 'kɔnfɪˌtʃʊə] *s.* confitura, dulce.

conflagrant [kən'fleɪgrənt] *s.* ardiente, llameante.

conflagration [ˌkɑnflə'greɪʃən, B ˌkɔn-] *s.* conflagración, incendio; (fig.) conflagración, guerra.

conflation [kən'fleɪʃən] *s.* combinación, fusión (esp. de dos variantes de un texto en una versión definitiva).

conflict ['kɑnˌflɪkt, B 'kɔn-] *s.* 1. conflicto, contienda, combate, lucha. 2. (fig.) conflicto, pugna, oposición. — [kən'flɪkt] *v.i.* (gen. fig.) pugnar, estar en pugna.

conflicting [kən'flɪktɪŋ] *a.* incompatible, opuesto, contrario (intereses, ideas, etc.).

conflict of interest, conflicto de intereses (gen. en casos de funcionarios públicos que tienen intereses particulares).

confluence ['kɑnˌfluəns, B 'kɔn-] *s.* 1. confluencia (de ríos, caminos, etc.). 2. confluencia, concurrencia (de gente).

confluent [-ənt] *a.* confluente (ríos, caminos). —*s.* río confluente, tributario.

conflux [-ˌflʌks] *s.* confluencia.

conform [kən'fɔrm, B -'fɔm] *v.t.* conformar, ajustar, concordar. —*v.i.* (con *to*) conformarse (a, con), amoldarse; acatar, someterse.

conformability [-ˌfɔrmə'bɪlətɪ, B ˌfɔmə-] *s.* conformabilidad.

conformable [kən'fɔrməbəl, B -'fɔmə-] *a.* 1. (con *to*) conforme, acorde (con), similar (a). 2. dócil, tratable.

conformably [-blɪ] *adv.* conformemente, en conformidad; dócilmente; sumisamente.

conformal [-məl] *a.* (mat., topog.) conforme (representación, proyección, mapa, etc.).

conformance [-məns] *s.* conformidad.

conformation [ˌkɑnfɔr'meɪʃən, B ˌkɔnfɔ'-] *s.* 1. conformación, disposición, estructura; figura, forma. 2. ajuste, adaptación. 3. formación.

conformism [kən'fɔrˌmɪzəm, B -'fɔˌ-] *s.* conformismo.

conformist [-məst] *s.* conformista; (relig., G.B.) conformista.

conformity [-mətɪ] *s.* conformidad; avenencia, concordancia.

confound [kən'faʊnd] *v.t.* 1. maldecir, abominar, detestar, esp. en **c. it!** ¡maldito sea! 2. confundir, enredar, embrollar. 3. aturrullar, atolondrar.

confounded [-əd] *a.* 1. atolondrado, aturdido. 2. (fam.) maldito, detestable, odioso.

confoundedly [-ədlɪ] *adv.* execrablemente; detestablemente, odiosamente.

confraternity [ˌkɑnfrə'tɜrnətɪ, B ˌkɔn'tɜnɪtɪ] *s.* confraternidad, cofradía, hermandad, sociedad.

confrere ['kɑnˌfrɛr, B 'kɔnfrɛə] *a.* colega, compañero.

confront [kən'frʌnt] *v.t.* 1. confrontar, enfrentar, carear. 2. confrontar, cotejar, comparar.

confrontation [ˌkɑnfrən'teɪʃən, B ˌkɔn-] *s.* confrontación, careo, enfrentamiento.

Confucian [kən'fjuʃən] *a., s.* confuciano, partidario de Confucio.

Confucianism [-ˌɪzəm] *s.* confucianismo, doctrina de Confucio.

Confucianist [-əst] *a., s.* confuciano, confucianista.

Confucius [kən'fjuʃəs] *s.* Confucio.

confuse [kən'fjuz] *v.t.* 1. confundir, desconcertar, desorientar. 2. confundir, desordenar, mezclar. 3. turbar, ofuscar (la vista); borrar (ej., contorno). 4. (con *with*) confundir (con otra persona o cosa).

confusedly [-ədlɪ] *adv.* confusamente, atropelladamente.

confusedness [-ədnəs] *s.* confusión, perplejidad, estado confuso.

confusing [-ɪŋ] *a.* desconcertante, que causa confusión, ej., *all this is very c.,* todo esto me causa gran confusión.

confusingly [-lɪ] *adv.* de un modo confuso, confusamente.

confusion [kən'fjuʒən] *s.* 1. confusión, desorden. 2. confusión, desorientación, perturbacion, perplejidad. 3. vergüenza.

confutation [ˌkɑnfjʊ'teɪʃən, B ˌkɔn-] *s.* confutación.

confute [kən'fjut] *v.t.* confutar, refutar, invalidar.

conga ['kɑŋgə, B 'kɔŋgə] *s.* 1. conga (danza). 2. bongó.

con game [kɑn-, B kɔn-] (jer.) estafa, timo, embaucamiento.

congé ['kɑnʒeɪ, B 'kɔn-] *s.* (fr.) despedida, adiós; cortesía.

congeal [kən'dʒil] *v.t.* 1. cuajar, coagular (sangre, etc.). 2. congelar, helar. —*v.i.* 1. coagularse, cuajarse. 2. (fig.) petrificarse (sociedad, pensamientos, etc.).

congealable [-əbəl] *a.* congelable.

congealment [-mənt] *s.* congelamiento.

congeal point, (quím.) punto de solidificación.

congelation [ˌkɑndʒə'leɪʃən B ˌkɔn-] *s.* congelación.

congener ['kɑndʒənər, B 'kɔn-ə] *s.* (planta o animal) congénere.

congeneric [ˌkɑndʒə'nɛrɪk, B ˌkɔn-] **congenerous** [kən'dʒɛnərəs] *s., a.* congénero, congenérico.

congenial [kən'dʒinjəl] *a.* 1. congenial. 2. compatible (con). 3. agradable, conveniente. 4. sociable, simpático.

congeniality [-ˌdʒinɪ'ælətɪ] *s.* congenialidad, afinidad; compatibilidad.

congenital [kən'dʒɛnətəl] *a.* congénito, hereditario, de nacimiento (díc. esp. de enfermedades, defectos, etc.).

conger eel ['kɑŋgər-, B 'kɔŋ-] (ict.) congrio; anguila.

congeries ['kɑndʒəˌriz, kɑn'dʒɪriz, B kɔn'dʒɪəriz] *s.* congerie, cúmulo, montón.

congest [kən'dʒɛst] *v.t.* congestionar, apiñar, aglomerar. —*v.i.* (med.) congestionarse.

congestion [-'dʒɛstʃən] *s.* (med.) congestión; (fig.) congestión, acumulación (de tráfico, población, etc.).

congestive [-tɪv] *a.* (med.) congestivo.

conglobate ['kɑnglоʊˌbeɪtʲ kɑn'gloʊ-, B 'kɔngloʊ-] *v.t., v.i.* conglobar(se). —*a.* conglobado.

conglobation [ˌkɑngloʊ'beɪʃən, B ˌkɔn-] *s.* conglobación.

conglomerate [kən'glɑmərət, B -'glɔm-] *a.* conglomerado. —*s.* 1. conglomeración. 2. (geol.) conglomerado. — [-ˌreɪt] *v.t., v.i.* conglomerar(se), amontonar(se).

conglomeration [-ˌglɑmə'reɪʃən, B -ˌglɔm-] *s.* conglomeración.

conglutinate [kən'glutənˌeɪt] *v.t., v.i.* conglutinar(se); pegar(se); reunir(se). —*a.* conglutinado.

conglutination [-ˌglutən'eɪʃən] *s.* conglutinación.

Congo ['kɑŋgoʊ, B'kɔŋ-] *s.* Congo.

Congolese [ˌkɑŋgə'liz, B ˌkɔŋ-] *a.* congoleño, congolés. —*s.* (*pl.* CONGOLESE) 1. natural del Congo, congoleño. 2. idioma congoleño.

Congo red, (quím., tej.) rojo Congo.
congou ['kaŋgu, B 'kɔŋ-] *s.* (especie de) té negro de la China.
congratulate [kən'grætʃə,leɪt] *v.t.* congratular, cumplimentar, felicitar.
congratulation [-,grætʃə'leɪʃən] *s.* congratulación, felicitación; **congratulations!** ¡felicidades! ¡enhorabuena!
congratulatory [-'grætʃələ,tɔrɪ, B -lətərɪ] *a.* congratulatorio.
congregate ['kaŋgrɪ,geɪt, B 'kɔŋ-] *v.t., v.i.* congregar(se), juntar(se), reunir(se).
congregation [,kaŋgrɪ'geɪʃən, B ,kɔŋ-] *s.* 1. congregación, asamblea, reunión. 2. (relig.) congregación. 3. (relig.) grey, feligreses, fieles.
congregational [-əl] *a.* 1. perteneciente a una congregación. 2. **C.,** congregacional.
congregationalism [-,ɪzəm] *s.* 1. congregacionalismo. 2. **C.,** (relig.) congregacionalismo.
Congregationalist [-əst] *a., s.* congregacionalista.
congress ['kaŋgrəs, B 'kɔŋgrɛs] *s.* 1. congreso; asamblea, reunión, convención, concilio. 2. ayuntamiento (carnal). 3. **C.,** (E.U.) Congreso, Asamblea Nacional.
congressional [kən'grɛʃənəl, B kɔŋ-] *a.* de o del congreso.
congressional district, (E.U.) distrito electoral (que elige a un diputado para la cámara de representantes).
Congressional Record, (E.U.) diario de sesiones del Congreso.
congressman ['kaŋgrəsmən, B 'kɔŋgrɛs-] *s.* 1. congresista. 2. diputado al congreso. 3. (E.U.) miembro de la Cámara de Representantes.
congresswoman [-,wʊmən] *s.* 1. congresista (*f.*). 2. diputada al congreso.
congruence [kən'gruəns, 'kaŋgruəns, B 'kɔŋgrʊ-] *s.* 1. congruencia, concordancia. 2. (mat., geom.) congruencia.
congruency [-ənsɪ] *s.* (*pl.* CONGRUENCIES) *var. de* **congruence.**
congruent [-ənt] *a.* 1. congruente, concorde. 2. (mat., geom.) congruente.
congruently [-lɪ] *adv.* congruentemente, armónicamente.
congruity [kən'gruətɪ, B kɔŋ-] *s.* congruidad, concordancia; (mat., geom.) congruencia.
congruous ['kaŋgrʊəs, B 'kɔŋ-] *a.* congruo, congruente, conveniente; (mat., geom.) congruente.
congruously [-lɪ] *adv.* congruamente, congruentemente.
congruousness [-nəs] *s.* calidad o carácter congruente.
conic ['kanɪk, B 'kɔn-] *a.* cónico. —*s.* (*pl.*) (mat.) geometría de las cónicas.
conical [-əl] *a.* cónico.
conical flask, (quím.) matraz cónico.
conically [-əlɪ] *adv.* en forma cónica.
conicalness [-əlnəs] *s.* conicidad.
conic section, (geom.) cónica, sección cónica.
conidial [kə'nɪdɪəl] *a.* (bot.) conídico.
conidiophore [-ɪə,fɔr, B -,fɔ] *s.* (bot.) conidióforo.
conidium [kə'nɪdɪəm] *s.* (*pl.* CONIDIA [-ɪə]) (bot.) conidio.
conifer ['kanəfər, 'kounə-, B 'kounɪfə] *s.* (bot.) conífero.
coniferous [kou'nɪfərəs, kə-] *a.* (bot.) conífero.
coniform ['kounə,fɔrm, B -,fɔm] *a.* coniforme, cónico.
conine ['kou,nin, -nɪn] *s.* (quím.) conicina, cicutina.
conirostral [,kounɪ'rastrəl, B -'rɔs-] *a.* (orn.) conirrostro.
conium [kou'naɪəm, 'kounɪəm, B kou'naɪ-] *s.* (bot.) conio, cicuta.
conj. *abrev. de* **conjunction,** conjunción (conj.).
conjecturable [kən'dʒɛktʃərəbəl] *a.* conjeturable, presumible.
conjectural [-'dʒɛktʃərəl] *a.* conjetural.
conjecturally [-əlɪ] *adv.* conjeturalmente, presumiblemente.
conjecture [kən'dʒɛktʃər, B -tʃə] *s.* conjetura, suposición. —*v.t.* conjeturar, suponer. —*v.i.* andarse en conjeturas.
conjoin [kən'dʒɔɪn] *v.t., v.i.* juntar(se), unir(se), asociar(se), combinar(se).
conjoint [-'dʒɔɪnt, B 'kɔndʒɔɪnt] *a.* conjunto, unido, asociado.
conjointly [-lɪ] *adv.* conjuntamente, mancomunadamente.
conjugal ['kandʒɪgəl, kən'dʒugəl, B 'kɔnd-ʒʊ-] *a.* conyugal.
conjugally [-ɪ] *adv.* conyugalmente.
conjugant ['kandʒɪgənt, B 'kɔn-] *s.* (biol.) gameto conyugante.
conjugate [-gɪt, -,geɪt] *a.* 1. conjugado, acoplado. 2. (bot.) conyugado, conjugado. 3. (gram.) congénere. 4. (mat.) conjugado. —*s.* palabra congénere. — [-,geɪt] *v.t.* 1. juntar, unir, acoplar (esp. sexualmente). 2. (gram.) conjugar (un verbo). —*v.i.* 1. unirse, copularse. 2. (gram.) conjugarse (un verbo).
conjugation [,kandʒə'geɪʃən, B ,kɔn-] *s.* 1. conjunción, unión. 2. (gram.) conjugación. 3. (biol.) conjugación o fusión.
conjunct [kən'dʒʌŋkt] *a.* conjunto, unido, combinado.
conjunction [-'dʒʌŋkʃən] *s.* 1. conjunción, unión, conexión 2. coyuntura, concurrencia (de eventos, circunstancias, etc.). 3. (astr., gram., bot., lóg.) conjunción.
conjunction of purpose, (gram.) conjunción final.
conjunctiva [,kandʒʌŋk'taɪvə, B ,kɔn-] *s.* (*pl.* CONJUNCTIVAS O CONJUNCTIVAE [-'taɪvi]) (anat.) cojuntiva.
conjunctival [-'taɪvəl] *a.* (anat.) conjuntival.
conjunctive [kən'dʒʌŋktɪv] *a.* 1. conjuntivo. 2. (gram.) conjuntivo. —*s.* (gram). 1. conjunción, palabra conjuntiva. 2. modo conjuntivo, subjuntivo.
conjunctively [-lɪ] *adv.* conjuntivamente, conjuntamente.
conjunctivitis [kən,dʒʌŋktɪ'vaɪtɪs] *s.* (med.) conjuntivitis.
conjuncture [kən'dʒʌŋktʃər, B -tʃə] *s.* 1. coyuntura, ocasión. 2. conjunción, unión.
conjuration [,kandʒə'reɪʃən, B ,kɔn-] *s.* 1. conjuración, conspiración. 2. conjuro, imprecación. 3. hechizo, encanto, palabra mágica; acto de prestidigitación. 4. conjuro, súplica, imploración.
conjure [kən'dʒʊr, B -'dʒʊə] *v.t.* 1. conjurar, implorar, suplicar. 2. ['kandʒər, 'kʌn-, B 'kʌndʒə] invocar (demonio, espíritus, etc.). 3. **c. away,** exorcizar; hacer desaparecer (por magia), escamotear; **c. up,** evocar (en la imaginación); inventar, idear. — ['kan-, 'kʌn-, B 'kʌn-] *v.i.* invocar un demonio o espíritu; practicar la magia, hacer juegos de manos.
conjurer, conjuror ['kandʒərər, 'kʌn-, B 'kʌndʒərə] *s.* mago, nigromante, prestidigitador.
conk [kaŋk, kɔŋk, B kɔŋk] *s.* (jer.) 1. nariz. 2. coco, cabeza. —*v.t.* (jer.) golpear en la cabeza. —*v.i.* **c. out,** (jer.) dejar de funcionar, fallar, estropearse (motor, máquina); desmayarse.
conker ['kaŋkər, 'kɔŋk-, B 'kɔŋkə] *s.* (fam., G.B.) castaño de Indias (esp. en un juego de niños).
con man [kan-, B kɔn-] (fam.)*abrev. de* **confidence man,** timador, estafador (que se aprovecha de la confianza del otro).
conn [kan, B kɔn] *v.t.* (mar.) gobernar (un buque). —*s.* gobierno (de un buque).
Conn. *abrev. de* **Connecticut,** Connecticut (E.U.).
connnate [ka'neɪt, 'kan,eɪt, B 'kɔn-] *a.* 1. congénito, innato. 2. (bot., zool.) connato.
connatural [kə'nætʃərəl] *a.* connatural, innato, congénito.
connaturality [-,nætʃə'rælətɪ] *s.* lo connatural, lo congénito.
connaturally [kə'nætʃərəlɪ] *adv.* connaturalmente.
connect [kə'nɛkt] *v.t.* 1. (con *with* o *to*) conectar, juntar, unir. 2. (con *with*) relacionar (con). 3. (elec.) conectar. 4. (mec.) conectar, ensamblar, acoplar. —*v.i.* 1. (pr. con *with*) juntarse, unirse (con). 2. (pr. con *with*) empalmar, entroncar (trenes, líneas); cambiar a (otro tren). 3. **c. with,** asociarse, relacionarse con; comunicarse con (ej., un cuarto con otro).
connected [-əd] *a.* 1. unido. 2. conexo, relacionado; asociado. 3. coherente. 4. **c. with,** relacionado con.
connectedly [-lɪ] *adv.* coherentemente, con ilación o relación.
connecter, *var. de* **connector.**
Connecticut [kə'nɛtɪkət] *s.* Connecticut, estado de los E.U.
connecting link, nexo, eslabón.
connecting rod, 1. (mot.) biela, biela motriz. 2. (f.c.) barra de conexión.
connection, (pr. G.B.) **connexion** [kə'nɛkʃən] *s.* 1. conexión, unión, enlace. 2. conexión, coherencia. 3. respecto, referencia, ej., *in this c.,* a este respecto, en cuanto a esto; **in c. with,** con respecto a. 4. relaciones, ej., *a salesman with good connections,* un vendedor con buenas relaciones. 5. cópula. 6. (f.c.) empalme, entronque (de trenes, líneas). 7. (mec.) acoplamiento, junta, unión. 8. (elec.) conexión. 9. (jer.) traficante callejero de drogas. 10. **to cut the c.,** (fig.) cortar los lazos o vínculos; **to miss the c.,** perder la conexión (de un tren, etc.).
connective [kə'nɛktɪv] *a.* conectivo, conexivo, conjuntivo. —*s.* (gram.) conjunción, palabra conjuntiva.
connective tissue, (anat.) tejido conectivo.
connector [-tər, B -tə] *s.* (elec., mec.) conector, empalmador.
conning tower ['kanɪŋ-, B 'kɔn-] (mar.) torre blindada de mando (de un buque de guerra); torrecilla (de un submarino).
conniption [kə'nɪpʃən] *s.* (fam.) acceso de furia o histeria, rabieta.
connivance [-'naɪvəns] *s.* connivencia, confabulación; permiso tácito.
connive [kə'naɪv] *v.i.* hacer la vista gorda; disimular, tolerar, consentir; **c. with,** confabular, conspirar (con).
connivent [-ənt] *a.* (anat., bot.) connivente.
conniver [kə'naɪvər, B -ə] *s.* cómplice; conspirador.
connoisseur [,kanə'sɜr, -'sʊr, B ,kɔnə'sɜ] *s.* (fr.) conocedor, perito (esp. en las artes).
connotation [,kanə'teɪʃən, B ,kɔn-] *s.* connotación.
connotative ['kanə,teɪtɪv, kə'noutətɪv, B 'kɔnə-] *a.* connotativo.
connote [kə'nout, B kɔ-] *v.t.* connotar, significar indirectamente; implicar (condiciones o consecuencias).

connubial [kə'nubɪəl, B -'nju-] *a.* connubial, conyugal, matrimonial.
conoid ['koʊˌnɔɪd] *a.* (geom.) conoidal, conoideo. —*s.* (geom.) conoide.
conoidal [koʊ'nɔɪdəl] *a.* (geom.) conoidal, conoideo.
conquer ['kɑŋkər, B 'kɔŋkə] *v.t.* 1. conquistar (país, pueblo, montaña, cumbre, etc.). 2. (fig.) vencer, superar (temores, dificultades, etc.). —*v.i.* triunfar, vencer, ser victorioso.
conquerable [-kərəbəl] *a.* conquistable; vencible, superable, domable.
conqueror [-kərər, B -ə] *s.* conquistador; triunfador, vencedor.
conquest ['kɑnˌkwɛst, 'kɑŋ-, B 'kɔŋ-] *s.* conquista; **the C.,** la conquista (de Inglaterra por Guillermo el Conquistador); **to make a c. (of),** (fig.) conquistar (a una persona).
conquistador [kɔŋ'kistəˌdɔr, kɑn'kwɪs-, B kɔŋ'kɪstəˌdɔ] *s.* conquistador, esp. los españoles que conquistaron Perú y México en el siglo XVI.
consanguine [kɑn'sæŋgwɪn, B kɔn-] **consanguineous** [ˌkɑnˌsæn'gwɪnɪəs, -ˌsæŋ-, B ˌkɔnsæŋ-] *s.* consanguíneo.
consanguinity [-'gwɪnətɪ] *s.* consanguinidad.
conscience ['kɑntʃəns, B 'kɔnʃəns] *s.* conciencia; **for c. 'sake,** para tener la conciencia tranquila; **in all c.,** en conciencia, en justicia; sin duda; **to have a bad c.,** no tener la conciencia tranquila; **to have a guilty c.,** sentirse culpable; **to have c. for (someone's feelings,** etc.), tener consideración o respeto para con (las sensibilidades, etc. de otro); **to have on one's c.,** tener un cargo de conciencia.
conscienceless [-ləs] *a.* desalmado, sin conciencia.
conscience money, dinero donado para tranquilizarse la conciencia (esp. después de actuar sin honradez).
conscience-stricken [-ˌstrɪkən] *a.* arrepentido, remordido por la conciencia.
conscientious [ˌkɑntʃɪ'ɛntʃəs, B ˌkɔnʃɪ'ɛnʃəs] *a.* 1. concienzudo, escrupuloso. 2. concienzudo, cuidadoso, meticuloso.
conscientiously [-lɪ] *adv.* concienzudamente, a conciencia.
conscientiousness [-nəs] *s.* rectitud, equidad; escrupulosidad.
conscientious objector, pacifista, objetor de conciencia (esp. que rehúsa combatir como soldado).
conscious ['kɑntʃəs, B 'kɔnʃəs] *a.* 1. consciente, sabedor. 2. consciente de sí mismo. 3. intencional, ej., *a hardly c. movement,* un movimiento apenas intencional, *a c. lie,* una mentira intencional. 4. **to be c.,** tener conocimiento; **to be c. of,** tener conciencia de; **to become c.,** volver en sí, recobrar el conocimiento; **to become c. of,** darse cuenta de.
consciously [-lɪ] *adv.* conscientemente, con conocimiento, a sabiendas.
consciousness [-nəs] *s.* 1. conocimiento, sentido, estado consciente. 2. conciencia. 3. **to lose c.,** perder el conocimiento o el sentido; **to regain c.,** volver en sí, recobrar el conocimiento.
conscript [kən'skrɪpt] *v.t.* reclutar, alistar. —['kɑnˌskrɪpt, B 'kɔn-] *a.* alistado. —*s.* quinto, recluta, conscripto.
conscription [kən'skrɪpʃən] *s.* reclutamiento, alistamiento, quinta, conscripción.
consecrate ['kɑnsəˌkreɪt, B 'kɔn-] *v.t.* 1. consagrar, santificar. 2. consagrar, dedicar. —*a.* consagrado, santificado.
consecration [ˌkɑnsə'kreɪʃən, B ˌkɔn-] *a.* consagración.
consecrator ['kɑnsəˌkreɪtər, B 'kɔn-ə] *s.* consagrante.
consecratory [-krəˌtɔrɪ, B -ˌkreɪtərɪ] *a.* consagratorio.
consecution [ˌkɑnsə'kjuʃən, B ˌkɔn-] *s.* secuencia, sucesión, ilación; (gram.) secuencia (de palabras, tiempos del verbo, etc.).
consecutive [kən'sɛkjətɪv] *a.* consecutivo, sucesivo.
consecutively [-lɪ] *adv.* consecutivamente.
consensual [kən'sɛntʃʊəl, B -'sɛnʃʊ-] *a.* (der.) consensual (contrato); (fisiol.) consensual.
consensus [-'sɛnsəs] *s.* 1. consenso, asenso general. 2. (fisiol.) relación consensual (de los órganos). 3. **c. of opinion,** opinión general, consenso general.
consent [kən'sɛnt] *s.* consentimiento, aquiescencia, anuencia, asenso; **by common c.,** de mutuo acuerdo; según la opinión unánime; **silence gives c.,** quien calla otorga. —*v.i.* consentir, condescender, acceder; **c. to,** consentir en.
consentaneous [ˌkɑnsən'teɪnɪəs, B 'kɔn-] *a.* 1. acorde, conforme. 2. unánime.
consentient [kən'sɛntʃənt, B -'sɛnʃənt] *a.* consintiente, anuente.
consequence ['kɑnsəˌkwɛns, -kwəns, B 'kɔnsɪkwəns] *s.* 1. consecuencia, resultado. 2. consecuencia, importancia, consideración. 3. rango, distinción (social), ej., *persons of c.,* personas de rango, gente de distinción. 4. **in c.,** por consiguiente; **in c. of,** como resultado de; **of no c.,** de ninguna importancia; **to take the consequences,** aceptar las consecuencias.
consequent [-kwənt, -ˌkwɛnt] *s.* 1. consecuencia. 2. (lóg., mat., gram.) consecuente. —*a.* consecuente, consiguiente; lógico; **c. upon,** consiguiente a.
consequential [ˌkɑnsə'kwentʃəl, B ˌkɔnsɪ'kwenʃəl] *a.* 1. consecuente, consiguiente. 2. consecuente, lógico, racional. 3. de consecuencia, importante. 4. pomposo, altivo.
consequently ['kɑnsəˌkwentlɪ, -kwəntlɪ, B 'kɔnsɪ-] *adv.* por lo tanto, en consecuencia, por consiguiente, por ende.
conservancy [kən'sɜrvənsɪ, B -'sɜvən-] *s.* 1. conservación, preservación (esp. de los bosques, ríos, salud pública). 2. área reservada, vedado (para la preservación de riquezas naturales). 3. (G.B.) comisión portuaria (para regular la pesca y la navegación).
conservation [ˌkɑnsər'veɪʃən, B ˌkɔnsə'-] *s.* conservación, preservación (esp. de bosques, ríos y demás recursos naturales).
conservationist [-əst] *s.* conservacionista; partidario de la conservación de los recursos naturales.
conservation of energy, (fís.) conservación de la energía.
conservation of mass, (fís.) conservación de la masa.
conservatism [kən'sɜrvəˌtɪzəm, B -'sɜvə-] *s.* conservatismo, conservadurismo, tendencia conservadora.
conservative [-tɪv] *a.* 1. conservativo, moderado. 2. (pol.) conservador. —*s.* 1. agente conservativo o preservativo. 2. conservador, tradicionalista; (pol.) conservador.
conservative party, (pol.) partido conservador.
conservator [kən'sɜrvətər, 'kɑnsərˌveɪtər, B 'kɔnsəˌveɪtə] *s.* 1. conservador, defensor, protector. 2. conservador, curador (de un museo, etc.).
conservatory [kən'sɜrvəˌtɔrɪ, B -'sɜvətrɪ] *s.* 1. (mús.) conservatorio. 2. invernadero, invernáculo, jardín de invierno.
conserve ['kɑnˌsɜrv, B kən'sɜv] *s.* (*gen. pl.*) conserva, compota, dulce. — [kən'sɜrv, B -'sɜv] *v.t.* conservar, preservar.
consider [kən'sɪdər, B -ə] *v.t.* 1. considerar, pensar en. 2. considerar, tener o tomar en cuenta. 3. mirar, examinar. 4. considerar, juzgar, estimar. 5. **all things considered,** considerándolo bien; **c. oneself,** considerarse. —*v.i.* considerar, reflexionar, pensar, deliberar.
considerable [-ərəbəl] *a.* 1. considerable, notable. 2. considerable, cuantioso.
considerably [-əblɪ] *adv.* considerablemente.
considerate [kən'sɪdərət] *a.* considerado, atento, cortés.
considerately [-lɪ] *adv.* consideradamente.
considerateness [-nəs] *s.* consideración, miramiento.
consideration [kənˌsɪdə'reɪʃən] *s.* 1. consideración, deliberación, reflexión. 2. consideración, miramiento, tacto. 3. aspecto, motivo, consideración. 4. gratificación, recompensa. 5. **for a c.,** por una gratificación; **in c. of,** en consideración a, en reconocimiento de; **on no c.,** bajo ningún concepto, de ninguna manera; **to take into c.,** tomar en consideración; **under c.,** en consideración, en estudio; **without due c.,** sin reflexión.
considered [-'sɪdərd, B -əd] *a.* considerado.
considering [-'sɪdərɪŋ] *prep.* considerando, teniendo en cuenta, en atención a, en vista de. —*adv.* en las circunstancias, considerándolo todo.
consign [kən'saɪn] *v.t.* 1. consignar, confiar, entregar. 2. consignar, dirigir, encomendar (paquete, envío, etc.). 3. consignar, depositar (dinero). 4. (com.) consignar, dar en consignación (mercadería).
consignatary [-'sɪgnəˌtɛrɪ, B -nətərɪ] *s.* consignatario, depositario.
consignation [ˌkɑnˌsaɪ'neɪʃən, -sɪg-, B ˌkɔnsaɪ-] *s.* consignación.
consignee [-ˌsaɪ'ni] *s.* (com.) consignatario, destinatario.
consignment [kən'saɪnmənt] *s.* (com.) 1. consignación; mercancía consignada. 2. lote, envío. 3. **on c.,** en consignación.
consignor [-'saɪnər, B -nə] *s.* (com.) consignador.
consist [kən'sɪst] *v.i.* 1. (con *in*) consistir, estribar (en). 2. (con *of*) consistir (de, en), constar, componerse, estar compuesto (de), estar constituido (por). 3. (con *with*) concordar, ser compatible, armonizar (con).
consistence [-əns] *var. de* **consistency,** consistencia.
consistency [-ənsɪ] *s.* 1. consistencia, solidez; coherencia. 2. persistencia, firmeza (de carácter).
consistent [-ənt] *a.* 1. consistente, denso, uniforme. 2. (con *with*) consistente, compatible (con). 3. consecuente (persona). 4. firme.
consistently [-lɪ] *adv.* firmemente, sin cejar.
consistorial [ˌkɑnˌsɪs'tɔrɪəl, B ˌkɔn-] *a.* consistorial.
consistory [kən'sɪstərɪ] *s.* (*pl.* CONSISTORIES) consistorio; junta, asamblea, congreso.
consociate [kən'soʊʃɪˌeɪt] *v.t., v.i.* asociar(se), unir(se). —*a.* asociado, unido. —*s.* consocio, socio, miembro, asociado.
consociation [-ˌsoʊʃɪ'eɪʃən] *s.* asociación, sociedad.
consolation [ˌkɑnsə'leɪʃən, B ˌkɔn-] *s.* consolación, consuelo, alivio, solaz.
consolation prize, premio (de) consuelo.
consolatory [kən'soʊləˌtɔrɪ, -'sɑl-, B -'sɔlətərɪ] *a.* consolador, consolatorio.

console [kən'soʊl] *v.t.* consolar, confortar.
console ['kɑnˌsoʊl, B 'kɔn-] *s.* 1. (arq.) cartela, ménsula. 2. caja del órgano. 3. consola, mesa de consola. 4. (elec.) tablero de mando, tablero de distribución.
consoler [kən'soʊlər, B -ə] *s.* consolador, confortador.
console table, consola.
consolidate [kən'sɑləˌdeɪt, B -'sɔl-] *v.t.* consolidar. *—v.i.* consolidarse, esp. fusionarse; endurecerse.
consolidated balance sheet, (ten.) balance general consolidado.
consolidation [-ˌsɑlə'deɪʃən, B -ˌsɔl-] *s.* consolidación, conjunción, unión.
consols [kən'sɑlz, B -'sɔlz] *s. pl.* (G.B.) *forma abrev. de* **consolidated annuities,** títulos de la deuda consolidada nacional.
consommé [ˌkɑnsə'meɪ, B kən'sɔmeɪ] *s.* consomé, caldo.
consonance ['kɑnsənəns, B 'kɔn-] **consonancy** [-nənsɪ] *s.* consonancia, armonía, conformidad.
consonant ['kɑnsənənt, B 'kɔn-] *a.* 1. consonante, armonioso, conforme. 2. (mús., gram.) consonante. *—s.* (gram.) consonante.
consonantal [ˌkɑnsə'næntəl, B ˌkɔn-] *a.* (gram.) consonántico, de consonante(s).
consonantly ['kɑnsənəntlɪ, B 'kɔn-] *adv.* en consonancia, consonantemente.
consort ['kɑnˌsɔrt, B 'kɔnˌsɔt] *s.* 1. consorte, asociado. 2. (mar.) buque de reserva, escolta. 3. consorte, cónyuge. — [kən'sɔrt, B -'sɔt] *v.t.* asociar, juntar. *—v.i.* **c. with,** asociarse (con); concordar, armonizar (con).
consort ['kɑnˌsɔrt, B 'kɔnˌsɔt] *s.* asociación; **in c. with,** conjuntamente con.
consortium [kən'sɔrʃɪəm, B -'sɔtjəm] *s.* (*pl.* CONSORTIA [-ʃɪə, B -tɪə]) consorcio.
conspecific [ˌkɑnspɪ'sɪfɪk, B ˌkɔn-] *a.* (biol.) de la misma especie.
conspectus [kən'spɛktəs] *s.* sinópsis; vista general (de un objeto, escena, etc.), cuadro sinóptico, sumario.
conspicuous [kən'spɪkjʊəs] *a.* conspicuo, sobresaliente, llamativo.
conspicuously [-lɪ] *adv.* patentemente, visiblemente, manifiestamente; notoriamente.
conspicuousness [-nəs] *s.* carácter conspicuo, evidencia, claridad.
conspiracy [kən'spɪrəsɪ] *s.* (*pl.* CONSPIRACIES) conspiración, complot, conjura, conjuración, cábala.
conspirator [-ətər, B -ə] *s.* conspirador.
conspiratorial [kənˌspɪrə'tɔrɪəl] *a.* de conspirador, misterioso.
conspiratress [-'spɪrətrəs] *s.* conspiradora.
conspire [kən'spaɪr, B -'spaɪə] *v.i.* conspirar, conjurar(se), complotar. *—v.t.* maquinar, tramar, urdir.
constable ['kɑnstəbəl, B 'kʌn-] *s.* 1. (G.B.) policía (*m.*), guardia (*m.*). 2. alguacil. 3. (hist.) condestable.
constabulary [kən'stæbjəˌlɛrɪ, B -jʊlərɪ] *s.* policía, guardia civil (de un distrito, condado, país). *—a.* policial.
constancy ['kɑnstənsɪ, B 'kɔn-] *s.* 1. constancia, perseverancia. 2. fidelidad, lealtad. 3. continuidad, invariabilidad.
constant [-stənt] *a.* 1. constante, continuo, invariable. 2. constante, fiel, firme, leal. *—s.* (fís., mat.) constante (*f.*).
constant boiling, (quím.) de temperatura de ebullición constante.
Constantinople [ˌkɑnstæntə'noʊpəl, B ˌkɔn-] *s.* Constantinopla, antiguo nombre de Estambul.
constantly ['kɑnstəntlɪ, B 'kɔn-] *adv.* constantemente, continuamente, de continuo, incesantemente.
constellate ['kɑnstəˌleɪt, B 'kɔn-] *v.t., v.i.* (astr.) formar(se) una constelación.
constellation [ˌkɑnstə'leɪʃən, B ˌkɔn-] *s.* 1. (astr., astrol.) constelación. 2. (fig.) pléyade (de personas destacadas y brillantes).
consternate ['kɑnstərˌneɪt, B 'kɔnstəˌ-] *v.t.* consternar; **to be consternated,** consternarse.
consternation [ˌkɑnstər'neɪʃən, B ˌkɔnstə'-] *s.* consternación.
constipate ['kɑnstəˌpeɪt, B 'kɔn-] *v.t.* (med.) estreñir.
constipated [-əd] *s.* (med.) estreñido.
constipation [ˌkɑnstə'peɪʃən, B ˌkɔn-] *s.* (med.) estreñimiento, constipación de vientre.
constituency [kən'stɪtʃʊənsɪ, B -'stɪtjʊ-] *s.* (pol.) distrito electoral; grupo de votantes.
constituent [-ənt] *a.* 1. constituidor, constituyente, componente (elemento, etc.). 2. (pol.) constituyente. *—s.* 1. constitutivo, componente, elemento. 2. (pol.) votante, elector. 3. (der.) poderdante, mandante.
constituent assembly, (pol.) asamblea constituyente.
constitute ['kɑnstəˌtut, B 'kɔn-ˌtjut] *v.t.* 1. constituir. 2. designar, nombrar. 3. dar forma legal a, redactar debidamente.
constitution [ˌkɑnstə'tuʃən, B ˌkɔnstɪ'tju-] *s.* 1. constitución, establecimiento. 2. constitución, físico (de una persona). 3. (pol., der.) constitución (de un estado).
constitutional [-əl] *a.* constitucional; (pol., der.) constitucional. *—s.* caminata, paseo (para conservar el buen estado físico).
constitutional diagram, (quím.) diagrama de fases.
constitutionalism [-əlˌɪzəm] *s.* constitucionalismo.
constitutionalist [-ələst] *s.* perito en constituciones; adherente a los principios constitucionales, constitucionalista.
constitutionality [-ˌtuʃə'nælətɪ, B -ˌtju-] *s.* constitucionalidad.
constitutionally [-'tuʃənəlɪ, B -'tju-] *adv.* 1. mentalmente, temperamentalmente, ej., *he is c. unable to understand it,* él es mentalmente incapaz de comprenderlo. 2. físicamente, ej., *c. he is a weakling,* físicamente él es un canijo. 3. en estructura, fundamentalmente. 4. (pol., der.) constitucionalmente.
constitutional monarchy, monarquía constitucional.
constitutive ['kɑnstəˌtutɪv, B 'kɔnstɪˌtjut-] *a.* 1. constitutivo, esencial. 2. constituyente, constructivo, componente.
constrain [kən'streɪn] *v.t.* 1. constreñir, compeler, obligar. 2. restringir; detener; encerrar. 3. apretar, incomodar.
constrained [-'streɪnd] *a.* forzado, artificial, ej., *c. smile,* risa forzada o artificial.
constrainedly [-nədlɪ] *adv.* forzadamente.
constraint [kən'streɪnt] *s.* 1. constreñimiento, coacción, apremio, compulsión. 2. represión. 3. embarazo, encogimiento. 4. **under c.,** bajo compulsión.
constrict [-'strɪkt] *v.t.* apretar, estrechar, encoger.
constriction [-'strɪkʃən] *s.* constricción, encogimiento, contracción.
constrictive [-'strɪktɪv] *a.* constrictivo.
constrictor [-tər, B -tə] *s.* 1. (anat.) constrictor, músculo constrictor. 2. (zool.) serpiente constrictora, boa común o constrictora.
constringe [kən'strɪndʒ] *v.t.* constreñir, comprimir.
constringent [-'strɪndʒənt] *a.* constringente.
construct [kən'strʌkt] *v.t.* construir, edificar, fabricar; (geom., gram.) construir.
construction [-'strʌkʃən] *s.* 1. construcción, edificación, estructura. 2. obra construida; estructura. 3. interpretación, esp. en *to put a (good, bad) c. upon,* dar una interpretación (favorable, desfavorable) a, tomar en (buena, mala) parte. 4. (gram.) construcción. 5. **under c.,** en construcción.
constructional [-əl] *a.* de construcción, estructural.
construction crane, grúa-torre.
constructionist [-əst] *s.* interpretador; persona que interpreta, esp. la ley, de una manera específica.
construction plant, maquinaria de construcción, equipo de trabajo.
construction work, construcción, trabajo de edificación.
constructive [kən'strʌktɪv] *a.* 1. constructivo, ej., *c. criticism,* crítica constructiva. 2. (der.) inferido, implícito.
constructiveness [-nəs] *a.* carácter constructivo, aptitud mecánica, ingeniosidad.
constructivism [-tɪˌvɪzəm] *s.* (arte) constructivismo.
constructor [kən'strʌktər, B -tə] *s.* constructor (esp. naval).
construe [kən'stru] *v.t.* 1. (gram.) construir. 2. (gram.) analizar (frase, oración, etc.); traducir textualmente. 3. interpretar, explicar. *—v.i.* prestarse al análisis, ej., *this sentence does not c.,* este pasaje no se presta al análisis. *—s.* texto que debe ser traducido textualmente.
consubstantial [ˌkɑnsəb'stænʃəl, B ˌkɔn-'stænʃəl] *a.* (relig.) consubstancial.
consubstantiate [-tʃɪˌeɪt, B -'stænʃɪ-] *v.t., v.i.* unir(se) en una sola sustancia o naturaleza.
consubstantiation [-ˌstæntʃɪ'eɪʃən, B -ˌstænʃɪ-] *s.* (relig.) consubstanciación.
consuetude ['kɑnswɪˌtud, B 'kɔnswɪˌtjud] *s.* costumbre, hábito (esp. la que ha adquirido fuerza legal).
consuetudinary ['kɑnswɪ'tudənˌɛrɪ, B ˌkɔnswɪ'tjudənərɪ] *a.* consuetudinario. *—s.* manual de costumbres (esp. de un monasterio o catedral).
consul ['kɑnsəl, B 'kɔn-] *s.* 1. (hist.) cónsul, magistrado supremo. 2. (dipl.) cónsul, representante comercial.
consular [-sələr, B -sjʊlə] *a.* consular.
consular invoice, factura consular.
consulate [-lət] *s.* 1. consulado, oficina de un cónsul. 2. (hist., fr.) Consulado, gobierno consular.
consul general, (*pl.* CONSULS GENERAL) cónsul general.
consulship ['kɑnsəlˌʃɪp, B 'kɔn-] *s.* consulado, puesto o dignidad de cónsul.
consult [kən'sʌlt] *v.t.* consultar; **c. one's pillow,** consultar con la almohada. *—v.i.* (con *with*) consultar, conferenciar con.
consultant [-'sʌltənt] *s.* consultor; consejero.
consultation [ˌkɑnsəl'teɪʃən, B ˌkɔn-] *s.* consulta, consultación, conferencia.
consultative [kən'sʌltətɪv] *a.* consultivo.
consulting [-'sʌltɪŋ] *a.* consultor, consultivo, consultante.
consulting office, consultorio.
consulting physician, médico consultor, médico de apelación.
consultor [kən'sʌltər, B -tə] *s.* (relig.) consultor, consejero espiritual.

consumable [kən'suməbəl, B -'sjum-] *a.* consumible, de consumo. —*s.* (*pl.*) artículos de consumo.
consume [-'sum, B -'sjum] *v.t.* consumir, devorar, gastar; **c. time,** tomar u ocupar tiempo; **to be consumed with,** (fig.) comerse de (envidia, ira), estar consumido o devorado por (pasión), estar carcomido por (envidia). —*v.i.* consumirse.
consumedly [-ədlɪ] *adv.* excesivamente, extremadamente.
consumer [kən'sumər, B -'sjumə] *s.* consumidor.
consumer credit, crédito otorgado al consumidor, crédito para comprar a plazos.
consumer goods, mercancía de consumo, artículos de consumo, efectos de consumo, bienes de consumo.
Consumer Price Index *s.* indice de precios al consumo, indice de precios al consumidor.
consumer tax, impuesto de consumo, impuesto al consumidor.
consummate [kən'sʌmət, 'kɑnsə-, B kən's-ʌmɪt] *a.* 1. consumado, completo, cabal, perfecto. 2. de remate, perfecto, ej., *c. ass,* tonto de remate. ['kɑnsəˌmeɪt, B ˌkɔn-] *v.t.* 1. consumar. 2. satisfacer (deseo). 3. (der.) consumar (el matrimonio).
consummation [ˌkɑnsə'meɪʃən, B ˌkɔn-] *s.* consumación; (der.) consumación de un contrato (esp. del matrimonio).
consummative ['kɑnsəˌmeɪtɪv, kən'sʌ-mət-, B 'kɔnsəˌmeɪt-] *a.* consumativo.
consumption [kən'sʌmʃən] *s.* 1. consunción, consumición, gasto, destrucción. 2. consumo (de comestibles, de agua, etc.). 3. (med.) consunción, tisis, tuberculosis.
consumption graph, diagrama o gráfico de consumo.
consumption tax, impuesto de consumo, impuesto al consumo.
consumptive [-'sʌmptɪv] *a.* 1. consuntivo, destructivo. 2. (med.) hético, tísico. —*s.* tísico.
contact ['kɑnˌtækt, B 'kɔn-] *s.* 1. contacto. 2. (*pl.*) contactos, relaciones. 3. (med.) contacto, portador contacto. 4. (geom.) contacto. 5. (elec.) contacto; tomacorriente. 6. **to be in c. with,** estar en contacto con; **to break c.,** (elec.) interrumpir el contacto. [-ˌtækt, B kən'tækt] *v.t.* 1. hacer contacto con. 2. (E.U.) ponerse en contacto o al habla con (personas o entidades comerciales o sociales). —*v.i.* tocarse.
contact breaker, (elec.) interruptor automático.
contact carrier, (med.) portacontactos.
contact catalysis, (quím.) catálisis heterogénea.
contact fire, (min.) explosión por contacto.
contact flying, (aer.) vuelo con visibilidad.
contact lens, lente de contacto.
contact light, (nav.) luz de referencia.
contact man, representante (de empresa, etc.).
contact mine, (mil.) mina de contacto.
contactor ['kɑnˌtæktər, B 'kɔn-tə] *s.* (elec.) contactor, interruptor automático.
contact print, (foto.) copia por contacto.
contact rail, (f.c.) carril conductor, tercer riel.
contact shoe, (elec.) zapata.
contagion [kən'teɪdʒən] *s.* contagio, contaminación; infección.
contagious [-dʒəs] *a.* contagioso, infeccioso.
contagious abortion, (vet.) aborto contagioso, brucelosis del ganado.
contagiousness [-nəs] *s.* contagiosidad.
contagium [kən'teɪdʒɪəm] *s.* (*pl.* CONTAGIA [-dʒɪə]) virus, contaminación, infección.
contain [kən'teɪn] *v.t.* contener, abarcar, incluir; (mat.) contener, ser exactamente divisible; (mil.) contener, retener; **c. oneself,** refrenarse, contenerse.
container [-ər, B -ə] *s.* envase; recipiente, vasija; caja.
containerize [-ərˌaɪz] *v.t.* embalar (carga general) en grandes recipientes de tamaño estándar, para facilitar el trasbordo.
containerization [-ˌteɪnərə'zeɪʃən, B -əraɪ-] *s.* embalaje de carga general en grandes recipientes.
containment [-'teɪnmənt] *s.* 1. contención. 2. (pol.) contención, refrenamiento, represión (de un poder o ideología hostil).
contaminant [kən'tæmənənt] *s.* contaminador (materia, sustancia), contaminante.
contaminate [-ˌneɪt] *v.t.* contaminar; contagiar; depravar, pervertir, corromper.
contamination [-ˌtæmə'neɪʃən] *s.* contaminación; contagio; depravación, perversión; (filol.) contaminación.
contaminator [-'tæməˌneɪtər, B -ə] *s.* contaminador (persona).
contd. *abrev. de* **continued,** sigue.
conte [koʊnt] *s.* (fr.) cuento, narración breve.
contemn [kən'tɛm] *v.t.* desdeñar, despreciar, menospreciar.
contemplate ['kɑntəmˌpleɪt, B 'kɔntɛm-] *v.t.* 1. contemplar, reflexionar. 2. proponerse, tener la intención de. —*v.i.* meditar, sumirse en contemplación.
contemplation [ˌkɑntəm'pleɪʃən, B ˌkɔn-tɛm-] *s.* 1. contemplación, meditación. 2. proyecto, intención.
contemplative [kən'tɛmplətɪv, 'kɑntəmˌpleɪ-, B 'kɔntɛm-] *a.* contemplativo.
contemplator ['kɑntəmˌpleɪtər, B 'kɔn-tɛm-ə] *s.* contemplador.
contemporaneity [kənˌtɛmpərə'niətɪ] *s.* contemporaneidad.
contemporaneous [-'reɪnɪəs] *a.* contemporáneo.
contemporaneously [-lɪ] *adv.* contemporáneamente.
contemporaneousness [-nəs] *s.* contemporaneidad.
contemporary [kən'tɛmpəˌrɛrɪ, B -pərərɪ] *a.* 1. contemporáneo. 2. coetáneo. —*s.* 1. contemporáneo. 2. coetáneo.
contemporize [-ˌraɪz] *v.t., v.i.* contemporizar, volver(se) contemporáneo.
contempt [kən'tɛmpt] *s.* 1. desdén, desprecio. 2. (der.) desacato. 3. **to hold in c.,** despreciar.
contempt of congress, (der.) desacato, rebeldía contra el poder legislativo.
contempt of court, (der.) desacato al tribunal, contumacia, rebeldía.
contemptibility [-ˌtɛmptə'bɪlətɪ] **contemptibleness** [-'tɛmptəbəlnəs] *s.* ruindad, vileza, bajeza.
contemptible [-'tɛmptəbəl] *a.* despreciable, desdeñable.
contemptuous [kən'tɛmptʃʊəs, B -tjʊ-] *a.* desdeñoso, despreciativo, despectivo.
contemptuously [-lɪ] *adv.* desdeñosamente.
contemptuousness [-nəs] *s.* desdén, desprecio.
contend [kən'tɛnd] *v.i.* 1. (con *with*) luchar, contender. 2. rivalizar, pugnar, competir (pasiones, emociones, etc.). 3. (con *with*) contender, disputar, argüir (con alguien). —*v.t.* 1. mantener, sostener (argumento, creencia, etc.). 2. disputar.
contender [-ər, B -ə] *s.* contendiente, contendor, competidor.
contending [-ɪŋ] *a.* litigante, contendiente.
contending parties, (der.) partes litigantes, partes contendientes.
content ['kɑnˌtɛnt, B 'kɔn-] *s.* 1. (*pl.*) contenido (de un recipiente, libro, documento, etc.); índice, tabla de materias. 2. contenido, capacidad (de un recipiente, envase, etc.), volumen (de un sólido); extensión, tamaño. 3. (fig.) contenido, sustancia (de una obra de arte).
content [kən'tɛnt] *a.* contento, satisfecho, complacido. —*v.t.* contentar, complacer, satisfacer. —*s.* 1. contento, satisfacción. 2. (G.B.) voto en pro (en la Cámara de los Lores); **contents,** votos afirmativos; votantes en pro; **not c.,** voto en contra. 3. **to one's heart's c.,** a gusto, a sus anchas.
contented [-əd] *a.* contento, satisfecho.
contentedly [-lɪ] *adv.* contentamente, con satisfacción, tranquilamente.
contention [kən'tɛntʃən, B -'tɛnʃən] *s.* 1. contención, contienda, disputa. 2. argumento, punto de vista.
contentious [-tʃəs, B -'tɛnʃəs] *a.* 1. contencioso, altercador, pendenciero, disputador. 2. disputable. 3. (der.) contencioso.
contentiously [-lɪ] *adv.* contenciosamente.
contentiousness [-nəs] *s.* pugnacidad, espíritu de contradicción, carácter pendenciero.
contentment [kən'tɛntmənt] *s.* contento, contentamiento, satisfacción.
conterminous [-'tɜrmənəs, B kən'tɜmɪ-] *a.* 1. contérmino, colindante. 2. coextensivo (en espacio, tiempo o significado).
contest ['kɑnˌtɛst, B 'kɔn-] *s.* 1. certamen, competencia, concurso; contienda, lid, torneo. 2. debate, discusión, disputa. — [kən'tɛst] *v.t.* disputar, debatir (afirmación, tesis, etc.), disputar (la victoria, escaño en parlamento, etc.). —*v.i.* **c. against,** combatir, luchar contra; **c. for,** contender, luchar por; **c. with,** contender con, trabarse en lucha con.
contestable [kən'tɛstəbəl] *a.* contestable, discutible, disputable.
contestant [-tənt] *s.* 1. contendiente, competidor, contrincante. 2. disputador, disputante.
contestation [ˌkɑntɛs'teɪʃən, B ˌkɔn-] *s.* 1. (der.) contestación. 2. controversia, competencia.
context ['kɑnˌtɛkst, B 'kɔn-] *s.* contexto.
contextual [kən'tɛkstʃʊəl] *a.* del contexto.
contexture [-tʃər, B -tʃə] *s.* contextura.
contiguity [ˌkɑntə'gjuətɪ, B ˌkɔn-] *s.* contigüidad, proximidad, inmediación, vecindad.
contiguous [kən'tɪgjʊəs] *a.* contiguo, adyacente, colindante, próximo, vecino.
contiguously [-lɪ] *adv.* contiguamente.
contiguousness [-nəs] *s.* carácter contiguo, contigüidad.
continence ['kɑntənəns, B 'kɔnt-] *s.* continencia, castidad, moderación, templanza.
continent ['kɑntənənt, B 'kɔn-] *a.* continente, casto; moderado. —*s.* (geog.) continente; **the C.,** la Europa continental.
continental [ˌkɑntən'ɛntəl, B ˌkɔnt-] *a.* 1. continental. 2. (E.U.) continental (díc. de las colonias confederadas durante la revolución). —*s.* 1. europeo, habitante de Europa. 2 (hist.) soldado en el ejército de las colonias confederadas. 3. (hist., E.U.) moneda emitida por la Confederación. 4. **not worth a c.,** no vale un comino.
continental divide, divisoria continental.
continental drift, (geol.) deriva de los continentes (debido a variaciones geológicas en la capa suboceánica).
continental shelf, (geog.) plataforma continental.
contingency [kən'tɪndʒənsɪ] *s.* 1. contingencia, eventualidad. 2. evento contingente, evento fortuito, suceso posible.
contingency fund, (com.) fondo de contingencia, fondo de previsión.
contingent [-dʒənt] *a.* contingente, eventual, casual, fortuito, accidental; (esp., der.) condicional; **c. on** (o **upon**), dependiente de. —*s.* 1.

contingencia, contingente. 2. (mil.) contingente (de tropas).
contingent legacy, (der.) legado condicional.
contingent liability, (ten.) pasivo eventual o contingente.
contingently [-lɪ] *adv.* contingentemente, casualmente, accidentalmente.
continual [kən'tɪnjʊəl] *a.* continuo, incesante, constante.
continually [-ɪ] *adv.* continuamente, incesantemente, constantemente.
continuance [-'tɪnjʊəns] *s.* 1. continuación, prolongación. 2. (con *in*) permanencia (en un lugar o condición). 3. (der.) aplazamiento (de un juicio).
continuant [-jʊənt] *s.* (mat.) continuante.
continuation [kən,tɪnjʊ'eɪʃən] *s.* continuación, prolongación, extensión.
continuative [-'tɪnjʊ,eɪtɪv, B -jʊətɪv] *a.* continuativo.
continuator [-,eɪtər, B -ə] *s.* continuador.
continue [kən'tɪnju] *v.i.* 1. continuar, proseguir. 2. mantenerse, permanecer, quedar; (con *in*) quedarse (en un lugar, condición o estado). 3. durar, prolongarse. 4. seguir camino, ej., *we continued along the river,* seguíamos camino a lo largo del río. 5. **c. to (do),** seguir, continuar (haciendo). —*v.t.* 1. continuar (algo), seguir (haciendo). 2. retener (en un empleo, puesto, etc.). 3. (der.) aplazar (juicio).
continued [-'tɪnjud] *a.* 1. continuo, prolongado. 2. continuado. 3. **to be c.,** continuará.
continued fraction, (mat.) fracción continua.
continued quantity, (mat.) cantidad continua.
continuing [kən'tɪnjʊɪŋ] *a.* continuo, continuado, constante, duradero, durable.
continuity [,kɑntə'nuətɪ, B ,kɔntɪ'nju-] *s.* 1. continuidad. 2. (cine., rad., t.v.) guión, libreto. 3. (rad., t.v.) intervalo musical o de comentarios (entre programas). 4. trama o diálogo (de historietas cómicas).
continuo [kən'tɪnjʊ,oʊ] *s.* (*pl.* CONTINUOS) (mús.) bajo continuo.
continuous [-jʊəs] *s.* continuo, ininterrumpido.
continuous current, (elec.) corriente continua o directa.
continuously [-lɪ] *adv.* continuamente.
continuous spectrum, (fís.) espectro continuo.
continuous wave, (fís.) onda continua (esp. de los rayos laser).
continuum [kən'tɪnjʊəm] *s.* (*pl.* CONTINUA [-jʊə]) 1. continuo. 2. (mat.) continuo. 3. (quím.) medio continuo.
contort [kən'tɔrt, B -'tɔt] *v.t.* 1. torcer, retorcer. 2. contraer (el rostro, las facciones). —*v.i.* (fig.) desfigurarse, demudarse (el rostro).
contortion [-'tɔrʃən, B -'tɔʃən] *s.* contorsión, torsión (de una parte del cuerpo); demudación (esp. de la cara).
contortionist [-əst] *s.* contorsionista.
contour ['kɑn,tʊr, B 'kɔn,tʊə] *s.* contorno, perfil; (cart.) curva de nivel. —*v.t.* contornear, perfilar.
contour feather, (orn.) pluma de contorno, penna, pena.
contour interval, (top.) distancia vertical entre los planos de nivel.
contour line, (top.) curva de nivel, línea de nivel (en un mapa o una carta).
contour map, (top.) plano topográfico, mapa acotado.
contour plowing, (agr.) surcado en contorno.
contra ['kɑntrə, B 'kɔn-] *prep.* **contra; pro and c.,** a favor y en contra.
contraband [-,bænd] *s.* 1. contrabando. 2. (hist., E.U.) esclavo negro fugitivo (durante la guerra civil). —*a.* de contrabando, ilegal, prohibido.
contrabandist [-,bændəst] *s.* contrabandista.
contraband of war, contrabando de guerra (material bélico que embarga uno de los beligerantes).
contrabass ['kɑntrə,beɪs, B 'kɔn-] *s.* (mús.) contrabajo (instrumento).
contrabassist [-,beɪsəst] *s.* (mús.) contrabajo (músico).
contrabassoon [,kɑntrəbə'sun, B ,kɔn-] *s.* (mús.) contrabajón.
contraception [-'sɛpʃən] *s.* contracepción, anticoncepción.
contraceptive [-'sɛptɪv] *a.* de contracepción. —*s.* contraceptivo, preservativo, anticonceptivo.
contract ['kɑn,trækt, B 'kɔn-] *s.* 1. contrato, pacto, convenio, trato. 2. (gram.) contracción. 3. (bridge) contrato. — ['kɑn-, kən'trækt, B kən'trækt] *v.t.* 1. contratar, pactar. 2. contraer (deudas, etc.). 3. contraer, encoger. 4. reducir; concentrar. 5. fruncir. 6. (gram.) contraer. —*v.i.* 1. (con *with*) hacer un contrato (con); (con *for*) contratar, hacer un contrato (por o para). 2. contraerse (músculo, nervio, etc.); encogerse; (fig.) reducirse, encogerse.
contract bridge, bridge contrato.
contractibility [kən,træktə'bɪlətɪ] *s.* contractibilidad.
contractible [-'træktəbəl] *a.* contractable, contráctil.
contractile [-təl, B -taɪl] *a.* contráctil (músculo, metal, etc.).
contractility [,kɑn,træk'tɪlətɪ, B ,kɔn-] *s.* contractilidad, contractibilidad.
contracting ['kɑn,træktɪŋ, B kən'træktɪŋ] *a.* contrayente; contratante; contractivo.
contracting parties, (der.) partes contratantes.
contraction [kən'trækʃən] *s.* 1. contración. 2. (gram.) contracción. 3. (econ.) reducción de actividad comercial.
contractive [-'træktɪv] *a.* contractivo.
contractor ['kɑn,træktər, kən'træk-, B kən'træktə] *s.* 1. contratante, contratista, concesionario. 2. cosa que se contrae (esp. un músculo).
contractual [kən'træktʃʊəl] *a.* contractual.
contracture [-tʃər, B -tʃə] *s.* (med.) contractura.
contradict [,kɑntrə'dɪkt, B ,kɔn-] *v.t.* contradecir; refutar, desmentir; oponerse; **c. oneself,** contradecirse.
contradictable [-'dɪktəbəl] *a.* controvertible.
contradiction [-'dɪkʃən] *s.* contradicción.
contradictious [-ʃəs] *a.* 1. contradictorio, opuesto. 2. contradictor, pendenciero.
contradictor [-'dɪktər, B -tə] *s.* contradictor.
contradictorily [-'dɪktərəlɪ] *adv.* contradictoriamente.
contradictoriness [-ɪnəs] *s.* carácter contradictorio, espíritu de contradicción.
contradictory [-'dɪktərɪ] *a.* contradictorio, contrario. —*s.* (lóg.) contradictoria.
contradistinction [,kɑntrədɪs'tɪŋkʃən, B ,kɔn-] *s.* distinción por contraste (de cualidades opuestas).
contradistinguish [-'tɪŋgwɪʃ] *v.t.* distinguir por el contraste de calidades.
contrail ['kɑn,treɪl, B 'kɔn-] *s.* (aer.) estela de vapor o condensación.
contraindicant [,kɑntrə'ɪndəkənt, B ,kɔn-] *s.* (med.) contraindicante, contraindicación.
contraindicate [-,keɪt] *v.t.* (med.) contraindicar.
contraindication [-,ɪndə'keɪʃən] *s.* (med.) contraindicación.
contralto [kən'træl,toʊ] *s.* (mús.) contralto, la voz femenina de registro más bajo. —*a.* de contralto.
contraposition [,kɑntrəpə'zɪʃən, B ,kɔn-] *s.* contraposición, contraste, oposición; (lóg.) contraposición, antítesis.
contraption [kən'træpʃən] *s.* (fam.) artificio, dispositivo, artefacto.
contrapuntal [,kɑntrə'pʌntəl, B ,kɔn-] *a.* (mús.) de contrapunto; polifónico.
contrapuntist [-əst] *s.* (mús.) contrapuntista.
contrariety [,kɑntrə'raɪətɪ, B ,kɔn-] *s.* 1. contrariedad; oposición. 2. desacuerdo.
contrarily ['kɑn,trɛrəlɪ, kən'trɛr-, B 'kɔntrərɪlɪ, kən'trɛər-] *adv.* contrariamente, opuestamente.
contrariness [-ɪnəs] *s.* 1. contrariedad, oposición. 2. desobediencia, rebeldía (esp. de un niño).
contrariwise [-,waɪz] *adv.* 1. al contrario. 2. al revés, a la inversa, viceversa. 3. obstinadamente, tercamente.
contrary ['kɑn,trɛrɪ, B 'kɔntrərɪ] *a.* 1. contrario, opuesto. 2. adverso, desfavorable (viento, clima, etc.). 3. [kən'trɛrɪ, B -'trɛərɪ] díscolo, recalcitrante, desobediente, rebelde. —*s.* 1. contrario, contradicción. 2. (lóg.) contraria. 3. **on the c.,** al contrario, por el contrario; **to the c.,** en contra, en contrario; no obstante. —*adv.* en contrario; **c. to,** en contra de, en oposición a.
contrast ['kɑn,træst, B 'kɔn,trɑst] *s.* contraste. — [kən'træst, B -'trɑst] *v.i.* contrastar, estar en contraste, mostrar diferencias. —*v.t.* poner en contraste, hacer contrastar.
contrasting [kən'træstɪŋ, B -'trɑst-] *a.* contrastante.
contrasty ['kɑn,træstɪ, kən'træstɪ, B kɔn'-trɑstɪ] *a.* (foto.) de marcados contrastes.
contravallation [,kɑntrəvə'leɪʃən, B ,kɔn-] *s.* (fort.) contravalación.
contravene [,kɑntrə'vin, B ,kɔn-] *v.t.* 1. contravenir, infringir, desobedecer (la ley). 2. disputar, oponerse a (una afirmación).
contravener [-'vinər, B -ə] *s.* contraventor.
contravention [-'vɛntʃən, B -'vɛnʃən] *s.* contravención, infracción, oposición, desobediencia.
contredanse ['kɑntrə,dæns, B 'kɔntrɔ,-dɑns] *s.* contradanza.
contretemps ['kɑntrə,tɑn, B 'kɔntrə'tɑŋ] *s.* (fr.) contratiempo.
contribute [kən'trɪbjət, -jut, B -jut] *v.t.* contribuir, aportar. —*v.i.* (con *to*) contribuir (a), cooperar, colaborar (con), ayudar (a).
contribution [,kɑntrə'bjuʃən, B ,kɔn-] *s.* 1. contribución, aportación; donación, donativo. 2. cuota, dádiva. 3. contribución literaria a una publicación.
contributive [kən'trɪbjətɪv] *a.* contributivo, contribuyente.
contributor [-tər, B -tə] *s.* contribuyente, contribuidor, colaborador.
contributory [-,tɔrɪ, B -tərɪ] *a.* contribuyente, cooperante, contribuidor. —*s.* 1. contribuidor. 2. factor contribuyente.
contrite ['kɑn,traɪt, kən'traɪt, B 'kɔn,t-raɪt] *a.* contrito, pesaroso, arrepentido.
contritely [-lɪ] *adv.* contritamente, con pesar.
contrition [kən'trɪʃən] *s.* contrición, arrepentimiento.
contrivable [kən'traɪvəbəl] *a.* 1. imaginable. 2. realizable, factible.
contrivance [-vəns] *s.* 1. invención; artificio, maquinación. 2. invento, artefacto, dispositivo, artilugio.
contrive [kən'traɪv] *v.t.* 1. inventar, idear, ingeniar. 2. (con *to*) procurar, ingeniarse (a); lograr (a). —*v.i.* formar planes; maquinar.

contrived [-'traɪvd] *a.* artificial, fabricado.
contriver [-'traɪvər, B -ə] *s.* autor, inventor, tramador.
control [kən'troʊl] *v.t.* (*pret., p.p.* CONTROLLED; *p.pr.* CONTROLLING) 1. controlar, dominar, gobernar, manejar. 2. controlar, comprobar, inspeccionar, verificar. 3. **c. oneself,** dominarse, controlarse. —*s.* 1. control, dominio, gobierno, manejo. 2. control, comprobación, inspección, verificación. 3. (*pl.*) (mec., aut., aer.) mandos, controles. 4. (aer.) puesto de control. 5. (aut.) puesto o tramo de control (en carreras). 6. (fís.) testigo, patrón de comparación (para verificar los resultados de una experimentación). 7. **to bring under c.,** reducir (*a un insubordinado*); **to get under c.,** conseguir dominar; **to be in c. of,** dominar, estar al mando de.
control board, (tec.) tablero de mando o de control.
control box, (tec.) caja de mando.
control desk, (elec.) pupitre de distribución.
control devise, (ing.) instrumento de regulación.
control experiment, (fís.) control de factores.
control gear, (aut.) mecanismo de accionamiento de la caja de cambio.
control gondola, (avia.) cabina de mando.
control knob, botón de mando, perilla de control; (ing.) botón de reglaje.
controllable [kən'troʊləbəl] *a.* 1. dominable, gobernable, manejable. 2. comprobable.
controllable pitch, (ing.) de paso controlable.
controllable trim, (ing.) de compensación controlable.
controlled spin [-'troʊld-] (acrob.) barrena mandada.
controlled variable, (ing.) variable controlada.
controller [-'troʊlər, B -ə] *s.* 1. contralor, veedor, interventor. 2. contralor, jefe de contaduría (de una empresa, institución, etc.). 3. director, superintendente, inspector. 4. (elec.) combinador. 5. (mec.) regulador, controlador. 6. senescal, mayordomo (de la casa real).
controllership [-ˌʃɪp] *s.* contraloría, veeduría; oficina del contralor.
control lever, palanca de mando.
controlling [kən'troʊlɪŋ] *a.* mandante, gobernante; predominante; determinante, decisivo.
controlling interest, interés dominante, interés predominante o superior.
control panel, (tec.) tablero de control o de gobierno.
control post, puesto de control, puesto de mando.
control room, sala o cámara de control o de mando, cabina de control.
control station, puesto de mando o de control.
control stick, (avia.) palanca de mando.
control surface, (avia.) superficie de mando.
control switch, (elec.) interruptor de mando.
control tower, (aer.) torre de control o de mando.
control valve, 1. (hidr.) válvula de maniobra. 2. (rad.) válvula de control.
controversial [ˌkantrə'vərʃəl, B ˌkɔntrə'vɜʃəl] *a.* 1. discutible, polémico, disputable, problemático (tema, asunto, personalidad, etc.). 2. contencioso, disputador, discutidor, problemático (persona).
controversialist [-əst] *s.* polemista, disputador, controversista.
controversy ['kantrəˌvərsɪ, B 'kɔntrəˌvɜsɪ] *s.* controversia, debate, polémica, disputa; **without o beyond c.,** incuestionable, sin lugar a dudas.
controvert [-ˌvərt, ˌkantrə'vərt, B 'kɔntrəˌvɜt] *v.t.* controvertir, rebatir, debatir, disputar, contradecir.
controvertible [-əbəl] *a.* controvertible, rebatible, discutible.
controvertist [-əst] *s.* controversista, argumentador, polemista.
contumacious [ˌkantə'meɪʃəs, B ˌkɔntjʊ-] *a.* contumaz, insubordinado, desobediente.
contumaciously [-lɪ] *adv.* contumazmente.
contumacy [kən'tuməsɪ, 'kantə-, B 'kɔntjʊməsɪ] *s.* contumacia, terquedad; (der.) contumacia.
contumelious [ˌkantə'milɪəs, B ˌkɔntjʊ-] *a.* contumelioso, ofensivo, injurioso, afrentoso, oprobioso, insolente.
contumely [kən'tuməlɪ, 'kantəˌmilɪ, B 'kɔntjʊmlɪ] *s.* contumelia, injuria, ofensa, afrenta, oprobio.
contuse [kən'tuz, B -'tjuz] *v.t.* contundir, magullar, contusionar.
contusion [-'tuʒən, B -'tju-] *s.* contusión, magullamiento.
conundrum [kə'nʌndrəm] *s.* acertijo, adivinanza; cuestión intrincada, asunto difícil.
conurbation [ˌkanər'beɪʃən, B ˌkɔnə'-] *s.* conjunto de distritos urbanos (de una ciudad) densamente poblado.
convalesce [ˌkanvə'lɛs, B ˌkɔn-] *v.i.* convalecer.
convalescence [-əns] *s.* convalecencia.
convalescent [-ənt] *a., s.* convaleciente.
convalescent home, casa para convalecientes; clínica de reposo.
convection [kən'vɛkʃən] *s.* 1. conducción, transmisión. 2. (fís.) convección.
convector [-'vɛktər, B -tə] *s.* (elec.) convector; transmisor.
convene [kən'vin] *v.t.* 1. convocar, citar. 2. (der.) emplazar. —*v.i.* juntarse, congregarse, reunirse, convenir.
convenience [kən'vinjəns] *s.* 1. conveniencia, comodidad; provecho, utilidad. 2. dispositivo, mecanismo útil. 3. (*pl.*) comodidades (materiales). 4. **at your c.,** según le convenga, cuando guste; **at your earliest c.,** a su más pronta conveniencia, tan pronto como le sea posible; **it's a great c.,** es de gran comodidad; **to suit one's c.,** convenirle algo a uno; hacer uno lo que le guste.
conveniency [-jənsɪ] *s.* (*pl.* CONVENIENCIES) (ant.) *var. de* **convenience.**
convenient [-jənt] *a.* conveniente, oportuno, útil; cómodo.
conveniently [-lɪ] *adv.* convenientemente.
convent ['kanvənt, -ˌvɛnt, B 'kɔn-] *s.* convento.
convent church, iglesia conventual.
conventicle [kən'vɛntɪkəl] *s.* (hist.) conventículo; conciliábulo (religioso).
convention [kən'vɛntʃən, B -'vɛnʃən] *s.* 1. convención, asamblea, congreso, junta. 2. convenio, pacto, acuerdo, contrato. 3. convención, costumbre, uso, regla convencional. 4. (bridge) convención.
conventional [-əl] *a.* 1. convencional, estipulado, convenido. 2. convencional, acostumbrado, corriente.
conventionalism [-ˌɪzəm] *s.* convencionalismo, formalismo.
conventionalist [-əst] *s.* formalista.
conventionality [kənˌvɛntʃə'nælətɪ, B -ˌvɛnʃə-] *s.* convencionalismo, formalidad, formalismo, regla impuesta por la costumbre.
conventionalize [-'vɛntʃənəlˌaɪz, B -vɛnʃən-] *v.t.* 1. hacer convencional. 2. (arte) tratar (un tema, estilo, etc.) en forma convencional.
conventionally [-əlɪ] *adv.* convencionalmente, formalmente.
conventioneer [kənˌvɛntʃə'nɪr, B -ˌvɛnʃə'nɪə] *s.* delegado a o miembro de una convención.
conventual [-'vɛntʃʊəl, B -tjʊəl] *a.* conventual. —*s.* miembro de un convento.
converge [kən'vərdʒ, B -'vɜdʒ] *v.i.* convergir, converger. —*v.t.* hacer convergir.
convergence [-'vərdʒəns, B -'vɜdʒəns] **convergency** [-dʒənsɪ] *s.* convergencia.
convergent [-dʒənt] *a.* convergente.
conversable [kən'vərsəbəl, B -'vɜs-] *a.* conversable, tratable, sociable, afable, comunicable.
conversableness [-nəs] *s.* sociabilidad.
conversably [-səblɪ] *adv.* afablemente, amablemente; socialmente.
conversance [-'vərsəns, B -'vɜs-] **conversancy** [-ənsɪ] *s.* (con *with*) familiaridad (con), conocimiento (de).
conversant [-ənt] *a.* (con *with*) versado (en), experimentado, familiarizado (con), conocedor (de), al corriente (de).
conversation [ˌkanvər'seɪʃən, B ˌkɔnvə'-] *s.* 1. conversación, plática. 2. (der.) trato carnal, ej., *criminal c.,* adulterio. 3. **to make c.,** dar conversación, charlar.
conversational [-əl] *a.* 1. conversador. 2. propio de la conversación (estilo, etc.); por conversación (método, etc.).
conversationalist [-ələst] *s.* conversador.
conversationally [-əlɪ] *adv.* a modo de conversación.
conversation piece, 1. (pint.) estilo de pintura popular en el siglo XVIII. 2. objeto curioso o interesante que sirve de tema de conversación.
converse [kən'vərs, B -'vɜs] *v.i.* conversar, platicar, hablar. —*s.* conversación, plática.
converse [kən'vərs, 'kanˌvərs, B 'kɔnˌvɜs] *a.* inverso, opuesto, contrario. — ['kanˌvərs, B 'kɔnˌvɜs] *s.* 1. (lóg.) conversa, recíproca. 2. (mat.) recíproca.
conversely [-lɪ] *adv.* a la inversa, vice-versa.
conversion [kən'vərʒən, -ʃən, B -'vɜʃən] *s.* 1. conversión, transformación, mudanza. 2. (lóg., mat.) conversión. 3. (relig.) conversión. 4. (der.) apropiación ilícita. 5. (com.) conversión, canje (de valores, acciones, etc.). 6. (baloncesto, fútbol) conversión (de un tiro libre en un tanto).
convert [-'vərt, B -'vɜt] *v.t.* 1. convertir, transformar, cambiar (en cuanto a opinión, fe, etc.). 2. (lóg.) convertir (una proposición). 3. (com.) convertir, cambiar (valores, acciones, etc.). 4. (metal.) convertir, cementar. 5. (baloncesto, fútbol) convertir (tiros en tantos). —*v.i.* 1. convertirse. 2. (fútbol, baloncesto) lograr un tanto.
convert ['kanˌvərt, B 'kɔnˌvɜt] *s.* converso, neófito.
converter [kən'vərtər, B -'vɜtə] *s.* 1. (metal.) convertidor. 2. (elec., rad., t.v.) (**t. convertor**) convertidor. 3. persona o cosa que convierte.
convertibility [-ˌvərtə'bɪlətɪ, B -ˌvɜtə-] *s.* convertibilidad.
convertible [-'vərtəbəl, B -'vɜt-] *a.* 1. convertible, transmutable; transformable. 2. (com.) convertible (díc. de la moneda que se puede cambiar por otra o por oro). 3. (aut.) convertible. —*s.* (aut.) automóvil convertible.
convertiplane, convertaplane [-əˌpleɪn] *s.* (aer.) avión convertible (que despega y aterriza verticalmente, como un helicóptero).
convex [kan'vɛks, 'kanˌvɛks, B 'kɔn'vɛks] *a.* convexo.
convexity [kən'vɛksətɪ, kan-, B kɔn-] *s.* 1. convexidad. 2. (*pl.* CONVEXITIES) superficie convexa.

convexly [-lɪ] *adv.* convexamente.
convexo-concave [-ˌvɛksoʊˌkɑn'keɪv, B -'kɔn-] *a.* cóncavo-convexo.
convexo-convex [-kɑn'vɛks, B -'kɔn-] *a.* biconvexo.
convey [kən'veɪ] *v.t.* 1. transportar, llevar, acarrear. 2. conducir, llevar (sonido, corriente, agua, etc.). 3. transmitir, llevar (infección, enfermedad, etc.). 4. transmitir, impartir, comunicar (idea, sentido, recado, etc.), dar a entender. 5. (der.) transferir, traspasar (propiedad); ceder (un título). 6. (ant.) robar.
conveyable [-əbəl] *a.* conductible; transmisible; comunicable; (der.) transferible, traspasable.
conveyance [-əns] *s.* 1. conducción, transporte, acarreo. 2. transmisión, comunicación (de ideas, recados, etc.). 3. cesión, traspaso; escritura de traspaso, título traslativo de dominio. 4. vehículo, carruaje.
conveyancer [-ənsər, B -sə] *s.* (der.) escribano que hace escrituras de traspaso.
conveyancing [-ənsɪŋ] *s.* (der.) preparación de escrituras de traspaso, de dominio.
conveyer, conveyor [kən'veɪər, B -ə] *s.* 1. (der.) cedente. 2. (mec.) correa transportadora; transportador. 3. conductor; portador.
conveyor belt, (mec.) correa transportadora.
conveyor chain, (mec.) cadena sin fin.
convict ['kɑnˌvɪkt, B 'kɔn-] *s.* convicto, presidiario, penado. — [kən'vɪkt] *v.t.* 1. condenar, declarar culpable, declarar convicto. 2. hacer admitir, hacer darse cuenta de (culpa, error, etc.).
conviction [kən'vɪkʃən] *s.* 1. condena (por un delito, etc.). 2. convencimiento, creencia firme, persuasión. 3. convicción, convencimiento. 4. fallo condenatorio. 5. **to carry c.,** sonar convincente (voz); parecer convincente (argumento, razón, etc.).
convince [kən'vɪns] *v.t.* convencer, persuadir, reducir.
convincible [-əbəl] *a.* convencible.
convincing [-ɪŋ] *a.* convincente, convencedor, persuasivo.
convincingly [-lɪ] *adv.* convincentemente.
convivial [kən'vɪvɪəl] *a.* jovial, festivo, sociable, convival.
conviviality [-ˌvɪvɪ'ælətɪ] *s.* jovialidad, buen humor.
convivially [-'vɪvɪəlɪ] *adv.* jovialmente.
convocation [ˌkɑnvə'keɪʃən, B ˌkɔn-] *s.* 1. convocación, llamamiento. 2. asamblea. 3. convocación religiosa o académica.
convoke [kən'voʊk] *v.t.* convocar, citar, llamar.
convolute ['kɑnvəˌlut, B 'kɔn-] *s.* enroscadura. —*a.* 1. enrollado; (bot., zool.) convoluto. 2. (ing.) espiral. —*v.t., v.i.* enrollar, arrollar; convolverse.
convoluted [-əd] *a.* 1. arrollado, enrollado (en forma curva o tortuosa, esp. que tiene convoluciones). 2. complicado, intrincado, confuso.
convolution [ˌkɑnvə'luʃən, B ˌkɔn-] *s.* 1. (anat.) circunvolución (del cerebro, estómago, etc.). 2. enroscadura, repliegue, enrollamiento.
convolve [kən'vɑlv, B -'vɔlv] *v.t., v.i.* arrollar(se), enrollar(se), retorcer(se), enroscar(se).
convolvulus [kən'vɑlvjələs, B -'vɔl-] *s.* (*pl.* CONVOLVULUSES o CONVOLVULI [-ˌlaɪ]) (bot.) convólvulo.
convoy ['kɑnˌvɔɪ, kən'vɔɪ, B 'kɔnˌvɔɪ] *v.t.* 1. convoyar, escoltar (barcos mercantes o de pasajeros, etc.). 2. (ant.) conducir (huéspedes, damas, etc.). — ['kɑnˌvɔɪ, B 'kɔn-] *s.* 1. convoy, escolta. 2. convoy, flota, tren.
convulse [kən'vʌls] *v.t.* 1. convulsionar. 2. crispar. 3. **to be convulsed with laughter,** desternillarse de risa; **to be convulsed with pain, rage, etc.,** crisparse de dolor, rabia, etc. —*v.i.* agitarse violentamente.
convulsion [-'vʌlʃən] *s.* 1. (med.) convulsión, espasmo. 2. (*pl.*) ataque, paroxismo (de risa). 3. (fig.) convulsión, conmoción, agitación (esp. social o política). 4. (geol.) cataclismo.
convulsionary [-ʃənˌɛrɪ, B -ʃənərɪ] *a.* convulsionario.
convulsive [-sɪv] *a.* convulsivo, espasmódico, convulso.
convulsively [-lɪ] *adv.* convulsivamente.
cony ['koʊnɪ] *s.* 1. (zool.) conejo. 2. conejuna. 3. especie de damán. 4. piel de conejo.
coo [ku] *v.t., v.i.* arrullar (palomas, enamorados); **to bill and coo,** acariciarse, arrullarse (los enamorados). —*s.* arrullo; caricia.
cook [kʊk] *s.* cocinero, cocinera; **too many cooks spoil the broth,** demasiados cocineros arruinan el puchero. —*v.t.* 1. cocer, cocinar, guisar. 2. tramar, maquinar, urdir. 3. alterar, falsear, falsificar cuentas, etc.). 4. **c. up,** preparar; (fam.) inventar, tramar. —*v.i.* 1. atender la cocina, cocinar, ser cocinero o cocinera. 2. cocer. 3. pasar, ocurrir, ej., *what's cooking?* ¿qué pasa?
cookbook ['kʊkˌbʊk] *s.* libro de recetas de cocina.
cooker [-ər, B -ə] *s.* 1. estufa, hornillo, cocina. 2. hervidor; olla para cocinar, puchero.
cookery ['kʊkərɪ] *s.* cocina, arte práctico o trabajo culinario.
cookhouse [-ˌhaʊs] *s.* lugar destinado a la cocina; recinto para cocinar; cabina, cocina de un barco.
cookie ['kʊkɪ] *s.* 1. (E.U.) galletita, bizcochito, pastelito dulce. 2. (jer.) mujer atractiva.
cooking ['kʊkɪŋ] *s.* 1. cocción. 2. arte de cocinar; cocina, sazón. 3. **her c. is very good,** ella cocina muy bien. —*a.* para cocinar, de cocina (utensilios, elementos, etc.); **c. oil,** aceite de cocina.
cookout [-ˌaʊt] *s.* comida campestre; picnic; comida cocinada al aire libre.
cookroom [-ˌrum, -ˌrʊm] *s.* (mar.) cuarto-cocina de un buque.
cooky, *var. de* **cookie.**
cool [kul] *a.* 1. fresco, moderadamente frío. 2. sereno, tranquilo. 3. indiferente, tibio. 4. fresco, insolente, audaz, ej., *a c. hand,* persona audaz. 5. (fig.) fresco (color, vestido, etc.). 6. débil. 7. (jer.) superior, excelente. 8. **a c. thousand dollars,** nada menos que mil dólares; **(as) c. as a cucumber,** (tan) fresco como una lechuga; **play it c.,** (fam.) mantenerse ecuánime, tomarlo con calma. —*s.* 1. frescura. 2. (fam.) calma, cachaza; aplomo. —*v.t., v.i.* 1. refrescar(se), enfriar(se), entibiar(se), orear(se). 2. apaciguar(se), atemperar(se), moderar(se). 3. **c. one's heels,** (fam.) hacer antesala, estar esperando mucho tiempo; **c. off,** refrescar; (fam.) serenarse, tranquilizarse; **cool it!** ¡cálmate! ¡tranquilízate!
coolant ['kulənt] *s.* enfriador, líquido enfriador; elemento refrigerante.
cooler [-ər, B -ə] *s.* 1. enfriador; (E.U.) refrigeradora. 2. refresco, bebida refrescante. 3. (fam.) chirona, calabozo, cana (Am.).
cool-headed [-'hɛdəd] *a.* sereno, tranquilo, juicioso, sensato.
coolie ['kulɪ] *s.* culí, peón (en China e India).
cooling ['kulɪŋ] *a.* refrescante, refrigerante. —*s.* enfriamiento, refrigeración.
cooling coil, serpentín refrigerante.
cooling system, sistema de refrigeración.
coolish ['kulɪʃ] *a.* (fam.) un tanto fresco, fresquillo.
coolly [-lɪ] *adv.* 1. fríamente; serenamente, tranquilamente; indiferentemente. 2. con frescura, con descaro; con aplomo.
coolness [-nəs] *s.* 1. frescura. 2. tranquilidad, serenidad. 3. indiferencia. 4. sangre fría, aplomo.
coon [kun] *s.* 1. (zool., E.U.) mapache, oso lavador (*var. de* **racoon**). 2. **c. skin,** piel de mapache. 3. (hist. E.U.) (miembro del partido) republicano (en la época de la Revolución). 4. (jer.) patán, bruto, estúpido. 5. (jer., despec.) negro.
cooncan ['kunˌkæn] *s.* conquián (juego de naipes).
coon cat, 1. (dial.) gato de angora. 2. (zool.) cacomistle; coatí.
coonhound [-ˌhaʊnd] *s.* sabueso de cazar mapaches.
coon's age, mucho tiempo.
coonskin [-ˌskɪn] *s.* piel de mapache. —*a.* de piel de mapache.
coop [kup] *s.* 1. jaula de gallina; corral, gallinero, caponera. 2. casilla, cabina. 3. (G.B.) canasta colocada sobre ave clueca. 4. (fam.) chirona, reja, caponera, cana. 5. **to fly the c.,** (fam.) evadirse, fugarse. —*v.t.* (gen. con *up*) enjaular; encerrar, emparedar.
co-op ['koʊˌɑp, B -ˌɔp] *s.* (fam.) cooperativa.
co-op apartment, (departamento en) propiedad horizontal o condominio.
cooper ['kupər, 'kʊp-, B 'kupə] *s.* barrilero, tonelero. —*v.t.* fabricar o reparar (barriles).
cooperage [-ərɪdʒ] *s.* barrilería, tonelería.
cooperate [koʊ'ɑpəˌreɪt, B -'ɔp-] *v.i.* cooperar, colaborar; **c. in (doing),** cooperar a (hacer); **c. to,** cooperar para.
cooperation [-ˌɑpə'reɪʃən, B -ˌɔp-] *s.* cooperación; (econ. pol.) acción cooperativa.
cooperative [-'ɑpərətɪv, -əˌreɪt-, B -'ɔpərət-] *a.* cooperativo, coadyuvante. —*s.* cooperativa (empresa o compañía).
cooperator [-ˌreɪtər, B -ə] *s.* cooperador, colaborador.
cooper's hatchet, hachuela de tonelero.
co-opt [-'ɑpt, B -'ɔpt] *v.t.* elegir por votación (de los miembros de un comité, sociedad, etc.); nombrar sumariamente; apropiar.
co-optation [ˌkoʊˌɑp'teɪʃən, B -ɔp-] *s.* elección (por votación colectiva); nombramiento sumario; apropiación.
coordinate [koʊ'ɔrdənət, -ˌneɪt, B -'ɔdənɪt] *a.* coordinado; (gram.) coordinada (oración). —*s.* semejante, igual; (mat.) coordenada, coordinada. — [-'ɔrdəˌneɪt, B -'ɔd-] *v.t.* coordinar, armonizar. —*v.i.* coordinarse.
coordinate geometry, geometría de las coordenadas, geometría analítica.
coordinately [-lɪ] *adv.* coordinadamente.
coordinate paper, papel cuadriculado.
coordinates [-nəts, -ˌneɪts, B -nɪts] *s., pl.* (cart.) coordenadas.
coordination [-ˌɔrdə'neɪʃən, B -ˌɔd-] *s.* coordinación, orden.
coordinative [-'ɔrdənətɪv, -ˌneɪt-, B -'ɔd-] *a.* coordinativo.
coordinator [koʊ'ɔrdəˌneɪtər, B -'ɔdɪˌneɪtə] *s.* coordinador.
coot [kut] *s.* 1. (orn.) negreta, fulica, foja. 2. (fam.) bobalicón, simple.
cootie ['kutɪ] *s.* (fam.) piojo.
cop [kɑp, B kɔp] *s.* 1. (hilandería) husada, canilla. 2. (E.U., fam.) agente de policía. 3. (dial.) cumbre, cima; penacho. —*v.t.* (*pret., p.p.* COPPED ; *p.pr.* COPPING) 1. (jer.) prender, capturar. 2. (jer.) hurtar, robar. 3. **c. it,** (jer.) merecerse castigo, merecerse un regaño; meterse en un lío; encontrar la muerte; **cop a plea,** declararse culpable, entregarse, rendirse.
copaene [koʊ'peɪˌin] *s.* (quím.) copaína.

copaiba [koʊ'paɪbə, -'peɪ-, B -'paɪ-] *s.* 1. (bot.) copaiba, copayero. 2. (farm.) bálsamo de copaiba.
copaifera [ˌkoʊpeɪ'ɪfərə] *s.* (bot.) copayero.
copal ['koʊpəl, koʊ'pæl] *s.* (farm.) copal (resina).
coparcenary [koʊ'pɑrsəˌnɛri, B -'pɑsɪnərɪ] *s.* 1. (der.) copropiedad, coparticipación. 2. (der.) herencia conjunta.
coparcener [-nər, B -nə] *s.* (der.) coheredero.
copartner [ˌkoʊ'pɑrtnər, B -'pɑtnə] *s.* consocio, copartícipe.
copartnership [-ˌʃɪp] *s.* coparticipación; asociación.
cope [koʊp] *v.i.* darse abasto; **c. with,** manejárselas con, arreglárselas con, salir adelante con (un problema); dar o darse abasto para. —*v.t.* (const.) rebajar, recortar. —*s.* 1. recorte, rebajada; 2. (relig.) capa consistorial. 3. (arq.) albardilla, coronamiento; arco, bóveda, cúpula.
copeck, *var. de* **kopeck, kopek.**
Copenhagen [ˌkoʊpən'heɪgən] *s.* Copenhague, capital de Dinamarca.
copepod ['koʊpəˌpɑd, B -ˌpɔd] *s., a.* (zool.) copépodo.
Copernican [koʊ'pɜrnɪkən, B -'pɜnɪ-] *a.* copernicano, perteneciente o relativo a las teorías del astrónomo Copérnico.
copestone ['koʊpˌstoʊn] *s.* 1. piedra de remate, piedra de albardilla. 2. (fig.) remate, última mano; culminación.
copier ['kɑpɪər, B 'kɔpɪə] *s.* 1. copiador, copista; imitador, plagiario. 2. (com.) máquina copiadora.
copilot ['koʊˌpaɪlət] *s.* (aer., aut.) copiloto, piloto segundo.
coping ['koʊpɪŋ] *s.* (arq.) albardilla, broca.
coping stone, (arq.) piedra de albardilla, piedra de remate.
copious ['koʊpɪəs] *a.* 1. copioso, abundante, caudaloso, cuantioso. 2. rico, de extenso vocabulario (idioma), florido (estilo).
copiously [-lɪ] *adv.* copiosamente.
copiousness [-nəs] *s.* copiosidad, abundancia.
coplanar [koʊ'pleɪnər, B -nə] *a.* (geom.) coplanar, coplanario, en un mismo plano.
copolymer [-'pɑləmər, B -'pɔlɪmə] *s.* (quím.) copolímero.
copolymerize [ˌkoʊpə'lɪməˌraɪz, B -'pɔlɪ-] *v.t., v.i.* (quím.) copolimerizar (dos o más sustancias polímeras).
cop-out ['kɑpˌaʊt, B 'kɔp-] *s.* (fam.) entrega, rendición, retractación.
cop out, *v.i.* (fam.) rehusar comprometerse; retractarse; retirarse.
copper ['kɑpər, B 'kɔpə] *s.* 1. (fam., E.U.) agente de policía. 2. cobre. 3. vellón, calderilla. 4. caldera, calderón (de cobre o hierro para cocina o lavandería). —*v.t.* 1. cubrir o revestir de cobre. 2. (E.U.) apostar contra. —*a.* cobreño, de cobre, cobrizo.
copperas [-ərəs] *s.* (quím.) caparrosa verde, vitriolo verde, aceche, acije.
copper-bearing [-ˌbɛrɪŋ, B -əˌbɛər-] *a.* cuprífero, cobrizo.
copper bit, cautil, cautín (de soldador).
copper-bottomed [-ˌbɑtəmd, B -ˌbɔt-] *a.* de fondo de cobre (nave, caldera).
copper-colored [-ˌkʌlərd, B -əd] *a.* cobrizo.
copper glance, (min.) calcosina, sulfuro de cobre.
copperhead [-ˌhɛd] *s.* 1. (zool.) especie de víbora norteamericana. 2. **C.,** (E.U., hist.) habitante de los estados del norte que simpatizaba con los confederados del sur.
copper loss, (elec.) pérdida en el cobre.
copper nickel, (min.) niquelina.
copper ore, mineral cuprífero, mineral de cobre.
copperplate ['kɑpərˌpleɪt, B 'kɔpəˌ-] *s.* lámina de cobre (para grabar); grabado en cobre. —*a.* nítido (díc. de la caligrafía).
copper pyrites, pirita de cobre, calcopirita, sulfato de cobre.
coppersmith [-ˌsmɪθ] *s.* calderero; el que elabora objetos o instrumentos de cobre.
copper sulfate, sulfato de cobre, cobre quemado, vitriolo azul.
copper work, cobrería.
coppice ['kɑpəs, B 'kɔpɪs] *s.* soto, matorral, maleza, monte bajo, bosque pequeño.
copra ['koʊprə, 'kɑp-, B 'kɔp-] *s.* copra, almendra del coco seco.
coprolite ['kɑprəˌlaɪt, B 'kɔp-] *s.* (pal.) coprolito, excremento fósil.
coprology [kɑ'prɑlədʒɪ, B kɔ'prɔl-] *s.* estudio de la pornografía en arte y literatura.
coprophagous [kɑ'prɑfəgəs, B kə'prɔf-] *a.* coprófago.
coprophagy [-ədʒɪ] *s.* coprofagia.
coprophilia [ˌkɑprə'fɪlɪə, B ˌkɔp-] *s.* coprofilia, atracción anormal hacia las materias fecales.
cops and robbers, ladrones y celadores; **to play c. and r.,** jugar a ladrones y celadores.
copse [kɑps, B kɔps] *var. de* **coppice.**
Copt [kɑpt, B kɔpt] *s.* (relig.) copto.
copter ['kɑptər, B 'kɔptə] *s. forma abrev. de* **helicopter,** helicóptero.
Coptic [-tɪk] *a.* (relig.) cóptico, copto. —*s.* copto (idioma).
Coptic church, Iglesia copta.
copula ['kɑpjələ, B 'kɔp-] *s.* 1. cópula, lazo, ligamento. 2. (lóg., gram.) cópula. 3. (der.) cópula, unión.
copulate [-ˌleɪt] *v.i.* 1. copularse; unirse. 2. tener relaciones sexuales.
copulation [ˌkɑpjə'leɪʃən, B ˌkɔp-] *s.* 1. cópula, copulación, coito. 2. acoplamiento, unión. 3. (gram.) enlace (de palabras).
copulative ['kɑpjəˌleɪtɪv, B 'kɔpjʊlətɪv] *a.* copulativo; (gram.) copulativo. —*s.* (gram.) palabra copulativa.
copulative conjunction, (gram.) conjunción copulativa.
copy ['kɑpɪ, B 'kɔpɪ] *s.* 1. copia, imitación, remedo. 2. ejemplar (de un libro, periódico, revista, etc.), ej., *have you got a c. of "Time"?* ¿tiene un ejemplar de (la revista) "Time"? 3. modelo (para una reproducción). 4. (impr.) original, material; originales, manuscritos, textos. 5. texto de propaganda, texto de un anuncio (periodístico). 6. **fair o clean c.,** copia en limpio; **it will make good c.,** se puede escribir un artículo interesante sobre esto; **rough c.,** borrador; **to make a fair c. of,** pasar en limpio. —*v.t.* (*pret., p.p.* COPIED; *p.pr.* COPYING) 1. copiar. 2. imitar, copiar, remedar. —*v.i.* 1. hacer copias. 2. copiar (en un examen). 3. prestarse a ser copiado.
copybook [-ˌbʊk] *s.* 1. cuaderno de escritura, cuaderno de ejercicios. 2. (com.) libro copiador. 3. libro de modelos de caligrafía. 4. **to blot one's c.,** (fig.) manchar su hoja de servicios. —*a.* (despec.) convencional, trivial.
copyboy [-ˌbɔɪ] *s.* mensajero, mandadero (en una editorial o un periódico).
copycat [-ˌkæt] *s.* (fam.) imitador, remedador. —*v.t.* imitar, remedar.
copydesk [-ˌdɛsk] *s.* mesa de redacción.
copy-edit [-ˌɛdət] *v.t.* revisar, corregir un manuscrito original.
copy editor, 1. revisor de manuscritos. 2. jefe (del departamento) de redacción (de un periódico).
copygraph [-ˌgræf, B -ˌgrɑf] *s.* hectógrafo.
copyhold [-ˌhoʊld] *s.* (der.) posesión por enfiteusis; tierras poseídas por enfiteusis.
copyholder [-ər, B -ə] *s.* 1. (der.) enfiteuta. 2. (impr.) lector de pruebas. 3. (impr.) atril, sujetacuartillas (para sostener el original).
copying ink[-ɪŋ-] tinta comunicativa, tinta de copiar.
copying machine, copiador, multicopista, polígrafo.
copyist ['kɑpɪəst, B 'kɔp-] *s.* 1. copista, copiante. 2. imitador, plagiario.
copyreader [-ˌridər, B -ə] *s.* corrector (de manuscritos); redactor de mesa.
copyright [-ˌraɪt] *s.* derechos de autor, propiedad literaria o artística, propiedad intelectual, derecho de reproducción. —*v.t.* registrar como propiedad literaria o artística (una obra, etc.). —*a.* protegido por los derechos de autor (texto, libro, invento, etc.).
copywriter [-ər, B -ə] *s.* redactor de textos publicitarios o anuncios.
coq au vin [kɔkoʊ'væn] (fr., cocina) pollo al vino.
coq feathers, (cost.) plumas de gallo para adornar tocados.
coquet [koʊ'kɛt, B kɔ-] *a.* coquetón; coqueta. —*v.i.* (*pret., p.p.* COQUETTED ; *p.pr.* COQUETTING) coquetear; jugar (con idea, etc.).
coquetry ['koʊkətrɪ, koʊ'kɛtrɪ, B 'kɔkə-] *s.* coqueteo, coquetería.
coquette [koʊ'kɛt, B kɔ-] *s.* coqueta, casquivana.
coquettish [-'kɛtɪʃ] *a.* coquetón, coquetona.
coquettishly [-lɪ] *adv.* coquetonamente, con coquetería.
coquettishness [-nəs] *s.* carácter coquetón, coquetería.
coquina [koʊ'kinə] *s.* (zool.) coquina.
coquito palm [koʊ'kitoʊ-] (bot.) coquito.
Cor. *abrev. de* **Corinthians,** Epístola de San Pablo a los Corintios (Cor.).
coraciiform [ˌkɔrə'saɪəˌfɔrm, kə'ræsɪə-, B ˌkɔrəˌsaɪfˌɔm] *a.* (orn.) coracido.
coracle ['kɔrəkəl, 'kɑr-, B 'kɔr-] *s.* (G.B.) pequeño bote de mimbre y cuero o encerado.
coracoid ['kɔrəˌkɔɪd, 'kɑr-, B 'kɔr-] *a.* (anat.) coracoideo. —*s.* hueso coracoides.
coral ['kɔrəl, 'kɑr-, B 'kɔr-] *s.* coral; rojo coral. —*a.* coralino, de coral, como coral.
coralliferous [ˌkɔrə'lɪfərəs] *a.* coralífero.
coralline ['kɔrəˌlaɪn, 'kɑr-, B 'kɔr-] *a.* coralino, coral; de color rojo coral. —*s.* 1. (bot.) coralina, musgo marino. 2. (quím., t. **corallin**) coralina.
corallite [-ˌlaɪt] *s.* 1. coral fósil; esqueleto de coral (de pólipos). 2. mármol coralino.
coralloid [-ˌlɔɪd] **coralloidal** [ˌkɔrəlɔɪdəl] *a.* coraliforme; coralino.
coral pink, rosado coral (color).
coral reef, arrecife o banco de coral.
Coral Sea, Mar del Coral, en el S. del Océano Pacífico.
coral snake, (zool.) coral, víbora de coral; coralillo.
corban ['kɔrˌbæn, B 'kɔˌ-] *s.* (relig.) corbán, ofrenda.
corbeil ['kɔrbəl, B 'kɔbəl] *s.* (arq.) canasta modelada (de flores, frutas, etc.).
corbel [-bəl] *s.* (arq.) voladizo, ménsula, cartela, can, canecillo, modillón. —*v.t.* (*pret., p.p.* CORBELED O CORBELLED ; *p.pr.* CORBELING O CORBELLING) proveer de voladizos; moldear en ménsulas.
corbeling, corbelling [-ɪŋ] *s.* (arq.) vuelo, acartelamiento.

corbie ['kɔrbɪ, B 'kɔbɪ] *s.* (esco.) cuervo; cuervo negro europeo.
corbie gable, (arq.) gablete escalonado.
corbie step, (arq.) saliente escalonado.
corbina [kɔr'binə, B kɔ'-] *s.* (ict.) corvina.
cord [kɔrd, B kɔd] *s.* 1. cordel, cuerda, cordón. 2. (anat.) cuerda (vocal). 3. (anat.) cordón, cordoncillo (umbilical). 4. (fig.) lazo. 5. (tej.) pana inglesa; (*pl.*) pantalones de pana. 6. cuerda (medida de leña, gen. 128 pies cúbicos, o sea 3,625 metros cúbicos). 7. (elec.) cordón o cable (flexible). —*v.t.* 1. encordelar, encordonar, acordonar. 2. amontonar en cuerdas (leña).
cordage ['kɔrdɪdʒ, B 'kɔdɪdʒ] *s.* 1. (mar.) cordaje, cordelería, jarcias. 2. cantidad de cuerdas (de leña).
cordate ['kɔrˌdeɪt, B 'kɔˌ-] *a.* acorazonado, en forma de corazón, cordiforme.
cordeau [kɔr'doʊ, B kɔ'-] *s.* mecha de tubería de plomo llena de pólvora detonante.
corded ['kɔrdəd, B 'kɔdɪd] *a.* 1. encordelado, encordonado, acordonado. 2. (tej.) con nervaduras o cordoncillos.
cordelier [ˌkɔrdə'lɪr, B ˌkɔdɪ'lɪə] *s.* cordelero (fraile franciscano).
cordial ['kɔrdʒəl, B 'kɔdjəl] *s.* 1. cordial (licor). 2. (G.B.) jugo concentrado de fruta; jarabe de fruta. —*a.* cordial, afectuoso, amistoso.
cordiality [ˌkɔrdʒɪ'æləti, -'dʒæl-, B ˌkɔdɪ'æl-] *a.* cordialidad, amabilidad.
cordially ['kɔrdʒəlɪ, B 'kɔdjəlɪ] *adv.* cordialmente, atentamente, sinceramente.
cordierite ['kɔrdɪəˌraɪt, B 'kɔd-] *s.* (min.) cordierita.
cordiform ['kɔrdəˌfɔrm, B 'kɔdɪˌfɔm] *a.* (bot.) cordiforme.
cordilleran [ˌkɔrdəl'jɛrən, -'dɪlərən, B ˌkɔdɪl'jɛərən] *a.* montañés, cordillerano (Am.).
cordite ['kɔrˌdaɪt, B 'kɔˌ-] *s.* (quím.) cordita (explosivo).
cordless ['kɔrdləs] *adj.* inalámbrico.
cordless telephone, teléfono inalámbrico, teléfono sin hilos.
cordoba ['kɔrdəbə, B 'kɔdəvə] *s.* córdoba (unidad monetaria de Nicaragua).
cordon [-ən] *s.* 1. cordón, cíngulo. 2. (arq.) cordón. 3. cordón (de soldados, policías, etc.). —*v.t.* 1. adornar con cordón. 2. (gen. con *off*) aislar con cordón policial; formar cordón alrededor de.
Cordovan [-əvən] *s., a.* 1. cordobés, de Córdoba, España. 2. cordobán, cuero fino, gen. color rojizo oscuro.
cord tire, (aut.) neumático acordonado, neumático de cuerdas.
corduroy ['kɔrdəˌrɔɪ, B 'kɔd-] *s.* (tej.) pana, terciopelo de cordoncillos; (*pl.*) pantalones de pana; **c. road,** camino de rollizos.
cordwainer [-ˌweɪnər, B -nə] *s.* 1. zapatero. 2. (ant.) cordobanero.
cordwood [-ˌwʊd] *s.* leña apilada o que se vende en cuerdas.
CORE *s.* **Congress of Racial Equality** congreso de igualdad racial.
core [kɔr, B kɔ] *s.* 1. (bot.) corazón (de frutas). 2. parte central, centro, núcleo. 3. (fig.) meollo, médula, esencia. 4. (med.) foco (de infección o de absceso). 5. (elec.) núcleo (magnético). 6. alma, ánima, eje (de cable). 7. (miner., petróleo) muestra de sondaje. 8. (fund.) macho o ánima (de molde). 9. **English to the c.,** inglés hasta la médula. —*v.t.* 1. quitar el corazón de (una manzana, piña, etc.). 2. (fund.) formar con macho.
core barrel, (fund.) linterna para machos, alma tubular de macho; portatestigo; sacanúcleo.
core bit, barrena tubular, sacanúcleo; barrena cortanúcleo.
core diameter, (mec.) diámetro mínimo.
core drill, barrena o taladro tubular, barrena sacanúcleos; perforadora de coronas, sonda de núcleos.
corelate, corelation, etc., (pr. G.B.) *var. de* **correlate, correlation,** etc.
coreligionary [ˌkoʊrɪ'lɪdʒəˌnɛrɪ, B -ənərɪ] *s. var. de* **coreligionist.**
coreligionist [-ənəst] *s.* correligionario.
coreopsis [ˌkɔrɪ'ɑpsəs, B -'ɔp-] *s.* (bot.) coreopsidina, coreopsis (*m.*).
corer ['kɔrər, B -ə] *s.* despepitador(a).
corespondent [ˌkoʊrɪ'spɑndənt, B -'spɔn-] *s.* (der.) cómplice del demandado (en un juicio de divorcio por adulterio).
corf [kɔrf, B kɔf] *s.* (*pl.* CORVES [kɔrvz, B kɔvz]) (G.B.) canasta grande (usada en minería.).
corgi ['kɔrgɪ, B 'kɔgɪ] *s.* (zool.) pequeño perro galés.
coriaceous [ˌkɔrɪ'eɪʃəs] *a.* coriáceo, correoso.
coriander ['kɔrɪˌændər, ˌkɔrɪ'æn-, B ˌkɔrɪ'ændə] *s.* (bot.) coriandro, cilantro, culantro.
corindon [kə'rɪndən] (miner.) corindón.
Corinthian [kə'rɪnθɪən] *a., s.* 1. (hist., arq.) corintio, corintia, coríntico. 2. sibarita, persona que ama el lujo y la molicie. 3. deportista.
Corinthian Order, (arq.) orden corintio, el más elaborado de la arquitectura clásica griega.
coriolis force [ˌkɔrɪ'oʊləs-] *s.* (fís.) fuerza de Coriolis.
corium ['kɔrɪəm] *s.* corión, dermis, piel.
cork [kɔrk, B kɔk] *s.* 1. corcho, corteza del alcornoque. 2. corcho, tapón (de botella). 3. flotador de corcho (en la pesca). —*v.t.* 1. encorchar. 2. taponar, tapar con corcho. 3. tiznar (con corcho quemado).
corkage ['kɔrkɪdʒ, B 'kɔk-] *s.* recargo de licores (que se cobra en restaurantes, hoteles, bares, etc. por servir licores comprados fuera del establecimiento).
corked [kɔrkt, B kɔkt] *a.* 1. taponado (con corcho), encorchado. 2. tiznado (con corcho quemado). 3. avinagrado (vino por encorchamiento defectuoso de la botella).
corker ['kɔrkər, B 'kɔkə] *s.* 1. encorchador (persona); encorchadora (máquina). 2. (fam.) argumento concluyente. 3. (fam.) persona excelente; cosa extraordinaria. 4. (fam.) mentira grande.
corking [-kɪŋ] *a.* (jer.) excelente, rico, extraordinario.
cork jacket, cinturón o chaleco salvavidas (de corcho).
cork oak, (bot.) alcornoque.
corkscrew ['kɔrkˌskru, B 'kɔk-] *s.* tirabuzón, sacacorchos. —*v.i., v.t.* serpentear (camino, pista, río, etc.); retorcer, arrollar (en espiral).
cork tree, (bot.) alcornoque.
corkwood [-ˌwʊd] *s.* (bot.) balso.
corky [-ɪ] *a.* 1. suberoso, como el corcho. 2. (fam.) frívolo, vivaz, caprichoso.
corm [kɔrm, B kɔm] *s.* (bot.) bulbo, tallo bulboso, cebolla.
cormel ['kɔrməl, B 'kɔməl] *s.* (bot.) bulbo pequeño o secundario (producido por uno más grande).
cormorant ['kɔrmərənt, B 'kɔmə-] *s.* 1. (orn.) cuervo marino, cormorán, corvejón, viguá. 2. glotón; persona avara.
corn [kɔrn, B kɔn] *s.* 1. grano, cereal. 2. (E.U.) maíz; (G.B.) trigo; (Irl., Esco.) avena. 3. (fam.) música o broma de mal gusto o trillada. 4. callo (en los pies, manos). —*v.t.* 1. curar, salar (carne). 2. granular. 3. alimentar con granos (caballo, etc.).
cornaceous [kɔr'neɪʃəs, B kɔ'-] *a.* (bot.) cornáceo.
cornball ['kɔrnˌbɔl, B 'kɔn-] *a.* (jer.) banal, cursi, anticuado.
Corn Belt, (E.U.) 1. zona maicera; zona central famosa por sus maizales. 2. (fig.) lo cursi y chabacano que se le atribuye a dicha región.
corn borer, (ento.) pintón, plaga del maíz.
corn bread, pan o torta de maíz.
corncake [-ˌkeɪk] *s.* (E.U.) panecillo de maíz, torta de maíz.
corn chandler, (G.B.) vendedor de granos al por menor.
corncob [-ˌkɑb, B -ˌkɔb] *s.* mazorca de maíz, tusa de maíz, elote.
corn cockle, (bot.) neguilla, neguillón, candileja, lucérnula.
corncrake [-ˌkreɪk] *s.* (orn.) rascón, rey de codornices, ave zancuda de los maizales.
corncrib [-ˌkrɪb] *s.* hórreo o granero para almacenar maíz.
cornea ['kɔrnɪə, B 'kɔnɪə] *s.* (anat.) córnea.
corned [kɔrnd, B kɔnd] *a.* acecinado, curado con sal o salmuera; **c. beef,** cecina.
cornel ['kɔrnəl, B 'kɔn-] *s.* (bot.) cornejo, corno.
cornelian [kɔr'niljən, B kɔ'-] *s.* (min.) cornalina, cornelina.
cornelian cherry, (bot.) cornejo macho.
corneous ['kɔrnɪəs, B 'kɔnɪ-] *a.* córneo, calloso.
corner ['kɔrnər, B 'kɔnə] *s.* 1. esquina (esp. de calles), rincón (de un cuarto, etc.), ángulo. 2. escondrijo, lugar retirado. 3. rincón, región (de la tierra, de un país, etc.). 4. (com.) acaparamiento, monopolio. 5. (dep.) tiro de esquina. 6. **around the c.,** a la vuelta (de la esquina); **in a c.,** (fig.) en un aprieto, en una situacion difícil; **on the c.,** esquinero; **out of the c. of one's eye,** con el rabillo del ojo; **to cut corners,** tomar atajos; hacer un trabajo más rápido y barato, pero más chapucero; reducir gastos; **to drive into a c.,** arrinconar; **to turn the c.,** doblar la esquina; (fig.) pasar el punto crítico (en una enfermedad, etc.). —*v.t.* 1. arrinconar, poner en un aprieto. 2. atrapar, lograr abordar (a alguien para que escuche a uno). 3. (com.) acaparar, monopolizar. —*v.i.* 1. rematar o formar esquina. 2. dar la vuelta, doblar; tomar la curva (ej., un automóvil). —*a.* 1. de esquina, ej., *c. room,* cuarto de esquina, *c. table,* mesa de esquina. 2. de la esquina, ej., *the c. newstand,* el puesto (o quiosco) de periódicos de la esquina.
corner brace, taladro angular, barbiquí para rincones.
corner chisel, formón de ángulo, escoplo angular.
cornered [-nərd, B -nəd] *a.* 1. (*ú. en palabras compuestas*) de (cierta calidad o cierto número de) esquinas, rincones, ángulos o picos, ej., *a three-c. hat,* un sombrero de tres picos. 2. (*ú. en palabras compuestas*) con (cierto número de) participantes, entre (cierto número de) rivales, ej. *a four-c. dispute,* una disputa con cuatro participantes, *a three-c. competition,* un concurso entre tres rivales. 3. (fig.) atrapado, acorralado, a raya.
corner grocery store, tienda de la esquina.
corners of the mouth, comisura de los labios.
cornerstone ['kɔrnərˌstoʊn, B 'kɔnəˌ-] *s.* 1. (arq.) piedra angular; primera piedra (de un edificio). 2. (fig.) piedra angular.

cornerwise [-ˌwaɪz] **cornerways** [-ˌweɪz] *adv.* diagonalmente.
cornet [kɔr'nɛt, B 'kɔnɪt] *s.* 1. (mús.) corneta. 2. cucurucho. 3. barquillo; cartucho; (G.B.) cono (de helado). 4. (mil.) corneta (músico). 5. (relig.) toca grande de color blanco (de las Hermanas de la Caridad). 6. (mil., G.B.) portaestandarte. 7. (mar.) banderín de señales.
cornetist, cornettist [kɔr'nɛtəst, B kɔ'-] *s.* corneta (músico).
corn exchange, bolsa o lonja de granos.
cornfed ['kɔrnˌfɛd, B 'kɔn-] *a.* 1. alimentado de maíz. 2. (jer.) saludable, fuerte y campechano.
cornfield [-ˌfild] *s.* (E.U.) maizal; (G.B.) trigal.
cornflakes [-ˌfleɪks] *s.* copos de maíz.
corn flour, (G.B.) almidón de maíz; harina de maíz.
cornflower [-ˌflaʊər, B -ə] *s.* (bot.) 1. aciano, aciano menor, liebrecilla. 2. neguilla, neguillón.
cornhusk [-ˌhʌsk] *s.* perfolla del maíz; totomoxtle (Mex.).
cornhusking [-ˌhʌskɪŋ] *s.* deshojadura (de la perfolla) del maíz; fiesta con esa ocasión.
cornice ['kɔrnɪs, B 'kɔnɪs] *s.* 1. (arq.) cornisa, cornija. 2. sobrepuerta.
corniche ['kɔrnɪʃ, B 'kɔnɪʃ] *s.* (fr.) carretera a lo largo del frente de un acantilado.
corniculate [kɔr'nɪkjələt, B kɔ'-] *a.* (bot.) corniculado.
Cornish ['kɔrnɪʃ, B 'kɔnɪʃ] *a.* de Cornualles, natural de Cornualles, Inglaterra. —*s.* idioma de Cornualles.
corn liquor, whiski de maíz, chicha.
cornmeal ['kɔrn'mil, B 'kɔn-] *s.* harina de maíz.
corn on the cob, mazorca tierna de maíz, choclo (Am.).
corn plaster, emplasto para los callos.
corn pone, (S. de E.U.) pan o borona de maiz hecho con agua.
corn popper, tostador de rositas de maíz.
corn poppy, (bot.) amapola.
corn rose, (bot.) 1. amapola. 2. neguilla.
corn salad, (bot.) colleja, hierba de los canónigos, valerianilla.
corn sheller, 1. desgranadora de maíz. 2. (jer.) fusil de repetición.
corn silk, barba del maíz, pelusa.
cornstalk ['kɔrnˌstɔk, B 'kɔn-] *s.* tallo del maíz.
cornstarch [-ˌstɑrtʃ, B -ˌstɑtʃ] *s.* almidón de maíz, maicena.
corn sugar, dextrosa de almidón de maíz.
corn syrup, jarabe de maíz.
cornu ['kɔrnu, B 'kɔnju] *s.* (*pl.* CORNUA [-ə]) (anat.) cornu, cuerno.
cornucopia [ˌkɔrnə'koʊpɪə, B ˌkɔnjʊ-] *s.* cornucopia, cuerno de la abundancia.
cornupete ['kɔrnjəˌpit, B 'kɔn-] *a.* (numis.) cornupeta.
cornute [kɔr'nut, B kɔ'njut] *s.* (lóg.) argumento cornuto.
cornuted [-əd] *a.* cornudo; corniforme.
cornuto [-oʊ] *s.* (ital.) cornudo, marido engañado.
corn whisky, whiski de maíz.
corny ['kɔrnɪ, B 'kɔnɪ] *a.* 1. cargado de granos. 2. (jer.) vulgar, trillado; banal, cursi, sentimental (música, drama, etc.).
corny *a.* calloso, corneo.
corolla [kə'rɑlə, B -'rɔlə] *s.* (bot.) corola.
corollaceous [ˌkɔrə'leɪʃəs, ˌkɑr-, B ˌkɔr-] *a.* (bot.) coroláceo.
corollary ['kɔrəˌlɛrɪ, 'kɑr-, B kə'rɔlərɪ] *s.* corolario; consecuencia natural, resultado.
corona [kə'roʊnə] *s.* 1. (anat.) corona (de un diente, etc.). 2. (arq.) corona, alero (de una cornisa). 3. (astr., meteor.) corona, halo (alrededor del sol o de la luna). 4. (bot.) corona (en el ápice de algunos pétalos). 5. (elec.) corona (descarga luminosa de un conductor). 6. candelabro o araña circular (que cuelga de la bóveda de una iglesia). 7. (tipo de) cigarro o tabaco habano.
Corona Australis [-ɔ'streɪləs] (astr.) corona austral.
Corona Borealis [-'bɔrɪ'æləs, B -'eɪlɪs] (astr.) corona boreal.
coronach ['kɔrənək] *s.* (Esco., Irl.) endecha; canto o lamentación fúnebre, gen. tocado a la gaita.
coronal ['kɔrənəl, 'kɑr-, B 'kɔr-] *s.* corona, cerco (esp. de oro o de piedras preciosas); guirnalda. —*a.* (anat.) coronal (hueso); (bot.) coronal, de la corona.
coronary ['kɔrəˌnɛrɪ, 'kɑr-, B 'kɔrənərɪ] *a.* coronario; (anat.) coronario.
coronary thrombosis, (med.) trombosis coronaria, oclusión coronaria.
coronate ['kɔrəˌneɪt, 'kɑr-, B 'kɔr-] **coronated** [-əd] *a.* (bot., zool.) coronado.
coronation [ˌkɔrə'neɪʃən, ˌkɑr-, B ˌkɔr-] *s.* coronación.
coroner ['kɔrənər, 'kɑr-, B 'kɔrənə] *s.* (der.) pesquisidor que investiga la causa de un fallecimiento.
coronet [ˌkɔrə'nɛt ˌkɑr-, 'kɔrəˌnɛt, B 'kɔrənɪt] *s.* 1. corona pequeña (esp. la que denota rango inferior al de soberano). 2. guirnalda, cintillo (esp. material precioso para adornar tocas de mujeres). 3. corona (del casco del caballo), diadema.
coronium [kə'roʊnɪəm] *s.* (astr.) coronio.
Corp. *abrev. de* 1. **Corporal,** cabo. 2. **Corporation,** corporación.
corpora ['kɔrpərə, B 'kɔpərə] *pl. de* **corpus.**
corporal [-pərəl] *a.* 1. corporal, físico, ej., *c. punishment,* castigo corporal. 2. corpóreo, material. —*s.* 1. (relig.) corporal. 2. (mil.) cabo, caporal.
corporality [ˌkɔrpə'rælətɪ, B ˌkɔpə-] *s.* 1. corporalidad, corporeidad. 2. existencia corporal, condición material.
corporally ['kɔrpərəlɪ, B 'kɔpərə-] *adv.* corporalmente.
corporal of the guard, cabo de guardia.
corporate ['kɔrpərət, B 'kɔpə-] *a.* corporativo; incorporado, colectivo; social.
corporately [-lɪ] *adv.* corporativamente, colectivamente.
corporate name, (com.) nombre de una corporación, compañía, etc.
corporation [ˌkɔrpə'reɪʃən, B ˌkɔpə-] *s.* 1. corporación, cuerpo de asociados. 2. (der., com.) sociedad anónima, sociedad por acciones, corporación. 3. (G.B.) cabildo, ayuntamiento.
corporative ['kɔrpəˌreɪtɪv, B 'kɔpərə-] *a.* corporativo.
corporator [-ˌreɪtər, B -ˌreɪtə] *s.* miembro de una corporación.
corporeal [kɔr'pɔrɪəl, B kɔ'-] *a.* 1. corpóreo, material, tangible, palpable, físico. 2. (der.) material (posesión); corporal (bien).
corporeality [-ˌpɔrɪ'ælətɪ] *s.* corporeidad, materialidad.
corporeally [-'pɔrɪəlɪ] *adv.* materialmente, físicamente, corporalmente.
corporeity [ˌkɔrpə'riətɪ, B ˌkɔpə-] *s.* corporeidad, naturaleza física; materialidad.
corposant ['kɔrpəˌsænt, -ˌzænt, B 'kɔpəˌzænt] *s.* (mar.) fuego de San Telmo (manifestación de una descarga atmosférica en los mástiles).
corps [kɔr, B kɔ] (*pl.* CORPS [kɔrz, B kɔz]) *s.* cuerpo, corps, asociación, conjunto de integrantes; **c. de ballet,** cuerpo de baile; **Army C.,** cuerpo o unidad del ejército (sanidad, señales, etc.); **diplomatic c.,** cuerpo diplomático.
corpse [kɔrps, B kɔps] *s.* 1. cadáver, difunto. 2. (fig.) despojos, restos.
corpulence ['kɔrpjələns, B 'kɔpjʊ-] **corpulency** [-lənsɪ] *s.* corpulencia, robustez.
corpulent [-lənt] *a.* corpulento, robusto, grueso.
corpus ['kɔrpəs, B 'kɔpəs] *s.* (*pl.* CORPORA, [-pərə]) 1. (anat.) cuerpo; cuerpo, cadáver. 2. cuerpo, colección (de escritos, leyes, etc.). 3. (der.) cuerpo principal, caudal (esp. de un fondo o hacienda testamentaria).
corpus callosum [-kə'loʊsəm] (*pl.* CORPORA CALLOSA [-sə]) (anat.) cuerpo calloso.
Corpus Christi [-'krɪstɪ] *a.* (relig.) Corpus Christi, Corpus.
corpuscle ['kɔrˌpʌsəl, B 'kɔˌ-] *s.* 1. corpúsculo. 2. (bot., quím., fís.) corpúsculo. 3. (fisiol.) corpúsculo, glóbulo, célula, ej., *red corpuscles,* corpúsculos o glóbulos rojos (de la sangre), *colostrum c.,* corpúsculo o célula del colostro.
corpuscular [kɔr'pʌskjələr, B kɔ'-lə] *a.* (anat., filos.) corpuscular.
corpus delicti [-dɪ'lɪkˌtaɪ] (der.) cuerpo del delito.
corpus juris [-'dʒʊrəs, B -'jʊrəs] (der.) cuerpo de leyes.
corpus luteum [-'lutɪəm] (anat.) cuerpo amarillo o lúteo.
corpus striatum [-straɪ'eɪtəm] (anat.) cuerpo estriado del cerebro.
corrade [kə'reɪd] *v.t., v.i.* (geol.) erosionar(se), corroer(se).
corral [kə'ræl, B kɔ'rɑl] *s.* 1. corral, aprisco. 2. cercado de carros (para defensa y seguridad). —*v.t.* (*pret., p.p.* CORRALLED ; *p.pr.* CORRALLING) 1. acorralar (ganado). 2. formar un cercado de (carros). 3. conseguir, capturar.
correct [kə'rɛkt] *v.t.* 1. corregir; enmendar, subsanar, rectificar. 2. corregir, reprender, castigar. —*a.* 1. correcto, exacto, justo. 2. correcto, cumplido.
correction [kə'rɛkʃən] *s.* 1. corrección, enmienda, rectificación. 2. corrección, reprensión, castigo, censura.
correctional [-əl] *a.* correccional, penal, reformatorio.
correctitude [kə'rɛktəˌtud, B -ˌtjud] *s.* exactitud, corrección (esp. en el comportamiento).
corrective [-tɪv] *a.* correctivo, correccional. —*s.* medio o agente correctivo; remedio; castigo; medida correctiva.
correctly [kə'rɛktlɪ] *adv.* correctamente, bien.
corrector [-tər, B -tə] *s.* corrector, revisor, corregidor, reformador.
correlate ['kɔrəˌleɪt, 'kɑr-, B 'kɔr-] *s.* concepto correlativo. —*v.t.* correlacionar, poner en correlación. —*v.i.* ser correlativos, estar en relación recíproca. —*a.* correlativo.
correlation [ˌkɔrə'leɪʃən, ˌkɑr- B ˌkɔr-] *s.* correlación.
correlative [kə'rɛlətɪv] *a.* correlativo; (gram.) correlativo. —*s.* (gram.) palabra correlativa.
correspond [ˌkɔrə'spɑnd, ˌkɑr-, B ˌkɔrɪ'spɔnd] *v.i.* 1. (con *to*) corresponder, convenir (a); tocar (a). 2. (con *with*) comunicarse, mantener correspondencia, corresponderse (con).
correspondence [-'spɑndəns, B -'spɔn-] *s.* 1. correspondencia, relación. 2. correspondencia, correo.
correspondence course, curso por correspondencia.
correspondence school, escuela por correspondencia.

correspondency [-dənsɪ] *s.* correspondencia, relación, reciprocidad.
correspondent [-dənt] *a.* correspondiente. —*s.* 1. cosa correspondiente, cosa correlativa. 2. (periodismo, com.) corresponsal.
corresponding [-dɪŋ] *a.* correspondiente, perteneciente.
correspondingly [-lɪ] *adv.* correspondientemente.
corridor ['kɔrədər, 'kɑr-, -ˌdɔr, B 'kɔrɪˌdɔ] *s.* corredor, pasillo, pasadizo; (pol., geog.) corredor, territorio de una nación que pasa por el de otra (esp. para dar acceso a un puerto).
corrie ['kɔrɪ, 'kɑrɪ, B 'kɔrɪ] *s.* (Esco.) hondonada circular (en la ladera de un cerro o de una montaña).
corrigendum [ˌkɔrə'dʒɛndəm, ˌkɑr-, B ˌkɔr-] *s.* (*pl.* CORRIGENDA [-də]) error o falta que debe ser corregida en un manuscrito o impreso; (*pl.*) fe de erratas.
corrigibility [-dʒə'bɪlətɪ] *s.* corregibilidad.
corrigible ['kɔrədʒəbəl, 'kɑr- B 'kɔr-] *a.* corregible, enmendable.
corrival [kə'raɪvəl] *s.* rival, competidor, émulo. —*a.* rival.
corroborant [kə'rɑbərənt, B -'rɔb-] *a.* (ant.) corroborante, tónico, fortaleciente.
corroborate [-ˌreɪt] *v.t.* corroborar, confirmar.
corroboration [kəˌrɑbə'reɪʃən, B -ˌrɔb-] *s.* corroboración, confirmación.
corroborative [kə'rɑbəˌreɪtɪv, -rətɪv, B -'rɔb-] *a.* corroborativo, corroborante, confirmativo.
corroborator [-ˌreɪtər, B -ə] *s.* corroborante.
corroboratory [-rəˌtɔrɪ, B -rətərɪ] *a.* corroborativo, confirmativo, corroborante.
corroboree [-əˌri] *s.* (Aust.) 1. festividad nocturna de los aborígenes. 2. jarana, bullicio, alboroto.
corrode [kə'roʊd] *v.t.* 1. corroer, desgastar. 2. menoscabar. —*v.i.* corroerse, desgastarse, oxidarse.
corrodible [-əbəl] *a.* corrosible.
corrosion [kə'roʊʒən] *s.* corrosión, desgaste, oxidación.
corrosive [-sɪv, -zɪv] *a.* 1. corrosivo. 2. (fig.) mordaz, cáustico. —*s.* sustancia corrosiva.
corrosively [-lɪ] *adv.* corrosivamente.
corrosive sublimate, (quím.) sublimado corrosivo.
corrugate ['kɔrəˌgeɪt, 'kɑr-, B 'kɔrʊ-] *v.t., v.i.* arrugar, fruncir, encarrujar; acanalar.
corrugated [-əd] *a.* corrugado, acanalado, arrugado, encogido.
corrugated culvert, alcantarilla corrugada.
corrugated iron, hierro acanalado, corrugado u ondulado.
corrugation [ˌkɔrə'geɪʃən, ˌkɑr-, B ˌkɔrʊ-] *s.* corrugación, arruga, ondulación, acanaladura.
corrupt [kə'rʌpt] *v.t.* corromper; pervertir; contaminar; alterar (texto). —*v.i.* corromperse. —*a.* 1. corrompido, corrupto. 2. (ant.) contaminado, podrido. 3. inmoral, pervertido, depravado. 4. errado, alterado (texto).
corrupter, corruptor [-ər, B -ə] *s.* corruptor, depravador.
corruptibility [kəˌrʌptə'bɪlətɪ] *s.* corruptibilidad.
corruptible [kə'rʌptəbəl] *a.* corruptible, pervertible.
corruptibly [-blɪ] *adv.* corruptiblemente.
corrupting [-tɪŋ] *a.* corruptor, corrompedor.
corruption [kə'rʌpʃən] *s.* 1. corrupción, corruptela. 2. (ant.) influencia corruptora.
corruptive [kə'rʌptɪv] *a.* corruptivo.
corruptly [kə'rʌptlɪ] *adv.* corrompidamente, corruptamente.
corruptness [-nəs] *s.* corrupción, corruptela.
corsage [kɔr'sɑʒ, -'sɑdʒ, B kɔ'sɑʒ] *s.* 1. corpiño, blusa (de un vestido de mujer). 2. ramillete (para llevarse al pecho o a la cintura).
corsair ['kɔrˌsɛr, B 'kɔsɛə] *s.* 1. corsario, pirata. 2. corsario, barco pirata.
corse [kɔrs, B kɔs] *s.* (poét.) cadáver.
corselet ['kɔrslət, B 'kɔs-] *s.* 1. peto de armadura. 2. [ˌkɔrsə'lɛt, B 'kɔslɪt] corsé ligero sin ballenas.
corset ['kɔrsət, B 'kɔsɪt] *s.* corsé, cotilla. —*v.t.* poner un corsé, vestir con un corsé.
corset cover, cubrecorsé, corpiño, canesú, justillo.
corsetiere [ˌkɔrsə'tɪr, -'tjɛr, B ˌkɔsɪ'tɪə] *s.* corsetera.
Corsican ['kɔrsɪkən, B 'kɔsɪ-] *a., s.* corso, de Córcega (isla francesa en el Mediterráneo).
cortege [kɔr'tɛʒ, B kɔ'teɪʒ] *s.* cortejo, comitiva, séquito, procesión.
Cortes ['kɔrˌtɛz, kɔr'tɛz, B 'kɔtɛs] *s.* (las) Cortes, cuerpo legislativo de España.
cortex ['kɔrˌtɛks B 'kɔtɛks] *s.* (*pl.* CORTICES [-təˌsiz] o CORTEXES) 1. (bot.) corteza. 2. (anat.) corteza (esp. del cerebro); capa externa de un órgano.
cortical ['kɔrtɪkəl, B 'kɔt-] *a.* (bot., anat.) cortical.
corticate ['kɔrtəkət, -ˌkeɪt, B 'kɔtɪkɪt] **corticated** [-ˌkeɪtəd] *a.* cortezudo.
corticoid [-ˌkɔɪd] *s.* (bioquím.) corticoide; corticosteroide.
corticose [-ˌkoʊs] *a.* (bot.) corticoso.
corticosteroid [ˌkɔrtə'kɑstəˌrɔɪd, -koʊ'stɪrˌɔɪd, B ˌkɔtɪ'kɔstəˌrɔɪd] *s.* (bioquím.) corticosteroide; corticoide.
corticosterone [-ˌroʊn] *s.* (bioquím.) corticosterona.
corticotrophin [ˌkɔrtɪkoʊ'troʊfən, B ˌkɔtɪ-] **corticotropin** [-'troʊpən] *s.* (fisiol.) corticotrofina, corticotropina.
cortin ['kɔrtən B 'kɔt-] *s.* (bioquím.) cortina, corticina.
cortisone ['kɔrtəˌsoʊn, -ˌzoʊn, B 'kɔtɪˌzoʊn] *s.* (bioquím.) cortisona.
corundum [kə'rʌndəm] *s.* (min.) corindón.
coruscant [kə'rʌskənt] *a.* coruscante, brillante, resplandeciente.
coruscate ['kɔrəˌskeɪt, 'kɑr-, B 'kɔr-] *v.i.* coruscar, resplandecer, relucir, brillar.
coruscation [ˌkɔrə'skeɪʃən, ˌkɑr-, B ˌkɔr-] *s.* 1. fulgor, brillo, resplandor. 2. (fig.) destellos, chispazos (de ingenio), agudezas.
corvée [kɔr'veɪ, B 'kɔveɪ] *s.* 1. (hist.) labor o servidumbre no remunerada (de un vasallo). 2. labor comunal obligatoria (exigida por las autoridades públicas, esp. para construcción de carreteras, etc.).
corves, *pl. de* **corf.**
corvette [kɔr'vɛt, B kɔ'-] *s.* (mar.) corbeta.
corvina [kɔr'vinə, B kɔ'-] (ict.) corvina.
corvine ['kɔrˌvaɪn, B 'kɔˌ-] *a.* corvino, perteneciente al cuervo.
Corvus ['kɔrvəs, B 'kɔvəs] *s.* (astr.) Cuervo.
corydalis [kə'rɪdələs] *s.* (bot.) corídalo.
Corydon ['kɔrədən, 'kɑr-, B 'kɔr-] *s.* (lit.) Coridón, nombre tradicional de un pastor en la poesía bucólica.
corymb ['kɔrɪm, -ɪmb, 'kɑr-, B 'kɔr-] *s.* (bot.) corimbo.
corymbous [kə'rɪmbəs] **corymbose** [-ˌboʊs] *a.* (bot.) 1. corimbífero (planta). 2. corimbiforme (inflorescencia).
coryphaeus [ˌkɔrə'fiəs, ˌkɑr, B ˌkɔrɪ-] *s.* (*pl.* CORYPHAEI [-'fiˌaɪ]) corifeo.
coryphée [ˌkɔrɪ'feɪ] *s.* (raro) primera bailarina; bailarina.
coryza [kə'raɪzə] *s.* (med.) coriza, catarro nasal.
cos *abrev. de* **cosine,** coseno (cos).
C.O.S. *abrev. de* **cash on shipment,** pago contra embarque.
Cosa Nostra ['koʊsə'noʊstrə] *s.* (E.U.) sindicato criminal relacionado con la mafia siciliana.
cosec *abrev. de* **cosecant,** cosecante (cosec).
cosecant [koʊ'sikənt, -ˌkænt] *s.* (geom.) cosecante.
cosh [kɑʃ, B kɔʃ] *s.* (jer., G.B.) cachiporra corta.
cosher ['kɑʃər, B 'kɔʃə] *v.t.* (Irl.) acariciar, mimar. —*v.i.* (fam.) comadrear, chismear.
cosignatory [koʊ'sɪgnəˌtɔrɪ, B -nətərɪ] *s.* firmante conjunto, cosignatario.
cosily, *var. de* **cozily.**
cosine ['koʊˌsaɪn] *s.* (geom.) coseno.
cosiness, *var. de* **coziness.**
cosmetic [kɑz'mɛtɪk, B kɔz-] *a.* cosmético. —*s.* cosmético, afeite.
cosmetician [ˌkɑzmə'tɪʃən, B ˌkɔz-] *s.* fabricante, vendedor de cosméticos; cosmetólogo.
cosmetologist [-'tɑlədʒəst, B -'tɔl-] *s.* cosmetólogo, cosmetóloga.
cosmetology [-ədʒɪ] *s.* cosmetología.
cosmic ['kɑzmɪk, B 'kɔz-] *a.* 1. cósmico. 2. vasto, infinito.
cosmic dust, (astr.) polvo cósmico.
cosmic radiation, (fís.) radiación cósmica.
cosmic ray, (fís.) rayo cósmico.
cosmism [ˌkɑzˌmɪzəm, B 'kɔz-] *s.* teoría de la evolución cosmogónica.
cosmogonic [ˌkɑzmə'gɑnɪk, B ˌkɔzmə'gɔn-] **cosmogonical** [-ɪkəl] *a.* cosmogónico.
cosmogonist [kɑz'mɑgənəst, B kɔz'mɔg-] *s.* especialista en cosmogonía.
cosmogony [-ənɪ] *s.* cosmogonía.
cosmographer [-rəfər, B -ə] *s.* cosmógrafo.
cosmographic [ˌkɑzmə'græfɪk, B ˌkɔz-] **cosmographical** [-ɪkəl] *a.* cosmográfico.
cosmography [kɑz'mɑgrəfɪ, B kɔz'mɔg-] *s.* cosmografía.
cosmologic [ˌkɑzmə'lɑdʒɪk B ˌkɔzmə'lɔdʒ-] **cosmological** [-ɪkəl] *a.* cosmológico.
cosmologist [kɑz'mɑlədʒəst, B kɔz'mɔl-] *s.* cosmólogo.
cosmology [-ədʒɪ] *s.* cosmología.
cosmonaut ['kɑzməˌnɔt, -ˌnɑt, B 'kɔzməˌnɔt] *s.* cosmonauta, astronauta.
cosmonautics ['kɑzmə'nɔtɪks, -'nɑt-, B ˌkɔzmə'nɔt-] *s.* cosmonáutica.
cosmopolis [kɑz'mɑpələs, B kɔz'mɔp-] *s.* ciudad cosmopolita.
cosmopolitan [ˌkɑzmə'pɑlətən, B ˌkɔzmə'pɔl-] *a.* cosmopolita. —*s.* cosmopolita, ciudadano del mundo.
cosmopolitanism [-ˌɪzəm] *s.* cosmopolitismo.
cosmopolite [kɑz'mɑpəˌlaɪt, B kɔz'mɔp-] *s.* cosmopolita; (bot., zool.) cosmopolita, que crece o se da en cualquier región.
cosmorama [ˌkɑzmə'rɑmə, -'ræmə, B ˌkɔz-] *s.* cosmorama, panorama o exhibición de fotos de diversas partes del mundo.
cosmos ['kɑzməs, B 'kɔz-] *s.* 1. cosmos, universo. 2. (bot.) planta parecida a la dalia.
cosmotron [-məˌtrɑn, B -ˌtrɔn] *s.* (fís.) cosmotrón, acelerador de alta potencia.
Cossack ['kɑsæk, -ək, B 'kɔsæk] *a., s.* cosaco.
cosset ['kɑsət, B 'kɔsɪt] *s.* ovejita doméstica; animal favorito. —*v.t.* acariciar, mimar, regalar.
cost [kɔst] *s.* 1. coste, costo, costa. 2. costo, precio. 3. (*pl.*) (der.) costas, gastos (de un juicio). 4. **at any c., at all costs,** a toda costa, a raja tabla;

at c., (com., ten.) al costo, a precio de costo; **at the cost of,** a costa de; **to count the c.,** calcular los riesgos (antes de actuar); **to my (your, his,** etc.) **c.,** a mis (sus) expensas. —*v.i.* (*pret., p.p.* COST ; *p.pr.* COSTING) costear; **c. what it may,** cueste lo que cueste. —*v.t.* calcular el costo de.

costa ['kɑstə, B 'kɔstə] *s.* (*pl.* COSTAE [-ti, -taɪ]) (anat.) costilla.

cost accounting, (com.) contabilidad de costos.

costal ['kɑstəl, B 'kɔstəl] *a.* (anat.) costal.

co-star ['koʊˌstɑr, B -ˌstɑ] *s.* actor o actriz que comparte la mención estelar en el elenco. —*v.i.* compartir la mención estelar. —*v.t.* presentar dos estrellas en una obra.

costard ['kɑstərd, B 'kʌstəd, 'kɔs-] *s.* 1. variedad de manzana inglesa. 2. (ant.) cabeza.

Costa Rica [ˌkɑstə'rikə, ˌkos-, B ˌkɔs-] *s.* Costa Rica.

Costa Rican [-'rikən] *s., a.* costarricense, de Costa Rica.

costate ['kɑsˌteɪt, B 'kɔstət] *a.* con costillas; estriado, surcado.

costeaning [kɑ'stinɪŋ, B kɔ-] *s.* (min.) cateo, calas de prueba, calicatas; reconocimiento.

coster ['kɑstər, B 'kɔstə] *s.* (G.B.) *forma abrev. de* **costermonger.**

costermonger [-ˌmʌŋgər, -ˌmɑŋ-, B -ˌmʌŋgə] *s.* (G.B.) frutero, vendedor ambulante (de frutas, pescado, etc.).

costive ['kɑstɪv, B 'kɔs-] *a.* 1. (med.) estreñido, estíptico. 2. (fig.) estreñido, tacaño, mezquino. 3. lerdo.

costively [-lɪ] *adv.* estreñidamente.

costiveness [-nəs] *s.* estreñimiento.

costliness ['kɔstlɪnəs] *s.* carestía, alto precio, calidad de costoso, suntuosidad.

costly ['kɔstlɪ] *a.* (COSTLIER; COSTLIEST) 1. costoso, caro; valioso, de gran valor. 2. (E.U.) espléndido, suntuoso, magnífico. 3. (ant.) extravagante.

costmary [-ˌmɛrɪ, B -ˌmɛərɪ] *s.* (bot.) atanasia, hierba de Santa María, hierba romana.

cost of living, costo de vida.

cost of living index, índice del costo de vida.

cost-plus [-'plʌs] *s.* costo de producción más margen de utilidad fija (ú. como base para compras estatales).

cost price, precio de costo.

costrel ['kɑstrəl, B 'kɔs-] *s.* (dial.) botella (de piel, arcilla o madera) con correas para colgarla al hombro.

costume ['kɑsˌtum, B 'kɔsˌtjum] *s.* 1. traje (esp. de cierto país, época, clase, etc.). 2. disfraz, traje de máscara; vestuario de teatro. 3. traje de chaqueta, traje sastre (de mujer). 4. estilo (de vestirse, de peinado). —*v.t.* vestir, disfrazar.

costume ball, baile de disfraces, baile de máscaras.

costume jewelry, joyas de fantasía, bisutería.

costume piece, (teat.) obra histórica (con trajes de época).

costumer [-ər, B -ə] **costumier** [kɑs'tumiər, B kɔs'tjumɪə] *s.* 1. sastre de máscaras o disfraces. 2. mascarero, mascarera. 3. sastre de teatro.

costusroot ['kɔstəsˌrut, 'kɑs-, B 'kɔs-] *s.* (bot.) costo.

cosy, *var. de* **cozy.**

cot [kɑt, B kɔt] *s.* 1. catre, camilla. 2. (G.B.) cuna; cama (en un hospital infantil). 3. cabañita, choza. 4. dedil (funda para cubrir la cura de un dedo).

cot. *abrev. de* **cotangent,** cotangente (cotg.).

cotangent [koʊ'tændʒənt] *s.* (geom.) cotangente.

cote [koʊt] *s.* 1. corral, aprisco, abrigo, cobertizo (para animales domésticos). 2. (G.B.) cabaña, casita.

cotemporaneous [koʊˌtɛmpə'reɪnɪəs] *var. de* **contemporaneous.**

cotenancy [koʊ'tɛnənsɪ] *s.* coinquilinato de una propiedad colectiva.

cotenant [-ənt] *s.* coinquilino.

coterie ['koʊtərɪ] *s.* camarilla, círculo, tertulia.

coterminal [koʊ'tɜrmənəl, B -'tɜm-] *a.* con término, confinante.

coterminous [-ənəs] *a.* 1. contérmino, confinante. 2. coextenso.

cothurnus [koʊ'θɜrnəs, B -'θɜnəs] *s.* (*pl.* COTHURNI [-ni]) coturno, estilo sublime de tragedia romana o griega.

cotidal line [koʊ'taɪdəl-] línea de mareas coincidentes (en un mapa).

cotillion, cotillon [koʊ'tɪljən, B kə-] *s.* cotillón, baile de gran realce.

cotta ['kɑtə, B 'kɔtə] *s.* (relig.) sobrepelliz corta.

cottage ['kɑtɪdʒ, B 'kɔt-] *s.* casita de campo; cabaña amena y cómoda.

cottage cheese, requesón, queso fresco.

cottage pudding, especie de budín con salsa dulce.

cottager [-ər, B -ə] *s.* 1. veraneante (que alquila una casa de campo). 2. (G.B.) jornalero de campo.

cottar, cotter ['kɑtər, B 'kɔtə] *s.* (Esco.) jornalero de campo, campesino escocés que por su trabajo recibe en pago una pequeña porción de tierra y una cabaña.

cotter, *s.* (mec.) chaveta, llave, pasador, clavija.

cotter drill, taladro ranurador.

cotter pin, (mec.) clavija hendida, chaveta de dos patas.

cottier ['kɑtɪər, B 'kɔtɪə] *s.* (Irl.) jornalero de campo; campesino arrendatario.

cotton ['kɑtən, B 'kɔtən] *s.* 1. (bot.) algodón. 2. (fibra o tela de) algodón. —*v.i.* prosperar, tener éxito; **c. on to,** comprender, aceptar (un hecho, idea, etc.); **c. to,** armonizar, simpatizar (con), coger cariño (a una persona); aficionarse, gustar (de una cosa, idea, etc.).

cotton batting, algodón en hoja o en rama.

Cotton Belt, región algodonera (del sur de los E.U.).

cotton braid, (elec.) trenza de algodón, algodón trenzado.

cotton cake, torta de orujo de algodón para alimento del ganado.

cotton candy, algodón de azúcar, confección populachera que se vende en los parques de diversiones.

cotton flannel, (tej.) franela de algodón, muletón.

cotton gin, despepitadora de algodón, desmotadora (Am.).

cotton moth, (ento.) mariposa del gusano del algodón.

cottonmouth ['kɑtənˌmaʊθ, B 'kɔt-] *s.* (zool.) mocasín de agua (reptil).

cotton picker, 1. recolectora de algodón (máquina), cosechadora de algodón (Am.). 2. peón que recoge el algodón en las plantaciones.

cotton-picking, *a.* (jer., despec.) despreciable, detestable.

cotton plant, (bot.) algodonero.

cotton plantation, algodonal, plantación de algodón.

cotton press, prensa para embalar algodón.

cotton print, tejido fino de algodón, estampado.

cottonseed ['kɑtənˌsid, B 'kɔt-] *s.* semilla del algodón.

cottonseed meal, harina de orujo de algodón.

cottonseed oil, aceite de semillas de algodón.

cottontail [-ˌteɪl] *s.* (zool.) liebre de rabo blanco; (E.U.) conejo común.

cotton thistle, (bot.) cardo borriqueño, cardo yesquero, toba, acantio.

cotton tree, (bot.) viburno; ceiba; álamo y otros árboles bombáceos.

cotton waste, estopa de algodón, desperdicios de hilaza de algodón.

cottonweed [-ˌwid] *s.* (bot.) lanaria, perpetua.

cottonwood [-ˌwʊd] *s.* (bot., E.U.) álamo, chopo.

cotton wool, 1. algodón en rama; algodón (usado para envolturas). 2. (med.) algodón, algodón absorbente. 3. (fig.) algodones, vida de mimo y delicadeza; ej., *brought up in cotton wool,* criado entre algodones.

cottony ['kɑtənɪ, B 'kɔt-] *a.* 1. algodonoso, suave. 2. velloso.

cotunnite [kə'tʌnˌaɪt] *s.* cotunita, cloruro de plomo nativo.

cotyla ['kɑtələ, B 'kɔt-] *s.* (anat.) cótila.

cotyledon [ˌkɑtəl'idən, B ˌkɔt-] *s.* (bot.) cotiledón; **C.,** cotiledóneas.

cotyledonary [-'idənˌɛrɪ, B -ənərɪ] *a.* (bot.) cotiledonario.

cotyledonous [-ənəs] *a.* (bot.) cotiledóneo.

couch [kaʊtʃ] *v.t.* 1. (*ú. en p.p. en voz pasiva*) recostar. 2. bordar con hilos de oro. 3. bajar, enristrar (la lanza para el ataque). 4. formular, expresar. 5. (med.) batir (las cataratas o nubes de los ojos). 6. **c. oneself,** acostarse. 7. (ant.) esconder, ocultar. —*v.i.* 1. acostarse; dormir con, yacer con (persona del otro sexo). 2. estar al acecho, agacharse. 3. recogerse (animal en su guarida). —*s.* 1. canapé, sofá; lecho. 2. cubil, guarida (esp. de la nutria).

couchant ['kaʊtʃənt] *a.* (her.) acostado.

couch grass, (bot.) grama, bermuda, gramilla colorada.

couch potato, (jer.) haragán.

cougar ['kugər, -ˌgɑr, B 'kugə] *s.* (zool.) puma.

cough [kɔf] *v.i.* toser. —*v.t.* (con *out, up*) expectorar, esputar; decir tosiendo; **c. up, (jer.) aflojar, soltar (la mosca), dar (dinero); revelar de mala gana. —*s.*** tos; carraspera.

cough drop, 1. pastilla contra la tos. 2. (fam.) persona graciosa y animada.

could [kʊd, kəd] *v. aux. defectivo* (**pret. y condicional de can**) pude, podría.

couldn't ['kʊdənt] *contr. de* **could not.**

coulee ['kulɪ] *s.* 1. (pr. Oeste E.U.) quebrada, cañada. 2. (geol.) arroyo de lava.

coulisse [ku'lis] *s.* 1. (teat.) bastidor, bastidores. 2. corredera, guía; desagüe.

coulomb ['kuˌlɑm, -ˌloʊm, B 'kulɔm] *s.* (fís.) culombio.

coulter, *var. de* **colter.**

coumarin ['kumərən] *s.* (quím.) cumarina.

coumarone ['kuməˌroʊn] *s.* (quím.) cumarona.

coumarou ['kuməru] *s.* (bot.) haba tonca.

council ['kaʊnsəl] *s.* 1. concilio, consejo, asamblea, junta. 2. (relig.) concilio. 3. ayuntamiento, concejo. 4. **city c.,** concejo municipal.

councillor, councillorship, *vars. de* **councilor, councilorship.**

councilman [-mən] *s.* concejal, regidor.

council of ministers, consejo de ministros.

councilor ['kaʊnsələr, B -lə] *s.* concejal, consejero; (relig.) conciliar.

councilorship [-ˌʃɪp] *s.* cargo o dignidad de consejero.

counsel ['kaʊnsəl] *s.* 1. consejo, parecer, opinión. 2. abogado consultor, asesor legal; abogado. 3. consultor. 4. (ant.) designio, propósito, trama; secreto, sigilo. 5. **to keep one's (own) c.,** ser reservado, guardar silencio, callar; **to take c. (with),** pedir consejo (a), consultar. —*v.t.* (*pret., p.p.* COUNSELED O COUNSELLED ; *p.pr.* COUNSELING O COUNSELLING) aconsejar; dirigir, guiar, asesorar. —*v.i.* hacer consultas, pedir consejo, aconsejarse.

counseling [-ɪŋ] *s.* asesoramiento.

counselor, counsellor ['kaʊnsələr, B -lə] *s.* 1. consejero. 2. abogado; asesor legal.

count [kaʊnt] *v.t.* 1. contar. 2. considerar, estimar, juzgar. 3. tomar en cuenta, tener en cuenta. 4. **c. in,** incluir; **c. off,** separar contando; **c. out,** contar uno por uno; (boxeo) declarar vencido (a un pugilista que no puede levantarse después de contársele los diez segundos); (fig.) eliminar; excluir, omitir, no incluir. —*v.i.* 1. contar, hacer cuentas. 2. valer. 3. **c. against,** influir en contra, pesar contra; **c. down,** contar al revés; **c. for,** valer por, equivaler a; importar; **c. on** o **upon,** contar con; confiar en, depender de; **c. up to,** ascender a, sumar. —*s.* 1. cuenta; cómputo, recuento. 2. suma, total. 3. (der.) cargo. 4. (tej.) número (del hilo); diámetro (del hilo de trama o de urdimbre). 5. conde. 6. **on all counts,** en todo respecto; **to keep c.,** llevar la cuenta; **to lose c.,** perder la cuenta.

countable ['kaʊntəbəl] *a.* contable, contadero.

countdown [-ˌdaʊn] *s.* cuenta regresiva, cuenta al revés (de los segundos, ej., para el lanzamiento de un cohete).

countenance ['kaʊntənəns] *s.* 1. semblante, talante, expresión (de la cara). 2. serenidad, compostura. 3. apoyo, aprobación. 4. **to change c.,** cambiar de semblante, cambiar de aspecto; **to give c. to,** prestar apoyo a; aprobar; **to keep one's c.,** contenerse, guardar serenidad, no perder la seriedad; **to lose one's c.,** agitarse, conturbarse; **to put out of c.,** desconcertar, avergonzar. —*v.t.* tolerar, aprobar, favorecer, sancionar.

counter ['kaʊntər, B -ə] *s.* 1. contador, computador, calculista. 2. contador, máquina contadora (en juegos, etc.). 3. ficha, tanto. 4. mostrador, bar. 5. lo opuesto, contrario. 6. (mar.) bovedilla. 7. contrafuerte (del zapato). 8. contragolpe. 9. (esgr.) contra, parada circular (en que la espada sigue a la del contrincante). 10. pecho del caballo. 11. (tip.) blanco interno, profundidad central (del ojo del tipo). 12. **over the c.,** (vendido) por medio de corredores (díc. de ciertos valores de bolsa o acciones); **under the c.,** (fig.) subrepticiamente, a escondidas. —*a.* 1. contrario, opuesto. 2. de contragolpe. 3. duplicado. —*adv.* en sentido opuesto, al revés, contrariamente; (con *to*) en contra (de), en oposición (a); **to run c. to, go c. to,** oponerse a, estar en contra de. —*v.t.* 1. oponerse a, contender, combatir. 2. contradecir, replicar —*v.i.* (con *with*) contestar, desquitarse (con); oponerse.

counteraccusation ['kaʊntərˌækjʊ'zeɪʃən] *s.* contraacusación.

counteract [ˌkaʊntər'ækt] *v.t.* contrarrestar, frustrar, neutralizar; contrariar, impedir.

counteraction [-ækʃən] *s.* acción contraria, contrarresto, neutralización, oposición; impedimento.

counteractive [-'æktɪv] *a.* contrario, opuesto.

counterapproach ['kaʊntərəˌproʊtʃ] *s.* (fort.) contraaproches; contratrinchera.

counterattack [-əˌtæk] *s.* (mil.) contraataque. —*v.t., v.i.* contraatacar.

counterattraction [-ə'trækʃən] *s.* atracción contraria; atracción rival (en una feria, parque de diversiones, etc.).

counterbalance [-ˌbæləns B 'kaʊntəˌ-] *s.* contrabalanza, contrapeso. — [ˌkaʊn-'bæləns] *v.t., v.i.* contrabalancear, contrapesar, equilibrar; compensar.

counterblast ['kaʊntərˌblæst, B -əˌblɑst] *s.* réplica violenta.

counterbore [-ˌbɔr, B -ˌbɔ] *s.* ensanchamiento, contrataladro. —*v.t.* abocardar con fondo plano, contrataladrar.

counterbrace [-ˌbreɪs] *s.* (mec.) barra de contratensión; (mar.) contrabraza, contraamantillo. —*v.t.* (mar.) contrabracear.

counterchange [ˌkaʊntər'tʃeɪndʒ, B ˌkaʊntə'-] *v.t.* trocar, cambiar, intercambiar.

counterchanged [-'tʃeɪndʒd] *a.* (her.) contrabandado, contracuartelado.

countercharge ['kaʊntərˌtʃɑrdʒ, B 'kaʊntəˌtʃɑdʒ] *s.* 1. (der.) reconvención. 2. (mil.) contraataque. —*v.t.* 1. (der.) reconvenir. 2. (mil.) contraatacar.

countercheck [-ˌtʃɛk] *s.* obstáculo, traba; segunda comprobación. —*v.t.* 1. contrarrestar, contrastar, estorbar. 2. comprobar por segunda vez.

counter check, cheque de mostrador o en blanco.

counterclaim [-ˌkleɪm] *s.* contrademanda. —*v.t., v.i.* contrademandar.

counterclaimant [-ənt] *s.* contrademandante.

counterclockwise [ˌkaʊntər'klɑkˌwaɪz, B -tə'klɔk-] *a., adv.* en sentido contrario al de las manecillas del reloj.

countercurrent ['kaʊntərˌkɜrənt, B -ə-ˌkʌrənt] *s.* (elec., geog., mar.) contracorriente.

counter electromotive force, (elec.) fuerza contraelectromotriz.

counterespionage [ˌkaʊntər'ɛspɪəˌnɑʒ] *s.* contraespionaje.

counterfeit ['kaʊntərˌfɪt, B -təˌ-] *a.* falso, falsificado; fingido, espurio. —*s.* 1. falsificación, contrahechura. 2. imitación, falsificación, cosa falsificada; moneda falsa. 3. (ant.) impostor. —*v.t., v.i.* contrahacer, falsificar, falsear; disimular, fingir.

counterfeiter [-ər, B -ə] *s.* falsificador, contrahacedor, falsario; imitador.

counterflange [-ˌflændʒ] *s.* contrabrida.

counterfoil [-ˌfɔɪl] *s.* matriz, talón (ej., de un cheque).

counterfort [-ˌfɔrt, B ˌfɔt] *s.* (arq.) contrafuerte, estribo, machón.

counterguard [-ˌgɑrd, B -ˌgɑd] *s.* (fort.) contraguardia.

counterinformation [ˌkaʊntərˌɪnfər'meɪʃən, B -fə'-] *s.* contraaviso.

counterintelligence [-ɪn'tɛlədʒəns] *s.* (mil.) contraespionaje.

counterirritant [-'ɪrətənt] *s.* (med., fig.) contrairritante, repulsivo.

counterjumper ['kaʊntər'dʒʌmpər, B -əˌdʒʌmpə] *s.* (fam., despec.) vendedor de tienda, dependiente.

counterlight [-ˌlaɪt] *s.* contraluz, trasluz.

counterman [-ˌmæn] *s.* vendedor de tienda, dependiente.

countermand [ˌkaʊntər'mænd, B -ə'mɑnd] *v.t.* 1. contramandar, revocar (una orden anterior). 2. hacer volver. 3. cancelar, anular (pedido, etc.). — ['kaʊntərˌmænd, B -əˌmɑnd] *s.* contramandato, contraorden.

countermarch ['kaʊntərˌmɑrtʃ, B -əˌmɑtʃ] *v.i.* (mil.) contramarchar. —*s.* (mil.) contramarcha.

countermark [-ˌmɑrk, B -ˌmɑk] *v.t.* contramarcar, resellar. —*s.* contramarca, contrasello, contraseña.

countermeasure [-ˌmɛʒər, B -ə] *s.* medida preventiva; represalia.

countermine [-ˌmaɪn] *s.* (mil.) contramina. —*v.t., v.i.* (mil., fig.) contraminar.

countermove [-ˌmuv] *s.* jugada defensiva, parada; contraataque. —*v.i.* contraatacar.

counteroffensive ['kaʊntərəˌfɛnsɪv] *s.* (mil.) contraofensiva.

counteropening [-ˌoʊpənɪŋ] *s.* (med.) contraabertura, contrapunción.

counterpane ['kaʊntərˌpeɪn, B 'kaʊntəˌ-] *s.* cubrecama, colcha, corbertor.

counterpart [-ˌpɑrt, B -ˌpɑt] *s.* 1. contraparte, duplicado, complemento. 2. (teat.) contrafigura.

counterplea [-ˌpli] *s.* (der.) reconvención.

counterplot [-ˌplɑt, B -ˌplɔt] *s.* contratreta. —*v.i.* (*pret., p.p.* COUNTERPLOTTED ; *p.pr.* COUNTERPLOTTING) conspirar. —*v.t.* contraminar.

counterpoint [-ˌpɔɪnt] *s.* (mús.) contrapunto.

counterpoise [-ˌpɔɪz] *s.* 1. contrapeso. 2. balance, equilibrio. —*v.t.* contrabalancear, contrapesar, equilibrar.

counterpoison [-ˌpɔɪzən] *s.* contraveneno, antídoto.

counterproposal [-prəˌpoʊzəl] *s.* contraproposición, contrapropuesta, contraoferta.

counterproposition ['kaʊntərˌprɑpə'zɪʃən, B -əˌprɔp-] *s.* contraproposición.

counterpunch [-ˌpʌntʃ] *s.* contragolpe (en el boxeo).

counterreformation ['kaʊntəˌrɛfər'meɪʃən, B -fə'-] *s.* contrarreforma.

counterrevolution [-ˌrɛvə'luʃən] *s.* contrarrevolución.

counterrevolutionary [-'luʃəˌnɛrɪ, B -ʃənərɪ] *a., s.* contrarrevolucionario.

counterrevolutionist [-ʃənəst] *s.* contrarrevolucionario.

counterscarp ['kaʊntərˌskɑrp, B -əˌskɑp] *s.* (fort.) contraescarpa.

counterseal [-ˌsil] *v.t.* contrasellar. —*s.* contrasello.

countersense [-ˌsɛns] *s.* contrasentido, sentido opuesto.

countershaft [-ˌʃæft, B -ˌʃɑft] *s.* (mec.) contraeje, eje de transmisión intermedia, árbol auxiliar o de contramarcha, contraárbol.

countersign [-ˌsaɪn] *s.* 1. refrendata, contraseña. 2. (mil.) santo y seña. —*v.t.* refrendar.

countersignature ['kaʊnter'sɪgnətʃər, B -ə'sɪgnətʃə] *s.* refrendata.

countersink ['kaʊntərˌsɪŋk, B 'kaʊntəˌ-] *v.t.* avellanar, abocardar; meter (un tornillo) en un agujero avellanado. —*s.* 1. agujero avellanado. 2. avellanador, abocardo, broca de avellanar.

counterslope [-ˌsloʊp] *s.* contratalud.

counterspy [-ˌspaɪ] *s.* agente de contraespionaje.

counterstroke [-ˌstroʊk] *s.* contragolpe.

countersunk [-ˌsʌŋk] *a.* 1. avellanado, abocardado. 2. de cabeza embutida o perdida (clavo, tornillo, etc.).

countertenor [-ˌtɛnər, B -ə] *s.* (mús.) contralto (hombre).

countertorque [-ˌtɔrk, B -ˌtɔk] *s.* (ing.) momento de torsión antagónico; cupla antagónica.

countertype [-ˌtaɪp] *s.* tipo opuesto; tipo paralelo.

countervail [ˌkaʊntər'veɪl, B 'kaʊntəˌ-] *v.t., v.i.* contrapesar, compensar; contrarrestar.

counterweigh [ˌkaʊntər'weɪ, B -ə'-] *vt., v.i.* contrapesar, contrabalancear.

counterweight ['kaʊntərˌweɪt, B -əˌ-] *s.* contrapeso; peso equivalente. —*v.t.* poner contrapeso a, proveer de contrapeso.

counter word, *s.* palabra que expresa aprobación o desaprobación sin relación a su exacto significado (terrible, increíble, etc.).
counterwork [-ˌwɜrk, B -ˌwɜk] *s.* (fort.) (*pl.*) contrafuertes, contraataques; contraaproches, contratrincheras. —*v.t.* contrarrestar, contrariar, contraminar.
countess ['kaʊntəs] *s.* condesa.
countinghouse ['kaʊntɪŋˌhaʊs] *s.* contaduría, oficina de contabilidad; despacho, oficina, escritorio.
counting room, *var. de* **countinghouse.**
countless ['kaʊntləs] *a.* innumerable, incontable, sin cuento.
count palatine, conde palatino.
countrified, countryfied ['kʌntrɪˌfaɪd] *a.* campesino, rústico, rural, campestre.
country ['kʌntrɪ] *s.* 1. región, distrito; territorio, tierra. 2. país, patria, tierra. 3. campo. 4. (fig.) pueblo, nación. 5. (geol.) formación. 6. **in the c.,** en el campo; **to go to the c.,** (G.B., fig.) convocar a elecciones después de disolver el parlamento. —*a.* rural, rústico, campesino, campestre.
country club, club campestre, donde se practican actividades sociales y deportivas.
country cousin, provinciano (que visita la ciudad).
country-dance [-ˌdæns, B -ˌdɑns] *s.* baile campestre; (especie de) contradanza.
country estate, heredad, hacienda (Am.).
coupist ['kupɪst] *s.* golpista (S.A.).
countryfolk [-ˌfoʊk] *s.* gente del campo.
country gentleman, country squire, caballero de provincia; dueño de finca rural.
country house, casa de campo, quinta, villa.
countryman [-mən] *s.* 1. habitante, natural (de cierta región). 2. compatriota, paisano, coterráneo, conciudadano. 3. campesino, paisano, aldeano.
country music, estilo de música y canciones folklóricas.
country people, campesinos, provincianos, aldeanos; gente del campo.
country road, camino rural.
country rock, 1. (min.) roca madre, roca de caja. 2. (mús., E.U.) estilo de música popular.
countryseat [ˌkʌntrɪ'sit, B 'kʌn-] *s.* finca, heredad campestre, villa, quinta.
countryside ['kʌntrɪˌsaɪd] *s.* campo, campiña, ambiente rural.
countrywoman [-ˌwʊmən] *s.* 1. habitante (mujer), natural (de cierta región). 2. compatriota, paisana, coterránea, conciudadana. 3. campesina, paisana, aldeana.
county ['kaʊntɪ] *s.* condado, distrito, partido; los habitantes de un condado; **the c.,** (G.B.) los notables del condado.
county agent, (E.U.) asesor estatal y federal en agricultura y economía doméstica para las zonas rurales.
county clerk, secretario del condado.
county court, juzgado del distrito.
county palatine, palatinado, condado palatino.
county seat, cabeza de partido o distrito, capital de condado.
coup [ku] *s.* (*pl.* COUPS [kuz]) 1. golpe maestro; estratagema. 2. (bridge) jugada; golpe.
coup de grâce [ˌkudə'grɑs] (*pl.* COUPS DE GRACE [-'grɑs]) (fr.) golpe de gracia, puñalada de misericordia.
coup de main [-'mæn] (*pl.* COUPS DE MAIN [-'mæn]) (fr.) ataque de sorpresa, ataque violento.
coup d'état [-'tɑ, B 'kudeɪ-] (*pl.* COUPS D'ETAT [-'tɑz]) (fr.) golpe de estado.
coup d'oeil [ku'dɛɪ] (fr.) mirada, vistazo, ojeada.
coupé, coupe [ku'peɪ, B 'kupeɪ] *s.* 1. cupé (coche o automóvil). 2. (f.c., G.B.) medio compartimiento (al extremo del coche).
couple ['kʌpəl] *s.* 1. pareja. 2. par. 3. traílla doble (para juntar dos perros). 4. yunta (de bueyes, etc.). 5. (elec., mec.) par (de fuerzas), ej., *voltaic c.,* par voltaico. 6. **a c. of,** un par de, unos pocos, unos cuantos. —*v.t.* acoplar, conectar, unir, empalmar, juntar; unir en matrimonio; formar pares o parejas. —*v.i.* 1. copularse. 2. unirse, juntarse. —*a.* dos.
coupler ['kʌplər, B -lə] *s.* 1. (mec., rad.) acoplador; (elec.) acoplamiento. 2. (f.c.) enganche, enganchador, manguito.
couplet [-lət] *s.* 1. pareado, dos versos pareados, dístico. 2. copla, cuplé. 3. par, pareja, gemelos.
coupling [-lɪŋ] *s.* 1. pareo. 2. cópula (esp. sexual). 3. (mec.) acoplamiento, empalme, acopladura, empalmadura, unión. 4. (elec.) acoplamiento. 5. (f.c.) enganche.
coupling box, collar de acoplamiento, caja de cambios.
coupling clutch, embrague de manguito.
coupling coefficient, (elec.) coeficiente de acoplamiento.
coupling coil, (rad.) bobina de acoplamiento.
coupling condenser, (rad.) condensador de acoplamiento.
coupling flange, brida de acoplamiento.
coupling pin, (f.c.) pasador de enganche.
coupling rod, (f.c.) biela paralela.
coupon ['kuˌpɑn, 'kju-, B 'kuˌpɔn] *s.* cupón, talonario.
courage ['kɜrɪdʒ, 'kʌrɪdʒ, B 'kʌ-] *s.* valor, intrepidez, denuedo, valentía, ánimo; **to have the c. of one's convictions,** tener valor para poner en práctica sus convicciones; **to lose c.,** acobardarse; **to take c.,** cobrar ánimo, envalentonarse; **to take one's c. in both hands,** apelar a todo su valor.
courageous [kə'reɪdʒəs] *a.* valiente, valeroso, animoso, intrépido, denodado, arrojado.
courageously [-lɪ] *adv.* valientemente, animosamente.
courageousness [-nəs] *s.* ánimo, valor, valentía, intrepidez, denuedo, brío, arrojo.
courante [kʊ'rɑnt, -'rænt] *s.* antiguo baile francés de salón y su música.
courbaril ['kʊrbərəl, B 'kʊəbər-] *s.* (bot.) curbaril, anime.
courier ['kʊrɪər, 'kʌ-, B 'kʊrɪə] *s.* 1. mensajero, posta; estafeta; correo (esp. diplomático). 2. enlace (de espías).
courlan ['kʊrlən, B 'kʊələn] *s.* (orn.) carrao, caraú.
course [kɔrs, B kɔs] *s.* 1. curso, paso; transcurso, marcha. 2. dirección, rumbo. 3. punto, rumbo (de la brújula). 4. camino, vía, ruta, recorrido, trayectoria. 5. pista (esp. de hipódromo, velódromo, etc.); campo (de golf). 6. corriente (de agua); conducto (de agua). 7. plato (de una comida). 8. proceder, procedimiento; (línea de) conducta. 9. curso, asignatura (de estudios). 10. (mar.) vela baja. 11. (aer.) rumbo, derrota, derrotero. 12. (arq.) mampuesta, hilada (de ladrillos, piedras, cemento, etc.). 13. (min.) galería. 14. **by c. of,** por el procedimeinto regular de (la ley, etc.); **in due c.,** a su debido tiempo; **in the c. of,** en el transcurso de; durante; **(a) matter of c.,** cosa común, cosa corriente, cosa de cajón; **of c.,** por supuesto, desde luego, naturalmente; claro, ya lo creo; **the last c.,** el postre (en una comida); **to change c.,** cambiar de rumbo; **to hold one's c.,** mantener el rumbo; **to take its c.,** seguir su curso (cosa, evento, etc.). —*v.t.* 1. cazar con perros; poner (perros) a la caza. 2. recorrer, atravesar. 3. perseguir, pisar los talones. —*v.i.* correr, seguir su curso.
course light, (aer.) faro o luz de ruta.
courser ['kɔrsər, B 'kɔsə] *s.* 1. cazador. 2. perro de caza. 3. (poét.) corcel, caballo ligero. 4. (orn.) ave corredora, avefría.
coursing [-sɪŋ] *s.* 1. cacería, caza de liebres. 2. (min.) ventilación.
court [kɔrt, B kɔt] *s.* 1. corte (de un rey, soberano, etc.). 2. corte, comitiva, séquito, cortejo. 3. patio, atrio. 4. callejuela, plazuela, plazoleta. 5. cortejo, galanteo; cortesía, homenaje, ej., *to pay c. to,* galantear, cortejar; adular, lisonjear; rendir homenaje a. 6. tribunal, juzgado, corte (Am.); juez, audiencia; sala de justicia. 7. (dep.) pista, campo. 8. **in open c.,** ante el tribunal en pleno, en audiencia pública; **out of c.,** fuera de consideración; (der.) fuera de litigio, extrajudicialmente; inadmisible; **to go to c.,** acudir a los tribunales. —*v.t.* 1. hacer la corte a, cortejar, galantear, enamorar. 2. engatusar, adular. 3. buscar, solicitar, procurar (favor, oportunidad, etc.). 4. buscar, provocar (aplauso, etc.). 5. (con *into, to*) inducir, incitar (a). 6. arriesgar, exponerse a (desastre, muerte, irrisión, etc.). —*v.i.* hacer la corte, cortejar.
court card, figura (sota, caballo o rey en los naipes).
court day, (der.) día hábil; día en que se reúne el tribunal.
courteous ['kɜrtɪəs, B 'kɜtjəs] *a.* cortés, atento, comedido.
courteously [-lɪ] *adv.* cortésmente.
courteousness [-nəs] *s.* cortesía, comedimiento, urbanidad.
courtesan ['kɔrtəzən, B ˌkɔtɪ'zæn] *s.* cortesana.
courtesy ['kɜrtəsɪ, B 'kɜt-] *s.* 1. cortesía, urbanidad, cortesanía. 2. finura. 3. gracia, reverencia, merced, favor. 4. **by c.,** por cortesía.
courtesy call, visita de cumplido, visita de cortesía.
courtesy light, (aut.) luz interior.
courtesy title, título de cortesía.
court hand, (hist.) caligrafía, letra de curia (que se usaba en documentos oficiales), letra gótica.
courthouse ['kɔrtˌhaʊs, B 'kɔt-] *s.* 1. palacio de justicia, edificio de los tribunales. 2. (E.U.) sede o asiento del tribunal; capital de distrito.
courtier ['kɔrtɪər, B 'kɔtjə] *s.* 1. cortesano, palaciego. 2. lisonjero, adulador, galante, obsequioso.
courtliness [-lɪnəs] *s.* 1. cortesanía, urbanidad; elegancia. 2. obsequiosidad.
courtly [-lɪ] *a.* 1. cortesano; elegante. 2. obsequioso, lisonjero, adulón. —*adv.* cortesanamente; cortésmente, galantemente.
courtly love, amor cortesano, amor cortés.
court-martial ['kɔrtˌmɑrʃəl, B 'kɔt'mɑʃəl] *s.* (*pl.* COURTS-MARTIAL O COURT-MARTIALS) consejo de guerra, tribunal militar. —*v.t.* (*pret., p.p.* COURT-MARTIALED O COURT-MARTIALLED ; *p.pr.* COURT-MARTIALING O COURT-MARTIALLING) procesar en consejo de guerra.
Court of Appeals, tribunal de apelación, sala de apelaciones.
Court of Claims, (E.U.) tribunal que investiga las demandas contra el gobierno.
Court of Inquiry, tribunal convocado para investigar y presentar un informe acerca de alguna cuestión militar.
court of justice, sala de justicia.
court of last resort, tribunal de última instancia.

court of probate, tribunal testamentario, corte de sucesiones.
court order, orden judicial.
court plaster, esparadrapo, tafetán inglés.
courtroom [-ˌrum, -ˌrʊm] *s.* sala de tribunal.
courtship [-ˌʃɪp] *s.* 1. corte (*f.*), cortejeo, galanteo, enamoramiento, galantería. 2. (ant.) cortesanía, cortesía.
courtyard [-ˌjɑrd, B -ˌjɑd] *s.* patio, atrio; corral.
couscous ['kuskus] *s.* plato del norte de África hecho de trigo molido, legumbres y carne.
cousin ['kʌzən] *s.* primo, prima; **first c.,** primo hermano o carnal; **second c.,** primo segundo.
cousin-german [ˌkʌzən'dʒɜrmən, B -'dʒɜmən] *s.* (*pl.* COUSINS-GERMAN) primo hermano o carnal, prima hermana.
cousinhood ['kʌzənˌhʊd] **cousinship** [-ˌʃɪp] *s.* primazgo, parentesco de primo o prima.
couth [kuθ] *a.* pulido, mundano.
couture [ku'tʊr, B 'tʊə] *s.* (fr.) costura, arte de diseñar ropa femenina.
couturier [-ɪər, -ɪˌeɪ, B -ˌtʊr'jɛə] *s.* (fr.) costurero, diseñador, el que diseña y confecciona ropa femenina.
couvade [ku'vɑd] *s.* (antrop.) covada.
covalence [koʊ'veɪləns] **covalency** [-lənsɪ] *s.* (quím.) covalencia.
covalent [-lənt] *a.* covalente.
covalent bond, (quím.) enlace covalente.
covariant [koʊ'vɛrɪənt, -'vær-, B -'vɛər-] *a.* (mat.) covariante.
cove [koʊv] *s.* 1. abra, ancón, caleta, cala, ensenada. 2. pequeño valle al costado de una montaña. 3. (arq.) bovedilla, moldura cóncava. —*v.t.* abovedar, arquear.
cove *s.* (jer. G.B.) tío, sujeto, tipo (Am.) ej., *a queer c.,* tipo raro, sujeto excéntrico.
coven ['kʌvən] *s.* reunión, mitin (esp. de brujas).
covenant ['kʌvənənt] *s.* 1. contrato, acuerdo, convenio, pacto. 2. (bíbl.) alianza; promisión. —*v.t., v.i.* convenir, pactar, estipular; hacer acuerdo formal; prometer.
covenantee [ˌkʌvəˌnæn'ti] *s.* contratante, pactante; garantizado.
covenanter ['kʌvəˌnæntər, B -nəntə] *s.* 1. contratante, pactante. 2. **C.,** (hist.) firmante del pacto escocés de la reforma religiosa.
covenantor [-ər, B -ə] *s.* obligado, garantizador, el que debe cumplir lo estipulado en un pacto.
Coventry ['kʌvəntrɪ, 'kɑv-, B 'kɔv-] *s.* (fig.) estado de ostracismo; **to send (someone) to C.,** rehusar asociarse con (alguien).
cover ['kʌvər, B -ə] *v.t.* 1. cubrir, tapar. 2. cubrir, vestir, revestir; cubrirse (la cabeza); forrar (un libro, etc.). 3. (fig.) cubrir, investir (de gloria, etc.). 4. cubrir, fecundar (animal). 5. empollar, incubar (huevos). 6. cubrir, comprender, incluir, abarcar, abrazar; ocupar. 7. proteger, amparar; cobijar; vigilar. 8. (gen. con *up*) disimular, ocultar (sentimientos, etc.); encubrir (delitos, etc.). 9. copar, igualar (apuesta, banca, etc. en el juego). 10. apuntar (arma de fuego) contra (alguien). 11. (mil.) cubrir (flanco, retirada, etc.); dominar (terreno, estrecho, etc.). 12. (com.) cubrir, asegurar, proteger contra (riesgo); cubrir (deuda, cheque, etc.); compensar, indemnizar. 13. recorrer, atravesar, andar (distancias, etc.). 14. (periodismo) informar, hacer un reportaje. 15. **c. over,** cubrir por completo; **c. up one's tracks,** no dejar huellas; **c. up,** cubrir por completo; disimular, encubrir. —*v.i.* cubrir; **c. for,** reemplazar, substituir; **c. up for (a friend,** etc.), servir de pantalla a, ocultar la verdad para proteger a (un amigo, etc.). —*s.* 1. cubierta, tapa; cobertor (de cama), colcha. 2. cubierto, techo; refugio, escondite; escondrijo, guarida. 3. amparo, protección. 4. pretexto, excusa. 5. envoltura, cubierta, sobre (postal). 6. cubierto (de mesa). 7. funda, forro; portada (de una revista, etc.). 8. **to break c.,** salir al aire libre, salir a campo raso, salir del escondite; **to take c.,** ocultarse, ponerse a cubierto; **under c.,** bajo techo; a cubierto; escondido; protegido; **under c. of,** al abrigo de, so pretexto de; **under separate c.,** por correo aparte.
coverage ['kʌvərɪdʒ] *s.* 1. alcance. 2. circulación (de un periódico, etc.). 3. reportaje. 4. (rad., t.v.) cobertura. 5. (fin.) respaldo (de dinero en circulación); fondos (de un cheque, etc.). 6. (seguros) cobertura, extensión de una póliza. 7. (fig.) protección, amparo.
coveralls ['kʌvərˌɔlz] *s. pl.* mono, traje de faena, overol.
cover charge, precio del cubierto (en restaurantes, centros nocturnos, etc.).
cover crop, (agr.) siembra de abono, siembra de protección.
covered wagon, (E.U.) galera, carromato, carro con toldo.
cover girl, modelo (cuya fotografía aparece en la portada de una revista).
covering ['kʌvərɪŋ] *s.* cubierta, envoltura, cobija; pelaje; ropa, abrigo.
covering action, (mil.) misión de cobertura.
covering fire, (mil.) fuego de protección.
covering letter, carta acompañante, carta explicatoria.
coverlet ['kʌvərlət, B -ələt] *s.* colcha, sobrecama, cubrecama.
coversed sine ['koʊˌvɜrst-, B -ˌvɜst-] (trig.) coseno-verso.
covert ['kʌvərt, 'koʊ-, B 'kʌvət] *a.* 1. secreto, furtivo; disimulado. 2. abrigado, protegido, amparado (del viento, etc.). 3. (der.) casada y bajo la protección del marido (mujer). —*s.* 1. refugio, amparo, cubierta, abrigo. 2. espesura, guarida. 3. (orn.) tectriz, bobija. 4. tela asargada e impregnada.
covertly [-lɪ] *adv.* secretamente, furtivamente; disimuladamente, en secreto.
coverture ['kʌvərˌtʃʊr, -tʃər, B -ətjʊə] *s.* 1. cubierta, abrigo, refugio. 2. (der.) estado de casada (de la mujer).
cover-up ['kʌvərˌʌp] *s.* (jer.) coartada; encubrimiento.
covet ['kʌvət] *v.t.* codiciar, desear, ambicionar; envidiar, desear lo ajeno. —*v.i.* sentir deseo o codicia.
coveter [-ər, B -ə] *s.* codicioso.
covetous [-əs] *a.* codicioso, ambicioso, avariento.
covetously [-lɪ] *adv.* codiciosamente, avariciosamente.
covetousness [-nəs] *s.* codicia, avidez, ambición, avaricia.
covey ['kʌvɪ] *s.* 1. pollada, nidada; bandada. 2. grupo; montón.
cow [kaʊ] *s.* 1. vaca. 2. hembra (de algunos animales). 3. (jer.) mujer obesa y desaliñada. 4. **to wait till the cows come home,** esperar interminablemente. —*v.t.* acobardar, amedrentar, intimidar, atemorizar.
coward ['kaʊəd, B -əd] *s.* cobarde.
cowardice [-əs] *s.* cobardía.
cowardliness [-lɪnəs] *s.* carácter o naturaleza cobarde.
cowardly [-lɪ] *a.* cobarde, propio de un cobarde; llamón (Mex.). —*adv.* cobardemente.
cowbane ['kaʊˌbeɪn] *s.* (bot.) cicuta.
cowbell [-ˌbɛl] *s.* cencerro, esquila.
cowberry [-ˌbɛrɪ] *s.* (bot.) arándano rojo.
cowbird [-ˌbɜrd, B -ˌbɜd] *s.* (orn.) garrapatero.
cowboy [-ˌbɔɪ] *s.* (E.U.) vaquero, gaucho, jinete ganadero.
cowcatcher [-ˌkætʃər, -ˌkɛtʃ-, B -ˌkætʃə] *s.* (E.U.) rastrillo, trompa, quitapiedras (en la delantera de una locomotora), guardarrieles.
cower ['kaʊər, B -ə] *v.i.* 1. agacharse, agazaparse. 2. encogerse (de miedo o frío), alebrarse.
cowfish ['kaʊˌfɪʃ] *s.* 1. (ict.) (pez) cofre, variedad de delfín. 2. (zool.) manatí.
cowgirl [-ˌgɜrl, B -ˌgɜl] *s.* vaquera.
cowhand [-ˌhænd] *s.* vaquero.
cowherd [-ˌhɜrd, B -ˌhɜd] *s.* pastor de vacas, vaquero.
cowhide [-ˌhaɪd] *s.* 1. cuero o piel de vaca. 2. látigo de cuero, zurriago, penca. —*v.t.* azotar, zurriagar.
cowhiding [-ɪŋ] *s.* azotaina, cueriza, zurra.
cowl [kaʊl] *s.* 1. cogulla (de monje); capucha, capuz. 2. sombrerete (de chimenea). 3. (aut.) capó, cubretablero, bóveda del tablero. 4. (aer.) capota, cubierta del motor de un avión. —*v.t.* poner cogulla a, encapuchar.
cowled [kaʊld] *a.* 1. encapuchado. 2. (bot.) cuculifoliado, cuculiforme. 3. (zool.) cuculiforme.
cowlick ['kaʊˌlɪk] *s.* remolino, mechón de pelo (que cae sobre la frente).
cowling ['kaʊlɪŋ] *s.* (aer.) capota, cubierta del motor de un avión.
cowman ['kaʊmən] *s.* 1. ganadero, hacendado. 2. vaquero, pastor de ganado (vacuno).
co-worker ['koʊˌwɜrkər, B -ˌwɜkə] *s.* coadjutor, colaborador, compañero de trabajo.
cowpea ['kaʊˌpi] *s.* 1. (bot.) caupí. 2. semilla de caupí (especie de garbanzo).
Cowper's gland ['kaʊpərz-, 'ku-, B -pəz-] (anat.) glándula de Cowper.
cowpoke ['kaʊˌpoʊk] *s.* (fam., E.U.) vaquero.
cow pony, caballo adiestrado para reunir o encerrar el ganado.
cowpox [-ˌpɑks, B -ˌpɔks] *s.* (med.) vacuna.
cowpuncher [-ˌpʌntʃər, B -tʃə] *s.* (fam., E.U.) vaquero.
cowrie, cowry ['kaʊrɪ] *s.* 1. cauri. 2. ciprea o porcelana (molusco).
cow shark, tiburón gris.
cowshed ['kaʊˌʃɛd] *s.* establo para vacas.
cowslip [-ˌslɪp] *s.* (bot.) prímula, primavera, vellorita.
cox [kɑks, B kɔks] *s.* (fam.) timonel. —*v.t., v.i.* actuar como timonel.
coxa ['kɑksə, B 'kɔk-] *s.* (*pl.* COXAE [-ˌsi]) (anat.) cadera; hueso coxal.
coxal [-səl] *a.* (anat.) coxal, de la cadera.
coxalgia [kɑk'sældʒɪə, B kɔk-] *s.* (med.) coxalgia.
coxalgic [-dʒɪk] *a.* coxálgico.
coxcomb ['kɑksˌkoʊm, B 'kɔks-] *s.* 1. fanfarrón, jactancioso, farfante. 2. (ant.) gorro de bufón.
coxcombical [kɑks'koʊmɪkəl, B kɔks-] *a.* fanfarrón, fachendoso; presumido, fatuo.
coxcombry ['kɑksˌkoʊmrɪ, B 'kɔks-] *s.* fanfarronería, presunción, fachenda; jactancia.
coxswain ['kɑksən, -ˌsweɪn, B 'kɔk-] *s.* 1. (mar.) patrón de bote o lancha, batelero. 2. timonel (de bote de remo).
coy [kɔɪ] *a.* 1. reservado, tímido, esquivo, modesto. 2. gazmoño, afectado. 3. evasivo.
coyly ['kɔɪlɪ] *adv.* 1. tímidamente. 2. afectadamente. 3. evasivamente.
coyness [-nəs] *s.* 1. modestia, timidez. 2. afectación, gazmoñería. 3. esquivez.
coyote ['kaɪˌoʊt, kaɪ'oʊtɪ, B 'kɔɪoʊt] *s.* (zool.) coyote.

coypu ['kɔɪpu] *s.* (zool.) coipo (roedor sudamericano parecido a la nutria).
coz [kʌz] *s.* (fam.) primo, prima.
cozen ['kʌzən] *v.t.* engañar, defraudar, trampear.
cozenage [-ɪdʒ] *s.* trampa, fraude, engaño, superchería.
cozener [-ər, B -ə] *s.* engañador, defraudador, embaucador.
cozily ['koʊzəlɪ] *adv.* cómodamente, amenamente, acogedoramente.
coziness [-zɪnəs] *s.* comodidad, amenidad; intimidad.
cozy ['koʊzɪ] *a.* (COZIER; COZIEST) 1. cómodo, acogedor, agradable. 2. íntimo, afable, sociable. 3. **to play it c.,** (jer.) actuar cautelosamente. — **to c. up to,** (fam.) tratar de caerle bien (a alguien); tratar de trabar amistad. —*s. pl.* (COZIES) cubierta tejida de una tetera (para mantener el té caliente).
CP *abrev. de* 1. **Communist Party,** Partido Comunista. 2. **Command Post,** comandancia.
CPA *abrev. de* **certified public accountant,** contador público.
Cpl. *abrev. de* **Corporal,** cabo.
cpm *abrev. de* **cycles per minute,** ciclos por minuto (cpm).
CPO *abrev. de* **Chief Petty Officer,** contramaestre.
cps *abrev. de* **cycles per second,** ciclos por segundo (cps).
cr. *abrev. de* **credit,** crédito.
Cr *símb. de* **chromium,** cromio (Cr).
craal, *var. de* **kraal.**
crab [kræb] *s.* 1. (zool.) cangrejo, cámbaro, jaiba. 2. (mec.) grúa, cabria. 3. (astr.) **C.,** Cáncer. 4. (aer.) derrape. 5. **to catch a c.,** hundir demasiado el remo, o no tocar con él en el agua. —*v.t.* (*pret., p.p.* CRABBED; *p.pr.* CRABBING) (aer.) hacer derrapar (un avión). —*v.i.* 1. (aer.) derrapar. 2. correr oblicuamente. 3. pescar cangrejos.
crab, *s.* (fam.) gruñón, cascarrabias. —*v.t.* 1. avinagrar, agriar, exasperar. 2. (fam.) criticar, censurar; reprender. 3. (fam.) estropear, arruinar, frustrar. —*v.i.* (fam.) refunfuñar, rezongar, quejarse; regañar.
crab apple, 1. (bot.) manzano silvestre, maguillo, maíllo. 2. manzana silvestre, maílla.
crabbed ['kræbəd] *a.* 1. avinagrado, áspero, huraño, agrio, ceñudo, hosco. 2. intrincado, enredado, complicado (escritura, letras, texto).
crabber [-ər, B -ə] *s.* 1. pescador de cangrejos, cangrejero. 2. bote para pescar cangrejos. 3. (fam.) regañón, cascarrabias.
crabbily [-əlɪ] *adv.* malhumoradamente, gruñonamente.
crabbiness [-ɪnəs] *s.* mal genio, malhumor, gruñonería.
crabby ['kræbɪ] *a.* (CRABBIER; CRABBIEST) malhumorado, de mal genio, quejumbroso, gruñón.
crab grass, (bot.) garranchuelo, yerba mala gramínea.
crab louse, (ento.) ladilla, piojo del pubis.
crab's eyes, ojos de cangrejo (piedrezuelas calcáreas que crían interiormente los cangrejos).
crabstick ['kræbˌstɪk] *s.* 1. garrote, porra, bastón de manzano silvestre. 2. (ant.) regañón, tipo quejumbroso.
crab tree, (bot.) manzano silvestre.
crack [kræk] *v.i.* 1. romperse, partirse, abrirse. 2. rajarse, resquebrajarse, agrietarse, cuartearse. 3. estallar, restallar, crujir. 4. cascarse, quebrarse (la voz). 5. avanzar a toda vela, correr a todo vapor; correr velozmente. 6. (gen. con *up*) ceder, rendirse, darse por vencido; fallar; debilitarse, ceder a las emociones, perder el control (sobre sí). 7. volverse loco, enloquecer. 8. fraccionarse, descomponerse (petróleo, aceites). 9. (esco., N. de Ingl.) charlar, parlotear; chismear. 10. **at a cracking pace,** a todo correr; a un ritmo veloz; **c. down (on),** (fam. E.U.) tomar medidas enérgicas (contra); reprimir drásticamente; actuar con dureza; **c. up,** estrellarse, destrozarse, hacerse pedazos; reírse ruidosamente; (fig.) descomponerse; enloquecer; perder la razón; **get cracking!** (jer.) ¡muévete! ¡manos a la obra! —*v.t.* 1. romper, partir. 2. rajar, resquebrajar, agrietar. 3. pegar, golpear. 4. abrir, destapar (una botella para beber); abrir, estudiar (un libro). 5. resolver (problema), explicar (misterio), descifrar (código). 6. derribar, vencer (una barrera). 7. robar, ej., *c. a safe,* robar una caja fuerte (abriéndola). 8. trastornar, estorbar (calma, etc.); enloquecer. 9. craquear, fraccionar (petróleo, aceites). 10. **c. a joke,** gastar una broma o chiste; **c. a smile,** sonreír; **c. a whip,** chasquear un látigo; **c. up,** destrozar, hacer pedazos; arruinar; elogiar, pintar, ej., *it's not what it's cracked up to be,* no es (tan bueno) como lo pintan. —*s.* 1. ruptura, hendedura, grieta, raja, rajadura, resquebrajadura, cuarteadura. 2. chasquido, traquido, estallido, crujido; estrépito, estruendo, trueno. 3. gallo (de la voz). 4. instante, momento, ej., *in a c.,* en un instante. 5. golpe fuerte. 6. intento, ensayo. 7. agudeza, sutileza; sarcasmo, réplica insolente, insolencia. 8. robo, escalamiento (de una casa). 9. campeón, jugador excelente. 10. chiflado, tipo raro. 11. (pr. dial., G.B.) murmuración, chismeo. 12. (*drug*) cocaína dura. 13. **at the c. of dawn,** al romper el alba; **c. of doom,** día del Juicio Final; **dirty c.,** observación o comentario maligno; **to take a c. at,** asestar un golpe a, pegar; probar, ensayar. —*a.* excelente, superior, de primera.
crackajack ['krækəˌdʒæk] *a. var. de* **crackerjack.**
crackbrain ['krækˌbreɪn] *s.* chiflado, mentecato.
crackbrained [-'breɪnd] *a.* alocado, mentecato, chiflado.
crackdown [-ˌdaʊn] *s.* medidas enérgicas, castigo violento.
cracked [krækt] *a.* 1. cuarteado, agrietado. 2. chiflado, loco.
cracker ['krækər, B -ə] *s.* 1. galleta, galletita. 2. petardo, triquitraque; bombón sorpresa. 3. cascanueces. 4. (S. de E.U., gen. despec.) blanco pobre; **C.,** natural de Florida o Georgia.
crackerbarrel [-ˌbærəl] *a.* (fam.) parecido a o característico de una discusión informal en una hostería.
crackerjack [-ˌdʒæk] *a.* (jer., E.U.) excelente, superior, de marca mayor, de primera. —*s.* cosa excelente; persona habilísima, campeón.
Cracker Jack (TM), Cracker Jack (dulce).
crackers ['krækərz, B -əz] *a.* (jer., G.B.) loco, chiflado, turulato.
crack house, casa donde venden la cocaína dura.
cracking ['krækɪŋ] *a.* (fam.) extraordinario, grande. —*adv.* muy, sumamente.
cracking, *s.* (quím.) craqueo, fraccionamiento.
cracking distillation, destilación pirogénica.
crackle ['krækəl] *v.i.* crepitar, crujir, chisporrotear. —*v.t.* estrujar (papeles, etc.). —*s.* 1. crepitación, crujido, chisporroteo. 2. (pint.) grieta, raja.
crackleware [-ˌwɛr, B -ˌwɛə] *s.* artículos (de alfarería, porcelana, vidrio, etc.) de superficie estriada o agrietada.
crackling ['kræklɪŋ] *s.* 1. crepitación, chisporroteo, crujido. 2. (*gen. pl.*) chicharrón de pellejo, chicharrón. —*a.* crepitante, chisporroteante, crujiente.
crackly [-lɪ] *a.* crepitante; quebradizo, frágil.
cracknel [-nəl] *s.* 1. galleta dura, rosca quebradiza. 2. (*gen. pl.*) chicharrón.
crackpot ['krækˌpɑt, B -ˌpɔt] *s.* (fam.) chiflado, destornillado. —*a.* (fam.) alocado, chiflado, excéntrico.
cracksman ['kræksmən] *s.* 1. (fam.) ladrón, escalador. 2. ladrón de cajas fuertes.
crackup ['krækˌʌp] *s.* 1. (fam.) colapso (físico o mental); fracaso. 2. colisión, choque.
cracky ['krækɪ] *interj.* (reg., E.U.) gen. usado en la frase **by cracky!** ¡ caracoles! ¡caramba!
cradle ['kreɪdəl] *s.* 1. cuna. 2. (fig.) infancia, niñez. 3. (fig.) cuna, origen. 4. (mec.) soporte, cuna, apoyo, cama. 5. gancho, horquilla (de teléfono). 6. armadura (de guadaña). 7. (mar.) basada, cuna (de botadura). 8. (med.) tablilla (para componer fracturas), arco de protección. 9. (min.) artesa oscilante (para lavar oro). 10. (const.) plataforma colgante. 11. (aer.) soporte (de aeronave en construcción). 12. **from the c.,** desde la cuna; **to rob the c.,** (fam.) tener un(a) esposo(a) o novio(a) más joven que uno mismo. —*v.t.* 1. acunar, mecer. 2. meter en la cuna. 3. abrigar, proteger. 4. segar con guadaña armada. 5. (min.) lavar (oro) con artesa oscilante. —*v.t.* mecer en la cuna; segar con guadaña gavilladora.
cradle car, vagoneta basculante, carro decauville.
cradle scythe, guadaña con armadura, guadaña agavilladora.
cradle snatcher, cradle robber, (fam.) persona que se casa con o que corteja a alguien de menor edad.
cradlesong [-ˌsɔŋ] *s.* canción de cuna, arrullo.
craft [kræft, B krɑft] *s.* 1. arte, habilidad, destreza, pericia. 2. oficio, trabajo manual, ocupación. 3. gremio. 4. astucia, maña, artimaña, artificio. 5. (*pl.* **craft**) nave, embarcación, barco, vehículo (marítimo o aéreo); aeronave. 6. **the C.,** la masonería.
craftily ['kræftəlɪ, B 'krɑf-] *adv.* astutamente, mañosamente, artificiosamente.
craftiness [-tɪnəs] *s.* astucia, artificio, maña.
craftsman ['kræftsmən, B 'krɑfts-] *s.* artesano; artífice.
craftsmanship [-ˌʃɪp] *s.* 1. artesanía; habilidad, destreza (de alguien). 2. ejecución, acabado, artificio (de algo); mano de obra.
craft union, gremio de artesanos de un mismo oficio.
crafty ['kræftɪ, B 'krɑf-] *a.* (CRAFTIER; CRAFTIEST) 1. astuto, taimado, artificioso, ladino, mañoso. 2. (pr. dial., G.B.) diestro, hábil.
crag [kræg] *s.* despeñadero, risco, peñasco escarpado.
cragged ['krægəd] *a.* escabroso, peñascoso, escarpado, fragoso.
cragginess [-ɪnəs] *s.* escabrosidad, aspereza, fragosidad.
craggy [-ɪ] *a.* escabroso, peñascoso, escarpado, fragoso.
cragsman ['krægzmən] *s.* escalador experto (de despeñaderos o peñascos).
crake [kreɪk] *s.* (orn.) rascón, rey de codornices.
cram [kræm] *v.t.* (*pret., p.p.* CRAMMED ; *p.pr.* CRAMMING) 1. rellenar, atestar, embutir (un baúl, un cajón, etc.); (fig.) llenar, cargar (la cabeza con información o datos). 2. embaular (ropa en canasta, etc.), meter (ej., dinero en el bolsillo). 3. embocar, engullir (la comida); atracar (a alguien de comida). 4. preparar (a un estudiante) o repasar apresuradamente (para un examen). 5. **c. down one's throat,** (fig.) reiterarle (mentiras, etc.) a uno porfiadamente. —*v.i.* 1. embutirse la comida, hartarse, atracarse. 2. empollar, estudiar

o prepararse apresuradamente (para un examen), aprender a la carrera. —*s.* 1. apretura, apretón (de gente). 2. estudio o repaso apresurado (para un examen).

crambo ['kræmbou] *s.* (*pl.* CRAMBOES) 1. juego de salón en el que hay que encontrar consonante a una palabra. 2. (despec.) rima cursi.

crammer ['kræmər, B -ə] *s.* 1. (mec.) comprimidor, apretador. 2. (fam.) mentiroso; engaño.

cramoisy, cramoisie ['kræm,ɔɪzɪ] *a.* (ant.) carmesí. —*s.* (ant.) tela color carmesí.

cramp [kræmp] *s.* 1. calambre, rampa. 2. (*gen. pl.*) calambre abdominal, retortijón. 3. grapa, grapón, laña. 4. (carp.) cárcel, corchete. 5. (fig.) traba, restricción. —*v.t.* 1. dar calambre a, entorpecer (los músculos, etc.). 2. trabar; (fig.) entorpecer. 3. torcer, girar (ruedas de un vehículo estacionado). 4. engrapar. 5. **c. one's style,** (jer.) cortarle las alas a uno; molestarle a uno. —*v.i.* acalambrarse.

cramped [kræmpt] *a.* 1. estrecho, angosto, apretado, confinado, restringido. 2. indescifrable, ilegible (escritura, palabra).

crampfish ['kræmp,fɪʃ] *s.* (ict.) torpedo, tremielga.

crampon ['kræm,pɑn, B -pən] *s.* 1. (*gen. pl.*) (mec.) tenazas de garfios. 2. (*gen. pl.*) tacos (en la suela del calzado para andar sobre el hielo); trepadores, garfios de trepar.

crampoon [kræm'pun] *var. de* **crampon.**

cranage ['kreɪnɪdʒ] *s.* (const.) derechos de grúa.

cranberry ['kræn,bɛrɪ, B -bərɪ] *s.* (*pl.* CRANBERRIES) 1. (bot.) arándano, agrio, ráspano. 2. baya de arándano.

cranberry bush, (bot.) viburno.

cranch [krɑntʃ] *var. de* **craunch.**

crane [kreɪn] *s.* 1. (orn.) grulla. 2. (mec.) grúa, cabria. 3. cigüeña, aguilón (de chimenea). 4. (cine, t.v.) jirafa (para sostener cámara o micrófono). 5. (mar.) pescante; arbotante; abanico. 6. sifón (para sacar licor de una vasija). —*v.t.* 1. levantar con grúa. 2. estirar, extender (el cuello). —*v.i.* estirarse el cuello (para ver mejor).

crane boom, aguilón o pluma de grúa.

crane derrick, grúa giratoria con aguilón horizontal y trole corredizo.

crane fly, (ento.) (especie de) típula, zancudo.

crane girder, viga portagrúa.

craneman ['kreɪnmən] *s.* maquinista de grúa.

cranesbill ['kreɪnz,bɪl] *s.* (bot.) geranio.

craneway ['kreɪn,weɪ] *s.* carrilera de grúa.

cranial ['kreɪnɪəl] *a.* craneal, craneano, craniano.

cranial index, (anat.) índice cefálico.

cranial nerve, (anat.) nervio craneal.

craniate ['kreɪnɪət, B -,eɪt] *a., s.* (zool.) craniado.

craniological [,kreɪnɪə'lɑdʒɪkəl, B -'lɔdʒ-] *a.* craneológico.

craniologist [-'ɑlədʒəst, B -'ɔi-] *s.* craneólogo.

craniology [-dʒɪ] *s.* craneología, estudio científico de las características del cráneo.

craniometer [-'ɑmətər, B -'ɔmɪtə] *s.* craneómetro, instrumento para medir el cráneo.

craniometric [-ə'mɛtrɪk] *a.* craneométrico.

craniometry [-'ɑmətrɪ, B -'ɔm-] *s.* craneometría.

craniosacral [-ou'sækrəl, -'seɪ-, B -'seɪ-] *a.* 1. relativo al cráneo y al sacro. 2. parasimpático.

cranioscopy [-'ɑskəpɪ, B -'ɔs-] *s.* craneoscopia.

craniotomy [-'ɑtəmɪ, B -'ɔt-] *s.* (med.) craneotomía; perforación del cráneo.

cranium ['kreɪnɪəm] *s.* (*pl.* CRANIUMS O CRANIA [-nɪə]) (anat.) cráneo.

crank [kræŋk] *s.* 1. manivela, manubrio, manija. 2. (mec.) cigüeña; codo. 3. capricho, antojo, chifladura. 4. maniático, extravagante, chiflado. 5. gruñón, cascarrabias. —*v.t.* 1. acodillar. 2. dar vueltas (al cigüeñal) con la manivela, hacer arrancar (el motor). —*v.i.* girar la manivela. —*a.* 1. flojo, descompuesto (aparato, máquina, etc.). 2. (mar.) celoso (barco).

crank arm, (mot.) manivela, brazo del cigüeñal.

crank axle, (mot.) eje acodado, cigüeñal.

crank brace, berbiquí.

crankcase ['kræŋk,keɪs] *s.* (mot.) cárter del cigüeñal.

crank handle, (aut.) manivela de arranque.

crankily ['kræŋkəlɪ] *adv.* 1. caprichosamente, excéntricamente. 2. irritablemente.

crankiness [-kɪnəs] *s.* 1. irritabilidad, mal humor. 2. calidad de caprichoso, excentricidad. 3. chifladura.

crankle ['kræŋkəl] *v.t., v.i.* (ant.) encorvar, doblar, zigzaguear, serpentear.

crankless engine ['kræŋkləs-] motor sin cigüeñales.

crankpin ['kræŋk,pɪn] *s.* (mot.) gorrón de manivela, muñón o muñequilla del cigüeñal, clavija de la cigüeña.

crank pit, (mec.) pozo de cigüeña.

crankshaft [-,ʃæft, B -,ʃɑft] *s.* (mot.) cigüeñal.

crankshaft gear, (mot.) engranaje del cigüeñal, piñón del cigüeñal.

crank windlass, (mec.) cabria de manivela.

cranky ['kræŋkɪ] *a.* (CRANKIER; CRANKIEST) 1. caprichoso, excéntrico; chiflado, lunático, maniático. 2. irritable, malhumorado. 3. (raro) tortuoso, torcido, sinuoso (camino, etc.). 4. defectuoso, en mal estado, de mal funcionamiento. 5. (mar.) celoso (barco).

crannied ['krænid] *a.* grietoso, hendido.

cranny [-ɪ] *s.* abertura, raja, hendidura, grieta.

crap [kræp] *s.* 1. tiro perdedor (en juego de dados). 2. (jer., vulg.) insensatez, disparate; mentiras, exageración. 3. mercadería de inferior calidad, cosa baladí, basura; (vulg.) mierda. —*v.i.* (*pret., p.p.* CRAPPED ; *p.pr.* CRAPPING) 1. tirar dados. 2. (gen. con *out*) pasarse (en el juego de dados). 3. (vulg.) cagar.

crape [kreɪp] *s.* 1. crespón. 2. crespón de luto, paño de luto (en sombrero o brazo). —*v.t.* cubrir con crespón, vestir de luto.

crape fish ['kreɪp,fɪʃ] *s.* bacalao seco.

crapehanger, *var. de* **crepehanger.**

crappie ['kræpɪ] *s.* (ict.) pomosio.

craps [kræps] *s. pl.* (*pl. en const.*) juego de dados; **to shoot c.,** jugar a los dados, tirar los dados.

crapshooter ['kræp,ʃutər, B -ə] *s.* jugador de dados.

crapulence ['kræpjələns] *s.* crápula.

crapulent [-lənt] *a.* crapuloso.

crapulous [-ləs] *a.* crapuloso.

crash [kræʃ] *v.t.* 1. romper, hacer pedazos. 2. estrellar. 3. (fam.) entrar, colarse o asistir sin ser invitado, ej., *c. a party,* colarse a una fiesta (sin ser invitado). 4. invadir, irrumpir en. 5. **c. one's way through,** abrirse paso violentamente; **c. a pad,** (jer., E.U.) quedarse a dormir en la casa de alguien. —*v.i.* 1. estallar, quebrar con estrépito. 2. detonar, dar un estampido. 3. derrumbarse. 4. (con *into*) estrellarse contra; entrar violentamente, irrumpir, bruscamente. 5. caer, estrellarse (avión). 6. (com.) quebrar. —*s.* 1. estallido, estampido, estrépito, fragor. 2. choque, colisión; caída (de un avión). 3. derrumbe; (com.) bancarrota, quiebra. 4. (tej.) cutí burdo (usado para vestidos de verano, cortinas, toallas). —*a.* (fam.) intensivo, de urgencia, ej., *a c. course,* un curso intensivo.

crash dive, descenso, sumersión rápida, sumergimiento de emergencia (de un avión, buzo, submarino).

crash-dive ['kræʃ'daɪv] *v.i.* (*pret., p.p.* CRASH-DIVED ; *p.pr.* CRASH-DIVING) sumergirse rápidamente (submarino).

crash helmet, casco protector (de motociclista, etc.).

crashing [-ɪŋ] *a.* 1. (fam.) completo, perfecto, ej., *he's a c. bore,* es un perfecto aburrido. 2. gran, rotundo, ej., *c. success,* gran éxito.

crash-land [-'lænd] *v.t., v.i.* (aer.) aterrizar de emergencia (dañando el avión).

crash landing, (aer.) aterrizaje de emergencia con o por avería.

crash pad, (jer., E.U.) apartamento, lugar donde dormir, gen. improvisado, ocasional o comunal, usado por los *hippies.*

crash program, programa o proyecto intensivo, de urgencia.

crasis ['kreɪsəs] *s.* (*pl.* CRASES [-,siz]) (gram.) crasis, contracción, sinalefa.

crass [kræs] *a.* 1. craso (error, disparate). 2. torpe, estúpido, insensato. 3. basto, tosco. 4. grueso, espeso.

crassly ['kræslɪ] *adv.* 1. crasamente. 2. torpemente, insensatamente.

crassness [-nəs] *s.* 1. enormidad (del error, etc.). 2. torpeza, tosquedad.

crassulaceous [,kræsjə'leɪʃəs] *a.* (bot.) crasuláceo.

crate [kreɪt] *s.* 1. embalaje de tablas, canasta, banasta, jaba (Am.), guacal o huacal. 2. (fam.) automóvil viejo. —*v.t.* embalar en banasta o jaba.

crater ['kreɪtər, B -ə] *s.* 1. cráter, boca de volcán. 2. (mil.) cráter (formado por una explosión). 3. (gen. **krater**) (arqueol.) crátera. 4. (astr.) Cráter, Copa.

C ration, (mil., E.U.) ración enlatada para campaña.

craunch [krɔntʃ, krɑntʃ] *v.t., v.i., var. de* **crunch.**

cravat [krə'væt] *s.* corbata, corbatín.

crave [kreɪv] *v.t.* 1. suplicar, implorar, pedir encarecidamente. 2. apetecer, anhelar, ansiar, desear vehementemente. —*v.i.* (gen. con *for*) sentir deseo vehemente (por), anhelar.

craven ['kreɪvən] *a.* acobardado, amilanado, temeroso. —*s.* cobarde, pusilánime. —*v.t.* (ant.) amilanar, acobardar, intimidar.

cravenly [-lɪ] *adv.* cobardemente, pusilánimemente.

cravenness [-nəs] *s.* cobardía, amilanamiento.

craving ['kreɪvɪŋ] *s.* antojo, ansia, anhelo, regosto.

craw [krɔ] *s.* buche.

crawfish ['krɔ,fɪʃ] *s.* 1. (zool.) cangrejo de río, ástaco. 2. (zool.) langostín, langostino. —*v.i.* (fam., E.U.) recular, retroceder, echarse atrás; **c. out of,** abandonar la costumbre de; eludir el deber de; faltar a lo prometido.

crawl [krɔl] *v.i.* 1. arrastrarse, reptar. 2. gatear, andar a gatas. 3. andar paso a paso, marchar a paso de tortuga. 4. arrastrarse, trepar (las plantas). 5. hormiguear; sentir hormigueo. 6. (fig.) arrastrarse, humillarse. 7. (dep.) nadar estilo crol. 8. **c. along,** avanzar paso a paso; **c. by,** pasar lentamente (ej., horas, minutos, etc.); **c. under,** meterse debajo de; **c. with,** estar repleto de; sentir un hormigueo causado por; ej., *his skin crawled with fear,* el miedo le hizo correr un hormigueo por la piel. —*v.t.* arrastrarse sobre. —*s.* 1. arrastramiento; paso lento. 2. (G.B.) ronda de las tabernas. 3. (natación) estilo crol.

4. corral, atajadizo (para encerrar peces, tortugas etc. en acuarios, ríos o en la orilla del mar).
crawler ['krɔlər, B -ə] *s.* 1. (t. **c. tractor**) tractor oruga. 2. oruga (de un tractor, tanque, etc.). 3. (G.B.) taxi desocupado (que se mueve lentamente en busca de pasajeros). 4. persona rastrera, servil. 5. reptil.
crawl space, espacio angosto que solamente permite el acceso de una sola persona.
crawly [-ɪ] *a.* (CRAWLIER; CRAWLIEST) (fam.) pavoroso, espeluznante, hormigueante.
crayfish ['kreɪˌfɪʃ] *s. var. de* **crawfish.**
crayon ['kreɪˌɑn, -ən, B -ɔn] *s.* 1. lápiz de color, creyón. 2. dibujo hecho a lápiz. —*v.t.* bosquejar o dibujar a lápiz o creyón.
craze [kreɪz] *v.t.* 1. enloquecer, enajenar. 2. cuartear, agrietar (el esmalte de la cerámica). —*s.* 1. manía, capricho; moda (pasajera); delirio, furor. 2. locura, demencia. 3. grieta menuda (en el esmalte de la cerámica, o en la superficie de pinturas).
crazily ['kreɪzəlɪ] *adv.* alocadamente, insensatamente.
craziness [-zɪnəs] *s.* locura, enajenación, insania, demencia; extravagancia.
crazy ['kreɪzɪ] *a.* (CRAZIER; CRAZIEST) 1. loco, enajenado, demente. 2. loco, fantástico, extravagante, absurdo (plan, gusto, etc.). 3. quebrantado; decrépito. 4. inclinado, torcido. 5. (jer., E.U.) nuevo; excelente; excitante; superior. 6. **to be c. about** (u **over**), estar loco por (algo o alguien).
crazy quilt, 1. (cost.) centón, manta hecha de gran número de piececitas de paño o tela de diversos colores y formas. 2. (fig.) chapucería, embrollo, maraña.
crazyweed [-ˌwid] *s.* (bot.) hierba mala, hierba venenosa.
creak [krik] *v.i.* crujir, rechinar, chirriar. —*s.* crujido, chirrido, rechinamiento.
creaky ['krikɪ] *a.* (CREAKIER; CREAKIEST) 1. crujiente, crujidero, chirriador. 2. decrépito.
cream [krim] *s.* 1. crema, nata (de la leche). 2. (fig.) crema, nata, flor, flor y nata. 3. crema (de licor). 4. crema, ej., *chocolate c.*, crema de chocolate. 5. crema (cosmética). 6. color crema. —*a.* cremoso, color crema. —*v.i.* 1. formarse crema; cubrirse de crema. 2. espumar. —*v.t.* 1. desnatar, sacar la nata de. 2. batir, hacer crema de (ej., mantequilla y azúcar). 3. añadir crema a (té, café, etc.), cubrir de crema (torta, manjar, etc.).
cream cheese, queso crema, queso de nata.
creamcups ['krimˌkʌps] *s. pl.* (*sing. o pl. en const.*) (bot.) especie de amapola o pamplina.
creamer ['krimər, B -ə] *s.* 1. jarrita para crema. 2. desnatadora.
creamery [-ərɪ] *s.* lechería, quesería, mantequería.
cream of tartar, (quím.) cremor tártaro.
cream puff, 1. bollo de crema. 2. (jer.) hombre o joven afeminado, marica. 3. (jer.) auto de uso en buenas condiciones.
cream sauce, salsa de crema.
creamy [-ɪ] *a.* (CREAMIER; CREAMIEST) cremoso.
crease [kris] *s.* 1. pliegue, doblez, arruga, plegadura, raya. 2. (dep.) línea de base (en criquet); círculo de portería (en hockey). —*v.t.* plegar, doblar, arrugar; (enc.) filetear. —*v.i.* arrugarse.
creaser ['krisər, B -ə] *s.* 1. (enc.) fileteador. 2. (cost.) marcador, plegador.
create [krɪ'eɪt] *v.t.* 1. crear, procrear, producir, engendrar. 2. causar, originar, ocasionar. 3. crear, elegir, nombrar, constituir, establecer. 4. componer, representar (un papel de teatro). —*v.i.* (jer. G.B.) quejarse, hacer alharacas. —*a.* (ant., poét.) creado.
creatine ['kriəˌtin, B -ˌtaɪn] *s.* (bioquím.) creatina.
creatinine [krɪ'ætəˌnin, B -ˌnaɪn] *s.* (bioquím.) creatinina.
creation [krɪ'eɪʃən] *s.* 1. creación (esp. del mundo); universo. 2. creación, elección, nombramiento. 3. creación, fundación, presentación (de una nueva concepción artística). 4. creación, obra, cosa creada. 5. (cost.) diseño, modelo.
creationism [-ˌɪzəm] *s.* (teol.) creacionismo, doctrina que sostiene que el mundo, la materia, las especies, etc. fueron creadas por Dios y no por la evolución.
creative [krɪ'eɪtɪv] *a.* creativo, creador, productivo.
creatively [-lɪ] *adv.* con ingenio creativo, de modo creador, creadoramente.
creativeness [-nəs] *s.* facultad creadora, genio inventivo.
creativity [ˌkrieɪ'tɪvətɪ] *s.* habilidad o facultad creadora.
creator [krɪ'eɪtər, B -ə] *s.* creador, criador; **the C.,** el Creador.
creatural ['kritʃərəl] *a.* del ser creado; humano.
creature [kritʃər, B -tʃə] *s.* 1. criatura, cosa creada, ser viviente. 2. animal (esp. doméstico). 3. hombre, tipo. 4. ser de aspecto o naturaleza anómala o extraña.
creature comforts, comodidad material.
crèche [krɛʃ, B kreɪʃ] *s.* 1. (fr.) jardín de infancia. 2. inclusa, casa de expósitos. 3. belén, nacimiento.
credence ['kridəns] *s.* 1. creencia, fe. 2. asenso, crédito, ej., *to give c. to,* dar asenso o crédito a, creer. 3. (relig.) credencia.
credendum [krɪ'dɛndəm] *s.* (*pl.* **credenda** [-də]) (relig.) un artículo o cuestión de la religión.
credent ['kridənt] *a.* (ant.) creyente, crédulo; creíble.
credential [krɪ'dɛntʃəl, B -'dɛnʃəl] *a.* credencial. —*s.* credencial, carta credencial; (*pl.*) credenciales.
credenza [krɪ'dɛnzə] *s.* aparador, estantería, anaquel.
credibility [ˌkrɛdə'bɪlətɪ] *s.* credibilidad, verosimilitud.
credible [krɛdəbəl] *a.* creíble, verosímil.
credit ['krɛdət] *s.* 1. crédito, fe, asenso, confianza. 2. crédito, reputación, buen nombre; (com.) crédito, plazo. 3. (ten.) crédito, asiento de crédito; haber. 4. mérito. 5. reconocimiento. 6. motivo de orgullo, ej., *he's a c. to his friends,* él es motivo de orgullo para sus amigos. 7. influencia. 8. marca, nota (que se acumula como condición previa para adquirir un grado académico). 9. **on c.,** a crédito, a plazos, al fiado; **to do (someone) c.,** decir mucho a favor de (alguien), ej., *his truthfulness does him c.,* su veracidad dice mucho a su favor; **to get c. for,** recibir reconocimiento por; **to give c.,** dar crédito, conceder crédito; dar reconocimiento; hacer justicia; nombrar (una obra que se cita); **to give (someone) c. for,** reconocer los méritos de (alguien); (com.) abonar o acreditar en cuenta a (alguien); **to give c. to,** dar crédito a, dar asenso a; **to take c. for,** atribuirse el mérito de. —*v.t.* 1. dar crédito a, creer, reconocer. 2. acreditar, abonar en (cuenta, etc.). 3. atribuir, acreditar (a). 4. **c. (someone) with,** atribuir a (alguien) el mérito de.
creditability [ˌkrɛdətə'bɪlətɪ] *s.* crédito, reputación; credibilidad.
creditable ['krɛdətəbəl] *a.* 1. digno de crédito. 2. apreciable, estimable, loable, honroso (esfuerzo, actuación, etc.). 3. respetable, de buena reputación. 4. (con *to*) debido, atribuible (a).
creditably [-blɪ] *adv.* honorablemente, honrosamente.
credit balance, (ten., com.) saldo acreedor.
credit bureau, agencia que suministra información acerca del crédito de presuntos clientes.
credit card, tarjeta de crédito.
credit line, 1. nota de reconocimiento (al autor, productor, etc. en una obra). 2. (com.) límite de crédito.
credit memorandum, c. note (com.) nota de crédito, nota de abono.
creditor ['krɛdətər, B -ə] *s.* acreedor, impago (Am.).
credit rating, cálculo de la cantidad de crédito que se puede conceder a un individuo o compañía.
credit union, banco cooperativo, asociación cooperativa de crédito.
credo ['kridoʊ, 'kreɪd-] *s.* (*pl.* CREDOS) 1. credo, doctrina, profesión de fe. 2. **C.,** credo de los apóstoles.
credulity [krɪ'dulətɪ, B -'dju-] *s.* credulidad.
credulous ['krɛdʒələs, B 'krɛdjʊ-] *a.* crédulo.
credulously [-lɪ] *adv.* crédulamente.
credulousness [-nəs] *s.* credulidad.
Cree [kri] *s.* (E.U.) cri (indio de una tribu algonquina); su idioma.
creed [krid] *s.* 1. credo, creencia, profesión de fe, doctrina; **the C.,** el credo de los apóstoles. 2. resumen de principios, doctrina profesada (en una ciencia, política, etc.).
creek [krik, krɪk, B krik] *s.* 1. (pr. G.B.) cala, caleta, ensenada. 2. (E.U.) riachuelo, arroyo. 3. (dial., pr. G.B.) llanura estrecha (entre montañas). 4. **up the c.,** (jer.) en apuros.
Creek [krik] *s.* (E.U.) crik (indio de una confederación de tribus de habla muskogee).
creel [kril] *s.* 1. nasa, cesta de pescador, jaula de mimbres. 2. (tej.) fileta.
creep [krip] *v.i.* (*pret., p.p.* CREPT [krɛpt]; *p.pr.* CREEPING) 1. arrastrarse; reptar; gatear, andar a gatas. 2. moverse lentamente, avanzar tímidamente o cautelosamente. 3. humillarse, someterse abyectamente. 4. trepar (las plantas). 5. sentir hormigueo. 6. (mec.) resbalarse, correrse (faja en polea, rodamiento sobre eje, etc.). 7. (f.c.) deslizarse (rieles). 8. **c. by,** pasar lentamente (tiempo); **c. in,** entrar cautelosamente o furtivamente; **c. into,** insinuarse en, comenzar a notarse; entrar cautelosamente o furtivamente en (un cuarto, etc.); **c. out,** salir furtivamente, escurrirse; **c. up,** trepar; subir lentamente; **c. upon,** acercarse inadvertidamente a. —*s.* 1. arrastramiento; gateamiento. 2. hormigueo. 3. (jer.) persona detestable y desagradable, chinche (fig.). 4. (mec.) resbalamiento (de una correa, rodamiento, etc.). 5. (f.c.) deslizamiento (de rieles). 6. (geol.) movimiento paulatino del terreno. 7. **the creeps,** (fam.) miedo, pavor, sobrecogimiento, ej., *he gives me the creeps,* (él) me da grima, repugnancia.
creepage ['kripɪdʒ] *s.* (elec.) escurrimiento, corrimiento.
creeper [-ər, B -ə] *s.* 1. persona o animal que se arrastra. 2. (bot.) enredadera, planta trepadora. 3. (orn.) trepador, ave trepadora. 4. garfio, garabato (para sacar objetos de un pozo o estanque). 5. (*gen. pl.*) ramplones, espolones de zapato (para andar sin resbalar sobre el hielo); trepadores (para subir postes telegráficos, etc.). 6. (*pl.*) (especie de) pelele (para niños). 7. (aut.) camilla

(sobre ruedas para trabajo debajo del automóvil).
creepie ['kripɪ] *s.* (dial., G.B.) banquillo o taburete de tres patas.
creepiness ['kripɪnəs] *s.* carácter pavoroso, aire tétrico (de un lugar).
creeping barrage [-ɪŋ-] (mil.) barrera rasante, barrera de fuego móvil.
creeping paralysis, (med.) parálisis progresiva.
creep limit, (metal.) límite del flujo.
creepy ['kripɪ] *a.* (CREEPIER; CREEPIEST) 1. rastrero. 2. grimoso, tétrico, lúgubre, inquietante (lugar, ambiente, etc.).
creese [kris] *s.* cris, arma blanca de forma serpenteada usada en Filipinas.
cremate ['kriˌmeɪt, krɪ'meɪt, B krɪ'meɪt] *v.t.* cremar, incinerar, quemar.
cremation [krɪ'meɪʃən] *s.* cremación, incineración.
cremator ['kriˌmeɪtər, krɪ'meɪt-, B krɪ'meɪtə] *s.* 1. el que incinera cadáveres. 2. crematorio.
crematorium [ˌkrimə'tɔrɪəm, B ˌkrɛm-] *s.* (*pl.* CREMATORIUMS o CREMATORIA [-ɪə]) crematorio, horno crematorio.
crematory ['krimə,tɔrɪ, B 'krɛmətərɪ] *s.* crematorio; horno crematorio o de incineración. —*a.* crematorio.
crème [krɛm, krim, B kreɪm, krɛm] *s.* 1. (fr.) (cocina) crema. 2. crema, licor (espeso).
crème de la crème [ˌkrɛmdəla'krɛm] (fr.) lo mejor de lo mejor, la crema y nata.
Cremona [krɪ'moʊnə] *s.* (mús.) violín de Cremona.
cremone bolt [-'moʊn-] falleba.
crenate ['kriˌneɪt] **crenated** [-əd] *a.* (bot.) crenado, dentado.
crenation [krɪ'neɪʃən] *s.* (bot.) crenación, formación dentada.
crenature ['krɛnətʃər, B -tʃə] *s.* (bot.) diente (en el borde de una hoja).
crenel ['krɛnəl] *s.* (fort.) almena, almenas, aspillera.
crenelate [-ˌeɪt] *v.t.* almenar. —*a.* 1. (fort.) almenado. 2. (arq.) denticulado.
crenelated [-əd] *a.* almenado.
crenelation [ˌkrɛnə'leɪʃən] *s.* almenaje; almena.
crennellate, crenellated, crenellation, crenelle [krə'nɛl] *vars. de* **crenelate, crenelated, crenelation, crenel.**
crenulate ['krɛnjələt, -ˌleɪt] *a.* (bot.) crenulado.
Creole ['kriˌoʊl] *s.* 1. criollo. 2. (E.U.) blanco de ascendencia francesa o española. 3. (E.U.) negro criollo. 4. (E.U.) francés dialectal (hablado en Luisiana). —*a.* criollo.
creolized language [-əˌlaɪzd-] tipo de idioma mezclado que se desarrolla con el contacto de un grupo dominante y otro subordinado que hablan diferentes idiomas.
creosol ['kriəˌsɔl, -ˌsoʊl, B -ˌsɔl] *s.* (quím.) creosol.
creosote [-ˌsoʊt] *s.* (quím.) creosota. —*v.t.* creosotar (madera para impedir que se pudra). —*a.* creosotado.
creosote bush, (bot.) variedad de arbusto de madera resinosa.
crepe [kreɪp] *s.* 1. (tej.) crespón, crepé. 2. crespón de luto.
crepe de Chine [ˌkreɪpdə'ʃin] crespón o crepé de China, crespón de seda.
crepe paper, papel rizado, papel cresponado, papel de China, papel crepé (Am.).
crepe rubber, caucho crudo de superficie arrugada (para suela de zapatos).
crepitant ['krɛpətənt] *s.* crepitante.
crepitate [-ˌteɪt] *v.i.* crepitar, chasquear, chisporrotear.
crepitation [ˌkrɛpə'teɪʃən] *s.* crepitación, chasquido, chisporroteo; (med.) crepitación.
crept [krɛpt] *pret., p.p. de* **creep.**
crepuscular [krɪ'pʌskjələr, B -lə] *a.* crepuscular, crepusculino.
crepuscule [-kjul, B 'krɛpəskjul] *s.* crepúsculo.
crescendo [krɪ'ʃɛndoʊ] *a., s.* (*pl.* CRESCENDOS) (mús.) crescendo.
crescent ['krɛsənt] *s.* 1. luna creciente. 2. media luna (de Turquía y del Islamismo). 3. (fig.) islamismo; el poderío turco. 4. semicírculo (de objetos). 5. (her.) creciente. 6. panecillo (en forma de media luna). —*a.* creciente.
crescent truss, armadura de lúmula.
cresol ['kriˌsɔl, -ˌsoʊl, B -ˌsɔl] *s.* (quím.) cresol.
cress ['krɛs] *s.* (bot.) 1. mastuerzo. 2. berro.
cresset ['krɛsət] *s.* fanal, farol, fogaril, almenar, tedero.
crest [krɛst] *s.* 1. cresta, copete, penacho. 2. crestón, cimera. 3. (her.) timbre. 4. cresta, cumbre, cima (de una montaña); cresta (de una ola). 5. (arq.) cumbrera. 6. (anat.) borde (alrededor de la superficie de un hueso). —*v.t.* 1. coronar; adornar (con una cimera). 2. alcanzar la cumbre de. 3. (her.) timbrar. —*v.i.* encrestarse, encresparse (las olas).
crested ['krɛstəd] *a.* 1. crestado, penachudo, coronado. 2. (her.) timbrado.
crested flycatcher, (orn.) papamoscas.
crested lark, (orn.) cogujada, copada, cotovía, galerita, vejeta.
crestfallen ['krɛstˌfɔlən] *a.* cabizbajo, cabizcaído, con las orejas gachas, abatido.
crestless [-ləs] *a.* 1. sin cresta; sin cimera; sin divisa; sin escudo. 2. (fig.) de humilde linaje.
crest valve, (elec.) valor máximo.
cresylic [krə'sɪlɪk] *a.* (quím.) cresílico.
cretaceous [krɪ'teɪʃəs] *a.* 1. gredoso. 2. **C.,** (geol.) cretáceo. —*s.* **C.,** cretáceo.
Cretan ['kritən] *a., s.* cretense, crético, de la isla griega de Creta.
cretin ['kritən, 'krɛ-] *s.* 1. (med.) cretino. 2. (fig.) cretino, estúpido, necio.
cretinism [-ˌɪzəm] *s.* (med.) cretinismo.
cretinous [-əs] *a.* (med.) cretino.
cretonne ['kriˌtɑn, krɪ'tɑn, B krɛ'tɔn] *s.* (tej.) cretona.
crevasse [krɪ'væs] *s.* 1. grieta, hendedura o fisura profunda (esp. en un ventisquero o glaciar). 2. (E.U.) rajadura (en un dique o malecón).
crevice ['krɛvəs] *s.* grieta, hendedura, rajadura, fisura, resquebradura, resquebrajadura.
creviced [-əst] *a.* agrietado.
crew [kru] *s.* 1. personal, dotación, equipo. 2. tripulación (de un barco o avión). 3. cuadrilla, banda.
crew [kru] (G.B.) *pret. de* **crow.**
crew cut, corte alemán, corte cepillo, corte militar (de pelo masculino).
crewel ['kruəl] *s.* estambre, hilo de lana (para tejer, bordar, etc.).
crew neck, cuello de cisne (de una prenda de vestir).
crib [krɪb] 1. cuna, camita con barandillas (para niño). 2. establo, cuadra. 3. choza, casucha; cuartucho, chiribitil. 4. canasta, cesto, capacho. 5. granero (esp. para maíz). 6. pesebre. 7. (min., const.) cofre, encofrado, cajón. 8. (fam.) ratería. 9. (fam.) plagio. 10. (fam.) chuleta, traducción para uso de escolares (esp. no autorizada). 11. (jer.) caja fuerte, bóveda (de bancos). 12. (naipes) cartas descartadas (en el juego de "cribbage"). —*v.t.* (*pret., p.p.* CRIBBED ; *p.pr.* CRIBBING). 1. enjaular, encerrar (en sitio reducido). 2. almacenar (en granero). 3. proveer o reforzar con encofrado. 4. (fam.) apropiarse de, plagiar (ideas, texto, etc.). —*v.i.* 1. plagiar, usar plagios. 2. (fam.) usar chuleta o trampa (en examen escolar).
cribbage ['krɪbɪdʒ] *s.* juego de naipes que se juega utilizando un tablero de puntuación.
cribbing ['krɪbɪŋ] *s.* vicio (de los caballos) de morder el borde del pesebre.
crib dam, presa de cajón, azud de encofrado.
cribriform ['krɪbrəˌfɔrm, B -ˌfɔm] *a.* semejante a una criba, agujereado.
cribwork [-ˌwɜrk B -ˌwɜk] *s.* cajón o armazón de apoyo hecho de listones de madera.
cricetid [kraɪ'sitəd, -'sɛt-] *s.* (zool.) cricétido, cualquier roedor.
crick [krɪk] *s.* tortícolis; calambre (esp. en el cuello o la espalda). —*v.t.* causar calambre en (cuello o espalda).
cricket ['krɪkət] *s.* (ento.) grillo.
cricket, *s.* (dep.) criquet. 2. (fam., fig.) juego limpio, rectitud, imparcialidad ú. esp. en **it's not c.,** no es correcto. 3. taburete, banquillo bajo (de madera). —*v.t.* jugar al criquet.
cricketer [-ər, B -ə] *s.* jugador de criquet.
cricoid ['kraɪˌkɔɪd] *a.* (anat.) cricoides.
crier ['kraɪər, B -ə] *s.* pregonero, baladrero.
crime [kraɪm] *s.* 1. crimen, delito, fechoría. 2. actividad criminal.
Crimean [kraɪ'miən, B -'mɪən] *a.* perteneciente a la Crimea, península en el Mar Negro.
crime wave, ola de crímenes.
criminal ['krɪmənəl] *a.* criminal; penal. —*s.* criminal, reo, delincuente, malhechor.
criminal charge, (der.) acusación criminal.
criminal code, (der.) código penal.
criminal conversation, (der.) coito ilegal, adulterio.
criminal court, (der.) tribunal penal.
criminality [ˌkrɪmə'nælətɪ] *s.* criminalidad.
criminal law, derecho penal o criminal, ley penal.
criminal lawyer, (abogado) penalista, criminalista.
criminally ['krɪmənəlɪ] *adv.* 1. criminalmente. 2. según el derecho penal, de acuerdo al derecho penal, ej., *c. insane,* demente según el derecho penal.
criminal negligence, (der.) negligencia criminal.
criminal offense, (der.) delito penal.
criminal record, antecedentes penales.
criminate ['krɪməˌneɪt] *v.t.* 1. incriminar, acriminar, acusar. 2. censurar (fuertemente).
crimination [ˌkrɪmə'neɪʃən] *s.* incriminación, acriminación, acusación.
criminative ['krɪməˌneɪtɪv, -nətɪv] **criminatory** [-nəˌtɔrɪ, B -tərɪ] *a.* acusatorio.
criminological [ˌkrɪmənəl'ɑdʒɪkəl, B -'ɔdʒ-] *a.* criminológico.
criminologist [-ə'nɑlədʒəst, B -'nɔl-] *s.* criminalista, experto en criminología.
criminology [-dʒɪ] *s.* criminología.
criminous ['krɪmənəs] *s.* criminoso, criminal, delictivo.
crimmer, *var. de* **krimmer.**
crimp [krɪmp] *v.t.* 1. rizar, encrespar; ondular, corrugar, arrugar. 2. hacer cortes o incisiones (en carne, pescado). 3. doblar hacia adentro (el borde de un cartucho); estrechar (un tubo); dar forma doblando. 4. (fam., E.U.) limitar, estorbar, obstaculizar (acción, plan, etc.). —*s.* 1. rizado, encrespado (del pelo). 2. (fam., E.U.) obstáculo,

restricción, impedimento. 3. (cost.) plegado, plisado. 4. **to put a crimp in,** limitar, estorbar, obstaculizar (acción, plan, etc.).
crimp, *s.* enganchador, reclutador (de marineros o soldados contra su voluntad). —*v.t.* reclutar, enganchar (marineros y soldados contra su voluntad).
crimper ['krɪmpər, B -ə] *s.* 1. enganchador, reclutador (de marineros o soldados). 2. (mec.) plegador de cápsulas, tenazas para detonador; herramienta de plegar.
crimple ['krɪmpəl] *v.t., v.i.* arrugar, corrugar, estrujar.
crimpy [-pɪ] *a.* rizado, encrespado, arrugado.
crimson ['krɪmzən] *s., a.* carmesí. —*v.t.* teñir de carmesí. —*v.i.* enrojecerse, sonrojarse.
crimson clover, (bot.) trébol encarnado, trébol rosado, trébol anual.
cringe [krɪndʒ] *v.i.* 1. contraerse, encogerse (por el frío, viento, etc.). 2. encogerse, arrastrarse, recular (por temor o humildad servil). 3. humillarse, rebajarse, adular servilmente. —*s.* postración, saludo servil.
cringer ['krɪndʒər, B -ə] *s.* adulador.
cringle ['krɪŋgəl] *s.* (mar.) garrucho.
crinite ['kraɪ,naɪt] *a.* (bot., zool.) crinado, crinito, peludo, peloso. —*s.* (zool.) fósil crinoideo.
crinkle ['krɪŋkəl] *v.i.* 1. serpentear. 2. arrugarse, rizarse, encresparse. 3. crujir (como la seda), crepitar. —*v.t.* arrugar, rizar, encrespar. —*s.* arruga, pliegue.
crinkly [-klɪ] *a.* 1. arrugado; ondulado. 2. crujiente.
crinoid ['kraɪ,nɔɪd] *a., s.* (zool.) crinoideo.
crinoline ['krɪnələn, B -in] *s.* 1. (tej.) crinolina. 2. miriñaque, ahuecador.
cripes [kraɪps] *interj.* ¡caracoles!
cripple ['krɪpəl] *a.* lisiado, tullido, baldado. —*s.* lisiado, tullido, inválido. —*v.t.* 1. lisiar, tullir, baldar, mutilar. 2. (fig.) debilitar, incapacitar.
crippling ['krɪplɪŋ] *s.* (const.) abarquillamiento, desgarramiento; inestabilidad local.
crisis ['kraɪsəs] *s.* (*pl.* CRISES [-,siz]) 1. (med.) crisis. 2. crisis, punto crucial, momento crítico.
crisp [krɪsp] *a.* 1. crespo, rizado, ondulado. 2. quebradizo, frágil. 3. agudo, claro, preciso, tajante, bien definido. 4. vivo, brillante. 5. fresco y firme (ej., lechuga). 6. vigorizador, tonificante (aire, frío). 7. tostado. —*s.* (*pl.*) (G.B.) patatas fritas en rajas delgadas. —*v.t.* 1. rizar, encrespar; tostar. 2. hacer quebradizo o frágil; tostar(se). —*v.i.* 1. encresparse; rizarse. 2. volverse quebradizo; tostarse.
crispate ['krɪspeɪt] *a.* crespo, rizado, ondulado.
crispation [krɪs'peɪʃən] *s.* 1. rizado, encrespadura, ondulación. 2. crispatura, contracción. 3. crispadura nerviosa.
crispness ['krɪspnəs] *s.* 1. textura o consistencia tostada o quebradiza. 2. claridad, precisión (en lenguaje, etc.). 3. frescura.
crispy [-pɪ] *a.* (CRISPIER; CRISPIEST) 1. rizado, crespo. 2. frágil, tostado, quebradizo. 3. fresco, vigorizante.
crisscross ['krɪs,krɔs] *s.* 1. red de líneas cruzadas, red intrincada. 2. (fig.) enredo, enmarañamiento. —*v.t.* 1. marcar con líneas cruzadas. 2. formar una red de líneas en. 3. atravesar o cruzar en todas direcciones. —*v.i.* moverse o pasar en todas direcciones. —*a.* entrecruzado, enmarañado. —*adv.* contrariamente, en cruz.
cristate ['krɪs,teɪt] **cristated** [-əd] *a.* crestado.
criterion [kraɪ'tɪrɪən, B -'tɪər-] *s.* (*pl.* CRITERIA [-ɪə]) criterio, norma, juicio, discernimiento.
critic ['krɪtɪk] *s.* 1. crítico; censor. 2. criticón.
critical [-ɪkəl] *a.* 1. crítico, criticador, criticón. 2. crítico, de crítica (ej., obras). 3. crítico, decisivo. 4. crítico, arriesgado, precario. 5. (fís., mat.) crítico.
critical angle, (ópt., aer.) ángulo crítico, ángulo mínimo de reflexión total.
critical damping, (elec.) amortiguación crítica.
critically [-kəlɪ] *adv.* 1. críticamente. 2. peligrosamente.
critical mass, (fís.) masa crítica.
criticalness [-kəlnəs] *s.* carácter crítico o peligroso (de una situación, etc.).
critical point, (fís.) punto crítico.
critical state, (fís.) estado crítico.
critical temperature, (fís., quím.) temperatura crítica.
criticaster ['krɪtɪ,kæstər, B -,kɑstə] *s.* criticastro; crítico o cronista incompetente.
criticism ['krɪtə,sɪzəm] *s.* crítica; censura; juicio crítico.
criticizable [-,saɪzəbəl] *a.* criticable, censurable.
criticize [-,saɪz] *v.i.* criticar. —*v.t.* 1. criticar, juzgar. 2. criticar, censurar, hallar faltas.
criticizer [-ər, B -ə] *s.* crítico, criticador, criticón.
critique [krɪ'tik] *s.* crítica; ensayo o estudio crítico.
critter ['krɪtər, B -ə] *s.* (dial.) criatura; bicho, animal.
croak [kroʊk] *v.i.* 1. croar (la rana); graznar (el cuervo). 2. (fig.) gruñir; hablar con voz ronca. 3. pronosticar, presagiar (algo malo). 4. (jer.) morir. —*v.t.* 1. proferir o gritar en voz ronca; (fig.) agorar, presagiar. 2. (jer.) matar. —*s.* 1. graznido (del cuervo); canto (de ranas). 2. gruñido, graznido, grito bronco.
croaker ['kroʊkər, B -kə] *s.* 1. gruñón, refunfuñador; agorero, profeta de mal agüero. 2. (ict.) roncador. 3. (jer.) médico, cirujano.
Croat [kroʊt, 'kroʊ,æt, B 'kroʊət] *var. de* **Croatian.**
Croatian [kroʊ'eɪʃən] *s.* 1. croata, natural de Croacia, Yugoslavia. 2. lengua croata. —*a.* croata.
crocein ['kroʊsɪɪn] *s.* (quím.) croceína.
crochet [kroʊ'ʃeɪ, B 'kroʊʃeɪ] *s.* tejido o labor de gancho, crochet. —*v.t., v.i.* tejer con gancho, hacer ganchillo (Esp.).
crochet file, lima finísima puntiaguda.
crochet hook, gancho para tejer, aguja de gancho, aguja de crochet.
crocidolite [kroʊ'sɪdəl,aɪt, B 'krɔsɪd-] *s.* (min.) crocidolita.
crock [krɑk, B krɔk] *s.* 1. tarro de loza, olla de barro. 2. cazuela, tiesto. 3. (dial.) hollín, suciedad. 4. (jer.) tontería. —*v.t.* (dial.) ensuciar. —*v.i.* desteñirse (ej., el cuero al ser frotado).
crock, *s.* 1. (fam.) tullido, decrépito, inválido. 2. (G.B.) matalón, rocinante. 3. (esco.) oveja vieja. 4. **to be an old c.,** estar hecho un cascajo. —*v.t.* tullir, estropear. —*v.i.* estropearse, averiarse.
crocked [krɑkt, B krɔkt] *a.* (jer.) borracho.
crockery ['krɑkərɪ, B 'krɔk-] *s.* loza; cacharros, vasijas y platos de barro.
crocket ['krɑkət, B 'krɔkɪt] *s.* (arq.) follaje; ornamento en forma de hojas y flores.
crocodile ['krɑkə,daɪl, B 'krɔk-] *s.* (zool.) cocodrilo.
crocodile bird, (orn.) especie de chorlito africano (que se alimenta de insectos parasitarios del cocodrilo).
crocodile shear, cortador de palanca.
crocodile squeezer, cinglador de quijadas.
crocodile tears, (fig.) lágrimas de cocodrilo; **to shed c. t.,** llorar con sentimiento fingido; deplorar (algo) hipócritamente.
crocodilian [,krɑkə'dɪlɪən, B ,krɔk-] *s.* (zool.) crocodílido. —*a.* 1. falso, fingido. 2. propio de un cocodrilo (andar, movimientos, etc.).
crocoite ['krɑkoʊ,aɪt, B 'kroʊ-] **crocoisite** [-wə,zaɪt] *s.* (min.) crocoíta.
crocus ['kroʊkəs] *s.* (*pl.* CROCUSES) 1. (bot.) (*pl. t.* CROCI [-,ki, -,kaɪ]) azafrán, azafrán croco. 2. (quím.) rojo de pulir, polvo de óxido de hierro.
crocus cloth, arpillera, cañamazo.
Croesus ['krisəs] *s.* (fig.) creso, hombre rico.
croft [krɔft] *s.* (G.B) pequeño terreno rústico cercado; pequeña granja (trabajada por el arrendatario).
crofter ['krɔftər, B -ə] *s.* (G.B.) colono, agricultor (que es inquilino de un pequeño terreno).
croissant [krwɑ'sɑnt, B -'sɑn] *s.* (*pl.* CROISSANTS) (cocina) panecillo de media luna.
Cro-Magnon [kroʊ'mægnən, -'mænjən, B -'mænjɔŋ] *s.* Cro-Magnon, tipo humano prehistórico.
cromlech ['krɑm,lɛk, B 'krɔm-] *s.* (arqueol.) 1. crómlech, crónlech, monumento megalítico. 2. dolmen.
crone [kroʊn] *s.* (fam.) vieja fea, bruja.
crony ['kroʊnɪ] *s.* (*pl.* CRONIES) camarada, compinche.
crook [krʊk] *s.* 1. gancho, garfio. 2. curva; recodo (de un río, camino, etc.). 3. corva (de la pierna). 4. (fam.) estafador, fullero, ladrón. 5. cayado (de pastor u obispo). —*v.t.* 1. encorvar, doblar, torcer. 2. (fam.) estafar; conseguir por estafa. —*v.i.* 1. torcer, serpentear (río, camino, etc.). 2. torcerse, encorvarse.
crookback ['krʊk,bæk] *s.* (ant.) joroba; jorobado.
crooked ['krʊkəd] *a.* 1. corvo, encorvado, torcido, doblado. 2. deshonesto, fraudulento. 3. **to go c.,** apartarse de la buena senda, volverse un malhechor.
crookedly [-lɪ] *adv.* 1. torcidamente, de través. 2. deshonradamente, fraudulentamente.
crookedness [-nəs] *s.* 1. encorvadura; sinuosidad. 2. deshonestidad, fraude, maldad.
Crookes tube ['krʊks-] (elec.) tubo de Crookes.
crookneck ['krʊk,nɛk] *s.* (bot.) variedad de calabaza (de cuello retorcido).
croon [krun] *v.i.* cantar, canturrear (esp. canciones sentimentales). —*v.t.* cantar con voz suave. —*s.* canturreo.
crooner ['krunər, B -ə] *s.* cantante popular de estilo romántico.
crop [krɑp, B krɔp] *s.* 1. cosecha, siega; cultivo, labranza. 2. (fig.) cosecha, acopio; (p. ext.) lote, montón. 3. empuñadura de látigo; látigo de jinete. 4. buche (de aves e insectos). 5. piel de res curtida. —*v.t.* 1. cortar corto (el cabello); podar (arbustos, seto vivo, etc.); desmochar (ramas, etc.); cortar (césped). 2. marcar, cortar la oreja de (un animal). 3. cosechar, segar. 4. cultivar, labrar. —*v.i.* 1. pacer. 2. dar frutos, rendir. 3. **c. out** o **c. up,** aflorar; asomarse, dejarse ver, aparecer, ej., *errors c. up,* aparecen (hay) errores.
crop dusting, aerofumigación.
crop-eared ['krɑp'ɪrd, B 'krɔp'ɪəd] *a.* desmochado, con el extremo de las orejas cortadas; con el cabello corto de modo que se destaquen las orejas.
cropper [-ər, B -ə] *s.* 1. labrador, cultivador. 2. segador, cosechador.
cropper, *s.* 1. caída brusca o aparatosa (ej., de un caballo). 2. fracaso, colapso. 3. **to come a c.,** caer aparatosamente; (fig.) fracasar.
croquet [kroʊ'keɪ, B 'kroʊkeɪ] *s.* (dep.) croquet. —*v.t.* echar fuera (la bola del adversario en el juego de croquet).

croquette [kroʊ'kɛt, B krɔ-] *s.* (cocina) croqueta.
croquis [kroʊ'ki] *s.* (*pl.* CROQUIS [-'kiz]) croquis, boceto, esbozo, bosquejo.
crosier ['kroʊʒər, B -ʒə] *s.* 1. (relig.) báculo (de obispo, abad o abadesa). 2. (bot.) fronda circinada (de los helechos).
cross [krɔs] *s.* 1. cruz, crucifijo. 2. revés, frustración; molestia, vejamen. 3. cruzamiento (de razas, etc.); híbrido, mezcla. 4. fraude, engaño, estafa (ú. esp. en: *on the c.,* fraudulentamente). 5. (elec.) cruce, contacto accidental (de líneas). 6. (boxeo) golpe cruzado. 7. (astr.) la Cruz del Norte; la Cruz del Sur. 8. **the C.,** la Cruz, la Santa Cruz; **to be a c. between,** ser una mezcla de (dos cosas); **to bear one's c.,** (fig.) cargar uno con su cruz; **to make the sign of the c.,** hacer la señal de la cruz, santiguarse. —*v.t.* 1. cruzar, formar una cruz en. 2. cruzar (las piernas, los brazos). 3. cruzar, atravesar, pasar al otro lado de (río, mar, puente, etc.). 4. cruzar, cruzarse con, encontrarse con (alguien). 5. persignar, santiguar. 6. marcar con una cruz. 7. cruzar (animales, plantas, razas, etc.). 8. obstruir, impedir; oponerse a, volverse contra; frustrar. 9. **c. each other,** cruzarse (ej., cartas); **c. my heart and hope to die,** que me muera si miento; **c. oneself,** persignarse, santiguarse; **c. one's fingers,** (fig.) cruzar los dedos; **c. one's heart,** (fig.) jurar; **c. one's mind,** ocurrírsele a uno; **c. one's t's,** poner los puntos sobre las íes, ser muy preciso; **c. out** (o **off**), tachar, borrar; **c. (someone's) path,** (fig.) cruzar el camino de (alguien); **c. swords,** quebrar lanzas, medir las armas; (fig.) reñir, contender. —*v.i.* 1. cruzar, pasar de través. 2. cruzarse, entrecruzarse, formar una cruz. 3. cruzarse (cartas, personas). 4. (con *over*) cruzar al otro lado; (teat.) cruzar el escenario. —*a.* 1. cruzado. 2. transversal. 3. contrario, opuesto, adverso. 4. malhumorado, de mal genio, irascible; airado, enfadado. 5. cruzado, híbrido.
crossbar ['krɔsˌbɑr, B -ˌbɑ] *s.* 1. travesaño; tirante, listón. 2. tranca, aldaba (en puerta o ventana); cruceta (de la ventana). 3. palo o madero horizontal (de una cruz). 4. tubo horizontal (del cuadro de una bicicleta). 5. apoyo (del florete). 6. (impr.) crucero, medianil. 7. (dep.) travesaño (de la portería).
crossbeam [-ˌbim] *s.* 1. (arq.) viga transversal. 2. palo o madero transversal (de una cruz).
cross bearer, barrote transversal.
crossbill [-ˌbɪl] *s.* (orn.) piquituerto.
cross bit, barrena de filo en cruz.
crossbones [-ˌboʊnz] *s. pl.* (figura de dos) huesos cruzados (como símbolo de la muerte).
crossbow [-ˌboʊ] *s.* ballesta (arma).
cross bracing, arriostramiento transversal.
crossbred [-'brɛd] *a.* cruzado (de raza); híbrido; mestizo, mixto. — [-ˌbrɛd] *s.* cruzado, híbrido.
crossbreed [-ˌbrid, -'brid] *v.t.* cruzar, entrecruzar (animales o plantas). —*v.i.* crear híbridos. — [-ˌbrid] *s.* híbrido, cruzado.
cross bun, bollo marcado con una cruz (que se come en semana santa).
cross-country [-'kʌntrɪ] *a.* a campo traviesa; a través del país.
cross-country race, (dep.) carrera a campo traviesa.
crosscurrent [-'kɜrənt, -'kʌrənt, B -'kʌ-] *s.* contracorriente; movimiento o tendencia encontrada o contraria.
crosscut [-ˌkʌt, -'kʌt] *v.t.* aserrar transversalmente, tronzar. — [-ˌkʌt] *s.* 1. atajo. 2. traviesa, crucero (en mina). 3. corte transversal.
crosscut file, lima de doble talla.
crosscut saw, sierra tronzadera, sierra de tumba, sierra de través.
crosse [krɔs] *s.* (dep.) vilorto (palo con que se juega a la vilorta o lacrosse).
cross-examination [ˌkrɔsɪgˌzæmə'neɪʃən] *s.* (der.) repreguntas, interrogatorio riguroso (que se hace a un testigo).
cross-examine [-'zæmən] *v.t.* (der.) repreguntar, interrogar, examinar (sobre lo declarado).
cross-examiner [-ənər, B -ənə] *s.* (der.) examinador, el que interroga o repregunta.
cross-eye ['krɔsˌaɪ] *s.* bizquera, estrabismo.
cross-eyed [-'aɪd] *a.* ojituerto, bizco, bisojo.
cross-fertilization [-ˌfɜrtələ'zeɪʃən, B -ˌfɜtɪlaɪ-] *s.* (bot., zool.) fecundación o fertilización cruzada (de una planta con otra o de un organismo con otro).
cross-fertilize [-'fɜrtəlˌaɪz, B-'fɜt-] *v.t., v.i.* fecundar(se) por fertilización cruzada.
cross-file [-'faɪl] *v.i., v.t.* (pol., E.U.) registrar(se) (para las elecciones primarias) como candidato de más de un partido político.
cross fire, (mil.) fuego cruzado; ataque por varios lados.
cross-grained [-'greɪnd] *a.* 1. repeloso, de fibras cruzadas, de contrafibra (madera). 2. intrincado, enmarañado (problema, etc.). 3. irritable, intratable, terco.
cross hairs, (ópt.) hilo del retículo (en el foco del ocular en instrumentos de óptica).
crosshatch [-ˌhætʃ] *v.t., v.i.* (dib.) sombrear, rayar con líneas que se entrecrucen.
crosshead [-ˌhɛd] *s.* 1. (maq.) cruceta de cabeza, cruceta. 2. (impr.) subtítulo de columna (de un periódico, etc.).
cross-index [-'ɪndɛks] *v.t., v.i.* habilitar (un libro, catálogo, etc.) con un índice de referencia sistemática.
crossing ['krɔsɪŋ] *s.* 1. travesía. 2. cruzamiento (de plantas o animales). 3. cruce, intersección (de caminos, vías férreas, etc.); paso, vado (de un río); paso para peatones (en una calle, camino, etc.).
crossing gate, (f.c.) barrera de cruce, tranquera de cruce, barrera de paso a nivel.
cross-legged ['krɔsˌlɛgəd, -ˌlɛgd, B -ˌlɛgd] *a.* con las piernas cruzadas.
crosslet [-lət] *s.* (her.) crucecita.
cross-link [-ˌlɪŋk] *s.* eslabón (de átomos, etc.) en cruz. —*v.t.* unir al través.
crossly ['krɔslɪ] *adv.* malhumoradamente, airadamente, con enfado.
cross member, (aut.) travesaño.
crossness [-nəs] *s.* mal humor, enfado, irascibilidad.
cross of Lorraine, cruz de Lorena (de dos barras horizontales, siendo la inferior más larga).
crossover ['krɔsˌoʊvər, B -və] *s.* 1. cruce, travesía (de un lado, nivel, vía, etc., a otro). 2. (biol.) cruzamiento.
crossover network, (rad.) red de discriminación (en altoparlante).
crosspatch [-ˌpætʃ] *s.* (fam.) cascarrabias, gruñón.
crosspiece [-ˌpis] *s.* 1. pieza transversal, cruceta, atravesaño, travesaño, travesero, crucero. 2. (mar.) cabillero.
cross-pollinate [-'pɑləˌneɪt, B -'pɔl-] *v.t., v.i.* fecundar por polinización cruzada.
cross-pollination [ˌkrɔsˌpɑlə'neɪʃən, B -ˌpɔl-] *s.* (bot.) polinización cruzada (de una planta con otra).
cross-purpose ['krɔs'pɜrpəs, B -'pɜpəs] *s.* propósito distinto o contrario; **to be at cross-purposes,** no comprenderse uno a otro; estar en pugna; **to talk at cross-purposes,** hablar sin entenderse uno a otro.
cross-question [-'kwɛstʃən] *v.t.* repreguntar. —*s.* pregunta (hecha durante un interrogatorio).
crossrail [-ˌreɪl] *s.* 1. travesaño (ej., de una silla). 2. mesa (de acepilladora). 3. peinazo intermedio (de puerta).
cross-refer [ˌkrɔsrɪ'fɜr, B -'fɜ] *v.t., v.i.* hacer una referencia (a), de una página a otra (al lector).
cross-reference ['krɔs'rɛfərəns] *s.* referencia recíproca, remisión (de una parte de un texto a otra). —*v.t.* proveer de remisiones.
crossroad [-ˌroʊd, -'roʊd] *s.* 1. vía o camino transversal. 2. (*pl.*) encrucijada. 3. **at the crossroads,** (fig.) en la encrucijada.
crossruff [-ˌrʌf, -'rʌf] *v.t., v.i.* (juego de cartas) fallar en cruz. —*s.* fallo en cruz.
cross section, 1. sección o corte transversal. 2. muestra representativa de un total (de población, etc.).
cross-staff [-ˌstæf, B -ˌstɑf] *s.* 1. (relig.) guión. 2. (astr.) cruz geométrica, ballestilla. 3. (top.) escuadra de agrimensor.
cross-stitch [-ˌstɪtʃ] *s.* (cost.) punto cruzado o de cruz; bordado de punto cruzado. —*v.t.* bordar con puntos cruzados.
cross street, travesía, calle traviesa, por media calle.
cross talk, 1. interferencia telefónica. 2. (rad.) diafonía, interferencia. 3. intercambio de agudezas.
crosstie [-ˌtaɪ] *s.* (f.c.) traviesa, durmiente (Am.).
cross-town [-ˌtaʊn] *a.* que atraviesa una ciudad o población (un ómnibus, etc.).
crosstrees [-ˌtriz] *s., pl.* (mar.) crucetas, baos de gavia.
cross-up [-ˌʌp] *s.* (jer.) traición a un cómplice.
cross vault, (arq.) bóveda de aristas, arco crucero.
crosswalk [-ˌwɔk] *s.* cruce para peatones (en una calle o avenida).
crossway [-ˌweɪ] *s.* (*gen. pl.*) encrucijada.
crossways [-ˌweɪz] *adv.* 1. de través, al través, transversalmente. 2. (ant.) en forma de cruz.
crosswind [-ˌwɪnd] *s.* viento transversal, viento de costado.
cross wire, (ópt.) hilo de retículo (en el foco del ocular en instrumentos de óptica).
crosswise [-ˌwaɪz] *adv.* 1. de través, al través, transversalmente. 2. (ant.) en forma de cruz. —*a.* transverso, oblicuo.
crossword puzzle [-ˌwɜrd-, B -ˌwɜd-] crucigrama, palabras cruzadas.
crotch [krɑtʃ, B krɔtʃ] *s.* 1. horca de madera. 2. horcadura (de árbol); bifurcación. 3. (anat.) bragadura, entrepiernas. 4. (const. naval) pique.
crotchet ['krɑtʃət, B 'krɔtʃ-] *s.* 1. capricho, rareza, excentricidad. 2. (mús., G.B.) negra. 3. (ant.) ganchito, corchete; broche.
crotchety [-ɪ] *a.* caprichoso, extravagante, excéntrico.
croton ['kroʊtən] *s.* (bot.) crotón; buenavista.
Croton bug, (ento.) (especie de) cucaracha pequeña (que vive frecuentemente alrededor de las tuberías de agua caliente).
crouch [kraʊtʃ] *v.i.* 1. agacharse, agazaparse, acuclillarse. 2. (fig.) rebajarse, encogerse, arrastrarse servilmente. —*v.t.* doblar, inclinar.
croup [krup] *s.* anca, nalgas, grupa (del caballo); cadera (de vaca).
croup, *s.* (med.) crup, crup catarral, garrotillo, difteria.
croupier ['krupɪər, -ˌeɪ, B -ə] *s.* crupié, crupier (ayudante del banquero en los casinos).
croupy ['krupɪ] *a.* (med.) crupal.

crouse [krus] *a.* (dial.) confiado, engreído; vivo, activo.
crouton ['kru,tɑn, B kru'tɔn] *s.* cubito de pan tostado (que se sirve sobre sopas, etc.).
crow [kroʊ] *s.* 1. (orn.) cuervo; corneja; grajo; chova. 2. (mec.) pie de cabra, alzaprima. 3. (despec.) negro. 4. **as the c. flies,** en línea recta; **to eat c.,** (E.U.) cantar la palinodia; aceptar la derrota. —*v.i.* (*pret.* CREW O CROWED) 1. cacarear, cantar (el gallo). 2. dar gritos de placer; gritar con entusiasmo (muchedumbre, etc.). 3. (fig.) (esp. con **over** o **about**) exultar, gloriarse, relamerse (de); jactarse. —*s.* 1. cacareo, quiquiriquí, canto (del gallo). 2. grito de placer.
crowbar ['kroʊ,bɑr, B -,bɑ] *s.* (mec.) pata de cabra, alzaprima, palanca.
crowd [kraʊd] *v.i.* arremolinarse, agolparse, apiñarse; **c. into,** entrar por fuerza; **c. on the heels of,** pisar los talones a; **c. through,** abrir paso a empellones. —*v.t.* 1. sobrecargar, agobiar, abrumar. 2. atestar, llenar hasta el tope, rellenar. 3. apiñar; comprimir. 4. urgir, apremiar. 5. arrimarse a, acercarse a. 6. **c. each other,** agolparse, apiñarse (imágenes, memorias, cambios, etc.); **c. out,** empujar o empellar fuera; (fig.) desalojar, desplazar; **c. one's luck,** confiar uno demasiado en su suerte; **c. (on) sail** (o **canvas**), (mar.) hacer fuerza de vela. —*s.* 1. multitud, muchedumbre, tropel, gentío. 2. (fig.) montón, mar, infinidad (de cosas). 3. gente, compañía, grupo. 4. (mús.) antiguo instrumento musical de origen céltico, parecido al violín. 5. **the c.,** el populacho, la turba, el vulgo; **to follow the c.,** hacer lo que hacen los demás.
crowded ['kraʊdəd] *a.* 1. lleno, atestado, abarrotado, de bote en bote. 2. apretado, apiñado, amontonado, tupido.
crowfoot ['kroʊ,fʊt] *s.* (*pl.* CROWFEET [-,fit]) 1. (bot.) (*pl. gen.* CROWFOOTS) pata de gallo; ranúnculo, botón de oro. 2. (*pl.*) patas de gallo (en los ojos). 3. (mar.) araña.
crown [kraʊn] *s.* 1. corona (de monarca, del vencedor, etc.); diadema, guirnalda, premio. 2. (anat.) corona, coronilla (de la cabeza); corona (del diente). 3. corona, cima, cumbre (de montaña, colina, etc.); copa (de árbol o arbusto); copa (de sombrero). 4. (fig.) corona, coronamiento (de una obra). 5. (fig.) corona, monarca; monarquía. 6. corona (nombre de varias monedas, en G.B.). 7. (zool.) cresta (de un ave). 8. (bot.) corona. 9. (mar.) diamante (del ancla). 10. (her.) coronel, corona. —*v.t.* 1. coronar. 2. (fig.) coronar, premiar, recompensar. 3. (fig.) coronar, completar, perfeccionar. 4. (juego de damas) coronar. 5. poner una corona (postiza) a (diente). 6. (jer.) golpear (a alguien) en la cabeza. —*v.i.* 1. (juego de damas) convertirse en dama (un peón). 2. (med.) coronarse (el feto).
crown colony, colonia de la Corona (la que no tiene autonomía completa en la Comunidad Británica).
crowned head, testa coronada (monarca).
crowned pigeon, (orn.) gura.
crowner ['kraʊnər, B -ə] *s.* 1. coronador, colmo, culminación, punto culminante, remate. 2. cabezada, golpe en la cabeza; caída de cabeza.
crown glass, crown glass, vidrio (para vidrieras de ornamentación e instrumentos ópticos).
crown grafting, injerto de corona, injerto de coronilla.
crowning [-ɪŋ] *s.* remate, coronamiento, coronación.
crown land, (G.B.) patrimonio y bienes raíces de la Corona.
crown law, (G.B.) derecho penal o procesal.
crown lens, lente convergente de crown (de una lente acromática).
crownpiece [-,pis] *s.* remate, ápice.
crown prince, príncipe heredero.
crown princess, 1. esposa del príncipe heredero. 2. princesa heredera.
crown saw, sierra tubular giratoria.
crown wheel, (mec.) rueda coronaria o de escape, corona dentada.
crownwork [-'wɜrk, B -,wɜk] *s.* 1. (med.) corona artificial de los dientes, trabajo en coronas artificiales. 2. (anat., fort.) obra de corona, obra coronada.
crow's-foot ['kroʊz,fʊt] *s.* 1. pata de gallo (arruga en el extremo del ojo). 2. (mil.) abrojo.
crow's-nest [-,nɛst] 1. (mar.) nido de cuervo (cofa para la vigía). 2. torre de vigía (en tierra).
croze [kroʊz] *s.* 1. jable (de toneles y cubas), ruñaderas. 2. argollera, jabladera (para ruñar las cubas).
crozier, *var. de* **crosier.**
cruces, *pl. de* **crux.**
crucial ['kruʃəl] *a.* 1. crucial, grave, decisivo, crítico. 2. (ant.) crucial, cruciforme, en forma de cruz, cruzado, atravesado.
crucially [-ɪ] *adv.* críticamente, severamente.
cruciate ['kruʃɪ,eɪt] *a.* 1. cruciforme, en forma de cruz. 2. (bot.) crucífero. 3. (ento.) cruzada (díc. de las alas de algunos insectos).
crucible ['krusəbəl, B 'krʊ'sɪ-] *s.* 1. crisol. 2. (fig.) crisol, prueba severa, tribulación.
crucible steel, acero de crisol.
crucifer ['krusəfər, B -fə] *s.* 1. (relig.) cruciferario, crucífero, crucero. 2. (bot.) planta crucífera.
Cruciferae [kru'sɪfə,ri] *s. pl.* (bot.) crucíferas.
cruciferous [-rəs] *a.* (bot.) crucífero.
crucified ['krusə,faɪd] *p.p. de* **to crucify.** —*a.* crucificado.
crucifix [-,fɪks] *s.* crucifijo.
crucifixion [,krusə'fɪkʃən] *s.* 1. crucifixión. 2. (fig.) crucifixión, prueba dolorosa, sufrimiento intenso. 3. **the C.,** la Crucifixión.
cruciform ['krusə,fɔrm, B -,fɔm] *a.* cruciforme.
crucify [-,faɪ] *v.t.* (*pret., p.p.* CRUCIFIED ; *p.pr.* CRUCIFYING) 1. crucificar. 2. martirizar, atormentar. 3. (fig.) crucificar, mortificar; criticar acerbamente.
crud [krʌd] *s.* 1. sedimento de grasa, mugre; impureza. 2. mal, dolencia (no identificada). 3. (jer.) persona indigna y despreciable. 4. (jer.) enfermedad imaginaria. —*v.t., v.i.* (dial., poét.) cuajar, coagular, condensar.
crude [krud] *a.* 1. crudo, sin cocinar. 2. crudo, no sazonado, verde (frutas). 3. (fig.) crudo, sin acabar, tosco, imperfecto. 4. crudo, vulgar. 5. grosero, inculto, falto de tino. —*s.* substancia cruda (esp. petróleo crudo).
crudely ['krudlɪ] *adv.* crudamente, rudamente.
crudeness [-nəs] *s.* crudeza; grosería, falta de tino.
crude oil, petróleo bruto, petróleo crudo; aceite bruto; aceite pesado.
crudity [-ətɪ] *s.* crudeza, grosería, tosquedad.
cruel ['kruəl, 'krʊəl] *a.* (CRUELER O CRUELLER; CRUELEST O CRUELLEST) cruel, cruento, despiadado, atroz, inhumano, feroz, inclemente.
cruelly [-ɪ] *adv.* cruelmente.
cruelty [-tɪ] *s.* crueldad.
cruet ['kruət] *s.* ampolleta para aceite o vinagre; angarillas, vinagreras, convoy de mesa.
cruet stand, angarillas, vinagreras, convoy de mesa.
cruise [kruz] *v.i.* 1. (mar.) cruzar. 2. hacer un crucero por mar. 3. ambular, deambular, vagar, pasear; circular (ej., un taxi). 4. (mar., aer.) navegar o volar a velocidad de crucero. —*v.t.* 1. navegar (por). 2. inspeccionar (un bosque) para estimar la madera en pie. —*s.* crucero, viaje por mar o aire, excursión.
cruiser ['kruzər, B -ə] *s.* 1. (mar.) crucero. 2. *forma abrev. de* **cabin c.,** pequeño yate de motor. 3. taxi circulante; carro patrullero (de policía). 5. (jer.) ramera, prostituta. 4. inspector de bosque (que estima la cantidad de madera en pie).
cruising radius [-ɪŋ-] (mar., aer.) radio de acción; autonomía de vuelo.
cruising range, radio de acción (a velocidad de crucero).
cruising speed, 1. (mar., aer.) velocidad de crucero. 2. (aut.) velocidad de viaje.
cruller ['krʌlər, B -ə] *s.* buñuelo, churro; cohombro (fruta de sartén).
crumb [krʌm] *s.* 1. migaja, migajón, miaja, miga, mendrugo. 2. (jer.) desgraciado. —*v.t.* 1. migar, desmigar, desmigajar. 2. (cocina) cubrir con migajas, empanar. 3. limpiar de migas (ej., la mesa).
crumble ['krʌmbəl] *v.t.* desmenuzar, desmigar, desmigajar, desboronar (Am.). —*v.i.* desmoronarse, desintegrarse, derrumbarse. —*s.* escombros menudos.
crumbliness [-blɪnəs] *s.* 1. tendencia a desmoronarse. 2. estado ruinoso.
crumblings [-blɪŋz] *s. pl.* escombros menudos; migajas.
crumbly [-blɪ] *a.* desmoronadizo, desmenuzable, friable.
crumbum [-,bʌm] *s.* persona inútil, inservible.
crumby ['krʌmɪ] *a.* blando, miguero.
crummie ['krʌmɪ] *s.* (esco., N. de Ingl.) vaca (esp. con cuernos torcidos).
crummy ['krʌmɪ] *a.* (CRUMMIER; CRUMMIEST) (jer.) 1. miserable, de mala muerte, mísero, ej., *a c. joint,* un lugar miserable o de mala muerte. 2. gastado, trillado, ej., *a c. joke,* un chiste gastado.
crummy, *var. de* **crummie.**
crump [krʌmp] *v.i.* (pr. G.B.) 1. ronzar, roznar, detonar; cascar con los dientes. 2. estallar con estrépito. —*s.* 1. roznido, batacazo, detonación. 2. bomba, granada.
crumpet ['krʌmpət] *s.* 1. buñuelo o bollo blando frito. 2. (fam.) coco, cabeza.
crumple ['krʌmpəl] *v.t.* arrugar, apañuscar, estrujar. —*v.i.* 1. contraerse, encogerse, arrugarse. 2. (gen. con *up*) desplomarse. —*s.* arruga, pliegue.
crunch [krʌntʃ] *v.t.* 1. ronzar, roznar, ronchar, tascar; masticar (ruidosamente). 2. aplastar o pisar con ruido crujiente. —*v.i.* crujir. —*s.* 1. roznido, mascadura. 2. crujido.
crunchy ['krʌntʃɪ] *a.* (CRUNCHIER; CRUNCHIEST) 1. quebradizo. 2. crujiente.
cruor ['kruɔr, B -ɔ] *s.* (fisiol.) crúor, coágulo sanguíneo.
crupper ['krʌpər, 'krʊp-, B 'krʌpə] *s.* 1. baticola. 2. anca, grupa; (fam.) nalgas.
crural ['krʊrəl] *a.* (anat.) crural, femoral.
crus [krʌs, krus] *s.* (anat.) caña de la pierna; pedúnculo.
crusade [kru'seɪd] *s.* 1. cruzada. 2. (fig.) cruzada. —*v.i.* hacer una cruzada o campaña (por algo o contra algo).
crusader [-ər, B -ə] *s.* cruzado.
cruse [kruz, krus, B kruz] *s.* cántaro, jarra, botijo (para agua, aceite, etc.); cantarillo, botellita, frasco.
crush [krʌʃ] *v.t.* 1. apretar, estrujar, comprimir. 2. apiñar, apretar. 3. magullar, machacar, triturar. 4. aplastar, abrumar. 5. oprimir, pesar sobre, agobiar; anonadar, ej., *I was crushed by what you told me,* lo que me dijiste me anonadó. 6. (ant.)

beber. 7. **c. out,** extinguir (apretando, ej., cigarrillo). —*v.i.* 1. aplastarse, romperse. 2. (con *forward, toward, through,* etc.) avanzar a empellones. —*s.* 1. presión fuerte, apretadura violenta; destrucción. 2. apretón, apretadura (de gente); gentío, muchedumbre apiñada. 3. recepción o fiesta concurrida (en la que se agolpan los invitados). 4. (jer.) amorío, pasión, ej., *to have a c. on,* estar enamorado de, estar perdido por, tener una pasión por. 5. (jer.) amor, querido, querida.

crushed rock, c. stone, grava, gravilla.

crusher ['krʌʃər, B -ə] *s.* 1. (mec.) bocarte, trituradora, quebrantadora. 2. golpe violento. 3. (fam.) réplica aplastante; respuesta contundente.

crush hat, clac, sombrero de copa plegable.

crushing ['krʌʃɪŋ-] *a.* aplastante.

crushing strength, resistencia a la compresión.

crust [krʌst] *s.* 1. costra, corteza. 2. corteza de pan, mendrugo, corteza de un pastel. 3. capa (de nieve, suciedad, etc.); (geol.) capa exterior (de la tierra). 4. (zool.) concha, carapacho, tegumento duro. 5. sarro (en la superficie interior de las botellas de vino). 6. (jer.) desfachatez, impudencia, cara. —*v.t., v.i.* encostrar(se), revestir(se), incrustar(se).

crustacean [ˌkrʌs'teɪʃən] *a., s.* (zool.) crustáceo.

crustaceous [-ʃəs] *a.* (zool., bot.) crustáceo, que tiene carapacho, conchado.

crustal ['krʌstəl] *a.* de la corteza (terrestre o lunar).

crustation [ˌkrʌs'teɪʃən] *s.* costra, incrustación, formación de costras, cobertura.

crustification [-təfə'keɪʃən] *s.* encostradura, incrustación.

crustily ['krʌstəlɪ] *adv.* rudamente, ásperamente.

crustiness [-tɪnəs] *s.* 1. dureza de la costra. 2. mal genio, aspereza.

crusty ['krʌstɪ] *a.* 1. costroso, que parece costra. 2. de corteza dura (pan). 3. sarroso. 4. rudo, brusco, áspero.

crutch [krʌtʃ] *s.* 1. muleta. 2. (fig.) muleta, soporte, sostén. 3. horca, horcón, horqueta. 4. arzón (de la silla de montar); soporte ahorquillado (del sillón de montar). 5. (anat.) entrepiernas, bragadura. 6. (mar.) pique, candelero de horquilla. —*v.t.* ahorquillar, apuntalar. —*v.i.* andar con muletas, cojear.

crux [krʌks, krʊks, B krʌks] *s.* (*pl.* CRUXES o CRUCES ['kruˌsiz]) 1. enigma, problema arduo. 2. punto capital; punto crucial o crítico; el quid, lo esencial. 3. (her.) cruz. 4. **C.,** (astr.) Cruz.

cruzeiro [kru'zeɪroʊ, B krʊ-] *s.* cruzeiro (unidad mónetaria del Brasil).

cry [kraɪ] *v.i.* (*pret., p.p.* CRIED ; *p.pr.* CRYING) 1. gritar, exclamar, vocear, pregonar. 2. llorar, lamentarse. 3. aullar, bramar, ladrar. 4. **c. aloud,** llorar sollozando; **c. for,** clamar; **c. for mercy,** pedir gracia o misericordia; **c. for joy,** llorar de alegría; **c. off,** (pr. G.B.) retirarse; deshacer, romper (un contrato); **c. off from,** (G.B.) excusarse de tomar parte en, retirarse de (trato, juego); **c. out,** clamar, exclamar (con dolor, miedo, sorpresa, etc.); **c. out against,** clamar o protestar contra; **c. out for,** gritar por; **c. out to,** gritar a (alguien); **c. to heaven,** clamar al cielo; **it's no use to c. over spilt milk,** a lo hecho, pecho. —*v.t.* 1. decir a gritos, gritar, pedir, clamar, reclamar, implorar. 2. pregonar. 3. llorar. 4. **c. down,** menospreciar, despreciar; hacer callar a fuerza de gritos; **c. one's eyes** (o **heart**) **out,** llorar amargamente; **c. oneself to sleep,** llorar hasta quedarse dormido; **c. out,** pregonar, anunciar en voz alta, publicar; **c. quits,** dar por empatada la pelea, dar por terminada la discusión; **c. up,** alabar, elogiar; exaltar. —*s.* (*pl.* CRIES) 1. grito; exclamación. 2. clamor. 3. bramido; aullido. 4. grito, voz. 5. llanto. 6. moda, boga. 7. **a far c.,** gran distancia; mucha diferencia; **in full c.,** en plena persecución; (fig.) en plena marcha; **to have a good c.,** desahogarse llorando.

crybaby ['kraɪˌbeɪbɪ] *s.* llorón, llorona.

crying [-ɪŋ] *a.* llorón, quejumbroso. —*s.* lamento, grito.

crymotherapy [ˌkraɪmə'θɛrəpɪ] *s.* (med.) crimoterapia.

cryogen ['kraɪədʒən] *s.* (med.) criógeno.

cryogenic [ˌkraɪə'dʒɛnɪk] *a.* (med.) criogénico, criógeno.

cryogenics [-ɪks] *s. pl.* (*gen. sing. en const.*) criogenia.

cryohydrate [-'haɪˌdreɪt] *s.* (quím.) criohidrato.

cryolite ['kraɪəˌlaɪt] *s.* (min.) criolita.

cryometer [kraɪ'ɑmətər, B -'ɔmɪtə] *s.* criómetro.

cryophilic [ˌkraɪə'fɪlɪk] *a.* criófilo.

cryoscopy [kraɪ'ɑskəpɪ, B -'ɔs-] *s.* (fís.) crioscopia.

cryostat ['kraɪəˌstæt] *s.* (fís.) crióstato.

cryotherapy [ˌkraɪə'θɛrəpɪ] *var. de* **crymotherapy.**

crypt [krɪpt] *s.* 1. cripta, bóveda (subterránea). 2. (anat.) cripta, folículo, cavidad glandular.

cryptanalysis [ˌkrɪptə'næləsəs] *s.* criptoanálisis, análisis criptográfico.

cryptanalyst [-'tænələst] *s.* descifrador de criptogramas.

cryptic ['krɪptɪk] **cryptical** [-tɪkəl] *a.* misterioso, enigmático, secreto.

cryptically [-ɪkəlɪ] *adv.* misteriosamente, enigmáticamente.

cryptoclastic [ˌkrɪptə'klæstɪk] *a.* (geol.) criptoclástico.

cryptocrystalline [-toʊ'krɪstələn, B-laɪn] *a.* (fís., quím.) criptocristalino.

cryptogam ['krɪptəˌgæm] *s.* (bot.) criptógama.

Cryptogamia [ˌkrɪptə'gæmɪə] *s. pl.* (bot.) acotiledóneas.

cryptogamic [-'gæmɪk] **cryptogamous** [kri-p'tɑgəməs, B -'tɔg-] *a.* (bot.) criptógamo.

cryptogenic [-'dʒɛnɪk] *a.* criptogénico; de origen obscuro, ignorado.

cryptogram ['krɪptəˌgræm] *s.* criptograma; cifra, clave.

cryptograph [-ˌgræf, B -ˌgrɑf] 1. *var. de* **cryptogram.** 2. dispositivo para escribir o descifrar claves.

cryptographer [krɪp'tɑgrəfər, B -'tɔgrəfə] *s.* criptógrafo.

cryptographic [ˌkrɪptə'græfɪk] *a.* criptográfico.

cryptography [krɪp'tɑgrəfɪ, B -'tɔg-] *s.* criptografía.

cryptomeria [ˌkrɪptə'mɪrɪə, B -'mɪər-] *s.* (bot.) cedro del Japón.

cryptozoite [-'zoʊˌaɪt] *s.* (med.) criptozoíto.

crystal ['krɪstəl] *s.* 1. (min.) cristal (de roca). 2. cristal (de hielo, sal, etc.). 3. cristal, vidrio. 4. (electrón.) cristal. —*a.* 1. cristalino, transparente. 2. de cristal.

crystal ball, bola de cristal (del adivino).

crystal detector, (rad.) detector de cristal.

crystal gazing, 1. adivinación por medio de la bola de cristal. 2. (fig.) predicción del resultado de unas elecciones.

crystalliferous [ˌkrɪstə'lɪfərəs] *a.* cristalífero.

crystalline ['krɪstəlɪn, B -laɪn] *a.* 1. cristalino, claro, transparente. 2. de cristal.

crystalline lens, (anat.) cristalino (del ojo).

crystallite [-ˌlaɪt] *s.* (min.) cristalito.

crystallizable [-ˌlaɪzəbəl] *a.* cristalizable.

crystallization [ˌkrɪstələ'zeɪʃən, B -laɪ-] *s.* cristalización.

crystallize ['krɪstəˌlaɪz] *v.t., v.i.* (lit. y fig.) cristalizar(se).

crystallographer [ˌkrɪstə'lɑgrəfər, B -'lɔgrəfə] *s.* cristalógrafo.

crystallography [-fɪ] *s.* cristalografía.

crystalloid ['krɪstəˌlɔɪd] *a.* cristaloide. —*s.* (fís., bot.) cristaloide.

crystalloidal [ˌkrɪstə'lɔɪdəl] *a.* (fís.) cristaloideo.

crystal set, (rad.) receptor (con detector) de cristal.

crystal violet, (quím.) violeta cristal.

Cs *símb. de* **cesium,** cesio (Cs).

csc *abrev. de* **cosecant,** cosecante (cosec).

ctenoid ['tɛnˌɔɪd B 'tiˌnɔɪd] *a.* (ict.) serrada (escama); de escamas serradas.

ctenophoran [tɪ'nɑfərən, B -'nɔf-] *s., a.* (zool.) ctenóforo.

ctenophore ['tɛnəˌfɔr, B -ˌfɔ] *s.* (zool.) ctenóforo.

cu *abrev. de* **cubic,** cúbico.

Cu *símb. de* **cuprum,** cobre (Cu).

cub [kʌb] *s.* 1. cachorro (de mamífero); cría de ballena o tiburón; ballenato. 2. joven inexperto, inexperta. 3. aprendiz, principiante, novato.

Cuba ['kjubə] *s.* Cuba.

Cuban [-bən] *a., s.* cubano.

cubature ['kjubətʃər, B -tʃə] *s.* 1. (geom.) cubicación. 2. contenido cúbico, volumen.

cubby ['kʌbɪ] **cubbyhole** [-ˌhoʊl] *s.* 1. cuarto pequeño, chiribitil, cuartito. 2. casilla, compartimiento (de un armario, estantería, etc.).

cube [kjub] *s.* 1. (geom.) cubo. 2. (mat.) cubo, tercera potencia (de una cantidad). —*v.t.* cubicar, elevar al cubo (una cantidad).

cube, *s.* (bot.) verbasco, barbasco.

cubeb ['kjuˌbɛb] *s.* 1. (bot.) cubeba. 2. cigarrillo (medicinal) de cubeba.

cube root, (mat.) raíz cúbica.

cubic ['kjubɪk] *a.* cúbico; (mat., geom.) cúbico.

cubical [-bɪkəl] *a.* cúbico (esp. de forma de cubo).

cubically [-kəlɪ] *adv.* cúbicamente.

cubic capacity, cubicaje.

cubic content, volumen o capacidad cúbica.

cubic equation, ecuación cúbica o de tercer grado.

cubicle [-bɪkəl] *s.* 1. cubículo, recodo de una habitación. 2. compartimiento, recinto para el estudio individual (en biblioteca).

cubic measure, medida de capacidad.

cubiculum [kjʊ'bɪkjələm] *s.* cubículo (catacumbas), tumba.

cubiform ['kjubəˌfɔrm B -ˌfɔm] *a.* de forma cúbica.

cubism [-ˌbɪzəm] *s.* (arte) cubismo (estilo y escuela).

cubist [-bəst] *s., a.* (arte) cubista.

cubit ['kjubət] *s.* codo (medida antigua).

cubital [-bətəl] *a.* 1. cubital. 2. codal (que mide un codo).

cuboid ['kjuˌbɔɪd] *a.* cuboideo. —*s.* 1. (mat.) paralelepípedo rectangular. 2. (anat.) cuboides.

cuboidal [kju'bɔɪdəl] *a.* cúbico, cuboideo.

cuboid bone, (anat.) hueso cuboides.

cub scout, (E.U.) niño explorador (de 8 a 10 años).

cucking stool['kʌkɪŋ-] silla de chapuzar (utilizada antiguamente para castigar).

cuckold ['kʌkəld, B -oʊld] *s.* cornudo, cabrón. —*v.t.* encornudar, hacer cornudo (a un marido).

cuckoo ['ku,ku, B 'kʊku] *s.* 1. (orn.) cuclillo, cuco. 2. cucú (canto del cuclillo). 3. (fam.) tonto, loco. —*v.i.* (*pret., p.p.* CUCKOOED; *p.pr.* CUCKOOING) cantar como un cuclillo. —*v.t.* repetir monótonamente. —*a.* (fam.) loco, chiflado, tonto.
cuckoo clock, reloj de cuclillo o de cuco.
cuckooflower [-,flaʊər, B -ə] *s.* (bot.) 1. cardámina. 2. acederilla.
cuckoopint [-,pɪnt] *s.* (bot.) aro europeo, tragontina.
cuckoo spit, c. spittle, (ento.) baba de cuclillo.
cuculiform [kə'kjulə,fɔrm, B kjʊ'kʌlɪ,fɔm] *a.* (orn.) cuculiforme.
cucullate ['kjukə,leɪt] **cucullated** [-əd] *a.* cuculado; en forma de capucha.
cucumber ['kjukʌmbər, B -bə] *s.* (bot.) pepino, cohombro (fruta y planta); **cool as a c.,** sereno, sosegado; (fam.) fresco como una lechuga.
cucumber tree, (bot.) magnolia (magnolia acuminata).
cucumiform [kjʊ'kjumə,fɔrm, B -,fɔm] *a.* en forma de pepino.
cucurbit [kju'kɜrbət, B -'kɜbɪt] *s.* 1. cucúrbita, retorta. 2. (bot.) cucurbitácea.
cucurbitaceous [kjʊ,kɜrbə'teɪʃəs, B -,kɜbɪ-] *a.* (bot.) cucurbitáceo.
cud [kʌd] *s.* 1. bolo alimenticio (que los rumiantes mastican por segunda vez). 2. (fam.) mascada de tabaco. 3. **to chew the c.,** rumiar; (fig.) reflexionar, meditar.
cudbear ['kʌd,bɛr, B -,bɛə] *s.* 1. (bot.) orchilla. 2. orcina (materia colorante).
cuddle ['kʌdəl] *v.t.* abrazar, acariciar, abrigar; mimar. —*v.i.* juntarse, arrimarse (por frío, cariño, etc.).
cuddlesome [-səm] *a.* amable, atractivo, cautivador.
cuddy ['kʌdɪ] *s.* 1. (mar.) camarote de proa. 2. (mar.) pañol, despensa (en una embarcación pequeña). 3. cuartito; alacena pequeña.
cuddy, *s.* (esco.) burro; tonto, mentecato, zopenco.
cudgel ['kʌdʒəl] *s.* garrote, porra, estaca; **to take up the cudgels for,** (fig.) entrar en la lucha (por), salir en defensa. —*v.t.* (*pret., p.p.* CUDGELED O CUDGELLED; *p.pr.* CUDGELING O CUDGELLING) aporrear, apalear, tundir; **c. one's brains,** devanarse los sesos.
cudgel play, (esgr.) asalto con bastones.
cue [kju] *s.* 1. (teat.) pie, apunte. 2. indicación, señal. 3. cola (de personas que esperan). 4. trenza, coleta (de cabello). 5. taco (de billar). 6. **to take one's c. (from),** guiarse, dejarse guiar uno (por). —*v.t.* (*pret., p.p.* CUED; *p.pr.,* CUING O CUEING) 1. trenzar; entrelazar, entretejer; enroscar. 2. apuntar, (fig.) dar el pie a (los técnicos o actores). 3. **c. in,** insertar. —*v.i.* 1. (gen. con *up*) hacer cola (esperando). 2. golpear con taco (de billar).
cue ball, (billar) pinta.
cue rest, (billar) diablo.
cuff [kʌf] *s.* 1. puño (de camisa, etc.). 2. doblez, vuelta (en el pantalón). 3. (*pl.*) esposas. 4. **off the c.,** (jer.) improvisado, espontáneo, extemporáneo; improvisadamente, extemporáneamente; **on the c.,** (jer.) a crédito, a plazos. —*v.t.* 1. poner puños en (vestido). 2. esposar.
cuff, *v.t.* abofetear, dar golpes, golpear con la mano abierta. —*v.i.* trenzarse a golpes. —*s.* bofetón, manotada (Am.).
cuff button, botón del puño.
cuff links, gemelos, yugos (Am.), yuntas, mancuernas, cuencas.
Cufic ['kjufɪk] *a.* cúfico (alfabeto, escritura).
cuirass [kwɪ'ræs] *s.* 1. coraza, armadura, peto de armadura. 2. (zool.) coraza. —*v.t.* armar de coraza, poner armadura.
cuirassier [,kwɪrə'sɪr, B -'sɪə] *s.* coracero.
cuish [kwɪʃ] *var. de* **cuisse.**
cuisine [kwɪ'zin] *s.* cocina; arte culinario.
cuisse [kwɪs] *s.* (arm.) muslera, quijote.
culch, *var. de* **cultch.**
cul-de-sac [,kʌldə'sæk, ,kʊl-, B 'kʊl-, 'kʌl-] *s.* callejón sin salida.
culet ['kjulət] *s.* 1. (joy.) pequeña faceta plana (que constituye el fondo de un brillante, paralela a la faceta del haz). 2. escarcela (de una armadura).
culex ['kju,lɛks] *s.* (ento.) mosquito común.
culicid [kju'lɪsəd] *s.* (ento.) culícido.
culinary ['kʌlə,nɛrɪ, 'kju-, B 'kʌlɪnərɪ] *a.* culinario.
cull [kʌl] *v.t.* recoger; escoger, entresacar, seleccionar. —*s.* pieza desechada, desecho.
cullender ['kʌləndər, B -də] *s.* coladera, colador, espumadera, escurridor.
cullet ['kʌlət] *s.* vidrio de desecho.
cullion ['kʌljən] *s.* (ant.) pícaro, tunante.
cullis ['kʌləs] *s.* (arq.) canal (en el tejado).
cully ['kʌlɪ] *s.* (raro) bobo, tonto, incauto, simplón. —*v.t.* (*pret., p.p.* CULLIED; *p.pr.* CULLYING) (ant.) engañar, tomar el pelo.
culm [kʌlm] *s.* polvo o desperdicios de carbón, cisco; antracita inferior.
culm, *s.* (bot.) caña, tallo (propio de las gramas).
culminant ['kʌlmənənt] *a.* culminante.
culminate [-,neɪt] *v.i.* culminar; (astr.) culminar; **c. in,** conducir a, terminar en. —*v.t.* hacer culminar, llevar al punto culminante.
culmination [,kʌlmə'neɪʃən] *s.* culminación, apogeo; (astr.) culminación.
culottes [kʊ'lɑts, B kjʊ'lɔts] *s. pl.* falda pantalón.
culpa ['kʊlpə, 'kʌl-] *s.* (der.) negligencia, culpabilidad.
culpability [,kʌlpə'bɪlətɪ] *s.* culpabilidad.
culpable ['kʌlpəbəl] *a.* culpable.
culpableness [-nəs] *s.* culpabilidad.
culpably [-blɪ] *adv.* culpablemente.
culprit ['kʌlprət] *s.* culpado, acusado; delincuente, reo, criminal.
cult [kʌlt] *s.* 1. (relig.) culto. 2. secta, cofradía, círculo.
cultch [kʌltʃ] *s.* 1. ripio o desperdicio (como conchas de ostras) en que se fijan los embriones (en un ostrero). 2. hueva de molusco.
cultigen ['kʌltədʒən] *s.* planta cultivada (esp. la que no tiene variedad silvestre).
cultism ['kʌlt,ɪzəm] *s.* 1. devoción a un culto. 2. cultismo, culteranismo; (lit.) gongorismo.
cultist [-əst] *s.* devoto, cultor.
cultivable ['kʌltəvəbəl] *a.* cultivable.
cultivatable [-,veɪtəbəl] *a.* cultivable.
cultivate [-,veɪt] *v.t.* 1. cultivar, labrar (la tierra). 2. cultivar (plantas). 3. criar (ej., ostras, gusanos de seda, etc.). 4. (fig.) cultivar (amistad, estilo). 5. asociarse con (gente); frecuentar (compañía).
cultivated [-əd] *a.* 1. culto, cultivado, refinado; ilustrado, instruido (personas). 2. (agr.) cultivado, labrado.
cultivation [,kʌltə'veɪʃən] *s.* 1. cultivación, cultivo. 2. cultura, refinamiento.
cultivator ['kʌltə,veɪtər, B -ə] *s.* 1. cultivador. 2. labrador, agricultor. 3. (agr.) extirpador.
cultrate ['kʌl,treɪt] **cultrated** [-əd] *a.* afilado; puntiagudo, que tiene forma de cuchillo.
cultural ['kʌltʃərəl] *a.* cultural, perteneciente a la cultura o al cultivo.
culture [-tʃər, B -tʃə] *s.* 1. cultura. 2. cultivo, labranza (de la tierra); cría (de ostras, gusanos de seda, etc.), cultivo (de perlas, plantas, etc.). 3. (biol.) cultivo (de bacterias omicroorganismos). 4. civilización. —*v.t.* 1. cultivar, labrar. 2. (biol.) cultivar (microorganismos, etc.). 3. educar, enseñar, refinar.
cultured [-tʃərd, B -tʃəd] *a.* 1. culto, refinado. 2. cultivado, de cultivo (perlas, bacterias, etc.).
cultus ['kʌltəs] *s.* culto (esp. religioso).
culver ['kʌlvər, B -və] *s.* paloma, pichón.
culverin [-vərən] *s.* (arm.) 1. culebrina. 2. mosquete primitivo.
culvert [-vərt, B -vət] *s.* alcantarilla, atarjea.
cum [kʊm, B kʌm] *prep.* con; combinado con; junto con; **c. laude,** con honor. —*a.* (com.) que incluye dividendo. —*adv.* con dividendo incluso.
cumber ['kʌmbər, B -bə] *v.t.* embarazar, molestar, estorbar, impedir, obstaculizar. —*s.* molestia, estorbo, impedimento, obstáculo.
cumbersome [-səm] *a.* pesado, embarazoso, engorroso, incómodo, molesto, difícil de manejar.
cumbersomely [-lɪ] *adv.* embarazosamente, pesadamente.
cumbersomeness [-nəs] *s.* carácter embarazoso, pesadez.
cumbrance ['kʌmbrəns] *s.* (ant.) carga, peso, molestia, impedimento, obstáculo.
cumbrous [-brəs] *a.* pesado, embarazoso, engorroso, incómodo.
cumbrously [-lɪ] *adv.* embarazosamente, pesadamente.
cumbrousness [-nəs] *s.* carácter embarazoso, pesadez.
cumin ['kʌmən] *s.* (bot.) comino.
cuminol ['kjumə,nɔl] *s.* (quím.) cuminol.
cummer ['kʌmər, B -ə] *s.* (esco.) madrina; amiga; mujer, niña.
cummerbund ['kʌmər,bʌnd, B -ə,-] *s.* faja ancha (que se usa alrededor de la cintura).
cumquat, *var. de* **kumquat.**
cumshaw ['kʌm,ʃɔ] *s.* propina; regalo, obsequio, presente (esp. en el Oriente).
cumulate ['kjumjə,leɪt] *v.t., v.i.* acumular(se), cumular(se).
cumulation [,kjumjə'leɪʃən] *s.* acumulación, cumulación.
cumulative ['kjumjələtɪv, -,leɪt-] *a.* acumulativo; (fin.) acumulativo, acumulable (dividendo, interés); (der.) cumulativo (prueba); acumulada (condena).
cumulatively [-lɪ] *adv.* acumulativamente.
cumuliform [-lə,fɔrm, B -,fɔm] (meteor.) cumuliforme.
cumulocirrus [,kjumjəloʊ'sɪrəs] *s.* (meteor.) cirrocúmulo, cúmulo cirro.
cumulonimbus [-'nɪmbəs] *s.* (meteor.) cumulonimbo.
cumulostratus [-'streɪtəs] *s.* (meteor.) cumulostrato.
cumulous ['kjumjələs] *a.* (meteor.) en forma de un cúmulo, parecido a un cúmulo, compuesto de cúmulos.
cumulus [-ləs] *s.* 1. montón, acumulación. 2. (meteor.) cúmulo.
cunctation [,kʌŋk'teɪʃən] *s.* demora, tardanza.
cuneal ['kjunɪəl] *a.* cuneiforme.
cuneate [-,eɪt] *a.* (bot.) cuneiforme (hoja)
cuneatic [,kjunɪ'ætɪk] *a.* cuneiforme.
cuneiform [kju'niə,fɔrm, 'kjunɪə-, B 'kjuniɪ,fɔm] *a.* cuneiforme (escritura). —*s.* 1. carácter o inscripción cuneiforme. 2. (ant.) (hueso) cuneiforme, cuña.
cuneus ['kjunɪəs] *s.* (*pl.* CUNEI [-nɪi]) cúneo (en teatros antiguos).
cunner ['kʌnər, B -ə] *s.* (ict.) un pez lábrido.

cunnilingus [ˌkʌnɪ'lɪŋgəs] **cunnilinctus** [-'lɪŋktəs] *s.* cunilinguo (actividad sexual que comprende el contacto bucal con los órganos genitales femeninos).
cunning ['kʌnɪŋ] *a.* 1. astuto, artero, socarrón. 2. (E.U.) gracioso, lindo, mono. 3. hábil, diestro, ingenioso, sagaz. —*s.* 1. habilidad, destreza. 2. astucia, artimaña, artificio, ardid. 3. (ant.) conocimiento, erudición.
cunningly [-lɪ] *adv.* 1. hábilmente, diestramente. 2. astutamente, arteramente. 3. graciosamente.
cunningness [-nəs] *s.* astucia.
cunt [kʌnt] *s.* 1. (vulg.) coño, concha, chocho, chocha, pucha. 2. (depec.) hija de puta.
cup [kʌp] *s.* 1. taza; jícara. 2. taza, contenido de una taza. 3. (*pl.*) borrachera. 4. (relig.) cáliz; vino eucarístico. 5. (med.) ventosa (empleada para atraer la sangre a la superficie del cuerpo). 6. (bot.) cáliz. 7. copa, trofeo. 8. (golf) caja de metal (dentro del hoyo); hoyo, agujero. 9. **bitter c.,** cáliz de amargura; **his c. was full,** su felicidad (o desgracia) era completa; **in one's cups,** borracho; **it is not my c. of tea,** esto no es de mi interés o agrado. —*v.t.* (*pret., p.p.* CUPPED; *p.pr.* CUPPING) 1. (med.) aplicar ventosas a. 2. ahuecar (esp. la mano) en forma de taza. 3. poner en una taza o copa.
cup anemometer, anemómetro de semiesferas.
cup barometer, (meteor.) barómetro de cubeta.
cupbearer ['kʌpˌbɛrər, B -ˌbɛərə] *s.* copero, escanciador.
cupboard ['kʌbərd, B -əd] *s.* aparador, alacena.
cupcake ['kʌpˌkeɪk] *s.* pastelito horneado en molde de forma de taza.
cupel [kju'pɛl, B 'kjupəl] *s.* (metal.) copela. —*v.t.* (*pret., p.p.* CUPELLED O CUPELED; *p.pr.* CUPELLING O CUPELING) (metal.) copelar.
cupellation [ˌkjupə'leɪʃən] *s.* (metal.) copelación.
cupful ['kʌpˌfʊl] *s.* (contenido de una) taza; (cocina) taza (media pinta).
cup grease, grasa lubricante, grasa de copa.
Cupid ['kjupəd] *s.* (mitol.) Cupido; **c.,** figura de Cupido.
cupidity [kjʊ'pɪdətɪ] *s.* 1. codicia, avaricia. 2. (ant.) concupiscencia.
Cupid's bow, 1. arco de Cupido. 2. labios pintados en forma de corazón.
cupola ['kjupələ] *s.* 1. (arq.) cúpula, domo. 2. (metal.) cubilote. 3. (mar.) cúpula (de un acorazado). 4. (anat., zool.) cúpula. 5. (geol.) bóveda.
cupped [kʌpt] *a.* acopado, en forma de copa; (vet., bot.) acopado.
cupper ['kʌpər, B -ə] *s.* aplicador de ventosas.
cupping [-ɪŋ] *s.* (med.) aplicación de ventosas.
cupreous ['kjuprɪəs] *a.* (metal.) cobrizo.
cupric [-prɪk] *a.* (quím.) cúprico.
cupriferous [kju'prɪfərəs] *a.* (quím.) cuprífero.
cuprite ['kjuˌpraɪt] *s.* (min.) cuprita.
cupronickel [ˌkjuproʊ'nɪkəl] *s.* cuproníquel.
cuprous ['kjuprəs] *a.* (quím.) cuproso.
cuprum [-prəm] *s.* (quím.) cobre.
cupulate ['kjupjəˌleɪt] **cupular** [-lər, B -lə] *a.* acopado, en forma de cúpula, que tiene cúpula.
cupule ['kjupjul] *s.* (bot.) cúpula.
cur [kɜr, B kɜ] *s.* 1. perro cruzado. 2. hombre vil, canalla.
curability [ˌkjʊrə'bɪlətɪ, B ˌkjʊər-] *s.* curabilidad, capacidad para ser curado.
curable ['kjʊrəbəl, B 'kjʊər-] *a.* curable.
curableness [-nəs] *s.* curabilidad.
curaçao [ˌkjʊrə'soʊ, -'saʊ, B ˌkjʊərə'soʊ] **curaçoa** [-'soʊə] *s.* curasao, curazao (licor).
curacy ['kjʊrəsɪ, B 'kjʊər-] *s.* (relig.) curato.
curare, curari [kjʊ'rɑrɪ] *s.* (bot.) curare, planta venenosa.
curarine [-ən, B 'kjʊərəˌraɪn] *s.* (quím.) curarina.
curarization [-ˌrɑrə'zeɪʃən, B ˌkjʊrəraɪ-] *s.* tratamiento con curare, aplicación del curare.
curarize [-'rɑrˌaɪz, B 'kjʊərəˌraɪz] *v.t.* tratar con curare, aplicar curare a.
curassow ['kjʊrəˌsoʊ, B 'kjʊər-] *s.* (orn.) guaco.
curate ['kjʊrət, B 'kjʊər-] *s.* 1. (relig.) cura, asistente de párroco. 2. párroco, cura (*m.*).
curative [-ɪv] *a.* curativo. —*s.* remedio.
curator [kjʊ'reɪtər, B kjʊə-ə] *s.* 1. conservador, encargado (de museo). 2. guardián, celador (ej., en un jardín zoológico). 3. (E.U.) miembro del cuerpo administrativo (de una universidad); (esco.) miembro del cuerpo elector (de profesores en una universidad). 4. (der. romano y esco.) curador, ecónomo, tutor.
curatorship [-ˌʃɪp] *s.* 1. oficio o puesto de conservador (de museo). 2. (der. romano y esco.) curaduría, tutela.
curb [kɜrb, B kɜb] *s.* 1. barbada (del freno del caballo). 2. (fig.) freno, restricción. 3. reborde. 4. brocal (del pozo). 5. encintado, bordillo, flanco (de la acera), orilla. 6. (mec.) camisa, envolvente. 7. (econ.) bolsa exterior, bolsa de la calle. 8. **to put a c. on,** (fig.) poner freno a. —*v.t.*contener, refrenar, controlar.
curb bit, bocado (de la brida).
curbing ['kɜrbɪŋ, B 'kɜb-] *s.* reborde, material para reborde.
curb service, servicio que se ofrece a clientes que permanecen en su automóvil.
curbstone [-ˌstoʊn] *s.* guardacantón, reborde, piedra de cordón; canto (de acera); brocal (de pozo).
curculio [kər'kjulɪˌoʊ, B kə'-] *s.* (*pl.* CURCULIOS) (ento.) curculio, gorgojo.
curcuma ['kɜrkjəmə, B 'kɜkjʊ-] *s.* (bot.) cúrcuma.
curd [kɜrd, B kɜd] *s.* cuajada, requesón. —*v.t., v.i.* coagular(se), cuajar(se).
curdle ['kɜrdəl, B 'kɜd-] *v.t., v.i.* coagular(se), cuajar(se), espesar(se); **c. one's blood,** (fig.) helarse la sangre (de miedo), ej., *my blood curdled at the sight,* se me heló la sangre al verlo.
curdy [-ɪ] *a.* cuajado, coagulado.
cure [kjʊr, B kjʊə] *s.* 1. remedio, cura; método curativo. 2. curación, cura. 3. cura, cura de almas, atención espiritual. 4. cura, curación (de carnes, pescado, pieles, etc.); curtido (de pieles); cura (de tabaco, madera, tela). —*v.t.* 1. curar, sanar. 2. remediar (un mal). 3. curar (carne, pieles, madera); vulcanizar (goma). —*v.i.* curarse.
curé [kjʊ'reɪ, B 'kjʊreɪ] *s.* cura (*m.*), párroco.
cure-all ['kjʊrˌɔl, B 'kjʊər-] *s.* curalotodo, panacea.
cureless [-ləs, B 'kjʊələs] *a.* incurable.
curer [-ər, B -rə] *s.* preservador, preparador (de salazones y conservas).
curettage [ˌkjʊrə'tɑʒ, B kjʊ'rɛtɪdʒ] *s.* (med.) raspado, curetaje.
curette [kjʊ'rɛt] *s.* (med.) cureta. —*v.t.* (med.) raspar (con una cureta), hacer un curetaje a.
curfew ['kɜrfju, B 'kɜfju] *s.* 1. queda. 2. toque de queda.
curia ['kjʊrɪə, B 'kjʊər-] *s.* (*pl.* CURIAE [-ɪˌi]) 1. (hist. romana) curia. 2. corte del rey. 3. curia, tribunal. 4. (relig.) **C.,** Curia romana.
curial [-ɪəl] *a.* curial.
curie ['kjʊri, B 'kjʊərɪ] *s.* (fís.) curio.
Curie's law, (fís.) ley de Curie.
curio ['kjʊrɪˌoʊ, B 'kjʊər-] *s.* (*pl.*) curiosidad, objeto (de arte) curioso; bibelot.
curiosa [ˌkjʊrɪ'oʊsə, B ˌkjʊər-] *s. pl.* curiosidades, rarezas (esp. libros de temas extraños, a menudo eróticos).
curiosity [-'ɑsətɪ, B -'ɔs-] *s.* 1. curiosidad; **c. killed the cat,** el pez por su boca muere. 2. curiosidad, rareza.
curious ['kjʊrɪəs, B 'kjʊər-] *a.* 1. curioso, indiscreto. 2. curioso, raro, interesante. 3. (ant.) cuidadoso, exacto, minucioso.
curiously [-lɪ] *adv.* curiosamente.
curiousness [-nəs] *s.* curiosidad.
curite ['kjʊrˌaɪt, B 'kjʊər-] *s.* (min.) curita.
curium [-ɪəm] *s.* (quím.) curio.
curl [kɜrl, B kɜl] *v.t.* 1. rizar, ondear, ensortijar; encrespar. 2. arrollar, enrollar. 3. torcer (ej., los labios). 4. **c. up,** arrollar; **c. up in a ball,** ovillar. —*v.i.* 1. rizarse, ondear (pelo, etc.). 2. salir o ascender en espiral (humo, etc.). 3. serpentear, retorcerse. 4. jugar al "curling". 5. **c. up,** arrollarse; encogerse, acurrucarse; **c. up in a ball,** ovillar. —*s.* 1. rizo, bucle, tirabuzón (de pelo). 2. ondulación, espiral (de humo, etc.); sinuosidad. 3. torcedura, torcimiento. 4. veta espiral (en maderas). 5. (bot.) zarcillo. 6. (bot.) alechugamiento anormal (de hojas).
curled [kɜrld, B kɜld] *a.* (bot.) rizada (col).
curler ['kɜrlər, B 'kɜlə] *s.* 1. rizador, encrespador. 2. (*gen. pl.*) tenacillas (para rizar el pelo). 3. jugador de "curling".
curlew ['kɜrlu, B 'kɜlju] *s.* (orn.) sarapito, sarapico.
curlicue ['kɜrlɪˌkju, B 'kɜlɪ-] *s.* plumada, voluta. —*v.t.* trazar plumadas, adornar con volutas.
curliness ['kɜrlɪnəs, B 'kɜlɪ-] *s.* ensortijamiento.
curling [-lɪŋ] *s.* (dep.) juego escocés sobre hielo en el que se hace deslizar piedras hacia una meta.
curling iron, tenacillas, rizador, encrespador (de cabello).
curlpaper ['kɜrlˌpeɪpər, B 'kɜl-pə] *s.* rollete de papel usado para rizar el pelo.
curly ['kɜrlɪ, B 'kɜlɪ] *a.* (CURLIER; CURLIEST) crespo, rizo, rizado, ensortijado, encrespado.
curlycue, *var. de* **curlicue.**
curly grain, fibra ondulada.
curmudgeon [kər'mʌdʒən, B ˌkɜ'-] *s.* 1. malgenioso, cascarrabias. 2. (ant.) tacaño, cicatero.
curn [kɜrn, B kɜn] *s.* (esco.) grano; gránulo.
curr [kɜr, B kɜ] *v.i.* murmurar, arrullar.
currant ['kɜrənt, B 'kʌr-] *s.* 1. (bot.) pasa de Corinto. 2. grosellero; uva crespa, uva espina. 3. grosella.
currency ['kɜrənsɪ, B 'kʌr-] *s.* (*pl.* CURRENCIES) 1. moneda, moneda corriente, dinero en circulación. 2. valor corriente. 3. aceptación o uso general.
currency expansion, (fin.) expansión del circulante.
current ['kɜrənt, B 'kʌr-] *a.* 1. corriente, actual, en curso. 2. corriente, de actualidad, popular, de moda. 3. (com.) corriente, abierto (crédito, cuenta, etc.). —*s.* 1. corriente (de agua, río, aire, etc.). 2. corriente, flujo, curso. 3. corriente, tendencia (de opiniones, etc.). 4. (elec.) corriente.
current account, (ten.) cuenta corriente.
current assets, (com.) activo corriente o realizable.
current breaker, (elec.) interruptor de corriente, cortacorriente, interruptor eléctrico.
current density, (elec.) densidad de corriente.
current events, sucesos del momento, actualidades, asuntos de actualidad.
current exchange, (com.) cambio corriente.

current liabilities, (com.) pasivo corriente o exigible.
currently [-lɪ] *adv.* 1. corrientemente, con fluidez. 2. actualmente, presentemente.
current meter, 1. (hidr.) contador de corriente, correntímetro, hidrómetro. 2. (elec.) contador de intensidad.
current money, (econ.) moneda nacional, moneda (de curso) legal, moneda corriente.
currentness [-nəs] *s.* actualidad, aceptación general.
current price, precio corriente o actual.
current rate, (com.) curso; precio, tarifa, etc. corriente.
curricle ['kɜrɪkəl, B 'kʌrɪ-] *s.* silla volante, carrocín.
curricular [kə'rɪkjələr, B -lə] *a.* curricular, del plan de estudios.
curriculum [-ləm] *s.* (*pl.* CURRICULA [-lə] CURRICULUMS) currículum, plan o programa de estudios.
curriculum vitae [-'vaɪtɪ] curriculum vitae, historial personal, sumario personal y profesional, resumen.
currier ['kɜrɪər, B 'kʌrɪə] *s.* 1. almohazador (de caballos). 2. (curtiduría) adobador (de pieles).
curriery [-ərɪ] *s.* (curtiduría) sobadero, tenería.
currish ['kɜrɪʃ] *a.* 1. perruno. 2. arisco, regañón.
currishly [-lɪ] *adv.* ásperamente, malhumoradamente.
curry ['kɜrɪ, B 'kʌrɪ] *v.t.* (*pret., p.p.* CURRIED; *p.pr.* CURRYING) 1. sobar, adobar (cuero curtido). 2. almohazar (caballos o ganado). 3. sobar, zurrar, castigar. 4. cocinar o sazonar con cari. 5. **c. favor,** buscar favores de una manera servil; **c. favor with,** congraciarse con (alguien). —*s.* cari, pimienta de la India.
currycomb [-ˌkoʊm] *s.* almohaza, rascadera. —*v.t.* almohazar.
curry powder, polvo de curry o cari.
curse [kɜrs, B kɜs] *s.* 1. maldición, imprecación, juramento, blasfemia. 2. (relig.) anatema, excomunión. 3. maleficio, hechizo maligno. 4. mal, aflicción, calamidad, azote. 5. **the c.,** (jer.) menstruación; **curses on . . . !** ¡mal haya(n) . . . !; **c. on him!** ¡maldito sea!; **under a c.,** hechizado. —*v.t.* 1. maldecir, imprecar. 2. (relig.) execrar, anatematizar. 3. **to be cursed with,** estar afligido o angustiado por. —*v.i.* blasfemar, jurar, renegar.
cursed ['kɜrsəd, kɜrst, B 'kɜsɪd] *a.* 1. maldito; execrable, abominable. 2. hechizado. 3. (dial. gen. **curst**) pendenciero, avieso.
cursedness [-nəs] *s.* malicia, abominación.
cursing ['kɜrsɪŋ, B 'kɜsɪŋ] *s.* imprecación, blasfemia, maldición. —*a.* maldiciente, blasfemador.
cursive ['kɜrsɪv, B 'kɜsɪv] *a.* cursiva (letra, escritura). —*s.* letra cursiva; (tip.) cursiva.
cursorial [kər'sɔrɪəl B kə'-] *a.* (zool.) corsorípedo.
cursorily ['kɜrsərəlɪ, B 'kɜs-] *adv.* superficialmente, de paso, de carrera, precipitadamente.
cursoriness [-rɪnəs] *s.* precipitación, superficialidad.
cursory ['kɜrsərɪ, B 'kɜs-] *s.* superficial, sumario.
curst [kɜrst, B kɜst] (*pret. y p.p. ant. de* **curse**) *var. de* **cursed.**
curt [kɜrt, B kɜt] *a.* 1. breve, corto, lacónico. 2. brusco, rudo. 3. (ant.) acortado.
curtail [kər'teɪl, B kɜ'-] *v.t.* acortar, cercenar, reducir, abreviar.
curtailment [-mənt] *s.* acortamiento, reducción, abreviación, restricción.
curtain ['kɜrtən, B 'kɜtən] *s.* 1. cortina. 2. (fig.) cortina, pantalla (de humo, lluvia; de seguridad; de mentiras, disimulo, etc.). 3. (teat.) telón; bajada del telón, fin (de un acto o escena). 4. (fig.) acto final, última escena. 5. (*pl.*) fin (esp. muerte), ej., *it's curtains for him,* esto es el fin para él. 6. (arq.) lienzo (de pared). 7. (fort.) cortina, lienzo (entre dos bastiones o baluartes). 8. **behind the c.,** (fig.) entre bambalinas, en secreto, en privado; **the c. falls** (o **drops,** o **is dropped**), baja el telón (al fin del acto y fig.); **the c. rises** (o **is raised**), sube el telón (al comienzo del acto y fig.); **to draw the c.,** (fig.) correr la cortina (para descubrir u ocultar algo); **to raise the c.,** alzar el telón. —*v.t.* 1. poner cortina(s) en, cubrir con cortina(s). 2. (fig.) cubrir, tapar. 3. **c. off,** separar con (o por) cortina(s).
curtain call, (teat.) llamada a escena (al final de la representación para recibir aplausos).
curtain lecture, reprimenda conyugal, regaño de la mujer (al marido).
curtain of fire, (mil.) cortina de fuego.
curtain raiser, 1. (teat.) entremés, pequeña obra preliminar. 2. corta introducción.
curtain speech, (teat.) discurso pronunciado delante del telón al final de una representación.
curtain wall, (teat.) paneles.
curtal ['kɜrtəl, B 'kɜtəl] (ant.) *a.* 1. mocho, con rabo cortado. 2. vestido de túnica corta. —*s.* animal mocho (con el rabo cortado, esp. el caballo).
curtal ax, *var. de* **cutlass.**
curtate [-ˌteɪt] *a.* abreviado, acortado, reducido.
curtation [kər'teɪʃən, B kə'-] *s.* (astr.) curtación.
curtesy, *var. de* **courtesy.**
curtilage ['kɜrtəlɪdʒ, B 'kɜt-] *s.* (der.) propiedad cercada.
curtly ['kɜrtlɪ, B 'kɜt-] *adv.* brevemente, lacónicamente, fríamente.
curtness [-nəs] *s.* brevedad, laconismo; frialdad.
curtsy, curtsey ['kɜrtsɪ, B 'kɜt-] *s.* (*pl.* CURTSIES o curtseys) reverencia (ant. hecha esp. por mujeres o niñas); **to make** (o **to drop**) **a.,** hacer una reverencia. —*v.i.* (*pret., p.p.* CURTSIED o CURTSEYED; *p.pr.* CURTSYING o CURTSEYING) hacer una reverencia.
curule ['kjʊrˌul] *a.* (hist. romana) curul (díc. de una silla romana utilizada por los ediles).
curvaceous [kər'veɪʃəs, B kə'-] *a.* de curvas marcadas, curvilíneo (cuerpo femenino).
curvature ['kɜrvətʃər, B 'kɜvətʃə] *s.* 1. curvatura. 2. combadura; (med.) encorvamiento (esp. anormal). 3. (arq.) cintras.
curve [kɜrv, B kɜv] *a.* (ant.) curvo, curvado. —*s.* 1. curva; (mat.) curva. 2. (*pl.*) curvas (de la figura femenina). 3. (béisbol) curva (de la trayectoria que sigue una pelota). —*v.i.* 1. curvarse, doblarse, encorvarse. 2. torcerse, describir una curva (camino, etc.). —*v.t.* doblar, encorvar.
curved [kɜrvd, B kɜvd] *a.* curvo, encorvado, torcido.
curvet [kər'vɛt B kɜ'-] *s.* corveta, corcovo. —*v.t.* (*pret., p.p.* CURVETTED o curveted; *p.pr.* CURVETTING o CURVETING) 1. corvetear, corcovar. 2. juguetear, retozar, brincar.
curvilinear [ˌkɜrvə'lɪnɪər, B ˌkɜvɪ-ə] **curvilineal** [-ɪəl] *a.* curvilíneo.
curving ['kɜrvɪŋ, B 'kɜvɪŋ] *s.* encorvamiento, curvatura. —*a.* que se curva o encorva.
curvometer [kər'vɑmətər, B kə'vɔmɪtə] *s.* curvímetro.
curvy ['kɜrvɪ B 'kɜvɪ] *a.* 1. que tiene curvas, curvilíneo. 2. curvado, encorvado, torcido.
cusec ['kjuˌsɛk] *s.* un pie cúbico por segundo.
cushat ['kʌʃət] *s.* (orn.) paloma torcaz.
cushaw [kə'ʃɔ] *s.* (variedad invernal de) calabaza de cuello torcido.
cushily ['kʊʃəlɪ] *adv.* fácilmente, cómodamente.
cushion ['kʊʃən] *s.* 1. cojín, almohada, almohadilla. 2. (billar) banda, baranda. 3. (mec.) cojín, colchón, amortiguador. 4. (impr.) mantilla, franela. —*v.t.* 1. asentar o poner sobre un cojín. 2. cubrir con cojines, poner cojines en; suavizar. 3. acojinar, acolchar. 4. (fig.) ocultar, disimular. 5. (mec.) amortiguar.
cushy ['kʊʃɪ] *a.* (jer.) fácil, seguro, agradable, cómodo (esp. un empleo, una situación, etc.); **a c. job,** un trabajo fácil.
cusk [kʌsk] *s.* (ict.) variedad de pez parecido al bacalao.
cusk eel, (ict.) martina.
cusp [kʌsp] *s.* 1. cúspide, ápice, pico, cima. 2. (geom.) cúspide, vértice. 3. (astr.) punta, cuerno (de la luna u otro astro). 4. (arq.) vértice (de un arco). 5. (odont.) cúspide. 6. (bot.) punta (de la hoya).
cuspate ['kʌsˌpeɪt, -pət] **cuspated** [-ˌpeɪtəd] **cusped** [kʌspt] *a.* (bot.) cuspidado, cuspídeo.
cuspid ['kʌspəd] *s.* (anat.) diente canino, colmillo.
cuspidal [-pədəl] *a.* puntiagudo.
cuspidate [-pəˌdeɪt] **cuspidated** [-əd] *a.* (bot.) cuspidado, cuspidiforme.
cuspidor ['kʌspəˌdɔr, B -ˌdɔ] *s.* escupidera.
cuss [kʌs] *s.* 1. (fam. E.U.) maldición, imprecación. 2. (gen. hum.) tipo, tío. —*v.t., v.i.* (fam.) maldecir, imprecar, blasfemar.
cussed ['kʌsəd] *a.* (fam.) maldito, abominable.
cussedly [-lɪ] *adv.* miserablemente, abominablemente.
cussedness [-nəs] *s.* obstinación, terquedad, empecinamiento.
custard ['kʌstərd, B -təd] *s.* flan, natilla.
custard apple 1. (bot.) anona, guanábano, chirimoyo. 2. anón, anona (fruta), guanábana, chirimoya. 3. (bot.) asimina.
custodial [ˌkʌs'toʊdɪəl] *a.* perteneciente a la custodia. —*s.* (relig.) sagrario.
custodian [-ɪən] *s.* custodio, guardián.
custodianship [-ˌʃɪp] *s.* custodia, guardanía.
custody ['kʌstədɪ] *s.* (*pl.* CUSTODIES) custodia, guardia; **to be in c.,** estar detenido, estar bajo arresto; **to be in the c. of,** estar bajo la custodia de; estar al cuidado de; **to take into c.,** detener, arrestar.
custom ['kʌstəm] *s.* 1. costumbre, usanza, uso, hábito. 2. costumbres, prácticas (que rigen la vida social). 3. (*pl.*) aduana; derechos de aduana; **to go through customs,** pasar por la aduana. 4. (der.) costumbre, usanza. 5. clientela, parroquia (de una tienda, etc.). —*a.* (hecho) a la medida, ej., *c. made clothes,* ropa a la medida, *c. tailor,* sastre que hace ropa a la medida.
customable [-əbəl] *a.* (ant.) sujeto a derechos de aduana, aforable.
customarily [ˌkʌstə'mɛrɪlɪ, B 'kʌstəmər-] *adv.* comúnmente, habitualmente, ordinariamente.
customariness ['kʌstəˌmɛrɪnəs, B -mər-] *s.* frecuencia, carácter habitual, costumbre.
customary ['kʌstəˌmɛrɪ, B -mərɪ] *a.* 1. usual, acostumbrado, habitual. 2. (der.) consuetudinario.
custom-built ['kʌstəm'bɪlt] *a.* fabricado según diseño del comprador; de diseño particular; hecho o fabricado a la orden o por encargo.
customer ['kʌstəmər, B -mə] *s.* 1. cliente, parroquiano, marchante (Am.). 2. (fam.) tipo, persona, individuo, ej., *an ugly-looking c.,* un tipo de mala catadura.

custom-free [ˈkʌstəmˈfri] *a.* libre o exento de derechos aduaneros.
customhouse [-ˌhaʊs] *s.* aduana, oficinas de aduana.
customhouse broker, agente de aduana.
customhouse officer, inspector o vista de aduana.
customhouse seal, marchamo.
customize [-ˌaɪz] *v.t.* construir, fabricar, acomodar o alterar según especificaciones.
custom-made [-ˈmeɪd] *a.* hecho a la medida, hecho a la orden.
customs declaration, (com.) declaración de aduana, declaración aduanera.
customs officer, aduanero, oficial de aduana.
customs union, unión aduanera.
cut [kʌt] *v.t.* (*pret., p.p.* CUT; *p.pr.* CUTTING) 1. cortar. 2. tallar, labrar, grabar (madera, piedras preciosas, etc.); grabar (discos de gramófono); (cost.) cortar (vestido, tela, etc.). 3. segar, cortar (trigo), talar (árboles), recortar (césped). 4. acortar, cercenar, reducir (gastos, libro, texto); rebajar (precios). 5. atravesar, cruzar (una línea). 6. cortar, acortar (camino). 7. dividir (ganancias, botín, etc.). 8. diluir (líquidos, etc.). 9. (esp. con **across**) dar un golpe cortante (a, a través de). 10. penetrar, atravesar, ej., *the wind c. him to the bone,* el viento le penetró hasta los huesos. 11. (fig.) herir, lastimar (sensibilidad). 12. negar el saludo (a un conocido). 13. (fam.) dejarse de, terminar con (*ú. esp. en imper.*) ej., *c. the nonsense!* ¡déjate de tonterías! 14. (cine.) cortar una toma. 15. (aut.) parar (el motor). 16. (fam.) faltar a, fumarse (la clase); **to c. class,** pirárselas. 17. (naipes) cortar (la baraja); robar, tomar (una carta de la pila). 18. **c. a caper,** hacer cabriolas; (fig.) andar de parranda; divertirse; **c. across,** cortar a través; **c. adrift,** desatar; **c. a (poor, brilliant,** etc.) **figure,** causar una (mala, magnífica, etc.) impresión; **c. asunder,** separar (cortando), dividir; **c. a tooth,** salirle un diente a uno; **c. away,** recortar, cercenar (parte superflua, etc.); **c. back,** podar, mondar; acortar; reducir, disminuir (gastos, etc.); **c. corners,** tomar atajos; hacer un trabajo más rápido y barato, pero más chapucero; reducir gastos; **c. down,** reducir (gastos, etc.); derribar, abatir; **c. down to size,** (fig.) reducir a proporciones normales, privar de importancia exagerada; **c. in,** insertar; conectar (tanque, motor, etc.); (cinem.) insertar en una secuencia; (elec.) intercalar; **c. in on,** incluir en, hacer partícipe en (ganancias, etc.); **c. it fine,** no dejar margen (de tiempo, para error, etc.), calcular con demasiada precisión; **c. it out!** ¡déjese de eso! ¡basta ya!; **c. loose,** soltar, desatar; **c. no ice,** carecer de importancia; carecer de influencia o autoridad; **c. off,** cortar, segar; amputar; cercenar; matar; obstruir (la vista); interrumpir, cortar, interceptar (retirada, comunicaciones, abastecimiento, etc.); aislar, separar; desconectar; (aut.) parar (el motor), cortar (la ignición); (tele.) cortar la comunicación a; desheredar; **c. one's teeth,** echar los dientes; **c. one's teeth on,** pasar la novatada, iniciar su carrera con (algún estudio o actividad); **c. one's throat,** (fig.) arruinarse, destruirse; **c. open,** abrir con un corte; **c. out,** recortar; quitar o sacar cortando; cavar, excavar; (cost.) cortar (vestido, etc.); omitir, excluir, eliminar; suplantar; dejar de hacer; despojar, privar; desconectar; separar del rebaño (a un animal); **c. short,** interrumpir; terminar o acabar prematuramente con; **c. the ground from under,** quitar el fundamento a (razonamiento, teoría, etc.); **c. the knot,** (fig.) cortar el nudo (gordiano); **c. to the bone,** (fig.) reducir a un mínimo; **c. to the heart, c. to the quick,** herir en lo vivo; **c. to pieces,** despedazar; aniquilar, diezmar (ej., un ejército); (fig.) hacer pedazos, hacer trizas; **c. up,** despedazar, cortar en pedazos; acuchillar, apuñalar (a alguien); disecar; destrozar, criticar mordazmente; **to be c. out for,** estar hecho para, estar destinado para; venir de perilla para; **to be c. up (about),** estar angustiado o afligido (por); **to c. a long story short,** para abreviar, en suma, en fin. —*v.i.* 1. cortar (bien, mal, etc.). 2. cortarse, dejarse cortar. 3. cortar, penetrar (frío, viento, etc.). 4. correr, pasar rápidamente. 5. dividir el botín, ir a medias. 6. salir, brotar (diente). 7. **c. across,** atravesar, pasar a través de; atajar por; (fig.) rebasar; **c. and run,** dejar todo y huir, largarse de prisa, levar anclas (un barco); **c. back (to),** reanudar la narración de episodio anterior (en libro, filme, etc.); **c. both** (o **two**) **ways,** (fig.) ser de dos filos (argumento, observación, etc.); **c. down,** economizar, reducir gastos, personal, etc.; **c. down on,** reducir; **c. in,** entremeterse; interrumpir, interpolar (en conversación, debate, etc.); irrumpir en (cuarto, etc.); cerrar el paso (un vehículo a otro); conectarse, entrar en funcionamiento; **c. in on,** interrumpir (conversación, etc.); interrumpir (a una pareja que baila) para cambiar de pareja; (naipes) entrar en (el juego); **c. into,** acortar, reducir; **c. loose,** escaparse, zafarse; desmedirse; jaranear, andar de parranda; **c. off,** marcharse, largarse; pararse, dejar de funcionar (motor, etc.); **c. out,** irse de prisa; salir de la fila (de vehículos); (naipes) salir del juego; dejar de funcionar (motor, etc.); **c. through,** atravesar; atajar por; **c. to the right (left),** doblar a la derecha (izquierda); **c. up,** alardear. —*s.* 1. corte, cortadura, incisión; herida. 2. corte (de tela, seda, etc.); tajada (de carne), rebanada (de pan, etc.); segmento. 3. parte, porción. 4. atajo. 5. figura, talle. 6. corte (de un vestido, traje, etc.). 7. estilo (de ropas, peinado, etc.). 8. reducción, rebaja (de precios, salarios, etc.). 9. inasistencia (a clase). 10. sarcasmo, observación mordaz. 11. (med.) talla, incisión. 12. (bot.) entrada (en el borde de la hoja). 13. (geog.) ría, ensenada. 14. (joy.) talla (de un diamante o piedra preciosa). 15. (t.v., cine., rad.) corte, interrupción; cambio brusco. 16. corte de pelo. 17. (impr.) clisé, cliché; grabado, estampa, ilustración. 18. (naipes) corte, alza. 19. **cold cuts,** fiambres; **c. of one's jib,** (fig.) fisonomía, semblante, aspecto; **short c.,** atajo; **to be a. c. above,** ser superior a. —*a.* 1. cortado (díc. esp. de flores). 2. reducido, rebajado (precio). 3. tallado (piedra preciosa, vidrio). 4. (bot.) recortado (borde de hojas, etc.).
cut-and-dried [ˌkʌtənˈdraɪd] **cut-and-dry** [-ˈdraɪ] *a.* planeado, preparado o convenido de antemano; rutinario, sin originalidad, estereotipado.
cutaneous [kjʊˈteɪnɪəs] *a.* cutáneo.
cutaway [ˈkʌtəˌweɪ] *a.* recortado (díc. de una máquina u otro objeto al que se ha recortado una parte para mostrar su interior). —*s.* chaqué.
cutback [ˈkʌtˌbæk] *s.* 1. reducción (de pedidos, personal, etc.). 2. (t.v., cine, rad.) segmento del episodio anterior.
cutch [kʌtʃ] *s.* (quím.) cato, cachú.
cute [kjut] *a.* (fam.) lindo, mono, atractivo, encantador.
cutely [ˈkjutlɪ] *adv.* graciosamente, encantadoramente.
cuteness [-nəs] *s.* gracia, encanto, monada.
cut gear, (mec.) engranaje fresado, engranaje, tallado.
cut glass, cristal tallado.
cut-grass [ˈkʌtˌgræs, B -ˌgrɑs] *s.* (bot.) variedad de hierba con hojas bordeadas de diminutas espinas encorvadas.
cuticle [ˈkjutɪkəl] *s.* (bot., anat.) cutícula.
cuticular [kjʊˈtɪkjələr, B -lə] *a.* cuticular.
cutie [ˈkjutɪ] *s.* (jer.) muchacha agraciada, joven guapa.
cutin [ˈkjutən] *s.* (bioquím.) cutina.
cutis [ˈkjutəs] *s.* (*pl.* CUTES [-ˌtiz] o CUTISES) (anat.) dermis, cutis, vera.
cutlass, cutlas [ˈkʌtləs] *s.* alfanje; machete.
cutler [-lər, B -lə] *s.* cuchillero.
cutlery [-lərɪ] *s.* 1. cuchillería. 2. cuchillos, tijeras, instrumentos cortantes. 3. cubiertos.
cutlet [ˈkʌtlət] *s.* (cocina) chuleta, costilla.
cutoff [ˈkʌtˌɔf] *s.* 1. corte, cesación; limitación. 2. atajo. 3. agua estancada (que queda cuando el río cambia de cauce). 4. (hidr.) muro interceptador. 5. (mec.) cortavapor, punto de expansión, cierre de la admisión. 6. (elec.) cortacircuito. 7. (impr.) tamaño de corte; placa divisoria.
cutoff frequency, (rad.) frecuencia crítica.
cutoff valve, (mec.) válvula de cierre, válvula de estrangulación.
cutoff voltage, (elec.) tensión final, voltaje final.
cutout [-ˌaʊt] *s.* 1. recorte. 2. figura recortable (con que juegan los niños). 3. (elec.) cortacircuito, interruptor, disyuntor. 4. (aut.) válvula de escape libre. 5. (jer.) salida a escape. 6. (mec.) estrangulador.
cutover [-ˌoʊvər, B -və] *a.* despoblado, desmontado (terreno).
cutpurse [-ˌpɜrs, B -ˌpɜs] *s.* carterista, ratero.
cut-rate [ˈkʌtˈreɪt] *a.* 1. de precio(s) rebajado(s), de tarifa reducida. 2. barato.
cutter [-ər, B -ə] *s.* 1. cortador (en sastrería, zapatería, etc.), tallador, grabador. 2. máquina cortadora. 3. (mar.) cúter, balandra; (E.U.) guardacostas pequeño. 4. trineo ligero.
cutter bar, portacuchilla, portahierro.
cutthroat [-ˌθroʊt] *s.* asesino, criminal, degollador. —*a.* 1. asesino, criminal. 2. cruel, despiadado, implacable. 3. (naipes) a tres manos (bridge, etc.).
cutting [ˈkʌtɪŋ] *s.* 1. cortadura, corte. 2. (G.B.) recorte (de periódico). 3. (agr.) estaca, rampollo, esqueje, mugrón (para plantar). 4. alce de naipes. 5. (cinem.) montaje. —*a.* 1. cortante, cortador. 2. penetrante (frío, etc.). 3. mordaz, hiriente, sarcástico.
cutting edge, filo o arista cortante.
cutting iron, cortafrío.
cuttingly [-lɪ] *adv.* mordazmente, sarcásticamente.
cutting tool, herramienta cortante, herramienta de corte.
cuttlebone [ˈkʌtəlˌboʊn] *s.* jibión.
cuttlefish [-ˌfɪʃ] *s.* (zool.) jibia, sepia.
cutty stool [ˈkʌtɪ-] (esco.) 1. taburete bajo. 2. (hist.) asiento de pecadores (en las antiguas iglesias).
cutup [ˈkʌtˌʌp] *s.* 1. (jer.) persona traviesa o cómica. 2. (*pl.*) dibujos para recortar.
cutwater [-ˌwɔtər, -ˌwɑt-, B -ˌwɔtə] *s.* tajamar, espolón (de un buque o puente).
cutwork [-ˌwɜrk, B -ˌwɜk] *s.* (cost.) calado, bordado abierto.
cutworm [-ˌwɜrm, B -ˌwɜm] *s.* (ento.) (variedad de) oruga nocturna.
cuvette [kjuˈvɛt] *s.* tubo, probeta.
cwt. *abrev. de* **hundredweight,** quintal (ql.).
cyanamide [saɪˈænəməd, -ˌmaɪd] **cyanamid** [-məd] *s.* (quím.) cianamida.
cyanate [ˈsaɪəˌneɪt] *s.* (quím.) cianato.

cyanic [saɪ'ænɪk] *a.* 1. (quím.) ciánico. 2. (bot.) cianíctero, de matiz azul; cianoficeo (alga).
cyanic acid, (quím.) ácido ciánico.
cyanide ['saɪəˌnaɪd] *s.* (quím.) cianuro. —*v.t.* cianurar, tratar con cianuro.
cyanide process, (metal.) cianuración.
cyanine [-ˌnin, B -ˌnaɪn] *s.* (quím.) cianina.
cyanite [-ˌnaɪt] *s.* (min.) cianita.
cyanocobalamin [ˌsaɪənoʊkə'bələmən] *s.* (med.) cianocobalamina, cianoblamina.
cyanogen [saɪ'ænədʒən] *s.* (quím.) cianógeno.
cyanosis [ˌsaɪə'noʊsəs] *s.* (med.) cianosis.
cyanotic [-'nɑtɪk, B -'nɔt-] *a.* (med.) cianótico.
cyanotype [saɪ'ænəˌtaɪp] *s.* copia azul, copia heliográfica (de planos, mapas, dibujos).
cyanurate [ˌsaɪə'njʊrˌeɪt] *s.* (quím.) cianurato.
cyanuric [-'njʊrɪk] *a.* (quím.) cianúrico.
Cybele ['sɪbəli] *s.* (mitol.) Cibeles, diosa de la tierra.
cybernetic [ˌsaɪbər'nɛtɪk, B -bə'-] *a.* (fisiol., electrón.) cibernético.
cybernetics [-ɪks] *s. pl.* (*sing. o pl. en const.*) (fisiol., electrón.) cibernética.
cycad ['saɪkəd] *s.* (bot.) cicadácea.
Cycadaceae [ˌsaɪkə'deɪsɪˌi] *s. pl.* (bot.) cicadáceas.
cycas ['saɪkəs] *s.* (bot.) cica.
Cyclades ['sɪkləˌdiz] *s. pl.* Cícladas, islas griegas.
cyclamate ['saɪkləˌmeɪt, 'sɪk-] *s.* (quím.) ciclamato.
cyclamen [-mən, B 'sɪk-] *s.* (bot.) ciclamino, pamporcino, artanica.
cycle ['saɪkəl] *s.* 1. ciclo, período. 2. círculo, circuito. 3. órbita (celeste). 4. (lit.) ciclo. 5. (biol., bot.) ciclo. 6. (elec.) ciclo, período. 7. bicicleta; velocípedo; triciclo; motocicleta. —*v.i.* 1. pasar por un ciclo. 2. producirse en ciclos. 3. montar o ir en bicicleta.
cycler ['saɪklər, B -lə] *s.* ciclista.
cyclic ['saɪklɪk, 'sɪk-] **cyclical** [-lɪkəl] *a.* cíclico.
cyclic rate, cadencia cíclica.
cycling ['saɪklɪŋ] *s.* (dep.) ciclismo.
cyclist [-ləst] *s.* ciclista.
cyclohexane [ˌsaɪkloʊ'hɛkˌseɪn] *s.* (quím.) ciclohexano.
cycloid ['saɪˌklɔɪd] *s.* (geom.) cicloide. —*a.* dispuesto en círculos; cicloidal.
cycloidal [saɪ'klɔɪdəl] *a.* cicloidal, cicloideo.
cyclometer [-'klɑmətər, B -'klɔmɪtə] *s.* ciclómetro, odómetro, cuentarrevoluciones.
cyclometric [ˌsaɪkloʊ'mɛtrɪk] *a.* ciclométrico.
cyclometry [saɪ'klɑmətrɪ, B -'klɔm-] *s.* ciclometría.
cyclone ['saɪˌkloʊn] *s.* ciclón.
cyclonic [saɪ'klɑnɪk, B -'klɔn-] *a.* ciclónico.
cyclopaedia, *var. de* **cyclopedia.**
cyclopean [ˌsaɪklə'piən, B saɪ'kloʊpjən] *a.* 1. **C.,** ciclópeo. 2. (fig.) ciclópeo, gigantesco, enorme.
cyclopedia [ˌsaɪklə'pidɪə] *s.* enciclopedia.
cyclopedic [-ɪk] *a.* enciclopédico.
cyclopedist [-əst] *s.* enciclopedista.
Cyclopic [saɪ'klɑpɪk, B -'klɔp-] *a.* ciclópico.
cycloplegia [ˌsaɪklə'plidʒɪə] *s.* (med.) cicloplejía.
cyclopropane [-'proʊˌpeɪn] *s.* (quím.) ciclopropano.
cyclops ['saɪˌklɑps, B -ˌklɔps] *s.* 1. **C.,** (*pl.* CYCLOPES [saɪ'kloʊpiz]) Cíclope. 2. (med.) (*pl.* CYCLOPES) cíclope, ciclope. 3. (zool.) (*pl.* CYCLOPS) pulga de agua.
cyclorama [ˌsaɪklə'ræmə, B -'rɑmə] *s.* ciclorama, panorama.
cycloramic [-'ræmɪk] *a.* ciclorámico.
cyclosis [saɪ'kloʊsəs] *s.* (fisiol.) ciclosis.
Cyclostoma [-'klɑstəmə, B -'klɔs-] **Cyclostomata** [ˌsaɪklə'stɑmətə, B -'stoʊm-] *s. pl.* (ict.) ciclóstomas.
cyclostomate [-ˌmeɪt] **cyclostomatous** [ˌsaɪklə'stɑmətəs, B -'stoʊm-] *a.* (zool.) ciclóstomo.
cyclostome ['saɪkləˌstoʊm] *a.* (zool.) ciclóstomo. —*s.* (*zool.*) ciclóstoma, ciclóstomo.
cyclostyle [-ˌstaɪl] *s.* ciclostilo.
cyclothymia [ˌsaɪklə'θaɪmɪə] *s.* (psic.) ciclotimia.
cyclothymic [-mɪk] *a., s.* ciclotímico.
cyclotron ['saɪkləˌtrɑn B -ˌtrɔn] *s.* (fís.) ciclotrón.
cyder, (G.B.) *var. de* **cider.**
cygnet ['sɪgnət] *s.* pichón de cisne.
Cygnus [-nəs] *s.* (astr.) Cisne.
cylinder ['sɪləndər, B -də] *s.* cilindro, rodillo; (geom., mec., impr.) cilindro. —*v.t.* cilindrar.
cylinder block, (mot.) bloque de cilindros.
cylinder bore, diámetro interior del cilindro.
cylinder head, culata del cilindro, cabeza del cilindro.
cylinder saw, taladro.
cylindrical [sɪ'lɪndrɪkəl] **cylindric** [-drɪk] *a.* cilíndrico.
cylindrically [-kəlɪ] *adv.* cilíndricamente.
cylindroid [-'sɪlənˌdrɔɪd] *s.* (mat.) cilindroide. —*a.* cilindroideo.
cyma ['saɪmə] *s.* (arq.) cimacio, gola.
cymar [sɪ'mɑr, B -'mɑ] *s.* prenda femenina usada en el medioevo.
cyma reversa [saɪmərɪ'vɜrsə, B -'vɜsə] talón.
cymatium [saɪ'meɪʃɪəm] *s.* (*pl.* CYMATIA, [-ʃɪə]) (arq.) cimacio (de una cornisa clásica).
cymbal ['sɪmbəl] *s.* (mús.) címbalo, platillo.
cymbalist [-əst] *s.* cimbalista, cimbalero.
cyme [saɪm] *s.* (bot.) cima.
cymene ['saɪˌmin] *s.* (quím.) cimeno.
cymophane [-məˌfeɪn] *s.* (min.) cimófana; variedad de crisoberilo.
cymoscope [-ˌskoʊp] *s.* (elec.) cimoscopio.
cymose [-ˌmoʊs] *a.* (bot.) cimoso.
Cymric ['kɪmrɪk] *a.* cambriano, cámbrico, galés. —*s.* grupo de lenguas célticas (esp. galés).
Cymry [-rɪ] *s. pl.* cámbricos, los galeses (colectivamente).
cynegetic [ˌsɪnə'dʒɛtɪk] *a.* cinegético.
cynegetics [-ɪks] *s. pl.* (*sing. en const.*) cinegética.
cynic ['sɪnɪk] *s.* cínico; **C.,** (filos.) cínico. —*a.* cínico.
cynical [-ɪkəl] *a.* cínico; sarcástico, capcioso.
cynically [-kəlɪ] *adv.* cínicamente; sarcásticamente.
cynicism ['sɪnəˌsɪzəm] *s.* 1. **C.,** cinismo, doctrina de los cínicos. 2. cinismo, actitud o expresión cínica.
cynosure ['saɪnəˌʃʊr, B 'sɪnəzjʊə] *s.* 1. **C.,** (astr., mitol.) Cinosura. 2. (fig.) blanco (de todas las miradas); centro de atención.
cypher, (pr. G.B.) *var. de* **cipher.**
cypress ['saɪprəs] *s.* 1. (bot.) ciprés. 2. (madera de) ciprés. 3. rama de ciprés (usada como señal de duelo). 4. (ant.) especie de tela negra usada como señal de duelo.
cyprian ['sɪprɪən] *s.* 1. **C.,** chipriota. 2. (ant.) prostituta. 3. (ant., fig.) lujurioso.
cyprinodont [sə'prɪnəˌdɑnt, B -'praɪnəˌdɔnt] *a., s.* (ict.) ciprinodonte.
cyprinoid ['sɪprəˌnɔɪd, B sɪ'praɪ-] *a.* (ict.) ciprinoideo.
Cypriot ['sɪprɪət] **Cypriote** [-ˌoʊt] *a., s.* cipriota, chipriota, ciprio, de la isla de Chipre.
cypripedium [ˌsɪprə'pidɪəm] *s.* (bot.) cipripedio.
Cyprus ['saɪprəs] *s.* Chipre, isla del Mediterráneo.
cypsela ['sɪpsələ] *s.* (*pl.* CYPSELAE [-li]) cipsela.
Cyrenaic [ˌsɪrə'neɪɪk, B ˌsaɪərə-] *a., s.* (filos.) cirenaico.
Cyrillic [sə'rɪlɪk] *a.* cirílico (alfabeto, letra, escritura).
cyst [sɪst] *s.* 1. (med.) quiste. 2. (biol.) espora (en ciertas algas); vesícula de aire (en ciertas hierbas). 3. (zool.) quiste (de parásitos).
cysteine ['sɪsˌtiən] *s.* (quím.) cisteína.
cystectomy [sɪs'tɛktəmɪ] *s.* (cir.) cistotomía.
cystic ['sɪstɪk] *a.* 1. (med., anat.) cístico. 2. (zool.) enquistado.
cysticercoid [ˌsɪstə'sɜrˌkɔɪd, B -'sɜˌ-] *s.* (zool.) cisticercoide.
cysticercosis [-sər'koʊsəs, B -sə'-] *s.* (med.) cistercosis.
cysticercus [-'sɜrkəs, B -'sɜkəs] *s.* (*pl.* CYSTICERCI [-'sɜrˌsaɪ, B -'sɜˌsi]) (zool.) cisticerco.
cystic fibrosis, (med.) fibrosis cística.
cystine ['sɪsˌtin, B -ˌtaɪn] *s.* (bioquím.) cistina.
cystitis [sɪs'taɪtəs] *s.* (med.) cistitis.
cystocarp ['sɪstəˌkɑrp, B -ˌkɑp] *s.* (bot.) cistocarpo.
cystocele [-ˌsil] *s.* (med.) cistocele.
cystoid [-ˌtɔɪd] *a., s.* (med., pal.) cistoide.
cystolith [-təˌlɪθ] *s.* 1. (bot.) cistolito. 2. (med.) cistolito, cálculo de la vejiga.
cystoma [sɪs'toʊmə] *s.* (med.) cistoma.
cystoscope ['sɪstəˌskoʊp] *s.* (med.) cistoscopio.
cystoscopy [sɪs'tɑskəpɪ, B -'tɔs-] *s.* (med.) cistoscopia.
cystotomy [-'tɑtəmɪ, B -'tɔt-] *s.* (cir.) cistotomía.
cytase ['saɪˌteɪs] *s.* (bioquím.) citasa.
Cytherea [ˌsɪθə'riə] *s.* (mitol.) Citerea, uno de los nombres de Afrodita.
Cytherean [-'riən] *a.* (poét.) citereo, perteneciente a Afrodita.
cytochemistry [ˌsaɪtoʊ'kɛməstrɪ] *s.* (bioquím.) citoquímica.
cytochrome ['saɪtəˌkroʊm] *s.* (bioquím.) citocromo.
cytogenetics [ˌsaɪtədʒə'nɛtɪks] *s. pl.* (biol.) citogenética.
cytokinesis [-kə'nisəs] *s.* (biol.) citocinesis.
cytological [-'lɑdʒɪkəl, B -'lɔdʒ-] **cytologic** [-ɪk] *a.* (biol.) citológico.
cytologist [saɪ'tɑlədʒəst, B -'tɔl-] *s.* citólogo.
cytology [-dʒɪ] *s.* (biol.) citología.
cytolysin [-sən] *s.* citolisina.
cytolysis [-səs] *s.* (biol.) citólisis.
cytolytic [ˌsaɪtə'lɪtɪk] *a.* (biol.) citolítico.
cytophagy [saɪ'tɑfədʒɪ, B -'tɔf-] *s.* (biol.) citofagia.
cytoplasm ['saɪtəˌplæzəm] *s.* (biol.) citoplasma.
cytoplasmic [ˌsaɪtə'plæzmɪk] *a.* citoplasmático.
cytoplast ['saɪtəˌplæst] *s.* (biol.) citoplastina.
cytoplastic [ˌsaɪtə'plæstɪk] *a.* (biol.) citoplástico.
C.Z. *abrev. de* **Canal Zone,** Zona del Canal.
czar [zɑr, B zɑ] *s.* zar, czar, nombre que daba Rusia a sus emperadores.
czardas ['tʃɑrˌdæʃ, B 'tʃɑˌ-] *s.* (*pl.* CZARDAS) chardas, danza folklórica húngara y su música.
czarina [zɑ'rinə] *s.* zarina, czarina, nombre que se daba en Rusia a la emperatriz.
czarism ['zɑrˌɪzəm] *s.* 1. zarismo. 2. (fig.) gobierno autocrático, autocracia.
Czech [tʃɛk] *s.* 1. checo. 2. checo, idioma checo. —*a.* checo.
Czechoslovak [ˌtʃɛkə'sloʊˌvɑk, B -ˌvæk] *s., a.* checoslovaco.
Czechoslovakia [-sloʊ'vɑkɪə, -'væk-] *s.* Checoslovaquia.

D

D [di] *s.* 1. d, cuarta letra del alfabeto inglés. 2. (mús.) re. 3. número romano que indica 500.

d. *abrev. de* 1. **date,** fecha. 2. **daughter,** hija. 3. **died,** muerto.

D.A. *abrev. de* **District Attorney,** fiscal del distrito.

dab [dæb] *s.* 1. golpe ligero, palmada, golpecito, toque suave. 2. pequeña masa (esp. de pintura), brochazo, untadura. 3. **a d. (of),** una pizca, un poquito de). —*v.t.* (*pret., p.p.* DABBED; *p.pr.* DABBING) 1. golpear o tocar ligeramente, dar toques a, retocar suavemente. 2. dar brochadas de, aplicar con brochazos (esp. pintura). —*v.i.* (con *at*) dar toques (a).

dab, *s.* (ict.) lenguado, platija, barbado.

dabber ['dæbər, B -ə] *s.* (impr.) bala, tampón, almohadilla, cojincillo (usado para entintar).

dabble ['dæbəl] *v.t.* salpicar, rociar. —*v.i.* chapotear; **d. in** (o **at**) ocuparse superficialmente (en, de), meterse (en), tener un ligero interés (por), jugar (a), ej., *d. in politics,* meterse en política, *d. in stocks,* jugar a la Bolsa.

dabbler [-ələr, B -lə] *s.* aficionado, diletante; el que se dedica a algún negocio, arte, etc., de modo superficial.

dabchick [-ˌtʃɪk] *s.* (orn.) zambullidor, colimbo, castañero; somorgujo castaño o menor.

dabster [-stər, B -stə] *s.* 1. (fam.) aficionado; amateur. 2. (dial.) perito, experto.

dace [deɪs] *s.* (*pl.* DACE) (ict.) leucisco, albur, dardo, breca (pez pequeño de los arroyos).

dacha ['dɑtʃə] *s.* dacha, casa de campo rusa.

dachshund ['dɑksˌhʊnt, -ˌhʊnd, B 'dæks-,-hʊnd] *s.* (*pl.* DACHSHUNDS O DACHSHUNDE [-ˌhʊndə]) (zool.) dachshund, especie de perro pachón o raposero, perro salchicha (Am.).

Dacian ['deɪʃən, B -sjən] *a., s.* dacio, natural de la antigua Dacia, hoy Rumania.

dacron ['deɪˌkrɑn, 'dæ-, B -ˌkrɔn] *s.* (tej.) dacrón (tejido hecho de fibra de polyester); marca de fábrica.

dacryocystitis [ˌdækrɪˌoʊsɪs'taɪtəs] *s.* (med.) dacriocistitis.

dactyl ['dæktəl] *s.* (poét.) dáctilo.

dactylic [dæk'tɪlɪk] (poét.) *a.* dactílico. —*s.* verso dactílico.

dactyliology [ˌdæktɪlɪ'ɑlədʒɪ B -'ɔl-] **dactylology** [-tə'lɑl-, B -'lɔl-] *s.* dactiliología, dactilolalia (uso de las manos y los dedos para expresar ideas, como el alfabeto de los sordomudos).

dactylion [dæk'tɪlɪˌɑn, B -ˌɔn] *s.* (mús.) dactilión.

dactylography [ˌdæktə'lɑgrəfɪ, B -'lɔg-] *s.* dactiloscopia, sistema de identificación individual por las huellas digitales.

dactyloscopic [-ˌtɪlə'skɑpɪk, B -'skɔp-] *a.* dactiloscópico, referente a las huellas digitales.

dactyloscopy [-tə'lɑskəpɪ, B -'lɔs-] *s.* dactiloscopia, examen o clasificación de las huellas digitales.

dad [dæd] *s.* (fam.) papá.

Dada ['dɑdɑ] *forma abrev. de* **dadaism.**

Dadaism [-ˌɪzəm] *s.* (arte) dadaísmo, movimiento precursor del surrealismo en Europa.

Dadaist [-əst] *s.* dadaísta, integrante del movimiento Dada en las artes.

daddy ['dædɪ] *s.* (fam.) papaíto, papito, papacito (Am.).

daddy longlegs [-'lɔŋˌlɛgz] *s. pl.* (*sing. o pl. en const.*) (ento.) típula; segador, falangio (arácnido).

dado ['deɪdoʊ] *s.* 1. (arq.) dado, neto. 2. friso (pintado de la pared), revestimiento de madera, friso, rodapié.

daedal ['didəl] *a.* 1. intrincado, completo. 2. ingenioso, primoroso, artístico. 3. (poét.) rico, variado.

Daedalian, Daedalean [dɪ'deɪljən] *a.* dedálico, concerniente o relativo a Dédalo, inventor del Laberinto en la mitología griega.

Daedalus ['dɛdələs, B 'did-] *s.* (mitol.) Dédalo, arquitecto del Laberinto e inventor de las alas de Ícaro.

daemon, *var. de* **demon.**

daff [dæf] *v.i.* (esco.) bromear; juguetear. —*v.t.* (ant.) echar de lado, descartar.

daffodil ['dæfəˌdɪl] *s.* (bot.) narciso trompon o atrompetado.

daffodilly [-ˌdɪlɪ] (dial., poét.) *var. de* **daffodil.**

daffy ['dæfɪ] *a.* (jer.) chiflado, loco, imbécil.

daft [dæft, B dɑft] *a.* 1. necio, tonto, bobo, venático, loco. 2. (esco.) casquivano; alegre.

dag [dæg] *s.* 1. colgadura, gen. en forma de pico. 2. mechón de lana apelmazado o sucio (en una oveja).

dagger ['dægər, B -ə] *s.* 1. daga, puñal. 2. (tip.) cruz, obelisco. 3. **to be at dagger's point,** estar a punto de pelear; **to look daggers at,** mirar con odio.

daggle ['dægəl] *v.t., v.i.* (ant.) enfangar, embarrar, enlodar, ensuciar arrastrando.

daglock ['dægˌlɑk, B -ˌlɔk] *s.* mechón sucio o apelmazado (ej., de oveja o perro).

dago ['deɪgoʊ] *s.* (*pl.* DAGOS O DAGOES) 1. (despec., E.U.) italiano, persona de ascendencia italiana. 2. (despec., G.B.) español, gallego.

daguerreotype [də'gɛrəˌtaɪp] *s.* daguerrotipo. —*v.t.* daguerrotipar.

daguerreotypy [-ɪ] *s.* daguerrotipia, daguerrotipo.

dahabeah, dahabeeyah [ˌdɑhə'biə] *s.* barco de transporte que se usa en el Nilo.

dahlia ['dæljə, 'dɑl-, B 'deɪl-] *s.* (bot.) dalia, planta y flor.

Dahoman [də'hoʊmən] *s., a.* dahomeyano, natural de Dahomey (t. **Dahomedan, Dahomean).**

Dahomey [-mɪ] *s.* Dahomey.

daily ['deɪlɪ] *a.* diario, cotidiano, diurno; de todos los días (uso, gasto, salario, ejercicio, comida, etc.). —*s.* (*pl.* DAILIES) 1. diario, periódico. 2. (fam. G.B.) sirvienta (que no reside en la casa). —*adv.* diariamente, todos los días, día por día.

daily double, apuesta combinada para dos carreras (de caballos), dupleta (Am.).

daily grind, jornal.

daimio ['daɪmɪˌoʊ] *s.* (*pl.* DAIMIO O DAIMIOS) (hist.) daimio, barón feudal del antiguo Japón.

daimon ['daɪˌmoʊn] *s.* (*pl.* DAIMONES [-məˌniz] O DAIMONS) demonio.

daimonic [daɪ'mɑnɪk, B -'mɔn-] *a.* demoníaco.

daintily ['deɪntəlɪ] *adv.* delicadamente, finamente.

daintiness [-ɪnəs] *s.* delicadeza, finura.

dainty ['deɪntɪ] *a.* (DAINTIER; DAINTIEST) 1. delicado, exquisito. 2. delicioso, apetitoso. 3. fino, refinado. 4. melindroso, afectado. —*s.* (*pl.* DAINTIES) golosina, gollería, bocado exquisito.

daiquiri ['daɪkərɪ, 'dæk-] *s.* daiquirí (coctel de origen cubano, elaborado con ron, limón y azúcar).

dairy ['dɛrɪ, B 'dɛərɪ] *s.* 1. lechería, quesería, vaquería. 2. granja lechera. 3. vacada, vaquería.

dairy cattle, ganado lechero, vacas lecheras.

dairy farm, granja lechera.

dairying [-ɪŋ] *s.* negocio de lechería.

dairymaid [-ˌmeɪd] *s.* lechera, vaquera.

dairyman [-mən, -ˌmæn] *s.* lechero, vaquero.

dairy products, productos lácteos.

dais ['deɪəs, 'daɪ-, B 'deɪ-] *s.* estrado, tablado, grada; palio, dosel, pabellón.

daisy ['deɪzɪ] *s.* 1. (bot.) margarita. 2. (fam.) joya, primor, cosa de primera clase.

daisy chain, guirnalda o rama de margaritas entretejidas; cualquier serie así eslabonada.

daisy wheel, margarita.

daisy wheel printer, impresora de margarita.

Dakar [də'kɑr, 'dækˌɑr, B 'dækə, -ɑ] *s.* Dakar, capital del Senegal.

Dakin's solution ['deɪkənz-] (farm.) solución antiséptica de Dakin.

dale [deɪl] *s.* valle, vallecico.

dalesman ['deɪlzmən] *s.* (G.B.) habitante de un valle (esp. en el norte de Ingl.).

dalliance ['dælɪəns] *s.* 1. regodeo; coqueteo, retozo. 2. frivolidad. 3. tardanza, dilación.

dally ['dælɪ] *v.i.* (*pret., p.p.* DALLIED; *p.pr.* DALLYING) 1. juguetear, divertirse. 2. perder tiempo, holgar, tardar, demorarse. 3. **d. with,** coquetear, flirtear (con), perder el tiempo (en algo); (fig.) acariciar (idea, etc.); tomar a la ligera, ej., *d. with an important matter,* tomar un asunto importante a la ligera.

Dalmatian [dæl'meɪʃən] *a.* dálmata, natural de Dalmacia (región de Yugoslavia). —*s.* 1. dálmata, habitante de Dalmacia. 2. perro dálmata o dalmático.

dalmatic [-'mætɪk] *s.* dalmática (vestidura imperial de los antiguos, hoy usada como casulla por los eclesiásticos).

Daltonism ['dɔltənˌɪzəm] *s.* (med.) daltonismo.

dam [dæm] *s.* 1. dique, presa, represa. 2. embalse, agua contenida por un dique. 3. (odont.) dique (para mantener seco un diente durante una operación). 4. (metal.) dama (muro que cierra el crisol de un horno). 5. madre (de animales cuadrúpedos). —*v.t.* (*pret., p.p.* DAMMED; *p.pr.* DAMMING) (gen. con *up*) represar, estancar, embalsar (agua); (fig.) represar, bloquear, obstruir.

damage ['dæmɪdʒ] *s.* 1. daño, avería, lesión, deterioro. 2. (con *to*) perjuicio, detrimento, desdoro (de la reputación). 3. (*pl.*) (der.) (indemnización de) daños y perjuicios. —*v.t.* 1. dañar,

estropear; averiar, lesionar, lastimar; deteriorar. 2. damnificar, perjudicar. —*v.i.* deteriorarse; dañarse.
damageable [-əbəl] *a.* susceptible de daño o detrimento, deteriorable.
damaging [-ɪŋ] *a.* perjudicial, dañoso.
daman ['dæmən] *s.* (zool.) damán, especie de marmota de Asia y África.
damascene ['dæməˌsin ˌdæmə'sin] *s.* 1. **D.,** damasceno, natural de Damasco. 2. damasquinado, ataujía. —*a.* 1. **D.,** damasceno, natural de Damasco. 2. damasquino, ataujiado. —*v.t.* damasquinar, ataujiar; incrustar oro o plata sobre acero.
Damascus [də'mæskəs, B -'mɑs-] *s.* Damasco, capital de Siria.
damask ['dæməsk] *s.* 1. (tej.) damasco. 2. acero damasquino. 3. damasquinado, ataujía. 4. color morado. —*a.* 1. damasquino (tela, arma). 2. morado. 3. damasquinado, adamascado.
damaskeen [-əˌskin, ˌdæmə'skin] *v.t.* hacer labor de ataujía; damasquinar, adamascar.
damask rose, (bot.) rosa de Damasco, rosa de las cuatro estaciones.
damask steel, acero damasquino.
damassin ['dæməsɪn] *s.* (tej.) damasquillo, damasina.
dam dike, dique de contención.
dame [deɪm] *s.* 1. dama, señora. 2. matrona, señora de edad. 3. (jer.) mujer. 4. **D.,** (G.B.) (como tratamiento de una mujer condecorada con la Orden del Imperio Británico) Dama.
dame's violet, (bot.) juliana.
dammar, dammer ['dæmər, B -ə] *s.* damarina, resina de damara.
damn [dæm] *v.t.* 1. condenar a pena eterna, execrar. 2. condenar, reprobar, censurar severamente. 3. maldecir, blasfemar. 4. desacreditar, deslucir, arruinar, (ej., una obra artística criticándola acerbamente). 5. **(I'll be) damned, if I know,** no tengo ni idea (de eso); **d. it!** ¡maldito sea!; **I'll be damned!** ¡caramba! quién lo hubiera creído. —*v.i.* maldecir, jurar, blasfemar. —*s.* 1. **d.! ¡maldición! 2. a d.,** un comino, un pepino, un pito, ej., *I don't care* (o *give*) *a d.,* no me importa un pito o un comino. —*adv.* muy, sumamente, ej., *you know d. well what I mean,* tú sabes muy bien lo que quiero decir. —*a.* maldito, perdido, arruinado.
damnable ['dæmnəbəl] *a.* 1. condenable. 2. detestable, abominable, execrable, infame.
damnably [-blɪ] *adv.* detestablemente, infamemente.
damnation [dæm'neɪʃən] *s.* 1. condenación, damnación. 2. (teo.) condenación a castigo eterno. —*interj.* ¡maldición!
damnatory ['dæmnəˌtɔrɪ, B -nətərɪ] *a.* condenatorio.
damned [dæmd] *a.* (DAMNEDEST) 1. maldito, condenado. 2. infernal, detestable, abominable, infame. 3. completo, tremendo (imbécil, disparate, etc.). 4. (*ú. sólo en el super.*) extraordinario, increíble. 5. **the d.,** los condenados (a pena eterna). —*adv.* muy, sumamente, extraordinariamente.
damnify ['dæmnəˌfaɪ] *v.t.* (*pret., p.p.* DAMNIFIED; *p.pr.* DAMNIFYING) damnificar, perjudicar, dañar.
damning ['dæmɪŋ] *a.* 1. mortal (pecado). 2. concluyente, probatorio (prueba).
Damocles ['dæməˌkliz] *s.* (hist.) Damocles; **sword of D.,** espada de Damocles, amenaza, peligro.
damp [dæmp] *s.* 1. humedad. 2. mofeta (en minas). 3. (fig.) abatimiento, desaliento. —*v.t.* 1. humedecer, mojar ligeramente. 2. sofocar, ahogar. 3. desanimar, desalentar, deprimir; disminuir, moderar, apagar (entusiasmo, alegría, etc.). 4. (mús., fís., elec.) amortiguar (oscilaciones, ondas). 5. **damp down the fire,** cubrir el fuego. —*v.i.* 1. humedecerse, mojarse algo. 2. ir disminuyéndose (onda sonora, vibración, etc.). 3. **d. off,** (bot.) pudrirse por el pie (plantas a causa de honguillos). —*a.* 1. húmedo, ligeramente mojado. 2. desanimado, deslucido, aburrido, tedioso.
dampen ['dæmpən] *v.t.* 1. humedecer, mojar. 2. (fig.) deprimir, desanimar; disminuir, moderar, apagar. 3. (mús., fís., elec.) amortiguar. —*v.i.* 1. humedecerse, mojarse algo. 2. (fig.) disminuirse, apagarse.
dampener [-ənər, B -ənə] *s.* (fís., elec.) amortiguador.
damper ['dæmpər, B -pə] *s.* 1. compuerta de tiro, regulador de tiro (en un tubo de caldera, chimenea, etc.). 2. apagador (en el piano). 3. (G.B.) amortiguador. 4. (fig.) freno, influencia moderadora, ej., *to put a d. on,* desanimar, desalentar, apagar (el entusiasmo, etc.).
damping [-pɪŋ] *s.* (fís., elec.) amortiguamiento, disminución de la amplitud de onda.
damping-off [ˌdæmpɪŋ'ɔf] *s.* (bot.) enfermedad de los almácigos.
damping piston, émbolo amortiguador.
dampish ['dæmpɪʃ] *a.* algo húmedo.
damply ['dæmplɪ] *adv.* húmedamente.
dampness [-nəs] *s.* humedad.
damsel ['dæmzel] *s.* damisela, mocita, doncella.
damson ['dæmzən, -sən, B -zən] *s.* 1. (bot.) ciruelo damasceno, amaceno. 2. ciruela damascena, amacena.
dance [dæns, B dɑns] *v.i.* 1. bailar, danzar. 2. (fig.) brincar (de alegría, dolor, etc.). —*v.t.* 1. hacer bailar (oso, etc.). 2. bailar. 3. **d. attendance on,** atender a alguien con mucha deferencia y atención. —*s.* 1. baile, danza. 2. baile (reunión).
dance band, orquesta de baile, orquesta bailable, orquestina.
dance floor, pista de baile.
dance hall, salón de baile.
dance music, música de baile, música bailable.
dancer ['dænsər, B 'dɑnsə] *s.* bailarín, bailarina.
dance school, academia de baile.
dancing girl ['dænsɪŋ-, B 'dɑns-] bayadera, corista.
dancing partner, pareja de baile (uno con respecto a otro).
dancing slippers, zapatillas de baile.
dandelion ['dændəˌlaɪən] *s.* (bot.) amargón, diente de león.
dander ['dændər, B -də] *s.* 1. caspa. 2. (fam.) cólera, mal genio, ira. 3. **to get one's d. up,** irritar o enojar a uno, enojarse, enfadarse.
dandiacal [dæn'daɪəkəl] *a.* demasiado elegante, propio de un dandi o petimetre.
Dandie Dinmont [ˌdændɪ'dɪnˌmɑnt, B -ˌmɔnt] (zool.) terrier de patas cortas y cuerpo largo.
dandify ['dændɪˌfaɪ] *v.t.* (*pret., p.p.* DANDIFIED; *p.pr.* DANDIFYING) vestir como un dandi o petimetre.
dandle ['dændəl] *v.t.* mecer (a un niño en los brazos o rodillas), mimar, acariciar, hacer fiestas (a).
dandruff ['dændrəf, B -drʌf] *s.* caspa.
dandy ['dændɪ] *s.* (*pl.* DANDIES) 1. dandi, petimetre, lechuguino, gomoso, caballerete. 2. (fam.) lindura, cosa excelente. 3. (mar.) balandra de dos palos. —*a.* 1. currutaco. 2. (fam.) primoroso, rebueno, de rechupete.
dandy fever, (med.) dengue.
dandyish [-ɪʃ] *a.* alechuguinado, currutaco; elegantón.
dandyism [-ˌɪzəm] *s.* dandismo.
dandy roll, d. roller, cilindro para impartir al papel la marca de aqua.
Dane [deɪn] *s.* 1. danés, dinamarqués, de Dinamarca. 2. (zool.) (perro) danés, alano.
daneweed ['deɪnˌwid] **danewort** [-ˌwɜrt, B -ˌwɜt] *s.* (bot.) cimicaria, yezgo.
danger ['deɪndʒər, B -dʒə] *s.* peligro, riesgo; **in d. of,** en peligro de; **there is no d.,** no hay cuidado, no hay temor.
dangerous [-dʒərəs, B -dʒrəs] *a.* peligroso, arriesgado, de cuidado.
dangerously [-lɪ] *adv.* peligrosamente, arriesgadamente.
dangerousness [-nəs] *s.* peligrosidad, riesgo.
danger signal, señal de peligro.
dangle ['dæŋgəl] *v.i.* 1. pender, colgar, suspender. 2. (con *after, about, around*) rondar, ir tras de. —*v.t.* 1. balancear (piernas, etc.). 2. (fig.) dejar entrever. 3. (gram.) estar inconexo (en la frase).
dangling [-glɪŋ] *a.* pendiente, colgante.
Danish ['deɪnɪʃ] 1. *a., s.* danés, dinamarqués. 2. *var. de* **Danish pastry.**
Danish pastry, bollo cubierto de azúcar glaseado y frutas o nueces.
dank [dæŋk] *a.* desagradablemente húmedo, mojado, liento.
dankness ['dæŋknəs] *s.* humedad desagradable.
danse macabre ['dɑnsmə'kɑbrə] (fr.) danza macabra, danza de la muerte.
danseuse [dɑn'sʌz, -'sʊz, B -'sɜz] *s.* (fr.) bailarina (de ballet).
Dantean ['dæntɪən, B dæn'tiən] *a.* dantesco.
Dantesque [dæn'tɛsk] *a.* dantesco (relativo al infierno que describió Dante en *La Divina Comedia*).
Danube ['dænjub] *s.* Danubio (río); **blue D.,** Danubio azul.
Danubian [dæ'njubɪən] *a.* danubiano (del río Danubio).
dap [dæp] *v.i.* (*pret., p.p.* DAPPED; *p.pr.* DAPPING) 1. pescar con carnada flotante. 2. zambullirse; rebotar, brincar. —*v.t.* 1. hacer rebotar (en el agua). 2. (carp.) hacer muescas en (la madera). —*s.* muesca (en la madera).
daphne ['dæfnɪ] *s.* (bot.) rododafne, adelfa.
dapper ['dæpər, B -ə] *a.* 1. pulido, aseado; apuesto, gallardo. 2. vivaz, vivaracho.
dapple ['dæpəl] *s.* 1. mancha moteada. 2. apariencia moteada. 3. animal de piel moteada. —*v.t.* manchar, motear, salpicar, abigarrar con manchas. —*v.i.* volverse manchado, moteado o abigarrado.
dappled [-əld] *a.* tordo, moteado, habado; manchado, pinto.
dapple-gray ['dæpəl'greɪ] *a.* (zool.) tordillo, rodado, rucio (díc. de los cuadrúpedos).
darb [dɑrb, B dɑb] *s.* (jer., Can.) maravilla, lindura, ejemplar insuperable.
Dardan ['dɑrdən, B 'dɑd-] **Dardanian** [dɑr'deɪnɪən, B dɑ'-] *a.* dardanio, dárdano. —*s.* dárdano, troyano.
Dardanelles [ˌdɑrdə'nɛlz B ˌdɑdə-] *s. pl.* Dardanelos (el estrecho entre el mar Egeo y el de Mármara).
dare [dɛr, dær, B dɛə] *v.i.* osar, atreverse. —*v. aux.* (ú.sin *to*) atreverse a. —*v.t.* 1. retar, desafiar. 2. provocar, ej., *d. someone's anger,* provocar la ira de alguien. 3. arrostrar, hacer frente a, arrostrarse con. 4. aventurar, arriesgar. 5. **I d. say,** probablemente; (irón.) ya lo creo, muy probable. —*s.* 1. desafío, reto, provocación. 2. arrojo, bravura.

daredevil [ˈdɛrˌdɛvəl, ˈdær-, B ˈdɛəˌ-] *s.* atrevido. *—a.* atrevido, temerario, osado.
daredeviltry [-trɪ] *s.* atrevimiento, osadía.
daresay [ˌdɛrˈseɪ, ˌdær-, B ˈdɛəˈ-] *v.t., v.i.* (*ú. sólo en la primera persona sing. del presente*) creer, no dudar, suponer, ej., *I d. he's right,* creo (supongo, no dudo) que tiene razón.
Dar es Salaam [ˌdɑrˌɛssəˈlɑm] *s.* Dar-es-Salaam, capital de Tanzania.
daring [ˈdɛrɪŋ, ˈdær-, B ˈdɛər-] *s.* osadía, bravura, arrojo, audacia. *—a.* temerario, intrépido, osado, audaz, emprendedor.
daringly [-lɪ] *adv.* intrépidamente, osadamente, audazmente.
dark [dɑrk, B dɑk] *a.* 1. obscuro. 2. (fig.) obscuro, negro, sombrío, tenebroso, misterioso. 3. (fig.) malvado, malo, siniestro. 4. (fig.) obscuro, confuso, incomprensible. 5. secreto, oculto. 6. ignorante, poco civilizado. 7. moreno; negro, ej., *d. bread,* pan negro. 8. **to become, get** o **grow d.,** obscurecerse; anochecer. —*s.* 1. obscuridad; tinieblas, anochecer, noche. 2. (pint.) color obscuro, sombra. 3. **at d.,** al caer la noche, al anochecer; **leap in the d.,** salto a ciegas; **to be in the d.,** (lit., fig.) estar a obscuras; **to be left in the d.,** quedarse a obscuras, quedarse en ayunas; **to keep (something** o **someone) in the d.,** ocultar (algo o alguien). *—v.t., v.i.* (ant.) obscurecer(se), opacar(se), ensombrecer(se).
dark adaptation, (ópt.) adaptación de la vista a la obscuridad.
dark-adapted [ˌdɑrkəˈdæptəd, B ˌdɑkə-] *a.* adaptado para ver con luz débil o mortecina.
Dark Ages, Edad Media, medioevo, edad del oscurantismo.
dark beer, cerveza parda, cerveza negra.
dark-complexioned [-kəmˈplɛkʃənd, B ˈdɑk-] *a.* de tez oscura, moreno.
Dark Continent, África.
darken [ˈdɑrkən, B ˈdɑk-] *v.i.* obscurecerse; ensombrecerse, ponerse o volverse obscuro. *—v.t.* 1. obscurecer, volver obscuro. 2. ofuscar, nublar (el entendimiento), confundir, embrollar. 3. ennegrecer, manchar; empañar. 4. ensombrecer, entristecer. 5. **d. one's door** (o **doorstep**), pisar el umbral de la casa de uno, ej., *never d. my door* (o *doorstep*) *again,* nunca vuelvas a pisar el umbral de esta casa.
dark-eyed [-ˈaɪd] *a.* de ojos negros, oji-negro.
dark-field microscope [-ˌfild-] (ópt.) ultramicroscopio.
dark horse, 1. caballo con pocas posibilidades (de ganar); ganador insospechado. 2. (pol.) candidato desconocido; candidato de posibilidades incalculables.
darkie [ˈdɑrkɪ, B ˈdɑkɪ] *s. var. of* **darky.**
darkish [-kɪʃ] *a.* obscurecido, un tanto obscuro.
dark lantern, linterna sorda, linterna flamenca.
darkle [-kəl] *v.i.* obscurecerse, volverse obscuro; nublarse; quedar oculto en la obscuridad.
darkling [-klɪŋ] *adv.* (poét.) a obscuras. *—a.* obscuro, obscurecido, tenebroso; (que está o sucede) en la obscuridad.
darkly [ˈdɑrklɪ, B ˈdɑk-] *adv.* obscuramente, secretamente, misteriosamente.
darkness [-nəs] *s.* 1. obscuridad, opacidad, tinieblas, sombra. 2. ofuscación, ignorancia. 3. tenebrosidad, tinieblas, tristeza. 4. ceguera.
darkroom [-ˌrum, -ˌrʊm] *s.* (foto.) cámara obscura, cuarto obscuro, cuarto de revelar.
darksome [-səm] *a.* (poét.) obscuro, sombrío, opaco.
dark star, (astr.) estrella obscura (invisible).
darky, *s.* [ˈdɑrkɪ, B ˈdɑkɪ] (despec., ant.) negro.
darling [ˈdɑrlɪŋ, B ˈdɑlɪŋ] *s.* querido, amor, tesoro; favorito. *—a.* 1. querido, muy amado. 2. (fam.) amable, encantador; gracioso, lindo.
darn [dɑrn, B dɑn] *v.t.* 1. zurcir. 2. eufem. por **damn.** *—v.i.* hacer zurcidos. *—s.* 1. zurcido, lugar zurcido (acto o resultado de zurcir). 2. bledo, comino, ej., *I don't give a d.,* no me importa un bledo.
darn, darned, *a., adv., interj.* eufem. por **damn, damned,** ej., *a darned sight more,* muchísimo más.
darnel [ˈdɑrnəl, B ˈdɑn -] *s.* (bot.) cizaña, joyo, cominillo.
darner [ˈdɑrnər, B ˈdɑnə] *s.* 1. zurcidor. 2. máquina zurcidora. 3. (ento.) libélula.
darning ball, d. egg [-ɪŋ-] huevo de zurcir.
darning needle, 1. aguja de zurcir. 2. (ento., jer., E.U.) libélula.
dart [dɑrt, B dɑt] *s.* 1. dardo, saeta. 2. movimiento rápido. 3. punzada (de dolor). 4. (cost.) sisa, pinza. 5. aguijón. *—v.t.* lanzar, arrojar, tirar. *—v.i.* correr, lanzarse, volar rápidamente.
dartboard [ˈdɑrtˌbɔrd, B ˈdɑtˌbɔd] *s.* blanco, tabla vertical contra la cual se lanzan los dardos.
darter [-ər, B -ə] *s.* 1. animal o cosa que se lanza rápidamente. 2. (orn.) pájaroculebra. 3. (ict.) variedad americana de perca. 4. flechador, lanzador.
darting nail [-ɪŋ-] clavo de flecha, tachuela flechadora.
dartle [-əl] *v.t., v.i.* lanzar(se) repetidamente.
darts [dɑrts, B dɑts] *s. pl.* (*sing. en const.*) juego de dardos (que se lanzan contra un blanco vertical de superficie plana).
Darwinian [dɑrˈwɪnɪən, B dɑˈ-] *a.* darviniano, propio de Darwin.
Darwinism [ˈdɑrwənˌɪzəm B ˈdɑwɪn-] *s.* darvinismo, teoría de la evolución de las especies.
Darwinist [-əst] *s., a.* darvinista, relativo a, o que cree en el darvinismo.
dash [dæʃ] *v.t.* 1. lanzar, arrojar, tirar. 2. salpicar (algo con agua, pintura, etc.). 3. diluir, mezclar. 4. arruinar, destruir, frustrar, desvanecer (esperanzas, ilusiones, etc.). 5. confundir, desconcertar, deprimir. 6. **d. against,** arrojar contra; **d. down,** anotar, escribir de prisa; **d. off,** hacer rápidamente (dibujo, esquicio, composición, etc.); tragar, beber de prisa; **d. to the ground,** (fig.) echar por tierra. *—v.i.* lanzarse, apresurarse, avanzar o pasar rápidamente; **d. against,** lanzarse contra; estrellarse contra; **d. away,** partir corriendo, marcharse de prisa; **d. by,** pasar corriendo; **d. in (out),** entrar (salir) corriendo; entrar (salir) como un rayo; **d. off,** salir de prisa. —*s.* 1. plumada, trazo (de la pluma); pincelada, toque (de la brocha). 2. chorro (de agua). 3. pizca, poquito. 4. avance rápido, arranque, arremetida. 5. brío, garbo, donaire. 6. carrera de velocidad, carrera corta. 7. guión, raya. 8. (teleg.) raya (como parte de una letra en la clave Morse). 9. (*forma abrev. de* **dashboard**) (aut.) tablero de instrumentos; guardafango. 10. **at a d.,** de un golpe; **to make a d. at,** arremeter; **to make a d. to** (o **for**), correr para alcanzar, echarse a correr para alcanzar, darse prisa para; **to make a d. for it,** tratar de escapar, echarse a correr huyendo.
dashboard [ˈdæʃˌbɔrd, B -ˌbɔd] *s.* 1. (aut.) guardabarros, guardalodos, guardafango (Am.). 2. (aut., aer.) tablero de instrumentos.
dash coat, capa lanzada contra el concreto por brochón.
dasher [-ər, B -ə] *s.* 1. batidora, agitadora (en una mantequera, mezcladora, etc.). 2. (fam.) persona briosa o impetuosa.
dashing [-ɪŋ] *a.* 1. vigoroso, animoso, brioso, garboso, lucido. 2. vistoso, elegante, ostentoso.
dash line, (dib.) línea de rayas o de trazos.
dashpot [ˈdæʃpɔt] *s.* amortiguador.
dassie [ˈdɑsɪ, B ˈdæsɪ] *s.* (zool.) damán de Sudáfrica.
dastard [ˈdæstərd, B -təd] *s.* cobarde, hombre vil.
dastardliness [-lɪnəs] *s.* cobardía, vileza, alevosía.
dastardly [-lɪ] *a.* miserable, cobarde, vil.
dasyure [ˈdæsɪˌjʊr, B -jʊə] *s.* (zool.) dasiuro.
data [ˈdeɪtə, ˈdætə, ˈdɑtə, B ˈdeɪtə, ˈdɑtə] *pl. de* **datum.**
data bank, banco de datos.
database [ˈdeɪtəbeɪs] *s.* base de datos.
data capture, (comput.) formulación de datos, toma de datos.
data dictionary, guía de datos.
data directory, guía de datos.
data file, archivo de datos.
data link, (comput.) medio de transmisión de datos.
data preparation, preparación de datos.
data processing, proceso de datos.
data procesor, procesador de datos.
data protection, protección de datos.
data transmission, transmisión de datos, telemática.
datary [ˈdeɪtərɪ] *s.* (relig.) 1. datario. 2. dataría (tribunal que investiga la idoneidad de candidatos a beneficios populares).
date [deɪt] *s.* 1. fecha. 2. fecha, día, momento; época, período. 3. duración. 4. cita, compromiso (a una fecha y hora señaladas). 5. (fig.) compañero, compañera, persona (del sexo opuesto) con quien se tiene cita. 6. **at an early d.,** en fecha próxima; **out of d.,** anticuado, atrasado; atrasado de noticias; **to d.,** hasta la fecha; **to have a d. with,** tener una cita o compromiso con; **to make a d. with,** concertar una cita con; **up to d.,** al día; al corriente; a la moda; hasta la fecha; **what's the d. today?** ¿a qué fecha estamos hoy?. *—v.t.* 1. datar, fechar. 2. asignar fecha a, estimar el período de (objeto de arte, etc.). 3. estimar, computar (desde un día o fecha). 4. revelar o fijar la edad de, ej., *style dates a house,* el estilo revela la edad de una casa. 5. dar cita a, hacer un compromiso con; salir con, ej., *he's been dating her for a long time,* ha estado saliendo con ella desde hace mucho tiempo. *—v.i.* 1. fijar o estimar la fecha; poner o imprimir la fecha (una máquina, un aparato, etc.). 2. volverse anticuado. 3. **d. back to,** pertenecer a la época (pasada) de, ser del tiempo (pasado) de; originarse a (o en), tener su comienzo u origen en, remontarse a; **d. from,** datar de (una época o período).
date, *s.* 1. (bot.) datilero, palma datilera. 2. dátil.
dated [ˈdeɪtəd] *a.* pasado de moda, anticuado; fechado.
dateless [-ləs] *a.* 1. sin fecha (carta, etc.). 2. sin tiempo señalado. 3. sin compañero o compañera.
date line, línea de cambio de fecha (que cruza el meridiano 180 y que cambia la fecha a medianoche).
dateline [-ˌlaɪn] *s.* fecha y lugar de origen (que precede a un parte periodístico). *—v.t.* fechar (un artículo, reportaje, etc.).
date mussel, (zool.) dátil de mar.
date palm, (bot.) palmera de dátiles, palmera datilera.
dater [ˈdeɪtər, B -ə] *s.* (sello) fechador.
dating [-ɪŋ] *s.* fechación.
dating service, agencia de contactos.
dative [ˈdeɪtɪv] *a.* (gram.) dativo; (caso) dativo.
datum [ˈdeɪtəm, ˈdæt-, ˈdɑt-, B ˈdeɪt-, ˈdɑt-] *s.* (*pl.* DATA [-ə]) 1. dato, referencia, fundamento. 2. (*pl.*) datos, detalles, información.

datum line, (top.) línea de referencia.
datum plane, (top.) plano de referencia o de comparación.
datura [də'tʊrə, B -'tjʊərə] *s.* (bot.) datura.
daub [dɔb] *v.t.* 1. embadurnar, embarrar. 2. enlucir, cubrir de argamasa o mortero (pared). 3. pintarrajar, pintarrajear, pintorretear. —*v.i.* pintorrear. —*s.* 1. argamasa, mortero, yeso. 2. embarradura, unto. 3. pintarrajo. 4. mancha.
dauber ['dɔbər, B -ə] *s.* 1. pintamonas, pintor de brocha gorda. 2. cepillo para dar betún al calzado.
dauby [-ɪ] *a.* 1. pintarrajeado. 2. pegajoso, viscoso.
daughter ['dɔtər, B -ə] *s.* hija.
daughter cell, (biol.) célula hija.
daughter-in-law [-ərən,lɔ] *s.* (*pl.* DAUGHTERS-IN-LAW) nuera, hija política.
daughterly [-ərlɪ, B -əlɪ] *a.* filial, propio de una hija.
daunt [dɔnt, dɑnt, B dɔnt] *v.t.* acobardar, intimidar, atemorizar, amilanar.
dauntless ['dɔntləs, 'dɑnt-, B 'dɔnt-] *a.* intrépido, impávido, arrojado, valiente.
dauntlessly [-lɪ] *adv.* intrépidamente, arrojadamente.
dauntlessness [-nəs] *s.* intrepidez, valor, arrojo.
dauphin ['dɔfən] *s.* (hist.) delfín (título dado al hijo mayor del rey de Francia).
dauphine [-fin, B -fɪn] *s.* (hist.) delfina (título dado a la esposa del delfín).
davenport ['dævən,pɔrt, B -,pɔt] *s.* 1. (G.B.) escritorio pequeño. 2. sofá grande tapizado (a veces convertible en cama).
davit ['dævɪt, 'deɪ-, B 'dæ-] *s.* (mar.) pescante (para alzar botes); serviola (para colgar anclas).
Davy Jones ['deɪvɪ'dʒoʊnz] (poét.) espíritu del mar; demonio del mar.
Davy Jones's locker, (poét). el fondo del mar.
Davy lamp, (ant.) lámpara de Davy (usada en minas), lámpara aflogistica.
daw [dɔ] *s.* (orn.) corneja.
dawdle ['dɔdəl] *v.i.* 1. perder el tiempo, haraganear. 2. demorarse, tardar. —*v.t.* (gen. con *away*) gastar, malgastar (tiempo, años, etc.).
dawdler ['dɔdlər, B -lə] *s.* 1. haragán, holgazán. 2. tardón, demorón (Am.).
dawn [dɔn] *v.i.* 1. amanecer, rayar (el día); rayar el alba, alborear. 2. (fig.) amanecer (uso de la razón, civilización, etc.); esbozarse, bosquejarse, asomarse (ej., sonrisa en la cara). 3. (con *on* o *upon*) caer uno en cuenta, empezar a comprender, ej., *it dawned on me* (*him, her,* etc.) *that,* comencé (comenzó) a darme (se) cuenta de que, empecé (empezó) a comprender que. —*s.* 1. amanecer, alba, madrugada. 2. (fig.) albor, albores, aurora, principio. 3. **d. breaks,** quiebra, raya o rompe el alba.
day [deɪ] 1. día. 2. (*ú. t. en pl.*) período, tiempo, época, ej., *in our day,* en nuestro tiempo. 3. **all d.,** todo el día; **all d. long,** todo el día, todo el santo día; **any d.,** cualquier día; **a rainy d.,** (fig.) tiempos difíciles; **at the close of the d.,** al caer el día, al atardecer; **break of d.,** alba, amanecer; **by d.,** de día; **by the d.,** a jornal; **d. after d.,** día tras día; **d. after tomorrow,** pasado mañana; **d. before yesterday,** anteayer, antier; **d. by d.,** día por día; **d. in d. out,** día por día, día tras día; **d. off,** día libre, asueto; **every d.,** cada día, todos los días; **every other d.,** un día sí y otro no, cada tercer día; **from d. to d.,** de día en día; **from one d. to the next,** de un día al otro; **from this d. onward,** de hoy en adelante; **in the days of,** la época de; **it's all in a day's work,** son gajes del oficio; **one d.,** un día (indeterminado); **one of these days,** un día de éstos; **some d.,** algún día (en el futuro); **the d. after,** al día siguiente; **the d. before,** el día anterior, un día antes; la víspera de, ej., *he left on Saturday but I saw him the d. before,* se fue el sábado pero yo lo vi el día anterior (o un día antes); **the other d.,** el otro día; **this very d.,** hoy mismo, en este mismo día; **to call it a d.,** dar por terminado el día; **to carry** (o **win**) **the d.,** triunfar, salir airoso; **to know the time of d.,** saber cuántas son cinco; **to pass the time of d.,** pasar el rato, las horas; **to work d. and night,** trabajar día y noche; **twice (three times,** etc.) **a d.,** dos veces (tres veces, etc.) al día.
Dayak ['daɪ,æk] *s.* dayak, miembro de las tribus indonesias de Borneo; (t. **Dyak**).
daybed ['deɪ,bɛd] *s.* sofá cama.
daybook [-,bʊk] *s.* (ten.) diario.
day boy, (G.B.) escolar externo.
daybreak [-,breɪk] *s.* alba, aurora, amanecer, apuntar del día, romper del día.
day care, servicio de guardería infantil.
day care center, guardería infantil.
day coach, (f.c.) coche de viajeros de segunda.
daydream [-,drim] *s.* ensueño, ilusión; (*pl.*) castillos en el aire. —*v.i.* fantasear, soñar despierto, ilusionarse.
daydreamer [-ər, B -ə] *s.* iluso, soñador.
day fly, (ento.) cachipolla, efímera.
day hostel, casa de aseo.
day laborer, jornalero, gañán, peón, bracero.
day letter, carta telegrama (menos costosa pero más demorada que un telegrama corriente).
daylight ['deɪ,laɪt] *s.* 1. luz del día, luz natural. 2. amanecer, alba. 3. luz, distancia (entre botes en una regata). 4. **at d.,** a primera luz, al amanecer; **in d.,** (lit., fig.) a la luz del día; **in broad d.,** en pleno día; **to scare (beat, knock) the living daylights out of,** asustar o pegar fuertemente a; **to see d.,** llegar a comprender; **to throw d. on,** aclarar; sacar a luz.
daylight saving, aprovechamiento de la luz solar (adelantando los relojes en la primavera).
daylight-saving time, hora de verano (aprovechamiento de la luz solar adelantando los relojes en verano).
day lily, (bot.) azucena amarilla, azucena anteada.
daylong [-'lɔŋ] *a.* de todo el día. —*adv.* todo el día, el día entero.
day nursery, guardería (para infantes y niños); jardín de infantes, escuela de párvulos.
Day of Atonement, (relig.) día de la expiación.
Day of Judgement, (relig.) día del juicio, día del juicio final.
day school, externado, escuela o colegio para externos.
day shift, turno de día.
days of grace, días de gracia (que se conceden para el pago de una letra después de su vencimiento).
dayspring ['deɪ,sprɪŋ] *s.* (poét.) aurora, alba.
daystar [-,stɑr, B -,stɑ] *s.* 1. estrella matutina, lucero. 2. (poét.) el sol.
daytime [-,taɪm] *s.* día, luz del día.
daze [deɪz] *v.t.* aturdir, atontar, ofuscar. —*s.* ofuscamiento, aturdimiento, atolondramiento; **in a d.,** aturdido, ofuscado.
dazedly ['deɪzədlɪ] *adv.* atolondradamente, aturdidamente.
dazzle ['dæzəl] *v.t.* (lit., fig.) deslumbrar, encandilar. —*v.i.* brillar, deslumbrar. —*s.* 1. deslumbramiento, ofuscamiento. 2. luz o reflejo deslumbrante.
db *abrev. de* **decibel,** decibel, decibelio.
D.B.E., *abrev. de* **Dame Commander of (the Order of) the British Empire,** Dama de la Orden del Imperio Británico.
dbl. *abrev. de* **double,** doble.
DC *abrev. de* **direct current,** corriente continua.
D.C. *abrev. de* **District of Columbia,** Distrito de Columbia.
D.C.L. *abrev. de* **Doctor of Civil Law,** Doctor en Derecho Civil.
D.D. *abrev. de* **Doctor of Divinity,** Doctor en Teología.
D-day ['di,deɪ] 1. (mil.) día de desembarco (de las fuerzas aliadas en Francia durante la segunda guerra mundial). 2. (fig.) fecha acordada en secreto para realizar algo extraordinario.
D.D.S. *abrev. de* **Doctor of Dental Surgery,** Dentista Cirujano.
DDT ['didi'ti] D.D.T., siglas de diclorodifeniltricloretano, un insecticida muy eficaz.
deaccentuator ['diæk'sɛntʃʊ,eɪtər, B -'sɛntjʊ-ə] *s.* (rad.) circuito desacentuador.
deacon ['dikən] *s.* diácono. —*v.t.* 1. (E.U.) entonar leyendo (los salmos antes de cantarlos). 2. empacar (ej., fruta) colocando la mejor encima. 3. adulterar, alterar.
deaconess [-əs] *s.* diaconisa.
deaconry [-rɪ] *s.* diaconado, diaconato.
deaconship [-,ʃɪp] *s.* diaconado, diaconato (puesto y oficio).
deactivate [di'æktɪ,veɪt] *v.t.* desactivar, hacer inactivo o ineficaz.
dead [dɛd] *a.* 1. muerto. 2. entumecido, insensible (mano, dedos, etc.). 3. inanimado, inerte (materia). 4. insensible, indiferente. 5. extinto, extinguido (fuego, volcán, etc.), apagado (horno, etc.). 6. agotado, cansadísimo, muerto (fig.). 7. estéril, árido (suelo). 8. muerto, apagado, opaco (color), sordo, apagado (sonido). 9. estancado, inmóvil (aire, agua, etc.). 10. agotado (pozo de petróleo, mina, etc.); descargado (batería). 11. muerto, anticuado (idioma, lengua, costumbre, etc.). 12. aburrido, monótono. 13. seguro, certero (tirador, etc.). 14. absoluto, completo (silencio, quietud; certeza, seriedad, etc.), total (pérdida); exacto (centro, etc.). 15. repentino, brusco (ej., parada). 16. (der.) sin efecto (ley). 17. (com.) muerto (capital, mercado). 18. (elec.) sin corriente, inactivo, desconectado (alambre, aparato, etc.). 19. (mec.) inmóvil (husillo de torno, eje, etc. de máquina). 20. (impr.) usado, muerto, para tirar (tipos, planchas, composición, etc.). 21. (dep., naipes) fuera de juego. 22. (golf) muy cerca del hoyo (pelota). 23. **d. as a doornail,** muerto de remate; **d. men tell no tales,** los muertos no hablan (ú. como argumento para matar al que posee un secreto); **d. to the world,** (jer.) completamente borracho o dormido; **more d. than alive,** más muerto que vivo; **to be in d. earnest,** obrar o hablar con toda seriedad; **to come to a d. stop,** pararse en seco; **to fall d.,** caer muerto; encalmarse (viento); **to fall in a d. faint,** caer desmayado como muerto; **to go d.,** dejar de funcionar; volverse mudo (radio, altoparlante, teléfono, línea telegráfica, etc.). —*s.* (*pl.* DEAD) 1. **the d.,** los muertos. 2. quietud, profundo silencio. 3. **d. of night,** plena noche, altas horas de la noche; **the d. of winter,** pleno invierno, lo más recio del invierno. —*adv.* 1. completamente, absolutamente. 2. bruscamente, de golpe. 3. (G.B., dial.) muy, sumamente. 4. **to be d. set against,** ser completamente opuesto a; **to stop d.,** parar en seco.
dead-air space ['dɛd'ɛr-, B -'ɛə-] espacio cerrado, espacio sin ventilación.
dead angle, ángulo muerto.
deadbeat [-,bit] *a.* (elec., rad.) aperiódico, que se detiene sin oscilar (galvanómetro, antena). —*s.* (jer., E.U.) gorrón, aprovechado.

dead-burned plaster [-ˌbɜrnd- ˌB- ˌbɜnd-] yeso anhidro.
dead center, 1. (mot.) punto muerto. 2. (mec.) punta fija (en máquinas o herramientas). 3. *(exact center)* el mismo centro; **in d.** justo en el centro.
dead-clamp [-ˌklæmp] *s.* (elec.) abrazadera terminal, grapa de anclaje.
dead-drunk [-'drʌŋk] *a.* hecho una uva, borracho como una cuba.
deaden ['dɛdən] *v.t.* 1. amortiguar, amortecer (color, pasión, pesar, etc.); apagar, ahogar (sonido). 2. disminuir (la velocidad de un barco). 3. aislar contra el ruido (ej., una pared). *—v.i.* 1. morir(se). 2. amortiguarse, disminuirse.
dead end, (lit., fig.) callejón sin salida; extremo cerrado.
dead-end [-ˌɛnd] *a.* 1. que tiene sólo una salida. 2. sin oportunidad de progresar o realizarse (plan, proyecto, etc.).
dead-end street, callejón sin salida, calle cerrada, calle ciega.
deadening ['dɛdənɪŋ] *s.* aislante (para paredes, pisos, etc.).
deadeye ['dɛdˌaɪ] *s.* (mar.) vigota.
deadfall [-ˌfɔl] *s.* trampa (en que un peso cae sobre la presa).
dead freight, flete falso.
dead ground, (elec., rad.) conexión perfecta a tierra, tierra perfecta.
dead hand, (der.) manos muertas.
deadhead [-ˌhɛd] *s.* 1. (fam.) persona que recibe entradas gratis (para teatros, actuaciones públicas, etc.). 2. (fam.) persona aburrida. 3. (metal.) mazarota (en el molde). 4. (mec.) contrapunta. 5. (mar.) bloque de madera sumergido; boya de madera; poste de amarre. *—v.i.* 1. hacer el viaje de vuelta sin carga (camión, vagón, etc.). 2. hacer uso de pases o entradas gratis. *—adv.* sin carga ni pasajeros.
dead heat, carrera en la que dos o más competidores empatan.
dead language, lengua muerta.
dead letter, 1. (der.) ley que sin estar abolida no está en vigencia. 2. (fig.) carta que no se puede entregar al destinatario ni devolver al expedidor por falta de direcciones correctas. 3. letra muerta.
deadlight [-ˌlaɪt] *s.* 1. (mar.) cuartel o tapa de escotilla; lumbrera de cubierta. 2. claraboya hecha para no abrirse.
deadline [-ˌlaɪn] *s.* 1. línea vedada (en E.U. esp. la que marca en una prisión el límite que los prisioneros no deben pasar). 2. límite de tiempo, fin de plazo (esp. en periodismo, para entregar un artículo o cerrar una edición).
deadliness ['dɛdlɪnəs] *s.* efecto o carácter mortífero.
dead load, carga fija, carga muerta.
deadlock [-ˌlɑk, B -ˌlɔk] *s.* 1. estancación, estancamiento. 2. empate. 3. cerradura dormida. *—v.t., v.i.* estancar(se), parar(se); empatar(se).
deadly ['dɛdlɪ] *a.* (DEADLIER; DEADLIEST) 1. mortífero, mortal. 2. mortal, implacable (enemigo, lucha, odio, etc.). 3. devastador, aniquilador (crítica, palabra, etc.). 4. nocivo, pernicioso, deletéreo (hábito, práctica, efecto, etc.). 5. certero, seguro (tirador). 6. cadavérico (palidez, blancura, etc.). 7. (fam.) extremo, absoluto. *—adv.* sumamente, extraordinariamente, extremadamente; **to be d. enemies,** ser enemigos a muerte.
deadly nightshade, (bot.) belladona.
deadly sins, los siete pecados capitales.
deadman ['dɛdˌmæn] *s.* macizo de anclaje, anclaje.
dead march, (mil.) marcha fúnebre.
deadpan [-ˌpæn] *a., adv.* (jer.) inexpresivo, inalterado, impasible. *—s.* (jer.) cara impasible, semblante inexpresivo.
dead point, (mec.) punto muerto.
dead reckoning, 1. (mar.) navegación a estima. 2. conjetura.
dead rising, (mar.) delgado, racel, rasel.
Dead Sea, Mar Muerto (entre Israel y Jordania).
Dead Sea Scrolls, manuscritos del Mar Muerto (que contienen antiguos textos hebreos).
dead spindle, (mec.) husillo fijo.
dead-stick landing ['dɛdˌstɪk-] (aer.) aterrizaje con motor parado, aterrizaje con hélice calada.
dead-thimble [-ˌθɪmbəl] *s.* (elec.) guardacabo terminal.
dead tonnage tonelaje de carga, porte bruto, carga bruta.
dead wall, pared sin vanos.
dead weight, peso muerto.
dead wind, (mar.) viento a proa.
deadwood ['dɛdˌwʊd] *s.* 1. madera seca (en el árbol). 2. (fig.) mercancía inservible; gente inútil (en una organización, etc.). 3. (mar.) durmientes (vigas horizontales en la proa y la popa de una embarcación). 4. (dep.) bolos derribados (que quedan en la pista de juego).
dead works, (teo.) obras muertas.
deaerate [dɪ'ɛrˌeɪt, B -'eɪər-] *v.t.* desaerear.
deaf [dɛf] *a.* 1. sordo. 2. (fig. con *to*) sordo, insensible (a). 3. **d. and dumb,** sordomudo; **d. as a post,** sordo como una tapia; **to turn a d. ear (to),** cerrar los oídos (a), hacerse el sordo (antc), hacer oídos de mercader (a, ante).
deaf-and-dumb ['dɛfən'dʌm] *s., a.* sordomudo.
deafen ['dɛfən] *v.t.* 1. ensordecer, asordar. 2. aislar contra el ruido (pared, cielo raso, etc.).
deafening [-ɪŋ] *a.* ensordecedor, atronador.
deaf-mute ['dɛf'mjut] *s., a.* sordomudo.
deafness [-nəs] *s.* sordera.
deal [dil] *s.* 1. cantidad; buena o gran cantidad. 2. negocio, trato, pacto. 3. trato, tratamiento (recibido). 4. arreglo, amarre. 5. (naipes) distribución; turno de dar; mano. 6. tabla de pino o abeto. 7. **a great** (o **good**) **d.,** un montón, una gran cantidad; mucho, ej., *that's a great d. of money,* esto es un montón (o una gran cantidad) de dinero, *he knows a great d. about her,* él sabe mucho (o muchas cosas) de ella; **it's a d.!** ¡trato hecho!; **raw d.,** trato injusto, mal trato; mala suerte; **square d.,** trato justo, trato honesto; **to make a great d. of,** (fig.) tratar (a alguien) con mucha atención; hacer mucho ruido acerca de (algo o alguien).
deal [dil] *v.t.* (*pret., pp.* DEALT [dɛlt]; *p.pr.* DEALING) 1. (gen. con *out*) distribuir, repartir, dar. 2. proporcionar, asestar (golpe, etc.). 3. distribuir, dar (naipes). *—v.i.* (naipes) distribuir, dar, repartir; **d. in,** traficar, comerciar, negociar (en); **d. with,** tratar o versar sobre, abordar (un tema, etc.), encargarse de (un asunto); tratar o asociarse con (persona, gente); habérselas con (alguien); tratar (bien o mal); dar trato (severo, etc.) a alguien o algo.
dealate [di'eɪˌleɪt] *s., a.* insecto despojado de alas, sin alas.
dealer ['dilər, B -ə] *s.* 1. negociante, comerciante, traficante. 2. (naipes) banquero, tallador.
dealership [-ʃɪp] *s.* (com.) representación, concesión.
dealing [-ɪŋ] *s.* 1. comportamiento, conducta. 2. (*pl.*) tratos, relaciones; negocios, transacciones.
deaminate [di'æməˌneɪt] *v.t.* (quím.) separar las aminas de (un compuesto).
deamination [diˌæmə'neɪʃən] *s.* (quím.) desaminación.
dean [din] *s.* 1. (relig.) deán; sacerdote supervisor de un distrito diocesano. 2. (E.U.) decano (de universidad); director administrativo (de un colegio o universidad). 3. decano (ej., del cuerpo diplomático).
deanery ['dinərɪ] *s.* 1. (relig.) deanato, deanazgo. 2. decanato (en una universidad o colegio).
deanship [-ˌʃɪp] *s.* decanato (dignidad de decano).
dear [dɪr, B dɪə] *a.* 1. amado, querido; apreciado, estimado, precioso, valioso. 2. amable. 3. caro, costoso. 4. sincero, profundo (deseo, rezo, amor, etc.). 5. **d. me! oh d.!** ¡Dios mío! ¡válgame Dios!; **D. Sir,** estimado señor, muy señor mío (nuestro); **for d. life,** como para salvar la vida misma; **my d. Smith,** mi querido Smith; **to be d. to,** ser muy amado por, ej., *the cause of freedom is d. to me,* la causa de la libertad es muy preciada para mí, *my brother is very d. to me,* amo mucho a mi hermano. *—s.* querido, querida, amor; **like a d.,** tan amable, ej., *help me carry these things, like a d.,* sea tan amable y ayúdeme a llevar estas cosas; **my d.,** querido mío, querida mía, amor mío. *—adv.* caro, caramente, ej., *to buy* (o *to sell*) *d.,* comprar (o vender) caro.
dearly ['dɪrlɪ, B 'dɪəlɪ] *adv.* 1. profundamente, ej., *to love d.,* amar profundamente. 2. caro, caramente.
dearness [-nəs] *s.* 1. amabilidad, dulzura. 2. alto precio, carestía.
dearth [dɜrθ, B dɜθ] *s.* carestía, escasez, ej., *d. of news,* carencia de noticias, *there's a d. of competent accountants,* hay escasez de contadores competentes.
death [dɛθ] *s.* 1. muerte, fallecimiento. 2. (fig.) muerte, fin; extinción. 3. **at d.'s door,** a las puertas de la muerte; **d. to (the tyrant,** etc.)! ¡muera (el tirano, etc.)!; **pale as d.,** pálido como un muerto; **to be the d. of,** matar, llevar a la tumba; **to catch one's d. of cold,** pescarse un resfrío grave; **to d.,** sumamente, en extremo, ej., *I am tired to d.,* estoy sumamente cansado, estoy muerto de cansancio; **to put to d.,** dar muerte a, ejecutar; **to the d.,** hasta la muerte.
death adder, (zool.) víbora australiana.
deathbed ['dɛθˌbɛd] *s.* lecho de muerte.
death benefit, indemnización o beneficios por muerte, cuota mortuoria.
deathblow [-ˌbloʊ] *s.* golpe mortal.
death certificate, partida de defunción; certificado de defunción.
death chamber, cámara de gas.
death cup, (bot.) canaleja, hongo venenoso.
death-dealing [-ˌdilɪŋ] *a.* mortífero.
death house, pabellón de los condenados; **to be in the d. h.,** (fam.) estar en capilla.
death knell, 1. doble, toque de difuntos, toque a muerto. 2. (fig.) golpe de gracia.
deathless ['dɛθləs] *a.* inmortal, imperecedero.
deathlessness [-nəs] *s.* inmortalidad.
deathlike [-ˌlaɪk] *a.* quedo, inmóvil, silencioso, como muerto, aletargado, cadavérico.
deathly [-lɪ] *a.* 1. mortal, mortífero, fatal. 2. cadavérico (palidez, etc.). *—adv.* 1. mortalmente, gravemente. 2. como un muerto (pálido).
death mask, mascarilla (vaciado del rostro de un cadáver).
death notice, aviso fúnebre.
death penalty, (der.) pena de muerte.
death point, (biol.) punto de muerte, límite de supervivencia (para especies, organismos, etc.).
death rate, índice de mortalidad.
death rattle, estertor agónico (de los moribundos).

death roll, lista de bajas (de un ejército, etc.).
death row, corredor de la muerte.
death's-head [ˈdɛθsˌhɛd] *s.* 1. calavera (como símbolo de la muerte). 2. (ento.) calavera, mariposa de la muerte.
death tax, impuesto a la sucesión.
deathtrap [ˈdɛθˌtræp] *s.* trampa mortal (díc. de un barco viejo, un teatro sin puertas de escape, etc.).
Death Valley, Valle de la Muerte (en California), nivel más bajo en el Hemisferio Occidental.
death warrant, 1. (der.) decreto o sentencia de muerte; orden de ejecución. 2. (fig.) golpe mortal.
deathwatch [-ˌwɑtʃ, B -ˌwɔtʃ] *s.* 1. vigilia a los moribundos; velorio. 2. guardia que acompaña a un condenado a muerte.
deb [dɛb] *s.* (jer.) debutante, joven que es presentada en sociedad.
debacle [dɪˈbɑkəl, -ˈbæk-, B deɪˈbɑk-] *s.* 1. debacle, fracaso, fiasco, desplome. 2. caída, derrota (de un ejército, etc.). 3. deshielo, rompimiento del hielo (en un río).
debar [dɪˈbɑr, B -ˈbɑ] *v.t.* (*pret., p.p.* DEBARRED; *p.pr* DEBARRING) (gen. con *from*) excluir (de), privar (de); impedir.
debark [dɪˈbɑrk, B -ˈbɑk] *v.t., v.i.* desembarcar(se).
debarkation [ˌdiˌbɑrˈkeɪʃən, B -ˌbɑˈ-] *s.* desembarco.
debarment [-mənt] *s.* exclusión; prohibición.
debase [dɪˈbeɪs] *v.t.* 1. degradar, rebajar, envilecer; deteriorar. 2. desvalorar, desvalorizar.
debasement [-mənt] *s.* degradación, rebajamiento, envilecimiento.
debatable [dɪˈbeɪtəbəl] *a.* discutible, disputable.
debate [-ˈbeɪt] *s.* debate, discusión, disputa. —*v.i.* debatir, discutir, argüir. —*v.t.* 1. debatir, discutir, disputar. 2. reflexionar, deliberar, considerar.
debater [-ər, B -ə] *s.* polemista, controversista.
debauch [dɪˈbɔtʃ] *v.t.* corromper, viciar, seducir, pervertir. —*v.i.* entregarse a los placeres. —*s.* 1. corrupción, perversión. 2. orgía, libertinaje.
debauchee [dɪˌbɔtʃˈi, B ˌdɛbɔˈtʃi] *s.* libertino, licencioso, disoluto.
debauchery [dɪˈbɔtʃərɪ] *s.* 1. disolución, libertinaje, corrupción; sensualidad. 2. (*pl.*) orgias.
debenture [dɪˈbɛntʃər, B -tʃə] *s.* (com., fin.) bono de deuda; pagaré, orden de pago del gobierno; vale, obligación, bono.
debilitate [dɪˈbɪləˌteɪt] *v.t.* debilitar, extenuar.
debilitation [-ˌbɪləˈteɪʃən] *s.* debilitación, extenuación.
debility [-ˈbɪlətɪ] *s.* debilidad, languidez, flojedad.
debit [ˈdɛbət] *s.* (com., ten.) 1. débito, cargo. 2. pasivo, debe (de una cuenta). —*v.t.* (com., ten.) cargar, adeudar, cargar (suma) a la cuenta de (alguien).
debit balance, (com., ten.) saldo deudor.
debit entry, (ten.) asiento de cargo o débito.
debit memo, debit note (com., ten.) nota de débito, nota de cargo.
debonair [ˌdɛbəˈnɛr, B -ˈnɛə] *a.* 1. garboso, airoso, agraciado. 2. alegre, festivo, jovial. 3. afable, cortés.
debonairly [-lɪ] *adv.* airosamente; festivamente, con donaire.
debouch [dɪˈbuʃ, -ˈbaʊtʃ] *v.i.* desembocar, emerger, salir.
debouchment [-mənt] *s.* 1. desembocadura (de un río, canal, etc.); desembocadero, desemboque (de una calle, un camino, etc.). 2. salida.
debridement [dəˈbridmənt] *s.* (med.) desbridamiento.
debrief [dɪˈbrif, ˈdi-] *v.t.* interrogar, someter a un interrogatorio (a piloto al regresar a su base, a funcionario que vuelve de una misión oficial en el extranjero, etc.).
debris [dəˈbri, B ˈdeɪˌbri] *s.* (*pl.* DEBRIS) 1. escombro, desecho, desperdicio, restos. 2. (geol.) deyección, detrito, morena, morrena.
debris cone, (geol.) abanico de deyección.
debt [dɛt] *s.* deuda, adeudo, obligación; **in d.,** adeudado; **out of d.,** libre de deudas; **to be deeply in d.,** estar lleno de deudas; **to be in (someone's) d.,** estar endeudado con (alguien); **to go into d.,** endeudarse, adeudarse.
debtor [ˈdɛtər, B -ə] *s.* deudor.
debunk [diˈbʌŋk] *v.t.* (fam.) bajar del pedestal, desdorar, desprestigiar.
deburr [diˈbɜr, B -ˈbɜ] *v.t.* (mec.) quitar las rebabas.
debut [ˈdeɪˌbju, dɪˈbju, B ˈdeɪbu] *s.* estreno, debut; **to make one's d.,** estrenarse, debutar.
debutant [ˈdɛbjʊˌtɑnt, B -tɑŋ] *s.* principiante, debutante.
debutante [-ˌtɑnt] *s.* debutante, (muchacha) joven que se presenta en la sociedad.
Dec. *abrev. de* **December,** diciembre (dic.).
deca-ampere [ˌdɛkəˈæmˌpɪr, B -ˌpɛə] *s.* (elec.) decaamperio.
decade [ˈdɛkˌeɪd, -əd, dɛˈkeɪd] *s.* 1. década, decena. 2. década, decenio. 3. diez (del rosario).
decadence [ˈdɛkədəns, dɪˈkeɪdəns] *s.* decadencia, deterioro, declinación; período de decadencia.
decadent [-ənt] *a.* decadente; decadentista (autor). —*s.* (lit.) decadentista.
decaffeinated [dəˈkæfəˌneɪtəd] *a.* descafeinado.
decaffeinated coffee, cafe descafeinado.
decagon [ˈdɛkəˌgɑn, B -gən] *s.* (geom.) decágono.
decagonal [dɪˈkægənəl] *a.* decagonal.
decagram, (pr. G.B.) **decagramme** [ˈdɛkəˌgræm] *s.* decagramo.
decahedral [ˌdɛkəˈhidrəl] *a.* (geom.) decaedral.
decahedron [ˌdɛkəˈhidrən] *s.* (geom.) decaedro.
decal [dɪˈkæl, ˈdikæl] *s.* calcomanía.
decalcification [diˌkælsəfəˈkeɪʃən] *s.* descalcificación.
decalcify [-ˈkælsəˌfaɪ] *v.t.* descalcificar (huesos).
decalcomania [dɪˌkælkəˈmeɪnɪə] *s.* calcomanía.
decalescence [ˌdikəˈlɛsəns] *s.* (fís.) decalescencia.
decalin [ˈdɛkəlɪn] *s.* decalina.
decaliter, (pr. G.B.) **decalitre** [ˈdɛkəˌlitər, B -ə] *s.* decalitro.
Decalogue [-ˌlɔg, -ˌlɑg, B -ˌlɔg] *s.* (bíbl.) Decálogo, los Diez Mandamientos.
decameter, (pr. G.B.) **decametre** [ˈdɛkəˌmitər, B -ə] *s.* decámetro.
decamp [dɪˈkæmp] *v.i.* 1. decampar, levantar el campamento (un ejército, etc.). 2. (fig.) tomar las de Villadiego.
decampment [-mənt] *s.* salida del campamento.
decane [ˈdɛkˌeɪn] *s.* (quím.) decano.
decanoic acid [ˌdɛkəˈnoʊɪk-] *s.* (quím.) ácido cáprico.
decant [dɪˈkænt] *v.t.* decantar (vino, líquido), trasegar.
decantation [ˌdikænˈteɪʃən] *s.* decantación, trasiego.
decanter [dɪˈkæntər, B -ə] *s.* garrafa (de vino o licores).
decapitate [dɪˈkæpəˌteɪt] *v.t.* decapitar, degollar, descabezar.
decapitation [-ˌkæpəˈteɪʃən] *s.* decapitación, degüello, descabezamiento.
decapitator [-ˈkæpəˌteɪtər, B -ə] *s.* degollador.
decapod [ˈdɛkəˌpɑd, B -ˌpɔd] *s., a.* (zool.) decápodo.
Decapoda [dɪˈkæpədə] *s. pl.* (zool.) decápodos.
decarbonate [diˈkɑrbəˌneɪt, B -ˈkɑbə-] *v.t.* (fís.) descarbonatar.
decarbonation [-ˌkɑrbəˈneɪʃən, B -ˌkɑbə-] *s.* (quím.) descarbonatación.
decarbonization [-nəˈzeɪʃən, B -naɪ-] *s.* (quím.) descarburación.
decarbonize [diˈkɑrbəˌnaɪz, B -ˈkɑbə-] *v.t.* (quím.) descarbonizar, descarburar.
decarboxylate [ˌdiˌkɑrˈbɑksəˌleɪt, B -ˌkɑˈbɔk-] *v.t.* (quím.) quitar el carboxilo.
decarburization [diˌkɑrbərəˈzeɪʃən, B -ˌkɑbjʊraɪ-] *s.* (quím.) descarburación.
decarburize [-ˈkɑrbəˌraɪz, B -ˈkɑbjʊ-] *v.t.* (quím.) descarbonizar, descarburar.
decare [ˈdɛkˌɛr, B -ˌɛə] *s.* decárea, medida de superficie.
decastere [-əˌstɪr B -əˌstɪə] *s.* decastéreo (medida de masa).
decasyllabic [ˌdɛkəsəˈlæbɪk] *a.* decasílabo.
decasyllable [ˈdɛkəˌsɪləbəl] *s.* decasílabo, verso decasílabo; palabra decasílaba.
decathlon [dɪˈkæθlən, -ˌlɑn, B -ˌlɔn] *s.* (dep.) decatlón.
decay [dɪˈkeɪ] *v.i.* 1. pudrirse, descomponerse (fruta, etc.); cariarse (dientes). 2. deteriorarse, arruinarse, destruirse; desmoronarse. 3. degenerarse, decaer, declinar, empeorar, ir a menos. 4. disminuir, debilitarse (sonido, intensidad, etc.). —*v.t.* arruinar, destruir; descomponer. —*s.* 1. descomposición, podredumbre, putrefacción; caries (de los dientes). 2. deterioro, ruina, dilapidación, desmoronamiento. 3. degeneración, declinación, decaimiento. 4. disminución (del sonido, de la intensidad, etc.). 5. (fís.) desintegración espontánea (de una sustancia radiactiva).
decay chain, (fís.) cadena de desintegración.
decease [dɪˈsis] *s.* fallecimiento, deceso, muerte, defunción. —*v.i.* fallecer, morir.
deceased [-ˈsist] *a.* muerto, difunto, fallecido, finado; **the d.,** el finado, la finada, el difunto, la difunta.
decedent [-ˈsidənt] *s.* (der.) difunto, finado.
deceit [dɪˈsit] *s.* 1. engaño, fraude, superchería, embuste, artificio. 2. dolo, falsedad, decepción.
deceitful [-fəl] *a.* engañoso, falso, falaz, mentiroso.
deceitfully [-fəlɪ] *adv.* fraudulentamente, engañosamente, falsamente, falazmente.
deceitfulness [fəlnəs] *s.* falsedad, falacia, engaño.
deceivable [-ˈsivəbəl] *a.* engañadizo, cándido.
deceive [dɪˈsiv] *v.t.* engañar, alucinar, embaucar. —*v.i.* obrar engañosamente.
deceiver [-ər, B -ə] *s.* impostor, el que engaña, burlador.
deceivingly [-ɪŋlɪ] *adv.* engañosamente
decelerate [diˈsɛləˌreɪt] *v.t., v.i.* disminuir la velocidad (de), retardar(se).
deceleration [-ˌsɛləˈreɪʃən, B ˈdi-] *s.* reducción o disminución de la velocidad.
decelerator [-ˈsɛləˌreɪtər, B -ə] *s.* reductor de velocidad.
deceleron [-ˌrɑn, B -ˌrɔn] *s.* (aer.) freno de aire combinado con alerones.
December [dɪˈsɛmbər, B -bə] *s.* diciembre.

decemvir [-'sɛmvər, B -və] *s.* (hist.) decenviro, decenvir.
decemviral [-vərəl] *a.* (hist.) decenviral.
decemvirate [-rət] *s.* (hist.) decenvirato.
decency ['disənsɪ] *s.* 1. decencia, decoro, propiedad; pudor. 2. normas de conducta, buenos modales, buenas costumbres.
decennary [dɪ'sɛnərɪ] *s.* decenario, decenio. —*a.* decenario; decenal.
decennial [-ɪəl] *a.* decenal. —*s.* aniversario decenal, decenio, fiestas decenales.
decennially [-əlɪ] *adv.* cada diez años.
decennium [-ɪəm] *s.* (*pl.* DECENNIUMS O DECENNIA [-ɪə]) decenio, década.
decent ['disənt] *a.* 1. decente, decoroso, respetable, propio. 2. adecuado, apropiado, aceptable; suficiente, razonable. 3. (fam.) gentil, amable, ej., *that was very d. of you,* esto fue muy gentil (o amable) de su parte (Ud.). 4. (fam.) visible, vestido, presentable, ej., *may I come in? are you d.?* ¿puedo entrar? ¿estás vestido?
decently [-lɪ] *adv.* decentemente, con honestidad.
decentralization [di,sɛntrələ'zeɪʃən, B -laɪ-] *s.* descentralización.
decentralize [di'sɛntrə,laɪz] *v.t.* descentralizar.
deception [dɪ'sɛpʃən] *s.* decepción, engaño, impostura, superchería.
deceptive [-'sɛptɪv] *a.* engañoso, falaz, ilusorio.
deceptively [-lɪ] *adv.* engañosamente.
deceptiveness [-nəs] *s.* apariencia engañosa, aspecto ilusorio.
dechlorinate [di'klɔrə,neɪt] *v.t.* desclorinar, desclorar.
dechristianize [di'krɪstʃə,naɪz, B -'krɪstjə-] *v.t.* descristianizar.
deciampere [,dɛsɪ'æm,pɪr, B -,pɛə] *s.* (elec.) deciamperio.
deciare ['dɛsɪ,ɛr, B -,ɛə] *s.* deciárea, medida de superficie.
decibel ['dɛsə,bɛl, -bəl] *s.* (fís., electrón.) decibel, decibelio.
decidable [dɪ'saɪdəbəl] *a.* determinable, resoluble.
decide [dɪ'said] *v.t.* 1. decidir. 2. decidirse a, resolverse a, determinar(se). —*v.i.* enunciar una decisión, juzgar, sentenciar.
decided [-əd] *a.* 1. decidido, determinado, resuelto. 2. indiscutible, indudable.
decidedly [-lɪ] *a.* 1. decididamente, resueltamente. 2. indiscutiblemente, indudablemente.
decidedness [-nəs] *s.* determinación, resolución.
decidua [dɪ'sɪdʒʊə, B -'sɪdjʊə] *s.* (*pl.* DECIDUAE [-,i]) (anat.) decidua, caduca.
deciduous [-ʊəs, B -jʊəs] *a.* (bot., zool.) deciduo, caedizo, caduco; efímero.
decigram, (pr. G.B.) **decigramme** ['dɛsə,græm] *s.* decigramo.
deciliter, (pr. G.B.) **decilitre** [-,litər, B -ə] *s.* decilitro.
decimal ['dɛsəməl] *a.* decimal. —*s.* decimal, fracción decimal.
decimal fraction, fracción decimal.
decimalize [-,aɪz] *v.t.* decimalizar, convertir al sistema decimal.
decimal point, punto decimal, coma decimal.
decimal system, sistema decimal.
decimate ['dɛsə,meɪt] *v.t.* diezmar.
decimation [,dɛsə'meɪʃən] *s.* pérdida, muerte o ejecución, esp. de la décima parte (de tropas, población, etc.).
decimeter, (pr. G.B.) **decimetre** ['dɛsə,mitər, B -ə] *s.* decímetro.
decipher [dɪ'saɪfər, B -fə] *v.t.* descifrar; (fig.) descifrar, traducir.
decipherable [-fərəbəl] *a.* descifrable.
decipherment [-fərmənt, B -fəmənt] *s.* descifre.
decision [dɪ'sɪʒən] *s.* 1. decisión, resolución, conclusión. 2. fallo, decreto, auto, sentencia. 3. decisión, determinación, firmeza.
decisive [dɪ'saɪsɪv] *a.* 1. decisivo, conclusivo, concluyente, terminante. 2. decidido, firme.
decisively [-lɪ] *adv.* concluyentemente, terminantemente.
decisiveness [-nəs] *s.* carácter decisivo; firmeza, resolución.
decistere ['dɛsə,stɪr, B -,stɪə] *s.* decistéreo (medida de masa).
deck [dɛk] *s.* 1. (mar.) cubierta. 2. plataforma, superficie plana (ej., de un avión); (f.c.) techo (de vagón); (impr.) piso (de una rotativa). 3. (naipes) baraja, monte. 4. **below decks,** en (o a) la bodega (de un buque); **between d.,** entrepuente; **on d.,** (mar.) sobre cubierta; (fam., dep.) en reserva, a la mano, listo; **to clear the decks,** (fig.) alistarse para la pelea. —*v.t.* 1. vestir. 2. (gen. con *out*) ataviar, engalanar; adornar, embellecer. 3. (jer.) derribar.
deck beam, 1. viga T con nervio o bordón. 2. (mar.) bao de cubierta.
deck bridge, (f.c.) puente de tablero superior.
deck chair, silla de cubierta, silla de buque, silla de extensión.
decker ['dɛkər, B -ə] *s. ú. en palabras compuestas para expresar* más de una cubierta o capa, más de un puente o estrato, ej., *a two-d. ship,* un navío de dos puentes, *a double-d. sandwich,* un emparedado doble (con tres rebanadas de pan).
deckhand ['dɛk,hænd] *s.* marinero (que trabaja en la cubierta).
deckhouse [-,haʊs] *s.* (mar.) caseta sobre cubierta.
decking [-ɪŋ] *s.* piso, tablero.
deckle ['dɛkəl] *s.* 1. forma (para fabricar papel de mano o de cuba). 2. barba (del papel de mano).
deckle edge, barba, borde picoteado o plumillado (del papel de mano).
deckle-edged[-'ɛdʒd] *a.* con borde de barbas, de borde picoteado (papel).
declaim [dɪ'kleɪm] *v.i.* 1. declamar. 2. perorar, arengar. —*v.t.* declamar, recitar.
declamation [,dɛklə'meɪʃən] *s.* declamación, recitación.
declamatory [dɪ'klæmə,tɔrɪ, B -ətərɪ] *a.* declamatorio.
declarable [dɪ'klærəbəl, -'klɛr-, B -'klɛər-] *a.* declarable.
declaration [,dɛklə'reɪʃən] *s.* 1. declaración; manifestación, enunciación. 2. declaración, manifiesto (escrito). 3. (der.) declaración; primer alegato (en un proceso). 4. (bridge) declaración.
declaration of bankruptcy, declaración de quiebra.
Declaration of Independence, (E.U.) Declaración de la Independencia, adoptada en 1776.
declarative [dɪ'klærətɪv, -'klɛr-, B -'klær-] *a.* 1. declarativo. 2. (gram.) enunciativo, aseverativo.
declaratory [-ə,tɔrɪ, B -ətərɪ] *a.* (der.) declaratorio (fallo, auto, estatuto, etc.).
declare [dɪ'klɛr, B -'klɛə] *v.t.* 1. declarar; manifestar, enunciar. 2. (der.) declarar (ante el juez, bajo juramento, etc.). 3. (bridge) declarar. 4. **d. oneself,** hacer una declaración, manifestar uno su opinión; declararse. —*v.i.* hacer una declaración; **d. against,** declarar o testificar en contra de; **d. for,** declarar, testificar a favor de; **well, I d.!** ¡no me diga!
declaredly [-ədlɪ, B -'klɛər-] *adv.* explícitamente, manifiestamente.
declarer [-ər, B -ə] *s.* declarante; (bridge) declarante.
declass [di'klæs, B 'di'klɑs] *v.t.* degradar, rebajar de clase, perder rango.
declassify [-'klæsə,faɪ] *v.t.* suspender el carácter confidencial o secreto de (un dato o documento); desclasificar.
declension [dɪ'klɛnʃən] *s.* 1. declinación, declive, declividad. 2. declinación, decadencia, deterioro. 3. (gram.) declinación (de sustantivos, adjetivos, etc.); desinencia.
declinable [dɪ'klaɪnəbəl] *a.* declinable.
declination [,dɛklə'neɪʃən] *s.* 1. declinación, inclinación, descenso. 2. declinación, decadencia, deterioro. 3. rechazo (esp. cortés). 4. declinación de la aguja, declinación magnética. 5. (astr.) declinación.
declination compass, declinatorio, brújula de declinación.
declinatory [dɪ'klaɪnə,tɔrɪ, B -ətərɪ] *a.* que indica excusa o renuncia.
decline [dɪ'klaɪn] *v.i.* 1. declinar, desviarse. 2. declinar, inclinarse hacia abajo. 3. declinar (el sol, el día). 4. declinar, decaer, deteriorarse. 5. rehusar, excusarse. 6. **d. to (do),** negarse a hacer; **d. with thanks,** (gen. irón.) rechazar desdeñosamente. —*v.t.* 1. (gram.) declinar. 2. inclinar (hacia abajo), doblar. 3. rechazar (cortésmente), rehusar, no aceptar. —*s.* 1. declinación, descenso, decaimiento, decadencia. 2. disminución; baja (de precios). 3. declive, inclinación, pendiente. 4. caída (de la tarde), ocaso (del sol, de la vida, etc.). 5. (med.) tuberculosis pulmonar, consunción. 6. **to be on the d.,** estar en decadencia.
declining [-ɪŋ] *a.* declinante (fuerzas, poder, etc.); **one's d. years,** los últimos años de la vida de uno.
declinograph [-ə,græf] *s.* declinógrafo.
declinometer [,dɛklə'nɑmətər, B -'nɔmɪtə] *s.* declinómetro.
declivitous [dɪ'klɪvətəs] *a.* inclinado, algo escarpado.
declivity [-ətɪ] *s.* declive, declividad, pendiente, inclinación.
declutch [di'klʌtʃ, B 'di-] *v.t.* (mec.) desembragar.
decoct [dɪ'kɑkt, B -'kɔkt] *v.t.* reducir mediante decocción, condensar, hacer un cocimiento de.
decoction [-'kɑkʃən, B -'kɔk-] *s.* decocción, cocimiento; extracto (obtenido por cocción).
decode [di'koʊd] *v.t.* descifrar (mensaje en clave); (ling.) descodificar.
decoder [-ər, B -ə] *s.* 1. descifrador (persona). 2. máquina de descifrar. 3. (rad.) aparato detector estereofónico. 4. (comput.) descodificador.
decoding [ɪŋ] *s.* (comput.) descodificación.
decoherence [,dikoʊ'hɪrəns, B -'hɪər-] *s.* (elec.) descohesión.
decoherer [-ər, B -ə] *s.* (rad.) descohesor.
decohesion [-'hiʒən] *s.* (rad.) descohesión.
decollate [dɪ'kɑl,eɪt, B -'kɔl-] *v.t.* degollar, decapitar.
decollation [,di,kɑ'leɪʃən, B -,kɔ-] *s.* degollación, degüello, decapitación.
décolletage [deɪ,kɑlə'tɑʒ, B -'kɔltɑʒ] *s.* (cost.) 1. escote. 2. traje o vestido escotado.
décolleté [-'teɪ, B -'kɔlteɪ] *a.* (cost.) 1. escotado. 2. vestido con traje escotado.
decolor [di'kʌlər, B -ə] *v.t.* descolorar.
decolorant [-ərənt] *a.* descolorante, decolorante, blanqueador. —*s.* decolorante, substancia descolorante o blanqueadora.

decolorization [-ˌkʌlərəˈzeɪʃən, B -raɪ-] *s.* descoloramiento, decoloración.

decolorize [-ˈkʌləˌraɪz] *v.t.* descolorar, decolorar, blanquear.

decompensation [diˌkɑmpənˈseɪʃən, B -ˌkɔm-] *s.* (med.) descompensación (cardíaca), falta de compensación; ataque cardíaco.

decomposable [ˌdikəmˈpoʊzəbəl] *a.* descomponible, corruptible.

decompose [-ˈpoʊz] *v.t.* 1. descomponer, desintegrar. 2. pudrir, corromper. —*v.i.* descomponerse, corromperse.

decomposition [-ˌkɑmpəˈzɪʃən, B -ˌkɔm-] *s.* descomposición, corrupción, putrefacción.

decompound [ˌdiˈkɑmˌpaʊnd, B ˌdikəmˈpaʊnd] *a.* (bot.) bicompuesto. —*v.t.* descomponer, separar en constituyentes.

decompress [-kəmˈprɛs] *v.t.* descomprimir.

decompression [-ˈprɛʃən] *s.* descompresión.

decompression chamber, cámara de descompresión.

decompression sickness, aeroembolismo.

decontaminate [ˌdikənˈtæməˌneɪt] *v.t.* desinfectar, descontagiar (esp. de gases venenosos, radiación atómica, etc.).

decontamination [-ˌtæməˈneɪʃən] *s.* desinfección, descontaminación.

decontrol [ˌdikənˈtroʊl] *v.t.* liberar de controles (economía, venta de artículos, etc.). —*s.* supresión de controles.

décor, decor [deɪˈkɔr, B ˈdeɪkɔ] *s.* 1. decoración (esp. interior). 2. (teat.) decoración (escénica), decorado, escenografía.

decorate [ˈdɛkəˌreɪt] *v.t.* 1. decorar, adornar, ataviar. 2. condecorar.

decoration [ˌdɛkəˈreɪʃən] *s.* 1. decoración, ornamentación. 2. decoración, adorno, ornamento. 3. condecoración, insignia, medalla. 4. **D. Day,** (E.U.) 30 de mayo en que se decoran las tumbas de los soldados.

decorative [ˈdɛkərətɪv, -ˌreɪt-, B -rət-] *a.* decorativo, ornamental.

decoratively [-lɪ] *adv.* en forma decorativa.

decorator [-ˌreɪtər, B -ə] *s.* decorador.

decorous [ˈdɛkərəs, dɪˈkɔrəs] *a.* decoroso, decente, propio, apropiado, correcto.

decorously [-lɪ] *adv.* decorosamente, correctamente, apropiadamente.

decorousness [-nəs] *s.* decoro, recato, corrección.

decorticate [diˈkɔrtəˌkeɪt, B -ˈkɔt-] *v.t.* descortezar, descascarar, pelar, mondar.

decortication [-ˌkɔrtəˈkeɪʃən, B -ˌkɔt-] *s.* descortezamiento.

decorticator [-ˈkɔrtəˌkeɪtər, B -ˈkɔt-ə] *s.* descortezador.

decorum [dɪˈkɔrəm] *s.* decoro, decencia, recato, corrección.

decoupling [diˈkʌplɪŋ] *s.* (rad.) desacoplamiento, desacoplo.

decoy [dɪˈkɔɪ, ˈdiˌkɔɪ] *s.* 1. señuelo, cimbel, reclamo, añagaza. 2. (fig.) señuelo, añagaza. — [B dɪˈkɔɪ] *v.t.* 1. reclamar (a las aves). 2. (fig.) atraer con señuelo o añagaza.

decrease [dɪˈkris, ˈdikris] *v.t., v.i.* disminuir(se), reducir(se), aminorar(se). —*s.* 1. disminución, decrecimiento. 2. mengua, merma.

decreasingly [-ɪŋlɪ] *adv.* en escala decreciente.

decree [dɪˈkri] *s.* decreto, edicto, mandato. —*v.t., v.i.* decretar, mandar.

decrement [ˈdɛkrəmənt] *s.* decremento, disminución, diminución, decrecimiento, merma; (mat., fís.) decremento.

decrepit [dɪˈkrɛpət] *a.* decrépito, caduco, senil.

decrepitate [-əˌteɪt] *v.i.* crepitar, decrepitar. —*v.t.* asar o calcinar (una sal) produciendo decrepitación.

decrepitation [-ˌkrɛpəˈteɪʃən] *s.* decrepitación.

decrepitly [-ˈkrɛpətlɪ] *adv.* decrépitamente.

decrepitude [-ˌtud, B -ˌtjud] *s.* decrepitud, senectud.

decrescendo [ˌdikrəˈʃɛndoʊ, ˌdeɪ-, B ˈdi-] *a., s.* (mús.) decrescendo.

decrescent [dɪˈkrɛsənt] *a.* decreciente, menguante.

decretal [dɪˈkritəl] *a.* decretal. —*s.* 1. decretal, decreto (papal). 2. (*pl.*) (relig.) decretales.

decretist [-əst] *s.* decretista, decretalista.

decretive [-ɪv] *a.* imperativo, autoritario, perentorio, decretal.

decretory [ˈdɛkrəˌtɔrɪ, B dɪˈkritərɪ] *a.* 1. propio de un decreto; imperativo. 2. decretorio, decisivo, crítico.

decrial [dɪˈkraɪəl] *s.* desaprobación, reprobación, censura, vituperio.

decry [dɪˈkraɪ] *v.t.* (*pret., p.p.* DECRIED; *p.pr.* DECRYING) 1. desaprobar, despreciar, censurar, condenar. 2. menospreciar, quitar importancia a. 3. depreciar, desvalorar, desvalorizar (moneda).

decubitus [dəˈkjubətəs] *s.* (med.) decúbito.

decumbency [dɪˈkʌmbənsɪ] *s.* decúbito, postura decumbente.

decumbent [-bənt] *a.* 1. decumbente, recostado, reclinado. 2. (bot.) (brote o tallo) decumbente.

decuple [ˈdɛkjəpəl] *a., s.* décuplo. —*v.t.* decuplicar, decuplar.

decurion [dɪˈkjʊrɪən] *s.* (hist. romana) decurión, oficial a cargo de diez hombres.

decurrent [diˈkɜrənt, B -ˈkʌr-] *a* (bot.) decurrente.

decurved [diˈkɜrvd, B -ˈkɜvd] *a.* (bot.) decurvado.

decury [ˈdɛkjʊrɪ] *s.* (hist.) decuria, escuadra de diez soldados en la antigua Roma.

decussate [ˈdɛkəˌseɪt, diˈkʌsˌeɪt] *v.t., v.i.* cruzar(se), entrecruzar(se). —*a.* 1. entrecruzado; decusata (cruz). 2. (bot.) decusado, decuso.

decussation [ˌdɛkəˈseɪʃən, ˌdi-, B ˌdɛ-] *s.* 1. cruzamiento. 2. (anat.) decusación, entrecruzamiento.

dedicate [ˈdɛdɪkət, B -ˌkeɪt] *a.* consagrado, dedicado. — [-ˌkeɪt] *v.t.* 1. dedicar, consagrar (gloria, etc.). 2. dedicar, aplicar, destinar (a un uso o empleo determinado). 3. dedicar (libro u obra de arte).

dedication [ˌdɛdɪˈkeɪʃən] *s.* 1. dedicación, consagración. 2. dedicatoria. 3. dedicación, aplicación, esmero. 4. dedicación, destinación.

dedicative [ˈdɛdɪˌkeɪtɪv, -kət-] *a.* dedicativo, dedicatorio.

dedicator [-ˌkeɪtər, B -ə] *s.* consagrante, dedicante.

dedicatory [-kəˌtɔrɪ, B -kətərɪ] *a.* dedicatorio.

deduce [dɪˈdus, B -ˈdjus] *v.t.* deducir, inferir, concluir, derivar.

deducible [-əbəl] *a.* deducible.

deduct [dɪˈdʌkt] *v.t.* deducir, restar, substraer, rebajar, descontar.

deductible [-əbəl] *a.* deducible, descontable.

deduction [-ˈdʌkʃən] *s.* 1. deducción, substracción, rebaja, descuento. 2. deducción, conclusión, inferencia.

deductive [-ˈdʌktɪv] *a.* deductivo.

deductively [-lɪ] *adv.* deductivamente, por inferencia, por deducción.

dee [di] *s.* (fís.) electrodo (hueco) en forma de D (en un ciclotrón).

deed [did] *s.* 1. acto, hecho, acción. 2. hazaña, proeza. 3. ejecución, realización, obra. 4. (der.) escritura; título de propiedad. 5. **good d.,** buena obra; **in d.,** de hecho; en verdad; de veras; **in word and d.,** de palabra y obra. —*v.t.* traspasar por escritura.

deem [dim] *v.t., v.i.* juzgar, opinar, considerar, creer, pensar.

deep [dip] *s.* 1. profundidad, abismo, sima. 2. lo (más) profundo. 3. (*gen. pl.*) partes más profundas (del mar). 4. (mar.) división de la sondaleza (entre los nudos). 5. **the d.,** (poét.) el piélago, el mar. —*a.* 1. profundo, hondo. 2. de hondo; de profundidad, ej., *water ten feet d.,* agua de diez pies de profundidad. 3. astuto, sagaz. 4. subido, intenso, obscuro (díc. de un color). 5. grave, profundo (sonido, voz). 6. **d. in debt,** lleno de deudas; **in d. mourning,** de luto riguroso; **knee-d.,** (que llega) hasta las rodillas; **to be d. in (thought, a book, a pursuit,** etc.), estar absorto en, estar totalmente embebido en (pensamientos, un libro, una ocupación, etc.); **to get in d. water,** meterse en honduras, verse mezclado en dificultades; **to go off the d. end,** (fig.) actuar precipitadamente, obrar temerariamente, correr riesgos; (G.B.) salir (uno) de sus casillas, ponerse furioso. —*adv.* 1. profundamente. 2. hasta tarde, hasta bien avanzado, ej., *d. in the night,* hasta tarde (o bien avanzada) la noche. 3. **d. down,** en el fondo; **to drink d.,** apurar el trago hasta las heces; **still waters run d.,** del agua mansa líbreme Dios.

deep-chested [ˈdipˈtʃɛstəd] *a.* de pecho corpulento; voz grave.

deep-dyed [-ˈdaɪd] *a.* total, consumado, absoluto.

deepen [ˈdipən] *v.t., v.i.* profundizar(se), ahondar(se); intensificar(se); hacerse más intenso.

deepening [-ənɪŋ] *s.* (meteor.) caída de presión.

deep etch, (impr.) regrabado.

deepfreeze [-ˈfriz] *s.* 1. congelación (rápida). 2. congelador. 3. **in d.,** (fig., fam.) paralizado (proyecto, plan, etc.). —*v.t.* congelar, helar.

deep freezer, congelador, heladora.

deepfry [-ˈfraɪ] *v.t.* freír en aceite abundante.

deep-laid [-ˈleɪd] *a.* astutamente elaborado (plan, etc.); hecho con sagacidad.

deeply [ˈdiplɪ] *adv.* 1. profundamente, hondamente, a fondo. 2. sumamente, en sumo grado, intensamente, muy. 3. gravemente, seriamente (comprometido, afectado, etc.).

deep mourning, luto riguroso.

deepness [-nəs] *s.* profundidad, hondura; intensidad.

deep page, (impr.) página vertical.

deep-rooted [-ˈrutəd] *a.* profundamente arraigado; inveterado.

deep-sea [-ˈsi] *a.* 1. de aguas profundas (peces, corriente, etc.). 2. de alta mar (pesca, pescador, remolcador, etc.).

deep-sea fishing, pesca de alta mar, pesca de altura.

deep-seated [-ˈsitəd] *a.* 1. de origen profundo (terremoto, etc.); de origen interno (enfermedad, etc.). 2. profundamente arraigado.

deep-set [-ˈsɛt] *a.* hundido (ojos); colocado profundamente, fijo, sólidamente establecido.

deep space, intergaláctico, interplanetario.

deep structure, (ling.) estructura profunda.

deepwater [-ˈwɔtər, -ˈwɑt-, B -ˈwɔtə] *a.* 1. profundo, de aguas profundas (canal, pozo, etc.). 2. de alta mar (pesca, navegación, etc.). —*s.* dificultad, apuro, ej., *to get into deepwater,* meterse en camisa de once varas.

deep waterline, (mar.) línea de carga máxima.

deer [dɪr, B dɪə] *s.* (*pl.* DEER) (zool.) ciervo, venado.

deerfly [ˈdɪrˌflaɪ, B ˈdɪəˌ-] *s.* (ento.) variedad de tábano.

deerhound [-ˌhaʊnd] *s.* galgo para cazar venados.

deer lick, charco impregnado de sal (que los venados suelen lamer), salegar.

deerskin [-ˌskɪn] *s.* gamuza, cuero de venado; prenda de vestir de cuero de venado.

deerstalker [-ˌstɔkər, B -ə] *s.* 1. cazador al acecho. 2. gorra de cazador (con visera delante y detrás).

deerstalking [-ɪŋ] *s.* caza de venado al acecho.

deeryard [-ˌjɑrd, B -ˌjɑd] *s.* invernadero de ciervos.

de-escalate ['di'ɛskəleɪt] *v.t.* desescalar, desacelerar.

de-escalation ['di'ɛskə'leɪʃən] *s.* desescalada.

deface [dɪ'feɪs] *v.t.* 1. desfigurar, deformar; mutilar, estropear. 2. desacreditar. 3. hacer borroso o ilegible, borrar (escritura, etc.).

defacement [-mənt] *s.* desfiguración, deformación, deterioro; estropeo, mutilación.

de facto [dɪ'fæktoʊ, di-] *adv., a.* defacto, de hecho.

defalcate [dɪ'fælˌkeɪt, -'fɔl-, B 'difæl-] *v.i.* desfalcar, malversar.

defalcation [ˌdiˌfæl'keɪʃən, -ˌfɔl-] *s.* desfalco, malversación.

defalcator [dɪ'fælˌkeɪtər, -'fɔl-, B 'difæl-ə] *s.* desfalcador.

defamation [ˌdɛfə'meɪʃən] *s.* difamación, calumnia.

defamatory [dɪ'fæməˌtɔrɪ, B -ətərɪ] *a.* difamatorio, infamatorio, calumnioso.

defame [dɪ'feɪm] *v.t.* difamar, denigrar, calumniar.

defamed [-'feɪmd] *a.* difamado, calumniado.

defamer [-'feɪmər, B -ə] *s.* difamador, calumniador.

default [dɪ'fɔlt] *s.* 1. omisión, descuido; incumplimiento (ej., de pago). 2. falta, ausencia. 3. (der.) rebeldía, contumacia, ej., *judgement by d.*, juicio en rebeldía. 4. (dep.) falta de no presentarse, abandono (de una contienda). 5. (ant.) falta, ofensa; error, equivocación. 6. **by d.,** (der.) en rebeldía, en contumacia; (dep.) por abandono, por no presentarse; **in d. of,** por falta de, por faltar a; **in d. whereof,** (der.) en cuyo defecto. —*v.i.* 1. faltar, dejar de cumplir (díc. con referencia a un contrato, acuerdo u obligación, esp. de pago). 2. (der.) caer en rebeldía o contumacia. 3. (dep.) dejar de presentarse (para una contienda); abandonar la contienda; perder por incumplimiento o abandono. —*v.t.* 1. (der.) declarar (a alguien) en rebeldía. 2. perder (una contienda) por abandono o por no presentarse. 3. dejar de pagar (ej., un préstamo).

defaulter [-ər, B -ə] *s.* 1. (der.) rebelde, contumaz. 2. malversador, desfalcador. 3. (com.) deudor, delincuente. 4. (G.B.) soldado culpable de una ofensa militar.

defeasance [dɪ'fizəns] *s.* (der.) revocación, anulación, abrogación.

defeasance clause, (der.) cláusula resolutoria.

defeasibility [dɪˌfizə'bɪlətɪ] *s.* revocabilidad.

defeasible [-'fizəbəl] *a.* anulable, revocable.

defeat [dɪ'fit] *v.t.* 1. derrotar, vencer. 2. frustrar, privar de esperanza. 3. (der.) anular. 4. (ant.) deshacer, destruir. —*s.* 1. derrota. 2. frustración. 3. (der.) anulación. 4. (ant.) destrucción.

defeatism [-ˌɪzəm] *s.* derrotismo.

defeatist [-əst] *s., a.* derrotista; (el) que se declara vencido o impotente, o desea la derrota (de la patria, causa, etc.).

defecate ['dɛfɪˌkeɪt] *v.t.* 1. defecar, depurar, purificar. 2. defecar, expeler (los excrementos). —*v.i.* defecar, evacuar el vientre.

defecation [ˌdɛfɪ'keɪʃən] *s.* 1. defecación, depuración, purificación. 2. defecación, evacuación (de excrementos).

defecator ['dɛfɪˌkeɪtər, B -ə] *s.* defecadora (de azúcar).

defect ['diˌfɛkt, dɪ'fɛkt] *s.* defecto, desperfecto, falla, tacha. — [dɪ'fɛkt] *v.i.* desertar, abandonar.

defection [dɪ'fɛkʃən] *s.* defección, deserción, abandono, apostasía.

defective [dɪ'fɛktɪv] *a.* defectivo, defectuoso, imperfecto; (gram.) defectivo (verbo). —*s.* 1. (psic.) persona anormal generalmente de poca capacidad intelectual. 2. (gram.) verbo defectivo.

defectively [-lɪ] *adv.* defectuosamente, deficientemente.

defectiveness [-nəs] *s.* imperfección, estado defectuoso, deficiencia.

defence, (G.B.) *var. de* **defense.**

defend [dɪ'fɛnd] *v.t.* 1. defender, proteger, amparar. 2. defender, sostener (una tesis, teoría, etc.). 3. (der.) defender (a un acusado). 4. **d. oneself,** defenderse; asumir su propia defensa. —*v.i.* hacer una defensa.

defendant [-ənt] *s.* (der.) acusado (en causa criminal); demandado (en causa civil).

defender [-ər, B -ə] *s.* defensor, protector; campeón; (der.) defensor.

defending champion [-ɪŋ-] (dep.) campeón titular (actual o de ese momento).

defenestration [diˌfɛnə'streɪʃən] *s.* defenestración.

defense, (pr. G.B.) **defence** [dɪ'fɛns] *s.* 1. defensa, protección, amparo. 2. defensa, sustentación (de una tesis, teoría, etc.). 3. (der.) defensa. 4. (ajedrez, bridge, dep.) defensa.

defenseless [-ləs] *a.* indefenso, sin defensa, desamparado.

defenselessly [-lɪ] *adv.* indefensamente.

defenselessness [-nəs] *s.* estado indefenso, vulnerabilidad.

defense mechanism, 1. (biol.) mecanismo de defensa (orgánica, propia, etc.). 2. (psic.) mecanismo de defensa (ej., rechazo).

defense post, (mil.) puesto defensivo.

defensibility [dɪˌfɛnsə'bɪlətɪ] *s.* posibilidad de defensa.

defensible [-'fɛnsəbəl] *a.* defendible.

defensive [dɪ'fɛnsɪv] *a.* defensivo, de defensa. —*s.* defensiva, posición defensiva; **to be** (o **stand) on the d.,** estar a la defensiva.

defensive fire, (mil.) tiro de defensa, fuego defensivo.

defensively [-lɪ] *adv.* a la defensiva.

defer [dɪ'fɜr, B -'fɜ] *v.t.* (*pret., p.p.* DEFERRED; *p.pr.* DEFERRING) diferir, dilatar, retrasar, posponer, postergar. —*v.i.* tardarse, demorarse (Am.).

defer, *v.t.* delegar (función, asunto); someter (opinión, fallo, etc.) a consideración. —*v.i.* (con *to*) deferir (a).

deference ['dɛfərəns] *s.* deferencia, acatamiento, consideración, condescendencia; **in d. to,** por deferencia o consideración a.

deferent [-ənt] *a.* (raro) deferente, respetuoso, cortés.

deferent, *a.* (anat.) deferente (conducto, arteria, canal).

deferential [ˌdɛfə'rɛntʃəl, B -'rɛnʃəl] *a.* deferente, respetuoso, cortés.

deferentially [-ɪ] *adv.* respetuosamente, con deferencia, deferentemente.

deferment [dɪ'fɜrmənt, B -'fɜmənt] *s.* postergación, aplazamiento (en E.U. esp. del servicio militar).

deferrable [-'fɜrəbəl] *a.* postergable, aplazable. —*s.* (E.U.) persona con opción a aplazamiento (del servicio militar).

deferred [dɪ'fɜrd, B -'fɜd] *a.* 1. aplazado, diferido. 2. (ten., com.) diferido (activo, pasivo).

deferred payment, pago aplazado, pago a plazos.

deferred stock, (fin.) acciones diferidas, acciones de dividendo diferido.

deferrer [dɪ'fɜrər, B -ə] *s.* tardador, hombre moroso.

defervescence [ˌdifər'vɛsəns, B -fə'vɛs-] *s.* (med.) defervescencia, declinación de una fiebre.

defiance [dɪ'faɪəns] *s.* 1. desafío, reto, provocación. 2. obstinación, resistencia porfiada. 3. **in d. of,** a despecho de; **to bid d. to,** desafiar, despreciar.

defiant [-ənt] *a.* desafiador, desafiante, provocador, insolente.

defiantly [-lɪ] *adv.* insolentemente.

deficiency [dɪ'fɪʃənsɪ] *s.* (*pl.* DEFICIENCIES) deficiencia, imperfección, insuficiencia, falta; (fin.) déficit.

deficiency disease, (med.) enfermedad por carencia.

deficiency judgment, (der.) fallo de deficiencia.

deficient [dɪ'fɪʃənt] *a.* 1. (con *in*) deficiente, incompleto, falto (de). 2. insuficiente. 3. imbécil, de mentalidad deficiente. —*s.* persona de mentalidad deficiente.

deficiently [-lɪ] *adv.* deficientemente, insuficientemente.

deficit ['dɛfəsət] *s.* (fin., ten., com.) déficit, descubierto.

deficit spending, (fin.) gasto deficitario; dícese de la política que consiste en usar (gastar) fondos obtenidos en préstamo.

defier [dɪ'faɪər, B -ə] *s.* desafiador, retador.

defilade ['dɛfəˌleɪd, B ˌdɛfɪ'leɪd] *v.t., v.i.* (fort.) desenfilar. —*s.* (mil.) desenfilada.

defile [dɪ'faɪl] *v.t.* 1. manchar, ensuciar. 2. contaminar, corromper. 3. profanar. 4. deshonrar, mancillar (reputación, etc.). 5. violar (mujer).

defile [dɪ'faɪl, diˌfaɪl, B dɪ'faɪl] *v.i.* (mil.) desfilar, marchar o ir en filas.

defile [dɪ'faɪl, 'diˌfaɪl] *s.* desfiladero, garganta de montaña.

defilement [dɪ'faɪlmənt] *s.* 1. contaminación, profanación; corrupción. 2. violación (de una mujer).

defiler [-ər, B -ə] *s.* contaminador, profanador; corruptor.

definable [dɪ'faɪnəbəl] *a.* definible.

define [dɪ'faɪn] *v.t.* 1. definir, circunscribir. 2. definir, explicar, interpretar. 3. definir, determinar.

definer [-ər, B -ə] *s.* definidor.

defining clause [-ɪŋ-] (gram.) oración relativa determinativa.

definite ['dɛfənət] *a.* 1. definido, determinado. 2. claro, exacto, preciso. 3. (gram.) definido, determinado (artículo).

definite article, (gram.) artículo definido o determinado.

definite integral, (mat.) integral definida.

definitely [-lɪ] *adv.* claramente, precisamente, exactamente; indudablemente, positivamente.

definiteness [-nəs] *s.* 1. carácter definido o determinado. 2. exactitud, precisión.

definition [ˌdɛfə'nɪʃən] *s.* 1. definición. 2. nitidez, claridad (de dibujo, del sonido, etc.).

definitive [dɪ'fɪnətɪv] *a.* 1. definitivo, decisivo, perentorio, terminante, concluyente, final. 2. definidor. —*s.* lo que define.

definitive host, *s.* (biol.) huésped definitivo, huésped primario.

definitively [-lɪ] *adv.* definitivamente, en definitiva, decisivamente.
definitiveness [-nəs] *s.* carácter definitivo (de una respuesta, sentencia, etc.).
definitude [dɪ'fɪnəˌtud, B -ˌtjud] *s.* precisión, exactitud.
deflagrate ['dɛfləˌgreɪt] (quím.) *v.i.* deflagrar. —*v.t.* hacer deflagrar.
deflagration [ˌdɛflə'greɪʃən] *s.* deflagración.
deflagrator ['dɛfləˌgreɪtər, B -ə] *s.* deflagrador.
deflate [dɪ'fleɪt] *v.t.* 1. desinflar, deshinchar. 2. (fig.) rebajar (la vanidad, el orgullo, etc.); reducir (las esperanzas), bajarle (a uno) los humos. 3. (fin.) desinflar (precios, volumen de crédito). —*v.i.* desinflarse.
deflation [-'fleɪʃən] *s.* 1. deshinchadura. 2. (fin.) deflación. 3. (geol.) deflación.
deflationary [-ˌɛrɪ, B -ərɪ] *a.* (fin.) deflatorio, deflacionario (tendencia, política, etc.).
deflator [-'fleɪtər, B -ə] *s.* (fin.) índice de deflación.
deflect [dɪ'flɛkt] *v.t., v.i.* desviar (se), apartar(se).
deflection, (pr. G.B.) **deflexion** [-'flɛkʃən] *s.* 1. desviación, desvío, torcimiento. 2. (fís.) desviación (de la aguja en un instrumento), deflección; (arq.) flecha; (naveg.) desviación.
deflection angle, ángulo de desviación.
deflection correction, (nav.) corrección de desviación.
deflective [-'flɛktɪv] *a.* desviador, que desvía, deflector.
deflector [-tər, B -tə] *s.* 1. deflector, desviador, placa de guía (ej., en un horno). 2. (hidr.) muro de salto.
deflexed [-'flɛkst] *a.* (bot.) deflexo (tallo, rama).
defloration [ˌdɛflə'reɪʃən, B ˌdiflɔ-] *s.* desfloración, desfloramiento, desvirgamiento.
deflower [di'flaʊər, B -e] *v.t.* 1. desflorar, desvirgar. 2. desflorar, ajar.
defluxion [dɪ'flʌkʃən] *s.* (med.) deflujo, defluxión, destilación, reuma.
defoliant [di'foʊlɪənt] *s.* líquido que causa defoliación, defoliante.
defoliate [-ˌeɪt] *v.t.* deshojar. —*a.* deshojado.
defoliation [diˌfoʊlɪ'eɪʃən] *s.* defoliación.
deforce [di'fɔrs, B -'fɔs] *v.t.* (der.) usurpar, detentar (tierras); desahuciar forzosamente.
deforcement [-mənt] *s.* (der.) usurpación, detentación.
deforciant [di'fɔrʃənt, B -'fɔʃənt] *s.* (der.) detentador, despojante.
deforest [di'fɔrəst, -'fɑr-, B -'fɔr-] *v.t.* desmontar, desforestar, talar, despoblar.
deforestation [-ˌfɔrəs'teɪʃən, -ˌfɑr-, B -ˌfɔr-] *s.* desmonte, desforestación, tala.
deform [dɪ'fɔrm, B -'fɔm] *v.t.* deformar, desfigurar. —*v.i.* deformarse, desfigurarse.
deformation [ˌdifɔr'meɪʃən, B -fɔ'-] *s.* deformación, desfiguración.
deformed [dɪ'fɔrmd, B -'fɔmd] *a.* deforme, deformado, disforme, desfigurado.
deformedness [-'fɔrmədnəs, B -'fɔməd-] *s.* aspecto deforme, deformidad.
deformity [-mətɪ] *s.* 1. deformidad, disformidad. 2. deformidad, cosa fea. 3. defecto (moral o estético).
defraud [dɪ'frɔd] *v.t.* defraudar, estafar, engañar.
defraudation [ˌdiˌfrɔ'deɪʃən] *s.* defraudación.
defrauder [dɪ'frɔdər, B -ə] *s.* defraudador, estafador, timador.
defray [dɪ'freɪ] *v.t.* sufragar, costear (gasto), subvenir.
defrayal [-əl] *s.* pago o subvención (de gastos).
defrock [di'frɑk, B -'frɔk] *v.t.* (relig.) expulsar, deponer, degradar (a un cura, monja, etc.).
defrost [dɪ'frɔst] *v.t.* deshelar, descongelar.
defroster [-ər, B -ə] *s.* descongelador, deshelador.
defrosting [-ɪŋ] *s.* descongelación (esp. de refrigeradores).
deft [dɛft] *a.* diestro, hábil, experto, ducho.
deftly ['dɛftlɪ] *adv.* diestramente, hábilmente.
deftness [-nəs] *s.* destreza, habilidad, maña.
defunct [dɪ'fʌŋkt] *a.* difunto, muerto. —*s.* (raro) difunto.
defy [dɪ'faɪ] *v.t.* (*pret., p.p.* DEFIED; *p.pr.* DEFYING) 1. desafiar, retar, provocar. 2. contravenir, resistir. 3. atreverse con, no admitir. —*s.* (fam.) reto, desafío.
deg. *abrev. de* **degree,** grado.
degas [di'gæs] *v.t.* degasificar, limpiar de gases (un lugar).
degauss [di'gaʊs] *v.t.* hacer antimagnético, desimantar; neutralizar el campo magnético de (un barco); (mar.) desgausar.
degeneracy [dɪ'dʒɛnərəsɪ] *s.* degeneración, degradación, depravación; (biol.) degeneración.
degenerate [-rət] *a.* degenerado, degradado, depravado; (biol.) degenerado. —*s.* degenerado. — [-ˌreɪt] *v.i.* degenerar, degradarse; (biol.) degenerar.
degenerateness [-nəs] *s.* carácter degenerado, condición degenerada.
degeneration [dɪˌdʒɛnə'reɪʃən] *s.* degeneración, deterioración; (biol.) degeneración, reacción negativa.
degenerative [-'dʒɛnəˌreɪtɪv, -ərətɪv] *a.* degenerativo.
deglutinate [dɪ'glutənˌeɪt] *v.t.* extraer el gluten de (trigo, etc.).
deglutition [ˌdiglu'tɪʃən] *s.* deglución.
degradation [ˌdɛgrə'deɪʃən] *s.* 1. degradación, deposición (de grado o condición). 2. degradación, degeneración, deterioración. 3. (fís., geol.) degradación.
degrade [dɪ'greɪd] *v.t.* 1. degradar, deponer. 2. degradar, envilecer, corromper. 3. rebajar, mermar (la calidad). 4. (geol.) degradar, desgastar (por erosión). 5. (biol.) hacer degenerar. 6. (quím.) reducir, descomponer.
degraded [-əd] *a.* degenerado, depravado, degradado, rebajado.
degrading [-ɪŋ] *a.* degradante.
degree [dɪ'gri] *s.* 1. grado (de frío o calor, de fiebre, de parentesco, de culpabilidad, en todas sus acepciones). 2. grado, paso. 3. grado, rango, categoría. 4. grado, rango académico. 5. (fís., mat., geom., mús., gram.) grado. 6. (ant.) grada, peldaño. 7. **by degrees,** paso a paso, poco a poco, gradualmente; **to a d.,** hasta cierto punto, algo; (fam.) en sumo grado, muchísimo; **to a high d.,** en alto grado; **to take a d.,** optar o recibir un grado o título (académico).
degree of bank, (avia.) ángulo de viraje.
degree of freedom, (quím.) grado de libertad, número de grados de libertad de un sistema.
degree of latitude, (nav.) grado de latitud.
degression [dɪ'grɛʃən] *s.* decrecimiento; descenso; disminución gradual (en los impuestos).
degum [di'gʌm] *v.t.* desgomar, desengomar (tejidos, esp. seda).
degust [dɪ'gʌst] *v.t.* gustar, catar (alimentos, licores).
degustation [ˌdigə'steɪʃən] *s.* degustación, gustación.
dehisce [dɪ'hɪs] *v.i.* (bot.) hendirse, abrirse (fruta).
dehiscence [-əns] *s.* (bot., biol.) dehiscencia.
dehiscent [-ent] *a.* (bot., biol.) dehiscente.
dehorn [di'hɔrn, B -'hɔn] *v.t.* descornar (a un animal).
dehumanization [diˌhjumənə'zeɪʃən, B -mənaɪ-] *s.* deshumanización, embrutecimiento.
dehumanize [-'hjuməˌnaɪz] *v.t.* deshumanizar, embrutecer.
dehumidify [ˌdihju'mɪdəˌfaɪ] *v.t.* deshumedecer, desecar.
dehydrate [di'haɪˌdreɪt] *v.t.* 1. deshidratar. 2. (fig.) marchitar, desecar.
dehydration [ˌdiˌhaɪ'dreɪʃən] *s.* deshidratación, desecación.
dehydrogenase [-'drɑdʒəˌneɪs, B di'haɪdrədʒə-] *s.* (biol.) deshidrogenasa.
dehydrogenate [-ˌneɪt] *v.t.* (quím.) deshidrogenar.
dehydrogenation [-ˌdrɑdʒə'neɪʃən, B diˌhaɪdrədʒə-] *s.* deshidrogenación.
dehypnotize [di'hɪpnəˌtaɪz, B 'di-] *v.t.* deshipnotizar.
deice [di'aɪs] *v.t.* (aer.) deshelar, descongelar.
de-icer [-ər B -ə] *s.* descongelador; (avia.) dispositivo antihielo.
deicidal [ˌdiə'saɪdəl] *a.* deicida.
deicide ['diəˌsaɪd] *s.* 1. deicida. 2. deicidio.
deictic ['daɪktɪk] *a.* (lóg.) demostrativo, que señala directamente.
deific [di'ɪfɪk] *a.* deífico, divino, apoteósico.
deification [ˌdiəfə'keɪʃən] *s.* deificación, divinización; apoteosis.
deiform ['diəˌfɔrm, B -ˌfɔm] *a.* deiforme, divino.
deify ['diəˌfaɪ] *v.t.* (*pret., p.p.* DEIFIED; *p.pr.* DEIFYING) deificar, divinizar, endiosar.
deign [deɪn] *v.t.* permitir, conceder, dignarse dar. —*v.i.* dignarse, condescender.
deism ['diˌɪzəm] *s.* (filos.) deísmo.
deistic [di'ɪstɪk] **deistical** [-əl] *a.* (filos.) deísta.
deity ['diətɪ] *s.* (*pl.* DEITIES) 1. deidad, naturaleza o rango divino. 2. deidad, dios, diosa. 3. **the D.,** el Ser Supremo.
déjà vu [ˌdeɪʒɑ'vu] *s.* (fr.) ilusión de haber experimentado una situación que en realidad se presenta por primera vez.
deject [dɪ'dʒɛkt] *v.t.* abatir, desanimar, desalentar, afligir, descorazonar.
dejecta [dɪ'dʒɛktə] *s. pl.* (fisiol.) deyecciones, excrementos.
dejected [dɪ'dʒɛktəd] *a.* abatido, desalentado, acongojado, desanimado, deprimido.
dejectedly [-lɪ] *adv.* abatidamente, afligidamente.
dejectedness [-nəs] *s.* abatimiento, desaliento.
dejection [dɪ'dʒɛkʃən] *s.* 1. depresión, aflicción, abatimiento. 2. (fisiol.) deyección, evacuación (de excrementos); (*pl.*) deyecciones.
de jure [di'dʒʊrɪ, B -'dʒʊərɪ] (lat.) de ley, legítimamente, de derecho.
Del. *abrev. de* **Delaware,** Delaware (E.U.).
delaine [də'leɪn] *s.* (tej.) muselina de lana, muselina de lana con algodón.
delaminate [di'læməˌneɪt] *v.i.* (biol.) dividirse en láminas.
delamination [-ˌlæmə'neɪʃən] *s.* (biol.) delaminación.
delate [dɪ'leɪt] *v.t.* (pr. esco.) delatar, acusar, denunciar.
delation [-'leɪʃən] *s.* (pr. esco.) delación, denuncia, acusación.
delator [-'leɪtər, B -ə] *s.* (pr. esco.) delator, denunciador, denunciante.
Delaware ['dɛləˌwɛr, B -ˌwɛə] *s.* 1. Delaware, estado de los E.U. 2. (E.U.) delavar (indio de la tribu algonquina).
delay [dɪ'leɪ] *v.t.* 1. demorar, retardar, dilatar, atrasar; detener, retener. 2. aplazar, posponer, postergar. —*v.i.* demorarse, dilatarse, tardar. —*s.*

1. dilación, tardanza, demora, retraso; largona (Chile, Perú). 2. detención, retención.
delay-action [-'ækʃən] **delayed-action** [dɪ'leɪd-] *a.* de acción retardada (bomba, mina, trampa, etc.).
delayer [-'leɪər, B -ə] *s.* tardón, tardador.
delay fuse, (mil.) espoleta de retardo.
delaying [dɪ'leɪŋ] *a.* dilatorio.
dele ['dili] *v.t.* (impr.) suprimir; marcar con un dele. —*s.* dele, deleátur.
delectability [dɪˌlɛktə'bɪlətɪ] *s.* 1. sabor delicioso. 2. (*gen. en pl.*) cosa deleitable, delicia.
delectable [-'lɛktəbəl] *a.* deleitable, deleìtoso, delicioso.
delectableness [-nəs] *s.* sabor, calidad de delicioso.
delectably [-blɪ] *adv.* deleitosamente.
delectate [-ˌteɪt] *v.t.* deleitar, agradar, encantar.
delectation [ˌdiˌlɛk'teɪʃən] *s.* 1. deleite, delicia. 2. goce, fruición.
delegacy ['dɛlɪgəsɪ] *s.* delegación.
delegate ['dɛlɪgət, -ˌgeɪt] *s.* 1. delegado. 2. (E.U.) diputado, comisionado (de un territorio en la Cámara de Representantes). — [-ˌgeɪt] *v.t.* delegar, diputar, comisionar.
delegation [ˌdɛlɪ'geɪʃən] *s.* delegación, diputación.
delete [dɪ'lit] *v.t.* suprimir, borrar, tachar.
deleterious [ˌdɛlə'tɪrɪəs, B -'tɪər-] *a.* deletéreo, nocivo, dañoso, pernicioso.
deleteriously [-lɪ] *adv.* perniciosamente.
deletion [dɪ'liʃən] *s.* supresión, borradura, tacha.
delft [dɛlft] **delftware** ['dɛlftˌwɛr, B -ˌwɛə] *s.* 1. porcelana de Delft. 2. vajilla barnizada; loza fina.
deliberate [dɪ'lɪbərət] *a.* 1. deliberado, premeditado, pensado. 2. deliberado, intencional. 3. pausado, ponderativo. — [-ˌreɪt] *v.t.* deliberar, meditar, considerar. —*v.i.* deliberar.
deliberately [-lɪ] *adv.* 1. deliberadamente, con premeditación; intencionalmente. 2. pausadamente.
deliberateness [-nəs] *s.* 1. carácter intencional (ej., de un acto). 2. deliberación, ponderación.
deliberation [dɪˌlɪbə'reɪʃən] *s.* deliberación, reflexión, ponderación.
deliberative [-'lɪbəˌreɪtɪv, B -ərətɪv] *a.* deliberativo.
deliberator [-ˌreɪtər, B -ə] *s.* deliberante.
delible ['dɛləbəl] *a.* deleble.
delicacy ['dɛlɪkəsɪ] *s.* (*pl.* DELICACIES) 1. delicadeza, finura, exquisitez. 2. delicadeza, gentileza, tino, consideración, discreción; ternura, suavidad. 3. sensibilidad, precisión (de instrumentos). 4. delicadez, debilidad, fragilidad. 5. melindrería. 6. carácter delicado (de un tema, una situación, etc.). 7. golosina, bocado delicado. 8. (ant.) lujo, regalo.
delicate ['dɛlɪkət] *a.* 1. delicado, fino, exquisito. 2. delicado, gentil, atento; discreto; tierno, suave. 3. sensible, preciso (díc. de instrumentos). 4. delicado, débil, frágil. 6. melindroso. 7. delicado, difícil, precario (tema, situación, etc.). 8. (poét.) delicioso.
delicately [-lɪ] *adv.* delicadamente, sutilmente.
delicateness [-nəs] *s.* delicadeza.
delicatessen [ˌdɛlɪkə'tɛsən] *s.* delicatessen (tienda de comestibles preparados, fiambrería).
delicious [dɪ'lɪʃəs] *a.* delicioso, sabroso; exquisito, agradable, placentero, rico.
deliciously [-lɪ] *adv.* deliciosamente.
deliciousness [-nəs] *s.* sensación o sabor delicioso.
delict [dɪ'lɪkt] *s.* delito; **in flagrant d.,** en flagrante, in fraganti.
delight [dɪ'laɪt] *s.* deleite, delicia, encanto; **to find** (o **take**) **d. in,** encontrar deleite en. —*v.t.* deleitar, regalar, encantar. —*v.i.* deleitarse; **d. in,** deleitarse en o con.
delighted [-əd] *a.* encantado, satisfecho, contento; **to be d. to (know, accept an invitation,** etc.), tener mucho gusto en, estar encantado de (conocer, aceptar una invitación, etc.).
delightful [-fəl] *a.* delicioso, encantador, muy agradable.
delightfully [-fəlɪ] *adv.* deliciosamente.
delightfulness [-fəlnəs] *s.* encanto, naturaleza encantadora.
delightsome [-'laɪtsəm] *a.* encantador, placentero, ameno.
delightsomely [-lɪ] *adv.* amenamente.
delightsomeness [-nəs] *s.* amenidad.
Delilah [dɪ'laɪlə] *s.* (bíbl.) Dalila.
delimit [dɪ'lɪmət] *v.t.* 1. delimitar, deslindar, limitar. 2. trazar, marcar (frontera).
delimitate [-əˌteɪt] *v.t.* delimitar, deslindar.
delimitation [-ˌlɪmə'teɪʃən] *s.* delimitación, deslinde.
delimitative [-'lɪməˌteɪtɪv] *a.* deslindante, limitativo; deslindador, limitador.
delineate [dɪ'lɪnɪˌeɪt] *v.t.* 1. delinear, trazar, bosquejar, esbozar. 2. (fig.) retratar, pintar; describir, relatar.
delineation [-ˌlɪnɪ'eɪʃən] *s.* delineación, delineamiento, bosquejo, esbozo; descripción.
delineative [-'lɪnɪˌeɪtɪv] *a.* delineante.
delineator [-ər, B -ə] *s.* 1. delineador, diseñador (de planos, etc.). 2. luces de demarcación (esp. al borde de carreteras).
delinquency [dɪ'lɪŋkwənsɪ] *s.* 1. delincuencia, criminalidad. 2. (com., ten.) morosidad; deuda en mora.
delinquent [-kwənt] *a.* 1. delincuente, criminal. 2. (com., ten.) moroso (deudor). —*s.* delincuente, criminal.
delinquently [-lɪ] *adv.* criminalmente.
deliquesce [ˌdɛlɪ'kwɛs] *v.i.* 1. licuarse, liquidarse; derretirse. 2. (bot.) ramificarse (como las venas de una hoja).
deliquescence [-'kwɛsəns] *s.* (quím.) delicuescencia.
deliquescent [-ənt] *a.* delicuescente.
deliration [ˌdɛlə'reɪʃən] *s.* (raro) delirio; desvarío.
delirious [dɪ'lɪrɪəs] *a.* delirante, desvariado.
deliriously [-lɪ] *adv.* delirantemente, desvariadamente.
deliriousness [-nəs] *s.* estado o condición delirante.
delirium [dɪ'lɪrɪəm] *s.* delirio, desvarío, devaneo.
delirium tremens [-'trimənz] (med.) delírium tremens.
delitescence [ˌdɛlə'tɛsəns] *s.* (med.) delitescencia.
deliver [dɪ'lɪvər, B -ə] *v.t.* 1. (con *from*) librar, libertar; redimir, rescatar (de). 2. dar, depositar, entregar, confiar. 3. recitar, pronunciar (sermón, etc.), dictar (una conferencia); rendir (cuentas). 4. dar, asestar, descargar (un golpe). 5. despachar (un pedido); transmitir (energía); repartir, distribuir (el correo, etc.). 6. (fam.) procurar o lograr (votos). 7. (med.) partear. 8. **d. the goods,** (fam.) cumplir, hacer lo prometido; **d. oneself of,** aliviarse de (un secreto, opinión, etc.); **d. over** (o **up**), ceder, entregar; **to be delivered of (a child),** alumbrar, parir; dar a luz, dar nacimiento a.
deliverable [-ərəbəl] *a.* (com.) disponible.
deliverance [-ərəns] *s.* 1. rescate, liberación; redención, salvación. 2. dictamen, declaración. 3. (der.) veredicto, dictamen.
deliverer [-ərər, B -ə] *s.* 1. entregador, librador, libertador. 2. salvador, redentor. 3. depositador.
delivery [dɪ'lɪvərɪ] *s.* (*pl.* DELIVERIES) 1. liberación, rescate. 2. entrega, transferencia. 3. alumbramiento, parto. 4. ejecución, modo o forma de expresarse, estilo de hablar o de hacer. 5. recitación, lectura (de un discurso). 6. reparto, distribución. 7. (com.) expedición, remisión (de pedidos).
deliveryman [-mən] *s.* recadero, repartidor, mozo de reparto, entregador.
delivery room, sala de partos, sala de alumbramiento (en un hospital).
delivery truck, camión de reparto.
dell [dɛl] *s.* valle pequeño; cañada.
delocalize [di'loʊkəˌlaɪz] *v.t.* sacar o mudar de su lugar o localidad.
Delos ['diˌlɑs, B -ˌlɔs] *s.* Delos (isla griega del Egeo, patria de Apolo).
delouse [di'laʊs, B 'di-] *v.t.* espulgar, despiojar.
Delphian ['dɛlfɪən] **Delphic** [-fɪk] *a.* (hist., mitol.) délfico, de Delfos.
delphinine ['dɛlfəˌnin, B -ˌnaɪn] **delphinin** [-nɪn] *s.* (quím.) delfinina (alcaloide venenoso del delfinio).
delphinium [dɛl'fɪnɪəm] *s.* (bot.) delfinio, espuela de caballero.
Delphinus [-'faɪnəs] *s.* (astr.) Delfín.
delta ['dɛltə] *s.* 1. delta (cuarta letra del alfabeto griego). 2. delta (de un río). 3. (mat.) incremento finito de una variable.
delta connection, (elec.) conexión en triángulo.
delta current, (elec.) corriente en triángulo.
deltaic [dɛl'teɪɪk] *a.* deltaico.
delta ray, (fís.) rayo delta.
delta voltage, voltaje delta, voltaje polifásico.
delta-wing ['dɛltəˌwɪŋ] *a.* (aer.) de ala delta.
deltoid ['dɛlˌtɔɪd] *a.* deltoide. —*s.* (anat.) deltoides.
deltoideus [dɛl'tɔɪdɪəs] *s.* (*pl.* DELTOIDEI [-dɪˌaɪ]) (anat.) deltoides.
delude [dɪ'lud] *v.t.* 1. deludir, despistar, alucinar, engañar. 2. (ant.) frustrar, desilusionar, eludir, evadir.
deluder [-ər, B -ə] *s.* delusor, engañador.
deludingly [-ɪŋlɪ] *adv.* delusoriamente, engañosamente.
deluge ['dɛljudʒ] *s.* 1. diluvio, inundación. 2. chubasco, aguacero. 3. (fig.) diluvio, torrente (de palabras, injurias, etc.). 4. **the D.,** el Diluvio (universal). —*v.t.* 1. inundar, anegar. 2. (fig., con *with*) inundar de (cartas, visitantes, ejemplos, etc.).
delusion [dɪ'luʒən] *s.* 1. ilusión, concepto falso. 2. decepción, engaño. 3. (psic., med.) delirio (ej., de grandeza).
delusional [-əl] *a.* de alucinaciones, alucinatorio (estado, ideas, enfermedad, etc.).
delusive [dɪ'lusɪv] *a.* delusivo, engañoso, delusorio, falaz.
delusively [-lɪ] *adv.* delusoriamente.
delusiveness [-nəs] *s.* carácter o aspecto delusivo, falsedad.
delusory [dɪ'lusərɪ] *a.* delusorio, engañoso.
deluxe [dɪ'lʊks, -'lʌks] *a.* de lujo, lujoso, suntuoso. —*adv.* con todo lujo.
delve [dɛlv] *v.i.* 1. cavar. 2. (fig.) sondear, inquirir. 3. **d. into,** (fig.) cavar, ahondar en. —*v.t.* 1. (ant.) excavar. 2. explorar. —*s.* (raro) cavidad; depresión (en carretera, terreno).
Dem. *abrev. de* **Democrat** (miembro del partido demócrata de los E.U.).
demagnetization [diˌmægnətə'zeɪʃən, B -taɪ-] *s.* desimantación, desimanación.
demagnetize [di'mægnəˌtaɪz, B 'di-] *v.t.* desimantar, desimanar.

demagogic [ˌdɛmə'gɑdʒɪk, -'gɑg-, B -'gɔg-] **demagogical** [-ɪkəl] *a.* demagógico.
demagogically [-ɪkəlɪ] *adv.* demagógicamente.
demagogism ['dɛməˌgɑgˌɪzəm, B -ˌgɔg-] *s.* demagogia.
demagogue, demagog ['dɛməˌgɑg, B -ˌgɔg] *s.* demagogo.
demagoguery [-ərɪ] *s.* demagogia.
demagogy ['dɛməˌgɑdʒɪ, -ˌgoʊ-ʲ -ˌgɑgɪ, B -ˌgɔgɪ] *s.* demagogia.
demand [dɪ'mænd, B -'mɑnd] *v.t.* 1. exigir, demandar. 2. requerir, necesitar. 3. (der.) demandar, reclamar (un derecho, propiedad, etc.). —*s.* 1. demanda, exigencia. 2. (der.) demanda, reclamación. 3. (econ.) demanda. 4. **in d.,** con demanda o salida; popular; **in great d.,** de mucha demanda; **on d.,** a solicitud; (com.) a presentación; **to be in d.,** tener demanda.
demandable [-əbəl] *s.* exigible, demandable.
demandant [-ənt] *s.* (der.) demandante, demandador.
demand bill, d. draft, (fin.) giro o letra (pagadero) a la vista.
demand deposit, (com.) depósito disponible, depósito a la vista.
demander [-ər, B -ə] *s.* exactor, demandador.
demanding [-ɪŋ] *a.* exigente.
demand loan, préstamo pagadero a la demanda.
demantoid [dɪ'mænˌtɔɪd] *s.* (min.) andradita verde.
demarcate [dɪ'mɑrˌkeɪt, 'diˌmɑr-, B 'dimɑˌ-] *v.t.* 1. demarcar, deslindar. 2. distinguir, diferenciar.
demarcation [ˌdiˌmɑr'keɪʃən, B -ˌmɑ'-] *s.* demarcación, deslinde.
démarche [deɪ'mɑrʃ, B 'deɪmɑʃ] *s.* gestión, maniobra o representación diplomática.
demark [dɪ'mɑrk, B -'mɑk] *v.t.* demarcar, deslindar.
dematerialize [ˌdimə'tɪrɪəˌlaɪz, B -ˌtɪərɪə-] *v.t., v.i.* despojar(se) o ser despojado de cualidades materiales; perder la forma material, hacer(se) espiritual.
demean [dɪ'min] *v.t.* 1. rebajar, degradar; 2. (*gen. ú. refl.*) comportar(se), portar(se). 3. **d. oneself,** rebajarse, degradarse, deshonrarse.
demeanor, demeanour [dɪ'minər, B -ə] *s.* comportamiento, conducta, proceder; porte, semblante.
dement [dɪ'mɛnt] *v.t.* dementar, enloquecer.
demented [-əd] *a.* demente, desvariado, loco.
dementedly [-lɪ] *adv.* locamente, con demencia.
dementedness [-nəs] *s.* demencia.
dementia [dɪ'mɛntʃə, B -'mɛnʃɪə] *s.* (med.) demencia.
dementia praecox [-'priˌkɑks, B -ˌkɔks] (med.) demencia precoz.
demerit [di'mɛrət] *s.* 1. desmerecimiento, demérito, falta. 2. nota de reprobación. 3. (ant.) ofensa.
demesne [dɪ'meɪn, -'min] *s.* 1. (der.) posesión (de tierra); heredad. 2. tierra solariega. 3. dominio, reino. 4. región. 5. **land held in d.,** heredad.
Demeter [dɪ'mitər, B -ə] *s.* (mitol.) Deméter, diosa de la agricultura y fertilidad.
demibastion [ˌdɛmɪ'bæstʃən, B -tɪən] *s.* (fort.) medio bastión (compuesto de un frente y un flanco).
demigod ['dɛmɪˌgɑd, B -ˌgɔd] *s.* semidiós.
demigoddess [-əs] *s.* semidiosa.
demijohn [-ˌdʒɑn, B -ˌdʒɔn] *s.* damajuana, garrafón, castaña.
demilitarization [diˌmɪlətərə'zeɪʃən, B 'di-tərai-] *s.* desmilitarización.
demilitarize [di'mɪlətəˌraɪz, B ˌdi-] *v.t.* (mil.) desmilitarizar.
demilitarized zone [-ˌraɪzd-] *s.* (mil.) zona desmilitarizada.
demilune ['dɛmɪˌlun] *s.* (fort.) media luna.
demimondaine [ˌdɛmɪˌmɑn'deɪn, B -ˌmɔn-] *s.* cortesana elegante.
demimonde ['dɛmɪˌmɑnd, B -'mɔnd] *s.* mujeres de la vida airada; gente de reputación dudosa.
demineralization [diˌmɪnərələ'zeɪʃən, B -laɪ-] *s.* (med.) desmineralización.
demipique ['dɛmɪˌpik] *a.* (hist.) de perilla baja. —*s.* (hist.) silla (militar) de perilla baja.
demirelief [ˌdɛmɪrɪ'lif] *s.* (esco.) medio relieve.
demirep ['dɛmɪˌrɛp] *s.* (jer.) mujer de reputación dudosa, aventurera.
demise [dɪ'maɪz] *s.* 1. fallecimiento, defunción. 2. transmisión (de la corona). 3. (der.) traspaso (de una propiedad). —*v.t.* (der.) transferir por arriendo; transmitir por sucesión o herencia; legar, dejar en testamento. —*v.i.* 1. transmitirse por sucesión o herencia. 2. morir, (fig.) desaparecer.
demisemiquaver [ˌdɛmɪ'sɛmɪˌkweɪvər, B 'dɛmɪsɛm-ə] *s.* (mús.) fusa.
demission [dɪ'mɪʃən] *s.* dimisión, abdicación, renuncia.
demit [dɪ'mɪt] *v.t.* (*pret., p.p.* DEMITTED; *p.pr.* DEMITTING) 1. (pr. esco.) dimitir. 2. (ant.) despedir. —*v.i.* presentar uno su renuncia.
demitasse ['dɛmɪˌtæs, B -ˌtɑs] *s.* tacita; tacita de café.
Demiurge [-ˌɜrdʒ, B 'dimɪˌɜdʒ] *s.* (filos.) demiurgo, creador del mundo material.
demivolt, demivolte ['dɛmɪˌvoʊlt, B -ˌvɔlt] *s.* (equit.) media vuelta con las patas delanteras levantadas.
demob [di'mɑb, B 'di'mɔb] *v.t.* (*pret., p.p.* DEMOBBED; *p.pr.* DEMOBBING) (fam., pr. G.B.) licenciar (a soldado).
demobilization [dɪˌmoʊbələ'zeɪʃən, B 'di-laɪ-] *s.* (mil.) licenciamiento, desmovilización.
demobilize [dɪ'moʊbəˌlaɪz, B di-] *v.t.* (mil.) licenciar, desmovilizar (las tropas, soldado).
democracy [dɪ'mɑkrəsɪ, B -'mɔk-] *s.* (*pl.* DEMOCRACIES) 1. democracia, gobierno democrático. 2. democracia, país democrático.
democrat ['dɛməˌkræt] *s.* 1. demócrata. 2. **D.,** miembro del Partido Demócrata de los E.U.
democratic [ˌdɛmə'krætɪk] *a.* democrático.
democratically [-ɪkəlɪ] *adv.* democráticamente.
Democratic Party, (E.U.) Partido Demócrata, uno de los dos partidos políticos más importantes.
democratization [dɪˌmɑkrətə'zeɪʃən, B -ˌmɔkrətaɪ-] *s.* democratización.
democratize [dɪ'mɑkrəˌtaɪz, B -'mɔk-] *v.t.* democratizar, hacer democrático.
Democritus [dɪ'mɑkrətəs, B -'mɔk-] *s.* Demócrito, filósofo de la Grecia antigua.
démodé [ˌdeɪˌmoʊ'deɪ, B -'moʊdeɪ] *a.* (fr.) fuera de moda; anticuado.
demoded [di'moʊdəd] *a.* fuera de moda, pasado de moda.
demodulate [di'mɑdʒəˌleɪt, B -'mɔdjʊ-] *v.t.* (rad.) desmodular.
demodulation [diˌmɑdʒə'leɪʃən, B -'mɔdjʊ-] *s.* (rad.) desmodulación, demodulación, detección.
demographer [dɪ'mɑgrəfər, B -'mɔgrə-fə] *s.* demógrafo.
demographic [ˌdimə'græfɪk] *a.* demográfico.
demography [dɪ'mɑgrəfɪ, B -'mɔg-] *s.* demografía.
demoiselle [ˌdɛmwə'zɛl] *s.* 1. damisela, doncella. 2. (orn.) grulla de Numidia; zaida. 3. (ento.) caballito del diablo.
demolish [dɪ'mɑlɪʃ, B -'mɔl-] *v.t.* demoler, derribar, derruir; destruir, aniquilar.
demolisher [-ər, B -ə] *s.* demoledor; destructor.
demolition [ˌdɛmə'lɪʃən, ˌdi-] *s.* demolición; destrucción.
demolition charge, (mil.) carga de demolición, carga de destrucción (de una bomba).
demolition squad, escuadra de demolición, destacamento de demolición.
demon ['dimən] *s.* 1. demonio, diablo, espíritu maligno. 2. demonio, malvado. 3. relámpago, persona ágil, persona incansable, ej., *she's a d. for work,* ella es incansable en el trabajo.
demonetization [diˌmɑnətə'zeɪʃən, B -ˌmʌnɪtaɪ-] *s.* (econ.) desmonetización.
demonetize [di'mɑnəˌtaɪz, B -'mʌnɪ-] *v.t.* (econ.) 1. desmonetizar. 2. invalidar (un billete, una moneda).
demoniac [dɪ'moʊnɪˌæk] *a.* demoníaco, endemoniado. —*s.* endemoniado, energúmeno.
demonic [di'mɑnɪk, B -'mɔn-] *a.* demoníaco.
demonism ['dimənˌɪzəm] *s.* demonismo, creencia en demonios, demoniolatría.
demonize [-ˌaɪz] *v.t.* convertir en (un) demonio.
demonolater [ˌdimə'nɑlətər, B -'nɔlətə] *s.* demonólatra.
demonolatry [-ətrɪ] *s.* demonolatría.
demonology [-ədʒɪ] *s.* demonología.
demonstrability [dɪˌmɑnstrə'bɪlətɪ, ˌdɛmən- B ˌdɛmən-, dɪˌmɔn-] *s.* calidad de demostrable, demonstrabilidad.
demonstrable [dɪ'mɑnstrəbəl, 'dɛmən-, B 'dɛmən-, dɪ'mɔn-] *a.* demostrable.
demonstrably [-blɪ] *adv.* demostrablemente.
demonstrant [dɪ'mɑnstrənt, B -'mɔn-] *s.* manifestante.
demonstrate ['dɛmənˌstreɪt] *v.t.* 1. demostrar, probar (la verdad de algo). 2. demostrar, mostrar (el manejo, funcionamiento, etc.; afecto, sentimientos, etc.). —*v.i.* estar con (los) manifestantes; **d. against,** hacer una manifestación contra.
demonstration [ˌdɛmən'streɪʃən] *s.* 1. demostración, prueba (de una verdad). 2. demostración, exposición (ej., de las ventajas de una mercancía). 3. demostración, expresión (de sentimientos, etc.). 4. manifestación (pública).
demonstrative [dɪ'mɑnstrətɪv, B -'mɔn-] *a.* 1. demonstrativo. 2. (gram.) demostrativo. 3. que muestra sus sentimientos, expansivo, efusivo. —*s.* (gram.) pronombre o adjetivo demostrativo.
demonstrative pronoun, (gram.) pronombre demostrativo.
demonstrator ['dɛmənˌstreɪtər, B -ə] *s.* 1. demostrador. 2. modelo de muestra. 3. manifestante.
demoralization [dɪˌmɔrələ'zeɪʃən, -ˌmɑr-, B -ˌmɔrəlaɪ-] *s.* desmoralización.
demoralize [dɪ'mɔrəˌlaɪz, -'mɑr-, B -'mɔr-] *v.t.* 1. desmoralizar, corromper. 2. desmoralizar, desalentar, socavar la moral de (ej., tropas).
demoralizer [-ər, B -ə] *s.* desmoralizador.
demoralizing [-ɪŋ] *a.* desmoralizador (efecto, enseñanza, etc.).
demos ['diˌmɑs, B 'dimɔs] *s.* 1. (hist. griega) demos, pueblo. 2. populacho, chusma.
Demosthenes [dɪ'mɑsθəˌniz, B -'mɔs-] *s.* Demóstenes, orador y político griego.
Demosthenic [ˌdiməs'θɛnɪk, B ˌdɛm-] *a.* demostino, relativo a Demóstenes.
demote [dɪ'moʊt] *v.t.* (E.U.) degradar, rebajar en clase (de rango o categoría).
demotic [dɪ'mɑtɪk, B -'mɔt-] *s.* demótico, forma de griego moderno. —*a.* 1. demótico, popular. 2. (arqueol.) demótico (escritura).

demotion [dɪ'moʊʃən] *s.* degradación, descenso de rango.

demount [di'maʊnt] *v.t.* desmontar, desarmar (ej., máquinas).

demountable [-əbəl] *a.* desmontable, desarmable.

demulcent [dɪ'mʌlsənt] *a., s.* (med.) demulcente, emoliente, calmante, dulcificante.

demur [dɪ'mɜr, B -'mɜ] *v.i.* (*pret., p.p.* DEMURRED; *p.pr.* DEMURRING) 1. (con *at*) objetar (a), poner reparo (a). 2. (der.) interponer objeción, alegar excepción. 3. (ant.) tardar, demorar, vacilar. —*s.* 1. objeción, reparo. 2. (ant.) vacilación.

demure [dɪ'mjʊr, B -'mjʊə] *a.* 1. modesto, reservado, tímido, púdico, pacato. 2. gazmoño, recatado.

demurely [-lɪ] *adv.* modestamente; con gazmoñería.

demureness [-nəs] *s.* 1. modestia. 2. timidez. 3. gazmoñería, recato.

demurrage [dɪ'mɜrɪdʒ, B dɪ'mʌrɪdʒ] *s.* 1. demora, detención. 2. (com.) estadía, estadías.

demurral [dɪ'mɜrəl, B -'mʌrəl] *s.* objeción, reparo.

demurrer [-'mɜrər, B -'mʌrə] *s.* 1. (der.) excepción (de demanda insuficiente). 2. objeción, reparo.

demy [dɪ'maɪ] *s.* (*pl.* DEMIES) papel (de) marquilla (aproximadamente 40 x 53 cm.).

demyelinate [di'maɪələ,neɪt] *v.t.* (quím., biol.) desmielinizar, eliminar o destruir la mielina de.

demyelination [di,maɪələ'neɪʃən] *s.* (quím., biol.) desmielinación, desmielinización.

den [dɛn] *s.* 1. cubil, guarida, madriguera; caverna, escondrijo. 2. cuchitril, pocilga. 3. cuarto privado, cuarto de trabajo, rincón. —*v.i.* (*pret., p.p.* DENNED; *p.pr.* DENNING) morar, habitar (en lugar sucio, incómodo, etc.).

denarius [dɪ'nærɪəs, B -'nɛər-] *s.* (*pl.* DENARII [-ɪ,aɪ]) denario.

denary ['dɛnərɪ, B 'di-] *a.* denario; decimal.

denationalization [di,næʃənələ'zeɪʃən, B 'di-laɪ-] *s.* 1. desnacionalización, pérdida de la nacionalidad. 2. devolución (de industrias, tierra) a particulares.

denationalize [-'næʃənəl,aɪz] *v.t.* 1. desnacionalizar, desnaturalizar (personas). 2. desnacionalizar, devolver a particulares (industria, tierra).

denaturalization [di,nætʃərələ'zeɪʃən, B -laɪ-] *s.* desnaturalización.

denaturalize [-'nætʃərə,laɪz] *v.t.* 1. desnaturalizar (ciudadano). 2. desnaturalizar, pervertir, desfigurar.

denaturant [di'neɪtʃərənt] *s.* (quím., fís.) desnaturalizante.

denaturation [-,neɪtʃə'reɪʃən] *s.* (quím.) desnaturalización.

denature [-'neɪtʃər, B -tʃə] *v.t.* (quím.) desnaturalizar (el alcohol, una proteína, material radioactivo).

denatured alcohol, alcohol de quemar, alcohol desnaturalizado.

denaturize [-tʃə,raɪz] *v.t., var. de* **denature.**

denazification [di,nɑtsəfə'keɪʃən] *s.* (pol.) desnacificación.

denazify [di'nɑtsə,faɪ] *v.t.* (*pret., p.p.* DENAZIFIED; *p.pr.* DENAZIFYING) desnacificar (desarraigar elementos o influencias nazis).

dendriform ['dɛndrə,fɔrm, B -,fɔm] *a.* dendriforme (en forma de árbol).

dendrite ['dɛn,draɪt] *s.* 1. (min.) dendrita, planta fósil. 2. (anat.) dendrita.

dendritic [dɛn'drɪtɪk] **dendritical** [-ɪkəl] *a.* dendrítico; ramificado (forma de árbol).

dendrochronology [,dɛndroʊkrə'nɑlədʒɪ, B -'nɔl-] *s.* dendrocronología (medición del tiempo en troncos de árboles).

dendrographic [-drə'græfɪk] *a.* dendrográfico.

dendrography [dɛn'drɑgrəfɪ, B -'drɔg-] *s.* dendrografía (tratado de los árboles).

dendroid ['dɛn,drɔɪd] *a.* (bot.) dendroideo, arborescente.

dendrologic [,dɛndrə'lɑdʒɪk, B -'lɔdʒ-] **dendrological** [-ɪkəl] *a.* (bot.) dendrológico.

dendrology [dɛn'drɑlədʒɪ, B -'drɔl-] *s.* (bot.) dendrología (estudio científico de los árboles).

dendron ['dɛn,drɑn, B -,drɔn] *s.* (anat.) dendrita.

dene [din] *s.* (G.B.) valle boscoso.

Denebola [dɪ'nɛbələ] *s.* (astr.) Denébola (estrella de la constelación del León).

denegation [,dɛnɪ'geɪʃən] *s.* denegación.

dengue ['dɛŋgɪ, -,geɪ, B -gɪ] *s.* (med.) dengue.

deniable [dɪ'naɪəbəl] *a.* negable.

denial [dɪ'naɪəl] *s.* 1. negación, negativa, desmentida. 2. repudiación, rechazo. 3. abnegación. 4. (der.) denegación, negación.

denicotinize [di'nɪkə,ti,naɪz] *v.t.* quitar (al tabaco) parte de su nicotina.

denier [də'nɪr, B -'nɪə] *s.* (numis.) denier (moneda de plata de Francia).

denier ['dɛnjər, B 'dɛnɪeɪ] *s.* (tej.) dinero, diner, unidad de peso del hilo de seda, rayón, etc.

denier [dɪ'naɪər, B -ə] *s.* negador, contradictor.

denigrate ['dɛnɪ,greɪt] *v.t.* denigrar, manchar, empañar, mancillar (reputación, etc.); ennegrecer.

denigration [,dɛnɪ'greɪʃən] *s.* denigración.

denigratory ['dɛnɪgrə,tɔrɪ, B -,greɪtərɪ] *a.* denigrativo.

denim ['dɛnəm] *s.* 1. (tej.) dril de algodón. 2. (*pl.*) mono, traje de faena, mameluco (Am.), overol (Am.).

denitration [,di,naɪ'treɪʃən] *s.* (quím.) denitración.

denitrification [di,naɪtrəfə'keɪʃən] *s.* (quím.) desnitrificación.

denitrify [-'naɪtrə,faɪ] *v.t.* (quím.) desnitrificar.

denizen ['dɛnəzən] *s.* 1. habitante, ciudadano. 2. residente (extranjero). 3. planta o animal naturalizado; palabra incorporada (en un idioma).

Denmark ['dɛn,mɑrk, B -,mɑk] *s.* Dinamarca.

denominate [dɪ'nɑmənət, B -'nɔm-] *a.* (mat.) denominado (díc. del número concreto). — [-,neɪt] *v.t.* denominar, nombrar, titular, intitular.

denominate number, (mat.) número denominado, número complejo.

denomination [dɪ,nɑmə'neɪʃən, B -,nɔm-] *s.* 1. denominación, título. 2. categoría, clase, grupo. 3. secta, creencia. 4. valor, denominación, ej., *notes of high d.,* billetes de gran valor o de alta denominación.

denominational [-əl] *a.* 1. religioso, ej., *d. education,* educación religiosa. 2. sectario, partidista, parcial.

denominationalism [-,ɪzəm] *s.* sectarismo.

denominationally [-əlɪ] *adv.* sectariamente.

denominative [dɪ'nɑmənətɪv, B -'nɔm-] *a.* denominativo; (gram.) denominativo. —*s.* (gram.) palabra denominativa.

denominator [dɪ'nɑmə,neɪtər, B -'nɔmɪ,neɪtə] *s.* denominador; (mat.) denominador, divisor.

denotation [,dinoʊ'teɪʃən] *s.* 1. denotación; nombre, designación. 2. marca, señal, indicio. 3. indicación, significación. 4. (lóg.) denotación, extensión. 5. (gram.) denotación.

denotative ['dinoʊ,teɪtɪv, di'noʊtə-, B dɪ'noʊtə-] *a.* denotativo.

denote [dɪ'noʊt] *v.t.* 1. denotar, indicar, marcar. 2. señalar, simbolizar, significar. 3. (lóg., gram.) denotar.

denotement [-mənt] *s.* denotación; indicación.

denouement [,deɪ,nu'mɑn, B -'numɑŋ] *s.* éxito, desenlace, desenredo, solución (de una situación complicada).

denounce [dɪ'naʊns] *v.t.* 1. denunciar, delatar, censurar, reprobar. 2. dar por terminado (tratado, armisticio, etc.). 3. (der.) denunciar (criminal, delito, daño, etc.). 4. (ant.) presagiar, augurar; denunciar, declarar; acusar.

denouncement [-mənt] *s.* 1. denuncia, censura, reprobación, condena. 2. denuncia (de un tratado, armisticio, etc.). 3. (der.) denuncia.

denouncer [-ər, B -ə] *s.* 1. censurador, delator, crítico. 2. denunciador (de un tratado, etc.). 3. (der.) denunciante.

dense [dɛns] *a.* 1. denso, compacto, tupido, apretado, espeso. 2. torpe, estúpido. 3. craso, grave (ignorancia). 4. (foto.) relativamente opaco (negativo).

densely ['dɛnslɪ] *adv.* 1. densamente. 2. estúpidamente.

denseness [-nəs] *s.* 1. densidad, espesura. 2. estupidez.

densify ['dɛnsə,faɪ] *v.t.* (*pret., p.p.* DENSIFIED; *p.pr.* DENSIFYING) (carp.) densificar (madera).

densimeter [dɛn'sɪmətər, B -ə] *s.* (fís., quím.) densímetro.

densimetric [,dɛnsə'mɛtrɪk] *a.* (fís., quím.) densimétrico.

densimetry [dɛn'sɪmətrɪ] *s.* (fís., quím.) densimetría.

densitometer [,dɛnsə'tɑmətər, B -'tɔmɪtə] *s.* (foto., ocean.) densitómetro.

density ['dɛnsətɪ] *s.* 1. densidad. 2. (fís., elec.) densidad. 3. torpeza, estupidez (de la mente).

dent [dɛnt] *s.* 1. abolladura, mella, hendidura. 2. (fig.) mella, impacto, impresión. 3. (med.) diente, ranura, muesca. —*v.t., v.i.* abollar(se), mellar(se).

dental ['dɛntəl] *a.* dental, dentario; (fon.) dental (articulación, consonante). —*s.* (fon.) (consonante) dental.

dental floss, hilo dental, seda encerada.

dentalium [dɛn'teɪlɪəm] *s.* (*pl.* DENTALIA [-lɪə]) (zool.) dentalium.

dental plate, dentadura postiza.

dental surgeon, cirujano dental, cirujano dentista.

dental surgery, cirugía dental.

dental technician, fabricante de utensilios dentales, mecánico dental *or* dentista, técnico dental.

dentate ['dɛn,teɪt] *a.* (bot., zool.) dentado.

dentation [dɛn'teɪʃən] *s.* (bot.) borde dentado.

dent corn, (bot.) maíz dentado o hendido.

dentex ['dɛn,tɛks] *s.* (ict.) dentón.

denticle ['dɛntɪkəl] *s.* 1. dientecillo. 2. (arq.) dentículo.

denticular [dɛn'tɪkjələr, B -lə] *a.* denticular.

denticulate [-lət] **denticulated** [-,leɪtəd] *a.* 1. (bot., zool.) dentellado. 2. (arq.) denticulado.

denticulation [-,tɪkjə'leɪʃən] *s.* (bot., zool.) denticulación.

dentiform ['dɛntə,fɔrm, B -,fɔm] *a.* denticular.

dentifrice ['dɛntəfrəs] *s.* dentífrico.

dentigerous [dɛn'tɪdʒərəs] *a.* que tiene estructuras dentadas.

dentil ['dɛntəl] *s.* (arq., carp.) dentículo, dentellón.

dentilabial [ˌdɛntəˈleɪbɪəl] *a.* (fon.) labiodental (articulación, consonante). —*s.* (consonante) labiodental.
dentilingual [-ˈlɪŋgwəl] *a.* (fon.) dentilingual.
dentin [ˈdɛntən] **dentine** [-ˌtin] *s.* (anat.) dentina, marfil (de los dientes).
dentirostral [ˌdɛntəˈrɑstrəl, B -ˈrɔs-] *a.* (orn.) dentirrostro.
Dentirostres [-ˌtriz] *s. pl.* (orn.) dentirrostros.
dentist [ˈdɛntəst] *s.* dentista, odontólogo.
dentistry [-rɪ] *s.* odontología; dentistería (S.A.).
dentist's office, dentistería (S.A.).
dentition [dɛnˈtɪʃən] *s.* dentición.
denture [ˈdɛntʃər, B -tʃə] *s.* dentadura (esp. la artificial o postiza).
denuclearization [diˈnukliərəˈzeɪʃən] *s.* desnuclearización.
denudate [dɪˈnuˌdeɪt, B ˈdɛnjʊˌdeɪt] *var. de* **denude.**
denudation [ˌdinuˈdeɪʃən, B -nju-] *s.* 1. desnudamiento; desposeimiento. 2. (geol.) erosión.
denude [dɪˈnud, B -ˈnjud] *v.t.* 1. desnudar, desvestir. 2. (fig.) desnudar, despojar, desposeer. 3. (geol.) desgastar (por erosión).
denunciate [dɪˈnʌnsɪˌeɪt] *v.t., v.i.* denunciar.
denunciation [-ˌnʌnsɪˈeɪʃən] *s.* 1. censura, reprobación, condena. 2. denuncia, denunciación (de un tratado, armisticio, etc.). 3. (der.) denuncia (de un delito, daño, etc.), acusación.
denunciator [-ˈnʌnsɪˌeɪtər, B -ə] *s.* denunciador; (der.) denunciante.
denunciatory [-sɪəˌtɔrɪ, B -sɪətərɪ] *a.* denunciatorio.
denutrition [ˌdɪnuˈtrɪʃən, B -nju-] *s.* (med.) desnutrición.
deny [dɪˈnaɪ] *v.t.* (*pret. p.p.* DENIED; *p.pr.* DENYING) 1. negar (acusación, responsabilidad, conocimiento, etc.). 2. desconocer, repudiar (firma, palabra, etc. de uno). 3. decir no a, denegar, rechazar; no permitir, negarle a. 4. **to be denied** (**to**), no tener la suerte de, ej., *it was denied* (*to*) *me to have a son,* no tuve la suerte de tener un hijo; **d. oneself,** negarse a sí mismo, abstenerse, privarse; negarse (a visitantes).
deodar [ˈdiəˌdɑr, B -ˌdɑ] *s.* (bot.) cedro deodara, cedro de la India.
deodorant [diˈoʊdərənt] *a., s.* desodorante.
deodorize [dɪˈoʊdəˌraɪz] *v.t.* desodorizar.
deodorizer [-ər, B -ə] *s.* desodorante.
deontology [ˌdiˌɑnˈtɑlədʒɪ, B -ɔnˈtɔl-] *s.* deontología.
deoxidization [diˌɑksədəˈzeɪʃən, B -ˌɔksɪdaɪ-] *s.* (quím.) desoxidación.
deoxidize [diˈɑksəˌdaɪz, B -ˈɔk-] *v.t.* (quím.) desoxidar.
deoxidizer [-ər, B -ə] *s.* (quím.) desoxidante.
deoxycorticosterone [diˌɑksɪˌkɔrtɪˈkɑstəˌroʊn, B -ˌɔksɪˌkɔtɪˈkɔs-] *s.* (bioquím.) desoxicorticosterona.
deoxygenate [-ˈɑksɪdʒəˌneɪt, B -ˈɔk-] *v.t.* (quím.) desoxigenar.
deoxygenation [-ˌɑksɪdʒəˈneɪʃən, B -ˌɔk-] *s.* (quím.) desoxigenación.
dep. *abrev. de* **department,** departamento (Dep., Dept.).
depart [dɪˈpɑrt, B -ˈpɑt] *v.i.* 1. partir, irse. 2. (con *from*) desviarse (de), apartarse (de). 3. morir, fallecer. —*v.t.* (ant.) abandonar, salir de; **d. this life,** salir de este mundo. —*s.* (ant.) partida, muerte.
departed [-əd] *a.* 1. pasado (grandeza, gloria). 2. difunto, muerto.
department [dɪˈpɑrtmənt, B -ˈpɑt-] *s.* 1. departamento (de un gobierno, universidad, almacén, etc.). 2. departamento, provincia, territorio. 3. (fig.) esfera, campo. 4. (E.U.) ministerio, ej., *D. of Justice,* Ministerio de Justicia.
departmental [diˌpɑrtˈmɛntəl, B -ˌpɑt-] *a.* departamental; del departamento, ramo, etc.
departmentalize [-ˌaɪz] *v.t.* dividir en departamentos.
departmentally [-ˈmɛntəlɪ] *adv.* por departamentos; en departamentos.
Department of Labor, (E.U.) Ministerio de Trabajo.
Department of the Interior, (E.U.) Ministerio de la Gobernación, Ministerio de Gobierno.
Department of the Navy, (E.U.) Ministerio de Marina.
department store, grandes almacenes, tienda por departamentos, almacén grande (con numerosas secciones de venta).
departure [dɪˈpɑrtʃər, B -ˈpɑtʃə] *s.* 1. partida, salida. 2. (con *from*) desviación, abandono (de). 3. dirección, rumbo (esp. nuevo). 4. (mar.) punto de partida. 5. (mar.) diferencia de longitud (entre punto de partida y posición del barco). 6. (ant.) fallecimiento, defunción.
departure platform, (f.c.) andén de partida.
depasture [dɪˈpæstʃər, B diˈpɑstʃə] *v.t., v.i.* (ant.) pastar, apacentar, herbajar.
depauperate [dɪˈpɔpərət, B ˈdi-] *v.t.* empobrecer. —*a.* (med.) depauperado.
depauperation [-ˌpɔpəˈreɪʃən] *s.* (med.) depauperación.
depend [dɪˈpɛnd] *v.i.* 1. (con *on* o *upon*) depender de; contar con, necesitar, ej., *it depends on you,* depende de usted, *she depends upon her mother,* ella depende (es dependiente) de su madre, *I depend upon your help,* cuento con (o necesito) tu ayuda. 2. confiar en, ej., *you can depend on him to get this job well done,* puede confiar en que él haga bien el trabajo. 3. pender, colgar. 4. **you may d. on** (o **upon**) **it,** puede Ud. estar seguro, puede Ud. confiar en eso, pierda cuidado; **that depends,** eso depende.
dependability [dɪˌpɛndəˈbɪlətɪ] *s.* carácter cumplidor o responsable, carácter sólido, seriedad.
dependable [dɪˈpɛndəbəl] *a.* cumplidor, confiable, seguro, responsable.
dependableness [-nəs] *s.* carácter cumplidor o responsable; carácter sólido, seriedad.
dependant, *var. de* **dependent** (*s.*).
dependence [dɪˈpɛndəns] *s.* 1. dependencia. 2. (gen. con *on* o *upon*) confianza, apoyo (en), necesidad (de). 3. sostén, apoyo.
dependency [-dənsɪ] *s.* 1. dependencia, subordinación. 2. dependencia, posesión, colonia.
dependent [-dənt] *a.* 1. (con *on*) dependiente (de), subordinado, sujeto (a). 2. (gram.) subordinado. 3. **to be d. on (someone) for (something),** depender de (alguien) para (algo). —*s.* 1. dependiente. 2. persona a cargo.
dependent clause, (gram.) cláusula subordinada.
dependent variable, (mat.) variable dependiente.
deperm [diˈpɜrm, B -ˈpɜm] *v.t.* (mar.) reducir el magnetismo de (casco de acero de un barco).
depersonalization [diˌpɜrsənələˈzeɪʃən, B -ˌpɜsənəˌlaɪ-] *s.* 1. despersonalización. 2. pérdida del sentido de la identidad personal.
depersonalize [-ˈpɜrsənəˌlaɪz, B-ˈpɜsə-] *v.t.* 1. privar de personalidad. 2. hacer impersonal.
dephase [diˈfeɪz] *v.t.* (elec.) defasar, desfasar.
dephlegmate [dɪˈflɛgˌmeɪt] *v.t.* (quím.) deflegmar.
depict [dɪˈpɪkt] *v.t.* 1. retratar, pintar. 2. (fig.) retratar, representar, pintar, describir.
depiction [dɪˈpɪkʃən] *s.* 1. pintura. 2. descripción, representación.
depicture [-tʃər, B -tʃə] *v.t.* pintar, retratar, representar; describir; imaginar, concebir.
depigmentation [diˌpɪgmənˈteɪʃən] *s.* despigmentación.
depilate [ˈdɛpəˌleɪt] *v.t.* depilar.
depilation [ˌdɛpəˈleɪʃən] *s.* depilación.
depilatory [dɪˈpɪləˌtɔrɪ, B -ətərɪ] *a.* depilatorio. —*s.* depilatorio.
deplane [diˈpleɪn] *v.i.* bajar o desembarcar del avión.
depletable [dɪˈplitəbəl] *a.* agotable (provisiones, existencias, etc.).
deplete [dɪˈplit] *v.t.* 1. reducir, disminuir, agotar. 2. (med.) vaciar, evacuar (líquidos del cuerpo).
depletion [-ˈpliʃən] *s.* 1. reducción, disminución, agotamiento. 2. (med.) depleción. 3. (com.) disminución (del capital).
depletive [-plitɪv] *a.* (med.) depletivo.
deplorable [dɪˈplɔrəbəl] *a.* deplorable, lamentable.
deplorably [-əblɪ] *adv.* deplorablemente, lamentablemente.
deplore [dɪˈplɔr, B -ˈplɔ] *v.t.* deplorar, lamentar.
deploy [dɪˈplɔɪ] *v.t., v.i.* (mil.) desplegar(se) (tropas, fuerzas, etc.).
deployment [-mənt] *s.* (mil.) despliegue.
deplumation [diˌpluˈmeɪʃən] *s.* (zool.) desplumadura.
deplume [diˈplum] *v.t.* 1. desplumar. 2. (fig.) despojar (de bienes).
depolarization [ˌdiˌpoʊlərəˈzeɪʃən, B -ləraɪ-] *s.* (fís.) despolarización.
depolarize [diˈpoʊləˌraɪz] *v.t.* (fís.) despolarizar.
depolarizer [-ər, B -ə] *s.* (fís.) despolarizador.
depone [dɪˈpoʊn] *v.t., v.i.* (der.) deponer, atestiguar, testificar.
deponent [dɪˈpoʊnənt] *a.* (gram.) deponente (díc. de ciertos verbos griegos y latinos). —*s.* 1. (gram. latina y griega) (verbo) deponente. 2. (der.) deponente, declarante.
depopulate [diˈpɑpjəˌleɪt, B -ˈpɔp-] *v.t.* despoblar.
depopulation [diˌpɑpjəˈleɪʃən, B -ˌpɔp-] *s.* despoblación, despueble, despueblo.
depopulator [diˈpɑpjəˌleɪtər, B -ˈpɔp-ə] *s.* despoblador.
deport [dɪˈpɔrt, B -ˈpɔt] *v.t.* deportar, desterrar, expulsar. —*v.i.* comportarse, portarse, conducirse.
deportable [-əbəl] *a.* 1. sujeto a deportación. 2. punible con deportación (delito).
deportation [ˌdiˌpɔrˈteɪʃən B -pɔˈ-] *s.* deportación, destierro, expulsión.
deportee [-pɔrˈti, B -pɔˈ-] *s.* deportado, desterrado.
deportment [dɪˈpɔrtmənt, B -ˈpɔt-] *s.* porte, conducta, comportamiento.
deposal [dɪˈpoʊzəl] *s.* deposición, destitución, destronamiento.
depose [dɪˈpoʊz] *v.t.* 1. deponer, destituir, destronar. 2. (der.) deponer, atestiguar, testificar. —*v.i.* testificar, dar testimonio.
deposit [dɪˈpɑzət, B -ˈpɔzɪt] *v.t.* 1. depositar (bienes, valores, dinero; confianza, etc.). 2. depositar, posar, sedimentar. 3. poner, deponer (huevos). —*v.i.* depositarse, sedimentarse. —*s.* 1. depósito; **on d.,** en depósito. 2. (geol., min.) sedimento, yacimiento.
deposit account, (com.) cuenta de depósito.
depositary [dɪˈpɑzəˌtɛrɪ, B -ˈpɔzɪtərɪ] *s.* 1. depositario, guardián. 2. depositaría, albacea.
deposition [ˌdɛpəˈzɪʃən] *s.* 1. deposición, destitución, destronamiento. 2. (der.) deposición, declaración, testimonio. 3. depósito, sedimento.

depositor [dɪ'pɑzətər, B -'pɔzɪtə] *s.* depositante, depositador (esp. en un banco), cuentacorrentista.
depository [-ə,tɔrɪ, B -ɪtərɪ] *s.* 1. depositaría, depósito, almacén. 2. depositario, guardián.
depot ['dipoʊ, B 'dɛpoʊ] *s.* 1. depósito, almacén, bodega. 2. (E.U.) estación de ferrocarril o autobús. 3. (mil.) depósito (para suministros); cuartel, base (para el entrenamiento de los reclutas.).
depravation [,dɛprə'veɪʃən] *s.* depravación, corrupción, perversión, vicio.
deprave [dɪ'preɪv] *v.t.* 1. depravar, corromper, pervertir, envilecer. 2. (ant.) difamar, calumniar.
depraved [-'preɪvd] *a.* depravado, corrompido, pervertido, viciado, envilecido.
depravedly [-'preɪvədlɪ, -'preɪvdlɪ] *adv.* depravadamente, corrompidamente.
depraver [-'preɪvər, B -ə] *s.* depravador, corruptor.
depravity [dɪ'prævətɪ] *s.* 1. depravación, corrupción. 2. acto depravado, práctica corrupta.
deprecate ['dɛprɪ,keɪt] *v.t.* 1. deprecar. 2. desaprobar. 3. menospreciar, quitar importancia a.
deprecating [-ɪŋ] *a.* disculpador, modesto (sonrisa, gesto, etc.), deprecante.
deprecation [,dɛprɪ'keɪʃən] *s.* 1. deprecación, súplica. 2. desaprobación.
deprecative ['dɛprɪ,keɪtɪv] **deprecatory** [-kə,tɔrɪ, B -kətərɪ] *a.* disculpador, modesto *(sonrisa, gesto, etc.),* deprecatorio.
depreciable [dɪ'priʃɪəbəl] *a.* depreciable, abaratable.
depreciate [-,eɪt] *v.t.* 1. depreciar, abaratar, desvalorar. 2. menospreciar, despreciar, desestimar. —*v.i.* depreciarse.
depreciatingly [-ɪŋlɪ] *adv.* despreciativamente, con desestimación.
depreciation [dɪ,priʃɪ'eɪʃən] *s.* 1. depreciación, desvalorización. 2. desprecio, menosprecio, desestimación. 3. (com., ten.) depreciación (de un activo).
depreciative [dɪ'priʃɪ,eɪtɪv, -ʃɪətɪv] *a.* despreciativo, menospreciativo.
depreciatively [-lɪ] *adv.* despreciativamente.
depreciator [-,eɪtər, B -ə] *s.* desestimador, despreciador.
depreciatory [dɪ'priʃɪə,tɔrɪ, B -ʃjətərɪ] *a.* despreciativo, menospreciativo.
depredate ['dɛprə,deɪt] *v.t., v.i.* depredar, saquear, pillar.
depredation [,dɛprə'deɪʃən] *s.* depredación, pillaje, saqueo.
depredator ['dɛprə,deɪtər, B -ə] *s.* depredador, saqueador, pillo.
depredatory [dɪ'prɛdə,tɔrɪ, B -dətərɪ] *a.* saqueador, de depredación.
depress [dɪ'prɛs] *v.t.* 1. (fig.) deprimir, desalentar, desanimar. 2. oprimir, apretar (botón, tecla, etc.). 3. deprimir, hundir, bajar. 4. reducir, disminuir, bajar. 5. depreciar, desvalorar, rebajar.
depressant [-ənt] *a.* (med.) deprimente, debilitante. —*s.* (med.) sedativo, sedante.
depressed [-'prɛst] *a.* 1. deprimido, abatido, desanimado. 2. necesitado, desamparado (gente, proletariado, etc.). 3. (bot.) deprimido, hundido. 4. (zool., anat.) deprimido, aplanado. 5. (econ.) de depresión (período, área), en depresión (industria, comercio).
depressing [dɪ'prɛsɪŋ] *a.* deprimente, depresivo, desalentador.
depressingly [-lɪ] *adv.* depresivamente.
depression [dɪ'prɛʃən] *s.* 1. abatimiento, desaliento, desánimo. 2. depresión, hondonada, hueco, concavidad. 3. el apretar (de un botón, tecla, etc.). 4. baja (del mercurio en el termómetro); rebajamiento (del nivel de un camino, terreno, etc.). 5. (econ.) depresión, crisis. 6. (astr., meteor., top.) depresión. 7. (med.) depresión.
depression angle, (ópt., top.) ángulo de depresión.
depressive [dɪ'prɛsɪv] *a.* depresivo; deprimente.
depressively [-lɪ] *adv.* depresivamente.
depressor [-'prɛsər, B -ə] *s.* 1. (med.) depresor (músculo, nervio o aparato). 2. (min.) depresor antiflotante.
deprivable [dɪ'praɪvəbəl] *a.* amovible, revocable.
deprival [-vəl] *s.* privación, despojo.
deprivation [,dɛprə'veɪʃən] *s.* 1. privación, carencia, pérdida. 2. privación, desposeimiento (de un empleo, dignidad, oficio, etc.).
deprive [dɪ'praɪv] *v.t.* 1. privar, despojar. 2. privar, desposeer, deponer (de un oficio, dignidad, etc., esp. a un clérigo).
dept. *abrev. de* **department,** departamento (dep., dept.).
depth [dɛpθ] *s.* 1. profundidad (esp. del agua), hondura. 2. (*pl.*) aguas profundas; abismo, sima. 3. profundidad, gravedad (del sonido). 4. intensidad, obscuridad (de colores). 5. profundidad, lo más recóndito (del pensamiento o sentimientos). 6. sagacidad. 7. **in d.,** a fondo; (mil.) en profundidad; **in the d. of winter,** en la yema del invierno, en pleno invierno; **to be out of one's d.,** estar en aguas demasiado profundas; (fig.) estar fuera de ambiente; **to get out of one's d.,** (fig.) meterse en honduras, no tener piso.
depth charge, (arm.) carga de profundidad.
depth gauge, (mec.) calibre de profundidad; (hidr.) escala hidrométrica.
depthless ['dɛpθləs] *a.* 1. sin fondo, insondable; (fig.) inmensurable (miseria, pobreza, etc.). 2. bajo, poco profundo; (fig.) superficial.
depth of definition, (foto.) profundidad de foco.
depth of field, (foto.) profundidad de campo.
depth of focus, (foto.) profundidad de foco.
depth perception, 1. percepción de profundidad. 2. (avia.) sensación de relieve, percepción de fondo.
depth psychology, psicoanálisis, cualquier sistema de psicología que tenga que ver con el subconsciente.
depurate ['dɛpjə,reɪt] *v.t., v.i.* depurar(se), purificar(se), limpiar(se).
depuration [,dɛpjə'reɪʃən] *s.* depuración, purificación.
depurative ['dɛpjə,reɪtɪv] *a.* (med.) depurativo (medicamento). —*s.* (med.) depurador.
depurator [-ər, B -ə] *s.* (aparato) depurador.
deputation [,dɛpjə'teɪʃən] *s.* diputación, delegación.
depute [dɪ'pjut] *v.t.* diputar, delegar, comisionar.
deputize ['dɛpjə,taɪz] *v.t.* diputar, delegar, comisionar. —*v.i.* (con *for*) reemplazar, suplir (a), hacer las veces (de).
deputy ['dɛpjətɪ] *s.* 1. diputado, delegado, comisionado, enviado, agente. 2. asistente, suplente. 3. (pol.) diputado.
deputy governor, teniente gobernador.
deracinate [dɪ'ræsən,eɪt] *v.t.* desarraigar, arrancar de raíz; extirpar.
deracination [dɪ,ræsən'eɪʃən] *s.* desarraigo; extirpación.
deraign [dɪ'reɪn] *v.t.* (ant., der.) probar; decidir (esp. por medio de combate).
derail [dɪ'reɪl] *v.i.* descarrilar.
derailment [-mənt] *s.* descarrilamiento.
derange [dɪ'reɪndʒ] *v.t.* 1. desordenar, desarreglar, desconcertar. 2. perturbar, molestar. 3. trastornar, enloquecer.
deranged [-'reɪndʒd] *a.* trastornado, loco.
derangement [-'reɪndʒmənt] *s.* 1. desorden, desarreglo. 2. trastorno (mental), locura.
derby ['dɜrbɪ, B 'dɑbɪ] *s.* 1. sombrero hongo. 2. carrera, competencia. 3. **D.,** carrera (anual) de caballos en Epsom.
derelict ['dɛrə,lɪkt] *a.* 1. abandonado. 2. (E.U.) negligente, remiso. —*s.* 1. derelicto, barco abandonado (en alta mar). 2. (der.) tierra u objeto abandonado. 3. pelagatos, pelafustán, vago.
dereliction [,dɛrə'lɪkʃən] *s.* 1. abandono, desamparo. 2. negligencia, descuido, falta.
deride [dɪ'raɪd] *v.t.* ridiculizar, burlarse de, mofarse de, escarnecer.
derider [-ər, B -ə] *s.* burlón, zumbón, mofador, escarnecedor.
deridingly [dɪ'raɪdɪŋlɪ] *adv.* burlonamente, irónicamente.
de rigueur, (fr.) de rigor.
derisible [dɪ'rɪzəbəl] *a.* risible, irrisorio, ridículo.
derision [dɪ'rɪʒən] *s.* irrisión, mofa, escarnio, burla.
derisive [dɪ'raɪsɪv] *a.* burlón, mofador, irónico.
derisively [-lɪ] *adv.* burlonamente, irónicamente.
derisory [-'raɪsərɪ, -zə-] *a.* 1. burlón, irónico. 2. irrisorio, ridículo (oferta, etc.).
derivable [dɪ'raɪvəbəl] *a.* derivable, deducible.
derivate ['dɛrə,veɪt, B -vɪt] *var. de* **derivative.**
derivation [,dɛrə'veɪʃən] *s.* 1. derivación, deducción. 2. origen; descendencia. 3. (mat.) derivación. 4. (gram.) derivación; derivado.
derivative [dɪ'rɪvətɪv] *a.* derivativo, derivado. —*s.* 1. (gram.) derivado, palabra derivativa. 2. (mat.) derivada. 3. (quím.) derivado.
derive [dɪ'raɪv] *v.t.* 1. derivar, inferir, deducir. 2. derivar, recibir (nombre, etc.). 3. obtener (de una fuente u origen). 4. trazar (origen, descendencia). 5. (quím.) derivar (una substancia de otra). —*v.i.* derivarse, provenir.
derm [dɜrm, B dɜm] *s.* dermis, cutis.
derma ['dɜrmə, B 'dɜmə] *s.* (anat., zool.) dermis.
dermal [-məl] *a.* (anat., zool.) dérmico.
dermapteran [dər'mæptərən, B də'-] *s., a.* (ento.) dermáptero.
dermatitis [,dɜrmə'taɪtəs, B -dɜmə-] *s.* (med.) dermatitis, dermitis.
dermatologic [dər,mætə'lɑdʒɪk, B ,dɜmətə'lɔdʒ-] **dermatological** [-ɪkəl] *a.* (med.) dermatológico.
dermatologist [,dɜrmə'tɑlədʒəst, B ,dɜmə'tɔl-] *s.* dermatólogo.
dermatology [-dʒɪ] *s.* (med.) dermatología.
dermatome ['dɜrmə,toʊm, B 'dɜmə-] *s.* (fisiol.) dermatoma, neoplasma de la piel.
dermatophyte [dər'mætə,faɪt, B də'-] *s.* (med.) dermatófito.
dermatosis [,dɜrmə'toʊsəs, B ,dɜmə-] *s.* (*pl.* DERMATOSES [-,siz]) (med.) dermatosis.
dermic ['dɜrmɪk, B 'dɜmɪk] *a.* dérmico, cutáneo.
dermis [-məs] *s.* (anat.) dermis, cutis.
dermoid [-,mɔɪd] **dermoidal** [dər'mɔɪdəl, B də'-] *a.* (med.) dermoideo.
dermopteran [dər'mɑptərən, B də'mɔp-] *s.* (zool.) dermóptero, lémur o maqui volador.
dermopterous [-rəs] *a.* (zool.) dermóptero, dermatóptero.
dermotropic [,dɜrmə'trɑpɪk, B ,dɜmə'trɔp-] *a.* (med.) dermótropo (díc. esp. de los virus).
dernier cri [,dɛrn,jeɪ'kri, B ,dɜn-] (fr., fig.) el último grito (de la moda); la última palabra.
derogate ['dɛrə,geɪt] *a.* (raro) derogado. —*v.t.* 1. desacreditar, detraer, menospreciar. 2. (ant.) derogar, anular, abrogar. —*v.i.* (con *from*) quitar (parte) de, disminuir (méritos, derechos, etc.).

derogately [-lɪ] *adv.* (ant.) despreciativamente.
derogation [ˌdɛrə'geɪʃən] *s.* 1. derogación, disminución; detracción, menosprecio. 2. (raro) derogación, abolición.
derogative [dɪ'rɑgətɪv, 'dɛrəˌgeɪt-, B -'rɔgət-] *a.* despreciativo, detractor (de).
derogatorily [-ˌrɑgə'tɔrəlɪ, B -'rɔgətər-] *adv.* despreciativamente, despectivamente.
derogatory [-'rɑgəˌtɔrɪ, B -'rɔgətərɪ] *a.* despectivo, detractor, menospreciativo, despreciativo, desdeñoso.
derrick ['dɛrɪk] *s.* 1. grúa, cabria, malacate. 2. cabria, torre de taladrar, castillete (esp. sobre pozo de petróleo).
derrière [ˌdɛrɪ'ɛr, B -'ɛə] *s.* (fr.) las nalgas.
derring-do ['dɛrɪŋ'du] *s.* proeza; arrojo, intrepidez.
derringer ['dɛrəndʒər, B -dʒə] *s.* pistola de bolsillo (con cañón corto y grueso).
derry ['dɛrɪ] *s.* antigua balada.
dervish ['dɜrvɪʃ, B 'dɜvɪʃ] *s.* derviche.
desalination [diˌsælə'neɪʃən] *s.* desalación.
desalt [di'sɔlt] *v.t.* desalar.
desalter [-ər, B -ə] *s.* aparato para desalar, desalador.
desalting [-ɪŋ] *s.* desalazón.
descant ['dɛsˌkænt] *s.* 1. (mús.) contrapunto, discantus. 2. discurso, disertación, alocución. 3. (poét.) melodía, canción. — ['dɛs-, dɛskænt, B dɪs'kænt] *v.i.* 1. (mús.) discantar, cantar o tocar en contrapunto. 2. disertar, discurrir largamente. 3. **d. upon,** extenderse en la alabanza de (belleza, méritos, etc.).
descend [dɪ'sɛnd] *v.i.* 1. descender, bajar. 2. descender, provenir, derivarse (de una fuente u origen). 3. transmitirse por herencia, pasar de padres a hijos. 4. descender, ir a menos, decaer (en estima, estado social, etc.). 5. (astr.) declinar, ponerse. 6. **d. from,** descender de (antepasados, familia, etc.); **d. upon,** caer encima, acometer; invadir. —*v.t.* descender o bajar por.
descendant [-ənt] *s.* descendiente. —*a.* descendiente, descendente.
descendent, *var. de* **descendant.**
descender [-ər, B -ə] *s.* 1. descendente, persona o cosa que desciende. 2. (tip.) letra con trazo bajo.
descendible [-əbəl] *a.* 1. que permite el descenso. 2. heredable.
descension [dɪ'sɛntʃən, B -'sɛnʃən] *s.* 1. (astrol.) la parte del Zodíaco en que la influencia de un planeta es más débil. 2. (ant.) descensión, descenso.
descent [dɪ'sɛnt] *s.* 1. descenso, bajada. 2. (fig.) descenso, decaimiento (en virtud, valor, posición, etc.). 3. inclinación (hacia abajo), cuesta, declive, pendiente. 4. descendencia, generación, grado genealógico. 5. embestida, asalto; invasión, incursión. 6. (der.) sucesión, transmisión por herencia.
describable [dɪ'skraɪbəbəl] *a.* descriptible.
describe [-'skraɪb] *v.t.* 1. describir, relatar, narrar. 2. (geom.) describir, delinear, trazar (un círculo, elipse, etc.).
describer [-ər, B -ə] *s.* descriptor.
description [dɪ'skrɪpʃən] *s.* 1. descripción, representación. 2. clase, tipo, especie. 3. **to answer a d.,** corresponder a una descripción.
descriptive [-'skrɪptɪv] *a.* 1. descriptivo. 2 dado a la descripción (díc. de un escritor). 3. (gram.) (adjetivo) calificativo.
descriptive geometry, geometría descriptiva.
descriptively [-lɪ] *adv.* descriptivamente.
descriptiveness [-nəs] *s.* carácter descriptivo.
descry [dɪ'skraɪ] *v.t.* (*pret., p.p.* DESCRIED; *p.pr.* DESCRYING) columbrar, divisar; descubrir (por medio de una observación cuidadosa).
desecrate ['dɛsɪˌkreɪt] *v.t.* profanar.
desecration [ˌdɛsɪ'kreɪʃən] *s.* profanación.
desecrator ['dɛsɪˌkreɪtər, B -ə] *s.* profanador.
desegregate [di'sɛgrɪˌgeɪt] *v.t., v.i.* 1. abolir la segregación (en el servicio militar, en la educación, etc.). 2. integrar (una raza o individuo a la sociedad).
desegregation [-ˌsɛgrɪ'geɪʃən] *s.* 1. supresión de la segregación. 2. integración.
desensitize [di'sɛnsəˌtaɪz, B 'di-] *v.t.* desensibilizar, insensibilizar.
desensitizer [-ər, B -ə] *s.* 1. (med., fisiol.) desensibilizante. 2. (foto.) desensibilizador.
desensitizing etch [-ɪŋ-] (foto.) desensibilizador.
desert ['dɛzərt, B -zət] *s.* desierto, páramo. —*a.* desierto, baldío, desolado, yermo.
desert [dɪ'zɜrt, B -'zɜt] *s.* 1. merecimiento (de castigo o premio). 2. merecido. 3. (raro) mérito, valor. 4. **to get one's just deserts,** llevarse su merecido. —*v.t.* desertar de, abandonar, desamparar. —*v.i.* desertar, desbandarse.
deserter [-ər, B -ə] *s.* desertor.
desertion [dɪ'zɜrʃən, B -'zɜʃən] *s.* 1. deserción, defección. 2. abandono, desolación.
desert rat ['dɛzərt-, B -zət-] soldado de infantería que peleaba en el desierto norafricano durante la segunda guerra mundial.
deserve [dɪ'zɜrv, B -'zɜv] *v.t., v.i.* merecer, ser digno de (premio o castigo).
deserved [-'zɜrvd, B -'zɜvd] *a.* merecido, correspondiente, condigno.
deservedly [-'zɜrvədlɪ, B -'zɜvəd-] *adv.* merecidamente.
deserver [-'zɜrvər, B -'zɜvə] *s.* merecedor.
deserving [-vɪŋ] *s.* mérito, merecido. —*a.* 1. de mérito (persona); meritorio (acto). 2. (con *of*) digno (de alabanza, crítica, etc.).
deservingly [-lɪ] *adv.* merecidamente.
deservingness [-nəs] *s.* merecimiento.
desex [di'sɛks] *v.t.* 1. remover parte o la totalidad de los órganos sexuales; castrar. 2. suprimir o aminorar las características sexuales.
desexualization [diˌsɛkʃʊələ'zeɪʃən, B -sɛksjʊəlar-] *s.* (med.) desexualización.
desexualize [-'sɛkʃʊəˌlaɪz, B -'sɛksjʊə-] *v.t.* privar de caracteres sexuales o de potencial sexual.
deshabille [ˌdɛsə'bil, B 'dɛzæbil] (fr.) *var. de* **dishabille.**
desiccant ['dɛsɪkənt] *a., s.* desecante, secador, secante; deshidratante.
desiccate [-ˌkeɪt] *v.t.* 1. desecar, resecar, secar. 2. desecar, arrugar (cara, etc.). 3. desecar, deshidratar. —*v.i.* secarse, desecarse.
desiccation [ˌdɛsɪ'keɪʃən] *s.* desecación, deshidratación.
desiccative ['dɛsɪˌkeɪtɪv, B dɛ'sɪkət-] *a., s.* desecativo, deshidrativo.
desiccator ['dɛsɪˌkeɪtər, B -ə] *s.* desecador; (quím.) evaporadora, deshidratador.
desiderata, *pl. de* **desideratum.**
desiderate [dɪ'sɪdəˌreɪt, -zɪd-] *v.t.* echar de menos, extrañar (Am.); anhelar, añorar.
desideration [-ˌsɪdə'reɪʃən, -ˌzɪd-] *s.* antojo, anhelo, añoranza.
desiderative [-'sɪdəˌreɪtɪv, -'zɪd-, B -rətɪv] *s., a.* desiderativo.
desideratum [-ˌsɪdə'rɑtəm, -ˌzɪd-, -'reɪt-] *s.* (*pl.* DESIDERATA [-ə] desiderátum, algo que se anhela o apetece.
design [dɪ'zaɪn] *s.* 1. idea, concepción, invención. 2. propósito, intención, designio; complot, intriga, mala intención. 3. plan, planeamiento, proyecto. 4. diseño, dibujo; modelo. 5. (ing.) proyecto, estudio, desarrollo. 6. **by d.,** adrede, a propósito, intencionalmente; **to have designs on** (o **upon**), poner las miras en. —*v.t.* 1. concebir, idear, planear, inventar. 2. (con *for*) destinar, asignar, dedicar (a). 3. planear, proyectar, intentar. 4. diseñar, dibujar. —*v.i.* hacer diseños, dibujos o planos.
designate ['dɛzɪgˌneɪt, -nət] *a.* designado. — [-ˌneɪt] *v.t.* 1. señalar, indicar, determinar. 2. designar, denominar, nombrar. 3. designar, destinar.
designation [ˌdɛzɪg'neɪʃən] *s.* 1. designación, indicación, señalamiento. 2. denominación, nombre, descripción. 3. designación, nombramiento (para un puesto).
designative ['dɛzɪgˌneɪtɪv] *a.* indicativo, especificativo.
designedly [dɪ'zaɪnədlɪ] *adv.* adrede, a propósito; intencionadamente.
designee [ˌdɛzɪg'ni] *s.* persona designada o nombrada.
designer [dɪ'zaɪnər, B -ə] *s.* 1. dibujante, diseñador, delineante. 2. conspirador, intrigante, tramador. 3. (cost.) diseñador, modisto de alta costura. 4. (ing.) proyectista. —*a.* (*jeans, labels, furniture*) de diseño, de diseño exclusivo, muy exclusivo.
designing [-ɪŋ] *a.* intrigante, maquinador, artificioso, ej., *a d. woman,* una mujer intrigante. —*s.* el arte de diseñar.
designingly [-lɪ] *a.* insidiosamente.
desilverize [di'sɪlvərˌaɪz] *v.t.* desplatar, extraer o separar la plata de.
desinence ['dɛsɪnəns] *s.* (gram.) desinencia.
desirability [dɪˌzaɪrə'bɪlətɪ, B -ˌzaɪəre-] *s.* conveniencia; calidad de deseable; aspecto apetecedor.
desirable [dɪ'zaɪrəbəl, B -'zaɪərə-] *a.* 1. deseable, apetecible. 2. deseable, conveniente.
desirably [-blɪ] *adv.* deseablemente.
desire [dɪ'zaɪr, B -'zaɪə] *v.t.* 1. desear, anhelar, apetecer. 2. desear, querer. —*v.i.* tener o sentir deseo. —*s.* deseo, anhelo, apetencia.
desirous [dɪ'zaɪrəs, B -'zaɪər-] *a.* deseoso, anheloso.
desirously [-lɪ] *adv.* deseablemente, ansiosamente.
desist [dɪ'zɪst, -'sɪst] *v.i.* desistir; **d. from,** desistir de.
desistance [-'zɪstəns, -'sɪs-] *s.* desistencia, desistimiento.
desk [dɛsk] *s.* 1. escritorio, mesa de escribir, buró. 2. pupitre, atril. 3. mostrador, carpeta (en hotel).
desk clerk, recepcionista.
desk job, trabajo de oficina.
desk lamp, lámpara de escritorio.
desk pad, bloc de notas.
deskman ['dɛskˌmæn, -mən] *s.* redactor de mesa (en la redacción de un periodico).
desktop ['dɛsktɑp] *a.* (*computer, calculator*) de escritorio, de sobremesa.
desktop publishing, autoedición, edición electrónica.
desk work, trabajo de gabinete, trabajo de escritorio.
desman ['dɛzmən] *s.* (zool.) desmán, ratón almizclero.
desmid ['dɛzməd] *s.* (bot.) desmidia.
desmoid ['dɛsˌmɔɪd] *a.* (anat., med.) desmoide, fibroide, fibroso.
desolate ['dɛsələt, 'dɛz-, B 'dɛs-] *a.* 1. desolado, devastado, arruinado. 2. desierto, despoblado, solitario. 3. melancólico, sombrío. 4. desolado, afligido, desconsolado. — [-ˌleɪt] *v.t.* 1. desolar, devastar, arrasar, arruinar. 2. despoblar, abandonar. 3. afligir, desconsolar, angustiar.

desolateness [-nəs] *s.* desolación; soledad; melancolía.
desolater [-ˌleɪtər, B -ə] *s.* desolador, asolador.
desolation [ˌdɛsə'leɪʃən, ˌdɛz-, B ˌdɛs-] *s.* 1. desolación, asolación, devastación. 2. desolación, desconsuelo, aflicción, angustia. 3. desierto. 4. soledad, abandono.
desolator, *var. de* **desolater.**
despair [dɪ'spɛr, B -'spɛə] *v.i.* desesperanzarse, desesperarse; (con *of*) abandonar la esperanza (de). —*s.* desesperación, desesperanza.
despairing [-ɪŋ, B -rɪŋ] *a.* desesperado, desesperanzado; desalentado, abatido.
despairingly [-lɪ] *adv.* sin esperanzas, desalentadamente.
despatch, despatcher, *vars. de* **dispatch, dispatcher.**
desperado [ˌdɛspə'rɑdoʊ, -'reɪd-] *s.* (*pl.* DESPERADOES O DESPERADOS) (E.U.) malhechor o criminal peligroso.
desperate ['dɛspərət] *a.* 1. desesperado, desesperanzado. 2. desesperado, peligroso, ej., *a d. criminal,* un criminal temerario. 3. crítico, grave, difícil (problema, situación, etc.). 4. extremo. 5. **to be d. for,** necesitar desesperadamente, necesitar con suma urgencia.
desperately [-lɪ] *adv.* desesperadamente.
desperation [ˌdɛspə'reɪʃən] *s.* desesperación; temeridad, furor.
despicable [dɪ'spɪkəbəl, 'dɛspɪk-] *a.* despreciable, desdeñable, vil.
despicableness [-nəs] *s.* vileza, ruindad, bajeza.
despicably [-blɪ] *adv.* vilmente, bajamente.
despise [dɪ'spaɪz] *v.t.* despreciar, menospreciar, desdeñar.
despiser [-ər, B -ə] *s.* despreciador, desdeñoso.
despite [dɪ'spaɪt] *s.* 1. despecho, malicia, inquina. 2. desprecio, menosprecio. 3. insulto, afrenta. 4. **in d. of,** a despecho de. —*v.t.* (ant.) vejar, enfadar, molestar. —*prep.* a despecho de, a pesar de, no obstante.
despiteful [-fəl] *a.* (ant.) rencoroso, malicioso, vengativo, maligno.
despitefully [-fəlɪ] *adv.* maliciosamente, malignamente.
despitefulness [-fəlnəs] *s.* malignidad, malicia, rencor, odio, mala voluntad.
despoil [dɪ'spɔɪl] *v.t.* despojar, privar; robar, saquear, pillar.
despoiler [-ər, B -ə] *s.* saqueador, ladrón, pillador.
despoliation [dɪˌspoʊlɪ'eɪʃən] *s.* despojo, rapiña, pillaje, saqueo.
despond [dɪ'spɑnd, B -'spɔnd] *v.i.* desalentarse, desanimarse, desesperanzarse, descorazonarse.
despondence [-'spɑndəns, B -'spɔn-] **despondency** [-dənsɪ] *s.* desaliento, desánimo, abatimiento, melancolía.
despondent [-dənt] *a.* desalentado, abatido, desanimado, desesperanzado.
despondently [-lɪ] *adv.* desalentadamente.
despot ['dɛspət, -ˌpɑt, B -ˌpɔt] *s.* déspota, tirano, autócrata; (hist.) déspota.
despotic [dɛs'pɑtɪk, B -'pɔt-] *a.* despótico, tiránico, autocrático.
despotically [-ɪkəlɪ] *adv.* despóticamente.
despotism ['dɛspəˌtɪzəm] *s.* despotismo, tiranía, opresión, autocracia.
despumate [də'spjuˌmeɪt, 'dɛspjʊ-] *v.t.* despumar.
desquamate ['dɛskwəˌmeɪt] *v.i.* (med.) descamarse, exfoliarse.
desquamation [ˌdɛskwə'meɪʃən] *s.* (med.) descamación, exfoliación.
dessert [dɪ'zɜrt, B -'zɜt] *s.* postre; dulce.
dessertspoon [-ˌspun] *s.* cuchara de postre.
dessert wine, vino dulce, vino generoso.
destabilize [di'steɪbəˌlaɪz] *v.t.* hacer inestable, desestabilizar.
destain [di'steɪn] *v.t.* decolorar, desteñir (para facilitar el estudio microscópico).
desterilize [di'stɛrəˌlaɪz] *v.t.* 1. anular esterilización. 2. movilizar (las reservas de oro de un sistema monetario).
destination [ˌdɛstə'neɪʃən] *s.* 1. destino, meta, fin. 2. destinación.
destine ['dɛstən] *v.t.* predestinar, destinar; **destined for,** destinado para; con destino a.
destiny [-tənɪ] *s.* destino, suerte, hado, sino.
destitute ['dɛstəˌtut, B -ˌtjut] *a.* 1. necesitado, indigente, menesteroso. 2. (con *of*) desprovisto, carente o privado (de). 3. abandonado, desamparado.
destitution [ˌdɛstə'tuʃən, B -'tju-] *s.* miseria, indigencia, pobreza.
destrier ['dɛstrɪər, B -ə] *s.* (ant.) caballo de guerra.
destroy [dɪ'strɔɪ] *v.t.* 1. destruir, destrozar, desbaratar. 2. matar; aniquilar. 3. (fig.) arruinar (reputación, fama, etc.); anular (efecto, fuerza, etc.).
destroyer [-ər, B -ə] *s.* 1. destructor, destruidor, devastador. 2. (mar.) destructor, destróyer.
destroying angel [-ɪŋ-] (bot.) (variedad de) amanita venenosa.
destruct [dɪ'strʌkt] *s.* (astronáut.) destrucción deliberada de un cohete deficiente, después de su despegue. —*v.i.* destruirse.
destructibility [-ˌstrʌktə'bɪlətɪ] *s.* destructibilidad.
destructible [-'strʌktəbəl] *a.* destructible.
destruction [-'strʌkʃən] *s.* destrucción; ruina.
destructionist [-əst] *s.* destructor.
destructive [-'strʌktɪv] *a.* destructivo, destructor, destruyente.
destructive distillation, (quím.) destilación seca (de cuerpos sólidos).
destructively [-lɪ] *adv.* destructivamente.
destructiveness [-nəs] *s.* destructividad.
destructor [-'strʌktər, B -tə] *s.* 1. (G.B). incinerador de basura. 2. dispositivo para la destrucción de cohetes (durante pruebas).
desuetude ['dɛswɪˌtud, B dɪ'sjʊɪˌtjud] *s.* desuso.
desulfurization [diˌsʌlfərə'zeɪʃən, B -raɪ-] *s.* (quím.) desulfuración.
desulfurize [-'sʌlfəˌraɪz] *v.t.* (quím.) desulfurar, desazufrar.
desulphurize, desulphurization, *var. de* **desulfurize, desulfurization.**
desultorily [ˌdɛsəl'tɔrəlɪ, B 'dɛsəltər-] *adv.* sin plan ni ilación, sin método, inconexamente, vagamente.
desultoriness ['dɛsəlˌtɔrɪnəs, B -tər-] *s.* desconexión, inconsistencia.
desultory [-ˌtɔrɪ, B -tərɪ] *a.* vago, impensado, inconexo; ocasional, esporádico, ej., *a d. remark,* una observación inconexa o vaga, *d. reading,* lectura ocasional o esporádica.
detach [dɪ'tætʃ] *v.t.* 1. separar, apartar; desprender. 2. (mil.) destacar.
detachable [-əbəl] *a.* separable, desmontable, despegable.
detached [-'tætʃt] *a.* 1. separado, independiente (esp. casa). 2. indiferente; despreocupado; imparcial.
detached column, (arq.) columna aislada, columna exenta o suelta.
detachment [-'tætʃmənt] *s.* 1. separación. 2. desinterés, despreocupación, indiferencia. 3. (mil.) destacamento.
detail [dɪ'teɪl, 'diˌteɪl] *s.* 1. detalle, pormenor. 2. (arte, arq.) detalle. 3. (mil.) destacamento pequeño. 4. **in d.,** en detalle, con detalle(s); detallada o minuciosamente; **to go into details,** entrar en pormenores. —*v.t.* 1. detallar, particularizar, pormenorizar. 2. asignar. 3. (mil.) destacar (oficial, tropas, etc.).
detailed [dɪ'teɪld, 'diˌteɪld] *a.* detallado, minucioso, exacto; **d. drawing,** dibujo detallado, diseño completo.
detail man, 1. propagandista de artículos médicos y medicinas. 2. (const.) chapucero.
detain [dɪ'teɪn] *v.t.* 1. detener, arrestar. 2. retardar, retener, detener.
detainer [-ər, B -ə] *s.* 1. (der.) detentador, retenedor. 2. (der.) detención. 3. (der.) orden de detención (para mantener arrestada a una persona).
detect [dɪ'tɛkt] *v.t.* 1. descubrir, averiguar. 2. percibir (sonido), vislumbrar, advertir (movimiento, luz), hallar. 3. (rad.) rectificar.
detectable [-'tɛktəbəl] *a.* perceptible, averiguable.
detectaphone [-ˌfoʊn] *s.* aparato para escuchar las conversaciones telefónicas.
detection [-'tɛkʃən] *s.* 1. descubrimiento, averiguación. 2. (rad.) detección; rectificación.
detective [dɪ'tɛktɪv] *a.* 1. investigador, de investigación (habilidad, método, etc.). 2. policíaca, policial (novela). —*s.* detective, investigador.
detective story, novela o relato policial.
detector [-tər, B -tə] *s.* 1. descubridor. 2. (mec.) indicador. 3. (rad.) detector; rectificador.
detent ['diˌtɛnt, dɪ'tɛnt, B dɪ'tɛnt] *s.* (mec.) retén, fiador, trinquete; escape (de un reloj).
détente [deɪ'tɑnt, B -'tɔnt] *s.* distensión internacional.
detention [dɪ'tɛntʃən, B -'tɛnʃən] *s.* 1. detención. 2. arresto, retención. 3. (com., mar.) estadía. 4. (der.) detentación.
detention barracks, prisión militar, calabozo.
deter [dɪ'tɜr, B -'tɜ] *v.t.* (*pret., p.p.* DETERRED; *p.pr.* DETERRING) 1. refrenar, desanimar, disuadir, desviar. 2. impedir.
deterge [-'tɜrdʒ, B -'tɜdʒ] *v.t.* deterger, lavar, limpiar.
detergency [-'tɜrdʒənsɪ, B -'tɜdʒən-] *s.* poder o efecto detergente.
detergent [-dʒənt] *a., s.* detergente, abstergente.
deteriorate [dɪ'tɪrɪəˌreɪt, B -'tɪər-] *v.t., v.i.* deteriorar(se), desmejorar(se), empeorar(se), degenerar.
deterioration [-ˌtɪrɪə'reɪʃən, B -ˌtɪər-] *s.* deterioro, deterioración, empeoramiento, desmejora.
deteriorative [-'tɪrɪəˌreɪtɪv, B -'tɪər-] *a.* deteriorador, nocivo.
determent [dɪ'tɜrmənt, B -'tɜmənt] *s.* refrenamiento, disuasión.
determinable [-'tɜrmənəbəl, B -'tɜm-] *a.* determinable.
determinacy [-nəsɪ] *s.* exactitud; calidad de determinado.
determinant [-nənt] *a.* determinante. —*s.* 1. factor, causa determinante. 2. (mat., biol.) determinante.
determinate [dɪ'tɜrmənət, B -'tɜmɪ-] *a.* determinado, definido; resuelto, definitivo.
determinate cleavage, (biol.) segmentación determinada.
determinate growth, (bot.) crecimiento de inflorescencia limitada.
determination [dɪˌtɜrmə'neɪʃən, B -ˌtɜmɪ-] *s.* 1. determinación, definición. 2. determinación, firmeza, resolución. 3. (der.) resolución (judicial); conclusión, terminación (del debate, etc.). 4. (med.) determinación (de la sangre).

determinative [-'tɜrmə,neɪtɪv, -nət-, B -'tɜmɪnət-] *a.* determinativo, determinante. —*s.* 1. factor determinativo. 2. (gram.) adjetivo determinativo.
determinatively [-lɪ] *adv.* determinantemente, con tendencia o carácter determinativo.
determine [dɪ'tɜrmən, B -'tɜmɪn] *v.t.* 1. determinar, limitar. 2. determinar, fijar, establecer. 3. determinar, decidir, resolver. 4. terminar, concluir. 5. (der.) determinar, definir (un pleito, etc.).
determined [-mənd] *a.* determinado, fijado; decidido, resuelto; **to be d. to,** estar resuelto o decidido a.
determinedly [-lɪ] *adv.* determinadamente, resueltamente.
determinism [-'tɜrmə,nɪzəm, B -'tɜm-] *s.* (filos.) determinismo.
determinist [-nəst] *a., s.* (filos.) determinista.
deterministic [dɪ,tɜrmə'nɪstɪk, B -,tɜmɪ-] *a.* (filos.) determinista.
deterrence [dɪ'tɜrəns, B -'tɛr-] *s.* refrenamiento, disuasión.
deterrent [-ənt] *a.* disuasivo, impeditivo. —*s.* factor disuasivo, freno; **to act as a d.,** servir de freno.
detersion [dɪ'tɜrʃən, B -'tɜʃən] *s.* (med.) detersión.
detersive [-'tɜrsɪv, B -'tɜsɪv] *a., s.* detersivo, detersorio, abstergente.
detest [dɪ'tɛst] *v.t.* detestar, aborrecer, abominar, odiar.
detestable [-'tɛstəbəl] *a.* detestable, execrable, abominable.
detestably [-blɪ] *adv.* detestablemente, abominablemente.
detestation [,di,tɛs'teɪʃən] *s.* 1. detestación, aborrecimiento. 2. objeto de execración.
dethrone [dɪ'θroʊn] *v.t.* destronar, derrocar.
dethronement [-mənt] *s.* destronamiento.
detinue ['dɛtən,u, B -,ju] *s.* (der.) retención ilegal (de muebles, etc.); acción reivindicatoria.
detonable ['dɛtənəbəl] **detonatable** [-,eɪtəbəl] *a.* detonable, capaz de ser detonado.
detonate ['dɛtən,eɪt] *v.i.* detonar, explotar, estallar. —*v.t.* hacer detonar, explotar o estallar.
detonating [-ɪŋ] *a.* detonante.
detonating fuse, mecha detonante, cebo detonante.
detonating gas, mezcla detonante o explosiva.
detonation [,dɛtən'eɪʃən] *s.* detonación, estallido, estampido.
detonator ['dɛtən,eɪtər, B -ə] *s.* 1. detonador, fulminante. 2. (f.c.) señal detonante. 3. (mil.) detonador, espoleta.
detour ['di,tʊr, dɪ'tʊr, B 'di,tʊə] *v.i.* desviarse, dar un rodeo, tomar un desvío. —*v.t.* 1. desviar. 2. evitar; pasar de lado. —*s.* desvío, rodeo, vuelta; desviación; **to make a d.,** dar un rodeo.
detoxicate [di'tɑksə,keɪt, B -'tɔk-] *v.t.* 1. desintoxicar (a personas). 2. (med.) eliminar el veneno de (substancias).
detoxication [-,tɑksə'keɪʃən, B -,tɔk-] *s.* 1. desintoxicación (de personas). 2. (med.) destoxicación, destoxificación (de substancias venenosas).
detoxification [-fə'keɪʃən] *s.* 1. desintoxicación (de personas). 2. (med.) destoxificación, destoxicación (de substancias venenosas).
detoxify [di'tɑksə,faɪ, B -'tɔk-] *v.t.* (*pret., p.p.* DETOXIFIED; *p.pr.* DETOXIFYING) 1. desintoxicar (a personas). 2. (med.) eliminar el veneno de (substancias).
detract [dɪ'trækt] *v.t.* 1. apartar. 2. distraer. 3. (con *from*) disminuir, hacer desmerecer. 4. (ant.) detraer, denigrar; quitar (mérito o reputación).
detraction [-'trækʃən] *s.* detracción, denigración, calumnia, difamación.
detractive [-'træktɪv] *a.* detractor, difamatorio, denigrante.
detractor [-tər, B -tə] *s.* detractor.
detrain [di'treɪn] *v.t., v.i.* (hacer) bajar o desembarcar del tren, apearse.
detrainment [-mənt] *s.* bajada del tren.
detribalization [di,traɪbələ'zeɪʃən, B -laɪ-] *s.* desintegración de una tribu (esp. debido a influencias culturales).
detribalize [-'traɪbə,laɪz] *v.t.* apartar de una tribu, hacer perder las costumbres propias de una tribu.
detriment ['dɛtrəmənt] *s.* perjuicio, detrimento, daño, desmedro; **to the d. of,** en perjuicio de, con menoscabo de.
detrimental [,dɛtrə'mɛntəl] *a.* perjudicial, dañino, nocivo, desventajoso.
detrital [dɪ'traɪtəl] *a.* (geol.) detrítico.
detrition [-'trɪʃən] *s.* 1. (med.) detrición (de los dientes). 2. (geol.) desgaste, erosión, deslave.
detritus [-'traɪtəs] *s.* 1. (geol.) detrito, detritus. 2. detrito, escombros, despojos.
de trop [də'troʊ] *a.* (fr.) demasiado; superfluo.
detrude [dɪ'trud] *v.t.* 1. hundir, sumir, deprimir. 2. exprimir, expeler.
detruncate [dɪ'trʌŋ,keɪt, B di-] *v.t.* destroncar, truncar, cercenar, mutilar.
detruncation [,di,trʌŋ'keɪʃən] *s.* destroncamiento, mutilación.
detrusion [dɪ'truʒən] *s.* depresión, expulsión (de un cuerpo o elemento para abajo o hacia fuera).
deuce [dus, B djus] *s.* 1. dos (de naipes o dados). 2. (tenis) empate. 3. (golf) hoyo hecho en dos (golpes). 4. (esp. en imprecaciones) diablo, demonio, diantre. 5. algo muy grande, notable o excepcional, ej., *in a d. of a hurry,* a toda prisa, sumamente apremiado. 6. (jer.) dos dólares. 7. **what the d.?** ¿qué diablos?; **where the d. is he?** ¿dónde diablos está él? —*v.t.* (tenis) empatar (un juego o etapa).
deuced ['dusəd, B 'djust] *a.* maldito, tremendo.
deucedly [-lɪ, B 'djusɪd-] *adv.* muy, extremadamente.
deuces wild ['dusəz-, B 'dju-] juego de naipes en el que el dos hace de comodín.
deus ex machina [,deɪəs,ɛks'mækənə, B 'di-] (lat.) se usa para significar la intervención de un poder sobrenatural en el desenlace o resolución de una dificultad.
deuteragonist [,dutə'rægənəst, B ,djut-] *s.* deuteragonista (en el drama griego antiguo, actor que desempeñaba el segundo papel).
deuteranopia [-rə'noupɪə] *s.* (med.) deuteranopía.
deuterium [du'tɪrɪəm, B dju'tɪər-] *s.* (quím.) deuterio.
deuterium oxide, (quím.) agua pesada (compuesta de deuterio y oxígeno).
deuterocanonical [,dutəroukə'nanɪkəl, B ,dju-'nɔn-] *a.* (rel.) deuterocanónico.
deuterogamist [-'ragəməst, B -'rɔg-] *s.* (der.) deuterógamo.
deuterogamy [-mɪ] *s.* (der.) deuterogamia, matrimonio después de la muerte o divorcio del primer cónyuge.
deuteron ['dutə,ran, B 'djutə,rɔn] *s.* (fís.) deuterón.
Deuteronomy [,dutə'ranəmɪ, B ,djutə'-rɔn-] *s.* (bíbl.) Deuteronomio.
deuteropathy [-'rapəθɪ, B -'rɔp-] *s.* (med.) deuteropatía.
deuton ['du,tan, B 'dju,tɔn] *s.* (quím.) deutón.
deutoplasm ['dutə,plæzəm, B 'djut-] *s.* (biol.) deutoplasma.
deutoplasmic [,dutə'plæzmɪk, B ,djut-] *a.* (biol.) deutoplasmático.
deutoxide [du'tɑk,saɪd, B dju'tɔk-] *s.* (quím.) deutóxido.
devaluate [di'væljʊ,eɪt] *v.t.* desvalorar, desvalorizar, depreciar, devaluar (una moneda).
devaluation [-,væljʊ'eɪʃən, B ,di-] *s.* desvalorización, devaluación.
devalue [di'vælju, B 'di-] *v.t.* desvalorar, desvalorizar, depreciar, devaluar (la moneda).
devastate ['dɛvə,steɪt] *v.t.* devastar, asolar, desolar, arrasar.
devastating [-ɪŋ] *a.* 1. devastador, desolador. 2. abrumador, arrollador.
devastation [,dɛvə'steɪʃən] *s.* devastación, desolación, asolación, arrasamiento.
devel ['dɛvəl] *v.t.* (esco.) aturdir con un golpe. —*s.* golpe aturdidor.
develop [dɪ'vɛləp] *v.t.* 1. desarrollar. 2. adquirir, cobrar (gusto, odio, etc.); revelar (tendencia); dar señales de (falla, desperfecto, etc.); contraer (enfermedad). 3. urbanizar (terreno, distrito, etc.); explotar (mina). 4. (foto.) revelar. 5. (mat.) desarrollar. 6. (mús.) desarrollar, elaborar (un tema). 7. (mil.) desplegar. —*v.i.* 1. desarrollarse, evolucionar; crecer. 2. revelarse, descubrirse. 3. cobrar fuerza, crecer (interés, gusto, odio, etc.).
developer [-ər, B -ə] *s.* (foto.) revelador.
development [-mənt] *s.* 1. desarrollo. 2. tendencia, rumbo, ej., *a new d. in the arts,* una nueva tendencia (o nuevo rumbo) en las artes. 3. ocurrencia, suceso, acontecimiento, ej., *an unexpected d.,* un suceso o acontecimiento inesperado. 4. urbanización. 5. explotación (de una mina). 6. (*tract of new dwellings*) colonia (*un grupo de casas nuevas*). 7. (mat.) desarrollo. 8. (biol.) desarrollo, evolución. 9. (mús.) desarrollo, elaboración (de un tema). 10. (mil.) despliegue (de tropas). 11. (foto.) revelado.
developmental [-,vɛləp'mɛntəl] *a.* 1. de desarrollo (proceso, programa, etc.); para el desarrollo (concesión, ayuda, etc.). 2. experimental (prueba, estado, etc.).
developmental psychology, psicología del desarrollo.
deverbative [dɪ'vɜrbətɪv, B -'vɜbə-] *a.* (gram.) verbal, (derivado) de un verbo, deverbal.
devest [dɪ'vɛst] *v.t.* (der.) despojar.
deviance ['divɪəns] **deviancy** [-ənsɪ] *s.* desviación.
deviant [-ənt] *a.* desviado, descarriado, que no se adhiere a lo considerado normal en un grupo o sociedad. —*s.* persona cuya conducta difiere de lo establecido; invertido, homosexual.
deviate ['divɪ,eɪt] *v.i.* desviarse, apartarse (de una norma, tema, camino, etc.). —*v.t.* desviar. —[-vɪət, -,eɪt] *s.* extravagante; invertido (sexual). —*a.* desviado, extravagante.
deviation [,divɪ'eɪʃən] *s.* 1. desviación, extravío. 2. divergencia. 3. perversión. 4. (mat.) desviación.
deviation clock, (avia.) plataforma de compensación de brújulas.
deviationism [-,ɪzəm] *s.* desviacionismo, desviación de la línea del partido (ideología comunista).
deviation table, (avia.) tabla de desviación.
deviator ['divɪ,eɪtər, B -ə] *s.* desviador; desviacionista.
device [dɪ'vaɪs] *s.* 1. dispositivo, aparato, artefacto, artificio. 2. plan, ardid, estratagema. 3. figura, dibujo, diseño, modelo (de tela o bordado). 4. (her.) carga, emblema. 5. divisa, lema.

6. (*pl.*) voluntad, veleidad, (esp. en) **to leave (one) to one's own devices,** abandonar (a uno) a sus propios recursos, dejar (a uno) que se valga por sí mismo.

devil ['dɛvəl] *s.* 1. diablo. 2. demonio, espíritu maligno. 3. (fig.) diablo, fiera. 4. tío, tipo, ej., *he's a queer d.,* es un tipo raro. 5. *forma abrev. de* **printer's d.,** aprendiz de imprenta. 6. plato muy picante. 7. máquina de moler o triturar; máquina de desgranar; máquina deshilachadora. 8. tormenta de arena (en la India y África). 9. **a d. of a (thing),** (cosa) de todos los diablos, (algo) muy difícil o importuno, ej., *it's a d. of a job,* es un trabajo dificilísimo, *he's a d. of a fellow,* ¡hay que ver qué tipo! *we had a d. of a time there on the island,* pasamos muy mal allá en la isla; **between the d. and the deep blue sea,** entre la espada y la pared; **(to do it) for the d. of it,** (hacerlo) sólo por gusto, sólo porque le da la gana; **like the d.,** como poseído, como llevado por el diablo; **poor d.,** pobre diablo; **talk of the d. (and he will appear),** hablando del rey de Roma (y asomando la corona); **the d.!** ¡qué diablos!; **the d. and all,** por completo; **the d. take the hindmost,** el que se quede en zaga, con el diablo se las haya; quien se quede atrás, que pague el pato; **there will be the d. to pay,** habrá una de todos los diablos; **to be a d. for (drinking, gambling,** etc.), ser muy adicto a (la bebida, juegos de azar, etc.); **to give the d. his due,** para ser justo hasta con el diablo; **to go to the d.,** irse al demonio, arruinarse, ir a la ruina; (*imper.*) ¡váyase al diablo!; **to play the d. with,** estropear, frustrar; maltratar, arruinar; **to raise the d.,** armar la de San Quintín. —*v.t.* (*pret., p.p.* DEVILED o DEVILLED; *p.pr.* DEVILING o DEVILLING) 1. molestar, fastidiar, importunar. 2. (cocina) sazonar fuertemente con picantes; desmenuzar y condimentar. 3. deshilachar (ropas).

deviled eggs ['dɛvəld-] huevos rellenos sazonados.

devilfish ['dɛvəlˌfɪʃ] *s.* 1. (ict.) manta, mortaja voladora, raya murciélago. 2. (zool.) pulpo, octópodo.

devilish ['dɛvəlɪʃ] *a.* 1. diabólico, perverso, malvado. 2. (fam.) extremo, tremendo. —*adv.* (fam.) muy, excesivamente.

devilishly [-lɪ] *adv.* diabólicamente.

devilishness [-nəs] *s.* diablura, perversidad, maldad.

devilkin ['dɛvəlkən] *s.* 1. diablillo. 2. (fam.) niño travieso, picaruelo.

devil-may-care [ˌdɛvəlmeɪ'kɛr, B 'dɛv--'kɛə] *a.* 1. irresponsable, indisciplinado, bohemio. 2. temerario, audaz, osado.

devilment ['dɛvəlmənt] *s.* 1. diablura, travesura. 2. maldad, perversidad.

devilry [-rɪ] *s.* (*pl.* DEVILRIES) 1. maldad, iniquidad, crueldad, perversidad. 2. brujería, magia, arte diabólico. 3. diablura, travesura. 4. atrevimiento, osadía; picardía, diversión.

devil's advocate, (relig., fig.) abogado del diablo.

devil's cotton, (bot.) abroma.

devil's darning needle, 1. (ento.) caballito del diablo, libélula. 2. (bot.) peine de Venus.

devil's food cake, (cocina) torta de chocolate.

Devil's Island, Isla del Diablo (en la Guayana francesa).

deviltry ['dɛvəltrɪ] *var. de* **devilry,** picardía, diversión.

devilwood [-ˌwʊd] *s.* (bot.) variedad de pequeño olivo.

devious ['divɪəs] *a.* 1. (lit., fig.) tortuoso (camino, mente, persona, etc.). 2. desviado, descarriado, errado. 3. apartado, remoto. 4. insincero, engañoso.

deviously [-lɪ] *adv.* tortuosamente.

deviousness [-nəs] *s.* (lit., fig.) tortuosidad.

devisable [dɪ'vaɪzəbəl] *a.* 1. imaginable, lo que se puede idear. 2. (der.) transferible por herencia.

devisal [-zəl] *s.* (der.) legado (de bienes raíces).

devise [dɪ'vaɪz] *v.t.* 1. trazar, idear, inventar, ingeniar, planear. 2. (der.) legar (bienes raíces). —*s.* (der.) legado; testamento (por el que se legan bienes raíces).

devisee [ˌdɛvə'zi, dɪˌvaɪ-] *s.* (der.) legatario (que hereda bienes raíces).

deviser [dɪ'vaɪzər, B -ə] *s.* inventor, autor.

devisor [ˌdɛvə'zɔr, dɪ'vaɪzər, B ˌdɛvɪ'zɔ] *s.* (der.) testador (que deja un legado de bienes raíces).

devitalize [di'vaɪtəlˌaɪz] *v.t.* debilitar; restar vitalidad.

devitrify [di'vɪtrəˌfaɪ] *v.t.* (*pret., p.p.* DEVITRIFIED; *p.pr.* DEVITRIFYING) desvitrificar, quitar brillo o transparencia al vidrio.

devocalize [di'voʊkəˌlaɪz] *v.t.* (fon.) ensordecer.

devoice [di'vɔɪs, B 'di-] *v.t.* (fon.) ensordecer.

devoid [dɪ'vɔɪd] *a.* (con *of*) falto, desprovisto, exento, libre (de).

devoir [dəv'war, B 'dɛvˌwa] *s.* deber, obligación; (*pl.*) cumplidos, cortesía.

devolution [ˌdɛvə'luʃən, B ˌdi-] *s.* 1. (der.) entrega, traspaso, transferencia (esp. por herencia o sucesión), delegación (de trabajo o poder). 2. (der.) retrocesión. 3. (biol.) degeneración, desarrollo retrógrado.

devolve [dɪ'vɑlv, B -'vɔlv] *v.i.* 1. (con *to* o *upon*) tocar, incumbir, corresponder (a). 2. (ant.) rodar hacia adelante o hacia abajo. 3. recaer por derecho de sucesión (en alguien). —*v.t.* (con *upon*) traspasar, transferir (deber, trabajo, etc.); entregar; legar.

Devonian [dɪ'voʊnɪən, B dɛ-] *a.* (geol.) devoniano, devónico. —*s.* (geol.) devoniano; edad devoniana.

devote [dɪ'voʊt] *v.t.* dedicar; consagrar; **d. oneself to,** dedicarse a, entregarse a (una tarea, causa, etc.). —*a.* (ant.) dedicado.

devoted [-əd] *a.* 1. devoto, piadoso, ferviente. 2. devoto, leal (amigo). 3. (con *to*) dedicado, adicto, afecto (a). 4. (con *to*) destinado, dedicado, consagrado (a).

devotedly [-lɪ] *adv.* devotamente.

devotedness [-nəs] *s.* devoción, abnegación; dedicación, celo.

devotee [ˌdɛvə'ti, -'teɪ, B -'ti] *s.* devoto, partidario; fanático (esp. religioso).

devotion [dɪ'voʊʃən] *s.* 1. devoción, fervor. 2. (con *to*) dedicación (a), celo (en trabajo, estudio, etc.); lealtad (a un amigo), afecto (a familia, etc.). 3. (*pl.*) oraciones, súplicas. 4. **book of devotions,** devocionario.

devotional [-əl] *a.* devoto, piadoso. —*s.* oficio religioso de corta duración.

devotionally [-ɪ] *adv.* devotamente, piadosamente.

devour [dɪ'vaʊr, B -'vaʊə] *v.t.* 1. devorar, tragar. 2. (fig.) devorar, consumir; aniquilar. 3. (fig.) devorar (ej., un libro). 4. **to be devoured by,** estar consumido o agobiado por (ansiedad, miedo, etc.).

devourer [-ər, B -rə] *s.* devorador; tragón; destructor.

devouringly [-'vaʊrɪŋlɪ, B -'vaʊər-] *adv.* devoradoramente.

devout [dɪ'vaʊt] *a.* 1. devoto, piadoso, pío, fervoroso. 2. sincero, cordial (amigo, felicitación, etc.).

devoutly [-lɪ] *adv.* devotamente, piadosamente.

devoutness [-nəs] *s.* piedad, devoción.

dew [du, B dju] *s.* 1. rocío. 2. (fig.) flor, frescura (de la juventud, inocencia, etc.). 3. humedad que aparece en pequeñas gotas (ej., lágrimas, sudor, etc.). 4. (bot.) sudor (de las plantas). —*v.i.* rociar. —*v.t.* cubrir o bañar de rocío.

dewan [dɪ'wɑn] *s.* (India) oficial jefe o administrador; gobernador de distrito; primer ministro (de un estado).

dewar flask ['duər-, B 'djuə-] *s.* (quím.) frasco de Dewar.

dewberry ['duˌbɛrɪ, B 'dju-] *s.* 1. (bot.) zarza. 2. zarzamora.

dewclaw [-ˌklɔ] *s.* espolón (de ciervo, jabalí, etc.).

dewdrop [-ˌdrɑp, B -ˌdrɔp] *s.* gota de rocío.

Dewey decimal classification [ˌduɪ-, B 'djuɪ-] sistema de clasificación decimal de Dewey.

dewfall ['duˌfɔl, B 'dju-] *s.* 1. caída del rocío. 2. horas antes del amanecer (cuando cae el rocío).

dewlap [-ˌlæp] *s.* papada (de algunos animales, como buey, toro, perro); barba (de pájaros).

dewlapped [-ˌlæpt] *a.* papudo.

DEW line, (Distant Early Warning) grupo de estaciones de radar al norte del Océano Glacial Ártico.

dew point, (fís.) punto de rocío, temperatura de condensación (del vapor).

dew worm, lombriz de tierra (usada como carnada).

dewy ['duɪ, B 'djuɪ] *a.* 1. rociado. 2. (fig.) fresco, puro, virginal; radiante.

dewy-eyed [-'aɪd] *a.* inocente y confiado.

dexamyl ['dɛksəmɪl] *s.* (farm.) mezcla de dextroanfetamina y amobarbital que se usa para el tratamiento de la obesidad.

dexedrine [-ˌdrin] *s.* (farm.) dextroanfetamina.

dexiotropic ['dɛksɪə'trɑpɪk, B -'trɔp-] **dexiotropous** [-'ɑtrəpəs, B -'ɔ-] *a* (zool.) dextrotrópico, dexiotrópico.

dexter ['dɛkstər, B -stə] *a.* 1. diestro, derecho. 2. (her.) diestro (lado del escudo, a la derecha de la persona que lo lleva). 3. (ant.) diestro, propicio.

dexterity [dɛk'stɛrətɪ] *s.* 1. destreza, agilidad, maña, habilidad. 2. agilidad mental, prontitud. 3. (ant.) empleo de la mano derecha.

dexterous ['dɛkstərəs] *a.* diestro, hábil, experto, ducho, ágil.

dexterously [-lɪ] *adv.* diestramente, hábilmente.

dexterousness [-nəs] *s.* destreza, habilidad, acierto.

dextral ['dɛkstrəl] *a.* 1. derecho, diestro. 2. dextrómano.

dextrally [-strəlɪ] *adv.* diestramente.

dextran ['dɛkˌstræn, -strən] *s.* (quím.) dextran.

dextrin [-strən] **dextrine** [-ˌstrin, -strən] *s.* (quím.) dextrina.

dextroamphetamine [ˌdɛkstroʊæm'fɛtəˌmin] *s.* (farm.) dextroanfetamina (droga que se usa para controlar el apetito).

dextrocardia [ˌdɛkstrə'kɑrdɪə, B -'kɑd-] *s.* (med.) dexiocardia.

dextroglucose [-'gluˌkoʊs, -ˌkoʊz] *s.* (quím.) dextroglucosa.

dextrogyrate [-'dʒaɪrˌeɪt, B -'dʒaɪər-] **dextrogyratory** [-əˌtɔrɪ, B -ətərɪ] **dextrogyre** ['dɛkstrəˌdʒaɪr, B -ˌdʒaɪə] **dextrogyrous** [ˌdɛkstrə'dʒaɪrəs, B -dʒa-ɪər-] *s., a.* (fís.) dextrógiro, dextrorrotatorio.

dextrorotation [ˌdɛkstrəroʊ'teɪʃən] *s.* (fís., quím.) rotación hacia la derecha.

dextrorotatory [-'roʊtəˌtɔrɪ, B -tətərɪ] *a.* dextrorrotatorio, dextrógiro.

dextrorse ['dɛk,strɔrs, B -,strɔs] *a.* (bot.) dextrorso.
dextrose ['dɛk,strous] *s.* (quím.) dextrosa, dextroglucosa, azúcar de uva.
dextrous ['dɛkstrəs] **dextrously** [-lɪ] **dextrousness** [-nəs] *vars. de* **dexterous, dexterously, dexterousness.**
dey [deɪ] *s.* (hist.) dey, título del jefe o príncipe musulmán que gobernaba la regencia de Argel.
D.F.A. *abrev. de* **Doctor of Fine Arts,** Doctor en Bellas Artes.
dg. *abrev. de* **decigram,** decigramo (dg.).
dharma ['dɜrmə, B 'dɑmə] *s.* (hinduismo, budismo) dharma, orden cósmico que incluye los principios naturales y morales que atañen a los seres y las cosas.
dhole [doʊl] *s.* perro salvaje de la India.
dhoti, dhooti ['doʊtɪ] *s.* (India) prenda de atuendo masculino.
dhow [daʊ] *s.* embarcación árabe de un solo mástil.
dia *abrev. de* **diameter,** diámetro.
diabase ['daɪə,beɪs] *s.* (geol.) diabasa.
diabetes [,daɪə'bitiz, -əs, B -iz] *s.* (med.) diabetes.
diabetes insipidus [-ɪn'sɪpədəs] (med.) diabetes insípida.
diabetes mellitus [-'mɛlətəs] (med.) diabetes mellitus.
diabetic [-'bɛtɪk] *a., s.* diabético.
diablerie [dɪ'ɑbləri] *s.* (fr.) 1. hechicería, magia negra. 2. demonología. 3. diablura; temeridad.
diabolic [,daɪə'bɑlɪk, B -'bɔl-] **diabolical** [-ɪkəl] *a.* diabólico.
diabolically [-ɪkəlɪ] *adv.* diabólicamente.
diabolicalness [-kəlnəs] *s.* perversidad, carácter diabólico.
diabolism [daɪ'æbə,lɪzəm] *s.* 1. magia negra, hechicería, brujería. 2. demonolatría. 3. malevolencia, perversidad.
diabolist [-ləst] *s.* demonólatra.
diabolize [-,laɪz] *v.t.* representar como diabólico; someter a influencia diabólica.
diabolo [dɪ'æbə,loʊ, B -'ɑb-] *s.* (*pl.* DIABOLOS) diábolo.
diacaustic [,daɪə'kɔstɪk] *a.* (fís.) diacáustico.
diacetylmorphine [,daɪə,sitəl'mɔr,fin, B -'mɔ,-] *s.* (farm.) heroína.
diachrony [daɪ'ækrənɪ] *s.* (filol.) diacronía.
diachylon [-'ækə,lɑn, B -,lɔn] **diachylum** [-ləm] *s.* (farm.) diaquilón.
diacid [-'æsəd] *s.* (quím.) diácido.
diaconal [-'ækənəl] *a.* diaconal.
diaconate [-ənət] *s.* diaconato.
diacoustics [,daɪə'kustɪks] *s. pl.* (*sing. en const.*) diacústica.
diacritic [-'krɪtɪk] *a.* (med., fon.) diacrítico. —*s.* (fon.) signo diacrítico, punto diacrítico.
diacritical [-ɪkəl] *a.* (med., fon.) diacrítico.
diacritical mark, (gram.) signo diacrítico.
diactinic [,daɪ,æk'tɪnɪk] *a.* (fís.) diactínico.
diactinism [daɪ'æktə,nɪzəm] *s.* (fís.) diactinismo.
diadelphous [,daɪə'dɛlfəs] *a.* (bot.) diadelfo.
diadem ['daɪə,dɛm, -dəm] *s.* diadema. —*v.t.* adornar o coronar con una diadema.
diadromous [daɪ'ædrəməs] *a.* (ict.) diadromo.
diaeresis [daɪ'ɛrəsəs, B -'ɪər-] *s.* (*pl.* DIAERESES [-,siz]) (fon.) diéresis.
diageotropism [,daɪədʒɪ'ɑtrə,pɪzəm, B -'ɔ-] **diageotropy** [-pɪ] *s.* (bot.) diageotropismo.
diagnose ['daɪəg,noʊs, -,noʊz, B -,noʊz] *v.t.* diagnosticar. —*v.i.* hacer un diagnóstico.
diagnosis [,daɪəg'noʊsəs] *s.* (*pl.* DIAGNOSES [-,siz] 1. (med.) diagnosis. 2. (bot., zool.) diagnosis.

diagnostic [-'nɑstɪk, B -'nɔs-] *s., a.* (med.) diagnóstico.
diagnosticate [-tɪ,keɪt] *v.t., v.i.* diagnosticar.
diagnostician [-,nɑs'tɪʃən, B -,nɔs-] *s.* experto en hacer diagnósticos.
diagonal [daɪ'ægənəl] *a., s.* diagonal.
diagonally [-ɪ] *adv.* diagonalmente.
diagram ['daɪə,græm] *s.* diagrama, esquema. —*v.t.* (*pret., p.p.* DIAGRAMED O DIAGRAMMED; *p.pr.* DIAGRAMING O DIAGRAMMING) representar o demostrar por diagrama.
diagrammatic [,daɪəgrə'mætɪk] **diagrammatical** [-ɪkəl] *a.* esquemático, gráfico.
diagrammatically [-ɪkəlɪ] *adv.* gráficamente, por medio de diagramas.
diagraph ['daɪə,græf, B -,grɑf] *s.* diágrafo.
diakinesis [,daɪəkə'nisəs, -kaɪ-] *s.* (biol.) diacinesis.
diakinetic [-'nɛtɪk] *a.* (biol.) diacinético.
dial ['daɪəl] *s.* 1. cuadrante, esfera (de un instrumento, medidor, etc.); esfera, muestra (de reloj); cuadrante (del reloj solar). 2. disco selector, disco de marcar (del teléfono). 3. (rad.) cuadrante, dial. 4. botón regulador; (rad.) botón de sintonización. 5. (jer., G.B.) jeta, hocico, cara (de una persona). —*v.t.* (*pret., p.p.* DIALED O DIALLED; *p.pr.* DIALING O DIALLING) 1. llamar por teléfono. 2. (rad.) sintonizar (emisora, programa). —*v.i.* marcar un número de teléfono, hacer una llamada.
dialect ['daɪə,lɛkt] *s.* 1. dialecto. 2. jerga, lenguaje (de una profesión o ciencia).
dialectal [,daɪə'lɛktəl] *a.* dialectal.
dialectic [-tɪk] *s.* dialéctica; (*pl.*) dialéctica. —*a.* dialéctico.
dialectical [-tɪkəl] *a.* dialéctico.
dialectical materialism, (filos.) materialismo dialéctico, p. ext. marxismo.
dialectician [-,lɛk'tɪʃən] *s.* 1. dialéctico. 2. estudiante de dialectos.
dialecticism [-'ɛktə,sɪzəm] *s.* 1. práctica de la dialéctica. 2. dialectalismo.
dialectologist [-,lɛk'tɑlədʒəst, B -'tɔl-] *s.* especialista en dialectología.
dialectology [-dʒɪ] *s.* dialectología.
dial gage, indicador de cuadrante; (ing.) manómetro.
diallage ['daɪəlɪdʒ] *s.* (min.) diálaga.
dialogic [,daɪə'lɑdʒɪk, B -'lɔdʒ-] **dialogical** [-ɪkəl] *a.* dialogal, dialogístico.
dialogism [daɪ'ælə,dʒɪzəm] *s.* (ret.) dialogismo.
dialogist [-dʒəst] *s.* 1. dialoguista, escritor de diálogos. 2. interlocutor.
dialogistic [,daɪəloʊ'dʒɪstɪk] *a.* dialogístico.
dialogue, dialog ['daɪə,lɔg, -,lɑg, B -,lɔg] *s.* diálogo; interlocución, conversación, coloquio. —*v.i.* dialogar, dialogizar.
Dialogue Mass, (relig.) misa dialogada.
dial telephone, teléfono automático (de comunicación directa).
dial tone, (tele.) tono de marcar, señal de línea libre.
dialysis [daɪ'æləsəs] *s.* (*pl.* DIALYSES [-,siz]) (quím.) diálisis.
dialytic [,daɪə'lɪtɪk] *a.* (quím.) dialítico.
dialyze ['daɪə,laɪz] *v.t.* (quím.) dializar.
dialyzer [-,laɪzər, B -zə] *s.* (quím.) dializador.
diamagnet ['daɪə,mægnət] *s.* (fís.) substancia diamagnética.
diamagnetic [,daɪə,mæg'nɛtɪk] *a.* (fís.) diamagnético.
diamagnetism [-'mægnə,tɪzəm] *s.* diamagnetismo.
diamantiferous [-mən'tɪfərəs, B -mæn-] *a.* diamantífero.

diamantine [-'mæntaɪn, B -tɪn] *a.* diamantino.
diameter [daɪ'æmətər, B -ə] *s.* (geom.) diámetro.
diameter pitch, diámetro del círculo primitivo.
diametral [-ətrəl] *a.* diametral.
diametral pitch, (avia.) módulo.
diametric [,daɪə'mɛtrɪk] **diametrical** [-trɪkəl] *a.* diametral.
diametrically [-əlɪ] *adv.* diametralmente.
diamine ['daɪə,min, B -,maɪn] *s.* (bioquím.) diamina.
diamond ['daɪmənd, -əmənd] *s.* 1. diamante. 2. rombo, losange. 3. (béisbol) campo de juego; cuadrado. 4. (naipes) diamante, carró (Esp.). 5. (tip.) perla (tipo de letra de 4 o 41/2 puntos). 6. **d. in the rough,** (lit., fig.) diamante en bruto. —*v.t.* adornar con diamantes.
diamond anniversary, sexagésimo o septuagésimo quinto aniversario.
diamondback [-,bæk] *s.* (zool.) culebra de cascabel, crótalo. —*a.* de dorso con rombos (díc. de la culebra de cascabel y de la tortuga).
diamondback terrapin, (zool.) tortuga emis, emis de dorso con rombos.
diamond cutter, diamantista.
diamond-drill [-,drɪl] *s.* taladro de diamantes, broca con punta de diamantes.
diamond shape, (ing.) romboide.
Diana [daɪ'ænə] *s.* (mitol.) Diana, diosa de la luna y de la caza, identificada por los romanos con la griega Artemisa.
diandrous [-'ændrəs] *a.* (bot.) diandro.
dianoetic [,daɪənoʊ'ɛtɪk] *s.* (filos.) dianoética, dianoética.
dianthus [daɪ'ænθəs] *s.* (bot.) (cualquier especie de) clavel.
diapason [,daɪə'peɪzən, -'peɪs-] *s.* 1. (mús.) diapasón. 2. (fig.) notas, melodía. 3. diapasón, horquilla para afinar. 4. registro de fondo (del órgano).
diapause ['daɪə,pɔz] *s.* período de letargo (entre períodos de actividad, esp. en ciertos insectos).
diapedesis [,daɪəpə'disəs] *s.* (*pl.* DIAPEDESES [-,siz]) (med.) diapédesis.
diaper ['daɪpər, B -əpə] *s.* 1. pañal, culero, braga, metedor. 2. toalla, servilleta. 3. (tej.) lienzo adamascado. 4. (arte) arabesco, adorno de figuras repetidas (gen. geométricas). —*v.t.* 1. adornar con arabescos. 2. envolver en pañales (a una criatura).
diapered [-pərd, B -pəd] *a.* (her.) diapreado.
diaper rash, salpullido, escaldadura (en los bebés).
diaphaneity [daɪ,æfə'niətɪ] *s.* diafanidad, transparencia.
diaphanometer [daɪ,æfə'nɑmətər, B -'nɔmɪtə] *s.* (litog.) diafanómetro, opacímetro.
diaphanous [-'æfənəs] *a.* diáfano, transparente.
diaphanously [-lɪ] *adv.* diáfanamente.
diaphone ['daɪə,foʊn] *s.* 1. (mar.) sirena de niebla de dos tonos. 2. (fon.) doble tono.
diaphoresis [,daɪəfə'risəs] *s.* (*pl.* DIAPHORESES [-,siz]) (med.) diaforesis, sudor.
diaphoretic [-'rɛtɪk] *a.* (med.) diaforético, sudorífico. —*s.* agente diaforético o sudorífico.
diaphragm ['daɪə,fræm] *s.* 1. (anat., bot., zool.) diafragma. 2. diafragma anticonceptivo. 3. (tec., foto.) diafragma. —*v.t.* 1. proveer de diafragma. 2. (foto.) diafragmar.
diaphragmatic [,daɪə,fæg'mætɪk] *a.* diafragmático.
diaphragm pump, bomba de membrana, bomba de diafragma.
diaphyseal, diaphysial [-'fɪzɪəl] *a.* (anat.) diafisario.

diaphysis [daɪ'æfəsəs] *s.* (*pl.* DIAPHYSES [-ˌsiz]) (anat.) diáfisis.
diapophysis [ˌdaɪə'pɑfəsəs, B -'pɔf-] *s.* (*pl.* DIAPOPHYSES [-ˌsiz]) (anat., zool.) diapófisis.
diapositive [-'pɑzətɪv, B -'pɔz-] *s.* (foto.) diapositiva, transparencia.
diapsid [daɪ'æpsəd] *a.* (zool.) diápsido.
diarchy ['daɪˌɑrkɪ, B -ˌɑkɪ] *a.* diarquía, gobierno entre dos mandatarios.
diarist ['daɪərəst] *s.* diarista, persona que lleva un diario.
diarrhea, diarrhoea [ˌdaɪə'riə, B -'rɪə] *s.* (med.) diarrea.
diarrheal, diarrhoeal [-riəl] **diarrheic, diarrhoeic** [-ɪk] *a.* (med.) diarreico.
diarthrosis [ˌdaɪˌɑr'θroʊsəs, B -ˌɑ'-] *s.* (*pl.* DIARTHROSES [-ˌsiz]) (anat.) diartrosis.
diary ['daɪərɪ] *s.* diario (relación periódica).
diascordium [ˌdaɪə'skɔrdɪəm, B -'skɔd-] *s.* (farm.) diascordio.
Diaspora [daɪ'æspərə] *s.* diáspora, diseminación de los judíos por toda la extensión del mundo antiguo.
diaspore ['daɪəˌspɔr, B -ˌspɔ] *s.* (min.) diásporo.
diastase [-ˌsteɪs] *s.* (bioquím.) diastasa; enzima.
diastasis [daɪ'æstəsəs] *s.* (*pl.* DIASTASES [-ˌsiz]) (med.) diastasis.
diastatic [ˌdaɪə'stætɪk] *a.* (bioquím.) diastásico.
diastem ['daɪəˌstɛm] *s.* (geol.) diastema.
diastema [ˌdaɪə'stimə] *s.* (*pl.* DIASTEMATA [-tə]) (anat.) diastema, espacio interdental (esp. entre los caninos y los dientes laterales de la mandíbula superior).
diaster ['daɪˌæstər, B daɪ'æstə] *s.* (biol.) diáster.
diastole [daɪ'æstəli, B -lɪ] *s.* 1. (fisiol.) diástole (del corazón o las arterias). 2. (poét.) diástole.
diastolic [ˌdaɪə'stɑlɪk, B -'stɔl-] *a.* (fisiol.) diastólico.
diastrophism [daɪ'æstrəˌfɪzəm] *s.* (geol.) diastrofismo.
diastyle ['daɪəˌstaɪl] *s.* (arq.) diástilo.
diathermancy [ˌdaɪə'θɜrmənsɪ, B -'θɜmən-] *s.* (fís.) diatermancia.
diathermanous [-mənəs] *a.* (fís.) diatérmano, diatérmico.
diathermia [-mɪə] *var. de* **diathermy.**
diathermic [-mɪk] *a.* (fís.) diatérmico.
diathermize [-ˌmaɪz] *v.t.* tratar con diatermia.
diathermy ['daɪəˌθɜrmɪ, B -θəmɪ] *s.* (med.) diatermia.
diathesis [daɪ'æθəsəs] *s.* (*pl.* DIATHESES [-ˌsiz]) (med.) diátesis.
diathetic [ˌdaɪə'θɛtɪk] *a.* (med.) diatésico.
diatom ['daɪəˌtɑm, B -təm] *s.* (bot.) diatomea.
diatomaceous [ˌdaɪətə'meɪʃəs] *a.* (bot.) diatomáceas.
diatomaceous earth, (geol., min.) diatomita, tierra de infusorios.
diatomic [-'tɑmɪk, B -'tɔm-] *a.* (quím.) diatómico.
diatomite [daɪ'ætəˌmaɪt] *s.* (geol., pal.) diatomita, kieselguhr, harina de diatomeas, trípoli.
diatonic [ˌdaɪə'tɑnɪk, B -'tɔn-] *a.* (mús.) diatónico.
diatonically [-ɪkəlɪ] *adv.* (mús.) diatónicamente.
diatonicism [-əˌsɪzəm] *s.* diatonismo.
diatonic scale, (mús.) escala diatónica.
diatonic semitone, (mús.) semitono diatónico, semitono mayor.
diatribe ['daɪəˌtraɪb] *s.* diatriba.
diatropic [ˌdaɪə'trɑpɪk, B -'trɔp-] *a.* (bot.) diatrópico.
diatropism [daɪ'ætrəˌpɪzəm] *s.* (bot.) diatropismo.
diazine ['daɪəˌzin] *s.* (quím.) diazina.
diazonium [ˌdaɪə'zoʊnɪəm] *s.* (quím.) diazonio.
dib [dɪb] *v.i.* (*pret., p.p.* DIBBED; *p.pr.* DIBBING) pescar con carnada flotante.
dibasic [daɪ'beɪsɪk] *a.* (quím.) dibásico.
dibber ['dɪbər, B -ə] *var. de* **dibble.**
dibble ['dɪbəl] *s.* plantador, almocafre (para plantar). —*v.t.* 1. plantar con almocafre. 2. hacer huecos en (la tierra).
dibble, *v.i., var. de* **dib.**
Dibranchia [daɪ'bræŋkɪə] **Dibranchiata** [-ˌbræŋkɪ'ɑtə] *s. pl.* (zool.) dibranquio, dibranquios.
dibranchiate [-'bræŋkɪət] *a., s.* (zool.) dibranquio, dibranquial.
dibs [dɪbz] *s. pl.* (jer.) 1. dinero (esp. en pequeña cantidad). 2. (G.B.) cantillos, taba (juego). 3. **d. on (something),** demandas, reclamaciones, derechos (sobre algo).
dicast ['daɪˌkæst, B 'dɪ-] *s.* (hist.) dicasta, un jurado en la Atenas antigua.
dice [daɪs] *s.* (*pl.* DICE) dados, partida o juego de dados; **no d.,** (jer.) nada que hacer, de ninguna manera; **to load the d.,** hacer trampa. —*v.t.* 1. perder, malgastar (fortuna, etc.) jugando a los dados. 2. cortar (algo) en cubitos. 3. marcar con figuras de dados. —*v.i.* jugar a los dados.
dice box, cubilete (de dados).
dicentra [daɪ'sɛntrə] *s.* (bot.) dicentra.
dicer ['daɪsər, B -ə] *s.* 1. jugador de dados. 2. máquina cortadora (de frutas, patatas, zanahoria, etc.).
dichasial [daɪ'keɪʒəl, B -zɪəl] *a.* dicásico.
dichasium [-zɪəm] *s.* (*pl.* DICHASIA [-zɪə]) (bot.) dicasio.
dichlamydeous [ˌdaɪklə'mɪdɪəs] *a.* (bot.) diclamídeo.
dichloride [daɪ'klɔrˌaɪd] *s.* (quím.) compuesto diclorado, bicloruro.
dichogamous [-'kɑgəməs, B -'kɔg-] *a.* (bot.) dicógamo.
dichogamy [-mɪ] *s.* (bot.) dicogamia.
dichotomize [-'kɑtəˌmaɪz, B -'kɔt-] *v.t., v.i.* separar(se) o dividir(se) en dos.
dichotomous [-məs] *a.* dicotómico, dividido en dos.
dichotomy [-mɪ] *s.* (*pl.* DICHOTOMIES) (astr., biol., bot., lóg.) dicotomía.
dichroic [-'kroʊɪk] *a.* (fís.) dicroico.
dichroism ['daɪkroʊˌɪzəm] *s.* (fís.) dicroísmo, dicromatismo.
dichroite [-ˌaɪt] *s.* (min.) dicroíta, cordiorita.
dichromat [-ˌmæt] *s.* (med.) persona afectada por dicromatopsia.
dichromate [daɪ'kroʊˌmeɪt] *s.* (quím.) bicromato, dicromato.
dichromatic [ˌdaɪkroʊ'mætɪk] *a.* 1. (biol.) dicromático. 2. (fís.) dicroico.
dichromatism [daɪ'kroʊməˌtɪzəm] *s.* 1. (fís.) dicroísmo, dicromatismo. 2. (fisiol.) dicromatopsia.
dichromatopsia [-ˌkroʊmə'tɑpsɪə, B -'tɔp-] *s.* (fisiol.) dicromatopsia.
dichromic acid [-'kroʊmɪk-] (quím.) ácido bicrómico.
dichroscope ['daɪkrəˌskoʊp] *s.* (fís.) dicroscopio.
dick [dɪk] *s.* 1. (jer. & ant.) polizonte, detective. 2. (fam., vulg.) pene, verga, polla.
dickcissel [dɪk'sɪsəl] *s.* (orn.) calandria de pecho negro.
dickens ['dɪkənz] *s.* (fam.) diablo, demonio; **the d.!** ¡demontre! ¡diantre! ¡caramba!
Dickensian [dɪ'kɛnzɪən] *a.* perteneciente o relativo a los personajes en la obra de Charles Dickens, novelista inglés.
dicker ['dɪkər, B -ə] *v.i.* (E.U.) regatear, cambalachear, trocar. —*s.* 1. (E.U.) regateo, cambalache, trueque. 2. decena (de pieles o cueros).
dickey, dicky ['dɪkɪ] *s.* (*pl.* DICKEYS; DICKIES) 1. camisolín; pechera postiza. 2. (G.B.) delantal, mandil. 3. pajarito. 4. babero. 5. asno. 6. (aut., G.B.) asiento del conductor; asiento auxiliar trasero.
Dick test, (med.) prueba de Dick, para demostrar la inmunidad a la escarlatina.
dicky ['dɪkɪ] *a.* (jer., G.B.) decaído, débil, enfermizo.
diclinous [daɪ'klaɪnəs, B 'daɪklɪ-] *a.* (bot.) diclino.
dicot ['daɪˌkɑt, B -ˌkɔt] **dicotyl** [-əl] *formas abreviadas de* **dicotyledon.**
dicotyledon [ˌdaɪˌkɑtəl'idən, B -ˌkɔt-] *s.* (bot.) dicotiledón, dicotiledóneo.
dicotyledoneous [-əs] *a.* (bot.) dicotiledóneo.
dicoumarin [daɪ'kumərən] *s.* (quím., med.) dicumarol.
dicrotic [-'krɑtɪk, B -'krɔt-] *a.* (med.) dicroto.
dicrotism ['daɪkrəˌtɪzəm] *s.* (med.) dicrotismo.
dict. *abrev. de* **dictionary,** diccionario.
dicta ['dɪktə] *pl. de* **dictum.**
Dictaphone ['dɪktəˌfoʊn] *s.* dictáfono.
dictate ['dɪkˌteɪt, dɪk'teɪt, B dɪk'teɪt] *v.t.* 1. dictar (una carta, etc.). 2. ordenar, mandar. 3. imponer, prescribir, preceptuar, ej., *d. terms,* imponer condiciones. —*v.i.* 1. dictar una carta. 2. dar o imponer órdenes; imponerse. — ['dɪkˌteɪt] *s.* 1. (*gen. en pl.*) dictados (del corazón, de la razón, etc.). 2. mandato, precepto, orden.
dictating machine [-ɪŋ-] dictáfono.
dictation [dɪk'teɪʃən] *s.* 1. dictado (de una carta, etc.). 2. mandato, orden arbitraria. 3. **to take d.,** escribir al dictado, tomar dictado.
dictator ['dɪkˌteɪtər, dɪk'teɪt-, B dɪk'teɪtə] *s.* 1. dictador. 2. el que dicta (cartas, etc.).
dictatorial [ˌdɪktə'tɔrɪəl] *a.* dictatorial, dictatorio.
dictatorially [-ɪəlɪ] *adv.* dictatorialmente.
dictatorship [dɪk'teɪtərˌʃɪp, B -əˌʃɪp] *s.* dictadura.
diction ['dɪkʃən] *s.* dicción.
dictionary ['dɪkʃəˌnɛrɪ, B -ʃənrɪ] *s.* diccionario; **d. English,** inglés pedantesco; **walking** (o **living**) **d.,** enciclopedia ambulante.
Dictograph ['dɪktəˌgræf, B -ˌgrɑf] *s.* dictógrafo, aparato telefónico para grabar o escuchar conversaciones secretamente.
dictum ['dɪktəm] *s.* (*pl.* DICTA [-tə] O DICTUMS) 1. sentencia, máxima, aforismo. 2. (der.) dictamen legal.
dicyanine [daɪ'saɪəˌnin] *s.* (foto.) dicianina.
did [dɪd] *pret. de* **do.**
didact ['daɪdækt] *s.* didacta.
didactic [daɪ'dæktɪk, B dɪ-] **didactical** [-tɪkəl] *a.* didáctico.
didactically [-kəlɪ] *adv.* didácticamente.
didacticism [-təˌsɪzəm] *s.* 1. estilo o método didáctico. 2. pedantismo, pedantería.
didactics [-tɪks] *s. pl.* (*sing. en const.*) didáctica.
didapper ['daɪˌdæpər, B -ə] *s.* (orn.) somorgujo; colimbo.
diddle ['dɪdəl] *v.t.* 1. menear, agitar rápidamente. 2. desperdiciar, perder (tiempo). 3. (jer.) engañar, defraudar. —*v.i.* haronear, haraganear, malgastar el tiempo.
diddler ['dɪdlər, B -lə] *s.* embustero, impostor.
didelphic [daɪ'dɛlfɪk] *a.* 1. (anat.) didelfo. 2. (zool.) didelfo, marsupial.

didn't [ˈdɪdənt] *contr. de* **did not.**
dido [ˈdaɪdoʊ] *s.* (*pl.* DIDOES o DIDOS) (E.U.) travesura, jugarreta, treta.
didrachma [daɪˈdrækmə] *s.* (*pl.* DIDRACHMAS o DIDRACHMAE [-ˌmi]) (numis.) didracma.
didymium [-ˈdɪmɪəm, B dɪ-] *s.* (min.) didimio.
didymous [ˈdɪdəməs] *a.* (bot., zool.) dídimo.
didymus [-məs] *s.* (zool.) dídimo, testículo.
die [daɪ] *v.i.* (*pret., p.p.* DIED; *p.pr.* DYING) 1. morir; expirar, fallecer, fenecer. 2. extinguirse, acabarse, desaparecer. 3. (fig.) morirse, morir (de frío, sed, cansancio, etc.). 4. apagarse, pararse (ej., un motor). 5. **d. a hero, a martyr, a beggar,** etc., morir como un héroe, mártir, mendigo, etc.; **d. away,** extinguirse gradualmente (esp. sonido o fuego); desmayarse; **d. down,** apagarse, acabarse (lentamente), extinguirse gradualmente; amainar (viento); **d. from,** morir de; **d. hard,** persistir, perdurar (rumores, oposición), resistir tenazmente (conservatismo, etc.); **d. in (one's) bed,** morir en la cama (por vejez o enfermedad); **d. in one's boots, d. with one's boots on,** morir al pie del cañón; **d. laughing,** morirse de risa; **d. like flies,** morir como moscas; **d. off,** ir muriendo, morir uno tras otro; **d. out,** extinguirse (razas, especies); pasarse de moda; apagarse (fuego); **never say d.,** ¡nunca te rindas!; **to be dying for (someone o something),** morirse por (alguien o algo); **to be dying to (do something),** morirse por (hacer algo).
die, *s.* (*pl.* DICE [daɪs] o DIES [daɪz]) 1. (*pl.* DICE) dado (para jugar). 2. (*ú. gen. en pl.*) cubito, cubo pequeño (de carne, zanahoria, etc.). 3. (*pl.* DIES) (arq.) dado, neto. 4. (mec.) cuño, matriz, troquel; molde, estampa; hembra de terraja, cojinete de roscar. 5. **the d. is cast,** la suerte está echada. —*v.t.* (*pret., p.p.* DIED; *p.pr.* DIEING) cortar o estampar con troquel.
die-cast [ˈdaɪˌkæst, B -ˌkɑst] *v.t.* fundir al troquel, moldear en matriz, fundir a presión; troquelar, estampar.
diecious, dieciously, *var. de* **dioecious, dioeciously.**
diehard [-ˌhɑrd, B -ˌhɑd] *a.* intransigente, obcecado, empecinado. —*s.* intransigente, oposicionista, reacio; reaccionario.
dieldrin [ˈdiəldrən] *s.* (quím.) dieldrín, insecticida clorado.
dielectric [ˌdaɪəˈlɛktrɪk] *a., s.* (elec.) dieléctrico.
dielectric heating, (elec.) calentamiento dieléctrico.
diemaker [ˈdaɪˌmeɪkər, B -ə] *s.* (mec.) troquelista, ajustador, modelista.
diencephalic [daɪˌɛnsəˈfælɪk] *a.* (anat.) del diencéfalo.
diencephalon [ˌdaɪˌɛnˈsɛfəˌlɑn, B -ˌlɔn] *s.* (anat.) diencéfalo, cerebro intermedio.
dieresis, *var. de* **diaeresis.**
diesel engine [ˈdizəl-, -səl-, B -zəl-] *s.* (aut.) motor diesel, motor de aceite pesado.
diesel fuel, (aut.) aceite pesado, combustible de motor diesel.
dieselize [-ˌaɪz] *v.t.* equipar con motores diesel.
diesinker [ˈdaɪˌsɪŋkər, B -kə] *s.* grabador de cuños, moldeador.
diesinking [-kɪŋ] *s.* producción de matrices, moldeado.
diesis [ˈdaɪəsəs] *s.* (*pl.* DIESES [-ˌsiz]) 1. (mús., hist.) diesi. 2. (mús.) sostenido. 3. (tip.) obelisco doble.
diestock [ˈdaɪˌstɑk, B -ˌstɔk] *s.* (mec.) terraja, portacojinete.
diestrus [daɪˈɛstrəs] *s.* (vet.) diestro.
diet [ˈdaɪət] *s.* 1. dieta; régimen alimenticio (habitual o prescrito). 2. ración (de alimentos); comida. 3. **to be on a d.,** estar a dieta; **to put on a d.,** poner a dieta, adietar. —*v.i.* estar a dieta o régimen. —*v.t.* poner a dieta, adietar.
diet, *s.* dieta, asamblea; (hist.) dieta, asamblea legislativa.
dietary [ˈdaɪəˌtɛrɪ, B -tərɪ] *s.* dieta, ración alimenticia (en hospitales, instituciones, etc.). —*a.* dietético, de dieta.
dietetic [ˌdaɪəˈtɛtɪk] *a.* dietético.
dietetically [-ɪkəlɪ] *adv.* dietéticamente.
dietetics [-ɪks] *s. pl.* (*sing. o pl. en const.*) dietética.
diethylstilbestrol [ˌdaɪˌɛθəlˌstɪlˈbɛsˌtrəl] *s.* (bioquím.) dietilestilbestrol.
dietitian, dietician [ˌdaɪəˈtɪʃən] *s.* dietista.
differ [ˈdɪfər, B -ə] *v.i.* 1. (con *from*) diferir, diferenciarse, distinguirse (de). 2. (con *with*) disentir (con), discrepar (con), estar en desacuerdo (con). 3. **I beg to d. with you,** siento no estar de acuerdo con usted.
difference [ˈdɪfərəns, ˈdɪfrəns] *s.* 1. diferencia, desemejanza, desigualdad, disimilitud. 2. diferencia, distinción. 3. diferencia, discrepancia, desacuerdo. 4. (lóg.) diferencia. 5. (mat.) diferencia, residuo. 6. **it makes a great d.,** ¡ésa es otra cosa!; **it makes no d.,** no importa; **to make a d. between,** diferenciar entre, hacer distinción entre; **to split the d.,** dividir la diferencia, llegar a una transacción; **what d. does it make?** ¿qué más da? —*v.t.* diferenciar, distinguir.
different [ˈdɪfərənt, ˈdɪfrənt] *a.* diferente, distinto, disímil; (fig.) individualista.
differentia [ˌdɪfəˈrɛntʃɪə, B -ˈrɛnʃɪə] *s.* (*pl.* DIFFERENTIAE [-ˌi]) (lóg.) diferencia.
differentiable [-əbəl] *a.* que puede ser diferenciado, distinguible; (mat.) derivable.
differential [-ˈrɛntʃəl, B -ˈrɛnʃəl] *a.* diferencial; (mat., mec.) diferencial. —*s.* 1. (mat.) diferencial. 2. (elec.) devanado diferencial. 3. (mec.) diferencial. 4. índice diferencial, ej., *price differentials,* índices diferenciales de precios.
differential aileron, (avia.) alerón compensador.
differential calculus, (mat.) cálculo diferencial.
differential coefficient, (mat.) coeficiente diferencial.
differential equation, (mat.) ecuación diferencial.
differential gear, (maq.) engranaje diferencial.
differential pressure, (mot.) presión diferencial.
differential rate, tarifa diferencial (de transporte o de salario).
differentiate [ˌdɪfəˈrɛntʃɪˌeɪt, B -ˈrɛnʃɪ-] *v.t.* 1. diferenciar, distinguir. 2. diferenciar, modificar. 3. (mat.) derivar, diferenciar. —*v.i.* (biol.) diferenciarse.
differentiation [-ˌrɛntʃɪˈeɪʃən, B -ˌrɛnʃɪ-] *s.* diferenciación.
differently [ˈdɪfərəntlɪ, ˈdɪfrənt-] *adv.* diferentemente, de manera diferente.
difficile [dəˈfɪsəl, B ˈdɪfɪsil] *a.* dificultoso, obstructor, porfiado.
difficult [ˈdɪfɪˌkʌlt, B -kəlt] *a.* difícil; terco, obstinado.
difficulty [-ˌkʌltɪ, B -kəl-] *s.* 1. dificultad. 2. (*pl.*) apuro, aprieto. 3. obstáculo, tropiezo, molestia. 4. riña o pelea. 5. **to make difficulties,** crear dificultades, poner obstáculos; **with d.,** difícilmente, trabajosamente; **with great d.,** a duras penas.
diffidence [ˈdɪfədəns] *s.* apocamiento, timidez, (fig.) encogimiento.
diffident [-dənt] *a.* 1. tímido, apocado, inseguro. 2. (ant.) difidente, desconfiado.
diffidently [-lɪ] *adv.* tímidamente, modestamente.
diffract [dɪˈfrækt] *v.t.* (fís.) difractar.
diffraction [-ˈfrækʃən] *s.* (fís.) difracción.
diffraction grating, (ópt.) rejilla de difracción.
diffractive [-ˈfræktɪv] *a.* difrangente.
diffuse [dɪˈfjus] *a.* 1. difuso, difundido, esparcido, extendido. 2. (fig.) difuso, dilatado, verboso. — [-ˈfjuz] *v.t.* 1. difundir, esparcir (líquidos, conocimiento, rumor, etc.), despedir (calor). 2. (fig.) disolver, diluir (poder, fuerza). —*v.i.* difundirse, propagarse.
diffused light [-ˈfjuzd-] luz difusa.
diffusely [-ˈfjuslɪ] *adv.* difusamente.
diffuseness [-nəs] *s.* carácter o aspecto difuso; tenuidad.
diffuser [-ˈfjuzər, B -zə] *s.* difusor, atomizador.
diffuser vane, (mot.) álabe difusor.
diffusibility [-ˌfjuzəˈbɪlətɪ] *s.* (fís.) difusibilidad, atomicibilidad.
diffusible [-ˈfjuzəbəl] *a.* difusible, atomizable.
diffusion [dɪˈfjuʒən] *s.* 1. difusión, dispersión, diseminación. 2. prolijidad, difusión (del lenguaje). 3. (fís., quím.) difusión. 4. (mot.) difusión, atomización.
diffusive [-ˈfjusɪv] *a.* difusivo; difuso, difundido, atomizable.
diffusively [-lɪ] *adv.* difusamente.
diffusiveness [-nəs] *s.* difusión, prolijidad.
diffusor [-zər, B -zə] *var. de* **diffuser.**
dig [dɪg] *v.i.* (*pret., p.p.* DUG [dʌg]; ant. DIGGED [dɪgd]; *p.pr.* DIGGING) 1. cavar. 2. (jer., G.B.) alojarse. 3. **d. away at,** afanarse en; estudiar asiduamente; **d. down,** calar, penetrar, ahondar; **d. in,** (mil.) atrincherarse, afosarse; **d. into,** escudriñar, investigar (los hechos, un asunto, etc.). —*v.t.* 1. cavar, excavar. 2. (jer.) comprender, captar; reparar en; apreciar, gustar; admirar. 3. (jer.) burlarse de, mofarse de. 4. **d. a pit for,** (fig.) tender una trampa para; **d. in,** clavar (uñas en carne, espuelas en caballo, etc.); (jer.) empezar a comer; **d. in the ribs,** dar(le) un codazo (a uno); **d. into,** clavar, hundir (dedos en carne, pies en arena, etc.); **d. out,** desentrañar (un secreto, dato oculto, etc.); **d. up,** desenterrar (tesoro, secreto, etc.); remover con azada, roturar, barbechar (la tierra); desarraigar, arrancar (planta); (fig.) averiguar, descubrir (datos, información). —*s.* 1. empujón; codazo. 2. (*pl.*) (G.B., fam.) alojamiento, habitación. 3. (jer.) observación irónica. 4. excavación (arqueológica); lugar de excavaciones.
digametic [ˌdaɪgəˈmɛtɪk] *a.* que posee dos gametos, uno masculino y otro femenino.
digamy [ˈdɪgəmɪ] *s.* deuterogamia, segundas nupcias.
digastric [daɪˈgæstrɪk] *a.* (anat.) digástrico (músculo).
digenesis [daɪˈdʒɛnəsəs] *s.* (biol.) digénesis.
digenetic [ˌdaɪdʒəˈnɛtɪk] *a.* (biol.) digenético.
digest [ˈdaɪˌdʒɛst] *s.* 1. compendio, resumen, recolección; reseña (literaria). 2. (der.) digesto; compilación de reglas legales. — [daɪˈdʒɛst, də-] *v.t.* 1. digerir (los alimentos). 2. recopilar, clasificar, condensar. 3. (fig.) digerir, asimilar (mentalmente). 4. compendiar, resumir. 5. digerir, tolerar, aguantar (ofensa, opinión adversa, etc.). 6. (quím.) digerir. —*v.i.* digerirse (alimentos); digerir la comida.
digestant [daɪˈdʒɛstənt, də-] *s.* digestivo.
digester [-tər, B -tə] *s.* 1. compendiador. 2. digestivo. 3. digestor (vasija para calentar substancias bajo presión).
digestibility [-ˌdʒɛstəˈbɪlətɪ] *s.* digestibilidad.
digestible [-ˈdʒɛstəbəl] *a.* digestible, digerible.
digestion [-tʃən] *s.* 1. digestión. 2. (fig.) asimilación (de ideas, opiniones, etc.). 3. (quím.) digestión, absorción.

digestive [-tɪv] *a., s.* digestivo.
digestive gland, glándula digestiva (que segrega enzimas).
digestively [-lɪ] *adv.* con efecto digestivo.
digestive system, aparato digestivo.
digger ['dɪgər, B -ə] *s.* 1. cavador. 2. excavadora; azadón, almocafre. 3. **D.** (forma abrev. de **D. Indian**), indio norteamericano primitivo (que escarbaba la tierra buscando raíces para su alimentación). 4. (Aust., jer.) australiano.
digging [-ɪŋ] *s.* 1. cavadura, excavación. 2. (*pl.*) (lugar de) excavaciones. 3. (*pl.*) cosas excavadas. 4. (*pl.*) (jer., G.B.) alojamiento, habitación.
dight [daɪt] *v.t.* (poét.) adornar, embellecer, vestir; preparar, limpiar.
digit ['dɪdʒət] *s.* 1. (mat., astr.) dígito. 2. dedo (medida de longitud). 3. (zool.) dedo (de la mano o del pie); (hum.) dedo (de la mano).
digital [-əl] *a.* 1. digital; dactilar, del dedo. 2. dígito (número). —*s.* 1. (hum.) dedo. 2. tecla (de instrumento o máquina).
digital clock, reloj digital.
digital computer, ordenador digital.
digitalin [ˌdɪdʒə'tælən, B -'teɪl-] *s.* (quím.) digitalina.
digitalis [-əs] *s.* 1. (bot.) digital, dedalera. 2. (farm.) digital.
digitalism ['dɪdʒɪtəlˌɪzəm] *s.* (med.) digitalismo.
digitalization [ˌdɪdʒɪˌtælə'zeɪʃən, B -təlaɪ-] *a.* (med.) digitalización.
digitalize ['dɪdʒətəlˌaɪz] *v.t.* digitalizar.
digital scanner, lector digital.
digital watch, reloj digital.
digitate ['dɪdʒəˌteɪt] **digitated** [-əd] *a.* (zool., bot.) digitado, dispuesto como los dedos.
digitation [ˌdɪdʒə'teɪʃən] *s.* (biol., mús., mec.) digitación.
digitiform ['dɪdʒətəˌfɔrm, B -ˌfɔːm] *a.* digitiforme.
digitigrade [-ˌgreɪd] *a.* (zool.) digitígrado, que camina sobre los dedos de las patas (gatos, perros, etc.).
digitize ['dɪdʒəˌtaɪz] *v.t.* (com.) dar valores numéricos.
digitoxin [ˌdɪdʒə'tɑksən, B -'tɔk-] *s.* (quím.) digitoxina.
diglot ['daɪˌglɑt, B -ˌglɔt] *a.* bilingüe. —*s.* edición bilingüe (ej., de un libro).
diglyph [-ˌglɪf] *s.* (arq.) diglifo.
dignification [ˌdɪgnəfɪ'keɪʃən] *s.* dignificación.
dignified ['dɪgnəˌfaɪd] *a.* digno, serio, mesurado, señorial, decoroso, augusto, majestuoso.
dignifiedly [-lɪ] *adv.* seriamente, mesuradamente, con dignidad.
dignify ['dɪgnəˌfaɪ] *v.t.* (*pret., p.p.* DIGNIFIED; *p.pr.* DIGNIFYING) dignificar, ennoblecer, exaltar, elevar, honrar.
dignifying [-ɪŋ] *a.* dignificante, honroso.
dignitary ['dɪgnəˌterɪ, B -tərɪ] *s.* (*pl.* DIGNITARIES) dignatario.
dignity ['dɪgnətɪ] *s.* 1. dignidad, elevación, excelencia. 2. dignidad, decoro, gravedad, señorío. 3. dignidad, rango. 4. (ant.) dignatario, dignidad. 5. **to consider (something) beneath one's d.,** considerar (algo) como impropio de la dignidad de uno, tener (algo) a menos; **to stand on one's d.,** hacerse respetar.
digraph ['daɪˌgræf, B -ˌgrɑf] *s.* (fon.) digrama (grupo indivisible de dos letras y con un solo sonido como la *ch* española o la *th* inglesa).
digress [daɪ'grɛs, də-] *v.i.* divagar, hacer una digresión.
digression [-'grɛʃən] *s.* digresión, divagación (fuera del tema).
digressive [-'grɛsɪv] *a.* digresivo.
digressively [-lɪ] *adv.* digresivamente.
dihedral [daɪ'hidrəl] *a.* diedro. —*s.* (geom., aer.) diedro.
dihedrical [-drɪkəl] *a.* (aer.) diedro o decaedro.
dihedron [-'hidrən] *var. de* **dihedral.**
dihybrid [-'haɪbrəd] *a.* (biol.) dihíbrido.
dik-dik ['dɪkˌdɪk] *s.* (zool.) (especie de) pequeño antílope.
dike [daɪk] *s.* 1. dique, escollera, represa. 2. zanja, acequia. 3. terraplén; (G.B.) muro de piedra o tierra, malecón. 4. (fig.) dique, barrera. 5. (geol.) dique. —*v.t.* represar; canalizar; desaguar con zanjas, abrir un canal de desagüe.
diktat [dɪk'tɑt] *s.* orden o decreto dictatorial.
dilacerate [dɪ'læsəˌreɪt] *v.t.* dilacerar, desgarrar.
dilaceration [-ˌlæsə'reɪʃən] *s.* dilaceración, desgarramiento.
dilantin [dɪ'læntɪn] *s.* (quím.) dilantina.
dilapidate [də'læpəˌdeɪt] *v.t.* 1. arruinar, desmantelar. 2. dilapidar, malgastar. —*v.i.* arruinarse.
dilapidated [-'læpəˌdeɪtəd] *a.* dilapidado, ruinoso, arruinado, desmantelado.
dilapidation [-ˌlæpə'deɪʃən] *s.* dilapidación, arruinamiento, ruina, estado ruinoso.
dilatability [daɪˌleɪtə'bɪlətɪ, dɪ-] *s.* dilatabilidad, capacidad de dilatarse.
dilatable [-'leɪtəbəl] *a.* dilatable.
dilatant [-ənt] *a., s.* que se dilata, dilatador.
dilatation [ˌdɪlə'teɪʃən, B ˌdaɪleɪ-] *s.* 1. dilatación, ensanchamiento; prolijidad. 2. (fís.) dilatación, expansión. 3. (med.) dilatación (del corazón, estómago, etc.).
dilate [daɪ'leɪt, 'daɪˌleɪt, B daɪ'leɪt] *v.t.* dilatar, extender, expandir. —*v.i.* 1. dilatarse, explayarse. 2. dilatarse, expandirse.
dilated [-əd] *a,* dilatado.
dilation [daɪ'leɪʃən] *s.* 1. dilatación, ensanche, ensanchamiento. 2. (fís.) dilatación, expansión. 3. (med.) dilatación.
dilative [-'leɪtɪv] *a.* dilatativo.
dilatometer [ˌdɪlə'tɑmətər, B ˌdaɪ-'tɔmɪtə] *s.* (fís.) dilatómetro.
dilatometry [-ətrɪ] *s.* (metal.) dilatometría.
dilator [daɪ'leɪtər, dɪ-, B -ə] *s.* 1. (anat.) (músculo) dilatador. 2. dilatador (instrumento o droga).
dilatorily [ˌdɪlə'tɔrəlɪ, B 'dɪlətər-] *adv.* dilatoriamente, lentamente.
dilatoriness ['dɪləˌtɔrɪnəs, B -tər-] *s.* dilación, demora, tardanza, lentitud.
dilatory [-ɪ] *a.* dilatorio; tardón, demorón (Am.).
dildo ['dɪldoʊ] *s.* (vulg.) consolador, objeto en forma de pene.
dilemma [də'lɛmə] *s.* dilema; (lóg.) dilema, disyuntiva.
dilemmatic [ˌdɪlə'mætɪk] *a.* dilemático.
dilettante [ˌdɪlə'tɑnt, -'tɑntɪ, B -'tæntɪ] *a., s.* (*pl.* DILETTANTES o DILETTANTI [-i]) diletante, aficionado.
dilettantism [-'tanˌtɪzəm, B -'tæn-] *s.* diletantismo.
diligence ['dɪlədʒens] *s.* 1. diligencia, asiduidad, esmero. 2. prontitud, prisa, agilidad. 3. [ˌdɪlə'ʒɑns, B 'dɪlɪˌʒɑns] diligencia (coche).
diligent [-dʒənt] *a.* diligente, aplicado, asiduo, industrioso.
diligently [-lɪ] *adv.* diligentemente, asiduamente.
dill [dɪl] *s.* (bot.) eneldo, abesón.
dill pickle, (cocina) pepino encurtido sazonado con eneldo.
dilly ['dɪlɪ] *s.* (jer.) joya, perla, cosa o persona sobresaliente.
dillydally [-ˌdælɪ] *v.i.* (fam.) perder el tiempo; entretenerse en bagatelas; holgazanear; vacilar.
diluent ['dɪljʊənt] *a.* diluente, diluyente, disolvente. —*s.* (quím.) diluyente, disolvente.
dilute [daɪ'lut, də-, B -'ljut] *v.t.* 1. diluir, desleír, aguar. 2. aguar, atenuar, debilitar. —*v.i.* diluirse, desleírse. —*a.* diluido, aguado; debilitado, atenuado.
dilution [-'luʃən] *s.* 1. dilución, desleidura. 2. solución atenuada.
diluvial [də'luvɪəl, daɪ-] **diluvian** [-ən] *a.* diluvial, diluviano.
diluvium [-əm] *s.* (*pl.* DILUVIUMS o DILUVIA [-vɪə]) (geol.) diluvial.
dim [dɪm] *a.* (DIMMER; DIMMEST) 1. débil, mortecino (luz o sonido). 2. opaco, empañado, deslustrado. 3. indistinto, obscuro, poco claro. 4. (fig.) opaco, sombrío (futuro, expectativa, etc.). 5. lerdo, obtuso. 6. (jer.) aburrido, tedioso. 7. (fot.) velado. 8. **to take a d. view of,** (fam.) considerar con pesimismo; ver con desaprobación. —*v.t.* (*pret., p.p.* DIMMED; *p.pr.* DIMMING) 1. obscurecer, empañar, opacar. 2. amortiguar (luz o sonido). 3. (aut.) amortiguar la luz de, inclinar el haz de (los faros). —*v.i.* 1. obscurecerse, amortiguarse (luz). 2. (fig.) opacarse, desvanecerse (fama, belleza, etc.). —*s.* 1. (aut.) luz de cruce; luz de estacionamiento. 2. (ant.) oscuridad.
dime [daɪm] *s.* (E.U., Can.) (moneda de) diez centavos; **a d. a dozen,** (fam.) abundante y de fácil obtención; barato.
dime novel, (E.U.) novela barata y melodramática.
dimension [də'mɛntʃən, daɪ-, B -'mɛnʃən] *s.* 1. dimensión. 2. (*gen. pl.*) dimensión, dimensiones, extensión, tamaño. 3. (mat.) dimensión.
dimensional [-əl] *a.* dimensional.
dimensionalize [-ˌaɪz] *v.t.* medir, dimensionalizar.
dimeric [daɪ'mɛrɪk] *a.* 1. (bot., ento.) dímero. 2. (biol.) regido por dos factores.
dimerous ['dɪmərəs] *a.* (bot., ento.) dímero.
dime store, (E.U.) almacén de artículos baratos.
dimeter ['dɪmətər, B -ə] *s.* (poét.) dímetro.
dimethyl [daɪ'mɛθəl] *s.* (quím.) dimetilo.
dimidiate [dɪ'mɪdɪˌeɪt] *v.t.* dimidiar, demediar, promediar.
diminish [də'mɪnɪʃ] *v.t.* 1. disminuir, reducir, minorar, aminorar. 2. amenguar, rebajar, degradar. —*v.i.* disminuirse, menguar, minorarse, aminorarse, decrecer, degenerarse.
diminishable [-əbəl] *a.* que se puede disminuir, reducible.
diminished [-ɪʃt] *a.* disminuido; (mús.) disminuida, ej., *d. seventh,* séptima disminuida.
diminishingly [-ɪʃɪŋlɪ] *adv.* decrecientemente.
diminishing returns [-ɪŋ-] (econ.) renta decreciente, utilidad decreciente.
diminuendo [dəˌmɪnjʊ'ɛndoʊ] *a., adv.* (mús.) diminuendo. —*s.* (*pl.* DIMINUENDOS o DIMINUENDOES) (mús.) diminuendo.
diminution [ˌdɪmə'nuʃən, B -'nju-] *s.* disminución, atenuación, amenguamiento, rebaja, reducción, merma.
diminutive [də'mɪnjətɪv] *a.* 1. (gram.) diminutivo (vocablo, sufijo). 2. diminutivo, menudo, pequeñísimo. —*s.* (gram.) diminutivo.
diminutively [-lɪ] *adv.* 1. diminutivamente. 2. diminutamente.
dimissory ['dɪməˌsɔrɪ, B -sərɪ] *a.* dimitente, de dimisión; de despido.
dimissory letter, (relig.) dimisorias.
dimity ['dɪmətɪ] *s.* (tej.) cotonía.
dimly ['dɪmlɪ] *adv.* oscuramente; indistintamente (visto, percibido); débilmente (iluminado); nebulosamente (comprendido, recordado, etc.).

dimmer [-ər, B -ə] *s.* 1. reductor de luz. 2. (aut.) (*pl.*) luces de estacionamiento; luces de cruce o bajas.
dimness [-nəs] *s.* 1. oscurecimiento; oscuridad. 2. ofuscación, torpeza.
dimorphic [daɪ'mɔrfɪk, B -'mɔfɪk] *a.* (min., bot., zool.) dimorfo.
dimorphism [-ˌfɪzəm] *s.* (min., bot., zool.) dimorfismo.
dimorphous [-fəs] *a.* (min.) dimorfo.
dim-out ['dɪmˌaʊt] *s.* apagón, oscurecimiento parcial de luces (como medida de seguridad).
dimple ['dɪmpəl] *s.* 1. hoyuelo (esp. en las mejillas o barbilla). 2. depresión, hendidura (en el suelo). —*v.i.* mostrar o lucir hoyuelos. —*v.t.* formar hoyuelos en (mejillas, barbilla), ej., *laughter dimpled her cheeks,* la risa le formó hoyuelos en las mejillas.
dimply [-plɪ] *a.* lleno de hoyuelos.
dimwit ['dɪmˌwɪt] *s.* tonto, mentecato, estúpido.
dimwitted [-'wɪtəd] *a.* estúpido, torpe, lerdo.
dimwittedly [-lɪ] *adv.* estúpidamente.
dimwittedness [-nəs] *s.* estupidez, torpeza.
dimyarian [ˌdaɪˌmaɪ'ærɪən, B dɪmɪ'ɛər-] **dimyaric** [-'ærɪk] *a.* (zool.) dimiario.
din [dɪn] *s.* ruido fuerte, estrépito, batahola ensordecedora, estridencia, clamoreo, alboroto. —*v.t.* (*pret., p.p.* DINNED; DINNING) 1. ensordecer, asordar (el oído). 2. repetir insistentemente. 3. **d. into,** inculcar. —*v.i.* hacer un ruido estrepitoso.
dinar [dɪ'nɑr, B 'dinɑ] *s.* dinar, antigua moneda de oro (hoy unidad monetaria de varios países).
Dinaric Alps [dɪ'nærɪk-] Alpes Dináricos (en la costa del Adriático).
dine [daɪn] *v.i.* cenar, comer (en la noche); **d. out,** comer fuera de casa. —*v.t.* dar de comer; invitar o convidar a cenar.
diner ['daɪnər, B -nə] *s.* 1. comensal. 2. coche-comedor, vagón-restaurante (de un tren o ferrocarril). 3. restaurante popular, comedor.
dinette [daɪ'nɛt] *s.* (E.U.) pequeño comedor; pequeño juego de muebles para comedor.
ding [dɪŋ] *v.i.* repicar, (re)sonar, tañer (ej., campanas). —*v.t.* instar, reiterar porfiadamente, machacar.
ding-a-ling ['dɪŋəˌlɪŋ] *s.* tintín, tilín (sonido onomatopéyico).
dingbat ['dɪŋˌbæt] *s.* 1. (fam.) cualquier objeto pequeño que se puede lanzar. 2. (impr.) símbolo decorativo que inicia un párrafo.
dingdong [-ˌdɔŋ, -ˌdɑŋ, B -'dɔŋ] *s.* 1. talán talán (de las campanas). 2. campana; triángulo. —*v.i.* 1. retiñir, repiquetear. 2. hablar tediosa o insistentemente. —*a.* reñido, animado, feroz, disputado vigorosamente, ej., *d. race,* carrera reñida.
dinghy ['dɪŋɪ, B -gɪ] *s.* 1. dinga. 2. esquife, chinchorro, lancha, bote de remo. 3. balsa de caucho.
dingily ['dɪndʒəlɪ] *adv.* suciamente.
dinginess [-dʒɪnəs] *s.* estado sucio, escualidez; deslustre.
dingle ['dɪŋgəl] *s.* cañada, vallejuelo estrecho y umbroso.
dingo ['dɪŋgoʊ] *s.* (zool.) dingo, perro salvaje (de Australia).
dingus ['dɪŋəs, B -gəs] *s.* (jer.) cosa, chisme, sustitución humorística de un vocablo que se ha olvidado.
dingy ['dɪndʒɪ] *a.* (DINGIER; DINGIEST) manchado, sucio, empañado, deslustrado.
dining car ['daɪnɪŋ-] coche-comedor, vagón-restaurante.
dining hall, refectorio (en los colegios y conventos).
dining room, comedor.
dining-room suite [-ˌrum-, -ˌrʊm-] juego de comedor (muebles).
dinitrobenzene [daɪˌnaɪtroʊ'bɛnˌzin] *s.* (quím.) dinitrobencina.
dink [dɪŋk] *s.* nombre despectivo que dan los soldados norteamericanos a los miembros de las Fuerzas de Liberación Nacional del Vietnam del Sur.
dinkey ['dɪŋkɪ] *s.* (fam.) locomotora pequeña (para transportar carga, desviar carros, etc.).
dinkum ['dɪŋkəm] *a.* (Aust.) genuino, auténtico, legítimo.
dinky ['dɪŋkɪ] *a.* (DINKIER; DINKIEST) 1. (fam.) pequeño, diminuto; insignificante. 2. (pr. G.B.) bonito, lindo.
dinner ['dɪnər, B -ə] *s.* 1. cena; comida principal. 2. banquete. 3. cena completa a precio fijo.
dinner bell, campana de la cena.
dinner coat, d. jacket, smoking, esmoquin.
dinner dance, cena con baile, comida bailable.
dinner pail, fiambrera, portaviandas.
dinner party, cena, comida.
dinner plate, plato grande.
dinner roll, panecillo.
dinner table, mesa de comedor.
dinner theater, sala de espectáculos con servicio de restaurante.
dinner time, hora de cenar, hora de comer.
dinnerware [-ˌwɛr, B -ˌwɛə] *s.* servicio de mesa para la cena.
dinoceras [daɪ'nɑsərəs, B -'nɔ-] *s.* (pal.) dinoceras.
dinoflagellate [ˌdaɪnoʊ'flædʒələt, B -ˌleɪt] *s.* (*pl.* DINOFLAGELLATA) (biol.) dinoflagelado.
dinornis [daɪ'nɔrnəs, B -'nɔnɪs] *s.* (pal.) dinornis.
dinosaur ['daɪnəˌsɔr, B -ˌsɔ] *s.* (pal.) dinosaurio.
dinothere [-ˌθɪr, B -ˌθɪə] *s.* (pal.) dinoterio.
dint [dɪnt] *s.* 1. abolladura, depresión. 2. fuerza. 3. (ant.) golpe. 4. **by d. of, a** fuerza de, a puro. —*v.t.* abollar.
diocesan [daɪ'ɑsəsən, B -'ɔs-] *a.* (relig.) diocesano. —*s.* 1. diocesano. 2. (G.B.) feligrés.
diocese ['daɪəsəs, -sis] *s.* (*pl.* DIOCESES [-səsəz]) (relig.) diócesis, diócesi.
diode ['daɪˌoʊd] *s.* (rad.) diodo, válvula de dos electrodos.
dioecious [daɪ'iʃəs] *a.* (biol., bot., zool.) dioico.
Diogenes [daɪ'ɑdʒəˌniz, -'ɔdʒ-] *s.* Diógenes, filósofo griego de la escuela cínica.
dioicous [-'ɔɪkəs] *var. de* **dioecious.**
Diomedes [ˌdaɪə'midiz] *s.* (mitol.) Diomedes, héroe homérico de Troya.
Dionysia [-'nɪʒɪə, B -'nɪz-] *s. pl.* (hist., mitol.) dionisias, dionisíacas.
Dionysiac [-'nɪsɪˌæk] **Dionysian** [-ɪən, B -'nɪz-] *a.* dionisíaco, desenfrenado, orgiástico.
Dionysius [-'nɪsɪəs] *s.* Dionisio, tirano de Siracusa (Grecia antigua).
Dionysus [-'naɪsəs] *s.* (mitol.) Dionisos, dios del vino y la jarana, identificado con Baco.
diopside [daɪ'ɑpˌsaɪd, B -'ɔp-] *s.* (min.) diópsido.
dioptase [-ˌteɪs] *s.* (min.) dioptasa.
diopter, dioptre [-tər, B -tə] *s.* (ópt.) dioptría.
diopter scale, (ópt.) escala dióptrica.
dioptometer [-ˌɑp'tɑmətər, B -ˌɔp'tɔmɪtə] *s.* (ópt.) dioptómetro.
dioptric [-'ɑptrɪk, B -'ɔp-] **dioptrical** [-trɪkəl] *a.* (ópt.) dióptrico.
dioptrics [-trɪks] *s. pl.* (*sing. en const.*) (ópt.) dióptrica.
diorama [ˌdaɪə'ræmə, B -'rɑmə] *s.* 1. diorama. 2. representación con figuras y un fondo pintado.
dioramic [-'ræmɪk] *a.* diorámico.
diorite ['daɪəˌraɪt] *s.* (min.) diorita.
dioritic [ˌdaɪə'rɪtɪk] *a.* (min.) diorítico.
Dioscoreaceae [ˌdaɪəsˌkoʊrɪ'eɪsɪˌi, B daɪˌ-ɔs-] *s. pl.* (bot.) dioscóreas.
dioscoreaceous [-'eɪʃəs] *a.* (bot.) dioscóreo.
Dioscuri [daɪ'ɑskjəˌraɪ, B ˌdaɪə'skʊərˌaɪ] *s. pl.* (mitol.) Dioscuros, nombre colectivo de Cástor y Pólux.
diosmose [daɪ'ɑsˌmoʊs, B 'daɪɔs-] **diosmosis** [ˌdaɪɑs'moʊsəs, B -ɔs-] *s.* (fís.) ósmosis.
dioxide [daɪ'ɑkˌsaɪd, B -'ɔk-] *s.* (quím.) dióxido.
dip [dɪp] *v.t.* (*pret., p.p.* DIPPED; *p.pr.* DIPPING) 1. meter, sumergir (en un líquido). 2. bañar, mojar, humedecer. 3. zambullir. 4. (con *out* o *up*) sacar (un líquido) con cuchara o cucharón. 5. inclinar. 6. saludar con, bajar y volver a izar (la bandera). 7. (E.U.) frotar (rapé) en las encías. 8. **d. one's fingers into,** meter su cuchara en, entremeterse en, inmiscuirse en. —*v.i.* 1. sumergirse, hundirse y volver a salir. 2. declinar, inclinarse. 3. bajar temporalmente (precios, valores). 4. (aer.) inclinarse (el avión) repentinamente. 5. (geol.) buzar. 6. **d. into,** investigar superficialmente; meterse en, ocuparse superficialmente en (negocio, pasatiempo, etc.); hojear, leer superficialmente (un libro); **d. into one's purse** (o **pockets**), gastar dinero, rascarse el bolsillo. —*s.* 1. inmersión. 2. zambullida, baño corto. 3. declinación, inclinación. 4. declive, caída. 5. baja o caída temporal (de precios, valores). 6. vela de sebo. 7. baño (para limpieza, pintura, laqueado, etc. de un objeto). 8. (cocina) salsa. 9. (aer.) bajada corta y repentina (del avión). 10. depresión, hondonada (en el terreno); (mar.) depresión (de horizonte). 11. (geol.) buzamiento, descenso. 12. (fís.) inclinación, ángulo de inclinación (de la aguja). 13. (jer.) carterista, ratero.
dip equator, (ocean.) inclinación magnética cero.
diphase ['daɪˌfeɪz] **diphasic** [daɪ'feɪzɪk] *a.* (elec.) difásico, bifásico.
diphenyl [daɪ'fɛnəl] *s.* (quím.) difenilo.
diphenylamine [-ˌfɛnələ'min] *s.* (quím.) difenilamina.
diphosgene [-'fɑzˌdʒin, B -'fɔz-] *s.* (quím.) difosgeno.
diphtheria [dɪf'θɪrɪə, dɪp-, B -'θɪər-] *s.* (med.) difteria.
diphtherial [-ɪəl] **diphtherian** [-ɪən] **diphtheritic** [ˌdɪfθə'rɪtɪk, ˌdɪp-, B ˌdɪfθə-] *a.* (med.) diftérico.
diphtheritis [ˌdɪfθə'raɪtəs] *s.* (med.) difteritis.
diphthong ['dɪfˌθɔŋ, 'dɪp-] *s.* (fon.) diptongo.
diphthongal [dɪf'θɔŋgəl, dɪp-, -'θɔŋəl] *a.* de (o del) diptongo.
diphthongization [-ˌθɔŋə'zeɪʃən, B ˌdɪfθɔ-ŋgaɪ-, ˌdɪp-] *s.* diptongación.
diphthongize ['dɪfˌθɔŋˌaɪz, 'dɪp-, B -ˌgaɪz] *v.t., v.i.* diptongar(se).
diphycercal [ˌdɪfɪ'sərkəl, B -'səkəl] *a.* (zool.) dificercal.
diphyletic [ˌdaɪfaɪ'lɛtɪk, B ˌdɪfɪ-] *a.* (biol.) difilético.
diphyllous [daɪ'fɪləs] *a.* (bot.) difilo.
diphyodont [-'faɪəˌdɑnt, B 'dɪfɪəˌdɔnt] *a.* (zool.) difiodonte.
diplegia [daɪ'plidʒɪə] *s.* (med.) diplejía.
diplex ['daɪˌplɛks] *a.* (rad.) diplex.
diplobacillus [ˌdɪpləbə'sɪləs] *s.* (med.) diplobacilo, bacilo apareado.
diploblastic [-'blæstɪk] *a.* (biol.) diploblástico.
diplococcus [-'kɑkəs, B -'kɔk-] *s.* (*pl.* DIPLOCOCCI [-'kɑksaɪ, B -'kɔk-]) (bact.) diplococo.

diplodocus [də'plɑdəkəs, B -'plɔd-] *s.* (pal.) diplodoco.
diploe ['dɪploʊ,i] *s.* (anat.) diploe.
diploic [də'ploʊɪk] *a.* (anat.) diploico.
diploid ['dɪp,lɔɪd] *a.* (biol.) diploide. —*s.* célula diploide.
diploma [də'ploʊmə] *s.* diploma; **to give a d. to, to receive a d.,** diplomar.
diplomacy [-sɪ] *s.* 1. diplomacia. 2. (fig.) discreción, cautela, tacto.
diploma mill, (fig.) centro educativo que, por dinero, confiere títulos.
diplomat ['dɪplə,mæt] *s.* diplomático.
diplomatic [,dɪplə'mætɪk] *a.* 1. diplomático. 2. discreto.
diplomatically [-ɪkəlɪ] *adv.* diplomáticamente, discretamente.
diplomatic corps, cuerpo diplomático.
diplomatic immunity, inmunidad diplomática.
diplomatic pouch, valija diplomática.
diplomatics [-ɪks] *s. pl.* (*sing. en const.*) 1. diplomática (rama de la paleografía). 2. (ant.) diplomacia.
diplomatist [də'ploʊmətəst] *s.* diplomático.
diplont ['dɪp,lɑnt, B -,lɔnt] *s.* (biol.) planta diplonte.
diplophase ['dɪploʊ,feɪz, B -lə-] *s.* (biol.) fase diploide (en un ciclo de vida).
diplopia [dɪp'loʊpɪə] *s.* (med.) diplopía.
diplopod ['dɪplə,pɑd, B -,pɔd] *s.* (zool.) diplópodo.
diplopodous [dɪp'lɑpədəs, B -'lɔp-] *a.* (zool.) diplópodo.
dip needle, (fís.) aguja de inclinación.
dipnoan ['dɪpnoʊən] *a.* (zool.) dipneo, dipnoo. —*s.* (pez) dipnoo.
dipody [-ədɪ] *s.* (poét.) dipodia.
dipolar [daɪ'poʊlər, B -lə] *a.* (fís.) dipolar.
dipole ['daɪ,poʊl] *s.* 1. (fís., quím.) dipolo. 2. (rad.) (antena) dipolo, antena de media onda.
dipper ['dɪpər, B -ə] *s.* 1. cucharón, cuchara, cacillo; cazo, paleta; caldera de colada. 2. (t. **Big D.,**) (astr.) la Osa Mayor. 3. (orn.) zambullidor, mirlo de agua.
dipsacaceous [,dɪpsə'keɪʃəs] *a.* (bot.) dipsáceo.
dipso ['dɪpsoʊ] *s.* (*pl.* DIPSOS) (jer.) borrachín.
dipsomania [,dɪpsə'meɪnɪə] *s.* dipsomanía, alcoholismo.
dipsomaniac [-,æk] *s.* dipsómano, dipsomaníaco.
dipsomaniacal [-mə'naɪəkəl] *a.* dipsomaníaco, dipsómano.
dipstick ['dɪp,stɪk] *s.* varilla para medir la profundidad.
dipteral ['dɪptərəl] *a.* (ento.) díptero.
dipteran [-rən] *a.* (ento.) díptero.
dipterocarp ['dɪptərə,kɑrp, B -,kɑp] *s.* (bot.) dipterocarpea.
dipteron ['dɪptə,rɑn, B -,rɔn] *s.* (*pl.* DIPTERA [-rə]) (ento.) díptero.
dipterous [-rəs] *a.* (bot., zool.) díptero.
diptych ['dɪptɪk] *s.* (hist.) díptica, par de tablas plegables en forma de libro.
dire [daɪr, B 'daɪə] *a.* 1. terrible, horrendo, espantoso. 2. calamitoso, fatal, de mal agüero. 3. extremo, abrumador (necesidad, pobreza).
direct [də'rɛkt, daɪ-] *v.t.* 1. dirigir, guiar, orientar. 2. dirigir, gobernar, manejar. 3. dirigir, encaminar. 4. dirigir, aplicar (palabra, observación). 5. dirigir, sobrescribir (carta, envío, etc.). 6. mandar, ordenar. 7. asignar, dedicar. 8. (teat., cinem.) dirigir. 9. **d. against,** dirigir contra. —*v.i.* 1. dar dirección. 2. dirigir, actuar como director, ser director (de orquesta, coro, etc.). —*a.* 1. directo, derecho, recto. 2. directo, inmediato. 3. franco, sincero, natural. 4. exacto, todo (lo), ej., (*the*) *d. opposite,* todo lo contrario, exactamente lo opuesto. 5. (gram.) directo (complemento, discurso); textual, literal (cita). 6. (elec.) continua (corriente). —*adv.* directamente.
direct action, acción directa, métodos sindicalistas extremos (huelgas, sabotajes, uso de la fuerza).
direct current, (elec.) corriente continua, (abrev.) D.C.; **d. c. ammeter,** (elec.) amperímetro de corriente continua; **d. c. generator,** (elec.) generador de corriente continua.
direct drive, (mot.) toma directa, transmisión directa.
directed distance [-'rɛktəd-] (mat.) segmento dirigido (de recta en el que se ha marcado un sentido positivo).
direct examination, (der.) interrogatorio directo.
direct fire, (mil.) tiro directo.
direct hit, impacto directo.
direction [də'rɛkʃən, daɪ-] *s.* 1. dirección, orientación. 2. dirección, gobierno, manejo. 3. dirección, rumbo, curso; tendencia. 4. dirección (de una obra teatral, una orquesta, etc.). 5. (*pl.*) instrucciones. 6. sobrescrito. 7. **in the d. of,** con rumbo a, en la dirección de.
directional [-əl] *a.* 1. director, directriz. 2. (rad.) direccional (antena, emisora, fase, acoplamiento, receptor).
directional antenna, (rad., t.v.) antena dirigida.
directional radio, (rad.) radiogoniómetro.
directional signal, (aut.) intermitente.
directional stability, (avia.) estabilidad direccional, estabilidad de vuelo.
direction finder, (rad.) radiogoniómetro, antena indicadora de dirección.
direction finding, (avia., rad.) orientación, determinación del rumbo; radiogoniometría.
directive [-'rɛktɪv] *a.* 1. directivo, directorio. 2. indicativo, direccional. —*s.* orden, instrucción, directiva, mandato.
directive antenna, (avia., rad.) antena direccional, antena radiogoniométrica.
directivity [-,rɛk'tɪvətɪ] *s.* capacidad direccional, direccionalidad.
directly [də'rɛktlɪ, daɪ-] *adv.* 1. directamente. 2. exactamente, precisamente. 3. inmediatamente, al instante, ahora mismo, en seguida. 4. sin interferencia, ej., *to go d. from manufacturer to buyer,* ir directamente del fabricante al consumidor. —*conj.* (pr. G.B.) tan pronto como.
direct object, (gram.) complemento directo.
Directoire [dɪrɛk'twɑr, B -'rɛktwɑ] *s.* (hist.) Directorio, cuerpo de gobierno en Francia del período 1795-1799.
Directoire style, estilo Directorio.
director [də'rɛktər, daɪ-, B -tə] *s.* director, administrador, dirigente; director (de cine, teatro, etc.), regente.
directorate [-tərət] *s.* 1. directorio, dirección, directiva (de un banco, corporación, etc.). 2. cargo de director.
directorial [-,rɛk'tɔrɪəl] *a.* 1. directorio, directivo. 2. directoral, de director, del director. 3. del directorio.
directorship [-'rɛktər,ʃɪp, B -tə,-] *s.* cargo de director, dirección.
directory [-tərɪ] *a.* directivo, directorio. —*s.* 1. directorio, libro de instrucciones. 2. guía (comercial, profesional, telefónica, etc.) 3. directorio, (junta) directiva, mesa directiva, cuerpo de directores.
directress [-trəs] *s.* directora.
directrix [-trɪks] *s.* (*pl.* DIRECTRIXES O DIRECTRICES [,daɪrɛk'traɪsiz]) (geom.) directriz.
direct tax, contribución directa, impuesto directo.
direful ['daɪrfəl, B 'daɪəfəl] *a.* terrible, espantoso, pavoroso, calamitoso.
direfully [-fəlɪ] *adv.* terriblemente, pavorosamente.
direly [-lɪ] *adv.* espantosamente, fatalmente.
direness [-nəs] *s.* aspecto horrendo o espantoso.
dirge [dɜrdʒ, B dɜdʒ] *s.* 1. endecha, canto lúgubre. 2. treno, salmo de difuntos, canto fúnebre.
dirgeful ['dɜrdʒfəl, B 'dɜdʒ-] *a.* fúnebre, de luto.
dirham [dɪr'hæm, B dɪə'-] **dirhem** [-'hɛm] *s.* dirhem, unidad monetaria de Marruecos.
dirigible ['dɪrədʒəbəl, də'rɪdʒ-] *a.* dirigible. —*s.* (aer.) dirigible.
diriment ['dɪrəmənt] *a.* (der.) dirimente, anulatorio; **d. impediment,** impedimento dirimente (que anula un matrimonio).
dirk [dɜrk, B dɜk] *s.* daga, puñal. —*v.t.* apuñalar.
dirndl ['dɜrndəl, B 'dɜn-] *s.* traje tirolés (de doncella), vestido (femenino) a la bávara.
dirt [dɜrt, B dɜt] *s.* 1. suciedad, inmundicia, mugre, basura; barro, lodo (en la calle); excremento (de animales). 2. polvo, tierra. 3. (fig.) sordidez, bajeza. 4. (fig.) indecencia, obscenidad, porquería, cochinada. 5. (fig.) chisme malicioso, denuesto. 6. (jer.) información (esp. confidencial). 7. **to do d. to,** engañar, hacer una mala jugada a; **to eat d.,** (fig.) tragar insultos; **to fling** (o **throw**) **d. (at),** (fig.) echar lodo (a), lanzar denuestos (a); **to hit the d.,** (jer.) echarse a tierra (para protegerse de bombas aéreas o fuego de armas).
dirt-cheap ['dɜrt'tʃip, B 'dɜt-] *a.* (fam.) baratísimo, tirado.
dirt farmer, labrador que cultiva su propia tierra.
dirt track, (dep.) pista de ripio, pista de polvo de ladrillo (para carreras de motocicletas, etc.).
dirty ['dɜrtɪ, B 'dɜtɪ] *a.* (DIRTIER; DIRTIEST) 1. sucio, inmundo; enlodado, barroso (calle, etc.). 2. bajo, vil, atroz. 3. sórdido, indecente, obsceno (lenguaje, chiste, etc.). 4. sórdido, deshonesto (negocio, asunto, etc.). 5. malévolo, rencoroso (mirada). 6. ronco, turbio. 7. de precipitación radiactiva muy grande. 8. borrascoso, inclemente, abominable (tiempo). 9. **to do d. (on),** (jer.) jugar una mala pasada (a); **to do someone's d. work for him,** hacer el trabajo sucio de alguien; **to wash one's d. linen in public,** sacar los trapos al aire, sacar los trapitos al sol. —*v.t.* (*pret., p.p.* DIRTIED; *p.pr.* DIRTYING) 1. ensuciar, enlodar, emporcar. 2. (fig.) enlodar, manchar (nombre, reputación, etc.). 3. **d. oneself,** ensuciarse; (fig.) enfangarse. —*v.i.* ensuciarse.
dirty trick, mala jugada, mala pasada, faena; **to play a d. t. on,** hacerle (a alguien) una mala jugada.
disability [,dɪsə'bɪlətɪ] *s.* 1. incapacidad (física o mental), invalidez, inhabilidad. 2. impedimento.
disable [dɪs'eɪbəl, diz-] *v.t.* 1. (con *from* o *for*) incapacitar, inhabilitar (para). 2. baldar, lisiar.
disabled [-bəld] *a.* 1. incapacitado, inhabilitado. 2. inválido, lisiado, baldado. 3. roto, estropeado, fuera de combate.
disabled serviceman, mutilado o inválido de guerra.
disablement [-bəlmənt] *s.* 1. inhabilitación, incapacidad. 2. incapacitación, tullimiento.
disabuse [,dɪsə'bjuz] *v.t.* desengañar, desilusionar, sacar de un error.
disaccharide [daɪ'sækə,raɪd] *s.* (quím.) disacárido.

disaccord [ˌdisə'kɔrd, B -'kɔd] *v.i.* discordar. —*s.* desacuerdo.

disaccustom [-ə'kʌstəm] *v.t.* desacostumbrar, deshabituar.

disadvantage [-əd'væntɪdʒ, B -'vɑnt-] *s.* 1. desventaja. 2. menoscabo, detrimento. 3. **at a d.**, en situación desventajosa, en inferioridad de condiciones. —*v.t.* perjudicar.

disadvantaged [-ɪdʒd] *a.* de condición económica o social muy baja.

disadvantageous [-ˌædvən'teɪdʒəs, B -vɑn-] *a.* desventajoso, desfavorable.

disadvantageously [-lɪ] *adv.* desventajosamente.

disaffect [ˌdɪsə'fɛkt] *v.t.* indisponer, descontentar; enemistar, malquistar.

disaffected [-əd] *a.* enemistado, desleal. —*s.* desafecto.

disaffectedly [-lɪ] *adv.* con desafecto.

disaffection [-ə'fɛkʃən] *s.* desafecto, desafección, desafición, deslealtad, desamor.

disaffiliate [-ə'fɪlɪˌeɪt] *v.t.* desasociar. —*v.i.* terminar una afiliación.

disaffirm [ˌdɪsə'fɜrm, B -'fɜm] *v.t.* contradecir, negar, impugnar; (der.) negar, rechazar, repudiar; anular, renunciar, revocar.

disaffirmance [-əns] **disaffirmation** [-ˌæfər'meɪʃən, B -fə'-] *s.* confutación, impugnación; (der.) repudiación, renuncia; invalidación, anulación.

disafforest [-ə'fɔrəst -'fɑr-, B -'fɔr-] *v.t.* (G.B., der.) desacotar, convertir en tierra común (bosque acotado).

disagree [-dɪsə'gri] *v.i.* 1. disentir, diferir, desconvenir(se), no estar de acuerdo, discrepar. 2. **d. with,** sentar mal a, caer mal a, hacer daño a (apl. a comidas).

disagreeable [-'griəbəl, B -'grɪ-] *a.* 1. desagradable, ingrato, desapacible. 2. descortés, rudo; displicente, antipático.

disagreeably [-blɪ] *adv.* desagradablemente.

disagreement [-'grimənt] *s.* 1. desacuerdo, disconformidad. 2. desavenencia, discordia, discordancia, disensión. 3. altercado, altercación, disputa.

disallow [ˌdɪsə'laʊ] *v.t.* 1. desaprobar, rechazar, denegar. 2. negar, no admitir.

disallowable [-əbəl] *a.* negable, inadmisible, censurable.

disallowance [-əns] *s.* desaprobación, rechazo, denegación, prohibición, vedamiento.

disannul [-ə'nʌl] *v.t.* anular, invalidar.

disannulment [-mənt] *s.* anulación, invalidación.

disappear [ˌdɪsə'pɪr, B -'pɪə] *v.i.* desaparecer, desvanecerse, perderse de vista; extinguirse.

disappearance [-əns, B -'pɪərəns] *s.* desaparición, desvanecimiento.

disappoint [ˌdɪsə'pɔɪnt] *v.t.* desilusionar, decepcionar, desengañar, frustrar, chasquear.

disappointed [-əd] *a.* desilusionado, decepcionado, frustrado, chasqueado; **to be d. (at, in** o **with),** quedar desilusionado (de), llevarse un chasco (con).

disappointment [-mənt] *s.* desilusión, desengaño, decepción, chasco.

disapprobation [dɪsˌæprə'beɪʃən] *s.* desaprobación, censura.

disapprobatory [ˌdɪsə'proʊbəˌtɔrɪ, B -'æprəˌbeɪtərɪ] *a.* desaprobador, que desaprueba.

disapproval [-ə'pruvəl] *s.* desaprobación, censura.

disapprove [-ə'pruv] *v.t.* desaprobar, censurar, condenar. —*v.i.* no estar conforme, estar en contra; expresar (su) desaprobación; **d. of,** desaprobar, condenar, tener mala opinión de (alguien).

disapprovingly [-ɪŋlɪ] *adv.* con desaprobación.

disarm [dɪs'ɑrm, dɪz-, B -'ɑm] *v.t.* 1. desarmar; desguarnecer (ciudad, plaza, etc.). 2. (fig.) apaciguar, congraciarse con, ganar la voluntad de, cautivar. 3. (mec.) desarmar, desmontar. —*v.i.* deponer las armas; desanimarse.

disarmament [-'ɑrməmənt, B -'ɑmə-] *s.* desarme.

disarming [-mɪŋ] *a.* (fig.) apaciguador, cautivador (sonrisa, gesto, etc.).

disarrange [-dɪsə'reɪndʒ] *v.t.* desarreglar, desordenar, trastornar, desbarajustar.

disarrangement [-mənt] *s.* desarreglo, desorden.

disarray [-ə'reɪ] *v.t.* desordenar, desorganizar; desarreglar, desaliñar; (poét.) desnudar. —*s.* desarreglo, desorden, confusión; desaliño, desatavío.

disarticulate [-ɑr'tɪkjəˌleɪt, B -ɑ'-] *v.t., v.i.* desarticular(se), descoyuntar(se), desencajar(se).

disarticulation [-ˌtɪkjə'leɪʃən] *s.* (med.) desarticulación.

disassemble [-ə'sɛmbəl] *v.t.* desarmar, desmontar (reloj, máquina).

disassembly [-blɪ] *s.* (mec.) desarme, desmontaje.

disassimilate [ˌdɪsə'sɪməˌleɪt] *v.t.* (fisiol.) desasimilar.

disassimilation [-əˌsɪmə'leɪʃən] *s.* (fisiol.) desasimilación.

disassociate [-ə'soʊʃɪˌeɪt, -sɪ-] *v.t.* disociar, desasociar, desunir, separar.

disassociation [-əˌsoʊsɪ'eɪʃən] *s.* disociación.

disaster [dɪ'zæstər, B -'zɑstə] *s.* desastre, calamidad, catástrofe.

disastrous [-trəs] *a.* desastroso, calamitoso, catastrófico.

disastrously [-lɪ] *adv.* desastrosamente.

disavow [ˌdɪsə'vaʊ] *v.t.* repudiar, negar, desconocer, desaprobar, desautorizar.

disavowal [-əl] *s.* repudiación, desautorización.

disband [dɪs'bænd] *v.t.* dispersar; disolver, licenciar (tropas). —*v.i.* desbandarse, dispersarse.

disbandment [-mənt] *s.* desbandada, disolución, dispersión, licenciamiento.

disbar [-'bɑr, B -'bɑ] *v.t.* (der.) excluir del foro.

disbarment [-mənt] *s.* (der.) exclusión del foro.

disbelief [ˌdɪsbɪ'lif] *s.* incredulidad, descreimiento, escepticismo.

disbelieve [-'liv] *v.t.* descreer. —*v.i.* faltar a la fe, ser incrédulo.

disbeliever [-ər, B -ə] *s.* incrédulo.

disbranch [dɪs'bræntʃ, B -'brɑntʃ] *v.t.* desgajar, arrancar (las ramas) del tronco.

disbud [-'bʌd] *v.t.* 1. (bot.) desyemar (los capullos para mejorar la calidad de la floración). 2. (vet.) descornar (ganado).

disburden [-'bɜrdən, B -'bɜd-] *v.t.* descargar, aligerar, desembarazar; **d. one-self,** (fig.) desahogarse, aliviarse. —*v.i.* descargar (díc. de un barco).

disburdenment [-mənt] *a.* descargo, alivio.

disburse [dɪs'bɜrs, B -'bɜs] *v.t.* desembolsar, pagar, gastar.

disbursement [-mənt] *s.* desembolso, dispendio, gasto.

disburser [-ər, B -ə] *s.* pagador.

disc [dɪsk] *v.t.* (*pret., p.p.* DISCED [dɪskt]; *p.pr.* DISCING ['dɪskɪŋ]) grabar en disco (fonográfico), disco. —*var. de* **disk.**

disc. *abrev. de* **discount,** descuento.

discalced [dɪs'kælst] *a.* (relig.) descalzo.

discant ['dɪsˌkænt, B dɪs'kænt] *var. de* descant.

discard [dɪs'kɑrd, 'dɪsˌkɑrd, B dɪs'kɑd] *v.t.* 1. desechar (ropa); (fig.) descartar, desechar (ej., posibilidad), abandonar (hábito, costumbre, creencia, etc.). 2. (naipes) descartar. —*v.i.* (naipes) descartarse. — ['dɪsˌkɑrd, B -ˌkɑd] *s.* 1. (naipes) descarte; naipe(s) descartado(s). 2. desecho.

discern [dɪ'sɜrn, -'zɜrn, B -'sɜn, -'zɜn] *v.t.* discernir, percibir, columbrar, distinguir. —*v.i.* ser discernidor.

discerner [-ər, B -ə] *s.* discernidor.

discernible [-əbəl] *a.* discernible, perceptible, visible.

discernibly [-blɪ] *adv.* perceptiblemente, visiblemente.

discerning [-ɪŋ] *a.* juicioso, perspicaz, discernidor, penetrante.

discerningly [-lɪ] *adv.* juiciosamente, sagazmente.

discernment [-mənt] *s.* discernimiento, perspicacia, penetración, criterio.

discerptible [dɪ'sɜrptəbəl, B -'sɜp-] *a.* (raro) separable, divisible.

discharge [dɪs'tʃɑrdʒ, 'dɪsˌtʃɑrdʒ, B dɪs'tʃɑdʒ] *v.t.* 1. descargar (barco, camión; arma de fuego, arco). 2. (fig.) eximir, exonerar, desembarazar (de una obligación). 3. despedir, remover (de oficio, empleo). 4. librar, soltar, poner en libertad. 5. licenciar (a soldado); dar de alta (a paciente); disolver (jurado). 6. evacuar, secretar (pus, fluido). 7. ejecutar, desempeñar, cumplir con (deber). 8. saldar, cancelar, pagar (deuda). 9. descolorar, desteñir. 10. (elec.) descargar (batería). 11. (arq.) aligerar. —*v.i.* 1. descargar (ej., un barco). 2. dispararse (arma). 3. correrse (color). 4. salir, vaciarse (fluido). 5. descargar (río). — [B dɪs'tʃɑdʒ, 'dɪsˌtʃɑdʒ] *s.* 1. descarga, descargo (de un barco, de mercaderías). 2. descarga, disparo (de un arma); (mil.) descarga. 3. despedida, despido, destitución, deposición (de un funcionario, etc.); (mil.) licenciamiento, licencia absoluta; certificado de licencia. 4. satisfacción, pago (de deuda). 5. liberación (del prisionero). 6. cumplimiento, ejecución, desempeño (de un deber). 7. descargo, exoneración. 8. salida, evacuación; (med.) derrame, secreción (de pus, fluido). 9. (elec.) descarga.

discharge header, (aut.) colector de escape o de descarga.

discharge lamp, lámpara de descarga luminosa.

discharge nozzle, (aut.) tobera de descarga, boquilla de descarga; inyector.

discharger [-ər, B -ə] *s.* (elec.) descargador.

discharge tube, tubo luminoso (de neón).

discharge valve, (aut.) válvula de escape; válvula de desagüe o descargue.

discharging arch [-ɪŋ-] (arq.) arco de descarga, sobrearco.

disc harrow, (agr.) grada de discos, rastra de discos.

discifloral [ˌdɪsɪ'flɔrəl] *a.* (bot.) de flores discoidales.

disciform ['dɪsəˌfɔrm, B -ˌfɔm] *a.* discoidal.

disciple [dɪ'saɪpəl] *s.* 1. discípulo. 2. apóstol. 3. (fig.) seguidor, partidario, secuaz.

discipleship [-ˌʃɪp] *s.* discipulado.

disciplinable [ˌdɪsə'plɪnəbəl, B 'dɪsəˌplɪn-] *a.* disciplinable, dócil, educable.

disciplinal ['dɪsəplənəl] *a.* disciplinal.

disciplinarian [ˌdɪsəplə'nɛrɪən, B -'nɛər-] *a.* disciplinario. —*s.* ordenancista, persona que manda o enseña con rigor.

disciplinary ['dɪsəpləˌnɛrɪ, B -nərɪ] *a.* disciplinario, correctivo.

discipline ['dɪsəplən] *s.* 1. disciplina, orden. 2. castigo. 3. disciplina, ciencia, curso, materia (de estudio). —*v.t.* 1. disciplinar. 2. castigar, corregir, reformar.
disc jockey, (rad.) pinchadiscos, animador (de un programa de discos).
disclaim [dɪs'kleɪm] *v.t.* 1. repudiar, negar, renegar, desconocer. 2. (der.) renunciar; rechazar, desaprobar, desautorizar, declinar. —*v.i.* hacer renuncia o abandono.
disclaimer [-ər, B -ə] *s.* (der.) renuncia, abandono.
disclamation [ˌdɪsklə'meɪʃən] *s.* repudiación, desautorización; renuncia o abandono.
disclimax [dɪs'klaɪˌmæks] *s.* comunidad ecológica que ha cambiado, gen. por influencia del hombre.
disclose [-'kloʊz] *v.t.* 1. descubrir, revelar. 2. divulgar, revelar, publicar. 3. (ant.) abrir.
discloser [-ər, B -ə] *s.* descubridor, revelador.
disclosure [-'kloʊʒər, B -ʒə] *s.* revelación, divulgación; declaración.
disco ['dɪskoʊ] *s.* (*nightclub*) discoteca, disco.
discobolus [-'kɑbələs, B -'kɔb-] *s.* discóbolo, atleta que arroja el disco.
disco dancing, baile disco, baile discoteca.
discographer [-'kɑgrəfər, B -'kɔgrəfə] *s.* catalogador de discos (fonográficos).
discography [-fɪ] *s.* catálogo de discos (fonográficos).
discoid ['dɪsˌkɔɪd] *a.* (bot.) discoide, discoideo.
discoidal [dɪs'kɔɪdəl] *a.* (zool.) discoidal.
discolor, discolour [-'kʌlər, B -ə] *v.t., v.i.* descolorar(se), desteñir(se); manchar(se). —*a.* discoloro.
discoloration, discolouration [-ˌkʌlə'reɪʃən] *s.* descoloramiento; mancha.
discombobulate [ˌdɪskəm'bɑbjəˌleɪt, B -'bɔb-] *v.t.* (fam.) trastornar, perturbar, aturdir, confundir, desconcertar.
discomfit [dɪs'kʌmfət] *v.t.* 1. desconcertar, turbar; frustrar; embarazar. 2. (ant.) derrotar, vencer.
discomfiture [-fətʃər, B -tʃə] *s.* 1. desconcierto, embarazo, confusión. 2. derrota. 3. frustración, decepción. 4. perjuicio, daño.
discomfort [-'kʌmfərt, B -fət] *v.t.* 1. incomodar, molestar; desconcertar, turbar. 2. desanimar, afligir. —*s.* 1. incomodidad, molestia, inquietud. 2. aflicción, pesar.
discomfortable [-əbəl] *a.* (ant.) incómodo, molesto.
discommode [ˌdɪskə'moʊd] *v.i.* incomodar, molestar.
discommodity [-'mɑdətɪ, B -'mɔd-] *s.* (ant.) incomodidad, inconveniencia, inconveniente.
discompose [-kəm'poʊz] *v.t.* 1. disturbar, turbar, perturbar, desconcertar; trastornar, agitar; confundir, aturdir. 2. descomponer, desarreglar.
discomposure [-'poʊʒər, B -ʒə] *s.* perturbación, desconcierto, inquietud, desasosiego, destemple.
disco music, música disco.
disconcert [ˌdɪskən'sɜrt, B -'sɜt] *v.t.* desconcertar, descomponer, confundir, turbar, perturbar.
disconcerted [-əd] *a.* desconcertado, descompuesto, confundido.
disconcertedly [-lɪ] *adv.* desconcertadamente, turbadamente.
disconcerting [-ɪŋ] *a.* desconcertante.
disconformity [ˌdɪskən'fɔrmətɪ B -'fɔmɪ-] *s.* 1. (geol.) discordancia (esp. erosiva). 2. (ant.) disconformidad.
disconnect [ˌdɪskə'nɛkt] *v.t.* desunir, separar, desacoplar, disociar; (mec., elec.) desconectar.
disconnected [-əd] *a.* inconexo, incoherente, desconectado.
disconnectedly [-lɪ] *adv.* incoherentemente, sin conexión.
disconnection, (pr. G.B.) **disconnexion** [-'nɛkʃən] *s.* desunión, separación, desconexión, desembrague.
disconsolate [dɪs'kɑnsələt, B -'kɔn-] *a.* desconsolado, apesadumbrado, desolado, abatido, afligido, inconsolable.
disconsolately [-lɪ] *adv.* desconsoladamente.
disconsolateness [-nəs] *s.* desconsuelo, desconsolación, tristeza.
disconsolation [-ˌkɑnsə'leɪʃən, B -ˌkɔn-] *s.* desconsolación, desconsuelo, aflicción.
discontent [ˌdɪskən'tɛnt] *s.* 1. descontento, sinsabor, disgusto, desagrado. 2. malcontento, revoltoso. —*a.* descontento, malcontento, disgustado, insatisfecho. —*v.t.* descontentar, desagradar, disgustar.
discontended [-əd] *a.* descontento, disgustado; malcontento, insatisfecho.
discontentedly [-lɪ] *adv.* con ánimo descontento.
discontentedness [-nəs] *s.* descontento, mal humor.
discontentment [-'tɛntmənt] *s.* descontento, desagrado, mal humor.
discontinuance [ˌdɪskən'tɪnjʊəns] *s.* discontinuación, interrupción, intermisión; desunión, separación; (der.) descontinuación, sobreseimiento (de una acción judicial), cesación, suspensión.
discontinuation [-ˌtɪnjʊ'eɪʃən] *s.* descontinuación, cesación, interrupción, intermisión; desunión, separación.
discontinue [-'tɪnju] *v.t.* 1. discontinuar, descontinuar, interrumpir, suspender. 2. (der.) sobreseer. —*v.i.* 1. suspenderse, cesar. 2. (der.) sobreseer.
discontinuity [-ˌkɑntə'nuətɪ, B -ˌkɔntɪ'n-ju-] *s.* discontinuidad; interrupción, laguna.
discontinuous [-kən'tɪnjʊəs] *a.* discontinuo, interrumpido.
discontinuously [-lɪ] *adv.* interrumpidamente.
discophile ['dɪskəˌfaɪl] *s.* discófilo.
discord ['dɪsˌkɔrd, B -ˌkɔd] *s.* 1. discordia, desacuerdo, disensión, desavenencia; conflicto. 2. (mús.) discordancia, disonancia. 3. **to sow d.,** meter o sembrar cizaña. — [dɪs'kɔrd, B -'kɔd] *v.i.* discordar, discrepar, disconvenir, chocar.
discordance [dɪs'kɔrdəns, B -'kɔd-] **discordancy** [-ənsɪ] *s.* 1. discordia, desaacuerdo, disentimiento, disensión, disconformidad. 2. (mús.) disonancia, desentono.
discordant [-ənt] *a.* 1. discordante, discrepante (nota, opinión, parecer, etc.); discorde, en desacuerdo; (con *with*) contrario (a), opuesto (a), incompatible (con). 2. (mús.) discorde, disonante.
discordantly [-lɪ] *adv.* en tono discorde; con disonancia.
discotheque ['dɪskəˌtɛk] *s.* (fr.) discoteca, boite o cabaret que ofrece música grabada para bailar.
discount ['dɪsˌkaʊnt, dɪs'kaʊnt] *v.t.* 1. descontar, deducir. 2. rebajar, disminuir. 3. despreciar, desestimar, dar poca importancia a. 4. descartar, desechar, dejar a un lado. 5. considerar debidamente, anticipar. 6. (com.) descontar (letra de cambio, documento, etc.). —*v.i.* descontar letras de cambio, hacer descuentos. — ['dɪsˌkaʊnt] *s.* 1. descuento, deducción; rebaja. 2. (com.) descuento (de letra de cambio, documento, etc.). 3. **at a d.,** bajo par, al descuento; rebajado; depreciado.
discountable [-əbəl] *a.* descontable.
discountenance [dɪs'kaʊntənəns] *v.t.* 1. desconcertar, avergonzar, confundir. 2. desaprobar, poner mala cara a, condenar. —*s.* (raro) desaprobación.
discount house, 1. almacén o tienda que vende al descuento. 2. (G.B.) agente de letras.
discount rate, (com.) tasa o tipo de descuento.
discourage [dɪs'kɜrɪdʒ, -'kʌ-, B -'kʌ-] *v.t.* 1. desalentar, descorazonar, desanimar. 2. (con *from*) disuadir. 3. apartar, hacer desistir, desaprobar, oponerse a.
discouragement [-mənt] *s.* desaliento, desánimo.
discouraging [-ɪŋ] *a.* desalentador, deprimente.
discouragingly [-lɪ] *adv.* desalentadoramente.
discourse ['dɪsˌkɔrs, dɪs'kɔrs, B dɪs'kɔs, 'dɪsˌkɔs] *s.* 1. conversación, plática. 2. discurso, disertación, sermón. 3. discurso, tratado. — [B dɪs'kɔs] *v.i.* 1. conversar, platicar. 2. discurrir, disertar, hablar. —*v.t.* (ant.) discursar, proferir, pronunciar.
discourser [dɪs'kɔrsər, B -'kɔsə] *s.* disertante, orador.
discourteous [-'kɜrtɪəs, B -'kɜt-] *a.* descortés, desatento, grosero.
discourteously [-lɪ] *adv.* descortésmente, groseramente.
discourteousness [-nəs] *s.* descortesía, grosería.
discourtesy [-əsɪ] *s.* descortesía, desatención, grosería.
discover [dɪs'kʌvər, B -ə] *v.t.* 1. descubrir, revelar. 2. descubrir, hallar. 3. (ant.) exhibir, lucir, exponer a la vista.
discoverable [-ərəbəl] *a.* que se puede descubrir.
discoverer [-ərər, B -ərə] *s.* descubridor, explorador; inventor.
discovert [-ərt, B -ət] *a.* (der.) (mujer) soltera, divorciada o viuda.
discovery [dɪs'kʌvərɪ] *s.* 1. descubrimiento, hallazgo, encuentro. 2. (ant.) revelación.
Discovery Day, *var. de* **Columbus Day,** Día de la Raza (12 de Octubre).
discreate [-ˌkrɪ'eɪt] *v.t.* aniquilar, destruir.
discreation [-'eɪʃən] *s.* aniquilación, destrucción.
discredit [-'krɛdət] *v.t.* 1. descreer, no dar crédito a, dudar. 2. desacreditar, desprestigiar, deshonrar. 3. desautorizar, desvirtuar. —*s.* 1. descrédito, desprestigio, desestimación, deshonra. 2. desconfianza, duda. 3. **to bring d. on (a person),** deshonrar (a una persona); **to cast** (o **throw**) **d. on** (o **upon**) **(a theory, version,** etc.), hacer dudar, desacreditar (una teoría, versión, etc.).
discreditable [-əbəl] *a.* vergonzoso, deshonroso, desdoroso.
discreditably [-blɪ] *adv.* vergonzosamente, deshonrosamente.
discreet [dɪs'krit] *a.* discreto, prudente, mesurado, moderado, modesto.
discreetly [-lɪ] *adv.* discretamente.
discreetness [-nəs] *s.* discreción, prudencia, modestia.
discrepancy [-'krɛpənsɪ] *s.* discrepancia, diferencia, divergencia.
discrepant [-ənt] *a.* discrepante, diferente, discordante.
discrete [dɪs'krit] *a.* 1. separado, distinto. 2. inconexo, desunido, discontinuo. 3. (mat.) discreta (cantidad). 4. (med.) discreta (viruela).
discretely [-lɪ] *adv.* distintamente, separadamente.
discreteness [-nəs] *s.* distinción, separación.
discrete quantity, (mat.) cantidad discreta.
discretion [-'krɛʃən] *s.* 1. discreción, prudencia. 2. arbitrio, albedrío, sindéresis. 3. **age of d.,** edad de la razón, edad legal; **at d.,** a discreción;

at one's d., al albedrío de uno; **at the d. of,** a juicio de, según el deseo de.
discretionally [-əlɪ] *adv.* discrecionalmente, a discreción, a voluntad.
discretionary [-ˌɛrɪ, B -ərɪ] *a.* discrecional.
discretive [dɪs'kritəv] *a.* disyuntivo; separado; diferencial; que distingue.
discretively [-lɪ] *adv.* disyuntivamente, separadamente, de por sí.
discriminable [-'krɪmənəbəl] *a.* que puede ser discriminado, distinguible, discernible.
discriminant [-nənt] *s.* (mat.) discriminante.
discriminate [-'krɪməˌneɪt] *v.t.* diferenciar, distinguir, discriminar. *—v.i.* hacer distinción, discriminar; **d. against,** discriminar en contra de, dar trato inferior a; **d. between,** diferenciar o hacer distinción entre. — [-nət] *a.* 1. discernidor, que sabe escoger. 2. (ant.) preciso, definido, distinto.
discriminating [-ɪŋ] *a.* 1. discerniente, exigente. 2. distintivo (marca, señal, etc.). 3. discriminador, analítico. 4. discriminador, que demuestra favoritismo, preferente, parcial.
discrimination [dɪsˌkrɪmə'neɪʃən] *s.* 1. discriminación, sindéresis, distinción, diferenciación. 2. discernimiento, buen gusto. 3. (*racial, sexual*) discriminación.
discriminative [-'krɪməˌneɪtɪv, -nət-] *a.* 1. discerniente, discriminador, parcial, injusto. 2. diferencial, discriminatorio (tarifa, tasa, etc.).
discriminatively [-lɪ] *adv.* con discernimiento; con discriminación, con parcialidad.
discriminator [-ər, B -ə] *s.* 1. (rad.) discriminador (de frecuencia, amplitud). 2. discriminador (persona).
discriminatory [-nəˌtɔrɪ, B -tərɪ] *a.* 1. diferencial, discriminatorio (tarifa, impuesto). 2. discriminador, injusto, parcial.
discrown [dɪs'kraʊn] *v.t.* (ant.) destronar, derrocar, deponer.
discursive [-'kɜrsɪv B -'kɜsɪv] *a.* 1. digresivo, divagante, divagador. 2. razonado, meditado.
discursively [-lɪ] *adv.* razonablemente, con ilación.
discursiveness [-nəs] *s.* 1. tendencia digresiva. 2. carácter discursivo (de razonamiento).
discus ['dɪskəs] *s.* (*pl.* DISCUSES) 1. (dep.) disco; lanzamiento del disco. 2. (bot., anat., zool.) disco.
discuss [dɪs'kʌs] *v.t.* 1. discutir, debatir, argüir; tratar, ventilar. 2. (ant., fam.) probar, catar.
discussant [-'kʌsənt] *s.* participante en una discusión.
discussion [-'kʌʃən] *s.* discusión, debate, polémica, exposición.
disdain [dɪs'deɪn] *v.t.* 1. desdeñar, despreciar, menospreciar. 2. no dignarse. *—s.* desdén, desprecio, menosprecio.
disdainful [-fəl] *a.* desdeñoso, despectivo, despreciativo; altivo.
disdainfully [-fəlɪ] *adv.* desdeñosamente, altivamente, con desprecio.
disease [dɪ'ziz] *s.* enfermedad, mal, morbo, dolencia. *—v.t.* causar una enfermedad, enfermar, provocar un daño.
diseased [-'zizd] *a.* enfermo, morboso.
disembark [ˌdɪsəm'bɑrk, B -'bɑk] *v.t., v.i.* desembarcar(se).
disembarkation [-ɛmˌbɑr'keɪʃən, B -ˌbɑ'-] **disembarkment** [-əm'bɑrkmənt, B -'bɑk-] *s.* desembarque, desembarco.
disembarrass [-əm'bærəs] *v.t.* (con *of*) desembarazar (de), librar (de); (con *from*) desenredar, desenmarañar, sacar (de); zafar, despejar.
disembarrassment [-mənt] *s.* desembarazo, desenredo.
disembodied [dɪsəm'bɑdid, B -'bɔd-] *a.* incorpóreo (espíritu, idea, etc.).
disembodiment [-ɪmənt] *s.* 1. separación o liberación del cuerpo; incorporeidad. 2. (ant.) licenciamiento (de tropas).
disembody [-'bɑdɪ, B -'bɔdɪ] *v.t.* 1. separar o librar del cuerpo o existencia corporal. 2. (ant., mil.) licenciar (a las tropas), dispersar.
disembogue [-əm'boʊg] *v.i.* desembocar, desaguar (río). *—v.t.* **d. itself,** desembocar, desaguar (río).
disembosom [-əm'bʊzəm, -'buz-, B -'bʊz-] *v.t.* revelar, exponer, desembuchar (fam.), desahogarse.
disembowel [ˌdɪsəm'baʊəl] *v.t.* destripar, desentrañar.
disembowelment [-mənt] *s.* destripamiento, desentrañamiento.
disembroil [-ɪm'brɔɪl] *v.t.* desembrollar, desentrañar; restablecer el orden.
disemploy [-ɪm'plɔɪ] *v.t.* privar de empleo o de trabajo.
disenable [-ɪn'eɪbəl] *v.t.* incapacitar, inhabilitar, descalificar.
disenchant [ˌdɪsən'tʃænt, B -'tʃɑnt] *v.t.* desencantar, desilusionar.
disenchantment [-mənt] *s.* desencanto, desilusión.
disencumber [-ən'kʌmbər, B -bə] *v.t.* desembarazar, librar (de impedimento o estorbo).
disendow [ˌdɪsən'daʊ] *v.t.* privar de subvención o dote.
disendowment [-mənt] *s.* privación de subvención o dote.
disenfranchise [-ən'frænˌtʃaɪz] *v.t.* privar de derechos civiles; privar de franquicias u otros privilegios.
disenfranchisement [-mənt, B -tʃɪz-] *s.* privación de derechos civiles y franquicias.
disengage [-ən'geɪdʒ] *v.t.* 1. retirar, liberar. 2. quitar, desasir, soltar; separar, desprender. 3. (mec.) desembragar, desengranar. 4. (mil.) retirar del combate (tropas). *—v.i.* 1. separarse, libertarse, librarse, desligarse, zafarse. 2. (mil.) romper el contacto (con el enemigo). 3. (esgr.) hacer una finta.
disengagement [-mənt] *s.* 1. desembarazo, liberación, separación. 2. soltura, desenvoltura. 3. ruptura de compromiso matrimonial. 4. (mec.) desembrague, desengranaje. 5. (mil.) ruptura del combate.
disentail [ˌdɪsən'teɪl] *v.t.* (der.) desamortizar, liberar de vínculo (bienes), desvincular.
disentailment [-mənt] *s.* (der.) desamortización.
disentangle [-ən'tæŋgəl] *v.t., v.i.* desenredar(se), desembrollar(se), desenmarañar(se).
disentanglement [-mənt] *s.* desenredo, desembarazo.
disenthrall [-ən'θrɔl] *v.t.* liberar, libertar, librar, eximir (de una obligación).
disenthrone [-ən'θroʊn] *v.t.* destronar, derrocar, deponer.
disenthronement [-mənt] *s.* destronamiento.
disentitle [-ən'taɪtəl] *v.t.* privar de un título o derecho.
disentomb [ˌdɪsən'tum] *v.t.* desenterrar, exhumar.
disentombment [-mənt] *s.* desenterramiento, exhumación.
disentrance [-ən'træns, B -'trɑns] *v.t.* despertar de un trance, desencantar, desilusionar, hacer volver en sí.
disentwine [-ən'twaɪn] *v.t., v.i.* destorcer(se), desenredar(se), desenrollar(se).
disepalous [daɪ'sɛpələs] *a.* (bot.) disépalo.
disestablish [ˌdɪsə'stæblɪʃ] *v.t.* privar de posición o privilegio establecido, esp. separar (la iglesia) del estado.
disestablishment [-mənt] *s.* privación de posición o privilegio establecido; separación de la iglesia del estado.
disesteem [-ə'stim] *v.t.* desestimar, menospreciar, desairar. *—s.* descrédito, desprestigio, disfavor, desestima (ción).
diseuse [dɪ'zʌz, B -'zɜz] *s.* (*pl.* DISEUSES) recitadora profesional.
disfavor, (G.B.) **disfavour** [dɪs'feɪvər, B -və] *s.* 1. desagrado, desaprobación. 2. desgracia, desprestigio. 3. desventaja, detrimento. 4. desaire, descortesía. *—v.t.* desfavorecer; desaprobar.
disfeature [-'fitʃər, B -tʃə] *v.t.* desfigurar, desemejar, deformar.
disfiguration [-ˌfɪgjə'reɪʃən] *s.* desfigución, deformación; deformidad.
disfigure [-'fɪgjər, B -'fɪgə] *v.t.* desfigurar, deformar, afear.
disfigurement [-mənt] *s.* desfiguramiento, desfiguración; deformidad.
disforest [-'fɔrəst, -'fɑr-, B -'fɔr-] *v.t.* desmontar, talar; desacotar.
disforestation [-ˌfɔrə'steɪʃən, -ˌfɑr-, B -ˌfɔr-] *s.* tala, desmonte.
disfranchise [dɪs'frænˌtʃaɪz] *v.t.* privar de los derechos ciudadanos, privar de privilegios o franquicias.
disfranchisement [-mənt, B -tʃɪz-] *s.* privación de los derechos civiles, privación de privilegios e inmunidades.
disfrock [-'frɑk, B -'frɔk] *v.t.* expulsar, deponer (a clérigo).
disgorge [-'gɔrdʒ, B -'gɔdʒ] *v.t.* 1. vomitar. 2. (fig.) vomitar, arrojar de sí; derramar, verter (ej., pasajeros el tren). 3. descargar (sus aguas el río). *—v.i.* (fig.) vomitar, soltar, entregar, restituir (botín, ganancias mal habidas, etc.); desembuchar.
disgrace [dɪs'greɪs] *s.* 1. ignominia, deshonra, estigma, vergüenza, oprobio. 2. desgracia, desfavor. 3. **in d.,** en desgracia. *—v.t.* 1. deshonrar, desacreditar, difamar; degradar. 2. causar oprobio a.
disgraceful [-fəl] *a.* deshonroso, oprobioso, vergonzoso, ignominioso.
disgracefully [-fəlɪ] *adv.* ignominiosamente, vergonzosamente.
disgracefulness [-nəs] *s.* carácter o aspecto vergonzoso (de una situación, conducta, etc.).
disgruntle [-'grʌntəl] *v.t.* descontentar, enfadar, irritar.
disgruntled [-əld] *a.* descontento, malhumorado.
disguise [-'gaɪz] *v.t.* 1. disfrazar, enmascarar. 2. (fig.) disfrazar, encubrir, disimular, solapar (intención, opinión). 3. desfigurar. 4. **d. oneself as,** disfrazarse de. *—s.* 1. disfraz, máscara. 2. (fig.) simulación, velo, embozo.
disgust [dɪs'gʌst] *v.t.* repugnar, dar asco a, hastiar. *—s.* aversión; repugnancia, asco, hastío.
disgusted [-əd] *a.* asqueado, hastiado.
disgustedly [-lɪ] *adv.* desagradablemente, repugnantemente.
disgustful [-fəl] *a.* repulsivo, fastidioso, desagradable.
disgustfully [-fəlɪ] *adv.* desagradablemente, repulsivamente.
disgusting [-ɪŋ] *a.* repugnante, desagradable; odioso.
disgustingly [-lɪ] *adv.* repugnantemente.
dish [dɪʃ] *s.* 1. plato, fuente; (*pl.*) vajilla. 2. plato (manjar o vianda); (contenido de) un plato. 3. (jer.) gusto, preferencia, ej., *classical music is*

not my dish, la música clásica no es de mi gusto. 4. (jer.) muchacha atractiva. —*v.t.* 1. (gen. con *up*) servir (los alimentos en platos). 2. formar una concavidad en. 3. (jer., G.B.) engañar, dejar plantado; liquidar, arruinar. 4. **d. out,** (jer.) dar, soltar (información, noticias); asestar (golpes); infligir (castigo); pagar, gastar; **d. it out,** (jer.) gastar dinero; proferir insultos, infligir castigo.

dishabille [ˌdɪsə'bil] *s.* 1. bata, desabillé, deshabilé. 2. desorden, desaliño. 3. paños menores.

disharmonic [ˌdɪshɑr'mɑnɪk, B -hɑ'mɔn-] **disharmonious** [-'moʊnɪəs] *a.* inarmónico, desafinado, disonante.

disharmonize [dɪs'hɑrməˌnaɪz, B -'hɑmə-] *v.t., v.i.* hacer inarmónico, hacer disonante.

disharmony [-nɪ] *s.* disonancia, falta de armonía.

dishcloth ['dɪʃˌklɔθ, -ˌklɑθ, B -ˌklɔθ] *s.* 1. estropajo, fregador. 2. albero, paño para lavar los platos.

dishcloth gourd, (bot.) estropajo.

dishearten [dɪs'hɑrtən, B -'hɑt-] *v.t.* desanimar, desalentar, descorazonar.

disheartening [-ɪŋ] *a.* descorazonador, desalentador.

disheartenment [-mənt] *s.* desaliento, descorazonamiento, desánimo.

dished [dɪʃt] *a.* cóncavo, ahondado.

disherit [dɪs'hɛrɪt] *v.t.* desheredar.

dishevel [dɪ'ʃɛvəl] *v.t.* (*pret., p.p.* DISHEVELED o DISHEVELLED; *p.pr.* DISHEVELING o DISHEVELLING) desgreñar, desmelenar, despeinar (el cabello); desaliñar (a una persona), desarreglar.

disheveled, dishevelled [-əld] *a.* desgreñado, despeinado; desaliñado.

dishevelment [-əlmənt] *s.* despeluzamiento; desaliño.

dishful ['dɪʃˌfʊl] *s.* contenido de un plato lleno; fuente, fuentada.

dishonest [dɪs'ɑnəst, B -'ɔn-] *a.* deshonesto, fraudulento, falso, ímprobo.

dishonestly [-lɪ] *adv.* fraudulentamente, deshonestamente.

dishonesty [-ɪ] *s.* 1. improbidad, falta de honradez, deshonestidad. 2. dolo, fraude, falacia.

dishonor, (G.B.) **dishonour** [dɪs'ɑnər, B -'ɔnə] *s.* 1. deshonor, deshonra, ignominia, infamia. 2. (com.) rechazo (de un cheque, giro, etc.). —*v.t.* 1. deshonrar, difamar, afrentar. 2. (com.) rechazar, rehusar el pago de (un cheque, giro, etc.).

dishonorable [-nərəbəl] *a.* deshonroso, indecoroso, ignominioso, vil, vergonzoso, oprobioso.

dishonorableness [-bəlnəs] *s.* deshonor, ignominia, deshonra.

dishonorably [-blɪ] *adv.* ignominiosamente, deshonrosamente.

dishonorer [-'ɑnərər, B -'ɔnərə] *s.* deshonrador; seductor.

dishpan ['dɪʃˌpæn] *s.* pileta, fregadero o paila de fregar platos.

dish rack, escurreplatos.

dishrag [-ˌræg] *s.* estropajo, fregador.

dish towel, secador, paño para secar platos.

dishwasher [-ˌwɔʃər, -ˌwɑʃ-, B -ˌwɔʃə] *s.* 1. lavaplatos, lavador(a) de platos. 2. máquina de lavar platos, lavadora de platos, lavadora de vajilla.

dishwater [-ˌwɔtər, -ˌwɑt-, B -ˌwɔtə] *s.* agua en que se lavan los platos; agua sucia; **to taste like d.,** saber a agua sucia.

disillusion [ˌdɪsə'luʒən] *s.* desilusión, desencanto, desengaño. —*v.t.* desilusionar, desengañar, desencantar.

disimpassioned [-ɪm'pæʃənd] *a.* desapasionado, sin pasión, sereno.

disincentive [-ən'sɛntɪv] *s.* cosa disuasiva, sin incentivo.

disinclination [-ˌɪnklə'neɪʃən] *s.* renuencia, aversión, mala gana.

disincline [-ən'klaɪn] *v.t.* desinclinar, desviar la inclinación o afecto de alguno.

disinclined [-'klaɪnd] *a.* maldispuesto, renuente, averso.

disinfect [ˌdɪsən'fɛkt] *v.t.* desinfectar, desinficionar.

disinfectant [-ənt] *s.* desinfectante.

disinfection [-'fɛkʃən] *s.* desinfección.

disinfest [-ən'fɛst] *s.* limpiar de bichos o plagas (de ratas, etc.).

disinflation [ˌdɪsən'fleɪʃən] *s.* (fin.) deflación.

disingenuous [-ən'dʒɛnjʊəs] *a.* solapado, falso, doble.

disingenuously [-lɪ] *adv.* solapadamente, disimuladamente.

disingenuousness [-nəs] *s.* doblez, duplicidad, disimulo.

disinherit [-ən'hɛrət] *v.t.* desheredar.

disinheritance [-əns] *s.* desheredación.

disintegrability [dɪsˌɪntəgrə'bɪlətɪ] *s.* (fís., mec.) desintegrabilidad.

disintegrable [-'ɪntəgrəbəl] *a.* (fís., mec.) desintegrable.

disintegrate [-'ɪntəˌgreɪt] *v.t., v.i.* desintegrar(se), desagregar(se), disgregar(se), desmoronar(se), deshacer(se).

disintegration [-ˌɪntə'greɪʃən] *s.* desintegración, desagregación, disgregación, desmoronamiento.

disintegrative [-'ɪntəˌgreɪtɪv] *a.* disgregativo.

disintegrator [-ər, B -ə] *s.* (mec.) desintegrador.

disinter [ˌdɪsən'tɜr, B -'tɜ] *v.t.* desenterrar, exhumar.

disinterest [dɪs'ɪntrəst, -'ɪntərəst] *v.t.* (ant.) quitar interés a, privar de interés; **d. oneself,** desinteresarse. —*s.* 1. desinterés, desapego; imparcialidad. 2. (ant.) desventaja.

disinterested [-əd] *a.* desinteresado, imparcial, desprendido, indiferente.

disinterestedly [-lɪ] *adv.* desinteresadamente, imparcialmente.

disinterestedness [-nəs] *s.* desinterés, imparcialidad.

disinterment [ˌdɪsən'tɜrmənt, B -'tɜmənt] *s.* desenterramiento, exhumación.

disinvestment [-ən'vɛstmənt] *s.* (fin.) inversión negativa, gasto de capital.

disjoin [dɪs'dʒɔɪn] *v.t., v.i.* desunir(se), separar(se), despegar(se), desprender(se).

disjoint [-'dʒɔɪnt] *v.t.* dislocar, desarticular, desunir. —*v.i.* desunirse, separarse. —*a.* 1. (mat.) sin elementos comunes, disjunto. 2. dislocado, desarticulado.

disjointed [-əd] *a.* 1. inconexo, incoherente (lenguaje, habla). 2. dislocado, descoyuntado, desarticulado. 3. desunido, desordenado (comunidad, sociedad, etc.).

disjointedly [-lɪ] *adv.* incoherentemente.

disjointedness [-nəs] *s.* incoherencia.

disjunct [-'dʒʌŋkt] *a.* 1. descoyuntado, desunido, separado. 2. esporádico, disperso.

disjunction [-'dʒʌŋkʃən] *s.* 1. disyunción, separación. 2. (ret., lóg.) disyunción.

disjunctive [-tɪv] *a.* 1. disyuntivo, separativo. 2. (gram., ret., lóg.) disyuntivo. —*s.* 1. (gram.) conjunción disyuntiva. 2. (lóg.) proposición disyuntiva.

disjunctively [-lɪ] *adv.* disyuntivamente.

disk [dɪsk] *s.* 1. (dep.) disco. 2. (bot.) disco. 3. (mec.) disco, plato. 4. (gen. **disc**) disco (fonográfico). 5. (comput.) disco. —*v.t.* 1. (agr.) cultivar con escarificador de discos. 2. (G.B.) grabar en disco (fonográfico); **to cut a d.,** grabar un disco.

disk armature, (elec.) inducido de plato.

disk brake, freno de plato, freno de discos.

disk drive, unidad de disco, disquetera.

diskette [dɪs'kɛt] *s.* disquete, disquette.

disk flower, (bot.) flor tubular (en el disco de una planta compuesta).

disk harrow, (agr.) grada de discos, escarificador de discos.

disk jockey, *var. de* **disc jockey.**

disklike ['dɪskˌlaɪk] *a.* discoidal, semejante a un disco.

disk plow, arado de discos.

disk sander, (mec.) esmeriladora de disco, lijadora de plato.

disk saw, sierra circular, sierra de plato.

disk thrower, (dep.) discóbolo.

disk wheel, (aut.) rueda de disco; (mot.) rueda de plato, rueda llena.

dislikable [dɪs'laɪkəbəl] *a.* antipático.

dislike [-'laɪk] *v.t.* tener aversión a, ej., *they d. each other,* se tienen aversión (uno a otro); no gustarle a uno, ej., *I d. walking in the rain,* no me gusta caminar bajo la lluvia. —*s.* aversión, repugnancia, antipatía.

dislimn [-'lɪm] *v.t., v.i.* (poét.) borrar(se), desvanecer(se).

dislocate ['dɪsloʊˌkeɪt, dɪs'loʊ-, B 'dɪsloʊ-] *v.t.* 1. dislocar, descoyuntar (hueso). 2. desarreglar, trastornar (asuntos, planes, etc.).

dislocation [ˌdɪsloʊ'keɪʃən, -lə-] *s.* 1. dislocación, dislocadura, descoyuntamiento. 2. desarreglo, trastorno.

dislodge [dɪs'lɑdʒ, B -'lɔdʒ] *v.t.* desalojar, echar fuera (persona o cosa). —*v.i.* desatascarse, soltarse; mudarse.

dislodgment [-mənt] *s.* desalojamiento.

disloyal [-'lɔɪəl] *a.* desleal, infiel, falso, traidor.

disloyally [-əlɪ] *adv.* deslealmente.

disloyalty [-tɪ] *s.* deslealtad, infidelidad.

dismal ['dɪzməl] *a.* 1. depresivo, deprimente, desconsolador. 2. miserable, desconsolado, funesto, lúgubre. —*s.* (G.B., fam.) **the dismals,** esplín, morriña, murria, melancolía.

dismally [-məlɪ] *adv.* desconsoladamente; melancólicamente.

dismalness [-məlnəs] *s.* calidad de deprimente o lúgubre.

dismantle [dɪs'mæntəl] *v.t.* 1. desarmar, desguarnecer. 2. (mil.) desmantelar (una plaza). 3. (mar.) desmantelar, desaparejar, desarmar (una embarcación). 4. (mec.) desmontar, desarmar (un motor).

dismantlement [-mənt] *s.* desarmadura, desmantelamiento, desmontadura.

dismast [-'mæst, B 'dɪs'mɑst] *v.t.* (mar.) desarbolar.

dismay [dɪs'meɪ, dɪz-] *v.t.* consternar, desanimar, desalentar. —*s.* consternación, desánimo, desaliento; **in d.,** desalentado.

dismember [-'mɛmbər, B -bə] *v.t.* desmembrar, despedazar, destrozar.

dismemberment [-mənt] *s.* desmembramiento.

dismiss [dɪs'mɪs] *v.t.* 1. despedir, remover, destituir; licenciar (del ejército). 2. dejar ir, dar permiso para irse. 3. disolver (asamblea, junta, etc.); (mil.) mandar romper filas. 4. descartar, desechar (pensamiento, idea, etc.). 5. (der.) desechar, declarar sin lugar (caso, petición).

dismissal [-əl] *s.* 1. despedida, despido, remoción, destitución. 2. desolución (de una asamblea, junta, etc.). 3. abandono (de un pensamiento, idea, etc.).

dismount [-'maʊnt] *v.i.* 1. desmontar(se), apearse (esp. de caballería). 2. (poét.) descender, bajar. —*v.t.* 1. desmontar. 2. (mec.) desarmar. —*s.* desmonte.

disnature [-'neɪtʃər, B -tʃə] *v.t., v.i.* desnaturalizar(se).
disobedience [ˌdɪsə'bidɪəns] *s.* desobediencia.
disobedient [-ənt] *a.* desobediente.
disobediently [-lɪ] *adv.* desobedientemente.
disobey [ˌdɪsə'beɪ] *v.t., v.i.* desobedecer.
disoblige [-ə'blaɪdʒ] *v.t.* 1. no complacer. 2. incomodar, disgustar, ofender.
disobliging [-ɪŋ] *a.* poco complaciente, poco servicial; desagradable, ofensivo.
disomic [daɪ'soʊmɪk] *a.* (biol.) de cromosoma(s) duplicado(s).
disorder [dɪs'ɔrdər, B -'ɔdə] *s.* 1. desorden, desarreglo, desbarajuste. 2. desorden, barullo, alboroto. 3. desorden, indisposición, trastorno. —*v.t.* desordenar, desarreglar, descomponer, trastornar.
disordered [-dərd, B -dəd] *a.* desordenado, trastornado.
disorderliness [-dərlɪnəs, B -dəlɪ-] *s.* 1. falta de sentido de orden. 2. estado desordenado; carácter de desordenado, confusión.
disorderly [-lɪ] *a.* 1. desordenado, desarreglado. 2. turbulento, alborotador, escandaloso.
disorderly conduct, conducta escandalosa; (der.) alteración del orden público.
disorderly house, burdel; garito.
disorderly person, persona de conducta escandalosa.
disorganization [dɪsˌɔrgənə'zeɪʃən, B -ˌɔgənaɪ-] *s.* desorganización.
disorganize [-'ɔrgəˌnaɪz, B -'ɔgə-] *v.t.* desorganizar.
disorganizer [-ər, B -ə] *s.* desorganizador.
disorient [-'ɔrɪˌɛnt] *v.t.* desorientar.
disorientate [-ənˌteɪt, -ˌɛnˌteɪt] *v.t.* desorientar.
disorientation [-ˌɔrɪən'teɪʃən, -ɛn'teɪ-] *s.* desorientación.
disown [dɪs'oʊn] *v.t.* 1. repudiar, desconocer, no reconocer. 2. negar. 3. negar que es suyo, ej., *the accused disowned the murder weapon,* el acusado negó que el arma asesina fuera suya.
disparage [-'pærɪdʒ] *v.t.* 1. menospreciar, menoscabar. 2. desdorar, desacreditar.
disparagement [-mənt] *s.* 1. menosprecio, desestimación. 2. desdoro, detracción, descrédito.
disparager [-ər, B -ə] *s.* detractor.
disparaging [-ɪŋ] *a.* menospreciativo, detractivo.
disparagingly [-lɪ] *adv.* despectivamente, en tono menospreciativo.
disparate ['dɪspərət] *a.* desigual, desemejante, diferente, distinto.
disparately [-lɪ] *adv.* desigualmente.
disparity [dɪs'pærətɪ] *s.* disparidad, desemejanza, desigualdad.
dispart [-'pɑrt, B -'pɑt] *v.t., v.i.* (ant.) despartir, partir(se), separar(se).
dispassionate [-'pæʃənət] *a.* desapasionado, imparcial.
dispassionately [-lɪ] *adv.* desapasionadamente, imparcialmente.
dispatch [dɪs'pætʃ] *v.t.* 1. despachar, remitir, enviar. 2. despachar, matar. 3. despachar, expedir, aviar (una tarea, trabajo, etc.). 4. acabar con; despabilar, engullir (comida). —*v.i.* apurarse, darse prisa. —*s.* 1. despacho, envío. 2. despacho, mensaje, comunicación. 3. ejecución, matanza. 4. prontitud, eficiencia, diligencia.
dispatch boat, (mar.) barco aviso.
dispatcher [-ər, B -ə] *s.* despachador, expedidor.
dispel [dɪs'pɛl] *v.t.* (*pret., p.p.* DISPELLED; *p.pr.* DISPELLING) disipar, dispersar, desvanecer (niebla, obscuridad; temor, sospecha, etc.).
dispensability [-ˌpɛnsə'bɪlətɪ] *s.* calidad de dispensable o prescindible.
dispensable [-'pɛnsəbəl] *a.* 1. dispensable. 2. prescindible, innecesario.
dispensary [-'pɛnsərɪ] *s.* (med.) dispensario.
dispensation [ˌdɪspən'seɪʃən, -ˌpɛn-] *s.* 1. dispensación, distribución, reparto. 2. dispensación, dispensa, exención (de ley, voto o impedimento). 3. (teol.) designio divino, acto o plan providencial.
dispensator ['dɪspənˌseɪtər, B -ə] *s.* dispensador.
dispensatory [dɪs'pɛnsəˌtɔrɪ, B -tərɪ] *s.* 1. farmacopea. 2. (ant.) dispensario.
dispense [-'pɛns] *v.t.* 1. dispensar, distribuir, repartir. 2. aplicar (leyes, ordenanzas); administrar (justicia, sacramento). 3. dispensar, excusar, eximir, absolver. 4. hacer, preparar (medicamento con varios ingredientes). —*v.i.* otorgar dispensa; **d. with,** dispensar de, hacer caso omiso de; pasar sin, prescindir de; eliminar.
dispenser [-'pɛnsər, B -sə] *s.* 1. dispensador (de favores, etc.); administrador (de justicia). 2. farmacéutico. 3. surtidor. 4. distribuidor automático.
dispeople [-'pipəl] *v.t.* despoblar.
dispersal [dɪs'pɜrsəl, B -'pɜsəl] *s.* dispersión.
disperse [-'pɜrs, B -'pɜs] *v.t.* 1. dispersar, esparcir (multitud, etc.). 2. (fig.) dispersar, diseminar (noticias, etc.). 3. (fís.) dispersar (la luz); (quím.) dispersar (substancias). 4. disipar, desvanecer (vapor, olor). —*v.i.* dispersarse, desvanecerse.
dispersedly [dɪs'pɜrsədlɪ, B -'pɜsəd-] *adv.* en forma dispersa, esparcidamente.
disperser [-sər, B -sə] *s.* dispersador, diseminador.
dispersion [-ʒən, B -ʃən] *s.* dispersión, difusión, esparcimiento; (fís.) dispersión; (quím.) dispersión; substancia dispersa.
dispersive [-sɪv] *a.* dispersivo.
dispersoid [-ˌsɔɪd] *s.* (quím.) coloide.
dispirit [dɪ'spɪrət] *v.t.* desalentar, desanimar, descorazonar.
dispirited [-əd] *a.* desanimado, desalentado, decaído.
dispiritedly [-lɪ] *adv.* desanimadamente, desalentadamente.
dispiritedness [-nəs] *s.* desaliento, desánimo.
displace [dɪs'pleɪs] *v.t.* 1. desplazar; obligar a expatriarse; desalojar. 2. destituir, deponer. 3. substituir, suplantar, reemplazar. 4. desplazar (agua). 5. (quím.) desplazar.
displaced person [-'pleɪst-] expatriado, persona desplazada, forzada a dejar su país, esp. por una guerra.
displacement [-'pleɪsmənt] *s.* 1. desalojamiento. 2. destitución. 3. reemplazo, sustitución. 4. (mar., mec., quím.) desplazamiento. 5. (geol.) falla, dislocación (de las capas terrestres). 6. (psic.) desplazamiento.
displacer [-ər, B -ə] *s.* (quím.) colador.
displant [dɪs'plænt, B -'plɑnt] *v.t.* (ant.) desalojar, desarraigar.
display [dɪs'pleɪ] *v.t.* 1. exhibir, exponer, ostentar. 2. desplegar, revelar, mostrar. 3. (tip.) destacar, hacer resaltar. —*s.* 1. exhibición, exposición, despliegue. 2. demostración, muestra. 3. ostentación. 4. (tip.) resalto, destaque; presentación, disposición. 5. **on d.,** en exhibición; a la vista.
displayed [-'pleɪd] *a.* (her.) explayada, desplegada (águila).
display window, escaparate, vidriera (Am.).
displease [dɪs'pliz] *v.t.* disgustar, desplacer, molestar; **to be displeased (at, with),** estar disgustado o molesto (con). —*v.i.* causar molestia, desagradar.
displeasing [-ɪŋ] *a.* displicente, desagradable.
displeasure [-'plɛʒər, B -ə] *s.* 1. desagrado, disgusto. 2. incomodidad, molestia. 3. desaprobación.
displume [-'plum] *v.t.* (poét.) desplumar; deshonrar, infamar.
disport [-'pɔrt, B -'pɔt] *s.* (ant.) diversión, deporte, pasatiempo. —*v.t.* **d. oneself,** divertirse, entretenerse, distraerse. —*v.i.* juguetear, retozar.
disposable [dɪs'poʊzəbəl] *a.* 1. disponible. 2. desechable.
disposal [-zəl] *s.* 1. disposición. 2. eliminación (de basura), neutralización (de bombas, minas). 3. colocación, distribución. 4. **at the d. of,** a (la) disposición de; **at your d.,** a su disposición; **to have at one's d.,** disponer de, tener a su disposición.
disposal system, instalación evacuadora.
dispose [-'poʊz] *v.t.* 1. disponer, colocar, ordenar, acomodar. 2. disponer, ordenar, arreglar. 3. inclinar (a alguien el ánimo). 4. disponer, determinar (los acontecimientos). —*v.i.* 1. disponer, ej., *man proposes, God disposes,* el hombre propone y Dios dispone. 2 **d. of,** disponer de, decidir (el destino, condición, empleo, etc.) de; desembarazarse de; deshacerse de, librarse o zafarse de; quitarse de encima; poner fin a, terminar; consumir, comer; eliminar, destruir, matar; vender.
disposition [ˌdɪspə'zɪʃən] *s.* 1. disposición, mandato. 2. disposición, genio, constitución, carácter. 3. disposición, tendencia, inclinación, propensión. 4. disposición, ordenación, arreglo, colocación. 5. (*pl.*) planes, preparativos. 6. **at the d. of,** a (la) disposición de.
dispossess [-'zɛs] *v.t.* 1. desposeer, privar (de una posesión); desalojar, desahuciar; desterrar, expulsar. 2. **d. oneself of,** desprenderse de.
dispossession [-'zɛʃən] *s.* desposeimiento; desahucio, expulsión.
dispossessor [-'zɛsər, B -ə] *s.* desahuciador, desposeedor.
dispraise [dɪs'preɪz] *v.t.* menospreciar, despreciar; censurar, criticar. —*s.* menosprecio, desprecio; censura, crítica, desaprobación.
dispraisingly [-ɪŋlɪ] *adv.* con desaprobación.
disprize [dɪs'praɪz] *v.t.* (ant.) desapreciar, desestimar.
disproof [-'pruf] *s.* refutación, confutación.
disproportion [ˌdɪsprə'pɔrʃən, B -'pɔʃən] *s.* desproporción, desigualdad, disparidad. —*v.t.* desproporcionar, desigualar.
disproportional [-əl] *a.* desproporcionado, desigual.
disproportionate [-ət] *a.* desproporcionado, desigual, asimétrico.
disproportionately [-lɪ] *adv.* desproporcionadamente.
disprovable [dɪs'pruvəbəl] *a.* refutable.
disproval [-vəl] *s.* refutación, confutación.
disprove [-'pruv] *v.t.* refutar, confutar.
disputability [dɪsˌpjutə'bɪlətɪ] *s.* carácter disputable.
disputable [-'pjutəbəl, 'dɪspjə-] *a.* disputable, discutible.
disputant [-ənt] *a., s.* disputador.
disputation [ˌdɪspjə'teɪʃən] *s.* 1. disputa, controversia, debate. 2. (ant.) conversación, discusión.
disputatious [-ʃəs] *a.* 1. disputador. 2. disputable, problemático.
dispute [dɪs'pjut] *v.t.* 1. disputar, discutir, debatir, argüir. 2. pleitear, contender, altercar. —*v.i.* 1. disputar, contender, impugnar. 2. luchar por, disputar (título, candidatura, victoria, etc.). —*s.* 1. disputa, discusión, debate, polémica. 2.

(der.) pleito, litigio. 3. **beyond d.,** sin disputa; **in d.,** disputado.
disputer [-ər, B -ə] *s.* disputador, controversista.
disqualification [dɪsˌkwɑləfə'keɪʃən, B -ˌkwɔl-] *s.* 1. descalificación, inhabilitación. 2. motivo de descalificación.
disqualify [-'kwɑləˌfaɪ, B -'kwɔl-] *v.t.* descalificar, inhabilitar, incapacitar.
disquiet [-'kwaɪət] *v.t.* inquietar, desasosegar, intranquilizar, perturbar, preocupar. —*a.* (ant.) inquieto, intranquilo. —*s.* inquietud, desasosiego, intranquilidad, ansiedad.
disquieting [-ɪŋ] *a.* inquietante, alarmante.
disquietude [-'kwaɪəˌtud, B -ˌtjud] *s.* inquietud, desasosiego, ansiedad.
disquisition [ˌdɪskwə'zɪʃən] *s.* disertación, discurso, disquisición.
disrate [dɪs'reɪt] *v.t.* degradar.
disregard [ˌdɪsrɪ'gɑrd, B -'gɑd] *v.t.* desatender, descuidar, pasar por alto, hacer caso omiso de. —*s.* desatención, descuido, negligencia.
disregardful [-fəl] *a.* desatento, indiferente, descuidado, negligente.
disrelish [dɪs'rɛlɪʃ] *s.* disgusto, desazón, desabrimiento, inapetencia; repugnancia, aversión, antipatía. —*v.t.* no gustarle a uno; detestar; sentir aversión a.
disrepair [ˌdɪsrɪ'pɛr, B -'pɛə] *s.* mal estado, descompostura; **in d.,** en mal estado; **to fall into d.,** deteriorarse, descomponerse.
disreputability [dɪsˌrɛpjətə'bɪlətɪ] *s.* mala fama.
disreputable [-'rɛpjətəbəl] *a.* desacreditado, de mala fama, deshonroso, desdoroso; vergonzoso; desgarbado, de mala apariencia.
disreputably [-blɪ] *adv.* deshonrosamente.
disrepute [ˌdɪsrɪ'pjut] *s.* descrédito, desprestigio, deshonor, mala fama; **to bring into d.,** desprestigiar, desacreditar; **to fall into d.,** desprestigiarse; **to hold in d.,** desapreciar, desestimar.
disrespect [-rɪ'spɛkt] *s.* desacato, descortesía, desatención, irreverencia; falta de respeto. —*v.t.* desacatar, faltar al respeto a.
disrespectable [-əbəl] *a.* indecoroso.
disrespectful [-fəl] *a.* irrespetuoso, irreverente, descortés.
disrespectfully [-fəlɪ] *adv.* irrespetuosamente, descortésmente.
disrespectfulness [-nəs] *s.* descortesía.
disrobe [dɪs'roˌʊb] *v.t., v.i.* desnudar(se), desvestir(se).
disroot [-'rut] *v.t.* desarraigar, arrancar de raíz, descuajar.
disrupt [-'rʌpt] *v.t.* 1. romper. 2. desorganizar. 3. interrumpir.
disruption [-'rʌpʃən] *s.* 1. rotura, fractura. 2. desgarro. 3. disolución, desorganización. 4. interrupción.
disruptive [-tɪv] *a.* destrozador; desbaratador, desorganizador, disociador, desgarrador, destructor; rajante.
disruptive strength, (elec.) resistencia dieléctrica.
disruptive voltage, (elec.) tensión disruptiva.
dissatisfaction [dɪsˌsætəs'fækʃən, B 'dɪs-] *s.* descontento, desagrado, disgusto.
dissatisfactory [-'fæktərɪ] *a.* poco satisfactorio, nada satisfactorio.
dissatisfy [-'sætəsˌfaɪ] *v.t.* descontentar, desagradar, desplacer; no satisfacer.
disseat [dɪs'sit] *v.t.* (ant.) quitar o echar de un asiento; (equit.) desarzonar.
dissect [dɪ'sɛkt, daɪ-, B dɪ-] *v.t.* 1. anatomizar, disecar, dividir o cortar en pedazos. 2. (fig.) disecar, analizar minuciosamente.
dissected [-əd] *a.* 1. disecado, dividido. 2. (bot.) seccionado.
dissecting knife [-ɪŋ-] escalpelo.
dissecting room, sala de disección.
dissection [-'sɛkʃən] *s.* 1. disección, disecación. 2. espécimen disecado. 3. análisis anatómico.
dissector [-'sɛktər, B -ə] *s.* disector, disecador.
disseize, disseise [dɪs'siz] *v.t.* (der.) desposeer (de algo), desalojar; usurpar (bienes raíces).
disseizin, disseisin [-ən] *s.* (der.) usurpación (de tierras), desposesión.
disseizor, disseisor [-ər, B -ə] *s.* (der.) usurpador (de bienes raíces).
dissemblance [dɪ'sɛmbləns] *s.* 1. desemejanza, disimilitud, diferencia. 2. disimulación, disimulo, simulación, encubrimiento.
dissemble [-bəl] *v.t.* 1. disimular, encubrir. 2. simular, fingir, aparentar. —*v.i.* disimular, obrar con disimulo, ser hipócrita.
dissembler [-blər, B -blə] *s.* disimulador, hipócrita.
disseminate [dɪ'sɛməˌneɪt] *v.t.* diseminar, difundir, propagar. —*v.i.* diseminarse, difundirse.
dissemination [-ˌsɛmə'neɪʃən] *s.* diseminación, propagación, divulgación.
disseminative [-'sɛməˌneɪtɪv] *a.* diseminador.
disseminator [-ər, B -ə] *s.* difusor (ej., de noticias); propagador (ej., de enfermedades).
disseminule [-'sɛməˌnjul] *s.* (bot.) disemínulo.
dissension [dɪ'sɛntʃən, B -'sɛnʃən] *s.* disensión, desacuerdo, oposición; **to sow d.,** sembrar cizaña.
dissent [-'sɛnt] *v.i.* 1. disentir, diferir, discrepar, desconvenir. 2. (relig.) disidir. —*s.* 1. disenso, disentimiento, desavenencia, desacuerdo. 2. disidencia. 3. no conformismo, rechazo de las reglas establecidas.
dissenter [-ər, B -ə] *s.* 1. disidente. 2. no conformista.
dissentient [-'sɛntʃənt, B -'sɛnʃɪənt] *a.* disidente, disconforme. —*s.* disidente.
dissenting [-'sɛntɪŋ] *a.* 1. disidente. 2. rebelde, no conformista.
dissentious [-'sɛntʃəs, B -'sɛnʃəs] *a.* contencioso, pendenciero; faccioso, sedicioso, revoltoso.
dissepiment [dɪ'sɛpəmənt] *s.* (bot., pal.) disepimento.
dissert [dɪ'sɜrt, B -'sɜt] *v.i.* disertar, discurrir.
dissertate ['dɪsərˌteɪt, B -səˌ-] *v.i.* disertar, discurrir.
dissertation [ˌdɪsər'teɪʃən, B -sə'-] *s.* disertación (científica, histórica, etc.); tesis.
dissertator ['dɪsərˌteɪtər, B 'dɪsəˌ-ə] *s.* disertante, disertador.
disserve [dɪs'sɜrv, B -'sɜv] *v.t.* (raro) deservir, dañar, perjudicar.
disservice [-'sɜrvəs, B 'dɪs'sɜvɪs] *s.* mal servicio, perjuicio, daño.
dissever [dɪ'sɛvər, B -ə] *v.t.* separar; desmembrar, dividir. —*v.i.* separarse, desunirse.
disseverance [-ərəns] *s.* separación, división.
dissidence ['dɪsədəns] *s.* disidencia, desacuerdo.
dissident [-ənt] *a.* disidente, desconforme, disconforme. —*s.* disidente.
dissiliency [dɪ'sɪlɪənsɪ] *s.* (bot.) dehiscencia súbita.
dissilient [-ənt] *a.* (bot.) disiliente.
dissimilar [dɪ'sɪmələr, B -lə] *a.* disímil, desemejante, diferente, desigual, distinto.
dissimilarity [-ˌsɪmə'lærətɪ] *s.* desemejanza, disimilitud, diferencia, desigualdad, diversidad.
dissimilate [-'sɪməˌleɪt] *v.t., v.i.* hacer(se), tornar(se) disímil o diferente; (fon.) disimilar(se).
dissimilation [-ˌsɪmə'ləɪʃən] *s.* 1. (fon.) disimilación. 2. (biol.) catabolismo.
dissimilitude [ˌdɪsə'mɪləˌtud, B -ˌtjud] *s.* disimilitud, desemejanza.
dissimulate [dɪ'sɪmjəˌleɪt] *v.t.* disimular, fingir, encubrir. —*v.i.* obrar con disimulo, ser hipócrita.
dissimulation [-ˌsɪmjə'leɪʃən] *s.* disimulo, disimulación, hipocresía.
dissimulative [-'sɪmjəˌleɪtɪv] *a.* disimulador.
dissimulator [-ər, B -ə] *s.* disimulador.
dissipate ['dɪsəˌpeɪt] *v.t.* 1. disipar (niebla, nubes, etc.), dispersar (muchedumbre, etc.). 2. disipar, desvanecer (duda, sospecha, temores, etc.). 3. disipar, malgastar, desperdiciar (fortuna, dinero, herencia, energías, etc.). —*v.i.* 1. disiparse; dispersarse. 2. entregarse a los placeres; darse a la bebida.
dissipated [-əd] *a.* disipado, disoluto, relajado.
dissipatedly [-lɪ] *adv.* disipadamente, disolutamente.
dissipater [-ər, B -ə] *s.* disipador.
dissipation [ˌdɪsə'peɪʃən] *s.* 1. disipación, dispersión. 2. disipación, desperdicio. 3. disipación, vida disoluta, libertinaje. 4. distracción, diversión.
dissipative ['dɪsəˌpeɪtɪv] *a.* (elec.) disipador.
dissociability [dɪˌsoʊʃə'bɪlətɪ] *s.* disociabilidad.
dissociable [-'soʊʃəbəl] *a.* 1. disociable, separable. 2. insociable.
dissocial [-'soʊʃəl] *a.* insociable, huraño; egoísta.
dissociate [-'soʊʃɪˌeɪt] *v.t.* disociar, desunir, separar; (quím.) disociar. —*v.i.* disociarse.
dissociation [-ˌsoʊsɪ'eɪʃən] *s.* 1. disociación, separación, desunión, disgregación. 2. (quím.) disociación. 3. (med.) desdoblamiento (de la personalidad).
dissociative [-'soʊsɪˌeɪtɪv] *a.* disociador.
dissolubility [dɪˌsɑljə'bɪlətɪ, B -ˌsɔl-] *s.* disolubilidad.
dissoluble [-'sɑljəbəl, B -'sɔl-] *a.* disoluble, soluble.
dissolute ['dɪsəˌlut] *a.* disoluto, libertino, licencioso.
dissolutely [-lɪ] *adv.* disolutamente.
dissoluteness [-nəs] *s.* disipación, relajación, disolución.
dissolution [ˌdɪsə'luʃən] *s.* 1. disolución, descomposición, desagregación, desintegración, destrucción. 2. extinción de la vida; muerte. 3. disolución (de una asamblea, sociedad, matrimonio, parlamento, etc.).
dissolvable [dɪ'zɑlvəbəl, -'zɔl-, B -'zɔl-] *a.* disoluble, soluble.
dissolve [-'zɑlv, -'zɔlv, B -'zɔlv] *v.t.* 1. disolver, descomponer, desagregar, desintegrar. 2. (con *in*) disolver (en), mezclar (con). 3. disolver (una asamblea, sociedad, parlamento, matrimonio, etc.). 4. (cinem., t.v.) desvanecer una imagen gradualmente. 5. (der.) disolver, derogar, revocar, anular. 6. **dissolved in tears,** deshecho en lágrimas, bañado en lágrimas. —*v.i.* 1. disolverse, descomponerse, desintegrarse. 2. (con *in*) disolverse (en), mezclarse (con). 3. (cinem., t.v.) desvanecerse (imagen). —*s.* (cinem., t.v.) disolvencia.
dissolvent [-ənt] *s., a.* disolvente.
dissonance ['dɪsənəns] *s.* 1. disonancia. 2. (fig.) disonancia, desconcierto, desacuerdo. 3. (mús.) disonancia.
dissonant [-nənt] *a.* disonante, discordante; (mús.) disonante, desentonado.
dissuade [dɪ'sweɪd] *v.t.* disuadir, desaconsejar; desviar, apartar (a uno de su intento).

dissuader [-ər, B -ə] *s.* factor disuasivo, motivo de disuasión.
dissuasion [-'sweɪʒən] *s.* disuasión.
dissuasive [-'sweɪsɪv] *a.* disuasivo.
dissyllabic, dissyllable, *vars. de* **disyllabic, disyllable.**
dissymmetric [ˌdɪsə'mɛtrɪk] **dissymmetrical** [-rɪkəl] *a.* disimétrico, asimétrico.
dissymmetry [dɪ'sɪmətrɪ] *s.* disimetría, asimetría.
distaff ['dɪsˌtæf, B -ˌtɑf] *s.* 1. rueca. 2. quehaceres femeninos. 3. **the d. side,** línea o rama femenina (de la familia). —*a.* femenino.
distain [dɪs'teɪn] *v.t.* (ant.) descolorar, desteñir; manchar, deslustrar.
distal ['dɪstəl] *a.* (bot., anat.) distal, distante del centro.
distance ['dɪstəns] *s.* 1. distancia (de lugar o tiempo). 2. lontananza, lejanía. 3. (fig.) distancia, reserva, frialdad. 4. (mús.) distancia, intervalo (entre dos notas). 5. trecho, tirada (en el camino). 6. **a good d. off,** a buena distancia; **at this d.,** a esta distancia, desde tan lejos; después de tanto tiempo; **from a d.,** desde lejos; **in the d.,** en lontananza, a lo lejos; **to keep at a d.,** mantener a distancia, tratar con frialdad; **to keep one's d.,** guardar las distancias, no familiarizarse; **within striking d.,** al alcance de su puño; al alcance de la artillería, al alcance de los bombarderos, lo suficientemente cerca como para atacar. —*v.i.* 1. distanciar, apartar, poner a distancia. 2. dejar atrás, distanciarse de, aventajar.
distant [-tənt] *a.* 1. distante, apartado, alejado, remoto (lugar); distante, remoto, lejano (tiempo). 2. (fig.) lejano, ej., *a d. likeness,* un parecido lejano, *a d. relative,* un pariente lejano. 3. (fig.) reservado, frío, esquivo. 4. (fig.) abstraído. 5. **five miles d.,** a cinco millas de distancia.
distantly [-lɪ] *adv.* con una mirada vaga, con un aire distraído, con los ojos perdidos en el vacío; a distancia, de lejos; a lo lejos, en lontananza.
distaste [dɪs'teɪst] *v.t.* (ant.) aborrecer; desplacer, enfadar, ofender. —*s.* hastío, tedio, fastidio, aversión.
distasteful [-fəl] *a.* desagradable, enfadoso, repugnante.
distastefulness [-nəs] *s.* carácter desagradable, aspecto repugnante.
distemper [dɪs'tɛmpər, B -pə] *s.* 1. mal genio, mal humor. 2. mal, destemplanza, indisposición, enfermedad (de animales), esp. moquillo (en los perros). 3. perturbación, desorden, tumulto. 4. (pint.) templa, tempera. —*v.t.* 1. destemplar, desordenar, perturbar. 2. (ant.) enfermar (animales) de moquillo; desarreglar (mentalmente); malhumorar. 3. (pint.) pintar al temple; mezclar los colores para pintar al temple.
distemperature [-'tɛmprətʃər, -pərə-, B -tʃə] *s.* (ant.) destemplanza, indisposición, dolencia; perturbación, desorden (mental).
distend [-'tɛnd] *v.t.* 1. hinchar, inflar. 2. extender. 3. (med.) distender. 4. alargar, estirar. —*v.i.* inflarse; agrandarse.
distensibility [dɪsˌtɛnsə'bɪlətɪ] *s.* dilatabilidad; (med.) distensibilidad.
distensible [-'tɛnsəbəl] *a.* dilatable, que se puede inflar; (med.) distensible.
distension, *var. de* **distention.**
distent [-'tɛnt] *a.* (poét.) extendido, ensanchado; dilatado, hinchado.
distention [-'tɛntʃən, B -'tɛnʃən] *s.* expansión, dilatación; (med.) distensión.
distich ['dɪstɪk] *s.* (poét.) dístico.
distichous [-tɪkəs] *a.* (bot.) dístico.
distill, distil [dɪs'tɪl] *v.t.* (*pret., p.p.* DISTILLED; *p.pr.* DISTILLING) destilar, alquitarar, alambicar. —*v.i.* destilar, exudar, gotear.
distillable [-əbəl] *a.* destilable.
distillate ['dɪstəˌleɪt, -lət] *s.* (quím.) destilado.
distillation [ˌdɪstə'leɪʃən] *s.* 1. destilación. 2. (quím.) el destilado.
distiller [dɪs'tɪlər, B -ə] *s.* 1. destilador (esp. de alcoholes), refinador. 2. destiladera, alambique; condensador.
distillery [-ərɪ] *s.* destilería (esp. de licores alcohólicos).
distinct [dɪs'tɪŋkt] *a.* 1. claro, preciso, nítido. 2. distinto, diferente, diverso. 3. marcado, notable, señalado. 4. concreto, positivo; cierto, indudable. 5. **d. from,** distinto a, distinto de.
distinction [-'tɪŋkʃən] *s.* 1. distinción, discriminación, diferenciación. 2. distinción, diferencia. 3. distinción, honor, mérito. 4. distinción, eminencia. 5. **in d. from** o **to,** a distinción de; **without d.,** indistintamente.
distinctive [-'tɪŋktɪv] *a.* 1. distintivo, característico. 2. distinguido, elegante. 3. **d. to,** característico de.
distinctly [-lɪ] *adv.* distintamente, claramente.
distinctness [-nəs] *s.* claridad, nitidez; distinción.
distingué [ˌdɪsˌtæŋ'geɪ] *a.* (fr.) distinguido, elegante, de buen porte.
distinguish [dɪs'tɪŋgwɪʃ] *v.t.* 1. distinguir, diferenciar; clasificar; discernir. 2. distinguir, divisar. 3. distinguir, honrar. 4. **d. oneself,** distinguirse, descollar. —*v.i.* **d. between** o **among,** distinguir entre.
distinguishable [-əbəl] *a.* distinguible, discernible, perceptible.
distinguished [-gwɪʃt] *a.* 1. distinguido, ilustre, notable, prestigioso. 2. señalado, marcado. 3. **as d. from,** a diferencia de.
distinguishing [-gwɪʃɪŋ] *a.* distintivo, característico.
distomatosis [daɪˌstoʊmə'toʊsəs] *s.* (*pl.* DISTOMATOSES [-ˌsiz]) (med., vet.) distomatosis.
distomatous [-'stɑmətəs, B -'stɔ-] *a.* (zool.) dístomo.
distome ['daɪˌstoʊm] *s.* (zool.) gusano dístomo.
distort [dɪs'tɔrt, B -'tɔt] *v.t.* 1. torcer, retorcer, deformar. 2. (fig.) torcer, falsear (hechos, verdad, motivos, etc.); tergiversar, pervertir. 3. (fís.) distorsionar (sonido, ondas luminosas).
distorted [-əd] *a.* torcido, deformado; pervertido (idea, valor); distorsionado.
distortion [-'tɔrʃən, B -'tɔʃən] *s.* 1. distorsión, torsión. 2. deformación, falsificación (de hechos, de la verdad, etc.). 3. (fís.) distorsión.
distortional [-əl] *a.* de distorsión.
distract [dɪs'trækt] *v.t.* 1. distraer, divertir (atención, pensamientos, etc.). 2. perturbar, aturdir, confundir; trastornar.
distracted [-əd] *a.* aturdido, enloquecido, aturullado.
distractedly [-lɪ] *adv.* 1. distraídamente. 2. alocadamente.
distraction [-'trækʃən] *s.* 1. distracción, pasatiempo, entretenimiento. 2. confusión, aturdimiento, perturbación; frenesí, locura. 3. **to drive to d.,** volver loco.
distrain [dɪs'treɪn] *v.i., v.t.* (der.) embargar, secuestrar, enajenar.
distrainable [-əbəl] *a.* secuestrable, embargable.
distrainer [-ər, B -ə] *s.* embargador.
distraint [-'treɪnt] *s.* (der.) embargo, secuestro.
distrait [dɪs'treɪ] *a.* distraído.
distraught [-'trɔt] *a.* perturbado, aturdido, enloquecido.
distress [-'trɛs] *s.* 1. aflicción, congoja, angustia, zozobra. 2. apuro, infortunio, peligro. 3. miseria, necesidad, escasez. 4. (der.) embargo, secuestro. 5. **in d.,** (mar.) en peligro; **d. signals,** señales de socorro. —*v.t.* 1. afligir, angustiar, acosar. 2. (der.) embargar, secuestrar.
distressed [-'trɛst] *a.* 1. angustiado, acongojado, afligido. 2. agotado, extenuado. 3. en la miseria, en apuros; en peligro.
distress flag, (mar.) bandera morrón.
distressful [-'trɛsfəl] *a.* penoso, angustioso, acongojado.
distressing [-ɪŋ] *a.* penoso, aflictivo; embarazoso; inquietante, perturbador.
distressingly [-lɪ] *adv.* penosamente, acongojadamente.
distributary [dɪs'trɪbjəˌtɛrɪ, B -tərɪ] *s.* brazo de río que sirve de desaguadero.
distribute [-'trɪbjət] *v.t.* distribuir, repartir; clasificar, disponer; (com.) distribuir (productos, mercancías); (tip.) distribuir, desempastelar (tipos en las cajas respectivas).
distribution [ˌdɪstrə'bjuʃən] *s.* distribución, reparto, repartición; disposición, clasificatición; (com.) distribución (de productos, mercancías); (tip.) distribución (de tipos); (mat.) distribución.
distributional [-əl] *a.* de distribución.
distribution switchboard, tablero de distribución (de electricidad).
distributive [dɪs'trɪbjətɪv] *a.* distributivo; (gram., mat.) distributivo.
distributively [-lɪ] *adv.* distributivamente.
distributor [-ər, B -ə] *s.* distribuidor, repartidor, dispensador; (com.) distribuidor (de productos, mercancías); (mot.) distribuidor (de encendido); esparcidor.
district ['dɪstrɪkt] *s.* comarca, región, partido (de un territorio); barriada, barrio (de una ciudad); jurisdicción, distrito (administrativo). —*v.t.* dividir en distritos.
district attorney, (E.U.) fiscal de un distrito judicial.
District of Columbia (D.C.), (E.U.) Distrito Federal (Washington, D.F., la capital).
distrust [dɪs'trʌst] *v.t.* desconfiar de (alguien), sospechar, recelar; dudar de (algo o alguien). —*s.* desconfianza, recelo, duda, sospecha, suspicacia.
distrustful [-fəl] *a.* desconfiado, receloso, suspicaz, sospechoso.
distrustfully [-fəlɪ] *adv.* desconfiadamente.
distrustfulness [-fəlnəs] *s.* naturaleza recelosa.
disturb [dɪs'tɜrb, B -'tɜb] *v.t.* 1. molestar (a alguien). 2. turbar, conturbar, perturbar, inquietar (el sueño, la conciencia, etc.). 3. desordenar, desarreglar; alborotar, alterar. 4. agitar, mover, ej., *a light breeze disturbed the flowers,* una brisa ligera agitaba o movía las flores. 5. tocar, ej., *please do not d. (the articles on display),* se ruega no tocar (los artículos aquí exhibidos); se ruega no molestar. 6. **do not d. yourself,** no se moleste.
disturbance [-əns] *s.* 1. disturbio, alteración. 2. desarreglo, desorden. 3. tumulto, bullicio, conmoción, revuelo, alboroto. 4. **d. of the peace,** alteración del orden público.
disturbed [-'tɜrbd, B -'tɜbd] *a.* (psic.) desequilibrado.
disturbing [-'tɜrbɪŋ, B -'tɜb-] *a.* inquietante, perturbador; que distrae o molesta.
disulfide [daɪ'sʌlˌfaɪd] *s.* (quím.) disulfuro.
disunion [dɪs'junjən] *s.* 1. desunión, separación, disyunción. 2. (fig.) desunión, desacuerdo, disensión; discordia.
disunionist [-əst] *s.* (pol.) separatista; (E.U.) secesionista (como durante la Guerra Civil).

disunite [ˌdɪsju'naɪt] *v.t.* 1. desunir, separar. 2. (fig.) desunir, desavenir, disociar. —*v.i.* desunirse, separarse.
disunity [dɪs'junətɪ] *s.* desunión, separación; discordia, desavenencia.
disuse [dɪs'jus] *s.* desuso, deshabituación. — [-'juz] *v.t.* desusar, dejar de usar, desechar; desacostumbrar.
disutility [ˌdɪsjʊ'tɪlətɪ] *s.* 1. inconveniencia, incomodidad; impedimento. 2. (e.p.) desutilidad.
disvalue [dɪs'vælju] *v.t.* desvalorar, desapreciar, depreciar. —*s.* 1. desestimación. 2. valor negativo.
disyllabic [ˌdaɪsə'læbɪk, ˌdɪ-] *a.* (gram.) disílabo, bisílabo, disilábico.
disyllable ['daɪˌsɪləbəl, daɪ'sɪl-, B dɪ-] *s.* (gram.) bisílabo, disílabo.
disyoke [dɪs'joʊk] *v.t.* desuncir.
ditch [dɪtʃ] *s.* 1. zanja, cuneta, regadero, acequia. 2. (fort.) trinchera, foso, cárcava. 3. (hidr.) badén, presa. 4. **the D.,** jer., G.B.) el Canal de la Mancha o el Mar del Norte; **to the last d.,** hasta quemar el último cartucho. —*v.t.* 1. zanjar, acequiar. 2. hacer caer en la zanja (bicicleta, automóvil). 3. (jer.) hacer descender (avión) en el mar (en amaraje forzoso). 4. (jer., E.U.) abandonar, desembarazarse de; evadir.
ditch digger, zanjeador, acequiador.
ditcher ['dɪtʃər, B -ə] *s.* cavador de zanjas.
ditheism ['daɪθɪˌɪzəm] *s.* diteísmo, creencia en dos dioses.
ditheistic [ˌdaɪθɪ'ɪstɪk] *a.* diteísta, de la dualidad (creencia en dos dioses).
dither ['dɪðər, B -ə] *v.i.* 1. temblar, tiritar. 2. vacilar. —*s.* estado excitado, agitación; **to be all in a d.,** estar muy nervioso; estar preso de agitación o incertidumbre.
dithionic [ˌdaɪθaɪ'ɑnɪk, B -'ɔn-] *a.* (quím.) ditiónico.
dithyramb ['dɪθɪˌræm, -ˌræmb] *s.* ditirambo; himno y danza en honor a Dioniso en la Grecia antigua.
dithyrambic [ˌdɪθɪ'ræmbɪk] *a.* ditirámbico, dionisíaco, desenfrenado.
ditone ['daɪˌtoʊn] *s.* (mús.) dítono.
dittany ['dɪtənɪ] *s.* (bot.) díctamo.
ditto ['dɪtoʊ] *s.* (*pl.* DITTOS) 1. ídem, lo mismo, lo antedicho. 2. comillas vueltas, signo de repetición. 3. copia, duplicado. 4. **to say d. to,** (G.B.) concordar (con). —*adv.* de la misma manera, como se ha dicho. —*v.t.* repetir, reiterar (argumento, afirmación); copiar, duplicar.
ditty ['dɪtɪ] *s.* cantinela, cantilena, sonsonete.
ditty bag, d. box, (mar.) bolsa o caja para guardar cosas pequeñas.
diuresis [ˌdaɪjʊ'risəs, B -jʊə-] *s.* (*pl.* DIURESES [-ˌsiz]) (med.) diuresis.
diuretic [-rɛtɪk] *a., s.* (med.) diurético.
diurnal [daɪ'ɜrnəl, B -'ɜn-] *a.* 1. diurno, de día. 2. diario. 3. (astr.) diurno. —*s.* (ant.) diario.
diurnally [-ɪ] *adv.* de día; diariamente.
diva ['divə] *s.* (*pl.* DIVAS O DIVE [-veɪ]) diva, cantante consagrada, estrella de la ópera.
divagate ['daɪvəˌgeɪt] *v.i.* divagar, vagar; alejarse del tema.
divagation [ˌdaɪvə'geɪʃən] *s.* divagación, digresión; tangente.
divalent [daɪ'veɪlənt, B 'daɪˌveɪ-] *a.* (quím.) bivalente.
divan ['daɪˌvæn, dɪ'væn] *s.* 1. diván, consejo turco o lugar donde éste se reúne. 2. diván, sofá sin respaldo, otomana. 3. fumadero; cigarrería. 4. diván, colección de poesías esp. persas o árabes.
divaricate [daɪ'værəˌkeɪt, də-] *v.i.* bifurcarse, divergir; separarse. —*a.* divergente.
divarication [-ˌvæə'keɪʃən] *s.* 1. bifurcación, divergencia. 2. (fig.) divergencia, desacuerdo.
dive [daɪv] *v.i.* (*pret.* DIVED O DOVE [doʊv]; *p.p.* DIVED; *p.pr.* DIVING) 1. zambullirse, zabullirse; saltar (al agua). 2. sumergirse (submarino); caer por el aire. 3. (aer.) picar (el avión). 4. lanzarse; (fig.) meterse de lleno (en un asunto, problema, etc.). —*v.t.* ahondar, profundizar en, meter adentro. —*s.* 1. zambullida; salto (al agua). 2. inmersión, sumersión (del submarino). 3. (aer.) picado. 4. (E.U.) (jer.) tugurio, tabernucha, escondite del hampa. 5. (dep.) salto ornamental (al agua); estirada, clavado; salto con paracaídas sin abrirlo hasta estar cerca del suelo.
dive-bomber ['daɪvˌbɑmər, B -ˌbɔmə] *s.* (mil.) avión de bombardeo en picada.
dive-bombing [-ɪŋ] *s.* (mil.) bombardeo en picada.
diver ['daɪvər, B -və] *s.* 1. zambullidor. 2. buzo, buceador. 3. (orn.) somorgujo, clavador.
diverge [də'vɜrdʒ, daɪ-, B -'vɜdʒ] *v.i.* 1. divergir, desviarse. 2. (fig.) divergir, diferir. —*v.t.* desviar.
divergence [-'vɜrdʒəns, B -'vɜdʒəns] *s.* 1. divergencia, desviación. 2. (fig.) divergencia, desacuerdo.
divergency [-dʒənsɪ] *s. var. de* **divergence.**
divergent [-dʒənt] *a.* divergente; no convergente.
divergently [-lɪ] *adv.* de modo divergente.
divers ['daɪvərz, B -vəz] *a.* varios, diversos.
diverse [daɪ'vɜrs, də-, B daɪ'vɜs] *a.* variado, multiforme; diferente, disímil, distinto.
diversely [-lɪ] *adv.* variamente, diversamente.
diverseness [-nəs] *s.* diversidad, variedad.
diversification [-ˌvɜrsəfə'keɪʃən, B -ˌvɜ-sə-] *s.* diversificación; variación.
diversified [-'vɜrsəˌfaɪd, B -'vɜsə-] *a.* diversificado, variado.
diversiform [-ˌfɔrm, B -ˌfɔm] *a.* diversiforme.
diversify [-ˌfaɪ] *v.t.* (*pret., p.p.* DIVERSIFIED; *p.pr.* DIVERSIFYING) diversificar, variar, matizar; (com.) diversificar, extender las actividades de una compañía a nuevos ramos.
diversion [də'vɜrʒən, daɪ-, B -'vɜʃən] *s.* 1. desviación, diversión. 2. diversión, entretenimiento, distracción. 3. (mil.) diversión.
diversionary [-ˌɛrɪ, B -ərɪ] *a.* desviador; de distracción, ej., *d. attack,* (mil.) ataque de distracción o diversión.
diversionist [-əst] *s.* (pol.) desviacionista; agitador.
diversity [-'vɜrsətɪ, B -'vɜsə-] *s.* 1. diversidad, variedad. 2. diversidad, diferencia.
divert [-'vɜrt, B -'vɜt] *v.t.* 1. divertir, distraer, apartar (atención, mente, etc.). 2. desviar (río, etc.). 3. divertir, distraer, entretener. 4. **d. oneself,** divertirse, distraerse. —*v.i.* tomar un desvío.
diverter [-ər, B -ə] *s.* (mec., elec.) desviador.
diverticulitis [ˌdaɪvərˌtɪkjə'laɪtəs, B -vəˌ-] *s.* (med.) diverticulitis.
diverticulosis [-'loʊsəs] *s.* (med.) diverticulosis.
diverticulum [-'tɪkjələm] *s.* (*pl.* DIVERTICULA [-lə]) (biol.) divertículo.
divertimento [dɪˌvɜrtə'mentoʊ, B -ˌvətə-] *s.* (*pl.* DIVERTIMENTI [-ti] O DIVERTIMENTOS) (mús.) divertimento.
diverting [də'vɜrtɪŋ, daɪ-, B -'vɜt-] *a.* divertido, entretenido.
divertingly [-lɪ] *adv.* divertidamente, entretenidamente.
divertissement [dɪ'vɜrtəsmənt, B -'vɜtɪz-] *s.* (teat.) pieza o representación ligera, entretenimiento; (mús.) divertimiento; baturrillo.
divertor [-ər, B -ə] *s.* (elec.) desviador.
Dives ['daɪˌviz] *s.* (bíbl.) (personificación del) hombre acaudalado.
divest [daɪ'vɛst, də-] *v.t.* desnudar; despojar, desposeer (de algo); **d. oneself of,** deshacerse de, abandonar.
divestiture [-ətʃər, B -etʃə] *s.* desposeimiento, despojo.
divestment [-mənt] *s.* desnudamiento, despojamiento, desposeimiento.
dividable [də'vaɪdəbəl] *a.* divisible.
divide [-'vaɪd] *v.t.* 1. dividir, partir, separar. 2. dividir, repartir. 3. (fig.) dividir, desunir. 4. (mat.) dividir. 5. **d. and conquer,** divide y vencerás. —*v.i.* dividirse, separarse. —*s.* (geog.) divisoria (de dos cuencas o valles); **the Great D.,** (E.U.) los montes Rocosos.
divided [-əd] *a.* 1. dividido; desunido. 2. (bot.) seccionado.
dividend ['dɪvəˌdɛnd, -dənd] *s.* (mat.) dividendo; (com.) dividendo, cuota proporcional de ganancia.
divider [də'vaɪdər, B -ə] *s.* 1. divisor, separador; distribuidor, repartidor. 2. (*pl.*) compás de división. 3. división, tabique. 4. (arq.) riostra. 5. (agr.) púa (en la tabla de la cosechadora).
divider flange, (ing.) seccionador.
dividing [-ɪŋ] *a.* divisorio, divisor.
divi-divi [ˌdivɪ'divɪ, B ˌdɪvɪ'dɪvɪ] *s.* (bot.) dividivi.
dividual [də'vɪdʒʊəl, B -'vɪdjʊ-] *a.* (ant.) separado; distinto; divisible.
divination [ˌdɪvə'neɪʃən] *s.* 1. adivinación, pronóstico. 2. intuición.
divinatory [də'vɪnəˌtɔrɪ, B -tərɪ] *a.* adivinatorio.
divine [də'vaɪn] *a.* divino. —*s.* 1. sacerdote, clérigo, ministro del culto. 2. teólogo. —*v.t.* adivinar. —*v.i.* 1. hacer pronósticos, presagiar. 2. conjeturar, imaginarse.
Divine Liturgy, (relig.) liturgia ortodoxa.
divinely [-lɪ] *adv.* divinamente.
diviner [-ər, B -ə] *s.* adivinador, adivino, agorero; conjeturador; sibila, profetisa.
diving ['daɪvɪŋ] *a.* 1. zambullidor, zabullidor (ave). 2. de buceo, de buzo (aparato, traje, etc.). 3. (aer.) en picado, de picado. —*s.* buceo, zambullida; (aer.) picada.
diving bell, campana de buzo.
diving board, trampolín.
diving helmet, casco de buzo (parte de la escafandra).
diving suit, escafandra, escafandro; atuendo de bucear.
divining rod [də'vaɪnɪŋ-] vara divinatoria, varilla o varita mágica (para determinar la presencia de agua o minerales).
divinity [də'vɪnətɪ] *s.* 1. divinidad. 2. atributo divino. 3. deidad; **the D.,** Dios. 4. teología. 5. **d. fudge,** crema en pasta, típico postre del sur de E.U.
divinize ['dɪvəˌnaɪz] *v.t.* divinizar, endiosar.
divisibility [dəˌvɪzə'bɪlətɪ] *s.* divisibilidad.
divisible [-'vɪzəbəl] *a.* divisible; (der.) dividuo.
division [-'vɪʒən] *s.* 1. división; reparto, distribución. 2. compartimento, compartimiento; (com.) ramo, departamento, sección. 3. (fig.) división, discordia. 4. (mat., pol., lóg.) división. 5. (mil., mar.) división. 6. **armored d.,** división blindada (de un ejército).
divisional coin [-əl-] moneda fraccionaria.
Divisionism [-ˌɪzəm] *s.* (arte) divisionismo, puntillismo; rama del neo-impresionismo.

divisive [dəˈvaɪsɪv, -ˈvɪs-, B -ˈvaɪs-] *a.* divisivo, que crea desacuerdo o disensión.

divisor [dəˈvaɪzər, B -zə] *s.* (mat.) divisor.

divorce [dəˈvɔrs, B -ˈvɔs] *s.* 1. (der.) divorcio. 2. (fig.) separación. 3. **to get a d. from,** divorciarse de. —*v.t.* 1. divorciar (a los casados); divorciarse de (marido o mujer). 2. (fig.) separar, desunir.

divorcé [-ˌvɔrˈseɪ, -ˈsi, B -ˌvɔ'-] *s.* (fr.) hombre divorciado.

divorcée, divorcee [-ˈseɪ, -ˈsi, B -ˌvɔ'-] *s.* (fr.) mujer divorciada.

divorcement [-ˈvɔrsmənt, B -ˈvɔs-] *s.* separación, desunión.

divot [ˈdɪvət] *s.* 1. (esco.) tepe. 2. (golf) pedazo de tierra cortada (al dar un mal golpe con el palo).

divulgate [dəˈvʌlgeɪt] *v.t.* (ant.) divulgar, publicar.

divulgation [ˌdɪvəlˈgeɪʃən] *s.* divulgación, publicación.

divulge [dəˈvʌldʒ, daɪ-] *v.t.* 1. revelar (ej., secreto). 2. divulgar, pregonar.

divulgement [-mənt] *s.* revelación, divulgación.

divulgence [-ˈvʌldʒəns] *s.* revelación, divulgación.

divulsion [daɪˈvʌlʃən, də-] *s.* arrancamiento, desgarro; (med.) divulsión, dilaceración.

divvy [ˈdɪvɪ] *s.* (jer.) porción o pedazo. —*v.t.* (jer.) dividir.

diwan, *var. de* **dewan.**

Dixie [ˈdɪksɪ] *s.* (E.U.) (nombre dado a) los estados del Sur.

Dixiecrat [-ˌkræt] *s.* (pol., E.U.) demócrata disidente de los estados del Sur (esp. el que se opuso al programa del candidato demócrata sobre derechos civiles en las elecciones presidenciales de 1948).

Dixieland [-ˌlænd] *s.* (E.U.) estilo de jazz con ritmo acentuado, característico de los años veinte.

dixit [ˈdɪksət] *s.* aseveración dogmática, pronunciamiento sentencioso.

dizen [ˈdaɪzən] *v.t.* (ant.) vestir ostentosamente y sin gusto, emperejilar.

dizygotic [ˌdaɪzaɪˈgɑtɪk, B -ˈgɔt-] *a.* dicigótico, dicorial (díc. de mellizos).

dizzily [ˈdɪzəlɪ] *adv.* 1. aturdidamente. 2. vertiginosamente.

dizziness [-ɪnəs] *s.* vértigo, desvanecimiento, vahído; aturdimiento.

dizzy [ˈdɪzɪ] *a.* (DIZZIER; DIZZIEST) 1. mareado, tambaleante; confundido, aturdido. 2. vertiginoso (altura, carrera, etc.). 3. (fam.) tonto, chiflado.

DJ *abrev. de* **disk jockey,** animador de un programa de discos.

Djakarta, Jacarta [dʒəˈkɑrtə, B -ˈkɑtə] *s.* Yakarta, Jakarta, capital de Indonesia.

djin, djinn, djinni, *var. de* **jinn.**

dkg *abrev. de* **decagram,** decagramo (Dg).

dkl *abrev. de* **decaliter,** decalitro (Dl).

dkm *abrev. de* **decameter,** decámetro (Dm).

dl *abrev. de* **deciliter,** decilitro (dl).

D layer, (rad.) capa D, la capa más baja de la ionosfera.

D. Lit., D. Litt., *abrev. de* **Doctor of Literature,** Doctor en Literatura.

dm *abrev. de* **decimeter,** decímetro (dm).

DM *abrev. de* **Deutsche Mark,** marco alemán (DM).

DMZ *abrev. de* **demilitarized zone,** zona desmilitarizada (díc. esp. de la región en Vietnam).

DNA *abrev. de* **deoxyribonucleic acid,** ácido ribonucleico.

do [du] *v.t.* (*pret.* DID [dɪd]; *p.p.* DONE [dʌn]; *p.pr.* DOING [ˈduɪŋ]; tercera pers. sing. pres. DOES [dʌz, bəz]) 1. hacer, producir. 2. hacer, ejecutar, realizar; producir (una obra de teatro, película, etc.). 3. cumplir con (deber); desempeñar (papel). 4. dar, rendir (homenaje, etc.). 5. realizar (una suma); resolver (un problema). 6. arreglar, limpiar (una habitación, etc.); lavar, limpiar (los platos, etc.). 7. arreglar, peinar (el cabello). 8. escribir, preparar (un libro, una nueva edición, un artículo); trabajar en, ej., *the painters are now doing the house,* los pintores trabajan ahora en la casa. 9. estudiar, aprender (lección). 10. (con *for*) servir (de), ej., *this piece of cardboard will do you for a hat,* este pedazo de cartón te servirá de sombrero. 11. recorrer (distancia). 12. correr a (cierta velocidad), ej., *the car was doing fifty (miles an hour),* el coche estaba corriendo a cincuenta (millas por hora). 13. visitar, ver (museos, ciudad, etc.). 14. (fam.) cumplir (condena). 15. (fam.) engañar, estafar. 16. (fam. G.B.) tratar, agasajar, ej., *they did us well,* nos trataron o agasajaron bien. 17. **do again,** volver a hacer, hacer otra vez; **do credit to (one's intelligence, fairness,** etc.), hacer honor a, ser digno de (la inteligencia, imparcialidad, etc. de uno); **do (someone) harm,** hacer daño, ser perjudicial (a alguien); **do in,** (jer.) cansar, agotar; engañar; matar, despachar, liquidar; **do one credit,** decir mucho en su favor; **do one good,** hacer bien a uno, sentarle bien a uno; **do one's best,** hacer cuanto uno pueda; **do one's damnedest,** hacer lo mejor que uno pueda; **do one's worst,** hacer lo peor que uno pueda; **do oneself well,** darse gusto, darse buena vida; **d. out,** (fam.) robar; **do (someone) out of,** privar (a alguien) con engaño de; **do over,** revisar, reparar; retocar (un cuadro); **do over again,** volver a hacer desde el principio; **do (someone) right, do right by (someone),** tratar bien a (alguien); **do the (polite, magnanimous,** etc.), dárselas de (cortés, generoso, etc.); **do the trick,** (jer.) surtir efecto; **do time,** purgar una condena; **do to death,** matar, asesinar; (fam.) trillar; **do up,** atar, empaquetar, envolver; arreglar, ordenar, poner en orden; vestir, decorar; restaurar, reparar; lavar y planchar; **it isn't done,** (eso) no se hace, no está bien; **to be done,** estar terminado, estar listo; **do with,** hacer con, ej., *what shall I do with you here?* ¿qué haré contigo aquí?; **to be done for,** estar arruinado, estar perdido; **to be done in,** estar agotado, estar acabado; **to be done to a turn,** cocido, asado o frito en su punto; **to be well done,** estar bien cocido, asado o frito; **what can I do for you?** ¿en qué puedo servirle?; **what's done is done,** a lo hecho, pecho. —*v.i.* 1. hacer, actuar, obrar, comportarse, ej., *do as I say,* haz como te digo. 2. hallarse, estar, sentirse (bien, mal, etc.), ej., *how are you doing?* ¿cómo estás? ¿cómo te sientes? 3. irle a uno, ej., *how are you doing at your new job?* ¿cómo te va en tu nuevo empleo? 4. bastarse, servir, ser suficiente o adecuado (para un propósito). 5. suceder, pasar, ej., *what's doing there?* ¿qué sucede o pasa allí? 6. **do away with,** abolir, suprimir; eliminar; matar; **do badly,** irle mal; **d. for,** (fam.) arruinar; acabar con, liquidar (a alguien); (G.B.) trabajar como criada para; **don't!** ¡no lo haga(s)!; **do or die,** vencer o morir; **do unto,** (ant.) tratar; **do well,** prosperar, pasarlo bien; **do with,** tratar, entenderse con; **do without,** prescindir de; **done,** aceptado, de acuerdo, trato hecho; **have done with it,** terminar de una vez; **how do you do?** ¿cómo está Ud.?; **I could do with (a cigarette, a cup of tea,** etc.), no me vendría mal, me vendría bien (un cigarrillo, una taza de té, etc.); **in Rome do as the Romans do,** dondequiera que fueres, haz lo que vieres; **it won't do, it will never do,** eso no sirve, eso es inaceptable; no conviene, no es conveniente; **nothing doing,** (jer.) nada de eso, ni hablar, imposible (díc. al rehusar algo terminantemente); **that will do!** ¡basta ya! ¡cállese!; **to have done with,** haber terminado con; no tener más que ver con; **to have (nothing) to do with,** (no) tener (nada) que ver con; **to make (something) do,** hacer servir (algo), ej., *I'll have to make my old car do for another year,* tendré que hacer servir mi carro viejo otro año más. —*v. aux.* 1. *ú. para dar énfasis al significado del verbo,* ej., *I do like her,* seguro que ella me gusta. 2. *para indicar interrogación o negación en el pres. y pasado simples,* ej., *do you want a cigar?* ¿quiere Ud. un cigarro? *I did not see him,* no lo vi. 3. *para sustituir un verbo ya usado,* ej., *do you like grapes? yes, I do,* ¿le gustan las uvas? sí me gustan. 4. *para formar el imper. enfático,* ej., *do tell me,* dígame, por favor. 5. *en casos inversos,* ej., *rarely do I see you here,* pocas veces le veo por acá. —*s.* (*pl.* DOS o DO'S) 1. (fam. G.B.) festejo, fiesta, jarana, jaleo. 2. (jer. G.B.) estafa, timo. 3. (dial.) alharaca, agitación. 4. lo que se debe hacer, enseñanzas (morales o sociales), código (social, de costumbres, etc.). 5. **the do's and don'ts,** el código (de la sociedad, de una agrupación, grupo, organización), lo que se debe y lo que no se debe hacer.

do [doʊ] *s.* (mús.) do.

DOA *abrev. de* **dead on arrival,** muerto al llegar.

doable [ˈduəbəl] *a.* factible, realizable, practicable.

do-all [ˈduˌɔl] *s.* gerente general; factótum.

dobber [ˈdɑbər, B ˈdɔbə] *s.* (dial.) flotador (en una cuerda de pescar).

dobbin [ˈdɑbən, B ˈdɔb-] *s.* 1. caballo de campo. 2. caballo dócil; jamelgo, rocín.

dobra [ˈdoʊbrə] *s.* dobra (antigua moneda portuguesa).

dobson [ˈdɑbsən, B ˈdɔb-] *s.* (ento.) larva acuática de un insecto coridálido de Norte América (se la usa como carnada para pescar).

doc [dɑk, B dɔk] *s.* (fam., E.U.) doctor.

docent [ˈdoʊsənt, doʊˈsɛnt] *s.* maestro, profesor, docente (gen. adjunto al catedrático vigente).

Docetism [doʊˈsitˌɪzəm] *s.* (relig.) docetismo.

Docetist [-əst] *s.* (relig.) docetista, doceta, sostenedor del docetismo.

docile [ˈdɑsəl, B ˈdoʊˌsaɪl] *a.* dócil, sumiso.

docilely [-əlɪ, B -ˌsaɪlɪ] *adv.* dócilmente, obedientemente.

docility [dɑˈsɪlətɪ, doʊ-, B dou-] *s.* docilidad, obediencia.

docimastic [ˌdɑsəˈmæstɪk, B ˌdɔs-] *a.* (med., min.) docimástico.

docimasy [ˈdɑsəməsɪ, B ˈdɔs-] *s.* (med., min.) docimasia, docimástica.

dock [dɑk, B dɔk] *s.* 1. maslo (de la cola de un animal). 2. muñón de cola (cercenada). —*v.t.* 1. derrabar, descolar (animal); cercenar, desmochar (cola de un animal). 2. acortar, reducir (sueldo, texto, etc.). 3. deducir, descontar (de sueldo o salario); multar, castigar con una multa, ej., *I was docked for being late,* me castigaron con una multa por haber llegado tarde.

dock, *s.* (mar.) 1. dique. 2. desembarcadero, muelle, dársena. 3. banquillo del acusado. 4. (bot.) romaza. —*v.t.* (mar.) poner (un barco) en dique. —*v.i.* 1. entrar al dique, atracar. 2. (astronáut.) acoplar (dos vehículos en el espacio).

dockage [ˈdɑkɪdʒ, B ˈdɔk-] *s.* rebaja, reducción.

dockage, *s.* 1. (mar.) muellaje, derechos de atraque. 2. (mar.) conjunto de diques y muelles. 3. (mar.) entrada (de un buque) al dique. 4. reducción, rebaja, merma.

docked [dɑkt] *a.* (mar.) surto en el muelle.
docker [-ər, B -ə] *s.* estibador, obrero de muelles.
docket ['dɑkət, B 'dɔk-] *s.* 1. etiqueta, marbete, rótulo, cédula (que indica el contenido de un bulto, etc.). 2. (E.U.) agenda, orden del día. 3. (der.) sumario del procedimiento (en acción judicial); registro de sumarios de procedimiento; lista de causas por juzgar. —*v.t.* 1. rotular; marcar. 2. (der.) registrar en la lista de causas por juzgar. 3. resumir, extractar (asunto legal).
dockhand ['dɑkˌhænd, B 'dɔk-] *s.* estibador, cargador (en los muelles y puertos).
docking [-ɪŋ] *s.* (astronáut.) acoplamiento (de dos vehículos en el espacio).
dockmackie [-ˌmækɪ] *s.* (bot.) (variedad de) viburno.
dockyard [-jɑrd, B -jɑd] *s.* astillero, arsenal.
doctor ['dɑktər, B 'dɔktə] *s.* 1. médico, doctor. 2. doctor (título académico). 3. señuelo en forma de mosca (para pescar). —*v.t.* 1. medicinar, tratar, cuidar; curar. 2. reparar, componer. 3. manipular, alterar; falsear, falsificar. —*v.i.* (fam.) practicar la medicina, trabajar de médico.
doctoral [-tərəl] *a.* doctoral.
doctorate [-rət] *s.* doctorado.
doctrinaire [ˌdɑktrə'nɛr, B ˌdɔk-'nɛə] *a., s.* doctrinario.
doctrinairism [-ˌɪzəm, B -ˌrɪzəm] *s.* doctrinarismo.
doctrinal ['dɑktrənəl, B dɔk'traɪn-] *a.* doctrinal; didáctico.
doctrinally [-ɪ] *adv.* doctrinalmente, doctrinariamente.
doctrine ['dɑktrən, B 'dɔk-] *s.* doctrina, dogma, credo, creencia; teoría.
document ['dɑkjəmənt, B 'dɔk-] *s.* 1. documento. 2. (ant.) ejemplo, prueba. — [-ˌmɛnt] *v.t.* documentar, asesorar con pruebas o documentos.
documental [ˌdɑkjə'mɛntəl, B 'dɔk-] *a.* documental.
documentary [-ərɪ] *a.* documental. —*s.* (cinem.) documental.
documentation [-mən'teɪʃən] *s.* documentación.
dodder ['dɑdər, B 'dɔdə] *v.i.* tartalear, temblar, tambalearse. —*s.* (bot.) cúscuta, rascalino.
doddered [-ərd, B -əd] *a.* 1. sin ramas, ajado (árbol). 2. débil, debilitado.
doddering [-ərɪŋ] *a.* senil, chocho, decrépito.
dodecagon [doʊ'dɛkəˌgɑn, B -gən] *s.* (geom.) dodecágono.
dodecagonal [ˌdoʊdə'kægənəl] *a.* (geom.) dodecagonal.
dodecahedral [-ˌdɛkə'hidrəl] *a.* (geom.) dodecaédrico.
dodecahedron [-ˌdɛkə'hidrən, B 'doʊdɪkə'-hɛ-] *s.* (geom.) dodecaedro.
dodecaphonic [doʊˌdɛkə'fɑnɪk, B ˌdoʊdɪk-ə'fɔn-] *a.* (mús.) dodecafónico.
dodecaphonism [-'dɛkəˌfoʊnˌɪzəm] *s.* (mús.) dodecafonismo.
dodecasyllabic [ˌdoʊdɛkəsɪ'læbɪk] *a.* dodecasílabo.
dodge [dɑdʒ, B dɔdʒ] *v.i.* 1. regatear, esquivar el cuerpo, hacer un regate. 2. evadir el deber. 3. hacer uso de argucias, buscar escapatorias. —*v.t.* 1. esquivar (golpe), evadir (deber), eludir (encuentro). 2. evitar astutamente; rehuir (reclutamiento). 3. (foto.) desvanecer. —*s.* 1. regate. 2. truco, artificio. 3. esquive (en el boxeo). 4. plan ingenioso.
dodger ['dɑdʒər, B 'dɔdʒə] *s.* 1. marrullero, trampista. 2. (mar.) pantalla protectora (en el puente de un barco contra la espuma o rocío del mar). 3. (E.U.) volante, cartel o anuncio pequeño. 4. (E.U.) torta elaborada con harina de maíz. 5. **draft d.,** (E.U.) el que evade ser reclutado por las fuerzas armadas.
dodgery [-ərɪ] *s.* evasión, evasiva, trampería.
dodgy ['dɑdʒɪ, B 'dɔdʒɪ] *a.* evasivo, tramposo, marrullero.
dodo ['doʊdoʊ] *s.* (*pl.* DODOES O DODOS) 1. ave extinta, de la isla Mauricio. 2. (fam.) vejestorio.
doe [doʊ] *s.* (*pl.* DOES O DOE) (zool.) 1. gama. 2. coneja, cabra, hembra de la liebre, antílope o rata.
doer ['duər, B -ə] *s.* hacedor, agente, persona activa.
does [dʌz, dəz] *tercera persona del pres. de indic. de* **do.**
doeskin ['doʊˌskɪn] *s.* 1. ante, piel de gamo. 2. tejido fino de lana.
doesn't ['dʌzənt] *contr. de* **does not.**
doff [dɑf, dɔf, B dɔf] *v.t.* 1. quitarse (el sombrero, la ropa). 2. librarse de, desembarazarse de (algo superfluo o no deseado).
dog [dɔg, dɑg, B dɔg] *s.* 1. perro. 2. (macho de) zorro, lobo, etc. 3. canalla, sinvergüenza, perro (tipo o sujeto), ej., *he's a sly d.,* es un tipo socarrón. 4. desastre, horror (díc. por ej. de una mala obra de teatro). 5. (*gen. pl.*) morillos. 6. (mec.) grapa, grapón, laña, gancho, agarrador. 7. (astr.) Can Mayor o Can Menor. 8. (*pl.*) (jer.) pies. 9. (meteor.) (t. **sun d.**) parhelia. 10. **the dogs,** (fam., G.B.) carrera de galgos; **a dead dog** (fam.) una persona caída (que ha perdido su importancia o influencia); **d. eat d.,** competencia despiadada; **d. tired,** agotado, exhausto; **every d. has his day,** a cada uno le llega su turno; **let sleeping dogs lie,** dejar lo bueno en paz, peor es meneallo; **not to have a d.'s chance,** no tener la mínima posibilidad; **to die a d.'s death,** morir como un perro; **to go to the dogs,** arruinarse, echarse a perder; **to lead a d.'s life,** llevar una vida de perros; **to put on the d.,** (fam) darse aires; **to rain cats and dogs,** llover a cántaros; **to throw it to the dogs,** sacrificar desperdiciando; **you can't teach an old d. new tricks,** loro viejo no aprende a hablar. —*v.t.* (*pret., p.p.* DOGGED; *p.pr.* DOGGING) 1. seguir (los pasos a uno), perseguir, seguirle las pisadas a uno. 2. acosar, inquietar. 3. sujetar con grapa o grapón. —*a.* inferior, falso, fingido. —*adv.* (usado en combinación con otras palabras como en **dog-tired, dog-happy, dog-angry**) totalmente, completamente.
dog-ape ['dɔgˌeɪp, ˌdɑg-, B 'dɔg-] *s.* (zool.) mandril.
dogbane [-ˌbeɪn] *s.* (bot.) adelfa.
dogberry [-ˌbɛrɪ] *s.* 1. (bot.) cornejo. 2. baya de cornejo.
dog biscuit [-ˌbɪskət] *s.* canil, moyana.
dogbolt [-ˌboʊlt] *s.* (mec.) perno dobladizo (para unir piezas en ángulo recto).
dogcart [-ˌkɑrt, B -ˌkɑt] *s.* carruaje liviano de dos ruedas altas (con dos asientos dispuestos espalda con espalda).
dogcatcher [-ˌkætʃər, B -ə] *s.* lacero de perros (callejeros), perrero, recogedor de perros sueltos.
dog clutch, (maq.) embrague de garras.
dog collar, 1. collar (de perro). 2. (jer.) collar romano (de clérigos).
dog days, canícula, días de mucho calor.
doge [doʊdʒ] *s.* duque; dux (primer magistrado de las antiguas repúblicas de Venecia y Génova).
dogear ['dɔgˌɪr, ˌdɑg-, B 'dɔgˌɪə] *s.* punta doblada (de una página). —*v.t.* doblar la punta de una página.
dogeared [-ˌɪrd, B -ˌɪəd] *a.* 1. con las puntas dobladas (libro, etc.). 2. gastado, usado.
dogface [-ˌfeɪs] *s.* (jer.) soldado, esp. de infantería.
dog fennel, (bot.) manzanilla loca; brezo.
dogfight [-ˌfaɪt] *s.* 1. riña entre perros. 2. (aer.) refriega aérea. —*v.i.* combatir, reñir; entrar en una refriega (aviones).
dogfish [-ˌfɪʃ] *s.* (ict.) lija, melgacho; tollo, cazón, tiburón pequeño.
dogged ['dɔgəd, 'dɑg-, B 'dɔg-] *a.* obstinado, tenaz, persistente, insistente, terco.
doggedly [-lɪ] *adv.* tenazmente, obstinadamente, persistentemente, tercamente.
doggedness [-nəs] *s.* obstinación, persistencia, tenacidad.
dogger [-ər, B -ə] *s.* (mar.) dogre, urca.
doggerel ['dɔgərəl, 'dɑg-, B 'dɔg-] *a.* de estilo chabacano (verso); trivial, prosaico. —*s.* verso burlesco; coplas de ciego, aleluya.
doggery [-ərɪ] *s.* 1. comportamiento insolente; conducta soez. 2. perrería, perros (en conjunto). 3. la canalla, chusma. 4. (jer.) tabernucho; garito.
doggie ['dɔgɪ, 'dɑgɪ, B 'dɔgɪ] *s.* perrito.
doggish [-ɪʃ] *a.* 1. perruno; arisco, gruñón, regañón. 2. (jer.) de elegancia exagerada, aparatoso.
doggishly [-lɪ] *adv.* gruñonamente, de mala gana.
doggishness [-nəs] *s.* 1. carácter arisco. 2. (jer.) aspecto chillón.
doggo [-goʊ] *adv.* (jer.) escondidamente; **to lie d.,** estar escondido, no asomarse.
doggone ['dɑgˌgɑn, 'dɔgˌgɔn, B 'dɔgˌgɔn] **doggoned** [-ˌgɑnd, -ˌgɔnd, B -ˌgɔnd] *interj.* ¡caramba! —*a., s.* maldito, fastidioso.
doggy ['dɔgɪ, 'dɑgɪ, B 'dɔgɪ] *a.* (DOGGIER; DOGGIEST) 1. perruno, rel. al perro. 2. (fam.) de elegancia exagerada, aparatoso, chillón.
doghole [-ˌhoʊl] *s.* cuarto humilde, cuchitril.
doghouse [-ˌhaʊs] *s.* perrera, casa para perro; **to be in the d.,** (fam.) estar castigado, estar en desgracia.
dogie ['doʊgɪ] *s.* (Oeste de E.U.) becerro sin madre, becerro descarriado.
dog in the manger, (fam.) el perro del hortelano que ni come ni deja comer.
dog Latin, latinajo, latín macarrónico.
dogleg ['dɔgˌlɛg, 'dɑg-, B 'dɔg-] **doglegged** [-ˌlɛgd, -ˌlɛgəd] *a.* con la pierna doblada o torcida (tramo de vía con cierto ángulo de desviación). —*s.* ángulo agudo o curva parecida a la de las patas traseras de los perros.
dogma ['dɔgmə, 'dɑg-, B 'dɔg-] *s.* (*pl.* DOGMAS O DOGMATA [-mətə]) dogma.
dogmatic [dɔg'mætɪk, dɑg-, B dɔg-] **dogmatical** [-ɪkəl] *a.* dogmático.
dogmatically [-ɪkəlɪ] *adv.* dogmáticamente.
dogmatics [-ɪks] *s. pl.* (*sing. o pl. en const.*) (teo.) estudio de dogmas y doctrinas.
dogmatism ['dɔgməˌtɪzəm, 'dɑg-, B 'dɔg-] *s.* dogmatismo, aseveración categórica (esp. sin pruebas ni fundamento).
dogmatist [-təst] *s.* dogmatista.
dogmatization [ˌdɔgmətə'zeɪʃən, ˌdɑg-, B ˌdɔgmətaɪ-] *s.* declaración o escrito dogmatizante.
dogmatize ['dɔgməˌtaɪz, 'dɑg- B 'dɔg-] *v.t.* dogmatizar. —*v.i.* hablar o escribir en forma dogmática.
dogmatizer [-ər, B -ə] *s.* dogmatizante, dogmatizador.
do-gooder ['duˌgʊdər, B -ə] *s.* (fam.) persona que ofrece una ayuda, más que nada por prestigiarse de benefactora (úsase en sentido irónico).
dog racing, carreras de galgos.
dog rose, (bot.) rosal silvestre, agavanzo, zarzaperruna, galabardera.

dog show, exposición canina.
dog sled, dog sledge, trineo tirado por perros.
dogsleep ['dɔg,slip, 'dɑg-, B 'dɔg-] *s.* sueño ligero o intranquilo; sueño simulado.
dog socket, portapúa.
Dog Star, (astr.) 1. Canícula. 2. Proción.
dog's-tongue ['dɔgz,tʌŋ, 'dɑgz-, B 'dɔgz-] *s.* (bot.) cinoglosa.
dog tag, 1. chapa fiscal (placa de metal con la licencia de un perro). 2. (jer.) placa (metálica) de identificación (que llevan al cuello los soldados).
dog tent, (jer., mil.) tienda de campaña chica, carpa pequeña (Am.).
dog-tired ['dɔg'taɪrd, 'dɑg-, B 'dɔg'taɪəd] *a.* cansadísimo, muerto de cansancio.
dogtooth [-,tuθ] *s.* 1. colmillo, diente canino. 2. (arq.) diente de perro.
dogtooth violet, (bot.) diente de perro.
dogtrot [-,trɑt, B -,trɔt] *s.* 1. trote lento (como el del perro). 2. corredor, camino cubierto (entre dos alas de un edificio). —*v.i.* trotar lentamente, avanzar a trote lento.
dogvane [-,veɪn] *s.* (mar.) cataviento.
dogwatch [-,wɑtʃ, B -,wɔtʃ] *s.* (mar.) guardia de cuartillo, media guardia.
dog wheel, rueda de trinquete.
dogwood [-,wʊd] *s.* (bot.) cornejo, sanguiñuelo, cerezo silvestre.
doily ['dɔɪlɪ] *s.* 1. servilleta pequeña. 2. pequeño tapete (de mesa).
doing ['duɪŋ] *s.* 1. acción. 2. esfuerzo, ej., *it will take some d.,* requerirá bastante esfuerzo. 3. (*gen. pl.*) actividades, ocurrencias.
doit [dɔɪt] *s.* 1. antigua moneda holandesa. 2. pizca, ápice, nonada.
do-it-yourself ['duətjər'sɛlf, B -jɔ'-] *s.* la práctica de hacer las cosas uno mismo. —*a.* (jer.) diseñado para ser hecho o usado por un aficionado (opuesto a profesional).
dolce ['doʊl,tʃeɪ, B 'dɔltʃrɪ] *a.* (mús.) dolce, dulce.
dolce far niente [-,fɑrnɪ'ɛntɪ, B -,fɑnɪ-] (italiano) dulce ociosidad.
dolce vita [-'vitɑ] (italiano) (la) vida dulce (un modo de vida caracterizado por la disipación y promiscuidad).
doldrums ['doʊldrəmz, 'dɑl-, B 'dɔl-] *s. pl.* 1. murria, melancolía, depresión; **to be in the d.,** tener murria. 2. calmas ecuatoriales. 3. estancamiento, inactividad.
dole [doʊl] *s.* 1. distribución (esp. de comida o dinero), repartimiento (esp. en porciones pequeñas); limosna, dádiva. 2. socorro a desocupados. 3. (ant.) suerte, sino, destino. 4. (poét.) pesar, aflicción. 5. **on the d.,** viviendo del socorro dado a desocupados. —*v.t.* (con *out*) distribuir, dar, repartir (esp. limosnas).
doleful ['doʊlfəl] *a.* afligido, dolorido, triste; lúgubre, lastimoso.
dolefully [-fəlɪ] *adv.* tristemente.
dolefulness [-fəlnəs] *s.* tristeza, melancolía, dolor.
dolerite ['dɑlə,raɪt, B 'dɔl-] *s.* (min.) 1. dolerita. 2. diabasa.
dolesome ['doʊlsəm] *a.* (raro) afligido, dolorido, triste; lúgubre, lastimoso.
dolichocephalic [,dɑlɪkoʊsə'fælɪk, B 'dɔlɪkoʊkɛ-] *a.* (antrop.) dolicocéfalo, dolicocefálico.
dolichocephalism [-'sɛfə,lɪzəm] *s.* (antrop.) dolicocefalia.
dolichocranial [-'kreɪnɪəl] **dolichocranic** [-nɪk] *a.* (antrop.) dolicocranio, dolicocraneal.
doll [dɑl, dɔl, B dɔl] *s.* 1. muñeca. 2. (fig.) muñeca, mujer bonita. 3. (jer.) mujer. 4. (jer.) querida, amante, amiga. 5. (fam.) persona servicial y encantadora. —*v.t., v.i.* **d. up,** (fam.) engalanar(se), acicalar(se), emperifollar(se).
dollar ['dɑlər, B 'dɔlə] *s.* 1. dólar. 2. (jer. G.B.) corona, moneda de cinco chelines. 3. **half a d.,** media corona; **like a million dollars,** magníficamente, excelentemente.
dollar diplomacy, diplomacia del dólar (que utiliza el poder económico de los E.U. para incrementar su influencia política).
dollarfish [-,fɪʃ] *s.* (ict.) pequeño pez chato de aleta espinosa.
dollar gap, escasez de dólares o divisa norteamericana (debido a la desproporción entre lo importado y lo exportado).
dollar mark, d. sign, signo del dólar ($).
dollop ['dɑləp, B 'dɔl-] *s.* masa, bulto, burujo.
dolly ['dɑlɪ, B 'dɔlɪ] *s.* 1. muñequita. 2. madero para batir la ropa (mientras se lava). 3. (mec.) aguantadora, contrarremachador. 4. (min.) batidor (de mineral). 5. carretilla. 6. (cinem., t.v.) carro portacámara, pie rodante, travelín. 7. (f.c.) pequeña locomotora para maniobras. —*v.i.* (*pret., p.p.* DOLLIED; *p.pr.* DOLLYING) **d. in,** (cinem., t.v.) acercarse con la cámara (a la escena); **d. out,** (cinem., t.v.) alejarse con la cámara (de la escena).
dolly bar, sufridera de palanca, barra de entibar.
dolly tub, (min.) cubeta para lavar mineral.
dolman ['doʊlmən, 'dɑl-, B 'dɔl-] *s.* (*pl.* DOLMANS) 1. dormán. 2. manto o chaqueta con mangas perdidas.
dolman sleeve, (cost.) manga perdida (encajada en el hombro al sesgo).
dolmen ['doʊlmən, 'dɑl-, B 'dɔlmɛn] *s.* (arqueol.) dolmen.
dolomite ['doʊlə,maɪt, 'dɑl-, B 'dɔl-] *s.* (min.) dolomía, dolomita; **The Dolomites,** (las) Dolomitas, (los) Alpes Dolomíticos.
dolomitic [,doʊlə'mɪtɪk, ,dɑl-, B ,dɔl-] *a.* (geol.) dolomítico.
dolor, (esp. G.B.) **dolour** ['doʊlər, B -lə] *s.* (poét.) dolor, pena, angustia.
dolorous ['doʊlərəs, 'dɑl-, B 'dɔl-] *a.* doloroso, penoso, lastimoso; pesaroso, afligido, melancólico.
dolorously [-lɪ] *adv.* dolorosamente.
dolorousness [-nəs] *s.* aspecto penoso, desolación, aflicción.
dolphin ['dɑlfən, 'dɔl-, B 'dɔl-] *s.* 1. (zool.) delfín, golfín, arroaz, tonina. 2. (astr.) **D.,** Delfín. 3. (mar.) proís; boya de anclaje.
dolphin striker, (mar.) moco del bauprés.
dolt [doʊlt] *s.* bobalicón, tonto, bobo.
doltish ['doʊltɪʃ] *a.* lerdo, estúpido, mentecato, tonto.
doltishness [-nəs] *s.* estupidez, tontería, imbecilidad.
domain [doʊ'meɪn, də-] *s.* 1. dominio, imperio, soberanía. 2. dominio, territorio (sobre el que se ejerce soberanía); heredad, propiedad, finca. 3. dominio, campo de acción, esfera de influencia. 4. (mat.) dominio (de una función). 5. (fís.) dominio magnético, región de imantación uniforme.
dome [doʊm] *s.* 1. (arq.) domo, cúpula, cimborrio, dombo. 2. bóveda (de los árboles, del cielo, etc.); cima (de un cerro, etc.). 3. (jer.) cabeza. 4. (ant.) mansión, edificio majestuoso. —*v.t.* 1. cubrir con cúpula. 2. dar forma de cúpula a. —*v.i.* elevarse como una cúpula; abombarse.
dome head, (mot.) culata abovedada.
dome lamp, d. light, lámpara de techo, luz cenital.
domesday ['dumz,deɪ, 'doʊmz-, B 'dumz-] *var. de* **doomsday**.
Domesday Book, (hist.) registro de empadronamiento de tierras (hecho por Guillermo I de Inglaterra en 1086).
domestic [də'mɛstɪk] *a.* 1. doméstico. 2. casero, hogareño. 3. nacional, interior, interno. —*s.* doméstico, criado, sirviente.
domestically [-tɪkəlɪ] *adv.* domésticamente.
domesticate [-,keɪt] *v.t.* domesticar, amansar; civilizar. —*v.i.* volverse hogareño.
domestication [-,mɛstɪ'keɪʃən] *s.* domesticación.
domestic commerce, comercio interior.
domesticity [,doʊ,mɛs'tɪsətɪ, də-, B ,doʊ-] *s.* 1. domesticidad. 2. (*pl.*) asuntos domésticos.
domestic relations court, (E.U.) en algunos estados, tribunal con jurisdicción sobre relaciones familiares.
domestic science, economía doméstica.
domestic trade, comercio interior.
domical ['doʊmɪkəl] *a.* en forma de domo o cúpula; abombado.
domicile ['dɑmə,saɪl, 'doʊ-, B 'dɔmɪ-] *s.* domicilio, residencia; morada; (com.) domicilio. —*v.t.* domiciliar; dar domicilio a; establecer.
domiciliary [,dɑmə'sɪlɪ,ɛrɪ, ,doʊ-, B ,dɔmɪ'sɪljərɪ] *a.* domiciliario.
domiciliate [-'sɪlɪ,eɪt] *v.t.* domiciliar; dar domicilio a, establecer. —*v.i.* residir, tener domicilio.
dominance ['dɑmənəns, B 'dɔm-] **dominancy** [-nənsɪ] *s.* predominio, autoridad.
dominant [-nənt] *a.* dominante; (astrol., mús., biol.) dominante; **to be d. over,** dominar, ejercer influencia dominante sobre. —*s.* 1. (mús.) dominante. 2. factor o característica dominante.
dominate [-,neɪt] *v.t.* 1. dominar, tener dominio sobre. 2. dominar (a), predominar sobre, sobresalir a. —*v.i.* 1. ejercer dominio. 2. dominar, sobresalir.
domination [,dɑmə'neɪʃən, B ,dɔm-] *s.* 1. dominación, dominio, tiranía, autoridad. 2. (*pl.*) (teo.) dominaciones (espíritus bienaventurados que forman el cuarto coro).
dominative ['dɑmə,neɪtɪv, B 'dɔm-] *a.* dominativo, dominante, gobernante.
dominator [-ər, B -ə] *s.* dominador.
domineer [,dɑmə'nɪr, B ,dɔmɪ'nɪə] *v.i., v.t.* tiranizar, oprimir, tener actitud imperiosa.
domineering [-ɪŋ, B -'nɪər-] *s.* dominante, imperioso; avasallador; mandón, tiránico.
domineeringly [-lɪ] *adv.* imperiosamente, avasalladoramente.
dominical [də'mɪnɪkəl] *a.* dominical.
Dominican [-kən] *a., s.* (religioso) dominico, dominicano.
Dominican, *a.* dominicano, de Santo Domingo. —*s.* dominicano, natural de la República Dominicana.
Dominican Republic, República Dominicana.
dominie ['dɑmənɪ, 'doʊ-, B 'dɔm-] *s.* (esco.) dómine, maestro, preceptor; (E.U.) pastor protestante; (fam., E.U.) clérigo.
dominion [də'mɪnjən] *s.* 1. dominio, señorío, soberanía. 2. (der.) dominio. 3. dominio (de la Comunidad Británica de Naciones).
dominium [doʊ'mɪnɪəm, B də-] *s.* (der.) dominio.
domino ['dɑmə,noʊ, B 'dɔm-] *s.* (*pl.* DOMINOES O DOMINOS) 1. dominó (disfraz). 2. máscara, careta. 3. ficha de dominó. 4. (*pl.*) dominó (juego).
don [dɑn, B dɔn] *s.* 1. don (tratamiento español). 2. caballero español. 3. (G.B.) preceptor; rector (en las universidades de Oxford y Cambridge); catedrático. 4. (ant.) gran personaje. —*v.t.* (*pret., p.p.* DONNED; *p.pr.* DONNING) 1. ponerse, vestirse de. 2. (fig.) asumir (personalidad, maneras, etc.).
donate ['doʊ,neɪt, doʊ'neɪt, B -'neɪt] *v.t.* donar, contribuir. —*v.i.* hacer una donación.

donation [doʊ'neɪʃən] *s.* donación; donativo, dádiva.
Donatism ['dɑnəˌtɪzəm, 'doʊnə-, B 'doʊnə-] *s.* (relig.) donatismo.
Donatist [-təst] *s.* (relig.) donatista.
donative ['doʊnətɪv, 'dɑn-, B 'doʊnə-] *s.* donativo, regalo, dádiva.
donator ['doʊˌneɪtər, B doʊ'neɪtə] *s.* donador, donante.
done [dʌn] *p.p. de* **do.** —*a.* 1. acabado, completado. 2. gastado, usado, consumido. 3. agotado, cansadísimo. 4. (jer., G.B.) engañado, embaucado. 5. bien cocido o asado. 6. **d. for,** agotado, rendido; vencido; **d. up,** vestido, abrochado; envuelto.
donee [doʊ'ni] *s.* donatario.
dong [dɔŋ] *s.* 1. sonido que imita al de la campana. 2. [dɑŋ, B 'dɔŋ] unidad monetaria del Vietnam del Norte.
donjon ['dʌndʒən, 'dɑn-, B 'dɔn-] *s.* torre del homenaje (de un castillo).
donkey ['dɑŋkɪ, 'dɔŋ-, 'dʌŋ-, B 'dɔŋ-] *s.* (*pl.* DONKEYS), asno, burro, borrico; (fig.) asno, burro.
donkey boiler, caldera auxiliar.
donkey engine, locomotora pequeña (para maniobras de servicio); motor auxiliar.
donnish ['dɑnɪʃ, B 'dɔn-] *a.* erudito, pedantesco (aspecto, maneras, etc.).
donnishly [-lɪ] *adv.* pedantescamente.
donnishness [-nəs] *s.* pendantería.
donnybrook ['dɑnɪ, brʊk, B 'dɔn-] *s.* trifulca, camorra.
donor ['doʊnər, B -nə] *s.* donador, donante.
do-nothing ['duˌnʌθɪŋ] *s., a.* haragán, vagabundo.
donship ['dɑnˌʃɪp, B 'dɔn-] *s.* nobleza, caballerosidad.
don't [doʊnt] *contr. de* **do not.**
donut ['doʊˌnʌt] *s., var. de* **doughnut.**
doodad ['duˌdæd] *s.* (jer.) adminículo, chuchería; cosa (usado para substituir un nombre que se ha olvidado), comose-llama.
doodle ['dudəl] *s.* garabato (hecho mientras uno está distraído). —*v.i.* borrajear, garabatear. —*v.t.* llenar de garabatos.
doodlebug [-ˌbʌg] *s.* 1. (E.U.) larva de la hormiga león. 2. (fam., E.U.) vara divinatoria. 3. (fam., G.B.) bomba voladora.
doohickey ['duˌhɪkɪ] *s., var. de* **doodad.**
doom [dum] *s.* 1. fatalidad, sino, destino; ruina, muerte. 2. juicio, sentencia. 3. (hist.) estatuto, ley, decreto. 4. día del juicio final. —*v.t.* 1. condenar, sentenciar (a muerte). 2. predestinar a la destrucción. 3. **to be doomed,** estar definitivamente perdido, estar predestinado al fracaso.
doom palm, (bot.) duma.
doomsday ['dumzˌdeɪ] *s.* día del juicio final, día del fin del mundo.
door [dɔr, B dɔ] *s.* 1. puerta. 2. (fig.) puerta, entrada, camino. 3. **at death's d.,** a las puertas de la muerte; **behind closed doors,** a puertas cerradas; **from d. to d.,** de puerta en puerta; **front d.,** puerta de entrada, puerta principal; **next d. neighbor,** vecino más cercano; **next d. to,** (fig.) cerca de; casi; **out of doors,** afuera (de la casa), al aire libre; **three doors off,** (en la) tercera casa de al lado; **to close the d. upon,** cerrar la puerta a, hacer imposible; **to knock the d. down,** echar la puerta abajo; **to lay at the d. of,** echarle a uno la culpa de, hacer a uno responsable por; **to open a d. to,** (fig.) abrir la puerta a, hacer posible; **to show someone the d.,** enseñarle a uno la puerta (de la calle); **to show (someone) to the d.,** acompañar (a alguien) a la puerta.
doorbell ['dɔrˌbɛl, B 'dɔˌ-] *s.* timbre de llamada; campanilla (de la puerta).
door bolt, cerrojo (de puerta), falleba, pasador.
door butt, bisagra de puerta.
doorcase [-ˌkeɪs] *s.* contramarco, contracerco (de puerta).
door catch, golpete, cierre.
door check, amortiguador de puerta.
doorframe [-ˌfreɪm] *s.* revestimiento de la puerta, marco de puerta.
doorhead [-ˌhɛd] *s.* dintel, cabecero.
doorjamb [-ˌdʒæm] *s.* jamba, quicial, batiente.
doorkeeper [-ˌkipər, B -ˌpə] *s.* 1. portero. 2. (relig.) ostiario.
doorknob [-ˌnɑb, B -ˌnɔb] *s.* perilla (de puerta).
door latch, pestillo.
doorman [-ˌmæn, -mən] *s.* portero.
doormat [-ˌmæt] *s.* 1. alfombrilla, esterilla, felpudo (de puerta). 2. (fig.) uno que sufre sin protestar.
doornail [-ˌneɪl] *s.* clavo de cabeza ancha y grande (antiguamente usado en las puertas); **dead as a d.,** completamente muerto; **deaf as a d.,** sordo como una tapia.
doorplate [-ˌpleɪt] *s.* rótulo, placa de puerta (con el nombre del morador).
doorpost [-ˌpoʊst] *s.* jamba o quicial de puerta.
door pull, agarradera, tirador, manija.
doorsill [-ˌsɪl] *s.* umbral.
doorstep [-ˌstɛp] *s.* escalón de la puerta.
doorstop [-ˌstɑp, B -ˌstɔp] *s.* tope de puerta.
doorway [-ˌweɪ] *s.* entrada, vano o claro de puerta; portal.
dooryard [-ˌjɑrd, B -ˌjɑd] *s.* (E.U.) patio de entrada.
dope [doʊp] *s.* 1. compuesto lubricante (para cables, tubos, etc.); suavizador (de gasolina). 2. material absorbente (usado en la manufactura de la dinamita). 3. (aer.) barniz de revestimiento (aplicado a telas de globos, aeronaves, etc.). 4. tonto, bobo. 5. (jer.) narcótico, estimulante, droga. 6. (jer.) morfinómano. 7. (jer.) informes, datos (esp. confidenciales). 8. (dep.) droga, doping (para aletargar a un participante). —*v.t.* 1. narcotizar; adormecer, entorpecer. 2. (dep.) dopar. 3. (jer.) calcular, estudiar. 4. **d. out,** (jer.) deducir, resolver, concluir.
dope fiend, (jer.) morfinómano.
dope racket tráfico de narcóticos.
dope ring, cofradía de traficantes en drogas.
dope sheet, hoja volante que da información sobre los caballos que corren en el día.
dopester ['doʊpstər, B -stə] *s.* pronosticador (en las carreras de caballos).
dopey ['doʊpɪ] *s.* (DOPIER; DOPIEST) 1. (jer.) narcotizado; aletargado, estupefacto. 2. (fam., E.U.) torpe, tonto.
doping [-pɪŋ] *s.* dopaje, práctica inescrupulosa que consiste en administrar drogas estimulantes a participantes en un evento deportivo.
doppelgänger ['dɑpəlˌgæŋər, B 'dɔp-ə] *s.* fantasma, doble (de una persona).
Doppler effect ['dɑplər-, B 'dɔplə-] (fís.) efecto Doppler-Fizeu.
dorado [də'rɑdoʊ] *s.* (ict.) dorado; **D.,** (astr.) Dorado, Pez Dorado.
dorbeetle ['dɔrˌbitəl, B 'dɔˌ-] *s.* (ento.) escarabajo estercolero.
dorhawk [-ˌhɔk] *s.* (orn.) chotacabras europeo.
Dorian ['dɔrɪən] *a., s.* dorio.
Doric ['dɔrɪk, 'dɑr-, B 'dɔr-] *a.* 1. dórico, dorio. 2. (arq.) dórico. —*s.* dórico, dialecto de los dorios.
dorm [dɔrm, B dɔm] *s. forma abrev. de* **dormitory,** (fam.) dormitorio (esp. en internados, universidades, etc.).
dormancy ['dɔrmənsɪ, B 'dɔmən-] *s.* 1. inactividad, período inactivo. 2. (biol.) estado o vida latente.
dormant [-mənt] *a.* 1. durmiente. 2. inactivo (ej., volcán). 3. (biol.) latente. 4. (der.) en suspenso, suspendido. 5. (her.) echado (ej., león). 6. **to lie d.,** estar inactivo.
dormer ['dɔrmər, B 'dɔmə] *s.* buhardilla, buharda, ventanillo; gablete; **d. window,** ventana de gablete.
dormie, dormy ['dɔrmɪ, B 'dɔmɪ] *a.* (golf) en ventaja con tantos golpes como el número de hoyos por jugar, ej., *he stood d. 4,* tenía una ventaja de cuatro golpes quedando cuatro hoyos por jugar.
dormitory ['dɔrməˌtɔrɪ, B 'dɔmɪtrɪ] *s.* dormitorio (esp. el colectivo común en internado, etc.).
dormouse ['dɔrˌmaʊs, B 'dɔˌ-] *s.* (zool.) lirón.
dornick ['dɔrnɪk, B 'dɔnɪk] *s.* (dial.) piedra, roca, pedrejón.
dorp [dɔrp, B dɔp] *s.* (ant.) aldea, pueblo.
dorrbeetle, *var. de* **dorbeetle.**
dorsad ['dɔrˌsæd, B 'dɔˌ-] *adv.* (anat.) en el dorso, en la espalda.
dorsal [-səl] *a.* dorsal, espinal. —*s.* (anat.) vértebra dorsal.
dorsally [-səlɪ] *adv.* en el dorso.
dorsiventral [ˌdɔrsɪ'vɛntrəl, B ˌdɔsɪ-] *a.* (bot.) dorsiventral.
dorsolateral [-soʊ'lætərəl] *a.* (zool., anat.) dorsolateral.
dorsoventral [-'vɛntrəl] *a.* (zool., anat.) dorsoventral; (bot.) dorsiventral.
dorsum ['dɔrsəm, B 'dɔsəm] *s.* (*pl.* DORSA [-sə]) dorso, espalda, lomo.
dory ['dɔrɪ] *s.* 1. (mar.) esquife de fondo plano y costados acampanados. 2. (ict.) dorada, gallo, pez de San Pedro.
dos-à-dos ['doʊzɑˌdoʊ] *s.* (fr.) carruaje o sofá que da cabida a dos personas sentadas espalda contra espalda.
dosage ['doʊsɪdʒ] *s.* 1. (med., farm.) dosis, dosificación. 2. (fig.) dosis, porción.
dose [doʊs] *s.* 1. (med.) dosis. 2. (fig.) dosis, porción. 3. (jer.) infección de gonorrea o sífilis. —*v.t.* 1. medicinar, dar una dosis a enfermo. 2. dosificar (medicina). 3. encabezar (vino).
dosimeter [doʊ'sɪmətər, B -ə] *s.* (med.) dosímetro.
dosimetric [ˌdoʊsə'mɛtrɪk] *a.* (med.) dosimétrico.
dosimetry [doʊ'sɪmətrɪ] *s.* (med.) dosimetría.
dosing ['doʊsɪŋ] *s.* dosificación.
doss [dɑs, B dɔs] (pr. G.B., jer.) *s.* 1. camastro. 2. (t. **d. house**) hotel barato, posada de mala muerte. 3. sueño. —*v.i.* (t. **d. down**) dormir, pasar la noche (en cama improvisada, hotel barato, etc.).
dossal, dossel ['dɑsəl, B 'dɔs-] *s.* dosel.
dosser [-ər, B -ə] *s.* cuévano, serón.
doss house, (pr. G.B., jer.) posada de mala muerte; burdel.
dossier ['dɔsˌjeɪ, 'dɑsɪˌeɪ, B 'dɔsɪeɪ] *s.* expediente; documentos, historial.
dost [dʌst] (ant.) *segunda pers. sing. pres. de* **do.**
dot [dɑt, B dɔt] *s.* 1. punto. 2. (ortografía) punto (sobre letras). 3. pequeña cantidad. 4. (mat.) punto decimal. 5. (mús.) puntillo. 6. (teleg.) punto (en el alfabeto de Morse). 7. (der.) dote. 8. **off one's d.,** (jer., G.B.) alocado, loco; **on the d.,** puntualmente, a la hora exacta; en punto, ej., *it's now six o'clock on the d.,* ahora son las seis en punto. —*v.t.* (*pret., pp.* DOTTED; *p.pr.* DOTTING) 1. puntar, poner punto a (una letra).

2. puntear, salpicar. 3. (jer., G.B.) pegar, asestar (un golpe). 4. **d. one's i's and cross one's t's,** poner los puntos sobre las íes; **dotted with,** salpicado de; lleno de.

dotage ['doʊtɪdʒ] *s.* chochera, chochez, senectud.

dotal ['doʊtəl] *a.* (der.) dotal.

dotard ['doʊtərd, B -əd] *s.* viejo chocho, vieja chocha; persona ñoña.

dotation [doʊ'teɪʃən] *s.* dotación.

dote [doʊt] *v.i.* chochear; **d. on** (o **upon**), idolatrar, amar con exceso; caérsele la baba por.

doth [dʌθ] (ant.) *tercera pers. del sing. del pres. de* **do.**

doting ['doʊtɪŋ] *a.* 1. excesivamente afectuoso o cariñoso. 2. senil, chocho.

dotingly [-lɪ] *adv.* con afecto excesivo.

dotted line ['dɑtəd-, B 'dɔt-] línea de puntos (donde gen. se firman los formularios).

dotted swiss, muselina (adornada) con motas bordadas.

dotterel, dottrel ['dɑtərəl, -trəl, B 'dɔtrəl] *s.* 1. (orn.) avefría, frailecillo, chorlito. 2. (dial.) tonto, bobo, incauto.

dottle, dottel ['dɑtəl, B 'dɔt-] *s.* masa de tabaco no fumado (que queda en el fusique de una pipa); cabo de tabaco que se fuma en pipa.

dotty ['dɑtɪ, B 'dɔtɪ] *a.* 1. punteado. 2. esporádico. 3. inestable, tambaleante. 4. (fam.) mentecato, imbécil, loco.

doty ['doʊtɪ] *a.* 1. desteñido, descolorido (madera). 2. (esco.) chocho.

double ['dʌbəl] *a.* 1. doble, dúplice. 2. el doble de, ej., *I'll have to pay d. the original amount,* tendré que pagar el doble del monto original. 3. doble, ambiguo. 4. (bot.) doble. 5. (mús.) doble; contra, ej., *d. bass,* contrabajo, *d. bassoon,* contrabajón. 6. (impr.) doble. —*s.* 1. doble, duplo. 2. doble, doblez (en tela, etc.). 3. vuelta o giro repentino. 4. (teat.) doble, sustituto. 5. (naipes) contra, doblo (Esp.). 6. (carreras) apuesta combinada, quiniela. 7. (*pl.*) (dep.) dobles; (*sing.*) doble en béisbol, golpe con el que el bateador alcanza la segunda base. 8. **at the d.,** (mil.) a paso ligero, corriendo; **on the d.,** (jer.) inmediatamente, pronto, presto (ú. a menudo como orden). —*adv.* 1. doble, doblemente, dos veces. 2. dos (juntos), ej., *to ride d.,* montar dos en un caballo, *to sleep d.,* dormir dos en una cama. 3. **to see d.,** ver doble. —*v.t.* 1. doblar, duplicar (cantidad), redoblar (ej., esfuerzos). 2. doblar, plegar. 3. (gen. con *up*) hacer doblarse (en dos). 4. cerrar (el puño, la mano). 5. (teat.) actuar como doble de, reemplazar, sustituir; desempeñar (dos papeles). 6. (mar.) doblar (cabo, península, etc.). 7. (tej.) retorcer (hilo). 8. (naipes) doblar. 9. (billar) doblar (la bola). —*v.i.* 1. doblarse, duplicarse. 2. volver bruscamente. 3. servir a la vez como, ej., *the church doubled as a surgery room during the war,* la iglesia sirvió a la vez como sala de cirugía durante la guerra. 4. (mil.) correr a paso ligero. 5. (teat.) (con *for*) sustituir, reemplazar (a), actuar como doble (de). 6. **d. back,** volver atrás, retornar al punto de partida; **double in brass,** servir en capacidad doble; **d. round,** dar la vuelta por; **d. up,** doblarse, doblarse en dos, encogerse; acurrucarse; dormir (dos) en una misma cama; ocupar el mismo cuarto juntos (dos personas); **d. up laughing,** desternillarse de risa.

double-acting [-'æktɪŋ] *a.* de doble efecto.

double agent, doble agente.

double bar, (mús.) barra doble.

double-barreled, double-barrelled [-'bærəld] *a.* 1. de dos cañones (escopeta). 2. (fig.) de doble efecto.

double bass, (mús.) contrabajo, violón.

double bed, cama doble, cama camera.

double bill, (cinem., teat., dep.) programa doble.

double-bitt [-'bɪt] *v.t.* (mar.) abitar dos veces.

double boiler, marmita doble (cacerola para el baño de María).

doble bond, (quím.) ligazón doble.

double bottom, doble fondo; fondo falso.

double-breasted [-'brɛstəd] *a.* cruzado (abrigo, chaqueta, etc.).

double carnation, (bot.) clavel reventón.

double chin, papada, doble quijada, doble barba.

double cocoon, capullo ocal.

double consciousness, (psic.) doble personalidad.

double cross, (jer.) traición, trampa (hecha a un cómplice).

double-cross [-'krɔs] *v.t.* (jer.) traicionar (a un cómplice, etc.).

double-crosser [-ər, B -ə] *s.* (jer.) traidor (a un cómplice, etc.).

double-current [-'kɜrənt, -'kʌrənt, B -'kʌ-] *a.* de dos corrientes, continua y alterna (dínamo, etc.).

double-cut file ['dʌbəl,kʌt-] lima de doble talla, lima de picadura cruzada.

double-cut saw, serrucho de corte doble.

double dagger, (tip.) obelisco doble, cruz doble.

double date, salida de dos parejas (al teatro, cine, etc.) en conjunto.

double-date [-'deɪt] *v.t., v.i.* (gen. con *with*) salir dos parejas juntas; hacer cita para salir dos parejas.

double-dealer [-'dilər, B -ə] *s.* persona doble, traidor.

double-dealing [-lɪŋ] *s.* doblez, perfidia, doble juego. —*a.* doble, insincero, traidor.

double-deck [-,dɛk] **double-decked** [-'dɛkt] *a.* de dos pisos o cubiertas.

double-decker [-'dɛkər, B -ə] *s.* 1. navío de dos cubiertas. 2. ómnibus de dos pisos. 3. emparedado doble (con dos capas de relleno entre tres tostadas o rebanadas de pan).

double Dutch, (fam.) algarabía, palabrería incomprensible.

double-dyed ['dʌbəl'daɪd] *a.* 1. dos veces teñido. 2. (fig.) rematado, perdido, inveterado (bribón, etc.).

double-edged [-'ɛdʒd] *a.* (lit. y fig.) de dos filos (ej., cuchillo; argumento).

double ended, de extremos iguales.

double-ended drill [-'ɛndəd-] broca de dos puntas.

double-ended wrench, llave de dos bocas.

double ender, cosa que tiene dos extremos iguales (locomotora de dos direcciones; barco de timón en ambos extremos).

double entendre [,dublɑn'tɑndrə] doble sentido; locución de doble sentido.

double entry, (com.) partida doble.

double-entry bookkeeping, doble contabilidad.

double-faced ['dʌbəl'feɪst] *a.* 1. de dos caras. 2. (fig.) doble, hipócrita. 3. con acabado por ambos lados.

double-face hammer [-,feɪs-] martillo de dos cotillos.

double feature, (cinem.) programa o función doble.

double flat, (mús.) bemol doble.

double-flow turbine [-,floʊ-] turbina de doble efecto.

double frame, (impr.) chibalete doble.

double harness, doble guarnición (de caballo); (fig.) unión estrecha (como en el matrimonio).

double-header [-'hɛdər, B -ə] *s.* 1. (E.U., Can.) tren con dos locomotoras delante. 2. (dep.) dos partidos entre dos equipos, o dos diferentes pares de equipos (que se juegan en la misma ocasión).

double house, casa doble, morada separada de otra igual por una pared.

double-hung window [-,hʌŋ-] ventana de guillotina.

double image, (t.v.) imagen fantasma o repetida.

double indemnity, indemnización doble, póliza de seguro que garantiza el doble de la indemnización que consta en el contrato.

double-jointed [-'dʒɔɪntəd] *a.* con articulaciones dobles.

double-leaded [-'lɛdəd] *a.* (tip.) con dos interlíneas entre renglones.

double-lock [-'lɑk, B -'lɔk] *v.t.* dar dos vueltas a la cerradura.

double meaning, segunda intención, doble sentido.

double-minded [-'maɪndəd] *a.* vacilante, indeciso; engañoso, falso.

double negative, (gram.) construcción incorrecta que emplea dos negativos en lugar de uno, ej., *he didn't say nothing,* no dijo nada, en lugar de la forma correcta *he said nothing* o *he didn't say anything.*

double-park [,dʌbəl'pɑrk, B -'pɑk] *v.i., v.t.* estacionar(se) en doble fila.

double play, (béisbol) jugada en la que dos jugadores son puestos fuera de juego.

double-pole ['dʌbəl'poʊl] *a.* (elec.) bipolar.

double printing, (foto., tipo.) sobreimpresión fotomecánica, negativo doble.

double-quick [-'kwɪk] *a.* muy rápido, rapidísimo. —*adv.* al instante, sobre la marcha.

double-quick time, (mil.) a la carrera.

doubler ['dʌblər, B -lə] *s.* 1. (tej.) doblador, retorcedor, (persona); máquina de retorcer. 2. (rad.) doblador (de tensión, de frecuencia).

double-reed ['dʌbəl'rid] *a.* (mús.) con dos lengüetas (instrumento).

double refraction, (fís.) birrefringencia, refracción doble.

double rhyme, rima que comprende dos sílabas.

double-ripper [-'rɪpər, B -ə] *s.* (dial.) trineo doble (de dos rastras).

double riveting, remachado doble.

double room, cuarto para dos, habitación con dos camas.

double row engine, (avia.) motor radial de doble estrella.

double rule, (impr.) mediacaña.

double-runner [-'rʌnər, B -ə] *s.* 1. *var. de* **double-ripper.** 2. patín de dos cuchillas (para niños).

double sharp, (mús.) doble sostenido.

double snap roll, (acrob.) doble tonel rápido.

double-space [-'speɪs] *v.t.* escribir (a máquina) dejando dos espacios.

double standard, criterio moral que permite más libertad al hombre que a la mujer.

double star, (astr.) estrella doble.

double-stop [-'stɑp, B -'stɔp] *s.* (mús.) dos tonos (en un instrumento de cuerdas) que suenan en acorde. —*v.i.* tocar dos cuerdas simultáneamente.

doublet ['dʌblət] *s.* 1. (hist.) jubón, casaca, chaleco. 2. uno de un par; pareja. 3. (*pl.*) par de dados tirados a la vez con el mismo número. 4. (filol.) doblete. 5. (ópt.) combinación de dos lentes simples. 6. (rad.) antena dipolo. 7. (fís.) línea doble en el análisis espectral. 8. (joy.) piedra preciosa falsa.

double take, reacción tardía (a la importancia de algo que antes había pasado inadvertido).

double-talk ['dʌbəl'tɔk] *s.* lenguaje ambiguo, términos engañosos, galimatías.

double thread, (mec.) rosca de filete doble.

double-throw switch [-ˌθroʊ-] (elec.) interruptor de doble acción.
double time, 1. (mil.) paso ligero. 2. doble paga (como sobretiempo).
double-time [-ˌtaɪm] *v.i.* (mil.) correr a paso ligero.
doubleton ['dʌbəltən] *s.* (bridge) doblete (dos cartas del mismo palo).
double-tongue [-'tʌŋ] *v.i.* tocar staccato (ej., en la flauta). —*a.* falso, pérfido.
double-track [-'træk] *a.* de doble vía.
doubletree [-ˌtri] *s.* volea, travesaño (en un carruaje, arado, etc.).
double vision, (med.) vista doble, visión doble, diplopía.
double void, (bridge) doble fallo.
double wound, (elec.) bifilar, de doble arrollamiento.
doubling ['dʌblɪŋ] *s.* 1. pliegue, doblez, vuelta repentina para huir; rodeo, artificio. 2. (cost.) forro. 3. (mar.) embono; batidero.
doubloon [dʌ'blun] *s.* (numis.) doblón español.
doublure [du'blur, B -'bluə] *s.* (impr.) forro ornamental de la contratapa.
doubly ['dʌblɪ] *adv.* doblemente, al doble, por duplicado.
doubt [daʊt] *v.t.* 1. dudar. 2. desconfiar de, recelar(se) de. —*v.i.* dudar, estar en duda; **d. about,** dudar de; **d. of,** no tener fe en. —*s.* 1. duda, incertidumbre. 2. desconfianza, recelo. 3. **beyond d.,** indudable, fuera de duda; **in d.,** dudoso, incierto; **make no d. about it,** puedes creerme, puedes estar seguro; **no d.,** indudablemente; **there can be no d.,** no cabe duda; **to call in d.,** poner en duda, poner en tela de juicio; **to give someone the benefit of the d.,** dar a alguien el beneficio de la duda; **to have doubts about,** dudar de; **when in d.,** en caso de duda; **without d.,** sin duda.
doubtable ['daʊtəbəl] *a.* dudable.
doubter [-ər, B -ə] *s.* incrédulo, pesimista, el que duda.
doubtful ['daʊtfəl] *a.* 1. dudoso, incierto, equívoco, ambiguo. 2. dudoso, indeciso, vacilante, titubeante.
doubtfully [-fəlɪ] *adv.* dudosamente.
doubtingly [-ɪŋlɪ] *adv.* dudosamente, incrédulamente.
doubting Thomas, (un) Santo Tomás, incrédulo.
doubtless [-ləs] *a.* indudable, cierto. —*adv.* ciertamente, sin duda, indudablemente.
doubtlessly [-lɪ] *adv.* indudablemente.
douceur [du'sɜ] *s.* (fr.) dulzura; recompensa; soborno.
douche [duʃ] *s.* 1. ducha; (med.) ducha, irrigación. 2. jeringa. —*v.t., v.i.* aplicar un lavado a alguna parte del cuerpo, esp. la vagina.
dough [doʊ] *s.* 1. pasta, masa, amasijo, cochura. 2. (jer.) pasta, guita, plata, mosca (dinero). 3. (jer.) información, datos confidenciales.
doughboy ['doʊˌbɔɪ] 1. (fam., E.U.) soldado de infantería (de la Primera Guerra Mundial). 2. (pr. G.B.) bolita de pasta cocida.
doughface [-ˌfeɪs] *s.* (E.U., hist.) parlamentario norteño que no se oponía a la esclavitud en el Sur; norteño simpatizante con el Sur (antes o durante la Guerra de Secesión).
dough-faced [-'feɪst] *a.* de cara pastosa.
doughfoot [-ˌfʊt] *s.* (*pl.* DOUGHFEET [-ˌfit] o DOUGHFOOTS) (E.U.) soldado de infantería (término en desuso).
doughnut ['doʊˌnʌt] *s.* rosquita frita, buñuelo (en forma de rosca).
doughtily ['daʊtəlɪ] *adv.* valientemente, con denuedo.
doughtiness [-ɪnəs] *s.* valentía, denuedo.
doughty ['daʊtɪ] *a.* valiente, bravo, formidable.
doughy ['doʊɪ] *a.* pastoso, como mezcla pastelera.
Douglas fir ['dʌgləs-] (bot.) pino Oregón.
dour [daʊr, dʊr, B dʊə] *a.* 1. severo, duro, austero. 2. obstinado, terco. 3. hosco, agrio, malhumorado.
dourine [dʊ'rin] *s.* (vet.) durina, sífilis equina.
douse [daʊs] *v.t.* 1. mojar, empapar; meter en el agua, remojar, poner en remojo. 2. echar (agua, líquido). 3. extinguir. 4. (mar.) cerrar (portilla). 5. (mar.) estibar, recoger, arriar (velas). —*v.i.* 1. caer (al agua). 2. remojarse. —*s.* 1. empapamiento, mojada, mojadura. 2. (G.B.) golpe.
dove [dʌv] *s.* 1. paloma, palomo, tórtola. 2. (fig.) paloma. 3. (fig.) político o legislador pacifista. 4. **my d.,** mi querido, mi querida; persona a quien se considera inocentona, cándida; **the d. of peace,** la paloma (símbolo) de la paz.
dove [doʊv] *pret. de* **dive.**
dovecot ['dʌvˌkɑt, B -ˌkɔt] **dovecote** [-ˌkoʊt] *s.* palomar; **to flutter the dovecots,** alarmar a gente apacible.
dovekie ['dʌvkɪ] *s.* (orn.) alca.
dovetail ['dʌvˌteɪl] *s.* (carp.) ensambladura a cola de milano. —*v.t.* 1. cortar, machihembrar o ensamblar a cola de milano. 2. (fig.) ajustar, amoldar. —*v.i.* encajar, corresponder.
dovetail plane, cepillo de ensamblar.
dowager ['daʊədʒər, B -dʒə] *s.* 1. viuda que goza de título o bienes heredados del marido (apl. esp. a reinas, etc.). 2. señora mayor, matrona respetable.
dowdily ['daʊdəlɪ] *adv.* desaliñadamente.
dowdiness [-ɪnəs] *s.* desaliño.
dowdy ['daʊdɪ] *a.* (DOWDIER; DOWDIEST) desaliñado, mal vestido, desaseado (persona); sin atractivo, fuera de moda (vestido). —*s.* 1. mujer desaliñada, maritornes. 2. (E.U.) (t. **apple pandowdy**) (cierta clase de) pastel de frutas.
dowel ['daʊəl] *s.* 1. (carp.) clavija, espiga. 2. taco, tarugo (en la pared). —*v.t.* (*pret., p.p.* DOWELED o DOWELLED; *p.pr.* DOWELING o DOWELLING) (carp.) enclavijar, fijar con espiga.
dower ['daʊər, B -ə] *s.* 1. viudedad, parte de la herencia del marido asignada de por vida a la viuda. 2. dote, bienes dotales. 3. don natural, talento. —*v.t.* 1. asignar viudedad a. 2. (fig.) dotar, favorecer.
dowitcher ['daʊɪtʃər, B -tʃə] *s.* (orn.) agachadiza de pico largo.
down [daʊn] *adv.* abajo, hacia abajo, hasta el origen, (ú. con sentidos de movimiento, dirección, disminución, reducción, etc. así como en frases elípticas); **d. and out,** sin un real, arruinado; (boxeo) fuera de combate; **d. at heel,** andrajoso, desarrapado; **d. below,** abajo; allá abajo; **d. in the mouth,** deprimido; **d. the hatch!** (fam.) ¡de un solo trago! ¡hasta la última gota! ¡seco y volteado!; **d. the helm,** (mar.) ¡la caña a sotavento!; **d. to the ground,** (fig.) completamente; **d. under,** en Australia; en las antípodas; **d. with (the king,** etc.), abajo (el rey, etc.); **to be d.,** estar derribado, vencido o arruinado; estar agotado o reducido; venderse más barato, haber bajado de precio, ej., *sugar is d. this week,* el azúcar ha bajado de precio esta semana; **to be d. on,** tener inquina a; **to be d. with,** estar enfermo de; **to bear d.,** (mar.) navegar a sotavento; **to come d.,** bajar, descender; **to come d. in the world,** venir a menos; **to copy d.,** copiar; **to fall d.,** caer(se); **to get d. to (work),** aplicarse al (trabajo); **to go d.,** bajar (la comida); ponerse (el sol); hundirse (barco); **to hunt d.,** perseguir y capturar; **to jot d.,** apuntar rápidamente; **to lie d.,** acostarse; **to pay d.,** pagar al contado; pagar a cuenta; **to run d.,** perseguir y capturar; **to send d.,** (G.B.) expulsar de la universidad; **to take d.,** anotar, apuntar; **to thin d.,** diluir; **to water d.,** aguar, diluir; **to write d.,** anotar, apuntar; **up and d.,** de arriba a abajo; de un lado a otro. —*a.* 1. descendente; deprimido. 2. inicial, a cuenta, ej., *d. payment,* pago a cuenta, cuota inicial. 3. exhausto, cansado. 4. (fútbol, béisbol) fuera de juego, ej., *d. ball,* pelota fuera de juego. —*prep.* por, abajo; a lo largo de, a través de, ej., *d. the street,* calle abajo, *d. the centuries,* a través de los siglos; **d. the wind,** con el viento; **to go d. the road,** irse por el camino; **up and d. (the room,** etc.), de un lado a otro de (la habitación, etc.). —*v.t.* 1. beber, tragar; devorar. 2. suprimir, retener. 3. derribar, derrotar. 4. poner (en el suelo), bajar deponer. 5. **d. tools,** terminar el trabajo del día; entrar en huelga. —*s.* 1. baja, caída; bajo, punto bajo. 2. reverso, revés. 3. ojeriza. 4. (bridge) caída. 5. (fútbol) colocación de la pelota en el suelo para una rebatiña. 6. plumón, flojel. 7. vello (de frutas). 8. pelusa. 9. **ups and downs,** altibajos.
down-at-the-heel ['daʊnətðə'hil] *a.* 1. mezquino, pobre, barato. 2. desaseado, descuidado, zarrapastroso.
downbeat [-ˌbit] *s.* 1. (mús.) compás acentuado. 2. señal inicial del director de orquesta. 3. deterioro, depresión. —*a.* triste, sombrío, pesimista.
down-bow [-ˌboʊ] *s.* (mús.) movimiento hacia abajo del arco (de un instrumento de cuerdas).
downcast [-ˌkæst, B -ˌkɑst] *a.* cabizbajo, abatido, deprimido, afligido, desalentado, desanimado, alicaído. —*s.* (min.) pozo de ventilación.
downcomer [-ˌkʌmər, B -ə] *s.* tubo de descenso; (metal.) tubería de gases combustibles.
down current, (avia.) viento o corriente de aire descendente.
downdraft carburator [-ˌdræft-, B -ˌdrɑft-] (aut.) carburador de aspiración invertida.
downer ['daʊnər] *s.* 1. (*barbituate*) sedante, tranquilizante, amansalocos. 2. (jer.) (*depressing experience*) experencia deprimente, palo; **to be on a d.,** estar con la depre.
downfall ['daʊnˌfɔl] *s.* 1. caída, ruina. 2. chubasco, aguacero; nevada fuerte.
downflow [-ˌfloʊ] *s.* circulación descendente.
down gear, (avia.) tren de aterrizaje desplegado.
downgrade [-ˌgreɪd] *s.* bajada, descenso, pendiente; **on the d.,** (fig.) cuesta abajo, desmejorando. —*v.t.* degradar, disminuir (de categoría o importancia); desacreditar.
downhaul [-ˌhɔl] *s.* (mar.) briol, candaliza, cargadera.
downhearted [-'hɑrtəd, B -'hɑt-] *a.* descorazonado, abatido, deprimido.
downheartedly [-lɪ] *adv.* abatidamente.
downheartedness [-nəs] *s.* abatimiento, depresión.
downhill ['daʊn'hɪl] *adv.* cuesta abajo, ladera abajo; **to go d.,** (fig.) ir cuesta abajo, desmejorar; venir a menos. —*a.* en declive, inclinado. —*s.* declive, bajada.
down home *a.* del sur (*de los E.U.*); (*cooking*) casero; (*appearance*) rústico, de las cosas sencillas.
downiness ['daʊnɪnəs] *s.* vellosidad.
download ['daʊn'loʊd] *v.t.* (comput.) trasvasar, mandar por teléfono.
down payment, entrega inicial, entrada, pago al contado; **to make a d.** dar la entrega inicial.
downpour ['daʊnˌpɔr, B -ˌpɔ] *s.* aguacero, chaparrón, manga de agua.

downrange [-ˈreɪndʒ] *adv.* (mil.) a cierta distancia del lugar de lanzamiento (a lo largo de la zona de ensayo de cohetes), ej., *300 miles d.,* a 300 millas del lugar de lanzamiento.
downright [-ˌraɪt] *adv.* 1. claramente, llanamente, sin preámbulos. 2. completamente, sumamente. —*a.* 1. absoluto, completo, ej., *a d. lie,* una mentira completa. 2. brusco, franco, directo.
downrightness [-nəs] *s.* franqueza, rectitud.
downside [ˈdaʊnˈsɑɪd] *s.* inconveniente, desventaja.
downsize [ˈdaʊnˈsɑɪz] *v.t.* reducir el tamaño de.
downsizing [ˈdaʊnˈsaɪzɪŋ] *s.* (com.) despedida de empleados.
Down's syndrome, síndrome de Down, mongolismo.
downstage [ˈdaʊnˈsteɪdʒ] *adv.* (teat.) al frente del escenario, en las candilejas, hacia el proscenio. —*s.* proscenio, frente del escenario. —*a.* relativo al frente del escenario.
downstairs [-ˈstɛrz, B -ˈstɛəz] *adv.* abajo, en el piso bajo, escaleras abajo. —*a.* bajo, en la planta baja, ej., *d. room,* cuarto bajo o en la planta baja. —*s. pl.* piso bajo, planta baja, (los) bajos (Amer.).
downstream [-ˈstrim] *adv.* aguas o río abajo.
downstroke [-ˌstroʊk] *s.* 1. trazo (hecho) hacia abajo. 2. (mec.) carrera descendente.
downswing [-ˌswɪŋ] *s.* 1. (mec.) recorrido hacia abajo. 2. tendencia descendente (esp. en actividades comerciales).
downthrow [-ˌθroʊ] *s.* derribo.
down-to-earth [ˈdaʊntəˈɜrθ, B -ˈɜθ] *a.* práctico, realista.
downtown [-ˈtaʊn] *adv.* hacia o en el centro (comercial) de la ciudad. —*s.* (E.U.) (el) centro (comercial) de la ciudad. —*a.* del centro (comercial) de la ciudad.
downtrend [-ˌtrɛnd] *s.* tendencia descendente.
downtrick [-ˌtrɪk] *s.* (bridge) baza de caída.
downtrodden [-trɑdən, B -ˈtrɔd-] *a.* oprimido, esclavizado; pisoteado, atropellado.
downturn [-ˌtɜrn, B -ˌtɜn] *s.* 1. vuelta hacia abajo. 2. (fin.) baja, depresión (esp. del comercio).
downward [-wərd, B -wəd] *a.* 1. descendente, inclinado. 2. hacia abajo. —*adv., var. de* **downwards.**
downwards [-wərdz, B -wədz] *adv.* 1. hacia abajo, abajo. 2. **from . . . . . . d.,** empezando por, ej., *all tyrants from Napoleon d.,* todos los tiranos, empezando por Napoleón.
downwash [-ˌwɔʃ, -ˌwɑʃ, B -ˌwɔʃ] *s.* 1. (mec.) deflexión hacia abajo. 2. (avia.) torbellino descendente.
downwind [-ˈwɪnd] *adv.* con el viento, a favor del viento; **d. landing,** (avia.) aterrizaje con viento de cola.
downy [ˈdaʊnɪ] *a.* (DOWNIER; DOWNIEST) 1. velloso, aterciopelado. 2. (bot.) pubescente. 3. blando, suave, sosegador.
dowry [ˈdaʊrɪ, B ˈdaʊərɪ] *s.* (*pl.* DOWRIES) 1. dote. 2. arras. 3. talento, dote natural.
dowse, *var. de.* **douse.**
dowse [daʊz] *v.i.* buscar (agua o metales) con varita divinatoria.
dowser [ˈdaʊzər, B -ə] *s.* varita mágica, vara divinatoria.
doxology [dɑkˈsɑlədʒɪ, B dɔkˈsɔl-] *s.* (relig.) doxología, Gloria in excelsis, Gloria Patri.
doxy [ˈdɑksɪ, B ˈdɔk-] *s.* 1. mujerzuela, ramera. 2. (dial.) querida, amante. 3. opinión, parecer; doctrina, creencia.
doyen [ˈdɔɪən] *s.* decano (de un cuerpo o grupo).
doz. *abrev. de* **dozen,** docena (doc.).
doze [doʊz] *v.i.* dormitar; **d. off,** adormecerse, adormitarse. —*s.* sueño ligero.
dozen [ˈdʌzən] *s.* (*pl.* DOZEN O DOZENS) 1. (*pl.* DOZEN después de numerales o sus equivalentes) docena(s) (de), ej., *six d. apples,* seis docenas de manzanas, *several d.,* varias docenas, *how many d.?* ¿cuántas docenas? 2. (*pl.* DOZENS después de "*some*" y cuando significa un juego de doce) docena, ej., *some dozens of people,* algunas docenas de personas, *pack them in dozens,* empaquételos por docenas. 3. **cheaper by the d.,** más barato(s) por docena; **daily d.,** ejercicios físicos diarios; **dozens of times,** muchísimas veces; **to talk nineteen to the d.,** (G.B.) hablar por los codos, hablar incesantemente.
dozy [ˈdoʊzɪ] *a.* adormecido, soñoliento, amodorrado.
DP *abrev. de* **displaced person,** expatriado; apátrida.
D.Ph., D.Phil. *abrev. de* **Doctor of Philosophy,** Doctor en Filosofía.
dpt. *abrev. de* **department,** departamento.
Dr. *abrev. de* **Doctor,** Doctor (Dr.).
drab [dræb] *s.* 1. color pardusco. 2. tela gruesa de color gris o pardusco. 3. aspecto deslustrado; carácter monótono (de algo). 4. ramera; mujer desaliñada. —*a.* 1. pardusco. 2. opaco, deslustrado; monótono, ordinario.
drabble [ˈdræbəl] *v.t.* enfangar, embarrar; mojar. —*v.i.* enfangarse, embarrarse, arrastrar.
drably [ˈdræblɪ] *adv.* deslustradamente, monótonamente.
drabness [-nəs] *s.* deslustre; monotonía.
dracaena [drəˈsinə] *s.* (bot.) drago.
drachm [dræm] *var. de* **drachma.**
drachma [ˈdrækmə] *s.* (*pl.* DRACHMAS, DRACHMAE [-mi] O DRACHMAI [-maɪ]) 1. dracma (moneda). 2. (farm.) dracma (peso); gramo.
Draco [ˈdreɪkoʊ] *s.* 1. (hist.) Dracón. 2. (astr.) Dragón.
Draconian [dreɪˈkoʊnɪən] *a.* draconiano, severo, riguroso, cruel.
draconic [drəˈkɑnɪk, B -ˈkɔn-] *a.* 1. draconiano, severo, riguroso. 2. dragontino.
draff [dræf] *s.* desperdicios, heces; orujo.
draft, (pr. G.B.) **draught** [dræft, B drɑft] *s.* 1. corriente de aire, viento colado, chiflón (Amer.). 2. tiro; regulador de tiro (en una chimenea). 3. bosquejo, borrador, anteproyecto. 4. filtro, poción; dosis. 5. tracción, tiro. 6. extracción; succión, cantidad extraída (de un líquido). 7. (*pl.*) juego de damas. 8. (com.) letra de cambio, giro, cheque, libramiento, libranza. 9. (mar.) calado. 10. (mil.) reclutamiento, leva, conscripción (Am.). 11. **on d.,** sacada del barril (cerveza); **to make a d. on,** (com.) girar contra. —*a.* 1. de tiro (díc. de animales). 2. (sacado) del barril. 3. preliminar. —*v.t.* 1. hacer un borrador de, hacer un proyecto de; bosquejar, delinear, dibujar. 2. (mil.) reclutar, levar, quintar. 3. destacar, asignar.
draft beer, cerveza al grifo, cerveza a presión, cerveza de barril, cerveza tirada, cerveza servida directamente del tonel.
draft bill, anteproyecto de ley.
draft board, (mil.) junta de reclutamiento.
draft dodger, (mil.) el que rehúye el servicio militar obligatorio.
draftee [dræfˈti, B drɑf-] *s.* quinto, recluta, conscripto (Am.).
draft furnace, alto horno.
draft gauge, 1. (mec.) indicador de tiro. 2. (mar.) escala de calado.
draft horse, caballo de tiro.
drafting [ˈdræftɪŋ, B ˈdrɑft-] *s.* dibujo mecánico.
drafting board, tablero de dibujo.
draftsman, (pr. G.B.) **draughtsman** [ˈdræftsmən, B ˈdrɑfts-] *s.* 1. dibujante, diseñador, bosquejador. 2. peón o pieza en el juego de damas.
draftsmanship, (pr. G.B.) **draughtsmanship** [-ˌʃɪp] *s.* facultad de dibujar; arte del dibujante; ejecución gráfica.
draft treaty, proyecto de tratado.
drafty, (pr. G.B.) **draughty** [ˈdræftɪ, B ˈdrɑf-] *a.* expuesto a corrientes de aire (lugar, cuarto, etc.).
drag [dræg] *v.t.* (*pret., p.p.* DRAGGED; *p.pr.* DRAGGING) 1. arrastrar, halar (con dificultad). 2. (mar.) rastrear, dragar; pescar o coger (algo) con brancada. 3. caminar arrastrando, arrastrar (pie, cola, etc.). 4. (agr.) gradar, rastrillar. 5. (jer.) aburrir, molestar. 6. **d. in,** traer por los cabellos; **d. (someone) into an (argument, affair,** etc.), envolver (a alguien) contra su voluntad en una (disputa, asunto, etc.); **d. on,** prolongar tediosamente; **d. one's feet,** arrastrar los pies; (fam.) dejar de cumplir, faltar a su deber; **d. one's tail,** (fig.) estar alicaído; **d. out,** demorar, dilatar. —*v.i.* 1. arrastrarse (por el suelo). 2. atrasarse, rezagarse, quedarse atrás, ir a la zaga. 3. ir tirando, avanzar lenta, tediosa o penosamente; continuar interminablemente. 4. **d. on,** prolongarse tediosamente. —*s.* 1. arrastre, arrastramiento. 2. narria, rastra. 3. (jer.) fumada, chupada; trago. 4. (fig.) estorbo, traba. 5. carruaje, diligencia. 6. rastro, caza con perros que siguen un rastro, caza con perros que siguen un rastro artificial. 7. (metal.) marco inferior de una caja de moldear. 8. (min.) hierro para limpiar pozos. 9. (mar.) rastra, draga; brancada; ancla flotante. 10. (aer.) resistencia al avance. 11. (agr.) grada. 12. (jer.) cuña, influencia. 13. (jer.) calle, camino; **the main d.,** la calle principal. 14. (jer.) compañera (que uno escolta). 15. (jer., aut.) carrera de velocidad. 16. (jer.) baile, velada, reunión (social). 17. (jer.) machaca, persona pesada. — **in d.,** (jer.) vestido de mujer (transvestido).
drag anchor, (mar.) ancla flotante.
drag chain, (f.c.) cadena de acoplamiento.
drag coefficient, (avia.) coeficiente de resistencia al avance.
drag conveyor, transportador de paletas, transportador de cadena sin fin.
drag fold, (geol.) pliegue de arrastre.
dragger [ˈdrægər, B -ə] *s.* bote que pesca a la rastra.
draggle [ˈdrægəl] *v.t.* ensuciar, embarrar, emporcar (algo arrastrándolo por el suelo). —*v.i.* 1. ensuciarse, embarrarse (algo que se arrastra). 2. rezagarse, ir a la zaga.
draggletail [-ˌteɪl] *s.* mujer desaliñada.
draggy [ˈdrægɪ] *a.* perezoso, tardo, lerdo.
dragline [-ˌlaɪn] *s.* 1. cable de arrastre. 2. cuerda lateral de guía. 3. excavadora de cable de tracción, pala de cable de arrastre, draga cavadora.
drag link, 1. (mec.) contramanivela. 2. (aut.) contrabrazo. 3. (f.c.) barra de enganche.
dragnet [-ˌnɛt] *s.* 1. brancada, red barredera, boliche; (fig.) red barredera. 2. (fig.) pesquisa, sistema o artificio para recoger datos, redar personas sospechosas, etc.
dragoman [ˈdrægəmən] *s.* dragomán, trujamán, intérprete (en el Cercano Oriente).
dragon [ˈdrægən] *s.* 1. dragón, monstruo fabuloso. 2. (fig.) fiera (persona). 3. (bot.) dragontea. 4. (zool.) dragón. 5. (mil.) dragoncillo. 6. (astr.) **D.,** Dragón.

dragonet [-ət, ˌdrægə'nɛt, B 'drægənɪt] *s.* dragoncillo, pequeño dragón.
dragonfly ['drægənˌflaɪ] *s.* (ento.) libélula, caballito del diablo.
dragon gum, (carp.) goma tragacanto.
dragonhead [-ˌhɛd] *s.* (bot.) variedad de menta o hierbabuena.
dragonish [-ɪʃ] *a.* dragontino.
dragonnade [ˌdrægə'neɪd] *s.* 1. (hist.) (*pl.*) dragonadas. 2. persecución, invasión.
dragon's blood, (bot.) sangre de drago.
dragon's mouth, (bot.) dragón, boca de dragón.
dragon's tail, (astr.) nodo descendente (de un planeta).
dragon tree, (bot.) drago.
dragoon [drə'gun] *s.* (mil.) dragón. —*v.t.* 1. acosar, perseguir; tiranizar. 2. **d. (someone) into (doing something),** ordenar dictatorialmente (a alguien que haga algo).
drag queen, (coll.) loca.
drag race, (E.U., fam.) carrera donde se compara el poder de aceleración entre dos automóviles.
dragrope ['drægˌroʊp] *s.* cable de arrastre; (aer.) cable de remolque; sonda.
drag sail, d. sheet, (mar.) ancla flotante (hecha gen. de una vela).
dragsaw [-ˌsɔ] *s.* sierra de tiro; sierra de trozar.
drag strut, (ing.) montante de compresión.
drag wire, (avia.) cable de resistencia.
drain [dreɪn] *v.t.* 1. avenar, encañar, drenar, desaguar, desecar (tierra, terreno, etc.). 2. (gen. con *off* o *away*) encañar, drenar, variar (agua, etc.). 3. enjugar, escurrir. 4. apurar, vaciar (un vaso, etc.). 5. (fig.) (con *of*) desangrar, privar (de); disipar, consumir. 6. (fig.) agotar. —*v.i.* 1. escurrirse, desaguarse, desecarse. 2. vaciarse. 3. (fig.) disiparse. 4. desaguar (ríos). —*s.* 1. desagüe, desaguadero, canal o tubería de desagüe, escurridor, sumidero. 2. desagüe, drenaje. 3. (fig.) desgaste; carga, lastre; consumo, gasto. 4. (med.) dren. 5. **to be a d. on,** consumir, agotar.
drainable ['dreɪnəbəl] *a.* desaguable.
drainage [-ɪdʒ] *s.* 1. desagüe, avenamiento, drenaje. 2. saneamiento, alcantarillado. 3. cuenca (hidrográfica).
drainage basin, área colectora, área de drenaje (de un río).
drainboard [-ˌbɔrd, B -ˌbɔd] *s.* escurridero (para platos).
drain cock, llave o robinete de purga.
drainer [-ər, B -ə] *s.* 1. secador de platos, escurreplatos. 2. colador, coladera.
drainpipe [-ˌpaɪp] *s.* tubo, tubería o caño de desagüe.
drain plug, tapón de purga, tapón de evacuación, tapón de desagüe.
drain valve, válvula de purga.
drake [dreɪk] *s.* (zool.) pato; ánade (macho).
dram [dræm] *s.* 1. dracma (peso comercial). 2. traguito, copita (de licor). 3. pizca, triza, poquito (de algo).
drama ['drɑmə, 'dræmə, B 'drɑmə] *s.* 1. drama (pieza teatral; género dramático; suceso conmovedor). 2. (fig.) el arte escénico.
Dramamine ['dræməˌmin] *s.* (farm.) dramamina.
dramatic [drə'mætɪk] *a.* dramático.
dramatical [-ɪkəl] *a.* dramático.
dramatically [-kəlɪ] *adv.* dramáticamente.
dramatic art, arte escénico, arte dramático.
dramatics [-ɪks] *s. pl.* (*sing. o pl. en const.*) 1. arte dramático. 2. teatro, representación de piezas teatrales, ej., *he likes d.,* le gusta hacer teatro, le gusta actuar. 3. gestos melodramáticos, conducta melodramática.
dramatis personae ['dræmətəspər'soʊni, 'drɑm-, B -pə'soʊnaɪ] (teat.) personajes de un drama, lista de personajes en una obra escrita.
dramatist ['dræmətəst] *s.* dramaturgo, escritor (de obras de teatro).
dramatization [ˌdræmətə'zeɪʃən, B -taɪ-] *s.* dramatización, escenificación.
dramatize ['dræməˌtaɪz] *v.t.* 1. dramatizar. 2. escenificar, convertir en un drama, hacer una escena dramática de. 3. hacer resaltar. —*v.i.* actuar dramáticamente.
dramaturgist ['dræməˌtɜrdʒəst, B -ˌtɜdʒəst] *s.* dramaturgo.
dramaturgy [-dʒɪ] *s.* dramaturgia, dramática.
dramshop ['dræmˌʃɑp, B -ˌʃɔp] *s.* (ant., G.B.) cantina, taberna, bar.
drank [dræŋk] *pret. de* **drink.**
drape [dreɪp] *v.t.* 1. cubrir o adornar con colgaduras, vestir, entapizar, tapizar. 2. colgar. 3. formar pliegues artísticos en (un ropaje o colgaduras). 4. **d. oneself in,** (lit., fig.) cubrirse con, envolverse en. —*v.i.* plegarse, caer (ropaje, cortinas, colgaduras). —*s.* colgadura, cortina.
draper ['dreɪpər, B -pə] *s.* pañero.
drapery [-pərɪ] *s.* (*pl.* DRAPERIES) 1. colgaduras, tapicería, cortinaje. 2. (G.B.) mercería. 3. forro de muebles.
drastic ['dræstɪk] *a.* drástico, enérgico, riguroso, extremo; (med.) drástico, purgador. —*s.* (med.) drástico, purgante fuerte.
drastically [-tɪkəlɪ] *adv.* drásticamente, de modo drástico.
drat [dræt] *interj.* ¡maldita sea!
D ration, (mil., E.U.) ración (alimenticia) de emergencia.
draught, (pr. G.B.) *var. de* **draft.**
draughts [dræfts, B drɑfts] *s. pl.* (*sing. en const.*) (G.B.) juego de damas.
draughtsman ['dræftsmən, B 'drɑfts-] *s.* peón del juego de damas (t. **draftsman**).
Dravidian [drə'vɪdɪən] *a., s.* dravidiano, drávida (idioma y habitante de una región de la India).
draw [drɔ] *v.t.* (*pret.* DREW [dru]; *p.p.* DRAWN [drɔn]; *p.pr.* DRAWING) 1. tirar de, halar, arrastrar (carruaje, vagón, etc.). 2. correr (cortina, velo, etc.). 3. tirar de, atraer (ej., el imán al hierro); (fig.) atraer (público, etc.). 4. acarrear, traer consigo (consecuencias, ruina, etc.). 5. sacar, extraer (diente, clavo, corcho, cerveza del barril, etc.); sacar (espada, pistola). 6. provocar, aguijar (a alguien). 7. tomar (aliento, inspiración). 8. sacar (conclusión). 9. formular (opinión, juicio), hacer (comparación, distinción, etc.). 10. cobrar (sueldo, salario). 11. tirar, trazar, delinear, dibujar. 12. trazar, describir. 13. (gen. con *out* o *up*) redactar, extender (documento). 14. tirar, estirar (metal, alambre). 15. (jer.) encoger, fruncir, arrugar (cara). 16. tender (el arco). 17. empatar, igualar (juego, competencia, etc.). 18. hacer una infusión, destilar. 19. destripar, limpiar (aves, pescado). 20. (com.) girar (letra, cheque); retirar, sacar (fondos); ganar, devengar (intereses). 21. (mar.) tener un calado de (cierta profundidad). 22. (mil.) provocar (fuego del enemigo). 23. (caza) batir (monte, la guarida, etc.). 24. (naipes) robar, tomar (una carta). 25. (bridge) arrastrar (triunfos). 26. (billar) hacer retroceder (la bola). 27. (golf) desviar a la izquierda (la pelota). 28. **d. a line (between),** hacer distinción (entre); **d. a blank,** no encontrar nada; no tener éxito; **d. aside,** descorrer (la cortina, etc.); llamar a un lado, llevar aparte, apartar (a alguien); **d. asunder,** separar, dividir; **d. away,** quitar, llevar; distraer; **d. attention,** atraer o llamar la atención; **d. blood,** hacer sangrar; (fig.) tocar en lo vivo, llegarle a lo vivo; **d. down,** bajar (persiana, telón); **d. forth,** hacer salir, sacar; **d. in,** retraer; ganar la cooperación de; **d. in one's horns,** (fig.) obrar con más cautela; **d. into (dispute, conversation,** etc.), envolver en (disputa, conversación, etc.); **d. lots,** echar suertes; **d. off,** sacar, extraer; **d. on,** ocasionar, causar, producir; (com.) girar sobre (banco); **d. oneself up,** aderezarse, estirarse; erguirse con dignidad; **d. out,** sacar, extraer; estirar; alargar, dilatar; sonsacar, provocar; **d. rein,** tirar de las riendas; (fig.) refrenarse, detenerse; **d. straws,** echar la suerte; **d. (one's) sword against,** (fig.) atacar, acometer; **d. the curtain,** (lit., fig.) correr el telón; echar un velo; **d. the line,** fijar un límite; **d. the line at,** no estar dispuesto a seguir adelante; **d. tight,** apretar(se) (el cinturón, etc.); **d. together,** unir; **d. up,** levantar, tirar hacia arriba; redactar, extender (documento, contrato, etc.); (mil.) formar, ordenar (tropas). —*v.i.* 1. tirar, atraer. 2. sacar el arma, ej., *they drew and fired,* sacaron las armas y dispararon. 3. tirar (bien o mal, chimenea, pipa, etc.). 4. dibujar. 5. empatar. 6. echar (suertes), sacar (un premio). 7. hincharse (vela). 8. (mar.) calar. 9. (naipes) tomar una carta. 10. **d. against,** (com.) girar contra o sobre (cuenta, fondos); **d. aside,** apartarse, hacerse a un lado; **d. back,** retroceder, retirarse, recular; **d. in,** acortarse (día, etc.); economizar; **d. level (with),** dar alcance (a), igualar; **d. near,** acercarse; **d. off,** apartarse, retirarse; **d. on,** acercarse; girar sobre (fondos); servirse de, hacer uso de, recurrir a; **d. to an end** (o **close**), tocar o llegar a su fin; **d. together,** unirse; **d. up,** pararse, detenerse; **d. up short,** pararse en seco; **d. up to,** acercarse a; **d. upon,** girar sobre; servirse de, hacer uso de, recurrir a. —*s.* 1. tiro (de la pipa o la chimenea). 2. fumada, chupada. 3. sorteo (de una lotería). 4. atracción (de taquilla). 5. cantidad girada (de fondos). 6. empate, tablas. 7. (E.U.) tramo levadizo, arco giratorio (de ciertos puentes). 8. estiramiento (de alambre). 9. arroyo. 10. (póker) robo (de cartas). 11. habilidad para sacar el revólver, ej., *quick on the d.,* rápido en sacar y disparar; **to beat (someone) to the d.,** adelantarse (a alguien) en sacar el revólver; (fig.) adelantarse (a alguien).
drawback ['drɔˌbæk] *s.* 1. desventaja, inconveniente, impedimento. 2. descuento, reintegro, esp. de derechos de aduana.
drawband [-ˌbænd] *s.* abrazadera, zuncho de tensión.
drawbar [-ˌbɑr, B -ˌbɑ] *s.* (f. c.) enganche, barra de tracción.
drawbench [-ˌbɛntʃ] *s.* (mec.) banco de estirar.
drawbolt [-ˌboʊlt] *s.* perno de acoplamiento.
drawbridge [-ˌbrɪdʒ] *s.* puente levadizo, puente giratorio.
drawee [drɔ'i] *s.* (com.) librado, girado.
drawer [drɔr, B drɔ] *s.* 1. gaveta, cajón. 2. ['drɔər, B 'drɔə] dibujante, bocetista. 3. (com.) librador, girador (de una letra de cambio o un cheque). 4. (*pl.*) calzoncillos.
draw hook, gancho de tracción (para halar troncos).
drawing ['drɔɪŋ] *s.* 1. dibujo, diseño. 2. sorteo, rifa. 3. tiramiento, estiramiento. 4. sorteo (de lotería, jurado, etc.); extracción. 5. (metal.) revenido.
drawing account, (ten.) cuenta de adelantos.
drawing board, tablero de dibujo.
drawing card, (fig.) atracción.
drawing compass(es), compás portalápiz.
drawing frame, estirador, carda mecánica.

drawing knife, cuchilla (desbastadora) de dos mangos.
drawing paper, papel de dibujo.
drawing pen, tiralíneas.
drawing press, (mec.) prensa estiradora.
drawing room, 1. salón. 2. recepción (social); asistentes a una recepción. 3. (E.U.) compartimiento reservado (en un tren).
drawing-room comedy ['drɔɪŋ,rum-, -,rʊm-] (teat.) comedia de costumbres frívolas.
drawing triangle, (dib.) escuadra.
drawknife ['drɔ,naɪf] *s.* cuchilla (desbastadora) de dos mangos.
drawl [drɔl] *v.t.* pronunciar despacio. —*v.i.* arrastrar las palabras. —*s.* enunciación lenta.
drawler ['drɔlər, B -ə] *s.* persona que arrastra las palabras.
drawn [drɔn] *p.p. de* **to draw**. —*a.* 1. desenvainado (revólver, espada); destripado (pollo, pescado). 2. (dib.) trazado, tirada (línea). 3. (fig.) ojeroso, contraído (de dolor, fatiga, etc.). 4. (dep.) empatado. 5. abierto (puente levadizo).
drawn butter, (cocina) salsa de mantequilla derretida.
drawnwork ['drɔn,wɜrk B -,wɜk] *s.* (cost.) labor de calado.
drawplate ['drɔ,pleɪt] *s.* 1. (mec.) calibre de estirar, placa perforada de estirar. 2. plancha de enganche (de la locomotora).
draw poker, (naipes) póker cerrado.
draw press, prensa punzonadora.
drawshave [-,ʃeɪv] *s.* cuchilla (desbastadora) de dos mangos.
drawstring [-,strɪŋ] *s.* cerradero, cuerda o cinta que cierra una bolsa o prenda con ojales.
drawtube [-,tub, B -,tjub] *s.* tubo telescópico; portaocular (del microscopio).
dray [dreɪ] *s.* carro fuerte, carretón. —*v.t., v.i.* acarrear.
drayage ['dreɪɪdʒ] *s.* acarreo, arrastre; costo de acarreo.
dray horse, caballo de tiro.
drayman [-mən] *s.* acarreador, transportista.
dread [drɛd] *v.t.* temer, tener miedo de. —*s.* 1. temor, espanto, pavor. 2. (ant.) temor reverencial. —*a.* terrible, espantoso.
dreadful ['drɛdfəl] *a.* 1. terrible, espantoso; asombroso. 2. molesto, desagradable, pesado.
dreadfully [-fəlɪ] *adv.* terriblemente; extremamente.
dreadnought, dreadnaught [-,nɔt, -,nɑt, B -,nɔt] *s.* 1. paño doble; capote grueso. 2. (mar.) acorazado. 3. el que nada teme.
dream [drim] *s.* 1. sueño. 2. (fig.) sueño, ensueño, ilusión. 3. (fig.) sueño, maravilla; deseo inalcanzable, ambición. 4. **d. come true,** sueño hecho realidad; **d. reader,** intérprete de los sueños. —*v.i.* (*pret., p.p.* DREAMED o DREAMT [drɛmt] *p.pr.* DREAMING) 1. soñar. 2. (fig.) soñar, fantasear. 3. **d. of,** soñar con. —*v.t.* 1. soñar, soñar con. 2. **d. away one's time,** pasarse el tiempo fantaseando; **d. up** (fam.) inventar, improvisar; **not to d. of (doing),** (no hacer) ni en sueños, ej., *I would not d. of selling it,* ni en sueños se me ocurriría venderlo.
dreamer ['drimər, B -ə] *s.* soñador, visionario.
dreamily ['driməlɪ] *adv.* como de ensueño, vagamente.
dreaminess [-ɪnəs] *s.* 1. languidez, estado de ensueño. 2. aire de irrealidad.
dreamingly [-ɪŋlɪ] *adv.* de modo soñador.
dreamland ['drɪm,lænd] *s.* 1. país del ensueño, país de las hadas. 2. mundo de sueños, mundo imaginario. 3. sueño, ej., *he's in d.,* está soñando, está durmiendo. 4. **to be in a d. (of),** estar en un mundo de sueños, soñar (con).
dreamless [-ləs] *a.* libre de sueños; sin ilusión.
dreamlike [-,laɪk] *a.* como un sueño, de ensueño, irreal, iluso; vago, nebuloso.
dreamworld [-,wɜrld, B -,wɜld] *s.* (fig.) mundo de sueños, mundo de ensueños.
dreamt [drɛmt] *pret. y p.p. de* **to dream.**
dreamy ['drimɪ] *a.* (DREAMIER; DREAMIEST) 1. soñador, dado a los sueños, ilusionado. 2. lánguido, de ensueño. 3. vago, nebuloso. 4. encantador, maravilloso.
drear [drɪr, B drɪə] *a.* (poét.) melancólico, triste, lóbrego.
drearily ['drɪrəlɪ, B 'drɪər-] *adv.* 1. melancólicamente, pesadamente. 2. monótonamente, pesadamente.
dreariness [-ɪnəs] *s.* aspecto o aire melancólico, pesadez, monotonía.
dreary [-ɪ] *a.* 1. triste, melancólico, deprimente. 2. monótono, pesado, aburrido.
dredge [drɛdʒ] *s.* draga; (mar.) rastra —*v.t.* 1. dragar, rastrear. 2. (cocina) espolvorear.
dredger ['drɛdʒər, B -ə] *s.* 1. (mar.) draga. 2. (cocina) implemento para espolvorear.
dredging machine [-ɪŋ-] draga.
dree [dri] *v.t.* (*pret., p.p.* DRED; *p.pr.* DREEING) (pr. esco.) aguantar, sufrir.
dreg [drɛg] *s.* 1. (*gen. pl.*) hez, poso, sedimento, borra. 2. (fig.) (*pl.*) escoria, ej., *the dregs of society,* la escoria de la sociedad. 3. (fig.) vestigio, ej., *there's not a d. of truth in it,* no tiene ni un vestigio de verdad. 4. **to drink** (o **drain**) **to the dregs,** apurar la copa hasta las heces.
drench [drɛntʃ] *s.* 1. remojo, remojón, mojadura. 2. (vet.) dosis o poción purgativa. 3. solución para curtir pieles. —*v.t.* 1. empapar, mojar. 2. remojar, sopetear. 3. (fig.) empaparse de (conocimientos, ideas, etc.). 4. bañar (animales). 5. (curtiduría) remojar, adobar, aderezar (las pieles). 6. (vet.) purgar a la fuerza. 7. (ant.) saciar, abrevar, hacer beber con exceso.
dress [drɛs] *s.* 1. vestido, traje. 2. (fig.) atuendo, ropa. —*v.t.* (*pret., p.p.* DRESSED; *p.pr.* DRESSING) 1. vestir. 2. adornar, ataviar. 3. arreglar, peinar (el cabello). 4. preparar, alistar. 5. almohazar (las caballerías). 6. curar (las heridas). 7. podar o cultivar (los árboles, el jardín). 8. cepillar, desbastar, labrar (madera); labrar, tallar (piedra). 9. (curtiduría) curar, curtir (pieles). 10. (tej.) aprestar (el tejido); encolar, engomar (la urdimbre). 11. (cocina) aliñar, aderezar. 12. (mil.) alinear. 13. (mar.) empavesar, engalanar (el buque). 14. **d. down,** poner a uno las orejas coloradas, calentar a uno las orejas; **dressed to kill,** vestida muy elegantemente; **d. up,** vestir con esmero, vestir de etiqueta, vestir elegantemente; disfrazar; **(to be) dressed up to the nines,** (estar) de tiros largos, (estar) de punta en blanco. —*v.i.* 1. vestirse. 2. (mil.) alinearse. 3. **d. up,** vestirse de etiqueta; endomingarse, emperejilarse; disfrazarse. —*a.* 1. perteneciente o relativo al vestir. 2. de fiesta (vestido). 3. de etiqueta, ceremonioso.
dress ball, baile de etiqueta, baile suntuoso.
dress circle, (teat.) galería principal de palcos.
dress coat , frac.
dresser ['drɛsər, B -ə] *s.* 1. ayudante (de cirujano). 2. (teat.) ayuda de cámara (de actores y actrices). 3. aparador; tocador; cómoda con espejo. 4. **to be a good d.,** vestir con buen gusto.
dressiness [-ɪnəs] *s.* elegancia exagerada, acicalamiento.
dressing [-ɪŋ] *s.* 1. aderezo, aliño, salsa; relleno. 2. (med.) vendaje, hilas. 3. abono, estercoladura.
dressing case, neceser (de tocador).
dressing chisel, desbastador.
dressing down, regaño, reprimenda; **to give (someone) a d. d.,** poner (a uno) las orejas coloradas, calentar (a uno) las orejas, regañar a uno.
dressing gown, bata, peinador.
dressing room, camarín (de teatro); cuarto de vestir.
dressing station, puesto de primeros auxilios; hospital de sangre, hospital de campaña.
dressing table, tocador.
dressmaker ['drɛs,meɪkər, B -ə] *s.* modista, costurera.
dressmaking [-ɪŋ] *s.* el arte y oficio de la costura.
dressmaking school, academia de corte y confección.
dress parade, (mil.) desfile de gala, parada (Amer.).
dress rehearsal, (teat.) ensayo general.
dress-shield ['drɛs,ʃild] *s.* (cost.) sobaquera.
dress shirt, camisa de etiqueta.
dress suit, traje o vestido de etiqueta.
dress sword, espadín, espada de ceremonia.
dress uniform, (mil.) uniforme de media gala.
dressy ['drɛsɪ] *a.* (DRESSIER; DRESSIEST) 1. acicalado, peripuesto (persona). 2. vistoso, de moda, elegante (ropa). 3. de etiqueta, propio de ocasiones de gala.
drew [dru] *pret. de* **draw**.
dribble ['drɪbəl] *v.i.* 1. gotear, escurrir. 2. babear. 3. (fig.) gotear. 4. (dep.) driblar, avanzar driblando. —*v.t.* 1. dejar caer gota a gota. 2. (gen. con *out*) repartir o divulgar poco a poco. 3. (dep.) driblar con (la pelota). 4. **d. away,** desperdiciar. —*s.* 1. goteo; hilo, chorro delgado (de agua, etc.). 2. llovizna, garúa (Amer.). 3. pizca, bicoca. 4. (dep.) habilidad de driblar; finta.
driblet [-lət] *s.* pizca, gota, insignificancia.
dribs and drabs ['drɪbzən'dræbz] en cantidades pequeñas; intermitente.
dried [draɪd] *pret., p.p. de* **dry**. —*a.* paso, seco, deshidratado (higo, ciruela, etc.).
dried beef, cecina, tasajo.
dried-up ['draɪd'ʌp] *a.* seco; apergaminado, acartonado.
drier ['draɪər, B -ə] *s.* 1. enjugador; desecante, secante. 2. (pint.) secante, desecador. 3. (t. **dryer**) secadora (aparato).
drift [drɪft] *s.* 1. cosas arrastradas por la corriente. 2. flujo o corriente lenta. 3. humo, lluvia, nieve o arena llevada por el viento. 4. amontonamiento (de arena, nieve, hielo); ventisquero; duna, médano. 5. rumbo, tendencia. 6. tenor, significado (de un discurso o escrito). 7. desviación (de un proyectil, de un vehículo). 8. inacción, inercia, indecisión. 9. (mar.) deriva, desvío (de la nave). 10. (aer.) deriva, velocidad lateral (del avión). 11. (elec.) deriva. 12. (rad.) desplazamiento, desviación. 13. (geol.) terreno de acarreo, morena. 14. (min.) socavón, galería, túnel horizontal. 15. (mec.) ensanchador, martillo punzón, broca, mandril cuadrado. 16. vado (en el África del S.). 17. **to get the d. of,** comprender el significado de. —*v.i.* 1. flotar, ser arrastrado por la corriente. 2. (mar.) ir a la deriva, derivar. 3. (fig.) ir o vivir sin rumbo. 4. amontonarse (por efecto del viento o del agua). —*v.t.* 1. arrastrar, llevar la corriente (algo). 2. amontonar, apilar. 3. (mec.) ensanchar, escariar (un agujero).
driftage ['drɪftɪdʒ] *s.* 1. (mar., aer.) deriva. 2. cosas arrastradas por la corriente o arrojadas a la orilla.
drift anchor, ancla flotante.
drift angle, (aer.) ángulo de deriva.
drift avalanche, alud.
drift bar, (avia.) retículo del derivómetro.

driftbolt [-ˌbouIt] *s.* perno largo; botador, clavo o perno para sacar pernos empujándolos.
drift computer, (avia.) calculador o computador de derivas.
drifter [ˈdrɪftər, B -ə] *s.* 1. barco que usa una red flotante. 2. persona sin rumbo, sin ocupación fija. 3. (min.) perforadora de galería. 4. barco de pesca con red rastrera.
drift indicator, d. meter, (aer.) indicador de deriva, derivómetro.
drifting [-ɪŋ] *a.* 1. (avia., mar.) a la deriva. 2. (fig.) sin rumbo ni meta.
drift net, red rastrera.
driftpin [ˈdrɪftˌpɪn] *s.* broca pasadora, mandril de ensanchar, cola de rata.
driftway [-ˌweɪ] *s.* 1. (min.) galería de dirección, galería horizontal de avance. 2. (mar.) curso a la deriva (de la nave).
driftweed [-ˌwid] *s.* alga marina flotante.
driftwood [-ˌwud] *s.* 1. madera flotante, madera de acarreo, madera arrojada a la playa (por la corriente). 2. (fig., jer.) peso muerto, impedimento; basura.
drill [drɪl] *s.* 1. taladro, broca, barrena. 2. (min.) sonda. 3. ejercicio, entrenamiento. 4. (mil.) instrucción, adiestramiento, ejercicio. 5. (pr. G.B.) procedimiento correcto, conducta correcta. —*v.t.* 1. taladrar, perforar, barrenar, horadar, agujerear. 2. instruir, entrenar, ejercitar en forma repetida e insistente. 3. (mil.) adiestrar (en las artes militares). 4. (con *into*) inculcar (en). 5. **d. a hole in,** (jer.) matar a bala. —*v.i.* 1. hacer un hueco. 2. (mil.) adiestrarse, hacer ejercicios.
drill, *v.t.* plantar o sembrar en surcos o hileras. —*s.* 1. surco (donde se siembra). 2. hilera de semilla sembrada en un surco. 3. sembradora mecánica. 4. (zool.) dril, mono del África, más pequeño que el mandril. 5. (tej.) dril, tela fuerte de algodón.
drill chuck, (mec.) portabroca, portabarrena, portamecha, mandril de broca.
driller [ˈdrɪlər, B -ə] *s.* 1. taladrador. 2. entrenador, instructor.
drill gage, (mec.) diámetro de la broca.
drilling [-ɪŋ] *s.* 1. barrenado, perforación, taladro, horadación. 2. instrucción, adiestramiento. 3. (mil.) ejercicio.
drillmaster [-ˌmæstər, B -ˌmustə] *s.* instructor militar; el que instruye bajo una estricta disciplina.
drill press, (mec.) prensa taladradora, taladradora, perforadora.
drill sergeant, (mil.) sargento instructor de reclutas.
drillstock [-ˌstɑk, B -ˌstɔk] *s.* portataladro.
drill yard, (f.c.) playa de maniobras.
drily *var. de* **dryly.**
drink [drɪŋk] *v.t.* (*pret.* DRANK [dræŋk]; *p.p.* DRUNK [drʌŋk] o (ant.) DRUNKEN [ˈdrʌŋkən]; *p.pr.* DRINKING) 1. beber. 2. (con *in* o *up*) embeber, absorber. 3. **d. away,** beberse (el sueldo, fortuna, etc.); **d. (someone) down,** tener mejor cabeza para las bebidas alcohólicas que (alguien); **d. (something) down,** beber de una vez, beber de un trago; **d. in,** (fig.) embeberse en, contemplar o escuchar con deleite; beberse, absorber (palabras, conocimiento, etc.); **d. off** (o **up**), bebérselo todo de un trago; **d. oneself out of a job,** perder uno su puesto por afición a la bebida; **d. oneself to death,** alcoholizarse hasta morir; **d. (someone) under the table,** hacer emborracharse (a alguien). —*v.i.* 1. beber. 2. beber (con exceso), empinar el codo. 3. **d. deep,** tomar un gran trago; ser un gran bebedor; **d. hard** (o **heavily**), beber con exceso, beber mucho; **d. like a fish,** beber como una cuba; **d. out of,** beber de o en (un arroyo, un sombrero, etc.); **d. to,** beber o brindar a o por. —*s.* 1. bebida, trago. 2. (el) beber. 3. (jer.) mar, agua. 4. **soft d.,** refresco, bebida no alcohólica; **to carry one's d. well,** tener buena cabeza; **to take a d.,** echar o tomar un trago; **to take to d.,** darse a la bebida.
drinkable [ˈdrɪŋkəbəl] *a.* bebible, potable. —*s.* (*gen. pl.*) bebida.
drinker [-ər, B -ə] *s.* 1. bebedor, borrachín. 2. bebedero (para pájaros, aves domésticas, etc.).
drinking [-ɪŋ] *s.* acción de beber.
drinking bout, (juerga de) borrachera.
drinking cup, taza para beber.
drinking fountain, surtidor de agua, fuente de agua (en lugares públicos, oficinas, etc.).
drinking horn, cuerna, aliara.
drinking party, fiesta o reunión en la que se sirven bebidas alcohólicas.
drinking song, 1. canción de taberna. 2. brindis cantado.
drinking trough, abrevadero, aguaje.
drinking water, agua potable.
drip [drɪp] *v.t.* (*pret. p.p.* DRIPPED O DRIPT; *p.pr.* DRIPPING) verter gota a gota, hacer gotear. —*v.i.* gotear, rezumar, chorrear; **d. with,** chorrear (sangre, agua, etc.); **dripping wet,** empapado. —*s.* 1. goteo, gotera, humedad condensada. 2. (arq.) alero, vierteaguas. 3. (jer.) sentimiento empalagoso, melosidad. 4. (jer.) chinche, pesado.
drip coffee, café colado.
drip cup, (aut.) colector de aceite.
drip-drip [ˈdrɪpˌdrɪp] *s.* goteo continuo.
drip-dry [-ˈdraɪ] *a.* que seca rápido (ej., ropa de nilón). —*v.i.* secarse rápidamente (al estar colgado).
drip feed, (aut.) alimentación por gotas, engrase por goteo.
drip pan, (aut.) colector de aceite, recogegotas; grasera, pringuera.
dripping [ˈdrɪpɪŋ] *s.* 1. goteo. 2. (*gen. pl.*) pringue, grasa y jugo (de un asado).
drippy [-ɪ] *a.* (DRIPPIER; DRIPPIEST) 1. lluvioso, pluvioso, llovioso. 2. empalagoso, sentimental (persona).
dripstone [-ˌstoun] *s.* 1. (arq.) alero, vierteaguas, escurridero de piedra. 2. (formaciones de) estalactita o estalagmita.
drive [draɪv] *v.t.* (*pret.* DROVE [drouv]; *p.p.* DRIVEN [ˈdrɪvən]; *p.pr.* DRIVING) 1. empujar, impulsar, impeler; llevar (cosas el viento o el agua). 2. arrear (animales). 3. mover, accionar, impulsar, poner en movimiento (máquina, etc.). 4. conducir, guiar, manejar (un vehículo); llevar (a alguien) en coche. 5. (con *to* o *into*) inducir; compeler, obligar, forzar. 6. hacer trabajar fuertemente. 7. (con *to* o *into*) hacer entrar por fuerza; clavar (ej., un poste en la tierra). 8. perforar (un túnel). 9. registrar (territorio) en busca de caza; levantar (caza). 10. (dep.) golpear fuertemente. 11. **d. against,** lanzar contra; **d. a good bargain,** hacer un buen negocio; **d. a hard bargain,** regatear mucho; **d. a point home,** (fig.) remachar el clavo; **d. away,** echar, alejar; **d. back,** hacer retroceder, rechazar; **d. crazy,** privar de juicio, sacar de sus casillas; **d. from,** echar o desalojar forzosamente de; **d. mad,** volver loco; **d. off,** ahuyentar; **d. oneself,** trabajar demasiado; **d. out,** expulsar, echar fuera; **d. out of one's mind** (o **senses**), hacer perder el juicio, volver loco; **d. to the wall,** poner entre la espada y la pared. —*v.i.* 1. manejar un vehículo, conducir un coche. 2. viajar o ir en coche. 3. **d. at,** proponerse, querer decir; **d. away,** irse, partir (en coche); **d. back,** volver, regresar (en coche); **d. by,** pasar por (en coche); **d. in,** entrar (en coche) en; **d. into,** entrar (en coche) en; chocar con (en coche); **d. into someone,** atropellar a alguien; **d. off,** irse (en coche); (golf) ejecutar el golpe inicial; **d. on,** seguir avanzando, no parar, pasar de largo (en coche); **d. through,** atravesar, pasar por (en coche); **d. up,** llegar (en coche); **d. up to,** llegar a, parar delante de (en coche). —*s.* 1. paseo, excursión o viaje (en vehículo). 2. camino particular (de una casa); autopista. 3. impulso, instinto. 4. campaña (contra o por una causa, de propaganda, etc.). 5. empuje, vigor, fuerza, energía. 6. apremio, apuro. 7. conducción, flotación (de leños). 8. montón de leños (que flotan río abajo). 9. (mec.) propulsión, accionamiento. 10. (aut.) transmisión; mecanismo de mando o de transmisión; conducción, ej., *left-hand d.,* conducción por la izquierda. 11. ofensiva, expansión (política). 12. (mil.) ataque vigoroso, ataque a viva fuerza. 13. (caza) batida. 14. (tenis, criquet) golpe fuerte (que se da a la pelota); (golf) golpe inicial. 15. (naipes) torneo (de bridge o whist).
drive belt, correa de transmisión.
drive bracket, (elec.) palomilla para clavar.
drive chain, (aut.) cadena de mando; (mec.) cadena de impulsión.
drive gear, (mec.) engranaje impulsor o transmisor.
drive-in [ˈdraɪvˌɪn] *a.* con servicio para automovilistas (banco, restaurante); al aire libre (cine). —*s.* banco o restaurante con servicio para automovilistas; cine al aire libre (en que los espectadores se quedan sentados en sus automóviles).
drive-in motion picture theater, motocine, auto-teatro, cine de verano, autocine (Chile).
drivel [ˈdrɪvəl] *v.i.* (*pret., p.p.* DRIVELED O DRIVELLED; *p.pr.* DRIVELING O DRIVELLING) 1. babear, echar la baba. 2. bobear, tontear. —*s.* 1. bobería, bobada, estupidez. 2. (ant.) baba. —*v.t.* 1. pronunciar bobamente (palabras). 2. (gen. con *away*) desperdiciar, gastar (tiempo).
driveler, driveller [-ər, B -ə] *s.* simple, baboso, tonto.
driven [ˈdrɪvən] *p.p. de* **drive.**
driver [ˈdraɪvər, B -və] *s.* 1. piloto, conductor, cochero, maquinista. 2. (mec.) rueda motriz; engranaje motor. 3. (dep.) un palo de golf (que lanza la pelota a mayor distancia). 4. mazo. 5. (jer.) jefe que exige que sus empleados trabajen duramente (t. **slave d.**).
driver ant, (ento.) hormiga devastadora (de África).
driver's license, licencia para conducir, licencia de chófer, licencia para manejar (Amer.), brevete (Amer.).
driver's seat, (fig.) posición de autoridad; asiento del conductor.
drive shaft, (mec.) árbol o eje propulsor o impulsor, eje de transmisión.
driveway [ˈdraɪvˌweɪ] *s.* camino particular (de una casa, para coches).
driving [ˈdraɪvɪŋ] *a.* 1. impulsor, motor, motriz. 2. enérgico, dinámico (persona). 3. violento, azotador (tempestad), torrencial (lluvia). —*s.* 1. conducción, manejo (de un vehículo). 2. (golf) ejecución del golpe inicial.
driving axle, (mec.) árbol o eje propulsor o impulsor.
driving belt, d. band, correa de transmisión.
driving drum, (mec.) tambor de transmisión.
driving iron, un palo de golf (con cabeza casi recta).
driving mirror, espejo retrovisor.

driving school, autoescuela, escuela de choferes, academia de choferes.
driving spindle, (mec.) árbol o eje de transmisión.
driving wheel, rueda motriz.
drizzle ['drɪzəl] *v.i.* lloviznar, molliznar, garuar (Amer.), briznar (Ven.). —*v.t.* asperjar, regar, rociar, salpicar. —*s.* llovizna, mollizna, garúa (Amer.), brizna (Ven.).
drizzly ['drɪzlɪ] *a.* de frecuentes lloviznas (día, etc.).
drogue [droʊg] *s.* 1. (mar.) boya (al extremo de la cuerda de un arpón). 2. (mar.) ancla arrastradiza, ancla flotante. 3. (aer.) ancla flotante, ancla de manga cónica. 4. (aer., astronáut.) paracaídas usado para frenar un objeto veloz, esp. una cápsula espacial al reintegrarse a la atmósfera.
droit [drɔɪt] *s.* (der.) derecho.
droll [droʊl] *a.* risible, chistoso, gracioso; raro, extraño. —*s.* bromista, burlón, bufón. —*v.i.* bromear, chancearse.
drollery ['droʊlərɪ] *s.* 1. bufonería, chuscada. 2. cuadro o dibujo cómico. 3. humorismo, agudeza.
dromedary ['drɑməˌdɛrɪ, B 'drʌmədərɪ] *s.* (zool.) dromedario.
dromond ['drɑmənd, B 'drɔm-] *s.* (mar.) dromón, galeaza, galeón.
drone [droʊn] *s.* 1. zángano, abejón. 2. (fig.) zángano, haragán, holgazán, parásito. 3. orador monótono. 4. zumbido, sonido monótono. 5. (mús.) roncón (de gaita); gaita. 6. avión o embarcación sin piloto (teledirigida). —*v.i.* 1. zumbar (como una abeja o gaita); hablar monótonamente. 2. flojear, obrar indolentemente. —*v.t.* 1. (con *out*) pronunciar monótonamente. 2. (con *away*) desperdiciar, gastar ociosamente (el tiempo).
drone bass, (mús.) bajo continuo.
drool [drul] *v.i.* 1. babear. 2. (fig.) caérsele la baba, hacérsele a uno agua la boca. 3. **d. over,** caérsele a uno la baba por. —*v.t.* (gen. con *out*) decir en tono empalagoso, decir tonterías. —*s.* bobería, bobada, estupidez.
droop [drup] *v.i.* 1. inclinarse, colgar, pender. 2. languidecer, extenuarse, flaquear, decaer. —*v.t.* dejar caer (orejas, cabeza). —*s.* inclinación, encorvadura; postura lánguida.
drooping ['drupɪŋ] *a.* 1. inclinado, pendiente. 2. caído, ej., párpados.
droopy [-ɪ] *a.* lánguido; flojo, flácido.
drop [drɑp, B drɔp] *s.* 1. gota. 2. (fig.) gota, pizca. 3. traguito (de licor). 4. pendiente (*m.*), arete; adorno colgante. 5. caramelo, bombón; pastilla. 6. caída. 7. descenso (en paracaídas), distancia en sentido vertical. 8. baja (de precios, temperatura). 9. pendiente (*f.*), declive, precipicio. 10. escotillón, trampa. 11. (med.) (*pl.*) (dosis en) gotas. 12. (teat.) (telón de) fondo; (t. **d. curtain**) telón. 13. (mar.) caída (de una vela). 14. (fútbol) (t. **d. kick**) puntapié dado a la pelota cuando ésta rebota del suelo. 15. **d. in a bucket,** (fig.) una bicoca, una cosa insignificante; **a d. in the ocean,** (fig.) una gota de agua en el mar; **at the d. of a hat,** (fig.) al dar la señal, al instante, en el acto; de buena gana, con gusto; **d. by d.,** gota a gota; **to have taken a d. too much,** estar borracho; **to take a d.,** tomar un traguito (de licor). —*v.t.* (*pret., p.p.* DROPPED; *p.pr.* DROPPING) 1. dejar caer; hacer caer. 2. bajar (la voz, los precios, etc.). 3. dejar caer, soltar (una palabra, sugerencia, etc.). 4. mandar (una carta, tarjeta, etc.). 5. excluir (de un club, del equipo, etc.); despedir. 6. dejar, abandonar, renunciar a (idea, plan, proyecto, etc.). 7. dejar de asociarse con (una persona). 8. omitir, suprimir (letra, palabra, sílaba); dejar de pronunciar (una letra). 9. derribar, tumbar. 10. llevar y dejar (un paquete, etc. en su destino). 11. parir (díc. de un animal). 12. (cocina) escalfar (huevos). 13. (teat.) bajar (el telón). 14. (dep.) conceder, perder (juegos, puntos, etc.). 15. (fútbol) patear (la pelota) cuando rebota; marcar (un tanto) con tiro hecho al rebotar la pelota. 16. (jer.) perder (dinero, esp. en el juego o en la bolsa de valores), ej., *I dropped a packet,* perdí un dineral. 17. (jer.) matar (a una persona). 18. **d. a curtsy,** hacer una reverencia; **d. a hint,** hacer una alusión, soltar una indirecta; **d. a line,** escribir (sólo) unas palabras; avisar (por carta); **d. anchor,** echar anclas; **d. a subject,** poner fin a una cuestión, cambiar de asunto o de tema; **d. it!** ¡basta ya!; **d. one's eyes,** bajar (uno) la mirada; **d. off,** dejar (*un pasajero*). —*v.i.* 1. caer. 2. descender, bajar (ej., un camino). 3. bajar (la voz, precios, producción, etc.). 4. dejarse caer; desplomarse. 5. caerse muerto, morir. 6. escapar (una observación, un reniego, etc.). 7. **d. around, by** u **over,** entrar o visitar al pasar, hacer una visita casual; ir o venir a ver; **d. asleep,** caer dormido; **d. away,** retirarse uno a uno (ej., socios de un club, etc.); **d. back,** retroceder, cejar; retirarse; **d. back into,** volver a acostumbrarse a; **d. behind,** retrasarse; **d. dead,** caer muerto; **d. in,** entrar al pasar, entrar o visitar de paso, ir o venir a ver; **d. in on,** visitar inesperadamente; **d. into,** caer en; entrar (al azar) en (una taberna, tienda, etc.); coger la costumbre de; **d. off,** adormecerse, caer dormido; disminuir, decrecer, ir a menos; morir; **d. out (of),** retirarse (de), separarse (de); **d. on,** reprender, reñir; **d. on one's knees,** caer de rodillas.
drop annunciator, (elec.) indicador de disco.
drop-bottom bucket ['drɑpˌbɑtəm-, B 'drɔpˌbɔt-] (const.) cucharón de descarga por debajo.
drop-bottom car, (f.c.) vagón de trampilla.
drop box, 1. (tej.) caja ascendente; caja de caballeros, caja de agujas. 2. buzón.
drop-box loom [-ˌbɑks-, B -ˌbɔks-] (tej.) telar de cajas ascendentes.
drop-center rim [-ˌsɛntər-, B -ə-] *s.* llanta de canal.
drop cord, (elec.) cordón de suspensión.
drop cover, tapa caediza.
drop curtain, (teat.) telón.
drop-forge ['drɑp'fɔrdʒ, B 'drɔp'fɔdʒ] *v.t.* forjar a martinete o a troquel.
drop forging, forjadura a martinete o a troquel.
drop hammer, (mec.) martinete, martillo pilón, martillo de caída libre, martillo de fragua.
drophead [-ˌhɛd] *s.* 1. tabla hundible (en un escritorio o mesa para máquina de coser o de escribir). 2. (G.B., aut.) convertible.
dropkick [-ˌkɪk] (fútbol) *s.* puntapié dado a la pelota cuando ésta rebota del suelo. —*v.i.* patear la pelota cuando rebota. —*v.t.* marcar (un tanto) con tiro hecho al rebotar la pelota.
drop leaf, hoja o tabla plegadiza de una mesa.
drop-leaf table [-ˌlif-] mesa de hojas plegadizas.
droplet ['drɑplət, B 'drɔp-] *s.* gotita.
droplet infection, (med.) infección por gotas de Pfflüger.
drop letter, carta local (que se entrega al destinatario en la misma estafeta donde fue despachada).
droplight [-ˌlaɪt] *s.* lámpara movible, lámpara de extensión.
drop-off [-ˌɔf] *s.* bajada escarpada, bajada perpendicular.
drop-out [-ˌaʊt] *s.* 1. abandono, deserción (esp. de estudios o entrenamiento). 2. estudiante que no termina el curso. 3. persona que abandona sus deberes sociales y se dedica a una vida bohemia; hippie.
drop-out voltage, (elec.) voltaje de disparo, tensión de desenganche.
droppage ['drɑpɪdʒ, B 'drɔp-] *s.* fruta que cae del árbol antes de la cosecha.
dropper [-ər, B -ə] *s.* cuentagotas, gotero (Amer.).
dropping [-ɪŋ] *s.* 1. (*gen. pl.*) gota caída (ej., de cera). 2. (*pl.*) deyecciones (de animales).
dropping angle, (avia.) ángulo de caída.
drop press, 1. prensa punzadora. 2. martinete forjador.
drop shot, 1. perdigones (hechos por el procedimiento de rociar metal fundido desde una altura). 2 (tenis) tiro con efecto (que hace caer bruscamente la pelota muy cerca de la red).
drop shutter, (foto.) obturador de guillotina.
dropsical ['drɑpsɪkəl, B 'drɔp-] *a.* 1. hidrópico. 2. (fig.) hinchado.
dropsonde ['drɑpˌsɑnd, B 'drɔpˌsɔnd] *s.* (rad.) radiosonda de paracaídas (soltada por un avión que vuela a gran altura).
dropsy ['drɑpsɪ, B 'drɔp-] *s.* (med., vet.) hidropesía.
drop valve, válvula de cierre por gravedad.
drop wire, (rad., avia.) antena de cable colgante.
dropwort ['drɑpˌwɜrt, B 'drɔpˌwɜt] *s.* (bot.) filipéndula.
Droseraceae [ˌdrɑsə'reɪsɪˌi, B ˌdrɔs-] *s. pl.* (bot.) droseráceas.
droshky ['drɑʃkɪ, B 'drɔʃ-] *s.* droski (carruaje ruso, bajo y de cuatro ruedas).
drosometer [droʊ'sɑmətər, B drɔ'sɔmɪtə] *s.* drosómetro.
drosophila [droʊ'sɑfələ, B -'sɔf-] *s.* (ento.) drosófila.
dross [drɔs, drɑs, B drɔs] *s.* 1. escoria (de metal fundido). 2. impurezas, desechos, desperdicios, basura.
drossy ['drɔsɪ, 'drɑsɪ, B 'drɔsɪ] *a.* 1. cubierto de escoria. 2. impuro, inmundo.
drought [draʊt] **drouth** [draʊθ] *s.* sequía, seca.
droughty ['draʊtɪ] **drouthy** ['draʊθɪ] *a.* 1. árido, seco. 2. (dial.) sediento.
drove [droʊv] *s.* 1. hato, manada, rebaño, vacada, piara. 2. multitud, gentío, muchedumbre. 3. cincel desbastador. —*v.t.* (G.B.) 1. arrear. 2. acabar o retocar (una piedra) con cincel desbastador.
drove [droʊv] *pret. de* **drive**.
drover ['droʊvər, B -və] *s.* ganadero, persona que conduce ganado; mercader de ganado.
drown [draʊn] *v.i.* ahogarse. —*v.t.* 1. ahogar (a una persona, animal, etc.). 2. ahogar, encharcar, inundar (tierra, etc.). 3. empapar, mojar. 4. (fig.) ahogar (sonido, ruido; miseria, pesar, etc.). 5. **d. oneself in,** (fig.) sumirse en, sumergirse en (trabajo, etc.).
drowse [draʊz] *v.t.* 1. adormecer, adormitar. 2. (con *away*) pasar dormitando (el tiempo, la tarde, etc.). —*v.i.* 1. dormitar, adormitarse. 2. **d. off,** adormecerse. —*s.* sueño ligero.
drowsily ['draʊzəlɪ] *adv.* soñolientamente.
drowsiness [-zɪnəs] *s.* somnolencia, modorra, pereza.
drowsy [-zɪ] *a.* soñoliento, adormecido, amodorrado.
drub [drʌb] *v.t.* (*pret. de* DRUBBED; *p.pr.* DRUBBING) 1. apalear, tundir, zurrar. 2. (dep.) derrotar por completo (en un partido). 3. (con *into* o *out of*) machacar (una idea, etc.). 4. golpear (con un palo).
drubbing ['drʌbɪŋ] *s.* 1. paliza, zurra, tunda, azotaina. 2. (dep.) derrota severa.

drudge [drʌdʒ] *v.i.* afanarse, trabajar como un esclavo. —*s.* esclavo del trabajo, trabajador servil.
drudgery ['drʌdʒərɪ] *s.* trabajo fatigoso, labor monótona.
drug [drʌg] *s.* 1. droga, medicina, medicamento. 2. narcótico, estupefaciente. 3. **to be a d. on the market,** ser invendible; ser indeseable la presencia de (uno). —*v.t.* (*pret., p.p.* DRUGGED: *p.pr.* DRUGGING) 1. narcotizar, dopar. 2. adulterar con drogas (alimentos, bebidas, etc.). —*v.i.* tomar drogas.
drug addict, narcómano.
drug addiction, narcomanía.
drug fiend, narcómano.
drugget ['drʌgət] *s.* 1. (tej.) droguete. 2. alfombra de algodón y lana.
druggist ['drʌgəst] *s.* farmacéutico, boticario; droguero, droguista.
drug habit, narcomanía.
drugstore [-ˌstɔr, B -ˌstɔ] *s.* 1. (E.U.) tienda de medicamentos, refrescos, revistas y artículos menudos. 2. droguería, farmacia, botica.
druid ['druəd] *s.* (hist.) druida, sacerdote de una orden religiosa céltica.
druidism [-ˌɪzəm] *s.* druidismo, religión y conceptos filosóficos de los druidas (antigua orden céltica).
drum [drʌm] *s.* 1. (mús.) tambor. 2. tambor, cilindro (como recipiente); carrete, bobina. 3. tambor, cilindro (de un revólver). 4. (anat.) tímpano (del oído). 6. (arq.) tambor, vaso de capitel, cuerpo de columna. 7. **to beat the d. (for),** hacer propaganda (a o por). —*v.i.* (*pret., p.p.* DRUMMED; *p.pr.* DRUMMING) 1. tocar el tambor. 2. tamborear, tamborilear, tabalear. —*v.t.* 1. (gen. con *up*) convocar, juntar, reunir (a toque de tambor). 2. **d. a lesson into (someone),** meterle (a uno) la lección en la cabeza; **d. into,** inculcar, imbuir; **d. out,** expeler ignominiosamente, expulsar; **d. up trade,** solicitar o fomentar ventas.
drumbeat ['drʌmˌbit] *s.* toque de tambor.
drumbeater [-ər, B -ə] *s.* defensor vociferante (de una causa).
drumbeating [-ɪŋ] *s.* defensa vociferante (de una causa).
drumfire ['drʌmˌfaɪr, B -ˌfaɪə] *s.* fuego graneado.
drumhead [-ˌhɛd] *s.* 1. parche o piel de tambor. 2. (mar.) sombrero (de un cabrestante).
drumhead court-martial, (mil.) consejo de guerra celebrado en marcha o en el campo de batalla.
drumlin ['drʌmlən] *s.* (geol.) colina oval alargada (formada por el viento o depósitos de origen pluvial).
drum major, (mil.) tambor mayor, cachiporrero.
drum majorette, (E.U.) muchacha que marcha al frente de una banda de músicos (en desfiles, etc.), guaripolera (Amer.), cachiporrera.
drummer ['drʌmər, B -ə] *s.* 1. tambor, el que toca el tambor. 2. (E.U.) viajante, agente viajero.
drumming [-ɪŋ] *s.* tamboreo, tamborileo.
drum mixer, (quím.) mezclador cilíndrico.
drumstick [-ˌstɪk] *s.* 1. baqueta o palillo de tambor. 2. (fam.) muslo (de ave cocida).
drumstick tree, (bot.) cañafístula.
drunk [drʌŋk] *p.p. de* **drink**. —*a.* borracho, embriagado, ebrio; **dead d., d. with (love, success, power,** etc.), (fig.) embriagado de (amor, éxito, poder, etc.). —*s.* 1. borracho, borrachín. 2. borrachera, parranda.
drunkard ['drʌŋkərd, B -kəd] *s.* borracho, borrachín, bebedor.
drunken [-kən] *a.* 1. borracho, embriagado. 2. de borrachos, entre borrachos, ej., *a d. brawl,* una reyerta de o entre borrachos. 3. inestable, tambaleante, precario.
drunkenly [-lɪ] *adv.* ebriamente.
drunkenness [-nəs] *s.* embriaguez.
drunkometer [ˌdrʌŋ'kɑmətər, B -'kɔmɪtə] *s.* aparato para medir el porcentaje de alcohol en la sangre.
drupaceous [dru'peɪʃəs] *a.* (bot.) drupáceo.
drupe [drup] *s.* (bot.) drupa.
drupelet ['druplət] *s.* (bot.) drupéolo, drupéola.
druse [druz] *s.* 1. (min.) drusa. 2. (med.) inflamación.
Druze, Druse [druz] *s.* druso; miembro de una secta musulmana del Oriente Medio.
dry [draɪ] *a.* (DRIER; DRIEST) 1. seco, árido. 2. desecado. 3. en seco (mampostería, construcción). 4. sediento. 5. (servido) sin mantequilla (pan, tostada). 6. seco (vino, champaña, etc.). 7. (fig.) seco (hombre, humor, carácter, estilo, etc.). 8. simulado, de práctica (tiro, prueba, etc.). 9. pesado, aburrido (relato, descripción, etc.). 10. (fam.) seco, que prohíbe la venta de bebidas alcohólicas. 11. **d. run,** práctica, ensayo; **on d. land,** en seco, en tierra firme; **to go d.,** secarse; (fig.) prohibir la venta de bebidas alcohólicas. —*v.t.* (*pret., p.p.* DRIED; *p.pr.* DRYING) secar, desecar; **d. up,** secar totalmente. —*v.i.* secarse, desecarse; **d. up,** desecarse; (fig.) callarse; **d. up!** ¡cállate la boca! —*s.* (*pl.* DRYS) 1. sequedad. 2. lugar seco. 3. (fam., E.U.) partidario de la ley seca.
dryad ['draɪəd, -ˌæd] *s.* (mitol.) dríada, dríade; ninfa del bosque.
dry-as-dust ['draɪəzˌdʌst] *a.* aburrido, tedioso, prosaico. —*s.* pedante.
dry assay, (quím.) determinación por método seco.
dry battery, (elect.) batería seca, pila seca.
dry beef, cecina, charqui, tasajo.
dry-bulb thermometer [-'bʌlb-] termómetro de bola seca.
dry casting, fundición en arena seca.
dry cell, (elec.) celda seca, pila seca, elemento seco.
dry-clean [-ˌklin] *v.t.* limpiar en seco, lavar en seco.
dry cleaner, tintorero, lavandero, limpiador en seco.
dry cleaning, limpieza o lavado en seco.
dry clutch, (aut.) embrague seco.
dry concentration, (meteor.) concentración en seco o por venteo.
dry cup, (med.) ventosa seca.
dry distillation, (quím.) destilación seca.
dry dock, dique de carena, dique seco.
dry-dock ['draɪˌdɑk, B -ˌdɔk] *v.t., v.i.* encarenar(se), carenar(se), entrar (a dique de carena).
dryer, dryest *var. de* **drier, driest.**
dryer ['draɪər, B -ə] *s.* 1. persona o cosa que seca. 2. secadora (aparato).
dry-eyed [-ˌaɪd] *a.* ojiseco, que no llora.
dry farm, granja de cultivo sin riego.
dry farmer, granjero que se dedica al cultivo seco.
dry farming, (agr.) cultivo seco (sin riego).
dry fly, (pesca) mosca artificial flotante.
dry fruit, frutas pasas, frutas secas.
dry goods, (com., E.U.) mercancías generales (esp. telas, paños, ropa); lencería, mercería.
dry goods store, tienda de tejidos.
drygulch ['draɪˌgʌltʃ] *v.t.* (jer.) 1. asesinar, matar en una emboscada. 2. dejar saber, revelar el propósito de (sin proponérselo).
dry ice, hielo seco; (quím.) nieve carbónica.
drying ['draɪɪŋ] *a.* desecante, secante, secador, desecativo.
drying oil, aceite secante o cocido.
dry kiln, horno, secadero (para secar y curar madera aserrada).
dry land, tierra firme.
dry law, (E.U.) ley seca (contra el expendio de bebidas alcohólicas).
drylot ['draɪˌlɑt, B -ˌlɔt] *s.* corral pequeño para cebar ganado.
dryly ['draɪlɪ] *adv.* secamente, fríamente.
dry masonry, mampostería en seco, mampostería a hueso.
dry measure, medida para áridos; (ing.) medida de volumen.
dryness [-nəs] *s.* sequedad, aridez.
dry nurse, ama seca, niñera (que cuida a un bebé sin darle de mamar).
dry-nurse[-'nɜrs, B -'nɜs] *v.t.* 1. ser niñera de, criar un bebé sin darle de mamar. 2. (fig.) cuidar demasiado, tratar como a un niño.
dry plate, (foto.) placa o plancha seca.
dry point, 1. (arte) grabado a buril. 2. (quím.) punto final de ebullición.
dry rot, 1. (agr.) podredumbre seca (de la madera). 2. (fig.) deterioro, desintegración, corrupción interna y oculta (de las costumbres, moralidad, etc.).
dry run, (mil.) pasada de tiro simulado; sesión de práctica o prueba; (teat.) ensayo final sin utilería ni vestuario.
dry-salt ['draɪˌsɔlt] *v.t.* curar (viandas, carnes, etc.) en seco con sal.
dry scall, sarna.
dry season, temporada que precede a las lluvias otoñales.
dry-shod [-'ʃɑd, B -'ʃɔd] *a.* a pie enjuto.
dry sump, (mec.) colector seco.
dry wall, muro construido de piedras encajadas sin mezcla cohesiva.
dry wash, 1. ropa lavada y secada (pero no planchada). 2. arroyo seco.
dry weight, 1. (ing.) peso en vacío. 2. (quím.) peso seco.
DST *abrev. de* **daylight-saving time,** hora de verano.
DTH *abrev. de* **Doctor of Theology,** Doctor en Teología.
DT's ['di'tiz] *s.* (jer.) delírium tremens.
duad ['duˌæd, B 'dju-] *s.* par, pareja; (quím.) díada.
dual ['duəl, B 'dju-] *a.* doble, dual, binario; (gram.) dual. —*s.* dual, número dual.
dual citizenship, dual nationality, (der.) doble nacionalidad.
dual control, (aer., aut.) mando doble, control de doble mando.
dual drive, (aut.) mando doble.
dual ignition, (mec.) encendido doble.
dualism ['duəlˌɪzəm, B 'dju-] *s.* dualismo, dualidad.
dualist [-əst] *s.* dualista.
dualistic [ˌduə'lɪstɪk, B ˌdju-] *a.* dualístico.
duality [du'ælətɪ, B dju-] *s.* dualidad.
dualize ['duəlˌaɪz, B 'dju-] *v.t.* hacer binario o doble.
dual personality, (psic.) personalidad doble o múltiple.
dual-purpose [ˌduəl'pɜrpəs, B 'dju'pɜpəs] *a.* de doble aprovechamiento, de doble uso, de doble función.
dub [dʌb] *v.t.* (*pret., p.p.* DUBBED; *p.pr.* DUBBING) 1. armar, hacer (caballero). 2. apellidar, apodar; titular, llamar. 3. (jer.) chapucear, frangollar. 4. (golf, jer.) golpear en falso (la pelota).
dub [dʌb] *v.t.* 1. alisar, estregar, suavizar (cueros). 2. (carp.) aparar, desbastar (madera) con la azuela. 3. tamborilear. 4. golpear, empujar. 5.

apellidar, poner apodo. 6. (cinem.) doblar (una película), sonorizar. 7. (gen. con *in*) mezclar o intercalar (música auxiliar, voces, efectos sonoros, etc.). —*s.* 1. (fam.) chambón, persona torpe. 2. golpe, empuje. 3. toque de tambor.

dubbing [ˈdʌbɪŋ] *s.* 1. ceremonia en que se arma caballero (a alguien). 2. adobo (para engomar las telas, o curtir pieles). 3. (cinem.) doblaje de películas, sonorización.

dubiety [duˈbaɪətɪ, B dju-] **dubiosity** [ˌdubɪˈɑsətɪ, B djubɪˈɔs-] *s.* duda, incertidumbre; irresolución.

dubious [ˈdubɪəs, B ˈdjubjəs] *a.* 1. dudoso, dudable. 2. dudoso, indeciso, irresoluto.

dubiously [-lɪ] *adv.* dudosamente.

dubiousness [-nəs] *s.* duda, incertidumbre.

dubitable [ˈdubətəbəl, B ˈdju-] *a.* dudable, dudoso, cuestionable.

dubitation [ˌdubəˈteɪʃən B ˌdju-] *s.* (ant.) duda, vacilación.

dubitative [ˈdubəˌteɪtɪv, B ˈdjubɪtətɪv] *a.* dubitativo; (gram.) dubitativo.

dubitative conjunction, (gram.) conjunción dubitativa.

dubitatively [-lɪ] *adv.* dubitativamente.

Dublin [ˈdʌblən] *s.* Dublín, capital de Irlanda.

ducal [ˈdukəl, B ˈdju-] *a.* ducal; perteneciente al duque.

ducat [ˈdʌkət] *s.* 1. ducado (moneda de oro). 2. (jer.) dinero. 3. (jer.) entrada (al cine, teatro, etc.).

duchess [ˈdʌtʃəs] *s.* duquesa.

duchy [ˈdʌtʃɪ] *s.* ducado.

duck [dʌk] *s.* 1. (orn.) pato, ánade; pata. 2. (carne de) pato. 3. (fam., G.B.) pichona, querida. 4. (jer.) tipo, tipa, tío, tía, persona. 5. (tej.) dril, brin, lona fina, loneta. 6. (*pl.*) (fam.) traje de dril, pantalón de dril. 7. (E.U., mil.) camión anfibio. 8. **fine day for young ducks,** (irón.) tiempo lluvioso; **in two shakes of a d.'s tail,** en un dos por tres; **like water off a d.'s back,** sin producir efecto alguno; **to take (to a thing) like a d. to water,** estar a gusto con, hallarse en su elemento con, tomar (algo) como una cosa natural.

duck [dʌk] *v.t.* 1. zambullir, sumergir. 2. bajar, hundir o agachar repentinamente (la cabeza). 3. esquivar, evitar (un golpe) bajando la cabeza; (fig.) eludir (problema, dificultad, etc.). —*v.i.* 1. zambullirse, chapuzarse. 2. agacharse, regatear. 3. (gen. con *out*) escaparse. 4. **d. out on,** eludir, evadir (pago, responsabilidad, deber, etc.). —*s.* 1. zambullida. 2. agachada, regate.

duckbill [ˈdʌkˌbɪl] *s.* (zool.) ornitorrinco.

duckboard [-ˌbɔrd, B -ˌbɔd] *s.* (*ú. gen. en pl.*) caminillo de tablillas, tarima (sobre una superficie barrosa o mojada).

duck call, reclamo para llamar a patos.

ducker [ˈdʌkər, B -ə] *s.* (orn.) zambullidor, somorgujo.

duck hawk, (orn.) halcón peregrino.

duckie, (jer.) *var. de* **ducky.**

ducking [ˈdʌkɪŋ] *s.* zambullida; remojada, chapuzón.

ducking stool, (hist.) silla para zambullir al castigado en el agua.

duckling [ˈdʌklɪŋ] *s.* patito, anadino, anadeja.

duckpin [-ˌpɪn] *s.* bolo; (*pl.*) juego con bolos de madera.

ducks and drakes, duck and drake, juego de cabrillas; **to play d. and d.,** jugar a cabrillas; **play d. and d. with, make d. and d. of,** (fig.) despilfarrar, derrochar, malgastar.

duck soup, (fam.) cosa fácil, juego de niños.

duckweed [-ˌwid] *s.* (bot.) lenteja de agua.

ducky [ˈdʌkɪ] *a.* 1. (jer.) grato, placentero; bonito, mono, lindo. 2. (fam.) querido, amada, corazón.

duct [dʌkt] *s.* conducto, canal, tubo; (anat.) conducto. —*v.t.* conducir (gas, agua, etc.) por un tubo.

ductile [ˈdʌktəl, B -taɪl] *a.* 1. dúctil, flexible (díc. esp. de metales). 2. (fig.) dúctil, blando, dócil.

ductility [ˌdʌkˈtɪlətɪ] *s.* ductilidad; docilidad.

ducting [ˈdʌktɪŋ] *s.* sistema de conductos; material para hacer conductos.

ductless gland [ˈdʌktləs-] (anat.) glándula endocrina, glándula de secreción interna.

ductule [ˈdʌkˌtul, B -ˌtjul] *s.* (anat.) dúctulo, conducto pequeño.

dud [dʌd] *s.* 1. bomba o granada que no estalla. 2. fracaso, fiasco; fracasado (persona); cosa inútil. 3. (*pl.*) (fam.) ropas. 4. (*pl.*) (fam.) trapos, andrajos, ropa gastada y vieja; pertenencias. —*a.* falsificado; inútil; insatisfactorio.

dude [dud, B djud] *s.* (E.U.) 1. petimetre, pisaverde, currutaco, lechuguino. 2. (jer.) persona oriunda del Este; ciudadano, habitante de la ciudad. 3. (jer.) fulano, tío.

dudeen [duˈdin] *s.* (Irl.) pipa corta.

dude ranch, (E.U.) hacienda o rancho para (entretenimiento de) turistas.

dudgeon [ˈdʌdʒən] *s.* 1. inquina, enojo, ojeriza. 2. (ant.) daga con empuñadura de madera; mango, puño o asa de madera.

due [du, B dju] *a.* 1. vencido, pagadero (letra, obligación, etc.). 2. debido, merecido, propio (respeto, premio, pena, etc.). 3. debido, adecuado, suficiente (prueba, consideración, etc.). 4. esperado, aguardado, que debe llegar, ej., *the train is d. at six,* el tren debe llegar a las seis. 5. **d. to,** debido a, a causa de; **in d. course, in d. time,** a su debido tiempo; **to be d. to (do),** deber, ej., *he is d. to speak tonight,* él debe hablar esta noche; **to be d. to (someone),** corresponder a (alguien), tocar a (alguien); **to become d., to fall d.,** vencer (letra, obligación). —*s.* 1. derecho. 2. (*pl.*) derechos, impuestos. 3. cuota (de socio de un club, etc.). 4. **to get one's d.,** llevar su merecido; **to give someone his d.,** ser justo con alguien; **to give the devil his d.,** ser justo hasta con el diablo (tengo que reconocer que, etc.). —*adv.* directamente; **d. north,** (mar.) proa al norte.

due bill, (com.) pagaré, abonaré (gen. con mercancías o servicios).

due date, (com.) fecha de vencimiento.

duel [ˈduəl, B ˈdju-] *s.* duelo; combate; **d. to the death,** duelo a muerte; **to fight a d.,** batirse a duelo. —*v.i.* (*pret., p.p.* DUELED o DUELLED; *p.pr.* DUELING o DUELLING) batirse a duelo.

dueler, dueller [-ər, B -ə] **duelist, duellist** [-əst] *s.* duelista.

duello [duˈɛloʊ, B dju-] *s.* (*pl.* DUELLOS) 1. duelo. 2. código del duelo, código de honor.

duenna [duˈɛnə, B dju-] *s.* acompañante, dama de compañía; chaperona.

due process of law, (der.) proceso legal establecido.

duet [duˈɛt, B dju-] *s.* (mús.) dúo, dueto (composición e intérpretes).

duff [dʌf] *s.* 1. (esco., E.U.) mantillo, tierra vegetal (en los bosques). 2. polvo de carbón, cisco. 3. budín de harina, cocido al vapor. —*v.t.* 1. (jer., G.B.) retocar, transformar, cambiar la apariencia de (cosas robadas). 2. (Aust.) robar ganado, cambiar la marca a (reses). 3. (golf) dar un golpe en falso a (la pelota).

duff [dʌf] *v.t.* 1. (jer., G.B.) retocar, transformar, cambiar la apariencia de (cosas robadas). 2. (Aust.) robar ganado, cambiar la marca a (reses). 3. (golf) dar un golpe en falso a (la pelota).

duffel [ˈdʌfəl] *s.* 1. (tej.) muletón, paño de lana basta. 2. (fam., E.U.) equipo, pertrechos, suministros.

duffel bag, talego de lona o piel flexible para efectos personales.

duffel coat, abrigo tres cuartos con capuchón.

duffer [ˈdʌfər, B -ə] *s.* 1. (jer.) estúpido, inútil, incompetente, chabacano; chambón (en el juego). 2. (jer.) (gen. **old d.**) viejo chocho. 3. (jer.) vendedor ambulante (de artículos de fantasía); buhonero, baratillero. 4. (jer.) bicoca, cosa inútil.

duffle, *var. de* **duffel.**

dug [dʌg] *pret., p.p. de* **dig.** —*s.* pezón, tetilla.

dugong [ˈduˌgɔŋ, -ˌgɑŋ, B -ˌgɔŋ] *s.* (zool.) dugongo, dugong.

dugout [ˈdʌgˌaʊt] *s.* 1. piragua. 2. (mil.) refugio subterráneo, trinchera cubierta. 3. (dep.) cobertizo de espera (para los jugadores de béisbol). 4. (jer., G.B.) oficial retirado llamado a servicio.

duiker [ˈdaɪkər, B -ə] *s.* (zool.) pequeño antílope africano.

duke [duk, B djuk] *s.* 1. duque. 2. (*pl.*) (jer.) manos, puños.

dukedom [ˈdukdəm, B ˈdjuk-] *s.* ducado.

dulcet [ˈdʌlsət] *a.* 1. melodioso, melifluo, dulcísono. 2. agradable, calmante. 3. (ant.) dulce (al paladar). —*s.* (mús.) registro del órgano de tono dulce.

dulcification [ˌdʌlsəfəˈkeɪʃən] *s.* dulcificación.

dulcify [ˈdʌlsəˌfaɪ] *v.t.* (*pret., p.p.* DULCIFIED; *p.pr.* DULCIFYING) 1. dulcificar, endulzar. 2. apaciguar, ablandar.

dulcimer [ˈdʌlsəmər, B -mə] *s.* (mús.) dulcémele.

dulia [duˈlaɪə, B dju-] *s.* (relig.) dulía, culto que se rinde a ángeles y santos.

dull [dʌl] *s.* 1. estúpido, torpe, obtuso, tardo (de comprensión). 2. lerdo, lento. 3. romo, embotado, obtuso, sin punta, sin filo. 4. opaco, deslustrado, empañado, desvaído (color). 5. débil, apagado (fuego, lumbre). 6. apagado, sordo (sonido). 7. sordo (dolor). 8. deprimido, alicaído, desanimado. 9. insípido, insulso, soso. 10. aburrido, tedioso, monótono. 11. nublado, nubloso, nebuloso. 12. sin demanda (mercancía); inactivo, muerto (comercio, temporada). —*v.t., v.i.* 1. embotar(se), entorpecer(se) (sentidos, intelecto). 2. embotar(se), desafilar(se). 3. opacar(se), deslustrar(se), empañar(se). 4. apagar(se) (un sonido). 5. moderar(se), mitigar(se) (dolor, pena, etc.). 6. volver(se) aburrido, tedioso o monótono. 7. **d. the edge of,** (fig.) embotar, debilitar, quitar la fuerza a.

dullard [ˈdʌlərd, B -əd] *s.* estúpido, estólido.

dullish [-ɪʃ] *a.* 1. bastante estúpido. 2. algo opaco, sin mucho brillo (color); algo apagado o sordo (sonido). 3. algo tedioso, bastante aburrido.

dullness, dulness [-nəs] *s.* 1. estupidez, torpeza. 2. falta de filo o punta. 3. deslustre, opacidad. 4. pesadez, monotonía. 5. (com.) depresión, desinterés.

dull-witted [-ˈwɪtəd] *a.* lerdo, estúpido.

dully [ˈdʌlɪ] *adv.* 1. torpemente, estúpidamente; lentamente. 2. monótonamente, tediosamente, aburridamente.

dulse [ˈdʌls] *s.* variedad de alga marina roja (usada como alimento).

duly [ˈdulɪ, B ˈdjulɪ] *adv.* 1. debidamente, correctamente, adecuadamente, apropiadamente, convenientemente. 2. puntualmente, a tiempo.

Duma [ˈdumə] *s.* duma, parlamento de la Rusia zarista.

dumb [dʌm] *a.* 1. mudo. 2. (fig.) mudo, silencioso, reticente, callado, taciturno. 3. (fam.) tonto, estúpido. 4. **the d.,** los mudos; **to strike d.,** dejar mudo (de sorpresa, etc.). *—v.t.* 1. enmudecer. 2. entorpecer, aturdir.
dumb ague, (cierta clase de) fiebre intermitente.
dumb alphabet, abecedario manual, abecedario de los sordos.
dumb animal, bestia, animal.
dumbbell ['dʌm,bɛl] *s.* 1. pesas (de gimnasia). 2. (jer.) estúpido, tonto, zopenco.
dumbfound [,dʌm'faʊnd] **dumbfounder** [-'faʊndər, B -də] *var. de* **dumfound.**
dumbly ['dʌmlɪ] *adv.* 1. silenciosamente, en silencio; mudamente. 2. (fam.) tontamente, estúpidamente.
dumb motions, señas.
dumbness [-nəs] *s.* 1. mudez. 2. (fam.) estupidez.
dumb piano, piano mudo para practicar.
dumb show, 1. signos y gestos (sin palabras). 2. pantomima.
dumbstruck ['dʌm,strʌk] *a.* pasmado, atónito, sin habla.
dumb-waiter [-'weɪtər, B -ə] *s.* montaplatos, pequeño montacargas; ascensor giratorio para transportar platos y comida de un piso a otro.
dum-dum ['dʌm,dʌm] *s.* dumdum, bala de expansión.
dum-dum bullet, bala expansiva.
dumfound [,dʌm'faʊnd] *v.t.* enmudecer, pasmar, dejar sin habla, dejar atónito, dejar turulato.
dummy ['dʌmɪ] *s.* 1. estúpido, imbécil. 2. testaferro, hombre de paja. 3. maniquí (para vestidos). 4. substituto, imitación. 5. (impr.) maqueta (de un libro). 6. (naipes) muerto (jugador o mano). 7. (ing.) maqueta, modelo, plantilla. 8. **to be the d.,** (naipes) hacer de muerto. *—a.* 1. postizo, imitado, simulado, falso. 2. nominal. 3. (jer.) mudo.
dummy ammunition, (mil.) munición de fogueo.
dummy antenna, (rad.) antena fantasma.
dummy reversal, (bridge) inversión del muerto.
dump [dʌmp] *s.* (dial. G.B.) 1. trozo grueso, masa deforme. 2. ficha de plomo (usada en ciertos juegos infantiles). 3. (*gen. pl.*) tristeza, melancolía, desánimo, morriña, murria. 4. **in the dumps,** deprimido, alicaído.
dump [dʌmp] *v.t.* 1. vaciar, descargar de golpe, arrojar. 2. abandonar, deshacerse de; dejar a su suerte, plantar. 3. (jer.) derribar, tumbar. 4. (com.) inundar el mercado con, vender a bajo costo. *—v.i.* desplomarse, caer pesadamente. *—s.* 1. montón de basura; basurero, muladar. 2. (fam., fig.) pocilga; casucha; chabola. 3. (mil.) depósito provisional. 4. (impr.) galerón, galerón de pruebas, portagaleras.
dump body, carrocería de camión volquete, caja de volteo.
dumpiness ['dʌmpɪnəs] *s.* gordura (de persona pequeña).
dumping [-ɪŋ] *s.* 1. vaciadura, vaciada, descarga. 2. (com.) inundación del mercado (con productos a bajo precio).
dumping bank, (impr.) comodín, galerador.
dumping car, carro o vagón de volteo o de fondo caedizo, camión de volquete.
dumpish [-ɪʃ] *a.* triste, melancólico, desanimado.
dumpling ['dʌmplɪŋ] *s.* 1. bola de masa hervida (para sopa, etc.). 2. fruta envuelta en pasta y horneada, pastelito de fruta. 3. (fam.) persona o animal regordete.
dump trailer, remolque volcador.
dump truck, camión basculante o de volteo, volquete, camión de tumba.
dump valve, (mec.) válvula de descarga.
dumpy ['dʌmpɪ] *a.* 1. regordete, rechoncho. 2. hosco; descontento; triste.
dumpy level, (top.) nivel rígido o de anteojo corto.
dun [dʌn] *v.t.* (*pret., p.p.* DUNNED; *p.pr.* DUNNING) 1. demandar, urgir (a un deudor) para que pague. 2. acosar, importunar. *—s.* 1. acreedor importuno. 2. demanda urgente de pago. 3. (arqueol.) loma fortificada.
dun, *a.* pardo grisáceo, bruno. *—s.* 1. caballo pardo. 2. (ento.) mosca de mayo; cachipolla, efímera. 3. (pesca) señuelo artificial.
dunce [dʌns] *s.* zopenco, burro, estúpido.
dunce cap, coroza (para los escolares no estudiosos).
dunderhead ['dʌndər,hɛd B -də,-] *s.* bodoque, alcornoque, zopenco.
dunderheaded [-əd] *a.* estúpido, tonto.
dune [dun, B djun] *s.* duna, médano, marisma.
dung [dʌŋ] *s.* estiércol, excremento (de los animales). *—v.t.* abonar, fertilizar o cubrir con estiércol.
dungaree [,dʌŋgə'ri] *s.* 1. tela tosca de algodón para hacer tiendas, velas, etc. 2. (*pl.*) pantalones de tela tosca; mono, traje de faena, overol (Am.).
dung beetle, (ento.) escarabajo, bolero, escarabajo pelotero.
dungeon ['dʌndʒən] *s.* 1. mazmorra, calabozo. 2. (hist.) torre del homenaje. *—v.t.* (gen. con *up*) encalabozar, meter en un calabozo o mazmorra.
dunghill ['dʌŋ,hɪl] *s.* montón de estiércol, estercolar, estercolero, muladar.
dungon ['duŋ,ɔn, B 'dun,gɔn] *s.* (bot.) dongón.
dungy ['dʌŋɪ] *a.* lleno de estiércol; sucio, inmundo.
dunk [dʌŋk] *v.t.* sopetear, ensopar, remojar (pan, galleta en leche, *té,* café, etc.). *—v.i.* tirarse al agua, zambullirse.
dunnage ['dʌnɪdʒ] *s.* 1. (mar.) abarrotes, maderos de estibar, material para sujetar la carga. 2. equipaje; efectos personales.
dunning letter ['dʌnɪŋ-] carta de requerimiento, carta de cobranza.
dunnite ['dʌn,aɪt] *s.* dunita, explosivo Dunn (explosivo compuesto en gran parte de ácido pícrico).
duo ['duoʊ, B 'djuoʊ] *s.* (*pl.* DUOS) 1. (mús.) dúo, dueto. 2. pareja, dúo (de acróbatas, artistas, etc.).
duodecimal [,duə'dɛsəməl, B ,djuə-] *a.* duodecimal.
duodecimo [-,moʊ] *s.* (*pl.* DUODECIMOS) (tamaño de) libro en dozavo. *—a.* dozavo.
duodenal [-'dinəl] *a.* (anat.) duodenal; **d. ulcer,** úlcera en el duodeno.
duodenum [-'dinəm] *s.* (*pl.* DUODENA [-'dinə]) (anat.) duodeno.
duograph ['duə,græf, B 'djuə,grɑf] *s.* (litog.) bitono, dobletono.
duogravure [-grə'vjʊr, B -'vjʊə] *s.* fotograbado en un color con dos placas.
duologue [-,lɔg, -,lɑg, B -,lɔg] *s.* diálogo entre dos personas; drama con dos actores.
duopoly [du'ɑpəlɪ, B dju'ɔp-] *s.* (com.) duopolio.
duopsony [-sənɪ] *s.* (com.) duopsonio.
duotone ['duə,toʊn, B 'djuə-] **duotoned** [-,toʊnd] *a.* de dos tonos o colores.
duotype [-,taɪp] *s.* ilustración hecha con dos fotograbados a media tinta.
dupable ['dupəbəl, B 'djup-] *a.* crédulo, inocentón, que se puede engañar.
dupe [dup, B djup] *s.* incauto, primo, víctima de engaño o dolo, inocentón. *—v.t.* engañar, embaucar.
duper ['dupər, B 'djupə] *s.* embaucador.
dupery [-ərɪ] *s. superchería, añagaza, impostura.*
dupion ['dupɪ,oʊn, B 'dju-ən] *s.* capullo ocal.
duple ['dupəl, B 'dju-] *a.* doble, duplo.
duple time, (mús.) compás binario.
duplex ['du,plɛks, B 'dju-] *a.* 1. doble, duplo, dúplice, de dos partes; (tec.) dúplex. 2. (tec.) gemelo (compresor, torno, etc.). *—s.* (E.U.) casa para dos familias; departamento de dos pisos.
duplexer [-ər, B -ə] *s.* (rad.) comunicador dúplex.
duplex lathe, (mec.) torno doble.
duplex lock, cerradura de dos cilindros.
duplex process, (metal.) dúplex.
duplex pump, (mec.) bomba de doble efecto.
duplex telegraphy, telegrafía dúplex.
duplicate ['duplɪkət, B 'dju-] *a.* 1. duplicado; doble. 2. (bridge) por equipos. *—s.* duplicado (de un documento, etc.); **in d.,** por duplicado. — [-,keɪt] *v.t.* 1. duplicar. 2. copiar, reproducir.
duplicate part, pieza de recambio o de repuesto.
duplication [,duplɪ'keɪʃən, B ,dju-] *s.* 1. duplicación. 2. duplicado, copia.
duplicative ['duplɪ,keɪtɪv, B 'dju-] *a.* duplicativo.
duplicator [-ər, B -ə] *s.* (máquina) duplicadora, copiadora.
duplicity [du'plɪsətɪ, B dju-] *s.* duplicidad, doblez, engaño, segunda intención.
durability [,dʊrə'bɪlətɪ, B ,djʊər-] *s.* durabilidad; estabilidad, permanencia.
durable ['dʊrəbəl, B 'djʊər-] *a.* durable, duradero.
durable goods, (*pl.*) artículos o mercancías duraderos; (com.) géneros pesados.
durableness [-nəs] *s.* durabilidad; estabilidad, permanencia.
durably [-blɪ] *adv.* duraderamente.
dural ['dʊrəl, B 'djʊər-] *a.* (anat.) dural.
duralumin, duraluminium [dʊ'ræljəmən, B djʊə-] *s.* (metal.) duraluminio (nombre de fábrica), cuproaluminio, aleación de aluminio y cobre.
dura mater ['dʊrə,meɪtər, B 'djʊərə'-meɪtə] (anat.) duramáter, duramadre.
duramen [dʊ'reɪmən, B djʊə-] *s.* (bot.) duramen.
duramold ['dʊrə,moʊld, B 'dʊər-] *s.* (metal.) duramolde, molde de duraluminio.
durance ['dʊrəns, B 'djʊər-] *s.* 1. prisión, cautividad, cautiverio. 2. (tej.) sempiterna, tela fuerte de lana.
duration [dʊ'reɪʃən, B djʊə-] *s.* duración, ej., *for the d. of the war,* hasta el término de la guerra, por la duración del conflicto.
durbar ['dɜr,bɑr, B 'dɜ,bɑ] *s.* sala de recepción; corte de un príncipe; recepción formal de príncipes (en la India).
duress [dʊ'rɛs, B djʊə-] *s.* 1. prisión, encierro, cautividad. 2. coacción, compulsión; (der.) coacción. 3. **under d.,** bajo coacción.
during ['dʊrɪŋ, B 'djʊər-] *prep.* durante, mientras.
durmast ['dɜr,mæst, B 'dɜ,mɑst] *s.* roble negro, roble villano, melojo.
duro ['dʊroʊ, B 'dʊər-] *s.* (*pl.* DUROS) duro (moneda española de cinco pesetas).
durometer [dʊ'rɑmətər, B djʊə'rɔmɪtə] *s.* durómetro.
durra ['dʊrə] *s.* (bot.) durra, zahína, maíz de Guinea.
durst [dɜrst, B dɜst] (ant.) *pret. de* **dare.**
durum ['dʊrəm, B 'djʊər-] *s.* (bot.) trigo fanfarrón, trigo duro con el que se elabora la semolina.

dusk [dʌsk] *a.* (poét.) obscuro, fusco; moreno. —*v.i.* obscurecerse. —*v.t.* 1. obscurecer. 2. (fig.) ensombrecer. —*s.* 1. crepúsculo. 2. sombra, obscuridad, tinieblas. 3. **d.-to-dawn,** de(l) anochecer a (la) madrugada; **at d.,** al anochecer.

duskily [ˈdʌskəlɪ] *adv.* obscuramente.

duskiness [-kɪnəs] *s.* 1. obscuridad. 2. (poét.) color moreno (de la piel).

dusky [ˈdʌskɪ] *a.* (DUSKIER; DUSKIEST) 1. obscuro, en sombras. 2. negruzco; moreno. 3. (fig.) melancólico, apesadumbrado.

dust [dʌst] *s.* 1. polvo. 2. polvareda. 3. (fig.) cenizas, restos (mortales). 4. confusión, barullo, alboroto. 5. (cocina) pizca (de polvo). 6. (G.B.) basura, tamo, barredura. 7. (jer.) droga en polvo. 8. **in the d.,** muerto, sepultado; **to bite the d.,** (fig.) morder el polvo; **to kick up (a) d.,** armar un alboroto; **to lay (someone) in the d.,** hacer(le) morder el polvo (a alguien); **to lick the dust,** postrarse, humillarse; **to make** (o **to raise**) **a d.,** levantar una polvareda; **to settle the d.,** arreglar un asunto; **to throw d. in one's eyes,** echarle a uno polvo en los ojos; embaucar. —*v.t.* 1. empolvar, polvorear, espolvorizar. 2. desempolvar, quitar el polvo a. 3. **to d. off,** reacondicionar, volver a poner en uso; **d. one's jacket for him,** (fam.) sacudirle el polvo a alguien, dar una paliza a alguien. —*v.i.* bañarse en arena o tierra (las aves).

dustbin [ˈdʌstˌbɪn] *s.* (G.B.) cubo para basura; latón de la basura.

dust boot, (mec.) funda guardapolvo.

dust bowl, región de sequía (en que se producen a veces grandes ventarrones de polvo).

dust cartridge, filtro de polvo.

dustcloth [-ˌklɔθ] *s.* 1. trapo para limpiar. 2. guardapolvo.

dust cloud, polvareda.

dustcoat [-ˌkoʊt] *s.* (pr. G.B.) guardapolvo (para proteger el traje).

dust cover, 1. guardapolvo (para proteger muebles u otros objetos). 2. sobrecubierta (de libros).

dust devil, remolino de arena o de polvo.

duster [ˈdʌstər, B -ə] *s.* 1. plumero; (G.B.) trapo para limpiar. 2. guardapolvo (para proteger el traje). 3. pulverizador, rociador (para insecticidas).

duster plane, (avia., agr.) avión fumigador.

dustiness [-ɪnəs] *s.* calidad de polvoriento (lo viejo o seco).

dusting [-ɪŋ] *s.* 1. desempolvoradura. 2. capa (fina) de polvo. 3. (fam., G.B.) tunda, zurra. 4. **to give (someone) a d.,** (fam., G.B.) darle una tunda a (alguien); **to give (something) a d.,** desempolvar, quitar el polvo a (algo).

dust jacket, sobrecubierta (de un libro).

dustman [-mən] *s.* (G.B.) basurero, barrendero.

dustpan [-ˌpæn] *s.* pala para recoger la basura.

dust storm, tolvanera, tempestad de polvo.

dust-up [ˈdʌstˌʌp] *s.* pelea, riña, pleito.

dust wrap, guardapolvo (para proteger muebles u otros objetos).

dusty [ˈdʌstɪ] *a.* (DUSTIER; DUSTIEST) 1. polvoriento, polvoroso (camino, etc.); cubierto de polvo, empolvado (cara, ropa, etc.); lleno de polvo (cuarto, etc.). 2. en polvo. 3. (G.B.) vago, indeterminado (respuesta, etc.).

dusty miller, 1. mosca artificial (para pescar salmón). 2. (bot.) aurícula, oreja de oso.

Dutch [dʌtʃ] *a.* 1. holandés. 2. (jer., ant.) alemán. —*s.* holandés (idioma); **in D.,** (jer., E.U.) en desgracia; **the D.,** los holandeses; **to go D.,** ir a medias, pagar a la inglesa; **to beat the D.,** ser cosa sorprendente o inaudita.

Dutch brass, metal dorado, tombac (aleación de zinc y cobre).

Dutch clover, (bot.) trébol blanco, trébol rastrero.

Dutch courage, (fam.) valentía que resulta de haber bebido.

Dutch door, puerta dividida horizontalmente, puerta de dos paneles que se pueden abrir por separado.

Dutch foil, D. leaf, D. gold, hoja de latón (que se usa para decorar juguetes o papeles).

Dutch hoe, azadón de pala.

Dutch liquid, (quím.) dicloroetano.

Dutchman [ˈdʌtʃmən] *s.* 1. holandés. 2. (jer.) alemán. 3. (mar.) nave holandesa. 4. **or I'm a D., I'm a D. if,** sin lugar a equivocarme.

Dutchman's-breeches [-mənzˈbrɪtʃəz] *s. pl.* (*sing. o pl. en const.*) (bot.) (variedad de) dicentra.

Dutchman's-pipe [-ˈpaɪp] *s.* (bot.) (variedad de) aristoloquía.

Dutch metal, latón (esp. en hojas.).

Dutch oven, (E.U.) caldera de hierro para asar; parrilla para asar.

Dutch roll, (acrob.) barril holandés.

Dutch treat, (fam.) convite a escote, convite a la inglesa.

Dutch uncle, (fam.) mentor o crítico severo; **to talk to one like a D. u.,** reprender a alguien severamente, poner a uno las orejas coloradas.

duteous [ˈdutɪəs, B ˈdjut-] *a.* obediente, respetuoso, sumiso, obsequioso.

duteously [-lɪ] *adv.* debidamente, obedientemente.

duteousness [-nəs] *s.* cumplimiento del deber, obediencia.

dutiable [ˈdutɪəbəl, B ˈdjut-] *a.* (der.) sujeto al pago de impuestos, que paga derechos de aduana.

dutiful [ˈdutɪfəl, B ˈdjut-] *a.* 1. cumplidor, concienzudo. 2. obediente, respetuoso.

dutifully [-ɪ] *adv.* debidamente, cumplidamente; obedientemente.

dutifulness [-nəs] *s.* afán de cumplir con los deberes; obediencia, sumisión, respeto.

duty [ˈdutɪ, B ˈdjutɪ] *s.* 1. deber, obligación; tarea, cargo. 2. respeto, acatamiento, obediencia. 3. impuesto, derecho; arancel, derecho de aduana. 4. (relig.) oficios. 5. (mil.) servicio, facción. 6. (agr.) dotación, alema, coeficiente de riego. 7. (mec.) servicio, trabajo; rendimiento (de una máquina). 8. **in d. bound,** moralmente obligado; **in line of d.,** en cumplimiento de (mis, sus, etc.) deberes; **off d.,** franco, libre de servicio; **on d.,** de servicio; (mil.) de facción, de guardia; **to do d. for,** servir de, pasar por; **to do one's d.,** cumplir con su deber; **to take up one's duties,** entrar en funciones.

duty-free [-ˈfri] *a.* libre o franco de derechos.

duty roster, (mil.) lista de facción.

duumvirate [duˈʌmvərət, B dju-] *s.* (hist. romana) duunvirato, autoridad compartida por dos personas.

duvetyn, duvetine, duvetyne [ˈduvəˌtin] *s.* (tej.) tela suave aterciopelada (hecha de lana mezclada con seda, algodón, o ambos).

DVM *abrev. de* **Doctor of Veterinary Medicine,** Doctor en Medicina Veterinaria.

dwarf [dwɔrf, B dwɔf] *s.* (*pl.* DWARFS o DWARVES [dwɔrvz, B dwɔvz]) 1. enano, pigmeo. 2. (t. **d. star**) (astr.) estrella enana. —*v.t.* impedir el crecimiento o desarrollo de; empequeñecer, achicar. —*v.i.* empequeñecerse, achicarse. —*a.* diminuto, enano, pigmeo.

dwarf alder, (bot.) (variedad de) espino enano.

dwarf elder, (bot.) 1. actea, yezgo; mundillo, sauquillo. 2. aralia.

dwarfish [ˈdwɔrfɪʃ, B ˈdwɔf-] *a.* diminuto, pigmeo, enano, pequeño.

dwarfishness [-nəs] *s.* pequeñez.

dwarfism [-ˌɪzəm] *s.* (med.) enanismo.

dwarfness [-nəs] *s.* 1. pequeñez. 2. (med.) enanismo.

dwarf oak, (bot.) chaparro, mata parda.

dwell [dwɛl] *v.i.* (*pret., p.p.* DWELT [dwɛlt] o DWELLED [dwɛld]; *pr.p.* DWELLING) 1. habitar, morar, residir, vivir. 2. **d. on** (o **upon**), dilatarse, extenderse en (materia o asunto).

dweller [ˈdwɛlər, B -ə] *s.* morador, habitante.

dwelling [-ɪŋ] *s.* morada, residencia, domicilio, casa, vivienda.

dwelling place, morada, residencia.

dwindle [ˈdwɪndəl] *v.i.* menguar, disminuirse, consumirse. —*v.t.* amenguar, disminuir, mermar.

Dy *símb. de* **dysprosium,** disprosio (Dy).

dyad [ˈdaɪˌæd, -əd] *s.* 1. grupo de dos, par, pareja. 2. (biol.) díade. 3. (quím.) díada.

Dyak [-ˌæk] *s. var. de* **dayak.**

dyarchy [ˈdaɪˌɑrkɪ, B -ˌɑkɪ] *s.* diarquía, gobierno de dos.

dye [daɪ] *s.* tinte, tintura; **of the deepest** (o **blackest**) **d.,** (el) más infame, de la clase más vil (crimen, criminal). —*v.t.* (*pret., p.p.* DYED; *p.pr.* DYEING) teñir, tintar, tinturar, colorar; **d. in the grain** (o **in the wool**), teñir en rama (lana). —*v.i.* teñirse, tintarse, colorarse.

dyed-in-the-wool[ˈdaɪdənðəˈwʊl] *a.* 1. teñida en bruto o en rama (lana). 2. (fig.) completamente compenetrado (con una idea). 3. acérrimo o intransigente.

dyeing [ˈdaɪɪŋ] *p.pr. de* **dye.** —*s.* tinte, tintura, teñido.

dyer [ˈdaɪər, B -ə] *s.* tintorero.

dyer's alkanet, (bot.) onoquiles, orcaneta, palomilla.

dyer's-broom [ˈdaɪərzˈbrum, B ˈdaɪəz-] *s.* (bot.) retama de tintes o de tintoreros.

dyer's rocket, (bot.) gualda.

dyer's-weed [-ˌwid] *s.* (bot.) retama de tintes, hierba pastel.

dyestuff [ˈdaɪˌstʌf] *s.* materia colorante, pigmento.

dyewood [-ˈwʊd] *s.* (bot.) palo de Campeche, fustete, (cualquier) madera de tinte.

dying [ˈdaɪɪŋ] *p. pr. de* **die.** —*a.* moribundo, agonizante, mortal; mortecino; hecho o dicho en los últimos momentos de vida.

dyke, *var. de* **dike.**

dynameter [daɪˈnæmətər, B -tə] *s.* (ópt.) dinámetro.

dynamic [-ˈnæmɪk] *a.* dinámico, enérgico, vigoroso.

dynamically [-ɪkəlɪ] *adv.* con dinamismo, enérgicamente.

dynamic clamper, (mec.) amortiguador dinámico o de vibraciones.

dynamic head, (hidr.) carga dinámica, carga de velocidad.

dynamic range, gama dinámica (del sonido).

dynamics [daɪˈnæmɪks] *s. pl.* (*sing. en const.*) dinámica.

dynamic speaker, (rad.) altavoz electrodinámico.

dynamic thrust, (ing.) tracción dinámica.

dynamism [ˈdaɪnəˌmɪzəm] *s.* 1. (filos.) dinamismo. 2. dinamismo, energía activa.

dynamist [-məst] *s.* (filos.) dinamista.

dynamistic [ˌdaɪnəˈmɪstɪk] *a.* (filos.) dinamista.

dynamite [ˈdaɪnəˌmaɪt] *s.* dinamita. —*v.t.* dinamitar.

dynamiter [-ər, B -ə] *s.* dinamitero.

dynamo [ˈdaɪnəˌmoʊ] *s.* (*pl.* DYNAMOS) 1. (elec.) dinamo, dínamo (Am.). 2. (fig., jer.) dínamo, persona eficiente y enérgica.

dynamoelectric [ˌdaɪnəmoʊəˈlɛktrɪk] *a.* dinamoeléctrico.
dynamogenesis [-ˈdʒɛnəsəs] *s.* (psic.) dinamogénesis. actividad muscular debida a estimulación de los sentidos.
dynamometer [-ˈmɑmətər, B -ˈmɔmɪtə] *s.* (mec., fís.) dinamómetro.
dynamometric [ˌdaɪnəmoʊˈmɛtrɪk] *a.* (mec., fís.) dinamométrico.
dynamometry [-ˈmɑmətrɪ, B -ˈmɔm-] *s.* (mec., fís.) dinamometría.
dynamotor [ˈdaɪnəˌmoʊtər, B -ə] *s.* (elec.) dinamotor.
dynast [ˈdaɪˌnæst, -nəst, B ˈdɪnəst] *s.* dinasta, señor, gobernante, esp. en un cargo hereditario.
dynastic [daɪˈnæstɪk, B dɪ-] *a.* dinástico.
dynasty [ˈdaɪnəstɪ, B ˈdɪn-] *s.* dinastía.
dynatron [ˈdaɪnəˌtrɑn, B -ˌtrɔn] *s.* (elec.) dinatrón.
dyne [daɪn] *s.* (fís.) dina.
dynode [ˈdaɪˌnoʊd] *s.* (rad.) dinodo.
dysacousia [ˌdɪsəˈkuʒə, B -zɪə] **dysacousis** [-ˈkusəs] *s.* (med.) disecea.
dysarthria [dɪsˈɑrθrɪə, B -ˈɑθrɪə] *s.* (med.) disartria.
dyschromatopsia [dɪsˌkroʊməˈtɑpsɪə, B -ˈtɔp-] *s.* (med.) discromatopsia.
dyscrasia [dɪsˈkreɪʒə, B -zjə] *s.* (med.) discrasia.
dysenteric [ˌdɪsənˈtɛrɪk] *a.* (med.) disentérico.
dysentery [ˈdɪsənˌtɛrɪ, B -trɪ] *s.* (med.) disentería.
dysergia [dɪsˈɜrdʒɪə, B -ˈɜdʒ-] *s.* (med.) disergia.
dysesthesia [ˌdɪsɛsˈθiʒə, B -zjə] *s.* (med.) disestesia.
dysfunction [dɪsˈfʌŋkʃən] *s.* (med.) disfunción, disergia.
dysgenesis [-ˈdʒɛnəsəs] *s.* (biol.) disgénesis, disgenesia.
dysgenic [-ɪk] *a.* (biol.) disgenético.
dysgenics [-ɪks] *s. pl.* (*sing. en const.*) (biol.) disgenesia, disgenia.
dyslalia [dɪsˈleɪlɪə] *s.* (med.) dislalia.
dyslexia [-ˈlɛksɪə] *s.* (med.) dislexia (impedimento para la lectura por defecto congénito o por lesión cerebral).
dyslogistic [ˌdɪsləˈdʒɪstɪk] *a.* despreciativo, despectivo.
dyslogistically [-tɪkəlɪ] *adv.* despreciativamente, despectivamente.
dysmenorrhea [dɪsˌmɛnəˈriə] *s.* (med.) dismenorrea.
dysmetria [-ˈmɛtrɪə] *s.* (med.) dismetría.
dysmnesia [-ˈniʒə, B -zjə] *s.* (med.) dismnesia.
dysorexy [ˌdɪsəˈrɛksɪ] *s.* (med.) disorexia.
dyspepsia [dɪsˈpɛpʃə, B -sɪə] *s.* (med.) dispepsia.
dyspepsy [-ˈpɛpsɪ] *s.* dispepsia.
dyspeptic [-ˈpɛptɪk] *a., s.* (med.) dispéptico.
dyspeptically [-tɪkəlɪ] *adv.* (fig.) malhumoradamente, coléricamente.
dysphagia [dɪsˈfeɪdʒɪə] *s.* (med.) disfagia.
dysphagic [-ˈfædʒɪk] *a.* (med.) disfágico.
dysphasia [-ˈfeɪʒə, B -ˈfeɪzjə] *s.* (med.) disfasia.
dysphonia [-ˈfoʊnɪə] *s.* (med.) disfonía.
dysphoria [-ˈfɔrɪə] *s.* (psic.) disforia.
dysplasia [-ˈpleɪʒə, B -zɪə] *s.* (med.) displasia.
dyspnea [ˈdɪspnɪə, B dɪspˈniə] *s.* (med.) disnea.
dyspneic [dɪspˈniɪk] *a.* (med.) disneico.
dysprosium [-ˈproʊzɪəm] *s.* (quím.) disprosio.
dystocia [-ˈtoʊʃɪə] *s.* (med.) distocia.
dystocial [-ʃəl] *a.* (med.) distócico.
dystrophia [-ˈtroʊfɪə] *var. de* **distrophy**.
dystrophic [-ˈtrɑfɪk, -ˈtroʊ-, B -ˈtrɔ-] *a.* (med.) distrófico.
dystrophy [ˈdɪstrəfɪ] *s.* (med., biol.) distrofia.
dysuria [dɪsˈjʊrɪə] *s.* (med.) disuria.
dysuric [-ɪk] *a.* (med.) disúrico.
dz. *abrev. de* **dozen**, docena (doc).

E

E [i] *s.* 1. e, quinta letra del alfabeto inglés. 2. (mús.) mi.

E *abrev. de* 1. **East,** este. 2. **Earth,** la tierra. 3. **Engineer, Engineering,** ingeniero, ingeniería. 4. **English,** (idioma) inglés. 5. **Excellent,** (nota escolar) excelente.

E *símb. de* **einsteinium,** einstenio (Es).

ea. *abrev. de* **each,** cada uno (c/u).

each [itʃ] *a.* cada, ej., *e. child received a toy,* cada niño recibió un juguete. *—pron.* 1. cada uno, cada cual, ej., *e. of the children received a toy,* cada uno de los niños recibió un juguete. 2. **e. for himself,** cada cual por su cuenta; **e. other,** el uno al otro, mutuamente, entre sí (*a veces se traduce sólo por* se) ej., *they love e. other,* se aman, *they look at e. other,* se miran (el uno al otro), *they said good-by to e. other,* se dijeron adiós; **to e. his own,** a cada cual lo suyo. *—adv.* por persona, por cabeza, por pieza, cada uno, ej., *they cost ten cents e.,* cuesta diez centavos cada uno.

eager ['igər, B 'igə] *a.* ansioso, deseoso, anhelante; afanoso, impaciente, codicioso.

eager beaver, (jer.) persona que trata de impresionar con su exagerada dedicacíon, iniciativa o entusiasmo.

eagerly [-lɪ] *adv.* ansiosamente, vehementemente, afanosamente.

eagerness [-nəs] *s.* ansia, anhelo; afán, avidez, vehemencia.

eagle ['igəl] *s.* 1. águila. 2. (E.U.) moneda de oro de 10 dólares. 3. (golf) hoyo jugado en dos golpes menos que el "par".

eagle boat, especie de cazasubmarinos.

eagle-eyed [-ˌaɪd] *a.* con ojo de lince, ojo avizor; **to be e.-e.,** tener vista de águila.

eagle owl, (orn.) tinge, buharro, curuca.

eagle ray, (ict.) águila.

Eagle Scout, el rango más alto en la organizacion de Niños Exploradores.

eaglestone [-ˌstoʊn] *s.* (min.) etites, etita.

eaglet ['iglət] *s.* 1. aguilucho. 2. (hist.) L'Aiglon, el Aguilucho (hijo de Napoleón).

eaglewood ['igəlˌwʊd] *s.* (bot.) palo de áloe, palo de águila.

eagre ['igər, B 'eɪgə] *s.* creciente de la marea, ola que forma la subida de la marea.

ear [ɪr, B ɪə] *s.* 1. oído. 2. oreja. 3. oído, sentido musical. 4. asa (de una jarra, etc.). 5. atención, reparo. 6. (periodismo) oreja (atención e intuicíon). 7. **by e.,** de oído; **in** (o **into**) **one's e.,** (fig.) al oído; **over head and ears (in),** (fig.) hundido (en), abrumado (por); **to be all ears,** ser todo oídos; **to fall on deaf ears,** caer en oídos sordos; **to give e. (to),** hacer caso (a); **to go in one e. and out the other,** entrar por un oído y salir por el otro; **to have a good e.,** tener buen oído; **to have an e. for music;** tener oído (para la música); **to have a person's e.,** tener la atención o confianza de una persona; **to keep an e. to the ground,** estar alerta; **to lend an e. (to),** prestar oídos (a), escuchar (a); **to open one's ears,** abrir los oídos; **to play (it) by e.,** improvisar, tocar de oído; **to prick up one's ears,** abrir o aguzar los oídos, parar la oreja (Amer.); **to set (persons) by the ears,** enemistar; **to turn a deaf e. (to),** hacer oídos de mercader (a), cerrar los oídos (a), hacerse el sordo (ante); **up to the ears (in),** (fig.) hundido (en), abrumado (por).

ear, *s.* mazorca (del maíz), espiga (de cereales). *—v.i.* espigar.

earache ['ɪrˌeɪk, B 'ɪər-] *s.* dolor de oído.

ear canal, conducto auditivo.

ear cup, (rad.) audífono.

eardrop ['ɪrˌdrɑp, B 'ɪəˌdrɔp] *s.* pendiente, arete, zarcillo, dormilona.

eardrum [-ˌdrʌm] *s.* (anat.) tímpano, membrana del oído.

eared [ɪrd, B ɪəd] *a.* 1. en mazorca, en espiga. 2. **long-eared,** de orejas largas.

earflap ['ɪrˌflæp, B 'ɪəˌ-] *s.* 1. (anat.) pabellón de la oreja. 2. orejera (protector contra el frío, etc.).

earful [-ˌfʊl] *s.* (jer.) 1. noticias, rumores. 2. arenga, admonición.

earing ['ɪrɪŋ, B 'ɪər-] *s.* (mar.) empuñidura.

earl [ɜrl, B ɜl] *s.* (G.B.) conde.

earlap ['ɪrˌlæp, B 'ɪəˌ-] *s.* (anat.) pabellón de la oreja.

earldom ['ɜrldəm, B 'ɜl-] *s.* título, condición y propiedad de conde en G. B.

earlier ['ɜrlɪər, B 'əlɪə] *a., adv. comp. de* **early,** más temprano, antes; anterior, antiguo.

earliest, *a., adv. super. de* **early,** más temprano; más antiguo, más remoto; antiguo, primitivo.

earliness [-nəs] *s.* precocidad, anticipación; presteza, prontitud; calidad de temprano.

earlobe ['ɪrˌloʊb, B 'ɪəˌ-] *s.* (anat.) pulpejo, lóbulo (de la oreja), pallar de la oreja (Am.).

early ['ɜrlɪ, B 'ɜlɪ] *a.* 1. temprano (visita, hora, fruta, etc.); prematuro (muerte). 2. primitivo, antiguo (colonos, habitantes, arte, herramienta, etc.). 3. primero (noticias, días, etc.). 4. cercano, próximo, ej., *at an e. date,* en una fecha próxima o cercana. 5. pronto, rápido (respuesta, mejora, etc.). 6. **at your earliest convenience,** a la mayor brevedad, tan pronto como le sea posible; **e. bird,** (fig.) madrugador; uno que llega antes de la hora señalada; **e. life,** juventud, primeros años (de la vida); **e. part,** principio, comienzos, inicios; **e. riser,** madrugador; **e. show,** (cinem.) primera función; **since e. childhood,** desde la infancia; **the e. bird gets the worm,** al que madruga, Dios le ayuda; **the e. hours of the morning,** las primeras horas de la madrugada; **the e. morning,** las primeras horas de la mañana. *adv.* temprano, tempranamente, pronto; prematuramente; **as e. as possible,** lo más pronto posible, cuanto antes; **earlier on,** antes, previamente, anteriormente; **e. in the morning,** a primeras horas de la mañana; **much earlier,** mucho antes; **one hour (day,** etc.) **e.,** con una hora (día, etc.) de anticipación; **to be e.,** llegar temprano, llegar antes de la hora; **to die e.,** morir prematuramente; **to rise e.,** madrugar, levantarse temprano; **too e.,** demasiado temprano; prematuramente.

Early English style, (arq.) inglés primitivo.

early Middle Ages, Alta Edad Media.

early retirement, jubilación anticipada.

early stages, (ento.) estados inmaduros.

early warning system, sistema de alarma anticipada, sistema de alerta previa, sistema de alerta avanzada.

earmark ['ɪrˌmɑrk B 'ɪəˌmɑk] *s.* 1. marca en la oreja. 2. señal, indicio; característica, distintivo. *—v.t.* 1. marcar en la oreja. 2. dejar su marca en. 3. (con *for*) destinar (a), designar (a), señalar (para); asignar (ej., fondos) (a), ej., *this sum is earmarked for you,* esta suma está destinada para ti.

earmuff [-ˌmʌf] *s.* orejera (protección contra el frío).

earn [ɜrn, B ɜn] *v.t.* 1. ganar (dinero, etc.); devengar (intereses). 2. merecer, ganar, ganarse (estima, honra, etc.). 3. **e. one's living,** ganarse el pan, ganarse la vida.

earnest ['ɜrnəst, B 'ɜnɪst] *s.* seriedad, ahínco, empeño, intensidad; **in e.,** en serio, con seriedad; de veras. *—a.* 1. serio, formal (persona). 2. serio, grave (situación, asunto). 3. intenso, vivo (atención, deseo, etc.).

earnest, *s.* 1. arras; pago a cuenta. 2. (fig.) prenda, fianza.

earnestly [-lɪ] *adv.* 1. seriamente. 2. intensamente, de veras.

earnest money, caparra; adelanto.

earnestness [-nəs] *s.* 1. seriedad, formalidad (de una persona). 2. seriedad, gravedad (de una situación, un asunto).

earnings ['ɜrnɪŋz, B 'ɜnɪŋz] *s.* 1. ingresos, salario, paga, estipendio, jornal. 2. (com.) ganancia(s), utilidad(es).

earphone ['ɪrˌfoʊn, B 'ɪəˌ-] *s.* auricular; audífono.

earpick [-ˌpɪk] *s.* limpiaoídos, escarba-oreja.

earring [-ˌrɪŋ] *s.* pendiente, arete, zarcillo.

earshell [-ˌʃɛl] *s.* (zool.) abalone, oreja de mar, oreja de San Pedro.

earshot [-'ʃɑt, B -'ʃɔt] *s.* alcance del oído; **out of e.,** fuera del alcance del oído; **within e.,** al alcance del oído.

earsplitting [-ˌsplɪtɪŋ] *a.* ensordecedor, atronador, estridente.

ear stone, (med.) otolito.

earth [ɜrθ, B ɜθ] *s.* 1. tierra. 2. mundo. 3. tierra, suelo. 4. tierra firme. 5. madriguera. 6. (quím.) tierra rara. 7. (elec., rad.) (pr. G.B.) tierra. 8. (poét.) país, región. 9. **down to e.,** práctico; prosaico; **to come back to e.,** (fig.) bajarse de las nubes; **to move heaven and e.,** (fig.) mover cielo y tierra; **why on e.?** ¿por qué diantres? *—v.t.* 1. enterrar, cubrir con tierra (raíz de plantas). 2. acosar (a una zorra, etc.) en su madriguera. 3. (elec., rad.) (pr. G.B.) conectar a tierra. *—v.i.* esconderse en su madriguera (animal).

earthboard ['ɜrθˌbɔrd, B 'ɜθˌbɔd] *s.* orejera del arado.

earthborn [-ˌbɔrn, B -ˌbɔn] *a.* 1. terrígeno, mortal. 2. terrestre, humano. 3. de humilde cuna.

earthbound [-ˌbaʊnd] *a.* 1. apegado a la tierra. 2. prosaico, pedestre. 3. con rumbo a la tierra.

earthen ['ɜrθən, B 'ɜθən] *a.* 1. terrenal, terreno. 2. térreo, terrizo, de barro.
earthenware [-ˌwɛr, B -ˌwɛə] *s.* loza de barro; objetos o cacharros de alfarería.
earth flax, (min.) asbestos.
earthiness [-θɪnəs] *s.* 1. robustez; desenvoltura, desenfado. 2. calidad de lo práctico, verdadero o físico.
earthlight ['ɜrθˌlaɪt, B 'ɜθ-] *s.* (astr.) luz cenicienta, luz cinérea.
earthliness [-lɪnəs] *s.* terrenidad, mundanalidad; condición de laico, de lo secular.
earthling [-lɪŋ] *s.* 1. habitante de la tierra; ser humano. 2. persona mundana.
earthly ['ɜrθlɪ, B 'ɜθ-] *a.* 1. terrenal, terreno, terrestre; mundano, temporal. 2. concebible. 3. **it's of no e. use,** (fam.) no sirve para nada; **there's no e. reason,** no hay razón concebible.
earthmover [-ˌmuvər, B -ə] *s.* máquina excavadora.
earthnut [-ˌnʌt] *s.* (bot.) cacahuete, cacahuate, cacahué, maní.
earth oil, (min.) petróleo.
earthquake [-ˌkweɪk] *s.* terremoto, temblor de tierra, sismo.
earthshaking [-ˌʃeɪkɪŋ] *a.* estremecedor (anuncio, noticia, etc.); importantísimo (descubrimiento, suceso, etc.).
earthshine [-ˌʃaɪn] *s.* (astr.) luz cenicienta, luz cinérea.
earthward ['ɜrθwərd, B 'ɜθwəd] **earthwards** [-wərdz, B -wədz] *adv.* hacia la tierra.
earthwork [-ˌwɜrk, B -ˌwɜk] *s.* 1. obra (s) de tierra. 2. (fort.) terraplén, obra accesoria, obra accidental.
earthworm [-ˌwɜrm, B -ˌwɜm] *s.* 1. lombriz o gusano de tierra. 2. (ant.) persona vil, canalla.
earthy ['ɜrθɪ, B 'ɜθɪ] *a.* 1. terroso, térreo, terrizo. 2. robusto. 3. vulgar, grosero. 4. sin inhibiciones, sensual, atrevida (mujer). 5. terrestre, terrenal, mundano.
ear trumpet, trompetilla (acústica).
earwax ['ɪrˌwæks B 'ɪəˌ-] *s.* (fisiol.) cerilla o cera de los oídos, cerumen.
earwig [-ˌwɪg] *s.* (ento.) tijereta, cortapicos, forfícola, gusano del oído. *—v.t.* molestar o tratar de influenciar (a una persona) con cuchicheos.
ease [iz] *s.* 1. tranquilidad, serenidad, reposo. 2. comodidad. 3. alivio, desahogo, sosiego. 4. desembarazo, desenvoltura, naturalidad. 5. facilidad, holgura. 6. **a life of e.,** una vida desahogada; **at e.,** tranquilo, cómodo; con desahogo; (mil.) ¡descansen!; en posición de descanso; **to do (something) at one's e.,** hacer (algo) sin apremio; **to feel at one's e.,** sentirse cómodo; **to put (someone) at e.,** tranquilizar; hacer que (alguien) se sienta cómodo; **to stand at e.,** (mil.) descansar, estar en posición de descanso; **to take one's e.,** descansar, holgar; **with e.,** fácilmente, con facilidad. *—v.t.* 1. aliviar, mitigar, templar, moderar. 2. aligerar, descargar, desembarazar. 3. aflojar, soltar. 4. facilitar. 5. (mar.) (gen. con *off, away, down*) lascar, arriar (cable, cadena, etc.). 6. **e. her,** (mar.) reducir la velocidad (del barco); **e. one's mind,** tranquilizarse, dejar de preocuparse; **e. the helm, e. the rudder,** (mar.) retomar un poco el rumbo anterior. *—v.i.* 1. dar alivio. 2. (gen. con *off* o *up*) aliviarse, disminuir, aflojar; apaciguarse. 3. (gen. con *along, over,* etc.) moverse o pasar lentamente.
easel ['izəl] *s.* 1. caballete de pintor; atril. 2. (foto.) marco para ampliación.
easement ['izmənt] *s.* 1. alivio; apoyo; descarga. 2. (der.) servidumbre, derecho de vía o de paso.
easily ['izəlɪ] *adv.* 1. fácilmente, aína, sin dificultad. 2. sobradamente, con mucho. 3. probablemente, con alguna seguridad.
easiness ['izɪnəs] *s.* 1. facilidad. 2. suavidad; soltura, gracia; holgura. 3. tranquilidad, quietud.
east [ist] *s.* 1. este, oriente, levante. 2. **the E.,** el Oriente; el Este (países del bloque soviético); (E.U.) el Este, la región al este del Misisipí. *—a.* oriental, de oriente, del este. *—adv.* hacia el este, al este.
eastbound ['istˌbaʊnd] *a.* con rumbo al este.
east by north, este cuarta al nordeste.
east by south, este cuarta al sudeste.
Easter ['istər, B -tə] *s.* (relig.) Pascua de Resurrección, Pascua Florida.
Easter egg, huevo de Pascua (chocolate o dulce en forma de huevo).
Easter eve, noche de Sábado Santo o de Gloria; víspera de Pascua Florida.
easterly ['istərlɪ, B -təlɪ] *a.* oriental, que viene desde el este; que va hacia el este. *—adv.* desde el este; hacia el este.
easterly wind, viento de levante, solano.
eastern [-tərn, B -tən] *a.* oriental, de oriente. *—s.* 1. oriental, natural del Oriente. 2. miembro de la Iglesia Oriental. 3. (astr.) ortivo.
Easterner [-ər, B -ə] *s.* 1. oriental, natural del este. 2. (E.U.) habitante de la región este del país.
Eastern Hemisphere, Hemisferio Oriental.
easternmost [-ˌmoʊst] *a.* (el) más oriental, más al este.
Eastern Seabord, (E.U.) los estados de la costa del Atlántico.
Eastern standard time, Eastern time, (E.U.) hora oficial del Este (cinco horas anterior a la de Greenwich).
Easter Saturday, Sábado Santo o de Gloria.
Easter Sunday, Domingo de Resurrección.
Eastertide ['istərˌtaɪd, B -təˌ-] *s.* aleluya, tiempo de Pascua, tiempo pascual.
East Germany, (hist.) Alemania Oriental.
East Indian, *a., s.* natural del archipiélago y península de Malaya; (G.B.) de la India.
easting ['istɪŋ] *s.* 1. (mar.) avance en dirección al este. 2. distancia longitudinal desde un meridiano hacia un punto al este. 3. dirección este.
east-northeast ['istˌnɔrθ'ist, -ˌnɔr'ist, B -ˌnɔθ-] *s.* estenordeste.
East Pakistan, Paquistán Oriental (hoy Bangladesh).
east-southeast [-ˌsaʊθ'ist -ˌsaʊ'ist] *s.* estesureste.
eastward ['istwərd, B -wəd] *a., adv.* hacia el este. *—s.* este.
eastwardly [-lɪ] *a.* que va hacia el este; que viene desde el este (viento). *—adv.* hacia el este; (de vientos) desde el este.
eastwards [-wərdz, B -wədz] *adv.* hacia el este.
easy ['izɪ] *a.* (EASIER; EASIEST) 1. fácil (problema, tarea, etc.; víctima, presa, mujer, etc.). 2. liviano, leve (castigo, pena, etc.). 3. suave, moderado (declive, pendiente, etc.). 4. cómodo, agradable (vida, circunstancias, etapa, paseo, etc.). 5. simple, sencillo, claro (estilo, lenguaje). 6. suave, natural (maneras, trato); complaciente (persona, disposición); desenvuelto, natural (conducta). 7. suave, lento, moderado (ritmo, paso, etc.). 8. confortable, cómodo (mueble, calzado, etc.). 9. fácil, dócil, manejable, obediente (niño, etc.). 10. (com.) de menos o poca demanda (valores, mercaderías); bajo (tipo de interés); abundante (dinero); flojo (mercado). 11. (bridge) distribuido igualmente (ej., ases en las manos). 12. (jer.) agradable, placentero, ej., *e. on the eyes,* agradable a la vista. 13. **an e.,** unos buenos, ej., *that fat fellow weighs an e. two hundred pounds,* ese tipo gordo pesa unas buenas doscientas libras; **e. come, e. go,** así como viene se va (dinero fácil, etc.); **e. does it,** (fam.) no te apresures; **e. to (do),** fácil de (hacer); **free and e.,** suelto, desenvuelto, despreocupado; con naturalidad; **lady of e. virtue,** mujer de vida alegre; **on e. street,** en buenas circunstancias, acomodado; **to be e. on,** tratar con lenidad. *—adv.* 1. fácilmente. 2. despacio. 3. **e.!** ¡despacio! ¡tranquilo!; **to go e. with** (u **on**), no usar o gastar mucho, tener cuidado con (ej., agua, mantequilla, etc.); **to take it e.,** tomarlo con calma, dejar de preocuparse, aceptar la vida tal cual es; **to take things e.,** no exaltarse por cualquier cosa.
easy chair, sillón, poltrona.
easy-going ['izɪ'goʊɪŋ] *a.* 1. de paso lento y suave (caballo). 2. despacioso, pausado. 3. despreocupado, plácido, calmado. 4. indolente, descuidado. 5. **to be (very) e.-g.,** ser fácil de tratar, tener buena disposición.
easy mark, (fam.) inocentón, fácil de embaucar.
easy money, dinero fácil de ganar.
easy street, (jer.) abundancia, riqueza, buenas circunstancias.
easy terms, facilidades (de pago); condiciones favorables (de un convenio).
eat [it] *v.t.* (*pret.* ATE [eɪt, B ɛt]; *p.p.* EATEN ['itən]; *p.pr.* EATING) 1. comer. 2. (fig.) devorar, tragar. 3. (gen. con *away*) (fig.) comer, consumir (gradualmente); corroer; gastar. 4. (jer.) molestar, preocupar. 5. **e. breakfast,** desayunarse; **e. crow,** tragar saliva, aceptar la derrota; **e. dinner,** cenar, comer (Amer.); **e. dirt,** humillarse, someterse a críticas severas o insultos; **e. humble pie,** humillarse y dar excusas, retractarse; **e. lunch,** almorzar; **e. one's fill,** comer bien, hartarse; **e. one's heart out,** sufrir amargamente; **e. one's words,** retractarse, desdecirse, cantar la palinodia; **e. (someone) out,** reprender (a alguien); **e. supper,** cenar; **e. up,** devorar, tragar, comer del todo, deleitarse en; (fig.) absorber; tragar, aceptar sin crítica. *—v.i.* 1. comer; alimentarse. 2. **e. away,** comer a sus anchas; **e. into,** corroer; (fig.) hacer estragos en; **e. out,** comer fuera (de casa).
eatable ['itəbəl] *a.* comestible, comedero; comible. *—s.* comestible; (*pl.*) comestibles, víveres, vituallas, alimentos.
eater ['itər, B 'itə] *s.* 1. comedor; comilón. 2. (G.B.) fruta de mesa (esp. manzana).
eatery [-ərɪ] *s.* (fam., E.U.) fonda, comedor público.
eating [-ɪŋ] *s.* 1. la acción de comer. 2. comida. *—a.* de comer; para comer.
eating house, restaurante, comedor, bodegón.
eau de Cologne [ˌoʊdəkə'loʊn, B 'oʊ-] agua de Colonia.
eaves [ivz] *s. pl.* (*sing.* EAVE) alero, socarrén, tejaroz.
eaves board, (arq.) ristrel, contrapar, guardacabio.
eavesdrop ['ivzˌdrɑp, B -ˌdrɔp] *v.i.* (*pret., p.p.* EAVESDROPPED; *p.pr.* EAVESDROPPING) escuchar furtivamente, ponerse a escuchar disimuladamente (conversación, etc.), escuchar secretamente por medio de dispositivos electrónicos.
eavesdropper [-ər, B -ə] *s.* escuchador furtivo.
eaves trough, (arq.) canaleta, canalón.
ebb [ɛb] *s.* 1. (mar.) menguante, reflujo. 2. decadencia, declinación; **at a low e.,** en decadencia, en un punto bajo; decaído. *—v.i.* 1. menguar o bajar (la marea). 2. (fig.) menguar, decaer, declinar, disminuir, irse consumiendo (algo).
ebb and flow, flujo y reflujo.
ebbet ['ɛbət] *s.* (zool.) salamandra verde (del E. de E.U.).

ebb tide, 1. (mar.) marea menguante, marea descendente, aguas de menguante, reflujo. 2. (fig.) tendencia decadente, (período de) decadencia.
Ebenaceae [ˌɛbəˈneɪsɪˌi] *s. pl.* (bot.) ebenáceas.
ebenaceous [-ˈneɪʃəs] *a.* (bot.) ebenáceo.
Ebionite [ˈɛbɪəˌnaɪt, B ˈibjə-] *s.* (relig.) Ebionita.
Ebionitic [ˌɛbɪəˈnɪtɪk, B ˌibjə-] *a.* (relig.) ebionita.
E b N *abrev. de* **east by north,** este cuarta al nordeste.
ebon [ˈɛbən] *a.* (poét.) de ébano; negro como el ébano.
ebonite [-ˌaɪt] *s.* (quím.) ebonita, vulcanita.
ebonize [-ˌaɪz] *v.t.* ebonizar; teñir de negro.
ebony [-ɪ] *s.* 1. (bot.) ébano, abenuz. 2. (madera de) ébano. —*a.* 1. de ébano, hecho de ébano. 2. negro, de color del ébano.
ebracteate [ɪˈbræktɪˌeɪt] **ebracteated** [-əd] *a.* (bot.) ebracteado.
E b S *abrev. de* **east by south,** este cuarta al sudeste.
ebullience [ɪˈbʊljəns, ɪˈbʌl-] *s.* ebullición; exaltación, entusiasmo, efervescencia, exuberancia.
ebullient [-jənt] *a.* 1. hirviente, rebosante. 2. exaltado, entusiasta, efervescente, exuberante.
ebulliently [-lɪ] *adv.* exaltadamente; con entusiasmo.
ebulliometer [ɪˌbʌlɪˈɑmətər, B -ˈɔmɪtə] *s.* (fís.) ebullómetro.
ebullioscope [ɪˈbʌljəˌskoʊp] *s.* (fís.) ebulloscopio.
ebullioscopy [ɪˌbʌlɪˈɑskəpɪ, B -ˈɔs-] *s.* (quím.) ebulloscopía.
ebullition [ˌɛbəˈlɪʃən] *s.* 1. ebullición, hervor. 2. entusiasmo; arranque, arrebato (de pasión, etc.).
eburnated [ˈɛbərˌneɪtəd, B ˈɛbəˌ-] *a.* (med.) endurecido como hueso.
eburnation [ˌɛbərˈneɪʃən, B ˌɛbəˈ-] *s.* (med.) eburnación.
eburnean [ɪˈbɜrnɪən, B ɪˈbɜn-] *a.* ebúrneo, marfileño.
ecarinate [iˈkærəˌneɪt, -nət] *a.* (bot.) carente de quilla, sin carina (una flor).
écarté [ˌeɪkɑrˈteɪ, B eɪˈkɑteɪ] *s.* (naipes) ecarte.
ecce homo [ˈɛkeɪˈhoʊmoʊ, B ˈɛksɪ-] *m.* ecce-homo, imagen de Cristo lacerado; (fig.) persona lacerada de aspecto lastimoso.
eccentric [ɪkˈsɛntrɪk, ɛk-] *a.* 1. (geom., mec.) excéntrico. 2. excéntrico, extravagante, estrafalario, irregular. —*s.* 1. excéntrico, persona extravagante. 2. (mec.) excéntrica.
eccentrically [-trɪkəlɪ] *adv.* excéntricamente.
eccentricity [ˌɛksɛnˈtrɪsətɪ] *s.* 1. excentricidad, extravagancia. 2. (geom., mec.) excentricidad.
ecchondroma [ˌɛkənˈdroʊmə] *s.* (med.) econdrosis.
ecchymosis [ˌɛkɪˈmoʊsəs] *s.* (med.) equimosis.
eccl. *abrev. de* **ecclesiastic,** eclesiástico.
Eccles. *abrev. de* **Ecclesiastes,** Eclesiastés (Ecl.).
ecclesia [ɪˈkliʒɪə, B -zjə] *s.* 1. (hist.) asamblea popular (esp. de los atenienses). 2. (relig.) iglesia, cuerpo o grupo de los fieles.
Ecclesiastes [ɪˌkliziˈæstɪz] *s.* (bíbl.) Eclesiastés (libro canónico del Antiguo Testamento, escrito por Salomón).
ecclesiastic [-tɪk] *a.* eclesiástico. —*s.* eclesiástico, clérigo, sacerdote, cura.
ecclesiastical [-tɪkəl] *a.* eclesiástico.
ecclesiastically [-kəlɪ] *adv.* eclesiásticamente.
ecclesiasticism [-təˌsɪzəm] *s.* clericalismo, espíritu eclesiástico.
Ecclesiasticus [-tɪkəs] *s.* (bíbl.) Eclesiástico, Sabiduria de Jesús.
ecclesiolatry [ɪˌklizɪˈɑlətrɪ, B -ˈɔl-] *s.* devoción excesiva a la Iglesia.
ecclesiology [-ədʒɪ] *s.* ciencia que estudia el arte, arquitectura y decorado de las iglesias.
eccrine [ˈɛkrən, -ˌraɪn] *a.* (fisiol.) ecrina (glándula).
eccrinology [ˌɛkrəˈnɑlədʒɪ, B -ˈnɔl-] *s.* (fisiol.) ecrinología, ecrisiología.
ecdysiast [ɛkˈdɪzɪˌæst] *s.* (hum., E.U.) desnudista, bataclana, bailarina que se desnuda durante su número; persona entusiasta de dicho espectáculo.
ecdysis [ˈɛkdəsəs] *s.* (zool.) ecdisis, muda (de los ofidios, crustáceos, etc.).
ecesis [ɪˈsisəs] *s.* (biol.) ecesis.
ECG *abrev. de* **electrocardiogram,** electrocardiograma.
echelon [ˈɛʃəˌlɑn, B -ˌlɔn] *s.* 1. (mil.) escalón. 2. jerarquía, categoría, grado; grupo. —*v.t., v.i.* (mil.) escalonar(se).
echidna [ɪˈkɪdnə, B ɛ-] *s.* (zool.) equidna, mamífero.
echinate [ɪˈkaɪnət, B ˈɛkənət] *a.* erizado, cubierto de púas o cerdas.
echinite [ˈɛkəˌnaɪt] *s.* erizo de mar fósil.
echinococcosis [ɪˌkaɪnəkəˈkoʊsəs] *s.* (med.) equinococosis.
echinococcus [-ˈkɑkəs, B -ˈkɔk-] *s.* equinococo, larva de la tenia.
echinoderm [ɪˈkaɪnəˌdɜrm, B -ˌdɜm] *s.* (zool.) equinodermo.
echinodermatous [ɪˌkaɪnəˈdɜrmətəs, B -ˈdɜm-] *a.* (zool.) equinodermo.
echinoid [ɪˈkaɪˌnɔɪd, ˈɛkə-] *s., a.* (zool.) equinoideo.
echinulate [ɪˈkɪnjələt, -ˌleɪt] *a.* (bact.) equinulado.
echinus [ɪˈkaɪnəs] *s.* (*pl.* ECHINI [-ˌnaɪ]) 1. (zool.) equino, erizo de mar. 2. (arq.) equino (moldura convexa en el capitel dórico); gallón, agallón.
echo [ˈɛkoʊ] *s.* (*pl.* ECHOES) 1. eco. 2. (radar) eco; (t.v.) imagen, eco, imagen fantasma. 3. imitador. 4. (fig.) eco, acogida favorable. 5. **E.** (astronáut.) (satélite) Eco. —*v.t.* hacer eco a; repetir o imitar (palabras). —*v.i.* producir eco, reverberar, resonar.
echo chamber, (rad.) cámara de resonancia.
echoic [ɪˈkoʊɪk, ɛ-] *a.* 1. ecoico. 2. onomatopéyico; imitativo.
echolalia [ˌɛkoʊˈleɪlɪə] *s.* (med.) ecolalia.
echolocation [-loʊˈkeɪʃən] *s.* detección por sonda ecoica, detección por ultrasonidos.
echo sounder, sonda ecoica, sonda acústica.
ECLA *abrev. de* **Economic Commission for Latin America,** Comisión Económica para América Latina (CEPAL).
éclair [eɪˈklɛr, B ˈeɪklɛə] *s.* pastel pequeño con relleno de crema.
eclampsia [ɛˈklæmpsɪə] *s.* (med.) eclampsia.
éclat [eɪˈklɑ, B ˈeɪklɑ] *s.* 1. resplandor, brillo. 2. bombo, publicidad. 3. éxito resonante; aplauso, aclamación.
eclectic [ɛˈklɛktɪk, ɪ-] *a., s.* ecléctico.
eclectically [-tɪkəlɪ] *adv.* eclécticamente.
eclecticism [-təˌsɪzəm] *s.* eclecticismo.
eclipse [ɪˈklɪps] *s.* (astr.) eclipse; (fig.) eclipse, desaparición, obscurecimiento. —*v.t.* 1. (astr.) eclipsar, eclipsarse. 2. (fig.) eclipsar, opacar, empañar. 3. superar (belleza, brillo, honor, etc.).
ecliptic [ɪˈklɪptɪk] (astr.) *s.* eclíptica. —*a.* eclíptico.
ecliptic coordinates, (nav.) coordinadas eclípticas.
eclogue [ˈɛkˌlɔg, -ˌlɑg, B -ˌlɔg] *s.* (poética) égloga.
eclosion [ɪˈkloʊʒən] *s.* eclosión.
ecocide [ˈɛkəˌsaɪd] *s.* ecocidio.
ecological [ˌɛkəˈlɑdʒɪkəl, B -ˈlɔdʒ-] *a.* ecológico.
ecologist [ɪˈkɑlədʒəst, B ɪˈkɔl-] *s.* ecólogo, experto en ecología.
ecology [-dʒɪ] *s.* ecología.
econ. *abrev. de* **economics, economy,** economía; **economist,** economista.
econometrics [ɪˌkɑnəˈmɛtrɪks, B ɪˌkɔn-] *s. pl.* (*sing. en const.*) econometría.
economic [ˌɛkəˈnɑmɪk, ˌikə-, B -ˈnɔm-] *a.* económico.
economical [-ɪkəl] *a.* económico, frugal, módico, ahorrativo.
economics [-ɪks] *s. pl.* (*gen. sing. en const.*) 1. economía (ciencia y estudio). 2. economía, aspecto económico.
economic speed, (aut., avia.) velocidad de crucero.
economist [ɪˈkɑnəməst, B ɪˈkɔn-] *s.* economista.
economize [-ˌmaɪz] *v.t.* economizar, ahorrar. —*v.i.* ser ahorrativo, economizar.
economy [-mɪ] *s.* 1. economía, sistema económico (de un país, período, etc.). 2. economía, ahorro, frugalidad. 3. economía, estructura, sistema orgánico, organización. 4. (relig.) designio divino.
economy class, segunda clase (en avión o barco).
ECOSOC *abrev. de* **Economic and Social Council of the United Nations,** Consejo Económico y Social de las Naciones Unidas (ECOSOC).
ecotone [ˈɛkoʊˌtoʊn] *s.* (ecol.) área de transición (entre dos comunidades adyacentes que presenta especies comunes a ambas).
ecru [ˈɛkru, B ˈeɪ-] *a.* de color crudo, sin blanquear. —*s.* género de lino crudo; color de lino sin blanquear.
ecstasied [ˈɛkstəsid] *a.* extático, extasiado.
ecstasy [-sɪ] *s.* éxtasis, rapto, arrobamiento, embeleso. —*v.t.* provocar el éxtasis en, arrobar, embelesar.
ecstatic [ɛkˈstætɪk, ɪk-] *a.* extático. —*s.* exaltado.
ecstatical [-ɪkəl] *a.* extático.
ectasis [ˈɛktəsəs] *s.* 1. (poética) éctasis. 2. (med.) ectasia.
ecthyma [ɛkˈθaɪmə] *s.* (med.) ectima.
ectoblast [ˈɛktəˌblæst] *s.* (biol.) ectoblasto, ectodermo.
ectoblastic [ˌɛktəˈblæstɪk] *a.* ectoblástico.
ectocommensal [-toʊkəˈmɛnsəl] *s.* (biol.) ectocomensal.
ectoderm [ˈɛktəˌdɜrm, B -ˌdɜm] *s.* (biol.) ectodermo, ectoblasto.
ectodermal [ˌɛktəˈdɜrməl, B -ˈdɜməl] **ectodermic** [-mɪk] *a.* ectodérmico.
ectogenic [-ˈdʒɛnɪk] **ectogenous** [ɛkˈtɑdʒənəs, B -ˈtɔdʒ-] *a.* (bact.) ectógeno.
ectomere [ˈɛktəˌmɪr, B -ˌmɪə] *s.* (biol.) ectómetro.
ectomorphic [ˌɛktəˈmɔrfɪk, B -ˈmɔfɪk] *a.* (antrop.) ectomórfico.
ectomorphy [ˈɛktəˌmɔrfɪ, B -ˌmɔfɪ] *s.* (antrop.) ectomorfía.
ectoparasite [ˌɛktoʊˈpærəˌsaɪt] *s.* ectoparásito.
ectopia [ɛkˈtoʊpɪə] *s.* (med.) ectopia.
ectoplasm [ˈɛktəˌplæzəm] *s.* 1. (biol.) ectoplasma, exoplasma. 2. (espiritismo) emanación que se supone exhala el médium.
ectoplasmic [ˌɛktəˈplæzmɪk] *a.* ectoplasmático.

ectosarc [ˈɛktəˌsɑrk, B -ˌsɑk] *s.* (biol.) ectosarco.
ectotherm [-ˌθɜrm, B -ˌθɜm] *s.* animal de sangre fría; organismo de sangre fría.
ectropion [ɛkˈtroʊpɪˌɑn, B -ɪən] *s.* (med.) ectropión.
ectypal [ˈɛktəpəl] *a.* ectípico.
ectype [-ˌtaɪp] *s.* ectipo, copia.
Ecuador [ˈɛkwəˌdɔr, B ˌɛkwəˈdɔ] *s.* (el) Ecuador.
Ecuadoran [ˌɛkwəˈdɔrən] **Ecuadorean, Ecuadorian** [-ɪən] *a., s.* ecuatoriano.
ecumenical [ˌɛkjəˈmɛnɪkəl, B ˌikjʊ-] *a.* ecuménico, universal.
ecumenical council, (relig.) concilio ecuménico.
ecumenically [-kəlɪ] *adv.* ecuménicamente.
ecumenism [ˈɛkjəməˌnɪzəm, ɛˈkju-] *s.* movimiento ecuménico, principios o prácticas de acercamiento entre las religiones cristianas.
eczema [ɪgˈzimə, ˈɛksə-, B ˈɛksɪ-] *s.* eczema, eccema.
eczematous [ɪgˈzɛmətəs, B ɛkˈsɛm-] *a.* eczematoso, eccematoso.
edacious [ɪˈdeɪʃəs] *a.* voraz, devorador, goloso.
edacity [ɪˈdæsətɪ] *s.* voracidad, gula.
Edam [ˈidəm, B ˈidæm] *s.* queso de Edam, queso de bola.
edaphic [ɪˈdæfɪk] *a.* (ecol.) edáfico.
edaphology [ˌɛdəˈfɑlədʒɪ, B -ˈfɔl-] *s.* edafología.
EDC *abrev. de* **European Defense Community,** Comunidad Defensiva Europea (CDE), Mancomunidad de Defensa Europea (MDE).
Edda [ˈɛdə] *s.* (lit.) Edda, colección de literatura escandinava.
eddo [ˈɛdoʊ] *s.* (*pl.* EDDOES) (bot.) taro (planta o raíz).
eddy [ˈɛdɪ] *s.* 1. remolino. 2. contracorriente, contraflujo, revesa. —*v.t.* remolinear. —*v.i.* remolinar(se), remolinear.
eddy current, (elec.) corriente parásita de Foucault.
edelweiss [ˈeɪdəlˌwaɪs, B -ˌvaɪs] *s.* (bot.) edelweiss, planta alpina y pirenaica.
edema [ɪˈdimə] *s.* (med.) edema, hidropesía.
edematous [ɪˈdɛmətəs] *a.* (med.) edematoso.
Eden [ˈidən] *s.* (bíbl., fig.) edén.
Edenic [ɪˈdɛnɪk] *a.* edénico.
Edentata [ˌidɛnˈteɪtə] *s. pl.* (zool.) edentados, desdentados.
edentate [iˈdɛnˌteɪt] *a., s.* (zool.) edentado, desdentado.
edentulous [-tʃələs] *a.* edentado, desdentado.
edge [ɛdʒ] *s.* 1. filo, corte (ej., de un cuchillo). 2. borde, margen, orilla, arcén; canto (de mesa, tabla, pirámide, moneda, etc.); afueras, contornos (de una ciudad, etc.). 3. (fig.) estímulo; sabor. 4. **on e.,** de canto; (fig.) impaciente, ansioso; nervioso, irritable; **to have the e. on,** llevar (una pequeña) ventaja a; **to put an e. on,** afilar (cuchillo, etc.); **to set (one's) teeth on e.,** irritar (a uno); **to set (one's) nerves on e.,** ponerle (a uno) los nervios de punta; **to take the e. off,** embotar; (fig.) suavizar, mitigar, templar. —*v.t.* 1. afilar, aguzar. 2. poner o formar bordes en (ej., el jardín); bordear, ribetear; cantear (madera). 3. (dep.) inclinar, poner de canto (el esquí). 4. **e. on,** aguijar, incitar, estimular; **e. one's way (through),** abrirse paso poco a poco (por); **e. oneself in,** introducirse paulatinamente. —*v.i.* (con *away, off, out,* etc.) apartarse o alejarse paso a paso.
edgebone [ˈɛdʒˌboʊn] *var. de* **aitchbone.**
edged [ɛdʒd] *p.p. de* **to edge.** —*a.* (mec.) afilado, cortante.
edge tool, 1. herramienta cortante. 2. tiracantos.
edgeways [ˈɛdʒˌweɪz] *var. de* **edgewise.**
edge weld, soldadura de cantos.
edgewise [-ˌwaɪz] *adv.* de filo, de canto, de lado; **to get a word in e.,** lograr decir una palabra (cuando el interlocutor es muy hablador).
edginess [ˈɛdʒɪnəs] *s.* nerviosidad, nerviosismo, inquietud.
edging [-ɪŋ] *s.* borde, margen, orla, ribete, pestaña.
edging knife, (impr.) chifla, cuchilla serpeta.
edgy [-ɪ] *a.* (EDGIER; EDGIEST) 1. agudo, afilado, aguzado. 2. nervioso, inquieto.
edible [ˈɛdəbəl] *a.* comestible, comible, comedero. —*s.* comestible.
edibleness [-nəs] *s.* condición de comestible.
edict [ˈidɪkt] *s.* edicto, bando, decreto, mandato, ordenanza.
edification [ˌɛdəfəˈkeɪʃən] *s.* edificación (enseñanza, beneficios espirituales).
edificatory [ɪˈdɪfəkəˌtɔrɪ, B ˈɛdɪfɪˌkeɪtərɪ] *a.* edificante, edificativo, formativo.
edifice [ˈɛdəfəs] *s.* 1. edificio. 2. (fig.) estructura.
edifier [ˈɛdəˌfaɪər, B -ə] *s.* edificador.
edify [-ˌfaɪ] *v.t.* (*pret., p.p.* EDIFIED; *p.pr.* EDIFYING) edificar, incitar a la virtud.
edifying [-ɪŋ] *a.* edificante, virtuoso.
Edinburgh [ˈɛdənˌbɜrə, B -bərə] *s.* Edimburgo, capital de Escocia.
edit [ˈɛdət] *v.t.* 1. arreglar y preparar para la publicación; corregir, repasar. 2. preparar una edición de. 3. redactar, dirigir (un periódico). 4. (cinem.) hacer el montaje de, montar (una película). 5. **e. out,** recortar, suprimir (un artículo, etc.).
edition [ɪˈdɪʃən] *s.* 1. edición. 2. tirada, tiraje (de un periódico). 3. (fig.) edición, versión.
editor [ˈɛdətər, B -ə] *s.* 1. director, redactor titular (de un periódico). 2. editor (de textos literarios, de películas, etc.).
editorial [ˌɛdəˈtɔrɪəl] *a.* de redacción (oficina, etc.). —*s.* artículo de fondo, editorial (Amer.).
editorial board, comité de redacción.
editorialist [-əst] *s.* periodista que escribe artículos de fondo, editorialista (Amer.).
editorialize [-ˌaɪz] *v.t.* escribir artículos de fondo, escribir editoriales (Amer.).
editorially [-əlɪ] *adv.* 1. en un artículo de fondo, en un editorial (Amer.). 2. como editor, editorialmente.
editorial staff, cuerpo de redacción (de un periódico).
editor in chief, (*pl.* EDITORS IN CHIEF) jefe de redacción.
editorship [ˈɛdətərˌʃɪp, B -əˌ-] *s.* dirección o redacción (de una revista o periódico).
editor's note, nota de redacción, nota del redactor.
EDT *abrev. de* **eastern daylight time,** hora de verano del este.
educ. *abrev. de* **education,** educación.
educable [ˈɛdʒəkəbəl, B ˈɛdjʊ-] *a.* educable, entrenable.
educate [-ˌkeɪt] *v.t.* 1. educar, instruir, enseñar. 2. desarrollar, mejorar (facultades, etc.). 3. adiestrar, amaestrar (animales).
educated [-əd] *a.* educado, instruido; culto; entrenado (díc. de animales); informado, probable, ej., *his estimate was an educated guess,* su pronóstico fue una conjetura informada.
education [ˌɛdʒəˈkeɪʃən, B ˌɛdjʊ-] *s.* 1. educación, instrucción, enseñanza. 2. educación, cultura. 3. adiestramiento (de animales).
educational [-əl] *a.* educacional, educativo.
educationally [-ɪ] *adv.* desde el punto de vista educacional, para la educación.
educationist [-əst] *s.* educador, educacionista.
educative [ˈɛdʒəˌkeɪtɪv, B ˈɛdjʊkə-] *a.* educativo, educador, instructivo.
educator [-ˌkeɪtər, B -ə] *s.* educador, maestro, pedagogo, instructor.
educatory [-kəˌtɔrɪ, B -ˌkeɪtərɪ] *a.* educativo, educador.
educe [ɪˈdus, B ɪˈdjus] *v.t.* educir, sacar, extraer, deducir.
educible [-əbəl] *a.* deducible.
educt [ˈidʌkt] *s.* (quím.) educto.
eductor [ɪˈdʌktər, B -tə] *s.* (mec.) eductor, eyector.
edulcorate [ɪˈdʌlkəˌreɪt] *v.t.* 1. (fig.) dulcificar, suavizar (carácter, etc.). 2. (ant.) edulcorar (substancias).
Edwardian [ɛdˈwɑrdɪən, B -ˈwɔdjən] *a.* (hist., G.B.) eduardiano (período, estilo, arte, literatura, decoración, modas).
EE *abrev. de* **Electrical Engineer,** ingeniero electrotécnico.
E.E.C. *abrev. de* **European Economic Community,** Comunidad Económica Europea (CEE) Mercado Común Europeo (MCE).
EEG *abrev. de* **electroencephalogram,** electroencefalograma.
eel [il] *s.* 1. (ict.) anguila, anguilla. 2. (zool.) anguilula. 3. **to be as slippery as an eel,** escurrirse como una anguila.
eelgrass [ˈilˌgræs, B -ˌgrɑs] *s.* (E.U., bot.) zostera marina.
eelpot [-ˌpɑt, B -ˌpɔt] *s.* nasa para anguilas; anguilera.
eelpout [-ˌpaʊt] *s.* (ict.) pez zoarcido.
eelworm [-ˌwɜrm, B -ˌwɜm] *s.* (zool.) anguilula.
e'en [in] *adv. contr. de* **even.**
e'er [ɛr, B ɛə] *adv. contr. de* **ever.**
eerie, eery [ˈɪrɪ, B ˈɪərɪ] *a.* 1. misterioso, pavoroso, espectral. 2. (pr. esco.) miedoso, espantado, atemorizado.
efface [ɪˈfeɪs] *v.t.* 1. tachar, borrar. 2. (fig.) destruir, arrasar. 3. sobrepasar, superar, eclipsar. 4. **e. oneself,** retirarse, ponerse de lado.
effaceable [-əbəl] *a.* deleble.
effacement [-mənt] *s.* 1. tachadura, borradura. 2. destrucción. 3. modestia, humildad.
effect [ɪˈfɛkt] *s.* 1. efecto, resultado, consecuencia. 2. vigor, vigencia. 3. eficacia, efectividad. 4. (*pl.*) efectos, bienes, posesiones. 5. efecto, impacto, impresión. 6. **for e.,** para causar efecto; **in e.,** en efecto, en realidad, efectivamente; en vigor; **no effects,** sin fondos (escrito por el banco en un cheque rechazado); **of no e.,** sin resultado; ineficaz; **personal effects,** efectos personales; **special effects,** (cinem., t.v.) efectos especiales; **to bring to e., to carry into e.,** llevar a cabo, realizar; **to give e. to,** hacer efectivo, llevar a efecto; **to go into e.,** entrar en vigor; **to no e.,** inútilmente; **to put into e.,** poner en vigor; **to take e.,** volverse efectivo, hacer efecto; entrar en vigor; **to the e. that,** en el sentido de que; con el propósito de; **to this e.,** en este sentido; con este propósito. —*v.t.* efectuar, realizar, ejecutar; producir, hacer.
effective [ɪˈfɛktɪv] *a.* 1. efectivo, actual, real. 2. eficaz. 3. impresionante. 4. vigente, en vigencia, en vigor. 5. (mil.) efectivo, disponible. —*s.* (*pl.*) efectivos.
effective bore, (arm.) ánima resultante.
effectively [-lɪ] *adv.* 1. efectivamente, en efecto. 2. eficazmente. 3. con efecto.
effectiveness [-nəs] *s.* 1. eficacia. 2. vigencia (de la ley).
effective nucleus, (quím.) núcleo de átomo.
effective pitch, (avia.) paso efectivo de la hélice.
effective range, (arm.) alcance eficaz.
effective weight, peso útil.

effector [ɪ'fɛktər, B -tə] *s.* (fisol.) efector.
effectual [-tʃʊəl] *a.* eficaz, adecuado; válido, obligatorio.
effectually [-əlɪ] *adv.* eficazmente, efectivamente; con validez.
effectualness [-nəs] *s.* eficacia; validez.
effectuate [ɪ'fɛktʃʊˌeɪt] *v.t.* efectuar, obrar, realizar.
effectuation [ɪˌfɛktʃʊ'eɪʃən] *s.* ejecución, realización.
effeminacy [ɪ'fɛmənəsɪ] *s.* afeminamiento, afeminación.
effeminate [-nət] *a.* 1. afeminado, mujeril, adamado. 2. afeminado, decadente (civilización, etc.). —*s.* afeminado. — [-ˌneɪt] *v.t.* afeminar(se), adamar(se).
effeminately [-lɪ] *adv.* afeminadamente.
effeminateness [-nəs] *s.* carácter afeminado.
effendi [ɛ'fɛndɪ] *s.* (*pl.* EFFENDIS) efendi (título honorífico usado entre los turcos).
efferent ['ɛfərənt] *a.* (fisiol.) eferente.
effervesce [ˌɛfər'vɛs, B ˌɛfə'-] *v.i.* (lit., fig.) estar en efervescencia.
effervescence [-əns] *s.* efervescencia.
effervescent [-ənt] *a.* efervescente.
effete [ɛ'fit, ɪ-] *a.* 1. exhausto, gastado, agotado. 2. estéril. 3. débil, incapaz. 4. decadente, superfino (persona).
effeteness [-nəs] *s.* debilidad, incapacidad; decadencia.
efficacious [ˌɛfə'keɪʃəs] *a.* eficaz.
efficaciously [-lɪ] *adv.* eficazmente.
efficacy ['ɛfɪkəsɪ] *s.* eficacia.
efficiency [ɪ'fɪʃənsɪ] *s.* eficiencia, habilidad; (mec.) rendimiento.
efficiency apartment, apartamento de una habitación que incluye una pequeña cocina.
efficiency engineer, ingeniero coordinador (cuya tarea es mejorar el rendimiento de una fábrica, etc.).
efficient [-ənt] *a.* 1. eficiente, competente, capaz. 2. (mec.) de gran rendimiento.
efficient cause, (filos.) causa eficiente.
efficiently [-lɪ] *adv.* 1. eficientemente. 2. (mec.) con buen rendimiento.
effigy ['ɛfədʒɪ] *s.* (*pl.* EFFIGIES) efigie, imagen; **to burn (hang) in e.,** quemar (colgar) en efigie.
effloresce [ˌɛflə'rɛs, B ˌɛflɔ-] *v.i.* 1. (lit., fig.) florecer. 2. (quím.) eflorecerse.
efflorescence [-əns] *s.* 1. florescencia, florecimiento. 2. (med., quím.) eflorescencia.
efflorescent [-ənt] *a.* 1. floreciente. 2. (quím.) eflorescente.
effluence ['ɛflʊəns] *s.* efluencia, emanación, efusión, efluvio.
effluent [-ənt] *a.* efluente. —*s.* chorro o corriente que sale.
effluvium [ɛ'fluvɪəm] *s.* (*pl.* EFFLUVIA [-vɪə] o EFFLUVIUMS) efluvio, exhalación, emanación.
efflux ['ɛfˌlʌks] *s.* 1. efluvio, emanación. 2. efusión, flujo.
effort ['ɛfərt, B -ət] *s.* 1. esfuerzo. 2. (fam.) producto, producción. 3. (fís.) fuerza efectiva, fuerza eficaz. 4. **to make every effort (to),** hacer lo posible (por).
effort arm, (ing.) palanca de fuerza.
effortless [-ləs] *a.* fácil, sin esfuerzo; suave.
effrontery [ɪ'frʌntərɪ] *s.* desvergüenza, descaro, desfachatez, insolencia.
effulge [ɪ'fʌldʒ, ɛ-] *v.i.* fulgir, fulgurar, brillar, resplandecer.
effulgence [-'fʌldʒəns] *s.* refulgencia, resplandor.
effulgent [-dʒənt] *a.* refulgente, resplandeciente, radiante, esplendoroso.
effuse [ɪ'fjuz, ɛ-] *v.t.* derramar, esparcir, verter. —*v.i.* (fís.) fluir, emanar. — [-'fjus] *a.* (bot.) esparcido, difuso.
effusion [-'fjuʒən] *s.* 1. efusión, derrame. 2. (fig.) efusión, expansión, desahogo.
effusive [-'fjusɪv] *a.* efusivo, expansivo; (geol.) efusivo.
effusively [-lɪ] *adv.* efusivamente.
effusiveness [-nəs] *s.* naturaleza efusiva o expansiva.
eft [ɛft] *s.* (zool.) tritón, lagartija acuática.
EFTA *abrev. de* **European Free Trade Association,** Asociación Europea de Libre Comercio (AELC).
e.g. *abrev. de* **exempli gratia,** por ejemplo (p. ej., *vg., v.g., v.gr.*).
egad [ɪ'gæd] *interj.* ¡pardiez!
egalitarian [ɪˌgælə'tɛrɪən, B -'tɛər-] *a.* igualitario; partidario de la igualdad social, política y civil.
egalitarianism [-ˌɪzəm] *s.* igualitarismo, la doctrina de la igualdad.
egest [ɪ'dʒɛst] *v.t.* excretar, expeler.
egesta [ɪ'dʒɛstə] *s. pl.* deyecciones, excrementos.
egestion [ɪ'dʒɛstʃən] *s.* defecación.
egg [ɛg] *s.* 1. huevo. 2. (jer.) tío, tipo, sujeto. 3. **bad e.,** huevo podrido; (jer.) calavera, sinvergüenza, tipo vicioso; **boiled e.,** huevo pasado (por agua), huevo tibio (Amer.); **fried e.,** huevo frito, huevo estrellado; **good e.,** (jer.) buen tipo; **hard-boiled e.,** huevo duro; **in the e.,** en embrión; **poached e.,** huevo escalfado; **scrambled eggs,** huevos revueltos; **to put** o **have all one's eggs in one basket,** jugárselo todo a una carta; **to lay an e.,** fracasar completamente (en un chiste, obra de teatro, etc.); **to walk (tread) on eggs,** conducirse con extremo cuidado; estar en terreno peligroso.
egg [ɛg] *v.t.* 1. (gen. con *on*) urgir, instar, incitar. 2. (cocina) envolver en huevo. 3. (jer.) arrojar huevos (a una persona).
egg and dart, e. and anchor, e. and tongue, (arq.) óvolos.
eggbeater ['ɛgˌbitər, B -ə] *s.* 1. batidor de huevos. 2. (jer.) helicóptero.
egg cell, (biol.) óvulo.
egg cleavage, (biol.) segmentación del óvulo.
egg cup, huevera.
egger ['ɛgər, B -ə] *s.* (variedad de) polilla, alevilla.
egg flip, ponche de huevo, batido con jerez u oporto.
egghead [-ˌhɛd] *s.* (jer., E.U.) (gen. despec.) intelectual.
eggnog [-ˌnɑg, B -ˌnɔg] *s.* ponche de leche y huevo.
eggplant [-ˌplænt, B -ˌplɑnt] *s.* (bot.) berenjena.
egg roll, rollo relleno de carne o pollo picado con verduras, típico plato de la cocina china adaptada a la norteamericana.
egg-shaped [-ˌʃeɪpt] *a.* ovoide, ovoideo, aovado, oviforme.
eggshell [-ˌʃɛl] *s.* cáscara de huevo, cascarón. —*a.* 1. tenue y frágil. 2. ligeramente lustroso. 3. **e. finish,** (pint.) acabado mate.
egg tooth, (orn.) diamante (en el pico del pájaro embrionario para romper la cáscara).
egg-whisk [-'hwɪsk, -ˌwɪsk] *s.* (G.B.) batidor de huevos.
egg white, clara de huevo.
egis ['idʒəs] *var. de* **aegis.**
eglantine ['ɛglənˌtaɪn] *s.* (bot.) escaramujo oloroso, agavanzo; eglantina.
ego ['igoʊ, B 'ɛgoʊ] *s.* (*pl.* EGOS) 1. (filos.) yo; conciencia (humana). 2. (psic.) ego. 3. (fam.) egoísmo.
egocentric [ˌigoʊ'sɛntrɪk, B ˌɛg-] *a., s.* egocéntrico.
egocentrism [-ˌtrɪzəm] *s.* egocentrismo.
egoism ['igoʊˌɪzəm, B 'ɛg-] *s.* egoísmo.
egoist [-əst] *s.* egoísta.
egoistic [ˌigoʊ'ɪstɪk, B ˌɛg-] **egoistical** [-tɪkəl] *a.* egoísta.
egoistically [-tɪkəlɪ] *adv.* egoísticamente, con egoísmo.
egomania [-'meɪnɪə] *s.* preocupación obsesiva o patológica con el ego.
egotism ['igəˌtɪzəm, B 'ɛg-] *s.* 1. egotismo. 2. egoísmo.
egotist [-təst] *s.* 1. egotista. 2. ególatra.
egotistic [ˌigə'tɪstɪk, B ˌɛg-] **egotistical** [-tɪkəl] *a.* 1. egotista. 2. ególatra, egolátrico.
egotize ['igəˌtaɪz, B 'ɛg-] *v.i.* hablar o escribir mucho de sí mismo.
egregious [ɪ'gridʒəs] *a.* extraordinario, tremendo, atroz, insigne (error, estupidez, disparate, tonto, etc.).
egregiously [-lɪ] *adv.* tremendamente (estúpido, equivocado, etc.).
egress ['iˌgrɛs, B 'igrəs] *s.* salida. — [i'grɛs] *v.i.* salir.
eggression [i'grɛʃən] *s.* salida, emergencia.
egret ['igrət, ɪ'grɛt, B 'igrɛt] *s.* (orn.) airón, moño, penacho.
Egypt ['idʒəpt] *s.* Egipto.
Egyptian [ɪ'dʒɪpʃən] *a.* 1. egipcio, natural u oriundo de Egipto. 2. gitano. 3. (tip.) egipcio. —*s.* 1. egipcio. 2. gitano.
Egyptian clover, (bot.) trébol de Alejandría.
Egyptian vulture, (orn.) abando, abanto, alimoche.
Egyptological [iˌdʒɪptə'lɑdʒɪkəl, B -'lɔdʒ-] *a.* egiptológico.
Egyptologist [ˌidʒɪp'tɑlədʒəst, B -'tɔl-] *s.* egiptólogo.
Egyptology [-dʒɪ] *s.* egiptología.
eh [eɪ, ɛ] *interj.* ¡eh!
eider ['aɪdər, B -ə] *s.* (orn.) eíder, eidero, pato de flojel.
eiderdown [-ˌdaʊn] *s.* edredón; plumón; colcha rellena con plumas.
eider duck, (orn.) pato del flojel, eíder.
eidetic [aɪ'dɛtɪk] *a.* (psic.) eidético.
eidograph ['aɪdəˌgræf, B -ˌgrɑf] *s.* pantógrafo.
eidolon [aɪ'doʊlən, B -lɔn] *s.* (*pl.* EIDOLONS o EIDOLA [-lə]) imagen; fantasma.
Eiffel ['aɪfəl] **Tower,** Torre Eiffel.
eigen value ['eɪgən-] (quím.) valor propio o específico.
eight [eɪt] *s.* 1. ocho (número). 2. bote de ocho remeros; automóvil o motor de ocho cilindros. 3. **the Eights,** (G.B.) carreras de botes de ocho remeros en Oxford y Cambridge; **to have one over the e.,** (jer., G.B.) emborracharse.
eight ball, 1. (billar) bola negra numerada con un "8". 2. **to be behind the e.b.,** (jer., E.U.) estar en apuros, estar en una situación desventajosa o desconcertante.
eighteen ['eɪ'tin] *s., a.* dieciocho, diez y ocho.
eighteenmo [-ˌmoʊ] *s.* (impr.) tamaño décimo octavo.
eighteenth [-'tinθ] *s.* 1. décimoctavo, dieciocheno. 2. dieciocho (en fechas). —*a.* décimoctavo, dieciocheno.
eightfold ['eɪtˌfoʊld] *a.* óctuplo, óctuple. —*adv.* ocho veces.
eighth [eɪtθ] *s.* 1. octavo. 2. ocho (en fechas). 3. (mús.) octava; corchea. —*a.* octavo.
eighth note, (mús.) corchea.
eight hundred, ochocientos.

eight hundredth, octingentésimo.
eightieth ['eɪtɪəθ] *s., a.* octogésimo, ochentavo.
eighty ['eɪtɪ] *a.* ochenta. —*s.* ochenta; **the eighties,** (*pl.*) los años ochenta, la novena década del siglo pasado.
eightyfold [-ˌfoʊld] *a., adv.* ochenta veces.
eikon ['aɪˌkɑn, B -ˌkɔn] *s. var. de* **icon,** icono.
einkorn ['aɪnˌkɔrn, B -ˌkɔn] *s.* (bot.) carraón.
einsteinium [aɪn'staɪnɪəm] *s.* (quím.) einstenio.
either ['iðər, 'aɪ-, B -ðə] *a.* 1. uno u otro, cualquiera de los dos. 2. ambos. —*pron.* uno de dos, el uno o el otro. —*conj.* o; **either . . . . . . or,** o . . . . . . o. —*adv.* (después de una negación) tampoco.
ejaculate [ɪ'dʒækjəˌleɪt] *v.t.* 1. (fisiol.) eyacular, expeler. 2. pronunciar súbitamente, exclamar. —*v.i.* 1. (fisiol.) hacer una eyaculación. 2. exclamar.
ejaculation [ɪˌdʒækjə'leɪʃən] *s.* 1. (fisiol.) eyaculación. 2. exclamación.
ejaculative [ɪ'dʒækjəˌleɪtɪv, B -lətɪv] *a.* jaculatorio.
ejaculatory [-ləˌtɔrɪ, B -lətərɪ] *a.* 1. (fisiol.) eyaculatorio. 2. jaculatorio (oración, etc.). 3. vocinglero.
ejaculatory prayer, jaculatoria.
eject [ɪ'dʒɛkt] *v.t.* expeler; echar, arrojar (de lugar, oficina o propiedad); expulsar, echar (del colegio); (aer.) expeler (piloto de un avión incendiado, etc.).
ejecta [ɪ'dʒɛktə] *s. pl.* (geol.) deyección, eyecto (ej., de un volcán), (*pl.*) materias expelidas.
ejection [ɪ'dʒɛkʃən] *s.* 1. expulsión. 2. eyección (del cartucho de un arma).
ejection seat, (aer.) asiento proyectable, asiento eyectable.
ejective [ɪ'dʒɛktɪv] *a.* 1. expulsivo (fuerza, etc.). 2. (fon.) explosivo. 3. (geol.) eyecto (ej., de un volcán).
ejectment [-mənt] *s.* expulsión; (der.) lanzamiento, desahucio.
ejector [-ər, B -ə] *s.* 1. (arm.) expulsor. 2. (mec.) eyector, bomba de chorro.
ejector seat, (aer.) asiento proyectable, asiento eyectable.
eke [ik] *v.t.* 1. (ant.) aumentar; añadir. 2. **e. out,** suplir, complementar; ganarse (la vida) a duras penas; hacer bastar o durar (provisiones, víveres, cierta suma, etc.) con economía.
EKG *abrev. de* **electrocardiogram,** electrocardiograma.
ekistics [ɪ'kɪstɪks] *s.* estudios de la planificación de ciudades y comarcas con todos sus servicios.
el [ɛl] *s.* (fam.) ferrocarril elevado.
elaborate [ɪ'læbərət] *a.* 1. detallado, esmerado. 2. trabajado. 3. complejo, complicado. —[-ˌreɪt] *v.t.* 1. elaborar, desarrollar con cuidado (plan, invención). 2. elaborar, fabricar. —*v.i.* 1. explicarse en detalle. 2. **e. (up)on,** explayarse (en un tema).
elaborately [-lɪ] *adv.* 1. detalladamente, esmeradamente. 2. en forma compleja, de un modo complicado.
elaborateness [-nəs] *s.* 1. esmero. 2. complejidad; primor, perfección.
elaboration [ɪˌlæbə'reɪʃən] *s.* elaboración, obra acabada.
elaborator [ɪ'læbəˌreɪtər, B -ə] *s.* artífice.
elaeagnaceous [ˌɛlɪˌæg'neɪʃəs] *a.* (bot.) eleagnáceo.
élan [eɪ'lɑn, B -'lɑŋ] *s.* pujanza, brío; ánimo; donaire.
eland ['ilənd] *s.* (variedad de) antílope africano.
elapid ['ɛləpəd] *s.* (zool.) elápido.
elapse [ɪ'læps] *v.i.* pasar, transcurrir, mediar (el tiempo).
elapsed time [ɪ'læpst-] duración, lapso, tiempo transcurrido.
elasmobranch [ɪ'læzməˌbræŋk] *s., a.* (ict.) elasmobranquio.
elastic [ɪ'læstɪk] *a.* 1. elástico. 2. (fig.) elástico. flexible, adaptable. —*s.* elástico.
elastically [-tɪkəlɪ] *adv.* elásticamente.
elastic chuck, (mec.) mandril de garras.
elasticity [ɪˌlæs'tɪsətɪ, B ˌɛlæs-] *s.* 1. elasticidad. 2. (fig.) elasticidad, flexibilidad, adaptabilidad. 3. (fís.) elasticidad.
elasticized [ɪ'læstəˌsaɪzd] *a.* elastizado (tejido, género, etc.).
elastin [ɪ'læstən] *s.* (bioquím.) elastina.
elastomer [-təmər, B -mə] *s.* (quím.) elastómero.
elate [ɪ'leɪt] *v.t.* exaltar; enorgullecer; regocijar, alborozar; alentar, entusiasmar.
elated [-əd] *a.* exaltado; regocijado; entusiasmado.
elater ['ɛlətər, B -ə] *s.* 1. (bot.) elátero. 2. (ento.) elatérido.
elaterin [ɪ'lætərɪn] *s.* (quím.) elaterina.
elaterite [-ˌraɪt] *s.* (min.) elaterita.
elaterium [ˌɛlə'tɪrɪəm, B -'tɪər-] *s.* (farm.) elaterio.
elation [ɪ'leɪʃən] *s.* elación, júbilo, alegría, exaltación.
E layer, (rad.) capa E (de la ionosfera).
elbow ['ɛlboʊ] *s.* 1. codo. 2. (zool.) codillo. 3. curva, recodo. 4. codo, tubo en ángulo. 5. **at one's e.,** muy cerca, a la mano; **out at elbows,** gastado, desgastado (chaqueta, abrigo); (fig.) pobre, necesitado (una persona); **to bend, crook, o lift an e.,** alzar, levantar, o empinar el codo; **to rub elbows with,** codearse con; **up to the elbows,** hasta los codos. —*v.t* 1. dar codazos a; empujar con el codo. 2. **e. one's way,** abrirse paso a codazos; **e. out,** empujar afuera (a alguien); (fig.) sacar, eliminar. —*v.i.* 1. codear. 2. formar un ángulo, dar una vuelta.
elbow-bending [-ˌbɛndɪŋ] *s.* el beber, la bebida, tragos.
elbow grease, energía física, afán.
elbow lever, (ing.) palanca ahorquillada.
elbowroom [-ˌrum, -ˌrʊm] *s.* espacio amplio, campo suficiente.
eld [ɛld] *s.* (ant., poét.) vejez, senectud; los ancianos; la antigüedad, los tiempos pasados.
elder ['ɛldər, B -də] *a.* mayor, más viejo; **the E.,** el viejo, ej., *Brueghel the E.,* Brueghel el Viejo. —*s.* 1. mayor. 2. (relig.) anciano. 3. (*pl.*) mayores, ancianos, antepasados. 4. (bot.) saúco.
elderberry [-ˌbɛrɪ] *s.* 1. baya del saúco. 2. (bot.) saúco.
elderly [-lɪ] *a.* entrado en años, de avanzada edad.
eldership ['ɛldərˌʃɪp, B -dəˌ-] *s.* (relig.) oficio de anciano.
elder statesman, ilustre estadista; estadista jubilado.
eldest [-dəst] *a.* primogénito; (el) mayor, (el) más viejo.
eldest hand, elder hand, (naipes) mano, primer jugador (a la izquierda del que reparte).
El Dorado [ˌɛldə'rɑdoʊ] El Dorado, El-dorado, comarca imaginaria abundante en riquezas, que los exploradores europeos soñaban encontrar en el Nuevo Mundo.
Eleatic [ˌɛlɪ'ætɪk] *a., s.* (filos.) 1. eleático (natural de Elea). 2. perteneciente o relativo a la escuela filosófica que floreció en Elea, Grecia antigua.
Eleaticism [-əˌsɪzəm] *s.* (filos.) eleatismo.
elec. *abrev. de* 1. **electric, electrical,** eléctrico. 2. **electrician,** electricista. 3. **electricity,** electricidad.
elecampane [ˌɛlɪˌkæm'peɪn] *s.* (bot.) helenio, énula campana, olivarda, raíz del moro, atarraga, hierba del ala.
elect [ɪ'lɛkt] *a.* 1. escogido, selecto. 2. electo. 3. (teo.) elegido. 4. **the e.,** (teo.) los elegidos. —*v.t.* 1. elegir, sacar (por medio del voto). 2. escoger, seleccionar, elegir. 3. (teo.) elegir. —*v.i.* elegir, optar por (gen. seguido por un verbo).
election [ɪ'lɛkʃən] *s.* 1. elección, selección. 2. elección, nombramiento; (pol.) elección. 3. (teo.) elección (divina), predestinación.
electioneer [ɪˌlɛkʃə'nɪr, B -'nɪə] *v.i.* solicitar votos, hacer campaña electoral.
elective [ɪ'lɛktɪv] *a.* 1. electivo. 2. elector, electoral. 3. selectivo. —*s.* curso electivo, asignatura electiva.
elective affinity, (quím.) afinidad electiva.
electively [-lɪ] *adv.* electivamente.
electiveness [-nəs] *s.* electividad.
elector [-tər, B -tə] *s.* 1. elector, votante. 2. (hist.) elector. 3. (E. U.) elector, miembro del colegio electoral.
electoral [-tərəl] *a.* electoral.
electoral college, colegio electoral.
electorate [-tərət] *s.* 1. electorado. 2. distrito electoral. 3. (hist.) electorado.
Electra [ɪ'lɛktrə] *s.* (mitol.) Electra, hija de Agamenón y hermana de Orestes.
Electra complex, (psic.) complejo de Electra (tendencia inconsciente de una hija de ser apegada al padre y hostil hacia su madre).
electress [ɪ'lɛktrəs] *s.* (hist.) electriz.
electric [ɪ'lɛktrɪk] *a.* 1. eléctrico. 2. (fig.) electrizante, excitante. —*s.* (raro) tranvía o ferrocarril eléctrico.
electrical [-trɪkəl] *a.* 1. eléctrico. 2. (fig.) electrizante, excitante.
electrical engineer, ingeniero electrotécnico.
electrical engineering, ingeniería eléctrica, electrotecnia.
electrical supplies, materiales o efectos eléctricos.
electric appliance, electrodoméstico, aparato eléctrico, objeto práctico que son electroactivado; (*pl.*) artefactcos eléctricos.
electric balance, electrómetro de balanza; puente de Wheatstone.
electric blanket, manta eléctrica, colcha térmica.
electric blue, azul acerado, azul eléctrico.
electric boiler, electrocaldera.
electric bulb, bombillo (a), bulbo, foco.
electric cable, cable conductor.
electric car, tranvía.
electric cell, pila eléctrica.
electric chair, silla eléctrica (pena capital en E.U.).
electric clock, reloj eléctrico.
electric column, (fís.) pila voltaica.
electric cooker, cocina eléctrica.
electric current, corriente eléctrica.
electric drill, taladro eléctrico.
electric drive, accionamiento eléctrico, electropropulsión.
electric eel, (ict.) anguila eléctrica, que produce descargas eléctricas.
electric eye, ojo fotoeléctrico, célula fotoeléctrica, pila fotoeléctrica, ojo mágico.
electric field, campo eléctrico.
electric fire, (G.B.) estufa eléctrica.
electric fixtures, instalación eléctrica (de lámpara, aparato, etc.).
electric furnace, horno eléctrico, electro-horno.

electric generator, generador eléctrico, dinamo.
electric guitar, guitarra eléctrica.
electric heating, calefacción eléctrica.
electrician [ɪˌlɛk'trɪʃən] *s.* electricista.
electricity [-'trɪsətɪ] *s.* electricidad.
electric light, luz eléctrica.
electric lighting, alumbrado eléctrico.
electric locomotive, (f.c.) locomotora eléctrica.
electric meter, contador eléctrico.
electric motor, motor eléctrico, electromotor.
electric needle, electrodo acicular (usado en cirugía).
electric percolator, cafetera eléctrica.
electric phonograph, electrófono.
electric power, fuerza, energía o potencia eléctrica.
electric power plant, central generadora, planta eléctrica, planta de energía.
electric ray, (ict.) raya eléctrica, torpedo, tremielga, tembladera.
electric razor, **e. shaver,** afeitadora.
electric refrigerator, nevera, refrigerador (eléctrico).
electric shock, 1. descarga eléctrica. 2. (med.) electrochoque.
electric shock treatment, (med.) tratamiento por electrochoque.
electric starter, (aut.) arranque eléctrico.
electric steel, acero de horno eléctrico.
electric strength, (elec.) resistencia dieléctrica, resistencia aisladora.
electric switch, interruptor eléctrico.
electric tape, cinta aisladora.
electric thermometer, termómetro eléctrico, pirómetro eléctrico.
electric typewriter, máquina de escribir eléctrica.
electric vane, molinete eléctrico.
electric varnish, barniz aislador.
electric wave, onda eléctrica o herziana.
electric welding, soldadura eléctrica o electrosoldadura.
electric wiring, instalación eléctrica.
electrification [ɪˌlɛktrəfə'keɪʃən] *s.* electrificación.
electrify [ɪ'lɛktrəˌfaɪ] *v.t.* (*pret., p.p.* ELECTRIFIED; *p.pr.* ELECTRIFYING) 1. electrizar. 2. electrificar (ferrocarril, máquina, fábrica, etc.). 3. (fig.) electrizar, excitar, exaltar (el ánimo).
electrifying [ɪŋ] *a.* electrizante.
electrize [ɪ'lɛktraɪz] *v.t.* electrizar.
electrizer [-ər, B -ə] *s.* electrizador.
electroacoustics [ɪˌlɛktroʊə'kustɪks] *s. pl.* (*sing. en const.*) electroacústica.
electroanalysis [-ə'næləsəs] *s.* (quím.) electroanálisis.
electrobus [ɪ'lɛktroʊˌbʌs] *s.* electrobús.
electrocapillar [ɪˌlɛktroʊ'kæpələr, B -lə] *a.* (quím.) electrocapilar.
electrocardiogram [-'kɑrdɪəˌgræm, B -'kɑd-] *s.* (med.) electrocardiograma.
electrocardiograph [-ˌgræf, B -ˌgrɑf] *s.* (med.) electrocardiógrafo.
electrocardiography [-ˌkɑrdɪ'ɑgrəfɪ, B -ˌkɑdɪ'ɔg-] *s.* (med.) electrocardiografía.
electrochemical [ɪˌlɛktroʊ'kɛmɪkəl] *a.* electroquímico.
electrochemistry [-əstrɪ] *s.* electroquímica.
electrocoagulation [-koʊˌægjə'leɪʃən] *s.* (med.) electrocoagulación.
electrocute [ɪ'lɛktrəˌkjut] *v.t.* electrocutar.
electrocution [ɪˌlɛktrə'kjuʃən] *s.* electrocución.
electrode [ɪ'lɛkˌtroʊd] *s.* (elec.) electrodo.
electrodeposit [ɪˌlɛktroʊdɪ'pɑzət, B -'pɔz-] *s.* electrodepósito. —*v.t.* depositar electrolíticamente.
electrodeposition [-ˌdɛpə'zɪʃən] *s.* electrodeposición.
electrodialysis [-daɪ'æləsəs] *s.* (quím.) electrodiálisis.
electrodynamic [-daɪ'næmɪk] *a.* electrodinámico.
electrodynamics [-ɪks] *s.* (*sing. en const.*) electrodinámica.
electrodynamometer [-ˌdaɪnə'mɑmətər, B -'mɔmɪtə] *s.* electrodinamómetro.
electroencephalogram [-ɛn'sɛfələˌgræm] *s.* (med.) electroencefalograma.
electroencephalograph [-ˌgræf, B -ˌgrɑf] *s.* (med.) electroencefalógrafo.
electroencephalography [ɪˌlɛktroʊˌɛnˌsɛfə'lɑgrəfɪ, B -'lɔg-] *s.* (med.) electroencefalografía.
electroform [ɪ'lɛktrəˌfɔrm, B -ˌfɔm] *v.t.* formar (artículos moldeados) por electrodeposición.
electroforming [-ɪŋ] *s.* (quím.) galvanoplastia.
electrograph [-ˌgræf, B -ˌgrɑf] *s.* electrógrafo, pantelégrafo.
electrogun [-ˌgʌn] *s.* (fís.) cañón de electrones.
electrokinetic [ɪˌlɛktroʊkə'nɛtɪk, B -kaɪ-] *a.* electrocinético.
electrokinetics [-ɪks] *s. pl.* (*sing. en const.*) electrocinética.
electrolier [-trə'lɪr, B -'lɪə] *s.* candelabro o araña de lámparas eléctricas.
electrolysis [-'trɑləsəs, B -'trɔl-] *s.* electrólisis.
electrolyte [ɪ'lɛktrəˌlaɪt] *s.* (quím., fís.) electrólito.
electrolytic [ɪˌlɛktrə'lɪtɪk] *a.* (quím., fís.) electrolítico.
electrolyzation [-lə'zeɪʃən, B -laɪ-] *s.* (quím., fís.) electrolización.
electrolyze [ɪ'lɛktrəˌlaɪz] *v.t.* (quím., fís.) electrolizar.
electrolyzer [-ər, B -ə] *s.* (quím., fís.) electrolizador.
electromagnet [ɪˌlɛktroʊ'mægnət] *s.* (fís.) electroimán.
electromagnetic [-ˌmæg'nɛtɪk] *a.* electromagnético.
electromagnetic field (fís.) campo electromagnético.
electromagnetic spectrum, (fís.) espectro electromagnético.
electromagnetic wave, (fís.) onda electromagnética.
electromagnetism [-'mægnəˌtɪzəm] *s.* electromagnetismo.
electromechanical [-mə'kænəkəl] *a.* electromecánico.
electromechanics [-ɪks] *s. pl.* (*sing. en const.*) electromecánica.
electrometallurgical [-ˌmɛtə'lɜrdʒɪkəl, B -'lɜdʒ-] *a.* electrometalúrgico.
electrometallurgy [-'mɛtəlˌɜrdʒɪ, B -ˌɜdʒɪ] *s.* electrometalurgia, electrosiderurgia.
electrometer [ɪˌlɛk'trɑmətər, B -'trɔmɪtə] *s.* electrómetro.
electrometric [-trə'mɛtrɪk] *a.* electrométrico.
electrometry [-'trɑmətrɪ, B -'trɔm-] *s.* electrometría.
electromotion [-trə'moʊʃən] *s.* movimiento producido por la energía eléctrica.
electromotive [-'moʊtɪv] *a.* electromotor, electromotriz.
electromotive force, fuerza electromotriz.
electromotor [-'moʊtər, B -ə] *s.* motor eléctrico, electromotor.
electron [ɪ'lɛkˌtrɑn, B -ˌtrɔn] *s.* (fís., quím.) electrón.
electron beam (fís., **rad.**) **haz electrónico.**
electron current, corriente electrónica.
electronegative [ɪˌlɛktroʊ'nɛgətɪv] *a.* (fís.) electronegativo.
electron gun, lanzador o disparador de electrones.
electronic [-'trɑnɪk, B -'trɔn-] *a.* electrónico.
electronically [-ɪkəlɪ] *adv.* electrónicamente.
electronic brain, cerebro electrónico, computador.
electronic mail, correo electrónico.
electronics [-ɪks] *s. pl.* (*sing. en const.*) electrónica.
electronic shell, (fís.) capa electrónica.
electron lens, lente electrónico.
electron microscope, microscopio electrónico.
electron multiplier, multiplicadora electrónica o fotoeléctrica.
electronography [ɪˌlɛktrə'nɑgrəfɪ, B -'nɔg-] *s.* (impr.) electronografía.
electron tube, (rad., electrón.) tubo electrónico, tubo de vacío, válvula termoiónica.
electron-volt, (fís.) electrón-voltio, voltio electrónico.
electropathic [-'pæθɪk] *a.* electroterápico.
electropathy [-'trɑpəθɪ, B -'trɔp-] *s.* electroterapia.
electrophoresis [ɪˌlɛktrəfə'risəs] *s.* (fís., quím.) electroforesia.
electrophorus [-'trɑfərəs, B -'trɔf-] *s.* (*pl.* ELECTROPHORI [-ˌraɪ]) (fís.) electróforo.
electrophysiology [-troʊˌfɪzɪ'ɑlədʒɪ, B -'ɔl-] *s.* (fís.)electrofisiología.
electroplate [ɪ'lɛktrəˌpleɪt] *v.t.* galvanizar (mediante galvanoplastia).
electroplating [-ɪŋ] *s.* galvanoplastia, electrodeposicion, electrochapeado, electroplastia.
electropositive [ɪˌlɛktroʊ'pɑzətɪv, B -'pɔz-] *a.* (fís.) electropositivo.
electropuncture [-'pʌŋktʃər, B -tʃə] *s.* (med.) electropuntura.
electrorefining [-rɪ'faɪnɪŋ] *s.* (quím.) refinación electrolítica.
electroscope [ɪ'lɛktrəˌskoʊp] *s.* electroscopio.
electroshock [-ˌʃɑk, B -ˌʃɔk] *s.* (med.) electrochoque.
electroshock therapy, terapia de electrochoque.
electrostatic [ɪˌlɛktrə'stætɪk] *a.* electrostático, electroestático.
electrostatic generator, generador electrostático.
electrostatic induction, (elec.) inducción electrostática o eléctrica.
electrostatic precipitator, (quím.) filtro eléctrico.
electrostatics [-ɪks] *s. pl.* (*sing. en cons.*) electrostática.
electrosurgery [-troʊ'sɜrdʒərɪ, B -'sɜdʒ-] *s.* (med.) electrocirugía.
electrosynthesis [-'sɪnθəsəs] *s.* electrosíntesis.
electrotechnical [-'tɛknɪkəl] *a.* electrotécnico.
electrotechnics [-nɪks] *s. pl.* (*sing. en const.*) electrotecnia.
electrotherapeutic [-ˌθɛrə'pjutɪk] **electrotherapeutical** [-ɪkəl] *a.* electroterapéutico.
electrotherapeutics [-ɪks] *s.* electroterapia.
electrotherapist [ɪˌlɛktroʊ'θɛrəpəst] *s.* electroterapeuta.
electrotherapy [-'θɛrəpɪ] *s.* (med.) electroterapia, electroterapéutica.
electrothermal [-'θɜrməl, B -'θɜməl] **electrothermic** [-mɪk] *a.* electrotérmico.
electrothermics [-mɪks] *s.* (quím.) electrotermia.
electrotonic [ɪˌlɛktrə'tɑnɪk, B -'tɔn-] *a.* (fisiol.) electrotónico.

electrotonus [-'trɑtənəs, B -'trɔt-] *s.* (fisiol.) electrotono.
electrotype [ɪ'lɛktrəˌtaɪp] *s.* electrotipo, electrotipia, galvano, plancha electrotípica o galvánica. —*v.t.* galvanotipar. —*v.i.* prestarse (bien o mal) a reproducción electrotípica.
electrotyper [-ər, B -ə] *s.* el que hace electrotipos, baños para la electrotipia.
electrotypic [ɪˌlɛktrə'tɪpɪk] *a.* electrotípico.
electrotyping [ɪ'lɛktrəˌtaɪpɪŋ] *s.* electrotipia.
electrotypy [-ˌtaɪpɪ] *s.* electrotipia.
electrovalence [ɪˌlɛktroʊ'veɪləns] əλəčɪrσ-ᵛ λəŋčʸ [-lənsɪ] *s.* (fís., quím.) electrovalencia.
electrovalent [-lənt] *s.* (quím.) electrovalente.
electrowinning [-'wɪnɪŋ] *s.* (quím.) extracción electrolítica.
electrum [ɪ'lɛktrəm] *s.* 1. (min.) electro. 2. (min.) oro argentífero. 3. (ant.) ámbar, electro.
electuary [ɪ'lɛktʃʊˌɛrɪ, B -tjʊərɪ] *s.* (fam.) electuario.
eleemosynary [ˌɛlɪ'mɑsənˌɛrɪ, B ˌɛlɪɪ'mɔsɪnərɪ] *a.* 1. limosnero, caritativo. 2. de caridad.
elegance ['ɛlɪgəns] *s.* elegancia.
elegancy [-gənsɪ] *s., var. de* **elegance.**
elegant [-gənt] *a.* 1. elegante, refinado. 2. (fam.) excelente, magnífico. —*s.* persona elegante.
elegantly [-lɪ] *adv.* elegantemente.
elegiac [ˌɛlə'dʒaɪək] *a.* 1. elegíaco. 2. triste, plañidero. —*s.* (hist.) verso, pentámetro o dístico elegíacos.
elegiacal [-əkəl] *a.* elegíaco.
elegist ['ɛlədʒəst] *s.* autor o compositor de una elegía.
elegit [ɪ'lidʒət] *s.* (der.) decreto judicial que ordena el embargo y la entrega de los efectos del demandado al demandante en garantía de una deuda.
elegize ['ɛləˌdʒaɪz] *v.t.* lamentar en una elegía; deplorar, lamentar. —*v.i.* escribir elegías.
elegy [-dʒɪ] *s.* elegía.
element ['ɛləmənt] *s.* 1. (quím.) elemento, cuerpo simple. 2. (mat., geom., fís., biol., astr., anat., elec.) elemento. 3. elemento, medio natural, ambiente. 4. (*pl.*) elementos, fuerzas de la naturaleza, agentes naturales. 5. elemento, parte, componente, ingrediente; algo, (un) grano, ej., *there was an e. of truth in what he said,* había algo (un grano) de verdad en lo que dijo. 6. (*pl.*) elementos, principios, rudimentos. 7. (relig.) (*pl.*) especies eucarísticas. 8. **the four elements,** los cuatro elementos; **the elements,** los elementos, las fuerzas naturales; **to be in (out of) one's e.,** estar en (fuera de) su elemento.
elemental [ˌɛlə'mɛntəl] *a.* 1. elemental. 2. a los elementos, ej., *e. religion, e. worship,* culto a los elementos. 3. elemental, primario, rudimentario. 4. (quím.) elemental. —*s.* espíritu, aparición.
elementally [-ɪ] *adv.* elementalmente.
elementarily [ˌɛləmɛn'tɛrəlɪ, B -'mɛntərɪlɪ] *adv.* elementalmente.
elementariness [-'mɛntərɪnəs] *s.* carácter o índole elemental, simplicidad.
elementary [-'mɛntərɪ, -trɪ] *a.* elemental, simple, rudimentario, primordial, fundamental.
elementary particle, (fís.) partícula elemental.
elementary school, escuela primaria.
elemi ['ɛləmɪ] *s.* elemí, resinas de árboles tropicales para fabricar barnices, tintas, etc.
elenchus [ɪ'lɛŋkəs] *s.* (*pl.* ELENCHI) [-ˌkaɪ-] (filos.) elenco.
eleoptene [ˌɛlɪ'ɑptin, B -'ɔp-] *s.* (quím.) eleópteno.
elephant ['ɛləfənt] *s.* (zool.) elefante.
elephant fish, (ict.) pez elefante, pez gallo, achagual.
elephant grass, (bot.) (variedad de) espadaña.
elephantiac [ˌɛlə'fæntɪˌæk] *a., s.* (med.) elefancíaco, elefantiásico.
elephantiasis [-fən'taɪəsəs] *s.* (med.) elefantiasis.
elephantine [-'fænˌtin, B -ˌtaɪn] *a.* 1. elefantino. 2. enorme, inmenso. 3. torpe, pesado, sin gracia, ej., *e. gestures,* ademanes torpes, *e. humor,* humor pesado o sin gracia.
elephant seal, (zool.) elefante marino, león marino, foca elefante.
elephant's-ear ['ɛləfəntsˌɪr, B -ˌɪə] *s.* (bot.) 1. begonia. 2. taro.
elephant's-foot [-ˌfʊt] *s.* (bot.) (variedad de) ñame de Sudáfrica.
Eleusinia [ˌɛljʊ'sɪnɪə] *s. pl.* (hist.) eleusinias (fiestas que se celebraban en Eleusis en honor de la diosa Deméter).
Eleusinian [-ɪən] *a.* eleusino.
Eleusinian mysteries, (hist.) misterios eleusinos.
elev. *abrev. de* **elevation,** elevación.
elevate ['ɛləˌveɪt] *v.t.* 1. elevar, alzar, levantar. 2. alzar (vista, voz, etc.). 3. subir (el volumen de una radio, etc.). 4. (fig.) elevar, ascender (en un empleo). 5. levantar, exaltar, ennoblecer. —*a.* (poét.) elevado.
elevated [-əd] *a.* 1. elevado, alzado. 2. (fig.) elevado, exaltado. 3. (fam.) achispado, ajumado. —*s.* (fam.) ferrocarril elevado.
elevated railroad, e. railway, ferrocarril elevado.
elevation [ˌɛlə'veɪʃən] *s.* 1. elevación, alzamiento; alza. 2. elevación, altura, altitud. 3. (fig.) elevación, exaltación. 4. elevación (de una pieza de artillería). 5. (astr., arq.) elevación. 6. **the E.,** (relig.) la elevación (de la hostia o del cáliz).
elevator ['ɛləˌveɪtər, B -ə] *s.* 1. (E.U.) ascensor. 2. elevador (de granos, tierra, etc.); montacargas. 3. silo, almacén o depósito de granos. 4. (aer.) timón de profundidad.
eleven [ɪ'lɛvən] *s.* once; (dep.) (equipo de) once (jugadores). —*a.* once.
elevenfold [-ˌfoʊld] *a.* undécuplo. —*adv.* once veces.
elevens [-ənz] əλəᵛəŋšəš [-ənzəz] *s. pl.* (fam. G.B.) refrigerio (a las once de la mañana).
eleventh [-ənθ] *a.* onceno, undécimo, onzavo; **at the e. hour,** a la hora undécima, al último momento. —*s.* 1. undécimo, onceno, onzavo. 2. once (en fechas).
elf [ɛlf] *s.* (*pl.* ELVES [ɛlvz]) 1. elfo, elfina, duende, trasgo. 2. enano. 3. diablillo, trasgo, niño travieso.
elfin ['ɛlfən] *a.* 1. de duendes; semejante a un duende. 2. (fig.) mágico, encantador. 3. travieso, chancero. —*s.* 1. duendecillo, elfo. 2. diablillo, niño travieso.
elfish [-fɪʃ] *a.* 1. parecido a un elfo, propio de un elfo. 2. travieso.
elfland ['ɛlfˌlænd] *s.* país de las hadas.
elflock [-ˌlɑk, B -ˌlɔk] *s.* (*ú. gen. en pl.*) greña (de pelo).
elf-struck [-ˌstrʌk] *a.* embrujado, hechizado.
Elgin marbles ['ɛlgən-] mármoles de Elgin (colección de antiguas esculturas atenienses en el Museo Británico).
elicit [ɪ'lɪsət] *v.t.* 1. sacar, sonsacar. 2. educir, deducir. 3. evocar, producir (recuerdos, memorias, respuesta, etc.).
elicitation [ɪˌlɪsə'teɪʃən] *s.* sonsacamiento, extracción.
elicitor [ɪ'lɪsətər, B -ə] *s.* sonsacador (de informaciones, datos, etc.).
elide [ɪ'laɪd] *v.t.* 1. omitir, suprimir; pasar por alto (vocal o sílaba en la enunciación). 2. (gram.) elidir. 3. (der., esco.) anular.
eligibility [ˌɛlɪdʒə'bɪlətɪ] *s.* elegibilidad, aceptabilidad, idoneidad, capacidad.
eligible ['ɛlɪdʒəbəl] *a.* 1. elegible. 2. aceptable, idóneo, apto. —*s.* 1. persona elegible. 2. buen partido.
eliminate [ɪ'lɪməˌneɪt] *v.t.* eliminar; excluir, suprimir, quitar; (mat., quím.) eliminar; (fisiol.) eliminar, expeler (del organismo).
elimination [ɪˌlɪmə'neɪʃən] *s.* eliminación.
eliminative [ɪ'lɪməˌneɪtɪv, B -nət-] *a.* (fisiol.) eliminador (órgano).
eliminator [-ər, B -ə] *s.* eliminador.
eliminatory [-nəˌtɔrɪ, B -tərɪ] *a.* eliminatorio.
elision [ɪ'lɪʒən] *s.* 1. (gram.) elisión. 2. (poét.) omisión de una vocal o sílaba para conservar la métrica.
elite [eɪ'lit, ɪ-, B eɪ-] *s.* 1. (ú. con *the*) la élite, lo selecto, lo mejor, lo escogido, la flor y nata. 2. élite (tipo de letra pequeña de máquina de escribir).
elixir [ɪ'lɪksər, B -sə] *s.* elíxir.
Elizabethan [ɪˌlɪzə'biθən] *a., s.* isabelino.
elk [ɛlk] *s.* (*pl.* ELK) 1. (zool.) alce, ante, anta. 2. (E.U.) uapití.
elkhound ['ɛlkˌhaʊnd] *s.* (zool.) galgo noruego.
ell [ɛl] *s.* ana (antigua medida de longitud).
ell, *s.* 1. (arq.) pabellón, ala (de un edificio). 2. cosa en forma de L. 3. **an ellshaped room,** cuarto con un recodo.
ellipse [ɪ'lɪps] *s.* (geom.) elipse.
ellipsis [ɪ'lɪpsəs] *s.* (*pl.* ELLIPSES [-ˌsiz]) 1. (gram.) elipsis. 2. (imp.) elipsis, estrellas o puntos suspensivos.
ellipsograph [-səˌgræf, B -ˌgrɑf] *s.* elipsógrafo.
ellipsoid [-ˌsɔɪd] *s.* (geom.) elipsoide.
ellipsoid [-ˌsɔɪd] **ellipsoidal** [ɪˌlɪp'sɔɪdəl] *a.* (geom.) elipsoidal.
elliptic [ɪ'lɪptɪk] **elliptical** [-tɪkəl] *a.* (geom., gram.) elíptico.
elliptically [-tɪkəlɪ] *a.* elípticamente.
ellipticity [ɪˌlɪp'tɪsətɪ] *s.* elipticidad, forma elíptica.
elliptic spring, (mec.) ballesta elíptica o doble.
elm [ɛlm] *s.* (bot.) olmo.
elm bark beetle, especie de escarabajo dañino a la corteza del olmo.
elmy ['ɛlmɪ] *a.* ulmáceo.
elocution [ˌɛlə'kjuʃən] *s.* elocución, declamación.
elocutionary [-ʃəˌnɛrɪ, B -nərɪ] *a.* declamatorio.
elocutionist [-nəst] *s.* orador, declamador, recitador.
eloign [ɪ'lɔɪn] *v.t.* (der.) trasladar, esconder (mercancías sujetas a embargo).
elongate [ɪ'lɔŋˌgeɪt, B 'ilɔŋ-] *v.t., v.i.* alargar(se); extender(se); estirar(se), prolongar(se). —*a.* alargado, extendido, estirado.
elongation [ɪˌlɔŋ'geɪʃən, ˌi-, B ˌilɔŋ-] *s.* 1. alargamiento, prolongación, extensión. 2. (astr.) elongación.
elope [ɪ'loʊp] *v.i.* 1. fugarse con un amante. 2. huir, escaparse, evadirse.
elopement [-mənt] *s.* fuga de amantes, rapto; escapada, huida.
eloquence ['ɛləkwəns] *s.* elocuencia, oratoria, facundia; (fam.) labia.
eloquent [-kwənt] *a.* elocuente.
El Salvador [ɛl'sælvəˌdɔr, B -dɔ] la república de El Salvador.

else [ɛls] *a.* otro; diferente; más; **anyone e., anybody e.,** alguien más, alguna otra persona; **anything e.,** algo más, cualquier otra cosa; **everyone e.,** todos los demás; **nobody e., no one e.,** ningún otro, nadie más; **nothing e.,** nada más; **something e.,** algo diferente, algo más; **what e. could I say?** ¿qué otra cosa (o qué más) podría decir?; **who e.?** ¿quién más? —*adv., conj.* de otro modo, de otra manera; más, además; en vez de; **nowhere e.,** en ningún otro lugar, en ninguna parte más; **or e.,** o bien, o en su lugar; de otro modo, en otro caso; o si no, ej., *you must tell me what you know, or e.,* tienes que decirme lo que sabes, o si no (sufrirás las consecuencias).

elsewhere [ˈɛlsˌhwɛr, -ˌwɛr, B -ˈwɛə, -ˈhwɛə] *adv.* en otra parte, a otra parte.

elucidate [ɪˈlusəˌdeɪt] *v.t.* elucidar, poner en claro, aclarar, dilucidar.

elucidation [ɪˌlusəˈdeɪʃən] *s.* elucidación, aclaración, dilucidación.

elucidative [ɪˈlusəˌdeɪtɪv] *a.* explicativo, aclaratorio.

elucidator [-ər, B -ə] *s.* dilucidador.

elucidatory [-dəˌtɔrɪ, B -ˌdeɪtərɪ] *a.* explicativo, aclaratorio, dilucidatorio.

elude [ɪˈlud] *v.t.* eludir, evadir, esquivar, evitar (golpe, peligro, dificultad, obligación, etc.); escapársele a uno (atención, penetración, etc.).

eludible [-əbəl] *a.* eludible, evitable.

elusion [ɪˈluʒən] *s.* 1. evasión (de un deber, obligación, problema, etc.). 2. escape, fuga.

elusive [ɪˈlusɪv] *a.* evasivo, esquivo, escurridizo.

elusively [-lɪ] *adv.* evasivamente, vagamente, esquivamente.

elusory [ɪˈlusərɪ] *a.* evasivo, esquivo.

elute [ɪˈlut] *v.t.* extraer; esp. levigar, lavar (material absorbido) por medio de un disolvente.

elution [ɪˈluʃən] *s.* levigación, limpieza por medio de un disolvente.

elutriate [ɪˈlutrɪˌeɪt] *v.t.* elutriar, purificar por medio del lavado; decantar, colar.

elutriation [ɪˌlutrɪˈeɪʃən] *s.* elutriación, levigación.

eluvial [ɪˈluvɪəl] *a.* (geol.) eluvial.

eluviation [ɪˌluvɪˈeɪʃən] *s.* (geol.) eluviación.

eluvium [ɪˈluvɪəm] *s.* (geol.) eluvio.

elver [ˈɛlvər, B -və] *s.* (ict.) angula.

elves [ɛlvz] *pl. de* **elf.**

elvish [ˈɛlvɪʃ] *var. de* **elfish.**

Elysian [ɪˈlɪʒən, B ɪˈlɪzɪən] *a.* 1. elíseo, elisio. 2. ameno, delicioso, paradisíaco.

Elysian Fields, (mitol.) Campos Elíseos.

Elysium [ɪˈlɪzɪəm] *s.* (myth.) Elíseo; (fig.) paraíso.

elytrum [ˈɛlətrəm] ɜλʏɪˈrɔŋ [-ˈtrɑn, B -ˌtrɔn] *s.* (*pl.* ELYTRA [-trə]) (ento.) élitro.

Elzevir, Elzevier [ˈɛlzəvɪr, B -vɪə] *a.* elzeviriano. —*s.* (tip.) 1. romana de Elzevir. 2. elzevirio, elzevir, perteneciente a la tradición de un antiguo estilo gráfico.

em [ɛm] *s.* (*pl.* EMS) 1. (la letra) eme. 2. (tip.) eme; pica. 3. cosa en forma de eme.

'em [əm] *pron. contr. de* **them**

emaciate [ɪˈmeɪʃɪˌeɪt, -sɪ-] *v.t.* 1. demacrar, enflaquecer. 2. empobrecer (el suelo). —*v.i.* demacrarse, enflaquecerse.

emaciated [-əd] *a.* enflaquecido, flaco, (med.) extenuado; **to be emaciated,** estar en huesos.

emaciation [ɪˌmeɪʃɪˈeɪʃən, -sɪˈeɪ-] *s.* enflaquecimiento, demacración.

E-mail [ˈimeɪl] *abrev. de* **electronic mail** , *s.* correo electrónico.

emanant [ˈɛmənənt] *a.* emanante.

emanate [ˈɛməˌneɪt] *v.i.* emanar, surgir, brotar, provenir, proceder, originarse. —*v.t.* emitir, irradiar.

emanation [ˌɛməˈneɪʃən] *s.* emanación, efluvio.

emanationism [-ʃəˌnɪzəm] *s.* (filos.) emanantismo.

emanationist [-nəst] *s.* emanantista.

emanative [ˈɛməˌneɪtɪv] *a.* emanante, relativo a la emanación.

emancipate [ɪˈmænsəˌpeɪt] *v.t.* 1. (der.) emancipar (de la tutela o patria potestad). 2. libertar, emancipar (esp. de restricciones morales, sociales, intelectuales). 3. manumitir.

emancipation [ɪˌmænsəˈpeɪʃən] *s.* emancipación; liberación; manumisión.

emancipationist [-ʃənəst] *s., a.* antiesclavista.

emancipator [ɪˈmænəsəˌpeɪtər, B -ə] *s.* emancipador; libertador.

emarginate [ɪˈmɑrdʒənət, -ˌneɪt, B ɪˈmɑdʒɪnət] **emarginated** [-əd] *a.* (bot., zool.) emarginado, sin margen, recortado.

emasculate [ɪˈmæskjəˌleɪt] *v.t.* 1. emascular, castrar, capar. 2. (fig.) castrar, afeminar, enervar. 3. (fig.) desvirtuar, mutilar (una obra literaria). — [-lət] *a.* castrado, capado; enervado, afeminado.

emasculation [ɪˌmæskjəˈleɪʃən] *s.* 1. emasculación, castración, mutilación. 2. (fig.) afeminamiento, enervación.

emasculator [ɪˈmæskjəˌleɪtər, B -ə] *s.* emasculador, castrador, capador.

emasculatory [-ləˌtɔrɪ, B -lətərɪ] *a.* emasculador.

embalm [ɪmˈbɑm] *v.t.* 1. embalsamar. 2. (fig.) preservar, conservar (recuerdo, memoria, etc.). 3. (poét.) perfumar.

embalmer [-ər, B -ə] *s.* embalsamador.

embalmment [-ˈbɑmmənt] *s.* embalsamamiento.

embank [ɪmˈbæŋk] *v.t.* represar; terraplenar.

embankment [-mənt] *s.* terraplén, malecón, dique, presa.

embargo [ɪmˈbɑrgoʊ, B ɛmˈbɑgoʊ] *s.* (*pl.* EMBARGOES) 1. (der., mar.) embargo. 2. restricción (en venta de mercancías); impedimento; prohibición. —*v.t.* embargar, detener.

embark [ɪmˈbɑrk, B -ˈbɑk] *v.t.* 1. embarcar. 2. invertir, emplear (ej., capital, dinero, etc.). —*v.i.* 1. embarcarse. 2. (con *in, upon*) aventurarse, lanzarse (en una acción política, empresa o aventura).

embarkation [ˌɛmbɑrˈkeɪʃən, B -bɑˈ-] *s.* embarco (de personas), embarque (de mercancías, etc.).

embarrass [ɪmˈbærəs] *v.t.* 1. avergonzar, desconcertar, confundir, turbar. 2. estorbar, embarazar. 3. poner en apuros económicos.

embarrassing [-ɪŋ] *a.* vergonzoso, desconcertante; embarazoso.

embarrassingly [-lɪ] *adv.* embarazosamente.

embarrassment [-mənt] *s.* 1. vergüenza, desconcierto, turbación, perplejidad, confusión. 2. embarazo, impedimento.

embassador [ɪmˈbæsədər, B -ə] *var. de* ambassador.

embassage [ˈɛmbəsɪdʒ] *s.* embajada, mensaje.

embassy [-sɪ] *s.* embajada.

embattle [ɪmˈbætəl] *v.t.* 1. formar en orden de batalla. 2. (fort.) fortificar; almenar.

embattlement [-mənt] *s.* almenaje, almenado.

embay [ɪmˈbeɪ] *v.t.* 1. (mar.) encerrar, guarecer o abrigar (una embarcación) en una bahía; obligar (el viento a una embarcación) a entrar en bahía. 2. (fig.) rodear, encerrar, cercar.

embayment [-mənt] *s.* ensenada, bahía.

embed [ɪmˈbɛd] *v.t.* (*pret., p.p.* EMBEDDED; *p.pr.* EMBEDDING) 1. embutir, incrustar, engastar; empotrar, encajar. 2 (fig.) fijar, plantar.

embedded column [-əd-] (arq.) columna embebida, columna entregada.

embellish [ɪmˈbɛlɪʃ] *v.t.* hermosear, embellecer, adornar, ornamentar; exornar (lenguaje, narración, etc.).

embellishment [-mənt] *s.* 1. embellecimiento, adornamiento. 2. embellecimiento, adorno, ornamento, ornato.

ember [ˈɛmbər, B -bə] *s.* (*gen. pl.*) ascua, brasa; pavesa.

Ember days, (relig.) témporas.

embezzle [ɪmˈbɛzəl] *v.t.* desfalcar, malversar, apropiarse ilícitamente.

embezzlement [-mənt] *s.* desfalco, peculado, malversación.

embezzler [-ˈbɛzlər, B -lə] *s.* desfalcador, malversador.

embitter [ɪmˈbɪtər, B -ə] *v.t.* 1. amargar, dar sabor amargo a. 2. (fig.) amargar, agriar el carácter de (una persona). 3. agravar, exacerbar.

emblaze [ɪmˈbleɪz] *v.t.* 1. engalanar, adornar, embellecer. 2. iluminar o alumbrar con fuego; encender. 3. (ant.) blasonar.

emblazon [-ən] *v.t.* 1. blasonar. 2. esmaltar, adornar de vivos colores. 3. (fig.) celebrar, ensalzar, enaltecer.

emblazonry [-rɪ] *s.* 1. blasón. 2. adorno o decoración brillante.

emblem [ˈɛmbləm] *s.* 1. emblema; símbolo. 2. (hist.) emblema. —*v.t.* simbolizar, representar por emblemas.

emblematic [ˌɛmbləˈmætɪk] **emblematical** [-ɪkəl] *a.* emblemático, simbólico.

emblematically [-ɪkəlɪ] *adv.* emblemáticamente, simbólicamente.

emblematicize [ɛmˌblɛˈmætəˌsaɪz] *v.t.* dar carácter emblemático; alegorizar.

emblematize [-ˈblɛməˌtaɪz] *v.t.* simbolizar, representar por emblemas.

emblement [ˈɛmbləmənt] *s.* (der.) (*gen. pl.*) frutos cultivados, frutos de la tierra; derecho del arrendatario a su cosecha.

embodiment [ɪmˈbɑdɪmənt, B -ˈbɔd-] *s.* 1. encarnación, personificación. 2. incorporación, inclusión. 3. organización en cuerpo; incorporación.

embody [-ˈbɑdɪ, B -ˈbɔdɪ] *v.t.* (*pret., p.p.* EMBODIED; *p.pr.* EMBODYING) 1. encarnar, personificar. 2. incorporar, incluir, comprender, englobar. 3. dar cuerpo o forma perceptible (a una idea, etc.). 4. organizar en cuerpo. —*v.i.* unirse formando cuerpo o masa.

embolden [ɪmˈboʊldən] *v.t.* envalentonar, animar.

embolectomy [ˌɛmbəˈlɛktəmɪ] *s.* (med.) embolectomía.

embolic [ɛmˈbɑlɪk, B -ˈbɔl-] *a.* (med.) causado por émbolo(s); embolísmico.

embolism [ˈɛmbəˌlɪzəm] *s.* 1. (astr.) embolismo, intercalación (de ciertos días, meses o años). 2. (med.) embolia. 3. (med.) émbolo.

embolismic [ˌɛmbəˈlɪzmɪk] *a.* (astr.) embolismal, ej., *e. year,* año embolismal o de trece lunaciones.

embolus [ˈɛmbələs] *s.* (*pl.* EMBOLI [-ˌlaɪ, -ˌli]) (med.) émbolo.

emboly [ˈɛmbəlɪ] *s.* (med.) embolia.

embonpoint [ˌɑnbɔnˈpwæn, B ˌɔmbɔmˈpwɛŋ] *s.* adiposidad, gordura, corpulencia.

emborder [ɛmˈbɔrdər, B -ˈbɔdə] *v.t.* enmarcar, guarnecer con marco o borde.

embosom [ɪmˈbuzəm] *v.t.* 1. abrigar, encerrar, proteger, ocultar en el seno. 2. ensenar, abrazar, acariciar.

embosomed [-əmd] *a.* rodeado, encerrado.
emboss [ɪm'bɑs, -'bɔs, B -'bɔs] *v.t.* 1. repujar, grabar o tallar en relieve. 2. adornar, embellecer.
embosser [-ər, B -ə] *s.* grabador en relieve.
embossment [-mənt] *s.* 1. relieve, repujado. 2. grabado en relieve. 3. bulto, protuberancia.
embouchure [ˌɑmbʊ'ʃʊr, B ˌɔmbʊ'ʃʊə] *s.* 1. embocadura, desembocadura (de unrío). 2. (mús.) embocadura; aplicación de los labios a la embocadura.
embow [ɪm'boʊ] *v.t.* enarcar, curvar, abovedar.
embowel [ɪm'baʊəl] *v.t.* (*pret., p.p.* EMBOWELED O EMBOWELLED; *p.pr.* EMBOWELING O EMBOWELLING) desentrañar, sacar las entrañas, destripar.
embower [ɪm'baʊər, B -'baʊə] *v.t.* emparrar, enramar; encerrar, abrigar.
embrace [ɪm'breɪs] *v.t.* 1. abrazar. 2. (fig.) adoptar, abrazar (doctrina, modo de vida, etc.). 3. (fig.) aprovecharse de (oportunidad). 4. (fig.) abarcar, abrazar, comprender. 5. sobornar, cohechar (un tribunal, etc.). —*v.i.* abrazarse. —*s.* 1. abrazo. 2. (fig.) adopción, aceptación.
embracement [-mənt] *s.* abrazo, abrazamiento.
embraceor, embracer [-'breɪsər, B -sə] *s.* 1. (der.) sobornador, cohechador. 2. el que abraza.
embracery [-sərɪ] *s.* (der.) soborno; cohecho.
embracing [-sɪŋ] *a.* abrazador (que incluye). —*s.* abarcamiento, abrazamiento.
embranchment [ɪm'bræntʃmənt, B -'brɑntʃ-] *s.* brazo (de río, etc.).
embrangle [ɪm'bræŋgəl] *v.t.* enredar, embrollar, enmarañar.
embranglement [-mənt] *s.* enredo, embrollo, complicación.
embrasure [ɪm'breɪʒər, B -ʒə] *s.* 1. (arq.) alféizar. 2. (fort.) aspillera, tronera, cañonera, saetera.
embrittle [-'brɪtəl] *v.t.* (metal.) hacer quebradizo.
embrocate ['ɛmbrəˌkeɪt] *v.t.* (med.) embrocar, humedecer y frotar una parte del cuerpo.
embrocation [ˌɛmbrə'keɪʃən] *s.* (med.) embrocación; friega, frotación.
embroider [ɪm'brɔɪdər, B -ə] *v.t.* 1. bordar, recamar. 2. (fig.) embellecer, adornar (ej., una narración); exagerar. 3. **embroidered by hand,** bordado a mano. —*v.i.* hacer bordado o labor.
embroiderer [-ərər, B -ərə] *s.* bordador, recamador.
embroidery [-ərɪ] *s.* bordado, recamado, labor.
embroidery hoop, e. frame, bastidor para bordar.
embroil [ɪm'brɔɪl] *v.t.* 1. embrollar, confundir (las cosas). 2. enredar, envolver (a alguien en dificultades, etc.), enemistar (a una persona con otra).
embroilment [-mənt] *s.* 1. embrollo, alboroto, confusión. 2. envolvimiento.
embrown [ɪm'braʊn] *v.t.* 1. obscurecer, sombrear. 2. embazar, volver amarillento (hojas, etc.). —*v.i.* obscurecerse, ponerse moreno o pardo.
embrue, *var. de* **imbrue.**
embryectomy [ˌɛmbrɪ'ɛktəmɪ] *s.* embriectomía.
embryo ['ɛmbrɪˌoʊ] *s.* (biol., bot.) embrión; **in e.,** (fig.) en embrión. —*a.* incipiente, embrionario.
embryogenesis [ˌɛmbrɪoʊ'dʒɛnəsəs] *s.* (biol.) embriogenia.
embryogenetic [-dʒə'nɛtɪk] *a.* (biol.) embriogenético.
embryogenic [-'dʒɛnɪk] *a.* (biol.) embriogénico.
embryogeny [ˌɛmbrɪ'ɑdʒənɪ, B -'ɔdʒ-] *s.* (biol.) embriogenia.
embriologic [-ə'lɑdʒɪk, B -ə'lɔdʒ-] **embriological** [-ɪkəl] *a.* embriológico.
embryologist [-'ɑlədʒəst, B -'ɔl-] *s.* embriólogo.
embryology [-dʒɪ] *s.* embriología.
embryon ['ɛmbrɪˌɑn, B -ˌɔn] *s.* embrión.
embryonal ['ɛmbrɪənəl] *a.* (biol.) embrionario, embrional.
embryonated [-əˌneɪtəd] *a.* (bot.) embrionado.
embryonic [ˌɛmbrɪ'ɑnɪk, B -'ɔn-] *a.* 1. (biol.) embrionario, embrional. 2. (bot.) embriónico. 3. (fig.) embrionario, incipiente, rudimentario.
embryonically [-ɪkəlɪ] *adv.* embrionariamente.
embryonic membrane, (biol.) membrana embrionaria.
embryophyte ['ɛmbrɪəˌfaɪt] *s.* (bot.) embriófita.
embryotic [ˌɛmbrɪ'ɑtɪk, B -'ɔt-] *a.* (fig.) embrionario, incipiente, rudimentario.
emcee ['ɛm'si] *s.* maestro de ceremonias, animador. —*v.i.* (*pret., p.p.* EMCEED; *p.pr.* EMCEEING) actuar de maestro de ceremonias.
emeer, emeerate, *var. de* **emir, emirate** .
emend [ɪ'mɛnd] *v.t.* enmendar, corregir, (esp. una obra literaria).
emendable [-əbəl] *a.* enmendable, corregible.
emendandum [ˌimɛn'dændəm] *s.* (*pl.* EMENDANDA [-də]) error por corregir (en un libro, manuscrito, etc.).
emendate ['iˌmɛnˌdeɪt] *v.t.* enmendar, corregir.
emendation [ˌimɛn'deɪʃən] *s.* enmienda, enmendación, enmendadura, corrección.
emendator ['iˌmɛnˌdeɪtər, B -ə] *s.* corrector, enmendador.
emendatory [i'mɛndəˌtɔrɪ, B -ətərɪ] *a.* enmendador; de corrección o enmienda.
emerald ['ɛmərəld] *s.* esmeralda. —*a.* de color esmeralda, esmeraldino.
Emerald Isle, Irlanda.
emerge [ɪ'mərdʒ, B ɪ'mədʒ] *v.i.* emerger, brotar, salir, surgir (del agua, etc.); (fig.) emerger, surgir.
emergence [ɪ'mərdʒəns, B ɪ'mərdʒəns] *a.* emergencia, salida, surgimiento, aparición; (bot.) emergencia, prominencia, aguijón.
emergency [-dʒənsɪ] *s.* emergencia; aprieto, apuro, situación crítica; caso de urgencia.
emergency barrage, (mil.) barrera de urgencia.
emergency brake, freno de emergencia, freno de seguridad.
emergency cells, (elec.) elementos de urgencia.
emergency exit, salida de emergencia.
emergency landing, (aer.) aterrizaje forzoso.
emergency ration, (mil.) ración de reserva, ración seca.
emergency stop, parada de emergencia.
emergent [-dʒənt] *a.* 1. emergente, saliente, naciente. 2. repentino, imprevisto.
emeritus [ɪ'mɛrətəs] *a.* emérito, jubilado. —*s.* (*pl.* EMERITI [-ˌtaɪ, -ˌti]) persona (clérigo, profesor, etc.) emérita.
emersed [ɪ'mərst, B ɪ'məst] *a.* (bot.) emergido.
emersion [ɪ'mərʒən, B ɪ'məʃən] *s.* emersión, salida; (astr.) reaparición.
emery ['ɛmərɪ] *s.* esmeril.
emery board, lima de uñas.
emery cloth, tela de esmeril.
emery grinder, esmeriladora, muela o amoladora de esmeril.
emery paper, papel de lija, papel (de) esmeril.
emery stone, piedra de esmeril.
emesis ['ɛməsɪs] *s.* (med.) vómito.
emetic [ɪ'mɛtɪk] **emetical** [-ɪkəl] *a., s.* emético, vomitivo.
emetine ['ɛməˌtin, -tɪn, B -ˌtaɪn] *s.* (quím.) emetina.
emigrant ['ɛmɪgrənt] *a.* emigrante, migratorio. —*s.* emigrante; emigrado.
emigrate ['ɛməˌgreɪt] *v.i.* emigrar, expatriarse. —*v.t.* ayudar (a alguien) a emigrar.
emigration [ˌɛmə'greɪʃən] *s.* emigración.
émigré [-'greɪ, B 'ɛmɪgreɪ] *s.* emigrado.
eminence ['ɛmənəns] *s.* 1. eminencia, altura, elevación. 2. eminencia, superioridad, distinción (social, intelectual, etc.). 3. eminencia, persona eminente. 4. **E.,** Eminencia (como título de cardenales).
eminency [-nənsɪ] *s.* eminencia, distinción.
eminent [-nənt] *a.* 1. eminente, elevado, prócer. 2. (fig.) eminente, distinguido, notable.
eminent domain, (der.) dominio eminente, dominio supremo.
eminently [-lɪ] *adv.* eminentemente.
emir, emeer [ɪ'mɪr, B ɛ'mɪə] *s.* emir, amir.
emirate [-ət, -ˌeɪt, B -rət] *s.* emirato.
emissary ['ɛməˌsɛrɪ, B -sərɪ] *s.* emisario, enviado, agente.
emissary duct, (anat.) conducto deferente.
emission [ɪ'mɪʃən] *s.* (fís., quím., med.) emisión, emanación; (com.) emisión (ej., de papel moneda); (mec.) escape, desprendimiento; (elec.) emisión (de electrones).
emission spectrum, (ópt.) espectro de emisión.
emissive [ɪ'mɪsɪv] *a.* (fís.) emisivo, emisor, de emisión o irradiación.
emissivity [ˌɛmə'sɪvətɪ, B ˌimɪ-] *s.* (fís.) emisividad.
emit [ɪ'mɪt] *v.t.* (*pret., p.p.* EMITTED; *p.pr.* EMITTING) 1. emitir, despedir (gases, luz, rayos, olor, etc.). 2. (com.) emitir, poner en circulación. 3. emitir, expresar, proferir (opinión, etc.).
emitter [-ər, B -ə] *s.* (elec., rad.) emisor.
emmenagogic [ə'mɛnəˌgɑgɪk, B ə'minəˌgɔg-] *a.* (med.) emenagogo.
emmenagogue [-ˌgɑg, B -ˌgɔg] *s.* (med.) emenagogo.
emmer ['ɛmər, B -ə] *s.* (bot.) escandia, espelta.
emmet ['ɛmɪt] *s.* (pr. dial.) hormiga.
emmetropia [ˌɛmə'troʊpɪə] *s.* emetropía.
emmetropic [-'trɑpɪk, B -'trɔp-] *a.* emétrope.
emollient [ɪ'mɑljənt, B ɪ'mɔl-] *a., s.* emoliente.
emolument [-jəmənt] *s.* emolumento, salario, retribución, estipendio.
emote [ɪ'moʊt] *v.i.* (teat., cinem.) actuar con demasiada emoción.
emotion [ɪ'moʊjən] *s.* emocion.
emotional [-əl] *a.* 1. emocional. 2. emotivo, conmovedor. 3. impresionable.
emotionalism [-ˌɪzəm] *s.* 1. sentimentalismo. 2. (sociol.) emocionalismo.
emotionality [ɪˌmoʊʃə'nælətɪ] *s.* (sociol.) emocionabilidad.
emotional life, vida afectiva.
emotionally [ɪ'moʊʃənəlɪ] *adv.* emocionalmente, en forma emocionante, con emoción.
emotional quotient (E.Q.), coeficiente emocional.
emotive [ɪ'moʊtɪv] *a.* emotivo, emocionante.
emotively [-lɪ] *adv.* emotivamente, de manera emotiva.
empale, *var. de* **impale.**
empanel [ɪm'pænəl] *v.t.* (der.) eligir, seleccionar (un jurado), inscribir (un jurado) en la lista de los jurados.
empathy ['ɛmpəθɪ] *s.* (psic.) empatía.
empennage [ˌɑmpə'nɑʒ, ˌɛm-, B ɛm'pɛnɪdʒ] *s.* (aer.) empenaje, cola (de avión).
emperor ['ɛmpərər, -prər, B -pərə, -prə] *s.* emperador.
emperor moth, (ento.) mariposa nocturna grande; pavón.

empery ['ɛmpərɪ] *s.* dominio absoluto; soberanía; imperio.
emphasis ['ɛmfəsəs] *s.* (*pl.* EMPHASES [-ˌsiz]) énfasis; acento, intensidad, fuerza, relieve.
emphasize [-ˌsaɪz] *v.t.* recalcar, destacar, hacer hincapié en, acentuar, subrayar, poner de relieve.
emphatic [ɪm'fætɪk] *a.* 1. enfático. 2. categórico, enérgico, fuerte, acentuado, marcado.
emphatically [-ɪkəlɪ] *adv.* enfáticamente.
emphysema [ˌɛmfə'simə] *s.* (med.) enfisema.
emphysematous [-'sɛmətəs, -'sim-] *a.* (med.) enfisematoso.
emphyteusis [-'tjusəs] *s.* (der.) enfiteusis.
emphyteuta [-'tjutə] *s.* (der.) enfiteuta.
emphyteutic [-tɪk] *a.* (der.) enfitéutico.
empire ['ɛmˌpaɪr, B -ˌpaɪə] *s.* imperio. —*a.* **E.**, imperio, de estilo imperio, ej., *E. furniture,* muebles de estilo imperio.
empire cloth, tela barnizada aisladora.
Empire State, (E.U.) nombre dado al estado de Nueva York.
empiric [ɛm'pɪrɪk, ɪm-] *a.* empírico. (ant.) farsante, curandero, charlatán.
empirical [-ɪkəl] *a.* empírico.
empirical formula , (quím.) fórmula empírica.
empirically [-ɪkəlɪ] *adv,* empíricamente.
empiricism [ɛm'pɪrəˌsizəm, ɪm-] *s.* empirismo.
emplace [ɪm'pleɪs] *v.t.* emplazar, situar.
emplacement [ɪm'pleɪs] *s.* emplazamiento, colocación, ubicación; (fort.) emplazamiento (del cañón).
emplane [ɪm'pleɪn, ɛm-] *v.i., var. de* **enplane.**
employ [ɪm'plɔɪ] *v.t.* 1. emplear, usar. 2. emplear, dar trabajo a. 3. **e. oneself in,** emplearse de o como, ocuparse en. —*s.* empleo, puesto, cargo, ocupación; **in the e. of,** empleado por, al servicio de.
employable [-əbəl] *a.* empleable, utilizable.
employee, employe [ɪmˌplɔɪ'i, -'plɔɪˌi, ɛm-] *s.* empleado.
employer ɪm'plɔɪər, B -ə] *s.* empleador, patrón, patrona.
employment [-mənt] *s.* 1. empleo, uso, destino. 2. empleo, contratación. 3. profesión, oficio, ocupación.
employment agency, agencia de colocaciones.
empoison [ɪm'pɔɪzən] *v.t.* 1. (fig.) ponzoñar. 2. (ant.) envenenar.
empoisonment [-mənt] *s.* (fig.) emponzoñamiento.
emporium [ɛm'pɔrɪəm] *s.* (*pl.* EMPORIUMS o EMPORIA [-rɪə]) 1. emporio. 2. almacén, tienda, bazar.
empower [ɪm'paʊər, B -ə] *v.t.* facultar, habilitar, comisionar, autorizar.
empowerment [ɛm'paʊərmənt] *s.* otorgamiento de poderes.
empress ['ɛmprəs] *s.* emperatriz.
empressement [ˌɑnprɛs'mɑn] *s.* cordialidad.
emprise [ɛm'praɪz] *s.* (ant.) empresa; aventura.
emptier ['ɛmptɪər, B -ə] *s.* vaciador, vertedor.
emptily [-təlɪ] *adv.* vacuamente.
emptiness [-tɪnəs] *s.* 1. vacío, vacuidad. 2. (fig.) futilidad.
empting [-tɪŋ] *s.* (*pl.*) (fam.) heces de la cerveza usadas como levadura.
empty ['ɛmptɪ] *a.* 1. vacío, vacuo; desocupado. 2. (fig.) vacío, ocioso. 3. (fig.) vacío, vano, frívolo. 4. falto, desprovisto (de talento, conocimientos, significado, etc.). 5. (fig.) hueco, vano, sin sentido (palabras, lenguaje, etc.). 6. ignorante. 7. hambriento. —*v.t.* (*pret., p.p.* EMPTIED; *p.pr.* EMPTYING) 1. vaciar (botella, cajón, bolsillo, etc.). 2. vaciar, verter (contenido), sacar, desalojar (muebles, animales, etc.), descargar (sacos, basura, etc.). 3. despojar (de significado, sentido, etc.). 4. **e. itself,** vaciarse; vaciar, desaguar (un río). —*v.i.* 1. vaciarse. 2. vaciar, desaguar, desembocar (un río). —*s.* (*pl.* EMPTIES) recipiente o envase vacío.
empty-handed [ˌɛmptɪ'hændəd] *a.* con las manos vacías.
empty-headed [-'hɛdəd] *a.* frívolo, necio, tonto.
emptying culvert ['ɛmptɪɪŋ-] (mar.) conducto de vaciamiento, ladrón de desagüe (de dique seco).
empurple [ɪm'pɜrpəl, B -'pɜpəl] *v.t.* purpurar, teñir de púrpura.
empyema [ˌɛmˌpaɪ'imə] *s.* (*pl.* EMPYEMATA [-mətə])(med.) empiema.
empyemic [-mɪk] *a.* (med.) empiemático.
empyreal [ˌɛmˌpaɪ'riəl, ɛm'pɪrɪ-] *a.* empíreo.
empyrean [-ən] *s.* 1. empíreo, cielo de los bienaventurados, paraíso. 2. cielo, firmamento. —*a.* empíreo.
empyreuma [ˌɛmpə'rumə] *s.* empireuma.
empyreumatic [-ˌru'mætɪk] *a.* empireumático.
emu ['imju] *s.* (orn.) emú.
emulate ['ɛmjəˌleɪt] *v.t.* emular, imitar, competir con, rivalizar con.
emulation [ˌɛmjə'leɪʃən] *s.* emulación.
emulative ['ɛmjəˌleɪtɪv, B -jʊlə-] *a.* emulador, émulo.
emulator [-ˌleɪtər, B -ə] *s.* émulo, emulador, rival.
emulgent [ɪ'mʌldʒənt] *a.* (anat.) emulgente.
emulgent vein, (anat.) vena emulgente.
emulous ['ɛmjələs] *a.* 1. émulo, emulador, rival; imitador. 2. deseoso (de fama, renombre, etc.).
emulously [-lɪ] *a.* con emulación, en competencia, a porfía.
emulsifiable [ɪ'mʌlsəˌfaɪəbəl] **emulsible** [-səbəl] *a.* emulsionable.
emulsification [ɪˌmʌlsəfə'keɪʃən] *s.* emulsionamiento.
emulsifier [ɪ'mʌlsəˌfaɪər, B -ə] *s.* 1. emulsionador, substancia emultiva. 2. emulsor, aparato para emulsionar.
emulsify [-səˌfaɪ] *v.t.* (*pret., p.p.* EMULSIFIED; *p.pr.* EMULSIFYING) emulsionar.
emulsion [-ʃən] *s.* (farm., quím., foto.) emulsión.
emulsive [-sɪv] *a.* (farm.) emulsivo.
emulsoid [-ˌsɔɪd] *s.* (quíum.) emulsoide.
emunctory [ɪ'mʌŋktərɪ] *s.* (anat.) emuntorio. —*a.* (anat.) excretorio.
en [ɛn] *s.* (*pl.* ENS) 1. (la letra) ene. 2. (tip.) ene. 3. cosa en forma de N.
enable [ɪn'eɪbəl] *v.t.* 1. habilitar, capacitar, hacer posible, permitir, facilitar, poner en situación de. 2. autorizar, facultar, permitir.
enact [ɪn'ækt] *v.t.* 1. promulgar, aprobar y sancionar (una ley); convertir en ley, poner en ejecución (una ley). 2. decretar, estatuir, establecer. 3. (teat.) representar, ejecutar. —*v.i.* (teat.) representar, ejecutar. —*v.i.* (teat.) actuar.
enactable [-əbəl] *a.* que puede ser estatuido, legalizado, decretado o representado.
enactment [-mənt] *s.* 1. promulgación, aprobación y sanción (de una ley). 2. ley, estatuto, norma, decreto.
enallage [ɛn'ælədʒɪ] *s.* (gram.) enálage.
enamel [ɪ'næməl] *s.* esmalte; (anat., fig.) esmalte. —*v.t.* (*pret., p.p.* ENAMELED o ENAMELLED; *p.pr.* ENAMELING o ENAMELLING) esmaltar.
enameler, enameller [-ər, B -ə] **enamelist, enamellist** [-əst] *s.* esmaltador.
enameling [-ɪŋ] *s.* esmaltadura, esmaltado, esmalte; charolado.
enamelware [-ˌwɛr, B -ˌwɛə] *s.* utensilios de hierro esmaltado.
enamel work, esmalte (obra u objeto).
enamor, (pr. G.B.) **enamour** [ɪn'æmər, B -ə] *v.t.* enamorar, encantar, fascinar, cautivar.
enamored, enamoured [-ərd, B -əd] *a.* (con *of* o *with*) enamorado; prendado (de).
enanthic [ɛn'ænθɪk] *a.* (quím.) enántico.
enantiomorph [ɪn'æntɪəˌmɔrf, B -ˌmɔf] *s.* (quím.) enantiomorfo.
enantiomorphic [ɪnˌæntɪə'mɔrfɪk, B -'mɔfɪk] *a.* (quím.) enantiomorfo.
enantiomorphism [-ˌfɪzəm] *s.* (quím.) enantiomorfismo.
enantiomorphus [-fəs] *a.* (quím.) enantiomorfo.
enarthrosis [ˌɛnɑr'θroʊsəs, B ˌɛnɑ'-] *s.* (anat.) enartrosis.
enate ['iˌneɪt] *s.* cognado, pariente por descendencia materna.
enation [ɪ'neɪʃən] *s.* parentesco por madre.
en bloc [ɑn'blɑk, ɛn-, B 'ɔn'blɔk] en bloque, en masa, en una pieza; por mayor.
encaenia [ɛn'sinjə] *s.* 1. (hist.) encenia, festival conmemorativo. 2. (G.B.) ceremonia conmemorativa anual (de la Universidad de Oxford).
encage [ɪn'keɪdʒ] *v.t.* enjaular.
encamp [ɪn'kæmp] *v.i., v.t.* acampar(se).
encamping [-ɪŋ] *s.* (mil.) castrametación.
encampment [-mənt] *s.* campamento, acampamento.
encapsulate [ɪn'kæpsəˌleɪt, B -sjʊ-] *v.t., v.i.* encerrar(se) en una cápsula.
encase [ɪn'keɪs] *v.t.* encajar, encajonar, encerrar; embutir.
encasement [-mənt] *s.* encierro, encajonamiento.
encastré [ɑnkæs'treɪ, B ɔn-] *a.* empotrado.
encaustic [ɛn'kɔstɪk] (pint.) *a.* encáustico. —*s.* 1. pintura al encausto. 2. encausto, encauste.
encaustic painting, pintura al encausto.
encaustic tile, azulejo de colores.
encave [ɪn'keɪv, ɛn-] *v.t.* encorvar, embodegar.
enceinte [ɑn'sænt, -'seɪnt, B -'sɛnt] *a.* (fr.) encinta, preñada, embarazada.
enceinte, *s.* (fort.) recinto, ciudadela.
encephalic [ˌɛnsə'fælɪk, B ˌɛnkə-] *a.* (anat.) encefálico.
encephalitic [ɛnˌsɛfə'lɪtɪk, B ɛnˌkɛf-] *a.* (med.) encefalítico.
encephalitis [-ˌlaɪtəs] *s.* (med.) encefalitis.
encephalogram [ɛn'sɛfələˌgræm] *s.* (med.) encefalograma.
encephalograph [-ˌgræf, B -ˌgrɑf] *s.* 1. (med.) encefalógrafo. 2. (med.) electroencefalografía, encefalograma.
encephalography [ɛnˌsɛfə'lɑgrəfɪ, B -'lɔg-] *s.* (med.) encefalografía.
encephaloma [-'loʊmə] *s.* (med.) encefaloma.
encephalomyelitis [-loʊˌmaɪə'laɪtəs] *s.* (vet.) encefalomielitis.
encephalon [ɛn'sɛfəˌlɑn, B -ˌlɔn] *s.* (*pl.* ENCEPHALA [-lə]) (anat.) encéfalo.
encephalopathy [-ˌsɛfə'lɑpəθɪ, B -'lɔp-] *s.* (med.) encefalopatía.
enchain [ɪn'tʃeɪn] *v.t.* 1. encadenar, engrillar. 2. (fig.) cautivar (atención, emociones).
enchainment [-mənt] *s.* encadenamiento.
enchant [ɪn'tʃænt, B -'tʃɑnt] *v.t.* (lit., fig.) encantar, hechizar.
enchanter [-ər, B -ə] *s.* 1. encantador, hechicero, brujo. 2. (fig.) hechizo.
enchanting [-ɪŋ] *a.* encantador, fascinante, fascinador.
enchantingly [-lɪ] *adv.* encantadoramente.
enchantment [-mənt] *s.* 1. encantamiento, hechicería, hechizo. 2. (fig.) encanto, fascinación, embeleso.

enchantress [ɪn'tʃæntrəs, B -'tʃɑn-] *s.* 1. encantadora, maga, bruja. 2. (fig.) encantadora, seductora, hechicera.
enchase [ɪn'tʃeɪs] *v.t.* 1. engastar (una piedra preciosa), montar (en un marco). 2. repujar, estampar en relieve. 3. taracear, incrustar.
enchiridion [ˌɛnkaɪ'rɪdɪən] *s.* enquiridión, manual, prontuario.
enchondroma [ˌɛnkɑn'droʊmə, B -kən-] *s.* (*pl.* ENCHONDROMATA [-mətə] ENCHONDROMAS) (med.) encondroma.
enchorial [ɛn'kɔrɪəl] *a.* peculiar de un país, demótico; endémico, indígena, autóctono.
encina [ɛn'sinə] *s.* (bot.) encina, roble (árbol y madera).
encipher [ɪn'saɪfər, B -fə] *v.t.* cifrar, poner en cifra.
encircle [ɪn'sɜrkəl, B -'sɜkəl] *v.t.* circundar, circunscribir, abrazar, rodear, cercar, circunvalar; (mil.) envolver (tropas); poner cerco a (una ciudad).
encirclement [-mənt] *s.* encerramiento, encierro, circunvalación; (mil.) envolvimiento (de tropas); cerco (puesto a una ciudad).
enclasp [ɪn'klæsp, B -'klɑsp] *v.t.* abrazar.
enclave ['ɛnˌkleɪv] *s.* 1. enclave, región o zona enclavada en territorio extranjero. 2. barrio o distrito habitado por extranjeros o destinado a un objeto especial. 3. (anat.) órgano enclavado en otro. —*v.t.* establecer o encerrar en territorio extranjero.
enclisis ['ɛŋkləsɪs] *s.* (gram.) énclisis.
enclitic [ɛn'klɪtɪk, B ɪn-] *a.* (gram.) enclítico. —*s.* enclítica.
enclose [ɪn'kloʊz] *v.t.* 1. cercar, circunvalar, circundar, encerrar. 2. incluir, adjuntar. 3. englobar, meter en. 4. **enclosed herewith,** adjunto a la presente; **our check is enclosed,** nuestro cheque va adjunto; **to e. here** (o **herewith**), remitir adjunto.
enclosure [-'kloʊʒər, B -ʒə] *s.* 1. cercamiento, encerramiento. 2. cercado, vallado, tapia, coto, cerca, recinto. 3. carta adjunta, documento adjunto, anexo.
encode [ɪn'koʊd] *v.t.* poner en código, codificar.
encomiast [ɛn'koʊmɪˌæst] *s.* encomiasta, panegirista, elogiador.
encomiastic [ɛnˌkoʊmɪ'æstɪk] *a.* encomiástico.
encomium [ɛn'koʊmɪəm] *s.* (*pl.* ENCOMIUMS o ENCOMIA [-mɪə]) encomio, elogio, alabanza encarecida.
encompass [ɪn'kʌmpəs] *v.t.* 1. circuir, circundar, cercar, rodear. 2. abarcar, incluir, contener, encuadrar. 3. envolver. 4. ejecutar, realizar, llevar a cabo. 5. **e. the globe,** dar la vuelta al mundo.
encompassment [-mənt] *s.* cercamiento; abarcamiento.
encore ['ɑnˌkɔr, B ɔŋ'kɔ] *s.* (teat.) (pedido de) repetición, bis. —*interj.* ¡que se repita! —*v.t.* (teat.) pedir la repetición de.
encounter [ɪn'kaʊntər, B -ə] *v.t.* 1. encontrar, salir al encuentro de. 2. dar, topar o tropezar con. —*s.* 1. encuentro, choque; combate, batalla. 2. encuentro, entrevista.
encourage [ɪn'kɜrɪdʒ, -'kʌrɪdʒ, B -'kʌ-] *v.t.* 1. animar, alentar, fortalecer, dar alas. 2. estimular, fomentar, ayudar, favorecer. 3. incitar, aconsejar.
encouragement [-mənt] *s.* 1. aliento, animación. 2. estimulo, incentivo, pábulo.
encouraging [-ɪŋ] *a.* animador, alentador, halagueño, favorable.
encouragingly [-lɪ] *adv.* alentadoramente.
encrimson [ɪn'krɪmzən] *v.t.* teñir de carmesí.
encrinite ['ɛnkrɪˌnaɪt] *s.* (pal.) encrinita, encrino fósil.
encroach [ɪn'kroʊtʃ] *v.i.* traspasar los límites; cometer intrusión; **e. on** (o **upon**), inmiscuirse en; invadir (territorio, posesiones, soledad, etc.); usurpar (derechos).
encroacher [-ər, B -ə] *s.* usurpador, intruso.
encroachment [-mənt] *s.* intrusión, intromisión, invasión, usurpación.
encrust [ɪn'krʌst] *v.t.* incrustar, encostrar. —*v.i.* encostrar(se).
encrustation [-ˌkrʌs'teɪʃən] *s.* incrustatación.
encumber [ɪn'kʌmbər, B -bə] *v.t.* 1. recargar, sobrecargar. 2. embarazar, estorbar, impedir. 3. gravar, afectar (con obligaciones, hipoteca, etc.). 4. (fam.) entrampar.
encumbrance [-brəns] *s.* 1. embarazo, impedimento, traba, estorbo. 2. carga, gravamen. 3. **free from encumbrances,** libre de gravamen.
encumbrancer [-brənsər, B -sə] *s.* acreedor hipotecario.
encyclic [ɪn'sɪklɪk, ɛn-] **encyclical** [-lɪkəl] *a.* circular, general. —*s.* encíclica.
encyclopedia, encyclopaedia [ɪnˌsaɪklə'pidɪə, B ɛn-] *s.* enciclopedia.
encyclopedic, encyclopaedic [-ɪk] **encyclopedical, encyclopaedical** [-ɪkəl] *a.* enciclopédico.
encyclopedism, encyclopaedism [-'piˌdɪzəm] *s.* enciclopedismo.
encyclopedist, encyclopaedist [-'pidəst] *s.* enciclopedista.
encyst [ɪn'sɪst, ɛn-] *v.t., v.i.* enquistar(se).
encystment [-mənt] **encystation** [ˌɛnˌsɪs'teɪʃən] *s.* enquistamiento.
end [ɛnd] *s.* 1. fin, final, término; muerte. 2. fin, final, extremidad, extremo, punta, cabo. 3. fin, finalidad, propósito, objeto. 4. (*pl.*) remanente, sobrante. 5. parte, fase, aspecto (de un negocio, organización, etc.), ej., *the propaganda e. of commerce,* el aspecto propagandístico del comercio. 6. **and that's the e. of it (u of the matter),** y se acabó; **at loose ends,** desocupado; **at the e. of,** al extremo de (la calle, sala, etc.); al fin de, al cabo de; **at the e. of (the week, month, year),** a fines de (la semana, del mes, del año); **e. on,** con la punta de frente; **to e.,** punta con punta, topando; **from e. to e.,** de un extremo a otro, de cabo a rabo, de punta a cabo, de principio a fin; **in the e.,** a la larga, al fin y al cabo; **no e.,** (fam.) sumamente, muy; **no e. of,** muchísimo(s), un sin fin de, la mar de; **odds and ends,** fragmentos, sobrantes, retazos; **on e.,** derecho, de pie; sin interrupción, incesantemente, ej., *it rained for weeks on e.,* llovía por semanas sin interrupción o incesantemente; seguido, consecutivo, ej., *for six days (weeks, months,* etc.) *on e.,* por seis días (semanas, meses, etc.) seguidos o consecutivos; **to be at an e.,** tocar a su fin (asunto, etc.); **to be at one's wits' e.,** no saber ya qué hacer; **to come to an e.,** terminarse, acabarse; **to gain one's ends,** lograr uno sus propósitos; **to go off the deep e.,** perder los estribos; encolerizarse; correr riesgos; **to keep one's e. up,** no aflojar, cumplir con su parte, hacer lo que a uno corresponde, defenderse; **to make an e. of,** acabar con; **to make (both) ends meet,** (poder) vivir uno de sus ingresos; **to no e.,** inútilmente, en vano; **to put an e. to,** poner fin a, poner término a; **to stand on e. (hair),** erizarse (los cabellos), ej., *his hair stood on e.,* se le erizaron los cabellos; **to the e. that,** a fin de que, para que, con objeto de que; **to what e.?** ¿a qué propósito? ¿con qué finalidad? —*v.t.* 1. terminar, finalizar, acabar. 2. marcar el fin de, concluir. 3. acabar con, ej., *a war to e. all wars,* una guerra para acabar con las guerras. —*v.i.* 1. terminar(se), acabarse, cesar. 2. terminar la vida, morir. 3. **e. by,** llegar a (hacer), concluir con (hacer); terminar por; **e. in,** terminar en; **e. up,** concluir, terminar (diciendo, haciendo); **e. up (doing),** terminar (haciendo o por hacer); **e. up in (jail,** etc.), ir a parar en, terminar en (la cárcel, etc.).
end-all ['ɛndˌɔl] *s.* conclusión definitiva, punto final.
endamage [ɪn'dæmɪdʒ] *v.t.* dañar, perjudicar.
endamoeba [ˌɛndə'mibə] *s.* (*pl.* ENDAMOEBAE, [-bi] o ENDAMOEBAS) endamoeba.
endanger [ɪn'deɪndʒər, B -dʒə] *v.t.* poner en peligro, hacer peligrar, arriesgar, comprometer.
endarch ['ɛnˌdɑrk, B -ˌdɑk] *a.* (biol.) formado o producido fuera del centro.
endbrain ['ɛndˌbreɪn] *s.* (anat.) cerebro terminal, telencéfalo.
end bulb, (anat.) bulbo terminal.
end cells, (elec.) elementos de regulacíon.
endear [ɪn'dɪər, B -'dɪə] *v.t.* hacer querer, hacer apreciar o estimar; **e. oneself to,** congraciarse con.
endearing [-ɪŋ, B -'dɪərɪŋ] *a.* cautivador, atractivo.
endearingly [-lɪ] *adv.* cariñosamente.
endearment [-'dɪrmənt, B -'dɪə-] *s.* 1. encariñamiento. 2. caricia, cariño. 3. lo que excita el cariño o afecto.
endeavor, endeavour [ɪn'dɛvər, B -ə] *v.i.* esforzarse; **e. to (do),** tratar de (hacer). —*s.* esfuerzo, empeño, intento, tentativa.
endemic [ɛn'dɛmɪk] *a.* endémico. —*s.* endemia.
endemical [-ɪkəl] *a.* endémico.
endemically [-ɪkəlɪ] *adv.* de manera endémica.
endemicity [ˌɛndə'mɪsətɪ] *s.* (med.) endemicidad.
endenizen [ɛn'dɛnəzən] *v.t.* naturalizar; franquear, hacer libre.
endermic [-'dɜrmɪk, B -'dɜmɪk] *a.* (med.) endérmico.
endgame ['ɛnd'gem] *s.* final.
end grain, contrahílo.
end hauling, transporte longitudinal.
ending ['ɛndɪŋ] *s.* 1. final, terminacíon, conclusíon. 2. (gram.) terminacíon, desinencia. 3. (mús.) coda.
endive ['ɛnˌdaɪv, B -dɪv] *s.* (bot.) escarola, endibia.
endless ['ɛndləs] *a.* 1. infinito, interminable, eterno. 2. incesante, inacabable, continuo. 3. (mec.) sin fin.
endlessly [-lɪ] *adv.* infinitamente, perpetuamente, sin cesar; sin fin.
endlong ['ɛndˌlɔŋ] *adv.* (ant.) longitudinalmente, a lo largo.
end mill, (hidr., mec.) fresa escariadora o de espiga.
endmost [-ˌmoʊst] *a.* último, extremo.
endobiotic [ˌɛndoʊbaɪ'ɑtɪk, B -'ɔt-] *a.* (bot.) endobiótico.
endoblast ['ɛndəˌblæst, B -ˌblɑst] *s.* (biol.) endoblasto.
endoblastic [ˌɛndə'blæstɪk] *a.* (biol.) endoblástico.
endocardial [ˌɛndoʊ'kɑrdɪəl, B -'kɑd-] *a.* (anat.) endocardíaco.
endocarditis [-kɑr'daɪtəs, B -kɑ'-] *s.* (med.) endocarditis.
endocardium [-'kɑrdɪəm, B -'kɑd-] *s.* (*pl.* ENDOCARDIA [-dɪə]) (anat.) endocardio.
endocarp ['ɛndəˌkɑrp, B -ˌkɑp] *s.* (bot.) endocarpio.

endocline [-ˌklaɪn] *a.* (geol.) endoclinal.
endocranium [ˌɛndoʊ'kreɪnɪəm] *s.* (*pl.* ENDOCRANIA [-nɪə]) (anat.) endocráneo.
endocrine ['ɛndəkrən, -ˌkraɪn, -ˌkrin, B -ˌkraɪn] *a.* (fisiol.) endocrino. —*s.* glándula endocrina.
endocrinic [ˌɛndə'krɪnɪk] **endocrinous** [ɛn'dɑkrənəs, B -'dɔ-] *a.* endócrino.
endocrinologist [ˌɛndəkrɪ'nɑlədʒəst, B -'nɔl-] *s.* endocrinólogo.
endocrinology [-dʒɪ] *s.* (fisiol.) endocrinología.
endoderm ['ɛndəˌdɜrm, B -ˌdɜm] *s.* (biol.) endodermo.
endodermal [ˌɛndə'dɜrməl, B -'dɜməl] **endodermic** [-mɪk] *a.* (biol.) endodérmico.
endodermis [-məs] *s.* (bot.) endodermis.
endodontia [-'dɑntʃə, B -'dɔnʃɪə] *s.* (med.) endodoncia.
endodyne ['ɛndəˌdaɪn] *a.* (rad.) autoheterodino; endodino.
endoenzyme [ˌɛndoʊ'ɛnzaɪm] **endoenzym** [-zɪm] *s.* (bioquím.) endoenzima.
endogamous [ɛn'dɑgəməs, B -'dɔg-] *a.* endogámico.
endogamy [-mɪ] *s.* endogamia.
endogen ['ɛndədʒən] *s.* (bot.) planta endógena.
endogenous [ɛn'dɑdʒənəs, B -'dɔdʒ-] *a.* (biol., bot.) endógeno.
endogenously [-lɪ] *adv.* (biol., bot.) endogénicamente.
endogeny [-nɪ] *s.* (biol.) endogénesis.
endolymph ['ɛndəˌlɪmf] *s.* (anat.) endolinfa.
endometritis [ˌɛndəmə'traɪtəs] *s.* (med.) endometritis, inflamacíon de la mucosa uterina.
endomixis [-'mɪksəs] *s.* (biol.) endomixis.
endomorph ['ɛndəˌmɔrf, B -ˌmɔf] *s.* (min.) cristal endomorfo.
endomorphic [ˌɛndə'mɔrfɪk, B -'mɔfɪk] *a.* (min., antrop.) endomórfico.
endomorphism [-ˌfɪzəm] *s.* (geol.) endomorfismo.
endomorphy ['ɛndəˌmɔrfɪ, B -ˌmɔfɪ] *s.* (min., antrop.) endomorfia.
endoparasite [ˌɛndoʊ'pærəˌsaɪt] *s.* (biol.) endoparásito.
endophyte ['ɛndəˌfaɪt] *s.* (bot.) endófito.
endoplasm [-ˌplæzəm] *s.* (biol.) endoplasma.
endopodite [ɛn'dɑpəˌdaɪt, B -'dɔp-] *s.* (zool.) endopodito.
endorse [ɪn'dɔrs, B -'dɔs] *v.t.* 1. (com.) endosar (ej., un cheque). 2. aprobar, sancionar. 3. confirmar (declaración, etc.), apoyar. 4. respaldar, hacer suyo. 5. **e. over,** transferir (bienes).
endorsee [-ˌdɔr'si, ˌɛn-, B ˌɛndɔ'-] *s.* endorsatario, endosado.
endorsement [-dɔrsmənt, B -'dɔsmənt] *s.* 1. (com.) endoso, endose. 2. aprobación, sanción, apoyo, respaldo.
endorser [-sər, B -sə] *s.* endosante.
endosarc ['ɛndəˌsɑrk, B -ˌsɑk] *s.* (biol.) endosarco, endoplasma.
endoscope [-ˌskoʊp] *s.* (med.) endoscopio.
endoscopy [ɛn'dɑskəpɪ, B -'dɔs-] *s.* (med.) endoscopia.
endoskeletal [ˌɛndoʊ'skɛlətəl] *a.* (anat., zool.) endoesquelético.
endoskeleton [-ətən] *s.* (anat., zool.) endoesqueleto, neuroesqueleto.
endosmometer [ɛnˌdɑs'mɑmətər, B -ˌdɔz'mɔmɪtə] *s.* (fís.) endosmómetro.
endosmosis [ˌɛnˌdɑs'moʊsəs, -ˌdɑz-, B -ˌdɔz-] *s.* (fisiol., fís., quím.) endosmosis.
endosmotic [-'mɑtɪk, B -'mɔt-] *a.* (fisiol., fís., quím.) endosmótico.
endosperm ['ɛndəˌspɜrm, B -ˌspɜm] *s.* (bot.) endosperma.
endospermous [ˌɛndə'spɜrmɪk, B -'spɜmɪk] *a.* (bot.) endospérmeo.
endospore ['ɛndəˌspɔr, B -ˌspɔ] *s.* (bact., bot.) endóspora.
endosporic [ˌɛndə'spɔrɪk] *a.* (bact., bot.) endospórico.
endosporous [-əs] *a.* (bot.) endosporado.
endosternite [ˌɛndoʊ'stɜrˌnaɪt, B -'stɜˌ-] *s.* (ento.) endosternito.
endosteum [ɛn'dɑstɪəm, B -'dɔs-] *s.* (*pl.* ENDOSTEA [-tɪə]) (anat.) endostio.
endostosis [ˌɛndɑs'toʊsəs, B -dɔs-] *s.* (anat.) endostosis.
endothecium [ˌɛndoʊ'θisɪəm, -ʃɪəm] *s.* (*pl.* ENDOTHECIA [-sɪə, -ʃɪə]) (bot.) endotecio.
endothelial [ˌɛndə'θilɪəl] *a.* (anat.) endotelial.
endothelioma [-ˌθilɪ'oʊmə] *s.* (*pl.* ENDOTHELIOMATA [-mətə] o ENDOTHELIOMAS) (med.) endotelioma, endotelioinoma.
endothelium [-'θilɪəm] *s.* (*pl.* ENDOTHELIA [-lɪə]) (anat.) endotelio.
endotheloid [-'θiˌlɔɪd] *a.* (anat.) endoteloide.
endotherm ['ɛndəˌθɜrm, B -ˌθɜm] *s.* animal de sangre caliente.
endothermic [ˌɛndə'θɜrmɪk, B -'θɜmɪk] *a.* (quím.) endotérmico.
endotoxic [ˌɛndoʊ'tɑksɪk, B -'tɔk-] *a.* (bact.) endotóxico.
endotoxin [-sən] *s.* (bact.) endotoxina.
endow [ɪn'daʊ] *v.t.* dotar, donar; **e. with,** (fig.) dotar de (cualidades, hermosura, etc.).
endower [-ər, B -ə] *s.* dotador.
endowment [-mənt] *s.* 1. dotación, fundación. 2. dote, prenda, talento.
endowment insurance, (seguros) póliza dotal.
endozoic [ˌɛndə'zoʊɪk] *a.* (bot.) endozoico.
endpaper ['ɛndˌpeɪpər, B -pə] *s.* (enc.) guarda.
end plate, (anat.) placa terminal.
end platform, (f.c.) andén de cabeza.
end play, (mec.) juego longitudinal.
end post, (f.c.) montante o poste extremo.
end product, producto final.
end table, mesita colocada al lado de un sofá; mesa auxiliar.
endue [ɪn'du, B -'dju] *v.t.* 1. dotar, proveer. 2. (con *with*) vestir de (ropas); (fig.) revestir de (virtudes), dotar de (cualidades). 3. investir. 4. ponerse (un vestido, etc.).
endurable [-'dʊrəbəl, B -'djʊər-] *a.* soportable, aguantable, tolerable.
endurance [-əns] *s.* aguante, resistencia, paciencia; **beyond e.,** más de lo soportable.
endure [ɪn'dʊr, B -'djʊə] *v.t.* 1. soportar, aguantar, resistir, sobrellevar. 2. sufrir, tolerar. —*v.i.* 1. perdurar, durar. 2. continuar firmemente, seguir sin rendirse.
enduring [-ɪŋ, B -'djʊər-] *a.* 1. paciente, sufrido, constante. 2. perdurable, durable, permanente. 3. resistente.
endways ['ɛndˌweɪz] **endwise** [-ˌwaɪz] *adv.* de punta, de pie; longitudinalmente; con la punta al frente, cabeza con cabeza.
end zone, (dep.) diagonal.
ENE *abrev. de* **east-northeast,** estenordeste (ENE).
enema ['ɛnəmə] *s.* (*pl.* ENEMAS) (med.) enema, lavativa, ayuda.
enemy ['ɛnəmɪ] *s.* enemigo, adversario, antagonista; **the E.,** el Enemigo, el Diablo, Satanás; la Muerte, el Tiempo.
Eneolithic [ˌɛnɪoʊ'lɪθɪk] *a.* (pal.) eneolítico.
energesis [ˌɛnər'dʒisəs, B ˌɛnə'-] *s.* (bot.) energesis.
energetic [-'dʒɛtɪk] **energetical** [-ɪkəl] *a.* 1. enérgico, vigoroso. 2. muy eficaz. 3. (fís.) energético.
energetically [-ɪkəlɪ] *adv.* 1. enérgicamente. 2. (fís.) energéticamente.
energetics [-'dʒɛtɪks] *s.* (*sing. o pl. en const.*) (fís.) energética.
energid ['ɛnərdʒɪd, B 'ɛnədʒɪd] *s.* (bot.) enérgida.
energize [-ˌdʒaɪz] *v.i.* desplegar energía; actuar con energía. —*v.t.* 1. impartir energía a, activar, vigorizar. 2. (elec.) excitar. 3. (metal.) energizar, acelerar.
energizer [-ər, B -ə] *s.* 1. (elec.) excitador. 2. (metal.) acelerador.
energumen [ˌɛnər'gjumən, B ˌɛnə'-] *s.* energúmeno, endemoniado.
energy ['ɛnərdʒɪ, B -ədʒɪ] *s.* 1. energía, vigor; tesón, carácter. 2. (fís., elec., mec.) energía, fuerza, potencia.
energy absorber, amortiguador de energía.
energy crisis, crisis de energía, crisis energética.
energy efficiency, (elec.) rendimiento de vatihoras.
energy level, (fís.) nivel de energía.
enervate ['ɛnərˌveɪt, B 'ɛnəˌ-] *v.t.* 1. enervar, debilitar, privar de fuerza, desvirtuar. 2. cortar los nervios o tendones. — [ɪ'nɜrvət, B ɪ'nɜvɪt] *a.* debilitado, enervado, endeble, falto de vigor (físico, moral, literario, artístico o mental).
enervating [-ɪŋ] *a.* enervante, debilitante.
enervation [ˌɛnər'veɪʃən, B ˌɛnə'-] *s.* enervación, debilidad.
enface [ɛn'feɪs] *v.t.* escribir, estampar, imprimir (en un billete, giro, letra, etc.).
enfant terrible [ˌɑnfɑntɛ'riblə] *s.* (**fr.**) niño insoportable, por demás inquieto y travieso; (fam.) persona embarazosa por sus imprudencias.
enfeeble [ɪn'fibəl] *v.t.* debilitar, enflaquecer.
enfeeblement [-mənt] *s.* debilidad, endeblez, enflaquecimiento, desfallecimiento.
enfeoff [ɪn'fɛf, -'fif, ɛn-] *v.t.* (der.) enfeudar; dar en vasallaje.
enfeoffment [-mənt] *s.* (der.) enfeudamiento, enfeudación.
enfetter [ɪn'fɛtər, B -ə] *v.t.* engrillar, encadenar.
enfilade ['ɛnfəˌleɪd, B ˌɛnfɪ'leɪd] *s.* (mil.) fuego o tiro de enfilada, ringlera, hilera doble. —*v.t.* 1. (mil.) enfilar. 2. disponer en doble hilera.
enflame, *var. de* **inflame.**
enfleurage [ˌɑnflɜr'ɑʒ] *s.* extracción de perfume (por absorción de las exhalaciones de las flores).
enfold [ɪn-foʊld] *v.t.* 1. envolver, arrollar. 2. abrazar.
enforce [ɪn'fɔrs, B -'fɔs] *v.t.* 1. dar fuerza a, reforzar. 2. exigir. 3. imponer, hacer valer. 4. hacer cumplir (ley, etc.), poner en vigor. 5. forzar (paso, etc.).
enforceable [-əbəl] *a.* exigible; (der.) que se puede hacer cumplir.
enforcement [-mənt] *s.* 1. imposición, coacción de una ley; (der.) ejecución. 2. acción de hacer valer (razones, etc.). 3. constreñimiento.
enforcer [-ər, B -ə] *s.* el que impone o hace cumplir una ley, disposición, etc.
enfranchise [ɪn'frænˌtʃaɪz] *v.t.* 1. libertar, manumitir (ej., a un esclavo). 2. dar franquicia a. 3. conceder derechos de sufragio, derechos políticos; (G.B.) otorgar derechos municipales a (un pueblo); dar carta de naturaleza.
enfranchisement [-tʃɪzmənt] *s.* 1. manumisión, liberación. 2. concesión de derechos de sufragio y políticos.
eng. *abrev. de* **engineer,** ingeniero (ing.).
engage [ɪn'geɪdʒ] *v.t.* 1. comprometer, empeñar (su palabra, fortuna, etc.). 2. emplear, contratar (servidor o servicios); reservar (sitio en teatro,

habitación, etc.); alquilar (un coche). 3. requerir, demandar (esfuerzo, fuerza, etc.). 4. atraer, cautivar (a personas); ocupar, tener ocupada (atención, mente, etc.). 5. librar o trabar (combate); emplear (tropas) en combate; trabar combate con (enemigo). 6. (arq.) entregar (ej., un pilar). 7. (mec.) hacer engranar, embragar. 8. **e. oneself,** comprometerse (esp. en matrimonio). —*v.i.* 1. comprometerse, dar la palabra, obligarse. 2. trabarse en combate. 3. (mec.) engranar, encajar, endentar. 4. **e. for,** garantizar; **e. in,** participar (en); meterse, ocuparse (en política, negocio, etc.).

engaged [-'geɪdʒd] *a.* 1. prometido, comprometido (esp. en matrimonio). 2. ocupado, atareado. 3. empleado, contratado. 4. (arq.) (parcialmente) empotrado, embebido. 5. (mec.) engranado, endentado, encajado. 6. **to be e. to,** estar comprometido (en matrimonio) con.

engaged column, (arq.) columna adosada, columna embebida, columna entregada.

engaged signal, señal de ocupado.

engagement [ɪn'geɪdʒmənt] *s.* 1. obligación, compromiso. 2. esponsales, compromiso. 3. cita. 4. contratación; empleo. 5. (*pl.*) (com.) obligaciones pecuniarias. 6. (mil.) acción, batalla, combate. 7. (mec.) engranaje.

engagement book, agenda de trabajo.

engagement ring, anillo, sortija de compromiso, anillo de pedida.

engaging [-ɪŋ] *a.* atractivo, cautivador (sonrisa, etc.); agraciado, gracioso, simpático (persona).

engagingly [-lɪ] *adv.* graciosamente.

engarland [ɪn'garlənd, B -'galənd] *v.t.* enguirnaldar.

engender [-'dʒɛndər, B -də] *v.t.* engendrar, procrear; (fig.) engendrar, causar, producir (celos, odio, etc.). —*v.i.* engendrarse, formarse, nacer, producirse.

engine ['ɛndʒən] *s.* 1. máquina (de vapor); motor (de combustión). 2. locomotora, máquina. 3. máquina, maquinaria (de guerra). —*v.t.* poner motor a (un barco, etc.).

engine block, (aut.) bloque del motor.

engine-driver [-'draɪvər, B -və] *s.* (G.B.) maquinista.

engineer [ˌɛndʒə'nɪr, B -'nɪə] *s.* 1. ingeniero. 2. (E.U., f.c.) maquinista; operador, mecánico. 3. (mil.) ingeniero. 4. (fig.) artífice. —*v.t.* 1. diseñar, construir o dirigir como ingeniero. 2. gestionar, manejar; guiar; planear; realizar; fraguar, tramar. 3. darse maña.

Engineer Corps, (E.U.) Cuerpo de Ingenieros del ejército o de la armada.

engineering [-ɪŋ, B -'nɪər-] *s.* 1. ingeniería; técnica. 2. manejo, dirección.

engineering alidade, alidada de topógrafo.

engineer's chain, (top.) cadena para ingenieros (de cien pies).

engineer's level, nivel de agrimensor, nivel de anteojo.

engineer's scale, (dib.) escala decimal o de ingeniero.

engine fitter, montador.

enginehouse ['ɛndʒənˌhaʊs] *s.* 1. sala o cuarto de máquinas. 2. cobertizo de locomotoras. 3. cuartel de bomberos.

engine lathe, torno corriente, torno de engranaje para roscar.

engineman [-mən] *s.* maquinista.

engine room, cámara o cuarto de máquina.

engine runner, maquinista, operador.

engird [ɪn'gɛrd, B -'gɛd] *v.t.* cercar, rodear, ceñir, circundar.

engirdle [-əl] *v.t.* circundar, cercar, encerrar en un círculo, atar con una correa o cinturón.

englacial [ɛn'gleɪʃəl] *a.* empotrado en un glaciar.

England ['ɪŋglənd] *s.* Inglaterra.

Englander [-ər, B -ə] *s.* natural de Inglaterra.

English ['ɪŋglɪʃ] *a.* inglés. —*s.* 1. inglés (idioma). 2. (E.U., billar) efecto (lateral). 3. (tip.) atanasia. 4. **in plain E.,** con palabras sencillas; **the E.,** los ingleses; **the king's E., the queen's E.,** inglés correcto. —*v.t.* 1. traducir al inglés. 2. (E.U., billar) impartir efecto a (la bola).

English bond, aparejo inglés.

English Channel, Canal de la Mancha.

English daisy, (bot.) margarita, flor de primavera, maya.

English hawthorn, (bot.) marjoleto, majoleto.

English horn, (mús.) corno inglés.

Englishism [-ˌɪzəm] *s.* 1. costumbre inglesa, peculiaridad inglesa. 2. anglicismo.

English ivy, (bot.) hiedra inglesa.

Englishman [-mən] *s.* inglés, hombre inglés.

English muffin, especie de panecillo que se sirve en rodajas y tostado.

English setter, perro perdiguero.

English shepherd, perro ovejero inglés.

English-Spanish *a.* angloespañol.

English sparrow, (orn.) gorrión.

English-speaking, angloparlante.

English springer, espaniel de aguas de raza inglesa.

English type, (impr.) atanasia.

English walnut, 1. (bot.) nogal. 2. nuez.

English white, pigmento de blanco de España.

Englishwoman [-ˌwʊmən] *s.* inglesa, mujer inglesa.

English yew, (bot.) tejo.

englut [ɪn'glʌt] *v.t.* engullir.

engorge [-'gɔrdʒ, B -'gɔdʒ] *v.t.* 1. engullir, devorar, tragar a dos carrillos. 2. hartar, atiborrar, dar un atracón a. 3. (med.) congestionar (ej., una vena). —*v.i.* atiborrarse de sangre (insectos); comer con voracidad.

engoulée, engoulé [ˌɑngʊ'leɪ, B ˌɛn-] **engouled** [-'guld] *a.* (her.) engolado.

engraft [ɪn'græft, B -'grɑft] *v.t.* (agr.) injertar; (fig.) inculcar (ej., principios); incorporar.

engraftment [-mənt] *s.* injerto.

engrail [-'greɪl] *v.t.* dentar. —*v.i.* tener o formar borde dentellado o angrelado.

engrailed [-'greɪld] *a.* angrelado.

engrain, *v.t. var. de* **ingrain.**

engram, engramme ['ɛnˌgræm] *s.* (biol., psic.) engrama.

engrave [ɪn'greɪv] *v.t.* 1. grabar, cincelar, burilar, tallar (en metal, madera o piedra). 2. imprimir con plancha(s) grabada(s). 3. (fig.) imprimir, grabar (en la memoria).

engraver [-ər, B -ə] *s.* grabador.

engraving [-ɪŋ] *s.* 1. grabado, grabación. 2. (impr.) grabado, lámina grabada; plancha, clisé. 3. grabado, estampa.

engross [ɪn'groʊs] *v.t.* 1. escribir (documento) con caracteres grandes; copiar o transcribir en forma legal, poner en limpio. 2. acaparar (mercancías, productos, etc.), absorber (tiempo, atención de una persona). 3. monopolizar (conversación).

engrosser [-ər, B -ə] *s.* 1. pendolista, calígrafo. 2. monopolista, acaparador.

engrossed [-'groʊst] *a* absorto, enfrascado, engolfado.

engrossing [-'groʊsɪŋ] *a.* fascinate, absorbente, monopolizador.

engrossment [-mənt] *s.* 1. monopolización (de pensamientos, atención, etc.), abstracción, preocupación. 2. documento caligrafiado.

engulf [ɪn'gʌlf] *v.t.* 1. sumergir, sumir, sorber, absorber. 2. (biol.) rodear (el alimento).

enhance [ɪn'hæns, B -'hɑns] *v.t.* aumentar, intensificar (placer, sabiduría, poder, etc.); incrementar; acrecentar (importancia, peligro, etc.). 2. aumentar el valor de (hacienda, etc.). 3. realzar, mejorar (apariencia, belleza, etc.). 4. (ant.) subir, alzar. 5. (comput.) (*image*) procesar.

enhanced [-'hænst] *a.* mejorado: (comput.) (*image*) procesado.

enhancement [-mənt] *s.* aumento, acrecentamiento; intensificación, realce.

enharmonic [ˌɛnhɑr'mɑnɪk, B -hɑ'mɔn-] *a.* (mús.) enarmónico.

enhearten [ɛn'hɑrtən, B -'hɑt-] *v.t.* alentar, animar.

eniac ['ɛnɪˌæk] *s.* calculador electrónico para la solución rápida de problemas matemáticos.

enigma [ɪ'nɪgmə] *s.* 1. enigma, acertijo, adivinanza. 2. enigma, persona enigmática.

enigmatic [ˌɛnɪg'mætɪk] **enigmatical** [-ɪkəl] *a.* enigmático, inexplicable, inescrutable.

enigmatically [-ɪkəlɪ] *adv.* enigmáticamente.

enigmatize [ɪ'nɪgməˌtaɪz] *v.i.* usar enigmas.

enisle [ɪn'aɪl] *v.t.* (poét.) aislar.

enjambment, enjambement [ɪn'dʒæmmənt] *s.* (poét.) encabalgamiento.

enjoin [-'dʒɔɪn] *v.t.* mandar, ordenar, prescribir, imponer; (der., esp. E.U.) prohibir, interdecir.

enjoy [ɪn'dʒɔɪ] *v.t.* 1. gozar de, disfrutar de (vacaciones, estadía, buena salud, etc.). 2. gustarle a uno (libro, película, etc.). 3. gozar, poseer (usufructo, renta). 4. gustarle a uno, gozar(se) en, complacerse en (hacer algo), ej., *he enjoys swimming,* le gusta nadar. 5. **e. one's food,** saborear (uno) la comida; **e. oneself,** deleitarse, divertirse, gozar.

enjoyable [-əbəl] *a.* deleitable, deleitoso, agradable, grato, ameno.

enjoyably [-blɪ] *adv.* agradablemente, amenamente.

enjoyment [-mənt] *s.* 1. goce, disfrute, deleite, placer. 2. uso, usufructo.

enkindle [ɪn'kɪndəl] *v.t., v.i.* encender(se), inflamar(se), arder.

enlace [ɪn'leɪs] *v.t.* 1. cercar, rodear, envolver. 2. enredar, enlazar, entrelazar, entretejer.

enlacement [-mənt] *s.* enlazamiento, enlazadura, entrelazamiento.

enlarge [ɪn'lɑrdʒ, B -'lɑdʒ] *v.t.* 1. agrandar, abultar. 2. (fig.) extender, ensanchar, expandir. 3. (foto.) ampliar. —*v.i.* 1. agrandarse, crecer, extenderse. 2. (con *on, upon*) explayarse (en), dilatarse (en).

enlargement [-mənt] *s.* 1. agrandamiento, extensión. 2. (fig.) ensanchamiento, expansión. 3. (foto.) ampliación.

enlarger [-ər, B -ə] *s.* (foto.) ampliadora.

enlighten [ɪn'laɪtən] *v.t.* 1. iluminar, instruir, ilustrar. 2. aclarar, esclarecer (la mente y el espíritu).

enlightener [-ər, B -ə] *s.* esclarecedor, instructor.

enlightenment [-mənt] *s.* 1. esclarecimiento, ilustración, instrucción. 2. **The Age of E.,** el siglo de las luces.

enlist [ɪn'lɪst] *v.i.* 1. alistarse, enrolarse, engancharse. 2. (con *in*) participar, meterse (en). —*v.t.* 1. reclutar, alistar. 2. alistar, listar, sentar en lista. 3. asegurarse, conseguir (apoyo, ayuda, etc. de personas, ciencias, fuerzas naturales).

enlisted [-əd] *a.* alistado; de recluta(s), enrolado.

enlisted man, (E.U., mil.) miembro de las fuerzas armadas sin rango de oficial.

enlistment [-mənt] *s.* alistamiento, reclutamiento.

enliven [ɪn'laɪvən] *v.t.* 1. vivificar, avivar, animar, alentar. 2. despabilar, despertar.

en masse [ɑn'mæs, ɛn-, B ɑŋ-] (fr.) en masa, en conjunto, en cuerpo.

enmesh [ɪn'mɛʃ] *v.t.* enredar, enmarañar, coger en la red.

enmity ['ɛnmətɪ] *s.* enemistad, hostilidad; aborrecimiento, antagonismo.

ennead ['ɛnɪˌæd] *s.* conjunto o serie de nueve (libros, discursos, etc.).

enneagon ['ɛnɪəˌgɑn, B -ˌægən] *s.* (geom.) eneágono.

enneagonal [ˌɛnɪ'ægənəl, B 'ɛnɪˌæ-] *a.* (geom.) eneágono.

enneasyllabic [ˌɛnɪəsɪ'læbɪk] *s.* (poét.) eneasílabo.

ennoble [ɪ'noʊbəl] *v.t.* 1. ennoblecer, hacer noble (a una persona). 2. (fig.) ennoblecer, elevar, dignificar.

ennoblement [-bəlmənt] *s.* ennoblecimiento.

ennobling [-blɪŋ] *a.* ennoblecedor. —*s.* ennoblecimiento.

ennui ['ɑn'wi] *s.* (fr.) lasitud; displicencia; aburrimiento, tedio, fastidio.

enol ['iˌnɔl] *s.* (quím.) enol.

enolic [i'nɑlɪk, B i'nɔl-] *a.* (quím.) enólico.

enological, enologist, enology, *vars. de* **oenological, oenologist, oenology.**

enormity [ɪ'nɔrmətɪ, B ɪ'nɔmə-] *s.* 1. enormidad, monstruosidad, atrocidad. 2. inmensidad, enormidad, demasía.

enormous [-məs] *a.* enorme, descomunal, inmenso, desmesurado.

enormously [-lɪ] *adv.* enormemente.

enormousness [-nəs] *s.* enormidad, inmensidad.

enostosis [ˌɛnɑs'toʊsəs, B -ɔs-] *s.* (med.) enostosis.

enough [ɪ'nʌf, ə'nʌf] *a.* Bastante, suficiente, harto. —*adv.* Bastante, harto, suficientemente; **oddly e.,** por raro que parezca, por extraño que resulte; **sure e.,** ciertamente, sin duda alguna, en efecto; **well e.,** Bastante Bien; muy Bien. —*s.* lo Bastante, lo suficiente; **e.!** Basta ya, no siga, no diga más; **e. and to spare,** de soBra, de más; **e. of this (folly, arguments,** etc.), Basta de (tonterías, argumentos, etc.); **to cry e.,** darse por vencido; **to have had e. (of),** estar harto (de); **you have done more than e.,** ha hecho Ud. demasiado.

enounce [i'naʊns] *v.t.* 1. enunciar, exponer, expresar, declarar. 2. proferir, pronunciar.

enouncement [-mənt] *s.* enunciación, declaración.

enow [ɪ'naʊ] *a., adv. forma ant. de* **enough.**

en passant [ɑnpæ'sɑn, B ɑm'pæsɑŋ] *adv.* (fr.) de paso; (ajedrez) al paso.

enplane [ɪn'pleɪn] *v.i.* tomar el avión; abordar el avión.

enquire, enquiry, *var. de* **inquire, inquiry.**

enrage [-'reɪdʒ] *v.t.* enfurecer, encolerizar, irritar.

en rapport [ɑnræ'pɔr, B -'pɔ] (fr.) en armonía.

enrapt [ɪn'ræpt] *a.* arrebatado, cautivado, arrobado, embelesado, extasiado, enajenado.

enrapture [-'ræptʃər, B -tʃə] *v.t.* arrebatar, arrobar, embelesar, extasiar.

enregister [ɪn'rɛdʒəstər, B -stə] *v.t.* registrar, inscribir, alistar.

enrich [ɪn'rɪtʃ] *v.t.* 1. enriquecer. 2. (fig.) enriquecer; adornar, embellecer. 3. (agr.) abonar, enriquecer, fertilizar.

enrichment [-mənt] *s.* (agr.) enriquecimiento, abono; (arq.) enriquecimiento.

enrobe [ɪn'roʊb] *v.t.* cubrir con un manto, vestir, abrigar.

enrockment [ən'rɑkmənt, ɛn-, B -'rɔk-] *s.* enrocamiento.

enroll, enrol [ɪn'roʊl] *v.t.* 1. alistar, empadronar, inscribir, matricular. 2. registrar. 3. envolver, enrollar. —*v.i.* alistarse, inscribirse.

enroller, enroler [-ər, B -ə] *s.* registrador, empadronador.

enrollment, enrolment [-mənt] *s.* alistamiento, empadronamiento, inscripción, matrícula; registro.

enroot [ɪn'rut] *v.t.* arraigar, implantar.

en route [ɑn'rut] *adv.* en o durante el camino; **e. r. to,** camino de, con rumbo a.

ens [ɛnz] *s.* (*pl.* ENTIA ['ɛnʃɪə]) (filos.) ente, ser.

ensanguine [ɪn'sæŋgwən] *v.t.* ensangrentar.

ensate ['ɛnˌseɪt] *a.* (bot.) ensiforme.

ensconce [ɪn'skɑns, B -'skɔns] *v.t.* 1. resguardar, proteger, esconder, ocultar. 2. acomodar, asentar, situar.

ensemble [ɑn'sɑmBəl] *s.* 1. totalidad. 2. conjunto (de músicos, de ballet, de piezas de vestido, etc.).

ensepulcher, ensepulchre [ɪn'sɛpəlkər, B -kə] *v.t.* sepultar.

ensheathe [-'ʃið] *v.t.* envainar.

enshrine [ɪn'ʃraɪn] *v.t.* 1. encerrar en un relicario. 2. (fig.) abrigar, envolver, conservar; venerar, guardar como algo precioso.

enshrinement [-mənt] *s.* conservación; veneración.

enshroud [-'ʃraʊd] *v.t.* amortajar, envolver; tapar, velar, ocultar.

ensiform ['ɛnsəˌfɔrm, B -ˌfɔm] *a.* (anat., bot., zool.) ensiforme.

ensign ['ɛnˌsaɪn, -sən] *s.* 1. enseña, estandarte, bandera, pabellón; insignia, divisa. 2. [-'ɛnsən] (mar.) alférez, subteniente. 3. (mil., ant.) abanderado, portaestandarte.

ensigncy [-sɪ] **ensignship** [-ˌʃɪp] *s.* alferazgo, alferecía.

ensilage ['ɛnsəlɪdʒ] *s.* (agr.) ensilaje.

ensile [ɛn'saɪl] *v.t.* (agr.) ensilar.

ensky [ɪn'skaɪ] *v.t.* levantar hacia el cielo; exaltar, ensalzar.

enslave [ɪn'sleɪv] *v.t.* esclavizar, avasallar.

enslavement [-mənt] *s.* esclavitud, avasallamiento, servidumbre.

enslaver [-ər, B -ə] *s.* avasallador, esclavizador.

ensnare [ɪn'snɛr, B -'snɛə] *v.t.* 1. entrampar, atrapar. 2. tender un lazo a, seducir, engañar.

ensnarl [-'snɑrl, B -'snɑl] *v.t.* enmarañar, enredar, confundir.

ensorcell, ensorcel [-'sɔrsəl, B -'sɔsəl] *v.t.* embrujar, encantar, hechizar; fascinar, arrobar, embelesar.

ensoul [-'soʊl] *v.t.* infundir alma en, animar.

ensphere [-'sfɪr, B -'sfɪə] *v.t.* encerrar, abarcar, rodear.

ensue [ɪn'su, B -'sju] *v.i.* seguirse, resultar, sobrevenir.

ensuing [-ɪŋ] *a.* 1. resultante, consecuente. 2. siguiente, próximo.

ensuingly [-lɪ] *adv.* (ant.) seguidamente, consecutivamente, después.

en suite [ɑn'swit] en serie o conjunto; en sucesión.

ensure [ɪn'ʃʊr, B -'ʃʊə] *v.t.* asegurar.

enswathe [-'swɑð, B -'sweɪð] *v.t.* envolver, enrollar; vender.

entablature [ɪn'tæblətʃər, ɛn-, B -tʃə] *s.* (arq.) entablamento, cornisamento, cornijamiento, cornijamento, cornijón.

entail [ɪn'teɪl] *v.t.* 1. acarrear, ocasionar, causar. 2. (der.) vincular, sujetar a vínculo (bienes). —*s.* (der.) vinculación, vínculo; propiedad sujeta a vínculo.

entailment [-mənt] *s.* (der.) vinculación.

entangle [ɪn'tæŋgəl] *v.t.* enredar, embrollar, intrincar, enmarañar.

entanglement [-mənt] *s.* 1. enredo, embrollo, maraña, enmarañamiento. 2. (mil.) alambrada.

entangler [-glər, B -glə] *s.* enredador, embrollador.

entasis ['ɛntəsɪs] *s.* (arq.) éntasis.

enté ['ɛnteɪ] *a.* (her.) entado.

entelechy [ɛn'tɛləkɪ] *s.* (filos.) entelequia.

entente [ɑn'tɑnt] *s.* convenio, acuerdo, pacto, entente; alianza.

enter ['ɛntər, B -ə] *v.i.* 1. entrar. 2. (teat.) entrar, salir a escena. 3. **e. into,** entrar en o a; participar en, formar parte de; celebrar (ej., un contrato); **e. on (o upon),** comenzar, emprender; tomar posesión de. —*v.t.* 1. entrar en o a (cuarto, etc.). 2. entrar en o a, introducirse en, penetrar. 3. (fig.) entrar en o a, tomar parte en, participar en (conversación, concurso, negocio, conspiración, etc.); afiliarse, hacerse miembro de (un club, etc.); entrar en, abrazar (una profesión, carrera, etc.). 4. matricular, inscribir. 5. registrar, anotar, asentar; poner, publicar (anuncio en periódico). 6. presentar (petición, reclamo, etc.). 7. (com.) declarar, aduanar. 8. (ten.) asentar. 9. (mil.) entrar (ciudad, fortaleza, etc.). 10. (crim.) allanar (Chile). 11. **e. an order,** (com.) asentar un pedido; **e. a protest,** elevar una protesta; dejar constancia de una protesta; **e. one's head,** cruzar la mente a uno, ocurrírsele a uno.

enteral ['ɛntərəl] *a.* (med.) enteral, entérico.

enteralgia [ˌɛntə'rældʒɪə] *s.* (med.) enteralgia.

enteric [ɛn'tɛrɪk] *a.* (med.) entérico, intestinal.

enteric fever, (med.) fiebre entérica, fiebre tifoidea.

entering ['ɛntərɪŋ] *a.* que entra, de entrada. —*s.* allanamiento (Chile).

entering edge, (aer.) borde de ataque.

entering wedge, (fig.) primer paso; operación que abre camino o prepara el terreno.

enteritidis [ˌɛntə'rɪtədəs] *s.* (vet.) enteritis.

enteritis [-'raɪtəs] *s.* (med.) enteritis.

enterococcus [-roʊ'kɑkəs, B -'kɔk-] *s.* (*pl.* ENTEROCOCCI [-'kɑkaɪ, -i, B -'kɔk-]) (med.) enterococo.

enterocoele, enterocoel ['ɛntəroʊˌsil] *s.* (med.) enterocelo.

enterocoelic [ˌɛntəroʊ'silɪk] *a.* (med.) enterocelíaco.

enterocolitis [-kə'laɪtəs] *s.* (med.) enterocolitis.

enterogastrone [-'gæstroʊn] *s.* (fisiol.) enterogastrona.

enterohepatitis [-ˌhɛpə'taɪtəs] *s.* (vet.) enterohepatitis.

enterokinase [-'kɪnˌeɪs, -'kaɪn, B -ˌeɪz] *s.* (fisiol.) enteroquinasa, enterocinasa.

enterologist [-'rɑlədʒɪst, B -'rɔl-] *s.* enterólogo.

enterology [-dʒɪ] *s.* enterología.

enteron ['ɛntəˌrɑn, B -ˌrɔn] *s.* (anat.) canal intestinal.

enterostomy [ˌɛntə'rɑstəmɪ, B -'rɔs-] *s.* (med.) enterostomía.

enterprise ['ɛntərˌpraɪz, B -təˌ-] *s.* 1. empresa, proyecto; aventura; arresto, carácter emprendedor. 2. resolución, iniciativa. 3. empresa, sociedad (comercial o industrial).

enterpriser [-ˌpraɪzər, B -zə] *s.* empresario; hombre de empresa.

enterprising [-zɪŋ] *a.* emprendedor, acometedor, decidido, esforzado.

entertain [ˌɛntər'teɪn, B -tə'-] *v.t.* 1. agasajar, hospedar. 2. entretener, divertir, distraer. 3. abrigar, acariciar (idea, esperanza, etc.). —*v.i.* dar comidas o fiestas, invitar, recibir invitados.

entertainer [ˌɛntər'teɪnər, B ˌɛntə'-ə] *s.* 1. anfitrión, festejador, animador. 2. artista, actor de variedades.
entertaining [-ɪŋ] *a.* entretenido, divertido, gracioso, jovial.
entertainingly [-ɪŋlɪ] *adv.* entretenidamente, divertidamente.
entertainment [-mənt] *s.* 1. recibimiento, hospitalidad; agasajo, festín. 2. entretenimiento, diversión. 3. espectáculo, función. 4. consideración, contemplación (de una idea, propuesta, etc.).
entertainment allowance, gastos de representación.
entertainment guide, agenda cultural.
enthalpy ['ɛnˌθælpɪ, ɛn'θæl-] *s.* (fís.) entalpia, contenido de calor.
enthetic [ɛn'θɛtɪk] *a.* (med.) entético.
enthrall, enthral [ɪn'θrɔl] *v.t.* 1. (ant.) esclavizar, subyugar, avasallar. 2. cautivar, encantar, hechizar.
enthrallment, enthralment [-mənt] *s.* 1. subyugación, sometimiento. 2. encantamiento, hechizo.
enthrone [ɪn'θroʊn] *v.t.* (lit., fig.) entronar, entronizar.
enthronement [-mənt] *s.* entronización.
enthuse [ɪn'θuz, B -'θjuz] *v.t.* (fam.) entusiasmar. —*v.i.* entusiasmarse; hablar con entusiasmo.
enthusiasm [-'θuzɪˌæzəm, B -'θju-] *s.* 1. entusiasmo, fervor. 2. (ant.) fanatismo religioso.
enthusiast [-ˌæst] *s.* entusiasta; fanático.
enthusiastic [-ˌθuzɪ'æstɪk, B -ˌθju-] *a.* entusiasta, entusiástico; caluroso; entusiasmado.
enthymematic [ˌɛnθəmə'mætɪk] **enthymematical** [-ɪkəl] *a.* (lóg.) entimemático.
enthymeme ['ɛnθəˌmim] *s.* (lóg.) entimema.
entice [ɪn'taɪs] *v.t.* atraer, tentar, seducir; halagar; engatusar (fam.).
enticement [-mənt] *s.* 1. tentación, incitación, seducción. 2. aliciente, atractivo, añagaza.
enticer [-ər, B -ə] *s.* tentador, seductor, incitador.
enticing [-ɪŋ] *a.* tentador, incitador, seductor.
enticingly [-ɪŋlɪ] *adv.* seductoramente, tentadoramente.
entire [ɪn'taɪr, ɛn-, B -'taɪə] *a.* 1. entero, completo, cabal; intacto, total, íntegro; continuo, indiviso. 2. (bot.) entero, liso (díc. de las hojas). 3. (zool.) no castrado. —*s.* 1. caballo semental. 2. (ant.) todo, totalidad.
entirely [-lɪ] *adv.* 1. enteramente, completamente, totalmente, del todo, por completo. 2. únicamente, exclusivamente, ej. *it's my mistake e.,* es exclusivamente mi error, el error es únicamente mío.
entireness [-nəs] *s.* totalidad, estado o condición de entero.
entirety [-'taɪrətɪ, B -'taɪər-] *s.* totalidad, suma total; **in its e.,** íntegramente, enteramente.
entitle [ɪn'taɪtəl] *v.t.* 1. intitular, titular. 2. dar derecho a, tener derecho a, habilitar, autorizar; calificar, acreditar.
entitlement [-mɛnt] *s.* derecho, autorización; (before *s*) *(program)* de ayuda social.
entity ['ɛntətɪ] *s.* entidad; ente, ser.
entoblast ['ɛntəˌblæst, B -ˌblɑst] *s.* (biol.) endoblasto, entoblasto.
entoderm [-ˌdɜrm, B -ˌdɜm] *s.* (biol.) endodermo.
entoil [ɪn'tɔɪl] *v.t.* (ant.) entrampar, enmarañar.
entomb [ɪn'tum] *v.t.* sepultar, enterrar.
entombment [-mənt] *s.* sepultura, entierro.
entomogenous [ɛntə'mɑdʒənəs, B -'mɔdʒ-] *a.* (bot.) que crece en el cuerpo de los insectos.

entomologic [ˌɛntəmə'lɑdʒɪk, B -'lɔdʒ-] **entomological** [-ɪkəl] *a.* entomológico.
entomologically [-ɪkəlɪ] *adv.* entomológicamente.
entomologist [-'mɑlədʒəst, B -'mɔl-] *s.* entomólogo.
entomologize [-ˌdʒaɪz] *v.i.* estudiar entomología; coleccionar insectos (para estudio).
entomology [-dʒɪ] *s.* entomología.
entomophagous [-'mɑfəgəs, B -'mɔf-] *a.* (bot., zool.) entomófago, insectívoro.
entomophilous [-'mɑfələs, B -'mɔf-] *a.* (bot.) entomófilo.
entomophily [-əlɪ] *s.* entomofilia.
entomostracan [-'mɑstrɪkən, B -'mɔs-] *a., s.* (zool.) entomostráceo.
entophyte ['ɛntəˌfaɪt] *s.* (bot.) endófito.
entoproct [-ˌprɑkt, B -ˌprɔkt] *s.* (zool.) entoprocto.
entourage [ˌɑntʊ'rɑʒ, B ˌɔn-] *s.* (fr.) 1. séquito, cortejo; acompañantes. 2. (ant.) medio ambiente, alrededores.
entozoa [ˌɛntə'zoʊə] *s., pl.* (zool.) entozoos, entozoarios, endoparásitos.
entozoal [-'zoʊəl] *a.* (zool.) entozoico.
entozoan [-ən] *s.* (zool.) entozoario, endoparásito.
entozoic [-'zoʊɪk] *a.* (zool.) entozoico.
entr'acte ['ɑnˌtrækt, B 'ɔn-] *s.* (teat.) entreacto, intermedio.
entrails ['ɛnˌtreɪlz, -trəlz, B -treɪlz] *s. pl.* entrañas, vísceras, tripas, intestinos.
entrain [ɪn'treɪn] *v.t.* 1. embarcar (esp. tropas) en tren, subir a un tren, tomar el tren. 2. (quím.) transportar un líquido en suspensión por medio de la evaporación y destilación. —*v.i.* ir en tren.
entrained air, (const.) aire arrastrado, aire retenido.
entrainment [-'treɪnmənt] *s.* (hidr.) arrastre.
entrance ['ɛntrəns] *s.* 1. entrada, ingreso. 2. admisión, permiso de entrada. 3. entrada, puerta, acceso, paso. 4. (teat.) salida (de un actor) a escena. 5. (mús.) entrada. 6. **no e.,** se prohíbe la entrada.
entrance [ɪn'træns, B -'trɑns] *v.t.* 1. embelesar, fascinar, extasiar. 2. poner en estado hipnótico.
entrance examination ['ɛntrəns-] examen de ingreso, examen de admisión.
entrance fee, derechos de admisión.
entrancement [ɪn'trænsmənt, B -'trɑns-] *s.* 1. embelesamiento, embeleso. 2. estado hipnótico.
entrancing [-ɪŋ] *a.* embelesador, encantador, fascinador.
entrant ['ɛntrənt] *s.* 1. entrante. 2. participante, concursante, postulante.
entrap [ɪn'træp] *v.t.* 1. entrampar, atrapar; *(trick, deceive)* hacer caer en la trampa. 2. (der.) incitar a la comisión de un delito.
entrapment [-mɛnt] *s.* (der.) incitación por agentes de la ley a la comisión de un delito.
entreat [ɪn'trit] *v.t.* suplicar, implorar, rogar, pedir, instar. —*v.i.* hacer una súplica, pedir un favor.
entreatingly [-ɪŋlɪ] *adv.* suplicantemente.
entreaty [-ɪ] *s.* súplica, petición, ruego, instancia.
entre côte [ˌɑntrə'koʊt, B 'ɔntrəkoʊt] (fr., cocina) bistec de costilla.
entrée ['ɑntreɪ, B 'ɔn-] *s.* 1. entrada, ingreso. 2. (libre) acceso. 3. (cocina) plato principal.
entremets ['ɑntrəˌmeɪ, B 'ɔn-] *s. pl.* (*sing. o pl. en const.*) (cocina) entremés.
entrench [ɪn'trɛntʃ] *v.t.* 1. atrincherar, proteger con trincheras. 2. (fig.) afianzar, arraigar. 3. **e. oneself,** atrincherarse. —*v.i.* 1. atrincherarse. 2. (con *on* o *upon*) invadir, infringir.

entrenchment [-mənt] *s.* atrincheramiento, trinchera, parapeto de tierra.
entrepôt ['ɑntrəˌpoʊ, B 'ɔn-] *s.* almacén; centro comercial o de distribución.
entrepreneur [ˌɑntrəprə'nɜr, B ˌɔn-'nɜ] *s.* empresario, contratista.
entresol ['ɛntərˌsɑl, -trə-, B 'ɔntrəˌsɔl] *s.* entresuelo.
entropion [ɛn'troʊpɪˌɑn, B -ən] *s.* (med.) entropión, inversión de los párpados.
entropy ['ɛntrəpɪ] *s.* (fís.) entropía.
entrust [ɪn'trʌst] *v.t.* encargar, encomendar, recomendar; **e. to,** confiar a; **e. (someone) with (something),** confiar o encargar (algo) a (alguien).
entry ['ɛntrɪ] *s.* 1. entrada, ingreso. 2. acceso, admisión, paso. 3. entrada, vestíbulo, portal. 4. anotación, registro; ítem. 5. vocablo, artículo (en un diccionario, etc.). 6. concursante. 7. (der.) toma de posesión; allanamiento (de morada). 8. (ten.) asiento, partida, ej., *double e. bookkeeping,* teneduría de libros por partida doble. 9. (mar.) entrada, declaración (a la aduana.).
entwine [ɪn'twaɪn] *v.t.* entrelazar, entretejer.
entwist [ɪn'twɪst] *v.t.* enrollar, trenzar, enroscar.
enucleate [ɪ'nuklɪˌeɪt, B ɪ'nju-] *v.t.* 1. (cir.) enuclear, extirpar (un tumor, etc.). 2. (biol.) privar del núcleo. 3. (ant.) aclarar, explicar. —*a.* sin núcleo.
enucleation [ɪˌnuklɪ'eɪʃən, B ɪˌnju-] *s.* (med.) enucleación.
enumerable [ɪ'numərəbəl, B ɪ'nju-] *a.* enumerable.
enumerate [-ˌreɪt] *v.t.* 1. enumerar. 2. contar, numerar.
enumeration [ɪˌnumə'reɪʃən, B ɪˌnju-] *s.* 1. enumeración. 2. recuento, cómputo o relación numeral, censo. 3. (ret.) recapitulación.
enumerative [ɪ'numəˌreɪtɪv, B ɪˌnumərətɪv] *a.* enumerativo.
enumerator [-ˌreɪtər, B -ə] *s.* empadronador, enumerador.
enunciable [ɪ'nʌnsɪəbəl, B -ʃɪ-] *a.* enunciable.
enunciate [-sɪˌeɪt] *v.t.* 1. enunciar, declarar, proclamar. 2. pronunciar, articular.
enunciation [ɪˌnʌnsɪ'eɪʃən] *s.* 1. enunciación, manifiesto, declaración. 2. pronunciación, articulación.
enunciative [ɪ'nʌnsɪˌeɪtɪv, B -ʃɪətɪv] *a.* enunciativo, declarativo.
enunciator [-sɪˌeɪtər, B -ə] *s.* declarador; portavoz, vocero.
enure, *var. de* **inure.**
enuresis [ˌɛnjʊ'risəs] *s.* (med.) enuresis.
envelop [ɪn'vɛləp] *v.t.* envolver, rodear; cubrir, esconder; (mil.) envolver (al enemigo).
envelope ['ɛnvəˌloʊp, 'ɑn-, B 'ɛn-] *s.* 1. sobre, cubierta. 2. envoltura, capa. 3. (bot., zool.) túnica, envoltura. 4. (mat., aer.) envolvente. 5. (astr.) nebulosa alrededor del núcleo de un cometa. 6. (rad.) ampolla de válvula.
envelope distortion, (rad.) deformación del envolvente.
envelopment [ɪn'vɛləpmənt] *s.* envolvimiento.
envenom [ɪn'vɛnəm] *v.t.* (lit., fig.) envenenar, emponzoñar.
enviable ['ɛnvɪəbəl] *a.* envidiable.
enviably [-blɪ] *adv.* envidiablemente.
envier [-ər, B -ə] *s.* envidioso.
envious [-əs] *a.* envidioso.
enviously [-lɪ] *adv.* envidiosamente.
enviousness [-nəs] *s.* envidia.
environ [ɪn'vaɪrən, B -'vaɪərən] *v.t.* rodear, envolver; circundar, cercar; sitiar.

environment [-mənt] *s.* 1. medio ambiente, ambiente; cercanía. 2. circunstancias, condiciones externas.
environmental [ɪn,vaɪrən'mɛntəl B -,vaɪərən-] *a.* ambiental.
environs [ɪn'vaɪrənz, B 'ɛnvirənz] *s. pl.* alrededores, cercanías, inmediaciones; afueras, suburbios.
envisage [ɪn'vɪzɪdʒ] *v.t.* 1. contemplar, considerar. 2. concebir, imaginar, visualizar.
envision [-'vɪʒən] *v.t.* imaginar, prever.
envoi, envoy ['ɛnvɔɪ, 'ɑn-, B 'ɛn-] *s.* (poét.) tornada, envío (en un poema); post scriptum (de un ensayo o libro).
envoy, *s.* 1. enviado, mensajero. 2. agente o representante diplomático.
envy ['ɛnvɪ] *s.* 1. envidia. 2. persona o cosa más envidiada, ej., *his new car is the e. of the neighborhood,* su automóvil nuevo es la envidia de la vecindad. —*v.t.* (*pret. p.p.* ENVIED; *p.pr.* ENVYING) envidiar. —*v.i.* tener o mostrar envidia.
envyingly [-ɪŋlɪ] *adv.* envidiosamente.
enwind [ɪn'waɪnd] *v.t.* enrollar.
enwomb [ɪn'wum] *v.t.* (fig.) sepultar o esconder.
enwrap [ɪn'ræp] *v.t.* 1. envolver, rodear. 2. (fig.) absorber (atención, pensamiento).
enwreathe [ɪn'rið] *v.t.* enguirnaldar; entrelazar.
enzootic [,ɛnzoʊ'ɑtɪk, B -'ɔtɪk] (vet.) *a.* enzoótico. —*s.* enzootia.
enzygotic [,ɛnzaɪ'gɑtɪk, B -'gɔt-] *a.* encigótico, del mismo óvulo (gemelos).
enzymatic [-'mætɪk] **enzymic** [ɛn'zaɪmɪk] *a.* (quím.) enzimático.
enzyme ['ɛnzaɪm] *s.* (quím.) enzima.
enzymologist [,ɛnzaɪ'mɑlədʒəst, B -'mɔl-] *s.* especialista en enzimología.
enzymology [-dʒɪ] *s.* (quím.) enzimología.
Eocene ['iə,sin] *a., s.* (geol.) eoceno.
eohippus [,ioʊ'hɪpəs] *s.* (pal.) eohippus.
Eolian, Eolic, eonian, *vars. de* **Aeolian, Aeolic, aeonian.**
eolipile [i'ɑlə,paɪl, B -'ɔl-] *var. of* **aeolipile,** (fís.) eolípila.
eolith ['iəlɪθ] *s.* (arqueol.) eolito.
eolithic [,iə'lɪθɪk] *a.* (geol.) eolítico.
eon ['iən, 'i,ɑn, B 'iən, 'i,ɔn] *var. de* **aeon,** eón.
eosin ['iəsən] ɘɔɘ̃ɪŋɘ [-sən, B -sin] *s.* (quím.) eosina.
eosinophil [,iə'sɪnə,fɪl] **eosinophile** [-,faɪl] *s.* (biol.) célula eosinófila.
eosinophilic [,iə,sɪnə'fɪlɪk] *a.* (biol.) eosinófilo.
Eozoic [-'zoʊɪk] *a., s.* (geol.) eozoico.
EP *abrev. de* **extended play,** de duración prolongada.
epact ['i,pækt] *s.* (astr.) epacta.
eparch ['ɛpɑrk, B 'ɛpɑk] *s.* eparca.
eparchy [-ɪ] *s.* eparquía.
epaulet, epaulette ['ɛpə,lɛt, ,ɛpə'lɛt] *s.* (mil.) charretera, hombrera; **to win his epaulettes,** (mil.) obtener el ascenso al grado de oficial.
épée ['eɪ,peɪ, B eɪ'peɪ] *s.* (dep.) espada.
épéeist [-əst] *s.* (dep.) esgrimista, experto en el uso de la espada.
epeirogenic [ɪ,paɪrə'dʒɛnɪk] *a.* (geol.) epirogenético, epeirogénico.
epencephalon [,ɛpɛn'sɛfə,lɑn, B -lən] *s.* (anat.) epencéfalo.
ependyma [ɛ'pɛndɪmə] *s.* (anat.) epéndimo.
epenthesis [ɛ'pɛnθəsəs] *s.* (gram.) epéntesis.
epenthetic [,ɛpɛn'θɛtɪk] *a.* (gram.) epentético.
epergne [ɪ'pɜrn, B ɪ'pɜn] *s.* centro o adorno de mesa.
epexegesis [ɛp,ɛksə'dʒisəs] *s.* (ret.) epexégesis.
ephebe [ɪ'fib, 'ɛf,ib] ɘbʎɘƃ š [ɪ'fibəs] *s.* (*pl.* EPHEBI [-,baɪ]) (hist.) efebo, joven griego.
ephedra [ə'fɛdrə, 'ɛfə-] *s.* (bot.) belcho, canadillo.
ephedrine [ɪ'fɛdrən, B 'ɛfə,drin] *s.* (farm.) efedrina.
ephemera [ɪ'fɛmərə] *s.* (*pl.* EPHEMERAE [-ə,ri] o EPHEMERAS) 1. (zool.) efímera, cachipolla. 2. cosa efímera.
ephemeral [-ərəl] *a.* efímero, pasajero. —*s.* planta efímera.
ephemeral fever, (vet.) fiebre efímera o efémera.
ephemerally [-ərəlɪ] *adv.* efímeramente.
ephemerid [-ərəd] *s.* (zool.) efímera, cachipolla.
ephemeris [-ərəs] *s.* (*pl.* EPHEMERIDES [,ɛfə'mɛrə,diz]) 1. efemérides astronómicas. 2. (ant.) efemérides, diario.
ephemeron [-ə,rɑn, B -ə,rɔn] *s.* (*pl.* EPHEMERA [-ərə] o EPHEMERONS) (zool.) efímera.
ephemerous [-ərəs] *a.* efímero, pasajero, de corta duración.
Ephesian [ɪ'fiʒən, B -ʒjən] *a., s.* efesino, efesio, de Éfeso.
Ephesus ['ɛfəsəs] *s.* Éfeso, ciudad griega, famosa por el antiguo templo de Artemisa.
ephete ['ɛf,it] *s.* (hist.) éfeta, juez griego.
Ephialtes [,ɛfɪ'æltiz] *s.* (mitol.) Efialtes, Efialto; opresión nocturna, pesadilla.
ephod ['ɛf,ɑd, B 'ifɔd] *s.* efod, vestiduras que usaban los sacerdotes israelitas.
ephor ['ɛfər, -,ɔr, B 'ɛfə] *s.* (*pl.* EPHORS, EPHORI [-ə,raɪ]) (hist.) éforo (magistrado griego); superintendente de obras públicas.
Ephraimite ['ifrɪəm,aɪt] *s.* (bíbl.) efraimita, miembro de la tribu israelita de Efraín.
epiblast ['ɛpə,blæst] *s.* (anat.) epiblasto.
epic ['ɛpɪk] *a.* épico. —*s.* epopeya.
epical [-ɪkəl] *a.* épico.
epically [-ɪkəlɪ] *adv.* épicamente.
epicalyx [,ɛpə'keɪlɪks, -'kæl-] *s.* (bot.) epicáliz, sobrecáliz.
epicardial [-'kɑrdɪəl, B -'kɑd-] *a.* (anat.) epicárdico.
epicardium [-ɪəm] *s.* (*pl.* EPICARDIA [-ɪə]) (anat.) epicardio.
epicarp ['ɛpə,kɑrp, B -,kɑp] *s.* (bot.) epicarpio.
epicedium [,ɛpə'sidɪəm] *s.* (*pl.* EPICEDIA [-dɪə]) epicedio, elegía.
epicene ['ɛpə,sin] *a.* 1. (gram.) epiceno. 2. asexual. 3. afeminado. —*s.* persona afeminada.
epicenism [-,ɪzəm] *s.* afeminamiento.
epicenter, epicentre ['ɛpə,sɛntər, B -ə] *s.* epicentro.
epicentrum [,ɛpə'sɛntrəm] *s.* (*pl.* EPICENTRA [-trə]) epicentro.
epicotyl [,ɛpə'kɑtəl B -'kɔt-] *s.* (bot.) epicotilo o epicotilo.
epicranial [-'kreɪnɪəl] *a.* (med.) epicraneal.
epicritic [-'krɪtɪk] *a.* (fisiol., psic.) epicrítico.
epicure ['ɛpɪ,kjʊr, B -,kjʊə] *s.* 1. gastrónomo. 2. (ant.) epicúreo.
Epicurean [,ɛpɪkjʊ'riən, -'kjʊrɪ- B -kjʊ'ri-] *a.* epicúreo. —*s.* 1. epicúreo. 2. **e.,** gastrónomo, sibarita.
Epicureanism [-,ɪzəm] *s.* (filos.) epicureísmo.
epicurism ['ɛpɪkjʊr,ɪzəm, B -kjʊər-] *s.* gastronomía.
epicycle ['ɛpə,saɪkəl] *s.* (astr., geom.) epiciclo.
epicyclic [,ɛpə'saɪklɪk, -'sɪk-] *a.* epicíclico.
epicyclic train, (mec.) tren epicicloidal.
epicycloid [-'saɪ,klɔɪd] *s.* (geom.) epicicloide.
epicycloidal [-saɪ'klɔɪdəl] *a.* epicicloidal.
epicycloidal wheel, (mec.) rueda epicicloidal.
epidemic [,ɛpə'dɛmɪk] *a.* epidémico, epidemial. —*s.* epidemia.
epidemical [-ɪkəl] *a.* epidémico. epidemial.
epidemically [-ɪkəlɪ] *adv.* epidémicamente.
epidemicity [-,dɛm'ɪsətɪ] *s.* epidemicidad.
epidemiologist [,ɛpə,dimɪ'ɑlədʒəst, B -'ɔl-] *s.* epidemiólogo.
epidemiology [-dʒɪ] *s.* (med.) epidemiología.
epidendrum [,ɛpə'dɛndrəm] **epidendron** [-drən] *s.* (bot.) epidendrum.
epidermal [-'dɜrməl, B -'dɜməl] **epidermic** [-mɪk] *a.* epidérmico.
epidermis [-məs] *s.* (anat., zool.) epidermis, cutícula; (bot.) epidermis.
epidermoid [-,mɔɪd] **epidermoidal** [-dər'mɔɪdəl, B -də'-] *a.* epidermoide.
epidiascope [,ɛpə'daɪə,skoʊp] *s.* 1. epidiascopio, epidiascopo. 2. episcopio.
epididymis [-'dɪdəməs] *s.* (anat.) epidídimo.
epidote ['ɛpə,doʊt] *s.* (min.) epidota.
epigastric [,ɛpə'gæstrɪk] *a.* (anat.) epigástrico.
epigastrium [-trɪəm] *s.* (*pl.* EPIGASTRIA [-trɪə]) (anat.) epigástrico.
epigeal [,ɛpə'dʒiəl] **epigean** [-ən] *a.* (bot.) epigeo.
epigene ['ɛpə,dʒin] *a.* (geol.) epigénico.
epigenesis [,ɛpə'dʒɛnəsəs] *s.* (biol., geol.) epigénesis.
epigenetic [-dʒə'nɛtɪk] *a.* (geol.) epigenético.
epigeous [,ɛpə'dʒiəs] *a.* (bot.) epigeo.
epiglottal [-'glɑtəl, B -'glɔt-] **epiglottic** [-ɪk] *a.* (anat.) epiglótico.
epiglottis [-əs] *s.* (anat., zool.) epiglotis, epiglosis.
epigone ['ɛpə,goʊn] *s.* epígono.
epigram [-,græm] *s.* epigrama.
epigrammatic [,ɛpɪgrə'mætɪk] **epigrammatical** [-ɪkəl] *a.* epigramático, epigramatorio.
epigrammatically [-ɪkəlɪ] *adv.* epigramáticamente.
epigrammatist [-'græmətəst] *s.* epigramista, epigramatario, epigramatista, epigramático.
epigrammatize [-,taɪz] *v.t.* hacer un epigrama; expresar epigramáticamente. —*v.i.* escribir epigramas.
epigraph ['ɛpə,græf, B -,grɑf] *s.* epígrafe.
epigrapher [ɪ'pɪgrəfər, B -fə] *s.* epigrafista.
epigraphic [,ɛpə'græfɪk] **epigraphical** [-ɪkəl] *a.* epigráfico.
epigraphist [ɪ'pɪgrəfəst] *s.* epigrafista.
epigraphy [-fɪ] *s.* epigrafía.
epigynous [ɪ'pɪdʒənəs] *a.* (bot.) epigino.
epilate ['ɛpɪleɪt] *v.t.* depilar.
epilation [,ɛpə'leɪʃən] *s.* depilación.
epilepsy ['ɛpə,lɛpsɪ] *s.* (med.) epilepsia.
epileptic [,ɛpə'lɛptɪk] *a., s.* epiléptico.
epileptiform [-tə,fɔrm, B -,fɔm] *a.* (med.) epileptiforme.
epileptoid [-,tɔɪd] *a.* (med.) epileptoide.
epilogic [-'lɑdʒɪk, B -'lɔdʒ-] *a.* epilogal.
epilogue ['ɛpə,lɔg, -,lɑg, B -,lɔg] *s.* epílogo.
epimorphosis [,ɛpə'mɔrfəsəs, B -'mɔf-] *s.* (med.) epimorfosis.
epimysium [-'mɪzɪəm] *s.* (anat.) epimisio.
epinastic [-'næstɪk] *a.* (bot.) epinástico.
epinasty ['ɛpə,næstɪ] *s.* (bot.) epinastia.
epinephrine, epinephrin [,ɛpə'nɛf,rin, -rɪn] *s.* (biol.) epinefrina.
epineurium [-'nʊrɪəm, B -'njʊr-] *s.* (anat.) epineurio, epineuro.
epinicion [,ɛpɪ'nɪsɪən] *s.* epinicio (himno triunfal).
Epiphany [ɪ'pɪfənɪ] *s.* 1. (relig.) Epifanía, día de los Reyes Magos. 2. **e.,** epifanía, manifestación, aparición (esp. divina).
epiphenomenalism [,ɛpəfɪ'nɑmənəl,ɪzəm, B -'nɔm-] *s.* (filos.) epifenomenismo.

epiphenomenon [-'nɑmə,nɑn, B -'nɔmɪnən] *s.* (med., filos.) epifenómeno.
epiphonema [-foʊ'nimə] *s.* (ret.) epifonema.
epiphora [ɪ'pɪfərə] *s.* (med.) epífora.
epiphragm ['ɛpə,fræm] *s.* (zool.) epifragma.
epiphysis [ɪ'pɪfəsəs] *s.* (*pl.* EPIPHYSES [-,siz]) (anat.) epífisis.
epiphyte ['ɛpə,faɪt] *s.* (bot.) epifita.
epiphytic [,ɛpə'fɪtɪk] *a.* (bot.) epífito, epifito.
epiphytotic [-faɪ'tɑtɪk, B -'tɔt-] *a.* (bot.) epifitótico.
epiploon [ɪ'pɪplə,ɑn, B -ɔn] *s.* (anat.) epiplón.
epirogeny, epirogenic, *vars. de* **epeirogeny, epeirogenic.**
episcopacy [ɪ'pɪskəpəsɪ] *s.* (relig.) episcopado.
episcopal [-pəl] *a.* 1. episcopal. 2. **E.,** Episcopal.
episcopalian [ɪ,pɪskə'peɪljən] *a., s.* episcopalista.
episcopalism [ɪ'pɪskəpəl,ɪzəm] *s.* (relig.) episcopalismo.
episcopate [-pət, -,peɪt] *s.* episcopado, obispado.
episcope ['ɛpə,skoʊp] *s.* episcopio.
episode [-,soʊd] *s.* episodio; incidente, lance.
episodic [,ɛpə'sɑdɪk, B -'sɔd-] **episodical** [-ɪkəl] *a.* episódico.
episodically [-ɪkəlɪ] *adv.* episódicamente.
epispastic [-'spæstɪk] *a., s.* (med.) epispástico, vesicante, vejigatorio.
epistasy [ɪ'pɪstəsɪ] *s.* (med.) epistasia, epistasis.
epistaxis [,ɛpə'stætsəs] *s.* (med.) epistaxis.
epistemological [ɪ,pɪstəmə'lɑdʒɪkəl, B -'lɔdʒ-] *a.* epistemológico.
epistemologist [-'mɑlədʒəst, B -'mɔl-] *s.* epistemólogo.
epistemology [-dʒɪ] *s.* epistemología.
episternum [,ɛpə'stɜrnəm, B -'stɜnəm] *s.* (*pl.* EPISTERNA [-nə]) (zool.) episternón.
epistle [ɪ'pɪsəl] *s.* 1. epístola, carta, misiva. 2. (poét.) epístola. 3. **E.,** (bíbl.) Epístola.
epistler [ɪ'pɪslər, B -lə] *var. de* **epistoler.**
epistolary [-tə,lɛrɪ, B -lərɪ] *a.* epistolar. —*s.* epistolario.
epistoler [-tələr, B -lə] *s.* 1. (t. **epistolist**) epistológrafo. 2. epistolero.
epistolographer [ɪ,pɪstə'lɑgrəfər, B -'lɔgrəfə] **epistolographist** [-fəst] *s.* epistológrafo.
epistrophe [ɪ'pɪstrəfɪ] *s.* (ret.) epístrofe; (mús.) estribillo.
epistyle ['ɛpə,staɪl] *s.* (arq.) epistilo, arquitrabe.
epitaph ['ɛpə,tæf, B -,tɑf] *s.* epitafio.
epitasis [ɪ'pɪtəsəs] *s.* (teat.) epítasis.
epithalamic [,ɛpəθə'læmɪk] *a.* epitalámico.
epithalamium [-'leɪmɪəm] *s.* epitalamio.
epithelial [,ɛpə'θilɪəl] *a.* epitelial.
epithelioid [-,ɔɪd] *a.* epitelioide.
epithelioma [-,θilɪ'oʊmə] *s.* (med.) epitelioma.
epitheliomatous [-'ɑmətəs, B -'ɔm-] *a.* (med.) epiteliomatoso.
epithelium [,ɛpə'θilɪəm] *s.* (anat., biol., bot.) epitelio.
epithem ['ɛpə,θɛm] *s.* (med.) epítema, epítima.
epithet ['ɛpə,θɛt, -θət] *s.* epíteto.
epitome [ɪ'pɪtəmɪ] *s.* epítome, resumen, sumario, compendio.
epitomize [-,maɪz] *v.t.* epitomar, resumir, compendiar.
epitrope [ɪ'pɪtrəpɪ] *s.* (ret.) epítrope.
epizoic [,ɛpə'zoʊɪk] *a.* (zool.) epizoico, epizoario.
epizoite [-'zoʊ,aɪt] *s.* (bot.) planta epizoica.
epizoon [-,ɑn, B -,ɔn] *s.* (*pl.* EPIZOA [-'zoʊə]) (zool.) epizoario, ectoparásito.
epizootic [-zoʊ'ɑtɪk, B -'ɔ-] *a.* epizoótico. —*s.* (vet.) epizootia, enfermedad epizoótica.

e pluribus unum [,i,plʊrəbəs'junəm] (lat.) muchos forman uno solo (lema de los Estados Unidos).
epoch ['ɛpək, 'ɛpɑk, B 'ipɔk] *s.* época, era, edad, período; (astr., geol.) época.
epochal ['ɛpəkəl, B 'ɛpɔkəl] *a.* trascendental, memorable.
epoch-making [-,meɪkɪŋ, B 'ipɔk-] *a.* trascendental, memorable; **to be e.-m.,** hacer época.
epode ['ɛp,oʊd] *s.* (poét.) epodo, epoda.
eponym ['ɛpə,nɪm] *s.* epónimo.
eponymic [,ɛpə'nɪmɪk] **eponymous** [ɪ'pɑnəməs, B ɪ'pɔn-] *a.* epónimo.
epopee ['ɛpə,pi] *s.* epopeya, poema épico.
epos ['ɛp,ɑs, B 'ɛpɔs] *s.* poesía épica.
epoxide [ɛp'ɑk,saɪd, B -'ɔk-] *s.* (quím.) epóxido.
epoxidize [-sə,daɪz] *v.t.* convertir en epóxido.
epoxy [ɛp'ɑksɪ, B -'ɔk-] *a.* (quím.) epoxia.
epoxy resin, resina epoxídica.
epsilon ['ɛpsə,lɑn, -lən, B ɛp'saɪlən] *s.* épsilon, quinta letra del alfabeto griego.
epsomite ['ɛpsə,maɪt] *s.* epsomita, sulfato de magnesio natural.
Epsom salt ['ɛpsəm-] (quím.) sal de Epsom, sal de la higuera, epsomita.
equability [,ɛkwə'bɪlətɪ, ˌik-] *s.* 1. uniformidad, constancia. 2. tranquilidad, ecuanimidad.
equable ['ɛkwəbəl, 'ik-] *a.* 1. uniforme, constante, estable. 2. tranquilo, quieto, ecuánime.
equableness [-nəs] *s.* 1. uniformidad, constancia. 2. tranquilidad, ecuanimidad.
equably [-blɪ] *adv.* 1. uniformemente. 2. tranquilamente.
equal ['ikwəl] *a.* 1. igual; mismo. 2. equilibrado, constante, balanceado. 3. liso, parejo, a nivel. 4. (ant.) igual, indistinto. 5. **to be e. to you,** ser igual a ti; **to be e. to the task,** ser suficiente para, ser capaz de, poder hacer frente a (ocasión, etc.), poder desempeñar (tarea, etc.). —*s.* 1. igual, persona igual (en rango o condición). 2. cantidad o número igual. —*v.t.* (*pret., p.p.* EQUALED O EQUALLED; *p.pr.* EQUALING O EQUALLING) 1. igualar, poner al igual con; igualarse a, con. 2. igualar, equivaler, emparejar.
equaling file, lima paralela ligeramente combada.
equalitarian [ɪ,kwɑlə'tɛrɪən, B ɪ,kwɔlɪ'tɛər-] *a.* igualitario. —*s.* persona igualitaria.
equality [ɪ'kwɑlətɪ, B ɪ'kwɔl-] *s.* igualdad, uniformidad, paridad; **to be on an e. with,** estar al mismo nivel de, tratar de igual a igual.
equalization [,ikwələ'zeɪʃən, B -laɪ-] *s.* igualamiento, igualación, compensación.
equalize ['ikwə,laɪz] *v.t.* igualar, emparejar, uniformar; (dep.) igualar (el marcador).
equalizer [-ər, B -ə] *s.* 1. (mec.) igualador, compensador, balancín. 2. (elec.) igualador, compensador. 3. (jer.) pistola, revólver.
equalizing [-ɪŋ] *a.* igualador; compensador, de compensación.
equally ['ikwəlɪ] *adv.* igualmente, por igual.
equal mark (sign), (mat.) signo de igualdad (=).
equal rights, igualdad de derechos.
equanimity [,ɛkwə'nɪmətɪ, ˌik-] *s.* ecuanimidad, equilibrio.
equate [ɪ'kweɪt] *v.t.* 1. igualar, considerar idéntico (a). 2. (mat.) igualar, poner en ecuación (con).
equation [ɪ'kweɪʒən, -ʃən] *s.* 1. ecuación. balanceo; equilibrio. 2. (mat., astr., quím.) ecuación.
equational sentence [-əl] (gram.) oración nominal.
equator [ɪ'kweɪtər, B -ə] *s.* (geog., astr.) ecuador, línea ecuatorial.

equatorial [,ikwə'tɔrɪəl, ˌɛk-] *a.* ecuatorial. —*s.* (astr.) ecuatorial.
equerry ['ɛkwərɪ, ɪ'kwɛrɪ] *s.* 1. caballerizo de la casa real, palafrenero mayor. 2. ayuda de cámara (de uno de los miembros de una casa real británica).
equestrian [ɪ'kwɛstrɪən] *a.* ecuestre. —*s.* jinete.
equestrianism [-,ɪzəm] *s.* equitación.
equestrienne [ɪ,kwɛstrɪ'ɛn] *s.* amazona (esp. de circo).
equiangular [,ikwɪ'æŋgjələr, B -lə] *a.* (geom.) equiángulo.
equiaxed ['ikwə,ækst] *a.* (metal.) equidimensional.
equidifference [-'dɪfrəns, -ərəns] *s.* (mat.) equidiferencia.
equidistance [,ikwə'dɪstəns] *s.* equidistancia.
equidistant [-tənt, B 'ik-] *a.* equidistante.
equidistantly [-lɪ] *adv.* a igual distancia.
equilateral [-'lætərəl, B 'ik-] *a.* (geom.) equilátero. —*s.* (geom.) lado equilátero (de una figura); figura equilátera.
equilibrant [ɪ'kwɪləbrənt] *s.* (fís.) fuerza equilibrante.
equilibrate [-,breɪt, B ,ikwɪ'laɪbreɪt] *v.t.* equilibrar, poner en equilibrio, balancear, contrapesar. —*v.i.* equilibrarse, estar en equilibrio.
equilibration [ɪ,kwɪlə'breɪʃən, B ,ikwɪlaɪ-] *s.* equilibrio; (tec.) equilibración.
equilibrator [ɪ'kwɪlə,breɪtər, B ,ikwɪ'laɪ-ə] *s.* equilibrador.
equilibrist [ɪ'kwɪləbrəst] *s.* equilibrista, acróbata.
equilibrium [,ikwə'lɪbrɪəm] *s.* (*pl.* EQUILIBRIUMS O **equilibria** [-rɪə]) equilibrio, balance.
equimolecular [-mə'lɛkjələr, B -lə] *a.* (fís.) equimolecular.
equine ['i,kwaɪn, 'ɛk-] *a.* equino, caballar, hípico; (zool.) équido. —*s.* equino, caballo.
equinoctial [,ikwə'nɑkʃəl, B -'nɔk-] *a.* equinoccial. —*s.* 1. (astr.) equinoccial. 2. tempestad equinoccial.
equinoctial circle, e. line, (astr.) línea equinoccial, ecuador celeste.
equinox ['ikwə,nɑks, B -,nɔks] *s.* (astr.) equinoccio.
equip [ɪ'kwɪp] *v.t.* (*pret., p.p.* EQUIPPED; *p.pr.* EQUIPPING) equipar, pertrechar, proveer, aviar; **e. oneself,** equiparse.
equipage ['ɛkwəpɪdʒ] *s.* 1. equipaje, equipo; tren. 2. carruaje.
equipment [ɪ'kwɪpmənt] *s.* 1. equipo, provisión, aprovisionamiento. 2. equipo, pertrechos, aparatos. 3. equipaje, bagaje. 4. (fig.) capacidad, talento (mental). 5. (f.c.) equipo rodante, material móvil. 6. (aut.) accesorios, aditamentos.
equipoise ['ɛkwə,pɔɪz, 'ik-] *s.* 1. equilibrio. 2. contrapeso, contrabalanza. —*v.t.* 1. equilibrar. 2. contrabalancear, contrapesar, compensar.
equipollence [,ikwə'pɑləns, B -'pɔl-] **equipollency** [-ənsɪ] *s.* equipolencia, equivalencia.
equipollent [-ənt] *a.* equipolente, equivalente. —*s.* equivalente.
equiponderance [-'pɑndərəns, B -'pɔn-] **equiponderancy** [-ənsɪ] *s.* equiponderancia.
equiponderant [-ənt] *a.* equiponderante.
equiponderate [-'pɑndə,reɪt, B -'pɔn-] —*v.i.* equiponderar. —*v.t.* contrapesar, igualar en peso (dos cosas).
equipotential [-pə'tɛntʃəl, B -'tɛnʃəl] *a.* (fís.) equipotencial.
Equisetaceae [,ɛkwəsɪ'teɪsɪ,i] *s. pl.* (bot.) equisetáceas.

equisetaceous [-'teɪʃəs] *a.* (bot.) equisetáceo.
equisetum [-'sitəm] *s.* (*pl.* EQUISETUMS O EQUISETA [-ə]) (bot.) equiseto, cola de caballo.
equitable ['ɛkwətəbəl] *a.* equitativo, justo, imparcial.
equitableness [-nəs] *s.* equidad.
equitably [-blɪ] *adv.* equitativamente.
equitant ['ɛkwətənt] *a.* (bot.) equitante.
equitation [ˌɛkwə'teɪʃən] *s.* equitación.
equites ['ɛkwəˌtiz] *s. pl.* (hist.) équites.
equity ['ɛkwətɪ] *s.* (*pl.* EQUITIES) 1. equidad, imparcialidad. 2. (der.) equidad, justicia natural (por oposición a la letra de la ley positiva). 3. sindicato de actores. 4. (G.B.) (*pl.*) acciones de interés variable.
equity capital, (com.) acciones, capital propio.
equivalence [ɪ'kwɪvələns] *s.* equivalencia; (quím.) equivalencia; valencia.
equivalency [-lənsɪ] *s.* (*pl.* EQUIVALENCIES) *var. de* **equivalence.**
equivalent [-lənt] *a.* equivalente (mat., geom., quím.) equivalente. —*s.* equivalente.
equivalently [-lɪ] *adv.* equivalentemente.
equivocal [ɪ'kwɪvəkəl] *a.* 1. equívoco, ambiguo. 2. dudoso, sospechoso. 3. incierto, indeciso.
equivocally [-əkəlɪ] *adv.* equívocamente, con equívoco.
equivocalness [-əkəlnəs] *s.* ambigüedad, carácter equívoco.
equivocate [-əˌkeɪt] *v.i.* emplear lenguaje equívoco o ambiguo, usar de equívocos (esp. con intención de engañar).
equivocation [ɪˌkwɪvə'keɪʃən] *s.* empleo de equívocos, lenguaje ambiguo, equivocación.
equivocator [ɪ'kwɪvəˌkeɪtər, B -ə] *s.* equivoquista.
equivoque, equivoke ['ɛkwəˌvoʊk] *s.* 1. equívoco; término ambiguo; ambigüedad. 2. doble sentido; juego de palabras, anfibología.
Er *símb. de* **erbium,** erbio (Er).
era ['ɪrə, 'ɛrə, 'irə, B 'ɪərə] *s.* era, época; período (histórico); (geol.) era, edad.
eradiate [i'reɪdɪˌeɪt] *v.t.* radiar, irradiar.
eradiation [iˌreɪdɪ'eɪʃən] *s.* radiación.
eradicable [ɪ'rædɪkəbəl] *a.* extirpable.
eradicate [ɪ'rædəˌkeɪt] *v.t.* erradicar, desarraigar, extirpar.
eradication [ɪˌrædə'keɪʃən] *s.* erradicación, extirpación, desarraigo.
eradicator [ɪ'rædəˌkeɪtər, B -ə] *s.* 1. extirpador. 2. quitamanchas (de tinta o tinte).
erasable [ɪ'reɪsəbəl, B ɪ'reɪzə-] *a.* borrable.
erase [ɪ'reɪs, B ɪ'reɪz] *v.t.* 1. borrar. 2. remover, suprimir (grabación de cinta magnetofónica). 3. (jer.) matar.
eraser [ɪ'reɪsər, B -zə] *a.* goma de borrar, borrador.
eraser head, (electrón.) cabeza supresora (de una grabadora de cinta magnetofónica).
erasion [ɪ'reɪʒən] *s.* (med.) extirpación o eliminación por raspadura.
Erasmian [ɪ'ræzmɪən] *a., s.* erasmiano, erasmista.
Erasmianism [-ˌɪzəm] *s.* (filos.) erasmismo.
Erasmus [ɪ'ræzməs] *s.* Erasmo, escritor, humanista y filólogo holandés.
Erastian [ɪ'ræstɪən] *a.* (rel.) erastiano.
Erastianism [-ˌɪzəm] *s.* (rel.) erastianismo.
erasure [ɪ'reɪʃər, B ɪ'reɪʒə] *s.* borradura; raspadura.
Erato ['ɛrəˌtoʊ] *s.* (mitol.) Erato, musa de la poesía lírica, esp. la erótica.
erbium ['ɜrbɪəm, B 'ɜbɪ-] *s.* (quím.) erbio.
ere [ɛr, B ɛə] (poét., ant.) *prep.* antes de. —*conj.* antes que.
Erebus ['ɛrəbəs] *s.* (mitol.) Erebo; (poét.) infierno.
erect [ɪ'rɛkt] *a.* 1. erecto, levantado, derecho, vertical. 2. erguido, enhiesto, engallado. 3. erizado (cabello). —*v.t.* 1. erigir, levantar, edificar, construir. 2. (fig.) constituir, establecer. 3. (mec.) armar, montar, instalar.
erectile [ɪ'rɛktəl, B -taɪl] *a.* eréctil.
erectility [ɪˌrɛk'tɪlətɪ] *s.* erectilidad.
erecting eye piece, ocular de imagen recta.
erection [ɪ'rɛkʃən] *s.* 1. erección, construcción. 2. estructura. 3. (fisiol.) erección (del pene).
erection bolts, pernos de montaje o de armar, bulones de montaje.
erection plan, dibujo de montaje.
erector [-tər, B -tə] *s.* erector; (anat.) erector.
E region, (astr.) región E (de la ionosfera).
erelong [ɛr'lɔŋ, B ɛə'-] *adv.* (ant., poét.) antes de mucho, dentro de poco tiempo.
eremite ['ɛrəˌmaɪt] *s.* eremita, ermitaño.
eremitic [ˌɛrə'mɪtɪk] **eremitical** [-ɪkəl] *a.* eremítico, solitario.
erenow [ɛr'naʊ, B ɛə'-] *adv.* (ant., poét.) antes de ahora.
erepsin [ɪ'rɛpsən] *s.* (bioquím.) erepsina.
erethism ['ɛrəˌθɪzəm] *s.* (med.) eretismo.
erethismic [ˌɛrə'θɪzmɪk] *a.* (med.) eretísmico.
erewhile [ɛr'hwaɪl, -'waɪl, B ɛə'-] *adv.* (ant.) antes, hasta ahora.
erg [ɜrg, B ɜg] *s.* (fís.) ergio, unidad de energía.
ergastulum [ər'gæstʃələm, B ə'-] *s.* (*pl.* ERGASTULA [-lə]) (hist.) ergástulo, ergástula.
ergo ['ɜrgoʊ, 'ɛr-, B 'ɜgoʊ] *adv.* ergo, por tanto, luego.
ergograph ['ɜrgəˌgræf, B 'ɜgəˌgrɑf] *s.* (med.) ergógrafo.
ergometer [ər'gɑmətər, B ɜ'gɔmɪtə] *s.* (med.) ergómetro.
ergonovine [ˌɜrgə'noʊˌvin, B ˌɜgə'-] *s.* (farm.) ergonovina.
ergosterol [-'gɑstəˌroʊl, B -'gɔstəˌrɔl] *s.* (bioquím.) ergosterol, ergosterina.
ergot ['ɜrgət, B 'ɜgət] *s.* (bot.) cornezuelo del centeno.
ergotamine [ər'gɑtəˌmin, B ɜ'gɔt-] *s.* (farm.) ergotamina.
ergotic [-ɪk] *a.* (quím.) ergótico (ácido).
ergotin['ɜrgətɪn, B 'ɜgət-] *s.* (farm.) ergotina.
ergotinine [ər'gɑtəˌnin, B ɜ'gɔt-] *s.* (quím.) ergotinina.
ergotism ['ɜrgətˌɪzəm, B 'ɜgət-] *s.* 1. (med.) ergotismo. 2. (filos.) ergotismo.
ergotize [-ˌaɪz] *v.i.* (filos.) ergotizar.
erica ['ɛrɪkə] *s.* (bot.) erica.
Ericaceae [ˌɛrə'keɪsɪˌi] *s. pl.* (bot.) ericáceas.
ericaceous [-'keɪʃəs] *a.* (bot.) ericáceo.
Eric the Red, Erico el Rojo, explorador noruego, colonizador de Groenlandia.
Eridanus [ɪ'rɪdənəs] *s.* (astr.) Erídano.
Erin ['ɛrən, B 'ɪərɪn] *s.* (poét.) Erín (antiguo nombre de Irlanda).
Erinyes [ɪ'rɪnɪˌiz] *s. pl.* (mitol.) Erinias, las Furias.
eristic [ɪ'rɪstɪk, B ɛ-] **eristical** [-tɪkəl] *a.* erístico, polémico.
ermine ['ɜrmən, B 'ɜmɪn] *s.* 1. (zool.) armiño. 2. toga de juez; judicatura. 3. (her.) armiño.
ermined [-mənd] *a.* armiñado.
ermines [-mənz] **erminees** [-məˌniz] *s.* (her.) contraarmiño.
erne, ern [ɜrn, B ɜn] *s.* (orn.) águila marina, águila de cola blanca.
erode [ɪ'roʊd] *v.t.* corroer, roer; gastar, desgastar (suelo, roca, etc.). —*v.i.* desgastarse, sufrir erosión.
erodent [-ənt] *a.* (med.) corrosivo, cáustico.
erodible [-əbəl] *a.* capaz o susceptible de ser corroído; gastable.
erogenous [ɪ'rɑdʒənəs, B ɪ'rɔdʒ-] **erogenic** [ˌɛrə'dʒɛnɪk] *a.* (psic.) erógeno, que despierta el deseo sexual.
Eros ['ɛrˌɑs, 'ɪr-, B 'ɪərɔs] *s.* (mitol., astr.) Eros.
erose [ɪ'roʊs] *a.* (bot.) lacerado (borde de la hoja).
erosible [-əbəl] *a.* capaz o susceptible de ser corroído; gastable.
erosion [ɪ'roʊʒən] *s.* erosión; corrosión, desgaste.
erosive [-sɪv] *a.* (geol.) erosivo.
erotic [ɪ'rɑtɪk, B ɪ'rɔt-] *a.* erótico; que estimula el instinto sexual; **e. poems,** poemas eróticos.
erotica [-ɪkə] *s. pl.* obra(s) o colección erótica(s).
erotical [-ɪkəl] *a.* erótico.
erotically [-ɪkəlɪ] *adv.* eróticamente.
eroticism [-əˌsɪzəm] **erotism** ['ɛrəˌtɪzəm] *s.* 1. lo erótico, aspecto erótico. 2. erotismo.
erotogenic [ɪˌroʊtə'dʒɛnɪk, ɪˌrɑtə-, B ɪˌroʊtə-] *a.* erotogénico, erotógeno, erógeno; susceptible a la estimulación sexual.
erotomania [-'meɪnɪə] *s.* (med.) erotomanía.
erotomaniac [-ɪˌæk] *s.* erotómano.
err [ɜr, ɛr, B ɜ] *v.i.* 1. errar (en), errarse, equivocarse. 2. pecar, descarriarse.
errancy ['ɛrənsɪ] *s.* propensión a errar.
errand ['ɛrənd] *s.* 1. mandado, diligencia. 2. (ant.) mensaje, recado. 3. **to run** (o **go on**) **errands,** hacer diligencias, hacer mandados; **to send on an e.,** mandar hacer una diligencia, enviar a un recado.
errand-boy [-ˌbɔɪ] *s.* mandadero, recadero; mensajero.
errant ['ɛrənt] *a.* 1. errante, errabundo; andante (caballero). 2. descarriado. 3. caprichoso (brisa, ráfaga de viento, etc.).
errantry [-rɪ] *s.* vida errante, vagabundeo.
errata [ɛ'rɑtə, ɛ'reɪtə] *s.* (*pl. de* ERRATUM) erratas; fe de erratas.
erratic [ɪ'rætɪk] *a.* 1. excéntrico, caprichoso, irregular. 2. (med.) errático, errante (dolor, calentura). 3. (geol.) errático.
erratically [-ɪkəlɪ] *adv.* erráticamente, de modo errático; irregularmente, caprichosamente.
erratum [ɛ'rɑtəm, ɛ'reɪt-] *s.* (*pl.* ERRATA [-ə]) errata.
erring ['ɜrɪŋ, 'ɛr-, B 'ɜr-] *a.* errado; descarriado; errante.
erroneous [ɪ'roʊnɪəs, ɛ-] *a.* erróneo, errado, incorrecto.
erroneously [-lɪ] *adv.* erróneamente.
erroneousness [-nəs] *s.* error, calidad de erróneo.
error ['ɛrər, B 'ɛrə] *s.* 1. error, equivocación, yerro. 2. pecado, falta, ofensa, transgresión. 3. (mat.) error. 4. **in e.,** por error; errado; **to fall into the e. (of),** caer en el error (de).
ersatz ['ɛrˌzɑts, B 'ɛəˌzæts] *s.* sucedáneo, substituto. —*a.* artificial, sintético.
Erse [ɜrs, B ɜs] *s.* gaélico (antiguo idioma de Irlanda).
erst [ɜrst, B ɜst] *adv.* (ant.) en otro tiempo, antes.
erstwhile ['ɜrstˌhwaɪl, -ˌwaɪl, B 'ɜst-] *adv.* antiguamente, en otro tiempo. —*a.* antiguo, anterior, de otro tiempo.
erubescence [ˌɛrʊ'bɛsəns] *s.* erubescencia, rubor.
erubescent [-ənt] *a.* erubescente, ruboroso.
eruct [ɪ'rʌkt] **eructate** [-ˌteɪt] *v.t., v.i.* 1. eructar, erutar, regoldar. 2. (fig.) arrojar, expeler.
eructation [ˌirʌk'teɪʃən] *s.* eructación, eructo, eruto, regüeldo.
erudite ['ɛrəˌdaɪt, -jʊ-, B 'ɛrʊ-] *a.* erudito, letrado, instruido, culto.

eruditely [-lɪ] *adv.* eruditamente, con erudición.

erudition [ˌɛrəˈdɪʃən, -jʊ-, B ˌɛrʊ-] *s.* erudición, conocimientos (esp. históricos, literarios o críticos).

erupt [ɪˈrʌpt] *v.i.* hacer erupción (volcán), salir o brotar. —*v.t.* arrojar, expeler (lava, gases, etc.).

eruption [ɪˈrʌpʃən] *s.* 1. erupción (de un volcán); irrupción, brote (de una enfermedad, guerra, pasión, etc.). 2. (med.) erupción.

eruptive [-tɪv] *a.* eruptivo.

eryngo [ɪˈrɪŋgoʊ] *s.* (bot.) eringe, cardo corredor.

erysipelas [ˌɛrəˈsɪpələs, ˈɪr-, B ˌɛr-] *s.* (med.) erisipela.

erysipelatous [-sɪˈpɛlətəs] *a.* erisipelatoso.

erythema [ˌɛrəˈθimə] *s.* (med.) eritema.

erythemal factor [-ˈθiməl-] (ilum.) factor de eficiencia eritémica.

erythema solare, (med.) eritema solar.

erythematous [-ˈθɛmətəs, -ˈθi-] **erythematic** [-θɪˈmætɪk] **erythemic** [-ˈθimɪk] *a.* (med.) eritematoso.

erythrin [ɛˈrɪθrɪn] *s.* (quím.) eritrina.

erythrism [ɪˈrɪθˌrɪzəm] *s.* (med., zool.) eritrismo.

erythrite [-ˌraɪt] *s.* (min., quím.) eritrina, flor de cobalto.

erythritol [ɪˈrɪθrəˌtoʊl, B -ˌtɔl] *s.* (quím.) eritrita.

erythroblast [-ˌblæst, B -ˌblɑst] *s.* (anat.) eritroblasto.

erythrocyte [-ˌsaɪt] *s.* (anat.) eritrocito.

erythrocytometer [ɪˌrɪθrəˌsaɪˈtɑmətər, B -ˈtɔmɪtə] *s.* eritrocitómetro, hematímetro.

erythromycin [-ˈmaɪsən] *s.* (med.) eritromicina.

erythron [ˈɛrəˌθrɑn, B -ˌθrɔn] *s.* (fisiol.) eritrón.

erythropoiesis [ɪˌrɪθrəˌpɔɪˈisəs] *s.* (fisiol.) eritropoyesis.

erythrosin, erythrosine [ɪˈrɪθrəsən] *s.* (quím.) eritrosina.

Erythroxylaceae [ˌɛrəˌθrɑksəˈleɪsɪˌi, B -ˈθrɔksɪ-] *s. pl.* (bot.) eritroxiláceas.

erythroxylaceous [-ˈleɪʃəs] *a.* (bot.) eritroxíleo, eritroxiláceo.

Es *símb. de* **einsteinium,** einstenio (Es).

escadrille [ˈɛskəˌdrɪl] *s.* (mil.) escuadrilla (naval o aérea).

escalade [ˈɛskəˌleɪd, B ˌɛskəˈleɪd] *s.* (mil.) escalada. —*v.t.* escalar.

escalate [ˈɛskəˌleɪt] *v.t.* intensificar (esp. la guerra).

escalation [ˌɛskəˈleɪʃən] *s.* escalada, intensificación (esp. de la guerra).

escalator [ˈɛskəˌleɪtər, B -ə] *s.* escalera mecánica.

escalator clause, (der.) cláusula de ajuste proporcional (de sueldo, alquiler, etc., en un contrato).

escalop, escallop [ɪsˈkɑləp, -ˈkæl-, B -ˈkɔl-] *vars. de* **scallop,** venera.

escapable [ɪsˈkeɪpəbəl] *a.* evitable.

escapade [ˈɛskəˌpeɪd, B ˌɛskəˈpeɪd] *s.* escapada, travesura, aventura.

escape [əˈskeɪp, ɪsˈkeɪp, B ɪs-] *v.i.* 1. escaparse, fugarse, huir. 2. escaparse, salirse (gas, líquido, etc.). 3. (bot.) volverse silvestre. —*v.t.* 1. escapar de, librarse de, salvarse de, evitar (la muerte, infortunio, pena, castigo, etc.). 2. eludir, esquivar, evadir (a una persona, hacer algo, etc.). 3. escapársele (a uno), ej., *nothing escapes her,* no se le escapa nada a ella. 4. olvidársele (a uno), ej., *his name escaped me,* se me olvidó su nombre. 5. salírsele (a uno), ej., *a scream escaped her lips,* se le salió un grito. —*s.* 1. escape, evasión, huida, fuga. 2. escape (de gas, líquido, etc.). 3. (fig.) evasión, escape (de la realidad o rutina). 4. **to have a narrow e.,** escaparse por un pelo. —*a.* 1. de evasión, de escape (literatura, etc.). 2. de escape (válvula, etc.). 3. de salvedad (cláusula, etc.).

escape clause, cláusula de un contrato que libera al firmante de ciertas responsabilidades en determinadas circunstancias.

escapee [ˌɛskeɪˈpi, əˈskeɪpi] *s.* prófugo, fugitivo, esp. prisionero evadido.

escape hatch, (mar.) escotilla de emergencia.

escape mechanism, (psic.) mecanismo de escape.

escapement [əˈskeɪpmənt, ɪsˈkeɪp-, B ɪs-] *s.* escape (del reloj).

escape velocity, (astr.) velocidad de escape, velocidad de liberación.

escapism [-ˌɪzəm] *s.* escapismo.

escapist [-əst] *s.* escapista.

escarole [ˈɛskəˌroʊl] *s.* (bot.) escarola.

escarp [ɪsˈkɑrp, ɛs-, B -ˈkɑp] *s.* escarpa, escarpadura; (fort.) escarpa. —*v.t.* (fort.) escarpar.

escarpment [-mənt] *s.* acantilado, escarpa; (fort.) escarpa.

eschalot [ˈɛʃəˌlɑt, B -ˌlɔt] *s.* (bot.) chalote, escaloña.

eschar [ˈɛsˌkɑr, B -ˌkɑ] *s.* (med.) escara, costra.

eschar, *var. de* **esker.**

escharotic [ˌɛskəˈrɑtɪk, B -ˈrɔt-] *a., s.* (med.) escarótico.

eschatological [ˌɛsˌkætəˈlɑdʒɪkəl, ˌɛskətə-, B -ˈlɔdʒ-] *a.* escatológico.

eschatology [ˌɛskəˈtɑlədʒɪ, B -ˈtɔl-] *s.* escatología.

escheat [ɪsˈtʃit] *s.* (der.) reversión (de los bienes del que muere intestado) al rey o al estado; bienes mostrencos que revierten al rey o al estado. —*v.t., v.i.* hacer revertir al estado (bienes del que muere intestado), confiscar.

escheatable [-əbəl] *a.* (der.) revertible.

escheatage [-ɪdʒ] *s.* (der.) derecho de confiscación (de propiedad del que muere intestado).

eschew [ɪsˈtʃu, ɛs-] *v.t.* evitar, abstenerse de, evadir.

eschewal [-əl] *s.* evitación, abstención (de cierto acto, conducta, alimento, etc.).

escort [ˈɛsˌkɔrt, B -ˌkɔt] *s.* escolta, convoy, acompañante. — [ɪsˈkɔrt, B -ˈkɔt] *v.t.* escoltar, acompañar.

escort carrier, (mil.) buque-escolta; portaviones de escolta.

escort fighter, (mil.) caza de escolta (avión).

escrow [ˈɛsˌkroʊ, B ɛsˈkroʊ] *s.* (der.) plica; **in e.,** en depósito, en custodia (de tercera persona). —*v.t.* (der.) entregar en depósito (a tercera persona).

escudo [ɛsˈkudoʊ] *s.* escudo (unidad monetaria de Chile y Portugal).

esculent [ˈɛskjələnt] *a., s.* comestible.

escutcheon [ɪsˈkʌtʃən] *s.* 1. escudo de armas. 2. escudo, escudete (de cerradura); placa ornamental. 3. (mar.) espejo de popa. 4. **a blot on one's e.,** (fig.) un baldón o una mancha en la reputación de uno.

escutcheoned [-ənd] *a.* blasonado.

ESE *abrev. de* **east-southeast,** estesudeste (ESE).

eserine, eserin [ˈɛsəˌrin] *s.* (quím.) eserina.

esker [ˈɛskər, B -kə] *s.* (geol.) lomo o caballón de cascajo.

Eskimo [ˈɛskəˌmoʊ] *s.* (*pl.* ESKIMO O ESKIMOS) 1. esquimal. 2. idioma esquimal. —*a.* esquimal; **e. dog,** perro esquimal.

Eskimoan [ˌɛskəˈmoʊən] *a.* esquimal.

ESL *abrev. de* **English as a Second Language,** inglés como secunda lengua.

esophageal [ɪˌsɑfəˈdʒiəl, ˌisəˈfædʒɪ-, B iˈsɔfədʒiəl] *a.* (anat.) esofágico.

esophagus [ɪˈsɑfəgəs, B ɪˈsɔf-] *s.* (*pl.* ESOPHAGI [-ˌgaɪ, -ˌdʒaɪ]) (anat., zool.) esófago.

esoteric [ˌɛsəˈtɛrɪk] *a.* 1. esotérico, abstruso, recóndito. 2. privado, particular, confidencial.

esoterica [-ɪkə] *s. pl.* artículos esotéricos.

ESP *abrev. de* **extrasensory perception,** percepción extrasensorial.

espadrille [ˈɛspəˌdrɪl] *s.* alpargata, esparteña.

espagnolette [ɛˈspænjəˌlɛt] *s.* falleba, tarabilla.

espalier [ɪsˈpæljər, B -jə] *s.* espaldera, enrejado, encañado, arriste. —*v.t.* aparrar (ramas de un árbol).

esparto grass [ɛsˈpɑrtoʊ-, B -ˈpɑt-] (bot.) esparto, hierba de España o de Argel, atocha, atochón.

especial [ɪsˈpɛʃəl] *a.* especial, particular.

especially [-ɪ] *adv.* especialmente, particularmente.

Esperantist [ˌɛspəˈræntəst, -ˈrɑn-] *s.* esperantista.

Esperanto [-oʊ] *s.* esperanto.

espial [ɛsˈpaɪəl, ɪs-] *s.* acecho, observación, vigilancia.

espionage [ˈɛspɪəˌnɑʒ, -nɪdʒ, B ˌɛspɪəˈnɑʒ] *s.* espionaje.

esplanade [ˌɛspləˈneɪd, ˈɛs-ˌnɑd, B ˌɛs-ˈneɪd] *s.* 1. explanada. 2. terraplén costañero. 3. (fort.) explanada.

espousal [ɪsˈpaʊzəl] *s.* 1. (*gen. pl.*) esponsales. 2. boda, matrimonio. 3. (fig.) adopción, apoyo (de una teoría, doctrina, etc.), adhesión (a una causa).

espouse [ɪsˈpaʊz] *v.t.* 1. desposar, casarse con; casar, dar en matrimonio. 2. (fig.) abrazar (una causa), adoptar (una doctrina).

espresso [ɛsˈprɛsoʊ] *s.* expreso, café exprés *or* expreso (café preparado en cafetera a presión).

esprit [ɛsˈpri, B ˈɛspri] *s.* (fr.) espíritu, ingenio, agudeza.

esprit de corps [-dəˈkɔr, B -ˈkɔ] (fr.) solidaridad, espíritu de equipo, armonía en un conjunto de personas.

espy [ɪsˈpaɪ, ɛs-] *v.t.* (*pret., p.p.* ESPIED; *p.pr.* ESPYING) divisar, columbrar, espiar.

Esquimau, *var. de* **eskimo.**

esquire [ˈɛskwaɪr, ɪsˈkwaɪr, B ɪsˈkwaɪə] *s.* 1. (ant.) escudero. 2. terrateniente. 3. **Esq.** (abrev. que se usa como título de cortesía y se agrega a un nombre sin anteponer ningún otro título), señor, ej., *John Smith, Esq.,* Sr. John Smith.

essay [ˈɛsˌeɪ] *s.* 1. ensayo, prueba, intento, tentativa. 2. (lit.) ensayo. 3. ensayo, composición (escolar). 4. (impr.) prueba (de un diseño no aceptado de un sello postal o billete). 5. (ant.) muestra. — [ɛˈseɪ, ˈɛsˌeɪ] *v.t.* 1. probar, someter a prueba (a persona o cosa). 2. probar, intentar, ensayar (una tarea, etc.); tratar de (hacer algo).

essayist [ˈɛsˌeɪəst] *s.* ensayista, escritor de ensayos.

essence [ˈɛsəns] *s.* 1. esencia, substancia, naturaleza intrínseca, médula. 2. ente. 3. (filos.) esencia. 4. (quím.) esencia, extracto. 5. **in e.,** en esencia; esencialmente; **of the e.,** esencial, indispensable.

Essene [ˈɛsˌin, ɛˈsin] *s.* (hist.) esenio, miembro de una antigua secta hebrea.

essential [əˈsɛntʃəl, B ɪˈsɛnʃəl] *a.* 1. esencial. 2. esencial, intrínseco, inherente. —*s.* 1. elemento esencial, base. 2. cosa indispensable, necesidad fundamental. 3. **to stick to essentials,** ir al grano.

essentiality [ɪˌsɛntʃɪˈælətɪ, B ɪˌsɛnʃɪ-] *s.* esencialidad.

essentially [ə'sɛntʃəlɪ, B ɪ'sɛnʃ-] *adv.* esencialmente.
essential mineral, mineral básico o esencial.
essential oil, aceite esencial o volátil.
essoin [ɪs'ɔɪn] *s.* 1. (G.B., der.) excusa para no presentarse ante una corte. 2. (ant.) excusa, demora, tardanza.
essonite ['ɛsən,aɪt] *s.* (min.) esonita, grosularia canela.
EST *abrev. de* **eastern standard time,** hora oficial del Este.
establish [ə'stæblɪʃ, B ɪs'tæb-] *v.t.* 1. establecer, afirmar (principio, verdad, hecho, teoría, etc.). 2. establecer, constituir (gobierno, negocio, etc.). 3. establecer, fundar, instituir (colonia, estado, etc.). 4. reconocer, oficializar (una religión). 5. (naipes) afirmar, establecer (un palo, una carta). 6. probar, demostrar, ej., *to e. one's case at law,* probar uno su caso ante la ley. 7. **e. (someone) in,** establecer (a alguien) en (negocio, oficio, casa, etc.); **e. oneself in,** establecerse en (un negocio, posición favorable, casa, etc.). —*v.i.* aclimatarse (planta).
established church, iglesia oficial o reconocida.
establisher [-lɪʃər, B -ə] *s.* establecedor.
establishment [-mənt] *s.* 1. establecimiento. 2. (mil.) efectivos. 3. **the E.,** (G.B.) la Iglesia Anglicana. 4. clase o círculo que gobierna una nación, una institución, etc. 5. pensión o renta vitalicia.
estafet, estafette [,ɛstə'fɛt] *s.* estafeta, correo montado, correo.
estate [ə'steɪt, B ɪs'teɪt] *s.* 1. estado, condición. 2. estado, orden, clase (plebeyo, eclesiástico, etc.). 3. bienes (raíces o inmuebles), fortuna, propiedades. 4. hacienda, finca, heredad. 5. (der.) testamentaría, caudal hereditario, cuerpo de la herencia. 6. **the fourth e.,** (fam.) el cuarto poder (la prensa); **the Three Estates,** los tres estados, los tres órdenes (el clero, la nobleza y el pueblo). —*v.t.* (ant.) legar; dotar.
esteem [ə'stim, B ɪs'tim] *v.t.* 1. estimar, apreciar, respetar. 2. considerar, juzgar. 3. creer, opinar. 4. (ant.) valorar, evaluar. —*s.* 1. estimación, consideración, estima, aprecio. 2. (ant.) valorización, tasación; reputación, rango. 3. **to hold in e.,** tener en estima, estimar, apreciar.
ester ['ɛstər, B -tə] *s.* (quím.) éster.
esterase [-tə,reɪs] *s.* (bioquím.) estearasa, esterase.
esterify [ɛs'tɛrə,faɪ] *v.t., v.i.* (quím.) convertir(se) en éster.
esthesia [ɛs'θiʒə, B -'θizɪə] *s.* (med.) estesia, sensibilidad.
esthesiometer [ɛs,θizɪ'ɑmətər, B -'ɔmɪtə] *s.* estesiómetro.
esthesis [ɛs'θisəs] *s.* estesia.
esthete, esthetic, *var. de* **aesthete, aesthetic.**
esthetically [ɛs'θɛtɪkəlɪ] *adv.* estéticamente.
esthetics [-ɪks] *s.* (filos.) estética.
esthiomene [ɛs'θaɪə,min] *s.* (med.) estiómeno.
estimable ['ɛstəməbəl] *a.* 1. estimable, calculable. 2. (ant.) valioso.
estimableness [-nəs] *s.* estimabilidad.
estimate ['ɛstə,meɪt] *v.t.* 1. estimar, valorar, avaluar, tasar. 2. estimar, juzgar. — [-mət] *s.* 1. estimación, valoración, tasación. 2. cálculo, calculación; presupuesto. 3. juicio, opinión.
estimation [,ɛstə'meɪʃən] *s.* 1. estimación, valoración, cálculo. 2. juicio, opinión. 3. estimación, estima, aprecio. 4. **to hold in e.,** hacer estimación de, estimar, tener en (alta) estima.
estimator ['ɛstə,meɪtər, B -ə] *s.* tasador, estimador.
estival, estivate, estivation, *var. de* **aestival, aestivate, aestivation.**

Estonia [ɛs'toʊnɪə] *s.* Estonia.
Estonian [-nɪən] *s.* 1. estonio, natural de Estonia. 2. (idioma) estonio.
estop [ɛ'stɑp, B ɛ'stɔp] (*pret., p.p.* ESTOPPED; *p.pr.* ESTOPPING) *v.t.* 1. (der.) impedir, prevenir (afirmación o negación de lo que por acción previa ha sido admitido, implicado o determinado como lo contrario).
estoppel [-əl] *s.* (der.) (recurso de) impedimento para que alguien no pueda alegar o negar algo que él mismo, en efecto o por implicación, ha afirmado, negado o alegado anteriormente.
estovers [ɛ'stoʊvərz, B -vəz] *s. pl.* (der.) abastecimientos necesarios; árboles que se tiene derecho a cortar en un predio arrendado; asignación que se da a una mujer divorciada.
estrade [ɛ'strɑd] *s.* estrado, tarima.
estradiol [,ɛstrə'daɪ,əl] *s.* (bioquím.) estradiol.
estrange [ɪs'treɪndʒ, ɛs-] *v.t.* enajenar; **e. from,** malquistar, enemistar (con); apartar, separar (de).
estrangement [-mənt] *s.* 1. extrañamiento, desavenencia. 2. separación, alejamiento.
estray [ɪs'treɪ] *s.* (der.) animal doméstico descarriado. —*v.i.* (ant.) vagar, alejarse (de su sitio).
estreat [ɪs'trit, ɛs-] *s.* (der.) copia fiel del original; duplicado o extracto del original. —*v.t.* 1. (der.) extractar de los archivos de la corte para procesar o hacer cumplir la ley. 2. exigir tributo; multar.
estrin ['ɛstrən] *s.* (bioquím.) estrona.
estriol ['ɛs,traɪ,əl] *s.* (bioquím.) estriol.
estrogen ['ɛstrədʒən] *s.* (bioquím.) estrógeno.
estrogenic [,ɛstrə'dʒɛnɪk] *a.* (bioquím.) estrógeno.
estrone ['ɛs,troʊn] *s.* (bioquím.) estrona, foliculina.
estrus ['ɛstrəs] *s.* (vet.) estro; (fig.) estro, estímulo, inspiración.
estuarine ['ɛstʃʊə,raɪn] *a.* (geol.) estuarino, del estuario, formado o depositado en el estuario (de un río).
estuary [-,ɛrɪ, B -ərɪ] *s.* (*pl.* ESTUARIES) estuario, estero, ría.
esurience [ɪ'sʊrɪəns, B ɪ'sjʊr-] **esuriency** [-ənsɪ] *s.* hambre, voracidad; codicia.
esurient [-ənt] *a.* hambriento, voraz, glotón; anhelante, codicioso.
Et *símb. de* **ethyl,** etilo.
ET *abrev. de* **Eastern Time,** hora del Este.
eta ['eɪtə, 'itə, B 'itə] *s.* eta, séptima letra del alfabeto griego.
ETA *abrev. de* **estimated time of arrival,** hora prevista de llegada.
étagère, etagere [,eɪtɑ'ʒɛr, B -'ʒɛər] *s.* (fr.) juguetero, estante abierto para exhibir objetos pequeños.
et cetera [ɛt'sɛtərə] etcétera, lo demás, lo que resta, lo que sigue, y así sucesivamente.
etcetera [-ərə] *s.* 1. enumeración, lista (de personas o cosas no especificadas). 2. (*pl.*) cositas, cachivaches.
etch [ɛtʃ] *v.t., v.i.* grabar al agua fuerte.
etcher ['ɛtʃər, B -ə] *s.* grabador, aguafuertista.
etching [-ɪŋ] *s.* 1. grabado. 2. aguafuerte.
ETD *abrev. de* **estimated time of departure,** hora prevista de partida.
eternal [ɪ'tɜrnəl, B ɪ'tɜn-] *a.* 1. eterno, eternal, sempiterno, perpetuo, perenne. 2. (fam.) eterno, incesante, constante, repetido. —*s.* 1. **the E.,** el Eterno, el Padre Eterno. 2. (*pl.*) cosas eternas.
Eternal City, (ú. con *the*) la Ciudad Eterna (Roma).
eternally [-ɪ] *adv.* eternamente, perpetuamente, por siempre.

eternalness [-nəs] *s.* carácter eterno, naturaleza eterna.
eternity [-nətɪ] *s.* (*pl.* ETERNITIES) eternidad, perpetuidad, perennidad.
eternize [-,naɪz] *v.t.* 1. eternizar, perpetuar, prolongar indefinidamente. 2. inmortalizar.
etesian [ɪ'tiʒən] *a.* etesio, anual (apl. a ciertos vientos mediterráneos). —*s.* (viento) etesio.
ethane ['ɛθ,eɪn] *s.* (quím.) etano.
ethanol ['ɛθə,nɔl] *s.* (quím.) etanol.
ethene ['ɛθ,in] *s.* (quím.) etileno.
ether ['iθər, B 'iθə] *s.* 1. éter (las altas regiones del espacio). 2. (quím.) éter. 3. (fís.) éter (medio hipotético constitutivo del espacio por el cual se propagan las ondas luminosas y electro-magnéticas).
ethereal [ɪ'θɪrɪəl, B ɪ'θɪər-] *a.* 1. etéreo, celestial; tenue. 2. (quím., fís.) etéreo.
ethereality [ɪ,θɪrɪ'ælətɪ, B ɪ,θɪər-] *s.* carácter etéreo; espiritualidad, tenuidad.
etherealize [ɪ'θɪrɪə,laɪz, B ɪ'θɪər-] *v.t.* volver etéreo, espiritualizar.
ethereally [-lɪ] *adv.* de manera etérea.
etheric [ɪ'θɛrɪk] *a.* etéreo, celestial.
etherification [ɪ,θɛrəfə'keɪʃən] *s.* (quím.) eterificación.
etherify [ɪ'θɛrə,faɪ] *v.t.* (*pret., p.p.* ETHERIFIED; *p.pr.* ETHERIFYING) (quím.) eterificar.
etherism ['iθə,rɪzəm] *s.* (med.) eterismo.
etherization [,iθərə'zeɪʃən, B -raɪ-] *s.* (med.) eterización.
etherize ['iθə,raɪz] *v.t.* 1. (med.) eterizar. 2. (fig.) insensibilizar, entorpecer.
ethic ['ɛθɪk] *s.* 1. (*pl.*) (*sing. o pl. en const.*) ética, sistema ético. 2. (*gen. pl.*) ética, moralidad. —*a.* ético.
ethical [-ɪkəl] *a.* ético, moral.
ethically [-ɪkəlɪ] *adv.* éticamente, moralmente.
ethicize ['ɛθə,saɪz] *v.t.* volver ético, dar carácter ético a. —*v.i.* tratar acerca de la ética; hablar sobre la moral.
ethics [-ɪks] *s. pl.* ética, moral.
Ethiop ['iθɪ,ɑp, B -,ɔp] *a., s.* etíope, etiope.
Ethiopia [,iθɪ'oʊpɪə] *s.* Etiopía.
Ethiopian [-pɪən] *a.* etiópico, etíope, etiope. —*s.* 1. etíope, etiopio, natural de Etiopía. 2. (ant.) negro.
Ethiopic [-'ɑpɪk, -'oʊpɪk, B -'ɔp-] *a.* etiópico. —*s.* lengua etiópica clásica.
ethmoid ['ɛθ,mɔɪd] **ethmoidal** [ɛθ-'mɔɪdəl] *a.* (anat.) etmoides, etmoidal. —*s.* (anat.) etmoides.
ethnarch [-,nɑrk, B -,nɑk] *s.* (hist.) etnarca.
ethnarchy [-,nɑrkɪ, B -,nɑkɪ] *s.* (hist.) etnarquía.
ethnic ['ɛθnɪk] *a.* étnico.
ethnical [-nɪkəl] *a.* 1. étnico. 2. etnológico.
ethnically [-kəlɪ] *adv.* étnicamente; etnológicamente.
ethnic cleansing, limpieza étnica.
ethnocentrism [,ɛθnoʊ'sɛn,trɪzəm] *s.* etnocentrismo.
ethnogeny [ɛθ'nɑdʒənɪ, B -'nɔdʒ-] *s.* etnogenia.
ethnographer [-'nɑgrəfər, B -'nɔgrəfə] *s.* etnógrafo.
ethnographic [,ɛθnə'græfɪk] **ethnographical** [-ɪkəl] *a.* etnográfico.
ethnography [ɛθ'nɑgrəfɪ, B -'nɔg-] *s.* etnografía.
ethnologic [,ɛθnə'lɑdʒɪk, B -'lɔdʒ-] **ethnological** [-ɪkəl] *a.* etnológico.
ethnologically [-ɪkəlɪ] *adv.* etnológicamente.
ethnologist [ɛθ'nɑlədʒəst, B -'nɔl-] *s.* etnólogo.

ethnology [-dʒɪ] *s.* etnología.
ethology [ɪ'θɑlədʒɪ, B ɪ'θɔl-] *s.* (biol.) etología.
ethos ['iˌθɑs, B 'iˌθɔs] *s.* carácter distintivo, genio (de un grupo humano).
ethyl ['ɛθəl] *s.* (quím.) etilo.
ethyl acetate, (quím.) acetato de etilo.
ethyl alcohol, (quím.) alcohol etílico.
ethylamine ['ɛθələˌmin] *s.* (quím.) etilamina.
ethylate ['ɛθəˌleɪt] *v.t.* (quím.) etilar.
ethylation [ˌɛθə'leɪʃən] *s.* (quím.) etilación.
ethyl cellulose, (quím.) celulosa de etilo.
ethyl chloride, (quím.) cloruro de etilo.
ethylene ['ɛθəˌlin] *s.* (quím.) etileno.
ethylene glycol, (quím.) etilenglicol.
ethyl ether, (quím.) éter etílico.
ethyl fluid, plomo tetraetilo.
ethylic [ɛ'θɪlɪk] *a.* etílico.
etiolate ['itɪəˌleɪt] *v.t., v.i.* blanquear, emblanquecer, descolorar, palidecer(se).
etiolation [ˌitɪə'leɪʃən] *s.* descoloramiento, descolorimiento, descoloración, decoloración.
etiologic [ˌitɪə'lɑdʒɪk, B -'lɔdʒ-] **etiological** [-ɪkəl] *a.* etiológico.
etiology [-'ɑlədʒɪ, B -'ɔl-] *s.* (filos., med.) etiología.
etiquette ['ɛtɪkət, B -ˌkɛt] *s.* etiqueta, ceremonia.
Etna ['ɛtnə] *s.* Etna, volcán de Sicilia.
Etnean [ɛt'niən] *a.* etneo, perteneciente al Etna.
Eton collar ['itən-] cuello ancho almidonado (que usan los estudiantes del Colegio de Eton, Inglaterra).
Eton jacket, chaqueta negra corta con solapas (que visten los estudiantes del Colegio de Eton, Inglaterra).
Etrurian [ɪ'trʊrɪən, B ɪ'trʊər-] *var. de* **Etruscan.**
Etruscan [ɪ'trʌskən] *a.* etrusco. *—s.* 1. etrusco, habitante de Etruria. 2. (idioma) etrusco.
étude ['eɪˌtud, B eɪ'tjud] *s.* (mús.) estudio, composición para instrumento solo.
etui [eɪ'twi, B ɛ-] *s.* (fr.) estuche, cajita.
etymological [ˌɛtəmə'lɑdʒɪkəl, B -'lɔdʒ-] *a.* etimológico.
etymologically [-kəlɪ] *adv.* etimológicamente.
etymologist [-'mɑlədʒəst, B -'mɔl-] *s.* etimologista, etimólogo.
etymologize [-ˌdʒaɪz] *v.t., v.i.* etimologizar, sacar o averiguar etimologías, estudiar las etimologías.
etymology [-dʒɪ] *s.* etimología.
etymon ['ɛtəˌmɑn, B -ˌmɔn] *s.* (*pl.* ETYMONS O ETYMA [-mə]) (gram.) étimo, raíz.
Eu *símb. de* **europium,** europio (Eu).
Euboean [jʊ'biən] *a., s.* eubeo, euboico.
Euboic [-'boʊɪk] *a.* eubeo, euboico.
eucaine ['juˌkeɪn] *s.* (quím., farm.) eucaína.
eucalypt ['jukəˌlɪpt] *s.* (bot.) eucalipto.
eucalyptol [ˌjukə'lɪptɔl] *s.* (quím., farm.) eucaliptol.
eucalyptus [-təs] *s.* (*pl.* EUCALYPTI [-ˌtaɪ] O EUCALYPTUSES) (bot.) eucalipto.
Eucharist ['jukərəst] *s.* (relig.) Eucaristía.
Eucharistic [ˌjukə'rɪstɪk] **Eucharistical** [-ɪkəl] *a.* eucarístico.
euchology [ˌju'kɑlədʒɪ, B -'kɔl-] *s.* (rel.) eucologio.
euchre ['jukər, B -kə] *s.* juego de naipes. *—v.t.* 1. dar codillo, en el juego de "euchre". 2. (jer.) burlar, engañar, timar.
euchromatin [ju'kroʊmətən] *s.* (biol.) eucromatina.
euchromosome [-ˌsoʊm] *s.* (biol.) eucromosoma.
Euciliata [ˌjusɪlɪ'eɪtə] *s. pl.* (zool.) eucilistos.
euciliate [ju'sɪlɪət] *s.* (zool.) euciliado.
euclase ['juˌkleɪs] *s.* (min.) euclasa.
Euclid ['juklɪd] *s.* Euclides, matemático griego.
Euclidean, Euclidian [ju'klɪdɪən] *a.* euclidiano, relativo a las teorías de Euclides.
Euclidean algorithm, (geom.) algoritmo de Euclides.
Euclidean geometry, geometría de Euclides.
eudaemonia [ˌjudɪ'moʊnɪə] *s.* (filos.) eudemonía.
eudaemonism [ju'diməˌnɪzəm] *s.* (filos.) eudemonismo, doctrina que sostiene que la felicidad es el sumo bien.
eudaemonist [-nəst] *s.* (filos.) eudemonista.
eudiometer [ˌjudɪ'ɑmətər, B -'ɔmɪtə] *s.* (quím.) eudiómetro.
eudiometric [-ə'mɛtrɪk] **eudiometrical** [-trɪkəl] *a.* (quím.) eudiométrico.
eudiometry [-'ɑmətrɪ, B -'ɔm-] *s.* (quím.) eudiometría.
eugenia [ju'dʒinɪə, jʊ-] *s.* (bot.) acona.
eugenic [jʊ'dʒɛnɪk] *a.* eugenésico.
eugenicist [-əsəst] *s.* (med.) eugenista.
eugenics [-ɪks] *s. pl.* eugenesia.
eugenism [-ˌɪzəm] *var. de* **eugenics.**
eugenol ['judʒəˌnɔl] *s.* (quím.) eugenol.
euglena [jʊ'glinə] *s.* (zool.) euglena.
eulogist ['julədʒəst] *s.* panegirista, encomiasta, elogiador.
eulogistic [ˌjulə'dʒɪstɪk] *a.* laudatorio, elogiador, encomiástico, panegírico.
eulogistically [-tɪkəlɪ] *adv.* laudatoriamente, de manera encomiástica.
eulogium [jʊ'loʊdʒɪəm] *s.* (*pl.* EULOGIUMS O EULOGIA [-dʒɪə]) elogio, encomio, apología, preconización, ensalzamiento.
eulogize ['juləˌdʒaɪz] *v.t.* elogiar, preconizar, ensalzar, panegirizar, loar, encomiar.
eulogizer [-ər, B -ə] *s.* panegirista.
eulogy [-dʒɪ] *s.* 1. elogio, encomio, apología, ensalzamiento. 2. oración de alabanza, panegírico.
Eumenides [jʊ'mɛnəˌdiz] *s. pl.* (mitol., lit.) Euménides (las Furias).
eunuch ['junək] *s.* eunuco; capón.
eupatheoscope [jʊ'pæθɪəˌskoʊp] *s.* eupateoscopio.
eupatorium [ˌjupə'tɔrɪəm] *s.* (bot.) eupatorio.
eupatrid [jʊ'pætrəd] *s.* (hist.) eupátrida.
eupepsia [-'pɛpʃə, B ju-sɪə] *s.* (med.) eupepsia.
eupeptic [-'pɛptɪk] *a.* eupéptico.
euphemism ['jufəˌmɪzəm] *s.* (ret.) eufemismo.
euphemistic [ˌjufə'mɪstɪk] *a.* eufemístico.
euphemistically [-tɪkəlɪ] *adv.* en forma eufemística, de modo eufemístico.
euphemize ['jufəˌmaɪz] *v.t., v.i.* (ret.) hacer uso del eufemismo, expresar(se) con eufemismos.
euphonic [jʊ'fɑnɪk, B -'fɔn-] *a.* eufónico.
euphonically [-ɪkəlɪ] *adv.* eufónicamente.
euphonious [-'foʊnɪəs] *a.* eufónico, de sonido agradable.
euphonium [-əm] *s.* (mús.) especie de tuba tenor.
euphonize ['jufəˌnaɪz] *v.t.* eufonizar, harmonizar.
euphony [-nɪ] *s.* (ret.) eufonía.
euphorbia [jʊ'fɔrbɪə, B -'fɔbɪə] *s.* (bot.) euforbio.
Euphorbiaceae [-ˌfɔrbɪ'eɪsɪˌi, B -ˌfɔbɪ-] *s. pl.* (bot.) euforbiáceas.
euphorbiaceous [-'eɪʃəs] *a.* (bot.) euforbiáceo.
euphorbium [-'fɔrbɪəm, B -'fɔbɪ-] *s.* (farm.) euforbio.
euphoria [jʊ'fɔrɪə] *s.* euforia.
euphoric [-ɪk] *a.* eufórico.
euphoriant [-ɪənt] *a., s.* (med.) estimulante.
euphrasy ['jufrəsɪ] *s.* (bot.) eufrasia.
Euphrates [jʊ'freɪtiz] *s.* río Eufrates, Éufrates.
euphuism ['jufjʊˌɪzəm] *s.* (lit.) eufuismo, culteranismo.
euphuist [-əst] *s.* (lit.) eufuista.
euphuistic [ˌjufjʊ'ɪstɪk] **euphuistical** [-tɪkəl] *a.* eufuístico, culterano.
euphuistically [-tɪkəlɪ] *adv.* de manera eufuística, en forma culterana.
euploid ['juˌplɔɪd] *a.* (biol.) euploide.
eupnea, eupnoea ['jupnɪə, B jup'niə] *s.* (fisiol.) eupnea.
Eur. *abrev. de* 1. **Europe,** Europa. 2. **European,** europeo.
Eurasia [jʊ'reɪʒə, -ʃə] *s.* (geog.) Eurasia.
Eurasian [-ʒən, -ʃən] *a.* eurasiático.
EURATOM, *abrev. de* **European Atomic Energy Community,** Comunidad Europea de Energía Atómica.
eureka [jʊ'rikə] *interj.* ¡eureka! (¡lo encontré!).
Euripidean [jʊˌrɪpə'diən] *a.* (propio) de Eurípides.
Euripides [-'rɪpəˌdiz] *s.* Eurípides, uno de los grandes dramaturgos de la Grecia antigua.
Eurodollar ['jʊrəˌdɑlər] *s.* eurodólar.
Europe ['jʊrəp, B 'jʊər-] *s.* Europa.
European [ˌjʊrə'piən, B ˌjʊər-] *a., s.* europeo, natural de Europa.
European bunting, (orn.) hortelano.
European Economic Community, (t. **Common Market**) Mercado Común Europeo.
Europeanize [-ˌaɪz] *v.t.* europeizar.
European plan, (sistema de tarifas en hoteles) alojamiento sin comidas.
europium [jʊ'roʊpɪəm] *s.* (quím.) europio.
Eurovision ['jʊrə'vɪʒən] *s.* Eurovisión (red europea de televisión).
eurybathic [ˌjʊrɪ'bæθɪk] *a.* que vive en el fondo del agua.
Eurydice [jʊ'rɪdəˌsi] *s.* (mitol.) Eurídice (esposa de Orfeo).
euryhaline [ˌjʊrɪ'heɪlaɪn] *a.* capaz de vivir en aguas salinas.
eurypterid [jʊ'rɪptərəd] *s.* (pal.) euriptérido.
eurytherm ['jʊrɪˌθɜrm, B -ˌθɜm] *s.* (biol.) organismo euritermo.
eurythermal [ˌjʊrɪ'θɜrməl, B -'θɜməl] **eurythermic** [-mɪk] **eurythermous** [-məs] *a.* (biol.) euritérmico, euritermo.
eurythmic [jʊ'rɪðmɪk] *a.* (arq., mús.) eurítmico.
eurythmics [-mɪks] *s. pl.* euritmia (el arte).
eurythmy [-mɪ] *s.* euritmia (el movimiento armonioso).
Eustachian tube [jʊ'steɪʃən-, -'steɪkɪən-, B jʊs'teɪʃjən-] (anat.) trompa de Eustaquio.
eustatic [jʊ'stætɪk] *a.* (geog.) eustático.
eustyle ['jʊstaɪl] *s.* (arq.) éustilo.
eutectic [jʊ'tɛktɪk] *a., s.* (fís.) eutéctico.
eutectoid [-ˌtɔɪd] *s., a.* (quím.) eutectoide.
euthanasia [ˌjuθə'neɪʒə, B -zjə] *s.* eutanasia, muerte sin dolor (teoría que sostiene que es más compasivo terminar la vida de un enfermo incurable que dejarle sufrir).
euthenics [jʊ'θɛnɪks] *s. pl.* euténica, ciencia que trata de mejorar las especies y razas a través del control del medio ambiente.
eutrophic [-'trɑfɪk, B -'trɔf-] *a.* (ecol.) eutrófico.
eutrophy ['jutrəfɪ] *s.* (ecol.) eutrofia.
Eutychian [jʊ'tɪkɪən] *s., a.* (hist., relig.) eutiquiano.
Eutychianism [-ˌɪzəm] *s.* eutiquianismo.
euxenite ['juksəˌnaɪt] *s.* (min.) euxenita.
EV *abrev. de* **electron volt,** electronvoltio.
evacuant [ɪ'vækjʊənt] *a., s.* (med.) evacuante, evacuativo.

evacuate [-ˌeɪt] *v.t.* 1. evacuar, desocupar. 2. evacuar, vaciar, expeler (humores o excrementos). 3. (mil.) evacuar (tropas, heridos, civiles, etc.); dejar (las tropas, una plaza o un lugar). —*v.i.* 1. retirarse. 2. excretar.
evacuation [ɪˌvækjʊˈeɪʃən] *s.* 1. evacuación (de tropas; ciudad, plaza, etc.). 2. evacuación, defecación. 3. deyección.
evacuative [ɪˈvækjʊˌeɪtɪv] *a.* (med.) evacuatorio.
evacuator [-ər, B -ə] *s.* evacuador.
evacuee [ɪˌvækjʊˈi] *s.* persona que una autoridad retira de un lugar peligroso o inconveniente; persona desplazada.
evadable [ɪˈveɪdəbəl] *a.* eludible.
evade [ɪˈveɪd] *v.t.* evadir, eludir, evitar, esquivar, rehuir. —*v.i.* 1. usar evasivas o subterfugios. 2. (mil.) efectuar una acción o maniobra evasiva.
evader [-ər, B -ə] *s.* evasor (ej., de impuestos).
evaginate [ɪˈvædʒəˌneɪt] *v.t.* volver al revés, volver de adentro afuera.
evagination [ɪˌvædʒəˈneɪʃən] *s.* (med.) evaginación.
evaluate [ɪˈvæljʊˌeɪt] *v.t.* 1. evaluar, avaluar, valuar, valorar, tasar. 2. (mat.) hallar el valor numérico.
evaluation [ɪˌvæljʊˈeɪʃən] *s.* evaluación, valuación, avalúo, valoración.
evanesce [ˌɛvəˈnɛs, B ˌiv-] *v.i.* desvanecerse, disiparse, esfumarse, evaporarse.
evanescence [-əns] *s.* desvanecimiento, disipación, evaporación.
evanescent [-ənt] *a.* evanescente.
evangel [ɪˈvændʒəl] *s.* (ant.) 1. evangelio. 2. evangelista. 3. doctrina, principio.
evangelic [ˌivænˈdʒɛlɪk] *a.* evangélico.
evangelical [-ɪkəl] *a.* evangélico.
Evangelicalism [-ˌɪzəm] *s.* evangelismo.
evangelically [-ɪkəlɪ] *adv.* evangélicamente.
evangelism [ɪˈvændʒəˌlɪzəm] *s.* 1. evangelización, predicación del evangelio. 2. celo ardiente, gen. en una causa religiosa.
evangelist [-ləst] *s.* 1. evangelista, evangelizador; predicador del evangelio. 2. **E.,** evangelista.
evangelistic [ɪˌvændʒəˈlɪstɪk] *a.* evangélico.
evangelization [-ləˈzeɪʃən, B -laɪ-] *s.* evangelización.
evangelize [ɪˈvændʒəˌlaɪz] *v.t.* evangelizar. —*v.i.* predicar el evangelio.
evangelizer [-ər, B -ə] *s.* evangelizador.
evanish [ɪˈvænɪʃ] *v.i.* (poét.) desvanecerse, desaparecer.
evaporable [ɪˈvæpərəbəl] *a.* evaporable.
evaporate [-əˌreɪt] *v.t., v.i.* (lit., fig.) evaporar, evaporarse.
evaporated milk [-əd-] leche evaporada.
evaporating dish [-ɪŋ-] (lab.) cápsula de evaporación, evaporadora.
evaporation [ɪˌvæpəˈreɪʃən] *s.* evaporación.
evaporative [ɪˈvæpəˌreɪtɪv] *a.* evaporatorio.
evaporative condenser, condensador de evaporación.
evaporator [-ər, B -ə] *s.* evaporador.
evaporimeter [ɪˌvæpəˈrɪmətər, B -tə] əv þɔ-rɑmɘɪɘr [-ˈrɑm-, B -ˈrɔm-] *s.* (fís.) evaporímetro.
evaporize [ɪˈvæpəˌraɪz] *v.t., v.i.* vaporizar.
evapotranspiration [-oʊˌtrænspəˈreɪʃən] *s.* (agr.) evapo-transpiración.
evasion [ɪˈveɪʒən] *s.* 1. evasión, fuga, huida, escape. 2. escapatoria, evasión, efugio, salida. 3. evasión (de impuestos).
evasive [ɪˈveɪsɪv] *a.* evasivo.
evasively [-lɪ] *adv.* evasivamente.
eve [iv] *s.* 1. víspera. 2. (poét.) atardecer, anochecer, noche. 3. **Christmas E.,** Nochebuena; **on the e. of,** la víspera de, en vísperas de.

evection [ɪˈvɛkʃən] *s.* (astr.) evección.
even [ˈivən] *a.* 1. plano, llano. 2. liso. 3. a nivel, paralelo. 4. igual. 5. parejo, regular, uniforme. 6. balanceado, constante. 7. ecuánime, apacible, tranquilo. 8. exacto, cabal, justo. 9. (mat.) par. 10. (com.) saldado. 11. **e. with,** al nivel de, al mismo nivel de; a nivel con, parejo con, a la par con; **on an e. keel,** (mar.) sin diferencia de calados; (fig.) firme, estable; equilibrado; **to be e. (with),** estar en paz (con), haberse vengado (de), estar mano a mano; **to break e.,** recuperar los gastos (en negocio); ni ganar ni perder (en el juego); **to get e. with,** desquitarse de, vengarse de, saldar las cuentas con; **to make e.,** allanar, igualar, aplanar, compensar; **to stand an e. chance,** tener un cincuenta por ciento de probabilidad; **to stay e.,** cubrir los gastos, mantenerse a flote. —*adv.* 1. aun, hasta, ej., *e. he knows it,* aun (o hasta) él lo sabe. 2. siquiera. 3. aún, todavía, ej., *he knows it e. better,* él lo sabe aún (o todavía) mejor. 4. **e. as,** aun como; lo mismo que, al igual que; al mismo tiempo que, mientras; **e. if,** aun cuando; **e. so,** aun así, no obstante; **e. though,** aunque, aun cuando; **e. when,** aun cuando; **not e.,** ni siquiera. —*v.t.* igualar, emparejar, nivelar; **e. up,** balancear (cuentas). —*v.i.* igualarse, emparejarse, nivelarse; **e. up on,** desquitarse de (alguien). —*s.* (poét., ant.) atardecer, anochecer, noche.
evenfall [-ˌfɔl] *s.* (poét.) crepúsculo, anochecer, caída de la tarde.
evenhanded [-ˈhændəd] *a.* justo, imparcial, equitativo.
evening [ˈivnɪŋ] *s.* 1. tarde, atardecer, anochecer, primeras horas de la noche. 2. (fig.) ocaso (de la vida, gloria, etc.). 3. noche, velada, ej., *musical evenings,* veladas musicales. 4. **Good evening!** ¡buenas tardes! ¡buenas noches! —*a.* vespertino; de noche.
evening dress, traje de etiqueta o de ceremonia; traje de noche.
evening gown, vestido de noche, vestido formal de mujer.
evening performance, función nocturna.
evening prayer, (rel.) oración vespertina (vísperas).
evening primrose, (bot.) hierba del asno.
evenings [ˈivnɪŋz] *adv.* por las tardes (repetidamente); en cualquier tarde.
evening star, estrella vespertina, lucero de la tarde.
evening wear, vestido de etiqueta.
evenly [ˈivənlɪ] *adv.* 1. igualmente, con igualdad, en forma pareja. 2. imparcialmente, equitativamente. 3. tranquilamente, suavemente.
evenness [-nəs] *s.* 1. igualdad, equilibrio. 2. uniformidad, regularidad. 3. ecuanimidad.
even number, número par.
evensong [ˈivənˌsɔŋ] *s.* (relig.) vísperas, oraciones vespertinas.
even-steven [-ˈstivən] *adv.* (jer.) mano a mano. —*a.* empatado.
event [ɪˈvɛnt] *s.* 1. evento, acontecimiento, suceso, incidente. 2. caso, contingencia. 3. (dep.) contienda, competencia. 4. **at all events,** de todos modos; **double e.,** (dep.) programa doble; **in any e.,** en todo caso; **in the e. of,** en caso de; **quite an e.,** todo un acontecimiento, una cosa extraordinaria.
even-tempered [ˌivənˈtɛmpərd, B -pəd] *a.* calmado, sereno, plácido, sosegado.
eventful [ɪˈvɛntfəl] *a.* 1. lleno de acontecimientos (día, época, etc.). 2. memorable, extraordinario.
eventfully [-fəlɪ] *adv.* de modo memorable.

eventide [ˈivənˌtaɪd] *s.* (poét.) atardecer, anochecer, noche.
eventual [ɪˈvɛntʃʊəl] *s.* 1. final, subsiguiente. 2. (ant.) eventual.
eventuality [ɪˌvɛntʃʊˈælətɪ, B -tjʊ-] *s.* (*pl.* EVENTUALITIES) eventualidad, contingencia.
eventually [ɪˈvɛntʃʊəlɪ] *adv.* finalmente, con el tiempo, a la larga.
eventuate [-ˌeɪt, B -tjʊ-] *v.i.* 1. acontecer, acaecer, suceder. 2. terminarse, resultar (bien, mal, etc.).
ever [ˈɛvər, B -ə] *adv.* 1. siempre. 2. alguna vez, una vez, ej., *have you e. been in New York?* ¿ha estado Ud. alguna vez en Nueva York? *if I e. catch him,* si lo llego a agarrar alguna vez. 3. jamás, nunca, en la vida. 4. ú. para dar énfasis y no se traduce en castellano o queda traducido con el verbo *poder* o con *nunca* o *jamás,* ej., *how did I e. lose it?* ¿cómo pude perderlo? *will you e. finish?* ¿no terminará usted nunca? *who has e. seen such a thing?* ¿quién ha visto jamás cosa igual? 5. **better than e.,** mejor que nunca; **did you e.?** ¿habráse visto? ¡qué ocurrencia!; **e. since,** desde que, desde entonces; **e. so,** muy, sumamente; **e. so much,** muchísimo, ej., *it's e. so much easier,* es muchísimo más fácil; **for e.,** para siempre, por siempre, eternamente; **for e. and e., for e. and a day,** por los siglos de los siglos, por siempre jamás; **hardly e., scarcely e.,** casi nunca; **nor e.,** ni nunca; **not e.,** nunca; **what e. do you want?** ¿qué más quiere? ¿qué diablos quiere?
everblooming [ˌɛvərˈblumɪŋ, B ˌɛvə-] *a.* siempre floreciente, siempre lozano.
everglade [ˈɛvərˌgleɪd, B ˈɛvəˌ-] *s.* terreno pantanoso cubierto de hierba; **The Everglades,** (E.U.) región pantanosa en la Florida.
evergreen [-ˌgrin] *a.* (bot.) siempre verde. —*s.* 1. (bot.) árbol o planta siempre verdes. 2. (*pl.*) adorno de ramas de plantas siempre verdes.
everlasting [ˌɛvərˈlæstɪŋ, B ˌɛvəˈlɑs-] *a.* 1. eterno, sempiterno, perpetuo. 2. (fig.) eterno, perdurable, duradero. 3. (fig.) eterno, interminable, tedioso. —*s.* 1. eternidad. 2. **the E.,** Dios, el Ser eterno. 3. (bot.) siempreviva, perpetua. 4. (tej.) sempiterna (especie de tela muy duradera y resistente).
everlasting flower, (bot.) perpetua amarilla, siempreviva.
everlastingly [-lɪ] *adv.* eternamente, perpetuamente.
everlastingness [-nəs] *s.* duración eterna e interminable.
evermore [ˌɛvərˈmɔr, B ˈɛvəˈmɔ] *adv.* para siempre; **for e.,** por siempre jamás, eternamente.
eversion [ɪˈvɜrʒən, B ɪˈvɜʃən] *s.* (med.) eversión.
evert [ɪˈvɜrt, B ɪˈvɜt] *v.t.* (med.) volver de dentro hacia afuera (ej., intestino, párpado).
every [ˈɛvrɪ] *a.* 1. cada, ej., *e. three days,* cada tres días. 2. todo, ej., *e. citizen,* todo ciudadano. 3. todos los (las), ej., *e. night,* todas las noches. 4. todo, completo, entero, ej., *e. confidence,* toda o completa confianza. 5. **e. bit,** todo, ej., *e. bit a gentleman (soldier, etc.),* todo un caballero (soldado, etc.); **e. day,** todos los días; **e. man for himself,** cada cual por su cuenta; sálvese quien pueda; **e. now and then,** de cuando en cuando, de vez en cuando; **e. once in a while,** una que otra vez; **e. one,** cada uno, cada cual; **e. other,** cada dos, uno sí y otro no; **e. other day,** un día sí y otro no; **e. so often,** una que otra vez; **e. time,** cada vez; (fam.) siempre; **e. way,** en todo respecto; **e. which way,** (fam.) por todas partes, en toda dirección; desordenadamente.

everybody [-ˌbɑdɪ, B -ˌbɔdɪ] *pron.* cada uno, cada cual; todos; todo el mundo; **e. for himself,** cada cual por su cuenta; sálvese quien pueda.
everyday [-ˌdeɪ] *a.* 1. diario, cotidiano. 2. común, corriente.
everyone [-ˌwʌn] *pron.* todo el mundo, todos; cada uno, cada cual.
everyplace [-ˌpleɪs] *adv.* (fam.) *var. de* **everywhere.**
everything [-ˌθɪŋ] *pron.* todo, toda cosa.
everywhere [-ˌhwɛr, -ˌwɛr, B -ˌwɛə, -ˌhwɛə] *adv.* en todas partes, por todas partes, a todas partes, por donde quiera.
evict [ɪ'vɪkt] *v.t.* 1. desalojar, echar. 2. (der.) desahuciar (al inquilino o arrendatario). 3. excluir, expulsar.
eviction [ɪ'vɪkʃən] *s.* (der.) desahucio, evicción; desalojamiento.
eviction notice, (der.) notificación de desahucio.
evidence ['ɛvədəns] *s.* 1. evidencia. 2. (der.) prueba; testimonio, declaración. 3. **in e.,** visible, manifiesto, notorio; **to be in e.,** estar a la vista, ser conspicuo; **to give e.,** dar testimonio, deponer, declarar; **to show e. (of),** dar o presentar señales (de); **to turn state's e.,** (E.U.) **to turn King's e., to turn Queen's e.,** (G.B.) dar testimonio en contra de sus cómplices. *—v.t.* evidenciar, probar, atestiguar.
evident [-ənt] *a.* evidente, patente, manifiesto; **to be e.,** ser evidente, obvio; resaltar, destacarse.
evidential [ˌɛvə'dɛntʃəl, B -'dɛnʃəl] *a.* indicativo, probatorio, comprobatorio.
evidently ['ɛvədəntlɪ] *adv.* evidentemente. patentemente. manifiestamente.
evil ['ivəl] *a.* malo; maligno, perverso, malvado; nocivo, perjudicial; pernicioso; **e. tongue,** mala lengua, lengua viperina; **social e.,** lacra social; **the E. One,** el Malo, el Maligno, el diablo. *—s.* mal; maldad, perversidad. *—adv.* mal, malignamente.
evildoer [-ˌduər, B -'duə] *s.* malhechor, persona malvada.
evildoing [-ɪŋ] *s.* fechoría.
evil eye, aojo, mal de ojo.
evil-eyed [-ˌaɪd] *a.* aojador, que hace mal de ojo.
evilly ['ivəlɪ] *adv.* malvadamente, perversamente.
evil-minded ['ivəl'maɪndəd] *a.* malintencionado, maligno, de mala índole.
evilness [-nəs] *s.* maldad.
evil repute, pésima fama.
evil spirit, espíritu maligno.
evince [ɪ'vɪns] *v.t.* demostrar, revelar, convencer, imponer su opinión.
evincible [ɪ'vɪnsəbəl] *a.* demostrable.
evincibly [-blɪ] *adv.* convincentemente, demostrablemente.
evincive [-sɪv] *a.* demostrativo, convincente.
eviscerate [ɪ'vɪsəˌreɪt] *v.t.* destripar, desentrañar.
evisceration [ɪˌvɪsə'reɪʃən] *s.* destripamiento, desentrañamiento.
evitable ['ɛvətəbəl] *a.* evitable, eludible.
evocable ['ɛvəkəbəl] *a.* evocable.
evocation [ˌɛvoʊ'keɪʃən] *s.* 1. evocación. 2. (der.) avocación.
evocative [ɪ'vɑkətɪv, B ɪ'vɔk-] *a.* evocador (narración, descripción, etc.).
evoke [ɪ'voʊk] *v.t.* 1. evocar (recuerdos, sentimientos o espíritus). 2. (der.) avocar.
evolute ['ɛvəˌlut, 'ivə-] *s.* (geom.) evoluta.
evolution [ˌɛvə'luʃən, ˌivə-] *s.* 1. evolución, desarrollo, desenvolvimiento. 2. (biol.) evolución; evolucionismo. 3. (mar., mil.) maniobra, evolución. 4. (mat.) extracción de raíces; evolución (de una curva). 5. (quím., fís.) emisión (de gas, calor, etc.).
evolutionary [-ʃəˌnɛrɪ, B -nərɪ] *a.* evolucionista, evolutivo; (mil.) evolucionario.
evolutionism [-ˌnɪzəm] *s.* (biol.) evolucionismo, teoría de la evolución.
evolutionist [-nəst] *s.* (biol.) evolucionista.
evolutive ['ɛvəˌlutɪv, 'ivə-] *a.* evolutivo.
evolve [ɪ'vɑlv, B ɪ'vɔlv] *v.t.* 1. desarrollar, deducir (teorías, etc.). 2. desenvolver, despedir, emitir (gas, calor, etc.). *—v.i.* evolucionar, desarrollarse.
evolvement [-mənt] *s.* 1. desenvolvimiento, desarrollo, evolución. 2. desarrollo, deducción (de teorías, etc.). 3. despedida, emisión (de gas, calor, etc.).
evulsion [ɪ'vʌlʃən] *s.* (med.) evulsión, extracción, extirpación.
ewe [ju] *s.* oveja hembra.
ewe lamb, ovejita, corderita.
ewe-necked ['juˌnɛkt] *a.* de cuello delgado.
ewer ['juər, B -ə] *s.* aguamanil, jarra.
ex [ɛks] *prefijo,* ex, que fue, ej., *ex-minister,* ex ministro. *—prep.* (com.) ex, en, puesto en, ej., *goods ex works,* mercancías puestas en fábrica. *—s.* (fam.) ex-marido, ex-mujer (separados o divorciados).
exacerbate [ɪg'zæsərˌbeɪt B ɛk'sæsəˌ-] *v.t.* 1. exacerbar, agravar, avivar (dolor, pasión, molestia). 2. exacerbar, exasperar, irritar (a una persona).
exacerbation [-ˌzæsər'beɪʃən, B -ˌsæsə'-] *s.* irritación, exasperación.
exact [ɪg'zækt] *a.* 1. exacto, preciso, riguroso. 2. exacto, certero, acertado. *—v.t.* exigir.
exactable [-əbəl] *a.* exigible.
exacter [-ər, B -ə] *s. var. de* **exactor.**
exacting [-ɪŋ] *a.* 1. exigente (persona). 2. pesado, cargante (tarea, trabajo, etc.).
exaction [-'zækʃən] *s.* 1. exacción; extorsión. 2. impuesto excesivo.
exactitude [-'zæktəˌtud, B -ˌtjud] *s.* exactitud, precisión.
exactly [-'zæktlɪ] *adv.* exactamente, precisamente.
exactness [-nəs] *s.* exactitud, precisión.
exactor [-ər, B -ɔ] *s.* exactor, cobrador de impuestos.
exaggerate [ɪg'zædʒəˌreɪt] *v.t.* exagerar.
exaggerated [-əd] *a.* exagerado.
exaggeratedly [-lɪ] *adv.* exageradamente.
exaggeration [-ˌzædʒə'reɪʃən] *s.* exageración.
exaggerative [-'zædʒəˌreɪtɪv, -rətɪv] *a.* exagerativo.
exaggerator [-ər, B -ə] *s.* exagerador.
exalt [ɪg'zɔlt] *v.t.* 1. exaltar, elevar (en grado, distinción, etc.). 2. exaltar, enaltecer, engrandecer, ensalzar, alabar. 3. realzar, avivar (un color).
exaltation [ˌɛgzɔl'teɪʃən] *s.* 1. exaltación, elevación, enaltecimiento. 2. arrebato, éxtasis, júbilo. 3. (astrol.) casa o signo ascendente.
exalted [ɪg'zɔltəd] *a.* 1. exaltado. 2. elevado (estilo, etc.), eminente (personaje). 3. muy favorable (opinión, parecer, etc.).
exaltedly [-lɪ] *adv.* exaltadamente.
exam [ɪg'zæm] *s.* (fam.) examen.
examen [-'zeɪmən, B ɛg-mɛn] *s.* 1. (relig.) examen de conciencia. 2. (lit.) ensayo crítico.
examinable [-'zæmənəbəl] *a.* examinable.
examinant [-nənt] *s.* examinador.
examination [ɪgˌzæmə'neɪʃən] *s.* 1. examen. 2. registro, inspección, análisis. 3. (der.) interrogatorio. 4. **to take an e.,** tomar un examen; **to take an e. in,** examinarse de; **to give an e. in,** dar un examen de.
examinational [-əl] *a.* de examen (método, procedimiento, etc.).
examinatorial [-nə'tɔrɪəl] *a.* de examen; de examinador.
examine [ɪg'zæmən] *v.t.* 1. examinar. 2. registrar, revisar. *—v.i.* interrogar, inquirir.
examinee [-ˌzæmə'ni] *s.* examinando.
examiner [-'zæmənər, B -nə] *s.* examinador.
example [ɪg'zæmpəl, B -'zɑm] *s.* 1. ejemplo. 2. ejemplar, tipo. 3. problema, ejercicio (matemático, etc.). 4. **beyond e.,** sin ejemplo, sin precedente; **for e.,** por ejemplo, verbigracia; **to follow the e. of,** seguir el ejemplo de; **to make an e. of,** hacer un ejemplo de, infligir castigo ejemplar a; **to set an e. (for),** dar o sentar ejemplo (a, para); **without e.,** sin ejemplo, sin precedente.
exanimate [-'zænəmət] *a.* 1. exánime, muerto. 2. sin animación, apagado.
exanimation [-ˌzænə'meɪʃən] *s.* exanimación, muerte; desmayo.
exanthem [ɪg'zænθəm, B ɛk'sæn-] *var. de* **exanthema.**
exanthema [ˌɛgzæn'θimə, B ˌɛksæn-] *s.* (*pl.* EXANTHEMATA [-tə] O EXANTHEMAS) (med.) exantema.
exanthematous [-'θɛmətəs, B -'θi-] *a.* (med.) exantemático, eruptivo.
exarch ['ɛkˌsɑrk, B -ˌsɑk] *s.* (hist.) exarca. *—s.* (hist., relig.) exarcado.
exarchate [-ˌsɑrkət, B -sɑˌkeɪt] *s.* (hist., relig.) exarcado.
exasperate [ɪg'zæspəˌreɪt, B -'zɑs-] *v.t.* 1. exasperar, exacerbar; agravar. 2. enojar, irritar.
exasperation [ɪgˌzæspə'reɪʃən, B -ˌzɑs-] *s.* exasperación, provocación, enojo; recargo.
ex-cathedra [ˌɛkskə'θidrə] *a.* ex cátedra.
excavate ['ɛkskəˌveɪt] *v.t.* excavar, cavar; desenterrar, zanjar.
excavation [ˌɛkskə'veɪʃən] *s.* excavación.
excavator ['ɛkskəˌveɪtər, B -ə] *s.* 1. excavador. 2. (máquina) excavadora.
exceed [ɪk'sid] *v.t.* 1. exceder, superar. 2. propasar, exceder (límite, autoridad, etc.), rebasar. *—v.i.* excederse, propasarse.
exceeding [-ɪŋ] *a.* excesivo, sumo, extremo, extraordinario.
exceedingly [-lɪ] *adv.* sumamente, extremadamente, extraordinariamente.
excel [ɪk'sɛl] *v.t.* (*pret., p.p.* EXCELLED; *p.pr.* EXCELLING) aventajar, superar. *—v.i.* sobresalir, distinguirse.
excellence ['ɛksələns] *s.* excelencia.
excellency [-lənsɪ] *s.* 1. excelencia. 2. **E.,** Excelencia (título honorífico). 3. **His E.,** Su Excelencia.
excellent [-lənt] *a.* excelente, sobresaliente.
excellently [-lɪ] *adv.* excelentemente.
excelsior [ɪk'sɛlsɪər, B -sɪɔ] *a., interj.* más alto, siempre arriba. *—s.* viruta de madera (para empaquetar y rellenar).
excentric, *var. de* **eccentric.**
except [ɪk'sɛpt] *v.t.* exceptuar, excluir. *—v.i.* (der.) recusar, exceptuar; **e. against,** objetar a. *—prep.* excepto, salvo; a excepción de; **e. for,** si no fuera por, a no ser por; aparte de, ej., *e. for a few mistakes it's all right,* aparte de unos cuantos errores está bien; **e. that,** (fam.) sólo que, ej., *I'd buy it, e. that I've no money,* lo compraría, sólo que no tengo dinero. *—conj.* sino, fuera de que.
excepting [-ɪŋ] *prep.* a excepción de, salvo, fuera de.
exception [-'sɛpʃən] *s.* 1. excepción, salvedad. 2. objeción, reparo, crítica. 3. (der.) excepción; recusación. 4. **the e. proves the rule,** la excepción confirma la regla; **to take e. to,** objetar,

oponerse a, criticar; **with the e. of,** a excepción de, excepto.
exceptionable [-ʃənəbəl] *a.* impugnable, recusable, tachable.
exceptional [-ʃənəl] *a.* excepcional, extraordinario, poco común, superior.
exceptionally [-ɪ] *adv.* excepcionalmente.
exceptive [ɪk'sɛptɪv] *a.* 1. exceptivo. 2. (ant.) susceptible, quisquilloso.
excerpt [ɛk'sɜrpt, 'ɛkˌsɜrpt, B ɛk'sɜpt] *v.t.* 1. extractar, condensar (un libro, un escrito). 2. (con *from*) seleccionar, citar (de). — ['ɛkˌsɜrpt, B -ˌsɜpt] *s.* 1. excerpta, extracto, resumen (de un libro, escrito, etc.). 2. pasaje, cita.
excerption [ɛk'sɜrpʃən, B -'sɜp-] *s.* selección, cita literaria.
excess [ɪk'sɛs, 'ɛkˌsɛs] *s.* 1. exceso, demasía, superfluidad. 2. exceso, abuso (en placeres, afectos, etc.). 3. exceso, excedente. 4. **in e. of,** más que; **to e.,** en exceso. —*a.* excesivo, excedente, sobrante.
excess baggage, e. luggage, exceso de equipaje.
excessive [ɪk'sɛsɪv] *a.* excesivo, inmoderado, desmedido.
excessively [-lɪ] *adv.* excesivamente, inmoderadamente, desmedidamente.
excess profits tax, impuesto sobre utilidades excedentes, impuesto sobre ganancias excesivas.
excess weight, exceso de peso.
exchange [ɪks'tʃeɪndʒ] *s.* 1. cambio, intercambio, trueque, canje (de mercancías, prisioneros, golpes, palabras, etc.). 2. ejemplar de canje (de revista, etc.). 3. bolsa, lonja, mercado, plaza o casa de contratación. 4. central de teléfonos. 5. (com.) tipo de cambio. 6. (*pl.*) (com.) documentos cambiarios. 7. (ajedrez) calidad. 8. **in e. for,** a cambio de; **to win the e.,** (ajedrez) ganar la calidad. —*v.t.* cambiar, canjear, permutar; **e. greetings,** cambiar saludos; **e. signs, courtesies,** hacerse señas, cortesías; **e. words,** cruzar palabras. —*v.i.* (con *for*) ser cambiado (por), cambiarse (por).
exchangeable [-əbəl] *a.* cambiable, intercambiable.
exchange control (com., **fin.**) **control de devisas.**
exchangee [ˌɛksˌtʃeɪn'dʒi] *s.* participante en un programa de intercambio (de estudiantes).
exchanger [ɪks'tʃeɪndʒər, B -ə] *s.* cambista.
exchange rate, (com.) tipo o tarifa de cambio.
exchange student, estudiante de intercambio.
exchequer ['ɛksˌtʃɛkər, B ɪks'tʃɛkə] *s.* 1. real hacienda, erario, tesorería. 2. **E.,** (G.B.) tribunal de hacienda. 3. medios económicos, fondos (propios); dinero, capital.
exchequer bill, (G.B.) pagaré de la Tesorería.
excide [ɪk'saɪd] *v.t.* escindir, recortar.
excipient [-'sɪpɪənt] *s.* (farm.) excipiente.
excisable [-'saɪzəbəl, 'ɛkˌsaɪ-, B ɛk'saɪ-] *a.* sujeto a impuesto de consumo o de sisa.
excise ['ɛkˌsaɪz, -ˌsaɪs, B ɛk'saɪz] *s.* 1. impuesto de consumo o de sisa. 2. alcabala. —*v.t.* gravar con impuesto de consumo.
excise [ɛk'saɪz] *v.t.* cortar, extirpar (tumor, etc.).
exciseman ['ɛkˌsaɪzmən, ɪk'saɪz-, B -ˌmæn] *s.* (G.B.) tasador de impuesto de consumo.
excise tax ['ɛkˌsaɪz-, -ˌsaɪs-, B ɛk'saɪz-] impuesto al consumo, impuesto sobre el consumo.
excision [ɛk'sɪʒən] *s.* (med.) excisión, extirpación.
excitability [ɪkˌsaɪtə'bɪlətɪ] *s.* excitabilidad.
excitable [-'saɪtəbəl] *a.* excitable.
excitant [-'saɪtənt, 'ɛksətənt] *s., a.* estimulante, excitante.
excitation [ˌɛksaɪ'teɪʃən, B -sɪ-] *s.* excitación.
excitative [ɪk'saɪtətɪv] *a.* excitativo.
excitatory [-əˌtɔrɪ, B -ətərɪ] *a.* excitador, excitativo.
excite [ɪk'saɪt] *v.t.* excitar, estimular, provocar; (elec.) excitar (un electroimán); (fisiol.) excitar, estimular (funcionamiento de un órgano o tejido); **e. oneself,** excitarse.
excited [-əd] *a.* excitado; agitado, acalorado; **to get e.,** alterarse, acalorarse, enojarse; excitarse sexualmente.
excitedly [-lɪ] *adv.* agitadamente, acaloradamente.
excitement [-mənt] *s.* excitación; agitación, conmoción.
exciter [-ər, B -ə] *s.* 1. excitador, agitador, instigador. 2. (elec.) excitador, excitatriz, máquina excitadora. 3. (rad.) encendedor.
exciting [ɪk'saɪtɪŋ] *a.* 1. excitante, estimulante, incitante. 2. emocionante.
exciting coil, (elec.) carrete excitador, bobina excitadora.
excitingly [-lɪ] *adv.* de modo excitante o provocativo.
excitor [-ər, B -ə] *s.* 1. (fisiol.) nervio, excitomotor. 2. (elec.) excitador, excitatriz.
exclaim [ɪks'kleɪm] *v.i.* exclamar, lanzar una exclamación (de ira, dolor, sorpresa, etc.); **e. against, at** o **upon,** protestar o clamar contra. —*v.t.* proclamar.
exclamation [ˌɛksklə'meɪʃən] *s.* exclamación; (gram.) interjección.
exclamation point, e. mark, signo de admiración, signo de exclamación (!).
exclamatory [ɪks'klæməˌtɔrɪ, B -tərɪ] *a.* exclamatorio, exclamativo.
exclave ['ɛksˌkleɪv] *s.* parte de un país separada por territorio extranjero.
exclosure [ɪks'kloʊʒər, B -ʒə] *s.* cercamiento, lugar resguardado con una barrera artificial (a prueba de ganado, roedores, insectos, etc.).
exclude [-'klud] *v.t.* excluir, sacar, exceptuer.
exclusion [-'kluʒən] *s.* exclusión; **to the e. of,** con exclusión de.
exclusionist [-əst] *s.* el que quiere excluir a otros de sus derechos o privilegios.
exclusion principle, (fís.) principio de exclusión (de Pauli).
exclusive [ɪks'klusɪv] *a.* 1. exclusivo, único. 2. reservado, apartado (persona). 3. selecto, distinguido, elegante. —*s.* exclusiva, noticia o artículo de exclusividad, esp. de un periódico.
exclusively [-lɪ] *adv.* exclusivamente.
exclusiveness [-nəs] *s.* exclusividad.
exclusivism [ɛks'klusɪvˌɪzəm] *s.* exclusivismo.
exclusivist [-əst] *s.* exclusivista.
exclusivity [ˌɛksklu'sɪvətɪ] *s.* 1. exclusividad. 2. (com.) exclusiva, derechos exclusivos (de uso, venta, reproducción, etc.).
excogitate [ɛks'kɑdʒəˌteɪt, B -'kɔdʒ-] *v.t.* excogitar, inventar, idear mediante meditación intensa.
excogitation [-ˌkɑdʒə'teɪʃən, B -ˌkɔdʒ-] *s.* invención.
excogitative [-'kɑdʒəˌteɪtɪv, B -'kɔdʒ-] *a.* inventivo.
excommunicable [ˌɛkskə'mjunəkəbəl] *a.* digno de excomunión.
excommunicate [-nɪkət, B -ˌkeɪt] *a., s.* excomulgado. — [-ˌkeɪt] *v.t.* excomulgar, anatematizar.
excommunication [-ˌmjunə'keɪʃən] *s.* excomunión.
excommunicative [-'mjunəˌkeɪtɪv] *a.* partidario de la excomunión; de excomunión.
excommunicator [-ər, B -ə] *s.* excomulgador.
excommunicatory [-kəˌtɔrɪ, B -tərɪ] *a.* de excomunión, excomunicatorio.
ex-con [ˌɛks'kɑn] (fam.) *abrev. de* **ex-convict.**
ex-convict ['ɛks'kɑnvɪkt, B -'kɔn-] *s.* ex presidario, ex convicto.
excoriate [ɛk'skɔrɪˌeɪt] *v.t.* 1. excoriar, desollar. 2. (fig.) reprender, vituperar, criticar mordazmente.
excoriation [-ˌskɔrɪ'eɪʃən] *s.* 1. excoriación, desolladura. 2. crítica mordaz, vituperio.
excorticate [-'skɔrtəˌkeɪt, B -'skɔt-] *v.t.* descortezar, pelar.
excortication [-ˌskɔrtə'keɪʃən, B -ˌskɔt-] *s.* mondadura.
excrement ['ɛkskrəmənt] *s.* excremento.
excremental [ˌɛkskrə'mɛntəl] *a.* excremental.
excrementitious [-ˌmɛn'tɪʃəs] *a.* excrementicio, excrementoso.
excrescence [ɪks'krɛsəns] *s.* excrecencia, excrescencia, carnosidad.
excrescency [-ənsɪ] *s. var. de* **excrescence.**
excrescent [-ənt] *a.* 1. saliente; superfluo. 2. (gram.) epentético.
excreta [ɛks'kritə] *s. pl.* (fisiol.) excreta, excreciones.
excrete [-'krit] *v.t.* excretar.
excretion [-'kriʃən] *s.* excreción.
excretory ['ɛkskrəˌtɔrɪ, B ɛks'kritərɪ] *a.* excretorio, excretor. —*s.* órgano excretorio.
excruciate [ɪks'kruʃɪˌeɪt] *v.t.* atormentar, torturar; afligir, angustiar.
excruciating [-ɪŋ] *a.* 1. agudísimo, extremo. 2. dolorosísimo, penosísimo.
excruciatingly [-lɪ] *adv.* extremadamente; dolorosamente, penosamente.
excruciation [-ˌkruʃɪ'eɪʃən] *s.* tormento, tortura, suplicio.
exculpable [ɛk'skʌlpəbəl] *a.* disculpable.
exculpate ['ɛkskʌlˌpeɪt, ɪk'skʌl-, B 'ɛkskʌl-] *v.t.* exculpar, disculpar, excusar, sincerar.
exculpation [ˌɛkskʌl'peɪʃən] *s.* exculpacion, disculpa.
exculpatory [ɛk'skʌlpəˌtɔrɪ, B -tərɪ] *a.* justificativo, sincerador, disculpable.
excurrent [ɛk'skɜrənt, B ɪk'skʌrənt] *a.* 1. que brota, manante (díc. de la sangre). 2. (bot.) excurrente. 3. (zool.) excurrente, apopilo.
excursion [ɪk'skɜrʒən, B -'skɜʃən] *s.* 1. excursión, paseo, romería. 2. desviación, digresión. 3. (mec., astr.) excursión. 4. (ant., mil.) salida, expedición.
excursionist [-əst] *s.* excursionista.
excursion train, tren de recreo (de tarifa rebajada).
excursive [-'skɜrsɪv, B -'skɜsɪv] *a.* divagador, digresivo, errante.
excursively [-lɪ] *adv.* de modo divagador, con digresiones.
excursiveness [-nəs] *s.* divagación.
excursus [ɪk'skɜrsəs, B -'skɜsəs] *s.* apéndice explicativo; digresión.
excusable [ɪk'skjuzəbəl] *a.* excusable, disculpable, perdonable.
excusably [-blɪ] *adv.* disculpablemente.
excusatory [-ˌtɔrɪ, B -tərɪ] *a.* de excusa, apologético.
excuse [-'skjuz] *v.t.* 1. excusar, disculpar, perdonar. 2. excusar, dispensar, exonerar, exentar, eximir. 3. dejar irse, despedir. 4. **e. me!** ¡perdóneme! ¡discúlpeme!; **e. oneself (from),** excusarse (de). — [-'skjus] *s.* 1. excusa, disculpa. 2. excusa, pretexto.

exeat ['ɛksɪæt] *s.* (G.B.) permiso para ausencia temporal (de un colegio, monasterio, etc.).
exec [ɪg'zɛk] *s.* (jer., mil.) segundo comandante.
exec. *abrev. de* **executive,** ejecutivo.
execrable ['ɛksɪkrəbəl] *a.* execrable, abominable, detestable.
execrably [-blɪ] *adv.* execrablemente.
execrate ['ɛksə,kreɪt] *v.t.* execrar, abominar, detestar; maldecir.
execration [,ɛksə'kreɪʃən] *s.* execración, abominacion, detestación, maldición.
execrative ['ɛksə,kreɪtɪv] *a.* execrativo.
execrator [-ər, B -ə] *s.* execrador.
execratory [-krə,tɔrɪ, B -tərɪ] *a.* execratorio.
executable ['ɛksə,kjutəbəl] *a.* ejecutable.
executant [ɪg'zɛkjətənt] *s.* ejecutante (esp. de música).
execute ['ɛksə,kjut] *v.t.* 1. ejecutar, llevar a cabo, realizar. 2. ejecutar, ajusticiar (reo). 3. (der.) celebrar, finiquitar, formalizar (contrato, documento); ejecutar, cumplir (testamento, contrato, etc.). 4. (mús.) ejecutar, interpretar. 5. (com.) servir, ejecutar (pedido).
executer [-ər, B -ə] *s.* ejecutor; verdugo.
execution [,ɛksə'kjuʃən] *s.* 1. ejecución, realización. 2. ejecución, ajusticiamiento, pena de muerte. 3. (der.) celebración, ejecución, cumplimiento. 4. (mús.) ejecución, interpretación.
executioner [-ər, B -ə] *s.* verdugo, ejecutor de la justicia.
executive [ɪg'zɛkjətɪv] *a.* 1. ejecutivo, directivo, administrativo. 2. (pol.) ejecutivo. —*s.* 1. (pol.) poder ejecutivo. 2. ejecutivo, funcionario. 3. (com.) ejecutiva, junta directiva.
executive board, e. committee, junta directiva, consejo de dirección, comité ejecutivo.
Executive Mansion, (E.U.) 1. palacio presidencial, palacio de gobierno. 2. residencia (oficial) del primer mandatario o gobernador (de un estado).
executive officer, (mil.) segundo comandante; (com.) ejecutivo de alto rango.
executive power, poder ejecutivo, gobierno.
executive privilege, privilegio presidencial.
executive session, (pol.) sesión ejecutiva (esp. de un cuerpo legislativo) cerrada para el público.
executor [ɪg'zɛkjətər, B -ə] *s.* 1. ejecutor. 2. (der.) albacea, testamentario, ejecutor testamentario.
executorial [-,zɛkjə'tɔrɪəl] *a.* 1. ejecutorio, ejecutivo. 2. (der.) testamentario.
executory [-'zɛkjə,tɔrɪ, B -tərɪ] *a.* 1. ejecutivo. 2. ejecutorio (contrato, etc.). 3. administrativo.
executrix [-trɪks] *s.* (der.) mujer albacea, testamentaria.
exedra ['ɛksədrə] *s.* (arq.) exedra; banco de piedra.
exegesis [,ɛksə'dʒisəs] *s.* (*pl.* EXEGESES [-,siz]) exégesis, explicación, interpretación crítica (esp. de los libros de la Biblia).
exegete ['ɛksə,dʒit] *s.* exegeta, exégeta.
exegetic [,ɛksə'dʒɛtɪk] **exegetical** [-ɪkəl] *a.* exegético.
exegetically [-ɪkəlɪ] *adv.* exegéticamente.
exegetics [-ɪks] *s.* (ciencia de la) exégesis.
exemplar [ɪg'zɛm,plɑr, B -plə] *s.* ejemplar, modelo, tipo; dechado.
exemplarily [,ɛgzəm'plɛrəlɪ, B ɪg'zɛmplər-] *adv.* ejemplarmente.
exemplariness [ɪg'zɛmplərɪnəs] *s.* ejemplaridad.
exemplary [-plərɪ] *a.* ejemplar.
exemplary damages, (der.) daños punitivos, daños ejemplares impuestos al demandado como castigo.
exemplification [-,zɛmpləfə'keɪʃən] *s.* 1. ejemplificación. 2. (der.) copia certificada.
exemplify [ɪg'zɛmplə,faɪ] *v.t.* (*pret., p.p.* EXEMPLIFIED; *p.pr.* EXEMPLIFYING) 1. ejemplificar, ilustrar. 2. (der.) trasladar, copiar.
exempli gratia [-plɪ'grɑtɪ,ɑ, B -'greɪʃɪə] verbi gratia, verbigracia, por ejemplo.
exemplum [-pləm] *s.* (*pl.* EXEMPLA [-plə]) 1. ejemplo, modelo, muestra. 2. anécdota o narración breve (usada para destacar un punto moral o sustentar un argumento).
exempt [ɪg'zɛmpt] *a.* 1. exento, libre, franco, exonerado. 2. (ant.) cortado, separado. —*s.* persona exonerada (de una obligación o tributos). —*v.t.* 1. exentar, eximir, exonerar, franquear, liberar (de obligación). 2. (ant.) poner aparte.
exemptible [-əbəl] *a.* exento, libre, privilegiado.
exemption [-'zɛmpʃən] *s.* exención, franquicia, exoneración, liberación.
exenterate [ɛk'sɛntə,reɪt] *v.t.* (med.) retirar, extraer (un órgano); (raro, fig.) desentrañar.
exenteration [-,sɛntə'reɪʃən] *s.* (med.) extracción, extirpación; desentrañamiento, destripamiento.
exequatur ['ɛksə,kweɪtər, B ,ɛksɪ'kweɪtə] *s.* exequátur, documento oficial que acredita a un cónsul o agente.
exequies ['ɛksəkwɪz] *s. pl.* (*sing.* EXEQUY [-kwɪ]) exequias, honras, funerales.
exercisable ['ɛksər,saɪzəbəl, B -sə,-] *a.* ejercitable.
exercise ['ɛksər,saɪz, B -sə,-] *s.* 1. ejercicio, uso (de órgano, facultad, derecho, etc.). 2. ejercicio, práctica, entrenamiento. 3. ejercicio, composición (escolar, etc.). 4. (*pl.*) ceremonia (académica, etc.). 5. (*pl.*) (rel.) ejercicios espirituales. 6. (mil.) ejercicio; maniobra. —*v.t.* 1. ejercer, emplear, usar (órgano, facultad, derecho, etc.). 2. ejercitar, entrenar. 3. preocupar, inquietar. 4. ejercer, desempeñar (función, oficio, etc.). 5. **e. caution (tact,** etc.), proceder con cuidado (discreción, etc.). —*v.i.* ejercitarse, entrenarse, hacer ejercicios.
exercise bike, bicicleta fija, bicicleta de ejercicio.
exercised [-,saɪzd] *a.* intranquilo, agitado, inquieto; esforzado.
exerciser [-,saɪzər, B -ə] *s.* 1. ejercitante. 2. mozo de cuadra. 3. aparato gimnástico.
exercitation [ɪg,zɜrsə'teɪʃən, B -,zɜsɪ-] *s.* ejercicio, ejercitación, práctica.
exergue ['ɛk,sɜrg, B ɛk'sɜg] *s.* (numis.) exergo.
exert [ɪg'zɜrt, B -'zɜt] *v.t.* 1. ejercer, emplear (fuerza, habilidad, presión, influencia, etc.). 2. **e. oneself (for, to do),** esforzarse (por algo, en hacer algo), afanarse (por algo, por hacer algo); **e. pressure on,** aplicar presión a.
exertion [-'zɜrʃən, B -'zɜʃən] *s.* 1. ejercicio, empleo (de fuerza, facultad, etc.). 2. esfuerzo.
exeunt ['ɛksɪ,ʌnt, -,ʊnt, B -,ʌnt] *s.* (teat.) éxeunt (voz latina para indicar que dos o más actores salen de la escena).
exeunt omnes [-'ɑmniz, B -'ɔm-] (teat.) frase latina para indicar que todos los actores salen de la escena.
exfiltration [,ɛksfɪl'treɪʃən] *s.* exfiltración.
exfoliate [ɛks'foʊlɪ,eɪt] *v.t.* 1. exfoliar. 2. (fig.) desplegar, desdoblar. —*v.i.* 1. exfoliarse. 2. (fig.) desdoblarse, multiplicarse.
exfoliation [-,foʊlɪ'eɪʃən] *s.* exfoliación.
exfoliative [-'foʊlɪ,eɪtɪv] *a.* deshojable, desplegable.
exhalant, exhalent [-'heɪlənt] *a.* exhalador. —*s.* conducto o tubo exhalador.
exhalation [,ɛksə'leɪʃən, ˌɛkshə-] *s.* exhalación, espiración; vapor, vaho, tufo, emanación, efluvio.
exhale [ɛks'heɪl, ɛk'seɪl, B ɛks'heɪl] *v.t.* exhalar, espirar (aire, vapores, gases, etc.). —*v.i.* 1. disiparse, evaporarse. 2. exhalar.
exhaust [ɪg'zɔst] *v.t.* 1. agotar, extraer, vaciar. 2. agotar, causar. 3. agotar, gastar (surtido, fuerzas, recursos, tema, etc.). 4. empobrecer (tierra). —*s.* (mot.) 1. escape, descarga. 2. gases de escape. 3. tubo de escape.
exhaust cam, (mot.) leva de escape.
exhaust collector, (ing.) múltiple de escape.
exhaust duct, conducto eductor, canal de escape.
exhausted [-əd] *a.* exhausto, agotado, postrado, rendido.
exhauster [-ər, B -ə] *s.* (mec.) aspirador.
exhaust fan, ventilador aspirador, abanico extractor, abanico eductor.
exhaustible [-əbəl] *a.* agotable.
exhausting [-ɪŋ] *a.* agotador, cansador.
exhaustion [ɪg'zɔstʃən] *s.* agotamiento.
exhaustive [-tɪv] *a.* exhaustivo, detallado, minucioso.
exhaustively [-lɪ] *adv.* detalladamente, minuciosamente.
exhaustless [-'zɔstləs] *a.* inagotable; incansable.
exhaustlessly [-lɪ] *adv.* de manera inagotable, incansablemente.
exhaust manifold, (aut.) múltiple de escape.
exhaust pipe, (mot., aut.) tubo de escape.
exhaust stroke, (mot.) carrera o tiempo de escape, golpe de expulsión.
exhaust valve, válvula de descarga.
exhibit [ɪg'zɪbət] *v.t.* 1. exhibir, exponer, presentar. 2. mostrar, revelar (miedo, curiosidad, etc.). 3. (der.) exhibir, presentar (documento, pruebas, etc.). —*v.i.* exponer, dar una exhibición. —*s.* 1. exhibición, exposición. 2. objeto exhibido. 3. (der.) prueba instrumental.
exhibiter [-ər, B -ə] *var. de* **exhibitor.**
exhibition [,ɛksə'bɪʃən] *s.* 1. exhibición, exposición, presentación. 2. (G.B.) beca. 3. **to make an c. of oneself,** dar un espectáculo desagradable, hacer un papelón (Amer.).
exhibitioner [-ər, B -ə] *s.* (G.B.) becario.
exhibitionism [-,ɪzəm] *s.* (psic.) exhibicionismo.
exhibitionist [-əst] *s.* (psic.) exhibicionista.
exhibitive [ɪg'zɪbətɪv] *a.* (con *of*) representativo (de).
exhibitor [-ər, B -ə] *s.* exhibidor, expositor.
exhibitory [-,tɔrɪ, B -tərɪ] *a.* exhibitorio.
exhilarant [ɪg'zɪlərənt] *a.* regocijador; vivificante, estimulante, vigorizante.
exhilarate [-,reɪt] *v.t.* alegrar, regocijar, alborozar; animar, vivificar, estimular.
exhilarating [-ɪŋ] *a.* regocijador; vivificante, estimulante, vigorizante.
exhilaratingly [-lɪ] *adv.* regocijadamente, estimulantemente.
exhilaration [ɪg,zɪlə'reɪʃən] *s.* regocijo, alegría, alborozo.
exhilarative [-'zɪlə,reɪtɪv, B -ərətɪv] *a.* refrescante, vigorizante, estimulante.
exhort [-'zɔrt, B -'zɔt] *v.t.* exhortar; aconsejar. —*v.i.* dar consejo o advertencias, amonestar; urgir, instar.
exhortation [,ɛgzɔr'teɪʃən, ˌɛksər-, B ,ɛgzɔ'-] *s.* exhortación.
exhortative [ɪg'zɔrtətɪv, B -'zɔt-] *a.* exhortativo.
exhorter [-ər, B -ə] *s.* exhortador.
exhumation [,ɛkshju'meɪʃən] *s.* exhumación, desenterramiento.
exhume [ɪgz'jum, B ɛks'hjum] *v.t.* exhumar, desenterrar.

exhumer [-ər, B -ə] *s.* exhumador, desenterrador.
exigence ['ɛksədʒəns] *var. de* **exigency.**
exigency [-dʒənsɪ, ɛk'sɪdʒən-] *s.* 1. exigencia, necesidad. 2. emergencia, urgencia.
exigent ['ɛksədʒənt] *a.* 1. exigente. 2. urgente, crítico.
exigently [-lɪ] *adv.* exigentemente, con exigencia, insistentemente.
exigible [-dʒəbəl] *a.* exigible.
exiguity [ˌɛksə'gjuətɪ] *s.* exigüidad, escasez, parvedad.
exiguous [ɛg'zɪgjʊəs] *a.* exiguo, escaso, reducido; diminuto, menudo.
exiguousness [-nəs] *s.* escasez, poquedad; parquedad.
exile ['ɛgˌzaɪl, 'ɛkˌsaɪl] *s.* 1. exilio, destierro. 2. desterrado, exiliado, exilado. 3. **the E.,** el cautiverio (de los judíos en Babilonia). —*v.t.* desterrar, deportar, exiliar, exilar.
EXIMBANK *abrev. de* **Export and Import Bank of Washington,** Banco de Exportaciones e Importaciones de Washington.
exist [ɪg'zɪst] *v.i.* existir, vivir, ser; subsistir.
existence [-əns] *s.* existencia, vida; ente, entidad, ser.
existent [-ənt] *a.* existente, viviente.
existential [ˌɛgzɪs'tɛntʃəl, B -'tɛnʃəl] *a.* existencial.
existentialism [-ˌɪzəm] *s.* (filos.) existencialismo.
existentialist [-əst] *s.* (filos.) existencialista.
exit ['ɛgzət, 'ɛksət] *s.* 1. (teat.) salida (de un actor de la escena), mutis. 2. salida, partida; muerte. 3. salida, salidero. 4. (teat.) éxit (voz latina para indicar que un actor sale de la escena). —*v.i.* salir, morir.
ex libris [ɛks'librəs, B -'laɪ-] *s.* ex libris (inscripción que en un libro indica su dueño).
exobiology ['ɛksoʊbaɪ'ɑlədʒɪ, B -'ɔl-] *s.* astrobiología, biología espacial.
exocarp [-ˌkɑrp, B -ˌkɑp] *s.* (bot.) exocarpio, exocarpo.
exocrine [-səkrən, -ˌkrin] *a.* (anat.) exocrino.
Exod. *abrev. de* **Exodus,** Éxodo (Éx.).
exoderm [-ˌdɜrm, B -ˌdɜm] *s.* exodermo, ectodermo.
exodermis [ˌɛksoʊ'dɜrməs, B -'dɜmɪs] *s.* (bot.) exodermis.
exodontia [-sə'dɑntʃə, B -'dɔnʃə] *s.* (med.) exodoncia.
exodus ['ɛksədəs] *s.* éxodo, salida, emigración; **E.,** Éxodo (segundo libro del Pentateuco); **the E.,** (bíbl.) el Éxodo (de los israelitas).
exoenzyme [ˌɛksoʊ'ɛnˌzaɪm] *s.* (biol.) exoencima.
exoergic [-'ɜrdʒɪk, B -'ɜdʒɪk] *a.* (quím.) exoérgico.
ex officio [ˌɛksə'fɪʃɪˌoʊ] *adv.* ex-oficio, por virtud de oficio o posición.
exogamy [ɛk'sɑgəmɪ, B -'sɔg-] *s.* (sociol., biol.) exogamia.
exogen ['ɛksədʒɛn] *s.* (bot.) planta exógena, dicotiledónea.
exogenous [ɛk'sɑdʒənəs, B -'sɔdʒ-] *a.* (biol., bot., med.) exógeno.
exogenously [-lɪ] *adv.* de manera exógena.
exonerate [ɪg'zɑnəˌreɪt, B -'zɔn-] *v.t.* 1. exonerar, descargar (de obligación, responsabilidad, etc.). 2. disculpar, exculpar, excusar.
exoneration [-ˌzɑnə'reɪʃən, B -ˌzɔn-] *s.* 1. exoneración, descargo. 2. disculpa, exculpación.
exonerative [-'zɑnəˌreɪtɪv, B -'zɔnərət-] *a.* exonerativo, exonerante.
exophthalmic [ˌɛksɑf'θælmɪk, B -sɔf-] *a.* (med.) exoftálmico.
exophthalmos [-məs, B -mɔs] **exophthalmus** [-məs] *s.* (med.) exoftalmía, exoftalmos.
exorability [ˌɛksərə'bɪlətɪ] *s.* exorabilidad.
exorable ['ɛksərəbəl] *a.* exorable, fácil de persuadir.
exorbitance [ɪg'zɔrbətəns, B -'zɔbɪt-] **exorbitancy** [-ənsɪ] *s.* exorbitancia, desmesura, exceso.
exorbitant [-ənt] *a.* exorbitante, excesivo, desmedido, desmesurado.
exorbitantly [-lɪ] *adv.* exorbitantemente, excesivamente, desmesuradamente.
exorcise ['ɛksɔrˌsaɪz, B -sɔˌ-] *v.t.* exorcizar, conjurar.
exorciser [-ər, B -ə] *s.* exorcista, conjurador.
exorcism [-ˌsɪzəm] *s.* exorcismo, conjuro.
exorcist [-ˌsɪst] *s.* exorcista, conjurador.
exordial [ɪg'zɔrdɪəl, B ɛk'sɔd-] *a.* (ret.) introductor, previo, preliminar.
exordium [-əm] *s.* (ret.) exordio, preámbulo.
exoskeleton [ˌɛksoʊ'skɛlətən] *s.* (zool.) dermatosqueleto, dermatoesqueleto.
exosmosis [-ˌsɑs'moʊsəs, B -ˌsɔz-] **exosmose** [-sɑs'moʊs, B 'ɛksəzˌmoʊs] *s.* (fís., quím., anat.) exósmosis, exosmosis.
exosmotic [-'mɑtɪk, B -'mɔt-] **exosmic** [ɛk'sɑsmɪk, B -'sɔz-] *a.* (fís., quím., anat.) exosmótico.
exosphere ['ɛksoʊˌsfɪər, B -ˌsfɪə] *s.* (astr.) exosfera.
exospheric [ˌɛksoʊ'sfɛrɪk] *a.* (astr.) exosférico.
exospore ['ɛksəˌspɔr, B -ˌspɔ] *s.* (biol.) exospora.
exostosis [ˌɛksɑs'toʊsəs, B -sɔs-] *s.* (med.) exostosis.
exoteric [-sə'tɛrɪk] *a.* exotérico, accesible, no exclusivo, público.
exothermic [-soʊ'θɜrmɪk, B -'θɜmɪk] *a.* (quím.) exotermico, exotermo.
exotic [ɪg'zɑtɪk, B -'zɔt-] *a.* exótico, extraño, fascinante. —*s.* planta exótica; palabra exótica.
exotically [-ɪkəlɪ] *adv.* exóticamente.
exoticism [-əˌsɪzəm] **exotism** ['ɛksəˌtɪzəm, B 'ɛgzə-] *s.* exotiquez, exotismo, exoticidad; objeto, costumbre o palabra exótica.
exotoxin [ˌɛksoʊ'tɑksən, B -'tɔk-] *s.* (bioquím.) exotoxina.
expand [ɪk'spænd] *v.i.* 1. extenderse, estirarse. 2. agrandarse; expandirse, dilatarse, hincharse. 3. (fig.) expansionarse, soltarse. —*v.t.* 1. extender, estirar. 2. agrandar; dilatar, ensanchar, hinchar. 3. (mat., lóg.) desarrollar.
expandable [-əbəl] *a.* expansible, extensible, dilatable.
expanded metal [-əd-] (met., arq.) metal desplegado o estirado.
expander [-ər, B -ə] *s.* (mec.) mandril de expansión, expandidor, ensanchador.
expanding [-ɪŋ] *a.* dilatable, ensanchable, extensible, expansible; regulable.
expanding brake, freno de expansión.
expanding pulley, polea de diámetro regulable.
expanding reamer, (mec.) escariador expansivo.
expanse [ɪk'spæns] *s.* extensión, espacio.
expansibility [-ˌspænsə'bɪlətɪ] *s.* expansibilidad.
expansible [-'spænsəbəl] *a.* expansible, extensible, dilatable.
expansion [ɪk'spæntʃən, B -'spænʃən] *s.* 1. expansión, extensión, ensanche. 2. (mat.) desarrollo (de una operación). 3. (mec.) expansión.
expansionary [-ˌɛrɪ, B -ərɪ] *a.* (fin.) expansionista (economía, método, etc.); de expansión (factor, etc.).
expansion bend, curva de dilatación, codo compensador.
expansion bolt, perno de expansión.
expansion gap, (f.c.) entrecarril compensador, codo compensador.
expansionism [ɪk'spæntʃənˌɪzəm, B -'spænʃən-] *s.* (com., pol.) expansionismo; la política de ampliar un territorio nacional o su esfera de influencia, a base de subyugación o coloniaje.
expansionist [↓ᵊšɪ] *a., s.* (com., pol.) expansionista; el que propone extender un territorio nacional o su esfera de influencia.
expansionistic [-ˌspæntʃə'nɪstɪk, B -ˌspænʃə-] *a.* expansionista.
expansion joint, junta de expansión o de dilatación; unión o acoplamiento de expansión.
expansive [ɪk'spænsɪv] *a.* 1. expansivo. 2. (fig.) expansivo, efusivo. 3. extensivo. 4. opulento.
expansively [-lɪ] *adv.* 1. expansivamente. 2. (fig.) expansivamente, efusivamente. 3. opulentamente.
expansiveness [-nəs] *s.* 1. carácter expansivo; generosidad. 2. (fís.) expansibilidad, dilatabilidad.
expansivity [ˌɛkspæn'sɪvətɪ] *s.* expansibilidad, dilatabilidad.
expatiate [ɛk'speɪʃɪˌeɪt] *v.i.* explayarse, extenderse; vagar libremente, sin rumbo.
expatiation [-ˌspeɪʃɪ'eɪʃən] *s.* explayamiento, dilatación.
expatriate [ɛks'peɪtrɪət, -ˌeɪt, B -'pætrɪˌeɪt] *a., s.* expatriado, exiliado, exilado, desterrado. — [-ˌeɪt] *v.i.* expatriarse, desterrarse. —*v.t.* desterrar.
expatriation [-ˌpeɪtrɪ'eɪʃən, B -ˌpæ-] *s.* expatriación, destierro, exilio.
expect [ɪk'spɛkt] *v.t.* esperar, aguardar; contar con (algo o alguien). —*v.i.* 1. (fam.) pensar, suponer. 2. **to be expecting,** (fam.) estar embarazada, estar encinta.
expectance [-'spɛktəns] *var. de* **expectancy.**
expectancy [-tənsɪ] *s.* expectativa, esperanza.
expectant [-tənt] *a.* 1. aspirante (a un oficio, etc.). 2. expectante (medicina, tratamiento, etc.). 3. embarazada, encinta, preñada, ej., *e. mothers,* mujeres embarazadas. 4. (der.) expectante, en expectativa (beneficiario, propiedad). —*s.* aspirante, candidato.
expectantly [-lɪ] *adv.* a la expectativa.
expectation [ˌɛkspɛk'teɪʃən] *s.* 1. expectación, expectativa. 2. esperanza; (*pl.*) expectativas de herencia. 3. **beyond e.,** más allá de toda esperanza; más de lo esperado; **contrary to e.,** contra toda expectativa.
expectative [ɪk'spɛktətɪv] *a.* que se espera, contingente.
expectorant [-'spɛktərənt] *a., s.* (med.) expectorante.
expectorate [-ˌreɪt] *v.t.* expectorar, esputar. —*v.i.* escupir.
expectoration [-ˌspɛktə'reɪʃən] *s.* expectoración.
expectorative [-'spɛktəˌreɪtɪv, B -rət-] *a.* expectorante.
expedience [ɪk'spidɪəns] *var. de* **expediency** .
expediency [-ənsɪ] *s.* 1. conveniencia, oportunidad. 2. ventaja o utilidad momentánea.
expedient [-ənt] *a.* conveniente, oportuno, apropiado; util, ventajoso. —*s.* expediente, arbitrio, recurso.
expediential [-ˌspidɪ'ɛntʃəl, B -ˌspɛdɪ'ɛnʃəl] *a.* oportuno, conveniente.
expediently [-'spidɪəntlɪ] *adv.* convenientemente, oportunamente.

expedite ['ɛkspə,daɪt] *v.t.* 1. dar curso a. 2. despachar, expedir. 3. facilitar. 4. acelerar, apresurar.
expediter [-ər, B -ə] *s.* coordinador (en una fábrica); despachador, expedidor.
expedition [,ɛkspə'dɪʃən] *s.* 1. expedición, excursión, viaje. 2. expedición, despacho, prontitud. 3. expedición, envío, despacho.
expeditionary [-ə,nɛrɪ, B -nərɪ] *a.* expedicionario.
expeditionary force, (mil.) cuerpo expedicionario.
expeditious [,ɛkspə'dɪʃəs] *a.* expedito, expeditivo, pronto.
expeditiously [-lɪ] *adv.* prontamente, expeditamente.
expeditiousness [-nəs] *s.* prontitud, velocidad.
expel [ɪk'spɛl] *v.t.* (*pret., p.p.* EXPELLED; *p.pr.* EXPELLING) 1. expeler, echar, arrojar. 2. expulsar (a un alumno, socio, etc.).
expellable [-əbəl] *a.* expulsable.
expellant [-ənt] *a.* expelente. —*s.* medicina expelente, purgante.
expellent [-ənt] *a.* expelente.
expeller [-ər, B -ə] *s.* expulsor.
expend [ɪk'spɛnd] *v.t.* 1. gastar, derrochar (tiempo, energía, dinero, fortuna, etc.). 2. (mar.) enrollar (soga de repuesto) alrededor de la verga.
expendable [-'spɛndəbəl] *a.* gastable, disponible; derrochable; (mil.) fungible; sacrificable. —*s.* (*gen. pl.*) materiales o bienes fungibles.
expenditure [-dɪtʃər, B -tʃə] *s.* 1. gasto, desembolso. 2. expendio, consumo (de tiempo, energía, etc.).
expense [ɪk'spɛns] *s.* 1. gasto, dispendio, desembolso; costo. 2. (*pl.*) expensas, gastos. 3. detrimento, pérdida. 4. **at the e. of,** a expensas de, a costa de; **spare no e.,** no escatime gastos; **to go to the e. of,** meterse a gastar en; **to laugh at someone's e.,** reír a costillas de otro; **to meet (the) expenses (of),** hacer frente a los gastos (de).
expense account, cuenta de gastos reembolsables (a un empleado).
expensive [-'spɛnsɪv] *a.* costoso, dispendioso, caro.
expensively [-lɪ] *adv.* costosamente.
expensiveness [-nəs] *s.* precio elevado, alto costo, carestía.
experience [ɪk'spɪrɪəns, B -'spɪər-] *s.* experiencia, práctica; **by e.,** por experiencia propia. —*v.t.* 1. experimentar; sentir. 2. (con *that, how,* etc.) aprender por experiencia, observar.
experienced [-ənst] *a.* experimentado, hábil, experto, perito, versado.
experiential [-,spɪrɪ'ɛntʃəl, B -,spɪərɪ'ɛnʃəl] *a.* experimental, empírico.
experientially [-tʃəlɪ, B -ʃəlɪ] *adv.* experimentalmente.
experiment [ɪk'spɛrəmənt, -'spɪr-, B -'spɛr-] *s.* experimento, prueba, ensayo. — [-,mɛnt] *v.i.* experimentar, hacer experimentos.
experimental [-,spɛrə'mɛntəl, -,spɪr-, B -,spɛr-] *a.* experimental, empírico; deprueba, de ensayo.
experimentalism [-,ɪzəm] *s.* (filos.) experimentalismo, pragmatismo.
experimentalist [-əst] *s.* experimentador (esp. científico); (filos.) experimentalista.
experimentally [-ɪ] *adv.* experimentalmente.
experimentation [ɪk,spɛrəmən'teɪʃən, -,mɛn-, B -,mɛn-] *s.* experimentación, prueba, ensayo.
experimenter [-'spɛrə,mɛntər, -'spɪr-, B -'spɛr-ə] *s.* experimentador, ensayador.
experiment station, estación experimental.
expert ['ɛk,spɜrt, ɪk'spɜrt, B 'ɛk,spɜt, ɛk'spɜt] *a.* experto, experimentado, perito. — ['ɛk,spɜrt, B -,spɜ'-] *s.* experto, perito.
expertise [,ɛk,spɜr'tiz, B -,spɜ'-] *s.* pericia, práctica, experiencia; juicio, mesura.
expertly ['ɛk,spɜrtlɪ, ɪk'spɜrt-, B 'ɛk,s-pɜt-] *adv.* expertamente, hábilmente, con destreza.
expertness [-nəs] *s.* pericia, habilidad, destreza.
expiable ['ɛkspɪəbəl] *a.* capaz de ser expiado (pecado, culpa), expiable.
expiate [-,eɪt] *v.t.* expiar; satisfacer, reparar.
expiation [,ɛkspɪ'eɪʃən] *s.* expiación.
expiative ['ɛkspɪ,eɪtɪv] *a.* expiativo, expiatorio.
expiator [-ər, B -ə] *s.* le que expía o hace expiacion.
expiatory [-ə,tɔrɪ, B -tərɪ] *a.* expiatorio.
expiration [,ɛkspə'reɪʃən, B -spaɪə-] *s.* 1. espiración (de aire, humo, etc.). 2. expiración, terminación. 3. muerte, expiración. 4. (com.) vencimiento, cumplimiento.
expiration date, (med.) fecha de caducidad.
expiratory [ɛk'spaɪrə,tɔrɪ, B -'spaɪərətərɪ] *a.* 1. (anat., zool.) espirador (músculo). 2. (fon.) de intensidad espiratoria (acento). 3. ref. a la expiración.
expire [ɪk'spaɪr, B -'spaɪə] *v.t.* espirar, expeler (el aire, humo, etc.). —*v.i.* 1. expirar, morir. 2. expirar, terminar, caducar, vencer (documento, plazo, etc.).
expiry [-'spaɪrɪ, 'ɛkspərɪ, B ɪks'paɪərɪ] *s.* expiración, terminación (de documento, período, etc.).
explain [ɪk'spleɪn] *v.t.* explicar, aclarar, dilucidar; **e. away,** disculpar dando explicaciones; **e. oneself,** explicar uno lo que quiere decir; explicar uno su conducta o presencia. —*v.i.* dar explicaciones.
explainable [-əbəl] *a.* explicable.
explainer [-'spleɪnər, B -ə] *s.* explicador.
explanation [,ɛksplə'neɪʃən] *s.* explicación, aclaración.
explanative [ɪk'splænətɪv] *a.* explicativo.
explanatorily [-,splænə'tɔrəlɪ, B -'splænətər-] *adv.* de manera explicativa, como explicación.
explanatory [-'splænə,tɔrɪ, B -ətərɪ] *a.* explicativo.
explant [ɛks'plænt, B -'plɑnt] *v.t.* (med.) hacer una explantación de (tejido).
explantation [,ɛksplæn'teɪʃən] *s.* (med.) explantación.
expletive ['ɛkspləṭɪv, B ɛks'plitɪv] *a.* (gram.) expletivo. —*s.* 1. reniego, imprecación. 2. (gram.) voz expletiva.
explicable ['ɛksplɪkəbəl, ɛks'plɪk-] *a.* explicable.
explicate ['ɛksplə,keɪt] *v.t.* explicar, exponer, desarrollar (noción, principio, etc.).
explication [,ɛksplə'keɪʃən] *s.* explicación, exposición, descripción detallada.
explication de texte [ɛksplɪkɑ'sjoun-də'tɛkst] (fr.) exposición textual (método de crítica literaria); análisis por ese método; conferencia o lección sobre ese método.
explicative [ɛks'plɪkətɪv, 'ɛksplə,keɪt-] *a.* explicativo.
explicator ['ɛksplə,keɪtər, B -ə] *s.* explicador, expositor, narrador.
explicatory [ɛks'plɪkə,tɔrɪ, 'ɛksplɪk-, B ɛks'plɪkətərɪ] *a.* explicativo.
explicit [ɪk'splɪsət] *a.* explícito, claro, inequívoco.
explicitly [-lɪ] *adv.* explícitamente, claramente.
explicitness [-nəs] *s.* claridad, precisión.
explode [ɪk'sploud] *v.t.* 1. detonar, estallar, volar, hacer explosión. 2. refutar, desacreditar, demostrar la falsedad de (teoría, sofisma, etc.). —*v.i.* 1. detonar, estallar, hacer explosión. 2. (fig.) reventar, estallar (una persona). 3. **e. with laughter,** desternillarse de risa.
exploded view [-əd-] (tec.) vista esquemática (con las partes separadas de una máquina, aparato, etc.).
explodent [-ənt] *s.* (fon.) sonido explosivo, consonante explosiva.
exploder [-ər, B -ə] *s.* 1. detonador; el que causa una explosión. 2. (fig.) el que destruye una teoría o un sofisma.
exploit ['ɛksplɔɪt] *s.* proeza, hazaña. — [ɪk'splɔɪt] *v.t.* 1. sacar utilidad de (mina, etc.). 2. explotar, aprovecharse de (persona, trabajo de otros, etc.). 3. promover, despertar interés en (producto, obra teatral, etc.).
exploitable [ɪk'splɔɪtəbəl] *a.* explotable. aprovechable.
exploitation [,ɛksplɔɪ'teɪʃən] *s.* explotación, aprovechamiento.
exploitative [ɪk'splɔɪtətɪv] *a.* de explotación, explotador.
exploiter [-ər, B -ə] *s.* explotador.
explorable [-'splɔrəbəl] *a.* explorable.
exploration [,ɛksplə'reɪʃən, B -plɔ-] *s.* 1. exploración. 2. (med.) exploración, sondeo.
explorative [ɪk'splɔrətɪv] **exploratory** [-ə,tɔrɪ, B -tərɪ] *a.* exploratorio.
explorator ['ɛksplə,reɪtər, B -ə] *s.* explorador.
explore [ɪk'splɔr, B -'splɔ] *v.t.* 1. explorar. 2. (med.) examinar, sondear. —*v.i.* hacer una investigación.
explorer [-ər, B -rə] *s.* 1. explorador; sondeador. 2. (med.) explorador.
explosion [ɪk'splouʒən] *s.* 1. explosión, detonación, estallido. 2. (fig.) explosíon (de risa, ira, etc.). 3. (fon.) explosión.
explosion engine, motor o máquina de explosión.
explosive [-'splousɪv, -zɪv] *a.* explosivo; (fon.) explosivo (sonido, consonante). —*s.* 1. explosivo, fulminante. 2. (fon.) explosiva.
explosively [-lɪ] *adv.* coléricamente; explosivamente.
explosiveness [-nəs] *s.* 1. carácter explosivo (de una situación, etc.). 2. disposición colérica, iracundia.
exponent [-'spounənt] *s.* 1. (mat.) exponente, índice. 2. expositor, intérprete, ejecutante (de música, arte, etc.). 3. exponente, representante (de una teoría, escuela de arte, etc.).
exponential [,ɛkspə'nɛntʃəl, B -'nɛnʃəl] *a.* (mat.) exponencial.
export [ɛk'spɔrt, 'ɛk,spɔrt, B ɛk'spɔt] *v.t.* exportar. — ['ɛk,spɔrt, B -,spɔt] *s.* exportación; (*pl.*) artículos de exportación. —*a.* de exportación, para la exportación.
exportable [-əbəl] *a.* exportable, apto para la exportación.
exportation [,ɛkspɔr'teɪʃən, B -pɔ'-] *s.* (com.) exportación.
export duty, derechos de exportación.
exporter [ɛk'spɔrtər, B -'spɔtə] *s.* exportador.
exporting [-ɪŋ] *a.* exportador.
expose [ɪk'spouz] *v.t.* 1. exponer, arriesgar, poner en peligro. 2. abandonar (a un niño). 3. exponer, exhibir, mostrar. 4. desenmascarar, poner al descubierto (crimen, criminal, etc.), revelar, descubrir (faltas, secreto, etc.). 5. (foto.) exponer. 6. (naipes) descubrir (una carta).
exposé [,ɛkspou'zeɪ, B ɛks'pouzeɪ] *s.* 1. exposición, declaración. 2. revelación (de un escándalo, crimen, etc.).

exposed [ɪk'spoʊzd] *a.* expuesto, descubierto; al descubierto, en peligro, sin protección.

exposer [-'spoʊzər, B -ə] *s.* descubridor, revelador.

exposition [ˌɛkspə'zɪʃən] *s.* 1. exposición, presentación; descripción; comentario. 2. abandono (de un niño). 3. exhibición, exposición (de productos, obras de arte, etc.). 4. (mús.) exposición, exordio.

expositive [ɪk'spɑzətɪv, B -'spɔz-] *a.* expositivo; descriptivo; explicativo.

expositor [-ər, B -ə] *s.* expositor; explicador; comentador, comentarista.

expository [-əˌtɔrɪ, B -tərɪ] *a.* expositor, expositivo; explicativo.

expostulate [ɪk'spɑstʃəˌleɪt, B -'spɔstjʊ-] *v.i.* objetar, reclamar, protestar; **e. with (someone),** reconvenir a, reprender a (alguien).

expostulation [-ˌspɑstʃə'leɪʃən, B -ˌspɔstjʊ-] *s.* reconvención, recriminación, protesta.

expostulator [-'spɑstʃəˌleɪtər, B -'spɔstjʊ-ə] *s.* objetador, recriminador.

expostulatory [-ləˌtɔrɪ, B -tərɪ] *a.* recriminador, objetante.

exposure [ɪk'spoʊʒər, B -ʒə] *s.* 1. exposición (a los elementos, peligro, etc.). 2. revelación (de un secreto), descubrimiento (de un criminal, etc.). 3. frente, ej., *a room with western e.,* un cuarto con frente al oeste. 4. (foto.) exposición.

exposure meter, (foto.) exposímetro, fotómetro, medidor de exposición.

exposure test, prueba de intemperismo.

expound [ɪk'spaʊnd] *v.t.* 1. exponer, detallar, enunciar. 2. explicar, interpretar (esp. la Biblia).

expounder [-ər, B -ə] *s.* expositor, intérprete.

express [ɪk'sprɛs] *a.* 1. expreso, claro, explícito. 2. exacto, preciso. 3. expreso, específico. 4. expreso, rápido (tren, ascensor, etc.). 5. (G.B.) de entrega inmediata (carta, etc.). *—adv.* expresamente, especialmente; por expreso; rápidamente. *—s.* 1. transporte rápido; compañía de transporte rápido. 2. (G.B.) mensajero especial. 3. (G.B.) entrega inmediata. 4. tren expreso. 5. rifle que dispara balas con gran velocidad inicial. *—v.t.* 1. expresar, formular, manifestar. 2. extraer, sacar (zumo, etc.); extraer por fuerza (una confesión). 3. (E.U.) enviar por expreso. 4. (mat.) expresar, representar. 5. **e. oneself,** expresarse.

expressage [-ɪdʒ] *s.* servicio de transporte expreso, porte de transporte expreso.

expresser [-ər, B -ə] *s.* expositor.

expressible [-əbəl] *a.* 1. expresable (emoción, etc.). 2. exprimible (jugo, etc.).

expression [ɪk'sprɛʃən] *s.* 1. expresión, manifestación. 2. expresión, locución. 3. expresión, aspecto (del rostro); expresión, entonación (de la voz). 4. expresión, estrujamiento (de jugo, zumo, etc.). 5. (mat.) expresión, representación. 6. (arte) expresión.

expressionism [-ˌɪzəm] *s.* (arte) expresionismo.

expressionist [-əst] *s., a.* (arte) expresionista.

expressionless [-ləs] *a.* inexpresivo.

expressive [ɪk'sprɛsɪv] *a.* 1. de expresión (método, medios, etc.). 2. (con *of*) que expresa, ej., *e. of joy,* que expresa regocijo. 3. expresivo, significativo (palabras, gesto, etc.).

expressively [-lɪ] *adv.* expresivamente, vívidamente.

expressiveness [-nəs] *s.* fuerza o intensidad de expresión.

expressivity [ˌɛksprɛs'ɪvətɪ] *s.* 1. fuerza expresiva. 2. (biol.) expresividad.

expressly [ɪk'sprɛslɪ] *adv.* 1. expresamente, adrede, intencionalmente. 2. expresamente, explícitamente.

expressman [-ˌmæn, -mən, B -ˌmæn] *s.* (E.U.) empleado de una compañía de transporte expreso.

express train, tren expreso.

expressway [-ˌweɪ] *s.* autopista, supercarretera.

expropriate [ɛks'proʊprɪˌeɪt] *v.t.* expropiar, enajenar.

expropriation [-ˌproʊprɪ'eɪʃən] *s.* expropiación, enajenamiento.

expropriator [-'proʊprɪˌeɪtər, B -ə] *s.* (der.) expropiador, expropiante.

expropriatory [-əˌtɔrɪ, B -tərɪ] *a.* expropiatorio.

expugnable [ɛk'spjunəbəl, B ɛks'pʌg-] *a.* expugnable (plaza, fortificación, etc.).

expulse [ɪk'spʌls] *v.t.* expulsar; despedir; expeler, echar, arrojar.

expulsion [-'spʌlʃən] *s.* expulsión.

expulsive [-'spʌlsɪv] *a.* (med.) expulsivo.

expunction [ɪk'spʌŋkʃən] *s.* borradura; omisión.

expunge [-'spʌndʒ] *v.t.* 1. tachar, borrar, cancelar. 2. erradicar; destruir.

expurgate ['ɛkspərˌgeɪt, B -pɜˌ-] *v.t.* expurgar, purificar; tachar, cancelar (párrafos de un libro o escrito).

expurgation [ˌɛkspər'geɪʃən, B -pɜ'-] *s.* expurgación, purificación.

expurgator ['ɛkspərˌgeɪtər, B -pɜˌgeɪtə] *s.* expurgador, purificador.

expurgatorial [ɪksˌpɜrgə'tɔrɪəl, ɛks-, B ɛksˌpɜgə-] *a.* expurgatorio.

expurgatory [-'pɜrgəˌtɔrɪ, B -'pɜgətərɪ] *a.* expurgatorio.

exquisite ['ɛkskwɪzət, ɪks'kwɪzət] *a.* 1. exquisito, primoroso; fino, delicado. 2. agudo, vivo, intenso (dolor, placer, sensibilidad, etc.). *—s.* petimetre, pisaverde, lechuguino.

exquisitely [-lɪ] *adv.* exquisitamente, primorosamente.

exquisiteness [-nəs] *s.* exquisitez, primor; delicadeza, refinamiento, excelencia; intensidad, agudeza.

exsanguinate [ɛks'sæŋgwəˌneɪt] *v.t.* desangrar, extraer la sangre.

exsanguination [-ˌsæŋgwə'neɪʃən] *s.* exanguinación, desangramiento.

exsanguine [ɛks'sæŋgwɪn] *a.* (med.) exangüe, anémico.

exscind [ɛk'sɪnd] *v.t.* escindir, cortar, cercenar, extirpar, amputar.

exsect [ɛk'sɛkt] *v.t.* escindir, amputar, cortar, extirpar.

exsection [ɛk'sɛkʃən] *s.* recorte, escisión, amputación, extirpación.

exsert [ɛk'sɜrt, B -'sɜt] *v.t.* sacar, empujar hacia afuera.

exserted [-'sɜrtəd, B -'sɜtɪd] *a.* (bot.) exerto.

exsertion [-'sɜrʃən, B -'sɜʃən] *s.* protuberancia.

exsiccant [-'sɪkənt] *a., s.* desecante, desecativo.

exsiccate ['ɛksɪˌkeɪt] *v.t., v.i.* desecar, secar; desaguar.

exsiccation [ˌɛksɪ'keɪʃən] *s.* desecación.

exsiccative ['ɛksɪˌkeɪtɪv] *a., s.* desecante.

exsiccator [-ˌkeɪtər, B -ə] *s.* desecador.

exstipulate [ɛks'stɪpjələt, -ˌleɪt] *a.* (bot.) no estipulada (hoja).

ext. *abrev. de* **extension,** extensión; **external,** externo; **extinct,** extinto; **extract,** extracto.

extant ['ɛkstənt, ɪk'stænt] *a.* existente, sobreviviente, en existencia, ej., *e. dialects,* dialectos sobrevivientes.

extemporal [ɛk'stɛmpərəl, ɪk-] (ant.) *var. de* **extemporaneous.**

extemporaneous [-ˌstɛmpə'reɪnɪəs] *a.* improvisado, (hecho) sin preparación; provisional; ocasional, impremeditado.

extemporaneously [-lɪ] *adv.* improvisadamente.

extemporaneousness [-nəs] *s.* carácter improvisado.

extemporarily [ɪk'stɛmpə'rɛrəlɪ, B ɪks'tɛmpərərɪlɪ] *adv.* improvisadamente.

extemporary [ɪk'stɛmpəˌrɛrɪ, B -pərərɪ] *a.* 1. improvisado, (hecho) sin preparación; provisional, ocasional. 2. repentino, impremeditado.

extempore [ɪk'stɛmpərɪ] *adv.* de improviso, improvisadamente, sin previo estudio. *—a.* improvisado, sin previo estudio.

extemporization [-ˌstɛmpərə'zeɪʃən, B -raɪ-] *s.* improvisación.

extemporize [ɪk'stɛmpəˌraɪz] *v.t., v.i.* improvisar.

extemporizer [-ər, B -ə] *s.* improvisador, repentista.

extend [ɪk'stɛnd] *v.t.* 1. extender, ensanchar, ampliar, agrandar, alargar. 2. extender, alargar (mano); estirar (cuerpo); extender (brazo, ala, etc.); tender (vela). 3. prorrogar (plazo, período, etc.). 4. prolongar (tiempo, visita, etc.). 5. ofrecer, brindar (simpatía, hospitalidad, ayuda, etc.); (com.) conceder (crédito). 6. diluir, mezclar, adulterar (esp. alimentos). 7. exigir al máximo (las capacidades de un atleta, etc.). 8. (mil.) extender, desplegar (filas). 9. (G.B.) tasar, avaluar (inmueble); (G.B., der.) embargar. 10. **e. oneself,** esforzarse; gastar más de lo que se debe. *—v.i.* 1. extenderse, alcanzar, llegar. 2. sobresalir, proyectarse. 3. (mil.) extenderse, desplegarse; seguir en servicio activo.

extended [-əd] *a.* 1. extendido, extenso. 2. intenso (esfuerzo, curso, etc.). 3. prolongado, dilatado (estadía, visita, etc.). 4. tendido (galope). 5. (mil.) extendido (frente, líneas, etc.); desplegada (formación); abierto (orden). 6. (impr.) extraancho, de ojo extraancho, abierto.

extendedly [-ədlɪ] *adv.* extendidamente; prolongadamente.

extender [-ər, B -ə] *s.* (quím.) diluente, sustancia que sirve para diluir o adulterar; material que se añade a algo para alargarlo o ensancharlo.

extendible [-əbəl] *a.* extensible.

extensibility [ɪkˌstɛnsə'bɪlətɪ] *s.* extensibilidad.

extensible [ɪk'stɛnsəbəl] *a.* extensible, extensivo.

extensile [-səl, B -ˌsaɪl] *a.* extensible.

extension [-'stɛntʃən, B -'stɛnʃən] *s.* 1. extensión, ampliación, ensanche, ensanchamiento. 2. extensión, superficie. 3. prolongación. 4. anexo (de una casa); extensión (teléfono). 5. (com.) prórroga. 6. (lóg., gram., elec., fís., med.) extensión.

extension bar, alargadera (de un compás).

extension bit, barrena de extensión, barrena de expansión.

extension ladder, escalera extensible.

extension stock, (mil.) estuche-culatín.

extensity [ɪk'stɛnsətɪ] *s.* extensión, alcance.

extensive [ɪk'stɛnsɪv] *a.* extensivo; extenso, amplio, dilatado.

extensive cultivation, (agr.) cultivo extensivo.

extensively [-lɪ] *adv.* extensamente, por extenso.

extensometer [ɛkˌstɛn'sɑmətər, B -'sɔmɪtə] *s.* extensómetro, dispositivo para medir la resistencia de dilatación o de extensión de un material (metal, etc.).

extensor [ɪk'stɛnsər, B -sə] *s.* (anat.) (músculo) extensor.

extent [ɪk'stɛnt] *s.* 1. extensión, área. 2. alcance; grado, medida, punto. 3. (der.) ejecución, embargo. 4. **to a certain e.,** hasta cierto punto;

to a great e., en gran parte; substancialmente, en alto grado; **to a lesser e.,** en menor grado; **to such e. (that),** hasta tal grado (que); **to that, e.,** hasta tal punto; **to the e. of,** hasta el punto de; **to the full e. of,** hasta el máximo de (la capacidad, poder, etc. de uno); **to what e.?** ¿hasta qué punto? ¿hasta dónde?

extenuate [ɪk'stɛnjʊˌeɪt] *v.t.* 1. atenuar, mitigar, minorar, paliar, excusar. 2. extenuar, debilitar.

extenuating [-ɪŋ] *a.* atenuante, mitigante, paliativo; **e. circumstances,** circunstancias atenuantes.

extenuation [ɪkˌstenjʊ'eɪʃən] *s.* atenuación, mitigación; extenuación.

extenuative [ɪk'stɛnjʊˌeɪtɪv, B -ətɪv] *a.* mitigante, disminuyente.

extenuator [-ˌeɪtər, B -ə] *s.* mitigador.

exterior [ɪk'stɪrɪər, B ɛks'tɪərɪə] *s.* 1. exterior, aspecto, apariencia. 2. (arte) paisaje. 3. (cinem.) (*pl.*) exteriores. —*a.* exterior, extrínseco.

exteriority [ɛkˌstɪrɪ'ɔrətɪ, B -ˌstɪərɪ-] *s.* exterioridad; posición exterior.

exteriorization [ɛkˌstɪrɪərə'zeɪʃən, B -ˌstɪərɪəraɪ-] s. exteriorización.

exteriorize [ɪk'stɪrɪəˌraɪz, B ɛks'tɪərɪə-] *v.t.* 1. exteriorizar. 2. dar forma tangible a.

exteriorly [-'stɪrɪərlɪ, B -'stɪərɪəlɪ] *adv.* exteriormente.

exterminate [ɪk'stɜrməˌneɪt, B -'stɜm-] *v.t.* exterminar, aniquilar, destruir; extirpar.

extermination [ɪkˌstɜrmə'neɪʃən, B -ˌstɜmɪ-] *s.* exterminio, aniquilación, extirpación.

exterminator [ɪk'stɜrməˌneɪtər, B -'stɜmɪˌneɪtə] *s.* exterminador; fumigador (persona o elemento químico contra roedores, insectos, etc.).

exterminatory [-nəˌtɔrɪ, B -nətərɪ] *a.* exterminante, exterminatorio.

extern, externe ['ɛksˌtɜrn, B -ˌstɜn] *s.* 1. médico no residente, médico consultor (en un hospital). 2. externo (alumno).

external [ɛk'stɛrnəl, B -ˌstɜn-] *a.* 1. externo, exterior. 2. accidental, superficial. —*s.* (*gen. pl.*) partes externas, aspectos externos; exterioridad, apariencia.

external combustion, (aut.) combustión externa.

externalism [-ˌɪzəm] *s.* externalismo.

externality [ˌɛkstər'nælətɪ, B ˌɛkstə'-] *s.* 1. objetividad, imparcialidad. 2. (*gen. pl.*) exterioridades, apariencias externas.

externalization [ɛkˌstɜrnələ'zeɪʃən B -ˌstɜnəlaɪ-] *s.* 1. exteriorización. 2. existencia externa; encarnación.

externalize [ɛk'stɜrnəˌlaɪz, ɪk-, B -'stɜnə-] *v.t.* 1. exteriorizar. 2. atribuir existencia externa a, dar forma o cuerpo.

externally [-əlɪ] *adv.* externamente.

external respiration, (biol.) respiración externa.

exteroceptive [ˌɛkstəroʊ'sɛptɪv] *a.* (fisiol.) exteroceptivo.

exteroceptor [-tər, B -tə] *s.* (fisiol.) exteroceptor.

exterritorial [ˌɛksˌtɛrə'tɔrɪəl] *a.* extraterritorial.

exterritoriality [-ˌtɔrɪ'ælətɪ] *s.* extraterritorialidad.

exterritorially [-'tɔrɪəlɪ] *adv.* extraterritorialmente.

extinct [ɪk'stɪŋkt] *a.* 1. extincto. 2. extinguido, apagado. 3. desaparecido, destruido. 4. abolido, suprimido. 5. **to become e.,** extinguirse, consumirse.

extinction [ɪk'stɪŋkʃən] *s.* 1. extinción. 2. supresión, destrucción. 3. abolición.

extinctive [-'stɪnktɪv] *a.* extintivo.

extinguish [ɪk'stɪŋgwɪʃ] *v.t.* 1. extinguir, apagar (fuego, luz, sonido, etc.). 2. (fig.) extinguir, aniquilar (esperanza, vida, etc.). 3. eclipsar, oscurecer, deslucir. 4. (der.) extinguir, anular, derogar, abolir.

extinguishable [-əbəl] *a.* extinguible.

extinguisher [-ər, B -ə] *s.* extintor, apagador, matacandelas.

extinguishment [-mənt] *s.* 1. extinción, apagamiento, destrucción. 2. aniquilamiento, anulación.

extirpate ['ɛkstərˌpeɪt, B 'ɛkstəˌ-] *v.t.* extirpar, erradicar, exterminar; arrancar, desarraigar.

extirpation [ˌɛkstər'peɪʃən, B ɛkstə'-] *s.* extirpación, excisión.

extirpator ['ɛkstərˌpeɪtər, B 'ɛkstəˌpeɪtə] *s.* (agr.) extirpador, arrancador.

extol, extoll [ɪk'stoʊl] *v.t.* (*pret., p.p.* EXTOLLED; *p.pr.* EXTOLLING) ensalzar, exaltar, alabar, elogiar.

extoller [-ər, B -ə] *s.* alabador, elogiador.

extolment [-mənt] *s.* exaltación, alabanza, elogio.

extort [ɪk'stɔrt, B 'stɔt] *v.t.* 1. extorsionar. 2. arrancar, arrebatar, usurpar, quitar por fuerza.

extorter [-ər, B -ə] *s.* usurpador.

extortion [-'stɔrʃən, B -'stɔʃən] *s.* extorsión; exacción, concusión.

extortionary [-ˌɛrɪ, B -ərɪ] *a.* lo que implica extorsión o exacción.

extortionate [-ət] *a.* 1. de extorsión. 2. exorbitante, gravoso, excesivo (precio, etc.).

extortioner [ɪk'stɔrʃənər, B -'stɔʃənə] ɘ¸ɿoᵞɿɪoɳɪšɿ [-əst] *s.* usurpador; concusionario, opresor.

extra ['ɛkstrə] *a.* 1. extraordinario, suplementario, adicional. 2. óptimo, superior; de calidad superior. —*s.* 1. recargo, sobreprecio. 2. extra, gasto extraordinario. 3. edición extra o extraordinaria (de un diario). 4. extra, adehala, yapa, ñapa. 5. (trabajador) supernumerario. 6. (teat., cinem.) extra, comparsa; (*pl.*) comparsa. —*adv.* extraordinariamente, excepcionalmente, extra (grande, largo, etc.).

extra-base hit [-'beɪs-] (béisbol) golpe que permite alcanzar más de una base.

extrabold [-'boʊld] *s.* (impr.) (tipo) extranegro.

extracellular [ˌɛkstrə'sɛljələr, B -lə] *a.* (biol.) extracelular.

extra charge, recargo.

extract [ɪk'strækt] *v.t.* 1. extraer, sacar (dinero, verdad, diente, etc.). 2. extractar, compendiar (pasajes de un libro, etc.). 3. deducir, inferir. 4. (quím.) extraer, destilar. 5. (mat.) extraer (una raíz). — ['ɛkstrækt] *s.* 1. extracto, fragmento, selección. 2. (quím.) extracto, esencia.

extractable, extractible [-əbəl] *a.* que se puede extraer, extraíble.

extraction [ɪk'strækʃən] *s.* 1. extracción, sacamiento. 2. extracción, origen, linaje, descendencia. 3. (quím.) extracción.

extractive [ɪk'stræktɪv] *a.* extractivo. —*s.* substancia extraíble o destilable; elemento insoluble de una mezcla o un extracto.

extractor [-ər, B -ə] *s.* 1. extractor, exprimidera. 2. extractador. 3. (arm.) sacatrapos; extractor de cartuchos, sacabalas.

extracurricular [ˌɛkstrəkə'rɪkjələr, B -lə] *a.* extracurricular, fuera del plan de estudios, fuera del programa de actividades; **e. activity,** (jer.) aventura amorosa de una persona casada.

extraditable ['ɛkstrəˌdaɪtəbəl] *a.* sujeto a la extradición.

extradite ['ɛkstrəˌdaɪt] *v.t.* entregar por extradición; obtener la extradición de, extraditar (Am.).

extradition [ˌɛkstrə'dɪʃən] *s.* extradición.

extrados ['ɛkstrəˌdɑs, -ˌdoʊs, B ɛks'treɪdɔs] *s.* (*pl.* EXTRADOS O EXTRADOSES) (arq.) extradós, trasdós.

extragalactic [ˌɛkstrəgə'læktɪk] *a.* (astr.) extragaláctico.

extrajudicial [-dʒu'dɪʃəl] *a.* extrajudicial, fuera de la jurisdicción de un tribunal.

extrajudicially [-'dɪʃəlɪ] *adv.* extrajudicialmente.

extrajudicial opinion, (der.) dictamen interpolado.

extralegal [-'ligəl] *a.* (der.) extralegal, extrajurídico.

extramundane [-ˌmʌn'deɪn, B -'mʌndeɪn] *a.* extramundano, fuera de este mundo.

extramural [ˌɛkstrə'mjʊrəl, B -'mjʊərəl] *a.* de extramuros, situado extramuros; fuera del recinto (de una institución).

extraneous [ɛk'streɪnɪəs] *a.* 1. extraño, externo, ajeno. 2. accidental.

extraneously [-lɪ] *adv.* accidentalmente, contingentemente.

extraneousness [-nəs] *s.* carácter extraño.

extranuclear [ˌɛkstrə'nuklɪər, B -'njuklɪə] *a.* (biol.) extranuclear.

extraordinarily [ɪk'strɔrdənˌɛrəlɪ, ˌɛkstrə'ɔrd-, B -'trɔdnərɪlɪ] *adv.* extraordinariamente.

extraordinary [ɪk'strɔrdənˌɛrɪ, ˌɛkstrə'ɔrd-, B -'trɔdənrɪ] *a.* 1. extraordinario, raro. 2. extraordinario, notable. 3. extraordinario, especial (enviado, diplomático, etc.).

extrapolate [ɪk'stræpəˌleɪt] *v.t., v.i.* (mat.) extrapolar.

extrapolation [ɪkˌstræpə'leɪʃən] *s.* (mat.) extrapolación.

extraprofessional [ˌɛkstrəprə'fɛʃənəl] *a.* fuera de la profesión o ajeno a ella.

extrasensory [ˌɛkstrə'sɛnsərɪ] *a.* extrasensorial (percepción).

extrasystole [-'sɪstəlɪ] *s.* (med.) extrasístole.

extraterritorial [-ˌtɛrə'tɔrɪəl] *a.* extraterritorial, fuera de los confines de un estado.

extraterritoriality [-ˌtɛrəˌtɔrɪ'ælətɪ] *s.* extraterritorialidad (jurisdicción de un país sobre sus súbditos en el extranjero, e.g. sus diplomáticos).

extrauterine [-'jutərən, B -ˌraɪn] *a.* (med.) extrauterino.

extravagance [ɪk'strævəgəns] *s.* 1. extravagancia, disparate. 2. exceso, profusión, derroche, despilfarro; lujo desmedido.

extravagancy [-ɪ] *s. var. de* **extravagance.**

extravagant [ɪk'strævəgənt] *a.* 1. extravagante, estrafalario. 2. inmoderado, desmedido, excesivo. 3. pródigo, manirroto, gastador, disipador. 4. costoso, exorbitante.

extravagantly [-lɪ] *adv.* 1. extravagantemente, disparatadamente. 2. inmoderadamente, desmedidamente, excesivamente. 3. pródigamente.

extravaganza [ɪkˌstrævə'gænzə] *s.* obra (musical o literaria) espectacular o muy elaborada.

extravasate [-'strævəˌseɪt] *v.t., v.i.* (fisiol.) extravasar(se), trasvenar(se), extravenar(se) (sangre, linfa, etc.).

extravasation [ɪkˌstrævə'seɪʃən] *s.* (fisiol.) extravasación.

extravascular [ˌɛkstrə'væskjələr, B -lə] *a.* (anat.) extravascular.

extraversion, extravert, *vars. de* **extroversión, extrovert** .

extreme [ɪk'strim] *a.* extremo, sumo, extremado. —*s.* extremo, extremidad, fin, cabo; **extremes meet,** los extremos se tocan; **in the e.,** en

extremo, extremadamente; **to go from one e. to the other,** pasar de un extremo al otro; **to go to extremes,** excederse; tomar medidas extremas.
extremely [-lɪ] *adv.* extremadamente, extremamente, excesivamente, en extremo.
extreme unction, (relig.) extremaunción.
extremism [-ˌɪzəm] *s.* extremismo, radicalismo.
extremist [ɪk'striməst] *s.* extremista, radical.
extremity [ɪk'strɛmətɪ] *s.* (*pl.* EXTREMITIES) 1. extremidad, punto extremo. 2. necesidad, apuro, adversidad, grave peligro. 3. medida extrema. 4. el fin de la vida. 5. extremidad, miembro (pie o mano).
extremum [ɪk'striməm] *s.* (*pl.* EXTREMA [-mə]) (mat.) extremo (de una función).
extricable ['ɛkstrɪkəbəl] *a.* que puede resolverse o desenredarse (problema, situación).
extricate ['ɛkstrəˌkeɪt] *v.t.* 1. desenredar, desembrollar. 2. sacar (de una dificultad). 3. (quím.) liberar (gas, etc.).
extrication [ˌɛkstrə'keɪʃən] *s.* desenredo; liberación, desembarazo.
extrinsic [ɛk'strɪnsɪk] *a.* extrínseco, externo.
extrinsically [-sɪkəlɪ] *adv.* extrínsecamente.
extrorse [ɛk'strɔrs, 'ɛkˌstrɔrs, B ɛk'strɔs] *a.* (bot.) extrorso, vuelto hacia afuera.
extroversion [ˌɛkstrə'vɜrʒən, -ʃən, B -'vɜʃən] *s.* 1. (med.) extroversión, extrofia. 2. (psic.) extraversión, extroversión.
extrovert ['ɛkstrəˌvɜrt, B -ˌvɜt] *a., s.* (psic.) extravertido, extrovertido.
extroverted [-əd] *a.* (psic.) extravertido, extrovertido.
extrude [ɪk'strud] *v.t.* 1. empujar fuera, expulsar. 2. (metal.) extruir, moldear por extrusión. 3. moldear por eyección (plástico). —*v.i.* sobresalir.
extrusion [ɪk'struʒən] *s.* 1. expulsión. 2. (med.) protuberancia. 3. (metal.) extrusión. 4. eyección (de plástico). 5. (geol.) efusión (de lava).
extrusive [-'strusɪv] *a.* (geol.) efusivo, eruptivo, volcánico.
extubate [ɛks'tuˌbeɪt, B -'tju-] *v.t.* (med.) sacar un tubo o cánula de (ej., de la laringe).
exuberance [ɪg'zubərəns, B ɪg'zju-] *s.* 1. exuberancia, superabundancia, profusión. 2. efusión. 3. alegría, vivacidad. 4. prolijidad (de lenguaje).
exuberant [-bərənt] *a.* 1. exuberante, superabundante, prufuso. 2. efusivo, desbordante. 3. alegre, vivaz. 4. prolijo (lenguaje).
exuberate [-bəˌreɪt] *v.i.* 1. (raro) abundar, rebosar. 2. (con *in*) regocijarse (por), complacerse (en, con).
exudate ['ɛksjəˌdeɪt, ɪg'zu-, B 'ɛksjʊ-] *s.* (med.) exudado, materia exudada.
exudation [ˌɛksjə'deɪʃən, B -ju-] *s.* exudación.
exude [ɪg'zud, B ɪg'zjud] *v.i., v.t.* exudar; rezumar.
exult [ɪg'zʌlt] *v.i.* exultar, regocijarse, alborozarse.
exultance [-əns] **exultancy** [-ənsɪ] *s.* exultación, regocijo, júbilo, alborozo.
exultant [ɪg'zʌltənt] *a.* exultante, jubiloso.
exultantly [-lɪ] *adv.* jubilosamente, con exultación.
exultation [ˌɛgzəl'teɪʃən, ˌɛksəl-] *s.* exultación, regocijo, júbilo, alborozo.
exurb ['ɛksˌɜrb, B -ˌɜb] *s.* zona residencial (más allá de los suburbios y habitada gen. por familias acomodadas).
exurbanite [ɛks'ɜrbəˌnaɪt, B -'ɜbə-] *s.* residente o habitante de las zonas residenciales semirrurales.
exurbia [ɛks'ɜrbɪə, B -'ɜbɪə] *s. pl.* conjunto de zonas residenciales más allá de los suburbios.
exuviae [ɪg'zuvɪˌi, B -'zju-] *s. pl.* despojos (de los animales).
exuviate [-ˌeɪt] *v.t., v.i.* mudar, echar, soltar (piel, caparazón o plumas).
exuviation [ɪgˌzuvɪ'eɪʃən, B -ˌzju-] *s.* exuviación, muda.
eyas ['aɪəs] *s.* (ornith.) halcón niego.
eye [aɪ] *s.* 1. (anat.) ojo. 2. (fig.) ojo (de la aguja, en el queso, en la patata, de la tormenta, en las plumas de la cola del pavo real). 3. ojo, anillo (en herramientas), (cost.) corcheta; presilla. 4. (jer.) detective, investigador. 5. **an e. for an e.,** ojo por ojo; **apple of the e.,** niña de los ojos; **e. of the morning,** astro del día,; **e. of the storm,** ojo o centro de la tempestad; **before one's eyes,** delante de los ojos de uno; **eyes right (left),** (mil.) vista a la derecha (a la izquierda); **if you had half an e.,** si tuvieras dos dedos de frente; **in the eyes of,** a juicio de; **in the mind's e.,** en la imaginación; **in the public e.,** muy visto en público; muy conocido (persona, etc.); **in the wind's e., in the e. of the wind,** (mar.) contra el viento; **keep your eyes peeled! ¡pela el ojo! ¡ojo alerta!; not to take one's eyes off,** no quitar los ojos de; **one only has to open one's eyes to see it,** no hay más que abrir los ojos y verlo; **to be all eyes,** mirar con gran atención; **to catch one's e.,** atraerle a uno la atención; **to give one the glad e.,** (jer.) echarle una mirada coqueta; **to give (a person) the e.,** (jer.) coquetear con los ojos; **to have an e. for,** tener ojo (habilidad, capacidad, gusto) para; **to have an e. to,** estar a la mira de, estar atento a; **to have eyes for,** admirar, anhelar (algo o alguien); **to have good eyes,** tener buena vista; **to have one's eyes on,** tener los ojos en; tener los ojos puestos en; **to have one's e. on everything,** estar en todo; **to keep an e. on,** tener ojo a, no perder de vista, vigilar; **to keep one's eyes glued to the ground,** tener los ojos clavados en el suelo; **to keep one's eyes open** (o **skinned**), abrir uno el ojo, permanecer ojo avisor; **to lay (set) eyes on,** avistar, alcanzar a ver; **to leap to the e.,** saltar a los ojos; **to make eyes at,** hacerle ojos a, dirigir miradas amorosas a; **to open one's eyes to,** abrirle los ojos a uno; **to roll one's eyes,** poner uno los ojos en blanco; **to ruin one's eyes,** acabarse los ojos; **to see e. to e. with,** estar completamente de acuerdo con; **to set one's e. on,** echar el ojo a, echar tanto ojo a; **to shut one's eyes to,** hacer la vista gorda ante; **to speak with the eyes,** hablar con los ojos; **to turn a blind e. to,** hacer la vista gorda ante; **to view with a friendly e.,** mirar con buenos ojos; **with an e. to,** con miras a, con la intención de. —*v.t.* (*pret., pp.* EYED; *p.pr.* EYING O EYEING) mirar, contemplar, observar, ojear.
eyeball ['aɪˌbɔl] *s.* globo del ojo, globo ocular.
eye bank, (med.) banco de ojos (donde se conservan ojos de cadáveres para injertos).
eyebolt ['aɪˌboʊlt] *s.* (mec.) tornillo o perno de ojo, armella, hembrilla; (mar.) cáncamo, cáncamo de ojo.
eyebright [-ˌbraɪt] *s.* (bot.) eufrasia; anagálide, murajes.
eyebrow ['aɪˌbraʊ] *s.* ceja.
eye-catcher ['aɪˌkætʃər, B -ə] *s.* cosa que llama la atención (visualmente).
eye-catching [-ɪŋ] *a.* que llama la atención, que atrae la vista.
eyecup ['aɪˌkʌp] *s.* ojera, lavaojos.
eyed [aɪd] *a.* de ojos, ej., *blue-e.,* de ojos azules.
eyedropper ['aɪˌdrɑpər, B -ˌdrɔpə] *s.* cuentagotas, gotero (Amer.).
eyeflap [-ˌflæp] *s.* anteojera (de las caballerías).
eyeful ['aɪˌfʊl] *s.* 1. (un) buen vistazo; buena ojeada. 2. persona de apariencia atractiva, esp. mujer muy guapa.
eyeglass [-ˌglæs, B -ˌglɑs] *s.* 1. monóculo. 2. (*pl.*) anteojos, gafas, espejuelos, lentes. 3. ojera, lavaojos.
eyehole [-ˌhoʊ] *s.* 1. órbita o cuenca del ojo. 2. atisbadero.
eyelash [-ˌlæʃ] *s.* pestaña.
eyeless ['aɪləs] *a.* sin ojos, ciego.
eyelet [-lət] *s.* 1. ojete, ojalillo reforzado del bordado. 2. ojillo, ojo pequeño. 3. abertura, atisbadero, resquicio. —*v.t.* ojetear.
eyelid ['aɪˌlɪd] *s.* párpado; **to hang on by the eyelids,** (G.B.) agarrarse por un pelo.
eye-opener ['aɪˌoʊpənər, B -nə] *s.* 1. sorpresa, revelación. 2. (fam.) trago, bebida.
eyepatch ['aɪpætʃ] *s.* parche.
eyepiece ['aɪˌpis] *s.* (ópt.) ocular (de un aparato óptico).
eye rhyme, rima imperfecta (de coincidencia ortográfica pero no fonética, ej., *move y love*).
eye-shade [-ˌʃeɪd] *s.* visera.
eye shadow, *s.* sombreador (cosmético).
eyeshot [-ˌʃɑt, B -ˌʃɔt] *s.* alcance de la mirada, vista.
eyesight ['aɪˌsaɪt] *s.* el sentido y alcance de la vista.
eyesore [-ˌsɔr, B -ˌsɔ] *s.* cosa que ofende la vista.
eyespot [-ˌspɑt, B -ˌspɔt] *s.* (zool.) mancha ocular.
eyestalk [-ˌstɔk] *s.* (zool.) pedúnculo movible (que sostienen los ojos de los crustáceos).
eyestrain ['aɪˌstreɪn] *s.* (med.) fatiga visual, vista fatigada.
eyestring [-ˌstrɪŋ] *s.* (anat.) músculo o nervio del ojo.
eyetooth ['aɪˌtuθ] *s.* (anat.) colmillo; **to cut one's eyeteeth,** (fig.) adquirir experiencia; volverse ducho; **to give one's eyeteeth for (something),** beber los vientos (o aires) por (algo).
eye tuning indicator, (rad.) ojo indicador visual de sintonía.
eyewash [-ˌwɔʃ, -ˌwɑʃ, B -ˌwɔʃ] *s.* 1. colirio, loción para los ojos. 2. (jer.) tontería, idiotez, disparate. 3. (jer.) lisonja, zalamería, adulación engañosa.
eyewater [-ˌwɔtər, -'wɑt-, B -ˌwɔtə] *s.* 1. colirio, loción para los ojos. 2. lágrimas. 3. bebida espirituosa.
eyewink ['aɪˌwɪŋk] *s.* guiño, guiñada.
eyewinker [-ər B -ə] *s.* pestaña.
eyewitness ['aɪ'wɪtnəs] *s.* testigo ocular, testigo presencial.
eyre [ɛr, B ɛə] *s.* (hist., G.B.) vuelta, circuito; **justices in e.,** juccεs que hacen el circuito de los distintos pueblos para presidir las sesiones de los tribunales.
eyrie, eyry, *vars. de* **aerie.**

F

F [ɛf] *s.* 1. f, sexta letra del alfabeto inglés. 2. (mús.) fa.
F *abrev. de* 1. **Fahrenheit,** Fahrenheit. 2. **farad,** farad, faradio. 3. **failing grade,** nota deficiente en un examen. 4. **focal length,** distancia focal. 5. **force,** fuerza.
F *símb. de* **flourine,** flúor (F).
fa [fɑ] *s.* (mús.) fa, cuarta nota de la escala.
FA *abrev. de* **fine arts,** bellas artes.
FAA *abrev. de* **Federal Aviation Agency,** Agencia Federal de Aviación.
fab [fæb] *a.* (jer.) colosal, fabuloso, excelente.
fabaceous [fə'beɪʃəs] *a.* (bot.) fabácea (planta).
Fabian ['feɪbɪən] *a.* fabiano, contemporizador, dilatorio.
Fabian, *s.* fabiano, miembro de la Sociedad Fabiana de socialistas británicos.
Fabian Society, Sociedad Fabiana, organización británica para promover el desarrollo del socialismo.
fable ['feɪbəl] *s.* 1. fábula, apólogo, conseja, leyenda, mito. 2. fábula, mentira, falsedad. —*v.i.* (ant.) fantasear, inventar o contar fábulas. —*v.t.* (*ú. gen. en voz pasiva*) **it is fabled that,** según la leyenda, ej., *it is fabled that Caesar lived in this house,* según la leyenda César vivió en esta casa.
fabled [-bəld] *a.* legendario, mítico; ficticio, fabuloso.
fabler [-blər, B -blə] *s.* 1. fabulista. 2. mentiroso, cuentista.
fabliau ['fæblɪˌoʊ] *s.* (*pl.* FABLIAUX [-ˌoʊz]) (hist.) fabliau, breve verso picaresco (en Francia medieval).
fabric ['fæbrɪk] *s.* 1. tejido, textura, trama (de una tela). 2. tela, paño, género. 3. edificio, fábrica, estructura. 4. (fig.) red, maraña (de mentiras, embustes, etc.).
fabricant ['fæbrɪkənt] *s.* (ant.) fabricante.
fabricate [-ˌkeɪt] *v.t.* 1. fabricar, construir, manufacturar. 2. (fig.) fabricar, inventar (mentiras, etc.); falsificar (documento).
fabrication [ˌfæbrɪ'keɪʃən] *s.* 1. invención, mentira. 2. (raro) fabricación, manufactura.
fabricator ['fæbrɪˌkeɪtər, B -ə] *s.* 1. embustero, farsante, fabricador (de mentiras, etc.). 2. (raro) fabricante, constructor.
fabulist ['fæbjələst] *s.* 1. fabulista. 2. embustero, mentiroso.
fabulous [-ləs] *a.* 1. fabuloso, legendario, ficticio, imaginario. 2. fabuloso, maravilloso, increíble.
fabulously [-lɪ] *adv.* fabulosamente.
fabulousness [-nəs] *s.* fabulosidad.
façade [fə'sɑd] *s.* 1. (arq.) fachada, frente. 2. (fig.) apariencia.
face [feɪs] *s.* 1. cara, rostro. 2. faz, superficie. 3. fachada, frente. 4. haz, derecho (de una tela); cara (de un documento); frente (de un pliego de papel); esfera (del reloj). 5. cariz, aspecto, apariencia. 6. apariencias, prestigio. 7. desfachatez, descaro. 8. mueca, gesto. 9. (geom.) cara, lado. 10. (impr.) ojo (del tipo); arista de impresión (de una raya o filete); cara (de una matriz). 11. (mec.) frente, paramento (de una presa); cotillo (del martillo); cara, ancho (de una polea). 12. **f. to f.,** cara a cara, frente a frente; **f. to f. with,** enfrentándose a; **f. value,** valor nominal (de un cheque, acción, letra de cambio, etc.); **in the f. of,** a pesar de; haciendo frente a; **in the f. of day,** abiertamente, públicamente; **on the f. of it,** a primera vista; **to fly in the f. of,** oponerse a, desafiar, no hacer caso de, desobedecer abiertamente; **to keep a straight f.,** contener la risa; **to look (someone) in the f.,** mirar de frente, enfrentar (a alguien); **to lose f.,** perder prestigio, quedar mal; **to make a wry f.,** torcer el gesto; **to make** (o **pull**) **faces,** hacer muecas; **to one's f.,** en la cara de uno, abiertamente; **to pull** (o **wear**) **a long f.,** poner cara larga, poner mala cara, estar cariacontecido; **to put a good f. on (the matter),** hacer que (el asunto) luzca bien; **to put a new f. on,** cambiar el aspecto de; **to save f.,** salvar las apariencias; **to set one's f. against,** oponerse a, mostrarse contrario a; **to show one's f.,** asomar la cara; **to tell someone to his f.,** decir a uno a rajatablas; **to turn red in the f.,** ponérsele roja la cara (a uno). —*v.t.* 1. estar enfrente de. 2. hacer frente a, mirar hacia, dar a. 3. enfrentar, ponerse de cara a, dar cara a, encararse con, habérselas con. 4. afrontar, arrostrar, enfrentar (peligro, riesgo, enemigo, etc.). 5. revestir, recubrir (superficie, muro, etc.). 6. voltear, descubrir, poner boca arriba (naipe, etc.). 7. guarnecer (prenda de vestir). 8. (mampostería) revestir, forrar, acerar. 9. (tec.) labrar, alisar, cepillar. 10. **f. about,** (mil.) hacer dar media vuelta; **f. down,** resistir firmemente (agresión, rebelión, etc.); eliminar resueltamente (oposición, etc.); **f. one another,** encontrarse cara a cara; **f. the music,** (fam.) dar la cara, afrontar las consecuencias; **f. (someone) with,** carear, confrontar (a alguien) con (prueba, los hechos, alternativa, etc.). —*v.i.* 1. mirar (hacia el sur, norte, etc.). 2. volver el rostro (hacia la derecha, izquierda). 3. (mil.) volverse (hacia la derecha o izquierda). 4. **f. about,** volver la cara; (mil.) dar media vuelta; **f. up to,** encararse con, afrontar.
face ache, neuralgia facial.
face brick, ladrillo de fachada o exterior.
face bushing, (mec.) boquilla sin reborde, casquillo de asiento.
face cam, (mec.) leva de cara o de asiento.
face card, (naipes) figura.
face cloth, 1. sudario. 2. paño para lavar la cara.
face cutter, (mec.) fresa de refrentar.
facedown ['feɪs'daʊn] *adv.* boca abajo, ten dido de bruces.
face gear, (mec.) engranaje de dientes laterales, engranaje de corona.
face guard, careta, careta protectora.
face hammer, (mec.) combo de cotillo plano, martillo de cara plana.
face-harden ['feɪsˌhɑrdən, B -ˌhɑd-] *v.t.* (mec.) templar superficialmente por cementación.
face lathe, (mec.) torno sin contrapunta, torno al aire, torno de plato.
faceless ['feɪsləs] *a.* 1. que no tiene identidad propia. 2. anónimo, desconocido, que no puede identificarse (ladrón, asesino). 3. sin cara (aparición, espectro, fantasma).
face lift o **face lifting,** *s.* 1. cirugía plástica facial, facioplastia. 2. (fig.) embellecimiento, modernización, reforma.
face mask, (*for diving*) máscara; (dep.) barra del casco.
face-mill [-ˌmɪl] *s.* (mec.) fresa de refrentar.
face milling, (mec.) fresado de refrentar.
face-pack [-ˌpæk] *s.* (cosmética) máscara de belleza.
faceplate [-ˌpleɪt] *s.* 1. (mec.) placa de recubrimiento; plato, disco, placa de sujeción (de torno). 2. (elec.) chapa de pared, escudete.
face powder, polvo para la cara, polvo de tocador.
face pressure, (hidr.) presión frontal o de asentamiento (en compuertas).
facer ['feɪsər, B -sə] *s.* 1. el o lo que pule o labra. 2. (pr. G.B.) revés o derrota demoledora; dificultad inesperada. 3. (pr. G.B.) bofetada.
face-saving ['feɪsˌseɪvɪŋ] *a.* que guarda las apariencias.
face shield, careta de soldador, pantalla.
facet ['fæsət] *s.* 1. faceta, cara (de un poliedro o piedra preciosa). 2. (fig.) faceta, aspecto. 3. (anat.) faceta (de un hueso). 4. (arq.) filete (entre las estrías de una columna). 5. (zool.) faceta (de un ojo compuesto). —*v.t.* labrar facetas en; cortar en facetas.
faceted [-əd] *a.* facetado, labrado en facetas; de facetas.
facetiae [fə'siʃɪˌi] *s. pl.* bromas, chistes; libros humorísticos.
facetious [-'siʃəs] *a.* jocoso, humorístico, chistoso (esp. de modo inoportuno).
facetiously [-lɪ] *adv.* chistosamente, jocosamente.
facetiousness [-nəs] *s.* jocosidad, agudeza.
face to face *a. & adv.* cara a cara, frente a frente.
faceup ['feɪs'ʌp] *adv.* boca arriba, tendido de espaldas.
face value, valor nominal (de un cheque, acción, letra de cambio, etc.); valor facial (de una moneda, sello, etc.).
facial ['feɪʃəl] *a.* facial. —*s.* (fam.) masaje o tratamiento facial.
facial angle, (antrop.) ángulo facial.
facial index, (antrop.) índice cefálico.
facies ['feɪʃɪˌiz] *s.* (*pl.* FACIES) (bot., geol., med.) facies.
facile ['fæsəl, B 'fæsaɪl] *a.* 1. fácil (tarea, triunfo, solución, etc.). 2. superficial, frívolo. 3. de verbo ágil; listo. 4. fácil, acomodaticio (carácter, disposición, etc.).
facilitate [fə'sɪləˌteɪt] *v.t.* facilitar, ayudar, expedir.
facilitation [-ˌsɪlə'teɪʃən] *s.* facilitación.
facility [fə'sɪlətɪ] *s.* (*pl.* FACILITIES) 1. facilidad (de una tarea, triunfo, solución, etc.). 2. facilidad, destreza, habilidad. 3. (*pl.*) facilidades, oportunidades, medios. 4. (*pl.*) medios (de transporte), servicios públicos.
facing ['feɪsɪŋ] *s.* 1. guarnición (en prenda de vestir). 2. (*pl.*) vueltas, bocamangas (en uniformes). 3. (arq.) revestimiento, paramento.

facing ashlar, (const.) sillar de hoja.
facing cutter, fresa de refrentar.
facsimile [fæk'sɪməlɪ] *s.* facsímil, facsímile.
fact [fækt] *s.* hecho; realidad; **as a matter of f.,** en realidad, de hecho, realmente; **facts of life,** verdades de la vida, las realidades de la procreación; **in f., in point of f.,** en realidad, de hecho, realmente; **in the very f.,** en el mero hecho; **the f. of the matter is (that),** la verdad es (que); **the f. remains (that),** a pesar de todo.
fact-finding ['fækt,faɪndɪŋ] *a.* de investigación, de indagación.
faction ['fækʃən] *s.* 1. facción, camarilla, pandilla, bando. 2. facción, parcialidad.
factional [-əl] *a.* 1. de una facción, sectario (líder). 2. partidista, sectario.
factionalism [-,ɪzəm] 1. partidarismo, sectarismo. 2. proliferación de facciones.
factious ['fækʃəs] *a.* 1. faccioso. 2. partidista, faccionario, sectario.
factiously [-lɪ] *adv.* facciosamente.
factiousness [-nəs] *s.* 1. tendencia o espíritu facciosos. 2. sectarismo.
factitious [fæk'tɪʃəs] *a.* artificial, artificioso.
factitiously [-lɪ] *adv.* artificialmente, artificiosamente.
factitiousness [-nəs] *s.* artificialidad.
factitive ['fæktətɪv] *a.* (gram.) factitivo (verbo).
factor ['fæktər, B -tə] *s.* 1. factor, circunstancia. 2. factor, agente, comisionado. 3. (mat., fisiol., foto., biol.) factor. 4. (esco.) hacedor. *—v.t.* (mat.) descomponer o dividir en factores.
factorage [-tərɪdʒ] *s.* (com.) 1. factoraje. 2. comisión de factor.
factorial [fæk'tɔrɪəl] *s.* (mat.) factorial.
factorization [,fæktərə'zeɪʃən, B -raɪ-] *s.* (mat.) descomposición en factores.
factorize ['fæktə,raɪz] *v.t.* (mat.) factorizar, descomponer en factores.
factory ['fæktərɪ] *s.* 1. factoría, fábrica, manufactura. 2. factoría, taller.
factory outlet, (com.) lugar donde se venden saldos o muestras de fábrica a precio de mayorista.
factotum [fæk'toʊtəm] *s.* 1. factótum, dije. 2. (ant.) entrometido, refitolero.
factual ['fæktʃʊəl] *a.* basado en hechos, real, verdadero, objetivo; cierto.
factuality [,fæktʃʊ'ælətɪ] **factualness** ['fæktʃʊəlnəs] *s.* objetividad, imparcialidad.
facture ['fæktʃər, B -tʃə] *s.* factura, ejecución (esp. en una obra literaria, musical o artística).
facula ['fækjələ] *s.* (*pl.* FACULAE [-,li]) (astr.) fácula.
facultative ['fækəl,teɪtɪv, B -tətɪv] *a.* 1. facultativo; permisivo, potestativo, opcional; contingente, fortuito, eventual. 2. (biol.) facultativo.
faculty ['fækəltɪ] *s.* (*pl.* FACULTIES) 1. facultad, aptitud, potencia, habilidad. 2. facultad, poder, autoridad. 3. facultad, cuerpo docente (de una universidad). 4. (psic.) facultad, poder mental.
fad [fæd] *s.* moda, furor, novedad; manía, capricho.
faddish ['fædɪʃ] *a.* novelero; caprichoso, maniático.
faddism [-,ɪzəm] *s.* novelería, manía, tendencia a seguir los caprichos de la moda o de las costumbres.
faddist [-əst] *s.* novelero.
faddy ['fædɪ] *a.* 1. novelero. 2. caprichoso, maniático.
fade [feɪd] *v.i.* 1. marchitarse. 2. descolorarse, desteñirse. 3. palidecer, obscurecerse. 4. apagarse (sonido). 5. (fig.) reducirse, decaer, debilitarse (interés, etc.). 6. (jer.) irse, retirarse. 7. **f. away,** desvanecerse, desaparecer; **f. in,** (cine., t.v.) aparecer progresivamente (imagen); (rad.) crecer gradualmente en volumen (sonido); **f. out,** (cinem., t.v.) disolverse en negro (imagen); (rad.) desvanecerse gradualmente (sonido). *—v.t.* 1. marchitar. 2. descolorar, desteñir. 3. obscurecer, poner pálido. 4. **f. in,** (cine., t.v.) dar entrada gradualmente a (imagen); (rad.) aumentar gradualmente el volumen de (sonido); **f. out,** (cine., t.v.) disolver en negro (imagen). *—s.* (cine., t.v.) disolvencia.
fade-in ['feɪdɪn] *s.* fundido, entrada disuelta.
fadeless ['feɪdləs] *a.* inmarcesible, inmarchitable.
fade-out ['feɪdaʊ] *s.* fundido de cierre, salida disuelta.
fading [-ɪŋ] *s.* (rad.) desvanecimiento, disminución (de señales, del sonido).
F. Adm. *abrev. de* **fleet admiral,** almirante supremo.
faecal, *var. de* **fecal.**
faeces, *var. de* **feces.**
faerie ['feɪərɪ, 'fɛrɪ, B 'feɪ-] *s.* (ant.) 1. país de las hadas. 2. hada, duende, trasgo. *—a.* (ant.) imaginario, fantástico.
faery, *s. var. de* **faerie.**
fag [fæg] *v.i.* (*pret., p.p.* FAGGED; *p.pr.* FAGGING) 1. fatigarse, trabajar duramente, afanarse. 2. (G.B.) atender, servir (al estudiante de grado superior). *—v.t.* (gen. con *out*) agobiar, fatigar, cansar; **to be fagged out,** estar con los huesos molidos. *—s.* 1. (pr. G.B.) faena, trabajo duro; agotamiento. 2. (G.B.) estudiante que sirve a otro de grado superior (en escuelas). 3. (jer., despec.) maricón, marica. 4. (fam.) cigarrillo.
fagaceous [fə'geɪʃəs] *a.* (bot.) fagáceo.
fag end, 1. cadille (parte burda al final de la urdimbre de la tela). 2. chicote, cabo. 3. residuo, remanente, retal. 4. remate, punta, extremo. 5. (G.B.) colilla.
fagot, faggot ['fægət] *s.* 1. gavilla, haz de palos o ramas, fajina. 2. paquete de barras (de acero). 3. (jer., despec.) maricón, marica. *—v.t.* liar, hacer un haz o gavilla de, atar en un haz.
fagoting, faggoting [-ɪŋ] *s.* (cost.) vainicas.
Fahrenheit thermometer ['færən,haɪt-] termómetro de Fahrenheit.
faience [feɪ'ɑns, faɪ-] *s.* alfarería de Faenza, loza fina.
fail [feɪl] *v.i.* 1. fallar, faltar, fracasar. 2. decaer, desfallecer. 3. menguar, debilitarse, apagarse. 4. averiarse, parar, dejar de funcionar. 5. (com.) fracasar, quebrar. 6. **f. to (do),** dejar de (hacer), no lograr (hacer), ej., *he failed to come,* dejó de venir, *I failed to find the book,* no logré encontrar el libro. *—v.t.* 1. abandonar, desertar, dejar solo (persona, causa); descuidar (obligación, deber, etc.). 2. desaprobar, suspender, catear, reprobar (en un examen). 3. faltarle a uno, hacer falta a uno, ej., *words f. me,* me faltan palabras, no tengo palabras. *—s.* falla, falta; **without f.,** sin falta.
failing ['feɪlɪŋ] *a.* menguante; decadente, declinante. *—s.* flaqueza, debilidad, punto débil, defecto. *—prep.* a falta de; en caso de no.
failingly [-lɪ] *adv.* deficientemente, negligentemente, descuidadamente; débilmente, menguadamente.
faille [faɪl, B feɪl] *s.* (tej.) faya; anafaya, anafalla.
fail-safe ['feɪl,seɪf] *a.* 1. capaz de compensar errores automáticamente, que detiene un ataque militar. 2. (*dependable*) que no falla, a toda prueba, infalible.
fail-safe device, mecanismo de seguridad.
failure [-jər, B -jə] *s.* 1. falta, omisión, descuido. 2. fracaso, fiasco, malogro. 3. defecto, deficiencia, falla; deterioro, declinación. 4. suspenso (en un examen). 5. fracasado, frustrado, malogrado (persona). 6. (med.) paro, ataque (al corazón, etc.). 7. (com.) quiebra, bancarrota. 8. **f. to (do),** (el) dejar de (hacer).
fain [feɪn] *a.* (ant.) 1. contento, alegre, satisfecho. 2. dispuesto, llano, deseoso. 3. constreñido, obligado. *—adv.* (ant.) alegremente, gustosamente, voluntariamente, de buena gana, ej., *I would f. (do it),* me alegraría (hacerlo).
fainéant ['feɪnɪənt] *a.* (fr.) inactivo, indolente, ocioso. *—s.* haragán, ocioso, holgazán.
faint [feɪnt] *a.* 1. timorato, tímido, acobardado, medroso. 2. tenue, débil, lánguido. 3. desmayado, desfallecido, debilitado, mareado. 4. pálido, indistinto, borroso (perfil, línea, etc.); vago (recuerdo, idea, etc.). 5. opresivo (aire, perfume, etc.). 6. **to feel f.,** sentirse mareado. *—s.* desmayo, desfallecimiento; **to fall in a dead f.,** desplomarse inconsciente; **to fall into a f.,** desmayarse. *—v.i.* 1. desmayarse. 2. palidecer, perder brillo. 3. (poét., ant.) debilitarse. 4. (ant.) desalentarse; acobardarse.
faint-hearted ['feɪnt'hɑrtəd, B -'hɑt-] *a.* tímido, medroso, pusilánime, temeroso, cobarde.
faintheartedly [-lɪ] *adv.* tímidamente, medrosamente, cobardemente.
faintheartedness [-nəs] *s.* timidez, pusilanimidad, miedo, cobardía.
faintish ['feɪntɪʃ] *a.* desfalleciente, tenue, débil.
faintly [-lɪ] *adv.* 1. tenuemente, débilmente. 2. desmayadamente. 3. indistintamente. 4. vagamente.
faintness ['feɪntnəs] *s.* 1. desmayo, debilidad. 2. palidez, falta de claridad.
faints [feɪnts] *s. pl.* productos impuros de la destilación (del whisky u otro licor).
fair [fɛr, B fɛə] *a.* 1. bello, hermoso. 2. agradable, ameno. 3. cortés, amable, suave. 4. considerable, adecuado; amplio. 5. razonable. 6. posible, probable. 7. justo, imparcial. 8. honrado, legítimo, justo. 9. según las reglas, correcto, limpio (juego). 10. limpio, puro, inmaculado. 11. claro, legible. 12. rubio (cabello); blanco (tez). 13. típico, característico (ejemplo, etc.). 14. bastante bueno; regular. 15. favorable, bueno (tiempo); favorable (viento, marea; perspectiva); bonancible (viento, brisa). 16. **all's f. in love and war,** en el amor y la guerra todo está permitido; **by f. means,** por medios honrados; por medios pacíficos; **by f. means or foul,** a todo trance, a toda costa; **f. and square,** honrado a carta cabal; honrada y abiertamente; **f. to middling,** bastante bueno, así así; bastante bien; **in a f. fight,** en buena lid, en buena ley; **the f. sex,** el sexo bello; **to be in a f. way to (do),** estar en buen camino de (hacer); **to give f. warning,** prevenir, advertir. *—adv.* 1. cortésmente. 2. honradamente, con rectitud; abiertamente. 3. correctamente, con corrección. 4. directamente, justamente. 5. **to bid f. to,** ser probable que (suceda algo); **to fight f.,** pelear limpio; **to play f.,** jugar limpio, observar las reglas de juego; comportarse honradamente. *—s.* (ant.) 1. hermosura, belleza. 2. mujer; amante, querida. 3. feria. 4. **a day after the f.,** demasiado tarde. *—v.i.* (dial.) aclarar, ponerse claro (el tiempo). *—v.t.* alisar; (ing., aer.) fuselar.
fair ball, (béisbol) batazo al campo interior o al cuadro.
fair copy, copia corregida, copia en limpio; **to make a f.c. (of),** pasar en limpio.
fair game, 1. caza no vedada. 2. (fig.) cosa o persona que se puede cazar o perseguir en buena lid.

fairground [ˈfɛrˌgraʊnd, B ˈfɛəˌ-] *s.* terreno para ferias, circos, etc.
fair-haired [-ˈhɛrd, B -ˈhɛəd] *a.* 1. pelirrubio. 2. (fam.) favorito, predilecto.
fairing [ˈfɛrɪŋ, B ˈfɛər-] *s.* (G.B.) (*ú. gen. en pl.*) ferias, regalos hechos en una feria.
fairing, *s.* (ing., aer.) fuselado fusiforme; **engine f.,** carenado del motor.
fairish [-ɪʃ] *a.* regular, bastante grande; bastante bueno.
fairlead [ˈfɛrˌlid, B ˈfɛəˌ-] **fairleader** [-ər, B -ə] *s.* (mar.) galápago guía.
fairly [-lɪ] *adv.* 1. primorosamente, lindamente. 2. limpiamente, claramente (escrito). 3. absolutamente, totalmente, completamente. 4. definitivamente, distintamente, claramente, indudablemente. 5. imparcialmente, objetivamente. 6. legítimamente, justificadamente. 7. moderadamente, bastante. 8. (ant.) cortésmente. 9. (ant.) suavemente, blandamente.
fair-minded [-ˈmaɪndəd] *a.* imparcial, justo, equitativo.
fair-mindedness [-nəs] *s.* imparcialidad, equidad.
fairness [-nəs] *s.* 1. imparcialidad, justicia, equidad; rectitud. 2. hermosura, belleza. 3. legitimidad. 4. serenidad, limpieza (del cielo). 5. pureza, limpidez. 6. blancura (de la tez). 7. **in all f.,** para ser justo.
fair play, juego limpio, jugada limpia.
fair sex, el bello sexo, la mujer.
fair shake, (jer.) buena oportunidad, tratamiento justo.
fair-spoken [ˈfɛrˈspoʊkən, B ˈfɛəˈ-] *a.* cortés, bien hablado.
fair trade, práctica comercial en la que el fabricante fija un precio mínimo para la venta de su producto.
fair-trade [-ˈtreɪd] *v.t.* comerciar bajo reciprocidad.
fair-trade agreement [-ˈtreɪd-] acuerdo de regulacion de precios de venta, acuerdo de comercio bajo reciprocidad.
fair warning, aviso, advertencia con plazo oportuno para tomar medidas correctivas.
fairway [-ˌweɪ] *s.* 1. (mar.) canalizo, paso navegable. 2. (golf) pista (entre el punto de partida y el hoyo).
fair-weather [-ˈwɛðər, B -ˌwɛðə] *a.* 1. para uso en el buen tiempo. 2. mudadizo, inconstante. 3. **f.-w. friend,** amigo por interés, amigo en la prosperidad.
fairy [ˈfɛrɪ, B ˈfɛərɪ] *s.* 1. hada, duende. 2. (jer.) maricón, homosexual. —*a.* 1. de hadas, de duendes. 2. imaginario, ficticio.
fairy godfather, (fig.) bienhechor; (jer.) patrocinador, financiador.
fairy godmother, (fig.) hada madrina, bienhechora; (jer.) patrocinadora, financiadora.
fairyland [-ˌlænd] *s.* tierra o país de las hadas; mundo mágico, lugar maravilloso, paisaje encantador.
fairylike [-ˌlaɪk] *a.* parecido a las hadas; delicado, fino, frágil; etéreo, intangible.
fairy ring, banda circular de hierbas más oscuras o de hongos (en un prado).
fairy tale, 1. cuento de hadas. 2. (fam.) cuento de viejas, patraña, embuste.
fait accompli [ˌfɛtækɔnˈpli, B ˌfeɪtɑ-] (fr.) hecho consumado.
faith [feɪθ] *s.* 1. fe (en Dios). 2. fe, creencia, religión. 3. fe, confianza. 4. fidelidad, lealtad. 5. **in bad f.,** de mala fe; **in f.,** en verdad; **in good f.,** de buena fe; **to break** (o **violate**) **one's f.,** faltar a la palabra dada; **to break f. with,** engañar; **to give (pledge** o **plight) one's f.,** dar su palabra, comprometerse; **to keep one's f.,** cumplir su palabra; **upon my f.,** a fe mía. —*interj.* en verdad.
faith cure, curación por la fe.
faithful [ˈfeɪθfəl] *a.* 1. creyente, fiel. 2. leal, fiel, constante. 3. firme (promesa). 4. fiel, exacto. 5. **the f.,** los fieles o creyentes (de una religión); los partidarios leales (de una causa o idea).
faithfully [-fəlɪ] *adv.* 1. fielmente, lealmente. 2. fielmente, exactamente. 3. **to deal f. with,** decir cuatro verdades a, decir las verdades del barquero a; **to promise f.,** prometer firmemente; **yours f.,** atentamente suyo (se emplea como fórmula de despedida en cartas).
faithfulness [-fəlnəs] *s.* fidelidad, lealtad; exactitud.
faith healer, curador por fe, curandero, santero.
faith healing, curación por fe.
faithless [-ləs] *a.* 1. incrédulo, sin fe, infiel. 2. falso, desleal, pérfido.
faithlessly [-lɪ] *adv.* 1. incrédulamente, con incredulidad. 2. deslealmente.
faithlessness [-nəs] *s.* deslealtad, infidelidad, perfidia.
fake [feɪk] *v.t.* 1. falsificar, contrahacer. 2. simular, fingir. 3. (mar.) adujar. —*s.* 1. falsificación, impostura; copia, imitación. 2. farsante, impostor. 3. truco (de un mago). 4. (mar.) aduja de cable. —*a.* 1. falso, falsificado, contrahecho, fraudulento. 2. fingido, simulado.
faker [ˈfeɪkər, B -ə] *s.* 1. (fam.) falsificador. 2. falsario, estafador; impostor, farsante.
fake vault, (arq.) bóveda fingida.
fakir [fəˈkɪr, B ˈfeɪkɪə] *s.* faquir, derviche, monje mahometano; santón, religioso mendicante (esp. en la India).
Falange [ˈfeɪlændʒ] *s.* (pol.) Falange, partido político fundado en España en 1933.
Falangist [fəˈlændʒəst] *s.* (pol.) falangista.
falcate [ˈfælˌkeɪt] **falcated** [-əd] *a.* falcado, encorvado.
falcation [fælˈkeɪʃən] *s.* encorvadura.
falchion [ˈfɔltʃən] *s.* 1. (hist.) falce (espada medieval ancha y encorvada). 2. (poét., ant.) espada.
falciform [ˈfælsəˌfɔrm, B -ˌfɔm] *a.* falciforme, falcado, encorvado.
falcon [ˈfælkən, ˈfɔl-, B ˈfɔl-, ˈfɔkən] *s.* 1. (orn.) halcón. 2. (arm., hist.) falcón.
falconer [-ər, B -ə] *s.* (caza) halconero, cetrero.
falconet [-ˌɛt] *s.* 1. (arm.) falconete. 2. (orn.) variedad de halcón enano.
falcon-gentle [-ˈdʒɛntəl] *s.* (orn.) hembra de halcón peregrino.
falconry [-rɪ] *s.* (caza) halconería, cetrería.
falderal [ˈfɑldəˌrɑl, ˈfɔldəˌrɔl, B ˈfældəˈræl] *var. de* **folderol.**
faldstool [ˈfɔldˌstul] *s.* 1. faldistoric, atril de los obispos. 2. facistol. 3. (G.B.) reclinatorio (esp. el usado por el rey durante su coronación).
Falkland Islands [ˈfɔklənd-] (las) Islas Malvinas.
fall [fɔl] *v.i.* (*pret.* FELL [fɛl]; *p.p.* FALLEN [ˈfɔlən]; *p.pr.* FALLING) 1. caer, caerse. 2. bajar (temperatura, barómetro, precios, marea, presión, mercado, etc.). 3. caer (noche, tarde). 4. caer (fecha), ocurrir, suceder. 5. bajar (ojos, mirada, voz), ej., *her eyes fell,* (ella) bajó los ojos, *his voice fell to a whisper,* bajó la voz hasta el susurro. 6. apenarse, entristecerse (rostro). 7. pecar, caer (en pecado); perderse, perder la honra (mujer). 8. caer, morir (esp. en batalla). 9. caer (gobierno, ministro, etc.); caer, ser capturado (fortaleza, ciudad). 10. desplomarse (casa, edificio). 11. cesar, cejar (conversación, ira, viento, etc.). 12. quedarse, volverse (mudo, callado, etc.). 13. nacer (cordero). 14. (ant.) resultar. 15. **f. aboard,** (mar.) abordar; **f. across,** dar con, encontrarse casualmente con; **f. apart,** caerse a pedazos; **f. a prey (victim) to,** ser presa (víctima) de; **f. asleep,** quedarse dormido, dormirse; **f. astern,** (mar.) rezagarse; **f. asunder,** caer a pedazos; **f. away,** cesar, eliminarse; desertar; apostatar; declinar, debilitarse; inclinarse, ir en declive (terreno); (mar.) desaparecer, perderse de vista (tierra); disolverse (muchedumbre); **f. back,** retroceder, retirarse; quedarse atrás, rezagarse; **f. back on** o **upon,** recurrir a, pedir ayuda a, echar mano de; (mil.) replegarse hacia; **f. backward,** caer de espaldas; **f. behind,** quedarse atrás, quedarse en zaga; quedarse detrás de; **f. down,** caer al suelo; (fam.) fracasar; **f. due,** (com.) vencerse, ser pagadero (letra, préstamo, etc.); **f. flat,** fracasar por completo, no tener éxito; pasar inadvertido, no surtir efecto; **f. flat on one's face,** caer de bruces, dar de narices en el suelo; **f. foul** o **afoul of,** chocar contra; pelear con, reñir con; ponerse a malas con; (mar.) chocar con; **f. for,** admirar a, estar cautivado por, prendarse de; acaramelarse con, enamorarse de; gustarle mucho, agradarle mucho (algo a uno); quedar engañado o embaucado por (un truco, etc.); **f. from,** caerse de; **f. from grace,** caer en desgracia; **f. from the grace of,** perder el favor de; **f. in,** caer dentro, desplomarse hacia dentro; **f. in!** (mil.) ¡a formar!; **f. in (line),** (mil.) alinearse, formar; formar cola; (fig.) conformarse, seguir el ejemplo, obedecer; **f. in love,** enamorarse; **f. in price,** bajar de precio; **f. into the hands of (the police, swindlers,** etc.), caer en manos de (la policía, estafadores, etc.); **f. in with,** encontrarse con; acceder a, dar su conformidad a, estar de acuerdo con, estar conforme con (idea, propuesta, etc.); convenir con (persona); **f. into,** caer en; iniciar, trabar (conversación, etc.); desembocar en el mar (díc. de ríos); **f. into a rage,** ponerse furioso; **f. into the habit of,** adquirir el hábito o la costumbre de; **f. off,** caerse, desprenderse; disminuir, menguar, decaer, perder fuerza; empeorarse; (mil.) retirarse; dejar de; (mar.) abatir, derivar; **f. on,** caer de (cabeza, espaldas, etc.); caer en, recaer en, cargar en (díc. del acento); caer en (domingo, una fecha, día feriado, etc.); tocar a, corresponder a; acometer, asaltar, embestir (enemigo, etc.); caer sobre (comida); emprender, empezar; recurrir a; **f. on one's sword,** atravesarse con su propia espada; **f. out,** reñir, luchar, querellar, pelear; resultar; (mil.) romper filas; **f. out,** (mil.) ¡rompan filas!; **f. out of,** abandonar (un hábito); **f. over,** caerse; volcarse, desertar; **f. overboard,** caerse por la borda; (fam.) adular, colmar de atenciones; **f. over oneself,** afanarse demasiado; **f. short,** resultar deficiente o insuficiente; quedarse corto; no alcanzar el blanco (un proyectil); **f. short of,** no llegar a; **f. sick,** enfermarse; **f. through,** fracasar, fallar, abortar; **f. to,** tocar a, corresponder a; comenzar a; echarse a pelear; caer en manos de; tirarse sobre; **f. to one's lot** o **share,** caber o caer en suerte a uno; **f. to pieces,** caerse a pedazos; **f. to the ground,** desplomarse, caerse; fracasar, arruinarse (planes); **f. under,** ser incluido en (categoría, etc.); incurrir, caer en o bajo de; **f. upon,** recaer en, tocar; acometer, embestir (al enemigo, etc.); tropezar con; **f. on one's feet** (o **legs**), (fig.) caer de pies, salir bien del paso; **f. within,** ser incluido en; **fallen arches,** pies planos; **to have fallen out,** estar peleado, estar de monos. —*s.* 1. caída. 2. (fig.)

caída, degradación, decandencia, ruina. 3. caída, captura (de una fortaleza, ciudad). 4. otoño. 5. caída, pecado. 6. baja, descenso (de precios, temperatura, presión, marea, etc.). 7. (*gen. pl.*) catarata, cascada, salto de agua. 8. cantidad caída (de lluvia, etc.). 9. declive, inclinación, pendiente. 10. desembocadura de un río. 11. (mar.) tira de aparejo. 12. adorno del atuendo femenino, ej., postizo de cabello lacio; adorno de encaje o gasa que cuelga de un vestido; velo que cuelga de un sombrero. 13. **the F.** (bíbl.) La Caída; **to ride for a f.,** correr peligro o estar destinado a fracasar. —*a.* otoñal, del otoño, ej., *a f. coat,* un abrigo de otoño.

fallacious [fəˈleɪʃəs] *a.* 1. engañoso, delusorio, erróneo (razonamiento, etc.). 2. falaz; sofístico; ilógico.

fallaciously [-lɪ] *adv.* 1. engañosamente, erróneamente. 2. falazmente, ilógicamente.

fallaciousness [-nəs] *s.* falacia, engaño, error, sofisma.

fallacy [ˈfæləsɪ] *s.* 1. error, idea falsa. 2. carácter erróneo. 3. (lóg.) falacia, falsedad, sofisma.

fal-lal [fæˈlæl, B ˈfælˈlæl] *s.* faralá, farfalá. —*a.* afectado, aficionado a los faralás.

fallback [ˈfɔlˌbæk] *s.* 1. reserva, base; refugio. 2. retirada.

fallen [ˈfɔlən] *a.* 1. caído, postrado, arruinado. 2. perdido, deshonrado, degradado. 3. **the f.,** los caídos, los muertos (en el campo de batalla).

faller [ˈfɔlər, B -lə] 1. talador. 2. (mec.) maza (en un batán, bombo, etc.). 3. (tej.) segmento de bajada; barrita.

fall guy, (jer., E.U.) 1. pagote, pagano, cabeza de turco. 2. ingenuo, crédulo.

fallibility [ˌfæləˈbɪlətɪ] *s.* falibilidad.

fallible [ˈfæləbəl] *a.* falible.

fallibly [-blɪ] *adv.* faliblemente.

falling [ˈfɔlɪŋ] *s.* 1. caída, descenso, desplazamiento, disminución (volumen, valor). 2. (med.) prolapso. 3. **f. away,** enflaquecimiento; apostasía; **f. down,** postración; hundimiento, derrumbe; **f. in,** desmoronamiento, caída.

falling evil, f. sickness, epilepsia, mal caduco.

falling leaf, (avia.) caída de hoja.

falling-out [ˌfɔlɪŋˈaʊt] *s.* desacuerdo entre dos personas, distanciamiento, enfriamiento de relaciones, pelea.

falling star, estrella fugaz, meteoro.

fall line, 1. línea geográfica que indica el comienzo de una meseta. 2. (dep.) línea de descenso directo (en esquís).

falloff [ˈfɔlˌɔf] *s.* declinación, menoscabo.

Fallopian tube [fəˈloʊpɪən-] (anat.) trompa de Falopio.

fallout [ˈfɔlˌaʊt] *s.* precipitación radioactiva en la atmósfera (después de una explosión nuclear), lluvia radioactiva, polvillo radiactivo; (fig.) repercusiones, beneficios secundarios.

fallout shelter, refugio antiatómico.

fallow [ˈfæloʊ] *s.* barbecho, rastrojo, añojal. —*a.* 1. barbechado, sin cultivar. 2. (fig.) durmiente, inactivo. 3. flavo, leonado. 4. **to lie f.,** estar en barbecho. —*v.t.* barbechar.

fallow deer, (zool.) gamo, paleto, corzo.

fallow finch, (orn.) triguero.

fallowing [-ɪŋ] *s.* barbechera.

fall wheat, trigo sembrado en el otoño.

false [fɔls] *a.* 1. falso, incorrecto. 2. falso, traicionero, desleal. 3. falso, falsificado (diamante, moneda, billete); postizo (diente, peluca, seno). 4. (mec., arq.) falso, provisional, no permanente. 5. (mús.) falso, discordante. 6. **f. pretenses,** dolo; **under f. pretenses,** con engaños, por medios fraudulentos. 7. **to bear f. witness,** jurar en falso, perjurarse. —*adv.* con engaño, engañosamente; **to play (someone) f.,** engañar, traicionar (a alguien).

false acacia, (bot.) acacia falsa, acacia blanca.

false alarm, falsa alarma.

false arrest, (der.) arresto ilegal.

false bottom, doble fondo.

false cirrus, (meteor.) cirro falso.

false claim, (der.) reclamación fraudulenta.

false colors, (fig.) pretextos falsos.

false door, puerta simulada.

false face, máscara, esp. cómica o grotesca.

false floor, subsuelo.

falsehearted [ˈfɔlsˈhɑrtəd, B -ˈhɑt-] *a.* pérfido, traicionero, alevoso.

falsehood [-ˌhʊd] *s.* 1. falsedad, mentira. 2. carácter falso o traicionero.

false horizon, (mar., aer.) horizonte artificial.

false imprisonment, (der.) prisión o encarcelamiento ilegal.

false indigo, (bot.) amorfa.

false keel, (mar.) sobrequilla, zapata.

false loop, (avia.) rizo falso.

falsely [ˈfɔlslɪ] *adv.* falsamente, con falsedad.

falseness [-nəs] *s.* falsedad.

false pregnancy, embarazo psicológico, embarazo fantasma.

false ribs, (anat.) costillas falsas, costillas flotantes.

false spar, (avia.) larguero falso o volado.

false step, paso en falso, desliz, error, imprudencia.

false teeth, dientes postizos.

falsetto [fɔlˈsɛtoʊ] *s.* (*pl.* FALSETTOS) (mús.) 1. falsete. 2. falsetista. —*a.* de falsete. —*adv.* en falsete.

false wind, (meteor.) corriente de aire descendente.

false witness, falso testimonio.

falsework [ˈfɔlsˌwɜrk, B -ˌwɜk] *s.* (const.) andamiaje.

falsidical [fɔlˈsɪdəkəl] *a.* que da impresiones falsas; imaginario; (psic.) ilusorio.

falsie [ˈfɔlsɪ] *s. gen. pl.* (fam.) senos postizos (en forma de sostén).

falsification [ˌfɔlsəfəˈkeɪʃən] *s.* falsificación.

falsifier [ˈfɔlsəˌfaɪər, B -ə] *s.* falsificador.

falsify [-faɪ] *v.t.* (*pret., p.p.* FALSIFIED; *p.pr.* FALSIFYING) 1. falsificar; adulterar. 2. refutar, desmentir, probar la falsedad de. 3. frustrar (esperanzas, promesas, etc.). —*v.i.* decir mentiras, mentir.

falsity [-tɪ] *s.* 1. falsedad, carácter falso. 2. falsedad, mentira.

faltboat [ˈfɑltˌboʊt] *s.* bote plegable.

falterer [-tərer, B -tərə] *s.* persona vacilante.

faltering [-tərɪŋ] *s. vacilación, titubeo.* —*a.* vacilante, titubeante.

falteringly [-lɪ] *adv.* en forma vacilante, con titubeo.

falx cerebelli [ˈfælksˌsɛrəˈbəlaɪ] (anat.) hoz del cerebelo.

falx cerebri [-ˈsɛrəbrɪ, B -braɪ] (anat.) hoz del cerebro.

fam. *abrev. de* 1. **familiar,** familiar. 2. family, familia.

fame [feɪm] *s.* fama, reputación, renombre; **house of ill f.,** prostíbulo, lupanar, mancebía. —*v.t.* afamar, celebrar.

famed [feɪmd] *a.* famoso, afamado, renombrado.

familial [fəˈmɪljəl] *a.* familiar, de familia.

familiar [-jər, B -jə] *a.* 1. familiar, conocido. 2. fresco. 3. **to be f. to,** ser familiar a; **to be f. with,** estar familiarizado con (alguien o algo); estar versado en, saber de (una cosa o materia). —*s.* 1. familiar, compañero. 2. familiar, espíritu protector. 3. (relig.) familiar (ministro de la Inquisición). 4. parroquiano, miembro de una parroquia.

familiarity [fəˌmɪlˈjærətɪ, B -ˌmɪlɪˈær-] *s.* (*pl.* FAMILIARITIES) 1. familiaridad, intimidad, confianza. 2. familiaridad (con), conocimiento (de). 3. (*pl.*) libertades (en el trato).

familiarize [fəˈmɪljəˌraɪz] *v.t.* familiarizar, acostumbrar a, habituar a; **f. oneself with,** familiarizarse con.

familiarly [-jərlɪ, B -jəlɪ] *adv.* familiarmente, amistosamente.

family [fæməlɪ] *s.* familia; linaje, cuna; (zool., bot.) familia; **Holy F.,** la Sagrada Familia; **in the f. way,** (fam.) embarazada, encinta. —*a.* familiar, casero, de la familia.

family Bible, Biblia, familiar.

family circle, 1. medio familiar, círculo familiar. 2. (teat.) galería, segundo balcón de asientos.

family doctor, médico de cabecera.

family man, hombre doméstico, hombre casero; padre de familia.

family name, apellido, nombre de familia.

family planning, planificación familiar.

family resemblance, aire de familia.

family skeleton, secreto o escándalo en una familia.

family tree, árbol genealógico.

famine [ˈfæmən] *s.* 1. hambre, hambruna (Amer.). 2. escasez; carestía.

famish [ˈfæmɪʃ] *v.t.* hambrear; **famished,** famélico, muerto de hambre. —*v.i.* morir(se) de hambre; hambrear; **to be famishing,** (fam.) estar famélico, estar muerto de hambre.

famous [ˈfeɪməs] *a.* 1. famoso, afamado, célebre, renombrado. 2. (fam.) famoso, excelente, magnífico. 3. (ant.) desacreditado.

famulus [ˈfæmjələs] *s.* (*pl.* FAMULI [-ˌlaɪ]) fámulo.

fan [fæn] *s.* 1. abanico. 2. ventilador. 3. (agr.) bieldo; aventadora. 4. (aer., jer.) hélice. 5. aspas reguladoras (en molinos de viento). 6. **suction f.,** ventilador aspirante; **extraction f.,** ventilador extractor; **vacuum f.,** ventilador de vacío. —*v.t.* (*pret., p.p.* FANNED; *p.pr.* FANNING) 1. abanicar. 2. avivar (fuego, llama, pasiones, etc.), excitar (curiosidad, interés, etc.). 3. soplar sobre. 4. (agr.) beldar, bieldar, aventar. 5. (jer.) zurrar. 6. (béisbol, jer.) obligar a salir (al bateador). 7. **f. oneself,** abanicarse; **f. the air,** dar un golpe en el aire, sin tocar blanco. —*v.i.* (ú. gen. con *out*) 1. abrirse como un abanico. 2. desplegarse; ramificarse. 3. (béisbol, jer.) retirarse, fallar (tres veces) (el bateador).

fan, *s.* (fam.) aficionado, hincha (Amer.) (de un atleta, artista, etc.); aficionado, entusiasta (de un deporte, de la música, etc.); admirador (de una persona, un actor, etc.).

fanatic [fəˈnætɪk] *a., s.* fanático.

fanatical [-ɪkəl] *a.* fanático.

fanatically [-kəlɪ] *adv.* fanáticamente.

fanaticism [fəˈnætəˌsɪzəm] *s.* fanatismo.

fanaticize [-ˌsaɪz] *v.t.* fanatizar.

fan belt, correa del ventilador.

fan blower, ventilador.

fancied [ˈfænsid] *a.* imginado, imaginario.

fancier [ˈfænsɪər, B -ə] *s.* 1. aficionado, conocedor (que cultiva una afición, como la cría de cierta raza de animales finos, etc.). 2. soñador, iluso.

fanciful [-sɪfəl] *a.* 1. extravagante, irreal, fantástico. 2. caprichoso, antojadizo.

fancifully [-fəlɪ] *adv.* caprichosamente.

fancily [ˈfænsəlɪ] *adv.* estrambóticamente, estrafalariamente; aparatosamente.

fanciness [-sɪnəs] *s.* 1. floridez (de estilo). 2. extravagancia.

fan-cooled motor ['fæn,kuld-] (elec.) motor enfriado por aire.

fancy ['fænsɪ] *s.* (*pl.* FANCIES) 1. inclinación, tendencia, afición. 2. capricho, antojo. 3. gusto, preferencia. 4. cariño, afecto. 5. imaginación, fantasía. 6. idea, concepción, concepto. 7. (ant.) fantasma, aparición. 8. **to catch** (o **take,** o **strike**) **the f. of,** gustarle a, agradarle a; **to take a. f. to** (o **for**), aficionarse a, prendarse de, coger cariño a (una persona); tomar gusto a (una cosa). —*v.t.* (*pret., p.p.* FANCIED; *p.pr.* FANCYING) 1. gustar; gustar de. 2. imaginar, concebir. 3. imaginarse, creer, suponer. 4. tener afecto a, gustarle a uno. 5. **f. (that)!** ¡imagínese! ¡qué sorpresa!; **f. meeting you here,** qué milagro encontrarle aquí; **f. oneself,** ser engreído, tener buena opinión de sí mismo; **f. oneself (an actor, dead,** etc.), imaginarse (actor, muerto, etc.). —*a.* (FANCIER; FANCIEST) 1. ornamental; de adorno. 2. selecto, fino, de lujo. 3. de fantasía, de imitación. 4. imaginario, irreal; de imaginación, imaginado. 5. caprichoso, extravagante; estrafalario, estrambótico. 6. excesivo (precio).

fancy ball, baile de trajes, baile de disfraces.

fancy dive, (dep.) salto acrobático ornamental.

fancy diving, (dep.) saltos acrobáticos ornamentales.

fancy dress, disfraz, traje de época, traje de fantasía.

fancy-free ['fænsɪ'fri] *a.* despreocupado, alegre; sin preocupaciones amorosas.

fancy goods, géneros o artículos de lujo.

fancy man, chulo, tercero.

fancy skating, patinaje artístico.

fancy woods, maderas preciosas.

fancywork ['fænsɪ,wɜrk, B -,wɜk] *s.* (cost.) labor ornamental.

fandango [fæn'dæŋgoʊ] *s.* fandango (baile y música de origen andaluz).

fan delta, (geol.) abanico aluvial.

fane [feɪn] *s.* (poét., ant.) templo, santuario.

fanfare ['fæn,fɛr, B -,fɛə] *s.* 1. (mús.) fanfarria, charanga; toque de trompetas. 2. (fig.) bombo y platillos.

fanfaron ['fænfə,rɑn, B -,rɔn] *s.* fanfarrón, baladrón.

fanfaronade [,fænfærə'neɪd, -'nɑd] *s.* fanfarronada, fanfarria, baladronada, bravata, jactancia.

fang [fæŋ] *s.* 1. colmillo (de animal), diente (de serpiente). 2. raíz, punta de la raíz (de un diente).

fanged [fæŋd] *a.* con colmillos.

fangless ['fæŋləs] *a.* sin colmillos.

fanhead engine ['fæn,hɛd-] (mec.) motor de válvulas laterales.

fanion ['fænjən] *s.* (fr., mil.) banderola, estandarte.

fanlight ['fæn,laɪt] *s.* (arq.) abanico, montante.

fanlike [-,laɪk] *a.* en forma de abanico; parecido a un abanico.

fan mail, cartas a un artista, deportista, etc. de parte de sus admiradores.

fan marker, (avia.) marcador de molinete.

fanner ['fænər, B -ə] *s.* 1. ventilador. 2. (agr.) aventadora.

fanning mill [-ɪŋ-] (agr.) aventadora.

fanny ['fænɪ] *s.* (jer.) trasero, nalgas, culo; (G.B., vulg.) coño.

fanon ['fænən] *s.* (rel.) fanón (ornamento en el atuendo eclesiástico).

fan palm, (bot.) miraguano.

fan-shaped ['fæn,ʃeɪpt] *a.* en forma de abanico.

fan sticks, varillas de abanico.

fantail [-,teɪl] *s.* 1. (orn.) (variedad de) paloma colipava; papamoscas de Australia. 2. (ict.) variedad de carpa dorada. 3. mechero de mariposa. 4. (carp.) cola de milano. 5. (mar.) bovedilla. 6. cola, parte (de un objeto o animal) en forma de abanico.

fantail burner, mechero de mariposa.

fantail pigeon, (orn.) paloma colipava.

fan-tan ['fæn,tæn] *s.* 1. juego de azar chino (en que se apuesta a adivinar el número de monedas escondidas bajo una escudilla). 2. juego de azar con naipes.

fantasia [fæn'teɪʒə, ˌfæntə'ziə, B fæn't-eɪzjə] *s.* (mús.) fantasía, pot-pourrí.

fantasm, *var. de* **phantasm.**

fantast ['fæn,tæst] *s.* visionario, soñador.

fantastic [fæn'tæstɪk, fən-] **fantastical** [-tɪkəl] *a.* 1. fantástico, imaginario, irreal, quimérico. 2. fantástico, grotesco, extravagante, extraño.

fantastically [-tɪkəlɪ] *adv.* fantásticamente.

fantasticate [-,keɪt] *v.t.* hacer fantástico.

fantasy ['fæntəsɪ, -əzɪ] *s.* 1. fantasía, imaginación. 2. fantasía, ensueño, noción fantástica. 3. (mús.) fantasía. —*v.t.* imaginar. —*v.i.* fantasear.

fanto, *var. de* **phantom.**

fan tracery, (arq.) tracería decorativa de bóvedas de abanico.

fan wheel, ventilador.

fan window, (arq.) abanico, ventana en forma de abanico.

fanwise ['fæn,waɪz] *adv.* en abanico.

fanwort [-,wɜrt, B -,wɜt] *s.* (bot.) cabomba.

FAO *abrev. de* **Food and Agriculture Organization,** Organización de las Naciones Unidas para la Agricultura y la Alimentación.

far [fɑr, B fɑ] *adv.* (FARTHER ['fɑrðər, B 'fɑðə] O FURTHER ['fɜr-, B 'fɜðə]; FARTHEST O FURTHEST) 1. lejos, a lo lejos, en lontananza. 2. muy; mucho. 3. **as f. as,** hasta, tan lejos como; **as f. as I am concerned,** por lo que a mí me toca, en lo que a mí respecta, por mi parte; **as f. as I know,** que yo sepa; **f. along in,** muy entrado, ej., *f. along in March,* muy entrado marzo; **f. and away,** mucho, por mucho, decididamente; **f. and near,** por todas partes; **f. and wide,** por todas partes; **f. away,** a lo lejos, a gran distancia; **f. be it from me,** yo sería incapaz de; **f. better,** mucho mejor; **f. different,** muy diferente; **(to be) f. from,** (estar, ser) lejos de (ser, hacer); no ser nada, ni ser . . . ni mucho menos, ej., *f. from being easy, it turned out to be quite difficult,* lejos de ser fácil, resultó ser bien difícil, *f. from believing it, I examined his statement very carefully,* lejos de creer en ello, examiné su declaración con mucho cuidado; **f. from it,** lejos de eso, ni mucho menos, muy al contrario; **f. gone,** avanzado, muy enfermo, muy débil; completamente loco; muy borracho; **f. into,** hasta muy adentro de; hasta muy tarde de, hasta altas horas de (la noche, etc.); hasta muy avanzado (el verano, etc.); **f. more,** mucho más; **f. too much,** demasiado; **few and f. between,** muy raro, muy escaso; **how f.?** ¿a qué distancia? ¿hasta dónde?; **in so f. as,** en cuanto, en cuanto que; **on the f. side of,** al otro lado de; **so f.,** hasta ahora, hasta la fecha; **so f. so good,** hasta ahora todo va bien; **the f. side,** el otro lado, el otro extremo; **thus f.,** hasta ahora; **to carry f.,** llegar lejos, oírse de lejos; **to carry (something) too f.,** llevar (algo) al exceso, insistir demasiado, exagerar; **to go f.,** (fig.) llegar lejos, realizar mucho; **to go f. towards,** contribuir mucho a, ayudar mucho en; **to go too f.,** pasarse de la raya, excederse, extralimitarse. —*s.* distancia, lugar distante; **by f.,** con mucho, con una gran diferencia; **from f.,** de lejos, desde gran distancia. —*a.* 1. lejano, distante, remoto. 2. largo (viaje, trayecto, etc.). 3. **f. cry,** gran diferencia, gran distancia; **f. out,** (fam.) muy avanzado, novedoso, arriesgado, no conformista.

farad ['fær,æd, B -əd] *s.* (elec.) faradio, farad, farádico, unidad electromagnética de capacidad eléctrica.

Faraday cage ['færə,deɪ-, -dɪ-] (elec.) jaula de Faraday.

faradic [fə'rædɪk] *a.* (elec.) farádico.

faradism ['færə,dɪzəm] **faradization** [,færədə'zeɪʃən, B -daɪ-] *s.* (med.) faradización.

faradize ['færə,daɪz] *v.t.* (med.) tratar con corriente farádica, faradizar.

faradizer [-ər, B -ə] *s.* instrumento usado para la faradización.

faradmeter ['færæd,mitər, B -əd,mitə] *s.* (elec.) faradímetro, instrumento usualmente graduado en microfaradios utilizado para medir la potencia electromotriz inducida.

farandole ['færən,doʊl] *s.* (mús.) farándula, farandola.

faraway ['fɑrə,weɪ] *a.* 1. lejano, alejado, distante, remoto. 2. abstraído, distraído, soñador (dic. de la mirada o de los ojos).

farce [fɑrs, B fɑs] *v.t.* 1. (teat.) meter morcillas en, rellenar (escrito, comedia, etc.) de pasajes o citas jocosas. 2. (ant., cocina) rellenar, embutir. —*s.* 1. (cocina) embutido, relleno de carne. 2. (teat.) farsa, entremés, sainete. 3. (fig.) farsa, enredo, tramoya.

farceur [fɑr'sɜr, B fɑ'sɜ] *s.* 1. bromista, burlón, chancero. 2. farsante, comediante. 3. farsista.

farcical ['fɑrsɪkəl, B 'fɑsɪ-] *a.* burlesco, ridículo, bufo, absurdo, asainetado.

farcicality [,fɑrsɪ'kælətɪ, B ,fɑsɪ-] *s.* carácter ridículo o absurdo.

farcically ['fɑrsɪkəlɪ, B 'fɑsɪ-] *adv.* ridículamente.

farcy ['fɑrsɪ, B 'fɑsɪ] *s.* (vet.) muermo.

fard [fɑrd, B fɑd] *v.t.* (ant.) afeitar, pintar, maquillar (el rostro).

fardel ['fɑrdəl, B 'fɑd-] *s.* 1. lío, atado, paquete. 2. (ant.) carga. 3. (ant.) miscelánea (de objetos).

fare [fɛr, B fɛə] *v.i.* 1. viajar; pasar. 2. irle (bien o mal) a uno, tener (buena o mala) suerte, prosperar. 3. alimentarse, comer. 4. **f. forth,** emprender viaje, ponerse en camino; **how did you f.?** ¿cómo le fue a usted? —*s.* 1. tarifa de viaje, pasaje (precio). 2. pasajero. 3. comida, alimentos. 4. (fig.) régimen, dieta. 5. **bill of f.,** menú, lista de platos; **light f.,** algo ligero, frívolo o alegre (como pieza de teatro, etc.).

Far East, Lejano Oriente, Extremo Oriente.

farer ['fɛrər, B 'fɛərə] *s.* viajero, viajante.

fare-thee-well [,fɛrði'wɛl, B ,fɛəði-] *f* ɾə-ʏʊ-ɯəλλ [-jə'wɛl] *s.* 1. (estado de) perfección. 2. el sumo grado, non plus ultra. 3. **to a f.-y.-w.,** a la perfección, completamente, a fondo.

farewell ['fɛr'wɛl, B 'fɛə'-] *interj.* ¡adiós! ¡vaya con Dios! ¡que le vaya bien! —*s.* despedida, adiós; salida; **to bid f. to, to take f. of,** despedirse de. —*a.* de despedida; final; **f. performance,** función de despedida.

far-famed ['fɑr'feɪmd, B 'fɑ'-] *a.* de gran fama.

farfetched [-'fɛtʃt] *a.* forzado, traído de los cabellos, improbable.

far-flung [-'flʌŋ] *a.* 1. vasto, extenso. 2. remoto, distante.

farina [fə'rinə, B -'raɪ-] *s.* 1. harina de cereales, patatas o nueces (para hacer gachas o budines). 2. fécula, almidón, (esp. de patatas). 3. (G.B., bot.) polen.

farinaceous [ˌfærəˈneɪʃəs] *a.* farináceo, harinoso; seco, pastoso.
farinose [ˈfærəˌnoʊs] *a.* 1. farináceo, harinoso. 2. (bot.) farináceo. 3. (bot., zool.) cubierto de polvo harinoso.
farkleberry [ˈfɑrkəlˌbɛrɪ, B ˈfɑkəl-] *s.* (bot.) batodendrón.
farm [fɑrm, B fɑm] *s.* 1. granja, finca, hacienda. 2. plantación; cultivo (acuático). 3. (béisbol) club subsidiario (de otro de primera división). —*v.t.* 1. cultivar, labrar (la tierra). 2. (béisbol) poner de reserva en un club subsidiario (a un jugador). 3. **f. out,** dar en contrato, ceder por contrato; encargar un trabajo de fábrica u oficina para hacerse fuera; **f. (land) out (with),** agotar (tierra) con el cultivo (de). —*v.i.* cultivar la tierra, ser agricultor o granjero; administrar una granja.
farmer [ˈfɑrmər, B ˈfɑmə] *s.* granjero, agricultor, hacendado; labrador, labriego, campesino, colono.
farmerette [ˌfɑrməˈrɛt, B ˌfɑmə-] *s.* (fam.) agricultora, labradora.
farmhand [ˈfɑrmˌhænd, B ˈfɑm-] *s.* peón de granja, mozo de labranza; campesino, labrador.
farmhouse [-ˌhaʊs] *s.* alquería, cortijo, casa hacienda (Amer.).
farming [-ɪŋ] *a.* agrícola, de labranza, para cultivo. —*s.* cultivo, labranza, agricultura.
farmland [-ˌlænd] *s.* terreno (apto) para cultivo.
farm produce, productos agrícolas.
farmstead [-ˌstɛd] *f* rmšɿə đɩŋ̰ [-ɪŋ] *s.* granja, alquería y sus dependencias; cortijo.
farmyard [-ˌjɑrd, B -ˌjɑd] *s.* corral de una granja.
faro [ˈfɛroʊ, B ˈfɛər-] *s.* faraón (juego de naipes parecido al monte).
far-off [ˈfɑrˈɔf] *a.* lejano, distante, remoto.
farouche [fəˈrʊʃ] *a.* indómito, hosco.
farraginous [fəˈrædʒənəs] *a.* (raro) farragoso, formado de varios materiales; mezclado.
farrago [fəˈrɑgoʊ, -ˈreɪ-] *s.* (*pl.* FARRAGOES) fárrago, miscelánea, broza, mezcla, mescolanza.
far-reaching [ˈfɑrˈritʃɪŋ, B ˈfɑˈ-] *a.* de mucho alcance, trascendente, de largo alcance.
farrier [ˈfærɪər, B -ə] *s.* herrador; (G.B.) veterinario de caballos.
farriery [-ɪərɪ] *s.* herrería; veterinaria.
farrow [ˈfæroʊ] *s.* 1. lechigada de puercos. 2. parto de la marrana. —*v.t.*, *v.i.* parir (la marrana). —*a.* horra, machorra (díc. de la vaca).
farseeing [ˈfɑrˈsiɪŋ, B ˈfɑˈ-] *a.* 1. prudente, previsor, precavido. 2. capaz de ver claramente en la distancia.
farsighted [-ˈsaɪtəd] *a.* 1. prudente, previsor, perspicaz, sagaz. 2. présbita, présbite, hipermétrope.
farsightedly [-lɪ] *adv.* prudentemente.
farsightedness [-nəs] *s.* 1. prudencia, previsión, sagacidad, perspicacia. 2. presbicia, hipermetropía.
fart [fɑrt, B fɑt] *s.* (vulg.) 1. pedo. 2. (*person*) **a boring old f.** un pesado de mierda. —*v.i.* (vulg.) peer, echarse un pedo, tirarse un pedo.
farther [ˈfɑrðər, B ˈfɑðə] *a.* (*comp. de* FAR) más lejano; ulterior, más alejado, más distante. —*adv.* 1. más lejos, a mayor distancia; más adelante. 2. además de, ulteriormente. 3. **f. on,** más adelante.
farthermost [-ˌmoʊst] *a.* (*super. de* FAR) más remoto, más lejano.
farthest [-ðəst] *a.* (*super. de* FAR) más lejano o remoto; más largo o extendido. —*adv.* más lejos, a la mayor distancia.
farthing [ˈfɑrðɪŋ, B ˈfɑðɪŋ] *s.* 1. (G.B.) cuarto de penique. 2. (fig.) pitoche, bicoca, comino, ej., *it doesn't matter a f.,* no importa un comino, *it isn't worth a f.,* no vale un pitoche.
farthingale [-ˌgeɪl] *s.* verdugado, miriñaque, guardainfante.
F.A.S., f.a.s. *abrev. de* **free alongside ship,** franco al costado del vapor.
fasces [ˈfæsiz] *s. pl.* (*sing. o pl. en const.*) (hist.) fasces, símbolo de autoridad en la antigua Roma.
fascia [ˈfæʃɪə, ˈfeɪʃə] *s.* 1. faja, tira. 2. (med.) venda, vendaja. 3. (arq.) faja, imposta. 4. (anat.) fascia. 5. (zool.) faja o franja (de color). 6. (astr.) faja alrededor de un planeta.
fascial [ˈfæʃəl, ˈfeɪʃ-] *a.* (anat.) fascial, aponeurótico.
fasciate [ˈfæsɪˌeɪt] **fasciated** [-əd] *a.* 1. (zool.) fasciado, listado. 2. (bot.) fasciculado. 3. (bot.) fasciado, aplanado. 4. vendado, atado o envuelto en tiras.
fasciation [ˌfæʃɪˈeɪʃən] *s.* 1. (bot.) fasciación. 2. vendaje.
fascicle [ˈfæsɪkəl] *s.* 1. fascículo, cuaderno (de una publicación por entregas). 2. (bot.) fascículo. 3. (anat.) fascículo (de fibras, nervios, etc.). 4. racimo, manojo.
fascicled [-kəld] *a.* (bot., anat.) fasciculado.
fascicular [fəˈsɪkjələr, B -lə] *a.* (bot.) fascicular.
fasciculate [-ˌleɪt] **fasciculated** [-əd] *a.* fascicular, fasciculado.
fasciculation [fəˌsɪkjəˈleɪʃən] *s.* (anat.) fasciculación.
fascicule [ˈfæsɪˌkjul] *s.* 1. fascículo, cuaderno (de una publicación por entregas). 2. (anat.) fascículo.
fasciculus [fəˈsɪkjələs] *s.* (*pl.* FASCICULI [-ˌlaɪ]) 1. fascículo, cuaderno (de una publicación por entregas). 2. (anat.) fascículo.
fascinate [ˈfæsənˌeɪt] *v.t.* 1. fascinar, hipnotizar. 2. (fig.) fascinar, hechizar, encantar, cautivar. 3. (ant.) fascinar, hechizar, aojar, embrujar. —*v.i.* ejercer fascinación.
fascinating [-ɪŋ] *a.* fascinador, fascinante, hechicero, cautivador.
fascination [ˌfæsənˈeɪʃən] 1. fascinación, hechizo, encanto. 2. (ant.) fascinación, embrujamiento, aojo.
fascinator [ˈfæsənˌeɪtər, B -ə] *s.* 1. persona o cosa fascinante. 2. mantilla ligera de ganchillo.
fascine [fæˈsin] *s.* (fort.) fajina; haz.
fascism [ˈfæʃˌɪzəm, ˈfæs-] *s.* (pol.) fascismo.
fascist [-əst] *s., a.* (pol.) fascista.
fascistic [fæˈʃɪstɪk] *a.* (pol.) fascista.
fash [fæʃ] *v.t.* (pr. esco.) fastidiar, irritar.
fashion [ˈfæʃən] *s.* 1. moda, boga. 2. manera, modo, estilo. 3. costumbre, uso, hábito. 4. distinción, buen tono. 5. (ant.) conducta, proceder; clase, especie. 6. **after** (o **in**) **a fashion,** hasta cierto punto, en cierto modo; **after one's f.,** a su manera (de uno); **after the f. of,** a manera de; **in f.,** en boga, de moda; **latest f.,** última moda; **out of f.,** pasado de moda, fuera de moda; **there was a f. for it,** estaba de moda; **to come into f.,** ponerse de moda; **to go out of f.,** pasar de moda; **to set the f.,** dictar la moda. —*v.t.* 1. formar, labrar, moldear. 2. amoldar, ajustar, adaptar. 3. (ant.) idear, inventar.
fashionable [-əbəl] *a.* de moda, en boga, elegante, de buen tono. —*s.* persona elegante.
fashionableness [-nəs] *s.* carácter elegante, buen tono.
fashionably [-blɪ] *adv.* a la moda.
fashion designer, modisto.
fashionmonger [-ˌmʌŋgər, -ˌmaŋ-, B -ˌmʌŋgə] *s.* petimetre, pisaverde, lechuguino.
fashion plate, 1. figurín (dibujo de moda). 2. figurín, pisaverde, gomoso; mujer esclava de la moda.
fashion shop, casa o tienda de modas.
fast [fæst, B fɑst] *a.* 1. rápido, veloz. 2. firme, estable, seguro. 3. firme, constante (amigo, amistad, etc.). 4. adelantado (reloj). 5. disoluto, disipado, inmoral. 6. cerrado (puerta, ventana, etc.); atascado (cajón, puerta, tapa, etc.). 7. (en palabras compuestas) a prueba de, resistente a, ej., *acid-f.,* a prueba de ácidos. 8. (foto.) rápido (obturador, objetivo), de alta sensibilidad (película). 9. **to make f.,** asegurar, amarrar, sujetar firmemente; **to play f. and loose with,** tratar irresponsablemente; gastar atolondradamente (dinero, herencia, etc.); burlarse de, jugar con (sentimientos, ideales, etc.); **to pull a f. one,** (jer.) hacer una bribonada. —*adv.* 1. firmemente, seguramente. 2. completamente, bien, perfectamente. 3. rápidamente, velozmente. 4. disipadamente, ej., *to live f.,* vivir disipadamente. 5. (ant., poét.) cerca, ej., *f. by,* muy cerca de, *f. behind,* siguiendo muy de cerca. 6. **f. aground,** encallado (barco); **f. asleep,** profundamente dormido; **f. shut,** perfectamente cerrado, bien cerrado; **to go f.,** correr velozmente; adelantar(se) (reloj); **to hold f.,** mantenerse firme; no moverse; **to sit f.,** no moverse de su asiento o sitio; **to sleep f.,** dormir profundamente; **to stand f.,** no ceder, no cejar. —*v.i.* ayunar. —*s.* 1. ayuno, abstinencia, ej., *to break one's f.,* romper el ayuno. 2. (mar.) amarra; noray.
fastback [ˈfæstˌbæk, B ˈfɑst-] *s.* automóvil moderno de techo en forma de curva ininterrumpida.
fast buck, (jer.) dinero ganado fácil y rápidamente.
fast color, color firme (que no se destiñe).
fast day, día de ayuno.
fasten [ˈfæsən, B ˈfɑsən] *v.t.* 1. fijar, afirmar. 2. atar, ligar; clavar. 3. cerrar, asegurar (puerta, cinturón de seguridad, etc.). 4. **f. down,** sujetar; **f. in** o **up,** encerrar; **f. on** o **upon,** fijar (mirada, pensamiento, etc.) en; cifrar (esperanzas) en; imputar, echar (culpa) a; atribuir (responsabilidad) a; **f. oneself upon,** pegarse a, no moverse del lado de. —*v.i.* 1. fijarse, afirmarse. 2. quedar cerrado, cerrarse. 3. **f. on** o **upon,** fijarse en; agarrarse de; asirse de.
fastener [-ər, B -ə] *s.* sujetador, fiador, fijador; **toggle f.,** sujetador articulado; **cowling f.,** fijador de carenaje; **threaded f.,** tornillo.
fastening [-ɪŋ] *s.* sujetador, fiador; aldabilla, cierre, cerrojo; broche.
faster [ˈfæstər, B ˈfɑstə] *s.* el que ayuna.
fasti [ˈfæsti] *s. pl.* (hist.) fastos, registros, anales.
fastidious [fæsˈtɪdɪəs, fəs-] *a.* quisquilloso, descontentadizo; remilgado, melindroso, dengoso; exigente.
fastidiously [-lɪ] *adv.* melindrosamente.
fastidiousness [-nəs] *s.* melindre, dengue.
fastigiate [fæsˈtɪdʒɪət, B -ˌeɪt] **fastigiated** [-ˌeɪtəd] *a.* (bot.) **fastigiado.**
fastigium [-ɪəm] *s.* (med.) fastigio.
fastness [ˈfæstnəs, B ˈfɑst-] *s.* 1. firmeza, fijeza. 2. rapidez. 3. disipación, inmoralidad. 4. adelanto (del reloj). 5. constancia, perseverancia (de amistad, etc.). 6. firmeza (de colores, tintes). 7. resistencia (a materias tóxicas, ácidos, etc.). 8. fortaleza, plaza fuerte.
fat [fæt] *a.* (FATTER; FATTEST) 1. gordo, obeso, grueso. 2. graso, grasiento, grasoso, mantecoso. 3. repleto, bien lleno, bien abastecido. 4. (fig.) pingüe, lucrativo, provechoso. 5. fértil, productivo. 6. abundante; rico. 7. lerdo, torpe. 8. (impr.) negro, ancho (tipo). 9. (jer., irón.) poco, ej., *a f. lot!* ¡vaya qué poco! 10. **to cut it f.,** hacer un despliegue u ostentación; **to get f.,** ponerse gordo; **f. chance!** (jer.) ¡ni en sueños (lograrás

eso)! —*s.* 1. grasa, sebo; manteca. 2. (fig.) lo mejor, la mejor parte. 3. gordura, obesidad. 4. (quím.) grasa. 5. (G.B., teat.) grato papel. 6. **the f. is in the fire,** la situación es crítica; **to chew the f.,** (fam.) platicar, charlar; **to live on (off) one's f.,** consumir uno sus reservas, vivir uno consumiendo sus reservas; **to live on (off) the f. of the land,** tener lo mejor de todo, vivir en la opulencia. —*v.t.* engordar, cebar.

fatal ['feɪtəl] *a.* fatal; funesto, mortífero, mortal; **the f. sisters,** (mitol.) las parcas.

fatalism [-ˌɪzəm] *s.* (filos.) fatalismo.

fatalist [-əst] *s.* fatalista.

fatalistic [ˌfeɪtəl'ɪstɪk] *a.* fatalista.

fatality [feɪ'tælətɪ, fə-] *s.* 1. fatalidad (de un suceso, circunstancia, etc.). 2. fatalismo. 3. fatalidad, calamidad, desgracia. 4. muerte violenta; muerto, víctima.

fatally ['feɪtəlɪ] *adv.* fatalmente.

fata morgana ['fɑtəmɔr'gɑnə, B -mɔ'-] fatamorgana, espejismo.

fatback ['fætˌbæk] *s.* tocino.

fat cat, (jer., E.U.) pez gordo, potentado.

fate [feɪt] *s.* 1. hado, sino, suerte, destino; muerte, parca. 2. estrella, fortuna. 3. **F.,** diosa del destino. 4. **to decide (fix o seal) one's f.,** sellar su destino; **to meet one's f.,** encontrar la muerte. —*v.t.* predestinar.

fated ['feɪtəd] *a.* 1. fatal; aciago, de mal agüero. 2. predestinado.

fateful [-fəl] *a.* 1. fatal; irrevocable. 2. fatídico, ominoso.

fatefully [-fəlɪ] *adv.* fatídicamente, ominosamente.

fatefulness [-fəlnəs] *s.* fatalidad; irrevocabilidad.

fathead ['fætˌhɛd] *s.* (jer.) bobalicón, estúpido, lerdo.

father ['fɑðər, B -ə] *s.* 1. padre. 2. **F.** (relig.) Padre. 3. padre, sacerdote, religioso. 4. (t. **church f.**) (relig.) padre de la Iglesia. 5. (fig.) padre, autor, inventor. 6. **like f., like son,** de tal palo tal astilla. —*v.t.* 1. engendrar, procrear. 2. (fig.) fundar; inventar; producir, originar. 3. prohijar; proteger, apadrinar.

father confessor, confesor, padre espiritual.

father figure, figura paterna, persona que se finge dotada de las cualidades paternales.

fatherhood [-ˌhʊd] *s.* paternidad.

father image (psic.) idealización del padre de uno (que a menudo se transfiere a otra persona a quien uno busca como protector).

father-in-law ['fɑðərənˌlɔ] *s.* (*pl.* FATHERS-IN-LAW) 1. suegro. 2. (raro) padrastro.

fatherland ['fɑðərˌlænd, B 'fɑðəˌ-] *s.* patria.

fatherless [-ləs] *a.* sin padre, huérfano de padre.

fatherlike [-ˌlaik] *a.* paternal. —*adv.* paternalmente.

fatherliness [-lɪnəs] *s.* carácter o disposición paternal.

fatherly [-lɪ] *a.* paternal. —*adv.* (ant.) paternalmente.

Father's Day, día del Padre.

Father Time, el Tiempo, representado por un anciano con una guadaña.

fathom ['fæðəm] *s.* (mar.) braza. —*v.t.* 1. sondear, sondar. 2. (fig.) penetrar en, comprender; profundizar, desentrañar.

fathomable [-əbəl] *a.* 1. sondeable. 2. (fig.) penetrable, comprensible.

Fathometer [fæðɑmətər, B -'ðɔmɪtə] *s.* (marca registrada) de una sonda de ultra sonidos, sondímetro.

fathomless ['fæðəmləs] *a.* 1. insondable. 2. (fig.) insondable, incomprensible; impenetrable.

fatidic [feɪ'tɪdɪk, fə-] *f* ɹɪʤɪč ʎ [-ɪkəl] *a.* fatídico, profético.

fatigability [ˌfætɪgə'bɪlətɪ] *s.* (med.) fatigabilidad.

fatigable ['fætɪgəbəl] *a.* fatigable.

fatigue [fə'tig] *s.* 1. fatiga. 2. (mec.) fatiga (del metal u otro material). 3. (mil.) faena, fajina; (*pl.*) traje de faena, mono. 4. (fisiol.) fatiga. —*v.t., v.i.* (*pret., p.p.* FATIGUED; *p.pr.* FATIGUING) fatigar(se), cansar(se), agotarse(se).

fatigue clothes, (mil.) traje de faena, mono.

fatigue detail, (mil.) destacamento de fajina.

fatigue duty, (mil.) servicio de fajina.

fatigue resistance, (mec.) resistencia a la fatiga (de metales).

fatiguing [fə'tigɪŋ] *a.* fatigoso, agotador.

Fatimid ['fætəmɪd] ɹɪᵐʇɪə [-ˌmaɪt] *a., s.* (hist.) fatimí, fatimita, dinastía mahometana de la antigüedad.

fatling ['fætlɪŋ] *s.* cebón, animal que se ceba para que rinda más carne.

fatly [-lɪ] *adv.* ricamente, copiosamente; corpulentamente.

fatness [-nəs] *s.* 1. gordura, obesidad. 2. oleosidad, untuosidad. 3. riqueza, fertilidad, abundancia.

Fats [fæts] ɹšʊ ['fætsoʊ] *s.* (despec.) gordo, gordiflón (apodo).

fat-soluble ['fætˌsɑljəbəl, B -'sɔl-] *a.* soluble en grasas.

fatten ['fætən] *v.t.* 1. engordar, cebar. 2. fertilizar, abonar, enriquecer (la tierra). 3. (póquer) añadir fichas a la puesta. —*v.i.* engordar, echar carnes.

fattener [-ər, B -ə] *s.* 1. engordador, cebadero. 2. cebón.

fattening [-ɪŋ] *a.* engordador, cebador. —*s.* ceba, engorde (del ganado).

fattiness ['fætɪnəs] *s.* 1. gordura, obesidad. 2. gordura, grasa, gordo, sebo.

fattish [-ɪʃ] *a.* gordiflón, regordete; algo grasoso.

fatty [-ɪ] *a.* (FATTIER; FATTIEST) 1. grasiento, seboso, grasoso. 2. (quím.) graso. 3. gordinflón, regordete, adiposo. —*s.* gordo, gordito, gordinflón.

fatty acid, (quím.) ácido graso.

fatty degeneration, (med.) degeneración grasosa.

fatty tissue, tejido adiposo.

fatty tumor, (med.) tumor adiposo, lipoma.

fatuitous [fə'tuətəs, B -'tju-] *a.* fatuo, estúpido.

fatuity [-tɪ] *s.* 1. fatuidad, simpleza, estupidez, necedad. 2. (ant.) idiotez, demencia.

fatuous ['fætʃʊəs, B 'fætjʊəs] *a.* fatuo, tonto; necio, presumido; ilusorio, fantasioso.

fatuously [-lɪ] *adv.* fatuamente, neciamente.

fatuousness [-nəs] *s.* fatuidad, tontería, inanidad.

fat-witted ['fæt'wɪtəd] *a.* tonto, estúpido, torpe.

fat wood, madera resinosa.

faubourg [foʊ'bʊr, B 'foʊbʊəg] *s.* (fr.) barrio, suburbio (esp. de una ciudad francesa).

faucal ['fɔkəl] *a.* 1. (anat.) faucal. 2. (fon.) faucal, gutural.

fauces ['fɔˌsiz] *s. pl.* (anat.) fauces.

faucet ['fɔsət] *s.* llave, grifo, espita, canilla.

faugh [fɔ] *interj.* ¡fo! (expresa asco, desprecio o disgusto).

fault [fɔlt] *s.* 1. falta, falla, imperfección, defecto, desperfecto. 2. error, yerro, omisión. 3. culpa, responsabilidad. 4. (geol., min.) falla, paraclasa. 5. (caza) pérdida del rastro o pista→stro perdido. 6. (elec.) fuga, escape (de corriente). 7. (tenis) falta. 8. (ant.) carencia, necesidad. 9. **at f.,** culpable; (caza) que ha perdido el rastro; (fig.) confundido, perplejo; **in f.,** culpable, responsable; **to a f.,** excesivamente, exageradamente; **to find f. with,** desaprobar, censurar, criticar. —*v.i.* 1. hallar defecto en, encontrar defectuoso. 2. culpar. 3. (geol.) producir una falla. —*v.t.* 1. errar, equivocarse, fallar. 2. (geol.) fracturarse, quebrarse (produciendo una falla).

faultfinder ['fɔltˌfaɪndər, B -də] *s.* criticón, reparón, persona que censura o se queja constantemente.

faultfinding [-dɪŋ] *s.* 1. crítica o censura mezquina. 2. criticón, reparón.

faultily ['fɔltəlɪ] *adv.* imperfectamente, defectuosamente, erradamente.

faultiness [-ɪnəs] *s.* defecto, falta, imperfección.

faultless [-ləs] *a.* sin falta, sin defecto, sin tacha, sin falla, perfecto, impecable, acabado.

faultlessly [-lɪ] *adv.* perfectamente, impecablemente, correctamente.

faultlessness [-nəs] *s.* perfección, impecabilidad.

faulty ['fɔltɪ] *a.* 1. imperfecto, defectuoso, inacabado, incompleto, falto. 2. (ant.) culpable, responsable.

faun [fɔn] *s.* (mitol.) fauno.

fauna ['fɔnə] *s.* (*pl.* FAUNAS O FAUNAE [-ˌi]) (zool.) fauna.

faunal ['fɔnəl] *a.* fáunico.

Faunus ['fɔnəs] *s.* (mitol.) Fauno, dios de la naturaleza.

faute de mieux [ˌfoʊt də'mjɜ] (fr.) a falta de otra cosa mejor.

fauteuil [fɔ'tɜɪ, B 'foʊtɜɪ] *s.* (fr.) sillón, poltrona.

fauvism ['foʊˌvɪzəm] *s.* (pint.) fauvismo, escuela pictórica que surgió a principios del siglo.

faux-bourdon ['foʊ'bʊrdən, B -'bʊədən] *s.* (mús.) fabordón.

faux pas ['foʊ'pɑ] (fr.) metida de pata.

faveolate [fə'vɪəˌleɪt] *a.* (bot.) faveolado.

favonian [-'voʊnɪən] *a.* 1. relativo al viento oeste. 2. suave, gentil, propicio.

favor, (G.B.) **favour** ['feɪvər, B -və] *s.* 1. favor, servicio. 2. favor, aprecio, estimación. 3. privilegio, concesión. 4. (*pl.*) favores (de una mjucr). 5. (com., pr. G.B.) atenta, grato escrito, carta. 6. cinta, emblema. 7. (ant.) apariencia, talento. 8. (ant.) ayuda, apoyo. 9. (ant.) permiso, indulgencia. 10. **in f. of,** en favor de, en proyecho de; en respaldo de; (com.) a favor de; **out of f.,** en desgracia, desfavorecido, en desuso; **out of f. with,** no grato a; **to be in f. of,** estar por, ser partidario de, estar a favor de, abogar por; **to be in f. with,** disfrutar del favor de; ser grato a; **to be in someone's f.,** gozar de la buena voluntad de alguien; **to find f. in the eyes of,** gustarle a, ser acogido favorablemente por; **to find f. with,** caer en gracia a, granjearse la buena voluntad de. —*v.t.* 1. favorecer, apoyar. 2. preferir, privilegiar. 3. cuidar. 4. ser favorable a o para. 5. asemejarse a, parecerse a, ej., *f. one's father,* parecerse a su padre. 6. **f. (someone) with,** regalar, donar (a alguien); dotar (a alguien) de (inteligencia, belleza, etc.).

favorable, (G.B.) **favourable** [-vərəbəl] *a.* favorecedor, patrocinador.

favorableness [-nəs] *s.* carácter favorable.

favorably [-blɪ] *adv.* favorablemente.

favored, (G.B.) **favoured** ['feɪvərd, B -vəd] *a.* 1. favorecido, ayudado, preferido. 2. dotado, agraciado. 3. **f. with,** dotado o agraciado de (inteligencia, belleza, etc.).

favorite, (G.B.) **favourite** [-vərət] *a.* favorito, preferido, predilecto. —*s.* favorito, protegido.

favorite son, 1. hijo predilecto, ciudadano distinguido. 2. (pol.) candidato favorito dentro de su partido.

favoritism[-ˌɪzəm] *s.* favoritismo.
favus ['feɪvəs] *s.* (med., vet.) favo.
fawn [fɔn] *s.* 1. (zool.) cervato, corzo o ciervo joven; gamo o gama en su primer año. 2. color de cervato. 3. **in f.,** preñada (cierva). —*v.i.* 1. hacer fiestas (el perro). 2. (con *on* o *upon*) adular servilmente, halagar, lisonjear. 3. parir (la cierva).
fawning ['fɔnɪŋ] *a.* adulón, lisonjero, servil. —*s.* adulación, servilismo.
fawningly [-lɪ] *adv.* lisonjeramente.
fax [fæks] *s.* fax, telefax, telefacsímil. —*v.t.* faxear, mandar por telefacsímil.
fax machine, telereproductor de imágenes.
fay [feɪ] *v.t., v.i.* (*pret., p.p.* FAYED; *p.pr.* FAYING) (const. naval) juntar(se), encajar(se), empalmar(se). —*s.* 1. (ant.) fe. 2. hada, duende, elfo.
fayalite ['feɪəˌlaɪt] *s.* (min.) fayalita.
faze [feɪz] *v.t.* (fam., E.U.) desconcertar, perturbar, molestar, preocupar.
FB *abrev. de* **freight bill,** conocimiento de embarque.
FBI *abrev. de* **Federal Bureau of Investigation,** (E.U.) Departamento Federal de Investigación Criminal, FBI, Brigada de Investigación Criminal.
FCC *abrev. de* **Federal Communications Commission,** (E.U.) Comisión Federal de Comunicaciones.
F.D. *abrev. de* **fire department,** cuerpo de bomberos.
FDA *abrev. de* **Food and Drug Administration,** (E.U.) Dirección de Alimentos y Medicinas.
Fe *símb. de* **ferrum,** hierro (Fe).
fealty ['fiəltɪ] *s.* 1. fidelidad (de un vasallo o terrateniente a su señor feudal). 2. homenaje, lealtad, fidelidad.
fear [fɪr, B fɪə] *s.* 1. miedo, temor. 2. preocupación, ansiedad. 3. peligro. 4. **f. of the Lord,** temor al Señor; **for f. (that),** por miedo de que; **for f. of,** por miedo de, por temor de; **in f. of one's life,** con tremendo temor; **to be in f.,** tener miedo. —*v.t.* temer, tener miedo de, recelar. —*v.i.* tener miedo; **f. for,** temer por; **f. to (do),** tener miedo de (hacer); **never f.!** ¡pierda cuidado! ¡quién dijo miedo!
fearful ['fɪrfəl, B 'fɪəfəl] *a.* 1. miedoso, medroso, temeroso, aprensivo; tímido, timorato. 2. terrible, espantoso, alarmante. 3. (fam.) terrible, tremendo, enorme.
fearfully [-fəlɪ] *adv.* 1. miedosamente, medrosamente, temerosamente. 2. (fam.) terriblemente, tremendamente, sumamente.
fearfulness [-fəlnəs] *s.* 1. aspecto terrible. 2. timidez, pusilanimidad, apocamiento.
fearless ['fɪrləs, B 'fɪəlɪs] *a.* intrépido, impertérrito, valiente, bravo, arrojado, osado.
fearlessly [-lɪ] *adv.* intrépidamente, impertérritamente, valientemente.
fearlessness [-nəs] *s.* intrepidez, valentía, arrojo, osadía.
fearnought, fearnaught ['fɪrˌnɔt, B 'fɪəˌ-] *s.* 1. (tej.) blanquita; abrigo de dicha lana gruesa. 2. (mar.) frisa.
fearsome [-səm] *a.* 1. terrible, temible. 2. tímido, timorato, apocado.
fearsomely [-lɪ] *adv.* 1. terriblemente, temiblemente. 2. tímidamente.
feasance ['fizəns] *s.* (der.) cumplimiento (de una condición, deber, etc.).
feasibility [ˌfizə'bɪlətɪ] *s.* viabilidad, carácter factible.
feasible ['fizəbəl] *a.* 1. factible, hacedero, viable. 2. conveniente, servible. 3. razonable, aceptable, posible.
feasibleness [-nəs] *s.* viabilidad.
feasibly [-blɪ] *adv.* factiblemente.
feast [fist] *s.* 1. banquete, festín. 2. fiesta, festividad (de la Iglesia), ej., *movable f.,* fiesta movible. 3. (fig.) gozo, deleite. —*v.t.* 1. agasajar, banquetear. 2. deleitar, complacer. 3. **f. one's eyes on,** regalarse la vista con. —*v.i.* 1. banquetear, comer opíparamente. 2. gozar, deleitarse.
feaster ['fistər, B -ə] *s.* banqueteador.
feastful [-fəl] *a.* (ant.) festivo, alegre, jubiloso.
feat [fit] *s.* 1. hazaña, proeza. 2. acto (de destreza, magia, etc.).
feather ['fɛðər, B -ə] *s.* 1. pluma (de ave). 2. plumaje. 3. moño o fleco de pelos (en la corva de perros). 4. nube (en piedras preciosas). 5. plumas (de una flecha). 6. condición, estado; humor. 7. (fig.) nimiedad, pequeñez. 8. (med.) nubécula (en el ojo). 9. (mar.) espiga, tope (del palo). 10. (mec.) cuña, llave; pestaña, reborde. 11. (carp.) lengüeta, barbilla. 12. **a f. in one's cap,** (fam.) triunfo, motivo de orgullo; **birds of a f.,** gente de la misma calaña, lobos de la misma camada; **birds of a f. flock together,** Dios los cría y ellos se juntan; **to show the white f.,** volver las espaldas, revelar cobardía. —*v.t.* 1. emplumar. 2. vestir o ataviar con plumas. 3. cubrir o forrar con plumas. 4. machihembrar. 5. alzar y poner horizontal la pala del (remo). 6. dar o proveer de alas; reducir a la finura de una pluma. 7. (aer.) poner en bandera (hélice). 8. (caza) quitarle plumas (a un pájaro) sin matarlo. 9. (impr.) extender la tinta. 10. (avia.) empenar. 11. **f. one's nest,** hacer su agosto, enriquecerse (esp. a expensas de otro). —*v.i.* 1. emplumar. 2. flotar, ondear (como plumas). 3. extenderse o crecer como plumas; ramificarse.
feather bed, lecho de plumas, colchón de plumas, plumón.
featherbed [-ˌbɛd] *v.i.* contratar obreros innecesarios, o retardar un trabajo (por indicación de un sindicato).
featherbedding [-ɪŋ] *s.* imposición (por parte de un sindicato) de trabajadores o trabajos innecesarios.
feather board, tabla o tablero de cantos biselados.
featherbone [-ˌboʊn] *s.* imitación de barbas de ballena (para corsé).
featherbrain [-ˌbreɪn] *s.* cabeza de chorlito, bobo, tonto, imbécil, disparatado.
featherbrained [-ˌbreɪnd] *a.* tonto, bobo, imbécil; frívolo, casquivano.
feathercut [-ˌkʌt] *s.* estilo de corte de cabello en el que los rizos dan la impresión de plumas y rodean la cara formando una especie de halo.
feather duster, plumero (como instrumento de limpieza).
feathered ['fɛðərd, B -əd] *a.* 1. emplumado, cubierto con plumas o alas. 2. (poét.) alado; penígero; veloz, ligero.
featheredge ['fɛðərˌɛdʒ] *s.* 1. filo finísimo (que se rompe o dobla fácilmente). 2. (mec.) canto biselado, bisel.
featheredged [-ˌɛdʒd] *a.* (mec.) biselado.
feather grass, (bot.) espolín.
featherhead ['fɛðərˌhɛd, B əˌ] *s.* imbécil, tonto, bobo.
featherheaded [-əd] *a.* imbécil, tonto, bobo; frívolo, casquivano.
feathering ['fɛðərɪŋ] *s.* 1. plumaje. 2. plumas (de una flecha). 3. (mús.) método especial y delicado de usar el arco del violín. 4. moño o fleco de pelos (en la corva del perro). 5. posición horizontal de las palas del remo.
feathering float, f. paddle, (hidr.) álabe o paleta movible.
feathering propeller, (avia.) hélice empenable; **f. the propeller,** poner la hélice en bandera.
feathering wheel, f. screw, rueda o hélice de aspas movibles.
feather joint, (carp.) junta de lengüeta postiza.
feather key, lengüeta paralela o postiza.
featherless ['fɛðərləs, B -əlɪs] *a.* implume, desplumado.
feather mattress, colchón de plumas.
feather palm, (bot.) palmera de hojas pinadas.
feather star, (zool.) lirio de mar.
featherstitch [-ˌstɪtʃ] *s.* (cost.) punto ruso; punto de espina o de París. —*v.t.* bordar con este punto.
feather-veined [-ˌveɪnd] *a.* (bot.) pinatinervio.
featherweight [-ˌweɪt] *s.* 1. peso muy liviano. 2. (boxeo) peso pluma. —*a.* 1. de poco peso, muy liviano. 2. (boxeo) de peso pluma. 3. (fig.) insignificante (persona o cosa).
featherweight paper, papel pluma, papel ligero o liviano.
feathery ['fɛðərɪ] *a.* 1. plumoso. 2. como plumas; liviano, ligero, leve.
featly ['fitlɪ] *adv.* (ant.) 1. atractivamente, primorosamente. 2. hábilmente, graciosamente. —*a.* gracioso, hábil, diestro.
feature ['fitʃər, B -tʃə] *s.* 1. aspecto, peculiaridad, característica. 2. rasgo, facción; (*pl.*) facciones, fisonomía, rostro. 3. figura, talla (de alguien). 4. película principal (de un programa), largometraje; artículo principal; fotografía, crónica o sección especial (en un periódico, diario o revista). —*v.t.* 1. ofrecer, tener en su programa (una película principal, atracción especial, etc.). 2. caracterizar. 3. representar, mostrar. 4. destacar, hacer resaltar. 5. imaginar, concebir. —*v.i.* destacarse, tener un papel (importante).
featured [-tʃərd, B -tʃəd] *a.* 1. (ú. en palabras compuestas) encarado (bien, mal) de rasgos, de facciones, ej., *ill-f.,* mal encarado, *heavy-f.,* de facciones toscas. 2. principal, prominente (actor, atractivo, etc.), estelar (papel, actuación, etc.); de primera plana (artículo, reportaje, etc. en una revista o periódico). 3. (ant.) formado, moldeado.
feature-length ['fitʃərˌlɛŋθ, -ˌlɛŋkθ, B -tʃəˌ-] *a.* de largo metraje (película); largo (artículo, reportaje, etc.).
featureless [-ləs] *a.* sin rasgos característicos; monótono, tedioso, aburrido.
feaze [fiz, feɪz] *var. de* **faze.**
Feb. *abrev. de* **February,** febrero (feb.).
febricity [fə'brɪsətɪ] *s.* (med.) fiebre, calentura.
febrifugal [fɪ'brɪfjəgəl] *a.* (med.) febrífugo, febricida.
febrifuge ['fɛbrəˌfjudʒ] *s., a.* (med.) febrífugo.
febrile ['fɛbrəl, B 'fibraɪl] *a.* (med.) febril.
February ['fɛbrʊˌɛrɪ, 'fɛbjʊ-, B 'fɛbrʊərɪ] *s.* febrero.
fecal ['fikəl] *a.* fecal, relativo a los excrementos.
feces ['fisiz] *s. pl.* heces, excrementos, materia fecal.
feckless ['fɛkləs] *a.* 1. ineficaz, incompetente, incapaz. 2. fútil, inútil. 3. indiferente, indolente; irresponsable.
fecklessly [-lɪ] *adv.* 1. ineficazmente, incompetentemente. 2. inútilmente, sin efecto. 3. indiferentemente, indolentemente; con irresponsabilidad.
fecklessness [-nəs] *s.* 1. ineficacia, incompetencia, incapacidad. 2. futilidad, inutilidad. 3. indiferencia, indolencia; irresponsabilidad.
feculence ['fɛkjələns] *s.* 1. condición feculenta; fetidez. 2. suciedad, inmundicia; heces.
feculent [-lənt] *a.* feculento; fétido, inmundo; fecal.

fecund ['fikənd, 'fɛk-] *a.* fecundo.

fecundate ['fikən,deɪt, 'fɛk-] *v.t.* 1. fecundar, fecundizar, fertilizar. 2. (biol.) fecundar.

fecundation [,fikən'deɪʃən, ,fɛk-] *s.* (biol.) fecundación.

fecundity [fɪ'kʌndətɪ] *s.* fecundidad, fertilidad, productividad.

fed[fɛd] *pret. y p.p. de* **feed.**

fed, Fed [fɛd] *s.* (jer., E.U.) oficial o agente federal.

Fed, *abrev. de* (E.U.) **Federal Reserve Board,** Junta de Gobernadores de la Reserva Federal.

fedayeen [fɛ'dɑjin] *s.* (árabe) guerrillero palestino.

federacy ['fɛdərəsɪ] *s.* (ant.) federación, confederación, alianza.

federal ['fɛdərəl] *a.* 1. federal, federativo. 2. **F.,** (E.U., hist.) federalista (durante la guerra civil). 3. (E.U.) relativo al gobierno o a las instituciones del país. 4. (E.U.) partidario del sistema federal. —*s.* 1. **F.,** (E.U., hist.) federalista (durante la guerra civil). 2. (E.U.) agente u oficial federal.

Federal Bureau of Investigation, (E.U.) Negociado *or* Departamento Federal de Investigaciones, Brigada de Investigación Criminal.

Federal Communications Commission, (E.U.) Comisión Federal de Comunicaciones.

Federal Distric, distrito federal (D. F.).

federalism ['fɛdərə,lɪzəm] *s.* (pol.) federalismo.

federalist [-ləst] *s.* 1. (pol.) federalista. 2. (E.U., hist.) federalista (partidario de una unión federal entre las ex-colonias).

federalist, federalistic [fɛdərə'lɪstɪk] *a.* (pol.) federalista.

federalization [-lə'zeɪʃən, B -laɪ-] *s.* federalización.

federalize ['fɛdərə,laɪz] *v.t.* 1. confederar, federar, federalizar. 2. poner bajo la autoridad de un gobierno central.

federally [-rəlɪ] *adv.* federalmente.

Federal Republic of Germany, República Federal de Alemania.

Federal Reserve Board, (E.U.) Junta de Gobernadores de la Reserva Federal.

Federal Reserve note, (E.U.) papel moneda, dólar.

Federal Reserve System, (E.U.) sistema (bancario) de la reserva federal.

Federal Trade Commission, (E.U.) agencia gubernamental que regula y supervisa métodos y prácticas comerciales.

federate ['fɛdərət] *a.* confederado, federado, aliado. — [-,reɪt] *v.t., v.i.* federar(se), confederar(se).

federation [,fɛdə'reɪʃən] *s.* federación, confederacion.

federative ['fɛdə,reɪtɪv, -ərətɪv] *a.* federativo.

fedora [fɪ'dɔrə] *s.* (E.U.) sombrero de fieltro de ala ancha y copa hundida a capricho.

fed up ['fɛd'ʌp] *a.* 1. harto, hastiado. 2. disgustado, aburrido. 3. **to be f. up,** estar hasta la coronilla, estar hasta los pelos; **to be f. up with,** estar harto de; estar disgustado con.

fee [fi] *s.* 1. honorarios; estipendio, remuneración, gratificación; derechos. 2. cuota de ingreso (en museos, clubes, etc.). 3. (hist.) feudo. 4. (der.) bienes, herencia, patrimonio. 5. **in f.,** en propiedad. —*v.t.* 1. recompensar, gratificar. 2. (esco.) emplear, contratar.

feeble ['fibəl] *a.* 1. débil, enfermizo, endeble. 2. débil, ineficaz, inadecuado. 3. débil, tenue.

feebleminded ['fibəl'maɪndəd] *a.* 1. imbécil, mentecato; ido. 2. (ant.) irresoluto, vacilante.

feeblemindedly [-lɪ] *adv.* imbécilmente.

feeblemindedness [-nəs] *s.* 1. imbecilidad, debilidad mental. 2. (ant.) irresolución.

feebleness [-nəs] *s.* debilidad.

feebly [-blɪ] *adv.* débilmente.

feed [fid] *v.t.* (*pret., p.p.* FED [fɛd]; *p.pr.* FEEDING) 1. alimentar, nutrir, dar de comer a. 2. (fig.) alimentar, dar pábulo a (deseo, esperanza, sentido de humor, etc.); fomentar (egotismo, vanidad, rumores, etc.). 3. pastar (ganado). 4. (mec.) alimentar, avanzar. 5. (elec., rad.) alimentar. 6. (teat.) apuntar (palabras a un actor). 7. (fútbol) dar pases a (jugador). 8. **f. a cold,** comer bien para curarse de un resfrío; **to be fed up with,** estar hastiado o harto de; **f. up,** engordar; saciar, hartar. —*v.i.* alimentarse, comer; pacer, pastar (ganado); **f. on, upon** u **off,** alimentarse de; (fig.) derivar satisfacción de (alabanzas, lisonjas, dolor ajeno, etc.). —*s.* 1. forraje, pienso. 2. alimentación, comida (esp. de animales). 3. (fam.) comilona. 4. (mec.) avance (mecanismo); alimentación (proceso); alimento (materia). 5. (elec., rad.) alimentación. 6. **out at f.,** pastando.

feedback ['fid,bæk] *s.* 1. (elec.) realimentación, regeneración, retroacción. 2. información acerca del resultado de un proceso; reacción, contrarreacción.

feedback amplifier, (elec., rad.) amplificador de reacción positiva o de retroacción.

feedback coil, (elec., rad.) amplificador realimentado, bobina de regeneración, de realimentación o de retroacción.

feed bag, cebadera, morral (del caballo).

feedboard [-,bɔrd, B -,bɔd] *s.* 1. (impr.) tablero de alimentación, metedor, marcador. 2. (elec.) tablero de contactos o de distribución.

feedbox [-,bɑks, B -,bɔks] *s.* (mec.) caja de avance.

feed cock, f. tap, grifo de alimentación, llave de llenar.

feeder ['fidər, B -ə] *s.* 1. alimentador (de ganado, etc.). 2. (mec.) alimentador, avanzador, dispositivo de avance. 3. corriente tributaria, afluente (de un río). 4. cebón, animal alimentado para la matanza. 5. (elec.) conductor de alimentación, alimentador. 6. (min.) filón ramal. 7. (teat.) actor o papel que sirve de pie a otro. 8. (f.c.) ramal tributario. 9. (impr.) alimentador, marcador (persona).

feeder road, camino secundario.

feeding [-ɪŋ] *s.* forraje, pasto, alimento. —*a.* de alimentación, alimenticio.

feeding bottle, biberón, botella para alimentar a los bebés.

feeding device, (maq.) aparato de alimentacion.

feeding dish, f. trough, comedero (de animales).

feed motor, motor de sobrecarga; (elec.) motor de avance.

feed pipe, tubo alimentador, caño de alimentación, tubo abastecedor.

feed pump, bomba de alimentación.

feed rack, 1. pesebre, comedero. 2. (elec.) estante de contactos.

feed roll, (maq.) rodillo de alimentación.

feedstuff ['fid,stʌf] *s.* forraje, alimentos para ganado.

feed valve, válvula de alimentación.

feed wire, (elec.) alambre alimentador, conductor de alimentación.

feel [fil] *v.t.* (*pret., p.p.* FELT [fɛlt]; *p.pr.* FEELING) 1. sentir, percibir, experimentar. 2. tocar, palpar; manosear. 3. quedar afectado o conmovido por, ej., *I felt his death deeply,* quedé profundamente afectado o conmovido por su muerte. 4. **f. it in one's bones (that),** tener la corazonada (de que); **f. one's legs** (o **feet**), encontrar suelo firme; **f. one's oats,** estar lleno de vigor, estar muy vivaracho; **f. one's way,** palpar, andar a tientas; (fig.) actuar con cautela; **f. out,** sondear, sondar, averiguar; **f. (quite) oneself,** sentirse bien, estar en plena posesión de sus facultades; **f. the need of,** sentir la necesidad de; **f. the pulse of,** tomar el pulso a; (fig.) tomar el pulso a una situación. —*v.i.* 1. tener el sentido del tacto. 2. sentirse, encontrarse, hallarse (bien, mal, etc.). 3. (con *about, around*) tentar, ir palpando. 4. tener (frío, sed, hambre, etc.). 5. estar (enfadado, disgustado, contento, etc.). 6. **f. bad,** sentirse mal; estar triste o incómodo; **f. bad about,** lamentar, sentir; **f. cheap,** sentirse mezquino; **f. for,** buscar tentando; condolerse de; compadecerse de; **f. like,** parecer al tacto, ej., *it feels like wood,* parece madera (al tacto); **f. like (doing),** tener ganas de (hacer); **f. like (something),** apetecer, tener ganas de (algo); **f. sorry,** arrepentirse, sentirlo; **f. sorry for,** compadecer a; **f. up to,** sentirse con ánimo para; estar como para; **f. with,** compadecerse de; **how do you f. about this?** ¿qué tal le parece eso? ¿qué opina Ud. de eso? —*s.* 1. tacto. 2. sensación. 3. pálpito, intuición. 4. **to get the f. of,** coger el tino de, coger el truco de.

feeler ['filər, B -ə] *s.* 1. tentáculo; palpo (de animales), antena (de insectos). 2. sondeo, tentativa. 3. **to put out** (o **send out) a f.,** soltar una especie, hacer una prueba (para enterarse de algo); **to put out feelers,** (fig.) hacer sondeos o investigaciones.

feeler gauge, galga; (aut.) indicador de holgura; (mec.) calibrador de hojillas; sonda.

feeler rod, (aut.) varilla de comprobación, sonda.

feeling [-ɪŋ] *s.* 1. tacto, sentido del tacto. 2. sensación, sensibilidad. 3. sentimiento, emoción. 4. (*pl.*) sentimientos, susceptibilidad. 5. simpatía, conmiseración; ternura. 6. sensación (de seguridad, peligro, etc.). 7. presentimiento, corazonada. 8. parecer, opinión. 9. efecto emocional (producido por una obra de arte). 10. **hard feelings,** resentimiento; **to hurt someone's feelings,** herir los sentimientos o la susceptibilidad de alguien. —*a.* 1. sensible, tierno. 2. lleno de sentimiento, conmovedor.

feelingly [-lɪ] *adv.* con mucha emoción, con sentimiento.

feertype ['fɪr,taɪp, B 'fɪə,-] *s.* (foto.) ferrotipia.

fee simple, (der.) pleno dominio, dominio absoluto (de una herencia o patrimonio).

fee splitting, pago de comisión por un especialista al médico general que le ha enviado el paciente.

feet [fit] *pl. de* **foot.**

fee tail, (der.) dominio limitado a herederos directos.

feeze [fiz, feɪz, B fiz] *s.* (dial.) alarma, alboroto.

Fehling solution ['feɪlɪŋ-] (quím.) licor de Fehling.

feign [feɪn] *v.t.* 1. aparentar, simular, disimular, fingir. 2. (ant.) idear, imaginar, inventar. —*v.i.* fingir.

feigned [feɪnd] *a.* fingido, ficticio; falso, irreal.

feigner ['feɪnər, B -ə] *s.* fingidor.

feint [feɪnt] *s.* 1. finta, amago. 2. (mil.) maniobra fingida. 3. **to make a f. of (doing),** fingir (hacer). —*v.i.* hacer una finta. —*v.t.* amagar (un golpe, ataque, etc.).

feints, *var. de* **faints.**

feldspar ['fɛld,spɑr, 'fɛl,spɑr, B -,spɑ] *s.* (min.) feldespato.

feldspathic [fɛld'spæθɪk] **feldspathose** [-'spæθ,oʊs, B 'fɛld,spæθoʊs] *a.* (min.) feldespático.

felicific [,filə'sɪfɪk] *a.* regocijante, alegrante.

felicitate [fɪ'lɪsəˌteɪt] *a.* (ant.) regocijado, feliz, dichoso. —*v.t.* 1. felicitar, cumplimentar, dar el parabién o la enhorabuena. 2. (ant.) alegrar, regocijar.

felicitation [-ˌlɪsə'teɪʃən] *s.* felicitación, enhorabuena, parabién.

felicitous [-'lɪsətəs] *a.* 1. feliz, oportuno, apto (observación, idea, etc.). 2. elocuente, persuasivo (orador).

felicitously [-lɪ] *adv.* aptamente, certeramente, con buenos resultados.

felicity [fɪ'lɪsətɪ] *s.* 1. felicidad, dicha, bienaventuranza. 2. aptitud, gracia (de expresión). 3. dicho feliz, ocurrencia.

felid ['filəd] *s.* (zool.) félido.

feline ['fiˌlaɪn] *a.* 1. (zool.) felino. 2. felino, gatuno, gatesco (movimiento, aspecto, etc.). 3. (fig.) felino, ágil; astuto; grácil. —*s.* felino.

feline enteritis, (vet.) enteritis o tifoidea felina.

felinely [-lɪ] *adv.* (fig.) felinamente, furtivamente.

fell [fɛl] *v.t.* 1. talar, cortar. 2. derribar, tumbar. 3. (cost.) sobrecargar, sobrecoser. —*s.* 1. tala, corte de monte; madera cortada en una estación. 2. costura sobrecargada, costura sobrecosida. 3. cuero, piel, pellejo. 4. (G.B.) colina; páramo; duna.

fell [fɛl] *pret. de* **fall.**

fell, *a.* 1. cruel, fiero, feroz. 2. maligno, siniestro.

fellah ['fɛlə] *s.* (*pl.* FELLAHIN, FELAHEEN [ˌfɛlə'-hin] fellahs) felá, labrador egipcio, campesino árabe.

fellatio [fə'leɪʃɪˌoʊ, -'lɑtɪoʊ] **fellation** [-'leɪʃən] *s.* felatorismo, irrumación, estimulación oral del pene.

feller ['fɛlər, B -ə] *s.* 1. talador, leñador. 2. máquina taladora. 3. (cost.) accesorio para hacer sobrecosturas. 4. (fam., pr. G.B.) tipo, tío, sujeto; muchacho.

fellmonger ['fɛlˌmʌŋgər, B -gə] *s.* 1. (G.B., curtiduría) depilador. 2. mercader de pieles.

fellmongering [-gərɪŋ] ƒəλλmση‿əry [-gərɪ] *s.* (G.B., curtiduría) depilación.

fellness ['fɛlnəs] *s.* 1. crueldad, ferocidad. 2. malignidad.

felloe ['fɛloʊ] *var. de* **felly,** pina camón (de una rueda).

fellow ['fɛloʊ, -ə] *s.* 1. compañero, camarada. 2. socio, asociado. 3. pareja, par. 4. igual (en poder, rango, carácter), congénere. 5. (fam.) tipo, tío, sujeto; mozo, muchacho. 6. miembro (de una sociedad científica o literaria); miembro del consejo de gobierno (de algunas universidades). 7. graduado o catedrático becado (para realizar investigación). 8. (ant.) patán, rústico; payo, siervo. 9. **a good f.,** (fam.) un buen chico, una buena persona; **old f.,** viejo; **poor f.,** pobre; **the f.,** (despec.) ese tipo. —*v.t.* (ant.) aparear, emparejar. —*a.* asociado; igual, parecido, correspondiente.

fellow being, prójimo, semejante.

fellow boarder, comensal, compañero de pupilaje.

fellow citizen, conciudadano.

fellow commoner, 1. (G.B.) estudiante que recibe el privilegio de comer en la mesa de los miembros de la facultad. 2. el que tiene los mismos derechos que otro.

fellow countryman, compatriota, paisano.

fellow creature, criatura del Señor (persona o animal); hijo de Dios (persona); prójimo, semejante.

fellow feeling, sentimiento de afinidad, compañerismo.

fellow heir, coheredero.

fellow laborer, colaborador, trabajador asociado.

fellowman ['fɛloʊ'mæn] *s.* prójimo, semejante.

fellow member, consocio (en un club), compañero.

fellow partner, colega, asociado.

fellow passenger, compañero de viaje.

fellowship ['fɛloʊˌʃɪp] *s.* 1. camaradería, compañerismo. 2. comunidad (de intereses, etc.). 3. compañía, confraternidad, grupo. 4. (relig.) comunión, hermandad (entre los miembros de la Iglesia). 5. (educ.) beca, pensión (concedida a graduados o catedráticos para realizar investigaciones); fundación (universitaria) de becas. 6. concejo directivo, concejo de gobierno (de algunas universidades). 7. **good f.,** espíritu de paz y confraternidad.

fellowship holder, becado, becario.

fellow student, condiscípulo.

fellow traveler, (fig.) compañero de viaje; (pol.) simpatizante (esp. de los comunistas); correligionario.

felly ['fɛlɪ] *adv.* cruelmente, ferozmente, fieramente. —*s.* (mec.) pina, camón (de una rueda).

felo-de-se [ˌfɛloʊdə'seɪ, B 'filoʊdi'si] *s.* (der.) 1. suicida. 2. suicidio.

felon ['fɛlən] *a.* felón, criminal, traidor; malvado. —*s.* 1. (der.) criminal, felón. 2. (med.) panadizo, uñero.

felonious [fə'loʊnɪəs] *a.* 1. (der.) criminal, culpable, culposo. 2. felón, traicionero, malvado, perverso.

felonious assault, (der.) asalto con propósito criminal.

felonious intent, (der.) propósito criminal.

feloniously [-lɪ] *adv.* 1. criminalmente, culpablemente. 2. (ant.) malvadamente, traicioneramente, perversamente.

felonry ['fɛlənrɪ] *s.* picaresca; pillería, conjunto de pillos; presidiarios (en conjunto).

felony ['fɛlənɪ] *s.* (der.) felonía, delito mayor, crimen.

felsite ['fɛlˌsaɪt] *s.* (min.) petrosílice, felsita.

felspar [-ˌspɑr, B -ˌspɑ] *var. de* **feldspar.**

felt [fɛlt] *pret., p.p. de* **feel.** —*s.* (tej.) fieltro. —*v.t.* 1. fieltrar, verter en fieltro. 2. cubrir con fieltro. 3. espesar, trabar. —*a.* de fieltro.

felt hat, sombrero de fieltro.

felt tip pen, rotulador, marcador.

felting ['fɛltɪŋ] *s.* 1. (tej.) fieltrado. 2. (material de) fieltro.

felucca [fə'lukə, B -'lʌkə] *s.* (mar.) faluche, haloque, falúa.

fem. *abrev. de* **feminine,** femenino (f.).

female ['fiˌmeɪl] *s.* 1. hembra (persona o animal del sexo femenino). 2. mujer. 3. (bot.) (planta) hembra, planta pistilada. 4. (mec.) hembra, hembrilla. —*a.* 1. hembra, ej., *a f. giraffe,* una girafa hembra. 2. femenino, mujeril. 3. (bot.) gineceo, pistilado (díc. de las plantas). 4. (mec.) hembra, matriz.

female screw, tuerca, hembra de tornillo.

female sex, sexo femenino.

feme [fɛm, B fim] *s.* 1. (her.) figura femenina. 2. (der.) mujer.

feme covert, (der.) mujer casada.

feme sole, (der.) mujer soltera; viuda; mujer casada completamente independizada de su marido en materia de bienes.

feminacy ['fɛmənəsɪ] *s.* (raro) femineidad.

femineity [ˌfɛmə'niətɪ] *s.* femineidad.

feminine ['fɛmənən] *a.* 1. femenino, femenil, femíneo. 2. afeminado, femenil, mujeril. 3. (gram.) femenino. —*s.* (gram.) (género) femenino.

femininely [-lɪ] *adv.* femenilmente.

femininity [ˌfɛmə'nɪnətɪ] *s.* 1. femineidad. 2. sexo femenino, las mujeres.

feminism ['fɛməˌnɪzəm] *s.* 1. (pol.) feminismo, movimiento a favor de los derechos de la mujer. 2. características femeninas.

feminist [-nəst] *s., a.* (pol.) feminista.

feminity [fɛ'mɪnətɪ] *var. de* **femininity.**

feminization [ˌfɛmənə'zeɪʃən, B -naɪ-] *s.* afeminacón; proceso de afeminarse.

feminize ['fɛməˌnaɪz] *v.t., v.i.* afeminar(se).

femme [fɛm, B fæm] *s.* (fr.) esposa; mujer.

femme fatale [ˌfɛmfə'tæl, -'tɑl, B ˌfæm-] (fr.) vampiresa.

femoral ['fɛmərəl] *a.* (anat.) femoral.

femur ['fimər, B -mə] *s.* (*pl.* FEMURS O FEMORA ['fɛmərə]) (anat.) fémur.

fen [fɛn] *s.* marjal, ciénaga, pantano; **the Fens,** los marjales, distritos bajos y pantanosos en algunos condados ingleses.

fence [fɛns] *s.* 1. cerca, cercado, valla, vallado, seto. 2. (jer.) perista, reducidor (Amer.). 3. (dep.) esgrima. 4. (mec.) guarda, guía. guia. 5. **on the f.,** (fig.) entre dos aguas, neutral, sin tomar partido (en una disputa, política, etc.). —*v.t.* 1. cercar, vallar. 2. (con *from* o *against*) defender, proteger, guardar (de). 3. **f. in,** encerrar con cerca; **f. off,** separar con cerca, levantar cerca alrededor de; **f. out,** excluir con cerca. —*v.i.* 1. esgrimir. 2. evadir la respuesta directa, usar tácticas evasivas. 3. traficar con artículos robados. 4. saltar la valla (caballo). 5. **f. with,** dar respuestas evasivas a.

fenceless ['fɛnsləs] *a.* sin cercar, indefenso.

fencer ['fɛnsər, B -ə] *s.* 1. esgrimidor, esgrimista. 2. cercador. 3. caballo ágil que salta bien las cercas.

fence season, tiempo de veda.

fence stake, f. rail, várgano.

fencible [-səbəl] *a.* (esco.) defendible. —*s.* (ant., mil.) (*gen. pl.*) soldado que presta servicios sólo dentro del territorio nacional.

fencing [-sɪŋ] *s.* 1. (dep.) esgrima; técnica de esgrimir. 2. materiales para cercas; cercado, vallado, valladar. 3. (jer.) tráfico con mercancías robadas.

fencing bout, encuentro de esgrima.

fencing foil, florete.

fencing master, maestro de esgrima.

fencing school, escuela de esgrima.

fen cress, (bot.) berro de pantanos.

fend [fɛnd] *v.t.* 1. (gen. con *off*) parar, detener (golpe, etc.); tener a raya; repeler. 2. (ant.) defender. —*v.i.* 1. ingeniarse. 2. (dial., G.B.) esforzarse, luchar. 3. **f. for,** mantener, sustentar; **f. for oneself,** valerse, mirar por sí; sustentarse, ganarse la vida. —*s.* (esco., dial.) esfuerzo (en el interés propio); recurso, expediente.

fender ['fɛndər, B -də] *s.* 1. defensa, dispositivo de protección. 2. guardafuego (de la chimenea). 3. (aut.) guardabarro, guardalodo, guardafango. 4. (f.c.) trompa, quitapiedras. 5. (mar.) defensas, andullo, pallete.

fender bar, f. rail, batayola.

fender beam, espolón.

fender bender, (jer., hum.) topetón, topetazo.

fender pile, pilote de protección.

fender stone, marmolillo.

fen duck, ánade silvestre.

fenestella [ˌfɛnə'stɛlə] *s.* 1. (arq.) ventanilla. 2. sepulcro (en un altar).

fenestra [fɪ'nɛstrə] *s.* (*pl.* FENESTRAE [-tri, -ˌtraɪ]) 1. (anat.) ventana, esp. ventana oval (del oído). 2. (ento.) mancha transparente (en el ala de ciertas mariposas). 3. orificio a modo de ventana.

fenestra ovalis [-oʊ'vælɪs, B -'veɪ-] (anat.) ventana oval.

fenestra rotunda [-roʊ'tʌndə] (anat.) ventana redonda.
fenestrate [fɪ'nɛsˌtreɪt, 'fɛnəˌstreɪt, B fɪ'nɛsˌtreɪt] **fenestrated** [-əd] *a.* (bot., zool.) fenestrado.
fenestration [ˌfɛnə'streɪʃən] *s.* 1. (med.) fenestración. 2. (arq.) ventanaje.
fen fire, fuego fatuo.
Fenian ['finɪən] *s.* (pol., hist.) feniano, miembro de una sociedad revolucionaria irlandesa fundada en Nueva York a mediados del siglo XIX.
fenianism [-ˌɪzəm] *s.* (pol., hist.) fenianismo.
fennec ['fɛnɪk] *s.* (zool.) feneco, zorro africano.
fennel ['fɛnəl] *s.* 1. (bot.) hinojo. 2. (bot.) cáñamo de la India.
fennelflower [-ˌflaʊər, B -ə] *s.* (bot.) neguilla, neguillón, candileja.
fennel giant, (bot.) cañaheja.
fenny ['fɛnɪ] *a.* pantanoso, palustre, cenagoso.
fenugreek ['fɛnjəˌgrik] *s.* (bot.) alholva, fenegreco.
feod [fjud] *s.* (ant.) estado feudal; beneficio feudal.
feodal ['fjudəl] *a.* feudal.
feoff [fɛf, fif] *v.t.* (der., ant.) enfeudar.
feoffee [fɛ'fi, fi'fi] *s.* (hist., der.) feudatario.
feoffer ['fɛfər, 'fif-, B -ə] *var. de* **feoffor.**
feoffment [-mənt] *s.* (hist., der.) enfeudación, feudo.
feoffor [-ər, B fɛ'fɔ] *s.* (hist.) persona que enfeuda.
feracious [fə'reɪʃəs] *a.* (raro) feraz, fértil.
feracity [-'ræsətɪ] *s.* (raro.) feracidad, fecundidad, fertilidad.
feral ['fɪrəl, B 'fɪər-] *a.* feral, salvaje, cruel; (poét.) fúnebre.
ferbam ['fɜrˌbæm, B 'fɜˌbæm] *s.* (quím.) fungicida, usado esp. para árboles frutales.
fer-de-lance [ˌfɛrdə'læns, B ˌfɛədə'lɑns] *s.* (zool.) mapanare.
feria ['fɪrɪə, 'fɛr-, B 'fɪər-] *s.* (*pl.* FERIAE [-ɪˌi]) (relig.) feria (cualquier día de la semana menos los de fiesta o ayuno).
ferine ['fɪrˌaɪn, B 'fɪər-] *a.* ferino, salvaje, sin domesticar.
ferity ['fɛrətɪ] *s.* calidad de lo fiero, salvaje o indomable.
fermata [fɛr'mɑtə, B fɛə'-] *s.* (mús.) fermata, calderón.
ferment ['fɜrˌmɛnt, B 'fɜˌ-] *s.* 1. fermento. 2. fermentación. 3. (fig.) fermentación, agitación, tumulto. —*v.i.* 1. fermentar. 2. (fig.) fermentar, agitarse. [fər'mɛnt, B fə'-] *v.t.* 1. fermentar. 2. (fig.) fermentar, agitar, fomentar.
fermentable [fər'mɛntəbəl, B fə'-] *a.* fermentable.
fermentation [ˌfɜrmən'teɪʃən, -ˌmɛn-, B ˌfɜˌmɛn-] *s.* fermentación; (fig.) fermentación, agitación.
fermentative [fər'mɛntətɪv, B fə'-] *a.* fermentativo, fermentante.
fermium ['fɛrmɪəm, B 'fɜmɪ-] *s.* (quím.) fermio (elemento).
fern [fɜrn, B fɜn] *s.* (bot.) helecho, polipodio.
fernery ['fɜrnərɪ, B 'fɜn-] *s.* 1. florero para guardar helechos. 2. colección de helechos. 3. helechal.
fernlike [-ˌlaɪk] *a.* parecido al helecho.
fern seed, espora de helecho.
ferny [-ɪ] *a.* cubierto de helechos.
ferocious [fə'roʊʃəs] *a.* feroz, fiero, enfurecido, brutal.
ferociously [-lɪ] *adv.* ferozmente, fieramente, brutalmente.
ferociousness [-nəs] *s.* ferocidad, ensañamiento.
ferocity [fə'rɑsətɪ, B -'rɔs-] *s.* ferocidad, fiereza, crueldad.
ferrate ['fɛrˌeɪt] *s.* (quím.) ferrato.
ferreous ['fɛrɪəs] *a.* (quím.) ferroso, férreo.
ferret ['fɛrət] *s.* (cost.) listón, bocadillo, hiladillo, dobladillo, ribete.
ferret, *s.* (zool.) hurón. —*v.t., v.i.* 1. huronear, cazar con hurones. 2. (fig.) huronear. 3. **f. out,** indagar, averiguar, descubrir (secretos criminales, etc.).
ferreter [-ər, B -ə] *s.* 1. huronero, el que caza con hurón. 2. (fam.) que gusta de divulgar secretos ajenos.
ferriage ['fɛrɪɪdʒ] *s.* barcaje (que se paga por pasar de una orilla a otra en una barca o lanchón).
ferric ['fɛrɪk] *a.* 1. (quím.) férrico; **f. oxide,** óxido férrico. 2. (min.) hematita.
ferricyanic [ˌfɛraɪˌsaɪ'ænɪk, B ˌfɛrɪ-] *a.* (quím.) ferricianhídrico.
ferricyanide [-'saɪəˌnaɪd] *s.* (quím.) ferricianuro.
ferriferous [fə'rɪfərəs] *a.* ferrífero, que contiene hierro.
Ferris Wheel ['fɛrəs-] noria, vuelta al mundo, rueda gigante o giratoria, rueda de Chicago (Amer.).
ferrite ['fɛrˌaɪt] *s.* 1. (petrografía, min.) ferrita. 2. (quím.) ferrito.
ferroalloy [ˌfɛroʊ'ælˌɔɪ] *s.* (metal.) ferroaleación.
ferrocalcite [-'kælˌsaɪt] *s.* (min.) ferrocalcita.
ferrocerium [-'sɪrɪəm, B -'sɪər-] *s.* (metal.) ferrocerio.
ferroconcrete [-'kɑnˌkrit, -kɑn'krit, B -'kɔŋkrit] *s.* hormigón armado.
ferrocyanic [-ˌsaɪ'ænɪk] *a.* (quím.) ferrociánico.
ferrocyanide [-'saɪəˌnaɪd] *s.* (quím.) ferrocianuro.
ferromagnesian [-ˌmæg'niʃən, -ʒən, B -'nizjən] *a.* (min.) ferromagnesiano.
ferromagnetic [-ˌmæg'nɛtɪk] *a.* (fís.) ferromagnético.
ferromagnetism [-'mægnəˌtɪzəm] *s.* (fís.) ferromagnetismo.
ferromanganese [-'mæŋgəˌnis, B -ˌniz] *s.* ferromanganeso.
ferrosilicon [-'sɪlɪkən] *s.* ferrosilicio.
ferrotype ['fɛrəˌtaɪp] *s.* ferrotipia. —*v.t.* (foto.) satinar o pulir (una fotografía mientras está aún mojada, restregándola contra una placa de hierro esmaltado).
ferrous ['fɛrəs] *a.* de hierro; (quím.) ferroso.
ferrous oxide, (quím.) protóxido de hierro.
ferrous sulfate, (quím.) sulfato ferroso, caparrosa.
ferruginous [fə'rudʒənəs] *a.* 1. ferruginoso, ferrugíneo. 2. de color de la herrumbre; mohoso, aherrumbrado.
ferrule ['fɛrəl, B 'fɛrul] *s.* 1. regatón, casquillo (de bastón). 2. (mec.) virola, dedal, contera; férula, casquillo (de caldera). 3. (elec.) tapa de contacto. —*v.t.* encasquillar.
ferry ['fɛrɪ] *v.t.* (*pret., p.p.* FERRIED; *p.pr.* FERRYING) 1. barquear, balsear (un río, etc.). 2. transportar (de una a otra orilla) en barco. 3. conducir (un avión) desde la fábrica hasta su punto de entrega. 4. transportar (tropas, municiones, etc.) por avión. —*s.* 1. transbordador, barco de transbordo, barco de paso, barco de pasaje, pontón de transbordo (para cruzar un río, una bahía, etc.). 2. embarcadero, balsadero. 3. servicio de pilotaje (para llevar aviones desde la fábrica hasta el punto de entrega.).
ferryboat [-ˌboʊt] *s.* transbordador, barco de transbordo, barca de pasaje, pontón de transbordo (para pasajeros, vehículos y mercancías a través de un río, lago, bahía o brazo de mar).
ferry bridge, puente transbordador, puente corredizo.
ferrying [-ɪŋ] *s.* transporte por barco o lancha; transbordo.
ferryman [-mən] *s.* balsero, barquero; dueño de un barco de transbordo.
fertile ['fɜrtəl, B 'fɜtaɪl] *a.* 1. fértil, feraz, fecundo; productivo. 2. (fig.) fértil (imaginación, etc.). 3. (bot., biol.) fecundo.
fertilely [-ɪ] *adv.* fértilmente.
fertileness [-nəs] *s.* fertilidad; fecundidad.
fertility [ˌfɜr'tɪlətɪ, B fɜ'-] *s.* fertilidad; fecundidad.
fertilization [ˌfɜrtələ'zeɪʃən, B ˌfɜtɪlaɪ-] *s.* fertilización; (bot., biol.) fecundación.
fertilize ['fɜrtəˌlaɪz, B 'fɜt-] *v.t.* fertilizar, embonar (Am.); fecundar.
fertilizer [-ˌlaɪzər, B -zə] *s.* fertilizante, abono.
ferula ['fɛrələ] *s.* (*pl.* FERULAE [-ˌli]) 1. (bot.) férula, cañaheja. 2. férula, palmeta; cetro.
ferulaceous [ˌfɛrʊ'leɪʃəs] *a.* feruláceo.
ferule ['fɛrəl, B 'fɛrul] *s.* 1. férula, palmeta. 2. (fig.) disciplina escolar. —*v.t.* castigar con la férula.
fervency ['fɜrvənsɪ, B 'fɜvən-] *s.* fervor, ardor, calor; celo, devoción.
fervent [-vənt] *a.* ferviente, fervoroso, ardiente.
fervently [-lɪ] *adv.* fervientemente, fervorosamente.
fervid ['fɜrvəd, B 'fɜvɪd] *a.* férvido, fervoroso, ardiente, celoso.
fervidly [-lɪ] *adv.* férvidamente, fervorosamente, ardientemente.
fervidness [-nəs] *s.* fervor, devoción, ardor, calor, celo.
fervor (G.B.) **fervour** ['fɜrvər, B 'fɜvə] *s.* 1. fervor, calor. 2. (fig.) fervor, celo ardiente, vehemencia, devoción.
Fescennine ['fɜsəˌnaɪn] *a.* indecente, procaz, obsceno.
fescue ['fɛskju] *s.* 1. puntero, varita (que usan los maestros o profesores como indicador). 2. (t. **fescue grass**) (bot.) cañuela; lastón (planta gramínea).
fess, fesse [fɛs] *s.* (her.) faja.
festal ['fɛstəl] *a.* festivo, de fiesta.
fester ['fɛstər, B -tə] *v.i.* supurar, ulcerarse, enconarse; pudrirse. —*v.t.* enconar, emponzoñar. —*s.* llaga, úlcera, pústula.
festinate ['fɛstəˌneɪt] *a.* apresurado, de prisa. —*v.t.* apresurar, festinar (Amer.).
festival ['fɛstəvəl] *a.* festivo. —*s.* fiesta, festividad; festival (de música, etc.).
festive [-tɪv] *a.* 1. festivo, alegre, regocijado. 2. festivo, solemne.
festively [-lɪ] *adv.* festivamente, jubilosamente.
festivity [fɛs'tɪvətɪ] *s.* (*pl.* FESTIVITIES), festividad.
festoon [fɛs'tun] *s.* festón, guirnalda; (arq., esc.) festón. —*v.t.* festonear; formar festones de.
festooned [-'tund] *a.* afestonado, festoneado.
festoonery [-'tunərɪ] *s.* adorno o serie de festones.
fetal, foetal ['fitəl] *a.* (anat., zool.) fetal.
fetation [fɪ'teɪʃən] *s.* (anat., zool.) fetación gestación.
fetch [fɛtʃ] *v.t.* 1. ir a buscar, ir a traer, ir por. 2. traer, buscar y traer; (caza) cobrar (las presas). 3. proferir (grito, gemido, etc.); tomar (aliento); arrancar (lágrimas, suspiros, etc.). 4. venderse a (un precio). 5. tirar, ganar, devengar, cobrar (sueldo, salario, etc.); rendir, devengar (intereses). 6. interesar, atraer. 7. (fam.) asestar (un golpe). 8. **f. and carry,** llevar y traer (cosas); **f. around** (o **to**), hacer recobrase, hacer volver en

sí; **f. down,** abatir; traer abajo; **f. in,** meter, incluir; **f. one's breath,** tomar aliento; **f. (one) out,** hacer salir (a uno); **f. round to,** convencer de la corrección de (opinión, etc.); **f. up,** producir; recobrar (tiempo perdido); criar, educar (niños); parar, llegar a. —*v.i.* 1. (mar.) navegar, pasar. 2. **f. about, around** o **round,** dar la vuelta, circuir; **f. and carry for,** hacer mandatos para, servir a; **f. away,** (mar.) desamarrarse (buque); deslizarse, moverse (carga, etc.); **f. sternway,** (mar.) retroceder, ir atrás; **f. to windward,** (mar.) ganar el barlovento. —*s.* 1. (caza) cobranza. 2. treta, estratagema, truco. 3. (mar.) abra (de una bahía, etc.). 4. aparición, espectro (de una persona viva).

fetcher ['fɛtʃər, B -ə] *s.* el que va por algo.

fetching ['fɛtʃɪŋ] *a.* atractivo, encantador.

fete, fête [feɪt] *s.* fiesta (gen. al aire libre). —*v.t.* festejar.

feterita [ˌfɛtə'ritə] *s.* (bot.) variedad de sorgo, zahína.

fetial ['fiʃəl] *s.* (hist. romana) fecial, el que entre los romanos intimaba la paz y la guerra.

fetich, fetichism, fetichist, *vars. de* fetish, fetishism, fetishist.

feticidal [ˌfitə'saɪdəl] *a.* feticida.

feticide ['fitəˌsaɪd] *s.* feticidio.

fetid ['fɛtəd, 'fit-] *a.* fétido, hediondo.

fetidness [-nəs] *s.* fetidez, hediondez.

fetish ['fɛtɪʃ, 'fit-] *s.* fetiche.

fetishism [-ˌɪzəm] *s.* fetichismo.

fetishist [-əst] *s.* fetichista.

fetishistic [ˌfɛɪʃ'ɪstɪk, ˌfit-] *a.* fetichista.

fetlock ['fɛtˌlɑk, B -ˌlɔk] *s.* (zool.) 1. espolón (del menudillo de caballerías). 2. cerneja. 3. (t. **f. joint**) menudillo.

fetor ['fitər, B -ə] *s.* hedor, fetidez.

fetter ['fɛtər, B -ə] *s.* 1. (*gen. pl.*) grillo, grillete, cadena, pihuela (para una persona); traba, maniota, apea (para un animal). 2. (fig.) traba, impedimento. 3. (*pl.*) (fig.) cautiverio. —*v.t.* 1. engrillar, encadenar, apiolar. 2. (fig.) poner trabas a, inmovilizar, sujetar.

fetter-bush [-ˌbʊʃ] *s.* (bot.) variedad de brezo.

fetterlock [-ˌlɑk, B -ˌlɔk] *var. de* **fetlock.**

fettle ['fɛtəl] *v.t.* 1. (dial.) ordenar, arreglar. 2. esturgar (piezas de barro el alfarero). 3. (metal.) cubrir con brasca (esp. horno de reverbero). —*s.* 1. condición, estado. 2. *var. de* **fettling.** 3. **in good** (o **fine**) **f.,** en buena condición (física); dispuesto, de buen talante.

fettling [-əlɪŋ] *s.* (metal.) brasca.

fetus ['fitəs] *s.* (*pl.* FETUSES) (anat.) feto.

feud [fjud] *s.* 1. (der.) feudo, dominio. 2. enemistad inveterada, lucha encarnizada (entre dos familias, clanes o tribus). —*v.i.* luchar, pelear sin tregua.

feudal [-əl] *a.* feudal.

feudalism [-ˌɪzəm] *s.* feudalismo, sistema feudal.

feudalistic [ˌfjudəl'ɪstɪk] *a.* feudal.

feudality [fju'dæləti] *s.* 1. feudalidad. 2. feudo.

feudalization [ˌfjudələ'zeɪʃən, B -laɪ-] *s.* enfeudación.

feudalize ['fjudəˌlaɪz] *v.t.* enfeudar.

feudal system, feudalismo.

feudatory [-ˌtɔrɪ, B -tərɪ] *s.* 1. feudatorio, vasallo feudal. 2. dueño de un feudo. 3. feudo, estado feudal. —*a.* feudatorio.

feudist ['fjudəst] *s.* 1. (der.) feudista; experto en ley feudal. 2. (E.U.) camorrista, buscapleitos.

feuilleton [fɜjə'toʊn, B 'fɜɪtɔŋ] *s.* (fr.) 1. folletín. 2. novela publicada por entregas. 3. folletín, novela popular.

fever ['fivər, B -və] *s.* 1. (med.) fiebre, calentura, temperatura. 2. (fig.) fiebre, frenesí, agitación. —*v.t.* causar fiebre.

fever blister, (med.) herpe febril, herpe catarral (fuegos en los labios).

fevered [-vərd, B -vəd] *a.* febril.

feverfew [-vərˌfju, B -vəˌ-] *s.* (bot.) matricaria, magarza, expillo.

fever heat, 1. calentura, estado febril. 2. (fig.) intensidad febril.

feverish ['fivərɪʃ] *a.* 1. febril, febricitante, calenturiento. 2. ardoroso, desasosegado.

feverishly [-lɪ] *adv.* febrilmente.

feverishness [-nəs] *s.* calentura, estado febril.

feverous ['fivərəs] *var. de* **feverish.**

fever pitch, paroxismo; **to be at f.,** estar al rojo vivo.

fever sore, (med.) úlcera labial; escupidera, fuegos en la boca o los labios.

fever therapy, (med.) termoterapia.

fever tree, (bot.) eucalipto.

feverwort ['fivərˌwɜrt, B -vəˌwɜt] *s.* (bot.) eupatorio.

few [fju] *a., pron.* (FEWER; FEWEST) 1. pocos; unos cuantos, algunos, ej., *a man of f. words,* hombre de pocas palabras, *he spoke a f. words,* dijo algunas o unas cuantas palabras, *f. men have tried it,* pocos (hombres) lo han intentado, *a f. men have tried it,* algunos (hombres) lo han intentado. 2. **every f. days,** cada cierto tiempo; **f. and far between,** pocos y esparcidos. —*s.* 1. pocos; unos cuantos, algunos, ej., *f. have managed to escape,* pocos lograron escapar, *only a f. came,* solamente unos cuantos (o algunos) vinieron. 2. **not a f.,** no pocos; **quite a f.,** un buen número, una gran parte; **the f.,** la minoría, esp. un grupo pequeño y selecto.

fewness ['fjunəs] *s.* poquedad, escasez, cortedad.

fey [feɪ] *a.* 1. (pr. esco.) predestinado a la muerte; moribundo; aciago, de mal agüero. 2. visionario. 3. extraño, excéntrico; fantasioso.

fez [fɛz] *s.* fez, gorro de fieltro rojo y borla negra que usan los árabes y moros.

FGA, fga *abrev. de* **free of general average,** libre de avería general.

FHA (E.U.) *abrev. de* **Federal Housing Administration,** Dirección Federal de la Vivienda.

fiacre [fɪ'ɑkrə] *s.* fiacre, el típico coche de alquiler en Francia.

fiancé [ˌfiˌɑn'seɪ, fɪ'ɑnˌseɪ, B fɪ'ɑn-] *s.* novio, prometido.

fiancée [ˌfiˌɑn'seɪ, fɪ'ɑnˌseɪ, B fi'ɑn-] *s.* novia, prometida.

fiasco [fɪ'æskoʊ] *s.* (*pl.* FIASCOES o FIASCOS) fiasco, fracaso.

fiat ['faɪˌæt, -ət] *s.* fiat, autorización; mandato, orden, edicto, decreto.

fiat money, moneda fiduciaria; billetes emitidos por decreto sin respaldo de reservas en metal.

fib [fɪb] *s.* 1. mentirilla, filfa, trufa. 2. (G.B.) golpe, trompada. —*v.i.* (*pret., p.p.* FIBBED; *p.pr.* FIBBING) decir mentirillas, mentir. —*v.t.* (G.B.) golpear, aporrear.

fibber ['fɪbər, B -ə] *s.* mentiroso, inventor, trapacero, trufador.

fiber, (G.B.) **fibre** ['faɪbər, B -bə] *s.* 1. fibra, filamento, hebra, hilo. 2. (bot., anat.) fibra. 3. (fig.) carácter, temperamento, índole. 4. (quím.) fibra vulcanizada.

fiberboard, (G.B.) **fibreboard** [-ˌbɔrd, B -ˌbɔd] *s.* lámina, cartón o tabla de fibra.

fiberfill [-ˌfɪl] *s.* material sintético usado como relleno (de colchones, edredones, etc.).

Fiberglass (TM) [-ˌglæs, B -ˌglɑs] *s.* Fiberglass, vidrio fibroso, fibras de vidrio.

fiber optic, de fibra óptica.

fiber optic cable, cable de fibra óptica.

fiber optics, trasmisión por fibra óptica.

fiber sandal, alpargata; abarca de esparto.

fibriform ['faɪbrəˌfɔrm, B -ˌfɔm] *a.* de aspecto fibroso; (bot.) fibriforme.

fibril ['faɪbrəl] *s.* (anat., bot.) fibrilla, fibrila.

fibrillar [-brələr, B -lə] *a.* (anat.) fibrilar.

fibrillation [ˌfɪbrə'leɪʃən, B ˌfaɪ-] *s.* 1. (anat.) fibrilación. 2. (med.) fibrilación, temblor muscular; arritmia.

fibrillose ['faɪbrəˌloʊs] *a.* (anat., bot.) fibriloso.

fibrin ['faɪbrən] *s.* (bioquím.) fibrina.

fibrinogen [faɪ'brɪnədʒən, -ˌdʒɛn] *s.* (bioquím.) fibrinógeno.

fibrinogenous [ˌfaɪbrə'nɑdʒənəs, B -'nɔdʒ-] **fibrinogenic** [-noʊ'dʒɛnɪk] *a.* (bioquím.) fibrinógeno.

fibrinolysin [-'nɑləsən, B -'nɔl-] *s.* (bioquím.) fibrinolisina.

fibrinolysis [-əsəs] *s.* (bioquím.) fibrinólisis.

fibrinous ['faɪbrənəs] *a.* fibrinoso.

fibroblast [-ˌblæst] *s.* (biol.) fibroblasto, fibrocito.

fibroblastic [ˌfaɪbrə'blæstɪk] *a.* (biol.) fibroblástico.

fibrocartilage [-broʊ'kɑrtəlɪdʒ, B -'kɑt-] *s.* (anat.) fibrocartílago.

fibrocartilaginous [-ˌkɑrtə'lædʒənəs, B -ˌkɑt-] *a.* (anat.) fibrocartilaginoso.

fibrocyte ['faɪbrəˌsaɪt] *s.* (med.) fibrocito, fibroblasto.

fibroid ['faɪˌbrɔɪd] *a.* fibroide, fibriforme. —*s.* (med.) fibroide, fibroma, tumor fibroso.

fibroin ['faɪbroʊən] *s.* (bioquím.) fibroína.

fibroma [faɪ'broʊmə] *s.* (*pl.* FIBROMAS o FIBROMATA [-mətə]) (med.) fibroma.

fibromatous [-mətəs] *a.* (med.) fibromatoide.

fibrosis [faɪ'broʊsəs] *s.* (med.) fibrosis.

fibrositis [ˌfaibrə'saɪtəs] *s.* (med.) fibrositis.

fibrotic [faɪ'brɑtɪk, B -'brɔt-] *a.* (med.) fibrótico.

fibrous ['faɪbrəs] *a.* fibroso.

fibrous tissue, (anat., biol.) tejido fibroso.

fibrovascular [ˌfaɪbroʊ'væskjələr, B -lə] *a.* (bot.) fibrovascular.

fibster ['fɪbstər, B -stə] *s.* (jer.) persona que dice mentirillas.

fibula ['fɪbjələ] *s.* (*pl.* FIBULAS o FIBULAE [-ˌli]) 1. (arqueol.) fíbula, hebilla, broche. 2. (anat., zool.) fíbula, peroné.

fibular [-lər, B -lə] *a.* (anat.) fibular, peroneo.

fichu ['fɪʃu, B 'fiʃu] *s.* fichú, pañoleta triangular.

fickle ['fɪkəl] *a.* inconstante, inestable, veleidoso, voluble.

fickleness [-nəs] *s.* inconstancia, inestabilidad, veleidad.

fico ['fikoʊ] *s.* (*pl.* FICOES) (ant.) pizca, comino, pitoche.

ficoid ['fiˌkɔɪd] (bot.) *a.* ficóideo. —*s.* ficóidea.

Ficoideae [fi'kɔɪdɪˌi] *s. pl.* (bot.) ficóideas.

fictile ['fɪktəl, B -ˌtaɪl] *a.* (cerám.) figulino, plástico.

fiction ['fɪkʃən] *s.* 1. ficción, invención. 2. literatura novelesca, novelística. 3. embuste, fábula. 4. (der.) ficción; **legal f.,** ficción de derecho o legal.

fictional [-əl] *a.* ficticio, novelesco.

fictionalize [-ˌaɪz] *v.t.* convertir en ficción; novelizar.

fictionally [-ɪ] *adv.* ficticiamente, fingidamente.

fictioneer [ˌfɪkʃə'nɪr, B -'nɪə] *s.* novelista comercializado.

fictionist ['fɪkʃənəst] *s.* novelista, cuentista, narrador.

fictionize [-ˌnaɪz] *var. de* **fictionalize.**

fictitious [fɪk'tɪʃəs] *a.* ficticio, imaginario, fingido.

fictitiously [-lɪ] *adv.* ficticiamente, fingidamente.
fictitiousness [-nəs] *s.* carácter ficticio.
fictive ['fɪktɪv] *a.* fingido, ficticio.
fictively [-lɪ] *adv.* ficticiamente, fingidamente.
fid [fɪd] *s.* 1. (mar.) cuña de mastelero; barra de sostén. 2. (mar.) burel, pasador de cabo (para abrir los cordones de los cabos).
fiddle ['fɪdəl] *s.* 1. (fam.) violín. 2. (mar.) reborde de mesa (para impedir que se resbale y caiga la vajilla en un temporal). 3. **fit as a f.,** sano como una manzana, listo y dispuesto; **to play first f.,** llevar la batuta, llevar la voz cantante; **to play second f. (to),** desempeñar un papel secundario (al lado de). —*v.i.* 1. tocar el violín. 2. jugar nerviosamente (con dedos o manos). 3. ocuparse en fruslerías. 4. **f. around,** perder el tiempo, cazar moscas; **f. at,** chafallar; **f. away,** desperdiciar, malgastar; **f. with,** jugar con, manosear (algo) nerviosamente. —*v.t.* 1. tocar (una tonada, etc.) en el violín. 2. malgastar.
fiddle block, (mec.) motón violín, motón de dos ejes con poleas diferenciales.
fiddle bow, arco de violín.
fiddle-dee-dee [ˌfɪdəldɪ'di] *interj.* ¡tonterías! ¡qué disparate!
fiddle-faddle ['fɪdəlˌfædəl] *s.* (fam.) disparate, tontería, estupidez, bobería. —*interj.* ¡tonterías! ¡disparates! —*v.i.* ocuparse en fruslerías, desperdiciar el tiempo.
fiddle-footed [-'fʊtəd] *a.* 1. saltón, inquieto, asustadizo (caballo, etc.). 2. vagabundo, errante.
fiddlehead [-ˌhɛd] *s.* (mar.) mascarón de proa en forma de espiral del mástil de un violín.
fiddler ['fɪdlər, B -lə] *s.* 1. violinista. 2. (jer.) chanchullero.
fiddler crab, (zool.) barrilete, cangrejo de mar.
fiddlerfish [-ˌfɪʃ] *s.* (ict.) tipo de raya.
fiddlestick ['fɪdəlˌstɪk] *s.* 1. arco de violín. 2. (*pl.*) disparate. —*interj.* (*gen. pl.*) ¡tonterías! ¡boberías! ¡disparate!
fiddlestring [-ˌstrɪŋ] *s.* (fam.) cuerda de violín.
fiddling ['fɪdlɪŋ] *a.* (fam.) frívolo, fútil, insignificante.
fideicommissary [ˌfaɪdɪaɪ'kɑməˌsɛrɪ, B -'kɔmɪsərɪ] *a., s.* (der., G.B.) fideicomisario.
fideicommissor [-kə'mɪsər, B -ə] *s.* (der., G.B.) fideicomitente.
fideicommissum [-'mɪsəm] *s.* (*pl.* FIDEICOMMISSA [-ə]) (der., G.B.) fideicomiso.
fideism ['fideɪˌɪzəm, B 'faɪdɪ-] *s.* (filos.) fideísmo.
Fidelismo [ˌfidelˌizmoʊ] *s.* Fidelismo, adherencia a la política o las ideas de Fidel Castro.
fidelity [fə'dɛlətɪ, faɪ-] *s.* 1. fidelidad, exactitud, corrección. 2. fidelidad, lealtad. 3. (electrón., rad.) fidelidad.
fidget ['fɪdʒət] *v.i.* agitarse, inquietarse, cazcalear; **f. with,** manosear. —*v.t.* 1. inquietar, molestar. 2. jugar con. —*s.* 1. (*pl.*) impaciencia, agitación, inquietud. 2. persona inquieta.
fidgetiness [-ɪnəs] *s.* intranquilidad, carácter inquieto.
fidgety [-ɪ] *a.* intranquilo, inquieto, impaciente, agitado, nervioso.
fiducial [fə'duʃəl, B -'dju-] *a.* 1. de confianza. 2. fiduciario. 3. (fís., mat., astr.) fiducial.
fiduciary [-ʃɪˌɛrɪ, -ʃərɪ, B -ʃjə-] *a.* fiduciario. —*s.* fiduciario, persona de confianza.
fie [faɪ] *interj.* (poét.) ¡qué vergüenza!
fief [fif] *s.* (der.) feudo; estado feudal.
field [fild] *s.* 1. campo, campiña, sembrado, campo cultivado. 2. campaña; campo (de hielo, nieve, etc.), extensión (del mar, del cielo). 3. (min., geol.) yacimiento(s) (de petróleo, carbón, etc.). 4. (fig.) campo, esfera (de alguna actividad), campo, ramo (de ciencia, erudición, etc.). 5. (fig.) curso, ej., *the whole f. of history,* todo el curso de la historia. 6. franja (de bandera). 7. (fís.) campo (magnético o eléctrico). 8. (ópt.) campo de visión. 9. (mat.) cuerpo, campo. 10. (her.) campo (del escudo). 11. (mil.) campo de batalla. 12. (dep.) campo (de juego); (béisbol) jardín. 13. (dep.) participantes (en una carrera o competencia), conjunto de jugadores; (criquet, béisbol) equipo en el campo (opuesto al que tiene el bate); resto de los competidores (que no alcanzan los primeros puestos o no son favoritos para ello). 14. **a good f.,** buena concurrencia, numerosos competidores (esp. en carrera de caballos); **in the f.,** (mil.) en campaña; trabajar en el campo de acción de una obra (ingeniero, geólogo, etc.); **to hold the f.,** mantener su posición, no ceder terreno; **to keep the f.,** mantenerse firme, continuar la batalla; **to take the f.,** empezar una campaña. —*a.* 1. campal, campestre, campesino. 2. campestre, silvestre. 3. de campo; (mil.) de campaña. —*v.t.* 1. (dep.) parar y devolver la pelota, poner (un equipo o ciertos jugadores) en el campo. 2. (fig.) contestar satisfactoriamente (preguntas). —*v.i.* estar de jugador en el campo.
field army, (mil.) ejército de operaciones, ejército en campaña, fuerzas combatientes.
field artillery, (mil.) artillería de campaña, artillería rodada, artillería de batalla.
field battery, (mil.) batería de campaña.
field book, manual o cuaderno de agrimensor; (mil.) libreta de campo.
field camomile, (bot.) manzanilla loca, albihar, abiar.
field coil, (elec.) bobina de campo.
field corn, variedad de maíz utilizado como forraje.
field day, 1. (mil.) día de ejercicios, día de maniobras. 2. día de competencias atléticas, día de gala (en colegios). 3. (fig.) día de actividades exitosas o interesantes; **to have a f.,** obtener un gran éxito, triunfar, hacer su agosto; divertirse muchisimo, darse gusto haciendo algo.
fielder ['fildər, B -ə] *s.* (dep.) jardinero (en béisbol); servidor (en criquet).
field eryngo, (bot.) cardo corredor, cardo estelado corredor.
field events, (dep.) competencias de salto y lanzamiento.
fieldfare ['fildˌfɛr, B -ˌfɛə] *s.* (orn.) tordella, zorzal.
field flower, flor de los prados, flor caminera.
field forces, (mil.) fuerzas en campaña.
field glasses, gemelos de campaña.
field goal, (baloncesto) doble; (fútbol) tiro libre ejecutado con éxito.
field grade, (mil.) grado superior (de mayor, teniente coronel o coronel).
field gray, (mil.) gris de campaña.
field gun, (mil.) cañón de campaña.
field hand, peón de campo, bracero.
field hockey, (dep.) hockey de campo, hockey sobre hierba.
field hospital, hospital de sangre; hospital de campaña, ambulancia fija.
field intensity, (elec.) intensidad de campo.
field kitchen, (mil.) cocina móvil o de campaña.
field magnet, (fís.) imán inductor, imán del campo (para detectar el hierro).
fieldman ['fildmən] *s.* (criquet) jugador.
field marshal, (*pl.* FIELD MARSHALS) (mil.) mariscal de campo.
field mouse, (zool.) ratón del campo.
field music, (mil., nav.) banda militar de campaña; conjunto de cornetines y tambores.
field mustard, (bot.) mostaza silvestre.
field officer, (mil.) oficial superior (con rango de) coronel, teniente coronel o comandante.
field of force, (fís.) campo de fuerza.
field of honor, 1. campo del honor (en que tiene lugar un duelo). 2. (mil.) campo de batalla.
field of vision, campo visual.
field pea, (bot.) guisante común.
fieldpiece ['fildˌpis] *s.* (mil.) pieza móvil de artillería.
field pole, (elec.) polo del campo.
field scabious, (bot.) escabiosa, viuda.
field-strip [-ˌstrɪp] *v.t.* desmontar un arma de fuego para su limpieza e inspección.
field telephone, (mil.) teléfono de campaña.
field-test [-tɛst] *v.t.* someter a prueba (un método, artefacto, etc.) en la práctica, a diferencia de un test en un laboratorio.
field trip, excursión (esp. de escolares) con el propósito de recoger datos para una clase.
field winding, (elec.) arrollamiento inductor.
fieldwork ['fildˌwɜrk, B -ˌwɜk] *s.* 1. trabajo de campo o en el terreno. 2. (mil.) obras de campo.
fiend [find] *s.* 1. loco, monomaníaco. 2. fiera, arpía; espíritu malévolo. 3. fanático; adicto, vicioso. 4. **to be a f. at,** ser un genio en o para; **to be a f. for (work,** etc.), ser una fiera para (el trabajo, etc.).
fiendish ['findɪʃ] *a.* diabólico, perverso, malvado, cruel.
fiendishly [-lɪ] *adv.* perversamente, cruelmente.
fiendishness [-nəs] *s.* perversidad, crueldad, maldad.
fiendlike ['findˌlaɪk] *a.* perverso, cruel, malvado, diabólico.
fierce [fɪrs, B fɪəs] *a.* 1. fiero, feroz, cruel. 2. furioso, rabioso. 3. violento, (esfuerzo, dolor, etc.). 4. impetuoso, ardiente (deseo, etc.).
fiercely ['fɪrslɪ, B 'fɪəs-] *adv.* ferozmente, furiosamente.
fierceness [-nəs] *s.* fiereza, ferocidad, crueldad.
fieri facias [ˌfiərɪ'feɪkɪˌæs] (der.) auto ejecutorio.
fierily ['faɪrəlɪ, B 'faɪər-] *adv.* ardientemente, vehementemente.
fieriness [-ɪnəs] *s.* ardor, vehemencia.
fiery [-ɪ] *a.* 1. ardiente, flameante. 2. caliente; picante (comida, salsa). 3. (fig.) ardiente, enardecido, vehemente (mirada, discurso, debate, etc.). 4. (fig.) apasionado, irritable (carácter, persona, etc.). 5. fogoso, brioso (caballo, etc.). 6. inflamable (gas, vapores, etc.). 7. inflamado. 8. ígneo (ej., meteoro).
fiery cross, (E.U.) cruz ardiente (símbolo de terror del Ku Klux Klan).
fiesta [fɪ'ɛstə] *s.* fiesta, festival.
fife [faɪf] *s.* (mús.) pífano, flautín, chistu. —*v.i.* tocar el pífano.
fifer ['faɪfər, B -ə] *s.* el que toca el pífano, chistulari.
fife rail, (mar.) guindaste, cabillero.
fifteen [fɪf'tin, 'fɪf-] *s., a.* quince.
fifteenth [-'tinθ] *s.* 1. decimoquinto. 2. quince (en fechas). —*a.* decimoquinto.
fifth [fɪfθ] *s.* 1. quinto. 2. cinco (en fechas). 3. (mús.) quinta. 4. (mús.) dominante, quinta nota (de la escala). 5. (E.U.) quinto de galón (medida de líquido). —*a.* quinto.
Fifth Amendment, (E.U.) quinta enmienda a la Constitución que enumera los derechos de los acusados, esp. invalidando la auto-incriminación.
fifth column, (pol.) quinta columna; (fig.) el enemigo en casa.
fifth columnist, (pol.) quintacolumnista.

fifthly ['fɪfθlɪ] *adv.* en quinto lugar.
fifth wheel, 1. rodete (del coche). 2. rueda de repuesto. 3. (fig.) quinta rueda, persona o elemento superfluo.
fiftieth ['fɪftɪəθ] *a., s.* quincuagésimo.
fifty ['fɪftɪ] *s.* (*pl.* FIFTIES) 1. cincuenta. 2. grupo de cincuenta (personas o cosas). 3. **by fifties,** en grupos de cincuenta; **f.-f.,** a partes iguales, mitad y mitad; **the fifties,** la década de los cincuenta (de la vida o de un siglo); **to go f.-f.,** ir a partes iguales, ir a medias. —*a.* cincuenta, ej., *some f. children,* unos cincuenta niños, una cincuentena de niños.
fiftyfold [-ˌfoʊld] *adv.* cincuenta veces. —*a.* de cincuenta veces.
fig [fɪg] *s.* 1. higo, breva. 2. (bot.) higuera (árbol). 3. bledo, comino, pepino, ej., *I don't give a f.,* me importa un bledo (comino o pepino).
fig, *v.t.* (*pret., p.p.* FIGGED; *p.pr.* FIGGING) (gen. con *out* o *up*) dopar, dar estimulantes a (un caballo). —*s.* 1. (fam.) atavío, vestido. 2. condición, forma. 3. **in full f.,** (estar) vestido de veinticinco alfileres; **in good f.,** en buena condición.
figeater ['fɪgˌitər, B -ˌitə] *s.* escarabajo grande (del Sur de los E.U.).
fight [faɪt] *v.i.* (*pret., p.p.* FOUGHT [fɔt] *p.pr.* FIGHTING) 1. luchar, pelear, pugnar. 2. reñir, pelear. 3. **f. about,** luchar o pelear por; **f. against,** luchar contra; **f. against odds,** luchar con desventaja; **f. back,** defenderse, devolver golpe por golpe; **f. shy of,** evitar, mantenerse apartado de; **f. with,** luchar con, pelear con. —*v.t.* 1. combatir, luchar con. 2. disputar, luchar contra, oponerse a. 3. hacer pelear (a gallos). 4. **f. a battle,** dar o librar una batalla; **f. down,** reprimir (deseo, repugnancia, temor, etc.); **f. it out,** decidirlo peleando; **f. out,** pelear para decidir (algo); aguantar (ej., barco una tempestad); **f. one's way (through),** abrirse paso a la fuerza (a través de); **f. off,** repeler, rechazar; **f. windmills,** luchar con molinos de viento, combatir males imaginarios. —*s.* 1. lucha, pelea, pugna, lid. 2. ánimo; belicosidad, combatividad. 3. **sham f.,** (G.B., mil.) simulacro de combate; **to look like a f.,** oler a chamusquina; **to pick a f. with,** meterse con, armar camorra a; buscar la lengua a (uno); **to put up a f.,** ofrecer resistencia.
fighter ['faɪtər, B -ə] *s.* 1. luchador, combatiente, guerrero; peleador; batallador; duelista. 2. (dep.) boxeador, púgil, pugilista.
fighter bomber, (mil., aer.) caza-bombardero (avión).
fighter pilot, piloto de caza.
fighter plane, (mil.) avión de caza o combate.
fighter squadron, (mil., aer.) escuadrón de caza o de combate.
fighting chance ['faɪtɪŋ-] buena probabilidad de éxito (que se logra luchando); buena probabilidad de sobrevivir.
fighting cock, gallo de pelea; persona pugnaz.
fighting power, (mil.) potencia combatiente.
fighting top, (mar.) cofa militar.
fig leaf, 1. hoja de higuera. 2. (arte) hoja de parra, atuendo mínimo de las estatuas.
fig marigold, (bot.) doca.
figment ['fɪgmənt] *s.* invención, ficción.
figpecker ['fɪgˌpɛkər, B -ə] *s.* (orn.) becafigo, oropela.
figuline ['fɪgjʊlɪn, -ˌlaɪn] *s.* 1. arcilla figulina. 2. alfarería. 3. estatuilla de arcilla.
figural ['fɪgjərəl] *a.* 1. figurativo (cuadro, composición, etc.). 2. figurado (lenguaje, expresión, etc.).
figurant [-rənt] *s.* (*f.* FIGURANTE), (teat.) comparsa, figurante.
figurate ['fɪgjərət, B -reɪt] *a.* figurado; (mús.) floreado, embellecido.
figuration [ˌfɪgjə'reɪʃən] *s.* 1. figuración. 2. contorno, perfil, forma. 3. (mús.) (uso de) contrapunto figurado.
figurative ['fɪgjərətɪv, 'fɪgər-] *a.* 1. figurado, metafórico (lenguaje, sentido, etc.). 2. de estilo figurado (escritor). 3. figurativo (dibujo, escultura).
figuratively [-lɪ] *adv.* 1. figuradamente. 2. figurativamente.
figure ['fɪgjər, B 'fɪgə] *s.* 1. figura, forma, perfil. 2. figura, talle, cuerpo. 3. figura, trazado (hecho por patines en el hielo, avión en el aire, etc.). 4. figura, diseño, dibujo. 5. ilustración (en libro, revista, etc.). 6. cifra, número; (*pl.*) cálculo, operaciones aritméticas. 7. precio. 8. personaje, figura prominente. 9. (geom., ret., lóg., mús.) figura. 10. figura (de baile). 11. **at a low (high) f.,** a un precio bajo (alto); **f. of fun,** figura, persona grotesca; **good at figures,** hábil para sacar cuentas; **to cut a f.,** descollar, hacer figura; **to cut a (good, poor,** etc.) **f.,** hacer (buen, mal, etc.) papel; producir (buena, mala, etc.) impresión; **to keep one's f.,** guardar la línea, no engordar. —*v.t.* 1. figurar, representar. 2. adornar con figuras o diseño. 3. marcar con números, numerar. 4. idear. 5. imaginar, figurarse. 6. calcular, considerar. 7. (mús.) cifrar (el bajo). 8. (jer.) comprender. 9. **f. oneself,** imaginarse; **f. out,** deducir, resolver, explicarse; **f. to oneself,** figurarse, calcular. —*v.i.* 1. aparecer, parecer. 2. destacar, sobresalir, ser conspicuo. 3. calcular, hacer cálculos. 4. (jer.) parecer razonable, ser posible o probable, esperarse (que algo suceda), ej., *it figures,* era de esperarse. 5. **f. as,** pasar por; **f. on,** contar con; proponerse, planear (hacer algo); **f. out (at),** dar el total (de), sumar, calcular, ascender (a).
figured [-jərd, B 'fɪgəd] *a.* 1. figurado, representado. 2. decorado con figuras. 3. figurado (lenguaje, etc.). 4. (mús.) cifrado (bajo).
figure dance, baile de figuras.
figurehead ['fɪgjərˌhɛd, B 'fɪgəˌ-] *s.* 1. (mar.) mascaron de proa. 2. testaferro, líder o caudillo títere (que figura solamente, sin tener autoridad).
figure-of-eight knot [-əv'eɪt-, B 'fɪgər-] (mar.) nudo cruzado simple (en forma de 8).
figure skater, patinador artístico.
figure of speech, (ret.) figura o tropo de dicción, forma de expresión.
figure skating, patinaje artístico.
figurine [ˌfɪgjə'rin, B 'fɪgjʊˌrin] *s.* figurilla, figurina, estatuilla.
figwort ['fɪgˌwɜrt, B -ˌwɜt] *s.* (bot.) escrofularia.
Fijian ['fidʒɪən, B fi'dʒɪ-] *a., s.* fidjiano, fiyiano, nativo de las islas Fiji.
fila ['faɪlə] *pl. de* **filum.**
filagree, *var. de* **filigree.**
filament ['fɪləmənt] *s.* 1. filamento, hilillo, hilaza. 2. (bot., elec.) filamento.
filamentary [ˌfɪlə'mɛntərɪ] *a.* formado o compuesto de filamentos.
filament current, (rad.) corriente de filamento.
filament lamp, lámpara incandescente.
filamentous [-'mɛntəs] *a.* filamentoso.
filander [fə'lændər, B -də] *s.* (zool.) filandria (lombriz).
filar ['faɪlər, B -lə] *a.* reticulado (ocular), con ocular reticulado (microscopio).
filaria [fɪ'lɛrɪə, B -'lɛər-] *s.* (*pl.* FILARIAE [-ɪ,i]) (zool.) filaria.
filarial [-ɪəl] **filarian** [-ɪən] *a.* (zool.) filárico.
filariasis [ˌfɪlə'raɪəsəs] *s.* (med.) filariasis, filariosis.
filature ['fɪlətjər, B -tʃə] *s.* 1. devanado (de hilos de seda). 2. devanadera (para hilar la seda). 3. hilandería (deseda).
filbert ['fɪlbərt, B -bət] *s.* 1. (bot.) avellano. 2. avellana.
filch [fɪltʃ] *v.t.* ratear, hurtar, escamotear.
filcher ['fɪltʃər, B -tʃə] *s.* hurtador, escamoteador.
file [faɪl] *s.* 1. archivo, registro (de documentos, periódicos, etc.). 2. carpeta; fichero; archivador. 3. hilera, fila. 4. (ajedrez) columna. 5. (mil.) fila, columna (de soldados). 6. (ant.) acta, protocolo; lista. 7. **in single** (o **Indian**) **f.,** en fila india; a la hila; **on f.,** archivado, en el archivo, registrado. —*v.t.* 1. clasificar, ordenar. 2. archivar. 3. protocolizar, protocolar. 4. registrar, presentar, entablar. 5. **f. a claim,** entablar un reclamo; **f. a complaint,** (der.) sentar una denuncia; **f. a suit,** (der.) entablar juicio; **f. an appeal,** (der.) presentar una apelación. —*v.i.* 1. marchar en fila. 2. **f. by,** desfilar; pasar uno por uno; **f. in,** entrar uno por uno, entrar uno tras otro; **f. off** (o **out**), irse en fila; salir uno por uno.
file [faɪl] *s.* 1. lima, escofina. 2. (jer.) zorro, persona astuta. —*v.t.* 1. limar. 2. (fig.) limar, pulir. 3. **f. away,** limar, quitar con la lima (número, marca, etc.).
file brush, carda limpialimas.
file cabinet, archivo, fichero.
file card, 1. ficha, tarjeta (de un fichero). 2. limpialimas.
file clerk, archivista, archivero.
file cutter, (mec.) picador de limas.
filefish ['faɪlˌfɪʃ] *s.* (ict.) variedad de pez ballesta, lija.
file-hard ['faɪlˌhɑrd B -ˌhɑd] *a.* a prueba de lima.
filer [-ər, B -ə] *s.* 1. archivero. 2. limador.
file-soft [-ˌsɔft] *a.* que puede ser limado.
filet [fɪ'leɪ, B 'fɪlɪt] *s.* 1. filete (de carne o pescado). 2. encaje de malla cuadrada (t. **f. lace**).
filet mignon [-mi'noʊn] *s.* filete, solomillo de ternera, lomo.
filial ['fɪlɪəl, 'fɪljəl] *a.* filial.
filial generation, (biol.) generación filial.
filially [-ɪ] *adv.* filialmente.
filiation [ˌfɪlɪ'eɪʃən] *s.* 1. filiación (de un hijo con sus progenitores). 2. filiación, procedencia. 3. rama, derivado. 4. (der.) filiación.
filibuster ['fɪləˌbʌstər, B -tə] *s.* 1. filibustero; pirata, aventurero. 2. (E.U., pol.) obstruccionista. 3. (E.U., pol.) obstrucción; obstruccionismo. —*v.i.* 1. ser un filibustero. 2. (E.U.) obstruir la aprobación de una ley, practicar el obstruccionismo (en un cuerpo legislativo). —*v.t.* obstruir (moción, prospuesta).
filicidal [ˌfɪlə'saɪdəl] *a.* filicida.
filicide ['fɪləˌsaɪd] *s.* 1. filicidio. 2. filicida, el que mata a su propio hijo.
filiform ['fɪləˌfɔrm, B 'faɪlɪˌfɔm] *a.* filiforme.
filigree ['fɪləˌgri] *s.* filigrana. —*v.t.* afiligranar; adornar con filigrana.
filing ['faɪlɪŋ] *s.* 1. (*gen. pl.*) limaduras, limalla. 2. colocación en el archivo; **to do f.,** archivar (correspondencia oficinesca).
filing cabinet, archivador, gabinete de archivo.
filing card, ficha, tarjeta de archivo.
filing system, sistema de archivar.
Filipino [ˌfɪlə'pinoʊ] *a., s.* (*pl.* FILIPINOS), filipino, natural de las islas Filipinas.
fill [fɪl] *v.t.* 1. llenar. 2. llenar, saciar, hartar. 3. ocupar, llenar, desempeñar (sitio, lugar, puesto, oficio, vacante). 4. llenar, tapar (hoyo, agujero, etc.). 5. rellenar (dulce, pastel, etc.). 6. empastar, emplomar (diente). 7. enchapar, chapear (de oro,

etc.). 8. verter (vino, agua); echar, poner (ej., carbón en carbonera). 9. (E.U.) preparar (receta). 10. (ing. civil) terraplenar, rellenar (terreno bajo). 11. (com.) ejecutar, despachar (un pedido). 12. (mar.) hinchar (vela); orientar (una verga). 13. **f. away,** (mar.) orientar (una verga); **f. 'er up!** ¡llénelo! (el tanque del automóvil con gasolina); **f. in,** completar con (detalles, cifras, etc.); llenar (un formulario); rellenar (hoyo, agujero, zanja, etc.); **f. (someone) in (on),** dar (a alguien) la información necesaria (sobre, acerca de), explicar (algo a alguien); **f. one's shoes,** ocupar el puesto de uno; **f. out,** ensanchar, redondear; completar; llevar a cabo; extender (cheque, etc.); **f. the bill,** llenar los requisitos, servir, ser suficiente; **f. up,** llenar hasta el tope. —*v.i.* 1. llenarse. 2. (mar.) hincharse (vela). 3. **f. in,** estar o trabajar de reemplazo; **f. in for,** reemplazar a, tomar el lugar de; **f. out,** llenarse (mejillas), engordar (cuerpo); (mar.) hincharse (vela). —*s.* 1. abundancia; hartura, hartazgo. 2. (ing. civil) terraplén, relleno. 3. **to drink (weep, read,** etc.) **one's f.,** beber (llorar, leer, etc.) hasta no poder más; **to have one's f. (of),** saciarse (de); darse un hartazgo (de).

filled gold [fɪld-] (joy.) oro enchapado.

filled milk, leche desnatada enriquecida (por la adición de aceites vegetales).

filler ['fɪlər, B -ə] *s.* 1. relleno. 2. (arq., ing.) plancha, lámina o bloque de relleno. 3. (pint.) aparejo, tapaporos. 4. tripa (del cigarro).

filler cap, (aut.) tapón de llenado; tapón del radiador.

filler coat, (pint.) mano de aparejo.

filler metal, metal de aporte (para soldaduras).

filler neck, (aut.) boca de llenado.

filler rod, varilla para soldadura.

filler wall, (const.) pared de relleno, antepecho.

fillet ['fɪlət] *s.* 1. banda, faja, cinta (para el cabello). 2. (anat.) lemnisco, cinta de fibras (esp. de materia blanca en el cerebro). 3. (arq.) filete, listel; mediacaña. 4. (enc.) filete (en la cubierta de un libro). 5 [fɪ'leɪ, B 'fɪlɪt] (cocina) filete, solomillo (de carne o pescado). — ['fɪlət] *v.t.* 1. ceñir con banda, faja o cinta. 2. filetear. 3. (cocina) cortar en filetes.

filling ['fɪlɪŋ] *s.* 1. relleno, adición. 2. (cocina) relleno. 3. empaste (de diente). 4. (ing. civil) terraplén. 5. (tej.) trama (del tejido). 6. lo que llena o satisface el estómago o el apetito.

filling station, estación gasolinera, estación de servicio de gasolina.

fillip ['fɪləp] *v.t.* 1. dar un capirotazo a, tirar o impeler con un capirotazo. 2. (fig.) incitar, estimular, impulsar. —*s.* 1. capirotazo, papirote. 2. (fig.) estímulo, aguijón.

fillister ['fɪləstər, B -stə] *s.* (carp.) guillame.

fillister head, (carp.) cabeza cilíndrica ranurada.

fill-up ['fɪl,ʌp] *a.* (fig.) relleno (en un disco de gramófono, revista, etc.).

filly ['fɪlɪ] *s.* 1. potranca. 2. (fam.) muchacha vivaz y agraciada.

film [fɪlm] *s.* 1. película, telilla. 2. tela o nube (en el ojo). 3. (foto.) película; (cinem.) película, filme, film. 4. **to shoot a f.,** (cinem.) rodar una película. —*v.t.* 1. cubrir con una película. 2. filmar, rodar (una novela, una escena). —*v.i.* 1. cubrirse de una telilla. 2. tomar una película; (cinem.) rodar una película. 3. adaptarse (bien o mal) para ser fotografiado.

filmdom ['fɪlmdəm] *s.* industria cinematográfica; el mundo del cine.

film-goer [-,goʊər, B -ə] *s.* aficionado al cine.

filmic ['fɪlmɪk] *a.* del cine, cinematográfico, fílmico.

filminess [-mɪnəs] *s.* 1. opacidad, nubosidad. 2. diafanidad, tenuidad.

filming [-mɪŋ] *s.* (cinem.) filmación, rodaje.

film library, filmoteca.

film pack, (foto.) paquete de planchas fotográficas.

film play, drama cinematográfico.

film star, estrella de cine.

filmstrip [-,strɪp] *s.* tira de película.

film studio, estudio cinematográfico.

filmy ['fɪlmɪ] *a.* (FILMIER; FILMIEST) 1. tenue, diáfano. 2. nuboso, opaco. 3. membranoso, pelicular.

filopodium [,fɪlə'poʊdɪəm, ˌfaɪlə-] *s.* (biol.) filópodo, filopodio.

filose ['faɪ,loʊs] *a.* 1. filamentoso. 2. filiforme.

filter ['fɪltər, B -tə] *s.* filtro; (fís., elec., ópt., foto.) filtro. —*v.t.* filtrar. —*v.i.* 1. filtrarse. 2. (con *into*) infiltrarse. 3. (con *through* u *out*) (fig.) trascender, traslucirse (noticia, secreto, etc.).

filterable [-tərəbəl] *a.* filtrable.

filterable virus, (med.) virus filtrable.

filter bed, lecho filtrante o de filtración.

filter capacitor, (rad.) condensador de filtro.

filter cartridge, cartucho filtrante.

filter cloth, tela de filtrar, paño de filtro.

filter paper, papel de filtrar, papel de filtro.

filter press, prensa de filtrar, filtro-prensa.

filter tip, boquilla con filtro (de cigarrillo), cigarrillo con filtro.

filth [fɪlθ] *s.* suciedad, inmundicia, mugre; basura; (fig.) obscenidad.

filthily ['fɪlθəlɪ] *adv.* suciamente, asquerosamente.

filthiness [-θɪnəs] *s.* inmundicia, suciedad.

filthy [-θɪ] *a.* (FILTHIER; FILTHIEST) 1. sucio, puerco, asqueroso, inmundo, escuálido. 2. (fig.) sucio, obsceno. 3. (fig.) de perros, malo, ej., *f. weather,* tiempo de perros, *f. temper,* humor de perros. 4. **f. rich,** (jer.) podrido en dinero.

filtrability [,fɪltrə'bɪlətɪ] *s.* filtrabilidad.

filtrable ['fɪltrəbəl] *a.* filtrable.

filtrate [-,treɪt] *v.t., v.i.* filtrar (se). — [-trət, -,treɪt] *s.* (quím.) filtrado.

filtration [fɪl'treɪʃən] *s.* (quím.) filtración, destilación.

filum ['faɪləm] *s.* (*pl.* FILA [-lə]) filum, estructura filamentosa; filamento.

fimbriate ['fɪmbrɪ,eɪt] **fimbriated** [-əd] *a.* (bot., zool.) fimbriado, franjeado. —*v.t.* franjear, ribetear.

fimbrillate [-,leɪt] *a.* (bot.) orillado con fimbrilla.

fin [fɪn] *s.* 1. aleta (de peces, de carrocería, etc.). 2. (aer.) plano de deriva. 3. (mot.) aleta. 4. (mec.) rebaba. 5. (jer.) billete de cinco dólares. 6. (jer.) mano, brazo —*v.t.* (*pret., p.p.* FINNED; *p.pr.* FINNING) proveer de aletas. —*v.i.* aletear, nadar aleteando.

finable ['faɪnəbəl] *a.* que se puede multar.

finagle [fə'neɪgəl] *v.t.* (jer.) lograr, conseguir u obtener por maña. —*v.i.* 1. maquinar, tramar. 2. (naipes) renunciar.

final ['faɪnəl] *a.* final, último; conclusivo, decisivo; terminante. —*s.* 1. (dep.) final. 2. (*gen. pl.*) exámenes finales. 3. (fam.) edición de última hora, última edición (de un periódico).

final cause, (filos.) causa final, fin, propósito.

finale [fə'nælɪ, B -'nɑlɪ] *s.* 1. (mús.) final, último movimiento. 2. (teat.) último acto, última parte. 3. (fig.) el final de un asunto.

finalist ['faɪnələst] *s.* finalista (en un concurso o competencia).

finality [faɪ'nælətɪ, fə-, B faɪ-] *s.* 1. finalidad, inalterabilidad, irrevocabilidad. 2. carácter concluyente (de una decisión, etc.). 3. (filos.) doctrina finalista. 4. **with an air of f.,** de modo concluyente, en tono conclusivo; **to speak (say,** etc.) **with f.,** hablar (decir, etc.) de modo concluyente.

finalization [,faɪnələ'zeɪʃən, B -laɪ-] *s.* finiquito, conclusión.

finalize ['faɪnə,laɪz] *v.t.* finalizar, finiquitar, concluir.

finally [-lɪ] *adv.* finalmente, en conclusión, por último.

finance [fə'næns, 'faɪ,næns, B faɪ'næns] *s.* 1. (*gen. pl.*) fondos, recursos, finanzas (esp. de un gobierno). 2. finanzas, ciencia financiera. —*v.t.* financiar, costear.

finance bill, (pol.) ley de presupuestos.

finance company, sociedad financiera.

financial [fə'nænʃəl, faɪ-] *a.* financiero.

financier [,fɪnən'sɪr, ˌfaɪ,næn-, B -'nænsɪə] *s.* financiero, financista, rentista. —*v.i.* realizar prácticas financieras dudosas.

financing [fə'nænsɪŋ, 'faɪ,næns-, B faɪ'næns-] *s.* financiación, financiamiento.

finback ['fɪn,bæk] *s.* (zool.) rorcual, yubarta, ballena, cachalote.

finch [fɪntʃ] *s.* (orn.) pinzón.

find [faɪnd] *v.t.* (*pret., p.p.* FOUND [faʊnd]; *p.pr.* FINDING) 1. encontrar, hallar. 2. descubrir. 3. hallar, notar. 4. (gen. con *in*) proporcionar; proveer (de), abastecer (de). 5. (der.) pronunciar (veredicto, sentencia); fallar, decidir. 6. **f. fault with,** desaprobar, censurar, criticar; **f. favor with,** caer en gracia a, granjearse la buena voluntad de; **f. it in one's heart to (do),** sentirse capaz de (hacer); **f. its mark,** dar en el blanco (díc. de un proyectil); **f. one's feet,** empezar a caminar (niño); (fig.) empezar a poner en práctica sus aptitudes; **f. one's way to,** encontrar el camino a, (fig.) darse maña para; **f. oneself,** hallarse, encontrarse a sí mismo, descubrir su verdadero talento; **f. out,** descubrir (secreto, la verdad, etc.); averiguar; llegar a saber, enterarse de, darse cuenta de; descubrir, desenmascarar (delito, criminal, etc.); **you must take us as you f. us,** tiene que aceptarnos como somos. —*v.i.* **f. for,** (der.) fallar a favor de. —*s.* hallazgo, descubrimiento.

finder ['faɪndər, B -də] *s.* 1. hallador. 2. (ópt.) buscador (que se acopla a un telescopio). 3. (foto.) visor. 4. (com.) agente de financiamiento.

finder's fee [-dərz-, B -dəz-] (com.) comisión de agente o intermediario.

fin de siècle [,fændə'sjɛkəl] (fr.) del fin del siglo XIX; decadente.

finding ['faɪndɪŋ] *s.* 1. hallazgo, descubrimiento, invención. 2. (*pl.*) herramientas, avíos o materiales que usa un artesano. 3. (der.) informe; veredicto, fallo, decisión.

fine [faɪn] *a.* (FINER; FINEST) 1. fino. 2. bueno (tiempo, clima, etc.). 3. muy bueno, excelente, magnífico; lindo, bello, bonito. 4. (irón.) lindo, bonito. 5. **one f. day, one of these f. days,** un buen día; **that's f.!** ¡de acuerdo! ¡está bien!; **f. and dandy,** ¡estupendo!; **her finest hour,** el momento más sublime de ella. —*adv.* 1. muy bien. 2. finamente. —*v.t.* 1. (gen. con *down*) refinar, purificar, aclarar. 2. afilar, aguzar. —*v.i.* 1. aclararse, purificarse (líquido). 2. (gen. con *away* o *down*) refinarse, adelgazar.

fine, *s.* 1. multa. 2. (der.) traspaso de tierras (por medio del arreglo de un juicio ficticio). 3. **in f.,** en fin, en resumen. —*v.t.* multar.

fine arts, bellas artes.

fine-draw ['faɪn'drɔ] *v.t.* 1. coser (dos trozos de tela) con puntada invisible. 2. estirar al máximo. 3. (fig.) sutilizar (ej., un argumento).

fine-grained [-'greɪnd] *a.* de grano fino; denso, tupido.

finely [-lɪ] *adv.* finamente; primorosamente; sutilmente.
fine mesh, malla fina.
fineness [-nəs] *s.* 1. fineza, pureza. 2. finura, delicadeza, primor. 3. agudeza, sutileza. 4. ley (de un metal precioso).
fine print, letra menuda.
finery ['faɪnərɪ] *s.* 1. adorno, aderezo, atavío, galas. 2. (raro) elegancia, elegancia exagerada. 3. refinería de hierro.
finespun [-'spʌn] *a.* 1. hilado muy finamente. 2. atenuado, sutil, insubstancial, visionario.
finesse [fə'nɛs] *s.* 1. finura, delicadeza, tino, tacto. 2. astucia, sutileza; estratagema, treta, truco. 3. (bridge) finesse. —*v.i.* (bridge) hacer un finesse. —*v.t.* 1. lograr por trucos; trampear, burlar. 2. (bridge) hacer un finesse con (una carta).
fine-tooth comb ['faɪnˌtuθ-] **fine-toothed comb** [-ˌtuθt-] peine de dientes muy finos; **to go over with a f.-t. c.,** escudriñar minuciosamente.
fine tune, poner a punto, ajustar, afinar.
finger ['fɪŋgər, B -gə] *s.* 1. dedo (de la mano). 2. manecilla (del reloj). 3. (el ancho de un) dedo (como medida). 4. (mec.) uña, saliente, linguete, trinquete. 5. **his fingers are all thumbs,** es muy torpe con las manos; **my fingers itch,** estoy ansioso o impaciente; **not to lift** (o **stir**) **a f.,** no mover un dedo; **to burn one's fingers,** (fig.) quemarse los dedos; **to have a f. in the pie,** estar metido en el asunto; **to keep** o **(have) one's fingers crossed,** esperar o anhelar lograr algo; **to lay** (o **put**) **one's f. on,** dar con, acertar; **to let slip through one's fingers,** escapársele a uno de las manos; **to look through one's fingers at,** fingir no ver; **to put one's f. on the sore spot,** poner el dedo en la llaga; **to put the f. on (someone),** (jer.) marcar, señalar (a alguien) para ser asesinado; dar informaciones sobre (un criminal), delatar (a alguien) a la policía; **to twist** (o **turn**) **around one's (little) f.,** meter (a alguien) en el bolsillo, manejar fácilmente (a alguien), dominar (a alguien) con halagos. —*v.t.* 1. tocar con los dedos, manosear, palpar, juguetear con. 2. hurtar, robar, birlar. 3. (mús.) tocar, pulsar, tañer o teclear; digitar (las notas). —*v.i.* 1. (mús.) mover los dedos (al tocar); requerir una (cierta) digitación (instrumento). 2. (gen. con *across, out, through,* etc.) extenderse, alargarse (a través de, por, etc.).
fingerboard [-ˌbɔrd, B -ˌbɔd] *s.* (mús.) 1. diapasón (de los instrumentos de cuerda). 2. teclado (del piano u órgano).
finger bowl, aguamanil (para enjuagarse los dedos en la mesa).
fingerbreadth [-ˌbrɛdθ] *s.* anchura de un dedo.
fingered ['fɪŋgərd, B -gəd] *a.* 1. con dedos; (en palabras compuestas) de dedos, ej., *short-f.,* de dedos cortos. 2. (mús.) digitado (notas).
finger hole, agujerito.
fingering [-gərɪŋ] *s.* 1. manoseo. 2. (mús.) dedeo. 3. (mús.) digitación.
fingerless [-gərləs, B -gəlɪs] *a.* adáctilo, sin dedos.
fingerling [-lɪŋ] *s.* 1. pececillo. 2. cualquier objeto pequeño.
fingernail ['fɪŋgərˌneɪl, B 'fɪŋgəˌ-] *s.* uña (de un dedo de la mano).
fingernail polish, esmalte para las uñas.
finger painting, técnica de pintar con los dedos; cuadro pintado con los dedos.
finger plate, chapa de guarda (en puertas, etc.).
finger post, poste indicador (ej., en cruce de caminos); (fig.) indicación.
fingerprint ['fɪŋgərˌprɪnt, B -gəˌ-] *s.* huella digital, impresión dactilar o dactiloscópica. —*v.t.* tomar las impresiones dactilares a (alguien).
fingerstall [-ˌstɔl] *s.* dedil, protección (para un dedo lastimado).
fingertip [-ˌtɪp] *s.* 1. yema o punta del dedo. 2. dedil. 3. **to have at one's fingertips,** tener a la mano, saber al dedillo.
finger wave, peinado al agua.
finial ['fɪnɪəl, B 'faɪnɪəl] *s.* (arq.) florón.
finical ['fɪnɪkəl] *a.* melindroso, remilgado, dengoso.
finically [-kəlɪ] *adv.* melindrosamente, remilgadamente.
finickiness [-kɪnəs] *s.* melindro, remilgo, dengue.
finicking [-kɪŋ] *var. de* **finicky.**
finicky ['fɪnɪkɪ] *a.* melindroso, remilgado, dengoso.
finish ['fɪnɪʃ] *v.t.* 1. terminar, finalizar, acabar, concluir. 2. perfeccionar; retocar, pulir, dar la última mano a. 3. consumir, agotar; vencer, aplastar (en contienda); arruinar; liquidar, matar. 4. **f. off,** acabar, completar (algo); acabar con, liquidar, ultimar (Am.), matar (a alguien); **f. up,** terminar (de hacer algo, de comer, limpiar, etc.). —*v.i.* 1. terminar(se), acabarse. 2. **f. by** o **in (doing),** acabar por (hacer); **f. with,** romper con, terminar con (alguien); acabar (un trabajo, etc.). —*s.* 1. conclusión, fin, final, término. 2. fin, ruina, muerte. 3. acabado. 4. perfección. 5. perfeccionamiento (de cultura, educación o buenos modales); urbanidad, buenos modales. 6. (dep.) meta, (línea de) llegada. 7. **to be in at the f.,** (fig.) llegar a los finales; estar presente en el momento culminante; **to fight to a** (o **the**) **f.,** luchar hasta lo último, luchar hasta el fin; **to have a rough f.,** estar sin pulir.
finished [-ɪʃt] *a.* 1. concluido, completo, terminado. 2. fabricado. 3. pulido, consumado, perfecto. 4. acabado, liquidado, arruinado.
finisher [-ɪʃər, B -ɪʃə] *s.* 1. acabador (persona). 2. acabadora (máquina).
finishing nail[-ɪʃɪŋ-] alfilerillo, agujuela, puntilla francesa.
finishing post, poste de llegada (en carreras).
finishing school, escuela particular para señoritas, que las prepara para la vida social.
finishing touch, último toque, última mano; **to give the f. t. to,** dar la última mano a, pulir, refinar; (fig.) rematar, concluir.
finite ['faɪˌnaɪt] *a.* 1. finito, limitado, delimitado. 2. (gram.) que denota tiempo, número y persona (verbo). 3. (mat.) finito. —*s.* cosa o ser finito.
finitely [-lɪ] *adv.* finitamente, limitadamente.
finitude ['fɪnəˌtud, B 'faɪnɪˌtjud] *s.* carácter finito; condición finita.
fink [fɪŋk] *s.* 1. (jer.) delator, soplón, denunciador. 2. (jer.) rompehuelga, esquirol; persona detestable.
Finland ['fɪnlənd] *s.* Finlandia.
Finlander [-ləndər, B -də] *s.* finlandés.
Finn [fɪn] *s.* finlandés, finés, natural de Finlandia.
finnan haddie, f. haddock, merluza ahumada.
finnicking, finnicky, *var. de* **finicking,** finicky.
Finnish ['fɪnɪʃ] *a.* finlandés, finés (pueblo, raza o idioma). —*s.* finlandés, finés (idioma).
Finno-Ugric [ˌfɪnoʊ'ugrɪk, B -'jugrɪk] *a., s.* finougrio, grupo lingüístico que comprende el finlandés, húngaro, samoyedo. etc.
fiord, fjord [fjɔrd, fɪ'ɔrd, B fjɔd, fɪ'ɔd] *s.* (geog.) fiordo.
fir [fɜr, B fɜ] *s.* (bot.) abeto; pino, picea, pinsapo.
fire [faɪr, B 'faɪə] *s.* 1. fuego. 2. incendio. 3. brillo (del diamante, etc.). 4. (fig.) fuego, ardor, pasión. 5. fuego, descarga (de armas de fuego); andanada (de palabras, insultos, etc.). 6. (hist.) pena o suplicio del fuego. 7. (poét.) rayo, relámpago, trueno. 8. **between two fires,** entre dos fuegos, entre la espada y la pared; **f.!** (mil.) ¡fuego!; **on f.,** ardiendo; ardiente, ansioso; **out of the frying pan into the f.,** salir de Guatemala para entrar en guatepeor; **there is no smoke without f.,** cuando el río suena, piedras trae; **to catch f.,** encenderse, prenderse; **to catch on f.,** incendiarse; **to go through f. and water,** afrontar todos los peligros; **to lay the f.,** preparar la lumbre; **to light the f.,** prender el fuego; **to miss f.,** fallar (arma de fuego); **to open f.,** (mil.) romper fuego; **to play with f.,** jugar con fuego; **to put out the f.,** apagar el fuego; extinguir el incendio; **to set f. to,** pegar o prender fuego a; **to set on f.,** incendiar; (fig.) excitar; **to set the world on f.,** hacer algo extraordinario, realizar una hazaña; hacerse famoso; **to strike f.,** sacar chispas; **to take f.,** encenderse, inflamarse; **under f.,** bajo fuego, (fig.) bajo presión, fogoneado; **with f. and sword,** a sangre y fuego. —*v.t.* 1. encender. 2. prender fuego a, incendiar. 3. (fig.) inflamar, incitar (pasión), excitar (imaginación), inspirar, estimular (ambición). 4. alumbrar. 5. arrojar, tirar (piedras, etc.), lanzar (torpedo, bombas); (fig.) proferir (insultos). 6. despedir, echar (empleado, servidor, etc.). 7. hacer detonar, explotar. 8. disparar, tirar, descargar (bala, proyectil, arma, etc.). 9. cocer (cerámica, ladrillos, esmalte, etc.). 10. cauterizar. 11. enrojecer. 12. desecar calentando (hojas de té, tabaco, etc.). 13. (raro) ahuyentar con fuego. 14. **f. a salute,** tirar una salva; **f. off,** (fig.) despachar enseguida (carta, tarjeta, etc.); **f. questions at,** bombardear con preguntas; **f. up,** calentar (horno), cargar (el hogar). —*v.i.* 1. encenderse. 2. enrojecerse. 3. irritarse, encolerizarse. 4. hacer fuego, hacer disparo(s), disparar. 5. cuidar del fogón (de un vapor, etc.). 6. **f. away,** disparar sin cesar; **f. away!** (fig.) ¡proceda! ¡diga sin reparos!; **f. on,** hacer un disparo a (alguien o algo); hacer fuego sobre (la multitud, etc.); **f. up,** (fig.) irritarse, encolerizarse.
fire alarm, alarma de incendio.
fire-and-brimstone ['faɪrən'brɪmˌstoʊn, B 'faɪər-stən] *a.* infernal, del fuego del infierno.
firearm [-ˌɑrm, B -ˌɑm] *s.* arma de fuego.
fireback [-ˌbæk, B 'faɪəˌbæk] *s.* 1. pared posterior de un horno u hogar. 2. (orn.) faisán de Sumatra.
fireball [-ˌbɔl] *s.* 1. bola de fuego. 2. bólido, meteoro (en forma de bola de fuego). 3. (mil.) bola (llena de pólvora o de otro combustible). 4. (jer.) tipo eficiente o ambicioso.
fire beetle, (ento.) cocuyo, carbunco.
firebird [-ˌbɜrd, B -ˌbɜd] *s.* (orn.) oriol; oropéndola; tanagra escarlata.
fireboat [-ˌboʊt] *s.* barco bomba (equipado) para extinguir incendios.
fire bomb, (mil.) bomba incendiaria.
firebox [-ˌbɑks, B -ˌbɔks] *s.* caja de fuego (de hornos, calderas de vapor, etc.).
firebrand [-ˌbrænd] *s.* 1. tizón, tea. 2. agitador, revolucionario.
firebreak [-ˌbreɪk] *s.* cortafuego, barrera contra incendios (gen. zona talada para impedir la propagación del fuego).
firebrick [-ˌbrɪk] *s.* ladrillo refractario.
fire brigade, (pr. G.B.) cuerpo de bomberos.
firebug ['faɪrˌbʌg, B 'faɪəˌ-] *s.* 1. (ento.) mariquita. 2. (ento., dial.) cocuyo. 3. (fam.) incendiario, piromaniático.
fire call, toque de incendio.
fire chief, (E.U.) el jefe a cargo de un cuerpo de bomberos.

fire clay, arcilla refractaria (usada para hacer ladrillos y crisoles).
fire company, cuerpo de bomberos.
fire control, 1. conducción del tiro (de artillería). 2. control o extinción de incendios.
fire controller, (mil.) director de fuego (mecanismo).
firecracker [-ˌkrækər, B -ə] *s.* triquitraque, cohete, petardo.
fire-cure [-ˌkjʊr, B -ˌkjʊə] *v.t.* curar (tabaco) al humo (sobre fuego abierto).
fire curtain, cortina de fuego.
firedamp [-ˌdæmp] *s.* (min.) grisú, mofeta inflamable.
fire department, cuerpo de bomberos, servicio de incendios.
firedog [-ˌdɔg] *s.* morillo (del hogar).
fire door, 1. puerta contrafuego, puerta a prueba de incendio. 2. puerta de fuego, puerta del hogar, puerta del horno, boca de carga.
firedrake [-ˌdreɪk] *s.* (mitol.) dragón.
fire drill, 1. ejercicio contra incendios, simulacro. 2. práctica que se da a los ocupantes de un edificio para enseñarles la mejor manera de escapar en caso de incendio.
fired-up ['faɪrdˌʌp, B 'faɪəd-] *a.* (jer.) airado, enojado.
fire-eater ['faɪrˌitər, B 'faɪərˌitə] *s.* 1. pirófago (en circo, ferias, etc.). 2. (fam.) buscapleitos, picapleitos, matamoros, valentón.
fire engine, bomba de incendios, autobomba, carrobomba (Chile).
fire escape, escalera de escape de incendios, escalera de salvamento o de emergencia.
fire extinguisher, extinguidor de incendios, matafuego, extintor, apagaincendios, apagallamas.
fire fighter, (fam.) bombero.
firefly ['faɪrˌflaɪ, B 'faɪəˌ-] *s.* (ento.) luciérnaga.
fireguard [-ˌgɑrd, B -ˌgɑd] *s.* 1. pantalla (de chimenea), guardafuego. 2. cortafuego, zona talada para impedir la propagación del fuego. 3. guardián contra incendios.
fire hose, manguera para incendios.
firehouse [-ˌhaʊs] *s.* estación de bomberos.
fire hydrant, boca de incendio, hidrante (Amer.).
fire insurance, seguro contra incendio.
fire irons, 1. utensilios para el hogar (como badil, tenazas, atizador, etc.). 2. (*gen. pl.*) morillos.
firelight [-ˌlaɪt] *s.* lumbre, luz del hogar (esp. de chimenea).
fire lily, (bot.) azucena anteada.
firelock [-ˌlɑk, B -ˌlɔk] *s.* 1. llave de fusil (de pedernal). 2. trabuco de pedernal o de chispa.
fireman [-mən] *s. 1. bombero. 2. fogonero, paleador. 3. (E.U.) marino (que presta servicios en la sala de máquinas). 4. (béisbol) lanzador de reserva.*
fire opal , (mi.) ópalo de fuego, girasol.
fire pan , brasero.
fire pink , (bot.) especie de pegamoscas.
fireplace ['faɪrˌpleɪs, B 'faɪəˌ-] *s.* chimenea francesa; hogar.
fireplug [-ˌplʌg] *s.* boca de incendio, poste de incendios, boca toma-agua, hidrante (Amer.).
firepower [ˌpaʊər, B -ˌpaʊə] *s.* (mil.) potencia de fuego.
fireproof ['faɪrˌpruf, B 'faɪəˌ-] *a.* a prueba de fuego, incombustible (material, substancia, etc.); a prueba de incendio, contrafuego, contra incendios (puerta, instalación, etc.); refractario (arcilla, ladrillo, etc.). —*v.t.* hacer incombustible; revestir con material incombustible.
fire-resistive [-rɪ'zɪstɪv] *a.* resistente al fuego.
fire risk , riesgo, peligro o posibilidad de incendios.
fire sale , (com.) liquidación (de mercancías dañadas) por incendio.
fire screen , pantalla de chimenea.
fire ship, (mil.) brulote, nave infernal.
fireside [-ˌsaɪd] *s.* 1. sitio junto al fuego o chimenea. 2. (fig.) hogar, casa. —*a.* íntimo, informal.
fire station, estación de bomberos.
firestone [-ˌstoʊn] *s.* 1. (min.) pirita de hierro; pedernal. 2. piedra refractaria.
fire support, (mil.) apoyo de artillería.
fire tower, torre con atalaya para detectar incendios.
firetrap ['faɪrˌtræp, B 'faɪəˌ-] *s.* edificio sin medios adecuados de escape en caso de incendio.
fire wall, cortafuego, muro cortafuego, muro refractario, muro a prueba de incendio, parallamas.
firewarden [-ˌwɔrdən, B -ˌwɔdən] *s.* oficial o guardia encargado de la prevención de incendios.
firewater [-ˌwɔtər, -ˌwɑt-, B -ˌwɔtə] *s.* (hum.) aguardiente, cualquier licor fuerte.
fireweed [-ˌwid] *s.* (bot.) chamico, higuera loca.
firewood [-ˌwʊd] *s.* 1. leña. 2. (bot.) palo hacha.
firework [-ˌwɜrk, B -ˌwɜk] *s.* 1. (*gen. pl.*) fuegos artificiales. 2. (fig.) (*pl.*) excitación. 3. **there will be fireworks,** habrá Montescos y Capuletos, habrá líos.
fire worship, adoración del fuego.
firing ['faɪrɪŋ, B 'faɪər-] *s.* 1. descarga, disparo (de armas); descarga, detonación (de minas, bombas, etc.). 2. carga del hogar, alimentación del fuego. 3. despedida (de un empleado, etc.). 4. combustible, leña. 5. (vet.) cauterio, cauterización. 6. (cerám.) cocción. 7. (aut.) encendido.
firing angle, (mil.) ángulo de dirección (del fuego).
firing chamber, (arm.) recámara.
firing chart, (mil.) plano director artillero.
firing line, 1. (mil.) línea de fuego. 2. frente, puesto delantero o de vanguardia (en cualquier actividad).
firing mechanism, (arm.) mecanismo de disparo.
firing order, (mot., aut.) orden del encendido.
firing pin, percutor, percusor, aguja de percusión (de un arma de fuego).
firing squad, 1. piquete de salvas. 2. pelotón de fusilamiento, piquete de ejecución.
firkin ['fɜrkən, B 'fɜkɪn] *s.* 1. cuñete, barrilito (de madera). 2. (como medida de capacidad) cuarta parte de un barril.
firm [fɜrm, B fɜm] *a.* 1. firme, fuerte, fijo, estable. 2. firme, sólido. 3. firme, constante, decidido. 4. (com.) firme (mercado, valores, etc.). —*adv.* firmemente; **to hold** (o **stand**) **f.,** mantenerse firme, no ceder; **to hold f. to,** agarrar bien, no soltar; (fig.) mantenerse firme en (opinión, convicción, etc.). —*v.t.* 1. poner firme, solidificar. 2. afianzar, afirmar, asegurar. 3. (gen. con *up*) fortalecer (ánimo, etc.). 4. perfeccionar, finiquitar (un contrato, etc.). —*v.i.* 1. ponerse firme, solidificarse, adquirir solidez; endurecerse. 2. (com.) (gen. con *up*) afirmarse (mercado, precios, etc.). —*s.* 1. firma, casa, empresa (comercial). 2. razón social.
firmament ['fɜrməmənt, B 'fɜmə-] *s.* firmamento, bóveda celeste, cielo.
firmamental [-fɜrmə'mentəl, B ˌfɜmə-] *a.* del firmamento.
firman ['fɜrmən, fər'mɑn, B ˌfɜ'mɑn] *s.* (*pl.* FIRMANS) firmán, decreto real (en el Oriente).
firmer chisel [ˌfɜrmər-, B 'fɜmə-] escoplo-punzón, formón.
firmly ['fɜrmlɪ, B 'fɜm-] *adv.* firmemente, fijamente.
firmness [-nəs] *s.* 1. firmeza, consistencia, estabilidad, solidez. 2. firmeza, determinación, decisión.
firn [fɪrn, B fɪən] *s.* nieve granular.
firry ['fɜrɪ] *a.* hecho de abeto; abundante en abetos.
first [fɜrst, B fɜst] *a.* 1. primero, primario. 2. primitivo, prístino; original, delantero, temprano. 3. excelente, principal, sobresaliente. 4. menor, mínimo, ej., *I haven't the f. idea,* no tengo la menor idea. 5. (astr.) de primera magnitud (estrella). 6. **at first sight,** a primera vista; **f. thing,** lo primero, antes de todo; **in the f. place,** en primer lugar, en primer término; **not to know the f. thing about (something),** no saber absolutamente nada de (algo); **the f. (three),** los primeros (tres). —*adv.* 1. primero, primeramente, en primer lugar. 2. antes, más bien, primero. 3. **f. and foremost,** antes que nada; **f. and last,** desde todos los puntos de vista; **f. of all,** ante todo, primero que nada; **f. or last,** tarde o temprano, algún día; **head f.,** de cabeza. —*s.* 1. (con *the*) el primero, el principal. 2. (gen. con *the*) la primera cosa, la primera noticia, ej., *the f. he knew, he was out of a job,* la primera cosa que supo fue que había perdido el empleo. 3. (*pl.*) (com.) artículos de primera calidad. 4. primera edición (de un libro). 5. nota sobresaliente (en examen), ej., *he took a f. in Greek,* obtuvo nota sobresaliente en griego. 6. (mús.) primera voz (de dueto, trío, etc.); primer violín, primera viola, etc. (en orquesta). 7. (dep.) primer puesto (en una carrera). 8. (esgr.) primera. 9. **at f.,** al principio; **from f. to last,** de principio a fin, durante todo el tiempo; **from the f.,** desde el principio; **that's the f. I've heard about it,** recién me entero, es la primera noticia que tengo; **to be the f. to (congratulate, lament,** etc.), ser el primero (de los primeros) en (felicitar, lamentar, etc.).
first aid, primeros auxilios, primera cura o ayuda.
first-aid ['fɜrstˌeɪd, B 'fɜst-] *a.* de primeros auxilios, de primera ayuda.
first-aid kit, botiquín.
first-aid station, casa de socorro, puesto de primera intención.
first base, 1. (béisbol) primera base. 2. **not to get to f. b.,** no tener ningún éxito, no llegar a nada.
first blood, (fig.) ventaja inicial.
first-born [-'bɔrn, B -ˌbɔn] *a., s.* primogénito.
first class, primera clase (en barcos, trenes, etc.).
first-class [-'klæs, B -'klɑs] *a.* de primera clase, excelente, superior.
first cousin, primo hermano; **f. c. once removed,** primo hermano del padre de uno.
first day, 1. (filat.) primer día, día de emisión (de un sello postal). 2. (relig.) domingo.
first-day cover [-ˌdeɪ-] (filat.) sobre del primer día de emisión.
first dog watch, (mar.) primer cuartillo.
first floor, (E.U.) planta baja, primer piso (Amer.), piso bajo (Esp.); (G.B.) segundo piso (Amer.), piso principal (Esp.).
first fruits, primicias, primeros frutos.
firsthand ['fɜrst'hænd, B 'fɜst-] *a.* de primera mano, directo, sin intermediario, de fuentes originales; **at. f.,** directamente. —*adv.* directamente (de la fuente original).
first lady, (E.U.) primera dama (esposa del presidente de la república).
first lieutenant, (mil., mar.) teniente primero; teniente.

firstling ['fɜrstlɪŋ, B 'fɜst-] *s.* 1. primicia, primer producto; primer fruto. 2. primogénito.
firstly [-lɪ] *adv.* primeramente, en primer lugar, primero.
first mate, (mar.) segundo oficial.
first mortgage, primera hipoteca.
first-mortgage [-'mɔrgɪdʒ, B -'mɔgɪdʒ] *a.* de primera hipoteca.
first name, nombre de pila.
first night, (teat.) noche de estreno; estreno.
first-nighter [-naɪtər] *s.* persona que asiste habitualmente a los estrenos o funciones de gala (de teatro, ópera, etc.).
first officer, (mar.) primer piloto.
first papers, (E.U.) documentos preliminares de nacionalización (en que un inmigrante declara su intención de tomar carta de ciudadanía).
first person, (gram.) primera persona.
first quarter, cuarto creciente (de la luna); (dep.) primer período.
first-rate ['fɜrst'reɪt, B 'fɜst-] *a.* de primera clase, de primer orden; (fam.) excelente, magnífico, buenísimo, muy bueno. *—adv.* (fam.) muy bien.
first-run movie[-ˌrʌn] *s.* película de estreno.
first sergeant, (mil.) sargento.
first-string [-'strɪŋ] *a.* 1. regular, ordinario, normal (a diferencia de un substituto). 2. de primera clase, de primer orden; excelente.
first watch, (mar.) guardia de prima.
first water, 1. la mejor calidad, el más alto grado de pureza (díc. de piedras preciosas, esp. diamantes y perlas). 2. (fig.) primera clase, grado sumo.
firth [fɜrθ, B fɜθ] *s.* brazo de mar, estuario.
fisc [fɪsk] *s.* fisco, erario, hacienda pública.
fiscal ['fɪskəl] *a.* fiscal, perteneciente al fisco, rentístico. *—s.* (der.) fiscal.
fiscal year, año fiscal.
fish [fɪʃ] *s.* (*gen. pl.* FISH; para referirse a distintas especies: FISHES) 1. pez. 2. (carne de) pescado. 3. **F.,** Piscis, constelación y signo del zodíaco. 4. (f.c.) eclisa, mordaza. 5. (fam.) tipo tonto, bobo. 6. (mar.) pescante de ancla; jimelga, gemelo. 7. (mec.) refuerzo. 8. **an odd f.,** (fam.) un tipo raro; **drunk as a f.,** borracho como una cuba; **f. out of water,** gallina en corral ajeno, como pez fuera del agua; **neither f. nor fowl,** ni chicha ni limonada; **pretty kettle of f.,** bonito lio; **to drink like a f.,** beber con exceso; **to have other f. to fry,** tener cosas más importantes que hacer. *—v.i.* 1. pescar. 2. (fig.) (gen. con *for*) pescar (cumplidos, etc.). 3. **f. in troubled waters,** pescar en río revuelto. *—v.t.* pescar, coger; **f. out,** agotar los peces en (un lago, etc.); sacar (algo, ej., del bolsillo); sonsacar (secreto, opinión, etc.); **f. the anchor,** (mar.) enjimelgar el ancla.
fishable ['fɪʃəbəl] *a.* en que se puede pescar, en que se permite la pesca (río, aguas).
fish and chips, pescado con papas fritas.
fish bait, cebo para pescar, carnada.
fish ball, f. cake, albóndiga o fritura de pescado (gen. bacalao).
fish-bellied [-ˌbɛlid] *a.* en forma de pescado (díc. esp. de los rieles).
fishbolt [-ˌboʊlt] *s.* (f.c.) perno de eclisa.
fishbone [-ˌboʊn] *s.* espina de pescado.
fishbowl [-ˌboʊl] *s.* 1. pecera. 2. (fig.) lugar visible.
fish car, (f.c.) furgón para llevar pescado; vivero.
fish carver, cuchillo especial para cortar y servir pescados.
fish culture, piscicultura; crianza industrial de peces.
fish day, (relig.) día de vigilia.
fisher ['fɪʃər, B -ə] *s.* 1. pescador. 2. barco pesquero. 3. (zool.) pekán, marta de América; la piel de este animal.
fisherman [-mən] *s.* 1. pescador. 2. barco pesquero.
fisherman's bend [-mənz-] nudo utilizado para asegurar una argolla o un gancho.
fisherman's knot, nudo utilizado para unir dos cuerdas.
fishery ['fɪʃərɪ] *s.* 1. pesca, pesquería. 2. pesquera, zona pesquera, pesquería. 3. (der.) derecho de pesca.
fish-eye [-ˌaɪ] *a.* 1. suspicaz, receloso (mirada. etc.). 2. de 180 grados (lente, objetivo fotográfico).
fish flour, harina de pescado.
fishgig [-ˌgɪg] *s.* tridente para pescar, fisga.
fish glue, colapez, cola de pescado, colapiscis, colapiz (Amer.).
fish hatchery, criadero, vivero de peces.
fish hawk, (orn.) águila osífraga, quebrantahuesos, halieto, pigargo (t. **osprey**).
fishhook [-ˌhʊk] *s.* anzuelo, hamo, garfio.
fishing ['fɪʃɪŋ] *s.* 1. pesca. 2. pesquera, pesquería, zona pesquera.
fishing bank, f. ground, lugar en donde la pesca es abundante.
fishing barge, gánguil.
fishing boat, barca pesquera.
fishing expedition, (der.) interrogación preliminar del testigo para descubrir pruebas comprometedoras.
fishing fly, mosca artificial (para carnada).
fishing line, cuerda o hilo de pescar, pita.
fishing net, red para pescar.
fishing rod, caña o vara de pescar.
fishing tackle, avíos, aparejos de pesca.
fish joint, (f.c.) junta de eclisa, junta de mordaza.
fish kettle, caldera grande para cocinar el pescado entero.
fishlike ['fɪʃˌlaɪk] *a.* pisciforme.
fishline [-ˌlaɪn] *s.* sedal, hilo de pescar.
fish market, pescadería.
fish meal, harina de pescado (substancia alimenticia utilizada como forraje).
fishmonger [-ˌmʌŋgər, -ˌmɑŋ-, B -ˌmʌŋgə] *s.* 1. (pr. G.B.) pescadero. 2. (fam.) persona inculta, soez.
fish oil, aceite de pescado (esp. el de bacalao, foca, ballena o tiburón).
fishplate [-ˌpleɪt] *s.* (f.c.) eclisa, mordaza, plancha de unión de dos rieles.
fish pole, caña de pescar.
fishpond ['fɪʃˌpɑnd, B -ˌpɔnd] *s.* 1. estanque para peces, piscina. 2. (hum.) (el) mar.
fishpound [-ˌpaʊnd] *s.* (E.U.) cañal, red tendida entre palos para atrapar peces.
fish scale, escama.
fishskin [-ˌskɪn] *s.* piel de pescado, piel de lija.
fish-spear [-ˌspɪr, B -ˌspɪə] *s.* arpón, dardo.
fish stick, (cocina) lasca de pescado empanizado.
fish story, (fam.) fábula, cuento increíble.
fishtail [-ˌteɪl] *a.* de forma o movimiento similar a la cola de los peces. *—v.i.* (fam., aer.) colear, mecer (un avión) la cola (para reducir la velocidad al aterrizar); (aut.) colear.
fishtail cutter, fresa cola de pescado.
fish torpedo, torpedo submarino pisciforme.
fish trap, nasa, garlito.
fishwife [-ˌwaɪf] *s.* (*pl.* FISHWIVES) 1. pescadera. 2. (fig.) verdulera, rabanera; mujer gritona o soez.
fish wire, (elec.) alambre en tubo.
fishworm [-ˌwɜrm, B -ˌwɜm] *s.* gusano usado como carnada.
fishy ['fɪʃɪ] *a.* (FISHIER; FISHIEST) 1. a pescado (sabor, olor). 2. (fam.) dudoso, improbable, inverosímil. 3. sin brillo (díc. de los ojos); sin viso, mate (díc. de las joyas). 4. **there's something f. here,** aquí hay gato encerrado.
fissate ['fɪsˌeɪt] *a.* agrietado, hendido.
fissile ['fɪsəl, B -ˌaɪl] *a.* fósil, hendible; (fís.) fisionable.
fission ['fɪʃən] *s.* (biol.) fisión, escisión (del cuerpo, células, etc.); (fís., quím.) fisión (de un núcleo atómico). *—v.t., v.i.* (fís.) fisionar(se) (el átomo).
fissionable [-əbəl] *a.* fisionable. *—s.* materia fisionable.
fission bomb, bomba de fisión nuclear.
fissiparism [fɪ'sɪpəˌrɪzəm] **fissiparity** [ˌfɪsɪ'pærətɪ] (biol.) reproducción por división, fisiparidad.
fissiparous [-rəs] *a.* (biol., bot.) fisíparo.
fissiparousness [-nəs] *s.* (biol., bot.) fisiparidad.
fissiped ['fɪsəˌpɛd] *a., s.* (zool.) fisípedo.
Fissipedia [ˌfɪsə'pidɪə] *s. pl.* (zool.) fisípedos.
fissirostral [ˌfɪsə'rɑstrəl, B -'rɔs-] *a.* (orn.) fisirrostro (grupo de aves que tienen el pico profundamente hendido).
fissirostres [-ˌtriz] *s. pl.* (orn.) fisirrostros.
fissure ['fɪʃər, B -ə] *s.* 1. fisura, grieta, rajadura, hendidura. 2. (anat.) fisura, cisura. *—v.t., v.i.* hender(se), agrietar (se), cuartear(se).
fist [fɪst] *s.* 1. puño. 2. (hum.) mano. 3. (impr.) llamada, manecilla, mano (☞). 4. **to shake one's f. at,** amenazar con (el puño); **to strike with the f.,** dar puñetazos; **with clenched fists,** con los puños cerrados. *—v.t.* 1. apretar, cerrar (el puño). 2. apuñar, asir. 3. (G.B.) apuñear, dar puñetazos a. 4. (mar.) manejar (velas, remos, etc.).
fistic ['fɪstɪk] *a.* 1. (fam.) a puño cerrado, a puñetazos. 2. pugilístico, relativo al boxeo.
fisticuff [-tɪˌkʌf] *s.* 1. puñada, puñetazo, golpazo, trompada (Amer.). 2. pelea a puñetazos, pugilato, boxeo, trompeadura (Amer.).
fisticuffer [-ər, B -ə] *s.* púgil, pugilista, boxeador.
fistula ['fɪstʃələ, B 'fɪstjʊ-] *s.* (*pl.* FISTULAS O FISTULAE [-ˌli]) (med., vet.) fístula.
fistular [-lər, B -lə] *a.* (med., vet.) fistular.
fistulous [-ləs] *a.* 1. (med., vet.) fistuloso. 2. hueco; tubular.
fit [fɪt] *s.* 1. ataque, acceso (de histerismo, tos, epilepsia, etc.); paroxismo. 2. arranque (de cólera, energía, devoción, etc.), ataque (de risa). 3. humor, capricho. 4. **by fits and starts,** a tontas y a locas, a empujones; **to give one a f.,** dar rabia a uno; **to go off into fits of laughter,** desternillarse de risa; **to have a f.,** tener un arranque de cólera; **to throw a fit,** patalear, rabiar.
fit, *a.* (FITTER; FITTEST) 1. apto, idóneo, capaz. 2. adecuado, apropiado, propio, digno, ej., *a dinner f. for a king,* una comida digna de un rey. 3. conveniente, a propósito. 4. correcto, justo. 5. preparado, listo, dispuesto. 6. en buen estado físico, (díc. de un atleta, caballo de carrera, etc.). 7. sano, de buena salud. 8. **f. as a fiddle,** sano como una manzana; **f. for, f. to,** bueno para; ej., *water f. to drink,* agua potable; **(is) f. to be tied,** (está) fuera de sí; (está) loco de atar; **to be f. for,** estar capacitado para; **to see** (o **think**) **f. to (do),** tener a bien (hacer). *—v.t.* (*pret., p.p.* FITTED; *p.pr.* FITTING) 1. convenir a, venir bien a. 2. sentar bien a; quedar o caer (bien o mal) a. 3. ser apto para. 4. corresponder a, cuadrar con (descripción, etc.). 5. encajar en, servir para, ajustarse a. 6. acomodar, colocar. 7. ajustar,

adaptar, amoldar, adecuar; entallar (vestido). 8. equipar, aviar, proveer. 9. (con *for* o *to*) habilitar, preparar, aprestar (para). 10. tomar las medidas a, ej., *she was fitted for a new dress,* se le tomaron las medidas para un vestido nuevo. 11. (bridge) complementar (mano de pareja). 12. **f. on,** probar (vestido, etc.); **f. out** (o **up**), equipar (completamente), pertrechar. —*v.i.* 1. ajustarse, amoldarse, adaptarse. 2. sentar o caer (bien o mal), entallar (vestido). 3. encajar. 4. corresponder. 5. (bridge) completarse (manos de las parejas). 6. **f. in** (o **into**), encajar en, caber en; **f. in with,** concordar, estar en armonía con. —*s.* 1. ajuste, encaje. 2. talle (de vestido). 3. concordancia. 4. (ant.) canto, parte o estrofa de un poema o canción.

fitch [fɪtʃ] **fitchet** ['fɪtʃət] **fitchew** [-u] *s.* (zool.) mofeta, turón.

fitful ['fɪtfəl] *a.* espasmódico, intermitente, irregular; incierto, vacilante; caprichoso.

fitfully [-fəlɪ] *adv.* por intervalos, irregularmente; caprichosamente.

fitfulness ['fəlnəs] *s.* irregularidad, intermitencia.

fitly [-lɪ] *adv.* adecuadamente, propiamente, convenientemente, aptamente.

fitment [-mənt] *s.* (pr. G.B.) 1. equipo, material. 2. (*pl.*) avíos, guarniciones, accesorios.

fitness [-nəs] *s.* 1. aptitud, idoneidad. 2. propiedad; conveniencia, corrección. 3. buena salud. 4. **physical f.,** aptitud física, buenas condiciones físicas.

fitted ['fɪtəd] *a.* hecho a medida, entallado; **to be f. for** (*a job or profession*) ser apto para o tener talento para (*un trabajo o una profesión.*).

fitter ['fɪtər, B -ə] *s.* 1. ajustador. 2. (mec.) ajustador, armador, montador. 3. proveedor. 4. (cost.) probador.

fitting [-ɪŋ] *s.* 1. ajuste, encaje. 2. prueba (de una prenda de vestir). 3. (*pl.*) avíos, guarniciones, accesorios; herrajes; muebles. —*a.* propio, apropiado, digno, correcto, conveniente.

fittingly [-lɪ] *adv.* propiamente, apropiadamente.

fittingness [-nəs] *s.* propiedad, carácter apropiado o razonable.

five [faɪv] *s.* 1. cinco. 2. (dep.) quinteto (de jugadores, esp. de baloncesto). 3. (billete de) cinco dólares. 4. (*pl.*) juego de pelota inglés. 5. **bunch of fives,** mano favorable en juego de naipes. —*a.* cinco.

five-and-ten-cent store [ˌfaɪvən'tɛn'sɛnt-] *s.* almacén de artículos variados (en el que originalmente la mercancía costaba cinco o diez centavos de dólar).

five-day week [-ˌdəɪ-] semana de cinco días laborables.

five-eight time ['faɪv'eɪt-] (mús.) compás de cinco por ocho.

five-finger [-ˌfɪŋgər, B -gə] *s.* 1. (bot.) cincoenrama, quinquefolio; prímula; trébol; enredadera de Virginia. 2. (zool.) estrella de mar (de cinco puntas).

fivefold [-ˌfoʊld] *a.* quíntuplo.

five hundred, 1. quinientos. 2. cierto juego de naipes.

five hundredth, quingentésimo.

fiver ['faɪvər, B -və] *s.* (jer.) billete de cinco dólares o libras.

five-spot ['faɪvˌspɑt, B -ˌspɔt] *s.* (jer.) 1. billete de cinco dólares o libras. 2. naipe con cinco puntos. 3. bola de billar marcada con el número cinco.

five-year [-'jɪr, B -'jɜ] *a.* quinquenal.

five-year plan, (econ.) plan quinquenal (esp. en Rusia).

fix [fɪks] *v.t.* 1. fijar, asegurar, asentar. 2. fijar, establecer. 3. fijar, decidir, determinar. 4. preparar (bebida, alimento, etc.). 5. arreglar, reparar, componer. 6. resolver, solucionar. 7. (fam.) sobornar; arreglar (resultado de una carrera, elecciones, etc.). 8. desquitarse con, ajustar las cuentas a. 9. (quím.) fijar (sustancia volátil o gaseosa). 10. (foto.) fijar (negativo, etc.). 11. (mil.) calar, armar (bayoneta). 12. castrar (a un animal doméstico). 13. **f. on** o **upon,** fijar, clavar (ojos, mirada, atención; etc.) en; fijar, establecer (culpa, etc.) de; **f. oneself,** establecerse, radicarse; **f. up,** reparar, componer; curar; organizar, hacer arreglos para; arreglar; resolver; **f. (someone) up,** (jer.) proveer (a alguien) de lo necesario; conseguirle una cita a alguien; **f. (someone) up with (something),** proporcionar, dar (algo a alguien). —*v.i.* 1. fijarse, estabilizarse, afirmarse. 2. **f. on** o **upon,** fijarse en; convenir en; decidirse por, elegir; **f. oneself up,** arreglarse, vestirse, emperifollarse. —*s.* 1. (fam.) apuro, aprieto, dificultad, dilema. 2. (rad.) determinación de posición. 3. (mar., aer.) punto de posición. 4. (jer.) arreglo, soborno, cohecho. 5. (jer.) inyección de narcótico. 6. **in a tight** (o **bad**) **f.,** en un aprieto, en apuros.

fixable ['fɪksəbəl] *a.* fijable.

fixate [-ˌseɪt] *v.t.* 1. estancar, entorpecer, volver estático. 2. (psic.) fijar, dirigir (libido). —*v.i.* 1. (gen. con *on* o *upon*) fijarse en, fijar la mirada en. 2. estancarse.

fixation [fɪk'seɪʃən] *s.* 1. (psic.) fijación, obsesión. 2. (quím., foto.) fijación.

fixative ['fɪksətɪv] *a.* fijador. —*s.* fijativo, fijador.

fixed [fɪkst] *p.p. de* **fix.** —*a.* 1. fijo, firme, asegurado, permanente, arraigado, estable. 2. (quím.) fijo. 3. (fam.) bien provisto esp. de dinero. 4. (jer.) con el resultado arreglado deshonestamente de antemano. 5. **with f. bayonets,** con la bayoneta calada.

fixed acid, (quím.) ácido fijo.

fixed charge, (com.) gasto fijo.

fixed disk, (comput.) disco fijo.

fixed idea, (psic.) idea fija; obsesión.

fixed interest, a interés fijo.

fixedly ['fɪksədlɪ] *adv.* fijamente, ciertamente, firmemente.

fixedness [-nəs] *s.* firmeza, estabilidad, inmovilidad, inmutabilidad, constancia.

fixed star, (astr.) estrella fija.

fixer [-sər, B -sə] *s.* 1. (quím., foto.) fijador, fijativo. 2. componedor de dificultades, arbitrador, mediador. 3. cohechador, sobornador. 4. (jer.) vendedor ilegal de drogas.

fixing [-sɪŋ] *s.* 1. fijación. 2. (*pl.*) (fam.) accesorios, guarniciones, adornos.

fixing bath, (foto.) baño de fijado.

fixity [-sətɪ] *s.* 1. fijeza, firmeza; estabilidad. 2. accesorio.

fixture ['fɪkstʃər, B -tʃə] *s.* 1. fijación, afirmación. 2. accesorio, aditamento, pertenencia. 3. artefacto, dispositivo. 4. instalación fija; elemento permanente. 5. (dep.) fecha de competencia, competencia, encuentro (programado). 6. (fam.) persona o cosa que ha estado en un sitio por largo tiempo.

fixture hanger, (elec.) colgador de artefactos.

fizgig ['fɪzˌgɪg] *s.* 1. especie de fuego artificial, cohetecillo, buscapiés, carretilla, buscapique (Amer.). 2. trompo, peón, peonza. 3. (ant.) moza callejera, coqueta.

fizz [fɪz] *v.i.* hacer un ruido sibilante; chisporrotear; estar en efervescencia (líquido). —*s.* 1. ruido sibilante; chisporroteo. 2. gaseosa, champaña, bebida gaseosa.

fizzle ['fɪzəl] *v.i.* 1. hacer un ruido sibilante, chisporrotear. 2. (fam.) (gen. con *out*) quedar mal, fracasar; (fig.) desinflarse. —*s.* (fam.) fiasco, fracaso.

fjeld [fjɛl] *s.* (geog.) planicie desolada (en las tierras altas de Escandinavia).

fjord [fjɔrd, B fjɔd] *s.* (geog.) fiord, fiordo.

Fla. *abrev. de* **Florida,** Florida (E.U.).

flab [flæb] *s.* (fam.) pellejo, carne flácida y colgante.

flabbergast ['flæbərˌgæst, B -əˌgɑst] *v.t.* dejar sin habla, pasmar, aturullar, asombrar.

flabbily ['flæbəlɪ] *adv.* flojamente, blandamente, sin firmeza.

flabbiness [-ɪnəs] *s.* flojedad, blandura, flaqueza.

flabby [-ɪ] *a.* 1. flojo, lacio, fláccido, flácido, fofo, blando. 2. (fig.) débil, enfermizo, enclenque.

flabellate [flə'bɛlət] **flabelliform** [-əˌfɔrm, B -ˌfɔm] *a.* flabelado, flabeliforme, en forma de abanico.

flabellum [-əm] *s.* (*pl.* FLABELIA [-ə]) 1. (anat.) flabelo. 2. (relig.) flabelo (abanico grande con mango largo llevado delante del Papa en las grandes ceremonias).

flaccid ['flæksəd, 'flæsəd, B 'flæk-] *a.* fláccido, flácido, flaco, flojo, blando.

flaccidity [flæk'sɪdətɪ, flæ'sɪd-, B flæk-] *s.* flaccidez, flacidez, flojedad, flaqueza.

flack [flæk] *s.* (jer.) agente de publicidad. —*v.i.* servir de agente de publicidad.

flacon ['flækən] *s.* (fr.) frasco pequeño; perfumador de bolsillo.

flag [flæg] *s.* 1. bandera, pabellón, estandarte. 2. buque insignia, capitana. 3. almirante al mando. 4. (*pl.*) plumas largas (de la parte baja de las patas de ciertos halcones, lechuzas, etc.); plumas secundarias del ala (de las aves). 5. cola, rabo (de ciertos perros perdigueros y sabuesos); cola de venado. 6. rabo (de notas musicales). 7. (impr.) letra invertida. 8. **to dip the f.,** bajar la bandera momentáneamente en señal de saludo, respeto o bienvenida; **to hoist one's f.,** levantar o alzar bandera(s), tomar el mando; **to strike one's f.,** arriar (la) bandera (para rendirse); batir banderas (en saludo); (fig.) dejar o ceder el mando. —*v.t.* (*pret., p.p.* FLAGGED; *p.pr.* FLAGGING) 1. embanderar. 2. hacer señales con una bandera a; (t. con *down*) hacer señal de parada a (tren o taxi). 3. señalar (mensaje) con banderas.

flag *s.* (bot.) 1. lirio cárdeno. 2. espadaña, gladiolo. 3. laja, lancha, lastra, losa. —*v.t.* (*pret., p.p.* FLAGGED; *p.pr.* FLAGGING) pavimentar con lajas, enlosar. —*v.i.* 1. colgar, pender. 2. flaquear, amilanarse, debilitarse, languidecer. 3. decaer, aflojar (interés, atención, etc.).

flag captain, (mar.) capitán de bandera.

Flag Day, 1. (E.U.) día de la bandera, junio 14, aniversario de la ratificación del emblema norteamericano por el Congreso. 2. (G.B.) día en que se recaudan fondos para fines benéficos dándose banderitas a los contribuyentes.

flagellant ['flædʒələnt, flə'dʒɛ-] *s.* flagelante. —*a.* 1. fustigante (discurso, etc.). 2. flagelante, flagelador. 3. (relig.) disciplinante, azotado.

flagellantism [-lənˌtɪzəm] *s.* flagelantismo.

flagellate ['flædʒəˌleɪt] *v.t.* flagelar, azotar.

flagellate [-lət, B -ˌleɪt] **flagellated** [-ˌleɪtəd] *a.* (bot., biol.) flagelado.

flagellation [ˌflædʒə'leɪʃən] *s.* flagelación, azotamiento.

flagellator ['flædʒəˌleɪtər, B -tə] *s.* flagelador, azotador.

flagelliform [flə'dʒɛləˌfɔrm B -ˌfɔm] *a.* (bot., biol.) flageliforme.

flagellum [-əm] *s.* (*pl.* FLAGELLUMS O FLAGELLA [-ə]) (biol.) flagelo.

flageolet [ˌflædʒəˈlɛt] *s.* (mús.) caramillo, chirimía, dulzaina.
flagging [ˈflægɪŋ] *s.* enlosado. —*a.* lánguido, flojo, débil.
flaggingly [-lɪ] *adv.* lánguidamente, débilmente.
flagitious [fləˈdʒɪʃəs] *a.* flagicioso, facineroso, infame, abominable, atroz.
flagitiousness [-nəs] *s.* maldad, infamia, perversidad, vileza, felonía.
flagman [ˈflægmən] *s.* 1. abanderado. 2. (f.c.) guardavía, guardafrenos.
flag officer, (mar.) oficial general de la marina (en la armada de E.U. tiene el rango de comodoro, en la de G.B. el de almirante, vicealmirante o contralmirante).
flag of Spain (the), el rojo y gualda (de la nación).
flag of truce, bandera de tregua, bandera blanca.
flagon [ˈflægən] *s.* 1. jarro; botella grande (de vino), frasco. 2. la cantidad de líquido que contiene dicho recipiente.
flagpole [ˈflægˌpoʊl] *s.* asta o mástil de bandera.
flagrancy [ˈfleɪgrənsɪ] **flagrance** [-grəns] *s.* enormidad, notoriedad.
flagrant [-grənt] *a.* 1. notorio, descarado, impudente, enorme. 2. (ant.) ardiente, flagrante, encendido.
flagrant crime, flagrante delicto [fləˈgræntɪdəˈlɪktoʊˌ] (der.) delito flagrante.
flagrantly [ˈfleɪgrəntlɪ] *adv.* impudentemente, descaradamente.
flagship [ˈflægˌʃɪp] *s.* (mar.) buque insignia, capitana, navío almirante.
flagstaff [-ˌstæf, B -ˌstɑf] *s.* (*pl.* FLAGSTAFFS) (mar.) asta de bandera.
flag station, 1. (f.c.) estación de bandera, apeadero. 2. (aer.) escala opcional.
flagstone [-ˌstoʊn] *s.* laja, lancha, lastra, losa, baldosa.
flag stop, *var. de* **flag station.**
flag waver, patriotero, persona que exalta su país exageradamente.
flag-waving [-ˌweɪvɪŋ] *s.* patriotería.
flail [fleɪl] *s.* mayal, desgranador. —*v.t.* 1. golpear (con un mayal); desgranar. 2. golpear, azotar. 3. agitar, sacudir (brazos, piernas). —*v.i.* **f. away at,** trabarse a golpes con.
flair [flɛr, B flɛə] *s.* 1. (fam.) estilo, elegancia, cachet. 2. instinto, aptitud; disposición.
flak [flæk] *s.* (mil.) artillería antiaérea; fuego antiaéreo.
flake [fleɪk] *s.* 1. copo (de nieve); hojuela, escama. 2. chispa, brasa diminuta; pedacito. 3. (bot.) clavel rayado. 4. cañizo; bastidor (para secar alimentos). 5. (mar.) aduja. —*v.t.* 1. quitar las escamas a, limpiar de escamas. 2. cubrir de copos o escamas. —*v.i.* descamarse; descascararse, desprenderse en escamillas (pintura, pared, etc.); **to f. out,** (jer.) quedarse dormido o inconsciente; rendirse de cansancio.
flake of fire, centella, chispa.
flake of ice, carámbano, astilla de hielo.
flake white, (pint.) albayalde, blanco de plomo.
flakily [ˈfleɪkəlɪ] *adv.* en forma escamosa o laminosa.
flakiness [-ɪnəs] *s.* aspecto escamoso, consistencia laminosa.
flaky [ˈfleɪkɪ] *a.* escamoso; laminoso, hojaldrado.
flam [flæm] *s.* 1. falsedad, engaño, truco, soflama, fraude. 2. farsa, patraña, embuste, bola. 3. toque de tambor. —*v.t., v.i.* (*pret., p.p.* FLAMMED; *p.pr.* FLAMMING) mentir, engañar, timar, estafar, trampear, enfullar.
flambeau [ˈflæmˌboʊ] *s.* (*pl.* FLAMBEAUS o FLAMBEAUX [-ˌboʊz]) 1. antorcha, hachón. 2. candelabro ornamentado.
flamboyance [flæmˈbɔɪəns] *s.* 1. resplandor. 2. floridez. 3. ostentación, aparato, extravagancia.
flamboyant [-ənt] *a.* 1. (arq.) flamígero, flameante (díc. de un estilo de la arquitectura gótica). 2. flamante, resplandeciente. 3. florido, recargado. 4. llamativo, ostentoso, aparatoso, extravagante. —*s.* flamboyán (árbol).
flamboyantly [-lɪ] *adv.* floridamente; ostentosamente, con extravagancia.
flame [fleɪm] *s.* 1. llama. 2. (*pl.*) fuego. 3. flama, fulgor, brillo, reflejo. 4. (fig.) llama, fuego, pasión. 5. enamorado, enamoradá. 6. **to burst into flames,** inflamarse, incendiarse; empezar a arder; **to fan the flames,** avivar el fuego; **to go up in flames,** ser presa de las llamas o del fuego, quemarse; **to pour oil on the flames,** echar leña al fuego. —*v.i.* 1. arder, llamear, flamear. 2. fulgurar, brillar. 3. **f. up,** inflamarse, hacer llama, levantar llama; (fig.) inflamarse, encenderse. —*v.t.* 1. marcar con llamas. 2. flamear (vasijas, etc.); abrasar, destruir por fuego (maleza, hierbas malas, etc.); chamuscar. 3. iluminar.
flame cell, (zool.) bulbo ciliado (de platelmintos, etc.).
flame-hardened [ˈfleɪmˌhɑrdənd, B -ˌhɑd-] *a.* (met.) templado en fragua, templado a llama.
flameless [-ləs] *a.* sin llamas.
flamen [ˈfleɪmən, B -mɛn] *s.* (hist. romana) flamen, sacerdote romano dedicado al culto de un dios en particular.
flamenco [fləˈmɛŋkoʊ] *s.* (*pl.* FLAMENCOS) flamenco (danza, estilo o canto andaluz).
flameout [ˈfleɪmˌaʊt] *s.* (aer.) detención del motor de un avión a chorro.
flameproof [-ˌpruf] *a.* 1. incombustible. 2. a prueba de fuego.
flame resistant, ignífugo, resistente al fuego.
flame retardant, de combustión lenta.
flame thrower (mil.) lanzallamas.
flame tree, (bot.) árbol de Australia de flores rojas y brillantes.
flaming [ˈfleɪmɪŋ] *a.* 1. llameante, ardiente. 2. fulgurante, resplandeciente. 3. (fig.) ardiente, apasionado, fogoso. 4. (jer., G.B.) maldito.
flamingly [-lɪ] *adv.* radiantemente; fogosamente, ardientemente.
flamingo [fləˈmɪŋgoʊ] *s.* (*pl.* FLAMINGOS o FLAMINGOES) (orn.) flamenco.
flammability [ˌflæməˈbɪlətɪ] *s.* inflamabilidad, combustibilidad.
flammable [ˈflæməbəl] *s.* substancia inflamable. —*a.* inflamable, combustible.
flamy [ˈfleɪmɪ] *a.* 1. de color de llama. 2. llameante.
flan [flæn] *s.* 1. (cocina) flan. 2. **cospel** (molde para fundir monedas); tejo, disco de metal.
flanched [flæntʃt, B flɑntʃt] *a.* (her.) flanqueado.
flânerie [flɑnˈri, B ˈflɑnri] *s.* (fr.) ociosidad, holgazanería.
flaneur [flɑˈnɜr, B ˈflɑˌnɜ] *s.* (fr.) holgazán, azotacalles; hombre de mundo.
flange [flændʒ] *s.* (maq.) pestaña, reborde, oreja; brida (de tubo), ala, cabeza (de viga), pestaña, ceja, bordón, realce (de rueda); base, patín (de riel). —*v.t.* (mec.) rebordear, embridar.
flange coupling, (mec.) acoplamiento de bridas, acoplamiento de pestaña.
flange joint, (mec.) junta de pestañas remachadas o empernadas.
flange nut, (mec.) tuerca de reborde, tuerca de ceja.
flange pipe, (mec.) tubo con pestaña.
flanger [ˈflændʒər, B -dʒə] *s.* (mec.) pestañador.
flange rail, riel vignola, riel en T.
flange steel, acero dulce.
flange turner, (mec.) rebordeador.
flange union, (mec.) unión de brida.
flange wheel, (f.c.) rueda de ceja, rueda de pestaña.
flanging press [ˈflændʒɪŋ-] (mec.) prensa de rebordear.
flank [flæŋk] *s.* 1. costado, lado (de un animal). 2. (cocina) espaldilla (de res). 3. flanco, costado, lado, parte lateral. 4. (mil., mar., fort.) flanco (de un ejército, flota, escuadra, etc.). —*v.t.* 1. (mil.) flanquear. 2. flanquear, lindar con, confinar con, bordear.
flanker [ˈflæŋkər, B -ə] *s.* 1. (fútbol) flanqueador. 2. (mil.) fortificación de los flancos.
flank guard, (mil.) guardaflanco.
flanking [-ɪŋ] *s.* (mil.) flanqueo. —*a.* flanqueador, flanqueante.
flanking wind, viento de flanco.
flannel [ˈflænəl] *s.* 1. franela, muletón. 2. (*pl.*) ropa interior de franela, vendas de franela. 3. (*pl.*) pantalones de franela. 4. toallita (para lavarse); trapo o paño de franela (para limpiar el piso). 5. (jer., G.B.) carantoñas, lisonja.
flannelette [ˌflænəlˈɛt] *s.* (tej.) franela fina.
flannelly [ˈflænəlɪ] *a.* como la franela.
flannel-mouthed [-ˌmaʊθt, B -maʊðd] *a.* 1. de habla poco clara. 2. de palabra fácil y engañosa.
flap [flæp] *s.* 1. falda, faldilla, faldón (de prendas de vestir), ala (de sombrero), oreja (de zapato), solapa (del bolsillo), hoja plegadiza (de mesa), faldón (de silla), solapa (de la sobrecubierta de un libro), tapa (del sobre), corbata (de neumático). 2. alazo, aletazo, aletada, golpe de ala o aleta. 3. palmada, bofetada. 4. (med.) colgajo (de piel); labio (de una herida). 5. (bot., zool.) opérculo. 6. (aer.) alerón, flap. 7. (fon.) golpe de lengua (que se da al pronunciar la r). 8. (*pl.*) (jer.) orejas. 9. (jer.) concusión, conmoción, excitación; crisis. —*v.t.* (*pret., p.p.* FLAPPED; *p.pr.* FLAPPING) 1. dar una palmada a, abofetear. 2. batir, menear, sacudir, agitar (alas, aletas, etc.). —*v.i.* 1. aletear; oscilar, sacudirse. 2. (mar.) gualdrapear (vela).
flapdoodle [ˈflæpˌdudəl] *s.* (fam.) disparate, tontería.
flapdragon [-ˌdrægən] *s.* caimada, quemadillo, brandy o aguardiente encendido (bebida festiva que t. contiene fruta o golosinas).
flap-eared [-ˌɪrd, B -ˌɪəd] *a.* de orejas caídas (perro, etc.).
flapjack [-ˌdʒæk] *s.* 1. hojuela, torta de masa (frita en una plancha metálica). 2. polvera llana.
flapper [ˈflæpər, B -ə] *s.* 1. batidor. 2. matamoscas. 3. patito, anadino, perdiz joven. 4. (fam.) jovencita descocada, esp. en la década de los 20. 5. colgajo. 6. aleta ancha; cola (de ciertos crustáceos). 7. (jer.) mano.
flapping [-ɪŋ] *s.* 1. aleteo, aletazo, batimiento. 2. (mar.) socollada, gualdrapazo.
flare [flɛr, B flɛə] *v.i.* 1. arder, llamear. 2. fulgurar, lucir, brillar. 3. (gen. con *up*) inflamarse, destellar; (fig.) inflamarse, encolerizarse. 4. ensancharse, acampanarse, abrirse. 5. ondear, flamear. —*v.t.* 1. hacer llamear. 2. ensanchar, acampanar, abrir, abocinar. 3. señalar con fuego o luces. 4. exhibir ostentosamente. —*s.* 1. llamarada, fogarada. 2. fulgor, brillo. 3. señal luminosa, luz de bengala. 4. arrebato (de cólera), irritación, enfurecimiento. 5. abocinamiento, ensanchamiento, ensanche; vuelo (de falda). 6. estallido (de sonido). 7. (foto., ópt.) reflejo.
flareback [ˈflɛrˌbæk, B ˈflɛəˌ-] *s.* 1. llamarada que surge inesperadamente. 2. (mil.) fogonazo por la culata.

flare-up ['flɛr,ʌp, B 'flɛər-] *s.* llamarada; estallido, arrebato (de cólera), explosión (de rabia).
flaring [-ɪŋ] *a.* 1. rutilante, flamante, fulgurante, resplandeciente. 2. llamativo, chillón. 3. acampanado, abocinado.
flaring tool, abocardadora, abocinadora.
flash [flæʃ] *v.i.* 1. chispear, llamear, brillar, destellar, fulgurar, relampaguear. 2. echar chispas, fulgurar, brillar (los ojos). 3. pasar o cruzar como un relámpago, moverse aprisa. 4. estallar (en palabras), hablar con precipitación. 5. **f. upon (one),** comprender de repente, caer en la cuenta. —*v.t.* 1. enviar de prisa (o como un rayo), despachar (por radio o telégrafo). 2. despedir, lanzar (rayo de luz, destellos, etc.). 3. blandir, blandear (cuchillo, etc.). 4. (fam.) ostentar, alardear, fachendear, pregonar. 5. revestir con láminas de plomo o cinc (los cantos del techo para protegerlos contra la lluvia). 6. (ind.) cubrir (un cristal) con una película de otro color. —*s.* 1. destello, fulguración, resplandor, relumbrón, fogonazo. 2. rayo (de esperanza, etc.). 3. instante, tris, momento. 4. iluminación, acceso (de alegría); ráfaga, golpe (de luz); rasgo (de ingenio). 5. ostentación, boato. 6. ojeada, vistazo. 7. sonrisa repentina. 8. mensaje urgente, despacho telegráfico. 9. señal luminosa; señal de banderas. 10. (fam.) linterna. 11. (quím.) colorante (para los licores). 12. (foto.) flash, luz instantánea. 13. (ant.) jerga de los rateros. 14. (ant.) saetín, abertura de presa, golpe de agua. 15. **f. in the pan,** fogonazo, esfuerzo inútil. —*a.* 1. chillón, llamativo. 2. rápido, vivo. 3. majo, elegante. 4. chulo, picaresco; ratero, ladronesco.
flashback ['flæʃ,bæk] *s.* 1. narración retrospectiva (en una novela, etc.). 2. (cinem.) escena retrospectiva. 3. retroceso de la llama (en soldador).
flashboard [-,bɔrd, B -,bɔd] *s.* (hidr.) alza removible, tabla de quitapón.
flash bulb, (foto.) lámpara flash, lámpara de destello, bombilla de luz instantánea, bombilla de magnesio.
flash burn, quemadura ocasionada por la exposición pasajera a altas radiaciones.
flash burner, mechero de gas con encendedor eléctrico.
flasher ['flæʃər, B -ə] *s.* 1. (ict.) lobote. 2. caldera rápida, caldera instantánea. 3. (elec.) destellador, pulsador. 4. semáforo de luz intermitente.
flasher sign, anuncio intermitente.
flash flood, inundación repentina, torrente.
flashgun [-,gʌn] *s.* (foto.) disparador de destello.
flashily [-əlɪ] *adv.* 1. brillantemente. 2. ostentosamente, en forma llamativa o chillona.
flashiness [-ɪnəs] *s.* 1. ostentación. 2. carácter llamativo, aspecto chillón.
flashing ['flæʃɪŋ] *s.* 1. vierteaguas, botaguas, placas escurridizas. 2. tapajuntas, sello. 3. proceso de fusión de dos colores en los cristales. —*a.* centelleante, centellador; relampagueante.
flash lamp, (foto.) lámpara de relámpago.
flashlight [-,laɪt] *s.* 1. rayo, destello; luz intermitente o giratoria (esp. de un faro). 2. fanal de destellos. 3. linterna eléctrica (de bolsillo). 4. (foto.) luz instantánea, luz relámpago; fotografía tomada con luz relámpago.
flashover [-,oʊvər, B -və] *s.* (elec.) brinco de la corriente.
flash point, (fís.) punto de inflamación.
flash test, 1. (fís.) prueba del punto de inflamación. 2. (elec.) ensayo momentáneo del aislamiento.
flash wheel, rueda de cangilones para elevar agua.
flashy ['flæʃɪ] *a.* (FLASHIER; FLASHIEST) 1. brillante, relampagueante, fulgurante. 2. llamativo, ostentosamente vulgar, chillón, de relumbrón. 3. impetuoso, fogoso (temperamento).
flask [flæsk, B flɑsk] *s.* 1. frasco, redoma, matraz; frasco de bolsillo. 2. polvorín (del cazador). 3. (metal.) caja de moldear.
flasket ['flæskət, B 'flɑs-] *s.* 1. frasquito. 2. (G.B., dial.) cofre, cesta ancha y poco honda.
flat [flæt] *a.* (FLATTER; FLATTEST) 1. plano, llano. 2. tendido. 3. extendido, estirado; postrado. 4. liso, raso. 5. tendido, desenrollado. 6. (fig.) postrado. 7. chato, aplastado. 8. categórico, terminante, perentorio, positivo. 9. fijo, exacto; redondo (precio). 10. inanimado, abatido, aburrido. 11. insulso, insípido, desabrido. 12. sin efervescencia (champán, cerveza, etc.). 13. mate, deslustrado, sin brillo. 14. sordo, apagado (sonido, voz); desentonado (canto, etc.). 15. fijo, uniforme; sencillo (tarifa, tasa). 16. (com.) parado, inactivo, bajo (un mercado). 17. (mús.) bemol. 18. (pint.) uniforme (tono, color, matiz); sin relieve (cuadro, fotografía). 19. (gram.) sin terminación flexional (palabra). 20. (fon.) (vocal) llana. 21. (mar.) tieso, tesado (díc. de una vela). 22. (aut.) desinflado (neumático). 23. **as f. as a pancake,** llano como la palma de la mano; **to fall f.,** fracasar por completo, no tener éxito; pasar inadvertido, no surtir efecto; **to fall f. on one's face,** salir mal parado, pasar vergüenza; **to leave (someone) f.,** dar el esquinazo a (alguien). —*adv.* 1. horizontalmente, de plano. 2. exactamente, precisamente, determinadamente. 3. totalmente, completamente. 4. (fin.) sin recargo de intereses. 5. (mús.) desentonadamente, desafinadamente. —*s.* 1. nivel, plano, llanura; planicie. 2. bajo, bajío, banco, escollo. 3. cara (parte plana de algo), palma (de la mano). 4. (vagón de) plataforma. 5. barco o bote de fondo plano. 6. (mús.) bemol. 7. (teat.) bastidor. 8. (aut.) neumático desinflado. 9. (agr.) semillero de cajón. 10. (metal.) planchuela, platina, barra chata, solera. 11. (min.) filón horizontal. 12. (jer.) primo, zonzo. 13. (G.B.) apartamento, departamento, piso. 14. **double f.,** (mús.) doble bemol; **sharps and flats,** sostenidos y bemoles (de un piano). —*v.t.* (*pret., p.p.* FLATTED; *p.pr.* FLATTING) 1. (mús.) bemolar, bajar de tono. 2. (ant.) allanar, aplastar, achatar, aplanar; deslustrar. —*v.i.* 1. (mús.) desafinar por lo bajo. 2. (ant.) aplastarse, achatarse; allanarse.
flat arch, (arq.) arco adintelado, arco a nivel, bóveda rebajada.
flatbed ['flæt,bɛd] *s.* 1. (impr.) prensa (de imprimir) plana. 2. (aut.) remolque plano o de plataforma.
flatboat [-,boʊt] *s.* chalana, barcaza, barca chata, lanchón.
flat-bottomed [-'bɑtəmd, B -'bɔt-] *a.* de fondo plano.
flat broke, (jer.) completamente pelado, sin un centavo en el bolsillo.
flatcar [-,kɑr, B -,kɑ] *s.* (f.c.) plataforma; carro plano o de plataforma, vagón de plataforma, vagón raso.
flat file, lima plana o chata.
flatfish [-,fɪʃ] *s.* (ict.) rodaballo, platija, lenguado, cualquier pez pleuronecto.
flatfoot [-,fʊt] *s.* 1. (med.) pie plano. 2. (jer.) policía, detective.
flat-footed [-'fʊtəd] *a.* 1. de base plana (riel). 2. de pies planos. 3. (jer.) firme; determinado, inflexible. 4. (jer.) desprevenido, ej., *to catch one f.-f.,* coger a uno desprevenido, sorprender; coger a uno con las manos en la masa.
flat-hat [-,hæt] *v.i.* (aer., jer.) volar a ras de los árboles; volar bajo o en vuelo rasante.
Flathead [-,hɛd] *s.* 1. miembro de una de las varias tribus de indios norteamericanos que achataban las cabezas de sus niños artificialmente. 2. **f.,** pez de cabeza chata.
flathead rivet, (mec.) remache de cabeza achatada, roblón de cabeza chata.
flathead screw, (mec.) tornillo de cabeza perdida.
flatiron [-,aɪərn, B -,aɪən] *s.* plancha (para ropa).
flatiron holder, almohadilla.
flat knot, nudo de rizos, nudo llano.
flatland [-,lænd] *s.* llano, llanura.
flatling ['flætlɪŋ] **flatlings** [-lɪŋz] *adv.* (ant.) de plano.
flatly [-lɪ] *adv.* 1. de plano, categóricamente, rotundamente; perentoriamente. 2. completamente, totalmente, directamente. 3. (fig.) monótonamente, aburridamente. 4. sin relieve. 5. horizontalmente.
flatness [-nəs] *s.* 1. llanura, igualdad de superficie. 2. chatedad. 3. monotonía, deslustre.
flat nose, nariz chata.
flat race, (dep.) carrera en plano (de caballos).
flat rate, tarifa fija; precio alzado.
flat roof, azotea.
flat spin, (aer.) barrena plana, tirabuzón plano.
flat tax, impuesto único.
flatten ['flætən] *v.t.* 1. allanar, aplanar, aplastar; achatar. 2. deslustrar, quitar el brillo a (ej., pintura). 3. (fig.) postrar, arruinar. 4. (jer.) derribar, tumbar. —*v.i.* 1. allanarse, aplanarse. 2. perder el sabor, tornarse insípido; perder la efervescencia (cerveza, gaseosa, etc.). 3. (aer.) ponerse horizontal, enderezar el vuelo, enderezarse. 4. **f. out,** aplanar, achatar.
flatter ['flætər, B -ə] *s.* 1. (metal.) calibre de estirar. 2. (herrería) yunque de estampar; tas. —*v.t.* 1. halagar, lisonjear, adular, celebrar. 2. favorecer (díc. de un adorno, vestido, etc.). 3. embellecer, mejorar (un pintor o fotógrafo a la persona retratada). 4. **f. oneself (with),** hacerse ilusiones (con), complacerse (con). —*v.i.* emplear lisonjas.
flatterer [-ərər, B -ərə] *s.* adulador, lisonjero, zalamero.
flattering [-ərɪŋ] *a.* lisonjero, halagador.
flatteringly [-lɪ] *adv.* lisonjeramente, halagüeñamente.
flattery [-ərɪ] *s.* adulación, lisonja, halago, zalamería.
flat tire, (aut.) neumático desinflado, llanta reventada, goma ponchada (Ecuad., Cuba).
flattish ['flætɪʃ] *a.* achatado, bastante chato.
flattop [-,tɑp, B -,tɔp] *s.* (jer.) 1. casa plana, de superficie rasa. 2. barco portaaviones. 3. (fam.) corte de pelo cuadrado.
flatulence ['flætʃələns, B 'flætjʊ-] **flatulency** [-lənsɪ] *s.* 1. flatulencia, gases estomacales. 2. (fig.) hinchazón, pomposidad; vanidad.
flatulent [-lənt] *a.* 1. flatulento. 2. (fig.) hinchado, pomposo; vanidoso.
flatulently [-lɪ] *adv.* (fig.) pomposamente; vanidosamente.
flatus ['fleɪtəs] *s.* (med.) flato, gas producido en el estómago o en el intestino.
flatware ['flæt,wɛr, B -,wɛə] *s.* cubiertos, utensilios de mesa.
flatwise [-,waɪz] **flatways** [-,weɪz] *adv.* de plano, con el lado plano hacia abajo; tocando con el lado plano.
flatwork [-,wɜrk, B -,wɜk] *s.* artículos que pueden ser planchados con planchadora mecánica (como sábanas, toallas, manteles).
flatworm [-,wɜrm, B -,wɜm] *s.* (zool.) platelminto, gusano plano.
flaunt [flɔnt] *v.t.* 1. ostentar, hacer gala de, hacer alarde de. 2. mofarse de (reglas, disposiciones, etc.). —*v.i.* 1. ondear orgullosamente (bandera, etc.). 2. pavonearse. —*s.* ostentación, alarde.

flauntingly ['flɔntɪŋlɪ] *adv.* ostentosamente.
flautist ['flɔtəst, 'flaʊt-, B 'flɔt-] *s.* flautista.
flavescent [flə'vɛsənt] *a.* (poét.) flavescente, amarillento.
flavin ['fleɪvən] *s.* (bioquím.) flavina.
flavone ['fleɪˌvoʊn] *s.* (quím.) flavona.
flavonol [-vəˌnɔl] *s.* (quím.) flavonol.
flavoprotein [ˌfleɪvoʊ'proʊˌtin, -tɪən] *s.* (bioquím.) flavoproteína, enzima amarilla de Warburg.
flavopurpurin [-'pɜrpərən, B -'pɜpjʊr-] *s.* (quím.) flavopurpurina.
flavor, (pr. G.B.) **flavour** ['fleɪvər, B -və] *s.* 1. sabor, gusto, sazón. 2. condimento, salsa, sainete, aderezo. 3. (fig.) sabor, cualidad. —*v.t.* saborear, sazonar, condimentar.
flavorful, (pr. G.B.) **flavourful** [-fəl] *a.* sabroso, rico, gustoso.
flavoring, (pr. G.B.) **flavouring** ['fleɪvərɪŋ] *s.* condimento, sainete, aderezo.
flavorless, (pr. G.B.) **flavourless** [-ləs, B -vəlɪs] *a.* insípido, soso, sin sabor.
flavorous [-vərəs] *a.* (fig.) sabroso, delicioso; fragante.
flaw [flɔ] *s.* 1. grieta, hendedura. 2. defecto, imperfección; falta, tacha. 3. ráfaga de viento. —*v.t., v.i.* agrietar(se), rajar(se); ponerse defectuoso.
flawless ['flɔləs] *a.* perfecto, impecable, sin tacha.
flawlessly [-lɪ] *adv.* perfectamente, impecablemente.
flawlessness [-nəs] *s.* perfección, impecabilidad.
flawy ['flɔi] *a.* 1. agrietado. 2. defectuoso; lleno de faltas. 3. (mar.) propenso a rachas.
flax [flæks] *s.* 1. (bot.) lino. 2. lino, fibra de lino.
flax brake, (agr.) agramadera.
flax comb, rastrillo.
flax dresser, rastrillador.
flax dressing, rastrilleo del lino.
flaxen ['flæksən] *a.* 1. de lino. 2. color pajizo; rubio.
flax oil, aceite de linaza.
flax packing, (mec.) empaquetadura de lino.
flaxseed [-ˌsid] *s.* semilla de lino, linaza.
flaxy [-sɪ] *a.* parecido al lino.
flay [fleɪ] *v.t.* 1. desollar, despellejar, excoriar. 2. (fig.) despojar, pelar. 3. vituperar, reprender, criticar severamente.
flayer ['fleɪər, B -ə] *s.* desollador, descortezador.
flaying [-ɪŋ] *s.* desolladura, desuello, despellejadura.
flea [fli] *s.* pulga; **a f. in one's ear,** amonestación desagradable, reprensión severa; to **send someone off with a f. in his ear,** echar (o despedir) a uno a cajas destempladas.
fleabag ['fliˌbæg] *s.* (jer.) hotel o pensión de mala muerte.
fleabane [-ˌbeɪn] *s.* (bot.) hierba pulguera, coniza.
flea beetle, (ento.) escarabajuelo.
fleabite [-ˌbaɪt] *s.* 1. picadura de pulga. 2. (fig.) molestia insignificante.
flea-bitten [-ˌbɪtən] *a.* 1. picado de pulgas. 2. blanco mosqueado en colorado (díc. del caballo); salpicado. 3. (jer.) apolillado; desvencijado.
flea circus, circo de pulgas, pulgas amaestradas.
fleam [flim] *s.* (med.) lanceta; (vet.) fleme, ballestilla.
flea market, rastro (mercado callejero de artículos baratos o de segunda mano).
fleawort ['fliˌwɜrt, B -ˌwɜt] *s.* (bot.) pulguera, zaragatona, arta de agua.
flèche [flɛʃ, B fleɪʃ] *s.* 1. (arq.) aguja (esp. sobre la intersección de la nave y crucero de una iglesia). 2. (fort.) flecha.
fleck [flɛk] *s.* punto de color o luz; lunar, mancha, peca; vedija; partícula. —*v.t.* puntear, vetear, motear, salpicar, abigarrar, varetear.
fleckless ['flɛkləs] *a.* sin mancha, limpio; inocente.
flection, (pr. G.B.) **flexion** [-ʃən] *s.* 1. flexión, corvadura, inclinación. 2. (gram.) flexión, inflexión.
flectional, (pr. G.B.) **flexional** [-əl] *a.* (gram.) flexional.
fled [flɛd] *pret., p.p. de* **flee.**
fledge [flɛdʒ] *v.i.* emplumecer, emplumar, echar plumas (aves). —*v.t.* 1. criar (un ave) hasta que pueda volar. 2. emplumar, poner plumas a (ej., una flecha).
fledgling ['flɛdʒlɪŋ] *s.* 1. volantón, pajarito, pichón. 2. bisoño, novato, inexperto.
fledgy [-ɪ] *a.* cubierto de plumas, emplumado.
flee [fli] *v.i.* (*pret., p.p.* FLED, *p.pr.* FLEEING) 1. huir (del peligro). 2. apartarse de, apresurarse; **to f. with,** alzar. —*v.t.* 1. huir, escapar de. 2. esquivar, evadir.
fleece [flis] *s.* 1. vellón. vellocino. 2. capa blanda (de nieve, etc.). 3. tela de lanilla alta. 4. **the golden f.,** el vellocino de oro. —*v.t.* 1. esquilar. 2. (fam.) desplumar, pelar, despojar (por fraude, robo, etc.). 3. cubrir con, salpicar de (nudos de lana).
fleeced [flist] *a.* 1. cubierto de vellón. 2. velludo, aterciopelado. 3. engañado, víctima de robo o estafa.
fleecy ['flisɪ] *a.* lanudo, cubierto de lana; parecido al vellón.
fleer [flɪr, B flɪə] *s.* 1. persona que huye. 2. burlón, burlador. 3. sonrisa burlona, mueca, pulla. —*v.i.* hablar o sonreír burlonamente, mofarse.
fleet [flit] *s.* armada, fuerza naval; flota, escuadra (de barcos, aeroplanos, dirigibles o vehículos que se mueven juntos). —*a.* veloz, ligero, rápido; evanescente, efímero. —*v.i.* 1. apresurarse, pasar velozmente, volar, desaparecer. 2. (mar.) mover, desplazar.
fleet admiral, almirante de flota.
fleet-footed ['flit'fʊtəd] *a.* ligero de pies.
fleeting [-ɪŋ] *a.* efímero, fugaz, transitorio, pasajero, huidizo, momentáneo.
fleetingly [-ɪŋlɪ] **fleetly** [-lɪ] *adv.* velozmente, fugazmente.
fleetness [-nəs] *s.* velocidad, ligereza, rapidez; agilidad.
Fleet Street, (G.B.) vieja calle de Londres; (fig.) la prensa de Inglaterra (por encontrarse en dicha calle varios periódicos e imprentas).
fleet-winged [-ˌwɪŋd] *a.* alígero; veloz.
Fleming ['flɛmɪŋ] *s.* flamenco, natural de Flandes.
Flemish [-ɪʃ] *a.* flamenco, natural de Flandes. —*s.* flamenco (idioma), gen. hablado en el N. de Bélgica.
flench [flɛntʃ] *var. de* **flense.**
flense [flɛns, B flɛnz] *v.t.* cortar en tiras, despedazar grasa o piel de (ballenas); desollar, despellejar (focas).
flesh [flɛʃ] *s.* 1. carne. 2. pulpa, carne (de fruta); parte comestible (de una raíz, tallo, etc.). 3. género humano; naturaleza humana. 4. parentesco, consanguinidad; parientes, parentela. 5. gordura, grasa. 6. **f. and blood,** de carne y hueso; **f. side,** lado interno (de un cuerpo); **in the f.,** vivo; en persona; **one's own f. and blood,** (los de) su propia carne, descendientes o parientes de uno; **to make someone's f. creep,** aterrorizar, horrorizar. —*v.t.* 1. alimentar con carne. 2. enterrar, clavar (cuchillo, etc.). 3. acostumbrar, habituar, templar; iniciar en la matanza. 4. descarnar (pieles). 5. (ant.) engordar, cebar. —*v.i.* (gen. con *out* o *up*) engordar, volverse corpulento, ganar peso.
flesh brush, cepillo para friccionar la piel.
flesh-colored ['flɛʃˌkʌlərd, B -əd] *a.* encarnado, de color carne.
flesh-eating [-ˌitɪŋ] *a.* carnívoro.
flesh flick, (jer., E.U.) película de desnudos o pornográfica.
flesh fly, (ento.) mosca de la carne, moscarda.
fleshiness [-ɪnəs] *s.* carnosidad, corpulencia.
fleshings [-ɪŋz] *s. pl.* 1. calzas de punto color carne. 2. raspaduras o descarnaduras de pieles y cueros (usadas para hacer cola); piltrafas.
fleshless [-ləs] *a.* descarnado, sin carne.
fleshliness [-lɪnəs] *s.* carnalidad.
fleshly [-lɪ] *a.* 1. corpóreo, carnal. 2. sensual, lascivo. 3. carnudo, carnoso, regordete.
fleshpot [-ˌpɑt B -ˌpɔt] *s.* 1. olla, marmita (en la que se cocina carne). 2. antro de placer; abundancia.
flesh wound, herida ligera superficial.
fleshy ['flɛʃɪ] *a.* 1. carnoso, de carne. 2. carnudo, carnoso, corpulento, grueso. 3. (bot.) carnoso, pulposo, suculento (como ciertas frutas).
fletch [flɛtʃ] *v.t.* emplumar, poner plumas a (una saeta).
fletcher ['flɛtʃər, B -ə] *s.* (ant.) flechero, el que hace flechas.
Fletcherism [-əˌrɪzəm] *s.* práctica de masticar los alimentos lenta y completamente para ayudar a la buena digestión.
fleur-de-lis [ˌflɜrdə'li, -'lis, B ˌflɜdə-] *s.* (*pl.* FLEURS-DE-LIS [-'liz]) flor de lis.
fleuron ['flɜrˌɑn, B 'flʊərˌɔn] *s.* (arq.) florón.
flew [flu] *pret. de* **fly.**
flewed [flud] *a.* boquihendido.
flews [fluz] *s. pl.* belfos (de los perros, caballos, etc.).
flex [flɛks] *v.i., v.t.* doblar(se), encorvarse. —*s.* 1. flexión, doblez, encorvadura. 2. (G.B.) cordón eléctrico.
flexibility [ˌflɛksə'bɪlətɪ] *s.* flexibilidad; docilidad.
flexible ['flɛksəbəl] *a.* 1. flexible, doblegable. 2. (fig.) flexible, dócil, adaptable.
flexible coupling, (elec.) acoplamiento universal.
flexibly [-blɪ] *adv.* flexiblemente, dócilmente.
flexile ['flɛksəl, B -ˌsaɪl] *a.* flexible, adaptable, doblegable; plástico, cimbreante.
flexion, flexional, *vars. de* **flection, flectional.**
flexor [-sər, B -sə] *s.* (anat.) músculo flexor.
flexuose, *var. de* **flexuous.**
flexuosity [ˌflɛkʃʊ'ɑsətɪ, B ˌflɛksjʊ'ɔs-] *s.* tortuosidad, sinuosidad, ondulación.
flexuous ['flɛkʃʊəs, B 'flɛksjʊ-] *a.* 1. flexuoso, tortuoso, sinuoso, ondulante. 2. flexible, adaptable. 3. inconstante, vario. 4. (bot.) flexuoso.
flexuously [-lɪ] *adv.* tortuosamente, sinuosamente.
flexural ['flɛkʃərəl] *a.* 1. flexional. 2. flexible.
flexure [-ʃər, B -ʃə] *s.* 1. flexión, curvatura. 2. curva, doblez.
flibbertigibbet ['flɪbərtɪ'dʒɪbət, B -ətɪ-] *s.* (fam., E.U.) chismoso, charlador, frívolo.
flick [flɪk] *s.* 1. golpecito, latigazo suave. 2. mancha pequeña, salpicadura. 3. tris, ruido ligero. 4. (jer.) película, filme. —*v.t.* 1. golpear rápida y ligeramente; chasquear (un látigo). 2. (con *away* u *off*) quitar con un golpecito, sacudir. —*v.i.* revolotear, moverse rápida y ligeramente.
flicker ['flɪkər, B -ə] *v.i.* 1. aletear, revolotear. 2. flamear, lengüetear, titilar. 3. fluctuar, vacilar, oscilar. —*v.t.* hacer flamear, hacer oscilar, hacer

temblar. —*s.* 1. llama vacilante, luz oscilante; parpadeo (de la luz). 2. temblor momentáneo (de emoción). 3. (orn.) variedad de pájaro carpintero, picamaderos americano.
flickertail [-ˌtɔɪl] *s.* (zool.) ardilla de tierra.
flickery [-ərɪ] *a.* vacilante, oscilante; trémulo, tembloroso.
flicknife [-ˌnaɪf] *s.* navaja de muelle.
flicks [flɪks] *s. pl.* (jer.) cine; películas, filmes.
flier ['flaɪər, B -ə] *s.* 1. aviador. 2. tren expreso. 3. (fam.) empresa descabellada; operación arriesgada en la bolsa. 4. volante (de propaganda). 5. (arq.) escalón (de una escalera). 6. (fam.) cosa veloz (caballo, tren, etc.).
flight [flaɪt] *s.* 1. vuelo, volada. 2. viaje aéreo. 3. trayectoria. 4. paso fugaz (ej., del tiempo); ímpetu, arranque (ej., de la fantasía). 5. descarga (de flechas); bandada (de pájaros); (aer.) escuadrilla, formación (de dos o más aviones). 6. tramo (de escalera); piso, ej., *his room is three flights up,* su cuarto está tres pisos más arriba. 7. fuga, huida, evasión, escape; (fin.) fuga, éxodo (del capital); **to put to f.,** poner en fuga; **to take (to) f.,** fugar(se), huir. —*v.i.* ahuyentar; alzar vuelo o volar en bandadas. —*v.t.* 1. tirar al vuelo a (aves de caza). 2. levantar, hacer volar (aves de caza).
flight attendant, (*male*) aeromozo; (*female*) aeromoza, azafata.
flight control, 1. (aer.) control de vuelo (de un avión desde una estación en tierra, esp. por radio). 2. (aer.) sistema de instrumentos de mando (de un avión).
flight deck, 1. plataforma de vuelos, cubierta de aterrizaje (de un portaviones). 2. (aer.) compartimiento de pilotaje, cabina de mando.
flight engineer, (aer.) mecánico de a bordo, jefe mecánico, mecánico de vuelo.
flight feather, remera, plumas largas en que terminan las alas de las aves.
flight formation, (aer.) formación de vuelo.
flightily ['flaɪtəlɪ] *adv.* frívolamente.
flight indicator, indicador de vuelos.
flightiness [-ɪnəs] *s.* frivolidad, veleidad, liviandad, capricho.
flightless [-ləs] *a.* incapaz de volar (díc. de ciertas aves como el avestruz, casuario, ñandú).
flight line, (aer.) área de estacionamiento y servicio para aviones.
flight path, (aer.) trayectoria de vuelo (de un avión).
flight plan, carta de vuelo.
flight strip, (aer.) pista auxiliar de aterrizaje.
flight surgeon, (aer.) médico de aviación.
flight-test [-ˌtɛst] *v.t.* probar, ensayar, (un avión) en vuelo.
flighty ['flaɪtɪ] *a.* 1. ligero, frívolo, veleidoso, volátil. 2. alocado, casquivano. 3. fugaz, efímero, pasajero.
flimflam ['flɪmˌflæm] *s.* 1. bagatela, fruslería; fatuidad. 2. trampa, fraude, engaño, embaucamiento. 3. tontería, farsa. —*v.t.* (*pret., p.p.* FLIMFLAMMED; *p.pr.* FLIMFLAMMING) (fam.) engañar, trampear, embaucar.
flimflammer [-ər, B -ə] *s.* (fam.) tramposo, embaucador.
flimsily ['flɪmzəlɪ] *adv.* débilmente, superficialmente, endeblemente.
flimsiness [-zɪnəs] *s.* endeblez, falta de solidez, fragilidad.
flimsy [-zɪ] *a.* (FLIMSIER; FLIMSIEST) 1. débil, endeble, frágil. 2. baladí, trivial, fútil, frívolo. —*s.* 1. papel de seda, papel de cebolla; papel delgado. 2. (jer., G.B.) billete (de banco); telegrama.
flinch [flɪntʃ] *v.i.* acobardarse, echarse atrás; (con *from*) desistir de miedo (de algo), recular, retroceder (ante un peligro, riesgo, etc.). —*a.* 1. reculada, titubeo, vacilación. 2. juego de naipes en que se colocan las cartas en la mesa en cierto orden numérico.
flinder ['flɪndər, B -də] *s.* (*gen. pl.*) astilla, fragmento, trozo; **broken to flinders,** roto en astillas. astillado.
fling [flɪŋ] *v.t.* (*pret., p.p.* FLUNG, [flʌŋ] *p.pr.* FLINGING) 1. arrojar, tirar, despedir, lanzar, echar. 2. (t. con *about*) menear, agitar (brazos, piernas, etc.). 3. (t. con *out*) echar (reniegos, imprecaciones, etc.). 4. **f. aside,** dejar a un lado, abandonar (cuidado, prudencia, etc.); **f. away,** tirar, desechar, botar; **f. down,** tirar, echar al suelo; **f. in one's face,** echar en cara, reprochar a uno; **f. into (prison, river,** etc.), echar a (la cárcel, río, etc.); **f. one's money about,** prodigar su propio dinero; **f. oneself at someone,** afanarse descaradamente para conquistar a alguien; **f. oneself into (boat, well,** etc.), echarse al (barco, pozo, etc.); **f. (door, window,** etc.) **open,** abrir (puerta, ventana, etc.) de golpe; **f. out,** echar fuera; echar a viva fuerza; despedir, echar (a alguien); abrir (los brazos); **f. (door, window,** etc.) **shut,** cerrar (puerta, ventana, etc.) de golpe; **f. up,** levantar (ej., polvo). —*v.i.* 1. menearse. 2. agitarse. 3. precipitarse, lanzarse. 4. **f. into (room,** etc.), irrumpir en, entrar precipitadamente en (cuarto, etc.); **f. off,** dispararse, partir repentinamente; **f. out of (room,** etc.), salir violenta o precipitadamente. —*s.* 1. tiro, echada, echamiento. 2. (fam.) prueba, ensayo, esfuerzo, tentativa. 3. indirecta, sarcasmo, pulla, burla. 4. baile de compás muy rápido. 5. **to have a f. at,** probar, aventurar (algo); escarnecer (a una persona); **to have one's f.,** hacer una calaverada, correrla, echar una cana al aire.
flint [flɪnt] *s.* 1. (min.) pedernal. 2. pedernal, piedra (de chispa) (en gatillo de armas, encendedor). 3. cosa sumamente dura. 4. **to skin a f.,** ser miserable o avariento; **to wring water from a f.,** sacar aceite a un ladrillo, obrar milagros.
flint corn, (bot.) tipo de maíz de granos duros.
flint glass, cristal; cristal de roca.
flint-hearted ['flɪntˌhɑrtəd, B -ˌhɑt-] *a.* cruel, inflexible; de corazón de piedra.
flintily [-əlɪ] *adv.* inflexiblemente, inexorablemente.
flintiness [-ɪnəs] *s.* 1. calidad de pedernalino, dureza. 2. (fig.) dureza, inexorabilidad.
flintlock [-ˌlɑk, B -ˌlɔk] *s.* 1. llave de chispa. 2. pedreñal, trabuco de chispa.
flint paper, papel de lija de pedernal.
flinty ['flɪntɪ] *a.* 1. pedernalino, de pedernal, apedernalado. 2. (fig.) inflexible, inexorable.
flip [flɪp] *v.t.* (*pret., p.p.* FLIPPED; *p.pr.* FLIPPING) 1. lanzar, soltar, echar (ej., una moneda al aire). 2. dar un capirotazo a (oreja, etc.), dar un golpe rápido a; quitar de un golpecito. 3. **f. one's lid,** (jer.) enfurecerse, perder el control, ponerse furioso. —*v.i.* 1. moverse a tirones o sacudidas. 2. **f. at,** dar un golpe ligero a; dar golpes rápidos a; (jer.) quedarse boquiabierto. —*s.* 1. capirotazo, tirón. 2. salto mortal, vuelta de campana, vuelta de carnero. 3. (fútbol) pase corto. 4. bebida de vino o ron con azúcar, especias y, a veces, huevo batido. —*a.* (fam.) petulante, descarado; frívolo.
flip coil, (elec.) bobina exploradora.
flip-flop ['flɪpˌflɑp, B -ˌflɔp] *s.* 1. (ruido o movimiento de) aleteo. 2. voltereta hacia atrás sobre las manos. 3. cambio brusco (de dirección, punto de vista, etc.).
flippancy ['flɪpənsɪ] *s.* petulancia, impertinencia, ligereza.
flippant [-ənt] *a.* petulante, impertinente; sin seriedad.
flippantly [-lɪ] *adv.* petulantemente, impertinentemente.
flipper ['flɪpər, B -ə] *s.* 1. aleta (de foca, ballena, etc.). 2. (jer.) mano. 3. (*in a pinball machine*) flipper.
flip side, contraportada del disco.
flirt [flɜrt, B flɜt] *v.i.* 1. flirtear, coque tear, galantear, pololear (Chile). 2. moverse a sacudidas, corretear, bromear, chancear. 3. (con *with*) soñar con, dejarse tentar por (una idea, etc.). —*v.t.* agitar (algo), mover rápidamente, mover de un tirón; abrir o cerrar algo con ligereza. —*s.* 1. coqueta; galanteador. 2. golpe o meneo rápido.
flirtation [flər'teɪʃən, B flə'-] *s.* coquetería, coqueteo, flirteo.
flirtatious [-ʃəs] *a.* coqueta; galanteador.
flirtatiously [-lɪ] *adv.* coquetamente.
flirter ['flɜrtər, B 'flɜtə] *s.* galanteador; coqueta.
flirting [-ɪŋ] *s.* flirteo, galanteo.
flit [flɪt] *v.i.* (*pret., p.p.* FLITTED; *p.pr.* FLITTING) 1. volar, revolotear; pasar rápidamente. 2. (dial.) irse, marcharse; cambiar de puesto. —*v.t.* (ant.) transferir, remover. —*s.* movimiento rápido y ligero; aleteo, revoloteo.
flitch [flɪtʃ] *s.* 1. lonja de tocino, costado de puerco salado y curado. 2. costero, costanera; (carp.) tablón de viga ensamblada. —*v.t.* cortar en lonjas o tiras; aserrar en costeros.
flitter ['flɪtər, B -ə] *var. de* **flutter.**
flittermouse [-ˌmaʊs] *s.* (zool.) murciélago.
flitting ['flɪtɪŋ] *s.* fuga, vuelo rápido. —*a.* fugaz.
flivver ['flɪvər, B -ə] *s.* 1. (jer.) automóvil o acroplano pequeño y barato; automóvil viejo. 2. (jer.) fiasco, pifia. —*v.i.* (jer.) fracasar.
flix [flɪks] *s.* pelusa, plumón; bozo, vello.
float [floʊt] *s.* 1. flotador. 2. plataforma flotante; balsa, boya, salvavidas. 3. corcho (de caña de pescar, redes, etc.). 4. flotador (de hidroavión). 5. flote, flotación. 6. carro alegórico, carromato o carroza decorada (para espectáculos o desfiles públicos). 7. (ict.) vejiga natatoria. 8. (teat.) (*gen. pl.*) candilejas, luces del proscenio o escenario. 9. (const.) regla o tabla aplanadora, aplanadera, llana de enlucir. 10. bebida gaseosa con helado. 11. **to be floating in it,** (jer.) nadar en riquezas, estar podrido de plata. —*v.i.* flotar, boyar; sobrenadar, nadar; fluctuar, ser inestable, estar suelto. —*v.t.* 1. poner, mantener o llevar a flote. 2. cubrir con agua, inundar. 3. (com.) emitir, poner en circulación (bonos); lanzar (una empresa); negociar (un préstamo).
floatable ['floʊtəbəl] *a.* flotable, capaz de flotar.
floatage, floatation, *var. de* **flotage, flotation.**
float board, (mec.) álabe, paleta de rueda hidráulica.
float chamber, (ant.) cubeta del carburador, cuba del flotador.
floater [-ər, B -ə] *s.* 1. flotador. 2. (fam.) el que a menudo cambia de empleo, domicilio o partido político. 3. (E.U.) persona que vota fraudulentamente en varios sitios. 4. (com.) título al portador. 5. (jer., G.B.) despropósito, disparate, patochada. 6. (fís.) instrumento utilizado para registrar el nivel de los líquidos.
float-feed [-ˌfid] *a.* (aut.) de alimentación por flotador (carburador).
floating ['floʊtɪŋ] *a.* 1. flotante, boyante, a flote. 2. flotante, fluctuante, variable (población, etc.). 3. (mec.) flotante (eje, mandril, etc.). 4. (med.) flotante (costilla, riñón). 5. (com.) flotante

(deuda, capital). 6. **f. crap game,** (jer.) juego de dados que se realiza cada día en lugar distinto (para eludir a la policía); **f. on air,** (jer.) en las nubes, sumamente feliz.
floating battery, (elec.) acumulador compensador o flotante.
floating bridge, puente flotante, puente de barcas.
floating charge, (elec.) carga continua y lenta.
floating crane, grúa flotante.
floating debt, (com.) deuda flotante.
floating dock, dique flotante.
floating dry dock, dique de carena flotante.
floating grid, (rad., electrón.) rejilla libre.
floating heart, pequeña planta acuática de flores blancas y con hojas en forma de corazón.
floating island, 1. isla flotante o artificial. 2. (cocina) natillas con copos flotantes de merengue o crema batida.
floating kidney, (med.), riñón flotante.
floating light, (mar.) buque faro.
floating policy, póliza (de seguro) flotante o abierta.
floating rib, (anat.) costilla flotante.
floating supply, (com.) surtido corriente.
floating taper, mariposa (llamita flotante en un vaso de aceite).
floatplane ['floʊt,pleɪn] *s.* (aer.) hidroavión de (uno o dos) flotadores.
floatstone [-ˌstoʊn] *s.* 1. variedad esponjosa de ópalo capaz de flotar en el agua. 2. (const.) piedra utilizada para suavizar las curvas.
float valve, (mec.) válvula de flotador.
floc [flɑk, B flɔk] *s.* (fís., quím.) masa flocosa.
floccose ['flɑk'oʊs, B 'flɔk-] *a.* 1. (med.) flocoso. 2. (bot.) flocoso, tormentoso, velludo.
flocculant [-jələnt] *s.* (med.) agente de floculación.
flocculate [-ˌleɪt] *a.* (fís., quím.) floculado. —*v.t., v.i.* condensar(se) en pequeñas masas floculentas (ej., sedimentos).
flocculation [ˌflɑkjə'leɪʃən, B ˌflɔk-] *s.* (fís., quím.) floculación.
floccule ['flɑk,jul, B 'flɔk-] *s.* grumito, parte de un líquido que se coagula.
flocculence [-jələns] *s.* vellosidad.
flocculent [-lənt] *a.* 1. floculento, lanudo, velludo. 2. (bot.) floculento.
flocculus [-ləs] *s.* (*pl.* FLOCCULI [-ˌlaɪ]) 1. grumito. 2. (anat.) flóculo. 3. (astr.) mancha solar; flóculo.
floccus ['flɑkəs, B 'flɔk-] *s.* (*pl.* FLOCCI [-ˌsaɪ]) fleco, copo (ej., de lana).
flock [flɑk, B flɔk] *s.* 1. congregación, multitud, muchedumbre, gentío; agregado, conjunto, grupo, colleción (de cosas). 2. hato, manada, rebaño (de animales), bandada (de aves). 3. grey, rebaño (de fieles); congregación. 4. **flocks and herds,** ganado lanar y vacuno. —*v.i.* afluir, congregarse, juntarse, reunirse; moverse como en rebaño(s); **f. in,** entrar en tropel; **f. out,** salir en tropel. —*s.* 1. copo, mechón (de lana o pelo). 2. borra, tamo, flojel, pelillo (de lana o algodón usado para rellenar cojines, almohadones, etc.). 3. (fís., quím.) *var. de* **floc.** —*v.t.* rellenar, cubrir o revestir con borra, tamo o flojel.
flock bed, colchón de borra.
flock paper, papel aterciopelado.
flock wool, borra de lana.
flocky ['flɑkɪ, B 'flɔkɪ] *a.* flocoso, floculento, lanudo, velludo.
floe [floʊ] *s.* témpano o capa de hielo flotante.
flog [flɑg, B flɔg] *v.t.* (*pret., p.p.* FLOGGED; *p.pr.* FLOGGING) 1. azotar, flagelar, dar latigazos a. 2. agotar, cansar. 3. forzar, obligar. 4. (jer., G.B.) vender; cambalachear. 5. **f. a dead horse,** (fig.) desperdiciar energías; tratar de despertar interés en un asunto viejo, discutir un tema agotado. —*v.i.* gualdrapear (ej., velas).
flogger ['flɑgər, B 'flɔgə] *s.* azotador, castigador.
flogging [-ɪŋ] *s.* 1. azotamiento. 2. (pena de) azotes, flagelación, tunda, vapuleo, zurra.
flood [flʌd] *s.* 1. crecida, creciente, avenida, inundación, diluvio. 2. (t. **f. tide**) pleamar. 3. (fig.) correntada, chorro, flujo; torrente (de palabras, injurias, luz, lluvia, etc.). 4. (fam.) *abrev. de* **floodlight.** 5. (min.) aguada. 6. **the F.,** (bíbl.) el Diluvio. —*v.t.* 1. inundar, anegar, apantanar. 2. (fig.) inundar, colmar, abrumar. —*v.i.* desbordarse, salir a raudales.
flood control, (ing.) control de las crecidas, hidráulica fluvial.
floodgate ['flʌd,geɪt] *s.* compuerta (de esclusa, presa, dique, canal, etc.).
flooding [-ɪŋ] *s.* 1. inundación. 2. (med.) hemorragia uterina. 3. (com.) abarrotamiento. —*a.* inundante.
flood lamp, lámpara inundante.
floodlight [-ˌlaɪt] *s.* 1. luz de faro, luz de proyector. 2. proyector de haz disperso, reflector, proyector. —*v.t.* iluminar por (luz de) proyector(es) o reflectores.
flood lighting, sistema de iluminación intensiva sin sombras.
floodmark [-ˌmɑrk, B -ˌmɑk] *s.* nivel de la marea alta.
flood plain *s.* 1. área de inundación. 2. terreno aluvial, terreno de aluvión.
flood tide 1. pleamar, **creciente del mar. 2. (fig.) cantidad abrumadora; punto alto; cima, cumbre, pico.**
floodwater [-ˌwɔtər, -ˌwɑt-, B -ˌwɔtə] *s.* caudal de una crecida o creciente.
floodway [-ˌweɪ] *s.* cauce de alivio (para desviar las aguas de una crecida).
floor [flɔr, B flɔ] *s.* 1. piso, suelo, pavimento. 2. fondo (del mar, de un río, etc.); plataforma (de puente o de una estructura similar); piso (de automóvil). 3. piso (de un edificio). 4. hemiciclo (de una asamblea o parlamento). 5. nivel mínimo (ej., de precios). 6. (mar.) varenga. 7. **the f.,** uso de la palabra; **to have the f.,** tener la palabra; **to take the f.,** tomar la palabra. —*v.t.* 1. solar, pavimentar, entarimar, enladrillar. 2. derribar, tumbar, echar al suelo; derrotar, vencer. 3. revolcar, dejar confundido, arrumbar. 4. abrumar; asombrar. 5. pisar a fondo (acelerador).
floorage ['flɔrɪdʒ] *s.* área (útil) de un piso o suelo.
floor beam, (const.) viga, vigueta, tirante (de un edificio); travesaño, viga transversal, viga de tablero (de un puente).
floorboard [-ˌbɔrd, B 'flɔ,bɔd] *s.* 1. tabla del piso. 2. piso (de un automóvil, etc.); **floorboards,** suelo de tarima.
floorcloth [-ˌklɔθ] *s.* linóleo.
floorer ['flɔrər, B -ə] *s.* 1. persona que coloca pisos. 2. golpe o persona que derriba o abruma. 3. argumento o noticia desconcertante; pregunta difícil de contestar.
flooring [-ɪŋ] *s.* 1. solado. 2. entarimado, entablado, pavimento. 3. material para pisos.
floor lamp, lámpara de pie.
floor leader, (E.U.) líder parlamentario (de los diputados de un partido).
floor-length ['flɔr,lɛŋθ, -ˌlɛŋkθ, B 'flɔ,-] *a.* que llega al suelo (cortina, vestido, etc.); **f.-l. gown,** traje largo (hasta el suelo).
floor plan, (const.) plano de piso, planta del piso.
floor polish, cera de lustrar el piso.
floor show, programa de espectáculos (en un club nocturno o cabaret).
floor slab, losa de piso.
floor tile, baldosa, loseta, baldosín.
floorwalker [-ˌwɔkər, B -ə] *s.* (E.U.) jefe de sección, superintendente de sección o departamento (de una tienda o almacén).
floozie, *var. de* **floozy.**
floozy ['fluzɪ] *s.* (jer.) prostituta, callejera; mujer inmoral.
flop [flɑp, B flɔp] *v.i.* (*pret., p.p.* FLOPPED; *p.pr.* FLOPPING) 1. aletear, agitarse (algo plano). 2. desplomarse, dejarse caer, caer de rodillas o echarse flojamente. 3. volverse, moverse o cambiarse bruscamente. 4. (jer.) fallar, fracasar. 5. (jer.) acostarse, ir a la cama. —*v.t.* 1. dejar caer. 2. mover torpemente. 3. (jer., G.B.) batir, pegar, golpear fuerte o torpemente. —*s.* 1. aleteo; sonido sordo (hecho al aletear o golpear). 2. (jer.) fracaso, fiasco.
flophouse ['flɑp,haʊs, B 'flɔp-] *s.* (jer., E.U.) posada de mala muerte.
flopover [-ˌoʊvər, B -və] *s.* (t.v.) deriva vertical (de la imagen).
flopperoo, floperoo [-ə'ru] *s.* (jer.) fracaso; error, metida de pata.
floppy ['flɑpɪ, B 'flɔpɪ] *s.* (fam.) flojo, blando, flexible, fofo, colgante.
floppy disk, (comput.) disco flexible, disco floppy.
flora ['flɔrə] *s.* (*pl.* FLORAS O FLORAE [-ˌi]) flora.
floral ['flɔrəl] *a.* floral.
floral emblem, (E.U.) planta o flor reconocida como símbolo de una nación, estado o territorio.
Floral Games, (hist. rom.) juegos florales.
Floralia [flɔ'reɪlɪə] *s. pl.* fiestas florales (en honor de Flora, diosa romana).
floral leaf, 1. (bot.) hoja modificada (ej., sépalo o pétalo) del periantio de una flor. 2. (bot.) bráctea.
Floreal ['flɔrɪəl] *s.* (hist.) floreal, octavo mes del calendario de la Revolución Francesa.
Florentine ['flɔrən,tin, B -ˌtaɪn] *a.* florentino, de Florencia, Italia. —*s.* 1. florentino, habitante de Florencia. 2. clase de seda cruzada o sarga.
Florentine iris, (bot.) flor de lis blanca o (azul) celeste.
florescence [flɔ'rɛsəns] *s.* 1. (bot.) florescencia; eflorescencia, floración. 2. (fig.) florecimiento, prosperidad.
florescent [-ənt] *a.* floreciente.
floret ['flɔrət] *s.* (bot.) flósculo, florecita (de una flor compuesta).
floretum [flɔ'ritəm] *s.* jardín destinado al cultivo y al estudio científico de las flores.
floriate ['flɔrɪ,eɪt] *v.t.* florear, decorar con flores.
floriated [-əd] *a.* floreado; en forma de flor.
floricultural [ˌflɔrə'kʌltʃərəl] *a.* de floricultura.
floriculture ['flɔrə,kʌltʃər, B -tʃə] *s.* floricultura.
floriculturist [ˌflɔrə'kʌltʃərəst] *s.* floricultor.
florid ['flɔrəd, 'flɑr-, B 'flɔrɪd] *a.* 1. florido, ornamentado, recargado de adornos. 2. vivo, encarnado, rojo (díc. de la tez).
Florida [-ədə] *s.* (la) Florida, estado de E.U.
Florida Keys, (E.U.) (geog.) cayos de la Florida.
Floridan [-ədən] *a., s.* floridano.
Florida Strait, (E.U.) Estrecho de (la) Florida, Canal de la Florida.
Florida water, agua florida, agua perfumada.
Florida wood, madera de taracear.
floridity [flə'rɪdətɪ] **floridness** ['flɔrədnəs, 'flɑr-, B 'flɔr-] *s.* 1. floridez (de estilo). 2. rubicundez.
floridly ['flɔrədlɪ, 'flɑr-, B 'flɔr-] *adv.* floridamente.

floriferous [flɔ'rɪfərəs] *a.* florífero (díc. de las semillas o plantas).
florigenic [ˌflɔrə'dʒɛnɪk, ˌflɑr-, B ˌflɔr-] *a.* (bot.) florígeno.
florin ['flɔrən, 'flɑr-, B 'flɔr-] *s.* florín (moneda de oro o plata de diverso valor).
florist ['flɔrəst, 'flɑr-, B 'flɔr-] *s.* florista; **f.'s shop,** florería.
floristic [flɔ'rɪstɪk] *a.* florístico.
floristics [-tɪks] *s. pl.* (*sing. en const.*) florística.
floruit ['flɔrjʊət, 'flɑr-, B 'flɔrʊ-] *s.* período (aproximado) de vida.
floscule ['flɑskjul, B 'flɔs-] *s.* (bot.) flósculo.
floss [flɔs, flɑs, B flɔs] *s.* 1. borra o cadarzo (del capullo). 2. seda azache. 3. seda vegetal. 4. (bot.) barbas (del maíz). 5. **dental f.,** seda dental.
flossflower ['flɔsˌflaʊər, 'flɑs-, B 'flɔs- -ə] *s.* (bot.) agérato.
floss silk, seda floja.
flossy [-ɪ] *a.* 1. lene; velloso, suave, ligero. 2. (jer.) elegante, encantador.
flotage ['floʊtɪdʒ] *s.* 1. flotación, flotabilidad, flotadura, flotamiento, flote. 2. pecios; materia flotante.
flotation [floʊ'teɪʃən] *s.* 1. flotación. 2. (com., fin.) flotación, lanzamiento (de una empresa o negocio). 3. (metal.) flotación.
flotilla [-'tɪlə] *s.* (*pl.* FLOTILLAS) flotilla, flota de barcos pequeños; flota pequeña.
flotsam ['flɑtsəm, B 'flɔt-] *s.* 1. pecio; pecios, restos flotantes (de un naufragio). 2. personas a la deriva, vagos. 3. fruslerías, baratijas.
flounce [flaʊns] *v.i.* 1. andar con movimientos exagerados. 2. contonearse. 3. forcejar, forcejear, sacudirse (caballo en barro, pájaro en agua, etc.). 4. **f. out,** salir airadamente. —*s.* 1. volante, farfalá, cairel. 2. contorsión, sacudida (del cuerpo). —*v.t.* (cost.) adornar con volantes, guarnecer con caireles.
flouncing ['flaʊnsɪŋ] *s.* (cost.) tira (de género) para volantes; tira rizada o plisada.
flouncy [-sɪ] *a.* recargado de volantes (vestido).
flounder ['flaʊndər, B -də] *v.i.* 1. forcejar o forcejear torpemente (como un caballo empantanado); caminar torpemente (como cuando se vadea un río). 2. proceder con dificultad, perder el hilo (al hablar). 3. **f. through,** atravesar a duras penas, pasar con muchos tropiezos. —*s.* 1. tropiezo, tumbo. 2. (ict.) platija, lenguado, rodaballo.
flounderingly [-dərɪŋlɪ] *adv.* torpemente; inciertamente, con dificultad, a empujones.
flour [flaʊr, B 'flaʊə] *s.* harina; harina de trigo. —*v.t.* 1. enharinar, espolvorear (con harina). 2. moler, tamizar, convertir en harina.
flour bin, harinero (recipiente).
flour bolt, f. sieve, tamiz, cedazo.
flour dealer, comerciante en harinas.
flourish ['flɔrɪʃ, B 'flʌrɪʃ] *v.i.* 1. florecer, prosperar. 2. medrar (animales y plantas). 3. jactarse, vanagloriarse. 4. (mús.) ejecutar floreos. —*v.t.* 1. florear; adornar, embellecer. 2. blandir, esgrimir. —*s.* 1. (fig.) florecimiento, prosperidad. 2. gesto ceremonioso. 3. (mús.) floreo. 4. toque decorativo; plumada, adorno; rúbrica (después de una firma). 5. belleza retórica; expresión florida. 6. floreo (con una espada, etc.).
flourishing [-ɪŋ] *a.* floreciente, próspero, vigoroso.
flour mill, molino harinero.
flour moth, (ento.) polilla de la harina.
floury ['flaʊrɪ, B 'flaʊərɪ] *a.* harinoso, farináceo.
flout [flaʊt] *v.t.* burlar, zumbar, escarnecer; insultar; despreciar. —*v.i.* (ú. con *at*) burlarse, mofarse, reírse de. —*s.* mofa, burla; insulto, escarnio.
flouter ['flaʊtər, B -ə] *s.* mofador, burlón.
floutingly [-ɪŋlɪ] *adv.* burlonamente, con escarnio, con mofa, con sorna.
flow [floʊ] *v.i.* 1. fluir, manar, correr (agua), circular (sangre); pasar (gente). 2. subir, crecer (la marea). 3. flotar, ondear, ondular (bandera, etc.). 4. derramarse, correr (la sangre). 5. (fisiol.) menstruar (esp. profusamente). 6. **f. away,** deslizarse, pasar, irse; **f. from,** brotar de, salir de; (fig.) manar de, nacer de; **f. into,** afluir, desembocar, desaguar a; **f. over,** rebosar, desbordar; **f. together,** confluir (ríos); **f. with,** abundar en, nadar en, rebosar en. —*v.t.* inundar; hacer fluir. —*s.* 1. flujo, salida; corriente. 2. flujo creciente (de la marea). 3. derrame (de sangre). 4. (fig.) flujo, caudal, abundancia. 5. ondulación (de banderas, etc.). 6. (fís.) fluidez (de cuerpos líquidos). 7. (fisiol.) flujo, menstruación. 8. (hidr.) gasto, cantidad que sale o pasa por unidad de tiempo. 9. **f. of ideas,** caudal o racha de ideas.
flowage ['floʊɪdʒ] *s.* 1. inundación, derrame. 2. caudal de una creciente. 3. (min.) deformación estructural.
flow chart, (com.) diagrama de fabricación (que muestra el progreso del material a través de un proceso manufacturero).
flower ['flaʊər, B -ə] *s.* 1. flor. 2. (fig.) flor, crema, nata. 3. flor, nata (que hace el vino, etc.). 4. (*pl.*) (quím.) flor, ej., *flowers of sulphur,* flor de azufre. 5. (ret.) flor, imagen rebuscada, perífrasis. 6. (ant.) menstruación. 7. **in f.,** en flor. —*v.i.* 1. florecer, florar, dar flor, florear (Amer.). 2. (fig.) florecer. 3. **f. into,** desarrollarse en. —*v.t.* 1. florear, floretear, adornar con flores. 2. hacer florecer. —*a.* floral; de flores.
flowerage [-ərɪdʒ] *s.* floración, florecimiento, florescencia, (conjunto de) flores; adorno floral.
flower arrangement, arreglo floral.
flowerbed [-ˌbɛd, B 'flaʊəˌ-] *s.* arriate (de flores), era de jardín, macizo.
flower bud, capullo, botón de flor.
flower-de-luce [-də'lus] *s.* (her.) flor de lis, iris.
flowered ['flaʊərd, B -əd] *a.* floreado, adornado con flores.
floweret [-ərət] *s.* 1. *var. de* **floret.** 2. (poét.) florecilla, florecita.
flower girl 1. florista, **vendedora callejera de flores. 2. niña que lleva un ramillete de flores en una boda.**
flower head, (bot.) capítulo.
flowerily [-ərəlɪ] *adv.* floridamente.
floweriness [-ərɪnəs] *s.* 1. floridez, abundancia de flores. 2. (fig.) floridez (del estilo, etc.).
flowering [-ərɪŋ] *a.* floreciente, florido, en flor. —*s.* florecimiento, floración, florescencia.
flowering rush, (bot.) junco florido.
flowerless ['flaʊərləs, B 'flaʊəlɪs] *a.* sin flores, yermo; (bot.) criptógamo.
flower piece, (pint.) cuadro que representa flores.
flowerpot [-ˌpɑt, B -ˌpɔt] *s.* tiesto, maceta de flores.
flower show, exposición o concurso de floricultura.
flowery ['flaʊərɪ] *a.* 1. florido, lleno de flores. 2. floreado, floreteado, florido. 3. (fig.) florido (estilo, oratoria, etc.).
flowing ['floʊɪŋ] *a.* fluido, corriente, manante; ondeante, colgante; suelto. —*s.* flujo, derrame, corriente.
flowingly [-lɪ] *adv.* fluidamente, con fluidez; copiosamente.
flowingness [-nəs] *s.* fluidez.
flowing sheet, (mar.) escota floja.
flowmeter [-ˌmitər, B -ə] *s.* contador, medidor de corriente.
flown [floʊn] *p.p. de* **fly.** —*a.* 1. (ant.) abochornado, hinchado. 2. exaltado, excitado. 3. vidriado.
flow sheet, (ind.) diagrama de fabricación.
fl. oz. *abrev. de* **fluid ounce,** onza fluida.
flu [flu] *s.* (fam.) influenza, gripe.
flub [flʌb] *v.t.* (*pret., p.p.* FLUBBED; *p.pr.* FLUBBING) (jer.) estropear, echar a perder; chapucear, chafallar. —*s.* estropicio, fracaso.
flubdub ['flʌbˌdʌb] *s.* (jer.) faramalla, tontería, disparate.
fluctuant ['flʌktʃʊənt] *a.* fluctuante, fluctuoso.
fluctuate [-ˌeɪt] *v.i.* fluctuar, vacilar, oscilar, variar. —*v.t.* hacer fluctuar.
fluctuating current [-ɪŋ-] (elec.) corriente fluctuante.
fluctuation [ˌflʌktʃʊ'eɪʃən] *s.* fluctuación, vacilación, oscilación, variación.
flue [flu] *s.* 1. humero, cañón de chimenea. 2. tubo de caldera. 3. (mús.) caño de boca, caño de flauta (del órgano); hendidura del fondo (de un caño de boca); caño, tubo sonoro (de un instrumento de viento). 4. (mec.) conducto, canal.
flue, *s.* 1. (un tipo de) red barredera. 2. pelusa, borra, hilacha, tamo.
flue boiler, (mec.) caldera de conductores interiores o de tubos de humo.
fluency ['fluənsɪ] *s.* fluidez; facundia, labia.
fluent [-ənt] *a.* 1. fluente, fluyente. 2. fluido, corriente, fácil. 3. (fig.) fluente; facundo. 4. (raro) variable.
fluently [-lɪ] *adv.* 1. fluidamente. 2. con fluidez; afluentemente, con facundia.
flue pipe, (mús.) caño de flauta, caño de boca (del órgano).
flue stop, (mús.) registro de caños de boca (en un órgano).
fluff [flʌf] *s.* 1. plumón, flojel; vello, pelillo; pelusa, borra, lanilla, mota, tamo. 2. bozo, vello (sobre el labio o mejilla). 3. (teat., rad.) olvido, blanco. 4. **bit of f.,** (jer.) mujercita, polluela. —*v.i.* 1. volverse velloso o fofo, esponjarse, ahuecarse. 2. (teat., rad.) olvidarse, equivocarse (en su parte). —*v.t.* 1. mullir; esponjar, ahuecar. 2. (teat., rad.) olvidar, equivocar (parte). 3. (jer.) chapucear, estropear, chafallar.
fluffily ['flʌfəlɪ] *adv.* blandamente, suavemente, mansamente; de manera esponjosa.
fluffiness [-ɪnəs] *s.* 1. vellosidad; blandura, suavidad, mansedumbre. 2. esponjosidad.
fluffy [-ɪ] *a.* (FLUFFIER; FLUFFIEST) 1. velloso, velludo; cubierto de plumón. 2. mullido; ahuecado; esponjoso.
fluid ['fluəd] *a.* 1. fluido, fluente; móvil, variable. 2. fluido, fácil (lenguaje o estilo). —*s.* fluido.
fluidal [-əl] *a.* (geol., min.) fluidal.
fluid diet, dieta líquida, régimen de alimentos líquidos.
fluid dram, dracma, un octavo de onza líquida.
fluid drive, (aut.) transmisión hidráulica, turboembrague.
fluidextract [ˌfluəd'ɛkˌstrækt] *s.* (farm.) extracto alcohólico concentrado (de un producto vegetal).
fluidify [flu'ɪdəˌfaɪ] *v.t.* (*pret., p.p.* FLUIDIFIED; *p.pr.* FLUIDIFYING) rendir fluido; licuar.
fluidity [-'ɪdətɪ] *s.* fluidez; liquidez.
fluidize ['fluəˌdaɪz] *v.t.* fluidificar, fluidizar.
fluidizer [-ər B -ə] *s.* fluidizador.
fluidly ['fluədlɪ] *adv.* fluentemente, con fluidez.
fluid mechanics, (*sing. en const.*) mecánica de los fluidos.
fluidness [-nəs] *s.* fluidez; estado fluido.
fluid ounce, (farm.) onza líquida (en E.U. equivale a 29,6 cc., en Ingl. a 28,4 cc.).

fluke [fluk] *s.* 1. (ict.) platija, lenguado. 2. (zool.) trematodo, gusano, parásito aplanado. 3. uña u oreja (del ancla o del arpón). 4. aleta de la cola (de la ballena).
fluke, *s.* 1. (fam.) chiripa (en el billar). 2. chiripa, ganga, chamba, suerte. 3. **to win by** (o **through**) **a f.,** ganar de chiripa. —*v.i., v.t.* chiripear, ganar por chiripa; ganar por suerte.
fluky ['flukɪ] *a.* de chiripa, de suerte. 2. cambiadizo, inseguro, caprichoso.
flume [flum] *s.* (E.U.) 1. barranco, barranca, garganta, desfiladero, quebrada, cañada (por donde pasa un río). 2. (hidr.) saetín, caz, acequia, zanja, tragante.
flummery ['flʌmərɪ] *s.* 1. (cocina) gachas de avena. 2. (cocina) especie de flan. 3. insipidez; farsa, patarata.
flummox ['flʌməks] *v.t.* (jer.) enredar, despistar, enmarañar, embrollar.
flump [flʌmp] *v.i.* sentarse, moverse o caerse de golpe o con pesadez. —*v.t.* dejar caer de golpe.
flung [flʌŋ] *pret., p.p. de* **fling.**
flunk [flʌŋk] (fam.) *v.i.* fallar, fracasar (en un examen o curso); **f. out,** retirarse por miedo (de una empresa); abandonar sus estudios por incapacidad. —*v.t.* 1. colgar, reprobar, desaprobar, suspender (al examinando). 2. fallar en (curso, examen). 3. **f. out,** obligar a abandonar sus estudios. —*s.* (fam.) calabaza, suspenso, fracaso (en un examen).
flunky, flunkey ['flʌŋkɪ] *s.* lacayo, adulador, quitamotas.
flunkyism [-kɪˌɪzəm] *s.* servilismo.
fluor ['fluər, -ˌɔr, B -ɔ] *s.* (min.) fluorita.
fluoresce [ˌfluər'ɛs] *v.i.* despedir rayos de luz fluorescente.
fluorescein [-ɪən] *s.* (quím.) fluoresceína.
fluorescence [-əns] *s.* fluorescencia.
fluorescent [-ənt] *a.* fluorescente.
fluorescent lamp, tubo fluorescente.
fluoric [flu'ɔrɪk] *a.* (quím.) fluórico.
fluoridate ['flʊrəˌdeɪt, 'flɔr-, B 'fluəraɪ-] *v.t.* (quím.) fluorizar (el agua potable), tratar con (un) fluoruro.
fluoride ['flʊərˌaɪd] *s.* (quím.) fluoruro.
fluorimeter [ˌflʊə'rɪmətər, B -tə] *var. de* fluorometer.
fluorinate ['flʊrəˌneɪt, 'flɔr-, B 'flʊər-] *v.t.* (quím.) tratar o combinar con flúor.
fluorine ['flʊrˌin, 'flɔr-, B 'flʊər-] *s.* (quím.) (elemento) flúor.
fluorite [-ˌaɪt] *s.* (min.) fluorita, espato flúor.
fluorization [ˌflʊrə'zeɪʃən, ˌflɔr-, B ˌflʊəraɪ-] *s.* (quím.) fluorización (del agua potable).
fluorocarbon [-oʊ'kɑrbən, B -'kɑbən] *s.* (quím.) fluorocarburo.
fluorography [-'ɑgrəfɪ, B -'ɔg-] *s.* (fís.) fluorografía, fotofluorografía.
fluorometer [-'ɑmətər, B -'ɔmɪtə] *s.* (fís.) fluorómetro.
fluoroscope ['flʊrəˌskoʊp, 'flɔr-, B 'flʊər-] *s.* (med.) fluoroscopio.
fluoroscopy [flʊr'ɑskəpɪ, B flʊər'ɔs-] *s.* (fís., med.) fluoroscopía.
fluorosis [-'oʊsəs] *s.* (med.) fluorosis.
fluorspar ['flʊərˌspɑr, B 'flʊəˌspɑ] *s.* (min.) espato flúor, fluorita, fluoruro natural.
flurry ['flɜrɪ, B 'flʌrɪ] *s.* 1. racha, ráfaga (de viento). 2. nevisca; chubasco. 3. agitación, conmoción, excitación, tole; aturdimiento. 4. (com.) actividad repentina, subida o baja pasajera (de los precios o valores). —*v.t.* (*pret., p.p.* FLURRIED; *p.pr.* FLURRYING) agitar, excitar; confundir, aturdir. —*v.i.* agitarse, excitarse.
flush [flʌʃ] *s.* 1. flujo repentino, chorro; salto, golpe de agua. 2. baldeo, lavamiento, limpieza (con agua). 3. copia, afluencia, abundancia, crecimiento. 4. brote, floración repentina (de plantas). 5. acceso (de emoción). 6. rubor, sonrojo, bochorno, chapa (*en las mejillas*). 7. ardor, exaltación. 8. (med.) acaloramiento. 9. (naipes) flux. —*v.i.* 1. fluir con violencia, brotar, salir (agua, etc.). 2. enrojecerse, ruborizarse, sonrojarse, abochornarse. 3. brotar, echar renuevos (una planta). —*v.t.* 1. sacar o verter agua sobre; llenar de agua; inundar (pradera, etc.). 2. baldear, lavar a chorro, limpiar con un chorro de agua; desatancar, desatascar. 3. enrojecer, sonrojar, abochornar. 4. exaltar, inflamar. —*a.* 1. rebosante, lleno. 2. copioso, abundante. 3. opulento; pródigo, generoso. 4. ruboroso, encendido; robusto, vigoroso, lozano. 5. igual, parejo, ras, nivelado, arrasado. 6. directo, dado en pleno (golpe). 7. (impr.) alineado al margen, sin sangrar. 8. **f. with,** rebosante de, lleno de; al nivel de, a ras de, a flor de; **to make f.,** empotrar. —*adv.* 1. directamente, en línea recta. 2. rotundamente, en pleno, directamente. 3. al mismo nivel, ras con ras.
flush, *v.i.* levantarse repentinamente, echar a volar (como un pájaro asustado). —*v.t.* 1. volar (a un pájaro), levantar (caza). 2. (arq.) enrasar, nivelar, igualar.
flush bolt, cerrojo embutido; pasador de embutir, perno embutido.
flush box, (elec.) caja de inspección e introducción de conductores subterráneos.
flush deck, (mar.) cubierta corrida, cubierta rasa.
flusher ['flʌʃər, B -ə] *s.* baldeadora, cilindro perforado para lavar a chorro.
flush joint junta lisa o llana, **ensambladura enrasada.**
flush outlet, (elec.) toma de embutir, tomacorriente embutido.
flush pipe, (mec.) tubo de baldeo.
flush rivet, (mec.) remache de cabeza rasa.
flush switch, (mec.) interruptor embutido; llave de embutir.
flush tank, sifón de lavado automático, depósito de baldeo; tanque de inundación (de inodoro).
flush valve, válvula baldeadora; válvula de aspersión.
fluster ['flʌstər, B -tə] *v.t.* aturdir, confundir, turbar, encender (el rostro la bebida). —*v.i.* andar o moverse con agitación o nerviosidad. —*s.* 1. agitación, confusión, aturdimiento. 2. (ant.) acaloramiento, vehemencia (causada por borrachera).
flustered [-tərd, B -təd] *a.* confundido, turbado, aturdido.
flute [flut] *s.* 1. (mús.) flauta. 2. (cost.) pliegue, doblez (de una tela). 3. (arq.) estría (de columna). 4. (mús.) flautado (registro del órgano). —*v.i.* tocar la flauta. —*v.t.* 1. tocar, silbar o cantar suavemente; decir en tono aflautado. 2. estriar, acanalar (una columna). 3. plegar, doblar, alechugar (una tela).
fluted ['flutəd] *a.* 1. aflautado. 2. acanalado, estriado; ondulado.
fluter [-ər, B -ə] *s.* 1. acanalador (instrumento). 2. (ant.) flautista.
fluting [-ɪŋ] *s.* 1. estría, estriadura, acanaladura. 2. pliegue, doblez, plisado.
fluting plane, (carp.) cepillo bocel.
flutist ['flutəst] *s.* flautista.
flutter ['flʌtər, B -ə] *v.i.* 1. aletear, revolotear. 2. flamear, ondear (velamen, bandera); latir, palpitar (arteria, corazón, etc.). 3. obrar confusamente. 4. agitarse, temblar (de excitación). —*v.t.* 1. agitar, menear, sacudir; batir (las alas). 2. confundir, aturdir. 3. decir confusamente, balbucear. —*s.* 1. aleteo, revoloteo; flameo, ondulación; latido, palpitación, vibración. 2. alboroto, confusión, agitación; aturdimiento. 3. (aer.) flameo, oscilaciones aeroelásticas. 4. (rad., t.v.) vibración (del sonido, de la imagen); (electrón.) trémolo (del sonido). 5. (jer., pr. G.B.) operación azarosa, especulación. 6. **to be in a f.,** estar excitado o en un estado de confusión, estar alborotado.
flutterboard [-ˌbɔrd, B -əˌbɔd] *s.* tabla rectangular que usan los nadadores para practicar los movimientos de las piernas.
flutteringly [-ərɪŋlɪ] *adv.* agitadamente, inquietamente.
flutter kick, patada oscilante (que se ejecuta al nadar al estilo crol).
fluttery ['flʌtərɪ] *a.* 1. oscilante, vibrante. 2. confundido, agitado.
fluvial ['fluvɪəl] *a.* fluvial, perteneciente a los ríos.
fluviomarine [ˌfluvɪˌoʊmə'rin] *a.* (geol.) fluviomarino (díc. del depósito que forman conjuntamente el mar y los ríos en su desembocadura).
fluviometer [-'ɑmətər, B -'ɔmɪtə] *s.* (meteor.) fluviómetro.
flux [flʌks] *s.* 1. flujo, corriente. 2. mudanza o cambio continuo, fluctuación. 3. flujo (de la marea). 4. (med.) flujo. 5. (metal.) fundente, flujo (para metales); castina (para minerales). 6. (fís., elec.) flujo. —*v.t.* 1. derretir, fundir, fluidificar. 2. aplicar fundente a. —*v.i.* derretirse, fluidificarse.
flux density, (elec.) densidad de flujo.
flux gate, aparato indicador (de la dirección) del campo magnético terrestre.
fluxion ['flʌkʃən] *s.* 1. flujo, mudanza o cambio continuo. 2. (mat.) fluxión, derivada, diferencial. 3. (med.) fluxión.
fluxional [-əl] *a.* (mat.) variable; inconstante.
fluxionally [-əlɪ] *adv.* a manera de flujo.
fly [flaɪ] *v.i.* (*pret.* FLEW [flu]; *p.p.* FLOWN [floʊn]; *p.pr.* FLYING) 1. volar. 2. huir. 3. desvanecerse, desaparecer. 4. correr o pasar (rápidamente); lanzarse, precipitarse. 5. flotar, ondear (en el aire). 6. saltar (chispas, astillas). 7. viajar en avión. 8. (*pret., p.p.* FLIED [flaɪd]) (béisbol) pegar una planchita. 9. (caza) cazar con halcón; atacar (en vuelo) como un halcón. 10. **f. at,** arrojarse o lanzarse sobre; **f. away,** irse volando; escaparse; **f. from,** huir de; **f. high,** ser ambicioso; **f. into a rage,** montar en cólera; **f. off,** irse a la carrera; desprenderse; **f. off the handle,** (fam.) perder los estribos, encolerizarse; **f. open,** abrirse repentinamente; **f. out,** explotar en lenguaje (acción) violento; **f. over,** volar sobre; **f. up,** subir volando; **to let f. (at),** abrir fuego (sobre), disparar (contra); echar reniegos (contra); **to send flying,** echar a rodar. —*v.t.* 1. hacer volar (algo); hacer flotar; elevar (cometa, etc.); enarbolar, hacer flamear, desplegar, tener izada (bandera, etc.). 2. huir de, evadir, evitar. 3. llevar o transportar en avión; atravesar en avión. 4. manejar, dirigir (un avión). 5. cazar (con o como halcón). 6. **f. a kite,** conseguir dinero por medio de un pagaré de favor; (fig.) probar cómo sopla el viento; **go, f. a kite!** (jer.) ¡váyase! ¡no me moleste!; **to let f.,** disparar (un proyectil). —*s.* 1. vuelo (de un proyectil, pelota, etc.). 2. cabriolé, calesín, volanta. 3. pliegue (para cubrir botones); bragueta (abertura delantera de los pantalones). 4. toldo (de una tienda de campaña); lona que cubre o tapa la puerta de una tienda de campaña. 5. parte de la bandera más distante del asta; ancho o envergadura de una bandera. 6. (impr.) guarda (de un libro). 7. (mec.) rueda volante; brazo de romana; escape de reloj; brazo de veleta; lanzadera. 8. (teat.) (*pl.*) bambalinas.
fly, *s.* 1. (ento.) mosca. 2. (pesca) mosca artificial. 3. (impr., ant.) sacapliegos. 4. **a f. in the ointment,** pequeño incidente que estropea el encanto (de

algo); **to die like flies,** morir como moscas. —*a.* (jer., **G.B.**) instruido, hábil, entendido; astuto, ladino; vivo, listo.
flyable ['flaɪəbəl] *a.* apto para hacerlo volar; voladero.
fly agaric, (bot.) agárico, amanita.
flyaway [-əˌweɪ] *a.* 1. veleidoso, casquivano. 2. voladizo. 3. listo para el vuelo (avión en fábrica).
fly ball, (béisbol) pelota bateada que sigue la trayectoria de un arco.
flybelt [-ˌbɛlt] *s.* zona infestada por la (mosca) tse-tsé.
flyblow [-ˌbloʊ] *s.* cresa, larvas o huevos de moscas. —*v.t., v.i.* corromper depositando cresas; contaminar, inficionar.
flyblown [-ˌbloʊn] *a.* 1. cubierto con manchas de mosca. 2. contaminado, inficionado.
flyboat [-ˌboʊt] *s.* filibote, especie de buque rápido.
fly-boy [-ˌbɔɪ] *s.* (jer.) aviador, miembro de la fuerza aérea.
flyby [-ˌbaɪ] *s.* (astronáut.) vuelo de inspección (de un vehículo espacial).
fly-by-night ['flaɪbəˌnaɪt] *a.* fugaz, efímero; engañador; irresponsable.
fly casting, lanzamiento de moscas artificiales (en la pesca).
flycatcher [-ˌkætʃər, B -ə] *s.* (orn.) papamoscas, cazamoscas, doral, muscaria, moscareta.
flyer, *var. de* **flier.**
fly-fish [-ˌfɪʃ] *v.i.* pescar con moscas (artificiales o reales).
flyflap [-ˌflæp] *s.* mosqueador, espantamoscas, mosquero.
flying ['flaɪɪŋ] *a.* 1. volante, volador. 2. veloz, rápido. —*s.* 1. vuelo; viaje por avión. 2. aviación; pilotaje (de un avión).
flying boat, (aer.) hidroavión, hidroavión de casco.
flying bomb, (aer.) bomba volante.
flying bridge, puente superior o volante de un vehículo o embarcación.
flying buttress, (arq.) botarel con arbotante, contrafuerte, arco botarete.
flying club, aeroclub.
flying colors, (fig.) éxito completo; **to come off with f. c.,** quedar lucido, salir victorioso.
flying column, (mil.) cuerpo o columna volante.
flying corps, (mil.) fuerza aérea.
flying dragon, (zool.) dragón.
flying field, campo de aterrizaje.
flying fish, (ict.) volador, pez volador; milano.
flying fortress, (aer., mil.) fortaleza volante, fortaleza aérea.
flying fox, (zool.) zorro volante, panique, bermejizo, murciélago frugívoro.
flying frog, (zool.) rana voladora.
flying gurnard, (ict.) variedad de pez volador.
flying jib, (mar.) petifoque, cuarto foque.
flying jib boom, (mar.) botalón de petifoque.
flying lemur, (zool.) lémur o maqui volador.
flying machine, (aer.) aparato volador, máquina voladora (en la época experimental de la aeronáutica).
flying mare, (lucha) llave de brazo (con que el agresor agarra por la muñeca a su oponente y dándose vuelta, de un tirón le hace volar sobre su espalda).
flying saucer, platillo volador (t. **UFO**).
flying squadron, escuadra ligera.
flying squirrel, (zool.) ardilla voladora, guiguí.
flying start, (dep.) salida lanzada (en carrera de relevos); **to get off to a f. s.,** (fig.) empezar con mucho brío; tener un comienzo brillante (empresa, negocio, etc.).
flying wing, (aer.) ala volante (especie de avión sin cola ni fuselaje, que se asemeja a un ala).
flyleaf ['flaɪˌlif] *s.* (enc.) guarda.
fly net, mosquitero.
flyover [-ˌoʊvər, B -və] *s.* 1. (aer.) vuelo de demostración a baja altura (de uno o más aviones). 2. (G.B.) paso a desnivel.
flypaper [-ˌpeɪpər, B -ə] *s.* mosquero, papel atrapamoscas.
fly press, (mec.) prensa de tornillo.
fly sheet, volante de propaganda.
flyspeck [-ˌspɛk] *s.* mancha de mosca, cagada de mosca. —*v.t.* cubrir con manchas de mosca.
fly swatter, matamoscas.
flytrap [-ˌtræp] *s.* 1. (bot.) sarracenia. 2. (bot.) atrapamoscas, dionea. 3. mosquero.
flyway ['flaɪˌweɪ] *s.* ruta de migración (de las aves migratorias).
flyweight [-ˌweɪt] *s.* 1. (boxeo) peso mosca. 2. (aer.) contrapeso del regulador.
flywheel [-ˌhwil, -ˌwil] *s.* (mec.) volante.
FM ['ɛf'ɛm] (rad.) modulación de frecuencia, frecuencia modulada.
fm. *abrev. de* **fathom,** braza.
Fm *símb. de* **fermium,** fermio (Fm).
F-number, (foto.) número índice de abertura útil.
F.O. *abrev. de* **Foreign Office,** Ministerio de Relaciones Exteriores.
foal [foʊl] *s.* potro, potrillo (de caballo); pollino (de asno). —*v.t., v.i.* parir (una yegua o burra).
foam [foʊm] *s.* 1. espuma. 2. (poét.) (el) mar. —*v.i.* espumar, echar espuma; **f. at the mouth,** espumajear, (fig.) echar humo (de ira). —*v.t.* hacer espumoso o esponjoso.
foamily ['foʊməlɪ] *adv.* a modo de espuma.
foaminess [-ɪnəs] *s.* espumosidad.
foam rubber, caucho esponjoso, espuma de caucho.
foamy ['foʊmɪ] *a.* espumoso, espumajoso; lleno de espuma.
fob [fɑb, B fɔb] *s.* 1. faltriquera de reloj. 2. leontina, leopoldina. 3. dije (usado en la cadena del reloj). —*v.t.* (*pret., p.p.* FOBBED; *p.pr.* FOBBING) 1. embolsar, poner en la faltriquera de reloj. 2. (ant.) engañar, embaucar. 3. **f. (someone) off,** evadir con engañifas (a alguien); **f. (something) off upon (someone),** encajar (una cosa) a (alguien).
F.O.B., f.o.b. *abrev. de* **free on board,** franco a bordo (FAB, fab).
focal ['foʊkəl] *a.* focal, céntrico.
focal distance, f. length, (ópt.) distancia focal, longitud focal.
focal infection, (med.) infección focal.
focalization [ˌfoʊkələ'zeɪʃən, B -laɪ-] *s.* 1. enfoque. 2. (med.) localización.
focalize ['foʊkəˌlaɪz] *v.t.* 1. enfocar. 2. (med.) localizar, limitar a un área circunscrita. —*v.i.* 1. enfocarse, concentrarse. 2. (med.) quedar localizado.
focal point, foco, punto focal.
fo'c's'le ['foʊksəl] (mar.) *abrev. de* **forecastle.**
focus ['foʊkəs] *s.* (*pl.* FOCUSES o FOCI ['foʊˌsaɪ]) 1. (mat., fís., med., ópt., foto.) foco. 2. (ópt.) distancia focal, ajuste (del ojo u ocular). 3. foco, punto central (de actividad, atracción, epidemia, terremoto, tormenta, etc.). 4. **in f.,** enfocado; **out of f.,** fuera de foco, desenfocado; **to bring into f.,** enfocar. —*v.t.* (*pret., p.p.* FOCUSED o FOCUSSED; *p.pr.* FOCUSING o FOCUSSING) 1. enfocar; concentrar. 2. ajustar el foco de (ojo, lente, etc.). —*v.i.* enfocarse, concentrarse.
focus glass, f. lense, (foto.) enfocador.
focusing [-ɪŋ] *s.* (foto.) enfoque.
fodder ['fɑdər, B 'fɔdə] *s.* forraje, pienso, pastura; **cannon f.,** carne de cañón. —*v.t.* dar forraje a.
foe [foʊ] *s.* enemigo, adversario, antagonista.
foehn, föhn [fɜn] *s.* (meteor.) fohn, viento seco de las montañas (esp. los Alpes).
foelike ['foʊˌlaɪk] *a.* hostil.
foeman ['foʊmən] *s.* enemigo (en guerra).
foetal, foetus, *vars. de* **fetal, fetus.**
foetid ['fitəd] *var. de* **fetid.**
fog [fɔg, fɑg, B fɔg] *s.* 1. niebla, neblina, bruma. 2. (fig.) nebulosidad (mental), confusión, ej., *in a f.,* confundido, desorientado. 3. (foto.) velo (que obscurece el negativo). —*v.t.* (*pret., p.p.* FOGGED; *p.pr.* FOGGING). 1. envolver en niebla, obscurecer; empañar. 2. (fig.) confundir, aturdir. 3. (foto.) velar. —*v.i.* 1. ponerse brumoso; empañarse. 2. (foto.) velarse.
fog, *s.* 1. segundo crecimiento o cosecha (del pasto o hierba). 2. (esco.) (cualquier) musgo.
fog bank, brumazón, masa densa de niebla.
fog bell, campana de nieblas o de alarma.
fogbound ['fɔg, baʊnd, 'fɑg- B 'fɔg-] *a.* rodeado o cubierto de niebla; detenido (el tránsito o un barco) por la niebla.
fogbow [-ˌboʊ] *s.* arco de luz blanca o amarillenta que algunas veces se ve en la niebla.
fogdog [-ˌdɔg] *s.* punto luminoso que se ve algunas veces en la niebla cerca del horizonte.
foggily [-əlɪ] *adv.* nebulosamente.
fogginess [-ɪnəs] *s.* nebulosidad, bruma.
foggy ['fɔgɪ, 'fɑgɪ, B 'fɔgɪ] *a.* (FOGGIER; FOGGIEST). 1. neblinoso, brumoso, caliginoso. 2. (fig.) nebuloso, indistinto, confuso. 3. (foto.) velado.
foghorn [-ˌhɔrn, B -ˌhɔn] *s.* (mar.) bocina o sirena de niebla; (fig.) voz ronca y fuerte.
fogy, fogey ['foʊgɪ] *s.* (*pl.* FOGIES), vejestorio, persona de ideas y costumbres anticuadas o muy conservadoras.
fogyism [-ˌɪzəm] *s.* cosas de viejo, afición a las ideas anticuadas.
foible ['fɔɪbəl] *s.* 1. punto débil, punto vulnerable, punto flaco, debilidad, flaqueza. 2. parte más débil de la hoja de una espada (entre el medio y la punta).
foil [fɔɪl] *v.t.* 1. frustrar, contrarrestar, anular, hacer inútil (esfuerzo, planes, intento, etc.). 2. (caza) hollar, pisar, pisotear (el rastro o pista). —*s.* 1. florete; (*pl.*) esgrima con florete. 2. (ant.) fracaso, derrota, frustración. 3. (ant.) huella, pista, rastro (de un animal).
foil, *s.* 1. hojuela, chapa, pan (de oro, plata u otro metal), oropel (de latón). 2. azogado (de espejo). 3. (arq.) lóbulo. 4. (joy.) hoja de realce, pan (que se coloca debajo de una gema falsa). 5. (fig.) contraste (que sirve para realzar algo). 6. aluminio doméstico, papel de aluminio, papel de plata. 7. (esgr.) florete. —*v.t.* 1. azogar, platear. 2. realzar. 3. (arq.) adornar con lóbulos.
foiled [fɔɪld] *a.* (arq.) lobulado.
foil paper, papel de aluminio o estaño.
foilsman ['fɔɪlzmən] *s.* floretista.
foil-wrapped ['fɔɪlˌræpt] *a.* envuelto en papel de aluminio o estaño.
foist [fɔɪst] *v.t.* (con *in*) meter clandestinamente, introducir de contrabando (algo ilegítimo); **f. (something) off on** (o **upon**), encajar (algo) a; **f. on** (o **upon**), imponer a, atribuir falsamente a.
folacin ['foʊləsən] *s.* (quím.) ácido fólico.
fold [foʊld] *v.t.* 1. doblar, plegar. 2. cruzar (los brazos); enlazar (las manos). 3. envolver, cubrir. 4. **f. down,** bajar (asiento de silla, etc.); **f. up,** cerrar (ej., un mapa plegadizo); liquidar (negocio). —*v.i.* 1. doblarse, plegarse, cerrarse; desplomarse. 2. fracasar, liquidarse, dejar de funcionar (esp. un negocio o una obra de teatro). —*s.* 1. doblez, pliegue, arruga. 2. pliego (en

impreso). 3. (geol.) pliegue, plegamiento. 4. (anat.) pliegue. —*a.* en determinado número de partes, ej., *two-fold,* dos partes, doble.

fold, *s.* 1. redil, corral, aprisco (para ovejas). 2. rebaño (de ovejas). 3. (fig.) rebaño (de los fieles). —*v.t.* arredilar, cerrar, encerrar, meter en el redil.

foldaway ['fouldə,weɪ] *a.* plegadizo (puerta, cama).

foldboat [-,bout] *s.* bote plegable.

folder ['fouldər, B -də] *s.* 1. plegador, doblador. 2. carpeta (para hojas sueltas). 3. cuadernillo, folleto (no cosido sino doblado). 4. plegadera (del encuadernador, grabador, etc.).

folderol ['fɑldə,rɑl, B 'fɔldə,rɔl] *s.* 1. bagatela, friolera, chuchería. 2. tontería, disparate, patochada.

folding ['fouldɪŋ] *a.* plegable, plegadizo; doblador, plegador.

folding bed, cama plegadiza.

folding camera, cámara de fuelle.

folding chair, silla de tijera, silla plegable, perezoso (Urug.).

folding door, puerta plegadiza.

folding knife, navaja, cuchilla plegadiza.

folding machine, máquina de plegar.

folding money, (jer.) billetes (en contraste a monedas).

folding rule, metro plegadizo, metro de tramos, regla plegadiza.

folding screen, biombo.

folding seat, traspuntín, trasportín, asiento plegadizo (en carros, automóviles, etc.).

folding top, (aut.) capota plegadiza.

folia, *pl. de* **folium.**

foliaceous [,foulɪ'eɪʃəs] *a.* (bot., min.) foliáceo; laminado.

foliage ['foulɪɪdʒ] *s.* follaje, fronda; (arq.) follaje.

foliage plant, planta decorativa (cultivada por su follaje).

foliar ['foulɪər, B -ə] *a.* (bot.) foliar.

foliate ['foulɪət] *a.* 1. (bot.) foliado; hojoso. 2. (bot.) foliforme. —[-,eɪt] *v.t.* 1. cubrir con amalgama de estaño, azogar (vidrio para hacer espejos). 2. foliar (un libro, manuscrito, etc.). 3. batir (metal). 4. (arq.) adornar con hojas o lóbulos. —*v.i.* hojear (metal), exfoliarse (mineral, hueso, etc.).

foliation [,foulɪ'eɪʃən] *s.* 1. foliación (de las plantas). 2. foliación (de un libro, manuscrito, etc.). 3. azogamiento (de vidrio para hacer espejos). 4. (arq.) foliación, ornamentación con follaje; follajería. 5. (metal.) batimiento (de un metal para formar una lámina u hoja delgada). 6. (min.) estructura laminar.

foliature ['foulɪətʃər, B -tʃə] *s.* foliatura.

folic ['foulɪk] *a.* (quím.) fólico.

folio ['foulɪ,ou] *s.* 1. folio, hoja, foja. 2. pliego de papel doblado una vez. 3. libro en folio, infolio. 4. (ten.) folio. 5. (der.) unidad de 100 (en G.B. 72 ó 90) palabras de un documento. 6. (impr.) folio, número de la página; título de fecha; (*pl.*) foliación, numeración de las páginas. —*a.* en folio. —*v.t.* (*pret.* y *p.p.* FOLIOED; *p.pr.* FOLIOING) foliar, paginar.

foliolate ['foulɪə,leɪt] *a.* (bot.) foliolado.

foliose ['foulɪ,ous] **folious** [-əs] *a.* (bot.) foliado, foliáceo; frondoso.

folium ['foulɪəm] *s.*(*pl.* FOLIUMS O FOLIA [-lɪə]) 1. (geol.) estrato delgado (esp. en rocas metamórficas). 2. (geom.) curva, vuelta.

folk [fouk] *s.* (*pl.* FOLK O FOLKS) 1. gente. 2. (fam.) (*pl.*) padres, parientes, parentela. 3. (ant.) nación, raza, pueblo. —*a.* tradicional, popular.

folk air, aire popular.

folk dance, baile folklórico.

folkish ['foukɪʃ] *a.* 1. de carácter popular. 2. folklórico.

folklore ['fouk,lɔr, B -,lɔ] *s.* folklore, tradiciones y leyendas populares.

folkloric [-,lɔrɪk] *a.* folklórico.

folklorist [-,lɔrəst] *s.* folklorista.

folk medicine, remedios caseros (esp. con hierbas).

folkmoot ['fouk,mut] **folkmote, folkmot** [-,mout] *s.* (hist.) asamblea, convención; (der. anglosajón) asamblea general del pueblo.

folk music, música folklórica.

folk rock, música de ritmo *rock* combinada con letra de temas folklóricos.

folksiness ['fouksɪnəs] *s.* familiaridad empalagosa.

folk singer, cantante de música folklórica.

folk song, canción popular, canción tradicional.

folksy ['fouksɪ] *a.* muy informal o familiar; de trato social simple y campechano.

folk tale, cuento popular.

folkway [-,weɪ] *s.* costumbre tradicional (de un pueblo).

follicle ['fɑlɪkəl, B 'fɔl-] *s.* (bot., anat.) folículo.

follicle mite, (zool.) acárido que vive en folículos pilosos.

follicle-stimulating hormone [-,stɪmjə,leɪtɪŋ-] (med.) hormona folicular, estrina.

follicular [fə'lɪkjələr, B -lə] *a.* (bot., anat.) folicular.

folliculin [-'lɪkjələn] *s.* (med.) foliculina.

follies ['fɑliz, B 'fɔl-] *pl. de* **folly,** revista teatral.

follow ['fɑlou, B 'fɔl-] *v.t.* 1. seguir, andar tras de, ir detrás de. 2. perseguir, buscar. 3. seguir, observar (instrucciones, política, etc.). 4. copiar, imitar. 5. proseguir, continuar por (camino, rumbo); seguir (llamamiento, vocación). 6. seguir a, suceder a. 7. seguir el hilo de (argumento, etc.); comprender (el razonamiento de). 8. seguir con la mirada o los ojos. 9. (dial.) acompañar. 10. **f. the leader,** juego en que todos imitan al guía; **f. on,** seguir más tarde, subsequir; **f. one's nose,** seguir su propio instinto; **f. out,** perseguir hasta el fin; llevar a cabo; ejecutar; **f. suit,** (fig.) imitar el ejemplo, hacer lo mismo; **f. the herd,** dejarse llevar de la corriente, irse con la corriente; **f. the hounds,** cazar; **f. up,** perseguir con ahínco; continuar (una acción con otra); dar más detalles de, continuar el relato de (noticias, suceso, etc.). —*v.i.* 1. ir detrás, venir después. 2. seguirse, derivarse, desprenderse, resultar. 3. **as follows,** como sigue; **f. in one's steps,** seguir las huellas de, imitar el ejemplo de; **f. in the wake of,** venir o llegar como secuela de; **f. on,** (criquet) continuar en juego; **f. through,** (dep.) completar el movimiento (después de golpear la pelota, efectuar el lanzamiento, etc.); continuar la acción, proseguir uno su objetivo. —*s.* 1. seguimiento, continuación. 2. (billar) (tacada con) efecto hacia adelante.

follower ['fɑlouər, B 'fɔlouə] *s.* 1. seguidor, secuaz, partidario, adherente, discípulo; acompañante, sirviente, criado, ayudante; subalterno, dependiente. 2. (fam.) galán, cortejo. 3. (mec.) embutidor, falso pilote; casquillo (de prensaestopas); contrabrida (de tubería); engranaje impulsado; polea mandada; seguidor. 4. (*pl.*) séquito, cortejo. 5. **camp f.,** soldadera, cantinera.

followership [-,ʃɪp] *s.* séquito, comitiva.

following ['fɑlouɪŋ, B 'fɔl-] *a.* 1. siguiente, próximo. 2. **the f.,** lo siguiente; los siguientes. —*s.* séquito, comitiva, cortejo; secuaces, partidarios. —*prep.* después de, a raíz de.

follow-through [-'θru] *s.* (dep.) movimiento complementario (ejecutado después de haber golpeado la pelota, efectuado el lanzamiento, etc.). — **to f.-t.,** llevar a cabo (un plan, etc.) hasta el final.

follow-up [-,ʌp] *a.* consecutivo, recordatorio. —*s.* 1. tratamiento complementario (de un enfermo curado). 2. continuación, nuevo artículo (sobre noticias ya comentadas). 3. (com.) recordatorio (díc. de una nueva carta o diligencia a un posible cliente).

folly ['fɑlɪ, B 'fɔlɪ] *s.* (*pl.* FOLLIES) 1. locura, insensatez, tontería; extravagancia, idea disparatada. 2. empresa alocada, acto de un loco.

foment [fou'mɛnt] *v.t.* 1. fomentar, provocar, excitar, instigar. 2. (med.) fomentar, dar paños calientes a (con agua o líquidos medicinales).

fomentation [,foumən'teɪʃən] *s.* 1. excitación, provocación, instigación. 2. (med.) fomentación (aplicación de paños calientes húmedos al cuerpo para calmar el dolor); fomento (loción así aplicada).

fomenter [fou'mɛntər, B -ə] *s.* fomentador.

fond [fɑnd, B fɔnd] *a.* 1. tierno, cariñoso, afectuoso; demasiado indulgente. 2. caro (anhelo, íntimo deseo). 3. ingenuo, inocente, cándido. 4. **to be f. of,** estar encariñado con, tener cariño para con (una persona); ser aficionado a, ser amigo de; gustarle a uno; **to become** (o **get**) **f. of,** cobrar afición a, aficionarse a.

fondant ['fɑndənt, B 'fɔn-] *s.* pasta de azúcar (que sirve de base a muchos confites).

fondle ['fɑndəl, B 'fɔn-] *v.t.* mimar, acariciar, hacer fiestas o halagos a. —*v.i.* mostrarse cariñoso.

fondler [-dlər, B -dlə] *s.* acariciador, mimador.

fondly ['fɑndlɪ, B 'fɔnd-] *adv.* cariñosamente, tiernamente, afectuosamente.

fondness [-nəs] *s.* 1. afecto, afectuosidad, cariño, ternura. 2. afición, inclinación.

fondue, fondu [fɑn'du, B fɔn'dju] *s.* 1. queso derretido (sazonado con vino o aguardiente). 2. flan hecho con queso y miga de pan.

font [fɑnt, B fɔnt] *s.* 1. fuente, pila bautismal, pila de bautismo; pila de agua bendita. 2. (poét.) fuente, manantial; (fig.) fuente, origen. 3. depósito para combustible de una lámpara. 4. (impr.) fundición (de tipos); fuente (de tipos); torta.

fontanel, fontanelle [,fɑntə'nɛl, B ,fɔnt-] *s.* (anat.) fontanela.

food [fud] *s.* 1. comida, alimento, vianda. 2. (fig.) alimento, nutrimento (mental, intelectual). 3. **f. for thought,** materia de reflexión; **to be f. for worms,** estar muerto.

food chain, (ecol.) secuencia de organismos en que cada uno se alimenta del inmediato inferior, ej., yerba, conejo, zorro.

food cycle, (ecol.) todas las secuencias de organismos alimenticios en una comunidad.

food poisoning, (med.) intoxicación alimentaria.

food stamp, cupón federal, estampilla gubernamental que sirve como dinero para comprar alimentos.

foodstuff ['fud,stʌf] *s.* producto o substancia alimenticia, comida, alimento.

food value, valor nutritivo, valor alimenticio.

foofaraw ['fufə,rɔ] *s.* 1. ringorrangos, faralá. 2. ajetreo innecesario, alharaca.

fool [ful] *s.* 1. tonto, bobo, simplón, inocente, bobalicón, necio. 2. bufón, payaso. 3. (G.B.) (cocina) dulce hecho de fruta cocida y crema batida. 4. **no f. like an old f.,** no hay peor tonto que un viejo tonto (díc. esp. de viejos enamorados); **to be no** o **nobody's f.,** no tener pelo de tonto; **to make a f. of (someone),** poner en ridículo (a alguien); **to make a f. of oneself,** hacer un papelón (Amer.), ponerse en ridículo; **to play the f.,** hacerse el tonto; hacer payasadas, bromear. —*v.i.* 1. bromear, chancear, tontear. 2. **f. around,** bromear, tontear; ocuparse en cosas frívolas; **f. (around) with,** jugar con; meterse con. —*v.t.* 1. engañar, embaucar. 2. **f. away,** malgastar, gastar tontamente (el tiempo, dinero, etc.); **f. (someone) into (doing something),** persuadir (a alguien) fraudulentamente para que (haga algo); **f. (someone) out of (something),** sacar o despojar con maña (algo) de (alguien). —*a.* tonto, fatuo, bobo, disparatado.

foolery [ˈfulərɪ] *s.* (*pl.* FOOLERIES) tontería, bobería, bufonada.

foolhardily [-ˌhardəlɪ, B -ˌhɑdɪ-] *adv.* temerariamente, arriesgadamente.

foolhardiness [-dɪnəs] *s.* temeridad.

foolhardy [-ˌhardɪ, B -ˌhɑdɪ] *a.* arriesgado, temerario, aventurado, audaz.

fooling [ˈfulɪŋ] *s.* broma, chacota, humorada; engaño; **no f.,** (fam.) hablando en serio.

foolish [-ɪʃ] *a.* tonto, necio, simple, disparatado; imprudente; absurdo, ridículo, descabellado.

foolishly [-lɪ] *adv.* tontamente, simplemente.

foolishness [-nəs] *s.* tontería, necedad, simpleza, disparate, burrada, ridiculez.

foolproof [ˈfulˌpruf] *a.* a prueba de impericia, a prueba de mal trato; seguro, cierto, infalible.

foolscap, fool's cap [ˈfulzˌkæp] *s.* 1. gorro de bufón. 2. capirote de burro (que se suele poner al niño como castigo en la escuela). 3. (gen. **foolscap**) papel de oficio, hoja de papel de aproximadamente 33 cm. x 40 cm.

fool's errand, empresa descabellada, encargo o encomienda inútil; **to send on a f.'s. e.,** mandar a una encomienda inútil, hacer perder el tiempo.

fool's gold, pirita de hierro o cobre (parecida al oro en el color).

fool's paradise, felicidad engañosa.

fool's parsley, (bot.) perejil de perro, cicuta menor.

foot [fʊt] *s.* (*pl.* FEET [fit]) 1. pie, pata. 2. pie, medida lineal. 3. pie, parte inferior, parte baja (de cama, canapé, sofá, cerro, escalera, pared, lista, página, clase, etc.); peal (de calcetín, media, etc.). 4. (t. **presser f.**) (mec.) prensatelas, pisacosturas, horquilla (que sujeta la tela en la máquina de coser). 5. (mil., pr. G.B.) infantería. 6. (impr.) pie (de un tipo). 7. pie, unidad métrica. 8. (mar.) pujamen (de una vela). 9. **at one's feet,** a los pies de uno; sometido a uno; **my f.!** ¡tonterías! ¡qué disparate!; **on f.,** a pie, caminando, avanzando, en marcha; progresando, haciendo progresos; **on one's feet,** de pie; en pie, levantado, de buena salud; prosperando; **on the wrong f.,** con mal pie; **to carry off one's feet,** arrebatar, cautivar, entusiasmar (a uno); **to have one f. in the grave,** estar con un pie en el hoyo o en la sepultura; **to put one's best f. forward,** esmerarse, esforzarse, poner los cinco sentidos; andar con la mayor diligencia posible; correr tan rápido como pueda uno; **to put one's f. down,** (fig.) no ceder (más), ser firme; **to put one's f. in it** o **in one's mouth,** meter la pata, tirarse un planchazo; **to sweep off one's feet,** perder la cabeza; **to tread under f.,** pisotear, hollar; **under f.,** en el suelo, debajo de los pies; estorbando el paso. —*v.i.* avanzar rápido (un barco). —*v.t.* 1. bailar, danzar. 2. recorrer, pasar sobre. 3. (fam.) pagar, sufragar. 4. (G.B.) patear, cocear. 5. **f. it,** (fam.) andar, caminar; ir de pie; bailar; **f. the bill,** (lit., fig.) pagar la cuenta.

footage [ˈfʊtɪdʒ] *s.* longitud en pies, número de pies; (madera) pies de tablas; (cinem.) longitud en pies (de película filmada), metraje; película, ej., *much footage was wasted on superfluous scenes,* se desperdició mucha película en escenas superfluas.

foot-and-mouth disease [ˈfʊtənˈmaʊθ-] (vet.) fiebre aftosa, glosopeda.

football [-ˌbɔl] *s.* 1. (dep.) fútbol, fútbol americano; (*ball*) pelota de fútbol.

football field, campo de fútbol, cancha de fútbol (Amer.).

football player, futbolista, jugador de fútbol.

football pool, apuesta colectiva.

footbath [-ˌbæθ, B -ˌbɑθ] *s.* 1. baño de pies; pediluvio (que se toma por medicina). 2. bañera para lavar los pies.

footboard [-ˌbɔrd, B -ˌbɔd] *s.* 1. estribo; trasera (de coche); plataforma para los pies (del cochero). 2. (barandilla que forma el) pie de la cama.

footboy [-ˌbɔɪ] *s.* paje, lacayo, criado, sirviente, servidor.

foot brake, freno de pedal.

footbreadth [-ˌbrɛdθ] *s.* ancho del pie.

footbridge [-ˌbrɪdʒ] *s.* puente para peatones; pasarela.

foot-candle [ˈfʊtˈkændəl] *s.* (fotometría) bujía-pie o pie-bujía (unidad de iluminación).

footcloth [-ˌklɔθ] *s.* 1. gualdrapa. 2. (ant.) alfombra.

footed [ˈfʊtəd] *a.* con pies; (en palabras compuestas) de . . . pies o patas; de piernas, ej., *six-f.,* de seis pies o patas; **fleet-f.,** ligero de piernas.

footer [-ər, B -ə] *s.* 1. peatón. 2. (en palabras compuestas) hombre de . . . pies (de altura), ej., *a six-f.,* un hombre de seis pies. 3. (fam., G.B.) fútbol, balompié.

footfall [-ˌfɔl] *s.* paso (movimiento y ruido), pisada.

foot fault, (tenis) falta de pie.

footgear [-ˌgɪr, B -ˌgɪə] *s.* calzado.

foot guard, guardacascos (para los caballos); cualquier cosa que proteja los pies.

foothill [ˈfʊtˌhɪl] *s.* colina al pie de una montaña; estribo, estribación.

foothold [-ˌhoʊld] *s.* lugar firme, apoyo para el pie; posición firme o establecida; **to gain a f.,** encontrar apoyo; ganar pie, tener un pie adentro.

footing [ˈfʊtɪŋ] *s.* 1. pie, base, fundamento. 2. piso, suelo (donde se ponen los pies); posición establecida, base (para operación). 3. paso, baile, danza; marcha, curso, carrera; venida. 4. material para hacer pies (ej., de medias, etc.). 5. posición, situación, condición, relación. 6. (mat.) suma de una columna de guarismos. 7. (arq.) zarpa. 8. **on a friendly f.,** en relaciones amistosas; **on an equal f.,** por igual, igualmente, en un mismo pie de igualdad; **on a war f.,** en pie de guerra; **to gain a f.,** tener un pie (a) dentro; **to get a f.,** establecerse; **to lose one's f.,** perder pie, írsele los pies a uno.

footle [ˈfutəl] *v.i.* 1. chancear, hacerse el tonto; desperdiciar el tiempo. 2. decir tonterías. —*s.* disparate, estupidez.

footless [ˈfʊtləs] *a.* 1. sin pies. 2. sin fundamento, insubstancial. 3. (fam.) estúpido, tonto.

footlights [-ˌlaɪts] *s. pl.* 1. (teat.) candilejas, batería, luces del proscenio. 2. (fig.) (las) tablas, (el) teatro.

footling [ˈfutlɪŋ] *a.* 1. inepto, incapaz. 2. trivial, fútil; tonto; inútil.

footlocker [ˈfʊtˌlɑkər, B -ˌlɔkə] *s.* pequeño baúl para los efectos personales colocado generalmente al pie de la cama (en barracas, internados, etc.).

footloose [-ˌlus] *a.* libre, sin trabas ni obligaciones; desembarazado; **f. and fancy free,** libre, ligero y contento.

footman [-mən] *s.* 1. lacayo, criado, sirviente, mayordomo. 2. (raro) infante, soldado de a pie. 3. (ant.) caminante.

footmark [-ˌmɑrk, B -ˌmɑk] *s.* huella (de pisada).

footnote [ˈfʊtˌnoʊt] *s.* nota al pie de la página.

footpace [-ˌpeɪs] *s.* 1. paso lento, paso regular. 2. estrado, plataforma. 3. descanso de escalera.

footpad [-ˌpæd] *s.* salteador de caminos.

foot-pan [-ˌpæn] *s.* jofaina, palangana (para lavarse los pies).

footpath [-ˌpæθ, B -ˌpɑθ] *s.* senda para peatones; sendero, vereda.

foot patrol, (mil.) patrulla de a pie.

foot-pound [ˈfʊtˈpaʊnd] *s.* (mec.) pie-libra o libra-pie (unidad de energía o trabajo).

footprint [-ˌprɪnt] *s.* huella del pie, pisada, rastro.

footrace [-ˌreɪs] *s.* (dep.) carrera pedestre.

footrail [-ˌreɪl] *s.* rodapié.

footrest [-ˌrɛst] *s.* apoyo o descanso para los pies.

footrope [-ˌroʊp] *s.* (mar.) marchapié; relinga del pujamen.

foot-rule [-ˌrul] *s.* regla de un pie de longitud.

foots [fʊts] *s. pl.* sedimentos.

footscraper [ˈfʊtˌskreɪpər, B -ə] *s.* limpiabarros (a la entrada de una casa, para limpiar la suela de las botas).

footsie [ˈfʊtsɪ] *s.* **to play f. with,** flirtear tocando a escondidas (ej., debajo de la mesa) la pierna de; (fig.) estar en términos amistosos o íntimos con.

footslog [-ˌslɑg, B -ˌslɔg] *v.i.* caminar sobre lodo.

foot soldier, (mil.) infante, soldado de a pie, soldado de infantería.

footsore [-ˌsɔr, B -ˌsɔ] *a.* despeado, con los pies doloridos o lastimados.

footstalk [-ˌstɔk] *s.* (bot., zool.) pecíolo, pedúnculo, pedículo.

footstall [-ˌstɔl] *s.* 1. estribo (de montura) para mujer. 2. (arq.) plinto, base, pedestal (de una columna o pilar).

footstep [ˈfʊtˌstɛp] *s.* 1. paso, pisada; huella. 2. escalón, peldaño. 3. **to follow** (o **tread**) **in the footsteps of,** (fig.) seguir las huellas o los pasos de.

footstock [-ˌstɑk, B -ˌstɔk] *s.* (mec.) muñeca corrediza, cabeza móvil, contrapunta.

footstone [-ˌstoʊn] *s.* piedra fundamental; lápida al pie de una sepultura.

footstool [ˈfʊtˌstul] *s.* escabel, escañuelo.

foot stove, estufilla para los pies.

foot-ton [ˈfʊtˈtʌn] *s.* (mec.) pie-tonelada (unidad de energía o trabajo).

footwalk [-ˌwɔlk] *s.* senda, sendero (para peatones).

footwall [-ˌwɔl] *s.* 1. (min.) respaldo bajo. 2. (geol.) pared baja de una falla inclinada.

foot warmer, calentador de pies.

footway [-ˌweɪ] *s.* camino o senda angosta para peatones.

footwear [-ˌwɛr, B -ˌwɛə] *s.* calzado (botas, zapatos).

footwork [-ˌwɜrk, B -ˌwɜk] *s.* (dep.) juego o manejo de los pies (en el boxeo, fútbol, tenis, etc.).

footworn [-ˌwɔrn B -ˌwɔn] *a.* 1. despeado, de pies cansados o adoloridos. 2. trillado; gastado (camino, peldaño, etc.).

foozle [ˈfuzəl] *v.t.* pifiar, errar (golpe, tiro, etc.) de manera chambona. —*s.* chambonada, jugada fallida (ej., en golf); pifia (en billar).

fop [fɑp, B fɔp] *s.* mequetrefe, petimetre, currutaco, lechuguino. —*v.t.* (*pret., p.p.* FOPPED; *p.pr.* FOPPING) (ant.) engañar, embaucar.

foppery ['fɑpərɪ, B 'fɔp-] *s.* presunción o afectación en el vestir; perifollos.

foppish [-ɪʃ] *a.* alechuguinado; vanidoso, fatuo.

foppishly [-lɪ] *adv.* afectadamente.

foppishness [-nəs] *s.* presunción de currutaco.

for [fɔr, fər, B fɔ, fə] *prep.* 1. por (por razón de, a causa de, por motivo de), ej., *he refused f. fear of the consequences,* se ha negado por temor a las consecuencias, *she's famous f. her beauty,* es famosa por su belleza. 2. para (destinado a; por el bien de), ej., *he is the man f. the job,* es el hombre para el puesto, *they live f. each other,* viven el uno para el otro, *things look bad f. you,* las cosas se presentan mal para usted. 3. por (en vez de, en lugar o substitución de, en compensación de), ej., *an eye f. an eye,* ojo por ojo, *to take f. granted,* dar por seguro. 4. por, a favor de, ej., *I am f. reform,* estoy por (o a favor de) la reforma. 5. con, a pesar de, a despecho de, no obstante, ej., *f. all you say,* con todo lo que dice Ud., *f. all he did to her, she still loves him,* ella todavía lo ama, a pesar de todo lo que le hizo. 6. por (espacio de), para (mientras, durante), ej., *f. three nights he lay awake,* por (espacio de) tres noches estuvo despierto, *to walk f. miles,* caminar muchas millas, *I have enough work f. a year,* tengo trabajo para un año. 7. por, en busca de, ej., *to go f. a cab,* ir por (o en busca de) un taxi. 8. para, con destino a, hacia, ej., *he left f. England,* partió para (o con destino a) Inglaterra. 9. para (en vista de, considerando) ej., *he's tall f. his age,* es alto para su edad. 10. en cuanto (a), ej., *f. the rest,* en cuanto al resto. 11. por (al costo de, al precio de), ej., *six f. a dollar,* seis por un dólar, *I bought it f. a fortune,* lo compré por una fortuna. 12. por (indica igualdad o proporción entre números o cantidades cuando son comparados), ej., *f. one enemy he has a hundred friends,* por cada enemigo tiene cien amigos. 13. como, ej., *what shall we use f. a bed?* ¿qué usaremos como cama? 14. para que, ej., *there it is f. all to see,* allí está (eso) para que todos lo vean. 15. **f. a living,** para ganarse la vida; **f. all that,** con todo, a pesar de todo (eso); **for ever,** para siempre; **for ever and a day,** por siempre jamás; **f. good,** para siempre; **f. heaven's sake!** ¡por Dios!; **f. one thing,** primero, para mencionar una cosa; **f. sale,** en venta; **f. the fun of it,** por gusto; **f. the time being,** por ahora; **I f. one,** yo por ejemplo, yo personalmente; **it is f. you to (decide, act,** etc.), le toca a Ud. (decidir, obrar, etc.); **once and f. all,** de una vez y por todas; **(is) time f.,** (es) hora de; **to be (in) f. it,** (jer.) ser inevitable (molestia, castigo, peligro, etc.); **to go f. (someone),** (jer.) desear, gustar (una persona); **to go f. a walk,** ir de paseo, ir de caminata; **to sit f.,** representar, ser diputado por (una ciudad o distrito); **to take one's word f. it,** creer (a alguien), aceptar la palabra de uno; **word f. word,** palabra por palabra, literalmente; literal. *—conj.* porque, pues, puesto que.

forage ['fɔrɪdʒ, 'fɑr-, B 'fɔr-] *s.* forraje. *—v.t.* 1. forrajear; obtener forrajeando. 2. proveer forraje. 3. saquear, pillar. *—v.i.* 1. andar forrajeando. 2. merodear. 3. (gen. con *for*) buscar afanosamente.

forage acre, (medida equivalente a un) acre cubierto de forraje utilizable.

forage cap, (mil.) quepis, gorra con visera.

forage plant, planta forrajera.

forager [-ər, B -ə] *s.* forrajeador.

foraging [-ɪŋ] *s.* forraje.

foraging ant, (ento.) hormiga conductora.

foramen [fə'reɪmən, fɔ-] *s.* (*pl.* FORAMENS o FORAMINA [-'ræmənə]) (anat., zool., bot.) foramen, orificio, apertura.

foramen magnum, (anat.) foramen magnum.

foraminal [-'ræmənəl] *a.* (bot.) foraminal.

foraminate [-nət] **foraminated** [-ˌneɪtəd] *a.* (anat., zool., bot.) foraminado.

foraminifer [ˌfɔrə'mɪnəfər, B -ə] *s.* (zool.) foraminífero.

forasmuch as [ˌfɔrəz'mʌtʃəz] *conj.* puesto que, en vista de que, por cuanto que, ya que.

foray ['fɔrˌeɪ] *v.t.* saquear, despojar, pillar. *—v.i.* hacer correría(s) e incursión(es). *—s.* correría, incursión; pillaje, saqueo.

forb [fɔrb, B fɔb] *s.* mala hierba, maleza, cizaña.

forbade, forbad [fər'bæd, B fə'-] *pret. de* **forbid.**

forbear [fɔr'bɛr, B fɔ'bɛə] *v.t.* (*pret.* FORBORE; *p.p.* FORBORNE; *p.pr.* FORBEARING) 1. abstenerse de, desistir de, renunciar a. 2. (dial.) soportar, sufrir, tolerar. 3. evitar; dejar en paz, no meterse con. *—v.i.* 1. abstenerse, detenerse. 2. controlarse, contenerse, tener paciencia. 3. **f. with,** mostrar paciencia hacia, tener paciencia para con.

forbear, *var. de* **forebear.**

forbearance [-'bɛrəns, B -'bɛər-] *s.* 1. paciencia; dominio sobre sí mismo, refrenamiento. 2. abstención. 3. clemencia, indulgencia.

forbearing [-ɪŋ] *a.* tolerante, condescendiente, indulgente, paciente.

forbid [fər'bɪd, B fə'-] *v.t.* (*pret.* FORBADE o FORBAD; *p.p.* FORBIDDEN; *p.pr.* FORBIDDING) 1. prohibir, vedar. 2. excluir de, prohibir la entrada a. 3. **God f.!** ¡no lo permita Dios!; **to be forbidden,** estar prohibido (algo).

forbiddance [-'bɪdəns] *s.* prohibición.

forbidden [-'bɪdən] *a.* prohibido, vedado, ilícito.

forbidden fruit, (fig.) fruta prohibida, placer ilícito.

forbidding [-'bɪdɪŋ] *a.* 1. prohibitivo. 2. repugnante, repulsivo, aborrecible. 3. amenazante, ominoso, formidable.

forbiddingly [-lɪ] *adv.* en forma amenazante; ominosamente.

forbore [fɔr'bɔr, B fɔ'bɔ] *pret. de* **forbear.**

forborne [-'bɔrn, B -'bɔn] *p.p. de* **forbear.**

forby, forbye [fɔr'baɪ, B fɔ'-] *prep., adv.* (pr. esco.) además (de).

force [fɔrs, B fɔs] *s.* 1. fuerza, energía, vigor, reciedumbre, robustez. 2. fuerza; razón, peso, ej., *the f. of the argument,* la fuerza del argumento, *there's f. in what you say,* lo que Ud. dice tiene peso, hay (mucha) razón en lo que dice Ud. 3. (der.) vigencia, vigor, validez. 4. fuerza, violencia. 5. fuerza, poderío, capacidad. 6. (fís.) fuerza. 7. (mil.) fuerza, poderío bélico; cuerpo (de soldados, de policías); (*pl.*) fuerzas bélicas, poderío militar. 8. **by f.,** a la fuerza, por fuerza; **by f. of,** a fuerza de, por medio de; **in f.,** vigente, en vigor; (mil.) en gran número; **in great f.,** vigoroso, gallardo, airoso, resuelto; **the armed forces,** las fuerzas armadas; **the police f.,** la fuerza policial; **to join forces,** aliarse, unir fuerzas; **to put in f.,** poner en vigor. *—v.t.* 1. forzar, violentar (cerradura, puerta, cofre). 2. forzar, constreñir, obligar, coactar, compeler, coercer. 3. forzar, presionar, urgir. 4. forzar, aparentar (sonrisa, etc.). 5. forzar, violar (a una mujer). 6. (mil.) forzar (una plaza, etc.). 7. (agr.) forzar, hacer madurar a la fuerza o temprano. 8. (béisbol) poner (a un jugador en base) fuera de juego. 9. (naipes) forzar. 10. **f. away,** obligar a alejarse; **f. back,** rechazar, hacer retroceder; **f. down,** obligar a bajar; **f. from,** echar o sacar fuera por fuerza, arrancar violentamente; **f. in,** clavar o introducir por fuerza; **f. one's hand,** obligar a obrar o revelar sus planes prematuramente; **f. one's way,** abrirse paso a la fuerza; **f. oneself,** hacer esfuerzos violentos, esforzarse; **f. out,** arrancar, sacar u obtener (algo) por la fuerza; **f. the issue,** hacer que el asunto se discuta o se decida pronto; hacer que se vaya al grano sin demora; **f. through,** hacer penetrar por fuerza, llevar a cabo por fuerza; **f. (something) upon (someone),** obligar (a alguien) a tomar o aceptar (algo), hacer (a alguien) aceptar (algo).

forced [fɔrst, B fɔst] *a.* 1. forzado, forzoso, obligatorio, involuntario. 2. forzado, fingido, afectado, exagerado.

forced feed, (mot.) alimentación forzada, alimentación a presión.

forced labor, trabajo forzado.

forced landing, (aer.) aterrizaje forzoso.

forced march, (mil.) marcha forzada.

force-feed ['fɔrsˌfid, B 'fɔs-] *v.t.* alimentar forzadamente.

forceful ['fɔrsfəl, B 'fɔs-] *a.* enérgico, vigoroso, impresionante.

forcefully [-ɪ] *adv.* enérgicamente, vigorosamente.

forcefulness [-nəs] *s.* naturaleza enérgica, temperamento vigoroso; manera impresionante.

force majeure [-mɑ'ʒɜ] (fr.) fuerza mayor.

forcemeat [-ˌmit] *s.* (cocina) relleno, embutido, picadillo, salpicón.

force of inertia, (fís.) fuerza de inercia.

forceps ['fɔrˌsɛps, B 'fɔsɛps] *s.* (*pl.* FORCEPS; (raro) FORCEPSES) 1. (med.) forceps. 2. (odont.) gatillo. 3. pinzas, tenazas.

force pump, (mec.) bomba impelente o impulsora.

forcer ['fɔrsər, B 'fɔsə] *s.* 1. forzador; violador. 2. (mec.) émbolo.

forcible [-səbəl] *a.* 1. forzado, forzoso. 2. poderoso, fuerte, potente, vigoroso, enérgico. 3. eficaz, efectivo. 4. convincente, de peso, concluyente.

forcibleness [-nəs] *s.* fuerza, violencia, potencia.

forcibly [-blɪ] *adv.* forzosamente, fuertemente, violentamente.

forcing ['fɔrsɪŋ, B 'fɔsɪŋ] *s.* forzamiento.

ford [fɔrd, B fɔd] *s.* vado. *—v.t.* vadear, esguazar, atravesar.

fordable [-əbəl] *a.* vadeable.

fordo [fɔr'du, B fɔ'-] *v.t.* 1. agotar, extenuar. 2. (ant.) destruir, aniquilar; matar.

fore [fɔr, B fɔ] *adv.* 1. antes, delante, en la delantera, esp. (mar.) en o hacia proa. 2. (ant.) anteriormente, previamente. *—prep.* (ant.) ante, en presencia de (usado en juramentos, conjuros, etc.). *—conj.* (dial.) antes que, primero. *—a.* anterior, delantero; (mar.) proel, de proa. *—s.* 1. frente, cabeza, delantera; esp. (mar.) trinquete; la proa. 2. **to the f.,** en primer plano, destacado; a la mano; dispuesto; **to come to the f.,** destacarse, tener éxito, ganar fama. *—interj.* (golf) ¡ojo! ¡cuidado!

fore-and-aft [ˌfɔrən'æft, B -'ɑft] *a.* (mar.) longitudinal (díc. de la línea a lo largo del barco); de popa a proa.

fore and aft, (mar.) de popa a proa; de largo a largo (del barco); hacia popa y proa.

fore-and-after [-'æftər, B -'ɑftə] *s.* (fam., mar.) barco (esp. goleta) con aparejo longitudinal.

fore-and-aft rig, (mar.) aparejo de vela áurica, aparejo de vela cangreja o de cuchillo.

fore-and-aft sail, (mar.) vela cangreja, áurica o de cuchillo.

forearm ['fɔrˌɑrm, B -ˌɑm] *s.* antebrazo.

forearm [fɔr'ɑrm, B -'ɑm] *v.t.* 1. armar de antemano; preparar con anticipación armas y pertrechos. 2. prevenir.

forebear, forbear ['fɔrˌbɛr, B 'fɔˌbɛə] *s.* antepasado, ascendiente; (*pl.*) mayores.

forebode [fɔr'boud, B fɔ'-] *v.t.* 1. presagiar, agorar, ominar. 2. presentir.
foreboder [-ər, B -ə] *s.* agorero, pronosticador.
foreboding [-ɪŋ] *s.* presentimiento, corazonada; presagio. —*a.* agorero, presagioso.
forebrain ['fɔrˌbreɪn, B 'fɔˌ-] *s.* (anat.) cerebro anterior, prosencéfalo.
forecast [-ˌkæst, B -ˌkɑst] *v.t.* (*pret., p.p.* FORECAST O FORECASTED; *p.pr.* FORECASTING). 1. predecir, pronosticar. 2. presagiar. 3. (ant.) proyectar, planear. 4. **f. the weather,** pronosticar el tiempo. —*s.* 1. pronóstico, predicción; profecía. 2. (ant.) previsión; presciencia.
forecaster [-ər, B -ə] *s.* pronosticador (esp. del tiempo).
forecastle ['fouksəl, 'fɔrˌkæsəl, B 'fouksəl] *s.* (mar.) castillo, castillo de proa; camarote(s) en la proa.
forecited ['fɔrˌsaɪtəd, B 'fɔˌ-] *a.* precitado.
foreclose [fɔr'klouz, B fɔ'-] *v.t.* 1. excluir; impedir. 2. (der.) privar del derecho de redimir una hipoteca por incumplimiento de pagos. —*v.i.* (der.) ejecutar una hipoteca.
foreclosure [-'kluʒər, B -ʒə] *s.* 1. exclusión, privación. 2. (der.) juicio hipotecario, procedimiento ejecutivo hipotecario, ejecución de hipoteca, pérdida por el deudor hipotecario del derecho a redimir la hipoteca.
forecourse ['fɔrˌkɔrs, B 'fɔˌkɔs] *s.* (mar.) trinquete.
forecourt [-ˌkɔrt, B -ˌkɔt] *s.* (tenis) parte del campo cercana a la red.
foredate [fɔr'deɪt, B fɔ'-] *v.t.* fechar por adelantado.
foredeck ['fɔrˌdɛk, B 'fɔˌ-] *s.* (mar.) cubierta de proa.
foredo, *var. de* **fordo.**
foredoom [fɔr'dum, B fɔ'-] *v.t.* predestinar (el fracaso o la destrucción); condenar de antemano. — ['fɔrˌdum, B 'fɔˌ-] *s.* predestinación; sino, destino.
forefather ['fɔrˌfɑðər, B 'fɔˌfɑðə] *s.* antepasado, antecesor, ascendiente.
forefeel [fɔr'fil, B fɔ'-] *v.t.* presentir.
forefend, *var. de* **forfend.**
forefinger ['fɔrˌfɪŋgər, B 'fɔˌfɪŋgə] *s.* dedo índice.
forefoot [-ˌfʊt] *s.* 1. pata delantera, mano (de un animal). 2. (mar.) pie de roda, tajamar.
forefront [-ˌfrʌnt] *s.* frente, primera fila, vanguardia; **in the f.,** en primer plano; a la vanguardia.
foregather, *var. de* **forgather.**
forego [fɔr'gou, B fɔ'-] *v.t.* (*pret.* FOREWENT [-'wɛnt]; *p.p.* FOREGONE [-'gɔn] *p.pr.* FOREGOING) proceder, anteceder.
forego, *var. de* **forgo.**
foregoing [-ɪŋ] *a.* precedente, anterior; **the f.,** lo antedicho.
foregone ['fɔrˌgɔn, B 'fɔˌ-] *a.* pasado, anterior, predeterminado; inevitable.
foregone conclusion, conclusión sacada de antemano; resultado (considerado) inevitable.
foreground [-ˌgraʊnd] *s.* frente, delantera; primer término, primer plano; **in the f.,** en primer plano.
foregut [-ˌgʌt] *s.* (biol.) parte delantera del tubo digestivo en el embrión.
forehand [-ˌhænd] *s.* 1. cuarto delantero del caballo. 2. (tenis) golpe directo o derecho. 3. (ant.) posición superior, ventaja. —*a.* 1. (tenis) directo, derecho (golpe). 2. (ant.) hecho de antemano o anticipadamente.
forehanded ['fɔr'hændəd, B 'fɔ'-] *a.* 1. previsor, prudente; ahorrador. 2. acomodado, adinerado. 3. (tenis) directo, derecho (golpe).
fore hatching, (mar.) escotilla de proa.
forehead ['fɔrəd, 'fɑr-, -ˌhɛd, B 'fɔrɪd] *s.* 1. frente (de la cara). 2. parte delantera o frente.
foreign ['fɔrən, 'fɑr-, B 'fɔrɪn] *a.* 1. extranjero (ciudad, país, ciudadano, etc.). 2. extraño; ajeno, remoto.
foreign affairs, (pol.) asuntos exteriores, relaciones exteriores.
foreign bill, (der., com.) letra (de cambio) sobre el exterior.
foreign-born [-ˌbɔrn, B -ˌbɔn] *a.* nacido en el extranjero; extranjero de nacimiento.
foreign commerce, comercio (con el) exterior.
foreigner ['fɔrənər, 'fɑr-, B 'fɔrɪnə] *s.* extranjero, forastero; (pr. dial.) extraño.
foreign exchange, cambio exterior o extranjero; tipo de cambio; divisas.
foreignism [-ˌɪzəm] *s.* (raro) extranjerismo.
foreign legion, (mil.) legión extranjera.
foreign minister, ministro de relaciones exteriores, secretario de estado.
foreign mission, misión en el extranjero (diplomática, religiosa, de negocios).
foreignness [-nəs] *s.* lo extranjero, ajeno o extraño; carácter o aspecto exótico o extraño.
Foreign Office, (G.B.) ministerio de relaciones exteriores, secretaría de estado, cancillería.
foreign policy, política exterior.
Foreign Secretary, (G.B.) ministro de relaciones exteriores, secretario de estado.
Foreign Service, (E.U.) servicio diplomático y consular.
foreign trade, comercio exterior.
forejudge [fɔr'dʒʌdʒ, B fɔ'-] *v.t.* prejuzgar.
forejudgement [-mənt] *s.* prejuicio.
foreknow [-'nou] *v.t.* saber de antemano, tener presciencia de, prever.
foreknowledge ['fɔrˌnɑlɪdʒ, B 'fɔ'nɔl-] *s.* presciencia.
forelady [-ˌleɪdɪ] *s.* 1. capataz (mujer), encargada. 2. (der.) presidente de un jurado (t. **forewoman**).
foreland ['fɔrlənd, B 'fɔlənd] *s.* promontorio, punta, cabo.
foreleg [-ˌlɛg] *s.* pierna o pata delantera, brazo (del cuadrúpedo).
forelimb [-ˌlɪm] *s.* miembro delantero (de animales, insectos, etc.).
forelock [-ˌlɑk, B -ˌlɔk] *s.* 1. (mec.) chaveta; pezonera, sotrozo. 2. melena, mechón de pelo sobre la frente.
foreman ['fɔrmən, B 'fɔmən] *s.* 1. capataz, sobrestante, cabo de cuadrilla, aperador, mayoral, encargado, caporal. 2. (der.) presidente de un jurado. jurado 3. (impr.) regente.
foremanship [-ˌʃɪp] *s.* 1. cargo de capataz. 2. presidencia de un jurado.
foremast ['fɔrˌmæst, -məst, B 'fɔˌmɑst] *s.* (mar.) palo de trinquete.
forementioned [-ˌmɛntʃənd, B -ˌmɛnʃənd] *a.* antes mencionado, susodicho, antedicho.
foremilk [-ˌmɪlk] *s.* primera leche extraída (al ordeñar); calostro.
foremost [-ˌmoust] *a.* primero, principal; delantero. —*adv.* primero, en primer lugar; **first and f.,** ante todo, primero de todo.
forename [-ˌneɪm] *s.* nombre de pila, primer nombre.
forenamed [-ˌneɪmd] *a.* antedicho, precitado.
forenoon [-ˌnun] *s.* mañana, el día hasta el mediodía. —*a.* matinal.
forenoon watch, (mar.) guardia de la mañana.
forensic [fə'rɛnsɪk] *a.* forense.
forensically [-sɪkəlɪ] *adv.* de modo forense.
forensic medicine, medicina legal.
foreordain [ˌfɔrɔr'deɪn, B ˌfɔrɔ'-] *v.t.* preordinar, predestinar, predeterminar.
foreordination [fɔrˌɔrdən'eɪʃən, B fɔrˌɔd-] *s.* preordinación, predeterminación, predestinación.
forepart ['fɔrˌpɑrt, B 'fɔˌpɑt] *s.* parte delantera o primera; principio.
forepassed, forepast [-ˌpæst, B -ˌpɑst] *a.* pasado.
forepaw [-ˌpɔ] *s.* pata o zarpa delantera (del cuadrúpedo).
forepeak [-ˌpik] *s.* (mar.) bodega de proa.
foreplay [-ˌpleɪ] *s.* estimulación erótica que antecede al acto sexual.
forequarter [-ˌkwɔrtər, B -ˌkwɔtə] *s.* cuarto delantero (de una res).
forereach [fɔr'ritʃ, B fɔ'-] *v.i.* 1. (mar.) ganar barlovento. 2. ganar terreno. —*v.t.* 1. (mar.) alcanzar, dejar atrás (otra embarcación). 2. aventajar.
forerun [fɔr'rʌn, B fɔ'-] *v.t.* 1. preceder, adelantar. 2. presagiar, agorar. 3. anticiparse a.
forerunner ['fɔrˌrʌnər, B 'fɔˌrʌnə] *s.* 1. heraldo, precursor; **the F.,** San Juan Bautista, precursor de Cristo. 2. antepasado, predecesor. 3. (mil.) explorador.
foresaid [-ˌsɛd] *a.* antedicho, susodicho.
foresail [-ˌseɪl, -səl] *s.* (mar.) trinquete.
foresee [fɔr'si, B fɔ'-] *v.t.* prever, antever, barruntar.
foreseeable [-əbəl] *a.* previsible.
foreseer [-ər, B -ə] *s.* previsor.
foreshadow [-'ʃædou] *v.t.* presagiar, prefigurar, anunciar.
foreshank ['fɔrˌʃænk, B 'fɔˌ-] *s.* trozo de brazuelo.
foresheet [-ˌʃit] *s.* 1. (mar.) escota del trinquete. 2. (mar.) (*pl.*) parte delantera de un bote.
foreshock [-ˌʃɑk, B -ˌʃɔk] *s.* temblor de tierra que precede a un terremoto.
foreshore [-ˌʃɔr, B -ˌʃɔ] *s.* parte de la playa entre los límites de la pleamar y la bajamar.
foreshorten [fɔr'ʃɔrtən, B fɔ'ʃɔtən] *v.t.* 1. (pint.) escorzar. 2. condensar, reducir.
foreshortening [-ɪŋ] *s.* (pint.) escorzo.
foreshow [-'ʃou] *v.t.* 1. prefigurar, presagiar. 2. (ant.) demostrar, indicar. 3. exhibir de antemano.
foreside ['fɔrˌsaɪd, B 'fɔˌ-] *s.* 1. frente, parte anterior (de una cosa). 2. costa, franja de tierra que mira al mar.
foresight [-ˌsaɪt] *s.* 1. previsión, prudencia, providencia. 2. punto de mira (de armas).
foresighted [-əd] *a.* previsor, precavido; prudente; próvido.
foreskin [-ˌskɪn] *s.* (anat.) prepucio.
forespeak [fɔr'spik, B fɔ'-] *v.t.* predecir, pronosticar.
forest ['fɔrəst, 'fɑr-, B 'fɔr-] *s.* bosque, monte, selva, floresta. —*a.* forestal, selvático. —*v.t.* plantar o poblar (un terreno) de árboles, arbolar.
forestage ['fɔrˌsteɪdʒ, B 'fɔˌ-] *s.* (teat.) primer plano, proscenio, parte del escenario próxima al arco del proscenio.
forestal ['fɔrəstəl, 'fɑr-, B 'fɔr-] *a.* forestal.
forestall [fɔr'stɔl, B fɔ'-] *v.t.* 1. impedir, excluir, prevenir. 2. anticiparse a, adelantarse a. 3. (com.) acaparar, acopiar, monopolizar (feria, mercado, etc.). 4. acechar, interceptar, atajar, detener.
forestaller [-ər, B -ə] *s.* intermediario (en el comercio); acaparador; monopolizador.
forestallment [-mənt] *s.* 1. prevención. 2. anticipación. 3. acaparamiento.
forestation [ˌfɔrəs'teɪʃən, ˌfɑr-, B ˌfɔr-] *s.* forestación, repoblación forestal.
forestay ['fɔrˌsteɪ B 'fɔˌ-] *s.* (mar.) estay del trinquete.

forestaysail [-ˌseɪl, -səl] *s.* (mar.) contrafoque (de una goleta, queche, yola o cúter).
forested ['fɔrəstəd, 'fɑr-, B 'fɔr-] *a.* arbolado, boscoso, poblado o plantado de árboles.
forester [-ər, B -ə] *s.* 1. silvicultor. 2. guardabosques. 3. habitante de los bosques. 4. (ento.) especie de mariposa nocturna. 5. (Aust.) canguro gigante.
forest fire, incendio de bosques, incendio forestal.
forest green, verde oscuro.
forest ranger, guardabosque, guardamonte.
forestry ['fɔrəstrɪ, 'fɑr-, B 'fɔr-] *s.* 1. silvicultura, ingeniería forestal, ciencia forestal. 2. terreno poblado de bosques, terreno boscoso.
foreswear, foresworn, *var. de* **forswear,** forsworn.
foretackle [-ˌtækəl] *s.* aparejo de trinquete.
foretaste ['fɔrˌteɪst, B 'fɔˌ-] *s.* goce, sabor anticipado; anticipación. — [fɔr'teɪst, B fɔ'-] *v.t.* anticipar el goce o placer de; gustar o probar de antemano.
foretell [fɔr'tɛl, B fɔ'-] *v.t.* predecir, prenunciar, profetizar, presagiar, vaticinar, adivinar.
foreteller [-ər, B -ə] *s.* profeta, vaticinador.
forethought ['fɔrˌθɔt, B 'fɔˌ-] *s.* 1. deliberación, premeditación. 2. providencia, previsión, prudencia. —*a.* deliberado, premeditado, intencional.
foretime ['fɔrˌtaɪm B 'fɔˌ-] *s.* pasado; tiempos idos.
foretoken [-ˌtoʊkən] *s.* presagio, agüero. — [fɔr'toʊkən, B fɔ'-] *v.t.* presagiar, augurar, agorar.
foretooth [-ˌtuθ] *s.* (*pl.* FORETEETH) incisivo, diente incisivo.
foretop ['fɔrˌtɑp, B 'fɔˌtɔp] *s.* 1. copete (del caballo). 2. (mar.) cofa de trinquete.
fore-topgallant mast [-ˌgælənt-] (mar.) masterillo de proa.
fore-topgallant sail, (mar.) juanete de proa.
fore-topmast ['fɔrˌtɑpməst, B 'fɔˌtɔp-] *s.* (mar.) mastelero de proa o de velacho.
fore-topsail[-ˌseɪl, -səl] *s.* (mar.) velacho, velacho alto, gavia del trinquete.
forever [fɔ'rɛvər, B -ə] *adv.* por o para siempre, eternamente; **f. and ever,** por siempre jamás.
forevermore [-ˌrɛvər'mɔr, B -ˌrɛvə'mɔ] *adv.* por o para siempre, hasta la eternidad.
forewarn [fɔr'wɔrn, B fɔ'wɔn] *v.t.* avisar, advertir o prevenir.
forewarning [-ɪŋ] *s.* aviso, advertencia.
forewoman ['fɔrˌwʊmən, B 'fɔˌ-] *s.* (t. **forelady**) oficiala, supervisora (de taller o fábrica).
foreword [-ˌwɜrd, B -ˌwɜd] *s.* prefacio, prólogo, preámbulo, introducción, exordio.
foreyard ['fɔrˌjɑrd, B 'fɔˌjɑd] *s.* (mar.) verga del trinquete.
forfeit ['fɔrfət, B 'fɔfɪt] *s.* 1. multa, penalidad. 2. prenda. 3. (*pl.*) juego de prendas. —*a.* perdido o enajenado por falta, error o crimen. —*v.t.* 1. perder (cosa o derecho) como castigo. 2. confiscar. 3. (der.) comisar; decomisar.
forfeitable [-əbəl] *a.* perdible, confiscable, alienable; (der.) decomisable.
forfeiture ['fɔrfətʃər, B 'fɔfɪtʃə] *s.* 1. (der.) comiso, decomiso. 2. pérdida. 3. prenda perdida; multa.
forfend [fɔr'fɛnd, B fɔ'-] *v.t.* 1. (E.U.) proteger, amparar, preservar, resguardar, guardar, asegurar. 2. (ant.) prohibir, impedir, evitar; vedar.
forficate ['fɔrfəkət, -ˌkeɪt, B 'fɔfɪ-] *a.* (orn.) bifurcado (cola de ciertas aves).
forgather [fɔr'gæðər, B fɔ'gæðə] *v.i.* reunirse, juntarse, congregarse, encontrarse.
forgave [-'geɪv] *pret. de* **forgive.**
forge [fɔrdʒ, B fɔdʒ] *s.* 1. fragua. 2. herrería. 3. forja; hornaza. 4. forja, ferrería, fundición. —*v.t.* 1. fraguar, forjar. 2. (fig.) forjar, fraguar, fabricar, inventar (mentira, cuento, etc.). 3. falsificar, falsear, contrahacer. —*v.i.* avanzar firme; **f. ahead,** avanzar con ímpetu y firmeza.
forger ['fɔrdʒər, B 'fɔdʒə] *s.* 1. forjador, fraguador. 2. falsificador, falsario, embustero.
forgery [-ərɪ] *s.* 1. falsificación, adulteración (de documentos, billetes). 2. falsificación, documento falsificado, billete o moneda falsificada. 3. (poét.) invención, ficción.
forget [fər'gɛt, B fə'-] *v.t.* (*pret.* FORGOT [-'gɑt, B -'gɔt]; *p.p.* FORGOTTEN [-'gɑtən, B -'gɔt-] o (ant., poét.) FORGOT; *p.pr.* FORGETTING) 1. olvidar. 2. olvidarse de, olvidársele a uno. 3. **f. it!** ¡déjelo! pierda cuidado; **f. oneself,** olvidarse de sí mismo, ser desinteresado; propasarse, extralimitarse, descomedirse, desmandarse. —*v.i.* olvidar; **f. about,** descuidar, olvidarse de; **f. all about it,** olvidarse por completo.
forgetful [-fəl] *a.* 1. olvidadizo, desmemoriado. 2. descuidado, desatento.
forgetfully [-fəlɪ] *adv.* en forma olvidadiza, descuidadamente.
forgetfulness [-fəlnəs] *s.* falta de memoria; olvido, descuido.
forget-me-not [fər'gɛtmɪˌnɑt B fə'-ˌnɔt] *s.* 1. (bot.) nomeolvides (flor). 2. (bot.) raspilla, miosota.
forgettable [fər'gɛtəbəl, B fə'-] *a.* olvidable.
forging ['fɔrdʒɪŋ, B 'fɔdʒ-] *s.* forjadura, pieza forjada.
forgivable [fər'gɪvəbəl, B fə'-] *a.* perdonable.
forgive [fər'gɪv, B fə'-] *v.t.* (*pret.* FORGAVE [-'geɪv]; *p.p.* FORGIVEN [-'gɪvən]; *p.pr.* FORGIVNG) 1. perdonar, condonar (insulto, enemigo, culpable, etc.). 2. eximir, remitir, perdonar (deuda, obligación).
forgiveness [-nəs] *s.* perdón, indulgencia.
forgiving [-ɪŋ] *a.* perdonador, indulgente, clemente.
forgivingly [-lɪ] *adv.* indulgentemente, con clemencia o perdón.
forgivingness [-nəs] *s.* indulgencia, clemencia, perdón.
forgo [fɔr'goʊ, B fɔ'-] *v.t.* (*pret.* FORWENT [-'wɛnt]; *p.p.* FORGONE [-'gɔn]; *p.pr.* FORGOING [-'goʊɪŋ]) 1. renunciar a, abstenerse de, privarse de. 2. perder, desperdiciar (oportunidad, etc.). 3. desistir de, apartarse de.
forgot [-'gɑt, B -'gɔt] *pret.*, (ant., poét.) *p.p. de* **forget.**
forgotten [-ən] *p.p. de* **forget.**
forjudge, *var. de* **forejudge.**
fork [fɔrk, B fɔk] *s.* 1. tenedor (de mesa). 2. horca (de jardinero, etc.). 3. bieldo (para aventar), horcón, horqueta (para sostener ramas de un árbol). 4. bifurcación, ramificación (de caminos, etc.); horcajo, confluencia (de ríos); horquilla, horqueta (que forman las ramas y el tronco del árbol). 5. horquilla (de bicicleta). 6. (*pl.*) (jer., G.B.) dedos. —*v.t.* 1. ahorquillar. 2. levantar, hacinar o echar con una horca. 3. (ajedrez) atacar (dos piezas) a la vez (dic. del caballo o del peón). 4. **f. out** (o **up** u **over**), (jer.) pagar a disgusto, pagar con dificultad; aflojar o soltar dinero. —*v.i.* bifurcarse; ahorquillarse.
fork beam, (mar.) bao de horquilla.
forked [fɔrkt, B fɔkt] *a.* ahorquillado, bifurcado; (bot.) bífido.
forked tongue, (E.U.) conversación o información falsa o engañosa; **to speak with f. t.,** hablar con malicia, decir mentiras.
forkful ['fɔrkˌfʊl, B 'fɔk-] *s.* lo que abarca un tenedor.
forkhead [-ˌhɛd] *s.* lengüeta de flecha o saeta.
forklift [-ˌlɪft] *s.* elevador de carga (con barras de acero que encajan bajo el bulto, cajón, etc.).
forklift truck, carretilla de horquilla, carretilla elevadora.
forky [-ɪ] *a.* bifurcado.
forlorn [fər'lɔrn, B fə'lɔn] *a.* 1. desierto, solitario, desolado. 2. abandonado, desamparado. 3. desesperanzado; desesperado; acongojado, afligido, infeliz, desdichado; calamitoso (de apariencia).
forlorn hope, 1. destacamento de asalto. 2. empresa desesperada, sin esperanza de éxito. 3. esperanza lejana.
forlornly [-lɪ] *adv.* solitariamente; desesperadamente.
forlornness [-nəs] *s.* 1. soledad. 2. abandono, desamparo. 3. desesperación; miseria.
form [fɔrm, B fɔm] *s.* 1. forma, figura, conformación, configuración, contorno, perfil. 2. figura, (perfil del) cuerpo. 3. fórmula. 4. conducta, comportamiento, modales, ej., *bad f.,* malos modales. 5. formalidad, ceremonia, ritual; formalismo, convencionalismo. 6. forma, orden, arreglo (de una composición literaria o musical). 7. clase, especie, variedad. 8. forma, estado o condición física (esp. de atletas o caballos). 9. madriguera (del conejo). 10. banca, asiento largo sin respaldo. 11. forma, molde, horma. 12. maniquí (para probar ropa). 13. formulario. 14. (filol.) forma. 15. (educ.) grado, clase escolar. 16. (gram.) forma (de inflexión, ortografía, etc.). 17. (impr.) forma. 18. (ant.) belleza, hermosura. 19. **he was in great f.,** estaba muy animado, estaba en su elemento; **to lose one's f.,** (dep.) perder la forma. —*v.t.* 1. formar; moldear, modelar. 2. formar, desarrollar; contraer, adquirir (un hábito). 3. constituir (ej., una cláusula). 4. (mil.) formar, colocar en orden. 5. (gram.) formar (el pretérito, gerundio, etc.); constituir (una nueva palabra). —*v.i.* (gen. con *up*) 1. formarse, constituirse. 2. tomar forma, surgir. —*sufijo* **-form,** -forme; que tiene un número específico de formas, ej., *triform,* triforme.
formal ['fɔrməl, B 'fɔməl] *a.* 1. formal, en forma. 2. formal, convencional, regular. 3. de etiqueta (vestido). 4. formulario, nominal. 5. ceremonial, ceremonioso. 6. formal, explícito, expreso. 7. (filos.) esencial, constitutivo. —*s.* 1. baile de gala. 2. vestido de etiqueta; **go f.,** (fam.) ir en traje de etiqueta.
formal attire, f. dress, traje de etiqueta.
formal call, visita de cumplido o cortesía; (dip.) visita oficial.
formaldehyde [fɔr'mældəˌhaɪd, B fɔ'-] *s.* (quím.) formaldehído, aldehído fórmico.
Formalin ['fɔrmələn, B 'fɔmə-] *s.* (quím.) formalina (marca de fábrica).
formalism ['fɔrməˌlɪzəm, B 'fɔmə-] *s.* formalismo.
formalist [-ləst] *s.* formalista.
formalistic [ˌfɔrmə'lɪstɪk, B ˌfɔmə-] *a.* formalista.
formality [fɔr'mælətɪ, B fɔ'-] *s.* 1. formalidad, seriedad, ceremonia. 2. formalidad, ceremonia, ceremonial, etiqueta. 3. formalidad, norma, regla. 4. **as a mere f.,** por cumplir, por mera cortesía.
formalization [ˌfɔrmələ'zeɪʃən, B ˌfɔməlaɪ-] *s.* formalización.
formalize ['fɔrməˌlaɪz, B 'fɔmə-] *v.t.* 1. formalizar, concretar, formar, dar forma a. 2. formalizar, afectar, volver formal.
formal logic, (lóg.) lógica formal (que estudia las formas o estructuras generales del pensamiento).

formally [-mǝlɪ] *adv.* 1. formalmente, según la forma; en debida forma. 2. formalmente, expresamente. 3. ceremoniosamente.
formant ['fɔrmǝnt, -ˌmænt, B 'fɔmǝnt] *s.* (gram.) cualquiera de las ondas de sonido que caracteriza a una vocal determinada.
format ['fɔrˌmæt B 'fɔˌ-] *s.* 1. (impr.) formato, forma, tamaño (de un impreso). 2. plan o estructura general (de un programa de t.v., etc.).
formate [-ˌmeɪt] *s.* (quím.) formiato.
formation [fɔr'meɪʃǝn, B fɔ'-] *s.* 1. formación, desarrollo. 2. formación, forma, figura; estructura. 3. (geol., mil., aer.) formación. 4. disposición, arreglo.
formative ['fɔrmǝtɪv, B 'fɔmǝ-] *a.* 1. formativo, formante. 2. (gram.) formante. —*s.* (gram.) formante.
form class, (gram.) grupo de formas lingüísticas (que tienen una o varias estructuras morfológicas o sintácticas comunes).
former ['fɔrmǝr, B 'fɔmǝ] *a.* 1. precedente, antecedente, anterior. 2. antiguo, pasado, ej., *in f. times,* en tiempos pasados. 3. (con *the*) (el) primero, aquél; (la) primera, aquélla; (los) primeros, (las) primeras, aquéllos, aquéllas. 4. ex, que fue, ej., *former president,* ex-presidente. —*s.* formador; matriz, molde.
formerly [-lɪ] *adv.* antes, en otro tiempo, en tiempos pasados; antiguamente.
formfitting ['fɔrmˌfɪtɪŋ, B 'fɔm-] *a.* ceñido o ajustado al cuerpo; entallado.
formic ['fɔrmɪk, B 'fɔmɪk] *a.* (quím.) fórmico, hormigoso.
Formica (TM) [fɔr'maɪkǝ, B fɔ'-] *s.* formica, fórmica, plástico laminado, resistente al calor, que imita maderas, mármoles, etc. (marca de fábrica).
formic acid, (quím.) ácido fórmico.
formicary ['fɔrmǝˌkerɪ, B 'fɔmɪkǝrɪ] *s.* hormiguero, nido de hormigas.
formicate ['fɔrmǝˌkeɪt, B 'fɔmɪ-] *v.i.* hormiguear.
formication [ˌfɔrmǝ'keɪʃǝn, B ˌfɔmɪ-] *s.* hormigueo; (med.) formicación.
formidability [ˌfɔrmǝdǝ'bɪlǝtɪ, B ˌfɔmɪd-] *s.* dificultad formidable.
formidable ['fɔrmǝdǝbǝl, fɔr'mɪd-, B 'fɔmɪd-] *a.* formidable, temible; tremendo.
formidableness ['fɔrmǝdǝbǝlnǝs, B 'fɔmɪd-] *s.* aspecto o carácter formidable.
formidably [-blɪ] *adv.* formidablemente; horriblemente, terriblemente; asombrosamente.
formless ['fɔrmlǝs, B 'fɔm-] *a.* informe, sin forma; amorfo.
formlessly [-lɪ] *adv.* de manera informe, sin forma.
formlessness [-nǝs] *s.* falta de forma (regular); amorfia.
form letter, (com.) carta pre-impresa, a la cual se le añade el nombre, la fecha, etc.
formula ['fɔrmjǝlǝ, B 'fɔmjʊ-] *s.* (*pl.* FORMULAS O FORMULAE [-ˌli, -ˌlaɪ]) 1. fórmula (de palabras). 2. fórmula, receta. 3. fórmula, regla, norma (convencional). 4. fórmula, transacción. 5. (quím., mat.) fórmula.
formularize [-ˌraɪz] *v.t.* expresar en fórmula(s), formular.
formulary [-ˌlerɪ, B -lǝrɪ] *s.* 1. formulario. 2. ritual, fórmula, forma prescrita. 3. (farm.) formulario, recetario. —*a.* formular, formulario.
formulate [-ˌleɪt] *v.t.* 1. formular. 2. idear, concebir (un plan, etc.). 3. preparar según fórmula.
formulation [ˌfɔrmjǝ'leɪʃǝn B ˌfɔmjʊ-] *s.* formulación.
formulator ['fɔrmjǝˌleɪtǝr, B 'fɔmjʊˌleɪtǝ] *s.* formulador.
formulism [-ˌlɪzǝm] *s.* formulismo.
formulistic [ˌfɔrmjǝ'lɪstɪk, B ˌfɔmjʊ-] *a.* formulista.
formulization [-lǝ'zeɪʃǝn, B -laɪ-] *s.* formulación.
formulize ['fɔrmjǝˌlaɪz, B 'fɔmjʊ-] *v.t.* formular.
formulizer [-ǝr, B -ǝ] *s.* formulador.
form word, (gram.) palabra que expresa principalmente relación gramatical (ej., una conjunción o una preposición).
formyl ['fɔrˌmɪl, B 'fɔmɪl] *s.* (quím.) formilo.
fornicate ['fɔrnǝˌkeɪt, B 'fɔnɪ-] *v.i.* fornicar.
fornicated [-ǝd] *a.* (arq.) fornicado, abovedado.
fornication [ˌfɔrnǝ'keɪʃǝn, B ˌfɔnɪ-] *s.* fornicación.
fornicator ['fɔrnǝˌkeɪtǝr, B 'fɔnɪˌkeɪtǝ] *s.* fornicador.
fornicatrix [-ˌkeɪtrɪks] *s.* fornicadora, concubina.
fornix ['fɔrnɪks, B 'fɔnɪks] *s.* (*pl.* FORNICES [-nǝˌsiz]) (anat.) fórnix; (arq.) bóveda.
forrader, forrarder ['fɑrǝdǝr, B 'fɔrǝdǝ] *adv.* (pr. G.B., fam.) más adelante.
forsake [fǝr'seɪk, B fǝ'-] *v.t.* (*pret.* FORSOOK [-'sʊk]; *p.p.* FORSAKEN [-'seɪkǝn]; *p.pr.* FORSAKING) 1. dejar, abandonar, desamparar (a alguien). 2. abandonar, dejar, desechar (vicio, hábito, etc.). 3. **to be forsaken by God,** estar dejado de la mano de Dios.
forsooth [fǝr'suθ, B fǝ'-] *adv.* (irón.) en verdad, ciertamente, de veras, vaya.
forspent [-'spɛnt] *a.* (ant.) exhausto, fatigado.
forswear [fɔr'swɛr, B fɔ'swɛǝ] *v.t.* (*pret.* FORSWORE; *p.p.* FORSWORN) 1. abjurar, renunciar o rechazar solemnemente. 2. repudiar o negar bajo juramento. 3. **f. oneself,** perjurarse, jurar en falso. —*v.i.* perjurar, jurar en falso.
forsworn [-'swɔrn, B -'swɔn] *a.* perjuro.
forsythia [fɔr'sɪθɪǝ, B fɔ'saɪθjǝ] *s.* (bot.) forsitia.
fort [fɔrt, B fɔt] *s.* fuerte, fortaleza, castillo; **hold the f.,** (fam.) mantener algo en operación; permanecer en el puesto.
fortalice ['fɔrtǝlǝs, B 'fɔt-] *s.* (ant.) fortín.
forte [fɔrt, 'fɔrˌteɪ, B fɔt] *s.* 1. fuerte (talento o facultad en que uno se distingue). 2. fuerte (la parte más fuerte de la hoja de una espada).
forte ['fɔrteɪ, -tɪ, B 'fɔtɪ] *a., adv., s.* (mús.) forte, fuerte.
forth [fɔrθ, B fɔθ] *adv.* 1. delante, adelante, hacia adelante, en adelante, más allá. 2. fuera, afuera. 3. (ant.) fuera, afuera, lejos, ausente. 4. **and so f.,** y así sucesivamente; **back and f.,** de un lado a otro; de acá para allá; **from this time f.,** de ahora en adelante, en lo sucesivo; **to go f.,** salir, ir hacia delante. —*prep.* (ant.) de, desde; fuera de.
forthcoming [fɔrθ'kʌmɪŋ, B fɔθ-] *a.* 1. próximo, venidero, que viene. 2. amigable, afable. —*s.* aparición, acercamiento, proximidad.
forthright ['fɔrθˌraɪt, B 'fɔθ-] *a.* directo, derecho; franco. —*adv.* 1. directamente, francamente. 2. (ant.) inmediatamente, enseguida.
forthwith [-'wɪθ] *adv.* inmediatamente, sin dilación, sin tardanza.
fortieth ['fɔrtɪǝθ, B 'fɔt-] *s., a.* cuadragésimo, cuarentavo; cuarenta (ordinal).
fortifiable ['fɔrtǝˌfaɪǝbǝl, B 'fɔtɪ-] *a.* fortificable.
fortification [ˌfɔrtǝfǝ'keɪʃǝn, B ˌfɔtɪ-] *s.* 1. fortalecimiento, fortificación. 2. (mil.) (*gen. pl.*) fortificación, fortaleza, plaza fuerte.
fortifier ['fɔrtǝˌfaɪǝr, B 'fɔtɪ-ǝ] *s.* fortificador; fortalecedor.
fortify [-ˌfaɪ] *v.t.* (*pret., p.p.* FORTIFIED; *p.pr.* FORTIFYING). 1. fortificar, fortalecer (a persona, salud, etc.). 2. (fig.) fortificar, fortalecer, reforzar (idea, argumento, etc.). 3. encabezar (vinos), enriquecer (alimentos). 4. (mil.) fortificar (ciudad, plaza, etc.). —*v.i.* construir defensas.
fortissimo [fɔr'tɪsǝˌmoʊ, B fɔ'-] *a., adv.* (mús.) fortísimo, muy fuerte.
fortitude ['fɔrtǝˌtud, B 'fɔtɪˌtjud] *s.* fortaleza, ánimo, entereza, firmeza.
fortitudinous [ˌfɔrtǝ'tudǝnǝs, B ˌfɔtɪ'tjud-] *a.* animoso, valiente.
fortnight ['fɔrtˌnaɪt, B 'fɔt-] *s.* quincena, quince días, dos semanas.
fortnightly [-lɪ] *a.* quincenal, bisemanal. —*adv.* quincenalmente, cada quince días. —*s.* revista o periódico quincenal.
FORTRAN ['fɔrtræn, B 'fɔtræn] *s.* lenguaje digital de computadoras parecido al álgebra.
fortress ['fɔrtrǝs, B 'fɔtrɪs] *s.* fuerte, fortaleza, plaza fuerte. —*v.t.* fortificar.
fortuitous [fɔr'tuǝtǝs, B fɔ'tju-] *a.* fortuito, casual, accidental, eventual, impensado.
fortuitously [-lɪ] *adv.* fortuitamente, casualmente, accidentalmente.
fortuitousness [-nǝs] *s.* carácter fortuito (de un suceso); eventualidad, casualidad.
fortuity [-ǝtɪ] *s.* caso fortuito, accidente, casualidad.
fortunate ['fɔrtʃǝnǝt, B 'fɔtʃǝn-] *a.* afortunado, venturoso, bienhadado, fausto, feliz.
fortunately [-lɪ] *adv.* afortunadamente, felizmente.
fortune ['fɔrtʃǝn, B 'fɔtʃǝn] *s.* 1. fortuna, suerte. 2. buena suerte, buenaventura. 3. fortuna, riqueza, bienes, caudal. 4. **F.,** (diosa de la) Fortuna. 5. **to cost a f.,** costar un ojo de la cara; **to make a f.,** ganarse una fortuna, volverse rico; **to make one's f.,** tener éxito, prosperar; **to marry a f.,** casarse con una heredera; **to tell one's f.,** decirle a uno la buenaventura; **to try one's f.,** probar fortuna. —*v.t.* (ant.) dotar con una fortuna. —*v.i.* (ant.) suceder, acontecer.
fortune cookie, galletica de la fortuna, galletita china (con una máxima o una predicción impresa y colocada al centro).
fortune hunter, buscador de dotes, cazador de dotes, aventurero, cazafortuna.
fortuneless [-lǝs] *a.* sin fortuna, sin bienes, sin futuro.
fortuneteller [-ˌtɛlǝr, B -ǝ] *s.* adivino, sortílego, agorero, nigromante.
forty ['fɔrtɪ, B 'fɔtɪ] *a., s.* (*pl.* FORTIES) cuarenta; **the forties,** década de los cuarenta (de la vida o de un siglo).
forty-five [-'faɪv] *s.* 1. pistola de calibre 45. 2. disco fonográfico de 45 rpm.
forty-niner [ˌfɔrtɪ'naɪnǝr, B ˌfɔtɪ-ǝ] *s.* (fam., E.U.) persona que fue a California durante la fiebre del oro de 1849.
forty winks, siesta corta (esp. después de la comida).
forum ['fɔrǝm] *s.* (*pl.* FORUMS O FORA [-rǝ]) 1. foro, tribunal. 2. (fig.) plaza, foro (de discusión pública). 3. (hist. romana) foro.
forward ['fɔrwǝrd, B 'fɔwǝd] *a.* 1. delantero. 2. adelantado, precoz; prematuro. 3. avanzado, extremo, exagerado, radical (opiniones, ideas, educación, etc.). 4. listo, propenso. 5. atrevido, audaz, impertinente. 6. (com.) al futuro (compra, venta); para entrega futura (productos, etc.). 7. (mil.) avanzado (zona, posición, etc.). 8. (mar.) proel, de proa. —*adv.* 1. adelante, hacia adelante, en la delantera. 2. (mar.) hacia proa. 3. **to bring f.,** traer a colación; (ten.) llevar; (ten., mat.) van;

to come f., adelantarse, ofrecerse, presentarse (para una tarea, trabajo, etc.); **to look f.**, mirar hacia adelante; **to look f. to**, esperar con ilusión; **to put** o **set f.**, alegar, aducir; **to put oneself f.**, hacerse conspicuo, llamar la atención hacia sí mismo. —*s.* (dep.) delantero (en fútbol, baloncesto, polo). —*v.t.* 1. adelantar, patrocinar, fomentar, promover. 2. reenviar, transmitir. 3. remitir, expedir.
forward delivery, (com.) entrega en fecha futura.
forwarder [-ər, B -ə] *s.* (com.) agente de transportes, embarcador, agente expedidor.
forwarding [-ɪŋ] *s.* despacho, transporte, embarque (esp. de mercancías); servicio de transportes.
forward line, (dep.) línea delantera.
forward-looking [-ˌlʊkɪŋ] *a.* prevenido, apercibido; progresivo.
forwardly [-lɪ] *adv.* 1. ufanamente, confiadamente, presumidamente, descaradamente. 2. hacia adelante.
forwardness [-nəs] *s.* 1. adelantamiento. 2. precocidad. 3. ansia, ahínco. 4. impertinencia, descaro, audacia.
forward pass, (dep.) pase en profundidad.
forwards ['fɔrwərdz, B 'fɔwədz] *adv.* adelante, hacia adelante, en la delantera.
forwent [fɔr'wɛnt, B fɔ'-] *pret. de* **forego, forgo.**
fossa ['fɑsə, B 'fɔsə] *s.* (*pl.* FOSSAE [-i]) (anat.) fosa, cavidad.
fosse [fɔs, fɑs, B fɔs] *s.* (*pl.* FOSSES) foso, canal, hoyo, excavación profunda; (fort.) foso, cárcava, trinchera.
fossette [fɔ'sɛt] *s.* fosa pequeña, hoyuelo.
fossick ['fɑsɪk, B 'fɔs-] *v.i.* (Aust.) 1. explorar, escudriñar. 2. recoger oro en puntos aislados, en trabajos abandonados, etc.; robar oro de un yacimiento ajeno.
fossil ['fɑsəl, B 'fɔs-] *a.* 1. fósil (plantas, resinas, conchas). 2. (fig.) fósil, anticuado. —*s.* 1. fósil. 2. (fig.) fósil, persona de opiniones anticuadas.
fossiliferous [ˌfɑsə'lɪfərəs, B ˌfɔsɪ-] *a.* fosilífero.
fossilist ['fɑsələst, B 'fɔs-] *s.* paleontólogo.
fossilization [ˌfɑsələ'zeɪʃən, B ˌfɔsɪlaɪ-] *s.* fosilizacion.
fossilize ['fɑsəˌlaɪz, B 'fɔsɪ-] *v.t., v.i.* 1. fosilizar(se), convertir(se) en fósil; petrificar(se). 2. (fig.) hacer(se) anticuado.
fossilology [ˌfɑsɪ'lɑlədʒɪ, B ˌfɔsɪ'lɔl-] *s.* paleontología.
fossorial [fɑ'sɔrɪəl, B fɔ'-] *a.* cavador.
fossorial wasp, avispa cavadora.
foster ['fɔstər, 'fɑs-, B 'fɔstə] *v.t.* 1. criar, nutrir, cuidar. 2. fomentar, incitar, animar, alentar. —*a.* adoptivo, aplícase comúnmente a nombres que denotan parentesco debido a crianza o adopción.
fosterage [-tərɪdʒ] *s.* 1. crianza de niños ajenos. 2. entrega (de niños) a padres adoptivos. 3. fomento, promoción (de una obra o proyecto).
foster brother, hermano de crianza, hermano de leche, hermanastro.
foster child, hijo adoptivo, hija adoptiva; hijastro, hijastra; entenado, entenada.
foster daughter, hija adoptiva, hijastra, entenada.
foster earth, (agr.) tierra de almáciga.
foster family, familia de acogida.
foster father, padre adoptivo, padrastro.
foster home, casa de crianza.
fostering [-ɪŋ] *a.* fomentador. —*s.* fomento.
fosterling [-lɪŋ, B -təlɪŋ] *s.* niño adoptivo.
foster mother, madre adoptiva, madrastra.
foster nurse, nodriza.
foster parent, padre adoptivo, madre adoptiva.
foster son, hijo adoptivo, hijastro, entenado.
Foucault current [fu'koʊ-] (elec.) corriente de Foucault.
foudroyant [fu'drɔɪənt] *a.* 1. tonante, fulminante, magnífico, sorprendente, deslumbrador. 2. (med.) fulminante.
fought [fɔt] *pret., p.p. de* **fight.**
foul [faʊl] *a.* 1. asqueroso, puerco; fétido (aliento); hediondo; impuro, inmundo, sucio; viciado (aire), pestilente; abombado, contaminado (ej., agua); podrido. 2. atascado, atorado (cañón de fusil, etc.). 3. enredado, embrollado. 4. lodoso (camino). 5. estropeado por enmendaduras, lleno de correcciones (manuscrito, prueba de galera). 6. malo, desagradable (tiempo). 7. contrario (viento, marea). 8. obsceno, grosero, indecente (lenguaje, etc.). 9. execrable, detestable, vil. 10. deshonroso, ímprobo, fraudulento (acto, práctica, medios, etc.). 11. (fam., G.B.) abominable, pésimo. 12. (dep.) sucio (golpe, jugada, etc.). 13. (béisbol) fuera del cuadrado. 14. **by fair means or f.**, a buenas o a malas; **to fall (o run) f. of,** (mar.) chocar contra; pelear con, reñir con; ponerse a malas con. —*adv.* contra las reglas, suciamente, de una manera sucia; **to play (someone) f.**, traicionar (a alguien). —*s.* 1. choque, colisión; enredo, enmarañamiento. 2. (dep.) falta, incorrección, jugada vedada o sucia. 3. (béisbol) pelota que cae fuera del cuadrado. —*v.t.* 1. ensuciar, emporcar; contaminar, corromper. 2. deshonrar, difamar, profanar. 3. atorar, atascar, obstruir (el calibre de un arma de fuego). 4. (mar.) abordar; chocar contra, enredarse en. 5. incrustar (las lapas, etc. el fondo de un barco). 6. (dep.) cometer una falta contra; (boxeo) golpear debajo del cinturón (al antagonista); (béisbol) volear (la pelota lanzada) fuera del cuadrado. 7. **f. the anchor,** (mar.) enceparse en el ancla (cable, etc.). —*v.i.* 1. ensuciarse; corromperse. 2. atascarse, atorarse. 3. enredarse (sogas, cuerdas). 4. cubrirse con una incrustación (fondo de un barco). 5. chocar (embarcaciones). 6. (dep.) cometer una falta, hacer una jugada vedada; (béisbol) volear la pelota fuera del cuadrado.
foulard [fu'lɑrd, B -'lɑd] *s.* 1. (tej.) fular, tela fina de seda o algodón estampada. 2. corbata o bufanda de esta tela.
foul ball, (béisbol) pelota que cae fuera del cuadrado.
foul bill of health, (mar.) patente sucia.
foul breath, aliento fétido.
foulbrood ['faʊlˌbrud] *s.* loque (de las abejas).
foul dealing, mala fe, dolo.
fouled-up ['faʊld'ʌp] *a.* confuso, enmarañado, estropeado.
foul language, lenguaje obsceno o soez.
foul line, (dep.) línea que marca las áreas prohibidas en los campos de deportes.
foully ['faʊllɪ] *adv.* 1. suciamente, obscenamente. 2. vilmente, execrablemente. 3. burdamente.
foulmouthed ['faʊl'maʊðd] *a.* malhablado, deslenguado.
foulness [-nəs] *s.* 1. asqucrosidad, porquería, fetidez. 2. obscenidad. 3. maldad, vileza.
foul play, 1. (dep.) juego sucio, jugada prohibida. 2. (fig.) juego sucio, maniobras sucias; engaño, perfidia, traición.
foul smelling, hediondo, maloliente.
foul tip, (béisbol) pelota mal bateada que, si llega a las manos del jugador que defiende una base, es considerada válida.
foul-up ['faʊlˌʌp] *s.* (fam.) 1. confusión, atolondramiento, revoltijo; chapucería, chambonada. 2. falla mecánica.
foul weather, mal tiempo.
found [faʊnd] *v.t.* 1. fundar (una ciudad, institución, negocio, etc.). 2. fundamentar, cimentar (edificio, etc.). 3. (fig.) fundar, fundamentar, cimentar (argumento, teoría, etc.). 4. fundir, derretir (metal, etc.). —*v.i.* fundarse, basarse; (raro) **f. on** (o **upon**), fundar, basar en o sobre.
found, *pret., p.p. de* **find.**
foundation [faʊn'deɪʃən] *s.* 1. fundación (de una ciudad, institución, negocio, etc.). 2. fundamento, cimiento (de un edificio, etc.); (arq.) cimientos. 3. dotación o fondos (con que se funda una institución). 4. fundación, institución. 5. (fig.) fundamento, base (de una teoría, afirmación, razonamiento, etc.). 6. (ing.) firme, afirmado, asiento (de una carretera, etc.). 7. (cost.) tejido de fondo. 8. (cost.) forro, refuerzo. 9. base para maquillaje.
foundational [-əl] *a.* fundamental, de fundamento.
foundation garment, corsé con sostén.
foundation stone, piedra fundamental.
founder ['faʊndər, B -də] *v.i.* 1. mancarse, despearse (el caballo). 2. caerse, desplomarse; irse a tierra. 3. fallar, fracasar. 4. (mar.) zozobrar, irse a pique o al fondo. —*v.t.* 1. mancar (a un caballo). 2. (mar.) hacer zozobrar (un barco), hundir. 3. (golf) golpear (la pelota) contra la tierra. —*s.* 1. fundador. 2. (metal.) fundidor. 3. (vet.) laminitis, infosura, despeadura.
foundering [-dərɪŋ] *s.* (mar.) zozobra.
founderous, foundrous ['faʊndərəs, -drəs] *a.* no practicable, lodoso (díc. de un camino).
foundling ['faʊndlɪŋ] *s.* (niño) expósito, niño abandonado; inclusero.
foundling hospital, inclusa, casa de expósitos.
foundry ['faʊndrɪ] *s.* 1. fundición (de metales, vidrio). 2. fundición (fábrica en que se funden metales o vidrio).
foundry man, fundidor, moldeador.
foundry proof, (impr.) prueba de fundición (en la cual se hace la última corrección antes de hacer las placas para la tirada).
fount [faʊnt] *s.* 1. fuente, manantial. 2. (poét.) fontana, manantial. 3. (G.B., impr.) fundición (de tipos); fuente (de tipos).
fountain ['faʊntən] *s.* 1. fuente, manantial; nacimiento de un río. 2. fuente (artificial), surtidor. 3. (fig.) fuente, origen, inicio. 4. tanque, estanque, depósito (para líquidos). 5. fuente de soda.
fountainhead [-ˌhɛd] *s.* 1. nacimiento (de río), manantial. 2. (fig.) fuente primera, origen.
Fountain of Youth, la Fuente de la Juventud.
fountain pen, estilográfica, pluma de fuente.
four [fɔr, B fɔ] *s.* 1. (número) cuatro. 2. cuatro (grupo, naipe, dominó, dado). 3. (dep.) bote de cuatro remos. 4. **fours,** regata para botes de cuatro remos; **on all fours,** a gatas, en cuatro pies; (fig.) completamente análogo o correspondiente. —*a.* cuatro; **f. corners of the earth,** últimos confines de la tierra; **f. figures,** número de cuatro cifras.
fourchette [fʊr'ʃɛt, B fʊə'-] *s.* 1. (anat.) horquilla vulvar. 2. (orn.) quilla (de un pájaro). 3. (zool.) ranilla (del casco de las caballerías). 4. (bridge) tenaza.
four-color ['fɔrˌkʌlər, B 'fɔˌkʌlə] *a.* (impr., foto.) cuadricolor, cuadricromático.
four-cornered [-'kɔrnərd, B -'kɔnəd] *a.* cuadrangular.
four-cycle [-ˌsaɪkəl] *a.* (mec.) de cuatro tiempos.
four-dimensional [-də'mɛntʃənəl, B -'mɛnʃən-] *a.* de cuatro dimensiones.
four flush, (póker) flux de cuatro naipes.

four-flush ['fɔrˌflʌʃ, B fɔˌ-] *v.i.* 1. (póker) hacer finta teniendo un flux de cuatro naipes. 2. (fam.) fingir, disimular, aparentar; baladronear, fanfarronear.
four-flusher [-ər, B -ə] *s.* fanfarrón, baladrón, pretencioso, impostor.
fourfold [-ˌfoʊld] *a.* cuádruple. —*adv.* cuatro veces.
four-footed [-'fʊtəd] *a.* (zool.) cuadrúpedo.
fourgon [fʊr'goʊn, B fʊə'gɔn] *s.* (f.c.) furgón.
four-handed ['fɔr'hændəd, B fɔ'-] *a.* 1. (zool.) cuadrúmano. (díc. de los monos). 2. para cuatro jugadores. 3. (mús.) a cuatro manos.
four hundred, cuatrocientos; **the F.H.,** (E.U.) la alta sociedad, la flor y nata de la sociedad.
Fourierism ['fʊrɪəˌrɪzəm] *s.* furierismo, fourierismo (el sistema de reforma social abogado por F. M. Charles Fourier).
Fourierist [-rəst] *s.* furierista.
Fourierite ['fʊrɪəˌraɪt] *var. de* **Fourierist.**
Fourier series ['fʊrɪeɪ-] (mat.) serie de Fourier.
four-in-hand ['fɔrənˌhænd] *s.* 1. coche o carruaje tirado por cuatro caballos. 2. corbata larga de nudo corredizo.
four-leaf clover [-ˌlif-, B 'fɔˌ-] trébol de cuatro hojas (que trae buena suerte al que lo encuentra).
four-letter word [-'lɛtər-, B -ə-] mala palabra, palabra obscena.
four-motor [-'moʊtər, B -ə] *a.* cuatrimotor.
four-oared [-'ɔrd, B 'fɔr'ɔd] *a.* de cuatro remos.
four-o'clock ['fɔrəˌklɑk, B -ˌklɔk] *s.* (bot.) maravilla, dondiego de noche, dompedro, arrebolera, donjuán.
four-part ['fɔr'pɑrt, B 'fɔ'pɑt] *a.* (partitura) para cuatro voces.
fourpence ['fɔrpəns, B 'fɔpəns] *s.* (moneda de) cuatro peniques.
fourpenny [-ˌpɛnɪ, B 'fɔpənɪ] *s.* moneda de cuatro peniques. —*a.* de cuatro peniques, que cuesta o vale cuatro peniques.
four-poster [-'poʊstər, B -tə] *s.* cama imperial de cuatro postes que generalmente sostienen un dosel o cortinaje.
fourscore [-'skɔr, B -'skɔ] *a., s.* ochenta.
foursome [-səm] *s.* 1. cuaternidad, grupo de cuatro (personas o cosas). 2. dos parejas; partida de cuatro; reunión de cuatro. 3. (golf) partido doble.
foursquare [-'skwɛr, B -'skwɛə] *a.* 1. cuadrado, cuadrangular. 2. franco, sincero, inequívoco, sin ambages. —*adv.* francamente, sin ambages.
four-star [-'stɑr, B -'stɑ] *a.* (mil.) 1. de cuatro estrellas (general). 2. importantísimo, altamente recomendable.
fourteen ['fɔr'tin, B 'fɔ'-] *s., a.* catorce.
fourteenth [-'tinθ] *s.* 1. decimocuarto, catorzavo. 2. catorce (en fechas). —*a.* decimocuarto, catorzavo.
fourth [fɔrθ, B fɔθ] *s.* 1. cuarto, cuarta parte. 2. cuatro (en fechas). 3. (mús.) cuarta; cuarta nota, subdominante. 4. (aut.) cuarta (velocidad). —*a.* cuarto.
fourth dimension, (mat.) cuarta dimensión.
fourth-dimensional [-də'mɛntʃənəl, B -'mɛnʃən-] *a.* de la cuarta dimensión, cuatridimensional.
fourth estate, el cuarto poder, la prensa.
fourthly [-lɪ] *adv.* en cuarto lugar.
four-way ['fɔr'weɪ, B 'fɔ'-] *a.* 1. de cuatro direcciones; de cuatro pasos. 2. con cuatro participantes (conversaciones, etc.).
four-wheel [-ˌhwil, -ˌwil] *a.* de cuatro ruedas, en las cuatro ruedas.
four-wheel drive, (aut.) doble tracción, transmisión en las cuatro ruedas, propulsión total.
four-wheeler [-'hwilər, -'wilər, B -ə] *s.* vehículo de cuatro ruedas.
fovea ['foʊvɪə] *s.* (*pl.* FOVEAE [-ˌi]) 1. (anat.) fóvea, esp. fóvea central. 2. (bot.) fóvea.
fovea centralis [-sɛn'treɪləs] (anat.) fóvea central.
foveate ['foʊvɪˌeɪt, -ət] *a.* hoyoso, que tiene fóveas o fosas.
foveola [fə'viələ] *s.* (*pl.* FOVEOLAE [-ˌli]) (anat.) fovéola, esp. fovéola gástrica.
foveolate ['foʊvɪələt, -ˌleɪt] **foveolated** [-ˌleɪtəd] *a.* (bot., zool.) hoyoso, que tiene fovéolas.
foveole ['foʊvɪˌoʊl] *s.* (anat.) fovéola.
fowl [faʊl] *s.* 1. ave(s) doméstica(s); ave(s) de corral; gallo, gallina, pollo. 2. carne de ave (esp. de las domésticas). 3. (raro) ave (en general). —*v.i.* cazar aves; atrapar aves.
fowler ['faʊlər, B -ə] *s.* cazador de aves.
fowling [-ɪʌ] *s.* caza de aves.
fowling net, red para cazar aves.
fowling piece, escopeta ligera para caza menor.
fox [fɑks, B fɔks] *s.* 1. (zool.) zorro, raposa. 2. zorro, piel de la zorra. 3. (fig.) zorro, taimado. 4. (mar.) rebenque. 5. (ant.) clase de espada. —*v.t.* 1. engañar con astucia, embaucar, burlar. 2. dejar perplejo, deslumbrar. 3. remontar, reparar, remendar (zapatos, botas). 4. (ant.) embriagar, emborrachar. —*v.i.* disimular su intención.
fox-brush ['fɑksˌbrʌʃ, B 'fɔks-] *s.* (G.B.) rabo de zorra.
fox chase, f. hunt, caza de zorras.
foxed [fɑkst, B fɔkst] *a.* manchado, descolorido (hoja de libro, grabado antiguo, etc.).
fox fire, luz fosforescente de la madera podrida; hongo luminoso (que hace que la madera podrida resplandezca).
foxglove ['fɑksˌglʌv, B 'fɔks-] *s.* (bot.) dedalera, digital.
foxhole [-ˌhoʊl] *s.* (mil.) trinchera individual, pozo de tirador, hoyo de protección.
foxhound [-ˌhaʊnd] *s.* perro raposero, perro zorrero o jateo.
fox hunt, caza del zorro.
foxily ['fɑksəlɪ, B 'fɔksɪ-] *adv.* astutamente, taimadamente.
foxiness [-sɪnəs] *s.* zorrería, astucia, maña.
foxlike ['fɑksˌlaɪk, B 'fɔks-] *a.* astuto, taimado.
fox squirrel, ardilla negra.
foxtail [-ˌteɪl] *s.* 1. rabo de zorra, cola de zorra. 2. (bot.) rabo de zorra, cola de zorra, carricera.
foxtail millet, (bot.) panizo.
fox terrier, fox-térrier, perro raposero.
fox-trot ['fɑksˌtrɑt, B 'fɔksˌtrɔt] *s.* 1. trote corto (de un caballo). 2. fox trot (baile o música). —*v.i.* bailar el fox trot.
foxy ['fɑksɪ, B 'fɔk-] *a.* (FOXIER; FOXIEST) 1. astuto, taimado; inteligente. 2. rojizo, del color de la zorra. 3. descolorido, manchado (hoja de libro, grabado antiguo, etc.). 4. agrio, desagradable al paladar (vinos, cerveza, etc.).
foyer ['fɔɪər, -ˌeɪ, B -eɪ] *s.* salón de entrada; vestíbulo.
fps *abrev. de* **feet per second,** pies por segundo.
Fr *símb. de* **francium,** francio (Fr).
Fr. *abrev. de* **French,** francés.
fracas ['freɪkəs, 'fræk-, B 'frækˌɑ] *s.* (*pl.* FRACASES) tumulto, alboroto, pendencia, reyerta, altercado, riña, gresca, batahola.
fraction ['frækʃən] *s.* 1. fracción, fraccionamiento. 2. fracción, fragmento, porción. 3. (mat.) fracción, quebrado. 4. (quím.) fracción. 5. (raro) fractura, quebradura, rotura. —*v.t.* fraccionar.
fractional [-əl] *a.* 1. fraccionario, fraccionado, fragmentado. 2. minúsculo, insignificante. 3. (quím.) fraccionada (destilación, cristalización, etc.); de fraccionamiento (método, etc.). 4. (bolsa) fraccionario.
fractional currency, moneda divisionaria, moneda suelta, menudo.
fractionalize [-ˌaɪz] *v.t.* fraccionar, dividir, partir, frangir.
fractionate ['frækʃəˌneɪt] *v.t.* (quím.) fraccionar.
fractionation [ˌfrækʃə'neɪʃən] *s.* (quím.) fraccionamiento.
fractionize ['frækʃəˌnaɪz] *v.t., v.i.* fraccionar, fragmentar; dividir en partes pequeñas.
fractious [-ʃəs] *a.* 1. reacio, díscolo, indócil, rebelde, chúcaro (Amer.). 2. regañon, malhumorado, displicente; atravesado, avieso.
fractiousness [-nəs] *s.* 1. indocilidad, rebeldía. 2. malhumor, displicencia.
fractural [-tʃərəl] *a.* de fractura, causado por fractura.
fracture ['fræktʃər, B -tʃə] *s.* 1. fractura, ruptura, rompimiento. 2. brecha, grieta, hendedura, rajadura, rendija. 3. (min., geol.) disyunción. 4. (med.) fractura, rotura (de un hueso), desgarradura (de un cartílago). —*v.t.* 1. fracturar, romper (hueso, pierna, pieza en máquina, etc.). 2. (fig.) quebrantar (unidad, paz, etc.). 3. quebrar, violar (ley, etc.). —*v.i.* fracturarse, romperse.
fraenum, *var. de* **frenum.**
fragged [frægd] *a.* herido por una bomba de fragmentación.
fragile ['frædʒəl, B -aɪl] *a.* frágil, quebradizo; deleznable, friable; débil, delicado.
fragility [frə'dʒɪlətɪ] *s.* fragilidad; friabilidad.
fragment ['frægmənt] *s.* 1. fragmento, trozo. 2. casco (de granada o bomba). — [-ˌmɛnt] *v.t., v.i.* dividir, fragmentar.
fragmental [fræ g'mɛntəl] *a.* fragmentario.
fragmentary ['frægmənˌtɛrɪ, B -tərɪ] *a.* fragmentario; inconexo.
fragmentate [-ˌteɪt] *v.t., v.i.* fragmentar (se).
fragmentation [ˌfrægmən'teɪʃən] *s.* fragmentación.
fragmented ['frægˌmɛntəd] *a.* fragmentado.
fragmentize [-mənˌtaɪz] *v.t.* fragmentar, fraccionar.
fragrance ['freɪgrəns] *s.* fragancia, buen olor, perfume, aroma.
fragrancy [-grənsɪ] *s., var. ant. de* fragrance.
fragrant [-grənt] *a.* fragante, aromático.
fragrantly [-lɪ] *adv.* fragantemente.
frail [freɪl] *a.* 1. frágil, quebradizo; deleznable. 2. débil, endeble, delicado. —*s.* 1. canasta de mimbre para presentar frutas y nueces. 2. (jer.) muchacha, mozuela.
frailness ['freɪlnəs] *s.* fragilidad; debilidad.
frailty [-tɪ] *s.* flaqueza, debilidad, falla.
fraise [freɪz] *s.* 1. gorguera, lechuguilla (para el cuello). 2. (fort.) frisa.
framboesia [fræm'biʒə] *s.* (med.) frambesia, pian, bubas, mal de pinto.
frame [freɪm] *v.t.* 1. formar, formular, planear; construir. 2. forjar (ideas, etc.), concebir, inventar. 3. armar, ensamblar. 4. formar, moldear. 5. formular, expresar (respuesta, pensamientos, etc.). 6. ajustar, adaptar. 7. redactar (documento, proyecto de ley, etc.). 8. enmarcar (cuadro, espejo, etc.). 9. incriminar (a un inocente), acusar o hacer condenar fraudulentamente; formar un complot contra; inventar (pruebas). 10. arreglar, amañar (carrera, contienda, etc.). —*v.i.* (ant.) 1. proceder, ir. 2. hacer progresos, prosperar. 3. maquinar, ingeniarse. —*s.* 1. estructura,

armazón, esqueleto, montura. 2. cuerpo (humano o animal). 3. sistema, estructura. 4. marco (de cuadro, espejo, etc.); cerco, marco (de ventana, puerta). 5. (fig.) marco, fondo (en una novela, drama, etc.). 6. (mec., maq.) bastidor. 7. (mar.) cuaderna, costillas (de la nave). 8. (cine.) cuadro. 9. (t.v.) cuadro; panel. 10. (dep.) entrada, turno. —*a.* de tablas, de madera, de entramado.

frame house, casa de madera.

frame of mind, estado de ánimo, disposición, humor.

frame of reference, 1. esquema o marco de referencia. 2. (mat.) sistema de coordenadas, eje de coordenadas.

framer ['freɪmər, B -ə] *s.* 1. forjador. 2. redactor, autor. 3. inventor, constructor. 4. armador, ensamblador. 5. encuadrador. 6. (carp.) carpintero de obras de afuera; fabricante de marcos.

frame saw, sierra alternativa, sierra de bastidor.

frame-up [-ˌʌp] *s.* (jer.) treta, estratagema para incriminar a un inocente, acusación fraudulenta, complot.

framework [-ˌwɜrk, B -ˌwɜk] *s.* 1. armazón, entramado, esqueleto. 2. (fig.) estructura, sistema (de ideas, etc.).

framing [-ɪŋ] *s.* 1. construcción, formación. 2. (ing., arq.) armazón, armadura, tirantería, esqueleto, ensamblaje.

franc [fræŋk] *s.* franco, unidad monetaria de varios países de Europa y África.

France [fræns, B frɑns] *s.* Francia.

Franche-Comté [ˌfrɑnʃˌkoʊn'teɪ] *s.* (hist.) (el) Franco Condado.

franchise ['frænˌtʃaɪz] *s.* 1. franquicia, privilegio; exención, inmunidad. 2. derecho político. 3. sufragio, derecho de voto. 4. (com.) franquicia, licencia, concesión. —*v.t.* dar la concesión de; (*a retail outlet*) conceder en franquicia.

franchising ['frætʃaɪzɪŋ] *s.* concesión de franquicias, franchising.

Franciscan [fræn'sɪskən] *a., s.* (relig.) franciscano.

francium ['frænsɪəm] *s.* (quím.) francio.

Franco-German ['fræŋkoʊ'dʒɜrmən, B -'dʒɜmən] *a.* francoalemán.

francolin ['fræŋkələn] *s.* (orn.) francolín.

Francophile ['fræŋkəˌfaɪl] **Francophil** [-ˌfɪl] *a., s.* francófilo.

Francophilia [ˌfræŋkə'fɪlɪə] *s.* francofilia.

Francophobe ['fræŋkəˌfoʊb] *a., s.* francófobo.

Francophobia [ˌfræŋkə'foʊbɪə] *s.* francofobia.

franc-tireur [ˌfrɑnti'rɜ] *s.* (*pl.* FRANCSTIREURS) (mil.) francotirador, guerrillero.

frangible ['frændʒəbəl] *a.* frangible, frágil.

frangipani [ˌfrændʒə'pænɪ, -'pɑnɪ] (*pl.* FRANGIPANI O FRANGIPANIS) *s.* 1. (bot.) franchipaniero. 2. franchipán, pomada aromática. 3. dulce de almendras molidas.

franglais [fræn'gleɪ] *s.* franglés.

frank [fræŋk] *a.* 1. franco, sincero; ingenuo, natural, abierto. 2. (ant.) libre. 3. (ant.) liberal, generoso. —*v.t.* 1. enviar (carta, paquete, etc.). 2. llevar o transportar gratis; facilitar el libre paso a. 3. franquear, exceptuar, exentar de franqueo (por virtud de un permiso especial); libertar, liberar. —*s.* sello (indicador) de franquicia; franquicia, exención de los derechos de correos o de aduanas.

Frank, *s.* franco (miembro de las antiguas tribus de Germania).

Frankenstein ['fræŋkənˌstaɪn] *s.* Frankenstein, personaje literario destruido por un monstruo creado por él mismo. 2. (fig.) obra o trabajo que aniquila a su creador.

Frankforter, *var. de* **frankfurter.**

Frankfurt ['fræŋkfərt, B -fət] *s.* Francfort, ciudad de Alemania Occidental.

frankfurter [-ər, B -ə] *s.* salchicha alemana, perro caliente (fam.).

frankincense ['fræŋkənˌsɛns] *s.* incienso, olíbano.

Frankish ['fræŋkɪʃ] *a.* franco, de los francos. —*s.* franco, lengua de los francos.

franklin [-lən] *s.* (hist., G.B.) pequeño propietario (poseedor de un feudo franco).

franklinite [-ləˌnaɪt] *s.* (min.) franklinita.

Franklin stove, antigua estufa de hierro semejante a un hogar abierto.

frankly ['fræŋklɪ] *adv.* francamente, sinceramente.

frankness [-nəs] *s.* franqueza, sinceridad.

frankpledge [-ˌplɛdʒ] *s.* (der., ant., G.B.) 1. sistema que hacía responsable a cada miembro masculino de una decena de vecinos de la buena conducta de los otros miembros. 2. miembro de una decena de vecinos regida por este sistema.

frantic ['fræntɪk] *a.* 1. frenético, furioso, rabioso, enfurecido, desesperado. 2. (raro) desequilibrado, loco.

frantically [-ɪkəlɪ] *adv.* frenéticamente, furiosamente, desesperadamente.

frap [fræp] *v.t.* (*pret., p.p.* FRAPPED; *p.pr.* FRAPPING) (mar.) atortorar; asegurar, apretar (un cabo).

frappé [fræ'peɪ] *a.* helado, enfriado con hielo. —*s.* 1. refresco gen. de zumo de frutas, con hielo picado. 2. batido de leche. —*v.t.* (*pret., p.p.* FRAPPÉED; *p.pr.* FRAPPÉING) helar, refrescar.

frater ['freɪtər, B -ə] *s.* 1. (hist.) refectorio (en un monasterio). 2. miembro de una fraternidad u orden religiosa.

fraternal [frə'tɜrnəl, B -'tɜn-] *a.* 1. fraternal (amor, caridad, etc.). 2. fraterno (sociedad, etc.). 3. (biol.) fraterno, dicigótico, dicorial, biovular (díc. de gemelos que resultan de la fecundación simultánea de dos óvulos).

fraternalism [-ˌɪzəm] *s.* estado o sentimiento de fraternidad; teoría o práctica de las sociedades fraternas.

fraternally [-ɪ] *adv.* fraternalmente.

fraternity [-'tɜrnətɪ, B -'tɜnə-] *s.* 1. hermandad, hermanazgo, fraternidad, confraternidad. 2. congregación, hermandad, confradía; congregación de devotos. 3. (E.U.) asociación; club estudiantil (masculino). 4. sociedad, asociación, agrupación, gremio.

fraternization [ˌfrætərnə'zeɪʃən, B -ənaɪ-] *s.* fraternización.

fraternize ['frætərˌnaɪz, B -əˌ-] *v.i.* 1. fraternizar, confraternizar (Amer.), trabar amistad, codearse. 2. fraternizar con el enemigo. —*v.t.* (ant.) unir, juntar, ligar.

fratricidal [ˌfrætrə'saɪdəl, B ˌfreɪ-] *a.* fratricida.

fratricide ['frætrəˌsaɪd, B 'freɪ-] *s.* 1. fratricidio. 2. fratricida.

Frau [fraʊ] *s.* (alemán) ama de casa, señora, esposa.

fraud [frɔd] *s.* 1. fraude, artificio, truco, supercheria, impostura. 2. fraudulencia, engaño, dolo, trapacería, timo. 3. impostor, engañador, simulador. 4. (der.) defraudación, fraude. 5. **in f. of, to the f. of,** (der.) para defraudar.

fraudulence ['frɔdzələns, B -djʊ-] *s.* fraudulencia.

fraudulent [-lənt] *a.* fraudulento, engañoso, falaz.

fraudulently [-lɪ] *adv.* fraudulentamente, fraudulosamente, engañosamente.

fraught [frɔt] *s.* (ant.) carga, cargazón. —*v.t.* (ant.) fletar, cargar. —*a.* 1. cargado, lleno. 2. (ant.) fletado. 3. **f. with,** (fig.) lleno de, cargado de, preñado de, atestado de.

Fräulein ['frɔɪˌlaɪn] *s.* (alemán) chica, señorita.

fraxinella [ˌfræksə'nɛlə] *s.* (bot.) fresnillo, fraxinela, díctamo blanco.

fray [freɪ] *v.t.* 1. desgastar, deshilachar, ludir, frotar, tazar. 2. (fig.) irritar, exacerbar (los nervios). —*v.i.* desgastarse, deshilacharse. —*s.* 1. deshiladura; parte gastada o raída (de un tejido, etc.). 2. riña, pelea, combate, refriega, conflicto.

frayed [freɪd] *a.* raído, deshilachado, raboso.

frazzle ['fræzəl] *v.t.* 1. desgastar, deshilachar; hacer jirones. 2. agotar, rendir de cansancio. —*v.i.* deshilacharse, desgastarse, raerse. —*s.* 1. estado desgastado o deshilachado. 2. agotamiento, cansancio extremo. 3. **worn to a f.,** hecho jirones, desgastado por completo; (fig.) rendido de cansancio, completamente agotado; **to beat to a f.,** (dep.) ganar fácilmente.

freak [frik] *s.* 1. capricho, antojo. 2. anormalidad, rareza, curiosidad, monstruosidad; extravagante, tipo excéntrico. 3. (E.U.) hippie. 4. **f. of nature,** fenómeno, monstruo; **out of mere f.,** por puro capricho. —*a.* raro, estrafalario; inesperado.

freak, *v.t.* rayar, gayar, listar (esp. en colores). —*s.* raya o lista de color.

freakish ['frikɪʃ] *a.* 1. caprichoso, antojadizo. 2. extraño, raro, extravagante, estrafalario.

freakishness [-nəs] *s.* 1. carácter caprichoso. 2. monstruosidad, extrañeza, rareza.

freak out, (jer.) 1. experimentar los efectos alucinantes, etc., producidos por drogas sicodélicas. 2. experimentar efectos similares sin necesidad de drogas, a través de estímulos visuales y auditivos. 3. convertirse en **hippie.**

freckle ['frɛkəl] *v.t.* 1. hacer cubrir de pecas (rostro). 2. motear, salpicar. —*v.i.* cubrirse de pecas, ponerse pecoso. —*s.* peca.

freckle-faced [-ˌfeɪst] *a.* pecoso.

free [fri] *a.* 1. libre (elección, acuerdo, agente, acto, albedrío, etc.). 2. libre, independiente (hombre, institución, nación, mundo, etc.). 3. franco, libre (puerto), libre (economía, comercio, competencia). 4. libre, abierto, sin obstáculos. 5. liberal, generoso. 6. gratis, gratuito, franco. 7. suelto, flojo, desatado, (rueda, extremo de un cable, cuerda, etc.). 8. franco, abierto, sincero, directo, desembarazado. 9. permitido, permisible. 10. licencioso, impertinente. 11. aproximado, inexacto (palabra, término, habla). 12. libre (verso, traducción). 13. (quím.) puro (elemento, oxígeno, etc.). 14. (fís.) libre (energía, fuerza, etc.). 15. (mar.) abierto (viento). 16. **for f.,** gratis, sin costo; **f. and clear,** libre de trabas, libre de gravámenes; **f. and easy,** despreocupado; informal; **to be f. from,** estar libre de; estar exento de; **to be f. to,** tener libertad para (decidir, aceptar, rehusar, etc.); **to be f. with,** prodigar, ser generoso con; **to feel f. to,** no tener inconveniente o reparo en; **to give a f. hand,** dar plenos poderes, dar carta blanca; **to have a f. hand,** tener las manos libres (para); **to set f.,** libertar; **with a f. hand,** generosamente, liberalmente. —*adv.* 1. libremente, sin obstáculos. 2. gratuitamente, gratis. 3. (mar.) con viento abierto. —*v.t.* 1. libertar, dejar libre; soltar. 2. libertar, liberar, manumitir, rescatar. 3. **f. from,** librar de; eximir de; desenredar de; **f. of,** liberar de; desembarazar de.

free alongside ship, (com.) puesto al costado del barco, sobre muelle, franco muelle.

freeboard ['friˌbɔrd, B -ˌbɔd] *s.* 1. (mar.) obra muerta, franco bordo. 2. (aut.) espacio libre (entre el bastidor y el suelo).

freeboard deck, (mar.) cubierta superior que limita la medición de bordo libre, cubierta de franco bordo.
freeboot [-ˌbut] *v.i.* piratear, saquear.
freebooter [-ər, B -ə] *s.* pirata; saqueador.
freeborn [-ˌbɔrn, B -ˌbɔn] *a.* libre de nacimiento, nacido libre; propio o digno de un pueblo o persona libre.
Free Church, 1. iglesia separada del estado. 2. (G.B.) iglesia no conformista.
freedman ['fridmən] *s.* liberto, manumiso.
freedom ['fridəm] *s.* 1. libertad. 2. facilidad, fluidez, desenvoltura. 3. privilegio, derecho. 4. (ú. esp. con *from*) inmunidad, impunidad, exención. 5. (con *of*) libre acceso (a).
freedom from want, derecho a no sufrir indigencia.
freedom of speech, libertad de palabra.
freedom of the press, libertad de prensa.
freedom of the seas, libertad de los mares.
freedom of worship, libertad de cultos.
freedwoman ['fridˌwʊmən] *s.* liberta, manumisa.
free enterprise, libre empresa, libertad de competencia.
free fall, (fís.) caída libre.
free fight, refriega general; lucha libre.
free-for-all ['frifərˌɔl] *s.* pelotera, contienda general; altercado, alboroto.
free form, 1. (gram.) forma independiente (que tiene significado en sí misma y puede por lo tanto usarse sola). 2. forma libre, de forma irregular, arte abstracto.
free goods, (com.) mercancías exentas de derechos.
freehand [-ˌhænd] *a.* a pulso, hecho a pulso, sin ayuda de instrumentos o medidas (dibujos, diseños, etc.).
freehanded [-'hændəd] *a.* dadivoso, generoso, magnánimo.
freehearted [-'hɑrtəd, B -'hɑt-] *a.* 1. franco, abierto, cordial; espontáneo. 2. generoso, magnánimo.
freehold [-ˌhoʊld] *s.* 1. (der.) feudo franco. 2. dominio absoluto. 3. oficio o dignidad vitalicia.
freeholder [-ər, B -ə] *s.* 1. poseedor de feudo franco. 2. dueño, propietario absoluto de una finca, casa o heredad.
free labor, trabajadores no sindicalizados.
free lance, 1. persona que trabaja independientemente sin pertenecer a una empresa. 2. persona que actúa en forma política independiente (que no pertenece a ningún partido). 3. (hist.) caballero o soldado mercenario.
free-lance ['fri'læns, B -'lɑns] *v.i.* trabajar en forma independiente sin estar en una nómina permanente. *—a.* 1. mercenario. 2. independiente.
free liver, sibarita, persona incontinente.
free-living [-'lɪvɪŋ] *a.* de vida regalada, disoluto.
freeload [-ˌloʊd] *v.i.* (jer.) comer o beber a costa ajena, vivir de gorra; visitar o usar (algo) gratis.
free love, amor libre.
freely ['frilɪ] *adv.* 1. libremente, sin reserva; espontáneamente; desembarazadamente; francamente. 2. generosamente, liberalmente. 3. gratuitamente. 4. copiosamente, abundantemente.
freeman [-mən] *s.* hombre libre; ciudadano.
freemartin [-ˌmɑrtən, B -ˌmɑt-] *s.* ternera estéril.
Freemason [-'meɪsən, B -ˌmeɪ-] *s.* francmasón, masón.
freemasonry [-rɪ] *s.* 1. gen. **F.,** francmasonería, masonería. 2. (fig., p. ext.) compañerismo, fraternidad.
freeness ['frinəs] *s.* libertad.
free of charge, gratis, de balde.
free of duty, (com.) franco de derechos, libre de derechos.
free on board, (com.) franco a bordo.
free pass, pase, entrada libre; permiso de libre circulación.
free port, (com.) puerto franco, puerto libre.
freer [ˌfriər, B -ə] *s.* libertador. *—a. comp. de* **free,** más libre.
freesia ['friʒə] *s.* (bot.) fresia.
free silver, (econ.) acuñación sin límite de plata.
free soil, (hist., E.U.) territorio donde no se permitía la esclavitud.
free-spoken ['fri'spoʊkən] *a.* francote, sin reserva, sincero.
freestanding [-'stændɪŋ] *a.* (const.) autoestable.
freestone [-ˌstoʊn] *s.* 1. piedra franca, canto rodado, caliza o arenisca fácil de labrar. 2. fruta abridera; hueso de fruta abridera.
freestone peach, (bot.) abridero.
Freestone State, (el) estado de Connecticut (llamado así por sus canteras de piedra franca).
free-style wrestling ['fri'staɪl-] lucha libre.
freethinker [-'θɪŋkər, B -kə] *s.* librepensador.
freethinking [-kɪŋ] *s.* librepensamiento. *—a.* librepensador.
free thought, pensamiento racionalista, librepensamiento.
free throw, (baloncesto) tiro libre.
free time, 1. ratos perdidos, asueto. 2. (com.) tiempo sin sobreestadías.
Freetown ['friˌtaʊn] *s.* Freetown, capital de Sierra Leona.
free trade, comercio libre; librecambio.
free-trade [-'treɪd] *a.* librecambista.
free verse, verso libre, sin rima ni ritmo.
freeway [-ˌweɪ] *s.* autopista (esp. aquella en que no se paga peaje).
freewheel ['fri'hwil, -'wil] *s.* (mec.) rueda libre. *—v.i.* 1. correr en marcha libre, marchar desembragado; andar con rueda libre (esp. bicicleta). 2. llevar vida de bohemio, vivir sin responsabilidades.
free will, arbitrio, libre albedrío, libre voluntad, espontaneidad.
freeze [friz] *v.i.* (*pret.* FROZE [froʊz]; *p.p.* FROZEN ['froʊzən]; *p.pr.* FREEZING) 1. helarse, congelarse. 2. (fig.) helarse, quedarse muy frío. 3. volverse formal y frío (en el trato). 4. quedarse inmóvil. 5. **f. over,** congelarse la superficie, cubrirse de hielo (río, lago, etc.); **f. to death,** morirse de frío; (fig.) helarse. *—v.t.* 1. helar, congelar. 2. enfriar, refrigerar. 3. congelar (precios); congelar, inmovilizar (fondos extranjeros, cuentas, etc.). 4. tratar con frialdad. 5. **f. one's blood,** (fig.) helársele a uno la sangre; **f. out,** excluir (de un negocio, sociedad, club, etc.), eliminar; librarse de, deshacerse de; **f. up,** congelar completamente; **frozen to death,** muerto de frío. *—s.* 1. helada. 2. congelación, congelamiento. 3. (fig.) congelación (de precios); paralización, suspensión (de producción, etc.). 4. (jer.) trato frío, desaire.
freeze-dried [-ˌdraɪd] *a.* liofilizado.
freeze-dry ['frizˌdraɪ] *s.* (quím.) deshidratación por congelación. *—v.t.* liofilizar, deshidratar por congelación.
freezer ['frizər, B -ə] *s.* congelador, máquina frigorífica, heladera.
freezing [-ɪŋ] *a.* congelante; glacial. *—s.* congelación.
freezing point, (fís.) punto de congelación.
free zone, área de libre importación, zona franca.
freight [freɪt] *s.* 1. flete (que se paga por el transporte de mercaderías). 2. carga, cargamento, flete. 3. acarreo, transporte (de mercaderías). 4. tren de carga. *—v.t.* 1. cargar (buque, avión). 2. (fig., gen. con *with*) cargar (de), llenar (de). 3. llevar como carga, transportar. 4. fletar.
freightage ['freɪtɪdʒ] *s.* 1. flete. 2. carga, cargamento. 3. transporte, acarreo (de mercaderías). 4. capacidad total disponible para el transporte.
freight agent, (f.c.) agente de carga, factor.
freight car, (f.c.) carro de carga, vagón de mercancías.
freight elevator, ascensor o elevador de carga, montacargas.
freighter ['freɪtər, B -ə] *s.* 1. fletador. 2. embarcador, contratista de transportes. 3. buque de carga, carguero, fletero (Amer.); avión de carga.
freight prepaid, (com.) flete pagado, porte pagado.
freight station, (f.c.) estación de mercancías.
freight train, tren de carga.
freight yard, (f.c.) patio de carga, playa de carga (Amer.).
fremitus ['frɛmətəs] *s.* (med.) frémito, estremecimiento o vibración.
French [frɛntʃ] *a.* francés. *—s.* 1. (idioma) francés. 2. **the F.,** los franceses. *—v.t.* preparar alimentos a la francesa.
French bean, (pr. G.B.) judía verde, habichuela verde, vainita (Am.).
French Canadian, canadiense de ascendencia francesa.
French chalk, jabón de sastre, esteatita.
French chop, costilla de cordero.
French cuff, puño doble.
French door, puerta-ventana, puerta vidriera, puerta cristalera.
French dressing, salsa francesa, gen. para ensaladas.
French endive, (bot.) endibia, variedad de escarola.
French fry, freír en abundante grasa; **F. fries,** (fam.) papas fritas.
French heel, tacón alto y torneado (en el calzado femenino).
French horn, (mús.) corno francés, trompa de pistones.
Frenchification [ˌfrɛntʃəfə'keɪʃən] *s.* afrancesamiento.
Frenchify ['frɛntʃəˌfaɪ] *v.t.* (*pret., p.p.* FRENCHIFIED; *p.pr.* FRENCHIFYING) (fam.) afrancesar, agabachar, afranchutar.
French kiss, beso a la francesa (dándose la lengua).
French leave, despedida a la francesa, despedida desapercibida; **to take F. l.,** irse o despedirse a la francesa.
Frenchman [-mən] *s.* 1. francés. 2. buque (esp. de guerra) francés.
French marigold, (bot.) damasquina, clavel de la India.
French pastry, pasteles pequeños aderezados con abundante crema.
French roof, mansarda, tejado en voladizo.
French speaker, francófono.
French-speaking, francófono.
French telephone, microteléfono (aparato que reúne el auricular y el micrófono en una sola pieza).
French toast, torrija, torreja, rebanada de pan empapada de huevo y leche y frita, que se sirve con miel o jarabe.
French way, (jer.) felatorismo, irrumación, cópula oral.
French West Indies, Antillas Francesas (Martinica y Guadalupe).

French window, (arq.) puerta-ventana de dos hojas, (que da acceso a un balcón o terraza).
Frenchy ['frɛntʃɪ] *a.* afrancesado. —*s.* (jer.) franchute, gabacho.
frenetic [frə'nɛtɪk] **frenetical** [-ɪkəl] *a.* frenético.
frenetically [-ɪkəlɪ] *adv.* frenéticamente.
frenum ['frinəm] *s.* (*pl.* FRENUMS O FRENA [-nə]) (anat., zool.) frenillo.
frenzied ['frɛnzid] *a.* frenético, furioso, rabioso, loco, enloquecido; **a f. effort,** un esfuerzo frenético; **a f. rage,** una rabia loca.
frenzy [-zɪ] *s.* frenesí, locura, desvarío, desbarro; furor; **to drive to f.,** volver loco, enfurecer. —*v.t.* (*pret., p.p.* FRENZIED; *p.pr.* FRENZYING) enloquecer, volver loco, enfurecer.
Freon ['fri,ɑn, B -,ɔn] *s.* (quím.) freón, diclorodifluorometano.
frequency ['frikwənsɪ] *s.* 1. frecuencia; repetición. 2. (mat., fís., elec., rad.) frecuencia, ciclaje.
frequency band, (rad.) faja o banda de frecuencias.
frequency changer, (elec.) transformador, convertidor o cambiador de frecuencia.
frequency converter, (elec.) convertidor de frecuencia.
frequency distribution, (estadística) distribución de frecuencias.
frequency drift, (rad.) variación de frecuencia, oscilación.
frequency meter, (elec.) frecuencímetro.
frequency modulation, (rad.) modulación de frecuencia, frecuencia modulada.
frequency swing, (rad.) oscilación de la frecuencia.
frequent ['frikwənt] *a.* frecuente, repetido; habitual, usual, común, ordinario. — [fri'kwɛnt] *v.t.* frecuentar, visitar a menudo.
frequentation [,frikwɛn'teɪʃən] *s.* frecuentación.
frequentative [fri'kwɛntətɪv] *a., s.* frecuentativo.
frequenter [-ər, B -ə] *s.* frecuentador.
frequently ['frikwəntlɪ] *adv.* frecuentemente, repetidamente, regularmente, habitualmente.
frequent pulse, (med.) pulso acelerado.
fresco ['frɛskoʊ] *s.* (*pl.* FRESCOES O FRESCOS) fresco, pintura al fresco; **al f.,** al aire libre. —*v.t.* (*pret., p.p.* FRESCOED; *p.pr.* FRESCOING) pintar al fresco.
fresh [frɛʃ] *a.* 1. fresco, nuevo, reciente; recién terminado. 2. (con *from*) recién salido (del colegio, etc.). 3. dulce, potable (agua). 4. reciente, fresco (noticia, impresión, etc.). 5. fresco, puro, refrescante (aire). 6. fresco, refrescado, lozano; vigoroso. 7. novicio, nuevo, inexperto. 8. nuevo, otro. 9. parida (vaca). 10. (jer.) fresco, descarado, impertinente; atrevido. 11. (jer.) achispado, bebido. 12. **as f. as paint,** fresco como una lechuga; **in the f. air,** al fresco, al aire libre; **to begin a f. chapter,** (fig.) empezar un nuevo capítulo; **to break f. ground,** explorar un nuevo campo o terreno; **to make a f. start,** empezar de nuevo, probar otra vez. —*s.* 1. avenida, riada, crecida, inundación. 2. manantial, arroyo. —*adv.* frescamente; recientemente. —*v.t., v.i.* (gen. con *up*) refrescar(se).
freshen ['frɛʃən] *v.t.* 1. refrescar, refrigerar; hacer revivir. 2. (mar.) aliviar (un cabo, cambiándolo de sitio para que no roce). —*v.i.* 1. refrescarse. 2. avivarse, refrescar (el viento). 3. desalarse. 4. parir (una vaca).
freshet [-ət] *s.* 1. avenida, riada, crecida, inundación. 2. (ant.) arroyo, río. 3. corriente de agua dulce.
fresh gale, (meteor.) temporal; (mar.) viento duro (de 60 a 70 km. por hora).
freshly [-lɪ] *adv.* 1. frescamente, recientemente. 2. frescamente, vigorosamente. 3. impertinentemente, descaradamente, con frescura. 4. **f. made,** recién hecho.
freshman [-mən] *s.* (*pl.* FRESHMEN) 1. novato. 2. estudiante de primer año (de universidad, colegio superior, etc.).
freshness [-nəs] *s.* 1. frescura, frescor; lozanía, verdor. 2. descaro, impertinencia, frescura.
freshwater [-,wɔtər, -,wɑt-, B -,wɔtə] *a.* 1. de agua dulce. 2. (ant.) inexperto, bisoño (esp. marinero).
fret [frɛt] *v.t.* (*pret., p.p.* FRETTED; *p.pr.* FRETTING) 1. raer, rozar, corroer. 2. carcomer, raer por el uso. 3. agitar; rizar, ondear (agua). 4. irritar, molestar, vejar; preocupar, inquietar. —*v.i.* 1. gastarse, rozarse, consumirse, raerse. 2. impacientarse, inquietarse, irritarse, molestarse. 3. agitarse (una corriente de agua). 4. **f. and fume,** mostrar disgusto e impaciencia. —*s.* 1. roce, rozamiento; raspadura, desgaste. 2. rozadura, punto gastado o roído. 3. enojo, irritación, enfado.
fret, *s.* 1. calado, malla calada. 2. (arq.) greca, (adorno). 3. (mús.) traste (de guitarra, mandolina, etc.). —*v.t.* 1. bordar, recamar con oro o plata. 2. (arq.) adornar con grecas. 3. proveer de trastes (una guitarra, mandolina, etc.).
fretful ['frɛtfəl] *a.* irritable, displicente, descontentadizo, inquieto; incómodo, molesto.
fretfully [-fəlɪ] *adv.* con mal humor, de mala gana.
fretfulness [-fəlnəs] *s.* mal humor, mal genio; inquietud, desasosiego.
fret saw, sierra de marquetería, sierra de calar.
fretwork ['frɛt,wɜrk, B -,wɜk] *s.* 1. greca. 2. adorno calado o de relieve. 3. (her.) frete.
Freudian ['frɔɪdɪən] *a., s.* freudiano (de las teorías del fundador del psicoanálisis, Sigmund Freud).
Freudian slip, acto fallido.
Freudianism [-,ɪzəm] *s.* freudianismo.
Frey [freɪ] *s.* (mitol. escandinava) Freyr, dios de la fertilidad y de las cosechas, de la paz y la prosperidad.
Freya ['freɪə] *s.* (mitol. escandinava) Freya, diosa del amor y la belleza.
Fri. *abrev. de* **Friday,** viernes (vier.).
friability [,fraɪə'bɪlətɪ] *s.* friabilidad.
friable ['fraɪəbəl] *a.* friable, desmenuzable, deleznable, terroso (díc. del terreno).
friar ['fraɪər, B -ə] *s.* fraile (esp. de las cuatro órdenes mendicantes).
friarbird ['fraɪər,bɜrd, B -ə,bɜd] *s.* (orn.) pájaro de Australia que se alimenta de miel.
friar's balsam, tintura de benjuí.
friar's lantern, fuego fatuo.
friary ['fraɪrɪ, B 'fraɪərɪ] *s.* convento de frailes; orden de frailes.
fribble ['frɪbəl] *v.t.* malgastar, desperdiciar. —*a.* frívolo, vano. —*s.* fruslería.
fricandeau ['frɪkən,doʊ] *s.* (cocina) fricandó, guisado de carne mechada.
fricassee [,frɪkə'si, 'frɪkə,si] *s.* fricasé, plato hecho de ave, ternera u otra carne, cortada en pedazos y estofada en salsa o jugo. —*v.t.* (*pret., p.p.* FRICASSEED; *p.pr.* FRICASSEEING) guisar como fricasé; hacer fricasé.
fricative ['frɪkətɪv] *a.* (fon.) fricativo (díc. de ciertos sonidos). —*s.* fricativa, consonante fricativa.
friction ['frɪkʃən] *s.* 1. fricción, rozamiento, frotamiento, frotadura, frote, roce. 2. desavenencia, disensión, rozamiento, desacuerdo. 3. (mec.) fricción, rozamiento.
frictional [-əl] *a.* friccional, de fricción; producido por rozamiento o fricción (díc. por ej. de la electricidad).
friction brake, freno de fricción.
friction clutch, f. coupling, (mec.) embrague o acoplamiento de fricción.
friction drive, (aut.) impulsión o accionamiento por fricción, transmisión por fricción.
friction matches, fósforos, cerillas.
friction plate, rozadera, placa de fricción.
friction tape, (elec.) cinta aisladora o de fricción, cinta de empalme, cinta aislante.
Friday ['fraɪdɪ, -deɪ] *s.* viernes.
fridge [frɪdʒ] *s.* (fam., G.B.) refrigeradora, nevera.
fried [fraɪd] *pret., p.p.* de **fry.** —*a.* frito; (jer.) borracho.
friedcake ['fraɪd,keɪk] *s.* buñuelo.
fried egg, huevo frito, huevo estrellado.
friend [frɛnd] *s.* 1. amigo, amiga; compañero, compañera. 2. (fig.) amigo, partidario, favorecedor, aliado, adherente. 3. gente de paz (en respuesta al alto que echa el centinela). 4. **F.,** cuáquero. 5. (esco.) pariente. 6. **my honorable f.,** (G.B.) mi honorable amigo (fórmula con que se refiere un representante a otro en la Cámara de los Comunes); **my learned f.,** mi docto amigo (fórmula con que se dirige un abogado a otro en la corte o tribunal de justicia); **to be** (o **keep**) **friends with,** estar (o mantenerse) en buenos términos con; **to be close friends,** ser amigos íntimos; **to have a f. at court,** tener influencia; **to make friends,** trabar amistades; ganarse amigos. —*v.t.* (poét.) amparar, ayudar.
friendless ['frɛndləs] *a.* sin amigos, abandonado, desamparado, solitario.
friendlessness [-nəs] *s.* abandono, desamparo, soledad.
friendliness [-lɪnəs] *s.* amigabilidad, amistad, cordialidad, amabilidad.
friendly [-lɪ] *a.* (FRIENDLIER; FRIENDLIEST) 1. amigable, amistoso, amable, afable, cordial. 2. amigo, ej., *a f. nation,* una nación amiga. 3. favorable, propicio. —*s.* (*pl.* FRIENDLIES) miembro amigable (de una tribu de aborígenes). —*adv.* amigablemente, amistosamente.
friendly match, (dep.) partido amistoso.
friendship [-,ʃɪp] *s.* 1. amistad. 2. amigabilidad, bienquerencia.
Friesian ['friʒən, B -zjən] **Friesic** [-zɪk] *a.* frisio, frisón (de la región holandesa de Frisia).
frieze [friz] *s.* 1. (tej.) frisa, pañete. 2. (arq.) friso. 3. cenefa.
frig [frɪg] *v.t.* (jer.) copular; **f. around,** perder el tiempo, vagar sin objeto.
frigate ['frɪgət] *s.* (mar.) fragata.
frigate bird, (orn.) rabihorcado, pájaro burro, tijera.
fright [fraɪt] *s.* 1. miedo, susto, espanto, alarma. 2. espantajo; esperpento. 3. **to take f. (at),** asustarse (de). —*v.t.* (poét.) asustar.
frighten ['fraɪtən] *v.t.* 1. asustar, espantar, aterrorizar, alarmar, amedrentar, amilanar. 2. **f. away,** ahuyentar, espantar; **f. into (doing),** forzar (a hacer) con amenazas; **to be frightened at,** asustarse de; **to be frightened of,** tener miedo de.
frightened [-ənd] *a.* asustado, espantado, aterrorizado, atemorizado, alarmado, amedrentado, amilanado.
frightening [-ənɪŋ] *a.* aterrador, alarmante.
frightful [-fəl] *a.* 1. espantoso, pavoroso, terrible, horripilante. 2. (fam.) terrible, pésimo. 3. (fam.) tremendo, formidable, colosal.
frightfully [-fəlɪ] *adv.* 1. terriblemente, espantosamente. 2. (fam.) extremadamente, muy.

frightfulness [-fəlnəs] *s.* carácter o aspecto pavoroso.
frigid ['frɪdʒəd] *a.* 1. muy frío, helado (esp. clima o aire). 2. (fig.) indiferente; apático; altanero; hostil. 3. (med.) frígido (sexual).
frigidity [frə'dʒɪdətɪ] *s.* 1. frialdad, frío. 2. (fig.) frialdad, indiferencia. 3. (med.) frigidez.
frigidly ['frɪdʒədlɪ] *adv.* fríamente, indiferentemente.
frigidness [-nəs] *s.* 1. frialdad, frío. 2. (fig.) frialdad, indiferencia.
frigid zone, (geog.) zona glacial.
frigorific [ˌfrɪgə'rɪfɪk] *a.* frigorífico, refrigerante, enfriador.
frill [frɪl] *s.* 1. (cost.) lechuga, escarola, faralá, volante, chorrera. 2. (cocina) guarnición de papel (con que se adornan ciertos platos). 3. (fam.) ringorrango, adorno superfluo o extravagante; algo no esencial. 4. (*pl.*) aires o ademanes afectados, *ú. esp. en:* **to put on frills,** (despec.) darse tono, darse aires. 5. (zool.) gola de plumas o pelo (alrededor del cuello de ciertos animales). 6. (foto.) arrugamiento de la gelatina (en los bordes de una placa fotográfica). —*v.t.* 1. alechugar, escarolar. 2. guarnecer con escarola, faralá o chorrera. —*v.i.* (foto.) arrugarse (los bordes de una película).
frilling ['frɪlɪŋ] *s.* volantes, guarniciones.
frilly [-ɪ] *a.* (FRILLIER; FRILLIEST) 1. escarolado, rizado. 2. (fig.) frívolo; muy ornado.
Frimaire [fri'mɛr, B fri'mɛə] *s.* (hist.) frimario, tercer mes del año en el calendario de la Revolución Francesa.
fringe [frɪndʒ] *s.* 1. fleco, orla, borla, cenefa; pestaña, flequillo, cairel. 2. borde, margen; periferia. 3. grupo marginal; grupo extremista, ej., *criminal f.,* grupo marginal de criminales. 4. (ópt.) franja obscura o franja brillante (producida por la difracción de la luz). —*v.t.* 1. guarnecer con flecos, orlar, ribetear, cairelar. 2. (fig.) formar el borde de, bordear, orlar.
fringe area, (rad., t.v.) zona periférica (en que la recepción es débil o sufre distorsión).
fringe benefit, (com.) beneficio adicional o de menor cuantía, beneficios suplementarios; **f. benefits,** beneficios sociales, beneficio extrasalarial.
fringe effect, (rad.) efecto de borde.
fringillid [frɪn'dʒɪlɪd] *a.* (orn.) fringílido.
fringy ['frɪndʒɪ] *a.* floqueado.
frippery ['frɪpərɪ] *s.* 1. perejiles, perifollos. 2. fruslería, chuchería, baratija. 3. afectación (esp. en el estilo literario). 4. (ant.) ropa vieja; prendería, trapería.
Frisco ['frɪskoʊ] *s.* (jer., E.U.) la ciudad de San Francisco.
frisette [frɪ'zɛt] *s.* (ant.) flequillo artificial; rizos sobre la frente.
friseur [frɪ'zɜ] *s.* (fr.) peluquero.
Frisian ['frɪʒən, 'friʒən, B 'frɪzɪən] *a.* frisio, frisón. —*s.* 1. frisio, frisón. 2. (idioma) frisón (de una antigua tribu germana; de una región al N. de Holanda).
frisk [frɪsk] *a.* (ant.) retozón, vivaracho. —*s.* 1. brinco, retozo. 2. diversión. 3. (jer.) cacheo, registro. 4. (ant.) gambeta, cabriola. —*v.i.* retozar, cabriolar, brincar. —*v.t.* 1. zarandear, agitar. 2. (jer.) cachear, registrar; robar.
frisket ['frɪskət] *s.* (impr.) frasqueta.
friskily ['frɪskəlɪ] *adv.* juguetonamente, retozonamente.
friskiness [-ɪnəs] *s.* brío, vivacidad.
frisky [-ɪ] *a.* retozón, juguetón, vivaracho.
frit [frɪt] *s.* frita (mezcla semi-calcinada que se usa para fabricar vidrio y en la cerámica). —*v.t.* (*pret., p.p.* FRITTED; *p.pr.* FRITTING) fritar, derretir, calcinar, aglomerar (fabricación vidrio).
frith [frɪθ] *var. de* **firth.**
fritillaria [ˌfrɪtəl'ɛrɪə, B -'ɛər-] *s.* (bot.) fritilaria, corona imperial.
fritillary ['frɪtəlˌɛrɪ, B frɪ'tɪlərɪ] *s.* 1. (bot.) fritilaria, corona imperial. 2. (ento.) cierta mariposa con alas moteadas.
fritter ['frɪtər, B -ə] *s.* 1. fruta de sartén, fritura, frisuelo, buñuelo. 2. (raro) fragmento, triza. —*v.t.* desmenuzar, desmigajar; **f. away,** desperdiciar, malgastar.
fritz [frɪts] *s.* (jer.) boche, alemán, esp. soldado; **to be on the f.,** (jer., ant.) estar estropeado, estar caput.
Friulian [fri'ulɪən] *a., s.* friulano, lengua del Friul (antiguamente Venecia).
frivol ['frɪvəl] *v.i.* (*pret., p.p.* FRIVOLED O FRIVOLLED; *p.pr.* FRIVOLING O FRIVOLLING) obrar frívolamente, chancear(se). —*v.t.* **f. away,** desperdiciar (dinero, tiempo).
frivolity [frɪ'vɑlətɪ, B -'vɔl-] *s.* frivolidad, liviandad.
frivolous ['frɪvələs] *a.* 1. frívolo, baladí, fútil. 2. frívolo, liviano, ligero.
frivolously [-lɪ] *adv.* frívolamente.
frivolousness [-nəs] *s.* frivolidad.
frizz [frɪz] *v.t.* (*pret., p.p.* FRIZZED; *p.pr.* FRIZZING) rizar, encrespar, frisar (cueros). —*v.i.* rizarse, encresparse. —*s.* 1. rizo, bucle, crespo. bucle, crespo. 2. cabello rizado.
frizz, *v.t., v.i.* quemar(se) o chamuscar (se) produciendo chirrido o siseo; chirriar.
frizzily ['frɪzəlɪ] *adv.* rizadamente.
frizzle [-əl] *v.t.* 1. asar, freír, quemar. 2. rizar, encrespar. —*v.i.* 1. chirriar, sisear, crepitar. 2. (esp. con *up*) rizarse, encresparse. —*s.* crespo, rizo.
frizzly ['frɪzlɪ] *a.* rizado, muy ensortijado.
frizzy [-ɪ] *a.* rizado, frisado, encrespado, enmarañado.
fro [froʊ] *adv.* atrás, hacia atrás; **to and f.,** de aquí para allá, del tingo al tango.
frock [frɑk, B frɔk] *s.* 1. hábito, vestido talar (de los frailes o monjes). 2. túnica, saya, bata, manto. 3. jersey o camiseta de marinero. 4. vestido de mujer. —*v.t.* 1. vestir, cubrir con bata, túnica, vestido talar o hábito. 2. ordenar (a un sacerdote).
frock coat, levita.
froe [froʊ] *s.* cuña, hendedor (que se usa para partir duelas de barriles).
frog [frɔg, frɑg, B frɔg] *s.* 1. rana. 2. ronquera, carraspera, gallo (en la garganta). 3. ranilla, horquilla (del casco del caballo). 4. ojal, hebilla (cinturón), tahalí; alamar (presilla y botón en abrigos y vestidos). 5. talón (del arco de violín). 6. (despec.) gabacho, francés. 7. (f.c.) rana, crucero, corazón. —*v.i.* (*pret., p.p.* FROGGED; *p.pr.* FROGGING) cazar o coger ranas.
frogeye ['frɔgˌaɪ, 'frɑg-, B 'frɔg-] *s.* (agr.) moho azul (del tabaco).
frogfish [-ˌfɪʃ] *s.* (ict.) pejesapo, pescador, rape.
froggy [-ɪ] *a.* (FROGGIER; FROGGIEST) 1. (despec.) gabacho, francés. 2. abundante en ranas, lleno de ranas. 3. relativo o perteneciente a la rana.
froghopper [-ˌhɑpər, B -ˌhɔpə] *s.* (ento.) insecto escupidor.
frogman [-ˌmæn, B -mən] *s.* hombre rana, buceador.
frog-march [-ˌmɑrtʃ, B -ˌmɑtʃ] *v.t.* cargar boca abajo por los cuatro miembros a una persona.
frog's legs, (cul.) ancas de rana.
frog spit, 1. (ento.) baba del cuclillo. 2. (bot.) especie de alga.
frogtongue [-ˌtʌŋ] *s.* (med.) ránula; (vet.) alevosa, sapillo, barbilla, ránula.
frolic ['frɑlɪk, B 'frɔl-] *a.* juguetón, retozón, travieso; alegre. —*s.* 1. juego, jugarreta, retozo. 2. fiesta, holgorio. —*v.i.* (*pret., p.p.* FROLICKED; *p.pr.* FROLICKING) 1. juguetear, retozar. 2. jaranear.
frolicsome [-səm] *a.* juguetón, retozón, alegre.
frolicsomely [-lɪ] *adv.* alegremente, con viveza.
frolicsomeness [-nəs] *s.* vivacidad, alegría, disposición juguetona.
from [frɑm, frəm, B frɔm, frəm] *prep.* 1. de, desde. 2. por, a causa de, ej., *died f. exhaustion,* murió por (o a causa de) agotamiento. 3. a, ej., *they took the gun f. him,* le quitaron el revólver (a él). 4. **f. bad to worse,** de mal en peor; **f. beginning to end,** de principio a fin; **f. day to day,** diariamente, de día en día; **away f. home,** fuera de casa, lejos de casa; **f. his point of view,** desde su punto de vista, según él lo ve; **f. memory,** de memoria; **f. now on,** de ahora en adelante; **f. time to time,** ocasionalmente; **f. title to colophon,** del título al colofón, a lo largo de todo el libro; **f. A to Z,** completamente, de pe a pa.
fromenty ['froʊməntɪ] *var. de* **frumenty.**
frond [frɑnd, B frɔnd] *s.* (bot.) fronda, hoja (esp. de palma o palmera).
fronded ['frɑndəd, B 'frɔn-] *a.* frondoso, que tiene frondas.
frondose [-ˌdoʊs] *a.* (bot.) frondoso.
front [frʌnt] *s.* 1. frente (del rostro). 2. semblante, rostro, cara. 3. (fig.) fachada, apariencia. 4. (fig.) pantalla. 5. testaferro, figurante, figurón, títere. 6. posición, postura. 7. frente, delantera, vanguardia. 8. frente, asociación, agrupación. 9. pechera (de camisa), delantera (de prenda de vestir); camisolín. 10. postizos de pelo en la frente. 11. primera parte (ej., de un libro). 12. (fig.) campo (de actividades), frente. 13. (mil.) frente, frente de batalla, línea de combate. 14. (arq.) frente, fachada, frontispicio; frontal, portal, portada. 15. malecón, costanera. 16. (meteor.) frente. 17. (ant.) principio, comienzo. 18. **in f.,** en frente, delante; **in f. of,** delante de, frente a, en frente de; **out f.,** entre los espectadores, entre el auditorio; **to put up a f.,** disimular la verdad; **to show** (o **present**) **a bold f.,** mostrar firmeza. —*a.* 1. delantero, primero, frontero, frontal. 2. (fon.) anterior. —*v.t.* 1. hacer frente a, afrontar, arrostrar. 2. dar frente a, dar a, caer a. 3. estar al frente de. 4. poner frente a, fachada a. —*v.i.* 1. (con *on*) mirar (hacia), dar frente (a). 2. (con *for*) servir como títere o figurante (de); servir de fachada o pantalla (para).
frontage ['frʌntɪdʒ] *s.* 1. fachada, frente, frontis, frontispicio (de una construcción). 2. orientación, situación, vista, perspectiva. 3. terreno frontero. 4. (mil.) extensión frontal. 5. (der.) derecho de fachada.
frontal [-əl] *s.* 1. fachada. 2. frontal (de un altar). 3. (anat.) frontal, hueso frontal, músculo frontal. —*a.* frontal, de frente.
frontal bone, (anat.) hueso frontal o coronal.
frontal lobe, (anat.) lóbulo frontal.
frontal sinus, (anat.) seno frontal.
front bench, (G.B.) primera fila reservada a los ministros o a los antiguos ministros (en el parlamento).
front door, puerta principal.
front elevation, (arq.) alzado frontal, elevación frontal, elevación del frente.
frontier [ˌfrʌn'tɪr, B 'frʌntɪə] *s.* 1. frontera, confín, límite. 2. (E.U.) región fronteriza. 3. (ant.) plaza fuerte en una frontera. —*a.* fronterizo; limítrofe.

frontiersman [-'tɪrzmən, B -tɪəz-] *s.* habitante de la frontera; colonizador, explorador (esp. refiriéndose a los primeros pobladores del O. de E.U.).
frontispiece ['frʌntəs,pis] *s.* 1. (arq.) frontispicio, fachada, delantera (de un edificio). 2. (arq.) frontón (encima de puertas y ventanas). 3. portada, frontispicio (de un libro).
frontlet [-lət] *s.* 1. venda o cinta de adorno para la frente. 2. frente (de un animal o esp. de los pájaros cuando tienen plumaje de distinto color o textura). 3. frontalera (en el frontal del altar). 4. (bíbl.) filacteria.
front line, (mil.) línea del frente, primera línea.
front man, testaferro.
front matter, las páginas que anteceden al prólogo de un libro.
front office, ejecutivos, dirigentes (en conjunto) de una organización.
frontogenesis [,frʌntoʊ'dʒɛnəsəs] *s.* (meteor.) frontogénesis.
frontolysis [-'tɑləsəs, B -'tɔl-] *s.* (meteor.) frontolisis.
front page, primera plana (de un periódico); **f. p. news,** noticia extraordinaria.
front room, sala de estar, salón (principal de una residencia).
front row, delantera, primera fila (en teatro, estadio o iglesia); (fig.) posición de ventaja en un trato o situación.
front runner, puntero, corredor que va en cabeza; (pol.) favorito.
frontseat ['frʌnt'sit] *s.* asiento delantero o de primera fila.
front sight, (arm.) punto de mira.
frontstall [-,stɔl] *s.* (arm.) testera (del caballo).
front tooth, incisivo.
front view, vista o plano principal.
front vowel, (ling.) vocal frontal.
frontward [-wərd, B -wəd] **frontwards** [-wərdz, B -wədz] *adv.* hacia el frente; hacia adelante, en derechura.
front wheel drive, (aut.) transmisión o propulsión delantera.
frosh [frɑʃ, B frɔʃ] *s.* (fam.) estudiante de primer año (de universidad, colegio superior, etc.).
frost [frɔst, frɑst, B frɔst] *s.* 1. congelación. 2. helada, temperatura bajo cero. 3. escarcha, helada blanca. 4. (fig.) frialdad, indiferencia (en el trato). 5. (jer.) fracaso, fiasco. —*v.t.* 1. congelar; dañar, quemar (el frío). 2. (t. con *over*) cubrir con escarcha, empañar (lentes, ventana, etc.). 3. escarchar (ej., confituras, pasteles, tortas). 4. deslustrar, opacar (vidrio). —*v.i.* 1. helarse, congelarse. 2. cubrirse de escarcha, empañarse (lentes, ventana, etc.).
frostbite ['frɔst,baɪt, 'frɑst-, B 'frɔst-] *v.t.* helar, quemar por el frío o la helada (ej., una parte del cuerpo, plantas, etc.). —*s.* (med.) congelación.
frostbitten [-,bɪtən] *a.* helado, congelado, quemado (por el hielo o la escarcha).
frosted [-əd] *a.* 1. cubierto de escarcha. 2. escarchado (pastel, confitura). 3. empañado (ventana, vidrio). 4. deslustrado, mate (vidrio). 5. helado, congelado (alimentos). 6. cristalizado.
frostfish [-,fɪʃ] *s.* (ict.) bacalao pequeño, abadejo pequeño, falso merlán; capelán.
frost heave, levantamiento del pavimento o suelo (por congelación de la tierra).
frostily [-əlɪ] *adv.* (fig.) con frialdad, de manera fría y distante.
frostiness [-ɪnəs] *s.* (fig.) frialdad, frigidez.
frosting [-ɪŋ] *s.* 1. (cocina) capa de clara de huevo y azúcar. 2. acabado mate, (de metal o vidrio); imitación de escarcha (en metales); aspecto superficial cristalino (plásticos).
frostwork [-,wɜrk, B -,wɜk] *s.* flores de hielo, escarcha en las ventanas; erosión glaciar.
frosty [-ɪ] *a.* 1. escarchado. 2. helado; frío. 3. cano, canoso (cabello). 4. (fig.) frío, poco amistoso, poco cordial, indiferente.
froth [frɔθ, frɑθ, B frɔθ] *s.* 1. espuma. 2. espumarajo, espumajo. 3. frivolidad, palabras vanas. —*v.t.* 1. batir (un líquido) hasta que espume, hacer espumar. 2. mascullar furiosamente. 3. cubrir de espumarajo. —*v.i.* 1. espumar. 2. espumajear. 3. **f. at the mouth,** espumajear, echar espumarajos por la boca; (fig.) echar chispas (de ira).
frothily ['frɔθəlɪ, 'frɑθ-, B 'frɔθ-] *adv.* espumosamente, con espuma, frívolamente.
frothiness [-ɪnəs] *s.* 1. espumosidad. 2. frivolidad.
frothy [-ɪ] *a.* 1. espumoso; de espuma. 2. frívolo, vano, insustancial. 3. ligero, con encaje o tules (vestido). 4. poroso (aceros).
froufrou ['fru,fru] *s.* 1. frufrú. 2. faralá; ornamentación recargada y superflua.
frow [froʊ] *s.* (E.U.) cuña, hendedor.
froward ['froʊərd, -wərd, B 'froʊəd] *a.* indócil, rebelde, díscolo, refractario.
frown [fraʊn] *v.i.* 1. fruncir el entrecejo; arrugar la frente. 2. (con *at*) mirar con ceño. 3. (con *on, upon*) desaprobar. —*v.t.* desaprobar, expresar (esp. enojo) frunciendo el entrecejo. —*s.* 1. ceño, entrecejo; sobrecejo. 2. desagrado, enojo.
frowning ['fraʊnɪŋ] *a.* ceñudo, ceñoso.
frowningly [-lɪ] *adv.* ceñudamente, ceñosamente.
frowsty ['fraʊstɪ] *a.* (pr. G.B.) 1. mal ventilado, de aire pesado. 2. (fig.) anticuado (persona).
frowzily ['fraʊzəlɪ] *adv.* desaliñadamente, desaseadamente.
frowziness [-zɪnəs] *s.* desaliño, desaseo.
frowzy [-zɪ] *a.* 1. desaliñado; desaseado, sucio; mal peinado, despeinado. 2. maloliente, mal ventilado.
froze [froʊz] *pret. de* **freeze.**
frozen ['froʊzən] *a.* 1. helado, frío, gélido, frígido. 2. helado, congelado (alimento). 3. (fig.) frío, duro, insensible; inmóvil, rígido, petrificado. 4. congelado, fijo (precios, salarios). 5. (com.) congelado (crédito activo, etc.). 6. irreversible (reacciones).
Fructidor ['frʌktɪ,dɔr, B -,dɔ] *s.* (hist.) fructidor, duodécimo mes del año en el calendario de la Revolución Francesa.
fructiferous [frʌk'tɪfərəs] *a.* fructífero.
fructification [,frʌktəfə'keɪʃən] *s.* fructificación.
fructify ['frʌktə,faɪ] *v.i.* (*pret., p.p.* FRUCTIFIED; *p.pr.* FRUCTIFYING) fructificar, dar fruto (árboles y otras plantas). —*v.t.* fertilizar, fecundar.
fructose [-,toʊs] *s.* (quím.) fructosa, azúcar de frutas.
fructuous [-tʃʊəs] *a.* fructuoso, fecundo, fértil.
frugal ['frugəl] *a.* frugal, sobrio, económico, ahorrador.
frugality [fru'gælətɪ] *s.* frugalidad, sobriedad.
frugally ['frugəlɪ] *adv.* frugalmente.
frugalness [-gəlnəs] *s.* frugalidad.
frugivorous [fru'dʒɪvərəs] *a.* (zool.) frugívoro, fructívoro.
fruit [frut] *s.* 1. fruto (de las plantas). 2. fruta. 3. frutas, ej., *a diet of f.,* régimen de frutas. 4. (fig.) fruto, producto, resultado. 5. (jer.) homosexual, marica. —*v.i.* dar fruto, frutar, producir frutas. —*v.t.* hacer dar fruto.
fruitage ['frutɪdʒ] *s.* 1. fructificación. 2. (lit., fig.) fruto.
fruit bat, (zool.) bermejizo, murciélago frugívoro.
fruitcake [-,keɪk] *s.* pastel que contiene muchas variedades de fruta y nueces; **nuttier than a f.,** más loco que una cabra.
fruit dish, bandeja de fruta, frutero.
fruiter [-ər, B -ə] *s.* 1. barco frutero. 2. árbol frutal. 3. fruticultor.
fruiterer [-ərər, B -ərə] *s.* frutero, vendedor de fruta.
fruit fly, (ento.) mosca de las frutas, mosca mediterránea.
fruitful ['frutfəl] *a.* 1. fructífero, fructuoso, fértil, feraz, productivo, prolífico, fecundo. 2. (fig.) fructuoso, productivo, provechoso.
fruitfully [-fəlɪ] *adv.* fructiferamente, fructuosamente.
fruitfulness [-fəlnəs] *s.* 1. capacidad fructífera, fertilidad, fecundidad. 2. utilidad, carácter provechoso (de una empresa, etc.).
fruitiness [-ɪnəs] *s.* 1. olor o sabor a fruta. 2. (fig.) rico sabor (del estilo, de un dicho, etc.). 3. sonoridad, melosidad (de la voz). 4. salacidad (de un cuento). 5. (jer.) chifladura, locura.
fruiting body [-ɪŋ-] *s.* (bot.) órgano (de una planta) que produce esporas.
fruition [fru'ɪʃən] *s.* 1. fruición, complacencia, goce. 2. fructificación. 3. cumplimiento, realización.
fruit juice, jugo de frutas.
fruitless ['frutləs] *a.* 1. estéril, infecundo, infructífero, árido. 2. infructuoso, improductivo; vano, ineficaz.
fruitlessly [-lɪ] *adv.* estérilmente; infructuosamente, ineficazmente.
fruit piece, frutero; (pint.) naturaleza muerta.
fruit salad, 1. macedonia, ensalada de frutas. 2. (jer., mil.) condecoraciones.
fruit stand, puesto de fruta, frutería.
fruity ['frutɪ] *a.* 1. de olor o sabor de fruta (ej., vinos). 2. (fig.) sabroso, rico (estilo, dicho, etc.). 3. sonoro, meloso (voz). 4. (jer.) propio de maricas. 5. (jer.) chiflado.
frumentaceous [,frumən'teɪʃəs] *a.* frumenticio, frumentario, relativo a los cereales.
frumenty ['frumәntɪ] *s.* frangollo preparado con leche, azúcar, condimentos y pasas.
frump [frʌmp] *s.* 1. mujer desaliñada. 2. persona aburrida y de ideas anticuadas.
frumpish ['frʌmpɪʃ] *a.* 1. desaliñado. 2. pasado de moda, anticuado. 3. aburrido, malhumorado.
frustrate ['frʌs,treɪt, B frʌs'treɪt] *v.t.* frustrar, impedir, privar; anular.
frustrated [-əd] *a.* frustrado, malogrado.
frustration [frʌs'treɪʃən] *s.* frustración; desaliento.
frustule ['frʌs,tʃul] *s.* (bot., pal.) frústulo.
frustum ['frʌstəm] *s.* (*pl.* FRUSTUMS O FRUSTA [-tə]) (geom.) tronco (de cono, de pirámide, etc.).
frutescence [fru'tɛsəns] *s.* (bot.) consistencia frutescente.
frutescent [-ənt] *a.* (bot.) frutescente, arbustivo.
fruticose ['frutɪ,koʊs] *a.* (bot.) fruticoso, fruticuloso.
fry [fraɪ] *s.* (*pl.* FRY) 1. pececillos. 2. boliche, cardumen de peces pequeños. 3. cría, nidada. 4. (despec.) persona, individuo. 5. **small f.,** niños (pequeños); gente menuda; **young f.,** jovencitos, niños.
fry, *v.t.* (*pret., p.p.* FRIED; *p.pr.* FRYING) 1. freír. 2. (jer.) electrocutar, ejecutar en la silla eléctrica. —*v.i.* 1. freírse, achicharrarse. 2. (jer.) morir en la silla eléctrica. —*s.* 1. fritura, fritada, frito. 2. fritanga de pescado o carnes varias. 3. comida al aire libre a base de dichos platos.
fryer ['fraɪər, B -ə] *s.* 1. olla para freír, sartén. 2. pollito para freír.
frying pan, sartén; **to jump out of the f. into the fire,** salir de Guatemala para meterse en Guatepeor, salir de Guatemala y dar en Guatepeor.

f-stop ['ɛf,stɑp, B -,stɔp] *s.* (foto.) grado de abertura útil (del diafragma de una cámara).
ft. *abrev. de* **foot, feet,** pie, pies.
FTC *abrev. de* **Federal Trade Commission,** Comisión Federal de Comercio.
F2 layer, capa F2 (de la ionosfera).
fubsy ['fʌbzɪ] *a.* (raro) rechoncho, regordete, cachigordete.
fuchsia ['fjuʃə] *s.* (bot.) fucsia.
fuchsin, fuchsine ['fjuksən, 'fuk-, B 'fuk,-sin] *s.* (quím.) fucsina.
fuck [fʌk] *v.t., v.i.* (vulg.) joder, practicar el coito (con); **f. about** (o **around**), vagar, holgazanear; **f. off,** largarse, guillarse; **f. you Charley!** ¡fastídiate! ¡vete al diablo!
fucked-up ['fʌkt'ʌp] *a.* (vulg.) jodido, estropeado.
fucking ['fʌkiŋ] *a.* (vulg.) maldito, condenado. —*s.* (vulg.) joder, jodienda.
fuck-up ['fʌkʌp] *s.* (vulg.) lío, follón, pendejo.
fucoid ['fju,kɔɪd] *a.* (bot.) fucoideo. —*s.* planta marina fucoidea.
fucus [-kəs] *s.* (*pl.* FUCUSES o FUCI [-saɪ]) (bot.) fuco, ova.
fuddle ['fʌdəl] *v.t.* 1. embriagar. 2. atontar, confundir. —*v.i.* empinar el codo, chupar (Amer.). —*s.* 1. borrachera. 2. atontamiento, confusión.
fuddy-duddy ['fʌdɪ,dʌdɪ] *s.* tipo pomposo, viejo quisquilloso. —*a.* anticuado, pomposo, quisquilloso, estirado.
fudge [fʌdʒ] *s.* 1. embuste, mentira, dolo, cuento; tontería, disparate. 2. inserción de última hora (en un periódico). 3. dulce en pasta de chocolate o leche. —*interj.* ¡tonterías! ¡disparate! —*v.t.* 1. inventar; falsificar. 2. evadir. —*v.i.* (con *on*) dejar de cumplir (con).
Fuegian [fu'eɪdʒɪən, B fju'i-] *a., s.* fueguino, de la Tierra del Fuego.
fuel ['fjuəl] *s.* 1. combustible. 2. (fig.) pábulo, resorte, incentivo. 3. **to add f. to the fire,** (fig.) echar leña al fuego. —*v.t., v.i.* (*pret., p.p.* FUELED o FUELLED; *p.pr.* FUELING o FUELLING) abastecer(se) o aprovisionar(se) de combustible.
fuel cell, 1. compartimento de un tanque de combustible. 2. (elec.) célula electrógena, pila de Grove.
fuel gauge, (aut.) indicador (del nivel) de gasolina.
fuel oil, petróleo o aceite combustible.
fuel pump, (aut.) bomba de combustible; gasolinera, puesto o estación de gasolina.
fuel tank, depósito o tanque de combustible.
fug [fʌg] *s.* (pr. G.B.) aire viciado (en un cuarto, etc.). —*v.i.* no salir al aire libre, quedar en aire viciado. —*v.t.* viciar (el aire).
fugacious [fju'geɪʃəs] *a.* fugaz, evanescente, volátil; (bot.) fugaz.
fugacity [-'gæsətɪ] *s.* fugacidad.
fugal ['fjugəl] *a.* (mús.) al estilo de una fuga.
fugitive ['fjudʒətɪv] *a.* 1. fugitivo. 2. huidizo, huidero. 3. ambulante, errante, vagabundo. 4. pasajero, perecedero, transitorio, fugaz. 5. elusivo, volátil. 6. ocasional, efímero. —*s.* 1. fugitivo, prófugo. 2. refugiado.
fugitively [-lɪ] *adv.* como un fugitivo.
fugitiveness [-nəs] *s.* calidad de fugitivo; inestabilidad.
fugle ['fjugəl] *v.i.* 1. (ant.) servir de jefe de fila. 2. (fam.) servir de norma o modelo.
fugleman [-mən] *s.* 1. (mil.) jefe de fila. 2. (fig.) líder, dirigente.
fugue [fjug] *s.* 1. (mús.) fuga. 2. (psic.) amnesia temporal. —*v.i.* componer o tocar una fuga.
Führer, Fuehrer ['fjʊrər, B 'fjʊərə] *s.* (alemán) jefe supremo, caudillo.
Fula, Fulah ['fulə] *s.* (*pl.* FULA o FULAS, FULAH o FULAHS) fulah, fulbé, tribu musulmana del Sudán egipcio.
fulcrum ['fʊlkrəm, 'fʌl-] *s.* (*pl.* FULCRUMS o FULCRA [-krə]) 1. (mec.) fulcro, punto de apoyo. 2. (bot.) fulcro, apéndice.
fulfill, fulfil [fʊl'fɪl] *v.t.* (*pret., p.p.* FULFILLED; *p.pr.* FULFILLING) 1. cumplir, ejecutar (una promesa, orden, etc.); realizar (un proyecto, etc.). 2. satisfacer (un deseo, una necesidad, etc.); responder a (un ruego o propósito); cumplir con (una obligación); llenar (una condición, requisito, etc.). 3. completar, complementar. 4. **f. the contract,** cumplir el contrato.
fulfillment, fulfilment [-mənt] *s.* 1. cumplimiento, ejecución (de una promesa, orden, etc.). 2. realización (de un proyecto, etc.); satisfacción (de deseo, necesidad, etc.). 3. terminación.
fulgent ['fʌldʒənt, 'fʊl-, B 'fʌl-] *a.* fulgente, fúlgido, brillante, esplendoroso.
fulgurant [-gjərənt] *a.* fulgurante, brillante, resplandeciente.
fulgurate [-gjə,reɪt] *v.i.* fulgurar, resplandecer, brillar.
fulgurating [-ɪŋ] *a.* (med.) fulgurante (díc. de dolores).
fulguration [,fʌlgjə'reɪʃən, ,fʊl-, B ,fʌl-] *s.* fulguración.
fulgurite ['fʌlgjə,raɪt, 'fʊl-, B 'fʌl-] *s.* (geol.) fulgurita.
fulgurous [-rəs] *a.* fulguroso, fulgurante.
fulham ['fʊləm] *s.* dado cargado o trucado.
fuliginous [fjʊ'lɪdʒənəs, B fju-] *a.* fuliginoso, denegrido, tiznado.
full [fʊl] *a.* 1. lleno, llenado. 2. harto, repleto, saturado, saciado. 3. pleno, completo (cuota, cantidad, duración, poderes, etc.). 4. máximo (volumen, fuerza, etc.). 5. completo, abundante (comida), completo, detallado (informe). 6. amplio, ancho (falda, manga, vestido, etc.). 7. hinchado, rollizo, regordete. 8. carnal (hermano, hermana). 9. titular (socio, profesor, etc.). 10. de etiqueta (traje). 11. intenso (luz); profundo (color); intenso, concentrado (sabor). 12. lleno, desplegado (velas). 13. **at f. gallop,** a todo galope; **at f. length,** por completo, en toda su extensión; **at f. speed,** a toda velocidad; **f. details,** detalles completos; **f. of,** lleno de, colmado de (trabajo, preocupaciones, etc.); absorto en, abstraído en (problemas, intereses, etc.); **f. of beans** o **f. of prunes,** (jer.) equivocado, exagerado; vigoroso, vivaz, enérgico, lleno de vitalidad; **f. of fun,** muy alegre; muy divertido, muy chistoso; **full of shit,** (vulg.) equivocado; **full of piss and vinegar,** (vulg.) lleno de energía; **f. of play,** muy juguetón; **f. to the brim,** lleno hasta el borde; **f. up,** (fam.) lleno hasta el tope; **in f. blast,** a todo vapor, a toda máquina; **in f. detail,** con pelos y señales; **in f. force,** en pleno. —*s.* 1. lleno, colmo, plenitud, totalidad. 2. máximo. 3. suma íntegra. 4. **to pay in f.,** pagar íntegramente; **to the f.,** completamente, al máximo. —*adv.* 1. enteramente, plenamente, completamente. 2. muy, extremadamente. 3. exactamente, directamente. 4. **f. well,** perfectamente, muy bien. —*v.t.* llenar, dar amplitud a; (tej.) abatanar, enfurtir, apelmazar. —*v.i.* llegar al plenilunio (luna).
fullback ['fʊl,bæk] *s.* (fútbol) defensa, zaguero, back.
full-blast [-'blæst, B -'blɑst] *adv.* (fam.) rapidísimamente, a toda máquina, con gran intensidad.
full blood, de pura sangre, de pura casta.
full-blooded [-'blʌdəd] *a.* 1. rubicundo, pletórico. 2. de pura raza, de casta. 3. (fig.) robusto, vigoroso (estilo, narración). 4. exuberante. 5. legítimo, genuino.
full-blown [-'bloʊn] *a.* 1. (completamente) abierto, ej., *a f.-b. rose,* una rosa abierta. 2. maduro, desarrollado. 3. acabado, completo.
full-bodied [-'bɑdid, B -'bɔdɪd] *a.* 1. corpulento, corpudo. 2. espeso (ej., pintura). 3. rico, aromático (sabor, vino, gusto). 4. acabado, consumado.
full dress, traje de etiqueta, traje de noche; (mil.) uniforme de gala.
full-dress [-'drɛs] *a.* 1. de gala (uniforme), de etiqueta (traje). 2. (fig.) completo, cabal.
full employment, pleno empleo.
fuller ['fʊlər, B -ə] *s.* 1. (herrería) copador de fragua, degüello de fragua. 2. batanero, batán.
fuller's earth, tierra de batán, arcilla de batán.
fuller's teasel, 1. (bot.) cardencha, cardo de bataneros. 2. (tej.) carda.
fullface ['fʊl'feɪs] *s.* (impr.) negrita, negrilla, tipo negro.
full-fashioned [-'fæʃənd] **fully-fashioned** ['fʊlɪ-] *a.* (tej.) díc. del tejido de punto con menguados, que se amolda al cuerpo.
full-fledged [-'flɛdʒd] *a.* 1. desarrollado, maduro. 2. plumado, con plumaje completo (aves). 3. todo (un), ej., *a. f.-f. surgeon,* todo un cirujano.
full-grown [-'groʊn] *a.* crecido, maduro.
full hand, (póquer) (mano de) pierna más par.
fullhearted [-'hɑrtəd, B -'hɑt-] *a.* incondicional, completo, sincero (apoyo, reconocimiento, etc.).
full house, 1. (póquer) (mano de) pierna más par. 2. lleno (en teatro, circo, etc.).
full-length [-'lɛŋθ, -'lɛŋkθ] *a.* 1. de cuerpo entero (retrato, espejo, etc.). 2. de largo normal, de largo completo.
full-length picture, full-length movie o **full-length motion picture,** largometraje.
full load, carga máxima, plena carga; con toda la potencia.
full marks, (fig.) reconocimiento incondicional; **to give someone f. m.,** reconocer incondicionalmente el mérito de alguien, darle toda la razón a alguien.
full moon, luna llena, plenilunio.
fullmouthed [-'maʊðd, -'maʊθt, B -'maʊðd] *a.* 1. clamoroso, vociferante. 2. (vet.) con dentadura completa (esp. ganado).
fullness, fulness ['fʊlnəs] *s.* 1. plenitud, llenura. 2. abundancia. 3. saciedad. 4. **f. of time,** plenitud de los tiempos.
full pay, paga completa.
full-rigged [-'rɪgd] *a.* (mar.) de tres o más mástiles, de aparejo completo (buque), aparejado de fragata.
full-scale [-'skeɪl] *a.* 1. de, o en tamaño natural. 2. de gran envergadura. 3. sin restricciones; total, máximo.
full scope, 1. carta blanca, rienda suelta. 2. totalidad; alcance máximo.
full score, (mús.) partitura completa (de una composición coral o sinfónica).
full sentence, (gram.) oración completa.
full-sized [-'saɪzd] *a.* de tamaño natural.
full steam ahead, avante a toda máquina.
full stop, 1. (gram.) punto final. 2. (aut.) parada.
full-swing [-'swɪŋ] *adv.* a toda capacidad, a toda máquina; en plena actividad.
full tilt, a la velocidad, energía, fuerza, etc. total.
full-time [-'taɪm] *a.* 1. constante, incesante. 2. relativo a una jornada completa de trabajo o a un servicio permanente.
full toss, (criquet) bola lanzada que llega al bateador sin rebotar.
fully ['fʊlɪ] *adv.* enteramente, completamente; plenamente; de lleno.

fulmar ['fʊlmər, -ˌmɑr, B -mə] *s.* (orn.) fulmar, gaviota de las regiones árticas.

fulminant ['fʌlmənənt, 'fʊl-, B 'fʌl-] *a.* fulminante; (med.) fulminante (enfermedad).

fulminate [-ˌneɪt] *v.i.* fulminar, estallar, detonar; **f. against,** tronar contra. —*v.t.* 1. fulminar (censuras, sentencias, etc.). 2. hacer detonar. —*s.* 1. (quím.) fulminato. 2. pólvora fulminante.

fulminating powder [-ɪŋ-] (quím.) pólvora fulminante.

fulminator [-ər, B -ə] *s.* fulminador.

fulminatory [-nəˌtɔrɪ, B -ˌneɪtərɪ] *s.* fulminador, fulminante.

fulminic [fʌl'mɪnɪk, fʊl-, B fʌl-] *a.* (quím.) fulmínico (ácido).

fulminous ['fʌlmənəs] *a.* fulminoso, fulmíneo.

fulsome ['fʊlsəm, 'fʌl-, B 'fʊl-] *a.* 1. empalagoso, de mal gusto (lisonja, alabanza, etc.). 2. hipócrita; repugnante.

fulsomeness [-nəs] *s.* repugnancia; carácter hipócrita u ofensivo.

fulvous ['fʌlvəs] *a.* leonado; color terroso o castaño.

fumaric acid [fju'mærɪk-] (quím.) ácido fumárico.

fumarine ['fjuməˌrin, B -rɪn] *s.* (quím.) fumarina.

fumarole [-ˌroʊl] *s.* fumarola, grieta o fisura que arroja humo volcánico.

fumaryl ['fjuməˌrɪl] *s.* (quím.) fumarido.

fumatorium [ˌfjumə'tɔrɪəm] *s.* (*pl.* FUMATORIA [-[ɪə]) compartimiento para fumigación (de plantas en crecimiento).

fumble ['fʌmbəl] *v.i.* 1. (con *for, after*) tentar o buscar torpemente. 2. (con *at, with*) manipular desmañadamente; manosear torpemente. 3. fallar. 4. (con *along, about, around,* etc.) andar o moverse a tropezones. —*v.t.* 1. tocar o mover torpemente. 2. estropear; chapucear. 3. farfullar. 4. (dep.) perder, dejar caer (la pelota). —*s.* torpeza, desmaña, pifia (P. Rico), chapuz; (E.U., dep.) (*in football*) fumble.

fumbler [-blər, B -blə] *s.* chapucero, persona torpe o desmañada.

fume [fjum] *s.* 1. humo (del incienso, de la pipa, etc.); vaho. 2. emanación, tufo, gas. 3. cólera, enojo, enfado. —*v.i.* 1. humear, emitir vapores o gases. 2. (fig.) echar humo, echar rayos, irritarse. —*v.t.* 1. ahumar, fumigar, sahumar. 2. exhalar, arrojar (humo, vaho, vapor).

fumet ['fjumət] *f* ᵐəʇʇə [fju'mɛt, B 'fjumɛt] *s.* (fr., cocina) concentrado de carne, pescado, pollo, setas.

fumigant ['fjuməˌgənt] *s.* substancia fumigatoria.

fumigate [-ˌgeɪt] *v.t.* fumigar.

fumigation [ˌfjumə'geɪʃən] *s.* fumigación.

fumigator ['fjuməˌgeɪtər, B -ə] *s.* fumigador (persona o aparato).

fumingly ['fjumɪŋlɪ] *adv.* coléricamente.

fumitory ['fjuməˌtɔrɪ, B -tərɪ] *s.* (bot.) fumaria, palomilla, palomina.

fun [fʌn] *s.* diversión, entretenimiento, recreo; alegría, regocijo; **for f., in f.,** en broma; por gusto; **it's good f., it's great f.,** es muy divertido; **like f.,** (fam.) ¡ni hablar!; ni pensarlo, por cierto que no; **to have f.,** divertirse, pasar un buen rato; **to make f. of, to poke f. at,** burlarse, reírse de; **what f.!** ¡qué divertido! —*v.i.* (raro) bromear.

funambulist [fjʊ'næmbjələst] *s.* funámbulo, volatinero, equilibrista.

function ['fʌŋkʃən] *s.* 1. función; solemnidad. 2. ocupación, puesto. 3. funcionamiento, operación. —*v.i.* funcionar, desempeñar; ejercer.

functional [-əl] *a.* 1. (fisiol., gram., mat.) funcional. 2. funcional, práctico, útil. 3. (raro) oficial, formal.

functionalism [-ˌɪzəm] *s.* funcionalismo (la fusión de lo práctico y lo estético en diseño y construcción).

functionally [-ɪ] *adv.* funcionalmente.

functional shift, (gram.) cambio de función gramatical (de una palabra).

functionary [-ˌɛrɪ, B -ərɪ] *s.* funcionario (público, diplomático, etc.).

functionless [-ləs] *a.* sin función, sin aplicación; superfluo.

function word, (gram.) palabra que expresa principalmente una relación gramatical.

fund [fʌnd] *s.* 1. reserva, riqueza (de cosas materiales). 2. (fig.) fondo, caudal, acopio. 3. (com.) fondo, capital, reserva; (*pl.*) fondos, medios disponibles. 4. fondo, institución financiera, ej., *monetary f.,* fondo monetario. 5. **the funds,** (G.B.) títulos o bonos del estado. —*v.t.* 1. proveer de fondos, garantizar o respaldar (bonos, pensiones, etc.). 2. consolidar (una deuda); convertir (una deuda flotante) en deuda fija o perpetua. 3. (G.B.) invertir (dinero) en bonos del estado.

fundament ['fʌndəmənt] *s.* 1. fundamento, cimiento, base (de una teoría, etc.). 2. geofísica (de una región determinada). 3. nalgas, trasero; ano.

fundamental [ˌfʌndə'mɛntəl] *a.* 1. fundamental, básico, esencial. 2. (mús.) fundamental (tono en un acorde). 3. (fís.) fundamental (vibración). —*s.* 1. fundamento, principio, base. 2. (mús.) tono o nota fundamental.

fundamentalism [-ˌɪzəm] *s.* (relig.) fundamentalismo, creencia incondicional en la Biblia.

fundamentalist [-əst] *s.* (relig.) fundamentalista.

fundamental law, ley fundamental, constitución (de un país, estado, comunidad, etc.).

fundamentally [-ɪ] *adv.* fundamentalmente.

funded ['fʌndəd] *a.* consolidado; acumulado e invertido.

funded debt, (com.) deuda consolidada.

fundic ['fʌndɪk] *a.* (anat.) fúndico, relativo a un fondo.

fundus ['fʌndəs] *s.* (anat.) fondo, fundus.

funeral ['fjunərəl] *a.* funeral, fúnebre, funerario. —*s.* 1. funeral, funerales, exequias. 2. (fig.) fin, ruina. 3. entierro.

funeral director, empresario de pompas fúnebres.

funeral home, f. parlor, funeraria, agencia de funeraria.

funeral march, (mús.) marcha fúnebre.

funeral pile, pira, hoguera.

funeral service, funeral, pompas fúnebres.

funeral wake, llora (Ven.).

funerary ['fjunəˌrɛrɪ, B -rərɪ] *a.* funerario, funeral, fúnebre, funéreo.

funereal [fju'nɪrɪəl, B -'nɪər-] *a.* fúnebre, funéreo, funesto, lúgubre.

fungal ['fʌŋgəl] *a.* (bot.) fungino, fungal.

fungi, *pl. de* **fungus.**

fungible ['fʌndʒəbəl] *a.* 1. intercambiable. 2. (der.) fungible. —*s.* (*pl.*) (der.) bienes fungibles.

fungicidal [ˌfʌndʒə'saɪdəl] *a.* fungicida.

fungicide ['fʌndʒəˌsaɪd, 'fʌŋgə-, B 'fʌndʒɪ-] *s.* fungicida.

fungiform [-ˌfɔrm, B -ˌfɔm] *a.* fungiforme.

fungoid ['fʌŋˌgɔɪd] *a.* (bot.) fungoideo.

fungology [fʌŋ'gɑlədʒɪ, B -'gɔl-] *s.* fungología, estudio de los hongos.

fungosity [-'gɑsətɪ, B -'gɔs-] *s.* fungosidad.

fungous ['fʌŋgəs] *a.* 1. (bot.) fungino, fungal. 2. (med.) fungoide, fungoso.

fungus ['fʌŋgəs] *s.* (*pl.* FUNGUSES o FUNGI ['fʌnˌdʒaɪ, 'fʌŋˌgaɪ]) 1. (bot., bact.) hongo. 2. (med.) fungo, hongo. —*a.* fungoso, fungoideo; causado por hongos (enfermedad).

fun house, (fam.) atracción (en un parque de diversiones) que consiste en una serie de cuartos, pasadizos y cavernas con espejos de distorsión y figuras grotescas, destinados a sorprender y divertir al público.

funicular [fjʊ'nɪkjələr, B -lə] *a.* funicular. —*s.* (t. **f. railway**) ferrocarril funicular.

funiculate [-lət, -ˌleɪt] *a.* (anat., bot.) funiculado.

funiculus [-ləs] *s.* (*pl.* FUNICULI [-ˌlaɪ]) 1. (anat.) cordón umbilical. 2. (bot.) funículo.

funk [fʌŋk] *s.* 1. temor, pánico, amilanamiento. 2. cobarde. 3. **in a (blue) f.,** atemorizado, amilanado. —*v.i.* amilanarse, encogerse de miedo, retraerse con temor. —*v.t.* 1. temer, tener miedo a. 2. evadir por temor, dejar de cumplir por miedo (deber, tarea).

funk hole, 1. trinchera. 2. guarida, refugio.

funky ['fʌŋkɪ] *a.* 1. atemorizado. 2. maloliente, fétido.

funnel ['fʌnəl] *s.* 1. embudo. 2. túnel, cañon, humero. 3. chimenea (esp. de un vapor). —*v.t.* (*pret., p.p.* FUNNELED o FUNNELLED; *p.pr.* FUNNELING o FUNNELLING) verter por medio de un embudo; encauzar, dirigir; concentrar. —*v.i.* 1. tomar forma de embudo; estrecharse; ensancharse. 2. encauzarse, dirigirse.

funnelform [-ˌfɔrm, B -ˌfɔm] *a.* (bot.) infundibuliforme.

funnies ['fʌniz] *s. pl.* tiras cómicas; tebeos (Esp.).

funnily [-əlɪ] *adv.* 1. cómicamente, graciosamente. 2. extrañamente, de un modo raro.

funny ['fʌnɪ] *a.* (FUNNIER; FUNNIEST) 1. cómico, ridículo, risible. 2. divertido, chistoso, gracioso, ocurrente. 3. extraño, raro, curioso. 4. **to get f. with,** bromear con; **to strike one as f. (that),** encontrar uno extraño (que), parecerle a uno raro (que); **to find something f.,** hacerle algo gracia a uno.

funny bone, 1. cóndilo interno del húmero. 2. (fam.) sentido del humor.

funny business, f. stuff, 1. truco, trucos, picardías. 2. práctica fraudulenta.

funnyman [-ˌmæn] *s.* 1. cómico, comediante. 2. humorista.

funny papers, historietas cómicas, historietas gráficas; tebeos (Esp.).

fur [fɜr, B fɜ] *s.* 1. pelaje, pelo (del oso, castor, armiño, etc.). 2. piel (usada para hacer o adornar ropas de vestir). 3. abrigo de piel; guarnición de piel (en vestido). 4. sarro, saburra (en la lengua); sarro, borra (de vino, etc.). 5. pelusa (de ciertas telas). 6. (her.) forro. 7. **to make the f. fly,** armar camorra. —*a.* de piel, de pieles. —*v.t.* (*pret., p.p.* FURRED; *p.pr.* FURRING). 1. guarnecer, adornar, o forrar con pieles. 2. cubrir de sarro (esp. la lengua). 3. (const.) enrasar, enrasillar. —*v.i.* cubrirse de sarro (esp. la lengua).

furane ['fjʊrˌeɪn] **furan** ['fjʊræn, fjʊ'ræn] *s.* (quím.) furano, furfurano.

furbelow ['fɜrbəˌloʊ, B 'fɜbɪ-] *s.* faralá, volante, cairel. —*v.t.* adornar con faralás o volantes, recargar de caireles.

furbish ['fɜrbɪʃ, B 'fɜbɪʃ] *v.t.* 1. bruñir, acicalar, pulir. 2. (gen con *up*) renovar, restaurar.

furbisher [-ər, B -ə] *s.* (ant.) acicalador, pulidor.

furcate ['fɜrˌkeɪt, B 'fɜˌ-] *a.* bifurcado, ahorquillado, hendido (pezuña). —*v.i.* ahorquillarse, bifurcarse.

furcation [fər'keɪʃən, B fə'-] *s.* bifurcación.

fur coat, abrigo de pieles.

furcula ['fɜrkjələ, B 'fɜkjʊ-] *s.* (*pl.* FURCULAE [-ˌli]) 1. (anat.) fúrcula. 2. (orn.) espoleta.

furcular [-lər, B -lə] *a.* (anat.) furcular, furcal.

furfuraceous [ˌfɜrfjə'reɪʃəs, B ˌfɜf-] *a.* (bot.) furfuráceo, parecido al salvado.

furfural ['fɜrfəˌræl, B 'fɜfə-] *s.* (quím.) furfural, furfurol.

furfurane [-ˌreɪn] **furfuran** [-ˌræn] *var. de* **furan.**

furibund ['fjʊrəˌbʌnd, B 'fjʊər-] *a.* furibundo, furioso.

furious ['fjʊrɪəs, B 'fjʊər-] *a.* furioso, furibundo, rabioso.

furiously [-lɪ] *adv.* furiosamente, rabiosamente.

furl [fɜrl, B fɜl] *v.t.* arrollar, enrollar, plegar, recoger; (mar.) aferrar, acurrullar (velas, banderas). —*v.i.* arrollarse, plegarse. —*s.* enrollamiento; rollo.

furlong ['fɜrlɔŋ, B 'fɜˌ-] *s.* estadio, octava parte de una milla o 220 yardas.

furlough [-loʊ] *s.* (mil.) licencia, permiso. —*v.t.* 1. (mil.) dar licencia a. 2. suspender (obreros) temporalmente.

furnace ['fɜrnəs, B 'fɜnɪs] *s.* 1. horno. 2. calorífero. 3. reactor (atómico). 4. (fig.) caldera. —*v.t.* calentar en un horno.

furnaceman [-ˌmæn, B -mən] *s.* 1. hornero, fogonero. 2. instalador o reparador del calorífero.

furnace oil, petróleo de horno, combustible para calefacción.

furnish ['fɜrnɪʃ, B 'fɜnɪʃ] *v.t.* 1. proveer, surtir, suplir, suministrar. 2. amueblar. 3. proporcionar, procurar; aducir (pruebas).

furnisher [-ər, B -ə] *s.* 1. proveedor. 2. amueblador, decorador.

furnishing [-ɪŋ] *s.* (*ú. gen. en pl.*) 1. muebles, moblaje, mobiliario. 2. artículos de vestir. 3. accesorios.

furniture ['fɜrnɪtʃər, B 'fɜnɪtʃə] *s.* 1. muebles, moblaje. 2. accesorios, enseres. 3. (impr.) imposiciones, guarniciones, fornitura. 4. (mar.) armamento, aparejo. 5. **a piece of f.,** un mueble.

furniture van, carro o camión de mudanzas.

furor ['fjʊrˌɔr, B 'fjʊərɔ] *s.* 1. furor, furia, rabia. 2. entusiasmo, delirio (del público). 3. (ant., poét.) fervor, frenesí.

furore ['fjʊrˌɔr, B fjʊə'rɔrɪ] *s.* (G.B.) 1. furor, frenesí, locura momentánea (ej., de modas); sensación, excitación. 2. indignación violenta.

furred [fɜrd, B fɜd] *a.* 1. forrado, bordeado o cubierto de piel. 2. (med.) cubierto de sarro o saburra (la lengua). 3. (const.) enrasado, enrasillado.

furrier ['fɜrɪər, 'fʌrɪ-, B 'fʌrɪə] *s.* peletero, manguitero, comerciante en pieles de vestir.

furriness ['fɜrɪnəs] *s.* 1. vellosidad; lanosidad. 2. condición o estado sarroso.

furring ['fɜrɪŋ] *s.* 1. forro o guarnición de pieles. 2. (const.) enrasillado, costillaje; listones de enrasar; bloques de enrasillar. 3. incrustaciones (de una caldera). 4. sarro. 5. (arq.) revestimiento.

furrow ['fɜroʊ, B 'fʌroʊ] *s.* 1. surco, carril (del arado); (fig.) estela; huella, rastro. 2. surco, arruga (en el rostro). 3. (poét., fig.) labranza, labrado, tierras aradas, campo. 4. muesca; ranura, garganta (rosca, tornillo). 5. (arq.) estría. —*v.t.* 1. surcar (la tierra). 2. arrugar (la frente). —*v.i.* arrugarse (la frente).

furry ['fɜrɪ] *a.* 1. velloso, peludo; lanudo. 2. cubierto con pelo. 3. sarroso.

fur seal, (zool.) oso marino austral.

further ['fɜrðər, B 'fɜðə] *a.* 1. ulterior; nuevo, ej., *till f. notice,* hasta nueva orden o nuevo aviso. 2. más distante (lado, parte, etc.). 3. más amplio. 4. otro más, ej., *no f. proof is needed,* no hace falta otra prueba. 5. adicional (volumen, tomo, etc.). —*adv.* 1. más lejos, más allá. 2. además, además de eso. —*v.t.* promover, adelantar, favorecer, fomentar, apoyar.

furtherance [-ðərəns] *s.* fomento, promoción, adelanto, progreso; prima.

furtherer [-ðərər, B -ðərə] *s.* promotor, fomentador.

furthermore [-ðərˌmɔr, B -ðəˌmɔ] *adv.* además, a más de esto; (esp. en documentos legales) otrosí.

furthermost [-ˌmoʊst] *a.* lo más lejano, lo más remoto.

furthest ['fɜrðəst, B 'fɜðɪst] *a., adv.* más lejano, más distante; extremo.

furtive ['fɜrtɪv, B 'fɜtɪv] *a.* furtivo, sigiloso, disimulado, clandestino.

furtively [-lɪ] *adv.* furtivamente, disimuladamente, clandestinamente, a hurtadillas.

furtiveness [-nəs] *s.* carácter furtivo; disimulo.

furuncle ['fjʊrˌʌŋkəl, B 'fjʊər-] *s.* (med.) furúnculo, divieso, nacido (Mex., Cuba).

furuncular [fjʊ'rʌŋkjələr, B -lə] *a.* (med.) furuncular.

furunculosis [fjʊˌrʌŋkjə'loʊsəs] *s.* (med.) furunculosis.

fury ['fjʊrɪ, B 'fjʊərɪ] *s.* 1. furia, ira, furor. 2. (*pl.*) (fig.) las furias, espíritus, ánimos vengativos. 3. furia, virago colérica. 4. ferocidad, vehemencia. 5. frenesí, arrebatamiento, transporte. 6. **F.,** (mitol.) Furia. 7. **like f.,** como una furia; **to be in a f.,** estar furioso.

furze [fɜrz, B fɜz] *s.* (bot.) árgoma; tojo, aulaga; retama de escobas o negra.

fusain [fjʊ'zeɪn] *s.* (dib., pint.) carbón, carboncillo para dibujo; dibujo hecho al carbón.

fuscous ['fʌskəs] *a.* fosco, oscuro, de color gris oscuro.

fuse [fjuz] *v.t.* 1. fundir, derretir. 2. fundir, fusionar, amalgamar, juntar. —*v.i.* 1. fundirse, derretirse. 2. apagarse debido a cortocircuito (luces, focos). 3. fundirse, fusionarse. —*s.* 1. mecha, petardo de señales, espoleta. 2. (elec.) fusible; interruptor fusible, tapón de fusible. 3. **to blow a f.,** quemar un fusible.

fuseboard ['fjuzˌbɔrd, B -ˌbɔd] *s.* (elec.) tablero o cuadro de fusibles.

fuse box, caja de fusibles.

fused quartz, vidrio de cuarzo.

fusee [fju'zi] *s.* 1. fósforo de cartón. 2. caracol, husillo de reloj. 3. señal luminosa (de ferrocarril). 4. (med.) exostosis, tumor de un hueso de la pata del caballo. 5. espoleta.

fuselage ['fjusəˌlɑʒ, B 'fjuzɪ-] *s.* (aer.) fuselaje.

fusel oil ['fjuzəl-] (quím.) líquido que contiene alcohol amílico.

fusibility [ˌfjuzə'bɪlətɪ] *s.* fusibilidad.

fusible ['fjuzəbəl] *a.* fusible, fundible.

fusible metal, (metal.) aleación fusible.

fusiform [-ˌfɔrm, B -ˌfɔm] *a.* fusiforme, ahusado.

fusil ['fjuzəl] *s.* fusil de chispa.

fusilier, fusileer [ˌfjuzə'lɪr, B -'lɪə] *s.* 1. fusilero. 2. (*pl.*) (G.B.) fusileros (título que llevan ciertos regimientos británicos).

fusillade ['fjusəˌleɪd, -ˌlɑd, B ˌfjuzɪ'leɪd] *s.* 1. descarga de fusilería, rociada de balas. 2. fusilamiento. 3. (fig.) andanada, rociada. —*v.t.* 1. fusilar. 2. atacar con una descarga de fusilería.

fusilly ['fjuzəlɪ] *a.* (her.) fusado, fuselado.

fusion ['fjuʒən] *s.* 1. fusión, fundición, derretimiento. 2. fusión, unión, coalición. 3. (fís.) fusión; fusión nuclear.

fusion bomb, bomba termonuclear o de fusión.

fusionism [-ˌɪzəm] *s.* (pol.) fusionismo.

fusionist [-əst] *s., a.* (pol.) fusionista, unionista.

fusion welding, soldadura por fusión, fusiosoldeo.

fuss [fʌs] *s.* 1. nerviosidad, agitación por bagatelas. 2. pequeña disputa. 3. queja o protesta de una persona quisquillosa. 4. **to make a f. about,** hacer alharacas por, quejarse airadamente de; **to make a f. of** (u **over**), hacer fiestas a; alabar efusivamente; **without f. or feathers,** (fam.) a la llana, sin ostentación. —*v.i.* 1. preocuparse inquietarse, agitarse, afligirse por naderías. 2. zangolotear. 3. **f. over,** mimar, hacer fiestas a; **f. with,** manosear, repasar con exceso. —*v.t.* molestar, incomodar, fastidiar con tonterías.

fusser ['fʌsər, B -ə] *s.* quisquilloso, exigente.

fussily [-əlɪ] *adv.* minuciosamente, remilgadamente, melindrosamente.

fussiness [-ɪnəs] *s.* minuciosidad, remilgo, melindre.

fussy ['fʌsɪ] *a.* (FUSSIER; FUSSIEST) 1. exigente, minucioso. 2. melindroso, remilgado. 3. irritable, alharaquiento.

fustet [fʌ'stɛt, B 'fʌstɛt] *s.* (bot.) fustete.

fustian ['fʌstʃən, B -tɪən] *s.* 1. (tej.) fustán, pana, velludillo, pana acordonada. 2. rimbombancia, pomposidad, altisonancia. —*a.* 1. (hecho) de fustán, pana o velludillo. 2. ampuloso, rimbombante, pomposo, altisonante.

fustic ['fʌstɪk] *s.* 1. (bot.) fustete. 2. fustic, tinte procedente del fustete.

fustigate [-təˌgeɪt] *v.t.* fustigar.

fustily [-təlɪ] *adv.* de manera anticuada o pasada de moda.

fustiness [-tɪnəs] *s.* 1. moho, ranciedad. 2. aspecto o carácter anticuado.

fusty [-tɪ] *a.* 1. mohoso, rancio; manido, maloliente. 2. mal ventilado, sofocante. 3. mustio, marchito. 4. anticuado, pasado de moda, chapado a la antigua.

futile ['fjutəl, B -ˌtaɪl] *a.* fútil, inútil, vano, infructuoso, ineficaz; frívolo, insignificante, baladí.

futilely [-lɪ] *adv.* inútilmente, vanamente, infructuosamente, frívolamente.

futilitarian [fjʊˌtɪlə'tɛrɪən, B -'tɛər-] *a., s.* partidario de la doctrina de que todos los esfuerzos y aspiraciones humanas son en vano.

futility [-'tɪlətɪ] *s.* 1. futilidad, inutilidad, ineficacia. 2. frivolidad.

futtock ['fʌtək] *s.* (mar.) genol, singlón, ligazón, barraganete; arraigada.

futtock shrouds, (mar.) arraigadas, pernadas de las arraigadas.

futtock staff, (mar.) sotrozo.

future ['fjutʃər, B -tʃə] *a.* 1. futuro, venidero. 2. (gram.) futuro. —*s.* 1. (el o lo) futuro, (el) mañana, (el) porvenir, (el) más allá; **possible f.,** futurable, ej., *a woman is a possible f. president,* una mujer es una futurable presidente. 2. (*pl.*) (com.) artículos (comprados o vendidos) para entrega futura, entregas a término, entregas futuras. 3. (gram.) (tiempo) futuro. 4. **for the f.,** para el futuro, para el porvenir; **in the f.,** en lo sucesivo, de aquí en adelante.

futurism [-tʃərˌɪzəm] *s.* (arte) futurismo, movimiento que se opuso al tradicionalismo a raíz de la primera guerra mundial.

futuristic [ˌfjutʃər'ɪstɪk] *a.* (arte) futurista.

futurity [fjʊ'tʊrətɪ, B -'tjʊər-] *s.* 1. lo futuro, el porvenir, tiempo o estado venidero. 2. contingencia futura.

futz around [fʌtz-] (jer.) vagar sin objeto, holgazanear.

fuze [fjuz] *s.* espoleta, pebete, cebo, mecha, pajuela. —*v.t.* fijar o colocar una espoleta en.

fuzz [fʌz] *s.* 1. borra, tamo; pelusa, vello. 2. (E.U., despec.) policía, la policía. —*v.i.* volverse velloso. —*v.t* 1. cubrir con borra. 2. (fig.) anublar, empañar. 3. (gen. con *up*) confundir, turbar.

fuzzily ['fʌzəlɪ] *adv.* borrosamente, indistintamente.

fuzziness [-ɪnəs] *s.* vellosidad; aspecto borroso o indistinto.

fuzzy ['fʌzɪ] *a.* (FUZZIER; FUZZIEST) 1. velloso, velludo, cubierto de pelusa. 2. (fig.) borroso, confuso, indistinto. 3. rizado, encrespado.

fyke [faɪk] *s.* nasa (para pescar).

fylfot ['fɪlˌfɑt, B -ˌfɔt] *s.* svástica, cruz gamada.

G

G [dʒi] *s.* 1. g, séptima letra del alfabeto inglés. 2. (mús.) sol. 3. (fís.) (signo de la) gravedad. 4. (jer.) billete de mil dólares.
g. *abrev. de* 1. **acceleration of gravity,** aceleración de la gravedad (g.). 2. **gram,** gramo (g., gr.). 3. **gravity,** gravedad.
Ga *símb. de* **gallium,** galio.
Ga. *abrev. de* **Georgia,** Georgia (E.U.).
GA *abrev. de* **general average,** promedio general; avería gruesa.
gab [gæb] (*pret., p.p.* GABBED; *p.pr.* GABBING) *v.i.* (fam.) parlotear, charlar, picotear, cotorrear. —*s.* (fam.) parloteo, cháchara, cotorreo, palique; **stop your g.,** frena tu lengua. —*s.* (esco., fam. G.B.) boca.
gabardine ['gæbər,din, B 'gæbə,-] *s.* 1. gabardina, sobretodo. 2. gabardina (tela de varias fibras tejida al sesgo). 3. túnica, caftán.
gabber ['gæbər, B -ə] *s.* charlador, parlanchín, charlatán, chacharero.
gabble [-əl] *v.i., v.t.* 1. cotorrear, parlotear, garlar. 2. graznar (como ciertas aves). —*s.* 1. cotorreo, garla. 2. graznido.
gabbler ['gæblər, B -lə] *s.* charlatán, garlador, picotero.
gabbro ['gæbroʊ] *s.* (min.) gabro.
gabbroid [-,rɔɪd] *a.* (min.) semejante al gabro; gábrico.
gabby ['gæbɪ] *a.* (GABBIER; GABBIEST) (fam.) charlatán, parlanchín, hablador.
gabelle [gə'bɛl] *s.* 1. gabela, tributo, impuesto. 2. (hist., fr.) impuesto a la sal.
gaberdine ['gæbər,din, B 'gæbə,-] *s.* 1. tabardo. 2. túnica, caftán.
gaberlunzie [,gæbər'lʌnzɪ, B ,gæbə'-] *s.* (esco.) 1. mendigo, mendicante. 2. vagabundo, vagamundo.
gabfest ['gæb,fɛst] *s.* (fam.) charla prolongada; tertulia.
gabion ['geɪbɪən] *s.* (fort.) gavión, cestón.
gabionade [,geɪbɪə'neɪd, B 'geɪbɪə,neɪd] *s.* (fort.) obra hecha con gaviones.
gable ['geɪbəl] *s.* (arq.) gablete, faldón; aguilón, frontón.
gabled [-bəld] *a.* (arq.) de gablete, (provisto) con gabletes.
gable end, (arq.) hastial, alero.
gable roof, (arq.) tejado de caballete, techo de dos aguas (Amer.).
gablet ['geɪblət] *s.* (arq.) tímpano (espacio triangular entre las tres cornisas de un frontón).
gable window, (arq.) ventana en un gablete; ventana con gablete.
Gabon [gæ'boʊn] *s.* Gabón, república en África ecuatorial.
gaboon [gɑ'bun] *s.* (dial.) escupidera.
gaby ['geɪbɪ] *s.* (dial.) simplón, zonzo, tonto.
gad [gæd] *s.* 1. aguijón, puya. 2. (min.) cuña, punzón, piquetilla, taladro, barra aguzada. 3. vagancia, correteo, divagación. 4. **on the g.,** vagando; inquieto (ganado). —*v.i.* (*pret., p.p.* GADDED; *p.pr.* GADDING) deambular; **g. about,** callejear, viltrotear, andar de aquí para allá. —*interj.* (fam.) ¡por Dios! ¡pardiez! (usada como juramento leve).
gadabout ['gædə,baʊt] *a.* callejero, errante, vagabundo. —*s.* (fam.) azotacalles, trotacalles, placero.
gadarene ['gædə,rin, B ,gædə'rin] *a.* (fig.) arrojado, precipitado.
gadder ['gædər, B -ə] *s.* callejero, andariego.
gadding [-ɪŋ] *s.* holgazanería, briba, vagancia.
gadfly ['gæd,flaɪ] *s.* 1. (ento.) tábano, moscardón, mosca del caballo. 2. persona molestosa, latosa o pesada.
gadget ['gædʒət] *s.* 1. artilugio, artefacto, mecanismo. 2. (jer.) chatarra (cachivache inservible).
gadgeteer [,gædʒə'tɪr, B -'tɪə] *s.* persona muy aficionada a mecanismos; inventor de artefactos o cachivaches no siempre útiles.
gadgetry ['gædʒətrɪ] *s.* artilugios (conjunto de) artefactos; diseño o construcción de artefactos superfluos.
Gadhelic [gə'dɛlɪk] *var. de* **Goidelic.**
gadid ['geɪdɪd] *s.* (ict.) gádido.
gadoid [-,dɔɪd] *a., s.* (ict.) gádido.
gadolinite ['gædələ,naɪt] *s.* (min.) gadolinita.
gadolinium [,gædə'lɪnɪəm] *s.* (quím.) gadolinio.
gadroon [gə'drun] *s.* 1. (arq.) ornamento de talladura (hecho en una moldura redondeada). 2. especie de acanaladura o moldura ovalada (usada en vajilla de plata).
gadwall ['gæd,wɔl] *s.* (orn.) especie de pato zambullidor.
Gael [geɪl] *s.* gaélico (habitante de Escocia e Irlanda).
Gaelic ['geɪlɪk] *a., s.* gaélico (idioma celta de Escocia e Irlanda).
gaff [gæf] *s.* 1. arpón. 2. garfio (usado para izar peces muy pesados). 3. espolón de acero (con que se calza a los gallos de pelea). 4. garfio de trepar. 5. (mar.) cangrejo, pico de cangreja. 6. (jer., G.B.) disparate, tontería. 7. (jer., G.B.) (gen. **penny-g.**) teatro de mala muerte; cabaret de baja categoría. 8. (jer.) rudeza de trato; abuso; truco, fraude. 9. **to blow the g.,** (jer.) revelar el secreto; **to stand the g.,** aguantar la fatiga, tener resistencia; **to take (a great deal of) g.,** ser muy resistente (material); aguantar el maltrato. —*v.t.* 1. arponear, enganchar con arpón o garfio. 2. calzar con espolón de acero (a gallo de pelea). 3. (jer.) engañar, embaucar; pelar. 4. (jer.) arreglar, amarrar (juego, carrera, etc.); cargar (dados).
gaffe [gæf] *s.* error, metida de pata, paso en falso.
gaffer ['gæfər, B -ə] *s.* 1. viejo, vejete, vejestorio. 2. (G.B.) capataz, contramaestre, supervisor (de obreros).
gaff sail, (mar.) vela cangreja.
gaff-topsail [-'tɑp,seɪl, -səl, B -'tɔp-] *s.* (mar.) escandalosa.
gag [gæg] *v.t.* (*pret. p.p.* GAGGED; *p.pr.* GAGGING) 1. amordazar, poner mordaza a. 2. (fig.) amordazar, hacer callar. 3. hacer arquear, hacer nausear, basquear. 4. obstruir, atorar. 5. escribir chistes para, llenar de chistes (obra de teatro, película de cine, etc.). —*v.i.* 1. arquear, nausear, sentir náuseas. 2. (jer.) meter morcilla; (teat.) agregar chistes fuera del libreto. —*s.* 1. mordaza. 2. limitación del debate (en el parlamento). 3. cuento, tomadura de pelo, truco. 4. (teat.) morcilla, chiste, payasada.
gaga, ga-ga ['gɑ,gɑ] *a.* (jer.) 1. chocho, chalado; chiflado, tonto. 2. (con *over* o *about*) enloquecido, loco (por).
gage [geɪdʒ] *s.* 1. prenda, caución, garantía, fianza. 2. promesa, voto. 3. desafío, reto. 4. (bot.) ciruela verdal. —*v.t.* (ant.) dar o depositar (algo) en prenda; empeñar.
gage, *var. de* **gauge.**
gage pressure, (mec.) presión manométrica.
gager, *var. de* **gauger.**
gagger ['gægər, B -ə] *s.* 1. bromista, payaso. 2. escritor de chistes para comediantes o actores. 3. amordazador.
gaggle ['gægəl] *s.* 1. manada (esp. de gansos). 2. grupo, conjunto. 3. graznido. —*v.i.* graznar.
gagman ['gæg,mæn] *s.* escritor de chistes para comediantes o actores.
gag rule, (fam.) ley de la mordaza.
gagster [-stər, B -stə] *s.* 1. escritor de chistes para comediantes o actores. 2. (jer.) bromista, payaso.
gahnite ['gɑn,aɪt] *s.* (min.) gahnita.
Gaia ['geɪə] *s.* (mitol.) Gea, Ge (diosa de la Tierra entre los griegos).
gaiety ['geɪətɪ] *s.* 1. alegría, regocijo, alborozo, jovialidad. 2. entretenimiento, diversión alegre. 3. gala, adorno, atavío.
gaily ['geɪlɪ] *adv.* alegremente, jovialmente; vistosamente.
gain [geɪn] *s.* 1. ganancia, provecho, beneficio. 2. incremento, aumento. 3. adquisición, acumulación. 4. (elec., rad.) amplificación, ganancia; volumen. 5. (carp.) gárgol, ranura, muesca, entalladura. —*v.t.* 1. ganar (sustento, suma de dinero, fuerza, reputación, terreno, etc.). 2. obtener, conseguir, recibir. 3. ganar, alcanzar, llegar a (la cumbre, meta, etc.). 4. avanzar, progresar (cierta distancia). 5. cobrar (ímpetu, velocidad, etc.). 6. recobrar (equilibrio, etc.). 7. adelantar(se) por (un minuto, etc., un reloj). 8. **g. a point,** ganar un argumento; **g. ground,** ganar terreno; **g. strength,** reponerse, ganar fuerzas; **g. time,** ganar tiempo; **g. weight,** aumentar de peso. —*v.i.* 1. lucrar, sacar ventaja. 2. mejorar, recuperarse (enfermo). 3. crecer, aumentarse. 4. adelantar(se) (reloj). 5. **g. on,** acercarse a, ir alcanzando (meta, competidor, etc.).
gainer ['geɪnər, B -nə] *s.* 1. ganador, beneficiado. 2. (natación) patada (o puntapié) a la luna con salto mortal hacia atrás.
gainful ['geɪnfəl] *a.* ganancioso, remunerativo, lucrativo, ventajoso.
gainfully [-fəlɪ] *adv.* lucrativamente, ventajosamente, provechosamente.
gainfulness [-fəlnəs] *s.* carácter lucrativo, ganancia, provecho.
gainless [-ləs] *a.* infructuoso.
gainlessness [-nəs] *s.* infructuosidad.
gainliness ['geɪnlɪnəs] *s.* buena presencia; gracia.
gainly [-lɪ] *a.* de buen aspecto, bien formado; gracioso, agraciado.

gainsay [geɪn'seɪ] *v.t.* 1. contradecir, negar; oponerse a. 2. negar, prohibir.
gainsayer [-ər, B -ə] *s.* contradictor, negador, disputador.
gainsaying [-ɪŋ] *s.* contradicción, negación; oposición. —*a.* contradictorio, negativo.
'gainst, gainst [gɛnst, B geɪnst] (poét.) *vars. de* **against.**
gait [geɪt] *s.* modo de andar, marcha, andadura; paso (esp. del caballo). —*v.t.* adiestrar (a un caballo) a un trote regular.
gaited ['geɪtəd] *a.* (*ú. en palabras compuestas*) de (cierto) paso, ej., *slow-gaited,* de paso lento.
gaiter ['geɪtər, B -ə] *s.* 1. polaina. 2. borceguí, botín o botina con elástico por los costados.
gal [gæl] *s.* 1. (fís.) gal. 2. (fam.) muchacha, mujer.
Gal. *abrev. de* **Galatians,** Epístola de San Pablo a los Gálatas (Gál.).
gal. *abrev. de* **gallon,** galón.
gala ['geɪlə, 'gælə, B 'gɑlə] *s.* 1. fiesta, festival, celebración. 2. (ant.) vestido de gala, vestido de fiesta. —*a.* de gala, de fiesta.
galactagogue [gə'læktə,gɔg] *a.* (med.) galactagogo.
galactic [gə'læktɪk] *a.* 1. (med.) lácteo. 2. (astr.) galáctico.
galactic noise, ruido galáctico.
galactite [gə'læk,taɪt] *s.* galactita, galactites.
galactometer [,gælək'tɑmətər, B -'tɔmɪtə] *s.* galactómetro.
galactopoiesis [gə,læktə,pɔɪ'isəs] *s.* (fisiol.) galactopoyesis.
galactopoietic [-'ɛtɪk] *a.* (fisiol.) galactopoyético.
galactose [-'læk,toʊs] *s.* (quím.) galactosa.
galactoside [-tə,saɪd] *s.* (bioquím.) galactósido.
Galahad ['gælə,hæd] *s.* 1. Galahad, personaje de las leyendas del Ciclo de la Tabla Redonda. 2. (fig.) paladín exaltado.
galangal, galangale [gə'læŋgəl] *var. de* galingale.
galantine ['gælən,tin] *s.* (cocina) galantina.
galanty show [gə'læntɪ-] sombras chinescas.
Galapagos Islands [gə'lɑpəgəs-, B -'læp-] Islas Galápagos o Archipiélago de Colón (Ecuador).
galatea [,gælə'tiə] *s.* tela de algodón a rayas.
Galatea, *s.* (mitol.) Galatea, estatua de una doncella que cobró vida por obra de Afrodita, por intercesión de Pigmalión, su escultor.
Galatian [gə'leɪʃən] *a., s.* gálata, natural del Asia Menor.
Galatians [-ʃənz] *s. pl.* Epístola (de San Pablo) a los Gálatas.
galavant, *var. de* **gallivant.**
galaxy ['gæləksɪ] *s.* 1. **G.,** (astr.) Galaxia, Vía Láctea. 2. (astr.) galaxia. 3. (fig.) grupo representativo (de personas célebres); serie brillante (de cosas).
galbanum ['gælbənəm] *s.* gálbano.
galbulus ['gælbjələs] *s.* (*pl.* GALBULI [-laɪ]) (bot.) gálbula.
gale [geɪl] *s.* 1. ventarrón, viento muy fuerte. 2. (fig.) explosión (de risa). 3. (poét., ant.) brisa. 4. (bot.) mirto holandés, mirto de Brabante.
galea ['geɪlɪə] *s.* (*pl.* GALEAE [-lɪ,i]) (biol., bot.) gálea.
galeate [-,eɪt, B 'gælɪət] **galeated** [-,eɪtəd] *a.* (biol., bot.) galeado.
galeiform [gə'liə,fɔrm, B -,fɔm] *a.* (biol., bot.) galeiforme, galeado.
Galen ['geɪlən] Galeno, médico y filósofo de la Grecia antigua.
galena [gə'linə] *s.* (min.) galena.
Galenic [-'lɛnɪk] *a.* galénico, de Galeno.
galenical [-ɪkəl] *s.* (farm.) galénica (preparación medicinal esp. de origen vegetal). —*a.* **G.,** galénico, de Galeno (el médico y filósofo griego).
Galenism ['geɪlən,ɪzəm] *s.* (med.) galenismo, teorías o prácticas médicas descubiertas, establecidas y desarrolladas por Galeno.
Galenist [-əst] *s.* (med.) galenista, partidario del galenismo.
galenite [gə'linaɪt] *s.* (min.) galena.
Galicia [gə'lɪʃə] *s.* 1. Galicia (región de España). 2. Galitzia (región de Polonia).
Galician [-'lɪʃən] *a., s.* 1. gallego (de Galicia). 2. galiciano (de Galicia o Galitzia).
Galilean [,gælə'liən] *a.* 1. galileo, de Galilea. 2. de Galileo, galileano (de Galileo, científico y filósofo italiano). —*s.* 1. galileo, natural de Galilea. 2. galileo, cristiano. 3. **the G.,** el Galileo (Jesucristo).
Galilean transformation, (fís.) transformación de Galileo.
galilee ['gælə,li] *s.* galilea, pórtico (de iglesias).
Galilee, *s.* Galilea (región de Israel).
Galileo [,gælə'lioʊ, -'leɪ-] *s.* Galileo, científico y filósofo italiano del Renacimiento.
galimatias [,gælə'meɪʃɪəs, B -'mætɪəs] *s.* galimatías, jerigonza.
galingale ['gælən,geɪl, B -ɪŋ,geɪl] *s.* (bot.) 1. juncia. 2. galanga.
galiot, *var. de* **galliot.**
galipot ['gælə,pɑt, B -,pɔt] *s.* galipodio, trementina solidificada.
galium ['geɪlɪəm] *s.* (bot.) galio.
gall [gɔl] *s.* 1. bilis, hiel (esp. la del buey usada en artes y medicina). 2. (fig.) hiel, amargura, aspereza. 3. descaro, osadía, impudencia. 4. (bot.) agalla.
gall, *s.* 1. rozadura, matadura (ej., en el lomo de un caballo). 2. causa o estado de irritación; exasperación. 3. (ant.) punto débil, punto flaco; defecto. —*v.t.* 1. rozar, excoriar, desollar, ludir. 2. vejar, molestar, irritar, hostigar. —*v.i.* raerse, lastimarse rozando.
gallant ['gælənt] *a.* 1. garboso, vistoso, festivo, elegante. 2. imponente, gallardo, garboso. 3. bizarro, valiente, bravo, hazañoso. 4. [gə'læt] galante, cortesano. 5. galanteador, amoroso, amatorio. — ['gælənt, gə'lænt] *s.* 1. hombre garboso y elegante. 2. galán, galanteador, cortejador. 3. cortejo, amante. — [gə'lænt] *v.t.* galantear, requebrar, cortejar. —*v.i.* (raro) (con *with*) ser galante (con), flirtear (con).
gallantly [-lɪ] *adv.* 1. galantemente, cortesanamente. 2. valerosamente. 3. noblemente.
gallantry [-trɪ] *s.* 1. gallardía, valor, valentía. 2. galanteo. 3. galantería. 4. acto de cortesía. 5. (ant.) lujo, ostentación.
gallate ['gæleɪt] *s.* (quím.) galato.
gallbladder ['gɔl,blædər, B -ə] *s.* (anat.) vejiga de la bilis, vesícula biliar.
galleass ['gælɪes, -,æs] *s.* (hist., mar.) galeaza.
gallein ['gælɪən] *s.* (quím.) galeína.
galleon ['gælɪən] *s.* (hist., mar.) galeón.
galleried ['gælərid] *a.* (provisto) de galerías (sala, tribuna, etc.).
gallery ['gælərɪ] *s.* 1. galería, pórtico. 2. balcón largo; (S. de E.U.) veranda, porche, soportal. 3. galería, pasadizo subterráneo (hecho por animales o insectos); (fort., min.) galería. 4. pasadera, galería de servicio (alrededor de motores o máquinas grandes). 5. (arte) galería. 6. estudio de fotógrafo. 7. galería de tiro. 8. (teat.) galería, paraíso, cazuela; público de las galerías. 9. público, espectadores (en una competencia de tenis o de golf). 10. (mar.) galería. 11. **to play to the g.,** (fig.) complacer al vulgo. —*v.t.* hacer o perforar galerías en.
galley ['gælɪ] *s.* 1. galera. 2. fogón, cocina (de una embarcación o avión). 3. (impr.) galera.
galley proof, (impr.) prueba de galera, galerada.
galley slave, 1. galeote. 2. (fig.) ganapán, galopín.
galley-west [,gælɪ'wɛst] *adv.* (jer.) en estado aturdido; **he knocked the fellow g.-w.,** le propinó al tipo un tremendo golpe.
gallfly ['gɔl,flaɪ] *s.* (ento.) cinípido, cecidomido (insecto que produce agallas).
galliard ['gæljərd, B -ɪəd] *a.* (ant.) 1. intrépido, valiente. 2. vivo, alegre, galante. —*s.* gallarda (danza alegre del siglo XVI).
galliass, *var. de* **galleass.**
Gallic ['gælɪk] *a.* gálico, francés.
gallic ['gælɪk] *a.* (quím.) de galio, agállico, gálico.
gallic acid, (quím.) ácido gálico.
Gallican ['gælɪkən] *a.* galicano, galo.
Gallicanism [-kə,nɪzəm] *s.* galicanismo.
gallicism, Gallicism [-ə,sɪzəm] *s.* galicismo.
gallicize, Gallicize [-,saɪz] *v.t., v.i.* afrancesar(se).
gallicolous [gɔ'lɪkələs] *a.* 1. (bot.) galígeno, galífero. 2. (ento.) galícolo, galígeno.
galligaskins [,gælɪ'gæskənz] *s.* 1.(*pl.*) calzacalzón, botarga (esp. las que se usaban en el siglo XVII); calzones, pantalones holgados. 2. (dial., G.B.) polainas.
gallimaufry [-ə'mɔfrɪ] *s.* mezcolanza, revoltijo, masa confusa.
gallinaceous [-'neɪʃəs] *a.* (orn.) gallináceo.
galling ['gɔlɪŋ] *a.* irritante, exacerbante, exasperante, mortificante (para el espíritu).
gallingly [-lɪ] *adv.* irritantemente, exasperantemente.
gallinipper ['gælə,nɪpər, B -ə] *s.* 1. mosquito. 2. chinche.
gallinule [-,nul, B -,njul] *s.* (orn.) polla de agua, rey de las codornices.
galliot ['gælɪət] *s.* (mar.) galeota.
gallipot ['gælɪ,pɑt, B -,pɔt] *s.* 1. orza, vasija, pote (esp. para medicina). 2. (fam.) farmacéutico, boticario.
gallipot, *var. de* **galipot.**
gallium ['gælɪəm] *s.* (quím.) galio.
gallivant ['gælə,vænt, B ,gælɪ'vænt] *v.i.* 1. callejear, pindonguear. 2. galantear, flirtear.
gallnut ['gɔl,nʌt] *s.* agalla (en forma de nuez).
gallon ['gælən] *s.* galón.
gallonage [-ɪdʒ] *s.* cantidad en galones.
galloon [gə'lun] *s.* galoncillo, trencilla, (esp. de hilo de seda, oro o plata).
gallop ['gæləp] *v.i.* galopar; **to g. through,** (fig.) leer o recitar de prisa. —*v.t.* hacer galopar (a un caballo). —*s.* galope; at **full g.,** a galope tendido; **to go at a g.,** galopar, ir a galope, ir al galope (Amer.); (fig.) ir a (o de) galope.
gallopade [,gælə'peɪd] *s.* (baile, mús.) galop, galopa, caracoleo.
galloper ['gæləpər, B -ə] *s.* 1. jinete galopeador. 2. caballo galopeador. 3. (G.B.) edecán. 4. (G.B.) cañón de campaña ligero.
Gallophile ['gælə,faɪl] *s., a.* francófilo, galófilo.
Gallophobe [-,foʊb] *s., a.* galófobo, francófobo.
galloping ['gæləpɪŋ] *a.* galopante.
Galloway ['gælə,weɪ] *s.* (zool.) raza bovina de origen escocés.
gallows ['gæloʊz] *s.* (*pl.* GALLOWS O GALLOWSES [-əz]) 1. horca. 2. armazón, montante. 3. (*pl.*) (fam.) tirantes. 4. (impr.) caballete (de la máquina de imprimir). —*a.* que merece la horca, malvado.
gallows bird, (fam.) carne de horca.
gallows humor, humor negro, humor trágico, humor mórbido.

gallows tree, horca.
gallstone [ˈgɔlˌstoʊn] *s.* (med.) cálculo biliar.
gallus [ˈgæləs] *s.* (dial.) (*ú. gen. en. pl.*) tirantes (de los pantalones).
galoot [gəˈlut] *s.* (jer) tipo tosco, patán, palurdo; mamarracho.
galop [ˈgæləp] *s.* (baile, mús.) galop, galopa.
galore [gəˈlɔr, B -ˈlɔ] *a., adv.* en abundancia, en cantidad, muchísimo, a granel.
galosh [-ˈlɑʃ, B -ˈlɔʃ] *s.* 1. chanclo; zapato de caucho, bota impermeable. 2. (ant.) galocha, almadreña, zueco.
galumph [-ˈlʌmf] *v.i.* cabriolar, ir haciendo cabriolas.
galvanic [gælˈvænɪk] **galvanical** [-ɪkəl] *a.* 1. (elec.) galvánico. 2. (fig.) estimulante, excitante; convulsivo, nervioso; forzado.
galvanic battery, (elec.) batería galvánica, batería de pilas galvánicas.
galvanic couple, (fís.) par galvánico, par voltaico.
galvanic pile, (elec.) pila galvánica o voltaica.
galvanism [ˈgælvəˌnɪzəm] *s.* (fís., elec., med.) galvanismo.
galvanization [ˌgælvənəˈzeɪʃən, B -naɪ-] *s.* galvanización.
galvanize [ˈgælvəˌnaɪz] *v.t.* galvanizar.
galvanized iron [-ˌnaɪzd-] hierro galvanizado.
galvanizer [-ˌnaɪzər, B -ə] *s.* galvanizador.
galvanocautery [ˌgælvənoʊˈkɔtərɪ] *s.* (med.) galvanocauterio.
galvanometer [ˌgælvəˈnɑmətər, B -ˈnɔmɪtə] *s.* galvanómetro.
galvanometric [-noʊˈmɛtrɪk] *a.* galvanométrico.
galvanometry [-ˈnɑmətrɪ, B -ˈnɔm-] *s.* galvanometría.
galvanoplastic [-noʊˈplæstɪk] *a.* galvanoplástico. —*s. pl.* galvanoplástica.
galvanoplasty [ˈgælvənoʊˌplæstɪ] *s.* galvanoplastia.
galvanoscope [gælˈvænəˌskoʊp, B ˈgælvə-] *s.* galvanoscopio.
galvanoscopy [ˌgælvəˈnɑskəpɪ, B -ˈnɔs-] *s.* galvanoscopia.
galvanosurgery [-noʊˈsɜrdʒərɪ, B -ˈsɜdʒ-] *s.* (med.) galvanocirugía.
galvanotaxis [-ˈtæksəs] *s.* (med.) galvanotaxis.
galvanothermy [ˈgælvənoʊˌθɜrmɪ, B -ˌθɜmɪ] *s.* (med.) galvanotermia.
galvanotropism [ˌgælvəˈnɑtrəˌpɪzəm, B -ˈnɔt-] *s.* (med.) galvanotropismo, electrotropismo.
gam [gæm] *s.* (mar.) 1. grupo o cardumen de ballenas. 2. visita (esp. entre cazadores de ballenas) en alta mar. —*v.i.* (*pret., p.p.* GAMMED; *p.pr.* GAMMING) (mar.) reunirse en cardumen. —*v.t.* 1. visitar. 2. pasar (el tiempo, etc.) charlando.
gam, *s.* (jer.) pierna (esp. piernas bonitas de mujer).
gama grass [gɑmə-] (bot.) maicillo.
gamb [gæmb, gæm] *s.* (her.) pierna o zanca (de animal).
gamba [ˈgɑmbə, B ˈgæm-] *s.* (mús.) viola de gamba.
gambado [gæmˈbeɪdoʊ] *s.* (*pl.* GAMBADOES o GAMBADOS) 1. guardaestribos de cuero; polaina. 2. brinco o cabriola (del caballo). 3. calaverada.
gambe, *var. de* **gamb.**
gambeson [ˈgæmbɪsən] *s.* (hist.) manto acolchonado medieval.
gambier, gambir [ˈgæmˌbɪr, B -bɪə] *s.* (bot.) gambir.
gambit [ˈgæmbət] *s.* 1. (ajedrez) gambito. 2. (fig.) estratagema, maniobra.
gamble [ˈgæmbəl] *v.i.* 1. jugar por dinero. 2. correr (el) riesgo, aventurarse. —*v.t.* 1. apostar en el juego, jugar (una suma, etc.). 2. aventurar, arriesgar. 3. **g. away,** perder en el juego. —*s.* negocio arriesgado, acto riesgoso; jugada atrevida.
gambler [-blər, B -blə] *s.* 1. jugador, jugador inveterado. 2. tahúr, garitero.
gambling [-blɪŋ] *s.* 1. juego (por dinero). 2. tahurería.
gambling game, juego de envite.
gambling house, casa de juego, garito, tahureria.
gamboge [gæmˈboʊdʒ, B -ˈbuʒ] *s.* gomaguta o gutagamba.
gambol [ˈgæmbəl] *s.* cabriola, brinco, retozo. —*v.i.* (*pret., p.p.* GAMBOLED o GAMBOLLED; *p.pr.* GAMBOLING o GAMBOLLING) brincar, saltar, caracolear, cabriolar, retozar.
gambrel [ˈgæmbrəl] *s.* 1. (zool.) corvejón, tarso, jarrete (de animales). 2. caballete de suspensión (en mataderos). 3. (arq.) techo a la holandesa.
gambrel roof, (arq.) techo a la holandesa.
gambusia [gæmˈbjuʒɪə] *s.* (ict.) gambusino, guajacón.
game [geɪm] *s.* 1. deporte, juego. 2. juego, diversión, pasatiempo. 3. partido (de fútbol, tenis, etc.); partida (de naipes); certamen. 4. plan, estratagema. 5. profesión, línea. 6. (*esp. en pl.*) truco, treta, ardid. 7. (*pl.*) juegos atléticos, juegos públicos. 8. (tenis) juego (como parte de un partido). 9. (dep.) estilo de jugar (en golf, tenis, etc.). 10. (bridge) manga. 11. caza, animal(es) de caza. 12. carne salvajina. 13. **fair g.,** caza legal; (fig.) presa (de burlas, bajos instintos, etc.); **g. of tossing bottle caps,** chapas; **none of your games!** ¡nada de bromas! no me hagas trucos; **the g. is up,** (fig.) se acabó la jugada, todo está perdido; **to be on (off) one's g.,** (no) estar en forma; **to be on to someone's g.,** conocer el juego a alguien; **to give the g. away,** (fig.) descubrir las cartas; **to have thc g. in one's hands,** tener uno el juego en sus manos, estar uno seguro de ganar; **to make g. of,** burlarse de, ridiculizar; **to play a good** (o **poor**) **g.,** ser hábil (o torpe) en el juego; **to play the g.,** jugar limpio, observar las reglas; **to play one's g.,** hacer el juego de alguien. —*v.i.* jugar por dinero. —*v.t.* (ant.) disipar o dilapidar en el juego. —*a.* 1. animoso, valeroso. 2. montés; de caza o montería. 3. (fam.) cojo, lisiado.
gamebag [ˈgeɪmˌbæg] *s.* zurrón, morral, mochila de cazador.
game bird, ave de caza.
gamecock [-ˌkɑk, B -ˌkɔk] *s.* gallo de pelea.
game fish, pez que se pesca por deporte.
game fowl, raza dc gallo de pelea.
gamekeeper [-ˌkipər, B -pə] *s.* montaraz; guardabosque, guarda de coto.
gamelan [ˈgæməˌlæn] *s.* 1. gamelán (xilófono javanés). 2. (mús.) orquesta de flautas, cuerdas e instrumentos de percusión (del S.E. de Asia).
game laws, reglamentos de caza y pesca.
gamely [ˈgeɪmlɪ] *adv.* animosamente, valerosamente, resueltamente.
gameness [-nəs] *s.* resistencia, valor, ánimo, resolución.
game of chance, juego de azar.
game preserve, coto, vedado (de caza o pesca).
gamesmanship [ˈgeɪmzmənˌʃɪp] *s.* maestría en juegos (esp. del que usa trucos pero no viola las reglas).
gamesome [ˈgeɪmsəm] *a.* alegre, juguetón, retozón, travieso, bromista.
gamesomely [-lɪ] *adv.* alegremente, juguetonamente, por travesura, en broma.
gamesomeness [-nəs] *s.* alegría, festividad, retozo.
gamester [-stər, B -stə] *s.* jugador, tahúr, garitero.
gametangium [ˌgæməˈtændʒɪəm] *s.* (bot.) gametangio.
gamete [gəˈmit, ˈgæmˌit] *s.* (biol.) gameto.
game theory, técnica de aplicar la ley de la probabilidad a cualquier propósito.
gametic [gəˈmɛtɪk] *a.* (biol., bot.) gamético.
gametocyte [gəˈmitəˌsaɪt] *s.* (biol.) gametocito.
gametogenesis [-ˌmitəˈdʒɛnəsəs] *s.* (biol.) gametogénesis, gametogenia.
gametophore [-ˈmitəˌfɔr, B -ˌfɔ] *s.* (bot.) gametóforo.
gametophyte [-ˌfaɪt] *s.* (bot.) gametofita.
game warden, guardabosque, guarda de coto, montaraz.
gamic [-gæmɪk] *a.* (biol., bot.) gámico.
gamily [ˈgeɪməlɪ] *adv.* valerosamente, animosamente, resueltamente.
gamin [ˈgæmən] *s.* (fr.) pilluelo, golfo, rapazuelo.
gamine [gæˈmin] *s.* (fr.) pilluela, golfa, rapazuela.
gaming [ˈgeɪmɪŋ] *s.* juego, apuesta.
gaming house, casa de juego, garito.
gaming table, mesa de juego.
gamma [ˈgæmə] *s.* (*pl.* GAMMAS o GAMMA) 1. gamma, tercera letra del alfabeto griego. 2. (*pl.* GAMMA) microgramo. 3. (foto., t.v.) grado de contraste (de una impresión fotográfica o imagen televisada).
gammadion [gəˈmeɪdɪən] *s.* (*pl.* GAMMADIA [-dɪə]) cruz gamada (esp. la esvástica).
gamma globulin, (fisiol.) globulina gamma.
gamma particle, (fís.) partícula gamma.
gamma rays, (fís.) rayos gamma.
gammer [ˈgæmər, B -ə] *s.* vieja, vejarrona; (fam.) abuelita.
gammon [ˈgæmən] *s.* 1. lonja de tocino salado, parte inferior de la lonja de tocino; jamón ahumado o secado. 2. (chaquete) juego doble (ganado por el jugador que logra alejar todos sus peones sin que el adversario elimine ninguno). —*v.t.* 1. (chaquete) vencer ganando un juego doble. 2. (mar.) trincar (el bauprés a la roda).
gammon, *s.* (fam.) farsa, patraña, engaño, fraude, supercheria. —*v.i.* (fam.) hablar engañosamente; fingir. —*v.t.* (fam.) engañar, burlar.
gammoner [-ər, B -ə] *s.* farsante, embaucador.
gammy [ˈgæmɪ] *a.* (G.B., fam.) cojo, estropeado, lisiado.
gamogenesis [ˌgæməˈdʒɛnəsəs] *s.* (biol.) gamogénesis.
gamogenetic [-dʒəˈnɛtɪk] *a.* gamogenético.
gamogenetically [-ɪkəlɪ] *adv.* gamogenéticamente.
gamopetalous [ˌgæməˈpɛtələs] *a.* (bot.) gamopétalo.
gamophyllous [-ˈfɪləs] *a.* (bot.) gamofilo.
gamosepalous [-ˈsɛpələs] *a.* (bot.) gamosépalo.
gamp [gæmp] *s.* (G.B.) paraguas grande.
gamut [ˈgæmət] *s.* 1. (mús.) gama o escala musical. 2. (fig.) gama, serie.
gamy, gamey [ˈgeɪmɪ] *a.* (GAMIER; GAMIEST) 1. animoso, bravo. 2. de sabor a carne salvajina (esp. la cediza). 3. maloliente, apestoso. 4. escandaloso, indecente, salaz. 5. desdoroso, de mala fama.
gander [ˈgændər, B -də] *s.* 1. ganso, ánsar macho. 2. simplón, papanatas, zonzo, gaznápiro. 3. (jer.) mirada, ojeada; **to take a g. at,** echar una ojeada a.
gandy dancer [ˈgændɪ-] 1. ferroviario. 2. peón viajante. 3. bracero por temporadas.
ganef [ˈgɑnəf] *s.* (jer.) ladrón.
gang [gæŋ] *s.* 1. cuadrilla, brigada (de obreros, braceros, etc.). 2. banda, pandilla, gavilla (de malhechores, criminales, etc.). 3. (mec.) juego,

equipo (de herramientas, etc.). —*v.t.* 1. atacar en pandillas. 2. acoplar (partes mecánicas o electrónicas). 3. arreglar en juegos o serie. —*v.i.* (esco.) ir, andar. 2. **g. up,** agruparse, formar grupos; **g. up on,** (fam.) atacar en conjunto (a alguien); **g. up with,** unirse con, aliarse con.
gang, *var. de* **gangue.**
gang-bang ['gæŋ,bæŋ] *s.* (jer.) violación múltiple o colectiva (por parte de una pandilla de malhechores).
gang board, (mar.) rampa de embarque.
gang buster, (jer.) funcionario que reprime con ahínco el crimen organizado.
gang condenser, (rad.) condensador múltiple.
gang dies, matriz múltiple.
gang drill, taladro múltiple.
ganged circuits [gæŋd-] (rad.) circuitos de sintonía simultánea, circuitos acoplados.
ganger ['gæŋər, B -ə] *s.* (G.B.) capataz, obrajero, contramaestre.
Ganges ['gæn,dʒiz] *s.* Ganges, río de la India.
gang hook, (pesca) anzuelo múltiple.
gangland ['gæŋ,lænd] *s.* el hampa, mundo del crimen organizado.
ganglia, *pl. de* **ganglion.**
gangliated ['gæŋglɪ,eɪtəd] **gangliate** [-,eɪt] *a.* (anat., zool.) gangliado.
gangling ['gæŋglɪŋ] *a.* larguirucho, delgaducho.
ganglion ['gæŋglɪən] *s.* (*pl.* GANGLIA [-glɪə] o GANGLIONS) 1. (anat., zool.) ganglio. 2. (med.) ganglio. 3. (fig.) centro, foco (de energía, fuerza, etc.).
ganglionectomy [,gæŋglɪə'nɛktəmɪ] *s.* (med.) ganglionectomía, ganglictomía.
ganglionic [-'ɑnɪk, B -'ɔn-] *a.* ganglial, ganglionar.
gangly ['gæŋglɪ] *a.* (GANGLIER; GANGLIEST) larguirucho, delgaducho.
gangplank ['gæŋ,plæŋk] *s.* (mar.) plancha o pasarela de desembarco.
gang plow, arado de reja múltiple.
gang punch, punzón múltiple.
gangrel ['gæŋgrəl] *s.* (esco.) vagabundo.
gangrene ['gæŋ,grin, gæŋ'grin, B 'gæŋ,grin] *s.* (med.) gangrena. —*v.t., v.i.* volver(se) gangrenoso, gangrenar(se).
gangrenous ['gæŋgrənəs] *a.* gangrenoso.
gangster ['gæŋstər, B -stə] *s.* pandillero, pistolero, bandido.
gangsterism [-stə,rɪzəm] *s.* bandidaje, bandolerismo, crimen organizado.
gang switch, (elec.) interruptor acoplado.
gangue [gæŋ] *s.* (min.) ganga, blancarte.
gangway ['gæŋ,weɪ] *s.* 1. pasaje, camino (esp. el temporario sobre tablones). 2. (G.B.) corredor angosto, pasillo; corredor transversal (en la Cámara de los Comunes). 3. (mar.) portalón; plancha, escalera del portalón. 4. (mar.) pasarela. 5. (min.) nivel principal. —*interj.* (mar.) ¡abran paso! ¡paso libre!
ganister, gannister ['gænəstər, B -stə] *s.* 1. piedra arenosa silicosa (usada para fabricar ladrillos refractarios). 2. mezcla de cuarzo pulverizado y arcilla refractaria (para recubrir hornos metalúrgicos).
gannet ['gænət] *s.* (orn.) planga, planco, alcatraz.
ganof, *var. de* **ganef.**
ganoid ['gæn,ɔɪd] *a., s* (ict.) ganoideo.
gantlet ['gɔntlət, 'gænt-, B 'gɔnt-] *s.* (f.c.) vía traslapada, vía de garganta. —*v.t.* formar vía traslapada con (rieles).
gantlet, *var. de* **gauntlet.**
gantline ['gænt,laɪn] *s.* (mar.) cabo de labor.
gantry ['gæntrɪ] *s.* 1. caballete, poíno (para sustentar cubas o barriles). 2. (ing.) puente transversal de grúa corrediza. 3. (f.c.) puente transversal de señales, torre de señalización. 4. estructura de lanzamiento (de cohetes).
gantry crane, (ing.) grúa de pórtico, grúa de caballete.
Ganymede ['gænə,mid] *s.* 1. (mitol.) Ganimedes, copero de los dioses. 2. (fig.) ganimedes, copero, el que escancia. 3. (astr.) Ganimedes.
gaol, gaolbird, gaoler, (pr. G.B.) *vars. de* **jail, jailbird, jailer.**
gap [gæp] *s.* 1. boquete, abertura, raja, resquicio, brecha. 2. garganta, quebrada, barranca, cañada, hondonada, paso (entre montañas). 3. laguna, vacío; claro, intervalo. 4. (aer.) entreplanos. 5. (aut.) separación (de los electrodos en las bujías). 6. **to stop** (o **fill**) **a g.,** suplir o compensar una deficiencia o falta. —*v.t.* (*pret., p.p.* GAPPED; *p.pr.* GAPPING) hacer una brecha o abertura en. —*v.i.* abrirse; presentar una brecha.
gape [geɪp, gæp, B geɪp] *v.i.* 1. estar con la boca abierta, boquear. 2. bostezar. 3. embobarse, papar moscas, quedarse boquiabierto. 4. abrirse mucho, estar abierto. 5. **g. at,** mirar con la boca abierta. —*s.* 1. bostezo. 2. mirada atónita. 3. brecha, abertura. 4. anchura de la boca abierta; línea formada al cerrarse las mandíbulas de un pájaro. 5. **the gapes,** enfermedad de las aves de corral (cuyo síntoma es el pico abierto); (hum.), ataque de bostezos.
gaper ['geɪpər, 'gæp-, B 'geɪpə] *s.* 1. mirón, curioso. 2. (ict.) pez cabrilla. 3. (zool.) especie de molusco bivalvo.
gapeworm [-,wɜrm, B -,wɜm] *s.* (ento.) gusano parásito nematodo de color rojo (que causa una enfermedad de las aves de corral).
gaping [-ɪŋ] *a.* 1. abismal, profundo, vasto (precipicio, etc.). 2. boquiabierto.
gapped scale [gæpt-] (mús.) escala incompleta.
gar [gɑr, B gɑ] *s.* (ict.) 1. aguja de mar, pez aguja. 2. lucio, sollo.
garage [gə'rɑʒ, -'rɑdʒ, B 'gærɑdʒ, -rɪdʒ] *s.* 1. garaje, cochera (para automóviles). 2. taller para reparar automóviles. —*v.t.* (*pret., p.p.* GARAGED; *p.pr.* GARAGING) guardar o dejar (automóvil) en un garaje.
garageman [-,mæn] *s.* trabajador de garaje, mecánico.
garage sale, venta de garaje, venta de objetos usados en casa de su propietario, feria americana.
Garamond ['gærə,mɑnd, B -,mɔnd] *s.* (imp.) (tipo) garamond.
garb [gɑrb, B gɑb] *s.* 1. traje, vestido, vestidura, vestiduras. 2. (ant.) garbo, porte. 3. (ant.) moda, estilo de vestir. —*v.t.* vestir; adornar, ataviar.
garbage ['gɑrbɪdʒ, B 'gɑbɪdʒ] *s.* basura, desecho, desperdicios; (fig.) inmundicias, porquería; **don't throw out garbage,** (señal) prohibido tirar basura *or* se prohibe tirar basura.
garbage can, cubo para basura, tacho de basura (Amer.).
garbage collector, *s.* basurero (oficio).
garbage incinerator, incinerador de basura.
garbage truck, camión de la basura.
garbanzo [gɑr'bænzoʊ, B gɑ'-] *s.* garbanzo.
garble ['gɑrbəl, B 'gɑbəl] *v.t.* 1. seleccionar maliciosamente (partes de hechos, declaraciones, etc.); mutilar, confundir maliciosamente (texto, discurso, cuento, registro, etc.). 2. (raro) seleccionar lo mejor de, escoger. 3. (ant.) garbillar, cerner, cribar. —*s.* 1. impurezas de especias. 2. mutilación, torcimiento, confusión.
garbler [-blər, B -blə] *s.* 1. garbillador. 2. persona que tergiversa las razones o los hechos.
garboard ['gɑr,bɔrd, B 'gɑ,bɔd] *s.* (mar.) tablón de aparadura.
garboil [-,bɔɪl] *s.* (ant.) alboroto, tumulto, confusión.
garcinia [gɑr'sɪnɪə, B gɑ'-] *s.* (bot.) gutagamba.
garçon [gɑr'soʊn, B gɑ'sɔn] *s.* (fr.) camarero, mesero, mozo.
garden ['gɑrdən, B 'gɑd-] *s.* 1. jardín; huerto, huerta. 2. región fértil y bien cultivada. 3. lugar de recreo, parque público; jardín (botánico, zoológico). 4. (béisbol) campo situado fuera del diamante de juego. 5. **to lead up the g. (path),** (jer.) tentar, seducir; engañar. —*v.i.* cultivar o trabajar jardines o huertos. —*v.t.* cultivar (un terreno) como jardín o huerto. —*a.* 1. de jardín; de huerto. 2. (fig.) común, ordinario, corriente.
garden apartment, departamento en una unidad vecinal con amplios jardines.
garden balm, (bot.) melisa, toronjil, cidronela, abejera.
garden balsam, (bot.) balsamina, adomo, belén.
garden buttercup, (bot.) renúnculo de jardín, botón de oro.
garden cress, (bot.) lepidio.
garden dittany, (bot.) díctamo blanco.
garden-engine ['gɑrdən,ɛndʒən, B 'gɑd-] *s.* bomba impelente portátil para regadío.
gardener ['gɑrdnər, B 'gɑdnə] *s.* jardinero; hortelano.
garden heliotrope, (bot.) 1. valeriana. 2. heliotropo.
garden hose, manguera de jardín.
gardenia [gɑr'dinjə, B gɑ'-] *s.* (bot.) gardenia.
gardening ['gɑrdənɪŋ, B 'gɑd-] *s.* jardinería, horticultura.
gardenless [-ləs] *a.* sin jardín (es).
Garden of Eden, (bíbl.) jardín del Edén.
garden-party [-,pɑrtɪ, B -,pɑtɪ] *s.* reunión social en un jardín.
garden path, sendero en un jardín; **to lead someone up the g.,** embaucar a uno.
garden pink, (bot.) clavellina de pluma.
garden seat, banco de jardín.
garden shears, tijeras de jardín.
garden-variety [-və'raɪətɪ] *a.* común, corriente, ordinario; casero, campechano.
garden warbler, (orn.) papafigo, andahuertas.
garderobe ['gɑrd,roʊb, B 'gɑd-] *s.* (fr.) 1. guardarropa, armario para ropa. 2. vestuario, vestidos (de uno). 3. habitación privada; dormitorio. 4. retrete, excusado.
gardyloo [,gɑrdə'lu, B ,gɑdɪ-] *s.* (ant.) ¡agua va! (grito de advertencia al arrojar agua, etc., a la calle desde las ventanas).
garfish ['gɑr,fɪʃ, B 'gɑ,-] *s.* (ict.) aguja de mar, pez aguja.
garganey ['gɑrgənɪ, B 'gɑgə-] *s.* (orn.) cerceta europea, zarceta.
Gargantuan, gargantuan [gɑr'gæntʃʊən, B gɑ'gæntjʊən] *a.* enorme, gigantesco, muy grande.
garget ['gɑrgət, B 'gɑgət] *s.* (vet.) mastitis (del ganado).
gargle ['gɑrgəl, B 'gɑgəl] *v.t.* 1. limpiar (ej., la garganta) haciendo gárgaras. 2. decir (algo) como si se estuviera haciendo gárgaras. —*v.i.* gargarizar, hacer gárgaras. —*s.* 1. gárgara. 2. gargarismo.
gargoyle ['gɑr,gɔɪl, B 'gɑ,-] *s.* 1. (arq.) gárgola. 2. mascarón. 3. (fig.) carantamaula, carantoña.
gargoyled [-,gɔɪld] *a.* (arq.) (adornado) con gárgolas.
garibaldi [,gærə'bɔldɪ] *s.* garibaldina.
garish ['gɛrɪ, 'gær-, B 'gɛər-] *a.* chillón, deslumbrante; llamativo, extravagante.
garishly [-lɪ] *adv.* llamativamente, chillonamente.

garishness [-nəs] *s.* aspecto chillón; relumbrón, oropel.
garland ['gɑrlənd, B 'gɑlənd] *s.* 1. guirnalda, corona abierta (tejida de flores, hierbas o ramas). 2. crestomatía, antología, florilegio. 3. (mar.) estrobo, eslinga; roñada. —*v.t.* 1. enguirnaldar. 2. formar una guirnalda de.
garlic ['gɑrlɪk, B 'gɑlɪk] *s.* ajo.
garlicky [-ɪ] *a.* aliáceo, (con sabor u olor) a ajo.
garlic soup, sopa de ajo.
garment ['gɑrmənt, B 'gɑmənt] *s.* prenda de vestir, vestido, vestidura. —*v.t.* vestir.
garner ['gɑrnər, B 'gɑnə] *s.* granero, troj, troje. —*v.t.* 1. entrojar, almacenar (granos). 2. acumular, acopiar, reunir.
garnet ['gɑrnət, B 'gɑnɪt] *s.* 1. (min.) granate. 2. granate (color rojo). 3. (mar.) aparejo de estrinque, polispasto (gen. colocado en el estay mayor).
garnetiferous [ˌgɑrnət'ɪfərəs, B ˌgɑnət-] *a.* (min.) granatífero.
garnierite ['gɑrnɪəˌraɪt, B 'gɑnɪə-] *s.* (min.) garnierita.
garnish ['gɑrnɪʃ, B 'gɑnɪʃ] *v.t.* 1. adornar, decorar; guarnecer, engalanar. 2. (cocina) adornar, aderezar (los platos). 3. (der.) citar, emplazar (esp. a terceras partes); embargar, secuestrar. —*s.* 1. adorno, ornamento, decoración; (raro) vestido; vestimentas, prendas de vestir. 2. (cocina) adorno, aderezo; sazón. 3. (hist.) paga no autorizada (que demandaban los prisioneros antiguos o los trabajadores de una fábrica a los recién llegados).
garnishee [ˌgɑrnə'ʃi, B ˌgɑnɪ-] *s.* (der.) embargado; persona notificada de un embargo. —*v.t.* (*pret., p.p.* GARNISHEED; *p.pr.* GARNISHEEING) 1. (der.) embargar, secuestrar (la propiedad en juicio). 2. notificar, citar, emplazar.
garnisher ['gɑrnɪʃər, B 'gɑnɪʃə] *s.* 1. (cocina) aderezador. 2. (der.) embargador.
garnishment [-mənt] *s.* 1. adorno, ornamento. 2. (der.) citación o emplazamiento; embargo de bienes (de un deudor, en posesión de tercero); retención de sueldo (para satisfacer una deuda).
garniture ['gɑrnɪtʃər, B 'gɑnɪtʃə] *s.* adorno; gala; guarnición.
garotte, *var. de* **garrote.**
garpike ['gɑrˌpaɪk, B 'gɑˌ-] *s.* (ict.) pez aguja.
garret [ˌgærət] *s.* ático, desván, buhardilla.
garreteer ['gærə'tɪr, B -'tɪə] *s.* persona que vive en un desván o una buhardilla.
garrison ['gærəsən] *s.* (mil.) guarnición, plaza fuerte. —*v.t.* (mil.) guarnecer, guarnicionar.
garrison cap, (mil.) gorra de cuartel, cristina.
garrison house, (hist.) 1. casa fortificada; blanco, fortín. 2. casa colonial cuyo segundo piso era saledizo.
garrison state, estado sometido a disciplina militar.
garrote, garotte [gə'rɑt, -'rout, B -'rɔt] *s.* 1. garrote (pena e instrumento). 2. estrangulación (esp. ejecutada por salteadores). —*v.t.* (*pret., p.p.* GARROTED, GARROTTED O GAROTTED; *p.pr.* GARROTING, GARROTTING O GAROTTING) 1. agarrotar, dar garrote a. 2. estrangular, acogotar (esp. para robar).
garroter, garrotter [-ər, B -ə] *s.* verdugo (que ejecuta con garrote); salteador que acogota.
garrulity [gə'rulətɪ] *s.* garrulidad, locuacidad.
garrulous ['gærələs] *a.* gárrulo, locuaz, parlanchín.
garrulously [-lɪ] *adv.* gárrulamente, locuazmente.
garrulousness [-nəs] *s.* garrulidad, locuacidad.
garter ['gɑrtər, B 'gɑtə] *s.* 1. liga, jarretera. 2. **G.,** (insignia de la orden de la) Jarretera. —*v.t.* asegurar con liga, atar con jarrete (medias).
garter belt, portaligas.
garter snake, (zool.) variedad de culebra americana no venenosa.
garth [gɑrθ, B gɑθ] *s.* patio o jardín de claustro.
gas [gæs] *s.* (*pl.* GASES) 1. gas. 2. mezcla gaseosa; gas anestésico. 3. gasolina. 4. (min.) gas grisú. 5. (jer.) cháchara, garla, palique. 6. **to step on the g.,** apretar el acelerador; (fig.) apresurarse, acelerar el ritmo. —*v.t.* (*pret., p.p.* GASSED; *p.pr.* GASSING) 1. gasear (envenenar o asfixiar con gas). 2. (gen. con *up*) abastecer o proveer de gas. 3. (quím., tej.) gasear, tratar o saturar con gas. 4. (mil.) gasear, atacar con gases. —*v.i.* 1. despedir o desprender gas. 2. (jer.) chacharear. 3. (jer.) abrumar o engañar con cháchara.
gasbag ['gæsˌbæg] *s.* 1. bolsa de gas. 2. (aer.) cámara de gas. 3. (jer.) chacharero, charlatán.
gas black, negro de humo; negro de gas.
gas burner, mechero de gas, quemador de gas.
gas candle, (mil.) bengala de gas.
gas chamber, 1. (E.U.) cámara de gas (para ejecución de condenados a muerte). 2. cámara de gas en la que los nazis exterminaban a los judíos colectivamente durante la Segunda Guerra Mundial.
Gascon ['gæskən] *s.* 1. gascón, gasconés. 2. **g.,** fanfarrón, baladrón. —*a.* gascón.
gasconade [ˌgæskə'neɪd] *s.* fanfarronada, bravata. —*v.i.* fanfarronear, baladronear.
gasconader [-ər, B -ə] *s.* fanfarrón, bravucón.
gas engine, motor de gas.
gaseous ['gæsɪəs] *a.* 1. gaseoso; gaseiforme. 2. (fig.) tenue.
gas fitter, gasista, gasero.
gas fixture, artefacto de gas.
gas furnace, cocina, horno de gas.
gas gangrene, (med.) gangrena gaseosa.
gas generator, gasógeno, generador de gas.
gash [gæʃ] *v.t.* hacer un corte largo en, acuchillar. —*s.* corte largo, chirlo, cuchillada. —*a.* (jer.) chacharero; sabihondo.
gas helmet, (mil.) máscara antigás, careta antigás.
gasholder ['gæsˌhouldər, -də] *s.* gasómetro, tanque de gas.
gashouse [-ˌhaus] *s.* fábrica de gas.
gasifiable [ˌgæsə'faɪəbəl, B 'gæsɪˌfaɪ-] *a.* gasificable.
gasification [ˌgæsəfə'keɪʃən] *s.* gasificación.
gasifier ['gæsəˌfaɪər, B -ə] *s.* gasificador.
gasiform [-ˌfɔrm, B -ˌfɔm] *a.* gaseiforme; gaseoso.
gasify [-ˌfaɪ] *v.t.* (*pret., p.p.* GASIFIED; *p.pr.* GASIFYING) gasificar, convertir en gas. —*v.i.* gasificarse.
gas-jet [-ˌdʒɛt] *s.* quemador, mechero de gas; su llama.
gasket ['gæskət] *s.* 1. (mar.) tomador, baderna firme. 2. (mec.) empaquetadura, empaque, junta, arandela.
gaskin ['gæskən] *s.* 1. bragada. 2. (*pl.*) (ant.) polaina corta; calzacalzón.
gaslight ['gæsˌlaɪt] *s.* 1. luz de gas. 2. mechero o lámpara de gas.
gas lighter, encendedor de gas.
gas lighting, alumbrado, iluminación de gas.
gaslit [-ˌlɪt] *a.* iluminado por luz de gas.
gas log, calentador de gas que imita leña llameante y se usa en las chimeneas caseras.
gas main, cañería principal de gas, tubería maestra de gas.
gasman [-ˌmæn] *s.* 1. contralor de los medidores de gas. 2. fabricante de gas.
gas mask, máscara antigás, máscara protectora, careta antigás.
gas meter, contador de gas, medidor de gas.
gasogene ['gæsəˈdʒin] *s.* gasógeno.
gasolier [ˌgæsə'lɪr, B -'lɪə] *s.* araña o candelabro de gas.
gasoline, gasolene [ˌgæsə'lin, B 'gæsəˌlin] *s.* gasolina, gasoleno.
gasoline pump, (aut.) surtidor, bomba de gasolina.
gasometer [gæ'sɑmətər, B -'sɔmɪtə] *s.* gasómetro.
gasometry [-trɪ] *s.* (quím.) gasometría.
gas oven, horno de gas.
gasp [gæsp, B gɑsp] *v.i.* 1. jadear, acezar, resollar, anhelar. 2. quedar sin aliento, quedar boquiabierto (de asombro, susto, etc.). —*v.t.* (gen. con *out*) decir jadeando. —*s.* jadeo, resuello, boqueo; **at one's last g.,** a punto de dar el último suspiro.
gasper ['gæspər, B 'gɑspə] *s.* (jer., G.B.) pitillo (cigarrillo).
gas pipe, tubería de gas, tubo de conducción de gas, gasoducto (Amer.).
gas plant, 1. fábrica de gas. 2. (bot.) fresnillo.
gas pump, surtidor, bomba de gasolina.
gaspy [-pɪ] *a.* jadeante.
gas range, estufa de gas.
gas ring, hornillo de gas; hornilla (en una estufa de gas).
gassed [gæst] *a.* 1. (med.) gaseado. 2. (jer.) borracho, ebrio.
gasser ['gæsər, B -ə] *s.* 1. pozo petrolífero que produce gas. 2. (jer.) charlatán, chacharero. 3. (jer.) algo descollante, cosa fenomenal.
gas shell, (mil.) granada de gas.
gassing [-ɪŋ] *s.* 1. (quím.) saturación por gas. 2. gaseamiento (envenenamiento o asfixia por gases). 3. (mil.) ataque con gas.
gas station, estación de servicio para automotores; gasolinera (Amer.).
gassy [-ɪ] *a.* (GASSIER; GASSIEST) 1. lleno de gas, gaseoso. 2. gaseiforme. 3. (fam.) (lenguaje) vacío y verboso.
gas tank, 1. tanque de gas. 2. (aut.) tanque de gasolina, depósito de gasolina.
gasteropod ['gæstərəˌpɑd, B -ˌpɔd] *var. de* **gastropod.**
gastight ['gæs'taɪt] *a.* hermético, a prueba de gases.
gastral ['gæstrəl] *a.* (anat.) gastral.
gastralgia [gæs'trældʒɪə] *s.* (med.) gastralgia.
gastralgic [-dʒɪk] *a.* (med.) gastrálgico.
gastrectomy [-'trɛktəmɪ] *s.* (med.) gastrectomía.
gastric ['gæstrɪk] *a.* (med.) gástrico.
gastricism ['gæstrɪˌsɪzəm] *s.* (med.) gastricismo.
gastric juice, (fisiol.) jugo gástrico.
gastric ulcer, (med.) úlcera gástrica.
gastrin ['gæstrən] *s.* (bioquím.) gastrina.
gastritis [gæs'traɪtəs] *s.* (med.) gastritis.
gastrocoel, gastrocoele ['gæstrəˌsil] *s.* (anat.) gastrocelo.
gastrocolic [ˌgæstrou'kɑlɪk, B -'kɔl-] *a.* (fisiol.) gastrocólico.
gastroenteritis [-ˌɛntə'raɪtəs] *s.* (med.) gastroenteritis.
gastroenterologist [-'rɑlədʒəst, B -'rɔl-] *s.* gastroenterólogo.
gastroenterology [-dʒɪ] *s.* (med.) gastroenterología.
gastroenterostomy [-'rɑstəmɪ, B -'rɔs-] *s.* (med.) gastroenterostomía.
gastrogenic [ˌgæstrə'dʒɛnɪk] **gastrogenous** [gæs'trɑdʒənəs, B -'trɔdʒ-] *a.* (med.) gastrogénico.
gastrointestinal [-trouɪn'tɛstənəl] *a.* (med.) gastrointestinal; gastroentérico.

gastrolith ['gæstrə,lɪθ] *s.* (med.) cálculo gástrico.
gastrologist [gæs'trɑlədʒəst, B -'trɔl-] *s.* gastrólogo.
gastrology [-dʒɪ] *s.* (med.) gastrología.
gastronome ['gæstrə,noʊm] *s.* gastrónomo.
gastronomic [,gæstrə'nɑmɪk, B -'nɔm-] **gastronomical** [-ɪkəl] *a.* gastronómico.
gastronomically [-ɪkəlɪ] *adv.* gastronómicamente.
gastronomist [gæs'trɑnəməst, B -'trɔn-] *s.* gastrónomo.
gastronomy [-mɪ] *s.* gastronomía.
gastropod ['gæstrə,pɑd, B -,pɔd] *s., a.* (zool.) gasterópodo.
Gastropoda [gæs'trɑpədə, B -'trɔp-] *s. pl.*(zool.) gasterópodos.
gastropodan [-ədən] **gastropodous** [-əs] *a.* (zool.) gasterópodo.
gastroscope ['gæstrə,skoʊp] *s.* (med.) gastroscopio.
gastroscopic [,gæstrə'skɑpɪk, B -'skɔp-] *a.* (med.) gastroscópico.
gastroscopist [gæs'trɑskəpəst, B -'trɔs-] *s.* gastroscopista.
gastroscopy [-pɪ] *s.* (med.) gastroscopia.
gastrostomy [-'trɑstəmɪ, B -'trɔs-] *s.* (med.) gastrostomía.
gastrotomy [-'trɑtəmɪ, B -'trɔt-] *s.* (med.) gastrotomía.
gastrotrichan [-'trɑtrɪkən, B -'trɔ-] *s.* (zool.) gastrotico.
gastrovascular [,gæstoʊ'væskjələr, B -lə] *a.* (zool.) gastrovascular.
gastrula ['gæstrələ] *s.* (*pl.* GASTRULAS O GASTRULAE [-,li]) (embr.) gástrula.
gastrular [-lər, B -lə] *a.* gastrular.
gastrulate [-,leɪt] *v.i.* (embr.) convertirse en una gástrula.
gastrulation [,gæstrə'leɪʃən] *s.* (embr.) gastrulación.
gas turbine, turbina de gas.
gas welding, soldadura autógena.
gasworks ['gæs,wɜrks, B -,wɜks] *s. pl.* (*sing. en const.*) fábrica de gas.
gat [gæt] *s.* 1. canal o pasaje (natural o artificial) entre bancos de arena y acantilados. 2. (jer.) revólver, pistola.
gat, (ant., poét.) *pret. de* **get.**
gate [geɪt] *s.* 1. puerta, entrada, portalón (en un muro, cercado, etc.); portal (de una ciudad). 2. abra, garganta, paso. 3. válvula, compuerta. 4. taquilla, entrada. 5. (f.c.) barrera. 6. (metal.) vaciadero de un molde; conducto de colada. 7. (ant.) camino, vía, trayectoria. 8. (dial.) método, estilo. 9. **the g.,** (jer.) despido, despedida; **to give one the g.,** (jer.) despedir (del empleo); dar calabazas (mujer a su galán). —*v.t.* 1. proveer de puerta. 2. regular por válvula o compuerta. 3. (G.B.) confinar (a un alumno) dentro del colegio o universidad.
gateau [gɑ'toʊ] *s.* (fr.) pastel, bizcocho.
gate-crasher ['geɪt,kræʃər, B -ə] *s.* intruso (uno que entra sin pagar a un espectáculo o sin estar invitado a una reunión); zampón, colado (jer.), gorrero (Amer.).
gatefold [-,foʊld] *s.* lámina doble o múltiple (plegada e insertada en un libro o publicación).
gatehouse [-,haʊs] *s.* (f.c.) caseta de guardabarrera.
gatekeeper [-,kipər, B -pə] **gateman** [-mən] *s.* portero; (f.c.) guardabarrera.
gate-leg table [-,lɛg-] **gate-legged table** [-,lɛgd-] mesa plegable, mesa de alas abatibles.
gate money, taquilla, entradas, ingresos de entradas.
gatepost [-,poʊst] *s.* 1. pilar (de un portalón). 2. **between you and me and the g.,** en secreto, entre nosotros, en confianza.
gate valve, válvula de compuerta.
gateway [-,weɪ] *s.* entrada, puerta, paso; medio de acceso.
gather ['gæðər, B -ə] *v.t.* 1. recoger (flores, etc.); cosechar, recolectar. 2. recaudar (dinero). 3. acumular, reunir (a gente, dinero, etc.); acopiar (provisiones); cobrar (fuerzas, velocidad, etc.); tomar (aliento); concentrar, recoger (pensamientos); recoger, reunir (noticias). 4. ganar, adquirir. 5. juntar, unir (partes de algo). 6. cubrirse con (capa, sábana, etc.). 7. cubrirse de (moho, polvo, etc.). 8. deducir, inferir, colegir. 9. (cost.) fruncir, plegar. 10. **g. head,** cobrar fuerzas o ímpetu; (med.) madurar (un grano); **g. oneself together,** componerse, reanimarse, reponerse, cobrar fuerzas; **g. way,** (mar.) empezar a moverse; **I gather (that),** entiendo (que), tengo entendido (que); **rolling stone gathers no moss,** piedra que rueda no crea moho; agua que pasa no mueve molino. —*v.i.* 1. unirse, reunirse, juntarse, congregarse. 2. aumentarse. 3. amontonarse, acumularse, condensarse. 4. (med.) llenarse de pus. 5. (mar.) avanzar (barco). —*s.* 1. cosecha, colecta. 2. (cost.) pliegue, plegado, frunce.
gatherable [-ərəbəl] *a.* juntable; cosechable; deducible.
gatherer [-ərər, B -ərə] *s.* 1. segador, colector. 2. recaudador, recolector. 3. (cost.) fruncidor.
gathering [-ərɪŋ] *s.* 1. asamblea, reunión, tertulia, agrupación. 2. recolección, acopio, acopiamiento; colecta (de limosnas). 3. (cost.) fruncido, pliegue. 4. (med.) absceso.
GATT, *abrev. de* **General Agreement of Tariffs and Trade,** Acuerdo General sobre Aranceles Aduaneros y Comercio (GATT).
gauche [goʊʃ] *a.* (fr.) torpe, desmañado.
gauchely ['goʊʃlɪ] *adv.* torpemente, desmañadamente.
gaucheness [-nəs] *s.* torpeza.
gaucherie [,goʊʃə'ri, B 'goʊʃəri] *s.* torpeza, ineptitud.
gaucho ['gaʊtʃoʊ] *s.* gaucho, pampero (Amer.).
gaud [gɔd] *s.* charrada, charrería; prenda u objeto llamativo.
gaudery ['gɔdərɪ] *s.* charrerías, oropeles; perifollos.
gaudily [-əlɪ] *adv.* ostentosamente, con muchos adornos.
gaudiness [-ɪnəs] *s.* calidad de lo charro, chillón o llamativo.
gaudy [-ɪ] *a.* (GAUDIER; GAUDIEST) llamativo, charro, chillón; recargado (estilo). —*s.* (G.B.) fiesta, festín, banquete de fin de año (en una universidad).
gauffer, *var. de* **goffer.**
gauge [geɪdʒ] *s.* 1. medida, norma. 2. tamaño, capacidad, extensión. 3. regla de medir, aforador, medida de capacidad. 4. (gen. **gage**) manómetro, marcador, indicador (de presión, nivel, etc.). 5. (arm.) calibre. 6. (metal.) calibre, espesor (de hoja de metal). 7. (tej.) número de hilos (en una unidad). 8. (f.c.) (gen. **gage**) ancho de vía, entrevía, trocha; entrecarril. 9. (carp.) gramil. 10. (mec.) calibrador, cartabón. 11. (hidr.) nivel. 12. (impr.) guía (marginal, lateral, etc.); calibrador (de planchas). 13. (mar.) calado; arqueaje; posición relativa (del barco referente al viento o a otro barco). 14. lee (o **southerly**) **g.,** (mar.) sotavento; **to have the weather g. of,** (mar.) estar a barlovento de; (fig.) tener ventaja sobre; **to take the g. of,** (fig.) estimar, medir; **weather g.,** (mar.) barlovento. —*v.t.* 1. medir. 2. aforar (medir la capacidad de un recipiente). 3. estimar, apreciar, valuar (habilidad, carácter o fuerza). 4. graduar, calibrar. 5. tallar (piedras). 6. mezclar (el yeso) en ciertas proporciones.
gauge cock, llave de prueba, llave de nivel, robinete de prueba, grifo.
gauge glass, tubo indicador, vidrio de nivel.
gauge pin, perno de retención.
gauge pressure, presión manométrica.
gauger, gager ['geɪdʒər, B -ə] *s.* aforador; (pr. G.B.) aforador de aduana.
gauge rod, calibre cilíndrico de diámetros.
gauge stuff, (const.) mortero de cemento con yeso mate.
gauging [-ɪŋ] *s.* 1. aforo, aforamiento; medición. 2. (mar.) arqueaje.
Gaul [gɔl] *s.* 1. (hist.) Galia. 2. galo. 3. francés.
Gaulish ['gɔlɪ] *a.* galo. —*s.* galo, antigua lengua de la Galia.
gault [gɔlt] *s.* terreno arcilloso duro.
gaultheria [gɔl'θɪrɪə, B -'θɪər-] *s.* (bot.) gaultería, pirola.
gaunt [gɔnt] *a.* 1. demacrado, macilento, enjuto; flaco, adelgazado (por ayuno o sufrimiento). 2. desolado, solitario, sombrío.
gauntlet ['gɔntlət, 'gɑnt-, B 'gɔnt-] *s.* (mil., hist.) baqueta; **to run the g.,** pasar por baquetas; (fig.) sufrir desprecio o crítica general.
gauntlet, *s.* 1. guantelete, manopla. 2. guante industrial, guante protector. 3. guante de manopla (que cubre la muñeca). 4. **to fling** (o **throw**) **down the g.,** arrojar el guante; **to pick** (o **take**) **up the g.,** recoger el guante, aceptar el reto o desafío.
gauntlet, (f.c.) *var. de* **gantlet.**
gauntness ['gɔntnəs] *s.* extrema flacura.
gauntry ['gɔntrɪ] *var. de* **gantry.**
gaur [gaʊr, B gaʊə] *s.* (zool.) gaur.
gauss [gaʊs] *s.* (*pl.* GAUSS O GAUSSES) (elec.) gauss (unidad electromagnética).
gauze [gɔz] *s.* 1. gasa, cendal. 2. niebla, bruma.
gauzily ['gɔzəlɪ] *adv.* como gasa; nebulosamente.
gauziness [-zɪnəs] *s.* nebulosidad; diafanidad.
gauzy [-zɪ] *a.* (GAUZIER; GAUZIEST) brumoso, nebuloso; diáfano.
gavage [gə'vɑʒ] *s.* (med.) cebadura.
gave [geɪv] *pret. de* **give.**
gavel ['gævəl] *s.* 1. mazo (de albañil). 2. mallete, mazo, mallo (del presidente de una asamblea, tribunal, etc.); martillo (del subastador o martillero). —*v.t.* (*pret., p.p.* GAVELED O GAVELLED; *p.pr.* GAVELING O GAVELLING) 1. golpear con el mazo. 2. (fig.) abrumar, aplastar (oposición, etc.).
gavel, *s.* (G.B., hist.) gabela medieval.
gavelock ['gævlək, B 'gævə,lɔk] *s.* (dial. G.B.) pie de cabra, alzaprima, barreta.
gavotte [gə'vɑt, B -'vɔt] *s.* (mús.) gavota, antigua danza francesa más ligera que el minué.
gawk [gɔk] *s.* bobo, palurdo. —*v.i.* papar moscas, quedarse boquiabierto; **g. at,** quedarse abstraído mirando como un tonto.
gawkiness ['gɔkɪnəs] *s.* torpeza, desmaña.
gawkish [-kɪʃ] *a.* tonto, desgarbado.
gawky [-kɪ] *a.* (GAWKIER; GAWKIEST) desgarbado, desmañado, torpe.
gawsie, gawsy ['gɔsɪ] *a.* (esco.) próspero y guapo.
gay [geɪ] *a.* (GAYER; GAYEST) 1. gay, homosexual. 2. (ant.) (*cheerful*) alegre; (*color, appearance*) brillante, vistoso; (*life*) lleno de placeres. —*s.* gay, homosexual.

gayety, *var. de* **gaiety.**
Gay Liberation Movement, movimiento dirigido a proteger la homosexualidad.
gayly, *var. de* **gaily.**
gayness ['geɪnəs] *s.* 1. alegría, jovialidad. 2. vistosidad (en el vestir).
gazabo [gə'zeɪboʊ] *s.* (jer.) sujeto, tipo, tío.
gaze [geɪz] *v.i.* fijar la mirada; contemplar; **g. after,** seguir con una mirada fija; **g. at,** mirar fija o intensamente; mirar con curiosidad o asombro. —*s.* mirada fija o penetrante.
gazebo [gə'ziboʊ, -'zeɪ, B -'zi-] *s.* (*pl.* GAZEBOS o GAZEBOES) balcón, mirador, torre.
gazehound ['geɪzˌhaʊnd] *s.* perro que sigue la presa con la vista y no con el olfato, esp. galgo.
gazelle [gə'zɛl] *s.* (zool.) gacela.
gazette [-'zɛt] *s.* 1. gaceta, periódico oficial. 2. periódico. 3. (G.B.) comunicado oficial (en la gaceta). —*v.t.* (pr. G.B.) anunciar o publicar en la gaceta.
gazetteer [ˌgæzə'tɪr, B -'tɪə] *s.* 1. diccionario geográfico. 2. (ant.) gacetero.
gazogene ['gæzəˌdʒin] *var. de* **gasogene.**
G.B. *abrev. de* **Great Britain,** Gran Bretaña.
G.B.E. *abrev. de* **Knight** o **Dame of Grand Cross of The British Empire,** Caballero o Dama de la Gran Cruz del Imperio Británico.
GCA *abrev. de* **ground control approach,** aproximación controlada desde tierra.
G.C.D. *abrev. de* **greatest common divisor,** máximo común divisor.
G.C.F. *abrev. de* **greatest common factor,** máximo factor común.
g clef, (mús.) clave de sol.
GCT *abrev. de* **Greenwich civil time,** hora de Greenwich.
Gd *símb. de* **gadolinium,** gadolinio (Gd).
Ge *símb. de* **germanium,** germanio (Ge).
gean [gin] *s.* (especie de) cerezo dulce.
geanticline [dʒi'æntɪˌklaɪn] *s.* (geol.) gran arruga elevada de la corteza terrestre.
gear [gɪr, B gɪə] *s.* 1. vestidos, prendas. 2. equipo, pertrechos; utensilios, instrumentos. 3. aparejos de tiro; arneses (de caballos). 4. bienes móviles, utensilios caseros. 5. (mec.) aparato, mecanismo (de transmisión, de gobierno, etc.); rueda dentada; engranaje, tren de engranajes. 6. (mot., aut.) velocidad, marcha, ej., *in second g.,* en segunda velocidad, *in low g.,* en primera velocidad. 7. (mar.) aparejo. 8. (ant.) bienes, caudal, riqueza. 9. **in g.,** engranado; **out of g.,** desengranado; descompuesto, que funciona mal; **to change g.,** cambiar de velocidad; **to put in g.,** engranar; poner en marcha; **to throw out of g.,** desengranar. —*v.t.* 1. vestir, pertrechar, equipar, armar. 2. alistar, preparar. 3. aparejar, enjaezar. 4. (mec.) engranar, encajar, embragar. 5. **g. to,** ajustar a, amoldar a, adaptar a. —*v.i.* engranarse, funcionar (los engranajes).
gearbox ['gɪrˌbɑks, B 'gɪəˌbɔks] *s.* caja de engranajes, cárter de engranajes; (aut.) caja de velocidades, caja de cambios.
gear cutter, cortadora de engranajes, fresa para engranajes.
gear differential, (aut.) piñón diferencial.
gearing ['gɪrɪŋ, B 'gɪər-] *s.* (mec.) engranaje, tren de engranajes; mecanismo.
gearless ['gɪrləs, B 'gɪələs] *a.* sin engranaje.
gear pitch, (mec.) paso de engranaje.
gear rack, cremallera.
gear ratio, (aut.) coeficiente de reducción; relación de multiplicación.
gearshift [-ˌʃɪft] *s.* cambio de velocidades; aparato de cambios.
gearshift lever, (aut.) palanca de cambio.
gear wheel, (mec.) rueda dentada, rueda de engranaje.
gecko ['gɛkoʊ] *s.* (*pl.* GECKOS o GECKOES) (zool.) geco, salamanquesa.
gee [dʒi] *interj.* 1. (E.U.) ¡caramba! ¡cáspita! (expresión de sorpresa, descubrimiento, etc.); (eufem.) ¡Jesús! 2. (G.B.) ¡arre! ¡vamos! (voz de mando para un animal de tiro); g. up! ¡arre!
geegaw ['dʒiˌgɔ] *var. de* **gewgaw.**
geek [gik] *s.* (jer.) individuo de acciones grotescas y desalmadas.
geese [gis] *pl. de* **goose.**
gee whiz [-wɪz] *interj.* ¡corcholís! ¡recorcholís!
geezer ['gizər, B -zə] *s.* (jer.) viejo chiflado o excéntrico; tipo, tío.
gefilte fish [gə'fɪltə-] (cocina) **pescado** relleno.
Gehenna [gɪ'hɛnə] *s.* (bíbl.) **gehena,** infierno.
Geiger counter ['gaɪgər-, B -gə-] (fís.) contador de Geiger (para detectar partículas radioactivas).
Geiger tube, (fís.) tubo de Geiger.
geisha ['geɪʃə, 'gi-, B 'geɪ-] *s.* (*pl.* GEISHA o GEISHAS) geisha (muchacha japonesa entrenada en música y conversación para entretener a los hombres).
Geissler tube ['gaɪslər-, B -lə-] (fís.) tubo de Geissler.
geist [geɪst] *s.* espíritu; mente.
gel [dʒɛl] *s.* (quím.) gel. —*v.i.* (*pret., p.p.* GELLED; *p.pr.* GELLING) cuajarse (en forma de gel).
gelable ['dʒɛləbəl] *a.* (quím.) cuajable.
gelatin ['dʒɛlətən] *s.* gelatina, jaletina.
gelatinate [dʒə'lætəˌneɪt] *v.t., v.i.* convertir(se) en substancia gelatinosa.
gelatine ['dʒɛlətən, B ˌdʒɛlə'tin] *var. de* **gelatin.**
gelatinization [dʒəˌlætənə'zeɪʃən, B -naɪ-] *s.* gelatinización.
gelatinize [-'lætənˌaɪz] *v.t.* 1. convertir en gelatina o jalea. 2. (foto.) cubrir o tratar con gelatina. —*v.i.* convertirse en gelatina.
gelatinous [-əs] *a.* gelatinoso, viscoso.
gelation [-'leɪʃən] *s.* (quím.) gelación, congelación; el proceso de formación de un gel.
geld [gɛld] *v.t.* (*pret., p.p.* GELDED o GELT [gɛlt]; *p.pr.* GELDING) 1. castrar, capar. 2. privar, despojar (de algo esencial o vital). 3. aminorar, disminuir, mermar la fuerza de. —*s.* (hist.) impuesto pagado por los agricultores ingleses bajo los reyes anglosajones y normandos.
gelder ['gɛldər, B -də] *s.* castrador, capador.
gelding [-dɪŋ] *s.* 1. caballo castrado; animal castrado. 2. (ant.) eunuco, capón, espadón. 3. castración, capadura.
gelid ['dʒɛləd] *a.* gélido, helado, muy frío.
gelidity [dʒə'lɪdətɪ] *s.* frío extremo.
gelidly ['dʒɛlədlɪ] *adv.* fríamente, heladamente.
gelidness [-nəs] *s.* extrema frigidez.
gelignite ['dʒɛlɪgˌnaɪt] *s.* gelignita (explosivo).
gelsemium [dʒɛl'simɪəm] *s.* 1. (bot.) gelsemio, gelsemina. 2. gelsemina (alcaloide extraído de la raíz del gelsemio).
gelt [gɛlt] *pret., p.p. de* **geld.**
gelt [gɛlt] *s.* (jer.) dinero, plata, mosca, guita.
gem [dʒɛm] *s.* 1. gema, piedra preciosa. 2. (fig.) joya, preciosidad, tesoro (persona, cosa u obra). 3. bizcocho de harina gruesa. 4. (impr.) tipo antiguo de letra. —*v.t.* (*pret., p.p.* GEMMED; *p.pr.* GEMMING) adornar con piedras preciosas.
geminate ['dʒɛmənət, B -ˌneɪt] *a.* (bot.) geminado. — [-ˌneɪt] *v.t., v.i.* 1. duplicar, repetir. 2. (bot.) geminar.
geminated ['dʒɛməˌneɪtəd] *a.* (gram.) doble consonante.
gemination [ˌdʒɛmə'neɪʃən] *s.* 1. duplicación, repetición. 2. (odont.) geminación. 3. (gram.) geminación, duplicación (de una consonante).
Gemini ['dʒɛməˌni, -ˌnaɪ] *s.* (astr., astrol.) Géminis, Gemelos.
gemma ['dʒɛmə] *s.* (*pl.* GEMMAE [-ˌi]) (bot.) gema, yema.
gemmaceous [dʒɛ'meɪʃəs] *a.* (bot.) gemáceo.
gemmate ['dʒɛmˌeɪt] *a.* (bot.) 1. gemífero. 2. gemíparo. —*v.i.* producir gemas; reproducirse por gemas.
gemmation [dʒɛ'meɪʃən] *s.* (bot.) gemación.
gemmiferous [dʒɛ'mɪfərəs] *a.* (bot.) gemífero.
gemmiparous [-'mɪpərəs] *a.* (bot.) gemíparo.
gemmology, *var. de* **gemology.**
gemmulation [ˌdʒɛmjə'leɪʃən] *s.* (bot.) gemulación.
gemmule ['dʒɛmjul] *s.* (bot., zool.) gémula.
gemmy ['dʒɛmɪ] *a.* 1. duro y brillante (cristal, etc.). 2. (fig.) reluciente, resplandeciente.
gemology [dʒɛ'mɑlədʒɪ, B -'mɔl-] *s.* (bot.) estudio de las gemas.
gemsbok ['gɛmzˌbɑk, B -ˌbɔk] *s.* (zool.) variedad de órix, antílope sudafricano de cuernos largos y derechos.
gemstone ['dʒɛmˌstoʊn] *s.* piedra preciosa.
gemütlich [gə'mutlɪk] *a.* (alemán) amistoso, congeniable; cómodo, acogedor.
Gen. *abrev. de* 1. **General,** General (Gral.) 2. **Genesis,** el Génesis (Gén.).
gendarme ['ʒɑnˌdɑrm, B -dɑm] *s.* (fr.) gendarme.
gendarmery, gendarmerie [ʒɑn'dɑrmərɪ, B -'dɑm-] *s.* gendarmería.
gender ['dʒɛndər, B -də] *s.* 1. (gram.) género (masculino, femenino o neutro). 2. (fam.) sexo. 3. (ant.) clase, especie.
gender, *v.t., v.i.* engendrar(se), producir(se).
gene [dʒin] *s.* (biol.) gen.
genealogical [ˌdʒinɪə'lɑdʒɪkəl, ˌdʒɛn-, B -'lɔdʒ-] *a.* genealógico.
genealogically [-kəlɪ] *adv.* genealógicamente.
genealogical tree, árbol genealógico.
genealogist [ˌdʒinɪ'ɑlədʒəst, ˌdʒɛnɪ-, B -'æl-] *s.* genealogista.
genealogy [-dʒɪ] *s.* (*pl.* GENEALOGIES) genealogía.
gene mutation, (biol.) mutación de genes.
genera, *pl. de* **genus.**
generable ['dʒɛnərəbəl] *a.* generable.
general ['dʒɛnərəl] *a.* 1. general, total. 2. general, común. 3. general, usual, corriente. 4. vago (semejanza, idea, etc.). 5. **as a g. rule,** por regla general; **in a g. way,** de manera o de modo general; **in g.,** generalmente, en general, por lo general; **in g. terms,** en términos generales; **in the g. run of things,** comúnmente, generalmente; **the g. run of (people, persons,** etc.), la generalidad de (la gente, personas, etc.), la generalidad de (la gente, personas, etc.). —*s.* 1. (mil.) general. 2. (relig.) general, jefe de la orden. 3. (ant.) gente, público.
general anesthetic, (med.) anestesia general.
general assembly, 1. (E.U.) asamblea legislativa (de un estado). 2. (relig.) presbiterio, asamblea directiva (de los presbiterianos). 3. **G.A.,** Asamblea General (de las Naciones Unidas).
general average, (seguros) avería gruesa.
General Court, (E.U.) asamblea legislativa.
generalcy ['dʒɛnərəlsɪ] *s.* (mil.) generalato.
general delivery, lista de correos.
generalissimo [ˌdʒɛnərə'lɪsəˌmoʊ] *s.* (*pl.* GENERALISSIMOS) (mil.) generalísimo, comandante en jefe.
generalist ['dʒɛnərələst] *s.* hombre de aptitudes y conocimientos variados.
generality [ˌdʒɛnə'rælətɪ] *s.* (*pl.* GENERALITIES) 1. carácter general. 2. generalidad, vaguedad. 3. generalidad, mayoría, mayor parte.

generalization [ˌdʒɛnərələ'zeɪʃən, B -laɪ-] *s.* generalización.

generalize ['dʒɛnərəˌlaɪz] *v.t.* 1. generalizar. 2. (der., filos., mat.) generalizar, aplicar extensamente. —*v.i.* hablar en general.

generalized [-ˌlaɪzd] *a.* generalizado, indiferenciado.

generalizer [-ˌlaɪzər, B -ə] *s.* generalizador, generalizadora.

generally [-lɪ] *adv.* 1. generalmente. 2. en forma general, ej., *g. speaking,* hablando en forma general.

general meeting, junta general (de accionistas, etc.).

general officer, (mil., E.U.) oficial general (con un rango superior al de coronel).

general of the army, (mil., E.U.) general del ejército.

general paralysis, g. paresis, (med.) parálisis general, demencia paralítica, paresia, paresis.

general practitioner, médico general, internista.

general-purpose ['dʒɛnərəl'pɜrpəs, B -'pɜpəs] *a.* de uso general, de utilidad variada.

general reader, lector no especializado.

general relativity, (fís.) teoría de la relatividad (de Alberto Einstein).

general semantics, (psic.) doctrina (de Alfredo Korzubski) destinada a mejorar la conducta humana a través del empleo adecuado de signos y terminología.

general sessions, (E.U., der.) corte de jurisdicción general para causas criminales.

generalship [-ˌʃɪp] *s.* 1. generalato. 2. don de mando, dirección.

general staff, (mil.) estado mayor, plana mayor.

general store, tienda de artículos diversos, tienda de abarrotes (Amer.).

general strike, huelga general.

generate ['dʒɛnəˌreɪt] *v.t.* 1. engendrar, generar, procrear. 2. (fig.) engendrar, causar, ocasionar, producir. 3. (mat.) engendrar, generar. 4. (elec.) generar.

generating station [-ɪŋ-] (elec.) central generadora, planta generadora.

generation [ˌdʒɛnə'reɪʃən] *s.* 1. generación. 2. (mat., quím., mec.) generación, producción. 3. (elec.) generación. 4. (geom.) engendramiento. 5. progenitura; raza.

generation gap, barrera generacional, brecha generacional.

generative ['dʒɛnəˌreɪtɪv, -ərətɪv] *a.* generativo, genetivo; fecundo.

generative cell, (biol.) célula reproductora.

generator [-ər, B -ə] *s.* 1. procreador, engendrador. 2. (mec., elec.) generador, dínamo. 3. (geom.) (línea o figura) generatriz.

generator unit, generador con máquina impulsora.

generatrix [ˌdʒɛnə'reɪtrɪks, B 'dʒɛnəˌreɪ-] *s.* (*pl.* GENERATRICES [-ərə'traɪsiz, B -ˌreɪtrɪsiz]) 1. generatriz, procreadora, madre. 2. (geom.) generatriz.

generic [dʒə'nɛrɪk] **generical** [-ɪkəl] *a.* 1. genérico, general. 2. (biol.) genérico.

generically [-ɪkəlɪ] *adv.* genéricamente.

generosity [ˌdʒɛnə'rɑsətɪ, B -'rɔs-] *s.* 1. generosidad, largueza. 2. acto generoso.

generous ['dʒɛnərəs] 1. generoso, munífico, magnánimo. 2. abundante, amplio. 3. generoso (vino). 4. rico (régimen, dieta). 5. fértil (terreno). 6. (ant.) noble (de nacimiento).

generously [-lɪ] *adv.* generosamente, magnánimamente.

generousness [-nəs] *s.* generosidad, magnanimidad.

genesic [dʒə'nɛsɪk] *a.* genésico.

genesis ['dʒɛnəsəs] *s.* (*pl.* GENESIS [-ˌsiz]) 1. génesis, origen. 2. **G.,** (bíbl.) Génesis (primer libro del Pentateuco).

genet ['dʒɛnət] *s.* (zool.) jineta, ganeta, papialbillo, patialbillo.

genethliac [dʒɪ'nɛθlɪæk] **genethliacal** [ˌdʒɛnəθ'laɪəkəl] *a.* (astrol.) genetlíaco.

genethlialogical [-ˌnɛθlɪə'lɑdʒɪkəl, B -'lɔdʒ-] *a.* (astrol.) genetlíaco.

genethlialogy [ˌdʒɛnəθlɪ'ɑlədʒɪ, B -'æl-] *s.* (astrol.) genetlíaca.

genetic [dʒə'nɛtɪk] **genetical** [-ɪkəl] *a.* 1. (biol.) genético, genesíaco. 2. (bíbl.) genético.

genetically [-ɪkəlɪ] *adv.* genéticamente.

genetic code, código genético.

genetic engineering, ingeniería genética.

genetic fingerprint, huella genética.

genetic fingerprinting, identificación genética.

geneticist [dʒə'nɛtəsɪst] *s.* genetista, geneticista, especialista en genética.

genetics [-ɪks] *s.* (biol.) genética.

Geneva [dʒə'nivə] *s.* Ginebra, ciudad de Suiza.

Geneva cross, Cruz Roja.

Genevan [-vən] *s.* 1. ginebrino, ginebrés, natural de Ginebra. 2. calvinista. —*a.* ginebrino, ginebrés.

Genevese [ˌdʒɛnə'viz] *var. de* **Genevan.**

genial ['dʒinjəl] *a.* 1. afable, jovial, cordial. 2. suave, templado (clima, aire, etc.). 3. (raro) genial; ingenioso, brillante. 4. (ant.) nupcial, generativo; nativo, innato.

genial [dʒɪ'naɪəl] *a.* (anat., zool.) geniano.

geniality [ˌdʒinɪ'ælətɪ] *s.* afabilidad, complacencia, cordialidad.

genially ['dʒinjəlɪ] *adv.* afablemente, jovialmente.

genialness [-njəlnəs] *s.* 1. afabilidad, jovialidad. 2. suavidad, templanza (del clima, aire, etc.). 3. (raro) ingeniosidad.

genic ['dʒɛnɪk] *a.* (biol.) genético, genesíaco.

geniculate [dʒə'nɪkjələt] *a.* (bot., zool.) geniculado.

genie ['dʒinɪ] *s.* (*pl.* GENIES O GENII [-ˌaɪ]) genio (espíritu fantástico, esp. en el folklore árabe y mahometano).

genii, *pl. de* **genius, genie.**

genip [gə'nɪp, B 'dʒɛnɪp] *s.* (bot.) mamón.

genipap ['dʒɛnəˌpæp] *s.* (bot.) genipa, jagua.

genista [dʒɛ'nɪstə] *s.* (bot.) genista, retama.

genital ['dʒɛnətəl] *a.* genital; relativo a la reproducción.

genitalia [ˌdʒɛnə'teɪlɪə] **genitals** ['dʒɛnətəlz] *s.pl.* genitales, órganos externos de la reproducción.

genitival [ˌdʒɛnə'taɪvəl] *a.* (gram.) del genitivo.

genitive ['dʒɛnətɪv] *s.* (gram.) genitivo. —*a.* (gram.) de genitivo, en caso genitivo.

genitor ['dʒɛnətər, B -ə] *s.* genitor.

genitourinary [ˌdʒɛnətoʊ'jʊrəˌnɛrɪ, B -ənərɪ] *a.* (anat.) genitourinario.

genius ['dʒinjəs, 'dʒinɪəs] *s.* (*pl.* GENIUSES) 1. genio, don, talento, ingenio. 2. genio, lumbrera (persona). 3. espíritu, naturaleza, carácter (de una época, nación, pueblo). 4. (*pl.* GENII [-nɪˌaɪ]) (relig.) espíritu o deidad tutelar. 5. genio, espíritu de la naturaleza (esp. del fuego o del aire).

genocidal [ˌdʒɛnə'saɪdəl, B ˌdʒɛnoʊ-] *a.* de genocidio.

genocide ['dʒɛnəˌsaɪd] *s.* genocidio.

Genoese [ˌdʒɛnə'wiz, B -noʊ'iz] *a.* genovés. —*s.* (*pl.* GENOESE) genovés, natural de Génova, Italia.

genom ['dʒiˌnɑm, B -ˌnɔm] **genome** [-noʊm] *s.* (biol.) genoma.

genotype ['dʒinəˌtaɪp, B 'dʒɛnoʊ-] *s.* (biol.) genotipo.

Genovese [ˌdʒɛnə'viz, B -noʊ-] *a., s. var. de* **Genoese.**

genre ['ʒɑnrə, B 'ʒɑŋ-] *s.* 1. género, especie, clase, estilo, categoría. 2. pintura de género.

genre painter, pintor de género, especialista en un estilo determinado.

genro ['gɛn'roʊ] *s. pl.* genro (conjunto de sabios que asistían al Micado en Japón).

gens [dʒɛnz] *s.* (*pl.* GENTES ['dʒɛnˌtiz]) (hist. romana) gens (grupo de familias descendientes de un antecesor masculino común).

gent [dʒɛnt] *s.* (jer.) tipo, sujeto, tío, individuo, hombre; **the gents,** (jer.), retrete público para hombres. —*a.* (ant.) gracioso, agraciado, airoso.

genteel [dʒɛn'til] *a.* 1. urbano, cortés. 2. gracioso, agraciado, gallardo, airoso. 3. afectado, remilgado. 4. decoroso, discreto (pobreza, miseria, etc.). 5. bien nacido. 6. a la moda, elegante.

genteelly [-'tillɪ] *adv.* cortésmente, gentilmente.

genteelness [-nəs] *s.* 1. gentileza, gallardía, garbo; urbanidad, cortesía. 2. decoro.

gentian ['dʒɛntʃən, B 'dʒɛnʃɪən] *s.* (bot.) 1. genciana. 2. (t. **g. root**) raíz de genciana.

gentianaceous [ˌdʒɛntʃɪə'neɪʃəs, B ˌdʒɛnʃɪə-] *a.* (bot.) gencianáceo, gencianeo.

gentianella [-'nɛlə] *s.* (bot.) genciana acaule, gran genciana.

gentian violet, (tintura de) violeta de genciana.

gentile ['dʒɛnˌtaɪl] *s.* 1. (t. **G.**) cristiano, persona no judía, gentil (entre los judíos). 2. gentil, idólatra, pagano. 3. (t. **G.**) persona no mormona (entre los mormones). —*a.* 1. (t. **G.**) cristiano, no judío. 2. gentil, gentílico, pagano. 3. (gram.) gentilicio, étnico (adjetivo, nombre).

gentilesse [ˌdʒɛntəl'ɛs] *s.* (fr.) refinamiento, cultura, buena educación.

gentilism ['dʒɛnˌtaɪlˌɪzəm, B -tɪl-] *s.* (ant.) gentilismo, gentilidad, paganismo, idolatría.

gentility [dʒɛn'tɪlətɪ] *s.* 1. nobleza. 2. gentileza, cortesía, buenas maneras. 3. dignidad, decoro. 4. afectación, remilgo.

gentisic acid [dʒɛn'tɪsɪk-] (quím.) ácido gentísico.

gentle ['dʒɛntəl] *a.* 1. suave, tierno, dulce. 2. manso, dócil. 3. cortés, fino, comedido. 4. benévolo, benigno, bondadoso. 5. moderado; gradual. 6. suave, apacible. 7. bien nacido, noble, aristocrático. 8. honorable (por nacimiento, dignidad, posición, etc.). 9. (ant.) caballeroso. 10. **the g. craft,** deporte de la pesca; **the g. sex,** el sexo débil, el bello sexo. —*s.* (ant.) persona bien nacida, caballero. —*v.t.* 1. apaciguar, amansar. 2. moderar, suavizar. 3. enternecer, ablandar. 4. (ant.) ennoblecer.

gentle breeze, (meteor.) viento flojo (de 13 a 19 kilómetros por hora).

gentlefolk [-ˌfoʊk] **gentlefolks** [-ˌfoʊks] *s. pl.* gente bien nacida.

gentleman ['dʒɛntəlmən] *s.* (*pl.* GENTLEMEN [-mən]) 1. caballero, señor; hombre decente o bien nacido. 2. (*pl.*) caballeros, señores; (*en el encabezamiento de cartas*) muy señores míos, muy señores nuestros. 3. (hist.) gentilhombre (persona autorizada para llevar armas sin pertenecer a la nobleza). 4. sirviente (esp. camarero o paje). 5. **g. at large,** hombre de fortuna y posición social.

gentleman-at-arms [-ət'ɑrmz, B -'ɑmz] *s.* (*pl.* GENTLEMEN-AT-ARMS) caballero, miembro de la comitiva de un monarca.

gentleman in waiting, (G.B.) gentilhombre de cámara.

gentlemanlike [-ˌlaɪk] *a.* caballeroso, cortés, de buenos modales.

gentlemanliness [-lɪnəs] *s.* caballerosidad, hidalguía.
gentlemanly [-lɪ] *a.* caballeroso, propio de un caballero (naturaleza, conducta, maneras, etc.).
gentleman of fortune, caballero de industria, aventurero.
gentleman of the road, salteador de caminos, bandolero, atracador.
gentleman's agreement, gentlemen's agreement, pacto de caballeros (sin fuerza legal pero que obliga moralmente).
gentleman's gentleman, criado, camarero, paje, ayuda de cámara.
gentleness ['dʒɛntəlnəs] *s.* bondad, benignidad; apacibilidad, docilidad, mansedumbre; suavidad, dulzura, delicadeza.
gentle sex, el sexo débil.
gentlewoman [-ˌwʊmən] *s.* (*pl.* GENTLEWOMEN [-ˌwɪmən]) 1. señora, dama, mujer bien nacida. 2. (hist.) dama de honor o de compañía.
gently ['dʒɛntlɪ] *adv.* 1. suavemente, dulcemente. 2. mansamente, poco a poco, despacio. 3. con cariño, bondadosamente, cariñosamente.
gentrification ['dʒɛntrəfə'keɪʃən] *s.* aburguesamiento.
gentrify ['dʒɛntrəfaɪ] *v.t.* aburguesar.
gentry ['dʒɛntrɪ] *s.* 1. gente bien nacida, nobleza; gente bien educada; (G.B.) alta burguesía, clase media o acomodada. 2. (ant.) cortesía, generosidad, buena educación. 3. **landed g.,** la aristocracia provinciana.
genuflect ['dʒɛnjəˌflɛkt] *v.i.* hacer una genuflexión, doblar la rodilla (esp. en señal de reverencia).
genuflection, genuflexion [ˌdʒɛnjə'flɛkʃən] *s.* genuflexión.
genuine ['dʒɛnjʊən] *a.* 1. genuino, legítimo, auténtico, original. 2. verdadero, franco, sincero.
genuinely [-lɪ] *adv.* 1. legítimamente, auténticamente, genuinamente. 2. verdaderamente, sinceramente.
genuineness [-nəs] *s.* legitimidad, autenticidad.
genus ['dʒinəs] *s.* (*pl.* GENERA ['dʒɛnərə]) 1. (lóg., biol.) género. 2. género, especie, clase, categoría, orden, tipo.
geocentric [ˌdʒioʊ'sɛntrɪk] **geocentrical** [-trɪkəl] *a.* geocéntrico.
geochemical [-'kɛmɪkəl] *a.* geoquímico.
geochemistry [-əstrɪ] *s.* geoquímica.
geochronologic [-ˌkrɑnə'lɑdʒɪk, B -ˌkrɔnə'lɔdʒ-] **geochronological** [-ɪkəl] *a.* (geol.) geocronológico.
geochronology [-krə'nɑlədʒɪ, B -'nɔl-] *s.* (geol.) geocronología.
geochronometric [-ˌkrɑnə'mɛtrɪk, B -ˌkrɔn-] *a.* (geol.) geocronométrico.
geochronometry [-krə'nɑmətrɪ, B -'nɔm-] *s.* (geol.) geocronometría.
geode ['dʒiˌoʊd] *s.* (geol.) geoda.
geodesic [ˌdʒiə'dɛsɪk] *a.* (geol.) geodésico. —*s.* (geom.) geodésica.
geodesist [dʒɪ'ɑdəsəst, B -'ɔd-] *s.* (geol.) geodesta.
geodesy [-sɪ] *s.* (geol.) geodesia, ciencia geológica que estudia la forma y el tamaño de la Tierra.
geodetic [ˌdʒiə'dɛtɪk] **geodetical** [-ɪkəl] *a.* (geol.) geodésico.
geodynamic [-oʊdaɪ'næmɪk] **geodynamical** [-ɪkəl] *a.* (geol.) geodinámico.
geodynamics [-ɪks] *s. pl.* (*sing. en const.*) (geol.) geodinámica.
geognost ['dʒiˌɑgˌnɑst, B dʒi'ɔgnɔst] *s.* (geol.) geognosta.
geognostical [ˌdʒiɑg'nɑstɪkəl, B -ɔg'nɔs-] *a.* (geol.) geognóstico.
geognosy [dʒɪ'ɑgnəsɪ, B -'ɔg-] *s.* (geol.) geognosia, ciencia que estudia la estructura y composición de la Tierra.
geogonic [ˌdʒiə'gɑnɪk, B -'gɔ-] **geogonical** [-nɪkəl] *a.* (geol.) geogénico, geogónico.
geographer [dʒɪ'ɑgrəfər, B -'ɔgrəfə] *s.* geógrafo.
geographic [ˌdʒiə'græfɪk] **geographical** [-ɪkəl] *a.* geográfico.
geographical latitude, latitud geográfica o topográfica.
geographically [-ɪkəlɪ] *adv.* geográficamente.
geographical mile, milla marítima o geográfica.
geography [dʒɪ'ɑgrəfɪ, B -'ɔg-] *s.* geografía.
geoid ['dʒiˌɔɪd] *s.* geoide, la tierra considerada como sólido geométrico.
geol. *abrev. de* **geology,** geología.
geologic [ˌdʒiə'lɑdʒɪk, B -'lɔdʒ-] **geological** [-ɪkəl] *a.* geológico.
geologically [-ɪkəlɪ] *adv.* geológicamente.
geologist [dʒɪ'ɑlədʒəst, B -'ɔl-] *s.* geólogo.
geologize [-ˌdʒaɪz] *v.i.* estudiar la geología; hacer investigaciones geológicas; disertar sobre geología.
geology [-dʒɪ] *s.* 1. geología. 2. tratado de geología.
geom. *abrev. de* **geometry,** geometría.
geomagnetic [ˌdʒioʊmæg'nɛtɪk] *a.* geomagnético.
geomagnetism [-'mægnəˌtɪzəm] *s.* geomagnetismo.
geomancer ['dʒiəˌmænsər, B -sə] *s.* geomántico, adivinador.
geomancy [-sɪ] *s.* geomancia, geomancía, adivinación por medio de diseños geométricos.
geomantic [ˌdʒiə'mæntɪk] *a.* geomántico.
geometer [dʒɪ'ɑmətər, B -'ɔmətə] *s.* geómetra.
geometric [ˌdʒiə'mɛtrɪk] **geometrical** [-trɪkəl] *a.* geométrico.
geometrical horizon, (astr.) horizonte racional.
geometrically [-trɪkəlɪ] *adv.* geométricamente.
geometrician [dʒɪˌɑmə'trɪʃən, ˌdʒiəmə-, B ˌdʒiə-] *s.* geómetra.
geometric mean, media proporcional, media geométrica.
geometric progression, progresión geométrica, progresión por cociente.
geometric ratio, razón geométrica.
geometrid [dʒɪ'ɑmətrəd, B -'ɔm-] *s., a.* (ento.) geométrido.
geometrize [-ˌtraɪz] *v.i.* (raro) hacer deducciones mediante construcciones geométricas; obrar de acuerdo a los principios geométricos. —*v.t.* 1. representar geométricamente. 2. aplicar reglas geométricas a.
geometry [-trɪ] *s.* geometría; configuración geométrica de un objeto.
geomorphic [ˌdʒiə'mɔrfɪk, B -'mɔfɪk] *a.* (geol.) de (la) geomorfía, geomórfico.
geomorphologic [-ˌmɔrfə'lɑdʒɪk, B -ˌmɔfə-'lɔdʒ-] **geomorphological** [-ɪkəl] *a.* (geol.) geomorfológico.
geomorphology [-mɔr'fɑlədʒɪ, B -mɔ'fɔl-] *s.* (geol.) geomorfología, estudio de la evolución de la configuración física de la Tierra.
geophagism [dʒɪ'ɑfəˌdʒɪzəm, B -'ɔf-] *s.* geofagia, alimentación a base de elementos como la arcilla o la tierra.
geophagist [-dʒəst] *s.* geófago, el que come tierra o barro.
geophagy [-dʒɪ] *s.* geofagia.
geophysical [ˌdʒiə'fɪzɪkəl, B 'dʒi-] *a.* (geol.) geofísico.
geophysicist [-əsəst] *s.* (geol.) geofísico (el científico).
geophysics [-ɪks] *s.* (*sing. en constr.*) (geol.) geofísica, estudio físico de la Tierra.
geophyte ['dʒiəˌfaɪt] *s.* (bot.) geófito.
geopolitical [ˌdʒioʊpə'lɪtɪkəl] **geopolitic** [-'pɑləˌtɪk, B -'pɔl-] *a.* geopolítico.
geopolitically [-kəlɪ] *adv.* según la geopolítica.
geopolitician [-ˌpɑlə'tɪʃən, B -ˌpɔl-] *s.* experto o especialista en geopolítica.
geopolitics [-'pɑləˌtɪks, B -'pɔl-] *s. pl.* (*sing. en const.*) 1. geopolítica, estudio de las relaciones entre la geografía y la política. 2. doctrina expansionista de los nazis.
geoponic [-'pɑnɪk, B -'pɔn-] *a.* 1. geopónico, de la agricultura. 2. rural, bucólico.
geoponics [-ɪks] *s. pl.* (*sing. en const.*) geoponía, agricultura.
georgette [dʒɔr'dʒɛt, B dʒɔ'-] *s.* (tej.) crespón de seda diáfano.
Georgia ['dʒɔrdʒə, B 'dʒɔdʒjə] *s.* Georgia, estado del sur de los E.U.; Georgia, república soviética.
Georgian ['dʒɔrdʒən, B 'dʒɔdʒən] *s., a.* georgiano, perteneciente al estado de Georgia (E.U.) y a la república soviética de Georgia.
georgic [-dʒɪk] *a.* geórgico, rural, bucólico. —*s.* (poét.) geórgica.
geostatic [ˌdʒioʊ'stætɪk] *a.* geostático.
geostrophic [-'strɑfɪk, B -'strɔf-] *a.* (meteor.) geostrófico.
geosyncline [-'sɪnˌklaɪn] *a.* (geol.) geosinclinal.
geotaxis [-'tæksəs] *s.* (biol.) geotaxis, geotaxismo.
geotectonic [-ˌtɛk'tɑnɪk, B -'tɔn-] *a.* (geol.) geotectónico.
geothermal [-'θɜrməl, B -'θɜməl] **geothermic** [-mɪk] *a.* (geol.) geotérmico.
geotropic [ˌdʒiə'trɑpɪk, B -'trɔp-] *a.* (biol.) geotrópico.
geotropism [dʒɪ'ɑtrəˌpɪzəm, B -'ɔtrə-] *s.* (bot.) geotropismo.
geraniaceous [dʒəˌreɪnɪ'eɪʃəs] *a.* (bot.) geraniácco.
geraniol [-'reɪnɪˌɔl, -ˌoʊl, B -ˌɔl] *s.* (quím.) geraniol, rodonil.
geranium [-'reɪnɪəm, -njəm] *s.* (bot.) geranio, pico de cigüeña.
gerbil, gerbille ['dʒɜrbəl, B 'dʒɜbɪl] *s.* (zool.) gerbo, jerbo.
gerfalcon ['dʒɜrˌfælkən, -ˌfɔl-, B 'dʒɜˌfɔl-, -ˌfɔkən] *s.* (orn.) gerifalte, gerifalco.
geriatrician [ˌdʒɛrɪə'trɪʃən] *s.* (med.) geriatra.
geriatrics [-'ætrɪks] *s. pl.* (*sing. en const.*) (med.) geriatría, estudio de las dolencias de la vejez.
germ [dʒɜrm, B dʒɜm] *s.* 1. (bact., biol., bot.) germen. 2. (fig.) germen, origen.
German ['dʒɜrmən, B 'dʒɜmən] *s.* 1. alemán, germano. 2. idioma alemán. 3. cotillón; fiesta donde se baila el cotillón. —*a.* 1. alemán, germánico (país, pueblo o idioma). 2. **g.,** carnal, ej., *brother-g.,* hermano carnal, *cousin-g.,* primo carnal.
germander [dʒər'mændər, B dʒɜ'-də] *s.* (bot.) camedrio, germandría.
germane [-'meɪn] *a.* (ú. con *to*) pertinente, aplicable, relativo (a).
Germanic [-'mænɪk] *a.* germánico, alemán. —*s.* germánico (apl. a un grupo de las lenguas indoeuropeas).
Germanism ['dʒɜrməˌnɪzəm, B 'dʒɜmə-] *s.* 1. germanismo (idioma). 2. hábito o costumbre de Alemania. 3. admiración por Alemania o lo alemán.
Germanist [-nəst] *s.* germanista.
germanium [dʒər'meɪnɪəm, B dʒɜ'-] *s.* (quím.) germanio.

germanization [ˌdʒɜrmənə'zeɪʃən, B ˌdʒɜmənaɪ-] *s.* germanización.

germanize ['dʒɜrməˌnaɪz, B 'dʒɜmə-] *v.t.* 1. germanizar. 2. (ant.) traducir al alemán. —*v.i.* germanizarse.

German measles, (med.) rubéola, sarampión alemán.

Germanophile [dʒər'mænəˌfaɪl, B dʒə'-] *a., s.* germanófilo.

Germanophobe [-ˌfoʊb] *a., s.* germanófobo.

German script, letra gótica.

German shepherd, (perro) pastor alemán, perro policía.

German silver, plata alemana, maillechort.

Germany ['dʒɜrmənɪ, B 'dʒɜmə-] *s.* Alemania; **East G.,** (hist.) Alemania Oriental; **West G.,** (hist.) Alemania Occidental.

germ cell, (biol.) célula germinal, célula embrionaria.

germicidal [ˌdʒɜrmə'saɪdəl, B ˌdʒɜmə-] *a.* germicida.

germicide ['dʒɜrməˌsaɪd, B 'dʒɜmə-] *s.* (agente) germicida.

germinal ['dʒɜrmənəl, B 'dʒɜm-] *a.* germinal; (fig.) rudimentario.

germinal disk, (biol.) disco germinativo.

germinal vesicle, (biol.) vesícula germinal.

germinant ['dʒɜrmənənt, B 'dʒɜm-] *a.* germinante, germinador.

germinate [-ˌneɪt] *v.i.* germinar, brotar. —*v.t.* hacer germinar; hacer evolucionar.

germination [ˌdʒɜrmə'neɪʃən, B ˌdʒɜmə-] *s.* germinación.

germinative ['dʒɜrməˌneɪtɪv, B 'dʒɜmə-] *a.* germinativo.

germ plasm, g. plasma, (biol.) germen plasma.

germ warfare, guerra bacteriológica.

gerontocracy [ˌdʒɛrən'tɑkrəsɪ, B -'tɔk-] *s.* gerontocracia, gobierno de los mayores (personas de edad avanzada).

gerontology [-'tɑlədʒɪ, B -'tɔl-] *s.* gerontología, estudio del proceso del envejecimiento y de los problemas de la vejez.

gerrymander ['dʒɛrɪˌmændər, B -də] *v.t.* (E.U.) dividir (un estado, etc.) injusta o arbitrariamente en distritos electorales (para sacar ventaja de ello); manejar injustamente (los resortes políticos); tergiversar. —*s.* demarcación arbitraria e injusta de los distritos electorales; tergiversación.

gerund ['dʒɛrənd] *s.* (gram.) gerundio.

gerundial [dʒə'rʌndɪəl] *a.* (gram.) del gerundio.

gerundive [-dɪv] *s.* (gram.) gerundio adjetivado.

gesso ['dʒɛsoʊ] *s.* yeso, yeso mate, yeso de París (esp. el preparado para ser usado en pintura, etc.).

gest [dʒɛst] *s.* 1. gesta, hazaña, proeza, aventura. 2. gesta, romance.

gestalt [gə'ʃtɑlt] *s.* (psic.) gestalt, estructuralismo.

Gestalt psychology, gestaltismo, psicología de la forma o estructuralista.

Gestapo [-'stɑpoʊ, B gɛ-] *s.* gestapo, policía secreta (de Alemania bajo el régimen nazi).

gestate ['dʒɛsˌteɪt] *v.t.* 1. llevar (en el útero) durante la preñez. 2. (fig.) concebir (una idea).

gestation [dʒɛs'teɪʃən] *s.* 1. gestación, embarazo, preñez. 2. desarrollo, elaboración (de una idea, proyecto, etc.).

gestational [-əl] *a.* de (la) gestación.

gestatorial [ˌdʒɛstə'tɔrɪəl] *a.* gestatorio.

geste, *var. de* **gest.**

gestic ['dʒɛstɪk] **gestical** [-tɪkəl] *a.* que se expresa por gestos, gesticular.

gesticulate [dʒɛs'tɪkjəˌleɪt] *v.i.* gesticular, expresar por medio de gestos.

gesticulation [-ˌtɪkjə'leɪʃən] *s.* gesticulación, seña, gesto, ademán.

gesticulative [-'tɪkjəˌleɪtɪv] *a.* gesticulador, gestero, manoteador.

gesticulator [-ər, B -ə] *s.* gesticulante, manoteador, el que gesticula.

gesticulatory [-ləˌtɔrɪ, B -lətərɪ] *a.* gesticular, gesticulador.

gesture ['dʒɛstʃər, B -tʃə] *s.* 1. gesto, ademán. 2. gesto, acto de cortesía. 3. (ant.) presencia, porte, postura. —*v.i.* gesticular, hacer un ademán, hacer ademanes. —*v.t.* señalar a (alguien) con un ademán.

Gesundheit [gə'zʊntˌhaɪt] *interj.* (neol.) ¡salud! ¡Jesús! (después de un estornudo).

get [gɛt] *v.t.* (*pret.* GOT [gɑt, B gɔt]; *p.p.* GOT o esp. E.U., fam. GOTTEN ['gɑtən, B 'gɔt-]; *p.pr.* GETTING) 1. obtener, adquirir, conseguir. 2. lograr, conseguir. 3. dominar, señorear, ej., *a bad habit gets one at last,* una mala costumbre termina por dominarlo a uno. 4. arrinconar, acorralar, sorprender. 5. captar, coger; agarrar, atrapar, capturar. 6. pescar, cazar, ej., *g. a fine stag,* cazar un buen venado. 7. recibir, sufrir. 8. causar, hacer que, ocasionar, motivar. 9. inducir, persuadir, convencer, incitar. 10. (jer.) desconcertar, confundir. 11. (jer.) fastidiar, molestar, irritar. 12. ir por, ir a buscar, traer, ej., *let me g. my hat,* déjeme ir por mi sombrero. 13. llevar (ante la justicia). 14. tocar, alcanzar, ej., *g. it for me,* alcánzamelo. 15. (en *p.p.* con *have*) tener. 16. (en *p.p.* con *have* e *inf.*) tener que, ser obligado a, ej., *he has got to do it,* (fam.) tiene que hacerlo. 17. (con otro verbo en *p.p.*) hacer, hacer que, ej., *he got his beard shaved off,* se hizo afeitar la barba. 18. tener, obtener (como resultado). 19. aprender, ej., *g. by heart,* aprender de memoria. 20. (fam.) comprender, entender. 21. (fam.) conmover, impresionar. 22. extraer, sacar, ej., *g. coal,* extraer carbón. 23. preparar (almuerzo, etc.). 24. engendrar, procrear (animales). 25. (rad.) captar, sintonizar. 26. (dep.) poner fuera de juego (esp. en béisbol). 27. (jer.) dar a (uno), ej., *the blow got him in the mouth,* el golpe le dio en la boca, recibió el golpe en la boca. 28. (jer.) matar, destruir; vengarse, lastimar, herir. 29. **g. a footing (in),** establecerse (en); **g. a move on,** (jer.) darse prisa; **g. something across, hacer** comprender algo, lograr comunicación; **g. (something) away from,** quitar (algo) a; **g. back,** recuperar, recobrar; hacerse devolver; **g. (something) by,** lograr pasar (algo), conseguir que se deje pasar (algo); **g. (something) done,** lograr terminar (algo); mandar hacer (algo); **g. (one) down,** deprimir; cansar, agotar; **g. (something) down,** tragar; tener escrito; describir; **g. (something) going,** poner en marcha (algo); **g. hold of,** apoderarse de, coger, ponerse en contacto con (persona); comprometer, implicar (a alguien); lograr meter (un golpe); **g. in a word edgeways,** meter baza; **g. it,** recibir castigo o reprimenda; **g. it into one's head,** metérsele a uno en la cabeza; **g. it over,** acabar de una vez con ello, ej., *let's g. it over,* ¡acabemos de una vez con esto!; **g. off,** despachar; soltar (una observación, etc.); lograr la absolución o una pena leve para; quitarse (zapatos, ropa); **g. one's own back,** vengarse; **g. out,** sacar, hacer salir; publicar; editar; emitir; lograr pronunciar, soltar; **g. out of,** ayudar a partir o escapar; lograr sacar, sonsacar (información, etc.) a; obtener de, ganar de, sacar de; **g. (someone, something) out of the way,** sacar o quitar de en medio (algo, a alguien); **g. the better** o **the best of,** llevar ventaja a; engañar a, ganar a; **g. the sack,** (fam.) recibir calabazas; ser despedido de un empleo; **g. the start** o **the jump on,** coger la delantera a; **g. the upper hand,** imponerse, salir ganando; **g. the worst of,** llevar la peor parte, quedar mal parado, perder; **g. (one) to do (something),** lograr que, conseguir que (uno) haga (algo), ej., *he got us to pay the bill,* consiguió que nosotros pagáramos la cuenta; **g. together,** juntar, reunir; **g. (ship, project,** etc.) **under way,** poner (un buque, proyecto, etc.) en marcha; **g. up,** subir, montar; levantar; organizar, poner en marcha, producir; aderezar, acicalar; suscitar, despertar; familiarizarse con, estudiar; **g. up steam,** aumentar la presión (de una máquina para que funcione); (fig.) prepararse o disponerse para algo; encolerizarse; **g. wind of,** descubrir, recibir aviso de; **g. with child,** dejar embarazada, dejar encinta. —*v.i.* 1. llegar. 2. hacerse, ponerse, volverse; resultar; (*seguido de un a. o p.p. se traduce gen. con el verbo cuyo significado corresponde a estos últimos*), ej., *g. angry,* enfadarse, *g. better,* mejorar, *g. drunk,* embriagarse, *g. excited,* emocionarse, alegrarse, *g. hot,* sentir calor; apresurarse, animarse; excitarse; hacerse o resultar interesante, entusiasmarse, *g. married,* casarse, *g. rich,* enriquecerse, *g. tired,* fatigarse, *g. well,* restablecerse. 3. (*ú. gen. en imper.*) marcharse, largarse. 4. ganar dinero; enriquecerse. 5. **g. about,** ir a muchos sitios, viajar mucho; no estar ocioso; estar levantado (un convaleciente); circular, propalarse (rumores); **g. abroad,** difundirse, divulgarse; **g. across,** cruzar; (jer.) surtir efecto (en el auditorio); **g. after, perseguir; g. ahead,** prosperar; **g. ahead of,** adelantarse a, ganar la delantera a; **g. along,** irse, marcharse; seguir andando; tener éxito; sentirse o pasarla (bien o mal); progresar; arreglárselas; **g. along in years,** entrar en años, ponerse viejo; **g. along together,** llevarse (bien); **g. along with,** congeniar con, llevarse (bien o mal) con; **g. along without,** pasarla sin, poder prescindir de; **g. around,** adelantarse a; evitar; evadir, burlar (la ley, prohibición, etc.); engatusar; movilizarse, viajar; divulgarse; **g. around to,** encontrar tiempo u oportunidad para; tocar por fin (un tema, etc.); **g. at,** alcanzar; echar mano a, apoderarse de; dar a entender, querer decir; averiguar; sobornar; aplicarse (a), dedicarse (a); (jer.) atacar; intimidar; burlarse de; tratar de influir sobre; **g. away,** escaparse, evadirse, alejarse; irse, salir; ponerse en marcha; (*interj.*) ¡fuera!; **g. away from,** alejarse de; **g. away with,** cometer impunemente; **g. away with it,** salir triunfante, lograr hacerlo; quedar sin castigo, actuar con impunidad; **g. back,** regresar, volver; **g. back at,** vengarse de, desquitarse de; **g. behind,** atrasarse; rezagarse; penetrar (la máscara o apariencias de alguien); apoyar, respaldar; **g. by,** lograr pasar, pasar inadvertido; ir pasando, arreglárselas; **g. clear of,** desembarazarse o librarse de; **g. done with,** terminar con, acabar con; **g. down,** bajar, descender; desmontar, apearse; **g. down on,** cobrar aversión a; **g. down to,** echarse a trabajar en; proceder a examinar, pasar a considerar; **g. even with,** hacérselas pagar a, vengarse de, desquitarse de; **g. going,** ponerse en marcha; empezar; **g. home,** llegar a casa; llegar a la meta (en carreras o en juegos); **g. in,** (lograr) entrar; volver a casa; llegar; lograr meter (una observación o comentario, etc.); recibir (mercaderías); subir a (coche, etc.); ser elegido (para un oficio); (G.B.) ser elegido diputado; **g. in the habit of,** acostumbrarse a, contraer el hábito de;

g. in with, asociarse con, frecuentar la compañía de, amistarse con; **g. into,** entrar, penetrar; (fam.) ponerse (prendas); montar en (cólera, etc.); meterse en; subir a (coche); **g. nowhere,** (fig.) no llegar a nada, no lograr nada; **g. off,** desmontar, bajar de; levantarse de; bajar, apearse; salir, arrancar, partir; salir o librarse de (un compromiso); librarse, salvarse; recibir una pena liviana, ser absuelto; **g. off with,** amistarse o flirtear con; escaparse con (menor castigo, etc.); **g. on,** subir(se) a, montar; avanzar, progresar; prosperar, medrar; pasar (díc. del tiempo); pasarla, irle a uno (bien, mal, etc.); pasarlas, arreglárselas; reprender; **g. on one's legs,** recuperarse, levantarse; mejorar de fortuna; **g. on one's nerves,** irritar, cansar o fastidiar a uno; **g. on to,** caer en cuenta de, darse cuenta de, descubrir; ponerse en contacto con; **g. on with,** congeniar con, llevarse bien con; **g. on with it,** seguir adelante; acelerar (el paso, etc.); **g. out,** salir, escapar, salirse; bajar (de un vehículo); transpirar; difundirse, divulgarse; **g. out!** ¡fuera!; **g. out from under,** lograr escapar (de situación peligrosa, apuro, etc.); **g. out of,** evadir, escaparse de; librarse de, desligarse de, deshacerse de; perder, dejar (un hábito); evitar, eludir (hacer algo); bajar de (un vehículo); **g. out of the bed on the wrong side,** levantarse con el pie izquierdo; **g. out of hand,** escaparse del control (situación), desmandarse (muchedumbre, niños, etc.); **g. out of sight,** perderse de vista, desaparecer; marcharse, largarse; **g. out of the way,** quitarse de en medio; **g. over,** superar, vencer; cubrir (distancia); cumplir (tarea); pasar por alto; olvidar; recobrarse de (desengaño amoroso, enfermedad, etc.); **g. past,** lograr pasar, pasar inadvertido, filtrarse; **g. round,** persuadir, hacer aceptar; eludir (dificultad, etc.); **g. somewhere,** triunfar; hacer progreso, progresar; comprender, llegar a entender; **g. square with,** hacérselas pagar; **g. there,** (jer.) tener éxito, triunfar; **g. through,** atravesar; alcanzar la meta, llegar a su destino; pasar, ser aprobado (un proyecto de ley); pasar, ser aprobado (en los exámenes); pasar (tiempo); terminar; comunicarse, ser comprendido; **g. through to,** conseguir comunicación (esp. telefónica) con; **g. through with,** lograr llevar a cabo; **g. to,** comenzar, empezar; tener la oportunidad de; llegar a; afectar, conmover, influir en; **g. to (like, hate, know,** etc.), llegar a (cogerle el gusto a uno, odiar, conocer, etc.); **g. together,** reunirse, juntarse; **g. under,** meterse debajo de; **g. under way,** ponerse en marcha, ponerse en camino; (mar.) hacerse a la vela; **g. up,** ponerse de pie, levantarse (esp. de la cama); subir, montar (esp. a caballo); llegar cerca, acercarse; levantarse (el viento), ponerse bravo (el mar), desatarse (tempestad); **g. up!** ¡levántate! ¡arre!, **g. used to (doing** o **something), acostumbrarse a, hacerse a, habituarse a; g. used to it,** acostumbrarse; **g. wise to,** enterarse de, caer en cuenta de; (jer.) ponerse al día con (la moda, un nuevo estilo de vida, etc.); **g. with it!** ¡vamos! ¡de una vez! ¡ponte a tono!; **to be getting on,** estar entrado en años; hacerse tarde; **to be getting on (sixty,** etc.), estar entrando en (los sesenta, etc.); **to tell one where to g. off,** poner a uno en su sitio, cantárselas claras a uno.

get [gɛt] *s.* 1. cría, progenie (de un animal); raza. 2. engendro, engendramiento. 3. (dep.) devolución de un tiro difícil.

get-at-able [gɛt'ætəbəl] *a.* accesible, asequible, abordable, tratable.

getaway ['gɛtəˌweɪ] *s.* 1. escape, fuga. 2. partida (de una carrera, etc.). —*a.* perteneciente a los medios u objetos que se emplean para escapar, ej., *the getaway car,* el auto en que se escaparon.

Gethsemane [gɛθ'sɛmənɪ] *s.* 1. (bíbl.) Getsemaní. 2. (fig.) calvario.

getter ['gɛtər, B -ə] *s.* 1. (elec., electrón.) afinador de vacío. 2. (jer.) persona de empresa o iniciativa.

get-together ['gɛtəˌgɛðər, B -ə] *s.* reunión o fiesta informal.

get-up ['gɛtˌʌp] *s.* (fam.) 1. arreglo, disposición. 2. atavío, traje. 3. ambición, energía.

get up and go, (jer.) empuje, iniciativa.

get well card, tarjeta para un enfermo deseándole que se mejore.

geum ['dʒiəm] *s.* (bot.) gariofilea, yerba de San Benito, clavel silvestre.

gewgaw ['gjugɔ] *s.* chuchería, fruslería, futesa, miriñaque, bujería, friolera. —*a.* cursi, chillón, charro, pavoso (Amer.).

geyser ['gaɪzər, B -zə] *s.* 1. géiser. 2. [B 'gizə] (G.B.) calentador de agua.

geyserite [-zəˌraɪt] *a.* (min.) geyserita o geiserita.

Ghana ['gɑnə] *s.* Ghana, estado de África Occidental (ant. Costa de Oro).

gharry ['gærɪ] *s.* (anglo-ind.) coche de alquiler.

ghastliness ['gæstlɪnəs, B 'gɑst-] *s.* 1. palidez cadavérica. 2. enormidad (del error, crimen, etc.).

ghastly [-lɪ] *a.* 1. horrible, espantoso. 2. cadavérico, espectral, lívido, pálido. 3. enorme, atroz (error, mentira, crimen, etc.). 4. terrible, desagradable (asunto, tarea, etc.). 5. (ant.) aterrorizado, espantado. —*adv.* 1. horriblemente, espantosamente. 2. lívidamente, pálidamente. 3. extremadamente.

ghat, ghaut [gɔt, gɑt, B gɔt] *s.* (anglo-ind.) 1. desfiladero, abra. 2. (*pl.*) cordillera. 3. escalera a orillas de un río.

ghee, ghi[gi] *s.* (anglo-ind.) manteca clarificada de leche de búfalo.

gherkin ['gɜrkən, B 'gɜkɪn] *s.* (bot.) pepinillo, cohombrillo.

ghetto ['gɛtoʊ] *s.* (*pl.* GHETTOS o GHETTOES) 1. barrio pobre habitado por una minoría étnica o grupo social. 2. barrio judío, judería, ghetto.

Ghibelline ['gɪbəˌlin, B -ˌlaɪn] *a., s.* (hist.) gibelino.

ghillie ['gɪlɪ] *s.* zapato de sport entizado cuyos cordones terminan en borla.

ghost [goʊst] *s.* 1. espectro, fantasma, aparecido, ánima en pena. 2. alma. 3. (fig.) sombra, imagen, recuerdo, traza, asomo. 4. (t.v.) imagen eco, imagen fantasma. 5. (foto.) imagen falsa. 6. (ant.) espíritu, demonio. 7. **Holy G.,** Espíritu Santo; **not a g. of a doubt,** ni sombra de duda; **not the g. of a (chance, idea,** etc.), ni la más remota (posibilidad, idea, etc.); **to give up the g.,** entregar, dar o rendir el alma (a Dios). —*v.t.* 1. rondar por, vagar por (un lugar, díc. de un fantasma). 2. escribir como colaborador anónimo, escribir (discurso, etc.) para otro y en su nombre. —*v.i.* 1. flotar (fantasma, espectro). 2. escribir como colaborador anónimo.

ghost dance, danza de los espíritus (danza religiosa de los indios de N.A.).

ghost image, imagen secundaria, fantasma (en una pantalla de televisión).

ghostliness ['goʊstlɪnəs] *s.* carácter espectral.

ghostly [-lɪ] *a.* 1. espectral, fantasmal. 2. espiritual.

ghost ship, barco fantasma.

ghost story, cuento de fantasmas, cuento de aparecidos.

ghost town, pueblo desierto o abandonado.

ghost word, palabra creada por un error y que nunca ha sido incorporada al idioma.

ghostwrite ['goʊstˌraɪt] *v.i.* escribir para otro y en su nombre.

ghost-writer [-ər, B -ə] *s.* colaborador anónimo, autor que por dinero escribe obras para ser publicadas bajo otro nombre.

ghoul [gul] *s.* 1. espíritu o demonio que según las consejas se alimenta de cadáveres. 2. profanador de tumbas, ladrón de cementerios. 3. (fig.) persona que se deleita con lo repugnante y truculento.

ghoulish ['gulɪʃ] *a.* horrible, espantoso, brutal; repulsivo, truculento.

ghoulishly [-lɪ] *adv.* horriblemente, repulsivamente.

GHQ *abrev. de* **General Headquarters,** Cuartel General.

GI ['dʒi'aɪ] *abrev. de* **Government Issue,** emitido o aprobado por el gobierno; p. ext. todo lo que suministra el Ejército, incluso (jer.) el recluta; soldado americano, soldado raso. —*a.* de soldado.

giant ['dʒaɪənt] *s.* gigante. —*a.* gigante, gigantesco, de gran tamaño.

giant bass, (ict.) cherna.

giantess [-əs] *s.* giganta.

giant fennel, (bot.) cañaheja, férula.

giant fulmar, (orn.) quebrantahuesos, fulmar gigante, petrel gigante.

giantism [-ˌɪzəm] *s.* 1. gigantez. 2. (med.) gigantismo.

giant killer, matagigantes.

giant panda, panda gigante.

giant powder, variedad de dinamita.

giant reed, (bot.) caña brava, caña común.

giant sequoia, (bot.) secoya, wellingtonia.

giant size, de tamaño gigante.

giant star, (astr.) estrella gigante.

giant water lily, (bot.) irupé.

giaour [dʒaʊr, B 'dʒaʊə] *s.* infiel, cristiano (en países musulmanes).

gib [gɪb] *s.* 1. gato, esp. gato castrado. 2. (mec.) chaveta, cuña, contraclavija. —*v.t.* (*pret., p.p* GIBBED; *p.pr.* GIBBING) (mec.) enclavijar, acuñar, calzar, asegurar con chaveta.

gibber ['dʒɪbər, B -ə] *v.i.* farfullar, parlotear, cotorrear, disparatar. —*s.* guirigay, farfulla.

gibberish [-ərɪʃ, 'gɪb-] *s.* 1. algarabía, farfulla; guirigay, galimatías, monserga. 2. jerga, argot, germanía.

gibbet ['dʒɪbət] *s.* 1. horca, patíbulo. 2. picota (para exponer a reos ahorcados). —*v.t.* 1. ahorcar, ajusticiar en la horca. 2. exponer (a un criminal ejecutado) en la picota. 3. (fig.) ridiculizar, exponer al desprecio.

gibbon ['gɪbən] *s.* (zool.) gibón.

gibbose ['gɪboʊs] *var. de* **gibbous.**

gibbosity [dʒɪ'bɑsətɪ, gɪ-, B gɪ'bɔs-] *s.* gibosidad, giba, protuberancia; chichón, hinchazón.

gibbous ['dʒɪbəs, 'gɪb-, B 'gɪb-] *a.* 1. protuberante, hinchado, convexo. 2. giboso, corcovado, jorobado. 3. (astr.) casi llena (la luna).

gibbousness [-nəs] *s.* aspecto giboso; convexidad.

gibe [dʒaɪb] *v.t.* ridiculizar, escarnecer, vejar, burlarse de, mofarse de. —*v.i.* hacer mofa, mofarse. —*s.* sarcasmo, escarnio, burla, mofa.

giber ['dʒaɪbər, B -ə] *s.* burlador, escarnecedor, mofador.

giblet ['dʒɪblət] *s.* (*gen. pl.*) menudillo de las aves.

Gibraltar [dʒə'brɔltər, B -tə] *s.* 1. Gibraltar. 2. (fig.) fortaleza, plaza fuerte, fortificación inexpugnable.

Gibson ['gɪbsən] *s.* gibson (martini con una cebollita en lugar de aceituna).

Gibson girl, prototipo de la muchacha norteamericana de a principios del siglo, idealizada en los dibujos de Charles Dana Gibson.
gibus ['dʒaɪbəs] *s.* chistera, clac.
gid [gɪd] *s.* (vet.) modorra, nebladura, tornada, torneo.
giddap [gɪ'dæp] *interj.* ¡arre!
giddily ['gɪdəlɪ] *adv.* 1. vertiginosamente. 2. aturdidamente, atolondradamente. 3. frívolamente.
giddiness [-ɪnəs] *s.* 1. vértigo, vahído, mareo; aturdimiento. 2. frivolidad, veleidad.
giddy ['gɪdɪ] *a.* 1. mareado, aturdido, atontado, tambaleante. 2. vertiginoso. 3. casquivano, frívolo, inconstante, veleidoso, voluble. 4. **to play the g. goat,** hacer el tonto. —*v.t., v.i.* (*pret., p.p.* GIDDIED; *p.pr.* GIDDYING) aturdir(se), causar o tener vértigo; girar a gran velocidad.
giddy-head [-ˌhɛd] *s.* persona frívola, veleidosa.
gift [gɪft] *s.* 1. regalo, obsequio, presente, donación, oblación, dádiva. 2. don, dote, talento, facultad, genio, aptitud, inclinación, ejecutorio. 3. (jer., G.B.) breva. 4. **I would not have it as a g.,** no lo querría ni regalado. 5. **to have the g. of (the) gab** (fam.) tener: mucha labia. —*v.t.* 1. dotar (esp. de poder o facultad). 2. regalar, obsequiar.
gift certificate, cheque-regalo, cupón obsequio; vale canjeable por artículos en una tienda.
gifted ['gɪftəd] *a.* dotado, talentoso, genial.
gift-horse [-ˌhɔrs, B -ˌhɔs] *s.* caballo regalado; **don't look a g.-h. in the mouth,** a caballo regalado no se le mira el colmillo.
gift of gab, facilidad para hablar, verbosidad, elocuencia.
gift of tongues, (t. **glossolalia**) (relig.) letanía ininteligible del rito de ciertas sectas cristianas.
gift-wrap [-ˌræp] *v.t.* envolver como regalo.
gift wrapping [-ˌræpɪŋ] *s.* papel para regalo.
gig [gɪg] *s.* 1. arpón de pesca, fisga. 2. anzuelo múltiple en sedal (para enganchar por el cuerpo a los peces que no pican carnada). 3. calesa (de dos ruedas), quitrín. 4. (mar.) esquife, falúa. —*v.i.* (*pret., p.p.* GIGGED; *p.pr.* GIGGING) 1. pescar con anzuelo múltiple. 2. viajar en calesa o quitrín. —*v.t.* 1. arponear. 2. (fig.) aguijonear, provocar.
gig, *s.* (jer.) 1. informe oficial de una infracción menor (en escuela, etc.); demérito. 2. castigo por infracción menor. 3. reunión de músicos para una sesión de jazz. 4. contrato para tocar o cantar jazz. 5. cualquier trabajo o tarea asignada. —*v.t.* castigar por una infracción menor (en escuela, etc.).
gigantean [ˌdʒaɪgæn'tiən] *a.* gigantesco, enorme.
gigantesque [-'tɛsk] *a.* gigantesco.
gigantic [dʒaɪ'gæntɪk] **gigantical** [-tɪkəl] *a.* gigante, gigantesco, enorme, inmenso.
gigantism [-ˌtɪzəm] *s.* 1. gigantez. 2. (med.) gigantismo.
giggle ['gɪgəl] *v.i.* reír(se) tontamente, reír(se) falsa o nerviosamente. —*s.* risita entrecortada, risita tonta o falsa.
giggler [-ələr, B -lə] *s.* persona de risita falsa o nerviosa.
giggly [-lɪ] *a.* que se ríe fácilmente.
gigolo ['dʒɪgəˌlou, B 'ʒɪg-] *s.* 1. compañero de baile o acompañante profesional pagado. 2. gigolo, hombre que vive de una mujer que es su amante (gen. una rica).
gigot ['dʒɪgət] *s.* 1. pernil de carnero. 2. (cost.) manga afollada.
GI Joe, (fam.) soldado norteamericano, esp. en la Segunda Guerra Mundial; el recluta Pérez.
Gila monster ['hilə-] *s.* (zool., E.U.) monstruo de Gila, lagarto venenoso de Arizona.
gilbert ['gɪlbərt, B -bət] *s.* (fís.) gilbert (unidad de fuerza magnetomotriz o de potencial magnético).
gild [gɪld] *v.t.* (*pret., p.p.* GILDED o GILT [gɪlt]; *p.pr.* GILDING) 1. dorar, dar una capa de oro a. 2. dar brillo o lustre a; dar un brillo falso a. 3. (ant.) volver rojo, manchar (con sangre). 4. **g. the lily,** dorar la píldora.
gild, gildsman, *vars. de* **guild, guildsman.**
gilder ['gɪldər, B -ə] *s.* dorador.
gilding [-ɪŋ] *s.* 1. doradura, dorado. 2. oropel.
gill [dʒɪl] *s.* (medida para líquidos equivalente a la) cuarta parte de una pinta.
gill [gɪl] *s.* 1. agalla, branquia. 2. barba (del gallo, etc.); papada. 3. (bot.) lámina o membrana (debajo del sombrerillo del hongo). 4. (G.B.) arroyo, arroyuelo. 5. **blue** (o **green**) **around the gills,** con náuseas, mareado; **rosy about the gills,** de apariencia saludable. —*v.t.* 1. desentrañar (peces). 2. pescar o atrapar (peces) por las agallas en una red.
Gill [dʒɪl] *s.* moza, joven; **Jack and G.,** (E.U.) pareja de enamorados.
gill arch [gɪl-] (zool.) arco de la agalla de un pez o ave.
gillie ['gɪlɪ] *s.* 1. (esco.) criado, secuaz; ayudante o paje de un cazador. 2. seguidor, acompañante; criado, sirviente.
gill net [gɪl-] red rastrera vertical (con mallas que permiten pasar las cabezas de los peces pero que los sujetan por las agallas cuando intentan escapar).
gill slit [gɪl-] hendidura branquial.
gilly ['gɪlɪ] *s.* vagón de madera, carro o camión contratado para transportar equipos de circo.
gillyflower ['dʒɪlɪˌflauər, B -ə] *s.* (bot.) 1. gariofilea, betónica coronaria. 2. alhelí común de Europa; alhelí encarnado, alhelí amarillo.
gilsonite ['gɪlsəˌnaɪt] *s.* (min.) asfalto de Utah.
gilt [gɪlt] *s.* 1. dorado; oro en hojuelas, oropel. 2. (fig.) falso brillo. 3. (jer.) mosca, plata, guita (Amer.), dinero. 4. cerda, marrana joven. —*a.* dorado, áureo.
gilt [gɪlt] *pret., p.p. de* **gild.**
gilt-edged ['gɪlt'ɛdʒd] **gilt-edge** [-'ɛdʒ] *a.* 1. de cantos o cortes dorados. 2. de toda confianza, de lo mejor, ej., *g.-e. securities,* valores de primer orden, títulos de primera clase.
gilthead [-ˌhɛd] *s.* (ict.) dorada, doradilla.
gimbals ['gɪmbəlz, B 'dʒɪm-] *s. pl.* soporte cardánico, suspensión universal, balancines de la brújula.
gimcrack ['dʒɪmˌkræk] *s.* chucherías, baratija, cosa cursi. —*a.* cursi, de oropel, de fantasía.
gimcrackery [-ərɪ] *s.* 1. chucherías, baratijas (en general). 2. efectos o técnica rebuscada y artificial (en arte, literatura, etc.).
gimlet ['gɪmlət] *s.* 1. barrena de mano, barrenita, gusanillo. 2. coctel hecho con vodka o ginebra y jugo de limón verde. —*v.t.* barrenar.
gimlet-eyed [-ˌaɪd] *a.* de vista penetrante, de ojos de lince.
gimmal ['gɪməl, B 'dʒɪm-] *s.* (mec.) partes conectadas que se mueven una dentro de otra; par o serie de aros entrelazados.
gimmick ['gɪmɪk] *s.* 1. (jer.) artimaña, artefacto, artilugio. 2. (fam.) dispositivo secreto (para realizar un truco, amañar una ruleta, etc.). 3. trampa, dificultad oculta. 4. idea (brillante o novedosa para atraer la atención). —*v.t.* (fam.) usar artimañas, hacer trampas.
gimmickry [-rɪ] *s.* 1. artimañas, tretas, trampas, etc., colectivamente. 2. el uso de artimañas, etc.
gimp [gɪmp] *s.* 1. (tej.) trencilla o galón (para guarnecer piezas de vestir de lujo). 2. (fam.) espíritu, fuerza, vigor, brío. 3. (fam.) lisiado, baldado. —*v.t.* cojear.
gimp nail, tachuela para tapicería.
gimpy ['gɪmpɪ] *a.* (jer.) cojo, lisiado.
gin [dʒɪn] *s.* 1. ginebra, licor de enebro. 2. juego de naipes. 3. trampa, armadijo (para cazar). 4. (máquina) despepitadora, desmotadora (Amer.) (de algodón). 5. poste grúa, torno de izar. 6. (ant.) idea, artificio, ardid. —*v.t.* (*pret., p.p.* GINNED; *p.pr.* GINNING) 1. entrampar, coger en la trampa. 2. despepitar, alijar, desmotar (Amer.) (el algodón).
gin-fizz ['dʒɪnˌfɪz] *s.* bebida de ginebra, gaseosa y limón.
ginger ['dʒɪndʒər, B -dʒə] *s.* 1. (bot.) jengibre. 2. (cocina) jengibre, rizoma de jengibre. 3. (fam.) vivacidad, brío, ánimo, coraje. —*v.t.* 1. sazonar con jengibre. 2. (gen. con *up*) animar, avivar.
ginger ale, g. beer, gaseosa de jengibre.
gingerbread [-ˌbrɛd] *s.* 1. pan de jengibre. 2. adorno superfluo o cursi. —*a.* cursi, ostentoso, charro, relumbrón (díc. de los adornos).
gingerliness [-lɪnes] *s.* cautela, cuidado; remilgo.
gingerly [-lɪ] *adv.* 1. cuidadosamente, cautelosamente. 2. delicadamente, con afectación. —*a.* cuidadoso, cauteloso.
gingersnap [-ˌsnæp] *s.* galletita de sabor a jengibre.
gingery ['dʒɪndʒərɪ] *a.* 1. que sabe a jengibre, parecido al jengibre; sazonado con jengibre. 2. agudo, punzante (observación, etc.); picante.
gingham ['gɪŋəm] *s.* (tej.) guinga, zaraza.
gingili ['dʒɪndʒəlɪ] *s.* (bot.) sésamo.
gingiva [dʒɪn'dʒaɪvə] *s.* (*pl.* GINGIVAE [-ˌvi]) (anat.) encía.
gingival [-vəl, 'dʒɪndʒə-, B dʒɪn'dʒaɪ-] *a.* 1. (anat.) gingival. 2. (fon.) alveolar.
gingivitis [ˌdʒɪndʒə'vaɪtəs] *s.* (med.) gingivitis.
gingko, *var. de* **ginkgo.**
gink [gɪŋk] *s.* (jer.) tipo raro, tío.
ginkgo ['gɪŋkou] *s.* (*pl.* GINKGOES) (bot.) gingco.
gin mill, (jer.) cantina, taberna.
ginner ['dʒɪnər, B -ə] *s.* desmotador (de algodón).
gin rummy, juego de naipes.
ginseng ['dʒɪnˌsɛŋ] *s.* (bot.) ginseng, ginsén.
gin sling, bebida de ginebra fría sazonada y endulzada.
gipon [dʒɪ'pɑn, B -'pɔn] *s.* (hist.) jubón.
gipsy, *var. de* **gypsy.**
giraffe [dʒə'ræf, B -'rɑf] *s.* 1. (zool.) jirafa. 2. **G.,** (astr.) constelación Camelopardalis.
girandole ['dʒɪrənˌdoul] *s.* 1. girándula (de cohetes o fuegos artificiales) 2. candelabro ornamental de varios brazos. 3. girándula (en las fuentes de agua).
girasol, girasole ['dʒɪrəˌsɔl, -ˌsoul, B -ˌsɔl] *s.* 1. (bot.) girasol. 2. (min.) ópalo de fuego.
gird [gɜrd, B gɜd] *v.t.* (*pret., p.p.* GIRT [gɜrt, B gɜt] o GIRDED; *p.pr.* GIRDING) 1. atar, ceñir. 2. (con *with*) (fig.) investir (con), dotar (de) (poderes o atributos). 3. rodear, circundar, cercar. 4. **g. oneself,** aprestarse, prepararse.
gird [gɜrd, B gɜd] *v.t., v.i.* burlar(se), mofar(se), reír(se) de. —*s.* (ant.) burla, broma, mofa.
girder ['gɜrdər, B 'gɜdə] *s.* (const.) viga maestra, cuartón, trabe, jácena.
girder bridge, puente de vigas.
girder rail, riel de doble T para tranvías.
girdle ['gɜrdəl, B 'gɜd-] *s.* 1. faja, cintura, banda, cinto. 2. (fig.) cerco. 3. corte anular (en la corteza de un árbol). 4. faja, corsé. 5. (joy.)

borde de una gema cogida por el engaste. 6. (anat.) anillo óseo (que sostiene una extremidad). —*v.t.* 1. circundar, cercar. 2. atar con una correa o cinturón. 3. quitar (a un árbol) una tira circular de corteza.

girdler [-ələr, B -lə] *s.* 1. fabricante de fajas. 2. (ento.) escarabajo americano.

girl [gɜrl, B gɜl] *s.* 1. niña; muchacha, joven; soltera. 2. sirvienta, criada, doméstica. 3. novia, enamorada. 4. **old g.,** (fam.) vieja.

girl Friday, mano derecha, empleada eficiente y de confianza.

girl friend, enamorada, chica, novia; amiga.

girl guide, (G.B.) niña exploradora.

girlhood ['gɜrlˌhʊd, B 'gɜl-] *s.* niñez; juventud femenina.

girlie magazine, girly m. ['gɜrlɪ-, B 'gɜlɪ-] revista de desnudos femeninos.

girlie show, girly s., variedades frívolas, bataclán.

girlish [-lɪʃ] *a.* característico de una niña; aniñado.

girlishly [-lɪ] *adv.* como una niña.

girlishness [-nəs] *a.* carácter de niña, lo propio de una niña.

girl scout, (niña) exploradora, muchacha-guía.

girondist [dʒə'rɑndəst, B -'rɔn-] *s.* (hist.) girondino.

girt [gɜrt, B gɜt] *pret., p.p. de* **gird.**

girt [gɜrt, B gɜt] *v.i.* medir en circunferencia (díc. de árboles). —*v.t.* 1. ceñir, atar con cinturón. 2. medir la circunferencia de.

girth [gɜrθ, B gɜθ] *s.* 1. cincha. 2. circunferencia; dimensiones, tamaño. —*v.t.* cinchar, ceñir.

gismo ['gɪzmoʊ] *s.* (jer.) artilugio.

gist [dʒɪst] *s.* sustancia, esencia, quid.

gittern ['gɪtərn, B -ən] *s.* especie de guitarra medieval.

give [gɪv] *v.t.* (*pret.* GAVE [geɪv]; *p.p.* GIVEN ['gɪvən]; *p.pr.* GIVING) 1. dar, conceder, conferir, otorgar. 2. dar, entregar. 3. servir (un trago), administrar (sacramento). 4. dar, proferir (respuesta, opinión, razón, noticia); dar, impartir (orden). 5. dar, producir. 6. causar, trasmitir (enfermedad). 7. dedicar, consagrar. 8. presentar, mostrar. 9. dar (baile, comida, etc.). 10. dar, comunicar (pésame, enhorabuena, etc.). 11. indicar, marcar (temperatura, presión, etc. un termómetro, medidor, etc.). 12. venir con, ej., *don't g. me that tripe,* (jer.) ¡no me vengas con esas necedades! 13. **g. a cry,** dar un grito; **g. a good account of oneself,** salir bien, hacerlo bien; **g. a hand to,** ayudar (a), darle una mano (a); **g. a jump,** dar un salto; **g. a laugh,** soltar la risa; **g. a lift to (someone),** levantar los ánimos (a alguien); llevar en coche a alguien; **g. (somebody) a piece of one's mind,** cantarle las cuarenta (a alguien), regañar, reprender; **g. as good as one gets,** dar en la medida en que se recibe, replicar adecuadamente; **g. a thought to,** acordarse de, pensar en; **g. away,** regalar; entregar (la novia) al novio; revelar, descubrir; entregar (premios); **g. (someone) away,** poner en evidencia, traicionar, delatar (a alguien); **g. back,** devolver, restituir; **g. birth to,** dar a luz; (fig.) ocasionar, originar, dar lugar a; **g. chase,** salir en persecución de; **g. (an) ear,** escuchar; **g. effect to,** poner en ejecución; **g. forth,** emitir, publicar (noticia, etc.); despedir (olor, gas, etc.); **g. ground,** retirarse, ceder; **g. (one) his due,** reconocer (a alguien) sus méritos; **g. in,** entregar, rendir; **g. it to one,** castigar, reprender; **g. me the good old times,** a mí que me den los viejos tiempos; **g. mouth to,** proferir, expresar; **g. notice,** informar; renunciar (a empleo, puesto), despedir (de un empleo); **g. off,** emitir, despedir (vapor, olor, gas, etc.); **g. oneself (to),** darse (a), dedicarse (a); entregarse (mujer a hombre); **g. oneself airs,** darse aires (de grandeza, superioridad); **g. oneself away,** ponerse en evidencia; **g. oneself over to,** abandonarse a; **g. oneself trouble,** afanarse, esforzarse; **g. oneself up,** entregarse (a la policía, etc.); **g. oneself up to,** abandonarse a, entregarse a (desesperación, dolor, vicios, etc.); **g. out,** anunciar, emitir, proclamar; distribuir, repartir; **g. over,** abandonar, dejar de (hacer); desistir de; entregar, abandonar a; **g. rein,** dar rienda suelta; **g. rise to,** ocasionar, motivar; **g. (a child, etc.) something to (cry, etc.) for,** darle (a un niño, etc.) verdadero motivo para (llorar, etc.); **g. (one) the cold shoulder,** recibir (a uno) fríamente, ignorar, tratar fríamente (a uno); **g. the sack,** dar calabazas; despedir (de un empleo); **g. the slip,** dar el esquinazo, escapar; **g. tongue,** (caza) comenzar a ladrar (los sabuesos); **g. up,** rendir, entregar; abandonar (empleo, tentativa, etc.); retirarse de (negocios, etc.); desistir de, dejar de; renunciar a; **g. up the ghost,** morir; desistir; **g. up (time, a day,** etc.) **to,** dedicar o reservar (tiempo, un día, etc.) a; **g. vent to,** dar salida a, desatarse en; **g. way,** ceder, retroceder; ceder su puesto, hacer lugar; dejarse llevar por (angustia, dolor, etc.); **to be much given to,** ser aficionado a, gustarle mucho a uno, dedicarse mucho a; **would g. one's eyetooth,** daría cualquier cosa (por). —*v.i.* 1. dar, hacer donaciones o regalos. 2. ceder; aflojarse; desplomarse. 3. ablandarse (el tiempo); deshelarse (suelo). 4. (jer.) ocurrir, pasar, ej., *what gives?* ¿qué pasa? 5. (jer.) hablar, dar información. 6. **g. back,** devolver (a su dueño); **g. in,** ceder, acceder, asentir; **g. out,** acabarse, consumirse, terminarse, agotarse; pararse, detenerse (por agotamiento); **g. over,** dejar, no seguir, detenerse; **g. up,** resignarse, rendirse, darse por vencido.

give, *s.* flexibilidad; elasticidad, acción de ceder físicamente (un colchón, una superficie, etc.).

give-and-take ['gɪvən'teɪk] *s.* toma y daca, dares y tomares, concesiones mutuas.

giveaway [-əˌweɪ] *s.* 1. traición. 2. (fam.) revelación involuntaria. 3. premio. 4. (rad., t.v.) premio que se adjudica a los participantes u oyentes de un programa.

given ['gɪvən] *p.p. de* **give.** —*a.* 1. dado, otorgado, donado. 2. (con *to*) adicto (a), propenso (a). 3. determinado, cierto, ej., *in a g. moment,* en cierto momento, en un momento determinado. 4. dado, otorgado, fechado (esp. en documentos oficiales). 5. teniendo en cuenta, ej., *g. the present political situation,* teniendo en cuenta la actual situación política. 6. (mat., lóg.) dado, conocido; supuesto, pretendido.

given name, nombre de pila, nombre bautismal.

giver ['gɪvər, B -ə] *s.* donante, donador, dador.

gizmo, *var. de* **gismo.**

gizzard ['gɪzərd, B -əd] *s.* 1. molleja (de pájaro, ave). 2. (hum., fam.) entrañas, interior (de una persona). 3. **to fret one's g.,** preocuparse; **to stick in one's g.,** (fig.) ser inaceptable para uno.

glabella [glə'bɛlə] *s.* (anat.) glabela.

glabrous ['gleɪbrəs] *a.* (bot., zool.) glabro.

glacé [glæ'seɪ, B 'glæseɪ] *a.* 1. azucarado, almibarado, (cubierto) con una capa de azúcar (fruta, etc.). 2. glaseado, satinado (telas, cuero). —*v.t.* (*pret., p.p.* GLACÉED; *p.pr.* GLACÉING) 1. azucarar, almibarar, abrillantar (frutas, etc.). 2. glasear, satinar (telas).

glacial ['gleɪʃəl, B 'gleɪsjəl] *a.* 1. glacial, helado (viento, frío, etc.). 2. (fig.) glacial, frío, desafecto (mirada, recepción, etc.). 3. (quím.) glacial. 4. (geog.) glaciárico (erosión, lago, etc.). 5. **G.,** (geol.) glacial (época).

glacial acetic acid, ácido acético puro o glacial.

glacial epoch, g. era, g. period, época, era o período glacial.

glacialist [-əst] *s.* 1. (geol.) partidario de la teoría glacial. 2. estudiante de glaciares.

glacially [-ʃəlɪ] *adv.* glacialmente.

glaciate [-ʃɪˌeɪt, B -sɪˌeɪt] *v.t.* 1. helar, congelar. 2. (geol.) someter a la acción de los glaciares (rocas, etc.).

glaciation [ˌgleɪʃɪ'eɪʃən, -sɪ'eɪ-, B ˌglæ-] *s.* glaciación, helamiento, congelación.

glacier ['gleɪʃər, B 'glæsjə] *s.* glaciar, helero, ventisquero.

glaciered [-ʃərd, B -sjəd] *a.* glaciárico, cubierto de glaciares.

glaciology [ˌgleɪʃɪ'ɑlədʒɪ, -sɪ'ɑl-, B -'ɔl-] *s.* glaciología, estudio científico de los glaciares.

glacis ['gleɪsəs, B 'glæs-] *s.* (*pl.* GLACIS o GLACISES) 1. glacis, cuesta, explanada, ladera. 2. (fort.) glacis, explanada.

glad [glæd] *a.* (GLADDER; GLADDEST) 1. feliz, alegre, gozoso, contento. 2. halagüeño, feliz (hecho o noticia). 3. alegre, hermoso (naturaleza, día, etc.). 4. **to be g. (of** o **that),** alegrarse (de); **to be g. to,** tener mucho gusto en; **to give (someone) the g. eye,** (jer.) echar una mirada amorosa o provocativa (a alguien). —*v.t., v.i.* (*pret., p.p.* GLADDED; *p.pr.* GLADDING) (ant.) alegrar.

gladden ['glædən] *v.t.* alegrar, regocijar. —*v.i.* (ant.) alegrarse, regocijarse.

gladdon ['glædən] *s.* (G.B., bot.) jíride, lirio hediondo; espadaña.

glade [gleɪd] *s.* claro, claro umbroso (en un bosque).

glad hand, (fig.) bienvenida calurosa y fingidamente efusiva.

glad-hand ['glæd'hænd] *v.t.* dar una bienvenida calurosa o fingidamente efusiva.

gladiate ['glædɪˌeɪt, B 'gleɪdɪət] *a.* (bot.) gladiado.

gladiator ['glædɪˌeɪtər, B -ɔ] *s.* 1. (hist.) gladiador, gladiator. 2. contendor, polemista.

gladiatorial [ˌglædɪə'tɔrɪəl] *a.* gladiatorio.

gladiola [ˌglædɪ'oʊlə] *s.* (bot.) gladiolo, gladíolo, estoque.

gladiolus [-'oʊləs] *s.* (*pl.* GLADIOLI [-ˌlaɪ] o GLADIOLUSES) 1. (bot.) gladiolo, gladíolo, estoque. 2. (anat.) gladiolo.

gladly ['glædlɪ] *adv.* 1. alegremente, jubilosamente. 2. con mucho gusto, gustosamente, con placer.

gladness [-nəs] *s.* alegría, gozo, júbilo, regocijo.

glad rags, (jer.) vestido de gala, traje de vestir, traje dominguero.

gladsome [-səm] *a.* alegre, contento, gozoso, regocijado, jubiloso.

gladsomely [-lɪ] *adv.* jubilosamente, alegremente, regocijadamente.

gladsomeness [-nəs] *s.* alegría, regocijo, recreo, animación, júbilo, gozo.

Gladstone ['glædˌstoʊn, B -stən] *s.* carruaje de paseo de cuatro ruedas con dos asientos interiores.

Gladstone bag, maleta de viaje con costados flexibles y dos compartimientos iguales.

Glagolitic [ˌglægə'lɪtɪk] *a.* (lingüística) glagolítico. —*s.* alfabeto glagolítico.

glair [glɛr, B glɛə] *s.* 1. clara de huevo. 2. cola, encolado.

glairiness ['glɛrɪnəs, B 'glɛər-] *s.* viscosidad, pegajosidad, glutinosidad.

glairy [-ɪ] *a.* pegajoso, glutinoso, viscoso.

glaive [gleɪv] *s.* (ant.) espada, espadón.
glamorization [ˌglæmərə'zeɪʃən, B -raɪ-] *s.* embellecimiento; glorificación, exaltación, ensalzamiento; idealización romanticona.
glamorize, glamourize ['glæməˌraɪz] *v.t.* 1. embellecer. 2. ensalzar, alabar, glorificar; idealizar cándidamente.
glamorous, glamourous [-rəs] *a.* glamoroso, encantador, sugestivo.
glamour, glamor ['glæmər, B -ə] *s.* glamour, encanto, hechizo; fascinación, encantamiento, embeleso.
glamour girl, belleza exótica.
glance [glæns, B glɑns] *v.i.* 1. lanzar una mirada, echar un vistazo o una ojeada. 2. brillar, centellear, relampaguear. 3. deslizarse. 4. **g. at,** dar un vistazo a; aludir de paso a (lema, etc.); **g. off,** desviarse, rebotar (golpe, proyectil, etc.); **g. over,** leer a medias o por encima. —*v.t.* 1. avistar, divisar. 2. **g. off,** hacer rebotar o desviarse (proyectil, pelota lanzada, etc.). —*s.* 1. vistazo, ojeada, mirada; vislumbre. 2. fulgor, destello, centelleo, relampagueo. 3. desviación oblicua. 4. (min.) mineral lustroso. 5. **at a g.,** de un vistazo; **at first g.,** a primera vista.
glancing ['glænsɪŋ, B 'glɑn-] *a.* 1. incidental, indirecto. 2. no estudiado, informal, natural, fácil.
glancingly [-lɪ] *adv.* incidentalmente; informalmente.
gland [glænd] *s.* 1. (anat., bot.) glándula. 2. (mec.) collar, collarín; casquillo del prensaestopas.
glandered ['glændərd, B -dəd] *a.* (vet.) muermoso.
glanderous [-dərəs] *a.* (vet.) muermoso.
glanders [-dərz, B -dəz] *s. pl.* (vet.) muermo.
glandiferous [glæn'dɪfərəs] *a.* (bot.) glandífero, glandígero.
glandular ['gændʒələr, B -djʊlə] *a.* glandular, glanduloso.
glandulous [-ləs] *a.* (med.) glanduloso, adenoso, glandular.
glans [glænz] *s.* (*pl.* GLANDES ['glænˌdiz]) (anat.) glande, bálano (del pene); glande (del clítoris).
glare [glɛr, B glɛə] *v.i.* 1. relumbrar, fulgurar. 2. (con *at*) mirar con ira, lanzar miradas feroces (a). 3. (ant.) ser brillante o chillón (color), ser ostentoso o aparatoso. —*v.t.* expresar (odio, indignación) con la mirada. —*s.* 1. fulgor deslumbrante, relumbrón, luz intensa y molesta. 2. ostentación, boato. 3. mirada iracunda, mirada feroz. 4. (E.U.) superficie de hielo lisa y vidriosa.
glariness [-ɪnəs, B 'glɛər-] *s.* relumbre, resplandor, brillo.
glaring ['glɛrɪŋ, B 'glɛər-] *a.* 1. de mirada iracunda o feroz. 2. deslumbrante, deslumbrador; vívido, intenso, brillante. 3. conspicuo, evidente, notorio.
glaringly [-lɪ] *adv.* 1. furiosamente, penetrantemente. 2. evidentemente, notoriamente.
glary [-ɪ] *a.* deslumbrador, deslumbrante, relumbrante, resplandeciente, brillante.
glass [glæs, B glɑs] *s.* 1. vidrio, cristal. 2. cristalería; vajilla de cristal. 3. (*pl.*) lentes, espejuelos, anteojos, gafas. 4. vaso. 5. vaso (de), contenido de unvaso. 6. espejo. 7. barómetro. 8. telescopio, catalejo. 9. reloj de arena. 10. **he has had a g. too much,** está medio borracho. —*v.t.* 1. guardar en un recipiente de cristal; embotellar. 2. (poét.) reflejar. 3. cubrir o proteger con cristal. 4. hacer vítreo, vitrificar. —*v.i.* vitrificarse; vidriarse. —*a.* de cristal, de vidrio.
glass bead, abalorio, cuenta de cristal.
glass blower, vidriero, soplador de vidrio.
glass blowing, soplado del vidrio; fabricación de vidrio soplado.
glass case, 1. vitrina. 2. fanal, campana de cristal (con que se protegen del polvo ciertas cosas).
glass ceiling, techo de cristal; (fig.) tope, ej., **to go through the g.,** ir más allá del tope; **to help women break through the g. of promotion,** ayudar a las mujeres a romper las barreras que les impiden continuar ascendiendo.
glass cutter, cortavidrio, tallador de cristal.
glass door, puerta vidriera.
glass eye, 1. ojo de vidrio. 2. ojo de iris incoloro.
glass factory, g. shop, vidriería, cristalería.
glass flask, balón.
glassful ['glæsˌfʊl, B 'glɑs-] *s.* vaso (su contenido).
glass furnace, carquesa; horno de vidrio.
glasshouse [-ˌhaʊs] *s.* 1. vidriería; fábrica de vidrio o cristal. 2. (pr. G.B.) invernadero. 3. (jer., G.B.) prisión militar.
glassier's shop [-ɪərz-, B -ɪəz-] vidriería.
glassily [-əlɪ] *adv.* 1. como el vidrio. 2. con ojos vidriosos.
glassine [glæ'sin] *s.* papel cristal.
glassiness ['glæsɪnəs, B 'glɑs-] *s.* 1. vidriosidad. 2. lisura, tersura.
glassmaker [-ˌmeɪkər, B -ə] *s.* vidriero, fabricante de vidrio.
glassmaking [-ɪŋ] *s.* fabricación de vidrio.
glassman [-mən, -ˌmæn, B -mən] *s.* vidriero (el que vende o hace objetos de vidrio).
glass snake, (zool.) víbora de cristal.
glass sponge, esponja silícea.
glassware [-ˌwɛr, B -ˌwɛə] *s.* cristalería, vajilla de cristal.
glass window, ventana vidriera.
glass wool, cristal hilado, lana de vidrio, tela de vidrio.
glasswork [-ˌwɜrk, B -ˌwɜk] *s.* 1. (*pl.*) vidriería, cristalería, fábrica de vidrio o cristales, acrisolado. 2. fabricación de vidrio u objetos de cristal, decoración hecha a base de cristal o vidrio.
glassworker [-ˌwɜrkər, B -ˌwɜkə] *s.* vidriero (oficio).
glasswort [-ˌwɜrt, B -ˌwɜt] *s.* (bot.) barrilla, sosa, almarjo, almajo, armajo.
glassy ['glæsɪ, B 'glɑsɪ] *a.* 1. vítreo, cristalino, de vidrio o cristal. 2. (fig.) cristalino (agua); suave, transparente. 3. vidrioso, sin brillo (ojos).
Glaswegian [glæs'widʒən] *a.* de Glasgow. —*s.* natural o habitante de Glasgow, Escocia.
Glauber's salt ['glaʊbərz-, B -bəz-] (farm.) sal de Glauber.
glaucoma [glɔ'koʊmə, glaʊ-, B glɔ-] *s.* (med.) glaucoma.
glaucomatous [-təs] *a.* (med.) glaucomatoso.
glauconite ['glɔkəˌnaɪt] *s.* (min.) glauconita.
glaucous ['glɔkəs] *a.* 1. glauco, verdemar. 2. (bot.) cubierto de una pelusilla blanca azulosa.
glaucus ['glɔkəs] *s.* (zool.) glauco.
glaze [gleɪz] *v.t.* 1. poner vidrios a (una ventana o cuadro); guarnecer de ventanas con vidrios (un edificio). 2. vidriar, barnizar (lozas, etc.). 3. glasear, dar brillo a (papel, manjares, etc.), lustrar (tejidos); alisar, apomazar (una superficie). —*v.i.* vidriarse, nublarse (los ojos). —*s.* 1. barniz. 2. mogate (de alfareros). 3. capa vidriosa (en el suelo). 4. lustre, superficie lisa. 5. mirada vidriosa (de los ojos). 6. (meteor.) cellisca, aguanieve. 7. (pint.) capa transparente o semitransparente de pintura (aplicada sobre otra).
glazed earthenware [gleɪzd-] loza vidriada.
glazer ['gleɪzər, B -ə] *s.* satinador.
glazier ['gleɪʒər, -zɪər, B -zjə] *s.* vidriero.
glazier's nippers, (mec.) grujidor.
glazier's points, (mec.) puntas de vidriar.
glazing ['gleɪzɪŋ] *s.* 1. trabajo de vidriero. 2. vidriería, encristalado. 3. barniz, vidriado.
gleam [glim] *s.* 1. destello, fulgor, fulguración, viso, centelleo. 2. luz tenue o pasajera. 3. (fig.) rayo (de esperanza), punta (de ironía), chispa (de inteligencia). 4. (fig.) pizca, vestigio. —*v.i.* 1. destellar, centellear, brillar, fulgurar. 2. manifestarse breve o tenuemente.
gleamy ['glimɪ] *a.* centelleante, fulgurante.
glean [glin] *v.t.* 1. espigar, respigar. 2. recoger, juntar (noticias, hechos, cosas); coger, entresacar. —*v.i.* recoger espigas; espigar datos.
gleaner ['glinər, B -ə] *s.* 1. espigador, espigadera. 2. recogedor; investigador (de libros, datos, etc.).
gleaning [-ɪŋ] *s.* 1. espigueo; rebusco. 2. (*pl.*) conjunto de espigas, moraga.
glebe [glib] *s.* 1. (poét.) tierra, terrón, terruño, gleba. 2. (G.B.) tierras beneficiales. 3. (ant.) labrado, labranza.
glede [glid] **gled** [glɛd] *s.* (orn.) milano real.
glee [gli] *s.* 1. alegría, regocijo, júbilo. 2. (mús.) composición coral armonizada a contrapunto.
glee club, orfeón, coro, grupo coral.
gleed [glid] *s.* (dial., G.B.) carbón incandescente.
gleeful ['glifəl] *a.* alegre, regocijado, jubiloso.
gleefully [-fəlɪ] *adv.* alegremente, jubilosamente.
gleeman ['glimən] *s.* (ant.) cantor, trovador, juglar.
gleesome [-səm] *a.* (ant.) alegre, contento, feliz, regocijado, jubiloso.
gleet [glit] *s.* 1. (med.) blenorrea, gonorrea crónica, gota militar; pérdida, flujo mórbido. 2. (vet.) inflamación crónica de las cavidades nasales.
gleety ['glitɪ] *a.* (med.) blenorrágico.
glen [glɛn] *s.* hoya, hocino, valle estrecho y encerrado.
Glengarry [glɛn'gærɪ] *s.* gorra escocesa.
glenoid ['glɛnɔɪd, B 'glinɔɪd] *a.* (anat.) glenoideo.
gliadin ['glaɪədən] *s.* (quím.) gliadina.
glib [glɪb] *a.* 1. locuaz, verboso, suelto de lengua, de mucha labia (persona); fácil, insincero (habla, frase, etc.). 2. suelto, desenvuelto (movimiento); desahogado. 3. (dial.) liso, resbaladizo (superficie).
glibly ['glɪblɪ] *adv.* 1. con soltura, prontamente, sin reflexión. 2. con desenvoltura; desahogadamente.
glibness [-nəs] *s.* 1. locuacidad, facundia. 2. soltura, desenvoltura.
glide [glaɪd] *v.i.* 1. resbalar, deslizar, escurrirse. 2. (aer.) planear. 3. **g. along,** correr o pasar suavemente; **g. by,** pasarse, desvanecerse. —*v.t.* hacer deslizar. —*s.* 1. rebajamiento, deslizamiento, escurrimiento, desliz. 2. (aer.) planeo. 3. (danza) paso deslizado. 4. (mús.) ligadura. 5. (fon.) semivocal, pasaje gradual (de un sonido a otro).
glider ['glaɪdər, B -ə] *s.* 1. deslizador. 2. (aer.) planeador, deslizador. 3. columpio, mecedora.
gliding [-ɪŋ] *a.* deslizante.
gliding angle, (aer.) ángulo de planeo.
glim [glɪm] *s.* 1. vislumbre; luz. 2. (jer.) golpe de vista, ojeada, vistazo. 3. (jer.) ojo.
glimmer ['glɪmər, B -ə] *v.i.* rielar, centellear, brillar con luz tenue y vacilante. —*s.* 1. vislumbre, luz tenue y vacilante. 2. (fig.) rastro, pizca (de conocimientos, de verdad, etc.). 3. (fig.) vislumbre, idea fugaz, noción vaga.
glimmering [-ərɪŋ] *s.* 1. vislumbre, luz tenue y vacilante. 2. (fig.) pizca, rastro. 3. (fig.) vislumbre, idea fugaz, noción vaga. —*a.* vacilante, tenue, oscilante (luz, idea, etc.).

glimpse [glɪmps] *s.* vislumbre, vista fugaz, visión breve o momentánea; **to catch a g. of,** avistar brevemente; vislumbrar. —*v.t.* vislumbrar; avistar brevemente. —*v.i.* (con *at*) dar un vistazo a, echar una ojeada a.

glint [glɪnt] *s.* 1. destello, fulgor, centelleo, rayo, relumbrón, relumbre; viso, lustre. 2. (ant.) ojeada, vistazo. —*v.i.* 1. ser reflejado, saltar de rechazo (luz). 2. brillar, destellar. 3. (fig.) brillar (ojos con ira, etc.). —*v.t.* reflejar.

glioma [glaɪ'oʊmə] *s.* (*pl.* GLIOMATA [-mətə] o GLIOMAS) (med.) glioma.

glissade [glɪ'sɑd, -'seɪd] *s.* 1. descenso, deslizamiento (sobre una pendiente cubierta de nieve); resbalón, resbalamiento, patinazo. 2. (ballet) paso largo de lado. —*v.i.* resbalar, deslizar, patinar.

glissando [-'sɑndoʊ] *s.* (*pl.* GLISSANDI [-di] o GLISSANDOS) (mús.) glissando.

glisten ['glɪsən] *v.i.* relucir, resplandecer, brillar, centellear. —*s.* brillo, resplandor, viso, destello, centelleo.

glister ['glɪstər, B -tə] *v.i.* (poét.) brillar, lucir, resplandecer. —*s.* brillo, resplandor, viso.

glitch [glɪtʃ] *s.* (jer.) mal funcionamiento, desperfecto, falla.

glitter ['glɪtər, B -ə] *v.i.* rutilar, brillar, chispear, relumbrar, centellear, relucir; **all that glitters is not gold,** no todo lo que reluce es oro. —*s.* brillo, lustre, resplandor, viso.

glittery [-ərɪ] *a.* rutilante, brillante, relumbrante, resplandeciente.

glitz [glɪts] *s.* (jer.) oropel.

glitzy ['glɪtsi] *a.* (GLITZIER; GLITZIEST) (jer.) glamoroso, deslumbrante.

gloam [gloʊm] *s.* (poét.) crepúsculo vespertino, anochecer, anochecida.

gloaming ['gloʊmɪŋ] *s.* (poét.) anochecer, crepúsculo vespertino.

gloat ['gloʊt] *v.i.* 1. sentir un placer malicioso, exultar malignamente. 2. **g. at,** mirar con satisfacción maligna; **g. over,** contemplar con satisfacción perversa; regocijarse triunfalmente por; gozarse maliciosamente de. —*s.* placer maligno, satisfacción maliciosa o triunfal.

gloatingly ['gloʊtɪŋlɪ] *adv.* con placer maligno, con satisfacción maliciosa.

glob [glɑb, B glɔb] *s.* 1. gotita, bulbito. 2. terrón grande.

global ['gloʊbəl] *a.* 1. mundial. 2. global, total. 3. globoso, esférico.

global warming, calentamiento global, calentamiento del planeta.

globally [-bəlɪ] *adv.* 1. mundialmente. 2. globalmente, en conjunto.

globate [-ˌbeɪt] **globated** [-ed] *a.* globoso, esférico, globular.

globe [gloʊb] *s.* 1. globo, esfera, bola. 2. globo terráqueo o terrestre, esfera terrestre, orbe. 3. globo, globo terráqueo (mapa). 4. orbe (como insignia de soberanía). 5. (anat.) globo ocular. —*v.t., v.i.* (ant.) dar o tomar forma de globo.

globe amaranth, (bot.) amarantina, perpetua, perpetua encarnada.

globefish ['gloʊbˌfɪʃ] *s.* (ict.) orbe; erizo.

globeflower [-ˌflaʊər, B -ə] *s.* (bot.) calderona.

globe sight, (arm.) mira esférica.

globe-trotter [-ˌtrɑtər, B -ˌtrɔtə] *s.* trotamundos.

globe-trotting [-ɪŋ] *s.* viajes frecuentes por el mundo. —*a.* de trotamundos.

globe valve, válvula esférica.

globin ['gloʊbən] *s.* (bioquím.) globina.

globoid ['gloʊˌbɔɪd] *a.* globoso. —*s.* esferoide.

globose [-ˌboʊs] *a.* globoso, redondo, globular, esférico.

globosity [gloʊ'bɑsətɪ, B -'bɔs-] *s.* esfericidad, redondez.

globous ['gloʊbəs] *a.* globoso, redondo.

globular ['glɑbjələr, B 'glɔbjʊlə] *a.* 1. globular, globoso, redondo. 2. globular, compuesto de glóbulos. 3. mundial.

globulariaceous [ˌglɑbjəˌlærɪ'eɪʃəs, B 'glɔb-] *a.* (bot.) globulariáceo.

globule ['glɑbjul, B 'glɔb-] *s.* glóbulo, gota; (anat.) glóbulo.

globuliferous [ˌglɑbjə'lɪfərəs, B ˌglɔb-] *a.* (anat.) globulífero.

globulin ['glɑbjələn, B 'glɔb-] *s.* (bioquím.) globulina.

globulose ['glɑbjəloʊs, B 'glɔb-] **globulous** [-ləs] *a.* globuloso, esférico.

glochidiate [gloʊ'kɪdɪət] *a.* (bot.) provisto de gloquidios.

glochidium [-ɪəm] *s.* (*pl.* GLOCHIDIA [-ɪə]) (bot.) gloquidio.

glockenspiel ['glɑkənˌspil, B 'glɔkən-] *s.* (mús.) órgano de campanas; juego de timbres.

glom [glɑm, B glɔm] *v.t.* (*pret., p.p.* GLOMMED; *p.pr.* GLOMMING) (jer.) 1. hurtar, robar. 2. asir, agarrar, coger.

glomerate ['glɑmərət, B 'glɔm-] *a.* aglomerado, conglomerado.

glomeration [ˌglɑmə'reɪʃən, B ˌglɔm-] *s.* conglobación, conglomeración, aglomeración.

glomerular [glɑ'mɛrjələr, B glɔ'mɛəjʊlə] *a.* (biol.) glomerular.

glomerulate [-lət] *a.* racimoso.

glomerule ['glɑməˌrul, B 'glɔm-] *s.* (bot., anat.) glomérulo.

glomerulus [glɑ'mɛrjələs, B glɔ'mɛəjʊ-] *s.* (*pl.* GLOMERULI [-ˌlaɪ]) (anat.) glomérulo.

gloom [glum] *s.* 1. penumbra, lobreguez, tenebrosidad. 2 melancolía, abatimiento, tristeza, desaliento. 3. aspecto adusto o entristecido, mirada ceñuda. —*v.i.* 1. tener aspecto adusto, entristecido, desalentado o lúgubre. 2. obscurecerse, encapotarse (el cielo, etc.). 3. ser o parecer obscuro, sombrío o triste. —*v.t.* 1. obscurecer. 2. entristecer, ensombrecer, oscurecer.

gloomily ['glumәlɪ] *adv.* 1. obscuramente, tenebrosamente. 2. melancólicamente, tristemente.

gloominess [-mɪnəs] *s.* 1. obscuridad, tenebrosidad. 2. melancolía, tristeza.

glooming [-mɪŋ] *s.* (poét., ant.) penumbra; crepúsculo.

gloomy [-mɪ] *a.* 1. obscuro, lóbrego, sombrío, tenebroso; nublado, encapotado. 2. melancólico, triste, abatido, desalentado. 3. deprimente, desalentador.

gloria ['glɔrɪə] *s.* 1. nimbo, aureola. 2. gloria (tejido satinado).

glorification [ˌglɔrəfə'keɪʃən] *s.* 1. glorificación. 2. (fam., G.B.) fiesta, festividad.

glorifier ['glɔrəˌfaɪer, B -ˌfaɪə] *s.* glorificador.

glorify [-ˌfaɪ] *v.t.* (*pret., p.p.* GLORIFIED; *p.pr.* GLORIFYING) 1. glorificar, exaltar, ensalzar. 2. ensalzar por adulonería o con el propósito de engañar.

gloriole [-ɪˌoʊl] *s.* aureola, nimbo, halo.

glorious [-ɪəs] *a.* 1. glorioso, laudable, loable. 2. espléndido, brillante, resplandeciente. 3. (fam.) delicioso, magnífico.

gloriously [-lɪ] *adv.* gloriosamente; magníficamente, espléndidamente.

gloriousness [-nəs] *s.* gloria, calidad de glorioso.

glory ['glɔrɪ] *s.* 1. gloria, alabanza; honra, distinción; renombre, reputación, fama. 2. gloria, esplendor, magnificencia, pompa. 3. gloria, bienaventuranza. 4. cumbre de prosperidad o esplendor. 5. aureola, nimbo, halo. 6. **to be in one's g.,** estar uno en la gloria; **to go to g.,** morir(se); **to send to g.,** (hum.) matar. —*v.i.* (*pret., p.p.* GLORIED; *p.pr.* GLORYING) exultar, regocijarse; enorgullecerse, vanagloriarse.

gloss [glɑs, glɔs, B glɔs] *s.* 1. brillo, lustre; pulimento. 2. apariencia falaz, oropel. —*v.t.* 1. lustrar, pulir, barnizar. 2. (gen. con *over*) dar apariencia falaz a; paliar, encubrir, disimular (defecto, crimen, etc.).

gloss [glɑs, glɔs, B glɔs] *s.* 1. glosa, escolio, nota, comentario, observación, nota explicatoria, acotación, apostilla; glosario. 2. falsa interpretación; disculpa o pretexto engañoso. —*v.t.* 1. glosar, notar, comentar, acotar, apostillar. 2. interpretar falaz o especiosamente.

glossa ['glɑsə, 'glɔsə, B 'glɔsə] *s.* (*pl.* GLOSSAE [-ˌi]) (zool.) glosis.

glossal [-əl] *a.* (med.) glosiano.

glossarial [glɑ'sɛrɪəl, glɔ-, B glɔ'sɛər-] *a.* de glosario.

glossarist ['glɑsərəst, 'glɔs-, B 'glɔs-] *s.* glosador, comentador, escoliador, escoliasta.

glossary [-ərɪ] *s.* glosario.

glossectomy [glɑ'sɛktəmɪ, glɔ-, B glɔ-] *s.* (med.) glosectomía.

glosser ['glɑsər, 'glɔs-, B 'glɔsə] *s.* bruñidor.

glossily [-əlɪ] *adv.* brillantemente, lustrosamente.

glossiness [-ɪnəs] *s.* lustre, pulimento.

glossitis [glɑ'saɪtəs, glɔ-, B glɔ-] *s.* (med.) glositis, glotitis.

glossographer [-'sɑgrəfər, B -'sɔgrəfə] *s.* glosador.

glossography [-fɪ] *s.* 1. arte de glosar o de hacer glosarios. 2. (anat.) descripción de la lengua.

glossolalia [ˌglɑsə'leɪlɪə, ˌglɔs-, B ˌglɔs-] *s.* glosolalia, guirigay, farfulla, galimatías.

glossology [glɑ'sɑlədʒɪ, glɔ-, B glɔ'sɔl-] *s.* 1. (ant.) lingüística, glotología. 2. (ant.) nomenclatura, terminología.

glossy ['glɑsɪ, 'glɔsɪ, B 'glɔsɪ] *a.* 1. liso, brillante, lustroso, satinado. 2. especioso; cursi. —*s.* (foto.) fotografía en brillo.

glossy magazine, revista de portada atractiva y lujosa presentación.

glottal ['glɑtəl, B 'glɔt-] *a.* (anat.) glótico; (fon.) glotal, glótico.

glottal stop, (fon.) oclusión glótica, golpe de glotis; oclusiva glotal.

glottic [-ɪk] *a.* 1. (anat.) glótico, glotal. 2. (ant.) lingüístico.

glottis [-əs] *s.* (anat.) glotis.

glottologist [glɑ'tɑlədʒəst, B glɔ'tɔl-] *s.* lingüista (persona).

glottology [-dʒɪ] *s.* glotología, glosología, lingüística.

glove [glʌv] *s.* guante; guante de boxeo; **to be hand and g.,** ser uña y carne, ser inseparables; **to fit like a g.,** quedar (entallar, ajustar) como un guante; **to handle with kid gloves,** manejar o tratar con mucho cuidado; **to take up the g.,** (fig.) recoger el guante, aceptar el reto; **to throw down the g.,** (fig.) arrojar o lanzar el guante, retar; **with the gloves off,** sin piedad, sin miramientos, despiadadamente. —*v.t.* enguantar.

glove compartment, (aut.) gaveta para guantes, guantera (Amer.).

glover ['glʌvər, B -ə] *s.* guantero, guantera, persona que hace o vende guantes.

glove stretcher, ensanchador de guantes (artefacto).

glow [gloʊ] *v.i.* 1. brillar, resplandecer, fulgurar (con calor intenso pero sin llama); irradiar luz intensa y calor; brillar como algo incandescente; lucir color brillante. 2. (fig.) (gen. con *with*) enrojecerse o resplandecer (de calor, animación o agitación). 3. (fig.) (con *with*) abrasarse, quemarse, enardecerse o animarse (de calor o

pasión). —*v.t.* (ant.) enrojecer; hacer brillar. —*s.* 1. brillo (sin llama), resplandor. 2. luminosidad, viveza (de color). 3. calor agradable, sensación de calor (en el cuerpo). 4. rubor, color subido (de las mejillas); (fig.) ardor, fervor (de emociones).
glower ['glaʊər, B -ə] *v.i.* 1. tener la mirada ceñuda. 2. **g. at,** mirar con cólera o con ceño. —*s.* mirada colérica o ceñuda.
glowering [-ərɪŋ] *a.* ceñudo; de mirada colérica.
gloweringly [-lɪ] *adv.* (mirar) coléricamente o de manera ceñuda.
glowfly ['gloʊ͵flaɪ] *s.* (ento.) luciérnaga, cocuyo, gusano de luz.
glowing [-ɪŋ] *a.* 1. resplandeciente, incandescente. 2. radiante, vivo (color, rostro, etc.). 3. ardiente, fervoroso, entusiasta.
glow lamp, lámpara incandescente, lámpara de descarga luminosa.
glow plug, (mot.) tapón encendedor.
glowworm [-͵wɜrm, B -͵wɜm] *s.* (ento.) gusano de luz, luciérnaga, cocuyo.
gloxinia [glɑk'sɪnɪə, B glɔk-] *s.* (bot.) gloxínea.
gloze [gloʊz] *v.t.* 1. (gen. con *over*) atenuar, paliar. 2. (ant.) glosar. 3. (anat.) iluminar, abrillantar. —*v.i.* (ant.) ser lisonjero.
glucinum [glu'saɪnəm] **glucinium** [-'sɪnɪəm] *s.* (quím.) glucinio.
gluconic acid [-'kɑnɪk-, B -'kɔn-] (quím.) ácido glucónico.
glucoprotein [͵glukoʊ'proʊ͵tin, -tɪən] *var. de* **glycoprotein.**
glucose ['glukoʊs] *s.* (quím.) glucosa.
glucoside ['glukə͵saɪd] *s.* (quím.) glucósido.
glue [glu] *s.* cola; goma. —*v.t.* encolar, pegar con cola o goma; **g. (an eye, an ear) to,** (fig.) pegar (ojo, oreja) a (una ventana o pared para atisbar o escuchar).
gluey ['gluɪ] *a.* gomoso, pegajoso, viscoso, glutinoso.
glum [glʌm] *a.* melancólico, apenado, displicente, triste, sombrío.
glumaceous [glu'meɪʃəs] *a.* (bot.) glumáceo.
glume [glum] *s.* (bot.) gluma.
glumly ['glʌmlɪ] *adv.* displicentemente; tristemente.
glumness [-nəs] *s.* melancolía, displicencia, tristeza.
glut [glʌt] *v.t.* 1. saciar, hartar, ahitar. 2. (fig.) inundar, sobrecargar (el mercado). 3. **g. oneself,** hartarse. —*v.i.* saciarse, hartarse, ahitarse, comer con glotonería. —*s.* 1. hartazgo, surtido o provisión excesivos (de mercaderías). 2. (ant.) glotonería; hartura, plétora.
glutamate ['glutə͵meɪt] *s.* (quím.) glutamato.
glutamic acid [glu'tæmɪk-] *s.* (quím.) ácido glutámico.
glutamine ['glutə͵min] *s.* (quím.) glutamina.
gluteal [glu'tiəl] *a.* (anat.) glúteo.
gluten ['glutən] *s.* gluten.
gluten bread, pan de gluten.
glutenous [-əs] *a.* (bot.) 1. glutenoideo. 2. rico en gluten.
gluteus ['glutɪəs] *s.* (*pl.* GLUTEI [-͵aɪ]) (anat.) glúteo.
glutinous ['glutənəs] *a.* glutinoso, pegajoso.
glutinousness [-nəs] *s.* glutinosidad.
glutton ['glʌtən] *s.* 1. glotón, tragón, comilón, heliogábalo, comelón (Méx.). 2. (zool.) glotón.
gluttonous [-əs] *a.* glotón, voraz.
gluttonously [-lɪ] *adv.* glotonamente, vorazmente.
gluttony ['glʌtənɪ] *s.* gula, glotonería, voracidad.
glyceraldehyde [͵glɪsə'rældə͵haɪd] *s.* (quím.) aldehído glicérico, glicerosa.
glyceric acid [glɪ'sɛrɪk-, 'glɪsər-] (quím.) ácido glicérico.
glyceride ['glɪsə͵raɪd] *s.* (quím.) glicérido.
glycerin ['glɪsərən] *s.* (quím.) glicerina.
glycerinate [-rə͵neɪt] *v.t.* (quím.) glicerinar, tratar con glicerina.
glycerine [-rən, B ͵glɪsə'rin] *var. de* **glycerin.**
glycerol ['glɪsə͵rɔl, -͵roʊl, B -͵rɔl] *s.* (quím.) glicerol.
glyceryl [-rəl] *s.* (quím.) glicerilo.
glycine ['glaɪ͵sin] *s.* (quím.) glicina.
glycogen ['glaɪkədʒən, B 'glɪkədʒɛn] *s.* (bioquím.) glicógeno.
glycogenesis [͵glaɪkə'dʒɛnəsəs] *s.* (quím.) glicogénesis, glicogenia.
glycogenetic [-dʒə'nɛtɪk] *a.* (quím.) glicógeno, glucógeno.
glycogenic [-'dʒɛnɪk] *a.* (quím.) glicogénico, glucogénico.
glycol ['glaɪ͵kɔl, -͵koʊl, B -͵kɔl] *s.* (quím.) glicol.
glycolic [glaɪ'kɑlɪk, B -'kɔl-] *a.* (quím.) glicólico.
glyconic [glaɪ'kɑnɪk, B -'kɔn-] *a.* (poét.) glicomio.
glycoprotein [͵glaɪkoʊ'proʊ͵tin, -tɪən] *s.* (bioquím.) glicoproteína.
glycoside ['glaɪkə͵saɪd] **glycosid** ['glaɪkə͵sɪd] *s.* (quím.) glicósido, glucósido.
glycosuria [͵glaɪkoʊ'sʊrɪə, B -'sjʊər-] *s.* (med.) glicosuria, glucosuria.
glycosuric [-ɪk] *a.* (med.) glucosúrico.
glyph [glɪf] *s.* 1. (arq.) glifo. 2. (arqueol.) figura grabada, esp. jeroglífico maya.
glyphic ['glɪfɪk] *a.* (arq.) glífico, tallado.
glyptic ['glɪptɪk] *s.* glíptica.
glyptodont ['glɪptə͵dɑnt, B -͵dɔnt] *s.* (pal.) gliptodonte.
glyptograph [-͵græf, B -͵grɑf] *s.* inscripción grabada sobre gema; gema así grabada.
glyptographer [glɪp'tɑgrəfər, B -'tɔgrəfə] *s.* gliptógrafo, gliptólogo.
glyptographic [-tə'græfɪk] **glyptographical** [-ɪkəl] *a.* gliptográfico.
glyptography [-'tɑgrəfɪ, B -'tɔg-] *s.* 1. glíptica. 2. gliptografía; gliptología.
G. M. *abrev. de* 1. **grand master,** gran maestro. 2. **guided missile,** proyectil teledirigido.
gm. *abrev. de* **gram,** gramo (g., gr.).
G-man ['dʒi͵mæn] *s.* (E.U.) detective de la Oficina Federal de Investigación, agente de la policía secreta federal.
GMT *abrev. de* **Greenwich mean time,** hora media de Greenwich (HMG).
gnar, gnarr [nɑr, B nɑ] *v.i.* (onomatopeya) gruñir, refunfuñar.
gnarl [nɑrl, B nɑl] *v.t.* torcer, retorcer, deformar. —*s.* nudo (en la madera o en un árbol). —*v.i.* gruñir, refunfuñar.
gnarled [nɑrld, B nɑld] *a.* 1. nudoso, cubierto de protuberancias; retorcido, deforme. 2. rugoso (ej., corteza). 3. (fig.) áspero, escabroso.
gnarly ['nɑrlɪ, B 'nɑlɪ] *a. var. de* **gnarled.**
gnash [næʃ] *v.t.* hacer rechinar o crujir (los dientes). —*s.* rechinamiento, crujido (de los dientes).
gnat [næt] *s.* (ento.) mosquito, cénzalo, zancudo (Amer.), jején (Amer.).
gnathic ['næθɪk] *a.* (anat.) gnático.
gnathic index, indice gnático o alveolar.
gnathonic [næ'θɑnɪk, B -'θɔn-] *a.* lisonjero, halagüeño.
gnaw [nɔ] *v.t.* (*pret.* GNAWED; *p.p.* GNAWED o GNAWN [nɔn] *p.pr.* GNAWING) 1. roer, mordiscar, mordisquear, mascar. 2. corroer, raer; (fig.) consumir. 3. vejar, torturar, remorder. —*v.i.* (con *at*) mordiscar, roer; consumir.
gnawer ['nɔər, B -ə] *s.* roedor.
gnawing [-ɪŋ] *s.* (*gen. pl.*) retortijón o retorcijón (de hambre).
gneiss [naɪs] *s.* (geol.) gneis.
gneissic ['naɪsɪk] *a.* (geol.) gnéisico.
Gnetaceae [nə'teɪsɪ͵i] *s. pl.* (bot.) gnetáceas.
gnetaceous [-'teɪʃəs] *a.* (bot.) gnetáceo.
gnome [noʊm, B 'noʊmi] *s.* máxima, aforismo.
gnome [noʊm] *s.* gnomo, nomo.
gnome owl, (orn.) chucho.
gnomic ['noʊmɪk] **gnomical** [-ɪkəl] *a.* gnómico, nómico (poeta, poesía).
gnomology [noʊ'mɑlədʒɪ, B -'mɔl-] *s.* gnomología.
gnomon ['noʊ͵mɑn, B -͵mɔn] *s.* 1. gnomon (del reloj solar). 2. (geom.) gnomon.
gnomonic [noʊ'mɑnɪk, B -'mɔn-] *a.* gnomónico.
gnomonics [-ɪks] *s.* gnomónica.
gnosis ['noʊsəs] *s.* (filos.) gnosis, nosis.
Gnostic ['nɑstɪk, B 'nɔs-] *a., s.* gnóstico, nóstico.
Gnosticism [-tə͵sɪzəm] *s.* gnosticismo, nosticismo.
GNP *abrev. de* **gross national product,** producción o producto nacional bruto.
gnu [nu, B nju] *s.* (*pl.* GNU o GNUS) (zool.) ñu.
go [goʊ] *v.i.* (*pret.* WENT [wɛnt]; *p.p.* GONE [gɔn, gɑn, B gɔn]; *p.pr.* GOING ['goʊɪŋ]) 1. ir, moverse, proseguir, seguir adelante, marchar. 2. partir, irse, marcharse. 3. (t. **go about**) andar, caminar, estar (ej., desnudo, armado). 4. volverse, tornarse (loco, ciego, etc.). 5. ceder, irse abajo; romperse, averiarse, ej., *the mainmast went in the gale,* el palo mayor cedió con el viento; p. ext. (de personas) desmayarse; morir, morirse. 6. funcionar, marchar (negocio, máquina), ej., *a going concern,* empresa que marcha. 7. transcurrir, pasar, correr (el tiempo). 8. ser corriente, aceptado o conocido; circular (noticia, dinero). 9. estar en el promedio o término medio, ej., *he is a good author as authors go nowadays,* es un buen escritor comparado con el escritor promedio de hoy. 10. extenderse; ir, llegar (hasta), ej., *this road goes to London,* este camino va hasta Londres. 11. alcanzar, llegar, afectar, tener (cierto) efecto, ej., *will go a long way* (*to* o *towards*), tendrá mucho efecto (en), ayudará mucho (a); alcanzará para mucho, bastará por largo tiempo. 12. suceder, ocurrir, resultar. 13. rezar, decir, leerse (documento, etc.). 14. (con *to*) recurrir, acudir, apelar (a), ej., *go to court,* recurrir o acudir a los tribunales. 15. (con *to*) incurrir (en dificultades, gastos); proceder, actuar (de cierta manera). 16. venir, sentar o caer (bien o mal); acomodarse, adaptarse, congeniar. 17. entrar, penetrar; (con *in, on*) pertenecer (a), ir (en), tener su sitio (habitual) (en), ej., *success went to his head,* el éxito se le subió a la cabeza, el éxito le envaneció o le engrió; *the book goes on this shelf,* el libro va (tiene su sitio) en este anaquel. 18. valer, ser válido o aceptable, ej., *anything goes,* todo vale. 19. pasar, escaparse, ej., *go unobserved,* pasar inadvertido. 20. gastarse (el dinero); venderse (esp. en remate), ej., *the Picasso went for five thousand dollars,* el Picasso se vendió en cinco mil dólares. 21. **go about,** emprender, empezar a hacer; (soler) andar o caminar (ej., armado, hambriento); atender a, dedicarse a (asuntos propios); procurar; intentar; dar vueltas, ir de un sitio a otro; estar en circulación (dinero); (mar.) virar de bordo, cambiar de amuras; **go about** (o **around**) **with,** andar en compañía de, asociarse con; **go about one's business,** meterse uno en

lo que le importa; **go abroad,** ir al extranjero, partir o salir del país; divulgarse (alguna noticia); **go across,** cruzar; **go after,** seguir a, ir tras de, perseguir; ir por (algo); atacar; **go against,** oponerse a, ir en contra de; chocar con; **go ahead,** adelantar; ir delante; seguir, proseguir (sin titubeos); **go all out,** (fam.) ir hasta el tope, jugarse el todo por el todo; esforzarse al máximo; **go along,** seguir, continuar, proseguir; **go along with,** (E.U.) acompañar, ir con (alguien); estar de acuerdo con; (jer.) andar con (alguien); **go around,** dar vueltas, ir de un sitio a otro; (soler) andar (ej., armado, hambriento, etc.); bastar o alcanzar para todos, dar abasto; circular, propalarse (noticia, cuento, etc.); **go around with,** (jer.) tener citas frecuentes con; **go at,** emprender; atacar; acometer; **go away,** irse, marchar(se); pasar (dolor, etc.); **go away with,** llevarse (algo); robar; **go back,** retroceder, regresar; volverse atrás; desistir, cejar, ceder; **go back on,** traicionar, abandonar (principios, amigos, etc.); **go back on (upon) one's word,** faltar a su palabra, retractarse; **go back to,** remontarse hasta, datar de; **go before,** preceder; **go behind,** ir detrás o atrás de; investigar, reexaminar; **go better,** (póquer) subir la apuesta previa; (fam.) mejorar, sobrepasar; exceder; **go between,** interponerse entre, terciar, mediar entre; **go beyond,** ir más allá de, exceder, sobrepujar; **go by,** pasar, pasar por (un lugar); pasar al lado de; ajustarse a, atenerse a, regirse por; conocerse por (nombre, etc.); **go by the board,** ser abandonado, ser relegado (un asunto, proyecto); (fam.) perderse, arruinarse, irse al diablo; **go crazy,** enloquecerse; **go deep (into),** ahondar, profundizar (en); **go down,** hundirse (un barco); ponerse (el sol); bajar, descender; caer (ante un contendor); caerse; ser inscrito o registrado; tener acogida, ser aceptado; ser considerado; pasar a la historia; (G.B.) dejar la universidad; graduarse (en la universidad); **go down before,** sucumbir ante; **go down with,** enfermarse de, caer enfermo de; **go far,** ir lejos, servir de mucho; alcanzar para mucho; **go for,** ir a traer, ir por; (jer.) atacar, acometer, embestir; pasar por, ser tenido por; aprobar, aceptar; valer para; **go for (something o someone),** (jer.) gustarle (algo o alguien) a uno; **go forth,** salir; **go forward,** adelantar, adelantarse; **go from,** marcharse de, abandonar; **go hot and cold,** tener escalofríos; **go in,** entrar (como competidor); obscurecerse, ocultarse (el sol); entrar; encajar en; caber en; **go in for,** dedicarse a; tomar parte en; interesarse por, apoyar, favorecer; adherirse a; **go in with,** unirse con, aliarse con, compartir gastos con; **go into,** ponerse de (luto); entregarse a (histerismo, elogios, etc.); dedicarse a (una profesión); examinar, investigar; tocar (un asunto, etc.); caber en; **go mad,** enloquecerse; **go off,** hacer explosión; estallar; sonar; dispararse (un arma); desmayarse, perder el conocimiento; morirse; salir, resultar (bien o mal un asunto); irse, largarse; **go off one's head,** enloquecer, trastornarse; **go on,** continuar, proseguir; perseverar; ir adelante; suceder, ocurrir; encenderse (luz); **go on!** ¡qué va! ¡no me venga con cuentos!; **go on about,** seguir hablando de, hablar sin cesar de; **go on the stage,** hacerse actor o actriz; **go on strike,** declararse en huelga; **go on the air,** hablar o transmitirse por radio; **go on the town,** irse de juerga; **go on the streets,** echarse a la vida; **go out,** salir; salir de casa; apagarse, extinguirse; fallar (motor, etc.); (jer.) perder el conocimiento, desmayarse; **go out of fashion,** pasar de moda; **go out with,** pasar de moda junto con; **go over,** examinar; estudiar, repasar; repetir; ensayar; recorrer; pasar por encima de; ser acogido, salir (bien, mal); **go over to,** pasarse, cambiarse al (otro lado, partido, religión, etc.); **go over the top,** (mil.) salar de la trinchera para atacar al enemigo; **go past,** pasar, pasar de largo; **go places,** (jer.) tener éxito; **go straight,** vivir honradamente; **go through,** registrar, examinar cuidadosamente; pasar por, sufrir, desempeñar, ejecutar; atravesar; penetrar; aprobarse; **go through an inheritance,** dilapidar o derrochar una herencia; **go through with,** llevar a su término, llevar a cabo; **go through hell,** pasar las de Caín; **go together,** armonizar entre sí, avenirse; andar o ir juntos; **go to bed,** acostarse; **go to pieces,** abatirse, darse a la desesperación; sufrir un ataque de nervios; **go to sea,** hacerse marinero; **go to the bar,** hacerse abogado; **go under,** hundirse; fracasar; quebrar, quedar arruinado; sucumbir; ser arrollado o vencido; **go up,** subir; levantarse (edificios, construcciones, etc.); (G.B.) ir a la universidad; **go up in smoke,** (fam.) esfumarse; **go up the line,** (mil.) partir al frente (desde la base); **go with,** armonizar con, ir bien con; acompañar; (fam.) galantear; **go with the tide** (o **times**), dejarse llevar por la corriente, adaptarse a los tiempos; **go without,** pasarse sin, arreglárselas sin; **he is (still) going strong,** sigue actuando con vigor; **he's gone and done it,** (fam.) ¡ al fin lo hizo!; **he will go far,** llegará lejos, logrará éxito; **he would not go higher than 100 dollars,** no quiso dar, pagar u ofrecer más de 100 dólares; **to be going (to do),** ir a (hacer); **to be going on (thirty, five o'clock),** estar acercándose a (los treinta años, las cinco horas); **to be gone,** haberse agotado o gastado; haberse roto; haberse muerto, haber dejado de ser; **to go,** queda(n), ej., *there are five minutes to go before the match ends,* quedan cinco minutos antes que termine el partido; **to let go,** soltar; **to let go with,** (jer.) disparar (un arma); criticar, reprender severamente; **to let oneself go,** (fig.) soltarse. —*v.t.* 1. seguir (camino), emprender (viaje). 2. dar (la hora), ej., *the clock went five,* el reloj dio las cinco. 3. (fam.) soportar, sufrir, resistir, sobrellevar, tolerar, aguantar. 4. apostar, envidar (en juegos). 5. (bridge) declarar, ej., *he went four spades,* él declaró cuatro espadas. 6. **go (ten dollars,** etc.) **better,** ofrecer (diez dólares, etc.) más; **go halves** o **fifty fifty,** ir a medias; **go it,** (fam.) correrla, desenfrenarse; (imper.) ¡dale todo! ¡vamos! (ú. para alentar a alguien); **go it alone,** hacerlo solo, hacerlo sin ayuda; **go one's way,** proseguir uno su camino; **go the limit,** (fam.) ofrecer o apostar el máximo posible; jugar el todo por el todo; **go the way of all flesh,** pasar a mejor vida, morir. —*s.* (*pl.* GOES) 1. ánimo, energía, empuje. 2. (con *the*) (fam.) moda, usanza, boga. 3. (fam.) caso, incidente, situación, circunstancia. 4. empresa afortunada, éxito; ganga; negocio redondo, ej., *to make a go of,* tener éxito en, sacar adelante (un negocio). 5. (fam.) intento, intentona, ensayo, ej., *to have a go at,* hacer un intento, tentar, intentar, *a brief go at farming,* un breve ensayo en la agricultura. 6. (fam.) porción, dosis; copa, trago (de licor). 7. **is it a go?** ¿está resuelto? ¿estamos convenidos?; **it's a go,** trato hecho; **it's no go,** es inútil, esto no camina o marcha, es imposible, es un fracaso; **on the go,** en actividad, en movimiento, trajinando; en decadencia. —*a.* (fam.) listo (para entrar en acción), ej., *all planes are go,* todos los aviones están listos para entrar en acción.

goad [goʊd] *s.* 1. aguijada, aijada. 2. espuela, acicate, incitativo. —*v.t.* 1. aguijonear, aguijar. 2. (fig.) incitar, estimular, acicatear.

go-ahead [ˈgoʊəd,hɛd] *a.* emprendedor, activo, enérgico. —*s.* señal de pase; **to get** (o **give**) **the g.-a. signal,** recibir (o dar) la señal de permiso o de pase (para seguir adelante), o el visto bueno.

goal [goʊl] *s.* 1. meta, fin, objetivo, propósito, finalidad. 2. (dep.) portería, meta; gol, tanto.

goalee, goalie [ˈgoʊlɪ] *s.* (dep.) portero, guardameta, guardavalla.

goalkeeper [-,kipər, B -pə] o **goaltender** [ˈgoʊl,tɛndər] *s.* (dep.) portero, guardameta, guardavalla.

goal kick, (fútbol) tiro libre de meta.

goal line, (dep.) línea de gol, línea de meta.

goalpost [-,poʊst] *s.* (dep.) poste de la portería.

Goa powder [ˈgoʊə-] polvo de Goa, polvo de Bahía, polvo de araroba.

goat [goʊt] *s.* 1. cabra; macho cabrío, cabrón. 2. (fig.) libertino, disoluto. 3. (jer.) cabeza de turco. 4. **G.,** (astr.) Capricornio. 5. **to be the g.,** (jer.) pagar el pato, ser cabeza de turco; **to get one's g.,** (jer.) enojar, causar molestia, tomar el pelo a, hacer irritar a.

goatee [goʊˈti] *s.* perilla, pera, barbas de chivo.

goatfish [ˈgoʊt,fɪʃ] *s.* (ict.) lisa, mújol, mújil.

goatherd [-,hɜrd, B -,hɜd] *s.* cabrero, cabrerizo, pastor de cabras.

goatish [ˈgoʊtɪʃ] *a.* 1. caprino, cabruno, cabrerizo, cabrío. 2. (fig.) lascivo, lujurioso.

goatishness [-nəs] *s.* 1. parecido a cabras. 2. naturaleza lasciva.

goatlike [-,laɪk] *a.* de cabras(s), cabruno.

goat pepper, (bot.) pimiento de las Indias, guindilla, ají (Amer.), chile (Méx.).

goatsbeard [ˈgoʊts,bɪrd, B -,bɪəd] *s.* 1. (bot.) barba cabruna, barba de cabra, salsifí. 2. (bot.) barba de cabrón.

goatskin [ˈgoʊt,skɪn] *s.* piel de cabra.

goat's-rue [ˈgoʊts,ru] *s.* (bot.) galega, ruda cabruna.

goatsucker [ˈgoʊt,sʌkər, B -ə] *s.* (orn.) chotacabras.

gob [gɑb, B gɔb] *s.* 1. burujo, trocito; gota. 2. (jer.) marinero. 3. (jer. G.B.) boca. 4. (*pl.*) (fam.) gran cantidad, ej., *gobs of money,* mucho dinero.

gobbet [ˈgɑbət, B ˈgɔb-] *s.* 1. porción, pedazo, fragmento, trozo (de carne); masa (pequeña), bulto. 2. bocado.

gobble [ˈgɑbəl, B ˈgɔb-] *v.t.* 1.engullir, devorar, tragar apresuradamente. 2. (gen. con *up*) posesionarse ávidamente de. —*v.i.* 1. comer atropelladamente. 2. gluglutear, graznar (el pavo). —*s.* gluglú, graznido del pavo.

gobbledygook, gobbledegook [-dɪˈgʊk] *s.* (jer., E.U.) galimatías, guirigay, blablablá (Amer.).

gobbler [ˈgɑblər, B ˈgɔblə] *s.* 1. pavo (macho). 2. (jer.) glotón, tragón; tragador.

Gobelin [ˈgoʊbələn, ˈgɑbə-, B ˈgoʊbə-] *a.* gobelino, tapiz rico en diseños.

go-between [ˈgoʊbə,twin] *s.* intermediario, mediador; corredor; (jer.) alcahuete.

Gobi [ˈgoʊbɪ] *s.* Gobi, desierto del Asia Central.

gobioid [ˈgoʊbɪ,ɔɪd] *a.* (ict.) góbido.

goblet [ˈgɑblət, B ˈgɔb-] *s.* 1. copa. 2. (ant.) tazón (sin asas).

goblin [ˈgɑblən, B ˈgɔb-] *s.* duende, trasgo, gnomo, nomo.

gobo [ˈgoʊboʊ] *s.* (*pl.* GOBOS O GOBOES) 1. (cinem., t.v.) gobo, visera de cámara, pantalla a prueba de luz. 2. (rad.) gobo, pantalla antisonora.

goby [ˈgoʊbɪ] *s.* (ict.) gobio, cadoce.

go-by ['goʊˌbaɪ] *s.* (fam.) esquinazo, desaire.
go-cart ['goʊˌkɑrt, B -ˌkɑt] *s.* 1. andaderas. 2. cochecito para niños. 3. carretilla de mano. 4. (tipo de) coche ligero.
God [gɑd, B gɔd] *s.* 1. Dios. 2. **g.,** deidad, dios; hombre adorado como dios; ídolo. 3. (jer., teat.) espectador de cazuela; (*pl.*) paraíso, gallinero, cazuela. 4. **act of G.,** obra de Dios; (der.) fuerza mayor; **by G.!** ¡voto a Dios!; **for God's sake,** por amor de Dios; **G. bless you!** ¡que Dios le ayude!; **G. forbid,** no lo quiera Dios; **G. grant,** ojalá, permita Dios (que); **G. knows,** sabe Dios, sólo Dios lo sabe; no lo sé; llamo a Dios como testigo de que; **God's truth,** verdad absoluta; **G. willing,** Dios mediante, si Dios quiere; **(oh) my G.!** ¡Dios mío! ¡Dios!; **thank G.!** ¡gracias a Dios!; **with G.,** en el paraíso (díc. de los difuntos). *—v.t.* (*pret., p.p.* GODDED; *p.pr.* GODDING) (fig.) endiosar, deificar, divinizar.
god-awful ['gɑdˌɔfəl, B 'gɔd-] *a.* (jer.) atroz, inconcebible.
godchild [-ˌtʃaɪld] *s.* ahijado, ahijada.
goddam, goddamn [-'dæm] **goddamned** [-'dæmd] *a.* (vulg.) maldito. *—adv.* (vulg.) extremadamente. *—interj.* (vulg.) ¡maldición!, !carajo!.
goddaughter [-ˌdɔtər, B -ə] *s.* ahijada.
goddess ['gɑdəs, B 'gɔd-] *s.* 1. diosa. 2. (fig.) diosa, mujer de gran encanto. 3. mujer adorada como diosa.
go-devil ['goʊˌdɛvəl] *s.* 1. (mec.) tarugo, diablo. 2. (ind. petrolera) raspatubos, limpiatubos. 3. (E.U.) rastra, grada (usada en explotación forestal). 4. (f.c.) dresina, carrimano o automotor.
godfather ['gɑdˌfɑðər, B 'gɔd-ə] *s.* padrino. *—v.t.* apadrinar a; ser padrino de.
Godfearing [-ˌfɪrɪŋ, B -ˌfɪərɪŋ] *a.* pío, devoto.
Godforsaken [-fɔr'seɪkən, B -fəˌ-] *a.* 1. desolado, remoto, abandonado. 2. miserable, depravado; desesperado.
Godgiven [-ˌgɪvən] *a.* dado por Dios; que viene al pelo, de perilla, etc.; llovido del cielo.
godhead [-ˌhɛd] *s.* 1. deidad, esencia o naturaleza divina. 2. **the G.,** Dios.
godhood [-ˌhʊd] *s.* divinidad.
godless ['gɑdləs, B 'gɔd-] *a.* ateo, irreligioso, impío, sin Dios, sin religión.
godlessness [-nəs] *s.* ateísmo, irreligiosidad, impiedad.
godlike [-ˌlaɪk] *a.* deiforme; como Dios, divino.
godliness [-lɪnəs] *s.* piedad, devoción, santidad.
godling [-lɪŋ] *s.* deidad (inferior o puramente local).
godly ['gɑdlɪ, B 'gɔd-] *a.* (GODLIER; GODLIEST) 1. divino. 2. pío, devoto.
godmother [-ˌmʌðər, B -ə] *s.* madrina. *—v.t.* asistir como madrina; ser madrina de, amadrinar.
godown ['goʊˌdaʊn] *s.* almacén (en el E. de Asia, Filipinas, etc.).
godparent ['gɑdˌpærənt, -ˌpɛr-, B -ˌpɛər-] *s.* padrino o madrina (de bautizo).
godroon, *var. de* **gadroon.**
God's acre, camposanto, cementerio.
godsend ['gɑdˌsɛnd, B 'gɔd-] *s.* merced divina, cosa llovida del cielo, suerte inesperada, fortuna, buena suerte.
God's heaven, (fig.) paraíso, cazuela, gallinero (de un teatro).
God's house, iglesia, templo; sinagoga.
godson ['gɑdˌsʌn, B 'gɔd-] *s.* ahijado.
Godspeed [-'spid] *s.* bienandanza, buen viaje, buena suerte.
Godward [-wərd, B -wəd] **Godwards** [-wərdz, B -wədz] *adv.* hacia Dios.
godwit [-ˌwɪt] *s.* (orn.) agachadiza.
goer ['goʊər, B -ə] *s.* 1. corredor (díc. de un caballo). 2. (jer., G.B.) perito, experto.
goethite ['gɜrθaɪt, B 'gɜtaɪt] *s.* (min.) goetita.
goffer ['gɑfər, 'gɔf-, B 'goʊfə] *v.t.* 1. encañonar, encrespar, rizar (tela, cinta, papel, etc.). 2. (gen. **gauffer**) gofrar, repujar, ej., *goffered edges* (*of book*), cantos gofrados, bordes repujados (de un libro). *—s.* gofrador, (herramienta); ornamentación gofrada; rizado.
go-for ['goʊˌfɔr, B -ˌfɔ] *s.* (jer.) mensajero; lleva-y-trae.
go-getter ['goʊˌgɛtər, B -ə] *s.* (fam.) buscavidas, trafagón, persona dinámica.
goggle ['gɑgəl, B 'gɔg-] *v.i.* 1. salírsele a uno los ojos; (con *at*) mirar aturdidamente. 2. poner los ojos en blanco. *—a.* saltón, salido (díc. de los ojos).
goggle-eyed [-ˌaɪd] *a.* de ojos saltones.
goggles [-əlz] *s. pl.* gafas protectoras, anteojos de camino.
goglet ['gɑglət, B 'gɔg-] *s.* (anglo-ind.) alcarraza, botijo, cántaro.
go-go ['goʊˌgoʊ] *a.* go-go, vivaz, bullicioso al estilo de la juventud moderna.
go-go girl, go-go dancer, chica go-go, que baila en una discoteca o cabaret.
Goidelic [gɔɪ'dɛlɪk] *a., s.* gaélico.
going ['goʊɪŋ] *s.* 1. ida, partida, marcha. 2. (*gen. en pl.*) proceder, conducta. 3. estado del camino. 4. (ant.) paso, andar. *—a.* 1. en marcha, que funciona, activo, ej, *a g. concern,* un negocio que marcha. 2. que existe, obtenible. 3. corriente, actual (precio, etc.).
going-over [-'oʊvər, B -ə] *s.* 1. inspección rápida. 2. castigo severo.
goings-on [-ɪŋz'ɑn, B -'ɔn] *s. pl.* ocurrencias, sucesos, comportamiento, conducta.
goiter, goitre ['gɔɪtər, B -ə] *s.* (med.) bocio, coto (Amer.).
goitrogenic [ˌgɔɪtrə'dʒɛnɪk] **goiterogenic** [ˌgɔɪtəroʊ-] *a.* (med.) bocígeno.
goitrous ['gɔɪtrəs] *a.* que tiene bocio, cotudo (Amer.).
gola ['goʊlə] *s.* (arq.) gola, cimacio.
Golconda [gɑl'kɑndə, B gɔl'kɔn-] *s.* 1. Golconda, mina muy rica (de la India); p. ext. fuente de riqueza. 2. Golconda, nombre dado al movimiento del clero revolucionario de Sudamérica.
gold [goʊld] *s.* 1. oro. 2. monedas de oro. 3. (fig.) oro, riquezas, fortuna. 4. color del oro. *—a.* 1. de oro. 2. dorado, de color del oro.
gold-bearing ['goʊldˌbɛrɪŋ, B -ˌbɛər-] *a.* aurífero.
goldbeater [-ˌbitər, B -ə] *s.* batidor de oro, batihoja.
goldbeater's skin, venza (membrana del intestino grueso del buey que se usa para separar las hojas de oro al batirlas).
goldbeating ['goʊldˌbitɪŋ] *s.* arte de martillar el oro hasta convertirlo en hojas.
goldbrick [-ˌbrɪk] *s.* 1. oropel, cosa brillante pero sin valor. 2. (fam.) añagaza, embuste. 3. (jer., E.U.) soldado haragán; holgazán. 4. **to sell (someone) a g.,** dar gato por liebre (a alguien). *—v.i.* evitar el trabajo, faltar al trabajo. *—v.t.* embaucar, engañar.
Gold Coast, Costa de Oro, antiguo nombre de Ghana.
goldcrest [-ˌkrɛst] *s.* (orn.) reyezuelo moñudo.
gold digger, 1. buscador de oro. 2. (jer. E.U.) mujer vividora interesada en dinero y regalos; explotadora de hombres.
gold dust, oro en polvo, polvo de oro.
golden ['goʊldən] *a.* 1. áureo, de oro. 2. dorado, del color del oro; rubio. 3. precioso, excelente, muy valioso. 4. próspero, floreciente, feliz. 5. favorable, ventajoso.
Golden age, Edad de Oro; (fig.) siglo de oro, edad de oro (período de gran prosperidad y esclarecimiento).
golden anniversary, quincuagésimo aniversario.
golden buck, salsa de queso derretido con cerveza sobre tostadas con un huevo escalfado.
golden calf, (bíbl., fig.) becerro de oro; oro, riquezas como objetos de adoración.
golden chain, (bot.) lluvia de oro.
golden eagle, (orn.) águila real, águila dorada, águila leonada, águila caudal o caudalosa.
goldeneye ['goʊldənˌaɪ] *s.* (orn.) clángula.
Golden Fleece, 1. (mitol.) vellocino de oro. 2. toisón, toisón de oro.
golden glow, (bot.) rudbequia.
golden goose, gallina de los huevos de oro (en la fábula griega).
Golden Horde, (hist.) Horda de Oro (de los ejércitos mongoles).
Golden Horn, Cuerno de Oro (la bahía de Estambul).
golden mean, justo medio; moderación, prudencia.
golden nematode, (ento.) nematodo amarillento.
golden number, (astr.) número áureo.
golden oriole, (orn.) oropéndola, víreo, virio.
golden pheasant, (orn.) faisán dorado.
golden robin, (orn.) oriol (de Baltimore), oropéndola.
goldenrod ['goʊldənˌrɑd, B -ˌrɔd] *s.* (bot.) vara de oro, vara de San José, plumero amarillo.
golden rule, (mat.) regla de oro, regla áurea.
goldenseal [-ˌsil] *s.* (bot.) variedad de ranunculácea americana.
golden spoon, (bot.) peralejo.
golden thistle, (bot.) cardillo, tagarnina.
golden wattle, (bot.) acacia de flores doradas.
golden wedding, bodas de oro.
goldfield ['goʊldˌfild] *s.* yacimiento de oro.
gold-filled [-'fɪld] *a.* (joy.) revestido de oro, enchapado en oro.
gold filling, (odont.) orificación, obturación de oro.
goldfinch [-ˌfɪntʃ] *s.* (orn.) jilguero, cardelina, pintacilgo, pintadillo; pinzón.
goldfinny [-ˌfɪnɪ] *s.* (ict.) tordo de mar.
goldfish [-ˌfɪʃ] *s.* (ict.) 1. carpa dorada, pececillo de color. 2. (jer., mil.) salmón.
gold foil, (metal.) pan de oro, oro batido.
goldilocks ['goʊldɪˌlɑks, B -ˌlɔks] *s.* 1. persona rubia. 2. (bot.) especie de ranúnculo.
gold leaf, (metal.) pan de oro, hoja de oro (sumamente delgada).
gold mine, 1. mina de oro. 2. (fig.) mina (de información, etc.). 3. (fig.) mina de oro, fuente de gran riqueza o ganancias.
gold-of-pleasure ['goʊldəv'plɛʒər, B -ʒə] *s.* (bot.) camelina.
gold plate, lámina de oro.
gold-plated [-ˌpleɪtəd] *a.* dorado.
gold point, (com.) punto de oro.
gold reserve, (econ.) reservas de oro.
gold rush, 1. fiebre del oro. 2. (hist., E.U.) fiebre de oro, movimiento de buscadores de oro que se desplazaron hacia California en 1849.
goldsmith ['goʊldˌsmɪθ] *s.* orfebre, orífice.
gold standard, (com.) patrón de oro.
goldstone [-ˌstoʊn] *s.* (min.) venturina.
goldthread [-ˌθrɛd] *s.* (bot.) cúscuta.
golem ['goʊləm] *s.* (folklore judío) monstruo, hombre artificialmente creado por ritos cabalísticos; robot; hombre mecánico.
golf [gɑlf, gɔlf, B gɔlf] *s.* (dep.) golf. *—v.i.* jugar golf.
golf ball, bola o pelota de golf.

golf club, 1. (*stick*) palo de golf. 2. (*place*) club de golf.
golf course, campo de golf, cancha de golf.
golfer ['gɑlfər, 'gɔlf-, B 'gɔlfə] *s.* (dep.) jugador de golf, golfista.
golf link, campo de golf.
Golgotha ['gɑlgəθə, B 'gɔl-] *s.* 1. (bíbl.) Gólgota. 2. **g.,** calvario; cementerio.
goliard ['goʊljərd, B -jɑd] *s.* (hist.) goliardo; bufón medieval.
goliardic [goʊl'jɑrdɪk, B -'jɑd-] *a.* (hist.) goliardesco.
golliwog, golliwogg ['gɑlɪˌwɑg, B 'gɔlɪˌwɔg] *s.* 1. muñeco grotesco de color negro. 2. persona grotesca.
golly ['gɑlɪ, B 'gɔlɪ] *interj.* ¡Dios mío!
golosh, *var. de* **galosh.**
gombo, *var. de* **gumbo.**
gomphosis [gɑm'foʊsəs, B gɔm-] *s.* (anat.) gonfosis.
gomuti [goʊ'mutɪ, B gə-] *s.* 1. (bot.) gomuto, palmera gomuto. 2. fibras de gomuto.
gonad ['goʊˌnæd] *s.* (biol.) gónada.
gonadotropic [goʊˌnædə'trɑpɪk, B ˌgɔ-ə'-trɔpɪk] *a.* (bioquím.) gonadotrópico. gonadotrofico.
Gond [gɑnd, B gɔnd] *s.* gondo, habitante de la India Central.
Gondi ['gɑndɪ, B 'gɔn-] *s.* (filol.) gondo, gondi (dialecto de la India Central).
gondola ['gɑndələ, B 'gɔn-] *s.* 1. góndola. 2. (E.U.) barca pesada de fondo plano (usada esp. en Nueva Inglaterra). 3. (f.c., E.U.) batea. 4. (aer.) góndola, barquilla (de una aeronave).
gondolier [ˌgɑndə'lɪr, B ˌgɔndə'lɪə] *s.* gondolero.
gone [gɔn, gɑn, B gɔn] *p.p. de* **go.** —*a.* 1. ido, pasado, transcurrido, ej., *these ten years g.,* estos diez años pasados o transcurridos. 2. ido, apagado; perdido, arruinado. 3. embarazada, ej., *eight months g. with child,* embarazada de ocho meses, con ocho meses de embarazo. 4. agotado, cansadísimo. 5. muerto. 6. (jer., fig.) excelente, magnífico. 7. **far g.,** muy adelantado; muy comprometido; muy cansado; muy avanzado; **g. on,** (fam.) loco por, enamorado de.
gonef ['gɑnəf, B 'gɔn-] *s.* (jer.) ladrón.
goneness ['gɔnnəs, 'gɑn-, B 'gɔn-] *s.* agotamiento, desfallecimiento, debilidad.
goner ['gɔnər, 'gɑn-, B 'gɔnə] *s.* (fam.) enfermo desahuciado; persona perdida; persona arruinada.
gonfalon ['gɑnfələn, B 'gɔn-] *s.* confalón, gonfalón.
gonfalonier [ˌgɑnfələ'nɪr, B ˌgɔn-'nɪə] *s.* confalonier(o), gonfaloniero.
gong [gɑŋ, gɔŋ, B gɔŋ] *s.* 1. gong, batintín, tantán; campana en forma de platillo. 2. (jer., G.B.) medalla, condecoración.
Gongorism ['gɑŋgəˌrɪzəm, B 'gɔŋ-] *s.* (ht.) gongorismo, culteranismo.
Gongorist [-rəst] *s.* gongorino, gongorista.
Gongoristic [ˌgɑŋgə'rɪstɪk, B ˌgɔŋ-] *a.* gongorino, culterano.
gonidial [goʊ'nɪdɪəl] *a.* (bot.) gonidial.
gonidium [-ɪəm] *s.* (*pl.* GONIDIA [-ɪə]) (bot.) gonidio.
goniometer [ˌgoʊnɪ'ɑmətər, B -'ɔmɪtə] *s.* 1. goniómetro, escuadra de agrimensor. 2. (rad.) radiogoniómetro.
goniometric [-ə'mɛtrɪk] **goniometrical** [-trɪkəl] *a.* goniométrico.
goniometry [-'ɑmətrɪ, B -'ɔm-] *s.* goniometría.
gonion ['goʊnɪˌɑn, B -ˌɔn] *s.* (*pl.* GONIA [-nɪə]) (anat.) gonión, gonio.
gonium ['goʊnɪəm] *s.* (*pl.* GONIA [-nɪə]) (biol.) gonia.
gonococcal [ˌgɑnə'kɑkəl, B ˌgɔnə'kɔk-] **gonococcid** [-'kɑksɪk, B -'kɔk-] *a.* del gonococo, gonocócico.
gonococcus [-'kɑkəs, B -'kɔk-] *s.* (*pl.* GONOCOCCI [-'kɑkˌsaɪ, B -'kɔk-]) (bact.) gonococo.
gonocyte ['gɑnəˌsaɪt, B 'gɔnə-] *s.* (biol.) gonocito.
gonophore ['gɑnəˌfɔr, B 'gɔnəfɔ] *s.* (biol.) gonóforo.
gonopore ['gɑnəˌpɔr, B 'gɔnəˌpɔ] *s.* (zool.) gonóporo.
gonorrhea, gonorrhoea [ˌgɑnə'riə, B ˌgɔnə'rɪə] *s.* (med.) gonorrea.
gonorrheal, gonorrhoeal [-'riəl, B -'rɪ-] *a.* (med.) gonorreico.
goo [gu] *s.* (jer.) 1. substancia pegajosa. 2. lisonja, zalamería; sentimentalismo empalagoso.
goober ['gubər, B -ə] *s.* (dial.) cacahuete, cacahuate, maní (Amer.).
good [gʊd] *a.* (BETTER ['bɛtər, B -ə] BEST [bɛst]) 1. bueno. 2. (der.) válido (título, acto jurídico, causa). 3. **a g. deal,** mucho, bastante; **the g. life,** la buena vida; **a g. man for,** un hombre competente para (el trabajo, puesto, etc.); **a g. many,** un buen número; **a g. share,** una buena porción; **a g. turn,** un favor, una gracia; **a g. way,** un buen trecho, una buena distancia; **a g. while,** un buen rato; **all in g. time,** todo a su (debido) tiempo; **as g. as,** prácticamente, casi; **g. and,** bien, muy, sumamente, ej., *make the coffee g. and strong,* haga el café bien fuerte; **g. and late,** bien tarde; **g. and hard,** duro y parejo; **g. and tired,** muy cansado; **g. for a laugh,** hace reir; sirve para provocar risa; **g. for you!** ¡felicitaciones!; **g. old Joe!** (fam.) ¡mi viejo y querido Pepe!; **how g. of you!** ¡muy gentil de Ud.!; **in g. spirits,** de buen humor; **in g. standing,** de buena reputación, apreciado; **in g. time,** a buen tiempo, temprano; puntualmente; **that is a g. one,** (jer.) ¡un buen chiste! ¡qué buena mentira!; **to be g. at,** ser hábil en, tener talento para; **to be g. for,** ser bueno para, servir para; ser válido para o por; durar por (cierto tiempo); ser capaz de; ser capaz de pagar, tener crédito hasta por; sentirse capaz de; tener ganas de; **to be g. to (someone),** ser bueno para con (alguien), tratar bien a (alguien); **to be no g.,** ser inútil; ser un perdido; **to be so g. as to (do), to be g. enough to (do),** tener la bondad de (hacer); **to have a g. mind (to do),** sentirse inclinado (a hacer); **to have a g. night,** dormir bien, pasar una noche tranquila; **to have a g. time,** divertirse, pasarla bien; **to hold g. (for),** valer (para), tener validez (para); **to make g.,** compensar por; pagar (gastos); cumplir (promesa), realizar (propósito); comprobar (una acusación); reemplazar o restituir (objeto extraviado o dañado); lograr; tener éxito (esp. en negocios); **to say (o put in) a g. word for,** recomendar, hablar en favor de; **to take in g. part,** no molestarse por, recibir con serenidad. —*s.* 1. bien. 2. bien, beneficio, provecho, utilidad. 3. (e.p.) (*pl.*) bienes, hacienda, riqueza. 4. (*pl.*) géneros, mercancías, existencias, efectos. 5. (der.) bienes muebles. 6. (*pl.*) (jer.) prueba(s) de culpabilidad, ej., *to have the goods on (someone),* tener pruebas de la culpabilidad de (alguien). 7. **by goods,** (G.B.) por tren de carga; **for g.,** para siempre; **for g. and all,** de una vez por todas; **if it's to be of any g.,** si es que habrá de servir para algo; **the g.,** lo bueno; los (hombres) buenos; **the goods,** (der.) lo necesario; cualidades necesarias; **to be up to (o after) no g.,** llevar mala intención; **to catch with the goods,** coger con las manos en la masa; **to come to no g.,** terminar mal; **to do g.,** hacer el bien, ayudar a la gente; **to do (someone) g.,** hacer bien a (alguien); sentar o caer bien a (alguien); dar fuerzas a (alguien); **to the g.,** beneficioso, útil; en ventaja; a favor de uno, ej., *with my last winnings I am $20 to the g.,* con mis últimas ganancias estoy con 20 dólares a mi favor; **what g. will it do?** ¿de qué servirá? —*interj.* ¡bueno! ¡magnífico! ¡bien! ¡muy bien! —*adv.* (dial., fam.) bien; **to be doing g.,** hacerlo bien; **to be getting along g.,** prosperar.
good afternoon, buenas tardes.
Good Book, (la) Biblia.
good-by, good-bye [gʊd'baɪ] *interj.* adiós, hasta la vista, hasta pronto, hasta luego.
good cheer, 1. alegría, regocijo; ánimo, confianza. 2. buena mesa, comida rica. 3. **to be of g. c.,** alegrarse, regocijarse; tener confianza.
good day, buenos días (despedida).
good deal, buen negocio, negocio redondo.
good evening, buenas noches (al caer la tarde o a prima noche).
good fellow, buen amigo, buen chico, buen tipo; persona tratable.
good-fellowship [ˌgʊd'fɛloʊˌʃɪp] *s.* compañerismo, camaradería, sociabilidad.
good form, buena costumbre, buen uso, lo correcto.
good-for-nothing ['gʊdfərˌnʌθɪŋ, B -fəˌ-] *a.* inútil, inservible, sin valor. —*s.* haragán, gandul, tumbón.
good fortune, dicha, (buena) suerte.
Good Friday, Viernes Santo.
good graces, *s. pl.* favor, bienquerencia, consideración.
good gracious, ¡caramba! ¡cáspita!
goodhearted ['gʊd'hɑrtəd, B -'hɑt-] *a.* de buen corazón, bonachón.
goodheartedly [-lɪ] *adv.* sinceramente, bondadosamente.
goodheartedness [-nəs] *s.* bondad, sinceridad.
good heavens, ¡cielos!
good humor, buen humor, buen carácter.
good-humored [-'hjumərd, B -məd] *a.* jovial, de buen humor; alegre; festivo.
good-humoredly [-lɪ] *adv.* de buen humor, de buen grado, alegremente.
goodies ['gʊdiz] *s. pl.* dulces; (fam.) cosas atractivas.
goodish [-ɪʃ] *a.* 1. bastante bueno, regular. 2. bastante grande, abultado.
goodliness [-lɪnəs] *s.* bondad, gracia; buen talante.
good-looking [-'lʊkɪŋ] *a.* buen mozo, bien parecido, guapo.
good looks, apariencia atractiva (personal).
good luck, suerte, buena fortuna; que le vaya bien (fam.).
good luck charm, talismán de la buena suerte.
goodly ['gʊdlɪ] *a.* (GOODLIER; GOODLIEST) 1. bueno, agradable; de buena apariencia, carácter o cualidad. 2. grande, apreciable. considerable.
goodman [-mən, B -mæn] *s.* (ant.) 1. amo (de la casa); jefe de familia; esposo, marido. 2. señor (fórmula de tratamiento inferior a don o caballero).
good money, moneda genuina; (jer.) salario o sueldo elevado.
good morning, buenos días.
good nature, bondad, buen corazón.
good-natured ['gʊd'neɪtʃərd, B -tʃəd] *a.* bonachón, bondadoso, de buen corazón, generoso.
good-naturedly [-lɪ] *adv.* de buen humor, de buen grado.

good-naturedness [-nəs] *s.* afabilidad; bondad.
good-neighbor [-'neɪbər, B -bə] *a.* (pol.) de buen vecino, de buena vecindad.
good-neighborhood [-ˌhʊd] **good-neighborliness** [-lɪnəs] *s.* conducta amigable, conducta amistosa.
Good Neighbor Policy, política de (la) buena vecindad.
goodness ['gʊdnəs] *s.* bondad, virtud; **for g.' sake!** ¡por Dios!; **g. gracious!** ¡santo Dios! ¡Jesús, María y José!; **g. knows!** ¡Dios sabe!; **I wish to g.!** ¡ojalá!; **my g.!** ¡Dios mío!; **thank g.!** ¡gracias a Dios!; **to have the g. to,** tener la bondad de.
good night, buenas noches (despedida).
good offices, buenos oficios.
Good Samaritan, (bíbl.) buen samaritano.
goods and chattels, (der.) muebles y enseres.
good sense, sensatez, sabiduría práctica, sentido común.
Good Shepherd, (relig.) (El) Buen Pastor, Cristo.
good-sized ['gʊd'saɪzd] *a.* bastante grande, de regular tamaño.
good speed, buena suerte, éxito; buen viaje.
goods train [gʊdz-] (G.B.) tren de carga, tren de mercancías.
goods truck, g. wagon, (G.B.) vagón de carga, carro de carga, vagón de mercancías.
good-tempered ['gʊd'tɛmpərd, B -pəd] *a.* de buen corazón, de buen carácter.
good-temperedly [-lɪ] *adv.* de buen humor.
good thing, 1. buen negocio. 2. dicho ingenioso. 3. (*pl.*) golosinas.
goodtime Charlie [-'taɪm-] persona frívola, alegre y despreocupada en busca permanente de diversiones.
good turn, favor, acto amistoso de ayuda, bien. beneficio (que se da o se recibe).
goodwife [-ˌwaɪf] *s.* (ant., dial.) 1. ama de casa. 2. (buena) señora (fórmula de tratamiento inferior a doña o señora).
good will [-'wɪl] *s.* 1. buena voluntad. 2. benevolencia, bondad. 3. (der., com.) buen nombre, crédito; clientela (de un negocio); (fin.) plusvalía; fondo de comercio.
good word, palabra de recomendación.
goody ['gʊdɪ] *s.* 1. (ant.) tía (fórmula de tratamiento a una mujer, esp. casada, de clase baja). 2. dulce, golosina; cosa atractiva.
goody-goody [ˌgʊdɪ'gʊdɪ] *a.* santurrón, beato. —*interj.* delicioso, magnífico (en lenguaje infantil).
gooey ['guɪ] *a.* (fam.) viscoso, pegajoso; almibarado.
goof [guf] *s.* 1. papanatas, simplón. 2. disparate, error craso. —*v.i.* 1. meter la pata, equivocarse, cometer un error. 2. (jer.) (ú. gen. con *off*) holgazanear, haraganear. —*v.t.* estropear, chapucear.
goof ball, (jer.) 1. narcótico; marihuana. 2. narcómano. 3. sedante, calmante, tranquilizante (píldora). 4. papanatas, simplón; latoso.
goofily ['gufəlɪ] *adv.* tontamente, ridículamente.
goofiness [-ɪnəs] *s.* tontería, ridiculez; credulidad, simpleza.
goofy ['gufɪ] *a.* (GOOFIER; GOOFIEST) (jer.) tonto, zonzo, ridículo; crédulo, simple.
googol ['guˌgɔl] *s.* (mat.) el número uno seguido de cien ceros.
googolplex [-ˌplɛks] *s.* la cifra uno seguida por cien veces cien ceros.
goo-goo ['guˌgu] *s.* (E.U., hist.) partidario de una política reformista (en la época de Teodoro Roosevelt).
goo-goo eyes, (jer.) mirada amorosa o posesiva.
gook [gʊk, guk] *s.* (jer.) 1. basura, mugre, lodo, cieno. 2. (despec.) natural de las islas del Pacífico, Asia, África, Japón. 3. nombre despectivo que da el soldado norteamericano a los norvietnamitas y a los combatientes del Vietcong.
goon [gun] *s.* (jer., E.U.) 1. terrorista de alquiler, terrorista pagado, matón, guarura. 2. imbécil, estúpido, memo, ganso.
goop [gup] *s.* (jer.) persona pegajosa; cualquier materia pegajosa.
goosander [gu'sændər, B -də] *s.* (orn.) somorgujo, mergo.
goose [gus] *s.* (*pl.* GEESE [gis]) 1. ganso, ánsar. 2. gansa. 3. simplón, bobalicón. 4. (*pl.* GOOSES) plancha de sastre. 5. (ant.) juego de mesa. 6. **to cook one's g.,** malograrle los planes a uno, echarle a perder los planes a uno; arruinar a uno.
goose barnacle, (zool.) percebe, escaramujo.
gooseberry ['gusˌbɛrɪ, -bərɪ, 'guz-, B 'gʊzbərɪ] *s.* (*pl.* GOOSEBERRIES) 1. (bot.) grosellero silvestre, agrazón, uva crespa, uva espina. 2. grosella silvestre.
goose egg, (jer.) cero, falta de tantos (en juegos).
goosefish ['gusˌfɪʃ] *s.* (ict.) pejesapo, pescador.
gooseflesh [-ˌflɛʃ] *s.* carne de gallina (ocasionada por el frío o el miedo).
goosefoot [-ˌfʊt] *s.* (bot.) quenopodio, sayón.
gooseherd [-ˌhɜrd, B -ˌhɜd] *s.* ansarero, cuidador de gansos.
gooseneck [-ˌnɛk] *s.* 1. cuello de cisne, cuello de ganso (herramienta). 2. tubo en S. 3. (mar.) sustentante.
goose pimples, carne de gallina (ocasionada por frío, miedo o emotividad).
gooseskin [-ˌskɪn] *var. de* **gooseflesh.**
goose step, (mil.) paso de ganso (esp. de la infantería alemana).
goose-step [-ˌstɛp] *v.i.* (fam.) ir a paso de ganso.
goosey, goosy ['gusɪ] *a.* 1. de ganso, ansarino. 2. estúpido, tonto. 3. miedoso, con carne de gallina; friolento.
GOP *abrev. de* **Grand Old Party,** Partido Republicano (de los E.U.).
gopher ['goʊfər, B -fə] *s.* 1. (zool.) tuza. 2. (zool.) tortuga de tierra. 3. (zool.) ardilla de la tierra. 4. G., (E.U.) habitante del estado de Minnesota.
gopherwood [-ˌwʊd] *s.* 1. (bot.) fustete, árbol de madera amarilla. 2. madera no identificada, probablemente de ciprés, utilizada en la construcción del arca de Noé.
goral ['gɔrəl] *s.* (zool.) goral.
Gordian knot ['gɔrdɪən-, B 'gɔd-] nudo gordiano; **to cut the G. k.,** (fig.) cortar el nudo gordiano (resolver un problema en forma rápida y audaz).
Gordon setter ['gɔrdən-, B 'gɔd-] *s.* (zool.) perdiguero.
gore [gɔr, B gɔ] *s.* 1. (cost.) nesga, sesga, cuchillo. 2. (mar.) cuchillo. 3. pequeño terreno triangular. 4. sangre coagulada, cuajarón. —*v.t.* 1. acornear; coger (el toro). 2. cortar en forma triangular o ahusada. 3. (cost.) acuchillar, poner nesga en. 4. (ant.) agujerear o apuñalar (ej., con una espada).
gorge [gɔrdʒ, B gɔdʒ] *s.* 1. garganta, gorja, garguero, gola. 2. molleja (de halcón). 3. garganta, desfiladero, paso. 4. atasco, masa (ej., de hielo en un río). 5. (fort.) gola. 6. (ant.) estómago. 7. (ant.) especie de jarra de barro o arcilla. 8. **one's g. rises at (something),** (algo) le enferma a uno, (algo) le da asco a uno. —*v.i.* comer vorazmente, hartarse, empiparse; **g. on (books,** etc.), devorar (libros, etc.). —*v.t.* 1. atiborrar, hartar, saciar. 2. engullir, tragar con voracidad.
gorgeous ['gɔrdʒəs, B 'gɔdʒəs] *a.* 1. magnífico, brillante, espléndido, hermosísimo. 2. (fam.) encantador, delicioso.
gorgeously [-lɪ] *adv.* magníficamente, espléndidamente, brillantemente.
gorgeousness [-nəs] *s.* esplendor, magnificencia.
gorger ['gɔrdʒər, B 'gɔdʒə] *s.* devorador; tragón.
gorgerin ['gɔrdʒərɪn, B 'gɔdʒər-] *s.* (arq.) garganta, collarino.
gorget ['gɔrdʒət, B 'gɔdʒɪt] *s.* 1. (arm.) gola, gorguera, gorjal, colla, guardapapo. 2. gorguera (adorno de cuello). 3. toca. 4. (orn.) collar (en la garganta de aves).
Gorgon ['gɔrgən, B 'gɔgən] *s.* 1. (mitol.) Gorgona. 2. **g.,** (fig.) tarasca, mujeruca, esperpento, mujer muy fea.
gorgonia [gɔr'goʊnɪə, B gɔ'-] *s.* (*pl.* GORGONIAE [-i] o GORGONIAS) (zool.) gorgonia, abanico de mar.
Gorgonian [-nɪən] *a.* (mitol.) gorgóneo.
gorgonian [-nɪən] *s., a.* (zool.) gorgónido.
gorgonize ['gɔrgəˌnaɪz, B 'gɔgə-] *v.t.* petrificar, aturdir.
Gorgonzola [ˌgɔrgən'zoʊlə, B ˌgɔgən-] *s.* gorgonzola (queso italiano).
gorilla [gə'rɪlə] *s.* 1. (zool.) gorila. 2. (jer.) esperpento, hombre bruto y feo. 3. (jer.) matón, asesino pagado.
gormandize ['gɔrmənˌdaɪz, B 'gɔmən-] *v.t.* devorar, comer vorazmente. —*v.i.* glotonear. —*s.* (raro) glotonería, voracidad.
gormandizer [-ər, B -ə] *s.* glotón, tragón, tragador.
gorse [gɔrs, B gɔs] *s.* (bot.) tojo, aulaga.
gory ['gɔrɪ] *a.* (GORIER; GORIEST) 1. cubierto de sangre coagulada; manchado de sangre. 2. sangriento.
gosh [gɑʃ, B gɔʃ] *interj.* ¡Dios!; **by G.!** ¡por Dios!; **good G.!** ¡Santo Dios!; **my G.!** ¡Dios mío!
goshawk ['gɑsˌhɔk, B 'gɔs-] *s.* (orn.) accípitre, azor, milano.
Goshen ['goʊʃən] *s.* (fig.) tierra prometida; tierra o lugar de abundancia.
gosling ['gɑzlɪŋ, B 'gɔz-] *s.* 1. gansarón, ansarino, ansarón. 2. (fig.) calabaza, papanatas.
gospel ['gɑspəl, B 'gɔs-] *s.* 1. **G.,** Evangelio. 2. (fig.) evangelio, verdad indisputable. 3. (fig.) credo, programa. —*a.* 1. evangélico. 2. evangelizador. 3. del evangelio.
gospeller, gospeler [-pələr, B -lə] *s.* 1. lector del Evangelio; evangelistero, evangelista. 2. predicador protestante.
gospel oath, juramento por el Evangelio.
gospel truth, verdad indisputable, evangelio.
gospodin [ˌgɑspɑ'djin] *s.* señor (tratamiento cortés en Rusia).
gosport ['gɑsˌpɔrt, B 'gɔsˌpɔt] *s.* (aer.) tubo de comunicación flexible (entre las carlingas del avión).
gossamer ['gɑsəmər, B 'gɔsəmə] *s.* 1. telaraña (que flota en el aire); hilo de telaraña. 2. gasa muy fina. 3. (E.U.) tela de seda delgadísima; impermeable muy ligero. —*a.* sutil, finísimo, delgadísimo.
gossamery [-mərɪ] *a.* sutil, finísimo, delgadísimo.
gossip ['gɑsəp, B 'gɔs-] *s.* 1. chismorreo, charlatanería. 2. chismoso, chismero, charlatán. 3. **a piece of g.,** un chisme. —*v.i.* (*pret., p.p.* GOSSIPED; *p.pr.* GOSSIPING) chismear, murmurar.
gossiper [-ər, B -ə] *s.* chismoso, murmurador.
gossiping [-ɪŋ] *s.* 1. chismografía, murmuración. 2. (dial.) bautizo; fiesta de bautizo. —*a.* chismoso, murmurador.
gossipmonger [-'mʌŋgər, -'mɑŋ-, B -'mʌŋgə] *s.* chismoso, inveterado.
gossipry ['gɑsəprɪ, B 'gɔs-] *s.* murmuración, chismorreo.

gossipy [-əpɪ] *a.* chismoso.
gossoon [gɑ'sun, B gɔ-] *s.* (pr. Irl.) muchacho, mozo, esp. de servicio doméstico.
gossypin ['gɑsəpən, B 'gɔs-] *s.* (quím.) gosipina.
gossypol [-ˌpɔl] *s.* (quím.) gosipol.
got [gɑt, B gɔt] *pret. de* **get.**
Goth [gɑθ, B gɔθ] *s.* 1. godo. 2. (fig.) bárbaro, salvaje.
Gotham ['gɑθəm, B 'goʊθəm] *a.* neoyorquino, de Nueva York. *—m.* apodo de la ciudad de Nueva York.
Gothamite [-ˌaɪt] *s.* neoyorquino (apodo).
Gothic ['gɑθɪk, B 'gɔθ-] *a.* 1. gótico. 2. (arq.) gótico. 3. **g.,** (lit.) horripilante, cruel. 4. (impr.) grotesco, antiguo; gótico. 5. (ant.) teutónico, germánico. *—s.* 1. gótico, lengua de los godos. 2. (arq.) (estilo) gótico. 3. (impr.) tipo antiguo, tipo grotesco, tipo abastonado; (G.B.) tipo gótico, gótico alemán.
Gothicism [-əˌsɪzəm] *s.* 1. goticismo. 2. (fig.) rudeza, barbarie, falta de elegancia.
Gothicize [-ˌsaɪz] *v.t.* volver gótico, hacer de manera gótica.
gotten ['gɑtən, B 'gɔt-] *p.p. de* **get.**
gouache [gwɑʃ, gʊ'ɑʃ] *s.* (pint.) aguazo; aguada.
gouge [gaʊdʒ] *s.* 1. (carp.) gubia, formón de mediacaña. 2. acanaladura, estría, ranura; muesca, mella. 3. (min., geol.) salbanda. 4. (jer.) extorsión, estafa. *—v.t.* 1. excavar, escoplear (con una gubia); acanalar, estriar; mellar; cavar. 2. sacar, arrancar (un ojo a alguien). 3. (fam., E.U.) estafar, engañar.
goulash ['guˌlɑʃ, -ˌlæʃ] *s.* 1. gulash, guiso húngaro (de carne de vaca con verduras, condimentada con pimentón). 2. (naipes) distribución extraordinaria de naipes en una mano.
gourd [gɔrd, gʊrd, B gʊəd] *s.* 1. calabaza, calabacín. 2. (bot.) calabacera. 3. calabacino.
gourde [gʊrd, B gʊəd] *s.* gurdo, unidad monetaria de Haití.
gourmand ['gʊrˌmɑnd, B 'gʊəmənd] *a.* goloso.
gourmandise [gʊrmən'diz, B 'gɔməndaɪz] *s.* golosinería.
gourmandism ['gʊrˌmɑnˌdɪzəm, B 'gʊəmən-] *s.* gula, glotonería.
gourmet ['gʊrˌmeɪ, B 'gʊəˌ-] *s.* gastrónomo, epicúreo.
gout [gaʊt] *s.* 1. gota; salpicadura; tacha; grumo. 2. (med.) gota. 3. **rich man's g.,** gota debida al exceso de comida.
gouty ['gaʊtɪ] *a.* (med.) gotoso.
govern ['gʌvərn, B -ən] *v.t.* 1. gobernar; dirigir, controlar, manejar. 2. regir, guiar, regular, determinar. 3. (gram.) regir. 4. **g. oneself,** conducirse (en cierto modo), refrenarse, controlarse. *—v.i.* 1. prevalecer, prevaler, predominar. 2. gobernar.
governable [-ərnəbəl, B -ənə-] *a.* 1. gobernable. 2. manejable, dócil.
governance [-nəns] *s.* governación, gobierno, ejercicio del poder.
governess [-nəs] *s.* 1. institutriz, aya, gobernante (de niños). 2. gobernadora. 3. gobernadora; mujer del gobernador. *—v.t., v.i.* instruir o enseñar (como institutriz).
governing [-nɪŋ] *a.* gobernante, gubernativo, regulador.
governing class, clase gobernante.
governing hand, mano firme, dura; regla firme, dura.
government ['gʌvərnmənt, -əment, B 'gʌvən-, -əmənt] *s.* 1. gobierno, gobernación. 2. gobierno, sistema de gobierno. 3. gobierno, autoridad, dominio, poder. 4. territorio gobernado; división administrativa; provincia. 5. gobierno, cuerpo o poder ejecutivo, administración (del Estado). 6. (gram.) régimen, concordancia, relación sintáctica. 7. **to form a g.,** formar gabinete ministerial.
governmental [ˌgʌvərn'mɛntəl, B ˌgʌvən-] *a.* gubernamental, gubernativo.
governmentalism [-ˌɪzəm] *s.* (pol.) tendencia a extender la influencia del gobierno.
governmentalize [-ˌaɪz] *v.t.* someter al control del gobierno.
governmentally [-ɪ] *adv.* gubernativamente.
Government House, (G.B.) residencia oficial del gobernador.
Government Issue, (E.U.) equipo, uniformes, etc. expedidos por el ejército; p. ext. el recluta (en la jer. mil.).
government securities, bonos del gobierno.
governor ['gʌvənər, 'gʌvər-, B 'gʌvənə] *s.* 1. gobernador, jefe superior (de una provincia, ciudad, fortaleza). 2. alcaide (de una cárcel o prisión). 3. (E.U.) gobernador (de uno de los Estados); (G.B.) gobernador (de una dependencia). 4. administrador, director. 5. (jer.) padre, tutor (legal). 6. (jer.) jefe, patrón. 7. (mec.) regulador automático. 8. (ant.) tutor, ayo, instructor.
governor general, *s.* (*pl.* GOVERNORS GENERAL) gobernador general.
governorship [-ˌʃɪp] *s.* 1. gobierno, ministerio (de un gobernador). 2. (período de) gobierno. 3. (oficina de) gobierno.
govt. *abrev. de* **government,** gobierno.
gowk [gaʊk] *s.* 1. (esco.) cuclillo. 2. (fam. G.B.) simplón, simple, mentecato, tonto.
gown [gaʊn] *s.* 1. vestimenta, vestido, traje (de mujer). 2. toga (de magistrado, profesor, etc.). 3. (fig.) oficio, profesión. 4. bata. 5. ropa talar (de religioso). 6. (G.B.) miembros de la universidad (de Oxford o Cambridge, en conjunto).
gownsman ['gaʊnzmən] *s.* 1. togado. 2. (G.B.) universitario, miembro de una universidad.
goy [gɔɪ] *s.* (yiddish) (*pl.* GOYIM [-əm] o GOYS) hombre no judío, esp. cristiano; (*pl.*) los gentiles, los cristianos.
goyish [-ɪʃ] *a.* no judío (persona o cosa), gentil, cristiano.
G.P. *abrev. de* **general practitioner,** médico general.
GPO *abrev. de* **General Post Office,** Dirección General de Correos.
gr. *abrev. de* **gram,** gramo (g., gr.).
Graafian follicle ['grɑfɪən-, B 'greɪf-] (anat.) folículo de De Graaf, vesícula ovárica.
grab [græb] *v.t.* (*pret., p.p.* GRABBED; *p.pr.* GRABBING) 1. asir, agarrar, coger, arrebatar. 2. apresar, capturar, prender. 3. tomar algo apresuradamente, esp. comida, ej., *he grabbed a bite to eat,* comió un bocado a la carrera. 4. (gen. con *off*) apoderarse de, apropriarse de; posesionarse de. *—v.i.* **g. at,** tratar de agarrar o arrebatar. *—s.* 1. agarro, toma, asimiento. 2. rebatiña. 3. (mec.) gancho, garfio; garras. 4. **to be up for grabs,** (jer.) estar libre (presa), estar disponible (ej., el premio de un concurso). *—a.* 1. tomado al azar, ej., *g. sample,* muestra tomada al azar. 2. para sostenerse, ej., *g. rail, strap,* etc., barra, correa, etc., para sostenerse (en ómnibus, tranvía, etc.).
grab bag, paquete sorpresa.
grabble ['græbəl] *v.i.* 1. andar a tientas, andar a ciegas, buscar a tientas. 2. gatear, andar a gatas, andar en cuatro pies. 3. tenderse.
grab bucket, (mec.) cucharón de quijadas.
grabby ['græbɪ] *a.* (GRABBIER; GRABBIEST) codicioso, ávido, avaro.
grab link, (mec.) eslabón de retención.
grace [greɪs] *s.* 1. gracia, garbo, gracejo, donaire, donosura. 2. gracia, afabilidad, buen modo. 3. (*gen. en pl.*) gracia, benevolencia, buena voluntad. 4. gracia, favor, beneficio. 5. gracia, indulgencia (de tiempo, en pagos, etc.). 6. bendición (de la mesa); jaculatoria. 7. (teol.) gracia, don (de Dios). 8. (mús.) nota(s) de adorno. 9. **G.,** (G.B.) alteza, excelencia (como tratamiento de duques, duquesas o arzobispos y antiguamente de los soberanos ingleses), ej., *Your G.,* Vuestra Alteza (duque, duquesa); Vuecencia, Vuestra Excelencia (arzobispo). 10. (G.B.) permiso para recibir grado (en universidad). 11. (ant.) clemencia, misericordia. 12. **by (the) g. of,** gracias a; **by the g. of God,** por la gracia de Dios; **the Graces,** (mitol.) las tres Gracias; **to be in one's bad graces,** haber perdido la estima; **to be in one's good graces,** gozar del favor de uno; **to fall from one's graces,** caer de la gracia de uno; **to get in the good graces of,** congraciarse con; **to have the g. to,** tener la discreción de; tener la amabilidad o gentileza de; **to say g.,** bendecir la mesa; **with bad** (o **ill**) **g.,** de mal talante; **with good g.,** de buen talante. *—v.t.* 1. agraciar, adornar. 2. honrar, favorecer, distinguir (con título, dignidad, etc.). 3. (mús.) adornar, proveer de notas de adorno.
grace cup, último brindis (al fin de un banquete); copa para el último brindis.
graceful ['greɪsfəl] *a.* gracioso, lleno de gracia, garboso, elegante, agraciado, donairoso.
gracefully [-fəlɪ] *adv.* con gracia, con garbo, elegantemente.
gracefulness [-fəlnəs] *s.* gracia, donaire, garbo, elegancia.
graceless ['greɪsləs] *a.* 1. impío, depravado, réprobo. 2. desvergonzado. 3. sin gracia, desgarbado.
gracelessly [-lɪ] *adv.* desairadamente, desvergonzadamente.
gracelessness [-nəs] *s.* falta de gracia, garbo o elegancia; impiedad, depravación, reprobación; desvergüenza.
grace note, (mús.) nota de adorno, apoyatura.
gracile ['græsəl] *a.* grácil, sutil, ligero, menudo, delgado, delicado.
gracioso [ˌgrɑsɪ'oʊsoʊ, B ˌgreɪʃɪ-] *s.* gracioso, bufón, payaso; (ant.) favorito de la corte.
gracious ['greɪʃəs] *a.* 1. amable, benigno, benevolente, graciable. 2. condescendiente, indulgente (con los inferiores). 3. gracioso, gentil. 4. grato, placentero, ameno, confortable. 5. misericordioso (díc. de Dios). 6. (poét.) cortés. 7. (ant.) atractivo. 8. **good g.! my g.! g. me!** ¡válgame Dios! ¡Jesús!
graciously [-lɪ] *adv.* 1. amablemente, benignamente. 2. amenamente, confortablemente, gratamente.
graciousness [-nəs] *s.* gracia, graciosidad, gentileza, afabilidad, bondad.
grackle ['grækəl] *s.* (orn.) estornino de los pastores; quiscal.
grad [græd] *s.* (fam.) graduado (de una universidad).
gradate ['greɪˌdeɪt, B grə'deɪt] *v.t.* 1. graduar, ordenar en grados. 2. (pint.) degradar. *—v.i.* graduarse.
gradation [greɪ'deɪʃən, B grə-] *s.* 1. gradación, escalonamiento. 2. (ret., mús.) gradación. 3. (pint.) degradación.
gradational [-əl] *a.* gradual.
gradationally [-ɪ] *adv.* gradualmente.
grade [greɪd] *s.* 1. grado; clase, categoría. 2. grado, rango (militar). 3. declive, pendiente. 4. grado de inclinación (de una pendiente). 5. animal de raza mixta (esp. el que tiene sólo un

padre de pura raza). 6. (E.U.) grado, año (de estudios). 7. (E.U.) calificación, nota. 8. **at g.,** (E.U.) a nivel; **down (up) g.,** cuesta abajo (arriba); **to make the g.,** tener éxito. —*v.t.* 1. graduar, clasificar. 2. mejorar o elevar la calidad de. 3. dividir en grados (colegios). 4. (ing.) nivelar, explanar. 5. **g. down,** disminuir; **g. up,** mejorar la sangre de (caballos, perros, etc.); **to g. as,** graduar de (o por). —*v.i.* 1. ser o estar graduado. 2. ser de un grado. 3. **g. into,** convertirse gradualmente en.

grade crossing, (f.c.) paso a nivel, cruce a nivel.

graded aggregate ['greɪdəd-] (const.) agregado escalonado, agregado graduado.

grader [-ər, B -ə] *s.* 1. graduador. 2. nivelador, niveladora, explanador. 3. alumno de (cierto) grado, ej., *a fifth g.,* un alumno del quinto grado.

grade school, escuela primaria.

grade separation, cruce superpuesto (de carreteras o ferrocarriles).

gradient ['greɪdɪənt] *a.* descendiente, declinante. —*s.* 1. inclinación o declive (de un camino o ferrocarril). 2. rampa, cuesta. 3. tasa de aumento o disminución (de temperatura, potencial eléctrico. etc.). 4. (mat.) gradiente.

gradin ['greɪdən] **gradine** ['greɪˌdin, grə'din] *s.* grada.

gradometer [ˌgreɪ'dɑmətər, B -'dɔmɪtə] (top.) gradómetro.

gradual ['grædʒʊəl] *a.* gradual. —*s.* (relig.) gradual.

gradualism [-ˌɪzəm] *s.* política de proceder gradualmente.

gradualist [-əst] *s.* partidario del procedimiento gradual.

gradually [-əlɪ] *adv.* gradualmente; paulatinamente.

gradualness [-nəs] *s.* carácter gradual.

graduate ['grædʒʊət, -ˌeɪt] *a.* 1. graduado, titulado. 2. de o para estudiantes graduados. —*s.* 1. (estudiante) graduado. 2. probeta, pipeta o frasco graduado. — [-ˌeɪt] *v.t.* 1. graduar, conferir un grado a (esp. en las universidades). 2. graduar, marcar con grados o dividir en grados. —*v.i.* 1. graduarse. 2. **g. into,** convertirse gradualmente en; **g. to,** avanzar, pasar a (algo de más alta categoría).

graduate school, escuela universitaria de graduados.

graduate student, estudiante de escuela universitaria de graduados.

graduate studies, estudios avanzados (realizados por graduados).

graduation [ˌgrædʒʊ'eɪʃən, B ˌgrædjʊ-] *s.* 1. graduación (de un estudiante); ceremonia de graduación. 2. graduación, marca(s) (en un instrumento o vasija). 3. graduación, división (en grados).

graduator ['grædʒʊˌeɪtər, B 'grædjʊˌeɪtə] *s.* graduador.

gradus ['greɪdəs, B 'græ-] *s.* gradus, diccionario de versificación griega o latina.

graffito [græ'fitoʊ] *s.* (*pl.* GRAFFITI [-i]) 1. grafito, dibujo esgrafiado (esp. el trazado sobre los muros de las ciudades antiguas). 2. (*pl.*) inscripciones anónimas (generalmente) obscenas (en las paredes de retretes públicos, etc.).

graft [græft, B grɑft] *s.* 1. (agr.) injerto. 2. injeridura. 3. (med.) injerto. 4. chanchullo, concusión, mangoneo (Amer.); soborno, dinero malhabido (esp. por un político o funcionario público que aprovecha de su posición). —*v.t.* 1. (agr.) injertar (parte de una planta); aplicar un injerto a (planta, árbol). 2. tratar con injertos (flores, frutos). 3. (med.) injertar, transplantar (un pedazo de piel u otro tejido). 4. **g. on to,** vincular con; añadir a, sobreponer a. —*v.i.* 1. injertarse, ser injertado. 2. efectuar injertos. 3. cometer concusión o peculado; recibir sobornos, traficar (con los puestos públicos); mangonear (Amer.).

graftable ['græftəbəl, B 'grɑft-] *s.* injertable.

graftage [-ɪdʒ] *s.* práctica de hacer injertos.

grafter [-ər, B -ə] *s.* 1. injertador. 2. malversador, concusionario, mangoneador (Amer.).

graham cracker ['greɪəm-] *s.* galleta de harina de trigo entero.

graham flour, harina de trigo entero.

Grail [greɪl] *s.* Grial (en las leyendas medievales, plato o copa usada por J.C. en la última cena); cáliz.

grain [greɪn] *s.* 1. grano (semilla de cualquier cereal). 2. cereales, mieses. 3. grano, granillo (ej., de arena, azúcar, pólvora); pizca, ej., *without a g. of,* sin una pizca de. 4. (farm.) grano (medida de peso). 5. grana, cochinilla, quermes. 6. (ant.) grana, color rojo; tinte. 7. grano, superficie granulosa. 8. flor (del cuero). 9. fibra, hebra, trepa (de la madera). 10. grano, finura, textura (de una superficie); vena (de una piedra). 11. (fig.) genio, humor, disposición. 12. cristalización, granulación, coagulación. 13. (*pl.*) masa (cebada germinada que queda después de destilar o elaborar la cerveza). 14. (tej.) fibra (de una tela). 15. **against the g.,** contra la dirección de la fibra; (fig.) a contrapelo, contra el temperamento; **in g.,** en la raíz, arraigado, innato, auténtico, indeleble; **it goes against the g.,** va contra el carácter o la naturaleza (de uno); **to dye in the g.,** teñir de grana; teñir completamente; **(to take it) with a g. of salt,** tomarlo con cierto escepticismo. —*v.t.* 1. granular, granear, convertir en grano. 2. granelar (una piel). 3. vetear (la madera). 4. crispir (la pintura). 5. teñir de grana, teñir en rama. —*v.i.* volverse granulado.

grain alcohol, alcohol de grano.

grain elevator, silo de granos con elevador mecánico.

grainer ['greɪnər, B -ə] *s.* veteador (brocha).

grainfield [-ˌfild] *s.* sembrado de granos (de trigo, etc.).

grain moth, (ento.) palomilla, paulilla, polilla de los granos.

grain of paradise, 1. grana o grano del Paraíso, amomo. 2. pimienta de Chiapa, pimienta de Tabasco, malagueta (baya).

grain rust, roya de cereales.

grain sick, (vet.) carbunclo, grano malo o de oro.

grain weevil, (ento.) calapatillo, gorgojo de los granos.

grainy ['greɪnɪ] *a.* (GRAINIER; GRAINIEST) 1. graneado. 2. granoso. 3. granado, lleno de semillas. 4. granujoso, granuloso, granulado, granular. 5. veteado.

gram [græm] *s.* (bot.) variedad de garbanzo del Asia tropical.

gram [græm] *s.* gramo.

grama ['græmə, B 'greɪmə] **gramma** ['græmə] *s.* (bot.) grama.

gramarye, gramary ['græmərɪ] *s.* (ant.) magia, ciencias ocultas, nigromancia.

gram atom, gram-atomic weight ['græmə'tɑmɪk, B ə'tɔm-] (quím., fís.) átomo-gramo.

gram calorie, caloría.

gramercy [grə'mɜrsɪ, B -'mɜsɪ] *interj.* (ant.) ¡muchas gracias!

gramicidin [ˌgræmə'saɪdən] *s.* (med.) gramicidina.

gramineous [grə'mɪnɪəs, B greɪ-] *a.* (bot.) gramíneo.

graminivorous [ˌgræmə'nɪvərəs] *a.* (zool.) graminívoro.

grammar ['græmər, B -ə] *s.* 1. gramática. 2. (libro o tratado de) gramática. 3. elementos, rudimentos, principios (de cualquier ciencia o arte).

grammarian [grə'mɛrɪən, B -'mɛər-] *s.* gramático.

grammar school, 1. (E.U.) escuela primaria, escuela elemental. 2. (G.B.) escuela de segunda enseñanza; escuela de lenguas clásicas.

grammatical [grə'mætɪkəl] *a.* gramatical, gramático.

grammatical gender, (gram.) género, distinto del natural, aplicado a una palabra por excepción gramatical.

grammatically [-kəlɪ] *adv.* gramaticalmente.

gramme, *var. de* **gram.**

gram molecule, (quím., fís.) molécula-gramo.

Gram-negative ['græm'nɛgətɪv] *a.* (bact.) gramnegativo.

gramophone ['græməˌfoʊn] *s.* gramófono, fonógrafo.

gramophonic [ˌgræmə'fɑnɪk, B -'fɔn-] *a.* fonográfico.

Gram-positive ['græm'pɑzətɪv, B -'pɔz-] *a.* (bact.) grampositivo.

gramps [græmps] *s. sing.* (jer.) abuelo; viejo.

grampus ['græmpəs] *s.* (*pl.* GRAMPUSES) (zool.) orca, orco.

Gram's method ['græmz-] (bact.) coloración de Gram.

granadilla [ˌgrænə'dɪlə] *s.* (bot.) granadilla.

granary ['grænərɪ] *s.* 1. granero, hórreo, troj, troje. 2. (fig.) granero, región fértil en granos.

grand [grænd] *a.* 1. grande, magno, principal, primero, preeminente. 2. de mayor o gran importancia; comprensivo. 3. central, principal (piso, vestíbulo, salón, escalera de un edificio muy grande). 4. grandioso, magnífico, suntuoso, espléndido; imponente, impresionante, solemne; ilustre, augusto, noble, distinguido, encumbrado. 5. (fam.) maravilloso, excelente, admirable. —*s.* 1. piano de cola. 2. (jer.) mil dólares.

grandam ['grænˌdæm] **grandame** ['grænˌdeɪm] *s.* abuela; anciana, vieja.

grandaunt ['grænd'ænt, B -ˌɑnt] *s.* tía abuela.

Grand Canyon, (geog., E.U.) Gran Cañón (del Colorado).

grandchild [-ˌtʃaɪld] *s.* nieto, nieta.

grand conjunction, (astrol.) conjunción magna (de Júpiter y Saturno).

granddad ['grænˌdæd] *s.* (fam.) abuelo, abuelito.

granddaughter [-ˌdɔtər, B -ə] *s.* nieta.

grand duchess, gran duquesa.

grand duke, gran duque.

grandee [græn'di] *s.* noble, grande (esp. español o portugués).

grandeur ['grændʒər, B -dʒə] *s.* grandeza, grandiosidad, magnificencia, esplendor, fausto.

grandfather ['grænˌfɑðər, 'grænd-, B -ə] *s.* abuelo.

grandfather clock, grandfather's clock, reloj de caja, reloj de péndulo, reloj de pie.

grandfatherly [-lɪ] *a.* de abuelo; (fig.) benigno, benévolo.

grandiloquence [græn'dɪləkwəns] *s.* grandilocuencia.

grandiloquent [-kwənt] *a.* grandilocuente, grandílocuo.

grandiloquently [-lɪ] *adv.* grandilocuentemente.

Grand Inquisitor, (relig.) Inquisidor General.

grandiose ['grændɪˌoʊs] *a.* 1. grandioso, sobresaliente, magnífico. 2. ampuloso, hinchado, afectado, pomposo.

grandiosely [-lɪ] *adv.* 1. grandiosamente, magníficamente. 2. ampulosamente, pomposamente, afectadamente.
grandiosity [ˌgrændɪ'ɑsətɪ, B -'ɔs-] *s.* 1. grandiosidad. 2. ampulosidad, afectación.
grand jury, (der., E.U.) gran jurado de acusación.
Grand Lama, Gran Lama, Dalai Lama (padre espiritual de los monjes del Tibet).
grand larceny, (der.) robo de mayor cuantía.
grand lodge, gran oriente (de masones).
grandly ['grændlɪ] *adv.* grandiosamente, espléndidamente.
grandma ['grænmɑ] *s.* (fam.) abuela, abuelita.
grand mal ['græn'mɑl, B -ˌmæl] (med.) gran mal, epilepsia gravior.
grandmamma ['grændmɑˌmɑ] *s.* mamá-señora (Am.).
grand master, 1. Gran Maestre (de una orden militar). 2. Gran Maestro (de masones). 3. gran maestro (de ajedrez).
grandmother ['grænˌmʌðər, 'grænd-, B -ə] *s.* abuela.
grandmotherly [-lɪ] *a.* de abuela; (fig.) melindroso.
grandnephew [-'nɛfju, B -ˌnɛv-] *s.* resobrino, sobrino nieto.
grandniece [-ˌnis] *s.* resobrina, sobrina nieta.
Grand Old Party, (E.U., pol.) partido republicano.
grand opera, (mús.) gran ópera.
grandpa ['grænpɑ] *s.* (fam.) abuelo, abuelito.
grandparent ['grænˌpɛrənt, -ˌpær-, 'grænd-, B -ˌpɛər-] *s.* abuelo, abuela.
grand piano, piano de cola.
grand prix [grɑn'pri] (fr.) 1. competencia internacional (de caballos, automóviles). 2. primer premio en cualquier concurso o competencia.
grand prize, premio gordo.
grandsire ['grænˌsaɪr, 'grænd-, B -ˌsaɪə] *s.* (ant.) abuelo; antepasado; viejo.
grand slam, 1. (bridge) gran slam (Amer.), bola (Esp.). 2. (fig.) éxito completo.
grandson [-ˌsʌn] *s.* nieto.
grandstand [-ˌstænd] *s.* 1. tribuna principal (en los hipódromos, estadios, etc.). 2. espectadores, auditorio, público. —*v.i.* actuar o jugar para impresionar al público.
grandstand play, (fam.) 1. (dep.) juego vistoso para impresionar a los espectadores. 2. acto, discurso, truco tendiente a ganar simpatía y admiración.
granduncle ['grændˌʌŋkəl] *s.* tío abuelo.
grand vizier, gran visir.
grange [greɪndʒ] *s.* 1. granja, cortijo, alquería, hacienda. 2. (ant.) granero.
granger ['greɪndʒər, B -dʒə] *s.* 1. (pr. dial. E.U.) granjero, labriego. 2. (hist., E.U.) miembro de la sociedad de "Patrocinadores de la Agricultura".
grangerism [-dʒəˌrɪzəm] *s.* ilustración de un libro con material tomado de otro.
grangerize [-ˌraɪz] *v.t., v.i.* (G.B.) ilustrar (libro) con dibujos, pinturas, etc. tomados de otras fuentes; mutilar (libros, etc.) para obtener material para ilustrar otro libro.
graniferous [grə'nɪfərəs] *a.* (bot.) granífero.
granite ['grænət] *s.* 1. granito. 2. (fig.) firmeza, dureza, resistencia.
granite paper, papel granito (que contiene partículas de seda coloreada).
graniteware [-ˌwɛr, B -ˌwɛə] *s.* utensilios de hierro esmaltado.
granitic [græ'nɪtɪk] *a.* granítico.
granitite ['grænəˌtaɪt] *s.* (min.) granitita.
granitoid [-ˌɔɪd] *a.* granitoideo. —*s.* roca granitoidea.
granivorous [grə'nɪvərəs] *a.* granívoro.
granny, grannie ['grænɪ] *s.* 1. abuelita, abuela. 2. anciana, vieja. 3. (fam.) persona descontentadiza. 4. (S. de E.U.) ama, nodriza.
granny knot, granny's bend, granny's knot, (mar.) nudo de rizos mal cruzado e inseguro (hecho por un inexperto).
granodiorite [ˌgrænoʊ'daɪəˌraɪt] *s.* (geol.) granodiorita.
granolite ['grænoʊˌlaɪt] *s.* (geol.) roca ígnea granosa.
granolith [-ˌlɪθ] *s.* (const.) granolito.
granolithic [ˌgrænə'lɪθɪk] *a.* granolítico.
granophyre ['grænəˌfaɪr, B -ˌfaɪə] *s.* (min.) granófiro.
granophyric [ˌgrænə'fɪrɪk] *a.* (min) granofírico.
grant [grænt, B grɑnt] *v.t.* 1. conceder, otorgar, dar (permiso). 2. acordar, permitir, dispensar. 3. ceder, transferir, transmitir (título de propiedad, etc.). 4. admitir (como verdadero), ej., *I g. you,* te (le) admito (que), te acepto (que). 5. **granting that,** dado que, supuesto que; **to take for granted (that),** dar por sentado (que), dar por hecho (que). —*s.* 1. concesión. 2. otorgamiento, permiso. 3. dádiva, donación. 4. subvención. 5. transferencia (de propiedad por escritura). 6. (E.U.) división territorial menor (en Maine, Nueva Hampshire y Vermont).
grantable ['græntəbəl, B 'grɑnt-] *a.* concesible, dable, permisible.
grantee [grænt'i, B grɑnt'i] *s.* (der.) concesionario, cesionario, donatario.
granter ['græntər, B 'grɑntə] *s.* otorgante, otorgador, cedente, donador, donante.
grant-in-aid [ˌgræntən'eɪd, B ˌgrɑnt-] *s.* (*pl.* GRANTS-IN-AID) 1. pensión o subvención de fondos públicos (pagada por un gobierno central a uno local como ayuda para una obra pública). 2. subsidio, pensión (otorgada por una organización particular).
grantor ['græntər, B grɑn'tɔ] *s.* otorgante; (der.) otorgador, cedente, cesionista, donador.
granular ['grænjələr, B -lə] *a.* 1. granular. 2. (med.) granulado, granuloso.
granulate ['grænjəˌleɪt] *v.t.* granular, granear. —*v.i.* granularse; (med.) granularse.
granulated [-əd] *a.* granulado, granular.
granulation [ˌgrænjə'leɪʃən] *s.* 1. granulación. 2. (med.) granulación. 3. (astr.) grano de arroz, copo, flóculo (en la superficie del sol).
granulation tissue, (med.) tejido de granulación.
granulator ['grænjəˌleɪtər, B -ə] *s.* granuladora (de azúcar).
granule ['grænjul] *s.* 1. gránulo, granillo, granito. 2. (astr.) grano de arroz, copo, flóculo (en la superficie del sol).
granulite ['grænjəˌlaɪt] *s.* (min.) granulito, granulita.
granulitic [ˌgrænjə'lɪtɪk] *a.* (min.) granulítico.
granulocyte ['grænjəloʊˌsaɪt] *s.* (fisiol.) granulocito (tipo de glóbulo blanco).
granuloma [ˌgrænjə'loʊmə] *s.* (med.) granuloma.
granulose ['grænjəˌloʊs] *a.* granuloso, granilloso, granular.
grape [greɪp] *s.* 1. uva (fruto). 2. (bot.) vid, parra (planta). 3. metralla. 4. **the grapes are sour** or **sour grapes,** las uvas están verdes.
grapefruit ['greɪpˌfrut] *s.* (bot.) 1. toronjo. 2. toronja, pomelo.
grape hyacinth, (bot.) sueldacostilla; campanilla; almizcleña.
grape juice, jugo o zumo de uva.
grapery ['greɪpərɪ] *s.* invernadero para el cultivo de vides.
grapeshot [-ˌʃɑt, B -ˌʃɔt] *s.* metralla.
grapestone [-ˌstoʊn] *s.* semilla de uva.
grape sugar, azúcar de uva, glucosa, dextrosa.
grapevine [-ˌvaɪn] *s.* 1. (bot.) parra, vid. 2. rumor (esp. uno falso). 3. **the g.,** vía clandestina, medios secretos (para pasar o recibir información).
graph [græf, B graf] *s.* 1. gráfica, representación gráfica, diagrama. 2. (fon.) grafía, grafema. —*v.t.* dibujar la gráfica de, representar gráficamente. —**grafo,** sufijo que significa "escribir, grabar", ej., *telegraph, phonograph,* telégrafo, fonógrafo.
graphalloy ['græfəlɔɪ] *s.* grafito impregnado de metal.
grapheme ['græfˌim] *s.* 1. letra (de un alfabeto). 2. letra o combinación de letras que representan un fonema.
graphic ['græfɪk] *a.* gráfico. —*s.* 1. obra de arte gráfica. 2. (medio de) ilustración gráfica.
graphic accent, acento ortográfico.
graphical [-ɪkəl] *a.* gráfico.
graphically [-kəlɪ] *adv.* gráficamente, en forma gráfica.
graphic arts, artes gráficas.
graphic formula, fórmula gráfica.
graphics ['græfɪks] *s. pl.* (*sing. o pl. en const.*) 1. dibujo lineal; gráfico(s), gráfica(s). 2. cálculos matemáticos para preparar dibujos lineales, gráficos o gráficas.
graphic scale, escala gráfica.
graphite ['græfˌaɪt] *s.* (min.) grafito; lápiz de grafito.
graphitic [græ'fɪtɪk] *a.* grafítico.
graphitization [ˌgræfˌaɪtə'zeɪʃən, B -ɪtaɪ-] *s.* grafitización, grafitación.
graphitize ['græfəˌtaɪz] *v.t.* grafitizar, grafitar.
graphologic [ˌgræfə'lɑdʒɪk, B -lɔdʒ-] *a.* grafológico.
graphologist [græ'fɑlədʒəst, B -'fɔl-] *s.* grafólogo.
graphology [-dʒɪ] *s.* grafología.
graphomania [ˌgræfə'meɪnɪə] *s.* grafomanía.
graphomaniac [-'meɪnɪæk] **graphomaniacal** [-mə'naɪəkəl] *a.* grafomaníaco.
graphometer [græ'fɑmətər, B -'fɔmɪtə] *s.* grafómetro.
graphomotor ['græfəˌmoʊtər, B ˌgræfə'moʊtə] *a.* (med.) grafomotor.
Graphophone ['græfəˌfoʊn] *s.* grafófono (marca de fábrica).
graph paper, papel cuadriculado (para gráficas).
-graphy [-grəfɪ] -grafía, sufijo que significa "escrito, descripción o tratado", ej., *calligraphy, geography,* caligrafía, geografía.
grapnel ['græpnəl] *s.* (mar.) arpeo; rezón, anclote.
grapple ['græpəl] *s.* 1. lucha cuerpo a cuerpo. 2. (mar.) arpeo; rezón, anclote. —*v.t.* agarrar. —*v.i.* 1. luchar cuerpo a cuerpo; cogerse mutuamente. 2. **g. about,** tratar de coger algo; andar a tientas; **g. for,** tratar de pescar o coger; **g. to,** agarrar mediante un rezón; **g. with,** irse a las manos con; (fig.) tratar de resolver (problema), abordar (tema, asunto, etc.).
grappler ['græplər, B -lə] *s.* 1. (mar.) arpeo. 2. luchador.
grappling [-lɪŋ] *s.* (mar.) arpeo; rezón, anclote.
grappling iron, g. hook, (mar.) arpeo.
grapy ['greɪpɪ] *a.* 1. arracimado, racimal, racimado, en racimo. 2. que tiene sabor a uva (díc. de ciertos vinos). 3. hecho de uvas.

grasp [græsp, B grasp] *v.t.* 1. tomar o coger ansiosamente, asir, ej., *g. one's hand,* asir la mano de uno. 2. empuñar. 3. captar, comprender. —*v.i.* **g. at,** tratar de coger; agarrar ávidamente. —*s.* 1. cogedura, asimiento. 2. abrazo; apretón. 3. dominio, control. 4. alcance. 5. comprensión, facultad de comprender, capacidad mental. 6. **beyond (one's) g.,** fuera del alcance (de uno); **to have a good g. of,** saber a fondo, comprender bien; **within (one's) g.,** al alcance (de uno).

grasper ['græspər, B 'graspə] *s.* codicioso, hombre ávido, avaro.

grasping [-pɪŋ] *a.* avaro, codicioso, mezquino.

graspingly [-lɪ] *adv.* codiciosamente.

graspingness [-nəs] *s.* avaricia, mezquindad, codicia.

grass [græs, B gras] *s.* 1. hierba, yerba. 2. césped, grama (Amer.). 3. pasto, pastura (hierba y tierra de pastoreo). 4. (*pl.*) hoja de hierba. 5. (t.v.) hierba (variaciones de la base de tiempo). 6. (jer.) mariguana. 7. **not let the g. grow under one's feet,** no perder tiempo, ser muy activo; **to hear the g. grow,** tener oído finísimo. —*v.t.* 1. pastar (al ganado). 2. sembrar de hierba; cubrir con hierba. 3. tender (lino, tela) sobre la hierba. 4. derribar, tumbar. —*v.i.* producir hierba; enyerbarse.

grass cloth, (tej.) tela gruesa y fibrosa, ej., el yute (generalmente de fibras vegetales).

grass court, (G.B., tenis) cancha de césped.

grasshopper ['græs,hapər, B 'gras,hɔpə] *s.* (ento.) saltamontes, saltón, langosta, caballeta.

grassiness [-ɪnəs] *s.* 1. condición de estar cubierto de hierba. 2. lugar poblado de hierba, lugar herboso.

grassland [-,lænd] *s.* tierra de pastoreo; prado.

grassplot [-,plat, B -,plɔt] *s.* parcela de césped; prado.

grass roots, 1. suelo superficial, capa superficial del suelo. 2. (fig.) (el) fundamento mismo, (la) raíz misma (de un problema, asunto, etc.). 3. (pol.) comunidad rural.

grass-roots [-,ruts] *a.* de origen rural o popular.

grass seed, semilla de hierba.

grass snipe, (orn.) gallineta pectoral.

grass widow, 1. (jer., hum.) viuda (mujer separada temporalmente de su esposo). 2. divorciada; separada. 3. (ant.) querida abandonada.

grass widower, 1. hombre cuya esposa se halla ausente. 2. hombre divorciado o separado de su mujer.

grassy ['græsɪ, B 'grasɪ] *a.* (GRASSIER; GRASSIEST) 1. cubierto de hierba; herboso. 2. de color verde hierba.

grate [greɪt] *s.* 1. reja, verja, enrejado, parrilla. 2. hogar, chimenea. 3. tamiz o cernidor de minerales. 4. (ant.) jaula; prisión. —*v.t.* 1. enrejar. 2. rallar. 3. hacer rechinar (los dientes). 4. (fig.) rallar, exacerbar, irritar. 5. (ant.) arañar, raspar. —*v.i.* 1. rechinar, chirriar. 2. (con *on* o *upon*) exacerbar, irritar (los nervios, etc.).

grateful ['greɪtfəl] *a.* 1. agradecido, reconocido. 2. bienvenido; grato, agradable, reconfortante.

gratefully [-fəlɪ] *adv.* agradecidamente, con gratitud, con agradecimiento.

gratefulness [-fəlnəs] *s.* gratitud; agrado.

grater ['greɪtər, B -ə] *s.* rallador, raspador.

graticule ['grætɪ,kjul] *s.* 1. (ópt.) retículo, ocular cuadriculado. 2. red de las líneas de latitud y longitud (sobre las que se dibuja un mapa).

gratification [,grætəfə'keɪʃən] *s.* 1. gratificación, premio, recompensa. 2. satisfacción, placer, complacencia.

gratifier ['grætə,faɪər, B -,faɪə] *s.* gratificador.

gratify [-,faɪ] *v.t.* (*pret., p.p.* GRATIFIED; *p.pr.* GRATIFYING) 1. satisfacer, agradar, complacer, dar placer o satisfacción a. 2. (ant.) gratificar, remunerar, recompensar; corresponder, retornar (como prueba de gratitud).

gratifying [-ɪŋ] *a.* agradable, grato, satisfactorio.

gratin ['grætən, 'grat-, B 'grætɛŋ] *s.* (cocina) cubierta de salsa espesa y queso rallado o migajas de pan con mantequilla; **au g.,** al gratén.

grating ['greɪtɪŋ] *s.* 1. reja, verja, enrejado, rejilla; parrilla, emparrillado, emparrado. 2. (ópt.) red. —*a.* chirriante, áspero (sonido, voz).

gratingly [-lɪ] *adv.* con un sonido irritante.

gratis ['grætɪs, 'greɪt-] *adv.* gratis, de balde. —*s.* gratuito.

gratitude ['grætə,tud, B -,tjud] *s.* gratitud, agradecimiento.

gratuitous [grə'tuətəs, B -'tju-] *a.* 1. gratuito, de gracia. 2. gratuito, injustificado, sin fundamento. 3. no provocado. 4. (econ.) (bienes o beneficios) naturales (que no provienen del esfuerzo humano). 5. (der.) gratuito, gracioso.

gratuitous contract, (der.) contrato a título gratuito.

gratuitously [-lɪ] *adv.* gratuitamente, gratis.

gratuitousness [-nəs] *s.* gratuidad.

gratuity [grə'tuətɪ, B -'tju-] *s.* 1. dádiva, donación. 2. propina, gratificación.

gratulant ['grætʃələnt] *a.* que denota gratificación; congratulatorio.

gratulate [-,leɪt] (ant.) *v.t.* saludar calurosamente, congratular. —*a.* gratificante.

gratulation [,grætʃə'leɪʃən] *s.* (ant.) saludo, felicitación.

gratulatory ['grætʃələ,tɔrɪ, B 'grætjʊlətərɪ] *a.* congratulatorio.

graupel ['graʊpəl] *s.* granizo suave; gránulos de nieve.

gravamen [grə'veɪmən, B -mɛn] *s.* (*pl.* GRAVAMINA [-'væmənə, B -'veɪm-] o GRAVAMENS) 1. agravio, motivo de queja. 2. (der.) peso del agravio, materia de un cargo.

grave [greɪv] *a.* 1. grave, serio, importante. 2. grave, solemne. 3. sobrio, sombrío (color). 4. ['graveɪ] (mús.) grave, de tono bajo. 5. [B grav] (fon.) grave (acento). —*s.* acento grave.

grave [greɪv] *v.t.* (*pret.* GRAVED; *p.p.* GRAVED o GRAVEN ['greɪvən]; *p.pr.* GRAVING) 1. grabar, esculpir. 2. (fig.) grabar, fijar indeleblemente (en la mente, memoria, etc.). 3. (ant.) cavar, excavar.

grave [greɪv] *v.t.* (mar.) despalmar y calafatear (casco de un barco).

grave [greɪv] *s.* 1. sepultura, tumba, sepulcro. 2. **to have one foot in the g.,** tener un pie en la tumba; tener un pie en el hoyo; **would make one turn in his g.,** haría a uno revolverse en la tumba (de asombro o disgusto).

graveclothes ['greɪv,kloʊz, -,kloʊðz] *s. pl.* ropa de entierro (con que se viste al cadáver).

gravedigger [-,dɪgər, B -ə] *s.* sepulturero, enterrador.

gravel ['grævəl] *s.* 1. cascajo, ripio, grava, guijo. 2. (med.) gravela. 3. (ant.) arena. —*v.t.* (*pret., p.p.* GRAVELED o GRAVELLED; *p.pr.* GRAVELING o GRAVELLING) 1. enguijarrar, enripiar, recebar, cubrir con cascajo, ripio o grava. 2. (fam.) desconcertar, confundir, embarazar. 3. irritar.

gravel-blind [-,blaɪnd] *a.* cegato.

graveless ['greɪvləs] *a.* 1. insepulto. 2. (fig., poét.) inmortal.

gravelly ['grævəlɪ] *a.* 1. cascajoso, ripioso, guijoso, guijarroso. 2. ronco, áspero (sonido, voz).

gravel path, enarenado.

gravel pit ['grævəl-] cascajar, cascajal.

gravel road, camino de grava.

gravely ['greɪvlɪ] *adv.* gravemente; seriamente, severamente.

graven ['greɪvən] *a.* esculpido, grabado, tallado.

graveness ['greɪvnəs] *s.* gravedad, seriedad, severidad.

graven image ['greɪvən-] ídolo, fetiche; representación de la faz humana (prohibida por las religiones hebrea y musulmana).

graver [-vər, B -və] *s.* 1. grabador; escultor; cincelador. 2. buril; cincel; punzón.

Graves' disease ['greɪvz-] (med.) enfermedad de Graves, bocio exoftálmico.

gravestone ['greɪv,stoʊn] *s.* lápida sepulcral.

graveyard [-,jard, B -,jad] *s.* cementerio, camposanto, necrópolis, panteón (Amer.).

graveyard shift, (jer.) turno de medianoche; obreros del turno de medianoche.

gravid ['grævəd] *a.* 1. grávida, embarazada, encinta, preñada. 2. ominoso.

gravida ['grævədə] *s.* mujer grávida.

gravidity [grə'vɪdətɪ] *s.* gravidez, embarazo, gestación, preñez.

gravidly ['grævədlɪ] *adv.* ominosamente.

gravimeter [grə'vɪmətər, B -tə] *s.* (fís.) gravímetro.

gravimetric [,grævə'mɛtrɪk] **gravimetrical** [-trɪkəl] *a.* (fís.) gravimétrico.

gravimetry [grə'vɪmətrɪ] *s.* (fís.) gravimetría.

graving dock ['greɪvɪŋ-] dique seco, carenero.

gravitate ['grævə'teɪt] *v.i.* gravitar; **g. to** (o **toward**), (fig.) tender hacia, orientar sus pasos hacia.

gravitation [,grævə'teɪʃən] *s.* 1. (fís.) gravitación. 2. (fig.) tendencia, orientación.

gravitational [-əl] *a.* (fís.) de gravitación, gravitatorio.

gravitational constant, (fís.) constante de la gravitación.

gravitational field, (fís.) campo gravitatorio.

gravitational force, (fís.) fuerza de gravedad.

gravitational intensity, (fís.) intensidad de la gravedad.

gravitative ['grævə,teɪtɪv] *a.* (fís.) de gravitación, gravitatorio.

gravity ['grævətɪ] *s.* 1. gravedad, aire serio, sobriedad, solemnidad. 2. gravedad, seriedad (de una ofensa, situación, etc.). 3. (fís.) gravedad, pesantez. —*a.* de gravedad, por gravedad, a gravedad; por gravitación.

gravity anomaly, (geof.) anomalía gravimétrica.

gravity cell, (elec.) pila de gravedad.

gravity feed, (mec., mot.) alimentación por gravedad.

gravure [grə'vjʊr, greɪ-, B grə'vjʊə] *s.* (impr.) 1. calcografía, impresión en hueco. 2. fotograbado.

gravy ['greɪvɪ] *s.* 1. salsa, jugo (de la carne); grasa, pringue. 2. (jer.) ganga, breva. 3. (jer.) ganancia fácil.

gravy boat, salsera.

gravy train, (jer.) oportunidad para ganar dinero fácilmente; sinecura.

gray [greɪ] *a.* 1. gris, plomizo, pardo. 2. semi-obscuro, nuboso. 3. cano, encanecido. 4. (fig.) triste, lúgubre. 5. (fig.) maduro, antiguo. 6. dudoso, semi-legal (díc. de manejos comerciales secretos). —*s.* 1. (el color) gris. 2. vestido o traje gris; uniforme gris. 3. caballo tordo. —*v.t., v.i.* encanecer, poner(se) cano.

grayback ['greɪ,bæk] *s.* 1. ballena gris. 2. (jer.) piojo. 3. (hist., E.U.) soldado confederado en la guerra civil.

graybeard [-,bɪrd, B -,bɪəd] *s.* viejo, anciano.

gray eminence, eminencia gris, poder tras el trono.

grayfish [-ˌfɪʃ] *s.* (ict.) lija, cazón, melgacho, tollo.

Gray Friar, fraile franciscano.

gray goods, tejido en crudo, género crudo.

grayhound *var. de* **greyhound.**

gray iron, (metal.) fundición gris.

grayish [ˈgreɪɪʃ] *a.* 1. grisáceo, agrisado, plomizo, pardusco. 2. entrecano.

grayling [ˈgreɪlɪŋ] *s.* 1. (ict.) tímalo, timo. 2. (ento.) cierta clase de mariposa gris o parda.

gray manganese ore, mineral de manganeso gris, manganita.

gray matter, 1. (biol.) sustancia o materia gris. 2. (fam.) inteligencia, seso, materia gris.

grayness [ˈgreɪnəs] *s.* 1. color o colorido gris. 2. semi-obscuridad.

gray squirrel, (zool.) ardilla gris.

graywacke [ˈgreɪˌwæk] *s.* (geol.) grauvaca, grauwacka.

graze [greɪz] *v.t.* 1. apacentar, herbajar, pastorear. 2. rozar. 3. raspar. —*v.i.* 1. pacer, pastar. 2. rozar. —*s.* 1. pasto, pastadero, herbaje. 2. apacentamiento, pacedura. 3. rozamiento, roce. 4. raspadura, arañazo.

grazier [ˈgreɪʒər, B -zjə] *s.* 1. pastor, ganadero. 2. (Aust.) criador de ovejas (que ocupa tierras del estado).

grazing [ˈgreɪzɪŋ] *s.* 1. pasto, pastura, dehesa. 2. apacentamiento, pacedura.

grazioso [grɑˈtsjoʊsoʊ] *a., adv.* (mús.) con gracia, con soltura o ligereza.

grease [gris] *s.* 1. grasa, unto, pringue. 2. lana sucia. 3. (vet.) aguaja, úlcera (en los cascos de los caballos). — [griz, griz] *v.t.* 1. engrasar, untar, lubricar. 2. ensuciar o manchar con grasa. 3. **g. the palm of,** untar la mano de, sobornar.

grease box, vaso de engrase, engrasador.

grease cup, grasera de compresión, copilla de grasa, engrasador.

grease gun, engrasador de pistón, jeringa de grasa, pistola o inyector de grasa.

grease monkey, (jer.) 1. mecánico de automóviles. 2. (aer.) mecánico en tierra.

greasepaint [ˈgrisˌpeɪnt] *s.* (teat.) base del maquillaje.

greaser [ˈgrisər, ˈgriz-, B -ə] *s.* 1. engrasador. 2. (jer., despec., E.U.) mejicano; latinoamericano.

grease spot, g. stain, mancha de grasa, lámpara, lamparón (fam.).

grease trap, colector o separador de grasa.

grease wool, lana sucia.

greasily [ˈgrisəlɪ, -zə-] *adv.* grasosamente, untuosamente.

greasiness [-sɪnəs, -zɪ-] *s.* untuosidad.

greasy [ˈgrisɪ, -zɪ] *a.* 1. grasoso, grasiento, seboso, untuoso. 2. sucia (lana). 3. (fig.) zalamero. 4. (vet.) enfermo de aguaja.

greasy pole, cucaña, palo ensebado (juego).

greasy spoon, (jer.) restaurante pequeño y poco sanitario, que sirve comidas baratas.

great [greɪt] *a.* (GREATER; GREATEST) 1. grande, grandioso. 2. numeroso. 3. largo, prolongado, ej., *for a g. while,* por largo tiempo, por un buen rato. 4. principal (ej., escalera). 5. noble. 6. magno, (el) grande, ej., *Alexander the G.,* Alejandro Magno, Alejandro el Grande. 7. (con *with*) lleno (de) (orgullo, sabiduría, etc.). 8. (fam.) favorito. 9. excelente, magnífico, admirable. 10. (con *at, on*) (fam.) hábil, experto, perito (en). 11. (con *at, for, on*) aficionado (a); muy interesado (en). 12. (ant.) preñada. 13. **in g. detail,** con todos sus detalles, con muchos detalles; **the G.,** (fig.) los grandes. —*adv.* (fam.) muy bien, con éxito, ej., *it's going g.,* marcha muy bien. —*s.* (fig.) estrella, campeón, uno de los grandes (de la música, literatura, el fútbol, etc.).

great ape, mono antropoide.

great auk, (orn.) variedad de alca (ya desaparecida).

great-aunt [ˈgreɪtˈænt, B -ˈɑnt] *s.* tía abuela.

Great Basin, Gran Cuenca (en el O. de los E.U.).

Great Bear, (astr.) Osa Mayor.

Great Bear Lake, Gran Lago del Oso (Canadá).

Great Britain, Gran Bretaña.

great circle 1. (geom.) círculo máximo. 2. (geog.) meridiano terrestre, paralelo terrestre.

great-circle sailing [-ˈsɜrkəl-, B -ˈsɜkəl-] navegación en círculo máximo u ortodrómico.

greatcoat [ˈgreɪtˌkoʊt] *s.* (ant.) sobretodo, gabán, abrigo.

Great Dane, mastín danés, gran danés, dogo alemán.

great divide, 1. (geog.) divisoria continental, divisoria principal de aguas. 2. (fig.) línea divisoria (esp. entre la vida y la muerte).

Great Dog, (astr.) Can Mayor.

greaten [ˈgreɪtən] *v.t., v.i.* agrandar(se), engrandecer(se).

greater [-ər, B -ə] *comp. de* **great.** —*a.* mayor; se usa para designar una ciudad grande y sus suburbios, ej., *Greater New York,* la urbe neoyorquina; la ciudad de Nueva York y su área metropolitana.

Greater Antilles, Antillas Mayores.

greater weever, (ict.) dragón marino, peje araña.

greatest common divisor [-əst-] (mat.) máximo común divisor.

great go, (G.B.) examen final (en la Universidad de Oxford para obtener el grado de bachiller).

Great God! *interj.* ¡válgame Dios!

great-grandchild [ˈgreɪtˈgrænˌtʃaɪld, -ˈgrænd-] *s.* biznieto o biznieta.

great-granddaughter [-ˌdɔtər, B -ə] *s.* biznieta.

great-grandfather [-ˌfɑðər, B -ðə] *s.* bisabuelo.

great-grandmother [-ˌmʌðər, B -ðə] *s.* bisabuela.

great-grandparent [-ˌpærənt, -ˌpɛr-, B -ˌpɛər-] *s.* bisabuelo o bisabuela.

great-grandson [-ˌsʌn] *s.* biznieto.

great gross, doce gruesas.

great gun, (fig.) pájaro de cuenta, persona eminente.

great-hearted [ˈgreɪtˈhɑrtəd, B -ˈhɑt-] *a.* 1. valiente, intrépido. 2. magnánimo, generoso, noble.

great-heartedness [-nəs] *s.* magnanimidad, generosidad.

great horned owl, (zool.) búho real.

Great Lakes, Grandes Lagos (Superior, Michigan, Huron, Erie, Ontario).

greatly [ˈgreɪtlɪ] *adv.* muy, mucho; grandemente.

Great Mogul, Gran Mongol.

great-nephew [ˈgreɪtˈnɛfju, B -ˌnɛv-] *s.* sobrino nieto.

greatness [-nəs] *s.* grandeza.

great-niece [-ˈnis] *s.* sobrina nieta.

Great Plains, (E.U.) Zona de las Praderas (al E. de las Montañas Rocosas).

great power, (pol.) gran potencia.

great primer, (impr.) tipo texto (18 puntos).

Great Pyrenees, (zool.) mastín montañés de raza pirenaica, perro pastor vasco.

greats [greɪts] *s. pl.* (G.B.) examen final (en la Universidad de Oxford para obtener el grado de bachiller en estudios clásicos).

Great Salt Lake, (E.U.) Gran Lago Salado.

Great Scott! *interj.* ¡válgame Dios!

great seal, gran sello (de un reino o estado).

great titmouse, (orn.) paro carbonero, herrerillo, monje.

great toe, dedo gordo del pie.

great-uncle [ˈgreɪtˈʌŋkəl] *s.* tío abuelo.

Great Wall of China, Gran Muralla China.

Great War, Gran Guerra (primera guerra mundial).

Great Week, (Iglesia Ortodoxa) Semana Santa.

Great White Father, Gran Padre Blanco, nombre que daban los indios norte-americanos al presidente de los E.U.

Great White Way, Broadway (en Nueva York), la gran vía de la farándula y los teatros.

greave [griv] *s.* (arm.) (*gen. pl.*) greba, espinillera.

greaves [grivz] *s. pl.* (*sing. o pl. en const.*) chicharrones.

grebe [grib] *s.* (orn.) colimbo, castañero.

Grecian [ˈgriʃən] *s., a.* 1. griego, de Grecia. 2. helenista.

Grecian profile, perfil griego.

Grecism [-ˌsɪzəm] *s.* grecismo, helenismo.

Grecize [-ˌsaɪz] *v.t.* 1. helenizar. 2. (filol.) grecizar.

Greco-Latin [ˈgrikoʊˈlætən, B ˈgrɛ-] *a.* grecolatino.

Greco-Roman [-ˈroʊmən] *a.* grecorromano.

gree [gri] *s.* (esco.) superioridad; dominio, poder. —*v.i.* (G.B.) concordar.

Greece [gris] *s.* Grecia.

greed [grid] *s.* codicia, avidez, avaricia; voracidad, gula, glotonería.

greedily [ˈgridəlɪ] *adv.* 1. codiciosamente, ávidamente, avaramente. 2. vorazmente, golosamente, glotonamente.

greediness [-ɪnəs] *s.* codicia, avaricia; glotonería.

greedy [-ɪ] *a.* (GREEDIER; GREEDIEST) 1. codicioso, ávido, avaro. 2. voraz, goloso, glotón. 3. **g. for,** codicioso de.

Greek [grik] *s.* 1. griego, heleno, greco, natural de Grecia. 2. (idioma) griego. 3. (fig.) griego, chino (lenguaje ininteligible), ej., *it is (all) G. to me,* para mí eso es chino (o griego). 4. (E.U.) miembro de una asociación estudiantil universitario. —*a.* griego, helénico.

Greek calends, calendas griegas (época que nunca llegará).

Greek Catholic, católico de rito griego.

Greek cross, cruz griega (de aspas iguales).

Greek fire, fuego griego (composición química que empleaban los antiguos para incendiar barcos enemigos).

Greek Orthodox Church, Iglesia griega ortodoxa.

green [grin] *a.* 1. verde (de color). 2. verde, verdecido, cubierto de follaje; p. ext. sin nieve; templado. 3. verde, joven, lozano, vigoroso. 4. cetrino, pálido, de color enfermizo. 5. demudado (por la envidia). 6. verde, reciente, nuevo; fresco. 7. verde, inmaduro. 8. inexperto, novato. 9. crédulo, candoroso. 10. (ind.) crudo, sin tratar; no cocido. —*s.* 1. (el color) verde. 2. (*pl.*) verduras, legumbres verdes, hortalizas. 3. (*pl.*) hojas o ramos verdes (de adorno). 4. prado, pradera; césped. 5. (golf) césped que rodea al hoyo. —*v.i.* volverse verde; verdear.

green algae, algas verdes, verdín.

green-ass [ˈgrinˌæs] *s.* (jer., E.U.) inexperto, bisoño.

greenback [-ˌbæk] *s.* (E.U., fam.) papel moneda, billete de banco.

green bean, judía verde, habichuela verde.

greenbelt [-ˌbɛlt] *s.* zona sembrada (que provee de productos agrícolas a una urbe metropolitana).

greenbrier [-ˌbraɪər, B -ə] *s.* (bot.) zarzaparrilla.
green corn, maíz tierno, choclo (Amer.), elote (Amer.), jojoto (Amer.).
green crab, (zool.) cangrejo de mar.
green dragon, (bot.) dragón verde, dragontea, culebrilla, serpentaria, zumillo.
green earth 1. (pint.) verdacho, arcilla verde. 2. (min.) tierra verde.
greenery ['grinərɪ] *s.* (*pl.* GREENERIES) 1. verdor, follaje. 2. invernadero, invernáculo.
green-eyed ['grinˌaɪd] *a.* 1. de ojos verdes. 2. celoso, envidioso.
greenfinch [-ˌfɪntʃ] *s.* (orn.) verdecillo, verdezuelo, verderón, verderol.
green fingers, (fam.) destreza como jardinero.
greenfly [-ˌflaɪ] *s.* (G.B., ento.) pulgón verde (esp. del duraznero).
greengage [-ˌgeɪdʒ] *s.* ciruela verdal, reina claudia, ciruela claudia.
green grasshopper, (ento.) langostón.
greengrocer ['grinˌgroʊsər, B -sə] *s.* verdulero.
greengrocery [-sərɪ] *s.* (*pl.* GREENGROCERIES) verdulería.
green hand, novicio, novato, bisoño.
greenheart ['grinˌhɑrt, B -ˌhɑt] *s.* (bot.) bebeerú, especie de laurel de las Guayanas.
greenhorn [-ˌhɔrn, B -ˌhɔn] *s.* 1. novicio, aprendiz, novato, pipiolo. 2. bobo, simplón.
greenhouse [-ˌhaʊs] *s.* invernáculo, invernadero.
greenhouse effect, efecto invernadero.
greening ['grinɪŋ] *s.* 1. variedad de manzana de color verdoso. 2. acción de verdear.
greenish [-ɪʃ] *a.* verdoso, verdusco.
green jaundice, (med.) ictericia verdínica.
Greenland ['grinlənd] *s.* Groenlandia.
Greenlander [-ləndər, B -də] *s.* groenlandés.
Greenlandic [ˌgrin'lændɪk] *a.* groenlandés.
green laver, alga marina comestible.
green lead ore, (min.) plomo verde, piromorfita, fosfato de plomo.
greenlet ['grinlət] *s.* (zool.) vireo, virio, oropéndola.
green light, (fig.) luz verde (autorización para llevar adelante determinado proyecto).
greenling [-lɪŋ] *s.* (ict.) hexagramo.
greenmail ['grinmeɪl] *s.* (com.) una forma de chantaje: amenazas de vender un gran lote de acciones.
green man, guardián de los campos de golf.
green manure, (agr.) abono vegetal.
green meat, (G.B.) herbaje, forraje verde.
green mold, moho verde.
Green Mountain State, (E.U.) Estado de las Montañas Verdes (Vermont).
greenness ['grinnəs] *s.* 1. verdor. 2. inexperiencia.
greenockite ['grinəˌkaɪt] *s.* (min.) sulfuro de cadmio nativo.
green onion, cebolleta, cebollino, chalote.
green pepper, ají, pimiento dulce, pimiento verde.
greenroom ['grinˌrum, -ˌrʊm] *s.* (teat.) camarín, camerino; sala de espera.
greensand [-ˌsænd] *s.* 1. (geol.) arenisca verde. 2. (metal.) arena verde.
greenshank [-ˌʃæŋk] *s.* (orn.) caballero de pies verdes, lavandera, gallineta del Viejo Mundo.
greensick [-ˌsɪk] *a.* (med.) clorótico.
greensickness [-nəs] *s.* (med.) clorosis.
green snake, pequeña culebra inofensiva de N. América.
green soap, jabón verde, jabón suave (ú. para enfermedades de la piel).
greenstone ['grinˌstoʊn] *s.* 1. (geol.) roca verdosa eruptiva; diorita, dolerita. 2. nefrita, piedra nefrítica, jade.
green stuff, 1. hortalizas; verduras. 2. (jer.) dinero.
greensward [-ˌswɔrd, B -ˌswɔd] *s.* césped, prado.
green tail, (ento.) especie de mosca de agua.
green tea, té verde, té japonés.
green thumb, (fam.) destreza como jardinero, habilidad para la jardinería.
green turtle, (zool.) tortuga verde, tortuga franca.
green vegetable, hortaliza de hojas o tallos comestibles.
green vitriol, (quím.) caparrosa verde.
green weed, (bot.) retama de tintes.
Greenwich time ['grɛnɪtʃ-, B 'grɪnɪdʒ-] hora de Greenwich.
greenwood ['grinˌwʊd] *s.* floresta, bosque frondoso, selva frondosa.
green woodpecker, (orn.) pico verde, pito real.
greet [grit] *v.t.* 1. saludar, dar la bienvenida a. 2. recibir (con demostraciones, cariño, imprecaciones, etc.). 3. presentarse a (los ojos).
greeter ['gritər, B -ə] *s.* saludador.
greeting [-ɪŋ] *s.* salutación, saludo; cumplido por escrito, ej., *Christmas greetings,* saludo navideño, tarjeta de Navidad; **greetings!** ¡bienvenido!; (*in a letter*) recuerdos.
greeting card, tarjeta de saludo, tarjeta.
gregarine ['grɛgəˌraɪn, B -rɪn] *s.* (zool.) gregarínida.
gregarious [grɪ'gɛrɪəs, B -'gɛər-] *a.* 1. gregario, sociable. 2. (zool.) gregario. 3. (bot.) que crece en racimos o colonias.
gregariously [-lɪ] *adv.* gregariamente.
gregariousness [-nəs] *s.* carácter sociable.
grego ['grigoʊ, B 'greɪ-] *s.* (hist.) chaqueta o capa corta de tela gruesa con capucha.
Gregorian [grɪ'gɔrɪən] *a.* gregoriano.
Gregorian calendar, calendario gregoriano.
Gregorian chant, canto gregoriano.
greige [greɪʒ] *a.* (tej.) crudo, en crudo. *—s.* 1. tejido en crudo, género crudo. 2. (tej.) color entre gris y crema (de ciertas telas finas).
greisen ['graɪzən] *s.* (geol.) greisen.
gremial veil ['grimɪəl-] gremial (paño de seda que usan los obispos).
gremlin ['grɛmlən] *s.* duendecillo travieso que se mete en todo.
grenade [grə'neɪd] *s.* 1. (mil.) granada. 2. extintor de granada (para apagar incendios).
grenadier [ˌgrɛnə'dɪr, B -'dɪə] *s.* 1. (mil.) granadero. 2. (ict.) granadero, macrúrido.
grenadierial [-'dɪrɪəl, B -'dɪər-] *a.* de granaderos.
grenadine [ˌgrɛnə'din, 'grɛnəˌdin] *s.* 1. granadina (jarabe de zumo de granadas). 2. granadina (tela de seda).
Grenadines [ˌgrɛnə'dinz] *s. pl.* Granadinas, Granadillas, islas de Barlovento.
Gresham's law ['grɛʃəmz-] (e.p.) ley de Gresham.
gressorial [grɛ'sɔrɪəl] *a.* (orn.) ambulatorio, adaptado para andar (díc. de las patas de algunas aves).
Gretna Green marriage ['grɛtnə-] (G.B.) casamiento (de menores) sin consentimiento de los padres.
grew [gru] *pret. de* **grow.**
grewsome, *var. de* **gruesome.**
grey, greyback, greybeard, *vars. de* **gray,** grayback, graybeard.
greyhound ['greɪˌhaʊnd] *s.* galgo, perro galgo, lebrel.
greyhound race track, canódromo.
greyhound racing, carrera de galgos.
greyhound stadium, canódromo.
greyish, *var. de* **grayish.**
greylag ['greɪˌlæg] *s.* (orn.) ganso silvestre.
greyness, *var. de* **grayness.**
gribble ['grɪbəl] *s.* (zool.) limnoria.
grid [grɪd] *s.* 1. rejilla, parrilla. 2. (elec., rad.) rejilla. 3. (mil.) cuadrícula (de un mapa).
grid bias, (rad.) polarización de rejilla.
grid circuit, (rad.) circuito de rejilla.
grid condenser, (rad.) condensador de rejilla.
grid current, (rad.) corriente de rejilla.
griddle ['grɪdəl] *s.* (cocina) plancha, sartén plana (para asar a fuego directo).
griddlecake [-ˌkeɪk] *s.* (cocina) hojuela, torta delgada (cocida sobre una plancha).
gride [graɪd] *v.t.* raspar (esp. produciendo un sonido crujiente). *—s.* crujido.
gridiron ['grɪdˌaɪərn, B -ˌaɪən] *s.* 1. parrilla (para asar). 2. red (de vigas, tubos, rieles, etc.). 3. (mar.) andamiada de carenaje, parrilla. 4. (teat.) telar. 5. (mil.) maniobra naval. 6. (dep.) campo de fútbol (E.U.).
gridiron pendulum, (fís.) péndulo de compensación (con barras paralelas de diferentes metales).
gridiron tracks, (f.c.) vías de parrilla.
grid leak, (rad.) escape de rejilla, resistencia de escape de rejilla.
grief [grif] *s.* 1. pesar, aflicción, pena, pesadumbre. 2. desgracia, desastre. 3. **good g.!** ¡por vida del chápiro!; **to bring to g.,** apesadumbrar, afligir, arruinar; **to come to g.,** sufrir un quebranto; fracasar, arruinarse.
grief-stricken ['grifˌstrɪkən] *a.* desconsolado, afligido, apesadumbrado.
grievance ['grivəns] *s.* 1. motivo para quejarse. 2. agravio, resentimiento. 3. (ant.) aflicción, dolor.
grieve [griv] *v.t.* 1. apesadumbrar, apenar, afligir. 2. lamentar, dolerse de. *—v.i.* apesadumbrarse, dolerse, apenarse, afligirse. — **to be grieved at** (o **by**), afligirse con, por o de; **g. at** (o **about, for, u over**), lamentar, dolerse de.
grievous ['grivəs] *a.* 1. penoso, doloroso, lastimoso; deplorable. 2. severo, intenso (dolor, pena, etc.). 3. serio, grave (insulto, error, pérdida, etc.). 4. dolorido, apenado, afligido. 5. (ant.) atroz, horrible.
grievously [-lɪ] *adv.* 1. penosamente, dolorosamente, lastimosamente, deplorablemente. 2. seriamente, gravemente.
grievousness [-nəs] *s.* 1. carácter penoso o deplorable. 2. seriedad, gravedad.
griffe [grɪf] *s.* 1. (E.U.) cuarterón; mulato; mestizo de negro e indio. 2. (arq.) adorno en forma de garra (en la base de una columna).
griffin ['grɪfən] *s.* 1. (anglo-ind.) forastero, extranjero, europeo recién llegado. 2. (mitol.) *var. de* **griffon.**
griffon ['grɪfən] *s.* 1. (mitol.) grifo. 2. buitre. 3. (zool.) grifón (perro zorrero o raposero).
grift [grɪft] *s.* (jer.) dinero adquirido por embauco. *—v.t.* quitar (dinero) con maña o por ardides.
grifter ['grɪftər, B -ə] *s.* (jer., E.U.) trampista, embaucador.
grig [grɪg] *s.* 1. angula (cría de la anguila). 2. grillo, cigarra, saltamontes. 3. (fig.) persona alegre y vivaracha.
grigri, *var. de* **gris-gris.**
grill [grɪl] *v.t.* 1. asar a la parrilla. 2. torturar con fuego o calor. 3. interrogar severamente y sin tregua. *—v.i.* someterse a interrogatorio severo. *—s.* 1. parrilla. 2. comida asada a la parrilla. 3. restaurante que sirve comidas a la parrilla. 4. *var. de* **grille,** enrejado.
grillage ['grɪlɪdʒ] *s.* entramado, armazón de madera (para reforzar un suelo).
grille [grɪl] *s.* 1. enrejado, reja, rejilla. 2. verja (ventana con reja).

grilled [grɪld] *a.* 1. enrejado, provisto de una reja. 2. asado o cocido a la parrilla.
grilling ['grɪlɪŋ] *s.* interrogatorio severo.
grillroom [-ˌrum, -ˌrʊm] *s.* restaurante (esp. de un hotel) que se especializa en platos de carne asada a la parrilla.
grillwork [-ˌwɜrk, B -ˌwɜk] *s.* enrejado.
grilse [grɪls] *s.* (*pl.* GRILSE) (ict.) salmón primerizo (que vuelve del mar al agua dulce de un río para desovar por primera vez).
grim [grɪm] *a.* (GRIMMER; GRIMMEST) 1. torvo, ceñudo; repulsivo, siniestro. 2. desconsolador, sombrío, tétrico. 3. severo, inflexible. 4. (fam.) desagradable.
grimace [grɪ'meɪs, 'grɪməs, B grɪ'meɪs] *s.* mueca, gesto, sonrisa falsa. —*v.i.* hacer muecas.
grimalkin [grɪ'mælkən] *s.* 1. gata vieja. 2. (fig.) vieja malévola.
grime [graɪm] *s.* mugre, tizne. —*v.t.* ensuciar, tiznar.
Grimes Golden ['graɪmz-] manzana reineta.
grimily ['graɪməlɪ] *adv.* suciamente.
griminess [-mɪnəs] *s.* suciedad, mugre.
grimly ['grɪmlɪ] *adv.* 1. inflexiblemente, severamente. 2. tétricamente, sombríamente.
grimness [-nəs] *s.* 1. aspecto siniestro o tétrico. 2. inflexibilidad, severidad.
grimy ['graɪmɪ] *a.* (GRIMIER; GRIMIEST) sucio, mugriento, tiznado.
grin [grɪn] *v.i.* (*pret., p.p.* GRINNED; *p.pr.* GRINNING) sonreír (de manera falsa o forzada); hacer una mueca (de dolor, desdén, satisfacción); reír irónicamente o tontamente; **g. and bear it,** soportar estoicamente. —*v.t.* expresar con una sonrisa o mueca. —*s.* sonrisa, mueca.
grind [graɪnd] *v.t.* (*pret., p.p.* GROUND [graʊnd]; *p.pr.* GRINDING) 1. moler; triturar, aciberar; picar (carne). 2. amolar, afilar. 3. esmerilar, bruñir, pulir. 4. hacer rechinar o crujir (los dientes). 5. agobiar, oprimir. 6. tocar (organillo) con el manubrio; (con *out*) hacer (música) con un organillo. —*v.i.* 1. hacer molienda. 2. molerse. 3. triturarse, pulverizarse. 4. afilarse. 5. pulirse. 6. rozar, ludir. 7. (fam.) afanarse; empollar (estudiando). 8. (jer.) menear las caderas al bailar (esp. una desnudista). —*s.* 1. molienda. 2. (fam.) ajobo, zurra, trabajo penoso (esp. estudios). 3. (E.U.) empollón. 4. (G.B.) carrera agotadora; (*pl.*) (jer.) carrera de obstáculos. 5. (G.B.) transbordador (en Cambridge). 6. meneo de las caderas que hace la bailarina desnudista.
grinder ['graɪndər, B -də] *s.* 1. molendero, molinero, moledor; amolador; esmerilador. 2. (máq.) moledora, molinillo, molino; amoladora, afiladora; muela (para afilar); esmeriladora. 3. muela; (*pl.*) dientes, muelas. 4. (*sandwich*) (fam.) sándwich mixto de tamaño grande, emparedado hecho con una barra entera de pan.
grindery [-dərɪ] *s.* (G.B.) 1. materiales empleados por los guarnicioneros o zapateros. 2. tienda de amolador (que afila herramientas, etc.).
grindstone ['graɪnd,stoʊn] *s.* 1. muela (de molino). 2. piedra de amolar, amoladera, mollejón. 3. **to keep one's nose to the g.,** trabajar incesantemente.
gringo ['grɪŋgoʊ] *s.* (*pl.* GRINGOS) (despec.) gringo, forastero, extranjero (esp. norteamericano o inglés en Hispanoamér.).
grinningly ['grɪnɪŋlɪ] *adv.* entre sonrisas, haciendo muecas.
grip [grɪp] *s.* 1. agarro, asimiento. 2. apretón (de la mano). 3. (fig.) puño (fuerza de dominación, poder), control, dominio; capacidad, comprensión (ej., intelectual); garra (ej., de una enfermedad); fuerza, poder (de atracción). 4. dolor punzante. 5. modo de darse la mano (en las sociedades secretas). 6. agarradero, asidero, puño, mango. 7. (fam., E.U.) saco de mano, maletín. 8. (jer., teat.) tramoyista. 9. **to be at grips (with),** luchar cuerpo a cuerpo (con); (fig.) trabajar intensamente en (un problema, etc.); **to come to grips (with),** trabar combate (con); (fig.) abordar (un problema, etc.). —*v.t.* (*pret., p.p.* GRIPPED; *p.pr.* GRIPPING) 1. agarrar, asir, empuñar. 2. apretar firmemente (la mano). 3. absorber (la atención), cautivar (a los espectadores). 4. agarrarse de o a. 5. fijar, enganchar. —*v.i.* 1. engancharse (ej., un ancla). 2. cerrarse firmemente.
grip car, coche o vagón de arrastre por cable (de un funicular).
gripe [graɪp] *v.t.* 1. agarrar, empuñar. 2. acongojar, afligir. 3. dar cólico a, causar retortijones en (el estómago, entrañas). 4. (fam., E.U.) irritar, vejar, enfadar. 5. (mar.) amarrar. 6. (mec.) morder, sujetar. —*v.i.* 1. sentir retortijones (en el estómago, entrañas, etc.); padecer de cólicos. 2. (fam., E.U.) quejarse, refunfuñar. —*s.* 1. angustia, agobio, miseria, aprieto. 2. (*gen. pl.*) cólicos, retortijones. 3. agarradero, asidero, mango, manija. 4. (fam., E.U.) queja. 5. (mar.) trapas (para asegurar las lanchas de auxilio). 6. (mec.) uña, grapa; freno de malacate.
griper ['graɪpər, B -ə] *s.* (fam., E.U.) criticón, tipo quejumbroso.
grippal ['grɪpəl] *a.* (med.) gripal.
grippe [grɪp] *s.* (med.) gripe, influenza.
gripper ['grɪpər, B -ə] *s.* 1. el o lo que agarra. 2. (impr., mec.) uña.
gripping [-ɪŋ] *a.* que agarra (a uno), que absorbe la atención (díc. de una novela, cuento, etc.).
gripple ['grɪpəl] *a.* (dial.) avaro.
grippy ['grɪpɪ] *a.* griposo, propenso a la gripe.
gripsack ['grɪp,sæk] *s.* (E.U.) saco de mano, maletín.
grisaille [grɪ'zaɪ, B -'zeɪl] *s.* (pint.) grisalla; vidrio pintado en grisalla.
griseous ['grɪzɪəs] *a.* grisáceo, pardusco, plomizo, aplomado; entrecano (del pelo o persona).
grisette [grɪ'zɛt] *s.* costurera, modistilla (esp. de París).
gris-gris ['gri,gri] *s.* amuleto.
griskin ['grɪskɪn] *s.* (cocina, G.B.) filete o solomillo de cerdo.
grisliness ['grɪzlɪnəs] *s.* aspecto espantoso, carácter espeluznante.
grisly [-lɪ] *a.* (GRISLIER; GRISLIEST) espantoso, horrible, espeluznante.
grist [grɪst] *s.* 1. molienda (grano por moler o porción de grano molido). 2. masa de cebada. 3. (E.U.) montón, cantidad. 4. **all is g. that comes to his mill,** se sirve de todo; todo entra en su olla; **to bring g. to** (o **for**) **the mill,** ser provechoso.
gristle ['grɪsəl] *s.* cartílago, ternilla.
gristliness [-əlɪnəs] *s.* consistencia cartilaginosa.
gristly [-lɪ] *a.* cartilaginoso, ternilloso.
gristmill ['grɪst,mɪl] *s.* molino harinero.
grit [grɪt] *s.* 1. granos de arena. 2. dureza (de una piedra para amolar). 3. (geol.) asperón, arenisca silícea. 4. tesón, valor, coraje; resistencia. 5. (ant.) arena, cascajo. —*v.t., v.i.* (*pret., p.p.* GRITTED; *p.pr.* GRITTING) 1. cubrir o llenar de arena. 2. raspar, raer; pulir (mármol, etc.). 3. hacer rechinar o crujir (los dientes).
grith [grɪθ] *s.* (hist.) paz, seguridad; santuario; refugio, asilo.
grits [grɪts] *s. pl.* sémola, farro; (esp. E.U.) maíz a medio moler.
grittiness ['grɪtɪnəs] *s.* 1. contextura arenosa. 2. fortaleza, ánimo, perseverancia.
gritty [-ɪ] *a.* (GRITTIER; GRITTIEST) 1. arenoso, arenisco. 2. valiente, animoso, denodado, resuelto.
grivet ['grɪvət] *s.* (zool.) cercopiteco verde.
grizzle ['grɪzəl] *a.* gris, grisáceo, pardo. —*s.* 1. color gris. 2. (ant.) pelo canoso; peluca gris. —*v.t., v.i.* volver(se) grisáceo o entrecano. —*v.i.* (G.B.) lloriquear (esp. niños).
grizzled [-əld] *a.* gris, grisáceo, pardusco; entrecano.
grizzly [-lɪ] *a.* un poco gris, grisáceo, pardusco.
grizzly bear, (zool.) oso gris.
groan [groʊn] *v.i.* 1. gemir, plañir, quejarse. 2. gruñir. 3. crujir (bajo mucho peso, ej., una viga, una carreta, etc.). 4. **g. beneath** (o **under**), crujir bajo el peso de; (fig.) sufrir el peso de (una dictadura, etc.); **g. with,** estar repleto de, estar cargado de. —*v.t.* expresar con voz quejumbrosa, proferir entre gemidos. —*s.* 1. gemido, quejido. 2. gruñido.
groat [groʊt] *s.* (hist., G.B.) moneda antigua de plata de cuatro peniques.
groats [groʊts] *s. pl.* farro, sémola; grano desvainado (de trigo, avena, etc.) y molido grueso.
grocer ['groʊsər, B -sə] *s.* especiero, abacero, abarrotero, tendero, bodeguero (Amer.), pulpero (Amer.), almacenero (Amer.); **grocer's,** especiería, abacería, bodega, pulpería, tienda de abarrotes.
grocery ['groʊsərɪ] *s.* (*pl.* GROCERIES) 1. especiería, abacería, tienda de comestibles o ultramarinos; tienda de abarrotes, almacén, bodega. 2. (E.U.) (*gen. pl.*) comestibles, víveres, especierías, abarrotes (Amer.).
grog [grɑg, B grɔg] *s.* grog (mezcla de aguardiente o ron con agua); bebida alcohólica.
groggery ['grɑgərɪ, B 'grɔg-] *s.* tabernucha, chingana (Amer.), botiquín (Ven.).
grogginess [-ɪnəs] *s.* vacilación, inseguridad; debilidad; atontamiento (causado por un golpe).
groggy [-ɪ] *a.* (GROGGIER; GROGGIEST) vacilante, medio borracho, inseguro, tambaleante; débil, enervado; (dep.) atontado (díc. del púgil que recibe un fuerte golpe).
grogram ['grɑgrəm, B 'grɔg-] *s.* (tej.) gorgorán, cordellate.
grogshop ['grɑg,ʃɑp, B 'grɔg,ʃɔp] *s.* (pr. G.B.) tabernucha, chingana (Amer.), botiquín (Ven.).
groin [grɔɪn] *s.* 1. (anat.) ingle. 2. (arq.) arista de encuentro, esquina viva, aristón; rincón de encuentro. —*v.t.* (arq.) construir con aristas de encuentro.
groin vault, groined vault, (arq.) bóveda vaída.
grommet ['grɑmət, 'grʌm-, B 'grɔm-] *s.* 1. arandela de cabo; ojal de metal, anillo de cuerda. 2. (mar.) roñada, estrobo.
gromwell ['grɑm,wel, -wəl, B 'grɔm-] *s.* (bot.) variedad de borraja.
groom [grum, grʊm] *s.* 1. mozo de caballos o de cuadra. 2. (G.B.) camarero, caballerizo o ayuda de cámara (de la casa real). 3. novio. 4. (ant.) criado; hombre (esp. de condición humilde). —*v.t.* 1. cuidar, atender (caballos). 2. asear, acicalar; poner en orden. 3. (pol.) preparar (para una candidatura o para un cargo).
groomsman ['grumzmən, 'grʊmz-] *s.* padrino de boda.
grove [gruv] *s.* 1. ranura, acanaladura, muesca, rebajo. 2. garganta (de polea). 3. surco (del disco de gramófono). 4. (fig.) rutina, hábito arraigado. 5. (arq.) estría. 6. (tip.) cran, muesca, hendidura (en la base del tipo). 7. **in the g.,** (jer.) en vena (orador, escritor, etc.); en forma (deportista); **to get into a g.,** adquirir hábitos arraigados. —*v.t.*

ranurar, acanalar, estriar, muescar. —*v.i.* (jer.) disfrutar, deleitarse, transportarse, estar en onda, ej., *they g. to rock music,* ellos disfrutan con la música rock.
grooved [gruvd] *a.* acanalado.
groover ['gruvər, B -ə] *s.* ranurador, acanalador.
groove rail, riel de ranura, carril de canal.
grooving chisel [-ɪŋ-] cortafrío ranurador.
grooving machine, ranuradora.
grooving plane, (carp.) cepillo de ranurar, cepillo acanalador, guimbarda.
grooving saw, sierra ranuradora.
groovy ['gruvɪ] *a.* (GROOVIER; GROOVIEST) (jer., E.U.) atractivo, agradable; estupendo, excelente.
grope [groʊp] *v.t.* tentar (el camino en la obscuridad). —*v.i.* andar a tientas; **g. for** (o **after**), buscar tentando. —*s.* tiento (vacilante).
groping ['groʊpɪŋ] *a.* 1. escudriñador, inquisitivo. 2. vacilante, incierto.
gropingly [-lɪ] *adv.* 1. de modo escudriñador, en forma inquisitiva. 2. a tientas, a tiento.
grosbeak ['groʊs,bik] *s.* (orn.) picogordo, piñonero; pico grueso vespertino.
grosgrain ['groʊ,greɪn] *s.* (tej.) gro; gorgorán, cordellate.
gross [groʊs] *a.* 1. grande, voluminoso, abultado. 2. gordo, grueso, corpulento. 3. espeso, denso. 4. craso, grueso (error, mentira, etc.). 5. basto, tosco. 6. grosero, descortés. 7. vulgar, indecoroso, escandaloso, obsceno. 8. animal, sensual. 9. notorio, flagrante. 10. zafio, lerdo, estúpido, ignorante. 11. total, íntegro, entero; bruto (ganancia, producción, etc.). 12. general. 13. visible a simple vista; macroscópico. 14. (ant.) llano, simple; manifiesto; obvio. —*s.* 1. totalidad, total, suma total (de ingresos, gastos). 2. (*pl.* GROSS) gruesa, doce docenas. 3. (ant.) grueso, parte principal o mayor. 4. **by the g.,** al por mayor; **in the g.,** en grueso, en conjunto; (ant.) en líneas generales, en su totalidad. —*v.t.* sumar (ganancias) en bruto; rendir en bruto.
gross amount, importe bruto o total.
gross ignorance, ignorancia crasa.
grossly ['groʊslɪ] *adv.* 1. excesivamente. 2. vulgarmente. 3. groseramente, descortésmente. 4. más o menos, aproximadamente. 5. lerdamente, estúpidamente.
gross national product, producto nacional bruto, renta nacional íntegra; producción nacional bruta.
grossness [-nəs] 1. pesadez, magnitud (del cuerpo). 2. densidad, espesor. 3. vulgaridad. 4. descortesía, grosería. 5. torpeza, estupidez. 6. crasitud.
gross profit, (com.) ganancia o utilidad bruta, beneficio bruto.
gross ton, tonelada larga, tonelada bruta.
gross tonnage 1. tonelaje bruto. 2. (mar.) arqueo bruto.
grossulariaceous [,grɑsə,lɛrɪ'eɪʃəs B ,grɔs-] *a.* (bot.) grosulario.
grossularite ['grɑsələ,raɪt, B 'grɔs-] *s.* (min.) grosularita, grosularia, granate cálcico.
gross weight, peso bruto.
grosz [grɔʃ] *s.* unidad monetaria de Polonia.
grot [grɑt, B grɔt] *s.* (poét.) gruta; caverna.
grotesque [groʊ'tɛsk] *s.* 1. cosa grotesca. 2. (arte) obra grotesca. —*a.* 1. grotesco, ridículo, extravagante, fantástico. 2. (arte) grotesco. 3. (G.B., impr.) grotesco, griego, etrusco, de bastón.
grotesquely [-lɪ] *adv.* grotescamente.
grotesqueness [-nəs] *s.* carácter o aspecto grotesco.
grotesquerie, grotesquery [-'tɛskərɪ] *s.* 1. carácter grotesco. 2. objeto o trabajo grotesco.
grotto ['grɑtoʊ, B 'grɔt-] *s.* (*pl.* GROTTOES o GROTTOS) gruta, cueva, caverna.
grouch [graʊtʃ] *v.i.* estar de mal humor, refunfuñar, gruñir. —*s. 1. gruñón, cascarrabias. 2. mal humor. 3. rencor, inquina.*
grouchy ['graʊtʃɪ] *a.* (GROUCHIER; GROUCHIEST) malhumorado, refunfuñador, gruñón.
ground [graʊnd] *pret., p.p. de* **grind.** —*a.* molido, picado; pulverizado, triturado.
ground [graʊnd] *s.* 1. tierra, suelo. 2. territorio, terreno. 3. (*pl.*) terreno, área (de un edificio, etc.); jardines, parques. 4. campo (de batalla, desfile, etc.). 5. base, fundamento; causa, razón, motivo. 6. tema, asunto, tópico. 7. fondo. 8. (*pl.*) sedimento, poso, heces, concho (Am.). 9. (elec., rad.) tierra, toma de tierra. 10. (teat.) platea. 11. **above g.,** vivo; **down to the g.,** enteramente, por completo; **from the g. up,** desde el principio; completamente; **into the g.,** (fig.) hasta no poder más, al exceso; **on delicate g.,** en una situación que requiere tacto; **on the g.,** sobre el terreno; **to be on one's own g.,** estar en su propio elemento; **to break g.,** empezar a excavar; **to break new g.,** (fig.) investigar en terreno virgen, abrir nuevos horizontes (en una ciencia, etc.); **to cover much g.,** tratar sobre muchos asuntos, tratar extensamente el tema, abarcar muchos aspectos (de un tema, asunto, etc.); **to cover the g.,** recorrer el trecho o la distancia; (fig.) tratar (todo) el tema (extensamente, con muchos detalles, etc.); **to cut the g. from under one's feet,** socavar la posición de uno; destruirle las razones en una polémica; **to dash to the g.,** (fig.) dar en tierra con (esperanzas, etc.); **to fall to the g.,** (fig.) venirse al suelo o abajo, quedar en nada, fracasar; **to get off the g.,** alzar el vuelo; (fig.) ponerse en marcha; cobrar ímpetu; **to hold one's g.,** no ceder, mantenerse firme; **to lose g.,** perder terreno; **to run into the g.,** (fig.) abusar de; arruinar, agotar; **to take the g.,** varar, encallar; **to stand one's g.,** no ceder, resistir con éxito; **to the g.,** completamente, en todo respecto; **to touch g.,** (fig.) tocar tierra (en conversación, argumento, etc.). —*v.t.* 1. poner en tierra; traer a tierra. 2. descansar (armas). 3. (fig.) fundar, basar, apoyar, cimentar (argumentos, etc.). 4. (gen. con *in*) enseñar los elementos (de una materia, etc.) a. 5. (elec.) poner a tierra, conectar con tierra. 6. (mar.) varar. 7. (aer.) obligar a permanecer en tierra, impedir o imposibilitar el vuelo de (avión); impedir que despegue (avión o piloto); prohibir volar a, suspender (piloto). 8. (pint.) dar campo o fondo a (una superficie). 9. **well grounded,** bien fundado (razonamiento, juicio, etc.); **well grounded in,** bien versado en (una materia, etc.). —*v.i.* 1. (gen. con *on* o *upon*) tener fundamento o base; contar (con), confiar (en). 2. (mar.) encallar, varar. 3. (béisbol) golpear la pelota de modo que rebote en el suelo. —*a.* 1. a ras de tierra. 2. terrestre. 3. fundamental; primero, de base. 4. (elec.) a tierra.
ground bait, (pesca) cebo echado al fondo, carnada hundida por una plomada.
ground ball, (dep.) roletazo, tola.
ground bass, (mús.) bajo obstinado, continuo o rítmico.
ground cable, (elec.) cable de puesta a tierra, conductor a tierra.
ground-cherry ['graʊnd'tʃɛrɪ] *s.* (bot.) alquequenje, vejiga de perro; capulí (Am.).
ground connection, (elec., rad.) toma de tierra.
ground control, (aer.) control desde tierra (de personal y equipo).
ground-controlled approach [-kəntroʊld-] (aer.) aproximación controlada desde tierra.
ground cover, plantas pequeñas que cubren el suelo en un bosque.
ground crew, (aer.) tripulación o personal de tierra.
grounder ['graʊndər, B -də] *s.* (béisbol) golpe que hace rebotar la pelota en el suelo.
ground fire, fuego antiaéreo.
ground floor, planta baja, primer piso (Amer.), piso bajo (Esp.); **to get in on the g.,** (fig.) empezar por abajo.
ground glass, vidrio esmerilado o deslustrado.
groundhog ['graʊnd,hɔg, -,hɑg, B -,hɔg] *s.* (zool.) marmota americana.
Groundhog Day, día de la candelaria (2 de febrero).
ground ice, hielo de fondo.
grounding ['graʊndɪŋ] *s.* base, instrucción en los rudimentos; **a g. in** los rudimentos de, una base en.
ground itch, (med.) sarna causada por el anquilostoma.
ground ivy, (bot.) hiedra terrestre.
ground lead, (elec.) conductor a tierra.
groundless ['graʊndləs] *a.* infundado, sin fundamento, sin base, indefendible, insostenible.
groundlessly [-lɪ] *adv.* infundadamente, sin razón.
groundlessness [-nəs] *s.* falta de razón o fundamento.
ground level, nivel del suelo.
groundling [-lɪŋ] *s.* 1. que vive al fondo del agua (pez.). 2. (teat.) mosquetero. 3. persona de poco gusto.
ground loop, (aer.) caballito (vuelta violenta al aterrizar o despegar un avión).
groundmass [-,mæs] *s.* (min.) base vidriosa del pórfido.
ground mine, (mil.) mina de fondo.
groundnut [-,nʌt] *s.* 1. (bot.) chufa. 2. (bot., pr. G.B.) cacahuete, cacahuate, maní (Amer.).
ground pine, (bot.) 1. pinillo, hierba aromática. 2. licopodio.
ground pink, (bot.) musgo rosado.
ground plan, 1. planta, plano horizontal (de un edificio). 2. proyecto básico, plan fundamental.
ground plane, (dib.) plano geométrico.
ground plate, 1. (arq.) durmiente, solera de fondo. 2. (elec.) placa de conexión a tierra. 3. (f.c.) placa de base para traviesas o durmientes (Amer.).
ground plum, (bot.) especie de astrágalo o tragacanto.
ground rent, (pr. G.B.) renta (de la tierra), alquiler del terreno, censo.
ground rule, regla o norma de procedimiento.
groundsel ['graʊnsəl, 'graʊnd-] *s.* 1. (arq.) carrera inferior; solera, umbral. 2. (bot.) hierba cana, hierba caballar, zuzón.
groundsill ['graʊnd,sɪl] *s.* (arq.) carrera inferior; solera umbral.
grounds keeper['graʊndz-] persona encargada de cuidar estadios, cementerios, etc.; guardián, vigilante.
ground speed, (aer.) velocidad absoluta, velocidad respecto a tierra.
ground squirrel, (zool.) ardilla terrestre, ardilla listada, ardilla de la tierra.
ground staff, (aer.) personal de tierra.
ground steel, acero moldeado.
ground swell, mar de fondo, marejada de fondo.
ground target, (mil.) blanco terrestre.
ground-to-air ['graʊndtə'ɛr, B -'ɛə] *a.* de tierra a aire.

ground-to-ground [-tə'graʊnd] *a.* de tierra a tierra.
ground troops, (mil.) tropas terrestres.
ground water, agua subterránea, aguas freáticas, agua de pozo.
ground wave, (rad.) onda superficial, onda terrestre.
ground wire, (elec.) línea de tierra, conductor a tierra, alambre de masa.
groundwork ['graʊnd,wɜrk, B -,wɜk] *s.* fundamento, cimiento, base.
ground zero, punto en el terreno directamente encima o debajo de la explosión atómica.
group [grup] *s.* grupo, conjunto, agrupación. —*v.t.* agrupar, juntar, reunir; clasificar. —*v.i.* agruparse, armonizar(se).
group captain, (G.B., aer.) jefe de escuadrilla, capitán de grupo.
grouper ['grupər, B -ə] *s.* (*pl.* GROUPER O GROUPERS) (ict.) mero, cherna.
groupie ['grupi] *s.* (jer.) chica aficionada a los grupos de música popular; admiradora de músicos y cantantes estilo rock.
grouping ['grupɪŋ] *s.* agrupamiento, colocación, agrupación.
group insurance, seguro colectivo.
group practice, (med.) práctica colectiva.
group therapy, terapia en grupo.
grouse [graʊs] *s.* 1. (*pl.* GROUSE) (orn.) guaco, gallo de bosque, urogallo. 2. refunfuño, queja. —*v.i.* refunfuñar, quejarse.
grouse locust, (ento.) tetigonia.
grouser ['graʊsər, B -ə] *s.* gruñón.
grout [graʊt] *s.* 1. harina gruesa; (*pl.*) sémola, avena mondada. 2. (G.B.) (*gen. pl.*) sedimento, poso. 3. (const.) lechada, lechada de cemento. —*v.t.* enlechar.
grouty ['graʊtɪ] *a.* (fam., E.U.) regañón, huraño, arisco.
grove [groʊv] *s.* arboleda, bosquecillo, boscaje; huerto.
grovel ['grɑvəl, 'grʌv-, B 'grɔv-] *v.i.* (*pret., p.p.* GROVELED O GROVELLED; *p.pr.* GROVELING O GROVELLING) 1. serpear, arrastrarse. 2. (fig.) envilecerse, rebajarse. 3. deleitarse en lo bajo y abyecto. 4. **g. in the dust,** humillarse completamente.
groveler [-ələr, B -lə] **groveller** *s.* hombre servil y rastrero.
grovelingly, grovellingly [-əlɪŋlɪ] *adv.* servilmente, abyectamente.
grow [groʊ] *v.i.* (PRET. GREW [gru]; *p.p.* GROWN [groʊn]; *p.pr.* GROWING) 1. crecer. 2. medrar, prosperar, florecer. 3. desarrollarse, crecer (en tamaño), aumentar (en cantidad). 4. (fig.) crecer (en importancia, poder, etc.). 5. volverse (ej., rico), ponerse (ej., pálido); *cuando está seguido de un* a. *o* p.p. *se traduce a menudo con el verbo que corresponde en español a estos últimos,* ej., *g. old,* envejecer, *g. tired,* cansarse. 6. **g. accustomed,** acostumbrarse; **g. dark,** anochecer, obscurecerse; **g. from,** nacer de; derivarse de; **g. into,** hacerse o llegar a ser con los años (ej., un hombre fuerte, una mujer hermosa, etc.); **g. on one,** acostumbrarse a; arraigar en uno, ir apoderándose de uno (ej., un hábito); gustarle a uno cada vez más; **g. on trees,** abundar, encontrarse dondequiera, ej., *first-class players do not g. on trees,* los jugadores de primera clase no se encuentran dondequiera; **g. out of,** crecer, pasar de la edad para; perder (hábito, vicio, etc.); (fig.) originarse en, resultar de; **g. out of fashion,** pasar de moda; **g. together,** unirse, juntarse; **g. up,** madurar (en espíritu), volverse adulto; (fig.) crearse (situación, etc.); **g. up together,** criarse o crecer juntos; **to be grown over (with),** estar cubierto de cultivos (de). —*v.t.* 1. criar, cultivar, producir. 2. (fig.) cultivar; desarrollar (ej., una tendencia).
grower ['groʊər, B -ə] *s.* 1. cultivador; criador; agricultor. 2. uno que crece (rápido, lento), ej., *this flower is a fast g.,* esta flor crece rápido.
growing [-ɪŋ] *a.* 1. en crecimiento, ej., *a g. boy,* un muchacho en crecimiento; *a g. enterprise,* una empresa en crecimiento. 2. creciente (ej., ansiedad, sed, hambre, etc.). —*s.* 1. cultivo, cultivación. 2. cría. 3. crecimiento, aumento.
growing pains, dolores del crecimiento; (fig.) trastornos del desarrollo, dificultades del comienzo.
growl [graʊl] *v.i.* 1. gruñir (perro, etc.). 2. retumbar (cañón, etc.). 3. refunfuñar, rezongar, murmurar, quejarse. 4. **g. at,** recibir con gruñidos (ej., el perro a alguien). —*v.t.* expresar entre gruñidos (descontento, etc.). —*s.* 1. gruñido. 2. retumbo. 3. rezongo, refunfuño.
growler ['graʊlər, B -ə] *s.* 1. gruñidor, regañador, refunfuñador. 2. pequeño iceberg. 3. (elec.) probador de inducidos. 4. (E.U.) jarro (que sirve de medida) para la cerveza. 5. (G.B.) cabriolé de cuatro ruedas.
growling [-ɪŋ] *a.* 1. refunfuñador. 2. retumbante (trueno).
grown [groʊn] *a.* 1. crecido, desarrollado; maduro. 2. (en palabras compuestas) cubierto de, ej., *a violet-grown patch,* un sembrado cubierto de violetas.
grown-up ['groʊn'ʌp] *a.* 1. adulto, mayor. 2. serio, juicioso, propio de un adulto. —[-,ʌp]*s.* adulto.
growth [groʊθ] *s.* 1. crecimiento; desarrollo; aumento, expansión, agrandamiento. 2. amplitud, tamaño (máximo). 3. producción, producto; cultivo; planta; vegetación. 4. origen, ej., *of foreign g.,* de origen extranjero. 5. (med.) tumor. 6. **full g.,** desarrollo completo; tamaño máximo.
growth factor, factor de crecimiento o de expansión.
groyne [grɔɪn] *s.* espolón, rompeolas. —*v.t.* proveer (a una playa) de espolón o rompeolas.
grub [grʌb] *v.i.* (*pret., p.p.* GRUBBED; *p.pr.* GRUBBING) 1. cavar (laboriosamente); hozar (un cerdo). 2. afanarse, ajetrearse, atrafagarse. 3. (jer.) manducar, papar, comer. —*v.t.* 1. limpiar, desyerbar, desmalezar (un terreno). 2. (gen. con *up*) arrancar, desarraigar, extirpar. 3. (con *up* o *out*) (fig.) desenterrar, descubrir (datos, etc.). 4. (jer.) alimentar, nutrir. —*s.* 1. gusano, larva (esp. de gorgojo). 2. persona afanada, persona ajetreada; marmitón, galopín. 3. (jer.) comida.
grub ax, legón, picaza.
grubber ['grʌbər, B -ə] *s.* 1. desyerbador. 2. azadón.
grubbily [-əlɪ] *adv.* suciamente, descuidadamente.
grubbiness [-ɪnəs] *s.* 1. suciedad, roña, mugre. 2. desaliño, descuido.
grubby [-ɪ] *a.* (GRUBBIER; GRUBBIEST) 1. sucio, mugriento. 2. descuidado, desaliñado.
grub hoe, azada, azadón.
grubstake ['grʌb,steɪk] *s.* (E.U.) avío (anticipo de dinero, crédito que se da a un buscador de minerales o petróleo a cambio de una parte de sus descubrimientos, futuros). —*v.t.* aviar, subvencionar (a un buscador de minerales o petróleo).
Grub Street, (hist., G.B.) calle antigua en que vivían escritores mercenarios y necesitados; **to live on G.S.,** llevar la vida de un escritor mercenario.
grudge [grʌdʒ] *v.t.* 1. escatimar, dar de mala gana. 2. envidiar. —*v.i.* (ant.) refunfuñar, quejarse. —*s.* inquina, rencor, animosidad; **to bear one a g., to have a g. against one,** tener o guardar rencor a uno.
grudger ['grʌdʒər, B -ə] *s.* persona envidiosa.
grudgingly [-ɪŋlɪ] *adv.* de mala gana, a contrapelo.
gruel ['gruəl] *s.* (cocina) avenate, atole, gachas (de cereal o granos).
grueling, gruelling [-ɪŋ] *a.* agotador, abrumador. —*s.* castigo; zurra.
gruesome ['grusəm] *a.* horrible, horripilante, horroroso, horrendo.
gruesomely [-lɪ] *adv.* horriblemente.
gruesomeness [-nəs] *s.* carácter horrible; aspecto horroroso.
gruff [grʌf] *a.* 1. ceñudo, áspero, rudo. 2. ronco, desagradable (voz).
gruffly ['grʌflɪ] *adv.* ásperamente, rudamente.
gruffness [-nəs] *s.* aspereza, rudeza, severidad, mal humor.
grugru ['gru,gru] *s.* 1. (bot.) gri-grí. 2. (zool.) larva (comestible) de un gorgojo tropical.
grum [grʌm] *a.* áspero, severo, malhumorado.
grumble ['grʌmbəl] *v.i.* 1. refunfuñar, gruñir, rezongar, regañar. 2. rugir, retumbar (trueno, etc.). 3. **g. at, about u over,** gruñir a, quejarse de. —*v.t.* decir entre gruñidos, expresar rezongando. —*s.* 1. refunfuño, gruñido. 2. rugido, retumbo.
grumbler [-blər, B -blə] *s.* refunfuñador, gruñidor, rezongón.
grumblingly [-blɪŋlɪ] *adv.* refunfuñando, murmurando, rezongando.
grume [grum] *s.* (med.) grumo, cuajarón.
grummet ['grʌmət] *var. de* **grommet.**
grumose ['gru,moʊs] *a.* (bot.) granado, granilloso.
grumous [-məs] *a.* 1. grumoso. 2. (bot.) granado, granilloso.
grump [grʌmp] *s.* 1. (*pl.*) mal humor, morriña. 2. gruñón, rezongón.
grumpily ['grʌmpəlɪ] *adv.* malhumoradamente, de mal humor.
grumpiness [-pɪnəs] *s.* malhumor, aspereza.
grumpy [-pɪ] *a.* gruñón, malhumorado, rezongón.
Grundy ['grʌndɪ] *s.* gazmoña; **Mrs. Grundy,** (fig., G.B.) la gente, el mundo (como guardián de las convenciones sociales y la moral puritana).
grunion ['grʌnjən] *s.* (ict.) lisa de las costas de California.
grunt [grʌnt] *v.i.* gruñir. —*v.t.* (t. con *out*) expresar entre gruñidos. —*s.* 1. gruñido. 2. (ict.) roncador, ronco. 3. (E.U., jer.) soldado raso (en Vietnam).
grunter ['grʌntər, B -ə] *s.* 1. cerdo. 2. (ict.) ronco, roncador.
gruntingly [-ɪŋlɪ] *adv.* gruñendo, entre gruñidos.
Gruyère [gru'jɛr, gri-, B 'grujɛə] *s.* (queso) gruyere, tipo de queso suizo.
gr. wt. *abrev. de* **gross weight,** peso bruto.
gryphon, *var. de* **griffon** (mitol.).
G.S. *abrev. de* **General Staff,** Estado Mayor General.
GSC *abrev. de* **General Staff Corps,** Cuerpo del Estado Mayor.
GSO *abrev. de* **General Staff Officer,** oficial del Estado Mayor.
G-string ['dʒi,strɪŋ] *s.* taparrabo, pampanilla (esp. el que usan las bailarinas desnudistas).
G-suit [-'sut, B -'sjut] *s.* (aer., astronáut.) vestido anti-g (diseñado para contrarrestar los efectos fisiológicos de la aceleración).
GT *abrev. de* **gross ton,** tonelada bruta.

Gt. Brit. *abrev. de* **Great Britain,** Gran Bretaña.
guacamole [ˌgwɑkəˈmoʊleɪ] *s.* (cocina) guacamole (ensalada de aguacate, chile verde, cebolla picada y sal).
guacharo [ˈgwɑtʃəˌroʊ] *s.* (orn.) guácharo.
guaco [ˈgwɑkoʊ, B ˈgweɪ-] *s.* (bot.) guaco.
Guadeloupe [ˌgwɑdəˈlup, ˈgwɑdəlˌup, B ˌgwɑdəˈlup] *s.* Guadalupe (una de las islas francesas de las Antillas Menores).
guaiac [ˈgwaɪæk] *s.* guayaco (madera o resina).
guaiacol [ˈgwaɪəˌkɔl-ˌkoʊl, B -ˌkɔl] *s.* (farm., quím.) guayacol.
guaiacum [-kəm] *s.* 1. (bot.) guayacán. 2. guayaco (madera o resina).
Guam [gwɑm] *s.* Guam, isla del Pacífico, posesión de los E.U.
guama [gwəˈmɑ] *s.* (bot.) guamo, guabo, pacae, pacay.
guan [gwɑn] *s.* (orn.) guan, pavo de América.
guanaco [gwəˈnɑkoʊ, B -ˈneɪk-] *s.* (*pl.* GUANACOS O GUANACO) (zool.) guanaco.
guanidine [ˈgwɑnəˌdin, B ˈgwæn-] *s.* (quím.) guanidina.
guanine [ˈgwɑˌnin, B ˈgweɪnɪn] *s.* (quím.) guanina.
guano [ˈgwɑnoʊ] *s.* (*pl.* GUANOS) guano, abono que se obtiene del excremento de aves marinas.
Guarani [ˌgwɑrəˈni] *s.* (*pl.* GUARANI O GUARANIS) 1. guaraní (indio de Sud América). 2. guaraní (lengua). 3. **g.,** guaraní (unidad monetaria del Paraguay).
guarantee [ˌgærənˈti] *s.* (*pl.* GUARANTEES) 1. garantía, caución, fianza. 2. fiador, garante. 3. fiado, caucionado, persona afianzada. —*v.t.* garantizar; (com.) garantizar, avalar (una letra, obligación, etc.).
guarantee fund, caución de indemnidad.
guarantor [-ˈtɔr, ˈgærəntər, B ˌgærənˈtɔ] *s.* (der.) garante.
guaranty [ˈgærəntɪ] *s.* (*pl.* GUARANTIES) 1. garantia. 2. garante. —*v.t.* (*pret., p.p.* GUARANTIED; *p.pr.* GUARANTYING) garantizar; dar seguridad a.
guard [gɑrd, B gɑd] *v.t.* 1. proteger, defender, escudar. 2. guardar, custodiar, vigilar. 3. (cost.) orlar. 4. (ant.) escoltar. —*v.i.* vigilar, montar guardia; **g. against,** precaverse de, tomar precauciones contra. —*s.* 1. guardia, proteción, defensa, custodia, vigilancia. 2. (posición de) guardia (en esgr., boxeo, etc.). 3. guardia, guardián, centinela. 4. (*pl.*) (cuerpo de) guardia. 5. (f.c.) guardafrenos, guardabarrera. 6. (G.B., f.c.) conductor. 7. (mec.) guarda, defensa; pantalla o reja de protección. 8. guarda, guarnición (de espada). 9. (dep.) defensor. 10. (naipes) guarda. 11. **off g.,** desprevenido; **on g.,** en guardia, vigilante; (esgr.) en guardia; **to go on g. duty,** entrar de guardia; **to mount, stand** o **keep g.,** montar guardia; mantener vigilancia; **under g.,** a buen recaudo.
guard boat, barco de vigilancia, guardacostas.
guard-chain [ˈgɑrdˌtʃeɪn, B ˈgɑd-] *s.* cadena de seguridad.
guard dog, perro guardián.
guarded [ˈgɑrdəd, B ˈgɑd-] *a.* 1. cauteloso, cauto, mesurado. 2. guardado, protegido, vigilado.
guardedly [-lɪ] *adv.* cautelosamente.
guardedness [-nəs] *s.* cautela, cuidado, circunspección.
guarder [ˈgɑrdər, B ˈgɑdə] *s.* guardia; vigilante.
guardhouse [-ˌhaʊs] *s.* 1. cuartel de la guardia (esp. la que vigila una prisión). 2. cárcel militar.
guardian [ˈgɑrdɪən, B ˈgɑdjən] *s.* 1. guardián, custodio, vigilante. 2. (der.) tutor, curador. 3. (relig.) guardián (de un convento de franciscanos). —*a.* de guardia, custodio.
guardian angel, ángel custodio, ángel de la guarda.
guardianship [-ˌʃɪp] *s.* 1. (der.) tutela, tutoría, curatela, curaduría. 2. (fig.) tutela, amparo, protección. 3. (rel.) guardianía (en la orden de San Francisco).
guardrail [-ˌreɪl] *s.* 1. (f.c.) contrarriel, contracarril. 2. baranda, pasamanos (de una escalera o un balcón).
guardroom [-ˌrum, -ˌrʊm] *s.* (mil.) cuarto de la guardia.
guard ship, (mar.) navío de guardia, de ronda o de estación.
guardsman [ˈgɑrdzmən, B ˈgɑdz-] *s.* (mil.) guarda, guardia, centinela.
guard wire, (elec.) alambre de guardia.
Guatemala [ˌgwɑtəˈmɑlə] *s.* Guatemala.
Guatemalan [-lən] *a., s.* guatemalteco.
guava [ˈgwɑvə] *s.* (bot.) 1. guayabo. 2. guayaba.
guava apple, (bot.) guayaba.
guayule [gwaɪˈulɪ, B gwɑˈjul] *s.* (bot.) guayule.
gubernatorial [ˌgubərnəˈtɔrɪəl, B ˌgjubənə-] *a.* de gobernador, gubernativo; del gobernador.
guck [gʌk] *s.* (jer.) mugre; baba, substancia viscosa.
gudgeon [ˈgʌdʒən] *s.* 1. (mec.) gorrón, muñón. 2. (mar.) muñonera, hembra de gorrón, encastre de muñón. 3. (ict.) gobio, cadoce. 4. (jer.) papanatas, simplón. 5. (fig.) carnada, añagaza. —*v.t.* (ant.) engañar, embaucar.
gudgeon pin, 1. (mec.) pasador de émbolo, muñón del pie de la biela. 2. (aut.) bulón, eje de pistón.
guelder rose [ˈgɛldər-, B -də-] (bot.) mundillo, sauquillo, geldre.
Guelph, Guelf [gwɛlf] *s.* (hist.) güelfo.
Guernsey [ˈgɜrnzɪ, B ˈgɜn-] *s.* 1. ganado lechero (de la isla) de Guernsey. 2. **g.,** camisa o chaleco de lana ajustado.
guerrilla, guerilla [gəˈrɪlə] *s.* 1. guerrillero. 2. guerrilla. —*a.* de guerrilleros; de guerrilla.
guerrilla warfare, guerra de guerrillas.
guess [gɛs] *v.t.* 1. suponer, barruntar, conjeturar, opinar. 2. (pr. E.U.) creer, pensar. 3. adivinar, acertar. —*v.i.* suponer, hacer una conjetura; **I g. so,** me parece que sí, creo que sí. —*s.* suposición, conjetura, barrunto.
guesser [ˈgɛsər, B -ə] *s.* uno que siempre hace conjeturas, adivinador.
guessing game [-ɪŋ-] juego de adivinanzas, juego de ingenio.
guesstimate [ˈgɛstəˌmeɪt] *v.t.* (jer.) estimar o calcular al azar.
guesswork [ˈgɛsˌwɜrk, B -ˌwɜk] *s.* adivinación, conjetura.
guest [gɛst] *s.* 1. huésped. 2. invitado, convidado. 3. visita (persona). 4. (biol.) parásito (animal o vegetal). 5. (ant.) extranjero, extraño. —*v.t.* hospedar. —*v.i.* actuar como (artista, actor, etc.) visitante.
guest conductor, (mús.) director huésped, director visitante.
guesthouse [ˈgɛstˌhaʊs] *s.* casa de huéspedes.
guest of honor, huésped o invitado de honor.
guest room, cuarto de huéspedes.
guest rope, (mar.) (guía de) falsa amarra.
guff [gʌf] *s.* (jer.) farsa, patraña.
guffaw [gəˈfɔ] *s.* carcajada, risotada, risada. —*v.i.* reírse a carcajadas, reírse vulgarmente.
guggle [ˈgʌgəl] *v.i.* hacer gluglú, gorgotear. —*s.* gluglú, gorgoteo.
Guiana [gɪˈænə, -ˈɑnə, B gaɪˈænə] *s.* Guayana (francesa, holandesa, brasileña y venezolana), en S. América.
Guianan [-ˈænən, -ˈɑn-, B -ˈæn-] *var. de* **Guianese.**
Guianese [ˌgaɪəˈniz] *a.* guayanés. —*s.* (*pl.* GUIANESE) guayanés.
guib [gɪb, B gwɪb] *s.* (zool.) guiba, golango, ibanara, ungurungu.
guidable [ˈgaɪdəbəl] *a.* dirigible, manejable, dócil.
guidance [-əns] *s.* 1. guía, dirección, conducción, gobierno. 2. consejo, asesoramiento. 3. **for your g.,** para su (propio) gobierno.
guide [gaɪd] *v.t.* 1. guiar, conducir. 2. dirigir, encaminar, encauzar. 3. aconsejar, asesorar, orientar. 4. pilotear, manejar. —*v.i.* guiar, actuar o trabajar como guía. —*s.* 1. guía. 2. hito, poste de guía, poste indicador. 3. (mil.) guía. 4. guía, manual. 5. (mec.) guía, guiadera, montante, deslizadera, corredera, directriz.
guideboard [ˈgaɪdˌbɔrd, B -ˌbɔd] *s.* tablero de guía (en un poste indicador).
guidebook [-ˌbʊk] *s.* guía del viajero.
guided missile [-əd-] misil teledirigido.
guided tour, visita guiada.
guide line, pauta, principio, guía.
guidepost [ˈgaɪdˌpoʊst] *s.* 1. poste de guía, poste indicador. 2. (fig.) indicación, señal.
guider [-ər, B -ə] *s.* guía (de operaciones, de producción).
guide rope, 1. cuerda (lateral) de guía, cable-guía. 2. (aer.) cuerda de arrastre, arrastradera, cuerda freno.
guidon [ˈgaɪdˌɑn, B -ən] *s.* 1. (mil.) guión, banderola (que sirve de guía a las tropas para formarse). 2. (mil.) portaguión. 3. (her.) palón.
guild [gɪld] *s.* 1. gremio, agremiación, corporación, asociación, hermandad, sociedad, comunidad. 2. (bot.) comunidad vegetal, grupo ecológico de plantas.
guilder [ˈgɪldər, B -də] *s.* gulden, florín, unidad monetaria de Holanda.
guildhall [ˈgɪldˈhɔl] *s.* 1. (casa del) ayuntamiento, casa consistorial, concejo. 2. casa de un gremio.
guildship [-ˌʃɪp] *s.* 1. gremio. 2. condición de agremiado.
guildsman [ˈgɪldzmən] *s.* agremiado, asociado.
guild socialism, (e.p.) socialismo gremial, socialismo de los gremios, tipo de socialismo abogado a principios del siglo XX en Inglaterra.
guile [gaɪl] *s.* 1. maña, engaño, astucia, dolo, asechanza, superchería. 2. (ant.) estratagema, ardid. —*v.t.* (ant.) engañar, seducir, burlar.
guileful [ˈgaɪlfəl] *a.* engañoso, mañoso, doloso.
guilefully [-fəlɪ] *adv.* engañosamente, astutamente, dolosamente.
guilefulness [-fəlnəs] *s.* carácter o naturaleza mañosa, astucia.
guileless [ˈgaɪlləs] *a.* sencillo, cándido, inocente, sincero.
guilelessness [-nəs] *s.* sencillez, inocencia, candidez, sinceridad.
guillemot [ˈgɪləˌmɑt, B -ˌmɔt] *s.* (orn.) ave marítima de la familia de las alcas.
guilloche [gɪˈloʊʃ] *s.* (arq.) guilloquis.
guillotine [ˈgɪləˌtin, ˌgɪləˈtin] *s.* 1. guillotina. 2. (med., imp.) guillotina. 3. guillotina (método parlamentario). —*v.t.* guillotinar, decapitar (ejecutar a un condenado a muerte).
guillotine shears, cizalla de guillotina.
guilt [gɪlt] *s.* culpa, culpabilidad; delito, pecado; **g. feelings,** sentido de culpa, sentimiento de culpabilidad.
guilt complex, complejo de culpa.
guiltily [ˈgɪltəlɪ] *adv.* culpablemente.
guiltiness [-tɪnəs] *s.* culpabilidad.

guiltless ['gɪltləs] *a.* inocente, libre de culpa, sin tacha; **g. of,** inocente de; inexperto en, ignorante de; ajeno a; sin huellas de.
guiltlessly [-lɪ] *adv.* inocentemente.
guiltlessness [-nəs] *s.* inocencia.
guilty ['gɪltɪ] *a.* (GUILTIER; GUILTIEST) 1. culpable. 2. acusador, sucio, ej., *a g. look,* una mirada de culpa; apariencia acusadora, *g. conscience,* conciencia sucia. 3. **to have a g. conscience,** remorderle a uno la conciencia, tener sucia la conciencia.
guimpe [gɪmp, gæmp] *s.* 1. camiseta (usada debajo de un jersey o un delantal). 2. impla, griñon.
guinea ['gɪnɪ] *s.* 1. guinea (antigua moneda inglesa). 2. **G.,** Guinea.
Guinea corn, (bot.) 1. durra, variedad de sorgo. 2. maíz de Guinea, maíz morocho.
guinea fowl, (orn.) gallina de Guinea, pintada.
guinea grain, (bot.) (*gen. pl.*) granos del paraíso, amomo.
guinea hen, (orn.) gallina de Guinea, pintada.
guinea-hen weed ['gɪnɪˌhɛn-] (bot.) hierba de pipi.
Guinea pepper, pimiento de Guinea.
guinea pig, 1. (zool.) conejillo de Indias, cobayo, curiel, cuy (Amer.). 2. (fig.) conejillo de Indias, persona que otras utilizan para ensayar o probar algo nuevo o incierto.
Guinea worm, (zool.) especie de filaria.
Guinevere ['gwɪnəˌvɪr, B -ˌvɪə] *s.* Ginebra (según la leyenda, la esposa del rey Arturo y la amante de Lancelote).
guipure [gɪ'pjʊr, B 'gipʊə] *s.* (tej.) guipur.
guise [gaɪz] *s.* 1. apariencia, semejanza, aspecto, forma. 2. (fig.) máscara, color, pretexto. 3. traje, vestimenta. 4. **in the g. of,** disfrazado de; **in this g.,** (ant.) de este modo; **under the g. of,** so capa de, so pretexto de. —*v.t.* vestir, disfrazar. —*v.i.* (dial.) presentarse disfrazado.
guitar [gə'tɑr, B gɪ'tɑ] *s.* guitarra.
guitarfish [-ˌfɪʃ] *s.* (ict.) pez guitarra.
guitarist [-'tɑrəst] *s.* guitarrista.
gula ['gulə, B 'gjulə] *s.* (*pl.* GULAE [-li] o GULAS) (anat., arq.) gola.
gular [-lər, B -lə] *a.* de la garganta.
gulch [gʌltʃ, B gʌlʃ] *s.* (E.U.) barranco, quebrada, cañada, rambla.
gulden ['guldən, B 'gʊl-] *s.* gulden, unidad monetaria de Holanda, florín.
gules [gjulz] *s.* (her.) gules.
gulf [gʌlf] *s.* 1. golfo. 2. abismo, precipicio, sima. 3. vórtice, vorágine, torbellino, remolino. —*v.t.* sumir, sumergir; sorber, absorber.
Gulf of Mexico, Golfo de México.
Gulf Stream, Corriente del Golfo de México.
Gulf War, Guerra del Golfo.
gulfweed ['gʌlfˌwid] *s.* (bot.) sargazo.
gull [gʌl] *v.t.* engañar, embaucar, estafar, timar. —*s.* 1. bobo, incauto, simple, bodoque, primo. 2. (ant.) treta, engaño, ardid; fraude. 3. (orn.) gaviota, golondrina de mar, gaviotín.
gullable, gullability, *vars. de* **gullible, gullibility.**
Gullah ['gʌlə] *s.* dialecto inglés de grupos de negros que viven en la costa norte-americana de Carolina del Sur, Georgia y las islas cercanas.
gullet ['gʌlət] *s.* 1. esófago; garguero, gargüero, gola, gaznate, garganta. 2. entrediente, garganta (entre los dientes de una sierra). 3. (hidr.) canal.
gullibility [ˌgʌlə'bɪlətɪ] *s.* credulidad.
gullible ['gʌləbəl] *a.* crédulo, bobo, simple.
gullibly [-blɪ] *adv.* crédulamente.
gully ['gʌlɪ] *s.* (*pl.* GULLIES) arroyada, badén; barranco, hondonada. —*v.t.* (*pret., p.p.* GULLIED; *p.pr.* GULLYING) formar badén al arroyar (terreno).
gully erosion, (geol.) erosión producida por una corriente de agua.
gulosity [gju'lɑsətɪ, B -'lɔs-] *s.* glotonería, gulosidad.
gulp [gʌlp] *v.t.* engullir, tragar; **g. down,** engullir; sofocar (sollozos). —*v.i.* entrecortar el resuello; tragar en seco; no poder hablar. —*s.* gorgorotada, trago; **at a g.,** de un trago.
gulper ['gʌlpər, B -ə] *s.* engullidor, tragón.
gum [gʌm] *s.* 1. goma. 2. (*abrev. de* **chewing g.**) chicle, goma de mascar. 3. (*gen. pl.*) encía. 4. (*abrev. de* **g. tree**) árbol gomífero. 5. (*pl.*) (E.U.) chanclos, zapatos de goma; (*on eyelids*) legaña. —*v.t.* (*pret., p.p.* GUMMED; *p.pr.* GUMMING) 1. engomar, volver pegajoso. 2. (gen. con *down, together, up, in,* etc.) pegar con goma. 3. **g. up,** (jer.) estropear, echar a perder. —*v.i.* 1. exudar goma. 2. volverse gomoso. —*interj.* (G.B.) **by g.!** ¡válgame Dios!
gum ammoniac, goma amoníaco.
gum arabic, goma arábiga.
gum ball, chicle en forma de bola.
gumbo ['gʌmboʊ] *s.* (*pl.* GUMBOS) 1. (bot.) quingombó, quimbombó, abelmosco. 2. sopa de quingombó. 3. gumbo (suelo arcilloso y pegajoso). 4. jerga de negros (esp. los de Luisiana).
gumboil ['gʌmˌbɔɪl] *s.* (med.) flemón, párulis.
gum boot, (pr. G.B.) bota de goma, bota de agua.
gum dragon, (bot.) adraganto, tragacanto.
gumdrop [-ˌdrɑp, B -ˌdrɔp] *s.* pastilla de gelatina solidificada; caramelo.
gum elastic, goma elástica, caucho, jebe (Amer.).
gum elemi, elemí.
gum juniper, (bot.) sandáraca.
gumma ['gʌmə] *s.* (*pl.* GUMMATA [-tə]) (med.) goma, sifiloma.
gumminess ['gʌmɪnəs] *s.* gomosidad, calidad de pegajoso.
gummite ['gʌmaɪt] *s.* (min.) gumita.
gummosis [gʌ'moʊsəs] *s.* (bot.) gomosis.
gummous ['gʌməs] *a.* gomoso, pegajoso.
gummy [-ɪ] *a.* 1. gomoso. 2. pegajoso; viscoso. 3. (*eyelid*) legañoso.
gum plant, (bot.) planta de goma.
gumption ['gʌmpʃən] *s.* (fam.) 1. sentido común; perspicacia. 2. iniciativa, pujanza, brío.
gum resin, gomorresina.
gumshoe ['gʌmˌʃu] *s.* 1. zapato o chanclo de goma. 2. (jer.) detective, polizonte. —*v.i.* (jer., E.U.) andar furtiva o cautelosamente; fisgar.
gum succory, (bot.) condrila, ajonjera juncal.
gum tree, árbol gomífero.
gumwood [-ˌwʊd] *s.* madera de árbol gomífero.
gun [gʌn] *s.* 1. cañón, pieza de artillería. 2. fusil, rifle, escopeta, carabina. 3. revólver, pistola. 4. cañonazo (ej., para una salva o saludo). 5.pistolero, asesino pagado. 6. (mec.) inyector (ej., de grasa); pistola (pulverizadora, etc.). 7. (aer.) regulador; palanca del regulador. 8. **son of a g.,** (jer.) sinvergüenza, hijo del diablo; **to go great guns,** (jer.) obrar con rapidez y eficacia; **to jump** (o **beat**) **the g.,** no esperar la señal de partida, partir en falso (en carrera); **to spike one's guns,** reducir a uno a la impotencia, frustrar los planes de uno; **to stick to one's guns,** mantenerse firme en su posición. —*v.i.* (*pret., p.p.* GUNNED; *p.pr.* GUNNING) ir de caza (con escopeta); **g. for,** ir en basca de, buscar para matar; perseguir; aspirar a. —*v.t.* 1. disparar a, tirar a. 2. (aut.) acelerar fuertemente la marcha del (motor). 3. **g. down, g. to death,** matar a tiros.
gun apron, (arm.) cubichete.
gun barrel, cañón de fusil o de escopeta.
gun battery, (mil.) batería de cañones.
gunboat ['gʌnˌboʊt] *s.* (mar.) cañonero, lancha cañonera.
gunboat diplomacy, diplomacia de cañón, coerción que impone una nación poderosa a otra pequeña.
gun carriage, cureña.
guncase ['gʌnˌkeɪs] *s.* estuche o funda de un arma portátil.
guncotton [-ˌkɑtən, B -ˌkɔt-] *s.* algodón pólvora, pólvora de algodón, fulmicotón.
gun deck, (mar.) cubierta de batería.
gundog [-ˌdɔg] *s.* perro de ajeo, perro de muestra, perro de caza.
gun emplacement, (mil.) cañonera.
gunfight [-ˌfaɪt] *s.* pelea a tiros, tiroteo.
gunfire ['gʌnˌfaɪr, B -ˌfaɪə] *s.* 1. fuego (de artillería), disparo (de un arma de fuego); tiroteo. 2. (mil.) cañoneo.
gunflint [-ˌflɪnt] *s.* pedernal, piedra de chispa.
gung-ho ['gʌŋ'hoʊ] *a.* 1. (fam.) leal, entusiasta, fervoroso. 2. (mil.) (oficial o soldado) excesivamente oficioso y agresivo.
gunk [gʌŋk] *s.* (jer.) mugre, suciedad grasosa.
gunlock ['gʌnˌlɑk, B -ˌlɔk] *s.* llave de fusil.
gunman [-mən] *s.* pistolero, asesino pagado, abaleador (Amer.).
gun metal, bronce de cañon.
gun-metal [-ˌmɛtəl] *a.* 1. pavonado (acero). 2. de color de acero pavonado.
gun moll, (jer.) ladrona, mujer criminal; amante de un pistolero o pandillero.
gunnel ['gʌnəl] *s.* (zool.) blenia.
gunnel, *var. de* **gunwale.**
gunner ['gʌnər, B -ə] *s.* 1. artillero. 2. (mar.) condestable, cabo de artillería. 3. cazador.
gunnery [-ərɪ] *s.* artillería, uso de armas de fuego, empleo de la artillería.
gunnery officer, (mil.) oficial de tiro; (mar.) oficial de artillería.
gunning [-ɪŋ] *s.* 1. (dep.) caza, cacería. 2. persecución con intención de matar.
gunny ['gʌnɪ] *s.* (*pl.* GUNNIES) 1. yute (tejido para sacos). 2. arpillera, cáñamo tosco.
gunnysack [-ˌsæk] *s.* saco de yute.
gun permit, licencia de armas.
gun pin, (arm.) aguja de fogón.
gun pit, pozo de cañón.
gunplay ['gʌnˌpleɪ] *s.* tiroteo.
gun point, la punta de una pistola; **at g. p.,** a punta de pistola, a mano armada.
gunport [-ˌpɔrt, B -ˌpɔt] *s.* (mar.) cañonera.
gunpowder [-ˌpaʊdər, B -ə] *s.* 1. pólvora. 2. té verde chino.
gun room, 1. (mar., G.B.) alojamiento de proa para suboficiales. 2. sala de armas (en exhibición, en residencia, palacio, etc.).
gunrunner [-ˌrʌnər, B -ə] *s.* traficante de armas.
gunrunning [-ɪŋ] *s.* contrabando de armas.
gunsel ['gʌnsəl] *s.* (jer.) pandillero, pistolero.
gunshop [-ˌʃɑp, B -ˌʃɔp] *s.* armería, tienda de armas.
gunshot [-ˌʃɑt, B -ˌʃɔt] *s.* 1. tiro (de arma de fuego), escopetazo. 2. balazo. 3. alcance (de fusil u otra arma de fuego). 4. **out of g.,** fuera del alcance de tiro; **within g.,** a tiro de fusil. —*a.* de bala, ej., *g. wound,* herida de bala.
gun-shy [-ˌʃaɪ] *a.* 1. que se asusta de disparos, asustadizo (díc. esp. de perros); (fig.) miedoso. 2. (fig.) (ú. con *of*) desconfiado, receloso.
gunslinger [-ˌslɪŋər, B -ə] *s.* (jer.) pistolero, pandillero.
gunsmith [-ˌsmɪθ] *s.* armero, escopetero.
gunstock [-ˌstɑk, B -ˌstɔk] *s.* culata, caja (de un arma de fuego portátil).

Gunter's chain ['gʌntərz-, B -əz-] cadena de Gunter, cadena de agrimensor.
gunwale ['gʌnəl] *s.* (mar.) regala, borda.
guppy ['gʌpɪ] *s.* (*pl.* GUPPIES) (ict.) olomina.
gurge [gɜrdʒ, B gɜdʒ] *s.* (raro) remolino, torbellino. —*v.t., v.i.* arremolinar(se).
gurgitation [ˌgɜrdʒə'teɪʃən, B ˌgɜdʒɪ-] *s.* ebullición violenta; borbollón, borbotón, burbujeo.
gurgle ['gɜrgəl, B 'gɜgəl] *v.i.* 1. producir un gorgoteo, hacer gluglú (el agua). 2. gorgoritear, gorjear (un niño). —*v.t.* murmurar entre gorjeos. —*s.* gorgoteo, gluglú (del agua); gorjeo (de la voz).
gurjun tree ['gɜrdʒən-, B 'gɜdʒən-] (bot.) balao.
gurnard ['gɜrnərd, B 'gɜnəd] *s.* (ict.) rubio, escarcho.
gurry ['gɜrɪ, B 'gʌrɪ] *s.* desperdicios del pescado.
guru ['gʊru, gə'ru, B 'gʊru] *s.* 1. (angloind.) maestro; padre espiritual. 2. líder, guía.
gush [gʌʃ] *v.i.* 1. salir en chorros, salir a borbollones, surgir, brotar, manar. 2. hablar de manera efusiva. —*v.t.* echar, derramar, verter. —*s.* 1. chorro, borbollón. 2. (fig.) estallido, explosión (de sonido), derrame (de energías). 3. (fam.) efusión, palabras sentimentales.
gusher ['gʌʃər, B -ə] *s.* 1. persona efusiva. 2. pozo surtidor (de petróleo).
gushingly [-ɪŋlɪ] *adv.* efusivamente.
gushy ['gʌʃɪ] *a.* efusivo, extremo.
gusla ['guslə, B 'gʊs-] *s.* (mús.) guzla.
gusset ['gʌsət] *s.* 1. (const.) escudete, nesga. 2. (const.) escuadra de refuerzo, cartela, esquinero. 3. (mar.) curvatón. —*v.t.* **reforzar.**
gusset plate, escuadra de ensamble, placa nodal, placa de empalme.
gust [gʌst] *s.* 1. ventolera, ventolada, ráfaga, racha (de viento). 2. bocanada (de humo). 3. explosión (de ruido). 4. arrebato, acceso (de cólera, etc.). 5. (ant.) sazón, sabor, sainete, dejo; deleite, satisfacción; gusto, apetencia, placer. 6. **g. of rain,** aguacero; **to have a g. of,** apreciar. —*v.t.* (esco.) probar, gustar, paladear, saborear.
gustable ['gʌstəbəl] *a.* (ant.) 1. sabroso. 2. gustable, perceptible por el gusto.
gustation [gʌs'teɪʃən] *s.* gustación, gustadura.
gustative ['gʌstətɪv] *a.* gustativo.
gustatory [-ˌtɔrɪ, B -tətərɪ] *a.* gustativo.
gustily ['gʌstəlɪ] *adv.* 1. en ráfagas. 2. (fig.) tempestuosamente, explosivamente, impetuosamente.
gustiness [-tɪnəs] *s.* (fig.) impetuosidad.
gusto ['gʌstoʊ] *s.* 1. placer, deleite, apreciación. 2. vigor, vitalidad. 3. (ant.) gusto (artístico).
gusty ['gʌstɪ] *a.* 1. borrascoso, chubascoso, descompuesto (*viento*). 2. (fig.) tempestuoso, explosivo, impetuoso.
gut [gʌt] *s.* 1. (*pl.*) tripas, entrañas, intestinos. 2. barriga. 3. cuerda de tripa. 4. pasaje, desfiladero. 5. (mar.) pase, estrecho. 6. (*pl.*) (fig., fam.) agallas; coraje, valor, ánimo. —*v.t.* (*pret., p.p.* GUTTED; *p.pr.* GUTTING) 1. destripar, desentrañar; limpiar (el pescado). 2. vaciar (un lugar cerrado). 3. destruir (el fuego) el interior de (una casa, etc.); quemar, consumir el fuego. 4. extraer lo esencial de (un libro, etc.). 5. (fig.) destruir, arruinar. 6. hacer rodadas o baches en (suelo, camino). —*a.* (jer.) apremiante, básico y fundamental, ej., *the g. issues of a campaign,* los temas fundamentales de una campaña.
gutless ['gʌtləs] *a.* (jer.) cobarde, pusilánime.
gutlessness [-ləsnəs] *s.* (jer.) cobardía.
gutsy ['gʌtsɪ] *a.* (jer.) 1. atrevido, valeroso. 2. pujante, vigoroso.
gutta ['gʌtə] *s.* (*pl.* GUTTAE [-i]) (*ú gen. en. pl.*) (arq.) gotas (esp. en el estilo gótico).
gutta-percha [-'pɜrtʃə, B -'pɜtʃə] *s.* (quím.) gutapercha.**guttate** ['gʌˌteɪt] *a.* (zool., bot.) goteado; parecido a una gota.
gutter ['gʌtər, B -ə] *s.* 1. gotera, canal (de un tejado). 2. cuneta, zanja, arroyo (al lado de un camino). 3. canal, canalón, badén. 4. (impr.) margen del crucero, margen de medianil, margen interior (en un libro entre dos páginas). 5. (top.) cárcava. 6. (filat.) margen entre los sellos (en una hoja de sellos). 7. la clase social baja de una ciudad; el barrio bajo. 8. **to take (child,** etc.) **out of the g.,** rescatar (a un niño, etc.) de la calle. —*v.t.* acanalar, estriar. —*v.i.* 1. fluir, chorrear. 2. fundirse goteando (una vela). 3. arder con luz mortecina. 4. **g. out,** apagarse; (fig.) extinguirse.
guttersnipe [-ˌsnaɪp] *s.* 1. chico de la calle, pilluelo, pícaro, golfo. 2. vago, rufián.
gutter stick, (impr.) medianil.
guttiferous [gə'tɪfərəs] *a.* (bot.) gutífero.
guttle ['gʌtəl] *v.t., v.i.* glotonear.
guttler ['gʌtlər, B -lə] *s.* glotón.
guttural ['gʌtərəl] *a.* 1. gutural, de la garganta. 2. gutural, ronco. 3. (fon.) gutural. —*s.* sonido gutural.
gutturalization [ˌgʌtərələ'zeɪʃən, B -laɪ-] *s.* guturalización.
gutturalize ['gʌtərəˌlaɪz] *v.t.* 1. pronunciar guturalmente. 2. (fon.) guturalizar.
gutturally [-lɪ] *adv.* guturalmente.
gutty ['gʌtɪ] *a.* valiente, vigoroso.
guy [gaɪ] *s.* 1. sujeto, tipo, tío. 2. (G.B.) adefesio, mamarracho. 3. retenida, cable de retén, contraviento. 4. (mar.) obenque. —*v.t.* 1. ridiculizar, burlarse de. 2. atirantar, contraventar, sujetar con vientos o retenidas.
Guyana [gaɪ'ænə] *s.* Guyana (república de S. Amér., antes Guayana Inglesa).
guy wire, viento de alambre, retenida de alambre.
guzzle ['gʌzəl] *v.t.* tragar, engullir, devorar; beber a tragantadas. —*v.i.* empinar el codo, beber.
guzzler ['gʌzlər, B -lə] *s.* borrachín, borracho, bebedor.
gybe, *var. de* **jibe.**
gym [dʒɪm] *s.* (fam.) *abrev. de* **gymnasium,** gimnasio.
gymnasiarch [dʒɪm'neɪzɪˌɑrk, B -ˌɑk] *s.* (hist. griega) oficial que supervisaba los juegos atléticos, torneos y las escuelas.
gymnasiast [-ˌæst] *s.* 1. gimnasta. 2. estudiante o graduado de una escuela secundaria.
gymnasium [-əm] *s.* (*pl.* GYMNASIUMS O GYMNASIA [-ə]) gimnasio (el recinto).
gymnast ['dʒɪmˌnæst] *s.* gimnasta.
gymnastic [dʒɪm'næstɪk] *a.* gimnástico, atlético.
gymnastically [-tɪkəlɪ] *adv.* gimnásticamente, atléticamente.
gymnastics [-tɪks] *s. pl.* (*sing. en const.*) gimnasia, calistenia.
gymnosophist [dʒɪm'nɑsəfəst, B -'nɔs-] *s.* gimnosofista.
gymnosophy [-fɪ] *s.* gimnosofía.
gymnosperm ['dʒɪmnəˌspɜrm, B -ˌspɜm] *s.* (bot.) gimnosperma, gimnospérmeo.
gymnospermous [ˌdʒɪmnə'spɜrməs, B -'spɜməs] *a.* (bot.) gimnospermo.
gymnospore ['dʒɪmnəˌspɔr, B -ˌspɔ] *s.* (biol.) gimnosporo.
gym shoe, zapato o zapatilla de gimnasia.
gynaeceum [ˌdʒaɪnə'siəm, ˌdʒɪnə-] *s.* (*pl.* GYNAECEA [-'siə]) 1. (hist.) gineceo (aposentos de mujer). 2. (bot.) gineceo (verticilio de la flor).
gynaecocracy, gynaecocrat, *vars. de* **gynecocracy, gynecocrat.**
gynandromorph [dʒɪn'ændrəˌmɔrf, gaɪn-, B dʒaɪn-ˌmɔf] *s.* (biol.) ginandromorfo.
gynandromorphic [-ˌændrə'mɔrfɪk, B -'mɔfɪk] *a.* (biol.) ginandromorfo.
gynandromorphism [-ˌfɪzəm] *s.* (biol.) ginandromorfismo, hermafroditismo.
gynandrous [dʒɪn'ændrəs, gaɪn-, B dʒaɪn-] *a.* (bot.) ginandrio.
gynandry [-drɪ] *s.* (bot.) ginandria.
gynarchy ['dʒɪnˌɑrkɪ, 'dʒaɪˌnɑr-, B -ˌnɑkɪ] *s.* (*pl.* GYNARCHIES) ginecocracia.
gynecocracy [ˌdʒɪnɪ'kɑkrəsɪ, ˌgaɪn-, B ˌdʒɪnɪ'kɔk-] *s.* ginecocracia.
gynecocrat [dʒɪn'ikəˌkræt, B dʒaɪn-] *s.* ginecócrata.
gynecoid ['dʒɪnɪkɔɪd, 'gaɪn-, B 'dʒaɪn-] *a.* (med.) ginecoide.
gynecologic, gynaecologic [ˌgaɪnɪkə'lɑdʒɪk, ˌdʒɪn-, ˌdʒaɪn-, B ˌgaɪn-'lɔdʒ-] *a.* (med.) ginecológico.
gynecologist, gynaecologist [-'kɑlədʒəst, B -'kɔl-] *s.* ginecólogo.
gynecology, gynaecology [-dʒɪ] *s.* (med.) ginecología.
gyniatrics [-'ætrɪks] *s.* (med.) giniatría.
gynoecium [dʒɪn'isiəm, gaɪn-] *var. de* **gynaeceum.**
gynophore ['dʒɪnəˌfɔr, 'dʒaɪnə-, B -ˌfɔ] *s.* (bot.) ginóforo.
gynophoric [ˌdʒɪnə'fɔrɪk, ˌdʒaɪnə-, B ˌdʒaɪ-] *a.* (bot.) ginofórico.
gyp [dʒɪp] *s.* (G.B.) fámulo, sirviente (en las universidades de Oxford o Cambridge). —*v.t., v.i.* (*pret., p.p.* GYPPED; *p.pr.* GYPPING) (jer.) estafar, timar, trampear, embaucar.
gyp joint, (jer.) establecimiento donde se estafa al parroquiano.
gypseous ['dʒɪpsɪəs] *a.* yesoso.
gypseous alabaster, alabastro yesoso.
gypsiferous [dʒɪp'sɪfərəs] *a.* gipsífero.
gypsophila [dʒɪp'sɑfələ, B -'sɔf-] *s.* (bot.) gipsofila.
gypsum ['dʒɪpsəm] *s.* yeso. —*v.t.* tratar con yeso (suelos, agua, etc.).
Gypsy ['dʒɪpsɪ] *s.* (*pl.* GYPSIES, GIPSIES) 1. gitano. 2. (G.B., hum.) mujer de tez obscura; mujer vivaz y traviesa. 3. gitano, lengua gitana, caló. —*a.* gitano. — **g.,** *v.i.* (*pret., p.p.* GYPSIED; *p.pr.* GYPSYING) vagar, vivir o andar errante (como los gitanos).
gypsydom [-dəm] *s.* (antrop.) la gitanería, los gitanos.
gypsyhood [-ˌhʊd] *s.* condición gitana.
gypsy moth, (ento.) lagarta.
gyral ['dʒaɪrəl, B 'dʒaɪə-] *a.* giratorio.
gyrate ['dʒaɪreɪt, B 'dʒaɪərɪt] *a.* sinuoso, redondeado; curvo. — [B ˌdʒaɪə'reɪt] *v.i.* girar.
gyration [dʒaɪ'reɪʃən, B ˌdʒaɪə-] *s.* giro, movimiento giratorio, rotación.
gyrator ['dʒaɪˌreɪtər, B 'dʒaɪə-ə] *s.* rotador.
gyratory ['dʒaɪrəˌtɔrɪ, B 'dʒaɪərətərɪ] *a.* giratorio.
gyre [dʒaɪr, B 'dʒaɪə] *s.* 1. (poét) giro, rotación. 2. forma circular o espiral. —*v.i.* girar, moverse circularmente o en espiral.
gyrene ['dʒaɪrˌin, B 'dʒaɪər-] *s.* (jer.) soldado del Cuerpo de Infantería de Marina de E.U.
gyrfalcon *var. de* **gerfalcon.**
gyro ['dʒaɪroʊ, B 'dʒaɪər-] *s.* (*pl.* GYROS) (fam.) *abrev. de* **gyroscope, gyrocompass.**
gyrocompass [-ˌkʌmpəs, -ˌkɑm-, B -ˌkʌm-] *s.* (fís.) brújula giroscópica, compás giroscópico, girocompás (Am.).

gyromagnetic [ˌdʒaɪroʊmæg'nɛtɪk, B ˌdʒaɪə-] *a.* (fís.) giromagnético.
gyrometer [dʒaɪ'rɑmətər, B -'rɔmɪtə] *s.* girómetro.
gyron ['dʒaɪrən, B 'dʒaɪə-] *s.* (her.) jirón.
gyropilot [-roʊˌpaɪlət] *s.* (aer.) control automático, timonel mecánico, autopiloto.
gyroplane [-ˌpleɪn] *s.* (aer.) autogiro.
gyroscope ['dʒaɪrəˌskoʊp, B 'gaɪə-] *s.* (fís.) giroscopio.
gyroscopic [ˌdʒaɪrə'skɑpɪk, B ˌgaɪərə's-kɔp-] *a.* (fís.) giroscópico.
gyrose ['dʒaɪˌroʊs, B 'dʒaɪə-] *a.* marcado con líneas onduladas; ondulado; sinuoso.
gyrostabilizer [ˌdʒaɪroʊ'steɪbəˌlaɪzər, B ˌdʒaɪə-zə] *s.* (aer., mar.) giroestabilizador.
gyrostat ['dʒaɪrəˌstæt, B 'gaɪə-] *s.* (fís.) giróstato.
gyrostatic [ˌdʒaɪrə'stætɪk, B ˌgaɪə-] *a.* (fís.) girostático.
gyrostatically [-ɪkəlɪ] *adv.* girostáticamente.
gyrostatics [-ɪks] *s. pl.* (*sing. en const.*) (fís.) girostática.
gyrus ['dʒaɪrəs] *s.* (*pl.* GYRI [-ˌaɪ]) (anat.) circunvolución, esp. cerebral.
gyve [dʒaɪv] *s.* (*ú. gen. en pl.*) grillos, cadenas. —*v.t.* encadenar con grillos.

H

H [eɪtʃ] *s.* h, octava letra del alfabeto inglés.
H *símb. de* **hydrogen,** hidrógeno (H).
ha [hɑ] *interj.* ¡ah! ¡ja!
ha *abrev. de* **hectare,** hectárea (hect.).
habanera [ˌhɑbəˈnɛrə] *s.* (mús.) habanera.
habeas corpus [ˈheɪbɪəsˈkɔrpəs, B -ˈkɔp-] (der.) hábeas corpus.
haberdasher [ˈhæbərˌdæʃər, B -əˌdæʃə] *s.* 1. (E.U.) dueño de una tienda de ropa y accesorios para caballeros. 2. (G.B.) mercero; camisero.
haberdashery [-ərɪ] *s.* 1. (tienda de) ropa y accesorios para caballeros. 2. (G.B.) mercería, camisería; artículos de mercería.
habergeon [ˈhæbərdʒən, B -ədʒən] *s.* jaco; camisote; cota de malla sin mangas.
habile [ˈhæbəl] *a.* hábil, diestro, capaz, eficaz.
habiliment [həˈbɪləmənt] *s.* 1. (*gen. pl.*) traje, vestido, atuendo. 2. (ant.) (*gen. pl.*) avío, equipo, hábito, vestuario, ropa, vestidura.
habilitate [-ˌteɪt] *v.t.* 1. vestir, aviar. 2. equipar, proveer de equipo. 3. habilitar, pertrechar. —*v.i.* capacitarse, volverse apto, idóneo, competente.
habilitation [-ˌbɪləˈteɪʃən] *s.* 1. habilitación (para un oficio, etc.); aptitud. 2. rehabilitación (de un enfermo).
habit [ˈhæbət] *s.* 1. hábito, uso, costumbre, práctica (de personas); tendencia (de cosas); vicio. 2. hábito (de religioso, juez, etc.). 3. (t. **riding h.**) amazona, traje de montar. 4. carácter, disposición. 5. (bot.) forma de crecer; hábito. 6. (ant.) vestido, atuendo, atavío. 7. **by h.,** de vicio, por costumbre; **to be in the h. of (doing),** acostumbrar, tener la costumbre de (hacer); **to fall into the h. of,** adquirir el hábito o la costumbre de; **to kick the h.,** dejar de ser adicto (a una droga, etc.). —*v.t.* 1. vestir, arreglar. 2. (ant.) acostumbrar.
habitability [ˌhæbətəˈbɪlətɪ] *s.* habitabilidad.
habitable [ˈhæbətəbəl] *a.* habitable.
habitableness [-nəs] *s.* habitabilidad.
habitant [ˈhæbətənt] *s.* 1. habitante, morador. 2. [æbɪˈtɑn, B ˈhæbɪtɔŋ] (t. **habitan**) colono o hijo de colono francés (en el Canadá).
habitat [-ˌtæt] *s.* 1. hábitat, habitación, hogar natural (de una planta o animal). 2. (fig.) ambiente (natural o acostumbrado).
habitation [ˌhæbəˈteɪʃən] *s.* 1. habitación, ocupación (de un lugar, etc.). 2. habitación, morada, domicilio, residencia.
habit-forming [ˈhæbətˌfɔrmɪŋ, B -ˌfɔmɪŋ] *a.* que crea hábito, que envicia.
habitual [həˈbɪtʃʊəl, B -ˈbɪtjʊ-] *a.* habitual, acostumbrado, usual.
habitually [-ɪ] *adv.* habitualmente, usualmente.
habitualness [-nəs] *s.* costumbre, calidad de habitual.
habituate [-ˌeɪt] *v.t.* 1. habituar, acostumbrar. 2. (ant.) frecuentar.
habituation [həˌbɪtʃʊˈeɪʃən, B -ˌbɪtjʊ-] *s.* habituación (a estupefacientes, drogas, etc.).
habitude [ˈhæbəˌtud, B -ˌtjud] *s.* 1. hábito, costumbre; tendencia. 2. (ant.) carácter, disposición.
habitué [həˈbɪtʃʊˌeɪ, B -ˈbɪtjʊ-] *s.* parroquiano, concurrente, frecuentador.
habitus [ˈhæbətəs] *s.* (*pl.* HABITUS [-ˌtus]) hábito, predisposición, tendencia (esp. a ciertas enfermedades).
hachure [hæˈʃʊr, B -ˈʃjʊə] *s.* (arte) línea de sombra o declive. —*v.t.* sombrear con líneas.
hacienda [ˌhɑsɪˈɛndə, B ˌhæsɪ-] *s.* hacienda, fundo, propiedad rural.
hack [hæk] *v.t.* 1. cortar irregularmente, picar, tajar, acuchillar, machetear. 2. (fig.) recortar, mutilar (novela, relato, etc.). 3. (fútbol, Amer.) patear las canillas de (un jugador del equipo contrario). 4. **h. off,** cortar a hachazos; **h. to pieces,** cortar en pedazos, despedazar. —*v.i.* 1. (gen. con *at*) hachear; hacer cortes gruesos (en). 2. toser con tos seca. 3. (rugby) patear (las canillas de un jugador). —*s.* 1. pico, azadón, zapapico, hacha, cuchilla. 2. corte, hachazo. 3. mella, corte, incisión, cuchillada. 4. tos seca. 5. (rugby) puntapié en las canillas.
hack [hæk] *s.* 1. caballo de alquiler; caballo de silla. 2. jamelgo, rocín, matalón. 3. simón, coche de plaza, coche de alquiler; (fam.) taxi. 4. cochero, chófer (de taxi). 5. escritor mercenario; ganapán, alquiladizo. 6. (jer.) guardia penal, carcelero. —*v.t.* 1. usar a menudo, gastar, trillar, vulgarizar. 2. alquilar, dar en alquiler (ej., caballo). 3. (fam.) escribir como un escritor mercenario. —*v.i.* 1. cabalgar a paso normal, o por caminos (no a campo traviesa). 2. (fam.) trabajar como escritor mercenario o como chófer de taxi. —*a.* 1. de alquiler, alquiladizo. 2. mediocre, aburrido. 3. trillado, gastado, vulgarizado.
hack, *s.* 1. emparrillado para secar queso, pescado o ladrillos. 2. hilera o pila de ladrillos para ser secados. 3. comedero, esp. para halcones. —*v.t.* extender en un emparrillado para secar.
hackamore [ˈhækəˌmɔr, B -ˌmɔ] *s.* (E.U.) cabestro, ronzal, jáquima, cabezada.
hackberry [ˈhækˌbɛrɪ] *s.* 1. (bot.) álmez, almaizo, aligonero. 2. almeza, almecina (fruta).
hackbut [-ˌbʌt] **hagbut** [ˈhæg-] *s.* arcabuz (de culata encorvada).
hackbuteer [ˌhækbəˈtɪr, B -ˈtɪə] **hackbutter** [ˈhækˌbʌtər, B -ə] *s.* arcabucero.
hacker [ˈhækər] *s.* (comput.) (fam.) computomaníaco; (despec.) pirata informático.
hack hammer, martillo para desbastar piedra.
hackie [ˈhækɪ] *s.* (fam.) chófer de taxi; simón, cochero de alquiler.
hacking [-ɪŋ] *s.* (comput.) (despec.) piratería informática. —*a.* (*cough*) seco.
hackle [ˈhækəl] *s.* 1. rastrillo. 2. pluma o plumas del cuello (de ciertas aves, esp. del gallo). 3. (*pl.*) pelos eréctiles (del cuello del perro); **with his hackles up,** (fig.) de humor belicoso, listo para la pelea. 4. mosca artificial (para pescar). —*v.t.* 1. rastrillar (lino o cáñamo). 2. poner una mosca artificial en (un anzuelo).
hackle, *v.t.* machetear, cortar toscamente, romper en pedazos.
hackle fly, mosca artifical (para pescar).
hackler [ˈhæklər, B -lə] *s.* rastrillador.
hackly [-lɪ] *a.* mellado, dentado desigualmente.
hackman [-mən] *s.* chófer de taxi; simón, cochero de alquiler.
hackmatack [ˈhækməˌtæk] *s.* (bot.) alerce americano.
hackney [ˈhæknɪ] *s.* 1. caballo de silla. 2. **H.,** caballo fuerte de raza inglesa. 3. simón, coche de alquiler. 4. ganapán, alquiladizo. —*a.* 1. de alquiler. 2. común, trillado. —*v.t.* 1. trillar, gastar, vulgarizar. 2. alquilar.
hackney coach, simón, coche de alquiler.
hackneyed [-nid] *a.* común, gastado, trillado, vulgar.
hackneyed phrase, frase o dicho muy repetido, trillado.
hackneyed subject, asunto muy trillado, común, gastado.
hacksaw [ˈhækˌsɔ] *s.* sierra para (cortar) metales.
hack stand, sitio, punto, parada, piquera (de autos de alquiler).
hackwork [-ˌwɜrk, B -ˌwɜk] *s.* trabajo comercializado (literario, artístico o profesional); chapucería.
had [hæd] *pret., p.p. de* **have.** — (jer.) forma verbal que se emplea en la expresión interjectiva: **I've had it!** ¡no aguanto más! ¡no doy más!
haddock [ˈhædək] *s.* (ict.) anón, abadejo eglefino, bacalao de Saint-Pierre.
hade [heɪd] *s.* (geol.) buzamiento, recuesto, inclinación o ángulo (de un filón, o de una capa de terreno). —*v.i.* formar un buzamiento o un recuento.
Hades [ˈheɪdiz] *s.* 1. (mitol.) Hades, reino de los muertos. 2. (fam.) (t. **h.**) infierno.
hadj [hædʒ] *s.* peregrinación, esp. la de un musulmán a la Meca.
hadji [ˈhædʒi] *s.* peregrino musulmán (que ha ido a la Meca) (ú. t. como título).
Hadrian [ˈheɪdrɪən] *s.* (hist.) Adriano, emperador romano nacido en Itálica (España romana).
haem-, haema-, haemat-, haemato-, haemo-, *vars. de* **hem-, hema-, hemat-, hemato-, hemo.**
haffet, haffit [ˈhæfət] *s.* (esco.) mejilla, carrillo.
hafiz [hɑˈfɪz] *s.* musulmán que ha memorizado el Corán.
hafnium [ˈhæfnɪəm] *s.* (quím.) hafnio.
haft [hæft, B hɑft] *s.* mango, puño (de cuchillo, espada, etc.). —*v.t.* poner un mango o puño a.
hag [hæg] *s.* 1. bruja, hechicera. 2. (fig.) bruja, tarasca, mujeruca. 3. (ict.) lamprea glutinosa. 4. (ant.) hada, demonio, duende.
hagberry [ˈhægˌbɛrɪ] *var. de* **hackberry.**
hagborn [-ˌbɔrn, B -ˌbɔn] *a.* nacido de bruja o hechicera.
hagbut [ˈhægˌbʌt] *var. de* **hackbut.**
hagdon [ˈhægdən] *s.* (orn.) fulmar; frailecillo.
hagfish [-ˌfɪʃ] *s.* (ict.) lamprea glutinosa.
Haggada, Haggadah [həˈgɑdə] *s.* (*pl.* HAGGADOTH [-ˌdout]) haggadah, aggadah, libro que contiene la historia del Éxodo y el rito celebrado durante la pascua judía.
haggadic [həˈgædɪk] **haggadical** [-ɪkəl] *a.* de la haggadah.

haggadist [hə'gɑdəst] *s.* escritor o estudiante de la haggadah, talmudista.
haggard ['hægərd, B -əd] *a.* 1. macilento, ojeroso; consumido, demacrado. 2. montaraz, salvaje, intratable; (cetrería) zahareño. —*s.* halcón zahareño.
haggardly [-lɪ] *adv.* macilentamente.
haggardness [-nəs] *s.* aspecto macilento.
haggis ['hægəs] *s.* (esco.) manjar escocés (hecho con asaduras de carnero).
haggish ['hægɪʃ] *a.* de bruja o característico de una bruja.
haggle ['hægəl] *v.t.* tajar o cortar toscamente; machetear. —*v.i.* regatear; disputar, porfiar. —*s.* regateo.
haggler [-ələr, B -lə] *s.* regatón, regatero.
hagiarchy ['hægɪˌɑrkɪ, B -ˌɑkɪ] *s.* gobierno de sacerdotes.
hagiographer [ˌhægɪ'ɑgrəfər, B -'ɔgrəfə] *s.* hagiógrafo.
hagiographic [-ə'græfɪk] *a.* hagiográfico.
hagiography [-'ɑgrəfɪ, B -'ɔg-] *s.* hagiografía.
hagiolatry [-'ɑlətrɪ, B -'ɔl-] *s.* culto o adoración de los santos.
hagiologic [-ə'lɑdʒɪk, B -'lɔdʒ-] *a.* hagiológico.
hagiologist [-'ɑlədʒəst, B -'ɔl-] *s.* hagiólogo, hagiógrafo.
hagiology [-dʒɪ] *s.* hagiología.
hagioscope ['hægɪəˌskoʊp] *s.* hagioscopio.
hagridden ['hægˌrɪdən] *a.* 1. afligido, angustiado, atormentado, agobiado, vejado. 2. obsesionado.
hagseed [-ˌsid] *s.* prole de una bruja.
Hague [heɪg] *s.* **The H.,** La Haya, ciudad de Holanda, residencia del gobierno.
Hague Tribunal, Tribunal Internacional de La Haya.
hah, *var. de* **ha.**
ha-ha ['hɑˌhɑ] *s.* cerca hundida, pared hundida; foso con escarpa. [hɑ'hɑ] *interj.* ¡ ja, ja, ja!
haik [haɪk, hcɪk] *s.* jaique, pieza del atuendo típico del árabe.
haiku ['haɪku] *s.* (*pl.* HAIKU) hai kai (poema breve japonés).
hail [heɪl] *s.* 1. granizo. 2. (fig.) lluvia, ej., *h. of bullets,* lluvia de balas, *h. of stones,* lluvia de piedras. —*v.i.* granizar. —*v.t.* lanzar una andanada de (golpes, imprecaciones, etc.).
hail, *v.t.* 1. saludar, aclamar; dar vivas a; ej., *they hailed him king,* lo aclamaron rey. 2. llamar, clamar; (mar.) llamar (para atraer la atención). —*v.i.* **h. from,** venir de, ser oriundo de, proceder de. —*interj.* ¡salud! ¡salve! —*s.* 1. saludo, viva. 2. grito, llamada.
hail, (esco.) *var. de* **hale.**
hailer ['heɪlər, B -ə] *s.* aclamador.
hail-fellow [-ˌfɛloʊ] **hail-fellow-well-met** [-ˌwɛl'mɛt] *a., s.* (hombre) informal, cordial, simpático o demasiado afable.
Hail Mary, avemaría.
hailstone [-ˌstoʊn] *s.* gránulo de granizo, bola de granizo, granizo.
hailstorm [-ˌstɔrm, B -ˌstɔm] *s.* granizada.
hair [hɛr, B hɛə] *s.* 1. cabello, pelo; vello (humano); crin, cerda, pelo (animal). 2. pelillo, filamento (animal o vegetal). 3. cabellera (humana). 4. pelo, tris, pizca. 5. **against the h.,** (ant.) a contrapelo; **not to touch a h. on someone's head,** no tocarle el pelo a uno; **not to turn a h.,** no dar la menor muestra de cansancio o embarazo; **to a h.,** exactamente; **to do (put) up her h.,** peinarse (una mujer); **to get in (one's) h.,** (jer.) molestar, fastidiar, incomodar (a alguien); **to let down her h.,** soltarse el pelo (una mujer); **to let one's h. down,** (fig.) abandonar toda reserva; **to make one's h. stand on end,** poner los pelos de punta; **to split hairs,** hilar fino, hilar muy delgado, andar en quisquillas; **to tear one's hair,** tirarse el pelo, mesarse los cabellos.
hairband ['hɛrˌbænd, B 'hɛəˌ-] *s.* cinta o pañuelo para el cabello, vincha (Amer.).
hairbreadth [-ˌbrɛdθ] *s.* (fig.) pelo, tris; **by a h.,** por un pelo, por un tris. —*a.* muy estrecho; **a h. escape,** escape por un pelo, escape por un tris.
hairbrush [-ˌbrʌʃ] *s.* cepillo para el cabello o pelo.
haircloth [-ˌklɔθ] *s.* tela de crin.
haircut [-ˌkʌt] *s.* corte de pelo, peluqueada (Col., Ven.); **to have** (o **get**) **a h.,** cortarse el pelo o el cabello.
haircutter [-ər, B -ə] *s.* peluquero.
haircutting [-ɪŋ] *s.* peluquería, arte de cortar el pelo.
hairdo ['hɛrˌdu, B 'hɛəˌ-] *s.* (*pl.* HAIRDOS) peinado, tocado.
hairdresser [-ˌdrɛsər, B -ə] *s.* peinador, peluquero.
hairdressing [-ɪŋ] *s.* peluquería (como oficio).
hair dye, tinte para el cabello.
hair follicle, folículo piloso.
hairiness ['hɛrɪnəs, B 'hɛərɪ-] *s.* pilosidad.
hairless [-ləs, B 'hɛəlɪs] *a.* pelado, pelón, calvo, sin pelo; lampiño.
hairline [-ˌlaɪn] *s.* 1. línea delgada, rayita; trazo fino (de una letra). 2. tela rayada. 3. perfil del cuero cabelludo.
hair lock, rizo de pelo.
hairnet [-ˌnɛt] *s.* redecilla para el cabello.
hair part, raya del pelo.
hair pencil, pincel.
hair piece, tupé o peluca.
hairpin [-ˌpɪn] *s.* 1. horquilla, vincha, gancho (Amer.), ganchillo (Amer.). 2. curva cerrada (en un camino).
hair-raiser ['hɛrˌreɪzər, B 'hɛəˌ-zə] *s.* (jer.) novela o drama espeluznante.
hair-raising [-zɪŋ] *a.* horripilante, espeluznante.
hair-remover [-rɪ'muvər, B -ə] *s.* depilatorio.
hairsbreadth ['hɛrzˌbrɛdθ, B 'hɛəz-] *var. de* **hairbreadth.**
hair shirt, cilicio, camisa de crin.
hair space, (impr.) espacio pelo, espacio fino.
hairsplitter ['hɛrˌsplɪtər, B 'hɛəˌ-ə] *s.* persona quisquillosa.
hairsplitting [-ɪŋ] *a.* quisquilloso, nimio —*s.* quisquillas, sutilezas, sofismas.
hair spray, laca, gomina (para el pelo).
hairspring [-ˌsprɪŋ] *s.* pelo, espiral o muelle volante (de un reloj).
hairstreak [-ˌstrik] *s.* variedad de mariposa de listas transversales.
hair stroke, trazo fino (en la escritura o impresión).
hair style, diseño de un peinado.
hair styling, alta peluqueria.
hair switch, trenza o añadido postizo.
hair tonic, tónico para el cabello.
hair trigger, pelo (de armas de fuego).
hair-trigger ['hɛrˌtrɪgər, B 'hɛəˌ-ə] *a.* 1. impulsivo. 2. inmediato, violento (reacción). 3. delicado.
hairy ['hɛrɪ, B 'hɛərɪ] *a.* (HAIRIER; HAIRIEST) 1. piloso, peludo, velludo; lleno de pelo, cubierto con pelo; hirsuto. 2. de pelo, de crin. 3. (fam.) antiguo, ya conocido (díc. de chistes o cuentos). 4. (jer.) desagradable, peligroso.
hairy vetch, (bot.) veza, lagarroba.
Haiti ['heɪtɪ] *s.* Haití.
Haitian ['heɪʃən, 'heɪtɪən] *a., s.* haitiano.
haji, hajji, *var. de* **hadj, hadji.**
hakam [hɑ'kɑm] *s.* hacán, sabio o doctor entre los judíos.
hake [heɪk] *s.* (ict.) merluza, pescada, pijota.
hakenkreuz ['hɑkənˌkrɔɪts] *s.* cruz esvástica.
hakim [hə'kim] *s.* 1. (*pl.* HAKIMS) médico (en países islámicos). 2. ['hɑkəm] juez, legislador, gobernador (en países islámicos).
halation [heɪ'leɪʃən, B hə-] *s.* (foto., t.v.) halo.
halberd ['hælbərd, 'hɔl-, B -bəd] *s.* alabarda.
halberdier [ˌhælbər'dɪr, B -bə'dɪə] *s.* alabardero.
halcyon ['hælsɪən] *s.* 1. (orn.) alción. 2. (orn.) martín pescador. 3. **H.,** (mitol.) Alcione. —*a.* 1. calmo, pacífico, apacible. 2. feliz, próspero.
halcyon days, días felices, días tranquilos.
hale [heɪl] *v.t.* halar; arrastrar; **h. one to prison,** llevar (a uno) preso. —*a.* sano, saludable; robusto, vigoroso (díc. esp. de personas de edad).
haler ['hɑlər B -ə] *s.* moneda fraccionaria de Checoslovaquia.
half [hæf, B hɑf] *s.* (*pl.* HALVES [hævz, B hɑvz]) 1. mitad, medio. 2. parte, ej., *your h. is bigger than mine,* tu parte es mayor que la mía, *the larger h. of one's fortune,* la mayor parte de la fortuna de uno. 3. media hora, ej., *h. past* (o *after*) *six,* seis y media. 4. (G.B.) semestre (escolar). 5. (dep.) tiempo (primero o segundo de un partido). 6. (fútbol) medio, zaguero medio. 7. (G.B.) media pinta (esp. de cerveza). 8. (E.U.) medio dólar. 9. **better h.,** cara mitad, esposa; **by h.,** (jer.) demasiado, con mucho, ej., *too clever by h.,* demasiado listo, se pasa de listo; **by halves,** (hacer una cosa) a medias; **in h.,** en dos mitades, por la mitad; **to cry halves,** reclamar iguales derechos; **to go halves,** ir a medias. —*a.* 1. medio, ej., *h. share,* media parte, mitad, *a h. pound, h. a pound,* media libra. 2. a medias, ej., *h. owner,* dueño a medias. 3. **foresight is h. the battle,** con la previsión ya se tiene ganada la mitad de la batalla. —*adv.* 1. a medias, parcialmente, imperfectamente, ej., *h. done,* hecho a medias. 2. medio, a medio, ej., *h. clothed,* medio vestido, a medio vestir, *h. dead,* medio muerto. 3. **h. as much, h. as many,** (tanto como) la mitad; **h. price,** (fam.) a mitad de precio; **not h. bad,** (fam.) nada mal; **not h.,** (jer., G.B.) lo más posible, a más no poder, ej., *he was not h. running,* corría a más no poder, corría ¡y cómo!
half-and-half ['hæfən'hæf, B 'hɑfən'hɑf] *s.* mezcla de dos clases de cerveza, o de leche y crema. —*a.* a mitades, en igual proporción, igual. —*adv.* a medias, mitad y mitad, por partes iguales.
half-assed [-'æst] *a.* (jer., E.U.) bisoño; incompleto.
halfback [-ˌbæk] *s.* (fútbol) medio, medio zaguero.
halfback line, (dep.) línea media.
half-baked [-'beɪkt] *a.* 1. medio horneado, a medio hornear. 2. (fam.) precipitado, descabellado, absurdo, disparatado, a medio hacer.
half binding, (enc.) media pasta, encuadernación a la holandesa.
half blood, 1. relación entre dos personas que tienen un solo progenitor común. 2. mestizo.
half-blood [-ˌblʌd] *a.* medio, ej., *half-blood sister,* media hermana, *half-blood brother,* medio hermano.
half-blooded [-əd] *a.* que tiene solamente un progenitor común, media sangre, media casta, ej., *half-blooded sheep,* oveja media sangre o media casta.

half boot, botina.
half-bound ['hæf'baʊnd, B 'hɑf-] *a.* (enc.) encuadernado a la holandesa.
half-bred [-ˌbrɛd] *a., s.* media sangre, media casta.
half-breed [-ˌbrid] *a., s.* mestizo (esp. de blanco e indio americano).
half brother, medio hermano.
half-caste ['hæfˌkæst, B 'hɑfˌkɑst] *s.* 1. mestizo (de europeo y oriental). 2. mestizo (de razas diferentes). —*a.* mestizo.
half-close [-'kloʊz] *v.t.* entrecerrar.
half cock, at h. c., a medio armar, montado en seguro, medio amartillado; (G.B.) **to go off at h. c.,** hablar o actuar prematura o precipitadamente.
halfcocked [-'kɑkt, B -'kɔkt] *a.* 1. medio amartillado, en seguro. 2. (fam., E.U.) prematuro, precipitado; **to go off h.,** hablar o actuar prematura o precipitadamente.
half crown, (G.B.) media corona (dos chelines y medio).
half dollar, (E.U., Can.) medio dólar, moneda de cincuenta centavos.
half-done [-'dʌn] *a.* medio cocido; hecho a medias.
half eagle, (E.U., ant.) moneda de oro de cinco dólares.
half fare, medio pasaje, medio billete o boleto (Amer.).
half-full ['hæf'fʊl, B 'hɑf-] *a.* medio lleno, a medio llenar, mediado.
half gainer, (natación) (saltos ornamentales) patada a la luna con medio tirabuzón atrás.
half-hatched [-'hætʃt] *a.* casi empollado; (fig.) novato.
halfhearted [-'hɑrtəd, B -'hɑt-] *a.* frío, indiferente, sin ánimo o interés.
halfheartedly [-lɪ] *adv.* fríamente, indiferentemente.
halfheartedness [-nəs] *s.* frialdad, indiferencia.
half hitch, (mar.) cote, vuelta mordida (nudo).
half holiday, medio día de asueto, tarde de asueto.
half-hour ['hæf'aʊər, B 'hɑf'aʊə] *s.* media hora. —*a.* de media hora.
half-hourly [-lɪ] *a.* a cada media hora. —*adv.* cada media hora.
half-length [-'lɛŋθ, -'lɛŋkθ] *a.* de medio cuerpo, de busto (díc. de los retratos). —*s.* retrato de medio cuerpo.
half-life [-ˌlaɪf] (fís., quím.) período de semidesintegración, período de vida media, período medio (en que se desintegran la mitad de los átomos de un cuerpo radioactivo).
half-light [-ˌlaɪt] *s.* media luz, penumbra. —*a.* a media luz.
half line, (geom.) semirrecta.
half-long [-'lɔŋ] *a.* (fon.) semilarga (díc. de las vocales largas acortadas por su aparición en una sílaba no acentuada).
half-mast [-'mæst, B -'mɑst] *s.* media asta; **a flag at h.-m.,** bandera a media asta. —*v.t.* poner a media asta (banderas, etc.).
half measures, paños calientes, paños tibios, medidas a medias.
half-moon [-ˌmun] *s.* media luna.
half mourning, medio luto; vestido de medio luto (gris, morado o blanco).
half nelson, (lucha libre) llave de cuello (que consiste en pasar el brazo por debajo del sobaco del contrincante, colocando la mano sobre su nuca).
half note, (mús.) blanca, mínima.
half-opened ['hæf'oʊpənd, B 'hɑf-] *a.* entreabierto, a medio abrir.
half pay, media paga, medio sueldo (esp. de un oficial naval o del ejército cuando no está en servicio activo).
half-pay [-'peɪ] *a.* a media paga; a medio sueldo.
halfpenny ['heɪpənɪ, 'hæfˌpɛnɪ, B 'heɪpnɪ] *s.* (*pl.* HALFPENCE ['heɪpəns] o HALFPENNIES) (G.B.) medio penique. —*a. 1. de medio penique. 2. (fig.) insignificante.*
half pint, 1. líquido o medida equivalente a — de litro. 2. (jer.) arrancapinos. 3. persona diminuta.
half price, mitad de precio. —*adv.* a mitad de precio.
half relief, media talla, medio relieve.
half-round ['hæf'raund, B 'hɑf-] *a.* 1. semicircular. 2. de mediacaña.
half-seas over[-ˌsiz'oʊvər, B -və] (jer.) achispado, entre dos velas.
half sister, media hermana.
half-slip [-ˌslɪp] *s.* enagua(s), refajo corto que parte de la cintura.
half sole, media suela (de zapato).
half-sole [-'soʊl] *v.t.* poner media suela a (zapatos o botas).
half sovereign, (G.B., ant.) moneda (de oro) de diez chelines.
half-staff [-'stæf, B -'stɑf] *s.* media asta.
half-starved [-'stɑrvd, B -'stɑvd] *a.* medio muerto de hambre.
half step, 1. (mil.) medio paso, paso corto. 2. (mús.) semitono.
half tide, media marea.
half-timbered [-'tɪmbərd, B -bəd] *a.* (arq.) entramado; con muros de entramado de madera.
half time, (dep.) intermedio, medio tiempo (en fútbol, baloncesto).
half-timer [-'taɪmer, B -mə] *s.* el que trabaja sólo media jornada.
half title, (impr.) anteportada, portadilla; falsa portada; subtítulo.
halftone ['hæfˌtoʊn, B 'hɑf-] *s.* 1. (impr.) medio tono; grabado de medio tono; media tinta; grabado reticulado o de trama. 2. (mús.) semitono. 3. (*pl.*) (foto.) semitintes. —*a.* de medio tono o tramado (díc. de un fotograbado).
half-track [-ˌtræk] *s.* semicarril, semitractor, media oruga. —*a.* de media oruga.
half-tracked [-ˌtrækt] *a.* de media oruga.
half-truth [-ˌtruθ] *s.* verdad a medias, verdad incompleta, reticencia.
half volley (dep.) medio voleo.
half-volley [-'vɑlɪ, B -'vɔlɪ] *v.t., v.i.* (dep.) golpear (la pelota) en el rebote.
half-wave [-ˌweɪv] *s.* (elec.) de media onda.
halfway ['hæf'weɪ, B 'hɑf-] *a.* 1. equidistante, a medio camino. 2. incompleto, parcial. —*adv.* 1. en el medio, en la mitad. 2. a medio camino. 3. a medias, parcialmente, incompletamente. 4. **to do h.,** hacer a medias; **to meet h.,** encontrarse a medio camino, hacer concesiones a, hacer concesiones mutuas.
halfway house, 1. posada en la mitad del camino (entre dos ciudades). 2. (fig.) transición. 3. centro de rehabilitación, centro de reinserción social.
half-wit [-ˌwɪt] *s.* imbécil, tonto, mentecato.
half-witted [-'wɪtəd] *a.* deficiente mental; imbécil, tonto.
half-wittedly [-lɪ] *adv.* imbécilmente, neciamente, tontamente.
half year, semestre.
half-yearly ['hæf'jɪrlɪ, B 'hɑf'jəlɪ] *a.* semestral. —*adv.* semestralmente.
halibut ['hæləbət, 'hɑl-, B 'hæl-] *s.* (ict.) hipogloso, pez sin espinas de carne muy apetecida.
halide ['hælˌaɪd, 'heɪˌlaɪd] *s.* (quím.) haluro. —*a.* haloideo.
halidom ['hælədəm] **halidome** [-ˌdoʊm] *a.* (ant.) santidad, santimonia; lugar santo, santuario; reliquias.
halite ['hælˌaɪt, 'heɪˌlaɪt] *s.* (min.) halita.
halitosis [ˌhælə'toʊsəs] *s.* (med.) halitosis.
halitus ['hælətəs] *s.* hálito; exhalación; vapor.
hall [hɔl] *s.* 1. vestíbulo, recibidor, recibimiento, antecámara. 2. pasillo, corredor, zaguán. 3. edificio público; ayuntamiento. 4. sala (de sesiones o conferencias); paraninfo (de una universidad); edificio, comedor (de un colegio o universidad); (E.U.) edificio de una facultad. 5. (G.B.) casa señorial. 6. (hist.) habitación pública de un jefe o capitán teutónico.
hallelujah, halleluiah [ˌhælə'lujə] *s.* aleluya. —*interj.* ¡aleluya!
halliard, *var. de.* **halyard.**
hallmark ['hɔlˌmɑrk, B -ˌmɑk] *s.* 1. marca de contraste, marca de pureza. 2. (fig.) sello, distintivo. —*v.t.* estampar o marcar con sello de pureza.
Hall of Fame, edificio y galería en la ciudad de Nueva York donde se exhiben bustos de norteamericanos ilustres.
hallo, halloa [hə'loʊ] *var. de* **hollo.**
halloo [hə'lu] *s.* grito, llamada. —*v.i.* gritar (para azuzar a los perros). —*v.t.* (*pret., p.p.* HALLOOED; *p.pr.* HALLOOING) 1. gritar, llamar a gritos. 2. **do not h. until you are out of the wood,** no cantar victoria antes de tiempo.
hallow ['hæloʊ] *v.t.* 1. consagrar, santificar; hacer santo. 2. venerar, reverenciar.
hallow [hə'loʊ, 'hæloʊ] *var. de* **halloo.**
hallowed ['hæloʊd] *a.* sagrado, santo, santificado.
Halloween [ˌhælə'win, ˌhɑl-, B 'hæloʊ'in] *s.* víspera de Todos los Santos (la noche del 31 de octubre).
Hallowmas ['hæloʊˌmæs, -məs] *s.* (ant.) día de Todos los Santos, fiesta de Todos los Santos.
Hallstatt ['hɔlˌstæt, 'hɑlˌʃtɑt] *a.* (hist.) que designa a una cultura de Hallstatt.
hallucinate [hə'lusəˌneɪt] *v.t.* alucinar. —*v.i.* alucinarse, desvariar.
hallucination [həˌlusə'neɪʃən] *s.* alucinación, alucinamiento.
hallucinatory [hə'lusənəˌtɔrɪ, B -nətərɪ] *a.* alucinatorio, imaginario, irreal.
hallucinogen [hə'lusənədʒɛn] *s.* alucinógeno, droga que produce alucinaciones.
hallucinosis [həˌlusə'noʊsəs] *s.* alucinosis.
hallux ['hæləks] *s.* (*pl.* HALLUCES ['hæljəˌsiz]) (anat., orn.) hallus, hállux.
hallway ['hɔlˌweɪ] *s.* (E.U.) 1. vestíbulo; zaguán. 2. pasillo, corredor, pasadizo.
halm [hɔm, B hɑm] *var. de.* **haulm.**
halo ['heɪloʊ] *s.* (*pl.* HALOS O HALOES) 1. halo, aurora, resplandor; cerco luminoso, aureola, anillo lunar (en la madera). 2. gloria, nimbo. —*v.t., v.i.* aureolar, formar o rodear con un halo.
halobiont [ˌhæloʊ'baɪˌɑnt, B -ˌɔnt] *s.* (biol.) halobionte.
halogen ['hælədʒən] *s.* (quím.) halógeno.
halogenate ['hælədʒəˌneɪt] *v.t.* (quím.) halogenar.
halogenation [ˌhælədʒə'neɪʃən] *s.* (quím.) halogenación.
halogenous [hæ'lɑdʒənəs, B -'lɔdʒ-] *a.* halógeno.
halography [-'lɑgrəfɪ, B -'lɔg-] *s.* (quím.) halografía.
haloid ['hælɔɪd] *a., s.* (quím.) haloideo.
halophile ['hæləˌfaɪl] *s.* (biol.) organismo halófilo.
halophilic [ˌhælə'fɪlɪk] **halophilous** [hæ'lɑfələs, B -'lɔf-] *a.* (bot.) halófilo.
halophyte ['hæləˌfaɪt] *s.* (bot.) halófita.
halt [hɔlt] *s.* 1. alto, parada. 2. interrupción, detención. 3. (pr. G.B., f.c.) apeadero, paradero (Amer.). 4. **to bring to a h.,** parar, detener; **to**

call a h., mandar hacer alto; **to call a h. to,** poner coto a; **to come to a h.**, pararse; interrumpirse. —*v.i.* 1. hacer alto, pararse, detenerse. 2. interrumpirse, terminar. —*v.t.* 1. detener, parar. 2. interrumpir, terminar.

halt, *a.* (ant.) cojo, renco; lisiado. —*v.i.* 1. vacilar, titubear. 2. (ant.) cojear, renquear, claudicar. 3. tartamudear.

halter ['hɔltər, B -tə] *s.* 1. cabestro, ronzal, jáquima. 2. dogal, cuerda de ahorcar; muerte en la horca. 3. especie de corpiño. —*v.t.* 1. cabestrar; echar el ronzal a, poner el dogal a. 2. colgar, ahorcar. 3. trabar, echar trabas a, obstaculizar.

halter ['hɔltər, B 'hæltə] *s.* (*pl.* HALTERES) [hɔl'tɪriz, B hæl'tɪər-] (ento.) balancín, halterio.

halting ['hɔltiŋ] *a.* 1. claudicante. 2. vacilante, inseguro.

haltingly [-lɪ] *adv.* vacilantemente, inseguramente.

halvah [hɑl'vɑ] *s.* confite, golosina turca.

halve [hæv, B hɑv] *v.t.* 1. partir por la mitad; dividir o compartir entre dos; reducir por la mitad. 2. (golf) empatar (un hoyo o una partida). 3. (carp.) machihembrar.

halves [hævz, B hɑvz] *pl. de* **half.** 1. **by h.**, por mitades. 2. **go h.**, compartir por partes iguales, ir a medias.

halyard ['hæljərd, B -jəd] *s.* (mar.) driza.

ham [hæm] *s.* 1. jamón, pernil (del cerdo), nalgada. 2. (*gen. pl.*) (fam.) muslo, nalgas. 3. (jer.) comicastro, actor o artista aficionado; radioaficionado. 4. (anat.) corva. —*v.t.* (*pret., pp.* HAMMED; *p.pr.* HAMMING) (jer.) exagerar (un papel, escena o acto). —*v.i.* actuar melodramática o afectadamente.

hamadryad [ˌhæmə'draɪəd, -ˌæd] *s.* 1. (zool.) hamadríade, papión sagrado. 2. (zool.) cobra real, rey de las cobras.

hamal [hə'mɑl, -'mɔl] *s.* cargador; criado (en el Oriente).

hamamelidaceous [ˌhæməˌmɛlə'deɪʃəs] *a.* (bot.) hamamelidáceo.

hamamelin [ˌhæmə'milɪn] *s.* (farm.) hamamelina.

hamate ['heɪˌmeɪt] **hamated** [-əd] *a.* (anat.) hamoso, hamato, hamuloso.

hamatum [hə'meɪtəm] *s.* (*pl.* HAMATA [-ə]) (anat.) hamátum.

hamburger ['hæmˌbərgər, B -ˌbɜgə] *s.* 1. carne de res picada. 2. hamburguesa.

hamburger stand, hamburguesería.

hame [heɪm] *s.* horcate.

Hamite ['hæmˌaɪt] *s.* camita, hamita.

Hamitic [hæ'mɪtɪk, hə-] *a.* camítico. —*s.* lengua camítica.

Hamito-Semitic ['hæmətoʊsə'mɪtɪk] *a.* camito-semítico.

hamlet ['hæmlət] *s.* aldehuela, villorrio, caserío.

hamlet, *s.* (ict.) variedad de mero.

hammal, *var. de* **hamal.**

hammer ['hæmər, B -ə] *s.* 1. martillo. 2. martinete, macillo (de piano); macillo (para tocar instrumentos de percusión). 3. mazo, martillo (usado en subastas). 4. (anat.) martillo (del oído). 5. (dep.) martillo. 6. (arm.) gatillo, percusor. 7. **throwing the h.**, (dep.) lanzamiento de martillo; **to come under the h.**, ser subastado. —*v.t.* 1. martillar, golpear; batir. 2. clavar. 3. (fig.) machacar. 4. (fig.) elaborar trabajosamente. 5. hacer penetrar a martillazos. 6. **to h. an idea into (someone's) head,** (fig.) meterle una idea en la cabeza (a alguien); **h. one's brains,** devanarse los sesos; **h. out,** sacar a martillazos; formar a martillazos. —*v.i.* 1. martillar, dar golpes. 2. repiquetear. 3. (con *at*) trabajar asiduamente (en), dedicarse con ahínco (a). 4. **h. away (at),** seguir trabajando asiduamente (en); **h. away on the same subject,** estar siempre con la misma canción.

hammer and sickle, la hoz y el martillo, el emblema del partido comunista en algunos países, que significa la alianza de trabajadores y labriegos.

hammer and tongs, (fam.) con gran fuerza, con violencia; **to go at it h. and t.**, reñir violentamente; echarse a trabajar con ahínco.

hammer blow, martillazo.

hammer cloth, paño del pescante de un coche.

hammered work [-ərd-, B -əd-] obra repujada, obra martillada.

hammerer ['hæmərər, B -ərə] *s.* martillador.

hammerhead ['hæmərˌhɛd, B -əˌ-] *s.* 1. cabeza de martillo. 2. zoquete, zopenco. 3. (ict.) pez martillo, cornudilla.

hammering [-ərɪŋ] *s.* martilleo, ruido de martillazos.

hammerless ['hæmərləs, B -əlɪs] *a.* (arm.) sin martillo, de gatillo interior.

hammer lock, (dep.) llave al brazo, llave de candado (toma de lucha libre que consiste en doblar el brazo del adversario hacia su espalda).

hammertoe [-ˌtoʊ] *s.* (med.) dedo en martillo.

hammock ['hæmək] *s.* hamaca; (mar.) coy.

hammock, *s.* (S. de E.U.) región boscosa de tierra profunda y rica.

hammy ['hæmɪ] *a.* (HAMMIER; HAMMIEST) (jer.) digno de un comicastro (papel, actuación, etc.).

hamper ['hæmpər, B -pə] *s.* 1. capacho, cesto o canasta grande (gen. con tapa). 2. estorbo, obstáculo. 3. (mar.) aparejo, jarcias y motonería. —*v.t.* estorbar, embarazar, entorpecer, dificultar, impedir, obstar, poner trabas a.

hamshackle ['hæmˌʃækəl] *v.t.* 1. trabar (a un animal) con una cuerda desde la cabeza hasta la pata delantera. 2. contener, impedir.

hamster ['hæmstər, B -stə] *s.* (zool.) hámster, marmota de Alemania, rata del trigo, rata del algodón.

hamstring [-ˌstrɪŋ] *s.* (anat.) tendón de la corva; tendón del corvejón. —*v.t.* 1. desjarretar. 2. (fig.) incapacitar, paralizar; impedir.

hamulus ['hæmjələs] *s.* (*pl.* HAMULI [-ˌlaɪ]) 1. (anat.) hamulus. 2. (vet.) hámulo.

hanaper ['hænəpər, B -pə] *s.* (ant.) canasto para documentos.

hance [hæns, B hɑns] *s.* 1. (mar.) arqueo, brusca de las cubiertas. 2. (arq.) riñón.

hand [hænd] *s.* 1. mano. 2. (fig.) mano, autoridad, dirección. 3. (fig.) mano, dominio, posesión, ej., *in the hands of,* en manos de. 4. (fig.) participación, parte, interés, ej., *to have a h. in,* tener participación en. 5. lado, parte. 6. (fig.) mano, promesa de matrimonio (de la mujer), ej., *to give one's h. to,* conceder su mano a, hacer promesa de matrimonio a. 7. mano, habilidad, destreza, ej., *he has a h. for ceramics,* tiene mano (o habilidad) para cerámica. 8. firma, rúbrica; escritura, puño y letra, caligrafía. 9. (fig.) mano, ayuda, auxilio, asistencia, ej., *give me a h.,* dame una mano, ayúdame. 10. aplauso, ovación. 11. obrero, bracero, operario, peón, jornalero. 12. autor, pintor, ej., *two portraits by the same h.,* dos retratos por el mismo pintor. 13. experto, perito. 14. manecilla, mano (del reloj). 15. palmo menor (medida de 4 pulgadas). 16. (naipes) jugador; mano, juego; mano, dotación (de cartas). 17. manojo (de tabaco, etc.); mano (de plátanos). 18. (mar.) tripulante. 19. (ant.) obra de mano, confección, hechura. 20. **a (great, good,** etc.) **h. at,** hábil en, experto en; **all hands,** (mar.) toda la tripulación; **an old h.**, un experto; **at close h.**, muy de cerca; **at first h.**, de primera mano, de buena tinta; **at h.**, a la mano, cerca, inmediato, inminente; **second h.**, de segunda mano; **at the hands of,** por obra de, por; **by h.**, a mano; **clean hands,** (fig.) manos limpias, inocencia, honradez; **from h. to h.**, de mano en mano; **h. and foot,** completamente, totalmente; **h. in h.**, asidos de la mano, de las manos; juntos; de acuerdo; **hands down,** fácilmente, sin esforzarse; sin duda, indisputablemente; **hands off!** ¡no tocar!; **h. over h.**, **h. over fist,** pasando una mano sobre la otra (como al subir por una cuerda); (fig.) rápidamente, con progreso rápido o constante; **hands up!** ¡ manos arriba!; **in good hands,** en buenas manos; **in h.**, entre manos, a disposición de uno; dominado, controlado; (com.) en efectivo; **in one's own h.**, de su propio puño, de su puño y letra; **off one's hands,** fuera del cargo (de uno), desechado; despachado; **on h.**, a mano, disponible; en existencia; por hacer, pendiente; inminente; **on one's hands,** en mano(s) de uno, a cargo de uno; a la disposición de uno; **on the one h.**, por una parte; **on the other h.**, por otra parte; **out of h.**, incontenible, fuera de control; **to be h. in glove with,** ser uña y carne con, ser amigo inseparable de; estar de manga con; **to be in good hands,** estar en buenas manos; **to be in someone's hands,** estar (una cosa) en mano de alguien; estar (una persona) en manos de alguien; **to bear a h.**, dar una mano a, ayudar; **to bind one h. and foot,** atar de pies y manos; **to change hands,** mudar de manos, cambiar de dueño; **to clap hands,** batir palmas; **to do a h.'s turn,** esforzarse lo mínimo; **to eat out of one's hands** obedecer dócilmente a uno; **to fall from one's hands,** caérsele de la mano a uno; **to get one's h. in,** adquirir habilidad, aprender a hacerlo; **to get out of h.**, desmandarse (personas); escapar al control (situación, etc.); **to get** (o **have**) **the upper h.**, llevar ventaja, superar, dominar; **to go h. in h. with,** marchar de acuerdo con, guardar el paso con; **to have a free h.**, tener carta blanca; **to have a h. in,** tener mano en; **to have in one's h.**, (fig.) tener uno en su mano(s); **to have one's hands full,** tener muchísimo que hacer, estar ocupadísimo; **to have one's hands tied,** tener atadas las manos; **to hold out** (u **offer**) **one's h.**, tender la mano a, tender una mano a; **to join hands,** unirse en una causa común, combinar esfuerzos; **to keep** (o **have**) **one's h. in,** mantenerse en práctica; **to keep one's hands off,** to tocar; **to lay hands on,** tocar, echar mano a, agarrar; encontrar, localizar; **to leave in someone's hands,** dejar en manos de alguien; **to lend (someone) a h.**, echar una mano a, prestar ayuda a (alguien); **to lift** (o **raise**) **a h.**, hacer un esfuerzo; **to bite the h. that feeds one,** ser mal agradecido; **to place oneself in someone's hands,** ponerse en manos de alguien; **to play into the hands of,** hacerle el juego a, favorecer directamente; **to play one's own h.**, obrar uno en su propio interés; **to raise one's h. to (someone),** alzar la mano a (alguien); **to serve (someone) h. and foot,** servir (a alguien) asiduamente; **to shake hands (with),** estrecharse las manos; **to show one's h.**, revelar su intención, descubrir su juego; **to take in h.**, hacerse cargo de; emprender; **to tie one's hands,** atar las manos a uno; **to try one's h. at,** probar la mano en; **to wash one's hands of,** lavarse las manos de; **with a heavy h.**, opresivamente; **with a high h.**, osadamente, audazmente, arrogantemente. —*a.* de mano; manual, hecho a mano;

para la mano. —*v.t.* 1. dirigir, guiar o ayudar con la mano. 2. dar, entregar, pasar (con la mano); tender, ej., *she handed him the paper,* (ella) le tendió el papel. 3. (mar.) aferrar (velas). 4. (ant.) manipular. 5. **h. down,** transmitir; pasar de arriba abajo; (der.) anunciar (un fallo); **h. in,** presentar (renuncia, etc.); entregar; **h. in** (o **into**), dar la mano para entrar, ayudar a entrar; **h. it to someone,** (jer.) reconocer los méritos de alguien, cumplimentar o felicitar a alguien; **h. on,** transmitir, pasar a (otro); **h. out,** repartir, distribuir; aplicar (pena, castigo); **h. over,** entregar (el mando, etc.); ceder (privilegio, derecho).

handbag [ˈhændˌbæg] *s.* 1. bolsa de mano, bolso, cartera (Amer.) (de señora). 2. maletín, maletilla.

hand baggage, equipaje de mano.

handball [-ˌbɔl] *s.* (dep.) balonmano, pelota de frontón.

handbarrow [-ˌbæroʊ] *s.* andas, angarillas, parihuela.

handbell [-ˌbɛl] *s.* campanilla.

handbill [-ˌbɪl] *s.* volante (que se reparte a los transeúntes), cuartilla, octavilla.

handbook [ˈhændˌbʊk] *s.* 1. manual, libro de referencias; guía. 2. prontuario.

hand brake, freno de mano.

handbreadth [-ˌbrɛdθ -ˌbrɛtθ] *s.* palmo menor (medida de longitud); ancho de la mano.

handcar [-ˌkɑr, B -ˌkɑ] *s.* (f.c.) zorrilla, carrito de mano.

handcart [-ˌkɑrt, B -ˌkɑt] *s.* carro o carretilla de mano.

handclasp [-ˌklæsp, B -ˌklɑsp] *s.* apretón de manos.

handcraft [-ˌkræft, B -ˌkrɑft] *var. de* **handicraft.** —*v.t.* hacer a mano.

handcuff [-ˌkʌf] *s.* manilla; (*pl.*) esposas. —*v.t.* maniatar, esposar, poner manilla a, poner esposas a.

handed [ˈhændəd] *a.* (*ú. gen. en palabras compuestas*) 1. de . . . manos, ej., *a six-handed deity,* una deidad de seis manos. 2. a . . . manos, ej., *a three-h. card game,* un juego de naipes a tres manos.

handfast [-ˌfæst, B -ˌfɑst] *s.* 1. (ant.) contrato, convenio; esponsales. 2. firme apretón de mano.

handfasting [-ɪŋ] *s.* 1. (hist.) forma de matrimonio irregular y de prueba que se celebraba uniendo las manos y acordando vivir juntos. 2. (ant.) esponsales, desposorios.

handful [ˈhændˌfʊl] *s.* (*pl.* HANDFULS) 1. puñado, manojo. 2. puñado, poca cantidad, corto número.

hand glass, 1. espejo de mano. 2. lupa, lente de aumento para leer.

hand grenade, (mil.) granada de mano.

handgrip [-ˌgrɪp] *s.* 1. apretón de manos. 2. (*pl.*) combate, lucha cuerpo a cuerpo. 3. (*strap*) agarradera.

handgun [-ˌgʌn] *s.* arma de fuego que pueda dispararse con la mano; pistola.

handhold [-ˌhoʊld] *s.* 1. asimiento, agarro. 2. asidero, agarradero.

handicap [ˈhændɪˌkæp] *s.* 1. handicap (carrera, lucha o torneo en que se dan ciertas ventajas a los menos aventajados, para lograr una igualdad de condiciones; ventaja que se da o impedimento que se impone). 2. (fig.) desventaja, impedimento, obstáculo. —*v.t.* (*pret., p.p.* HANDICAPPED; *p.pr.* HANDICAPPING) 1. imponer impedimentos a; poner trabas u obstáculos a, estorbar; poner o situar en desventaja. 2. asignar obstáculos a (esp. a los caballos en las carreras).

handicapped [-kæpt] **person,** el minusválido físico y psíquico.

handicapper [-ər, B -ə] *s.* 1. oficial que asigna ventajas o impedimentos (en carreras). 2. pronosticador de carreras de caballos (para periódicos).

handicraft [-ˌkræft, B -ˌkrɑft] *s.* 1. destreza manual. 2. artesanía, oficio. 3. (ant.) artesano, artífice.

handicraftsman [-ˌkræftsmən, B -ˌkrɑfts-] *s.* artesano, artífice.

handily [ˈhændəlɪ] *adv.* 1. hábilmente, diestramente. 2. fácilmente. 3. convenientemente.

handiness [ˈhændɪnəs] *s.* 1. habilidad, destreza. 2. comodidad, conveniencia.

handiwork [-ˌwɜrk, B -ˌwɜk] *s.* 1. obra hecha a mano; obra manual. 2. obra de las manos (de uno). 3. (fig.) maniobra subrepticia.

handkerchief [ˈhæŋkərtʃəf, -ˌtʃif, B -kət-ʃɪf] *s.* 1. pañuelo (de mano), gasné (Mex.). 2. pañoleta. 3. **to throw the h. to,** expresar preferencia por (una persona); (en ciertos juegos) invitar (a una persona) a proseguir.

hand-knit [ˈhændˈnɪt] **hand-knitted** [-əd] *a.* tejido a mano.

handle [ˈhændəl] *v.t.* 1. tocar, palpar, manosear. 2. tratar, dar (buen o mal) trato a. 3. manejar, manipular, maniobrar. 4. (darse abasto para) recibir, ej., *the port of New York can h. much traffic,* el puerto de Nueva York puede (darse abasto para) recibir mucho tráfico. 5. dirigir, mandar. 6. (E.U.) tratar en, negociar en. —*v.i.* ser manejado, manejarse (de cierto modo). —*s.* 1. asa (de vasija, cesta, etc.), mango, manija (de instrumento o utensilio), puño (de bicicleta, bastón, espada, etc.), tirador (de cajón o gaveta), manigueta (de herramienta), astil (de hacha, azada, pico, etc.), manubrio (de organillo, ruedas, mecanismos). 2. (fig.) asidero, pretexto. 3. (jer.) nombre, apellido; apodo, alias. 4. total de apuestas. 5. **to fly off the h.,** salirse de sus casillas, perder los estribos.

handleable [-əbəl] *a.* manejable.

handlebar [-ˌbɑr, B -ˌbɑ] *s.* (*ú. gen. en pl.*) manillar, guía (de bicicleta).

handler [ˈhændlər, B -lə] *s.* 1. tratante. 2. (boxeo) entrenador.

handless [-ləs] *a.* 1. manco. 2. (fig.) torpe, desmañado.

handling [-lɪŋ] *s.* 1. manoseo; toqueteo. 2. manejo, manipulación. 3. desenvolvimiento, manera de desarrollar (un tema de arte, literatura, etc.).

handmade [ˈhændˈmeɪd] *a.* hecho a mano.

handmaid [-ˌmeɪd] *s.* sirvienta, doncella, vestidora, asistenta.

hand-me-down [-mɪˌdaʊn] *a.* 1. (ropa) hecha, barata, poco elegante. 2. de segunda mano (díc. esp. de las prendas de vestir). —*s.* ropa hecha o confeccionada; prenda de vestir barata, de poco gusto o de segunda mano.

hand organ, (mús.) organillo, aristón.

handout [ˈhændˌaʊt] *s.* 1. (jer., E.U.) comestibles o ropa que se dan de limosna. 2. volante, folleto gratuito. 3. información, noticias (distribuidas por una agencia de prensa). 4. parte oficial (a la prensa).

handpick [-ˈpɪk] *v.t.* escoger personalmente, seleccionar cuidadosamente.

hand pump, bomba de mano.

handrail [-ˌreɪl] *s.* pasamano, baranda, barandilla.

hand running, sin parar, consecutivamente.

handsaw [-ˌsɔ] *s.* sierra bracera, sierra de mano.

hands-down [ˈhændzˈdaʊn] *a.* 1. fácil, cómodo (victoria, triunfo, etc.). 2. indisputable, sin rival (favorito, etc.).

handsel [ˈhænsəl] *s.* 1. aguinaldo de año nuevo. 2. arras, anticipo. —*v.t.* (*pret., p.p.* HANDSELED O HANDSELLED; *p.pr.* HANDSELING O HANDSELLING) (pr. G.B.) 1. regalar, obsequiar (en señal de felicidad o buena suerte). 2. estrenar, inaugurar.

handset [ˈhændˌsɛt] *s.* (tele.) microteléfono combinado, aparato microtelefónico.

handshake [-ˌʃeɪk] *s.* apretón de manos.

hands-off [ˈhændzˈɔf] *a.* 1. (política o actitud) de no intervención o no interferencia. 2. (comput) automático.

handsome [ˈhænsəm] *a.* 1. hermoso, guapo, donoso, donairoso, bien parecido. 2. bondadoso, generoso, dadivoso. 3. considerable, amplio. 4. (dial.) adecuado, conveniente, apropiado; que sienta bien.

handsomely [-lɪ] *adv.* 1. hermosamente. 2. generosamente.

handsomeness [-nəs] *s.* 1. hermosura, gallardía. 2. generosidad.

hand's-on [ˈhændzˈɑn] *a.* práctico; (comput.) manual.

handspike [ˈhændˌspaɪk] *s.* palanca, barra.

handspring [-ˌsprɪŋ] *s.* salto mortal o voltereta sobre las manos.

handstand [-ˌstænd] *s.* (gimnasia) farol.

hand-to-hand [ˈhændtəˈhænd] *a.* de cerca, cuerpo a cuerpo.

hand-to-mouth [-ˈmaʊθ] *a.* imprevisor, impróvido; precario; **to live from h.-to-m.,** vivir al día.

hand-tooled [-ˈtuld] *a.* labrado a mano, damasquinado.

handwheel [-ˌhwil, -ˌwil] *s.* rueda de mano, volante, volante-manubrio.

handwork [-ˌwɜrk, B -ˌwɜk] *s.* trabajo a mano.

handwoven [ˈhændˈwoʊvən] *a.* tejido a mano.

handwrite [-ˌraɪt] *v.t.* escribir a mano.

handwriting [-ɪŋ] *s.* 1. escritura; letra, rasgo, carácter de letra; caligrafía. 2. (ant.) manuscrito.

handy [ˈhændɪ] *a.* (HANDIER; HANDIEST) 1. a la mano, cercano, próximo. 2. práctico, útil. 3. diestro, hábil. 4. (mar.) fácil de manejar, maniobrar o dirigir. 5. **to come in h.,** venir bien, ser o resultar útil.

handyman [-ˌmæn] *s.* factótum, criado para tareas diversas.

hang [hæŋ] *v.t.* (*pret., p.p.* HUNG [hʌŋ] O HANGED [hæŋd]; *p.pr.* HANGING) 1. suspender, colgar, enganchar en alto. 2. (*pret., p.p.* HANGED) ahorcar, colgar. 3. colgar, entapizar, adornar (con colgaduras y tapices). 4. pegar (empapelado). 5. inclinar, bajar (la cabeza). 6. hacer flotar, suspender (en el espacio). 7. ajustar, pegar, fijar equilibradamente (ej., un hacha a su mango). 8. (der.) impedir, con un dictamen discrepante, que el jurado pronuncie su fallo. 9. **h. it!** ¡caramba! ¡diablos! ¡maldito sea!; **h. one on,** (jer.) asestar un golpe a; pegarse una mona; **h. oneself,** colgarse; **h. out,** colgar fuera, tender (la ropa); desplegar (bandera); **h. up,** colgar (ropa, sombrero; auricular); **h. you!** ¡maldito seas!; **I'll be hanged if,** que me ahorquen si, de ninguna manera; **to be** (o **get**) **hung up (on something** o **someone),** obsesionarse o irritarse por algo o alguien. —*v.i.* 1. pender, colgar. 2. (*pret., p.p.* HANGED) ser ahorcado. 3. quedarse inmóvil, flotar (en el aire). 4. (gen. con *over*) cernerse (sobre); amenazar, ser inminente. 5. pender, estar en suspenso, estar por resolverse. 6. (con *on* o *to*) colgarse (de); pegarse (a), agarrarse (de); apoyarse (en). 7. (gen. con **on**) estar atento a, estar pendiente de. 8. (gen. con *about* o *around*) rondar, merodear, haraganear, holgazanear. 9. **h. back,** rezagarse, actuar con renuencia o de mala gana, hacerse el remolón; **h. behind,** rezagarse; **h. by a thread,** pender de un hilo; **h. down,** colgar, estar pendiente; **h. from,** colgar de; **h. heavy,** pasar lentamente (el tiempo); **h. in the balance,** estar en suspenso o en veremos, jugarse; **h. on,** depender de, confiar en; quedarse, permanecer; **h. on one's words,** estar colgado o pendiente de las palabras de uno; persistir; **h. on to,** colgarse de, aferrarse a; no soltar; **h. out,** (jer.) habitar, alojarse; vagar (por ciertos sitios); **h. together,** estar unidos, permanecer unidos; tener cohesión; **h. up** (tele.) colgar, cortar la comunicación; **h. upon,** escuchar ávidamente (palabras de uno). —*s.* 1. modo de colgar (una cosa); caída (de un vestido). 2. declive. 3. significado. 4. vacilación, pausa (en el movimiento). 5. comino, ardite, bledo. 6. **not to care** (o **give**) **a h.,** no importarle un bledo; **to get the h. of,** comprender, entender; aprender a usar o a hacer algo.

hangar ['hæŋər, -gər, B -ə, -gə] *s.* 1. cobertizo. 2. (aer.) hangar. —*v.t.* guardar en el hangar.

hangbird ['hæŋ,bɜrd, B -,bɜd] *s.* (orn.) cacique veranero.

hangdog [-,dɔg] *s.* desgraciado; solapado; canalla. —*a.* 1. avergonzado. 2. atemorizado, intimidado.

hanger ['hæŋər, B -ə] *s.* 1. verdugo. 2. empapelador. 3. alfanje. 4. colgadero, soporte; colgador de ropa, percha, gancho; presilla; barra de suspensión; faja de la que se suspendía una daga o espada. 5. (impr.) espito. 6. (aut.) soporte colgante.

hanger-on [-'ɑn, -'ɔn, B 'hæŋər'ɔn] *s.* (*pl.* HANGERS-ON) satélite, gorrista.

hanging ['hæŋɪŋ] *s.* 1. **ahorcadura,** ejecución en la horca. 2. (*gen. pl.*) colgaduras, cortinas; empapelado. —*a.* 1. suspendido, colgante, pendiente; inclinado. 2. que merece la horca, castigable por la horca (crimen). 3. (poét.) de apariencia lúgubre o triste.

hanging committee, comité que selecciona las obras que se exhiben (en un museo, exposición, etc.).

Hanging Gardens of Babylon, jardines colgantes de Babilonia.

hanging indention, (impr.) sangría francesa, párrafo francés.

hanging scaffold, andamio colgante, andamio volante.

hanging sleeve, (cost.) manga perdida.

hangman ['hæŋmən] *s.* verdugo.

hangnail [-,neɪl] *s.* (fam.) padrastro, cutícula inflamada o desgarrada.

hangout [-,aʊt] *s.* (fig.) nidal, lugar preferido (de una tertulia, un grupo consuetudinario de personas).

hangover [-,oʊvər, B -və] *s.* 1. sobrante, algo que queda. 2. malestar que se siente tras una borrachera, goma, cruda, ratón, guayabo (Amer.), resaca.

hang-up [-,ʌp] *s.* (jer.) algo que irrita u obsesiona; problema o dificultad emocional.

hank [hæŋk] *s.* 1. rollo, madeja; cadejo. 2. (mar.) garrucho, aro de madera. —*v.i.* adujar, hacer madejas.

hanker ['hæŋkər, B -kə] *v.i.* 1. (gen. con *for* o *after*) anhelar, desear.

hankering [-kərɪŋ] *s.* anhelo, deseo; **to have a h. for,** sentir anhelo por.

hankie, hanky ['hæŋkɪ] *s.* (*pl.* HANKIES) (fam.) pañuelo.

hanky-panky ['hæŋkɪ'pæŋkɪ] *s.* (fam.) trampería, manipuleo secreto, actividad dudosa.

Hanoi [hæ'nɔɪ] *s.* Hanoi, capital de Vietnam del Norte.

hansa ['hænsə] **hanse** [hæns] *s.* (hist.) liga hanseática o anseática; antigua unión mercantil entre ciertas regiones de Alemania.

Hansard ['hænsərd, -,sɑrd, B -,sɑd] *s.* (G.B.) informe oficial de las actas del Parlamento inglés.

Hanseatic [,hænsɪ'ætɪk] *a.* hanseático, anseático.

hansel, *var. de* **handsel.**

Hansen's disease ['hænsənz-] mal de Hansen, lepra.

hansom ['hænsəm] *s.* (hist.) cabriolé antiguo, coche ligero de dos ruedas (con el pescante elevado y a la zaga).

hap [hæp] *s.* azar, suerte, casualidad. —*v.i.* (*pret., p.p.* HAPPED; *p.pr.* HAPPING) (ant.) suceder, ocurrir, acontecer.

haphazard [,hæp'hæzərd, B 'hæp-əd] *s.* azar, accidente, capricho. —*a.* casual, fortuito, impensado. —*adv.* al azar, por casualidad.

haphazardly [-lɪ] *adv.* a la ventura, al azar, sin orden ni concierto.

hapless ['hæpləs] *a.* desafortunado, desventurado, sin suerte.

haplessness [-nəs] *s.* infortunio, mala suerte.

haplography [hæp'lɑgrəfɪ, B -'lɔg-] *s.* (filol.) haplografía.

haploid ['hæp,lɔɪd] *a.* (biol.) haploide.

haplology [hæp'lɑlədʒɪ, B -'lɔl-] *s.* haplología, simplificación de la escritura de una palabra compuesta, ej., *monomio* por mononomio.

haplont ['hæp,lunt, B -,lɔnt] *s.* (biol.) haplonte.

haply ['hæplɪ] *adv.* (ant.) casualmente, afortunadamente, accidentalmente.

happen ['hæpən] *v.i.* 1. acontecer, suceder. 2. ocurrir, ocurrir por casualidad. 3. llegar a suceder, resultar. 4. (ant., dial.) estar por casualidad (en algún lugar). 5. **as it happens,** da la casualidad que; **h. along,** pasar por casualidad por; **h. to (someone** o **something),** pasar a (alguien o algo); **h. to (be),** estar o encontrarse por casualidad; ser el caso que (cs, etc.), ej., *we happened to be there,* estábamos (o nos encontrábamos) allí por casualidad, *he happens to be a rich man,* resulta que él es un hombre rico; **h. to (do),** (hacer) por casualidad; resultar que (hago, etc.), ej., *I happened to hear,* oí por casualidad, *he happens to know you,* resulta que él te conoce; **I do not h. to (do),** el caso es que yo no (hago); **if anything should h. to me,** si algo me pasara; **it so happens (that),** da la casualidad (que); **no matter what happens,** suceda lo que suceda; **what happened?** ¿qué pasó?

happening [-ɪŋ] *s.* 1. hecho, suceso, acontecimiento. 2. espectáculo o representación improvisada.

happenstance [-,stæns] *s.* ocurrencia, circunstancia fortuita.

happily ['hæpəlɪ] *adv.* 1. por fortuna, afortunadamente. 2. felizmente. 3. acertadamente. 4. (ant.) por azar.

happiness [-ɪnəs] *s.* 1. felicidad, alegría, contento, dicha. 2. propiedad (de una expresión, etc.). 3. (ant.) buena suerte, buena fortuna, prosperidad.

happy ['hæpɪ] *a.* (HAPPIER; HAPPIEST) 1. feliz, contento, alegre; dichoso, afortunado; fausto. 2. apropiado, justo; acertado, feliz (ej., una expresión). 3. (fam. G.B.) achispado. 4. (*en palabras compuestas se usa con varios significados*) obsesionado; propenso, ej., *ski-h.,* obsesionado por el deporte de esquiar, *trigger-h.,* propenso a disparar impulsivamente. 5. **to be as h. as a lark,** estar más alegre que una pascua; **to be h. to,** alegrarse de, tener gusto en; **h. birthday,** feliz cumpleaños.

happy-go-lucky [-goʊ'lʌkɪ] *a.* descuidado, despreocupado, irresponsable. —*adv.* despreocupadamente, a la buena ventura.

hapten ['hæp,tɛn] **haptene** [-,tin] *s.* (quím.) hapteno.

hara-kiri [,hærə'kɪrɪ, ,hɑrə-, B 'hærə-] *s.* harakiri, voz japonesa con que se designa el suicidio ritual por desentrañamiento, como lo practicaba antiguamente la clase alta del Japón.

harangue [hə'ræŋ] *s.* arenga, perorata. —*v.t., v.i.* arengar, perorar.

harass [hə'ræs, 'hærəs, B 'hær-] *v.t.* 1. acosar, molestar. 2. saquear, pillar; asolar, desolar. 3. (mil.) hostilizar, hostigar.

harassment [-mənt] *s.* 1. acoso, apremio. 2. pillaje. 3. (mil.) hostigamiento.

harbinger ['hɑrbəndʒər, B 'hɑbɪndʒə] *s.* precursor, heraldo; presagio. —*v.t.* ser precursor de, presagiar, anunciar.

harbor (pr. G.B.) **harbour** ['hɑrbər, B 'hɑbə] *s.* 1. puerto, anclaje. 2. (fig.) puerto, refugio, asilo, amparo. —*v.t.* 1. hospedar, albergar. 2. albergar, encubrir (esp. criminales). 3. contener. 4. (fig.) albergar (malos pensamientos), abrigar (sospechas, desconfianza, etc.), guardar (sentimientos). —*v.i.* hospedarse, albergarse, habitar, refugiarse.

harborage, (pr. G.B.) **harbourage** [-bərɪdʒ] *s.* anclaje, puerto, fondeadero.

harborer, (pr. G.B.) **harbourer** [-bərər, B -bərə] *s.* albergador, amparador; encubridor.

harborless [-bərləs, B -bəlɪs] *a.* sin puerto; (fig.) desamparado, desabrigado.

harbor master, capitán de puerto.

harbor seal, foca peluda, de piel moteada.

hard [hɑrd, B hɑd] *a.* 1. duro, firme, sólido, compacto. 2. duro, fuerte, recio, resistente. 3. perseverante, asiduo, diligente, activo. 4. duro (trabajo), intenso (estudio). 5. duro, severo, cruel. 6. duro, obstinado. 7. rígido, inflexible. 8. inclemente, riguroso, crudo (tiempo, estación). 9. difícil (problema, cuestión, etc.). 10. duro, penoso (existencia, vida, etc.). 11. malo, adverso (suerte). 12. penetrante, inquisitivo (mirada, etc.). 13. (E.U.) fuerte, espirituoso, de alto contenido alcohólico (licores). 14. (fon.) sordo. 15. (fís.) duro (rayo, válvula). 16. **h. nut to crack,** (fig.) hueso duro de roer; **h. to deal with,** de trato difícil; **to be h. to (do),** ser difícil, ser malo de hacer; **to be h. on** (o **upon**), ser duro o severo con; criticar muy severamente; gastar (ropa, zapatos, etc.); **h. and fast,** estricto, rígido, sin excepción; **h. of hearing,** duro de oído, parcialmente sordo; **to do (it) the h. way,** hacer (algo) en forma complicada; **to have a h. time of it,** tener muchas dificultades, pasar por un mal momento; **to make it h. for,** hacerle las cosas difíciles a. —*adv.* 1. enérgicamente, vigorosamente. 2. violentamente. 3. fuertemente, mucho. 4. intensamente. 5. firmemente. 6. estrechamente. 7. con dificultad, penosamente. 8. severamente. 9. cerca, próximo. 10. **h. by,** muy cerca, a la mano; **h. on the heels of,** pisándole los talones a; **h. upon,** muy de cerca; **to be h. hit,** estar muy atribulado; estar severamente afectado, sufrir serias dificultades; **to be h. put to it,** estar en apuros; **to hold on h.,** agarrarse firmemente; **to run (someone) h.,** perseguir de cerca (a alguien); **to take it h.,** quedar muy acongojado, tomar algo muy en serio.

hard alee, (mar.) a orza todo.

hard aport, (mar.) a babor todo.
hardback ['hɑrd,bæk, B 'hɑd-] *s.* libro encuadernado.
hardball [-,bɔl] *s.* béisbol; **to play h.,** ser implacable, ser despiadado.
hard-bitten [-'bɪtən] *a.* recio, tenaz; aguerrido.
hard-boiled [-'bɔɪld] *a.* 1. duro, muy cocido (huevo). 2. inflexible, tenaz. 3. insensible, impasible, empedernido. 4. testarudo.
hard cash, moneda metálica, dinero contante; **to pay in h.,** pagar en metálico.
hard cider, sidra fermentada, sidra seca.
hard clam, (zool.) almeja redonda.
hard coal, carbón de antracita.
hard core, (fig.) núcleo duro (de un partido político, movimiento, etc.).
hard-core [-'kɔr, B -'kɔ] *a.* 1. incondicional, a ultranza del núcleo duro (de un partido político, movimiento, etc.). 2. patente, evidente; absoluto.
hard-core criminal, malhechor empedernido.
hard-core pornography, pornografía dura, explícito o crudo.
hard-core resistance, resistencia empedernida.
hard court, (tenis) cancha de ladrillo, cancha de arcilla.
hardcover [-'kʌvər] *s.* libro encuadernado.
hard currency, moneda firme.
hard disk, (comput.) disco duro, disco rígido.
hard-drawn [-'drɔn] *a.* estirado en frío (alambre).
harden ['hɑrdən, B 'hɑd-] *v.t.* 1. endurecer, hacer firme; solidificar; templar. 2. (fig.) endurecer, hacer insensible. 3. (fig.) robustecer, fortalecer; curtir (tropas, etc.). —*v.i.* 1. endurecerse, solidificarse. 2. (fig.) endurecerse, empedernirse; volverse duro de corazón. 3. (com.) estabilizarse, subir (precio, mercado).
hardener [-ər, B -ə] *s.* endurecedor (de pintura, barniz, cemento, etc.).
hardening [-ɪŋ] *s.* endurecimiento.
hard facts, hechos incontestables.
hard-featured ['hɑrd'fitʃərd, B 'hɑd'fitʃəd] *a.* de facciones duras, desagradables o innobles.
hard feelings, resentimiento, inquina.
hardfisted [-'fɪstəd] *a.* 1. de manos duras y callosas; fuerte, recio. 2. tacaño, manicorto, agarrado, cicatero.
hardfistedness [-nəs] *s.* tacañería.
hard-fought [-'fɔt] *a.* arduamente disputado, reñido, cruento.
hard goods, mercancía pesada (muebles, maquinaria, etc.).
hardhanded [-'hændəd] *a.* 1. de manos duras y callosas. 2. opresivo, tiránico, despótico.
hard hat, yelmo protector, hecho de metal o plástico duro, que usan los operarios de construcciones, mineros, etc.
hard-hat ['hɑrd,hæt, B 'hɑd-] *s.* (fam.) operario de construcciones. —*a.* relativo a obras de construcción o demolición; (jer., E.U.) contra los movimientos o grupos liberales (como los de intelectuales y estudiantes).
hardhead [-,hɛd] *s.* 1. porfiado, testarudo. 2. bodoque, estúpido. 3. (ict.) coto.
hardheaded [-'hɛdəd] *a.* 1. terco, obstinado, testarudo, tenaz. 2. práctico, realista; astuto.
hardheadedness [-nəs] *s.* terquedad, obstinación, testarudez; sagacidad.
hardhearted [-'hɑrtəd, B -'hɑt-] *a.* frío, indiferente, insensible; inclemente, despiadado, sin compasión.
hardheartedly [-lɪ] *adv.* indiferentemente; cruelmente, despiadadamente.
hardheartedness [-nəs] *s.* indiferencia; crueldad, inclemencia.
hardihood ['hɑrdɪ,hʊd, B 'hɑd-] *s.* 1. osadía, temeridad, audacia, intrepidez. 2. descaro, desvergüenza, impudencia. 3. robustez, vigor.
hardily [-əlɪ] *adv.* 1. osadamente, temerariamente, audazmente. 2. fuertemente, robustamente, de manera resistente.
hardiness [-ɪnəs] *s.* 1. robustez, resistencia, aguante. 2. audacia, osadía, atrevimiento; intrepidez.
hard labor, (der.) trabajos forzados.
hard-laid [-'leɪd] *a.* muy retorcido, de tejido apretado (cuerdas, tela, etc.).
hard landing, aterrizaje por impacto de un vehículo espacial que no está equipado para aterrizar lentamente.
hard liner, (pol.) partidario, político de línea dura.
hard liquor, licor de gran contenido alcohólico, esp. wiski, a diferencia de cerveza o vino.
hard luck, mala suerte.
hardly ['hɑrdlɪ, B 'hɑd-] *adv.* 1. difícilmente, a duras penas, con dificultad. 2. escasamente, apenas, casi no. 3. severamente, rigurosamente, ásperamente.
hard maple, (bot.) arce de azúcar.
hard-mouthed [-'maʊðd] *a.* que no responde al freno (caballo).
hardness [-nəs] *s.* 1. dureza, endurecimiento; firmeza, solidez. 2. (fig.) dureza, severidad, rigor.
hardness scale, (min.) escala de dureza.
hard-nosed ['hɑrd'noʊzd] *a.* duro, cabezón, terco.
hard of hearing, duro de oído.
hard-on [-,ɔn, -,ɑn, B -,ɔn] *s.* (vulg.) erección del pene; **to have a h.,** tenerla dura, tenerla parada, estar empalmado.
hard palate, (anat.) paladar duro, paladar óseo.
hardpan [-,pæn] *s.* (E.U.) 1. suelo resistente; capa dura debajo de terreno blando. 2. base sólida, parte firme o fundamental.
hard pressed, 1. apremiado, acosado. 2. en dificultades financieras. 3. **h. p. for money,** apurado de dinero.
hard rubber, ebonita, vulcanita, caucho endurecido, goma dura.
hards [hɑrdz, B hɑdz] *s. pl.* desechos del cáñamo o lino, estopa.
hard sauce, salsa espesa de repostería (elaborada con mantequilla, harina y mucha azúcar).
hard sell, actitud persistente y agresiva de un vendedor, método agresivo de vender.
hard-set ['hɑrd'sɛt, B 'hɑd-] *a.* 1. apremiado, acosado, apurado. 2. resuelto, firme, inflexible; obstinado.
hard-shell [-,ʃɛl] **hard-shelled** [-,ʃɛld] *a.* 1. con caparazón. 2. (fam., E.U.) intransigente, obstinado, inflexible.
hard-shell clam, almeja de concha muy dura que abunda en la costa occidental de N. América.
hard-shell crab, cangrejo de cáscara dura (antes de la muda), cangrejo de mar comestible, de caparazón duro.
hardship [-,ʃɪp] *s.* 1. penuria, privación. 2. fatiga, penas, trabajo arduo.
hard solder, soldadura fuerte, soldadura de alto punto de fusión.
hard-spun [-'spʌn] *a.* (tej.) firmemente enrollado (díc. del hilado).
hardstand [-,stænd] *s.* (aer.) terreno afirmado (para estacionamiento de aviones).
hard-surface [-'sɜrfəs, B '-sɜfɪs] *v.t.* afirmar, allanar (terreno, camino).
hardtack [-,tæk] *s.* galleta de munición o de marinero; sequete.
hard times, tiempos malos; vacas flacas; depresión económica.
hardtop ['hɑrd,tɑp, B 'hɑd,tɔp] *s.* automóvil que se asemeja a un convertible, pero de capota rígida.
hard-to-please [-tə'pliz] *a.* difícil de complacer, de mal contento.
hard up, (fam.) sin dinero o recursos; alcanzado, apurado.
hardware [-,wɛr, B -,wɛə] *s.* 1. quincalla, quincallería, cerrajería, ferretería. 2. (tec.) computadora utilizada para controlar vehículos espaciales, proceso de datos, etc.; equipo y accesorios de una computadora. 3. (fam.) armas.
hardware store, quincallería, ferretería.
hard water, agua cruda, agua gorda.
hard wheat, (bot.) trigo duro, trigo durillo, trigo fanfarrón, trigo moro, trigo moruno.
hard-won [-'wʌn] *a.* ganado a costa de mucho esfuerzo, ganado a pulso; logrado o conseguido con mucha dificultad.
hardwood [-,wʊd] *s.* 1. madera dura, madera brava. 2. árbol de madera dura. —*a.* de madera dura.
hard words, palabras mayores o injuriosas.
hard worker, trabajador muy constante.
hard-working [-'wɜrkɪŋ, B -'wɜk-] *a.* trabajador, industrioso.
hardy ['hɑrdɪ, B 'hɑdɪ] *a.* (HARDIER; HARDIEST) 1. fuerte, resistente, robusto. 2. valiente, bravo. 3. atrevido, audaz, temerario. 4. (agr.) resistente. —*s.* (herrería) cincel.
hare [hɛr, B hɛə] *s.* liebre; **mad as a March h.,** loco de remate, más loco que una cabra; **to run with the h. and hunt with the hounds,** ponerle una vela a Dios y otra al diablo, jugar con dos barajas; **to start a hare,** andarse por las ramas (en una discusión, etc.). —*v.i.* (pr. G.B.) correr.
hare and hounds, liebre y sabuesos.
harebell ['hɛr,bel, B 'hɛə,-] *s.* (bot.) 1. campánula, campanilla de hojas redondas. 2. jacinto de Escocia.
harebrained [-,breɪnd] *a.* atolondrado, tolondro, descuidado; estúpido.
harefoot [-,fʊt] *s.* pie de liebre; (poét.) corredor ágil.
harehound [-,haʊnd] *s.* perro lebrero, galgo, lebrel.
harelip [-'lɪp] *s.* labio leporino, labio hendido.
harelipped [-'lɪpt] *a.* labihendido, boquiconejuno, de labio leporino.
harem ['hɛrəm, 'hær-, B 'hɛər-] *s.* harén, harem, serrallo.
hare's ear, (bot.) perfoliada, perfoliata.
hare's foot, (bot.) pie de liebre, perfoliada.
haricot ['hærɪ,koʊ] *s.* 1. (bot.) judía, judía verde, habichuela. 2. guisado (esp. de carnero o de cordero).
hark [hɑrk, B hɑk] *v.i.* 1. atender, escuchar. 2. **h. back,** volver sobre la pista; volver al asunto; volver, retroceder, remontar. —*v.t.* escuchar, atender a.
harken, *var. de* **hearken.**
harl [hɑrl, B hɑl] *s.* hebra, filamento (esp. de lino o cáñamo).
Harlequin ['hɑrlɪkwən, B 'hɑlɪ-] *s.* 1. arlequín; payaso. 2. **h.,** diseño abigarrado. —*a.* arlequinesco; abigarrado; en dibujo a rombos de colores.
harlequinade [,hɑrlɪkwə'neɪd, B ,hɑlɪ-] *s.* arlequinada; payasada.
harlot ['hɑrlət, B 'hɑlət] *s.* ramera, prostituta. —*a.* meretricio, prostituido.
harlotry [-rɪ] *s.* 1. prostitución. 2. prostitutas (colectivamente).
harm [hɑrm, B hɑm] *s.* daño, perjuicio, mal; **out of h.'s way,** libre de peligro. —*v.t.* dañar, herir; perjudicar, estropear.

harmattan [ˌharmə'tæn, B hɑ'mætən] *s.* harmatán, terral, viento que azota el corazón de África en invierno.
harmful ['hɑrmfəl, B 'hɑm-] *a.* dañino, peligroso; perjudicial, nocivo.
harmfully [-ɪ] *adv.* perjudicialmente.
harmfulness [-nəs] *s.* calidad de dañino, pernicioso, peligroso.
harmless ['hɑrmləs, B 'hɑm-] *a.* inocente, sencillo, inofensivo, inocuo.
harmlessly [-lɪ] *adv.* inocuamente, inocentemente, sin intención de hacer daño.
harmlessness [-nəs] *s.* inocencia, inocuidad.
harmonic [hɑr'mɑnɪk, B hɑ'mɔn-] *a.* 1. (mús.) armónico. 2. (fig.) armónico, concordante. 3. (mat.) armónico, ej., *h. progression,* progresión armónica. —*s.* 1. (mús.) armónico. 2. (*pl.*) (rad., electrón.) armónicas, frecuencias armónicas.
harmonica [-ɪkə] *s.* (mús.) armónica, harmónica.
harmonically [-ɪkəlɪ] *adv.* armónicamente.
harmonic distortion, (rad., electrón.) distorsión armónica.
harmonic mean, (mat.) media armónica.
harmonicon [-ɪkən] *s.* (mús.) armonicón, organillo.
harmonics [hɑr'mɑnɪks, B hɑ'mɔn-] *s. pl.* (*sing. o pl. en constr.*) armonía, teoría física de los sonidos musicales.
harmonious [-'moʊnɪəs] *a.* armonioso.
harmoniously [-lɪ] *adv.* armoniosamente.
harmoniousness [-nəs] *s.* calidad de lo armonioso.
harmonist ['hɑrmənəst, B 'hɑmə-] *s.* 1. (mús.) armonista. 2. (bíbl.) experto en armonística.
harmonium [hɑr'moʊnɪəm, B hɑ'-] *s.* (mús.) armonio.
harmonization [ˌhɑrmənə'zeɪʃən, B 'hɑmənaɪ-] *s.* (mús.) armonización.
harmonize ['hɑrməˌnaɪz, B 'hɑmə-] *v.i.* armonizar, estar en armonía; compaginar, congeniar. —*v.t.* 1. armonizar, poner de acuerdo, concertar. 2. (mús.) armonizar (una melodía).
harmonizer [-ər, B -ə] *s.* (mús.) armonista.
harmony ['hɑrmənɪ, B 'hɑmə-] *s.* 1. (mús.) armonía, consonancia. 2. (fig.) armonía, concordancia (de opiniones, hechos, etc.). 3. armonística (concordancia de los evangelios).
harmotome ['hɑrməˌtoʊm, B 'hɑmə-] *s.* (min.) harmotoma.
harness ['hɑrnəs, B 'hɑnɪs] *s.* 1. arneses, arreos, guarniciones, montura. 2. equipo, enseres. 3. (tej.) remesa. 4. **in h.,** en servicio, trabajando; en pareja; **to die in h.,** morir al pie del cañón; **to get back in** (o **into**) **h.,** volver al trabajo, volver a la rutina. —*v.t.* 1. enjaezar, poner guarniciones a (una caballería). 2. (fig.) utilizar, aprovechar (fuerzas o recursos naturales). 3. (ant.) armar con un arnés.
harness cask, (mar.) barril para guardar la cecina.
harness hitch, as de guía (tipo de nudo marino).
harness horse, caballo de tiro.
harness maker, guarnicionero.
harness race, carrera de caballos de paso de andadura o trotadores enjaezados a un calesín.
harp [hɑrp, B hɑp] *s.* 1. (mús.) arpa. 2. **H.,** (astr.) Lira. —*v.i.* 1. tocar o tañer el arpa. 2. **h. on,** repetir, machacar, porfiar, insistir en.
harpins ['hɑrpɪnz, B 'hɑpɪnz] **harpings** [-pɪŋz] *s.* (mar.) cucharro.
harpist [-pəst] *s.* (mús.) arpista.
harpoon [hɑr'pun, B hɑ'-] *s.* arpón, fisga.
harpooner [-ər, B -ə] *s.* arponero, fisgador.
harpoon gun, cañón lanzaarpones.
harpsichord ['hɑrpsɪˌkɔrd, B 'hɑpsɪˌkɔd] *s.* (mús.) clavicordio, clave.
harpy ['hɑrpɪ, B 'hɑpɪ] *s.* (*pl.* HARPIES) 1. **H.,** (mitol.) arpía (ave fabulosa medio mujer, medio ave de rapiña). 2. (fig.) arpía.
harpy eagle, (orn.) arpía, águila real.
harquebus ['hɑrkwɪbəs, B 'hɑkwɪ-] *s.* (*pl.* HARQUEBUSES) arcabuz.
harquebusier [ˌhɑrkwɪbə'sɪr, B ˌhɑkwɪbə'sɪə] *s.* arcabucero.
harridan ['hærədən] *s.* vieja regañona, bruja.
harrier ['hærɪər, B -ə] *s.* 1. asolador, devastador. 2. (orn.) especie de halcón. 3. (zool.) perro lebrero, lebrel pequeño (adiestrado para cazar liebres). 4. corredor a campo traviesa.
harrier eagle, (orn.) atahorma, águila culebrera.
harrow ['hæroʊ] *s.* (maq.) grada, rastro, rastra, escarificador; **under the h.,** (fig.) atormentado, en el potro de tormentos. —*v.t.* 1. (agr.) gradar, rastrear, escarificar. 2. (fig.) inquietar, perturbar, atormentar.
harrowing [-ɪŋ] *a.* aflictivo, inquietante, atormentador; horripilante, desgarrador; **a h. experience,** una experiencia asoladora.
harry ['hærɪ] *v.t.* (*pret., p.p.* HARRIED; *p.pr.* HARRYING) 1. saquear, pillar, despojar, robar, expoliar; asolar. 2. perseguir, hostilizar, acosar; molestar, atormentar.
harsh [hɑrʃ, B hɑʃ] *a.* 1. áspero (superficie, licor), bronco, áspero (sonido, voz); acerbo, avinagrado. 2. chillón (color). 3. cruel, duro, severo (semblante, medidas, etc.).
harshen ['hɑrʃən, B 'hɑʃ-] *v.t.* hacer áspero; endurecer.
harshly [-lɪ] *adv.* 1. ásperamente. 2. desagradablemente, desapaciblemente. 3. cruelmente, severamente.
harshness [-nəs] *s.* 1. aspereza. 2. crueldad, rigor, severidad.
hart [hɑrt, B hɑt] *s.* (*pl.* HARTS O HART) (zool.) venado, ciervo, esp. de más de cinco años.
hartal [hɑr'tɑl, B 'hɑtɑl] *s.* en la India, cierre del comercio (esp. en señal de protesta).
hartebeest ['hɑrtəˌbist, B 'hɑt-] *s.* (zool.) caama, hartebeest, antílope de Sud-África.
hartshorn ['hɑrtsˌhɔrn, B 'hɑtsˌhɔn] *s.* 1. (bot.) cuerno de ciervo, estrellamar, hierba estrella. 2. (pr. dial.) amoníaco; carbonato amoníaco.
hartshorn plantain, (bot.) cuerno de ciervo, estrellamar, hierba estrella.
hart's tongue, (bot.) lengua cerval, lengua cervina, lengua de ciervo.
harum-scarum ['hɛrəm'skɛrəm, B 'hɛərəm'skɛər-] *a.* atolondrado, alocado, irresponsable. —*adv.* alocadamente; a troche y moche.
haruspex [hə'rʌsˌpɛks] *s.* (*pl.* HARUSPICES [-pəˌsiz]) (hist.) arúspice.
haruspicy [-pəsɪ] *s.* (hist.) aruspicina.
Harvardian [hɑr'vɑrdɪən, B hɑ'vɑd-] *a.* de Harvard. —*s.* estudiante (de la universidad) de Harvard.
harvest ['hɑrvəst, B 'hɑvɪst] *s.* 1. cosecha, recolección, agosto, siega. 2. cosecha, siega, fruto, producto. 3. (fig.) fruto, recompensa (de alguna acción o trabajo). —*v.t.* 1. recolectar (la cosecha). 2. (fig.) cosechar, recoger (el fruto de alguna acción o trabajo). —*v.i.* cosechar, segar, recolectar.
harvest bug, h. tick, (ento.) nigua, pique; garrapata; ácaro.
harvester [-ər, B -ə] *s.* 1. cosechero, segador. 2. cosechadora, segadora, máquina segadora.
harvester-thresher [-'θrɛʃər, B -ə] *s.* (maq.) segadora trilladora.
harvest festival, fiesta de la cosecha.
harvest fly, (ento.) cigarra, chicharra, cicada.
harvest home, 1. cosecha, recolección. 2. fiesta de segadores. 3. canción de segadores.
harvestman ['hɑrvəstmən, B 'hɑvɪstmæn] *s.* 1. cosechero, segador. 2. (ento.) segador, falangio.
harvest moon, luna llena, luna otoñal.
harvest mouse, ratón de campo.
harvest time, mies, tiempo de la siega.
Harveyize ['hɑrvɪˌaɪz, B 'hɑvɪ-] *v.t.* templar o endurecer (el acero, esp. el blindaje).
has [hæz, həz] *tercera pers. sing. pres. indic. de* **have.**
has-been ['hæzˌbɪn, B -ˌbin] *s.* (fam.) persona o cosa pasada de moda o de la que nadie se acuerda; persona venida a menos.
hash [hæʃ] *v.t.* 1. picar, desmenuzar. 2. embrollar, hacer un lío o revoltijo de. 3. **h. out,** discutir a fondo (un tema, etc.); **h. over,** (jer.) discutir, volver a discutir; **h. up,** enredar, embrollar. —*s.* 1. picadillo, salpicón, gigote. 2. mezcla, mezcolanza, revoltillo, lío, embrollo. 3. (gen. **old h.**) cosa vieja en nueva forma. 4. **to make a h. of,** estropear, confundir, embrollar, arruinar.
hash browns, (cul.) papas y cebolla doradas en la sartén.
hasheesh ['hæʃiʃ] *var. de* **hashish.**
hash-house, hashhouse ['hæʃˌhaʊs] *s.* (jer.) fonda, figón; restaurante de media caña.
Hashimite Kingdgom of Jordan ['hæʃəˌmaɪt-] Reino Hachemita de Jordania.
hashish ['hæʃˌiʃ, -ɪʃ] *s.* hachís, composición extraída de cierta variedad de cáñamo, mezclada con otras substancias aromáticas, que se usa como narcótico.
hash mark, (jer., mil.) galón (del uniforme).
hash-slinger, hashslinger ['hæʃˌslɪŋər, B -ə] *s.* (jer.) camarero, mozo (de restaurante de mala muerte).
Hasidism ['hæsəˌdɪzəm] *s.* (relig.) hasidismo, jasidismo (cierta secta y filosofía hebreas).
haslet ['hæslət, B 'heɪz-] *s.* asaduras o menudencias, esp. del cerdo.
hasp [hæsp, B hɑsp] *s.* aldaba de candado, broche. —*v.t.* cerrar con aldaba de candado, abrochar.
hassle ['hæsəl] *s.* 1. pugna o forcejeo; lío, confusión, barullo. 2. pleito, querella, reyerta, disputa.
hassock ['hæsək] *s.* 1. manojo de juncos; montecillo de hierbas o juncos. 2. almohadón o colchoncillo para apoyar los pies; colchoncillo para arrodillarse.
hast [hæst, həst] (ant.) *segunda pers. sing. pres. indic. de* **have.**
hastate ['hæsˌteɪt] *a.* (bot.) hastado (díc. de las hojas).
haste [heɪst] *s.* 1. prisa, presteza, celeridad. 2. precipitación, atolondramiento, arrebato. 3. urgencia. 4. **in h.,** de prisa; **more h. less speed,** despacio se va lejos, quien más corre menos vuela; **to make h.,** darse prisa. —*v.i.* (lit., dial.) apresurarse, darse prisa, afanarse.
hasten ['heɪsən] *v.t.* 1. apresurar, acelerar, apremiar; apretar (el paso). 2. precipitar. —*v.i.* apresurarse, darse prisa, apretar el paso.
hastily ['heɪstəlɪ] *adv.* apresuradamente, precipitadamente, de carrera, a la ligera.
hastiness [-tɪnəs] *s.* prisa, apuro, precipitación.
hasty [-tɪ] *a.* 1. apresurado. 2. precipitado, atropellado. 3. atolondrado, impaciente.
hasty pudding, (E.U.) gachas de harina de maíz; (G.B.) papilla, gachas de avena.
hat [hæt] *s.* 1. sombrero. 2. capelo, dignidad de cardenal. 3. **as black as my h.,** todo negro; **h. in hand,** humildemente, servilmente; **my h.!**

¡mentira, no lo creo!; **to do the h. trick,** (criquet) poner fuera de juego a tres jugadores consecutivos; (rugby, fútbol) marcar tres goles consecutivos (el mismo jugador); **to keep under one's h.,** callar, no divulgar; no decir nada; **to pass the h.,** hacer una colecta, solicitar donativos; **to put on one's h.,** ponerse el sombrero; **to take one's h. off to,** saludar, (fig.) felicitar; **to talk through one's h.,** disparatar, decir disparates, macanear (Amer.); **to throw** (o **toss**) **one's h. in the ring,** (fam.) anunciar uno su entrada en una contienda o debate. —*v.t.* (*pret., p.p.* HATTED; *p.pr.* HATTING) cubrir con sombrero.

hatband [ˈhætˌbænd] *s.* cinta del sombrero.

hatbox [-ˌbɑks, B -ˌbɔks] *s.* sombrerera, caja de sombreros.

hatch [hætʃ] *s.* 1. media puerta, compuerta. 2. escotillón, trampa. 3. (mar.) cuartel, tapadero de las escotillas. 4. (mar.) escotilla. 5. compuerta, esclusa. 6. **under hatches,** (mar.) bajo cubierta; (fig.) oculto, fuera de la vista; **down the h.!** (jer.) ¡salud! (brindis).

hatch, *v.t.* 1. empollar, incubar; sacar (pollos) del cascarón; criar (pollos). 2. (fig.) idear, maquinar, tramar, fraguar, urdir. —*v.i.* 1. empollarse, salir del cascarón. 2. (fig.) formarse, madurar. —*s.* 1. incubación; salida del cascarón. 2. cría, nidada, pollada.

hatch, (arte) *v.t.* plumear, sombrear. —*s.* plumeado, línea de sombreado.

hatchel [ˈhætʃəl] *s.* rastrillo (para limpiar cáñamo y lino). —*v.t.* (*pret., p.p.* HATCHELED O HATCHELLED; *p.pr.* HATCHELING O HATCHELLING) rastrillar (lino, cáñamo).

hatcher [ˈhætʃər, B -ə] *s.* 1. incubadora. 2. autor, maquinador, tramador (de planes, secretos, etc.).

hatchery [ˈhætʃərɪ] *s.* (*pl.* HATCHERIES) criadero (esp. de peces y aves de corral); incubadora, vivero.

hatchet [ˈhætʃət] *s.* 1. hachuela, hacheta, destral. 2. hacha bélica (de los pieles rojas). 3. **to bury the h.,** envainar la espada, hacer la paz; **to dig up the h.,** hacer la guerra.

hatchet face, cara de cuchillo, cara enjuta.

hatchet-faced [-ˌfeɪst] *a.* de facciones enjutas o delgadas.

hatchet job, (fam.) ataque malicioso y prejuzgado sobre el carácter o actividades de una persona, institución, etc.

hatchet man, (fam.) 1. asesino profesional, asesino a sueldo. 2. persona contratada por un superior o jefe para llevar a cabo tareas desagradables o inescrupulosas.

hatching [ˈhætʃɪŋ] *s.* (arte) sombreado, plumeado.

hatchling [-lɪŋ] *s.* pajarito recién salido del cascarón.

hatchment [-mənt] *s.* (her.) escudo de armas; panel con las armas de un caballero fallecido.

hatchway [-ˌweɪ] *s.* 1. escotillón; pasaje o escalera al sótano. 2. (mar.) escotilla.

hate [heɪt] *v.t.* 1. odiar. 2. aborrecer, detestar, abominar. 3. ser muy ingrato a, ej., *I h. to tell you,* me es muy ingrato decirle. —*v.i.* sentir odio. —*s.* odio, aborrecimiento; objeto de odio o de aversión.

hateable [ˈheɪtəbəl] *a.* que merece odiarse, detestarse, abominarse.

hateful [-fəl] *a.* 1. odioso, aborrecible, detestable, abominable. 2. maligno, malévolo; rencoroso.

hatefully [-fəlɪ] *adv.* odiosamente, aborreciblemente, detestablemente.

hatefulness [-fəlnəs] *s.* odiosidad.

hate monger, propagandista o incitador de prejuicios u odio, esp. entre grupos minoritarios.

hath [hæθ, həθ] (ant.) *tercera pers. sing. pres. indic. de* **have.**

Hathoric [hæˈθɔrɪk, B hə-] *a.* (arq.) hatórico (columna).

hatpin [ˈhætˌpɪn] *s.* agujón, alfiler de sombrero.

hatrack [-ˌræk] *s.* percha (de pared) para sombreros, cuelgacapas.

hatred [ˈheɪtrəd] *s.* odio, aborrecimiento, mala voluntad, aversión, enemistad, execración.

hat-stand [ˈhætˌstænd] *s.* percha de pie o pedestal (para sombreros).

hatter [ˈhætər, B -ə] *s.* sombrerero; **mad as a h.,** loco de atar, loco de remate.

hauberk [ˈhɔbərk, B -bɜk] *s.* (arm.) cota, camisote, plaquín.

haugh [hɔ] *s.* (esco.) prado a la vera de un río.

haughtily [ˈhɔtəlɪ] *adv.* altivamente, desdeñosamente, presuntuosamente.

haughtiness [-ɪnəs] *s.* altanería, altivez, presunción, arrogancia, desdén.

haughty [-ɪ] *a.* (HAUGHTIER; HAUGHTIEST) 1. altanero, altivo, presuntuoso, arrogante, desdeñoso. 2. (ant.) noble, exaltado.

haul [hɔl] *v.t.* 1. tirar de, halar; arrastrar; acarrear, transportar. 2. (mar.) virar (esp. para navegar hacia el viento). 3. **h. down one's colors,** (fig.) arriar la bandera; **h. in,** (jer.) detener, arrestar; **h. (one) over the coals,** (fig.) dar cuenta a (alguien). —*v.i.* 1. (con *at, upon*) dar un tiro (a), tirar (de). 2. (gen. *h. around*) cambiar de dirección (ej., el viento). 3. (mar.) virar. 4. **h. on the wind, h. to the wind, h. up,** (mar.) ceñir el viento, abarloar, virar para navegar ciñendo. —*s.* 1. tirón, estirón. 2. redada. 3. botín, presa; ganancia. 4. recorrido, trayecto. 5. arrastre, transporte. 6. carga, cargamento.

haulage [ˈhɔlɪdʒ] *s.* 1. acarreo, conducción, transporte; arrastre. 2. costo o gastos de acarreo, esp. (f.c.) costo de transporte (que pagan los vagones de una línea férrea por usar la vía de otra).

hauler [-ər, B -ə] *s.* 1. acarreador, transportador, conductor. 2. (G.B., min.) amainador.

haulm [hɔm] *s.* 1. tallo o caña (de planta). 2. paja, rastrojo.

haunch [hɔntʃ, hɑntʃ, B hɔntʃ] *s.* 1. cadera, anca, grupa; p. ext. (*pl.*) cuartos traseros. 2. pierna, pernil (de carnero, venado, cabrito). 3. (arq.) riñón de una bóveda.

haunch bone, cuadril (de cuadrúpedos).

haunt [hɔnt, hɑnt, B hɔnt] *v.t.* 1. frecuentar; rondar. 2. aparecerse en, vagar por (apl. a aparecidos y fantasmas). 3. perseguir, obsesionar (una idea a una persona). —*v.i.* 1. deambular, vagar. 2. persistir, quedarse. 3. aparecerse (fantasma). —*s.* 1. guarida, nidal, querencia, lugar predilecto. 2. [hænt] (dial.) fantasma, aparecido.

haunted [ˈhɔntəd, ˈhɑn-, B ˈhɔn-] *a.* 1. obsesionado, perturbado; inquieto, perseguido. 2. visitado por fantasmas (casa vieja, paraje solitario).

haunted house, casa de duendes.

haunting [-ɪŋ] *a.* 1. persistente, obsesionante. 2. inquietante, perturbador.

hauntingly [-lɪ] *adv.* persistentemente.

hausen [ˈhɔzən] *s.* (ict.) beluga, esturión blanco.

haustellum [hɔˈstɛləm] *s.* (*pl.* HAUSTELLA [-ə]) (ento.) trompa o sifón (de insectos).

haustorium [hɔˈstɔrɪəm] *s.* (*pl.* HAUSTORIA [-ɪə]) (bot.) haustorio.

hautbois, hautboy [ˈhoʊˌbɔɪ, ˈoʊ-] *s.* (*pl.* HAUTBOIS, HAUTBOYS) (mús.) oboe.

hauteur [hɔˈtɜr, hoʊ-, B oʊˈtɜ] *s.* (fr.) arrogancia, altivez, altanería; soberbia, orgullo.

Havana [həˈvænə] *s.* La Habana, capital de la isla de Cuba; **H. cigar,** puro habano, tabaco fino.

Havanan [-ˈvænən] *a., s.* habanero.

Havanese [ˌhævəˈniz] *a., s.* habanero.

have [hæv, həv] *v.t.* (*pret., p.p.* HAD [hæd, həd] *p.pr.* HAVING) 1. tener; poseer, ser dueño de. 2. (*seguido de infinitivo*) tener que, deber, haber de, ej., *he had to leave,* tuvo que salir. 3. parir, alumbrar; engendrar. 4. retener, conservar (en la memoria), tener (en la mente). 5. ejecutar, hacer, efectuar, poner en obra, ej., *h. your secretary call me,* haga que me llame su secretaria. 6. tener, ejercer, practicar (ej., la paciencia). 7. sostener, afirmar, asegurar. 8. obtener, adquirir. 9. saber (un idioma, etc.). 10. tolerar, permitir, ej., *I will not h. you say such things,* no toleraré que Ud. diga tales cosas. 11. causar, hacer, efectuar, ej., *I had him dismissed,* lo hice despedir. 12. tomar (alimentos), comer, ej., *I had a drink,* tomé un trago; *h. lunch,* almorzar. 13. gozar de, sufrir de (una causa externa). 14. (vulg.) (*gen. en pret. o futuro*) tener relaciones sexuales con. 15. (*v. aux.*) haber, ej., *I. h. worked,* he trabajado; *I shall h. eaten,* habré comido. 16. **had as soon (do),** preferiría (hacer); **had as well (do),** mejor sería que (haga); **h. a drink,** tomar o echar un trago; **h. at heart,** cuidar bien (intereses, etc. de alguien); **h. a try,** intentar; **h. a word with,** discutir brevemente, hablar unas palabras con; **h. done,** terminar, acabar; **h. (someone) in,** invitar, hacer entrar, dar alojamiento (a alguien); **h. in hand,** tener entre manos, estar ocupado con; **h. it,** ganar; acertar, dar con la solución; recibir (golpes, castigo); **h. it in for,** tenérselas juradas a; tenerle ganas a; **h. it in one,** ser capaz uno, tener capacidad uno (para); **h. it out (with),** poner las cosas en claro (a), cantarlas claras (a), habérselas (con); **h. it your own way,** haga Ud. lo que quiera, proceda como guste; **h. (something) made,** mandar hacer (algo); **h. no doubt,** no tener duda; **h. nothing on (someone),** no aventajar en nada (a alguien); no tener pruebas contra (alguien); **h. on,** llevar puesto (traje, vestido); **h. oneself,** gozar de, aprovecharse de; **h. to do with,** tener que ver con, tratar de, versar sobre; **he had his leg broken,** le rompieron la pierna; **he had me there,** me tenía vencido; **he has had it,** (jer.) (él) no aguanta más; **I had better do it myself,** mejor sería que lo hiciera yo mismo; **I had rather do it myself,** preferiría hacerlo yo mismo; **rumor has it (that),** se dice (que); **to be had,** obtenible, disponible; **to let (someone) h. it,** (jer.) golpear (a alguien); dispararle (a alguien), matar (a alguien); **you h. been had,** (jer.) te engañaron, te embaucaron.

havelock [ˈhævˌlɑk, -lək, B -ˌlɔk] *s.* cogotera.

haven [ˈheɪvən] *s.* 1. puerto, fondeadero, abra. 2. abrigo, asilo, refugio. —*v.t.* asilar, abrigar, dar abrigo o asilo a.

have-not [ˈhævˌnɑt, B -ˌnɔt] *s.* (fam.) pobre, desposeído (individuo, grupo o nación); **the haves and the have-nots,** los ricos y los pobres.

haven't [ˈhævənt] *contr. de* **have not.**

haversack [ˈhævərˌsæk, B -əˌsæk] *s.* barjuleta, morral; (mil.) mochila.

havoc [ˈhævək] *s.* estrago, devastación, destrucción; **to cry h.,** (hist.) dar la orden de saqueo y degüello; (fig.) dar la alarma, poner en guardia; **to play h. among** (o **with**), causar o hacer estragos entre (o en).

haw [hɔ] *s.* tosecilla, voz inarticulada (que indica vacilación al hablar). —*v.i.* dar tosecillas; **hem and h.,** tartalear, tartamudear; andar en rodeos. —*interj.* ¡aparta! (voz de mando a las caballerías para que se vuelvan a la izquierda).

haw, *s.* 1. (bot.) espino, marzoleto, marjoleto. 2. marzoleta, marjoleta, baya del espino. 3. (zool.) membrana nictitante, esp. cuando está inflamada.

Hawaii [hə'wɑi, -'waii, B hɑ-] *s.* Hawaii, Hawai, estado de los E.U.

Hawaiian [-'wɑjən, -'waɪ-, B hɑ'waɪ-] *a., s.* hawaiano, hauaiano.

hawfinch ['hɔˌfɪntʃ] *s.* (orn.) pico gordo, piñonero.

haw-haw ['hɔ'hɔ] *s.* risa, carcajada. —*v.i.* reír, reírse en voz alta.

hawk [hɔk] *s.* 1. (orn.) halcón. 2. (const.) esparavel. 3. partidario de la guerra. —*v.i.* practicar la cetrería o halconería; remontarse y atacar (como halcón).

hawk, *v.i.* carraspear, gargajear. —*v.t.* arrancar (flema) de la garganta por carraspeo. —*s.* carraspeo, gargajeo.

hawk, *v.t.* 1. pregonar (mercancías); vender como buhonero. 2. **h. about,** difundir (noticias, etc.). —*v.i.* ser buhonero.

hawker ['hɔkər, B -ə] *s.* 1. buhonero, mercachifle, quincallero, halconero. 2. cetrero, halconero.

hawk-eyed [-ˌaɪd] *a.* de ojo avizor, de ojos de lince; perspicaz.

hawk fly, (ento.) asilo.

hawking ['hɔkɪŋ] *s.* 1. halconería. 2. cetrería.

hawkish [-ɪʃ] *a.* 1. perteneciente o parecido al halcón. 2. dícese del partidario de la guerra y el militarismo, (fig.) partidario de las guerras expansionistas; partidario del militarismo, militarista.

hawkmoth [-ˌmɔθ] *s.* (ento.) esfinge.

hawk-nosed [-ˌnoʊzd] *a.* aguileño, de nariz prominente y encorvada.

hawksbill ['hɔksˌbɪl] *s.* 1. (zool.) carey, tortuga de mar. 2. **h. pliers,** pinzas de soldador.

hawkweed ['hɔkˌwid] *s.* (bot.) vellosilla, pelosilla, oreja de ratón.

hawse [hɔz] *s.* 1. (mar.) escobén; parte de la proa en que se hallan los escobenes. 2. (mar.) distancia entre la roda y el ancla. 3. (mar.) fondeo a barbas de gato.

hawsehole ['hɔzˌhoʊl] *s.* (mar.) escobén.

hawse pipe, (mar.) cañón de escobén.

hawser ['hɔzər, B -zə] *s.* (mar.) guindaleza, cable, estacha.

hawser-laid [-ˌleɪd] *a.* (mar.) colchado en guindaleza, acalabrotado, de tres cabos.

hawthorn ['hɔˌθɔrn, B -ˌθɔn] *s.* (bot.) espino, espinera, marzoleto, marjoleto.

hay [heɪ] *s.* 1. heno. 2. **to hit the h.,** acostarse; **to make h. (out) of,** poner de cabeza, alborotar; **to make h. while the sun shines,** golpear el hierro cuando está en ascua, aprovechar la ocasión. —*v.i.* henificar, hacer heno. —*v.t.* dar heno o forraje a (caballería).

haycock ['heɪˌkɑk, B -ˌkɔk] *s.* almiar, niara, montón de heno.

hay fever, (med.) fiebre del heno.

hayfield [-ˌfild] *s.* henar.

hayfork [-ˌfɔrk, B -ˌfɔk] *s.* horca, bieldo; elevador (mecánico) de heno.

haylift [-ˌlɪft] *s.* puente aéreo que deja caer alimentos a rebaños de ganado aislados por la nieve.

hayloft [-ˌlɔft] *s.* henal, henil.

haymaker [-ˌmeɪkər, B -kə] *s.* 1. henificador. 2. (jer., boxeo) golpe violento, golpazo.

haymow [-ˌmaʊ] *s.* henil, henal, acopio de heno.

hayrack [-ˌræk] *s.* 1. armazón que se monta en un carro para transportar heno, forraje, etc. 2. pesebre, comedero.

hayrick [-ˌrɪk] *s.* almiar, niara.

hayseed [-ˌsid] *s.* 1. semilla de heno (recolectada esp. del henil). 2. tamo, trocitos de heno. 3. (jer.) palurdo, rústico, paleto, campesino.

haystack [-ˌstæk] *s.* almiar, niara; **to look for a needle in a h.,** buscar una aguja en un pajar.

hayward [-wərd, B -wəd] *s.* (hist.) funcionario encargado del cuidado de las cercas para mantener al ganado fuera de los sembradíos.

haywire [-ˌwaɪr, B -ˌwaɪə] *s.* alambre que se usa para liar pacas de heno o paja. —*a.* (jer.) 1. loco. 2. desorganizado, confuso. 3. alocado, atolondrado. 4. **to go h.,** alocarse, volverse loco; desorganizarse, confundirse.

hazan ['hɑzən, B 'hɔz-] *s.* (*pl.* HAZANIM o HAZANS) 1. cantor de sinagoga. 2. (ant.) funcionario de sinagoga.

hazard ['hæzərd, B -əd] *s.* 1. peligro, riesgo. 2. acaso, azar, albur. 3. juego de azar a los dados. 4. (tenis) servicio ganador. 5. (G.B., billar) acción de entronerar; **winning h.,** acción de entronerar la bola (deseada); **losing h.,** acción de entronerar la pinta o su propia bola. 6. (golf) obstáculo. 7. **at h.,** en juego. —*v.t.* arriesgar, aventurar; correr o tomar el riesgo de.

hazardous [-əs] *a.* peligroso, arriesgado, aventurado.

hazardously [-lɪ] *adv.* peligrosamente, arriesgadamente.

hazardousness [-nəs] *s.* azar, peligro, riesgo.

haze [heɪz] *s.* 1. neblina, calina, niebla. 2. (fig.) confusión, vaguedad, ofuscamiento (mental). —*v.t., v.i.* anublar(se), obscurecer(se), empañar(se).

haze [heɪz] *v.t.* 1. fatigar, abrumar (con trabajos pesados o innecesarios). 2. (E.U.) dar novatada a (nuevo alumno). 3. (E. de E.U.) arrear (al ganado) a caballo.

hazel ['heɪzəl] *s.* 1. (bot.) avellano. 2. palo o estaca de avellano. 3. color de la avellana. —*a.* 1. de avellano, de madera de avellano. 2. de color de avellana.

hazelnut [-ˌnʌt] *s.* avellana.

hazily ['heɪzəlɪ] *adv.* nebulosamente, confusamente, vagamente.

haziness [-zɪnəs] *s.* 1. nebulosidad, calígine, calina. 2. (fig.) vaguedad, nebulosidad, imprecisión.

hazing ['heɪzɪŋ] *s.* 1. imposición de excesivo trabajo. 2. (E.U.) novatadas, cargadas. 3. paliza, zurra.

hazy ['heɪzɪ] *a.* 1. nebuloso, brumoso, calinoso. 2. (fig.) confuso, vago, obscuro, impreciso.

H.B.M. *abrev. de* **Her (His) Britannic Majesty,** Su Majestad Británica.

H-bomb ['eɪtʃˌbɑm, B -ˌbɔm] *s.* bomba H, bomba de hidrógeno.

H.C. *abrev. de* **House of Commons,** Cámara de los Comunes.

H.C.F. *abrev. de* **highest common factor,** máximo común divisor.

he [hi, hɪ] *pron.* él. —*s.* 1. hombre, varón, macho. 2. (ú. para indicar el animal macho) ej., *h.-goat,* macho cabrío.

H.E. *abrev. de* **His Excellency,** Su Excelencia (S.E.).

He *símb. de* **helium,** helio (He).

head [hɛd] *s.* 1. cabeza, testa. 2. cabeza, inteligencia, juicio, talento, aptitud, ej., *good h. for figures,* buena cabeza para las matemáticas. 3. cabeza, persona, individuo, ej., *two dollars a* (o *per*) *h.,* dos dólares por cabeza (o persona). 4. aplomo, serenidad, ej., *he kept his h.,* se mantuvo sereno. 5. cara (de una moneda), ej., *heads or tails?* ¿cara o cruz?, ¿águila o sol? (Méx.). 6. (*ú. t. con sentido de pl.*) res(es), cabeza(s) (de ganado), ej., *eight h. of cattle,* ocho cabezas de ganado. 7. provisión, existencias, ej., *a good h. of fish,* una buena provisión de pescado. 8. cabeza, cabecera, extremo superior, ej., *h. of a bed,* cabecera de cama. 9. cabeza (de familia, empresa); jefe, director (de una organización, instituto); director de escuela. 10. posición de comando, dirección. 11. culminación (de una crisis), ej., *to come to a h.,* llegar a su culminación, culminar, llegar al punto decisivo. 12. fuente, nacimiento, origen, ej., *h. of a stream,* origen de un curso de agua. 13. asta (de venado), ej., *deer of the first h.,* venado de primera asta. 14. carga o volumen de agua (en un depósito); presión, ej., *h. of steam,* presión de vapor. 15. encabezamiento, título. 16. cabeza, punta, tope; cabeza (de un libro); (mar.) gratil (de una vela). 17. tapa, fondo (de tonel, etc.). 18. promontorio, cabo. 19. extremo delantero; puño (ej., de bastón). 20. repollo (de plantas); cabezuela (de flores). 21. cabeza (de objeto, pieza o herramienta). 22. espuma, nata (de un líquido). 23. punto de ruptura (de un absceso maduro). 24. párrafo, división (de un discurso, tratado, etc.). 25. (bot.) capítulo (inflorescencia). 26. (mús.) parche (de tambor); clavijero (de violín, etc.); cabeza (de nota musical). 27. (mec.) cabezal, portaherramientas, cabezal revólver. 28. (maq.) culata (de cilindro). 29. (min.) galería, socavón. 30. (mil.) vanguardia, punta de lanza. 31. (mar.) proa (y partes adyacentes); letrina. 32. (jer.) boca, ej., *shut your h.,* cállate la boca. 33. **a crowned h.,** una testa coronada; **at the h. of,** a la cabeza de, al frente de; **by the h., down by the h.,** (mar.) capuzando, calando de proa; **from h. to foot,** de arriba abajo, completamente; **h. of hair,** cabellera (esp. abundante); **h. on,** de frente; cabeza con cabeza; **h. over heels,** patas arriba; a troche y moche, sin orden ni concierto; **I could do it on my h.,** (jer.) lo haría con una mano atada, es facilísimo; **not to make h. or tail of,** no encontrar ni pies ni cabeza a, no entender (algo); **off one's h.,** loco, demente, insensato; **on one's h.,** de cabeza; bajo la responsabilidad (de uno), sobre la conciencia (de uno), ej., *his blood will be on your h.,* su sangre pesará sobre tu conciencia; **out of one's h.,** (fig.) de la propia imaginación de uno; fuera de sí, delirante; **over one's h.,** por encima de uno, sin respetar la autoridad de uno; fuera del alcance de uno, ej., *he talks over our heads,* habla fuera de nuestro alcance; **to be h. over heels in love,** estar locamente enamorado; **to beat (someone's) h. off,** derrotar completamente (a alguien); **to bother one's h. about,** quebrarse la cabeza con, estar preocupado por; **to bring to a h.,** provocar una crisis en, forzar el desenlace de (un asunto); **to come into one's h.,** pasarle a uno por la cabeza; **to eat one's h. off,** comer hasta reventar; **to get it into one's h. (to do),** metérsele a uno la idea de (hacer); **to get (something) through one's h.,** enseñar (algo) a uno, hacer comprender (algo) a uno; **to give (horse, etc.) his h.,** dar rienda suelta; **to go h. and shoulders into,** meterse de cabeza; **to go to one's h.,** subírsele a la cabeza; **to hang** (o **hide**) **one's h.,** caérsele a uno la cara de vergüenza; **to keep one's h.,** no perder la cabeza, controlarse; **to keep one's h. above water,** mantenerse a flote, no llegar a fracasar o sucumbir; **to laugh one's h. off,** reír a mandíbula batiente; **to lay** (o **put**) **heads together,** intercambiar ideas, colaborar; **to lose one's h.,** perder la cabeza, perder los estribos; **to make h.,** avanzar, ganar terreno; **to put (something) into someone's h.,** meterle (algo) en la cabeza a alguien, sugerir (algo) a alguien; **to put (something) out of one's h.,** dejar de pensar en, olvidar (algo); **to stand on one's h.,** ponerse uno de cabeza; **to take it into one's h.,** metérsele a uno en la cabeza; **to talk one's h. off,** abrumar (a alguien) charlando; **to turn one's h.,** subírsele a la cabeza a uno; tenerle los sesos sorbidos a uno; **two heads are better than one,** más ven cuatro ojos que dos; **won by a h.,** ganado por una cabeza (carrera de caballos). —*a.* 1. principal, fundamental, primordial. 2. superior; delantero, a la cabeza. 3. de adelante; (mar.) de proa, ej., *h. sea,* marejada de proa. —*v.t.* 1. decapitar, descabezar. 2. desmochar, despuntar. 3. proveer de una cabeza (ej., una flecha), formar la cabeza de. 4. acaudillar, encabezar (Amer.). 5. dirigir (una empresa, etc.). 6. poner a la cabeza de, encabezar (lista, etc.). 7. ir a la cabeza de, ser el primero entre, descollar o sobresalir entre. 8. dirigir, enfilar, llevar hacia. 9. cortar (olas un vapor); marchar contra (la lluvia). 10. (dep.) ir a la punta de, aventajar (competidores). 11. (fútbol) cabecear (la pelota). 12. **h. back,** hacer regresar; **h. off,** atajar; cortar el paso a; desviar. —*v.i.* 1. desarrollar o formar cabeza; repollar. 2. dirigirse, ir. 3. originarse, tener fuente u origen. 4. **h. back,** regresar, volver; **h. for** (o **toward**), dirigirse hacia.

headache ['hɛd,eɪk] *s.* 1. dolor de cabeza, jaqueca. 2. (fig.) dolor de cabeza, preocupación, problema, situación difícil, asunto molesto.

headband [-,bænd] *s.* 1. venda, cinta o faja (para la cabeza), vincha (Amer.). 2. (impr.) cabecera; cabezada (de libro).

headboard [-,bɔrd, B -,bɔd] *s.* cabecera (esp. de cama).

head canal, (hidr.) canal de aducción, canal de acceso.

headcheese [-,tʃiz] *s.* (E.U.) queso de cerdo.

head cold, resfriado, resfrío.

headdress [-,drɛs] *s.* tocado.

headed ['hɛdəd] *a.* 1. encabezado; titulado. 2. provisto de cabeza, ej., *two-h. eagle,* águila bicéfala.

header ['hɛdər, B -ə] *s.* 1. encabezador (herramienta u obrero). 2. cámara de agua, colector. 3. (fam.) salto o caída de cabeza; zambullida. 4. (carp.) brochal. 5. (agr., mec.) cosechadora (de grano). 6. (const.) tizón, ladrillo puesto de canto. 7. **to take a h.,** irse de cabeza, caer de cabeza.

header course, (const.) hilera de tizones, hilera de cabezal.

head fast, (mar.) cabo de proa.

headfirst ['hɛd'fɜrst, B -'fɜst] **headforemost** [-'fɔr,moust, B -'fɔ,-] *adv.* de cabeza; precipitadamente, de sopetón; **to plunge in h.,** lanzarse al agua de cabeza.

headframe ['hɛd,freɪm] *s.* castillete.

head gate, 1. compuerta de aguas arriba, esclusa superior. 2. compuerta de toma, compuerta de cabecera.

headgear [-,gɪr, B -,gɪə] *s.* 1. tocado o sombrero. 2. cabezada (arnés).

headhunt [-,hʌnt] *s.* 1. caza de cabezas (entre tribus primitivas). —*v.i.* cazar cabezas; (fig.) buscar talentos.

head-hunter [-ər, B -ə] *s.* cazador de cabezas; (fig.) cazatalentos, cazador de cabezas.

headhunting [-iŋ] *s.* caza de cabezas; (fig.) caza de cabezas, caza de talentos (*búsqueda de ejecutivos y personal especializado*).

headhunting agency, agencia de caza de talentos.

headily ['hɛdəlɪ] *adv.* temerariamente; violentamente; obstinadamente.

headiness [-ɪnəs] *s.* 1. precipitación, impetuosidad. 2. efecto embriagante.

heading [-ɪŋ] *s.* 1. título, encabezamiento. 2. material para tapas (de toneles, barriles, etc.). 3. (mar., aer.) orientación, rumbo. 4. (min.) galería de avance; socavón; final de un pasaje.

head lamp, farol delantero, reflector, luz de cabeza; (aut.) faro delantero.

headland ['hɛdlənd] *s.* 1. promontorio, punta, cabo. 2. tierra no arada inmediata a los setos o cercados.

headledge [-,lɛdʒ] *s.* (const. naval) contrabrazola.

headless [-ləs] *a.* 1. sin cabeza, acéfalo. 2. decapitado, degollado. 3. (fig.) acéfalo, sin jefe o director. 4. (fig.) descabezado, imprudente, tonto.

headlight [-,laɪt] *s.* 1. farol delantero, reflector, luz de cabeza. 2. (aut.) faro delantero. 3. (mar.) farol de tope.

headline [-,laɪn] *s.* (*pl.* HEADLINES) 1. cabecera, encabezamiento, titular (de periódico). 2. título, titulillo. 3. (*pl.*) sumario de noticias. 4. **to hit the headlines,** hacerse famoso, ganar fama. —*v.t.* poner título a.

headliner [-,laɪnər, B -nə] *s.* 1. redactor de titulares (de periódicos). 2. actor o ejecutante de mucho cartel.

headlock [-,lak, B -,lɔk] *s.* (lucha) llave de cabeza.

headlong [-,lɔŋ] *adv.* 1. de cabeza. 2. precipitadamente, de sopetón, a toda prisa. 3. sin pensarlo, temeraria o imprudentemente. —*a.* 1. de cabeza. 2. arrojado, temerario, precipitado. 3. (poét.) escarpado, precipitoso.

headman [-mən, -,mæn] *s.* 1. jefe, caudillo, cacique, cabecilla. 2. (raro) ejecutor, verdugo.

headmaster [-,mæstər, B -'mastə] *s.* director, rector (de un colegio).

headmastership [-,ʃɪp] *s.* dirección (de un colegio), rectorado.

headmistress [-,mɪstrəs, B -'mɪs-] *s.* directora, rectora (de un colegio).

head money, 1. capitación. 2. premio o recompensa por la captura de un proscrito.

headmost [-,moust] *a.* delantero, primero, principal.

head of state, jefe de estado.

head-on ['hɛd'ɔn, -'an, B -'ɔn] *a.* 1. de frente (esp. una colisión). 2. frontal (ataque, aspecto, etc.).

headphone [-,foun] *s.* receptor o teléfono de cabeza, audífono, auricular, casco telefónico.

headpiece [-,pis] *s.* 1. yelmo, casco, morrión, bacinete. 2. (fig.) cabeza, juicio, inteligencia, ingenio. 3. (impr.) cabecera, viñeta.

headpin [-,pɪŋ] *s.* bolo delantero (en el juego de bolos).

headquarters [-'kwɔrtərz, B -'kwɔtəz] *s. pl.* (*sing. o pl. en const.*) 1. sede, oficina central, dirección general, centro de operaciones, administración, jefatura. 2. (mil.) cuartel general.

headrace [-,reɪs] *s.* canal de alimentación o de toma, canal de llegada, saetín, caz de caída, canal de carga.

headrail [-,reɪl] *s.* 1. larguero superior (de la puerta). 2. (mar.) brazal.

headrest [-,rɛst] *s.* apoyacabezas, apoyo para la cabeza.

headroom [-,rum, -,rʊm] *s.* altura de paso altura libre franqueo superior.

headsail [-,seɪl] *s.* (mar.) foque.

headscarf [-skarf] *s.* pañuelo de cabeza.

headset [-,sɛt] *s.* (tele.) juego de audífonos o auriculares.

headship [-,ʃɪp] *s.* jefatura, dirección, mando.

headshrinker [-,ʃrɪŋkər, B -kə] *s.* (jer.) psiquiatra, psicoanalista.

headsman ['hɛdzmən] *s.* 1. verdugo, degollador. 2. (mar.) patrón de ballenero. 3. (min.) minero de filón.

head spin, (lucha) maniobra (para escapar de una media nelson) que consiste en lanzar los pies al aire y dar vuelta a la cabeza.

headspring ['hɛd,sprɪŋ] *s.* fuente, origen, manantial.

headstall [-,stɔl] *s.* ronzal, cabestro, jáquima.

head stand, parada de cabeza.

head start, ventaja inicial.

headstock [-,stak, B -,stɔk] *s.* (mec.) muñeca fija, contrapunta de torno.

headstone [-,stoun] *s.* 1. (arq.) piedra angular, clave; primera piedra. 2. piedra sepulcral; lápida mortuoria.

headstream [-,strim] *s.* arroyo que da origen a un río; afluente principal.

headstrong [-,strɔŋ] *a.* voluntarioso, testarudo, terco, cabezudo, obstinado, indócil, reacio.

headstrongness [-nəs] *s.* terquedad, obstinación, testarudez.

head voice, (mús.) voz de cabeza, falsete.

headwaiter [-,weɪtər, B -ə] *s.* jefe de camareros, jefe de mozos; encargado del comedor.

headwater [-,wɔtər, -,wat-, B -,wɔtə] *s.* (*gen. pl.*) río arriba; naciente(s), cabeceras, aguas de cabecera, fuentes.

headway [-,weɪ] *s.* 1. ímpetu, avance, progreso; esp. salida (de un barco). 2. (arq.) espacio libre, altura libre, franqueo superior. 3. lapso o intervalo entre dos trenes en una misma vía. 4. **to make h.,** avanzar, progresar.

head wind, (mar.) viento de frente, viento de proa, viento en contra.

headword [-wɜrd] *s.* palabra cabeza de artículo, lema.

headwork [-,wɜrk, B -,wɜk] 1. *s.* trabajo mental o intelectual. 2. (arq.) adorno de clave.

heady ['hɛdɪ] *a.* (HEADIER; HEADIEST) 1. precipitado, impetuoso, vehemente. 2. arrojado, violento, temerario. 3. fuerte, embriagante, embriagador; cabezudo (vino). 4. (fam.) sesudo, sensato.

heal [hil] *v.t.* 1. curar, sanar, devolver la salud a. 2. cicatrizar (herida). 3. (fig.) remediar, enmendar, componer, reconciliar. —*v.i.* 1. sanar, recobrar la salud, curar(se). 2. cicatrizarse (herida). 3. (fig.) remediarse.

healable ['hiləbəl] *a.* sanable, curable.

healer ['hilər, B -lə] *s.* sanador, curador.

healing [-lɪŋ] *a.* curativo, sanador.

health [hɛlθ] *s.* 1. salud. 2. sanidad, salubridad, bienestar, prosperidad. 3. brindis. 4. **to be in bad (good) h.,** estar mal (bien) de salud; **to drink to the h. of,** beber a la salud de; **to your h.!** ¡a tu salud!

health certificate, certificado de salud.

health department, ministerio o secretaría de salubridad o de salud pública.

health food, alimentos naturales, alimentos macrobióticos.

healthful ['hɛlθfəl] *a.* saludable, sano, salubre.

healthfully [-fəlɪ] *adv.* saludablemente, con salud.

healthfulness [-fəlnəs] *s.* salubridad, sanidad.

healthily ['hɛlθəlɪ] *adv.* sanamente, saludablemente, con salud.

healthiness [-θɪnəs] *s.* sanidad, salud, goce de buena salud.

health insurance, seguro médico, seguro de enfermedad.

health measures, medidas sanitarias.

health officer, inspector de sanidad.

health resort, centro de salud, sanatorio, balneario (de aguas termales).

health station, estación sanitaria, puesto de salud (en un barrio o una comarca).

healthy ['hɛlθɪ] *a.* (HEALTHIER; HEALTHIEST) 1. sano, bien de salud, de buena salud. 2. sano, saludable, salubre. 3. considerable (parte), bueno (apetito). 4. robusto, floreciente. 5. sana (competencia), favorable (impresión).

heap [hip] *s.* 1. montón, pila, rimero. 2. (fam.) montón, cantidad, muchos. 3. (jer.) coche destartalado. —*v.t.* (*pret., p.p.* HEAPED o HEAPT; *p.pr.* HEAPING) 1. amontonar, apilar; acumular, atesorar, juntar. 2. colmar de, prodigar (elogios, insultos, etc.). 3. colmar, repletar (un recipiente, plato, etc.).

hear [hɪr, B hɪə] *v.t.* (*pret., p.p.* HEARD [hɜrd, B hɜd]; *p.pr.* HEARING) 1. oír. 2. oír, enterarse de. 3. oír, atender, prestar atención a. 4. oír, acceder, atender, conceder. 5. (der.) dar audiencia a; ver. 6. asistir a, estar presente en. 7. **h. (someone** o **something) doing** (o **do**), oír (a alguien o algo) hacer, oír que (alguien o algo) hace, ej., *he heard the dog barking* (o *bark*), oyó ladrar al perro, oyó que el perro ladraba; **h. it said,** oírlo decir; **h. (someone) out** (o **through**), oír (a alguien) hasta el final; **h. that,** oír decir que; **to be heard to (do),** oírse (hacer), ej., *the dog was heard to bark all night,* se oyó ladrar al perro toda la noche. —*v.i.* 1. oír. 2. oír, estar informado, tener noticia. 3. **he will not h. of it,** él no quiere ni oír hablar de ello, él no quiere aceptarlo (o permitirlo) de ningún modo; **hear! hear!** ¡bravo! ¡bravo!; **h. about** (u **of**), oír hablar de; enterarse de; **h. from,** tener noticias de, saber; **I never heard of such a thing,** jamás oí cosa igual; **you will h. of this,** ya oirá usted de esto, ya será Ud. reprendido por esto.

hearer ['hɪrər, B 'hɪərə] *s.* oyente, oidor.

hearing [-ɪŋ] *s.* 1. oído (sentido, aptitud); oída (acción de oír). 2. audiencia, audición. 3. alcance del oído. 4. (der.) audiencia; juicio, proceso. 5. **hard of h.,** duro de oído; **out of h.,** fuera del alcance del oído; **to give (someone) a fair h.,** escuchar (a alguien) con imparcialidad; **within h.,** al alcance del oído.

hearing aid, audífono, aparato del oído.

hearken ['hɑrkən, B 'hɑkən] *v.i.* escuchar, atender; prestar atención. —*v.t.* (ant.) oír; hacer caso de (o a).

hearsay ['hɪrˌseɪ, B 'hɪəˌ-] *s.* rumor, voz común; **by h.,** de o por oídas. —*a.* conocido de oídas.

hearsay evidence, (der.) testimonio o prueba de oídas, prueba por referencia.

hearse [hɜrs, B hɜs] *s.* 1. coche fúnebre, carroza fúnebre. 2. armazón con candeleros (que se usa durante los oficios de Tinieblas o sobre un ataúd en las iglesias). 3. (hist.) armazón adornada con versos o epitafios (que se ponía sobre un ataúd o tumba real). 4. (ant.) féretro, andas. —*v.t.* 1. llevar en coche fúnebre. 2. enterrar, sepultar. 3. (ant.) colocar en un ataúd.

heart [hɑrt, B hɑt] *s.* 1. corazón. 2. (fig.) corazón, riñón (de una región, etc.). 3. (fig.) corazón, ánimo, valor; espíritu, alma; buena voluntad, amor, benevolencia; compasión. 4. cogollo (de lechuga, berza, etc.). 5. (fig.) fondo, meollo, quid, ej., *h. of the matter,* el quid del asunto. 6. (*pl.*) (naipes) corazones, copas; juego parecido al whist. 7. **after (one's) own h.,** enteramente a su gusto, del completo agrado (de uno); **at h.,** en el fondo; **by h.,** de memoria; **change of h.,** cambio de opinión, cambio de actitud; **from one's h.,** de corazón; **have a h.,** (jer.) tenga piedad; **h. and hand,** entusiastamente; **h. and soul,** en cuerpo y alma, con toda el alma, de alma y corazón; **h. of oak,** valiente, hombre de valor; **h. to h.,** sincero, franco; **in one's h.,** en el fondo, en lo íntimo; **in one's h. of hearts,** en lo más recóndito del corazón de uno; **my h. was not in it,** no lo hice con entusiasmo; **my h. sank,** se me cayó el alma a los pies; **to be good at h.,** tener buen fondo, ser de buen corazón; **to break one's h.,** quebrar el corazón a uno, partir o arrancársele el alma a uno; **to cry one's h. out,** llorar a lágrima viva; **to die of a broken h.,** morir de pena; **to do one's h. good,** alegrar a uno, dar gusto a uno; **to eat one's h. out,** (fig.) recomerse, concomerse; **to get to the h. of,** entrar en el fondo de (un asunto, misterio, etc.); **to have (something) at h.,** velar por (algo); interesarse mucho por (algo); **to have h. trouble,** estar enfermo del corazón; **to have no h. for,** no gustarle a uno, no ser del agrado de uno; **to have not the h. to (do),** no poder ser tan cruel como para (hacer); **to have one's h. in one's mouth,** estar con el alma en un hilo, estar con el corazón en la boca; **to have one's h. in the right place,** tener el corazón bien templado, tener el alma bien puesta, ser un hombre sensato; **to lose h.,** caérsele (a uno) las alas del corazón, descorazonarse; **to lose one's h. to,** enamorarse de; **to one's h.'s content,** a sus anchas, sin restricción; **to open one's h. (to),** (fig.) descubrir el pecho (a), abrirse (con), aclarar; **to set one's h. on,** poner el alma en, ansiar; **to take h.,** tomar aliento, animarse, cobrar valentía; **to take to h.,** tomar a pecho; **to wear one's h. on one's sleeve,** manifestar sus sentimientos sin poder evitarlo; **with a heavy h.,** con el corazón oprimido, con el ánimo triste, con abatimiento; **with all one's h.,** de todo corazón. —*v.t.* (raro) animar, alentar; guardar (algo) en el corazón.

heartache ['hɑrtˌeɪk, B 'hɑt-] *s.* angustia, aflicción, pesar; congoja, tristeza.

heart attack, ataque al corazón, ataque cardiaco o cardíaco.

heartbeat [-ˌbit] *s.* latido (del corazón).

heart block, (med.) bloqueo del corazón, bloqueo cardiaco o cardíaco.

heartbreak [-ˌbreɪk] *s.* angustia o dolor abrumador.

heartbreaker [-ˌbreɪkər, B -kə] *s.* persona, suceso o cosa que causa angustia o dolor.

heartbreaking [-kɪŋ] *a.* angustioso; desgarrador, que parte el corazón, que parte el alma.

heartbroken [-ˌbroʊkən] *a.* transido de dolor, acongojado.

heartburn [-ˌbɜrn, B -ˌbɜn] *s.* 1. rescoldera, acedía, acidez (Amer.). 2. envidia, celos; amargura, rencor.

heartburning [-ˌbɜrnɪŋ, B -ˌbɜnɪŋ] *s.* envidia, celos; amargura, rencor.

heart cam, (mec.) leva (en forma de corazón).

heart disease, enfermedad del corazón, dolencia cardiaca o cardíaca.

hearten ['hɑrtən, B 'hɑt-] *v.t.* animar, alentar; confortar.

heart failure, (med.) insuficiencia cardíaca, fallo cardíaco.

heartfelt [-ˌfɛlt] *a.* sincero, sentido genuina y profundamente.

heart-free [-ˌfri] *a.* libre de compromiso amoroso.

hearth [hɑrθ, B hɑθ] *s.* 1. hogar, fogón; piso de chimenea o de horno. 2. (fig.) hogar, casa. 3. (metal.) crisol, hogar (de un alto horno); fondo, lecho (de un horno de reverbero); forja, horno de pudelar; fondo interno (de un cubilote u horno de manga).

hearthstone ['hɑrθˌstoʊn, B 'hɑθ-] *s.* 1. solera del hogar. 2. (fig.) hogar, casa.

heartily ['hɑrtəlɪ, B 'hɑt-] *adv.* 1. sinceramente, de corazón. 2. gustosamente, con entusiasmo. 3. abundantemente, copiosamente, mucho; completamente.

heartiness [-ɪnəs] *s.* 1. sinceridad, cordialidad, espontaneidad. 2. entusiasmo, vigor.

heartland [-ˌlænd] *s.* (pol.) zona de importancia decisiva.

heartless ['hɑrtləs, B 'hɑt-] *a.* 1. sin corazón, cruel, empedernido, duro, despiadado, desalmado. 2. (ant.) apocado, tímido, pusilánime.

heartlessly [-lɪ] *adv.* cruelmente, despiadadamente, desalmadamente.

heartlessness [-nəs] *s.* falta de corazón, crueldad.

heart-lung machine, bomba corazón-pulmón.

heart point, abismo o corazón de un escudo de armas.

heartrending ['hɑrtˌrɛndɪŋ, B 'hɑt-] *a.* congojoso, desconsolador.

hearts and flowers, sentimentalismo.

heart-searching [-hɑrtˌsɛrtʃɪŋ, B 'hɑtˌsɛtʃɪŋ] *s.* examen de conciencia.

heartsease ['hɑrtsˌiz, B 'hɑts-] *s.* 1. serenidad de ánimo, sosiego. 2. (bot.) pensamiento, trinitaria.

heartsick ['hɑrtˌsɪk, B 'hɑt-] *a.* desconsolado, muy abatido.

heartsickness [-nəs] *s.* desconsuelo, abatimiento.

heartsome [-səm] *a.* (esco.) 1. animoso. 2. vivificador, vigorizador. 3. alegre, divertido.

heartsore [-ˌsɔr, B -ˌsɔ] *a.* acongojado, dolorido, afligido.

heart-stricken [-ˌstrɪkən] *a.* afligido, transido, acongojado, angustiado.

heartstrings [-ˌstrɪŋz] *s. pl.* (fig.) fibras del corazón, las cuerdas del sentimiento (que alguien puede hacer vibrar).

heart-throb [-ˌθrɑb, B -ˌθrɔb] *s.* 1. latido del corazón. 2. (jer.) enamorado, enamorada.

heart-to-heart ['hɑrttə'hɑrt, B 'hɑttə'hɑt] *a.* íntimo, franco.

heart-whole [-ˌhoʊl] *a.* 1. libre de compromiso amoroso, libre de afectos. 2. sincero, verdadero.

heartwood [-ˌwʊd] *s.* duramen, médula, corazón de árbol.

hearty ['hɑrtɪ, B 'hɑtɪ] *a.* (HEARTIER; HEARTIEST) 1. sincero, cordial, espontáneo. 2. enérgico, vigoroso; sano, robusto. 3. nutritivo, substancioso; sabroso; abundante. 4. fértil, feraz (suelo). 5. **a h. eater,** un gran tragón, comilón. —*s.* (*pl.* HEARTIES) compañero (entre marinos); p. ext. marino.

heat [hit] *s.* 1. calor, temperatura alta; período de calor; aire caliente; calefacción. 2. (fig.) acaloramiento, ardor, ardimiento; vehemencia; exasperación, cólera; animosidad, ardor (en un discurso). 3. celo, brama (de los animales). 4. hornada, carga de un horno. 5. (jer.) presión extrema (ej., cuando la policía investiga un crimen). 6. (dep.) carrera; carrera eliminatoria. 7. **in h.,** en celo (animal); **to put the h. on (someone),** (jer.) presionar bajo amenazas a (alguien); exigir dinero bajo amenazas a (alguien); demandar mayor esfuerzo o un trabajo más intenso a (un empleado, etc.). —*v.t.* 1. calentar. 2. (fig.) acalorar, enardecer, excitar. 3. **h. up,** calentar, recalentar. —*v.i.* 1. calentarse. 2. **h. up,** recalentarse.

heat capacity, calor específico.

heatedly ['hitədlɪ] *adv.* acaloradamente, calurosamente, ardientemente.

heat energy, energía calórica.

heat engine, máquina térmica, termomotor, motor térmico.

heater ['hitər, B -ə] *s.* 1. calentador, calorífero; estufa. 2. (electrón., rad.) calefactor. 3. (jer.) revólver, pistola.

heat exchanger, (fís.) cambiador de calor, permutador térmico.

heat exhaustion, postración causada por el calor.
heath [hiθ] *s.* 1. terreno baldío; (G.B.) brezal, páramo. 2. (bot.) brezo común, urce.
heath aster, (bot.) aster común.
heathberry ['hiθ,bɛrɪ] *s.* baya de brezo.
heath cock, (orn.) gallo silvestre, urogallo.
heathen ['hiðən] *s.* 1. gentil, pagano; (bíbl.) idólatra. 2. salvaje, ignorante. —*a.* 1. pagano, ateo. 2. salvaje, inculto. 3. (fig.) libertino, hedonista.
heathenish [-ðənɪʃ] *a.* pagano, ateo, gentílico; bárbaro.
heathenism [-,ɪzəm] *s.* paganismo, idolatría; ateísmo.
heathenize [-,aɪz] *v.t.* convertir al paganismo o la idolatría.
heather ['hɛðər, B -ə] *s.* (bot.) brezo común, brecina, erica, urce.
heathery [-ərɪ] *a.* 1. cubierto de brezos, matoso. 2. salpicado de colores (tela).
heath grass, heather grass, (bot.) sieglingia decumbente.
heath hen, (orn.) gallina silvestre.
heathy ['hiθɪ] *a.* cubierto de brezos, matoso.
heating ['hitɪŋ] *a.* 1. calentador. 2. calorífico. —*s.* calefacción, caldeo.
heating appliance, (elec.) artefacto calentador.
heating coil, serpentín calentador.
heating element, elemento calentador, elemento de caldeo.
heating power, potencia calorífica, poder calorífico.
heating surface, superficie de calefacción, superficie de caldeo.
heatless ['hitləs] *a.* falto de calor, sin calefacción (vivienda, oficina, etc.).
heat lightning, relámpago de calor.
heatproof [-,pruf] *a.* a prueba de calor; (*ovenware*) refractario.
heat prostration, congestión debida al calor.
heat pump, compresor, bomba.
heat rash, salpullido o erupción causados por el calor.
heat-resistant [-rɪ,zɪstənt] *a.* resistente al calor, calorífugo.
heatstroke [-,strouk] *s.* (med.) insolación, golpe de calor.
heat treatment, (med.) tratamiento térmico.
heat unit, unidad térmica.
heat wave, 1. (fís.) onda calorífica. 2. ola de calor.
heaume [houm] *s.* tipo de yelmo grande.
heave [hiv] *v.t.* (*pret., p.p.* HEAVED O HOVE [houv] *p.pr.* HEAVING) 1. levantar, alzar (con esfuerzo). 2. exhalar, lanzar, emitir con esfuerzo, ej., *h. a sigh,* exhalar un suspiro. 3. henchir, abultar. 4. arrojar, tirar, echar. 5. arrojar, vomitar. 6. (mar.) izar. 7. (geol.) desplazar lateral u horizontalmente. 8. **h. the lead,** (mar.) sondar; **h. the log,** (mar.) echar la corredera. —*v.i.* 1. elevarse, levantarse, combarse (ej., el pavimento). 2. levantarse y bajar con movimientos alternativos (olas, el mar, etc.). 3. esforzarse. 4. jadear, acezar. 5. arquear, nausear. 6. (mar.) virar; halar o empujar; moverse (un barco). 7. **h. back,** (mar.) desvirar; **h. down,** (mar.) dar la quilla (de un buque); **h. in sight,** asomarse en el horizonte; **h. off,** (mar.) hacerse a la mar, alejarse de la costa; **h. out,** (mar.) largar las velas; **h. to,** (mar.) ponerse al pairo o en facha. —*s.* 1. esfuerzo para levantar algo, tirada, tiro. 2. echada, tiro. 3. elevación, levantamiento, movimiento hacia arriba (esp. rítmico). 4. (geol.) desplazamiento horizontal o lateral (por una falla), dislocación (de un filón). 5. (*pl.*) (vet.) huélfago. 6. **to give (something) a h.,** echar, arrojar, tirar (algo).
heaven ['hɛvən] *s.* 1. cielo. 2. (*pl.*) cielo, firmamento, bóveda celeste. 3. **H.,** cielo, cielos. 4. (fig.) paraíso; felicidad perfecta. 5. **by h.! good heavens!** ¡caramba! ¡cielos!; **for heaven's sake!** ¡por Dios!; **h. knows,** (sólo) Dios sabe, Dios es testigo, el cielo es testigo; **to move h. and earth,** mover cielo y tierra, hacer lo imposible.
heavenliness [-lɪnəs] *s.* excelencia, perfección.
heavenly [-lɪ] *a.* 1. celestial (música, coro, mansión, etc.). 2. celeste (cuerpo). 3. (fig.) celestial, delicioso, perfecto.
heavenward ['hɛvənwərd, B -wəd] *a.* dirigido al cielo. —*adv.* hacia el cielo.
heavenwards [-wərdz, B -wədz] *adv.* hacia el cielo.
heaver ['hivər, B -ə] *s.* 1. levantador, cargador. 2. (mar.) palanca de maniobra, espeque.
heavily ['hɛvəlɪ] *adv.* 1. pesadamente, con gran peso. 2. lentamente, laboriosamente, difícilmente. 3. fuertemente, en gran escala, excesivamente. 4. tristemente, melancólicamente, con pesadumbre.
heaviness [-ɪnəs] *s.* 1. pesadez, pesantez, peso, gravedad. 2. lentitud, tardanza, flema, torpeza. 3. desánimo, languidez, decaimiento, abatimiento; modorra, letargo.
Heaviside layer ['hɛvɪ,saɪd-] (rad., meteorol.) capa de Heaviside, ionosfera.
heavy ['hɛvɪ] *a.* (HEAVIER; HEAVIEST) 1. pesado, de mucho peso. 2. denso, espeso (líquido); denso (tráfico). 3. grueso (línea, cicatriz, etc.; tela, papel, etc.). 4. opresivo, duro, gravoso, penoso. 5. cargado, agobiado. 6. desalentado, abatido, triste. 7. grave, serio; de peso, importante, considerable. 8. pesado (sueño); profundo, intenso (silencio, etc.). 9. encinta, embarazada. 10. fuerte (tormenta, lluvia, nevada, etc.; olor, fragancia, etc.); abundante, copioso (cosecha, etc.). 11. pesado, lento, lerdo, tardo. 12. pesado, tedioso, aburrido, insulso. 13. pesado, difícil, laborioso (trabajo, tarea, avance, etc.). 14. cansado, agotado, atontado, amodorrado, soñoliento. 15. sombrío, nublado, encapotado (cielo). 16. grueso, bravo, borrascoso (mar), tormentoso (tiempo); cargado, sofocante (aire, atmósfera). 17. arcilloso, gredoso, pesado (camino). 18. empinado, escarpado (pendiente, etc.). 19. pesado, indigesto (comida); medio levantado (masa). 20. marcado (ritmo), intenso (cañoneo). 21. fuerte (pérdida, gastos, costo, etc.). 22. fuerte, grande (bebedor). 23. en gran escala (compras, comprador). 24. (com.) postrado (mercado). 25. (mil.) pesado; de armas pesadas. 26. (impr.) grueso, negro (carácter, letra, impresión). 27. (teat.) sombrío, grave (papel). 28. **h. with,** (fig.) preñado de (agua, noticias, etc.). —*adv.* pesadamente; con lentitud; **to hang h.,** pasar muy despacio (tiempo, horas), parecer como si se hubiera parado (el reloj); **to hang h. on one's hands,** esperar ansiosamente que pase (el tiempo), ej., *time hung h. on our hands,* esperábamos ansiosamente que pasara el tiempo; **to lie h. on,** pesar sobre (conciencia, etc.); **with a h. heart,** con el corazón apesadumbrado. —*s.* (*pl.* HEAVIES) 1. boxeador de peso pesado. 2. (*pl.*) caballería pesada; artillería pesada; bombarderos pesados. 3. ropa interior gruesa. 4. (teat.) villano, característico, (actor en) papel de antagonista.
heavy-armed ['hɛvɪ'ɑrmd, B -'ɑmd] *a.* que usa armadura pesada; que lleva armas pesadas.
heavy artillery, artillería gruesa.
heavy cream, crema doble, nata para montar.
heavy-duty [-'dutɪ, B -'djutɪ] *a.* para trabajo rudo o pesado; de servicio pesado.
heavy earth, (min.) barita, monóxido de bario.
heavy-footed [-'fʊtəd] *a.* 1. de pasos pesados. 2. (fig.) pesado, aburrido, soso (estilo literario, etc.).
heavy-handed [-'hændəd] *a.* 1. torpe, tosco, desgarbado. 2. (fig.) opresivo, autoritario, imperioso.
heavyhearted [-'hɑrtəd, B -'hɑt-] *a.* abatido, desesperanzado, acongojado.
heavy hydrogen, (fís., quím.) hidrógeno pesado.
heavy industry, industria pesada.
heavy-laden [-'leɪdən] *a.* recargado, agobiado.
heavy-set [-'sɛt] *a.* grueso, corpulento.
heavy spar, (min.) espato pesado, baritina, sulfato de bario.
heavy water, (quím.) agua pesada.
heavy weapons, (mil.) armas de acompañamiento, de apoyo.
heavyweight [-,weɪt] *s.* (boxeo) peso pesado; boxeador de peso pesado.
Heb. *abrev. de* 1. **Hebrew,** hebreo. 2. **Hebrews,** Epístola a los Hebreos (Hebr.).
hebdomad ['hɛbdə,mæd] *s.* hebdómada; grupo de siete; septenario.
hebdomadal [hɛb'dɑmədəl, B -'dɔm-] *a.* hebdomadario, semanal.
hebdomadally [-ɪ] *adv.* hebdomadariamente, semanalmente.
hebdomadary [-ə,dɛrɪ, B -ədərɪ] *s.* (relig.) hebdomadario.
Hebe ['hibɪ] *s.* 1. (mitol.) Hebe (diosa de la juventud y la primavera). 2. **h.,** (hum., G.B.) camarera, moza.
hebephrenia [,hibə'frinɪə] *s.* (med.) hebefrenia.
hebephrenic [-'frɛnɪk] *a.* (med.) hebefrénico.
hebetate ['hɛbə,teɪt] *v.t.* atontar, entorpecer, embrutecer.
hebetation [,hɛbə'teɪʃən] *s.* atontamiento, entorpecimiento, embrutecimiento.
hebetic [hɪ'bɛtɪk] *a.* hebético.
hebetude ['hɛbə,tud, B -,tjud] *s.* 1. torpeza, estupidez. 2. (med.) hebetud.
Hebraic [hɪ'breɪɪk] *a.* hebreo, hebraico.
Hebraism ['hibreɪ,ɪzəm] *s.* 1. hebraísmo, judaísmo, instituciones hebraicas. 2. espíritu hebraico, costumbre hebraica. 3. (filol.) hebraísmo, modismo hebraico.
Hebraist [-,breɪəst] *s.* hebraísta.
Hebraize [-,aɪz] *v.t.* hacer o volver hebreo. —*v.i.* hebraizar, usar hebraísmos.
Hebrew ['hibru] *s.* 1. hebreo, esp. israelí. 2. idioma hebreo. —*a.* hebreo, israelí.
Hebrew calendar, calendario judío o hebraico.
Hebrews [-,bruz] *s. pl.* (bíbl.) Hebreos, Epístola a los Hebreos.
Hebrides ['hɛbrə,diz] *s. pl.* Hébridas (archipiélago al O. de Escocia).
Hecate, Hekate ['hɛkətɪ] *s.* (mitol.) Hécate, diosa de la tierra y del infierno, vinculada a brujerías.
hecatomb ['hɛkə,toum, B -,tum] *s.* hecatombe, sacrificio en masa, matanza.
heck [hɛk] (jer.) 1. infierno; **what the h.!** ¡qué diablos! 2. **for the h. of it,** por gusto, de balde, a ver qué pasa.
heckle ['hɛkəl] *v.t.* 1. rastrillar. 2. interrumpir con preguntas molestas o insultos, provocar, fastidiar (a un orador). —*s.* rastrillo.
heckler ['hɛklər, B -lə] *s.* provocador, insultador (de un orador).
hectare ['hɛk,tɛr, -tər, B -tɑ] *s.* hectárea.
hectic ['hɛktɪk] *a.* 1. (med.) hético, tísico, en estado hético. 2. (fam.) agitado, turbulento, excitante. 3. ruborizado, rojizo. —*s.* 1. (med.) tisis, fiebre hética; hético, tísico (enfermo). 2. rubor hético.
hectic fever, (med.) fiebre hética.
hecto- ['hɛktou, -tə] *prefijo* que indica ciento.

hectocotylus [ˌhɛktəˈkɑtələs, B -ˈkɔt-] *s.* (*pl.* HECTOCOTYLI [-ˌlaɪ]) (zool.) hectocótilo.
hectogram [ˈhɛktəˌgræm] *s.* hectogramo.
hectograph [-ˌgræf, B -ˌgrɑf] *s.* hectógrafo, autocopia.
hectoliter [ˈhɛktəˌlitər, B -ə] *s.* hectolitro.
hectometer [-ˌmitər, B -ə] *s.* hectómetro.
hector [ˈhɛktər, B -tə] *s.* matón, fanfarrón, valentón. —*v.t.* amenazar, atormentar o intimidar con bravatas.
Hecuba [ˈhɛkjəbə] *s.* (mitol.) Hécuba, madre de Paris, Casandra y Héctor.
he'd [hid, id] *contr. de* **he had** o **he would.**
heddle [ˈhɛdəl] *s.* (tej.) lizo, malla de telar.
hedge [ˈhɛdʒ] *s.* 1. seto vivo; cerca, cercado, valla, vallado. 2. barrera, límite. 3. declaración evasiva. 4. (con *against*) seguro, defensa, protección (contra). 5. apuesta compensatoria. —*a.* 1. de seto, para seto (ej., plantas). 2. de la orilla. 3. clandestino. 4. malo, de mala calidad; bajo, de baja condición, de clase baja. —*v.t.* 1. cercar con un seto; rodear. 2. (gen. con *in* o *about*) encerrar; obstruir, entorpecer, impedir, poner trabas a, restringir. 3. proteger, guardar. 4. cubrirse contra, protegerse contra (una pérdida, etc.); compensar (apuestas). —*v.i.* 1. (con *against*) resguardarse, protegerse (contra). 2. dejarse una salida, eludir el compromiso (al hablar), hablar evasivamente. 3. hacer apuesta(s) compensatoria(s). 4. (fin., bolsa) compensar una jugada de bolsa, hacer operaciones de bolsa compensatorias (contra pérdidas).
hedge fumitory, (bot.) fumaria común.
hedge garlic, (bot.) aliaria.
hedgehog [ˈhɛdʒˌhɔg, -ˌhɑg, B -ˌhɔg] *s.* 1. (zool.) erizo; puerco espín. 2. (mil.) erizo, alambrada. 3. (fig.) persona intratable.
hedgehog parsley, (bot.) amores, bardana menor, cadillo.
hedgehop [-ˌhɑp, B -ˌhɔp] *v.i.* (*pret., p.p.* HEDGEHOPPED; *p.pr.* HEDGEHOPPING) (aer., jer.) volar a ras de los árboles o setos.
hedgehopper [-ər, B -ə] *s.* avión o piloto que vuela a ras de los árboles o setos.
hedge hyssop, (bot.) graciola, yerba del pobre.
hedge priest, (G.B.) cura iletrado.
hedger [ˈhɛdʒər, B -ə] *s.* 1. cercador, el que hace cercados o setos. 2. el que compensa o iguala sus apuestas. 3. el que vacila, titubea o elude.
hedgerow [ˈhɛdʒˌroʊ] *s.* seto vivo de árboles o arbustos en hilera.
hedge sparrow, (orn.) curruca, especie de gorrión.
hedonic [hɪˈdɑnɪk, B -ˈdɔn-] *a.* hedonista, que persigue los placeres como única finalidad.
hedonics [-ɪks] *s. pl.* (*sing. en const.*) (filos.) hedónica, ciencia del placer.
hedonism [ˈhidənˌɪzəm] *s.* hedonismo.
hedonist [-əst] *s.* hedonista.
hedonistic [ˌhidəˈnɪstɪk] *a.* hedonista, hedonístico.
heebie-jeebies [ˌhibɪˈdʒibiz] *s. pl.* (gen. **the h.-j.**) (jer.) inquietud, desasosiego, ataque nervioso; delirium tremens.
heed [hid] *v.t.* hacer caso de, atender a, escuchar; **to take (pay,** o **give) h. to,** prestar o poner atención a. —*v.i.* prestar atención, hacer caso. —*s.* cuidado, atención, mirada atenta.
heedful [ˈhidfəl] *a.* atento, cuidadoso, cauteloso.
heedfully [-fəlɪ] *adv.* atentamente, cautelosamente, cuidadosamente.
heedfulness [-fəlnəs] *s.* atención, cautela, cuidado.
heedless [-ləs] *a.* desatento, descuidado, incauto.
heedlessness [-nəs] *s.* inadvertencia, desatención, descuido, imprudencia.
hee-haw [ˈhiˌhɔ] *s.* 1. rebuzno (del asno). 2. carcajada, risotada. —*v.i.* 1. rebuznar. 2. reírse a carcajadas.
heel [hil] *s.* 1. talón, calcañar. 2. talón (de los cuadrúpedos); (*pl.*) patas traseras. 3. barra (del casco del caballo). 4. tacón (pieza exterior de un zapato); talón (parte de la media o el zapato que cubre el calcañar). 5. (fig.) restos; fin. 6. (mús.) talón (del arco del violín). 7. (mar.) talón (de la quilla). 8. (mar.) coz o pie (de palo). 9. (agr.) estaca, pie. 10. (golf) talón (del palo). 11. (jer. E.U.) bribón, sinvergüenza, infame. 12. **at h., at one's heels,** a los talones; **down at the h.,** con el talón muy gastado (zapatos); (fig.) andrajoso; desvalido, en una situación difícil (persona); **h. of Achilles,** talón de Aquiles, punto flaco; **heels over head, head over heels,** patas arriba, al revés; **on** (o **upon**) **the heels of,** a los talones de uno; **out at the heels,** andrajoso, destartalado; **to be at one's heels,** pisarle a uno los talones; **to cool one's heels,** esperar impacientemente; hacer antesala; **to dig one's heels in,** resignarse y prepararse; **to have by the heels,** (fig.) tener aprisionado, tener en su poder; **to h.,** a los talones, muy cerca; bajo control (díc. del perro); **to kick up one's heels,** mostrarse alegre y juguetón, echar una cana al aire; **to lay by the heels,** apresar; **to take to one's heels,** poner pies en polvorosa; **to turn on one's heels,** volverse o darse vuelta rápidamente. —*v.t.* 1. poner talón o tacón a (medias o zapatos). 2. perseguir o seguir de cerca. 3. poner espolones a (un gallo de pelea). 4. (golf) pegar (la pelota) con el talón del palo. 5. (fútbol) pasar (la pelota) con el tacón. 6. (jer., E.U.) proveer de dinero. —*v.i.* 1. taconear (en la danza). 2. (jer.) correr.
heel [hil] (mar.) *v.i.* inclinarse, tumbarse, escorar. —*v.t.* inclinar. —*s.* escora, inclinación (de un barco).
heel-and-toe race [ˌhilənˈtoʊ-] *s.* carrera de marcha.
heeled [hild] *a.* 1. que tiene talón. 2. (jer., E.U.) armado de un revólver. 3. **well-h.,** (jer., E.U.) bien provisto de dinero.
heeler [ˈhilər, B -lə] *s.* 1. taconero. 2. (fam. E.U.) (t. **ward h.**) muñidor, paniaguado de un cacique político.
heeling [-lɪŋ] *s.* 1. (mar.) recalada, inclinación. 2. talonaje (zapatos).
heelless [ˈhilləs] *a.* sin talón, sin tacón.
heelpiece [-ˌpis] *s.* talón (de un zapato).
heel plate, 1. (arm.) placa de la culata. 2. plancha de metal (en el talón del zapato).
heelpost [-ˌpoʊst] *s.* poste de quicio.
heeltap [-ˌtæp] *s.* 1. tapa (suela del tacón de los zapatos). 2. residuo (de licor que queda en un vaso después de beber).
heft [hɛft] *s.* 1. peso, pesadez. 2. (ant.) la mayor parte (de algo). 3. (ant.) esfuerzo violento. —*v.t.* 1. levantar, alzar. 2. sopesar.
hefty [ˈhɛftɪ] *a.* (HEFTIER; HEFTIEST). 1. bastante pesado. 2. (fam.) fornido, corpulento, robusto; fuerte, grande.
Hegelian [heɪˈgeɪlɪən, B -ˈgiljən] *a., s.* hegeliano, según la doctrina del filósofo alemán Hegel.
Hegelianism [-ˌɪzəm] *s.* (filos.) hegelianismo.
hegemonic [ˌhɛdʒəˈmɑnɪk, B -ˈmɔn-] *a.* hegemónico, predominante.
hegemony [hɪˈdʒɛmənɪ, ˈhɛdʒəˌmoʊnɪ, B hɪˈgɛmənɪ] *s.* (*pl.* HEGEMONIES) hegemonía, preeminencia, autoridad, influencia preponderante (esp. de un gobierno o estado).
hegira [hɪˈdʒaɪrə, ˈhɛdʒərə] *s.* hégira, héjira, égira, huida de Mahoma de la Meca; p. ext. fuga, huida, éxodo.
hegumen [hɪˈgjumɛn] *s.* (relig.) hegúmeno (superior de un monasterio de la Iglesia ortodoxa).
heifer [ˈhɛfər, B -ə] *s.* vaquilla, novilla.
heigh [haɪ, heɪ, B heɪ] *interj.* (para expresar estímulo, curiosidad, alegría) ¡ea! ¡ah! ¡tate!; (para llamar la atención) ¡eh! ¡oye! ¡hola!
heigh-ho [ˈhaɪˈhoʊ, ˈheɪ-, B ˈheɪ-] *interj.* (para expresar tedio, desengaño) ¡ay! ¡huy!; ¡bah! ¡puf! ¡uf!
height [haɪt] *s.* 1. altura, altitud, alto. 2. altura, elevación, eminencia, lugar alto; cima, cumbre. 3. estatura, talla. 4. (fig.) apogeo, cumbre (de la fama, fortuna, etc.); colmo (de la locura, estupidez, etc.); punto culminante, culminación (de un argumento, de deseos, pasiones, etc.). 5. (ant.) aristocracia; arrogancia, altivez. 6. **at its h.,** en su punto culminante; **to one's full h.,** en toda su talla, ej., *he drew himself up to his full h.,* se irguió en toda su estatura.
heighten [ˈhaɪtən] *v.t.* 1. aumentar, acrecentar. 2. intensificar, fortalecer, realzar. 3. (fig.) elevar, levantar, mejorar. 4. hacer más alto (edificio). 5. (ant.) exaltar, excitar. —*v.i.* aumentarse; intensificarse.
height to paper, (impr.) altura del tipo, altura tipográfica.
heinous [ˈheɪnəs] *a.* nefando, horrendo, horrible, infame.
heinously [-lɪ] *adv.* nefandamente, horrendamente, atrozmente, horriblemente, infamemente.
heir [ɛr, B ɛə] *s.* heredero. —*v.t.* (dial.) heredar.
heir apparent, (*pl.* HEIRS APPARENT) (der.) heredero forzoso.
heir at law, (der.) heredero legítimo, heredero legal.
heirdom [ˈɛrdəm, B ˈɛədəm] *s.* (ant.) herencia; condición de heredero.
heiress [-əs, B ˈɛər-] *s.* heredera; heredera de una fortuna.
heirloom [-ˌlum, B ˈɛəˌ-] *s.* 1. bienes muebles heredados inalienables. 2. reliquia o joya heredada. 3. (fig.) valor hereditario, herencia.
heir presumptive, (*pl.* HEIRS PRESUMPTIVE) (der.) presunto heredero.
heirship [-ˌʃɪp] *s.* derecho de heredar; condicion de heredero.
heist [haɪst] *v.t.* (jer.) 1. robar a mano armada; hurtar. 2. saltear, atracar. —*s.* (jer.) 1. robo; hurto. 2. salteo, atraco.
hejira, *var. de* **hegira.**
held [hɛld] *pret., p.p. de* **hold** .
Helen of Troy [ˈhɛlən-] (mitol.) Elena de Troya, Helena de Troya.
heliacal [hɪˈlaɪəkəl] (astr.) helíaco.
helianthemum [ˌhilɪˈænθəməm] *s.* (bot.) heliantemo.
helianthin [-ˈænθən] *s.* (quím.) heliantina.
helianthus [-ˈænθəs] *s.* (bot.) helianto, girasol.
helical [ˈhɛlɪkəl] *a.* helicoidal, espiral.
helices, *pl. de* **helix.**
helicoid [ˈhɛləˌkɔɪd] **helicoidal** [ˌhɛləˈkɔɪdəl] *a.* helicoidal, espiral. —*s.* (geom.) helicoide.
Helicon [-ˌkɑn, B -kən] *s.* 1. (mitol.) Helicón, monte que los griegos consagraron a las musas. 2. **h.,** (mús.) helicón, tuba mayor.
helicopter [ˈhɛləˌkɑptər, ˈhilə-, B ˈhɛlɪˌkɔptə] *s.* (aer.) helicóptero.
helio- [ˈhilɪˌoʊ, -lɪə] elemento compositivo que entra en la formación de algunas voces con el significado de "sol".

heliocentric [ˌhiliou'sɛntrɪk] *a.* (astr.) heliocéntrico.
heliochrome ['hilɪəˌkroum] *s.* fotocromo, fotografía en colores.
heliochromic [ˌhilɪə'kroumɪk] *a.* fotocrómico.
heliogram ['hilɪəˌgræm] *s.* heliograma.
heliograph [-ˌgræf, B -ˌgrɑf] *s.* 1. fotograbado. 2. instrumento para fotografiar el sol. 3. heliógrafo, heliotelégrafo. —*v.t.* comunicar por heliógrafo.
heliographic [ˌhilɪə'græfɪk] *a.* heliográfico.
heliography [ˌhilɪ'ɑgrəfɪ, B -'ɔg-] *s.* heliografía.
heliogravure [-ougrə'vjur, B -'vjuə] *s.* huecograbado, fotograbado en hueco.
heliolater [-'ɑlətər, B -'ɔlətə] *s.* heliólatra.
heliolatry [-trɪ] *s.* heliolatría, culto o adoración al sol.
heliometer [-'ɑmətər, B -'ɔmɪtə] *s.* (astr.) heliómetro.
heliometrical [-ou'mɛtrɪkəl] *a.* (astr.) heliométrico.
Helios ['hilɪˌɑs, B -ˌɔs] *s.* (mitol.) Helios, dios Sol, hijo de Hiperión.
helioscope [-əˌskoup] *s.* (astr.) helioscopio.
heliostat [-əˌstæt] *s.* helióstato.
heliotaxis [ˌhiliou'tæksəs] *s.* (biol.) heliotactismo, heliotaxismo.
heliotherapy [-'θɛrəpɪ] *a.* (med.) helioterapia.
heliotrope ['hiljəˌtroup, B 'hɛl-] *s.* 1. (bot.) heliotropo. 2. (bot.) valeriana oficinal, valeriana menor, hierba de los gatos. 3. (min.) heliotropo. 4. color rojiazul.
heliotropic [ˌhilɪə'troupɪk, -'trɑp-, B -'trɔp-] *a.* heliotrópico.
heliotropin [-'trɑpɪn, -'troup-, B -'trɔp-] *s.* (quím.) heliotropina.
heliotropism [-'ɑtrəˌpɪzəm, B -'ɔtrə-] *s.* (biol.) heliotropismo.
heliotypy ['hilɪəˌtaɪpɪ] *s.* heliotipia, fotograbado.
heliozoan [ˌhilɪə'zouən] *s.* (zool.) heliozoo. —*a.* heliozoide.
heliport ['hɛləˌpɔrt, B -ˌpɔt] *s.* helipuerto, aeropuerto para helicópteros.
helium ['hilɪəm] *s.* (quím.) helio.
helix ['hilɪks] *s.* (*pl.* HELICES ['hɛləˌsiz, 'hi-] o HELIXES) 1. (geom.) hélice, espiral. 2. (anat.) hélix o hélice. 3. (arq.) hélice, voluta. 4. (elec.) hélice.
hell [hɛl] *s.* 1. infierno. 2. fonducho; garito, timba (de juego). 3. (tip.) cajetín del diablo, cajetín de tipos inservibles. 4. (ant.) cajón de sastre. 5. **come h. or high water,** contra viento y marea; **(just) for the h. of it,** por (puro) gusto; **get the h. out of here!** ¡váyase de aquí¡; **go to h.!** váyase al infierno! ¡váyase al diablo!; **h. of a (thing),** (cosa) tremenda, extraordinaria; (cosa) pésima; **h.'s bells!** ¡caray! ¡caracoles!; **h. to pay,** pena severa, castigo duro; **in h. and beyond,** por los quintos infiernos; **like h.,** como el diablo, como un diablo, extremadamente, muchísimo, pésimamente; de ninguna manera, ni hablar, en absoluto; **sure as h.,** sin duda alguna, con toda seguridad; **the h. of it is that,** lo peor o lo raro en el asunto es que; **to be h. on,** ser muy nocivo para, ser pésimo para; **to go to h.,** ir a la ruina; echarse a perder; **to give (someone) h.,** criticar o censurar duramente (a alguien), gritarle (a alguien), decirle (a alguien) cuatro verdades; **to h. with it!** qué diablos! ¡qué me importa!; **to hope to h.,** esperar en serio; **to play** (o **raise**) **h. with,** echar a perder, hacer grandes estragos en, arruinar completamente; **to raise h.,** armar alboroto, armar escándalo; **what in h.!** ¡qué diablos!; **what the h.!** ¡qué me importa!; **who the h.?** ¿quién diablos?
he'll [hil, hɪl] *contr. de* **he will** o **he shall.**
Hellas ['hɛləs, B 'hɛlæs] *s.* (hist.) Hélade, Grecia.
hellbender ['hɛlˌbɛndər, B -də] *s.* 1. (zool.) salamandra gigante acuática. 2. (jer.) botarate. 3. (jer.) jumera, papalina.
hell-bent [-ˌbɛnt] *a.* 1. temerario, atolondrado. 2. corriendo a toda máquina o a todo vapor. 3. (con *on*) determinado a hacer, partidario decidido de (un plan, proyecto, etc.).
hellbox [-ˌbɑks, B -ˌbɔks] *s.* (tip.) cajetín del diablo, cajetín de tipos inservibles.
hellbroth [-ˌbrɔθ] *s.* poción infernal, poción mágica.
hellcat [-ˌkæt] *s.* 1. bruja. 2. arpía, mujer pendenciera y colérica.
hell-diver [-ˌdaɪvər, B -və] *s.* (orn.) zambullidor, colimbo pequeño.
hellebore ['hɛləˌbɔr, B -ˌbɔ] *s.* 1. (bot.) heléboro, eléboro, hierba de ballestero, hierba ballestera. 2. (bot.) verdegambre, veratro. 3. (farm.) eleboreína. 4. (hist.) eleborina.
Hellene ['hɛlin] *s.* heleno, griego.
Hellenic [hɛ'lɛnɪk, B -'lin-] *a.* helénico, heleno, greco. —*s.* griego clásico.
Hellenism ['hɛləˌnɪzəm] *s.* helenismo.
Hellenist [-nəst] *s.* helenista.
Hellenistic [ˌhɛlə'nɪstɪk] *a.* helenístico.
Hellenize ['hɛləˌnaɪz] *v.t., v.i.* helenizar.
heller ['hɛlər, B -ə] *s.* (*pl.* HELLER) 1. (numis.) heller (pequeña moneda austriaca de cobre; centavo de Checoslovaquia). 2. (jer.) muchacho travieso.
Hellespont ['hɛləˌspɑnt, B -ˌspɔnt] *s.* Helesponto, antiguo nombre del estrecho de los Dardanelos.
hellfire ['hɛlˌfaɪr, B -'faɪə] *s.* 1. fuego del infierno. 2. rencor o resentimiento vehemente.
hellgrammite ['hɛlgrəˌmaɪt] *s.* (ento.) larva de un coridálido acuático (ú. como carnada en la pesca).
hell-hole, hellhole ['hɛlˌhoul] *s.* (jer.) lugar desagradable o repugnante.
hellhound [-ˌhaund] *s.* 1. (mitol.) Cerbero, Cancerbero, perro guardián de los infiernos. 2. (fig.) monstruo, fiera (persona feroz).
hellion ['hɛljən] *s.* (fam.) pícaro, bribón, diablo.
hellish ['hɛlɪʃ] *a.* infernal; diabólico.
hellishly [-lɪ] *adv.* infernalmente; diabólicamente.
hellishness [-nəs] *s.* malicia infernal, diablura.
hellkite ['hɛlˌkaɪt] *s.* fiera, persona cruel.
hello [hə'lou, hɛ'-, B 'hɛ-] *interj.* ¡hola! ¡qué tal!; (al hablar por teléfono) ¡diga! ¡aló! —*s.* saludo, grito.
hell raiser, (jer.) camorrista.
hell's angel, ángel del infierno.
helm [hɛlm] *s.* 1. (mar.) timón, gobernalle, caña del timón. 2. (mar.) movimiento del timón. 3. (fig.) mando, dirección. 4. **down with the h.,** (mar.) toda la caña a sotavento; **ease the h.,** (mar.) menos caña; **to lee the h.,** (mar.) poner la caña a sotavento; **to take the h.,** (fig.) asumir el mando, hacerse cargo; **to weather the h.,** (mar.) poner la caña a barlovento; **up with the h.,** (mar.) toda la caña a barlovento. —*v.t.* gobernar (la nave); dirigir, guiar.
helm, *s.* yelmo, casco. —*v.t.* dar un yelmo a, cubrir con un yelmo.
helmet ['hɛlmət] *s.* 1. casco (de bombero, policía, buzo, soldado, etc.). 2. yelmo (de la armadura). 3. (esgr.) careta.
helmeted [-əd] *a.* cubierto con casco o yelmo.
helminth ['hɛlmɪnθ] *s.* (zool.) helminto, lombriz.
Helminthes [hɛl'mɪnθiz] *s. pl.* (zool.) helmintos.
helminthiasis [ˌhɛlmɪn'θaɪəsɪs] *s.* (med.) helmintiasis.
helminthic [hɛl'mɪnθɪk] *a.* helmíntico.
helminthologic [-ˌmɪnθə'lɑdʒɪk, B -'lɔdʒ-] *a.* helmintológico.
helminthology [ˌhɛlmɪn'θɑlədʒɪ, B -'θɔl-] *s.* helmintología.
helmsman ['hɛlmzmən] *s.* timonel, timonero, piloto.
Helot ['hɛlət] *s.* (hist.) 1. ilota (en Esparta). 2. **h.,** esclavo, siervo.
helotism [-ˌɪzəm] *s.* (hist.) 1. ilotismo. 2. servidumbre, esclavitud.
helotry [-rɪ] *s.* 1. los ilotas, la clase ilota. 2. servidumbre, esclavitud.
help [hɛlp] *v.t.* 1. ayudar, socorrer, asistir, auxiliar. 2. aliviar, mitigar. 3. remediar, evitar, prevenir, ej., *I can't h. that,* no puedo remediarlo, no puedo evitarlo, *it can't be helped,* no puede remediarse, no hay (más) remedio. 4. favorecer, beneficiar. 5. **(one, etc.) cannot h. (doing),** (uno, etc.) no puede menos que (hacer), ej., *I couldn't h. laughing,* no pude menos que reírme; **h. down,** ayudar a bajar; **h. forward,** adelantar, promover; **h. (someone) off with (coat,** etc.), ayudar (a alguien) a quitarse (el abrigo, etc.); **h. (someone) on with (coat,** etc.), ayudar (a alguien) a ponerse (el abrigo, etc.); **h. one (do),** ayudar a uno a (hacer); **h. oneself,** ayudarse; servirse; **h. oneself to (food, a drink),** servirse (alimentos, una bebida); tomar sin pedir permiso; **h. (someone) out,** ayudar, prestar ayuda a (uno); **h. (someone) out of (a difficulty,** etc.), ayudar (a alguien) a salir de (una dificultad) o a vencer (un obstáculo, etc.), ayudar a superar (una dificultad, crisis, etc.); **h. up,** ayudar a levantarse; ayudar a subir; **no more (longer, later,** etc.) **than one can h.,** no más (más lejos, más tiempo, etc.) que lo necesario; **so h. me God,** que Dios me castigue (si no digo la verdad). —*v.i.* 1. asistir. 2. servir, ser útil. 3. **h. out,** ser útil, ser de ayuda. —*s.* 1. ayuda, socorro, asistencia, auxilio. 2. remedio, ej., *there is no h. for it,* no hay remedio para eso. 3. ayudante, asistente, empleado; criado, peón, obrero; criados, peones, obreros; (G.B.) criada de medio día. 4. porción, ración (de comida). 5. **with the h. of,** con la ayuda de; **h.!** ¡socorro! ¡auxilio!; **to be a great h. to,** ser una gran ayuda para; **to be of h.,** ser útil, ayudar.
helper ['hɛlpər, B -ə] *s.* ayudante, asistente.
helpful [-fəl] *a.* útil, provechoso; beneficioso; servicial.
helpfully [-fəlɪ] *adv.* servicialmente.
helpfulness [-fəlnəs] *s.* utilidad; espíritu servicial.
helping [-ɪŋ] *s.* 1. ayuda, asistencia. 2. porción, ración (de comida).
helpless [-ləs] *a.* 1. desvalido, indefenso, débil. 2. inútil, incompetente. 3. impotente, incapacitado.
helplessly [-lɪ] *adv.* 1. desvalidamente, débilmente. 2. impotentemente.
helplessness [-nəs] *s.* 1. desamparo, debilidad. 2. impotencia.
helpmate [-ˌmeɪt] *s.* compañero, ayudante, asistente; compañera (esposa).
helpmeet [-ˌmit] *s.* compañera, esp. esposa.
Helsinki ['hɛlsɪŋkɪ, hɛl'sɪŋ-] *s.* Helsinki, capital de Finlandia.
helter-skelter ['hɛltər'skɛltər, B -tə'-tə] *adv.* (fam.) a troche y moche, cochite hervite, sin orden ni concierto. —*a.* precipitado, atropellado. —*s.* troche y moche, alboroto, confusión.
helve [hɛlv] *s.* mango, puño (de arma o herramienta). —*v.t.* poner mango a, encajar mango en.
Helvetia [hɛl'viʃɪə] *s.* Helvecia, nombre romano de la Suiza actual.

Helvetian [-ʃən] *a., s.* helvecio, suizo.
Helvetic [-'vɛtɪk] *a.* helvético, helvecio, suizo. —*s.* protestante suizo.
hem [hɛm] *s.* 1. bastilla, dobladillo, repulgo. 2. borde, margen. —*v.t.* (*pret., p.p.* HEMMED; *p.pr.* HEMMING) 1. dobladillar, bastillar, repulgar. 2. (gen. con *in*) rodear, encerrar, confinar, limitar, restringir.
hem [hɛm, B hm] *interj.* ¡ejem! —*s.* tos simulada; el sonido ¡ejem! —*v.i.* (*pret., p.p.* HEMMED; *p.pr.* HEMMING) decir ¡ejem!; simular tos, aclarar la garganta; **h. and haw,** tartalear, titubear, vacilar.
hemacytometer, *var. de* **hemocytometer.**
hemagglutinate, haemagglutinate [ˌhimə'glutənˌeɪt] *v.t.* causar la hemoglutinación de.
hemagglutination, haemagglutination [-ˌglutə'neɪʃən] *s.* (biol.) hemoglutinación.
hemagglutinin, haemagglutinin [-'glutənən] *s.* (biol.) hemoglutinina.
hemal, haemal ['himəl] *a.* 1. hemal, hemático, relativo a la sangre. 2. (zool.) hemal (del lado del corazón).
he-man ['hi'mæn] *s.* (fam.) hombre de pelo en pecho, hombre viril.
hematal, haematal ['hɛmətəl, 'himət-] *a.* (anat.) hemal, hemático.
hematein, haematein [ˌhimə'tiən, ˌhɛmə-] *s.* (quím.) hemateína.
hematemesis [-'tɛməsəs] *s.* (med.) hematemesis.
hematic, haematic [hɪ'mætɪk] *a.* hemático.
hematin, haematin ['hɛmətən, 'himə-] *s.* 1. (quím.) hemateína. 2. (bioquím.) hematina.
hematinic, haematinic [ˌhɛmə'tɪnɪk, ˌhimə-] *s., a.* (med.) hematínico.
hematite, haematite ['hɛməˌtaɪt, 'himə-, B 'hɛm-] *s.* (min.) hematita, hematites.
hematoblast, haematoblast ['hɛmətoʊˌblæst, 'himə-, B 'hi-] *s.* (biol.) hematoblasto.
hematocele, haematocele ['hɛmətoʊˌsil, 'himə-] *s.* (med.) hematocele.
hematocrit, haematocrit ['hɛmətoʊˌkrɪt, hɪ'mætə-, B 'hɛmətoʊ-] *s.* (fisiol.) hematocrito.
hematocryal [ˌhɛmə'tɑkrɪəl, B 'hɛmətoʊˌkraɪ-] *a.* (zool.) hematocrial.
hematogenous, haematogenous [ˌhɛmə'tɑdʒənəs, ˌhimə-, B -'tɔdʒ-] *s.* (fisiol.) hematógeno.
hematoid, haematoid ['himəˌtɔɪd, 'hɛmə-] *a.* (fisiol.) hematoideo.
hematologist, haematologist [ˌhɛmə'tɑlədʒəst, ˌhimə-, B -'tɔl-] *s.* (med.) hematólogo.
hematology, haematology [-dʒɪ] *s.* (med.) hematología.
hematoma, haematoma [ˌhimə'toʊmə, ˌhɛmə-] *s.* (*pl.* HEMATOMATA [-tə] o HEMATOMAS) (med.) hematoma.
hematophagous, haematophagous [-'tɑfəgəs, B -'tɔf-] *a.* hematófago.
hematopoiesis, haematopoiesis [ˌhɛmətoʊpɔɪ'isəs, ˌhimə-] *s.* (fisiol.) hematopoyesis, hemopoyesis.
hematopoietic, haematopoietic [-'ɛtɪk] *a.* (fisiol.) hematopoyético.
hematose, haematose ['himətoʊs, 'hɛmə-] *a.* (med.) hematoso.
hematosis, haematosis [ˌhimə'toʊsəs, ˌhɛmə-] *s.* (fisiol.) hematosis.
hematothermal [-toʊ'θɜrməl, B -'θɜməl] *a.* (zool.) hematotermo, de sangre caliente (mamíferos y pájaros).
hematoxylin [-'tɑksələn, B -'tɔk-] *s.* 1. (bot.) palo de Campeche. 2. hematoxilina.
hematozoal [ˌhɛmətə'zoʊəl, ˌhimə] **hematozoic** [-ɪk] *a.* (zool.) hematozoico.
hematozoon, haematozoon [ˌhɛmətə'zoʊˌɑn, ˌhimə-, B -ˌɔn] *s.* (*pl.* HEMATOZOA) (zool.) hematozoario, hematozoo.
hematuria, haematuria [ˌhimə'tʊrɪə, ˌhɛmə-, B -'tjʊr-] *s.* (med.) hematuria, hematuresis.
hemelytron [hɛ'mɛləˌtrɑn, B -ˌtrɔn] **hemelytrum** [-trəm] *s.* (*pl.* HEMELYTRA [-trə]) (ento.) hemélitro, hemiélitro.
hemeralopia [ˌhɛmərə'loʊpɪə] *s.* hemeralopía.
hemeralopic [-pɪk] *a.* hemerálope.
hemerocallis [-roʊ'kæləs] *s.* (bot.) hemerocala.
hemialgia [ˌhɛmɪ'ældʒɪə] *s.* (med.) hemialgia, dolor que afecta sólo a un lado del cuerpo.
hemic, haemic ['himɪk, 'hɛmɪk] *a.* hémico, hemático.
hemicellulose [ˌhɛmɪ'sɛljəloʊs] *s.* (quím.) hemicelulosa, afín al azúcar y a la celulosa.
hemicrania [-'kreɪnɪə] *s.* (med.) hemicránea, jaqueca.
hemicycle ['hɛmɪˌsaɪkəl] *s.* hemiciclo, semicírculo.
hemidemisemiquaver [ˌhɛmɪˌdɛmɪ'sɛmɪˌkweɪvər, B -və] *s.* (mús.) semifusa.
hemielytron [ˌhɛmɪ'ɛləˌtrɑn, B -ˌtrɔn] **hemielytrum** [-trəm] *vars. de* **hemelytron, hemelytrum.**
hemihedral [ˌhɛmɪ'hidrəl] *a.* hemiédrico.
hemihedrism [-drɪzəm] **hemihedry** [-drɪ] *s.* hemiedría.
hemihydrate [-'haɪˌdreɪt] *s.* (quím.) hemihidrato.
hemimetabolism [-mə'tæbəˌlɪzəm] *s.* (ento.) hemimetabolía, hemimetabolismo.
hemimorphic [-'mɔrfɪk, B -'mɔfɪk] *a.* hemimorfo.
hemimorphism [-ˌfɪzəm] *s.* hemimorfia, hemimorfismo.
hemimorphite [-ˌfaɪt] *s.* (min.) hemimorfita.
hemin, haemin ['himən] *s.* (bioquím.) hemina.
hemionus [hɪ'maɪənəs] *s.* (zool.) hemíono.
hemiparasite [ˌhɛmɪ'pærəˌsaɪt] *s.* (bot.) hemiparásito.
hemiplegia [-'plidʒə] *s.* (med.) hemiplejia.
hemiplegic [-dʒɪk] *a.* (med.) hemipléjico.
hemiplegy ['hɛmɪˌplidʒɪ] *s.* (med.) hemiplejia.
Hemiptera [hɪ'mɪptərə] *s. pl.* (ento.) hemípteros.
hemipteran [-rən] *s.* (ento.) hemíptero.
hemipteroid [-ˌrɔɪd] *a.* (ento.) hemipteroide.
hemipteron [-ˌrɑn, B -ˌrɔn] *s.* (ento.) hemíptero.
hemipterous [-rəs] *a.* (ento.) hemíptero.
hemisphere ['hɛməˌsfɪr, B -ˌsfɪə] *s.* 1. hemisferio, semiesfera. 2. (geog., astr.) hemisferio. 3. (fig.) campo, esfera. 4. (anat.) hemisferio (del cerebro o cerebelo).
hemispheric [ˌhɛmə'sfɪrɪk, B -'sfɛrɪk] **hemispherical** [-ɪkəl] *a.* hemisférico.
hemispheroid [-'sfɪrɔɪd] *s.* hemisferoide.
hemistich ['hɛmɪˌstɪk] *s.* (poét.) hemistiquio.
hemiterpene [ˌhɛmɪ'tɜrˌpin, B -'tɜˌ-] *s.* (quím.) hemiterpeno.
hemitrope ['hɛmɪˌtroʊp] *s.* (min.) hemítropo, macla.
hemitropic [ˌhɛmɪ'trɑpɪk, B -'trɔp-] *a.* (min.) hemítropo.
hemline ['hɛmˌlaɪn] *s.* bastilla, dobladillo, ruedo (de una falda, vestido, etc.).
hemlock ['hɛmˌlɑk, B -ˌlɔk] *s.* 1. (bot.) cicuta; cicuta mayor, cicuta de Sócrates; cicuta acuática, cicuta virosa. 2. (bot.) tsuga (esp. del Canadá); pinabete.
hemmer ['hɛmər, B -ə] *s.* repulgador, dobladillador.
hemoblast, haemoblast ['himəˌblæst, 'hɛmə, B 'himə-] *s.* (biol.) hemoblasto, hematoblasto.
hemocyanin, haemocyanin [ˌhimoʊ'saɪənən, ˌhɛmoʊ-] *s.* (quím.) hemocianina.
hemocyte, haemocyte ['himəˌsaɪt, 'hɛmə-] *s.* (biol.) hemocito, hematocito.
hemocytometer, haemocytometer [ˌhiməsaɪ'tɑmətər, ˌhɛmə-, B -'tɔmɪtə] *s.* hemocitómetro, hematímetro.
hemoflagellate, haemoflagellate [ˌhimoʊ'flædʒələt, ˌhɛmoʊ-] *s.* (zool.) hemoflagelado.
hemoglobin, haemoglobin ['himəˌgloʊbən, 'hɛmə-, B ˌhimə'gloʊ-] *s.* (bioquím.) hemoglobina.
hemoglobinous, haemoglobinous [ˌhimə'gloʊbənəs] *a.* (bioquím.) hemoglobinado.
hemoglobinuria, haemoglobinuria [-ˌgloʊbə'nʊrɪə, B -'njʊr-] *s.* (med.) hemoglobinuria.
hemoid, haemoid ['himɔɪd] *a.* (fisiol.) hemoide, hemoideo.
hemoleucocyte, haemoleucocyte, hemoleukocyte [ˌhimə'lukəˌsaɪt, B -'lju-] *s.* (anat.) hemoleucocito.
hemolysin, haemolysin [hɪ'mɑləsən, B ˌhimə'laɪsɪn] *s.* (bioquím.) hemolisina.
hemolysis, haemolysis [hɪ'mɑləsəs, B -'mɔl-] *s.* hemólisis.
hemolytic, haemolytic [ˌhimə'lɪtɪk, ˌhɛmə-] *a.* hemolítico.
hemopathy, haemopathy [hi'mɑpəθɪ, B -'mɔp-] *s.* (med.) hemopatía.
hemophile, haemophile ['himəˌfaɪl, 'hɛmə-] *a., s.* hemófilo (bacteria).
hemophilia, haemophilia [ˌhimə'fɪlɪə, ˌhɛmə-, B ˌhimə-] *s.* (med.) hemofilia.
hemophiliac, haemophiliac [-ɪˌæk] *a., s.* hemofílico.
hemophilic, haemophilic [-'fɪlɪk] *a.* 1. (med.) hemofílico (persona). 2. (biol.) hemófilo (bacteria).
hemoptysis, haemoptysis [hɪ'mɑptəsəs, B -'mɔp-] *s.* (med.) hemoptisis.
hemorrhage, haemorrhage ['hɛmərɪdʒ] *s.* (med.) hemorragia. —*v.i.* sangrar (profusamente).
hemorrhoid, haemorrhoid ['hɛməˌrɔɪd] *s.* (med.) (*ú. gen. en pl.*) hemorroide, almorrana.
hemorrhoidal, haemorrhoidal [ˌhɛmə'rɔɪdəl] *a.* (med.) hemorroidal.
hemorrhoidectomy, haemorrhoidectomy [-ˌrɔɪ'dɛktəmɪ] *s.* (med.) hemorroidectomía.
hemostatis, haemostatis [hɪ'mɑstəsəs, B ˌhimə'stæsɪs] *s.* (med.) hemostasia, hemostasis.
hemostat, haemostat ['himəˌstæt, 'hɛmə-] *s.* 1. (med.) hemostático. 2. hemóstato.
hemostatic, haemostatic [ˌhimə'stætɪk, ˌhɛmə-] *a., s.* (med.) hemostático.
hemp [hɛmp] *s.* 1. (bot.) cáñamo. 2. mariguana. 3. hachís, haschich, hachich; fibra de cáñamo.
hempen ['hɛmpən] *a.* cañameño (tela, etc.); cañamero (industria, etc.).
hemp nettle, (bot.) galeopsio.
hemp saddlebags, linches (Mex.).
hempseed ['hɛmpˌsid] *s.* cañamón.
hempy ['hɛmpɪ] (pr. esco.) *a.* travieso. —*s.* (*pl.* HEMPIES) carne de horca, bribón.
hemstitch ['hɛmˌstɪtʃ] *v.t.* (cost.) hacer una vainica en, adornar con vainicas. —*s.* (cost.) vainica.

hemstitcher [-ər, B -ə] *s.* vainiquera.
hen [hɛn] *s.* 1. gallina. 2. hembra de cualquier ave. 3. (jer.) mujer, esp. vieja.
hen and chickens, (bot.) 1. especie de siempreviva. 2. hiedra terrestre.
henbane ['hɛn,beɪn] *s.* beleño, beleño negro.
henbit [-,bɪt] *s.* (bot.) ortiga de hojas abrazadoras.
hence [hɛns] *adv.* 1. de aquí, de aquí a, desde aquí. 2. por (lo) tanto, por esto, en consecuencia. 3. **five years h.,** de aquí a cinco años; **h.!** (poét.) ¡fuera!; **h. with,** (ant.) fuera con, quiten de delante; **to go h.,** (poét.) morir, morirse; **years h.,** cuando hayan pasado muchos años.
henceforth ['hɛns,fɔrθ, B -'fɔθ] **henceforward** [-'fɔrwərd, B -'fɔwəd] *adv.* de aquí en adelante, en lo venidero, en lo futuro, en lo sucesivo.
henchman ['hɛntʃmən] *s.* 1. secuaz, paniaguado; muñidor. 2. partidario, defensor (de una idea, etc.). 3. (ant.) criado; escudero, paje.
hencoop ['hɛn,kup] *s.* gallinero.
hendecagon [hɛn'dɛkə,gɑn, B -gən] *s.* (geom.) endecágono.
hendecagonal [,hɛndə'kægənəl] *a.* (geom.) endecágono.
hendecasyllabic [hɛn,dɛkəsə'læbɪk] *a., s.* endecasílabo.
hendecasyllable [-'dɛkə,sɪləbəl, B 'hɛndɛkə,sɪl-] *s.* endecasílabo.
hendiadys [hɛn'daɪədəs] *s.* (ret.) endiadis, endíadis.
henequen ['hɛnɪkən] *s.* 1. (bot.) henequén, cáñamo. 2. fibra de henequén.
hen hawk, (orn.) águila pollera, águila de quema; gavilán pollero.
henhouse ['hɛn,haʊs] *s.* gallinero.
henna ['hɛnə] *s.* 1. (bot.) alcana, alheña. 2. alheña (tinte). 3. color de alheña. —*v.t.* (*pret., p.p.* HENNAED ['hɛnəd]; *p.pr.* HENNAING) alheñar, teñir con alheña.
hennery ['hɛnərɪ] *s.* 1. pollera, granja de pollos. 2. gallinero.
henotheism ['hɛnəθi,ɪzəm] *s.* (relig.) henoteísmo, creer en Dios sin afirmar que es uno sólo.
henotheist [-,θiəst] *s.* henoteísta.
hen party, (fam.) tertulia de mujeres.
henpeck ['hɛn,pɛk] *v.t.* fastidiar, dominar, tiranizar (al marido).
hen roost, *s.* gallinero.
henry ['hɛnrɪ] *s.* (elec.) henry, henrio.
hep [hɛp] *a.* 1. (jer.) moderno, avanzado. 2. (con *to*) aficionado (a), interesado (en). 3. (con *to*) enterado (de), informado (sobre), al tanto (de). 4. aficionado al jazz.
heparin ['hɛpərən] *s.* (bioquím.) heparina.
heparinize [-,aɪz] *v.t.* (med.) heparinizar (tratar con heparina).
hepatalgia [,hɛpə'tældʒɪə] *s.* (med.) hepatalgia, dolor intenso del hígado.
hepatic [hɪ'pætɪk] *a.* (biol., med., bot.) hepático. —*s.* (bot.) hepática.
hepatica [-ɪkə] *s.* (bot.) hepática.
hepatitis [,hɛpə'taɪtəs] *s.* (med.) hepatitis.
hepatization [,hɛpətə'zeɪʃən, B -taɪ-] *s.* (med.) hepatización.
hepatology [-'tɑlədʒɪ, B -'tɔl-] *s.* (med.) hepatología.
hepcat ['hɛp,kæt] *s.* (jer.) músico de jazz; aficionado al jazz.
hepped up [hɛpt-] (jer.) 1. entusiasmado, entusiasta. 2. excitado por una droga.
heptachord ['hɛptə,kɔrd, B -,kɔd] *s.* (mús.) 1. heptacordo, heptacordio. 2. lira de siete cuerdas.
heptad [-,tæd] *s.* heptada, septena.
heptagon [-tə,gɑn, B -gən] *s.* (geom.) heptágono.
heptagonal [hɛp'tægənəl] *a.* (geom.) heptagonal.
heptahedral [,hɛptə'hidrəl] *a.* (geom.) heptaédrico.
heptahedron [-drən] *s.* (geom.) heptaedro.
heptameter [hɛp'tæmətər, B -ə] *s.* (poét.) heptámetro.
heptane ['hɛp,teɪn] *s.* (quím.) heptano.
heptarch ['hɛptɑrk, B -tɑk] *s.* heptarca.
heptarchy [-,tɑrkɪ, B -,tɑkɪ] *s.* (*pl.* HEPTARCHIES) 1. heptarquía. 2. **the H.,** la Heptarquía anglosajona, los siete reinos aliados anglosajones.
heptasyllable ['hɛptə,sɪləbəl] *s.* heptasílabo.
Heptateuch ['hɛptə,tuk, B -,tjuk] *s.* (bíbl.) Heptateuco, los siete primeros libros del Antiguo Testamento.
heptose ['hɛp,toʊs] *s.* (quím.) heptosa.
her [hɜr, ɜr, B hɜ, ɜ] *pron.* (*acusativo o dativo de* **she**) la, le a ella. —*a. pos.* su(s), de ella.
Hera ['hirə, B 'hɪərə] *s.* (mitol.) Hera (Juno), diosa del matrimonio.
Heracles ['hɛrə,kliz] *s.* (mitol.) Heracles o Hércules, famoso por su estatura y su fuerza.
Heraclidae [,hɛrə'klaɪdɪ] *s. pl.* los heráclidas, descendientes de Hércules.
Heraclitus [,hɛrə'klaɪtəs] *s.* Heráclito, filósofo griego.
Herakles *var. de* **Heracles** .
herald ['hɛrəld] *s.* 1. heraldo. 2. mensajero. 3. portavoz, anunciador. 4. precursor. —*v.t.* 1. anunciar, presagiar. 2. proclamar, pregonar.
heraldic [he'rældɪk] *s.* heráldico.
heraldry ['hɛrəldrɪ] *s.* 1. heráldica. 2. blasón. 3. pompa o ceremonia heráldica.
herb [ɜrb, B hɜb] *s.* 1. hierba, yerba (esp. medicinal o aromática). 2. (ant.) césped, herbaje.
herbaceous [,hɜr'beɪʃəs, B ,hɜ'-] *a.* herbáceo.
herbage ['ɜrbɪdʒ, B 'hɜbɪdʒ] *s.* 1. herbaje, pasto. 2. hojas y tallos tiernos (de las plantas herbáceas). 3. (der.) herbaje (derecho que se cobra por el arrendamiento de dehesas).
herbal [-bəl] *a.* herbario, herbáceo. —*s.* (ant.) tratado de botánica.
herbalist [-bələst] *s.* 1. herbolario. 2. botánico, herbario.
herbarium [,hɜr'bɛrɪəm, B ,hɜ'bɛər-] *s.* (*pl.* HERBARIUMS O HERBARIA [-ɪə]) herbario (colección de hierbas; lugar donde se las guarda).
herb bennet, (bot.) gariofilea, clavel silvestre.
herbicide ['hɜrbə,saɪd, B 'hɜbə-] *s.* herbicida.
herbivore [-,vɔr, B -,vɔ] *s.* (zool.) herbívoro.
herbivorous [,hɜr'bɪvərəs, B ,hɜ'-] *a.* (zool.) herbívoro.
herb ivy, (bot.) pinillo oloroso.
herb Paris, (bot.) hierba de París.
Herculaneum [,hɜrkjə'leɪnɪəm, B ,hɜkjʊ-] *s.* Herculano, ciudad que, junto con Pompeya, fue destruida en la erupción del Vesubio.
herculean [-'liən] *a.* **1. H.,** hercúleo, de Hércules. 2. (fig.) hercúleo, enorme (fuerza, tarea, etc.). 3. de enorme tamaño, gigantesco.
Hercules ['hɜrkjə,liz, B 'hɜkjʊ-] *s.* (mitol., astr.) Hércules.
Hercules-club [-'klʌb] *s.* (bot.) aralia espinosa.
herd [hɜrd, B hɜd] *s.* 1. hato, rebaño, manada. 2. muchedumbre, multitud. 3. populacho, plebe, turba. —*v.i.* 1. reunirse en manada. 2. asociarse, agruparse, aglomerarse. —*v.t.* 1. (con *together*) reunir (el ganado) en hato o rebaño. 2. llevar al campo, guardar, pastorear (al ganado). 3. (esp. con *with*) agrupar (con). 4. **h. into,** meter en, apiñar en.
herd, herder ['hɜrdər, B 'hɜdə] *s.* pastor, zagal, vaquero, boyero, cabrero, porquerizo, ovejero.
herdic ['hɜrdɪk, B 'hɜd-] *s.* carruaje con asientos a los lados y entrada por la parte trasera.
herd's-grass ['hɜrdz,græs, B 'hɜdz,grɑs] *s.* (bot.) 1. fleo, semilla parda, grano plateado. 2. agróstide.
herdsman [-mən] *s.* 1. pastor, zagal, vaquero. 2. ganadero. 3. **H.,** (astr.) Bootes, Boyero.
here [hɪr, B hɪə] *adv.* 1. aquí, en este lugar. 2. acá, hacia acá. 3. aquí, en este punto. 4. en esta vida, en el estado presente. 5. **h.!** ¡presente!; **h. and there,** acá y allá; irregularmente; **h. below,** aquí en la tierra, acá abajo; **h. goes!** ahí va, allá va; ahora entro yo; **h. he is,** hele aquí; **here's to (you),** (brindis) a tu salud; **h., there and everywhere,** en todas partes; **h. we are!** ¡ya estamos! ¡ya llegamos!; **h. you are,** aquí tienes; **I don't belong h.,** no soy de aquí; no me encuentro a gusto aquí; **look h.,** escuche, atienda, mire Ud.; **(that's) neither h. nor there,** (eso) no viene al caso, (eso) no importa. —*s.* 1. este lugar, esta vida, ej., *the h. and the hereafter,* esta vida y la otra. 2. **from h.,** desde aquí; **to h.,** hasta aquí.
hereabout ['hɪrə,baʊt, B 'hɪər-] **hereabouts** [-ə,baʊts] *adv.* por aquí, en la vecindad, en estas cercanías, por aquí cerca, en estas inmediaciones.
hereafter [hɪr'æftər, B hɪər'ɑftə] *adv.* en lo futuro, de aquí en adelante, en lo sucesivo. —*s.* 1. el más allá. 2. el futuro.
hereat [-'æt] *adv.* a esto, por esto, en esto.
hereby ['hɪr'baɪ, B 'hɪə'-] *adv.* 1. por la presente, por este medio, por este acto, por éstas. 2. (ant.) muy cerca.
hereditable [hə'rɛdɪtəbəl] *a.* heredable.
hereditament [,hɛrə'dɪtəmənt] *s.* (der.) bienes heredables, herencia, patrimonio.
hereditarily [hə'rɛdə,tɛrəlɪ, B -tər-] *adv.* hereditariamente.
hereditary [-,tɛrɪ, B -tərɪ] *a.* hereditario.
hereditary disease, enfermedad hereditaria.
heredity [hə'rɛdətɪ] *s.* (biol.) herencia.
Hereford ['hɜrfərd, 'hɛrə-, B 'hɛrɪfəd] *s.* Hereford (raza de ganado bovino natural del condado inglés de Herefordshire).
herein [hɪr'ɪn, B 'hɪər-] *adv.* en esto; aquí dentro, incluso.
hereinabove [-,ɪnə'bʌv] *adv.* más arriba (en este escrito, documento, etc.).
hereinafter [,hɪrən'æftər, B 'hɪərɪn'ɑftə] *adv.* más abajo, después, más adelante, a continuación.
hereinbefore [-,ɪnbɪ'fɔr, B -'fɔ] *adv.* antes, arriba, más arriba, anteriormente, en lo precedente, en la parte anterior.
hereinbelow [-bɪ'loʊ] *adv.* más abajo (en este escrito, documento, etc.).
hereof [hɪr'ʌv, -'ɑv, B hɪər'ɔv] *adv.* de esto; acerca de esto.
hereon [-'ɔn, -'ɑn, B -'ɔn] *adv.* sobre esto, sobre este punto, acerca de esto, a esto.
heresiarch [hə'rizɪ,ɑrk, B hɛ-,ɑk] *s.* (*pl.* HERESIARCHS) heresiarca, hereje.
heresy ['hɛrəsɪ] *s.* (*pl.* HERESIES) herejía.
heretic ['hɛrə,tɪk] *s.* hereje. —*a.* herético.
heretical [hə'rɛtɪkəl] *a.* herético.
hereto [hɪr'tu, B 'hɪə'tu] *adv.* a esto, a las presentes, a la presente (escritura).
heretofore ['hɪrtə,fɔr, B 'hɪətu'fɔ] *adv.* hasta ahora, hasta aquí; en otro tiempo, antes, en tiempos pasados.
hereunder [hɪr'ʌndər, B hɪər'ʌndə] *adv.* 1. por las presentes, conforme a la presente (escritura). 2. más abajo, líneas abajo.

hereunto [-'ʌntu, B 'hɪərʌn'tu] *adv.* a esto, a las presentes, a la presente (escritura).
hereupon ['hɪrə,pɑn, B 'hɪərə'pɔn] *adv.* en esto; a esto, sobre esto; luego, por consiguiente.
herewith [hɪr'wɪð, -'wɪθ, B 'hɪə'-] *adv.* con esto, junto con esto, con la presente, incluso.
heriot ['hɛrɪət] *s.* (G.B., hist.) impuesto o tributo feudal pagadero al señor a la muerte de un arrendatario.
heritability [ˌhɛrətə'bɪlətɪ] *s.* condición de heredable.
heritable ['hɛrətəbəl] *a.* 1. heredable (bienes). 2. hereditario (vicio, enfermedad, etc.).
heritage ['hɛrətɪdʒ] *s.* herencia; patrimonio.
heritance [ˌəns] *s.* (ant.) herencia; patrimonio.
heritor [-ər, B -ə] *s.* 1. heredero. 2. (der., esco.) dueño de bienes heredables en una parroquia o feligresía.
herl [hɜrl, B hɜl] *s.* 1. cendal de pluma (usado para preparar moscas artificiales). 2. mosca artificial, con cendal (para la pesca).
herm [hɜrm, B hɜm] *s.* herma, busto sin brazos sobre un estípite.
hermaphrodism [hər'mæfrəˌdɪzəm, B hɜ'-] *s.* hermafroditismo.
hermaphrodite [-ˌdaɪt] *s., a.* 1. hermafrodita, andrógino. 2. (bot., zool.) hermafrodita.
hermaphrodite brig, (mar.) bergantín goleta.
hermaphroditic [-ˌmæfrə'dɪtɪk] *a.* hermafrodita.
hermaphroditism [-'mæfrəˌdaɪtˌɪzəm] *s.* (biol.) hermafroditismo.
hermeneutic [ˌhɜrmə'nutɪk, B ˌhɜmə'njut-] **hermeneutical** [-ɪkəl] *a.* hermenéutico.
hermeneutics [-ɪks] *s. pl.* (*sing. en const.*) hermenéutica, interpretación.
Hermes ['hɜrmiz, B 'hɜmiz] *s.* (mitol.) Hermes, mensajero de los dioses.
hermetic [hɜr'mɛtɪk, B hɜ-'] **hermetical** [-ɪkəl] *a.* hermético, impenetrable.
hermetically [-ɪkəlɪ] *adv.* herméticamente.
hermetic art, arte hermética, alquimia.
hermit ['hɜrmət, B 'hɜmɪt] *s.* 1. ermitaño, cenobita, eremita, anacoreta. 2. pasta de melaza con pasas y nueces picadas.
hermitage [-ɪdʒ] *s.* 1. morada del ermitaño, ermita. 2. residencia solitaria, retiro. 3. vida eremítica. 4. [ɛrmɪ'tɑʒ, B 'hɜmɪtɪdʒ] **H.,** una clase de vino francés.
hermit crab, (zool.) ermitaño, paguro.
hermitic [hɜr'mɪtɪk, B hɜ-'] **hermitical** [-ɪkəl] *a.* eremítico, anacorético.
hermit thrush, (orn.) tordo norteamericano.
hern [hɜrn, B hɜn] (dial.) *var. de* **heron.**
hernia ['hɜrnɪə, B 'hɜnjə] *s.* (*pl.* HERNIAS o HERNIAE [-ˌi]) (med.) hernia, quebradura.
hernial [-nɪəl] *a.* (med.) herniario.
herniate [-ˌeɪt] *v.i.* padecer de una hernia.
herniation [ˌhɜrnɪ'eɪʃən, B ˌhɜnɪ-] *s.* (med.) herniación.
hero ['hɪroʊ, B 'hɪər-] *s.* (*pl.* HEROES) 1. héroe. 2. (*sandwich*) (fam.) sándwich mixto de tamaño grande, emparedado hecho con una barra entera de pan.
Herod ['hɛrəd] *s.* (bíbl.) Herodes.
Herodian [hə'roʊdɪən] *a.* herodiano, relativo a Herodes.
Herodias [hə'roʊdɪəs, B hɛ-æs] *s.* (bíbl.) Herodías, madre de Salomé.
heroic [hɪ'roʊɪk] *a.* 1. heroico. 2. grande, poderoso, inmenso, impresionante. 3. extremo (ej., medidas). 4. (med.) heroico (medicamento); radical (tratamiento, etc.). —*s.* 1. heroida (poema o verso heroico). 2. (*pl.*) rimbombancia, ampulosidad, acto extravagante.
heroic age, edad heroica, tiempos heroicos; **the h. a.,** (hist. griega) la época heroica.
heroical [-ɪkəl] *var. de.* **heroic.**
heroically [-kəlɪ] *adv.* heroicamente.
heroic couplet, estrofa de dos versos heroicos pareados (de cinco yambos cada uno).
heroicomic [hɪˌroʊɪ'kɑmɪk, B -'kɔm-] *a.* heroico-cómico.
heroic verse, verso heroico.
heroin ['hɛroʊən] *s.* (farm.) heroína.
heroine ['hɛroʊɪn] *s.* heroína; protagonista.
heroism ['hɛroʊˌɪzəm] *s.* heroísmo, heroicidad, proeza, hazaña.
heron ['hɛrən] *s.* (orn.) garza.
heronry [-rɪ] *s.* criadero de garzas.
heron's bill, (bot.) pico de cigüeña.
hero sandwich, (fam.) sándwich mixto de tamaño grande, emparedado hecho con una barra entera de pan.
hero worship, adulación extrema (de una persona como modelo de perfección).
hero-worship ['hɪroʊˌwɜrʃəp, B 'hɪəroʊˌw-ɜʃɪp] *v.t.* idealizar, tratar con adulación extrema (a alguien).
herpes ['hɜrˌpiz, B 'hɜˌ-] *s.* (med.) herpe, herpes, erupción cutánea.
herpes labialis [-ˌleɪbɪ'æləs] (med.) herpe labial.
herpetic [hər'pɛtɪk, B hə'-] *a.* (med.) herpético.
herpetism ['hɜrpəˌtɪzəm, B 'hɜpə-] *s.* (med.) herpetismo.
herpetology [ˌhɜrpə'tɑlədʒɪ, B ˌhɜpə'tɔl-] *s.* (zool.) herpetología.
Herr [hɛr, B 'hɛə] **Herren** ['hɛrən, B 'hɛər-] *s.* (alemán) señor, señores.
herring ['hɛrɪŋ] *s.* (ict.) arenque.
herringbone [-ˌboʊn] *a.* de punto de espina; a punto de Hungría. —*s.* 1. espina de pescado (en telas, dibujos, etc.). 2. (cost.) punto de espina. 3. espinapez, punto de Hungría (en los entarimados). 4. (esquí) paso cruzado. —*v.t.* 1. producir un patrón de espina de pescado sobre (una superficie). 2. arreglar en forma de espina de pescado. 3. (cost.) hacer con punto de espina. —*v.i.* 1. hacer un patrón de espina de pescado. 2. (esquí) ascender a paso cruzado.
hers [hɜrz, B hɜz] *pron. pos.* suyo, suya, (el, la) de ella, el suyo, la suya, los suyos, las suyas (de ella).
herself [hər'sɛlf, B hɜ'-] *pron. de la tercera pers. f. del sing., forma enfática o reflexiva;* ella misma, sí misma, se, sí, ella, ej., *she h. told me,* ella misma me dijo, *she has blamed h.,* ella se ha echado la culpa a sí misma, *she has hurt h.,* ella se ha herido o lastimado; **with h.,** consigo misma.
hertz [hɜrts, B hɜts] *s.* (fís.) hertz, hertzio, unidad de frecuencia igual a un ciclo por segundo.
hertzian ['hɜrtsɪən, B 'hɜt-] *a.* hertziano.
hertzian wave, (elec.) onda hertziana, onda electromagnética.
he's [hiz] *contr. de* **he is** o **he has.**
hesitance ['hɛzətəns] *var. de* **hesitancy.**
hesitancy [-tənsɪ] *s.* vacilación, indecisión, titubeo, hesitación, duda.
hesitant [-tənt] *a.* vacilante, titubeante, indeciso.
hesitantly [-lɪ] *adv.* vacilantemente, con vacilación, con indecisión, con hesitación, con titubeo.
hesitate ['hɛzəˌteɪt] *v.i.* 1. vacilar, titubear. 2. tartamudear, balbucir.
hesitatingly [-ɪŋlɪ] *adv.* vacilantemente, con vacilación, con indecisión, con hesitación, con titubeo.
hesitation [ˌhɛzə'teɪʃən] *s.* 1. vacilación, titubeo, hesitación. 2. escrúpulo. 3. balbuceo.
hesitative ['hɛzəˌteɪtɪv] *a.* vacilante, titubeante, indeciso.
hesitatively [-lɪ] *adv.* vacilantemente, con vacilación, con indecisión, con titubeo, con hesitación.
Hesper ['hɛspər, B -pə] *var. de* **Hesperus.**
Hesperian [hɛs'pɪrɪən, B -'pɪər-] *a.* 1. hespéride, hespérido. 2. (poét.) hespérico, hespérido (occidental).
Hesperides [-'pɛrəˌdiz] *s. pl.* (mitol.) Hespérides, ninfas que guardaban el jardín de las manzanas de oro.
hesperidin [-dən] *s.* (quím.) hesperidina.
hesperidium [ˌhɛspə'rɪdɪəm] *s.* (*pl.* HESPERIDIA [-dɪə]) (bot.) hesperidio.
Hesperus ['hɛspərəs] *s.* (astr.) Héspero, Venus, lucero de la tarde.
Hessian ['hɛʃən, B 'hɛsɪən] *a.* de Hesse. —*s.* 1. natural o habitante de Hesse, Alemania. 2. (E.U., hist.) soldado mercenario alemán, p. ext. mercenario. 3. **h.,** harpillera, arpillera.
Hessian boot, (hist.) bota adornada con borlas (introducida en Inglaterra por los mercenarios alemanes).
Hessian fly, (ento.) cecidomio, mosca nociva para el trigo.
hessite ['hɛsˌaɪt] *s.* (min.) hesita.
hessonite [-əˌnaɪt] *s.* (min.) esonita, hesonita.
hest [hɛst] *s.* (ant.) mandamiento, precepto.
Hestia ['hɛstɪə] *s.* (mitol.) Hestia, diosa de la tierra y del hogar.
hetaera [hɪ'tɪrə, B -'tɪərə] *s.* (*pl.* HETAERAE [-ˌi] o HETAERAS) (hist.) hetera, hetaira, concubina, cortesana.
hetaerism [-'tɪrɪzəm] **hetairism** [-'taɪrɪz-] *s.* heterismo, concubinato.
hetaira [-'taɪrə] *s.* (*pl.* HETAIRAI [-raɪ] o HETAIRAS) *var. de* **hetaera.**
heterocercal [ˌhɛtəroʊ'sɜrkəl, B -'sɜkəl] *a.* (ict.) heterocerca.
heterochromatic [-krə'mætɪk] *a.* heterocromático, de diferentes colores.
heterochromatin [-'kroʊmətən] *s.* (biol.) heterocromatina.
heterochromatism [-ˌtɪzəm] *s.* (zool.) heterocromatismo.
heterochromosome [-ˌsoʊm] *s.* (biol.) heterocromosoma.
heteroclite ['hɛtərəˌklaɪt] *a.* heteróclito. —*s.* 1. (gram.) nombre heteróclito. 2. persona extraña; cosa irregular.
heterocyclic [ˌhɛtəroʊ'saɪklɪk, -'sɪklɪk] *a.* (quím.) heterocíclico.
heterodox ['hɛtərəˌdɑks, B -ˌdɔks] *a.* heterodoxo, disconforme con la doctrina oficial.
heterodoxy [-ˌdɑksɪ, B -ˌdɔk-] *s.* 1. heterodoxia. 2. doctrina u opinión heterodoxa.
heterodyne [-ˌdaɪn] *a.* (rad.) heterodino. —*v.t.* (rad.) heterodinar (la frecuencia).
heteroecious [ˌhɛtə'riʃəs] *a.* (biol.) heteroecio.
heteroecism [-'riˌsɪzəm] *s.* (biol.) heteroecia.
heterogamete [-roʊgə'mit, B -'gæˌmit] *s.* (biol.) heterogameto.
heterogamous [-'rɑgəməs, B -'rɔg-] *a.* (biol.) heterógamo.
heterogamy [-mɪ] *s.* (bot.) heterogamia.
heterogeneity [ˌhɛtəroʊdʒə'niətɪ] *s.* heterogeneidad.
heterogeneous [-rə'dʒinɪəs] *a.* heterogéneo.
heterogeneously [-lɪ] *adv.* en forma heterogénea.
heterogeneousness [-nəs] *s.* heterogeneidad.
heterogenesis [-roʊ'dʒɛnəsəs] *s.* (biol.) heterogénesis.
heterogenous [-'rɑdʒənəs, B -'rɔdʒ-] *a.* (biol., med.) heterógeno.
heterogeny [-nɪ] *s.* 1. (biol.) heterogénesis. 2. grupo o colección heterogénea.

heterogonous [ˌhɛtəˈrɑgənəs, B -ˈrɔg-] **heterogonic** [-rəˈgɑnɪk, B -ˈgɔn-] *a.* 1. (bot.) heterógono. 2. (biol.) alométrico.
heterogony [-nɪ] *s.* (biol., bot.) heterogonía.
heterography [-ˈrɑgrəfɪ, B -ˈrɔg-] *s.* heterografía, ortografía diferente de la corriente.
heterogynous [-ˈrɑdʒənəs, B -ˈrɔdʒ-] *a.* (zool.) (especie) caracterizada por dos hembras, una de ellas neutra.
heterologous [ˌhɛtəˈrɑləgəs, B -ˈrɔl-] *a.* (biol.) heterólogo.
heterology [-dʒɪ] *s.* (biol.) heterología.
heterolysis [-əsəs] *s.* (bioquím.) heterólisis.
Heteromera [-ˈrɑmərə, B -ˈrɔm-] **Heteromeri** [-rəˈmɪraɪ, B -ˈmɪər-] *s. pl.* (bot.) heterómeros.
heteromerous [-ˈrɑmərəs, B -ˈrɔm-] *a.* (bot.) heterómero.
heterometabolic [ˌhɛtəroʊˌmɛtəˈbɑlɪk, B -ˈbɔ-] **heterometabolous** [-məˈtæbələs] *a.* (ento.) heterometábolo.
heterometabolism [-məˈtæbəˌlɪzəm] *s.* (ento.) heterometabolia.
heteromorphic [-ˈmɔrfɪk, B -ˈmɔfɪk] **heteromorphous** [-fəs] *a.* (biol., quím., geol.) heteromorfo.
heteromorphism [-ˌfɪzəm] *s.* (biol., quím., geol.) heteromorfismo.
heteronomous [-ˈrɑnəməs, B -ˈrɔn-] *a.* heterónomo.
heteronomy [-mɪ] *s.* heteronomía.
heteropetalous [ˌhɛtəroʊˈpɛtələs] *a.* (bot.) heteropétalo.
heterophyllous [-ˈfɪləs] *a.* (bot.) heterófilo.
heterophylly [ˈhɛtəroʊˌfɪlɪ] *s.* (bot.) heterofilia.
heterophyte [-rəˌfaɪt] *s.* (bot.) heterófito.
heteroplasty [-ˌplæstɪ] *s.* (med.) heteroplastia.
heteroploid [-ˌplɔɪd] *a.* (biol.) heteroploide.
heteropolar [ˌhɛtərəˈpoulər, B -lə] *a.* (quím.) heteropolar.
heteropolarity [-roʊpəˈlærətɪ] *s.* (quím.) heteropolaridad.
heteropter [-ˈrɑptər, B -ˈrɔptə] *s.* (ento.) heteróptero.
Heteroptera [-tərə] *s. pl.* (ento.) heterópteros.
heteropterous [-tərəs] *a.* (ento.) heteróptero.
heterosexual [ˌhɛtəroʊˈsɛkʃʊəl, B ˈhɛ-ˈseksjʊ-] *a.* (biol.) heterosexual. *—s.* persona heterosexual.
heterosexuality [-ˌsɛkʃʊˈælətɪ, B -ˌseksjʊ-] *s.* (biol.) heterosexualidad.
heterosis [-ˈroʊsəs] *s.* (biol.) heterosis.
heterosporous [-rəˈspɔrəs] *a.* (bot.) heterósporo, heterospóreo.
heterotaxic [-ˈtæksɪk] *a.* heterotáxico.
heterotaxis [-ˈtæksəs] **heterotaxia** [-sɪə] *vars. de* **heterotaxy.**
heterotaxy [ˈhɛtərəˌtæksɪ] *s.* heterotaxia, heterotaxis.
heterothallic [ˌhɛtərəˈθælɪk] *a.* (bot.) heterotálico.
heterotopy [-ˈrɑtəpɪ, B -ˈrɔt-] *s.* (biol.) heterotopia.
heterotrophic [ˌhɛtərəˈtrɑfɪk, B -ˈtrɔf-] *a.* (fisiol.) heterotrofo.
heterozygosis [-roʊzaɪˈgoʊsəs] *s.* (biol.) heterocigosis.
heterozygote [-ˈzaɪˌgoʊt] *s.* (biol.) heterocigoto, heterócigo.
heterozygous [-gəs] *a.* (biol.) heterócigo.
hetman [ˈhɛtmən] *s.* (*pl.* HETMANS) atamán (jefe cosaco).
het up [hɛt-] (pr. dial.) excitado, agitado, turbado.
heulandite [ˈhjulənˌdaɪt] *s.* (min.) heulandita.
heuristic [hjʊˈrɪstɪk] *a.* heurístico. *—s.* heurística.
HEW (E.U.) *abrev. de* **(Department of) Health, Education and Welfare,** Ministerio de Salud, Educación y Bienestar Social.
hew [hju] *v.t.* (*pret.* HEWED; *p.p.* HEWED O HEWN [hjun]; *p.pr.* HEWING). 1. tajar, cortar. 2. hachear, desbastar. 3. labrar (madera, piedra); picar (piedra). 4. **h. asunder,** dividir de un hachazo; **h. down,** destroncar, talar, tumbar a hachazos (árbol); **h. one's way (through),** abrirse camino a hachazos o machetazos (por); **h. out,** separar a hachazos; modelar en bruto. *—v.i.* 1. hacer cortes, hachear, dar golpes con el machete. 2. (con *to*) conformarse (con), adaptarse (a). 3. **h. to the line,** irse con la corriente, conformarse; **h. right and left,** acuchillar a diestra y siniestra.
hewer [ˈhjuər, B -ə] *s.* cantero, desbastador.
hex [hɛks] *s.* 1. hechizo, maleficio, mal de ojo. 2. bruja, hechicera. *—v.t.* embrujar, hechizar, maleficiar.
hex- [hɛks] **hexa-** [ˈhɛksə] *prefijo* que significa seis.
hexabasic [ˌhɛksəˈbeɪsɪk] *a.* (quím.) hexabásico.
hexachord [ˈhɛksəˌkɔrd, B -ˌkɔd] *s.* 1. (mús.) hexacordo. 2. (mús.) hexacordio (instrumento).
hexad [ˈhɛkˌsæd] *s.* 1. grupo o serie de seis. 2. (quím.) átomo de seis valencias.
hexadic [hɛkˈsædɪk] *a.* en grupos o series de seis.
hexaemeron [ˌhɛksəˈɛmərˌɑn, B -ˈimərˌɔn] **hexahemeron** [-ˈhɛm-, B -ˈim-] *s.* hexamerón.
hexagon [ˈhɛksəˌgɑn, B -gən] *s.* (geom.) hexágono.
hexagonal [hɛkˈsægənəl] *a.* hexagonal.
hexagram [ˈhɛksəˌgræm] *s.* (geom.) hexagrama.
hexahedral [ˌhɛksəˈhidrəl, B ˈhɛksəˈhɛ-] *a.* (geom.) hexaédrico.
hexahedron [-drən] *s.* (*pl.* HEXAHEDRONS O HEXAHEDRA [-drə]) (geom.) hexaedro.
hexahydrate [-ˈhaɪˌdreɪt] *s.* (quím.) hexahidrato.
hexahydric [-drɪk] *a.* (quím.) hexahídrico.
hexamerous [hɛkˈsæmərəs] *a.* (bot., zool.) hexámero.
hexameter [-ˈsæmətər, B -ə] *s., a.* (poét.) hexámetro.
hexamethylenetetramine [ˌhɛksəˈmɛθəˌlinˈtɛtrəˌmin] *s.* (quím.) hexametilenotetramina.
hexane [ˈhɛkˌseɪn] *s.* (quím.) hexano.
hexapetalous [ˌhɛksəˈpɛtələs] *a.* (bot.) hexapétalo.
Hexapla [ˈhɛksəplə] *s.* (bíbl.) Hexapla.
hexaploid [ˈhɛksəˌplɔɪd] *a.* (biol.) hexaploide.
hexapod [-ˌpɑd, B -ˌpɔd] *a.* hexápodo. *—s.* (ento.) hexápodo.
hexapodous [hɛkˈsæpədəs] *a.* hexápodo.
hexapody [-ədɪ] *s.* (poét.) verso o grupo de seis pies.
Hexateuch [ˈhɛksəˌtuk, B -ˌtjuk] *s.* (bíbl.) Hexateuco.
hexose [ˈhɛkˌsoʊs] *s.* (quím.) hexosa.
hexyl [ˈhɛksəl] *s.* (quím.) hexil, hexilo.
hexylresorcinol [ˌhɛksəlrəˈzɔrsənˌɔl, B -ˈzɔs-] *s.* (quím.) hexilresorcina.
hey [heɪ] *interj.* ¡eh! ¡oiga! ¡oye!
heyday [ˈheɪˌdeɪ] *s.* 1. apogeo, auge; mejor época. 2. (ant.) alegría, júbilo.
hf *abrev. de* **high-frequency,** alta frecuencia.
Hf *símb. de* **hafnium,** hafnio (Hf).
Hg *símb. de* **hydrargyrium (mercury),** mercurio (Hg).
hg. *abrev. de* **hectogram,** hectogramo (hg.).
H.H. *abrev. de* 1. **Her** o **His Highness,** Su Alteza (S.A.). 2. **His Holiness,** Su Santidad.
H-Hour [ˈeɪtʃˌaʊr, B -ˌaʊə] *s.* (mil.) hora fijada para el ataque.
hi [haɪ] *interj.* (fam.) ¡hola!
hiatus [haɪˈeɪtəs] *s.* (*pl.* HIATUSES O HIATUS) 1. hiato, abertura. 2. (fig.) laguna, vacío. 3. (fon.) hiato.
hibachi [hɪˈbɑtʃɪ] *s.* brasero japonés.
hibernaculum [ˌhaɪbərˈnækjələm, B -bəˈ-] *s.* (*pl.* HIBERNACULA [-lə]) (bot., zool.) hibernáculo.
hibernal [haɪˈbɜrnəl, B -ˈbɜn-] *a.* hibernal, invernal.
hibernate [ˈhaɪbərˌneɪt, B -bəˌ-] *v.i.* invernar.
hibernation [ˌhaɪbərˈneɪʃən, B -bəˈ-] *s.* (biol.) hibernación, invernación.
Hibernian [haɪˈbɜrnɪən, B -ˈbɜnɪ-] *a., s.* hibernés, irlandés.
Hibernicism [-nəˌsɪzəm] *s.* modismo irlandés; calidad, carácter, rasgo o costumbre irlandesa.
hibiscus [haɪˈbɪskəs, B hɪ-] *s.* (bot.) hibisco.
hicatee [ˈhɪkəˌti] *s.* (zool.) hicotea, jicotea.
hiccough [ˈhɪkʌp] *var. de* **hiccup.**
hiccup [ˈhɪkʌp] *s.* hipo. *—v.i.* (*pret., p.p.* HICCUPED O HICCUPPED; *p.pr.* HICCUPING O HICCUPPING) hipar, tener hipo. *—v.t.* decir con hipos.
hick [hɪk] *s.* (fam.) patán, paleto, rústico. *—a.* rústico, campestre.
hickey [ˈhɪkɪ] *s.* 1. (elec.) doblador de tubos. 2. (elec.) casquillo conectador, buje de salida. 3. dispositivo, artefacto, artilugio. 4. (jer.) marca roja en la piel después de un beso o mordida. 5. barro o espinilla.
hickory [ˈhɪkərɪ] *s.* (bot.) nogal americano, pacana.
hick town, (fam.) población rural, aldea aburrida.
hid [hɪd] *pret., p.p. de* **hide.**
hidalgo [hɪˈdælgoʊ] *s.* hidalgo, noble español.
hidden [ˈhɪdən] *p.p. de* **hide** . *—a.* escondido, oculto, recóndito, secreto.
hiddenite [ˈhɪdənˌaɪt] *s.* (min.) hiddenita, piedra preciosa gris esmeralda.
hide [haɪd] *v.t.* (*pret.* HID [hɪd]; *p.p.* HIDDEN [ˈhɪdən] O HID; *p.pr.* HIDING) 1. esconder, ocultar. 2. encubrir, disimular (la verdad, etc.), guardar secreto (conocimiento, información, etc.). 3. tapar, ocultar. 4. volver (los ojos o la cara por disgusto o vergüenza). 5. **h. one's head,** (fig.) ocultarse avergonzado. *—v.i.* esconderse, ocultarse; **h. out,** estar escondido, refugiarse.
hide [haɪd] *s.* 1. cuero, piel, pellejo (de animal). 2. (hum.) piel humana. 3. **to have a thick h.,** tener la cara dura, no tener vergüenza; ser un descarado; **to save one's h.,** salvar uno el pellejo; **to tan the h. of,** darle una zurra a. *—v.t.* 1. sacar la piel de. 2. (fam.) azotar, dar latigazos.
hide-and-seek [ˌhaɪdənˈsik] *s.* juego de escondite, escondidas (Amer.); **to play h.-a.-s.,** jugar al escondite, jugar a las escondidas (Amer.).
hideaway [ˈhaɪdəˌweɪ] *s.* escondite, escondrijo; refugio.
hidebound [-ˌbaʊnd] *a.* 1. de piel dura, que tiene la piel pegada a los huesos (díc. de los animales). 2. obstinado, fanático. 3. (bot.) de corteza demasiado dura.
hideous [ˈhɪdɪəs] *a.* 1. horrible, espantoso. 2. feísimo, repugnante.
hideously [-lɪ] *adv.* horriblemente, terriblemente.
hideousness [-nəs] *s.* 1. horridez. 2. fealdad, deformidad.
hideout [ˈhaɪdˌaʊt] *s.* nidal, escondite, escondrijo.
hiding [-ɪŋ] *s.* 1. ocultación, encubrimiento. 2. escondite, retiro. 3. (fam.) tunda, zurra, paliza.

hiding place, escondite.
hidrosis [hɪ'droʊsəs] *s.* (fisiol., med.) hidrosis, sudor excesivo.
hidrotic [-'drɑtɪk, B -'drɔt-] *a.* (med.) hidrótico, que produce sudor.
hie [haɪ] *v.i.* (*pret., p.p.* HIED; *p.pr.* HYING O HIEING) apresurarse, darse prisa, apurarse; **h. thee home,** vuelve a casa pronto.
hiemal ['haɪəməl] *a.* hiemal, invernal.
hierarch ['haɪˌrɑrk, B -əˌrɑk] *s.* jerarca.
hierarchal [ˌhaɪ'rɑrkəl, B -ə'rɑkəl] *a.* jerárquico.
hierarchic [-kɪk] **hierarchical** [-kɪkəl] *a.* jerárquico.
hierarchically [-kɪkəlɪ] *adv.* jerárquicamente.
hierarchism ['haɪˌrɑrkɪzəm, B -əˌrɑkɪz-] *s.* jerarquía.
hierarchist [-kəst] *s.* jerarquista.
hierarchy [-kɪ] *s.* (*pl.* HIERARCHIES) jerarquía.
hieratic [ˌhaɪ'rætɪk, B -ə'ræt-] **hieratical** [-ɪkəl] *a.* 1. hierático, sagrado, sacerdotal. 2. (arqueol.) hierática (escritura egipcia).
hieratically [-ɪkəlɪ] *adv.* hieráticamente.
hierocracy [-'rɑkrəsɪ, B -'rɔk-] *s.* hierocracia.
hierodule ['haɪrəˌdul, B -ərəˌdjul] *s.* (hist.) hieródulo, esclavo al servicio de un templo.
hieroglyph [-ˌglɪf] *s.* jeroglífico.
hieroglyphic [ˌhaɪrə'glɪfɪk, B -ərə-] *a.* jeroglífico. —*s.* 1. jeroglífico. 2. (fig.) (*pl.*) garrapatos, garabatos, escarabajos, escritura ilegible.
hieroglyphically [-ɪkəlɪ] *adv.* jeroglíficamente.
hierology [-'rɑlədʒɪ, B -'rɔl-] *s.* hierología.
Hieronymite [-'rɑnəˌmaɪt, B -'rɔn-] *s.* jerónimo (monje de la Orden de San Jerónimo).
hierophant ['haɪrəˌfænt, B -ərə-] *s.* 1. (hist. griega) hierofante, hierofanta. 2. (fig.) hierofante, expositor, intérprete (de misterios).
hi-fi ['haɪ'faɪ] *a.* de alta fidelidad. —*s.* 1. (rad., electrón.) hi-fi, alta fidelidad. 2. sistema o equipo de alta fidelidad.
higgle ['hɪgəl] *v.t.* regatear, discutir por pequeñeces.
higgledy-piggledy ['hɪgəldɪ'pɪgəldɪ] *adv.* confusamente, sin orden ni concierto. —*a.* confuso, revuelto. —*s.* confusión, revoltillo, revoltijo.
higgler ['hɪglər, B -lə] *s.* regateador.
high [haɪ] *a.* 1. alto, elevado, de alto, de altura, ej., *h. hill,* colina alta, *one inch h.,* de una pulgada de alto, *ten stories h.,* de diez pisos de altura. 2. pleno; culminante, ej., *h. noon,* pleno mediodía, the *h. period of his work,* el período culminante de su obra. 3. grande, sumo, ej., *of h. antiquity,* de gran antigüedad. 4. alto, noble, ilustre. 5. alto, principal, superior, supremo (ej., tribunal), sumo (pontífice). 6. fuerte, violento (viento), alto, crecido (río), gruesa (mar). 7. violento, vehemente (pasión, etc.); extremo, sumo (placer, ansiedad, etc.). 8. arrogante, altanero. 9. serio, grave (delito, crimen). 10. caro. 11. manido, algo pasado (ej., carne); maloliente. 12. alegre, muy divertido, ej., *we had a h. time of it,* pasamos ratos muy divertidos, nos divertimos muchísimo. 13. agudo (sonido). 14. intenso (drama, aventura, etc.). 15. (geog.) alta (latitud). 16. (fon.) cerrada (vocal). 17. (jer.) borracho, achispado. 18. **h. and dry,** en seco; abandonado, desamparado, solo, sin recursos; **h. and low,** de toda clase (gente); **h. and mighty,** muy arrogante; **it's h. time,** ya es hora; **to be h.,** estar embriagado o intoxicado (esp. con drogas); **to get on one's h. horse,** volverse presumido, volverse estirado o mandón; **to ride the h. horse,** comportarse con arrogancia. —*s.* 1. alto, altura, elevación (en el terreno). 2. punto o nivel alto; extremo, máximum. 3. clases altas (de la sociedad). 4. (meteor.) área de alta presión (barométrica), anticiclón. 5. (aut.) directa, transmisión directa, toma directa. 6. **from on h.,** de o desde lo alto, del o desde el cielo; de los altos, de o desde un lugar elevado; **on h.,** en alto; en lo alto, en el cielo; en los altos, en un lugar elevado. —*adv.* 1. arriba; en alto. 2. lujosamente. 3. **h. and low,** por todas partes, dondequiera; **how h.?** ¿hasta qué altura? ¿hasta dónde?; ¿cuánto? (es el precio, etc.); **the higher one flies, the harder one falls,** a gran salto, gran quebranto; **to come** (o **cost**) **h.,** costar caro; **to fly h.,** tener metas muy ambiciosas; **to play h.,** jugar alto; jugar una carta alta; **to run h.,** tener una corriente fuerte, estar bravo (el mar); (fig.) estar exaltados (los ánimos).
high-alloy ['haɪ'ælˌɔɪ] *a.* (metal.) de aleación rica.
highball ['haɪˌbɔl] *s.* 1. licor (esp. whiski) con agua o gaseosa y hielo. 2. (f.c.) señal ferrocarrilera para que un tren prosiga a toda velocidad. —*v.i.* (jer.) proceder a gran velocidad.
high beam, (aut.) luz de gran alcance, luz de carretera, luz alta.
highbinder [-ˌbaɪndər, B -də] *s.* (E.U.) 1. pandillero, pistolero, bandido. 2. estafador, timador. 3. politicastro.
high blood pressure, (med.) hipertensión arterial; presión alta (fam.).
highborn [-'bɔrn, B -ˌbɔn] *a.* de ilustre cuna, de alta alcurnia, linajudo.
highboy [-ˌbɔɪ] *s.* cómoda de patas altas.
highbred [-'brɛd] *a.* de raza, de abolengo, de familia ilustre; aristocrático.
highbrow [-ˌbraʊ] *s., a.* (t. despec.) erudito, docto, intelectual.
highchair ['haɪˌtʃɛr, B -ˌtʃɛə] *s.* silla alta para infantes.
High Church, Alta Iglesia, iglesia ritualista (rama conservadora de la iglesia anglicana).
high-class [-'klæs, B -'klɑs] *a.* 1. de buen gusto, refinado. 2. de primera clase, de alta categoría; excelente.
high color, color subido, rubor.
high comedy, alta comedia, de temas y diálogo sofisticados.
high command, (mil.) alto mando, alto comando.
high commissioner, (G.B.) alto comisario (que representa en Londres a uno de los dominios británicos).
high-compression [-kəm'prɛʃən] *a.* de alta compresión.
high cost of living, (el) alto costo de la vida.
High Court, (der.) tribunal superior.
high day, (bíbl.) día de fiesta, día santo.
high diving, saltos desde grandes alturas.
higher ['haɪər, B -ə] *a. comp. de* **high,** más alto; superior (matemáticas, etc.).
higher criticism, alta crítica (esp. de la Biblia).
higher education, enseñanza superior.
higher-ups ['haɪərˌʌps] *s. pl.* (jer.) superiores, jefes; personas influyentes o importantes.
highest ['haɪəst] *a. super. de* **high,** más alto; sumo, supremo; mayor, máximo; de primer orden.
highest common divisor, (mat.) máximo común divisor.
high explosive, explosivo instantáneo, explosivo alto, explosivo rompedor.
highfalutin [ˌhaɪfə'lutən] *a.* pomposo, rimbombante, presuntuoso.
high fidelity, (rad.) alta fidelidad.
high-fidelity ['haɪfə'dɛlətɪ] *a.* de alta fidelidad (radio, tocadiscos, etc.).
highflier, highflyer [-'flaɪər, B -ə] *s.* 1. pájaro de alto vuelo. 2. empresa arriesgada. 3. (hist.) extremista, sumamente conservador.
high-flown [-'floʊn] *a.* 1. elevado, exaltado. 2. hinchado, ampuloso, pomposo.
highflying [-'flaɪɪŋ] *a.* 1. elevado, sublime. 2. pretencioso, ampuloso.
high-frequency [-'frikwənsɪ] *a.* (elec.) de alta frecuencia.
high gear, (aut.) transmisión directa, toma directa, marcha directa.
High German, alto alemán, el idioma alemán oficial y literario.
high-grade [-ˌgreɪd] *a.* de alta calidad, de calidad superior.
high hand, arbitrariedad, despotismo, altanería.
highhanded [-'hændəd] *a.* arbitrario, despótico, altanero.
highhandedly [-lɪ] *adv.* arbitrariamente, despóticamente, altaneramente.
high hat, chistera, sombrero de copa.
high-hat ['haɪ'hæt] *s.* presumido, esnob. —*a.* desdeñoso, encopetado, copetudo. —*v.t.* desairar, tratar con altanería (a otra persona).
high-hearted [-'hɑrtəd, B -'hɑt-] *a.* animoso, denodado.
high-heeled [-'hild] *a.* de tacón alto, de taco alto (Amer.).
highjack, highjacker, *vars. de* **hijack, hijacker.**
high jinks, high jinx, jarana, jaleo; farra, juerga; payasada, jugarreta, travesura.
high jump, (dep.) salto alto.
high-keyed [-'kid] *a.* impresionable; nervioso.
highland ['haɪlənd] *s.* región montañosa; (*pl.*) tierras altas; **the Highland,** región montañosa o tierras altas de Escocia.
highlander [-ləndər, B -də] *s.* 1. montañés. 2. **H.,** montañés de Escocia; soldado de un regimiento de montañeses en Escocia.
Highland fling, baile escocés muy animado.
highlandish [-dɪʃ] *a.* montañés.
high life, 1. vida aristocrática, gran mundo, alta sociedad. 2. danza africana.
highlight ['haɪˌlaɪt] *s.* 1. (arte) claro o toque de luz (en una pintura o fotografía). 2. (*pl.*) rasgos salientes, puntos salientes; atracciones principales, eventos más importantes. —*v.t.* 1. inundar de luz. 2. (fig.) realzar, destacar, poner de relieve.
high living, vida lujosa, vida costosa.
highly ['haɪlɪ] *adv.* 1. altamente, sumamente, muy, ej., *h. interesting,* sumamente interesante, *h. polished,* muy pulido. 2. muy bien, muy favorablemente, ej., *h. paid,* muy bien pagado, *to speak h. of,* hablar muy bien o muy favorablemente de.
highly placed, *a.* en alta posición, de alto rango.
highly seasoned, *a.* picante.
High Mass, (relig.) misa solemne, misa mayor.
high-minded ['haɪ'maɪndəd] *a.* 1. noble, magnánimo. 2. (ant.) arrogante, altivo, orgulloso.
high-mindedness [-nəs] *s.* 1. nobleza, magnanimidad. 2. (ant.) arrogancia, altivez.
high-necked [-'nɛkt] *a.* de escote subido.
highness ['haɪnəs] *s.* 1. altura, nivel. 2. **H.,** Alteza (título de honor).
high noon, 1. pleno mediodía. 2. (fig.) cenit, cumbre, punto culminante.
high-octane ['haɪ'ɑkˌteɪn, B -'ɔk-] *a.* de alto índice octánico, de alto octanaje (gasolina, nafta).
high-pass filter [-ˌpæs-, B -ˌpɑs-] (rad., electrón.) filtro pasaaltos, filtro de paso alto.
high-pitched [-'pɪtʃt] *a.* 1. agudo, estridente (voz). 2. empinado (techo). 3. (fig.) elevado, exaltado.
high place, (relig.) templo o altar semita (gen. en una colina).

high-powered [-ˈpaʊərd, B -əd] *a.* de gran potencia, extrafuerte.
high-pressure [-ˈprɛʃər, B -ə] *a.* 1. de alta presión. 2. urgente. 3. enérgico, tenaz; **h.-p. salesmanship,** arte de vender tenaz y decisivamente. —*v.t.* presionar o coaccionar tenazmente.
high pressure, altas presiones.
high-priced [-ˈpraɪst] *a.* de precio elevado, de alto precio; de alto costo; altamente remunerado (servicio).
high priest, sumo sacerdote.
high-proof [-ˈpruf] *a.* de alta concentración; de alto porcentaje alcohólico.
high-ranking [ˈhaɪˈræŋkɪŋ] *a.* alto, ej. *h. officer,* alto mando; ej. *h. position* alto cargo.
high relief, alto relieve.
high-rise [-ˈraɪz] *s.* edificio de muchos pisos, torre.
highroad [ˈhaɪˌroʊd] *s.* 1. (pr. G.B.) carretera, camino real. 2. (fig.) camino fácil.
high school, (E.U.) escuela de segunda enseñanza.
high sea, (*ú. gen. en pl.*) alta mar.
high sign, (jer.) señal secreta de aviso.
high society, alta sociedad, gran mundo, mundo elegante.
high-sounding [-ˈsaʊndɪŋ] *a.* altisonante, retumbante.
high-speed [-ˈspid] *a.* de alta velocidad; rápido.
high-speed drill, broca de alta velocidad.
high-speed emulsion, (foto.) emulsión rápida.
high-speed film, (foto.) película rápida.
high-speed steel, acero rápido, acero de alta velocidad.
high-spirited [-ˈspɪrətəd] *a.* 1. animoso, gallardo, valiente. 2. alegre, vivaz. 3. fogoso, brioso (ej., caballo).
high-spiritedly [-lɪ] *a.* 1. animosamente, gallardamente, valientemente. 2. alegremente, con vivacidad. 3. briosamente.
high-spiritedness [-nəs] *s.* 1. ánimo, gallardía, valentía. 2. alegría, vivacidad. 3. fogosidad.
high spirits, alegría, buen humor.
high spot, punto relevante o sobresaliente.
high-stepping [-ˌstɛpɪŋ] *a.* 1. pisador (caballo). 2. licencioso, desenfrenado.
high-strung [-ˈstrʌŋ] *a.* tenso, impresionable, excitable, muy nervioso, muy sensible.
hight [haɪt] *a.* (ant.) apellidado, llamado.
hightail [ˈhaɪˌteɪl] *v.i.* (jer.) escapar, irse apresuradamente.
high tea, merienda, colación (en que se sirven fiambres, platos calientes, etc., con el té).
high-tension [-ˈtɛntʃən, B -ˈtɛnʃən] *a.* (elec.) de alto voltaje, de alta tensión.
high-test [-ˌtɛst] *a.* de alta volatilidad, de alto octanaje (gasolina, nafta).
high-test gasoline, gasolina super.
high-test metal, metal de alta resistencia.
high tide, 1. marea alta o llena, aguas llenas, altas aguas, pleamar. 2. (fig.) culminación, momento culminante.
high time, 1. (fam.) juerga, fiesta. 2. hora de hacer algo, tiempo de no esperar más, ej., *it is h. t. we had dinner,* ya es hora de que cenemos.
high-toned [-ˈtoʊnd] *a.* 1. prestigioso, de categoría. 2. elevado, noble, de mucha dignidad. 3. elegante, a la moda, de buen tono. 4. (fam.) pretencioso, ampuloso, pomposo.
high treason, alta traición.
highty-tighty [ˌhaɪtɪˈtaɪtɪ] *var. de* **hoity-toity.**
high voltage, (elec.) alta tensión, alto voltaje.
high water, 1. marea alta o llena, altas aguas, pleamar. 2. crecida, creciente, avenida (de un río).
high-water line [ˈhaɪˈwɔtər-, -ˈwɑt-, B -ˈwɔtə-] **h.-w. mark,** 1. (mar.) línea de aguas altas; línea de la marea alta. 2. (fig.) cenit, punto culminante, apogeo.
highway [ˈhaɪˌweɪ] *s.* carretera, camino real; autopista.
highwayman [-mən] *s.* bandolero, salteador de caminos.
highway robbery, asalto, atraco.
high wire, cuerda floja.
high wire act, número en la cuerda floja.
high words, palabras airadas u ofensivas.
high-wrought [-ˈrɔt] *a.* 1. primorosamente labrado. 2. turbulento, revuelto, alborotado, agitado, excitado, inflamado.
hijack, highjack [-ˌdʒæk] *v.t.* 1. atracar, asaltar, saltear. 2. robar, hurtar. 3. forzar, coercer, obligar, constreñir. 4. secuestrar, forzar al piloto o chofer (de un avión, camión, etc.) a dirigir el vehículo a un sitio determinado por el asaltante.
hijacker, highjacker [-ər, B -ə] *s.* atracador, salteador, asaltador, asaltante; (aer.) secuestrador.
hike [haɪk] *v.i.* 1. marchar, caminar; pasear, dar una caminata, hacer excursión (en el campo). 2. viajar; transitar, trasladarse. 3. (gen. con *up*) arremangarse (ropa). —*v.t.* 1. subir, levantar. 2. subir de golpe (impuestos, precios, etc.). —*s.* 1. caminata, paseo, excursión. 2. aumento (de precios, salario, producción, etc.).
hiker [ˈhaɪkər, B -ə] *s.* excursionista.
hilar [ˈhaɪlər, B -lə] *a.* (anat.) hiliar.
hilarious [hɪˈlɛrɪəs, haɪ-, -ˈlær-, B hɪˈlɛər-] *a.* hilarante, divertidísimo, graciosísimo, muy chistoso.
hilariously [-lɪ] *adv.* muy chistosamente; **h. funny,** extremadamente chistoso; **to laugh h.,** reírse a carcajadas.
hilariousness [-nəs] *s.* hilaridad, alborozo, regocijo, júbilo.
hilarity [-ˈlærətɪ] *s.* hilaridad, júbilo, alegría.
hill [hɪl] *s.* 1. colina, collado, cerro. 2. montón, montoncillo, montículo. 3. (agr.) aporque, aporcadura, acogombradura; acobijo. 4. **to go over the h.,** (jer.) huir, evadirse; desertar; **to be over the hill,** estar en el ocaso, estar entrado en años. —*v.t.* 1. amontonar. 2. (agr.) recalzar, aporcar, acogombrar, acobijar, acohombrar.
hillbilly [ˈhɪlˌbɪlɪ] *s.* (*pl.* HILLBILLIES) (despec.) serrano, montañés; rústico, campesino.
hillbilly music, (E.U.) música de los montañeses y campesinos (esp. de los estados del sur).
hilliness [ˈhɪlɪnəs] *s.* montuosidad.
hillman [ˈhɪlˌmæn] *s.* serrano, montañés.
hill myna, (orn.) eulabes sagrado, mino.
hillock [ˈhɪlək] *s.* altillo, altozano, cerrejón, montecillo.
hillocky [-əkɪ] *a.* con muchos altillos (terreno).
hill of beans, (jer.) insignificante, de poca monta.
hillside [ˈhɪlˌsaɪd] *s.* ladera, flanco del cerro o de la colina.
hilltop [-ˌtɑp, B -ˌtɔp] *s.* cima, cumbre de una colina.
hilly [ˈhɪlɪ] *a.* (HILLIER; HILLIEST) 1. montuoso, cerril. 2. empinado, escarpado.
hilt [hɪlt] *s.* mango, puño, empuñadura (de arma blanca); **(up) to the h.,** por completo; a fondo. —*v.t.* proveer de mango, puño o empuñadura.
hilum [ˈhaɪləm] *s.* (*pl.* HILA [-lə]) 1. (bot.) hilo, núcleo. 2. (anat., zool.) hilio, hilo.
him [hɪm, ɪm] *pron.* (*acusativo o dativo de* **he**) le, lo, a él.
himation [hɪˈmætɪˌɑn, B -ˌɔn] *s.* (*pl.* HIMATIA [-ɪə]) (hist.) himatión.
himself [hɪmˈsɛlf] *pron. de la tercera pers. m. del sing., forma enfática o reflexiva;* él mismo, se, sí, ej., *he h. told me,* él mismo me lo dijo, *he has blamed h.,* él se ha echado la culpa a sí mismo, *he hurt h.,* él se lastimó; **by h.,** solo, por su cuenta; **for h.,** por su cuenta, por cuenta propia.
hind [haɪnd] *a.* trasero, posterior, zaguero. —*s.* 1. (G.B.) ranchero, labriego, campesino. 2. inculto, rústico, patán, palurdo. 3. (zool.) cierva. 4. (ict.) mero.
hind-bow [ˈhaɪndˌboʊ] *s.* borrén, trasero de la silla de montar.
hindbrain [ˈhaɪndˌbreɪn] *s.* (anat.) metencéfalo; rombencéfalo.
hinder [ˈhɪndər, B -də] *v.t.* 1. estorbar, obstaculizar, obstruir. 2. impedir, embarazar, molestar. 3. **h. someone from (doing),** impedir a alguien (hacer, que haga). —*v.i.* poner trabas u obstáculos, oponerse, ser un estorbo.
hinder [ˈhaɪndər, B -dər] *a.* trasero, posterior, zaguero.
hinderer [ˈhɪndərər, B -dərə] *s.* estorbador, obstructor.
hindgut [ˈhaɪndˌgʌt] *s.* parte posterior del canal alimenticio (en el embrión).
Hindi [ˈhɪndɪ] *s.* hindi (lengua).
hind leg, pata trasera (de un animal).
hindmost [ˈhaɪndˌmoʊst] *a.* postrero, último.
hindquarter [-ˌkwɔrtər, B -ˈkwɔtə] *s.* rabada, cuarto trasero (de reses de carnicería).
hindrance [ˈhɪndrəns] *s.* estorbo, embarazo, impedimento, obstáculo, obstrucción, óbice, traba.
hindsight [ˈhaɪndˌsaɪt] *s.* 1. (arm.) alza, mira posterior (de un arma). 2. percepción tardía o retrospectiva.
Hindu, Hindoo [ˈhɪndu] *s.* 1. hindú. 2. indio, indo, natural de la India. —*a.* hindú, indio.
Hinduism, Hindooism [-ˌɪzəm] *s.* hinduismo.
Hindustan [ˌhɪndʊˈstæn, -ˈstɑn] *s.* Indostán, Hindostán.
Hindustani, Hindostani [-ɪ] *a.* 1. indostanés, indostano (pueblo, persona). 2. indostánico, del Indostán. —*s.* (idioma) indostani.
hinge [hɪndʒ] *s.* 1. bisagra, gozne, charnela, gonce, pernio. 2. (fig.) punto esencial, eje, factor más importante. 3. (zool.) charnela (articulación de valvas de algunos moluscos). 4. (filat.) charnela. 5. (enc.) cartivana. 6. (ant.) eje de la tierra. —*v.t.* engoznar, enquiciar, poner bisagras. —*v.i.* 1. girar sobre un gozne. 2. **h. on,** depender de.
hinge joint, (anat.) gínglimo.
hinge post, quicialera.
hinny [ˈhɪnɪ] *s.* burdégano, burreño, mulo. —*v.i.* (raro) relinchar.
hint [hɪnt] *s.* 1. insinuación, alusión, indirecta, sugestión, indicación, indicio. 2. huella, pizca. 3. (ant.) oportunidad, ocasión. 4. **to drop a h.,** echar una indirecta; **to give one a h.,** darle una pista o clave a uno; **to take the h.,** darse por aludido, comprender la indirecta. —*v.t.* aludir, echar una indirecta, hacer una insinuación. —*v.i.* **h. at,** insinuar, dar a entender, aludir a.
hinter [ˈhɪntər, B -ə] *s.* insinuador, sugeridor.
hinterland [-ˌlænd] *s.* interior (de un país); región alejada (de los centros urbanos).
hip [hɪp] *s.* 1. cadera. 2. (arq.) caballete, lima tesa. 3. escaramujo (fruto). 4. **on** (o **upon**) **the h.,** (raro) en desventaja, acorralado, entre la espada y la pared. —*v.t.* (*pret., p.p.* HIPPED; *p.pr.* HIPPING) 1. (arq.) construir un techo a cuatro aguas. 2. (fam.) deprimir, desanimar. 3. inquietar, ofender, molestar. —*a.* (jer.) sofisticado, mundano; de moda, del momento.
hipbone [ˈhɪpˌboʊn] *s.* cía, hueso de la cadera.
hip joint, (anat.) articulación femorotibial.
hipparch [ˈhɪpɑrk, B -ɑk] *s.* (hist.) hiparca.

hipped [hɪpt] *a.* 1. ú. en palabras compuestas, ej., *large-h.,* de caderas grandes, *narrow-h.,* de caderas angostas. 2. renco, rengo. 3. (arq.) a cuatro vertientes, a cuatro aguas (techo). 4. (fam.) deprimido, desanimado. 5. (con *on*) obsesionado (por).
hippie ['hɪpɪ] *s.* (jer., E.U.) joven desilusionado de la sociedad convencional.
hippo ['hɪpoʊ] *s.* (*pl.* HIPPOS) (fam.) hipopótamo.
hippocampus [ˌhɪpə'kæmpəs] *s.* (*pl.* HIPPOCAMPI [-ˌpaɪ]) 1. (ict.) hipocampo, caballo de mar. 2. (anat.) hipocampo.
hippocras ['hɪpəˌkræs] *s.* (hist.) hipocrás, licor hecho con vino y especias.
Hippocrates [hɪ'pɑkrəˌtiz, B -'pɔk-] *s.* Hipócrates, médico de la antigua Grecia.
Hippocratic [ˌhɪpə'krætɪk] *a.* hipocrático.
Hippocratic oath, juramento hipocrático de honradez profesional prestado por los médicos.
Hippocrene ['hɪpəˌkrin, B ˌhɪpoʊ'krini] *s.* (mitol.) Hipocrene, fuente de la inspiración poética.
hippodrome ['hɪpəˌdroʊm] *s.* 1. (hist.) hipódromo. 2. campo de equitación. 3. (G.B.) teatro de variedades.
hippogriff [-ˌgrɪf] *s.* (mitol.) hipogrifo, animal fabuloso mitad grifo y mitad caballo.
Hippolyte [hɪ'pɑləti, B -'pɔl-] *s.* (mitol.) Hipólita, reina de las amazonas y amante de Teseo.
Hippolytus [-ətəs] *s.* (mitol.) Hipólito, hijo de Teseo.
Hippomenes [-'pɑməˌniz, B -'pɔm-] *s.* (mitol.) Hipómenes, joven que ganó la carrera a Atalanta.
hippophagy [hɪ'pɑfədʒɪ, B -'pɔ-] *s.* hipofagia.
hippopotamus [ˌhɪpə'pɑtəməs, B -'pɔt-] *s.* (*pl.* HIPPOPOTAMUSES o HIPPOPOTAMI [-ˌmaɪ]) (zool.) hipopótamo.
hippuric [hɪ'pjʊrɪk] *a.* (quím.) hipúrico.
hippurite ['hɪpjəˌraɪt] *s.* (zool.) hipurita.
hippy, *var. de* **hippie.**
hip roof, (arq.) techo a cuatro vertientes.
hipshot ['hɪpˌʃɑt, B -ˌʃɔt] *a.* renco, rengo, descaderado.
hipster [-stər, B -stə] *s.* (jer.) 1. joven desilusionado y extravagante. 2. músico de jazz; aficionado al jazz.
hircine ['hɜrsaɪn, B 'hɜsaɪn] *a.* hircino, cabrío, cabruno, caprino.
hire [haɪr, B haɪə] *s.* 1. alquiler, arrendamiento, arriendo. 2. empleo, contratación. 3. paga, sueldo. 4. **for h., to h.,** de alquiler; a sueldo. —*v.t.* 1. emplear, contratar (a alguien). 2. alquilar, arrendar, tomar en arriendo. —*v.i.* **h. out,** alquilarse, emplearse, prestar servicios pagados.
hireable, hirable ['haɪrəbəl, B 'haɪər-] *a.* alquilable, alquiladizo.
hired hand [haɪrd-, B 'haɪəd-] mozo de campo.
hired man, mozo de campo y plaza; criado.
hireling ['haɪrlɪŋ, B 'haɪəlɪŋ] *s.* (gen. despec.) alquilón, alquiladizo, mercenario. —*a.* mercenario, alquiladizo.
hire purchase, (G.B.) compra a plazos.
hirer [-ər, B -rə] *s.* alquilador, arrendador.
hiring hall [-ɪŋ-, B -rɪŋ-] oficina de empleos, esp. la que mantiene un sindicato obrero para sus miembros.
hirsute ['hɜrsut, B 'hɜsjut] *a.* 1. peludo, velludo. 2. hirsuto, cerdoso, erizado.
hirsuteness [-nəs] *s.* vellosidad.
hirsutulous [ˌhər'sutʃələs, B ˌhɜ'-] *a.* (bot.) hirsútulo.
hirtellous [-'tɛləs] *a.* (bot.) hirsútulo.
hirudin ['hɪrədən] *s.* (quím.) hirudina.
Hirudinea [ˌhɪrə'dɪnɪə] *s. pl.* (zool.) hirudíneas.
hirundine [hɪ'rʌndɪn] *a.* (orn.) hirundínido, de la familia de las golondrinas.
his [hɪz, ɪz] *a. pos.* su, de él. —*pron. pos.* suyo, suya, (el, la) de él; el suyo, la suya, los suyos, las suyas (de él).
Hispania [hɪs'pɑnɪə, B -'peɪ-] *s.* Hispania (nombre poético de España).
Hispanic [-'pænɪk] *a.* hispánico, hispano.
Hispanicism [-əˌsɪzəm] *s.* hispanismo, españolismo.
Hispanicist [-əsəst] *s.* hispanista.
Hispanist ['hɪspənəst] *s.* hispanista.
Hispano-Arabic [hɪs'pæˌnoʊ'ærəbɪk] *a.* hispanoárabe.
Hispanophile [-nəˌfaɪl] **Hispanophil** [-nəˌfɪl] *s.* hispanófilo.
Hispanophobe [-ˌfoʊb] *s.* hispanófobo.
hispid ['hɪspəd] *a.* (bot., zool.) híspido, hirsuto, cerdoso.
hispidulous [hɪs'pɪdʒələs] *a.* (bot., zool.) hispídulo.
hiss [hɪs] *v.i.* 1. silbar (serpiente). 2. sisear, silbar (para indicar desagrado, desaprobación, etc.). 3. (gen. con *from*) escapar silbando (aire, gas, vapor, etc.). —*v.t.* 1. sisear, silbar, recibir con siseos (a un actor, orador, etc.). 2. pronunciar o decir siseando. 3. **h. out (words,** etc.), hacer silbar (palabras, etc.). —*s.* 1. silbido, silbo (de serpiente, aire, gas, vapor, etc.). 2. siseo.
hissing ['hɪsɪŋ] *s.* siseo, silbido. —*a.* sibilante, chirriante.
hist [hɪst] *interj.* ¡chito! ¡chitón! ¡atención!
histaminase [hɪs'tæməˌneɪs] *s.* (farm.) histaminasa.
histamine ['hɪstəˌmin, -mən] *s.* (bioquím.) histamina.
histaminergic [ˌhɪstəmə'nɜrdʒɪk, B -'nɜd-ʒɪk] *a.* (fisiol.) activado por la histamina (dic. de las fibras de un nervio autónomo).
histaminic [-'mɪnɪk] *a.* (bioquím.) histamínico.
histidine ['hɪstəˌdin] *s.* (bioquím.) histidina.
histiocyte [-tɪəˌsaɪt] *s.* (fisiol.) histiocito, histocito.
histochemistry [ˌhɪstoʊ'kɛməstrɪ] *a.* (med.) histoquimia, histoquímica.
histogenesis [-tə'dʒɛnəsəs] *s.* (biol.) histogénesis, histogenia.
histogram ['hɪstəˌgræm] *s.* histograma.
histoid ['hɪstɔɪd] *a.* (med.) histoide, histoideo.
histological [ˌhɪstə'lɑdʒɪkəl, B -'lɔdʒ-] *a.* histológico.
histologist [hɪs'tɑlədʒəst, B -'tɔl-] *s.* histólogo.
histology [-dʒɪ] *s.* histología.
histolysis [-əsəs] *s.* (fisiol.) histólisis.
histolytic [ˌhɪstə'lɪtɪk] *a.* (fisiol.) histolítico.
histone, histon ['hɪsˌtoʊn] *s.* (bioquím.) histona.
histopathology [ˌhɪstoʊpə'θɑlədʒɪ, B -'θɔl-] *s.* (fisiol.) histopatología, histología patológica.
histophysiology [-ˌfɪzɪ'ɑlədʒɪ, B -'ɔl-] *s.* (fisiol.) histofisiología.
histoplasmosis [-təˌplæz'moʊsəs] *s.* (med.) histoplasmosis.
historian [hɪs'tɔrɪən] *s.* 1. historiador, historiógrafo. 2. cronista, analista.
historic [-'tɔrɪk, -'tɑr-, B -'tɔr-] *a.* histórico.
historical [-ɪkəl] *a.* histórico, historial.
historical linguistics, lingüística histórica.
historically [-kəlɪ] *adv.* históricamente.
historical materialism, materialismo histórico.
historicalness [-kəlnəs] *s.* historicidad.
historical present, historic present, (gram.) presente histórico.
historical school, (e.p.) escuela histórica.
historicism [hɪs'tɔrəˌsɪzəm, -'tɑr-, B -'tɔr-] *s.* (filos.) historicismo.
historicity [ˌhɪstə'rɪsətɪ] *s.* historicidad.
historicize [hɪs'tɔrəˌsaɪz, -'tɑr-, B -'tɔr-] *v.t.* representar como hecho histórico. —*v.i.* pensar o disertar históricamente.
historied ['hɪstərid] *a.* historiado, narrado como historia.
historiographer [hɪsˌtɔrɪ'ɑgrəfər, B -'ɔgrəfə] *s.* historiador, esp. por encargo, historiógrafo.
historiographical [-ɪə'græfɪkəl] *s.* historiográfico.
historiography [-ɪ'ɑgrəfɪ, B -'ɔg-] *s.* historiografía.
history ['hɪstərɪ] *s.* (*pl.* HISTORIES) 1. historia. 2. historial, reseña. 3. **ancient h.,** historia antigua; (hum.) cosa pasada de moda o anticuada; **to have a h.,** tener una historia (malos antecedentes); **to make h.,** adquirir importancia histórica; crear un precedente.
histrionic [ˌhɪstrɪ'ɑnɪk, B -'ɔn-] *a.* histriónico, teatral. —*s.* 1. (*pl.*) representación dramática. 2. histrionismo, teatralidad.
histrionical [-ɪkəl] *a.* histriónico, teatral.
histrionically [-kəlɪ] *adv.* teatralmente.
hit [hɪt] *v.t.* (*pret., p.p.* HIT; *p.pr.* HITTING) 1. golpear, pegar; dar (con fuerza), asestar. 2. afectar, conmover, alterar, ej., *the news h. him very hard,* la noticia lo afectó mucho. 3. atinar, acertar; dar con o en; encontrar, hallar, ej., *he h. the bull's eye,* acertó en el blanco, *they h. oil in the desert,* encontraron petróleo en el desierto. 4. llegar a, alcanzar, ej., *the price of wheat h. a new high,* el precio del trigo alcanzó un nuevo máximum, *the evening papers hit the newsstands at four thirty,* los diarios de la tarde llegaron a los puestos a las cuatro y treinta, *he h. town at nightfall,* llegó a la ciudad al anochecer. 5. convenir o cuadrar con, ajustarse o conformarse a. 6. representar, imitar, reproducir. 7. poner en marcha o funcionamiento. 8. (jer.) ganar (premio, dinero). 9. (jer.) echarse al (suelo, cama etc.). 10. **h. (someone) for,** dar un sablazo, pedir (a alguien); **h. home,** tocar un punto vulnerable; **h. it,** acertarlo; (jer.) irse, largarse; **h. it off,** avenirse, llevarse bien, hacer buenas migas; **h. it up,** tocar vigorosamente o con brío (una banda de músicos, etc.); jaranear, andar de parranda; **h. one's stride,** alcanzar su mejor estado o su máxima capacidad; **h. the books,** estudiar (esp. con ahínco); **h. the bottle,** darse a la bebida, dedicarse al trago; **h. the ceiling,** (fam.) agitarse, alterarse, encolerizarse; **h. the hay, h. the sack,** irse a dormir; **h. the high spots,** tocar los puntos sobresalientes (de un tema, materia, etc.); **h. the mark,** dar en el blanco; **h. the nail on the head,** dar en el clavo; **h. the road!** (jer.) ¡váyase!; **h. the spot,** (fam.) satisfacer plenamente; **to h. the trail,** (fam.) ponerse en marcha, partir; **to be hard h.,** estar severamente afectado, sufrir gran perjuicio. —*v.i.* 1. golpear, asestar golpes. 2. desatarse (tormenta, epidemia, etc.); atacar (enfermedad, tropas). 3. (mot.) encenderse. 4. (ant.) (con *with*) concordar (con), coincidir (con). 5. **h. and run,** morder y correr; asaltar y esconderse; **h. against,** tropezar con, chocar contra, dar contra; **h. below the belt,** asestar un golpe bajo; **h. on** (o **upon**), acertar, atinar; dar con, encontrar (solución, etc.); ocurrírsele (algo); **h. out,** asestar golpes duros, golpear duramente. —*s.* 1. golpe. 2. tiro certero. 3. acierto. 4. colisión, choque, impacto. 5. éxito. 6. **a lucky h.,** un golpe de suerte; una ocurrencia

feliz; **h. or miss,** al azar, a la buena de Dios, atolondradamente; **to make a h.,** tener éxito; **to make a h. with,** caer en gracia a, tener éxito con; **to score a h.,** apuntarse un triunfo, dar o acertar en el blanco; **to take a h. at,** (fig.) atacar, lanzar un ataque a.

hit-and-run ['hɪtən'rʌn] *a.* 1. (béisbol) díc. de la jugada en que el corredor de primera base corre hacia la siguiente base, mientras el lanzador empieza a lanzar y el bateador trata de golpear la pelota. 2. que atropella y se da a la fuga (conductor de auto, etc.).

hit-and-run driver, automovilista que huye después de atropellar a una persona.

hitch [hɪtʃ] *v.t.* 1. enganchar; amarrar, atar, ligar; uncir; asegurar. 2. mover a tirones. 3. (jer.) casar, unir. 4. **h. a ride,** (jer.) hacerse llevar en el coche de un amigo; **h. up,** arremangar, alzar de un tirón (pantalones). —*v.i.* 1. moverse a saltos o con vacilación; cojear. 2. (gen. con *together*) enredarse, resultar atrapado. 3. (fam.) congeniar, llevarse bien, armonizar. 4. (jer.) (gen. con *up*) casarse. —*s.* 1. tirón, sacudida. 2. cojera. 3. alto o parada súbita. 4. tropiezo, obstáculo, impedimento; dificultad, contratiempo. 5. enganche. 6. (jer.) trecho, período (esp. de servicio militar). 7. (mar.) vuelta de un cabo. 8. **without a h.,** sin tropiezo, sin dificultad.

hitched [hɪtʃt] *a.* (jer.) casado.

hitchhike ['hɪtʃ,haɪk] *v.i.* hacer auto-stop, viajar por auto-stop, hacerse llevar a trechos por vehículos que pasan; pedir pon (P. Rico), viajar a dedo (Amer.). —*v.t.* pedir ser llevado por vehículos que pasan.

hitchhiker [-ər, B -ə] *s.* autoestopista, turista que viaja por auto-stop.

hitchhiking [-ɪŋ] *s.* auto-stop, viaje a trechos en autos de paso.

hither ['hɪðər, B -ə] *adv.* acá, hacia acá; **h. and thither,** de acá para allá, acá y allá; **h. and yon,** de acá para allá. —*a.* de la parte de acá, más cercano; (tiempo) anterior; **on the h. side of,** aquende, de este lado.

hithermost [-,moʊst] *a.* (lo) más cercano o próximo.

hitherto [-,tu, ˌhɪðər'tu, B 'hɪðə'-] *adv.* 1. hacia acá. 2. hasta la fecha, hasta ahora, hasta aquí, todavía.

hitherward ['hɪðərwərd, B -əwəd] *adv.* hacia acá.

Hitlerism ['hɪtlə,rɪzəm] *s.* (hist.) hitlerismo.

Hitlerite [-,raɪt] *s., a.* hitlerista, nazi.

hit list, lista de los sentenciados a muerte; (*blacklist*) lista negra.

hit man, asesino a sueldo, pistolero, hombre del gatillo.

hit-or-miss ['hɪtər'mɪs, B -ɔ'mɪs] *a.* casual, fortuito, descuidado.

hit parade, (mús) relación de discos más populares, escala de éxitos.

hitter ['hɪtər, B -ə] *s.* golpeador.

Hittite ['hɪ,taɪt] *s., a.* (hist.) hitita o heteo.

hive [haɪv] *s.* 1. colmena. 2. enjambre de abejas. 3. (fig.) emporio, colmena, hormiguero. —*v.t.* 1. encorchar, meter (las abejas) en la colmena. 2. atesorar, acumular, guardar. 3. albergar (personas). —*v.i.* 1. entrar (el enjambre) en la colmena. 2. vivir apiñados.

hiver ['haɪvər, B -və] *s.* colmenero.

hives [haɪvz] *s. pl.* (*sing. o pl. en const.*) (med.) urticaria.

hi ya, hiya['haɪjə] (fam.) *var. de* **hi.**

hl. *abrev. de* **hectoliter,** hectolitro (hl).

H.L. *abrev. de* **House of Lords,** Cámara de los Lores.

H.M. *abrev. de* **Her** o **His Majesty,** Su Majestad (S.M.).

hm. *abrev. de* **hectometer,** hectómetro (hm.).

H.M.S. *abrev. de* **Her** o **His Majesty's Ship,** Buque de Su Majestad.

ho [hoʊ] *interj.* ¡cho! ¡so! ¡alto!

H.O. *abrev. de* **Home Office,** (G.B.) Ministerio del Interior.

Ho *símb. de* **holmium,** holmio (Ho).

hoagy, hoagie ['hoʊgɪ] *s.* (fam.) sándwich mixto de tamaño grande, emparedado hecho con una barra entera de pan.

hoar [hɔr, B hɔ] *a.* 1. (ant.) blanco, blanquecino, gris claro. 2. (ant.) cano, canoso, vetusto, envejecido; venerable. 3. (dial.) mohoso, rancio, pasado. —*s.* 1. escarcha. 2. blancura.

hoard [hɔrd, B hɔd] *s.* cúmulo, acumulación; dinero guardado, tesoro escondido, entierro (Amer.), tapado (Amer.). —*v.t.* atesorar, acumular, guardar. —*v.i.* acaparar alimentos (en tiempo de guerra o escasez).

hoarder ['hɔrdər, B 'hɔdə] *s.* atesorador, acumulador; acaparador.

hoarding [-ɪŋ] *s.* 1. atesoramiento, acumulación; acaparamiento; cúmulo, tesoro. 2. cerca provisional de tablas (alrededor de una construcción). 3. (G.B.) cartelera.

hoarfrost ['hɔr,frɔst, B 'hɔ'-] *s.* helada blanca, escarcha en agujas.

hoarhound, *var. de* **horehound.**

hoariness [-ɪnəs, B -rɪnəs] *s.* blancura; canicie.

hoarse [hɔrs, B hɔs] *a.* ronco, rauco; bronco, áspero, engolado; chirriante, discordante.

hoarsely ['hɔrslɪ, B 'hɔs-] *adv.* roncamente, ásperamente, discordantemente.

hoarsen [-ən] *v.t., v.i.* enronquecer(se).

hoarseness [-nəs] *s.* ronquera, carraspera.

hoary ['hɔrɪ] *a.* 1. blanco, blanquecino; cano, canoso; venerable. 2. remoto, antiguo. 3. (bot., zool.) canescente.

hoatzin [wɑt'sin, B hoʊ'ætsɪn] **hoactzin** [wɑkt-, B hoʊ'ækt-] *s.* (orn.) hoactzín, chenchena.

hoax [hoʊks] *s.* (*pl.* HOAXES) bola, pajarotada, engaño, fraude; truco, chanza, broma. —*v.t.* engañar, chasquear.

hoaxer ['hoʊksər, B -ə] *s.* bromista, chancero.

hob [hɑb, B hɔb] *s.* 1. (dial., G.B.) palurdo, rústico; bufón, payaso; hada, duende, trasgo. 2. (fam.) travesura, diablura.

hob [hɑb, B hɔb] *s.* 1. repisa interior de la chimenea, antehogar. 2. clavija de blanco, hito (en el juego de tejo). 3. tejo, chito, tángano. 4. (mec.) fresa, fresa madre. 5. **to play h. with,** arruinar, hacer daño a; falsear, torcer; **to raise h.,** andar de parranda; armar bochinche (Amer.); **to raise h. with,** enojarse mucho con, reprender severamente; arruinar, hacer daño a. —*v.t.* 1. clavetear con tachuelas. 2. (mec.) fresar.

hobbesian ['hɑbzɪən, B 'hɔb-] *a.* (filos.) característico del hobbismo; de Hobbes, filósofo inglés.

Hobbism [-ɪzəm] *s.* (filos.) hobbismo.

hobble ['hɑbəl, B 'hɔb-] *v.i.* cojear, renquear, renguear. —*v.t.* 1. hacer cojear, dejar cojo. 2. trabar, manear (caballos). 3. (fig.) impedir, obstruir, embarazar, entorpecer. —*s.* 1. cojera. 2. manea, traba, maniota. 3. (fig.) traba, obstáculo. 4. (ant.) dificultad, apremio.

hobblebush [-,bʊʃ] *s.* (bot.) lantana (americana).

hobbledehoy [-dɪ,hɔɪ] *s.* 1. adolescente, mozalbete. 2. joven desgarbado, muchacho torpe.

hobbler ['hɑblər, B 'hɔblə] *s.* cojo, renco, rengo.

hobble skirt, falda de medio paso.

hobby ['hɑbɪ, B 'hɔbɪ] *s.* (*pl.* HOBBIES) 1. pasatiempo favorito, afición; comidilla, tema favorito. 2. (orn.) alcotán.

hobbyhorse [-'hɔrs, B -,hɔs] *s.* 1. caballico, caballito de madera (juguete). 2. (fig.) caballo de batalla, tema favorito. 3. figura de caballo (en ciertas pantomimas).

hobgoblin ['hɑb,gɑblən, B 'hɔb,gɔb-] *s.* 1. duende, trasgo, diablillo. 2. (fig.) espantajo.

hobnail [-,neɪl] *s.* 1. tachuela (para clavetear suelas de zapatos o botas). 2. (ant.) rústico, patán, palurdo. —*v.t.* clavetear con tachuelas.

hobnailed [-,neɪld] *a.* claveteado con tachuelas.

hobnob [-,nɑb, B -,nɔb] *v.i.* (*pret., p.p.* HOBNOBBED; *p.pr.* HOBNOBBING). 1. codearse, tener trato familiar. 2. (ant.) beber juntos. —*s.* reunión, charla amistosa.

hobo ['hoʊboʊ] *s.* (*pl.* HOBOES o HOBOS). 1. vagabundo, vago. 2. trabajador errante.

hoboism [-,ɪzəm] *s.* vagabundeo, costumbre de vagabundear.

Hobson's choice ['hɑbsənz-, B 'hɔb-] opción ilusoria, elección sin alternativa, elección forzosa.

hock [hɑk, B hɔk] *s.* 1. corvejón, jarrete (de los cuadrúpedos); tarso (de las aves). 2. vino del Rin. 3. (jer.) prenda, señal, empeño; **in h.,** empeñado, pignorado; encarcelado. —*v.t.* desjarretar, mancar.

hockey ['hɑkɪ, B 'hɔkɪ] *s.* (dep.) hockey.

hockey stick, palo de hockey.

hock shop, (jer.) monte de piedad, casa de empeños.

hocus ['hoʊkəs] *v.t.* (*pret., p.p.* HOCUSED o HOCUSSED; *p.pr.* HOCUSING o HOCUSSING) 1. engañar, timar, trampear, defraudar. 2. adulterar, falsificar, falsear. 3. narcotizar, atontar con drogas; poner una droga en la bebida.

hocus-pocus [-'poʊkəs] *s.* 1. abracadabra, fórmula mágica, palabras mágicas. 2. truco, treta; farsa, burla, engaño. 3. tontería, adefesio. 4. (ant.) prestidigitador; prestidigitación, juego de manos. —*v.t.* (*pret., p.p.* HOCUS-POCUSSED o HOCUS-POCUSED; *p.pr.* HOCUS-POCUSSING o HOCUS-POCUSING) engañar, burlar.

hod [hɑd, B hɔd] *s.* 1. capacho de albañil, cuezo (para llevar yeso, argamasa, ladrillos, etc.). 2. cubo para carbón.

hod carrier, peón de mano, peón de albañil.

hodden ['hɑdən, B 'hɔd-] *s.* (esco.) tela basta sin teñir.

hodgepodge ['hɑdʒ,pɑdʒ, B 'hɔdʒ,pɔdʒ] *s.* bodrio, almodrote, baturrillo, mezcolanza.

hodman ['hɑdmən, B 'hɔd-] *s.* peón de mano, peón de albañil.

hodometer [hoʊ'dɑmətər, B hɔ'dɔmɪtə] *s.* odómetro.

hoe [hoʊ] *s.* azada, azadón. —*v.t., v.i.* azadonar, cavar o limpiar con azada o azadón.

hoecake ['hoʊ,keɪk] *s.* (S. de E.U.) torta de maíz.

hoedown [-,daʊn] *s.* (E.U.) contradanza; baile (festejo) de contradanzas.

hoer ['hoʊər, B -ə] *s.* azadonero.

hog [hɔg, hɑg, B hɔg] *s.* 1. puerco, cerdo, marrano, cochino, chancho (Amer.). 2. (fam.) puerco, cerdo, chancho, cochino, glotón. 3. (dial., G.B.) oveja joven (antes de su primera esquila). 4. **to go the whole h.,** (fam.) ir hasta el final, no quedarse a medio camino. —*v.t.* (*pret., p.p.* HOGGED; *p.pr.* HOGGING) 1. arquear, combar. 2. recortar (las crines de un caballo). 3. (jer.) abarcar, tomar para sí solo (todo o más de lo que corresponde). —*v.i.* combarse, arquearse (díc. de la quilla de las embarcaciones).

hogan ['hoʊ,gɑn, B -gən] *s.* (E.U.) típica choza de los indios navajos.

hogback ['hɔg,bək, 'hɑg-, B 'hɔg-] *s.* 1. cuchilla (cerro escarpado). 2. (geol.) pliegue.
hog cholera, peste porcina, cólera de los cerdos.
hogfish [-,fɪʃ] *s.* (ict.) escorpena, escorpina; ortopristis.
hoggish [-ɪʃ] *a.* puerco, cochino, sucio; voraz, egoísta; glotón.
hoggishly [-lɪ] *adv.* puercamente; vorazmente; glotonamente.
hoggishness [-nəs] *s.* porquería; voracidad; egoísmo, glotonería.
Hogmanay [,hɑgmə'neɪ, B 'hɔgmə,neɪ] *s.* (esco.) 1. víspera de año nuevo. 2. obsequio dado en la víspera de año nuevo.
hognose snake ['hɔg,noʊz-, 'hɑg-, B 'hɔg-] **hog-nosed snake** [-,noʊzd-] (zool.) heterodón.
hognut [-,nʌt] *s.* (bot.) 1. cotufa, chufa. 2. cacahuete, maní.
hog plum, (bot.) jobo.
hog's bristle, cerda (para hacer cepillos).
hog's fennel, (bot.) ervato, servato, hierba de Túnez.
hogshead ['hɔgz,hɛd, 'hɑgz-, B 'hɔgz-] *s.* 1. tonel grande. 2. unidad de medida equivalente a 238,5 litros.
hog-tie ['hɔg,taɪ, 'hɑg-, B 'hɔg-] *v.t.* (*pret., p.p.* HOG-TIED; *p.pr.* HOG-TYING) 1. atar juntas las patas de (un cerdo u otro animal). 2. (fig.) paralizar, inmovilizar.
hogwash [-,wɔʃ, -,wɑʃ, B -,wɔʃ] *s.* 1. bazofia (para cerdos), desperdicios. 2. (jer.) guirigay, galimatías, monserga.
hogweed [-,wid] *s.* (bot.) ambrosia; cerraja; manzanilla bastarda; cimarrona.
hog-wild [-,waɪld] *a.* (jer.) excitado en extremo.
hoicks [hɔɪks] **hoick** [hɔɪk] *interj.* (ú. para azuzar perros) ¡sus!
hoipolloi ['hɔɪpə'lɔɪ, B hɔɪ'pɔlɔɪ] *s. pl.* (las) masas, (el) populacho.
hoist [hɔɪst] *v.t.* (*pret., p.p.* HOISTED; *p.pr.* HOISTING) 1. levantar, elevar, alzar (esp. por medio de poleas). 2. enarbolar, izar (esp. banderas). 3. (jer.) alzarse o levantarse con, robar, hurtar. —*s.* 1. levantamiento, alzamiento; empujón hacia arriba. 2. montacargas, torno izador. 3. (pr. G.B.) ascensor de carga, elevador. 4. medida vertical de banderas o velas.
hoister ['hɔɪstər, B -ə] *s.* (min.) montacargas, torno izador o elevador.
hoity-toity ['hɔɪtɪ'tɔɪtɪ] *a.* 1. arrogante, altivo, altanero, engreído, petulante, desdeñoso. 2. atolondrado, voluble, caprichoso, veleidoso, inconstante. —*s.* (raro) conducta descabellada. —*interj.* ¡vaya arrogancia!
hokeypokey ['hoʊkɪ'poʊkɪ] *s.* 1. (ant.) helado barato (que se vende en las calles). 2. *var. de* **hocus-pocus.**
hokum ['hoʊkəm] *s.* 1. palabrería vana, faramalla, hojarasca. 2. trama sensiblera (de teatro); artificio para llegar al populacho.
holandric [hɑ'lændrɪk, B hɔ-] *a.* (biol.) holándrico.
Holarctic [-'lɑrktɪk, B -'lɑk-] *a.* (geog.) holártico.
hold [hoʊld] *v.t.* (*pret., p.p.* **HELD** [hɛld]; *p.pr.* HOLDING; *p.p. ant.* HOLDEN ['hoʊldən]) 1. agarrar, empuñar, asir. 2. tener, guardar (en poder); retener; conservar. 3. contener, dar cabida a. 4. sostener, sustentar, apoyar (opinión, teoría, etc.). 5. absorber, embargar, atraer (atención, interés). 6. detener, impedir (ataque, avance). 7. sujetar, ej., *a screw holds the axle,* un tornillo sujeta el eje. 8. obligar, hacer cumplir, ej., *h. one to his word,* hacer cumplir a uno su palabra. 9. considerar, juzgar, ej., *h. one guiltless,* considerar a uno libre de culpa. 10. abrigar, albergar (prejuicio, sentimiento, etc.). 11. sostener, tener, celebrar, mantener (conversación o reunión). 12. conducir, presidir, ej., *a judge holds court,* un juez preside un tribunal. 13. mantener, conducir o llevar (en determinada posición), ej., *he holds himself erect,* se mantiene erguido; *h. him at bay,* mantenerlo a raya, *h. him in suspense,* mantenerlo en suspenso. 14. soportar (un peso, etc.). 15. poseer (título, distinción, medalla, etc.), ser dueño, tenedor o arrendatario de (propiedades). 16. ocüpar (lugar; oficio; pensamientos de una persona). 17. reservar (un cuarto en hotel, asiento, etc.). 18. (mil.) conservar la posesión de, defender con éxito (un lugar). 19. tener (bajo custodia). 20. (ant.) sufrir, padecer, aguantar, tolerar. 21. **h. a candle to,** (fam.) poder compararse con; **h. a thing cheap,** menospreciar o no apreciar una cosa, no tener algo en estima o consideración; **h. a thing dear,** estimar una cosa, mirar algo con cariño o delectación; **h. back,** retener, sujetar; detener; **h. down,** (E.U.) seguir en, conservar, no perder (puesto, situación); **h. everything!** ¡un momento! ¡paren!; **h. hands,** estar cogidos de la mano (amigos o enamorados); **h. in,** contener, sujetar, retener, refrenar; **h. it!** ¡no te muevas! ¡espera! ¡aguanta!; **h. off,** mantener alejado; contener (enemigo, etc.); aplazar, diferir; **h. (a gun) on,** apuntar (con una pistola) a; **h. one's hand,** reprimirse, abstenerse; **h. one's head high,** llevar la cabeza muy alta; **h. one's ground, h. one's own,** mantenerse firme, no perder terreno; **h. one's liquor,** tener buena cabeza para el licor; **h. one's peace, h. one's tongue,** callar, guardar silencio; **h. out,** alargar, extender; ofrecer, proponer; **h. (something) over,** aplazar, diferir (algo); amenazar con (algo); **h. (one) responsible,** hacer responsable (a uno); **h. the bag, h. the sack,** (fam.) quedarse con las manos vacías; cargar con la responsabilidad; cargar con el muerto; (fam.) pagar el pato; **h. them up!** ¡arriba las manos!, **h. to,** agarrarse (bien) de; **h. together,** mantener unidos; **h. up,** levantar, alzar; sostener; exhibir, mostrar; (fam.) asaltar, atracar; detener, parar, impedir; no caerse; **h. up one's head,** no dejarse abatir; **h. water,** (fam.) ser lógico, estar bien fundado. —*v.i.* 1. mantenerse, sostenerse; soportar prueba, aguantar, no ceder. 2. asirse, agarrarse; pegarse, adherirse. 3. (con *of* o *from*) tener derecho o título. 4. valer, ser válido o valedero, estar en vigor, tener vigencia, ser aplicable. 5. (t. con *up*) seguir, continuar, durar, persistir. 6. ocurrir, tener lugar. 7. contenerse, detenerse, pararse. 8. **h. aloof,** mantenerse apartado; **h. back,** vacilar; abstenerse, detenerse, cohibirse; **h. by, h. to,** pegarse o adherirse a; **h. forth,** arengar, predicar; (despec.) perorar; **h. good,** valer, ser válido; **h. in,** abstenerse, contenerse; **h. off,** tardar, demorarse, mantenerse a distancia; **h. on,** tenerse bien agarrado, agarrarse bien; (fam.) ¡espere! ¡un momento! ¡no cuelgue! (el auricular del teléfono); **h. on there!** ¡paso a paso!; **h. out,** (jer.) negarse a trabajar o cumplir una obligación para exigir mejor sueldo o tratamiento; mantenerse firme, no ceder, aguantar; durar, persistir; **h. out for,** insistir en, no aceptar menos de; **h. out on (someone),** (fam.) tener secretos con, dejar a oscuras a (alguien); **h. over,** continuar desempeñando un cargo (cuando habría que dejarlo); **h. together,** mantenerse juntos, estar reunidos; no descomponerse; **h. with,** aprobar, dar el beneplácito a, convenir con. —*s.* 1. baluarte, fuerte, fortificación, plaza fuerte. 2. prisión, cárcel. 3. asidero, agarradero. 4. presa, asimiento, agarro. 5. autoridad, dominio; influencia, alcance. 6. (lucha) llave, presa. 7. (con *on* o *upon*) comprensión (de). 8. (mús.) pausa. 9. (ant.) custodia; posesión; protección. 10. **to get h. of,** agarrar, coger; encontrar; conseguir, apoderarse de; **to get h. on oneself,** dominarse; **to have a h. over,** tener en su poder, ejercer dominio o influencia sobre; **to loose one's h.,** desasirse; **to take h.,** afirmarse, afianzarse.
hold [hoʊld] *s.* 1. (mar.) bodega, cala. 2. (aer.) cabina de carga.
holdall ['hoʊld,ɔl] *s.* maletín, talega (para toda clase de cosas); esp. maleta de turista o de soldado.
holdback [-,bæk] *s.* 1. restricción, limitación; retención (de salario, etc.). 2. cejadero, cejador. 3. seguro (de puerta).
holden ['hoʊldən] (ant.) *p.p. de* **hold.**
holder ['hoʊldər, B -də] *s.* 1. sostén, soporte, sostenedor. 2. arrendatario, inquilino. 3. tenedor, posesor, poseedor. 4. boquilla. 5. portaplumas.
holdfast [-,fæst, B -,fɑst] *s.* 1. (mec.) grapa, laña; amarra; gancho de seguro. 2. (bot.) zarcillo, cirro. 3. (zool.) apéndice de adhesión al huésped de un organismo parásito.
holding ['hoʊldɪŋ] *s.* 1. posesión, tenencia (de tierras). 2. (*pl.*) valores en cartera; propiedades. 3. (dep.) uso ilegal de las manos o los brazos para detener al oponente.
holding company, (fin.) 1. holding, compañía tenedora, compañía de valores, compañía matriz. 2. sociedad de control.
holding fire, (mil.) fuego de contención.
holdover ['hoʊld,oʊvər, B -və] *s.* 1. remanente, resto, continuación. 2. empleado antiguo; miembro veterano (de un equipo, etc.). 3. temporada de una representación teatral que se extiende por éxito o aclamación.
holdup [-,ʌp] *s.* 1. detención, demora. 2. asalto a mano armada, atraco.
holdup man, atracador, asaltante.
hole [hoʊl] *s.* 1. agujero, abertura. 2. cavidad, hueco, hoyo. 3. caverna, cueva. 4. remanso, charco (de una corriente). 5. madriguera, guarida. 6. chiribitil, tabuco, cochitril; lugar aburrido, poblacho, pueblo de mala muerte. 7. defecto, imperfección, falta. 8. atolladero, aprieto, situación embarazosa. 9. (golf) hoyo. 10. **a h. to crawl out of,** salida, escapatoria; **h. in the wall,** (gen. despec.) tienda o habitación pequeña, cuchitril; **in a h.,** (jer.) en apuros, en un aprieto; **in the h.,** con puntaje negativo (en juegos); (jer.) adeudado; endeudado; **round peg in square h.,** persona fuera de lugar o no adecuada para su puesto; **to burn a h. in one's pocket,** írsele a uno (el dinero) de entre las manos; **to make a h. in,** gastar gran cantidad de; **to need like a h. in the head,** (fam.) ¡sólo eso faltaba!; **to pick holes,** encontrar errores. —*v.t.* 1. agujerear, cavar. 2. introducir en un hoyo o agujero. —*v.i.* 1. encuevarse, encovarse. 2. **h. out,** (golf) embocar, hacer entrar (la pelota) en un hoyo; **h. up in,** (jer.) esconder(se) (ej., de la policía); encontrar alojamiento temporal (ej., en un hotel).
holey ['hoʊlɪ] *a.* agujereado, hoyoso.
holiday, holyday ['hɑlə,deɪ, B 'hɔlədɪ] *s.* 1. día de fiesta, día feriado, día festivo, festivo. 2. vacaciones; (*pl.*) período de vacaciones. 3. **to take a h.,** irse de vacaciones, tomarse un descanso. —*a.* 1. de fiesta, festivo (vestido, espíritu, ambiente, etc.). 2. de vacaciones (tareas, etc.). —*v.i.* pasar las vacaciones, veranear.
holidays [-,deɪz, B -dɪz] *adv.* cada día feriado, durante los días feriados.

holier-than-thou ['hoʊlɪərðən'ðaʊ, B -əðən-] *a.* más papista que el papa; santurrón en un grado exagerado.
holily [-ləlɪ] *adv.* piadosamente, píamente, santamente.
holiness [-lɪnəs] *s.* 1. santidad, beatitud. 2. **His H., Your H.,** Su Santidad, Vuestra Santidad (tratamiento para el Papa).
holing ['hoʊlɪŋ] *s.* orificio, taladro, perforación.
holism ['hoʊˌlɪzəm, B 'hɔ-] *s.* (filos.) holismo.
holla ['hɑlə, B 'hɔlə] *interj. var. de* **hollo.**
Holland ['hɑlənd, B 'hɔl-] *s.* 1. Holanda. 2. (tej.) holanda, holán. 3. (tej.) holandilla, holandeta, mitán.
hollandaise [ˌhɑlən'deɪz, 'hɑlənˌdeɪʒ, B ˌhɔlən'deɪz] *s.* salsa holandesa (hecha con mantequilla, yema de huevo y vinagre o limón).
Hollander ['hɑləndər, B 'hɔləndə] *s.* holandés.
Hollands [-əndz] *s.* ginebra.
holler ['hɑlər, B 'hɔlə] *v.t., v.i.* gritar, vociferar. —*s.* grito.
hollo ['hɑloʊ, B 'hɔl-] *interj.* ¡alto! ¡eh! ¡hola! —*s.* grito. —*v.i.* (*pret., p.p.* HOLLOED; *p.pr.* HOLLOING) gritar, exclamar. —*v.t.* gritar, vociferar.
hollow ['hɑloʊ, B 'hɔl-] *a.* 1. hueco, ahuecado. 2. hundido, cóncavo. 3. sordo, apagado; retumbante, resonante (sonido). 4. (fig.) hueco (palabras, promesas, etc.), falso, insincero (elogio, etc.). 5. (fig.) vano (triunfo, festejo, etc.). 6. **his threats (words,** etc.) **rang h.,** sus amenazas (palabras, etc.) sonaban falsas. —*adv.* (fam.) enteramente, completamente, por completo, ej., *I beat him h.,* lo derroté por completo. —*s.* 1. cavidad; agujero. 2. hondonada, depresión; valle. —*v.t.* ahuecar, excavar, ahondar; **h. out,** ahuecar, excavar. —*v.i.* ahuecarse.
hollow-chested [-'tʃɛstəd] *a.* de pecho hundido.
hollow-eyed [-ˌaɪd] *a.* de ojos hundidos, ojeroso.
hollowhearted [-'hɑrtəd, B -'hɑt-] *a.* insincero, solapado, falso.
hollowly ['hɑloʊlɪ, B 'hɔl-] *adv.* sordamente, con resonancia sorda.
hollowness [-nəs] *s.* 1. hueco, cavidad. 2. doblez, falsía, simulación.
hollow organ, (anat.) órgano hueco.
hollow partition, (const.) tabique sordo.
hollow punch, sacabocado.
hollow ware, los objetos del servicio de mesa que gen. son de plata (bandejas, teteras, fruteros).
holly ['hɑlɪ, B 'hɔlɪ] *s.* (bot.) acebo, agrifolio, aquifolio.
hollyhock [-ˌhɑk, B -ˌhɔk] *s.* (bot.) malva real, malva arbórea, malva rósea, malva loca, malvarrosa.
holm [hoʊm] *s.* 1. isleta de río o lago, bajo de arena, mejana. 2. vega ribereña. 3. (bot.) encina, carrasca.
holmic ['hoʊlmɪk] *a.* (quím.) hólmico.
holmium [-mɪəm] *s.* (quím.) holmio.
holm oak, (bot.) encina, carrasca.
holoblastic [ˌhɑloʊ'blæstɪk, B ˌhɔl-] *a.* (embr.) holoblástico.
holocaine ['hɑləˌkeɪn, 'hoʊlə-, B 'hɔlə-] *s.* (farm.) holocaína.
holocaust ['hɑləˌkɔst, B 'hɔl-] *s.* 1. holocausto, sacrificio. 2. incendio voraz, abrasamiento total, destrucción completa por incendio. 3. **the H.,** el exterminio en masa de los judíos en la Segunda Guerra Mundial.
Holocene ['hɑləˌsin, 'hoʊlə-, B 'hɔlə-] *a.* (geol.) holocénico.
holocephalan [ˌhɑloʊ'sɛfələn, B ˌhɔl-] *a., s.* (ict.) holocéfalo.
Holocephali [-ˌlaɪ] *s. pl.* (ict.) holocéfalos.
holocrine ['hɑləkrən, -ˌkraɪn, B 'hɔl-] *a.* (fisiol.) holocrino.
hologamy [hə'lɑgəmɪ, B -'lɔg-] *s.* (biol.) hologamia.
hologram ['hoʊləgræm] *s.* holograma.
holograph ['hɑləˌgræf, 'hoʊlə-, B 'hɔləˌgrɑf] *a., s.* ológrafo, hológrafo.
holographic [ˌhɑlə'græfɪk, ˌhoʊlə-, B ˌhɔlə-] **holographical** [-ɪkəl] *a.* ológrafo, hológrafo.
holographic will, (der.) testamento ológrafo.
holography [ho'lɑgrəfi] *s.* holografía.
hologynic [-oʊ'dʒɪnɪk] *a.* (biol.) hologínico.
hologyny [hə'lɑdʒənɪ, B -'lɔdʒ-] *s.* (biol.) hologinia.
holohedral [ˌhɑlə'hidrəl, ˌhoʊlə-, B ˌhɔlə-] *a.* holoédrico (díc. de cristales).
holometabolism [-mə'tæbəˌlɪzəm] *s.* (ento.) holometabolismo.
holometabolous [-ləs] *a.* (ento.) holometábolo.
holometer [hə'lɑmətər, B -'lɔmɪtə] *s.* (top.) holómetro.
holomorphic [ˌhɑlə'mɔrfɪk, ˌhoʊlə-, B ˌhɔlə'mɔfɪk] *a.* olomórfico.
holophote ['hɑləˌfoʊt, B 'hɔlə-] *s.* holofoto, faro, reflector.
holophrastic [ˌhɑlə'fræstɪk, ˌhoʊlə-, B ˌhɔlə-] *a.* (filol.) holofrástico.
holophytic [-'fɪtɪk] *a.* (biol.) holofítico.
holosteric [-'stɛrɪk] *a.* holostérico.
holothurian [-'θʊrɪən, B -'θjʊr-] *s.* (zool.) holoturia, cohombro de mar.
holotype ['hɑləˌtaɪp, 'hoʊlə-, B 'hɔlə-] *s.* (biol.) holotipo.
holozoic [ˌhɑlə'zoʊɪk, ˌhoʊlə-, B ˌhɔlə-] *a.* (biol.) holozoico.
holp [hoʊlp] (ant., dial.) *pret. de* **help.**
holpen ['hoʊlpən] (ant., dial.) *p.p. de* **help.**
Holstein ['hoʊlˌstaɪn, -ˌstin, B -ˌstaɪn] *s.* variedad de ganado vacuno de origen frisón.
holster [-stər, B -stə] *s.* pistolera, funda de pistola, cañonera (Amer.).
holt [hoʊlt] *s.* (ant.) bosque; matorral; monte.
holus-bolus ['hoʊləs'boʊləs] *adv.* (fam.) todos a la vez; todos en montón; por completo; de un trago.
holy ['hoʊlɪ] *a.* (HOLIER; HOLIEST) 1. santo, sagrado, sacro; santificado, consagrado, bendito. 2. venerable, adorable. 3. asombroso, increíble. —*s.* (*pl.* HOLIES) santuario, lugar santo.
Holy Alliance, (hist.) Santa Alianza.
Holy Ark, (bíbl.) Arca de la Alianza.
Holy Bible, Santa Biblia.
Holy City, 1. Ciudad Santa (Jerusalén, Roma, Medina, etc.). 2. **h. c.,** cielo, mansión de Dios.
Holy Communion, (relig.) Santa Comunión, Sacramento de la Eucaristía.
holy cow, *interj.* (jer.) ¡cielo santo!.
holy day, fiesta (religiosa); día feriado (religioso); **h. of obligation** (relig.) fiesta de respeto, fiesta de precepto.
Holy Father, Santo Padre (el Papa).
Holy Ghost, (relig.) Espíritu Santo.
Holy Grail, Grial, Santo Grial.
Holy Land, Tierra Santa (Palestina).
Holy Office, (hist., relig.) Santo Oficio.
holy of holies, sanctasanctórum.
holy orders, (relig.) 1. orden, orden sacerdotal. 2. órdenes sagradas, órdenes mayores. 3. **to take h. o.,** ordenarse.
Holy Roman Empire, (hist.) Sacro Imperio Romano Germánico.
Holy Scripture, Sagradas Escrituras.
Holy See, Santa Sede.
holy smoke, *interj.* (fam.) ¡cielos! ¡caracoles!
Holy Spirit, Espíritu Santo.
holystone ['hoʊlɪˌstoʊn] *s.* (mar.) piedra bendita, piedra de cubierta, piedra de arena. —*v.t., v.i.* estregar con piedra de arena.
Holy Synod, Santo Sínodo.
holy terror, persona irresponsable, tipo exasperante; niño insoportable.
Holy Thursday, 1. (Iglesia Católica Romana) Jueves Santo. 2. (Iglesia Anglicana) día de la Ascensión.
holy water, agua bendita.
holy water sprinkler, hisopo.
Holy Week, Semana Santa.
homage ['hɑmɪdʒ, 'ɑm-, B 'hɔm-] *s.* 1. homenaje, reverencia. 2. (der.) homenaje, pleito homenaje. 3. **to pay h. to, to do h. to,** rendir homenaje a, acatar, honrar.
homager [-ɪdʒər, B -ə] *s.* vasallo, siervo.
homalographic [ˌhɑmələ'græfɪk, B ˌhɔm-] *a.* (cartografía) homolográfico.
homburg ['hɑmbərg, B 'hɔmbɜg] *s.* sombrero flexible.
home [hoʊm] *s.* 1. hogar; casa, residencia; domicilio; nido, lar. 2. patria; patria chica. 3. lugar de origen, país (de origen). 4. habitación, habitat, ambiente natural, elemento. 5. sede; base. 6. asilo, albergue (para ancianos, dementes, etc.). 7. (dep.) meta, gol. 8. **at h.,** en casa; de recibo; cómodo, confortable, sosegado; en su elemento, en su ambiente; **at h. in** (o **with**), conocedor de, familiarizado con; **away from h.,** lejos de la casa o de la patria; **make yourself at h.,** siéntase Ud. en su casa, está Ud. en su casa; **to make oneself at h.,** sentirse como en su casa, ponerse cómodo. —*a.* 1. doméstico, hogareño, casero. 2. nativo, indígena, natal. 3. nacional, local (industria, comercio, etc.), interno (mercado). 4. certero, eficaz, efectivo. —*adv.* 1. a casa; a la patria. 2. en casa. 3. al centro vital, a la base; (fig.) al corazón o médula. 4. al destino, al objetivo. 5. **nothing to write h. about,** (fam.) nada del otro mundo; **to bring h. to,** explicar, hacer ver claramente; **to come h.,** volver a casa; **to come h. to,** volverse claro para, hacerse comprender claramente; hacer impacto en, afectar profundamente; **to drive h.,** clavar, introducir (clavo, etc.) al máximo o al tope; **to drive a point h.,** (fig.) remachar el clavo; **to go h.,** ir a casa, volver a casa; dar en el blanco, ej., *the thrust went h.,* la pulla dio en el blanco; **to see h.,** acompañar a casa; **to strike h.,** dar en lo vivo; **to take h.,** llevar a casa. —*v.i.* ir o volver a casa; **h. in on, h. on to,** dirigirse hacia, estar guiado hacia (objetivo, blanco, etc., díc. de un proyectil teledirigido). —*v.t.* 1. guiar (a casa). 2. albergar, acomodar, cobijar.
home address, domicilio; **his h.,** las señas de su casa.
home base, (béisbol) base meta, base del bateador; (*headquarters*) base de operaciones.
homebody ['hoʊmˌbɑdɪ, B -ˌbɔdɪ] *s.* persona hogareña, persona casera.
home-bound [-'baʊnd] *a.* 1. camino de casa. 2. confinado en casa.
homeboy ['hoʊbɔɪ] *s.* (jer.) compinche, cuate.
homebred [-'brɛd] *a.* 1. doméstico, hecho en casa; casero, producido en el país. 2. sin pulir, rudo, inculto; sencillo.
home brew, bebida alcohólica hecha en casa, esp. cerveza.
homecoming [-ˌkʌmɪŋ] *s.* llegada, regreso (al hogar).
home computer, ordenador doméstico.

home cooking, cocina doméstica.
home counties, (G.B.) condados cercanos a Londres.
home economics, economía doméstica.
home front, frente civil (en una guerra).
homegrown [-ˈgroʊn] *a.* cultivado en casa (frutos, verduras, etc.).
home improvements, reformas mejores en la vivienda.
homeland [-ˌlænd] *s.* tierra natal, suelo patrio.
homeless [-ləs] *a.* sin hogar, sin casa; desamparado.
homelife [ˈhoʊmˌlaɪf] *s.* vida familiar, vida de familia.
homelike [-ˌlaɪk] *a.* como de casa, sosegado, abrigado, cómodo, agradable; casero, hogareño.
homeliness [-lɪnəs] *s.* 1. carácter doméstico o acogedor; intimidad, comodidad. 2. simplicidad, sencillez, llaneza. 3. (E.U.) fealdad.
home loan, préstamo para la vivienda.
homeloving [ˈhoʊmˌlʌvɪŋ] *a.* persona casera, persona hogareña.
homely [-lɪ] *a.* (HOMELIER; HOMELIEST) 1. casero, doméstico; acogedor, agradable. 2. (fig.) sencillo, llano, sin pretensiones. 3. gentil, bondadoso. 4. feo, de facciones ordinarias; liso, sin adornos.
homemade [-ˈmeɪd] *a.* casero, hecho en casa, de fabricación casera; producido en el país.
homemaker [-ˌmeɪkər, B -kə] *s.* ama de casa.
home movie, película casera.
homeochromatic [ˌhoʊmɪoʊkrəˈmætɪk] *a.* (ópt.) homocromático.
home office, 1. (com.) casa matriz; casa central, oficina principal. 2. **H.O.,** (G.B). Ministerio del (o de lo) Interior, Ministerio de la Gobernación, Ministerio de Gobierno.
homeomorphic [ˌhoʊmɪəˈmɔrfɪk, B -ˈmɔfɪk] *a.* (quím.) homeomorfo.
homeomorphism [-ˌfɪzəm] *s.* homeomorfismo.
homeopath, homoeopath [ˈhoʊmɪəˌpæθ] *s.* (med.) homeópata.
homeopathic [ˌhoʊmɪəˈpæθɪk] *a.* homeópata, homeopático.
homeopathically [-ɪkəlɪ] *adv.* homeopáticamente.
homeopathist [ˌhoʊmɪˈɑpəθəst, B -ˈɔp-] *s.* homeópata.
homeopathy [-əθɪ] *s.* homeopatía.
homeostasis [ˌhoʊmɪoʊˈsteɪsəs, B -ˈstæs-] *s.* (biol.) homeostasis.
homeostatic [-ˈstætɪk] *a.* (biol.) homeostático.
homeothermal [-ˈθɜrməl, B -ˈθɜməl] **homeothermic** [-mɪk] **homeothermous** [-məs] *a.* (zool.) homeotermo, homeotérmico.
homeotypic [-ˈtɪpɪk] *a.* (biol.) homeotípico.
home owner *s.* propietario de una vivienda; (*pl.*) propietarios de viviendas.
home plate, (béisbol) base meta, base del bateador.
home port, 1. puerto de origen. 2. base (naval).
homer [ˈhoʊmər, B -mə] *s.* 1. (fam.) (béisbol, Amer.) jonrón. 2. paloma mensajera.
Homer, *s.* Homero, poeta griego de la antigüedad.
Homeric [hoʊˈmɛrɪk] **Homerical** [-ɪkəl] *a.* homérico, perteneciente al poeta Homero o a sus obras.
homeroom [ˈhoʊmˌrum] *s.* clase del curso, sala donde los alumnos de una misma clase se reúnen con el fin de informar sobre sus actividades.
home rule, (pol.) autonomía, gobierno propio.
home run, (béisbol) jonrón (Amer.).
Home Secretary, (G.B.) Ministro de la Gobernación, Ministro de Gobierno, Ministro del (o de lo) Interior.
home shopping club, compras de la tele.
homesick [-ˌsɪk] *a.* nostálgico; **to be h. for,** sentir nostalgia de, echar de menos, añorar.
homesickness [-nəs] *s.* nostalgia, añoranza.
homespun [ˈhoʊmˌspʌn] *a.* 1. casero, doméstico, hecho en casa. 2. confeccionado con tela hecha en casa. 3. (fig.) simple, sencillo, llano. —*s.* 1. hilado doméstico, lienzo casero. 2. (ant.) rústico, campesino.
homestead [-ˌstɛd] *s.* 1. residencia, heredad, casa solariega. 2. (der.) hogar de familia, hogar seguro. —*v.t.* (E.U.) tomar posesión de (tierras) legalmente.
homesteader [-ər, B -ə] *s.* propietario de tierras, colono; (E.U.) que posee tierras garantizadas por leyes especiales.
homestead law, ley sobre inembargabilidad de hogares; ley de protección a las tierras de colonización; (E.U.) leyes que no autorizan la venta forzada de tierras de colonización.
homestretch [-ˈstrɛtʃ] *s.* (dep.) último trecho, recta final (de una carrera).
hometown [-ˈtaʊn] *s.* ciudad o pueblo natal.
homeward [-wərd, B -wəd] *a.* (que esta) en camino a casa, de regreso (a casa). —*adv.* hacia casa, con dirección a casa.
homeward bound, de regreso, de vuelta; hacia casa o al país natal.
homework [-ˌwɜrk, B -ˌwɜk] *s.* 1. ejercicio, tarea escolar (para la casa), deberes. 2. labor (fabril) hecha en casa.
homey, homy [ˈhoʊmɪ] *a.* doméstico, casero, hogareño; íntimo.
homicidal [ˌhɑməˈsaɪdəl, ˌhoʊ-, B ˌhɔ-] *a.* homicida.
homicide [ˈhɑməˌsaɪd, ˈhoʊ-, B ˈhɔmɪ-] *s.* 1. homicidio. 2. homicida.
homiletic [ˌhɑməˈlɛtɪk, B ˌhɔm-] **homiletical** [-ɪkəl] *a.* homilético, como una homilía, sermonario.
homiletics [-ɪks] *s. pl.* (*sing. en constr.*) (teo.) homilética.
homilist [ˈhɑməlǝst, B ˈhɔm-] *s.* homilista.
homily [-əlɪ] *s.* (*pl.* HOMILIES) 1. homilía, sermón. 2. (fig.) sermón, rapapolvo, rociada.
homing [ˈhoʊmɪŋ] *a.* 1. que retorna a casa. 2. guiado; autodirigido. 3. de guía, guiador; direccional. —*s.* 1. facultad o costumbre de regresar a casa (de animales). 2. (aer.) recalada.
homing beacon, (aer.) radiofaro direccional.
homing device, 1. mecanismo autodireccional (de proyectiles, cohetes). 2. (aer.) radioguía, indicador automático de ruta.
homing pigeon, paloma mensajera.
hominid [ˈhɑmənəd, B ˈhɔmɪ-] *a., s.* (antrop.) homínido (primate antecesor del Homo Sapiens).
hominoid [-ˌnɔɪd] *a., s.* hominoideo.
hominy [ˈhɑmənɪ, B ˈhɔm-] *s.* maíz machacado.
homo [ˈhoʊmoʊ] *s.* homo, género de primate que incluye al hombre.
homo, *s.* (jer.) maricón, homosexual.
homo-, *pref.* que significa el mismo o parecido, ej., *homologous,* homólogo.
homocentric [ˌhoʊməˈsɛntrɪk, ˌhɑmə-, B ˌhoʊmə-] *a.* (geom.) homocéntrico.
homocercal [-ˈsɜrkəl, B -ˈsɜkəl] *a.* (ict.) homocerco.
homochromatic [-krəˈmætɪk] **homochromous** [-ˈkroʊməs] *a.* (bot.) homocromático.
homochromosome [-ˈkroʊməˌsoʊm] *s.* (biol.) autosoma, cromosoma ordinario.
homoecious [hoʊˈmiʃəs] *a.* (bot., zool.) permanente (díc. de un parásito que tiene el mismo huésped durante toda su vida).
homoerotic [ˌhoʊmoʊɪˈrɑtɪk, B -ˈrɔt-] *a.* homosexual.
homoeroticism [-əˌsɪzəm] **homoerotism** [-ɪzəm] *s. homoerotismo, homosexualidad.*
homogamous [hoʊˈmɑgəməs, B -ˈmɔg-] *a.* (bot.) homógamo.
homogamy [-mɪ] *s.* (bot.) homogamia.
homogeneity [ˌhoʊmədʒəˈniətɪ, B ˌhɔmə-] *s.* homogeneidad.
homogeneous [-ˈdʒiniəs] *a.* homogéneo.
homogeneously [-lɪ] *adv.* homogéneamente.
homogeneousness [-nəs] *s.* homogeneidad.
homogenesis [-ˈdʒɛnəsəs] *s.* (biol.) homogénesis, homogenia.
homogenization [həˌmɑdʒənəˈzeɪʃən, B -ˌmɔdʒənaɪ-] *s.* homogeneización.
homogenize [həˈmɑdʒəˌnaɪz, B hɔˈmɔdʒ-] *v.t.* homogeneizar, hacer homogéneo.
homogenizer [-ər, B -ə] *s.* homogeneizador.
homogenous [-ənəs] *a.* (biol.) homógeno.
homogeny [-ənɪ] *s.* (biol.) homogenia.
homogonous [-ˈmɑgənəs, B -ˈmɔg-] *a.* (bot.) homógono.
homogony [-nɪ] *s.* (bot.) homogonía.
homograft [ˈhoʊməˌgræft, ˈhɑmə-, B ˈhɔməˌgrɑft] *s.* (med.) homoplastia, homoinjerto, homotrasplante.
homograph [-ˌgræf, B -ˌgrɑf] *s.* (filol.) homógrafo.
homographic [ˌhɑməˈgræfɪk, ˌhoʊmə-, B ˌhɔmə-] *a.* homógrafo.
homoiothermic [hoʊˌmɔɪəˈθɜrmɪk, B -ˈθɜmɪk] **homoiothermal** [-məl] **homoiothermous** [-məs] *a.* (fisiol., zool.) homotérmico, homotermo (con temperatura corporal uniforme); de sangre caliente.
Homoiousian [ˌhoʊmɔɪˈusɪən, B -ˈaʊsɪ-] *s.* (relig.) homoiusiano.
homologate [hoʊˈmɑləˌgeɪt, B hɔˈmɔl-] *v.t.* (der.) homologar.
homologation [-ˌmɑləˈgeɪʃən, B -ˌmɔl-] *s.* (der.) homologación.
homological [ˌhoʊməˈlɑdʒɪkəl, ˌhɑmə-, B ˌhɔmə-] *a.* homólogo.
homologize [hoʊˈmɑləˌdʒaɪz, B hɔˈmɔl-] *v.t.* homologar.
homologous [-əgəs] *a.* homólogo.
homolographic [ˌhɑmələˈgræfɪk, B ˌhɔm-] *a.* homolográfico.
homologue, homolog [ˈhɑməˌlɔg, ˈhoʊmə-, -ˌlɑg, B ˈhɔməlɔg] *s.* (biol.) elemento homólogo; (lóg.) término homólogo; (mat.) segmento homólogo; (quím.) compuesto homólogo.
homology [hoʊˈmɑlədʒɪ, B hɔˈmɔl-] *s.* (biol., lóg., mat., quím.) homología.
homolosine projection [-əˌsaɪn-, -əsɪn-] (geog.) proyección homolosenoidal.
homomorphic [ˌhoʊməˈmɔrfɪk, ˌhɑmə-, B ˌhɔməˈmɔfɪk] *a.* (biol., bot.) homomorfo.
homomorphism [-ˌfɪzəm] *s.* (biol., bot.) homomorfía, homomorfismo.
homomorphy [ˈhoʊməˌmɔrfɪ, ˈhɑmə-, B ˈhɔməˌmɔfɪ] *s.* (biol.) homomorfía.
homonym [ˈhɑməˌnɪm, ˈhoʊmə-, B ˈhɔmə-] *s.* homónimo.
homonymic [ˌhɑməˈnɪmɪk, ˌhoʊmə-, B ˌhɔmə-] *a.* homónimo.
homonymous [hoʊˈmɑnəməs, B hɔˈmɔnɪ-] *a.* homónimo.
homonymy [-mɪ] *s.* homonimia.
Homoousian [ˌhoʊmoʊˈusɪən, B -ˈaʊsɪ-] *s., a.* (relig.) homousiano.
homopetalous [-ˈpɛtələs] *a.* (bot.) homopétalo.
homophile [ˈhoʊmoʊˌfaɪl] *s.* homófilo.
homophobe [ˈhoʊmoʊˌfoʊb] *s.* homófobo.

homophobia [ˌhoʊmoʊ'foʊbɪə] *a.* homofobia.
homophobic [ˌhoʊmoʊ'foʊbɪk] *a.* homofóbico.
homophone ['hɑməˌfoʊn, 'hoʊmə-, B 'hɔmə-] *s.* palabra homófona; letra o letras homófonas.
homophonic [ˌhɑmə'fɑnɪk, ˌhoʊmə-, B ˌhɔmə'fɔnɪk] *a.* homófono; unísono.
homophonous [hoʊ'mɑfənəs, B hɔ'mɔf-] *a.* homófono.
homophony [-nɪ] *s.* homofonía.
homophyly ['hoʊməˌfaɪlɪ, B hɔ'mɔfəlɪ] *s.* homofilia, parecido debido a una ascendencia común.
homoplastic [ˌhoʊmə'plæstɪk, ˌhɑmə-, B ˌhɔmə-] *a.* (biol.) homoplástico.
homoplasy ['hoʊməˌpleɪsɪ, 'hɑmə-, B hɔ'mɔpləsɪ] *s.* (biol.) homoplasia.
homopolar [ˌhoʊmə'poʊlər, B -ə] *a.* (quím., elec.) homopolar.
Homoptera [hoʊ'mɑptərə, B -'mɔp-] *s. pl.* (ento.) homópteros.
homopteran [-tərən] *s.* (ento.) insecto homóptero.
homopterous [-əs] *a.* (ento.) homóptero.
homosexual [ˌhoʊmə'sɛkʃʊəl, B -'sɛksjʊ-] *a., s.* homosexual.
homosexuality [-ˌsɛkʃʊ'ælətɪ, B -ˌsɛksjʊ-] *s.* homosexualidad.
homosporous [-'spɔrəs, B hoʊ'mɔspərəs] *a.* (bot.) homósporo.
homotaxial [ˌhoʊmə'tæksɪəl, ˌhɑmə-, B ˌhɔmə-] *a.* (pal.) homotáxico.
homotaxis [-səs] *s.* (pal.) homotaxia.
homothallic [-'θælɪk] *a.* (bot.) homotálico.
homothallism [-'θælˌɪzəm] *s.* (bot.) homotalismo, homotalia.
homothetic [-'θɛtɪk] *a.* (mat.) homotético.
homothety [hoʊ'mɑθətɪ, B -'mɔθ-] *s.* (mat.) homotetismo, homotecia.
homotransplant [ˌhoʊmoʊ'trænsˌplænt, ˌhɑmə-, B ˌhɔmə-ˌplɑnt] *s.* (med.) homotransplante, homoinjerto.
homozygosis [-zaɪ'goʊsəs] *s.* (biol.) homocigosis.
homozygote [-'zaɪˌgoʊt] *s.* (biol.) homocigoto.
homozygotic [-zaɪ'gɑtɪk, B -'gɔt-] *a.* (biol.) homocigótico.
homunculus [hoʊ'mʌŋkjələs] *s.* (*pl.* HOMUNCULI [-laɪ]) homúnculo, hombrecillo, figurita; (hist.) homúnculo (de los alquimistas).
Hon. *abrev. de* **Honorable,** Honorable.
Honduran [hɑn'dʊrən, B hɔn'djʊər-] *a., s.* hondureño.
Honduras [-əs] *s.* Honduras.
hone [hoʊn] *s.* 1. piedra de afilar, piedra melodreña, amoladera. 2. muela de rectificar, muela de esmerilar. —*v.t.* 1. afilar. 2. asentar, agrandar o alisar con una amoladera; rectificar con piedra abrasiva; vaciar, pulir, esmerilar. —*v.i.* (dial.) gruñir, lamentarse; añorar; gemir.
honest ['ɑnest, B 'ɔn-] *a.* 1. honrado, íntegro, probo, derecho, recto, correcto. 2 veraz, franco, sincero; justo, equitativo; decente. 3. genuino, legítimo, sin adulterar. 4. (ant.) honorable, digno de crédito. 5. **to turn** (o **to earn**) **an h. penny,** ganarse unos centavos honradamente; **to make an h. woman out of,** casarse uno con una mujer que ha sido su querida; **h. dealing,** proceder de buena fe; **by h. means,** en buena lid.
honestly [-lɪ] *adv.* 1. honradamente, rectamente, correctamente. 2. francamente, sinceramente.
honesty [-əstɪ] *s.* 1. honradez, integridad, rectitud, probidad. 2. sinceridad, veracidad. 3. (bot.) lunaria. 4. (ant.) castidad.
honewort ['hoʊnˌwɜrt, B -ˌwɜt] *s.* (bot.) perejil de Macedonia, amomo vulgar.
honey ['hʌnɪ] *s.* 1. miel. 2. (fig.) dulzura. 3. (fig.) amor, encanto (persona). 4. (fam.) algo único, ej., *the inflation which followed the war was a h.,* la inflación que siguió a la guerra fue algo único. 5. (fam.) (*ú. como apelativo*) cariñito, amorcito. 6. **a h. of a,** (fam.) una maravilla de; **it's a h.,** es una maravilla, es una preciosidad. —*a.* 1. de miel, meloso, dulce. 2. (ant.) querido, precioso. —*v.t.* (*pret., p.p.* HONEYED O HONIED; *p.pr.* HONEYING) 1. endulzar, enmelar, almibarar. 2. (fig.) lisonjear, adular. —*v.i.* 1. portarse obsequiosamente. 2. **h. up to,** congraciarse con, engatusar.
honeybee [-ˌbi] *s.* abeja melífera.
honeycomb [-ˌkoʊm] *s.* 1. panal, bresca, ceras. 2. (const.) hormigueros, panales. 3. (metal.) escarabajo, sopladura. —*v.t.* 1. acribillar, agujerar, agujerear. 2. (fig.) impregnar, llenar. —*v.i.* agujerarse, agujerearse.
honeycomb coil, (rad.) bobina de panal, bobina de nido de abeja.
honeycombed [-ˌkoʊmd] *a.* apanalado, alveolar, lleno de agujeros.
honey creeper, (orn.) pitpit, pipí; azucarero.
honeydew [-ˌdu, B -ˌdju] *s.* 1. ligamaza, secreción dulce (de ciertas plantas e insectos). 2. especie de tabaco endulzado. 3. (poét.) ambrosía.
honeydew melon, melón dulce, melón de pulpa verdosa muy dulce.
honey eater, (orn.) tropidorinco; pájaro fraile; pájaro de Australia.
honeyed ['hʌnid] *p.p. de* **honey** . —*a.* 1. dulce, meloso, enmelado, melifluo. 2. (fig.) azucarado (palabras, frases, etc.), halagador.
honey locust, (bot.) acacia negra, corona de Cristo.
honeymoon ['hʌnɪˌmun] *s.* luna de miel. —*v.i.* pasar la luna de miel.
honeysucker [-ˌsʌkər, B -ə] *s.* (orn.) tropidorinco; pájaro fraile; pájaro de Australia.
honeysuckle [-ˌsʌkəl] *s.* 1. (bot.) madreselva. 2. (bot.) diervilla; azalea viscosa o de ciénaga. 3. (ant.) trébol.
honeywort [-ˌwɜrt, B -ˌwɜt] *s.* (bot.) ceriflor, aldeneja, becoquino.
hong [hɑŋ, B hɔŋ] *s.* establecimiento comercial extranjero, almacén o factoría (en China o Japón).
honied, *var. de* **honeyed.**
honk [hɑŋk, hɔŋk, B hɔŋk] *s.* 1. graznido (del ganso silvestre). 2. bocinazo (del automóvil). —*v.i.* 1. graznar. 2. tocar o sonar la bocina.
honkie, honky ['hɑŋkɪ, 'hɔŋ-, B 'hɔŋ-] *s.* (jer., despec.) una persona de raza blanca, el hombre blanco en gen. (u. por los negros en E.U.).
honkie-tonk [-ˌtɑŋk, -ˌtɔŋk, B ˌ-tɔŋk] *s.* (E.U.) tabernucho, chingana (Amer.). —*a.* propio o característico de taberna o cabaret barato y de poco fuste.
honor, (pr. G.B.) **honour** ['ɑnər, B 'ɔnə] *s.* 1. honor, honra, estimación, reputación, buen nombre, probidad, integridad. 2. honor, honradez. 3. (*pl.*) honores, distinciones. 4. señoría (título de ciertos cargos públicos), ej., *His H. the Mayor,* Su Señoría el Alcalde. 5. honor, honra (de una mujer). 6. (*pl.*) honores, actos de cortesía. 7. honor, motivo de orgullo, ej., *he is an h. to his profession,* él hace honor a su profesión. 8. condecoración. 9. (*pl.*) (educ.) distinción. 10. (*pl.*) (bridge) honores. 11. (golf) privilegio de jugar primero. 12. **bound in h.,** moralmente obligado; **code of h.,** código de honor; **h. bright,** por mi honor, a fe de caballero; **in h. of,** en honor de, en homenaje a; **military honors,** honores militares; **last** (o **funeral**) **honors,** honras fúnebres; **on my (his, her,** etc.) **h.,** por mi (su, etc.) honor; **to be on one's h.,** estar moralmente obligado (a hacer algo); **to do h. to,** hacer honor a; **to do the honors,** hacer los honores; **to regard as an h.,** tener a honra; **upon my h.,** ¡palabra de honor! ¡por mi honor!; **word of h.,** palabra de honor o de caballero. —*v.t.* 1. honrar, rendir honores a; adorar, reverenciar, respetar. 2. laurear, condecorar; promover (en rango o posición). 3. ennoblecer, exaltar. 4. hacer honor a, mantener uno su (palabra). 5. (com.) honrar, hacer honor a (firma, acuerdo, etc.); pagar, cancelar (letra, cheque, etc.).
honorable, (pr. G.B.) **honourable** [-ərəbəl] *a.* 1. honorable. 2. noble, ilustre, preclaro, insigne. 3. recomendable, loable, plausible. 4. honorífico, con honores. 5. honorable, honroso (acción, comportamiento, etc.). 6. (como tratamiento o título) honorable. 7. **to have h. intentions toward,** tener buenas intenciones respecto a.
honorable discharge, (mil.) licencia honrosa, licenciamiento honroso.
honorable mention, (mil.) mención honrosa, mención honorífica.
honorableness [-nəs] *s.* honradez, honorabilidad, hombría de bien, respetabilidad.
honorably [-ərəblɪ] *adv.* honorablemente, honrosamente.
honorarily [ˌɑnə'rɛrəlɪ, B 'ɔnərərɪlɪ] *adv.* honoríficamente.
honorarium [-'rɛrɪəm, B ˌɔnə'rɛər-] *s.* (*pl.* HONORARIA [-ɪə] O HONORARIUMS), honorarios, sueldo, gaje, estipendio.
honorary ['ɑnəˌrɛrɪ, B 'ɔnərərɪ] *a.* 1. honorario, honorífico, honroso. 2. honorario (puesto, cargo, socio, miembro, etc.). 3. de honor (una deuda).
honorer, (pr. G.B.) **honourer** [-ərər, B -ərə] *s.* honrador.
honorific [ˌɑnə'rɪfɪk, B ˌɔn-] *a.* honorífico (díc. esp. de tratamientos orientales). —*s.* antenombre, tratamiento honorífico.
honor point, (her.) punto de honor.
honors of war, (mil.) honores de guerra.
honor system, sistema que apela al sentido del honor de alumnos, empleados, reclusos, etc. para que cumplan ciertas normas sin necesidad de vigilancia.
honour, honourable, (pr. G.B.) *var. de* **honor, honorable.**
hooch [hutʃ] *s.* (jer., E.U.) bebida espirituosa, esp. de contrabando.
hood [hʊd] *s.* 1. capucho, capucha, capuchón, capilla. 2. muceta, capirote (en vestidos de académicos). 3. caperuza, anteojeras (de un caballo). 4. campana del hogar, sombrerete (de la chimenea). 5. (cetrería) capirote, caperuza, capillo. 6. (orn.) cresta, crestón, penacho. 7. (aut.) capó, cubierta. 8. (mec.) tapa, cubierta. 9. (mar.) caperuza de palo. —*v.t.* 1. encapuchar; cubrir con capirote o caperuza. 2. proveer de capucha. 3. tapar, cubrir, ocultar.
hood, *s.* (jer.) maleante, matón, rufián.
hooded ['hʊdəd] *a.* 1. encapuchado, con capucha. 2. (bot.) en forma de capucha. 3. (orn.) crestado, con cresta en forma de capucha. 4. (zool.) de capuchón, con capuchón. 5. (her.) caperuzado, capirotado, chaperonado.
hooded cobra, (zool.) cobra de capuchón, naja, cobracapelo.
hooded crow, (orn.) corneja cenicienta; chova.

hooded seal, (zool.) foca de capucha, gorro marino.
hoodie ['hʊdɪ] *s.* (orn.) corneja cenicienta.
hoodlum ['hudləm, 'hʊd-, B 'hud-] *s.* maleante, matón, rufián.
hoodman-blind [ˌhʊdmən'blaɪnd] *s.* (ant.) gallina ciega (juego).
hoodoo ['hudu] *s.* 1. vodú, vudú. 2. (fam.) aojo, mala sombra, mala suerte. 3. (O. de E.U.) montón natural de rocas de forma fantástica. —*v.t.* (*pret., p.p.* HOODOOED; *p.pr.* HOODOOING) (fam.) aojar, traer mala suerte a.
hoodwink ['hʊdˌwɪŋk] *v.t.* 1. burlar, engañar, embaucar. 2. vendar los ojos a (caballo, etc.). 3. (ant.) tapar, esconder, ocultar.
hoodwinker [-ər, B -ə] *s.* embaucador, embustero, petardista.
hooey ['huɪ] (jer., E.U.) *interj.* ¡música celestial! —*s.* música celestial, tontería, adefesio.
hoof [hʊf, huf, B huf] *s.* (*pl.* HOOFS o HOOVES [hʊvz, B huvz]) 1. casco, pezuña. 2. pata. 3. (hum.) pata, pie. 4. **on the h.,** en pie, vivo (ganado). —*v.i.* mover los pies, caminar, bailar. —*v.t.* 1. hollar, pisotear, pisar. 2. **h. it,** caminar, ir a pie; bailar; **h. out,** echar a puntapiés o patadas; (jer.) despedir, echar (a empleado, etc.).
hoofbeat ['hʊfˌbit, 'huf-, B 'huf-] *s.* ruido de cascos.
hoofbound [-ˌbaʊnd] *a.* corto de cascos.
hoofed [hʊft, B huft] *a.* ungulado.
hoofer ['hʊfər, 'huf-, B 'hufə] *s.* (jer.) zapateador, bailarín de zapateado.
hoofprint [-ˌprɪnt] *s.* huella o impresión de un casco.
hoo-ha ['huˌhɑ] *s.* (fam., G.B.) barahúnda; riña; alboroto.
hook [hʊk] *s.* 1. gancho, garfio, garabato, colgadero. 2. anzuelo, arpón. 3. hoz, segadera, segur. 4. corchete, prendedero. 5. (béisbol, golf) vuelo en curva (de la pelota). 6. (boxeo) gancho. 7. (mús.) rabo (de una nota). 8. (impr.) grapa, uña, cuña (para sujetar un grabado, etc.). 9. (jer.) (*pl.*) dedos, mano, ej., *to get one's hooks on* (*someone*), echar mano a (alguien). 10. **by h. or by crook,** a tuertas o a derechas, a todo trance; **to get (someone) off the h.,** sacar (a alguien) del apuro; **to go off the hooks,** (jer., G.B.) chiflarse, chalarse; **to swallow the h.,** (fig.) tragarse el anzuelo. —*v.t.* 1. encorvar, doblar, dar forma de gancho a. 2. enganchar, engrapar. 3. garfear; pescar, coger. 4. encornar, acornear, acornar. 5. (golf) desviar a la izquierda, golpear mal (la pelota, de modo que vuela en curva). 6. (boxeo) asestar un (golpe de) gancho a. 7. (béisbol, criquet) lanzar en curva (la pelota). 8. (jer.) atrapar. 9. **h. on,** enganchar, acoplar; **h. up,** abrochar, enganchar, unir; (elec.) acoplar; (rad.) conectar en red de circuitos (estaciones); **to get hooked on,** (jer.) aficionarse a, enviciarse con. —*v.i.* 1. doblarse, encorvarse. 2. engancharse, engraparse. 3. (boxeo) dar un (golpe de) gancho. 4. (golf) desviar la pelota. 5. (jer.) partir, largarse, irse. 6. **h. at,** dar cornadas a (díc. del toro, etc.); **h. on to,** pegarse a, seguir (a una persona).
hooka, hookah ['hʊkə] *s.* narguile, pipa turca.
hook and eye, (cost.) corchete (macho y hembra), broche y corchete.
hook and ladder, carro de bomberos en el que se llevan las escaleras de incendio.
hooked [hʊkt] *a.* 1. encorvado, ganchudo, ganchoso. 2. provisto de gancho(s); hecho con ganchos. 3. (jer.) atrapado, enviciado (por algo), sin poder prescindir (de algo, esp. estupefacientes).
hookedness ['hʊktnəs] *s.* encorvadura.
hooker ['hʊkər, B -ə] *s.* (mar.) balandra; **the old h.,** (despec.) barco viejo, carraca, urca.
hooker, *s.* 1. persona o cosa que engancha. 2. (jer., E.U.) ramera, prostituta.
hook-nosed [-ˌnoʊzd] *a.* de nariz aguileña.
hookup [-ˌʌp] *s.* 1. (elec.) acoplamiento; (rad., t.v.) sistema de conexión, red de circuitos; transmisión en circuito; **a h. with Eurovision,** una emisión conjunta con Eurovision; **a nationwide h.,** una cadena nacional; **a satellite h.,** una conexión vía satélite. 2. (pol.) (fam.) alianza, liga, coalición.
hookworm [-ˌwɜrm, B -ˌwɜm] *s.* (zool.) anquilostoma, lombriz intestinal.
hookworm disease, (med.) anquilostomiasis.
hooky ['hʊkɪ] *s.* **to play h.,** hacer novillos, hacer rabona, escaparse, faltar.
hooligan ['hulɪgən] *s.* rufián, truhán, matón, gamberro, pandillero. —*a.* rufianesco, truhanesco.
hooliganism [-ˌɪzəm] *s.* rufianismo, truhanería, matonería, pandillaje, gamberrismo.
hoop [hup, hʊp, B hup] *s.* 1. aro (en tonel, etc.; juguete); fleje, zuncho. 2. anilla, argolla. 3. (croquet) aro, argolla. 4. (*pl.*) aros, cercos (en miriñaque, tontillo, etc.). 5. **to go through the hoop(s),** pasar las de Caín. —*v.t.* 1. enarcar, enzunchar. 2. encorvar, arquear.
hooper ['hupər, 'hʊp-, B 'hupe] *s.* tonelero.
hoopla ['huplɑ, 'hʊp-] *s.* (jer.) 1. alboroto, conmoción, tumulto. 2. fanfarria, bombo.
hoopoe ['hupu, -poʊ, B -pu] *s.* (orn.) abubilla, upupa.
hoopskirt ['hupˌskɜrt, B -ˌskɜt] *s.* miriñaque, tontillo.
hooray [hʊ'reɪ] *var. de* **hurrah.**
hoosegow ['husˌgaʊ] *s.* (jer., E.U.) calabozo, cárcel, chirona, trena, gayola (Amer.).
Hoosier ['huʒər, B -ʒə] *s.* (E.U.) natural del estado de Indiana. —*a.* de Indiana.
hoot [hut] *v.i.* 1. ulular (el búho, etc.). 2. abuchear, huchear; dar grita. 3. (G.B.) tocar la bocina. —*v.t.* 1. abuchear. 2. gritar, dar grita a, manifestar a gritos (descontento, etc.). —*s.* 1. ululato, ululación. 2. grito, grita, clamor, protesta, rechifla. 3. **it's not worth a h.,** no vale un comino; **not to care a h.,** (jer.) no importarle a uno un bledo.
hootenanny ['hutənˌænɪ] *s.* (E.U.) ruidosa domingada en la que se presentan diversos grupos de música folklórica.
hooter [-ər, B -ə] *s.* sirena, bocina, señal acústica.
hoot owl, (orn.) alucón, cárabo, autillo.
hooves, *pl. de* **hoof.**
hop [hɑp, B hɔp] *v.i.* (*pret., p.p.* HOPPED; *p.pr.* HOPPING) 1. brincar, saltar; avanzar a saltitos; saltar a la pata coja, saltar en un pie. 2. (fam.) bailar, danzar. 3. ir (de prisa). 4. **h. to it,** meter manos a la obra, echar a trabajar; **hopping mad,** loco de cólera. —*v.t.* 1. saltar, brincar, cruzar de un salto. 2. (fam.) subir a (tren, taxi, etc.). 3. cruzar en avión; transportar o llevar en avión. —*s.* 1. salto, brinco, saltito (esp. sobre una sola pierna). 2. (fam.) baile, sarao, zamba, danza. 3. vuelo en avión; etapa de un vuelo.
hop, *s.* 1. (bot.) lúpulo. 2. (*pl.*) (frutos desecados del) lúpulo. 3. (jer.) estupefaciente, droga, narcótico. 4. (jer.) cuento fantástico, mentira, estupidez. —*v.t.* recoger el lúpulo; mezclar el lúpulo en la cerveza.
hope [hoʊp] *s.* 1. esperanza. 2. confianza, fe, seguridad. 3. perspectiva, posibilidad, promesa buena, ej., *a land of h.,* tierra de promisión. —*v.t.* 1. (gen. con *for*) esperar, abrigar esperanzas. 2. **to h. against h. (that),** aferrarse a la esperanza (de que); **h. in,** (ant.) confiar (en). —*v.i.* esperar.
hope chest, (fam.) arca con el ajuar de una soltera.
hopeful ['hoʊpfəl] *a.* 1. esperanzado, lleno de esperanzas, confiado, ilusionado. 2. lleno de promesas, prometedor. —*s.* 1. aspirante, candidato. 2. joven prometedor.
hopefully [-fəlɪ] *adv.* esperanzadamente, con optimismo.
hopefulness [-fəlnəs] *s.* 1. esperanza. 2. promisión.
hopeless ['hoʊpləs] *a.* 1. desesperanzado, desesperado. 2. desahuciado, incurable; imposible, irremediable; perdido, ej., *h. case,* caso perdido.
hopelessly [-lɪ] *adv.* sin esperanza, desesperadamente.
hopelessness [-nəs] *s.* 1. desesperación, desesperanza. 2. incurabilidad, carácter de irremediable.
hophead ['hɑpˌhɛd, B 'hɔp-] *s.* (jer.) toxicómano.
hoplite [-ˌlaɪt] *s.* (hist.) hoplita, soldado de infantería en la antigua Grecia.
hop-o'-my-thumb [ˌhɑpəmə'θʌm, B ˌhɔp-] *s.* enano, pigmeo.
hopped-up ['hɑpt'ʌp, B 'hɔpt-] *a.* (jer.) (E.U.) 1. excitado, eufórico. 2. drogado, excitado por las drogas. 3. (aut.) díc. del automóvil al que se ha aumentado la potencia.
hopper ['hɑpər, B 'hɔpə] *s.* 1. persona o cosa saltadora. 2. (ento.) insecto saltador; saltamontes, langosta, cigarra; mosca del queso. 3. tolva. 4. tragante (de un alto horno). 5. (mec.) tanque alimentador (que suelta el contenido a través de una tubería).
hopple ['hɑpəl, B 'hɔp-] *v.t.* poner trabas, trabar, atar las patas de. —*s.* traba, manea, maniota.
hopsack ['hɑpˌsæk, B 'hɔp-] *s.* (tej.) arpillera, cáñamo.
hopscotch [-ˌskɑtʃ, B -ˌskɔtʃ] *s.* infernáculo, a la pata coja, rayuela, tilíncampana, coxcojilla, reina mora (juego infantil).
hop, skip, and jump, salto triple; especie de rayuela (juego de niños).
hopvine [-ˌvaɪn] *s.* (bot.) 1. tallo del lúpulo. 2. lúpulo.
Horace ['hɔrəs, 'hɑr-, B 'hɔr-] *s.* Horacio, poeta latino.
horary ['hɔrərɪ] *a.* horario.
Horatian [hə'reɪʃən, B hɔ'reɪʃjən] *a.* (lit.) horaciano, de Horacio.
horde [hɔrd, B hɔd] *s.* 1. horda. 2. multitud (de personas); enjambre (de insectos); hato, manada (de animales); serie (de cosas).
hordein ['hɔrdɪən, B 'hɔd-] *s.* (bioquím.) hordeína.
horehound ['hɔrˌhaʊnd, B 'hɔˌ-] *s.* 1. (bot.) marrubio, asbatán. 2. extracto de marrubio; preparado o dulce de marrubio. 3. **h. drops,** pastillas para aliviar la irritación de la garganta.
horizon [hə'raɪzən] *s.* 1. horizonte. 2. (fig.) horizonte, perspectiva. 3. (geol.) horizonte, estrato, capa (correspondiente a determinada época). 4. (pint.) horizonte.
horizontal [ˌhɔrə'zɑntəl, ˌhɑr-, B ˌhɔrɪ'zɔnt-] *a.* horizontal. —*s.* 1. horizontal, línea horizontal. 2. barra o viga horizontal.
horizontal bar, (dep.) barra fija; (*pl.*) barras paralelas.
horizontally [-əlɪ] *adv.* horizontalmente.
horizontal stabilizer, (aer.) plano fijo horizontal, estabilizador.
hormonal [hɔr'moʊnəl, B hɔ'-] *a.* (fisiol.) hormonal.
hormone ['hɔrˌmoʊn, B 'hɔˌ-] *s.* (fisiol.) hormona, hormón.
hormonic [hɔr'mɑnɪk, B hɔ'mɔn-] *a.* (fisiol.) hormonal.
horn [hɔrn, B hɔn] *s.* 1. cuerno, asta, cacho (Amer.). 2. tentáculo (del caracol); cuerno, antena (de insectos). 3. cuerno, queratina. 4. cuerna; cuerno (de la abundancia, de pólvora,

etc.). 5. cuerno (del diablo). 6. cuerno (del cuarto creciente o menguante de la luna). 7. punta (del yunque). 8. promontorio. 9. alternativa (de un dilema). 10. (mús.) cuerno, trompa de caza, corneta, trompeta. 11. (aut., rad.) bocina. 12. **to blow one's own h.,** cantar sus propias alabanzas; **to blow the h.,** tocar la bocina; **to draw in one's horns,** (fig.) contenerse, moderarse; economizar. —*v.t.* 1. dar una cornada a, acornar. 2. (fig.) poner (los) cuernos a (marido). —*v.i.* **h. in (on),** (jer.) entremeterse o entrometerse (en), inmiscuirse (en).

hornbeam ['hɔrnˌbim, B 'hɔn-] *s.* (bot.) carpe, ojaranzo.

hornbill [-ˌbɪl] *s.* (orn.) cálao.

hornblende [-ˌblɛnd] *s.* (min.) hornablenda, horoblenda.

hornblendic [-ˌblɛndɪk] *a.* (min.) hornabléndico, hornablendífero.

hornbook [-ˌbʊk] *s.* cartilla o abecedario; p. ext. tratado rudimentario.

horned [hɔrnd, B hɔnd] *a.* cornudo, encornado, enastado; córneo.

horned nut, (mec.) tuerca con salientes.

horned pout, (ict.) siluro, bagre.

horned toad, (zool.) lagarto cornudo.

horned viper, (zool.) ceraste, hemorroo.

hornet ['hɔrnət, B 'hɔnɪt] *s.* (ento.) avispón, crabrón; **to stir up a h.'s nest,** (fig.) revolver el ajo, meterse en líos, alborotar el avispero, armar cisco.

hornito [hɔr'nitoʊ, B hɔ'-] *s.* (geol.) hornito.

hornless ['hɔrnləs, B 'hɔn-] *a.* sin cuernos, descornado.

hornlike [-ˌlaɪk] *a.* corniforme.

horn-mad [-'mæd] *a.* loco de ira, iracundo, furioso; delirante.

horn of plenty, cornucopia, cuerno de la abundancia.

hornpipe [-ˌpaɪp] *s.* 1. (mús.) chirimía. 2. danza folklórica inglesa ejecutada por una sola persona.

hornpout [-ˌpaʊt] *s.* (ict.) siluro, bagre.

horn-rimmed [-'rɪmd] *a.* de concha, de cuerno (o de imitación en pasta o plástico); **h.-r. glasses,** anteojos montados en armazón de carey.

horn silver, (min.) plata córnea, cerargirita.

hornstone [-ˌstoʊn] *s.* (min.) sílex córneo o negro, horsteno.

hornswoggle [-ˌswɑgəl, B -ˌswɔg-] *v.t.* (jer.) embaucar, engatusar, engañar.

horntail [-ˌteɪl] *s.* (ento.) sirícido.

hornwork [-ˌwɜrk, B -ˌwɜk] *s.* (fort.) hornabeque.

hornworm [-ˌwɜrm, B -ˌwɜm] *s.* (ento.) larva de los esfíngidos.

hornwort [-ˌwɜrt, B -ˌwɜt] *s.* (bot.) ceratófilo.

horny ['hɔrnɪ, B 'hɔnɪ] *a.* 1. córneo, hecho de cuerno. 2. cornudo. 3. duro, calloso. 4. semiopaco. 5. (vulg.) rijoso, lujurioso, sensual.

horologe ['hɔrəˌloʊdʒ, 'hɑr-, B 'hɔrəˌlɔdʒ] *s.* reloj (gen. reloj de sol, o de mecanismo primitivo).

horologer [hə'rɑlədʒər, B -'rɔlədʒə] *s.* relojero.

horologist [-dʒəst] *s.* relojero.

horology [-dʒɪ] *s.* horología, arte de hacer relojes, arte de medir el tiempo.

horopter [hə'rɑptər, B -'rɔptə] *s.* (ópt.) horópter.

horoscope ['hɔrəˌskoʊp] *s.* (astrol.) horóscopo; **to cast a h.,** sacar un horóscopo.

horoscopy [hə'rɑskəpɪ, B -'rɔs-] *s.* horoscopia.

horrendous [hɔ'rɛndəs] *a.* horrendo, espantoso, terrible, tremebundo, horrible.

horrendously [-lɪ] *adv.* horrendamente, espantosamente, terriblemente.

horrent ['hɔrənt, 'hɑr-, B 'hɔr-] *a.* (ant.) 1. erguido, erecto; tieso, rígido, erizado. 2. horrorizado; espantoso, terrible, horrible.

horrible ['hɔrəbəl, 'hɑr-, B 'hɔr-] *a.* horrible, horrendo, terrible, espantoso; chocante, repugnante.

horribly [-blɪ] *adv.* horriblemente, terriblemente, horrendamente, espantosamente; repugnantemente.

horrid [-əd] *a.* 1. horrible, hórrido, horrendo, espantoso; chocante, repugnante. 2. (fam.) desagradable, irritante, repulsivo. 3. (ant.) áspero, erizado, tieso, rígido.

horridly [-lɪ] *adv.* horriblemente, horrendamente.

horrific [hɔ'rɪfɪk] *a.* horrífico, horrendo, espantoso, tremebundo.

horrify ['hɔrəˌfaɪ, 'hɑr-, B 'hɔr-] *v.t.* (*pret., p.p.* HORRIFIED; *p.pr.* HORRIFYING) horrorizar, horripilar, espantar, aterrar.

horripilation [hɔˌrɪpə'leɪʃən] *s.* (med.) horripilación.

horror ['hɔrər, 'hɑr-, B 'hɔrə] *s.* 1. horror, espanto, pavor. 2. (con *of*) horror, repulsión (a). 3. (fam.) **the horrors,** melancolía, morriña; delírium tremens.

hors de combat [ˌɔrdəkoʊn'bɑ, B 'hɔdə'-kɔmbɑ] (fr.) fuera de combate.

hors d'oeuvre [ɔr'dɜv, B ɔ'dɜvrɜ] (fr.) (*pl.* HORS D'OEUVRES), entremés variado; tapas; canapés.

horse [hɔrs, B hɔs] *s.* 1. (zool.) caballo. 2. (carp.) caballete, burro, borrico. 3. (ajedrez) caballo. 4. (gimnasia) potro. 5. (mil.) caballería; soldados de caballería, caballo. 6. (min., geol.) caballo (masa de roca que intercepta un filón). 7. (const.) pila, caballete, armazón, machón; bastidor, castillete, pila. 8. (jer.) heroína (droga). 9. **don't look a gift h. in the mouth,** a caballo regalado no se le mira el colmillo; **hold your horses,** pare Ud. el carro, no hay prisa; **h. of a different color,** (fig.) harina de otro costal, otro cantar; **out of** (o **from**) **the h.'s mouth,** (fig.) de fuente fidedigna, de muy buena fuente; **to eat like a h.,** comer como un heliogábalo; **to mount** (o **ride**) **the high h.,** darse muchos aires, darse ínfulas, asumir una actitud altanera; **to play the horses,** apostar a los caballos; **to work like a h.,** trabajar como un esclavo. —*v.t.* 1. proveer de caballo(s); poner a caballo. 2. tirar o empujar a la fuerza. 3. (jer.) ridiculizar, burlarse de. —*v.i.* 1. estar en celo, estar salida (yegua). 2. **h. around,** chancear, bromear; gastar el tiempo innecesariamente. —*a.* 1. caballar, hípico, equino, caballuno. 2. (fig.) grande, basto, ordinario. 3. montado(s); para tropas montadas.

horse artillery, (mil.) artillería montada, artillería volante.

horseback ['hɔrsˌbæk, B 'hɔs-] *s.* 1. lomo del caballo. 2. (E.U.) loma, colina, cerro. 3. **on h.,** a caballo. —*adv.* a caballo; **to ride h.,** montar a caballo.

horse balm, (bot.) centinodia.

horsebean [-ˌbin] *s.* (bot.) haba caballar, haba caballuna, habón.

horse block, apeadero, montadero (para montar en caballerías o desmontarse de ellas).

horse-breaker [-ˌbreɪkər, B -ə] *s.* picador, amansador o domador de caballos.

horse butcher shop, carnicería de caballo.

horsecar [-ˌkɑr, B -ˌkɑ] *s.* (E.U.) tranvía tirado por caballos; vagón o carro de transportar caballos.

horse chestnut, (bot.) 1. castaña de Indias. 2. castaño de Indias.

horse dealer, chalán, tratante en caballos.

horse doctor, 1. (fam.) veterinario. 2. (jer.) matasanos.

horse-drawn ['hɔrsˌdrɔn, B 'hɔs-] *a.* arrastrado por caballos, de tracción a sangre.

horse fair, feria de caballos.

horseflesh [-ˌflɛʃ] *s.* 1. carne de caballo. 2. caballos (en general, como haberes).

horsefly [-ˌflaɪ] *s.* (ento.) tábano; mosca de burro, mosca de mula, mosca borriquera, moscardón.

Horse Guards, (mil.) 1. guardias montados (esp. la brigada de caballería de la Casa Real de Inglaterra). 2. (fam., G.B.) cuartel general del ejército.

horsehair [-ˌhɛr, B -ˌhɛə] *s.* 1. pelo o cerda de caballo. 2. tela de crin.

horsehide [-ˌhaɪd] *s.* piel o cuero de caballo.

horse latitudes, (mar.) calmas de Cáncer, zona de calmas tropicales.

horselaugh [-ˌlæf, B -ˌlɑf] *s.* risotada, carcajada.

horseleech [-ˌlitʃ] *s.* 1. (zool.) sanguijuela de caballo. 2. (ant.) veterinario, albéitar.

horseless ['hɔrsləs, B 'hɔs-] *a.* (ant.) sin caballo (díc. de los vehículos automotores); de propulsión mecánica.

horse mackerel, (ict.) atún; bonito; caballa, sarda; chicharro, jurel.

horseman [-mən] *s.* 1. jinete, caballero. 2. caballista; criador de caballos. 3. (ant.) soldado de caballería.

horsemanship [-ˌʃɪp] *s.* equitación, manejo.

horse marine, miembro de un cuerpo inexistente de caballería de marina; p. ext. persona fuera de su elemento; **tell it to the h. marines,** (fam.) cuéntaselo a tu abuela, a otro perro con ese hueso.

horsemint ['hɔrsˌmɪnt, B 'hɔs-] *s.* (bot.) 1. mastranzo nevado; hierbabuena rizada o morisca, sándalo de jardín. 2. monarda.

horse nettle, (bot.) especie americana de solano.

horse opera, (jer., cinem., t.v.) película de vaqueros.

horse pistol, (hist.) pistola de arzón.

horseplay [-ˌpleɪ] *s.* payasada, chanza pesada; juegos y bromas de carácter ruidoso.

horse pond, abrevadero de caballos.

horsepower ['hɔrsˌpaʊər, B -ə] *s.* caballo de vapor o de fuerza.

horsepower-hour [-ˌpaʊərˌaʊr, B -ˌaʊə] *s.* (mec.) caballo de fuerza por hora, caballo-hora.

horseradish [-ˌrædɪʃ] *s.* (bot.) rábano picante.

horse's ass, (jer.) necio, persona falta de tacto o sensatez.

horse sense, (fam.) sentido común.

horseshit['hɔrsˌʃɪt, B 'hɔs-] *s.* (vulg.) mentiras, exageración, insensatez, disparate.

horseshoe [-ˌʃu] *s.* 1. herradura. 2. (*pl.*) juego parecido al de tejos en que se tira a un hito con herraduras. —*v.t.* proveer de herraduras; herrar (a un caballo).

horseshoe arch, (arq.) arco de herradura.

horseshoe crab, (zool.) cangrejo bayoneta, límulo, cangrejo de las Molucas.

horseshoer [-ˌʃuər, B -ə] *s.* herrador.

horse show, concurso hípico.

horsetail [-ˌteɪl] *s.* 1. cola de caballo. 2. (bot.) cola de caballo, equiseto. 3. (bot.) corregüela hembra. 4. pendón turco que denota el rango de bajá.

horse thief, cuatrero.

horsetick [-ˌtɪk] *s.* (ento.) hipobosco.

horse trade regateo astuto con concesiones recíprocas.

horse-trade ['hɔrsˌtreɪd, B 'hɔs-] *v.i.* negociar astutamente.

horse trappings, arneses, gualdrapa.
horseweed [-ˌwid] *s.* (bot.) erigeron del Canadá.
horsewhip [-ˌhwɪp, -ˌwɪp] *s.* látigo, azote, fuete (Amer.). —*v.t.* azotar, dar latigazos a.
horsewoman [-ˌwʊmən] *s.* jinete; amazona.
horsiness ['hɔrsɪnəs, B 'hɔsɪ-] *s.* 1. aspecto caballar (rostro, etc.). 2. afición a los caballos.
horsing [-sɪŋ] *s.* 1. asiento del amolador de cuchillos. 2. vapuleo.
horsy [-sɪ] *a.* 1. caballar, caballuno, ej., *h. face,* cara de caballo. 2. equino, hípico. 3. aficionado a caballos o carreras de caballos.
hortative ['hɔrtətɪv, B 'hɔt-] *a.* exhortatorio, hortatorio; aconsejador.
hortatory [-ˌtɔrɪ, B -tərɪ] *a.* exhortatorio, hortatorio.
hortensial [hɔr'tɛnsɪəl, B hɔ'-] *a.* hortense, hortelano.
horticultural [ˌhɔrtə'kʌltʃərəl, B ˌhɔt-] *a.* hortícola.
horticulture ['hɔrtəˌkʌltʃər, B 'hɔt-tʃə] *s.* horticultura.
horticulturist [ˌhɔrtə'kʌltʃərəst, B ˌhɔt-] *s.* horticultor.
hosanna [hoʊ'zænə] *interj., s.* hosanna, gracias a Dios.
hose [hoʊz] *s.* (*pl.* HOSE o HOSES) 1. calceta, media, calcetín. 2. calza, calzón; pantalones hasta la rodilla. 3. (*pl.* HOSES) manguera, manga. —*v.t.* regar o lavar (con manguera).
hose reel, carretel de manguera.
hosier ['hoʊʒər, B 'hoʊzɪə] *s.* mediero, calcetero.
hosiery [-ɪ, B -rɪ] *s.* 1. medias, calcetas, calcetines. 2. (pr. G.B.) géneros de punto, calcetería.
hosp. *abrev. de* **hospital,** hospital.
hospice ['hɑspəs, B 'hɔs-] *s.* hospedería, hospicio.
hospitable [hɑs'pɪtəbəl, 'hɑspɪt-, B 'hɔs-] *a.* 1. hospitalario, acogedor, albergador. 2. receptivo.
hospitably [-blɪ] *adv.* hospitalariamente.
hospital ['hɑsˌpɪtəl, B 'hɔs-] *s.* 1. hospital, clínica. 2. (hist.) refugio, albergue.
hospital complex, ciudad sanitaria.
hospital cot, catre clínico (Chile).
Hospitaler, Hospitaller [-ər, B -ə] *s.* 1. (monje) hospitalario. 2. **h.,** (G.B.) capellán (en ciertos hospitales de Londres).
hospitality [ˌhɑspə'tælətɪ, B ˌhɔs-] *s.* hospitalidad.
hospitalization [ˌhɑspɪtələ'zeɪʃən, B ˌhɔspɪtəlaɪ-] *s.* hospitalización.
hospitalize ['hɑspɪtəlˌaɪz, B 'hɔs-] *v.t.* hospitalizar.
hospital ward, sala de hospital.
hospodar ['hɑspəˌdɑr, B ˌhɔspə'dɑ] *s.* hospodar (antiguo título de los príncipes de Moldavia).
host [hoʊst] *s.* 1. anfitrión, huésped; mesonero, posadero. 2. (biol.) huésped (animal o planta). 3. hueste, ejército. 4. multitud, muchedumbre; sinnúmero, montón. 5. **H.,** (relig.) hostia.
hostage ['hɑstɪdʒ, B 'hɔs-] *s.* rehén; **to be held (a) h., to be held as hostages,** quedar en rehenes; **to hold h.,** tener como rehén.
hostel ['hɑstəl, B 'hɔs-] *s.* 1. posada, hostería, hospedería, parador, hotel. 2. albergue (para jóvenes, esp. estudiantes).
hosteler [-tələr, B -tələ] *s.* 1. huésped en una posada o albergue. 2. (ant.) posadero, mesonero.
hostelry [-təlrɪ] *s.* fonda, mesón, posada, casa de huéspedes, hospedería, hostal.
hostess ['hoʊstəs] *s.* 1. anfitriona, huéspeda; dueña, ama. 2. jefa de comedor; maestra de ceremonias. 3. (avia.) azafata, aeromoza, camarera.
hostile ['hɑstəl, B 'hɔstaɪl] *a.* 1. hostil, enemigo. 2. (con *to*) hostil (a), contrario (a), adverso.
hostility [hɑs'tɪlətɪ, B hɔs-] *s.* (*pl.* HOSTILITIES) 1. hostilidad, enemistad. 2. (*pl.*) hostilidades (actos de guerra). 3. **to start hostilities,** comenzar las hostilidades.
hostler ['hɑslər, B 'ɔslə] *s.* palafrenero, mozo de cuadra, mozo de caballos.
hot [hɑt, B hɔt] *a.* (HOTTER; HOTTEST) 1. caliente, caluroso. 2. (fig.) caliente, acalorado, ardiente, vehemente. 3. violento, feroz (lucha, batalla). 4. febril, urgente. 5. (con *for*) ansioso (de). 6. fuerte, intenso (calor, colores, telas). 7. fresco, reciente (rastro, pista). 8. cercano, de cerca; apremiante (persecución). 9. picante (salsa, pimiento, etc.). 10. radiactivo. 11. (metal.) en caliente (remachado, laminado, etc.). 12. (jer.) rapidísimo, muy veloz (avión, automóvil, etc.). 13. (jer.) robado (joyas, etc.); de contrabando. 14. (jer.) muy rítmico, apasionante, excitante (música, esp. jazz). 15. (jer.) pasional, excitado, dominado por el deseo sexual. 16. de última hora (noticia, chisme). 17. (jer.) peligroso, inseguro (sitio, ciudad, etc. para alguien). 18. (jer.) buscado por la policía, fugitivo. 19. (jer.) bueno, excelente; competente, atractivo. 20. **h. on the track** (o **trail) of,** sobre la pista de, pisando los talones a; **h. under the collar,** molesto, abochornado; **not so h.,** (jer.) no tan bueno (como se esperaba); **to be h.,** sentir o tener calor; hacer calor; **to be h. on,** ser muy aficionado a; ser muy experto en; **to get h.,** estar cerca (de encontrar o descubrir algo); **to be in h. water,** estar metido en un lío; **to make it (too) h. for,** hacerle incómoda la situación a. —*adv.* 1. con calor, calurosamente; acaloradamente, ardientemente, con vehemencia; apasionadamente. 2. violentamente, ferozmente. 3. **h. and strong,** con vehemencia; **to blow h. and cold,** estar entre sí y no, mudar de humor a cada rato.
hot air, (jer.) 1. cháchara, palabrería; promesas falsas. 2. habla rimbombante o pomposa.
hot baths, termas, caldas.
hotbed ['hɑtˌbɛd, B 'hɔt-] *s.* 1. estercolero, almajara. 2. (fig.) semillero, foco, plantel, vivero. 3. cama de todos (por turnarse uno tras otro para dormir en ella).
hot-bent [-'bɛnt] *a.* doblado al fuego, doblado en caliente.
hot-blooded [-'blʌdəd] *a.* 1. ardiente, vehemente, fogoso, apasionado. 2. de pura sangre.
hotbox [-ˌbɑks, B -ˌbɔks] *s.* (f.c.) chumacera recalentada.
hot cake, tortitas calientes, panqueques (Amer.); **to sell like h. cakes,** venderse como pan caliente.
hotchpot ['hɑtʃˌpɑt, B 'hɔtʃˌpɔt] *s.* (der.) colación de bienes, caudal sucesorio.
hotchpotch [-ˌpɑtʃ, B -ˌpɔtʃ] *s.* 1. guiso hecho de varios ingredientes. 2. baturrillo, mezcolanza. 3. (der.) colación de bienes.
hot cockles, la gallina ciega (juego de niños o aldeanos).
hot cross bun, bollo marcado con una cruz de azúcar que se come esp. en Cuaresma.
hot dog, (fam.) perro caliente, perrito caliente; emparedado de salchicha de Francfort. —*interj.* (fam.) exclamación de entusiasmo.
hotel [hoʊ'tɛl] *s.* hotel; posada, fonda.
hotelier [ˌhoʊtɛl'jeɪ, B hoʊ'tɛlɪeɪ] *s.* (fr.) hotelero.
hot flash, (med.) acceso repentino de calor (gen. asociado con desequilibrio endocrino durante la menopausia).
hotfoot ['hɑtˌfʊt, B 'hɔt-] *adv.* (fam.) precipitadamente, rápidamente, impulsivamente, apresuradamente. —*v.i.* (fam.) apresurarse, darse prisa, precipitarse. —*v.t.* **h. it,** ir de prisa; apresurarse.
hothead [-ˌhɛd] *s.* persona arrojada o impetuosa, persona precipitada; exaltado, fanático.
hotheaded [-'hɛdəd] *a.* impetuoso, precipitado, arrojado, arrebatado, fogoso.
hotheadedly [-lɪ] *adv.* impetuosamente, precipitadamente.
hotheadedness [-nəs] *s.* impetuosidad, precipitación.
hothouse ['hɑtˌhaʊs, B 'hɔt-] *s.* 1. invernadero, invernáculo. 2. (ant.) casa de baños. 3. (ant.) burdel, lupanar. —*a.* 1. de invernadero, cultivado en invernadero. 2. (fig.) delicado, tierno; apañado, criado con esmero.
hot laboratory, laboratorio radiactivo.
hot line, (pol.) teléfono rojo, línea de emergencia; (*for the public*) línea directa, línea caliente.
hotly ['hɑtlɪ, B 'hɔt-] *adv.* acaloradamente, ardientemente, vehementemente; apasionadamente; violentamente, ferozmente.
hot money, (*stolen money*) dinero caliente.
hotness [-nəs] *s.* calidad del calor o lo caliente.
hot pants, (jer.) 1. satiriasis, erotomanía, pasión sexual. 2. erotómano, sátiro. 3. (fam., E.U.) pantalones muy cortos de mujer que alternan con la moda de la minifalda.
hot pepper, pimiento picante.
hot plate, hornillo; calentador portátil.
hot pot, (pr. G.B.) carne de vaca o carnero guisada con patatas en olla herméticamente tapada, cocido, guisado.
hot potato, (jer., fig.) asunto delicado, problema molesto, papa caliente (Amer.).
hot-press [-ˌprɛs] *s.* prensa de satinar papel en caliente. —*v.t.* satinar en caliente.
hot-pressed [-'prɛst] *a.* prensado en caliente.
hot pursuit, persecución encarnizada.
hot rod, automóvil veloz, coche de carrera (esp. el reconstruido o modificado).
hot seat, (jer., E.U.) silla eléctrica. 2. situación difícil.
hotshot ['hɑtˌʃɑt, B 'hɔtˌʃɔt] *s.* (jer.) pájaro de cuenta; tipo competente, brillante, emprendedor.
hot spot, (jer.) 1. apuros, situación precaria. 2. club nocturno popular, esp. con clientela alborotadora y programas atrevidos.
hot springs, baños o aguas termales.
hotspur [-ˌspɜr, B -ˌspɜ] *s.* hombre imprudente o impulsivo, temerario.
hot stuff, (jer.) 1. persona vivaz, persona vigorosa o enérgica. 2. programa sensacional (esp. lascivo o excitante). 3. botín, artículos robados. 4. persona o cosa interesante o atractiva.
hot tempered, arrebatado, de genio vivo.
Hottentot ['hɑtənˌtɑt, B 'hɔtənˌtɔt] *s., a.* hotentote, perteneciente a una tribu del S.E. de África.
hot tub, jacuzzi.
hot water, (fig.) aprieto, lío.
hot-water bottle ['hɑt'wɔtər-, -'wɑt-, B 'hɔt'wɔtə-] bolsa de agua caliente.
hot-wire cutter [-'waɪr-, B -'waɪə-] (elec.) cortador de alambre cargado.
hot words, palabras mayores.
Houdan ['huˌdæn] *s.* houdán (raza de gallinas francesas de cresta triple).
hound [haʊnd] *s.* 1. sabueso, podenco, galgo, lebrel. 2. perro (en gen.). 3. (fam.) canalla, tipo despreciable. 4. lebrero (en el juego de la caza de la liebre). 5. aficionado. 6. **the hounds,** la jauría; **to follow the hounds, to ride to hounds,** cazar con jauría. —*v.t.* 1. cazar con perros. 2. perseguir, acosar. 3. azuzar (perro).
hound, *s.* 1. (*pl.*) (mar.) cacholas. 2. (*pl.*) (en los vehículos) barras laterales que prestan rigidez a las partes que conectan.

hound's-tongue ['haʊndz,tʌŋ] *s.* (bot.) lengua de perro, lengua canina, cinoglosa, viniebla, lapilla.
houndstooth check, hound's-tooth check, [-,tuθ-] (tela con) diseño de cuadritos, o diseño pata de gallo.
hour [aʊr, B 'aʊə] *s.* 1. hora. 2. (*pl.*) (relig.) horas (rezos a ciertas horas del día). 3. hora o momento actual. 4. **after hours,** fuera de horas; **at all hours,** a todas horas; muy tarde; **at the eleventh h.,** a la hora undécima; **at this h.,** a esta hora; **by the h.,** por horas; **hours on end,** horas enteras; **on the h.,** a la hora en punto, a la hora exacta; **small hours,** horas que preceden a la madrugada; **to keep good (late) hours,** acostarse temprano (tarde); **to strike the h.,** dar la hora; **to work long hours,** trabajar muchas horas diarias.
hour angle, (astr.) ángulo horario.
hour circle, (astr.) círculo horario.
hourglass ['aʊr,glæs, B 'aʊə,glɑs] *s.* reloj de arena, reloj de agua, reloj de mercurio.
hour hand, horario (manecilla del reloj).
houri ['hʊrɪ, B 'hʊərɪ] *s.* (*pl.* HOURIS) hurí, mujer bella y seductora.
hourly ['aʊrlɪ, B 'aʊəlɪ] *adv.* a cada hora, por hora(s); frecuentemente, continuamente. —*a.* horario, de cada hora; frecuente; **on an h. basis,** por hora.
house [haʊs] *s.* 1. casa. 2. hogar, residencia, domicilio, morada, cobertura (de un animal); concha (del caracol). 3. casa, descendencia, linaje (esp. noble o ilustre), ej., *the h. of Windsor,* la casa de Windsor. 4. casa, familia. 5. fraternidad religiosa; convento. 6. facultad, escuela o colegio superior de una universidad; pensión o internado. 7. (teat.) sala, público, auditorio, concurrencia. 8. (pol.) cámara (del parlamento). 9. (com.) casa, firma. 10. (astrol.) casa (división del zodíaco). 11. especie de lotería. 12. **full h.,** teatro lleno; (póquer) full; **h. to h.,** de casa en casa; casa por casa; **like a h. on fire,** vigorosamente, rápidamente; **on the h.,** cortesía de la casa, pagado por la casa o por el dueño; **the H.,** (G.B.) la Cámara de los Comunes; la Cámara de los Lores; el Parlamento; (fam.) la bolsa de valores; (hist., G.B.) el hospicio; **to bring down the h.,** ser muy aplaudido; **to keep h.,** mantener un hogar; **to keep open h.,** dar hospitalidad; **to make a H.,** (G.B.), obtener quórum (en el parlamento); **to put** (o **set**) **one's h. in order,** arreglar uno sus asuntos; **to set up h.,** poner casa. —*v.t.* 1. alojar, hospedar, albergar. 2. guardar, almacenar; cubrir, poner a cubierto, proteger. 3. contener, encerrar. 4. (mar.) poner al abrigo, poner en lugar seguro, afianzar. 5. (mec.) encajar, envolver. — [haʊz] *v.i.* alojarse, hospedarse, albergarse.
house arrest, arresto domiciliario, detención domiciliaria.
houseboat ['haʊs,boʊt] *s.* casa flotante, barco habitación.
housebreak [-,breɪk] *v.t.* acostumbrar a un animal doméstico a excretar en un sitio determinado o fuera de casa.
housebreaker [-ər, B -ə] *s.* 1. ladrón que escala una casa, escalador. 2. (pr. G.B.) demoledor de edificios.
housebreaking [-ɪŋ] *s.* 1. escalo, escalamiento. 2. (pr. G.B.) demolición de un edificio.
housebroken [-,broʊkən] *a.* 1. entrenado en hábitos de limpieza, aseado (perro, etc.). 2. (fig.) amansado, dócil y respetuoso.
house-builder [-,bɪldər, B -də] *s.* constructor de casas.
house call, (med.) visita a domicilio.
housecarl [-,kɑrl, B -,kɑl] *s.* (hist.) guardia de corps o miembro de la casa de un rey o noble danés o inglés.
houseclean ['haʊs,klin] *v.i., v.t.* 1. limpiar (la casa); hacer limpieza de la casa. 2. (fig.) limpiar, deshacerse de (cosas o personas indeseables).
housecleaning [-ɪŋ] *s.* limpieza de la casa.
housecoat [-,koʊt] *s.* bata de casa.
housedress [-,drɛs] *s.* bata de casa.
house flag, (mar.) bandera del armador, bandera de la casa naviera.
housefly [-,flaɪ] *s.* mosca común o doméstica.
houseful ['haʊs,fʊl] *s.* lo que llena una casa, una casa llena, ej., *a h. of guests,* una casa llena de invitados.
house guest, invitado, huésped.
household [-,hoʊld] *s.* familia, casa. —*a.* 1. casero, familiar; doméstico, de la casa (tareas, quehaceres, gastos, etc.). 2. común, familiar.
householder [-ər, B -ə] *s.* amo o dueño de casa, padre o cabeza de familia.
household furniture, menaje de casa, ajuar de casa.
household goods, artículos de uso doméstico, artículos fundamentales de la comodidad hogareña.
household word, palabra del habla común, palabra del habla familiar, de uso corriente.
house sit, cuidar una casa mientras los propietarios estan ausentes.
housekeeper ['haʊs,kipər, B -ə] *s.* ama de llaves, ama de gobierno; casera.
housekeeping [-ɪŋ] *s.* manejo o gobierno de la casa.
houseleek ['haʊs,lik] *s.* (bot.) siempreviva mayor, hierba puntera.
houselights [-,laɪts] *s. pl.* luces de la sala (en un teatro).
houseline [-,laɪn] *s.* (mar.) piola.
housemaid ['haʊs,meɪd] *s.* empleada de hogar, criada, sirvienta, mucama (Amer.).
housemaid's knee, (med.) rodilla de fregona, bursitis de la rótula.
houseman [-mən] *s.* criado de casa, sirviente.
housemother [-,mʌðər, B -ə] *s.* directora en una residencia de jóvenes, niños o escolares.
house of assembly, (pol.) cámara baja.
house of assignation, casa de citas; prostíbulo.
house of cards, castillo de naipes; quimera.
House of Commons, Cámara de los Comunes (en G.B. y Canadá).
house of correction, correccional.
house of ill fame, burdel, lupanar.
House of Lords, (G.B.) Cámara de los Lores.
House of Representatives, (E.U., Aust.) Cámara de Representantes.
house of worship, casa de oración, casa de Dios, templo.
house organ, publicación informativa de una empresa; boletín (para empleados o clientes).
house painter, pintor de brocha gorda.
house party, 1. fiesta o convite de varios días. 2. el grueso de los invitados a dicha fiesta.
house physician, h. surgeon, médico residente (de un hospital).
house-raising ['haʊs,reɪzɪŋ] *s.* (en zonas rurales) construcción mancomunada de una casa (por un grupo de vecinos).
house rent, alquiler de una casa.
houseroom ['haʊs,rum, -,rʊm] *s.* alojamiento, cabida en una casa.
house sparrow, (orn.) gorrión, burrión.
house to house, de casa en casa, puerta a puerta.
housetop [-,tɑp, B -,tɔp] *s.* techado, techo, tejado; azotea; **to shout from the housetops,** pregonar a los cuatro vientos.
housewarming [-,wɔrmɪŋ, B -,wɔmɪŋ] *s.* fiesta o reunión que se celebra con motivo del estreno de una casa; **to have a h.** estrenar la casa.
housewife ['haʊs,waɪf] *s.* 1. ama de casa, madre de familia. 2. (G.B.) (gen. ['hʌzəf]) estuche de costura, alfiletero, agujetero. —*v.t., v.i.* (ant.) administrar prudentemente, administrar como una buena madre de familia.
housewifely [-lɪ] *a.* de ama de casa, casero, doméstico; económico, ahorrativo.
housewifery [-ərɪ] *s.* economía doméstica; quehaceres domésticos.
housework [-,wɜrk, B -,wɜk] *s.* quehaceres domésticos.
housing ['haʊzɪŋ] *s.* 1. alojamiento, aposentamiento; morada, estancia, residencia. 2. habitación, vivienda. 3. suministro de viviendas. 4. (mec.) envoltura, caja, bastidor. 5. (mar.) cuerpo interior del palo. 6. (arq.) muesca, encaje. 7. (aut.) cárter, caja.
housing, *s.* 1. gualdrapa, sudadero, mantilla, pellón. 2. (*pl.*) jaeces, aderezos, arreos (de caballo). 3. (mar.) piola, merlín.
housing development, colonia, urbanización, construcción de una comunidad de viviendas.
housing shortage, escasez de viviendas.
hove, *pret., p.p. de* **heave.**
hovel ['hʌvəl, 'hɑv-, B 'hɔv-] *s.* 1. cobertizo, tinglado. 2. barraca, choza, cabaña, cuchitril, chabola. 3. fábrica cónica (de un horno bajo). 4. (arq.) nicho. —*v.t.* (*pret., p.p.* HOVELED O HOVELLED; *p.pr.* HOVELING O HOVELLING) poner en cobertizo; albergar, proteger, abrigar.
hover ['hʌvər, 'hɑv-, B 'hɔvə] *v.i.* 1. cernerse, revolotear (ave). 2. estar en suspenso, flotar en el aire. 3. rondar, dar vueltas. 4. vacilar, oscilar. —*s.* 1. revoloteo. 2. grupo de truchas.
hovercraft [-,kræft, B -,krɑft] *s.* (G.B.) (mar.) hidrofoil, aerodeslizador.
how [haʊ] *adv.* 1. cómo, ej., *you know h. to do it,* sabes cómo hacerlo, *h. do you know it?* ¿cómo lo sabe Ud.? 2. cuán, qué, ej., *h. fast you go!* !cuán (o qué) rápido vas! *h. ugly!* ¡qué feo! *you do not realize h. late it is,* Ud. no se da cuenta de lo tarde que es (o cuán tarde es). 3. a qué precio, a cuánto, ej., *h. do you sell them?* ¿a cuánto los vende? *h. is cotton today?* ¿a cuánto (o a qué precio) está el algodón hoy? 4. **and h.!** (jer.) ¡y cómo! ¡así mismo es!; **here's h.!** ¡salud! ¡a su salud!; **h. about (a game of chess, a drink,** etc.)? ¿qué le parece (si jugamos una partida de ajedrez, tomamos un trago, etc.)?; **h. are you?** ¿cómo está Ud.? ¿cómo estás?; **h. come?** ¿cómo es eso? ¿cómo es posible?; **h. do you do?** buenos días, mucho gusto; **h. early?** ¿cuándo? ¿a qué hora?; **h. else?** ¿de qué otra manera?; **h. far?** ¿a qué distancia?; **h. fast?** ¿con qué rapidez?; **h. is that for (size, dancing,** etc.)? (fam.) ¿qué te parece (este tamaño, este baile, etc.)?; **h. late?** ¿a qué hora? ¿hasta qué hora? ¿cuándo?; **h. long?** ¿cuánto tiempo? ¿hasta cuándo?; **h. many?** ¿cuántos?; **h. much?** ¿cuánto?; **h. now?** ¿y bien? ¿pues qué? ¿qué significa esto?; **h. often?** ¿cuántas veces? ¿con qué frecuencia?; **h. old are you?** ¿cuántos años tienes?; **h. on earth (did you guess it, could I have known,** etc.)? ¿cómo diablos (lo adivinaste, podía saberlo yo, etc.)?; **h. soon?** ¿cuándo? —*conj.* como, que, ej., *he told me h. he found it,* me contó como (o que) lo encontró. —*s.* manera, modo, forma.
howdah ['haʊdə] *s.* castillo (sobre el lomo de un elefante).
howdie, howdy ['haʊdɪ] *s.* (Esco.) partera, comadrona. —*interj.* (E.U., reg.) ¡hola! ¡buenas!; **h., folks?** ¿qué tal, señores?

however [haʊ'ɛvər, B -ə] *adv.* 1. sin embargo, no obstante. 2. por . . . que, ej., *h. stupid they may be,* por tontos que sean. 3. de cualquier modo, como quiera que.
howff, howf [haʊf, hoʊf] *s.* (Esco.) guarida, nidal.
howitzer ['haʊətsər, B -sə] *s.* (mil.) obús, proyectil de artillería.
howl [haʊl] *v.i.* 1. aullar. 2. lamentarse, quejarse, llorar; hablar gritando, dar alaridos. 3. rugir, bramar. —*v.t.* 1. gritar, decir a gritos. 2. **h. down,** gritar, dar grita a (orador, etc.). —*s.* 1. aullido. 2. alarido, lamento; grito. 3. bramido (del viento). 4. **h. of laughter,** carcajada, risotada.
howler ['haʊlər, B -lə] *s.* 1. aullador, gritador. 2. (zool.) mono aullador. 3. (fam.) (*mistake*) plancha, gazapo, desacierto.
howlet [-lət] *s.* (ant.) lechuza.
howling [-lɪŋ] *a.* 1. aullador. 2. triste, melancólico. 3. (jer.) clamoroso, tremendo, ej., *a h. success,* un éxito clamoroso.
howling monkey, (zool.) mono aullador.
howsoever [ˌhaʊsoʊ'ɛvər, B -ə] *adv.* como quiera que; de cualquier modo; por muy.
hoy [hɔɪ] *s.* (mar.) lanchón; barcaza pesada; (ant.) buque costero.
hoy, *interj.* ¡hola! ¡oiga! ¡eh!
hoyden ['hɔɪdən] *s.* tunantuela. —*a.* tosca, ruda (díc. de una muchacha). —*v.i.* tunantear, tunear.
hoydenish [-ɪʃ] *a.* traviesa, revoltosa, tunanta (muchacha).
Hoyle [hɔɪl] *s.* libro con las reglas de juegos de naipes y de salón; **according to H.,** conforme a las reglas de juego, correctamente.
hp *abrev. de* **horsepower,** caballo de fuerza o vapor (CV).
HQ *abrev. de* **headquarters,** cuartel general; oficina central.
H.R. *abrev. de* **House of Representatives,** Cámara Baja, Cámara de Representantes.
H.R.H. *abrev. de* **Her** o **His Royal Highness,** Su Alteza Real (S.A.R.).
hrs. *abrev. de* **hours,** horas.
H.S. *abrev. de* **High School,** escuela secundaria.
HT, *abrev. de* **high-tension,** alta tensión.
hub [hʌb] *s.* 1. cubo (de rueda). 2. (fig.) centro, eje. 3. **the H.,** (E.U.) Boston.
hubba-hubba ['hʌbə'hʌbə] *interj.* ¡hurra! ¡bravo! ¡bien!
hubble-bubble ['hʌbəlˌbʌbəl] *s.* 1. especie de narguile (pipa turca). 2. sonido burbujeante. 3. parloteo confuso.
hubbub ['hʌbˌʌb] *s.* 1. grita, bullicio, vocerío, gritería. 2. tumulto, alboroto, confusión, batahola.
hubby ['hʌbɪ] *s.* (fam.) esposo, maridito.
hubcap ['hʌbˌkæp] *s.* (aut.) tapacubos.
hubris ['hjubrəs] *s.* (griego) arrogancia, presunción, engreimiento.
huckaback ['hʌkəˌbæk] *s.* (tej.) tela granito (para toallas).
huckle ['hʌkəl] *s.* (ant.) cadera, anca, grupa.
huckleberry [-ˌbɛrɪ] *s.* (*pl.* HUCKLEBERRIES) (bot.) gaylussacia.
hucklebone [-ˌboʊn] *s.* (anat.) 1. cía, hueso de la cadera. 2. taba, astrágalo.
huckster ['hʌkstər, B -stə] *s.* 1. buhonero, mercachifle, chalán, regatón, vendedor ambulante. 2. agente de publicidad, propagandista comercial (esp. por radio o televisión). —*v.i.* regatear el precio. —*v.t.* regatonear, vender al por menor.
huddle ['hʌdəl] *v.i.* 1. apiñarse, amontonarse, apilarse, arracimarse. 2. acurrucarse, agazaparse. 3. (E.U.) apelotonarse, agruparse (los jugadores de fútbol, etc. para planear las jugadas). —*v.t.* 1. apiñar, amontonar, atestar, apilar. 2. (G.B.) (con *over, through, up*) ejecutar apresuradamente. 3. (G.B.) (con *up*) atrabancar, frangollar, farfullar. 4. **h. oneself (up),** acurrucarse. —*s.* 1. tropel, turba, masa confusa. 2. confusión, baraúnda. 3. (E.U.) agrupamiento de jugadores (que planean jugadas en fútbol, etc.). 4. conferencia, reunión. 5. **to go into a h.,** agruparse o juntarse para conferenciar, reunirse en conferencia.
hue [hju] *s.* 1. color, tinte; matiz. 2. (ant.) forma, apariencia. 3. vocerío, clamor, grita, griterío esp. durante una cacería. 4. (ant.) gaceta policial.
hue and cry, 1. algazara, alboroto, vocerío, protesta ruidosa. 2. alarma; persecución pública de un delincuente.
hued ['hjud] *a.* (*ú. en palabras compuestas*) de color, de matiz, coloreado, matizado, ej., *violet-hued,* de color de violeta, violado, *many-h.,* multicolor, de varios matices.
huff [hʌf] *v.t.* 1. soplar. 2. hinchar; (fig.) inflar. 3. irritar, encolerizar, enfadar. 4. (juego de damas) soplar (una pieza). 5. tratar mal, ofender, injuriar; intimidar. 6. **to be huffed,** estar enojado, estar molesto. —*v.i.* 1. bufar, resoplar. 2. bravear, echar fieros. 3. (dial.) hincharse, abultarse. 4. ofenderse, resentirse. 5. **h. and puff,** estar muy indignado; bravear, echar fieros. —*s.* 1. enfado, arranque de cólera o enojo, malhumor. 2. (juego de damas) soplo (de una pieza). 3. **in a h.,** enojado, de mal humor.
huffily [-əlɪ] *adv.* irasciblemente, quisquillosamente.
huffiness [-ɪnəs] *s.* irascibilidad.
huffish ['hʌfɪʃ] *a.* resentido, enojadizo, irascible, petulante.
huffy ['hʌfɪ] *a.* (HUFFIER; HUFFIEST) 1. malhumorado, enojadizo, resentido. 2. (ant.) arrogante, altivo, desdeñoso.
hug [hʌg] *v.t.* (*pret., p.p.* HUGGED; *p.pr.* HUGGING) 1. abrazar, apretar con los brazos, estrechar entre los brazos. 2. aferrarse a. 3. (fig.) abrigar (ideas, esperanzas). 4. mantenerse cerca de, costear, ej., *the ship hugged the coast,* el barco se mantenía cerca de la costa, el barco costeaba. 5. adherirse a, ej., *the car hugs the road,* el carro se adhiere bien al camino. 6. **hug oneself,** (fig.) felicitarse, congratularse; **h. the wind,** (mar.) ceñir el viento, navegar de bolina. —*s.* 1. abrazo fuerte. 2. (fig.) estrujamiento, aprieto, abracijo.
huge [hjudʒ] *a.* enorme, muy grande, inmenso, vasto, gigantesco.
hugely ['hjudʒlɪ] *adv.* enormemente, inmensamente, vastamente.
hugeness [-nəs] *s.* enormidad, inmensidad, magnitud.
hugger-mugger ['hʌgərˌmʌgər, B 'hʌgəˌmʌgə] *s.* 1. confusión, desorden, embrollo, lío. 2. (ant.) misterio, secreto, clandestinidad. —*a.* 1. (ant.) secreto, disimulado, misterioso. 2. confuso, desordenado, desarreglado. —*v.t.* ocultar, mantener en secreto, encubrir. —*v.i.* actuar o confabular clandestinamente.
Huguenot ['hjugəˌnɑt, B -ˌnɔt] *s.* (hist., relig.) hugonote, calvinista, protestante francés.
hula ['hulə] **hula-hula** [-'hulə] *s.* hula, hula-hula (baile mímico de Hawai).
hulk [hʌlk] *s.* 1. casco de barco. 2. barco tosco o viejo, carraca. 3. (*ú. gen. en pl.*) pontón (que servía como prisión). 4. armatoste (cosa voluminosa, pesada o difícil de manejar). 5. hombre grandote; cuerpo pesado (de una persona). —*v.i.* mostrarse, vislumbrarse (díc. de objetos grandes).
hulking ['hʌlkɪŋ] *a.* voluminoso, corpulento, pesado; rústico, tosco; difícil de manejar.
hulky [-kɪ] *a.* (HULKIER; HULKIEST) *var. de* **hulking.**
hull [hʌl] *s.* 1. hollejo, vaina (de habas, guisantes, etc.), cáliz (de la fresa). 2. casco (de una nave o de un hidroavión). 3. casquillo (de un cartucho). 4. **h. down,** (mar.) con sólo el aparejo visible en el horizonte (díc. de un barco distante). —*v.t.* 1. mondar, desvainar, descascarar. 2. perforar o dar en el casco de (un barco, ej., un torpedo u otro proyectil).
hullabaloo, hullaballoo ['hʌləbəˌlu, B ˌhʌləbə'lu] *s.* 1. bullicio, alboroto; escándalo (esp. publicitario). 2. tumulto, batahola; **there was a big h.,** se armó la gorda (Mex.).
hullo [hə'loʊ, B 'hʌ'loʊ] (pr. G.B.) *var. de* **hello.**
hum [hʌm] *v.i.* (*pret., p.p.* HUMMED; *p.pr.* HUMMING) 1. zumbar, zurriar. 2. tararear, canturrear. 3. (fam.) estar muy activo o animoso, estar en plena actividad. 4. **h. and haw,** tartalear; titubear, vacilar; **to make things h.,** activar las cosas, hacer funcionar la maquinaria, meter prisa. —*v.t.* 1. tararear. 2. murmurar, expresar con un sonido inarticulado. 3. **h. to sleep,** arrullar, adormecer tarareando. —*s.* 1. zumbido. 2. murmullo, susurro.
human ['hjumən] *a.* humano. —*s.* humano, hombre.
human being, ser humano, persona.
humane [hju'meɪn] *a.* 1. humano, humanitario, caritativo, bondadoso, benévolo, compasivo, benigno. 2. humanístico (estudios).
humanely [-lɪ] *adv.* humanamente.
humaneness [-nəs] *s.* humanidad, benignidad.
humane studies, ciencias humanas, humanidades.
human interest, interés humano.
humanism ['hjuməˌnɪzəm] *s.* humanismo, humanidad.
humanist [-nəst] *s., a.* humanista.
humanistic [ˌhjumə'nɪstɪk] *a.* humanístico.
humanitarian [hjuˌmænə'tɛrɪən, B -'tɛər-] *s.* persona humanitaria, filántropo. —*a.* humanitario.
humanitarianism [-ˌɪzəm] *s.* humanitarismo, benevolencia, benignidad.
humanity [hju'mænətɪ] *s.* (*pl.* HUMANITIES) 1. humanidad, naturaleza humana; (*pl.*) características y atributos humanos. 2. humanidad, benevolencia, benignidad, filantropía. 3. humanidad, género humano, raza humana. 4. (*pl.*) humanidades, letras.
humanization [ˌhjumənə'zeɪʃən, B -naɪ-] *s.* humanización.
humanize ['hjuməˌnaɪz] *v.t.* humanizar, humanar, civilizar, refinar (costumbres).
humankind ['hjumənˌkaɪnd, B -'kaɪnd] *s.* humanidad, raza humana, género humano, especie humana.
humanly [-lɪ] *adv.* 1. humanamente; **all that is h. possible,** todo lo humanamente posible. 2. como un hombre; de un modo digno de un ser humano.
human nature, naturaleza humana.
humanness [-nəs] *s.* aspecto humano, calidad de humano.
humanoid [-məˌnɔɪd] *a.* de caracteres humanos, humanoide.
human resources, recursos humanos.
human rights, derechos humanos.
humate ['hjuˌmeɪt] *s.* (quím.) humato.
humble ['hʌmbəl] *a.* 1. humilde, modesto; sumiso. 2. humilde, bajo; insignificante. —*v.t.* humillar, abatir, degradar, rebajar.
humblebee [-ˌbi] *s.* (ento., G.B.) abejorro, abejón.

humbleness [-nəs] *s.* 1. humildad. 2. modestia.
humble pie, 1. empanada de menudo de venado. 2. **to eat h. p.,** humillarse, someterse.
humbling ['hʌmblɪŋ] *a.* humillador, humillante.
humbly [-blɪ] *adv.* humildemente.
humbug ['hʌm,bʌg] *s.* 1. farsa, hipocresía. 2. fraude, patraña, impostura, embuste, engaño. 3. farsante, embaucador, impostor, embustero. 4. (G.B.) bombón de menta. —*v.t.* (*pret., p.p.* HUMBUGGED; *p.pr.* HUMBUGGING) engañar, embaucar.
humbuggery [-ərɪ] *s.* fraude, engaño, patraña, trampería.
humdinger ['hʌm'dɪŋər, B -ə] *s.* (jer. E.U.) persona o cosa excelente, maravilla.
humdrum [-,drʌm] *a.* monótono, aburrido, cansado, pesado; ordinario, vulgar, común, trivial. —*s.* 1. posma, pelma, pelmazo (persona cargante o pesada). 2. monotonía, aburrimiento, pesadez.
humectant [hju'mɛktənt] *a., s.* humectante.
humectation [,hjumɛk'teɪʃən] *s.* (med.) humectación.
humeral ['hjumərəl] *a.* (anat., zool.) humeral. —*s.* humeral, velo humeral.
humeral veil, (relig.) humeral, velo humeral, cendal.
humerus [-ərəs] *s.* (*pl.* HUMERI [-,raɪ]) (anat., zool.) húmero.
humic ['hjumɪk] *a.* (quím.) húmico.
humic acid, (quím.) ácido húmico.
humid ['hjuməd, 'ju- B 'hju-] *a.* húmedo, mojado.
humidification [hju,mɪdəfə'keɪʃən] *s.* humedecimiento, humectación.
humidifier [-'mɪdə,faɪər, B -ə] *a.* humedecedor, humectante, que humedece. —*s.* humedecedor, humectador (aparato).
humidify [-,faɪ] *v.t.* (*pret., p.p.* HUMIDIFIED; *p.pr.* HUMIDIFYING) humedecer.
humidistat [-,stæt] *s.* humidistato, higróstato.
humidity [-'mɪdətɪ, ju-, B hju-] *s.* humedad.
humidly ['hjumədlɪ] *adv.* húmedamente.
humidor [-mə,dɔr, B -,dɔ] *s.* humidificador (recipiente que se usa para guardar tabaco o cigarros).
humifuse [-,fjus] *a.* (bot.) humifuso.
humiliate [hju'mɪlɪ,eɪt, ju-, B hju-] *v.t.* humillar, mortificar, avergonzar.
humiliating [-ɪŋ] *a.* humillante, degradante, vergonzoso.
humiliation [-,mɪlɪ'eɪʃən] *s.* humillación, mortificación.
humility [hju'mɪlətɪ] *s.* humildad, sumisión, rendimiento.
humin ['hjumɪn] *s.* (quím.) humina.
hummer ['hʌmər, B -ə] *s.* 1. zumbador. 2. colibrí, pájaro mosca.
humming [-ɪŋ] *a.* 1. zumbador. 2. (fam.) activo, animoso, vigoroso, enérgico; intenso, grande.
humming ale, tipo de cerveza fuerte.
hummingbird [-,bɜrd, B -,bɜd] *s.* (orn.) colibrí, pájaro mosca, tominejo, picaflor (Amer.), chupaflor (Amer.).
hummingly [-lɪ] *adv.* (fam.) activamente, vigorosamente.
hummock ['hʌmək] *s.* 1. montecillo, morón, mambla, mogote. 2. lomo o camellón de hielo. 3. (S. de E.U.) zona de tierra profunda y fértil.
humor, (pr. G.B.) **humour** ['hjumər, 'ju-, B 'hjumə] *s.* 1. humor, agudeza, gracia. 2. humor, disposición, genio, índole. 3. humorada, fantasía, capricho. 4. (biol.) humor. 5. carácter, talante. 6. **good h.,** buen humor; **ill h.,** mal humor; **out of h.,** de mal humor, de malas pulgas, disgustado; **to be in the h. for (doing),** tener ganas de (hacer). —*v.t.* 1. complacer, seguir o llevarle el humor a, dar gusto a; mimar. 2. acomodarse a, adaptarse a.
humoral ['hjumərəl] *a.* (med.) humoral.
humoresque [,hjumə'rɛsk] *s.* (mús.) capricho.
humorist, (G.B. t.) **humourist** ['hjumərəst, 'ju-, B 'hju-] *s.* 1. humorista. 2. bromista.
humoristic [,hjumə'rɪstɪk] *a.* 1. humorístico. 2. gracioso, chistoso, jocoso.
humorless, (pr. G.B.) **humourless** ['hjumərləs, 'ju-, B 'hjuməlɪs] *a.* 1. sin sentido del humor. 2. falto de gracia, seco.
humorous [-mərəs] *a.* chistoso, gracioso, ocurrente.
humorously [-lɪ] *adv.* humorísticamente, graciosamente, jocosamente.
humorousness [-nəs] *s.* jocosidad; gracejo, donaire.
hump [hʌmp] *s.* 1. joroba, giba, corcova. 2. mogote, mambla, montecillo, morón. 3. (jer., G.B.) esplín, morriña, murria, acceso de melancolía. 4. período crítico, fase más difícil. 5. (Aust.) caminata larga con un bulto en la espalda. 6. **to get over the h.,** superar el período crítico, dejar atrás la fase más difícil. —*v.t.* 1. encorvarse, doblar la espalda. 2. (Aust.) cargar en la espalda; p. ext. cargar. 3. **h. oneself,** (jer., E.U.) esforzarse. —*v.i.* 1. apresurarse, darse prisa, menearse. 2. correr a toda velocidad. 3. (vulg.) joder, copular.
humpback ['hʌmp,bæk] *s.* 1. giba, corcova, joroba. 2. jorobado, corcovado, curcuncho (Amer.). 3. (zool.) yubarta, ballena jorobada, rorcual de joroba.
humpbacked [-,bækt] *a.* jorobado, gibado, giboso, corcovado, curcuncho (Amer.).
humped [hʌmpt] *a.* jorobado, gibado, giboso, corcovado, curcuncho (Amer.).
humph [hʌmf] *interj.* (expresión de desprecio, duda o desagrado) ¡bah! ¡uh! ¡puf!
Humpty Dumpty ['hʌmptɪ'dʌmptɪ] hombrecillo rechoncho de un verso para niños, que personifica un huevo que cayó y se hizo añicos.
humpy ['hʌmpɪ] *a.* (HUMPIER; HUMPIEST) escabroso, lleno de protuberancias; giboso.
humus ['hjuməs, 'ju-, B 'hju-] *s.* humus, mantillo.
Hun [hʌn] *s.* 1. (hist.) huno. 2. vándalo. 3. (despec.) alemán (persona); **the Huns,** los alemanes.
hunch [hʌntʃ] *v.t.* 1. doblar (la espalda), encorvar. 2. empujar, dar empellones o codazos a. 3. **h. oneself up,** encorvarse; acurrucarse. —*v.i.* 1. moverse a empujones o a codazos. 2. encorvarse, agacharse, encogerse. —*s.* 1. pedazo o trozo grueso. 2. giba, corcova, joroba, protuberancia. 3. (fam.) corazonada, presentimiento, barrunto, pálpito (Amer.).
hunchback ['hʌntʃ,bæk] *s.* 1. corcova, joroba, giba. 2. corcovado, jorobado, gibado.
hunchbacked [-,bækt] *a.* corcovado, jorobado, gibado.
hundred ['hʌndrəd, -dərd, B -drəd] *s.* 1. ciento, centenar. 2. (billete de) cien dólares. 3. (hist., G.B.) división de un condado; (E.U.) pequeña circunscripción política. 4. **by the h., by the hundreds,** por centenares. —*a.* cien (antes de sustantivo); ciento.
hundredfold [-,foʊld] *a.* céntuplo. —*adv.* cien veces más. —*s.* céntuplo.
hundred-per-cent [-pər'sɛnt, B -pə'-] *a.* cabal, perfecto, puro, ciento por ciento.
hundredth ['hʌndrədθ, -drətθ] *a.* centésimo. —*s.* centésimo, céntimo, centavo.
hundredweight ['hʌndrəd,weɪt] *s.* quintal (E.U. 100 libras = 45,36 kg; G.B. 112 libras = 50,8 kg).
Hundred Years' War, (hist., G.B.) Guerra de los Cien Años.
hung [hʌŋ] *pret., p.p. de* **hang.**
Hungarian [hʌŋ'gɛrɪən, B -'gɛər-] *a.* húngaro, natural de Hungría. —*s.* 1. húngaro, natural de Hungría. 2. (idioma) húngaro.
Hungary ['hʌŋgərɪ] *s.* Hungría.
hung beef, tasajo, cecina, charqui (Amer.).
hunger ['hʌŋgər, B -gə] *s.* 1. hambre. 2. (fig.) hambre, anhelo, deseo. —*v.i.* 1. tener o padecer hambre, hambrear. 2. **h. for** (o **after**), tener hambre de; (fig.) anhelar, sentir anhelo por. —*v.t.* hambrear, hacer padecer hambre.
hunger strike, huelga de hambre.
hung jury, (der.) jurado en desacuerdo.
hungrily ['hʌŋgrəlɪ] *adv.* hambrientamente.
hungriness [-grɪnəs] *s.* hambre, sensación de hambre.
hungry ['hʌŋgrɪ] *a.* (HUNGRIER; HUNGRIEST) 1. hambriento. 2. (fig.) hambriento, deseoso, ganoso, codicioso. 3. pobre, estéril, árido. 4. (ant.) asolado o devastado por hambre. 5. **to be h.,** tener hambre; **to be h. for,** estar deseoso de; **to go h.,** pasar hambre.
hung up, (gen. con *on*) (jer.) 1. perturbado emocionalmente (por); neurótico. 2. desconcertado, frustrado (por). 3. adicto o sometido (a) u obsesionado (por).
hunk [hʌŋk] *s.* (fam.) buen pedazo, trozo grande; buena tajada, rebanada gruesa.
hunker ['hʌŋkər, B -kə] *v.i.* acurrucarse, agacharse.
hunkers [-kərz, B -kəz] *s. pl.* rabadas, cuartos traseros; (ú. esp. en) **on one's h.,** en cuclillas.
hunks [hʌŋks] *s. pl.* (*sing. o pl. en const.*) regañon, persona malhumorada; avaro, tacaño.
hunky ['hʌŋkɪ] *a.* (jer., E.U.) excelente, muy bien hecho, en buen estado. —*s.* (jer., E.U.) obrero extranjero; bracero o peón (esp. húngaro o yugoslavo).
hunky-dory [,hʌŋkɪ'dɔrɪ] *a.* (fam.) a pedir de boca, muy bien, excelente.
Hunnish ['hʌnɪʃ] *a.* 1. huno. 2. (fig.) bárbaro.
hunt [hʌnt] *v.t.* 1. cazar. 2. cazar en (bosque, pantano, etc.). 3. perseguir, acosar. 4. cazar con (perros, caballos, etc.). 5. **h. down,** acorralar, capturar; **h. out,** echar fuera; descubrir, averiguar; **h. the slipper,** un juego de salón; **h. up,** descubrir, averiguar; **h. up and down,** buscar por todas partes. —*v.i.* 1. cazar, ir de caza. 2. **h. for** (o **after**), buscar afanosamente; rebuscar, ir en busca de. —*s.* 1. caza, cacería, montería. 2. perseguimiento, persecución, acosamiento. 3. busca, búsqueda. 4. grupo de cazadores.
hunter ['hʌntər, B -ə] *s.* 1. cazador, montero. 2. buscador, escudriñador. 3. perro de caza, podenco; caballo de caza. 4. saboneta.
hunter's cap, montera, gorra de caza.
hunter's moon, luna llena después del equinoccio de otoño.
hunting [-ɪŋ] *s.* 1. caza, cacería, montería. 2. (elec.) fluctuación, variación, oscilaciones. —*a.* de caza.
hunting case, caja de saboneta.
hunting dog, perro de caza, podenco.
hunting horn, corneta de monte, trompa de caza.
hunting jacket, cazadora, chaqueta de caza.
hunting knife, cuchillo de monte o de caza.
hunting leopard, (zool.) leopardo cazador; guepardo, chita.
hunting lodge, pabellón de caza.
hunting match, partida de caza, cacería, batida, busca.
hunting scene, (pint.) cacería, montería.
hunting season, temporada de caza.

hunting watch, saboneta (reloj).
huntress ['hʌntrəs] *s.* cazadora; **Diana the H.,** Diana cazadora.
huntsman ['hʌntsmən] *s.* 1. cazador, montero. 2. montero mayor, persona que dirige la caza.
huntsman's-cup [-mənzˌkʌp] *s.* (bot.) sarracenia.
hunt's-up ['hʌntsˌʌp] *s.* tañido de la trompa de caza que llama a los cazadores; p. ext. (cualquier) tonada animosa.
huon pine ['hjuɑn-, B -ɔn-] (bot.) pino de Huon.
hurdies ['hɜrdiz, B 'hɜd-] *s. pl.* (esco.) nalgas, posaderas; rabadilla, ancas.
hurdle ['hɜrdəl, B 'hɜd-] *s.* 1. zarzo, valla, cañizo. 2. (fig.) obstáculo, dificultad. 3. (hist., G.B.) narria, rastra (para llevar a reos al patíbulo). 4. (dep.) valla; (*pl.*) carrera de vallas. —*v.t.* 1. cercar con palos, rodear de vallas. 2. saltar por encima de (vallas). 3. (fig.) remontar o vencer (un obstáculo). —*v.i.* saltar vallas; especializarse en carrera de vallas.
hurdler ['hɜrdlər, B 'hɜdlə] *s.* (dep.) corredor de vallas.
hurdle race, (dep.) carrera de vallas.
hurds [hɜrdz, B hɜdz] *s. pl.* agramiza, agramaduras; estopa.
hurdy-gurdy ['hɜrdɪ'gɜrdɪ, B 'hɜdɪˌgɜdɪ] *s.* (*pl.* HURDY-GURDIES) (mús.) organillo, gaita, zanfonía.
hurl [hɜrl, B hɜl] *v.t.* 1. lanzar, arrojar, tirar, echar. 2. soltar (invectivas, oprobios, etc.). 3. **h. oneself at,** lanzarse sobre. —*v.i.* 1. precipitarse, abalanzarse, arrojarse. 2. (béisbol) lanzar la pelota. —*s.* tiro, lanzamiento.
hurler ['hɜrlər, B 'hɜlə] *s.* lanzador (en béisbol).
hurley [-ɪ] *s.* 1. juego irlandés parecido al hockey. 2. palo de hockey.
hurling [-ɪŋ] *s.* juego irlandés parecido al hockey.
hurly [-ɪ] *s.* (ant.) alboroto, tumulto, batahola, baraúnda.
hurly-burly [-'bɜrlɪ, B -ˌbɜlɪ] *s.* alboroto, tumulto, batahola, baraúnda, confusión. —*a.* tumultuoso, alborotado; confuso.
hurrah [hʊ'rɔ, -'rɑ, B -'rɑ] *interj.* ¡hurra! ¡viva! —*s.* viva. —*v.i., v.t.* aclamar, vitorear, dar vivas.
hurray [-'reɪ] *var. de* **hurrah.**
hurricane ['hɜrəˌkeɪn, -ɪkən, 'hʌrə-, B 'hʌrɪkən] *s.* huracán.
hurricane deck, (mar.) cubierta superior (de un buque de pasajeros).
hurricane lamp, quinqué, linterna.
hurried ['hɜrid, 'hʌrid, B 'hʌrɪd] *a.* apresurado, apremiado; precipitado.
hurriedly [-lɪ] *adv.* apresuradamente, precipitadamente.
hurry ['hɜrɪ, 'hʌrɪ, B 'hʌ-] *v.t.* (*pret., p.p.* HURRIED; *p.pr.* HURRYING) 1. apresurar, dar prisa a. 2. acelerar; impulsar, adelantar, apremiar, incitar, acuciar. 3. llevar de prisa (a una persona). 4. **h. into (doing),** apresurar a, impeler a (hacer); **h. off,** hacer marchar o salir de prisa; llevar de prisa (a una persona); **h. on,** apresurar, hacer pasar rápidamente; **h. up,** apresurar. —*v.i.* apresurarse, darse prisa; obrar con escape o con precipitación; **h. after,** correr en pos de; **h. along,** pasar de prisa; **h. away,** irse de prisa, salir precipitadamente; **h. back,** volver de prisa; **h. off,** irse o marcharse de prisa; **h. on,** seguir caminando de prisa; **h. over to,** pasar rápidamente a, ir a ver de prisa a; **h. up,** apresurarse, darse prisa, meter prisa. —*s.* prisa, premura; apresuramiento, apremio; precipitación; **in a h.,** rápidamente; en caso de urgencia; (fam.) fácilmente; **to be in a h.,** tener prisa, estar de prisa; **what's the h.?** ¿qué prisa hay?
hurry-scurry, hurry-skurry [-'skɜrɪ, B -'skʌrɪ] *s.* precipitación, atropello; confusión. —*v.t., v.i.* (*pret., p.p.* HURRY-SCURRIED, HURRY-SKURRIED; *p.pr.* HURRY-SCURRYING, HURRY-SKURRYING) mover(se) o actuar precipitadamente; manejar confusamente; precipitarse, actuar a la desbandada. —*adv.* precipitadamente, atropelladamente.
hurst [hɜrst, B hɜst] *s.* 1. bosquecillo. 2. elevación de terreno.
hurt [hɜrt, B hɜt] *v.t.* (*pret., p.p.* HURT; *p.pr.* HURTING) 1. lastimar, herir, lisiar. 2. injuriar, ofender, agraviar. 3. estropear, dañar, perjudicar. 4. **h. oneself,** herirse, lastimarse, hacerse daño; **it hurts me,** me duele; **it won't h. you (him, her,** etc.) no te (le, etc.) hará daño; **my feelings are h.,** estoy resentido; **to get h.,** herirse, lastimarse. —*v.i.* 1. causar daño. 2. doler. 3. sufrir. —*s.* 1. lesión, herida, lastimadura. 2. vejación, perjuicio. 3. mal, daño.
hurtful ['hɜrtfəl, B 'hɜt-] *a.* dañoso, perjudicial, pernicioso, nocivo; injurioso, lesivo.
hurtfully [-fəlɪ] *adv.* dañosamente, perniciosamente, injuriosamente.
hurtle ['hɜrtəl, B 'hɜtəl] *v.i.* 1. moverse rápidamente; precipitarse, lanzarse, abalanzarse. 2. resonar con gran estruendo; moverse con gran estruendo. 3. (ant.) encontrarse con violencia, entrechocarse. —*v.t.* lanzar, arrojar.
hurtless [-ləs] *a.* (ant.) inocuo, inofensivo; ileso, libre de daño, intacto.
husband ['hʌzbənd] *s.* 1. marido, esposo. 2. (ant.) administrador. —*v.t.* 1. economizar, ahorrar, administrar con economía. 2. reservar, guardar (fuerza, energías). 3. utilizar, aprovechar. 4. (ant.) casar, conseguir marido a.
husbandman [-mən] *s.* (ant.) granjero, agricultor, labrador, cultivador.
husbandry [-bəndrɪ] *s.* 1. manejo, gobierno (atinado o desatinado); economía, conservación, ahorro. 2. labranza, agricultura. 3. (ant.) economía doméstica. 4. cría de animales domésticos.
hush [hʌʃ] *v.t.* 1. aquietar, apaciguar, calmar, sosegar, aplacar, mitigar. 2. acallar, imponer silencio. 3. **h. up,** callar, pasar en silencio, echar tierra a (asunto, escándalo, etc.). —*v.i.* estar quieto, callar(se), enmudecer. —*a.* (ant.) quieto, callado. —*s.* silencio, quietud (esp. la que sigue al ruido). —*interj.* ¡chito! ¡chitón! ¡chist!
hush-hush ['hʌʃ'hʌʃ] *a.* (fam.) muy secreto.
hush money, soborno, dádiva de dinero para asegurar que no se divulgue algo.
hush puppy, (reg.) torta de maíz frita.
husk [hʌsk] *s.* 1. cáscara, hollejo, vaina, pellejo; (E.U.) farfolla, chala (Amer.), (de maíz). 2. (fig.) cáscara, cubierta. —*v.t.* descascarar, deshollejar, desvainar, pelar, despellejar; espinochar, despinochar (el maíz).
husked [hʌskt] *a.* 1. que tiene cáscara, vaina u hollejo. 2. despellejado, desvainado.
husker ['hʌskər, B -kə] *s.* 1. operario o máquina que despinocha (el maíz). 2. descascarador, desgranador.
huskily ['hʌskəlɪ] *adv.* 1. roncamente. 2. secamente (hablar).
huskiness [-kɪnəs] *s.* 1. ronquera. 2. calidad de lo que tiene mucha cáscara o corteza.
husking [-kɪŋ] *s.* acción de descascarar, desvainar, pelar.
husking bee, (E.U.) reunión de vecinos para despinochar maíz.
husky ['hʌskɪ] *a.* (HUSKIER; HUSKIEST) 1. cascarudo, cortezudo. 2. ronco, bronco. 3. robusto, corpulento, fornido. —*s.* 1. esquimal (persona). 2. perro esquimal.
hussar [hə'zɑr, B hʊ'zɑ] *s.* (mil.) húsar.
Hussite ['hʌsˌaɪt] *a., s.* (relig.) husita.
hussy ['hʌzɪ, 'hʌsɪ] *s.* (*pl.* HUSSIES) 1. (despec.) mujer desvergonzada. 2. tunanta, pícara, buena pieza. 3. (dial.) estuche de costura.
hustings ['hʌstɪŋz] *s. pl.* (*sing. o pl. en const.*) 1. (G.B.) tribunal de autoridades municipales. 2. (G.B.) tribuna pública para discursos electorales. 3. proceso electoral, elecciones. 4. (fig.) plataforma, foro (político).
hustle ['hʌsəl] *v.t.* 1. empujar, impeler. 2. sacudir, menear. 3. apresurar. 4. conseguir, ganar. 5. (jer.) hurtar, robar; estafar. —*v.i.* 1. apresurarse, ir rápido. 2. trabajar con gran ahínco, menearse, ajetrearse. 3. andar a empellones. 4. (jer.) trabajar de prostituta. 5. **h. against,** chocar contra. —*s.* 1. empujón, empellón. 2. ajetreo, actividad enérgica. 3. (jer.) estafa; manera ilícita de ganarse la vida.
hustler ['hʌslər, B -lə] *s.* 1. trafagón, buscavidas. 2. (jer.) persona que se gana la vida por medios ilícitos; prostituta.
hut [hʌt] *s.* 1. choza, cabaña, casucha, cobertizo. 2. (mil.) barraca. —*v.t., v.i.* (*pret., p.p.* HUTTED; *p.pr.* HUTTING) alojar o vivir en una choza o cabaña; proveer de chozas.
hutch [hʌtʃ] *s.* 1. jaula (para conejos). 2. caja, cajón, cofre, arca. 3. choza, cabaña, casucha, cobertizo. 4. alacena. —*v.t.* lavar (minerales) en caja o cuba.
Huygens principle ['haɪgənz-] (ópt.) principio de Huygens.
huzza [hə'zɑ, B hʊ-] *interj.* ¡viva! ¡hurra! —*s.* viva. —*v.i., v.t.* (*pret., p.p.* HUZZAED; *p.pr.* HUZZAING) vitorear, dar vivas; aclamar, aplaudir (con vivas).
HV *abrev. de* **high voltage,** alta tensión.
hyacinth ['haɪəˌsɪnθ] *s.* 1. (bot.) jacinto. 2. (min.) jacinto. 3. color azul purpúreo.
Hyades ['haɪəˌdiz] **Hyads** [-ədz] *s. pl.* (mitol., astr.) Híadas, Híades.
hyaline ['haɪələn, B -ˌlaɪn] *a.* 1. vítreo. 2. hialino, diáfano, transparente, translúcido, transluciente. —*s.* 1. (poét.) el mar (manso, tranquilo); la atmósfera (diáfana, límpida); cosa transparente o diáfana. 2. (t. **hyalin**) (bioquím.) hialina.
hyaline cartilage, (anat.) cartílago hialino.
hyalite [-ˌlaɪt] *s.* (min.) hialita.
hyalogen [haɪ'ælədʒən] *s.* (bioquím.) hialógeno.
hyalograph [-'æloʊˌgræf, B -ˌgrɑf] *s.* hialógrafo.
hyalography [ˌhaɪə'lɑgrəfɪ, B -'lɔg-] *s.* hialografía.
hyaloid ['haɪəˌlɔɪd] *a.* (anat.) hialoideo.
hyaloid membrane, (anat.) membrana hialoidea.
hyalophane [haɪ'æləˌfeɪn] *s.* (min.) hialófana.
hyaloplasm [-ˌplæzəm] *s.* (biol.) hialoplasma.
hyaluronidase [ˌhaɪəljʊ'rɑnəˌdeɪs, B -'rɔn-] *s.* (bioquím.) hialuronidasa.
hybrid ['haɪbrəd] *s.* 1. (zool., bot.) híbrido. 2. (filol.) palabra híbrida. —*a.* híbrido.
hybridism [-ˌɪzəm] *s.* hibridismo.
hybridity [haɪ'brɪdətɪ] *s.* hibridismo, carácter híbrido, naturaleza híbrida.
hybridization [ˌhaɪbrədə'zeɪʃən, B -daɪ-] *s.* hibridación.
hybridize ['haɪbrəˌdaɪz] *v.t., v.i.* producir o generar híbridos; cruzar o mestizar.
hydatid ['haɪdətəd] (zool., med.) *s.* hidátide. —*a.* hidatídico, hidatidiforme.

hydra ['haɪdrə] *s.* (*pl.* HYDRAS O HYDRAE [-dri]) 1. **H.,** (mitol., astr.) Hidra. 2. (zool.) hidra (pólipo).
hydracid [haɪ'dræsəd] *s.* (quím.) hidrácido.
hydraemia, *var. de* **hydremia.**
hydrangea [-'dreɪndʒə] *s.* (bot.) hortensia, hidrangea.
hydrant ['haɪdrənt] *s.* boca de agua, toma de agua; boca de riego.
hydranth [-ˌdrænθ] *s.* (zool.) hidranto.
hydrargyric [ˌhaɪdrɑr'dʒɪrɪk, B -drɑ'-] *a.* hidrargírico, mercurial.
hydrargyrism [haɪ'drɑrdʒəˌrɪzəm, B -'drɑdʒɪ-] *s.* (med.) hidrargirismo.
hydrargyrum [-rəm] *s.* (quím.) hidrargiro, hidrargirio, mercurio.
hydrastine [-'dræsˌtin, B -ˌtaɪn] *s.* (quím.) hidrastina.
hydrastis [-təs] *s.* (quím.) hidrastina.
hydrate ['haɪˌdreɪt] *s.* (quím.) hidrato. —*v.t., v.i.* hidratar(se), combinar(se) con agua.
hydrated [-əd] *a.* (quím., min.) hidratado.
hydration [haɪ'dreɪʃən] *s.* (quím.) hidratación.
hydraulic [-'drɔlɪk, -'drɑ-, B -'drɔ-] **hydraulical** [-lɪkəl] *a.* hidráulico.
hydraulically [-kəlɪ] *adv.* hidráulicamente.
hydraulic brake, freno hidráulico.
hydraulic jack, gato hidráulico.
hydraulic lime, cal hidráulica.
hydraulic press, prensa hidráulica.
hydraulic ram, (ing.) ariete hidráulico.
hydraulics [-lɪks] *s. pl.* (*sing. o pl. en const.*) (fís.) hidráulica.
hydraulic turbine, turbina hidráulica.
hydrazine ['haɪdrəˌzin, B -ˌzaɪn] *s.* (quím.) hidrazina.
hydrazoic [ˌhaɪdrə'zoʊɪk] *a.* (quím.) hidrazoico.
hydremia [haɪ'drimɪə] *s.* (med.) hidrohemia, hidremia.
hydria ['haɪdrɪə] *s.* (hist.) hidria, antigua ánfora romana.
hydric [-drɪk] *a.* (quím.) hídrico.
hydride [-ˌdraɪd] *s.* (quím.) hidruro.
hydriodic [ˌhaɪdrɪ'ɑdɪk, B -'ɔd-] *a.* (quím.) hidriódico, yodhídrico.
hydriodic acid, (quím.) ácido hidriódico o yodhídrico.
hydro ['haɪdroʊ] *a.* hidroeléctrico.
hydro ['haɪdroʊ] *s.* (fam., G.B.) balneario de aguas medicinales; instituto hidroterápico.
hydro-airplane [ˌhaɪdroʊ'ɛrˌpleɪn, B -'ɛəˌ-] *s.* hidroplano, hidroavión.
hydrobomb ['haɪdroʊˌbɑm, B -ˌbɔm] *s.* torpedo lanzado al agua desde un avión.
hydrobromic [ˌhaɪdrə'broʊmɪk, B 'haɪ-] *a.* (quím.) hidrobrómico, bromhídrico.
hydrobromic acid, (quím.) ácido hidrobrómico o bromhídrico.
hydrobromide [-'broʊˌmaɪd] *s.* (quím.) bromhidrato.
hydrocarbon [-'kɑrbən, B -'kɑbən] *s.* (quím.) hidrocarburo.
hydrocele ['haɪdrəˌsil] *s.* (med.) hidrocele.
hydrocephaloid [ˌhaɪdrə'sɛfəˌlɔɪd] *a.* (med.) hidrocefaloide.
hydrocephalous [-'sɛfələs] *a.* (med.) hidrocéfalo, hidrocefálico.
hydrocephalus [-ləs] *s.* (med.) hidrocefalía.
hydrocephaly [-lɪ] *s.* (med.) hidrocefalía.
hydrochloric [-'klɔrɪk] *a.* (quím.) clorhídrico, hidroclórico.
hydrochloric acid, (quím.) ácido clorhídrico o hidroclórico.
hydrochloride [-ˌaɪd] *s.* (quím.) clorhidrato, hidroclorato.
hydrocortisone [ˌhaɪdrə'kɔrtəˌsoʊn, B -'kɔtɪˌzoʊn] *s.* (bioquím.) hidrocortisona.
hydrocyanic [-droʊsaɪ'ænɪk] *a.* (quím.) cianhídrico o prúsico.
hydrocyanic acid, ácido cianhídrico o prúsico.
hydrodynamic [-daɪ'næmɪk, B 'haɪ-] **hydrodynamical** [-ɪkəl] *a.* (fís.) hidrodinámico.
hydrodynamics [-ɪks] *s. pl.* (*sing. o pl. en const.*) (fís.) hidrodinámica.
hydroelectric [ˌhaɪdroʊɪ'lɛktrɪk] *a.* hidroeléctrico.
hydroelectricity [-ɪˌlɛk'trɪsətɪ] *s.* hidroelectricidad.
hydroelectric power station, central hidroeléctrica.
hydrofluoric [-flu'ɔrɪk] *a.* (quím.) fluorhídrico.
hydrofluoric acid, (quím.) ácido fluorhídrico.
hydrofoil ['haɪdrəˌfɔɪl] *s.* 1. (fís.) plano hidrodinámico. 2. aleta del submarino. 3. (mar.) hidrofoil, aereodeslizador.
hydroforming [-ˌfɔrmɪŋ, B -ˌfɔm-] *s.* hidroformación (de gasolina).
hydrogen ['haɪdrədʒən] *s.* (quím.) hidrógeno.
hydrogenate [haɪ'drɑdʒəˌneɪt, 'haɪdrədʒə-, B haɪ'drɔdʒ-] *v.t.* (quím.) hidrogenar, combinar con hidrógeno.
hydrogenation [haɪˌdrɑdʒə'neɪʃən, ˌhaɪdrədʒə-, B haɪˌdrɔdʒ-] *s.* (quím.) hidrogenación.
hydrogen bomb, bomba de hidrógeno, bomba H.
hydrogen ion, (quím.) hidrogenión, ión hidrógeno.
hydrogenous [haɪ'drɑdʒənəs, B -'drɔdʒ-] *a.* hidrogenado.
hydrogen peroxide, (quím.) agua oxigenada, peróxido de hidrógeno.
hydrogen sulfide, (quím.) sulfuro de hidrógeno, ácido sulfhídrico.
hydrographer [haɪ'drɑgrəfər, B -'drɔgrəfə] *s.* hidrógrafo.
hydrographic [ˌhaɪdrə'græfɪk] **hydrographical** [-ɪkəl] *a.* hidrográfico.
hydrography [haɪ'drɑgrəfɪ, B -'drɔg-] *s.* hidrografía.
hydroid ['haɪˌdrɔɪd] *a., s.* (zool.) hidroideo.
hydrokinetic [ˌhaɪdroʊkə'nɛtɪk] *a.* (fís.) hidrocinético.
hydrokinetics [-ɪks] *s. pl.* (*sing. o pl. en const.*) hidrocinética.
hydrologic [-drə'lɑdʒɪk, B -'lɔdʒ-] **hydrological** [-ɪkəl] *a.* hidrológico.
hydrologist [haɪ'drɑlədʒəst, B -'drɔl-] *s.* hidrólogo.
hydrology [-dʒɪ] *s.* hidrología.
hydrolysis [-səs] *s.* (*pl.* HYDROLYSES [-ˌsiz]) (quím.) hidrólisis.
hydrolyte ['haɪdrəˌlaɪt] *s.* substancia hidrolizada.
hydrolytic [ˌhaɪdrə'lɪtɪk] *a.* hidrolítico.
hydrolyzable ['haɪdrəˌlaɪzəbəl] *a.* (quím.) hidrolizable.
hydrolyze [-ˌlaɪz] *v.t., v.i.* (quím.) hidrolizar(se).
hydromancer [-ˌmænsər, B -sə] *s.* hidromántico.
hydromancy [-sɪ] *s.* hidromancia, hidromancía.
hydromechanical [ˌhaɪdroʊmə'kænɪkəl, B 'haɪ-] *a.* hidromecánico.
hydromechanics [-ɪks] *s. pl.* (*sing. o pl. en const.*) hidromecánica.
hydromedusa [-mə'dusə, B -'djusə] *s.* (*pl.* HYDROMEDUSAE [-ˌsi]) (zool.) hidromedusa.
hydromel ['haɪdrəˌmɛl] *s.* hidromel, hidromiel, aguamiel.
hydrometallurgical [ˌhaɪdrəˌmɛtə'lɜrdʒɪkəl, B -'lədʒɪ-] *a.* hidrometalúrgico.
hydrometallurgy [-'mɛtəlˌɜrdʒɪ, B -ˌədʒɪ] *s.* hidrometalurgia.
hydrometeor [-'mitɪər, B -ɪə] *s.* (meteor.) hidrometeoro.
hydrometeorology [-ˌmitɪə'rɑlədʒɪ, B -'rɔl-] *s.* hidrometeorología.
hydrometer [haɪ'drɑmətər, B -'drɔmɪtə] *s.* (fís.) areómetro, hidrómetro, densímetro de flotación.
hydrometric [ˌhaɪdrə'mɛtrɪk] **hydrometrical** [-trɪkəl] *a.* (fís.) areométrico, hidrométrico.
hydrometry [haɪ'drɑmətrɪ, B -'drɔm-] *s.* (fís.) areometría.
hydropath ['haɪdrəˌpæθ] *s.* (med.) hidrópata.
hydropathic [ˌhaɪdrə'pæθɪk] *a.* (med.) hidropático.
hidropathist [haɪ'drɑpəθəst, B -'drɔp-] *s.* (med.) hidrópata.
hydropathy [-θɪ] *s.* (med.) hidropatía.
hydrophane ['haɪdrəˌfeɪn] *s.* (min.) hidrófana.
hydrophilic [ˌhaɪdrə'fɪlɪk] **hydrophile** ['haɪdrəˌfaɪl] *a.* hidrofílico, hidrófilo.
hydrophilous [haɪ'drɑfələs, B -'drɔf-] *a.* (bot.) 1. hidrófilo. 2. hidrófito.
hydrophobe ['haɪdrəˌfoʊb] *s.* hidrófobo.
hydrophobia [ˌhaɪdrə'foʊbɪə] *s.* (med.) hidrofobia.
hydrophobic [-'foʊbɪk, -'fɑbɪk, B -'foʊbɪk] *a.* (med.) hidrofóbico, hidrófobo.
hydrophone ['haɪdrəˌfoʊn] *s.* (mar., hidr.) hidrófono.
hydrophyte [-ˌfaɪt] *s.* (bot.) hidrófita.
hydrophytic [ˌhaɪdrə'fɪtɪk] *a.* (bot.) hidrófito.
hydropic [haɪ'drɑpɪk, B -'drɔp-] *a.* (med.) hidrópico.
hydroplane ['haɪdrəˌpleɪn] *s.* 1. hidroplano (embarcación). 2. hidroavión, hidroplano; aleta de submarino. —*v.i.* deslizarse como un hidroplano; guiar (o viajar en) un hidroavión.
hydroponic [ˌhaɪdrə'pɑnɪk, B -'pɔn-] *a.* hidropónico.
hydroponics [-ɪks] *s. pl.* (*sing. o pl. en const.*) hidroponía, hidroponia, quimiocultura.
hydroponist [haɪ'drɑpənəst, B -'drɔp-] *s.* especialista en hidroponía.
hydropower ['haɪdrəˌpaʊər, B -ə] *s.* fuerza hidroeléctrica.
hydrops ['haɪˌdrɑps, B -ˌdrɔps] **hydropsy** [-ˌdrɑpsɪ, B -ˌdrɔp-] *s.* (med.) hidropesía.
hydroquinone [ˌhaɪdroʊkwɪ'noʊn, B 'haɪ-] *s.* (quím.) hidroquinona.
hydroscope ['haɪdrəˌskoʊp] *s.* hidroscopio.
hydrosilicate [ˌhaɪdrə'sɪləkət, -ˌkeɪt] *s.* (quím.) hidrosilicato.
hydrosol ['haɪdrəˌsɑl, B -ˌsɔl] *s.* (quím.) hidrosol.
hydrosphere [-ˌsfɪr, B -ˌsfɪə] *s.* hidrosfera.
hydrostat [-ˌstæt] *s.* hidrostato.
hydrostatic [ˌhaɪdrə'stætɪk] **hydrostatical** [-ɪkəl] *a.* hidrostático.
hydrostatic balance, balanza hidrostática.
hydrostatic joint, conexión hidrostática.
hydrostatics [-ɪks] *s. pl.* (*sing. o pl. en const.*) (fís.) hidrostática.
hydrosulfide [-'sʌlˌfaɪd] *s.* (quím.) hidrosulfuro, sulfhidrato.
hydrosulfite [-'faɪt] *s.* (quím.) hidrosulfito.
hydrosulfurous [ˌhaɪdroʊ'sʌlfərəs, -ˌsʌl'fjʊr-, B 'haɪ-'fjʊər-] *a.* (quím.) hidrosulfuroso.
hydrotaxis [-'tæksəs] *s.* (biol.) hidrotaxismo, hidrotaxis.
hydrotechny ['haɪdrəˌtɛknɪ] *s.* hidrotecnia.
hydrotherapeutic [ˌhaɪdroʊˌθɛrə'pjutɪk] *a.* (med.) hidroterápico.

hydrotherapeutics [-ɪks] *s. pl.* (*sing. o pl. en const.*) (med.) hidroterapia.
hydrotherapist [-'θɛrəpəst] *s.* hidrópata.
hydrotherapy [-pɪ] *s.* (med.) hidroterapia, hidiatría, hidropatía.
hydrothermal [-'θɝrməl, B -'θɜməl] *a.* hidrotermal, hidrotérmico.
hydrothoracic [-θə'ræsɪk] *a.* (med.) hidrotorácico.
hydrothorax [ˌhaɪdrə'θɔrˌæks] *s.* (med.) hidrotórax.
hydrotropic [-'trɑpɪk, B -'trɔp-] *a.* (biol.) hidrotrópico.
hydrotropism [haɪ'drɑtrəˌpɪzəm, B -'drɔt-] *s.* (biol.) hidrotropismo.
hydrous ['haɪdrəs] *a.* 1. acuoso, aguado. 2. (quím., min.) hidratado.
hydroxide [haɪ'drɑkˌsaɪd, B -'drɔk-] *s.* (quím.) hidróxido.
hydroxide ion, (quím.) ión hidroxilo u oxhidrilo.
hydroxyl [-səl] *s.* (quím.) hidroxilo, oxhidrilo.
hydroxylamine [-ˌdrɑksələ'min, B -'drɔkˌ-maɪn] *s.* (quím.) hidroxilamina.
hydrozoan [ˌhaɪdrə'zoʊən] *s., a.* (zool.) hidrozoo, hidrozoario.
hyena [haɪ'inə] *s.* (zool.) hiena.
hyetal ['haɪətəl] *a.* relativo a la lluvia.
hyetograph ['haɪətəˌgræf, B -ˌgrɑf] *s.* 1. hietógrafo, pluviógrafo. 2. mapa pluviométrico.
hyetographic [ˌhaɪətə'græfɪk] **hyetographical** [-ɪkəl] *a.* hietográfico.
hyetography [-'tɑgrəfɪ, B -'tɔg-] *s.* hietografía.
hyetology [-'tɑlədʒɪ, B -'tɔl-] *s.* hietología.
Hygeia [haɪ'dʒiə] *s.* (mitol.) Higía, diosa griega de la salud.
hygiene ['haɪˌdʒin] *s.* higiene.
hygienic [ˌhaɪdʒɪ'ɛnɪk, haɪ'dʒɛn-, B -'dʒin-] **hygienical** [-ɪkəl] *a.* higiénico.
hygienically [-ɪkəlɪ] *adv.* higiénicamente.
hygienics [-ɪks] *s.* higiene.
hygienist [haɪ'dʒinəst, B 'haɪdʒɪən-] *s.* higienista.
hygrograph ['haɪgrəˌgræf, B -ˌgrɑf] *s.* higrógrafo, higrómetro.
hygrometer [haɪ'grɑmətər, B -'grɔmɪtə] *s.* higrómetro.
hygrometric [ˌhaɪgrə'mɛtrɪk] *a.* higrométrico.
hygrometry [haɪ'grɑmətrɪ, B -'grɔm-] *s.* higrometría.
hygrophyte ['haɪgrəˌfaɪt] *s.* (bot.) higrófito, hidrófita.
hygrophytic [ˌhaɪgrə'fɪtɪk] *a.* (bot.) higrófito.
hygroscope ['haɪgrəˌskoʊp] *s.* higroscopio, instrumento que mide la humedad del aire.
hygroscopic [ˌhaɪgrə'skɑpɪk, B -'skɔp-] **hygroscopical** [-ɪkəl] *a.* higroscópico.
hygroscopicity [-skoʊ'pɪsətɪ] *s.* (fís.) higroscopicidad.
hygrothermograph [ˌhaɪgroʊ'θɝrməˌgræf, B -'θɜməˌgrɑf] *s.* (fís.) higrotermógrafo.
hyla ['haɪlə] *s.* (zool.) rana arbórea, rana de San Antonio.
hylomorphism [ˌhaɪlə'mɔrˌfɪzəm, B -'mɔˌ-] *s.* hilomorfismo.
hylotheism [-'θiˌɪzəm] *s.* (filos.) hiloteísmo.
hylozoism [-'zoʊˌɪzəm] *s.* hilozoísmo.
hylozoist [-əst] *s.* hilozoísta.
hymen ['haɪmən, B -mɛn] *s.* 1. (anat.) himen. 2. (ant.) himeneo, boda, casamiento. 3. (mitol.) **H.,** Himeneo, dios griego del matrimonio.
hymenal [-əl] *a.* (anat.) himenal.
hymeneal [ˌhaɪmə'niəl] *a.* nupcial. —*s.* (ant.) 1. (*pl.*) himeneo. 2. himno nupcial, epitalamio.
hymenium [haɪ'minɪəm] *s.* (*pl.* HYMENIA [-nɪə] o HYMENIUMS) (bot.) himenio.
Hymenoptera [ˌhaɪmə'nɑptərə, B -'nɔp-] *s. pl.* (ento.) himenópteros.
hymenopteran [-rən] *a., s.* (ento.) himenóptero.
hymenopteron [-ˌrɑn, B -rən] *s.* (*pl.* HYMENOPTERA [-tərə]) (ento.) himenóptero, insecto himenóptero.
hymenopterous [-rəs] *a.* (ento.) himenóptero.
hymn [hɪm] *s.* himno. —*v.t.* alabar con himnos; cantar (elogios, alabanzas, etc.) en himnos. —*v.i.* cantar himnos.
hymnal ['hɪmnəl] *a.* hímnico. —*s.* himnario.
hymnbook [-ˌbʊk] *s.* libro de himnos; himnario.
hymnist [-nəst] *s.* himnista.
hymnodist [-nədəst] *s.* himnoda.
hymnody [-nədɪ] *s.* 1. arte de cantar himnos. 2. colección de himnos (de una iglesia, época, etc.).
hymnologist [hɪm'nɑlədʒəst, B -'nɔl-] *s.* himnólogo.
hymnology [-dʒɪ] *s.* 1. himnología. 2. colección de himnos.
hyoglossal [ˌhaɪoʊ'glɑsəl, -'glɔs-, B -'glɔs-] *a.* (anat.) hiogloso.
hyoglossus [-əs] *s.* (*pl.* HYOGLOSSI [-aɪ]) (anat.) hiogloso.
hyoid ['haɪˌɔɪd] *a.* (anat., zool.) hioide, hioideo. —*s.* hioides, hueso hioides.
hyoid bone, (anat.) hueso hioides.
hyoscine ['haɪəˌsin, B -ˌsaɪn] *s.* (quím.) hioscina.
hyoscyamine [ˌhaɪə'saɪəˌmin, B -ˌmaɪn] *s.* (quím.) hiosciamina.
hyp. *abrev. de* **hypotenuse,** hipotenusa; **hypothesis,** hipótesis; **hypothetical,** hipotético.
hypaesthesia, hypaesthesic, *vars. de* **hypesthesia, hypesthesic.**
hypaethral [hɪp'iθrəl] *var. de* **hypetral.**
hypallage [haɪ'pælədʒɪ] *s.* (ret.) hipálage.
hypanthium [haɪ'pænθɪəm] *s.* (*pl.* HYPANTHIA [-θɪə]) (bot.) hipantio.
hype [haɪp] *s.* (jer.) 1. jeringa hipodérmica; inyección. 2. narcómano. —*v.t.* (jer.) excitar por medio de una inyección de droga estimulante.
hyperacid [ˌhaɪpər'æsəd] *a.* excesivamente ácido.
hyperacidity [-ə'sɪdətɪ] *s.* (med.) hiperacidez.
hyperactive [-'æktɪv] *a.* (med.) hiperactivo.
hyperaemia, hyperaemic, *vars. de* **hyperemia, hyperemic.**
hyperaesthesia, hyperaesthetic, *vars. de* **hyperesthesia, hyperesthetic.**
hyperalgesia [-æl'dʒizɪə] *s.* (med.) hiperalgesia.
hyperalgesic [-zɪk, B -'dʒɛsɪk] *a.* (med.) hiperalgésico.
hyperbatic [ˌhaɪpər'bætɪk, B -pə'-] *a.* (gram.) hiperbático.
hyperbaton [haɪ'pɝrbəˌtɑn, B -'pɜbəˌtɔn] *s.* (gram.) hipérbaton.
hyperbola [-bələ] *s.* (*pl.* HYPERBOLAS o HYPERBOLAE [-ˌli]) (geom.) hipérbola.
hyperbole [-bəlɪ] *s.* (ret.) hipérbole.
hyperbolic [ˌhaɪpər'bɑlɪk, B -pə'bɔl-] **hyperbolical** [-ɪkəl] *a.* (mat., ret.) hiperbólico.
hyperbolism [haɪ'pɝrbəˌlɪzəm, B -'pɜbə-] *s.* (ret.) uso frecuente de la hipérbole.
hyperboloid [-ˌlɔɪd] *s.* (geom.) hiperboloide.
hyperborean [ˌhaɪpər'bɔrɪən, B -pə'-] *a.* hiperbóreo.
hypercatalectic [-ˌkætəl'ɛktɪk] *a.* (poét.) hipercataléctico.
hyperchlorhydria [-ˌklɔr'haɪdrɪə, B -klɔ'-] *s.* (med.) hiperclorhidria.
hypercritic [-'krɪtɪk] **hypercritical** [-ɪkəl] *a.* hipercrítico.
hypercritically [-ɪkəlɪ] *adv.* hipercríticamente.
hyperdulia [-du'laɪə, B -dju-] *s.* (relig.) hiperdulía.
hyperemia [ˌhaɪpər'imɪə] *s.* (med., fisiol.) hiperemia, plétora, congestión.
hyperemic [-'imɪk] *a.* (med., fisiol.) hiperémico.
hyperesthesia [-ɛs'θiʒə, B -ɪs'θizjə] *s.* (med.) hiperestesia.
hyperesthetic [-'θɛtɪk] *a.* (med.) hiperestético.
hypereutectic [ˌhaɪpərjʊ'tɛktɪk, B -pəjʊ-] *a.* (fís., metal., quím.) hipereutéctico.
hyperfocal [-'foʊkəl] *a.* (foto.) hiperfocal (distancia).
hypergeometric [-ˌdʒiə'mɛtrɪk] *a.* (mat.) hipergeométrico.
hyperglycemia [-ˌglaɪ'simɪə] *a.* (med.) hiperglicemia.
hyperinsulinism [ˌhaɪpər'ɪnsələnˌɪzəm, B -'ɪnsjʊ-] *s.* (med.) hiperinsulinismo.
Hyperion [haɪ'pɪrɪən, B -'pɪər-] *s.* (mitol., astr.) Hiperión.
hyperirritable [ˌhaɪpər'ɪrətəbəl] *a.* (med.) hiperirritable.
hyperkeratosis [-ˌkɛrə'toʊsəs, B -pəˌ-] *s.* (med.) hiperqueratosis.
hyperkinesis [-kɪ'nisəs] *s.* (med.) hipercinesis.
hypermetric [-'mɛtrɪk] **hypermetrical** [-trɪkəl] *a.* (poét.) hipermétrico, que tiene una sílaba redundante; que se excede de la medida.
hypermetropia [-mɪ'troʊpɪə] *s.* (med.) hipermetropía.
hypermetropy [-'mɛtrəpɪ] *s.* (med.) hipermetropía.
hypermnesia [ˌhaɪpərm'niʒə, B -pəm'-nizjə] *s.* (med.) hipermnesia.
hypermorph ['haɪpərˌmɔrf, B -pəˌmɔf] *s.* (med.) hipermorfo.
hyperon ['haɪpəˌrɑn, B -ˌrɔn] *s.* (fís.) hiperón.
hyperope [-ˌroʊp] *s.* (med.) hipérope, hipermétrope.
hyperopia [ˌhaɪpər'oʊpɪə] *s.* (med.) hiperopía, hiperopsia, hipermetropía.
hyperostosis [-ˌɑs'toʊsəs, B -ˌɔs-] *s.* (*pl.* HYPEROSTOSES [-ˌsiz]) (anat., med.) hiperostosis.
hyperphysical [-'fɪzɪkəl, B -pə'-] *a.* hiperfísico.
hyperpituitarism [-pɪ'tuətəˌrɪzəm, B -'tju-] *s.* (med.) hiperpituitarismo.
hyperplasia [-'pleɪʒə, B -zɪə] *s.* (med., biol.) hiperplasia.
hyperplastic [-'plæstɪk] *a.* hiperplástico.
hyperploid ['haɪpərˌplɔɪd, B -pəˌ-] *a.* (biol.) hiperploide.
hyperpnea, hyperpnoea [ˌhaɪpər'niə, B -pə'-] *s.* (fisiol.) hiperpnea.
hyperpyrexia [-paɪ'rɛksɪə] *s.* (med.) hiperpirexia, hipertermia.
hypersensitive [-'sɛnsətɪv] *a.* hipersensible.
hypersensitiveness [-nəs] **hypersensitivity** [-ˌsɛnsə'tɪvətɪ] *s.* hipersensibilidad, hipersensitividad, sensibilidad exagerada.
hypersonic [-'sɑnɪk, B -'sɔn-] *a.* hipersónico.
hypersthene ['haɪpərˌsθin, B -pəˌ-] *s.* (min.) hipersteno, hiperstena.
hypersthenic [ˌhaɪpər'sθɛnɪk, B -pə'-] *a.* (min.) hipersténico.
hypertension [-'tɛnʃən, B -'tɛnʃən] *s.* (med.) hipertensión.
hypertensive [-'tɛnsɪv] *a.* (med.) hipertensivo.
hyperthyroid [-'θaɪˌrɔɪd] *s.* persona que padece de hipertiroidismo.
hyperthyroidism [-ˌɪzəm] *s.* (med.) hipertiroidismo, hipertiroidia.
hypertonic [-'tɑnɪk, B -'tɔn-] *a.* (fís., quím.) hipertónico.

hypertonicity [-tə'nɪsətɪ] *s.* (fís., quím.) hipertonicidad.
hypertrophic [-'trɑfɪk, B -'trɔf-] *a.* (med., biol.) hipertrófico.
hypertrophied [haɪ'pɜrtrəfid, B -'pɜtrə-] *a.* (med., biol.) hipertrofiado.
hypertrophy [-fɪ] *s.* (med., biol.) hipertrofia. —*v.i.* hipertrofiarse.
hyperventilation [ˌhaɪpərˌvɛntəl'eɪʃən, B ˌhaɪpəˌ-] *s.* (med.) hiperventilación.
hypervitaminosis [-ˌvaɪtəmə'noʊsəs] *s.* (*pl.* HYPERVITAMINOSES [-ˌsiz]) (med.) hipervitaminosis.
hypesthesia [ˌhɪpɛs'θiʒə, B -zjə] *s.* (med.) hipestesia.
hypesthesic [-'θisɪk, B -'θiz-] *a.* (med.) hipestésico.
hypethral [hɪ'piθrəl] *a.* 1. (arq.) hipetro. 2. (fig.) al aire libre.
hypha ['haɪfə] *s.* (*pl.* HYPHAE [-fi]) (bot.) hifa.
hyphal [-fəl] *a.* (bot.) hifal.
hyphen ['haɪfən] *s.* guión. —*v.t.* unir con guión; separar con guión.
hyphenate [-fəˌneɪt] *v.t.* unir con guión; separar con guión; escribir con guión.
hyphenated American, (E.U.) norteamericano de origen extranjero.
hyphenation [ˌhaɪfə'neɪʃən] *s.* separación (de sílabas) con guiones; unión (de palabras) con guiones.
hyphenization [ˌhaɪfənə'zeɪʃən, B -naɪ-] *s.* separación (de sílabas) con guiones; unión (de palabras) con guiones.
hypnoanalisys [ˌhɪpnoʊə'næləsəs] *s.* hipnoanálisis.
hypnogenesis [-'dʒɛnəsəs] *s.* hipnogénesis.
hypnogenetic [-dʒə'nɛtɪk] *a.* hipnogénico, hipnógeno.
hypnoid ['hɪpˌnɔɪd] **hypnoidal** [hɪp'nɔɪdəl] *a.* hipnoide, hipnoideo.
hypnologic [ˌhɪpnə'lɑdʒɪk, B -'lɔdʒ-] **hypnological** [-ɪkəl] *a.* hipnológico.
hypnologist [hɪp'nɑlədʒəst, B -'nɔl-] *s.* hipnólogo.
hypnology [-dʒɪ] *s.* hipnología, ciencia que estudia el fenómeno del sueño.
hypnopompic [ˌhɪpnə'pɑmpɪk, B -'pɔm-] *a.* hipnopómpico.
Hypnos ['hɪpˌnɑs, B -ˌnɔs] *s.* (mitol.) Hipnos, el dios del sueño.
hypnosis [hɪp'noʊsəs] *s.* (*pl.* HYPNOSES [-ˌsiz]) hipnosis.
hypnotherapy [ˌhɪpnoʊ'θɛrəpɪ] *s.* (med.) hipnoterapia.
hypnotic [hɪp'nɑtɪk, B -'nɔt-] *a.* hipnótico. —*s.* 1. hipnótico. 2. persona hipnotizada.
hypnotically [-ɪkəlɪ] *adv.* hipnóticamente.
hypnotism ['hɪpnəˌtɪzəm] *s.* hipnotismo; hipnosis.
hypnotist [-təst] *s.* hipnotizador, hipnotista.
hypnotization [ˌhɪpnətə'zeɪʃən, B -taɪ-] *s.* hipnotización.
hypnotize ['hɪpnəˌtaɪz] *v.t., v.i.* hipnotizar.
hypnotizer ['hɪpnəˌtaɪzər, B -ə] *s.* hipnotizador.
hypo ['haɪpoʊ] *s.* 1. (foto.) hiposulfito de sodio (ú. como agente fijador). 2. (fam.) hipocondría.
hypo, *s.* (*pl.* HYPOS) (fam.) 1. *abrev. de* **hypodermic injection** o **hypodermic syringe.** 2. estímulo. —*v.t.* (fam.) estimular.
hypoblast ['haɪpəˌblæst] *s.* (embr., zool.) hipoblasto.
hypoblastic [ˌhaɪpə'blæstɪk] *a.* hipoblástico.
hypocaust ['haɪpəˌkɔst] *s.* (arqueol.) hipocausto.
hypocenter [ˌhaɪpoʊ'sɛntər, B -ə] *s.* (fís. nuclear) hipocentro.
hypochlorite [-pə'klɔrˌaɪt] *s.* (quím.) hipoclorito.
hypochlorous [-'klɔrəs] *a.* (quím.) hipocloroso.
hypochlorous acid, (quím.) ácido hipocloroso.
hypochondria [-'kɑndrɪə, B -'kɔn-] *s.* (med.) hipocondría.
hypochondriac [-ˌæk] *a.* 1. (anat., zool.) hipocóndrico. 2. (med.) hipocondríaco, hipocóndrico. —*s.* (med.) hipocondríaco.
hypochondriacal [-kən'draɪəkəl] *a.* (med.) hipocondríaco, hipocóndrico.
hypochondriasis [-'draɪəsəs] *s.* (med.) hipocondría.
hypochondrium [-'kɑndrɪəm, B -'kɔn-] *s.* (*pl.* HYPOCHONDRIA [-drɪə]) (anat., zool.) hipocondrio.
hypocorism [haɪ'pɑkəˌrɪzəm, B -'pɔk-] *s.* (nombre) hipocorístico.
hypocoristic [ˌhaɪpəkə'rɪstɪk] **hypocoristical** [-tɪkəl] *a.* hipocorístico.
hypocotyl ['haɪpəˌkɑtəl, B -ˌkɔt-] *s.* (bot.) hipocotíleo, hipocótilo.
hypocrisy [hɪ'pɑkrəsɪ, B -'pɔk-] *s.* hipocresía.
hypocrite ['hɪpəˌkrɪt] *s.* hipócrita.
hypocritical [ˌhɪpə'krɪtɪkəl] *a.* hipócrita.
hypocritically [-kəlɪ] *adv.* hipócritamente.
hypocycloid [ˌhaɪpə'saɪˌklɔɪd, B 'haɪ-] *s.* (geom.) hipocicloide.
hypocycloidal [-saɪ'klɔɪdəl] *a.* (geom.) hipocicloidal.
hypoderm ['haɪpəˌdɜrm, B -ˌdɜm] *s.* (bot., zool.) hipodermis.
hypodermal [ˌhaɪpə'dɜrməl, B -'dɜməl] *a.* 1. (bot.) hipodermo. 2. (fisiol.) hipodérmico.
hypodermic [-mɪk] *a.* (fisiol.) hipodérmico, subcutáneo. —*s. forma abrev. de* **hypodermic injection** o **hypodermic syringe**.
hypodermic injection, inyección hipodérmica.
hypodermic needle, aguja hipodérmica.
hypodermic syringe, jeringuilla hipodérmica.
hypodermis [-məs] *s.* (bot., zool.) hipodermis.
hypoeutectic [ˌhaɪpoʊjʊ'tɛktɪk] *a.* (fís.) hipoeutéctico.
hypogastric [-pə'gæstrɪk] *a.* (anat.) hipogástrico.
hypogastrium [-trɪəm] *s.* (*pl.* HYPOGASTRIA [-trɪə]) (anat.) hipogastrio.
hypogeal [-'dʒiəl] *a.* (bot.) hipogeo.
hypogene ['haɪpəˌdʒin] *a.* (geol.) hipogénico, hipógeno.
hypogenous [haɪ'pɑdʒənəs, B -'pɔdʒ-] *a.* (bot.) hipogeo.
hypogeous [ˌhaɪpə'dʒiəs] *a.* (bot.) hipogeo.
hypogeum [-'dʒiəm] *s.* (*pl.* HYPOGEA [-'dʒiə]) (arq.) hipogeo.
hypoglossal [-'glɑsəl, -'glɔs-, B -'glɔs-] *a.* (anat.) hipogloso.
hypoglycemia [-glaɪ'simɪə] *s.* (med.) hipoglicemia.
hypognathous [haɪ'pɑgnəθəs, B -'pɔg-] *a.* (anat.) hipognato.
hypogynous [-'pɑdʒənəs, B -'pɔdʒ-] *a.* (bot.) hipógino.
hypogyny [-nɪ] *s.* (bot.) hipoginia.
hypomania [ˌhaɪpə'meɪnɪə] *s.* (med.) hipomanía.
hypomanic [-'mænɪk] *a.* (med.) hipomaníaco.
hypomorph ['haɪpəˌmɔrf, B -ˌmɔf] *s.* (med.) endomorfo.
hyponastic [ˌhaɪpə'næstɪk] *a.* (bot.) hiponástico.
hyponasty ['haɪpəˌnæstɪ] *s.* (bot.) hiponastia.
hyponitrite [ˌhaɪpoʊ'naɪˌtraɪt] *s.* (quím.) hiponitrito.
hyponitrous [-'naɪtrəs] *a.* (quím.) hiponitroso.
hyponitrous acid, (quím.) ácido hiponitroso.
hypopharynx [-'færɪŋks] *s.* (ento.) hipofaringe.
hypophosphate [ˌhaɪpə'fɑsˌfeɪt, B -'fɔs-] *s.* (quím.) hipofosfato.
hypophosphite [-ˌfaɪt] *s.* (quím.) hipofosfito.
hypophosphoric acid [-ˌfɑs'fɔrɪk-, B -ˌfɔs-] (quím.) ácido hipofosfórico.
hypophosphorous [-'fɑsfərəs, -fɑs'fɔr-, B -'fɔsfər-] *a.* (quím.) hipofosforoso.
hypophosphorous acid, (quím.) ácido hipofosforoso.
hypophyseal [haɪˌpɑfə'siəl, B -pə'fɪzɪəl] *a.* (anat., med.) hipofisario.
hypophysis [-'pɑfəsəs, B -'pɔf-] *s.* (anat.) hipófisis.
hypopituitarism [ˌhaɪpoʊpɪ'tuətəˌrɪzəm, B -'tju-] *s.* (med.) hipopituitarismo.
hypoplasia [-pə'pleɪʒə, B -zjə] *s.* (med.) hipoplasia.
hypoplastic [-'plæstɪk] *a.* (med.) hipoplástico.
hypoploid ['haɪpəˌplɔɪd] *a.* (biol.) hipoploide.
hypopyon [haɪ'poʊpɪˌɑn, B -ˌɔn] *s.* (med.) hipopión.
hyposensitize [ˌhaɪpoʊ'sɛnsəˌtaɪz] *v.t.* reducir la sensibilidad, desensibilizar.
hypostasis [haɪ'pɑstəsəs, B -'pɔs-] *s.* (*pl.* HYPOSTASES [-ˌsiz]) (teol., filos., med.) hipóstasis.
hypostatic [ˌhaɪpə'stætɪk] *a.* (filos., med.) hipostático; (teol.) (t. **hypostatical** [-ɪkəl]) hipostático.
hypostatization [haɪˌpɑstətə'zeɪʃən, B -ˌpɔstətaɪ-] *s.* (filos.) hipostatización.
hypostatize [-'pɑstəˌtaɪz, B -'pɔs-] *v.t.* (filos.) objetivar, atribuir existencia real a.
hyposthenia [-pə'sθinɪə] *s.* (med.) hipostenia.
hypostyle ['haɪpəˌstaɪl] *a.* (arq.) hipóstilo.
hyposulfite [ˌhaɪpə'sʌlˌfaɪt] *s.* (quím.) hiposulfito.
hyposulfurous [-sʌl'fjʊrəs, B -'sʌlfərəs] *a.* (quím.) hiposulfuroso.
hyposulfurous acid, (quím.) ácido hiposulfuroso.
hypotaxis [-'tæksəs] *s.* (gram.) hipotaxis.
hypotensión [-'tɛntʃən, B -'tɛnʃən] *s.* (med.) hipotensión.
hypotensive [-'tɛnsɪv] *a.* (med.) hipotensivo.
hypotenuse [haɪ'pɑtənˌus, B -'pɔtɪnˌjuz] **hypothenuse** [-'pɑθ-, B -'pɔθ-] *s.* (geom.) hipotenusa.
hypothalamus [ˌhaɪpoʊ'θæləməs] *s.* (*pl.* HYPOTHALAMI [-maɪ]) (anat.) hipotálamo.
hypothec [haɪ'pɑθɪk, B 'haɪpəθɛk] *s.* (der.) hipoteca.
hypothecary [-'pɑθəˌkɛrɪ, B -'pɔθɪkərɪ] *a.* (der.) hipotecario.
hypothecate [-ˌkeɪt] *v.t.* (der.) hipotecar, empeñar, pignorar.
hypothecation [-ˌpɑθə'keɪʃən, B -ˌpɔθ-] *s.* (der.) pignoración.
hypothecator [-'pɑθəˌkeɪtər, B -'pɔθ-ə] *s.* (der.) hipotecante.
hypothermia [ˌhaɪpə'θɜrmɪə, B -'θɜmɪə] **hypothermy** ['haɪpəˌθɜrmɪ, B -ˌθɜmɪ] *s.* hipotermia.
hypothesis [haɪ'pɑθəsəs, B -'pɔθ-] *s.* (*pl.* HYPOTHESES [-ˌsiz]) hipótesis.
hypothetic [ˌhaɪpə'θɛtɪk] **hypothetical** [-ɪkəl] *a.* hipotético.
hypothetically [-ɪkəlɪ] *adv.* hipotéticamente.
hypothyroid [ˌhaɪpoʊ'θaɪˌrɔɪd] *s.* (med.) hipotiroide, hipotiroideo.
hypothyroidism [-ˌɪzəm] *s.* (med.) hipotiroidismo, hipotiroidia.

hypotonic [-pə'tɑnɪk, B -'tɔn-] *a.* (fisiol.) hipotónico.
hypotonicity [-tə'nɪsətɪ] *s.* (fisiol.) hipotonía.
hypoxanthine [-poʊ'zæn,θin, B -'sæn,θaɪn] *s.* (quím.) hipoxantina.
hypoxia [haɪ'pɑksɪə, B -'pɔk-] *s.* (fisiol.) hipoxia, anoxemia moderada.
hypsographic [,hɪpsə'græfɪk] **hypsographical** [-ɪkəl] *a.* (geog.) hipsográfico.
hypsography [hɪp'sɑgrəfɪ, B -'sɔg-] *s.* (geog.) hipsografía.
hypsometer [-'sɑmətər, B -'sɔmɪtə] *s.* hipsómetro.
hypsometric [,hɪpsə'mɛtrɪk] *a.* hipsométrico.
hypsometry [hɪp'sɑmətrɪ, B -'sɔm-] *s.* hipsometría.
hyrax ['haɪr,æks, B 'haɪər-] *s.* (*pl.* HYRAXES o HYRACES [-ə,siz]) (zool.) hiráceo.
hyson ['haɪsən] *s.* té chino, té verde.
hyssop ['hɪsəp] *s.* 1. (bot.) hisopo. 2. (relig.) hisopo; aspersorio.
hysterectomize [,hɪstə'rɛktə,maɪz] *v.t.* extirpar el útero.
hysterectomy [-mɪ] *s.* (med.) histerectomía.
hysteresis [-'risəs] *s.* (*pl.* HYSTERESES) (fís.) histéresis.
hysteria [hɪs'tɛrɪə, -'tɪr-, B -'tɪər-] *s.* histeria; (med.) histerismo.
hysteric [-'tɛrɪk] *a.* histérico.
hysterical [-ɪkəl] *a.* 1. histérico. 2. sumamente emocional, violento.
hysterically [-kəlɪ] *adv.* de modo histérico.
hysterics [-ɪks] *s. pl.* (*sing. o pl. en const.*) ataque histérico.
hysterogenic [,hɪstəroʊ'dʒɛnɪk] *a.* (med.) histerógeno, histerogénico.
hysteroid ['hɪstə,rɔɪd] *a.* histeroide, histeroideo.
hysteron proteron [-,rɑn'prɑtə,rɑn, B -,rɔn'prɔtə,rɔn] (gram.) histerología.
hysterotomy [,hɪstə'rɑtəmɪ, B -'rɔt-] *s.* (med.) histerotomía.
hyzone ['haɪ,zoʊn] *s.* (quím.) hizono.

I

I [aɪ] *s.* i, novena letra del alfabeto inglés.
I [aɪ] *pron.* yo; **it is I.,** soy yo; **the I,** (filos.) el ego, el yo.
I *símb. de* (quím.) **iodine,** yodo (I).
Ia. *abrev. de* **Iowa,** Iowa (E.U.).
IADB *abrev. de* **Inter-American Defense Board,** Junta Interamericana de Defensa.
IAEA *abrev. de* **International Atomic Energy Agency,** Organismo Internacional de Energía Atómica (OIEA).
iamb ['aɪæmb, 'aɪæm] *var. de* **iambus.**
iambic [aɪ'æmbɪk] *a.* (poét.) yámbico. —*s.* (poét.) pie yámbico; verso yámbico.
iambus [-bəs] *s.* (*pl.* IAMBUSES o IAMBI [-ˌbaɪ]) (poét.) yambo.
Iapygia [ˌaɪə'pɪdʒɪə] *s.* (astr.) apygia, área del hemisferio austral de Marte.
IAS *abrev. de* **indicated airspeed,** velocidad relativa indicada.
IATA *abrev. de* **International Air Transport Association,** Asociación Internacional de Transporte Aéreo.
iatric [aɪ'ætrɪk] **iatrical** [-trɪkəl] *a.* médico, relativo a la medicina y a los medicamentos.
iatrogenic [aɪˌætrə'dʒɛnɪk] *a.* (med.) yatrogénico.
I beam, (const.) viga I, tirante I, viga doble T.
Iberia [aɪ'bɪrɪə, B -'bɪər-] *s.* Iberia, península ibérica (España y Portugal); nombre antiguo y poético de España.
Iberian [-ɪən] *a.* ibérico, ibero, iberio. —*s.* ibero.
Ibero-America [-oʊə'mɛrəkə] *s.* Iberoamérica.
Ibero-American [-kən] *a.* iberoamericano.
ibex ['aɪˌbɛks] *s.* (*pl.* IBEXES o IBICES [-bə-ˌsiz]) (zool.) íbice, cabra montés.
ibidem ['ɪbɪdəm, B ɪ'baɪdɛm] *adv.* (lat.) ibídem, allí mismo.
ibis ['aɪbəs] *s.* (*pl.* IBIS o IBISES) (orn.) ibis.
IBM *abrev. de* **International Business Machines,** Compañía Internacional de Máquinas de Oficina.
Ibsenism ['ɪbsəˌnɪzəm] *s.* ibsenismo, afición a las obras de Ibsen.
icaco plum [ɪ'kækoʊˌplʌm] (bot.) hicaco, icaco (planta y fruto).
ICAO *abrev. de* **International Civil Aviation Organization,** Organización de Aviación Civil Internacional (OACI).
Icarian [ɪ'kɛrɪən, aɪ-, B ɪ'kɛər-] *a.* 1. icario, icáreo. 2. (fig.) inadecuado; arriesgado.
Icarus ['ɪkərəs, B 'aɪk-] *s.* (mitol.) Icaro (personaje que intentando volar con alas de cera, cayó al mar, al derretirse éstas por el calor del sol).
ICBM *abrev. de* **intercontinental ballistic missile,** proyectil balístico intercontinental.
ice [aɪs] *s.* 1. hielo. 2. (t. *pl.*) granizado, sorbete. 3. (G.B.) helado. 4. (cocina) garapiña; capa dura de azúcar (hecha con clara de huevo). 5. (fig.) hielo, frialdad. 6. (jer.) diamantes; joyas. 7. **on thin i.,** en una situación precaria; **to break the i.,** (fig.) romper el hielo; abrir camino (siendo el primero en hacer algo); **to cut no i.,** (fam.) no surtir efecto; no importar nada; **to have on i.,** (jer.) tener asegurado, tener en el bolsillo (éxito, triunfo, etc.); **to keep on i.,** mantener helado (algo); (jer.) tener encarcelado (a alguien); **to put on i.,** (fam.) postergar. —*v.t.* 1. helar, refrigerar. 2. cubrir con hielo. 3. congelar. 4. (cocina) garapiñar; cubrir (pastel) con capa dura de azúcar. —*v.i.* 1. helarse. 2. (t. con *up*) cubrirse de hielo. —*a.* de hielo; glacial.
ice age, (geol.) período glaciar.
ice ax, pico de alpinista.
ice bag, (med.) bolsa de hielo, bolsa (de caucho) para hielo.
iceberg ['aɪsˌbɜrg, B -ˌbɜg] *s.* 1. iceberg, témpano de hielo flotante. 2. (fam.) témpano (persona muy reservada o fría).
iceblink [-ˌblɪŋk] *s.* resplandor en el horizonte debido a los hielos.
iceboat [-ˌboʊt] *s.* 1. (dep.) embarcación con patines, velero sobre hielo. 2. barco rompehielos, cortahielos.
icebound [-ˌbaʊnd] *a.* cercado por el hielo, detenido por el hielo.
icebox [-ˌbɑks, B -ˌbɔks] *s.* nevera, heladera (Am.), refrigerador(a) (Am.).
icebreaker [-ˌbreɪkər, B -kə] *s.* 1. rompehielos, cortahielos. 2. tajamar, espolón (de un puente).
icecap [-ˌkæp] *s.* casquete polar; manto de hielo; helero.
ice-cold ['aɪs'koʊld] *a.* helado, frío como el hielo.
ice cream, helado, mantecado.
ice-cream cone [-'krim-] barquillo de helado, cono, cucurucho de helado.
ice-cream freezer, sorbetera, garapiñera.
ice-cream parlor, heladería, salón de helados.
ice-cream soda, gaseosa o agua carbónica con helado.
ice cube, cubito de hielo.
ice-cube tray, cubeta de hielo.
iced [aɪst] *a.* helado; congelado, refrigerado; garapiñado; cubierto (pastel) con una capa dura de azúcar, cubierto con alfeñique.
icefall ['aɪsˌfɔl] *s.* 1. catarata congelada. 2. bloques de hielo de un glaciar.
ice field, 1. banco extenso de hielo flotante. 2. manto grande de hielo; helero.
ice floe, banco de hielo flotante; témpano tabular; campo de hielo abierto.
ice foot, faja de hielo costera (que se forma en las zonas glaciales).
ice hazard, riesgo o peligro ocasionado por el hielo.
ice hockey, hockey sobre hielo; hockey sobre patines.
icehouse [-ˌhaʊs] *s.* nevera, depósito de hielo; fábrica de hielo.
Iceland ['aɪslənd] *s.* Islandia.
Icelander [-ləndər -ˌlæn-, B -də] *s.* islandés.
Icelandic [aɪs'lændɪk] *a.* islandés. —*s.* islandés (lengua de Islandia).
Iceland moss, (bot.) liquen o musgo de Islandia.
Iceland spar, (min.) espato de Islandia.
ice-maker ['aɪsˌmeɪkər, B -ə] *s.* máquina de hacer hielo.
iceman ['aɪsˌmæn, -mən] *s.* vendedor de hielo; repartidor de hielo.
ice needle, (meteor.) aguja de hielo.
Iceni [aɪ'sinaɪ] *s. pl.* (hist.) icenos (antigua tribu de los celtas britanos que se sublevó contra los romanos).
ice pack, 1. banco de témpanos o hielos flotantes. 2. compresa de hielo.
ice paper, papel escarchado.
ice pick, punzón para romper hielo.
ice plant, (bot.) escarchada.
ice point, (fís.) punto de congelación.
ice rink, pista de hielo.
ice sheet, helero; capa de hielo; casquete glaciar.
ice shelf, capa espesa de hielo que se forma a lo largo de las costas polares.
ice-skate ['aɪsˌskeɪt] *v.i.* patinar sobre el hielo. —*s.* patín para hielo.
ice skate, patín de cuchilla.
ice skater, patinador.
ice skating, patinaje sobre hielo.
ice storm, tormenta de hielo.
ice tray, recipiente o cubeta para hielo.
ice water, agua helada.
ichneumon [ɪk'numən, B -'nju-] *s.* 1. (zool.) mangosta egipcia; rata de faraón; meloncillo, melón. 2. (ento.) (t. **i. fly**) icneumón.
ichnite ['ɪkˌnaɪt] *s.* huella o pisada fosilizadas.
ichnography [ɪk'nɑgrəfɪ, B -'nɔg-] *s.* (arq.) icnografía, ignografía.
ichnology [-'nɑlədʒɪ, B -'nɔl-] *s.* (pal.) el estudio científico de las huellas fósiles.
ichor ['aɪˌkɔr, -kər, B -kɔ] *s.* 1. (med.) icor. 2. (mitol.) sangre de los dioses.
ichthyic ['ɪkθiɪk] *a.* íctico, característico de los peces.
ichthyoid ['ɪkθɪˌɔɪd] *a.* ictioideo.
ichthyol [-ˌoʊl, -ˌɑl, B -ˌɔl] *s.* (farm.) ictiol.
ichthyological [ˌɪkθɪə'lɑdʒɪkəl, B -'lɔdʒ-] *a.* ictiológico.
ichthyologist [-'ɑlədʒəst, B -'ɔl-] *s.* ictiólogo.
ichthyology [-dʒɪ] *s.* ictiología.
ichthyophagous [-'ɑfəgəs, B -'ɔf-] *a.* ictiófago, que se alimenta de peces.
ichthyophagy [-dʒɪ] *s.* ictiofagia, alimentación a base de peces.
ichthyornis [-'ɔrnəs, B -'ɔnɪs] *s.* (pal.) ictiornis, pájaro prehistórico.
ichthyosaur ['ɪkθɪəˌsɔr, B -ˌsɔ] **ichthyosaurian** [ˌɪkθɪə'sɔrɪən] *s.* (pal.) ictiosauro, reptil prehistórico.
ichthyosis [ˌɪkθɪ'oʊsəs] *s.* (med.) ictiosis.
ichu ['itʃu] *s.* (bot.) icho, ichu (Am.).
icicle ['aɪsɪkəl] *s.* carámbano, cerrión, canelón.
icily ['aɪsəlɪ] *adv.* fríamente, glacialmente; con frialdad; frígidamente.
iciness [-sɪnəs] *s.* frialdad; frigidez.
icing [-sɪŋ] *s.* 1. (cocina) alcorza, capa dura de azúcar (hecha con clara de huevo). 2. (aer.) formación de hielo (sobre las alas o cuerpo de un avión).
ICJ *abrev. de* **International Court of Justice,** Tribunal Internacional de Justicia.
icker ['ɪkər, B -ə] *s.* (esco.) espiga de avena u otro cereal.

icky ['ɪkɪ] *a.* 1. (jer.) desagradablemente pegajoso o viscoso; repulsivo. —*s.* (jer.) el murmullo de un bebé.
icon ['aɪˌkɑn, B -ˌkɔn] *s.* (*pl.* ICONS o ICONES ['aɪkəˌniz]) 1. (relig.) icono. 2. (fig.) ídolo, ideal.
iconic [aɪ'kɑnɪk, B -'kɔn-] *a.* icónico.
iconoclasm [-'kɑnəˌklæzəm, B -'kɔn-] *s.* iconoclasia, iconoclastia.
iconoclast [-ˌklæst] *s.* iconoclasta, iconómaco.
iconoclastic [-ˌkɑnə'klæstɪk, B -ˌkɔn-] *a.* iconoclasta.
iconographic [-'græfɪk] **iconographical** [-ɪkəl] *a.* iconográfico.
iconography [ˌaɪkə'nɑgrəfɪ, B -'nɔg-] *s.* (*pl.* ICONOGRAPHIES) iconografía.
iconolater [-'nɑlətər, B -'nɔlətə] *s.* iconólatra.
iconolatrous [-trəs] *a.* iconólatra, que adora los iconos.
iconolatry [-trɪ] *s.* iconolatría.
iconological [ˌaɪˌkɑnə'lɑdʒɪkəl, B -ˌkɔnə'-lɔdʒ-] *a.* iconológico.
iconology [-kə'nɑlədʒɪ, B -'nɔl-] *s.* iconología, estudio de los iconos y representaciones simbólicas.
iconoscope [aɪ'kɑnəˌskoʊp, B -'kɔn-] *s.* (t.v.) iconoscopio.
iconostasis [ˌaɪkə'nɑstəsəs, B -'nɔs-] *s.* (*pl.* ICONOSTASES [-ˌsiz]) (relig.) iconostasio.
icosahedron [aɪˌkoʊsə'hidrən, B 'aɪkəsə'-hɛ-] *s.* (*pl.* ICOSAHEDRONS o ICOSAHEDRA [-drə]) (geom.) icosaedro.
icteric [ɪk'tɛrɪk] *a.* (med.) ictérico.
icterus ['ɪktərəs] *s.* (med.) ictericia.
Ictinus [ɪk'taɪnəs] *s.* Ictino, arquitecto que diseñó el Partenón.
ictus ['ɪktəs] *s.* 1. (med.) paroxismo; pulsación, latido. 2. (poét.) ictus (acento tónico).
icy ['aɪsɪ] *a.* (ICIER; ICIEST) 1. cubierto de hielo (ej., los mares). 2. glacial, frígido, helado.
id [ɪd] *s.* 1. (psic.) id (lo verdaderamente inconsciente). 2. (med.) id (erupción cutánea).
I'd [aɪd] *contr. de* **I had, I should** o **I would.**
ID 1. *abrev. de* **identification,** identificación. 2. **Intelligence Departament,** Departamento de Inteligencia.
IDA *abrev. de* **International Development Association,** Asociación Internacional de Fomento o Desarrollo (AIF o AID).
Ida. *abrev. de* **Idaho,** Idaho (E.U.).
Idaho ['aɪdəˌhoʊ] *s.* Idaho, estado de los E.U.
idea [aɪ'diə] *s.* 1. idea, noción, concepto. 2. idea, plan, propósito, proyecto. 3. idea, ingenio, imaginación. 4. (filos.) idea. 5. **man of ideas,** hombre de idea o ideas, hombre de imaginación; **I haven't the faintest idea,** no tengo la menor idea; **what's the big idea?** (E.U.) ¿qué cosa estás tramando?
ideal [aɪ'diəl, B -'dɪ-] *a.* 1. ideal. 2. ideado, imaginario. —*s.* 1. ideal, dechado; modelo de perfección. 2. meta, fin.
idealism [-ˌɪzəm] *s.* idealismo.
idealist [-əst] *s., a.* idealista.
idealistic [aɪˌdiə'lɪstɪk] *a.* idealista.
idealistically [-tɪkəlɪ] *adv.* de modo idealista.
ideality [ˌaɪdɪ'ælətɪ] *s.* 1. idealidad. 2. ideal; producto de la imaginación.
idealization [aɪˌdiələ'zeɪʃən, B -ˌdɪəlaɪ-] *s.* idealización.
idealize [-'diəˌlaɪz, B -'dɪ-] *v.t.* idealizar. —*v.i.* trabajar de modo idealista.
idealizer [-ˌlaɪzər, B -ə] *s.* persona idealizadora.
ideally [-lɪ] *adv.* 1. idealmente, mentalmente. 2. a la perfección, perfectamente.
idealness [aɪ'diəlnəs] *s.* idealidad.
ideate ['aɪdɪˌeɪt] *v.t.* idear, concebir, pensar.
ideation [ˌaɪdɪ'eɪʃən] *s.* ideación.
ideational [-ʃənəl] *a.* ideacional, relativo a las ideas.
idée fixe [ˌideɪ'fiks] (fr.) idea fija, obsesión.
idem ['aɪdɛm] *pron.* (lat.) ídem, el mismo, lo mismo.
identical [aɪ'dɛntɪkəl] *a.* 1. idéntico, igual. 2. mismo, ej., *the i. house we saw on our first trip,* la misma casa que vimos en nuestro primer viaje. 3. (biol.) idéntico (mellizo o gemelo).
identically [-ɪkəlɪ] *adv.* idénticamente.
identicalness [-kəlnəs] *s.* identidad, igualdad.
identifiable [aɪ'dɛntəˌfaɪəbəl] *a.* identificable.
identification [-ˌdɛntəfə'keɪʃən] *s.* identificación.
identification papers, documentos de identificación.
identification tag, (mil.) placa de identidad, ficha o medalla de identificación.
identifier [aɪ'dɛntəˌfaɪər, B -ə] *s.* signo o medio de identificación.
identify [-ˌfaɪ] *v.t.* (*pret., p.p.* IDENTIFIED; *p.pr.* IDENTIFYING) 1. identificar. 2. **i. oneself with,** identificarse con; unirse a (un grupo de negocios, partido político, etc.).
identity [-'dɛntətɪ] *s.* identidad.
identity card, cédula de identidad, cédula de vecindad, cédula personal.
identity papers, documentos de identidad.
ideogram ['ɪdɪəˌgræm, 'aɪdɪə-] *s.* ideograma, símbolo que representa una idea o un objeto.
ideograph [-ˌgræf, B -ˌgrɑf] *s.* ideograma.
ideographical [ˌɪdɪə'græfɪkəl, ˌaɪd-] *a.* ideográfico (apl. a la escritura formada por ideogramas).
ideography [-'ɑgrəfɪ, B -'ɔg-] *s.* ideografía.
ideologic [ˌaɪdɪə'lɑdʒɪk, ˌɪd-, B -'lɔdʒ-] **ideological** [-ɪkəl] *s.* ideológico.
ideologist [-'ɑlədʒəst, B -'ɔl-] *s.* ideólogo.
ideologue ['aɪdɪəˌlɔg, 'ɪd-, -ˌlɑg, B -ˌlɔg] *s.* ideólogo.
ideology [ˌaɪdɪ'ɑlədʒɪ, ˌɪd-, B -'ɔl-] *s.* (*pl.* IDEOLOGIES) ideología.
ideomotor [ˌaɪdɪə'moʊtər, ˌɪd-, B -ə] *a.* (psic.) ideomotor, perteneciente a la actividad causada por una idea.
ides [aɪdz] *s. pl.* idus (en el antiguo cómputo romano el día 15 de marzo, mayo, julio y octubre y el 13 de los demás meses).
idioblast ['ɪdɪəˌblæst] *s.* (biol., bot.) idioblasto.
idiocy ['ɪdɪəsɪ] *s.* 1. (*pl.* IDEOCIES) idiotez, imbecilidad. 2. majadería, necedad.
idiographic [ˌɪdɪə'græfɪk] *a.* (psic.) idiográfico.
idiolect ['ɪdɪəˌlɛkt] *s.* idiología (modo de hablar individual).
idiom ['ɪdɪəm] *s.* 1. lenguaje, dialecto, jerga, idioma peculiar (de una nación, comunidad, clase, etc.). 2. modismo, locución. 3. uso idiomático (de una lengua). 4. estilo, expresión característica (de un escritor o artista).
idiomatic [ˌɪdɪə'mætɪk] *a.* idiomático.
idiomatically [-ɪkəlɪ] *adv.* de modo idiomático.
idiomorphic [-'mɔrfɪk, B -'mɔfɪk] *a.* (cristalografía, min.) idiomorfo.
idiopathic [-'pæθɪk] *a.* (med.) idiopático, de causa desconocida (enfermedad).
idiopathy [ˌɪdɪ'ɑpəθɪ, B -'ɔp-] *s.* (med.) idiopatía.
idiophone ['ɪdɪəˌfoʊn] *s.* (mús.) instrumento idiofono o de percusión, como el triángulo.
idiophonic [ˌɪdɪə'fɑnɪk, B -'fɔn-] *a.* idiofono.
idioplasm ['ɪdɪəˌplæzəm] *s.* (biol.) idioplasma.
idioplasmatic [ˌɪdɪəˌplæz'mætɪk] *a.* (biol.) idioplasmático.
idiosyncrasy [-'sɪŋkrəsɪ] *s.* (*pl.* IDIOSYNCRASIES) 1. idiosincrasia. 2. (med.) idiosincrasia, hipersensibilidad individual (a una droga, comida u otro agente).
idiosyncratic [-ˌsɪn'krætɪk, B -ˌsɪŋ-] *a.* (med.) idiosincrásico.
idiot ['ɪdɪət] *s.* idiota, imbécil, necio, majadero.
idiotic [ˌɪdɪ'ɑtɪk, B -'ɔt-] **idiotical** [-ɪkəl] *a.* idiota, tonto, imbécil, necio.
idiotism ['ɪdɪəˌtɪzəm] *s.* idiotismo, modismo.
idle ['aɪdəl] *a.* 1. ocioso, perezoso, indolente, haragán, inactivo. 2. desocupado, sin colocación; sin uso apropiado (fondos, horas). 3. inútil, vano. 4. **in i. moments,** a ratos perdidos. —*v.i.* 1. holgazanear, haraganear, estar ocioso, holgar. 2. (mot.) marchar en vacío. —*v.t.* gastar ociosamente; desperdiciar; **i. away,** desperdiciar ociosamente (el tiempo).
idle current, (elec.) corriente devatiada.
idle fellow, holgazán.
idle life, vida ociosa.
idle money, dinero muerto, que no devenga provecho.
idler ['aɪdlər, B -lə] *s.* 1. holgazán, perezoso. 2. (mec.) polea de tensión, polea de guía, polea muerta o loca; rueda loca, rueda guía, rueda intermedia o de transmisión, engranaje intermedio. 3. furgón vacío. 4. (mar.) tripulante que no hace guardias.
idler pulley, (mec.) polea de tensión, polea de guía, polea muerta o loca.
idler wheel, (mec.) rueda loca, rueda guía, rueda intermedia, rueda de transmisión, engranaje intermedio.
idlesse ['aɪdlɪs] *s.* (ant.) ociosidad, pereza.
idle story, cuento de viejas.
idly [-lɪ] *adv.* ociosamente, inútilmente, fútilmente.
idocrase ['aɪdəˌkreɪs] *s.* (min.) idocrasa, vesubianita.
idol ['aɪdəl] *s.* 1. ídolo. 2. (fig.) ídolo. 3. (lóg.) falacia, falsa concepción. 4. (ant.) imagen; impostor.
idolater [aɪ'dɑlətər, B -'dɔlətə] *s.* idólatra.
idolatress [-trəs] *s.* mujer idólatra.
idolatrize [-ˌtraɪz] *v.i.* adorar ídolos, practicar culto idolátrico. —*v.t.* idolatrar.
idolatrous [-trəs] *a.* idolátrico.
idolatrously [-lɪ] *adv.* idolatradamente.
idolatrousness [-nəs] *s.* devoción idólatra.
idolatry [aɪ'dɑlətrɪ B -'dɔl-] *s.* idolatría.
idolism ['aɪdəlˌɪzəm] *s.* 1. idolatría, adoración de ídolos. 2. falacia, pensamiento falso.
idolization [ˌaɪdələ'zeɪʃən, B -əlaɪ-] *s.* idolatría (amor excesivo).
idolize ['aɪdəlˌaɪz] *v.t.* idolatrar, amar o admirar ciegamente. —*v.i.* practicar la idolatría.
idolizer [-ər, B -ə] *s.* idólatra.
Idomeneus [aɪ'dɑməˌnus, B -'dɔmɪˌnjus] *s.* (mitol.) Idomeneo, rey de Creta en la guerra con Troya.
Idun ['idun] *s.* (mitol. escandinava) Idún, diosa de la juventud y la primavera.
idyl, idyll ['aɪdəl, B 'ɪdɪl] *s.* idilio.
idyllic [aɪ'dɪlɪk] *a.* idílico, pastoral, bucólico.
idyllically [-ɪkəlɪ] *adv.* idílicamente.
idyllist ['aɪdələst] *s.* poeta idílico, egloguista; compositor de idilios.
i.e. *abrev. de* (lat.) **id est (that is),** es decir.
if [ɪf] *conj.* 1. si, en caso de, supuesto que, siempre que, con tal que. 2. si es, de ser, ej., *if true,* si es cierto, *if so,* si es así, de ser así. 3. si bien, aunque, ej., *a clever if uncouth fellow,* un tipo astuto si bien (o aunque) tosco. 4. **as if,** como

si, ej., *as if you did not know,* como si no lo supiera (Ud. lo sabe muy bien); **if anything,** quizás ej., *if anything he is thinner than ever,* él está quizás más delgado que nunca; **if at all,** si es que, ej., *I'll do it later, if at all,* si es que lo hago, lo haré más tarde; **if I only knew!** ¡ quién lo supiera! —*s.* 1. hipótesis, suposición. 2. estipulación, cláusula.
IF *abrev. de* **intermediate frequency,** frecuencia intermedia.
iffy ['ɪfɪ] *a.* (fam.) incierto, inseguro, problemático.
IFR *abrev. de* **instrument flight rules,** reglas de vuelo por instrumentos.
igloo, iglu ['ɪglu] *s.* iglú, habitación o choza esquimal construida con hielo.
Ignatian [ɪg'neɪʃɪən] *a.* ignaciano, perteneciente o relativo a S. Ignacio de Loyola.
igneous ['ɪgnɪəs] *a.* 1. (geol.) ígneo, volcánico, eruptivo (díc. de las rocas). 2. (fig.) ardiente, apasionado.
ignescent [ɪg'nɛsənt] *a.* ignífero.
igniferous [-'nɪfərəs] *a.* ignífero.
ignis fatuus ['ɪgnəs'fætʃʊəs, B -'fætju-] (*pl.* IGNES FATUI ['ɪgˌniz-ˌaɪ]) fuego fatuo.
ignitable [ɪg'naɪtəbəl] *a.* inflamable.
ignite [-'naɪt] *v.t.* encender, prender fuego a. —*v.i.* encenderse, inflamarse, enrojecerse, coger fuego, empezar a arder.
igniter, ignitor [-ər, B -ə] *s.* (mec.) deflagrador, dispositivo de encendido.
ignitible [-əbəl] *a.* inflamable.
ignition [ɪg'nɪʃən] *s.* 1. ignición, inflamación. 2. (mec.) encendido.
ignition coil, (aut.) bobina de encendido.
ignition distributor, (aut.) distribuidor del encendido.
ignition key, llave de contacto, llave de encendio.
ignition point, punto de inflamación, punto de combustión; (mot.) punto de encendido.
ignition spark, (mot.) chispa de combustión.
ignition stroke, (aut.) carrera de explosión.
ignitron [ɪg'naɪˌtrɑn, B -ˌtrɔn] *s.* (elec.) ignitrón.
ignivomous [-'nɪvəməs] *a.* (poét.) ignívomo.
ignobility [ˌɪgnoʊ'bɪlətɪ] *s.* villanía, bajeza.
ignoble [ɪg'noʊbəl] *a.* 1. innoble, deshonesto, bajo, miserable. 2. innoble, plebeyo.
ignobleness [-nəs] *s.* bajeza, ordinariez.
ignobly [-blɪ] *adv.* innoblemente, vilmente.
ignominious [ˌɪgnə'mɪnɪəs] *a.* ignominioso, deshonroso.
ignominiously [-lɪ] *adv.* ignominiosamente.
ignominy ['ɪgnəˌmɪnɪ] *s.* 1. ignominia, deshonra, oprobio, deshonor. 2. conducta ignominiosa.
ignoramus [ˌɪgnə'reɪməs] *s.* ignorante, zopenco.
ignorance ['ɪgnərəns] *s.* ignorancia, desconocimiento, carencia de conocimientos; **where i. is bliss 'tis folly to be wise,** donde reina la ignorancia es tonto ser sabio.
ignorant [-rənt] *a.* 1. ignorante. 2. (con *of* o *in*) ignorante, lego, desconocedor (de).
ignorantly [-lɪ] *adv.* ignorantemente.
ignore [ɪg'nɔr, B -'nɔ] *v.t.* 1. no hacer caso de, pasar por alto; desairar (a alguien). 2. (der.) rechazar, sobreseer, desechar.
Igorot [ˌigə'roʊt, ˌɪg-] *s.* igorrote (indio de la isla filipina de Luzón o su lengua).
iguana [ɪ'gwɑnə] *s.* (zool.) iguana.
iguanodont [-ˌdɑnt, B -ˌdɔnt] *s.* (pal.) iguanodonte, dinosaurio prehistórico de dos patas.
IHP *abrev. de* **indicated horsepower,** fuerza indicada en caballos.
ihram [ɪ'rɑm] *s.* ihram (atuendo especial usado por los peregrinos islámicos de la Meca).
I.H.S. (relig.) 1. *siglas de* **Iesus Hominum Salvator** (Jesús salvador de los hombres). 2. *siglas de* **In Hoc Signo Vinces** (con este signo vencerás). 3. *siglas de* **In Hoc Salus** (en esto se encuentra la salvación) (la cruz).
ikon, *var. de* **icon.**
ILA *abrev. de* **International Longshoremen's Association,** Asociación Internacional de Estibadores.
ilang-ilang ['ilɑŋˌ'ilɑŋ] *s.* 1. (bot.) ilang-ilang, variedad de anona. 2. (esencia de) ilang-ilang.
ileac ['ɪlɪˌæk] *a.* (anat.) iliaco, ilíaco.
Île de France [ˌildə'frɑns] Isla de Francia, antigua provincia del N. de Francia.
ileitis [ˌɪlɪ'aɪtəs] *s.* (med.) ileítis.
ileocaecal [-oʊ'sikəl] *a.* (med.) ileocecal.
ileum ['ɪlɪəm] *s.* (*pl.* ILEA [-ɪə]) (anat.) ilion, íleon.
ileus [-ɪəs] *s.* (*pl.* ILEUSES) (med.) íleo, cólico.
ilex ['aɪlɛks] *s.* (bot.) 1. encina. 2. acebo.
iliac ['ɪlɪˌæk] *a.* (anat.) iliaco, ilíaco.
Iliad ['ɪlɪəd] *s.* (lit.) La Ilíada, poema épico de Homero.
Ilian [-ən] *a.* (hist.) ilíaco, de Ilión.
Ilicaceae [ˌaɪlɪ'keɪsɪˌi] *s. pl.* (bot.) ilicíneas, ilicáceos.
ilium ['ɪlɪəm] *s.* (*pl.* ILIA [-ɪə]) (anat.) ilion, íleon.
Ilium ['ɪlɪəm, B 'aɪlɪ-] *s.* Ilión (nombre latino de Troya).
ilk [ɪlk] *s.* familia, clase, raza; **that same i.,** (esa) misma familia, clase o raza.
ill [ɪl] *a.* (WORSE [wɜrs, B wɜs]; worst [wɜrst, B wɜst]) 1. enfermo; indispuesto. 2. nocivo, malsano. 3. funesto, aciago, desafortunado. 4. torpe, inhábil, difícil. 5. **to do someone an i. turn,** hacer daño o perjudicar a alguien; **to fall i.,** caer enfermo; **to make someone i.,** enfermar a alguien (con comida, bebida); indisponer a alguien (con comida, bebida); indisponer a alguien (con disgusto o mala noticia); **an i. omen,** un mal presagio. —*adv.* 1. mal. 2. difícilmente, ej., *we can i. afford it,* difícilmente podríamos darnos el lujo, no podemos permitírnoslo. 3. **i. at ease,** turbado, incómodo; **to be i. spoken of,** tener mala reputación. —*s.* 1. mal, desgracia, infortunio. 2. enfermedad; indisposición. 3. (fig.) malestar, dificultad. 4. **to speak i. of someone,** hablar mal de alguien.
I'll [aɪl] *contr. de* **I will** o **I shall.**
Ill. *abrev. de* **Illinois,** Illinois (E.U.).
ill-advised ['ɪləd'vaɪzd] *a.* desatinado, malaconsejado, indiscreto, imprudente.
ill-assorted [-ə'sɔrtəd, B -'sɔt-] *a.* malsurtido, mal mezclado; mal diferenciado.
illation [ɪ'leɪʃən] *s.* ilación, inferencia, consecuencia.
illative ['ɪlətɪv, B ɪ'leɪtɪv] *a.* ilativo. —*s.* (gram.) conjunción ilativa, frase ilativa.
ill-behaved ['ɪlbɪ'heɪvd] *a.* de malos modales, de mala conducta.
ill-boding [-'boʊdɪŋ] *a.* de mal agüero, aciago.
ill-bred [-'brɛd] *a.* malcriado, mal educado; descortés.
ill-conceived [-kən'sivd] *a.* mal concebido, mal calculado.
ill-conditioned ['ɪlkən'dɪʃənd] *a.* 1. mal dispuesto; en malas condiciones. 2. irritable, de mal humor.
ill-considered [-kən'sɪdərd, B -əd] *a.* sin consideración, imprudente.
ill-defined [-dɪ'faɪnd] *a.* mal definido, poco claro.
illegal [ɪ'ligəl] *a.* ilegal, contra la ley, ilícito.
illegality [ˌɪli'gælətɪ] *s.* 1. ilegalidad, falta de legalidad; ilicitud. 2. acto ilegal.
illegally [ɪ'ligəlɪ] *adv.* ilegalmente, ilícitamente.
illegibility [ɪˌlɛdʒə'bɪlətɪ] *s.* ilegibilidad.
illegible [ɪ'lɛdʒəbəl] *a.* ilegible, indescifrable.
illegibly [-blɪ] *adv.* de modo ilegible, en forma indescifrable.
illegitimacy [ˌɪlɪ'dʒɪtəməsɪ] *s.* ilegitimidad.
illegitimate [-əmət] *a.* 1. ilegítimo, bastardo. 2. mal deducido, mal inferido, ilógico. 3. ilegal, ilegítimo, ilícito.
illegitimately [-lɪ] *adv.* ilegítimamente.
ill fame, mala fama, mala reputación.
ill-fated ['ɪl'feɪtəd] *a.* aciago, malaventurado, desafortunado, infausto, desdichado, siniestrado.
ill-favored, (pr. G.B.) **ill-favoured** [-'feɪvərd, B -vəd] *a.* feo; repulsivo, antipático, desagradable.
ill-founded [-'faʊndəd] *a.* mal fundado, sin fundamento (sospecha, acusación, etc.).
ill-gotten [-'gɑtən, B -'gɔt-] *a.* mal habido, mal conseguido.
ill-gotten gains, dinero mal habido.
ill-health [-'hɛlθ] *s.* mala salud.
ill humor, (pr. G.B.) **ill humour,** mal humor.
ill-humored, (pr. G.B.) **ill-humoured** [-'hjumərd, -'ju-, B -'hjuməd] *a.* malhumorado.
illiberal [ɪ'lɪbərəl] *a.* 1. iliberal, conservador. 2. (ant.) mezquino, tacaño.
illiberality [ɪˌlɪbə'rælətɪ] *s.* falta de liberalidad, intolerancia.
illiberally [ɪ'lɪbərəlɪ] *adv.* de modo iliberal, con intolerancia.
illicit [ɪ'lɪsət] *a.* ilícito, prohibido; ilegítimo.
illicitly [-lɪ] *adv.* ilícitamente, ilegalmente.
illicitness [-nəs] *s.* ilicitud, ilegalidad.
illimitable [ɪ'lɪmɪtəbəl] *a.* ilimitable; infinito, ilimitado, inmensurable, inconmensurable.
illimitably [-blɪ] *adv.* de modo ilimitable; ilimitadamente.
ill-informed ['ɪlɪn'fɔrmd, B -'fɔmd] *a.* mal informado.
illinium [ɪ'lɪnɪəm] *s.* (quím.) ilinio.
Illinois [ˌɪlə'nɔɪ] *s.* Illinois, estado de los E.U.
illiquid [ɪ'lɪkwəd] *a.* (com.) ilíquido (bien, reclamo, derecho, etc.), no realizable; (der.) sin fundamento legal, incierto.
illite ['ɪlˌaɪt] *s.* (min.) ilita.
illiteracy [ɪ'lɪtərəsɪ] *s.* 1. analfabetismo, incultura, ignorancia. 2. (gram.) barbarismo.
illiterate [-ərət] *a.* 1. analfabeto, ignorante. 2. iliterato, iletrado, indocto, inculto. —*s.* analfabeto, ignorante.
illiterateness [-nəs] *s.* analfabetismo, ignorancia.
ill-judged ['ɪl'dʒʌdʒd] *a.* insensato, temerario, tonto.
ill-kept [-'kɛpt] *a.* mal tenido, mal administrado, mal guardado.
ill-mannered [-'mænərd, B -əd] *a.* descortés, malcriado, incivil.
ill-mated [-'meɪtəd] *a.* desigual, disparejo, desparejo, dispar.
ill-minded [-'maɪndəd] *a.* maligno, de malas intenciones.
ill nature, mala disposición, mala intención, malevolencia.
ill-natured [-'neɪtʃərd, B -tʃəd] *a.* 1. maldispuesto, malévolo; malicioso. 2. malhumorado, enfadadizo, avieso.
illness ['ɪlnəs] *s.* 1. enfermedad, mal, afección, dolencia. 2. (ant.) maldad, iniquidad, perversidad; impiedad.
illogic [ɪ'lɑdʒɪk, B ɪ'lɔdʒ-] *s.* falta de lógica.
illogical [-ɪkəl] *a.* ilógica.

illogicality [ɪˌlɑdʒɪ'kælətɪ, B 'ɪlɔdʒ-] *s.* (*pl.* ILLOGICALITIES) falta de lógica.
illogically [-ɪkəlɪ] *adv.* ilógicamente.
illogicalness [-kəlnəs] *s.* falta de lógica.
ill-omened ['ɪl'oʊmənd] *a.* de mal agüero, aciago.
ill-pleased ['ɪl'plizd] *a.* descontento, insatisfecho.
ill repute, mala reputación.
ill-shaped [-'ʃeɪpt] *a.* contrahecho, deforme.
ill-spent [-'spɛnt] *a.* desperdiciado, malgastado.
ill-starred [-'stɑrd, B -'stɑd] *a.* malaventurado, malhadado, desdichado, desgraciado; de mal agüero (díc. de las creencias astrológicas).
ill-suited [-'sutəd, B -'sjut-] *a.* impropio, desacertado (observación, etc.); incompatible (pareja, etc.).
ill-tempered [-'tɛmpərd, B -pəd] *a.* de mal genio, áspero.
ill-timed [-'taɪmd] *a.* fuera de tiempo, inoportuno, intempestivo.
ill-treat ['ɪl'trit] *v.t.* maltratar, tratar cruelmente, abusar.
ill-treatment [-mənt] *s.* maltrato, maltratamiento.
ill turn, mala jugada.
illume [ɪ'lum, B ɪ'ljum] *v.t.* iluminar, aclarar.
illuminant [ɪ'lumənənt, B ɪ'ljumɪ-] *s.* iluminador; fuente de iluminación.
illuminate [-ˌneɪt] *v.t.* 1. iluminar, alumbrar. 2. aclarar, elucidar, dilucidar. 3. iluminar, ilustrar, adornar (con dibujos de oro, colores brillantes, letra inicial, etc.). 4. iluminar, decorar con luces (ej., edificios en acontecimientos de gala).
illuminati [ɪˌlumə'nɑtɪ] *s. pl.* (*sing.* ILLUMINATO [-oʊ]) 1. illuminados, alumbrados (miembros de una secta mística en España a fines del siglo XVI). 2. hombres ilustres.
illuminating gas[ɪ'lumə,neɪtɪŋ-, B ɪ'lju-] gas rico, gas de alumbrado.
illuminating oil, aceite de alumbrado.
illuminating projectile, (mil.) proyectil de iluminación, proyectil luminoso.
illumination [ɪˌlumə'neɪʃən, B ɪˌljumɪ-] *s.* 1. iluminación, alumbrado. 2. (*pl.*) luces, equipo de alumbrado. 3. esclarecimiento, inspiración (espiritual o mental). 4. iluminación, adorno (de una carta, manuscrito o libro, con colores brillantes, oro o plata). 5. (fís.) iluminancia.
illuminative [ɪ'lumə,neɪtɪv, B ɪ'ljumɪnətɪv] *a.* iluminativo.
illuminator [-ˌneɪtər, B -ə] *s.* 1. iluminador. 2. dispositivo de alumbrado.
illumine [-mən] *v.t.* iluminar, alumbrar; aclarar.
Illuminism [-ˌɪzəm] *s.* (filos., relig.) iluminismo.
illuminist [-əst] *s.* iluminado, iluminista.
illus. *abrev. de* **illustration,** ilustración.
ill-usage ['ɪl'jusɪdʒ] *s.* mal trato; abuso, injusticia, crueldad.
ill-use [-'juz, B -zɪdʒ] *v.t.* maltratar; abusar. —[-'jus] *s.* maltrato; abuso.
illusion [ɪ'luʒən] *s.* 1. ilusión; engaño, apariencia engañosa, ensueño, espejismo. 2. (tej.) cendal.
illusionary [-ˌɛrɪ, B -ərɪ] *a.* que produce ilusiones (efectos, trucos, etc.); ilusorio.
illusionism [-ˌɪzəm] *s.* 1. ilusionismo. 2. (filos.) idealismo.
illusionist [-əst] *s.* ilusionista, prestidigitador.
illusive [ɪ'lusɪv] *a.* ilusivo, falso, engañoso, aparente.
illusively [-lɪ] *adv.* ilusamente, engañosamente.
illusiveness [-nəs] *s.* carácter o aspecto ilusorio.
illusory [-sərɪ] *a.* ilusorio, engañoso.
illustrate ['ɪlə,streɪt, ɪ'lʌs,treɪt, B 'ɪləstreɪt] *v.t.* 1. ilustrar, aclarar, esclarecer, explicar (con ejemplos). 2. ilustrar, adornar (con grabados o láminas). 3. demostrar. 4. (ant.) iluminar, alumbrar; instruir.
illustration [ˌɪlə'streɪʃən] *s.* ilustración.
illustrative [ɪ'lʌstrətɪv, B 'ɪləs,treɪtɪv] *a.* ilustrativo, que ilustra, ilustrador.
illustratively [-lɪ] *adv.* de modo ilustrativo.
illustrator ['ɪləs,treɪtər, ɪ'lʌs-, B 'ɪləs-ə] *s.* ilustrador (de libros).
illustrious [ɪ'lʌstrɪəs] *a.* 1. ilustre, insigne, célebre, eminente. 2. (ant.) brillante, lustroso.
illustriously [-lɪ] *adv.* ilustremente, insignemente.
illustriousness [-nəs] *s.* grandeza, eminencia.
illuvial [ɪ'luvɪəl] *a.*(geog.) iluvial.
illuviation [ɪˌluvɪ'eɪʃən] *s.* (geog.) iluviación.
ill will, mala voluntad, malquerencia, inquina, tirria.
ill-wisher ['ɪl'wɪʃər, B -ə] *s.* el que desea mal (a otros), malicioso.
Illyria [ɪ'lɪrɪə] *s.* (hist.) Iliria, antiguo país al E. del mar Adriático.
Illyrian [-ɪən] *a.* ilirio, ilírico, natural de Iliria. —*s.* 1. ilirio. 2. ilírico (idioma).
ilmenite ['ɪlmə,naɪt] *s.* (min.) ilmenita, hierro titanado.
ILO *abrev. de* **International Labor Organization,** Organización Internacional del Trabajo (OIT).
ILS *abrev. de* **Instrument Landing System,** sistema de aterrizaje por instrumentos.
I'm [aɪm] *contr. de* **I am.**
image ['ɪmɪdʒ] *s.* 1. imagen. 2. (fam.) concepto, idea, ej., *the public i. of a statesman,* la idea o el concepto popular de un estadista. 3. (fís., psic.) imagen. 4. **in his own i.,** a su imagen; **to be the (very) i. of,** ser el vivo retrato de. —*v.t.* 1. formar imagen o idea de; retratar, pintar. 2. imaginar, concebir. 3. reflejar, representar. 4. simbolizar.
imagery [-rɪ, -ərɪ] *s.* (*pl.* IMAGERIES) 1. imágenes (en general). 2.imaginación, fantasía. 3. lenguaje figurado.
imaginable [ɪ'mædʒənəbəl] *a.* imaginable, concebible.
imaginably [-blɪ] *adv.* posiblemente, probablemente.
imaginal [ɪ'mædʒənəl] *a.* 1. imaginal. 2. (ento.) de imago.
imaginarily [ɪˌmædʒə'nɛrəlɪ, B ɪ'mædʒɪnərə-] *adv.* imaginariamente.
imaginary [ɪ'mædʒə,nɛrɪ, B -nərɪ] *a.* 1. imaginario, irreal, imaginado. 2. (mat.) imaginario. —*s.* (mat.) imaginaria, número imaginario.
imagination [ɪˌmædʒə'neɪʃən] *s.* 1. imaginación, fantasía. 2. imaginativa, inventiva.
imaginative [ɪ'mædʒənətɪv, -ˌneɪt-, B -nətɪv] *a.* imaginativo, lleno de fantasía, inventivo.
imaginatively [-lɪ] *adv.* con imaginación o inventiva.
imagine [ɪ'mædʒən] *v.t.* 1. imaginar, concebir, formar una idea de, representarse, figurarse. 2. imaginarse, suponer, pensar, ej., *I i. you are right,* me imagino (o supongo) que tiene Ud. razón. 3. discurrir, idear, concebir, fantasear, inventar. —*v.i.* formar imagenes, ejercitar la imaginación.
imagist ['ɪmɪdʒəst] *s.* (lit.) imaginista.
imago [ɪ'meɪgoʊ] *s.* (*pl.* IMAGOES O IMAGINES [-gə,niz, B ɪ'meɪdʒə-]) *s.* 1. (psic.) imago, imagen. 2. (ento.) imago.
imam [ɪ'mɑm] *s.* imán, jefe o sacerdote entre los musulmanes.
imamate [-ˌeɪt] *s.* 1. imanato (región o país gobernado por un imán). 2. función o cargo de un imán (jefe o guía espiritual de una comunidad musulmana).
imaret [ɪ'mɑrət] *s.* imareto (hostería turca).
imbalance [ɪm'bæləns] *s.* 1. desproporción, falta de equilibrio. 2. (com.) saldo desfavorable.
imbecile ['ɪmbəsəl, B -sil] *s., a.* imbécil, estúpido, idiota.
imbecility [ˌɪmbə'sɪlətɪ] *s.* 1. imbecilidad, debilidad mental. 2. imbecilidad, tontería, fatuidad. 3. disparate, estupidez, dicho o escrito disparatado.
imbed [ɪm'bɛd] *v.t.* (*pret., p.p.* IMBEDDED; *p.pr.* IMBEDDING) embutir, incrustar, engastar; empotrar, encajar; (fig.) fijar, plantar, meter, colocar dentro.
imbibe [ɪm'baɪb] *v.t.* 1. beber (esp. licor); embeberse en o de, asimilar (ideas). 2. inhalar (aire); absorber (humedad). 3. (ant.) saturar, mojar, empapar. —*v.i.* 1. beber (habitualmente), (fam.) empinar el codo. 2. ser absorbente.
imbiber [-ər, B -ə] *s.* bebedor.
imbibition [ˌɪmbə'bɪʃən] *s.* (fís., quím., foto.) imbibición.
imbricate ['ɪmbrɪkət] *a.* imbricado, sobrepuesto. [-ˌkeɪt] *v.t., v.i.* imbricar, solapar(se), trasplantar(se) (ej., tejas, escamas, etc.).
imbrication [ˌɪmbrə'keɪʃən] *s.* (arq.) imbricación, superposición.
imbroglio [ɪm'broʊljoʊ] *s.* (*pl.* IMBROGLIOS) 1. embrollo, lío, enredo, maraña. 2. embrollo, situación embarazosa, trance difícil.
imbrue [ɪm'bru] *v.t.* manchar, empapar, mojar (de sangre).
imbrute [-'brut] *v.t., v.i.* embrutecer(se).
imbue [ɪm'bju] *v.t.* 1. saturar; teñir completamente; impregnar, empapar; manchar. 2. imbuir, ej., *imbued with wisdom,* imbuido de sabiduría.
IMF *abrev. de* **International Monetary Fund,** Fondo Monetario Internacional (FMI).
imidazole [ˌɪmə'dæz,oʊl] *s.* (quím.) imidazol.
imide ['ɪm,aɪd] *s.* (quím.) imida.
imine [-ˌin] *s.* (quím.) imina.
imitability [ˌɪmətə'bɪlətɪ] *s.* calidad de imitable.
imitable ['ɪmətəbəl] *a.* imitable.
imitate [-ˌteɪt] *v.t.* imitar; copiar, plagiar; remedar.
imitation [ˌɪmə'teɪʃən] *s.* imitación; (mús.) imitación, repetición melódica; **in i. of,** a imitación de. —*a.* imitado, artificial, de imitación, imitación, ej., *i. leather,* imitación cuero.
imitation jewelry, estrás.
imitative ['ɪmə,teɪtɪv, B -tət-] *a.* imitativo, imitatorio.
imitatively [-lɪ] *adv.* de modo imitativo.
imitator [-ˌteɪtər, B -ə] *s.* imitador.
immaculacy [ɪ'mækjələsɪ] *s.* pureza, inocencia, limpieza.
immaculate [-lət] *a.* 1. inmaculado. 2. impecable, perfecto, sin mancha.
Immaculate Conception, (relig.) Inmaculada Concepción.
immaculately [-lɪ] *adv.* inmaculadamente.
immane [ɪ'meɪn] *a.* (ant.) enorme, muy grande; de carácter monstruoso, inhumano.
immanence ['ɪmənəns] *s.* inmanencia, inherencia.
immanency [-nənsɪ] *s.* (*pl.* IMMANENCIES) *var. de* **immanence.**
immanent [-nənt] *a.* inmanente, inherente.
immanentism [-ˌɪzəm] *s.* (teo.) inmanentismo.
immanently [-lɪ] *adv.* de modo inmanente o inherente.
immaterial [ˌɪmə'tɪrɪəl, B -'tɪər-] *a.* 1. inmaterial, incorpóreo. 2. baladí, insubstancial, sin importancia; **to be i.,** no importar, ser ajeno (al asunto).
immaterialism [-ˌɪzəm] *s.* (filos.) inmaterialismo.
immateriality [-ˌtɪrɪ'ælətɪ B -ˌtɪər-] *s.* inmaterialidad, incorporeidad.

immaterialize [-ˈtɪrɪə͵laɪz, B -ˈtɪər-] *v.t.* volver inmaterial.

immaterially [-lɪ] *adv.* inmaterialmente.

immature [͵ɪməˈtʊr, B -ˈtjʊə] *a.* 1. inmaturo, inmaduro, verde (frutos). 2. (ant.) prematuro.

immaturely [-lɪ] *adv.* sin madurez.

immatureness [-nəs] *s.* inmadurez, falta de madurez.

immaturity [-ˈtʊrətɪ, B -ˈtjʊər-] *s.* 1. inmadurez, falta de madurez. 2. chiquillada, niñería.

immeasurable [ɪˈmɛʒərəbəl] *a.* inmensurable, inconmensurable, inmenso, ilimitado.

immeasurableness [-nəs] *s.* inmensurabilidad, inconmensurabilidad, inmensidad.

immeasurably [-blɪ] *adv.* inmensamente, ilimitadamente.

immediacy [ɪˈmidɪəsɪ] *s.* 1. inmediación, proximidad, contigüidad. 2. necesidad primordial.

immediate [-ɪət, B -jət] *a.* 1. inmediato, cercano; perentorio, instantáneo; urgente. 2. directo, intuitivo.

immediately [-lɪ] *adv.* inmediatamente, seguidamente, prontamente. —*conj.* tan pronto como.

immediateness [-nəs] *s.* inmediación, proximidad, contigüidad.

immedicable [ɪˈmɛdɪkəbəl] *a.* inmedicable, incurable, irremediable.

Immelmann turn [ˈɪməlmən-] (aer.) vuelta de Immelmann.

immemorial [͵ɪməˈmɔrɪəl] *a.* inmemorial, inmemorable.

immemorially [-ɪəlɪ] *adv.* inmemorablemente.

immense [ɪˈmɛns] *a.* 1. inmenso, infinito, ilimitado; muy grande, vasto, enorme. 2. (jer.) excelente, espléndido.

immensely [-lɪ] *adv.* inmensamente.

immenseness [-nəs] *s.* inmensidad.

immensity [ɪˈmɛnsətɪ] *s.* 1. inmensidad, infinidad. 2. (fig.) coloso, cosa enorme.

immensurable [ɪˈmɛnsərəbəl, B -ʃərə-] *a.* inmensurable.

immerge [ɪˈmɜrdʒ, B ɪˈmɜdʒ] *v.i.* sumergirse, zambullirse. —*v.t.* (ant.) sumergir.

immerse [ɪˈmɜrs, B ɪˈmɜs] *v.t.* 1. sumergir, hundir (esp. en un fluido). 2. bautizar por inmersión. 3. (con *in*) absorber (en pensamiento); enfrascar (en trabajo, dificultades, etc.); sumir (en deudas).

immersed [ɪˈmɜrst B ɪˈmɜst] *a.* (bot.) sumergido.

immersible [ɪˈmɜrsəbəl, B ɪˈmɜs-] *a.* que puede ser sumergido en agua sin peligro; de inmersión.

immersion [ɪˈmɜrʃən, -ʒən, B ɪˈmɜʃən] *s.* 1. inmersión, esp. bautismo por inmersión. 2. (astr.) inmersión.

immersion heater, calentador de inmersión.

immesh [ɪˈmɛʃ] *var. de* **enmesh.**

immethodical [͵ɪməˈθɑdɪkəl, B -ˈθɔd-] *a.* (hecho) sin método; que no tiene método (para el trabajo, etc.), sin orden.

immigrant [ˈɪməgrənt] *s.* inmigrante. —*a.* inmigratorio.

immigrate [ˈɪmə͵greɪt] *v.i.* inmigrar.

immigration [͵ɪməˈgreɪʃən] *s.* inmigración.

immigratory [ˈɪməgrə͵tɔrɪ, B -͵greɪtərɪ] *a.* inmigratorio.

imminence [ˈɪmənəns] *s.* 1. inminencia. 2. peligro inminente.

imminency [-nənsɪ] *s.* (*pl.* IMMINENCIES) *var. de* **imminence.**

imminent [-nənt] *a.* inminente.

imminently [-lɪ] *adv.* de modo inminente.

immingle [ɪˈmɪŋgəl] *v.t., v.i.* mezclar(se) íntimamente; combinar(se), fundir(se); entremezclar(se).

immiscible [ɪˈmɪsəbəl] *a.* inmiscible, que no puede ser mezclado.

immiscibly [-blɪ] *adv.* inmisciblemente.

immitigable [ɪˈmɪtɪgəbəl] *a.* que no se puede mitigar.

immix [ɪˈmɪks] *v.t.* mezclar, inmiscuir.

immixture [ɪˈmɪkstʃər, B -tʃə] *s.* mezcla, mixtura, mistura.

immobile [ɪˈmoʊbəl, -͵bil, B -͵baɪl] *a.* inmóvil, inmovible, inmoble; sin movimiento; fijo.

immobility [͵ɪmoʊˈbɪlətɪ] *s.* inmovilidad.

immobilization [ɪ͵moʊbələˈzeɪʃən, B -laɪ-] *s.* inmovilización.

immobilize [ɪˈmoʊbə͵laɪz] *v.t.* inmovilizar, paralizar; (med.) inmovilizar (miembros fracturados, etc.); (fin.) inmovilizar (capital, fondos, etc.).

immoderacy [ɪˈmɑdərəsɪ, B ɪˈmɔd-] *s.* inmoderación, intemperancia, exceso.

immoderate [-ərət] *a.* 1. inmoderado, inmódico, excesivo. 2. (ant.) desmandado; intemperante; ilimitado.

immoderately [-lɪ] *adv.* inmoderadamente.

immoderateness [-nəs] *s.* inmoderación, falta de moderación.

immoderation [ɪ͵mɑdəˈreɪʃən, B ɪ͵mɔd-] *s.* inmoderación.

immodest [ɪˈmɑdəst, B ɪˈmɔd-] *a.* inmodesto; impúdico, indecente, indecoroso; jactancioso, pedante, presumido, presuntuoso.

immodestly [-lɪ] *adv.* inmodestamente; impúdicamente, presuntuosamente.

immodesty [-əstɪ] *s.* inmodestia; impudicia.

immolate [ˈɪmə͵leɪt] *v.t.* inmolar, sacrificar.

immolation [͵ɪməˈleɪʃən] *s.* inmolación.

immolator [ˈɪmə͵leɪtər, B -ə] *s.* inmolador.

immoral [ɪˈmɔrəl, ɪˈmɑr-, B ɪˈmɔr-] *a.* inmoral, deshonesto, obsceno, disoluto, licencioso, libertino; vicioso.

immoralist [-ələst] *s.* el que practica o defiende la inmoralidad.

immorality [͵ɪməˈrælətɪ, ͵ɪmɔ-] *s.* inmoralidad, deshonestidad, obscenidad.

immorally [-əlɪ] *adv.* de modo inmoral, licenciosamente.

immortal [ɪˈmɔrtəl, B ɪˈmɔt-] *a., s.* inmortal.

immortality [͵ɪmɔrˈtælətɪ, B ͵ɪmɔˈ-] *s.* inmortalidad, fama perdurable.

immortalization [ɪ͵mɔrtələˈzeɪʃən, B ɪ͵mɔtəlaɪ-] *s.* inmortalización.

immortalize [ɪˈmɔrtə͵laɪz, B ɪˈmɔt-] *v.t.* inmortalizar; perpetuar.

immortally [-əlɪ] *adv.* inmortalmente.

immortelle [͵ɪmɔrˈtɛl, B ͵ɪmɔˈ-] *s.* (bot.) siempreviva, perpetua.

immotile [ɪˈmoʊtəl, B -͵taɪl] *a.* inmoto, fijo.

immovability [ɪ͵muvəˈbɪlətɪ] *s.* 1. inmovilidad, inamovilidad. 2. impasibilidad, inmutabilidad.

immovable [ɪˈmuvəbəl] *a.* 1. inamovible; inmóvil, inmoble; fijo. 2. impasible, inmutable, inconmovible. 3. (der.) inmóvil. —*s. pl.* inmuebles, bienes raíces.

immovableness [-nəs] *s.* 1. inmovilidad, inamovilidad. 2. impasibilidad.

immovably [-blɪ] *adv.* inmutablemente, inalterablemente, impasiblemente.

immune [ɪˈmjun] *a.* inmune; **i. to,** inmune a (enfermedad, contagio, droga, medicamento, etc.); **i. from,** exento de, inmune de (gravamen, impuesto, etc.). —*s.* persona inmune.

immunity [-ətɪ] *s.* inmunidad; exención, dispensa.

immunization [͵ɪmjənəˈzeɪʃən, B -naɪ-] *s.* inmunización.

immunize [ˈɪmjə͵naɪz] *v.t.* inmunizar.

immunochemistry [͵ɪmjənoʊˈkɛməstrɪ] *s.* (med.) inmunoquímica.

immunogen [ɪˈmjunə͵dʒɛn] *s.* substancia. inmunógena.

immunogenic [͵ɪmjənoʊˈdʒɛnɪk] *a.* (med.) inmunógeno.

immunologist [-ˈnɑlədʒəst, B -ˈnɔl-] *a., s.* especialista en inmunología.

immunology [-dʒɪ] *s.* inmunología.

immunotherapy [͵ɪmjənoʊˈθɛrəpɪ] *s.* (med.) inmunoterapia.

immure [ɪˈmjʊr, B ɪˈmjʊə] *v.t.* 1. emparedar. 2. aprisionar, encarcelar, confinar. 3. empotrar. 4. sepultar entre paredes o muros. 5. **i. oneself,** encerrarse, emparedarse.

immurement [-mənt] *s.* 1. emparedamiento. 2. encarcelamiento. 3. empotramiento.

immutability [ɪ͵mjutəˈbɪlətɪ] *s.* 1. inmutabilidad, inalterabilidad. 2. firmeza, constancia.

immutable [ɪˈmjutəbəl] *a.* inmutable, inalterable; invariable.

immutably [-blɪ] *adv.* inmutablemente.

imp [ɪmp] *s.* 1. diablillo, trasgo, duende. 2. bribonzuelo, niño travieso. 3. (ant.) vástago, retoño; injerto; progenie. —*v.t., v.i.* (ant.) 1. reparar con pluma o plumas (las alas o cola del halcón). 2. reforzar, asegurar.

impact [ɪmˈpækt] *v.t.* fijar firmemente (en algo), embutir, engastar, incrustar. — [ˈɪm͵pækt] *s.* 1. impacto, choque; colisión. 2. (fig.) impacto, efecto.

impacted [-ˈpæktəd] *a.* (odont.) impactado.

impaction [-ˈpækʃən] *s.* (odont.) impacción; empotramiento.

impair [ɪmˈpɛr, B -ˈpɛə] *v.t.* deteriorar, dañar, perjudicar, empeorar, menoscabar (en cantidad, valor o fuerza). —*s.* (ant.) empeoramiento, deterioro, menoscabo.

impairment [-mənt] *s.* deterioro, menoscabo.

impale [ɪmˈpeɪl] *v.t.* 1. empalar, espetar. 2. (ant.) empalizar, cercar, vallar.

impalement [-mənt] *s.* empalamiento.

impalpability [ɪm͵pælpəˈbɪlətɪ] *s.* impalpabilidad.

impalpable [ɪmˈpælpəbəl] *a.* impalpable, intangible. —*s.* cosa impalpable.

impalpably [-blɪ] *adv.* de modo impalpable.

impanate [ɪmˈpeɪneɪt] *a.* (relig.) empanado, presente en el pan de la eucaristía.

impanation [͵ɪmpəˈneɪʃən] *s.* (relig.) empanación.

impanel [ɪmˈpænəl] *v.t.* (der.) eligir, selecctionar (un jurado), inscribir (un jurado) en la lista de los jurados.

imparadise [ɪmˈpærə͵daɪs] *v.t.* (fig.) convertir en un paraíso; colmar de felicidad.

imparidigitate [ɪm͵pærɪˈdɪdʒɪ͵teɪt, B -ətət] *a.* (zool.) imparidigitado.

imparity [ɪmˈpærətɪ] *s.* (*pl.* IMPARITIES) disparidad, imparidad, desigualdad, desproporción.

impark [ɪmˈpɑrk, B -ˈpɑk] *v.t.* (ant.) cerrar, encerrar (bestias) en un parque; cercar para convertir en parque.

impart [-ˈpɑrt, B -ˈpɑt] *v.t.* 1. impartir, repartir, conceder, dar, compartir. 2. decir, comunicar, difundir.

impartial [ɪmˈpɑrʃəl, B -ˈpɑʃəl] *a.* imparcial; equitativo, justo.

impartiality [-͵pɑrʃɪˈælətɪ, B -͵pɑʃɪ-] *s.* imparcialidad; equidad, justicia.

impartially [-ˈpɑrʃəlɪ, B -ˈpɑʃə-] *adv.* imparcialmente; equitativamente, justamente.

impartibility [ɪm͵pɑrtəˈbɪlətɪ, B -͵pɑt-] *s.* indivisibilidad.

impartible [-ˈpɑrtəbəl, B -ˈpɑt-] *a.* impartible, indivisible (bienes, propiedades).
impartibly [-blɪ] *adv.* indivisiblemente.
impartment [ɪmˈpɑrtmənt, B -ˈpɑt-] *s.* 1. impartición, repartimiento. 2. comunicación, transmisión, participación.
impassable [ɪmˈpæsəbəl, B -ˈpɑs-] *a.* intransitable, impracticable (caminos, monedas), infranqueable.
impasse [ˈɪmˌpæs, ɪmˈpæs, B æmˈpɑs] *s.* callejón sin salida; atolladero, dificultad insuperable, impase (Am.).
impassibility [ɪmˌpæsəˈbɪlətɪ] *s.* impasibilidad, insensibilidad.
impassible [-ˈpæsəbəl] *a.* impasible, insensible, empedernido.
impassibly [-blɪ] *adv.* impasiblemente, insensiblemente.
impassion [ɪmˈpæʃən] *v.t.* apasionar, enardecer; (fig.) inflamar.
impassioned [-ˈpæʃənd] *a.* apasionado, extremoso.
impassive [ɪmˈpæsɪv] *a.* 1. indiferente, impasible, estoico; apático, flemático; calmo, sereno. 2. (ant.) insensible.
impassively [-lɪ] *adv.* indiferentemente, insensiblemente.
impassiveness [-nəs] **impassivity** [ˌɪmpæˈsɪvətɪ] *s.* indiferencia, impasibilidad.
impaste [ɪmˈpeɪst] *v.t.* 1. convertir en pasta. 2. solidificar. 3. (pint.) empastar.
impasto [ɪmˈpæstoʊ, -ˈpɑs-] *s.* (pint.) empaste.
impatience [ɪmˈpeɪʃəns] *s.* impaciencia.
impatient [-ʃənt] *a.* 1. impaciente. 2. (con *of*) intolerante (con, para con); harto (de). 3. **to be i. to (do),** estar impaciente por (hacer).
impatiently [-lɪ] *adv.* impacientemente.
impavid [ɪmˈpævəd] *a.* (ant.) impávido.
impawn [ɪmˈpɔn] *v.t.* (ant.) empeñar, pignorar.
impeach [ɪmˈpitʃ] *v.t.* 1. encausar, inculpar, acusar, denunciar (esp. a un funcionario público). 2. poner en tela de juicio. 3. (der.) impugnar, recusar (testimonio, testigo, etc.), residenciar (a un juez, jurado, etc.).
impeachable [-əbəl] *a.* 1. acusable, censurable. 2. impugnable (testimonio, testigo, etc.).
impeacher [-ər, B -ə] *s.* delator, denunciador.
impeachment [-mənt] *s.* 1. acusación. 2. (der.) impugnación (de testimonio, testigo, etc.); residencia, denuncia, enjuiciamiento político, residenciamiento (contra un juez, jurado, etc.).
impearl [ɪmˈpɜrl, B -ˈpɜl] *v.t.* (poét.) aljofarar, adornar con perlas.
impeccability [-ˌpɛkəˈbɪlətɪ] *s.* impecabilidad.
impeccable [-ˈpɛkəbəl] *a.* impecable, inmaculado, sin defecto, perfecto.
impeccably [-blɪ] *adv.* impecablemente, inmaculadamente.
impeccant [-ˈpɛkənt] *a.* sin pecado, sin error, puro; honesto, justo.
impecunious [ˌɪmpɪˈkjunjəs] *a.* pobre, indigente, sin dinero.
impecuniously [-lɪ] *adv.* pobremente, sin dinero.
impecuniousness [-nəs] **impecuniosity** [-ˌkjunɪˈɑsətɪ, B -ˈɔs-] *s.* pobreza, indigencia, falta de dinero.
impedance [ɪmˈpidəns] *s.* (elec., electrón.) impedancia.
impede [ɪmˈpid] *v.t.* impedir, detener, estorbar, dificultar, obstruir.
impeder [-ər, B -ə] *s.* impedidor, obstructor.
impediment [-ˈpɛdəmənt] *s.* 1. impedimento, obstrucción, traba, obstáculo. 2. embarazo, defecto, ej., *i. in (one's) speech,* defecto del (o en el) habla (de uno). 3. (der.) impedimento.
impedimenta [-ˌpɛdəˈmɛntə] *s. pl.* 1. equipaje; efectos. 2. (der.) impedimentos legales. 3. (mil.) impedimenta.
impeditive [-ˈpɛdətɪv] *a.* impeditivo, obstructivo.
impel [ɪmˈpɛl] *v.t.* (*pret., p.p.* IMPELLED; *p.pr.* IMPELLING) 1. impulsar, impeler. 2. compeler, obligar, incitar, instigar. 3. empujar, mover.
impellent [-ənt] *a.* impelente. —*s.* agente o fuerza impelente.
impeller [-ər, B -ə] *s.* impulsor, propulsor, motor.
impend [ɪmˈpɛnd] *v.i.* amenazar, ser inminente, cernerse.
impendence [-əns] *s.* amago, amenaza, inminencia.
impending [-ɪŋ] **impendent** [-ənt] *a.* inminente, amenazante.
impenetrability [ɪmˌpɛnətrəˈbɪlətɪ] *s.* impenetrabilidad.
impenetrable [-ˈpɛnətrəbəl] *a.* 1. impenetrable, impermeable. 2. (fig.) impenetrable, inescrutable, insondable.
impenetrableness [-nəs] *s.* impenetrabilidad.
impenetrably [-blɪ] *adv.* impenetrablemente.
impenitence [ɪmˈpɛnətəns] *s.* impenitencia.
impenitent [-tənt] *a.* impenitente, no arrepentido.
impenitently [-lɪ] *adv.* de modo impenitente.
imperative [ɪmˈpɛrətɪv] *a.* 1. imperativo, autoritario, imperioso. 2. (gram.) imperativo, exhortatorio. 3. imperioso, perentorio, urgente. —*s.* (gram.) (modo) imperativo.
imperatively [-lɪ] *adv.* imperativamente, imperiosamente.
imperator [ˌɪmpəˈreɪtər, B -ˈrɑtɔ] *s.* (hist. romana) imperátor, nombre que se daba a un general victorioso.
imperatorial [ɪmˌpɛrəˈtɔrɪəl] *a.* imperatorio.
imperceptibility [ˌɪmpərˌsɛptəˈbɪlətɪ, B ˈɪmpəˌ-] *s.* imperceptibilidad.
imperceptible [-ˈsɛptəbəl] *a.* imperceptible.
imperceptibly [-blɪ] *adv.* imperceptiblemente.
imperceptive [-ˈsɛptɪv] *a.* carente de percepción.
imperceptiveness [-nəs] *s.* incapacidad de percibir.
imperfect [ɪmˈpɜrfɪkt, B -ˈpɜfɪkt] *a.* 1. imperfecto, defectuoso. 2. (gram., der.) imperfecto. —*s.* (gram.) (tiempo) imperfecto; pretérito imperfecto.
imperfect flower, (bot.) flor diclina.
imperfection [ˌɪmpərˈfɛkʃən, B ˌɪmpəˈ-] *s.* 1. imperfección. 2. desperfecto, falla, defecto.
imperfectly [ɪmˈpɜrfɪktlɪ, B -ˈpɜfɪkt-] *adv.* imperfectamente.
imperfectness [-nəs] *s.* imperfección.
imperforate [-ˈpɜrfərət, -ˌreɪt, B -ˈpɜfərɪt] *a.* 1. imperforado; sin abertura. 2. (filat.) sin perforaciones. —*s.* sello postal sin perforaciones.
imperforation [-ˌpɜrfəˈreɪʃən, B -ˌpɜfə-] *s.* (med.) imperforación, oclusión.
imperial [ɪmˈpɪrɪəl, B -ˈpɪər-] *a.* 1. imperial. 2. altivo, imperioso. 3. (fig.) soberbio, grandioso. —*s.* 1. perilla, pera (de barbilla). 2. antigua moneda rusa de 15 rublos. 3. imperial (techo de coche). 4. tamaño de papel. 5. imperial (juego de naipes).
imperial eagle, (ornit.) águila imperial, águila de los árboles.
imperial gallon, galón inglés (4,543 litros).
imperialism [-ɪzəm] *s.* 1. imperialismo. 2. gobierno, autoridad o sistema imperial.
imperialist [-əst] *s., a.* imperialista, expansionista.
imperialistic [-ˌpɪrɪəˈlɪstɪk, B -ˌpɪər-] *a.* imperialista.
imperialistically [-tɪkəlɪ] *adv.* de modo imperialista.
imperially [-ˈpɪrɪəlɪ, B -ˈpɪər-] *adv.* imperiosamente, imperialmente.
imperil [ɪmˈpɛrɪl] *v.t.* (*pret. p.p.* IMPERILED o IMPERILLED; *p.pr.* IMPERILING o IMPERILING) poner en peligro, arriesgar, exponer.
imperious [-ˈpɪrɪəs, B -ˈpɪər-] *a.* 1. imperioso, arrogante, autoritario, dominador. 2. imperativo, urgente.
imperiously [-lɪ] *adv.* imperiosamente, de modo imperativo.
imperiousness [-nəs] *s.* arrogancia, imperio, autoridad, mando.
imperishability [ˌɪmpɛrɪʃəˈbɪlətɪ] *s.* indestructibilidad.
imperishable [ɪmˈpɛrɪʃəbəl] *a.* eterno, indestructible, imperecedero.
imperishably [-blɪ] *adv.* indestructiblemente.
imperium [ɪmˈpɪrɪəm] *s.* (*pl.* IMPERIA [-ɪə]) 1. imperio, poder absoluto, dominio. 2. (der.) derecho de mando; soberanía, potestad, poder.
impermanence [ɪmˈpɜrmənəns, B -ˈpɜmə-] *s.* temporalidad, transitoriedad, inestabilidad.
impermanent [-nənt] *a.* temporal, transitorio, inestable, no permanente.
impermanently [-lɪ] *adv.* temporalmente, transitoriamente.
impermeability [ɪmˌpɜrmɪəˈbɪlətɪ B -ˌpɜmjə-] *s.* impermeabilidad.
impermeable [-ˈpɜrmɪəbəl, B -ˈpɜmjə-] *adv.* impermeable.
impermeably [-blɪ] *adv.* impermeablemente.
impermissibility [ˌɪmpərˌmɪsəˈbɪlətɪ, B -pəˌ-] *s.* intolerabilidad.
impermissible [-ˈmɪsəbəl] *a.* intolerable, no permisible.
impersonal [ɪmˈpɜrsənəl, B -ˈpɜs-] *a.* 1. impersonal. 2. (gram.) impersonal, unipersonal (verbo); indefinido (pronombre). —*s.* (gram.) verbo impersonal o unipersonal.
impersonality [-ˌpɜrsənˈælətɪ, B -ˌpɜs-] *s.* impersonalidad.
impersonalize [-ˈpɜrsənəˌlaɪz, B -ˈpɜs-] *v.t.* hacer impersonal.
impersonally [-ənəlɪ] *adv.* impersonalmente.
impersonate [-ˌneɪt] *v.t.* 1. (teat.) hacer el papel de, interpretar. 2. asumir la personalidad de, fingir ser o imitar a (otra persona). 3. (ant.) personificar.
impersonation [-ˌpɜrsəˈneɪʃən, B -ˌpɜs-] *s.* 1. (teat.) representación, papel; imitación. 2. (ant.) personificación.
impersonator [-ˈpɜrsəˌneɪtər, B -ˈpɜs-ə] *s.* (teat.) intérprete; actor, imitador; transformista (actor que hace mutaciones rápidas).
impertinence [ɪmˈpɜrtənəns, B -ˈ pɜt-] *s.* 1. impertinencia, importunidad, descortesía, incivilidad, insolencia, descaro. 2. impertinencia (palabra o acto).
impertinency [-ənsɪ] *s.* (*pl.* impertinencies) *var. de* **impertinence.**
impertinent [-ənt] *a.* impertinente, importuno, insolente.
impertinently [-lɪ] *adv.* impertinentemente, importunamente, insolentemente.
imperturbability [ˌɪmpərˌtɜrbəˈbɪlətɪ, B -pəˌtɜbə-] *s.* imperturbabilidad, serenidad, calma.
imperturbable [-ˈtɜrbəbəl, B -ˈtɜbə-] *a.* imperturbable; calmo, sereno.
imperturbably [-blɪ] *adv.* imperturbablemente, serenamente, calmadamente.

imperturbation [ˌɪmpərtər'beɪʃən, B -pətə'-] *s.* calma, serenidad, placidez.
impervious [ɪm'pɜrvɪəs, B -'pɜvjəs] *a.* (ú. con *to*) 1. impenetrable, impermeable (al agua, etc.). 2. (fig.) sordo (a crítica, reproches, etc.).
imperviously [-lɪ] *adv.* impenetrablemente.
imperviousness [-nəs] *s.* 1. impermeabilidad, impenetrabilidad. 2. (fig.) insensibilidad, indiferencia.
impetiginous [ˌɪmpə'tɪdʒənəs] *a.* (med.) impetigoso, exantematoso.
impetigo [-'taɪgoʊ] *s.* (med.) impétigo, empeine.
impetrate ['ɪmpəˌtreɪt] *v.t.* impetrar, solicitar.
impetration [ˌɪmpə'treɪʃən] *s.* impetración.
impetrator ['ɪmpəˌtreɪtər, B -ə] *s.* impetrador, impetrante.
impetratory [-trəˌtɔrɪ, B -trətərɪ] *a.* impetratorio.
impetuosity [ɪmˌpɛtʃʊ'ɑsətɪ, B -ˌpɛtjʊ'ɔs-] *s.* 1. impetuosidad, vehemencia, impulsividad. 2. acto impetuoso.
impetuous [ɪm'pɛtʃʊəs, B -'pɛtjʊ-] *a.* impetuoso, arrebatado, vehemente, impulsivo.
impetuously [-lɪ] *adv.* impetuosamente, vehementemente, impulsivamente.
impetuousness [-nəs] *s.* impetuosidad, vehemencia, impulsividad.
impetus ['ɪmpətəs] *s.* (*pl.* IMPETUSES) 1. ímpetu. 2. impulso, impulsión, incentivo, estímulo.
imphee ['ɪmfi] *s.* caña de azúcar africana.
impiety [ɪm'paɪətɪ] *s.* 1. impiedad, irreverencia, irreligiosidad. 2. acto impío.
impignorate [im'pignəreit] *v.t.* 1. pignorar, empeñar, dar en prenda. 2. pignorar, hipotecar, gravar (bienes raíces).
impignoration [ɪmˌpɪgnə'reɪʃən] *s.* pignoración, hipoteca, empeño.
impinge [ɪm'pɪndʒ] *v.i.* 1. (con *on, upon, against*) golpear, tropezar, chocar (con o contra); batir, dar con fuerza (sobre) (como la luz, el viento, la lluvia, etc.). 2. (con *on* o *upon*) interferir (con), inmiscuirse (en); violar. 3. (con *on* o *upon*) hacer impacto (en), causar o hacer efecto (en), impresionar.
impingement [-mənt] *s.* 1. choque, golpe, impacto. 2. infracción, violación.
impious ['ɪmpɪəs] *a.* impío, irreligioso, profano; irrespetuoso, irreverente; desobediente.
impiously [-lɪ] *adv.* impíamente, irreligiosamente; irrespetuosamente, irreverentemente.
impiousness [-nəs] *s.* impiedad, irreligiosidad; irreverencia.
impish ['ɪmpɪʃ] *a.* travieso, pícaro; endiablado.
impishly [-lɪ] *adv.* pícaramente, de manera traviesa o endiablada.
impishness [-nəs] *s.* travesura, diablura, picardía.
implacability [ɪmˌplækə'bɪlətɪ, -ˌpleɪkə-] *s.* implacabilidad, inexorabilidad.
implacable [-'plækəbəl, -'pleɪk-] *a.* implacable, inexorable.
implacably [-blɪ] *adv.* implacablemente, inexorablemente.
implacental [ˌɪmplə'sɛntəl] *a.* (zool.) implacentario.
implant [ɪm'plænt, B -'plɑnt] *v.t.* 1. implantar, arraigar, inculcar. 2. (med.) implantar. —*s.* (med.) injerto.
implantation [ˌɪmplæn'teɪʃən, B -plɑn-] *s.* 1. implantación, inculcación. 2. (med.) implantación.
implausible [ɪm'plɔzəbəl] *a.* poco plausible; improbable.
implead [ɪm'plid] *v.t., v.i.* (der.) demandar, poner pleito; acusar; defender (un pleito).
impleader [-ər, B -ə] *s.* (der.) demandante; defensor.
implement ['ɪmpləmənt] *s.* implemento, utensilio, instrumento, herramienta. — [-ˌmɛnt] *v.t.* 1. cumplir, llevar a cabo; poner en práctica; poner en ejecución (ej., un tratado). 2. equipar con aparejos; pertrechar.
implementation [ˌɪmpləmən'teɪʃən] *s.* ejecución, cumplimiento; puesta en práctica (plan, etc.).
implicate ['ɪmpləˌkeɪt] *v.t.* 1. implicar, envolver, embrollar, comprometer. 2. implicar, contener, significar. 3. (ant.) enredar, entrelazar.
implication [ˌɪmplə'keɪʃən] *s.* 1. insinuación, sugerencia. 2. inferencia, ilación, deducción. 3. (der.) implicación, complicidad.
implicative ['ɪmpləˌkeɪtɪv, ɪm'plɪkə-] *a.* implicatorio, que se infiere; insinuativo.
implicit [ɪm'plɪsət] *a.* 1. implícito, sobrentendido, tácito. 2. (con *in*) contenido (en), esencial (en). 3. completo, absoluto, ciego, ej., *i. faith,* fe ciega o absoluta.
implicitly [-lɪ] *adv.* implícitamente, tácitamente.
implicitness [-nəs] *s.* calidad de implícito.
implied [ɪm'plaɪd] *a.* incluido, implícito, tácito, sobrentendido.
implode [ɪm'ploʊd] *v.i.* implosionar, explosionar hacia dentro.
implore [ɪm'plɔr, B -'plɔ] *v.t.* implorar, suplicar, rogar, deprecar, invocar.
imploringly [-'plɔrɪŋlɪ] *adv.* implorantemente, suplicantemente.
implosion [ɪm'ploʊʒən] *s.* 1. estallido interno, reventón hacia adentro. 2. (fon.) implosión.
implosive [-'ploʊsɪv] *a.* (fon.) implosivo. —*s.* (sonido) implosivo.
impluvium [ɪm'pluvɪəm] *s.* (*pl.* IMPLUVIA [-vɪə]) (hist.) impluvio.
imply [ɪm'plaɪ] *v.t.* (*pret., p.p.* IMPLIED; *p.pr.* IMPLYING) 1. implicar, involucrar, contener, encerrar en sí, entrañar. 2. implicar, dar a entender, indicar, denotar, significar.
impolicy [ɪm'pɑləsɪ, B -'pɔl-] *s.* política indiscreta, imprudencia; inconveniencia; inoportunidad, impolítica.
impolite [ˌɪmpə'laɪt] *a.* descortés, incivil, grosero.
impolitely [-lɪ] *adv.* descortésmente, groseramente.
impoliteness [-nəs] *s.* descortesía, desatención, grosería.
impolitic [ɪm'pɑləˌtɪk, B -'pɔl-] *a.* impolítico, imprudente, impropio, inoportuno, indiscreto; inconveniente.
impoliticly [-lɪ] **impolitically** [ˌɪmpə'lɪtɪkəlɪ] *adv.* impolíticamente, imprudentemente, impropiamente, inoportunamente.
impoliticness [-nəs] **impoliticalness** [ˌɪmpə'lɪtɪkəl-] *s.* impolítica, imprudencia.
imponderability [ɪmˌpɑndərə'bɪlətɪ, B -ˌpɔn-] *s.* imponderabilidad.
imponderable [-'pɑndərəbəl, B -'pɔn-] *a.* imponderable. —*s.* substancia o elemento que no puede medirse o pesarse; (*pl.*) elementos (espirituales) imponderables.
imponderably [-blɪ] *adv.* imponderablemente.
imporosity [ˌɪmpə'rɑsətɪ, B -'rɔs-] *s.* falta de porosidad.
imporous [ɪm'pɔrəs] *a.* no poroso.
import [ɪm'pɔrt B -'pɔt] *v.t.* 1. significar, implicar, interesar, denotar. 2. introducir; (com.) importar (mercancías). 3. (ant.) tocar, interesar. —*v.i.* importar, convenir; tener importancia. — ['ɪmˌpɔrt, B -ˌpɔt] *s.* 1. sentido, significado, significación. 2. importancia, valor, peso, consecuencia. 3. (com.) mercancía importada; importación; (*pl.*) importaciones.
importable [-əbəl] *a.* (com.) importable.
importance [ɪm'pɔrtəns, B -'pɔt-] *s.* 1. importancia; significación. 2. consideración, consecuencia, alcance. 3. peso, valor.
important [-ənt] *a.* 1. importante, significativo; esencial, valioso, considerable. 2. pomposo, pretencioso, afectado; fachendoso. 3. (ant.) persistente, urgente.
importantly [-lɪ] *adv.* 1. importantemente. 2. pretenciosamente, pomposamente, engreídamente.
importation [ˌɪmpɔr'teɪʃən, B -pɔ'-] *s.* (com.) importación, entrada, internación; artículo importado.
import duties, derechos de entrada, impuestos de importación.
importer [ɪm'pɔrtər, B -'pɔtə] *s.* (com.) importador.
importunate [ɪm'pɔrtʃənət, B -'pɔtjʊ-] *a.* importuno, insistente (demandas, curiosidad, etc.); pesado, impertinente, apremiante.
importunately [-lɪ] *adv.* importunamente, importunadamente, insistentemente, impertinentemente.
importunateness [-nəs] *s.* importunidad, insistencia.
importune [-'pɔrtʃən, ˌɪmpər'tun, B -pɔtjun] *a.* importuno, insistente. —*v.t.* 1. importunar, cargar; apremiar, urgir, instar. 2. molestar, fastidiar. —*v.i.* ser importuno, porfiar, machacar.
importunely [-lɪ] *adv.* importunamente.
importuner [-ər, B -ə] *s.* importunador, posma, pelmazo.
importunity [ˌɪmpər'tunətɪ, B -pɔ'tjun-] *s.* importunidad, porfía, importunación, machaquería.
imposable [ɪm'poʊzəbəl] *a.* imponible.
impose [ɪm'poʊz] *v.t.* 1. imponer, gravar con (cargas, tributos, etc.); afectar, obligar. 2. (relig.) imponer (las manos en confirmación). 3. (impr.) imponer (las formas). 4. **i. oneself,** imponerse, hacerse aceptar; **i. oneself upon,** acompañar contra su voluntad a. —*v.i.* **i. on** (o **upon**), aprovecharse de; abusar de, engañar, embaucar.
imposer [-'poʊzər, B -zə] *s.* (impr.) imponedor.
imposing [-zɪŋ] *a.* imponente, grandioso, tremendo.
imposingly [-lɪ] *adv.* imponentemente, grandiosamente.
imposing stone, (imp.) piedra de imponer.
imposing table, (imp.) platina.
imposition [ˌɪmpə'zɪʃən] *s.* 1. imposición. 2. imposición, impuesto, gravamen, carga, gabela, tributo. 3. abuso, engaño, impostura, trama, embeleso. 4. (relig.) imposición (de las manos). 5. (impr.) imposición.
impossibility [ɪmˌpɑsə'bɪlətɪ, B -ˌpɔs-] *s.* 1. imposibilidad. 2. (cosa) imposible, ej., *request an i.,* pedir un imposible, pedir una cosa imposible?
impossible [-'pɑsəbəl, B -'pɔs-] *a.* 1. imposible, irrealizable, impracticable. 2. imposible, insoportable, intratable.
impossibleness [-nəs] *s.* imposibilidad.
impossibly [-blɪ] *adv.* imposiblemente.
impost ['ɪmˌpoʊst] *s.* 1. impuesto, esp. derecho de aduana, exacción, gabela, contribución. 2. (jer). handicap (en las carreras de caballos). 3. (arq.) imposta, salmer. —*v.t.* (E.U.) aforar (mercaderías).
impostor [ɪm'pɑstər, B -'pɔstə] *s.* impostor; engañador, embaucador.
imposture [-tʃər, B -tʃə] *s.* impostura; fraude; engaño, falsedad.
impotence ['ɪmpətəns] **impotency** [-ənsɪ] *s.* 1. impotencia, incapacidad. 2. (med.) impotencia, agenesia.

impotent [-ənt] *a.* 1. impotente, incapaz; débil. 2. (med.) impotente.
impotently [-lɪ] *adv.* impotentemente.
impound [ɪm'paʊnd] *v.t.* 1. acorralar, encerrar, aprisionar, restringir. 2. represar, embalsar, rebalsar. 3. (der.) secuestrar, embargar.
impounding [-ɪŋ] *s.* embalse, represa.
impoundment [-mənt] *s.* 1. acorralamiento, encierro. 2. embalse, represa. 3. (der.) secuestro, embargo.
impoverish [ɪm'pɑvərɪʃ, B -'pɔv-] *v.t.* 1. empobrecer, depauperar. 2. agotar, empobrecer (la tierra); menguar, esquilmar, deteriorar.
impoverishment [-mənt] *s.* empobrecimiento, depauperación.
impower, *var. de* **empower.**
impracticability [ɪm,præktɪkə'bɪlətɪ] *s.* 1. impracticabilidad. 2. cosa impracticable.
impracticable [-'præktɪkəbəl] *a.* 1. impracticable, irrealizable, imposible. 2. impracticable, intransitable. 3. (ant.) intratable, terco, irrazonable.
impracticableness [-nəs] *s.* impracticabilidad.
impracticably [-blɪ] *adv.* impracticablemente.
impractical [-'præktɪkəl] *a.* 1. que no es práctico; teórico, irreal. 2. quijotesco, soñador.
impracticality [ɪm,præktɪ'kælətɪ] **impracticalness** [-'præktɪkəlnəs] *s.* índole teórica (de un proyecto, etc.); falta de sentido práctico.
imprecate ['ɪmprɪ,keɪt] *v.t.* imprecar, maldecir. —*v.i.* blasfemar.
imprecation [,ɪmprɪ'keɪʃən] *s.* imprecación, maldición; vituperio, reniego, anatema.
imprecatory ['ɪmprɪkə,tɔrɪ, ɪm'prɛkə-, B 'ɪmprɪ,keɪtərɪ] *a.* imprecatorio, maldiciente.
imprecise [,ɪmprɪ'saɪs] *a.* impreciso, inexacto, indefinido.
imprecisely [-lɪ] *adv.* de modo impreciso, inexactamente.
impreciseness [-nəs] **imprecision** [-'sɪʒən] *s.* imprecisión, inexactitud.
impregnability [ɪm,prɛgnə'bɪlətɪ] *s.* calidad de inexpugnable.
impregnable [-'prɛgnəbəl] *a.* 1. inexpugnable, inconquistable; fuerte, firme. 2. (biol.) impregnable.
impregnably [-blɪ] *adv.* inexpugnablemente.
impregnate [ɪm'prɛgnət] *a.* preñada, embarazada; impregnado. — [-,neɪt] *v.t.* 1. preñar, empreñar, embarazar. 2. (con *with*) impregnar, saturar (con o de materia, líquido, etc.); imbuir (de o en una idea, etc.) 3. (biol.) fecundar, fertilizar, inseminar.
impregnation [,ɪmprɛg'neɪʃən] *s.* 1. impregnación, infusión. 2. (biol.) fertilización, fecundación.
impregnator [ɪm'prɛg,neɪtər, B -ə] *s.* 1. impregnador (de tejidos, etc.) 2. fertilizador, fecundador.
impresa [ɪm'preɪzə] **imprese** [-'priz] *s.* (hist.) lema, divisa (en un escudo).
impresario [,ɪmprə'sɑrɪoʊ, -'sɛr-, B -'sɑr-] *s.* (*pl.* IMPRESARIOS) (teat.) empresario, agente; administrador (de una compañia de ópera, ballet, etc.).
imprescriptible [,ɪmprɪ'skrɪptəbəl] *a.* imprescriptible, inalienable.
impress [ɪm'prɛs] *v.t.* 1. imprimir; marcar. 2. estampar, grabar. 3. (fig.) inculcar, fijar (idea, creencia, etc.). 4. impresionar, causar impresión en. 5. ejercer (fuerza). 6. (elec.) aplicar. —*v.i.* hacer impresión. — ['ɪm,prɛs] *s.* 1. impresión, huella. 2. marca, sello, estampa, señal. 3. (ant.) empresa, divisa, lema, mote.
impress, *v.t.* (mil.) reclutar, requisar, enganchar (esp. en la marina). — ['ɪm,prɛs] *s.* enganche, leva, requisa, conscripción (Am.).
impressibility [ɪm,prɛsə'bɪlətɪ] *s.* impresionabilidad, susceptibilidad.
impressible [-'prɛsəbəl] *a.* impresionable, susceptible; estampable.
impressing [-ɪŋ] *a.* impresionante, imponente.
impression [-'prɛʃən] *s.* 1. impresión. 2. (fig.) impresión, efecto, sensación, recuerdo vago. 3. (impr.) impresión; ejemplar, copia; placa (grabada); tiraje, edición. 4. estampa, siglación, marca, señal, huella. 5. **to be under the i. that,** tener la impresión de que; **to have the i.,** tener la impresión; **to make a good i.,** causar buena impresión.
impressionability [-,prɛʃənə'bɪlətɪ] *s.* impresionabilidad, susceptibilidad.
impressionable [-'prɛʃənəbəl] *a.* impresionable, susceptible, afectable.
impressional [-ənəl] *a.* perteneciente o relativo a la impresión.
impressionism [ɪm'prɛʃə,nɪzəm] *s.* (pint., lit., mús.) impresionismo (escuela, estilo).
impressionist [-nəst] *a.* (pint., lit., mús.) impresionista (artista y estilo).
impressionistic [-,prɛʃə'nɪstɪk] *a.* (pint., lit., mús.) impresionista.
impressive [ɪm'prɛsɪv] *a.* impresionante, emocionante, notable, solemne, grandioso.
impressively [-lɪ] *adv.* impresionantemente, imponentemente, grandiosamente.
impressiveness [-nəs] *s.* carácter impresionante, aspecto imponente, imponencia (Am.), solemnidad.
impressment [-'prɛsmənt] *s.* 1. expropiación (para uso público); requisición, requisa. 2. (mil.) leva, enganche (esp. para la marina).
impressure [-'prɛʃər, B -ə] *s.* (ant.) impresión, marca.
imprest ['ɪm,prɛst] *a.* anticipado, adelantado (dinero); prestado. —*s.* (com.) préstamo, anticipo (esp. el que otorga el erario).
imprimatur [,ɪmprə'mɑtər, B -'meɪtə] *s.* 1. (der.) imprimátur. 2. aprobación, permiso.
imprimis [ɪm'praɪməs] *adv.* en primer lugar, en principio.
imprint [ɪm'prɪnt] *v.t.* 1. imprimir, marcar, estampar. 2. fijar, grabar (en la memoria), puntualizar. — ['ɪm,prɪnt] *s.* 1. impresión, marca, huella. 2. (impr.) pie de imprenta; sello (editorial).
imprison [ɪm'prɪzən] *v.t.* encarcelar, aprisionar, encerrar.
imprisonment [-mənt] *s.* encarcelamiento, reclusión, prisión.
improbability [ɪm,prɑbə'bɪlətɪ, B -,prɔb-] *s.* improbabilidad, inverosimilitud.
improbable [-'prɑbəbəl, B -'prɔb-] *a.* improbable, inverosímil, increíble.
improbably [-blɪ] *adv.* improbablemente.
improbity [-'proʊbətɪ] *s.* improbidad, falta de probidad, de integridad o rectitud.
impromptu [ɪm'prɑmp,tu, B -'prɔmptju] *a.* improvisado, impremeditado. —*adv.* improvisamente, improvisadamente, de improviso; de repente, en el acto. —*s.* 1. (mús.) impromptu; improvisación. 2. (poét.) improvisación.
improper [-'prɑpər, B -'prɔpə] *a.* 1. impropio, inadecuado, inepto. 2. inexacto, injusto, incorrecto. 3. indecoroso, deshonesto.
improper fraction, (mat.) quebrado impropio, fracción impropia.
improperly [-lɪ] *adv.* 1. impropiamente, inadecuadamente. 2. inexactamente, injustamente, incorrectamente. 3. indecorosamente, sin honestidad.
impropriate [ɪm'proʊprɪɪt] *a.* secularizado. — [-,eɪt] *v.t.* secularizar, hacer secular (bienes eclesiásticos).
impropriation [ɪm,proʊprɪ'eɪʃən] *s.* secularización de bienes eclesiásticos.
impropriator [-'proʊprɪ,eɪtər, B -ə] *s.* secular que posee bienes eclesiásticos.
impropriety [,ɪmprə'praɪətɪ] *s.* 1. impropiedad (en el lenguaje), incongruencia. 2. deshonestidad, indecoro (en el vestir). 3. incorrección.
improvability [ɪm,pruvə'bɪlətɪ] *s.* capacidad para mejorar o enmendarse.
improvable [-'pruvəbəl] *a.* mejorable, perfectible, enmendable.
improve [-'pruv] *v.t.* 1. mejorar, perfeccionar, aumentar. 2. (E.U.) aumentar el valor de (un terreno, por medio de construcciones o urbanización). 3. beneficiar, abonar, embonar. (tierras). 4. (dial.) emplear, utilizar. —*v.i.* 1. mejorar(se), adelantar, hacer progresos. 2. **i. on** (o **upon**), mejorar, perfeccionar. 3. (com.) valorizarse, subir, encarecer, estar en alza.
improvement [-mənt] *s.* 1. mejoramiento, perfeccionamiento. 2. mejoría, mejora, medra. 3. adelanto, ventaja, progreso. 4. desarrollo, ampliación (ej., de una fábrica); urbanización.
improver [-ər, B -ə] *s.* aprendiz meritorio; el que aprende y adelanta.
improvidence [ɪm'prɑvədəns, B -'prɔv-] *s.* improvidencia, imprevisión, descuido.
improvident [-dənt] *a.* impróvido, imprevisor, descuidado, desprevenido.
improvidently [-lɪ] *adv.* impróvidamente, sin previsión.
improvisation [ɪm,prɑvə'zeɪʃən, B 'ɪmprəvaɪ-] *s.* improvisación.
improvisator [-'prɑvə,zeɪtər, B -'prɔvɪ-ə] *s.* improvisador, repentista.
improvisatorial [-,prɑvəzə'tɔrɪəl, B -,prɔvɪ-] *a.* improvisador, relativo a la improvisación.
improvisatory [-'prɑvəzə,tɔrɪ, B -'prɔvtərɪ] *a.* improvisador, relativo a la improvisación.
improvise ['ɪmprə,vaɪz] *v.t., v.i.* improvisar.
improviser, improvisor [-,vaɪzər, B -zə] *s.* improvisador, repentista.
imprudence [ɪm'prudəns] *s.* imprudencia, indiscreción, irreflexión, descuido, temeridad.
imprudent [-ənt] *a.* imprudente, indiscreto, irreflexivo, temerario.
imprudently [-lɪ] *adv.* imprudentemente, indiscretamente, irreflexivamente, temerariamente.
impudence ['ɪmpjədəns] *s.* impudencia, descaro, desvergüenza, atrevimiento, desfachatez.
impudent [-dənt] *a.* 1. impudente, descarado, atrevido. 2. (ant.) impúdico, inmodesto.
impudently [-lɪ] *adv.* descaradamente, con impudencia, insolentemente.
impudicity [,ɪmpju'dɪsətɪ] *s.* impudicicia, impudicia, impudor, desvergüenza.
impugn [ɪm'pjun] *v.t.* impugnar, combatir, poner en tela de juicio, contradecir.
impugnable [-əbəl] *a.* impugnable.
impugnation [,ɪmpəg'neɪʃən] *s.* impugnación.
impugner [ɪm'pjunər, B -ə] *s.* impugnador.
impuissance [ɪm'pjuəsəns, -'pwɪs-, B -'pjuəs-] *s.* impotencia, debilidad; incapacidad.
impuissant [-'pjuəsənt] *a.* impotente, débil, incapaz.
impulse ['ɪm,pʌls] *s.* 1. impulso, ímpetu, arranque, impulsión, inclinación repentina. 2. (elec., mec., fisiol.) impulso, impulsión. 3. **to act on i.,** obedecer a un impulso, actuar debido a un impulso; **under the i. of,** bajo el incentivo de. —*v.t.* impulsar.
impulse turbine, turbina de impulsión, turbina de acción.

impulsion [ɪm'pʌlʃən] *s.* impulsión, impulso.
impulsive [-sɪv] *a.* impulsivo.
impulsively [-lɪ] *adv.* impulsivamente.
impulsiveness [-nəs] *s.* impulsividad.
impunity [ɪm'pjunətɪ] *s.* impunidad.
impure [ɪm'pjʊr, B -'pjʊə] *s.* 1. impuro (agua, substancia, estilo, etc.). 2. obsceno, adulterado, impúdico (palabras, lenguaje). 3. (filol.) impuro (ej., un dialecto).
impurely [-lɪ] *adv.* impuramente.
impureness [-nəs] *s.* impureza, adulteración, inmundicia.
impurity [-ətɪ, B -'pjuər-] *s.* (*pl.* IMPURITIES) impureza.
imputability [ɪm,pjutə'bɪlətɪ] *s.* imputabilidad.
imputable [-'pjutəbəl] *a.* imputable, achacable.
imputation [,ɪmpjə'teɪʃən] *a.* imputación, atribución, insinuación, acusación, reproche.
imputative [ɪm'pjutətɪv] *a.* imputador, imputativo.
impute [ɪm'pjut] *v.t.* imputar, atribuir, achacar.
imputer [-ər, B -ə] *s.* imputador.
in [ɪn] *prep.* 1. en (indicando lugar o dirección), ej., *in New York,* en Nueva York, *put it in your pocket,* métalo en el bolsillo. 2. en, de (indicando condición, circunstancias, manera o modo), ej., *in the dark,* en la oscuridad, *in some respects,* en algunos aspectos, *in reply to,* en respuesta a, *dressed in white,* vestido de blanco. 3. con (indicando instrumento o medio), ej., *written in ink,* escrito con tinta. 4. en cada, de cada (indicando proporción), de (indicando dimensión), ej., *one in eight wins,* en cada ocho, uno gana, *four feet in length,* cuatro pies de largo. 5. en, por, de, dentro de, durante (indicando tiempo), ej., *in the morning,* por la mañana, de mañana, *in all my life,* en toda mi vida, *in an hour's time,* dentro de una hora, en una hora. 6. a (indicando acción, actividad) ej., *to spend one's time in reading,* dedicar su tiempo a la lectura. 7. **I do not suppose he has it in him,** no creo que él sea capaz de; **in-as-much as,** por cuanto, en cuanto, en vista de; **in itself,** en sí (mismo); aparte de todo lo demás; **in so far as,** en tanto que; **in that,** por cuanto, ya que, porque. —*adv.* 1. dentro, adentro, hacia adentro. 2. de moda, en su tiempo o estación, ej., *bikinis are in,* los bikinis están de moda. 3. **in and out,** yendo y viniendo; entrando y saliendo; **in here,** aquí dentro; **on the way in,** entrando, al entrar; **to be in,** estar (en su casa, en su oficina); haber llegado (tren, barco, verano); **to be in for,** estar expuesto a, no poder evitar; estar envuelto (complicado) en; (dep.) participar en (una competencia); **to be in for it,** estar en espera de dificultades; estar por recibir castigo o tareas pesadas; **to be in on,** tomar parte en, participar en; **to be** (o **to keep**) **in with,** gozar del favor de; **to have it in for (someone),** (jer.) enojarse con (alguien), desear vengarse de (alguien). —*a.* 1. interior, interno, de adentro, ej., *the in part,* la parte interior o interna, la parte de adentro. 2. en el poder, ej., *the in party,* el partido en el poder. 3. moderno, sofisticado (gente); de moda. 4. (algo o alguien) aceptado por personas importantes, influyentes, etc. 5. que pertenece a o es aceptado por un grupo específico de personas. 6. próximo, venidero; por llegar (ej., el tren). 7. **the in side,** (criquet) lado que batea. —*s.* 1. persona en funciones. 2. influencia (política, etc.). 3. **ins and outs,** pormenores, detalles, minucias; **the ins,** los que están en el poder (ej., los miembros de un partido político).
In *símb. de* **indium,** indio (In).
in. *abrev. de* **inch, inches,** pulgada(s).
inability [,ɪnə'bɪlətɪ] *s.* inabilidad, incapacidad, ineptitud; insuficiencia, impotencia, nulidad.
inaccessibility [,ɪnɪk,sɛsə'bɪlətɪ, B 'ɪnæk-] *s.* inaccesibilidad.
inaccessible [-'sɛsəbəl] *a.* inaccesible, inabordable.
inaccessibly [-blɪ] *adv.* inaccesiblemente.
inaccuracy [ɪn'ækjərəsɪ] *s.* inexactitud; incorrección; error, equivocación.
inaccurate [-jərət] *a.* inexacto; incorrecto, erróneo.
inaccurately [-lɪ] *adv.* inexactamente; incorrectamente.
inaction [ɪn'ækʃən] *s.* inacción; holgazanería; inercia, inactividad.
inactivate [-'æktə,veɪt] *v.t.* hacer inactivo.
inactivation [-,æktə'veɪʃən] *s.* (med.) inactivación.
inactive [ɪn'æktɪv] *a.* 1. inactivo, inerte; perezoso, indolente, pasivo, ocioso. 2. (fís., quím., med.) inactivo.
inactive list, escalafón de reserva.
inactively [-lɪ] *adv.* inactivamente.
inactive status, (mil.) situación de reserva.
inactivity [,ɪnæk'tɪvətɪ] *s.* inactividad; ociosidad.
inadaptability [,ɪnə,dæptə'bɪlətɪ] *s.* inadaptabilidad.
inadequacy [ɪn'ædɪkwəsɪ] *s.* insuficiencia, falta de adecuación.
inadequate [-kwət] *a.* inadecuado, deficiente, insuficiente.
inadequately [-lɪ] *adv.* inadecuadamente, insuficientemente.
inadequateness [-nəs] *s.* inadecuación.
inadmissibility [,ɪnəd,mɪsə'bɪlətɪ] *s.* inadmisibilidad.
inadmissible [-'mɪsəbəl] *a.* inadmisible, inaceptable.
inadmissibly [-blɪ] *adv.* inadmisiblemente.
inadvertence [,ɪnəd'vɜrtəns, B -'vɜt-] *s.* 1. inadvertencia, falta de atención, descuido. 2. falta, error.
inadvertency [-ənsɪ] *s.* inadvertencia, descuido, negligencia, error.
inadvertent [-ənt] *a.* 1. inadvertido, negligente, descuidado. 2. accidental, involuntario (acción).
inadvertently [-lɪ] *adv.* 1. inadvertidamente, negligentemente, descuidadamente. 2. accidentalmente, involuntariamente.
inadvisability [,ɪnəd,vaɪzə'bɪlətɪ] *s.* inconveniencia.
inadvisable [-'vaɪzəbəl] *a.* inconveniente, poco aconsejable, imprudente.
inalienability [ɪn,eɪljənə'bɪlətɪ] *s.* inalienabilidad.
inalienable [-'eɪljənəbəl] *a.* inalienable, inenajenable.
inalienably [-blɪ] *adv.* inalienablemente.
inalterability [ɪn,ɔltərə'bɪlətɪ] *s.* inalterabilidad.
inalterable [-'ɔltərəbəl] *a.* inalterable.
inalterably [-blɪ] *adv.* inalterablemente.
inamorata [ɪn,æmə'rɑtə] *s.* (*pl.* INAMORATAS) amada, enamorada, novia.
inamorato [-'rɑtoʊ] *s.* (*pl.* INAMORATOS) amado, enamorado, novio.
in-and-in ['ɪnənd'ɪn] *a.* endogámico.
inane [ɪn'eɪn] *a.* vacío, inane; necio, tonto, soso, anodino, insubstancial.
inanely [-lɪ] *adv.* insensatamente, neciamente.
inanimate [ɪn'ænəmət] *a.* 1. inanimado, muerto, exánime. 2. desanimado, apagado, abatido.
inanimately [-lɪ] *adv.* desanimadamente.
inanimateness [-nəs] *s.* falta de vida o vitalidad; desánimo, abatimiento.
inanition [,ɪnə'nɪʃən] *s.* inanición.
inanity [ɪn'ænətɪ] *s.* 1. inanidad, vaciedad. 2. insensatez, sandez.
inapparent [,ɪnə'pærənt] *a.* no aparente.
inappeasable [-'pizəbəl] *a.* inaplacable.
inappetence [ɪn'æpətəns] **inappetency** [-ənsɪ] *s.* inapetencia.
inappetent [-ənt] *a.* inapetente.
inapplicability [ɪn,æplɪkə'bɪlətɪ] *s.* falta de aplicabilidad.
inapplicable [-'æplikəbəl, ˌɪnə'plɪk-] *a.* inaplicable, inconveniente; fuera de lugar.
inapplicably [-blɪ] *adv.* inconvenientemente, inaplicablemente.
inapposite [ɪn'æpəzət] *a.* no apropiado, inoportuno, fuera de propósito, inconveniente.
inappositely [-lɪ] *adv.* inoportunamente, inconvenientemente.
inappreciable [,ɪnə'priʃəbəl] *a.* 1. inapreciable, insignificante, imponderable. 2. (ant.) invalorable, inestimable.
inappreciably [-blɪ] *adv.* imponderablemente.
inappreciative [-ʃətɪv, -ʃɪ,eɪt-] *a.* que no aprecia, ingrato.
inappreciatively [-lɪ] *adv.* sin mostrar (su) aprecio, ingratamente.
inappreciativeness [-nəs] *s.* falta de apreciación, ingratitud.
inapprehensible [,ɪnæprɪ'hɛnsəbəl] *a.* inteligible, incomprensible.
inapprehension [-'hɛntʃən, B -'hɛnʃən] *s.* falta de comprensión o de percepción.
inapprehensive [-sɪv] *a.* que no comprende o percibe.
inapproachability [,ɪnə,proʊtʃə'bɪlətɪ] *s.* inaccesibilidad.
inapproachable [-'proʊtʃəbəl] *a.* inaccesible, inasequible, inalcanzable.
inapproachably [-blɪ] *adv.* inaccesiblemente.
inappropriate [,ɪnə'proʊprɪət] *a.* inadecuado, impropio, no apropiado.
inappropriately [-lɪ] *adv.* impropiamente, fuera del caso.
inappropriateness [-nəs] *s.* impropiedad, incorrección.
inapt [ɪn'æpt] *a.* 1. inepto, inhábil, torpe. 2. inadecuado, inconveniente, impropio.
inaptitude [-'æptə,tud, B -,tjud] *s.* ineptitud, inhabilidad, insuficiencia, incapacidad.
inaptly [-lɪ] *adv.* 1. ineptamente, torpemente. 2. inadecuadamente.
inaptness [-nəs] *s.* 1. ineptitud, inhabilidad, torpeza. 2. inconveniencia.
inarable [-'ærəbəl] *a.* incultivable.
inarch [ɪn'ɑrtʃ, B -'ɑtʃ] *v.t.* (agr.) injertar por aproximación.
inarticulate [,ɪnɑr'tɪkjələt, B -ɑ'-] *a.* 1. inarticulado (sonido). 2. mudo, incapaz de articular; incapaz de expresarse. 3. (zool.) inarticulado.
inarticulately [-lɪ] *adv.* inarticuladamente.
inarticulateness [-nəs] *s.* incapacidad de articular o expresarse claramente, inarticulación.
inartificial [ɪn,ɑrtə'fɪʃəl, B -,ɑtɪ-] *a.* (ant.) 1. sin artificio, natural, sin arte, simple, sencillo, directo. 2. poco artístico, desmañado, chapucero.
inartistic, inartistical [-ɑr'tɪstɪk, B -ɑ'-] *a.* inartístico, sin arte, sin gusto artístico.
inasmuch as [,ɪnəz'mʌtʃəz] visto; puesto que; en vista de que, por cuanto; ya que.
inattention [,ɪnə'tɛntʃən, B -'tɛnʃən] *s.* inatención; desatención, distracción, inadvertencia.

inattentive [-'tɛntɪv] *a.* desatento, distraído, descuidado.
inattentively [-lɪ] *adv.* distraídamente, descuidadamente, sin atención.
inattentiveness [-nəs] *s.* descuido, inatención, falta de atención, distracción.
inaudibility [-ˌɔdə'bɪlətɪ] *s.* dificultad o incapacidad de ser oído.
inaudible [ɪn'ɔdəbəl] *a.* inaudible, imperceptible.
inaudibly [-blɪ] *adv.* imperceptiblemente.
inaugural [ɪn'ɔgjərəl, -gə-, B -gjʊ-] *a.* inaugural. —*s.* (E.U.) 1. discurso inaugural. 2. inauguración.
inaugurate [-ˌreɪt] *v.t.* 1. investir (de un cargo); introducir, instalar, consagrar. 2. inaugurar, empezar, iniciar. 3. inaugurar, principiar, originar, poner en marcha.
inauguration [-ˌɔgjə'reɪʃən, -gə-, B -gjʊ-] *s.* 1. inauguración; estreno. 2. instalación, investidura, toma de posesión.
inaugurator [-'ɔgjəˌreɪtər, -gə-, B -gjʊˌreɪtə] *s.* inaugurador.
inauspicious [ˌɪnɔ'spɪʃəs] *a.* poco propicio, desfavorable.
inauspiciously [-lɪ] *adv.* desgraciadamente, desfavorablemente, bajo malos auspicios.
inauspiciousness [-nəs] *s.* malos auspicios, desgracia.
inbeing ['ɪnˌbiɪŋ] *s.* inherencia, inseparabilidad, inmanencia; esencia, ser íntimo, ser profundo o esencial.
inboard [-ˌbɔrd, B -ˌbɔd] *adv.* 1. (mar.) hacia el interior del casco; dentro del casco. 2. (mec.) hacia dentro.
inborn [-'bɔrn, B -'bɔn] *a.* innato, ingénito, ínsito, connatural, congénito, de nacimiento.
inbound [-ˌbaʊnd] *a.* por llegar (buque, tren, etc.); que viene (de viaje); de llegada (estación); de entrada (puerto), entrante.
inbreathe [-'brið] *v.t.* inspirar, aspirar, inhalar.
inbred [-'brɛd] *a.* 1. ínsito, innato. 2. endogámico, nacido de padres consanguíneos o de razas muy semejantes.
inbreed [-'brid] *v.t.* 1. procrear dentro de una misma familia. 2. criar o producir dentro de una misma raza.
inbreeding [-ˌbridɪŋ] *s.* endogamia, generación sin mezcla de familias o razas.
Inc. *abrev. de* **incorporated,** incorporado.
Inca ['ɪŋkə] *s.* inca.
incage [ɪn'keɪdʒ] *v.t.* enjaular.
Incaic [ɪŋ'keɪɪk] *a.* incaico, incásico.
incalculability [ɪnˌkælkjələ'bɪlətɪ] *s.* calidad de incalculable.
incalculable [ɪn'kælkjələbəl] *a.* incalculable.
incalculably [-blɪ] *adv.* incalculablemente.
incalescence [ˌɪnkə'lɛsəns] *s.* (raro) calor creciente.
incalescent [-ənt] *a.* (raro) progresivamente caluroso.
Incan ['ɪŋkən] *a.* incaico, incásico.
incandesce [ˌɪnkən'dɛs, B 'ɪn-] *v.t., v.i.* encandecer(se), poner(se) incandescente.
incandescence [-əns] *s.* incandescencia, encendimiento.
incandescent [-ənt] *a.* incandescente, candente.
incandescent lamp, lámpara incandescente.
incantation [ˌɪnkæn'teɪʃən] *s.* conjuro, exorcismo, sortilegio, encantamiento, encanto.
incantatory [ɪn'kæntəˌtɔrɪ, B -tərɪ] *a.* mágico.
incapability [ɪnˌkeɪpə'bɪlətɪ] *s.* incapacidad; ineptitud.
incapable [ɪn'keɪpəbəl] *a.* 1. incapaz, incompetente, inhábil, inepto. 2. (con *of*) incapaz (de). 3. (der.) incapaz, sin aptitud legal; inelegible.
incapableness [-nəs] *s.* incapacidad.
incapably [-blɪ] *adv.* incompetentemente.
incapacious [ˌɪnkə'peɪʃəs] *a.* 1. estrecho, angosto, limitado. 2. (ant.) mentalmente deficiente.
incapacitate [-'pæsəˌteɪt] *v.t.* incapacitar, inhabilitar; (der.) incapacitar, imposibilitar.
incapacitation [-ˌpæsə'teɪʃən] *s.* 1. inhabilitación. 2. (der.) privación de la capacidad.
incapacity [-'pæsətɪ] *s.* incapacidad, inhabilidad, insuficiencia.
incarcerate [ɪn'kɑrsəˌreɪt, B -'kɑsə-] *v.t.* encarcelar; encerrar, aprisionar.
incarceration [-ˌkɑrsə'reɪʃən B -ˌkɑsə-] *s.* 1. encarcelación, encarcelamiento, prisión. 2. (cir.) estrangulación (de una hernia).
incarcerator [-'kɑrsəˌreɪtər, B -'kɑsə-tə] *s.* encarcelador.
incardinate [-'kɑrdəˌneɪt, B -'kɑdə-] *v.t.* (relig.) incardinar; elegir, instalar o nombrar cardenal.
incardination [-ˌkɑrdə'neɪʃən, B -ˌkɑdə-] *s.* (relig.) incardinación.
incarnadine [ɪn'kɑrnəˌdaɪn, -dən, B -'kɑnəˌdaɪn] *a.* encarnado, encardinado. —*s.* encarnado. —*v.t.* volver encarnado, enrojecer.
incarnate [-'kɑrnət, -ˌneɪt, B -'kɑnɪt] *a.* 1. encarnado, personificado. 2. encarnado, de color de carne. — [-ˌneɪt] *v.t.* 1. encarnar, dar cuerpo a, personificar. 2. realizar, dar realidad a.
incarnation [ˌɪnkɑr'neɪʃən, B ˌɪnkɑ'-] *s.* 1. encarnación, personificación. 2. **the I.,** (teo.) la Encarnación. 3. (cir.) encarnamiento.
incase [ɪn'keɪs] *var. de* **encase.**
incasement [-mənt] *s.* encaje, inclusión, encajonamiento, encierro, caja, cobertura.
incastellated [ɪn'kæstəˌleɪtəd] *a.* encastillado.
incatenation [-ˌkætə'neɪʃən] *s.* encadenamiento, concatenación.
incaution [ɪn'kɔʃən] *s.* falta de cautela o precaución; descuido, negligencia; imprudencia.
incautious [-ʃəs] *a.* incauto, descuidado, negligente, imprudente.
incautiously [-lɪ] *adv.* incautamente, descuidadamente.
incautiousness [-nəs] *s.* falta de cautela, descuido, imprevisión.
incavation [ˌɪnkə'veɪʃən] *s.* depresión, hueco, ahuecamiento.
incendiarism [ɪn'sɛndɪəˌrɪzəm] *s.* 1. (der.) incendio malicioso. 2. (psic.) manía incendiaria, piromanía.
incendiary [-dɪˌɛrɪ, B -dɪərɪ] *a.* 1. (der.) incendiario. 2. (fig.) incendiario, inflamatorio, sedicioso, subversivo. 3. incendiario, destinado a causar incendios (proyectil). —*s.* 1. incendiario, pirómano. 2. (fig.) incendiario, alborotador, agitador. 3. bomba o proyectil incendiario.
incendiary bomb, bomba incendiaria.
incense [ɪn'sɛns] *v.t.* exasperar, irritar, encolerizar, enfurecer, sulfurar, enfadar.
incense ['ɪnsɛns] *s.* 1. incienso; p. ext. perfume o aroma agradable. 2. (fig.) incienso, alabanza, elogio, encomio, loa; lisonja, halago, adulación. —*v.t.* incensar. —*v.i.* quemar u ofrecer incienso.
incensement [ɪn'sɛnsmənt] *s.* ira, furia, cólera.
incensory ['ɪnˌsɛnsərɪ] *s.* incensario.
incentive [ɪn'sɛntɪv] *a.* incitativo, incitador, incitante, estimulante. —*s.* incentivo, estímulo, aliciente, acicate; motivo.
incept [ɪn'sɛpt] *v.t.* 1. (biol.) ingerir. 2. (ant.) principiar, empezar. —*v.i.* (G.B.) obtener grado universitario para ejercer o enseñar una profesión (en la Universidad de Cambridge).
inception [-'sɛpʃən] *s.* 1. principio, comienzo, iniciación, inicio. 2. (biol.) ingestión.
inceptive [-tɪv] *a.* 1. incipiente, inicial. 2. (gram.) incoativo. —*s.* (gram.) verbo incoativo.
inceptor [-tər B -tə] *s.* 1. principiante, iniciador, introductor. 2. (G.B.) graduado (en la Universidad de Cambridge con grado de maestro o doctor).
incertitude [-'sɜrtəˌtud, B -'sɜtɪˌtjud] *s.* incertidumbre, duda; indecisión; inseguridad.
incessant [-'sɛsənt] *a.* incesante, incesable, continuo, ininterrumpido.
incessantly [-lɪ] *adv.* incesantemente, continuamente, ininterrumpidamente.
incest ['ɪnsɛst] *s.* incesto.
incestuous [ɪn'sɛstʃʊəs, B -tjʊ-] *a.* incestuoso.
incestuously [-lɪ] *adv.* incestuosamente.
inch [ɪntʃ] *s.* 1. pulgada (medida equivalente a 2,54 centímetros). 2. pizca, porción mínima. 3. **by inches,** poco a poco, paso a paso; **every i.,** en todo respecto; **give him an i. and he'll take a yard,** le das un dedo y se toma la mano; **i. by i.,** pulgada a pulgada, palmo a palmo; **to know every i. of,** conocer al dedillo, tener medido a palmos; **within an i. of,** a dos dedos de. —*v.t.* mover o llevar por pulgadas; **i. one's way,** avanzar lentamente. —*v.i.* (con *ahead, along, back, forward,* etc.) avanzar o recular poco a poco.
inch, *s.* 1. (Esco., Irl.) isla. 2. pequeño terreno aislado.
inched [ɪntʃt] *a.* de (cierto número de) pulgadas, ej., *a six-i. lever,* una palanca de seis pulgadas.
inchmeal ['ɪntʃˌmil] *adv.* gradualmente; (t. **by i.**) poco a poco.
inchoate [ɪn'koʊət, B 'ɪnkoʊˌeɪt] *a.* 1. incipiente, rudimentario o rudimental. 2. (der.) incoado. — ['ɪnkoʊˌeɪt] *v.t.* (ant.) incoar.
inchoately [-lɪ] *adv.* en el primer grado.
inchoation [ˌɪnkoʊ'eɪʃən] *s.* incoación, principio.
inchoative [ɪn'koʊətɪv, B 'ɪnkoʊˌeɪtɪv] *a.* incipiente, incoativo.
inchoative verb, (gram.) verbo incoativo.
inchworm ['ɪntʃˌwɜrm, B -ˌwɜm] *s.* (ento.) geometrino, oruga geómetra.
incidence ['ɪnsədəns] *s.* 1. incidencia, ocurrencia; frecuencia. 2. efecto. 3. (fís., geom.) incidencia.
incident [-dənt] *a.* 1. concomitante. 2. (fís., der.) incidente. 3. (raro) fortuito, accidental. 4. **to be i. to,** ser inherente a. —*s.* 1. incidente, acaecimiento, acontecimiento. 2. (der.) incidencia.
incidental [ˌɪnsə'dɛntəl] *a.* 1. incidental, fortuito, accidental, casual. 2. (com.) incidental, accesorio (gasto). 3. (der.) concomitante, accesorio (ej., poderes). 4. **to be i. to,** acompañar, ser consecuencia de. —*s.* elemento incidental; (*pl.*) imprevistos, detalles.
incidentally [-'dɛntlɪ, -əlɪ] *adv.* 1. entre paréntesis, a propósito, de paso. 2. incidentemente, incidentalmente.
incidental music, música de acompañamiento, fondo musical (en el teatro, etc.).
incinerate [ɪn'sɪnəˌreɪt] *v.t., v.i.* incinerar(se), quemar(se).
incineration [ɪnˌsɪnə'reɪʃən] *s.* incineración, cremación.
incinerator [-'sɪnəˌreɪtər, B -ə] *s.* incinerador, horno crematorio.
incipience [ɪn'sɪpɪəns] *s.* principio, comienzo, inicio.
incipiency [-ənsɪ] *s., var. de* **incipience.**
incipient [-ənt] *a.* incipiente, inicial.
incipiently [-lɪ] *adv.* incipientemente, al comienzo, inicialmente.
incipit ['ɪnsəpət] *s.* (hist.) incipit.

incise [ɪn'saɪz] *v.t.* 1. cortar; tallar, grabar. 2. (med.) incidir.
incised [-'saɪzd] *a.* 1. inciso, cortado. 2. (bot.) irregularmente denticular o serrado.
incision [ɪn'cɪʒən] *s.* 1. cortadura, corte, abscisión. 2. (med.) incisión; cisura, incisura.
incisive [ɪn'saɪsɪv] *a.* 1. incisivo, cortante. 2. (fig.) incisivo, mordaz, agudo.
incisively [-lɪ] *adv.* 1. (fig.) agudamente, mordazmente. 2. (fig.) tajantemente, decisivamente.
incisiveness [-nəs] *s.* 1. agudeza, sutileza, penetración (de espíritu). 2. mordacidad.
incisor [-'saɪzər, B -zə] *s.* (anat., zool.) incisivo (diente).
incisory [-zərɪ] *a.* incisorio.
incitation [,ɪnsaɪ'teɪʃən] *s.* incitación, instigación; estimulación.
incite [ɪn'saɪt] *v.t.* incitar, instigar, estimular, acuciar.
incitement [-mənt] *s.* 1. incitación, instigación, estímulo, incitamento. 2. aliciente.
inciter [-ər, B -ə] *s.* incitador, instigador.
inciting [-ɪŋ] *a.* incitante, provocativo.
incitingly [-ɪŋlɪ] *adv.* provocativamente, incitantemente.
incivility [,ɪnsə'vɪlətɪ] *s.* incivilidad, descortesía, desatención.
inclemency [ɪn'klɛmənsɪ] *s.* inclemencia.
inclement [-ənt] *a.* inclemente, duro, riguroso (tiempo); inclemente, severo, sin piedad (carácter).
inclemently [-lɪ] *adv.* de manera inclemente, severamente.
inclinable [ɪn'klaɪnəbəl] *a.* 1. (con *to*) propenso, inclinado (a); p. ext. favorablemente dispuesto (hacia). 2. inclinable.
inclination [,ɪnklə'neɪʃən] *s.* 1. inclinación, propensión, parcialidad; tendencia. 2. inclinación, reverencia, venia. 3. cuesta, pendiente, declive. 4. (geom.) inclinación.
inclinatory [ɪn'klaɪnə,tɔrɪ, B -tərɪ] *a.* inclinativo.
incline [ɪn'klaɪn] *v.i.* 1. inclinarse, hacer una venia o reverencia. 2. inclinarse, tender a, simpatizar con. 3. inclinarse, ladearse, sesgarse. —*v.t.* 1. inclinar, sesgar, doblar. 2. **i. one's ear to,** escuchar con simpatía. — ['ɪnklaɪn, B ɪn'klaɪn] *s.* declive, pendiente, cuesta.
inclined [-'klaɪnd] *a.* 1. inclinado, en declive, en cuesta, ladeado, oblicuo. 2. (fig.) inclinado, dispuesto, propenso, proclive. 3. **to be** (o **feel**) **i. to (do),** inclinarse a (hacer).
inclined plane, (mec.) plano inclinado.
incliner [-'klaɪnər, B -ə] *s.* inclinador.
inclinometer [,ɪnklə'nɑmətər, B -'nɔmɪtə] *s.* 1. inclinómetro. 2. clinómetro. 3. brújula de inclinación.
inclose, inclosure, *var. de* **enclose, enclosure.**
includable, includible [ɪn'kludəbəl] *a.* incluible.
include [ɪn'klud] *v.t.* 1. incluir, confinar. 2. incluir, comprender, abarcar, contener.
included [-əd] *a.* 1. incluido, incluso. 2. (bot.) incluso (díc. de estambres y pistilo).
inclusion [ɪn'kluʒən] *s.* 1. inclusión. 2. (geol.) inclusión. 3. (biol.) inclusión plasmática.
inclusion body, (med.) corpúsculo de inclusión.
inclusive [-sɪv] *a.* inclusivo; **i. of,** incluyendo, inclusive, ej., *chapters 7 and 8 i.,* incluyendo los capítulos 7 y 8, los capítulos 7 y 8 inclusive.
inclusively [-lɪ] *adv.* inclusivamente, inclusive, incluso.
inclusiveness [-nəs] *s.* inclusividad.
incoercible [,ɪnkoʊ'ɜrsəbəl, B -'ɜsɪ-] *a.* 1. incoercible. 2. (fís.) permanente (gas).
incogitable [ɪn'kɑdʒətəbəl, B -'kɔdʒ-] *a.* inconcebible.
incogitant [-tənt] *a.* irreflexivo, inconsiderado.
incognito [,ɪn,kɑg'nitoʊ, ɪn'kɑgnətoʊ, B ɪn'kɔg-] *a.* incógnito. —*adv.* de incógnito. —*s.* (*pl.* INCOGNITOS) incógnito.
incognizance [ɪn'kɑgnəzəns, B -'kɔg-] *s.* desconocimiento.
incognizant [-zənt] *a.* (con *of*) ignorante (de), inconsciente (de), ajeno (a).
incoherence [,ɪnkoʊ'hɪrəns, B -'hɪər-] *s.* incoherencia, inconexión.
incoherency [-ənsɪ] *s.* 1. incoherencia. 2. (*gen. pl.*) palabras incoherentes; cosa incoherente.
incoherent [-ənt] *a.* incoherente, inconexo, inconsistente.
incoherently [-lɪ] *adv.* incoherentemente, sin conexión.
incombustibility [,ɪnkəm,bʌstə'bɪlətɪ] *s.* incombustibilidad.
incombustible [-'bʌstəbəl] *a.* incombustible, no inflamable. —*s.* substancia incombustible.
income ['ɪn,kʌm] *s.* renta, rédito, utilidad; (com., ten.) ingreso(s), entrada(s).
income account, income statement (com.) cuenta de ingresos.
incomer [-ər, B -ə] *s.* (pr. G.B.) (dial.) inmigrante, recién llegado; intruso.
income tax, impuesto sobre la renta, impuesta sobre rentas, impuesto a las utilidades, impuesto sobre los réditos o los ingresos.
income tax return, declaración del impuesto sobre la renta.
incoming [-ɪŋ] *a.* entrante, que está por llegar; que empieza. —*s.* entrada, llegada, arribo.
incommensurability [,ɪnkə,mɛnsərə'bɪlətɪ, B 'ɪnkə,mɛnʃ-] *s.* inconmensurabilidad.
incommensurable [-'mɛnsərəbəl, B -'mɛnʃ-] *a.* inconmensurable. —*s.* cosa o cantidad inconmensurable.
incommensurate [-ərət] *a.* 1. desproporcionado; inadecuado, insuficiente. 2. inconmensurable.
incommensurately [-lɪ] *adv.* desproporcionadamente, inadecuadamente.
incommode [,ɪnkə'moʊd] *v.t.* incomodar, importunar; estorbar, molestar.
incommodious [-'moʊdɪəs] *a.* incómodo, molesto, inconveniente.
incommodiously [-lɪ] *adv.* incómodamente, inconvenientemente.
incommodiousness [-nəs] *s.* incomodidad; inconveniencia, molestia.
incommodity [-'mɑdətɪ, B -'mɔd-] *s.* 1. incomodidad, inconveniencia, molestia. 2. dificultad, estorbo; fastidio; desventaja.
incommunicability [,ɪnkə,mjunɪkə'bɪlətɪ] **incommunicableness** [-'mjunɪkəbəlnəs] *s.* incomunicabilidad.
incommunicable [-'mjunɪkəbəl] *a.* incomunicable, indecible.
incommunicado [-,mjunə'kɑdoʊ] *a., s.* incomunicado.
incommunicative [-'mjunə,keɪtɪv, B -kətɪv] *a.* taciturno, reservado; insociable.
incommunicativeness [-nəs] *s.* taciturnidad, reserva, insociabilidad, carácter intratable.
incommutability [,ɪnkə,mjutə'bɪlətɪ] *s.* inconmutabilidad.
incommutable [-'mjutəbəl] *a.* inconmutable, inmutable.
incommutably [-blɪ] *adv.* inconmutablemente.
incompact [,ɪnkəm'pækt] *a.* blando, fofo, suelto, esponjoso.
incomparability [ɪn,kɑmpərə'bɪlətɪ, B -,kɔm-] *s.* excelencia.
incomparable [-'kɑmpərəbəl, B -'kɔm-] *a.* 1. incomparable, sin igual, sin rival. 2. inconmensurable, sin paralelo.
incomparableness [-nəs] *s.* excelencia.
incomparably [-əblɪ] *adv.* incomparablemente.
incompatibility [,ɪnkəm,pætə'bɪlətɪ] *s.* incompatibilidad.
incompatible [-'pætəbəl] *a.* 1. incompatible, inconciliable. 2. (farm., med.) incompatible, antagónico. —*s.* 1. (*pl.*) medicinas antagónicas. 2. (lóg.) proposiciones incompatibles.
incompatibly [-blɪ] *adv.* de manera incompatible.
incompetence [ɪn'kɑmpətənt, B -'kɔm-] **incompetency** [-ənsɪ] *s.* 1. incompetencia, incapacidad, ineptitud, inhabilidad. 2. (der.) incompetencia.
incompetent [-ənt] *a.* 1. incompetente, incapaz, inepto. 2. (der.) incompetente. —*s.* persona incompetente o incapaz.
incompetently [-lɪ] *adv.* de manera incompetente.
incomplete [,ɪnkəm'plit] *a.* 1. incompleto; imperfecto, defectuoso. 2. (bot.) incompleto.
incompletely [-lɪ] *adv.* incompletamente.
incompletion [-'pliʃən] **incompleteness** [-'plitnəs] *s.* calidad de incompleto, estado incompleto.
incomplex [-kəm'plɛks] *a.* incomplejo, incomplexo.
incompliance [-'plaɪəns] **incompliancy** [-ənsɪ] *s.* 1. inflexibilidad, terquedad. 2. indocilidad, desobediencia.
incompliant [-ənt] *a.* 1. inflexible. 2. desobediente.
incompliantly [-lɪ] *adv.* 1. inflexiblemente. 2. indócilmente.
incomprehensibility [ɪn,kɑmprɪ,hɛnsə'bɪlətɪ, B -,kɔm-] *s.* incomprensibilidad.
incomprehensible [-'hɛnsəbəl] *a.* incomprensible, ininteligible, impenetrable.
incomprehensibleness [-nəs] *s.* incomprensibilidad.
incomprehensibly [-blɪ] *adv.* incomprensiblemente.
incomprehension [-'hɛntʃən, B -'hɛnʃən] *s.* incomprensión.
incomprehensive [-'hɛnsɪv] *a.* 1. incomprensivo. 2. limitado, que no incluye mucho.
incompressibility [,ɪnkəm,prɛsə'bɪlətɪ] *s.* incompresibilidad.
incompressible [-'prɛsəbəl] *a.* incompresible, incomprimible.
incomputable [,ɪnkəm'pjutəbəl] *a.* incalculable, incontable.
inconceivability [,ɪnkən,sivə'bɪlətɪ] **inconceivableness** [-'sivəbəlnəs] *s.* inconcebilidad.
inconceivable [-'sivəbəl] *a.* inconcebible, inimaginable; increíble.
inconceivably [-blɪ] *adv.* inconcebiblemente.
inconclusive [,ɪnkən'klusɪv] *a.* no concluyente, no decisivo, inconcluyente, que no convence.
inconclusively [-lɪ] *adv.* de manera no concluyente, inconclusamente.
inconclusiveness [-nəs] *s.* carácter inconcluyente.
incondensable [,ɪnkən'dɛnsəbəl] *a.* que no se puede condensar.
incondite [ɪn'kɑndət, -,daɪt, B -'kɔndaɪt] *a.* mal construido; imperfecto; tosco, mal acabado.
inconformity [,ɪnkən'fɔrmətɪ, B -'fɔmə-] *s.* inconformidad, desconformidad.
incongruence [ɪn'kɑŋgruəns, ,ɪnkən'gru-, B ɪn'kɔŋgrʊ-] *s.* incongruencia, inconexión.

incongruent [-ənt] *a.* incongruente, discordante, inconexo; inadecuado, inapropiado.
incongruently [ˌɪnkən'gruəntlɪ ɪn'kɑŋgrʊ- B -'kɔŋ-] *adv.* incongruente.
incongruity [ˌɪnkən'gruətɪ, B -kɔŋ-] *s.* incongruencia, inconsistencia, desacuerdo, discrepancia.
incongruous [ɪn'kɑŋgrʊəs, B -'kɔŋ-] *a.* incongruo, incongruente; incompatible; desacorde, discrepante; inadecuado, inapropiado; inconsistente, inarmónico.
incongruously [-lɪ] *adv.* incongruentemente, incongruamente.
incongruousness [-nəs] *s.* incongruencia.
inconsecutive [ˌɪnkən'sɛkjətɪv] *a.* no consecutivo.
inconsequence [ɪn'kɑnsəˌkwɛns, -kwəns, B -'kɔnsɪ-] *s.* inconsecuencia.
inconsequent [-ˌkwɛnt, -kwənt, B -kwənt] *a.* 1. inconsecuente, ilógico. 2. inconsiguiente. 3. inconexo, que no viene al caso, inaplicable.
inconsequential [-ˌkɑnsə'kwɛntʃəl, B -ˌkɔnsɪ'kwɛnʃəl] *a.* 1. insignificante, sin importancia, sin trascendencia. 2. inconsecuente, ilógico.
inconsequentiality [-ˌkwɛntʃɪ'ælətɪ, B -ˌkwɛnʃɪ-] *s.* 1. falta de importancia. 2. inconsecuencia.
inconsequentially [-'kwɛntʃəlɪ, B -'kwɛnʃəlɪ] *adv.* 1. sin importancia. 2. inconsecuentemente.
inconsequently [-'kɑnsəˌkwɛntlɪ, -kwənt-, B -kɔn-] *adv.* inconsecuentemente.
inconsiderable [ˌɪnkən'sɪdərəbəl] *a.* insignificante, baladí, trivial.
inconsiderableness [-nəs] *s.* trivialidad, insignificancia.
inconsiderably [-blɪ] *adv.* de manera insignificante.
inconsiderate [-'sɪdərət] *a.* 1. inconsiderado, precipitado, atolondrado. 2. desconsiderado, desatento.
inconsiderately [-lɪ] *adv.* 1. inconsideradamente, irreflexivamente, precipitadamente. 2. desconsideradamente.
inconsiderateness [-nəs] **inconsideration** [-ˌsɪdə'reɪʃən] *s.* 1. inconsideración, irreflexión; precipitación. 2. desconsideración.
inconsistence [-'sɪstəns] *var. de* **inconsistency.**
inconsistency [-tənsɪ] *s.* inconsistencia, incongruencia, contradicción, falta de armonía, incoherencia, falta de lógica.
inconsistent [-tənt] *a.* inconsistente, incongruente, inarmónico; incoherente, ilógico, contradictorio.
inconsistently [-lɪ] *adv.* en forma inconsistente, contradictoriamente.
inconsolability [ˌɪnkənˌsoʊlə'bɪlətɪ] *s.* desconsuelo.
inconsolable [-'soʊləbəl] *a.* inconsolable, desconsolado.
inconsolableness [-nəs] *s.* desconsuelo.
inconsolably [-blɪ] *adv.* inconsolablemente, desconsoladamente.
inconsonance [ɪn'kɑnsənəns, B -'kɔn-] *s.* disonancia, discordancia, desacuerdo.
inconsonant [-ənt] *a.* disonante, discordante.
inconsonantly [-lɪ] *adv.* disonantemente, discordantemente.
inconspicuous [ˌɪnkən'spɪkjʊəs] *a.* no conspicuo, poco aparente, indiscernible.
inconspicuously [-lɪ] *adv.* discretamente.
inconspicuousness [-nəs] *s.* indiscernibilidad.
inconstancy [ɪn'kɑnstənsɪ, B -'kɔn-] *s.* inconstancia, inestabilidad, veleidad.
inconstant [-stənt] *a.* inconstante, inestable, variable, voluble, veleidoso.
inconstantly [-lɪ] *adv.* inconstantemente, inestablemente, veleidosamente, volublemente.
inconsumable [ˌɪnkən'suməbəl, B -'sjumə-] *a.* inagotable, inacabable, inconsumible.
inconsumably [-blɪ] *adv.* inagotablemente.
incontestability [-ˌtɛstə'bɪlətɪ] *s.* incontestabilidad.
incontestable [-'tɛstəbəl] *a.* incontestable; indisputable, incontrovertible, incuestionable.
incontestably [-blɪ] *adv.* incontestablemente, indisputablemente.
incontinence [ɪn'kɑntənəns, B -'kɔnt-] *s.* 1. incontinencia; desenfreno, lascivia; 2. (med.) incontinencia.
incontinency [-ənsɪ] *s. var. de* **incontinence.**
incontinent [-ənt] *a.* incontinente; desenfrenado, lascivo, lujurioso; (med.) incontinente.
incontinently [-lɪ] *adv.* 1. incontinentemente, desenfrenadamente. 2. (ant.) sin demora, incontinenti.
incontrollable [ˌɪnkən'troʊləbəl] *a.* ingobernable, irrefrenable.
incontrollably [-blɪ] *adv.* sin poder dominarse, inconteniblemente.
incontrovertibility [ɪnˌkɑntrəˌvɜrtə'bɪlətɪ, B -ˌkɔntrəˌvɜt-] *s.* carácter o índole incontrovertible.
incontrovertible [-'vɜrtəbəl, B 'ɪnkɔntrə'-vɜt-] *a.* incontrovertible, indisputable.
incontrovertibly [-blɪ] *adv.* de manera incontrovertible, indisputablemente.
inconvenience [ˌɪnkən'vinjəns] *s.* inconveniencia, incomodidad, desconveniencia; molestia, estorbo, embarazo; **to put (someone) to i.,** causar molestia a (alguien). —*v.t.* causar inconvenientes a, incomodar; molestar, estorbar.
inconveniency [-jənsɪ] *s. var. de* **inconvenience.**
inconvenient [-jənt] *a.* 1. inconveniente, molesto, fastidioso, embarazoso, inoportuno, incómodo. 2. inapropiado, poco práctico.
inconveniently [-lɪ] *adv.* inconvenientemente.
inconvertibility [ˌɪnkənˌvɜrtə'bɪlətɪ, B 'ɪnkənˌvɜt-] *s.* inconvertibilidad.
inconvertible [ˌɪnkən'vɜrtəbəl, B -'vɜt-] *a.* inconvertible (esp. moneda).
inconvincible [-'vɪnsəbəl] *a.* inconvencible, incontrastable.
incoordinate [ˌɪnkoʊ'ɔrdənət, B -'ɔd-] **incoordinated** [-ˌeɪtəd] *a.* no coordinado, sin coordinación.
incoordination [-ˌɔrdən'eɪʃən, B -ˌɔd-] *s.* falta de coordinación, incoordinación.
incorporable [ɪn'kɔrpərəbəl, B -'kɔpərə-] *a.* incorporable, capaz de ser incorporado.
incorporate [-pərət] *a.* incorpóreo, espiritual.
incorporate *a.* 1. incorporado. 2. constituido en corporación. — [ɪn'kɔrpəˌreɪt, B -'kɔpə-] *v.t.* 1. (con *in*) incorporar (en o a); (con *with*) unir, combinar (con). 2. admitir como miembro (de una corporación, etc.). 3. constituir legalmente (una sociedad, etc.). 4. incorporar, dar cuerpo a. —*v.i.* 1. incorporarse, agregarse, asociarse, unirse. 2. constituirse legalmente (en corporación, etc.).
incorporated [-'kɔrpəˌreɪtəd, B -'kɔpə-] *a.* constituido legalmente (en corporación, etc.).
incorporation [ɪnˌkɔrpə'reɪʃən, B -ˌkɔpə-] *s.* incorporación, unión, asociación.
incorporator [-'kɔrpəˌreɪtər, B -'kɔpə-ə] *s.* 1. el que incorpora. 2. miembro fundador (de una corporación, sociedad, etc.).
incorporeal [ˌɪnkɔr'pɔrɪəl, B -kɔ'-] *a.* 1. incorpóreo, espiritual, inmaterial. 2. (der.) incorpóreo.
incorporeally [-əlɪ] *adv.* incorpóreamente.
incorporeity [ˌɪnkɔrpə'riətɪ, B -kɔpə-] *s.* incorporeidad, inmaterialidad.
incorrect [ˌɪnkə'rɛkt] *a.* 1. incorrecto. 2. impropio (vestido o prenda). 3. falso, inexacto, erróneo.
incorrectly [-lɪ] *adv.* incorrectamente.
incorrectness [-nəs] *s.* incorrección, impropiedad, inexactitud.
incorrigibility [ɪnˌkɔrədʒə'bɪlətɪ, -ˌkɑr- B -ˌkɔr-] *s.* incorregibilidad.
incorrigible [-'kɔrədʒəbəl, -'kɑr-, B -'kɔr-] *a.* incorregible, indócil, empecatado.
incorrigibleness [-nəs] *s.* incorregibilidad. indocilidad.
incorrigibly [-əblɪ] *adv.* incorregiblemente.
incorrupt [ˌɪnkə'rʌpt] *a.* incorrupto, puro, probo, íntegro.
incorruptibility [ˌɪnkəˌrʌptə'bɪlətɪ] *s.* incorruptibilidad.
incorruptible [-'rʌptəbəl] *a.* incorruptible, probo, íntegro.
incorruptibly [-blɪ] *adv.* incorruptiblemente.
incorruptly [-lɪ] *adv.* incorruptamente.
incorruptness [-nəs] *s.* incorrupción.
incrassate [ɪn'kræsˌeɪt] **incrassated** [-əd] *a.* (bot., zool.) engrosado, hinchado. —*v.t., v.i.* (ant.) encrasar(se), incrasar(se), espesar(se), condensar(se), engrosar(se).
incrassation [ˌɪnkræ'seɪʃən] *s.* (ant.) espesura, encrasación, engrasación, engrosamiento.
increasable [ɪn'krisəbəl] *a.* aumentable, acrecentable, crecedero.
increase [ɪn'kris] *v.i.* 1. crecer, arreciar, recrudecer, acrecentarse. 2. multiplicarse, propagarse. —*v.t.* 1. aumentar, agrandar. 2. multiplicar, extender, engrosar, abultar. — ['ɪnˌkris] *s.* 1. aumento, crecimiento, agrandamiento, acrecentamiento. 2. progenie. 3. (com., ten.) incremento, utilidad, ganancia. 4. **to be on the i.,** ir en aumento.
increaser [-ər, B -ə] *s.* 1. acrecentador, aumentador; reproductor. 2. (mec.) aumentador, tubo cónico de unión.
increasing [-ɪŋ] *a.* creciente, aumentativo, acrecentador.
increasingly [-lɪ] *adv.* cada vez más, crecientemente, en aumento, con creces, en creciente.
increate [ˌɪnkri'eɪt] *a.* increado.
incredibility [ɪnˌkrɛdə'bɪlətɪ] *s.* incredibilidad.
incredible [-'krɛdəbəl] *a.* increíble, inverosímil, fabuloso, milagroso.
incredibleness [-nəs] *s.* incredibilidad.
incredibly [-blɪ] *adv.* increíblemente.
incredulity [ˌɪnkrɪ'dulətɪ, B -'djʊl-] *s.* incredulidad.
incredulous [ɪn'krɛdʒələs, B -'krɛdjʊ-] *a.* incrédulo, escéptico, descreído.
incredulously [-lɪ] *adv.* incrédulamente.
incredulousness [-nəs] *s.* incredulidad.
increment ['ɪnkrəmənt, 'ɪŋ-] *s.* 1. incremento, aumento, crecimiento, acrecentamiento; añadidura. 2. (mat.) incremento. 3. (ret.) gradación, clímax.
incrementation [ˌɪnkrəmɛn'teɪʃən] *s.* aumento, incremento.
increscent [ɪn'krɛsənt] *a.* creciente (díc. esp. de la luna).
incretion [ɪn'kriʃən] *s.* (fisiol.) increción.
incriminate [ɪn'krɪməˌneɪt] *v.t.* incriminar, acriminar.

incriminating [-ɪŋ] *a.* acriminador, acusador.
incrimination [-ˌkrɪmə'neɪʃən] *s.* incriminación, acriminación.
incriminator [-'krɪməˌneɪtər, B -ə] *s.* acriminador.
incriminatory [-nəˌtɔrɪ, B -nətərɪ] *a.* acriminador, incriminador.
incrust [ɪn'krʌst] *v.t.* incrustar; encostrar.
incrustation [ˌɪnkrʌs'teɪʃən] *s.* incrustación; encostradura, costra, sarro.
incubate ['ɪŋkjəˌbeɪt, 'ɪn-] *v.t.* incubar, empollar; (fig.) pensar, madurar. —*v.i.* ser incubado.
incubation [ˌɪŋkjə'beɪʃən, ˌɪn-] *s.* incubación, empolladura; (med.) incubación.
incubation period, (med.) período de incubación, período de latencia.
incubative ['ɪŋkjəˌbeɪtɪv, 'ɪn-] *a.* incubador.
incubator [-ər, B -ə] *s.* incubadora, empolladora, incubador.
incubus ['ɪŋkjəbəs, 'ɪn-] *s.* (*pl.* INCUBI [-ˌbaɪ] o INCUBUSES) íncubo, carga, obligación; (med.) íncubo, pesadilla.
incudes, *pl. de* **incus.**
inculcate [ɪn'kʌlˌkeɪt, B 'ɪnkʌl-] *v.t.* inculcar.
inculcation [ˌɪnkʌl'keɪʃən] *s.* inculcación.
inculcator [ɪn'kʌlˌkeɪtər, 'ɪnkʌl-, B -ə] *s.* inculcador.
inculpable [ɪn'kʌlpəbəl] *a.* inculpable, inocente.
inculpableness [-nəs] *s.* inculpabilidad.
inculpably [-blɪ] *adv.* inculpablemente.
inculpate [ɪn'kʌlˌpeɪt, 'ɪnkʌl-] *v.t., v.i.* inculpar, incriminar, imputar, culpar.
inculpation [ˌɪnkʌl'peɪʃən] *s.* inculpación.
inculpatory [ɪn'kʌlpəˌtɔrɪ, B -tərɪ] *a.* que inculpa, acusador.
incumbency [ɪn'kʌmbənsɪ] *s.* 1. incumbencia. 2. ejercicio, goce (de un cargo, oficio, etc.).
incumbent [-bənt] *a.* 1. apoyado, sostenido, colocado. 2. (con *on* o *upon*) obligatorio, forzoso (para). 3. titular (juez, profesor, etc.). 4. (bot.) incumbente. 5. (geol.) incumbente, superyacente. 6. (ant.) pendiente, inminente. —*s.* 1. funcionario (que ejerce un oficio); titular. 2. residente, ocupante, inquilino.
incumber, incumbrance, *vars. de* **encumber, encumbrance.**
incunabula [ˌɪnkjə'næbjələ, B -kjʊ-] *s. pl.* (*sing.* INCUNABULUM [-ləm]) 1. incunables. 2. orígenes, principios.
incunabular [-lər, B -lə] *a.* incunable.
incur [ɪn'kɜr, B -'kɜ] *v.t.* (*pret., p.p.* INCURRED; *p.pr.* INCURRING) 1. incurrir en (castigo, culpa, error, etc.). 2. contraer (deuda).
incurability [ɪnˌkjʊrə'bɪlətɪ, B -ˌkjʊər-] *s.* incurabilidad.
incurable [-'kjʊrəbəl, B -'kjʊər-] *a.* incurable; irremediable. —*s.* enfermo incurable.
incurableness [-nəs] *s.* incurabilidad.
incurably [-əblɪ] *adv.* incurablemente; irremediablemente.
incuriosity [ˌɪnˌkjʊrɪ'ɑsətɪ, B -ˌkjʊərɪ'ɔs-] *s.* indiferencia, falta de curiosidad.
incurious [-'kjʊrɪəs, B -'kjʊər-] *a.* indiferente, sin curiosidad, descuidado.
incuriously [-lɪ] *adv.* indiferentemente, sin curiosidad ni esmero.
incuriousness [-nəs] *s.* indiferencia, falta de curiosidad o de interés.
incurrence [ɪn'kɜrəns, B -'kʌrəns] *s.* incurrimiento.
incurrent [-ənt] *a.* que fluye hacia adentro.
incursion [ɪn'kɜrʒən, B -'kɜʃən] *s.* incursión, correría.
incursive [-'kɜrsɪv, B -'kɜsɪv] *a.* invasor.
incurvate ['ɪnkɜrˌveɪt, B -kɜˌ-] *a.* curvado hacia adentro. —*v.t., v.i.* encorvar(se), esp. hacia adentro.
incurvation [ˌɪnkɜr'veɪʃən, B -kɜ'-] *s.* encorvadura (hacia adentro); curvatura.
incurvature [ɪn'kɜrvəˌtʃʊr, B -'kɜveˌtʃʊə] *s.* encorvadura (hacia adentro), curvatura.
incurve ['ɪnkɜrv, B 'ɪnkɜv] *s.* encorvadura, curvatura hacia adentro. — [ɪn'kɜrv, B -'kɜv] *v.t., v.i.* encorvar(se), esp. hacia adentro, doblar, torcer.
incus ['ɪŋkəs] *s.* (*pl.* INCUDES [ɪŋ'kjudiz]) (anat.) incus, yunque (del oído medio).
incuse [ɪn'kjuz] *a.* incuso, estampado (díc. esp. de las monedas antiguas). —*s.* estampado, incuso; figura incusa, diseño incuso. —*v.t.* estampar golpeando.
Ind [ɪnd] *s.* (gen. poét.) India, las Indias.
Ind. *abrev. de* **Indiana,** Indiana (E.U.).
indaba [ɪn'dɑbə] *s.* conferencia (entre los aborígenes de Sudáfrica).
indamine ['ɪndəˌmin, -mɪn] *s.* (quím.) indamina.
indebted [ɪn'dɛtəd] *a.* 1. endeudado, adeudado, empeñado, entrampado. 2. (fig.) (con *to*) endeudado con, obligado a, en deuda con.
indebtedness [-nəs] *s.* 1. obligación, agradecimiento. 2. (com.) obligaciones, deudas, adeudo.
indecency [ɪn'disənsɪ] *s.* indecencia, obscenidad, inmodestia.
indecent [-ənt] *a.* indecente, indecoroso, impropio, inmoral, obsceno.
indecent exposure, (der.) exhibición impúdica.
indecently [-lɪ] *adv.* indecentemente, indecorosamente; obscenamente.
indeciduous [ˌɪndɪ'sɪdʒʊəs, B -'sɪdjʊ-] *a.* 1. (bot.) persistente, perenne (díc. de las hojas). 2. (bot.) vivaz, perenne, siempreverde (díc. de los árboles).
indecipherability [ˌɪndɪˌsaɪfərə'bɪlətɪ] *s.* calidad de indescifrable, ininteligibilidad.
indecipherable [-'saɪfərəbəl] *a.* indescifrable, incomprensible, ininteligible.
indecision [ˌɪndɪ'sɪʒən] *s.* indecisión, irresolución, vacilación.
indecisive [ˌɪndɪ'saɪsɪv] *a.* 1. indeciso, irresoluto, vacilante. 2. incierto, dudoso; indefinido, vago.
indecisively [-lɪ] *adv.* indecisamente, con vacilación.
indecisiveness [-nəs] *s.* indecisión, irresolución.
indeclinable [ˌɪndɪ'klaɪnəbəl] *a.* 1. (gram.) indeclinable. 2. (ant.) inevitable, ineludible.
indecorous [ɪn'dɛkərəs] *a.* indecoroso, impropio, irrespetuoso.
indecorously [-lɪ] *adv.* indecorosamente.
indecorousness [-nəs] *s.* indecoro, falta de respeto.
indecorum [ˌɪndɪ'kɔrəm] *s.* indecoro, impropiedad.
indeed [ɪn'did] *adv.* verdaderamente, efectivamente, en verdad, en realidad, de veras, en efecto, seguramente, ya lo creo, claro está. —*interj.* ¡de veras! (expresando sorpresa, ironía, desprecio o incredulidad); **no i.** ¡de ninguna manera! ¡pues, no señor!
indefatigability [ˌɪndɪˌfætɪgə'bɪlətɪ] *s.* fuerza o energía inagotable.
indefatigable [-'fætɪgəbəl] *a.* infatigable, incansable.
indefatigableness [-nəs] *s.* fuerza o energía inagotable.
indefatigably [-blɪ] *adv.* infatigablemente, incansablemente.
indefeasibility [ˌɪndɪˌfizə'bɪlətɪ] *s.* irrevocabilidad.
indefeasible [-'fizəbəl] *a.* irrevocable, inabrogable, inquebrantable.
indefeasibly [-blɪ] *adv.* irrevocablemente.
indefectibility [ˌɪndɪˌfɛktə'bɪlətɪ] *s.* indefectibilidad.
indefectible [-'fɛktəbəl] *a.* indefectible, impecable.
indefectibly [-blɪ] *adv.* indefectiblemente.
indefensibility [ˌɪndɪˌfɛnsə'bɪlətɪ] *s.* calidad de indefendible, calidad de insostenible.
indefensible [-'fɛnsəbəl] *a.* 1. indefendible, insostenible. 2. inexcusable, injustificable.
indefensibly [-blɪ] *adv.* inexcusablemente.
indefinability [ˌɪndɪˌfaɪnə'bɪlətɪ] *s.* carácter o índole indefinible.
indefinable [-'faɪnəbəl] *a.* indefinible, indescriptible.
indefinably [-blɪ] *adv.* indefiniblemente.
indefinite [ɪn'dɛfənət] *a.* 1. indefinido, indeterminado, incierto, vago, impreciso. 2. (bot.) indefinido. 3. (gram., lóg.) indefinido, indeterminado.
indefinite article, (gram.) artículo indefinido, indeterminado o genérico.
indefinite integral, (mat.) integral indefinida o indeterminada.
indefinitely [-lɪ] *adv.* indefinidamente.
indefiniteness [-nəs] *s.* calidad de indefinido, indefinición.
indefinite pronoun, (gram.) pronombre indeterminado.
indehiscence [ˌɪndɪ'hɪsəns] *s.* (bot.) indehiscencia.
indehiscent [-ənt] *a.* (bot.) indehiscente.
indelibility [ɪnˌdɛlə'bɪlətɪ] *s.* indelebilidad.
indelible [ɪn'dɛləbəl] *a.* indeleble, imborrable.
indelibly [-blɪ] *adv.* indeleblemente.
indelicacy [ɪn'dɛlɪkəsɪ] *s.* falta de delicadeza, falta de tino.
indelicate [-kət] *a.* indelicado, indecoroso, desatinado.
indelicately [-lɪ] *adv.* de modo indelicado, indecorosamente.
indelicateness [-nəs] *s.* falta de delicadeza, indecoro.
indemnification [ɪnˌdɛmnəfə'keɪʃən] *s.* indemnización, compensación, resarcimiento, reparación.
indemnifier [ɪn'dɛmnɪˌfaɪər, B -ə] *s.* (com., der.) indemnizador, contrafiador.
indemnify [-ˌfaɪ] *v.t.* (*pret., p.p.* INDEMNIFIED; *p.pr.* INDEMNIFYING) indemnizar, compensar; resarcir, desagraviar, satisfacer.
indemnity [ɪn'dɛmnətɪ] *s.* (*pl.* INDEMNITIES) 1. indemnidad. 2. indemnización, compensación, resarcimiento, reparación.
indemonstrable [ˌɪndɪ'mɑnstrəbəl, B ɪn'dɛmən-] *a.* indemostrable.
indene ['ɪnˌdin] *s.* (quím.) indeno.
indent [ɪn'dɛnt] *v.t.* 1. dentar, endentar, hacer muescas en, mellar. 2. abollar. 3. machihembrar, ensamblar, encajar. 4. redactar o extender por duplicado (documento o pedido de mercaderías); cortar en zigzag (un documento hecho por duplicado). 5. (impr.) sangrar. —*v.i.* 1. formarse una depresión o muesca. 2. (pr. G.B.) expedir una orden escrita por duplicado. 3. (ant.) consentir por medio de escritura. 4. **i. upon (someone) for (something),** (pr. G.B.) requisar (algo) a (alguien); recurrir a (alguien) por (algo). — [ɪnˌdɛnt] *s.* 1. muesca, mella, hendidura, diente, ensambladura. 2. documento hecho por duplicado y cortado en zigzag; contrato, escritura. 3. (E.U.) certificado de deuda pública (emitido por el gobierno al final de la revolución por capital

o intereses). 4. (pr. G.B.) orden de requisición. 5. (com.) (pr. G.B.) pedido de mercaderías (esp. uno hecho desde el extranjero).

indentation [ˌɪndɛn'teɪʃən] *1. abolladura, depresión, hendidura. 2. muesca, hendidura, piquete, corte. 3. (impr.) sangría.*

indented [ɪn'dɛntəd] *a.* 1. dentado, dentellado, enmuescado, serrado. 2. (bot.) dentellado.

indention [ɪn'dɛntʃən] *s.* 1. (impr.) sangría. 2. (mec.) diente. 3. (ant.) muesca, hendidura, mella, abolladura.

indenture [-tʃər, B -tʃə] *s.* 1. documento hecho por duplicado y cortado en zigzag, escritura, contrato. 2. contrato de aprendizaje. 3. certificado, inventario, catálogo, lista oficial. 4. abolladura. —*v.t.* 1. (ant.) ligar por contrato (esp. un aprendiz a su maestro). 2. (ant.) abollar.

independence [ˌɪndə'pɛndəns] *s.* 1. independencia, autonomía, libertad. 2. suficiencia, holgura económica.

Independence Day, (E.U.) día de la independencia (4 de julio).

independency [-dənsɪ] *s.* 1. independencia, autonomía, libertad. 2. estado o provincia independientes. 3. **I.,** (rel.) doctrina y política de los independientes.

independent [-dənt] *a.* 1. independiente, libre. 2. adinerado, acomodado. 3. altivo, altanero. —*s.* 1. (pol.) independiente. 2. (G.B., relig.) congregacionista independiente.

independently [-lɪ] *adv.* independientemente.

indescribability [ˌɪndɪˌskraɪbə'bɪlətɪ] *s.* calidad de indescriptible.

indescribable [-skraɪbəbəl] *a.* indescriptible, inenarrable, inefable.

indescribably [-blɪ] *adv.* de manera indescriptible, inefablemente.

indestructibility [ˌɪndɪˌstrʌktə'bɪlətɪ] *s.* indestructibilidad.

indestructible [-'strʌktəbəl] *a.* indestructible.

indeterminable [-'tɜrmənəbəl, B -'tɜm-] *a.* indeterminable.

indeterminableness [-nəs] *s.* indeterminación.

indeterminancy principle [-nənsɪ-] (fís.) principio de incertidumbre, relación de indeterminación.

indeterminate [-nət] *a.* 1. indeterminado, indefinido, impreciso. 2. (mat.) indeterminado. 3. (bot.) racimoso.

indeterminately [-lɪ] *adv.* indeterminadamente.

indetermination [ˌɪndɪˌtɜrmə'neɪʃən, B -ˌtɜmɪ-] *s.* indeterminación, irresolución, duda, indecisión.

indetermined [-'tɜrmənd, B -'tɜm-] *a.* indeterminado, irresoluto.

indeterminism [-məˌnɪzəm] *s.* (filos.) indeterminismo.

indeterminist [-nəst] *s., a.* (filos.) indeterminista.

indeterministic [ˌɪndɪˌtɜrmə'nɪstɪk, B -ˌtɜmɪ-] *a.* (filos.) indeterminista.

index ['ɪnˌdɛks] *s.* (*pl.* INDEXES o INDICES [-dəˌsiz]) 1. índice, indicio, vestigio, señal. 2. (mat.) índice. 3. **I.,** (relig.) índice expurgatorio, índice de libros prohibidos. 4. (impr.) manecilla. 5. (mec.) índice, indicador. 6. (t. **i. finger),** (dedo) índice. —*v.t.* hacer un índice de; poner en un índice. —*v.i.* confeccionar un índice.

index card, tarjeta o ficha.

indexer [-ər, B -ə] *s.* confeccionador de índices.

Index Expurgatorius [-ɛksˌpɜrgə'tɔrɪəs, B -ˌpɜgə-] (*pl.* INDICES EXPURGATORII [-ɪˌaɪ]) (relig.) índice expurgatorio.

indexical [ɪn'dɛksɪkəl] *a.* indicativo; en forma de índice.

index number, (com.) número índice, número indicador.

index of refraction, (ópt.) índice de refracción.

India ['ɪndɪə] *s.* la India.

India ink, tinta china.

Indiaman [-mən] *s.* (mar.) barco que hace el comercio con la India, esp. el que pertenece a la Compañía de las Indias Orientales.

Indian ['ɪndɪən] *a.* indio, indiano, índico, indo. —*s.* 1. indio. 2. lengua india.

Indiana [ˌɪndɪ'ænə] *s.* Indiana, estado de los E.U.

Indian club, maza de gimnasia, clava para gimnasia.

Indian corn, maíz, panizo.

Indian corn meal, mañoco.

Indian cress, (bot.) capuchina, alcaparra de Indias.

Indian fig, (bot.) nopal, higuera de chomba, higuera de Indias; higo chumbo.

Indian file, fila india.

Indian giver, (fam., E.U.) regalador que espera recibir más en retorno; persona que quita o reclama un objeto después de regalarlo.

Indian hemp, (bot.) cáñamo de la India.

Indian licorice, (bot.) abro.

Indian-like ['ɪndɪənˌlaɪk] *a.* aindiado.

Indian meal, harina de maíz.

Indian millet, (bot.) 1. maíz de Guinea. 2. zahína, alcandía.

Indian Ocean, Océano Índico.

Indian paintbrush, (bot.) escrofularia.

Indian pudding, budín de maíz.

Indian red, almagre, colcótar.

Indian reed, I. shot, (bot.) cañacoro, caña de la India, caña de cuentas.

Indian reservation, reservación de indios (en los E.U.).

Indian sign, (E.U.) hechizo, encanto, ensalmo, aojo.

Indian summer, (E.U.) veranillo, veranillo de San Martín.

Indian tobacco, (bot.) lobelia silvestre.

Indian turnip, (bot.) aro.

India paper, papel de China.

India rubber, 1. caucho, goma elástica, jebe (Am.). 2. goma de borrar, borrador (Am.).

Indic ['ɪndɪk] *a.* índico, indio.

indican ['ɪndəˌkæn] *s.* 1. (quím.) indicano, indicán. 2. (bioquím.) indicán animal.

indicant [-kənt] *a., s.* indicante.

indicate ['ɪndəˌkeɪt] *v.t.* 1. indicar, señalar, denotar, significar. 2. recetar, recomendar (tratamiento o remedio).

indication [ˌɪndə'keɪʃən] *s.* 1. indicación, sugerencia. 2. indicación, indicio, señal, seña, signo.

indicative [ɪn'dɪkətɪv] *a.* 1. (gram.) indicativo. 2. indicativo, sugestivo. 3. **to be i. of,** revelar, indicar. —*s.* (gram.) (t. **i. mood)** (modo) indicativo.

indicatively [-lɪ] *adv.* 1. (gram.) en (modo) indicativo. 2. como (una) indicación, indicativamente.

indicator ['ɪndəˌkeɪtər, B -ə] *s.* 1. indicador, índice. 2. (mec., quím.) indicador.

indicator telegraph, telégrafo de agujas.

indicator weighing-machine, balanza automática.

indicatory [ɪn'dɪkəˌtɔrɪ, B -tərɪ] *a.* indicador, demostrativo.

indices, *pl. de* **index.**

indicia [ɪn'dɪʃɪə] *s. pl.* (*sing.* INDICIUM [-ɪəm]) 1. indicios, señales, indicaciones. 2. (E.U.) marca de franqueo impresa (usada en vez de sellos de correo).

indicial [-'dɪʃəl] *a.* 1. indicativo, que indica. 2. (anat.) índice, del índice.

indict [ɪn'daɪt] *v.t.* acusar; (der.) encausar, enjuiciar, procesar.

indictable [-əbəl] *a.* (der.) encausable, procesable.

indictee [ɪnˌdaɪt'i] *s.* (der.) acusado; procesado.

indicter, indictor [ɪn'daɪtər, B -ə] *s.* (der.) denunciante, acusador, fiscal.

indiction [-'dɪkʃən] *s.* (hist.) indicción.

indictment [-'daɪtmənt] *s.* 1. denuncia, acusación, proceso (esp. legal). 2. (der.) auto de acusación (formulado por el gran jurado).

Indies ['ɪndiz, B -dɪz] *s. pl.* **the I.,** las Indias; **the West I.,** las Indias Occidentales; **the East I.,** las Indias Orientales.

indifference [ɪn'dɪfrəns, -ərəns] *s.* indiferencia; apatía, insensibilidad.

indifferency [-rənsɪ] *s.* (ant.) indiferencia.

indifferent [-rənt] *a.* 1. indiferente. 2. de poca o ninguna importancia, insignificante (asunto, etc.). 3. mediocre, pobre, regular (calidad, calificaciones, etc.). 4. (quím., fís.) indiferente, neutro. 5. (biol.) sin diferenciación.

indifferentism [-ˌɪzəm] *s.* (filos., teo.) indiferentismo, indiferencia.

indifferentist [-əst] *s.* (filos., teo.) indiferentista.

indifferently [-lɪ] *adv.* 1. indiferentemente. 2. mediocremente, pobremente, regularmente.

indigen ['ɪndədʒɛn] *var. de* **indigene.**

indigence ['indɪdʒəns] *s.* indigencia, penuria, pobreza, inopia, necesidad.

indigene [-ˌdʒin] *s.* indígena, aborigen.

indigenous [ɪn'dɪdʒənəs] *a.* 1. indígena, nativo, autóctono, natural de. 2. ingénito, innato, inherente.

indigenously [-lɪ] *adv.* a la manera indígena.

indigenousness [-nəs] *s.* carácter nativo.

indigent ['ɪndɪdʒənt] *a., s.* indigente, necesitado, pobre.

indigently [-lɪ] *adv.* pobremente.

indigested [ˌɪndaɪ'dʒɛstəd, B -dɪ-] *a.* indigesto, no digerido; confuso, desordenado.

indigestibility [-ˌdʒɛstə'bɪlətɪ] *s.* calidad de indigestible; incapacidad para digerir.

indigestible [-'dʒɛstəbəl] *a.* indigestible.

indigestion [-'dʒɛstʃən] *s.* indigestión, empacho, ahíto.

indigestive [-tɪv] *a.* de mala digestión, dispéptico.

indign [ɪn'daɪn] *a.* (ant., poét.) indigno, despreciable, impropio.

indignant [ɪn'dɪgnənt] *a.* indignado.

indignantly [-lɪ] *adv.* con indignación.

indignation [ˌɪndɪg'neɪʃən] *s.* indignación, enojo, enfado.

indignity [ɪn'dɪgnətɪ] *s.* (*pl.* INDIGNITIES) 1. indignidad, insulto, oprobio, ultraje, injuria, afrenta. 2. desprecio, desdén.

indigo ['ɪndɪˌgoʊ] *s.* (*pl.* INDIGOS o INDIGOES) (bot., quím.) índigo, añil. —*a.* de color azul (de) añil.

indigo blue, color índigo, color azul (de) añil.

indigo-blue [-ˌblu] *a.* (de) añil, de color azul (de) añil.

indigo bunting, i. bird, (orn.) pequeño pinzón (del E. de E.U.); azulejo.

indigoid ['ɪndəˌgɔɪd] *s.* uno de los tintes que produce el azul (de) añil.

indigotin, indigotine [ɪn'dɪgətən, B 'ɪndɪˌgətɪn] *s.* (quím.) indigotina.

indirect [ˌɪndə'rɛkt, -daɪ-] *a.* 1. indirecto. 2. (fig.) torcido, desviado.

indirect discourse, (gram.) oración indirecta.

indirection [-'rɛkʃən] *s.* 1. tortuosidad, rodeo, falsedad. 2. falta de dirección; vaguedad.

indirect lighting, iluminación indirecta, alumbrado reflejado.
indirectly [-ˈrɛktlɪ] *adv.* indirectamente.
indirectness [-nəs] *s.* (fig.) oblicuidad, rodeo, tortuosidad; conducta torcida; indirecta.
indirect object, (gram.) complemento indirecto.
indirect tax, contribución indirecta, impuesto indirecto.
indiscernible [ˌɪndɪˈsɜrnəbəl, -ˈzɜr-, B -ˈsɜnə-] *a.* indiscernible, indistinguible, imperceptible.
indiscipline [ɪnˈdɪsəplən] *s.* indisciplina.
indiscreet [ˌɪndɪsˈkrit] *a.* indiscreto, poco juicioso, imprudente.
indiscreetly [-lɪ] *adv.* indiscretamente.
indiscreetness [-nəs] *s.* falta de discreción, indiscreción.
indiscrete [ˌɪndɪsˈkrit] *a.* no separado, unido, compacto.
indiscretion [-ˈkrɛʃən] *s.* indiscreción, imprudencia.
indiscriminate [-ˈkrɪmənət] *a.* sin distinción, indistinto; sin criterio.
indiscriminately [-lɪ] *adv.* indistintamente, promiscuamente.
indiscriminating [-ˌneɪtɪŋ] *a.* que no distingue, que no selecciona.
indiscriminatingly [-lɪ] *adv.* indistintamente.
indiscrimination [ˌɪndɪsˌkrɪməˈneɪʃən] *s.* falta de criterio.
indiscriminative [-ˈkrɪməˌneɪtɪv, B -nət-] *a.* que no distingue.
indispensability [ˌɪndɪsˌpɛnsəˈbɪlətɪ] *s.* indispensabilidad.
indispensable [-ˈpɛnsəbəl] *a.* indispensable, imprescindible; esencial, de rigor, forzoso.
indispensably [-blɪ] *adv.* indispensablemente.
indispose [ˌɪndɪsˈpoʊz] *v.t.* indisponer, inhabilitar.
indisposed [-ˈpoʊzd] *a.* indispuesto (de salud); falto de entusiasmo.
indisposition [ˌɪnˌdɪspəˈzɪʃən] *s.* 1. indisposición; malestar, destemplanza. 2. (con *to*) aversión (a).
indisputability [ˌɪndɪsˌpjutəˈbɪlətɪ, B ˈɪn-] *s.* indisputabilidad, incontestabilidad.
indisputable [-ˈpjutəbəl, ɪnˈdɪspjət-, B ˈɪndɪsˈpjut-] *a.* indisputable, irrefutable, incontestable.
indisputably [-blɪ, B ˌɪn-] *adv.* indisputablemente.
indissolubility [ˌɪndɪˌsɑljəˈbɪlətɪ, B -ˌsɔl-] *s.* indisolubilidad.
indissoluble [-ˈsɑljəbəl, B -ˈsɔl-] *a.* indisoluble, insoluble; estable, permanente.
indissolubleness [-nəs] *s.* indisolubilidad.
indissolubly [-blɪ] *adv.* indisolublemente.
indistinct [ˌɪndɪsˈtɪŋkt] *a.* indistinto, confuso, borroso, obscuro; indistinguible.
indistinctive [-ˈtɪŋktɪv] *a.* sin distinción, corriente; incapaz de distinguir.
indistinctively [-lɪ] *adv.* indistintamente; corrientemente.
indistinctly [-ˈtɪŋktlɪ] *adv.* indistintamente, obscuramente, confusamente.
indistinctness [-nəs] *s.* falta de claridad o nitidez.
indistinguishable [-ˈtɪŋgwɪʃəbəl] *a.* indistinguible, imperceptible.
indistinguishably [-blɪ] *adv.* de modo indistinguible, imperceptiblemente.
indite [ɪnˈdaɪt] *v.t.* 1. redactar. 2. poner por escrito. 3. (gen. hum.) escribir (ej., una carta). 4. (ant.) dictar.
inditement [-mənt] *s.* redacción, escrito.
inditer [-ər, B -ə] *s.* redactor, escritor.
indium [ˈɪndɪəm] *s.* (quím.) indio.
indivertible [ˌɪndəˈvɜrtəbəl, B -ˈvɜt-] *a.* que no se puede desviar.
indivertibly [-blɪ] *adv.* de modo que no se puede desviar.
individual [ˌɪndəˈvɪdʒʊəl, B -ˈvɪdjʊ-] *a.* individual; particular, singular. —*s.* 1. individuo, sujeto, persona. 2. (biol.) individuo.
individualism [-ˌɪzəm] *s.* individualismo.
individualist [-əst] *s., a.* individualista.
individualistic [-ˌvɪdʒʊəˈlɪstɪk, B -ˌvɪdjʊ-] *a.* individualista.
individuality [-ˈælətɪ] *s.* 1. individualidad. 2. característica. 3. personalidad.
individualization [-ələˈzeɪʃən, B -laɪ-] *s.* individualización; particularización.
individualize [-ˈvɪdʒʊəˌlaɪz, B -ˈvɪdjʊ-] *v.t.* 1. individualizar, individuar, hacer individual. 2. tratar o notar individualmente, particularizar.
individually [-əlɪ] *adv.* individualmente.
individuate [-ˌeɪt] *v.t.* 1. individuar. 2. dotar de individualidad.
individuation [-ˌvɪdʒʊˈeɪʃən, B -vɪdjʊ-] *s.* individuación.
indivisibility [ˌɪndəˌvɪzəˈbɪlətɪ, B ˈɪn-] *s.* indivisibilidad.
indivisible [-ˈvɪzəbəl] *a.* indivisible. —*s.* partícula indivisible.
indivisibly [-blɪ] *adv.* indivisiblemente.
Indo-American [ˌɪndoʊəˈmɛrəkən] *a., s.* indoamericano.
Indochina [-ˈtʃaɪnə, B ˈɪn-] *s.* Indochina.
Indo-Chinese [-ˈtʃaɪˈniz] *a., s.* indochino.
indocile [ɪnˈdɑsəl, B -ˈdoʊsaɪl] *a.* indócil, cerril; intratable; insociable.
indocility [ˌɪndɑˈsɪlətɪ, B -doʊ-] *s.* indocilidad.
indoctrinate [ɪnˈdɑktrəˌneɪt, B -ˈdɔk-] *v.t.* 1. adoctrinar, doctrinar, enseñar, inculcar. 2. imbuir de ideas partidistas o sectarias.
indoctrination [-ˌdɑktrəˈneɪʃən, B -ˌdɔk-] *s.* adoctrinamiento, inculcación, enseñanza.
indoctrinator [-ˈdɑktrəˌneɪtər, B -ˈdɔk-ə] *s.* adoctrinador, doctrinador.
Indo-European [ˌɪndoʊˌjʊrəˈpiən, B ˈɪn-] *a., s.* indoeuropeo.
indole [ˈɪnˌdoʊl] *s.* (quím.) indol.
indoleacetic acid [ˌɪndoʊləˈsitɪk-] (quím.) ácido indolacético.
indolebutyric acid [-bjuˈtɪrɪk-] (quím.) ácido indolbutírico.
indolence [ˈɪndələns] *s.* 1. indolencia, desidia, pereza, haraganería, flojera. 2. (med.) indolencia, insensibilidad.
indolent [-lənt] *a.* 1. indolente, flojo, desidioso, perezoso, haragán. 2. (med.) indoloro.
indolently [-lɪ] *adv.* indolentemente.
indomitability [ɪnˌdɑmətəˈbɪlətɪ, B -ˌdɔm-] *s.* indomabilidad, intrepidez.
indomitable [-ˈdɑmətəbəl, B -ˈdɔm-] *a.* indomable, indómito; invencible, insuperable, inconquistable.
indomitableness [-nəs] *s.* indomabilidad.
Indonesia [ˌɪndəˈniʒə, -ʃə, B -ˈnizjə] *s.* Indonesia.
Indonesian [-ʒən, -ʃən, B -zjən] *a., s.* indonesio.
indoor [ˈɪnˌdɔr, B -ˌdɔ] *a.* interno, interior; de puertas adentro; que se hace dentro de la casa o bajo techo.
indoor aerial, indoor antenna, (rad., t.v.) antena interior, antena de conejo.
indoor game, juego de salón.
indoors [ɪnˈdɔrz, B -ˈdɔz] *adv.* dentro, en casa, bajo techo.
indophenol [ˌɪndoʊˈfiˌnoʊl, B -ˌnɔl] *s.* (quím.) indofenol.
indorsable, indorse, indorsee, indorsement, indorser, *vars. de* **endorsable, endorse, endorsee, endorsement, endorser.**
indoxyl [ɪnˈdɑksəl, B -ˈdɔk-] *s.* (quím.) indoxilo.
indraft, indraught [ˈɪnˌdræft, B -ˌdrɑft] *s.* 1. atracción hacia el interior; corriente o fuerza que tira hacia dentro. 2. aspiración, aire aspirado, absorción, succión (del aire, agua, etc.).
indrawn [ˈɪnˈdrɔn] *a.* 1. inspirado. 2. reservado, introspectivo, introvertido.
indubitable [ɪnˈdubətəbəl, B -ˈdju-] *a.* indubitable, indudable; incuestionable, indisputable, indiscutible.
indubitableness [-nəs] *s.* certeza, certidumbre.
indubitably [-blɪ] *adv.* indubitablemente, indudablemente.
induce [ɪnˈdus, B -ˈdjus] *v.t.* 1. inducir, mover, incitar, persuadir. 2. efectuar, causar, producir. 3. (lóg.) inducir. 4. (fís.) inducir, producir por inducción.
inducement [-mənt] *s.* 1. inducimiento, inducción. 2. atractivo, móvil, aliciente, estímulo, incentivo. 3. (der.) introducción o preámbulo explicatorio (al alegato principal de la defensa).
inducer [-ər, B -ə] *s.* 1. inductor, el o lo que induce. 2. (mec.) alimentador de aire (en un compresor, etc.).
inducible [-əbəl] *a.* capaz de ser inducido.
induct [ɪnˈdʌkt] *v.t.* 1. instalar (en un cargo o función); admitir (en una sociedad). 2. incorporar, reclutar (en el ejército, etc.). 3. (con *into*) iniciar, instituir (en). 4. conducir, llevar. 5. (fís.) inducir.
inductance [-ˈdʌktəns] *s.* (elec.) inductancia.
inductance coil, (elec.) bobina o carrete inductor.
inductee [ˌɪndʌkˈti, ɪnˈdʌkˌti] *s.* (mil.) recluta (*m.*).
inductile [-ˈdʌktəl, B -taɪl] *a.* no dúctil; inflexible.
induction [ɪnˈdʌkʃən] *s.* 1. instalación (en un puesto, cargo, dignidad, etc.); admisión (en una sociedad). 2. (con *into*) iniciación, instrucción (en una materia). 3. incorporación (en el ejército). 4. (lóg., fís.) inducción. 5. (mot.) aspiración, inducción. 6. (ant.) introducción, preámbulo, prólogo.
induction balance, balanza de inducción.
induction coil, (elec.) bobina de inducción, carrete de inducción.
induction heating, calentamiento por inducción.
induction port, lumbrera de admisión.
induction valve, válvula de admisión.
inductive [ɪnˈdʌktɪv] *s., a.* 1. inductor, instigador, incitador. 2. inductivo (razonamiento, conciencia, etc.). 3. (elec.) inductivo, inductor, inductriz.
inductive load, (elec.) carga inductiva.
inductively [-lɪ] *adv.* inductivamente, de modo inductivo.
inductiveness [-nəs] *s.* capacidad inductiva.
inductivity [ˌɪndʌkˈtɪvətɪ] *s.* (elec.) inductividad.
inductor [-ˈdʌktər, B -tə] *s.* 1. instalador, iniciador. 2. (quím.) inductor. 3. (elec.) inductor.
indue, *var. de* **endue.**
indulge [ɪnˈdʌldʒ] *v.t.* 1. ser complaciente o indulgente con, mimar, consentir (a un niño, etc.). 2. ceder a (hábito, deseo, etc.). 3. (relig.) conceder dispensas o indulgencias. 4. **i. oneself,** darse el gusto, permitirse el placer, complacerse; **i. oneself in,** entregarse a, abandonarse a. —*v.i.* 1. (fam.) (pr. G.B.) darse a la bebida. 2. **i. in,**

gozarse en, complacerse en; entregarse a, abandonarse a.
indulgence [-'dʌldʒəns] *s.* 1. indulgencia, complacencia; capricho. 2. (com.) prórroga, extensión de plazo, moratoria. 3. (relig.) indulgencia. —*v.t.* (relig.) indulgenciar, conceder indulgencias a.
indulgent [-dʒənt] *a.* indulgente, condescendiente; complaciente; clemente.
indulgently [-lɪ] *adv.* indulgentemente.
indulgingly [-'dʌldʒɪŋlɪ] *adv.* indulgentemente.
induline ['ɪndjəˌlin, B -ˌlaɪn] *s.* (quím.) indulina.
indult [ɪn'dʌlt] *s.* (relig.) indulto, dispensa.
induplicate [ɪn'duplɪkət, B -'dju-] *a.* (bot.) induplicado.
indurate ['ɪndərət, B -djʊəreɪt] *a.* endurecido, duro (física o moralmente); (med.) indurado. — [-ˌreɪt] *v.t.* 1. endurecer, encallecer. 2. avezar, acostumbrar. 3. arraigar, establecer. —*v.i.* 1. endurecerse, encallecerse. 2. arraigar(se), establecerse, empedernirse.
induration [ˌɪndə'reɪʃən, B -djʊ-] *s.* 1. endurecimiento, induración. 2. dureza (de corazón), insensibilidad. 3. (med.) induración, dureza.
indurative ['ɪndəˌreɪtɪv, B -djʊ-] *a.* (med.) indurativo.
Indus ['ɪndəs] *s.* (astr.) Indo (constelación).
indusium [ɪn'duzɪəm, B -'dju-] *s.* (*pl.* INDUSIA [-zɪə]) (bot.) indusio.
industrial [ɪn'dʌstrɪəl] *a.* industrial. —*s.* 1. industrial. 2. (com.) (*pl.*) acciones de una sociedad industrial.
industrial arts, *pl.* (*sing. o pl. en const.*) artes mecánicas (enseñadas en los colegios).
industrial complex or **park,** complejo industrial, zona industrial.
industrial disease, (med.) enfermedad ocupacional.
industrialism [-ˌɪzəm] *s.* industrialismo.
industrialist [-əst] *s.* industrialista.
industrialization [-ˌdʌstrɪələ'zeɪʃən, B -laɪ-] *s.* industrialización.
industrialize [-'dʌstrɪəˌlaɪz] *v.t.* industrializar.
industrially [-əlɪ] *adv.* industrialmente.
industrial park, (econ.) parque o zona industrial.
industrial relations, (econ.) relaciones industriales (entre obreros y administradores).
Industrial Revolution, (econ.) revolución industrial.
industrial school, escuela industrial.
industrial union, sindicato industrial.
industrious [ɪn'dʌstrɪəs] *a.* 1. industrioso, aplicado, diligente, activo, hacendoso. 2. (ant.) diestro, hábil, experto.
industriously [-lɪ] *adv.* industriosamente, diligentemente.
industriousness [-nəs] *s.* diligencia, aplicación.
industry ['ɪndəstrɪ] *s.* (*pl.* INDUSTRIES) 1. aplicación, diligencia, laboriosidad. 2. industria (azucarera, del acero, etc.). 3. (ant.) industria, destreza, inteligencia.
indwell [ɪn'dwɛl] *v.t., v.i.* residir, morar, ser inherente (a).
indweller ['ɪnˌdwɛlər, B -ə] *s.* 1. residente, habitante. 2. espíritu o fuerza interior.
indwelling [-ɪŋ] *a.* morador, residente (díc. del espíritu o fuerza interior).
inebriant [ɪn'ibrɪənt] *a.* embriagante, embriagador. —*s.* bebida alcohólica; (fig.) lo que embriaga o transporta.
inebriate [-ət] *a.* 1. ebrio, borracho, bebido, tomado. 2. borracho, dado a la bebida. — [-ˌeɪt] *v.t.* 1. embriagar, emborrachar, inebriar. 2. (fig.) embriagar, enajenar, transportar. —*s.* beodo, borracho, borrachín.
inebriated [-ˌeɪtəd] *a.* embriagado.
inebriation [ɪnˌibrɪ'eɪʃən] *s.* ebriedad, embriaguez, borrachera.
inebriety [ɪnɪ'braɪətɪ] *s.* ebriedad, embriaguez, borrachera.
inedible [ɪn'ɛdəbəl] *a.* incomible, incomestible.
inedited [-'ɛdətəd] *a.* 1. inédito, no publicado. 2. sin redactar, no corregido (manuscrito, etc.).
ineducable [-'ɛdʒəkəbəl, B -'ɛdjʊ-] *a.* ineducable, que no puede educarse.
ineffability [ɪnˌɛfə'bɪlətɪ] *s.* inefabilidad.
ineffable [-'ɛfəbəl] *a.* inefable, inenarrable, indecible, inexpresable.
ineffableness [-nəs] *s.* inefabilidad.
ineffably [-blɪ] *adv.* inefablemente.
ineffaceable [ˌɪnə'feɪsəbəl] *a.* indeleble, imborrable.
ineffaceably [-blɪ] *adv.* indeleblemente.
ineffective [ˌɪnə'fɛktɪv] *a.* 1. ineficaz, sin efecto, vano, inútil, fútil. 2. ineficaz, incapaz.
ineffectively [-lɪ] *adv.* ineficazmente.
ineffectiveness [-nəs] *s.* ineficacia.
ineffectual [-'fɛktʃʊəl] *a.* ineficaz, inútil, vano, fútil.
ineffectuality [-ˌfɛktʃʊ'ælətɪ] *s.* ineficacia, futilidad.
ineffectually [ˌɪnə'fɛktʃʊəlɪ] *adv.* ineficazmente, futilmente.
ineffectualness [-nəs] *s.* ineficacia, futilidad.
inefficacious [ˌɪnˌɛfə'keɪʃəs] *a.* ineficaz, inadecuado.
inefficaciuosly [-lɪ] *adv.* ineficazmente.
inefficaciousness [-nəs] *s.* ineficacia.
inefficacy [ɪn'ɛfɪkəsɪ] *s.* ineficacia, falta de eficacia; futilidad, inutilidad.
inefficiency [ˌɪnə'fɪʃənsɪ] *s.* ineptitud, incompetencia, ineficacia; futilidad, inutilidad.
inefficient [-ənt] *a.* 1. no eficiente, incompetente, incapaz, inepto. 2. ineficaz, inútil. —*s.* persona poco eficiente.
inefficiently [-lɪ] *adv.* sin eficiencia, ineficazmente.
inelastic [ˌɪnə'læstɪk] *a.* inflexible, inconmovible; reacio, terco; inadaptable.
inelasticity [ˌɪnɪˌlæs'tɪsətɪ] *s.* falta de elasticidad.
inelegance [ɪn'ɛlɪgəns] *s.* inelegancia.
inelegancy [-gənsɪ] *s.* inelegancia, falta de gracia, falta de buen gusto.
inelegant [-gənt] *a.* inelegante, deslucido, desgarbado, tosco.
inelegantly [-lɪ] *adv.* de modo inelegante.
ineligibility [ɪnˌɛlədʒə'bɪlətɪ] *s.* inelegibilidad, calidad de inelegible.
ineligible [-'ɛlədʒəbəl] *a.* inelegible (para oficio, etc.); no apto (para servicio militar). —*s.* persona ineligible.
ineligibly [-blɪ] *adv.* de modo inelegible.
ineloquence [ɪn'ɛləkwəns] *s.* falta de elocuencia.
ineloquent [-kwənt] *a.* no elocuente, infacundo, de poca facilidad oratoria.
ineloquently [-lɪ] *adv.* sin elocuencia.
ineluctability [ˌɪnɪˌlʌktə'bɪlətɪ] *s.* calidad de ineluctable.
ineluctable [-'lʌktəbəl] *a.* ineluctable, inevitable, irresistible.
ineluctably [-blɪ] *adv.* ineluctablemente, inevitablemente, irresistiblemente.
ineludible [-'ludəbəl] *a.* ineludible.
inept [ɪn'ɛpt] *a.* 1. inepto, incapaz. 2. inadecuado, impropio, inapropiado. 3. absurdo, tonto, necio.
ineptitude [-'ɛptəˌtud, B -ˌtjud] *s.* ineptitud, incapacidad.
ineptly [-'ɛptlɪ] *adv.* ineptamente; neciamente.
ineptness [-nəs] *s.* ineptitud, incapacidad, inhabilidad.
inequality [ˌɪnɪ'kwɑlətɪ, B -'kwɔl-] *s.* 1. desigualdad, disparidad. 2. desigualdad social, injusticia. 3. desigualdad, desnivel (del terreno). 4. variabilidad, inconstancia (del clima, carácter, etc.). 5. (mat., astr.) desigualdad.
inequitable [ɪn'ɛkwətəbəl] *a.* injusto, sin equidad.
inequitably [-blɪ] *adv.* injustamente.
inequity [-wətɪ] *s.* inequidad, desigualdad; falta de equidad, injusticia.
inequivalve [ɪn'ikwəˌvælv] **inequivalved** [-ˌvælvd] *a.* de valvas disimétricas (molusco).
ineradicable [ˌɪnɪ'rædɪkəbəl] *a.* inextirpable; indeleble, imborrable.
ineradicably [-blɪ] *adv.* inextirpablemente; indeleblemente.
inerasable [-'reɪsəbəl, B -'reɪz-] *a.* imborrable, indeleble.
inerrability [ɪnˌɛrə'bɪlətɪ] *s.* infalibilidad, calidad de inerrable.
inerrable [-'ɛrəbəl] *a.* inerrable, infalible.
inerrancy [-'ɛrənsɪ] *s.* infalibilidad.
inerrant [-'ɛrənt] *a.* inerrable, infalible.
inert [ɪn'ɜrt, B -'ɜt] *a.* 1. inerte, inactivo. 2. inerte, perezoso, desidioso, flojo. 3. (farm., fís., quím.) inerte.
inert gas, (quím.) gas inerte.
inertia [-'ɜrʃə, B -'ɜʃjə] *s.* 1. inercia, inactividad. 2. (fís.) inercia.
inertial [-ʃəl] *a.* (fís.) de inercia.
inertial force, (fís.) fuerza de inercia.
inertial frame, (fís.) marco de inercia (de Newton).
inertial guidance, 1. (astronáut.) dirección por inercia (de cohetes). 2. (aer.) piloto automático.
inertial mass, (fís.) masa inerte.
inertial system, (fís.) sistema de inercia.
inertly [ɪn'ɜrtlɪ, B -'ɜt-] *adv.* sin movimiento; flojamente, indolentemente; pesadamente.
inertness [-nəs] *s.* inercia, flojedad; inactividad.
inescapable [ˌɪnə'skeɪpəbəl] *a.* ineludible, inevitable.
inescapably [-blɪ] *adv.* ineludiblemente, inevitablemente.
in esse [ɪn'ɛsɪ] (lat.) siendo; en existencia.
inessential [ˌɪnə'sɛntʃəl, B -'sɛnʃəl] *a.* no esencial, prescindible, sin importancia. —*s.* detalle sin importancia.
inestimable [ɪn'ɛstəməbəl] *a.* inestimable, inapreciable.
inestimably [-blɪ] *adv.* de modo inestimable.
inevitability [ɪnˌɛvətə'bɪlətɪ] *s.* inevitabilidad, fatalidad.
inevitable [-'ɛvətəbəl] *a.* inevitable, ineludible.
inevitably [-blɪ] *adv.* inevitablemente; fatalmente.
inexact [ˌɪnɪg'zækt] *a.* inexacto, incorrecto, erróneo.
inexactitude [-'zæktəˌtud, B -ˌtjud] *s.* inexactitud.
inexactly [-'zæktlɪ] *adv.* inexactamente.
inexactness [-nəs] *s.* inexactitud.
inexcusability [ˌɪnɪkˌskjuzə'bɪlətɪ] *s.* calidad de inexcusable.
inexcusable [-'skjuzəbəl] *a.* inexcusable, injustificable, imperdonable, indisculpable.
inexcusableness [-nəs] *s.* calidad de inexcusable.
inexcusably [-blɪ] *adv.* inexcusablemente.
inexhaustibility [ˌɪnɪgˌzɔstə'bɪlətɪ] *s.* calidad de inexhausto o inagotable.
inexhaustible [-'zɔstəbəl] *a.* inagotable; infatigable; inexhausto.

inexhaustibly [-blɪ] *adv.* inagotablemente.
inexhaustive [-tɪv] *a.* inagotable; infatigable.
inexhaustively, *adv.* de modo inexhausto.
inexistence [ˌɪnɪg'zɪstəns] *s.* inexistencia.
inexistent [-tənt] *a.* inexistente, nulo.
inexorability [ɪnˌɛksərə'bɪlətɪ] *s.* inexorabilidad.
inexorable [-'ɛksərəbəl] *a.* inexorable, inflexible, implacable.
inexorably [-blɪ] *adv.* inexorablemente, inflexiblemente.
inexpedience [ˌɪnɪk'spidɪəns] *s.* inoportunidad, inconveniencia; impracticabilidad.
inexpediency [-ənsɪ] *s., var. de* **inexpedience.**
inexpedient [-ənt] *a.* inoportuno, inconveniente; impráctico.
inexpediently [-lɪ] *adv.* inoportunamente, inconvenientemente; imprácticamente.
inexpensive [ˌɪnɪk'spɛnsɪv] *a.* barato, poco costoso.
inexpensively [-lɪ] *adv.* baratamente.
inexpensiveness [-nəs] *s.* baratura, bajo costo.
inexperience [ˌɪnɪk'spɪrɪəns, B -'spɪər-] *s.* inexperiencia, impericia.
inexperienced [-ənst] *a.* inexperto, novel, bisoño.
inexpert [ɪn'ɛkˌspɜrt, ˌɪnɪk'spɜrt, B ɪn'ɛkˌspɜt] *a.* inexperto, inhábil. —*s.* inexperto.
inexpertly [-lɪ] *adv.* a manera de aficionado; de modo inexperto; toscamente, torpemente.
inexpertness [-nəs] *s.* impericia, inexperiencia.
inexpiable [ɪn'ɛkspɪəbəl] *a.* inexpiable.
inexpiably [-blɪ] *adv.* de modo inexpiable.
inexplainable [ˌɪnɪk'spleɪnəbəl] *a.* inexplicable, incomprensible.
inexplicability [ɪnˌɛksplɪkə'bɪlətɪ, ˌɪnɪkˌsplɪk-] *s.* carácter inexplicable.
inexplicable [ɪn'ɛksplɪkəbəl, ˌɪnɪk'splɪk-] *a.* inexplicable, incomprensible.
inexplicably [-blɪ] *adv.* inexplicablemente.
inexplicit [ˌɪnɪk'splɪsət] *a.* no explícito, no definido, ambiguo.
inexpressibility [-ˌsprɛsə'bɪlətɪ] *s.* calidad de inexpresable, inefabilidad.
inexpressible [-'sprɛsəbəl] *a.* inexpresable, indecible, inefable, inenarrable.
inexpressibleness [-nəs] *s.* calidad de inexpresable, inefabilidad.
inexpressibly [-blɪ] *adv.* indeciblemente, inefablemente.
inexpressive [-'sprɛsɪv] *a.* 1. inexpresivo. 2. (ant.) indecible.
inexpressively [-lɪ] *adv.* inexpresivamente.
inexpressiveness [-nəs] *s.* falta de expresión.
inexpugnable [ˌɪnɪk'spʌgnəbəl, -'spjunə-, B -'spʌg-] *a.* inexpugnable, inconquistable.
inexpugnableness [-nəs] *s.* calidad de inexpugnable.
inexpugnably [-blɪ] *adv.* de modo inexpugnable.
inextensible [ˌɪnɪk'stɛnsəbəl] *a.* (fís.) inextensible.
in extenso [ˌɪnɪk'stɛnsoʊ] (lat.) en su totalidad, en toda su extensión.
inextinguishable [ˌɪnɪk'stɪŋgwɪʃəbəl] *a.* inextinguible, inapagable.
inextinguishably [-blɪ] *adv.* de modo inextinguible.
inextirpable [-'stɜrpəbəl, B -'stɜpə-] *a.* inextirpable.
in extremis [ˌɪnɪk'streɪməs, B -'strim-] (lat.) a punto de morir, en los últimos instantes de vida.
inextricability [ɪnˌɛkstrɪkə'bɪlətɪ] *s.* calidad de inextricable.
inextricable [ɪn'ɛkstrɪkəbəl, ˌɪnɪk'strɪk-] *a.* 1. inextricable, irresoluble. 2. intrincado, enmarañado.
inextricably [-blɪ] *adv.* intricadamente, de modo inextricable.
inf. *abrev. de* 1. **infantry,** infantería 2. **inferior,** inferior. 3. **infinitive,** infinitivo. 4. **influence,** influencia. 5. **information,** información.
infallibility [ɪnˌfælə'bɪlətɪ] *s.* infalibilidad.
infallible [-'fæləbəl] *a.* infalible.
infallibly [-blɪ] *adv.* infaliblemente.
infamous ['ɪnfəməs] *a.* 1. infame, vil. 2. infamatorio, ignominioso, vergonzoso. 3. de reputación y notoriedad escandalosa o infame. 4. (der.) infame, infamante (crimen, delito); infamante (pena).
infamously [-lɪ] *adv.* infamemente, ignominiosamente.
infamousness [-nəs] *s.* infamia, vileza, vergüenza.
infamy ['ɪnfəmɪ] *s.* 1. infamia, ignominia, oprobio, descrédito, deshonor. 2. acto infame, torpeza.
infancy ['ɪnfənsɪ] *s.* 1. infancia, niñez. 2. (der.) menor edad, minoridad, minoría. 3. **to be in its i.,** estar en pañales.
infant [-fənt] *s.* 1. infante, criatura. 2. (der.) menor. —*a.* 1. infantil, de niño; pequeño. 2. en su infancia, joven (estado, industria, etc.).
infanta [ɪn'fæntə] *s.* infanta (princesa en España y Portugal).
infante [ɪ] *s.* infante (príncipe en España y Portugal).
infanticidal [ɪnˌfæntəˌsaɪdəl] *a.* infanticida.
infanticide [-ˌsaɪd] *s.* 1. infanticidio. 2. infanticida.
infantile ['ɪnfənˌtaɪl, -təl, B -ˌtaɪl] *a.* infantil, pueril.
infantile paralysis, (med.) parálisis infantil.
infantile scurvy, (med.) escorbuto infantil o mal de Barlow.
infantilism [-ˌɪzəm] *s.* (med.) infantilismo.
infantine ['ɪnfənˌtaɪn] *a.* infantino, infantil.
infantry ['ɪnfəntrɪ] *s.* (mil.) infantería.
infantryman [-mən] *s.* soldado de infantería, infante.
infarct ['ɪnˌfɑrkt, B ɪn'fɑkt] *s.* (med.) infarto.
infarction [ɪn'fɑrkʃən, B -'fɑk-] *s.* (med.) infartación.
infare ['ɪnˌfær, B -ˌfɛə] *s.* 1. (dial.) tertulia para celebrar el estreno de una casa, esp. la de una novia. 2. recepción o fiesta postnupcial.
infatuate [ɪn'fætʃʊət, B -'fætjʊ-] *a.* 1. amartelado, locamente enamorado. 2. infatuado. —[-ˌeɪt] *v.t.* 1. amartelar, enamorar locamente. 2. infatuar, embobar, atontar.
infatuated [-ˌeɪtəd] *a.* locamente enamorado, amartelado; **to be i. with,** estar locamente enamorado de.
infatuatedly [-lɪ] *adv.* de modo infatuado; tontamente.
infatuation [ɪnˌfætʃʊ'eɪʃən, B -ˌfætjʊ-] *s.* 1. amartelamiento, amor obsesivo. 2. infatuación.
infeasibility [ɪnˌfizə'bɪlətɪ] *s.* impracticabilidad, infactibilidad.
infeasible [-'fizəbəl] *a.* impracticable; infactible.
infect [ɪn'fɛkt] *v.t.* 1. infectar, inficionar, contagiar, contaminar. 2. influir, influenciar. 3. **i. with,** (fig.) contagiar de (entusiasmo, idea, etc.).
infection [-'fɛkʃən] *s.* 1. infección; contagio, contaminación. 2. enfermedad infecciosa, infección. 3. agente infectante.
infectious [-ʃəs] *a.* infeccioso, infectivo, contagioso.
infectious disease, cocoliste (Mex.).
infectious hepatitis, (med.) hepatitis infecciosa o epidémica.
infectiously [-lɪ] *adv.* infecciosamente.
infectious mononucleosis, (med.) mononucleosis infecciosa o aguda.
infectiousness [-nəs] *s.* infección; calidad de infeccioso o infectivo.
infective [ɪn'fɛktɪv] *a.* infectivo, infeccioso.
infecund [ɪn'fikənd, -'fɛk-] *a.* infecundo, infructuoso, estéril.
infecundity [ˌɪnfɪ'kʌndətɪ] *s.* infecundidad, infructuosidad, esterilidad.
infelicitous [ˌɪnfɪ'lɪsətəs] *a.* 1. desatinado, desacertado, inapropiado. 2. infeliz, desgraciado, infortunado.
infelicitously [-lɪ] *adv.* 1. desatinadamente, desacertadamente, inapropiadamente. 2. infelizmente, infortunadamente, desgraciadamente.
infelicity [-tɪ] *s.* 1. desacierto, desatino. 2. infelicidad, infortunio, desgracia.
infer [ɪn'fɜr, B -'fɜ] *v.t.(pret., p.p.* INFERRED; *p.pr.* INFERRING) inferir, deducir, colegir, concluir. —*v.i.* hacer inferencias, sacar consecuencias.
inferable [-'fɜrəbəl] *a.* que puede inferirse.
inferably [-blɪ] *adv.* de modo que puede inferirse; consecuentemente.
inference ['ɪnfərəns] *s.* inferencia, deducción.
inferential [ˌɪnfə'rɛnʃəl, B -'rɛnʃəl] *a.* ilativo; deducido.
inferentially [-əlɪ] *adv.* por inferencia.
inferior [ɪn'fɪrɪər, B -'fɪərɪə] *a.* 1. inferior, más bajo. 2. inferior, subordinado, subalterno. 3. (de calidad) inferior; mediocre, deslucido. 4. (bot.) ínfero. 5. (impr.) debajo de la línea, a manera de subíndice (díc. de pequeñas letras o números). —*s.* inferior, subordinado.
inferiority [-ˌfɪrɪ'ɔrətɪ, -'ɑr-, B -ˌfɪərɪ'ɔr-] *s.* inferioridad.
inferiority complex, (psic.) complejo de inferioridad.
infernal [ɪn'fɜrnəl, B -'fɜn-] *a.* 1. infernal. 2. (fam.) infernal, detestable, abominable.
infernally [-əlɪ] *adv.* de modo infernal.
infernal machine, máquina infernal; trampa dañina o bomba de tiempo.
inferno [ɪn'fɜrnoʊ, B -'fɜnoʊ] *s.* infierno.
infertile [ɪn'fɜrtəl, B -'fɜtaɪl] *a.* infértil, estéril.
infertility [ˌɪnfər'tɪlətɪ, B -fə'-] *s.* infertilidad, esterilidad.
infest [ɪn'fɛst] *v.t.* infestar, plagar.
infestation [ˌɪnfɛs'teɪʃən] *s.* infestación.
infeudation [ˌɪnfjʊ'deɪʃən] *s.* (G.B., hist.) enfeudación.
infidel ['ɪnfədəl] *a.* infiel. —*s.* infiel, pagano, ateo.
infidelity [ˌɪnfə'dɛlətɪ] *s.* 1. infidelidad, carencia de fe. 2. deslealtad, traición, perfidia 3. infidelidad conyugal; adulterio.
infield ['ɪnˌfild] *s.* 1. campo cercano a los edificios de una granja. 2. (béisbol) cuadrado, diamante.
infielder [-ˌfildər, B -də] *s.* (béisbol) jugador de defensa (que juega dentro del diamante).
infighting ['ɪnˌfaɪtɪŋ] *s.* 1. boxeo o lucha cuerpo a cuerpo. 2. lucha interna (en una organización o partido).
infiltrate [ɪn'fɪlˌtreɪt, 'ɪnfɪl-] *v.t., v.i.* 1. infiltrar(se), calar(se). 2. (mil.) infiltrar(se). —*s.* (med.) infiltración.
infiltration [ˌɪnfɪl'treɪʃən] *s.* infiltración.
infiltrator [ɪn'fɪlˌtreɪtər, 'ɪnfɪl-, B -ə] *s.* infiltrado, espía.

infin. *abrev. de* **infinitive,** infinitivo (inf.).
infinite ['ɪnfənət] *a.* 1. infinito, ilimitado, indeterminado. 2. infinito, vasto, inmenso. 3. (mat.) infinito. —*s.* infinito; **the I.,** el Infinito (Dios).
infinitely [-lɪ] *adv.* infinitamente.
infiniteness [-nəs] *s.* infinidad, infinitud.
infinitesimal [ˌɪnˌfɪnə'tɛsəməl] *a.* infinitesimal. —*s.* (mat.) infinitésimo, cantidad infinitesimal.
infinitesimal calculus, (mat.) cálculo infinitesimal.
infinitesimally [-məlɪ] *adv.* infinitesimalmente.
infinitival [-'taɪvəl] *a.* (gram.) del (modo) infinitivo.
infinitive [ɪn'fɪnətɪv] *a., s.* (gram.) infinitivo.
infinitude [-ˌtud, B -ˌtjud] *s.* infinitud, infinidad.
infinity [ɪn'fɪnətɪ] *s.* 1. infinidad; infinitud; lo infinito; inmensidad. 2. (mat.) infinito.
infirm [ɪn'fɜrm, B -'fɜm] *a.* 1. débil, endeble, enfermizo. 2. débil (de carácter); irresoluto, titubeante, vacilante. 3. inestable; inseguro. —*v.t.* 1. infirmar, invalidar. 2. (ant.) debilitar, menoscabar.
infirmary [-ərɪ] *s.* enfermería, dispensario.
infirmity [-'fɜrmətɪ, B -'fɜmɪtɪ] *s.* 1. debilidad, endeblez, fragilidad. 2. enfermedad, dolencia, achaque. 3. flaqueza, lado flaco; defecto.
infirmly [-lɪ] *adv.* débilmente, enfermizamente.
infix ['ɪnˌfɪks, B ɪn'fɪks] *v.t.* 1. clavar, hincar, fijar; encajar; empotrar. 2. inculcar; instilar, infundir. 3. (gram.) insertar (letra o sonido) como infijo. — ['ɪnˌfɪks] *s.* (gram.) infijo, afijo (insertado en el cuerpo de una palabra).
inflame [ɪn'fleɪm] *v.t.* 1. inflamar, encender. 2. inflamar, enardecer, avivar (pasión, etc.). 3. encolerizar, enfurecer; enrojecer, congestionar (de ira, etc.). 4. (med.) inflamar. —*v.i.* 1. inflamarse, arder, encenderse; encolerizarse, enfurecerse. 2. (med.) inflamarse.
inflamer [-ər, B -ə] *s.* inflamador, agitador; incendiario.
inflammability [ɪnˌflæmə'bɪlətɪ] *s.* inflamabilidad.
inflammable [-'flæməbəl] *a.* 1. inflamable, combustible. 2. irascible, irritable. —*s.* substancia o cosa inflamable.
inflammableness [-nəs] *s. calidad de inflamable.*
inflammably [-blɪ] *adv.* de modo inflamable; irasciblemente.
inflammation [ˌɪnflə'meɪʃən] *s.* inflamación; (med.) inflamación.
inflammatory [ɪn'flæməˌtɔrɪ, B -tərɪ] *a.* 1. incendiario, sedicioso, incitante. 2. (med.) inflamatorio.
inflatable [ɪn'fleɪtəbəl] *a.* inflable, que puede inflarse, hinchable.
inflate [-'fleɪt] *v.t.* 1. inflar, distender, hinchar. 2. inflar, ensoberbecer, engreír. 3. (e.p.) causar la inflación de (la moneda). —*v.i.* inflarse, hincharse.
inflated [-əd] *a.* 1. inflado, distendido, hinchado. 2. pomposo, ampuloso, altisonante, rimbombante. 3. (e.p.) de inflación (precios, etc.); en inflación (moneda). 4. (bot.) hueco e hinchado (tallo, pedúnculo, cápsula); abierto y abultado (periantio).
inflater [-ər, B -ə] *s.* inflador.
inflating [-ɪŋ] *a.* inflativo.
inflation [ɪn'fleɪʃən] *s.* inflación; (e.p.) inflación (de la moneda).
inflationary [-ˌɛrɪ, B -ərɪ] *a.* (e.p.) inflacionario, inflacionista (política, economía, etc.); de inflación (precios, etc.).
inflationary spiral, (e.p.) espiral inflacionista, alza continua y acelerada del costo de vida.
inflationism [-ˌɪzəm] *s.* (e.p.) política inflacionista, inflacionismo.
inflationist [-əst] *s., a.* inflacionista.
inflator [-'fleɪtər, B -ə] *s.* inflador.
inflect [ɪn'flɛkt] *v.t.* 1. torcer, doblar; desviar. 2. modular (la voz, etc.). 3. (bot.) curvar hacia adentro o hacia el eje principal. 4. (gram.) inflexionar (una voz); declinar; conjugar.
inflection, (pr. G.B.) **inflexion** [-'flɛkʃən] *s.* 1. inflexión; curvatura. 2. inflexión, acento, modulación (de la voz). 3. (gram., mat.) inflexión, conjugación, declinación.
inflectional, (pr. G.B.) **inflexional** [-əl] *a.* (gram.) flexional; que tiene inflexiones.
inflectionally, (pr. G.B.) **inflexionally** [-ɪ] *adv.* por inflexión.
inflective [-'flɛktɪv] *a.* doblegable; (gram.) flexional.
inflexed ['ɪnˌflɛkst, B ɪn'flɛkst] *a.* 1. doblado, curvado. 2. (bot.) inflexo.
inflexibility [ɪnˌflɛksə'bɪlətɪ] *s.* inflexibilidad.
inflexible [ɪn'flɛksəbəl] *a.* 1. inflexible, rígido. 2. (fig.) inflexible, indoblegable, inexorable.
inflexibleness [-nəs] *s.* inflexibilidad.
inflexibly [-blɪ] *adv.* inflexiblemente.
inflict [ɪn'flɪkt] *v.t.* infligir (derrota), asestar (golpe), imponer (castigo, pena), causar (herida, dolor, sufrimiento); **i. oneself upon,** imponer (a otros) su propia compañía.
inflicter [-'flɪktər, B -tə] *s.* causante, autor.
infliction [-ʃən] *s.* 1. imposición. 2. molestia, fastidio. 3. pena, castigo.
inflictive [-tɪv] *a.* inflictivo, que se impone o inflige.
inflictor [-tər, B -tə] *s.* causante, autor.
inflorescence [ˌɪnflə'rɛsəns] *s.* (bot.) 1. inflorescencia. 2. florescencia.
inflorescent [-ənt] *a.* (bot.) floreciente.
inflow ['ɪnˌfloʊ] *s.* afluencia, flujo hacia dentro; entrada.
influence ['ɪnˌfluəns, B -flʊ-] *s.* 1. influencia, influjo. 2. (fig.) influencia, ascendencia, autoridad; **to peddle i.,** vender humos; 3. (astrol.) fluido etéreo; influencia. 4. (elec.) influencia. —*v.t.* influir en o sobre, inducir; persuadir.
influence peddler, vendehumos.
influent [-ənt] *a.* que fluye hacia dentro. —*s.* afluente (de un río).
influential [ˌɪnflʊ'ɛntʃəl, B -'ɛnʃəl] *a.* influyente, poderoso; **to be i.,** tener banca.
influentially [-'ɛntʃəlɪ, B -'ɛnʃ-] *adv.* influyentemente, con (mucha) influencia.
influenza [ˌɪnflʊ'ɛnzə] *s.* (med.) influenza, gripe.
influx ['ɪnˌflʌks] *s.* 1. afluencia, flujo hacia dentro. 2. desembocadura, salida (de un río).
info ['ɪnfoʊ] *s.* (jer.) información, dato.
infold, *v.t., var. de* **enfold.**
inform [ɪn'fɔrm, B -'fɔm] *v.t.* 1. informar, comunicar a, enterar. 2. (fig.) formar, moldear (opinión, etc.). 3. (gen. con *with*) inspirar, animar (con). 4. (ant.) entrenar, instruir; guiar, dirigir. 5. **to keep informed,** mantenerse informado. —*v.i.* 1. dar información. 2. **i. against** (u **on**), delatar, denunciar. —*a.* (ant.) 1. informe, deforme. 2. amorfo; no formado.
informal [-'fɔrməl, B -'fɔməl] *a.* informal; irregular, sin ceremonia, de confianza.
informality [ˌɪnfɔr'mælətɪ, B -fɔ'-] *s.* informalidad.
informally [ɪn'fɔrməlɪ, B -'fɔmə-] *adv.* informalmente, de manera informal.
informant [-mənt] *s.* 1. informante, informador. 2. soplón, delator; confidente (de la policía).
information [ˌɪnfər'meɪʃən, B -fə'-] *s.* 1. información. 2. denuncia, cargo. 3. (der.) acusación por el fiscal. 4. dato, conocimiento. 5. **for your i.,** para su gobierno, para que (Ud.) sepa.
informational [-əl] *a.* informativo.
information bureau, consultorio.
information storage, (comput.) informática.
informative [ɪn'fɔrmətɪv, B -'fɔmət-] *a.* informativo, instructivo.
informatively [-lɪ] *adv.* a título de información, de modo informativo.
informatory [-məˌtɔrɪ, B -tərɪ] *a.* informativo, informante.
informed [ɪn'fɔrmd, B -'fɔmd] *a.* informado, sabedor; culto; al corriente de, al tanto de; **to be i. of** o **about,** quedar o estar impuesto de.
informer [-'fɔrmər, B -'fɔmə] *s.* 1. informante, informador. 2. soplón, delator; confidente (de la policía).
infortune [ɪn'fɔrtʃən, B -'fɔtʃən] *s.* 1. (astrol.) infortuna, influjo adverso (de los planetas). 2. (ant.) infortunio.
infract [ɪn'frækt] *v.t.* (raro) infringir, transgredir, violar (derechos o leyes).
infraction [-'frækʃən] *s.* infracción, transgresión, violación.
infractor [-tər, B -tə] *s.* infractor, transgresor.
infra dig [ˌɪnfrə'dɪg] (fam.) indigno, degradante.
infrahuman [-'hjumən] *a., s.* infrahumano.
infralapsarian [-læp'sɛrɪən, B -'sɛər-] *a.* (relig.) infralapsariano.
infralapsarianism [-ˌɪzəm] *s.* (relig.) infralapsarismo (doctrina calvinista que afirma que Dios predestinó la redención y salvación de sólo algunos pecadores).
inframaxillary [-'mæksəˌlɛrɪ, B -mæk'sɪlərɪ] *a.* (anat.) inframaxilar. —*s.* (anat.) maxilar inferior.
infrangibility [ɪnˌfrændʒə'bɪlətɪ] *s.* calidad de infrangible.
infrangible [-'frændʒəbəl] *a.* 1. infrangible, irrompible. 2. (fig.) infrangible, inquebrantable, inviolable.
infrangibleness [-nəs] *s.* calidad de infrangible.
infraorbital [ˌɪnfrə'ɔrbətəl, B -'ɔbɪt-] *a.* (anat.) infraorbitario (situado debajo de la órbita del ojo).
infrared [-'rɛd] *a., s.* infrarrojo.
infrasonic [-'sɑnɪk, B -'sɔn-] *a.* (fís.) infrasónico.
infrastructure ['ɪnfrəˌstrʌktʃər, B -tʃə] *s.* infraestructura, fundamento.
infrequence [ɪn'frikwəns] *var. de* **infrequency.**
infrequency [-kwənsɪ] *s.* infrecuencia, rareza.
infrequent [-kwənt] *a.* infrecuente, poco común, raro, ocasional.
infrequently [-lɪ] *adv.* infrecuentemente, rara vez.
infringe [ɪn'frɪndʒ] *v.t.* 1. infringir, transgredir, violar. 2. (ant.) romper, destrozar; frustrar, anular. —*v.i.* (con *on* o *upon*) invadir, abusar de, usurpar, violar.
infringement [-mənt] *s.* 1. infracción, transgresión, violación. 2. usurpación (de derechos, etc.).
infringer [-ər, B -ə] *s.* infractor, violador, usurpador.
infundibular [ˌɪnfən'dɪbjələr, B -lə] **infundibulate** [-lət] *a.* 1. (bot.) infundibuliforme. 2. (anat.) infundibular.
infundibuliform [-ləˌfɔrm, B -ˌfɔm] *a.* (bot.) infundibuliforme.
infundibulum [-ləm] *s.* (*pl.* INFUNDIBULA [-lə]) (anat.) infundíbulo.

infuriate [ɪn'fjʊrɪət, B -'fjʊər-] *a.* furioso, enfurecido. — [-ˌeɪt] *v.t.* enfurecer, irritar.
infuriating [-ˌeɪtɪŋ] *a.* exasperante, irritante; que enfurece.
infuriatingly [-lɪ] *adv.* exasperantemente, irritantemente.
infuriation [ɪnˌfjʊrɪ'eɪʃən, B -ˌfjʊər-] *s.* furia, enfurecimiento.
infuse [ɪn'fjuz] *v.t.* 1. verter en, vaciar en. 2. infundir, instilar, inculcar (principios o cualidades). 3. hacer una infusión de. 4. **i. with,** imbuir de, llenar de.
infusibility [ɪnˌfjuzə'bɪlətɪ] *s.* infusibilidad.
infusible [-'fjuzəbəl] *a.* infusible.
infusion [ɪn'fjuʒən] *s.* infusión, instilación; (med., farm.) infusión; maceración.
infusionism [-ˌɪzəm] *s.* (teo.) infusionismo.
infusionist [-əst] *s.* (teo.) infusionista.
infusive [-'fjusɪv] *a.* inspirador; (teo.) infuso.
Infusoria [ˌɪnfju'sɔrɪə, B -'zɔr-] *s. pl.* (zool.) infusorios.
infusorial [-ɪəl] *a.* (zool.) infusorio, de infusorios (tierra).
infusorian [-ɪən] *a., s.* (zool.) infusorio.
ingather ['ɪnˌgæðər, ɪn'gæðər, B -ə] *v.t.* (ant.) recolectar, recoger (la cosecha). —*v.i.* reunirse.
ingathering ['ɪnˌgæðərɪŋ] *s.* 1. (ant.) recolección (de la cosecha). 2. reunión.
ingeminate [ɪn'dʒɛməˌneɪt] *v.t.* reduplicar, repetir; reiterar.
ingemination [-ˌdʒɛmə'neɪʃən] *s.* reduplicación, repetición.
ingenerate [ɪn'dʒɛnərət] *a.* ingénito, innato, connatural. — [-ˌreɪt] *v.t.* generar interiormente; causar, engendrar, producir.
ingenious [ɪn'dʒinjəs] *a.* ingenioso, genial.
ingeniously [-lɪ] *adv.* ingeniosamente, genialmente.
ingeniousness [-nəs] *s.* ingenio, ingeniosidad.
ingénue ['ɑndʒəˌnu, B ˌænʒeɪ'nju] *s.* (fr.) joven ingenua y candorosa; actriz que hace papeles de ingenua.
ingenuity [ˌɪndʒə'nuətɪ, B -'nju-] *s.* 1. ingenio, ingeniosidad, inventiva. 2. artefacto ingenioso.
ingenuous [ɪn'dʒɛnjʊəs] *a.* 1. ingenuo, inocente, candoroso; franco, sincero. 2. (ant.) noble, honorable.
ingenuously [-lɪ] *adv.* ingenuamente, cándidamente.
ingenuousness [-nəs] *s.* ingenuidad, candor, candidez.
ingest [ɪn'dʒɛst] *v.t.* 1. ingerir (alimento). 2. (fig.) absorber (ideas, pensamientos, etc.).
ingesta [-'dʒɛstə] *s. pl.* alimento tomado.
ingestion [-tʃən] *s.* ingestión.
ingestive [-tɪv] *a.* ingestivo.
ingle ['ɪŋgəl] *s.* 1. (G.B.) fuego, lumbre (del hogar). 2. hogar, chimenea.
inglenook [-ˌnʊk] *s.* (pr. G.B.) 1. rincón de la chimenea. 2. banco al lado de la chimenea.
inglorious [ɪn'glɔrɪəs] *a.* 1. ignominioso, vergonzoso, afrentoso. 2. (ant.) obscuro, sin fama.
ingloriously [-lɪ] *adv.* 1. ignominiosamente. 2. (ant.) obscuramente, sin fama.
ingloriousness [-nəs] *s.* ignominia.
ingoing ['ɪnˌgoʊɪŋ] *a.* entrante, que entra.
ingot ['ɪŋgət] *s.* 1. lingote, barra. 2. lingotera, molde de fundición.
ingot iron, hierro dulce, hierro de lingote.
ingraft [ɪn'græft, B -'grɑft] *v.t. var. de* engraft, injertar.
ingrain [ɪn'greɪn] *v.t.* fijar, impregnar; teñir en hilado o rama. — ['ɪnˌgreɪn] *a.* 1. teñido en rama. 2. (fig.) innato, inherente. —*s.* 1. fibra teñida antes de ser procesada. 2. cualquier tejido hecho con esa fibra, ej., alfombras.
ingrained [ɪn'greɪnd, 'ɪnˌgreɪnd] *a.* innato, inherente; inculcado, arraigado profundamente.
ingrate ['ɪnˌgreɪt, B ɪn'greɪt] *a.* (ant.) ingrato. —*s.* persona ingrata o desagradecida.
ingratiate [ɪn'greɪʃɪˌeɪt] *v.t.* congraciar, hacer aceptable; **i. oneself (with),** congraciarse (con).
ingratiating [-ɪŋ] *a.* congraciador.
ingratiatingly [-lɪ] *adv.* de modo congraciador.
ingratiation [-ˌgreɪʃɪ'eɪʃən] *s.* congraciamiento.
ingratiatory [-'greɪʃɪəˌtɔrɪ, B -ətərɪ] *a.* congraciador.
ingratitude [ɪn'grætəˌtud, B -ˌtjud] *s.* ingratitud, desagradecimiento.
ingravescent [ˌɪngrə'vɛsənt] *a.* (med.) ingravescente.
ingredient [ɪn'gridɪənt] *s.* ingrediente, componente. —*a.* componente, integrante.
ingress ['ɪnˌgrɛs] *s.* 1. ingreso, entrada. 2. paso, acceso. 3. lugar de entrada.
ingression [ɪn'grɛʃən] *s.* entrada, ingreso.
ingressive [-'grɛsɪv] *a.* entrante, esp. (gram.) incoativo.
in-group ['ɪnˌgrup] *s.* grupo de gente con creencias e intereses comunes que generalmente excluye a los que no forman parte del mismo; grupo excluyente (Am.).
ingrow ['ɪnˌgroʊ] *v.i.* crecer hacia dentro.
ingrowing [-ɪŋ] *a.* que crece hacia dentro.
ingrown [-ˌgroʊn] *a.* crecido hacia dentro; innato, congénito.
ingrown nail, uñero, uña encarnada o enterrada.
ingrowth [-ˌgroʊθ] *s.* crecimiento hacia dentro.
inguinal ['ɪŋgwənəl] *a.* (anat., med.) inguinal, inguinario, referente a la ingle.
inguinal canal, conducto inguinal.
ingulf, *var. de* **engulf.**
ingurgitate [ɪn'gɜrdʒəˌteɪt, B -'gɜdʒɪ-] *v.t., v.i.* ingurgitar; engullir.
ingurgitation [-ˌgɜrdʒə'teɪʃən, B -ˌgɜdʒɪ-] *s.* ingurgitación, voracidad, glotonería.
inhabit [ɪn'hæbət] *v.t.* habitar, poblar; vivir en, residir en. —*v.i.* (ant.) establecerse, radicarse.
inhabitability [-ˌhæbətə'bɪlətɪ] *s.* habitabilidad.
inhabitable [-'hæbətəbəl] *a.* (ant.) habitable.
inhabitancy [-ənsɪ] *s.* 1. habitación, la acción de habitar. 2. residencia, morada, domicilio.
inhabitant [-ənt] *s.* habitante, residente, poblador.
inhabitation [ɪnˌhæbə'teɪʃən] *s.* habitación, el acto de habitar.
inhabited [ɪn'hæbətəd] *a.* habitado, poblado.
inhabiter [-ər, B -ə] *s.* habitante.
inhalant [ɪn'heɪlənt] *a.* inhalante, adecuado para inhalaciones. —*s.* (med.) inhalador; inhalación, medicamento inhalante.
inhalation [ˌɪnhə'leɪʃən] *s.* inhalación; (med.) inhalación, medicamento inhalante.
inhalator ['ɪnhəˌleɪtər, B -ə] *s.* (med.) inhalador.
inhale [ɪn'heɪl] *v.t.* inspirar, aspirar; (med.) inhalar. —*v.i.* tragar el humo.
inhaler [-ər, B -ə] *s.* 1. persona que hace inhalaciones. 2. inhalador. 3. (fam.) copa ancha (que permite aspirar el aroma de un buen licor).
inharmonic [ˌɪnhɑr'mɑnɪk, B -hɑ'mɔn-] *a.* inarmónico, disonante, dísono; discordante.
inharmonious [-'moʊnɪəs] *a.* poco armonioso, discordante, disonante.
inharmoniously [-lɪ] *adv.* de manera inarmoniosa o discordante.
inharmoniousness [-nəs] *s.* inarmonía, discordancia.
inharmony [ɪn'hɑrmənɪ, B -'hɑmə-] *s.* inarmonía, discordia; disonancia, discordancia.
inhaul ['ɪnˌhɔl] **inhauler** [-ər, B -ə] *s.* (mar.) cargadera, briol, candaliza.
inhere [ɪn'hɪr, B -'hɪə] *v.i.* ser inherente o inmanente.
inherence [-əns, -'hɛr-, B -'hɪər-] *s.* inherencia, inmanencia.
inherency [-ənsɪ] *s.* 1. inherencia, inmanencia. 2. carácter o atributo inherente.
inherent [-ənt] *a.* inherente, inmanente; intrínseco.
inherently [-lɪ] *adv.* inherentemente, inmanentemente; intrínsecamente.
inherit [ɪn'hɛrət] *v.t.* heredar, recibir en herencia. —*v.i.* suceder, ser heredero.
inheritability [-ˌhɛrətə'bɪlətɪ] *s.* calidad de heredable.
inheritable [-'hɛrətəbəl] *a.* 1. heredable, hereditario; transmisible (ej., un título). 2. que puede heredar; con derecho a heredar.
inheritably [-blɪ] *adv.* hereditariamente, por herencia.
inheritance [-'hɛrətəns] *s.* 1. herencia, patrimonio, bienes; títulos o caracteres heredados. 2. (con *of*) sucesión (a). 3. (ant.) posesión, propiedad, heredad.
inheritance tax, (der.) impuesto de sucesión, impuesto a la herencia.
inheritor [-ər, B -ə] *s.* heredero.
inheritress [-ətrəs] **inheritrix** [-ətrɪks] *s.* heredera.
inhesion [ɪn'hiʒən] *s. var. de* **inherence.**
inhibit [ɪn'hɪbət] *v.t.* 1. inhibir, reprimir, impedir, detener. 2. (raro) prohibir, interdecir.
inhibiter [-ər, B -ə] *s.* inhibidor.
inhibition [ˌɪnhə'bɪʃən, ˌɪnə-] *s.* 1. inhibición, prohibición, restricción. 2. (psic.) inhibición, impedimento. 3. (fisiol.) inhibición (de un órgano).
inhibitive [ɪn'hɪbətɪv] *a.* inhibitorio.
inhibitor [-ər, B -ə] *s.* (fís., quím.) inhibidor, retardador.
inhibitory [-'hɪbəˌtɔrɪ, B -tərɪ] *a.* inhibitorio.
inhospitable [ɪn'hɑspɪtəbəl, ˌɪnhɑs'pɪt-, B -'hɔspɪt-] *a.* 1. inhospitalario, inhospitable. 2. inhóspito; desnudo, árido, desierto.
inhospitableness [-nəs] *a.* inhospitalidad.
inhospitably [-blɪ] *adv.* de manera inhospitalaria o inhóspita.
inhospitality [ɪnˌhɑspə'tælətɪ, B -ˌhɔs-] *s.* inhospitalidad.
in-house ['ɪnˌhaʊs] *a.* interno, de la casa, de dentro (de una organización, etc.).
inhuman [ɪn'hjumən, -'ju-, B -'hju-] *a.* inhumano, cruel, brutal; no humano, fuera de lo humano.
inhumane [ˌɪnhju'meɪn, ˌɪnju-, B -hju-] *a.* inhumano, falto de humanidad.
inhumanely [-lɪ] *adv.* inhumanamente.
inhumanity [-'mænətɪ] *s.* inhumanidad, crueldad, salvajismo.
inhumanly [ɪn'hjumənlɪ, ɪn'ju-, B -'hju-] *adv.* inhumanamente, cruelmente.
inhumation [ˌɪnhju'meɪʃən] *s.* inhumación, entierro.
inhume [ɪn'hjum] *v.t.* inhumar, sepultar, enterrar.
inhumer [-'hjumər, B -mə] *s.* sepulturero, enterrador.
inimical [ɪ'nɪmɪkəl] *a.* 1. enemigo, hostil, enemistoso (Am.). 2. (con *to*) opuesto (a); adverso (a).
inimically [-ɪkəlɪ] *adv.* enemigamente, con enemistad, hostilmente, enemistosamente (Am.).
inimitability [ɪnˌɪmətə'bɪlətɪ] *s.* calidad de inimitable.

inimitable [ɪn'ɪmətəbəl] *a.* inimitable, incomparable, incopiable.
inimitably [-blɪ] *adv.* inimitablemente, incomparablemente.
inion ['ɪnɪən] *s.* (anat.) inio, inión.
iniquitous [ɪn'ɪkwətəs] *a.* inicuo, injusto; malvado, perverso.
iniquitously [-lɪ] *adv.* inicuamente, injustamente; malvadamente, perversamente.
iniquitousness [-nəs] *s.* iniquidad, injusticia; perversidad, maldad.
iniquity [ɪn'ɪkwətɪ] *s.* 1. iniquidad, injusticia; perversidad, maldad. 2. ofensa; pecado.
initial [ɪ'nɪʃəl] *a.* inicial, incipiente; primero. —*s.* *inicial (letra).* —*v.t.* (*pret., p.p.* INITIALED O INITIALLED; *p.pr.* INITIALING O INITIALLING) poner iniciales a, firmar con las iniciales.
initially [-əlɪ] *adv.* primeramente, originalmente.
initiate [ɪ'nɪʃɪˌeɪt] *v.t.* 1. iniciar, principiar, empezar. 2. iniciar, instruir, enseñar. 3. iniciar, admitir (en una secta, sociedad secreta, etc.). — [-ɪət] *a., s.* iniciado.
initiation [ɪˌnɪʃɪ'eɪʃən] *s.* 1. iniciación, comienzo, principio. 2. iniciación, rito o ceremonia de admisión.
initiative [ɪ'nɪʃɪətɪv] *a.* iniciativo, iniciador; introductorio, preliminar. —*s.* 1. iniciativa. 2. (der., pol.) iniciativa, derecho de una asamblea o del pueblo, a introducir propuestas legislativas. 3. **on one's own i.,** por iniciativa propia; **to have i.,** tener iniciativa; **to take the i.,** tomar la iniciativa.
initiator [-ɪˌeɪtər, B -ə] *s.* iniciador.
initiatory [-əˌtɔrɪ, B -tərɪ] *a.* preliminar, introductorio; iniciativo, iniciador.
inject [ɪn'dʒɛkt] *v.t.* 1. inyectar, jeringar, meter (a la fuerza). 2. (med.) inyectar. 3. (fig.) introducir, infundir.
injection [-'dʒɛkʃən] *s.* inyección; (med.) inyección.
injector [-tər, B -tə] *s.* 1. (mec.) inyector. 2. (med.) inyector, jeringa.
injudicious [ˌɪndʒʊ'dɪʃəs] *a.* indiscreto, imprudente, poco juicioso.
injudiciously [-lɪ] *adv.* indiscretamente, imprudentemente.
injudiciousness [-nəs] *s.* indiscreción, imprudencia.
Injun ['ɪndʒən] *s.* (hum.) indio de los E.U.
injunction [ɪn'dʒʌŋkʃən] *s.* 1. mandato, orden, precepto. 2. amonestación. 3. (der.) requerimiento judicial; entredicho, interdicto.
injunctive [-'dʒʌŋktɪv] *a.* amonestador, preceptivo; inyuncto.
injure ['ɪndʒər, B -dʒə] *v.t.* 1. dañar, estropear, averiar, menoscabar. 2. lastimar, lesionar, herir. 3. injuriar, ofender, agraviar.
injured [-dʒərd, B -dʒəd] *a.* lesionado, herido; ofendido, siniestrado.
injurer [-dʒərər, B -dʒərə] *s.* perjudicador; injuriador.
injurious [ɪn'dʒʊrɪəs, B -'dʒʊər-] *a.* 1. perjudicial, dañino, lesivo. 2. injurioso, agravioso; calumnioso, difamatorio.
injuriously [-lɪ] *adv.* perjudicialmente; injuriosamente.
injuriousness [-nəs] *s.* carácter perjudicial o injurioso.
injury ['ɪndʒərɪ] *s.* (*pl.* INJURIES) 1. daño, perjuicio. 2. lesión, herida. 3. (der.) daño, perjuicio, agravio.
injustice [ɪn'dʒʌstəs] *s.* injusticia, arbitrariedad.
ink [ɪŋk] *s.* 1. tinta. 2. (zool.) tinta (de cefalópodo, esp. del calamar). —*v.t.* 1. entintar (tipos, rodillo, impresor, etc.). 2. (gen. con *in*) marcar con tinta. 3. (esp. con *over*) cubrir con tinta. 4. **i. up,** (impr.) batir la tinta.
inkberry ['ɪŋkˌbɛrɪ] *s.* (bot.) (especie de) acebo.
inkblot [-ˌblɑt, B -ˌblɔt] *s.* mancha de tinta; grupo de manchas de tinta, usado como prueba psicológica (prueba Rorschach).
inker ['ɪŋkər, B -kə] *s.* 1. el que entinta. 2. (impr.) rulo, rodillo.
ink fountain, (impr.) tintero de prensa.
inkhorn ['ɪnkˌhɔrn, B -ˌhɔn] *s.* tintero de cuerno. —*a.* pedantesco, pomposo.
inking ['ɪŋkɪŋ] *s.* (impr.) entintado, entintaje, tintaje.
inkle ['ɪŋkəl] *s.* cinta ancha de hilo.
inkling [-klɪŋ] *s.* 1. (gen. con *of*) indicio, vislumbre, sospecha. 2. noción vaga. 3. **to have no i.** (o **not an i.**) **(of),** no tener la menor idea (de).
ink pad, tampón, almo.
inkpot ['ɪŋkˌpɑt, B -ˌpɔt] *s.* tintero.
ink roller, inking r., (impr.) rodillo, rulo.
ink-slinger [-ˌslɪŋər, B -ə] *s.* (fam.) escritor, autor, periodista; chupatintas.
inkstand ['ɪŋkˌstænd] *s.* tintero, portatintero.
inkwell [-ˌwɛl] *s.* tintero.
inkwood [-ˌwʊd] *s.* árbol del trópico, de madera dura y oscura.
inky ['ɪŋkɪ] *a.* (INKIER; INKIEST) 1. entintado; parecido a la tinta. 2. (fig.) oscuro, negro.
inky cap, variedad de hongo.
inlaid ['ɪn'leɪd] *a.* taraceado, incrustado, embutido; (enc.) embutido.
inlaid floor, entarimado.
inland ['ɪnˌlænd, -lənd] *s.* interior (de un país). —*a.* 1. interior, interno. 2. (pr. G.B.) del país, local, nacional. — ['ɪnlænd] *adv.* tierra adentro.
inland duty, (G.B.) impuesto local o nacional.
inlander [-ˌlændər, -lən-, B -ləndə] *s.* el que habita tierra adentro; tierradentreño (Am.); (fig.) provinciano.
inland sea, 1. mar interior. 2. **I.S.,** mar del Japón.
inland trade, (G.B.) comercio interior.
inlaw [ɪn'lɔ] *v.t.* (G.B.) (der., ant.) anular una proscripción; poner bajo la protección de la ley.
in-law ['ɪnˌlɔ] *s.* pariente político, ej., *mother-in-law,* suegra, *father-in-law,* suegro, *sister-in-law,* cuñada, *brother-in-law,* cuñado.
inlay [ɪn'leɪ, B 'ɪn-] *v.t.* 1. embutir, taracear, incrustar. 2. montar (grabados). — ['ɪnˌleɪ] *s.* 1. embutido, taracea, incrustación. 2. (odont.) empaste (en un diente).
inlayer [-ər, B -ə] *s.* incrustador.
inlaying [-ɪŋ] *s.* incrustación, arte de taracear o incrustar.
inlet ['ɪnˌlɛt, -lət] *s.* 1. abra, caleta, cala, ensenada. 2. (mot., maq.) entrada, admisión. — [ɪn'lɛt] *v.t.* empotrar, embutir.
inlier ['ɪnˌlaɪər, B -ə] *s.* (geol.) asomo, área de afloramiento de rocas viejas completamente rodeada de rocas jóvenes.
inly ['ɪnlɪ] *adv.* (poét.) interiormente, internamente, en el corazón; cordialmente, de corazón; íntimamente.
inmate ['ɪnˌmeɪt] *s.* 1. residente, inquilino, huésped. 2. paciente, enfermo, hospitalizado. 3. recluso, preso, presidiario.
in memoriam [ˌɪnmə'mɔrɪəm] en memoria de, en recuerdo de (ú. gen. en epitafios).
inmesh, *var. de* **enmesh.**
inmost ['ɪnˌmoʊst] *a.* íntimo, profundo, recóndito.
inn [ɪn] *s.* posada, hospedería, fonda, mesón, hostería. —*v.i.* (raro) hospedar(se), alojar(se), parar en una hostería.
innards ['ɪnərdz, B -ədz] *s. pl.* 1. (fam.) entrañas, vísceras. 2. (fig.) entrañas, interior, centro.
innate [ɪ'neɪt, 'ɪneɪt, B 'ɪ'neɪt] *a.* innato, congénito, natural, connatural.
innately [-lɪ] *adv.* de manera innata, naturalmente, congénitamente.
innateness [-nəs] *s.* condición innata, carácter innato.
innatism ['ɪneɪˌtɪzəm] *s.* (filos.) innatismo (doctrina que sostiene que las ideas son connaturales a la razón y nacen con ella).
innavigable [ɪ'nævɪgəbəl] *a.* innavegable.
inner ['ɪnər, B -ə] *a.* 1. interior, interno. 2. íntimo. 3. recóndito, profundo, secreto. —*s.* 1. (fútbol) interior. 2. (arm.) la undécima zona (colindante con el centro del blanco).
inner city, sección central, esp. superpoblada o ruinosa, de una ciudad grande.
inner-directed [ˌɪnərdə'rɛktəd, B ˌɪnədɪ-] *a.* guiado por normas propias.
inner ear, (ant.) oído interno.
innermost ['ɪnərˌmoʊst, B 'ɪnəˌ-] *a.* más adentro, interior; más íntimo, más profundo o recóndito. —*s.* la parte más íntima.
innersole [ˌɪnər'soʊl, B ˌɪnə'-] *s.* plantilla, palmilla (del zapato).
inner space, (astronáut.) espacio interior.
innerspring ['ɪnərˌsprɪŋ, B 'ɪnəˌ-] *a.* de (con) resortes. —*s.* resorte interno.
innerspring mattress, colchón de resortes.
inner sternpost, (mar.) contracodaste.
inner tube, (aut.) cámara, tubo interior.
innervate [ɪ'nɜrˌveɪt, 'ɪnər-, B 'ɪnɜˌ-] *v.t.* 1. (fisiol.) inervar. 2. (anat.) proveer de nervios.
innervation [ˌɪnər'veɪʃən, B ˌɪnɜ'-] *a.* (anat., fisiol.) inervación.
innerve [ɪ'nɜrv, B ɪ'nɜv] *v.t.* inervar, estimular, vigorizar.
inning ['ɪnɪŋ] *s.* 1. (*pl.*) tierras ganadas al mar. 2. (*pl.*) (béisbol, criquet) (*sing. o pl. en const.*) turno, entrada. 3. (fig.) turno, período. 4. **to have a good (o long) i.,** (fig.) tener larga vida; tener (buena) suerte.
innkeeper ['ɪnˌkipər, B -pə] *s.* mesonero, posadero, hospedero, hostelero.
innocence ['ɪnəsəns] *s.* 1. inocencia. 2. (con *of*) ignorancia, desconocimiento (de). 3. (bot.) aciano.
innocency [-sənsɪ] *s.* (ant.) inocencia.
innocent [-sənt] *a.* 1. inocente, libre de culpa. 2. inocente, puro, inmaculado. 3. inocente, cándido; simple, ingenuo. 4. innocuo, inofensivo. 5. (con *of*) carente (de), libre (de); desprovisto (de). 6. (con *of*) ignorante (de), sin conocimientos (de). 7. legal, autorizado. —*s.* 1. inocente (persona, esp. niño); simple. 2. (*pl.*) (E.U., bot.) acianos.
innocently [-lɪ] *adv.* inocentemente; ingenuamente, cándidamente.
innocuous [ɪ'nɑkjʊəs, B ɪ'nɔk-] *a.* innocuo, inocuo, inofensivo.
innocuously [-lɪ] *adv.* de modo innocuo o inocuo, de manera inofensiva.
innocuousness [-nəs] *s.* innocuidad, inocuidad.
Inn of Court, (G.B.) (cuatro grupos de edificios de) gremios de abogados (en Londres, con derecho exclusivo para preparar candidatos en la profesión legal).
innominate [ɪ'nɑmənət, B ɪ'nɔm-] *a.* innominado, anónimo.
innominate bone, (anat.) hueso anónimo (coxal o ilíaco).
innovate ['ɪnəˌveɪt] *v.t.* innovar. —*v.i.* hacer cambios o innovaciones.
innovation [ˌɪnə'veɪʃən] *s.* innovación; cambio, novedad.
innovationist [-əst] *s.* innovador, partidario de las innovaciones.

innovative [ˈɪnəˌveɪtɪv] *a.* innovador, novedoso.
innovator [-ər, B -ə] *s.* innovador.
innoxious [ɪˈnɑkʃəs, B ɪˈnɔk-] *a.* innocuo, inocuo, inofensivo, no nocivo.
innuendo [ˌɪnjʊˈɛndoʊ] *s.* (*pl.* INNUENDOES) 1. alusión, indirecta, insinuación. 2. (ant.) a saber, es decir (término con que se introducía una explicación en documentos); paréntesis, explicación (en documentos).
innumerability [ɪˌnumərəˈbɪlətɪ, B ɪˌnjum-] *s.* innumerabilidad.
innumerable [ɪˈnumərəbəl, B ɪˈnjum-] *a.* innumerable; numeroso; indefinido.
innumerableness [-nəs] *s.* innumerabilidad.
innumerably [-blɪ] *adv.* innumerablemente.
innumerous [-ərəs] *a.* innumerable, innúmero.
innutrition [ˌɪnuˈtrɪʃən, B ˌɪnjʊ-] *s.* desnutrición; falta de alimentación.
innutritious [-əs] *a.* sin valor nutritivo.
inobservance [ˌɪnəbˈzɜrvəns, B -ˈzɜvəns] *a.* 1. (con *of*) inobservancia (de una ley, costumbre, etc.). 2. inatención, desatención, descuido.
inobservant [-vənt] *a.* 1. inobservante. 2. poco observador, distraído. 3. desatento.
inoculability [ɪˌnɑkjələˈbɪlətɪ, B ɪˌnɔk-] *s.* (med.) calidad de inoculable.
inoculable [ɪˈnɑkjələbəl, B ɪˈnɔk-] *a.* (med.) inoculable.
inoculant [-lənt] *s.* (med.) inóculo.
inoculate [-ˌleɪt] *v.t.* 1. (med.) inocular, vacunar. 2. (fig.) imbuir, inficionar (espíritu, mente, etc.). 3. (ant.) injertar.
inoculation [ɪˌnɑkjəˈleɪʃən, B ɪˌnɔk-] *s.* 1. (med.) inoculación, vacunación. 2. inóculo, vacuna.
inoculative [ɪˈnɑkjəˌleɪtɪv, B ɪˈnɔk-] *a.* (med.) de (la) inoculación, inoculador.
inoculator [-ər, B -ə] *s.* inoculador.
inoculum [-ləm] *s.* (*pl.* INOCULA [-lə]) (med.) inóculo.
inodorous [ɪnˈoʊdərəs] *a.* inodoro, sin olor.
inoffensive [ˌɪnəˈfɛnsɪv] *a.* inofensivo.
inoffensively [-lɪ] *adv.* inofensivamente, pacíficamente.
inoffensiveness [-nəs] *s.* inocuidad, carácter inofensivo.
inofficious [ˌɪnəˈfɪʃəs] *a.* (der.) inoficioso.
inoperable [ɪnˈɑpərəbəl, B -ˈɔp-] *a.* 1. impracticable. 2. (med.) inoperable.
inoperative [-ərətɪv, -əˌreɪtɪv, B -ərətɪv] *a.* inoperante, ineficaz; inaplicable, inválido (ley, decreto, etc.).
inoperativeness [-nəs] *s.* ineficacia; invalidez (de una ley, decreto, etc.).
inoperculate [ˌɪnoʊˈpɜrkjələt, B -əˈpɜkjʊ-] *a., s.* (zool.) inoperculado.
inopportune [-ˌɑpərˈtun, B -ˈɔpətjun] *a.* inoportuno, inconveniente, intempestivo.
inopportunely [-lɪ] *adv.* inoportunamente, intempestivamente.
inopportuneness [-nəs] *s.* inoportunidad, inconveniencia.
inordinacy [ɪnˈɔrdənəsɪ, B -ˈɔd-] *s.* desorden, desarreglo; exceso, inmoderación.
inordinate [-ənət] *a.* 1. excesivo, inmoderado. 2. inordenado, desordenado, irregular.
inordinately [-lɪ] *adv.* 1. excesivamente; inmoderadamente. 2. inordenadamente, desordenadamente, irregularmente.
inordinateness [-nəs] *s.* 1. exceso, demasía, inmoderación. 2. desorden, desarreglo.
inorganic [ˌɪnɔrˈgænɪk, B -ɔˈ-] *a.* inorgánico.
inorganical [-ɪkəl] *a.* inorgánico.
inosculate [ɪnˈɑskjəˌleɪt, B -ˈɔs-] *v.t.* (anat., bot.) unir por anastomosis (vasos o nervios); (fig.) unir o mezclar íntimamente. —*v.i.* anastomosarse.
inosculation [-ˌɑskjəˈleɪʃən, B -ˌɔs-] *s.* (anat., bot.) inosculación, anastomosis.
inosite [ˈɪnəˌsaɪt] *s.* (quím.) inosita.
inositol [ɪnˈoʊsəˌtɔl] *s.* (quím.) inositol.
inoxidizable [ɪnˈɑksəˌdaɪzəbəl, B -ˌɔksɪˈ-daɪz-] *a.* inoxidable.
inoxidize [-ˌdaɪz, B -ˈɔksɪ-] *v.t.* hacer inoxidable, inoxidar (Am.).
inpatient [ˈɪnˌpeɪʃənt] *s.* enfermo internado (en un hospital).
in petto [ɪnˈpɛtoʊ, B -ˈpɛtˌtoʊ] 1. secretamente, privadamente. 2. (relig.) no revelado, fuera de consistorio.
inphase [ˈɪnˌfeɪz] *a.* (elec.) fase.
inpour [ˌɪnˈpɔr, B -ˈpɔ] *v.i., v.t.* verter en o dentro de. —*s.* influjo, entrada.
input [ˈɪnˌpʊt] *s.* 1. (mec.) consumo, gasto, energía absorbida, potencia consumida. 2. (elec., electrón., rad.) entrada; potencia de entrada, energía de entrada.
input impedance, (elec., electrón., rad.) impedancia de entrada.
input power, (rad., electrón.) potencia de entrada.
input voltage, (elec., electrón.) tensión de entrada.
inquest [ˈɪnˌkwɛst] *s.* 1. (der.) encuesta, indagatoria, pesquisa; jurado indagatorio. 2. averiguación, investigación, examen.
inquietude [ɪnˈkwaɪəˌtud, B -ˌtjud] *s.* inquietud, turbación, agitación.
inquiline [ˈɪnkwəˌlaɪn, ˈɪŋ-] *a., s.* (biol.) huésped.
inquilinism [-ləˌnɪzəm, B -laɪ-] *s.* (biol.) inquilinismo.
inquilinous [ˌɪnkwəˈlaɪnəs] *a.* díc. de un animal que vive en el nido de otro.
inquirable [ɪnˈkwaɪrəbəl, B -ˈkwaɪər-] *a.* investigable.
inquire [-ˈkwaɪr, B -ˈkwaɪə] *v.t.* 1. preguntar por, averiguar, inquirir, indagar investigar. 2. (ant.) interrogar; cuestionar. —*v.i.* 1. hacer una pregunta, preguntar. 2. hacer una investigación o examen. 3. **i. about** o **after,** preguntar por **i. into (something),** investigar, inquirie (asunto).
inquirer [-ər, B -rə] *s.* inquiridor, investigador, averiguador; preguntador, encuestador (Am.).
inquiring [-ɪŋ, B -rɪŋ] *a.* inquisitivo, interrogativo.
inquiringly [-lɪ] *adv.* inquisitivamente, interrogativamente.
inquiring mind, mente despierta, lista a interesarse en cualquier asunto.
inquiry [ˈɪnˌkwaɪrɪ, -kwərɪ, B ɪnˈkwaɪərɪ] *s.* (*pl.* INQUIRIES) 1. pregunta, averiguación. 2. encuesta, investigación, indagación, pesquisa. 3. **i. into,** investigación de, estudio de.
inquisition [ˌɪnkwəˈzɪʃən] *s.* 1. inquisición, investigación (judicial u oficial). 2. I., (relig.) Inquisición, Santo Oficio.
inquisitional [-əl] *a.* inquisitorial.
inquisitive [ɪnˈkwɪzətɪv] *a.* 1. inquisitivo, inquisitorio. 2. curioso, preguntón, investigador.
inquisitively [-lɪ] *adv.* inquisitivamente.
inquisitiveness [-nəs] *s.* curiosidad; manía de preguntar.
inquisitor [-ətər, B -ə] *s.* 1. (relig.) inquisidor. 2. investigador, inquisidor oficial. 3. examinador, preguntador, inquiridor.
inquisitorial [-ˌkwɪzəˈtɔrɪəl] *a.* inquisitorial.
inquisitorially [-əlɪ] *adv.* inquisitorialmente.
in re [ɪnˈri, -ˈreɪ, B -ˈri] (der.) concerniente o relativo a.
I.N.R.I. *abrev. de* **Jesus of Nazareth, King of the Jews,** Jesús Nazareno, Rey de los Judíos (lat.).
inroad [ˈɪnˌroʊd] *s.* 1. incursión, correría, ataque inesperado, invasión; saqueo. 2. (fig.) intrusión, incursión.
inrush [-ˌrʌʃ] *s.* afluencia; flujo; irrupción, empuje, invasión.
INS *abrev. de* **International News Service,** Servicio Internacional de Noticias.
insalivate [ɪnˈsæləˌveɪt] *v.t.* (fisiol.) insalivar.
insalivation [-ˌsæləˈveɪʃən] *s.* (fisiol.) insalivación.
insalubrious [ˌɪnsəˈlubrɪəs] *a.* insalubre, malsano.
insalubrity [-brətɪ] *s.* insalubridad, falta de salubridad.
insane [ɪnˈseɪn] *a.* 1. insano, loco, demente. 2. rel. a enajenados mentales.
insane asylum, asilo para dementes, casa de orates, manicomio.
insanely [-lɪ] *adv.* locamente.
insaneness [-nəs] *s.* locura, demencia, insania, alienación mental.
insanitary [ɪnˈsænəˌtɛrɪ, B -tərɪ] *a.* insalubre, malsano, dañoso a la salud, antihigiénico.
insanity [-ˈsænətɪ] *s.* 1. locura, demencia. 2. (der.) insania. 3. (fig.) locura, desatino, insensatez, tontería.
insatiable [ɪnˈseɪʃəbəl] *a.* insaciable.
insatiableness [-nəs] *s.* insaciabilidad.
insatiably [-blɪ] *adv.* insaciablemente.
insatiate [-ˈseɪʃɪət] *a.* insatisfecho; insaciable.
insatiately [-lɪ] *adv.* insaciablemente.
inscribe [ɪnˈskraɪb] *v.t.* 1. inscribir, grabar (palabras, caracteres); grabar (letreros en metal, piedra, etc.). 2. inscribir (nombres, etc. en una lista). 3. dedicar, dirigir. 4. (geom.) inscribir. 5. (G.B.) registrar (los nombres de los poseedores de valores, acciones, etc.).
inscription [-ˈskrɪpʃən] *s.* 1. inscripción, registro. 2. rótulo, leyenda, inscripción, letrero. 3. dedicatoria (de un libro, etc.). 4. (G.B.) registro de valores; (*pl.*) acciones o valores registrados.
inscriptional [-əl] *a.* de inscripción.
inscriptive [-ˈskrɪptɪv] *a.* de (la) inscripción, inscrito, inscripto.
inscrutability [ɪnˌskrutəˈbɪlətɪ] *s.* inescrutabilidad.
inscrutable [-ˈskrutəbəl] *a.* inescrutable, insondable, impenetrable.
inscrutably [-blɪ] *adv.* inescrutablemente.
insculp [ɪnˈskʌlp] *v.t.* (ant.) grabar, cincelar, esculpir, tallar.
insect [ˈɪnsɛkt] *s.* 1. insecto. 2. (fig.) miserable, desgraciado.
insectarium [ˌɪnsɛkˈterɪəm, B -ˈtɛər-] *s.* (*pl.* INSECTARIA [-ɪə]) insectario.
insectary [ˈɪnˌsɛktərɪ, B ɪnˈsɛk-] *s.* insectario.
insecticidal [ɪnˌsɛktəˈsaɪdəl] *a.* insecticida.
insecticide [-ˈsɛktəˌsaɪd] *s.* insecticida.
insectifuge [-ˌfjudʒ] *s.* (loción, aceite) repelente (de insectos).
insectile [ɪnˈsɛktəl, B -ˌtaɪl] *a.* insectil.
Insectivora [ˌɪnsɛkˈtɪvərə] *s. pl.* (zool., bot.) insectívoros.
insectivore [ɪnˈsɛktəˌvɔr, B -ˌvɔ] *s.* (zool., bot.) insectívoro.
insectivorous [ˌɪnsɛkˈtɪvərəs] *a.* insectívoro.
insect powder, polvos insecticidas.
insecure [ˌɪnsɪˈkjʊr, B -ˈkjʊə] *a.* inseguro.
insecurely [-lɪ] *adv.* inseguramente; riesgosamente.
insecurity [-ˈkjʊrətɪ, B -ˈkjʊər-] *s.* 1. inseguridad, incertidumbre. 2. peligro, riesgo.
inseminate [ɪnˈsɛməˌneɪt] *v.t.* 1. sembrar, plantar. 2. inseminar, fecundar.
insemination [-ˌsɛməˈneɪʃən] *s.* inseminación, fecundación.
inseminator [-ˈsɛməˌneɪtər, B -ə] *s.* inseminador.

insensate [ɪn'sɛn,seɪt, -sət] *a.* 1. inconsciente, insensible. 2. insensato, tonto, fatuo.
insensately [-lɪ] *adv.* 1. insensiblemente. 2. insensatamente.
insensibility [-,sɛnsə'bɪlətɪ] *s.* 1. insensibilidad, incapacidad de sentir; inconsciencia. 2. insensibilidad, imperceptibilidad. 3. (con *to*) indiferencia (a). 4. insensibilidad, dureza, impasibilidad.
insensible [-'sɛnsəbəl] *a.* 1. insensible, incapaz de sentir; inanimado, inconsciente. 2. insensible, imperceptible. 3. (con *to*) indiferente (a); (con *of*) ignorante (de). 4. incomprensible, sin sentido. 5. insensible, duro, impasible. 6. (ant.) desprovisto de sentido, fatuo.
insensibly [-blɪ] *adv.* insensiblemente.
insensitive [ɪn'sɛnsətɪv] *a.* insensible, indiferente, insensitivo.
insensitively [-lɪ] *adv.* insensiblemente, insensitivamente.
insensitivity [-,sɛnsə'tɪvətɪ] **insensitiveness** [-'sɛnsətɪvnəs] *s.* insensibilidad, insensitividad.
insentience [ɪn'sɛntʃəns, B -'sɛnʃəns] *s.* insensibilidad, inconsciencia, falta de animación, inanimación.
insentient [-tʃənt, B -ʃənt] *a.* insensible, inanimado, inconsciente.
inseparability [ɪn,sɛpərə'bɪlətɪ] *s.* inseparabilidad.
inseparable [-'sɛpərəbəl] *a.* inseparable, indivisible. *—s.* (*gen. pl.*) amigo o compañero inseparable; cosa inseparable (de otra).
inseparableness [-nəs] *s.* calidad de inseparable, indivisibilidad.
inseparably [-blɪ] *adv.* inseparablemente.
insert [ɪn'sɜrt, B -'sɜt] *v.t.* insertar, introducir, meter, encajar; intercalar. — ['ɪn,sɜrt, B -,sɜt] *s.* 1. inserción; esp. (E.U.) hoja extra, circular, lámina intercalada (entre las hojas de un libro o periódico). 2. (cinem.) letrero explicativo proyectado sobre la pantalla.
inserted [-əd] *a.* (bot., zool.) inserto.
insertion [-'sɜrʃən, B -'sɜʃən] *s.* 1. inserción. 2. (cost.) entredós. 3. aparición (de un aviso en el periódico). 4. (zool., bot., anat.) inserción.
inset [ɪn'sɛt, 'ɪn,sɛt] *v.t.* (*pret., p.p.* INSET; (G.B.) INSETTED; *p.pr.* INSETTING) insertar, intercalar; embutir; meter. — ['ɪn,sɛt] *s.* 1. inserción, páginas insertadas (en un libro). 2. mapa insertado (dentro de otro más grande). 3. pedazo de tela intercalado (en un vestido). 4. comienzo, flujo (ej., de la marea).
inshore ['ɪn'ʃɔr, B -'ʃɔ] *a.* cercano a la orilla. *—adv.* cerca de la orilla; hacia la orilla.
inshrine, *var. de* **enshrine.**
inside ['ɪn'saɪd, 'ɪn,saɪd] *s.* 1. interior; lado o parte interior; contenido; (fam.) forro. 2. naturaleza o ser interior. 3. (*pl.*) entrañas. 4. mediados (de la semana, etc.). 5. (impr.) interior. 6. **i. out,** al revés; de dentro para fuera; a fondo, en todos sus detalles; **on the i.,** bajo edificio; **to be on the i.,** ocupar un puesto de confianza, tener acceso a información confidencial; **to turn i. out,** volver al revés. *—a.* 1. interior, interno. 2. confidencial; de confianza. 3. para trabajos en la casa. *—adv.* dentro, adentro, en el interior; **i. of,** (fam.) en menos de; dentro de. *—prep.* dentro de.
inside calipers, (mec.) compás de calibres.
inside job, (fig.) crimen (esp. robo) cometido por alguien en quien confiaba la víctima.
inside joke, chiste entre nosotros, chiste entre ellos.
inside lane, carril de la derecha; (G.B.) carril de la izquierda.
inside left, (dep.) interior izquierdo, entreala izquierdo.
insider ['ɪn'saɪdər, B -ə] *s.* 1. persona informada, persona enterada (de algo en particular). 2. miembro de un grupo o asociación.
inside right, (dep.) interior derecho, entreala derecho.
inside track, 1. (dep.) pista interior. 2. (fam.) ventaja, situación favorable (en competencia).
insidious [ɪn'sɪdɪəs] *a.* insidioso; engañoso, pérfido, aleve; traicionero, traidor; solapado, capcioso.
insidiously [-lɪ] *adv.* insidiosamente.
insidiousness [-nəs] *s.* insidia, asechanza.
insight ['ɪn,saɪt] *s.* penetración, perspicacia, discernimiento, agudeza de ingenio.
insightful [-fəl] *a.* perspicaz, agudo, clarividente.
insignia [ɪn'sɪgnɪə] *s.* (*pl.* INSIGNIA O INSIGNIAS) 1. insignia, señal, divisa honorífica. 2. distintivo, emblema, marca.
insignificance [,ɪnsɪg'nɪfɪkəns] *s.* insignificancia.
insignificancy [-kənsɪ] *s.* 1. insignificancia. 2. cosa insignificante.
insignificant [-kənt] *a.* insignificante; baladí; pequeño; mezquino.
insignificantly [-lɪ] *adv.* de manera insignificante.
insincere [,ɪnsɪn'sɪr, B -'sɪə] *a.* insincero; hipócrita, doble, simulado.
insincerely [-lɪ] *adv.* de modo insincero.
insincerity [-'sɛrətɪ] *s.* insinceridad, doblez.
insinuate [ɪn'sɪnjʊ,eɪt] *v.t.* 1. insinuar, introducir paulatinamente, infiltrar. 2. insinuar, sugerir, indicar, echar pullas o indirectas. 3. **i. oneself,** insinuarse, congraciarse.
insinuating [-ɪŋ] *a.* insinuante, insinuativo.
insinuatingly [-lɪ] *adv.* de modo insinuante.
insinuation [ɪn,sɪnjʊ'eɪʃən] *s.* 1. insinuación, sugestión, alusión, intimación. 2. insinuación, congraciamiento. 3. indirecta, pulla (fam.).
insinuative [-'sɪnjʊ,eɪtɪv] *a.* insinuativo, insinuante.
insinuator [-ər, B -ə] *s.* insinuador.
insipid [ɪn'sɪpəd] *a.* 1. insípido, soso, desabrido. 2. (fig.) insípido, insulso, poco interesante, falto de interés.
insipidity [,ɪnsə'pɪdətɪ] *s.* insipidez.
insipidly [ɪn'sɪpədlɪ] *adv.* insípidamente, insulsamente.
insipidness [-nəs] *s.* insipidez, sosería.
insipience [-'sɪpɪəns] *s.* insipiencia, ignorancia; estupidez, necedad.
insipient [-ənt] *a.* insipiente, ignorante.
insist [ɪn'sɪst] *v.i.* insistir; obstinarse, porfiar, persistir; **i. on (something),** insistir sobre o en (algo); **i. on (doing),** insistir en (hacer); **i. on (one's doing),** insistir en que (uno haga); **i. that,** insistir en que.
insistence [-'sɪstəns] **insistency** [-tənsɪ] *s.* insistencia, obstinación, persistencia; porfía; urgencia.
insistent [-tənt] *a.* insistente, porfiado, obstinado.
insistently [-lɪ] *adv.* insistentemente; obstinadamente.
in situ [ɪn'saɪtu, -'sɪ-] (latin) en el lugar de origen.
insnare, *var. de* **ensnare.**
insobriety [,ɪnsə'braɪətɪ, -soʊ-] *s.* intemperancia, embriaguez.
insociability [ɪn,soʊʃə'bɪlətɪ] *s.* insociabilidad, intratabilidad.
insociable [-'soʊʃəbəl] *a.* insociable, intratable, huraño, arisco.
insociably [-blɪ] *adv.* de modo insociable o intratable.
insofar as [,ɪnsə'fɑr-] en cuanto a, en lo que respecta a, hasta donde.
insolate ['ɪnsoʊ,leɪt] *v.t.* insolar; asolear.
insolation [,ɪnsoʊ'leɪʃən] *s.* 1. asoleo (para secar, blanquear, etc.). 2. (med.) insolación. 3. (meteor.) insolación.
insole ['ɪn,soʊl] *s.* plantilla, palmilla (del zapato).
insolence ['ɪnsələns] *s.* 1. insolencia, atrevimiento, descaro. 2. insolencia, insulto.
insolent [-lənt] *a.* insolente, descarado, procaz; soberbio, desvergonzado. *—s.* insolente, sinvergüenza.
insolently [-lɪ] *adv.* insolentemente.
in solido [ɪn'sɑlə,doʊ, B -'sɔl-] **in solidum** [-dəm] (der.) in sólidum (por entero, por el todo).
insolubility [ɪn,sɑljə'bɪlətɪ, B -,sɔl-] *s.* insolubilidad.
insoluble [-'sɑljəbəl, B -'sɔl-] *a.* insoluble.
insolubleness [-nəs] *s.* insolubilidad.
insolubly [-blɪ] *adv.* de modo insoluble.
insolvable [ɪn'sɑlvəbəl, B -'sɔl-] *a.* irresoluble, insoluble, que no se puede solucionar.
insolvency [-'sɑlvənsɪ, B -'sɔl-] *s.* insolvencia.
insolvency law, ley de insolvencia.
insolvent [-vənt] *a.* 1. insolvente (persona, deudor, etc.). 2. de insolvencia (ley, procedimiento, etc.). *—s.* persona insolvente.
insomnia [ɪn'sɑmnɪə, B -'sɔm-] *s.* insomnio.
insomniac [-,æk] *s.* persona insomne. *—a.* 1. del insomnio, debido al insomnio (ideas, inquietud, etc.). 2. insomne.
insomnious [-əs] *a.* insomne, desvelado.
insomuch [,ɪnsə'mʌtʃ, -soʊ-] *adv.* **i. that,** de tal modo que, hasta tal punto que; **i. as,** puesto que, ya que.
insouciance [ɪn'susɪəns] *s.* despreocupación, ligereza; indiferencia.
insouciant [-ənt] *a.* despreocupado; indiferente.
insouciantly [-lɪ] *adv.* en forma despreocupada, despreocupadamente.
insoul, *var. de* **ensoul.**
inspan [ɪn'spæn] *v.t., v.i.* (Sudáfrica) acoyundar, acoplar; enjaezar; armar con arnés.
inspect [ɪn'spɛkt] *v.t.* inspeccionar, examinar, revisar, registrar, intervenir; revistar (tropas, armas, etc.).
inspection [-'spɛkʃən] *s.* inspección, examen, reconocimiento, registro; revista (de tropas, armas, etc.).
inspectional [-əl] *a.* de inspección.
inspective [-'spɛktɪv] *a.* escudriñador (ej., mirada).
inspector [ɪn'spɛktər, B -tə] *s.* 1. inspector, supervisor. 2. inspector de policía.
inspectoral [-tərəl] *a.* de inspector, inspectorial.
inspectorate [-tərət] *s.* 1. distrito a cargo de un inspector. 2. cuerpo de inspectores.
inspectorship [-tər,ʃɪp, B -tə,-] *s.* cargo o rango de inspector; inspectoría.
insphere, *var. de* **ensphere.**
inspirable [ɪn'spaɪrəbəl, B -'spaɪə-] *a.* 1. capaz de ser inspirado (por ideas, etc.). 2. inhalable, respirable (aire, etc.).
inspiration [,ɪnspə'reɪʃən] *s.* 1. inspiración, aspiración (del aire, etc.). 2. inspiración, numen, musa, estro, aflato. 3. idea brillante. 4. (teo.) inspiración.
inspirational [-əl] *a.* 1. inspirado (ej., orador). 2. inspirante, inspirativo (discurso, conversación, etc.). 3. de inspiración divina.
inspirationally [-ɪ] *adv.* inspiradamente.
inspirator ['ɪnspə,reɪtər, B -ə] *s.* (med.) 1. inhalador. 2. respirador.

inspiratory [ɪn'spaɪrəˌtɔrɪ, B -'spaɪərətərɪ] *a.* (fisiol.) inspiratorio.

inspire [ɪn'spaɪr, B -'spaɪə] *v.t.* 1. inspirar, inhalar, aspirar. 2. inspirar, estimular. 3. influenciar. 4. inspirar, comunicar. 5. provocar, causar, producir. —*v.i.* 1. inspirar, inhalar. 2. comunicar inspiración.

inspirer [-ər, B -rə] *s.* inspirador.

inspiring [-ɪŋ, B -rɪŋ] *a.* 1. inspirante, inspirador. 2. inspirador, alentador, fortificante.

inspirit [ɪn'spɪrət] *v.t.* alentar, animar, confortar, avivar, vigorizar.

inspiriting [-ɪŋ] *a.* alentador, vigorizador, animador.

inspiritingly [-lɪ] *adv.* alentadoramente, vigorizadoramente.

inspissate [ɪn'spɪˌseɪt, 'ɪnspə-, B ɪn'spɪ-] *v.t., v.i.* espesar (se); condensar (se). — [ɪn'spɪsət, B -ˌseɪt] *a.* espeso; condensado.

inspissation [ˌɪnspə'seɪʃən] *s.* condensación, espesamiento.

inspissator [ɪn'spɪsˌeɪtər, B -ə] *s.* condensador.

inst. *abrev. de* 1. **instant,** (mes) corriente (cte.). 2. **institute; institution,** instituto; institución. 3. **instrument,** instrumento.

instability [ˌɪnstə'bɪlətɪ] *s.* inestabilidad, inconstancia.

instable [ɪn'steɪbəl] *a.* inestable, inconstante, mudable, variable.

install, instal [ɪn'stɔl] *v.t.* (*pret., p.p.* INSTALLED; *p.pr.* INSTALLING) instalar; colocar, montar.

installation [ˌɪnstə'leɪʃən] *s.* instalación.

installer [ɪn'stɔlər, B -ə] *s.* instalador, montador.

installment, instalment [-mənt] *s.* 1. instalación. 2. entrega, cuota; pago parcial.

installment plan, (com.) 1. pago a plazos, compra a plazos, mensualidades. 2. **on the i. p.,** con facilidades de pago; a pagar por cuotas.

instance ['ɪnstəns] *s.* 1. instancia, instigación, petición, sugerencia. 2. caso, ejemplo. 3. ocasión. 4. (der.) instancia, ej., *court of first i.,* tribunal de primera instancia. 5. (der.) pleito, proceso. 6. **for i.,** por ejemplo; **in the first i.,** en primer lugar, en primer término. —*v.t.* 1. mencionar como ejemplo, citar como ejemplo; citar, mencionar. 2. ilustrar, demostrar, ejemplificar.

instancy [-stənsɪ] *s.* 1. insistencia, instancia, urgencia, porfía. 2. (raro) inminencia. 3. (raro) inmediación, prontitud.

instant [-stənt] *a.* 1. inmediato, inminente. 2. corriente, actual, presente. 3. insistente, perentorio. 4. directo. 5. instantáneo, que se prepara en un instante, ej., *i. coffee,* café instantáneo. —*adv.* (poét.) inmediatamente, al instante. —*s.* 1. instante, momento, santiamén (fam.). 2. **the i.,** en el mismo momento en que, tan pronto como, ej., *I saw her the i. she entered,* la vi en el mismo momento en que entró, *I told him the i. I knew,* se lo dije tan pronto como lo supe.

instantaneous [ˌɪnstən'teɪnɪəs] *a.* 1. instantáneo, breve, fugaz. 2. instantáneo, inmediato. 3. (elec.) momentáneo (potencia, corriente, etc.).

instantaneously [-lɪ] *adv.* instantáneamente.

instantaneousness [-nəs] *s.* calidad de instantáneo, prontitud.

instant coffee, café instantáneo, café soluble.

instanter [ɪn'stæntər, B -ə] *adv.* inmediatamente, instantáneamente, en el acto.

instantiate [-'stæntʃɪˌeɪt, B -'stænʃɪ-] *v.t.* ejemplificar (una abstracción) concretamente.

instantly ['ɪnstəntlɪ] *adv.* instantáneamente, al instante, inmediatamente. —*conj.* tan pronto como.

instar [ɪn'stɑr, B -'stɑ] *v.t.* (*pret., p.p.* INSTARRED; *p.pr.* INSTARRING) (ú. con *with*) incrustar (piedras preciosas, etc.) en forma de estrellas en (ej., una corona o joya).

instar ['ɪnˌstɑr, B -ˌstɑ] *s.* (ento.) crisálida.

instate [ɪn'steɪt] *v.t.* 1. instalar, colocar, establecer, disponer, situar en empleo, cargo u oficio. 2. (ant.) investir, dotar; otorgar, conferir.

instauration [ˌɪnstɔ'reɪʃən] *s.* restauración, restablecimiento, renovación, renuevo.

instead [ɪn'stɛd] *adv.* en lugar, en vez, en cambio; más bien; **i. of,** en lugar de, en vez de.

instep ['ɪnˌstɛp] *s.* 1. empeine (del pie). 2. cara anterior de la caña del caballo.

instigate ['ɪnstəˌgeɪt] *v.t.* instigar, incitar, provocar, inducir; fomentar, promover, azuzar.

instigation [ˌɪnstə'geɪʃən] *s.* instigación, incitación; provocación.

instigative ['ɪnstəˌgeɪtɪv] *a.* instigador, incitador, provocador.

instigator [-ər, B -ə] *s.* instigador, incitador, provocador.

instill, instil [ɪn'stɪl] *v.t.* (*pret., p.p.* INSTILLED; *p.pr.* INSTILLING) 1. instilar, verter (un líquido) gota a gota. 2. (fig.) instilar, infundir, introducir gradualmente; inculcar.

instillation [ˌɪnstə'leɪʃən] *s.* instilación.

instillment, instilment [ɪn'stɪlmənt] *s.* instilación.

instinct ['ɪnstɪŋkt] *s.* instinto, impulso natural. — [ɪn'stɪŋkt] *a.* (con *with*) imbuido de o en, lleno de, saturado de.

instinctive [ɪn'stɪŋktɪv] *a.* instintivo, indeliberado, espontáneo.

instinctively [-lɪ] *adv.* instintivamente, espontáneamente.

institor ['ɪnstəˌtɔr, B -ˌtɔ] *s.* (der.) institor, factor mandatario comercial.

institute ['ɪnstəˌtut, B -ˌtjut] *v.t.* 1. instituir, establecer, fundar. 2. iniciar, entablar (acción judicial, etc.). 3. instituir, instalar. —*s.* 1. instituto, establecimiento. 2. (*pl.*) (der.) instituta, instituciones.

instituter, institutor [-ər, B -ə] *s.* fundador, institutor; profesor, pedagogo, maestro.

institution [ˌɪnstə'tuʃən, B -'tju-] *s.* 1. institución, organización, establecimiento. 2. (der.) institución, derecho, práctica o uso establecidos. 3. (relig.) institución (canónica, de beneficio eclesiástico, etc.). 4. instituto, plantel educativo. 5. lugar de confinamiento (como asilo mental, cárcel, etc.). 6. (der.) nombramiento de herederos.

institutional [-əl] *a.* 1. institucional. 2. dotado de instituciones (religión, iglesia). 3. de efecto duradero (díc. de propaganda que no está destinada a aumentar las ventas sino a crear prestigio para una compañía o fábrica).

institutionalism [-ˌɪzəm] *s.* institucionalismo, defensa de instituciones.

institutionalize [-ˌaɪz] *v.t.* 1. institucionalizar, estabilizar, dar una organización estable a. 2. confinar a alguien en una institución.

institutionally [-ɪ] *adv.* institucionalmente.

institutionary [ˌɪnstə'tuʃəˌnɛrɪ, B -'tjuʃənərɪ] *a.* institucional.

institutive ['ɪnstəˌtutɪv, B -ˌtjut-] *a.* 1. instituido. 2. aprobado (por el uso o por la ley).

institutress [-rəs] *s.* fundadora, institutora; institutriz, profesora, maestra.

instruct [ɪn'strʌkt] *v.t.* 1. instruir, enseñar, educar, adoctrinar. 2. ordenar, mandar, dar instrucciones a. 3. (der.) preparar el alegato para (abogado).

instruction [-'strʌkʃən] *s.* 1. instrucción, educación, enseñanza. 2. instrucción, orden. 3. conocimiento, saber. 4. lección.

instructional [-əl] *a.* de instrucción, de enseñanza.

instructive [-'strʌktɪv] *a.* instructivo, educativo, ilustrativo.

instructively [-lɪ] *adv.* instructivamente.

instructiveness [-nəs] *s.* carácter o efecto instructivos.

instructor [ɪn'strʌktər, B -tə] *s.* 1. instructor, profesor, maestro. 2. (E.U.) instructor (en colegios y universidades, grado inferior a profesor).

instructorship [-ˌʃɪp] *s.* oficio de instructor.

instructress [-'strʌktrəs] *s.* (raro) instructora, institutriz.

instrument ['ɪnstrəmənt] *s.* 1. instrumento, agente. 2. instrumento, herramienta, aparato. 3. (mús.) instrumento. 4. (der.) instrumento, documento, escritura. — [-ˌmɛnt] *v.t.* 1. solicitar por instrumento legal. 2. (mús.) orquestar, instrumentar. 3. equipar (con instrumentos).

instrumental [ˌɪnstrə'mɛntəl] *a.* 1. (con *to* o *in*) coadyutorio, útil (para). 2. (mús.) instrumental.

instrumentalism [-ˌɪzəm] *s.* (filos.) instrumentalismo.

instrumentalist [-əst] *s.* 1. (filos.) instrumentalista. 2. (mús.) instrumentista. —*a.* (filos.) instrumentalista.

instrumentality [-mən'tælətɪ] *s.* agencia, conducto, medio.

instrumentally [-'mɛntəlɪ] *adv.* instrumentalmente.

instrumentation [-mən'teɪʃən] *s.* 1. (mús.) instrumentación, orquestación. 2. equipo de instrumentos. 3. conducto, medio.

instrument board, (aer.) tablero, pizarra o cuadro de instrumentos.

instrument flying, (aer.) vuelo por instrumentos.

instrument landing, aterrizaje por instrumentos.

instrument panel, tablero, pizarra o cuadro de instrumentos.

instrument transformer, (elec.) transformador de medida.

insubordinate [ˌɪnsə'bɔrdənət, B -'bɔd-] *a.* insubordinado, rebelde, desobediente. —*s.* insubordinado.

insubordinately [-lɪ] *adv.* de modo insubordinado.

insubordination [-ˌbɔrdən'eɪʃən, B -ˌbɔd-] *s.* insubordinación, rebeldía, desobediencia.

insubstantial [ˌɪnsəb'stæntʃəl, B -'stænʃəl] *a.* insubstancial, insignificante; inmaterial, incorpóreo.

insubstantiality [-ˌstæntʃɪ'ælətɪ, B -ˌstænʃɪ-] *s.* insubstancialidad.

insufferable [ɪn'sʌfərəbəl] *a.* insufrible; intolerable.

insufferableness [-nəs] *s.* intolerabilidad.

insufferably [-blɪ] *adv.* insufriblemente.

insufficience [ˌɪnsə'fɪʃəns] *s.* (raro) insuficiencia.

insufficiency [-ənsɪ] *s.* 1. insuficiencia, incapacidad, ineptitud, inhabilidad. 2. insuficiencia, escasez, estrechez. 3. (med.) insuficiencia.

insufficient [-ənt] *a.* 1. insuficiente, escaso, corto. 2. incapaz, inepto.

insufficient funds, (com.) falta de fondos.

insufficiently [-lɪ] *adv.* de modo insuficiente.

insufflate ['ɪnsəˌfleɪt, ɪn'sʌfˌleɪt, B 'ɪnsəˌfleɪt] *v.t.* insuflar.

insufflation [ˌɪnsə'fleɪʃən] *s.* insuflación; (relig.) insuflación (soplo durante el bautismo).

insufflator ['ɪnsəˌfleɪtər, ɪn'sʌfˌleɪt-, B 'ɪnsəˌfleɪtə] *s.* insuflador.

insulant ['ɪnsələnt, B -sjʊ-] *s.* aislador, aislante.

insular ['ɪnsələr, -ʃə-, B -sjʊlə] *a.* 1. insular, isleño. 2. aislado, separado. 3. (fig.) iliberal, intolerante, estrecho de miras. 4. (med.) insular.
insularism [-lə,rɪzəm] *s.* estrechez de miras.
insularity [,ɪnsə'lærətɪ, B -sjʊ-] *s.* 1. insularidad, aislamiento. 2. (fig.) estrechez de conceptos.
insularly ['ɪnsələrlɪ, B -sjʊləlɪ] *adv.* aisladamente, insularmente.
insulate ['ɪnsə,leɪt, B -sjʊ-] *v.t.* aislar, separar, apartar; (fís., elec.) aislar.
insulating [-ɪŋ] *a.* aislador, aislante.
insulating glass, (elec.) vidrio aislador, cristal aislante.
insulating strength, (elec.) resistencia dieléctrica.
insulating tape, (elec.) cinta aislante, cinta de aislar.
insulation [,ɪnsə'leɪʃən, B -sjʊ-] *s.* (fís., elec.) aislamiento.
insulator ['ɪnsə,leɪtər, B 'ɪnsjʊ-ə] *s.* (elec.) aislador.
insulin ['ɪnsələn, B -sjʊ-] *s.* (bioquím.) insulina.
insulin shock, (med.) choque insulínico o hipoglicémico.
insult [ɪn'sʌlt] *v.t.* 1. insultar, injuriar, agraviar, afrentar, ofender. 2. (ant.) asaltar. —*v.i.* (ant.) insolentarse. — ['ɪnsʌlt] *s.* 1. insulto, ofensa, injuria, agravio, improperio, afrenta. 2. (med.) ataque, traumatismo.
insulter [-ər, B -ə] *s.* insultador.
insulting [-ɪŋ] *a.* insultante.
insultingly [-lɪ] *adv.* de modo insultante.
insuperability [ɪn,supərə'bɪlətɪ, B -,sju-] **insuperableness** [-'supərəbəlnəs, B -'sju-] *s.* calidad de insuperable.
insuperable [-'supərəbəl, B -'sju-] *a.* insuperable, inmejorable, invencible; inalcanzable.
insuperably [-blɪ] *adv.* inmejorablemente, de modo insuperable.
insupportable [,ɪnsə'pɔrtəbəl, B -'pɔt-] *a.* insoportable, inaguantable, insufrible, intolerable.
insupportableness [-nəs] *s.* calidad de insoportable; naturaleza inaguantable.
insupportably [-blɪ] *adv.* de modo insoportable; insoportablemente.
insuppressible [,ɪnsə'prɛsəbəl] *a.* que no se puede suprimir, irreprimible.
insuppressibly [-blɪ] *adv.* de modo irreprimible o insuprimible.
insurable [ɪn'ʃʊrəbəl, B -'ʃʊər-] *a.* asegurable.
insurance [-əns] *s.* 1. seguro, garantía; contrato de seguro. 2. prima (de seguro). 3. valor asegurado. 4. seguridad (medida o sistema de protección).
insurance agent, agente de seguros.
insurance bonds, bonos de inversión de fondos.
insurance broker, corredor de seguros.
insurance company, compañía aseguradora, compañía de seguros.
insurance policy, póliza de seguros.
insurance premium, prima o premio de seguro.
insurance rate, tipo o costo de seguro.
insurant [ɪn'ʃʊrənt, B -'ʃʊər-] *s.* el asegurado (en una póliza de seguros).
insure [-'ʃʊr, B -'ʃʊə] *v.t.* 1. asegurar (vida, joyas, etc.). 2. asegurar, afianzar. —*v.i.* asegurarse; vender o comprar seguros.
insured [-'ʃʊrd, B -'ʃʊəd] *s.* (*pl.* INSUREDS) asegurado (el protegido por una póliza de seguro). —*a.* asegurado (contra daños o perjuicios).
insurer [-'ʃʊrər, B -'ʃʊərə] *s.* asegurador (el que instituye o retiene una póliza).
insurgence [ɪn'sɜrdʒəns, B -'sɜdʒəns] *s.* insurrección, rebelión, levantamiento, sublevación.
insurgency [-dʒənsɪ] *var. de* **insurgence.**
insurgent [-dʒənt] *a., s.* insurgente, insurrecto, rebelde.
insurmountable [,ɪnsər'maʊntəbəl, B -sə'-] *a.* insuperable, invencible, infranqueable.
insurmountably [-blɪ] *adv.* de modo insuperable, insuperablemente.
insurrection [,ɪnsə'rɛkʃən] *s.* insurrección, rebelión, sublevación, levantamiento.
insurrectional [-əl] *a.* insurreccional.
insurrectionary [-ʃə,nɛrɪ, B -ʃənərɪ] *a., s.* rebelde, insurgente, revolucionario, insurrecto.
insurrectionism [-,nɪzəm] *s.* tendencia revolucionaria.
insurrectionist [-nəst] *s.* insurrecto, insurgente.
insusceptibility [,ɪnsə,sɛptə'bɪlətɪ] *s.* insensibilidad; falta de susceptibilidad.
insusceptible [-'sɛptəbəl] *a.* 1. insensible, inconmovible, no susceptible. 2. (con *to*) inmune (a).
insusceptibly [-blɪ] *adv.* de modo inconmovible, insensiblemente.
inswept ['ɪn,swɛpt] *a.* (aut.) más angosto adelante que atrás.
intact [ɪn'tækt] *a.* intacto, ileso; entero, completo, íntegro.
intaglio [ɪn'tæljoʊ, -'tal-] *s.* (*pl.* INTAGLIOS O INTAGLI [-ji]) 1. talla dulce, entalla, grabadura. 2. joya tallada o grabada, ej., un camafeo.
intake ['ɪn,teɪk] *s.* 1. admisión; toma; aspiración, absorción; entrada, orificio de entrada. 2. cantidad tomada o consumida; consumo. 3. (mec., mot.) admisión, aspiración. 4. (hidr.) toma, bocatoma. 5. personas admitidas, grupo admitido (a una organización, club, etc.).
intake gate, (hidr.) compuerta de toma.
intake manifold, 1. (aut.) múltiple de admisión. 2. (hidr.) tubería múltiple de toma.
intake port, (mec.) lumbrera de admisión.
intake stroke, (mot.) carrera de admisión, tiempo de aspiración.
intake valve, (mec., mot.) válvula de admisión.
intangibility [ɪn,tændʒə'bɪlətɪ] *s.* 1. intangibilidad. 2. cosa intangible.
intangible [-'tændʒəbəl] *a.* intangible, impalpable. —*s.* cosa intangible o impalpable.
intangibleness [-nəs] *s.* intangibilidad.
intangibly [-blɪ] *adv.* de modo intangible, intangiblemente.
intarsia [ɪn'tɑrsɪə, B -'tɑsɪə] *s.* taracea, marquetería, labor de incrustación.
intarsiate [-,eɪt] *a.* de taracea, de marquetería.
integer ['ɪntɪdʒər, B -dʒə] *s.* 1. entidad completa. 2. (mat.) entero, número entero.
integrable ['ɪntɪgrəbəl] *a.* (mat.) integrable.
integral ['ɪntɪgrəl] *a.* 1. integral. 2. completo, íntegro; esencial. 3. (mat.) integral. 4. **to be i. with,** formar un conjunto con, ser solidario con (díc. de parte de máquina, pieza, etc.). —*s.* (mat.) integral.
integral calculus, (mat.) cálculo integral.
integrality [,ɪntə'grælətɪ] *s.* integridad, totalidad.
integrally ['ɪntɪgrəlɪ] *adv.* integralmente.
integral root, (mat.) raíz entera.
integrand ['ɪntə,grænd] *s.* (mat.) integrando.
integrant [-grənt] *a., s.* constituyente, componente; integrante.
integrate [-,greɪt] *v.t., v.i.* 1. integrar, componer, constituir, formar, completar. 2. integrar, unificar. 3. (mat.) integrar.
integrated [-,greɪtəd] *a.* (*nonsegregated*) no segregacionista, integrado, sin separación racial; (*personality*) equilibrado, armonioso; (*forming a whole*) integrado, de conjunto, que forma un conjunto; (*component*) incorporado, integrado.
integrated circuit, (comput.) circuito integrado.
integrating factor [-ɪŋ-] (mat.) factor integrante.
integration [,ɪntə'greɪʃən] *s.* integración; (mat.) integración.
integrative ['ɪntə,greɪtɪv] *a.* integrante.
integrator [-ər, B -ə] *s.* (aparato) integrador.
integrity [ɪn'tɛgrətɪ] *s.* 1. integridad, entereza, probidad. 2. integridad, totalidad.
integument [ɪn'tɛgjəmənt] *s.* integumento, cubierta, túnica.
integumentary [-,tɛgjə'mɛntərɪ] *a.* integumentario.
intellect ['ɪntəl,ɛkt] *s.* 1. intelecto, entendimiento, inteligencia. 2. persona inteligente, intelectual.
intellection [,ɪntəl'ɛkʃən] *s.* 1. intelección, cognición, comprensión. 2. noción, idea, concepto.
intellective [-'ɛktɪv] *a.* intelectivo, intelectual, racional.
intellectively [-lɪ] *adv.* intelectualmente, racionalmente, de modo intelectivo.
intellectual [,ɪntəl'ɛktʃʊəl, B -'ɛktjʊ-] *a.* intelectual, del intelecto. —*s.* intelectual.
intellectualism [-,ɪzəm] *s.* (filos.) intelectualismo.
intellectualist [-əst] *s.* 1. (filos.) intelectualista. 2. intelectual.
intellectualistic [-,ɛktʃʊə'lɪstɪk, B -,ɛktjʊ-] *a.* (filos.) intelectualista.
intellectuality [-'ælətɪ] *s.* intelectualidad.
intellectualization [-ələ'zeɪʃən, B -laɪ-] *s.* intelectualización.
intellectualize [-'ɛktʃʊə,laɪz, B -'ɛktjʊ-] *v.t.* dar (un) carácter intelectual a; expresar en forma razonable, intelectualizar.
intellectually [-lɪ] *adv.* intelectualmente.
intelligence [ɪn'tɛlədʒəns] *s.* 1. inteligencia, intelecto, razón, entendimiento. 2. información, noticia; información secreta. 3. servicio de espionaje, servicio de información.
intelligence bureau, i. department, oficina o departamento de espionaje; oficina de información secreta.
intelligence officer, oficial del servicio de inteligencia del ejército o la marina.
intelligence quotient, cociente intelectual, cociente de inteligencia.
intelligencer [ɪn'tɛlədʒənsər, B -sə] *s.* (raro) informante; agente secreto, espía; noticiero, mensajero.
intelligence test, (psic.) prueba de inteligencia, prueba de nivel mental.
intelligent [-dʒənt] *a.* inteligente, ingenioso.
intelligential [-,tɛlə'dʒɛntʃəl, B -'dʒɛnʃəl] *a.* (psic.) intelectualista.
intelligently [-'tɛlədʒəntlɪ] *adv.* inteligentemente, ingeniosamente; con conocimiento del asunto.
intelligentsia [-,tɛlə'dʒɛntsɪə, -'gɛnt-] *s.* la intelectualidad, la clase intelectual.
intelligibility [ɪn,tɛlədʒə'bɪlətɪ] *s.* inteligibilidad, comprensibilidad, claridad.
intelligible [-'tɛlədʒəbəl] *a.* inteligible, comprensible, claro; (filos.) inteligible.
intelligibly [-blɪ] *adv.* inteligiblemente.
Intelsat ['ɪntɛl,sæt] *abrev. de* **International Telecommunications Satellite Consortium,** Consorcio Internacional de Intercomunicaciones por Vía Satélite (C.I.I.S.).

intemperance [ɪn'tɛmpərəns] *s.* intemperancia, destemplanza, inmoderación.
intemperate [-ət] *a.* 1. intemperante, destemplado, excesivo, inmoderado. 2. inclemente, violento, ej., *an i. wind,* un viento inclemente.
intemperately [-lɪ] *adv.* destempladamente, inmoderadamente.
intemperateness [-nɛs] *s.* intemperancia, inmoderación; demasía.
intend [ɪn'tɛnd] *v.t.* 1. proponerse, tener el propósito de. 2. pensar en. 3. querer hacer, ej., *they i. no harm,* no quieren hacer daño. 4. hacer a propósito, ej., *was this intended?* ¿hicieron esto a propósito? 5. querer decir, dar a entender, ej., *what do you i. by it?* ¿qué quiere decir con esto? 6. **i. for,** destinar a, dedicar a; reservar para; **to be intended for,** ser para, ej., *this film is not intended for children,* esta película no es para niños.
intendance [-'tɛndəns] *s.* gerencia, superintendencia; departamento administrativo; intendencia.
intendancy [-dɛnsɪ] *s.* intendencia.
intendant [-dənt] *s.* intendente; supervisor.
intended [-dəd] *a.* 1. intencional. 2. prometido, futuro. —*s.* prometido, prometida, novio, novia.
intendment [-'tɛndmənt] *s.* 1. (der.) intento, espíritu (de ley). 2. (ant.) intención, designio, propósito.
intenerate [ɪn'tɛnəˌreɪt] *v.t.* (raro) suavizar, ablandar.
inteneration [-ˌtɛnə'reɪʃən] *s.* ablandamiento.
intense [ɪn'tɛns] *a.* 1. intenso, fuerte, vivo. 2. intensivo, vehemente, ardiente; profundo. 3. (foto.) reforzado.
intensely [-lɪ] *adv.* intensamente, intensivamente.
intenseness [-nəs] *s.* intensidad.
intensification [ɪnˌtɛnsəfə'keɪʃən] *s.* intensificación, acrecentamiento.
intensifier [-'tɛnsəˌfaɪər, B -ə] *s.* 1. (elec., electrón.) intensificador. 2. (foto.) reforzador.
intensify [-ˌfaɪ] *v.t., v.i.* (*pret., p.p.* INTENSIFIED; *p.pr.* INTENSIFYING) 1. intensificar, acrecentar. 2. (foto.) reforzar (un negativo).
intension [ɪn'tɛntʃən, B -'tɛnʃən] *s.* 1. intensión, intensidad. 2. refuerzo, acrecentamiento, intensificación. 3. determinación. 4. (lóg.) contenido, comprensión.
intensity [-'tɛnsətɪ] *s.* 1. intensidad; fuerza, potencia. 2. (fís., elec.) intensidad. 3. (foto.) contraste (del negativo).
intensive [-sɪv] *a.* 1. intensivo; exhaustivo, concentrado, activo. 2. (agr.) intensivo (cultivo). 3. (gram.) intensivo (prefijo, sufijo, etc.). 4. (fís.) intensivo. —*s.* (gram.) palabra o afijo intensivo.
intensive care, terapia intensiva.
intensive care unit, unidad de cuidado intensivos *or* tratamiento intensivo *or* vigilancia intensiva.
intensively [-lɪ] *adv.* intensivamente.
intensiveness [-nəs] *s.* intensidad.
intent [ɪn'tɛnt] *a.* 1. atento, interesado. 2. (con *on*) dedicado (a), empeñado (en); resuelto (a). —*s.* 1. intento, intención, designio, propósito. 2. significado, sentido. 3. **to all intents and purposes,** prácticamente, en realidad, en el fondo.
intention [-'tɛntʃən, B -'tɛnʃən] *s.* 1. intención, propósito; (*pl.*) intenciones (que se declaran a una mujer con propósito de matrimonio). 2. (relig.) intención (de misa u oración). 3. (lóg.) concepto. 4. (med.) intención. 5. **by first (second) i.,** de o por primera (segunda) intención.
intentional [-əl] *a.* intencional, deliberado.
intentionally [-ɪ] *adv.* intencionalmente, intencionadamente, adrede, a propósito.
intently [ɪn'tɛntlɪ] *adv.* asiduamente; resueltamente.
intentness [-nəs] *s.* atención fija, asiduidad, aplicación.
inter [ɪn'tɜr, B -'tɜ] *v.t.* (*pret., p.p.* INTERRED; *p.pr.* INTERRING) enterrar, sepultar, inhumar.
interact [ˌɪntər'ækt] *v.i.* obrar recíprocamente, afectar uno a otro mutuamente. —*s.* (teat.) entreacto.
interaction [-'ækʃən] *s.* influencia recíproca, interacción, acción recíproca.
interactive [-'æktɪv] *a.* mutuo, recíproco.
inter alia [ˌɪntər'ɑliɑ] *adv.* (formal) entre otras cosas, entre otros.
interamerican ['ɪntərə'mɛrəkən] *a.* interamericano.
interarticular [-ɑr'tɪkjələr, B -ɑ'-lə] *a.* interarticular (díc. de lo que está dentro de la articulación).
interatomic [-ə'tɑmɪk, B -'tɔm-] *a.* interatómico.
interborough [ˌɪntər'bɜroʊ, -'bʌroʊ, 'ɪn-, B-tə'bʌrə] *a.* municipal, interseccional; entre distritos (de una ciudad).
interbrain ['ɪntərˌbreɪn, B -təˌ-] *s.* (anat.) diencéfalo.
interbreed [ˌɪntər'brid, B -tə'-] *v.i., v.t.* cruzar (animales de distinta especie); hibridar.
intercalary [ɪn'tɜrkəˌlɛrɪ, B -'tɜkələrɪ] *a.* 1. intercalado (día, mes); bisiesto (año). 2. inserto, interpuesto.
intercalate [-ˌleɪt] *v.t.* insertar, intercalar, interpolar, añadir.
intercalation [-ˌtɜrkə'leɪʃən, B -ˌtɜkə-] *s.* intercalación, interpolacíon, intercaladura, inserción.
intercede [ˌɪntər'sid, B -tə'-] *v.i.* interceder, mediar.
interceder [-ər, B -ə] *s.* intercesor.
intercellular [-sɛljələr, B -lə] *a.* (anat., bot.) intercelular.
intercept [-'sɛpt] *v.t.* 1. interceptar. 2. (mat.) intersecar. 3. (ant.) prevenir, detener, impedir. — ['ɪntərˌsɛpt, B -təˌ-] *s.* (mat.) intersección.
interception [-'sɛpʃən] *s.* 1. interceptación. 2. (mat.) intersección. 3. (mil.) interceptación.
interceptive [-'sɛptɪv] *a.* interceptor.
interceptor [-'tər, B -tə] *s.* avión de caza, avión interceptador; interceptor.
intercession [ˌɪntər'sɛʃən, B -tə'-] *s.* intercesión, mediación (esp. por oración).
intercessional [-əl] *a.* de intercesión, de mediación.
intercessor [-'sɛsər, B -ə] *s.* intercesor, mediador.
intercessory [-ərɪ] *a.* intercesor, mediador.
interchain [ˌɪntər'tʃeɪn, B -tə'-] *v.t.* encadenar; entrelazar.
interchange [-'tʃeɪndʒ] *v.t.* 1. intercambiar, trocar, permutar. 2. alternar, variar, cambiar. —*v.i.* cambiarse, alternarse. — ['ɪntərˌtʃeɪndʒ, B -təˌ-] *s.* 1. intercambio, trueque, permuta. 2. cruce, paso a desnivel.
interchangeability [-ˌtʃeɪndʒə'bɪlətɪ] *s.* calidad de intercambiable.
interchangeable [-'tʃeɪndʒəbəl] *a.* intercambiable, permutable.
interchangeableness [-nəs] *s.* calidad de intercambiable.
interchangeably [-blɪ] *adv.* de modo intercambiable, recíprocamente.
interchurch ['ɪntər'tʃɜrtʃ, B -tə'tʃɜtʃ] *a.* común a varias iglesias o a las iglesias.
interclavicle [ˌɪntər'klævɪkəl, B -tə'-] *s.* (zool.) hueso interclavicular.
interclavicular [-klə'vɪkjələr, B -lə] *a.* interclavicular (espacio).
intercoastal [-'koʊstəl] *a.* intercostero.
intercollegiate [-kə'lidʒɪət, -dʒət] *a.* interescolar, interuniversitario.
intercolumnar [-kə'lʌmnər, B -nə] *a.* (arq.) entre columnas.
intercolumniation [-kəˌlʌmnɪ'eɪʃən] *s.* (arq.) intercolumnio.
intercom ['ɪntərˌkɑm, B -təˌkɔm] *s.* sistema o circuito de intercomunicación; (*on a plane or ship*) interfono, intercomunicador; (*at a building entrance*) portero eléctrico.
intercommunicate [ˌɪntərkə'mjunəˌkeɪt, B -təkə-] *v.i.* 1. intercomunicar. 2. comunicarse (entre sí), ej., *the two lakes i.,* los dos lagos se comunican (entre sí).
intercommunication [-ˌmjunə'keɪʃən] *s.* intercomunicación.
intercommunication system, sistema de intercomunicación.
interconnect [-kə'nɛkt] *v.t.* interconectar, conectar entre sí.
interconnection [-'nɛkʃən] *s.* interconexión.
intercontinental [-ˌkɑntə'nɛntəl, B -ˌkɔn-] *a.* intercontinental.
intercontinental ballistic missile, cohete balístico intercontinental.
interconversion [ˌɪntərkən'vɜrʒən, -ʃən, B -təkən'vɜʃən] *s.* conversión mutua o recíproca.
interconvert [-'vɜrt, B -'vɜt] *v.t.* convertir entre sí.
intercostal [-'kɑstəl, B -'kɔs-] *a.* (anat., fisiol., bot.) intercostal.
intercostally [-təlɪ] *adv.* entre las costillas.
intercourse ['ɪntərˌkɔrs, B -təˌkɔs] *s.* 1. (*sexual relations*) coito, comercio sexual, trato sexual; **to have i. with,** tener comercio sexual con, tener relacionees sexuales con; 2. (ant.) trato social comercio, relaciones comerciales.
intercrop [ˌɪntər'krɑp, B -tə'krɔp] *v.t., v.i.* sembrar entre surcos, sembrar simultáneamente (dos cosechas distintas). —*s.* siembra de entre surcos; siembra accesoria de cosecha rápida.
intercross [-'krɔs] *v.t., v.i.* entrecruzar (se); hibridar. — ['ɪntərˌkrɔs, B -təˌ-] *s.* híbrido.
intercurrent [-'kɜrənt, -'kʌrənt, B -'kʌ-] *a.* 1. intercalado, interpuesto. 2. (med.) intercurrente.
intercutaneous [-kju'teɪnɪəs] *a.* intercutáneo.
interdenominational [-'dɪˌnɑmə'neɪʃənəl, B -ˌnɔm-] *a.* (relig.) intersectario.
interdental [-'dɛntəl] *a.* (fon.) interdental; interdentario.
interdepartmental [-dɪˌpɑrt'mɛntəl, B -ˌpɑt-] *a.* interdepartamental.
interdepend [ˌɪntərdɪ'pɛnd, B -tədɪ-] *v.i.* depender mutuamente.
interdependence [-'pɛndəns] *s.* interdependencia, dependencia recíproca.
interdependency [-dənsɪ] *var. de* **interdependence.**
interdependent [-dənt] *a.* interdependiente, de dependencia mutua.
interdependently [-lɪ] *adv.* de modo interdependiente.
interdict ['ɪntərˌdɪkt, B -təˌ-] *s.* 1. interdicción, prohibición, disposición prohibitiva. 2. (der.) interdicto. 3. (relig.) interdicto, entredicho. — [ˌɪntər'dɪkt, B -tə'-] *v.t.* 1. interdecir, prohibir, vedar. 2. (relig.) poner interdicto a.
interdiction [ˌɪntər'dɪkʃən, B -tə'-] *s.* interdicción, veto, veda, prohibición; (der., relig.) interdicto.

interdictive [-'dɪktɪv] *a.* prohibitivo.
interdictory [-tərɪ] *a.* prohibitorio, prohibitivo.
interdigital [-'dɪdʒətəl] *a.* (zool.) interdigital.
interdigitate [-'dɪdʒəˌteɪt] *v.t.* entretejer, entrelazar (como los dedos de las manos).
interdisciplinary [-'dɪsəpləˌnɛrɪ, B -plənərɪ] *a.* (educ.) interdisciplinario, que comprende más de una disciplina o campo de estudio.
interest ['ɪntrəst, 'ɪntərəst] *s.* 1. interés, participación. 2. interés, negocio. 3. interés, provecho, beneficio. 4. interés, atención, curiosidad. 5. (com.) interés, rédito. 6. **to put out at i.,** poner a interés; **to take an i. in,** tomar interés en; **with i.,** con interés. —*v.t.* interesar; **to be interested in,** interesarse por o en.
interested [-əd] *a.* interesado.
interestedly [-lɪ] *adv.* interesadamente.
interest group, grupo de intereses.
interesting [-ɪŋ] *a.* interesante; **to be in an i. condition,** (G.B.) estar embarazada, estar encinta.
interestingly [-lɪ] *adv.* interesantemente, de modo interesante, amenamente.
interface ['ɪntərˌfeɪs, B -təˌ-] *s.* zona interfacial, entrecara.
interfacial [ˌɪntər'feɪʃəl, B -tə'-] *a.* interfacial, que separa dos caras o regiones adyacentes.
interfaith ['ɪntərˌfeɪθ, B -təˌ-] *a.* entre personas de distintas religiones.
interfascicular [ˌɪntərfə'sɪkjələr, B ˌɪntəfə-lə] *a.* (anat.) interfascicular.
interfere [-'fɪr, B -'fɪə] *v.i.* 1. tropezarse, trastabillar (los caballos). 2. chocar (intereses, pretensiones, etc.). 3. (con *in*) mezclarse (en), meterse (en), intervenir (en). 4. (con *with*) interferir, obstruir, impedir, obstaculizar. 5. (der.) reclamar prioridad de invención. 6. (fís.) interferir.
interference [-'fɪrəns, B -'fɪər-] *s.* 1. tropiezo, traspié. 2. intromisión, entremetimiento, ingerencia. 3. (fís., rad.) interferencia. 4. (dep.) obstrucción.
interferential [-fə'rɛntʃəl, B -'rɛnʃəl] *a.* (fís.) de interferencia.
interferogram [-'fɪrəˌgræm, B -'fɪər-] *s.* (fís.) interferograma.
interferometer [-fə'rɑmətər, B -'rɔmɪtə] *s.* (fís.) interferómetro.
interferometry [-ətrɪ] *s.* (fís.) interferometría.
interferon [ˌɪntər'fɪrɑn, B -tə'fɪrɔn] *s.* (bioquím.) interferona.
interfertile [-'fɜrtəl, B -'fɜˌtaɪl] *a.* apto para cruzamiento (díc. de animales).
interfold [-'foʊld] *v.t.* interplegar; doblar o plegar varias veces.
interfuse [-'fjuz] *v.t.* 1. mezclar, amalgamar, unir. 2. infundir. —*v.i.* mezclarse, fundirse.
interfusion [-'fjuʒən] *s.* mezcla, compuesto, mixtura, combinación.
intergalactic [-gə'læktɪk] *a.* (astr.) situado entre galaxias, que ocurre entre galaxias; intergaláctico.
intergeneric [ˌɪntərdʒə'nɛrɪk, B -tədʒə-] *a.* (biol.) intergenérico.
interglacial [-'gleɪʃəl, B -sjəl] *a.* (geol.) interglacial.
intergradation [-greɪ'deɪʃən, B -grə-] *s.* mezcla o amalgamación graduales.
intergrade ['ɪntərˌgreɪd, B -təˌ-] *s.* forma intermedia o transitoria. — [ˌɪntər'greɪd, B -tə'-] *v.i.* mezclarse o unirse gradualmente.
interim ['ɪntərəm] *s.* 1. ínterin, intervalo, intermedio, entretanto. 2. **I.,** (relig., hist.) ínterin. 3. **in the i.,** entretanto, en el ínterin. —*a.* interino, provisorio, provisional, accidental.
interim certificate, certificado provisional.
interim dividend, (com.) dividendo provisorio o provisional.
interior [ɪn'tɪrɪər, B -'tɪərɪə] *a.* 1. interior, interno. 2. interior, de tierra adentro. —*s.* interior.
interior angles, (geom.) ángulos interiores.
interior decoration, decoración de interiores.
interior decorator, decorador de interiores.
interiority [-ˌtɪrɪ'ɔrətɪ, -'ɑr-, B -'ɔr-] *s.* interioridad.
interiorly [-'tɪrɪərlɪ, B -'tɪərɪəlɪ] *adv.* interiormente.
interjacent [ˌɪntər'dʒeɪsənt, B -tə'-] *a.* interyacente.
interject [-'dʒɛkt] *v.t.* interponer, interpolar.
interjection [-'dʒɛkʃən] *s.* 1. interpolación; intervención. 2. (gram.) interjección, voz interjectiva, exclamación.
interjectional [-əl] *a.* interjectivo.
interjectory [-'dʒɛktərɪ] *a.* interpuesto, interpolado.
interjoin [-'dʒɔɪn] *v.t.* incorporar, unir recíprocamente.
interlace [-'leɪs] *v.t.* entrelazar; entretejer. —*v.i.* entrelazarse.
interlaminate [ˌɪntər'læməˌneɪt, B -tə'-] *v.t.* insertar entre láminas, arreglar en láminas alternadas.
interlard [-'lɑrd, B -'lɑd] *v.t.* (con *with*) entreverar (con), mechar.
interleaf ['ɪntərˌlɪf, B -təˌ-] *s.* hoja interfoliada.
interleave [ˌɪntər'liv, B -tə'-] *v.t.* interfoliar, interpaginar (libro, etc.); intercalar (hoja).
interline [-'laɪn] *v.t.* 1. interlinear, entrerrenglonar. 2. (cost.) entretelar.
interlineal [-'lɪnɪəl] *a.* interlineal, interlineado, alternado.
interlineally [-əlɪ] *adv.* alternadamente, de modo interlineado.
interlinear [ˌɪntər'lɪnɪər, B ˌɪntə'-ə] *a.* interlineal, entrerrenglonado. —*s.* traducción interlinear.
interlineate [-ɪˌeɪt] *v.t., v.i.* interlinear, entrerrenglonar.
interlineation [-ˌlɪnɪ'eɪʃən] *s.* interlineación, entrerrenglonadura.
interlining ['ɪntərˌlaɪnɪŋ, B -təˌ-] *s.* 1. (cost.) entretela, entreforro. 2. (tip.) interlineación.
interlink [ˌɪntər'lɪŋk, B -tə'-] *v.t.* enlazar, eslabonar.
interlock [-'lɑk, B -'lɔk] *v.t.* 1. trabar, entrelazar. 2. (mec.) enclavar; (f.c.) enclavar, encerrojar (señales, etc.). —*v.i.* trabarse, entrelazarse. — ['ɪntərˌlɑk, B -təˌlɔk] *s.* (mec.) enclavamiento, entrecierre.
interlocking [-ɪŋ] *s.* 1. trabado, entrelazamiento. 2. (f.c.) sistema de enclavamiento, sistema de encerrojamiento.
interlocking armor, (elec.) blindaje cerrado, coraza trabada.
interlocking directorates, (com., fin.) juntas directivas vinculadas (por tener miembros comunes en varias empresas).
interlocking fire, (mil.) fuego entrecruzado.
interlocution [ˌɪntərloʊ'kjuʃən, B -təloʊ-] *s.* interlocución, conversación, plática, diálogo.
interlocutor [-'lɑkjətər, B -'lɔkjʊtə] *s.* interlocutor.
interlocutory [-jəˌtɔrɪ, B -jʊtərɪ] *a.* 1. dialogístico. 2. (der.) interlocutorio.
interlope [-'loʊp] *v.i.* 1. entrometerse. 2. traficar (sin licencia).
interloper [-ər, B -ə] *s.* 1. intruso, entrometido. 2. traficante (sin licencia).
interlude ['ɪntərˌlud, B -təˌ-] *s.* 1. intervalo. 2. (mús.) interludio. 3. (teat.) intermedio, entreacto. 4. entremés, farsa, comedia; drama o sainete corto, gen. con una ingenua moraleja.
interlunar [ˌɪntər'lunər, B -tə'lunə] *a.* del interlunio, interlunar.
interlunation [-ˌlu'neɪʃen] *s.* interlunio.
intermarriage [-'mærɪdʒ] *s.* matrimonio entre miembros de la misma familia o grupo; matrimonio entre miembros de razas distintas.
intermarry [-'mærɪ] *v.i.* 1. casarse entre sí (miembros de la misma familia o grupo). 2. unirse por matrimonio (casas reales, razas distintas, etc.).
intermaxillary [-'mæksəˌlɛrɪ, B -mæk'-sɪlərɪ] *a.* intermaxilar.
intermaxillary bone, (anat.) hueso intermaxilar.
intermeddle [ˌɪntər'mɛdəl, B -tə'-] *v.i.* inmiscuirse, entremeterse.
intermeddler [-'mɛdlər, B -lə] *s.* entremetido.
intermeddling [-lɪŋ] *s.* ingerencia, entremetimiento.
intermediacy [ˌɪntər'midɪəsɪ, B -tə'-] *s.* 1. calidad de intermedio. 2. intervención, mediación.
intermediary [-dɪˌɛrɪ, B -djərɪ] *a.* 1. medianero, intermedio. 2. mediador, intermediario. —*s.* (*pl.* INTERMEDIARIES) 1. mediador, intermediario. 2. forma o etapa intermedia.
intermediate [-'midɪət] *a.* medianero, intermedio. —*s.* 1. término o grado intermedio. 2. mediador, intermediario. 3. (quím.) compuesto o producto intermedio. — [-dɪˌeɪt] *v.t.* mediar, intermediar, interponerse.
intermediate frequency, (rad.) frecuencia intermediaria.
intermediately [-lɪ] *adv.* 1. medianamente. 2. indirectamente.
intermediateness [-nəs] *s.* calidad de medianero o de intermedio.
intermediate-range rocket [-'reɪndʒ-] cohete de alcance intermedio.
intermediation [ˌɪntərˌmidɪ'eɪʃən, B -təˌ-] *s.* intervención, mediación.
intermediator [-'midɪˌeɪtər, B -ə] *s.* mediador, intermediario.
intermedin [-'midən] *s.* (bioquím.) intermedina.
interment [ɪn'tɜrmənt, B -'tɜmənt] *s.* entierro, enterramiento, sepelio, sepultura.
intermezzo [ˌɪntər'mɛtsoʊ, -'mɛdzoʊ, B -tə'-] *s.* (*pl.* INTERMEZZI [-si, -zi] o INTERMEZZOS) 1. intermedio, entreacto. 2. (mús.) intermezzo.
interminable [ɪn'tɜrmənəbəl, B -'tɜmə-] *a.* interminable, inacabable.
interminably [-blɪ] *adv.* interminablemente.
interminate [-mənət] *a.* sin fin, ilimitado; inacabado.
intermingle [ˌɪntər'mɪŋgəl, B -tə'-] *v.t.* entremezclar, entreverar, entretejer. —*v.i.* entremezclarse.
intermission [-'mɪʃən] *s.* 1. (teat.) intermedio, entreacto. 2. intermisión, interrupción. 3. intervalo; pausa, respiro. 4. (med.) intermitencia.
intermissive [-'mɪsɪv] *a.* intermitente.
intermit [-'mɪt] *v.t.* (*pret., p.p.* INTERMITTED; *p.pr.* INTERMITTING) intermitir, interrumpir, discontinuar. —*v.i.* interrumpirse.
intermittence [-'mɪtəns] *s.* 1. intermitencia. 2. período recurrente.
intermittency [-ənsɪ] *s.* intermitencia.
intermittent [-ənt] *a.* intermitente, recurrente, periódico, regular.
intermittent current, (elec.) corriente intermitente.

intermittent fever, (med.) fiebre intermitente.
intermittently [-lɪ] *adv.* intermitentemente.
intermitter [-ər, B -ə] *s.* (mec.) intermisor.
intermix [ˌɪntər'mɪks, B -tə'-] *v.t., v.i.* entremezclar(se), juntar(se), entreverar(se), entretejer(se).
intermixture [-'mɪkstʃər, B -tʃə] *s.* 1. entremezcladura, mezcla, mixtura. 2. ingrediente adicional.
intermolecular [-mə'lɛkjələr, B -lə] *a.* intermolecular.
intermuscular [-'mʌskjələr, B -lə] *a.* intermuscular.
intern [ɪn'tɜrn, B -'tɜn] *v.t.* internar, recluir, encerrar. —*v.i.* trabajar como interno (en hospital). — ['ɪnˌtɜrn, B -ˌtɜn] *s.* 1. (t. **interne**) interno, médico prácticante, médico residente. 2. persona internada.
internal [-'tɜrnəl, B -'tɜn-] *a.* 1. interno. 2. inherente, intrínseco (ej., prueba). 3. doméstico, interno, intestino, nacional. 4. (psic.) interior, interno, subjetivo. —*s.* 1. (*pl.*) (anat.) órganos internos. 2. esencia, cualidad esencial.
internal-combustion engine [-kəm'bʌstʃən-] (mec.) motor de combustión interna.
internal gear, (mec.) engranaje de dientes interiores.
internality [ˌɪnˌtɜr'nælətɪ, B -ˌtɜ'-] *s.* calidad de interno, interioridad.
internalization [ɪnˌtɜrnələ'zeɪʃən, B -ˌtɜnəlaɪ-] *s.* incorporación, absorción.
internally [-'tɜrnəlɪ, B -'tɜn-] *adv.* internamente, interiormente.
internal medicine, medicina interna.
internal respiration, (fisiol.) respiración interna.
internal revenue, (E.U., econ.) rentas internas o interiores, rentas públicas.
Internal Revenue Service, Hacienda, Dirreción General Impositiva, Impuestos Internos, Superintendencia de Contribuciones.
internal rhyme, (poét., gram.) rima irregular o alterna.
internal secretion, (med.) secreción interna.
internation ['ɪntər'neɪʃən, B -tə'-] *s.* internación.
international [ˌɪntər'næʃənəl, B -tə'-] *a.* internacional. —*s.* **I.,** (t. **Internationale**) Internacional (asociación comunista o socialista mundial).
international code, (teleg.) código internacional.
International Court of Justice, Tribunal Internacional de Justicia.
International Date Line, línea internacional de cambio de fecha, línea horaria internacional.
Internationale [-ˌnæʃə'næl, B -'nɑl] *s.* La Internacional (himno mundial del proletariado comunista).
internationalism [-'næʃənəlˌɪzəm] *s.* internacionalismo.
internationalist [-əst] *s.* internacionalista.
internationality [ˌɪntərˌnæʃə'nælətɪ, B -təˌ-] *s.* internacionalidad.
internationalize [-'næʃənəlˌaɪz] *v.t.* internacionalizar.
International Labor Organization, Organización Internacional del Trabajo (de la O.N.U.).
international law, derecho internacional.
internationally [-əlɪ] *adv.* internacionalmente.
International Monetary Fund, Fondo Monetario Internacional.
International Phonetic Alphabet, Alfabeto Fonético Internacional.
international pitch, (mús.) diapasón bajo.
interne, *var. de* **intern.**
internecine [ˌɪntər'nɛsˌin, -'niˌsaɪn, B -tə'-] *a.* destructivo, mortífero; recíprocamente destructivo.
internee [ˌɪnˌtɜr'ni, B -ˌtɜ'-] *s.* persona internada, internado.
interneuron [ˌɪntər'nʊrɑn, B -tə'njʊrˌɔn] *s.* (fisiol.) neurona internuncial.
internist [ɪn'tɜrnəst, B -'tɜnɪst] *s.* (med.) internista.
internment [-'tɜrnmənt, B -'tɜn-] *s.* internación (de un súbdito de país enemigo); (mil.) internamiento.
internment camp, (mil.) campo de internación o internamiento.
internodal [ˌɪntər'noʊdəl, B -tə'-] *a.* (bot.) colocado entre dos nudos.
internode ['ɪntərˌnoʊd, B -təˌ-] *s.* (bot.) internodio, entrenudo.
inter nos [-'noʊs] (latín) entre nosotros.
internship ['ɪnˌtɜrnˌʃɪp, B -ˌtɜn-] *s.* servicio o práctica como interno.
internuncial [ˌɪntər'nʌnsɪəl, -'nʊn-, B -tə'nʌnʃəl] *a.* (fisiol.) internuncial.
internuncio [-sɪˌoʊ, B -ʃɪ-] *s.* 1. (dip. hist.) internuncio. 2. enviado, emisario papal.
interoceanic [ˌɪntərˌoʊʃɪ'ænɪk] *a.* interoceánico.
interoceptive [-təroʊ'sɛptɪv] *a.* (fisiol.) interoceptor.
interoceptor [-tər, B -tə] *s.* (fisiol.) interoceptor, visceroceptor.
interoffice [ˌɪntər'ɔfəs, -'ɑf-, B -'ɔf-] *a.* (de) entre oficinas (de una organización).
interosculate [-'ɑskjəˌleɪt, B -'ɔs-] *v.i.* 1. (biol.) interoscularse, cruzarse; tener características comunes (díc. de diferentes especies). 2. intercomunicarse.
interosseous [-'ɑsɪəs, B -'ɔs-] *a.* (anat.) interóseo.
interparietal [ˌɪntərpə'raɪətəl, B -təpə-] *a.* (anat.) interparietal.
interparliamentary [-ˌpɑrlə'mɛntərɪ, B -ˌpɑl-] *a.* interparlamentario.
interpellant [-'pɛlənt] *s.* interpelante.
interpellate [ˌɪntər'pɛleɪt, B ɪn'tɜpɛˌleɪt] *v.t.* interpelar, interrogar formalmente.
interpellation [-pə'leɪʃən, B ɪnˌtɜpə-] *s.* interpelación.
interpellator [-'pɛlˌeɪtər, B ɪn'tɜpɛlˌeɪtə] *s.* interpelante.
interpenetrate [ˌɪntər'pɛnəˌtreɪt, B -tə'-] *v.t.* penetrar en todas partes. —*v.i.* compenetrarse.
interpenetration [-ˌpɛnə'treɪʃən] *s.* compenetración.
interpersonal [-'pɜrsənəl, B -'pɜsə-] *a.* entre personas, personal.
interphone ['ɪntərˌfoʊn, B -təˌ-] *s.* interfono, teléfono de comunicación interna.
interplane [ˌɪntər'pleɪn, B -tə'-] *a.* situado entre dos planos.
interplanetary [-'plænəˌtɛrɪ, B -ətərɪ] *a.* interplanetario.
interplay ['ɪntərˌpleɪ, B -təˌ-] *s.* interacción, acción recíproca; influencia recíproca. — [ˌɪntər'pleɪ, B -tə'-] *v.i.* ejercer influencia recíproca.
interplead [ˌɪntər'plid, B -tə'-] *v.i.* (der.) pleitear uno con otro para decidir una causa que afecta a un tercero.
interpleader [-ər, B -ə] *s.* 1. (der.) procedimiento por el cual una persona puede obligar a dos o más personas, que le demandan por una misma cosa, a que previamente decidan quién de ellos tiene derecho a ella. 2. el que recurre a este procedimiento.
interpolate [ɪn'tɜrpəˌleɪt, B -'tɜpə-] *v.t.* 1. interpolar, intercalar. 2. adulterar o alterar con interpolaciones (texto). 3. (mat.) interpolar. —*v.i.* hacer interpolaciones.
interpolater, interpolator [-ər, B -ə] *s.* interpolador.
interpolation [-ˌtɜrpə'leɪʃən, B -ˌtɜpə-] *s.* interpolación.
interpolative [-'tɜrpəˌleɪtɪv, B -'tɜpə-] *a.* interpolativo.
interposal [ˌɪntər'poʊzəl, B -tə'-] *s.* interposición, mediación, intervención.
interpose [-'poʊz] *v.t.* 1. interpolar, interponer. 2. (cinem.) remplazar gradualmente una figura por otra. —*v.i.* 1. interponerse. 2. mediar, intervenir. 3. interrumpir.
interposer [-ər, B -ə] *s.* mediador.
interposition [-pə'zɪʃən] *s.* interposición.
interpret [ɪn'tɜrprət, B -'tɜprɪt] *v.t.* 1. interpretar, traducir. 2. interpretar, explicar, entender. 3. (teat.) interpretar, representar (papel, drama, etc.). —*v.i.* interpretar, traducir oralmente.
interpretable [-əbəl] *a.* 1. interpretable, traducible oralmente. 2. interpretable, explicable. 3. (teat.) interpretable, representable (papel, drama, etc.).
interpretation [-ˌtɜrprə'teɪʃən, B -ˌtɜprɪ-] *s.* 1. interpretación, traducción oral. 2. interpretación, sentido, entendimiento. 3. interpretación, representación (de un papel, drama, composición musical, etc.).
interpretational [-əl] *a.* de interpretación.
interpretative [ɪn'tɜrprəˌteɪtɪv, B -'tɜprɪtət-] *a.* 1. interpretativo. 2. debido a (la) interpretación (error, etc.).
interpreter [-ər, B -ə] *s.* 1. intérprete, traductor (oral). 2. intérprete (de una obra, composición, etc.).
interpretive [-'tɜrprətɪv, B -'tɜprɪt-] *a.* interpretativo.
interpretively [-lɪ] *adv.* interpretativamente.
interpupillary [ˌɪntər'pjupəˌlɛrɪ, B ˌɪntə'-lərɪ] *a.* (med.) interpupilar.
interracial [ˌɪntə'reɪʃəl] **interrace** [-'reɪs] *a.* interracial.
interregnum [-'rɛgnəm] *s.* (*pl.* INTERREGNUMS o INTERREGNA [-nə]) interregno; pausa, lapso.
interrelate [-rɪ'leɪt] *v.t., v.i.* correlacionar(se).
interrelated [-əd] *a.* con relación, vinculado, recíproco.
interrelation [-'leɪʃən] *s.* correlación.
interrogate [ɪn'tɛrəˌgeɪt] *v.t.* interrogar, preguntar. —*v.i.* hacer preguntas.
interrogatingly [-ɪŋlɪ] *adv.* interrogativamente.
interrogation [ɪnˌtɛrə'geɪʃən] *s.* interrogación.
interrogation point, i. mark, *var. of* **question mark.**
interrogative [ˌɪntə'rɑgətɪv, B -'rɔg-] *a.* interrogativo. —*s.* palabra o frase interrogativa.
interrogatively [-lɪ] *adv.* interrogativamente.
interrogator [ɪn'tɛrəˌgeɪtər, B -ə] *s.* interrogador, examinador.
interrogatorily [ˌɪntəˌrɑgə'tɔrəlɪ, B -tə'rɔgətər-] *adv.* interrogativamente.
interrogatory [-'rɑgəˌtɔrɪ, B -'rɔgətərɪ] *a.* interrogativo. —*s.* interrogatorio.
interrupt [ˌɪntə'rʌpt] *v.t.* interrumpir.
interruptedly [-ədlɪ] *adv.* interrumpidamente, discontinuamente.
interrupted screw [-əd-] tornillo de sectores interrumpidos.
interrupter, interruptor [-ər, B -ə] *s.* (elec.) interruptor, disyuntor.

interruption [-'rʌpʃən] *s.* 1. interrupción. 2. pausa, intervalo.
interruptive [-'rʌptɪv] *a.* interruptivo.
interscholastic [ˌɪntərskə'læstɪk, B -təskə-] *a.* interescolar.
inter se ['ɪntər'si, -'seɪ, B -tə'si] (latín) entre ellos mismos.
intersect [ˌɪntər'sɛkt, B -tə'-] *v.t.* cruzar, intersecar; cortar transversalmente. —*v.i.* intersecarse, cruzarse (líneas, vías, etc.).
intersecting line [-ɪŋ-] (geom.) línea transversal.
intersecting vault, (arq.) bóveda por arista.
intersection [-'sɛkʃən] *s.* 1. intersección, cruce, bocacalle. 2. (geom.) intersección, arista.
intersectional [-əl] *a.* interseccional.
intersession ['ɪntərˌsɛʃən, B -təˌ-] *s.* (E.U.) vacaciones semestrales universitarias.
intersex [-ˌsɛks] *s.* (biol.) individuo con características intersexuales.
intersexual [ˌɪntər'sɛkʃʊəl, B -tə'sɛksjʊ-] *a.* intersexual.
intersexuality [-ˌsɛkʃʊ'ælətɪ, B -ˌsɛksju-] *s.* intersexualidad.
interspace ['ɪntərˌspeɪs, B -tə'-] *s.* intervalo, intersticio, espacio intermedio. — [ˌɪntər'speɪs, B -tə'-] *v.t.* espaciar, separar por espacios.
interspatial [ˌɪntər'speɪʃəl, B -tə'-] *a.* intermedio, separado por espacios.
interspatially [-əlɪ] *adv.* intermediamente.
intersperse [-'spɜrs, B -'spɜs] *v.t.* entremezclar, intercalar, esparcir.
interspersion [-'spɜrʒən, -ʃən, B -'spɜʃən] *s.* entremezcladura, esparcimiento de una cosa entre otras.
interstate ['ɪntərˌsteɪt, B ˌɪntə'steɪt] *a.* interestatal, entre estados.
interstate highway, carretera interstatal, autopista interstatal, carretera nacional.
interstellar [ˌɪntər'stɛlər, B -tə'stɛlə] *a.* interestelar, intersideral.
interstellar flight, vuelo interestelar.
interstellar space, espacio interestelar.
interstice [ɪn'tɜrstəs, B -'tɜstɪs] *s.* intersticio, hendidura, grieta, rendija.
interstitial [ɪntər'stɪʃəl, B -tə'-] *a.* intersticial.
interstitially [-əlɪ] *adv.* en arreglo o forma intersticial.
interstratification [-ˌstrætəfə'keɪʃən] *s.* interestratificación.
interstratify [-'strætəˌfaɪ] *v.t., v.i.* interestratificar, insertar entre capas o estratos.
intertexture [-'tɛkstʃər, B -tʃə] *s.* entretejedura, entretejimiento, contexto.
intertidal [-'taɪdəl] *a.* (de) entre marea alta y baja (zona litoral).
intertrigo [ˌɪntər'traɪgoʊ, B -tə'-] *s.* (med.) intertrigo.
intertropical [-'trɑpɪkəl, B -'trɔp-] *a.* intertropical.
intertwine [-'twaɪn] *v.t., v.i.* entrelazar(se), entretejer(se).
intertwinement [-mənt] *s.* entrelazamiento.
intertwist [-'twɪst] *v.t., v.i.* entrelazar(se).
interurban [ˌɪntər'ɜrbən, B -'ɜbən] *a.* interurbano.
interval ['ɪntərvəl, B -təvəl] *s.* 1. intervalo, pausa, intermedio. 2. intervalo, claro, vacío, espacio. 3. (mús.) intervalo. 4. **at intervals,** a intervalos, de trecho en trecho.
intervale [-ˌveɪl] *s.* (E.U.) hondonada, tierras bajas.
intervallic [ˌɪntər'vælɪk, B -tə'-] *a.* espaciado, intermedio.
intervalometer [ˌɪntərvə'lɑmətər, B -təvə'lɔmɪtə] *s.* (foto.) intervalómetro.
intervene [-'vin] *v.i.* 1. intervenir. 2. ocurrir, sobrevenir, acontecer. 3. interponerse, mediar, terciar. 4. atravesarse, estar entre o en medio. 5. (der.) interponer tercería.
intervener [-'vinər, B -nə] *s.* interventor, mediador.
intervenient [-'vinjənt] *a.* interventor, mediador.
intervening [-'vinɪŋ] *a.* intermedio, intercurrente; interpuesto.
intervention [-'vɛntʃən, B -'vɛnʃən] *s.* 1. intervención, interposición, mediación. 2. intromisión, interferencia. 3. (der., pol.) intervención.
interventionism [-ˌɪzəm] *s.* (pol.) intervencionismo.
interventionist [-əst] *a., s.* (pol.) intervencionista.
intervertebral [ˌɪntər'vɜrtəbrəl, B -tə'vɜt-] *a.* (anat.) intervertebral.
intervertebral disk, (anat.) disco intervertebral.
interview ['ɪntərˌvju, B -təˌ-] *s.* entrevista, interviú. —*v.t.* entrevistar.
interviewee [ˌɪntərvju'i, B -təvju'i] *s.* entrevistado (el interrogado en una entrevista periodística o de solicitud de empleo).
interviewer ['ɪntərˌvjuər, B 'ɪntəˌ-ə] *s.* entrevistador, el que hace las preguntas en una entrevista.
intervocalic [ˌɪntərvoʊ'kælɪk, B -təvoʊ-] *a.* (fon.) intervocálico.
interweave [-'wiv] *v.t., v.i.* 1. entretejer(se). 2. entrelazar(se), entremezclar(se).
interweaving [-'wivɪŋ] *s.* entretejimiento, entrelazamiento.
interwoven [-'woʊvən] *a.* entrelazado, entretejido; vinculado.
interwreathe [-'rið] *v.t.* entrelazar en forma de guirnalda.
intestable [ɪn'tɛstəbəl] *a.* legalmente incapacitado para hacer testamento.
intestacy [-'tɛstəsɪ] *s.* (der.) falta de testamento; estado intestado.
intestate [-'tɛsˌteɪt, -tət] *a., s.* (der.) intestado.
intestate succession, (der.) sucesión intestada.
intestinal [-'təstənəl] *a.* intestinal.
intestinal fortitude, (fig.) nervio, fibra, tesón; coraje.
intestinal worm, (med.) lombriz intestinal.
intestine [ɪn'tɛstən] *a.* intestino, interior, interno. —*s.* intestino, tripa.
inthrall, inthral, *var. de* **enthrall.**
inthrone, *var. de* **enthrone.**
intima ['ɪntəmə] *s.* (*pl.* INTIMAE [-ˌmi]) (anat., zool.) íntima, túnica íntima.
intimacy [-təməsɪ] *s.* 1. intimidad, familiaridad; amistad íntima. 2. relaciones sexuales, contacto íntimo.
intimate ['ɪntəˌmeɪt] *v.t.* 1. intimar, anunciar, notificar. 2. sugerir, insinuar, dar a entender. — ['ɪntəmət] *a.* 1. íntimo; personal, privado. 2. estrecho, íntimo, entrañable. 3. profundo (conocimiento). 4. **to become i.,** intimarse, hacerse íntimo (de alguien). —*s.* íntimo, allegado.
intimately ['ɪntəmətlɪ] *adv.* íntimamente.
intimateness [-nəs] *s.* intimidad.
intimation [ˌɪntə'meɪʃən] *s.* 1. intimación. 2. insinuación, indicación, sugerencia. 3. indicio. 4. indirecta, pulla.
intimidate [ɪn'tɪməˌdeɪt] *v.t.* intimidar, amilanar, amedrentar.
intimidation [-ˌtɪmə'deɪʃən] *s.* intimidación.
intimidator [-'tɪməˌdeɪtər, B -ə] *s.* amedrentador.
intinction [ɪn'tɪŋkʃən] *s.* (relig.) el acto de dar la comunión mojando el pan o la hostia en vino.
intitle, *var. de* **entitle.**
intitule [ɪn'tɪtʃul, B -'tɪtjul] *v.t.* (G.B.) intitular, titular (ley, decreto, estatuto).
into ['ɪntu, -tə, B -tʊ] *prep.* 1. a, en; ej., *to come i. the garden,* entrar al jardín, *to get i. trouble,* meterse en dificultades. 2. hasta, ej., *watching far (on) i. the night,* velando hasta muy avanzada la noche. 3. dentro, adentro. 4. **i. the bargain,** por añadidura.
intolerability [ɪnˌtɑlərə'bɪlətɪ, B -ˌtɔl-] *s.* intolerabilidad.
intolerable [-'tɑlərəbəl, B -'tɔl-] *a.* intolerable, insufrible, inaguantable.
intolerableness [-nəs] *s.* intolerabilidad.
intolerably [-blɪ] *adv.* intolerablemente.
intolerance [ɪn'tɑlərəns, B -'tɔl-] *s.* intolerancia, intransigencia.
intolerant [-ənt] *a., s.* intolerante, intransigente.
intolerantly [-lɪ] *adv.* intolerantemente, sin tolerancia.
intomb, intombment, *var. de* **entomb, entombment.**
intonate ['ɪntəˌneɪt] *v.t.* entonar.
intonation [ˌɪntə'neɪʃən] *s.* entonación; (fon.) entonación.
intone [ɪn'toʊn] *v.t.* entonar. —*v.i.* salmodiar, recitar o cantar monótonamente.
intorsion, intortion [-'tɔrʃən, B -'tɔʃən] *s.* (bot.) intorsión.
intort [-'tɔrt, B -'tɔt] *v.t.* (bot.) enroscar, abrazar.
in toto [ɪn'toʊtoʊ] (latín) totalmente, todo.
intoxicant [ɪn'tɑksɪkənt, B -'tɔk-] *a.* 1. embriagante, embriagador. 2. intoxicante. —*s.* bebida embriagante, bebida alcohólica.
intoxicate [-kət] *a.* (ant.) ebrio, embriagado. — [-səˌkeɪt] *v.t.* 1. embriagar, emborrachar. 2. (fig.) (con *with*) embriagar (de); excitar (por), estimular (por). 3. (med.) intoxicar.
intoxicated [-səˌkeɪtəd] *a.* 1. ebrio, embriagado. 2. (fig.) (con *with*) embriagado (de), excitado (por).
intoxicating [-ɪŋ] *a.* embriagador, emborrachador, embriagante.
intoxication [-ˌtɑksə'keɪʃən, B -ˌtɔk-] *s.* 1. borrachera, embriaguez. 2. (med.) intoxicación. 3. (fig.) embriaguez, excitación.
intra-atomic [ˌɪntrəə'tɑmɪk, B -'tɔm-] *a.* intraatómico.
intracardiac [-'kɑrdɪˌæk, B -'kɑd-] *a.* (fisiol.) intracardíaco.
intracartilaginous [-ˌkɑrtəl'ædʒənəs, B -ˌkɑt-] *a.* (fisiol.) intracartilaginoso.
intracellular [-'sɛljələr, B -lə] *a.* (fisiol.) intracelular.
intracostal [-'kɑstəl, B -'kɔst-] *a.* (fisiol.) intracostal.
intracranial [-'kreɪnɪəl] *a.* (fisiol.) intracraneano.
intractability [ɪnˌtræktə'bɪlətɪ] *s.* intratabilidad, hurañería.
intractable [ɪn'træktəbəl] *a.* 1. intratable, huraño; ingobernable, indisciplinado, terco, obstinado. 2. refractario. 3. incurable (úlceras). 4. incultivable (terrenos). 5. difícil de trabajar (metales).
intractableness [-nəs] *s.* intratabilidad, hurañía.
intractably [-blɪ] *adv.* hurañamente.
intracutaneous test [ˌɪntrəkjʊ'teɪnɪəs-] (med.) prueba o reacción intracutánea.
intradermal [-'dɜrməl, B -'dɜməl] **intradermic** [-mɪk] *a.* (anat.) intradérmico, intracutáneo.
intrados ['ɪntrəˌdɑs, ɪn'treɪ-, B -ˌdɔs] *s.* (arq.) intradós.

intramolecular [ˌɪntrəmə'lɛkjələr, B -lə] *a.* intramolecular.
intramural [-'mjʊrəl, B -'mjʊər-] *a.* 1. intramuros, que ocurre o se halla en los límites de una ciudad, institución, edificio, o entre los estudiantes de una misma escuela. 2. (med.) intramural.
intramuscular [-'mʌskjələr, B -lə] *a.* (med.) intramuscular.
intransigence [ɪn'trænsədʒəns] *s.* intransigencia.
intransigency [-dʒənsɪ] *s.* (*pl.* INTRANSIGENCIES) *var. de* **intransigence.**
intransigent [-dʒənt] *s., a.* intransigente, intolerante, irreconciliable.
intransigently [-lɪ] *adv.* de modo intransigente, intransigentemente.
intransitive [ɪn'trænsətɪv] *a.* (gram.) intransitivo.
intransitively [-lɪ] *adv.* (gram.) intransitivamente.
intransitive verb, (gram.) verbo intransitivo, verbo neutro.
intransmutability [ˌɪntrænsˌmjutə'bɪlətɪ, -trænz-] *s.* intransmutabilidad.
intransmutable [-'mjutəbəl] *a.* intransmutable.
intrapsychic [ˌɪntrə'saɪkɪk] *a.* intrapsíquico.
intrastate [-'steɪt] *a.* que existe u ocurre dentro de los límites de un estado.
intrauterine [-'jutərən, -ˌraɪn] *a.* (med.) intrauterino.
intravenous [-'vinəs] *a.* (med.) intravenoso.
intravenously [-lɪ] *adv.* (med.) por vía intravenosa.
intreat, *var. de* **entreat.**
intrench, *var. de* **entrench.**
intrepid [ɪn'trɛpəd] *a.* intrépido, arrojado, valeroso.
intrepidity [ˌɪntrə'pɪdətɪ] *s.* intrepidez, arrojo, valor.
intrepidly [ɪn'trɛpədlɪ] *adv.* intrépidamente.
intrepidness [-nəs] *s.* intrepidez, arrojo, valor.
intricacy ['ɪntrɪkəsɪ] *s.* (*pl.* INTRICACIES) 1. intrincación, intrincamiento; embrollo, enredo. 2. detalle intrincado.
intricate [-kət] *a.* intrincado, confuso, embrollado, enredado; complicado.
intricately [-lɪ] *adv.* intrincadamente.
intricateness [-nəs] *s.* intrincación, embrollo, enredo.
intrigant [ˌɪntrɪ'gɑnt, B 'ɪntrɪgənt] *s.* hombre intrigante.
intrigante [ˌɪntrɪ'gænt] *s.* mujer intrigante.
intrigue [ɪn'trig] *v.t.* 1. engañar, trampear (mediante intrigas). 2. intrigar, atraer, interesar, despertar la curiosidad de. 3. confundir, dejar perplejo (a alguno). —*v.i.* 1. intrigar, tramar, complotar, maquinar. 2. tener intrigas amorosas. — ['ɪnˌtrig, B ɪn'trig] *s.* 1. intriga, trama, maquinación. 2. intriga amorosa. 3. intriga o trama (obra literaria, teatro, etc.).
intriguer [-ər, B -ə] *s.* intrigante, embrollón, maquinador.
intriguing [-ɪŋ] *a.* curioso, fascinante, intrigante, seductor.
intriguingly [-lɪ] *adv.* 1. de manera intrigante. 2. por medio de intrigas.
intrinsic [ɪn'trɪnʒɪk, -sɪk-] *a.* 1. intrínseco, esencial, inherente. 2. (anat.) intrínseco.
intrinsical [-zɪkəl, -sɪ-] *a.* intrínseco.
intrinsically [-kəlɪ] *adv.* intrínsecamente.
intrinsicalness [-kəlnəs] *s.* calidad de intrínseco.
introduce [ˌɪntrə'dus, B -'djus] *v.t.* 1. introducir (moda, novedad; industria; lema, etc.). 2. introducir, dar entrada a. 3. presentar (una persona a otra); introducir (una persona en la sociedad, corte, etc.). 4. introducir, meter, insertar. 5. proponer, presentar (proyecto de ley, etc.). 6. **to i. evidence,** presentar pruebas.
introducer [-ər, B -ə] *s.* introductor, presentador.
introduction [-'dʌkʃən] *s.* 1. introducción, prefacio, prologo, preámbulo. 2. presentación (de una persona a otra). 3. implantación.
introductive [-'dʌktɪv] *a.* introductorio, introductivo.
introductorily [-tərəlɪ] *adv.* como preliminar, de modo introductorio.
introductory [-tərɪ] *a.* introductorio, preliminar.
introit [ɪn'troʊət, 'ɪnˌtroʊ-, B -ˌtrɔɪt] *s.* (relig.) introito.
introjection [ˌɪntrə'dʒɛkʃən] *s.* (psic.) introyección.
intromission [-'mɪʃən] *s.* 1. (med.) intromisión. 2. intromisión, entremetimiento. 3. intromisión; introducción; admisión, iniciación.
intromit [-'mɪt] *v.t.* (*pret., p.p.* INTROMITTED; *p.pr.* INTROMITTING) 1. adjuntar, enviar adjunto; insertar. 2. admitir, dar pase o entrada. —*v.i.* entrometerse, intervenir.
introrse ['ɪnˌtrɔrs, ɪn'trɔrs, B -'trɔs] *a.* (bot.) introrso.
introrsely [-lɪ] *adv.* de modo introrso.
introspect [ˌɪntrə'spɛkt] *v.t.* examinar con introspección. —*v.i.* practicar la introspección.
introspection [-'spɛkʃən] *s.* introspección.
introspective [-'spɛktɪv] *a.* introspectivo.
introspectively [-lɪ] *adv.* de manera introspectiva, introspectivamente.
introspectiveness [-nəs] *s.* introspección.
introversion [-'vɜrʒən, -ʃən, B -'vɜʃən] *s.* introversión.
introversive [-'vɜrsɪv, -zɪv, B -'vɜsɪv] *a.* introverso.
introversively [-lɪ] *adv.* de forma introversa.
introvert ['ɪntrəˌvɜrt, ˌɪn-'vɜrt, B -'vɜt] *v.t.* 1. dirigir hacia sí mismo (pensamiento, agresividad, emoción, etc.); interesarse más en sí mismo y en su mundo interior que en el exterior. 2. (zool.) invaginar, doblar hacia adentro. — ['ɪn-ˌvɜrt, B -ˌvɜt] *s.* introvertido. —*a.* introverso.
introverted [-əd] *a.* introverso.
intrude [ɪn'trud] *v.t.* 1. (con *into*) clavar o meter por fuerza (en). 2. (con *upon*) imponer algo (a. alguien). —*v.i.* 1. entremeterse, inmiscuirse. 2. molestar. 3. **i. upon,** estorbar.
intruder [-ər, B -ə] *s.* intruso, incursor, entremetido.
intrusion [-'truʒən] *s.* 1. intrusión, entremetimiento, impertinencia. 2. (der.) intrusión, allanamiento; usurpación de propiedad. 3. (geol.) intrusión.
intrusional [-əl] **intrusive** [-'trusɪv] *a.* 1. intruso, entremetido. 2. introducido, insertado, enclavado. 3. (geol.) intrusivo, de inyección. 4. (filol.) añadido sin justificación etimológica.
intrusively [ɪn'trusɪvlɪ] *adv.* intrusamente.
intrusiveness [-nəs] *s.* tendencia a la intrusión.
intrust, *var. de* **entrust.**
intubate ['ɪntuˌbeɪt, B -tju-] *v.t.* (med.) intubar.
intubation [ˌɪntu'beɪʃən, B -tju-] *s.* (med.) intubación.
intuit [ɪn'tuət, B -'tju-] *v.t., v.i.* intuir, percibir por intuición.
intuition [ˌɪntʊ'ɪʃən, B -tjʊ-] *s.* intuición, aprehensión inmediata.
intuitional [-əl] *a.* 1. de la intuición, acerca de la intuición (teoría, etc.). 2. intuitivo.
intuitionally [-elɪ] *adv.* de forma intuitiva, intuitivamente.
intuitionism [-ˌɪzəm] *s.* (filos.) intuicionismo.
intuitionist [-əst] *a., s.* (filos.) intuicionista.
intuitive [ɪn'tuətɪv, B -'tju-] *a.* intuitivo.
intuitively [-lɪ] *adv.* intuitivamente.
intuitiveness [-nəs] *s.* poder intuitivo.
intumesce [ˌɪntʊ'mɛs, B -tjʊ-] *v.i.* hincharse, entumecerse.
intumescence [-əns] *s.* intumescencia, tumefacción, hinchazón.
intumescent [-ənt] *a.* intumescente, hinchado.
intussuscept [ˌɪntəsə'sɛpt] *v.t.* (med., biol.) invaginar.
intussusception [-'sɛpʃən] *s.* (med., biol.) intususcepción.
intussusceptive [-'sɛptɪv] *a.* (med., biol.) intususceptivo.
intwine, *var. de* **entwine.**
inula ['ɪnjələ] *s.* (bot.) coniza; atarraga, olivarda, énula.
inulin [-lən] *s.* (bioquím.) inulina.
inulinase [-ləˌneɪs] *s.* (bioquím.) inulinasa.
inunction [ɪn'ʌŋkʃən] *s.* 1. untura, unción, frotación. 2. (med.) inunción. 3. ungüento, linimento.
inundant [-'ʌndənt] *a.* inundante, que inunda.
inundate ['ɪnənˌdeɪt] *v.i.* inundar, anegar.
inundation [ˌɪnən'deɪʃən] *s.* inundación, aniego, desbordamiento.
inundator ['ɪnənˌdeɪtər, B -ə] *a.* que inunda.
inundatory [ɪn'ʌndəˌtɔrɪ, B -dətərɪ] *a.* inundante, con tendencia a inundar, que inunda.
inurbane [ˌɪnər'beɪn, B ˌɪnɜ'-] *a.* descortés, incivil.
inurbanity [-'bænətɪ] *s.* descortesía.
inure [ɪn'jʊr, B -'jʊə] *v.t.* habituar, acostumbrar, avezar; endurecer. —*v.i.* 1. (con *to*) redundar (en beneficio). 2. tener efecto, operar.
inurement [-mənt] *s.* habituación, endurecimiento; práctica, hábito, costumbre.
inurn [ɪn'ɜrn, B -'ɜn] *v.t.* poner en una urna; p. ext. enterrar.
inutile [ɪn'jutəl] *a.* inútil.
inutility [ˌɪnjʊ'tɪlətɪ] *s.* inutilidad.
invade [ɪn'veɪd] *v.t.* 1. invadir. 2. infringir, atropellar, violar (derechos, etc.). 3. permear, extenderse por.
invader [-ər, B -ə] *s.* invasor.
invaginate [ɪn'vædʒəˌneɪt] *v.t.* invaginar, envainar. —*v.i.* invaginarse.
invagination [-ˌvædʒə'neɪʃən] *s.* invaginación, enchufamiento.
invalid [ɪn'væləd] *a.* inválido, nulo, sin efecto.
invalid ['ɪnvələd, B -ˌlid] *a.* inválido, enfermizo, débil. —*s.* persona inválida, inválido. — [B ˌɪnvə'lid] *v.t.* 1. caer enfermo, lisiar. 2. dar de baja por invalidez. —*v.i.* 1. enfermarse, quedarse inválido. 2. retirarse por invalidez, impedimento o incapacidad.
invalidate [ɪn'væləˌdeɪt] *v.t.* invalidar, anular.
invalidation [-ˌvælə'deɪʃən] *s.* invalidación, anulación.
invalidity [ˌɪnvə'lɪdətɪ] *s.* 1. nulidad, invalidad, invalidez. 2. invalidez, inhabilitación, incapacidad.
invalidly [ɪn'vælədlɪ] *adv.* inválidamente.
invaluable [ɪn'væljʊəbəl] *a.* invalorable, inapreciable, inestimable, de incalculable valor.
invaluableness [-nəs] *s.* calidad de inestimable.
invaluably [-blɪ] *adv.* invalorablemente, inestimablemente, inapreciablemente.
invar [ɪn'vɑr, B -'vɑ] *s.* (metal.) invar.
invariability [ɪnˌvɛrɪə'bɪlətɪ, B -ˌvɛər-] *s.* invariabilidad.
invariable [-'vɛrɪəbəl, B -'vɛər-] *a.* invariable; constante, uniforme.
invariableness [-nəs] *s.* invariabilidad, constancia.

invariably [-blɪ] *adv.* invariablemente.
invariance [-ɪəns] *s.* (mat.) invariancia, invariación.
invariant [-ɪənt] *a.* invariable, constante. —*s.* (mat.) invariante.
invasion [ɪn'veɪʒən] *s.* invasión; infracción, violación.
invasion of privacy, invasión de la vida privada de una persona, con perjuicio de la misma.
invasive [-'veɪsɪv] *a.* invasor, hostil, agresivo.
invective [ɪn'vɛktɪv] *a.* insultante, ultrajante, injurioso. —*s.* invectiva, filípica, censura, vituperio.
invectively [-lɪ] *adv.* de manera insultante, injuriosamente.
inveigh [ɪn'veɪ] *v.i.* prorrumpir en invectivas; **i. against,** vituperar.
inveigher [-ər, B -ə] *s.* vituperador.
inveigle [ɪn'vigəl, -'veɪ-] *v.t.* 1. engatusar, embaucar; alucinar; seducir, engañar; sonsacar. 2. **i. into,** inducir artificiosamente o engatusar a alguien para que entre en un lugar o haga algo.
inveiglement [-mənt] *s.* engatusamiento, engañifa, embaucamiento.
inveigler [-glər, B -glə] *s.* seductor.
invent [ɪn'vɛnt] *v.t.* 1. inventar, crear; idear, discurrir. 2. (fig.) mentir, urdir.
inventable, inventible [ɪn'vɛntəbəl] *a.* que puede ser inventado.
invention [-'vɛnʃən, B -'vɛnʃən] *s.* 1. invención, invento. 2. invención, fabricación, falsedad. 3. inventiva, ingenio, ingeniosidad. 4. (mús.) invención. 5. (ant.) descubrimiento.
inventive [-'vɛntɪv] *a.* inventivo, ingenioso.
inventively [-lɪ] *adv.* ingeniosamente, con inventiva.
inventiveness [-nəs] *s.* inventiva, ingeniosidad.
inventor [-ər, B -ə] *s.* inventor, creador.
inventorial [ˌɪnvən'tɔrɪəl] *a.* del inventario.
inventorially [-ɪəlɪ] *adv.* mediante inventario, por inventario, con inventario.
inventory ['ɪnvənˌtɔrɪ, B -trɪ] *s.* (*pl.* INVENTORIES) 1. inventario. 2. existencias. —*v.t.* (*pret., p.p.* INVENTORIED; *p.pr.* INVENTORYING) hacer un inventario.
inveracity [ˌɪnvə'ræsətɪ] *s.* 1. falta de veracidad. 2. mentira, falsedad.
inverness [ˌɪnvər'nɛs, B -və'-] *s.* 1. macfarlán, macferlán, abrigo con capa larga separable. 2. **I.,** condado de Escocia.
inverse [ɪn'vɜrs, 'ɪnˌvɜrs, B -'vɜs] *a.* inverso; contrario, invertido. —*s.* lo inverso. — [ɪn'vɜrs, B -'vɜs] *v.t.* invertir.
inverse functions, (mat.) funciones inversas.
inversely [-lɪ] *adv.* inversamente.
inversely proportional, (mat.) inversamente proporcional.
inverse ratio, razón inversa.
inversion [ɪn'vɜrʒən, -ʃən, B -'vɜʃən] *s.* 1. inversión, trastrocamiento, transmutación. 2. (quím., meteor., mús., ret.) inversión. 3. (psic.) inversión sexual, homosexualidad.
inversive [-'vɜrsɪv, B -'vɜsɪv] *a.* inverso, inversivo.
invert [ɪn'vɜrt, B -'vɜt] *v.t.* 1. invertir, volver al revés. 2. invertir, cambiar el orden de, trastrocar, transponer. 3. (quím.) someter a inversión (azúcar, etc.). — ['ɪnˌvɜrt B -ˌvɜt] *a.* (quím.) invertido (díc. del azúcar). —*s.* (psic.) invertido, homosexual.
invertase [-'vɜrtˌeɪs, B -'vɜt-] *s.* (bioquím.) invertasa, invertina.
Invertebrata [-ˌvɜrtə'breɪtə, B -ˌvɜtɪ'b-rɑtə] *s. pl.* invertebrados.
invertebrate [-'vɜrtəbrət, -ˌbreɪt, B -'vɜt-] *a.* 1. invertebrado. 2. de poco carácter; de voluntad débil. —*s.* invertebrado.

inverted commas [-əd-] comillas.
inverter [ɪn'vɜrtər, B -'vɜtə] *s.* (elec.) inversor, transformador.
invertible [-əbəl] *a.* capaz de ser invertido.
invert sugar, azúcar invertida, invertasa.
invest [ɪn'vɛst] *v.t.* 1. investir, instalar (a alguien); conferir (autoridad, dignidad, etc.). 2. (fig.) (con *with*) cubrir (de), envolver (en). 3. (fig.) (con *with*) dotar (de), revestir (con o de), adornar (con o de). 4. invertir (capital, dinero, etc.), emplear, dedicar (tiempo, talento, etc.). 5. (mil.) sitiar, cercar. 6. (raro) vestir, ataviar. 7. **i. (someone) with (power, medal,** etc.), otorgar (poder, condecoración, etc.) a (alguien). —*v.i.* hacer una inversión.
investigable [ɪn'vɛstəgəbəl] *a.* investigable, averiguable, escudriñable.
investigate [-'vɛstəˌgeɪt] *v.t.* investigar, indagar, pesquisar, averiguar, escudriñar; estudiar o analizar.
investigation [-ˌvɛstɪ'geɪʃən] *s.* investigación, indagación, pesquisa, averiguación, encuesta; estudio, análisis.
investigative [-'vɛstəˌgeɪtɪv] *a.* 1. investigador (ej., científico). 2. de investigación (método, técnica, etc.).
investigator [-ər, B -ə] *s.* investigador, indagador.
investigatory [-tɪgəˌtɔrɪ, B -ˌgeɪtərɪ] *a.* investigador.
investitive [ɪn'vɛstətɪv] *a.* (der.) 1. que inviste, que da posesión. 2. de investidura.
investiture [-tʃər, B -tʃə] *s.* 1. investidura, instalación. 2. oficio, cargo, dignidad. 3. (der. feudal) investidura, entrega, acto de dar posesión, toma de posesión. 4. indumentaria, vestimenta, ropaje.
investment [ɪn'vɛstmənt] *s.* 1. inversión (de fondos). 2. investidura, instalación. 3. (mil.) sitio, bloqueo. 4. (ant.) vestimenta, ropas.
investment fund, fondo de inversiones (de una corporación o institución bancaria).
investment trust, sociedad inversionista, sociedad de cartera (que invierte dinero aportado por sus asociados).
investor [-'vɛstər, B -tə] *s.* inversionista, accionista, inversor.
inveteracy [ɪn'vɛtərəsɪ] *s.* hábito inveterado, costumbre arraigada.
inveterate [-'vɛtərət] *a.* 1. inveterado, inextirpable, crónico, arraigado, contumaz. (hábito, vicio, etc.). 2. empedernido (fumador, bebedor, etc.).
inveterately [-lɪ] *adv.* inveteradamente.
inviability [ɪnˌvaɪə'bɪlətɪ] *s.* (biol.) falta de viabilidad, incapacidad de sobrevivir.
inviable [-'vaɪəbəl] *a.* falto de viabilidad, incapaz de sobrevivir, no viable.
invidious [ɪn'vɪdɪəs] *a.* 1. difamante; denigrante. 2. que incita al odio; ofensivo, injusto. 3. (ant.) envidioso.
invidiously [-lɪ] *adv.* odiosamente, con intención de ofender o denigrar.
invidiousness [-nəs] *s.* odiosidad.
invigilate [ɪn'vɪdʒəˌleɪt] *v.i.* invigilar, vigilar; (G.B.) vigilar, supervisar (un examen).
invigilation [-ˌvɪdʒə'leɪʃən] *s.* vigilancia; (G.B.) supervisión.
invigorate [ɪn'vɪgəˌreɪt] *v.t.* vigorizar, fortificar, fortalecer; animar.
invigorating [-ɪŋ] *a.* vigorizador, fortaleciente.
invigoration [-ˌvɪgə'reɪʃən] *s.* tonificación, acto y efecto de vigorizar.
invigorator [-'vɪgəˌreɪtər, B -ə] *s.* tónico, agente vigorizador.

invincibility [ɪnˌvɪnsə'bɪlətɪ] *s.* invencibilidad.
invincible [-'vɪnsəbəl] *a.* invencible, inconquistable.
Invincible Armada, (hist.) Armada Invencible, díc. de la enviada por Felipe II de Esp. contra Inglaterra.
invincibleness [-nəs] *s.* invencibilidad.
invincibly [-blɪ] *adv.* invenciblemente.
inviolability [ɪnˌvaɪələ'bɪlətɪ] *s.* inviolabilidad; invulnerabilidad.
inviolable [-'vaɪələbəl] *a.* 1. inviolable, inquebrantable. 2. inviolable, invulnerable, inexpugnable.
inviolably [-blɪ] *adv.* inviolablemente.
inviolate [-lət, -ˌleɪt] *a.* inviolado, puro; intacto, íntegro.
inviolately [-lɪ] *adv.* en estado inviolado.
inviolateness [-nəs] **inviolacy** [-ləsɪ] *s.* estado inviolado.
invisibility [ɪnˌvɪzə'bɪlətɪ] *s.* invisibilidad.
invisible [-'vɪzəbəl] *a.* invisible; (com., fin.) invisible. —*s.* lo invisible; **the I.,** el mundo invisible; Dios.
invisible ink, tinta invisible o simpática.
invisibleness [-nəs] *s.* invisibilidad.
invisibly [-blɪ] *adv.* invisiblemente.
invitation [ˌɪnvə'teɪʃən] *s.* 1. invitación; convite. 2. sugerencia, proposición. 3. invitación, incentivo, estímulo; tentación.
invitational [-əl] *a.* (dep.) con participantes por invitación exclusiva (torneo, etc.).
invitatory [ɪn'vaɪtəˌtɔrɪ, B -tərɪ] *a.* invitador. *s.* (relig.) invitatorio.
invite [ɪn'vaɪt] *v.t.* 1. invitar, convidar, brindar. 2. instar, pedir, solicitar. 3. invitar, incitar, estimular; tentar; provocar. —*s.* (jer.) invitación.
inviter [-ər, B -ə] *s.* invitador, convidador.
inviting [-ɪŋ] *a.* tentador, atractivo, provocativo, incitante, seductor.
invitingly [-lɪ] *adv.* de modo tentador, tentadoramente.
invitingness [-nəs] *s.* carácter tentador o atractivo.
in vitro [ɪn'vitroʊ] *a.* (biol.) in vitro.
in vitro fertilization, fecundación in vitro.
invocation [ˌɪnvə'keɪʃən] *s.* 1. invocacion, plegaria, súplica. 2. conjuro. 3. (der.) suplicatorio, mandamiento, exhorto.
invocational [-əl] *a.* relativo a la invocación.
invocatory [ɪn'vɑkəˌtɔrɪ, B -'vɔkətərɪ] *a.* invocatorio, que sirve para invocar.
invoice ['ɪnˌvɔɪs] *s.* (com.) 1. factura, cuenta. 2. mercadería enviada o recibida (acompañada por factura). —*v.t.* facturar, pasar factura.
invoice price, invoiced price [-ˌvɔɪst-] (com.) precio de factura (sin descuentos).
invoke [ɪn'voʊk] *v.t.* 1. invocar, rogar, implorar, suplicar. 2. invocar, llamar, conjurar (al diablo, espíritus, etc.). 3. apelar a (clemencia, etc.).
invoker [-ər, B -ə] *s.* el que invoca o conjura.
involucel [ɪn'vɑljəˌsel, B -'vɔl-] *s.* (bot.) involucelo, involucro secundario.
involucral [ˌɪnvə'lukrəl] *a.* (bot.) involucral.
involucrate [-krət] *a.* (bot.) involucrado, dotado de involucro.
involucre ['ɪnvəˌlukər, B -kə] *var. de* **involucrum.**
involucrum [ˌɪnvəˌlukrəm] *s.* (bot., med.) involucro, envoltura.
involuntarily [ɪnˌvɑlən'tɛrəlɪ, B -'vɔləntər-] *adv.* involuntariamente.
involuntariness [-'vɑlənˌtɛrɪnəs, B -'vɔləntər-] *a.* involuntariedad.
involuntary [-ˌtɛrɪ, B -tərɪ] *a.* involuntario, no intencional, espontáneo.

involute ['ɪnvə,lut] *a.* 1. complicado, intrincado. 2. (bot.) involuto (díc. de la hoja enrollada hacia adentro). 3. (zool.) enrollado en espiral (díc. de los caracoles marinos). — [,ɪnvə'lut, B 'ɪnvə,lut] *v.i.* arrollar, enrollar.
involute ['ɪnvə,lut] *s.* (geom.) involuta, evolvente (curva).
involution [,ɪnvə'luʃən] *s.* 1. involución, envolvimiento. 2. complicación, enredo, embrollo. 3. (mat.) involución. 4. (biol., med.) involución. 5. (fisiol.) involución senil.
involutional [-əl] *a.* (med.) involutiva (melancolía).
involutionary [-ʃə,nɛrɪ, B -ʃənərɪ] *a.* involutivo.
involve [ɪn'vɑlv, B -'vɔlv] *v.t.* 1. envolver, complicar, comprometer. 2. complicar, intrincar, enredar. 3. comprender, abarcar, incluir. 4. entrañar, implicar. 5. absorber, preocupar. 6. (mat.) elevar a una potencia.
involved [-'vɑlvd, B -'vɔlvd] *a.* 1. complicado, complejo, intrincado. 2. confuso, enmarañado. 3. envuelto, implicado, afectado; comprometido (en una situación).
involvement [-'vɑlvmənt, B -'vɔlv-] *s.* envolvimiento; complicación, intrincación.
invulnerability [ɪn,vʌlnərə'bɪlətɪ] *s.* invulnerabilidad.
invulnerable [-'vʌlnərəbəl] *a.* invulnerable, inatacable, inexpugnable.
invulnerableness [-nəs] *s.* invulnerabilidad.
invulnerably [-blɪ] *adv.* de manera invulnerable, invulnerablemente.
inwall ['ɪnwɔl] *s.* pared interior (ej., de un horno). [ɪn'wɔl] *v.t.* amurallar, murar.
inward ['ɪnwərd, B -wəd] *a.* 1. interior, interno. 2. (ant.) doméstico, interno; familiar, íntimo. —*adv.* 1. hacia dentro, hacia el centro, hacia el interior. 2. dentro de la mente o espíritu. 3. (ant.) interiormente. —*s.* 1. lo que está dentro. 2. (*pl.*) (fam.) entrañas, vísceras.
inward-flow turbine [-'floʊ-] *turbina centrípeta.*
inwardly [-lɪ] *adv.* (lit. y fig.) internamente, interiormente, privadamente.
inwardness [-nəs] *s.* 1. calidad o naturaleza intrínseca, esencia. 2. introspección; espiritualidad. 3. familiaridad, intimidad.
inwards [-wərdz, B -wədz] *adv., var. de* inward.
inweave [ɪn'wiv] *v.t.* entretejer, entrelazar.
inwrap [ɪn'ræp] *var. de* **enwrap.**
inwreathe, *var. de* **enwreath.**
inwrought [-'rɔt] *a.* 1. labrado, incrustado; entretejido; bordado, brochado (telas). 2. (fig.) (con *with*) íntimamente mezclado (con).
iodate ['aɪə,deɪt] *v.t.* impregnar o tratar con yodo. —*s.* (quím.) yodato.
iodation [,aɪə'deɪʃən] *s.* (quím.) tratamiento con yodo.
iodic [aɪ'ɑdɪk, B -'ɔd-] *a.* (quím.) yódico.
iodic acid, (quím.) ácido yódico.
iodide ['aɪə,daɪd] *s.* (quím.) yoduro.
iodination [,aɪədə'neɪʃən] *s.* (quím.) tratamiento o impregnación con yodo.
iodine ['aɪə,daɪn, -dən, B -,din] **iodin** [-dən] *s.* (quím.) yodo.
iodism ['aɪə,dɪzəm] *s.* (med.) yodismo, envenenamiento causado por el yodo.
iodize [-,daɪz] *v.t.* (quím.) yodurar.
iodoform [aɪ'oʊdə,fɔrm, B -'ɔdə,fɔm] *s.* (quím.) yodopsina.
Iodol ['aɪə,doʊl, B -,dɔl] *s.* (quím.) yodol.
iodometry [,aɪə'dɑmətrɪ, B -'dɔm-] *s.* (quím.) yodometría.
iodoprotein [-doʊ'proʊtin, -'proʊtɪən] *s.* (bioquím.) proteína que contiene yodo.
iodopsin [-'dɑpsən, B -'dɔp-] *s.* (bioquím.) yodopsina.
iodosobenzene [-'doʊsoʊ'bɛn,zin] *s.* (quím.) yodoso-benceno.
iodous [aɪ'oʊdəs, 'aɪəd-, B aɪ'ɔd-] *a.* (quím.) yodoso.
iodyrite [aɪ'ɑdə,raɪt, B -'ɔd-] *s.* (min.) yodirita.
iolite ['aɪə,laɪt] *s.* (min.) iolita.
ion [,aɪən, -,ɑn, B -ən] *s.* (quím., fís.) ion.
ion exchange, (quím.) intercambio de iones.
Ionian [aɪ'oʊnɪən] *a.* (hist., arqueol., arq.) jonio, jónico.
Ionian Islands, Islas, Jónicas (de Grecia).
Ionian Sea, Mar Jónico (parte del Mediterráneo).
ionic [aɪ'ɑnɪk, B -'ɔn-] *a.* (quím., fís.) iónico, relativo a los iones.
Ionic, *s.* (arq., poét.) jónico. —*a.* jonio, jónico.
ionium [aɪ'oʊnɪəm] *s.* (quím.) ionio, isótopo radioactivo del torio.
ionization [,aɪənə'zeɪʃən, B -naɪ-] *s.* (quím., fís.) ionización, disociación.
ionization chamber, (fís.) cámara de ionización.
ionization constant, (quím., fís.) coeficiente de ionización.
ionize ['aɪə,naɪz] *v.t., v.i.* (quím., fís.) ionizar(se); separar en iones.
ionizer [-ər, B -ə] *s.* (quím., fís.) ionizazador.
ionone [-,noʊn] *s.* (quím.) ionona.
ionosphere [aɪ'ɑnə,sfɪr, B -'ɔnə,sfɪə] *s.* ionosfera, región de la atmósfera.
ionospheric [-,ɑnə'sfɪrɪk, B -,ɔnə'sfɛr-] *a.* de la ionosfera, ionosférico.
ionospheric wave, (rad.) onda reflejada.
ion trap, (t.v.) trampa de iones.
iota [aɪ'oʊtə] *s.* 1. iota, novena letra del alfabeto griego. 2. (fig.) jota, pizca, ápice. — **without an i. of,** sin una pizca de.
iotacism [-,sɪzəm] *s.* (fon.) iotacismo.
iota subscript, (gram. griega) iota subscrita (a las letras a, e, o).
IOU ['aɪ,oʊ'ju] *s. abrev. de* **I owe you,** vale, pagaré.
Iowa ['aɪoʊə] *s.* Iowa, estado de los E.U.
IPA *abrev. de* **International Phonetic Alphabet,** Alfabeto Fonético Internacional.
ipecac ['ɪpɪ,kæk] **ipecacuanha** [,ɪpə,kækjʊ'ænə] *s.* 1. (bot.) ipecacuana, bejuquillo. 2. (rizoma y raíces secas de) ipecacuana, tintura de ipecacuana.
Iphigenia [,ɪfədʒə'naɪə] *s.* (mitol.) Ifigenia, hija de Agamenón.
ipm *abrev. de* **inches per minute,** pulgadas por minuto.
ipomoea [,ɪpə'mɪə, B ,aɪpə-] *s.* (bot.) ipomea.
ips *abrev. de* **inches per second,** pulgadas por segundo.
IQ *abrev. de* **intelligence quotient,** cociente intelectual, índice de inteligencia.
Ir *símb. de* **iridium,** iridio (Ir).
IR *abrev. de* **internal revenue,** ingresos internos (devengados de los impuestos que recauda una nación).
IRA *abrev. de* **Irish Republican Army,** Ejército Republicano de Irlanda.
iracund ['aɪrə,kʌnd] *a.* (ant.) iracundo, irascible, colérico.
iracundity [,aɪrə'kʌndətɪ] *s.* (ant.) iracundia, enojo, cólera.
irade [ɪ'rɑdɪ] *s.* 1. (ant.) iradé (decreto de un soberano mahometano). 2. voluntad, deseo.
Irak, *var. de* **Iraq.**
Iran [ɪ'ræn, ɪ'rɑn, B ɪ'rɑn] *s.* Irán.
Iranian [ɪ'reɪnɪən, aɪ-] *a.* iranio, iraní, del Irán, de Persia, persa. —*s.* 1. iranio, iraní, nativo de Irán. 2. lengua irania; persa.
Iraq [ɪ'rɑk, ɪ'ræk, B ɪ'rɑk] *s.* Irak, Iraq.
Iraqui [-ɪ] *a.* perteneciente o relativo al Irak, iraquí. —*s.* natural y dialecto de Irak, iraquí.
Iraquian [-ən] *a.* iraquí.
irascibility [ɪ,ræsə'bɪlətɪ, aɪ-] *s.* irascibilidad.
irascible [ɪ'ræsəbəl, aɪ-] *a.* irascible, irritable, colérico.
irascibleness [-nəs] *s.* irascibilidad.
irascibly [-blɪ] *adv.* irasciblemente, de modo irascible, coléricamente.
irate [aɪ'reɪt] *a.* airado, furioso, sañoso, encolerizado.
irately [-lɪ] *adv.* airadamente, furiosamente.
IRBM *abrev. de* **intermediate range ballistic missile,** proyectil balístico de alcance intermedio.
ire [aɪr, B 'aɪə] *s.* ira, cólera, furia, saña.
Ire. *abrev. de* **Ireland,** Irlanda.
ireful [-fəl] *a.* iracundo, colérico, furioso.
irefully [-fəlɪ] *adv.* airadamente, con ira, furiosamente.
irefulness [-fəlnəs] *s.* calidad de iracundia, cólera.
Ireland ['aɪrlənd, B 'aɪələnd] *s.* Irlanda.
irenic [aɪ'rɛnɪk, B -'rinɪk] *a.* pacífico, conciliador.
irid ['airəd] *s.* (bot.) planta de la familia de las iridáceas.
iridaceous [,ɪrə'deɪʃəs, ,aɪrə-] *a.* (bot.) irídeo, iridáceo (a).
iridectomy [-'dɛktəmɪ] *s.* (med., oftal.) iridectomía, escisión de parte del iris.
iridescence [,ɪrə'dɛsəns] *s.* iridiscencia, irisación, cambiante, tornasol.
iridescent [-ənt] *a.* iridiscente, tornasolado.
iridescently [-lɪ] *adv.* con iridiscencia, iridiscentemente.
iridic [ɪ'rɪdɪk, aɪ-] *a.* 1. (quím.) del iridio. 2. (anat.) irídico, relativo al iris del ojo.
iridium [-ɪəm] *s.* (quím.) iridio.
iridosmine [,ɪrə'dɑz,min, B ,aɪrə'dɔz,-maɪn] iridosmium [-mɪəm] *s.* (min.) iridosmina, iridosmio.
iris ['aɪrəs, B 'aɪərɪs] *s.* (*pl.* IRISES o IRIDES -[rə,diz]) 1. (anat.) iris. 2. iris, arco iris. 3. (bot.) lirio. 4. **I.,** (mitol.) Iris. —*v.t.* irisar.
iris diaphragm, (ópt.) diafragma iris.
Irish ['aɪrɪʃ, B 'aɪər-] *a.* irlandés. —*s.* 1. irlandés, natural de Irlanda. 2. (idioma) gaélico irlandés. 3. **the I.,** los irlandeses.
Irish bull, despropósito, contrasentido.
Irish coffee, mezcla de café y whiski irlandés, coronada con un copo de nata o crema.
Irish daisy, (bot.) amargón, diente de león.
Irish Free State, Estado Libre de Irlanda.
Irish Gaelic, (idioma) gaélico de Irlanda.
Irishism [-,ɪzəm] *s.* locución irlandesa, modismo irlandés, uso o manera irlandesa.
Irish linen, irlanda (tela de lino).
Irishman [-mən] *s.* irlandés, natural de Irlanda.
Irish moss, (bot.) musgo de Irlanda.
Irish potato, patata blanca común.
Irish setter, perro perdiguero de raza irlandesa; perdiguero castaño rojizo.
Irish stew, guisado irlandés, estofado a la irlandesa, hecho con carne de cordero y patatas.
Irish terrier, terrier irlandés.
Irish whiskey, whiski o aguardiente irlandés que se destila de la cebada.
Irish wolfhound, galgo lobero irlandés.
Irishwoman ['aɪrɪʃ,wʊmən, B 'aɪər-] *s.* irlandesa.
iritic [aɪ'rɪtɪk] *a.* (med.) irítico.

iritis [-'raɪtəs] *s.* (med., oftal.) iritis, inflamación del iris del ojo.
irk [ɜrk, B ɜk] *v.t.* fastidiar, molestar; irritar; aburrir; cansar.
irksome ['ɜrksəm, B 'ɜk-] *a.* fastidioso, molesto, tedioso.
irksomely [-lɪ] *adv.* fastidiosamente, tediosamente.
irksomeness [-nəs] *s.* fastidio, molestia, tedio.
IRO *abrev. de* **International Refugee Organization,** Organización Internacional de Refugiados.
iron ['aɪərn, B -ən] *s.* 1. hierro, fierro (Am.). 2. arpón. 3. plancha (para planchar ropa). 4. (*pl.*) hierros, prisiones, grillos, esposas. 5. (fig.) fuerza, firmeza, poder. 6. (golf) (palo con cabeza de) hierro. 7. (jer.) revólver, pistola; (ant.) espada. 8. **in irons,** en grillos, preso; **into irons,** (mar.) incapaz de moverse o virar (velero, debido al ángulo que forman las velas y el viento); **to have many irons in the fire,** tener muchos asuntos entre manos; tener muchos recursos; **to strike while the i. is hot,** a hierro caliente batir de repente. —*a.* 1. (hecho) de hierro, férreo. 2. (fig.) férreo, de hierro, riguroso (disciplina, voluntad, etc.). —*v.t.* 1. herrar, guarnecer de hierro, revestir de hierro. 2. planchar (ropa). 3. **i. out,** (fig.) allanar (dificultad, obstáculo), subsanar (defecto, falla). —*v.i.* planchar ropas.
Iron Age, 1. (arqueol.) Edad de Hierro. 2. (mitol.) edad de hierro, la última y más corrupta de las cuatro edades del hombre.
ironbark [-ˌbɑrk, B -ˌbɑk] *s.* (bot.) eucalipto australiano.
ironbound [-'baʊnd] *a.* 1. zunchado; revestido de hierro. 2. escabroso, rocoso (costa, etc.). 3. férreo, duro, inflexible, rígido.
ironclad [-ˌklæd] *a.* 1. blindado, acorazado, armado. 2. (fam.) riguroso, exigente. —*s.* (mar., mil.) acorazado, buque blindado.
iron-core transformer [-ˌkɔr-, B -ˌkɔ-] (elec.) transformador de núcleo de hierro.
iron curtain, (fig.) cortina de hierro, telón de acero.
ironer ['aɪərnər, B -ənə] *s.* planchador, planchadora; máquina de planchar.
iron foundry, fundición de hierro.
iron gray, gris obscuro (que se parece al color del hierro fundido).
iron-gray [-'greɪ] *a.* (de) gris obscuro.
iron hand, mano de hierro, control firme, riguroso y severo.
iron horse, 1. (fam.) locomotora. 2. (E.U., hist.) caballo de hierro, nombre que daban los indios norteamericanos al ferrocarril. 3. triciclo.
ironic [aɪ'rɑnɪk, B -'rɔn-] **ironical** [-ɪkəl] *a.* irónico, mordaz, burlón.
ironically [-ɪkəlɪ] *adv.* irónicamente.
ironing ['aɪərnɪŋ, B 'aɪənɪŋ] *s.* planchado, ropa planchada o por planchar, acción de planchar.
ironing board, tabla de planchar.
ironist ['ɪrənəst] *s.* ironista (díc. gen. de escritores).
ironlike ['aɪərnˌlaɪk, B -ən-] *a.* férreo, como el hierro, ej., *i. will,* voluntad férrea.
iron lung, (med.) pulmón de hierro, pulmón de acero.
iron man, 1. (jer.) dólar, dólar de plata. 2. máquina que ejecuta un trabajo que anteriormente se hacía a mano.
ironmaster ['aɪərnˌmæstər, B -ənˌmɑstə] *s.* 1. (G.B.) maestro fundidor. 2. fabricante de hierro.
ironmonger [-ˌmʌŋgər, -ˌmɑŋ-, B -ˌmʌŋgə] *s.* (G.B.) quincallero, ferretero.
ironmongery [-gərɪ] *s.* (G.B.) ferretería, quincallería; quincalla.
iron-nickel storage battery [-'nɪkəl-] (elec.) acumulador de hierro-níquel.
iron ore, mineral de hierro.
iron pyrites, pirita de hierro.
ironside ['aɪərnˌsaɪd, B -ən-] *s.* 1. hombre fuerte, hombre de gran valor o resistencia. 2. (*pl.*) (mar.) acorazado. 3. **Ironsides,** (hist.) caballería de Oliverio Cromwell (en la guerra civil inglesa); nombre dado a Oliverio Cromwell. 4. (jer., E.U.) **old ironsides,** jefe disciplinario y malhumorado.
ironsmith [-ˌsmɪθ] *s.* herrero; herrador (de caballos).
ironstone [-ˌstoʊn] *s.* mineral de hierro, siderita, siderosa, espato ferrífero; hematita.
ironware [-ˌwɛr, B -ˌwɛə] *s.* 1. ferretería, artículos de ferretería. 2. conjunto de sartenes y ollas caseras de hierro.
ironweed [-ˌwid] *s.* (bot.) ambrosía; rompezaragüelles.
ironwood [-ˌwʊd] *s.* 1. (bot.) palo de hierro; quiebrahacha, jabí; tamarindo; cambrón; palo santo. 2. madera de estos árboles.
ironwork [-ˌwɜrk, B -ˌwɜk] *s.* 1. herraje, obra de hierro; carpintería metálica. 2. (*pl.*) fundición de hierro, herrería, ferrería, cerrajería.
ironworker [-ˌwɜrkər, B -ˌwɜkə] *s.* 1. herrero. 2. herrero de obra.
ironworks [-ˌwɜrks, B -ˌwɜks] *s.* ferrería, fundición de hierro.
ironwort [-ˌwɜrt, B -ˌwɜt] *s.* (bot.) samarilla.
irony ['aɪrənɪ, 'aɪərnɪ, B 'aɪərə-] *s.* (*pl.* IRONIES) ironía. — ['aɪərnɪ, B 'aɪənɪ] *a.* ferruginoso.
Iroquoian [ˌɪrə'kwɔɪən] *s.* iroqués.
Iroquois ['ɪrəˌkwɔɪ] *a.* iroqués, relativo o propio de los indios iroqueses. —*s.* (*pl.* IROQUOIS) 1. iroqués (miembro de un pueblo indígena de Norteamérica). 2. iroqués (lengua).
irradiance [ɪ'reɪdɪəns] *s.* irradiación; lustre, esplendor.
irradiancy [-ənsɪ] *s., var. de* **irradiance.**
irradiant [-ənt] *a.* radiante, esplendoroso.
irradiate [-ˌeɪt] *v.t.* 1. irradiar (luz, energía, etc.). 2. (fig.) iluminar (espíritu, intelecto, etc.). 3. iluminar, alumbrar (superficie, cara, etc.). 4. (med., quím.) tratar con irradiación. —*v.i.* (ant.) brillar, lucir. — [-ət, -ˌeɪt] *a.* resplandeciente, iluminado.
irradiation [ɪˌreɪdɪ'eɪʃən] *s.* irradiación; brillo; (med.) irradiación.
irradiative [ɪ'reɪdɪˌeɪtɪv] *a.* radiante.
irradiator [-ˌeɪtər, B -ə] *s.* irradiador.
irrational [ɪ'ræʃənəl] *a.* 1. irracional, irrazonable, absurdo, ilógico. 2. (mat.) irracional. —*s.* (mat.) número irracional.
irrationalism [-ˌɪzəm] *s.* (filos.) irracionalismo.
irrationality [ɪˌræʃə'nælətɪ] *s.* irracionalidad.
irrationally [ɪ'ræʃənəlɪ] *adv.* irracionalmente.
irrational root, (mat.) raíz irracional, raíz inconmensurable.
irreclaimability [ˌɪrɪˌkleɪmə'bɪlətɪ] *s.* calidad de irredimible.
irreclaimable [-'kleɪməbəl] *a.* irredimible, irreformable; incorregible, irrevocable, irremediable.
irreclaimably [-blɪ] *adv.* incorregiblemente, irrevocablemente, irremediablemente.
irreconcilability [ɪˌrɛkənˌsaɪlə'bɪlətɪ] *s.* calidad de irreconciliabilidad, intransigencia.
irreconcilable [-'saɪləbəl, ɪ'rɛkənˌsaɪ-] *a.* irreconciliable, incompatible, inconciliable; implacable; inconsistente. —*s.* persona irreconciliable o intransigente.
irreconcilableness [-nəs] *s.* calidad de irreconciliable, intransigencia.
irreconcilably [-blɪ] *adv.* irreconciliablemente.
irrecoverable [ˌɪrɪ'kʌvərəbəl] *a.* irrecuperable; incobrable; irreparable, irremediable.
irrecoverableness [-nəs] *s.* calidad de irrecuperable.
irrecoverably [-blɪ] *adv.* irreparablemente, irremediablemente.
irrecusable [-'kjuzəbəl] *a.* irrecusable.
irrecusably [-blɪ] *adv.* irrecusablemente.
irredeemable [-'diməbəl] *a.* 1. inconvertible (papel moneda); no amortizable; que no termina con el pago del capital. 2. irredimible; incorregible.
irredeemably [-blɪ] *adv.* de modo irredimible.
irredentism [ˌɪrɪ'dɛnˌtɪzəm] *s.* (hist., pol.) irredentismo, la causa del que lucha porque su patria recobre un terreno perdido.
irredentist [-təst] *s.* (hist., pol.) irredentista, el que milita en el irredentismo.
irreducibility [-ˌdusə'bɪlətɪ, B -ˌdju-] *s.* irreductibilidad.
irreducible [-'dusəbəl, B -'dju-] *a.* irreducible, irreductible.
irreducibly [-blɪ] *adv.* irreductiblemente.
irreformable [ˌɪrɪ'fɔrməbəl, B -'fɔmə-] *a.* irreformable.
irrefragability [ɪˌrɛfrəgə'bɪlətɪ] *s.* calidad de irrefragable, irrefragabilidad.
irrefragable [ɪ'rɛfrəgəbəl] *a.* 1. irrefragable, incontestable, incontrovertible, innegable, indisputable. 2. irrompible, indestructible, inviolable.
irrefragably [-blɪ] *adv.* irrefragablemente, de un modo innegable.
irrefrangible [ˌɪrɪ'frændʒəbəl] *a.* 1. irrompible, indestructible; inviolable. 2. (ópt.) irrefrangible, que no puede ser refractado.
irrefrangibly [-blɪ] *adv.* irrefrangiblemente.
irrefutability [-ˌfjutə'bɪlətɪ, B ɪˌrɛfjət-] *s.* irrefutabilidad.
irrefutable [ɪ'rɛfjʊtəbəl, ˌɪrɪ'fjut-] *a.* irrefutable, irrebatible.
irrefutably [-blɪ] *adv.* irrebatiblemente, irrefutablemente.
irregular [ɪ'rɛgjələr, B -lə] *a.* 1. irregular; anómalo, extraño; discontinuo, desigual; desordenado, disparejo; anormal, contranatural. 2. (gram.) irregular (esp. verbo). 3. (bot.) irregular (cáliz, corola, etc.). 4. (mil.) irregular. —*s.* (mil.) soldado que no pertenece al ejército regular; (*pl.*) tropas que no pertenecen al ejército de regulares, ej., guerrilleros, legionarios, milicianos; mercancía de ocasión por ser defectuosa.
irregularity [ɪˌrɛgjə'lærətɪ] *s.* (*pl.* IRREGULARITIES) 1. irregularidad; anomalía; desigualdad; exceso, demasía; error, falta. 2. (med.) estreñimiento.
irregularly [ɪ'rɛgjələrlɪ, B -ləlɪ] *adv.* irregularmente.
irregular verb, (gram.) verbo irregular.
irrelative [ɪ'rɛlətɪv] *a.* inconexo, impertinente, independiente.
irrelatively [-lɪ] *adv.* de modo inconexo.
irrelevance [ɪ'rɛləvəns] *s.* inconexión, falta de pertinencia.
irrelevancy [-vənsɪ] *s.* (*pl.* IRRELEVANCIES) 1. inconexión, falta de pertinencia. 2. cosa inconexa, asunto no pertinente, inaplicable, que no viene al caso.
irrelevant [-vənt] *a.* no pertinente, ajeno, inaplicable, improcedente, extraño.
irrelevantly [-lɪ] *adv.* fuera de propósito, inconexamente, sin pertinencia.

irrelievable [ˌɪrɪ'livəbəl] *a.* irremediable, no mitigable, irreparable.
irreligion [ˌɪrɪ'lɪdʒən] *s.* irreligión, irreligiosidad.
irreligionist [-əst] *s.* irreligioso.
irreligious [-'lɪdʒəs] *a.* irreligioso, impío; incrédulo, profano.
irreligiously [-lɪ] *adv.* irreligiosamente, impíamente.
irremeable [ɪ'rimɪəbəl] *a.* (ant.) irrevocable, irreversible.
irremediable [ˌɪrɪ'midɪəbəl] *a.* irremediable, irreparable; insubsanable.
irremediableness [-nəs] *s.* irremediabilidad.
irremediably [-blɪ] *adv.* irremediablemente.
irremissible [ˌɪrɪ'mɪsəbəl] *a.* irremisible, imperdonable; obligatorio.
irremissibly [-blɪ] *adv.* irremisiblemente; obligatoriamente.
irremovability [ˌɪrɪˌmuvə'bɪlətɪ] *s.* inamovilidad.
irremovable [-'muvəbəl] *a.* inamovible, que no puede ser privado de su cargo; inmutable.
irremovably [-blɪ] *adv.* de modo inamovible.
irreparability [ɪˌrɛpərə'bɪlətɪ] *s.* calidad de irreparable.
irreparable [ɪ'rɛpərəbəl] *a.* irreparable; irrecuperable; irremediable.
irreparably [-blɪ] *adv.* irreparablemente.
irrepealable [ˌɪrɪ'piləbəl] *a.* irrevocable, que no se puede abrogar.
irreplaceable [-'pleɪsəbəl] *a.* irreemplazable, irremplazable, insustituible.
irrepressibility [-ˌprɛsə'bɪlətɪ] *s.* espíritu irreprimible; temperamento irrefrenable, incontrolable, indomable.
irrepressible [-'prɛsəbəl] *a.* irreprimible, irrefrenable, indomable, incontrolable.
irrepressibly [-blɪ] *adv.* de modo irreprimible.
irreproachable [ˌɪrɪ'proʊtʃəbəl] *a.* irreprochable, irreprensible, intachable, incensurable.
irreproachably [-blɪ] *adv.* irreprochablemente.
irresistibility [ˌɪrəˌzɪstə'bɪlətɪ] *s.* calidad de irresistible.
irresistible [-'zɪstəbəl] *a.* irresistible.
irresistibleness [-nəs] *s.* calidad de irresistible.
irresistibly [-blɪ] *adv.* irresistiblemente.
irresoluble [ˌɪrɪ'zɑljəbəl, B ɪ'rɛzəljʊ-] *a.* irresoluble, insoluble, indisoluble.
irresolute [ɪ'rɛzəˌlut] *a.* irresoluto, indeciso, vacilante.
irresolutely [-lɪ] *adv.* de modo irresoluto.
irresoluteness [-nəs] *s.* irresolución, indecisión, vacilación.
irresolution [ɪˌrɛzə'luʃən] *s.* irresolución, indecisión, vacilación, duda.
irresolvable [ˌɪrɪ'zɑlvəbəl, B -'zɔlv-] *a.* irresoluble, insoluble; que no puede descomponerse.
irrespective [-'spɛktɪv] *a.* (raro) inconsiderado; **i. of,** sin consideración a (algo o alguien), prescindiendo de (algo o alguien), sin tener en cuenta.
irrespectively [-lɪ] *adv.* sin tomar en cuenta, sin tomar en consideración.
irrespirable [ɪ'rɛspərəbəl, ˌɪrɪ'spaɪr-] *a.* irrespirable.
irresponsibility [ˌɪrɪˌspɑnsə'bɪlətɪ, B -ˌspɔn-] *s.* irresponsabilidad.
irresponsible [-'spɑnsəbəl, B -'spɔn-] *a.* irresponsable; insolvente. —*s.* persona irresponsable.
irresponsibleness [-nəs] *s.* irresponsabilidad.
irresponsibly [-blɪ] *adv.* irresponsablemente, de modo o manera irresponsable.
irresponsive [-sɪv] *a.* que no responde, insensible; **to be i. to,** no responder a (tratamiento, etc.).
irresponsiveness [-nəs] *s.* falta de correspondencia, insensibilidad.
irretentive [ˌɪrɪ'tɛntɪv] *a.* no retentivo, que no retiene en la mente, desmemoriado.
irretraceable [-'treɪsəbəl] *a.* que no se puede desandar (camino o huella); que no se puede repasar (un trazado).
irretrievable [-'trivəbəl] *a.* irrecuperable, irreparable, incobrable.
irretrievably [-blɪ] *adv.* irreparablemente, irrecuperablemente.
irreverence [ɪ'rɛvərəns] *s.* irreverencia, falta de respeto, desacato.
irreverent [-ənt] *a.* irreverente, irrespetuoso; desatento.
irreverently [-lɪ] *adv.* irreverentemente.
irreversibility [ˌɪrɪˌvɜrsə'bɪlətɪ, B -ˌvɜsə-] *s.* inalterabilidad, invariabilidad.
irreversible [-'vɜrsəbəl, B -'vɜsə-] *a.* que no se puede volver atrás; irrevocable, inalterable, invariable.
irreversibly [-blɪ] *adv.* irrevocablemente, inalterablemente.
irrevocability [ɪˌrɛvəkə'bɪlətɪ] *s.* irrevocabilidad.
irrevocable [ɪ'rɛvəkəbəl] *a.* irrevocable; inapelable; inalterable, invariable.
irrevocableness [-nəs] *s.* irrevocabilidad.
irrevocably [-blɪ] *adv.* irrevocablemente.
irrigable ['ɪrəgəbəl] *a.* de regadío (terreno).
irrigate [-ˌgeɪt] *v.t.* 1. regar, mojar, humedecer. 2. (med.) irrigar.
irrigation [ˌɪrə'geɪʃən] *s.* 1. riego. 2. (med.) irrigación.
irrigational [-əl] *a.* 1. de riego (método, etc.). 2. (med.) de (la) irrigación.
irrigator ['ɪrəˌgeɪtər, B -ə] *s.* 1. regador (persona). 2. aparato para regar, regadera. 3. (med.) irrigador.
irriguous [ɪ'rɪgjʊəs] *a.* 1. (ant.) bien regado. 2. (que sirve) para regar.
irritability [ˌɪrətə'bɪlətɪ] *s.* 1. irritabilidad, impaciencia, mal genio, desasosiego. 2. (med., fisiol.) irritabilidad.
irritable ['ɪrətəbəl] *a.* 1. irritable, excitable. 2. (med., fisiol.) irritable.
irritableness [-nəs] *s.* irritabilidad; (med., fisiol.) irritabilidad.
irritably [-blɪ] *adv.* de modo irritable, con irritación.
irritancy ['ɪrətənsɪ] *s.* carácter o aspecto irritante.
irritant [-tənt] *a.* irritador, irritante. —*s.* 1. circunstancia irritante, motivo de irritación. 2. (med.) sustancia irritante. 3. (der.) irritante.
irritate [-ˌteɪt] *v.t.* 1. irritar, exacerbar, exasperar, encolerizar, enfadar, enojar. 2. (fisiol.) irritar. 3. (der.) irritar, anular.
irritated [-əd] *a.* 1. (fisiol.) irritado. 2. irritado, enfadado.
irritating [-ɪŋ] *a.* irritante, fastidioso, enojoso.
irritatingly [-lɪ] *adv.* de modo fastidioso, enojosamente, molestamente.
irritation [ˌɪrə'teɪʃən] *s.* 1. irritación, exasperación; molestia; ira, cólera, enojo, enfado. 2. (med.) irritación.
irritative ['ɪrəˌteɪtɪv] *a.* 1. irritador. 2. (med.) irritante.
irrupt [ɪ'rʌpt] *v.i.* 1. irrumpir; invadir. 2. (zool.) proliferar súbitamente (una especie animal).
irruption [ɪ'rʌpʃən] *s.* irrupción; invasión.
irruptive [-tɪv] *a.* 1. que irrumpe; invasor. 2. (geol.) intrusivo, plutónico (díc. de rocas ígneas).
IRS *abrev. de* **Internal Revenue Service,** Superintendencia de Contribuciones.
is [ɪz] *tercera pers. sing. del pres. de indic. de* **to be.**
is. *abrev. de* **island, isle,** isla.
isabelita [ˌɪzəbə'litə] *s.* (ict.) isabelita, especie de pez, común en las Antillas.
Isabella [ˌɪzə'bɛlə] *s.* Isabel I de España, la Católica; Isabel II de España.
isabelline [ˌɪzə'bɛlən, -ˌlaɪn] *a.* isabelino, de color pardo amarillento.
isacoustic [ˌaɪsə'kustɪk] *a.* de una misma intensidad (díc. del sonido).
isagoge ['aɪsəˌgoudʒɪ] *s.* isagoge, introducción, exordio.
isagogic [ˌaɪsə'gɑdʒɪk, B -'gɔdʒ-] *a.* isagógico, introductor. —*s. pl.* introduccíon a la exégesis; estudio crítico literario de la Biblia.
isallobar [aɪ'sæləˌbɑr, B -ˌbɑ] *s.* (meteor.) isalobara.
isatin ['aɪsətən] *s.* (quím.) isatina.
isba, izba [ɪz'bɑ, B 'ɪzˌbɑ] *s.* isba (vivienda rusa de madera con techo de paja).
Iscariot [ɪs'kɛrɪət, B -'kær-] *s.* (bíbl.) Iscariote (Judas).
ischemia, ischaemia [ɪs'kimɪə] *s.* (med.) isquemia, anemia local.
ischemic [-mɪk] *a.* (med.) isquémico.
ischiadic [ˌɪskɪ'ædɪk] **ischiatic** [-'æt-] **ischial** ['ɪskɪəl] *a.* (anat.) isquiático.
ischium ['ɪskɪəm] *s.* (*pl.* ISCHIA [-ə]) (anat.) isquión.
Iseult [ɪ'sult, B i'zult] *s.* (lit., mús.) Iseo, Isolda, princesa de Irlanda, amante de Tristán.
Ishmaelite ['ɪʃmɪəˌlaɪt] *s.* 1. ismaelita, descendiente de Ismael. 2. paria.
Ishmaelitic [ˌɪʃmɪə'lɪtɪk] *a.* ismaelita.
Isiac ['aɪsɪˌæk] *a.* (mitol.) isíaco, relativo al culto de Isis, la diosa egipcia.
isinglass ['aɪzənˌglæs, B -zɪŋˌglɑs] *s.* 1. colapez, colapiscis, colapiz (Am.). 2. (min.) mica.
Islam [ɪs'lɑm, ɪz-, 'ɪsˌlɑm, B 'ɪz-] *s.* Islam (la cultura y el pueblo musulmanes).
Islamic [ɪs'læmɪk, -'lɑm-, ɪz-, B -'læm-] *a.* islámico, musulmán.
Islamism [-ˌɪzəm, B 'ɪzləmɪz-] *s.* 1. islamismo, las doctrinas religiosas y sociales del pueblo musulmán. 2. nacionalismo islámico.
Islamite ['ɪsləˌmaɪt, 'ɪz-, B 'ɪz-] *s.* islamita, musulmán, mahometano.
Islamitic [ˌɪslə'mɪtɪk, ˌɪz-, B ˌɪz-] *a.* islamita, de Islam, de los pueblos musulmanes.
island ['aɪlənd] *s.* 1. isla, ínsula. 2. isla o zona de seguridad (en la calle). 3. (anat.) isla. 4. (mar.) superestructura, puente (en el lado de estribor de un portaaviones). —*v.t.* 1. aislar. 2. hacer una isla de. 3. (fig.) salpicar, motear.
islander [-ləndər, B -də] *s.* isleño, insular.
island-hop ['aɪləndˌhɑp, B -ˌhɔp] *v.t.* saltar de isla en isla, viajar entre un grupo de islas.
island universe, (astr.) universo aislado, galaxia externa.
isle [aɪl] *s.* (poét.) isla; isleta. —*v.t.* convertir en isla; poner en una isla.
Isle of Pines, Isla de Pinos (adyacente a Cuba).
islet ['aɪlət] *s.* isleta.
ism ['ɪzəm] *s.* ismo (doctrina o práctica de determinados principios religiosos, filosóficos, literarios, morales, etc.).
isn't ['ɪzənt] *contr. de* **is not.**
isoagglutination [ˌaɪsoʊəˌglutən'eɪʃən] *s.* (med.) isoaglutinación.
isoagglutinin [-ənən] *s.* (med.) isoaglutinina.
isoalloxazine [-ə'lɑksəˌzin, B -'lɔk-] *s.* (bioquím.) isoaloxazina.

isoantibody [-'æntɪˌbɑdɪ, B -ˌbɔdɪ] *s.* (bioquím.) isoanticuerpo.

isobar ['aɪsəˌbɑr, B -soʊˌbɑ] *s.* 1. (meteor.) isobara. 2. (quím.) isobaro.

isobaric [ˌaɪsə'bærɪk] *a.* (meteor., quím.) isobárico.

isobath ['aɪsəˌbæθ, B -ˌbɑθ] *s.* isóbato.

isobutylene [ˌaɪsoʊ'bjutəlˌin] *s.* (quím.) butileno gaseoso.

isocheim ['aɪsəˌkaɪm] *s.* (geog.) línea isoquímena.

isocheimal [ˌaɪsə'kaɪməl] **isocheimenal** [-mənəl] *a.* (geog.) isoquímeno.

isochor, isochore ['aɪsəˌkɔr, B -ˌkɔ] *s.* (fís.) línea isocórica, curva isocora.

isochromatic [ˌaɪsəkroʊ'mætɪk] *a.* 1. (ópt.) isocromático, isocrómico. 2. (foto.) ortocromático.

isochronal [aɪ'sɑkrənəl, B -'sɔk-] **isochronous** [-rənəs] *a.* (fís.) isócrono, de igual duración, (que ocurre) a intervalos regulares.

isochronism [-ˌnɪzəm] *s.* (fís.) isocronismo.

isochroous [aɪ'sɑkroʊəs, B -'sɔk-] *a.* isocre, de color uniforme.

isoclinal [ˌaɪsə'klaɪnəl] *a.* 1. isoclino, isoclínico, inclinado en la misma dirección, de la misma dirección. 2. (geol.) isoclinal. —*s.* línea isóclina.

isocline ['aɪsəˌklaɪn] *s.* (geol.) pliegue isoclinal.

isoclinic [ˌaɪsə'klɪnɪk] *a.* (geol.) isoclinal.

isoclinic line, (fís.) línea isóclina.

isocracy [aɪ'sɑkrəsɪ, B -'sɔk-] *s.* sistema de gobierno en el cual todas las personas tienen el mismo poder político.

isocyanate [ˌaɪsoʊ'saɪəˌneɪt] *s.* (quím.) isocianato.

isodiametric [-ˌdaɪə'mɛtrɪk] *a.* isodiamétrico, de igual diámetro.

isodimorphism [-daɪ'mɔrˌfɪzəm, B -'mɔˌ-] *s.* isodimorfismo (cristales).

isodose ['aɪsəˌdoʊs] *a.* (fís. nuclear) isodósico.

isodynamic [ˌaɪsoʊdaɪ'næmɪk] *a.* (fís.) isodinámico.

isoelectric [-ɪ'lɛktrɪk] *a.* (fís.) isoeléctrico.

isoelectronic [-ɪˌlɛk'trɑnɪk, B -'trɔn-] *a.* (fís.) isoelectrónico (átomos).

isogamete [-gə'mit, -'gæmˌit] *s.* (biol.) isogameto.

isogamous [aɪ'sɑgəməs, B -'sɔg-] *a.* (biol.) isógamo.

isogamy [-mɪ] *s.* (biol.) isogamia (reproducción).

isogenous [-'sɑdʒənəs, B -'sɔdʒ-] *a.* (biol.) isógeno, del mismo origen, genéticamente uniforme.

isogeny [-nɪ] *s.* (biol.) isogenia, isogénesis.

isogloss ['aɪsəˌglɑs, -ˌglɔs, B -ˌglɔs] *s.* (filol.) isoglosa.

isogonic [ˌaɪsə'gɑnɪk, B -'gɔn-] **isogonal** [aɪ'sɑgənəl, B -'sɔg-] *a.* (fís.) isógono, isogónico (cristales).

isogonic line, (fís.) isógona, línea isogónica.

isogram ['aɪsəˌgræm] *s.* (meteor.) isograma.

isohyet [ˌaɪsoʊ'haɪət] *s.* (meteor.) isohieta, isoyeta.

isohyetal [-əl] *a.* (meteor.) isohieto, isoyetico.

isolate ['aɪsəˌleɪt, 'ɪsə-, B 'aɪsə-] *v.t.* 1. aislar, separar, apartar. 2. (quím., med.) aislar. 3. (med.) poner en cuarentena.

isolation [ˌaɪsə'leɪʃən, ˌɪsə-, B ˌaɪsə-] *s.* 1. aislamiento, separación, incomunicación. 2. (med.) aislamiento por cuarentena.

isolation booth, (rad., t.v.) cabina insonorizada.

isolationism [-ˌɪzəm] *s.* (pol.) aislacionismo.

isolationist [-əst] *s.* (pol.) partidario del aislamiento político.

isolator ['aɪsəˌleɪtər, B -ə] *s.* 1. aislador. 2. (elec.) seccionador; aislador. 3. material para absorber las vibraciones.

Isolde [ɪ'soʊldə, ɪ'zoʊl-, B ɪ'zɔl-] *var. de.* **Iseult.**

isoleucine [ˌaɪsə'luˌsɪn, B -sɪn] *s.* (bioquím.) isoleucina.

isoline ['aɪsəˌlaɪn] *s.* (meteor.) isograma.

isologous [aɪ'sɑləgəs, B -'sɔl-] *a.* (quím.) isólogo.

isomagnetic [ˌaɪsoʊmæg'nɛtɪk] *a.* isomagnético, de igual magnetismo. —*s.* (geog.) línea isomagnética.

isomer ['aɪsəmər, B -mə] *s.* (fís., quím.) isómero.

isomeric [ˌaɪsə'mɛrɪk] *a.* (fís., quím.) isómero.

isomerism [aɪ'sɑməˌrɪzəm, B -'sɔm-] *s.* 1. (quím.) isomería. 2. (quím., bot.) isomerismo.

isomerous [-rəs] *a.* (quím., bot.) isómero.

isometric [ˌaɪsə'mɛtrɪk] *a.* 1. isométrico, que tiene la misma medida. 2. (min.) cúbico. 3. (dib.) de perspectiva isométrica.

isometric exercises, ejercicios isométricos.

isometric line, línea isométrica.

isometropia [ˌaɪsoʊmɪ'troʊpɪə] *s.* (ópt.) isometropía.

isometry [aɪ'sɑmətrɪ, B -'sɔm-] *s.* 1. igualdad de medidas. 2. (geog.) igualdad de altura sobre el nivel del mar.

isomorph ['aɪsəˌmɔrf, B -ˌmɔf] *s.* (biol., quím., min.) cuerpo isomorfo; ser o grupo isomorfo.

isomorphic [ˌaɪsə'mɔrfɪk, B -'mɔfɪk] *a.* (biol., quím., min.) isomorfo, isomórfico.

isomorphism [-ˌfɪzəm] *s.* (quím., min., biol.) isomorfismo.

isomorphous [-fəs] *a.* (biol., quím., min.) isomorfo, isomórfico.

isoniazid [ˌaɪsə'naɪəzəd] *s.* (quím., med.) isoniacida.

isonomy [aɪ'sɑnəmɪ, B -'sɔn-] *s.* igualdad de derechos políticos, isonomía.

isoperimetric [ˌaɪsəˌpɛrə'mɛtrɪk] **isoperimetrical** [-trɪkəl] *a.* (geom.) isoperímetro, de igual perímetro.

isopleth ['aɪsəˌplɛθ] *s.* (cartografía) línea isopleta.

isopod [-ˌpɑd, B -ˌpɔd] *a., s.* (zool.) isópodo.

isopodous [aɪ'sɑpədəs, B -'sɔp-] *a.* (zool.) isópodo.

isoprene ['aɪsəˌprin] *s.* (quím.) isopreno.

isosceles [aɪ'sɑsəˌliz, B -'sɔs-] *a.* (geom.) isósceles.

isosceles triangle, (geom.) triángulo isósceles.

isoseismal [ˌaɪsə'saɪzməl] *a.* (geol.) isosísmico. —*s.* (geol.) línea isosísmica.

isosmotic [ˌaɪˌsɑs'mɑtɪk, B -ˌsɔs'mɔt-] *a.* (fisiol.) isosmótico, que ejerce igual presión.

isospore ['aɪsəˌspɔr, B -ˌspɔ] *s.* (biol., bot.) isospora.

isosporous [ˌaɪsə'spɔrəs, B aɪ'sɔspər-] *a.* (biol., bot.) isospóreo.

isostasy [aɪ'sɑstəsɪ, B -'sɔs-] *s.* (geol.) isostasia.

isostatic [ˌaɪsə'stætɪk] *a.* (fís., geol.) isostático.

isotheral [aɪ'sɑθərəl, B -'sɔθ-] *a.* (meteor.) isótero.

isothere ['aɪsəˌθɪr, B -ˌθɪə] *s.* (meteor.) línea isótera.

isotherm [-ˌθɜrm, B -ˌθɜm] *s.* (fís., meteor.) isoterma.

isothermal [ˌaɪsə'θɜrməl, B -'θɜm-] *a.* isotermo, isotérmico.

isothermal line, (fís., meteor.) (línea) isoterma, línea isotérmica.

isotone ['aɪsəˌtoʊn] *s.* (quím.) isótono.

isotonic [ˌaɪsə'tɑnɪk, B -'tɔn-] *a.* (bioquím., fís.) isotónico, isótono.

isotonicity [-toʊ'nɪsətɪ] *s.* (bioquím., quím., fís.) isotonicidad.

isotope ['aɪsəˌtoʊp] *s.* (quím., fís.) isótopo.

isotopic [ˌaɪsə'tɑpɪk, B -'tɔp-] *a.* (quím., fís.) isotópico.

isotopy ['aɪsəˌtoʊpɪ, B aɪ'sɔtə-] *s.* (fís., quím.) isotopía.

isotropic [ˌaɪsə'trɑpɪk, B -'trɔp-] **isotropous** [aɪ'sɑtrəpəs, B -'sɔt-] *a.* 1. (min.) isótropo (cristal). 2. (biol.) isotrópico (huevo).

isotropy [aɪ'sɑtrəpɪ, B -'sɔt-] *s.* (min., biol.) isotropía.

Israel ['ɪzrɪəl, B -reɪ-] *s.* Israel.

Israeli [ɪz'reɪlɪ] *a.* israelí. —*s.* (*pl.* ISRAELIS o ISRAELI) israelí, del Estado de Israel.

Israelite ['ɪzrɪəˌlaɪt] *a., s.* (bíbl.) israelita.

Israelitic [ˌɪzrɪə'lɪtɪk] *a.* israelítico.

issei ['i'seɪ] *s.* (*pl.* ISSEI o ISSEIS) (E.U.) inmigrante japonés.

issuable ['ɪʃʊəbəl] *a.* 1. emisible. 2. discutible, disputable; en litigio.

issuance [-əns] *s.* emisión, promulgación; publicación; distribución, entrega (de un título, etc.).

issuant [-ənt] *a.* saliente, emergente.

issue ['ɪʃu] *s.* 1. emisión, emergencia. 2. salida, escape, paso. 3. resultado, consecuencia, secuela. 4. progenie, prole, sucesión. 5. (*pl.*) ganancia, rédito, utilidad. 6. tema (de discusión), punto, cuestión, problema. 7. emisión (de bonos, moneda, sellos postales, decretos, etc.); entrega (de abastecimientos, material, etc.); publicación (de un libro, edición, etc.). 8. producto (de la imaginación). 9. número (de periódico, revista, etc.). 10. (impr.) tirada, edición. 11. (med.) salida, emisión, pérdida (ej., de sangre). 12. (ant.) acto, hecho, obra. 13. **at i.,** en discusión (problema, asunto, etc.); en desacuerdo (personas); **cause at i.,** (der.) causa por sentenciarse; **i. of fact,** (der.) cuestión de hecho; **i. of law,** (der.) cuestión de derecho; **to bring to an i.,** llevar a un punto decisivo; **to force the i.,** forzar la decisión, insistir en la solución del problema; **to join i. with (someone) on (something),** disputar (algo) con (alguien), ponerse a discutir (algo) con (alguien); **to make an i. of,** hacer de un asunto o persona tema de discusión o controversia; machacar con un tema; crear un problema sobre; **to put to the i.,** someter a decisión; **to raise the i. of,** plantear el problema de; **to take i. with,** oponerse a, disentir de, discrepar de; **without i.,** sin prole, sin sucesión. —*v.i.* 1. salir, brotar, fluir. 2. surgir, emerger, surtir. 3. (con *from*) descender (de), proceder (de). 4. (gen. con *from*) derivarse (de), emanar (de), originarse (en), resultar (de). 5. ser emitido, publicado o proclamado. 6. **to i. in,** resultar en. —*v.t.* 1. echar, arrojar, expedir. 2. entregar, dar; proveer (a alguien de algo). 3. emitir (bonos, moneda, sellos postales, decretos, etc.); extender, librar (cheque); impartir (instrucciones, una orden, etc.); publicar (libro, etc.); dictar, expedir (un auto).

issued [-d] *a.* fecho.

issuer [-ər, B -ə] *s.* emisor, dador, distribuidor; otorgante, expedidor (de un documento, etc.).

issuing bank [-ɪŋ-] (fin., com.) banco emisor.

Istanbul [ˌɪstæm'bul, -tæn-, -tɑn-, B -tæn-] *s.* Estambul, nombre actual de Constantinopla (ciudad y puerto de Turquía).

isthmian ['ɪsmɪən, B 'ɪsθ-] *a.* ístmico. —*s.* 1. istmeño. 2. **I.,** panameño, natural de Panamá.

Isthmian Games, (hist.) juegos ístmicos de la Grecia antigua, en honor de Poseidón.
isthmus ['ɪsməs] *s.* (*pl.* ISTHMUSES o ISTHMI [-maɪ]) (geog., anat., zool.) istmo.
istle ['ɪstlɪ] *s.* sisal, pita, henequén.
it [ɪt] *pron. neutro tercera pers. sing., nominativo y acusativo,* ello; lo, la; eso, esto. Se usa como: 1. pron. de cosas inanimadas, animales de sexo indeterminado y bebés, ej., *I have seen it often on this shelf,* lo he visto a menudo en este anaquel (un libro, etc.), *we saw how it happened,* vimos cómo sucedió (ello). 2. pron. demostrativo, ej., *what is it?* ¿qué es eso? 3. no se le traduce cuando es sujeto gramatical de verbos y frases impersonales, ej., *it rains,* llueve, *it is warm,* hace calor, *it is late,* es tarde, *it is four o'clock,* son las cuatro, *it is silly to laugh so loud,* es tonto reírse tan fuerte. 4. antecedente de pron. rel., ej., *it was a hat that he bought,* fue un sombrero lo que compró, *it is you that I am looking for,* es a Ud. a quien busco. 5. antecedente del sujeto postergado que se introduce con la conj. *that,* ej., *it is useless that you quarrel with me,* es inútil que Ud. riña conmigo. 6. objeto indefinido de verbos, ej., *to foot it,* ir a pie, *it seems you have done it,* parece que ha metido Ud. la pata, *to run for it,* escapar corriendo. —*s.* 1. (en juegos de niños) el que la lleva. 2. (fam.) colmo. último grado, ej., *for shameless lying you really are it,* como mentiroso desvergonzado Ud. es el colmo. 3. (fam., ant.) atracción sexual, un no sé qué.
itacolumite [ˌɪtə'kɑljəˌmaɪt, B -'kɔl-] *s.* (geol.) itacolumita.
itaconic acid [-'kɑnɪk-, B -'kɔn-] (quím.) ácido itacónico.
Ital. *abrev. de* **Italian,** italiano.
Italian [ɪ'tæljən] *a., s.* italiano.
Italianate [-ət, -ˌeɪt] *a.* 1. de forma, índole o apariencia italiana. 2. italianizado. — [-ˌeɪt] *v.t.* italianizar, dar carácter italiano a.
Italianism [-ˌɪzəm] *s.* italianismo.
Italianization [ɪˌtæljənə'zeɪʃən, B -naɪ-] *s.* italianización.
Italianize [ɪ'tæljəˌnaɪz] *v.i., v.t.* italianizar(se).
Italic [ɪ'tælɪk] *a.* 1. itálico 2. **i.,** (tip.) cursivo, bastardillo. —*s.* 1. (filol.) itálico. 2. (*pl.*) (tip.) letras cursivas, bastardillas.
Italicism [-əˌsɪzəm] *s.* italianismo.
italicize [-əˌsaɪz] *v.t.* 1. imprimir con letra cursiva, bastardilla o itálica. 2. subrayar (letras, palabras); (fig.) dar énfasis.
Italo-Hispanic pidgin [ɪ'tæləhɪs'pænɪk] *s.* cocoliche (Am.).
Italy ['ɪtəlɪ] *s.* Italia.
itch [ɪtʃ] *s.* 1. comezón, picazón, prurito. 2. sarna. 3. (fig.) prurito, comezón, inquietud. —*v.i.* 1. picar, sentir comezón o picazón. 2. desear vehementemente, tener prurito por. 3. **to have an itching palm,** gustarle a uno recibir propinas, estar listo a aceptar un soborno.
itch mite, (ento.) ácaro de la sarna, arador.
itchy ['ɪtʃɪ] *a.* (ITCHIER; ITCHIEST) 1. picante, hormigante. 2. sarnoso. 3. (jer.) ansioso, impaciente (por hacer algo).
item ['aɪtəm] *adv.* (ant.) ítem, otrosí, además, más. —*s.* 1. ítem, artículo, noticia, detalle. 2. párrafo; suelto; partida. 3. (ant.) insinuación, aviso, advertencia.
itemize [-ˌaɪz] *v.t.* (E.U.) detallar; especificar, particularizar, pormenorizar, circunstanciar.
iterant ['ɪtərənt] *a.* iterativo, reiterativo.
iterate [-ˌreɪt] *v.t.* iterar, repetir, reiterar.
iteration [ˌɪtə'reɪʃən] *s.* iteración, repetición, reiteración.
iterative ['ɪtəˌreɪtɪv, -rət-] *a.* iterativo; (gram.) frecuentativo, repetidor.
Ithaca ['ɪθəkə] *s.* Itaca, una de las islas Jónicas (pertenecientes a Grecia).
ithyphallic [ˌɪθɪ'fælɪk] *a.* 1. (poét.) itifálico. 2. p. ext. lascivo, obsceno.
itineracy [aɪ'tɪnərəsɪ, ɪ-] **itinerancy** [-rənsɪ] *s.* peregrinación; viaje incesante; cambio frecuente de residencia.
itinerant [-rənt] *a.* ambulante, errante, viajero. —*s.* viandante.
itinerantly [-lɪ] *adv.* ambulantemente, errantemente.
itinerary [-ˌrɛrɪ, B -rərɪ] *a.* itinerario. —*s.* (*pl.* ITINERARIES) 1. itinerario, ruta. 2. relación de un viaje. 3. itinerario, guía de viajeros.
itinerate [-ˌreɪt] *v.t.* seguir una ruta o itinerario, visitar un distrito (predicando, etc.).
it'll ['ɪtəl] *contr. de* **it will.**
its [ɪts] *a. pos. neutro* su(s).
it's [ɪts] *contr. de* **it is** o **it has.**
itself [ɪt'sɛlf] *pron. de la tercera pers. del sing., forma enfática y reflexiva.* 1. mismo; él mismo, ella misma. 2. sí mismo, se, ej., *the baby hurt i.,* el bebé se lastimó a sí mismo. 3. de sí, de suyo, ej., *it is beautiful i.,* es hermoso por sí mismo. 4. solo, ej., *the frame i. is worth ten dollars,* el marco solo vale diez dólares. 5. **by i.,** solo; separado; **he is honesty i.,** es la honradez personificada.
itty-bitty ['ɪti'bɪti] *as.* (fam.) chiquitito, chiquitín, pequeñito.
I've [aɪv] (fam.) *contr. de* **I have.**
ivied ['aɪvid] *a.* cubierto de hiedra.
ivory ['aɪvərɪ] *s.* 1. marfil. 2. color del marfil; blancura (ej., de la tez). 3. colmillo (esp. de elefante). 4. (*pl.*) (jer.) dados; teclas (de piano); bolas de billar. 5. (*pl.*) (jer.) dientes. —*a.* marfileño, ebúrneo.
ivory black, negro de marfil (pigmento muy valioso que se obtiene del marfil tostado).
Ivory Coast, Costa de Marfil, república del África occidental.
ivory nut, (bot.) nuez de tagua, marfil vegetal.
ivory palm, (bot.) tagua.
ivory tower, (fig.) torre de marfil.
ivy ['aɪvɪ] *s.* (bot.) hiedra.
Ivy League, grupo de universidades en el noroeste de E.U., famosas por su prestigio académico y social.
iwis [ɪ'wɪs] *adv.* (ant.) ciertamente.
IWW *abrev. de* **Industrial Workers of the World,** Trabajadores Industriales del Mundo.
ixtle [ɪkstlɪ, B 'ɪst-] *var. de* **istle.**
izard [ɪzərd, B 'ɪzəd] *s.* (zool.) gamuza, especie de antílope.
izzard ['ɪzərd, B -əd] *s.* (dial.) la letra z; **from a to i.,** de cabo a rabo, completamente.

J

J [dʒeɪ] *s.* j, décima letra del alfabeto inglés.

J.A. *abrev. de* **Judge Advocate,** auditor, auditor de guerra.

jab [dʒæb] *v.t., v.i.* (*pret., p.p.* JABBED; *p.pr.* JABBING) pinchar, punzar, herir con arma blanca; **j. into,** hundir (puñal, dedo, etc.) de golpe en. —*s.* 1. punzada, pinchazo; estocada, puntazo. 2. (boxeo) golpe corto.

jabber ['dʒæbər, B -ə] *v.i.* parlotear, paliquear, barbullar. —*v.t.* farfullar, mascullar. —*s.* barbulla, jerigonza, guirigay.

jabberer [-ərər, B -ərə] *s.* farfullero, farfullador, parlanchín.

jabberwocky ['dʒæbərˌwɑkɪ, B -əˌwɔkɪ] *s.* jerigonza, guirigay.

jabiru [ˌdʒæbə'ru, B 'dʒæbɪˌru] *s.* (orn.) jabirú.

jaborandi [ˌdʒæbə'rændɪ] *s.* 1. (bot.) jaborandi. 2. (farm.) hojas (secas) del jaborandi.

jabot [ʒæ'boʊ, dʒæ-, B 'ʒæboʊ] *s.* (cost.) chorrera (cuello de encaje).

jaboticaba [dʒəˌbutɪ'kɑbə, B -ˌbɔt-] *s.* (bot.) jaboticaba.

jacamar ['dʒækəˌmɑr, B -ˌmɑ] *s.* (orn.) jacamara, jacamar.

jacana [ˌjæsən'æn, ˌʒɑsə'nɑ, B hɑ'kɑna] *s.* (orn.) jacana.

jacaranda [ˌdʒæke'rændə] *s.* (bot.) jacarandá.

jacinth [ˌdʒeɪsənθ, 'dʒæs-] *s.* 1. (min.) jacinto. 2. color (de) jacinto, (color) anaranjado claro.

jack [dʒæk] *s.* 1. (mec.) gato, cric. 2. sacabotas. 3. torno de asador. 4. marinero. 5. criador, jornalero. 6. boliche (en juego de bochas). 7. cantillo. 8. asno, burro. 9. (ict.) lucio (esp. pequeño). 10. (elec.) enchufe hembra. 11. (mar.) bandera de proa; bandera de señales. 12. (naipes) sota; (bridge) valet. 13. (jer.) mosca, plata, dinero. 14. aguardiente de fruta. 15. **every man j.,** todos sin excepción, hasta el último hombre. —*v.t.* (**ú.** gen. con *up*) 1. alzar con un gato, soliviar con un cric. 2. subir, aumentar (precios, etc.). 3. (fig.) elevar el nivel de, mejorar. 4. (fig.) edificar. 5. sermonear. —*v.i.* pescar con farol, cazar con antorcha.

jack, *s.* 1. cota de malla, esp. de cuero. 2. (ant.) odre, bota, boto, borracha, cuero, corambre. 3. (bot.) nanjea.

Jack, *s.* tipo, tío; compadre, amigo; **hey, J.!** ¡oiga amigo!

jack-a-dandy [ˌdʒækə'dændɪ] *s.* petimetre, sujeto vanidoso.

jackal ['dʒækəl, B -ɔl] *s.* 1. (zool.) chacal, adive, adiva. 2. (fig.) chacal, persona mercenaria, paniaguado.

Jack-a-Lent ['dʒækəˌlɛnt] *s.* 1. muñeco de trapo (al que se tira piedras por diversión). 2. simplón; nulidad, persona insignificante.

jackanapes [-ˌneɪps] *s.* 1. pisaverde, mequetrefe; persona engreída e impertinente. 2. (ant.) mono, simio.

jackaroo [ˌdʒækə'ru, B 'dʒækəˌru] *s.* (fam., Aust.) aprendiz, principiante.

jackass ['dʒækˌæs] *s.* 1. (zool.) asno, burro, borrico, garañón. 2. [B-ˌɑs] (fig.) asno, tonto, necio, imbécil.

jackassery [-ərɪ] *s.* estupidez, disparate, acto torpe.

jackboot [-ˌbut] *s.* bota fuerte (que pasa de la rodilla), bota de agua.

jackdaw [-ˌdɔ] *s.* (orn.) corneja, chova, grajo.

jacket ['dʒækət] *s.* 1. chaqueta, saco, jubón. 2. (E.U.) envoltura o forro (de un disco). 3. forro metálico, envoltura metálica (que cubre una bala de plomo). 4. (mec.) chaqueta, cubierta (de un cilindro). 5. sobrecubierta (de un libro). 6. piel, cáscara (de ciertos frutos como mango, naranja, banana, patata, etc.). 7. **to dust one's j.,** calentarle a uno las costillas, darle a uno una paliza. —*v.t.* poner una chaqueta, forro o cubierta a.

Jack Frost, (personificación del) tiempo frío.

jackfruit ['dʒækˌfrut] *s.* (bot.) nanjea.

jackhammer [-ˌhæmər, B -ə] *s.* 1. perforadora de mano, martillo perforador. 2. martillo neumático.

jack-in-office [-ən'ɔfəs, -'ɑf-, B -'ɔf-] *s.* (*pl.* JACKS-IN-OFFICE) oficial meticuloso (que da excesiva importancia a cosas insignificantes).

jack-in-the-box [-ðəˌbɑks, B -ˌbɔks] *s.* (*pl.* JACK-IN-THE-BOXES) muñeco de resorte en caja de sorpresa.

jack-in-the-pulpit [ˌdʒækənðə'pulpɪt] *s.* (*pl.* JACK-IN-THE-PULPITS) (bot.) arisema.

Jack Ketch, (G.B.) verdugo.

jackknife ['dʒækˌnaɪf] *s.* 1. navaja de bolsillo, navaja sevillana. 2. (natación) salto de carpa (que se ejecuta tocándose los pies antes de dar en el agua). —*v.t.* cortar con una navaja grande de bolsillo. —*v.i.* doblarse en el medio como en un salto de carpa; agacharse.

jackleg [-ˌlɛg] *s.* (fam.) aficionado. —*a.* 1. inescrupuloso, embustero. 2. improvisado, provisional, interino.

jacklight [-ˌlaɪt] *s.* antorcha o farol que se usa para pescar o cazar de noche.

jack-of-all-trades [ˌdʒækəv'ɔlˌtreɪdz] *s.* factótum, persona de muchas aptitudes.

jack-o'lantern ['dʒækəˌlæntərn, B -ən] *s.* (*pl.* JACK-O'-LANTERNS) 1. fuego fatuo; ilusión, quimera. 2. linterna hecha de una calabaza (cortada para imitar una cara humana, con una vela adentro).

jack plane, (carp.) garlopa, cepillo desbastador.

jackpot [-ˌpɑt, B -ˌpɔt] *s.* (póquer) puesta acumulada (para ganar la cual es necesario abrir juego por lo menos con un par de sotas); **to hit the j.,** (jer.) sacarse el premio gordo; (fig.) tener un éxito espectacular.

jack pudding, (G.B.) bufón, payaso.

jack rabbit, (zool.) liebre grande norte-americana.

jack rafter, (arq.) viga pequeña (en un techo a cuatro vertientes).

jackscrew ['dʒækˌskru] *s.* (mec.) gato de tornillo.

jackshaft [-ˌʃæft, B -ˌʃɑft] *s.* (aut.) contraeje, eje intermediario.

jacksnipe [-ˌsnɑɪp] *s.* (orn.) becada de los pantanos; gallineta de Guinea.

jack-spaniard [-ˌspænjərd, B -jəd] *s.* (ento.) camoatí.

jackstay [-ˌsteɪ] *s.* (mar.) nervio de envergue; estay de unión.

jackstone [-ˌstoʊn] *s.* 1. cantillo, taba, pito, taquín. 2. (*pl.*) cantillos, taba (juego).

jackstraw [-ˌstrɔ] *s.* 1. muñeco de paja, espantapájaros. 2. hombre insignificante. 3. (*pl.*) palitos chinos (juego).

jack-tar [-'tɑr, B -'tɑ] *s.* (fam.) marinero.

Jack the Ripper, (crim.) el destripador de Londres, Jack el Destripador.

jack towel, toalla sin fin, toalla que gira entre dos rollos.

Jacob ['dʒeɪkəb] *s.* (bíbl.) Jacob.

Jacobean [ˌdʒækə'biən] *a.* de Jacobo, jacobino (con ref. a Jacobo I, rey de Inglaterra). —*s.* escritor o estadista de la época de Jacobo I.

Jacobean architecture, arquitectura jacobina.

Jacobean lily, (bot.) flor de lis.

Jacobin ['dʒækəbən] *s.* 1. dominico. 2. (pol.) jacobino, p. ext., radical violento, demagogo. 3. **j.,** (orn.) jacobino, capuchino de cabeza negra.

Jacobinic [ˌdʒækə'bɪnɪk] **Jacobinical** [-ɪkəl] *a.* jacobínico; radical, demagógico.

Jacobinism ['dʒækəbəˌnɪzəm] *s.* 1. jacobinismo; radicalismo violento. 2. idea o carácter jacobínico.

Jacobite [-ˌbaɪt] *s.* (hist. G.B.) jacobita (partidario de la restauración de los Estuardos).

Jacobitical [ˌdʒækə'bɪtɪkəl] *a.* (hist.) jacobita.

Jacobitism ['dʒækəˌbaɪtˌɪzəm] *s.* (hist. G.B.) jacobitismo (partido legitimista que apoyó a Jacobo II).

Jacob's ladder, 1. (bíbl.) escalera de Jacob. 2. (bot.) polemonio (de flores azules). 3. (mar.) escala de gato, escala de jarcias, escala de viento.

jacobus [dʒə'koʊbəs] *s.* (hist.) moneda de oro (de 20 chelines del tiempo de Jacobo I de Ingl.).

jaconet ['dʒækəˌnet, B -nɪt] *s.* (tej.) chaconada, tela de algodón.

jacquard loom ['dʒækˌɑrd-, B -ˌɑd-] (tej.) jacquard, telar de Jacquard.

jacqueminot ['dʒækməˌnoʊ] *s.* (bot.) rosa perenne de color carmesí.

Jacquerie [ʒɑ'krɪ, B -kə'ri] *s.* 1. (hist.) revuelta de los campesinos franceses de 1358. 2. **j.,** cualquier revuelta de campesinos.

jactation [dʒæk'teɪʃən] *s.* 1. (med.) jactación, jactitación extrema. 2. jactancia, fanfarronería.

jactitation [ˌdʒæktə'teɪʃən] *s.* 1. (med.) jactitación, jactación. 2. (der.) jactancia; demanda o pretensión falsas. 3. (ant.) jactancia.

jaculate ['dʒækjəˌleɪt] *v.t., v.i.* lanzar, arrojar, tirar.

jaculation [ˌdʒækjə'leɪʃən] *s.* (ant.) lanzamiento.

jaculatory ['dʒækjələˌtɔrɪ, B -tərɪ] *a.* jaculatorio; disparado.

jaculatory prayer, (relig.) jaculatoria, fervorín.

Jacuzzi [dʒə'kuzi] *s.* Jacuzzi (marca de fábrica), baño de burbujas.

jade [dʒeɪd] *s.* 1. (min.) jade. 2. color verde jade. 3. jamelgo, rocín. 4. mujerzuela. —*v.t.* 1. cansar, agotar. 2. hastiar, ahitar. —*v.i.* cansarse.

jaded ['dʒeɪdəd] *a.* 1. cansado, agotado; rendido. 2. saciado, ahíto.
jade-green ['dʒeɪd,grin] *a.* de color verde jade.
jadeite ['dʒeɪdaɪt] *s.* (min.) jadeíta.
jadish ['dʒeɪdɪʃ] *a.* impúdica, licenciosa (mujer).
jaeger ['jeɪgər, B -gə] *s.* 1. cazador. 2. (*pl.*) (G.B.) calzoncillos largos de lana. 3. (orn.) gaviota de rapiña, skua.
jag [dʒæg] *s.* punta saliente, punta; diente, mella, muesca. —*v.t.* (*pret., p.p.* JAGGED; *p.pr.* JAGGING) 1. dentar, mellar. 2. (dial.) punzar, picar, pinchar.
jag, *s.* 1. (dial.) carga pequeña (de heno, etc.). 2. (jer.) borrachera, turca, mona; francachela, juerga; **to have a j. on,** (jer.) estar mamado, borracho.
jagged ['dʒægəd] *a.* dentado, mellado, serrado.
jaggedly [-lɪ] *adv.* en forma cerrada o intermitente.
jaggedness [-nəs] *s.* melladura.
jaggery ['dʒægərɪ] *s.* azúcar castaña de las Indias Orientales (extraída de la savia de la palmera).
jaggy ['dʒægɪ] *a.* (JAGGIER; JAGGIEST) mellado, dentellado, serrado.
jaguar ['dʒæg,wɑr, -jə,wɑr, B -jʊə] *s.* (zool.) jaguar.
jaguarundi [,dʒægwə'rʌndɪ] *s.* (zool.) yaguarundí, yaguareté.
jai alai ['haɪ,laɪ, ,haɪə'laɪ] jai alai, frontón (juego de pelota vasca).
jail [dʒeɪl] *s.* cárcel, prisión, calabozo, peni (Am.). —*v.t.* encarcelar, aprisionar.
jailbait ['dʒeɪlbeɪt] *s.* (fam.) chica menor de edad, con quien constituye delito tener relaciones sexuales.
jailbird ['dʒeɪl,bɜrd, B -,bɜd] *s.* (fam.) presidiario; criminal, malhechor.
jailbreak [-,breɪk] *s.* fuga de una prisión.
jail delivery, 1. liberación forzosa de prisioneros. 2. traslado de todos los presos (de una cárcel) a los tribunales (para ser juzgados).
jailer, jailor ['dʒeɪlər, B -lə] *s.* carcelero.
Jain [dʒaɪn] **Jaina** ['dʒaɪnə] *s.* (filos.) jaina, yaina (miembro del jainismo).
Jainism ['dʒaɪ,nɪzəm] *s.* (filos.) jainismo, yainismo (doctrina afín al budismo en la India).
Jakarta [dʒə'kɑrtə, B -'kɑtə] *s.* Yakarta, capital de Indonesia.
jake [dʒeɪk] *a.* (jer.) 1. correcto, perfecto. 2. arreglado.
jake leg, (jer.) parálisis alcohólica.
jalap ['dʒæləp] *s.* 1. (bot.) jalapa, mechoacán negro. 2. raíz de jalapa.
jalapin ['dʒæləpən] *s.* (quím.) jalapina.
jalopy [dʒə'lɑpɪ, B -'lɔpɪ] *s.* (*pl.* JALOPIES) (jer.) automóvil o avión destartalado.
jalousie ['dʒæləsi, B 'ʒælʊzi] *s.* (fr.) celosía, persiana, enrejado.
jam [dʒæm] *v.t.* (*pret., p.p.* JAMMED; *p.pr.* JAMMING) 1. apretar, estrujar. 2. apiñar, apretujar; llenar por completo, atestar (sala, etc.). 3. machucar, magullar (ej., la mano, un dedo, etc.). 4. obstruir, atorar, atascar (parte movible de una máquina). 5. (rad.) perturbar (una transmisión con señales interferentes). 6. **j. on the brakes,** dar un frenazo brusco. —*v.i.* 1. atorarse, atascarse; fijarse, quedar acuñado. 2. (mús.) participar en una sesión de música de jazz. —*s.* 1. estrujadura, estrujamiento, apretura. 2. apiñadura. 3. embotellamiento (de vehículos, etc.). 4. machucadura, machucamiento. 5. atascamiento, atoramiento. 6. (fam.) aprieto, lío, embrollo, enredo.
jam, *s.* 1. mermelada, confitura. 2. (jer., G.B.) delicia, deleite, algo delicioso.
Jamaica [dʒə'meɪkə] *s.* Jamaica.
Jamaica dogwood, (bot.) matasarna.
Jamaica ginger, 1. extracto (alcohólico) de jengibre. 2. polvo de jengibre (usado como infusión medicinal).
Jamaican [-kən] *a., s.* jamaicano, jamaiquino (Amer.), de Jamaica.
jamb [dʒæm] *s.* (arq.) jamba, quicial.
jambalaya [,dʒʌmbə'laɪə] *s.* 1. (cocina) paella de Luisiana. 2. (fig.) mezcolanza.
jambeau ['dʒæmboʊ] *s.* (fr.) (*pl.* JAMBEAUX [-boʊz]) (arm.) canillera, greba, espinillera.
jambo [-boʊ] *s.* (bot.) yambo.
jamboree [,dʒæmbə'ri] *s.* 1. reunión internacional de muchachos exploradores. 2. (jer.) jolgorio, francachela.
jam nut, contratuerca, tuerca de seguridad.
jam packed, repleto, hasta el tope.
jam session, (mús.) sesión de jazz improvisado; sesión de músicos que se reúnen para tocar por placer propio.
jam weld, soldadura de tope.
Jan. *abrev. de* **January,** enero (ene.).
jane [dʒeɪn] *s.* (jer.) muchacha; mujer joven.
Jane Doe ['dʒeɪn'doʊ] *s.* Fulana de Tal (nombre ficticio que substituye al verdadero cuando éste se desconoce).
jangle ['dʒæŋgəl] *v.i.* 1. cencerrear, sonar de manera discordante. 2. reñir, altercar. 3. (ant.) parlotear, cotorrear. —*v.t.* 1. hacer cencerrear. 2. dejar oír entre cencerreos. 3. irritar, crispar. —*s.* 1. sonido discordante, cencerreo. 2. parloteo, cháchara. 3. disputa, querella o riña ruidosas.
Janiculum [dʒə'nɪkjələm] *s.* Janículo (una de las colinas de Roma).
janissary ['dʒænə,serɪ, B -sərɪ] **janizary** [-,zerɪ, B -zərɪ] *s.* (hist.) 1. jenízaro (soldado de la guardia del sultán en Turquía). 2. partidario leal.
janitor ['dʒænətər, B -ə] *s.* 1. portero. 2. (E.U.) conserje (encargado del cuidado de un edificio).
janitorial [,dʒænə'tɔrɪəl] *a.* del conserje.
janitress ['dʒænətrəs] *s.* portera.
Jansenism ['dʒænsə,nɪzəm] *s.* (teo.) jansenismo.
Jansenist [-nəst] *s.* (teo.) jansenista.
Jansenistic [,dʒænsə'nɪstɪk] *a.* (teo.) jansenista.
January ['dʒænjʊ,erɪ, B -ərɪ] *s.* enero.
Janus ['dʒeɪnəs] *s.* (mitol.) Jano, dios de dos caras que veía el pasado y el porvenir.
Janus-faced [-,feɪst] *a.* de dos caras, falso, traidor.
Jap [dʒæp] *a., s.* (despec., jer.) japonés.
japan [dʒə'pæn] *s.* laca o barniz japonés; charol; obra charolada o de laca de estilo japonés. —*v.t.* (*pret., p.p.* JAPANNED; *p.pr.* JAPANNING) charolar con laca japonesa, aplicar laca japonesa a; laquear. —*a.* charolado, de laca.
Japan, *s.* el Japón.
Japanese [,dʒæpə'niz] *s.* 1. (*pl.* JAPANESE) japonés, nativo del Japón. 2. (idioma) japonés. —*a.* japonés.
Japanese beetle, (ento.) escarabajo japonés (que ataca los cultivos).
Japanese ivy, (bot.) higuera trepadora, hiedra.
Japanese lantern, linterna china o veneciana, farolito de papel.
Japanese pagoda tree, (bot.) sófora.
Japanese paper, papel japonés, papel de Japón (papel preparado a mano, de la corteza interior de la morera).
Japanese persimmon, (bot.) caqui.
Japanese quince, (bot.) camelia japonesa; membrillo japonés.
Japan globeflower, (bot.) mosqueta.
Japanize ['dʒæpə,naɪz] *v.t.* 1. dar carácter japonés a. 2. extender la influencia del Japón.
jape [dʒeɪp] *v.i.* bromear; burlarse, mofarse. —*v.t.* engañar, ridiculizar, mofar, burlarse de. —*s.* 1. broma; broma pesada, truco. 2. burla, mofa.
japer ['dʒeɪpər, B -pə] *s.* burlón.
japonica [dʒə'pɑnɪkə, B -'pɔn-] *s.* (bot.) 1. camelia japonesa. 2. membrillo japonés; membrillero japonés.
jar [dʒɑr, B dʒɑ] *s.* 1. tarro, jarra, pote, cántaro, tinaja. 2. (ant.) vuelta. 3. **on the j.,** entornado; entreabierto.
jar, *v.i.* (*pret.* y *p.p.* JARRED; *p.pr.* JARRING) 1. sonar con ruido desagradable, ser discordante. 2. sacudirse, vibrar. 3. desavenirse. 4. tener efecto desagradable. 5. **j. on** (o **upon**), irritar (nervios, oído, etc.); **j. with,** discrepar (de), divergir (de), discordar (con). —*v.t.* 1. sacudir, agitar, estremecer, hacer vibrar. 2. chocar, disgustar. —*s.* 1. estridor. 2. sacudida, estremecimiento. 3. discordia, pendencia, riña, choque. 4. (fig.) choque, sacudida; sobresalto.
jardiniere [,dʒɑrdən'ɪr, B ,ʒɑdɪ'njɛə] *s.* (fr.) 1. jardinera, florero. 2. tiesto, maceta grande de flores.
jargon ['dʒɑrgən, B 'dʒɑgən] *s.* jerga, jerigonza; vocabulario especial de ciertas profesiones o grupos sociales. —*v.i.* hablar jerigonza; hablar de modo ininteligible.
jargon [dʒɑr'gɑn, B 'dʒɑgən] *var. de* **jargoon.**
jargonize ['dʒɑrgə,naɪz, B 'dʒɑgə-] *v.i.* hablar jerga. —*v.t.* convertir en jerga.
jargoon [dʒɑr'gun, B dʒɑ'-] *s.* (min.) jergón, tipo de zircón opaco.
jarl [jɑrl, B jɑl] *s.* (hist.) jefe, capitán nórdico (que sigue en rango al rey).
jarosite ['dʒærə,saɪt] *s.* (min.) jarosita.
jarvey ['dʒɑrvɪ, B 'dʒɑvɪ] *s.* (*pl.* JARVEYS) 1. (G.B.) cochero de un coche o carruaje alquilado o de un tílburi irlandés. 2. (ant.) coche de alquiler.
jasmine ['dʒæzmən, B 'dʒæs-] *s.* (bot.) jazmín; jazmín amarillo, jazmín de Carolina, gelsemio.
Jason ['dʒeɪsən] *s.* (mitol.) Jasón, príncipe que, con ayuda de Medea su esposa, conquistó el vellocino de oro.
jasper ['dʒæspər, B -pə] *s.* (min.) jaspe.
jaspery [-pərɪ] *a.* jaspeado.
jato unit ['dʒeɪtoʊ-] (aer.) aparato para despegue con ayuda de cohetes.
jauk [dʒɔk] *v.i.* (esco.) juguetear, retozar, entretenerse; travesear, bromear, burlarse.
jaundice ['dʒɔndəs, dʒɑn-, B 'dʒɔn-] *s.* 1. (med.) ictericia. 2. (fig.) envidia, celos; displicencia, desazón. —*v.t.* 1. dar ictericia a. 2. avinagrar el genio a; predisponer, llenar de envidia; desazonar.
jaundiced [-dəst] *a.* 1. ictérico, ictericiado, aliacanado. 2. cetrino, amarillo. 3. (fig.) envidioso, celoso; displicente, desazonado, avinagrado.
jaunt [dʒɔnt, dʒɑnt, B dʒɔnt] *v.i.* 1. pasear, vagar, callejear, hacer una excursión. 2. (ant.) caminar cansadamente de un lado a otro. —*s.* 1. paseo, excursión. 2. (ant.) viaje aburrido, cansado, pesado.
jauntily [-əlɪ] *adv.* gallardamente, garbosamente; con desenvoltura.
jauntiness [-ɪnəs] *s.* garbo, desenvoltura; agilidad.
jaunting car [-ɪŋ-] tílburi irlandés.
jaunty [-ɪ] *a.* (JAUNTIER; JAUNTIEST) 1. gallardo, garboso; desenvuelto, despreocupado. 2. (ant.) gentil, cortés; elegante, vistoso.

jaup [dʒɔp] *v.t., v.i.* (esco.) chapotear; salpicar. —*s.* salpicadura.
Java ['dʒɑvə, 'dʒævə, B 'dʒɑvə] *s.* 1. Java, isla de Indonesia. 2. (jer.) café.
Javanese [ˌdʒævə'niz, B ˌdʒɑv-] *s.* (*pl.* JAVANESE) 1. javanés, natural de Java. 2. (idioma) javanés. —*a.* javanés.
Java sparrow, (orn.) gorrión de Java, tejedor.
javelin ['dʒævələn] *s.* 1. jabalina, venablo (de caza). 2. (dep.) jabalina.
Javelle water [ʒə'vɛl-] agua de javel.
jaw [dʒɔ] *s.* 1. maxilar inferior, mandíbula, quijada. 2. (*pl.*) fauces. 3. embocadura (de un valle, canal, etc.). 4. (*pl.*) (fig.) garras, ej., *in the jaws of death,* en las garras de la muerte. 5. (mec.) mandíbula, quijada; mordaza, telera. 6. (jer.) palabrería, charla; réplica insolente, insolencia. —*v.i.* (jer.) charlar, chacharear; reñir, regañar.
jaw, (esco.) *s.* ola, mar. —*vt., v.i.* salpicar, chapotear; verter, vaciar, caer copiosa o rápidamente.
jawbone ['dʒɔˌboʊn] *s.* (anat.) quijada, mandíbula (esp. el maxilar inferior). —*v.t.* (*fam*) persuadir en lugar de forzar.
jawbreaker [-ˌbreɪkər, B -kə] *s.* 1. (jer.) trabalenguas. 2. caramelo muy duro. 3. (maq.) triturador automático (de piedras, rocas, etc.).
jaw chuck, (mec.) mandril de quijadas, mandril de garras.
jaw clutch, (aut., maq.) embrague de mordaza, embrague de quijadas.
jaw coupling, (mec.) acoplamiento dentado, acoplamiento de garras.
jaw vise, (mec.) tornillo de mordazas.
jay [dʒeɪ] *s.* 1. (orn.) arrendajo, grajo, rendajo. 2. charlador, gárrulo, hablador. 3. (jer.) necio, tonto, simplón.
jayhawker ['dʒeɪˌhɔkər, B -kə] *s.* 1. guerrillero antiesclavista; p. ext., miliciano, guerrillero. 2. (E.U.) **J.,** nativo o residente del estado de Kansas.
jayvee ['dʒeɪ'vi] *s.* (jer., dep.) 1. equipo suplente (de una universidad). 2. miembro del equipo suplente.
jaywalk [-ˌwɔk] *v.i.* (fam.) cruzar una calle imprudentemente.
jaywalker [-ər, B -ə] *s.* (fam.) peatón imprudente que cruza la calle en medio del tránsito.
jaywalking [-ɪŋ] *s.* (fam.) cruce imprudente de una calle.
jazz [dʒæz] *s.* 1. (mús.) jazz, música popular sincopada. 2. (jer.) palabrería, palique; bola, cuentos. —*a.* 1. de jazz o relativo al jazz (música, aficionado, etc.). 2. discordante, chillón (colores, etc.). —*v.t.* 1. orquestar o armonizar en el estilo del jazz. 2. (jer.) (gen. con *up*) avivar, tonificar. 3. (jer.) acelerar. —*v.i.* 1. bailar o tocar jazz. 2. (gen. con *around*) andar de jarana.
jazz band, orquesta de jazz.
jazzist ['dʒæzəst] *s.* aficionado al jazz, fanático del jazz.
jazzman [-mən, -ˌmæn] *s.* (*pl.* JAZZMEN) músico de jazz.
jazzy ['dʒæzɪ] *a.* 1. propio de jazz; animado. 2. (jer.) ruidoso, estridente; chillón, llamativo.
J.C. *abrev. de* **Jesus Christ,** Jesucristo.
J.C.D. *abrev. de* **Doctor of Canon Law,** Doctor en Derecho canónico.
J.C.S. (mil., E.U.) *abrev. de* **Joint Chiefs of Staff,** Comando Conjunto.
J.D. *abrev. de* 1. **Doctor of Law,** Doctor en Derecho. 2. **juvenile delinquency,** delincuencia juvenil.
jealous ['dʒɛləs] *a.* 1. celoso. 2. envidioso, receloso, desconfiado.
jealously [-lɪ] *adv.* celosamente.
jealousy ['dʒɛləsɪ] *s.* (*pl.* JEALOUSIES) celos; desconfianza, recelo; envidia.
jean [dʒin, B dʒeɪn] *s.* 1. tela cruzada o asargada de algodón. 2. [B dʒinz] (*pl.*) pantalones (de tela) de algodón; mono, traje de faena, overol (Amer.).
Jeanne d'Arc [ʒɑn'dɑrk, B -'dɑk] (hist.) Juana de Arco.
Jebusite ['dʒɛbjəˌsaɪt, B -ˌzaɪt] *s.* (bíbl.) jebuseo.
Jebusitic [ˌdʒɛbjə'sɪtɪk, B -'zɪt-] **Jebusitical** [ɪkəl] *a.* (bíbl.) jebuseo.
jeep [dʒip] *s.* jeep, jip, yip, pequeño automóvil fuerte y práctico, propio para uso militar o rural.
jeer [dʒɪr, B dʒɪə] *v.i.* burlarse, mofar(se); **j. at,** burlarse de, escarnecer; tratar con desprecio. —*v.t.* befar, escarnecer. —*s.* mofa, befa, burla, escarnio, desprecio.
jeer, *s.* (mar.) (*gen. pl.*) guindaste con sus drizas, driza de verga.
jeerer ['dʒɪrər, B 'dʒɪərə] *s.* mofador, escarnecedor.
jeeringly [-ɪŋlɪ] *adv.* con escarnio o burla, burlonamente.
jehad, *var. de* **jihad.**
Jehoshaphat [dʒɪ'hɑsəˌfæt, B -'hɔʃə-] *s.* (bíbl.) Josafat.
Jehovah [-'hoʊvə] *s.* (bíbl.) Jehová (denominación de Dios en el Antiguo Testamento.).
Jehovah's Witnesses, (relig.) Testigos de Jehová.
Jehu ['dʒihju] *s.* 1. (bíbl.) Jehú. 2. (hum.) cochero, taxista.
jejune [dʒɪ'dʒun] *a.* 1. poco alimenticio. 2. (fig.) falto de interés, estéril, árido; aburrido. 3. inmaduro, insípido.
jejunely [-lɪ] *adv.* estérilmente, áridamente; aburridamente.
jejuneness [-nəs] *s.* aridez; inmadurez, insipidez.
jejunum [-'dʒunəm] *s.* (anat.) yeyuno.
jell [dʒɛl] *s.* (fam.) jalea. —*v.i.* 1. coagularse, cuajarse. 2. (fig.) cristalizarse; formarse (opinión, proyecto, etc.). —*v.t.* (fig.) formar, moldear.
jellied ['dʒɛlid] *a.* (cocina) gelatinado; en jalea, en gelatina; cuajado, solidificado.
jellied gasoline, gelatina de gasolina (incendiaria).
jellify ['dʒɛlɪˌfaɪ] *v.t., v.i.* (*pret., p.p.* JELLIFIED; *p.pr.* JELLIFYING) gelatinizar(se).
jelly ['dʒɛlɪ] *s.* 1. jalea. 2. substancia gelatinosa. —*v.t., v.i.* (*pret., p.p.* JELLIED; *p.pr.* JELLYING) convertir(se) en jalea, cuajar(se), solidificar(se).
jelly bean, 1. bombón o caramelo de gelatina (o goma) azucarada (en forma de frijol). 2. (jer.) alfeñique, (persona) débil.
jellyfish [-ˌfɪʃ] *s.* 1. (zool.) medusa, aguamar, aguamala, malagua (Amer.). 2. (jer.) calzonazos, braguetas.
jelly roll, bizcocho enrollado con relleno de jalea o crema, brazo gitano; pioquinto (Chile, Ecuador); pionono (Perú).
jemadar [ˌdʒɛmə'dɑr, B 'dʒɛməˌdɑ] *s.* (anglo-ind.) oficial de segunda graduación en una compañía de cipayos; oficial de la policía hindú.
jemmy ['dʒɛmɪ] *s.* (G.B., cocina) cabeza de oveja o carnero.
jennet ['dʒɛnət] *s.* jaca, jumenta.
jenny ['dʒɛnɪ] *s.* 1. hembra de ciertos animales, ej., *j. wren,* hembra del reyezuelo. 2. máquina para hilar.
jenny ass, burra, borrica.
jeopard ['dʒɛpərd, B -əd] **jeopardize** [-ərˌdaɪz, B -əˌ-] *v.t.* arriesgar, exponer, poner en peligro (futuro, vida, etc.); comprometer (buenas relaciones, etc.).
jeopardous [-ərdəs, B -əd-] *a.* expuesto, riesgoso, peligroso.
jeopardy [-ɪ] *s.* riesgo, peligro.
jequirity [dʒə'kwɪrətɪ] *s.* 1. (bot.) guayruro, jaquerita. 2. semilla del guayruro.
Jer. *abrev. de* **Jeremiah,** Jeremías (Jer.).
jerboa [dʒər'boʊə, B dʒɜ'-] *s.* (zool.) jerbo, gerbo.
jereed, jerid [dʒə'rid] *s.* jerid (especie de jabalina empleada por los musulmanes en maniobras o juegos militares).
jeremiad [ˌdʒɛrə'maɪəd] *s.* jeremíada, lamentación.
Jeremiah [-'maɪə] **Jeremias** [-'maɪəs] *s.* (bíbl.) Jeremías.
Jericho ['dʒɛrɪˌkoʊ] *s.* (bíbl.) Jericó.
jerk [dʒɜrk, B dʒɜk] *v.t.* 1. dar un tirón a, sacudir repentinamente. 2. tirar bruscamente. 3. **j. off,** quitar de un tirón; **j. out,** sacar de un tirón; decir de manera entrecortada o convulsiva. —*v.i.* 1. mover a tirones o empujones. 2. **j. off,** (vulg.) hacerse una paja, masturbarse. —*s.* 1. tirón, jalón (Amer.); empujón, sacudida. 2. dependiente de una fuente de soda. 3. tic, convulsión, espasmo. 4. (jer.) pelmazo, latoso. 5. **by jerks,** a sacudidas; **the jerks,** corea, baile de San Vito.
jerk, *v.t.* atasajar, tasajear, acecinar, charquear (Amer.).
jerked beef ['dʒɜrkt-, B 'dʒɜkt-] cecina, tasajo, charqui (Amer.).
jerkily ['dʒɜrkəlɪ, B 'dʒɜkɪ-] *adv.* espasmódicamente, bruscamente.
jerkin ['dʒɜrkən, B 'dʒɜkɪn] *s.* justillo, chaquetón; coleto de gamuza, sin mangas.
jerkwater ['dʒɜrkˌwɔtər, -ˌwɑt-, B 'dʒɜkˌwɔtə] *a.* (jer.) 1. remoto y sin importancia, insignificante (pueblo, localidad, etc.). 2. baladí, frívolo, trivial.
jerky ['dʒɜrkɪ, B 'dʒɜkɪ] *a.* (JERKIER; JERKIEST) 1. desigual (camino); que sacude, mal amortiguado (vehículo). 2. espasmódico; inestable. 3. (jer.) inepto, zonzo. —*s.* tasajo, cecina, charqui (Amer.).
jeroboam [ˌdʒɛrə'boʊəm] *s.* botella gigante (de champaña o vino).
jerreed, jerrid, *vars. de* **jereed.**
jerrican ['dʒɛrɪˌkæn] *s.* bidón, lata grande (de cinco galones, para gasolina, agua, etc.).
jerry ['dʒɛrɪ] *s.* (*pl.* JERRIES) (jer.) 1. soldado alemán. 2. orinal.
jerry, *a.* de inferior calidad, mal hecho, de pacotilla.
jerry-build [-ˌbɪld] *v.t.* construir o fabricar mal y a la carrera; producir mercancía de pacotilla.
jerry-built [-ˌbɪlt] *a.* 1. mal construido, de construcción barata. 2. de pacotilla, chapucero.
jersey ['dʒɜrzɪ, B 'dʒɜzɪ] *s.* 1. jersey, jubón o chaqueta de lana de tejido elástico, chompa (Amer.). 2. tela de lana, seda o hilo, tejida en forma de malla elástica. 3. **J.,** Jersey, raza de ganado lechero.
Jerusalem [dʒə'rusələm] *s.* Jerusalén, capital de Israel.
Jerusalem artichoke, 1. (bot.) topinambur, aguaturma, pataca. 2. cotufa, pataca, patata de caña (fruto).
Jerusalem sage, (bot.) matagallos, aguavientos.
Jerusalem thorn, (bot.) 1. espina santa, espina vera. 2. cinacina.
jess [dʒɛs] *s.* pihuela (con que se ata al halcón).
jessamine ['dʒɛsəmən] *var. de* **jasmine.**
jessant ['dʒɛsənt] *a.* (her.) emergente, reclinado (díc. de las figuras).
Jesse ['dʒɛsɪ] *s.* (bíbl.) Isaí.
jessed [dʒɛst] *a.* con la pihuela puesta (halcón).

jest [dʒɛst] *s.* 1. chanza, burla, broma, zumba; chiste, chunga. 2. (ant.) hazaña, proeza; gesta. 3. **in j.,** en broma. —*v.i.* bromear, chancear; mofarse.
jester ['dʒɛstər, B -ə] *s.* bufón, guasón, bromista.
jesting [-ɪŋ] *s.* bufonería. —*a.* juguetón, guasón, bromista.
jestingly [-lɪ] *adv.* en broma, juguetonamente, de guasa.
Jesu ['dʒizu, B -zju] *s.* (lit., poét.) Jesús.
Jesuit ['dʒɛʒuət, B 'dʒɛzjʊ-] *s.* 1. jesuita. 2. (despec.) jesuita, intrigante.
Jesuitic [ˌdʒɛʒʊ'ɪtɪk, B ˌdʒɛzjʊ-] **Jesuitical** [-ɪkəl] *a.* 1. jesuítico. 2. (despec.) jesuítico, solapado.
Jesuitically [-ɪkəlɪ] *adv.* (despec.) jesuíticamente, intrigantemente, solapadamente.
Jesuitism ['dʒɛʒuətˌɪzəm, B 'dʒɛzjʊ-] *s.* 1. jesuitismo. 2. (despec.) sofistería; sutileza, subterfugio, conducta solapada.
Jesuitry [-ətrɪ] *s.* (despec.) sofistería.
Jesuits' bark, (bot.) quina, cascarilla, corteza de quino.
Jesus ['dʒizəs] *s.* (bíbl., relig.) Jesús.
Jesus Christ, Jesucristo.
jet [dʒɛt] *s.* 1. (min.) azabache. 2. negro lustroso. 3. (ant.) mármol negro. —*a.* azabachado, negro azabache.
jet, *s.* 1. chorro, surtidor. 2. pitón, boca, boquilla, lanza; mechero. 3. (*abrev. de* **j. engine**) motor de reacción, motor de chorro, reactor. —*v.i.* (*pret. p.p.* JETTED; *p.pr.* JETTING) 1. salir a chorros, chorrear, brotar, surgir. 2. volar o viajar en avión de reacción. —*v.t.* echar o arrojar en chorro.
jet airplane, avión de propulsión a chorro, avión de reacción, jet, reactor.
jet-black ['dʒɛt'blæk] *a.* azabachado; negro azabachado, negro azabache.
jet bomber, (mil.) bombardero de reacción a chorro.
jet engine, motor a chorro, motor de reacción, reactor.
jet fighter, (aer.) (avión de) caza a chorro.
jet lag, jet-lag, desfase horario, cansancio del desfase (*debido a un largo viaje en avion*).
jetliner ['dʒɛtˌlaɪnər, B -nə] *s.* avión de reacción (de una compañía de aviación); jet comercial.
jetport [-ˌpɔrt, B -ˌpɔt] *s.* aeropuerto de pistas largas para los aviones jet.
jet-propelled [-prə'pɛld] *a.* (aer.) propulsado por motor de reacción.
jet propulsion, (aer.) propulsión a reacción, propulsión a chorro.
jet-propulsion [-'pʌlʃən] *a.* (aer.) de propulsión a chorro.
jetsam ['dʒɛtsəm] *s.* 1. (mar.) echazón. 2. (fig.) desecho, cosa desechada.
jet set, grupo social internacional que frecuenta los lugares de moda.
jet sprayer, pulverizador, rociador a presión.
jet stream, 1. (meteor.) corriente en chorro. 2. (aer.) chorro (proyectado por un motor de reacción).
jettison ['dʒɛtəsən, -zən] *s.* (mar.) echazón. —*v.t.* 1. echar al mar. 2. desechar, descartar. 3. (mil.) echar, tirar (equipo, armas, etc. para aligerar una aeronave, tanque, etc.).
jettisoning [-sənɪŋ, -zə-] *s.* (aer.) deslastre en vuelo.
jetton ['dʒɛtən] *s.* ficha, pieza que tiene un valor monetario (ej., para pagar el pasaje en un autobús, llamar por un teléfono público, etc.).
jetty ['dʒɛtɪ] *s.* espigón, rompeolas; muelle.
jetty, *a.* azabachado; muy negro.
jeu [ʒə] *s.* (fr.) juego; diversión.
jeu de mots [ʒədə'moʊ] (fr.) juego de palabras; retruécano.
jeu d'esprit [-dɛs'pri] (fr.) frase o escrito ingenioso o chistoso, dicho inteligente.
Jew [dʒu] *s., a.* judío. —*v.t.* **j.,** (despec.) 1. regatear tenazmente con (alguien). 2. (gen. con *down*) superar en el regateo (a alguien); bajar (el precio) después de un tenaz regateo.
Jew-baiting ['dʒuˌbeɪtɪŋ] *s.* persecución de los judíos.
jewel ['dʒuəl] *s.* 1. joya, alhaja. 2. piedra preciosa, gema. 3. rubí (en maquinaria de relojes). 4. (fig.) joya, perla (persona). —*v.t.* (*pret., p.p.* JEWELED O JEWELLED; *p.pr.* JEWELING O JEWELLING) 1. enjoyar. 2. (fig.) adornar, engalanar (con luces, estrellas, etc.).
jewel box, j. case, joyero, estuche de joyas.
jeweler, jeweller [-ər, B -ə] *s.* joyero (comerciante en joyas, relojes, etc.).
jewelly [-ɪ] *a.* 1. enjoyado. 2. lustroso, brillante (como una joya).
jewelry, (pr. G.B.) **jewellery** ['dʒuəlrɪ] *s.* 1. joyas, alhajas. 2. joyería.
jewelry store, joyería.
jewelweed [-ˌwid] *s.* (bot.) hierba de Santa Catalina.
Jewess ['dʒuəs] *s.* (despec.) judía.
jewfish ['dʒuˌfɪʃ] *s.* (*pl.* JEWFISH) (ict.) mero, cherna, guasa.
Jewish [-ɪʃ] *a.* judío, hebreo, israelita; judaico; ajudiado. —*s.* yiddish.
Jewishness [-nəs] *s.* carácter judío, naturaleza judía.
Jewry ['dʒurɪ, B 'dʒuərɪ] *s.* (*pl.* JEWRIES) 1. judíos, pueblo judío. 2. judería, ghetto.
jew's-harp ['dʒuzˌhɑrp, B -'hɑp] **jews' harp** (mús.) birimbao, trompa de París, trompa gallega.
Jezebel ['dʒɛzəˌbɛl, B -bəl] *s.* 1. (bíbl.) Jezabel. 2. suripanta, pelandusca, mujer impúdica.
jib [dʒɪb] *v.t., v.i.* (*pret., p.p.* JIBBED; *p.pr.* JIBBING) (mar.) cambiar(se) (vela, cable, botalón) de amura (al virar). —*s.* 1. (mar.) foque, vela triangular. 2. **the cut of one's j.,** corte de cara o figura, semblante, apariencia.
jib, *s.* aguilón, pescante, brazo de grúa. —*v.i.* plantarse (caballo), resistirse a avanzar, moverse hacia atrás o hacia los costados.
jibboom ['dʒɪb'bum] *s.* (mar.) botalón de bauprés, tormentín.
jibe [dʒaɪb] *v.i.* (mar.) 1. trasluchar, moverse de un lado a otro (una vela o su botavara). 2. cambiar el curso (de un barco) haciendo trasluchar la vela. —*v.t.* (mar.) hacer trasluchar (la vela o la botavara).
jibe, *v.i.* (fam., E.U.) concordar, armonizar, estar de acuerdo, ej., *his opinions do not j. with mine,* sus opiniones no están de acuerdo con las mías.
jibe, jiber, *vars. de* **gibe, giber,** asir con fuerza, duramente.
jiffy ['dʒɪfɪ] *s.* (*pl.* JIFFIES) (fam.) periquete, santiamén, instante, momento, ej., *I will be ready in a j.,* (fam.) estaré listo en un periquete, o en un santiamén.
jig [dʒɪg] *v.t.* (*pret., p.p.* JIGGED; *p.pr.* JIGGING) 1. cantar, tocar o bailar (la giga o jiga). 2. sacudir de abajo (hacia) arriba; mover con vaivén. 3. (mec.) formar o adaptar por medio de gálibos, patrones o guías. 4. (min.) separar minerales con criba. —*v.i.* 1. bailar una giga. 2. moverse a saltitos. 3. pescar con anzuelo de cuchara. 4. trabajar con la ayuda de un gálibo, patrón o guía. —*s.* 1. giga, jiga (baile y música). 2. anzuelo de cuchara o emplomado. 3. (mec.) gálibo, calibre, patrón, plantilla; montaje, guía. 4. (min.) clasificadora hidráulica, cribón de vaivén. 5. **the j. is up,** (jer.) el juego se acabó, se acabó la fiesta (llegó la hora de hacer las cuentas).
jig borer, taladradora de plantillas.
jig bushing, (mec.) boquilla de guía.
jigger ['dʒɪgər, B -ə] *s.* 1. bailador de giga. 2. vasito para medir licor (gen. de una onza y media o 42 ml). 3. artilugio, aparato, artefacto. 4. (pesca) anzuelo de cuchara o emplomado. 5. (billar, billas) tipo de puente. 6. (golf) palo de hierro con la cara angosta y bastante elevada 7. (min.) clasificadora hidráulica, cribón de vaivén. 8. (mar.) aparejuelo, aparejo liviano. 9. (mar.) pequeña embarcación (aparejada como una yola). 10. (elec.) transformador de oscilaciones. 11. (ento.) nigua, pique (Amer.).
jigger mast, (mar.) contramesana, palo de mesana.
jiggery-pokery ['dʒɪgərɪ'poʊkərɪ] *s.* (jer.) superchería, maniobras fraudulentas y taimadas.
jiggle ['dʒɪgəl] *v.t., v.i.* zangolotear(se), zangotear(se). —*s.* zangoloteo, zangoteo.
jiggly ['dʒɪglɪ] *a.* que se mueve a tirones o tiende a moverse de un lado a otro.
jigsaw ['dʒɪgˌsɔ] *s.* sierra caladora o para contornear, sierra de vaivén. —*v.t.* cortar o contornear con sierra caladora.
jigsaw puzzle, rompecabezas (hecho de una figura cortada en pedazos irregulares).
jigua ['higwə] *s.* (bot.) jigua.
jihad [dʒɪ'hɑd] *s.* 1. (hist.) jihad (guerra sagrada del Islam). 2. (fig.) cruzada.
jillet ['dʒɪlət] *s.* (esco.) coqueta, veleidosa, castigadora.
jilt [dʒɪlt] *s.* mujer coquetona que da calabazas al pretendiente. —*v.t.* dar calabazas o despedir a (un pretendiente); dejar plantado al novio o la novia a punto de casarse.
Jim Crow ['dʒɪm-] *s.* 1. (ant., despec.) negro. 2. discriminación contra el negro.
jim-dandy [-'dændɪ] *a.* (jer.) excelente, estupendo, maravilloso.
jimjams [-ˌdʒæmz] *s. pl.* (jer., E.U.) delírium tremens.
jimmy ['dʒɪmɪ] *s.* palanca, barreta, pata de cabra (usada por los ladrones), ganzúa. —*v.t.* (*pret., p.p.* JIMMIED; *p.pr.* JIMMYING) abrir con una palanca; forzar con palanca o barreta.
jimp [dʒɪmp] *a.* (esco.) cenceño, esbelto; garboso, apuesto; acicalado, ataviado.
jimsonweed ['dʒɪmsənˌwid] *s.* (bot.) chamico, estramonio.
jingal ['dʒɪngəl] *s.* mosquete largo y pesado o cañón rudimentario que se usaba en el Asia central.
jingle ['dʒɪŋgəl] *v.i.* 1. retiñir, cascabelear, sonar como campanillas. 2. rimar. —*v.t.* hacer retiñir. —*s.* 1. retintín, cascabeleo. 2. copla, estribillo; (rad., t.v.) anuncio comercial cantado. 3. carro cubierto de dos ruedas (usado en partes de **Irl.** y Aust.). 4. cascabel (sonaja de pandero).
jingly [-glɪ] *a.* metálico (sonido), cascabelero, tintineante.
jingo ['dʒɪŋgoʊ] *s.* (*pl.* JINGOES) 1. (hist., E.U.) jingoísta, patriotero. 2. **by j.,** (fam.) ¡caramba! —*a.* jingoísta.
jingoism [-ˌɪzəm] *s.* jingoísmo (forma de política reaccionaria y agresiva a todo elemento extranjero).
jingoist [-əst] *s.* jingoísta.
jingoistic [ˌdʒɪŋgoʊ'ɪstɪk] *a.* jingoísta.
jink [dʒɪŋk] *v.i.* esquivar, evadir, hacer quites, dar regates. —*s.* 1. regate, quite, evasiva. 2. (*pl.*) travesuras, jugarretas, juegos, (ú. esp. en) **high**

jinks, juegos o jugarretas bulliciosas, fiesta, holgorio.
jinker ['dʒɪŋkər, B -kə] *s.* (Aust.) carreta de dos o cuatro ruedas (usada para acarrear madera, leña, etc.).
jinn [dʒɪn] **jinni** [dʒə'ni, 'dʒɪnɪ, B dʒɪ'ni] *s.* (*pl.* JINNS o JINN) genio, espíritu fantástico, ser sobrenatural (según las creencias mahometanas).
jinrikisha [dʒɪn'rɪkʃɔ, -ʃɑ, B -ʃə] *s.* pequeño carruaje de dos ruedas y tirado por un hombre (usado originalmente en el Japón).
jinx [dʒɪŋks] *s.* (jer.) mal de ojo, aojo, mala suerte. —*v.t.* (jer.) aojar, traer mala suerte a.
jipijapa [ˌhipɪ'hɑpə] *s.* 1. (bot.) bombonaje. 2. sombrero jipijapa o panamá.
jiqui [hɪ'ki] *s.* (bot.) jigüe.
jitney ['dʒɪtnɪ] *s.* 1. auto destartalado, carcocha o carcacha, foyeque (Amer.). 2. pequeño ómnibus, colectivo (Amer.). 3. (jer.) (moneda de) cinco centavos, medio real (Amer.).
jitter ['dʒɪtər, B -ə] *v.i.* (jer.) estar nervioso; ponerse nervioso; actuar nerviosamente.
jitterbug [-ˌbʌg] *s.* 1. (E.U.) especie de baile de movimientos convulsivos popular en los años 40. 2. bailarín de dicho baile. 3. (fam., G.B.) pusilánime; persona nerviosa. —*v.i.* bailar con movimientos convulsivos.
jitters [-ərz, B -əz] *s. pl.* (jer.) nerviosidad extrema; nerviosismo, intranquilidad, desasosiego, agitación, ataque de nervios; **to give (someone) the j.,** poner nervioso (a alguien); **to have the j.,** estar muerto de miedo o muy nervioso.
jittery [-ərɪ] *a.* (jer., E.U.) nervioso, agitado, inquieto, muñequeado (Amer.).
jiujitsu, jiujutsu, *vars. de* **jujitsu.**
Jivaran ['hivərən] *a.* jíbaro.
Jivaro ['hivɑˌrɔ, B -vəˌroʊ] *s.* (*pl.* JIVAROS) jíbaro (miembro de una tribu de indios sudamericanos que momifican las cabezas humanas reduciéndolas al tamaño de un puño).
jive [dʒaɪv] *s.* 1. (E.U.) música de ritmo vigoroso y con improvisaciones (var. del jazz). 2. (jer.) jerga, jerigonza; cháchara, baladronada, palabrería, esp. entre músicos de jazz. —*v.i.* 1. tocar o bailar música de ritmo vigoroso. 2. (jer.) chacotear, burlarse; bromear, chancear. —*v.t.* (jer.) tomar el pelo a, burlarse de.
jo [dʒoʊ] *s.* (*pl.* JOES) (esco.) enamorado, novio.
Joan of Arc [ˌdʒoʊnəv'ɑrk, B -'ɑk] Juana de Arco.
job [dʒɑb, B dʒɔb] *s.* 1. tarea, trabajo, quehacer. 2. obra, trabajo. 3. lugar de trabajo. 4. arreglo, trato (ilegal o secreto). 5. empleo, puesto, posición, situación. 6. asunto. 7. (jer.) robo. 8. **bad j.,** cosa inútil; caso perdido; fracaso, fiasco; situación incómoda o difícil; **by the j.,** a destajo; **it's just the j.,** es justamente lo que necesitaba; **on the j.,** en el lugar de trabajo; (jer.) en acción, en su puesto, alerta; **to be out of a j.,** estar desocupado, estar sin trabajo; **to do a j. on (someone),** (jer.) hacer mucho daño a; **to do a person's j.,** arruinar a una persona. —*v.i.* (*pret., p.p.* JOBBED; *p.pr.* JOBBING) 1. trabajar a destajo. 2. tener empleo(s) ocasional(es). 3. trabajar como corredor, vender o comprar como corredor. —*v.t.* 1. comerciar con, especular con. 2. conseguir por arreglo o trato ilegal, conseguir por influencia (empleo público, obra municipal, etc.). 3. alquilar. 4. (jer.) engañar, estafar. —*a.* 1. (hecho) a destajo. 2. de trabajo (mercado, seguridad, etc.). 3. (G.B.) alquilado por (corto) tiempo; contratado para un (solo) trabajo.
job, *v.t., v.i.* (pr. dial.) punzar, aguijonear, herir (ligeramente) con arma blanca; pinchar, punzar a. —*s.* punzada, pinchazo.
Job [dʒoʊb] *s.* (bíbl.) Job.
job action, movilización (de trabajadores).
jobber ['dʒɑbər, B 'dʒɔbə] *s.* 1. corredor, intermediario. 2. trabajador a destajo, destajero, destajista. 3. (G.B.) corredor de bolsa. 4. funcionario deshonesto.
jobbery [-ərɪ] *s.* (pr. G.B.) corrupción (en alguna posición oficial o pública).
job control language, (comput.) lenguaje de control de trabajo.
jobholder [-ˌhoʊldər, B -də] *s.* 1. empleado. 2. (E.U.) empleado público.
job hunting, búsqueda de trabajo, busca de trabajo.
jobless [-ləs] *a.* desocupado, sin trabajo.
job lot, 1. lote de mercancías variadas o sueltas (comprado con fines de especulación), surtido mixto (de mercancías). 2. lote, surtido, grupo variado (de cosas).
job printer, (impr.) remendista.
job printing, (impr.) remendería (comercial); impresión de circulares, invitaciones, etc.
Job's comforter ['dʒoʊbz-] persona que aparentemente consuela pero que en realidad sólo agrava la pena de uno.
Job's tears, *pl.* (bot.) lágrimas de David o de Job, semilla de una gramínea.
job work, (impr.) remendería, remendería comercial, impresión de remiendos, trabajos de remiendo.
Jocasta [dʒoʊ'kæstə] *s.* (mitol.) Yocasta, madre y esposa de Edipo.
jock [dʒɑk, B dʒɔk] *s.* (fam.) 1. (*athlete*) deportista. 2. (*jockstrap*) suspensorio.
jockey ['dʒɑkɪ, B 'dʒɔkɪ] *s.* jinete (profesional), jockey. —*v.t.* 1. trampear, engañar, embaucar. 2. manejar. 3. manipular (con pericia o destreza). 4. montar (un caballo). 5. **j. into,** persuadir con intrigas a; meter con intrigas en, ej., *they jockeyed me into buying a useless thing,* me persuadieron con intrigas a que comprase una cosa inútil; **j. (someone) out of,** despojar fraudulentamente (a alguien) de. —*v.i.* 1. ser jinete (profesional), montar caballos (en carreras). 2. maniobrar.
jocko ['dʒɑkoʊ, B 'dʒɔk-] *s.* (*pl.* JOCKOS) (zool.) jocó, chimpancé.
jockstrap ['dʒɑkˌstræp, B 'dʒɔk-] *s.* suspensorio, suspensor.
jocose [dʒoʊ'koʊs, dʒə-] *a.* jocoso; festivo, juguetón; divertido, gracioso.
jocosely [-lɪ] *adv.* jocosamente.
jocoseness [-nəs] *s.* jocosidad.
jocosity [-'kɑsətɪ, B -'kɔs-] *s.* jocosidad; chiste.
jocular ['dʒɑkjələr, B 'dʒɔkjʊlə] *a.* jocoso, chistoso, humorístico, alegre.
jocularity [ˌdʒɑkjə'lærətɪ, B ˌdʒɔk-] *s.* jocosidad; chiste.
jocularly ['dʒɑkjələrlɪ, B 'dʒɔkjʊləlɪ] *adv.* jocosamente, chistosamente, alegremente.
jocund ['dʒɑkənd, B 'dʒɔk-] *a.* jocundo, plácido, alegre, agradable.
jocundity [dʒoʊ'kʌndətɪ] *s.* 1. jocundidad, alegría, jovialidad, apacibilidad. 2. chiste, dicho gracioso.
jocundly ['dʒɑkəndlɪ, B 'dʒɔk-] *adv.* alegremente.
jodhpur ['dʒɑdpər, B 'dʒɔdpʊə] *s.* pantalón de montar, ajustados a la pantorrilla.
Joe [dʒoʊ] *s.* 1. (jer.) tipo, hombre (esp. amigable o agradable). 2. (Esco.) novio.
joe-pye weed ['dʒoʊ'paɪ-] (bot.) eupatorio maculado; eupatorio purpúreo.
joey ['dʒoʊɪ] *s.* (Aust.) canguro joven; cría de animal.
jog [dʒɑg, B dʒɔg] *v.t.* (*pret., p.p.* JOGGED; *p.pr.* JOGGING) 1. empujar levemente; sacudir (con el codo o la mano); tocar ligera o disimuladamente; dar un codazo a. 2. estimular, refrescar (la memoria). —*v.i.* avanzar con ritmo lento; marchar a trote corto; moverse o ir despacio; cabalgar a trote corto; **j. along** (o **on**), cabalgar despacio, ir a trote corto; avanzar pausadamente. —*s.* 1. empujoncito, golpecito; sacudimiento ligero. 2. (E.U.) resalte, saliente (ej., en una pared). 3. trote corto.
jogger ['dʒɑgər] *s.* persona que hace footing.
jogging ['dʒɑgɪŋ] *s.* footing, futing, jogging.
jogging shoes, zapatillas de deporte.
jogging suit, chándal.
joggle ['dʒɑgəl, B 'dʒɔg-] *v.t.* 1. sacudir ligeramente, traquetear. 2. ensamblar, empalmar; sujetar o alinear con tarugos. —*v.i.* sacudirse, traquetear. —*s.* 1. sacudida ligera, traqueteo. 2. (carp.) nervadura, lengüeta, espiga (de una ensambladura).
joggle joint, (carp.) junta de ranura y lengua.
jog trot, 1. trote corto. 2. rutina; acto rutinario.
john [dʒɑn, B dʒɔn] *s.* 1. (jer., E.U.) retrete, excusado, inodoro. 2. cualquier sujeto, esp. aquél que se puede engañar fácilmente. 3. cliente de una prostituta.
John Barleycorn, (personificación de) el licor.
johnboat ['dʒɑnˌboʊt, B 'dʒɔn-] *s.* batea (de fondo plano y bordes rectos para navegar en ríos, canales, etc.).
John Bull, (personificación de) Inglaterra; el pueblo inglés; el inglés típico.
John Doe [-'doʊ] (der.) Fulano de Tal, Juan Pérez (nombre ficticio que substituye al verdadero cuando éste se desconoce).
John Dory [-'dɔrɪ] (ict.) ceo.
John Hancock [-'hænˌkɑk, B -ˌkɔk] **J. Henry** [-'hɛnrɪ] (fam.) autógrafo, firma (de una persona).
johnny ['dʒɑnɪ, B 'dʒɔnɪ] *s.* 1. (fam.) tipo, sujeto, tío. 2. chaqueta de mangas cortas y sin cuello con la abertura en la espalda (usada por los enfermos en el hospital).
johnnycake [-ˌkeɪk] *s.* (E.U.) torta o pan de maíz.
Johnny-come-lately [-ˌkʌm'leɪtlɪ] *s.* (fam.) recién llegado; (fig.) persona que se presenta tardíamente.
Johnny-jump-up [-'dʒʌmpˌʌp] *s.* 1. (bot.) pensamiento, trinitaria. 2. (bot.) violeta americana.
Johnny-on-the-spot [-ˌɑnðə'spɑt, -ˌɔn-, B -ˌɔnðə'spɔt] *s.* (fam.) factótum, hombre oficioso.
Johnny Reb [-'rɛb] (E.U., hist.) personificación del soldado confederado en la Guerra de Secesión.
Johnsonese [ˌdʒɑnsə'niz, B ˌdʒɔn-] *s.* (despec.) estilo literario pomposo, ampuloso y rimbombante.
Johnson grass ['dʒɑnsən-, B 'dʒɔn-] (bot.) sorgo de Alepo, hierba de Don Carlos, pasto Johnson.
Johnsonian [dʒɑn'soʊnɪən, B dʒɔn-] *a.* 1. johnsoniano, propio de (Dr. Samuel) Johnson, al estilo de Johnson. 2. (fig., despec.) pomposo, inflado, rimbombante. —*s.* discípulo o plagiario de Johnson.
John the Baptist [dʒɑn-, B dʒɔn] (bíbl.) San Juan Bautista.
joie de vivre [ˌʒwadə'vivrə] (fr.) gozo del vivir; deleite de la vida.
join [dʒɔɪn] *v.t.* 1. juntar, ligar, acoplar 2. afiliarse a, asociarse a (club, organización, etc.). 3. abrazar (un partido, religión, etc.). 4. alistarse en

(el ejército). 5. aunar, unir, unificar; agrupar, confederar, incorporar. 6. juntarse (río o camino) con otro. 7. lindar o colindar con. 8. (con *in* o *for*) acompañar (en o para). 9. **j. battle,** trabar combate; **j. forces with,** aliarse con; **j. hands,** darse las manos; (fig.) asociarse, ayudarse mutuamente (en una empresa, etc.); **j. the army,** alistarse en el ejército. —*v.i.* 1. unirse, juntarse; asociarse, confederarse. 2. colindar, lindar, tocarse. 3. confluir (ríos, caminos). 4. **j. in,** participar en; **j. up,** alistarse, enrolarse. —*s.* juntura.

joinder [ˈdʒɔɪndər, B -də] *s.* 1. unión, juntura, junta, conjunción. 2. (der.) acumulación de acciones, proceso acumulativo.

joiner [-ər, B -ə] *s.* 1. ebanista. 2. persona o cosa que une o junta. 3. persona que acostumbra a afiliarse a causas u organizaciones.

joinery [-ərɪ] *s.* (trabajo de) ebanistería.

joining [-ɪŋ] *s.* juntura, unión; bisagra de una puerta.

joint [dʒɔɪnt] *s.* 1. juntura, junta, unión. 2. (anat.) articulación, coyuntura; (bot.) articulación, nudo. 3. (anat.) artículo, segmento (interarticular); (bot.) entrenudo. 4. asado, carne cortada para asado. 5. (jer.) fonducho, garito. 6. (geol.) grieta, fractura de roca sin dislocamiento. 7. (mec.) articulación. 8. (carp.) empalme, ensamblaje. 9. (arq.) junta. 10. (jer.) cigarrillo de mariguana. 11. **out of j.,** dislocado; (fig.) confuso, en desorden; decepcionado, descontento; **to throw out of j.,** dislocarse, descoyuntarse (el codo, el brazo, etc.). —*a.* 1. unido, junto, combinado. 2. común, unido. 3. mancomunado. 4. conjunto, colectivo. 5. en común, ej., *during their j. lives,* durante su vida en común. —*v.t.* 1. acoplar, juntar con ensambles. 2. descuartizar (pato, pollo, etc.), cortar (carne). 3. articular, unir con articulación (es).

joint account, (com.) cuenta mancomunada, cuenta conjunta.

joint acquisition, (der.) coadquisición.

joint action, acción conjunta o mancomunada.

joint and several debt, (der.) obligación solidaria.

joint bar, (f.c.) eclisa.

joint box, (elec.) caja de empalme.

joint commission, (pol.) comisión mixta.

joint committee, comité mixto, comité conjunto.

joint creditor, (der.) coacreedor.

joint debtor, (der.) codeudor.

jointed [ˈdʒɔɪntəd] *a.* articulado; nudoso.

jointed charlock, (bot.) rabanillo, rabaniza, rábano silvestre.

joint employer, (der.) compatrono.

jointer [-ər, B -ə] *s.* 1. (carp.) juntera. 2. (mec., agr.) reja anterior, cuchilla de rozar o descuajar.

jointer gauge, (carp.) guía para cepillo mecánico.

jointer plane, (carp.) garlopa.

joint estate, copropiedad, propiedad mancomunada.

joint fir, (bot.) belcho, hierba de las coyunturas, canadillo, uva marina.

joint grass, (bot.) gramilla.

joint guarantor, (der.) cofiador.

joint heir, (der.) coheredero.

joint heiress, (der.) coheredera.

joint hinge, bisagra de paletas.

jointing plane [ˈdʒɔɪntɪŋ-] (carp.) juntera.

joint legatee, (der.) colegatario.

joint lessor, (der.) coarrendador.

joint litigant, (der.) colitigante.

jointly [ˈdʒɔɪntlɪ] *adv.* conjuntamente, colectivamente, mancomunadamente.

jointly and severally, (der.) mancomunada y solidariamente.

joint opinion, opinión conjunta.

joint owner, (der.) condueño, copropietario; condómino.

joint ownership, (der.) copropiedad, propiedad en común.

joint partner, copartícipe.

joint partnership, coparticipación; coasociación.

joint possession, (der.) coposesión.

joint possessor, (der.) coposesor.

joint proprietor, (der.) copropietario, condueño.

joint rate, (f.c.) tarifa consolidada, tarifa única.

joint resolution, resolución o decisión conjunta (de un cuerpo legislativo).

jointress [ˈdʒɔɪntrəs] *s.* (raro) viuda que goza de usufructo vitalicio de los bienes inmuebles dejados por el marido.

joint rule, correinado, sinarquía; regla de compañía.

joint session, sesión conjunta (de ambas cámaras legislativas).

joint stock, capital social, fondos en común.

joint-stock company [ˈdʒɔɪntˈstɑk-, B -ˌstɔk-] (der.) sociedad en comandita por acciones; sociedad de capitales; sociedad anónima.

joint tenancy, (der.) condominio, tenencia conjunta.

joint tenant, (der.) coarrendatario, coinquilino.

jointure [ˈdʒɔɪntʃər, B -tʃə] *s.* 1. (der.) (usufructo vitalicio por la viuda de los) bienes inmuebles dejados por el marido. 2. (hist.) condominio sobre una propiedad; propiedad en condominio. 3. (ant.) unión, juntura.

joint venture, empresa colectiva.

jointworm [ˈdʒɔɪntˌwɜrm, B -ˌwɜm] *s.* (ento.) larva de mosca calcídida.

joist [dʒɔɪst] *s.* 1. (arq.) cabio, cabrio, vigueta, viga. 2. abitaque, cuartón. —*v.t.* proveer de cabios.

joke [dʒoʊk] *s.* 1. chiste, agudeza, gracia. 2. broma, chanza, chasco. 3. **as a j.,** en broma; **it is no j.,** no es broma; **to play a j. on,** gastar una broma a; **to take as a j.,** tomar en broma; **to tell a j.,** contar un chiste. —*v.i.* bromear, chancearse; **joking aside** (o **apart**), **no joking,** bromas aparte, hablando en serio; **to be in a joking mood,** estar de broma; **to be joking,** andar de broma. —*v.t.* embromar, chasquear, gastar bromas a (alguien).

joker [ˈdʒoʊkər, B -kə] *s.* 1. bromista, burlón, guasón. 2. (naipes) mona, comodín. 3. (jer.) cláusula disimulada (en un proyecto de ley, en contratos, documentos, etc.). 4. (jer.) tipo, tío, sujeto.

jokingly [-kɪŋlɪ] *adv.* en broma.

jollier [ˈdʒɑlɪər, B ˈdʒɔlɪə] *s.* zalamero, candonguero, lisonjeador.

jollification [ˌdʒɑlɪfəˈkeɪʃən, B ˌdʒɔl-] *s.* (fam.) jolgorio, fiesta, festividad.

jollify [ˈdʒɑləˌfaɪ, B ˈdʒɔl-] *v.i.* (*pret. p.p.* JOLLIFIED; *p.pr.* JOLLIFYING) alegrar(se), regocijar(se). —*v.t.* festejar.

jollily [-əlɪ] *adv.* alegremente, jovialmente.

jolliness [ˈdʒɑlɪnəs, B ˈdʒɔl-] *s.* alegría, jovialidad.

jollity [-ətɪ] *s.* 1. regocijo, alegría, gozo, jovialidad. 2. (G.B.) jolgorio, fiesta.

jolly [ˈdʒɑlɪ, B ˈdʒɔlɪ] *a.* (JOLLIER; JOLLIEST) 1. alegre, festivo, jovial; divertido. 2. agradable, grato, placentero. 3. delicioso, exquisito, espléndido, ej., *a j. little house,* una casita deliciosa. 4. (fam., G.B.) achispado, alegre. 5. **a j. fool,** un gran tonto; **the j. God,** Baco. —*s.* 1. (G.B.) jarana, festividad. 2. (fam., G.B.) infante de marina. —*adv.* (fam.) muy, harto. —*v.t.* (*pret., p.p.* JOLLIED; *p.pr.* JOLLYING) animar, alegrar, estimular. —*v.i.* hacer burla, burlarse, dar vaya.

jolly boat, (mar.) esquife, serení, bote auxiliar.

Jolly Roger [ˌdʒɑlɪˈrɑdʒər, B ˌdʒɔlɪˈrɔdʒə] bandera pirata.

jolt [dʒoʊlt] *v.t.* 1. traquetear, sacudir. 2. estremecer (con un golpe fuerte, etc.). 3. (fig.) desconcertar, conmover, trastornar. —*v.i.* ir dando saltos, ir traqueteando (un vehículo). —*s.* 1. impacto, choque, sacudida. 2. (fig.) golpe, conmoción, trastorno, susto, sobresalto; desgracia, revés. 3. (boxeo) golpe potente. 4. poquito, pizca. 5. **to give** (o **deal**) **a j. (to),** (fig.) dar un sobresalto o susto (a), trastornar (a).

jolthead porgy [ˈdʒoʊltˌhɛd-] (ict.) bajonado.

Jonah [ˈdʒoʊnə] *s.* 1. (bíbl.) Jonás. 2. (fig.) ave de mal agüero.

Jonathan [ˈdʒɑnəθən, B ˈdʒɔn-] *s.* 1. Jonatás. 2. (E.U.) americano (esp. de Nueva Inglaterra). 3. (bot.) variedad de manzano rojo.

jongleur [ˈdʒɑŋglər, B ʒɔŋˈglɜ] *s.* (fr.) juglar, trovador.

jonquil [ˈdʒɑŋkwəl, ˈdʒɑn-, B ˈdʒɔŋ-] *s.* (bot.) junquillo.

jordan, jorden [ˈdʒɔrdən, B ˈdʒɔd-] *s.* (ant., dial.) vaso de noche, bacín, bacinilla.

Jordan [ˈdʒɔrdən, B ˈdʒɔd-] *s.* 1. Jordán (río). 2. Jordania (país).

Jordan almonds, almendras importadas de Málaga (usadas en pastelería).

Jordanian [dʒɔrˈdeɪnɪən, B dʒɔˈ-] *s., a.* jordano, de Jordania.

jorum [ˈdʒɔrəm] *s.* vaso grande, esp. ponchera.

joseph [ˈdʒoʊzəf, -səf, B -zɪf] *s.* (hist.) capa de montar de mujer (del siglo XVIII).

Joseph of Arimathaea [-əvˌærəməˈθiə] (bíbl.) José de Arimatea.

Joseph's coat, (bot.) papagayo, capa de rey.

josh [dʒɑʃ, B dʒɔʃ] *v.i.* (E.U.) bromear (se), candonguear. —*v.t.* zumbar, dar broma a. —*s.* (E.U.) chanza, guasa, broma, chunga.

josher [ˈdʒɑʃər, B ˈdʒɔʃə] *s.* bromista, guasón.

Joshua [ˈdʒɑʃʊə, B ˈdʒɔʃwə] *s.* (bíbl.) Josué, sucesor de Moisés.

Joshua tree, (bot.) yuca.

Josiah [dʒoʊˈsaɪə] **Josias** [-ˈsaɪəs] *s.* (bíbl.) Josías, rey de Judea.

joskin [ˈdʒɑskən, B ˈdʒɔs-] *s.* (jer.) rústico, palurdo.

joss [dʒɑs, B dʒɔs] *s.* dios chino; imagen venerada.

joss house, templo chino.

joss stick, pebete perfumado (que se quema ante divinidades chinas).

jostle [ˈdʒɑsəl, B ˈdʒɔs-] *v.t.* 1. empujar, empellar, dar empellones a. 2. forcejear con. 3. **j. one's way in (out),** entrar (salir) a empellones. —*v.i.* 1. codear, dar codazos. 2. abrirse paso a empellones. 3. **j. against,** chocar contra; **j. with,** mezclarse con (gente, muchedumbre, etc.); estar lado a lado con (una cosa). —*s.* 1. empellón, empujón. 2. encuentro.

jot [dʒɑt, B dʒɔt] *s.* jota, pizca, ápice; **I don't care a j.,** no me importa un bledo. —*v.t.* (*pret., p.p.* JOTTED; *p.pr.* JOTTING) (ú. gen. con *down*) anotar, tomar notas de, ej., *j. it down,* apúntalo.

jotting [ˈdʒɑtɪŋ, B ˈdʒɔt-] *s.* apunte, nota (de corta extensión).

jouk [dʒuk] *v.i., v.t.* (esco.) esquivar, evitar, escabullirse.

joule [dʒul, dʒaʊl] *s.* (fís.) julio, joule.

jounce [dʒaʊns] *v.t.* sacudir, traquetear. —*v.i.* dar tumbos (esp. viajando en vehículos). —*s.* sacudimiento, traqueteo, tumbo.

journal ['dʒɜrnəl, B 'dʒɜn-] *s.* 1. diario (personal). 2. diario de debates, acta del día (de un cuerpo legislativo). 3. diario, periódico; p. ext., revista. 4. (com., ten.) diario, libro diario. 5. (mec.) muñón.
journal box, (mec.) chumacera, muñonera; (f.c.) caja de engrase.
journalese [ˌdʒɜrnəl'iz, B 'dʒɜn-] *s.* (fam.) lenguaje o estilo periodístico.
journalism ['dʒɜrnəlˌɪzəm, B 'dʒɜn-] *s.* periodismo; la prensa (profesión).
journalist [-əst] *s.* periodista, cronista, articulista.
journalistic [ˌdʒɜrnəl'ɪstɪk, B ˌdʒɜn-] *a.* periodístico, propio de la prensa.
journalistically [-tɪkəlɪ] *adv.* de modo periodístico, periodísticamente.
journalize ['dʒɜrnəlˌaɪz, B 'dʒɜn-] *v.t.* 1. (com.) pasar al diario. 2. anotar, apuntar, narrar o describir en un diario.
journey ['dʒɜrnɪ, B 'dʒɜnɪ] *s.* 1. viaje. 2. (dial.) jornada, un día de viaje. —*v.i.* viajar; salir de viaje.
journeyer [-ər, B -ə] *s.* viajero, viandante, viajante.
journeyman [-mən] *s.* 1. oficial (obrero que ha terminado el aprendizaje). 2. (fig.) rutinero; alquiladizo.
journey tailor, oficial de sastre.
journeywork [-ˌwɜrk, B -ˌwɜk] *s.* 1. trabajo hecho por un oficial. 2. trabajo mediocre, trabajo rutinario.
joust [dʒaʊst] *v.i.* 1. justar, tornear. 2. (fig.) trabar combate. —*s.* justa, torneo.
jouster ['dʒaʊstər] *s.* justador, el que pelea en una justa o torneo.
Jove [dʒoʊv] *s.* (mitol., astr.) Jove, Júpiter; **by J.,** ¡por Dios!
jovial ['dʒoʊvɪəl] *a.* 1. jovial, alegre, festivo. 2. **J.,** jovial (relativo a Jove o Júpiter).
joviality [ˌdʒoʊvɪ'ælətɪ] *s.* jovialidad.
jovially ['dʒoʊvɪələ] *adv.* jovialmente.
jovialness [-nəs] *s.* jovialidad.
Jovian ['dʒoʊvɪən] *a.* joviano (relativo al planeta Júpiter).
jow [dʒaʊ] *v.t.* (esco.) tocar, tañer (una campana). —*v.i.* repicar (la campana).
jowl [dʒaʊl] *s.* 1. quijada, mandíbula. 2. mejilla. 3. **cheek by j.,** (fig.) cara a cara, en estrecha intimidad.
jowl, *s.* 1. carrillo, cachete. 2. papada. 3. barba (de gallo, pavo, etc.). 4. cabeza (y partes adyacentes) de un pescado (aderezado).
joy [dʒɔɪ] *s.* 1. alegría, júbilo, regocijo, alborozo. 2. felicidad, bienaventuranza. 3. placer, motivo de alegría o felicidad. —*v.i., v.t.* (poét.) alegrar(se), regocijar(se); (ant.) gozar de.
joyance ['dʒɔɪəns] *s.* (poét.) goce, placer; deleite; alegría, júbilo.
joy bells, campanas de alegría (que se hacen repicar en ocasiones festivas).
Joycean ['dʒɔɪsɪən] *a.* joiciano, de Joyce, al estilo de James Joyce, el escritor irlandés.
joyful ['dʒɔɪfəl] *a.* alegre, gozoso, contento, regocijado.
joyfully [-fəlɪ] *adv.* alegremente, gozosamente.
joyfulness [-fəlnəs] *s.* gozo, júbilo, alegría.
joyless ['dʒɔɪləs] *a.* sin alegría, triste, sin gozo, lúgubre.
joylessly [-lɪ] *adv.* tristemente, lúgubremente.
joylessness [-nəs] *s.* tristeza, melancolía, abatimiento.
joyous ['dʒɔɪəs] *a.* alegre, gozoso.
joyously [-lɪ] *adv.* alegremente, gozosamente.
joyousness [-nəs] *s.* alegría, regocijo, júbilo, gozo.
joy ride, (fam.) 1. paseo alocado en automóvil (muchas veces sin permiso del dueño), paseo en coche, vuelta en coche. 2. **they took the car for a j.,** robaron el coche para dar una vuelta; **to go on a j. r.,** (fig.) entregarse a una vida de holgorio y placeres.
joy stick, (jer., aer.) palanca de mando; (comput.) palanca de control, mando.
J.P. *abrev. de* **justice of the peace,** juez de paz.
Jr. *abrev. de* **junior,** hijo (calificativo en casos de nombres propios).
juba ['dʒubə] *s.* (mús.) juba (antigua danza típica de los negros de Luisiana).
jubbah ['dʒʊbə] *s.* aljuba (especie de gabán con mangas cortas y estrechas usado por los musulmanes).
jubilance ['dʒubələns] *s.* júbilo, alborozo.
jubilant [-ənt] *a.* jubiloso, alborozado.
jubilantly [-lɪ] *adv.* jubilosamente, alborozadamente.
jubilate ['dʒubəˌleɪt] *v.i.* exultar, alegrarse, regocijarse.
jubilation [ˌdʒubə'leɪʃən] *s.* júbilo, regocijo, alborozo, exultación.
jubilee ['dʒubəli, ˌdʒubə'li, B 'dʒubɪli] *s.* 1. (relig.) jubileo, indulgencia plenaria. 2. aniversario; quincuagésimo aniversario (de servicios, reinado, etc.). 3. (hist.) jubileo (fiesta que celebraban los israelitas cada cincuenta años). 4. júbilo, regocijo, alborozo, exultación.
Judaeo-Spanish [dʒuˌdeɪoʊ'spænɪʃ, B -'di-] *a., s.* judeo-español, sefardita.
Judah ['dʒudə] *s.* (bíbl.) Judá.
Judaic [dʒu'deɪɪk] **Judaical** [-əkəl] *a.* judaico.
Judaism ['dʒudəˌɪzəm, B -deɪ-] *s.* judaísmo, hebraísmo.
Judaist [-əst] *s.* hebraísta.
Judaize [-ˌaɪz] *v.i.* judaizar. —*v.t.* convertir al judaísmo.
Judaizer [-ər, B -ə] *s.* judaizante.
Judas ['dʒudəs] *s.* 1. (bíbl.) Judas Iscariote. 2. Judas, el apóstol. 3. (fig.) Judas, traidor. 3. **j.,** atisbadero en una puerta (esp. en prisión).
Judas kiss, beso de Judas.
Judas tree, (bot.) ciclamor, arjorán, algarrobo loco.
Judean, Judaean [dʒu'diən] *a., s.* judío, hebreo, israelí.
judge [dʒʌdʒ] *s.* 1. juez. 2. árbitro. 3. conocedor, crítico. 4. (hist.) juez (magistrado supremo del pueblo de Israel). 5. **to be no j. of,** no poder juzgar, no tener criterio para; **to be the j. of,** juzgar, decidir; calificar. —*v.t.* 1. juzgar (una causa o litigio). 2. juzgar, opinar, estimar. 3. (ant.) gobernar. —*v.i.* juzgar, estimar; formar una opinión sobre o de; **judging by** (o **from**), a juzgar por.
judge advocate, (*pl.* JUDGE ADVOCATES) (mil.) auditor de guerra; auditor de marina.
judge advocate general, auditor general (del ejército, marina o fuerza aérea).
judge-made ['dʒʌdʒˌmeɪd] *a.* creado por jueces o por decisión judicial.
judgement, *var. de* **judgment.**
Judges ['dʒʌdʒəz] *s. pl.* (*sing. en const.*) (bíbl.) Libro de los Jueces.
judgeship ['dʒʌdʒˌʃɪp] *s.* judicatura, magistratura, magistrado.
judgmatic [ˌdʒʌdʒ'mætɪk] **judgmatical** [-ɪkəl] *a.* (fam.) juicioso, cuerdo, sensato.
judgmatically [-ɪkəlɪ] *adv.* juiciosamente, cuerdamente, sensatamente.
judgment ['dʒʌdʒmənt] *s.* 1. juicio, criterio, discernimiento. 2. opinión, dictamen, decisión. 3. (der.) fallo, sentencia; ejecutoria. 4. (teo.) juicio (de Dios). 5. (ant.) justicia. 6. **in my j.,** en mi opinión, a mi juicio; **the Last J.,** (teo.) el juicio final; **to be a j. on (someone) for,** ser su castigo (de alguien) por.
Judgment Day, día del juicio final; el último día; día del juicio universal.
judgment debt, (der.) deuda por fallo, deuda por juicio.
judgment of God, (relig.) juicio de Dios.
judgment seat, tribunal.
judicable ['dʒudɪkəbəl] *a.* juzgable.
judicative [-dəˌkeɪtɪv, B -kət-] *a.* judicial.
judicator [-ər, B -ə] *s.* juez; juzgador.
judicatory [-dɪkəˌtɔrɪ, B -tərɪ] *a.* judicial. —*s.* (*pl.* JUDICATORIES) judicatura.
judicatory tribunals, tribunales judiciales.
judicature [-kətʃər, B -tʃə] *s.* 1. judicatura. 2. tribunal (de justicia).
judiciable [dʒu'dɪʃɪəbəl] *a.* juzgable.
judicial [dʒu'dɪʃəl] *a.* 1. judicial, de juez (poder, procedimientos; ropa, peluca, etc.). 2. crítico, discriminador (ojo, mente, etc.). 3. (G.B.) imparcial, equitativo, justo. 4. (teo.) debido a castigo divino.
judicially [-əlɪ] *adv.* judicialmente, por procedimiento judicial.
judiciary [-'dɪʃɪˌɛrɪ, B -ərɪ] *a.* judicial. —*s.* poder judicial; judicatura.
judicious [-'dɪʃəs] *a.* juicioso, cuerdo, sensato.
judiciously [-lɪ] *adv.* juiciosamente, cuerdamente, sensatamente.
judiciousness [-nəs] *s.* juicio, cordura, sensatez.
judo ['dʒudoʊ] *s.* judo, sistema japonés de defensa física, derivado del jiu-jitsu.
jug [dʒʌg] *s.* 1. jarra, botija, cántaro. 2. (jer.) chirona, gayola, cana (Amer.). —*v.t.* (*pret., p.p.* JUGGED; *p.pr.* JUGGING) 1. hervir o cocer en jarra o botija. 2. (jer.) encarcelar.
jugal ['dʒugəl] *a.* (anat., zool.) yugal, malar, cigomático.
jugate ['dʒuˌgeɪt, -gət] *a.* 1. (biol.) apareado, puesto en pares. 2. (bot.) yugado.
jugful ['dʒʌgˌfʊl] *s.* (*pl.* JUGFULS O JUGSFUL) cantidad contenida en una jarra, una jarra llena (de).
Juggernaut ['dʒʌgərˌnɔt, B -əˌ-] *s.* 1. Krisna, Krina o Visnú (dios hindú). 2. **j.,** institución o creencia que exige devoción ciega; fuerza inexorable e irresistible; monstruo destructivo.
juggins ['dʒʌgənz] *s.* (jer.) simplón, bobalicón, papanatas.
juggle ['dʒʌgəl] *v.i.* 1. hacer juegos malabares, escamotear. 2. (con *with*) engañar, hacer trampas (a); falsificar (los hechos). 3. **j. (someone) out of,** despojar (a alguien) por engaño de. —*v.t.* 1. engañar, embaucar, defraudar, trampear. 2. hacer malabares con, ej., *to j. knives,* hacer malabares con cuchillos. 3. **j. accounts,** falsear o alterar fraudulentamente las cuentas. —*s.* 1. juegos malabares, escamoteo. 2. truco, treta, ardid. 3. impostura, engaño, trampa.
juggler ['dʒʌglər, B -lə] *s.* 1. malabarista, prestidigitador. 2. (despec.) manipulador, maquinador. 3. (ant.) juglar, bufón.
jugglery [-lərɪ] *s.* (*pl.* JUGGLERIES) 1. prestidigitación, malabarismo. 2. (despec.) manipuleo, maquinación, manejo.
juggling [-lɪŋ] *s.* 1. prestidigitacíon, malabarismo. 2. (despec.) manipuleo, maquinación, manejo.
jughead ['dʒʌgˌhɛd] *s.* (jer.) bobalicón, estúpido.
juglandaceous [ˌdʒuglæn'deɪʃəs] *a.* (bot.) juglandáceo, juglándeo.
Jugoslav, *var. de* **Yugoslav.**
Jugoslavia, *var. de* **Yugoslavia.**
jugular ['dʒʌgjələr, B -lə] *a.* 1. (anat.) yugular. 2. del cuello, de la garganta. —*s.* (anat.) (vena) yugular.

jugular vein, (anat.) vena yugular.
jugulate ['dʒugjəˌleɪt, 'dʒʌg-] *v.t.* 1. degollar. 2. (med.) detener una enfermedad o proceso mediante procedimientos severos.
juice [dʒus] *s.* 1. jugo, zumo. 2. (jer.) electricidad; gasolina; aceite. 3. (jer.) licor esp. whiski. —*v.t.* 1. exprimir, extraer el jugo de. 2. hacer jugoso; poner en jugo. 3. **j. up,** (jer.) animar, vigorizar.
juiceless ['dʒusləs] *a.* seco, sin jugo.
juicer ['dʒusər, B -sə] *s.* exprimidera, exprimidero, exprimidor.
juicily [-səlɪ] *adv.* jugosamente.
juiciness [-sɪnəs] *s.* jugosidad; suculencia.
juicy [-sɪ] *s.* (JUICIER; JUICIEST) 1. jugoso, suculento. 2. (fam.) sabroso, picante.
jujitsu [dʒu'dʒitsu] *s.* jiu-jitsu, arte japonés de defensa física sin armas.
juju ['dʒudʒu] *s.* fetiche, talismán o amuleto africano; magia; poder o efecto mágico.
jujube ['dʒudʒub] 1. (bot.) azufaifo, azofaifo, guinjo, jinjolero. 2. azufaifa, azofaifa, guinja, jínjol (fruto). 3. jalea de azufaifa; pastilla de azufaifa.
jujutsu, *var. de* **jujitsu.**
jukebox ['dʒukˌbɑks, B -ˌbɔks] *s.* tocadiscos automático, máquina de discos, rocola (Amer.).
juke joint, (jer., E.U.) restaurant pequeño donde se baila al compás de la música de un tocadiscos automático.
julep ['dʒuləp, B -lɛp] *s.* 1. julepe. 2. (t. **mint j.**) julepe de menta (bebida).
Julian Alps ['dʒuljən-] Alpes Julianos.
Julian calendar, calendario juliano.
julienne [ˌdʒulɪ'ɛn] *s.* (fr., cocina) sopa juliana. —*a.* cortado en tiras delgadas (patata, zanahoria, etc.).
July [dʒʊ'laɪ, dʒu-] *s.* (*pl.* JULIES) julio (mes).
jumble ['dʒʌmbəl] *v.i.* pasar o mover en desorden. —*v.t.* (gen. con *up*) embarullar, mezclar, confundir. —*s.* 1. mezcla, revoltillo, revoltijo, mezcolanza. 2. rosquilla delgada y dulce.
jumble sale, venta de artículos donados.
jumbo ['dʒʌmboʊ] *s.* 1. coloso (cosa o animal enorme). 2. (const.) carro de perforadoras, vagón barrenador. 3. (mar.) trinquetilla. —*a.* enorme, colosal, gigantesco.
jump [dʒʌmp] *v.i.* 1. saltar, brincar, dar saltos; tirarse, lanzarse (de una altura). 2. rebotar; traquetear, sacudirse. 3. subir (repentinamente), ej., *the price jumped,* el precio subió repentinamente. 4. (con *with*) coincidir, concordar (con). 5. tener un sobresalto, sobresaltarse. 6. (bridge) saltar. 7. **go an j. in the lake,** váyase Ud. a freír espárragos; **j. at,** (fig.) aceptar en el acto, apresurarse a aceptar o a aprovechar (una oferta, una invitación); **j. down someone's throat,** estallar, enojarse de repente contra alguien, reprender severamente a alguien; **j. in,** saltar a (auto, etc.); **j. on,** saltar a (tren); **j. out,** saltar fuera; **j. over,** saltar o pasar por encima de, pasar de un salto; **j. to a conclusion,** sacar precipitadamente una conclusión; **j. to it!** (fam.) ¡apresúrate!; **j. up,** levantarse bruscamente; **j. upon,** caer encima a; acometer. —*v.t.* 1. saltar por encima de o al otro lado de. 2. acometer. 3. usurpar, tomar sin derecho, ej., *j. a claim,* usurpar un denuncio, esp. minero. 4. hacer saltar (a un caballo). 5. (E.U.) saltar a (un tren, etc.); saltar, salir fuera de, ej., *the train jumped the tracks,* el tren se descarriló. 6. no esperar, ej., *he jumped the green light,* no esperó el momento propicio. 7. adelantar en (hacer), ej., *j. the gun,* adelantarse (al otro) en sacar el revólver. 8. escapar de (prisión, etc.). 9. (elec.) desviar (conexión). 10. (damas) comer (una ficha). 11. (caza) hacer saltar (una liebre); hacer volar (una perdiz). 12. (ant.) arriesgar, aventurar, exponer. 13. **j. bail,** fugarse estando bajo fianza de arraigo. —*s.* 1. salto, brinco. 2. alza abrupta (de precio, etc.). 3. (fam.) ventaja. 4. sobresalto. 5. viaje corto (esp. en avión). 6. (damas) captura (de una ficha). 7. (dep.) salto (largo, alto). 8. (vulg.) coito, acto sexual. 9. **on the j.,** muy activo; muy ocupado, atareado; **the jumps,** nerviosidad, ataque de nervios; (jer., G.B.) corea, baile de San Vito; delírium tremens; **to have the j. on,** (fam.) tomar la delantera a, llevar ventaja a.
jump bid, (bridge) salto (declaración más alta de lo necesario).
jumper ['dʒʌmpər, B -pə] *s.* 1. saltador. 2. grada, rastra; trineo. 3. (elec.) alambre de cierre, cable de empalme, puente. 4. (mec.) barrena. 5. mono; jubón largo sin mangas ni cuello.
jumper cables, cables de arranque.
jumpiness [-pɪnəs] *s.* nerviosidad, nerviosismo.
jumping bean [-pɪŋ-] (bot.) frijol saltador o brincador.
jumping jack, títere, pelele.
jumping-off place [ˌdʒʌmpɪŋ'ɔf-] *s.* (fam.) 1. el rincón más remoto (de la tierra). 2. punto de partida.
jumping spider, (ento.) alguacil, alguacilillo.
jump-off ['dʒʌmpˌɔf] *s.* arranque, partida (en una carrera).
jump rope, cuerda de saltar, comba.
jump seat, asiento corredizo, asiento plegable (entre el asiento delantero y el trasero de un automóvil).
jump shot, (baloncesto) lanzamiento con salto.
jump spark, (elec.) chispa de entrehierro, chispa eléctrica.
jump start, hacer arrancar un coche haciendo un puente.
jump suit, 1. mono usado por paracaidistas, mecánicos, etc. 2. atuendo deportivo similar a un mono, que usan hombres y mujeres.
jumpy ['dʒʌmpɪ] *a.* (JUMPIER; JUMPIEST) 1. nervioso, aprensivo, asustadizo. 2. con mala amortiguación (coche, etc.).
juncaceous [ˌdʒʌŋ'keɪʃəs] *a.* (bot.) juncáceo.
junco ['dʒʌŋkoʊ] *s.* (*pl.* JUNCOS O JUNCOES) (orn.) (especie de) pinzón americano.
junction ['dʒʌŋkʃən] *s.* 1. unión, conexión. 2. (elec.) empalme. 3. (f.c.) empalme, entronque. 4. confluencia de dos o más vías.
junction box, (elec.) caja de empalme.
junctural ['dʒʌŋktʃərəl] *a.* (gram.) conjuntivo.
juncture [-tʃər, B -tʃə] *s.* 1. unión, juntura, junta. 2. coyuntura, articulación; conexión; costura. 3. coyuntura, ocasión, sazón, trance. 4. **at this j.,** en esta coyuntura, a esta sazón.
jundy, jundie ['dʒʌndɪ] *v.t., v.i.* (esco.) empujar, empellar, codear. —*s.* empujón, empellón.
June [dʒun] *s.* junio (mes).
June beetle, J. bug, (ento.) melolonta.
Juneberry ['dʒunˌbɛrɪ] *s.* (bot.) guillomo (árbol y fruto).
June grass, (bot.) poa de los prados, poa.
jungle ['dʒʌŋgəl] *s.* 1. selva, floresta, jungla. 2. (fig.) maraña, laberinto. 3. (jer., E.U.) campamento de vagos (en lugar despoblado). 4. lugar o situación en que la gente compite despiadadamente o lucha por sobrevivir.
jungle fever, (med.) fiebre palúdica, malaria.
jungle fowl, (orn.) bankiva; sonerat; gallo salvaje.
jungly [-glɪ] *a.* lleno de maraña, enmarañado.
junior ['dʒunjər, B -njə] *a.* 1. hijo (*gen. abrev.* **Jr.** o **jr.**), ej., *John Smith Jr.,* John Smith hijo. 2. joven. 3. juvenil (ej., novela). 4. menor, subalterno, ej., *j. partner,* socio menor, *j. officer,* oficial subalterno. 5. nuevo, recién nombrado (socio, senador, etc.). 6. de penúltimo año (en colegio o universidad). 7. de fecha reciente; secundario, inferior o posterior, ej., *j. writ,* (der.) escrito secundario o posterior. —*s.* 1. joven, menor (de edad). 2. (E.U.) estudiante de penúltimo año (en colegio o universidad). 3. (fam., E.U.) hijo, muchacho. 4. subordinado.
juniorate ['dʒunjəˌreɪt, -rət] *s.* 1. jovenado. 2. seminario jesuítico.
junior college, escuela semisuperior (gen. comprende los dos primeros años universitarios).
junior high school, escuela secundaria inferior (entre la primaria y la secundaria).
junior league, una rama de la organización norteamericana de mujeres ex-universitarias que se dedican a actividades de sociedad.
junior miss, jovencita.
junior officer, oficial subalterno.
juniper ['dʒunəpər, B -pə] *s.* (bot.) enebro, junípero común, cedro de Virginia.
juniper berry, enebrina, fruto del enebro.
juniper oil, aceite de enebro, aceite de cada.
juniper tar, juniper-tar oil [-ˌtɑr-] aceite de cada.
juniper tree, (bot.) enebro.
junk [dʒʌŋk] *s.* 1. jarcia trozada, cuerda gastada (usada para hacer estopa, felpudos, etc.). 2. chatarra, hierro viejo, vidrio o papel viejos, basura, trastos viejos, cachivaches, hojarascas. 4. (fig.) (fam.) hojarasca, tontería, disparate. 5. (pr. G.B.) trozo, pedazo, masa. 6. (mar.) cecina. 7. (jer.) droga, narcótico, esp. heroína. —*v.t.* (jer.) echar a la basura; reducir (aparato, máquina, etc.) a chatarra o hierro viejo.
junk, *s.* (mar.) junco (embarcación china).
junk art, arte tridimensional que utiliza materiales de desecho.
junk dealer, chatarrero.
Junker [juŋkər, B -kə] *s.* junker, miembro de la aristocracia en Prusia.
Junkerism [-kəˌrɪzəm] *s.* gobierno de los junkers.
junket ['dʒʌŋkət] *s.* 1. (cocina) crema de queso, manjar de cuajada y crema; especie de jalea. 2. fiesta, festejo, banquete; (E.U.) excursión o paseo (gastando fondos públicos). 3. (ant.) manjar, dulce. —*v.i., v.t.* festejar, agasajar; (E.U.) ir de paseo o de viaje (gastando fondos públicos).
junketeer [ˌdʒʌŋkə'tɪr, B -'tɪə] **junketer** ['dʒʌŋkətər, B -ə] *s.* (E.U.) funcionario deshonesto (que con el pretexto de hacer una visita de inspección, etc., se va de viaje gastando fondos públicos).
junk food, comida basura, porquerías, alimento chatarra.
junkie ['dʒʌŋkɪ] *s.* 1. (fam.) trapero. 2. (t. **junky**) (jer.) traficante de drogas. 3. (t. **junky**) (jer.) narcómano.
junk jewelery, (fam.) bisutería chabacana.
junk mail, correo de propaganda solicitando suscripciones, donaciones, etc. que se envía en grandes cantidades.
junk man, chatarrero, trapero.
junkyard ['dʒʌŋkˌjɑrd, B -ˌjɑd] *s.* almacén de trastos viejos, trapería; depósito de chatarra (o de objetos de desecho, papel de periódico, botellas vacías, etc. que usualmente son revendidos).
Juno ['dʒunoʊ] *s.* 1. (mitol.) Juno, diosa del matrimonio. 2. mujer de figura escultural.
Junoesque [ˌdʒunoʊ'ɛsk] *a.* propio o digno de Juno (belleza, figura, etc.).
junta ['hʊntə, 'dʒʌntə, B 'dʒʌntə] *s.* 1. junta, asamblea, concilio, tribunal o comité, esp. junta legislativa o administrativa (como en España). 2. cábala, cabildeo, camarilla.

junto ['dʒʌntoʊ] *s.* camarilla; facción (esp. política); cábala, cabildeo.
jupe [dʒup, B ʒup] *s.* (pr. esco.) 1. chaqueta o túnica de hombre. 2. camisa; corpiño; jubón.
Jupiter ['dʒupətər, B -ə] *s.* (mitol., astr.) Júpiter, dios de los dioses y el planeta mayor del sistema solar.
jupon ['dʒupɑn, B 'ʒupɔn] *s.* aljuba, jubón.
Jura ['dʒʊrə, B 'dʒuərə] *s.* (geol.) período jurásico.
jural ['dʒʊrəl, B 'dʒʊər-] *a.* legal, jurídico.
jurant [-ənt] *s.* persona que toma un juramento.
Jurassic [dʒʊ'ræsɪk] *a., s.* (geol.) jurásico.
jurat ['dʒʊr,æt, B 'dʒʊər-] *s.* 1. (hist.) persona bajo juramento; jurado. 2. (der.) certificado del notario; cláusula que da fe (de un juramento).
juratory ['dʒʊrə,tɔrɪ, B 'dʒʊərətərɪ] *a.* (der.) juratorio.
jurel [hu'rɛl, B hʊ-] *s.* (ict.) jurel; chicharro, caballa, furel, paro, sorel.
juridic [dʒʊ'rɪdɪk, B dʒʊə-] *a.* jurídico, judicial, legal.
juridical [-ɪkəl] *a.* 1. (der.) jurídico, judicial, del juez. 2. jurídico, legal.
juridically [-kəlɪ] *adv.* jurídicamente, judicialmente.
juridical days, días hábiles (durante los cuales funcionan los tribunales).
jurisconsult [,dʒʊrəs'kɑn,sʌlt, -kən'sʌlt, B 'dʒʊərɪskən,sʌlt] *s.* jurisconsulto, legista, jurista, jurisperito, abogado.
jurisdiction [-'dɪkʃən, B ,dʒʊərɪs-] *s.* jurisdicción.
jurisdictional [-əl] *a.* jurisdiccional.
jurisprudence [-'prudəns] *s.* jurisprudencia.
jurisprudent [-ənt] *s.* jurisprudente, jurisperito, jurisconsulto, jurista. —*a.* versado en jurisprudencia.
jurisprudential [-pru'dɛntʃəl, B -dɛnʃəl] *a.* de la jurisprudencia.
jurist ['dʒʊrəst, B 'dʒʊər-] *s.* jurista, jurisconsulto, legista.
juristic [dʒʊ'rɪstɪk, B dʒʊə-] *a.* jurídico.
juristical [-tɪkəl] *a.* jurídico.
juristically [-kəlɪ] *adv.* jurídicamente.
juror ['dʒʊrər, B'dʒʊərə] *s.* jurado (persona).
jury ['dʒʊrɪ, B 'dʒʊərɪ] *s.* 1. jurado, tribunal de jurados. 2. jurado, comité de examinadores.
jury, *a.* (mar.) improvisado, provisional, para uso temporal (esp. en una emergencia).
jury box, tribuna del jurado.
juryman [-mən] *s.* jurado (persona), miembro de un jurado.
jury mast, (mar.) bandola.
jury panel, lista de personas que integran el jurado; panel de jurados.
jury-rigged [-,rɪgd] *a.* (mar.) de aparejo provisional.
jus [jus, B dʒʌs] *s.* (*pl.* JURA ['jʊrə]) 1. ley; el cuerpo legislativo. 2. sistema legal particular. 3. principio o derecho legal.
jussive ['dʒʌsɪv] *a., s.* (gram.) imperativo.
just [dʒʌst] *a.* 1. justo, recto. 2. justo, justiciero, imparcial. 3. justo, merecido (recompensa, castigo, etc.). 4. justo, razonable, adecuado. 5. legítimo, genuino, ej., *a j. title,* un título legítimo. 6. justo, exacto, preciso. —*adv.* 1. precisamente, exactamente, ej., *j. at that spot,* precisamente en aquel lugar, *that is j. it,* eso es precisamente (el punto). 2. escasamente, apenas, casi, no más que. 3. allí mismo, ej., *j. around the corner,* allí mismo a la vuelta de la esquina. 4. solamente, sólo, ej., *it was j. an idea,* fue sólo una idea. 5. hace rato, hace poco; justamente, en este momento. 6. (fam.) simplemente, verdaderamente, ej., *it's j. splendid,* es simplemente espléndido, *all this is j. wonderful,* todo esto es verdaderamente maravilloso. 7. **j. about,** poco más o menos; o poco menos; más o menos, aproximadamente; **j. as,** al momento que, precisamente cuando; lo mismo que, al igual que; **j. as if,** lo mismo que si; **j. as you wish,** como Ud. quiera, como le guste; **j. as well,** da lo mismo; **j. beyond,** un poco más allá; **j. in case,** por si acaso; **j. in time,** justo a tiempo; **j. now,** en este momento; ahora mismo, hace poco; **j. so,** a su gusto, perfecto, ej., *he wants everything to be j. so,* él quiere que todo esté a su gusto (o perfecto); **to have j. (done),** acabar de (hacer), ej., *I have j. seen him pass,* acabo de verlo pasar.
just [dʒʌst] **juster** ['dʒʌstər, B -tə] *vars. de* **joust, jouster.**
justice ['dʒʌstəs] *s.* 1. justicia. 2. juez; magistrado. 3. imparcialidad, equidad. 4. rectitud. 5. (ant.) tribunal de justicia. 6. **to bring to j.,** capturar y enjuiciar; **to do j.,** actuar justamente, obrar con rectitud; **to do (food, liquor) j.,** comer o beber con gusto (manjar, licor); **to do j. to,** hacer pleno uso de, aprovechar plenamente; apreciar debidamente; **to do oneself j.,** rendir uno el máximo, estar a la altura de sus capacidades; **to do (someone) j.,** hacer justicia a (alguien), ser justo con (alguien), dar su merecido a (alguien).
justice of the peace, (der.) juez de paz.
justicer [-təsər, B -sə] *s.* (ant.) juez.
justiceship ['dʒʌstəs,ʃɪp] *s.* judicatura, justiciazgo.
justiciable [dʒʌs'tɪʃɪəbəl] *a.* justiciable.
justiciar [-ər, B -,ɑ] **justiciary** [-,ɛrɪ, B -ərɪ] *s.* (G.B.) (hist.) funcionario judicial (hasta el siglo XIII); alto funcionario real encargado de los asuntos judiciales.
justifiable ['dʒʌstə,faɪəbəl, ˌdʒʌstə'faɪ-] *a.* justificable.
justifiableness [-nəs] *s.* calidad de justificable.
justifiably [-blɪ] *adv.* justificadamente.
justification [,dʒʌstəfə'keɪʃən] *s.* 1. justificación; vindicación. 2. (impr.) justificación (de una máquina de componer). 3. (teo.) justificación (santificación del hombre por la gracia divina).
justification bar, (impr.) justificador.
justificative ['dʒʌstəfə,keɪtɪv] *a.* justificativo.
justificatory [,dʒʌs'tɪfɪkə,tɔrɪ, B 'dʒʌstɪfɪ,keɪtərɪ] *a.* justificador, vindicativo.
justifier ['dʒʌstə,faɪər, B -ə] *a.* justificador.
justify ['dʒʌstə,faɪ] *v.t.* (*pret., p.p.* JUSTIFIED; *p.pr.* JUSTIFYING) 1. justificar; vindicar. 2. (teo., der., impr.) justificar.
justly ['dʒʌstlɪ] *adv.* 1. justamente, rectamente, con justicia, cabalmente, a justo título. 2. debidamente, dignamente.
justness [-nəs] *s.* 1. justicia, equidad. 2. rectitud. 3. exactitud.
jut [dʒʌt] *v.i.* (*pret., p.p.* JUTTED; *p.pr.* JUTTING) sobresalir, proyectarse; **j. out,** resaltar, proyectarse, sobresalir. —*v.t.* sacar fuera, empujar hacia afuera. —*s.* resalto, saliente, salidizo, vuelo.
jute [dʒut] *s.* (bot.) yute, cáñamo de las Indias. —*a.* de yute.
Jutland ['dʒʌtlənd] *s.* Jutlandia, península de Dinamarca.
Jutlander ['dʒʌtləndər, B -də] *a., s.* jutlandés, de Jutlandia.
jutty ['dʒʌtɪ] *s.* (*pl.* JUTTIES) 1. (arq.) retallo, vuelo. 2. (ant.) malecón, rompeolas. —*v.t.* (ant.) hacer resaltar, proyectar.
jut window, mirador, tipo de ventana saliente.
juvenal ['dʒuvənəl] *a.* juvenil.
Juvenal, *s.* Juvenal, poeta satírico romano.
juvenescence [,dʒuvə'nɛsəns] *s.* 1. juventud. 2. parecer joven; aspecto juvenil.
juvenescent [-ənt] *a.* 1. joven. 2. juvenil. 3. rejuvenecedor (tónico, maquillaje).
juvenile ['dʒuvə,naɪl, -nəl, B ,naɪl] *a.* juvenil, joven; inmaduro. —*s.* 1. joven, mocito, mozuelo, mozalbete. 2. (teat.) actor que representa personajes juveniles. 3. libro para niños.
juvenile court, tribunal de menores; tribunal tutelar de menores.
juvenile delinquency, delincuencia de menores, delincuencia juvenil.
juvenile delinquent, menor delincuente, delincuente menor de edad, delincuente juvenil.
juvenile lead, (teat.) galán juvenil, galancete; papel de galán joven; **to play the j. l.,** desempeñar el papel de galán joven.
juvenilia [,dʒuvə'nɪlɪə] *s. pl.* obras de juventud (de un autor o compositor); producción inmatura (esp. literaria o artística).
juvenility [-ətɪ] *s.* carácter juvenil, mocedad, juventud.
juvia ['huvɪə, B 'ʒu-] *s.* (bot.) juvia.
juxtapose [,dʒʌkstə'poʊz, 'dʒʌkstə,poʊz] *v.t.* yuxtaponer.
juxtaposition [,dʒʌkstəpə'zɪʃən] *s.* yuxtaposición.

K

K [keɪ] *s.* k, undécima letra del alfabeto inglés.
k. *abrev. de* **kilo,** kilo (kg.).
K *símb. de* **kalium,** potasio (K).
ka [kɑ] *s.* el espíritu de los muertos, el otro yo (en la antigua religión de los egipcios).
Kaaba, Kaabeh ['kɑbə] *s.* Kaaba (santuario mahometano en la Meca).
kabala, kabbala, *var. de* **cabala.**
kabob, *var. de* **cabob.**
Kabul ['kɑbʊl, B 'kɔbəl] *s.* Kabul, capital de Afganistán.
Kabyle [kə'baɪl] *s.* cabila, beréber, berberisco; beduino de las tribus de Argelia y Túnez.
kadi ['kɑdɪ, 'keɪ-] *s.* cadí, juez civil entre los mahometanos.
Kaffir, Kafir ['kæfər, B -ə] *s.* 1. kafir, cafre. 2. infiel (entre los mahometanos).
kafir ['kæfər, B -ə] *s.* (bot.) (cierto cereal de) sorgo.
kaftan, *var. de* **caftan.**
kaiak, *var. de* **kayak.**
kailyard, *var. de* **kaleyard.**
kainite ['kaɪˌnaɪt] **kainit** [kaɪ'nit, B 'kaɪnɪt] *s.* (min.) cainita.
Kaiser ['kaɪzər, B -zə] *s.* káiser, emperador alemán o austríaco.
Kaiserism [-zəˌrɪzəm] *s.* gobierno absolutista del káiser.
kaka ['kɑkə] *s.* (orn.) loro de Nueva Zelandia.
kakapo [ˌkɑkə'poʊ] *s.* (orn.) kakapú.
kakemono [ˌkɑkɪ'moʊnoʊ, B ˌkækɪ-] *s.* kakemono (pintura japonesa sobre un rollo de seda o papel).
kaki ['kɑkɪ] *s.* (bot.) caqui, níspero del Japón.
kale [keɪl] *s.* (bot.) 1. col, berza común. 2. (esco.) sopa de legumbres. 3. (jer., E.U.) guita (Am.), plata (dinero).
kaleidoscope [kə'laɪdəˌskoʊp] *s.* caleidoscopio, calidoscopio.
kaleidoscopic [-ˌlaɪdə'skɑpɪk, B -'skɔp-] **kaleidoscopical** [-ɪkəl] *a.* calidoscópico; variado.
kalends, *var. de* **calends.**
kaleyard ['keɪlˌjard, B -ˌjɑd] *s.* (esco.) huerto pequeño.
kali ['kælɪ] *s.* (bot.) barrilla.
kalian [ˌkælɪ'ɑn, B kɑl'jɑn] *s.* narguile o pipa en que fuman los orientales.
kalif, *var. de* **caliph.**
kallikaks ['kæləˌkæks] *s.* familia, grupo o persona considerada inferior por la sociedad que le rodea.
kalmia ['kælmɪə] *s.* (bot.) kalmia.
Kalmuck, Kalmuk ['kælmʌk] *a., s.* calmuco, originario de Kalmuk, república autónoma de la Unión Soviética.
kalong ['kɑlɑŋ, B -lɔŋ] *s.* (zool.) murciélago frugívoro de Malaya.
kalpac, *var. de* **calpac.**
kalsomine, *var. de* **calcimine.**
kamala ['kʌmələ, kə'meɪlə, B 'kæmələ] *s.* (bot.) kamala.
Kamasutra [ˌkɑmə'sutrə] *s.* Kama-Sutra, tratado hindú sobre el amor sexual.
kame [keɪm] *s.* (geol.) morena (de origen glacial).
Kamerad [ˌkɑmə'rɑt, B 'kæmərɑd] *s.* camarada, palabra usada por los soldados alemanes en señal de rendición.
kamikaze [ˌkɑmɪ'kɑzɪ] *s.* 1. kamikaze, ataque suicida de los japoneses durante la Segunda Guerra mundial. 2. piloto suicida y su avión.
Kampala [kɑm'pɑlɑ, B kæm'pɑlə] *s.* Kampala, capital de Uganda.
kampilan [kɑm'piˌlɑn] *s.* (arm.) campilán.
kampong ['kɑmˌpɔŋ, B kæm'pɔŋ] *s.* aldea o villorrio malayo.
Kanaka [kə'nækə, B 'kænəkə] *s.* natural de las islas de Hawai, hawaiano; polinesio o melanesio.
kangaroo [ˌkæŋgə'ru] *s.* 1. (zool.) canguro. 2. (*pl.*) (fin., fam.) acciones o valores australianos.
kangaroo court, (jer., E.U.) tribunal improvisado, desautorizado e irresponsable.
kangaroo rat, (zool.) rata canguro.
Kans. *abrev. de* **Kansas,** Kansas (E.U.).
Kansas ['kænzəs] *s.* Kansas, estado de los E.U.
Kantian ['kæntɪən] *a.* kantiano. —*s.* kantiano, kantista, seguidor de Kant, el filósofo alemán.
Kantianism [-ˌɪzəm] *s.* kantismo, la filosofía y los conceptos de Kant.
kaolin, kaoline ['keɪələn] *s.* caolín, arcilla blanca que se emplea en la fabricación de la porcelana y del papel.
kaolinite [-ləˌnaɪt] *s.* (min.) caolinita.
Kapellmeister [kə'pɛlˌmaɪstər, B -stə] *s.* maestro de capilla; director de un coro.
kapok ['keɪˌpɑk, B -ˌpɔk] *s.* kapok, capoc, capoca, especie de lana de ceiba; fibra sedosa extraída del algodón.
kapok tree, (bot.) miraguano, capoquero.
kappa ['kæpə] *s.* kappa, décima letra del alfabeto griego.
kaput [kə'pʊt, -'put, B -'pʊt] *a.* (alemán) 1. aniquilado, acabado; arruinado; incapacitado. 2. descompuesto, malogrado (Am.). 3. fuera de moda.
Karaite ['kɛrəˌaɪt, B 'kɛər-] *s.* (hist.) karaíta, que practica el Karaísmo (doctrina religiosa originada en Persia).
karakul, karakule ['kærəkəl] *s.* 1. (zool.) cordero caracul. 2. piel del caracul, astracán.
karat, *var. de* **carat.**
karate [kə'rɑtɪ] *s.* karate (sistema japonés de defensa propia sin armas).
karma ['kɑrmə, 'kɜr-, B 'kɑmə, 'kɛmə] *s.* karma, sino, destino (en el budismo).
kaross [kə'rɑs, B -'rɔs] *s.* capa, alfombra o cobertor hecho de pieles (en S. África).
karroo, karoo [-'ru] *s.* (*pl.* KARROOS, KAROOS) (geol.) karroo, altiplanicie árida (de S. África).
karyokinesis [ˌkærɪoʊkə'nisəs] *s.* (biol.) cariocinesis, carioquinesis.
karyology [-'ɑlədʒɪ, B -'ɔl-] *s.* (fisiol.) cariología.
karyolymph ['kærɪəˌlɪmf] *s.* (fisiol.) cariolinfa.
karyomitome [ˌkærɪ'ɑməˌtoʊm, B -'ɔmɪ-] *s.* (biol.) cariomitoma.
karyoplasm ['kærɪəˌplæzəm] *s.* (biol.) carioplasma.
karyosome [-ˌsoʊm] *s.* (biol.) cariosoma.
karyotin [ˌkærɪ'oʊtɪn] *s.* (biol.) cariotina.
kasha ['kɑʃə] *s.* (ruso) gachas de trigo molido grueso.
kasher ['kɑʃər, B -ʃə] *var. de* **kosher.**
Kashmir ['kæʃmɪr, kæʃ'mɪr, B -'mɪə] *s.* Cachemira, región del Asia, entre Afganistán y Tibet.
Kashmir goat, (zool.) cabra de Cachemira, cabra tibetana.
Kashmiri [kæʃ'mɪrɪ, B -'mɪərɪ] *s.* cachemiro.
katharsis, *var. de* **catharsis.**
katydid ['keɪtɪˌdɪd] *s.* (ento.) saltamontes americano de chirrido agudo; chicharra, insecto ortóptero.
kauri ['kaʊrɪ] *s.* (bot.) pino de Nueva Zelandia y su resina.
kava ['kɑvə] *s.* 1. (bot.) kawa. 2. bebida embriagadora de las islas del Pacífico, hecha con kawa.
kayak ['kaɪæk] *s.* kayak (tipo de canoa que usan los esquimales).
kayo ['keɪ'oʊ] (jer., boxeo) *s.* golpe que pone fuera de combate. —*v.t.* poner fuera de combate (al contrincante).
kazoo [kə'zu] *s.* (tipo de) chicharra (instrumento).
kc *abrev. de* **kilocycle,** kilociclo.
K.C. *abrev. de* **King's Counsel,** prominente grupo de abogados elegidos como Consejo de la Corona Británica.
K.C.V.O. *abrev. de* **Knight Commander of the Victorian Order,** Caballero de la Orden Victoriana.
kea ['kiə, B 'keɪə] *s.* (orn.) kea, loro de Nueva Zelandia.
kebab, kebob, *vars. de* **cabob.**
kebbuck, kebbock ['kɛbək] *s.* (dial., G.B.) queso entero.
keck [kɛk] *v.i.* arquear, nausear, asquear.
keckle ['kɛkəl] *v.t.* (mar.) aforrar un cable.
keddah ['kɛdə] *s.* recinto para atrapar elefantes (en la India).
kedge [kɛdʒ] *s.* (mar.) anclote, ancla de lanzamiento, ancla pequeña. —*v.t.* espiar (embarcación) por un anclote.
keel [kil] *s.* 1. (mar., aer.) quilla. 2. (poét.) nave, navío. 3. (bot., zool.) carina, quilla. 4. barco de fondo plano. 5. (G.B.) barcaza, lanchón de carga, especialmente el que transporta carbón en el río Tyne. 6. (G.B.) medida de peso para carbón (igual a 21,2 toneladas largas). 7. creyón color bermejo (con que se marca a las ovejas, los maderos, etc.). —*v.t.* voltear (barco, para que la quilla quede arriba). —*v.i.* 1. volcarse. 2. **k. over,** (mar.) dar de quilla, tumbar (un barco); (fig.) caerse de repente, desplomarse, desmayarse.
keel, *v.t., v.i.* (dial.) enfriar (se), refrescar; enfriar un líquido revolviéndolo.
keelage ['kilɪdʒ] *s.* (mar.) derechos de quilla o de puerto.
keelboat ['kilˌboʊt] *s.* barco amplio, poco profundo, con quilla pero sin velas, usado para llevar materiales en los ríos.
keelhaul [-ˌhɔl] *v.t.* 1. (mar.) pasar por debajo de la quilla (antiguo castigo del cual salían vivos pocos marineros). 2. (fig.) castigar severamente.

keelson ['kɛlsən, 'kil-] *s.* (mar.) sobrequilla, palmejar.

keen [kin] *a.* 1. agudo, aguzado, puntiagudo; filudo, ej., *a k. razor,* una navaja filuda o con filo. 2. agudo, punzante (dolor); amargo; penetrante, ej., *a k. wind,* un viento penetrante. 3. picante, pungente; vívido, llamativo, fuerte, ej., *a k. scent,* un perfume fuerte. 4. ansioso, anhelante, vehemente; interesado o entusiasta; intenso (emoción, deseo, etc.). 5. agudo, sensitivo; fino (de oído, vista, olfato, etc.). 6. agudo (de mente), sutíl, vivo; perspicaz, sagaz; acre, mordaz, incisivo, ej., *k. questions,* preguntas incisivas. 7. **to be k. on,** ser muy aficionado a; estar muy encariñado con (alguien).

keen, *s.* (Irl.) endecha, canto fúnebre. —*v.t., v.i.* (Irl.) deplorar, llorar, lamentar(se), plañir (con cantos fúnebres o endechas).

keenly ['kinlɪ] *adv.* 1. agudamente, profundamente. 2. sutilmente. 3. con viveza.

keenness [-nəs] *s.* 1. agudeza, mordacidad. 2. sutileza. 3. perspicacia. 4. ansia, entusiasmo, anhelo.

keen-scented [-ˌsɛntəd] *a.* de olfato fino (ej., perro de caza).

keep [kip] *v.t.* (*pret., p.p.* KEPT [kɛpt] *p.pr.* KEEPING) 1. conservar, quedarse con; guardar (una cosa, etc.). 2. acatar, observar, cumplir (con), obedecer (ley, regla, código, compromiso, palabra, cita); respetar (tratado, acuerdo, etc.). 3. celebrar (sesión, fiesta, ceremonia, etc.). 4. guardar, proteger, defender (plaza fuerte, pueblo, portería en fútbol, etc.). 5. cuidar, mantener en orden; administrar, dirigir, manejar (negocio, tienda); llevar (diario, cuentas, registro); alojar, dar hospedaje a (por paga). 6. sostener, mantener, alimentar (familia, mujer); tener, criar (ganado, aves, abejas). 7. tener (habitualmente) en venta (mercadería). 8. conservar, mantener (en cierto estado). 9. demorar, detener (en custodia, prisión, etc.); (con *from*) no dejar, impedir. 10. (con *for*) reservar, guardar (para). 11. ocultar, guardar, disimular. 12. seguir, continuar por (pista, camino, dirección). 13. permanecer, quedarse en (cama, casa, etc.), ej., *k. one's house,* no salir, quedarse en casa. 14. (con *p.pr.*) hacer, ej., *k. one waiting,* hacer esperar a uno. 15. (ant.) atender regularmente. 16. **God k. you!** ¡Dios te guarde!; **k. away,** mantener alejado, impedir (venir, entrar, tocar algo); **k. back,** retener, impedir que avance; ocultar; **k. boarders,** tener (casa de) huéspedes; **k. company,** acompañar; (fam.) cortejar, galantear; **k. down,** sujetar, reprimir, sojuzgar; no dejar subir (precios, gastos); **k. in,** no dejar salir, mantener dentro, tener encerrado; disimular (disgusto, sentimientos); no dejar que se apague (el fuego); **k. in mind,** recordar; tener en cuenta; **k. it up,** no aflojar, no ceder; **k. off,** parar, desviar, detener, cerrar el paso a; **k. on,** mantener (algo) en uso, no quitarse (ropa); continuar; mantener (a alguien) en servicio; **k. out,** no dejar entrar; excluir; **k. tab(s) (of),** llevar cuenta (de); **k. tab(s) (on),** vigilar, tener bajo observación; **k. to one's word,** cogerle a uno la palabra; **k. (something) to oneself,** rehusar compartir (algo); no revelar (algo); **k. oneself to oneself,** apartarse, vivir retirado; **k. silence,** guardar silencio; **k. together,** mantener unidos o juntos; **k. under,** reprimir, oprimir; **k. up,** mantener (el nivel, correspondencia, etc.); no dejar bajar (precios); no dejar acostarse; conservar; sostener; **k. up appearances,** cubrir las apariencias; **k. up one's spirits,** no desalentarse. —*v.i.* 1. permanecer, quedar(se), ej., *k. in bed,* quedarse en cama, *k. friends,* quedar amigos. 2. (fam.) residir, habitar, morar, estar alojado. 3. conservarse, mantenerse (en), ej., *k. in good health,* mantenerse en buena salud. 4. proseguir, continuar (en dirección, curso, acción). 5. subsistir, perdurar; conservarse, durar sin dañarse (fruta, comida, etc.); admitir dilación, no tener urgencia (asunto, noticia, etc.). 6. (fam., E.U.) sesionar, reunirse. 7. (con *p.pr.*) seguir, persistir en (hacer algo), ej., *k. laughing,* seguir riendo, *k. going,* no parar, seguir caminando. 8. **k. at,** empeñarse en, persistir en (trabajo, tarea); **k. away,** no acercarse, mantenerse a distancia; no dejarse ver; **k. away from,** no meterse en; no mostrarse en, no dejarse ver en; dar de lado a, evitar el encuentro con, no meterse con (alguien); no tocar (cierto alimento, vino, licor, etc.); **k. back,** retardarse, quedarse atrás; no mostrarse; **k. cool,** tener calma, conservar la calma; **k. from,** abstenerse de; **k. in,** permanecer dentro, no salir de la casa; **k. in with,** conservar buenas relaciones con; **k. off,** mantenerse lejos o fuera de; no pisar (césped); no acercarse (a); **k. on,** continuar; **k. on at,** (fig.) regañar; **k. on (doing),** seguir (haciendo); **k. on with,** seguir o continuar con (trabajo, etc.); **k. out of,** no meterse en; **k. to,** seguir por (rumbo, dirección); mantener a (la derecha, izquierda); cumplir con (promesa, palabra); **k. together,** mantenerse juntos o reunidos; **k. up,** mantenerse firme, persistir, no cejar; **k. up with,** ir al paso de, marchar con, no quedarse atrás de; **k. up with the Joneses,** (fam., E.U.) luchar por tener tanto o más que el vecino; competir en la propia clase social; **that will k.!** ¡no hay prisa para eso! —*s.* 1. subsistencia, manutención. 2. torreón, alcázar; esp. torre del homenaje (de un castillo). 3. custodio, protector, defensor. 4. (*pl.*) (cierto tipo de) canicas. 5. (ant.) custodia, protección; guardia. 6. **for keeps** (fam.) para conservar(lo), para siempre; permanentemente; **to earn one's k.,** ganarse la vida; **to play for keeps,** jugar de veras.

keeper ['kipər, B -ə] *s.* 1. guardián, custodio, conserje. 2. carcelero; loquero; tenedor. 3. guardabosque. 4. patrono, patrona (de casa de huéspedes). 5. conservador (de museos). 6. (mec.) fijador, abrazadera; hembra de cerrojo, cerradero; armadura, contacto (de imán). 7. cosa que se conserva bien. 8. **k. of the keys,** llavero mayor; **k. of the records,** archivero; **k.'s lodge,** casilla.

keeping ['ɪŋ] *s.* 1. custodia, cuidado, ej., *in his k.,* en su custodia, a su cargo. 2. conservación, preservación. 3. observancia (de una regla). 4. mantenimiento. 5. conformidad; armonía, esp. en **in k. with,** en armonía con, de conformidad con. 6. **in safe k.,** en lugar seguro, en buenas manos.

keepsake [-ˌseɪk] *s.* recuerdo; prenda, regalo.

keet [kit] *s.* (orn.) gallina de Guinea, gallina pintada.

keeve [kiv] *s.* cubo donde se fermenta la cerveza.

kef [keɪf, B kɛf] *s.* 1. languidez, desfallecimiento; tranquilidad soñadora (ej., la causada por drogas). 2. (t. **keef** [ki'ef]) kif, narcótico de la India.

keg [kɛg] *s.* 1. cuñete, barrilito (gen. de 10 galones o menos). 2. (E.U.) medida de peso para clavos (equivalente a 45,36 kilogramos).

kegler ['kɛglər, B -lə] *s.* (fam.) jugador de bolos.

keir, *var. de* **kier.**

keloid ['kiˌlɔɪd] *s.* (med.) queloide.

kelp [kɛlp] *s.* 1. (bot.) kelp, alga marina. 2. cenizas de alga marina, de las que se obtiene potasio y yodo.

kelpie ['kɛlpɪ] *s.* 1. (esco.) ninfa, nereida. 2. (Aust.) perro pastor.

kelson ['kɛlsən] *var. de* **keelson.**

kelt [kɛlt] *s.* (ict.) salmón zancado.

Kelt [kɛlt] **Keltic** ['kɛltɪk] *var. de* **Celt, Celtic.**

kelter ['kɛltər, B -tə] *var. de* **kilter.**

Kelvin scale ['kɛlvən-] (fís.) escala absoluta (de temperaturas).

kempt [kɛmpt] *a.* limpio, arreglado.

ken [kɛn] *v.t.* (*pret., p.p.* KENNED; *p.pr.* KENNING) 1. (ant., esco.) saber; comprender, discernir, entender. 2. (pr. dial.) reconocer o admitir; (ant. excepto der. esco.) reconocer (como heredero). 3. (ant., dial.) reconocer (a primera vista). —*v.i.* (ant., dial.) saber (de o acerca de). —*s.* 1. vista, alcance de la vista; alcance de la comprensión. 2. conocimiento, comprensión.

kenaf [kə'næf] *s.* (bot.) variedad de cáñamo.

kench [kɛntʃ] *s.* (E.U.) recipiente para salar pescado o curar pieles.

Kendal green ['kɛndəl-] (tej.) paño de color verde (tejido en Kendal, G.B.).

kenilworth ivy ['kɛnəlˌwɜrθ-, B -ˌwɜθ-] (bot.) cimbalaria.

kennel ['kɛnəl] *s.* 1. perrera. 2. (*pl.*) criadero de perros. 3. jauría, recova. 4. arroyo (de la calle), canal, desagüe. —*v.i.* (*pret., p.p.* KENNELED O KENNELLED; *p.pr.* KENNELING O KENNELLING) yacer o guarecerse en perrera. —*v.t.* tener o encerrar en perrera.

kenning ['kɛnɪŋ] *s.* (esco.) pequeña porción o cantidad.

keno ['kinoʊ] *s.* lotería familiar que se juega con láminas.

kenogenesis [ˌkinoʊ'dʒɛnəsəs, B ˌkinə-] **kenogenetic** [-dʒə'nɛtɪk] *vars. de* **cenogenesis, cenogenetic.**

kenotron ['kɛnəˌtrɑn, B -ˌtrɔn] *s.* (elec.) kenotrón.

kentledge ['kɛntlɪdʒ] *s.* (mar.) enjunque, lastre de lingotes de hierro.

Kentucky [kən'tʌkɪ, B kɛn-] *s.* Kentucky, estado de los E.U.

Kentucky coffee tree, (bot.) raigón del Canadá.

Kenya ['kɛnjə, 'kin-] *s.* Kenya, Kenia, estado de África ecuatorial.

Kenyan [-jən] *s., a.* keniano, nativo de Kenya.

kep [kɛp] *v.t., v.i.* (esco., Irl.) coger, agarrar; interceptar.

kepi ['keɪpɪ, B 'kɛpɪ] *s.*(*pl.* KEPIS) (mil.) quepis, kepis (gorra de visera con copa plana).

kept [kɛpt] *pret. y p.p. de* **keep.**

kept woman, concubina, querida, manceba, mantenida (Guat., Mex.).

keratectomy [ˌkɛrə'tɛktəmɪ] *s.* (*pl.* KERATECTOMIES) (med.) queratectomía.

keratin ['kɛrətən] *s.* (bioquím.) queratina.

keratinous [kə'rætənəs] *a.* (bioquím.) queratinoso.

keratitis [ˌkɛrə'taɪtəs] *s.* (med.) queratitis, inflamación de la córnea.

keratoid ['kɛrəˌtɔɪd] *a.* (med.) queratoideo.

keratosis [ˌkɛrə'toʊsəs] *s.* (med.) queratosis, endurecimiento de la epidermis.

kerb, kerbstone, (G.B.) *vars. de* **curb, curbstone.**

kerchief ['kɜrtʃəf, B 'kɜtʃɪf] *s.* pañuelo, pañoleta (de cabeza, de adorno).

kerchiefed, kerchieft [-tʃɪft] *a.* cubierta (cabeza) con pañuelo.

kerf [kɜrf, B kɜf] *s.* 1. tajo, corte (que hace la sierra en la madera). 2. trozo cortado (de algo).

kermes ['kɜrmiz, B 'kɜmɪz] *s.* (ento.) quermes, kermes, carmes.

kermes insect, (ento.) quermes, grana.

kermes mineral, (quím.) quermes mineral.

kermes oak, (bot.) coscoja, coscojo, maraña, mata rubia.
kermess, kermis ['kɜrməs, B 'kɜmɪs] *s.* quermese; verbena, fiesta, bazar, romería.
kern [kɜrn, B kɜn] *s.* (hist.) 1. soldado de infantería medieval (irlandés o escocés) con armas ligeras. 2. patán, palurdo. 3. (tip.) hombro saliente, hombro de rebasa, perfil fuera de línea. —*v.t.* (tip.) 1. formar con perfil fuera de línea. 2. suavizar el hombro saliente.
kernel ['kɜrnəl, B 'kɜn-] *s.* 1. grano, semilla (de trigo o maíz). 2. almendra, pepita, meollo, semilla (de fruto). 3. (fig.) núcleo, médula, meollo.
kerneled [-əld] *a.* que tiene almendra, grano o pepita.
kernelly [-əlɪ] *a.* granado, que tiene pepitas o granos.
kernite ['kɜrˌnaɪt, B kɜˌ-] *s.* (min.) kernita.
kerogen ['kɛrədʒən] *s.* (min.) kerógeno.
kerosene, kerosine [-ˌsin, kɛrə'sin] *s.* queroséno, queroseno, petróleo destilado.
kerria ['kɛrɪə] *s.* (bot.) kerria.
Kerry ['kɛrɪ] *s.* raza irlandesa de ganado lechero pequeño y de color negro.
Kerry blue terrier, perro terrier de raza irlandesa y pelo color azulado.
kersey ['kɜrzɪ, B 'kɜzɪ] *s.* 1. (tej.) carisea, buriel. 2. (*pl.*) pantalones de carisea.
kerseymere [-ˌmɪr, B -ˌmɪə] *s.* (tej.) casimir.
kestrel ['kɛstrəl] *s.* (orn.) cernícalo, mochete.
ketch [kɛtʃ] *s.* (mar.) queche.
ketchup ['kɛtʃəp] *s.* salsa espesa hecha de tomate, sazonada con cebolla, sal, azúcar y otras especias (t. **catsup** o **catchup**).
ketene ['kitin] *s.* (quím.) queteno.
ketogenesis [ˌkitoʊ'dʒɛnəsəs] *s.* (quím., fisiol.) cetogénesis.
ketone ['kitoʊn] *s.* (quím.) quetona, acetona.
ketone body, (quím., fisiol.) cuerpo cetónico.
ketose ['kiˌtoʊs] *s.* (quím.) cetosa.
ketosis [kɪ'toʊsəs] *s.* (med.) cetosis, quetosis.
ketosteroid [ˌkitoʊ'stɛrˌɔɪd, -'stɪr-, B -'stɛr-] *s.* (med.) cetosteroide.
kettle ['kɛtəl] *s.* 1. marmita, olla, perol, paila; esp. tetera (para hervir agua), pava (Arg.). 2. (geol.) (t. **k. hole**) hueco o cavidad de pendiente escarpada sin drenaje superficial (esp. en un depósito de desecho glacial). 3. **a pretty (nice, fine) k. of fish,** (fam.) bonito lío; **k. of fish,** asunto, problema, situación embarazosa o difícil; **that's another k. of fish,** eso es otro cantar, eso es harina de otro costal.
kettledrum [-ˌdrʌm] *s.* (mús.) timbal, atabal, tímpano.
kettledrummer [-ər, B -ə] *s.* atabalero, timbalero.
kettleful [-fʊl] *s.* calderada.
kevel ['kɛvəl] *s.* (mar.) cornamusa, bita, manigueta.
Kewpie doll ['kjupɪ-] *s.* muñequita de juguete, regordeta de mejillas encarnadas (marca de fábrica).
key [ki] *s.* (*pl.* KEYS) 1. llave (para abrir o cerrar una cerradura). 2. (fig.) clave, llave (de un enigma, secreto, etc.); solución, explicación; clave (libro de soluciones). 3. persona o cosa principal. 4. tono (de la voz), ej., *plaintive k.,* tono (de voz) quejumbroso. 5. estilo (característico de un escrito, discurso, etc.). 6. tecla (de piano, órgano, máquina de escribir, etc.); llave, pistón (de instrumentos de viento). 7. (mús.) tono, tonalidad. 8. (mec.) llave, chaveta, clavija, cuña. 9. (arq.) (t. **keystone**) clave dovela. 10. (elec.) llave, interruptor, conmutador. 11. cayo, isleta. 12. **in k.,** afinado; (fig.) de acuerdo, en armonía; **off k.,** fuera de tono; desafinado. —*v.t.* 1. cerrar (con llave). 2. (mús.) regular el tono de (un instrumento), afinar las cuerdas de (un instrumento); (fig.) armonizar, acordar. 3. insertar clave en (avisos, para saber cuál de las respuestas corresponde a cada uno). 4. (mec.) enchavetar, acuñar, calzar. 5. (arq.) colocar la clave o dovela en (un arco). 6. **k. up,** elevar el tono de (un instrumento musical); (fig.) animar, excitar, agitar. —*a.* 1. principal, dominante. 2. fundamental (importancia, etc.). 3. clave, ej., *k. word,* palabra clave.
keyboard ['kiˌbɔrd, B -ˌbɔd] *s.* 1. teclado (de piano, órgano, linotipo, máquina de escribir, etc.). 2. tablero de llaves. —*v.t.* (impr.) componer (tipos manejando el teclado de una linotipia).
keyboarder ['kiˌbɔrdər] *s.* (comput.) operador.
key bugle, (mús.) corneta de llaves.
key club, (E.U.) club exclusivo para miembros que tienen una llave como identificación.
keyed [kid] *a.* 1. provisto de llaves to teclas. 2. (arq.) reforzado por una dovela. 3. (mús.) arreglado en (cierto) tono. 4. (fig. con *to*) adaptado (a), amoldado (a). 5. **k. up,** excitado, agitado.
key fruit, (bot.) sámara, fruto alado.
keyhole ['kiˌhoʊl] *s.* ojo de la cerradura, bocallave; *(of clock)* agujero de cuerda.
keyhole saw, sierra de calar, sierra de punta.
keyman [-ˌmæn] *s.* hombre clave, hombre indispensable.
keynote [-ˌnoʊt] *s.* 1. (mús.) tónica (de una llave o escala). 2. (fig.) principio fundamental, idea básica, piedra angular. —*v.t.* 1. (fig.) dar el rasgo característico a, caracterizar. 2. pronunciar el discurso de apertura de (una asamblea).
keynote address, k. speech, discurso de apertura (de una convención política).
keynoter [-ər, B -ə] *s.* orador que pronuncia el discurso principal.
keynote tone, (mús.) nota tónica (tocada).
key punch, máquina perforadora (de tarjetas con información para computadoras).
keypuncher [-ər] *s.* (comput.) perforista.
key rack, llavero, taquilla (artefacto).
key ring, llavero, portallaves (Mex., Ven.).
key seat, (mec.) cajera de cuña.
key signature, (mús.) armadura.
keystone ['kiˌstoʊn] *s.* 1. (arq.) clave, dovela. 2. (fig.) piedra angular, base, fundamento.
key valve, (mús.) válvula de pistón, válvula de llave (de instrumento de viento).
keyway [-ˌweɪ] *s.* 1. (mec.) chavetero, cuñero, cajera, ranura. 2. bocallave (de cerraduras).
Key West, (E.U.) Cayo Hueso (en la Florida).
key word, palabra clave.
kg *abrev. de* **kilogram,** kilogramo (kg).
K.G. *abrev. de* **Knight of the Garter,** Caballero de la Orden de la Jarretera.
kgps. *abrev. de* **kilogram per second,** kilogramo por segundo.
khaddar ['kɑdər, B 'kædə] **khadi** [-dɪ] *s.* tela de manufactura casera (en la India).
khaki ['kækɪ, 'kɑkɪ, B 'kɑkɪ] *a.* de color caqui. —*s.* caqui (tela y color).
khalif, khaliff, khalifa, khaleefate, khalifat, khalifate, *vars. de* **caliph, caliphate.**
khamsin, khamseen, kamsin [kæm'sin, B 'kæmsɪn] *s.* viento cálido proveniente del Sahara, kamsín.
khan [kɑn, kæn, B kɑn] *s.* 1. kan (título nobiliario en la India y en algunos países del Asia Central). 2. mesón o posada para caravanas.
khanate ['kɑneɪt, 'kæn-] *s.* kanato, reino o jurisdicción del kan.
Khartoum, Khartum [kɑr'tum, B kɑ-] *s.* Jartum, capital del Sudán.
khedive [kə'div] *s.* (ant.) jedive (virrey de Turquia).
Khmer [kmɛr, kə'mɛr, B -'mɛə] *s.* Kmer, uno de los pueblos más importantes de Camboya; su lengua.
Khmer rouge, (pol.) nacionalista camboyano.
kiang [kɪ'ɑŋ] *s.* (zool.) hemiono.
kiaugh [kjɑk] *s.* (esco.) perturbación, congoja; ansiedad.
kibble ['kɪbəl] *s.* borona, galleta desmenuzada.
kibbutz [kɪ'bʊts, -'buts, B -'buts] *s.* (*pl.* KIBBUTZIM [-ˌbʊt'sim, -ˌbut-, B -ˌbut-]) kibbutz (granja cooperativa en Israel).
kibbutznik [-nɪk] *s.* miembro de un kibbutz.
kibe [kaɪb] *s.* grieta en la piel; sabañón ulcerado (esp. en el talón).
kibed [kaɪbd] **kiby** ['kaɪbɪ] *a.* lleno de sabañones.
kibei ['ki'beɪ, B kɪ-] *s.* (*pl.* KIBEI O KIBEIS) hijo de padres japoneses nacido en E.U. y educado en el Japón.
kibitz ['kɪbəts] *v.i.* (fam., yiddish) estar de mirón; dar consejos no solicitados.
kibitzer [-ər, B -ə] *s.* (fam.) 1. mirón (en una partida de naipes u otro juego). 2. entremetido, metemuertos.
kibosh ['kaɪˌbɑʃ, kɪ'bɑʃ, B 'kaɪbɔʃ] *s.* (jer.) bagatela, tontería; **to put the k. on,** (jer.) desbaratar, imposibilitar; cancelar, eliminar.
kick [kɪk] *v.i.* 1. patear, cocear, tirar coces. 2. (fam.) mostrar oposición o mal genio; protestar vigorosamente, ej., *k. against a decision,* protestar vigorosamente contra una decisión. 3. dar coces, patear (Am.) (arma de fuego). 4. **k. about,** quejarse de (algo o alguien); estar sin uso; **k. back,** reaccionar inesperadamente; **k. in (with),** (jer.) hacer aporte (de); **k. in, k. off,** (jer.) estirar la pata, irse al otro mundo; **k. off,** (fútbol) dar el puntapié inicial; (fig.) comenzar, empezar; **k. up,** protestar, rebelarse; **k. up a dust** o **a row,** (fam.) armar un bochinche, alboroto, escándalo. —*v.t.* 1. dar un puntapié a; dar una patada a. 2. dar coz a, patear (Am.) (díc. de un arma de fuego). 3. (fútbol Am.) hacer (gol) de patada. 4. (jer.) librarse de (morfinomanía). 5. **k. around,** tratar en forma desconsiderada, maltratar; (jer.) dar vueltas a, pelotear con (problema, idea, etc.); **k. down,** echar abajo a puntapiés; **k. in,** romper a patadas o puntapiés; (jer.) aportar (dinero), pagar en parte; **k. off,** dejar caer (zapatos) sacudiendo el pie; poner en marcha, dar comienzo a; **k. oneself,** (fig.) reprocharse (por perder oportunidad, etc.); **k. out,** echar a patadas; **k. the bucket,** (fam.) estirar la pata, morirse; **k. up,** hacer saltar (piedras), levantar (polvo); subir, elevar (precios, etc.); **k. up a fuss,** (jer.) armar lío, armar bronca, causar disturbios; protestar; **k. up one's heels,** (fam.) retozar, jaranear, echar una cana al aire; **k. (one) upstairs,** rebajar (a uno) a un puesto menos deseable. —*s.* 1. puntapié, patada, coz. 2. (fig.) fuerza, vigor; elasticidad, ej., *he has no k. left in him,* no le queda fuerza, está exhausto. 3. reculada, culatazo, retroceso, coz (de un arma de fuego). 4. (jer.) queja, protesta. 5. (jer.) estímulo, aliento, efecto estimulante (ej., de una bebida alcohólica, droga, etc.); placer, gusto, sensación agradable o excitante; (*pl.*) diversión. 6. (jer.) aumento (de salario, etc.). 7. (jer.) bolsillo. 8. (jer.) despido. 9. (jer. G.B.) (moneda de) seis peniques. 10. **more kicks than halfpence,** (fig.) más rudeza que bondad; **to get a k. out of,** (jer.) hallar placer en.

kickback ['kɪk,bæk] *s.* 1. (fam.) reacción, esp. aguda o violenta. 2. (jer.) comisión confidencial (que se devuelve de una suma recibida, como salario, comisión, honorarios, etc.).
kicker [-ər, B -ə] *s.* 1. coceador, pateador. 2. (jer.) final sopresivo o irónico. 3. dificultad inesperada.
kickoff [-,ɔf] *s.* 1. (fútbol) puntapié inicial, inicio del juego. 2. (fig., fam.) comienzo.
kick plate, placa de protección (contra el roce de los pies).
kickshaw [-,ʃɔ] **kickshaws** [-,ʃɔz] s. 1. juguete, bagatela, fruslería. 2. bocado delicado, golosina.
kick stand, arrancador de pie o pedal (de motocicleta).
kick-turn [-,tɜrn, B -,tɜn] *v.i.* (esquí) cambiar de marcha bruscamente.
kickup ['kɪk,ʌp] *s.* (jer.) bochinche, alboroto, tumulto.
kid [kɪd] *s.* 1. cabrito, chivo, chivato. 2. (carne de) cabrito; cabritilla (piel). 3. (*pl.*) guantes o zapatos de cabritilla. 4. (fam.) chico, chica; muchachito, jovenzuelo. 5. gamella de madera. 6. (mar.) escudilla para rancho. —*a.* de piel de cabritilla, de piel fina. —*v.t.* (*pret., p.p.* KIDDED; *p.pr.* KIDDING) 1. engañar, embaucar. 2. tomar el pelo a (alguien); bromear con, embromar. —*v.i.* 1. bromear, chancear. 2. parir (la cabra o la hembra del antílope).
kidder ['kɪdər, B -ə] *s.* bromista, chancero.
Kidderminster [-,mɪnstər, B -stə] *s.* alfombra de Kidderminster (Ingl.).
kiddy, kiddie ['kɪdɪ] *s.* (fam.) *dim. de* **kid,** niño pequeño.
kid gloves, guantes de cabritilla, de piel fina; **to handle with k. gloves,** (fig.) manejar con guantes blancos, tratar con suma consideración o con finura.
kidnap ['kɪd,næp] *v.t.* (*pret., p.p.* KIDNAPED O KIDNAPPED; *p.pr.* KIDNAPPING O KIDNAPPING) secuestrar, raptar.
kidnaper, kidnapper [-ər, B -ə] *s.* secuestrador, raptor.
kidney ['kɪdnɪ] *s.* 1. (anat.) riñon. 2. temperamento; disposición; clase, especie, género, índole. 3. (*pl.*) (cocina) riñones, ej., *grilled kidneys,* riñones a la parrilla.
kidney bean, (bot.) 1. judía, habichuela, alubia, frejol o frijol (Am.), poroto (Am.). 2. judía escarlata, judía de España, frijol colorado; frijol caballero (Cuba).
kidney corpuscle, (anat.) corpúsculo de Malpighi.
kidney ore, (min.) riñon.
kidney-shaped, *a.* reniforme.
kidney stone, piedra nefrítica, cálculo renal.
kidney vetch, (bot.) vulneraria.
kidneywort ['kɪdnɪ,wɜrt, B -,wɜt] *s.* (bot.) ombligo de Venus.
kidskin ['kɪd,skɪn] *s.* cabritilla.
kier [kɪr, B kɪə] *s.* cuba o tanque de blanquear (para algodón u otras fibras).
kieselguhr, kieselgur ['kizəl,gʊr, B -gʊə] *s.* (geol.) kieselguhr, diatomita; tripol, trípoli, tierra de infusorios, harina fósil.
kif [kɪf] *var. de* **kef.**
kike [kaɪk] *s.* (despec., jer.) judío.
kilderkin ['kɪldərkən, B -dəkɪn] *s.* 1. barrilete, cubeta, pipote, tonelete. 2. antigua medida inglesa (equivalente a 18 galones).
kilerg ['kɪl,ɜrg, B -,ɜg] *s.* (fís.) kiloergio.
kill [kɪl] *v.t.* 1. matar, quitar la vida. 2. destruir, privar de vigor. 3. eliminar (competencia); neutralizar (un color). 4. descartar, rechazar, vetar (un proyecto de ley, etc.). 5. (fig.) matar, agotar. 6. detener, parar (motor, etc.). 7. (elec.) cortar (un circuito activo). 8. (impr.) suprimir. 9. (tenis) darle (a la bola) tan fuerte que no pueda ser devuelta; (fútbol) parar (la bola) en seco. 10. **k. off,** exterminar, acabar con; **k. time,** pasar el rato, matar el tiempo; **k. two birds with one stone,** matar dos pájaros de un tiro. —*v.i.* 1. matar, cometer homicidio. 2. **dressed to k.,** toda emperifollada. —*s.* 1. matanza. 2. cacería (animales muertos en la caza). 3. golpe mortal, ataque final. 4. (mil.) avión derribado. 5. (E.U.) riachuelo, arroyo; caleta.
killdeer ['kɪl,dɪr, B -,dɪə] *s.* (orn.) frailecillo norteamericano, especie de chorlito.
killer ['kɪlər, B -ə] *s.* 1. asesino, homicida. 2. (t. **k. whale**) (zool.) orca.
killick ['kɪlɪk] *s.* 1. anclote. 2. piedra para anclar (un bote de pesca).
killickinnic, killikinick [,kɪləkə'nɪk] *vars. de* **kinnikinnick.**
killing ['kɪlɪŋ] *s.* 1. matanza; asesinato, homicidio. 2. cacería (piezas obtenidas en la caza). 3. (fam.) triunfo, éxito notable (esp. en el mercado de valores). 4. **to make a k.,** hacer su agosto, ganar un montón de dinero (esp. en el mercado de valores). —*a.* 1. matador, destructivo. 2. abrumador, agotador (trabajo). 3. (fam.) irresistible, cautivador; sumamente divertido.
killjoy [-,dʒɔi] *s.* aguafiestas.
kiln [kɪln, kɪl] *s.* horno, estufa, horno de cochura, horno de calcinación, horno de cuba. —*v.t.* secar o cocer (ladrillos, etc.) en el horno.
kilndry ['kɪln,draɪ] *v.t.* secar al horno.
kilo ['kiloʊ] *s.* kilo, kilogramo.
kiloampere [,kɪloʊ'æm,pɪr, B -,pɛə] (elec.) kiloamperio.
kilocalorie ['kɪlə,kælərɪ] *s.* (fís.) kilocaloría.
kilocycle [-,saɪkəl] *s.* kilociclo.
kilogram, kilogramme [-,græm] *s.* kilogramo.
kilogram calorie, caloría grande, gran caloría.
kilogram-meter [-'mitər, B -ə] *s.* (mec., fís.) kilográmetro.
kilohertz [-,hɜrts] *s.* kilohertzio.
kilojoule ['kɪlə,dʒul, -,dʒaʊl] *s.* (fís.) kilojulio.
kiloliter, kilolitre ['kɪlə,litər, B -ə] *s.* kilolitro.
kilometer, kilometre [kɪ'lɑmətər, 'kɪlə,-mit-, B 'kɪl-ə] *s.* kilómetro.
kilometric [,kɪlə'mɛtrɪk] *a.* kilométrico.
kiloton ['kɪlə,tʌn] *s.* 1. kilotonelada corta, mil toneladas. 2. (fís. nuclear) kilotón.
kilovar [-,vɑr, B -,vɑ] *s.* (elec.) kilovoltamperio reactivo.
kilovolt [-,voʊlt] *s.* (elec.) kilovoltio, kilovolt.
kilovolt-ampere [-'æm,pɪr, B -,pɛə] *s.* (elec.) kilovoltamperio.
kilowatt ['kɪlə,wɑt, B -,wɔt] *s.* (elec.) kilovatio.
kilowatt-hour [-,aʊr, B -,aʊə] *s.* (elec.) kilovatio-hora.
kilt [kɪlt] *s.* tonelete escocés, falda del escocés. —*v.t.* 1. (dial.) plegar, hacer pliegues en una tela. 2. usar la falda (típica) del escocés, vestir de tonelete.
kilter ['kɪltər, B -tə] *s.* (fam., dial.) orden, arreglo; buena condición; **in k.,** arreglado, en orden, ordenado; **out of k.,** desarreglado, descompuesto.
kiltie, kilty [-tɪ] *s.* soldado escocés (que usa la falda típica).
kilting [-tɪŋ] *s.* (cost.) tableado.
kimmer ['kɪmər, B -ə] (esco., dial.) muchacha, doncella, moza.
kimono [kə'moʊnə, B -noʊ] *s.* quimono, kimono; bata de quimón.
kin [kɪn] *s.* 1. parentela, parientes, linaje. 2. familiar, pariente. 3. clan, tribu. 4. (ant.) parentesco. 5. **near of k.,** de parentesco cercano; **next of k.,** parientes más próximos; deudo más cercano; **of k.,** allegado. —*a.* pariente, allegado.
kinase ['kaɪn,eɪs, 'kɪn-] *s.* (bioquím.) cinasa.
kind [kaɪnd] *s.* 1. género, especie, clase, ej., *human k.,* especie humana. 2. clase, suerte, tipo, variedad, ej., *several kinds of people,* varios tipos de personas. 3. índole, carácter, ej., *different in k.,* de distinta índole. 4. clase, grupo. 5. (ant.) naturaleza. 6. **a. k. of,** cierto, ej., *I felt a k. of sadness,* sentí cierta tristeza; **all kinds of,** (jer.) gran variedad de; **in k.,** del mismo modo, de manera igual; en especie (no en dinero); **k. of,** en cierto modo; algo, un poco, ej., *I k. of expected it,* en cierto modo lo esperaba, *I felt k. of sorry for him,* en cierto modo me compadecí de él; **k. of slow,** algo lento, un poco lento; **of a k.,** de la misma clase, especie o valor; (despec.) una especie de, ej., *we had coffee of a k.,* tomamos una especie de café; **of the k.,** parecido, semejante, por el estilo; **something of the k.,** algo parecido, algo por el estilo; **to repay in k.,** (fig.) pagar con la misma moneda; **what k. of a,** qué clase de. —*a.* 1. bueno, benévolo, bondadoso, ej., *k. act,* acción bondadosa. 2. gentil, amable. 3. afectuoso, cordial, ej., *k. regards,* cordiales saludos. 4. (dial.) afectuoso, cariñoso. 5. (ant.) natural, nativo. 6. **to be k. to,** ser bueno (para) con; tratar bien.
kindergarten ['kɪndər,gɑrtən, -,gɑrd-, B -ə,gɑt-] *s.* kindergarten, jardín de infantes, escuela de párvulos, jardín infantil.
kindergartner [-,gɑrtnɛr, -,gɑrd-, B -,gɑtnə] *s.* maestro o alumno de un jardín de infantes o escuela de párvulos.
kindhearted ['kaɪnd'hɑrtəd, B -'hɑt-] *a.* de buen corazón, bondadoso.
kindheartedness [-nəs] *s.* bondad de corazón, bondad.
kindle ['kɪndəl] *v.t.* 1. encender, prender fuego a. 2. (fig.) encender, inflamar, excitar. 3. (fig.) iluminar. —*v.i.* 1. encenderse, prender, arder. 2. (fig.) excitarse, inflamarse, enardecerse. 3. (fig.) iluminarse; brillar.
kindle, *v.t., v.i.* (dial.) parir, alumbrar.
kindless ['kaɪndləs] *a.* falto de bondad.
kindliness [-lɪnəs] *s.* 1. benignidad. 2. benevolencia; amabilidad, afabilidad.
kindling ['kɪndlɪŋ] *s.* 1. leña. 2. encendimiento, ignición. 3. (fig.) enardecimiento. 4. (fig.) brillo, resplandor.
kindly ['kaɪndlɪ] *a.* 1. bondadoso, benévolo; compasivo; amable, afable, complaciente. 2. agradable, benigno (clima, estación, etc.). 3. (ant.) natural; nativo; hereditario. —*adv.* 1. bondadosamente, amablemente; afablemente, cordialmente. 2. naturalmente, normalmente; con soltura. 3. (fam.) por cortesía o favor, gentilmente, ej., *will you k. leave?* ¿puede hacer el favor de irse? 4. **to take (something) k.,** apreciar; **to take k. to,** acoger favorablemente, aceptar con agrado.
kindness [-nəs] *s.* 1. bondad, benevolencia; gentileza, amabilidad. 2. atención, favor, gracia. 3. (ant.) afecto. 4. **have the k. to,** tenga la bondad de.
kindred ['kɪndrəd] *s.* 1. pueblo, grupo; clan. 2. parentela, parientes; linaje. 3. (ant.) parentesco; afinidad. —*a.* 1. similar, semejante. 2. allegado; afín, congenial.
kine [kaɪn] *s. pl.* (ant., dial.) vacas; ganado.
kinematic [,kɪnə'mætɪk, -kaɪnə-] **kinematical** [-ɪkəl] *a.* (fís.) cinemático.

kinematics [-ɪks] *s. pl.* (*sing. en const.*) cinemática.
kinescope ['kɪnəˌskoʊp] *s.* (t.v.) cinescopio.
kinesics [kɪ'nisɪks] *s. pl.* el estudio de los movimientos del cuerpo, expresiones faciales, etc. como complemento a la comunicación humana.
kinesiology [kəˌnisɪ'ɑlədʒɪ, -zɪ-, B kaɪˌnisɪ'ɔl-] *s.* (med.) cinesiología.
kinesthesia [ˌkɪnəs'θiʒə, B ˌkaɪ-'θizjə] *s.* (*pl.* KINESTHESIAS) (fisiol.) cinestesia, sentido muscular, percepción de los movimientos musculares, propios.
kinesthesis [-'θisəs] *s.* (*pl.* KINESTHESES [-ˌsiz]) (fisiol.) cinestesia.
kinesthetic [-'θɛtɪk] *a.* (fisiol.) cinestético.
kinetic [kə'nɛtɪk, B kaɪ-] *a.* (fís.) cinético, dinámico.
kinetic energy, (fís.) energía cinética.
kinetics [-ɪks] *s. pl.* (*sing. en const.*) (fís.) cinética.
kinetograph [kə'nitəˌgræf, B kaɪ-ˌgrɑf] *s.* cámara fílmica.
kinfolk ['kɪnˌfoʊk] *var. de* **kinsfolk.**
king [kɪŋ] *s.* 1. rey. 2. (fig.) rey, monarca, soberano. 3. (naipes, ajedrez) rey; (damas) dama.
kingbird ['kɪŋˌbɜrd, B -ˌbɜd] *s.* (orn.) tirano.
kingbolt [-ˌboʊlt] *s.* 1. (aut.) pivote de dirección. 2. (f.c.) perno pinzote.
king cobra, serpiente grande y venenosa de la India.
king crab, (zool.) cangrejo de las Molucas, centolla.
kingcraft [-ˌkræft, B -ˌkrɑft] *s.* (el) arte de reinar.
kingcup [-ˌkʌp] *s.* (bot.) ranúnculo, botón de oro.
kingdom ['kɪŋdəm] *s.* reino; **k. come,** el otro mundo, el cielo.
kingfish [-ˌfɪʃ] *s.* 1. (ict.) (especie de) pez marino comestible de gran tamaño. 2. (fam.) jefe, amo.
kingfisher [-ər, B -ə] *s.* (orn.) martín pescador, pájaro polilla, guardarrío, alción.
kinghood [-ˌhʊd] *s.* dignidad de rey.
King James Version [-'dʒeɪmʒ-] Biblia traducida al inglés del hebreo y del griego bajo el auspicio del rey Jacobo I, t. llamada **Authorized Version,** versión autorizada.
kinglet ['kɪŋlət] *s.* 1. reyezuelo. 2. (orn.) reyezuelo, régulo, abadejo.
kingliness [-lɪnəs] *s.* realeza, majestuosidad.
kingly [-lɪ] *a.* real, regio; augusto, majestuoso; ilustre, noble. —*adv.* regiamente, majestuosamente.
kingpin [-ˌpɪn] *s.* 1. bolo central (en el juego de bolos), bolo delantero. 2. (fam.) persona principal (en un grupo o empresa). 3. (mec.) tornillo o perno maestro. 4. (ant.) pivote de dirección.
king post, (carp.) pendolón, pendolón sencillo; (arq.) nabo.
king-post bridge, k.-p. truss, puente o armadura triangular del pendolón.
king's bench, queen's bench, (G.B., hist.) tribunal supremo de derecho consuetudinario donde el rey administraba justicia personalmente.
king's bishop, (ajedrez) alfil rey.
king's blue, azul cobalto.
king's Counsel, Queen's Counsel, (G.B.) abogado prominente que integra el Consejo de la corona británica.
king's English, queen's English, inglés (lenguaje) aceptado (en G.B.).
king's evidence, queen's evidence, (G.B.) (der.) testimonio prestado por un testigo de cargo, (esp. el prestado por uno de los acusados contra sus cómplices).
king's evil, (med.) escrófula, lamparón.
kingship ['kɪŋˌʃɪp] *s.* 1. reino, monarquía. 2. majestad, dignidad real.
king-size [-ˌsaɪz] *a.* 1. de tamaño extra, extragrande, descomunal. 2. extralargo (díc. de los cigarrillos).
king-size bed, cama de gran tamaño.
king's knight, (ajedrez) caballo rey.
king's ransom, (fig.) suma enorme, toda una fortuna.
king's rook, (ajedrez) torre rey.
king's shilling, queen's shilling, (G.B., hist.) chelín que daba un oficial a un hombre (y que representaba su enrolamiento obligatorio en el ejército).
Kingston ['kɪŋstən] *s.* Kingston, capital de Jamaica.
king's yellow, (min.) oropimente, sulfuro natural de arsénico.
king truss, (carp.) cercha o armadura de pendolón.
kink [kɪŋk] *s.* 1. sortija, rulo, crespo, pasa (de pelo). 2. retorcimiento, ensortijamiento, enroscadura (de cabo, cuerda, hilo). 3. (med.) tortícolis. 4. (fam.) excentricidad, capricho, chifladura, manía. 5. falla, defecto. —*v.t., v.i.* retorcer(se), ensortijar(se), encarrujar(se) (Amer.).
kinkajou ['kɪŋkəˌdʒu] *s.* (zool.) kinkayú, mapache, especie de coatí.
kinkle ['kɪŋkəl] *s.* enroscadura pequeña.
kinkled [-kəld] *a.* retorcido, ensortijado, enroscado.
kinky [-kɪ] *a.* ensortijado, encarrujado (hilo, cuerda, etc.); crespo, grifo, pasudo (cabello, esp. el de los negros).
kinnikinnick, kinnikinic [ˌkɪnəkə'nɪk] *s.* (hist., E.U.) mezcla de hojas y corteza de zumaque (usada por los indios como substituto del tabaco).
kino ['kinoʊ] *s.* 1. (bot.) quino. 2. quino, quina (materia usada en medicina como astringente).
kinsfolk ['kɪnzˌfoʊk] *s. pl.* parentela, parientes, consanguíneos.
Kinshasa [kɪn'ʃɑsɑ] *s.* Kinshasa, capital de la República Democrática del Congo.
kinship ['kɪnˌʃɪp] *s.* parentesco.
kinsman ['kinzmən] *s.* pariente, deudo.
kinswoman [-ˌwʊmən] *s.* parienta, deuda.
kiosk ['kiˌɑsk, ki'ɑsk, B 'kiˌɔsk] *s.* 1. kiosco, quiosco, pabellón. 2. kiosko, quiosco (donde se venden periódicos, flores, etc.).
kip [kɪp] *s.* 1. piel de becerro; piel de res pequeña. 2. atado de pieles. 3. (peso de) mil libras, kilolibra. 4. (jer.) (casa de) pensión; alojamiento o cama en una pensión. —*v.i.* (jer.) dormir.
kipper ['kɪpər, B -ə] *s.* 1. salmón zancado. 2. salmón o arenque ahumado. 3. (jer., G.B.) compañero; chico; tío, tipo, sujeto. —*v.t.* ahumar (pescado).
kirk [kɜrk, B kɜk] *s.* 1. (esco., N. de Ingl.) iglesia. 2. (gen. **the K.**) la iglesia nacional de Escocia.
kirkman ['kɜrkmən, B 'kɜk-] *s.* 1. (esco.) eclesiástico, clérigo; miembro de una iglesia. 2. miembro de la Iglesia de Escocia.
kirmess, *var. de* **kermis.**
kirn [kɜrn, B kɜn] *s.* (esco.) 1. última gavilla recogida en la cosecha. 2. fiesta al final de la cosecha. 3. mantequera, mantequillera.
kirsch [kɪrʃ, B kɪəʃ] *s.* kirsch, licor de cerezas.
kirtle ['kɜrtəl, B 'kɜt-] *s.* (ant., hist.) 1. túnica, manto, capa (de hombre). 2. falda o faldilla corta (de mujer).
kismet ['kɪzmɛt, B 'kɪs-] *s.* hado, destino (en los países musulmanes).
kiss [kɪs] *v.t.* 1. besar. 2. tocar suavemente, acariciar; tocar o golpear ligeramente. 3. **k. away,** secar (lágrimas) con besos; consolar (pena, dolor) con besos; **k. hands** (o **the hand**), besar la mano; **k. one's hand to,** enviar un beso con la mano, mandar besos volados; **k. (something) goodbye,** (fam.) despedirse de (algo), renunciar (a algo), darse cuenta de que (algo) está perdido; **k. the book,** besar la Biblia (al prestar juramento); **k. the ground,** postrarse en señal de sumisión; (fig.) rebajarse; **k. the rod,** aceptar un castigo sumisamente. —*v.i.* besarse. —*s.* 1. beso. 2. contacto suave, roce leve. 3. (cocina) merengue pequeño. 4. (billar) beso (tocarse suavemente dos bolas).
kisser ['kɪsər, B -ə] *s.* 1. besador. 2. (fam.) besucón, besuqueador. 3. (jer.) boca; mentón; cara.
kissing bug [-ɪŋ-] (ento.) chupasangre.
kiss of death, cruz y raya; el beso de Judas.
kiss-off [-ˌɔf] *s.* (jer.) despido, destitución abrupta.
kist [kɪst] *s.* (esco., dial.) cofrecillo, caja, arca.
kit [kɪt] *s.* 1. equipaje, equipo; avíos, pertrechos. 2. juego de implementos; caja de herramientas, estuche de instrumentos, herramental. 3. juego de piezas (para armar). 4. grupo, conjunto. 5. gatito, gatita. 6. (mús.) violín pequeño (de tres cuerdas). 7. (dial., G.B.) cuba de madera. 8. **the whole k. and caboodle,** todo el lote, todos sin excepción.
kit bag, 1. bolsa (de marinero o soldado). 2. maletín de viaje.
kitchen ['kɪtʃən] *s.* 1. cocina (habitación, equipo y arte culinario). 2. (esco., dial.) condimento, aderezo. —*v.t.* (esco., dial.) condimentar, sazonar, aderezar.
kitchen boy, mozo de cocina, pinche.
kitchen cabinet, 1. alacena de cocina. 2. (fam.) camarilla (consejeros oficiosos del jefe de un gobierno).
kitchener [-ər, B -ə] *s.* 1. cocinero (de un convento). 2. (G.B.) cocina (aparato).
kitchenette [ˌkɪtʃə'nɛt] *s.* cocina pequeña; nicho equipado para cocinar.
kitchen garden, huerto.
kitchenmaid ['kɪtʃənˌmeɪd] *s.* moza de cocina, fregona.
kitchen midden, residuos de basura (que indican que allí existió una vivienda primitiva o prehistórica).
kitchen police, (mil.) 1. recluta que ayuda en la cocina. 2. faena de cocina, servicio de rancho.
kitchen sink, pila de cocina, fregadero; **Mary took everything but the k.,** (hum.) se fue con la casa a cuestas, María cargó hasta con el perico.
kitchen stove, k. range, cocina (aparato); fogón.
kitchen stuff, 1. alimentos, substancias alimenticias. 2. sobras, deshechos; grasa, mugre (que queda en las ollas, etc.).
kitchenware [-ˌwɛr, B -ˌwɛə] *s.* utensilios de cocina, batería de cocina.
kite [kaɪt] *s.* 1. cometa (*f.*), papalote (juguete). 2. (orn.) milano. 3. bribón, pillo, pícaro. 4. (com.) cheque sin fondo, letra o pagaré falso. 5. (aer.) planeador; (jer.) avión. 6. (*pl.*) (mar.) sobrejuanete, foque volante. 7. **go fly a k.** ¡vete! ¡piérdete! —*v.i.* 1. (fig.) volar, pasar a gran velocidad; subir vertiginosamente; (t. con *off*) marcharse, escapar. 2. obtener dinero por medio de cheques sin fondos, letras o pagarés falsos. —*v.t.* (com.) usar (cheques sin fondos, etc.) para obtener dinero en efectivo.
kite balloon, globo cometa.
kith and kin [kɪθ-] deudos y amigos; parientes.
kithe [kaɪð] *v.t.* (esco., dial.) manifestar, dar a conocer. —*v.i.* mostrarse, darse a conocer; aparecer.
kitsch [kɪtʃ] *s.* obra de arte, literatura, etc., pretensiosa, en el fondo frívola y destinada para el gusto popular.

kitten ['kɪtən] *s.* gatito, michino; **to have kittens,** (fam.) estar muy excitado; temblar de miedo. —*v.i.* parir (la gata).
kittenish [-ɪʃ] *a.* 1. retozón, juguetón. 2. coquetón.
kittiwake ['kɪtɪˌweɪk] *s.* (orn.) (especie de) gaviota.
kittle ['kɪtəl] (esco.) *a.* cosquilloso; espinoso, delicado. —*v.t.* 1. cosquillear, hacer cosquillas. 2. animar, alegrar. 3. confundir, aturdir, aturullar.
kitty ['kɪtɪ] *s.* 1. gatita, minino. 2. ponina, pozo, banco de apuestas (en juego de mesa). 3. colecta en reserva.
kitty cornered, (reg.) en diagonal.
kiva ['kivə] *s.* kiva, cámara ceremonial (de los indios de las tribus Hopi y Pueblo de Nuevo Méjico).
Kiwanian [kə'wɑnɪən] *s.* (E.U.) socio del club Kiwani, asociación internacional de profesionales.
kiwi ['kiwɪ] *s.* 1. (orn.) kiwí, pájaro áptero de Nueva Zelandia. 2. (*fruit*) kiwi.
KKK *abrev. de* **Ku Klux Klan,** Ku Klux Klan.
kl *abrev. de* **kiloliter,** kilolitro (kl).
Klamath weed ['klæməθ-] (bot.) hierba de San Juan, corazoncillo.
Klan [klæn] *s.* (el) Ku Klux Klan.
Klansman ['klænzmən] *s.* miembro del Ku Klux Klan.
klatch, klatsch [klɑtʃ, klætʃ, B klɑtʃ] *s.* (fam.) tertulia, corrillo.
Kleenex (TM) ['klinɛks] *s.* kleenex, pañuelo de papel.
klepht [klɛft] *s.* (hist.) klefto (guerrillero griego dedicado al bandolerismo).
kleptomania [ˌklɛptə'meɪnɪə] *s.* cleptomanía.
kleptomaniac [-nɪˌæk] *s.* cleptómano.
klieg light ['klig-] (cine) lámpara klieg.
klipspringer ['klɪpˌsprɪŋər, B -ə] *s.* (zool.) klipspringer, pequeño antílope.
kloof [kluf] *s.* (África del S.) valle profundo, barranca, hondonada.
klutz [klʌts] *s.* (jer.) torpe, ganso, patoso.
klystron ['klaɪˌstrɑn, B -ˌstrɔn] *s.* (fís.) klystron, clistron.
km *abrev. de* **kilometer,** kilómetro (km.).
knack [næk] *s.* 1. destreza, habilidad, don. 2. treta, truco; maña, tranquillo. 3. (ant.) artilugio, artificio; chuchería. 4. **to get the k. of,** cogerle el truco a.
knacker ['nækər, B -ə] *s.* (G.B.) 1. tratante o matarife de caballos. 2. tratante en chatarra o materiales de demolición.
knaggy ['nægɪ] *a.* nudoso, áspero.
knap [næp] *v.t.* (dial.) (*pret., p.p.* KNAPPED; *p.pr.* KNAPPING) 1. golpear, tocar; chasquear. 2. descantillar, astillar. 3. mordiscar, mordisquear; roer. —*s.* (dial.) cima, cumbre (de un cerro).
knapping ['næpɪŋ] *s. acción de quebrar o picar piedras.*
knapping hammer, martillo de picapedrero.
knapsack ['næpˌsæk] *s.* barjuleta; mochila (del soldado); alforja.
knapweed [-ˌwid] *s.* (bot.) centaura negra.
knar [nɑr, B nɑ] *s.* nudo (en la corteza de un árbol).
knarled [nɑrld, B nɑld] *a.* nudoso.
knave [neɪv] *s.* 1. bribón, tunante, pillo, pícaro, bellaco. 2. sota (de la baraja). 3. (ant.) criado, sirviente; hombre de origen o posición humilde.
knavery ['neɪvərɪ] *s.* 1. bribonada, pillada, fraude, bellaquería. 2. (ant.) travesura, jugarreta.
knavish [-ɪʃ] *a.* bribonesco, picaresco, bellaco.
knavishly [-lɪ] *adv.* bellacamente, de modo bribonesco o picaresco.
knavishness [-nəs] *s.* tunantería, picardía, bellaquería.
knead [nid] *v.t.* 1. amasar, sobar, heñir. 2. dar masaje a. 3. (fig.) formar, moldear.
kneader ['nidər, B -ə] *s.* amasador.
kneading machine [-ɪŋ-] amasadera, máquina de amasar.
kneading table, hintero.
kneading trough, amasadera, artesa.
knee [ni] *s.* 1. (anat.) rodilla. 2. rodillera (de una prenda). 3. (mec.) codo, codillo, escuadra. 4. **gone at the knees,** (fam. G.B.) decrépito; **knees up,** (jer. G.B.) jaleo; **to be on one's knees,** estar uno de rodillas; **to bend** (o **bow**) **the k.,** arrodillarse, doblar la rodilla; **to bring (someone) to his knees,** (fig.) poner (a alguien) de rodillas, vencer o subyugar (a alguien); **to fall** (o **go down**) **on one's knees,** caer de hinojos (esp. como expresión de súplica, adoración o sumisión). —*v.t.* golpear o tocar con la rodilla.
knee action, (aut.) suspensión independiente (de las ruedas delanteras).
knee brace, esquinal, cartela, cuadral, riostra angular.
knee breeches, pantalones cortos (hasta la rodilla).
kneecap ['niˌkæp] *s.* (anat.) rótula, choquezuela.
knee-crooking [-'krʊkɪŋ] *a.* obsequioso.
knee-deep [-'dip] *a.* 1. que llega hasta las rodillas, ej., *the water is only k.-d.,* el agua llega sólo hasta las rodillas. 2. hundido hasta las rodillas, ej., *troops k.-d. in snow,* tropas hundidas en la nieve hasta las rodillas. 3. (fig.) abismado, sumido.
knee-high [-'haɪ] *a.* 1. que sube o llega hasta las rodillas (díc. al describir estatura). 2. **k.-h. to a grasshopper,** muy bajo, pequeñito (niño, etc.).
kneehole ['niˌhoʊl] *s.* espacio (en mesa, escritorio) para acomodar las piernas.
knee jerk, reflejo rotuliano; (fig.) reacción instintiva, reacción automática; **a knee-jerk conservative** de derechas hasta la médula.
knee-joint [-ˌdʒɔɪnt] *s.* 1. (anat.) articulación de la rodilla. 2. (mec.) unión articulada.
kneel [nil] *v.i.* (*pret., p.p.* KNELT [nɛlt] O KNEELED; *p.pr.* KNEELING) arrodillarse, hincarse de rodillas, caer de hinojos, postrarse.
knee length, (*skirt*) hasta la rodilla; (*sock*) largo.
kneeler ['nilər, B -ə] *s.* el que está de rodillas, el que está arrodillado.
kneepad ['niˌpæd] *s.* rodillera.
kneepan [-ˌpæn] *s.* (anat.) rótula, choquezuela.
knee-sprung [-ˌsprʌŋ] *a.* (vet.) (díc. del animal) que tiene las rodillas dobladas (debido al esfuerzo, cansancio, etc.).
knee timber, madera para curvas.
knee tribute, genuflexión.
knell [nɛl] *v.t.* 1. anunciar o convocar repicando las campanas. 2. (ant.) tañer o doblar (la campana). —*v.i.* 1. doblar, tocar a muerto (la campana). 2. sonar (la campana) como mal presagio, sonar lúgubremente. —*s.* 1. toque a muerto, doble (de campanas). 2. sonido o indicio ominoso.
knelt [nɛlt] *pret., p.p. de* **kneel.**
knew [nu, B nju] *pret. de* **know.**
Knickerbocker ['nɪkərˌbɑkər, B -əˌbɔkə] *s.* 1. descendiente de los primeros colonizadores holandeses de Nueva York; p. ext. neoyorquino. 2. **knickerbockers,** pantalones bombachos (ceñidos bajo la rodilla).
knickers ['nɪkərz, B -əz] *s. pl.* 1. *abrev. de* **knickerbockers.** 2. (G.B.) bragas, calzón(es) (prenda de ropa interior femenina).
knicknack ['nɪkˌnæk] *s.* chuchería, baratija, brujería, miriñaque, friolera.
knife [naɪf] *s.* (*pl.* KNIVES [naɪvz]) 1. cuchillo, navaja. 2. (cir.) bisturí, escalpelo. 3. (mec.) cuchilla. 4. **to get one's k. into,** tener un pique con, tener inquina a, tener rabia a; **to go under the k.,** someterse a una operación (quirúrgica); **to have a horror of the k.,** tener miedo a operarse. —*v.t.* 1. acuchillar, apuñalar. 2. cortar con cuchillo. 3. (E.U.) traicionar, apuñalar por la espalda. —*v.i.* pasar como un rayo.
knife-edge ['naɪfˌɛdʒ] *s.* 1. filo de cuchillo o cuchilla. 2. (mec.) arista, filo; fiel de soporte, eje de apoyo (de una balanza).
knife grinder, afilador.
knifelike [-ˌlaɪk] *a.* 1. parecido a un cuchillo. 2. (fig.) incisivo, penetrante.
knife sharpener, 1. afilador, amolador. 2. afilacuchillos, afiladora de cuchillos (aparato).
knife switch, (elec.) interruptor de cuchilla.
knifing ['naɪfɪŋ] *s.* cuchillada, puñalada, agresión con cuchillo o puñal.
knight [naɪt] *s.* 1. caballero; campeón; noble. 2. (ajedrez) caballo. —*v.t.* 1. armar caballero. 2. (G.B.) conferir el título de **Sir,** caballero.
knight-errant ['naɪt'ɛrənt] *s.* caballero andante, caballero.
knight-errantry [-əntrɪ] *s.* 1. caballería andante. 2. acción quijotesca.
knighthead [-ˌhɛd] *s.* (mar.) tragante exterior del baupres, guardabauprés.
knighthood [-ˌhʊd] *s.* 1. rango de caballero. 2. caballería, cuerpo de caballeros. 3. caballerosidad.
knightliness [-lɪnəs] *s.* caballerosidad, hidalguía.
knightly [-lɪ] *a.* caballeroso, caballeresco. —*adv.* caballerosamente, caballerescamente.
Knights of Columbus, Caballeros de Colón (asociación fraternal católica).
Knight Templar, 1. templario, caballero del Temple. 2. (E.U.) masón (del rito York).
knit [nɪt] *v.t.* (*pret.* y *p.p.* KNIT O KNITTED; *p.pr.* KNITTING) 1. tejer, tejer a punto de aguja. 2. enlazar, unir, trabar. 3. fruncir (el entrecejo). 4. **k. up,** remendar (con punto de aguja); unir, trabar; (fig.) terminar, poner punto final a (una discusión). —*v.i.* 1. hacer punto, hacer malla. 2. soldarse (hueso).
knit goods, géneros de punto.
knitter ['nɪtər, B -ə] *s.* calcetero, mediero, tejedor de punto.
knitting [-ɪŋ] *s.* tejido, trabajo de punto, labor de punto.
knitting needle, aguja o agujeta de tejer, aguja de hacer calceta, aguja de punto.
knitwear [-ˌwɛr, B -ˌwɛə] *s.* artículos de punto.
knives [naɪvz] *pl. de* **knife.**
knob [nɑb, B nɔb] *s.* 1. botón, tirador, perilla (de puerta); botón (de aparato de radio, etc.). 2. prominencia, eminencia, protuberancia, bulto. 3. loma, montículo, cerro (esp. aislado). 4. (arq.) abollón, borlita, borlilla. 5. (pr. G.B.) terroncito (de azúcar), trocito (de carbón, hielo, etc.). 6. (ant.) cabeza.
knobby ['nɑbɪ, B 'nɔbɪ] *a.* 1. lleno de bultos, que tiene eminencias. 2. montañoso. 3. (fig.) intrincado, espinoso; duro, penoso.
knobkerrie [-ˌkɛrɪ] *s.* clava, mazo primitivo.
knock [nɑk, B nɔk] *v.t.* 1. golpear; tocar, llamar a una puerta. 2. terminar con, acabar con. 3. trastornar, inquietar, quitar la calma a. 4. (G.B.) impresionar, causar fuerte impresión en. 5. (E.U.) criticar duramente. 6. **k. about** (o **around**), golpear repetidamente (a alguien); (fig.) abofetear, tratar brutalmente; **k. back,** (pr. G.B., jer.) beber, mojar la garganta con (licor); **k. down,** derribar de un golpe; atropellar; tumbar, vencer; (fam.) rebajar (precio); rematar o asignar al mejor postor; (mec.) desarmar, desmontar

(aparato o máquina); **k. (someone) for a loop,** (jer.) hacer caer de espaldas (a alguien), hacer perder el conocimiento (gen. por una sorpresa); impresionar, asombrar; **k. in,** abollar; hacer entrar a golpes; **k. into,** hacer entrar a golpes; **k. it off!** (jer.) ¡ basta! ¡ deja eso!; **k. (someone's) block off,** (jer.) pegar (a alguien) fuertemente; hacer caer (a alguien) desvanecido; **k. (someone's) head off,** darle una buena paliza (a alguien); **k. off,** hacer saltar o desprender a fuerza de golpes; poner fin a; (fam.) liquidar, matar; descontar del precio; ejecutar (un trabajo) rápidamente, producir (obra literaria) con soltura y rapidez; suspender (trabajo); **k. on the head,** dar un golpe en la cabeza a; atontar, aturdir; (fig.) acabar con (plan, etc.); **k. out,** vaciar golpeando (pipa); dejar fuera de combate, dejar inconsciente (ej., a un púgil); **k. the bottom out of,** desfondar; (fig.) invalidar; frustrar; (jer.) echar a perder; **k. to pieces,** romper en pedazos; **k. together,** hacer chocar (ej., cabezas); darse un encontronazo en (ej., la cabeza); preparar o construir en forma precipitada o descuidada; **k. up,** despertar (a alguien) llamando a la puerta; (G.B.) fatigar, agotar; (vulg.) preñar, dejar preñada, embarazar. —*v.i.* 1. (con *on*) tocar (la puerta, ventana, etc.). 2. refunfuñar, criticar. 2. (mot.) pistonear. 4. **k. about** (o **around**), vagar, merodear; holgazanear, haraganear; llevar una vida irregular; **k. against,** dar contra, tropezar con; **k. at,** tocar a, llamar a (puerta, etc.); **k. into,** chocar con; **k. off,** suspender el trabajo; (jer.) estirar la pata; **k. under,** someterse, rendirse; **k. up,** (tenis) bolear; (jer.) (*to make pregnant*) dejar embarazada, hacerle un hijo a. —*s.* 1. golpe, toque; llamada, aldabonazo. 2. (fig.) golpe, revés. 3. (mot.) pistoneo. 4. (jer.) censura, crítica dura. 5. **k.k.,** tras, tras (ruido de golpes repetidos); **to take a k.,** sufrir un revés, sufrir una pérdida.

knockabout [nakəˌbaʊt, B ˈnɔk-] *a.* 1. informal (ropa, viajes, etc.). 2. bullicioso; tumultuoso, rudo. 3. vagabundo. —*s.* (mar.) yate pequeño (sin bauprés).

knockdown [-ˌdaʊn] *a.* 1. derribador, abrumador, irresistible. 2. (entregado) en piezas listas para armarse. —*s.* 1. golpe abrumador. 2. derribo. 3. cosa desmontada; cosa entregada en piezas y lista para armarse.

knockdown price, precio de saldo, precio de liquidación o remate.

knocker [-ər, B -ə] *s.* 1. aldaba, llamador. 2. (fam.) criticón. 3. (jer.) tipo, sujeto; ejemplar. 4. (E.U., vulg.) (*pl.*) senos muy prominentes.

knocking [-ɪŋ] *s.* 1. aldabonazo, aldabazo, llamada (a la puerta). 2. golpeteo.

knock-knee [-ˌni, -ˈni] *s.* pierna de panadero, pierna en forma de tijera o X.

knock-kneed [-ˈnid] *a.* patizambo, patituerto, patuleco (Am.).

knockout [-ˌaʊt] *a.* que desmaya, que pone fuera de combate, que noquea. —*s.* 1. (boxeo) knockout, fuera de combate; golpe decisivo. 2. (fam.) maravilla (persona o cosa atractiva); belleza deslumbrante (mujer). 3. **to be a k.,** (fam.) dar la hora, ser una maravilla.

knockout drops, gotas de narcótico.

knockwurst [ˈnakˌwɜrst, B ˈnɔkˌwɜst] *s.* salchicha alemana, gruesa y bien sazonada.

knoll [noʊl] *s.* loma, otero, morón.

knop [nap, B nɔp] *s.* prominencia o protuberancia ornamental, botón en relieve (ej., en el pie de un cáliz).

knot [nat, B nɔt] *s.* 1. nudo, atadura, ligadura. 2. (fig.) nudo, dificultad, problema. 3. nudo, lazo, vínculo (esp. del matrimonio). 4. lazo; escarapela; charretera. 5. haz (de fibras, nervios, etc.). 6. bulto, protuberancia. 7. corro, corrillo, grupo. 8. nudo (de planta, en maderas). 9. (mar.) nudo (división de la corredera; unidad de velocidad equivalente a una milla náutica por hora); p. ext. milla náutica. 10. (ant.) lazo (en cuadros de los jardines). 11. (orn.) canuto, tríngido. 12. **to tie oneself in knots,** enmarañarse, enredarse, crearse dificultades. —*v.t.* (*pret., p.p.* KNOTTED; *p.pr.* KNOTTING) 1. anudar, atar. 2. enredar, enmarañar, intrincar. 3. fruncir (las cejas). —*v.i.* 1. anudarse, enredarse. 2. tejer nudos (para flecos). 3. apiñarse, agruparse. 4. (gen. con *up*) contraerse espasmódicamente.

knotgrass [ˈnatˌgræs, B ˈnɔtˌgras] *s.* (bot.) 1. centinodia, correhuela, saucillo, altamandría, sanguinaria mayor. 2. grama.

knothole [-ˌhoʊl] *s.* agujero de nudo (que queda al desprenderse un nudo de la madera).

knot stitch, punto de bordado que forma líneas adornadas a intervalos con nudos; nudos del calado.

knotted [-əd] *a.* 1. anudado. 2. nudoso. 3. arreglado en lazos (cuadro en un jardín). 4. enmarañado, intrincado; confuso. 5. adornado con nudos o botones en relieve.

knotter [-ər, B -ə] *s.* 1. anudador (persona). 2. (tej.) aparato anudador.

knotty [ˈnatɪ, B ˈnɔtɪ] *a.* 1. nudoso, lleno de nudos, anudado. 2. difícil, intrincado, confuso, complejo.

knotty pine, (madera de) pino nudoso.

knotty rhatany, (bot.) ratania.

knotweed [-ˌwid] *s.* (bot.) 1. centáurea negra. 2. centinodia.

knout [naʊt] *s.* knut (tipo de látigo). —*v.t.* azotar con knut.

know [noʊ] *v.t.* (*pret.* KNEW [nu, B nju] *p.p.* KNOWN [noʊn] *p.pr.* KNOWING) 1. conocer, ej., *I k. him by sight,* lo conozco de vista. 2. discernir, distinguir, ej., *k. one from another,* distinguir al uno del otro. 3. reconocer, identificar, ej., *I knew him at once,* lo reconocí al instante. 4. conocer, comprender, entender. 5. saber. 6. (ant.) conocer (a una mujer carnalmente). 7. **k. a thing or two,** saber algo; **k. (one) for,** conocer (a uno) como, ej., *I knew him for an Englishman,* lo conocía como inglés; **k. (one) for what one is,** saber qué clase de persona es uno; **k. how many beans make five,** saber cuántas son cinco; **k. how to (do),** saber cómo (hacer); **k. one's (own) mind,** saber lo que uno quiere; no vacilar; **k. oneself,** conocerse a sí mismo; **k. (one) to be,** saber que (uno) es, ej., *we k. her to be an excellent cook,* sabemos que es una cocinera excelente; **k. what's what,** saber, estar enterado o preparado; **to be known to (be),** ser conocido como, ej., *he was known to be a liar,* era conocido como mentiroso; **to make (something) known,** hacer conocer (algo). —*v.i.* 1. saber, tener conocimiento, conocer. 2. tener información, estar informado. 3. **k. about,** conocer, tener conocimiento de, estar enterado de; **k. best,** ser el mejor juez, saber más que nadie; **k. better than that,** saber que no es así; **k. where the shoe pinches,** saber uno dónde le aprieta el zapato. —*s.* conocimiento; **to be in the k.,** estar al tanto, estar en el caso, andar en el ajo; tener información particular.

knowable [ˈnoʊəbəl] *a.* 1. conocible. 2. (G.B.) tratable, amable.

know-all [-ˌɔl] *var. de* **know-it-all.**

knower [ˈnoʊər, B -ə] *s.* conocedor.

know-how [-ˌhaʊ] *s.* pericia, conocimientos prácticos.

knowing [-iŋ] *s.* conocimiento. —*a.* 1. instruido, inteligente, hábil. 2. discernidor; perspicaz, sagaz; despierto.

knowingly [-lɪ] *adv.* 1. a sabiendas, intencionalmente, con conocimiento. 2. inteligentemente, hábilmente.

knowingness [-nəs] *s.* sabiduría, astucia.

know-it-all [ˈnoʊətˌɔl] *s.* sabihondo, sabelotodo.

knowledge [ˈnalɪdʒ, B ˈnɔl-] *s.* 1. conocimiento, comprensión, ej., *k. of the language will help you,* el conocimiento del idioma le será útil. 2. saber, conocimientos, ej., *a man of profound k.,* un hombre de profundo saber o de conocimientos profundos. 3. conocimiento, información, noticia, ej., *to have k. of,* tener conocimiento de. 4. (ant.) acto carnal. 5. **it has come to my k.,** me enteré, vine a saber; **not to my k.,** no que yo sepa; **to have a thorough k. of,** conocer a fondo; **to one's k.,** según lo que uno sabe; **to the best of my k.,** según mi entender.

knowledgeable [-əbəl] *a.* (fam.) inteligente, bien informado.

known [noʊn] *p.p. de* **know.**

know-nothing [ˈnoʊˌnʌθɪŋ] *s.* 1. ignorante. 2. agnóstico. 3. **K.-N.,** (E.U., hist.) miembro de un partido político secreto que abogaba por limitar el poder político de los extranjeros naturalizados.

Knt. *abrev. de* **Knight,** Caballero.

knuckle [ˈnʌkəl] *s.* 1. nudillo (de los dedos). 2. jarrete (usado para hacer sopa). 3. (*pl.*) llave inglesa, llave americana, manopla. 4. (mec.) charnela, junta de charnela, unión a charnela, articulación de bisagra. 5. (mar.) arista viva. 6. **near the k.,** escabroso, al borde de lo indecente o inmoral. —*v.i.* 1. (con *to*) ceder, someterse (a). 2. **k. down,** apoyar los nudillos en el suelo (para tirar las canicas); rendirse, ceder; **k. down to,** emprender con vehemencia (ej., un trabajo); **k. under,** rendirse, ceder. —*v.t.* apretar o frotar con los nudillos.

knuckle ball, (béisbol) tiro suave que se ejecuta agarrando la bola sólo con el pulgar y el meñique, presionándola con los nudillos de los demás dedos.

knucklebone [-ˌboʊn] *s.* 1. nudillo, articulación de los dedos; cóndilo (en los animales). 2. (*pl.*) taba (juego).

knuckle-duster [-ˌdʌstər, B -tə] *s.* (jer.) llave inglesa, llave americana, manopla.

knucklehead [-ˌhɛd] *s.* cabeza de alcornoque, persona estúpida o necia.

knuckle joint, 1. articulación del nudillo. 2. (mec.) junta de charnela, unión a charnela, articulación de bisagra.

knur [nɜr, B nɜ] *s.* nudo, protuberancia (en tronco de árbol).

knurl [nɜrl, B nɜl] *s.* 1. nudo (madera); protuberancia, bulto. 2. moleteado, cerrillado. 3. (esco.) hombrecillo rechoncho.

knurled [nɜrld, B nɜld] *a.* 1. nudoso. 2. moleteado, estriado (botón, tornillo, canto de moneda, etc.).

KO [ˈkeɪ, oʊ] (jer.) *a.* noqueado, puesto fuera de combate. —*v.t.* (*pret., p.p.* K. O.'D; *p.pr.* K. O'ING) noquear, dejar fuera de combate.

koala [koʊˈalə] *s.* (zool.) koala, especie de pequeño oso australiano.

kobold [ˈkoʊˌbɔld, B ˈkɔˌboʊld] *s.* kobold, duende de las minas; diablillo familiar.

Kodiak bear [ˈkoʊdɪˌæk-] (zool.) oso gigante de Kodiak, Alaska.

koel [ˈkoʊəl] *s.* (orn.) (especie de) cuclillo de India y Australia.

K. of C., *abrev. de* **Knights of Columbus,** Caballeros de Colón.

kohl [koʊl] *s.* alcohol (producto de tocador), polvillos negros que se usan en la India para dar sombra a los ojos.

kohlrabi [ˌkoʊl'rɑbɪ] *s.* (bot.) colirrábano, colinabo, nabicol.
Koine [kɔɪ'neɪ, 'kɔɪˌneɪ, B -ni] *s.* koiné (dialecto literario griego usado en el Nuevo Testamento).
kola, *var. de* **cola.**
kola nut, (bot., quím., farm.) nuez de cola.
kolinsky [kə'lɪnskɪ] *s.* (zool.) kolinski, visón de Siberia.
kolkhoz [kɑl'kɔz, B kɔl-] *s.* (*pl.* KOLKHOZY [-'kɔzɪ] o KOLKHOZES) koljoz, granja colectiva soviética.
koodoo, *var. de* **kudu.**
kook [kuk] *s.* (jer.) chiflado, majareta, excéntrico.
kookaburra ['kʊkəˌbɜrə, B -ˌbʌrə] *s.* (orn., Aust.) martín cazador.
kooky, kookie ['kukɪ] *a.* (jer.) alocado, excéntrico.
kopeck, kopek ['koʊˌpɛk] *s.* copec (moneda rusa).
kopje, koppie ['kɑpɪ, B 'kɔpɪ] *s.* (África del S.) colina o pequeño cerro.
Koran [kə'ræn, -'rɑn, B kɔ'rɑn] *s.* Corán, Alcorán, libro sagrado de los mahometanos.
Koranic [-'rænɪk] *a.* alcoránico, coránico.
Korea [kə'riə, kɔ-, B -'rɪə] *s.* Corea.
Korean [-'riən, B -'rɪ-] *s.* 1. coreano, natural de Corea. 2. (idioma) coreano. —*a.* coreano.
koruna ['kɔrəˌnɑ, koʊ'runɑ, B 'kɔrəˌnɑ] *s.* (*pl.* KORUNY [-ni] o KORUNAS) corona (moneda checoeslovaca).
kosher ['koʊʃər, B -ʃə] *a.* 1. (relig.) autorizado por la religión judía (alimentos). 2. (jer.) propio, correcto; legítimo, genuino. —*v.t.* (relig.) hacer o declarar autorizado (alimento).
Kotex (TM) ['koutɛks] *s.* kotex, compresa, toalla hygiénica.
koumis, koumiss, koumyss, *vars. de* **kumiss.**
kourbash, *var. de* **kurbash.**
kowtow ['kaʊ'taʊ, kaʊ-] *v.i.* 1. arrodillarse y tocar el suelo con la frente en señal de homenaje (costumbre china). 2. demostrar gran respeto. 3. (fig.) tratar (a persona) con deferencia servil. —*s.* reverencia, zalema (de rodillas y tocando el suelo con la frente).

kraal [krɑl, krɔl] (África del S.) *s.* 1. craal, corral, redil. 2. craal, población de hotentotes. —*v.t.* poner (el ganado) en el corral o redil.
kraft [kræft, B krɑft] *s.* papel kraft, papel fuerte (que sirve para hacer embalajes).
kraken ['krɑkən] *s.* monstruo marino mitológico de Escandinavia.
K ration, (E.U.) ración militar, paquete de alimentos concentrados.
Kraut [kraʊt] *s.* (jer., despec.) alemán; esp. soldado alemán.
Kremlin ['krɛmlən] *s.* Kremlin, sede del gobierno soviético en Moscú.
Kremlinologist [ˌkrɛmlən'ɑlədʒəst, B -'ɔl-] *s.* analizador de la política comunista rusa.
Kremlinology [-dʒɪ] *s.* análisis de la política comunista rusa.
kreuzer ['krɔɪtsər, B -sə] *s.* kreuzer (antigua moneda alemana o austríaca).
kris [kris] *s.* cris (especie de daga de Filipinas y Malasia).
Krishna ['krɪsʃnə] *s.* (mitol.) Krisna, principal avatar de Visnú.
Kriss Kringle ['krɪs'krɪŋgəl] Santa Claus.
krona ['kroʊnə] *s.* (*pl.* KRONOR [-ˌnɔr, B -ˌnɔ]) corona (moneda de Suecia).
krone ['kroʊnə] *s.* 1. (*pl.* KRONER [-nər, B -nə]) corona (moneda de Dinamarca y de Noruega). 2. corona, antigua moneda de Alemania y Austria-Hungría.
krypton ['krɪpˌtɑn, B -ˌtɔn] *s.* (quím.) criptón.
Kt. *abrev. de* **Knight,** Caballero.
Kuala Lumpur ['kwɑləlʊm'pʊr, B -'lʊmpʊə] *s.* Kuala Lumpur, capital de la Federación de Malasia.
kudos ['kuˌdɑs, B 'kjuˌdɔs] *s.* (*pl.* KUDOS [-ˌdoʊz]) gloria, celebridad; fama, renombre; alabanza.
kudu ['kudu] *s.* (zool.) kudu.
kudzu ['kʊdzu] *s.* (bot.) kudzú.
Ku Kluxer ['kuˌklʌksər, B 'kju-sə] miembro del Ku-Klux-Klan.
Ku-Klux Klan [-ˌklʌks'klæn] (E.U., pol., hist.) Ku Klux Klan, sociedad de blancos racistas que predomina en los estados del Sur.

kulak [ku'lɑk, -'læk, B 'kulæk] *s.* kulak, campesino acomodado (en Rusia).
Kultur [kʊl'tʊr, B -'tʊə] *s.* cultura como fuerza social, esp. la cultura alemana idealizada por los Nazis; hoy se usa irónicamente en relación a estructuras sociales sistematizadas.
kumiss ['kʊmɪs] *s.* kumiz (bebida alcohólica tártara hecha de leche).
kümmel ['kɪməl, B 'kʊm-] *s.* kummel, cúmel (licor).
kummerbund, *var. de* **cummerbund.**
kumquat ['kʌmˌkwɑt] *s.* (bot.) kuncuat, naranjita china, quinoto.
kunzite ['kʊntˌsaɪt] *s.* (min.) kunzita.
kurbash ['kʊrˌbæʃ, B 'kʊəˌ-] *s.* látigo de cuero crudo (usado en Turquía y Egipto). —*v.t.* azotar con látigo de cuero.
Kurd [kɜrd, kʊrd, B kɜd] *s.* curdo, kurdo, tribu nómada del Cáucaso.
Kurdish ['kɜrdɪʃ, 'kʊrd-, B 'kɜd-] *s., a.* curdo, kurdo.
kurtosis [kər'toʊsəs, B kɜ'-] *s.* (estadística) curtosis.
Kuwait [ku'weɪt, kə-, B kʊ-] *s.* Kuwait, estado árabe.
kuwaiti [-'weɪtɪ] *s., a.* kuwaiti, de o rel. a Kuwait.
kv *abrev. de* **kilovolt,** kilovoltio (kV.).
kva *abrev. de* **kilovolt-ampere,** kilovoltamperio.
kvar *abrev. de* **kilovar,** kilovoltamperio reactivo.
kvass [kə'vɑs, kvɑs, B kvɑs] *s.* kwas, kvas (cerveza rusa hecha de centeno).
kw. *abrev. de* **kilowatt,** kilovatio (kW.).
kwhr, kwh *abrev. de* **kilowatt hour,** kilovatio-hora (kWh.).
Ky. *abrev. de* **Kentucky,** Kentucky (E.U.).
kyack ['kaɪˌæk] *s.* 1. *var. de* **kayak.** 2. especie de alforja (que se lleva sobre el caballo).
kyanite ['kaɪəˌnaɪt] *var. de* **cyanite.**
kyle [kaɪl] *s.* (esco.) estuario, estero.
kymograph ['kaɪməˌgræf, B -ˌgrɑf] *s.* (med.) quimógrafo.
kymric, *var. de* **cymric.**
kyphosis [kaɪ'foʊsəs] *s.* (med.) cifosis.

L

L [ɛl] *s.* l, duodécima letra del alfabeto inglés.
L. *abrev. de* **Lady,** dama (título nobiliario), **Latin,** latín (idioma), **Lord,** lor.
l. *abrev. de* **liter,** litro (l.); **lake,** lago; **land,** tierra; **latitude,** latitud; **law,** derecho; **pound,** libra (como unidad monetaria).
la [lɑ] *s.* (mús.) la, sexta nota de la escala.
La *símb. de* **lanthanum,** lantano (La).
La. *abrev. de* **Louisiana,** Luisiana (E.U.).
L.A. *abrev. de* **Los Angeles,** Los Ángeles. (E.U.).
laager ['lɑgər, B -ə] *s.* (S. África) campamento (esp. el defendido por carromatos colocados en círculo). —*v.i.* formar un campamento (defendido por carromatos en círculo).
lab [læb] *s.* (fam.) laboratorio.
Lab. *abrev. de* **Labrador,** Labrador.
labarum ['læbərəm] *s.* (*pl.* LABARA [-rə]) (hist.) lábaro.
labdanum ['læbdənəm] *s.* (bot.) ládano.
labefaction [ˌlæbə'fækʃən] *s.* debilitamiento, decadencia; empeoramiento, deterioro.
label ['leɪbəl] *s.* 1. marbete, rótulo, etiqueta; marca (esp. de disco de gramófono). 2. cinta (de papel o tela para unir el sello a un escrito). 3. indicación, calificación, clasificación. 4. mote, apodo, sobrenombre. 5. (her.) lambel. 6. (arq.) ceja, alero: goterón. —*v.t.* (*pret., p.p.* LABELED O LABELLED; *p.pr.* LABELING O LABELLING) 1. poner marbete a, rotular, marcar. 2. calificar, clasificar. 3. apodar.
labellate [lə'bɛlət] *a.* (bot.) labelado.
labellum [-əm] *s.* (*pl.* LABELLA [-ə]) (bot.) labelo.
labia, *pl. de* **labium.**
labial ['leɪbɪəl] *a.* labial. —*s.* 1. (mús.) caño de boca, caño de flauta (del órgano); flauta labial. 2. (fon.) (consonante) labial.
labialism [-ˌɪzəm] *s.* (fon.) labialismo.
labialization [ˌleɪbɪələ'zeɪʃən, B -laɪ-] *s.* (fon.) labialización.
labialize ['leɪbɪəˌlaɪz] *v.t.* (fon.) labializar.
labia majora ['leɪbɪəmə'dʒərə] (anat.) labios mayores (vulva).
labia minora [-mɪ'nɔrə] (anat.) labios menores (vulva).
labiate ['leɪbɪət, -ˌeɪt] *a.* (bot.) labiado.
labile ['leɪbəl, B -baɪl] *a.* lábil, inestable, precario; (quím.) lábil.
labiodental [ˌleɪbɪoʊ'dɛntəl] (fon.) *a.* labiodental, dentolabial, dentilabial. —*s.* consonante labiodental.
labionasal [-'neɪzəl] (fon.) *a.* labionasal. —*s.* consonante labionasal.
labiovelar [-'vilər, B -lə] (fon.) *a.* labiovelar. —*s.* consonante labiovelar.
labium ['leɪbɪəm] *s.* (*pl.* LABIA [-bɪə]) 1. (bot., zool., ento.) labio. 2. (*pl.* anat.) labios.
labor, (pr. G.B.) **labour** ['leɪbər, B -bə] *s.* 1. labor, trabajo (mental o físico). 2. tarea, faena, ocupación. 3. (*pl.*) esfuerzos. 4. mano de obra. 5. clase obrera o trabajadora. 6. (med.) parto, dolores del parto. 7. (e.p.) trabajo. 8. **hard l.,** trabajos forzados o forzosos; **l. of love,** trabajo agradable, labor placentera; **lost l.,** trabajo inútil, trabajo sin frutos; **to be in l.,** estar de parto. —*v.i.* 1. trabajar duramente, esforzarse. 2. estar de parto. 3. funcionar con dificultad, obrar o avanzar penosamente. 4. (mar.) balancear, cabecear (un barco). 5. **l. for,** luchar por; **l. under,** sufrir, ser víctima de (malentendido, error, etc.). —*v.t.* 1. tratar minuciosamente, insistir en, ej., *I will not l. the point,* no quiero tratar minuciosamente el asunto, no insistiré en el asunto. 2. molestar, fatigar. 3. (pr. lit.) labrar, cultivar. 4. (ant.) hacer, ejecutar o producir laboriosamente. —*a.* 1. laboral, de trabajo (legislación, contrato, etc.). 2. de mano de obra (costo, disponibilidad, etc.). 3. obrero, laborista (prensa, dirigente, etc.); del partido laborista (candidato, política, etc.).
laboratory ['læbrəˌtɔrɪ, 'læbərə-, B lə'bɔrətərɪ] *s.* (*pl.* LABORATORIES) laboratorio.
labor camp, campo de trabajos forzados o forzosos.
labor conflicts, l. disputes, conflictos laborales.
Labor Day, (E.U.) día del trabajador (fiesta que se celebra el primer lunes de septiembre).
labored, (pr. G.B.) **laboured** ['leɪbərd, B -bəd] *a.* trabajoso, penoso, forzado.
laborer [-bərər, B -bərə] *s.* persona que labora (obrero, operario, trabajador, jornalero, bracero, labriego, etc.).
labor force, mano de obra; potencial laboral, ej., *recruiting has seriously depleted the l. f. of the country,* el reclutamiento ha reducido considerablemente el potencial laboral del país.
laboring, (pr. G.B.) **labouring** [-bərɪŋ] *a.* trabajador, que trabaja.
labor intensive, que requiere mucha mano de obra.
laborious [lə'bɔrɪəs] *a.* 1. laborioso, trabajoso, ímprobo. 2. laborioso, trabajador, industrioso, diligente.
laboriously [-lɪ] *adv.* laboriosamente.
laboriousness [-nəs] *s.* laboriosidad, diligencia; dificultad.
labor saving, que ahorra trabajo.
Labourite ['leɪbəˌraɪt] *s.* (G.B.) laborista, miembro del partido laborista.
labor laws, leyes laborales, legislación obrera.
labor leader, dirigente obrero, o dirigente laborista.
labor market, mano de obra disponible, mercado laboral.
Labour Party, (pol., G.B.) partido laborista.
labor-saving, (pr. G.B.) **labour-saving** ['leɪbərˌseɪvɪŋ, B -bəˌ] *a.* economizador de trabajo, que economiza esfuerzo.
labor shortage, escasez de mano de obra.
labor supply, disponibilidad de mano de obra.
labor troubles, conflictos laborales.
labor turnover, cambio del personal obrero, movimiento laboral.
labor union, sindicato o gremio obrero, central sindical.
labour, labourer, (G.B.) *vars. de* **labor,** laborer.
labradorite ['læbrədɔrˌaɪt] *s.* (min.) labradorita.
labret ['leɪbrət] *s.* adorno de los labios (pedazo de madera, concha o piedra que usan ciertas tribus primitivas).
labroid ['læbˌrɔɪd] *a.* (ict.) labroideo, labrido.
labrum ['leɪbrəm] *s.* (*pl.* LABRA [-brə]) 1. labio, borde (de una vasija, etc.). 2. (zool., ento.) labro.
laburnum [lə'bɜrnəm, B -'bɜnəm] *s.* (bot.) codeso de los Alpes, laburno.
labyrinth ['læbəˌrɪnθ] *s.* laberinto; dédalo.
labyrinthian [ˌlæbə'rɪnθɪən] **labyrinthic** [-θɪk] **labyrinthical** [-θɪkəl] *a.* laberíntico.
labyrinthine [-θən, -θin, B -θaɪn] *a.* laberíntico, intrincado, enmarañado.
lac [læk] *s.* laca, goma laca.
laccolith ['lækəˌlɪθ] *s.* (geol.) lacolito.
lace [leɪs] *s.* 1. encaje. 2. cordón, cinta (en prendas de vestir, para zapatos). —*v.t.* 1. atar (prendas o zapatos con cintas o cordones); ajustar (el cuerpo) con corsé; **l. up,** atar, atar el cordón de. 2. (fam.) golpear, azotar. 3. adornar con encajes o cordones. 4. entrelazar, entretejer. 5. rociar con licor (café, etc.). —*v.i.* 1. estar sujeto o atado con cordones o cintas. 2. usar cordones para ceñir la cintura.
lace bobbin, bolillo para hacer encajes.
Lacedaemonian, Lacedemonian [ˌlæsədə'moʊnɪən] *a.* lacedemonio, lacedemónico (apl. a cosas); lacedemón (apl. a personas). —*s.* lacedemón.
laced boot[leɪst-] borceguí.
laced ruffles, vuelos de encaje.
lace edging, *s.* puntilla, adorno de encaje.
lace frame, *s.* telar para hacer encajes.
lace maker, *s.* el que hace encajes, cordonero, pasamanero.
lace pillow, almohadilla para hacer encajes.
lacerate ['læsəˌreɪt] *v.t.* 1. lacerar, herir, desgarrar. 2. (fig.) atormentar; herir (sentimientos). — [-rət, -ˌreɪt] *a.* 1. lacerado, herido, desgarrado. 2. (fig.) atormentado, aturdido. 3. (bot., zool.) lacerado.
laceration [ˌlæsə'reɪʃən] *s.* laceración; herida, desgarradura, desgarro.
lacertilian [-ər'tɪlɪən, B -ə'-] *a., s.* (zool.) lacertilio.
lacewing ['leɪsˌwɪŋ] *s.* (ento.) crisopa.
lacework [-ˌwɜrk, B -ˌwɜk] *s.* filigrana, obra de filigrana.
laches ['lætʃəz, 'leɪtʃəz] *s.* (der.) negligencia, incuria; tardanza o demora indebida (para hacer valer un derecho y reclamar o pedir un privilegio).
Lachryma Christi ['lækrəmə'krɪstɪ] lácrima christi (vino).
lachrymal ['lækrəməl] *a.* 1. lacrimal. 2. (anat.) lagrimal, ej., *l. glands,* glándulas lagrimales. —*s.* 1. (*pl.*) órganos lagrimales. 2. (arqueol.) lacrimatorio.
lachrymator [-ˌmeɪtər, B -ə] *s.* substancia lacrimógena.
lachrimatory [-məˌtɔrɪ, B -mətərɪ] *s.* vaso lacrimatorio (que se encuentra en sepulcros antiguos). —*a.* 1. lacrimógeno. 2. lacrimatorio (vaso).
lachrymose [-ˌmoʊs] *a.* lacrimoso, lloroso.
lachrymosely [-lɪ] *adv.* lacrimosamente.
lacing ['leɪsɪŋ] *s.* 1. enlace, enlazamiento, enlazadura. 2. cordón, cordoncillo, cuerda. 3. pizca, poquito (de licor que se echa en el café y otras

bebidas o manjares). 4. tunda, zurra. 5. cordoncillos y galones.

laciniate [lə'sɪnɪət, -ˌeɪt] **laciniated** [-ˌeɪtəd] *a.* (bot.) laciniado.

lack [læk] *s.* falta, carencia, deficiencia, necesidad, menester; **for l. of,** por falta de, a falta de; **no l. of,** suficiente, bastante; **to supply the l.,** suplir la falta. —*v.i.* faltar, hacer falta; **l. in,** ser o estar deficiente en. —*v.t.* 1. faltarle a uno, hacerle falta a uno, necesitar. 2. carecer de.

lackadaisical [ˌlækə'deɪzɪkəl] *a.* lánguido, desganado; indiferente, distraído.

lackadaisically [-kəlɪ] *adv.* lánguidamente, con desgana, con indiferencia.

lackadaisicalness [-kəlnəs] *s.* languidez, desgana, indiferencia.

lackaday ['lækəˌdeɪ] *interj.* (ant.) ¡ay de mí! ¡mal día! ¡mal haya!

lacker, *var. de* **lacquer.**

lackey ['lækɪ] *s.* 1. lacayo, criado de librea, camarero. 2. (fig.) lacayo, adulador. —*v.t.* 1. servir obsequiosamente. 2. (fig.) adular.

lacking ['lækɪŋ] *a.* 1. deficiente, defectuoso. 2. faltante, carente. 3. (fam., G.B.) mentecato, estúpido. 4. **l. in,** carente de, falto de; **to be l.,** faltar, no haber, hacer falta.

lackluster, lacklustre [-ˌlʌstər, B -tə] *s.* falta de lustre o brillo. —*a.* deslustroso, sin brillo o lustre.

Laconian [lə'koʊnɪən] *a., s.* (hist.) laconio, de una antigua región del Peloponeso cuya capital era Esparta.

laconic [lə'kɑnɪk, B -'kɔn-] **laconical** [-ɪkəl] *a.* lacónico, breve, conciso, sucinto.

laconically [-ɪkəlɪ] *adv.* lacónicamente.

laconism ['lækəˌnɪzəm] *s.* laconismo, concisión; expresión breve y vigorosa.

lacquer ['lækər, B -ə] *s.* laca, barniz. —*v.t.* laquear, barnizar, cubrir con laca.

lacquerer [-ərər, B -ərə] *s.* barnizador.

lacquering [-ərɪŋ] *s.* acción de barnizar con laca; capa de barniz de laca.

lacquer ware, platos y objetos laqueados.

Lacrima Christi, *var. de* **lachryma christi.**

lacrimal, *var. de* **lachrymal.**

lacrimation [ˌlækrə'meɪʃən] *s.* (med.) lacrimación, lagrimeo.

lacrimator, lacrimatory, *vars. de* **lachrymator, lachrymatory.**

lacrimose, *var. de* **lachrymose.**

lacrosse [lə'krɔs] *s.* (dep.) juego originalmente practicado por los indios de Norteamérica, que se juega con una raqueta de mango largo.

lactalbumin [ˌlækˌtæl'bjumən] *s.* (bioquím.) lactalbúmina, albúmina de leche.

lactam ['læktæm] *s.* (quím.) lactama.

lactary ['læktərɪ] *a.* lácteo, lacticinoso, lechoso. —*s.* lechería.

lactase ['lækˌteɪs] *s.* (bioquím.) lactasa.

lactate [-ˌteɪt] *s.* (quím.) lactato. —*v.i.* (fisiol.) secretar leche, lactar.

lactation [læk'teɪʃən] *s.* 1. secreción de leche. 2. lactación, lactancia (período).

lacteal ['læktɪəl] *a.* 1. lácteo, lechoso. 2. (anat.) lácteo, quilífero. —*s.* (anat.) vaso lácteo, vaso quilífero.

lacteous [-tɪəs] *a.* lechoso, lácteo.

lactescence [læk'tɛsəns] **lactescency** [-ənsɪ] *s.* lactescencia.

lactescent [-ənt] *a.* 1. lactescente, de aspecto lechoso. 2. (bot.) lactescente.

lactic ['læktɪk] *a.* (quím.) láctico.

lactic acid, (quím.) ácido láctico.

lactiferous [læk'tɪfərəs] *a.* 1. lactífero. 2. (bot.) lechal.

lactobacillus [ˌlæktoʊbə'sɪləs] *s.* (med.) lactobacillus.

lactoflavin [-'fleɪvən] *s.* (quím.) lactoflavina.

lactogenic [-'dʒɛnɪk] *a.* lactógeno.

lactometer [læk'tɑmətər, B -'tɔmɪtə] *s.* lactómetro.

lactone ['lækˌtoʊn] *s.* (quím.) lactona.

lactoproteid [ˌlæktoʊ'proʊˌtid] **lactoprotein** [-ˌtin] *s.* (quím.) lactoproteína.

lactoscope ['læktəˌskoʊp] *s.* lactoscopio.

lactose ['lækˌtoʊs] *s.* (quím.) lactosa.

lactucarium [ˌlæktə'kɛrɪəm, B -tju'kɛər-] *s.* (farm.) lactucario.

lacuna [lə'kunə, B -'kju-] *s.* 1. laguna (en lo manuscrito o impreso), blanco, hueco, omisión (de un trozo). 2. (anat., biol.) laguna.

lacunal [-nəl] **lacunar** [-nər, B -nə] *a.* (anat., biol.) lacunar.

lacunar [-nər, B -nə] *s.* (arq.) lagunar, lacunario.

lacunary ['lækjəˌnɛrɪ, B lə'kjunərɪ] *a.* (anat.) lacunar.

lacunose [lə'kjuˌnoʊs] *a.* que tiene lagunas o claros.

lacustral [lə'kʌstrəl] **lacustrine** [-trən, B -ˌtraɪn] *a.* lacustre.

lacy ['leɪsɪ] *a.* (LACIER; LACIEST) 1. parecido al encaje; adornado con encaje. 2. (fig.) delicado, de filigrana.

lad [læd] *s.* 1. muchacho, joven, chico, mozo, mozalbete, mancebo, zagal. 2. amigo.

ladanum ['lædənəm] *var. de* **labdanum.**

ladder ['lædər, B -ə] *s.* 1. escala, escalera, escalerilla. 2. (fig.) escalón. 3. (pr. G.B.) carrera o línea de puntos (que se sueltan en la media). —*v.i.* soltarse la línea de puntos (en la media), correrse (la media).

ladder attenuator, (rad.) atenuador de escalera.

ladder-back [-ˌbæk] *a.* que tiene el espaldar semejante a una escala (ej., silla).

ladder ropes, (mar.) brandales.

ladder stitch, puntada de bordado en forma de travesaños.

ladder track, (f.c.) vía maestra, vía de enlace, vía de escala.

ladder truck, carro de escalera de bomberos.

laddie ['lædɪ] *s.* (Esco.) muchacho, joven, chico, mozo.

lade [leɪd] *v.t.* (*pret., p.p.* LADED O LADEN ['leɪdən] *p.pr.* LADING) 1. cargar. 2. (*ú. esp. en p.p.*) agobiar, abrumar 3. sacar con cucharón o pala. 4. achicar. 5. echar en. —*v.i.* tomar carga. —*s.* desembocadero, canal de desagüe.

laden ['leɪdən] *a.* 1. cargado. 2. abrumado, agobiado.

la-di-da ['lɑdɪ'dɑ] *a.* (fam.) amanerado, afectado, pretensioso; frívolo.

ladies' man, *var. de* **lady's man.**

ladies' mantle, (bot.) alquimila.

Ladin [lə'din] *s.* 1. (filol.) ladino, rético. 2. ladino (persona de habla ladina o rética).

lading ['leɪdɪŋ] *s.* 1. carga. 2. carguío, cargamento. 3. **bill of l.,** carta de porte, conocimiento (o póliza) de embarque.

Ladino [lə'dinoʊ] *s.* 1. (filol.) ladino, (lenguaje) judeo-español. 2. mestizo (de judío y español). 3. **l.,** (S.E. de E.U.) caballo mañoso.

ladkin ['lædkən] *s.* (ant.) jovencito, señorito.

ladle ['leɪdəl] *s.* 1. cazo, cucharón. 2. (fundición) caldero de colada. —*v.t.* sacar o servir (un líquido) con un cucharón.

lady ['leɪdɪ] *s.* (*pl.* LADIES) 1. dama, señora, señorita. 2. esposa, mujer. 3. **L.,** (G.B.) título que se antepone al nombre de la hija o esposa de un noble.

lady beetle, (ento.) mariquita.

ladybug [-ˌbʌg] *s.* (ento.) mariquita.

Lady Day, (relig.) Anunciación (25 de marzo).

lady doctor, doctora, médica.

ladyfinger [-ˌfɪŋgər, B -gə] *s.* bizcochuelo (en forma de dedo).

lady-in-attendance [-ɪnə'tɛndəns] *s.* camarera mayor.

lady-in-waiting [-'weɪtɪŋ] *s.* dama, azafata (de una reina o princesa).

lady-killer [-ˌkɪlər, B -ə] *s.* (fam.) tenorio, conquistador de mujeres, Don Juan.

ladykin ['leɪdɪkən] *s.* (ant.) pequeña dama.

ladylike [-ˌlaɪk] *a.* 1. bien criada o educada; de (una) dama, ej., *l. manners,* modales de dama. 2. delicado, fino, elegante. 3. afeminado, femenino, propio de mujer.

ladylove [-ˌlʌv] *s.* novia, dulce amiga; amante, querida.

lady's comb, *s.* (bot.) aguja, aguja de pastor, aguja de Venus.

ladyship ['leɪdɪˌʃɪp] *s.* 1. rango o posición de una dama. 2. (su) señoría (tratamiento que se da a las hijas o esposas de nobles).

lady's maid, doncella (al servicio de una dama).

lady's man, ladies' man, hombre galante y mujeriego.

lady's-slipper ['leɪdɪzˌslɪpər, B -ə] **lady-slipper** ['leɪdɪˌslɪp-] *s.* (bot.) chapín de Venus, zueco.

lady's-smock [-ˌsmɑk, B -ˌsmɔk] *s.* (bot.) cardamina, mastuerzo.

lady's-thumb [-ˌθʌm] *s.* (bot.) persicaria, durazníllo, hierba pejiguera.

lag [læg] *v.i.* (*pret., p.p,* LAGGED; *p.pr,* LAGGING) 1. retrasarse, atrasarse, demorarse, retardarse, rezagarse. 2. caminar o moverse lentamente, ir despacio. 3. remolonear, roncear. 4. tirar una canica (hacia una línea en el suelo) para determinar el orden de juego. —*s.* 1. retraso, atraso. 2. intervalo, demora. 3. (fís.) intervalo de retardación. 4. (elec.) retardo. 5. tiro para determinar el orden de juego (en canicas). 6. (ant.) plebe, populacho. —*a.* (dial.) último, final, postrero, trasero; atrasado, tardío, tardo, lento, moroso.

lag, *s.* 1. duela (de barril, cuñete, etc.). 2. listón de revestimiento (de un caldero). 3. (jer.) presidiario, malhechor. 4. (jer.) (duración de una) condena. —*v.t.* (*pret., p.p.* LAGGED; *p.pr.* LAGGING) 1. revestir, proveer de listones de revestimiento. 2. (jer.) confinar (a un criminal); enviar a la penitenciaría; arrestar, detener, poner preso.

lagan ['lægən] **lagend** [-ənd] *s.* (der.) mercancías echadas al mar y marcadas con una boya (para ser recogidas después).

lager ['lɑgər, B -ə] *s.* (especie de) cerveza añeja.

lager beer, cerveza reposada, cerveza de conserva.

laggard ['lægərd, B -əd] *a.* lento, calmoso, tardo, pesado; perezoso, haragán, holgazán. —*s.* rezagado; haragán, holgazán.

laggardly [-lɪ] *adv.* lentamente, perezosamente.

lagger ['lægər, B -ə] *s.* rezagado; haragán, holgazán.

lagging [-ɪŋ] *s.* 1. envoltura aisladora, camisa, revestimiento (de una caldera). 2. costillas, encostillado, estacas de revestimiento (en túneles). 3. entablado (de moldes). —*a.* rezagado, retrasado.

lagniappe, lagnappe ['lænˌjæp] *s.* (S. de E.U.) añadidura, adehala, refacción; yapa, ñapa (Amer.).

lagomorph ['lægəˌmɔrf, B -ˌmɔf] *s.* (zool.) lagomorfo.

lagoon [lə'gun] *s.* laguna (generalmente de agua dulce y de menores dimensiones que el lago).

Lagos ['leɪˌgɑs, B -ˌgɔs] *s.* Lagos, capital de Nigeria.

lag screw, (carp.) tirafondo; tornillo de cabeza cuadrada.
laic ['leɪɪk] *a., s.* laico, lego, seglar, secular.
laical [-əkəl] *a.* laico, laical.
laicism [-əˌsɪzəm] *s.* laicismo, laicidad.
laicization [ˌleɪəsə'zeɪʃən, B -saɪ-] *s.* laicización, laicalización (Amer.).
laicize ['leɪəˌsaɪz] *v.t.* laicizar, laicalizar (Amer.).
laid [leɪd] *pret., p.p. de* **lay.**
laid paper, papel vergé, papel vergueteado o verjurado.
laigh [leɪ] *a., adv.* (esco.) bajo, de poca altura; cerca del suelo. *—s.* tierra baja; fondo de una hondonada; depresión.
lain [leɪn] *p.p. de* **lie** (yacer).
lair [lɛr, B lɛə] *s.* cubil, guarida, madriguera. *—v.i.* amadrigar, recogerse (un animal) a su cubil o madriguera; descansar.
lair, *v.t.* (esco.) atollarse o hundirse (al vadear un fangal).
laird [lɛrd, B lɛəd] *s.* (esco.) hacendado, terrateniente.
laissez faire [ˌlesei'fɛr, B 'leɪseɪ'fɛə] (fr.) dejar hacer, política de no interferir o intervenir.
laissez-passer [-pæ'seɪ, B pɑ-] *s.* (fr.) permiso, pase, salvoconducto.
laity ['leɪətɪ] *s.* legos, laicos (en conjunto), laicado (Amer.).
lake [leɪk] *s.* lago; **The Great L.,** el Océano Atlántico; **The Great Lakes,** los Grandes Lagos; **to be like a l. (the sea),** estar en lecho (el mar).
lake, *s.* laca (color y pigmento); (pint.) laca.
lake dweller, habitante de construcciones lacustres.
lake dwelling, habitación lacustre, palafito (esp. de los tiempos prehistóricos).
lakelet ['leɪklət] *s.* laguito (por lo general de menores dimensiones que un lago pero mayor que una laguna).
Lake poets, poetas lakistas (Coleridge, Southey y Wordsworth), que se distinguieron por sus descripciones de la naturaleza.
laker ['leɪkər, B -kə] *s.* 1. (poét.) **L.,** lakista. 2. pez lacustre (esp. la trucha de lago). 3. embarcación lacustre.
lake trout, (ict.) trucha de los lagos.
lallan ['lælən] *a.* (esco.) de las tierras bajas.
lallation [læ'leɪʃən] *s.* (fonét.) lambdacismo.
lam [læm] *v.i.* (jer.) huir, fugarse (esp. de la policía). *—s.* (jer.) escape, huida, fuga; **on the l.,** prófugo; **to take it on the l.,** largarse.
lam, *v.t., v.i.* (*pret., p.p.* LAMMED; *p.pr.* LAMMING) (jer.) pegar, vapulear, zurrar.
lama ['lɑmə] *s.* lama (sacerdote del Tibet).
Lamaism [-ˌɪzəm] *s.* lamaísmo.
Lamaist [-əst] *a., s.* lamaísta, seguidor del lamaísmo.
Lamaistic [ˌlɑmə'ɪstɪk] *a.* lamaísta.
lamantin [lə'mæntən] *s.* (zool.) lamantino, manatí.
Lamarckian [lə'mɑrkɪən, B -'mɑkɪ-] *a.* (biol.) lamarquista, lamarquiano. *—s.* lamarquista, partidario del lamarquismo.
Lamarckism [-ˌkɪzəm] *s.* (biol.) lamarquismo, teoría de Lamarck.
lamasery ['lɑməˌserɪ, B -sərɪ] *s.* lamasería, monasterio budista.
lamb [læm] *s.* 1. cordero, borrego, carnero joven. 2. carne de cordero. 3. corderina, zamarro, piel de cordero. 4. (fig.) amor, niño bueno. 5. (fig.) cordero. 6. inocente, inocentón. 7. **like a l.,** mansamente; **we can as well be hanged for a sheep as for a l.,** preso por mil, preso por mil (y) quinientos. *—v.i.* (*pret., p.p.* LAMBED; *p.pr.* LAMBING) parir (la oveja).
lambaste [læm'beɪst, -'bæ st, B -'beɪst] *v.t.* (fam.) 1. pegar, zurrar, aporrear, golpear. 2. dar un jabón a, reprender o censurar con dureza.
lamb chop, chuleta de cordero.
lambda ['læmdə] *s.* lambda, undécima letra del alfabeto griego.
lambdoid [-ˌdɔɪd] **lambdoidal** [læm'dɔɪdəl] *a.* (anat.) lambdoideo.
lambency ['læmbənsɪ] *s.* (*pl.* LAMBENCIES) brillo suave (de las llamas).
lambent [-bənt] *a.* 1. de suave brillo (llama). 2. suavemente radiante (ojos, el cielo, etc.). 3. ligero, alegre, brillante (humor, genio o carácter).
lambently [-lɪ] *adv.* con brillo suave.
lambert [-bərt, B -bət] *s.* (fís.) lambert.
lambkin ['læmkən] *s.* 1. cordero o borrego pequeño. 2. amorcito (ú. como expresión de cariño).
lamblike [-ˌlaɪk] *a.* manso, dócil, sumiso; inocente.
Lamb of God, (El) Cordero de Dios, (El) Divino Cordero.
lambrequin ['læmbərkən, -brɪ-, B -bəkɪn] *s.* 1. (E.U.) guardamalleta, cenefa. 2. (hist.) cubierta de paño sobre el yelmo (para protegerlo del agua y el calor); rodete. 3. (her.) lambrequín.
lamb's fry, criadillas, escritillas.
lambskin ['læmˌskɪn] *s.* corderina, zamarro, piel de cordero; corderillo (piel adobada con su lana).
lamb's wool, añinos, lana de cordero.
lame [leɪm] *a.* 1. inválido, lisiado, paralizado. 2. cojo, renco, rengo. 3. pobre, débil, insatisfactorio, inaceptable (demostración, argumento, excusa). *—v.t.* 1. poner cojo. 2. lisiar, estropear.
lame [leɪm, læm] *s.* 1. lámina o plancha delgada. 2. (*pl.*) escamas (de la loriga).
lamé [lɑ'meɪ] *s.* lamé (tejido de oro o plata con seda, lana o algodón).
lame-brain ['leɪmˌbreɪn] *a.* (fam.) tonto, de pocas luces.
lame duck, 1. persona incapaz; cosa inútil. 2. corredor de bolsa insolvente. 3. (G.B.) barco averiado. 4. (E.U.) congresista o funcionario que no ha sido reelegido y que está a punto de terminar su período.
lame excuse, disculpa insatisfactoria o superficial.
lame expression, expresión incompleta o vana.
lamella [lə'mɛlə] *s.* 1. (zool.) lámina. 2. (bot.) laminilla, membrana (de hongo).
lamellar [-'mɛlər, B -ə] *a.* laminar.
lamellate ['læmələt, -ˌleɪt] **lamellated** [-ˌleɪted] *a.* 1. lamelado. 2. lameliforme.
lamellibranch [lə'mɛləˌbræŋk] *s.* (zool.) lamelibranquio.
Lamellibranchiata [ləˌmɛləˌbræŋkɪ'eɪtə] *s. pl.* (zool.) lamelibranquios.
lamellicorn [-'mɛləˌkɔrn, B -ˌkɔn] *a., s.* (ento.) lamelicornio.
lamelliform [-ˌfɔrm, B -ˌfɔm] *a.* (bot.) lameliforme.
lamellirostral [-ˌmɛlə'rɑstrəl, B -'rɔs-] **lamellirostrate** [-ˌtreɪt] *a.* (orn.) lamelirrostro.
lamellose [lə'mɛloʊs] *a.* (zool.) lameloso.
lamely ['leɪmlɪ] *adv.* débilmente, sin convicción; defectuosamente.
lameness [-nəs] *s.* 1. cojera. 2. debilidad, pobreza, imperfección (de un argumento, excusa, etc.).
lament [lə'mɛnt] *v.i.* lamentarse, dolerse. *—v.t.* lamentar, deplorar. *—s.* 1. lamento, lamentación, queja. 2. lamentación, elegía, treno.
lamentable ['læməntəbəl, lə'mɛntə-, B 'læmən-] *a.* lamentable, deplorable, lastimero, sensible.
lamentably [-blɪ] *adv.* lamentablemente, deplorablemente, lastimosamente.
lamentation [ˌlæmən'teɪʃən] *s.* lamentación, lamento.
lamented [lə'mɛntəd] *a.* llorado, lamentado (díc. de un muerto).
lamina ['læmənə] *s.* 1. lámina, hoja (de metal, madera, etc.). 2. (anat.) lámina laminilla. 3. (bot., geol.) lámina. 4. lámina, suela (del casco del caballo).
laminable [-nəbəl] *a.* laminable (metal).
laminar [-nər, B -nə] **laminal** [-nəl] *a.* laminar.
laminar flow, (fís.) flujo laminar, derrame laminar, régimen laminar.
laminaria [ˌlæmə'nɛrɪə, B -'nɛər-] *s.* (bot.) laminaria.
laminariaceous [-ˌnɛrɪ'eɪʃəs] *a.* (bot.) laminariáceo.
laminate ['læməˌneɪt] *a.* laminado. *—v.t.* laminar. *—v.i.* partirse en láminas. *—s.* producto laminado.
laminated [-əd] *a.* laminado.
lamination [ˌlæmə'neɪʃən] *s.* laminación, laminado.
laminitis [-'naɪtəs] *s.* (vet.) laminitis, despeadura.
laminous ['læmənəs] *a.* laminar; laminoso.
Lammas ['læməs] *s.* (t. **L. Day**) fiesta del primero de Agosto; (ant.) fiesta de la recolección de la cosecha; **latter L.,** fecha que nunca llegará; calendas griegas.
Lammastide [-ˌtaɪd] *s.* (G.B.) época del año alrededor del primero de Agosto.
lammergeier, lammergeyer ['læmərˌgaɪər, B -əˌgaɪə] *s.* (orn.) águila barbuda, quebrantahuesos.
lamp [læmp] *s.* 1. lámpara, candil, farol. 2. (*pl.*) (jer.) ojos. 3. (poét., fig.) antorcha. 4. **to pass on the l.,** llevar adelante una causa, pasar la antorcha de la cultura. *—v.t.* (jer.) avistar, mirar.
lampas ['læmpəs] *s.* 1. (tej.) tela decorativa (para amueblar o decorar), seda estampada. 2. (vet.) inflamación de la boca de los caballos.
lampblack [-ˌblæk] *s.* negro de humo (pigmento).
lamp burner, mechero.
lamp chimney, tubo de lámpara, chimenea del quinqué.
lamper eel ['læmpər-] (ict.) lamprea.
lamp globe, bombilla en forma de globo.
lamp holder, portalámpara.
lampion ['læmpɪən] *s.* lampión, lampeón; pequeña lámpara de aceite.
lamplight ['læmpˌlaɪt] *s.* luz de la lámpara, luz de un farol.
lamplighter [-ər, B -ə] *s.* farolero, lamparero.
lampoon [læm'pun] *s.* pasquín, libelo. *—v.t.* satirizar, pasquinar, ridiculizar.
lampooner [-ər, B -ə] *s.* libelista, satirista.
lamppost ['læmpˌpoʊst] *s.* poste de alumbrado, farol de la calle.
lamprey ['læmprɪ] *s.* (ict.) lamprea.
lampshade ['læmpˌʃeɪd] *s.* pantalla (de lámpara).
lampstand [-ˌstænd] **lamptable** [-ˌteɪbəl] *s.* velador, mesa de noche (Amer.).
lampwick [-ˌwɪk] *s.* 1. mecha de lámpara. 2. (bot.) candilera.
lanate ['leɪˌneɪt] **lanated** [-əd] *a.* lanoso, lanudo.
Lancasterian [ˌlænkæs'tɪrɪən, B ˌlæŋ-'tɪər-] **Lancastrian** [læn'kæstrɪən, B læŋ-] *a.* (educ.) lancasteriano.
lance [læns, B lɑns] *s.* 1. lanza, pica, asta. 2. lancero, lanza (soldado). 3. lanceta. *—v.t.* 1. alancear, lancear, abrir (con lanceta). 2. (poét.) arrojar, lanzar, tirar.

lance, *var. de.* **launce.**
lance coporal, (mil.) cabo interino (soldado raso que hace las veces de cabo).
lancelet ['lænslət, B 'lɑns-] *s.* (ict.) anfioxo.
Lancelot ['lænsə,lɑt, 'lɑn-, B 'lɑnslət] *s.* (lit.) Lanzarote (del Lago), Lancelote, amante de la reina Ginebra (Ciclo de la Tabla Redonda).
lanceolate ['lænsɪə,leɪt, -lət, B 'lɑn-] *a.* (bot., zool., arq.) lanceolado.
lancer ['lænsər, B 'lɑnsə] *s.* 1. lancero. 2. lanceros (baile parecido a la cuadrilla); música de este baile.
lance rest, l. socket, ristre.
lance sergeant, (mil.) sargento interino (cabo que hace las veces de sargento).
lancet [-sət] *s.* (med.) lanceta.
lancet arch, (arq.) arco apuntado.
lanceted [-əd] *a.* (arq.) con ojivas o ventanas lanceoladas.
lancet window, (arq.) ventana de arco de todo punto.
lancewood ['læns,wʊd, B 'lɑns-] *s.* (bot.) yaya, anona; palo de lanza.
lancinate ['lænsə,neɪt, B 'lɑn-] *v.t.* lancinar, punzar, pinchar.
lancinating ['lænsə,neɪtɪŋ, B 'lɑn-] *a.* lancinante (dolor).
lancination [,lænsə'neɪʃən, B ,lɑn-] *s.* dolor lancinante.
land [lænd] *s.* 1. tierra, suelo. 2. país, (fig.) reino (de los vivos, muertos, sueños, etc.). 3. país, población ej., *the whole l. rose against the tyrant,* todo el país (o toda la población) se levantó contra el tirano. 4. tierra, tierra firme. 5. tierra, terreno, terruño; campo; (*pl.*) tierras, fincas, predios, fundos, haciendas. 6. superficie entre surcos, parte plana entre ranuras o estrías (ej., en un disco de gramófono o en el ánima de un rifle). 7. (der.) bienes raíces. 8. (Sud África) terreno de labranza cercado. 9. **by l.,** por tierra; **to make l.,** tomar tierra (una nave); divisar tierra, avistar la costa; **to see how the l. lies,** catar el melón, tantear o reconocer el terreno, ver cómo están las cosas. —*v.t.* 1. desembarcar, poner en tierra; depositar (en un lugar determinado), bajar (de un vehículo). 2. coger, atrapar (ej., un pez); (fam.) conseguir, obtener (empleo, puesto); lograr agarrar. 3. (aer.) hacer aterrizar (avión). 4. (jer.) dar de lleno, asestar (golpe), ej., *he landed his opponent one in the eye,* le asestó a su adversario un golpe en el ojo. 5. **l. with,** dejar clavado con; **to be landed with,** quedarse clavado con. —*v.i.* 1. desembarcar, salir (de una embarcación), tocar tierra, atracar. 2. (aer.) aterrizar; amarar. 3. llegar (caballo a la meta en carrera), ganar (caballo la carrera). 4. ir a parar. 5. **l. on,** (fig.) caer encima; **l. on one's feet (head),** caer de pies (cabeza); **l. on the water,** amarizar.
land agent, 1. corredor de fincas. 2. (G.B.) administrador de hacienda (finca agrícola).
landau ['læn,daʊ, B -,dɔ] *s.* landó (coche de paseo tirado por caballos).
landaulet [,lændə'lɛt] *s.* 1. landó pequeño. 2. (aut.) landaulet.
land bank, 1. banco de fomento agrario. 2. (ant., G.B.) banco que emitía billetes garantizándolos con bienes raíces.
land based, (aer.) con base en tierra.
land breeze, terral, viento que sopla de tierra.
land-chain ['lænd,tʃeɪn] *s.* cadena de agrimensor.
land-crab [-,kræb] *s.* (zool.) cangrejo de tierra.
land defenses, (mil.) defensas terrestres.
landed ['lændəd] *a.* 1. terrateniente, hacendado. 2. que consiste en bienes raíces (díc. de propiedades). 3. **l. gentry,** la nobleza provinciana.
landed cost, (com.) costo o valor en tierra.
landfall ['lænd,fɔl] *s.* 1. (mar.) recalada, aterrada. 2. (aer.) aterrizaje. 3. (línea de la) costa (vista desde el mar).
land force, (mil.) fuerza terrestre, ejército de tierra.
landform [-,fɔrm, B -,fɔm] *s.* (geog.) forma terrestre, accidente geográfico.
land-grabber [-,græbər, B -ə] *s.* (Irl.) invasor de tierras, colono usurpador.
land grant, concesión o donación de tierras (por el gobierno).
landgrave ['lænd,greɪv] *s.* (hist.) landgrave, título de honor (en la antigua Germania).
landgraviate [-,greɪvɪət] **landgravate** [-vət] *s.* (hist.) landgraviato.
landgravine [-grə,vin] *s.* (hist.) la esposa de un landgrave.
landholder [-,hoʊldər, B -də] *s.* terrateniente, hacendado.
landholding [-dɪŋ] *s.* tenencia de tierra (s).
landing ['lændɪŋ] *s.* 1. aterraje, aterrizaje, amaraje (de un avión). 2. desembarco, desembarque (de pasajeros, tropas, etc.). 3. desembarcadero, lugar de desembarque; apeadero; plataforma o muelle de carga. 4. descansillo, rellano (de escaleras).
landing barge, (mil.) barcaza de desembarco.
landing craft, (mil.) embarcación de desembarco, lancha de desembarco.
landing deck, (mar.) cubierta de aterrizaje (en portaaviones).
landing field, (aer.) campo de aterrizaje.
landing force, (mil.) cuerpo expedicionario.
landing gear, (aer.) tren de aterrizaje.
landing net, salabardo, redeña.
landing party, (mil.) destacamento de desembarco o de exploración.
landing stage, embarcadero flotante.
landing strip, (aer.) pista de aterrizaje.
landing wheels, (aer.) ruedas de aterrizaje.
land-jobbing ['lænd,dʒɑbɪŋ, B -,dʒɔb-] *s.* especulación en tierras.
landlady ['lænd,leɪdɪ] *s.* (*pl.* LANDLADIES) 1. arrendadora, propietaria; casera. 2. patrona, hostelera.
landless [-ləs] *a.* sin tierras, que no posee tierras o bienes raíces.
landlocked [-,lɑkt, B -,lɔkt] *a.* 1. rodeado de tierra, cercado por tierra (como una bahía); sin salida al mar, sin litoral (país). 2. separado del mar, que vive en agua dulce (díc. de algunos peces).
landloper, landlouper [-,loʊpər, B -ə] *s.* (esco.) vago, vagabundo, golfo.
landlord ['lænd,lɔrd, B -,lɔd] *s.* 1. arrendador, propietario, casero. 2. patrón, hostelero.
landlordism [-,ɪzəm] *s.* (e.p.) sistema de terratenientes; hacendados en general.
landlubber [-,lʌbər, B -ə] *s.* (mar., despec.) 1. marinero bisoño; marinero de agua dulce. 2. hombre que vive en tierra.
landmark [-,mɑrk, B -,mɑk] *s.* 1. mojón, hito; señal, marca, guía. 2. acontecimiento importante, punto sobresaliente, hecho memorable, acontecimiento o fecha que hace época.
landmass [-,mæs] *s.* gran área de tierra.
land mine, (mil.) mina terrestre.
land office, oficina del catastro o catastral.
land-office business [-,ɔfəs-, -,ɑf-, B -,ɔf-] (fam., E.U.) negocios de gran volumen, negocio tremendo.
land of make-believe, país de los sueños; tierra de ensueños.
land of nod, (fam.) sueño.
Land of Promise, (bíbl.) Tierra de Promisión.
land of the midnight sun, país del sol de medianoche (Noruega).
land of the rising sun, país del sol naciente (Japón).
landowner ['lænd,oʊnər, B -nə] *s.* terrateniente, hacendado, propietario de tierras.
landownership [-,ʃɪp] *s.* posesión de tierras, tenencia de tierras.
land-poor [-,pʊr, B -,pʊə] *a.* (fam.) falto de fondos para trabajar sus tierras (pobres o gravadas).
land power, poderío militar terrestre (en contraste con el naval).
landrail ['lænd,reɪl] *s.* (orn.) rey de codornices.
landscape [-,skeɪp, 'læn,skeɪp] *s.* 1. paisaje, vista, panorama. 2. (pint.) paisaje. —*v.t.* mejorar (un paisaje) modificando y hermoseando el terreno. —*v.i.* dedicarse a la jardinería ornamental.
landscape architect, arquitecto que diseña jardines.
landscape gardener, experto en jardinería ornamental.
landscape gardening, jardinería ornamental.
landscapist ['læn,skeɪpəst, 'lænd-] *s.* (pint.) paisajista.
landside [-,saɪd] *s.* (agr.) dental (del arado).
landslide [-,slaɪd] *s.* 1. derrumbe, derrumbamiento, avalancha, desprendimiento (de tierra o rocas). 2. victoria aplastante (en una votación, esp. en elecciones).
landslip [-,slɪp] *s.* (pr. G.B.) derrumbe, derrumbamiento.
landsman ['lændzmən] *s.* 1. persona que vive en tierra. 2. (mar.) marinero bisoño. 3. (E.U.) compatriota.
land survey, land surveying, agrimensura, topografía geodésica.
land surveyor, agrimensor.
land target, (mil.) blanco terrestre.
land-tax ['lænd,tæks] *s.* impuesto sobre bienes raíces, impuesto predial, impuesto a los predios.
landward [-wərd, B -wəd] *a.* más próximo a la tierra; hacia la tierra.
landwards [-wərdz, B -wədz] *adv.* hacia tierra, en dirección a tierra.
land wind, terral, viento que sopla de tierra.
lane [leɪn] *s.* 1. sendero, senda. 2. callejuela, callejón. 3. faja, carril, pista (de carretera). 4. calle o paso (formado por dos hileras de personas). 5. ruta oceánica (de navegación). 6. (dep.) calle, pasillo (de la pista de carreras).
langbeinite ['læŋ,baɪ,naɪt] *s.* (min.) langbeinita.
langouste [lɑn'gust] *s.* langosta (marisco).
langrage, langridge ['æŋgrɪdʒ] **langrel** [-grəl] *s.* (hist.) metralla (que se disparaba para desgarrar las velas y aparejos de los barcos enemigos).
langsyne ['æŋ'zaɪn, B -'saɪn] (esco.) *adv.* hace mucho tiempo, tiempo ha, antaño. —*a.* (días, tiempo) pasados.
language ['læŋgwɪdʒ] *s.* 1. lengua, idioma, habla (de un pueblo o nación). 2. lenguaje, ej., *l. of flowers,* lenguaje de las flores. 3. lenguaje, palabras, ej., *bad l.,* palabras malas u obscenas, lenguaje obsceno, *strong l.,* lenguaje duro, palabras duras o fuertes. 4. lenguaje, vocabulario, terminología (de un arte o ciencia).
language barrier, barrera lingüística.
language laboratory, laboratorio de idiomas.
language school, academia de idiomas.
langue d'oc [lɑŋ'dɔk] (filol.) lengua de oc, lemosín (idioma de Provenza).

languedocian [ˌlæŋə'doʊʃən, B ˌlæŋgə-] *a.* languedociano, perteneciente o relativo a Languedoc (provincia de la antigua Francia).
langue d'oil [lɑŋdɔ'il, B -'dɔɪl] (filol.) lengua de oíl (idioma que se hablaba al N. del Loira en Francia).
languet, languette ['læŋgwət] *s.* lengüeta, orejeta.
languid ['læŋgwəd] *a.* lánguido, inerte, flojo; apático, indiferente.
languidly [-lɪ] *adv.* lánguidamente.
languidness [-nəs] *s.* languidez, flojedad, indiferencia.
languish ['læŋgwɪʃ] *v.i.* 1. languidecer, agostarse, marchitarse. 2. debilitarse, consumirse. 3. (fig.) decaer (conversación, interés, etc.). 4. (fig.) atascarse (proyecto, solicitud, etc.). 5. (fig.) pudrirse (en prisión, etc.) 6. **l. for,** suspirar por, penar por.
languishing [-ɪŋ] *a.* 1. lánguido, decaído. 2. enamorado; consumido (por amor). 3. lento; débil, sin interés. 4. prolongado, dilatado.
languishingly [-lɪ] *adv.* lánguidamente.
languishment [-mənt] *s.* (ant.) 1. languidez, debilidad, decaimiento; lasitud, desfallecimiento, cansancio. 2. aire de ternura.
languor ['læŋgər, B -gə] *s.* 1. desfallecimiento, debilidad, languidez, lasitud. 2. algo enervante, ej., *there's a certain l. in the air,* hay algo enervante en el aire.
languorous [-gərəs] *a.* lánguido; enervante.
languorously [-lɪ] *adv.* lánguidamente.
langur [lɑŋ'gʊr, B lʌŋ'gʊə] *s.* (zool.) (variedad de) mono de la India.
laniard, *var. de* **lanyard.**
laniary ['leɪnɪˌɛrɪ, B 'lænɪərɪ] *a., s.* (anat.) canino.
laniary teeth, caninos, colmillos.
lank [læŋk] *a.* 1. descarnado, flaco, delgado. 2. lacio (cabello). 3. pobre (césped).
lankiness ['læŋkɪnəs] *s.* delgadez, flacura.
lanky [-kɪ] *a.* (LANKIER; LANKIEST) larguirucho, delgaducho, langaruto.
lanner ['lænər, B -ə] *s.* (orn.) (hembra del) alfaneque o halcón lanero.
lanneret [ˌlænə'rɛt] *s.* (orn.) alfaneque, halcón lanero.
lanolin ['lænələn] *s.* (farm.) lanolina.
lanose ['leɪnoʊs] *a.* lanoso, lanudo.
lansdowne ['lænzdaʊn] *s.* tela de seda y lana, de trama fina y compacta.
lansquenet ['lænskəˌnɛt] *s.* 1. (hist.) lansquenete. 2. sacanete (juego de naipes).
lantana [læn'tɑnə] *s.* (bot.) lantana.
lantern ['læntərn, B -ən] *s.* 1. linterna, farol. 2. (t. **magic l.**) linterna de proyección. 3. (arq.) linterna, linternón, cupulino, cimborrio. 4. (mar.) faro, fanal.
lantern fly, (ento.) cocuyo.
lantern jaw, quijada larga y delgada.
lantern-jawed [-'dʒɔd] *a.* carilargo, de quijadas largas y delgadas.
lantern pinion, (mec.) piñón de linterna.
lantern slide, (foto.) diapositiva.
lantern wheel, (mec.) rueda de linterna.
lanthanide series ['lænθəˌnaɪd-] (quím.) series de los lantánidos.
lanthanum ['lænθənəm] *s.* (quím.) lantano.
lanthorn ['læntərn, B -ən] *s.* (ant.) linterna.
lanuginous [lə'nudʒənəs, B -'nju-] **lanuginose** [-ˌnoʊs] *a.* lanuginoso.
lanugo [-goʊ] *s.* pilosidad o lanosidad abundante; esp. (anat.) lanugo, vello del feto.
lanyard ['lænjərd, B -jəd] *s.* 1. (mar.) acolladar, cuerda, cabo. 2. (mil.) cuerda y gancho de disparo.
Lao [laʊ] *s.* laosiano (pueblo, individuo o lengua de Laos).
Laodicean [leɪˌɑdə'siən, B ˌleɪədɪ-] *a.* (fig.) tibio, indiferente. —*s.* 1. (hist.) laodicense (de Frigia). 2. cristiano apático, frío o indiferente.
Laos ['lɑoʊs, 'leɪɑs, B laʊz] *s.* Laos.
Laotian [leɪ'oʊʃən, B 'laʊʃɪən] *s.* laosiano, (pueblo, individuo o lengua de Laos).
lap [læp] *s.* 1. falda, regazo, enfaldo. 2. doblez, pliegue (en una prenda). 3. (ant.) falda, halda. 4. **in the l. of luxury,** rodeado de lujo; **to drop into one's l.,** venir a uno a la(s) mano(s).
lap, *v.t.* (*pret., p.p.* LAPPED; *p.pr.* LAPPING) 1. doblar, plegar, hacer pliegues en. 2. envolver, cubrir. 3. traslapar, solapar, superponer. 4. (carp.) ensamblar. 5. (mec.) pulir, alisar, pulimentar. 6. (carreras) sacar una vuelta (o vueltas) de ventaja a (los demás competidores). 7. (ant.) empaquetar, envolver. —*v.i.* 1. (con **over**) sobresalir. 2. superponerse, solapar. 3. cubrir la vuelta (caballo, corredor, etc.). —*s.* 1. traslapo, solapo, sobrepuesta. 2. trecho. 3. (mec.) muela pulidora, rueda de pulir, bruñidor, pulidor. 3. (dep.) vuelta (completa de pista).
lap, *v.i.* 1. lamer, dar lengüetazos. 2. chapalear suavemente. —*v.t.* 1. lamer, beber con la lengua. 2. (fig.) lamer, bañar (la playa, el mar, etc.). 3. **l. up,** beber (ávidamente) con la lengua; absorber con avidez; recibir con entusiasmo. —*s.* 1. lamedura, lametada, lengüetada. 2. chapaleteo suave. 3. bebida o manjar aguado.
laparotomy [ˌlæpə'rɑtəmɪ, B -'rɔt-] *s.* (*pl.* LAPARATOMIES) (med.) laparatomía.
La Paz [lɑ'pɑs, lə'pæz, B lɑ-] *s.* La Paz, sede del gobierno de Bolivia.
lapboard ['læpˌbɔrd, B -ˌbɔd] *s.* tabla faldera (usada en lugar de mesa por sastres y costureras).
lap dog, perrito faldero.
lap-eared [-'ɪrd, B -'ɪəd] *a.* de orejas pendientes o gachas.
lapel [lə'pɛl] *s.* solapa (de la chaqueta, etc.).
lapful ['læpˌfʊl] *s.* haldada (lo que cabe en la falda o regazo).
lapidarian [ˌlæpə'dɛrɪən, B -'dɛər-] *a.* lapidario, relativo a las piedras preciosas.
lapidary ['læpəˌdɛrɪ, B -dərɪ] *s.* (*pl.* LAPIDARIES) lapidario, el que labra o pule piedras preciosas. —*a.* 1. lapidario. 2. (fig.) lapidario, solemne y lacónico (díc. del estilo).
lapidate [-ˌdeɪt] *v.t.* (ant.) lapidar, apedrear, matar a pedradas.
lapidation [ˌlæpə'deɪʃən] *s.* lapidación, petrificación.
lapideous [lə'pɪdɪəs] *a.* lapídeo, de piedra.
lapidification [ləˌpɪdəfə'keɪʃən] *s.* (ant.) lapidificación.
lapidify [-'pɪdəˌfaɪ] *v.t.* (*pret., p.p.* LAPIDIFIED; *p.pr.* LAPIDIFYING) lapidificar, convertir en piedra.
lapin ['læpən] *s.* (fr.) 1. conejo, esp. conejo castrado. 2. piel de conejo teñida.
lapis ['læpəs] *s.* (lat.) piedra.
lapis lazuli, 1. (min.) lapislázuli. 2. azul de ultramar, azul ultramarino.
lap joint, empalme a media madera; junta de solapa, junta montada; solapada o de superposición.
lap-joint ['læpˌdʒɔɪnt] *v.t.* empalmar a media madera; hacer junta de solapa con.
Lapland ['læpˌlænd] *s.* (geog.) Laponia, la región más septentrional de Europa.
Laplander [-ˌlændər, B -də] *s.* lapón, lapona (de Laponia).
Lapp [læp] *s.* 1. lapón, lapona, natural de Laponia. 2. (idioma) lapón.
lappet ['læpət] *s.* 1. caída (de vestido), doblez (de una prenda de vestir). 2. lóbulo (de la oreja). 3. barba de (ciertas aves).
lap robe, manta de viaje (que se extiende sobre el regazo del viajero).
lapsable ['læpsəbəl] *a.* 1. susceptible a caer o a olvidarse. 2. (der.) prescriptible.
lapse [læps] *s.* 1. lapso, lapsus, desliz, traspié. 2. deterioración, declinación, baja. 3. interrupción, caída en desuso. 4. lapso, curso, transcurso (de tiempo). 5. (der.) caducidad, prescripción, lapso. —*v.i.* 1. (con *into*) deslizarse (en), caer (en). 2. errarse. 3. decaer, deteriorarse. 4. caer en desuso. 5. quedar interrumpido, suspenderse. 6. pasar, transcurrir (el tiempo). 7. (der.) caducar, extinguirse, prescribir.
lapsed [læpst] *a.* 1. caído. 2. cumplido, caducado. 3. prescrito.
lapstone ['læpˌstoʊn] *s.* piedra de zapatero.
lapstrake [-ˌstreɪk] **lapstreak** [-ˌstrik] *s.* bote de tingladillo. —*a.* de tingladillo.
lapsus ['læpsəs] *s.* (lat.) error, desliz.
lapsus linguae [-'lɪŋgwi, B -gwaɪ] *s.* (lat.) desliz verbal, error al hablar.
lapsus memoriae [-mɛ'mɔrɪˌi] *s.* (lat.) desliz de la memoria.
lapwing ['læpˌwɪŋ] *s.* (orn.) avefría, quincineta.
lapwork [-ˌwɜrk, B -ˌwɜk] *s.* obra de tingladillo, labor de entrelazado.
lar [lɑr, B lɑ] *s.* (*pl.* LARES ['lɛriz, B 'lɛər-]) (mitol.) lar (dios doméstico).
La Raza [lɑ'rɑsɑ] (E.U.) movimiento político-social de los norteamericanos de ascendencia mexicana (Chicanos).
larboard ['lɑrbərd, -ˌbɔrd, B 'lɑbəd] (mar.) *s.* babor. —*a.* de babor. —*adv.* a babor.
larcener ['lɑrsənər, B 'lɑsənə] **larcenist** [-əst] *s.* ladrón, ratero, caco (jer., Amer.).
larcenous [-əs] *a.* culpable de robo.
larceny [-ɪ] *s.* (*pl.* LARCENIES) 1. hurto, robo, latrocinio. 2. (der.) **petty l.,** ratería; **grand l.,** robo de mayor cuantía.
larch [lɑrtʃ, B lɑtʃ] *s.* (bot.) alerce, lárice.
lard [lɑrd, B lɑd] *s.* lardo; manteca (de cerdo); gordo (del tocino). —*v.t.* 1. (cocina) mechar; lardar, lardear. 2. (fig.) mezclar, sazonar (con algo para mejorar); adornar (ej., la conversación con expresiones jocosas o pintorescas).
larder ['lɑrdər, B 'lɑdə] *s.* despensa, almacén casero.
larder beetle, (ento.) dermesto.
larderer [-ərər, B -ərə] *s.* despensero.
lardon ['lɑrdən, B 'lɑdən] **lardoon** [lɑr'dun, B lɑ'-] *s.* (cocina) mecha, lonjilla (de tocino o de carne de cerdo).
lardy ['lɑrdɪ, B 'lɑdɪ] *a.* graso, grasoso, mantecoso.
lares and penates ['lɛriz-, B 'lɛər-] 1. (mitol. romana) lares y penates (dioses domésticos). 2. (fig.) efectos personales o domésticos, enseres.
large [lɑrdʒ, B lɑdʒ] *a.* 1. grande, amplio, extenso, vasto. 2. numeroso (público, familia, etc.). 3. (mar.) libre, favorable, bueno (viento). 4. **to take a l. view,** adoptar un punto de vista liberal. —*adv.* 1. (ant.) ampliamente, liberalmente. 2. (mar.) con viento largo, con viento a la cuadra. 3. **to talk l.,** (jer.) jactarse, hablar jactanciosamente. —*s.* 1. (mús.) máxima. 2. **at l.,** en libertad, suelto, sin restricciones; extensamente, detalladamente, minuciosamente (narrar, hablar); en general; (E.U.) que representa la totalidad de un estado (diputado, senador etc.); **gentleman at l.,** cortesano sin deberes específicos; persona sin ocupación; **in l., in the l.,** en gran escala.

large-handed ['lɑrdʒ'hændəd, B 'lɑdʒ-] *a.* 1. de manos grandes. 2. (fig.) generoso, dadivoso.
large-hearted ['lɑrdʒ'hɑrtəd, B 'lɑdʒ'hɑt-] *a.* generoso, magnánimo, desprendido.
large-heartedness [-nəs] *s.* magnanimidad, generosidad.
large intestine, (anat.) intestino grueso.
largely ['lɑrdʒlɪ, B 'lɑdʒ-] *adv.* 1. grandemente, ampliamente. 2. extensamente, en gran extremo. 3. mayormente, ej., *is l. due to,* se debe mayormente a.
large-minded [-'maɪndəd] *a.* de ideas liberales, tolerante, de criterio amplio.
large-mindedly [-lɪ] *adv.* liberalmente, tolerantemente.
largeness ['lɑrdʒnəs, B 'lɑdʒ-] *s.* magnitud, amplitud, gran tamaño.
large order, (fam.) empresa o tarea difícil.
large-scale [-'skeɪl] *a.* 1. en gran escala, en grande. 2. a gran escala (mapa, modelo, etc.).
large-size [-'saɪz] *a.* de tamaño grande (dimensión).
largess, largesse [lɑr'dʒɛs, 'lɑrdʒəs, B lɑ'dʒɛs] *s.* 1. largueza, generosidad, liberalidad. 2. donaciones, donativos, dádivas.
large-winged ['lɑrdʒ'wɪŋd, B 'lɑdʒ-] *a.* aludo, alón (Amer.).
larghetto [lɑr'gɛtoʊ, B lɑ'-] *a.* (mús.) larghetto (menos lento que largo).
largish ['lɑrdʒɪʃ, B 'lɑdʒ-] *a.* más bien grande; bastante largo.
largo ['lɑrgoʊ, B 'lɑgoʊ] *a., adv., s.* (mús.) largo.
lariat ['lærɪət] *s.* lazo, mangana (para atrapar el ganado); cuerda (para tener atado el ganado en el pasto).
lark [lɑrk, B lɑk] *s.* 1. (orn.) alondra. 2. (orn.) chirlota.
lark, *v.i.* (fam.) (ú. gen. con *about*) retozar, bromear, juguetear. —*s.* travesura; **to go on a l.,** echar una cana al aire, ir de jolgorio; **what a l.!** ¡qué divertido!
larkspur ['lɑrk,spɜr, B 'lɑk,spɜ] *s.* (bot.) consuelda, consólida real, espuela de caballero.
larrigan ['lærɪgən] *s.* (E.U., Can.) mocasín con pierna.
larrikin ['lærɪkən] *s.* (jer., Aust.) rufián, vago, callejero. —*a.* tosco, rudo; alborotador.
larrup ['lærəp] *v.t.* (dial.) 1. pegar, azotar, zurrar. 2. vencer, derrotar. —*s.* (dial.) golpe.
larva ['lɑrvə, B 'lɑvə] *s.* (*pl.* LARVAE [-vi]) (ento.) larva.
larval [-vəl] *a.* (ento.) larval.
larvicidal [,lɑrvə'saɪdəl, B ,lɑvɪ-] *a.* larvicida.
larvicide [-və,saɪd] *s.* larvicida.
laryngeal [lə'rɪndʒɪəl, ,lærən'dʒiəl] *a.* laríngeo.
laryngectomy [,lærən'dʒɛktəmɪ] *s.* laringectomía.
laryngitic [,lærən'dʒɪtɪk] *a.* (med.) laringítico.
laryngitis [-'dʒaɪtəs] *s.* (med.) laringitis.
laryngologic [lə,rɪŋgə'lɑdʒɪk, B -'lɔdʒ-] **laryngological** [-ɪkəl] *a.* (med.) laringológico.
laryngologist [,lærəŋ'gɑlədʒəst, B -'gɔl-] *s.* (med.) laringólogo.
laryngology [-dʒɪ] *s.* (med.) laringología.
laryngoscope [lə'rɪŋgə,skoʊp] *s.* laringoscopio.
laryngoscopic [-,rɪŋgə'skɑpɪk, B -'skɔp-] *a.* laringoscópico.
laryngoscopical [-ɪkəl] *a.* laringoscópico.
laryngoscopist [,lærəŋ'gɑskəpəst, B -'gɔs-] *s.* laringoscopista.
laryngoscopy [-pɪ] *s.* laringoscopía.
laryngotomy [-'gɑtəmɪ, B -'gɔt-] *s.* (med.) laringotomía.
larynx ['lærɪŋks] *s.* (*pl.* LARYNGES [lə'rɪndʒiz] o LARYNXES) (anat., zool.) laringe.
lasagna [lə'zɑnjə] *s.* (cocina) plato de pasta italiana, sazonado y horneado.
lascar ['læskər, B -kə] *s.* lascar (marinero de la India).
lascivious [lə'sɪvɪəs] *a.* lascivo, lujurioso, concupiscente.
lasciviously [-lɪ] *adv.* lascivamente, lujuriosamente, concupiscentemente.
lasciviousness [-nəs] *s.* lascivia, lujuria, concupiscencia.
laser ['leɪzər, B -zə] *s.* (fís.) láser.
laser beam, rayo láser, haz de láser.
laser gun, pistola de láser.
laser printer, (comput.) impresora láser.
laser rangefinder, telémetro lasérico.
laser scanning, lectura por lector óptico láser.
laser surgery, cirugía con láser.
lash [læʃ] *s.* 1. latigazo. 2. coletazo. 3. tralla (del látigo). 4. (fig.) sarcasmo, sátira. 5. pestaña. —*v.t.* 1. flagelar. 2. (fig.) azotar. 3. agitar, mover bruscamente; arrojar, lanzar. 4. impeler, impulsar. —*v.i.* 1. moverse súbitamente, lanzarse, precipitarse. 2. dar golpes. 3. **l. against,** chocar contra; azotar; **l. at,** dar un golpe a; (fig.) atacar (con crítica, etc.); increpar; **l. down,** caer con fuerza (lluvia, granizo); **l. out at,** dar un golpe o patada violenta a; (fig.) atacar ferozmente. —*v.t.* atar con soga, cuerda o cadena; ligar, enlazar.
lasher ['læʃər, B -ə] *s.* (G.B.) estanque bajo una represa (para aumentar el nivel de los ríos).
lashing [-ɪŋ] *s.* 1. castigo a latigazos, zurra; reprensión severa. 2. cuerda, soga; cadena.
lashings [-ɪŋz] *s. pl.* (jer. G.B.) (ú. con *of*) montones (de), gran abundancia o cantidad (de).
lash out [,læʃ'aʊt] *v.i., v.t.* desenfrenar (se), desordenar (se).
lash-up ['læʃ,ʌp] *s.* (jer.) artefacto improvisado, artilugio.
lass [læs] *s.* 1. muchacha joven. 2. enamorada. 3. (esco., dial.) sirvienta.
lassie ['læsɪ] *s.* 1. jovencita, mozuela. 2. **L.,** (cinem.) perra pastora famosa por sus actuaciones cinematográficas.
lassitude ['læsə,tud, B -,tjud] *s.* lasitud; cansancio, fatiga; sopor, languidez.
lasso ['læsoʊ, B læ'su] *s.* (*pl.* LASSOS o LASSOES) lazo, mangana (para lazar ganado y caballos). —*v.t.* (*pret., p.p.* LASSOED; *p.pr.* LASSOING) lazar, enlazar, manganear, coger con un lazo.
lassoer [-ər, B -ə] *s.* lazador, enlazador.
last [læst, B lɑst] *a.* 1. último, final, terminal, extremo, postrero, postrimero. 2. pasado, ej., *l. month,* el mes pasado. 3. último, inferior, menor, más bajo. 4. último, menos indicado, menos apropiado, menos propicio, menos posible, ej., *(it) is the l. thing to try,* es el último recurso, es lo único que queda por ensayar. 5. último, definitivo, concluyente, determinante. 6. sumo, extremo. 7. **every l. one,** hasta el último; cada (uno); **l. but not least,** el último en orden pero no en importancia; **l. but one,** penúltimo; **l. night,** anoche; **night before l.,** anteanoche, antes de anoche; **the l. thing,** lo último; **to be the l. to (do),** ser el último en (hacer); **year before l.,** (el) año antepasado. —*s.* 1. el o lo último. 2. fin. 3. el último día, ej., *the l. of October,* el último día de Octubre. 4. **at l., at long l.,** al fin, finalmente, por fin; **to breathe one's l.,** dar el último suspiro; **to see** (o **hear**) **the l. of,** no volver a ver (oír); **to speak one's l.** pronunciar su última palabra.
last, *v.i.* 1. durar, continuar. 2. permanecer. 3. perdurar, durar, sobrevivir. 4. existir, ser disponible. 5. bastar, alcanzar (dinero, etc.). 6. **l. out,** alcanzar, ser suficiente. —*v.t.* (gen. con *out*) aguantar, resistir, ej., *he will not l. (out) the winter,* no aguantará el invierno.
last, *s.* medida comercial de peso, capacidad o cantidad (variable según artículo y país, generalmente estimada en 4.000 libras).
last, *s.* horma de zapato; **stick to your l.,** zapatero, a tus zapatos. —*v.t.* ahormar, poner en horma.
last-ditch ['læst'dɪtʃ, B 'lɑst-] *a.* (fig.) hasta el último cartucho, desesperado.
last honors, honras fúnebres.
lasting ['læstɪŋ, B 'lɑs-] *s.* 1. tela fuerte de forro (para zapatos). 2. (ant.) larga vida.
lasting, *a.* duradero, durable, perdurable, permanente, constante.
lastingly [-lɪ] *adv.* permanentemente, duraderamente.
lastingness [-nəs] *s.* durabilidad, perdurabilidad, permanencia.
Last Judgment, (relig.) Juicio Final, Juicio Universal.
lastly ['læstlɪ, B 'lɑst-] *adv.* en último lugar, en conclusión; por fin, por último, finalmente.
last-minute [-'mɪnət] *a.* 1. de último minuto (planes, correcciones, etc.) 2. de última hora (ej., noticias).
last name, apellido.
last offices, (relig.) oficio de difuntos.
last quarter, cuarto menguante (de la luna).
last resort, última instancia, último recurso.
last sleep, la muerte.
last straw, to be the l. s., ser la gota que hizo desbordar el vaso, ser el colmo, ser el acabóse.
Last Supper, (bíbl.) (la) Última Cena.
last will and testament, (der.) última voluntad; testamento.
last word, 1. última palabra; lo mejor. 2. la última moda.
lat. *abrev. de* **latitude,** latitud (lat.).
Latakia [,lætə'kiə] *s.* clase superior de tabaco turco.
latch [lætʃ] *s.* aldabilla, picaporte, cerrojo, pasador, pestillo; **off the l.,** entreabierta; **on the l.,** junta (la puerta), cerrada sin estar con aldaba. —*v.t., v.i.* cerrar o asegurar con picaporte o cerrojo.
latchet ['lætʃət] *s.* (ant.) cordón para atar al pie un zapato o sandalia.
latchkey ['lætʃ,ki] *s.* 1. llave de picaporte. 2. llave de la puerta de la calle.
latchstring [-,strɪŋ] *s.* cordón del picaporte (para poder levantar el picaporte desde afuera).
late [leɪt] (LATER ['leɪtər, B -ə] o LATTER ['lætər, B -ə]; LATEST, LAST) *a.* 1. tarde. 2. tardío, ej., *l. dinner,* cena tardía. 3. avanzado (ej., la hora). 4. fallecido, difunto, el o la que fue; anterior, ej., *the l. prime minister,* el primer ministro anterior, o el que fue primer ministro, *my l. husband,* mi difunto marido, el que fue mi marido. 5. reciente, último, precedente. 6. antiguo, de antaño, ej., *l. enemies,* enemigos de antaño (que ya no lo son). 7. de fines, ej., *l. eighteenth-century architecture,* arquitectura de fines del siglo XVIII. 8. **of l. years,** en los últimos años; **to be l.,** llegar tarde (una persona); llegar con retraso, retrasarse (tren, avión); ser tarde (la hora); **to keep l. hours,** trasnochar, (soler) acostarse tarde. —*adv.* 1. tarde. 2. últimamente, recientemente. 3. **at the latest,** a más tardar; **better l. than never,** más vale tarde que nunca; **l. in,** hacia fines de

(la semana, mes, año, siglo); **l. in life,** a una edad avanzada; **l. in years,** de edad avanzada; **l. in the day,** (fam.) demasiado tarde; **later on,** más tarde, después; **of l.,** no hace mucho; **to sit** o **stay up l.,** quedarse en vela hasta avanzada la noche.
late arrival, recién llegado (persona, avión, correos, etc.).
late-comer ['leɪtˌkʌmər, B -ə] *s.* 1. recién llegado. 2. el que llega tarde, ej., *l. comers will not be admitted,* los que lleguen tarde no podrán entrar, a los que lleguen tarde se les prohibirá el ingreso.
lated [-əd] *a.* (poét.) atrasado, sorprendipo por la noche.
lateen [lə'tin] *a.* (mar.) latino. —*s.* (mar.) vela latina; embarcación de vela latina.
lateen-rigged [-ˌrɪgd] *a.* (mar.) de aparejo latino.
lateen sail, (mar.) vela latina o bastarda.
lateen yard, (mar.) entena.
late frost, helada tardía.
Late Greek, griego tardío, el del comienzo del imperio bizantino.
late lamented, malogrado, fallecido.
Late Latin, latín tardío, el del período postclásico.
lately ['leɪtlɪ] *adv.* recientemente, últimamente, no hace mucho.
laten ['leɪtən] *v.i.* hacerse tarde.
latency ['leɪtənsɪ] *s.* estado latente; (med.) latencia.
lateness [-nəs] *s.* tardanza, demora, atraso; ej., *due to the l. of the hour,* por lo tarde de la hora.
late-night ['leɪt'naɪt] *a.* (*pharmacy*) que está abierta por la noche: (*T.V. show*) de medianoche, de trasnoche.
latent ['leɪtənt] *a.* latente, oculto, escondido; dormido; no visible, no aparente. —*s.* huella digital latente.
latently [-lɪ] *adv.* ocultamente, latentemente.
latent period, (med.) latencia, período latente.
later ['leɪtər, B -ə] *adv., a. comp. de* **late.** —*adv.* (gen. con *on*) luego, más tarde, dentro de un rato.
lateral ['lætərəl] *a.* lateral, de (un) lado. —*s.* (min.) socavón lateral (paralelo a un socavón principal).
laterally [-ɪ] *adv.* lateralmente.
lateral pass, (fútbol) pase lateral (hecho en una dirección aproximadamente paralela a la línea del gol).
laterite ['lætəˌraɪt] *s.* (geol.) laterita.
laterization [ˌlætərə'zeɪʃən, B -raɪ-] *s.* (geol.) laterización.
latescent [lə'tɛsənt] *a.* (bot.) latescente, que se va ocultando.
late show, función de trasnoche.
latest ['leɪtəst] *adv., a. super. de* **late.** —*s.* **the l.,** lo último, lo más reciente o novedoso.
latex ['leɪˌtɛks] *s.* (*pl.* LATICES ['lætəˌsiz] o LATEXES) (bot.) látex.
lath [læθ, B lɑθ] *s.* listón (de madera); enlistonado, listonado, entablado de listones; listonería (conjunto de listones). —*v.t.* enlistonar, listonar.
lathe [leɪð] *s.* (mec.) 1. (t. **turning l.**) torno. 2. (t. **potter's l.**) torno o rueda de alfarero. —*v.t.* tornear, trabajar en el torno.
lathe, *s.* (tej.) batán (de mano).
lathe operator, tornero.
lather ['leɪðər, B -ə] *s.* (mec.) tornero; alfarero.
lather ['læðər, B 'lɑðə] *s.* 1. espuma (de jabón o de sudor). 2. (jer.) cólera; estado excitado, excitación; apuros. —*v.t.* 1. enjabonar. 2. (fam.) azotar, zurrar. 3. (gen. con **up**) excitar, agitar. —*v.i.* hacer espuma, espumar.
lathery [-ərɪ] *a.* espumoso, jabonoso.
lathing ['læθɪŋ, B 'lɑθ-] *s.* (const.) enlistonado.
lathing hammer, l. hatchet, (const.) hachuela de listonador o de media labor.
lathwork [-ˌwɜrk, B -ˌwɜk] *s.* enlistonado.
lathyrus ['læθərəs] *s.* (bot.) áfaca, áfaga.
latices, *pl. de* **latex.**
laticiferous [ˌlætə'sɪfərəs] *a.* (bot.) laticífero.
latifundium [-'fʌndɪəm] *s.* (*pl.* LATIFUNDIA [-dɪə]) latifundio.
Latin ['lætən] *a.* latino. —*s.* 1. latín (idioma). 2. latino, romano (persona).
Latin America, (la) América Latina, Latinoamérica.
Latin-American [-ə'mɛrəkən] *a.* latinoamericano, de la América Latina, ej., *I love L.-A. music,* me encanta la música latinoamericana.
Latin American, latinoamericano (persona), ej., *I married a L. A.,* me casé con un latinoamericano.
Latin cross, cruz latina (la clásica cruz que simboliza al Cristianismo, de aspa horizontal más corta que la vertical).
Latinism ['lætənˌɪzəm] *s.* latinismo (giro o expresión latina que se intercala en otro idioma).
Latinist [-əst] *s.* latinista, el que estudia o admira la cultura latina o el latín.
Latinity [læ'tɪnətɪ, lə-] *s.* 1. latinidad. 2. carácter latino.
latinization [ˌlætənə'zeɪʃən, B -ənaɪ-] *s.* latinización.
latinize ['lætənˌaɪz] *v.t.* latinizar. —*v.i.* latinar, latinear, latinizar.
Latino [læ'tino, lə-] *s.* (fam., E.U.) latinoamericano.
Latin Quarter, Barrio Latino (en París).
Latin square, (agr.) cuadrado latino.
latish ['leɪtɪʃ] *a.* algo tarde, un poco tarde.
latitude ['lætəˌtud, B -ˌtjud] *s.* 1. (astr. geol.) latitud. 2.(*gen. pl.*) latitudes, climas, regiones (esp. referidas a la temperatura) ej., *high latitudes,* altas latitudes. 3. libertad, anchura, amplitud.
latitudinal [ˌlætə'tudənəl, B -'tjud-] *a.* latitudinal.
latitudinally [-ɪ] *adv.* en sentido latitudinal, latitudinalmente.
latitudinarian [-ˌtudən'ɛrɪən, B 'lætɪˌt-judɪ'nɛər-] *a., s.* latitudinario.
latitudinarianism [-ˌɪzəm] *s.* (relig.) latitudinarismo.
latreutic [læ'trutɪk, B lə-] *a.* (teo.) latréutico.
latria [lə'traɪə] *s.* (relig.) latría, adoración.
latrine [lə'trin] *s.* letrina, (lugar) excusado, retrete (esp. en un campamento).
latten ['lætən] *s.* hoja de latón; hojalata.
latter ['lætər, B -ə] *a.* 1. posterior, (más) reciente, moderno. 2. segundo, último (de dos cosas, la mencionada en segundo lugar). 3. **the l.,** éste, este último, el o lo segundo; **the l. part (of the month, week,** etc.), fines (del mes, semana, etc.).
latter-day [-ˌdeɪ, B -ə'-] *a.* de nuestros días, de tiempos recientes.
Latter-day Saint, Santo del Último Día (mormón).
latterly [-lɪ] *adv.* recientemente, hace poco, últimamente.
lattermost [-ˌmoʊst] *a.* último, postrero.
lattice ['lætəs] *s.* 1. celosía, rejilla, enrejillado, enrejado; ventana, puerta o verja con enrejado. 2. (geom., mat.) reticulado, latis. 3. (fig.) reja. 4. (her.) celosía. —*v.t.* 1. hacer una celosía de, dar apariencia de enrejado a. 2. poner celosías a.
lattice bar, *s.* barra de celosía, barra de enrejado.
lattice girder, (cons.) viga de celosía, viga de alma abierta, viga de enrejado.
lattice truss, (const.) armadura de enrejado.
lattice web, *s.* (const.) alma de celosía.
lattice window, ventana de vidriera reticulada.
latticework [-ˌwɜrk, B -ˌwɜk] *s.* enrejado, celosía.
latticing [-ɪŋ] *s. celosía, enrejado.*
Latvia ['lætvɪə] *s.* (geog.) Letonia, Latvia (república de la U.R.S.S.).
Latvian [-vɪən] *a., s.* letón, latvio, de Latvia.
laud [lɔd] *s.* 1. loa, elogio, (canto de) alabanza. 2. (*pl.*) (relig.). (t. **Laudes**) laudes. —*v.t.* alabar, loar.
laudability [ˌlɔdə'bɪlətɪ] *s.* calidad loable.
laudable ['lɔdəbəl] *a.* 1. laudable, loable, elogiable. 2. (med.) sano, saludable, no nocivo (díc. de las secreciones).
laudableness [-nəs] *s.* calidad de elogiable.
laudably [-blɪ] *adv.* con encomio, loablemente.
laudanum ['lɔdnəm, -ənəm, B 'lɔdnəm] *s.* (farm.) láudano.
laudation [lɔ'deɪʃən] *s.* alabanza.
laudative ['lɔdətɪv] **laudatory** [-əˌtɔrɪ, B -ətərɪ] *a.* laudatorio, encomiástico, elogioso.
laugh [læf, B lɑf] *v.i.* 1. reír. 2. (fig.) reír, sonreír (el agua, paisaje, sembrados, etc.). 3. **he laughs best who laughs last,** el que ríe último ríe mejor, al freír será el reír; **l. at,** burlarse de, reírse de, mofarse de, ridiculizar; **l. up one's sleeve,** reír para su capote, reír secretamente; **l. in the face of,** desafiar (peligro, la muerte, etc.); **l. on the other side of one's face,** pasar de la risa al llanto; **l. out loud,** soltar una carcajada; **l. over,** reírse sobre (un asunto), discutir (un asunto) riéndose; **l. in one's face,** reírsele a uno en las barbas, reírsele a uno en la cara; **to die laughing,** morirse de risa. —*v.t.* 1. decir riendo. 2. **l. away,** dar por terminado (un tema o asunto) riéndose; echar a broma; ahogar en risa, olvidar riendo; **l. away time,** hacer pasar el tiempo con bromas; **l. down,** callar o acallar por medio de la risa; **l. off,** librarse de (vergüenza, timidez, etc.) riéndose o con una broma; tomar a risa; **l. one's head off,** reír a mandíbula batiente; **l. oneself,** (enfermarse o aturdirse) de tanto reír, ej., *he laughed himself sick,* se enfermó de tanto reír, *she laughed herself silly,* se ha aturdido de tanto reír; **l. someone out of,** burlarse de (alguien) hasta que abandone (hábito, mala costumbre, etc.). —*s.* 1. risa. 2. chiste, cosa ridícula. 3. (*pl.*) diversión, entretenimiento. **4. artificial l.,** risa falsa; **for laughs,** por diversión, para divertirse; **I'll have the l. on you yet!** ¡ un buen día yo me reiré de ti! ¡llegará el día en que me ría de ti!; **the l. is on you, them,** etc., se ríe a costa tuya, de ellos, etc.
laughable ['læfəbəl, B 'lɑf-] *a.* risible, ridículo, irrisorio.
laughableness [-nəs] *s.* aspecto ridículo, carácter irrisorio.
laughably [-blɪ] *adv.* irrisoriamente; ridículamente.
laugher [-ər, B -ə] *s.* reidor.
laughing [-ɪŋ] *a.* reidor, risueño, riente; **to be no l. matter,** no ser cosa de reír, no ser algo para tomar en broma.
laughing falcon, (orn.) macagua.
laughing gas, (quím.) gas hilarante o exhilarante.
laughing jackass, (orn.) martín pescador.
laughingly [-lɪ] *adv.* riendo, con risa.
laughingstock [-ˌstɑk, B -ˌstɔk] *s.* hazmerreír; objeto de ridículo.
laughter ['læftər, B 'lɑftə] *s.* risa; **to burst with l.,** reventar de risa; **to split one's sides with l.,** desternillarse de risa.
launce [lɔns, læns, B lɑns] *s.* (ict.) (especie de) anguila.

launch [lɔntʃ, lɑntʃ] *v.t.* 1. lanzar, arrojar, tirar, despedir. 2. botar, echar (un barco) al agua. 3. iniciar (a una persona) en algo. 4. acometer, emprender, comenzar, principiar, empezar, iniciar (una empresa). —*v.i.* 1. arrojarse, salir, lanzarse. 2. **l. forth, l. out,** salir, ponerse en marcha, emprender (negocio o tarea); **l. into,** lanzarse a; **l. into a discourse,** embarcarse en una peroración; **l. out,** gastar palabras, hablar mucho (de un tema). —*s.* botadura, lanzamiento (de un buque).
launch, *s.* (mar.) lancha, chalupa.
launcher ['lɔntʃər, 'lɑn-, B -tʃə] *s.* 1. lanzador. 2. iniciador. 3. (mil.) lanzagranadas. 4. (mil.) (t. **rocket l.**) lanzacohetes.
launching [-tʃɪn] *s.* 1. lanzamiento. 2. (mar.) botadura.
launching pad, plataforma de lanzamiento (de cohetes teledirigidos).
launching ramp, *s.* rampa de lanzamiento.
launder ['lɔndər, 'lɑn-, B -də] *s.* (min.) batea, artesa, lavadero, canalizo o regadera de colada. —*v.t.* lavar y planchar (la ropa). —*v.i.* resistir (bien o mal) el lavado (la ropa).
launderer [-dərər, B -dərə] *s.* lavandero.
laundress [-drəs] *s.* lavandera.
laundromat [-drəˌmæt] *s.* establecimiento público de lavadoras automáticas.
laundry ['lɔndrɪ, 'lɑn-] *s.* (*pl.* LAUNDRIES) 1. lavadero; lavandería (establecimiento). 2. ropa lavada, ropa para lavar. 3. (ant.) lavadura, lavado.
laundryman [-mən] *s.* lavandero; empleado de una lavandería.
laundrywoman [-ˌwʊmən] *s.* lavandera.
lauraceous [lɔ'reɪʃəs] *a.* (bot.) lauráceo.
laureate ['lɔrɪət, 'lɑr-, B 'lɔr-] *a.* laureado. —*s.* laureado (poeta, actor, científico, etc.). —[-ˌeɪt] *v.t.* laurear.
laureateship [-ˌʃɪp] *s.* dignidad de (poeta, actor, etc.) laureado.
laureation [ˌlɔrɪ'eɪʃən, ˌlɑr-, B ˌlɔr-] *s.* acto de laurear.
laurel ['lɔrəl, 'lɑr-, B 'lɔr-] *s.* 1. (bot.) laurel, lauro. 2. (E.U.) rododendro, azalea; calmia. 3. corona de laurel, lauréola; (fig.) laurel. 4. **to look to one's laurels,** no dormirse sobre sus laureles; **to reap** (o **win**) **laurels,** cargarse de laureles; **to rest on one's laurels,** dormirse en sus laureles. —*v.t.* (*pret., p.p.* LAURELED O LAURELLED; *p.pr.* LAURELING O LAURELLING) coronar con laureles, laurear.
Laurentian [lɔ'rɛntʃən, B -'rɛnʃən] *a.* (geol.) laurentino.
lauric acid ['lɔrɪk-, 'lɑr-, B 'lɔr-] (quím.) ácido láurico.
lauryl alcohol [-əl-] (quím.) alcohol laurilo.
lav. *abrev. de* **lavatory,** lavabo, retrete.
lava ['lɑvə, 'lævə, B 'lɑvə] *s.* lava.
lavabo [lə'vɑboʊ, B -'veɪ-] *s.* (*pl.* LAVABOES) 1. **L.,** (relig.) lavatorio (de manos). 2. lavabo, lavamanos.
lavage [lə'vɑʒ, 'lævɪdʒ, B læ'vɑʒ] *s.* (med.) lavado (de un órgano).
lavalava ['lɑvə'lɑvə] *s.* lavalava, falda de percal o calicó (usada por los habitantes de Samoa y Tonga).
lavaliere, lavalier [ˌlɑvə'lɪr, ˌlæv-, B -'lɪə] *s.* medallón formado por gemas a menudo colgado al cuello de una cadena.
lavaret [ˌlævə'rɛt, B 'lævəˌrɛt] *s.* (ict.) farra.
lavation [læ'veɪʃən, B lə-] *s.* lavado, limpieza.
lavatory ['lævəˌtɔrɪ, B -tərɪ] *s.* (*pl.* LAVATORIES) 1. lavatorio, lavabo, lavamanos. 2. excusado, retrete. 3. lavabo (cuarto). 4. (relig.) lavatorio.
lave [leɪv] *v.t.* (poét.) bañar, lavar. —*v.i.* bañarse, lavarse; lamer (río, mar) las orillas o costa.
lave, *s.* (ant., dial.) resto, sobrante, remanente.
laveer [lə'vɪr, B -'vɪə] *v.i.* (ant. mar.) navegar de bolina; cambiar de bordada.
lavender ['lævəndər, B -də] *s.* 1. (bot.) alhucema, lavándula, lavanda (Amer.), espliego. 2. color de lavándula. 3. **to lay up in l.,** guardar para uso futuro. —*a.* (del) color (de la) lavándula. —*v.t.* rociar con agua de lavanda; perfumar con lavándula.
lavender water, esencia de alhucema, agua de lavanda.
laver ['leɪvər, B -və] *s.* (bot.) ova.
laver, *s.* 1. (bíbl.) jofaina de abluciones (usada por los sacerdotes judíos). 2. (ant.) jofaina, palangana; aguamanil.
laverock ['lævərək] *s.* (esco.) alondra, calandria.
lavish ['lævɪʃ] *a.* 1. pródigo, malgastador, derrochador. 2. espléndido, generoso. 3. profuso, muy abundante. —*v.t.* prodigar, despilfarrar, derrochar.
lavishly [-lɪ] *adv.* pródigamente; despilfarradamente, derrochadoramente; profusamente, abundantemente, copiosamente.
lavishness [-nəs] *s.* prodigalidad; despilfarro, derroche; profusión, abundancia.
lavrock ['lævrək] *var. de* **laverock.**
law [lɔ] *s.* 1. ley, código, estatuto, legislacion, fuero. 2. derecho, leyes, jurisprudencia, ciencia jurídica. 3. abogacía, profesión legal, foro. 4. conocimiento legal. 5. (fig.) norma, regla, precepto, costumbre. 6. (fig.) juicio, justicia, administración de la justicia, acción de la ley, cortes o tribunales de justicia. 7. **the L.,** (t. **L. of Moses**) el Antiguo Testamento; **the l.,** (fam.) la policía; guardián de la ley, el policía; **according to l.,** conforme a la ley; **by l.,** según la ley; **in l. and equity,** en derecho y equidad, en equidad y justicia; **in point of l.,** desde el punto de vista legal; **l. and order,** el orden público; **learned in the l.,** versado en las leyes o en derecho; **the l. was made to be broken,** hecha la ley, hecha la trampa; **to be a l. unto oneself,** hacer lo que le da la gana, no observar las reglas convencionales; no reconocer autoridad sobre sí; **to enter the l.,** hacerse abogado; **to lay down the l.,** hablar en forma autoritaria, dictar las leyes, dar la orden; **to maintain l. and order,** mantener el orden público; **to practice l.,** ejercer (la profesión) de abogado; **to read l.,** estudiar derecho; **to take the l. into one's own hands,** aplicar la ley por mano propia. —*v.i.* pleitear, litigar. —*a.* legal, de ley; jurídico, judicial.
law-abiding ['lɔəˌbaɪdɪŋ] *a.* observante de la ley.
lawbook [-ˌbʊk] *s.* libro de texto que usan los estudiantes de derecho.
lawbreaker [-ˌbreɪkər, B -kə] *s.* infractor, violador de la ley.
lawbreaking [-kɪŋ] *s.* infracción de la ley. —*a.* infractor de la ley.
law court, tribunal de justicia.
law day, 1. día de vencimiento (para pagar una obligación). 2. día hábil.
law enforcement, ejecución de la ley; aplicación obligatoria de la ley.
lawful ['lɔfəl] *a.* 1. legal, legítimo. 2. constituido legalmente, autorizado por la ley, conforme a la ley, según derecho. 3. lícito, permitido; válido, justo.
lawfully [-fəlɪ] *adv.* legalmente, lícitamente, legítimamente.
lawfulness [-fəlnəs] *s.* legalidad, legitimidad.
lawgiver [-ˌgɪvər, B -ə] *s.* legislador.
law hand, (G.B.) estilo de caligrafía (usado en documentos legales).
law Latin, latín híbrido (usado en los primitivos estatutos legales ingleses).
lawless ['lɔləs] *a.* 1. sin ley, anárquico (ej., país o región). 2. desaforado, desenfrenado, incontrolado, revoltoso, desmandado (persona). 3. ilegal, ilícito.
lawlessly [-lɪ] *adv.* ilegalmente.
lawlessness [-nəs] *s.* 1. ilegalidad, anarquía. 2. desorden, licencia, desobediencia.
lawmaker ['lɔˌmeɪkər, B -kə] *s.* legislador.
lawmaking [-kɪŋ] *a.* legislativo. —*s.* legislación.
lawman [-mən] *s.* gendarme, comisario, alguacil, agente de policía.
law merchant, (*pl.* LAWS MERCHANT) derecho mercantil; derecho comercial; código de comercio.
lawn [lɔn] *s.* 1. césped, prado. 2. (tej.) linón, estopilla. 3. episcopado anglicano.
lawn hose, manguera de regar el césped.
lawn mower, cortadora o segadora de césped.
lawn sprinkler, rociador giratorio para regar el césped.
lawn tennis, lawn-tenis (tenis que se juega en canchas con césped).
lawny ['lɔnɪ] *a.* 1. parecido al césped. 2. cubierto de césped. 3. (hecho) de linón, vestido de linón. 4. parecido al linón.
law of diminishing returns, (econ.) ley de utilidad o rendimiento decreciente.
law of evidence, (der.) código de pruebas.
law office, oficina de abogados, bufete.
law-officer ['lɔˌɔfəsər, -ˌɑf-, B -ˌɔfɪsə] *s.* funcionario legal, policía; (G.B.) Procurador General.
law of limitations, (der.) ley de prescripción.
law of nations, derecho internacional.
law of nature, derecho o ley natural.
law of negotiable instruments, (der.) ley cambiaria.
law of procedure, (der.) derecho o ley procesal, leyes de enjuiciamiento.
law of retaliation, ley del talión.
law of supply and demand, (econ.) ley de la oferta y la demanda.
law of the jungle, ley de la selva.
law of the land, derecho común, ley de la nación.
law reports, compilación de decisiones judiciales.
law school, facultad de derecho.
law student, estudiante de derecho.
lawsuit ['lɔˌsut, B -ˌsjut] *s.* pleito, litigio, juicio, proceso.
law-term [-ˌtɜrm, B -ˌtɜm] *s.* término legal, palabra o expresión de uso jurídico.
lawyer ['lɔjər, 'lɔɪər, B 'lɔjə] *s.* 1. abogado, licenciado, letrado, jurista, jurisconsulto. 2. (dial., G.B.) zarza; tallo espinoso de un brezo.
lawyer's bill, minuta.
lawyer's office, estudio jurídico.
lax [læks] *a.* 1. relajado, laxo; débil, poco firme, no rígido (disciplina, moral, etc.). 2. descuidado, negligente. 3. (bot.) disperso, suelto, (panícula, panoja). 4. (fon.) corto, de corta duración (díc. de vocales). 5. suelto, flojo (díc. del estómago).
laxation [læk'seɪʃən] *s.* laxación, relajación.
laxative ['læksətɪv] *a.* 1. laxativo, laxante. 2. (raro) libre, suelto, incontinente, inmoderado. —*s.* medicina laxativa, laxante.
laxity ['læksətɪ] *s.* 1. laxitud, flojedad. 2. relajamiento, relajación. 3. descuido, negligencia.
laxly ['lækslɪ] *adv.* 1. relajadamente; flojamente. 2. negligentemente.
laxness [-nəs] *s.* 1. laxidad, laxitud, flojedad; relajamiento. 2. negligencia, descuido, indiferencia.

lay [leɪ] *pret. de* **to lie,** yacer.

lay [leɪ] *v.t.* (*pret., p.p.* LAID [leɪd]; *p.pr.* LAYING) 1. poner, colocar. 2. depositar, poner (en), meter, echar. 3. poner (en cierta posición o estado). 4. tender, postrar, dejar en el suelo; arrasar (la cosecha, el viento, la lluvia); alisar (lanilla de una tela). 5. asentar (el polvo); calmar, aquietar (viento, mar, recelo, etc.); conjurar (un fantasma). 6. poner (huevos, la mesa); disponer, arreglar (en cierto orden). 7. apostar, meter (dinero). 8. situar (la acción de una novela, drama, etc.). 9. presentar (reclamo, problema, etc.); formular, exponer, atribuir, imputar, achacar. 10. imponer (pena, carga, obligación); sobreponer. 11. (con *with*) cubrir, vestir, revestir (de color, alfombra, capa de metal, etc.). 12. formar, disponer, trazar (plan, argumento, etc.). 13. asestar (cañon, pieza de artillería). 14. (mar.) corchar. 15. (vulg., jer.) pisar, tirarse a, tumbar a, tener relaciones sexuales con. 16. **l. a cable,** tender un cable; **l. an egg,** poner un huevo (un ave); (jer.) fracasar; hacer el ridículo; **l. aside, l. by,** poner a un lado, abandonar; poner aparte; guardar (dinero), ahorrar; **l. away,** reservar, guardar, almacenar; apartar, desechar; **l. bare,** desnudar, revelar; **l. before,** someter a, exponer a; **l. by the heels,** poner en el cepo, aprisionar, trabar; derribar, echar al suelo; **l. claim,** reclamar, confirmar sus derechos; pretender; **l. down,** acostar, derribar; deponer (ej., armas); fundamentar, echar los cimientos de; poner la quilla de (barco); establecer, sentar, prescribir, dictar; abandonar, rendir, entregar, ceder; poner a curar (vino) en bodega; trazar, delinear, proyectar; **l. down one's arms,** rendirse, darse por vencido; **l. down one's life,** sacrificar su vida; **l. eyes on,** poner los ojos en, echar la vista encima; **l. fast,** amarrar, trabar; **l. great store upon,** apreciar mucho, darle mucha importancia; **l. hands on (someone),** meter mano a, coger (a alguien); descargar la mano sobre, golpear a (alguien); encontrar (algo); **l. heads together,** consultarse, conferenciar, confabular; **l. hold on** (u **of**), asirse de (una cosa); hacerse cargo de; **l. in,** proveerse de, surtirse de; **l. it on,** lisonjear, cantar las alabanzas de uno; recargar, aplicar exceso de algo; **l. it on thick,** colmar de lisonjas empalagosas y zalamerías; **l. low,** derribar; esconderse temporalmente, quedarse tranquilo o callado por el momento; **l. off,** poner fuera de servicio o acción; despedir, suspender (a un empleado); dejar, abandonar (vicio, etc.); trazar, marcar, señalar las medidas; (mar.) alejarse el buque de la costa; **l. on,** imponer (pena, carga, tributo); atacar, propinar golpes a; azotar (con látigo); aplicar, cubrir con (mano de pintura, etc.); instalar (tuberías, etc.); **l. one's hopes on,** cifrar uno sus esperanzas en; **l. oneself open to,** exponerse a; **l. oneself out,** (fam.) hacer cuanto se puede, molestarse, esforzarse mucho; **l. open,** abrir de un corte; poner al descubierto, revelar (defectos, secreto, etc.); exponer (a critica, ataque, etc.); **l. out,** tender, desplegar, extender; exhibir, poner a la vista; amortajar (a un difunto); desembolsar; gastar, expender (dinero); levantar el plano de (un terreno), planificar (terreno, jardín, etc.); (fam.) poner fuera de combate, derribar (en fútbol, boxeo, etc.); (jer.) matar; **l. over,** descansar, pernoctar, parar; diferir, aplazar; **l. siege to,** asediar, sitiar; **l. stress on,** poner énfasis en, acentuar; **l. the blame at his door,** echarle la culpa; **l. to,** (mar.) hacer ponerse en facha, pairar (el barco); **l. to sleep** o **rest,** acostar, hacer descansar; (fig.) enterrar; **l. up,** guardar, amontonar, acumular (provisiones, etc.); ahorrar, atesorar (dinero); (mar.) desarmar; **l. upon,** imponer a; **l. waste,** devastar, asolar; **to be laid up,** guardar cama, no poder salir (de la casa). —*v.i.* 1. poner huevos (gallina). 2. hacer una apuesta. 3. (mar.) ir, pasar, moverse. 4. **l. aboard,** (mar.) acostarse; **l. about, l. about one,** repartir golpes a diestra y siniestra; **l. for,** (jer.) acechar, emboscar; **l. into,** (jer.) apalear; **l. off,** (jer.) dejar de trabajar; desistir, dejar de molestar. —*s.* 1. capa, estrato. 2. cubil, madriguera. 3. configuración, contornos; (fig.) aspecto, cariz, ej., *the l. of the land,* la configuración o los contornos del terreno; (fig.) el aspecto o el cariz de las cosas. 4. plan, proyecto. 5. dirección, ubicación. 6. ocupación, actividad (esp. criminal). 7. (mar.) corcha. 8. (jer.) apuesta. 9. (vulg.) coito; mujer (considerada como participante en el acto sexual), ej., *an easy l.,* una mujer fácil.

lay [leɪ] *a.* 1. laico, lego. 2. secular, seglar. 3. lego, profano, no profesional. —*s.* canción, balada; romance; poema simple y corto.

lay [leɪ] *pret. de* **lie,** yacer.

layabout ['leɪə'baʊt] *s.* (G.B., fam.) vago, vagabundo.

lay brother, (relig.) donado, hermano lego.

lay-by [-ˌbaɪ] *s.* 1. (mar.) sección de un canal o río donde los barcos se detienen. 2. (G.B.) área al costado de la carretera para paradas de emergencia.

lay days, (*pl.*) días de estadía, días de demora (permitidos para cargar o descargar un barco).

layer ['leɪər, B -ə] *s.* 1. capa, estrato; tongada, camada. 2. (agr.) acodo, acodadura. 3. ostral. 4. (t. **good l.**) gallina ponedora. —*v.t., v.i.* (agr.) acodar, amugronar; acamarse (las mieses).

layerage [-ərɪdʒ] *s.* (agr.) acodadura.

layer cake, bizcocho de varias capas unidas con un relleno de crema o conserva.

layering [-ərɪŋ] *s.* (agr.) acodadura.

layette [leɪ'ɛt] *s.* canastilla (para el recién nacido); ajuar para bebé.

lay figure, 1. maniquí, figurín. 2. (fig.) títere, persona sin identidad propia.

laying ['leɪɪŋ] *s.* colocación, instalación. 2. tendido de (cables, etc.). 3. postura (de huevos). —*a.* situado, sito; (mar.) anclado.

laying on of hands, (relig.) imposición de manos.

laying press, (impr.) prensa de cepillo.

laying top, galapo.

laying walk, cordelería.

layman ['leɪmən] *s.* 1. lego, laico, seglar. 2. lego, profano (en una materia).

layoff [-ˌɔf] *s.* despido o suspensión de empleados; cierre, cesación de trabajo; paro forzoso.

layout [-ˌaʊt] *s.* 1. disposición, arreglo, esquema, plan, trazado. 2. equipo surtido. 3. (jer.) banquete, festín.

layover [-ˌoʊvər, B -və] *s.* escala; parada temporal (en un lugar).

lay reader, lego (anglicano o episcopal) al que se permite dar sermones y dirigir servicios religiosos.

lay sister, (relig.) donada, hermana lega.

laystall [-ˌstɔl] *s.* muladar, estercolero.

laywoman ['leɪˌwʊmən] *s.* mujer lega, seglar.

lazar ['læzər, 'leɪzər, B 'læzə] *s.* (ant.) lázaro; leproso, lazarino.

lazaret, lazarette [ˌlæzə'rɛt] **lazaretto** [-'rɛtoʊ] *s.* 1. lazareto, hospital de leprosos. 2. (mar.) despensa, pañol.

Lazarist ['læzərəst] **Lazarite** [-ˌraɪt] *s.* (relig.) lazarista.

laze [leɪz] *v.i.* darse al ocio, holgar, gandulear, holgazanear. —*v.t.* perder el tiempo holgazaneando.

lazily ['leɪzəlɪ] *adv.* perezosamente; indolentemente.

laziness [-zɪnəs] *s.* pereza, holgazanería, indolencia, desidia, flojera (Amer.).

lazuli ['læzjʊˌlaɪ, 'læʒ-, -ˌli, B 'læzjʊˌlaɪ] *s.* lapislázuli.

lazulite [-ˌlaɪt] *s.* (min.) lazulita, cianea, azul.

lazy ['leɪzɪ] *a.* (LAZIER; LAZIEST) 1. perezoso, holgazán, haragán, flojo, indolente. 2. lento, tardo. 3. acostada (díc. de las letras inclinadas del hierro de marcar ganado).

lazybones [-ˌboʊnz] *s.* holgazán, gandul.

lazy Susan [ˌleɪzɪ'suzən] *s.* 1. mesa pequeña de té de tres pisos. 2. bandeja giratoria con divisiones (en las que se ponen aderezos, entremeses, etc.).

lazy tongs, tenazas plegables que se extienden (para alcanzar un objeto).

lb. *abrev. de* **pound,** libra (lb).

L bar, L beam ['ɛl-] viga L, en forma de L, barra o vigueta en L.

lbs. *abrev. de* **pounds,** libras (lbs).

lc. *abrev. de* **lower case,** caja baja, minúsculas (letras).

L.C.D. *abrev. de* **lowest common divisor,** o **denominator,** mínimo común divisor (m.c.d.).

L.C.M. *abrev. de* **lowest common multiple,** mínimo común múltiplo (m.c.m.).

Ld. *abrev. de* 1. **limited,** limitado (ltdo.). 2. **Lord,** Lord.

lea [li] *s.* 1. (poét.) prado, pradera. 2. (tej.) madejita, troquillón.

leach [litʃ] *v.t.* 1. lixiviar (separar mediante un disolvente, una substancia soluble de otra insoluble). 2. **l. out,** extraer o separar por lixiviación. —*s.* 1. substancia para lixiviar. 2. lixiviación. 3. cenizas de lejía. 4. cuba para lixiviar.

leachable ['litʃəbəl] *a.* lixiviable.

leacher [-ər, B -ə] *s.* lixiviador.

leaching [-ɪŋ] *s.* lixiviación.

leaching vat, cuba para lixiviar.

leachy [-ɪ] *a.* permeable, poroso.

lead [lid] *v.t.* (*pret., p.p.* LED [lɛd]; *p.pr.* LEADING) 1. guiar, conducir, llevar. 2. dirigir, mandar; acaudillar; estar a la cabeza de, ej., *he leads all actors,* está a la cabeza de todos los actores. 3. llevar (buena o mala vida), ej., *l. a dog's life,* llevar una vida de perros. 4. conducir, llevar, ej., *these roads l. us to Boston,* estos caminos nos llevan a Boston, *it leads us to this conclusion,* nos lleva a esta conclusión. 5. inducir, impulsar, mover; tentar, atraer. 6. dirigir (una orquesta). 7. llevar ventaja sobre, aventajar a (competidor), ser el primero. 8. insinuar la respuesta al (testigo). 9. (boxeo) dirigir (un golpe al contendor). 10. (naipes) abrir o salir con (una carta, palo, etc.). 11. **l. along,** conducir, acompañar; **l. a new life,** enmendarse; **l. astray,** descarriar, llevar por mal camino; **l. by the nose,** manejar a su gusto; **l. on,** enseñar el camino a; (fig.) influenciar, seducir; inducir a proceder; **l. the fashion,** dictar la moda; **l. the way,** enseñar el camino, ir adelante; **l. (someone) to (do),** llevar o inducir (a alguien) a (hacer); **l. (a woman) to the altar,** llevar (una mujer) al altar; **to be led away by,** dejarse arrastrar por. —*v.i.* 1. guiar, enseñar el camino. 2. ser el primero, estar a la cabeza. 3. mandar, ser el jefe. 4. conducir, llevar (camino). 5. tender, dirigirse. 6. ir al frente, ir en la punta, puntear (Am.) (en carrera, etc.). 7. (naipes) principiar a jugar, ser mano; (bridge) atacar. 8. **l. off,** empezar, dar comienzo; **l. to,** (fig.) resultar en; **l. up to,** llevar a, servir de introducción para, culminar en; aproximarse gradualmente a (tema, tópico, etc.). —*s.* 1.

delantera, punta. 2. dirección, mando. 3. iniciativa. 4. pauta, ejemplo. 5. indicio, pista. 6. traílla, correa. 7. primacía, supremacía. 8. introducción, entradilla (a un artículo periodístico); artículo principal (en periódico); noticia principal (en la radio). 9. caz. 10. pasadizo libre (en bancos de hielo). 11. (mús.) tema o melodía principal. 12. (teat.) papel principal; protagonista. 13. (elec.) conductor. 14. (mec., elec.) avance. 15. (f.c.) arranque, avance. 16. (naipes) salida; mano, ej., *who has the l.?* ¿quién es mano?; (bridge) ataque. 17. (min.) filón, venero, veta. 18. (boxeo) primer golpe (del ataque continuado). 19. (mar.) extensión de cabo. 20. **to give one a l.,** darle una pista a uno, darle un indicio a uno; **to follow the l. of,** seguir el ejemplo de; **to take the l.,** tomar la delantera o el mando. —*a.* 1. de guía, de cabeza. 2. principal (noticia, artículo).

lead [lɛd] *s.* 1. plomo. 2. plomería, artículos de plomo. 3. plomada, plomo de la sonda, escandallo. 4. (*pl.*) engarces de plomo (de las vidrieras); (*pl.*) (G.B.) emplomado (de un techo). 5. grafito; mina (del lapicero o lápiz). 6. cerusa, albayalde, plomo blanco. 7. plomo, bala; balas (colectivamente). 8. (tip.) interlínea, regleta. —*a.* de plomo; plomizo. —*v.t.* 1. emplomar; lastrar o guarnecer con plomo. 2. tratar o mezclar con plomo. 3. (const.) emplomar (vidrieras). 4. (cerám.) vidriar con barniz al plomo. 5. (tip.) interlinear, regletear.

lead acetate, (quím.) acetato de plomo.

lead acetate water, (quím.) agua blanca, solución de acetato de plomo.

lead arsenate, (quím.) arseniato de plomo.

lead-coated [ˈlɛdˈkoʊtəd] *a.* emplomado.

lead colic, (med.) cólico de plomo, cólico de los pintores.

lead-colored [-ˌkʌlərd, B -əd] *a.* plomizo, plomoso.

leaded [-əd] *a.* 1. emplomado, guarnecido de plomo. 2. (impr.) interlineado.

leaden [ˈlɛdən] *a.* 1. de plomo, plúmbeo. 2. plomizo, de color plomo. 3. barato, ordinario. 4. abatido; lerdo, pesado, tardo, lento.

leaden-eyed [-ˈaɪd] *a.* soñoliento, de ojos soñolientos.

leaden-footed [-ˈfʊtəd] *a.* tardo, lento, pesado.

leaden-hearted [-ˈhɑrtəd, B -ˈhɑt-] *a.* duro, insensible.

leadenly [-lɪ] *adv.* abatidamente; pesadamente.

leadenness [-nəs] *s.* abatimiento; pesadez.

leaden sword, carabina de Ambrosio, cosa inútil.

leader [ˈlidər, B -ə] *s.* 1. guiador. 2. guía, conductor. 3. jefe, comandante; líder, caudillo. 4. guía, caballo de cabeza. 5. tubo, cañería, conducto. 6. (pesca) red guiadora; sotileza (parte fina del sedal donde va el anzuelo). 7. (com.) artículo de reclamo (que se ofrece barato para atraer al cliente). 8. (pr. G.B.) editorial, artículo de fondo (en periódico). 9. (mús.) director, conductor; instrumentista principal (ej., primer violín). 10. (mar.) guiacabos, guardacabos. 11. (tip.) (*pl.*) puntos conductores. 12. (min.) vena, filón.

leadership [-ˌʃɪp] *s.* dirección, jefatura, mando; caudillaje, liderazgo, liderato; dotes de mando.

lead glance [ˈlɛd-] (min.) galena.

lead glass [ˈlɛd-] cristal de sosa.

lead-in [ˈlidˌɪn] *a.* de entrada, de toma. —*s.* (rad.) bajada de antena, entrada.

leading [ˈlɛdɪŋ] *s.* 1. emplomadura, plomería. 2. (impr.) interlineación.

leading [ˈlidɪŋ] *s.* 1. dirección, guía, conducción. 2. sugerencia, insinuación. —*a.* 1. conductor, guiador, director. 2. principal, capital; dominante, sobresaliente.

leading article, artículo de fondo, editorial.

leading counsel, (der.) abogado principal.

leading current, (elec.) corriente avanzada, corriente en adelanto.

leading edge, (aer.) borde de ataque, borde anterior (de una hélice o superficie aerodinámica).

leading lady, (teat., cine) primera actriz, dama.

leading man, (teat., cine) primer galán, primer actor.

leading question, pregunta que sugiere o insinúa la respuesta.

leading-rein [ˈlidɪŋˌreɪn] *s.* cabestro, ramal.

leading role, (teat.) papel principal.

leading strings, andadores, tirantes (para sujetar a los niños cuando aprenden a andar).

leading tone, l. note, (mús.) séptima nota o tono (en la escala mayor y menor).

leading wheels, ruedas delanteras de una locomotora.

lead-in wire [ˈlidˌɪn-] (elec., rad.) alambre de entrada, bajada de antena.

lead line [ˈlɛd-] (mar.) sonda, sondaleza.

lead-off [ˈlidˌɔf] *a.* principiante, iniciativo, iniciador.

leadoff, *s.* 1. principio, comienzo. 2. jugador que comienza.

lead pencil [ˈlɛd-] lápiz de grafito, lapicero.

leadplant [-ˌplænt, B -ˌplɑnt] *s.* (bot.) amorfa.

lead poisoning [ˈlɛd-] saturnismo, plumbismo.

leadsman [ˈlɛdzmən] *s.* (mar.) sondeador.

lead time, plazo de entrega.

leadwork [ˈlɛdˌwɜrk, B -ˌwɜk] *s.* emplomadura, plomería.

leadwort [-ˌwɜrt, B -ˌwɜt] *s.* (bot.) belesa, dentelaria.

leady [ˈlɛdɪ] *a.* plomizo, plomoso, aplomado.

leaf [lif] *s.* (*pl.* LEAVES [livz]) 1. hoja, fronda. 2. pétalo. 3. follaje. 4. hoja, foja, folio. 5. hoja (de puerta, ventana, etc.); tablero (de mesa). 6. plancha, lámina. 7. (aut.) hoja de muelle o ballesta. 8. (dial., G.B.) ala (de sombrero). 9. **in l.,** con hojas; **to take a l. from someone's book,** imitar a alguien, seguir su ejemplo; **to turn over a new l.,** enmendarse, empezar nueva vida. —*a.* 1. foliáceo. 2. en rama, ej., *l. tobacco,* tabaco en rama. —*v.i.* echar hojas. —*v.t.* **l. through,** hojear (un libro, folleto, etc.).

leafage [ˈlifɪdʒ] *s.* follaje, frondas.

leaf blade, (bot.) lámina (parte ancha de la hoja).

leaf brass, oropel; latón en láminas.

leaf bud, (bot.) yema, botón de planta.

leaf fat, grasa abdominal (del cerdo).

leaf gold, oro en hojas.

leafhopper [ˈlifˌhɑpər, B -ˌhɔpə] *s.* (ento.) saltarilla.

leaf lard, manteca de cerdo (hecha de la grasa abdominal).

leafless [-ləs] *a.* deshojado; (bot.) áfilo.

leaflet [-lət] *s.* 1. hojuela, hojilla. 2. hoja suelta, volante; (impr.) folleto, panfleto. 3. (bot.) hojuela (de la hoja compuesta).

leaflike [-ˌlaɪk] *a.* foliforme.

leaf mold, 1. mantillo. 2. moho o añublo del follaje.

leaf spring, (aut.) ballesta, muelle de hojas.

leafstalk [-ˌstɔk] *s.* (bot.) pecíolo, rabillo (de una hoja).

leaf tobacco, tabaco en rama u hoja.

leafy [ˈlifɪ] *a.* (LEAFIER; LEAFIEST) 1. frondoso, hojoso. 2. en forma de hoja. 3. laminado.

league [lig] *s.* 1. legua; legua cuadrada. 2. liga, alianza, confederación; sociedad; **in l. with,** aliado o asociado con. —*v.i., v.t.* ligar(se); aliar(se), confederar(se).

leagued [ligd] *a.* ligado, en liga con, confederado.

League of Nations, Liga de las Naciones.

leaguer [ˈligər, B -gə] *s.* miembro de una liga, alianza o confederación.

leak [lik] *s.* 1. agujero, raja, grieta, abertura; gotera (en el techo). 2. salida, escape, fuga (de gas, agua, aire, etc.). 3. (fig.) divulgación no autorizada (de noticias, etc.); filtración; indiscreción. 4. (mar.) agua, vía de agua. 5. (elec.) pérdida, dispersión (de corriente). 6. **to spring a l.,** abrirse un agujero o escape (un tonel, vasija, etc.); (mar.) abrirse (una vía de) agua (un buque). —*v.i.* 1. escaparse, salirse (agua, gas, aire, etc.), filtrarse, rezumarse, gotear (líquido). 2. no cerrar bien, no ser estanco, tener agujero(s) o escape(s). 3. (mar.) hacer agua (buque). 4. (fig., gen. con *out*) trascender, divulgarse, saberse, filtrarse, traslucirse (noticia, secreto, etc.). —*v.t.* 1. dejar salir, dejar escapar; filtrar. 2. (fig.) dejar trascender, comunicar subrepticiamente. 3. **to take a l.,** (jer.) orinar.

leakage [ˈlikɪdʒ] *s.* 1. escape, filtración, derrame, goteo, fuga. 2. (elec.) dispersión. 3. merma, pérdida. 4. noticia oficiosa.

leakproof [-ˌpruf] *a.* a prueba de escapes o de filtración; estanco, hermético; a prueba de goteras.

leaky [ˈlikɪ] *a.* 1. agujereado, agrietado, que hace agua, que gotea. 2. llovedizo (bóveda, techo), permeable. 3. (ant.) indiscreto, locuaz.

leal [lil] *a.* (pr. esco.) leal, fiel, honrado.

lealty [ˈliltɪ] *s.* (pr. esco.) lealtad, fidelidad, honradez.

lean [lin] *v.i.* (*pret., p.p.* LEANED o (pr G.B.) LEANT [lɛnt]; *p.pr.* LEANING) 1. inclinarse, ladearse, apoyarse, reclinarse, encorvarse. 2. **l. against,** apoyarse contra; **l. back,** retreparse, recostarse; **l. forward,** inclinarse (hacia adelante); **l. on** o **upon,** recostarse, reclinarse o apoyarse sobre; (fig.) depender de; confiar en, necesitar el apoyo de; **l. out (of),** asomar la cabeza; **l. over,** inclinarse (hacia adelante); **l. over backwards,** (fam.) extremarse, esforzarse al máximo; **l. to,** inclinarse (hacia, a), propender (a); **l. toward,** inclinarse por. —*v.t.* inclinar, apoyar, recostar. —*s.* inclinación, disposición, propensión.

lean, *a.* 1. flaco, delgado, descarnado; enjuto, cenceño. 2. magro (díc. de la carne). 3. pobre, improductivo, deficiente, escaso, mezquino; de escasez, ej., *l. years,* años de escasez, (años de las) vacas flacas. 4. (aut.) pobre (díc. de la mezcla combustible). —*s.* carne magra. —*v.t.* (*pret., p.p.* LEANED; *p.pr.* LEANING) 1. (gen. con *down* o *out*) adelgazar. 2. (t. con *out*) (aut.) empobrecer (mezcla combustible). 3. separar la carne magra de (ballena).

leaning [ˈlinɪŋ] *s.* inclinación, propensión, tendencia. —*a.* inclinado, ladeado.

leanness [ˈlinnəs] *s.* 1. delgadez, flacura, magrura. 2. escasez, carestía, pobreza.

leant [lɛnt] (pr. G.B.) *pret., p.p. de* **lean.**

lean-to [ˈlinˌtu] *a.* (arq.) de una sola vertiente o agua. —*s.* (*pl.* LEAN-TOS) alpende, cobertizo, colgadizo.

lean-witted [-ˈwɪtəd] *a.* necio, tonto.

leap [lip] *v.i.* (*pret., p.p.* LEAPED o LEAPT [lipt]; *p.pr.* LEAPING) 1. saltar, brincar; brotar o salir con ímpetu. 2. dar un salto (corazón). 3. (fig.) saltar (de un tema al otro). 4. **l. at,** aceptar inmediatamente, apresurarse a aprovechar (la oportunidad); **l. over,** saltar, salvar (obstáculo); **l. to** o **into,** lanzarse a; **l. up,** levantarse de un salto. —*v.t.* 1. saltar, salvar. 2. hacer saltar (ej., a un caballo). 3. cubrir el macho a la hembra. —*s.* salto, brinco, cabriola, zapateta; **by leaps and bounds,** a saltos, a pasos agigantados; **l. in the dark,** salto a ciegas, salto en el vacío.

leaper ['lipər, B -pə] *s.* saltador, brincador.
leapfrog ['lip,frɔg, -,frɑg, B -,frɔg] *s.* pídola, fil derecho, salta cabrillas, salto de la muerte (juego de saltos). —*v.i.* (*pret., p.p.* LEAPFROGGED; *p.pr.* LEAPFROGGING) 1. jugar a la pídola. 2. (fig.) pasar de un salto, pasar de repente. 3. (fig.) alternarse en adelantar uno a otro (ej., vehículos en una carretera). —*v.t.* 1. saltar por encima de. 2. (mil.) pasar de línea, pasar de escalón.
leap year, año bisiesto.
learn [lɜrn, B lɜn] *v.t.* (*pret., p.p.* LEARNED O LEARNT [lɜrnt, B lɜnt]; *p.pr.* LEARNING) 1. aprender, estudiar, instruirse en. 2. enterarse de, imponerse de, saber (una noticia). 3. (dial.) enseñar. 4. **l. by heart, l. by rote,** aprender de memoria. —*v.i.* aprender, adquirir conocimientos, hacerse diestro; **to l. by doing,** aprender haciendo.
learnable ['lɜrnəbəl, B 'lɜnə-] *a.* que puede aprenderse.
learned [-nəd] *a.* 1. docto, erudito, culto, ilustrado, versado, sabio. 2. dirigido a los doctos, científico (revista, etc.).
learnedly [-lɪ] *adv.* doctamente, eruditamente, cultamente.
learned word, cultismo, palabra culta o erudita.
learned world, mundo de los eruditos.
learner ['lɜrnər, B 'lɜnə] *s.* principiante, aprendiz; estudiante, estudioso.
learning [-nɪŋ] *s.* 1. aprendizaje, entrenamiento, estudio. 2. erudición, saber, ciencia, instrucción.
learnt [lɜrnt, B lɜnt] *pret., p.p. de* **learn.**
leary, *var. de* **leery.**
lease [lis] *v.t.* arrendar, alquilar, dar o tomar en arriendo. —*s.* 1. arrendamiento, arriendo, alquiler, locación; contrato de arrendamiento. 2. inmueble que se da o toma en arriendo o alquiler. 3. **on l.,** en arriendo; **to have** (o **to take,** o **to be given**) **a new l. (on) life,** (fig.) prorrogar su vida; volver a la vida, nacer de nuevo; **to put out to l.,** dar en arriendo o alquiler.
leasehold ['lis,hoʊld] *a.* que se tiene en arriendo o alquiler (díc. de un inmueble). —*s.* 1. inquilinato, tenencia en arriendo; derecho de arrendamiento. 2. bienes raíces arrendados.
leaseholder [-ər, B -ə] *s.* arrendatario, locatario, inquilino.
leasehold estate, (der.) bienes forales.
leash [liʃ] *s.* 1. traílla, correa. 2. pihuela. 3. (caza) trío, grupo de tres (galgos, zorros, conejos, etc.). 4. **to hold in l.,** dominar, manejar; **to strain at the l.,** (fig.) tratar de sacudir el yugo. —*v.t.* atraillar.
least [list] *a. super. de* **little.** 1. menor. 2. mínimo. —*s.* 1. lo menor. 2. lo menos. 3. **at (the) l.,** al menos, por lo menos; **not in the l.,** en lo más mínimo, de ninguna manera; **to say the l. of it,** para decir lo menos, por no decir cosa peor. —*adv.* menos.
least common denominator, (mat.) mínimo común denominador.
least common multiple, (mat.) mínimo común múltiplo.
least flycatcher, (orn.) papamoscas.
leastways ['list,weɪz] *adv.* (dial.) al menos, por lo menos.
leastwise [-,waɪz] *adv.* (fam.) al menos, por lo menos.
leather ['lɛðər, B -ə] *s.* 1. cuero, piel, pellejo. 2. artículo de cuero. 3. pulpejo de la oreja de un perro (esp. de un sabueso). 4. pelota (de fútbol, béisbol). —*a.* de cuero. —*v.t.* 1. forrar o guarnecer con cuero. 2. (fam.) azotar, zurrar, dar una cueriza a (Amer.).
leatherback [-,bæk] *s.* (zool.) laúd (tortutuga gigante).
leather-bound [-,baʊnd] *a.* empastado o encuadernado en cuero.
leatherette [,lɛðə'rɛt] *s.* similicuero (papel o tela que imita al cuero).
leatherhead ['lɛðər,hɛd, B -ə,-] *s.* zopenco, tonto.
leathern [-ərn, B -ən] *a.* 1. de cuero. 2. como cuero, parecido al cuero, coriáceo.
leatherneck [-ər,nɛk, B -ə,-] *s.* (jer., E.U.) soldado de infantería de marina.
Leatheroid [-ə,rɔɪd] *s.* cartón cuero (marca de fábrica).
leathery [-ərɪ] *a.* correoso.
leave [liv] *v.t.* (*pret., p.p.* LEFT [lɛft]; *p.pr.* LEAVING) 1. dejar, ej., *it leaves much to be desired,* deja mucho que desear. 2. dejar estar, ej., *let's l. it at that,* dejémoslo así, dejemos las cosas como están, *l. him to himself,* déjenle estar, déjenle solo. 3. (con *to*) dejar, encomendar, confiar (a), ej., *I l. it to you,* se lo confío, lo dejo en sus manos, *l. it to me! ¡déjemelo Ud. a mí!* 4. dejar, legar. 5. salir de, abandonar, ej., *the king left the palace,* el rey salió del palacio, *we left the room together,* salimos del cuarto juntos. 6. dejar, abandonar, desamparar, ej., *they left him to his fate,* lo abandonaron a su suerte. 7. dejar de, parar. 8. **l. alone,** dejar tranquilo, dejar en paz, no meterse con; no tocar; **l. aside,** dejar de lado; **l. behind,** dejar atrás; irse o partir sin (algo); **l. (one) cold,** no alterar (a uno), no causar ninguna impresión (en uno); **l. go,** (vulg.) soltar, liberar; **l. hold of,** soltar; **l. holding,** dejar clavado con; **l. in the dark,** dejar a oscuras, dejar sin entender; **l. in the lurch,** (fam.) dejar plantado o colgado, dejar en la estacada, dar esquinazo a; **l. no stone unturned,** no escatimar esfuerzos; **l. off,** dejar, renunciar a (una costumbre, un vicio, etc.); no ponerse (una prenda de vestir); **l. off (doing),** dejar de (hacer); **l. out,** omitir, excluir, olvidar; **l. out in the cold,** (fam.) dejar colgado, olvidarse de, dejar de lado; **l. undone,** no hacer, dejar de hacer, dejar sin terminar; **l. word,** dejar dicho, dejar un recado; **to be left,** quedar(se), ej., *he was left alone in the house,* se ha quedado solo en la casa, *there's no more left,* no queda más; **to be left in the lurch,** (fam.) quedarse colgado; **to be left over,** quedar, sobrar. —*v.i.* 1. irse, marcharse, salir, ej., *he left a few minutes ago,* se fue hace unos minutos. 2. **l. for,** partir para, ej., *I'll l. for Europe tomorrow,* mañana partiré para Europa; **l. off,** cesar, pararse; terminar, dejar.
leave, *v.i.* (*pret., p.p.* LEAVED; *p.pr.* LEAVING) echar hojas (una planta o árbol).
leave [liv, B liv, lif] *s.* 1. permiso, autorización. 2. licencia (esp. militar), vacaciones. 3. adiós, despedida. 4. **by your l.,** con su permiso; **to be on l.,** estar de licencia, estar de vacaciones; **to give one l.,** darle permiso a uno; **to take l. of,** despedir; **to take (one's) l.,** despedirse; **to take l. of one's senses,** enloquecer, volverse loco.
leaved [livd] *a.* de hojas (ú. esp. en compuestos, ej., *red l.,* de hojas rojas).
leaven ['lɛvən] *s.* 1. levadura. 2. (fig.) fermento, incentivo. —*v.t.* 1. leudar, hacer fermentar. 2. (fig.) penetrar, entremezclar, impregnar, imbuir.
leavening [-ɪŋ] *s.* 1. fermentación. 2. fermento, levadura.
leave of absence ['liv-] licencia, permiso.
leaves [livz] *pl. de* **leaf.**
leave-taking ['liv,teɪkɪŋ] *s.* despedida, adiós.
leaving ['livɪŋ] *s.* (*ú. gen. en pl.*) 1. sobra(s), residuo(s). 2. desperdicios, basura(s).
Lebanese [,lɛbə'niz] *a.* libanés. —*s.* (*pl.* LEBANESE) libanés, libanesa.
Lebanon ['lɛbənən] *s.* (geog.) 1. (el) Líbano. 2. monte Líbano.
lebbek ['lɛ,bɛk] *s.* (bot.) **faurestina.**
lebensraum ['leɪbənz,raʊm] *s.* (pol.) espacio vital (de una nación).
lecher ['lɛtʃər, B -ə] *s.* libertino, lujurioso, disoluto.
lecherous [-ərəs] *a.* lujurioso, lascivo, salaz.
lecherously [-lɪ] *adv.* lujuriosamente, lascivamente.
lecherousness [-nəs] *s.* lujuria, lascivia, salacidad.
lechery [-ərɪ] *s.* (*pl.* LECHERIES) lujuria, lascivia, libertinaje.
lecithin ['lɛsəθən] *s.* (bioquím.) lecitina.
lecithinase [-θə,neɪs] *s.* (bioquím.) lecitinasa.
lectern ['lɛktərn, B -tən] *s.* atril, facistol.
lection ['lɛkʃən] *s.* 1. lección (versión de un texto). 2. (relig.) lección (trozo de las escrituras).
lectionary [-,ɛrɪ, B -ərɪ] *s.* (relig.) leccionario.
lectisternium [,lɛktə'stɜrnɪəm, B -'stɜn-] *s.* (hist.) lectisternio.
lector ['lɛktər, B -,tɔ] *s.* (relig.) lector.
lectorate [-tə,reɪt, -rət] *s.* (relig.) lectorado (orden); lectoría (oficio).
lecture ['lɛktʃər, B -tʃə] *s.* 1. disertación, conferencia; instrucción, clase. 2. reprimenda, admonición, amonestación, sermón. 3. **to read one a l.,** leerle la cartilla a uno. —*v.i.* disertar; dictar conferencias; **to l. on,** explicar. —*v.t.* 1. instruir, enseñar (por medio de conferencias); dar una conferencia o disertación a. 2. reprender, sermonear, reconvenir.
lecture hall, lecture room, aula, salón de actos o conferencias.
lecturer [-tʃərər, B -ə] *s.* conferenciante, conferencista (Amer.), disertante; catedrático.
lectureship [-tʃər,ʃɪp, B -tʃə,-] *s.* cargo o función de conferenciante.
led [lɛd] *pret., p.p. de* **lead.**
lederhosen ['leɪdər,hoʊzən, B -ə,-] *s.* (alemán) pantalones cortos de cuero (usados esp. en Baviera, Alemania).
ledge [lɛdʒ] *s.* 1. berma, reborde, saliente. 2. arrecife. 3. resalto, retallo, repisa. 4. (min.) filón o veta metalífera, vena.
ledger ['lɛdʒər, B -ə] *s.* 1. (ten.) libro mayor. 2. lápida sepulcral, losa funeraria. 3. solera (sobre la que se apoyan las almojayas) de un andamio. 4. (pesca) anzuelo, cordel o carnada de un tipo de avío en que la plomada descansa en el fondo del agua.
ledger bait, cebo de un cordel de pesca flotante y amarrado al banco.
ledger board, pasamano, baranda.
ledger date, (com., fin.) fecha de liquidación.
ledger line, 1. (pesca) cordel cuyo plomo descansa en el fondo del agua. 2. (mús.) línea auxiliar (del pentagrama).
ledger paper, (ten.) papel de cuentas, (esp. papel de cuentas del mayor).
ledger tackle, (pesca) avío en que la plomada descansa en el fondo del agua.
lee [li] *s.* 1. (mar.) sotavento, socaire. 2. abrigo, refugio, protección. —*a.* de sotavento, a sotavento.
leeboard ['li,bɔrd, B -,bɔd] *s.* (mar.) orza o quilla de deriva.
leech [litʃ] *s.* 1. (zool.) sanguijuela. 2. (fig.) gorrón, parásito, vividor. 3. (ant.) médico, curandero. 4. (mar.) caída, derribo (de la vela). 5. **to cling like a l.,** pegarse como ladilla, prenderse como una sanguijuela. —*v.t.* 1. sangrar (con sanguijuelas). 2. (fig.) sangrar, desangrar. 3. (ant.) curar, sanar, tratar médicamente.

leech-line ['litʃ,laɪn] *s.* (mar.) apagapenol.
leech rope, (mar.) relinga de caída.
leek [lik] *s.* (bot.) puerro, porro.
leer [lɪr, B lɪə] *v.i.* mirar de reojo, mirar de soslayo (esp. socarrona, maliciosa o lascivamente). —*s.* mirada de soslayo, mirada de reojo (esp. lasciva).
leeringly ['lɪrɪŋlɪ, B 'lɪər-] *adv.* con mirada de reojo o de soslayo; maliciosamente, lascivamente.
leery [-ɪ] *a.* sabido, astuto; receloso, desconfiado, suspicaz.
lees [liz] *s. pl.* heces, poso, zurrapa, sedimento, concho (Am.); **to drain to the l.,** apurar hasta la última gota, apurar hasta las heces.
lee shore, costa de sotavento.
lee side, (mar.) banda de sotavento.
lee tide, marea de sotavento.
leeward ['lɪwərd, 'luərd, B 'liwəd, 'luəd] (mar.) *a.* de sotavento. —*s.* banda de sotavento, sotavento; **on the l. of,** a sotavento de. —*adv.* a sotavento.
Leeward Islands, (geog.) Islas de Sotavento.
leeway ['li,weɪ] *s.* 1. (mar.) abatimiento, deriva. 2. (aer.) ángulo de deriva. 3. (fam.) libertad o campo de acción; margen, amplitud (de dinero, movimiento, etc.). 4. **to make up l.,** salir del atraso, recuperar lo perdido (tiempo, terreno, etc.).
left [lɛft] *pret., p.p. de* **leave.** —*a.* izquierdo; **to marry with the l. hand,** casarse morganáticamente. —*s.* 1. izquierda, lado izquierdo. 2. (pol.) izquierda. 3. (boxeo) (mano) izquierda; golpe de izquierda, izquierdazo. 4. **on** (o **to**) **the l.,** a (o por) la izquierda.
Left Bank, la parte de Paris que se encuentra sobre la orilla izquierda del Sena.
left field, (béisbol) jardín izquierdo.
left fielder, (béisbol) jardinero izquierdo.
left half, (dep.) medio izquierdo.
left-hand ['lɛft,hænd] *a.* 1. izquierdo, siniestro, a la izquierda. 2. zurdo.
left-hand drive, (aut.) conducción o mando por la izquierda.
left-handed ['lɛft'hændəd] *a.* 1. zurdo. 2. morganático, de la mano izquierda (matrimonio). 3. torpe, desmañado; insincero, malicioso, falso, ej., *l.-h. compliment,* falso halago. 4. (bot., zool.) sinistrorso, sinistrórsum.
left-handedly [-lɪ] *adv.* con la izquierda.
left-handedness [-nəs] *s.* zurdería.
left-handed screw, tornillo de rosca hacia la izquierda.
lefthander [-'hændər, B -də] *s.* 1. zurdo. 2. zurdazo, izquierdazo, golpe dado con la mano izquierda.
left-hand thread, (mec.) rosca zurda, rosca a la izquierda, filete de paso izquierdo.
leftism ['ləf,tɪzəm] *s.* (pol.) izquierdismo, tendencia izquierdista.
leftist [-təst] *a., s.* (pol.) izquierdista, radical.
leftover ['lɛft,oʊvər, B -və] *a.* sobrante. —*s.* (*ú. gen. en pl.*) sobras, restos.
left turn, giro o vuelta a la izquierda.
leftward [-wərd, B -wəd] *adv.* hacia la izquierda.
left wing, (pol.) izquierda, ala izquierda (de un partido político).
left-wing ['lɛft'wiŋ] *a.* (pol.) de la izquierda, izquierdista.
lefty ['lɛftɪ] *s.* (*pl.* LEFTIES) (fam.) 1. izquierdista, radical. 2. zurdo. —*a.* zurdo.
leg [lɛg] *s.* 1. pierna (de hombre o animal); pernil, pata (de animal). 2. pernil, pernera (de pantalón). 3. pata, poste, paral; soporte, sostén. 4. (mar.) bordada. 5. (mat.) cateto, lado (de un triángulo). 6. (dep.) tramo, trecho (en carrera de relevos, etc.). 7. (criquet) parte del campo a la espalda del bateador. 8. **to be all legs,** ser larguirucho, ser piernilargo; **to be on one's hind legs,** (hum.) estar de pie, esp. para hacer uso de la palabra; estar restablecido lo suficiente como para caminar; estar en situación próspera; **to be on one's own legs,** ser independiente, estar firmemente establecido; **to be on one's last legs,** estar en las últimas; agonizar; **to find one's legs,** recobrar el equilibrio; **to give one a l. up,** ayudar a trepar o subir; (fig.) ayudar, dar una mano a uno (para superar alguna dificultad); **not to have a l. to stand on,** no tener en qué basar o con qué defender un argumento; **to have the legs of,** poder ir más rápido que; **to keep one's legs,** mantenerse en pie, no caerse; **to pull one's l.,** tomar el pelo a uno, burlarse de uno, bromear con uno; **to shake a l.,** apresurarse, darse prisa; **to stand on one's own legs,** valerse por uno mismo; **to stretch one's legs,** estirar las piernas, dar un paseo; **to take to one's legs,** tomar las de Villadiego, poner pies en polvorosa, escapar. —*v.i.* (*pret., p.p.* LEGGED; *p.pr.* LEGGING) (ú. gen. con *it*) ir a pie, caminar; (jer.) largarse, irse.
leg. *abrev. de* **legal,** jurídico, legal; **legislative,** legislativo; **legislature,** legislatura.
legacy ['lɛgəsɪ] *s.* (*pl.* LEGACIES) 1. herencia. 2. (der.) legado, manda.
legacy duty, derechos de herencia.
legal ['ligəl] *a.* 1. legal, jurídico. 2. lícito, legítimo. 3. de la profesión legal. 4. dispuesto por ley. —*s.* (fin.) valor de inversión legal.
legal adviser, abogado consultor, asesor legal, consultor jurídico.
legal age, (der.) 1. mayoría de edad. 2. **of l. a.,** mayor de edad.
legal cap, papel de escribir tamaño folio (esp. para abogados).
legal capacity, l. status, (der.) personería, personalidad.
legal fees, honorarios de abogado.
legal holiday, día de fiesta oficial; día feriado legal.
legalism ['ligə,lɪzəm] *s.* rigorismo, estrictez legal o moral.
legalist [-ləst] *s., a.* legalista.
legalistic [,ligə'lɪstɪk] *a.* legalista.
legality [lɪ'gælətɪ] *s.* 1. legalidad; legitimidad. 2. observancia de la ley.
legalization [,ligələ'zeɪʃən, B -laɪ-] *s.* legalización.
legalize ['ligə,laɪz] *v.t.* legalizar, legitimar.
legally [-lɪ] *adv.* legalmente.
legal owner, propietario en derecho.
legal principle, precepto legal, principio o máxima de derecho.
legal reserve, (fin.) reserva legal, reserva estatutaria, encaje legal.
legal separation, (der.) separación legal.
legal status, (der.) estado civil, personalidad legal; personería.
legal tender, moneda legal, moneda de curso legal.
legate ['lɛgət] *s.* 1. legado, enviado papal. 2. legado, embajador, enviado, delegado. 3. (hist. romana) legado (gobernador provincial; asistente militar de un general).
legatee [,lɛgə'ti] *s.* (der.) legatario, asignatario.
legateship ['lɛgət,ʃɪp] *s.* legacía.
legatine ['lɛgə,tin, B -,taɪn] *a.* bajo la dirección de un legado (comisión, etc.); de un legado.
legation [lɪ'geɪʃən] *s.* legación (misión diplomática).
legato [lɪ'gɑtoʊ] *a., adv.* (mús.) ligado.
legator [lɪ'geɪtər, B -ə] *s.* (der.) testador.
legend ['lɛdʒənd] *s.* 1. leyenda (relato de sucesos tradicionales o maravillosos). 2. inscripción, leyenda. 3. (impr.) leyenda, pie de grabado, epígrafe.
legendary [-ən,dɛrɪ, B -dərɪ] *a.* legendario, fabuloso, de leyenda.
legendry [-əndrɪ] *s.* leyendas (colectivamente).
leger ['lɛdʒər, B -ə] *a.* (mús.) **l. lines,** líneas auxiliares del pentagrama; **l. space,** espacio comprendido entre ellas.
legerdemain [,lɛdʒərdə'meɪn, B -ədə-] *s.* 1. juego de manos, prestidigitación. 2. truco artificioso.
legerdemainist [-əst] *s.* prestidigitador.
legged ['lɛgəd, lɛgd] *a.* de patas o piernas (ú. esp. en compuestos, ej., *bandy-legged,* estevado, *three-l.,* de tres patas, *long-l.,* de piernas largas).
legging ['lɛgɪŋ] *s.* (*pr. pl.*), polaina, sobrecalza, escarpín.
leggy ['lɛgɪ] *a.* piernilargo.
leghorn ['lɛg,hɔrn, 'lɛgərn, B -,hɔn] *s.* 1. trenzado de paja toscana. 2. sombrero de paja toscana. 3. [B lɛ'gɔn] (orn.) Leghorn, raza de gallinas.
legibility [,lɛdʒə'bɪlətɪ] *s.* legibilidad.
legible ['lɛdʒəbəl] *a.* legible, descifrable, fácil de leer.
legibly [-blɪ] *adv.* legiblemente.
legion ['lidʒən] *s.* 1. legión (cuerpo de tropa). 2. legión, multitud; sinnúmero. 3. legión cívica de ex-combatientes.
legionary [-dʒə,nɛrɪ, B -nərɪ] *a.* legionario. —*s.* (*pl.* LEGIONARIES) legionario, miembro de una legión.
legionnaire [,lidʒə'nɛr, B -'nɛə] *s.* legionario, esp. miembro de legión cívica de ex-combatientes.
Legionnaires' disease, enfermedad del legionario, legionella.
Legion of Honor, Legión de Honor (sociedad fundada en Francia por Napoleón).
legis. *abrev. de* **legislation,** legislación; **legislative,** legislativo; **legislature,** legislatura.
legislate ['lɛdʒəs,leɪt] *v.i.* legislar, hacer leyes. —*v.t.* crear o disponer por ley.
legislation [,lɛdʒəs'leɪʃən] *s.* legislación.
legislative ['lɛdʒəs,leɪtɪv, B -lətɪv] *a.* legislativo. —*s.* poder o cuerpo legislativo.
legislatively [-lɪ] *adv.* de modo legislativo, legislativamente.
legislator [-,leɪtər, B -ə] *s.* legislador.
legislatorial [,lɛdʒəslə'tɔrɪəl] *a.* legislador, legislativo.
legislature ['lɛdʒəs,leɪtʃər, B -tʃə] *s.* poder legislativo; cuerpo legislativo, legislatura.
legist ['lidʒəst] *s.* legista, jurisconsulto.
legit [lɪ'dʒit] *a.* (jer.) *abrev. de* **legitimate,** legítimo.
legitimacy [-'dʒɪtəməsɪ] *s.* legitimidad.
legitimate [-mət] *a.* 1. legítimo (hijo, etc.). 2. legítimo, auténtico, genuino. 3. legítimo, legal, lícito. 4. válido, cierto, ej., *l. reasoning,* razonamiento válido o cierto. — [-meɪt] *v.t.* 1. legitimar (a un hijo). 2. legitimar, justificar, aprobar. 3. legitimar, autorizar.
legitimate drama, drama serio o clásico.
legitimately [-lɪ] *adv.* legítimamente.
legitimate stage, (teat.) las tablas, el teatro (a distinción del cine, vodevil, etc.).
legitimation [lɪ,dʒɪtə'meɪʃən] *s.* legitimación.
legitimatize [-'dʒɪtəmə,taɪz] *v.t.* legitimar.
legitimism [-,mɪzəm] *s.* (pol.) legitimismo.
legitimist [-məst] *a., s.* (pol.) legitimista.
legitimistic [-,dʒɪtə'mɪstɪk] *a.* (pol.) legitimista.

legitimization [-ˌdʒɪtəmə'zeɪʃən, B -maɪ-] *s.* legitimación.
legitimize [-'dʒɪtəˌmaɪz] *v.t.* legitimar.
leglen ['lɛglən] *s.* (esco.) balde para leche.
legless ['lɛgləs] *a.* sin pierna o piernas; sin patas.
legman [-ˌmæn, B -mən] *s.* 1. redactor de calle, recolector de noticias (para periódico). 2. asistente, mandadero.
leg of mutton, (cocina) pernil de carnero, pierna de carnero.
leg-of-mutton sail [-ə'mʌtən-] (mar.) vela triangular.
leg-of-mutton sleeve, (cost.) manga de jamón, manga afollada o de pernil.
legroom [-ˌrum, -ˌrʊm] *s.* espacio para las piernas (en un auto, etc.).
leg stump, (criquet) estaca de la derecha.
legume ['lɛgˌjum, lɪ'gjum, B 'lɛgjum] *s.* 1. legumbre, hortaliza, verdura. 2. planta leguminosa, esp. planta forrajera. 3. (bot.) legumbre.
legumin [lɪ'gjumən] *s.* (quím.) legúmina.
leguminous [lɪ'gjumənəs] *a.* leguminoso.
leg work, trabajo callejero; **to do the l.**, hacer los preparativos.
lehua [leɪ'huə, B lɪ-] *s.* lehua, mirto de Hawai.
lei [leɪ, 'leɪˌi, B -ˌi] *s.* guirnalda hawaiana, corona de flores.
leishmaniasis [ˌliʃmə'naɪəsəs] *s.* (med.) leishmaniasis, leishmaniosis.
leister ['listər, B -stə] *s.* arpón de tres dientes. —*v.t.* trinchar (pez) con arpón, arponear.
leisure ['liʒər, 'lɛz-, B 'lɛʒə] *s.* ocio, tiempo libre, ratos de ocio; **at l.**, desocupado; cómodamente, sin prisa; en ratos de ocio; **at one's l.**, cuando quiera uno, cuando uno tiene tiempo; a la comodidad o conveniencia de uno. —*a.* desocupado, libre, de ocio, ej., *l. hours, l. time,* horas libres, horas de ocio, ratos perdidos.
leisured [-ərd, B -əd] *a.* 1. con tiempo libre, desocupado; inactivo, ocioso. 2. sosegado, sereno. 3. pausado, deliberado.
leisureliness [-ərlɪnəs, B -əlɪ-] *s.* falta de prisa, comodidad (en obrar).
leisurely [-lɪ] *a.* pausado, cómodo. —*adv.* despacio, pausadamente; holgadamente.
leitmotif, leitmotiv ['laɪtmoʊˌtif] *s.* 1. (mús.) leitmotivo. 2. (fig.) tema o motivo principal.
leman ['lɛmən, 'lim-, B 'lɛm-] *s.* (ant.) enamorado, amante, esp. querida.
lemma ['lɛmə] *s.* 1. (*pl.* LEMMAS O LEMMATA [-tə]) lema; premisa; base. 2. (bot.) lemma, lema.
lemming ['lɛmɪŋ] *s.* (zool.) lemming, ratón de Noruega.
lemnaceous [ləm'neɪʃəs] *a.* (bot.) lemnáceo.
lemnad ['lɛmˌnæd] *s.* (bot.) lemnácea.
lemniscate [lɛm'nɪskət] *s.* (geom.) lemniscata.
lemniscus [-kəs] *s.* (*pl.* LEMNISCI [-'nɪsˌaɪ]) (anat.) lemnisco.
lemon ['lɛmən] *s.* 1. limón. 2. (bot.) limonero, (árbol del) limón. 3. color de limón, color cetrino. 4. (jer., E.U.) persona o cosa inútil, maula; aparato en malas condiciones, cacharro (esp. un automóvil). 5. (jer., G.B.) bagre, mujer fea. 6. **to hand (someone) a l.**, (jer.) hacer o dar (a alguien) algo desagradable (ej., un deber o trabajo). —*a.* 1. limonado, cetrino. 2. de limón.
lemonade [ˌlɛmə'neɪd] *s.* limonada.
lemon balm, (bot.) toronjil, abejera, melisa.
lemon drop, pastilla o confite de limón.
lemon geranium, (bot.) pelargonio o geranio de hojas (de olor semejante al del limonero).
lemon plant, (bot.) luisa, hierba luisa, yerbaluisa (Amer.).
lemon squash, jugo de limón; limonada.
lemon squeezer, exprimidor de limón.
lemon verbena, (bot.) luisa, hierba luisa, yerbaluisa (Amer.).
lemon yellow, color limón, amarillo limón.
Lemosi [ˌlɛmə'zi] *s.* (filol.) lemosín, lengua de oc, de la Provenza (Francia).
lemur ['limər, B -mə] *s.* (*pl.* LEMURS) (zool.) lémur, lemúrido, maqui, maki.
lemures ['lɛməˌreɪs, B -jʊˌriz] *s. pl.* (mitol.) lémures, espíritus de los muertos.
lemuroid ['lɛmjəˌrɔɪd] *a.* (zool.) lemúrido.
lend [lɛnd] *v.t.* (*pret., p.p.* LENT [lɛnt] *p.pr.* LENDING) 1. prestar (objetos, dinero, etc.). 2. dar, proveer, proporcionar. 3. **l. a hand, l. a helping hand,** ayudar, dar una mano, arrimar el hombro; **l. an ear,** dar oídos, prestar atención; **l. dignity,** añadir o dar dignidad; **l. itself (oneself) to,** prestarse a. —*v.i.* dar préstamos, prestar dinero.
lender ['lɛndər, B -ə] *s.* prestador; prestamista.
lending [-ɪŋ] *s.* otorgamiento de un préstamo.
lending library, biblioteca de préstamo a domicilio, biblioteca circulante.
lend-lease [-'lis] *s.* préstamo y arriendo. —*v.t.* dar en préstamo y arriendo.
Lend-Lease Act, (pol.) ley de préstamo y arriendo.
lene ['lini] *var. de* **lenis.**
length [lɛŋθ, lɛŋkθ] *s.* 1. longitud, largo, largura, extensión. 2. lapso, período, duración. 3. pieza, trozo, tramo, ej., *a l. of pipe,* un trozo de tubo. 4. (fon.) duración o cantidad (de una vocal o consonante). 5. (dep.) largo, cuerpo, ej., *the horse won by three lengths,* el caballo ganó por tres cuerpos, *the boat lost by one length,* el bote perdió por un largo. 6. **at arm's l.,** a prudente distancia; **at full l.,** a todo lo largo; sin ninguna omisión; **at great l.,** con muchos detalles, muy detalladamente; **at l.,** detalladamente, completamente; al fin; **to carry to (foolish, dangerous,** etc.) **lengths,** llevar a extremos (imprudentes, peligrosos, etc.); **to go (to) all (any) lengths,** darse al máximo, no escatimar esfuerzos, hacer todo lo posible; **to go (to) the l. of (doing),** llegar al extremo de (hacer); **to keep at arm's l.,** mantener a distancia, no dar confianza a.
lengthen ['lɛŋθən, 'lɛŋk-] *v.t., v.i.* alargar(se), estirar(se); prolongar(se).
lengthening [-ɪŋ] *s.* alargamiento, prolongación, extensión.
lengthening bar, l. tube, alargadera (de compás, retorta, etc.).
lengthily [-θəlɪ] *adv.* dilatadamente, prolijamente, prolongadamente.
lengthiness [-θɪnəs] *s.* prolijidad.
lengthways ['lɛŋθˌweɪz, 'lɛŋkθ-] *adv.* longitudinalmente, a lo largo, de largo a largo.
lengthwise [-ˌwaɪz] *adv.* longitudinalmente. —*a.* longitudinal.
lengthy ['lɛŋθɪ, 'lɛŋk-] *a.* (LENGTHIER; LENGTHIEST) 1. largo. 2. prolongado, dilatado, prolijo.
leniency ['linɪənsɪ, -njən-] **lenience** [-nɪəns, -njəns] *s.* lenidad, indulgencia, suavidad.
lenient [-nɪənt, -njənt] *a.* indulgente, clemente, misericordioso.
leniently [-lɪ] *adv.* indulgentemente, misericordiosamente.
Leninism ['lɛnəˌnɪzəm] *s.* (pol.) leninismo, el pensamiento y las doctrinas de Lenín.
Leninist [-nəst] **Leninite** [-ˌnaɪt] *s., a.* (pol.) leninista.
lenis ['linəs, 'leɪ-] *a.* (fon.) no aspirada, suave. —*s.* consonante no aspirada.
lenitive ['lɛnətɪv] *a.* lenitivo. —*s.* 1. (ant. med.) lenitivo. 2. (fig.) lenitivo, paliativo.
lenity [-ətɪ] *s.* lenidad, indulgencia, suavidad.
lens [lɛnz] *s.* (*pl.* LENSES) 1. lente, lupa, cristal (de gafa) 2. (anat., zool.) cristalino del ojo. 3. **contact lenses,** lentes de contacto.
lensman ['lɛnzmən] *s.* (jer.) fotógrafo.
Lent [lɛnt] *s.* (relig.) cuaresma, cuadragésima.
lent, *pret., p.p. de* **lend.**
Lenten ['lɛntən] *a.* 1. cuaresmal, de vigilia. 2. (fig.) parco, escaso, magro.
Lenten fare, vigilia, colación sin carne.
Lenten season, cuaresma.
lentic ['lɛntɪk] *a.* (biol., geol.) léntico.
lenticel ['lɛntəˌsɛl] *s.* (bot.) lenticela.
lenticular [lɛn'tɪkjələr, B -lə] **lentiform** ['lɛntəˌfɔrm, B -ˌfɔm] *a.* lenticular.
lenticulate [-lət, B -ˌleɪt] *v.t.* (foto.) cubrir con corpúsculos de color o reflectantes (película).
lenticule ['lɛntəˌkjul] *s.* (foto.) corpúsculo de color (en película a colores); corpúsculo reflectante (en película estereoscópica).
lentiginous [lɛn'tɪdʒənəs] *a.* 1. pecoso; casposo. 2. (bot.) lentiginoso.
lentil ['lɛntəl] *s.* (bot.) lenteja (planta y semilla).
lentisc, lentisk ['lɛntɪsk] **lentiscus** [lɛn'tɪskəs] *s.* (bot.) lentisco.
lento ['lɛntoʊ] *a.* (mús.) lento. —*adv.* lentamente.
lentoid ['lɛnˌtɔɪd] *a.* lentiforme.
Leo ['lioʊ] *s.* (astr., astrol.) Leo, León.
Leonardesque [ˌliəˌnɑr'dɛsk, ˌleɪ-, B ˌliəˌnɑ'-] *a.* al estilo de Leonardo da Vinci.
Leonese [ˌliə'niz] *a.* leonés, de León, España. —*s.* (*pl.* LEONESE) leonés, leonesa.
Leonid ['liənəd] *s.* (*pl.* LEONIDS O LEONIDES [li'ɑnəˌdiz, B -'ɔn-]) (astr.) leónida.
leonine ['liəˌnaɪn] *a.* leonino; (der.) leonino (contrato).
leontiasis [ˌliən'taɪəsəs] *s.* (med.) leonina (lepra).
leopard ['lɛpərd, B -əd] *s.* 1. (zool.) leopardo, pardal, pantera. 2. **can the l. change his spots?** ¿puede acaso enderezarse el árbol torcido?
leopardess [-əs] *s.* leopardo hembra.
leopard frog, (zool.) rana leopardo.
leopard's bane, (bot.) dorónico.
leotard ['liəˌtɑrd, B -ˌtɑd] *s.* malla de acróbatas y bailarines.
lepadid ['lɛpədəd] *s.* (zool.) lápade.
leper ['lɛpər, B -ə] *s.* leproso, lazarino.
lepidodendron [ˌlɛpɪdə'dɛndrən] *s.* (pal.) lepidodendro.
lepidolite [lɪ'pɪdəˌlaɪt] *s.* (min.) lepidolita.
lepidopteran [ˌlɛpə'dɑptərən, B -'dɔp-] *a.* lepidóptero.
lepidopterist [-əst] *s.* especialista en lepidópteros.
lepidosiren [ˌlɛpədoʊ'saɪrən] *s.* (ict.) lepidosirena.
leporid ['lɛpərɪd] *a., s.* (zool.) lepórido.
leporine ['lɛpəˌraɪn] *a.* leporino, lebruno.
leprechaun ['lɛprəˌkɔn, -ˌkɑn, B -ˌkɔn] *s.* (Irl.) duende, gnomo, nomo.
leprosarium [ˌlɛprə'sɛrɪəm, B -'sɛər-] *s.* leprosería, lazareto.
leprose ['lɛpˌroʊs] *a.* (bot., zool.) escamoso.
leprosy ['lɛprəsɪ] *s.* (med.) lepra.
leprous [-rəs] *a.* 1. leproso, lazarino. 2. léprico. 3. escamoso.
leptorrhine ['lɛptəˌraɪn] **leptorrhinian** [ˌlɛptə'rɪnɪən] *a.* (antrop.) leptorrino.
Lepus ['lipəs] *s.* (astr.) Liebre.
les [lɛz] *s.* (jer.) lesbiana.
Lesbian [lɛzbɪən] *a.* 1. lesbio, lesbiano, de Lesbos. 2. **l.**, lesbiano. —*s.* lesbiana, homosexual (mujer).
lesbianism [-ˌɪzəm] *s.* lesbianismo.

lese majesty ['liz'mædʒəstɪ] (der.) lesa majestad.
lesion ['liʒən] *s.* 1. lesión, herida, daño, perjuicio, detrimento. 2. (med., vet.) lesión.
lespedeza [ˌlɛspə'dizə] *s.* (bot.) trébol de los prados, esp. trébol del Japón.
less [lɛs] *a.* (LESSER; LEAST [list]) 1. menor, ej., *in a lesser degree,* en menor grado. 2. menos, ej., *drink less wine,* bebe menos vino, *l. than five,* menos de cinco. 3. **in l. time,** en menos tiempo; **in l. than no time,** (fam.) en el acto, en un abrir y cerrar de ojos; **no less a person than,** nada menos que. —*adv.* menos, en grado menor; **l. and l.,** de menos en menos, cada vez menos; **l. than,** menos de lo que; (hacer) menos que (otra persona); en menos que, ej., *it cost l. than I expected,* costó menos de lo que yo esperaba, *you eat l. than he does,* Ud. come menos que él, *I appreciate his astuteness l. than his honesty,* aprecio su astucia menos que su honradez; **more or l.,** más o menos; **none the l.,** no obstante, sin embargo; **the l., the better,** mientras menos mejor. —*s.* 1. menos, ej., *eat less,* come menos. 2. (el) menor, ej., *of two evils choose the l.,* escoge de dos males el menor. 3. **little l. than,** no menos que, poco menos que, casi; **nothing l.,** nada menos; **to take l.,** aceptar o tomar menos. —*prep.* menos, ej., *a month l. four days,* un mes menos cuatro días.
lessee [lɛ'si] *s.* (der.) arrendatario, inquilino, rentero.
lessen ['lɛsən] *v.i.* disminuir (se), decrecer, mermar. —*v.t.* disminuir, reducir, aminorar, achicar, mermar.
lesser ['lɛsər, B -ə] *a.* menor, más pequeño, inferior; **the l. of two evils,** el menor de (entre) dos males.
Lesser Bear, (astr.) Osa Menor.
lesser celandine, (bot.) celidonia menor.
Lesser Dog, (astr.) Can Menor.
lesser duckweed, (bot.) lenteja acuática.
lesser egret, (orn.) garceta.
lesser prophets, profetas menores.
lesser spearwort, (bot.) flámula.
lesson ['lɛsən] *s.* 1. lección, enseñanza. 2. clase, instrucción. 3. tarea, ejercicio, lección. 4. reprimenda, escarmiento, advertencia, amonestación, sermón. 5. **let this be a l. to you,** que te sirva (esto) de lección; **to give lessons in,** dar clases de, enseñar; **to take lessons in,** tomar clases de, aprender; **to teach (someone) a l.,** darle (a uno) una lección. —*v.t.* 1. aleccionar, dar lecciones a. 2. enseñar, amonestar; castigar, reprender.
lessor ['lɛsˌɔr, lɛ'sɔr, B -'sɔ] *s.* (der.) locador, arrendador, arrendante, alquilador.
lest [lɛst] *conj.* no sea que; para que no, por miedo de.
let [lɛt] *v.t.* (*pret., p.p.* LETTED; *p.pr.* LETTING) (ant.) obstruir, impedir, prevenir. —s. 1. (ant.) retardo, obstáculo, impedimento, (ú. en) **without l. or hindrance,** sin estorbo ni obstáculo. 2. (tenis) let (servicio correcto que rozó la red o rebotó en algún obstáculo).
let [lɛt] *v.t.* (*pret., p.p.* LET; *p.pr.* LETTING) 1. alquilar. 2. dar, asignar. 3. permitir, dejar, conceder; no impedir, tolerar, ej., *we l. them go,* les dejamos ir, *I was l. see her,* se me permitió verla. 4. dejar escapar, sacar, ej., *l. blood,* sacar sangre, sangrar. 5. (ant.) abandonar, dejar a (algo o alguien); *en uso moderno se emplea sólo con* **alone** *o* **be,** ej., *l. one alone, l. one be,* dejar en paz a uno, no molestar a uno. 6. (ant.) mandar hacer; *en uso moderno ocurre sólo en:* **l. one know,** hacer saber (a uno), informar o avisar a uno. 7. **l. alone,** menos aún; **l. (one) alone to (do),** confiar en (uno) para que (haga); **l. by,** dejar pasar; **l. bygones be bygones,** olvidar lo pasado; **l. down,** bajar; no cumplir con, decepcionar; **l. (one) down gently,** no humillar (a uno) de golpe; **l. fall,** dejar caer, soltar (una indirecta, palabra); **l. fly,** (fam.) soltar, disparar; **l. go,** soltar, liberar; **l. in,** dejar entrar, admitir; embutir, incrustar, taracear; **l. in for,** poner en (dificultades), exponer (algo) a (pérdida); **l. into,** embutir; iniciar en (un secreto, etc.); **l. it go at that,** conformarse con eso, no hacer o decir más; **l. loose,** desencadenar, desenfrenar (animal); soltar (ira, imprecación, etc.); **l. off,** disparar (arma); dejar escapar (fluido); perdonar; **l. off with,** castigar, sancionar con pena menor de la merecida o esperada; **l. on,** (jer.) dejar saber, revelar, soplar (fig.); **l. oneself go,** soltarse, desatarse, entusiasmarse; **l. oneself in,** entrar en la casa, abrir la puerta; **l. out,** dejar salir, poner en libertad; revelar, divulgar (secreto, noticia); ensanchar (vestido, prenda); alquilar (esp. a varios inquilinos); **l. out a shout,** pegar un grito; **l. slip,** dejar escapar, perder (oportunidad); **l. the cat out of the bag,** revelar el secreto; **l. through,** dejar pasar, dejar pasar por; **l. up,** (fam.) cesar; disminuir la tensión; **l. well enough alone,** dejar las cosas como están, dejarlas en paz. —*v.i.* 1. ser alquilado; alquilarse por, producir renta (de alquiler), ej., *to l.,* para alquilar; **to l.,** se alquila. **2. l. go,** desasirse, soltarse; **l. go of,** soltar; **l. into,** arremeter contra (alguien); **l. out,** lanzar un golpe, vociferar, vituperar; **l. up,** (fam.) cesar, desistir, disminuir, perder fuerza o severidad; **l. up on,** largar, aflojar. —*v. aux. ú. para formar las primeras y terceras personas del imperativo,* ej., *l. us play,* juguemos, *l. him read it,* (que) lo lea él; *l. A be equal to B,* supongamos que A sea igual a B.
letdown ['lɛtˌdaʊn, B -'daʊn] *s.* 1. disminución, aminoramiento. 2. (fam.) chasco, desilusión, frustración, disgusto. 3. (aer.) descenso.
lethal ['liθəl] *a.* letal, mortal, mortífero.
lethal gene, (biol.) gene letal.
lethargic [lɪ'θɑrdʒɪk, lɛ-, B -'θɑdʒɪk] **lethargical** [-ɪkəl] *s.* letárgico, apático, soñoliento.
lethargically [-ɪkəlɪ] *adv.* letárgicamente.
lethargize ['lɛθərˌdʒaɪz, B -əˌ-] *v.t.* (ant.) aletargar.
lethargy [-dʒɪ] *s.* letargo; inacción, apatía.
Lethe ['liθɪ] *s.* 1. (mitol.) Lete, Leteo (río del olvido). 2. **l.,** (fig.) olvido.
lethiferous [lɪ'θɪfərəs] *a.* (ant.) letal, mortal, mortífero, destructor.
let-out ['lɛtˌaʊt] *s.* (jer.) excusa plausible, escape (de una situación incómoda).
let's [lɛts] *contr. de* **let us.**
Lett [lɛt] *a., s.* letón (de Letonia o Latvia).
letter ['lɛtər, B -ə] *s.* 1. letra (del alfabeto). 2. (impr.) letra, tipo, carácter. 3. carta, epístola, misiva. 4. (*pr. pl.*) letras, literatura. 5. **a man of letters,** literato, letrado; **l. of the law,** letra de la ley, texto literal de la ley; **to the l.,** al pie de la letra. —*v.t.* estampar con letras; rotular, poner letras, título o letreros a.
letter, *s.* alquilador, el que alquila.
letter bomb, carta bomba.
letter book, (com.) (libro) copiador.
letter box, buzón, apartado o casilla (de correo).
letter carrier, (E.U.) cartero.
letter-case [-ˌkeɪs] *s.* cartera, carpeta.
letter drop, buzón (abertura por la que se echan las cartas).
lettered [-ərd, B -əd] *a.* 1. educado, instruido. 2. letrado, docto, erudito. 3. grabado, estampado con letras; 1. **in gold,** arcado con letras doradas.
letter file, clasificador, carpeta, archivo.
letterhead [-ərˌhɛd, B -əˌ-] *s.* 1. membrete. 2. (hoja de) papel membretado.
lettering [-ərɪŋ] *s.* 1. letrero, inscripción, leyenda, rótulo. 2. acción de poner letras o letreros.
letter-lock [-ərˌlɑk, B -əˌlɔk] *s.* candado de combinación.
letter of advice, (com.) notificación (ej., del consignador al consignatario).
letter of attorney, (carta de) poder, procuración.
letter of authorization, carta de autorización.
letter of commission, (der.) carta de comisión.
letter of credit, (com.) carta de crédito.
letter of introduction, carta de presentación o recomendación.
letter of license, carta de espera o moratoria.
letter of marque ['lɛtərəv'mɑrk, B -'mɑk] (mar.) carta de marca, patente de corso.
letter of marque and reprisal, (mar.) carta de contramarca.
letter opener, abrecartas.
letter paper, papel de cartas.
letter-perfect ['lɛtər'pɜrfɪkt, B -ə'pɜfɪkt] *a.* 1. exactísimo, letra por letra. 2. al dedillo.
letter press, prensa de copiar cartas.
letterpress [-ˌprɛs] *s.* 1. impresión tipográfica, impreso. 2. texto (a distinción de las ilustraciones). —*a.* hecho con tipos (a distinción de hecho con planchas o litografía).
letterpress printing, impresión con tipos.
letter scale, pesacartas.
letters patent, (der.) cédula o patente de privilegio, ejecutoria de nobleza.
letters requisitorial, (der.) exhorto.
letters rogatory, (der.) rogatoria.
letters testamentary, (der.) auto de authorización de albacea, carta testamentaria.
letter writer, 1. memorialista, escritor de cartas por oficio. 2. libro que contiene modelos de cartas, guía epistolar.
Lettic ['lɛtɪk] *a., s.* letón, letona (de Letonia o Latvia, U.R.S.S.).
Lettish [-ɪʃ] *a.* letón. —*s.* (idioma) letón.
lettre de cachet [ˌlɛtrədəkæ'ʃeɪ] (fr.) carta real sellada, decreto para arrestar a una persona sin proceso jurídico.
lettuce ['lɛtəs] *s.* 1. lechuga. 2. (jer.) dinero (en billetes).
lettuce opium, (farm.) lactucario, tridacio.
letup ['lɛtˌʌp] *s.* (fam.) diminución, cesación, interrupción; calma, descanso; **it rained without l.,** llovió sin cesar.
leu ['lɛʊ, B 'lɛʊ] *s.* (*pl.* LEI [leɪ]) leu (unidad monetaria de Rumania).
leucine ['luˌsin, -sɪn, B 'lju-] *s.* (bioquím.) leucina.
leucite [-ˌsaɪt] *s.* (min.) leucita.
leucocyte, *var. de* **leukocyte.**
leucocythemia [ˌlukəsaɪ'θimɪə, B ˌlju-] *s.* (med.) leucocitemia.
leucocytosis *var. de* **leukocytosis.**
leucoma [lu'koʊmə, B lju-] *s.* (med.) leucoma.
leucomaine ['lukəˌmaɪn, B lju'koʊməˌin] *s.* (bioquím.) leucomaína.
leucoplast ['lukəˌplæst, B 'ljukəˌplɑst] *s.* (bot.) leucoplasto.
leucoplastid [ˌlukə'plæstəd, B ˌljukə'plɑs-] *s.* (bot.) leucoplasto.
leud [lud, B ljud] *s.* (*pl.* LEUDS O LEUDES ['luˌdiz, B 'lju-]) (hist.) leude, siervo, vasallo feudal.
leukemia [lu'kimɪə, B lju-] *s.* (med.) leucemia.
leukocyte ['lukəˌsaɪt, B 'lju-] *s.* (fisiol.) leucocito.
leukocytic [ˌlukə'sɪtɪk, B ˌlju-] *a.* (fisiol.) leucocítico.

leukocytoblast [-'saɪtəˌblæst] *s.* (fisiol.) leucocitoblasto.
leukocytoid [-'saɪtˌɔɪd] *a.* leucocitoide.
leukocytosis [-ˌsaɪ'toʊsəs] *s.* (med.) leucocitosis.
leukoma, *var. de* **leucoma.**
leukopenia [-'pinɪə] *s.* (med.) leucopenia.
leukopoiesis [-ˌpɔɪ'isəs] *s.* (fisiol.) leucopoyesia.
leukopoietic [-'ɛtɪk] *a.* (fisiol.) leucopoyético.
leukorrhea [ˌlukə'riə, B ˌlju-] *s.* (med.) leucorrea.
leukosis [lu'koʊsəs, B lju-] *s.* (med.) leucemia, leucocitemia.
lev [lɛf] *s.* (*pl.* LEVA ['lɛvə]) lev (unidad monetaria de Bulgaria).
Lev. *abrev. de* **Leviticus,** Levítico (Lev.).
levant [lɪ'vænt] *s.* 1. **L.,** Levante. 2. levante, viento de Levante. 3. marroquín, tafilete. —*v.i.* (pr. G.B.) irse o desaparecer sin pagar su deuda.
Levanter [-ər, B -ə] *s.* 1. levante, viento de Levante. 2. levantino.
Levantine ['lɛvənˌtaɪn, -ˌtin] *a.* levantino. —*s.* 1. levantino (natural de uno de los países del Levante). 2. levantina (fuerte sarga de seda, originalmente manufacturada en el Oriente).
levant morocco, marroquí o tafilete de Levante.
levator [lɪ'veɪtər, B -ə] *s.* (anat.) elevador, levátor.
levee ['lɛvɪ] *s.* 1. (E.U.) malecón, dique (para prevenir inundaciones), muelle. 2. ribero, bordo (reparo de tierra para represar las aguas).
levee ['lɛvɪ, lə'vi, B 'lɛvɪ] *s.* 1. recepción matutina. 2. (G.B., Irl.) recepción real para hombres. 3. (E.U.) recepción, besamanos.
level ['lɛvəl] *s.* 1. nivel (instrumento). 2. nivel, altura. 3. grado, rango, categoría, posición (social, moral, intelectual, etc.). 4. llano, llanura, plano, ras. 5. **on a l. with,** del mismo nivel que, en la misma altura con; **on the l.,** (jer.) recto, honrado, sincero, serio, genuino; honradamente, de veras, sinceramente; **to find one's l.,** alcanzar u ocupar la posición que corresponde a uno. —*a.* 1. a nivel. 2. horizontal. 3. llano, plano. 4. igual (en rango, posición); parejo, a la par (con otro), igual, uniforme (en calidad, tono, estilo, importancia). 5. lleno a ras, raso, ej., *a l. teaspoon of,* una cucharadita rasa de (azúcar, sal, etc.). 6. (fam.) sereno. 7. (fís.) de nivel; equipotencial. 8. **to be l. with,** estar al nivel de, estar a ras o a flor de; **to do one's l. best,** realizar el máximo esfuerzo. —*v.t.* (*pret., p.p.* LEVELED O LEVELLED; *p.pr.* LEVELING O LEVELLING) 1. NIVELAR, IGUALAR, ALLANAR. 2. ASESTAR, APUNTAR (ARMA). 3. IGUALAR (EN CATEGORÍA, PRIVILEGIOS O DISTINCIONES). 4. AJUSTAR. 5. ARRASAR; DERRIBAR, ECHAR POR TIERRA. 6. EMPAREJAR (UN COLOR); ENRASAR. 7. (TOP.) DESLINDAR O MEDIR (TIERRAS), DEMARCAR (CON UN NIVEL DE AGRIMENSOR). 8. **l. down (up),** igualar a un nivel más bajo (alto). —*v.i.* 1. nivelarse. 2. emparejarse (colores). 3. **l. off,** (aer.) nivelarse para aterrizar. —*adv.* igualmente, llanamente; a nivel, a ras; en derechura.
level crossing, (G.B., f.c.) paso a nivel, cruce a nivel.
leveler [-ər, B -ə] *s.* 1. nivelador, igualador. 2. allanador, aplanador, aplanadera. 3. partidario de la igualdad (social).
level gage, indicador de nivel.
levelheaded [-'hɛdəd] *a.* sensato, juicioso. discreto, de buen sentido.
leveling [ɪŋ] *s.* nivelación, igualación. —*a.* nivelador, allanador.
leveling rod, l. staff, (top.) jalón, mira de nivelar.
leveling screws, tornillos niveladores.
leveller, (pr. G.B.) *var. de* **leveler.**
levelly ['lɛvəlɪ] *adv.* lisamente, llanamente.
levelness [-əlnəs] *s.* 1. igualdad, llanura. 2. uniformidad, lisura. 3. horizontalidad.
lever ['lɛvər, 'livər, B -və] *s.* 1. palanca, alzaprima, mangueta. 2. palanca de acción (en un arma de fuego portátil). 3. (mec.) palanca, barra, manubrio. —*v.t.* apalancar, levantar con palanca, palanquear (Am.).
leverage [-ərɪdʒ] *s.* 1. sistema de palancas. 2. apalancamiento; fuerza o ventaja mecánica. 3. (fig.) poder, eficacia, influencia, medios.
leveret ['lɛvərət] *s.* lebrato, liebre joven.
leviable ['ləvɪəbəl] *a.* exigible, recaudable, sujeto a impuestos, imponible (impuesto, tasa o castigo).
leviathan [lɪ'vaɪəθən] *s.* 1. **L.,** (bíbl.) Leviatán. 2. transatlántico grande. 3. (fig.) gigante, monstruo.
levier ['lɛvɪər, B -ə] *s.* imponedor (de contribuciones, etc.).
levigate ['lɛvəˌgeɪt] *v.t.* 1. levigar. 2. pulverizar. 3. pulir, pulimentar.
levigation [ˌlɛvə'geɪʃən] *s.* 1. levigación. 2. pulverización. 3. pulimiento.
levirate ['lɛvərət, B 'livə-] *s.* (hist.) levirato.
Levis['liˌvaɪz] *s.* (E.U.) (marca registrada) pantalones vaqueros, pantalones de mecánico (de dril azul).
levitate ['lɛvəˌteɪt] *v.i.* elevarse y flotar (en el aire) sin medios físicos, con el solo poder de la mente. —*v.t.* elevar y mantener flotando (en el aire).
levitation [ˌlɛvə'teɪʃən] *s.* levitación, suspensión o elevación sin medios físicos.
Levite ['liˌvaɪt] *s.* (bíbl.) levita.
Levitical [lɪ'vɪtɪkəl] *a.* (bíbl.) levítico.
Leviticus [-kəs] *s.* (bíbl.) Levítico.
levity ['lɛvətɪ] *s.* 1. frivolidad, futilidad, ligereza, falta de seriedad; inconstancia, veleidad. 2. ligereza, flotabilidad.
levoglucosan [ˌlivə'glukəˌsæn] *s.* (quím.) levoglucosa.
levogyrous [ˌlivə'dʒaɪrəs] **levogyrate** [-ˌreɪt] *a.* (fís., quím.) levógiro.
levorotation [ˌlivəˌroʊteɪʃən] *s.* (fís., quím.) levorrotación.
levorotatory [-'roʊtəˌtɔrɪ, B -tərɪ] *a.* (fís., quím.) levorrotatorio, levógiro.
levulin ['lɛvjʊlɪn] *s.* (quím.) levulina.
levulose [-ˌloʊs] *s.* (quím.) levulosa.
levy ['lɛvɪ] *s.* (*pl.* LEVIES) 1. recaudación (de impuestos); tasación, avalúo; imposición (de contribuciones). 2. suma recaudada. 3. embargo, ejecución. 4. leva, enganche, recluta, reclutamiento. 5. ejército reclutado. —*v.t.* (*pret., p.p.* LEVIED; *p.pr.* LEVYING) 1. recaudar, imponer impuesto. 2. reclutar, enganchar. 3. emprender, sostener, librar (guerra). 4. (der.) embargar, ejecutar, gravar. 5. **l. a fine,** (der.) transigir en un litigio por tierras.
levy en masse [-ɛn'mæs, -ɑn-, B -ɑŋ-] (der. internacional) movilización general y espontánea del pueblo ante la amenaza enemiga.
lewd [lud, B ljud] *a.* 1. lujurioso, sensual, lascivo, libidinoso. 2. (ant.) malvado, depravado; despreciable; ruin, vil.
lewdly ['ludlɪ, B 'ljud-] *adv.* lascivamente, sensualmente.
lewdness [-nəs] *s.* lascivia, lujuria, libertinaje.
lewis ['luəs] *s.* castañuela de cantera, loba de tres piezas (para levantar sillares).
Lewis gun, metralleta.
lewisite ['luəˌsaɪt] *s.* (mil.) lewisita.
lex [lɛks] *s.* (*pl.* LEGES ['leɪgeɪs]) ley.
lex. *abrev. de* **lexicon,** lexicón, diccionario.
lexical ['lɛksɪkəl] *a.* 1. léxico. 2. lexicográfico.
lexical meaning, (filol.) significado semántico del radical.
lexicographer [ˌlɛksə'kɑgrəfər, B -'kɔg-rəfə] *s.* lexicógrafo.
lexicographic [-koʊ'græfɪk] **lexicographical** [-ɪkəl] *a.* lexicográfico.
lexicography [-'kɑgrəfɪ, B -kɔg-] *s.* lexicografía.
lexicologic [-kə'lɑdʒɪk, B -'lɔdʒ-] **lexicological** [-ɪkəl] *a.* lexicológico.
lexicologist [-'kɑlədʒəst, B -'kɔl-] *s.* lexicólogo.
lexicology [-dʒɪ] *s.* lexicología.
lexicon ['lɛksɪkən, -səˌkɑn, B -kən] *s.* (*pl.* LEXICONS O LEXICA [-kə]) lexicón, diccionario; léxico, vocabulario.
Leyden jar ['laɪdən-, B 'leɪd-] (elec.) botella de Leyden o Leiden.
lf. *abrev. de* 1. (impr.) **lightface,** tipo común. 2. (fís.) **low frequency,** baja frecuencia.
lg. *abrev. de* **large,** grande.
L.H.D. *abrev. de* **Doctor of Humanities,** Doctor en Humanidades.
li [li] *s.* (*sing., pl.*) li (medida itineraria china que equivale a medio kilómetro aproximadamente).
Li *símb. de* **lithium,** litio (Li).
L.I. *abrev. de* **Long Island,** Long Island (en Nueva York).
liability [ˌlaɪə'bɪlətɪ] *s.* (*pl.* LIABILITIES). 1. responsabilidad, obligación (material, legal, etc.); obligación, posibilidad de incurrir en. 2. desventaja, impedimento. 3. riesgo, contingencia. 4. (com., ten.) pasivo. 5. (*pl.*) obligaciones, deudas; (ten.) pasivo.
liability insurance, seguro de (o contra) responsabilidad civil.
liable ['laɪəbəl] *a.* 1. (con *for*) sujeto (a), obligado (a), responsable (de), ej., *he is l. for the debt,* él es responsable de la deuda, *men l. for military service,* hombres obligados a servicio militar. 2. (con *inf.* o la *prep. to*) obligado (a hacer algo); expuesto (a riesgo, peligro, etc.), ej., *the goods are l. to suffer,* las mercaderías están expuestas a sufrir deterioro, *diseases to which man is l.,* enfermedades a las que el hombre está expuesto, *l. to err,* expuesto a errar.
liaise [lɪ'eɪz] *v.i.* (mil., jer.) establecer enlace, servir como oficial de enlace.
liaison ['liəˌzɑn, lɪ'eɪ-, B li'eɪzɔŋ] *s.* 1. vinculación, unión, enlace; coordinación, ej., *close l. between departments,* estrecha coordinación entre departamentos (de una oficina). 2. romance, aventura o relaciones ilícitas. 3. (mil.) enlace. 4. (fon.) unión de una consonante final a la vocal inicial de la palabra siguiente (en la lengua francesa).
liaison officer, (mil.) oficial de enlace.
liana [lɪ'ɑnə, -'ænə, B -'ɑnə] **liane** [-'ɑn, -'æn, B -'ɑn] *s.* (bot.) bejuco, liana.
liar ['laɪər, B -ə] *s.* mentiroso, embustero.
Lias [-əs] *s.* (geol.) lías.
Liassic [laɪ'æsɪk] *a.* (geol.) liásico.
libation [laɪ'beɪʃən] *s.* 1. libación; libamiento. 2. (hum.) potación, bebida, trago.
lib. *abrev. de* **liberal, liberal; liberation,** liberación; **librarian,** bibliotecario; **library,** biblioteca.
libel ['laɪbəl] *s.* 1. (der.) difamacion, calumnia. 2. (ant.) libelo, escrito difamatorio. —*v.t.* (*pret., p.p.* LIBELED O LIBELLED; *p.pr.* LIBELING O LIBELLING) 1. (der.) difamar, calumniar. 2. (fam.) denigrar, detractar, detraer.
libelant, libellant [-ənt] *s.* 1. demandante de una acción por calumnia o difamación. 2. libelista, difamador.

libelee, libellee [ˌlaɪbəˈli] *s.* difamador, calumniador, demandado por difamación.
libeler, libeller [ˈlaɪbələr, B -ə] *s.* difamamador, calumniador.
libelous, libellous [-əs] *a.* difamatorio, infamatorio.
libelously, libellously [-lɪ] *adv.* de modo difamatorio, injuriosamente.
liber [ˈlaɪbər, B -bə] *s.* 1. libro, registro público (esp. de propiedades e hipotecas). 2. (bot.) líber.
liberal [ˈlɪbərəl] *a.* 1. liberal, generoso, munífico, dadivoso. 2. amplio, copioso, abundante. 3. libre, aproximado, no literal (traducción, interpretación, etc.). 4. liberal, tolerante. 5. (pol.) liberal. 6. (ant.) libertino. —*s.* liberal; miembro del partido liberal.
liberal arts, humanidades, letras, artes liberales.
liberal education, educación humanista.
liberalism [ˈlɪbərəˌlɪzəm] *s.* liberalismo.
liberality [ˌlɪbəˈrælətɪ] *s.* 1. liberalidad, generosidad, munificencia. 2. donación generosa. 3. amplitud de criterio, liberalidad.
liberalization [-rələˈzeɪʃən, B -laɪ-] *s.* liberalización.
liberalize [ˈlɪbərəˌlaɪz] *v.t., v.i.* liberalizar(se), hacer(se) liberal.
liberally [-rəlɪ] *adv.* 1. liberalmente, generosamente. 2. ampliamente, abundantemente. 3. libremente, aproximadamente (traducido, interpretado, etc.).
liberal-minded [ˈlɪbərəlˈmaɪndəd] *a.* de ideas liberales; tolerante, de criterio amplio.
liberate [ˈlɪbəˌreɪt] *v.t.* 1. liberar, libertar, manumitir (esclavos, etc.). 2. liberar (país). 3. librar, eximir (de obligaciones, carga, etc.). 4. (quím.) liberar, separar (ej., gases).
liberation [ˌlɪbəˈreɪʃən] *s.* liberación.
liberator [ˈlɪbəˌreɪtər, B -ə] *s.* liberador, libertador, manumisor.
Liberia [laɪˈbɪrɪə, B -ˈbɪər-] *s.* Liberia.
Liberian [-ɪən] *a., s.* liberiano, liberiana.
libertarian [ˌlɪbərˈtɛrɪən, B -əˈtɛər-] *s.* partidario de la tesis del libre albedrío. —*a.* que sostiene la tesis del libre albedrío; libertario; liberal.
libertarianism [-ˌɪzəm] *s.* 1. tesis del libre albedrío. 2. liberalismo.
liberticide [lɪˈbɜrtəˌsaɪd, B -ˈbɜtɪ-] *a.* liberticida.
libertinage [ˈlɪbərˌtinɪdʒ, B -ətɪn-] *s.* libertinaje, desenfreno.
libertine [-ˌtin, B -ˌtaɪn] *s.* 1. libertino, disoluto. 2. (ant.) libertino, liberto. —*a.* libertino, disoluto, licencioso.
libertinism [-ˌɪzəm] *s.* libertinaje, licencia, desenfreno.
liberty [ˈlɪbərtɪ, B -ətɪ] *s.* (*pl.* LIBERTIES) 1. libertad. 2. permiso. 3. libertad, licencia, familiaridad. 4. (*pl.*) privilegios, prerrogativas, derechos. 5. (mar.) licencia, corto permiso. 6. **at l.,** libre, en libertad; desocupado, ocioso; **to be at l. to (do),** ser libre para (hacer), tener permiso para (hacer); **to set at l.,** poner en libertad, liberar, libertar; **to take liberties with,** tomarse o permitirse libertades con, tratar con familiaridad (a alguien); arriesgar (ej., la salud); **to take the l. to (do), to take the l. of (doing),** tomarse la licencia o libertad de (hacer); arriesgarse a (hacer).
Liberty Bell, (E.U.) campana de la libertad que se tocó el 4 de Julio de 1776, día de la independencia, en la ciudad de Filadelfia.
liberty cap, gorro frigio (símbolo de libertad).
liberty of conscience, libertad de credo, libertad de religión, libertad de conciencia.
Liberty Ship, (E.U.) (tipo de) nave transporte (de tropas y pertrechos).
libidinal [lɪˈbɪdənəl] *a.* de la libido, causado por la libido.
libidinous [-ənəs] *a.* libidinoso, lujurioso, lascivo.
libidinously [-lɪ] *adv.* libidinosamente, lujuriosamente, lascivamente.
libidinousness [-nəs] *s.* carácter libidinoso, libidinosidad.
libido [ləˈbidoʊ, -ˈbaɪd-] *s.* 1. libido, libídine. 2. (psic.) libido.
libra [ˈlaɪbrə, ˈli-] *s.* 1. (hist.) libra (unidad de peso en la Roma antigua). 2. (*pl.* LIBRAE [-ˌbri]) **L.,** (astr.) Libra.
librarian [laɪˈbrɛrɪən, B -ˈbrɛər-] *s.* bibliotecario, bibliotecaria.
librarianship [-ˌʃɪp] *s.* empleo o cargo de bibliotecario.
library [ˈlaɪˌbrɛrɪ, B -brərɪ] *s.* (*pl.* LIBRARIES) biblioteca; gabinete.
Library of Congress, (E.U.) Biblioteca del Congreso, una de las colecciones de libros y documentos más importantes del mundo.
library science, biblioteconomía.
librate [ˈlaɪˌbreɪt, B laɪˈbreɪt] *v.i.* balancear, oscilar; equilibrarse, quedar en equilibrio.
libration [laɪˈbreɪʃən] *s.* 1. libración, oscilación. 2. (astr.) libración.
libratory [ˈlaɪbrəˌtɔrɪ, B -tərɪ] *a.* 1. oscilatorio. 2. de libración.
librettist [ləˈbrɛtəst] *s.* (mús.) libretista, el que escribe el guión de una ópera o una composición coral.
libretto [-ˈbrɛtoʊ] *s.* (*pl.* LIBRETTOS O LIBRETTI [-ˌi]) (mús.) libreto.
libriform [ˈlaɪbrəˌfɔrm, B -ˌfɔm] *a.* (bot.) libriforme.
Libya [ˈlɪbɪə] *s.* Libia.
Libyan [-ɪən] *s.* libio (individuo o idioma de Libia). —*a.* líbico, libio.
lice [laɪs] *pl. de* **louse.**
license, licence [ˈlaɪsəns] *s.* 1. licencia, permiso. 2. libertad de acción. 3. licencia, autorización, permiso, matrícula, patente, título. 4. licencia, exceso de libertad, abuso de libertad; libertinaje. 5. licencia, libertad (ej., poética). —*v.t.* licenciar, dar licencia, facultar, autorizar.
licensee, licencee [ˌlaɪsənˈsi] *s.* (der.) concesionario, permisionario, titular de una licencia.
license plate, (aut.) chapa de matrícula (Esp., Urug.), chapa patente (Arg.), patente de automóvil (Chile), placa policíaca (Méx.), placa de inscripción (Perú).
licenser, licensor [ˈlaɪsənsər, B -sə] *s.* (der.) concedente (de la licencia).
licensure [-ʃər, B -ʃə] *s.* licenciamiento (esp. para la práctica de una profesión).
licentiate [laɪˈsɛntʃɪət, B -ˈsɛnʃɪ-] *s.* 1. licenciado, licenciada. 2. licenciatura.
licentious [-tʃəs, B -ˈsɛnʃəs] *a.* licencioso, atrevido; disoluto, libertino; libre (que no se sujeta a las normas establecidas).
licentiously [-lɪ] *adv.* licenciosamente.
licentiousness [-nəs] *s.* licencia, libertinaje, desenfreno, disolución, disipación.
licet [ˈlaɪsɛt] (latín) es permitido; es legal.
lich [lɪtʃ] *s.* (esco., dial.) cadáver, difunto.
lichen [ˈlaɪkən] *s.* (bot., med.) liquen. —*v.t.* cubrir con líquenes.
lichenin [-kənən] *s.* (quím.) liquenina.
lichenology [ˌlaɪkəˈnɑlədʒɪ, B -ˈnɔl-] *s.* (bot.) liquenología.
lichenous [ˈlaɪkənəs] *a.* liquenoso.
lich gate, *var. de* **lych gate.**
licit [ˈlɪsət] *a.* lícito.
licitly [-lɪ] *adv.* lícitamente.
lick [lɪk] *v.t.* 1. lamer. 2. (fam.) cascar, azotar, golpear, aporrear. 3. (fam.) vencer, derrotar (en contienda); superar, sobrepujar, ser más de lo que uno puede entender, ej., *that licks me,* no lo comprendo, me supera. 4. **l. into shape,** moldear; hacer presentable o eficiente; **l. one's chops,** (jer.) relamerse, esperar que suceda algo agradable; contemplar con satisfacción maligna la desgracia ajena; **l. one's lips,** lamerse los labios, relamerse; **l. one's shoes** o **boots,** adular servilmente a uno. —*v.i.* 1. lamer. 2. correr a toda velocidad. —*s.* 1. lamedura. 2. lengüetada. 3. golpe. 4. esfuerzo mínimo. 5. salegar, lamedero. 6. **to give a l. and a promise to,** dar un limpión a, jamerdar; hacer aprisa y mal; arreglar o limpiar superficialmente; **to have a l. and a promise,** lavarse como el gato.
licker [ˈlɪkər, B -ə] *s.* lamedor.
lickerish [ˈlɪkərɪʃ] *a.* 1. goloso, ansioso de placeres. 2. salaz, libidinoso. 3. (ant.) apetitoso, sabroso; exquisito.
lickety-split [ˌlɪkətɪˈsplɪt] *adv.* (jer.) muy rápidamente, rapidísimamente, a gran velocidad.
licking [ˈlɪkɪŋ] *s.* 1. lamedura, lengüetada. 2. (fam.) tunda, paliza. 3. (fam.) derrota. 4. **he took a l.,** recibió una paliza; tuvo un tremendo fracaso.
lickspittle [-ˌspɪtəl] *s.* quitamotas, adulón, parásito servil.
licorice [ˈlɪkərɪʃ, -rəs, B -rɪs] *s.* 1. (bot.) orozuz, regaliz, alcazuz. 2. zumo de orozuz. 3. palo dulce. 4. dulce de regaliz.
licorice root, palo dulce.
lictor [ˈlɪktər, B -tə] *s.* (hist.) lictor.
lid [lɪd] *s.* 1. tapa, tapadera; guardapolvo (de reloj). 2. párpado. 3. (jer.) sombrero, casco. 4. (fam.) sujeción, restricción, refrenamiento, represión. 5. (bot.) opérculo (en los musgos). 6. **to put the l. on,** (G.B., jer.) ser el colmo de; acabar definitivamente con; **with the l. off,** con todos los horrores o miserias al descubierto. —*v.t.* (*pret., p.p.* LIDDED; *p.pr.* LIDDING) tapar; poner tapa a, proveer de tapa.
lidless [ˈlɪdləs] *a.* 1. sin tapa. 2. (fig.) vigilante, despierto.
lido [ˈlidoʊ] *s.* lugar de veraneo, balneario.
lie [laɪ] *s.* 1. mentira, embuste, falsedad, impostura. 2. mentís, desmentida. 3. **to catch (someone) in a l.,** coger o pescar (a alguien) en una mentira; **to give the l. to (belief,** etc.), refutar, demostrar la falsedad de (una creencia, etc.); **to tell a l.,** decir una mentira, mentir. —*v.i.* (*pret., p.p.* LIED; *p.pr* LYING) mentir. —*v.t.* **l. away (reputation,** etc.), arruinar con mentiras (la buena reputación, etc.); **l. oneself out of,** conseguir salvarse de (algo) por una mentira.
lie *v.i.* (*pret.* LAY [leɪ] ; *p.p.* LAIN [leɪn]; *p.pr.* LYING) 1. echarse, tenderse, acostarse. 2. estar, hallarse, encontrarse, estar situado. 3. yacer, estar tendido o acostado; estar enterrado. 4. extenderse, dirigirse (ej., un camino). 5. (con *in*) estribar (en), consistir (en), radicar, residir, ej., *her strength lay in her weakness,* su fuerza consistía (o estaba) en su debilidad. 6. (der.) ser sostenible, ser admisible o ejecutable. 7. (ant.) pernoctar, alojarse, acampar (tropas, ejército). 8. **l. at, l. in,** yacer, estar enterrado en (tal lugar); **l. about,** estar por allí; estar esparcido; **l. by,** descansar; estar en desuso; mantenerse en reposo; estar cerca o a mano; **l. down,** echarse, acostarse; **l. down on the job,** holgazanear en el trabajo, abandonar las obligaciones, trabajar mal o indiferentemente; **l. hard on,** ser un peso

(en la conciencia); **l. in state,** estar (el difunto) en capilla ardiente; **l. low,** (fam.) esconderse temporalmente; esperar la ocasión; ocultar las intenciones; **l. off,** (mar.) estar a tal distancia de la costa o de otro barco; **l. on one's own bed,** atenerse a las consecuencias (de las propias acciones); **l. with,** yacer o acostarse con, tener relaciones sexuales con; corresponder o tocar a; ser problema de, ej., *it lies with you to (do),* ese es problema (o derecho) tuyo; **to let sleeping dogs l.,** dejar las cosas como están, no meterse en camisa de once varas; no revolver un asunto escabroso; **to take (it) lying down,** no ofrecer resistencia, aceptar abyectamente. —*s.* 1. dirección, posición, postura, orientación, sesgo, cariz. 2. madriguera, guarida (de un animal). 3. **l. of the land,** (fig.) estado de cosas.

lied [lid] *s.* canción lírica alemana.

Liederkranz ['lidər,krænts, B -ə,-] *s.* tipo de queso suave y de olor fuerte.

lie detector, detector de mentiras.

lie detector test, prueba con el detector de mentiras.

lief [lif] *a.* (ant.) querido, amado; gustoso, dispuesto. —*adv.* de buena gana, de buen grado; libremente.

liege [lidʒ] *a.* 1. ligio; feudatario, feudal. 2. que tiene derecho a feudo o vasallaje. 3. leal, fiel. —*s.* 1. señor feudal. 2. vasallo, súbdito.

Liège [li'eɪʒ] *s.* Lieja (Bélgica.).

liege lord, señor feudal.

liegeman ['lidʒmən] *s., a.* 1. vasallo. 2. p. ext. partidario, seguidor o secuaz fiel o leal.

lien [lin, 'liən, B 'lɪən] *s.* (der.) embargo preventivo; derecho de retención; gravamen, obligación.

lienal [laɪ'ɛnəl, B -'in-] *a.* (med.) lienal (del bazo).

lienteric [,laɪən'tɛrɪk] *a.* (med.) lientérico.

lientery ['laɪən,tɛrɪ, B -tərɪ] *s.* (med.) lientería, lientera.

lierne [lɪ'ɜrn, B -'ɜn] *s.* (arq.) nervio secundario (de bóveda gótica).

lieu [lu, B lju] *s.* lugar, sitio; **in l. of,** en lugar de, en vez de.

Lieut. *abrev. de* **Lieutenant,** teniente (tnte.).

lieutenant [lu'tɛnənt, B lɛf-] *s.* 1. lugarteniente. 2. (mil.) teniente. 3. [B le'tɛn-] (mar.) alférez de navío.

lieutenant colonel, (mil.) teniente coronel.

lieutenant commander, (mar.) capitán de corbeta.

lieutenant general, (mil.) teniente general.

lieutenant governor, (E.U.) vicegobernador; (G.B.) lugarteniente del gobernador general (en una colonia o un dominio).

lieutenant junior grade, (mar.) alférez de navío.

lieutenantship [lu'tɛnənt,ʃɪp, B lɛf-] *s.* (mil.) 1. lugartenencia. 2. tenencia.

life [laɪf] *s.* (*pl.* LIVES [laɪvz]) 1. vida, existencia, ser, vivir. 2. vida, animación; alma, animador, ej., *the l. of the party,* el alma de la fiesta. 3. vida, seres (colectivamente), ej., *marine l.,* vida marina. 4. duración, ej., *l. of a machine,* duración de una máquina. 5. vida, manera de vivir, ej., *night l.,* vida nocturna. 6. natural (modelo), ej., *a portrait from l.,* un retrato del natural. 7. biografía, ej., *Brief Lives,* Biografías Cortas (como título de un libro). 8. vigencia (de un documento, póliza, etc.). 9. carrera, existencia (política, etc.). 10. (jer.) cadena perpetua, prisión vitalicia. 11. **all my l.,** toda mi vida; **as large as l.,** de tamaño natural; en persona; **for dear l., for one's l.,** como para salvar la vida, como si fuera para salvar la vida; **for l.,** de por vida, por toda la vida; **for the l. of me,** a fe mía, en verdad; **matter of l. and death,** asunto de vida o muerte, cuestión vital; **not on your l.,** (jer.) ni en sueños, de ninguna manera; **nothing in l.,** nada en absoluto; **the cat has nine lives,** el gato tiene siete vidas; **to bring to l.,** resucitar; reanimar, vivificar; **to come to l.,** cobrar vida, animarse, recobrar los sentidos, volver en sí; empezar a funcionar (motor, etc.); **to depart from this l.,** fallecer, morir; **to have the time of one's l.,** divertirse de lo lindo; **to see l.,** correr mundo; **to take a l.,** matar; **to take one's l.,** suicidarse; **true to l.,** conforme a la realidad, tal cual. —*a.* 1. vital. 2. rel. a la vida, de la vida. 3. vitalicio, perpetuo, ej., *l. pension,* pensión vitalicia.

life-and-death [,laɪfən'dɛθ] *a.* a muerte (lucha, etc.).

life annuity, pensión o renta vitalicia.

life belt, cinturón salvavidas.

lifeblood ['laɪf,blʌd] *s.* 1. sangre vital. 2. alma, nervio (de un negocio, etc.); elemento vital (de una cosa).

lifeboat [-,boʊt] *s.* (mar.) bote salvavidas, lancha de salvamento.

life-breath [-,brɛθ] *s.* influencia inspiradora, principio animador.

life buoy, (mar.) cinturón salvavidas, cinturón de salvamento, boya de salvamento.

life cycle, (biol.) ciclo vital.

life expectancy, esperanza de vida, índice de longevidad.

life force, *s.* fuerza vital.

life-giving ['laɪf,gɪvɪŋ] *a.* vivificante, vivificativo; vigorizante, vigorizador.

lifeguard [-,gɑrd, B -,gɑd] *s.* salvavidas, guarda de playa (nadador experto empleado para labores de salvamento).

Life Guards, (G.B.) regimiento real de caballería.

life form, ser vivo; (*in science fiction*) ser.

life history, (biol.) historia (del ciclo) vital.

life imprisonment, cadena perpetua, prisión perpetua, prisión vitalicia.

life insurance, seguro de vida.

life interest, (der.) propiedad vitalicia.

life jacket, chaleco salvavidas.

lifeless ['laɪfləs] *a.* 1. sin vida, muerto; exánime. 2. (fig.) inanimado, inerte; falto de vigor; sin alma, sin poder; deslucido, apagado, flojo, insípido. 3. desierto, inhabitado.

lifelessly [-lɪ] *adv.* 1. sin vida. 2. (fig.) sin vigor, deslucidamente, sin ánimo.

lifelessness [-nəs] *s.* 1. falta de vida. 2. (fig.) falta de vigor, falta de animación.

lifelike ['laɪf,laɪk] *a.* que parece vivo, natural; fiel, de parecido fiel.

lifelikeness [-nəs] *s.* semejanza con la vida, semejanza con la naturaleza.

lifeline [-,laɪn] *s.* 1. (mar.) cuerda o cabo salvavidas, cabo de salvamento, andarivel de salvamento. 2. cuerda de seguridad (para los bañistas en las playas). 3. cuerda de comunicación (de buzos). 4. recurso vital, expediente principal. 5. línea vital de comunicación (para trasladar suministros vitales por vía marítima, terrestre, o aérea). 6. línea de la vida (quiromancia).

lifelong [-,lɔŋ] *a.* de toda la vida, vitalicio.

life member, miembro vitalicio o perpetuo.

life mortar, mortero lanza cabos.

life net, red o manta de salvamento (usada por bomberos).

life of leisure, vida de ocio.

life of Riley [-'raɪlɪ] (fig.) vida despreocupada y sibarítica, vida fácil, buena vida.

life preserver, 1. chaleco salvavidas. 2. cachiporra flexible.

lifer ['laɪfər, B -fə] *s.* (jer.) 1. presidiario de por vida, condenado a prisión perpetua. 2. soldado que hace del servicio militar una carrera.

life raft, balsa salvavidas.

lifesaver ['laɪf,seɪvər, B -və] *s.* 1. salvador (persona que salva la vida a otra). 2. miembro de una estación de salvamento. 3. (fig.) salvación. 4. (fam.) pastillita de menta.

lifesaving [-vɪŋ] *a.* de salvamento. —*s.* salvamento; servicio de salvavidas.

lifesaving gun, l. mortar, cañón o mortero lanzacabos, obús (para lanzar proyectiles de salvamento).

lifesaving station, estación de salvamento (en la costa).

life sentence, (der.) cadena perpetua, sentencia de prisión vitalicia.

life-size ['laɪf'saɪz] **life-sized** [-'saɪzd] *a.* de tamaño natural.

life span, duración (máxima) de vida; (*of a product, equipment*) vida útil.

life style, estilo de vida.

life support system, (aeroesp.) equipo de mantenimiento de vida; (med.) sistema de mantener la vida del enfermo, máquina corazón-pulmón.

life table, estadísticas de expectativa o promedio de vida.

lifetime [-,taɪm] *s.* vida, curso de la vida. —*a.* vitalicio, perpetuo, de por vida, que dura toda la vida.

life vest, chaleco salvavidas.

lifework ['laɪf'wɜrk, B -'wɜk] *s.* trabajo de toda la vida o que requiere toda la vida; obra principal de la vida de uno.

LIFO *abrev. de* **last in, first out,** lo que se recibe último se vende primero.

lift [lɪft] *v.t.* 1. alzar, levantar, elevar, izar. 2. exaltar, ensalzar, ascender (en estimación, honor, etc.), realzar o elevar a un plano superior. 3. (fam.) escamotear, levantarse con, robar, hurtar. 4. plagiar. 5. (E.U.) redimir, cancelar (una hipoteca). 6. sacar, recoger (frutos). 7. revocar, suprimir (prohibición, etc.). 8. levantar (bloqueo, sitio). 9. transferir (huella digital de una superficie). 10. transportar (tropas, pertrechos). 11. embellecer (la cara) por cirugía plástica. 12. (mil.) cambiar la dirección del (fuego de artillería). 13. (dial.) desenterrar (tesoro). 14. (dial.) cobrar, recaudar. 15. **l. a hand against,** poner la mano en (alguien); **l. one's hand,** levantar la mano (al prestar juramento); **l. one's voice,** alzar la voz; **l. up,** alzar. —*v.i.* 1. ascender, subir, elevarse, levantarse. 2. disiparse (la niebla, obscuridad, etc.). —*s.* 1. acción de elevar, levantar, alzar. 2. carga levantada. 3. ascenso (en posición o condición); avance, mejora; promoción; ayuda para levantar o elevar. 4. porte elevado (ej., de la cabeza). 5. exaltación, estímulo; elevación (del espíritu). 6. elevador, montacargas. 7. (G.B.) ascensor. 8. elevación, grado de elevación; altura de levantamiento. 9. alza (de precios). 10. transporte, transportación (de tropas, pertrechos, abastecimientos, etc.). 11. (aer.) fuerza ascensional, sustentación. 12. (min.) piso (en el filón). 13. **to give one a l.,** llevar a uno en vehículo; (fig.) ayudar a uno, alentar, animar.

lift attendant, (G.B.) ascensorista.

lift drag ratio, (aer.) rendimiento aerodinámico.

lifter ['lɪftər, B -ə] *s.* 1. levantador, alzador. 2. (fam.) ratero. 3. máquina o artefacto para levantar; aparato elevador; montacargas; elevador de granos; empujador (de válvulas); leva; máquina para la recolección (de cosechas); gancho para levantar (ej., tapas de ollas).

lifting [-ɪŋ] *s.* acción de alzar o elevar. —*a.* que levanta o eleva.

lifting force, l. power, fuerza ascensional, poder elevador.
lifting injector, inyector aspirante.
lifting jack, (mec.) cric, gato.
lifting rod, (mec.) vástago vertical que mueve el brazo de la válvula.
lift lock, esclusa.
lift-off [-ˌɔf] *s.* (aer.) despegue vertical (de un avión o de un cohete).
lift pump, (mec.) bomba aspirante.
lift shaft, (G.B.) pozo del ascensor.
lift truck, camión elevador, carro montacargas.
lift valve, (mec.) válvula de movimiento vertical.
lift van, cajón grande a prueba de agua (para transporte marítimo).
lift wire, (aer.) cable de sustentación.
ligament ['lɪgəmənt] *s.* 1. ligamento, ligamiento, ligadura, atadura, lazo, vínculo. 2. (anat.) ligamento.
ligamentary [ˌlɪgə'mɛntərɪ] **ligamentous** [-əs] **ligamental** [-əl] *a.* (anat.) ligamentoso.
ligan ['laɪgən] *var. de* **lagan.**
ligate ['laɪˌgeɪt, B laɪ'geɪt] *v.t.* (med.) ligar, atar con ligadura.
ligation [laɪ'geɪʃən] *s.* 1. ligación. 2. (med.) ligadura.
ligature ['lɪgətʃər, B -tʃʊə] *s.* 1. ligadura, ligación. 2. (mús.) ligado; ligadura. 3. (med.) ligadura. 4. (tip.) ligadura, ligado; letras ligadas. —*v.t.* ligar.
ligeance ['laɪdʒəns, 'lidʒ-] *s.* 1. (der. G.B.) jurisdicción o territorio de un señor feudal o de un soberano. 2. (ant.) lealtad, fidelidad.
light [laɪt] *s.* 1. luz. 2. luz del día, claridad. 3. luz, iluminación, ej., *it's not good to read in poor l.,* es malo leer con poca luz. 4. luz, ilustración, iluminación (mental). 5. (*pl.*) alcances, facultades, talento. 6. (*pl.*) entendimiento, modo de entender; preceptos. 7. luz, aspecto, ej., *to place (something) in a good l.,* hacer aparecer bajo una luz (o un aspecto) favorable. 8. candela, vela; lámpara, luz (eléctrica). 9. fanal, faro. 10. luz, claro, tragaluz. 11. lumbre, fuego; fósforo, ej., *to give one a l.,* dar lumbre o fuego a uno; *have you a l.?* ¿tiene Ud. una cerilla (o un fósforo)? 12. lumbrera, luminar, eminencia. 13. papel, ej., *he liked to appear in the l. of a ministering angel,* le gustaba aparecer en el papel de ángel guardián. 14. (*pl.*) (teat.) candilejas. 15. (pint.) luz. 16. (*pl.*) (jer.) ojos. 17. (ant.) vista, visión. 18. **against the l.,** contra la luz; al trasluz, ej., *look at it against the l.,* mírelo al trasluz; **by the l. of nature,** por instinto, sin la ayuda de conocimientos adquiridos; **in the l. of,** a la luz de; en vista de; **in this l.,** desde este punto de vista; **l. of one's eyes,** niña de los ojos (de uno); **l. of reason,** luz de la razón; **to bring to l.,** sacar a luz, revelar, descubrir; **to come to l.,** salir a luz, ser revelado, ser descubierto; **to see in a different l.,** mirar con otros ojos; **to see the l.,** ver la luz, nacer; ver la luz; convertirse; caer en cuenta; ver la solución (de un problema, etc.); **to see the l. of day,** ver la luz, nacer; **to stand in one's l.,** hacer sombra a uno, quitar la luz a uno; (fig.) hacer sombra a uno, cortar las posibilidades de uno; **to strike a l.,** encender una cerilla o fósforo; **to throw** o **to shed l. (up) on,** echar luz sobre. —*a.* 1. bien iluminado, claro. 2. claro (color). 3. de tez blanca. —*v.i.* (*pret., p.p.* LIGHTED O LIT [lɪt]; *p.pr.* LIGHTING) **l. up,** prender (fuego), encenderse; encender la luz; iluminarse (ej., la cara); encender la pipa. —*v.t.* 1. encender (lámpara, fuego). 2. **l. up,** iluminar (cuarto, calle, etc.).
light, *a.* ligero, liviano (peso, carga, coche, metal, vestido, etc.). 2. (fig.) ligero (alimento, almuerzo, té; sueño; espíritu; ejercicio, trabajo; toque; impresión, traza; herida; lluvia, viento; enfermedad, lectura, caballería; industria, etc.). 3. fácil, frívola (mujer). 4. licencioso, frívolo (cuento, conducta, etc.). 5. alegre (corazón, etc.). 6. de poca monta, de poca importancia. 7. de poco monto (impuesto, etc.). 8. inconstante, veleidoso (persona, afecto, etc.). 9. suelto, arenoso (terreno, tierra). 10. clara (voz). 11. de líneas graciosas o elegantes (edificio, etc.). 12. falto de peso (moneda). 13. sin carga (buque). 14. **l. on his feet,** ligero de pies; **to hold in l. esteem,** tener en poca estimación; **to make l. of,** no tomar en serio; burlarse de. —*adv.* 1. ligeramente, ej., *to travel l.,* viajar con poco equipaje, viajar ligero; (fig.) sin lastre. 2. (*ú. en palabras compuestas*) ligeramente, ej., *l-clad,* ligeramente vestido, *l.-footed,* de paso ágil. —*v.i.* (*pret., p.p.* LIGHTED O LIT [lɪt]; *p.pr.* LIGHTING) 1. (con *down*) desmontar, apearse. 2. (con *on* o *upon*) posar, reposarse, asentarse (ej., aves o nieve). 3. (con *on* o *upon*) tropezar (con), encontrar (por casualidad). 4. **l. into,** arremeter, atacar con fuerza; **l. out,** poner pies en polvorosa; tomar las de Villadiego.
light adaptation, (fisiol.) adaptación a la luz (de la retina).
light air, (mar.) ventolina.
light-armed ['laɪt'ɑrmd, B -'ɑmd] *a.* provisto de armas ligeras.
light artillery, (mil.) artillería ligera.
light beer, cerveza clara.
light breeze, (mar.) viento suave, brisa.
light bulb, bombilla (eléctrica), foco, bombillo (Amer.).
light buoy, boya o baliza luminosa.
light complexion, tez blanca.
light-duty [-'dutɪ, B -'djutɪ] *a.* para servicio liviano, para trabajo ligero.
lighten ['laɪtən] *v.i.* 1. iluminarse, brillar, fulgurar, destellar. 2. hacerse claro; aclararse, despejarse (cielo). 3. relampaguear, centellear. —*v.t.* 1. iluminar, alumbrar. 2. aclarar, avivar (color, etc.). 3. (ant.) iluminar (intelectual o espiritualmente); instruir, informar.
lighten, *v.t.* 1. (lit. y fig.) aligerar, aliviar (peso, carga, etc.; dolor, pena, etc.). 2. alijar, descargar (una embarcación). 3. alegrar, hacer agradable. 4. **l. one's mind,** ser un alivio para uno. —*v.i.* 1. aligerarse (de peso). 2. (fig.) aliviarse, volverse menos pesado (pena, aflicción, etc.). 3. tornarse más alegre (humor, etc.).
lightening ['laɪtnɪŋ, -ənɪŋ] *s.* 1. iluminación, alba, alborada. 2. aligeramiento, alivio. —*a.* 1. iluminador. 2. aligerador, aliviador.
lighter [-ər, B -ə] *s.* 1. encendedor (de fuegos). 2. mechero. 3. encendedor (de bolsillo). 4. (mar.) alijador, gabarra, barcaza, chalana, lanchón. —*v.t.* transportar en alijador.
lighterage ['laɪtərɪdʒ] *s.* (mar.) 1. alijo, lanchaje, gabarraje. 2. derechos de lanchaje o alijo.
lighterman [-ərmən, B -əmən] *s.* lanchonero, gabarrero.
lighter-than-air [ˌlaɪtərðən'ɛr, B -əðən'ɛə] *a.* más liviano que el aire.
lightface ['laɪtˌfeɪs] *s.* (tip.) letra fina o blanca (a distinción de la negra o negrita). —*a.* (tip.) fino, blanco, claro (apl. a caracteres, rayas o filetes).
lightfast [-ˌfæst, B -ˌfɑst] *a.* resistente a la luz (esp. colores).
light field artillery, artillería ligera, artillería montada o rodada.
light-fingered [-'fɪŋgərd, B -gəd] *a.* 1. largo de uñas, ligero de dedos. 2. diestro de manos.
light-footed [-'fʊtəd] **lightfoot** [-ˌfʊt] *a.* ligero de pies, de paso ágil.
light-footedly [-lɪ] *adv.* con ligereza de piernas.
light-footedness [-nəs] *s.* ligereza de paso o de pies.
light-haired ['laɪt'hɛrd, B -'hɛəd] *a.* pelirrubio, de cabello claro.
light-handed [-'hændəd] *a.* 1. ligero de manos. 2. (fig.) fácil, suave (estilo, manera, etc.). 3. (mar.) con poca tripulación.
lightheaded [-'hɛdəd] *a.* 1. mareado, aturdido. 2. atolondrado, ligero de cascos, casquivano; frívolo.
lightheadedly [-lɪ] *adv.* atolondradamente.
lightheadedness [-nəs] *s.* 1. mareo, aturdimiento. 2. frivolidad, ligereza.
lighthearted [-'hɑrtəd, B -'hɑt-] *a.* despreocupado, alegre, festivo, libre de cuidados.
lightheartedly [-lɪ] *adv.* despreocupadamente, con despreocupación, alegremente.
lightheartedness [-nəs] *s.* despreocupación, alegría, ánimo.
light heavyweight, (boxeo) peso semipesado.
light horse, (mil.) caballería ligera.
light-horseman ['laɪtˌhɔrsmən, B -'hɔs-] *s.* soldado de caballería ligera.
lighthouse [-ˌhaʊs] *s.* faro.
lighthouse keeper, guardafaro, torrero.
light infantry, infantería ligera.
lighting ['laɪtɪŋ] *s.* 1. encendido, ignición. 2. iluminación, incidencia de la luz (ej., en un cuadro). 3. alumbrado o luz (artificial).
lighting effects, (teat.) efectos de luz; iluminación escénica.
lighting fixtures, aparatos de alumbrado.
lighting technique, técnica lumínica, luminotecnia.
light keeper, guardafaro, torrero.
lightless ['laɪtləs] *a.* sin luz, obscuro.
lightly ['laɪtlɪ] *adv.* 1. levemente, gentilmente. 2. ligeramente, mesuradamente, moderadamente, ej., *he ate l.,* comió ligeramente. 3. superficialmente, a la ligera, sin seriedad. 4. ágilmente, graciosamente. 5. sin atención o cuidado. 6. alegremente, jovialmente. 7. (ant.) fácilmente.
light meter, (foto.) fotómetro.
light-minded [-'maɪndəd] *a.* frívolo; inconstante, voluble; atolondrado.
lightmindedly [-lɪ] *adv.* frívolamente, atolondradamente.
lightmindedness [-nəs] *s.* atolondramiento; frivolidad.
lightness ['laɪtnəs] *s.* 1. liviandad, poco peso, peso ligero. 2. (fig.) ligereza, levedad, liviandad, frivolidad; inconstancia, inestabilidad. 3. agilidad, delicadeza, gracia. 4. facilidad, suavidad (de estilo, manera de obrar, etc.).
lightness, *s.* 1. grado de iluminación, luminosidad. 2. claridad o claro (de color).
lightning ['laɪtnɪŋ] *s.* relámpago, rayo; relampagueo; **like l.,** como un rayo.
lightning arrester, pararrayos (en una instalación eléctrica).
lightning beetle, l. bug, (ento.) luciérnaga, cocuyo, bicho de luz.
lightning rod, pararrayos, barra pararrayos (en un edificio).
lightning stone, lightning tube, fulgurita, piedra de rayo.
lightning switch, (rad.) interruptor o conmutador de la conexión de la antena con la tierra.
light-o-love ['laɪtə'lʌv] *s.* persona inconstante en el amor; amante caprichosa y voluble.
light opera, (mús.) ópera ligera, opereta, zarzuela.
lightplane [-ˌpleɪn] *s.* avioneta.
light port, (mar.) portillo.
lightproof [-ˌpruf] *a.* a prueba de luz.

light pull, (elec.) cadenilla de tiro, tirador.
light quantum, (fís.) fotón.
light room, (mar.) pañol de faroles; linterna de faro.
lights [laɪts] *s. pl.* pulmones, bofes (de animales), livianos.
light shaft, toma de luz, lumbrera.
lightship ['laɪt,ʃɪp] *s.* (mar.) buque faro o fanal.
light sleep, sueño ligero.
light socket, portalámparas.
light soil, (agr.) tierra arija.
lightsome ['laɪtsəm] *a.* 1. iluminado; claro, luminoso; brillante. 2. airoso, gracioso, garboso; ágil, ligero. 3. alegre, festivo; animado, placentero. 4. frívolo, inconstante.
lightsomely [-lɪ] *adv.* 1. airosamente, graciosamente; ágilmente. 2. alegremente. 3. frívolamente.
lightsomeness [-nəs] *s.* 1. airosidad, gracia; agilidad. 2. alegría. 3. frivolidad.
lights-out ['laɪts'aʊt] *s.* retreta (toque militar para recogerse de noche); hora de acostarse.
light-struck ['laɪt,strʌk] *a.* (foto.) velado por la luz.
light switch, (elec.) apagador.
light trap, (foto.) trampa de luz.
light verse, parodia rimada.
light vessel, buque faro.
light wave, (fís.) onda luminosa.
lightweight ['laɪt,weɪt] *a.* de poco peso, ligero. —*s.* 1. persona de poco peso. 2. (boxeo) peso ligero, peso liviano; púgil de peso ligero. 3. (fam.) pelagatos, pelele.
lightwood [-,wʊd] *s.* (E.U.) leña (esp. de pino resinoso).
light-year [-,jɪr, B -,jɜ] *s.* (astr.) añoluz, año de luz.
lignaloe [laɪ'nælou] **lignaloes** [-oʊz] *s.* 1. (bot.) lináloe. 2. (farm.) áloe, aloe.
ligneous ['lɪgnɪəs] *a.* leñoso, lignario.
lignicole ['lɪgnəkoʊl] *a.* lignícola, que vive en la madera.
ligniferous [,lɪg'nɪfərəs] *a.* lignífero, leñífero.
lignification [,lɪgnəfə'keɪʃən] *s.* lignificación, conversión en madera.
lignify ['lɪgnə,faɪ] *v.t.* (*pret., p.p.* LIGNIFIED; *p.pr.* LIGNIFYING) (bot.) convertir en madera. —*v.i.* lignificarse.
lignin ['lɪgnən] *s.* (bot., quím.) lignina.
lignite [-,naɪt] *s.* (min.) lignito.
lignocellulose [,lɪgnoʊ'sɛljə,loʊs] *s.* (bot., quím.) lignocelulosa.
lignose ['lɪg,noʊs] *s.* (bot., quím.) lignosa.
lignum vitae ['lɪgnəm'vaɪti] 1. (bot.) guayaco, guayacán. 2. palo santo; palo de las Indias.
ligroin ['lɪgroʊən, B -rɔɪn] *s.* (quím.) ligroína (fracción de petróleo).
ligula ['lɪgjələ] *s.* (*pl.* LIGULAE [-,li] o LIGULAS), (bot., anat.) lígula.
ligulate [-lət] **ligulated** [-,leɪtəd] *a.* (bot.) ligulado.
ligule ['lɪgjul] *s.* (bot.) lígula.
Ligurian [lɪ'gjʊrɪən, B -'gjʊər-] *a., s.* ligurino, ligur, de Liguria, región de Italia.
likable ['laɪkəbəl] *a.* simpático, amable, agradable.
likableness [-nəs] *s.* simpatía, amabilidad.
like [laɪk] *a.* 1. semejante, similar, parecido, ej., *as l. as two peas in a pod,* tan parecido como dos gotas de agua, *in a l. manner,* de manera semejante. 2. equivalente, igual, ej., *to contribute a l. sum,* contribuir con una suma igual. 3. tal, igual a, parecido a, semejante a, típico de, característico de, ej., *l. father l. son,* de tal palo tal astilla, *it was l. him to talk so much,* era típico de él hablar tanto. 4. **l. hell,** (jer.) de ninguna manera; **l. that,** así como así; así no más (Am.); **nothing l. it,** no hay nada parecido, nada como eso; **something l.,** alrededor de, algo así como; **to feel l. (doing),** sentir deseos de (hacer); **to look l.,** parecerse a; parecer que, ej., *it looks l. good fishing today,* parece que hoy será un buen día para pescar; **what is he l.?** ¿qué tal es él? ¿qué aspecto tiene? —*s.* 1. semejante, igual; contraparte (cosa o persona), ej., *and the l.,* y cosas por el estilo; **his l., its l.,** otro igual; **the likes of us (them,** etc.), gente como nosotros (ellos, etc.); **the likes of you,** (fam.) personas como Ud. 2. (*ú. gen. en pl.*) gusto, simpatía, preferencia; afición; **likes and dislikes,** simpatías y antipatías; gustos y aversiones. —*v.i.* 1. querer, gustarle a uno, ej., *do as you l.,* haga como quiera, haga lo que guste. **2. if you l.,** si Ud. quiere, ej., *I am wrong if you l., but so is he,* estoy equivocado, si Ud. quiere, pero él también lo está. —*v.t.* 1. gustar de, gustarle a uno, ej., *I l. to swin (o swimming),* me gusta nadar (o la natación). 2. tener afecto a, serle simpático a uno, ej., *I l. him very much,* le tengo mucho afecto, él me es muy simpático. 3. agradarle a uno, ej., *I do not l. such subjects discussed,* no me agrada que se discuta sobre tales temas. 4. **I should (would) l. to (do),** me gustaría (hacer); **l. best,** gustarle más a uno; **l. better,** preferir. —*adv.* 1. probablemente, ej., *as l. as not it will rain,* probablemente lloverá. 2. (vulg.) casi, ej., *his manner was patronizing l.,* su conducta fue casi arrogante. —*prep.* 1. como, a manera (de), ej., *he talks l. a madman,* habla como un loco. 2. tal como, ej., *a painter like Gauguin,* un pintor como Gauguin (de su estilo o escuela). **3. l. anything,** vigorosamente, como loco. —*conj.* como, del mismo modo (que), *do it l. I told you,* hazlo como te dije (uso estrictamente fam.).
likeable, likeableness, *vars. de* **likable,** likableness.
likelihood ['laɪklɪ,hʊd] **likeliness** [-nəs] *s.* 1. probabilidad, ej., *it will rain in all l.,* con toda probabilidad lloverá; verosimilitud. 2. cosa probable.
likely [-lɪ] *a.* (LIKELIER; LIKELIEST) 1. probable, ej., *he is l. to come,* es probable que venga. 2. verosímil, creíble, ej., *a l. story,* una historia verosímil. 3. apto, idóneo, a propósito, calificado, ej., *a l. place to fish,* un lugar a propósito para pescar. 4. prometedor, que promete, ej., *three l. young fellows,* tres jóvenes que prometen. 5. **to be l. to (do),** ser probable que (haga), ej., *he's not l. to come today,* no es probable que él venga hoy. —*adv.* probablemente; **l. enough,** no sería extraño.
like-minded [-'maɪndəd] *a.* 1. del mismo parecer. 2. de la misma mentalidad.
liken [-ən] *v.t.* asemejar, comparar, equiparar.
likeness ['laɪknəs] *s.* 1. semejanza, similitud, parecido, aire. 2. apariencia, aspecto. 3. retrato, efigie, imagen. 4. **to be a good l.,** tener gran parecido, ser una imagen fiel.
like signs, (mat.) signos iguales.
like terms, (mat.) términos semejantes.
likewise [-,waɪz] *adv.* 1. asimismo, igualmente, del mismo modo, también. 2. además.
liking ['laɪkɪŋ] *s.* preferencia; simpatía; afecto; afición; gusto, agrado, inclinación, ej., *to one's l.,* de su agrado; **to take a l. to (something),** aficionarse a (algo); **to take a l. to (someone),** prendarse de, aficionarse a (alguien).
lilac ['laɪlək, -,lɑk, -,læk, B -lək] *s.* 1. (bot.) lila, lilac (arbusto y flor). 2. lila (color). —*a.* (de color de) lila.
Liliaceae [,lɪlɪ'eɪsɪ,i] *s. pl.* (bot.) liliáceas.
liliaceous [-'eɪʃəs] *a.* (bot.) liliáceo.
lilied ['lɪlid] *a.* 1. cubierto o adornado con lirios. 2. (ant.) como un lirio.
Lilliput ['lɪlɪ,pʌt, -pət] *s.* tierra habitada por los liliputienses (en el cuento de Swift, *Los viajes de Gulliver*).
Lilliputian [,lɪlə'pjuʃən] *a.* liliputiense, diminuto. —*s.* liliputiense, enano.
lilt [lɪlt] *s.* 1. música o canción alegre. 2. cadencia, deje, ritmo. 3. paso o movimiento ligero y airoso. —*v.i., v.t.* cantar alegremente, cantar airosamente.
lilting ['lɪltɪŋ] *a.* rítmico; animado, melodioso.
lily ['lɪlɪ] *s.* (*pl.* LILIES), 1. (bot.) lirio; azucena; cala, lirio de la pradera o del Canadá. 2. (her.) flor de lis, símbolo de Francia. 3. **to gild the l.,** tratar de hacer más hermoso lo hermoso. —*a.* 1. puro, blanco, pálido; delicado. 2. blanco, puro o delicado como un lirio.
lily iron, arpón con cabeza desmontable (usado para la pesca del pez espada).
lily-livered [-'lɪvərd, B -əd] *a.* débil; cobarde, ruin.
lily of the valley, (bot.) lirio del valle, muguete.
lily pad, (E.U.) hoja (flotante) del lirio de agua.
lily-white ['lɪlɪ'hwaɪt, -'waɪt] *a.* 1. lilial, blanquísimo, blanco como el lirio. 2. (fig.) puro, inocente.
lilywort [-,wɜrt, B -,wɜt] *s.* (bot.) liliácea.
Lima ['limə] *s.* Lima, capital del Perú.
Lima bean ['laɪmə-] (bot.) fríjol de media luna; judía o haba.
limaciform [laɪ'mæsə,fɔrm, B -,fɔm] *a.* (zool.) limaciforme.
limax ['laɪ,mæks] *s.* (zool.) babosa, babaza.
limb [lɪm] *s.* 1. miembro (brazo o pierna); extremidad. 2. rama (de árbol). 3. miembro, representante; agente. 4. vástago (de una planta, familia, etc.). 5. brazo (de cruz; del mar). —*v.t.* desmembrar, despedazar.
limb, *s.* 1. limbo (corona graduada que llevan los instrumentos destinados a medir ángulos). 2. (astr., bot.) limbo.
limbate ['lɪm,beɪt] *a.* (bot.) limbado.
limbed [lɪmd] *a.* (*ú. en palabras compuestas*) de miembros, ej., *large-l.,* de miembros grandes.
limber ['lɪmbər, B -bə] *a.* flexible, elástico, cimbreño, ágil. —*v.t.* (con *up*) poner flexible. —*v.i.* (con *up*) calentar el cuerpo, hacer ejercicios preliminares (ej., un atleta antes de competir).
limber, (mil.) *s.* avantrén de cureña, armón. —*v.i.* poner el avantrén. —*v.t.* colocar (el armón).
limberness [-nəs] *s.* flexibilidad, agilidad.
limbers ['lɪmbərz, B -bəz] *s. pl.* (mar.) imbornales (de varenga).
limbic ['lɪmbɪk] *a.* límbico, marginal.
limbless ['lɪmləs] *a.* 1. sin miembros, desmembrado. 2. sin ramas (árbol).
limbo ['lɪmboʊ] *s.* (*pl.* LIMBOES) 1. (teol.) limbo. 2. (fig.) prisión.
Limburger ['lɪm,bɜrgər, B -,bɜgə] *s.* queso de Limburgo.
limbus ['lɪmbəs] *s.* limbo; borde (en color, borde contrastante); orilla.
lime [laɪm] *s.* 1. ajonje, liga (materia viscosa para cazar aves). 2. cal. —*v.t.* 1. untar con liga; coger (pájaros) con liga. 2. encalar (pared, etc.); tratar con cal (ej., tierra para fertilizarla, velamen para blanquearlo, etc.); pelambrar (pieles). —*a.* de cal; calizo.
lime, *s.* 1. (bot.) limero agrio (árbol). 2. lima agria, limón verde, limoncillo (fruto). 3. lima (variedad de naranja). 4. tilo, tilia.

limeade [ˌlaɪm'eɪd, 'laɪm-] *s.* limonada hecha con jugo de limón verde o limoncillo.
lime-burner ['laɪmˌ B ɜrnər, B -ˌbɜnə] *s.* calero (oficio).
lime-cast [-ˌkæst, B -ˌkɑst] *s.* enlucido (de cal); enyesado o encalado de paredes.
lime-coated [-'koʊtəd] *a.* encalado.
lime-juicer [-ˌdʒusər, B -sə] *s.* (jer.) 1. barco inglés; marinero inglés. 2. inglés.
limekiln [-ˌkɪl, -ˌkɪln] *s.* calera (horno de cal).
limelight ['laɪmˌlaɪt] *s.* 1. luz de calcio. 2. (G.B., teat.) luz concentrada (para iluminar una parte del escenario). 3. **to be in the l.,** (fig.) ser objeto de la atención general, expuesto al público. —*v.t.* llamar la atención sobre, realzar, hacer resaltar.
limen ['laɪmən, B -mɛn] *s.* (psic., fisiol.) limen, umbral (de la conciencia).
lime-pit ['laɪmˌpɪt] *s.* 1. noque (estanque para curtir pieles). 2. calera.
limerick ['lɪmərɪk] *s.* (Irl.) quintilla jocosa o lira; refrán picaresco.
limestone ['laɪmˌstoʊn] *s.* caliza, piedra caliza.
lime sulfur, sulfuro de calcio (usado como fungicida o insecticida).
lime tree, (bot.) (árbol de) tila o tilo.
lime-twig [-ˌtwɪg] *s.* 1. vareta (untada con liga para cazar pájaros). 2. (fig.) trampa, lazo.
limewater [-ˌwɔtər, -ˌwɑt-, B -ˌwɔtə] *s.* agua de cal.
limey ['laɪmɪ] *s.* (jer.) marinero o soldado inglés; (despec.) inglés.
limicolous [laɪ'mɪkələs] *a.* (orn.) limícola.
liminal ['lɪmənəl, 'laɪ-, B 'lɪmɪn-] *a.* (psic.) liminal o liminar.
limit ['lɪmət] *s.* 1. límite, linde, lindero, frontera, confín. 2. límite, fin, término. 3. límite (de apuestas). 4. **the sky's the l.,** (fam.) todo es válido, no hay límite; **this (it) is the l.,** esto es el colmo; **to go to the l.,** (dep.) aguantar toda la contienda (ej., un púgil); (vulg.) tener trato carnal; **to know no l.,** no tener límite; **to the l.,** hasta más no poder; **without l.,** ilimitado, sin restricción. —*v.t.* 1. limitar, fijar; deslindar; restringir, coartar. 2. (der.) limitar, asignar dentro de límites. 3. **l. oneself (itself) to,** limitarse a.
limitable [-əbəl] *a.* limitable, restringible.
limitary ['lɪməˌtɛrɪ, B -tərɪ] *a.* (ant.) 1. que está limitado, sujeto a restricción (díc. de una autoridad). 2. limitáneo, fronterizo, limítrofe, confinante, aledaño. 3. limitador, restrictivo.
limitation [ˌlɪmə'teɪʃən] *s.* 1. limitación, restricción, coartación, acotamiento. 2. (der.) prescripción. 3. **to know one's limitations,** conocer las propias limitaciones, capacidades o fuerzas.
limitative ['lɪməˌteɪtɪv, B -tətɪv] *a.* limitativo, restrictivo.
limited ['lɪmɪtəd] *a.* 1. limitado, circunscrito. 2. reducido, estrecho, escaso. 3. (com., G.B.) de responsabilidad limitada, ej., *l. company* o *l. liability company,* sociedad de responsabilidad limitada.
limited divorce, divorcio restringido, (fam.) separación legal.
limited edition, edición especial de un libro del cual se imprime un número limitado de ejemplares.
limited monarchy, monarquía constitucional.
limited partnership, (com.) comandita, sociedad en comandita.
limiter ['lɪmətər, B -ə] *s.* limitador; (elec., electrón.) limitador.
limiting [-ɪŋ] *a.* 1. limitativo, restrictivo. 2. (gram.) determinativo, ej., *l. adjective,* adjetivo determinativo. 3. rayano, aledaño.
limiting factor, (ecol., biol.) factor ambiental que limita el crecimiento y desarrollo de organismos o de una colectividad humana.
limitless [-ləs] *a.* ilimitado, infinito.
limmer ['lɪmər, B -ə] *s.* 1. (esco.) mujercilla, muchacha descarada. 2. bribón, pícaro.
limn [lɪm] *v.t.* (*pret., p.p.* LIMNED; *p.pr.* LIMNING). 1. pintar, retratar, dibujar. 2. delinear, trazar, representar.
limner ['lɪmər, -nər, B -nə] *s.* pintor, retratista, dibujante.
limnetic [lɪm'nɛtɪk] *a.* (biol.) limnético.
limnite ['lɪmˌnaɪt] *s.* (min.) limnita.
limnology [lɪm'nɑlədʒɪ, B -'nɔl-] *s.* (biol.) limnología.
limo ['lɪmo] *s.* (fam.) limusina.
limonene ['lɪməˌnin] *s.* (quím.) limoneno.
limonite ['laɪməˌnaɪt] *s.* (min.) limonita.
limonitic [ˌlaɪmə'nɪtɪk] *a.* (min.) limonitizado (díc. de la roca impregnada de limonita).
limousine ['lɪməˌzin, ˌlɪmə'zin, B 'lɪmʊˌ-zin] *s.* (aut.) limusina, limosina.
limp [lɪmp] *a.* 1. flojo, relajado, laxo, fláccido, flácido, lacio. 2. flexible. 3. enervado, debilitado, agotado. 4. (fig.) débil, blando (de carácter). —*v.i.* cojear, renquear, renguear. —*s.* cojera, renquera, renguera.
limper ['lɪmpər, B -ə] *s.* cojo, renco, rengo.
limpet ['lɪmpət] *s.* 1. (zool.) lapa. 2. (fig.) persona (esp. empleado público) que se aferra a su puesto. 3. (mil.) mina magnética.
limpid ['lɪmpəd] *a.* límpido, claro, transparente, diáfano.
limpidity [lɪm'pɪdətɪ] *s.* limpidez, claridad, transparencia, diafanidad.
limpidly ['lɪmpədlɪ] *adv.* claramente, diáfanamente, transparentemente.
limpidness [-nəs] *s.* claridad, transparencia, diafanidad.
limping ['lɪmpɪŋ] *a.* 1. cojo. 2. que falla.
limpkin ['lɪmpkən] *s.* (orn.) caraú, carrao.
limply ['lɪmplɪ] *adv.* fláccidamente, de un modo laso.
limpness [-nəs] *s.* flojedad, flaccidez; debilidad, falta de firmeza.
limpsy ['lɪmpsɪ] *a.* (dial., E.U.) débil, debilitado, enervado.
limulus ['lɪmjələs] *s.* (*pl.* LIMULI [-ˌlaɪ]) (zool.) límulo.
limy ['laɪmɪ] *a.* 1. viscoso, pegajoso. 2. calizo.
Linaceae [laɪ'neɪsɪˌi] *s. pl.* (bot.) lináceas.
linaceous [-neɪʃəs] *a.* (bot.) lináceo.
linage ['laɪnɪdʒ] *s.* número de líneas (en un escrito o impreso); pago por líneas (escritas).
linalool [lɪ'næləˌoʊl, B -ˌɔl] *s.* (quím.) linalol.
linchpin ['lɪntʃˌpɪn] *s.* 1. sotrozo, pasador (de artillería). 2. pezonera, cabilla (de un carruaje). 3. (fig.) pieza clave, peón indispensable.
Lincoln ['lɪŋkən] *s.* raza inglesa de ganado lanar.
lindane ['lɪnˌdeɪn] *s.* (quím.) lindano (insecticida).
linden ['lɪndən] *s.* (bot.) tilo, tila, tilia.
line [laɪn] *s.* 1. línea. 2. cordel, cuerda, cordón, ej., *clothes l.,* tendedera, cuerda para tender la ropa. 3. (*pl.*) lindes, límites. 4. tubería, cañería (de agua, desagüe, etc.). 5. línea (telefónica, telegráfica, etc.). 6. sedal, cordel de pescar. 7. raya, línea, veta, banda, lista, franja. 8. arruga, línea (de la cara, las manos, etc.). 9. línea divisoria, límite. 10. lineamiento, rasgo, trazo, contorno. 11. plan. 12. renglón, línea; esquela, nota; (*pl.*) verso. 13. curso de acción, línea de conducta. 14. línea, linaje, estirpe; descendencia, ascendencia. 15. trayecto, trayectoria, curso. 16. línea, fila, hilera, cola. 17. renglón, ramo (de mercancías, negocios); especialidad, ocupación. 18. línea (de vapores, ómnibus, etc.). 19. (*pl.*) partida de matrimonio. 20. (*pl.*) (teat.) papel, parte (de un actor). 21. (*gen. pl.*) (arte) trazo(s), esquicio, esbozo. 22. (geog.) ecuador, línea geográfica. 23. (geom.) línea. 24. (mil.) trinchera; línea (de defensa, batalla, etc.). 25. (mús.) línea del pentagrama. 26. (mar.) cabo de remolque, estacha; manguera. 27. (f.c.) vía, ej., *branch l.,* vía lateral, ramal, *junction l.,* línea de empalme. 28. (ant.) sino, suerte. 29. **all along the l.,** en toda la línea, abarcándolo todo; **along these lines,** de esta manera, en estos términos; **by rule and l.,** con precisión; **in l.,** disciplinado; **in l. with,** de acuerdo con, en conformidad con; **on the l.,** sin retardo, al instante; en la línea divisoria, ni lo uno ni lo otro; en juego, en peligro, expuesto a peligro o riesgos, ej., *the life of a policeman is always on the l.,* la vida de un policía está siempre en peligro; **to be in l. for,** ser candidato para (promoción, aumento de sueldo, etc.); **to be out of l. with,** no concordar con, estar en desacuerdo con; **to be out of one's l.,** no ser de la especialidad de uno; carecer de interés para uno; **to bring into l.,** traer al orden; **to come into l.,** dejarse convencer o persuadir, abandonar su posición; **to do lines,** escribir líneas (como castigo en colegio); **to draw the l. at,** no ir más allá de; **to drop (one) a l.,** avisar (a uno), dejar una nota (para uno); **to feed (someone) a l.,** embaucar (a alguien); **to get (one) a l.,** conseguir línea (telefónica) para (uno); **to get a l. on,** (jer.) averiguar acerca de, conseguir información sobre; **to have a good l.,** (jer.) tener labia; ser convincente; **to lay it on the l.,** (jer.) entregar dinero (a alguien); hacer un pago; hablar con franqueza, poner las cartas sobre la mesa; **to read between the lines,** leer entre líneas; **to shoot a l.,** (jer.) jactarse; **to stand in l.,** hacer cola; **to take a (firm, etc.) l.,** tomar una actitud (firme, etc.); **to toe the l.,** obedecer. —*v.t.* 1. rayar, trazar líneas en. 2. delinear, dibujar; bosquejar, esbozar. 3. (con *up*) alinear, poner en fila. 4. arrugar (la cara, etc.). 5. **l. out,** marcar, trazar (ruta, etc.). —*v.i.* (gen. con *up*) alinearse, ponerse en fila, estar en fila, formarse.
line [laɪn] *v.t.* 1. forrar, aforrar. 2. revestir. 3. llenar (ej., el estómago, bolsillo, etc.). 4. (enc.) reforzar con el capricho (un libro). 5. **l. one's pockets,** llenarse los bolsillos (con dinero mal habido).
lineage ['lɪnɪɪdʒ] *s.* linaje, estirpe, raza.
lineage, *var. de* **linage.**
lineal ['lɪnɪəl] *a.* 1. lineal. 2. en línea directa (ascendiente o descendiente). 3. hereditario.
lineally [-əlɪ] *adv.* en línea recta.
lineament [-əmənt] *s.* lineamento, lineamiento, contorno o dibujo (de un cuerpo); (*pl.*) lineamentos (del rostro).
linear ['lɪnɪər, B -ə] *a.* linear, lineal; (zool., bot.) lineal, linear.
linear accelerator, (fís.) acelerador lineal.
linear B [-ˌbi] escritura descubierta en Creta (forma arcaica del griego).
linear coefficient, (mat.) coeficiente lineal.
linear equation, (mat.) ecuación de primer grado, ecuación lineal.
linear measure, medida de longitud.
linear perspective, perspectiva lineal.
lineate ['lɪnɪət] **lineated** [-ˌeɪtəd] *a.* (ant.) rayado, señalado con líneas, rayas o listas.
lineation [ˌlɪnɪ'eɪʃən] *s.* delineación; esbozo, bosquejo.
linebreed ['laɪnˌbrid] *v.t.* cruzar (descendientes) del mismo linaje.
linebreeding [-ɪŋ] *s.* cruzamiento entre descendientes del mismo linaje.
linecut [-ˌkʌt] *s.* (tip.) fotograbado de línea, clisé de línea (sin retícula).

lined [laɪnd] *a.* 1. rayado. 2. forrado.
lined paper, papel rayado.
line drawing, (tip.) dibujo lineal, dibujo a pluma.
line drop, (elec.) caída de potencial de línea.
line engraving, grabado al buril; plancha para grabado al buril; fotograbado.
line etcher, grabador al buril, fotograbador.
line fishing, pesca con sedal.
line gauge, (imp.) tipómetro, medida tipográfica, lineómetro.
line-haul ['laɪnˌhɔl] *s.* transporte (de artículos) entre terminales.
line keeper, (f.c.) guardavía.
line loss, (elec.) pérdida de transmisión.
lineman [-mən] *s.* 1. (E.U.) cadenero. 2. (elec.) guardalínea, instalador de líneas, recorredor de la línea. 3. (fútbol E.U.) delantero.
linen ['lɪnən] *s.* 1. lino; lienzo. 2. hilo de lino. 3. artículos de lino o hilo, lencería; ropa blanca. 4. papel de hilo o lino. 5. **to wash one's dirty l. at home,** lavar la ropa sucia en casa, no revelar las rencillas familiares; **to wash one's dirty l. in public,** sacar los trapitos al aire. *—a.* hecho de lino o cáñamo.
linen cambric, (tej.) batista, cambray holandés.
linen draper, lencero, vendedor de lencería.
line of action, curso de acción, modo de proceder, comportamiento.
line of battle, línea de combate.
line of circumvallation, (fort.) línea de circunvalación.
line of collimation, (fís., astr., top.) línea o eje de colimación.
line of contravallation, (fort.) línea de contravalación.
line of defense, línea de defensa.
line of departure, (mil.) dirección de salida de un proyectil.
line of duty, cumplimiento del deber.
line of elevation, (mil.) línea de tiro.
line officer, (mil.) oficial de línea, oficial combatiente; (mar.) oficial de navío.
line of fire, línea de tiro; (mil.) línea pieza-impacto, línea abierta al ataque.
line of flight, línea de vuelo.
line of force, (fís.) línea de fuerza.
line of induction, (fís.) línea de fuerza.
line of least resistance, (fig.) ley del menor esfuerzo; **to follow the l. of l. r.,** dejarse llevar por la corriente.
line of life, línea de la vida (quiromancia).
line of nodes, (astr.) línea de los nodos.
line of scrimmage, (dep.) línea imaginaria paralela a las líneas de gol (fútbol).
line of sight, 1. línea de mira. 2. visual.
line of vision, campo visual.
lineolate ['lɪnɪəˌleɪt] *a.* (zool., bot.) lineolado.
line printer, (comput.) impresora de línea.
liner ['laɪnər, B -nə] *s.* 1. revestidor. 2. forro, revestimiento. 3. rayador. 4. barco de travesía, transatlántico; avión de línea, avión de travesía. 5. (béisbol) pelota rasa, pelota rasante.
line shaft, árbol de transmisión.
linesman ['laɪnzmən] *s.* 1. (elec.) guardalínea, instalador de líneas, recorredor de la línea. 2. (tenis, fútbol) juez de línea. 3. (mil.) soldado de infantería de línea.
linesman's detector, galvanoscopio probador.
lines of communication, líneas de comunicaciones.
line spacer, interlineador (de máquina de escribir).
line squall, l. thunderstorm, (meteor.) chubasco de ceja, línea de turbonada.
line storm, (dial.) tormenta equinoccial.
line tester, (elec.) aparato probador de líneas.
linethrowing gun ['laɪnˌθroʊɪŋ-] cañón lanzacabos.
line-up, lineup ['laɪnˌʌp] *s.* 1. hilera de personas; formación. 2. (crim.) desfile de sospechosos, rueda de presos. 3. (dep.) formación, alineación (de un equipo).
ling [lɪŋ] *s.* 1. (bot.) brezo común. 2. (ict.) molva.
lingam ['lɪŋgəm] **linga** [-gə] *s.* (mitol.) lingam, símbolo fálico hindú.
linger ['lɪŋgər, B -gə] *v.i.* 1. demorar(se), quedarse, tardar en partir. 2. dilatarse, rezagarse; vacilar, titubear, estar ocioso. 3. persistir, subsistir; tardar en morirse. 4. pasearse. 5. **l. over upon,** meditar sobre, dilatarse en. *—v.t.* (con *away*) prolongar, dilatar, demorar.
lingerer [-gərər, B -gərə] *s.* el que se demora, el rezagado.
lingerie [ˌlɑndʒə'reɪ, -'ri, B 'læŋʒəˌri] *s.* lencería, ropa blanca; ropa interior (esp. de mujer).
lingering ['lɪŋgərɪŋ] *a.* persistente, prolongado.
lingo ['lɪŋgoʊ] *s.* (*pl.* LINGOES) (gen. *despec.*) idioma (esp. extranjero); dialecto; jerga.
lingua franca [-'fræŋkə] (*pl.* LINGUA FRANCAS o LINGUAE FRANCAE [-ˌgwaɪ-ˌkaɪ]) lengua franca; lenguaje híbrido que utiliza palabras de varios idiomas.
lingual [-gwəl] *a.* lingual; de la lengua; (fon.) lingual. *—s.* (fon.) (sonido) lingual.
lingue [-gweɪ] *s.* (bot.) lingue.
linguiform ['lɪngwəˌfɔrm, B -ˌfɔm] *a.* lingüiforme.
linguine [lɪŋ'gwinɪ] *s.* (ital.) macarrón plano y delgado.
linguist ['lɪŋgwəst] *s.* 1. lingüista (persona versada en lingüística). 2. poligloto, políglota (persona que sabe varias lenguas).
linguistic [lɪŋ'gwɪstɪk] **linguistical** [-tɪkəl] *a.* lingüístico.
linguistic atlas, atlas lingüístico.
linguistic form, (filol.) forma lingüística, unidad del habla.
linguistic geography, geografía dialectal.
linguistics [-tɪks] *s. pl.* (*sing. o pl. en const.*) lingüística.
linguistic science, lingüística, ciencia lingüística, ciencia del lenguaje.
linguistic stock, lengua madre de todos los dialectos que se derivan de ella.
lingulate ['lɪŋgjələt] *a.* lingüiforme; lingulado.
liniment ['lɪnəmənt] *s.* (farm.) linimento, embrocación, untura.
linin ['laɪnən] *s.* (quím., biol.) linina.
lining ['laɪnɪŋ] *s.* 1. forro, revestimiento interior. 2. (enc.) forro, guarnición. 3. (elec.) aislador.
link [lɪŋk] *s.* 1. eslabón (de cadena). 2. eslabón de agrimensor (que equivale a 20 cm). 3. vínculo, lazo, unión, conexión, enlace. 4. (*pl.*) gemelos (en los puños de la camisa). 5. (dial.) (*gen. pl.*) recodo (de una corriente de agua). 6. (elec.) fusible, plomo (de un cortacircuitos). 7. (mec.) eslabón, articulación, acoplador. 8. hacha de viento (antorcha de estopa y alquitrán). *—v.t., v.i.* (ú. gen. con *on, to, together, up*) vincular(se), unir(se), conectar(se), enlazar(se), eslabonar(se); **l. arms,** enlazar los brazos.
linkage ['lɪŋkɪdʒ] *s.* 1. eslabonamiento, unión, nexo, enlace, conexión; sistema de eslabones. 2. (quím.) enlace, afinidad. 3. (elec.) concadenamiento, enlace. 4. (mec.) varillaje, articulación, eslabonamiento, sistema articulado.
link belt, correa articulada.
link block, (mec.) taco del sector de la excéntrica.
linkboy ['lɪŋkˌbɔɪ] *s.* (hist.) paje de hacha.
linked [lɪŋkt] *a.* (biol.) asociado, unido.
link fuse, (elec.) fusible de cinta, fusible descubierto.
linking ['lɪŋkɪŋ] *s.* eslabonamiento, enlace.
linking verb, (gram.) verbo copulativo.
linkman [-mən] *var. de* **linkboy.**
link motion, (mec.) mecanismo o sistema de distribución por cuadrante oscilante.
links [lɪŋks] *s. pl.* 1. cancha de golf. 2. (esco.) dunas, médanos (esp. a la orilla del mar).
linkup ['lɪŋkˌʌp] *s.* 1. reunión, mitin. 2. enlace, conexión.
link verb, (gram.) verbo copulativo.
linkwork [-ˌwɜrk, B -ˌwɜk] *s.* 1. malla; cadena. 2. (mec.) varillaje, articulación, eslabonamiento.
linn [lɪn] *s.* (esco.) 1. balsa o laguna pequeña al pie de una cascada. 2. cascada, salto de agua. 3. barranca empinada.
Linnaean, Linnean [lə'niən] *a.* linneano, de Linneo (Karl Linnaeus, creador de la nomenclatura botánica).
linnet ['lɪnət] *s.* (orn.) pardillo, camachuelo; jilguero.
linocut ['laɪnoʊˌkʌt] *s.* dibujo cortado sobre una superficie de linóleo, grabado en linóleo.
linoleate [lə'noʊlɪˌeɪt] *s.* (quím.) linoleato.
linoleic [ˌlɪnə'lɪɪk] *a.* (quím.) linoleico.
linoleic acid, (quím.) ácido linoleico.
linoleum [lə'noʊlɪəm, -'noʊljəm] *s.* linóleo.
Linotype ['laɪnəˌtaɪp] *s.* (tip.) 1. linotipia (marca de fábrica). 2. (*type*) linotipo.
linotypist [-əst] *s.* linotipista.
linsang ['lɪnˌsæŋ] *s.* (zool.) linsang (especie de civeta de Borneo y Java).
linseed ['lɪnˌsid] *s.* linaza.
linseed cake, torta de linaza (que se usa como forraje).
linseed meal, harina de linaza.
linseed oil, aceite de linaza.
linsey-woolsey ['lɪnzɪ'wʊlzɪ] **linsey** ['lɪnzɪ] *s.* (tej.) paño burdo hecho de hilo y lana, o de algodón y lana. *—a.* basto; mezclado, que no es ni una cosa ni otra.
linstock ['lɪnˌstɑk, B -ˌstɔk] *s.* (hist.) botafuego, lanzafuego.
lint [lɪnt] *s.* 1. hilas (para curar llagas y heridas). 2. hilachas, pelusa, tamo. 3. (esco.) lino. 4. (E.U.) tejido de malla para redes de pescar.
lintel ['lɪntəl] *s.* (arq.) dintel, lintel; umbral.
linter ['lɪntər, B -ə] *s.* 1. máquina despelusadora (de semillas de algodón ya separadas de la fibra). 2. (*pl.*) pelusa de algodón, borra, tamo.
lintwhite ['lɪntˌhwaɪt, -ˌwaɪt] *s.* (orn.) pardillo; jilguero.
linty ['lɪntɪ] *a.* que parece pelusa; lleno o cubierto de pelusa o borra, hilachoso.
lion ['laɪən] *s.* 1. (zool.) leon. 2. (fig.) león (hombre audaz, valiente e impetuoso). 3. celebridad (persona muy festejada y admirada). 4. (astr., astrol.) Leo, León. 5. **in the lion's mouth,** en la boca del lobo, en situación peligrosa; **l. in the way,** obstáculo, esp. imaginario.
lioness [-əs] *s.* (zool.) leona.
lionet [-ˌɛt] *s.* (zool.) cachorro del león, leoncito.
lionheart [-ˌhɑrt, B -ˌhɑt] *s.* 1. persona valiente y magnánima. 2. (hist.) **L.,** Corazón de León (Ricardo I de Inglaterra).
lionhearted [-əd] *a.* valiente, intrépido.
lionization [ˌlaɪənə'zeɪʃən, B -naɪ-] *s.* homenajes y agasajos (que recibe la gente célebre, ej., al llegar a una ciudad).
lionize ['laɪəˌnaɪz] *v.t.* 1. celebrar, agasajar, festejar y alabar (a los famosos). 2. ver o visitar los puntos de interés en (un lugar).
lionlike ['laɪənˌlaɪk] *a.* de aspecto leonino.
lion's foot, (bot.) pata de león, pie de león, alquimila.
lion's share, (fam.) la mejor parte (de un negocio, reparto, etc.).

lip [lɪp] *s.* 1. labio. 2. (jer.) descaro, respuesta insolente. 3. labio, borde. 4. filo (de broca). 5. (bot., zool.) labelo, labium. 6. (mús.) embocadura, boquilla (de un instrumento). 7. (med.) labio, borde (de una llaga o herida). 8. (jer.) **none of your l.!** ¡nada de insolencias!; **to bite one's l.,** morderse los labios; **to curl one's l.,** fruncir los labios (mostrando desprecio o desdén); **to hang on someone's lips,** estar pendiente de los labios o palabras de otro; **to keep a stiff upper l.,** no perder el ánimo, obstinarse; **to lick** (o **smack**) **one's lips,** relamerse (o chasquear) los labios; **to open one's lips,** abrir la boca. —*a.* (*ú. en palabras compuestas*) 1. labial. 2. insincero, hipócrita. 3. (fon.) labial, formado o pronunciado con los labios (díc. de ciertas consonantes). —*v.t.* (*pret., p.p.* LIPPED; *p.pr.* LIPPING) 1. besar, tocar con los labios; lamer. 2. murmurar, susurrar. 3. (golf) hacer llegar la pelota hasta el borde del hoyo (sin que caiga en éste).

lipase [ˈlaɪpˌeɪs, ˈlɪp-, B ˈlaɪp-] *s.* (bioquím.) lipasa.

lip devotion, palabras vanas, insinceridad.

lipemia [ləˈpimɪə] *s.* (med.) lipemia.

lipide [ˈlɪpˌaɪd] **lipid** [-əd] *s.* (bioquím.) lípido.

lipodystrophy [ˌlɪpəˈdɪstrəfɪ] *s.* (med.) lipodistrofia.

lipoid [ˈlɪpˌɔɪd, ˈlaɪp-] *a.* (bioquím.) lipoideo.

lipolysis [lɪˈpɑləsəs, B -ˈpɔl-] *s.* lipólisis.

lipolytic [ˌlɪpəˈlɪtɪk] *a.* lipolítico.

lipoma [lɪˈpoʊmə] *s.* (*pl.* LIPOMATA [-tə] o LIPOMAS) (med.) lipoma.

lipoprotein [ˌlɪpəˈproʊˌtin, -tɪən] *s.* (bioquím.) lipoproteína.

lipothymy [ləˈpɑθəmɪ, B -ˈpɔθ-] *s.* (med.) lipotimia.

lipotropic [ˌlɪpəˈtrɑpɪk, B -ˈtrɔp-] *a.* (bioquím.) lipotrópico.

lipovaccine [-ˌvækˈsin, B -ˈvæksin] *s.* lipovacuna.

lipped [lɪpt] *a.* (*ú. en palabras compuestas*) de labios, ej., *thick-l.,* de labios gruesos.

lipper [ˈlɪpər, B -ə] *s.* (mar.) ligero encrespamiento del mar, mar rizado.

lippy [ˈlɪpɪ] *a.* (jer.) respondón, insolente.

lip-read [ˈlɪpˌrid] *v.t.* leer los labios. —*v.i.* leer los labios, hacer lectura labial (ej., un sordomudo).

lip reader, el que sabe leer los labios, el que hace lectura labial.

lip reading, labiomancia, lectura de los labios.

lipsalve [-ˌsæv, B -ˌsɑv] *s.* 1. ungüento para los labios. 2. (fig.) jarabe de pico.

lip service, jarabe de pico, alabanza o lealtad de dientes afuera; **to pay l. s. to,** alabar insinceramente, aparentar estar de acuerdo (con alguien).

lipstick [-ˌstɪk] *s.* lápiz de labios, lápiz labial.

liquate [ˈlaɪˌkweɪt, B ˈlɪ-] *v.t.* (metal.) licuar, licuefacer.

liquation [laɪˈkweɪʃən, B lɪ-] *s.* (metal.) licuación, licuefacción.

liquefacient [ˌlɪkwəˈfeɪʃənt] *s.* agente licuefaciente o licuefactivo.

liquefaction [-ˈfækʃən] *s.* licuefacción, licuación.

liquefiable [ˈlɪkwəˌfaɪəbəl] *a.* licuable.

liquefied petroleum gas [-ˌfaɪd-] gas licuado de petróleo.

liquefier [-ˌfaɪər, B -ə] *s.* licuador.

liquefy [ˈlɪkwəˌfaɪ] *v.t., v.i.* (*pret., p.p.* LIQUEFIED; *p.pr.* LIQUEFYING) licuar(se), licuefacer(se), derretir(se).

liquescence [lɪˈkwɛsəns] **liquescency** [-ənsɪ] *s.* licuescencia.

liquescent [-ənt] *a.* licuescente; fundente.

liqueur [lɪˈkɜr, B -ˈkjʊə] *s.* licor aromático (alcohólico), poscafé, pluscafé, bajativo (Amer.), cordial.

liqueur brandy, coñac aromático.

liquid [ˈlɪkwəd] *a.* 1. líquido, fluido. 2. límpido, transparente, translúcido. 3. claro, puro, suave (sonido). 4. (com.) líquido, corriente, circulante. 5. (fon.) líquida (consonante). 6. (fís.) líquido. —*s.* 1. líquido, fluido. 2. (fon.) consonante líquida.

liquid air, aire líquido.

liquidambar [-ˌæmbər, B -bə] *s.* 1. (bot.) liquidámbar, ocozol. 2. ámbar líquido, liquidámbar, copalmo.

liquid assets, (com., ten.) activo.

liquidate [ˈlɪkwəˌdeɪt] *v.t.* 1. liquidar (una firma, bienes, cuentas, deudas, etc.). 2. (fig.) liquidar, matar.

liquidation [ˌlɪkwəˈdeɪʃən] *s.* liquidación, disolución; **to go into l.,** entrar en liquidación (un negocio).

liquidator [ˈlɪkwəˌdeɪtər, B -ə] *s.* liquidador.

liquid crystal, cristal líquido.

liquid diet, dieta hídrica, dieta líquida.

liquid fire, (mil.) líquido incendiario (que arroja un lanzallamas).

liquidity [lɪˈkwɪdətɪ] *s.* liquidez, fluidez.

liquidize [ˈlɪkwəˌdaɪz] *v.t.* liquidar, licuar.

liquidly [-wədlɪ] *adv.* líquidamente.

liquid measure, medida para líquidos.

liquidness [-nəs] *s.* liquidez, fluidez.

liquid oxygen, líquido ligero, obtenido por fraccionamiento del aire líquido.

liquor [ˈlɪkər, B -ə] *s.* 1. licor, aguardiente. 2. licor, poscafé. 3. (farm.) licor (solución acuosa). 4. **in l.,** bebido, embriagado; **the worse for l.,** bastante borracho. —*v.i.* (gen. con *up*) (jer.) beber licor. —*v.t.* engrasar (cueros, zapatos).

liquor cabinet, licorera.

liquor case, (G.B.) licorera, frasquera.

liquor dealer, l. distiller, vendedor, fabricante de licores.

liquorice, (pr. G.B.) *var. de* **licorice.**

liquor store, licorería, tienda donde se venden vinos y licores al detalle.

lira [ˈlɪrə, B ˈlɪərə] *s.* (*pl.* LIRE [-eɪ, B -ɪ] o LIRAS) lira (unidad monetaria de Italia; moneda turca de oro).

liriodendron [ˌlɪrɪəˈdɛndrən] *s.* (*pl.* LIRIODENDRA [-drə]) (bot.) liriodendro, tulipanero.

liripipe [ˈlɪrəˌpaɪp] **liripoop** [-ˌpup] *s.* (ant., hist.) 1. cola larga de manga, capucha o sombrero. 2. esclavina, palatina; chalina; pañolón; capucha, caperuza.

Lisbon [ˈlɪzbən] *s.* Lisboa, capital de Portugal.

lisle [laɪl] *s.* (t. **l. thread**) hilo de Escocia.

lisp [lɪsp] *v.i.* 1. cecear. 2. balbucir. —*v.t.* pronunciar de manera balbuciente. —*s.* ceceo; balbuceo.

lis pendens [ˈlɪsˈpɛnˌdɛnz] (der.) litispendencia.

lisper [ˈlɪspər, B -ə] *s.* ceceoso, ceceosa, ceceante.

lisping [-ɪŋ] *a.* ceceante.

lispingly [-lɪ] *adv.* con ceceo.

lissome, lissom [ˈlɪsəm] *a.* flexible, elástico; ágil, veloz, ligero.

lissomely [-lɪ] *adv.* flexiblemente; ágilmente.

lissomeness [-nəs] *s.* flexibilidad, elasticidad; agilidad, ligereza.

list [lɪst] *s.* 1. lista, rol, nómina. 2. lista o raya de color. 3. (pr. G.B.) orilla, orillo, hirma (de tela). 4. (*pl.*) liza, palestra, arena, ej., *to enter the lists,* entrar en la liza, saltar a la palestra. 5. (arq.) listel, listón, filete. 6. (carp.) listón, esp. de albura. 7. (bolsa) **the l.,** lista de valores. 8. (ant.) banda, faja, tira. 9. (ant.) límite, linde; terreno cercado. —*v.t.* 1. alistar, inscribir, asentar, poner en lista; indicar, enumerar, hacer una lista de, catalogar. 2. surcar (la tierra de labranza). 3. (bolsa) inscribir (acciones o valores) en la lista. 4. (ant.) orlar, orillar, guarnecer con orlas u orillas.

list [lɪst] *v.i.* (*pret.* LISTED, *ant.* LIST; *p.p.* LISTED; *p.pr.* LISTING) 1. (mar.) escorar, inclinarse a la banda. 2. desear, antojarse, ej., *the wind blows where it lists,* el viento sopla donde se le antoja. —*v.t.* hacer escorar. —*s.* 1. inclinación; (mar.) escora. 2. (ant.) inclinación, deseo.

listed [ˈlɪstəd] *a.* 1. inscripto en la lista. 2. (com.) cotizado. 3. listado, rayado. 4. cercado (con valla).

listel [ˈlɪstəl] *s.* (arq.) listel, listón, filete.

listen [ˈlɪsən] *v.i.* 1. escuchar, oír. 2. **l. for,** estar atento a (ruido, sonido, etc.); **l. in,** escuchar a hurtadillas (ej., una conversación telefónica); escuchar por radio; **l. to,** escuchar, atender a, prestar atención a, hacer caso de; **l. to reason,** atender razones. —*v.t.* escuchar a, atender a. —*s.* escucha, oída.

listener [-ər, B -ə] *s.* 1. escuchante, escuchador, escuchadora. 2. oyente (ej., de radio), escucha.

listening key, l. plug [-ɪŋ-] clavija de intercalación para conectar con el circuito telefónico.

listening post, (mil.) puesto de escucha.

lister [ˈlɪstər, B -tə] *s.* 1. alistador. 2. (agr.) arado de doble vertedera.

lister drill, (agr.) arado sembrador.

listing [-tɪŋ] *s.* 1. alistamiento, inclusión en una lista. 2. ítem (listado). 3. orilla (de paño); cenefa.

listless [ˈlɪstləs] *a.* indiferente, apático, desganado.

listlessly [-lɪ] *adv.* indiferentemente, desganadamente, apáticamente.

listlessness [-nəs] *s.* indiferencia, desgano, apatía.

list price, (com.) precio de lista, precio de catálogo (sin descuento).

lit [lɪt] *pret., p.p. de* **light.** —*a.* (jer.) achispado, ahumado, picado (Amer.).

litany [ˈlɪtənɪ] *s.* (*pl.* LITANIES) letanía, oración en conjunto.

litchi [ˈlitʃi] *s.* (bot.) (t. **l. nut**) fruto del nefelio.

liter, (G.B.) **litre** [ˈlitər, B -ə] *s.* litro.

literacy [ˈlɪtərəsɪ] *s.* capacidad de leer y escribir, alfabetismo.

literacy campaign, campaña de alfabetización.

literal [ˈlɪtərəl] *a.* 1. literal, textual; al pie de la letra. 2. verdadero, exacto, preciso. 3. prosaico, realista, positivista. 4. literal (traducción).

literalism [-ˌɪzəm] *s.* atención exagerada a la letra o al sentido literal de un texto; (bellas artes) realismo exagerado.

literalist [-əst] *s., a.* literalista (escrupulosamente exacto).

literalistic [ˌlɪtərəˈlɪstɪk] *a.* pegado o aferrado a la letra.

literality [-ˈrælətɪ] *s.* literalidad; significado o interpretación literal.

literalize [ˈlɪtərəˌlaɪz] *v.t.* hacer literal; tomar o interpretar en sentido literal.

literally [-lɪ] *adv.* literalmente, al pie de la letra.

literalness [-rəlnəs] *s.* 1. literalidad, exactitud literal. 2. realismo, naturaleza prosaica.

literarily [ˌlɪtəˈrɛrəlɪ, B ˈlɪtərərɪlɪ] *adv.* literariamente.

literary [ˈlɪtəˌrɛrɪ, B -rərɪ] *a.* 1. literario. 2. literato.

literary agent, agente literario.

literary man, hombre de letras, literato.
literary property, propiedad literaria, propiedad intelectual.
literate [-rət] *a.* 1. que sabe leer y escribir. 2. literato, culto, educado, letrado. —*s.* 1. hombre letrado, persona culta. 2. persona que sabe leer y escribir.
literati [ˌlɪtə'rɑtɪ] *s. pl.* literatos, hombres de letras; (fam.) personas instruidas.
literatim [-'reɪtəm, B -'rɑt-] *adv.* (latín) literalmente, letra por letra.
literature ['lɪtərətʃər, -ˌtʃʊr, B -tʃə] *s.* 1. literatura, profesión literaria. 2. literatura (producción literaria). 3. (fam.) impresos, circulares, catálogos.
lith [lɪθ] *s.* (esco.) miembro, extremidad.
litharge ['lɪθˌɑrdʒ, B -ˌɑdʒ] *s.* (quím.) litargirio, almártaga, almártega.
lithe [laɪð] *a.* flexible, elástico; ágil.
lithely ['laɪðlɪ] *adv.* flexiblemente, de manera flexible, con movimientos elásticos; ágilmente, con gracia y ligereza.
lithemia [lɪ'θimɪə] *s.* (med.) litemia (exceso de ácido úrico y uratos en la sangre).
lithemic [-mɪk] *a.* (med.) litémico.
litheness ['laɪðnəs] *s.* flexibilidad, elasticidad; agilidad.
lithesome ['laɪðsəm] *var. de* **lissome.**
lithi ['litɪ] *s.* (bot.) litre.
lithia ['lɪθɪə] *s.* (quím.) litina.
lithiasis [lɪ'θaɪəsəs] *s.* (med.) litiasis.
lithia water, agua mineral litinada (especie de diurético).
lithic ['lɪθɪk] *a.* (quím., med.) lítico.
lithium [-ɪəm] *s.* (quím.) litio.
lithoclase ['lɪθəˌkleɪs] *s.* (geol.) litoclasa.
lithogenesis [ˌlɪθə'dʒɛnəsəs] **lithogenesy** [-əsɪ] *s.* litogénesis.
lithograph ['lɪθəˌgræf, B -ˌgrɑf] *v.t.* litografiar. —*s.* litografía.
lithographer [lɪ'θɑgrəfər, B -'θɔgrəfə] *s.* litógrafo.
lithographic [ˌlɪθə'græfɪk] **lithographical** [-ɪkəl] *a.* litográfico.
lithographically [-ɪkəlɪ] *adv.* litográficamente.
lithographic stone, (imp.) piedra litográfica.
lithography [lɪ'θɑgrəfɪ, B -'θɔg-] *s.* litografía.
lithoid ['lɪθɔɪd] **lithoidal** [lɪ'θɔɪdəl] *a.* litoideo.
lithologic [ˌlɪθə'lɑdʒɪk, B -'lɔdʒ-] **lithological** [-ɪkəl] *a.* litológico.
lithologist [lɪ'θɑlədʒəst, B -'θɔl-] *s.* litólogo.
lithology [-dʒɪ] *s.* 1. (geol.) litología. 2. (med.) tratado sobre los cálculos.
lithomarge ['lɪθəˌmɑrdʒ, B -ˌmɑdʒ] *s.* (min.) litomarga.
lithophagous [lə'θɑfəgəs, B -'θɔf-] *a.* (zool.) litófago.
lithophotography [ˌlɪθoʊfə'tɑgrəfɪ, B -'tɔg-] *s.* litofotografía.
lithophyte ['lɪθəˌfaɪt] *s.* 1. (bot.) planta litófila. 2. litófito.
lithopone [-ˌpoʊn] *s.* litopón.
lithoprint [-ˌprɪnt] *v.t.* imprimir por litografía.
lithoscope [-ˌskoʊp] *s.* (med.) litoscopio.
lithosperm [-ˌspɜrm, B -ˌspɜm] *s.* (bot.) litospermo.
lithosphere [-ˌsfɪr, B -ˌsfɪə] *s.* litosfera.
lithotint [-ˌtɪnt] *s.* cromolitografía, litografía en colores.
lithotome [-ˌtoʊm] *s.* (med.) litótomo.
lithotomic [ˌlɪθə'tɑmɪk, B -'tɔm-] **lithotomical** [-ɪkəl] *a.* (med.) litotómico.
lithotomy [lɪ'θɑtəmɪ, B -'θɔt-] *s.* (med.) litotomía, talla.
lithotrity [-rətɪ] *s.* (med.) litotricia.
Lithuania [ˌlɪθʊ'eɪnɪə, B -jʊ-] *s.* Lituania, república soviética en el Báltico.
Lithuanian [-nɪən] *a.* lituano. —*s.* lituano (lengua); lituano, lituana (natural de Lituania).
litigable ['lɪtɪgəbəl] *a.* que puede litigarse.
litigant [-gənt] *a., s.* litigante, contendiente.
litigate [-ˌgeɪt] *v.t.* litigar, pleitear, someter a juicio. —*v.i.* litigar, contender.
litigation [ˌlɪtə'geɪʃən] *s.* litigación; litigio, pleito; (fig.) disputa, discusión.
litigator ['lɪtəˌgeɪtər, B -ə] *s.* litigante, pleiteador.
litigious [lɪ'tɪdʒəs] *a.* 1. litigioso, contencioso. 2. litigioso, en litigio. 3. de litigios.
litigiously [-lɪ] *adv.* de modo litigioso, litigiosamente.
litigiousness [-nəs] *s.* inclinación a pleitear.
litmus ['lɪtməs] *s.* (quím.) tornasol.
litmus paper, (quím.) papel de tornasol.
litotes ['laɪtəˌtiz] *s.* (ret.) lítote.
litre, (G.B.) *var. de* **liter.**
litten ['lɪtən] *a.* (poét., ant.) iluminado, con luz.
litter ['lɪtər, B -ə] *s.* 1. litera (coche sin ruedas). 2. camilla, parihuelas. 3. camada, lechigada. 4. cama, mullido de paja (para los animales). 5. basura esparcida; tendalera, fárrago, revoltijo, desorden. 6. mantillo, humus. —*v.t.* 1. (gen. con *down*) preparar la cama a (los animales). 2. esparcir papeles u objetos menudos por (el suelo, etc.), dejar en desorden. 3. parir (animales). —*v.i.* parir una camada o lechigada.
litterateur [ˌlɪtərə'tɜr, B -'tɜ] *s.* literato, hombre de letras.
litter bearer, camillero, andero.
litterbug ['lɪtərˌbʌg, B -əˌ-] *s.* (E.U.) persona que arroja basuras en la vía pública.
littering ['lɪtərɪŋ] *s.* **no littering,** (señal) prohibido tirar basura *or* se prohibe tirar basura.
little ['lɪtəl] *a.* (LESS, LESSER; LEAST; *t.* SMALLER; SMALLEST; dial. y fam., LITTLER; LITTLEST) 1. pequeño, bajo, de poca estatura, ej., *a l. man,* un hombre pequeño. 2. poco, corto, breve (tiempo, lapso; trecho, distancia). 3. poco, poquito; ej., *give him a l. wine,* déle un poquito de vino. 4. insignificante, sin importancia, trivial, fútil; despreciable, mezquino, ej., *the l.,* gente insignificante. 5. *ú. para formar el diminutivo,* ej., *l. car,* carrito, *l. book,* librito. 6. **in l.,** en pequeña escala; **l. man,** (*ú. esp. como vocativo*) niño, joven; **l. ones,** gente menuda; **the l. people,** hadas, duendes. —*adv.* (LESS; LEAST) 1. poco; ligeramente; escasamente, ej., *l.-known authors,* autores poco conocidos. 2. (*delante de verbos*) no, nunca, nada, de ningún modo, ej., *l. did he think he was going to his doom,* él nunca pensó que iba a su perdición. 3. **not a l.,** muy. —*s.* 1. poco, algo (una pequeña cantidad; breve tiempo; corta distancia). 2. **he did what l. he could,** hizo lo poco que podía; **l. by l.,** poco a poco, gradualmente; **l. or nothing,** casi nada; **not a l.,** no poco, bastante; **to make l. of,** no tomar en serio, restar importancia a; **to think l. of,** tener en poco; no vacilar en.
little auk, (orn.) pequeña alca.
Little Bear, (astr.) Osa Menor.
little brain, (anat.) cerebelo.
Little Dipper, (astr.) Carro menor.
Little Dog, (astr.) Can menor.
Little Entente [-ɑn'tɑnt] (hist.) Pequeña Alianza.
little finger, meñique, dedo meñique; **to wrap (o twist) someone around one's l.,** meterse a alguien en el bolsillo.
Little Hours, (relig.) horas menores.
littleneck clam ['lɪtəlˌnɛk-] (zool.) almeja joven.
littleness [-nəs] *s.* 1. pequeñez, poquedad. 2. (fig.) pequeñez, bajeza, mezquindad, ruindad.
Little Office, (relig.) oficio parvo.
little owl, (orn.) mochuelo.
Little Red Ridinghood, Caperucita Roja.
Little Rhody [-'roʊdɪ] (fam.) Estado de Rhode Island.
Little Russian, ruteno, ucraniano, de la república soviética de Ucrania.
little slam, (bridge) pequeño slam (Amer.), semibola (Esp.).
little theater, teatro experimental.
littoral ['lɪtərəl] *a., s.* litoral.
lit up, (jer.) achispado, ahumado, algo beodo, picado (Am.).
liturgical [lə'tɜrdʒɪkəl, B -'tɜdʒɪ-] *a.* litúrgico.
liturgics [-dʒɪks] *s. pl.* (*sing. o pl. en const.*) liturgia.
liturgist ['lɪtərdʒəst, B -ədʒɪst] *s.* liturgista.
liturgy [-dʒɪ] *s.* (relig.) liturgia.
livability [ˌlɪvə'bɪlətɪ] *s.* viabilidad, expectativa de vida (esp. de aves de corral y ganado).
livable ['lɪvəbəl] *a.* 1. sufrible, soportable, ej., *he found life quite l.,* encontró la vida muy agradable. 2. habitable.
live [lɪv] *v.i.* 1. vivir, existir. 2. vivir, habitar, morar. 3. vivir, durar, perdurar. 4. sobrevivir (ej., un enfermo). 5. quedar a flote, salvarse (un barco). 6. **l. and learn,** vivir para ver; **l. and let l.,** vivir y dejar vivir; **l. by,** vivir de, ej., *l. by one's work,* vivir uno de su trabajo; **l. by one's wits,** vivir de gorra; **l. close,** vivir ajustadamente, vivir midiendo el centavo; **live fast,** vivir entregado a los placeres; **l. from hand to mouth,** vivir al día; **l. high,** vivir ostentosamente, darse la gran vida; **l. in,** vivir en la casa (del dueño, díc. de un sirviente, etc.); **l. in a small way,** vivir frugalmente, vivir moderadamente; **l. on,** seguir viviendo; vivir de, alimentarse de; vivir a cargo de, vivir a expensas de; **l. on air,** vivir de la nada, vivir del aire; comer muy poco; **l. on one's fame,** vivir uno de sus laureles; **l. through,** sobrevivir; **l. to oneself,** vivir aislado; **l. up to,** cumplir (promesa, palabra); vivir de acuerdo a, ser digno de; mantenerse fiel a; **l. well,** vivir bien, darse buena vida. —*v.t.* 1. pasar (hora, momentos, etc.), llevar (tal o cual vida). 2. practicar, poner en práctica. 3. sentir intensamente, gozar. 4. **l. a double life,** llevar doble vida; **l. down,** vivir hasta que se borre u olvide (una falta, error, etc.); **l. it up,** pasarse la gran vida; **l. out one's life,** pasar (el resto de) su vida; **l. out the night,** pasar la noche (con vida), amanecer con vida.
live [laɪv] *a.* 1. vivo, viviente. 2. vivo, encendido (fuego, combustibles, etc.). 3. (fig.) candente, palpitante. 4. (fig.) intenso, ej., *a l. fire,* un fuego intenso. 5. bullente, lleno de vida, vivaz; de interés, ej., *a l. topic,* un tema de interés. 6. vivo, brillante (díc. de los colores). 7. (min.) puro, nativo. 8. (elec.) cargado. 9. (aut.) impulsor. 10. (arm.) cargado (cartucho, munición, etc.). 11. (impr., periodismo) fresco; de actualidad; a componer. 12. (rad., t.v.) en directo, ej., *to broadcast l.* transmitir en directo. 13. (dep.) en juego (pelota).
liveable, *var. de* **livable.**
live assets [laɪv-] (com.) dinero disponible, mercaderías realizables.
live axle, eje motor o impulsor.
live bait, carnada viva (en anzuelo).
live-bearing ['laɪv'bɛrɪŋ, B -'bɛər-] *a.* vivíparo.

live box, portaobjetos para el examen microscópico; cajón perforado para conservar vivos los peces, etc.
live center, (mec.) centro de giro; punta giratoria (de tornos).
live coal, ascua, brasa.
live copy, (impr.) material para componer, original para componer.
live flame, llama ardiente.
livelihood [ˈlaɪvlɪˌhʊd] *s.* medios de vida, subsistencia, mantenimiento.
live-in [ˈlɪvˈɪn] *a.* residente.
live-in maid, criada con cama.
live-in partner, (*lover*) novio, novia, compañero, compañera, co-habitante.
liveliness [-nəs] *s.* vivacidad, viveza, animación, prontitud, agilidad, despejo.
live load, (arq., ing.) cargaviva, carga móvil.
livelong [ˈlɪvˌlɔŋ] *a.* todo; entero, largo (que tarda en pasar); **all the l. day,** todo el santo día.
lively [ˈlaɪvlɪ] *a.* (LIVELIER; LIVELIEST) 1. vivaz, vivaracho, vivo; bullicioso, vigoroso; enérgico, activo; animoso; vívido; agudo, penetrante. 2. vivificante, vivificador. 3. rápido, veloz. 4. gallardo, airoso. 5. gráfico, realista (idea, etc.). 6. (raro) que parece vivo, natural. —*adv.* vivamente, aprisa; vívidamente; enérgicamente.
lively step, paso muy ligero.
live matter [laɪv-] (impr.) composición para usar; composición para guardar.
liven [ˈlaɪvən] *v.t., v.i.* (fam.) animar (se).
live oak, (bot.) roble perenne (siempre verde).
liver [ˈlɪvər, B -ə] *s.* 1. (anat., zool.) hígado; (cocina) hígado. 2. morador, residente.
liver complaint, mal de hígado.
liver extract, (farm.) extracto de hígado.
liver fluke, (zool.) duela, pirhuín, saguaipe (Amer.).
liveried [ˈlɪvərid] *a.* en librea (conserje, bedel, etc.).
liverish [ˈlɪvərɪʃ] *a.* (fam.) 1. enfermo del hígado. 2. avinagrado, enojadizo.
Liverpudlian [ˌlɪvərˈpʌdlɪən, B -vəˈ-] *a.* de Liverpool. —*s.* natural o habitante de Liverpool, Inglaterra.
liverwort [ˈlɪvərˌwɜrt, B -əˌwɜt] *s.* (bot.) hepática, empeine.
liverwurst [-ˌwɜrst, B -ˌwɜst] *s.* salchicha o embutido de hígado.
livery [ˈlɪvərɪ] *s.* (*pl.* LIVERIES) 1. librea; uniforme. 2. facha, traza. 3. pensionado de caballos; (E.U.) caballeriza (donde se cuidan o alquilan caballos). 4. (der.) entrega. 5. (ant.) servidores; dependientes, sirvientes. 6. (ant.) ración.
livery company, (hist., G.B.) uno de los gremios o hermandades de Londres.
livery horse, caballo de alquiler.
liveryman [-mən] *s.* 1. (hist., G.B.) miembro de un gremio o hermandad. 2. dueño de una caballeriza o cuadra de carruajes de alquiler. 3. (ant.) criado de librea.
livery stable, caballeriza o pensión de caballos; cochera de carruajes de alquiler.
lives [laɪvz] *pl. de* **life.**
live spindle, (mec.) husillo giratorio.
live steam, vapor de la caldera; vapor activo.
livestock [ˈlaɪvˌstɑk, B -ˌstɔk] *s.* ganado, ganadería.
live wire, 1. (elec.) alambre cargado. 2. (jer.) trafagón (persona enérgica, persona activa y eficiente).
livid [ˈlɪvəd] *a.* 1. cárdeno, amoratado, lívido. 2. plomizo, ceniciento. 3. pálido, ceniciento, lívido.
lividity [lɪˈvɪdətɪ] **lividness** [ˈlɪvədnəs] *s.* lividez.
living [ˈlɪvɪŋ] *s.* 1. vida. 2. medios de vida, subsistencia, mantenimiento. 3. (G.B. relig.) beneficio. 4. (ant.) bienes; propiedades. 5. **for a l.,** para ganarse la vida; **good l.,** buena vida; **plain l. and high thinking,** vida frugal y filosófica; **to earn one's l., to make a l.,** ganarse la vida; **way of l.,** manera o modo de vivir. —*a.* 1. vivo, viviente. 2. activo; eficaz. 3. lleno de vida; vívido. 4. para vivir (ej., zona). 5. encendido, ardiente. 6. natural (roca, etc.); corriente (agua). 7. **the l.,** los vivos.
living allowance, gastos de estadía.
living death, muerte en vida (vida despojada de todo aquello que la hace llevadera).
living quarters, habitaciones, vivienda.
living room, sala, sala de estar, salón principal de un hogar.
living wage, (e.p.) salario vital, salario de subsistencia plena.
Livonian [lɪˈvoʊnɪən] *a., s.* livonio, de Livonia (región báltica de la U.R.S.S.).
lixiviate [lɪkˈsɪvɪˌeɪt] *v.t.* lixiviar.
lixiviation [lɪkˌsɪvɪˈeɪʃən] *s.* lixiviación.
lixivium [-ˈsɪvɪəm] *s.* lixivio.
lizard [ˈlɪzərd, B -əd] *s.* (zool.) lagarto, lagartija; saurio.
lizard fish, (ict.) lagarto.
lizzie [ˈlɪzɪ] *s.* coche barato, estropeado o viejo, (t. **tin lizzie**).
llama [ˈlɑmə] *s.* (zool.) llama.
llano [ˈlɑnoʊ] *s.* (*pl.* LLANOS) llano, llanura (en Sudamérica).
LL.B. *abrev. de* **Bachelor of Laws,** Licenciado en Derecho.
LL.D. *abrev. de* **Doctor of Laws,** Doctor en Derecho.
LL.M. *abrev. de* **Master of Laws,** Maestro en Derecho.
LMT *abrev. de* **local mean time,** hora media local.
lo [loʊ] *interj.* ¡he aquí! ¡ved aquí! ¡mirad! ú. gen. en **l. and behold!**
loach [loʊtʃ] *s.* (ict.) locha.
load [loʊd] *s.* 1. carga; cargamento. 2. (fig.) opresión, presión, peso. 3. carga (de un arma de fuego). 4. (*pl.*) montón, montones, gran cantidad, gran número, muchísimos. 5. tareas, deberes (anejos a un estado, empleo u oficio). 6. (elec.) carga. 7. (mec.) carga; resistencia. 8. (ing., mec., elec.) coeficiente de produción o rendimiento, producción. 9. (pint.) color blanco opacificante. 10. (jer.) trago (de bebida alcohólica). 11. **at full l.,** con carga completa; **to carry a l.,** (jer.) estar borracho; estar bajo la influencia de estupefacientes; **take (o get) a l. of this,** (jer.) ¡fíjese! ¡oiga esto! ¡escuche bien!; **to take a l. off one's mind,** quitarse un peso de encima. —*v.t.* 1. cargar (un vehículo, etc.). 2. agobiar, abrumar (por una carga). 3. cargar (arma de fuego, cámara fotográfica, etc.). 4. adulterar, poner narcótico en, ej., *l. wine,* adulterar el vino. 5. recargar (la prima de un seguro). 6. **l. with,** colmar de (trabajo, etc.). —*v.i.* 1. cargar; cargarse, recibir carga. 2. cargar un arma de fuego.
load displacement, (mar.) desplazamiento (de un barco) con carga total.
loaded [ˈloʊdəd] *a.* (jer.) 1. cargado (arma, cámara fotográfica, etc.). 2. rico, podrido en plata (Amer.). 3. ebrio, borracho. 4. **to get l.,** emborracharse.
loaded dice, dados cargados.
loader [-ər, B -ə] *s.* cargador (hombre); cargadora (máquina).
load factor, (elec.) factor de carga, coeficiente de aprovechamiento.
loading [-ɪŋ] *s.* 1. carga, cargamento. 2. (aer.) carga, volumen del tráfico. 3. (seguros) sobreprima, prima adicional. —*a.* que carga, de cargar, ej., *l. zone,* zona reservada para cargar mercancía.
loading coil, (elec.) bobina aumentadora de inductancia.
load line, (mar.) línea de carga.
loadstar, *var. de* **lodestar.**
loadstone, *var. de* **lodestone.**
loaf [loʊf] *s.* (*pl.* LOAVES [loʊvz]) 1. hogaza; pilón, pan (de azúcar). 2. (cocina) pastel de carne (en forma de hogaza). 3. (jer., G.B.) coco, cabeza. 4. (ant. dial.) pan. —*v.i.* haraganear, holgazanear; **l. around,** grandulear.
loafer [ˈloʊfər, B -fə] *s.* 1. haragán, holgazán, ocioso. 2. chinela; zapato estilo mocasín.
loaf sugar, azúcar de pilón.
loam [loʊm] *s.* 1. tierra negra; greda, barro, marga. 2. arcilla de moldeo. —*v.t.* cubrir o llenar con marga o arcilla.
loamy [ˈloʊmɪ] *a.* margoso.
loan [loʊn] *s.* préstamo, empréstito; **on l.,** prestado. —*v.t.* prestar, dar prestado.
loan [loʊn] *s.* (Filip.) loán (medida agraria).
loan office, casa de préstamos.
loan shark, (fam.) usurero, cuervo negro (Am.).
loanshift [ˈloʊnˌʃɪft] *s.* palabra extranjera que, cambiados algunos de sus morfemas, se adapta a otro idioma.
loan translation, palabra extranjera (traducida literalmente) que se adapta a otro idioma.
loanword [-ˌwɜrd, B -ˌwɜd] *s.* voz extranjera (adoptada de otro idioma).
loath [loʊθ] *a.* 1. poco dispuesto, reacio, renuente. 2. (ant.) odioso, repulsivo. 3. **l. to,** reacio a.
loathe [loʊð] *v.t.* abominar, detestar, aborrecer, odiar.
loathful [ˈloʊðfəl] *a.* aborrecible, detestable, repugnante.
loathing [-ɪŋ] *s.* aversión, repugnancia, hastío.
loathsome [-səm] *a.* repulsivo, repugnante; detestable, odioso.
loathsomely [-lɪ] *adv.* repugnantemente, repulsivamente.
loathsomeness [-nəs] *s.* repulsividad, aspecto detestable o repugnante.
loaves [loʊvz] *pl. de* **loaf.**
lob [lɑb, B lɔb] *v.t.* (*pret., p.p.* LOBBED; *p.pr.* LOBBING) (criquet) lanzar (la pelota) en trayectoria alta y con poca velocidad; (tenis) tirar (una pelota) por alto. —*v.i.* 1. moverse pesada o torpemente. 2. (tenis) darle a una pelota para que vaya por alto. —*s.* 1. (criquet) tiro alto y suave de la pelota (gen. con mucho efecto); (tenis) lanzamiento alto y tendido de la pelota. 2. lombriz para cebo, arenícola.
lobar [ˈloʊbər, -ˌbar, B -bə] *a.* lobar, lobular.
lobar pneumonia, (med.) neumonía lobar.
lobate [ˈloʊˌbeɪt] **lobated** [-əd] *a.* lobado, lobulado.
lobation [loʊˈbeɪʃən] *s.* 1. formación de lóbulos. 2. lóbulo, lobulillo.
lobby [ˈlɑbɪ, B ˈlɔbɪ] *s.* 1. pasillo, corredor; antecámara; vestíbulo, foyer (de un hotel). 2. (E.U., pol.) camarilla de cabilderos. —*v.i.* (E.U.) cabildear. —*v.t.* procurar la aprobación de (un proyecto de ley) por cabildeo.
lobbyism [-ˌɪzəm] *s.* (E.U., pol.) cabildeo.
lobbyist [-əst] *s.* (E.U., pol.) cabildero.
lobe [loʊb] *s.* 1. (anat.) lóbulo (de una víscera, etc.). 2. (aer.) saco de gas; compartimento.
lobectomy [loʊˈbɛktəmɪ] *s.* (med.) lobectomía.
lobed [loʊbd] *a.* lobado, lobulado (díc. esp. de las hojas).

lobelia [loʊ'biljə] *s.* (bot.) lobelia.
lobeliaceous [ˌloʊbilɪ'eɪʃəs] *a.* (bot.) lobeliáceo.
loblolly ['lɑbˌlɑlɪ, B 'lɔbˌlɔlɪ] *s.* 1. (dial.) gacha espesa. 2. (t. **l. pine**) (bot.) pino del incienso (árbol y madera). 3. lodazal.
loblolly bay, (bot.) árbol de la familia de las siemprevivas.
lobo ['loʊboʊ] *s.* (zool.) lobo gris (de E.U.).
lobotomy [loʊ'bɑtəmɪ, B -'bɔt-] *s.* (med.) lobotomía.
lobscouse ['lɑbˌskaʊs, B 'lɔb-] *s.* (mar.) olla, puchero.
lobster ['lɑbstər, B 'lɔbstə] *s.* 1. (zool.) langosta, bogavante. 2. (ant., despect.) soldado inglés. 3. **spiny l.,** langosta.
lobster joint, unión o conexión de piezas soldadas.
lobster Newburg [-'nuˌbɜrg, B -'njuˌbɜg] (cocina) plato que consiste en trozos de langosta cocidos en una rica salsa con jerez.
lobster pot, langostera (trampa para coger langostas).
lobster shift, l. trick, turno nocturno (de trabajadores, esp. de un periódico).
lobster tail, cola de langosta; la carne de esta parte.
lobster thermidor [-'θɜrməˌdɔr, B -'θɜmɪˌdɔ] plato que consiste en carne de langosta, setas, etc., que se sirve en el carapacho de la langosta.
lobular ['lɑbjələr, B 'lɔbjʊlə] *a.* lobular.
lobulate [-ˌleɪt] **lobulated** [-əd] *a.* (bot., zool.) lobulado.
lobule [-ˌjul] *s.* lobulillo.
lobworm ['lɑbˌwɜrm, B 'lɔbˌwɜm] *s.* (ento.) arenícola.
local ['loʊkəl] *a.* 1. local; regional, vecinal; (med.) local. 2. limitado, ej., *a. l. point of view,* un punto de vista limitado. —*s.* 1. tren, subterráneo o autobús local. 2. junta local (de confraternidad, gremio, etc.). 3. noticia de interés local. 4. (G.B., fam.) taberna o bar de barrio.
local anesthesia, (med.) anestesia local.
local anesthetic, anestésico local.
local attraction, 1. (top.) atracción local, perturbación de la brújula. 2. (fís.) atracción de la plomada.
local battery, (teleg.) pila o batería local, batería para instrumentos.
local call, (tele.) llamada urbana.
local color, (lit.) color local.
locale [loʊ'kæl, B -'kɑl] *s.* localidad, sitio; escena (de un crimen, etc.); situación.
local government, (pol.) gobierno municipal o regional; las personas elegidas para administrar este gobierno.
local horizon, horizonte sensible.
localism ['loʊkəˌlɪzəm] *s.* 1. localismo; costumbre o locución local. 2. predilección por cierto lugar. 3. provincialismo.
locality [loʊ'kælətɪ] *s.* localidad, lugar, sitio.
localization [ˌloʊkələ'zeɪʃən, B -lɑɪ-] *s.* localización.
localize ['loʊkəˌlaɪz] *v.t.* localizar.
locally [-kəlɪ] *adv.* localmente.
local option, (E.U.) poder discrecional territorial (para determinar si ciertas leyes son aplicables, esp. la venta de bebidas alcohólicas).
local remedy, remedio tópico o externo.
local time, hora local, tiempo local.
local value, (mat.) valor relativo (de una cifra).
locate ['loʊˌkeɪt, loʊ'keɪt, B -'keɪt] *v.t.* 1. situar, colocar, ubicar, establecer (algo en un lugar determinado). 2. localizar, dar con, dar con el paradero de. 3. (mat.) situar. —*v.i.* establecerse.

location [loʊ'keɪʃən] *s.* 1. ubicación, colocación, emplazamiento. 2. sitio, localidad; situación, posición. 3. (der.) contrato de alquiler o arrendamiento. 4. **on l.** (cinem.) (rodaje) exterior, fuera del estudio.
locative ['lɑkətɪv, B 'lɔk-] *a., s.* (gram.) locativo.
locator ['loʊˌkeɪtər, loʊ'keɪtər, B -ə] *s.* 1. (E.U.) localizador (de un terreno o una concesión minera). 2. detector de radio, radar.
loch [lɑk, B lɔk] *s.* (esco.) lago; ensenada, bahía o brazo de mar (casi cerrada por tierra).
lochia ['loʊkɪə, B 'lɔk-] *s. pl.* (med.) loquios.
lochial [-ɪəl] *a.* (med.) loquial.
loci ['loʊˌsaɪ, -ˌkaɪ] *pl. de* **locus.**
lock [lɑk, B lɔk] *s.* 1. cerradura, cerrojo, llave. 2. esclusa. 3. enlace, unión; abrazo fuerte. 4. cerrojo (del fusil). 5. traba; retén (para frenar las ruedas). 6. aglomeración (ej., de vehículos en la calle). 7. (ing.) antecámara (cajón neumático que sirve para conectar dos cámaras de diferentes presiones de aire). 8. (dep.) llave (en la lucha). 9. mechón, rizo, bucle (de cabello); (*pl.*) cabellera, cabellos. 10. vedija, vellón o borla (de lana, lino o algodón). 11. **l., stock and barrel,** (fam.) por completo, completamente; **under l. and key,** bajo llave. —*v.t.* 1. cerrar, echar llave a, cerrar con llave. 2. trabar. 3. entrecruzar, entrelazar. 4. (t. con *up*) inmovilizar, bloquear (capital, etc.). 5. hacer pasar por una esclusa. 6. **l. in,** encerrar (en); **l. off,** dividir (un canal) por esclusas; **l. (one) out,** cerrar la puerta a (uno), dejar (a uno) en la calle; dejar (a uno) sin trabajo; **l. up,** encerrar, poner bajo llave; encarcelar; (impr.) acuñar, cerrar (la forma). —*v.i.* 1. cerrarse (con llave). 2. unirse, enlazarse. 3. pasar por una esclusa.
lockage ['lɑkɪdʒ, B 'lɔk-] *s.* 1. paso (de una embarcación) por una esclusa. 2. portazgo (de esclusa). 3. serie o sistema de esclusas.
locker [-ər, B -ə] *s.* 1. cajón, gaveta. 2. alacena, armario, ropero; armario con llave. 3. cerrador. 4. congelador (para guardar alimentos a temperaturas bajo cero). 5. (mar.) cajonada, cajón.
locker room, vestuario, cuarto con roperos (en gimnasios, fábricas, etc.); (fam.) (*humor*) de machos.
locket ['lɑkət, B 'lɔk-] *s.* relicario, medallón, guardapelo.
locking ['lɑkɪŋ, B 'lɔk-] *s.* 1. cierre. 2. fijación, traba. —*a.* 1. fijador, de fijación. 2. de cierre, de traba.
locking gear, engranaje trabador.
locking plate, platillo fijador.
locking wire, (aer.) alambre fijador.
lockjaw ['lɑkˌdʒɔ, B 'lɔk-] *s.* (med.) trismo; tétanos, tétano.
lockmaster [-ˌmæstər, B -ˌmɑstə] *s.* persona encargada de una esclusa.
locknut [-ˌnʌt] *s.* (med.) tuerca de seguridad, contratuerca, tuerca de fijación, tuerca inaflojable.
lockout [-ˌaʊt] *s.* cierre forzoso (de una fábrica, etc., impuesto por los patronos a los empleados como medida de contrahuelga, o para que acepten alguna condición), huelga patronal.
lockscrew [-ˌskru] *s.* tornillo de seguridad, tornillo de traba.
lock-seaming ['lɑkˌsimɪŋ, B 'lɔk-] *s.* (mec.) engatillado.
locksman ['lɑksmən, B 'lɔks-] *s.* vigilante de la esclusa.
locksmith ['lɑkˌsmɪθ, B 'lɔk-] *s.* cerrajero.
locksmithery [-ərɪ] **locksmithing** [-ɪŋ] *s.* cerrajería.
lock step, marcha en filas cerradas.

lock stitch, cadeneta, doble pespunte.
lock strike, hembra de cerrojo, hembra de pestillo.
lockup ['lɑkˌʌp, B 'lɔk-] *s.* 1. encarcelamiento, cierre, encierro. 2. cárcel, calabozo.
lock washer, (mec.) arandela de seguridad, roldana de presión.
loco ['loʊkoʊ] *s.* 1. (bot.) loco. 2. (vet.) locoísmo. —*v.t.* 1. envenenar con locos. 2. (fam.) enloquecer, volver loco. —*a.* (jer.) loco, enloquecido.
loco disease, (vet.) locoísmo.
locoism [-ˌɪzəm] *s.* (vet.) locoísmo.
locomotion [ˌloʊkə'moʊʃən] *s.* locomoción.
locomotive [-'moʊtɪv, B 'loʊkəˌmoʊt-] *a.* locomotor, locomóvil. —*s.* locomotora.
locomotive boiler, (f.c.) caldera de locomotora.
locomotive engine, (máquina) locomotora.
locomotive engineer, (f.c.) maquinista.
locomotor [-'moʊtər, B -ˌmoʊtə] *a.* locomotor, locomotriz.
locomotor ataxia, (med.) ataxia locomotriz progresiva.
locoweed ['loʊkoʊˌwid] *s.* (bot.) loco, hierba leguminosa, loca.
locular ['lɑkjələr, B 'lɔkjʊlə] *a.* (bot., zool.) locular.
loculate [-lət, -ˌleɪt] **loculated** [-ˌleɪtəd] *a.* (bot.) loculado, loculoso.
locule ['lɑkjul, B 'lɔk-] *s.* (bot.) lóculo.
loculus ['lɑkjələs, B 'lɔk-] *s.* (*pl.* LOCULI [-ˌlaɪ]) 1. (bot.) lóculo. 2. (biol.) lóculo, celdilla, cavidad.
locum ['loʊkəm] *s.* (fam.) *abrev. de* **locum tenens.**
locum tenens [-'tiˌnɛnz] sustituto, interino, reemplazante (esp. de un médico o un clérigo).
locus ['loʊkəs] *s.* 1. lugar, sitio. 2. (mat.) lugar geométrico.
locust ['loʊkəst] *s.* 1. (ento.) langosta, saltamontes. 2. (ento.) cigarra. 3. (bot.) acacia blanca, acacia falsa, robinia; algarrobo; acacia negra.
locust bean, algarroba.
locution [loʊ'kjuʃən] *s.* locución, frase.
locutory ['lɑkjəˌtɔrɪ, B 'lɔkjʊtərɪ] *s.* locutorio.
lode [loʊd] *s.* 1. (dial., G.B.) vía acuática, canal o río navegable. 2. (min.) filón; veta.
loden ['loʊdən] *s.* (tej.) género fuerte de lana para confeccionar abrigos. —*a.* el color olivo oscuro de dicho paño.
lodestar ['loʊdˌstɑr, B -ˌstɑ] *s.* 1. estrella de guía; estrella polar. 2. (fig.) norte, guía.
lodestone [-ˌstoʊn] *s.* piedra imán, calamita, caramida.
lodge [lɑdʒ, B lɔdʒ] *s.* 1. pabellón de caza; casa de campo. 2. hotel, posada (gen. en el campo). 3. casita (del jardinero, portero). 4. logia (masónica). 5. guarida, cubil, madriguera. 6. tienda, choza, cabaña (de los indios de E.U.); familia de indios. 7. (ant., dial.) casucha, pocilga. —*v.t.* 1. alojar, hospedar, aposentar; albergar, cobijar. 2. colocar; introducir; fijar; plantar. 3. conferir, otorgar (autoridad), investir (de poderes). 4. depositar, dar a guardar. 5. sentar (una denuncia); comunicar (información). —*v.i.* 1. alojarse; hospedarse. 2. residir, morar (como huésped). 3. tenderse, echarse.
lodgement, *var. de* **lodgment.**
lodger ['lɑdʒər, B 'lɔdʒə] *s.* huésped, alojado; inquilino.
lodging [-ɪŋ] *s.* 1. alojamiento, hospedaje. 2. (*pl.*) cuartos, aposentos, habitaciones (esp. alquiladas); 3. **to take lodgings,** alojarse, hospedarse.
lodging house, albergue, casa de huéspedes.
lodgment [-mənt] *s.* 1. hospedamiento, alojamiento; habitación. 2. colocación, depósito. 3. amontonamiento, acumulación. 4. posición

firme, sitio establecido. 5. (mil.) toma (de una posición), conquista (de territorio), atrincheramiento.
lodicule ['lɑdɪˌkjul, B 'lɔd-] *s.* (bot.) lodícula, glumélula.
loess [lɛs, B 'loʊɪs] *s.* (geol.) loes.
loft [lɔft, lɑft, B lɔft] *s.* 1. desván, buhardilla, sobrado. 2. henal, henil. 3. (E.U.) piso superior (de un almacén). 4. galería, ej., *organ l.*, galería del órgano. 5. (golf) ángulo de la cara del mazo; golpe que eleva la bola. —*v.t.* 1. construir o equipar con un desván. 2. almacenar en un desván, granero o henil. 3. (golf) pegar a la pelota para que se eleve; darle ángulo a (la cara del mazo). —*v.i.* (golf) enviar la pelota por alto.
lofter ['lɔftər, 'lɑf-, B 'lɔftə] *s.* (golf) mazo de hierro para levantar la pelota.
loftily [-təlɪ] *adv.* altivamente, orgullosamente.
loftiness [-tɪnəs] *s.* 1. altura, elevación. 2. altivez, altanería, orgullo. 3. eminencia, distinción, majestad.
lofting iron [-tɪŋ-] *(golf) mazo de hierro para levantar la pelota.*
lofty [-tɪ] *a.* (LOFTIER; LOFTIEST) 1. alto, elevado, encumbrado; descollante, dominante. 2. altivo, orgulloso, soberbio. 3. eminente, excelso, distinguido.
log [lɔg, lɑg, B lɔg] *s.* 1. tronco, leño. 2. (mar.) corredera; barquilla de la corredera. 3. (mar.) cuaderno de bitácora, diario de navegación. 4. (aer.) diario de vuelo; registro de horas de vuelo, experiencias, etc. del piloto. 5. diario o registro del progreso o sucesos (de una expedición, experimento, etc.). 6. registro de rendimiento o funcionamiento (de motores, etc.). 7. **in the l.**, en bruto; **to heave** (o **throw**) **the l.**, medir la velocidad de una nave usando la corredera; **to sail by the l.**, calcular la posición de la nave usando la corredera; **to sleep like a l.**, dormir como un tronco. —*a.* de tronco; hecho de troncos. —*v.t.* (*pret., p.p.* LOGGED; *p.pr.* LOGGING) 1. cortar, derribar (árboles); aserrar (troncos), desmontar (terreno). 2. registrar (velocidad, etc.) en el cuaderno de bitácora. 3. cubrir, recorrer (cierta distancia), ej., *we have logged 100 miles*, hemos cubierto 100 millas. —*v.i.* dedicarse a la explotación forestal.
loganberry ['loʊgənˌbɛrɪ, B -bərɪ] *s.* (bot.) frambuesa americana (cruce de frambuesa con zarzamora).
loganiaceous ['loʊˌgeɪnɪ'eɪʃəs] *a.* (bot.) loganiáceo.
logaoedic [ˌlɑgə'idɪk, B ˌlɔg-] *a.* (poét.) logaédico.
logarithm ['lɔgəˌrɪðəm, 'lɑg-, B 'lɔgəˌrɪθ-] *s.* (mat.) logaritmo.
logarithmic [ˌlɔgə'rɪðmɪk, ˌlɑg-, B ˌlɔgə'rɪθ-] **logarithmical** [-mɪkəl] *a.* (mat.) logarítmico.
logarithmically [-mɪkəlɪ] *adv.* por logaritmos.
logarithm table, tabla de logaritmos.
logbook ['lɔgˌbʊk, 'lɑg-, B 'lɔg-] *s.* 1. (mar.) cuaderno de bitácora; diario de navegación. 2. (aer.) diario de vuelo. 3. diario (de una expedición, etc.).
log cabin, cabaña de troncos.
log chip, (mar.) barquilla de la corredera, guindola.
log driver, ganchero.
loge [loʊʒ] *s.* palco (de teatro).
logger ['lɔgər, 'lɑg-, B 'lɔgə] *s.* 1. maderero, explotador forestal; talador, leñero. 2. (mec.) cargadora de troncos.
loggerhead [-ˌhɛd] *s.* 1. (zool.) tortuga mordedora. 2. herramienta de hierro de mango largo terminado en una bola y que sirve para derretir brea o calentar líquidos. 3. necio, tonto, mentecato. 4. **at loggerheads,** en disputa, en desacuerdo.
loggerhead shrike, (orn.) alcaudón.
loggia ['lɑdʒɪə, 'lɔ-, B 'lɔdʒə] *s.* (arq.) logia, loggia, galería, pórtico.
logging ['lɔgɪŋ, 'lɑg-, B 'lɔg-] *s.* tala, corta (de árboles); explotación forestal; transporte de troncos.
logic ['lɑdʒɪk, B 'lɔdʒ-] *s.* lógica, dialéctica.
logical [-ɪkəl] *a.* 1. lógico, dialéctico. 2. consecuente, natural.
logicality [ˌlɑdʒə'kælətɪ, B ˌlɔdʒ-] *s.* carácter lógico.
logically [-kəlɪ] *adv.* lógicamente.
logical positivism, positivismo lógico.
logician [loʊ'dʒɪʃən] *s.* lógico, dialéctico.
logistic [-'dʒɪstɪk] *s.* (filos.) logística, lógica simbólica. —*a.* logístico.
logistical [-tɪkəlɪ] *a.* logístico.
logistician [loʊˌdʒɪs'tɪʃən] *s.* (mil.) experto en logística.
logistics [-'dʒɪstɪks] *s.* (mil.) logística; intendencia.
logjam ['lɔgˌdʒæm, 'lɑg-, B 'lɔg-] *s.* 1. masa de troncos estancados (en un río, etc.). 2. (fig.) obstrucción, estancamiento.
log line, (mar.) corredera; cordel de la corredera.
logo ['lɔgoʊ, 'lɑg-, B 'lɔg-] *s.* (tip.) forma abreviada de **logotipo.**
logogram [-əˌgræm] *s.* signo taquigráfico, fonograma (de una palabra, ej., *$* por pesos).
logograph [-ˌgræf, B -ˌgrɑf] *s.* fonograma.
logography [ˌloʊ'gɑgrəfɪ, B ˌlɔ'gɔg-] *s.* logografía.
logogriph ['lɔgəˌgrɪf, 'lɑg-, B 'lɔg-] *s.* logogrifo, anagrama.
logogriphic [ˌlɔgə'grɪfɪk, ˌlɑg-, B ˌlɔg-] *a.* logogrífico.
logomachy [loʊ'gɑməkɪ, B lɔ'gɔm-] *s.* 1. logomaquia, discusión sobre palabras. 2. juego anagramático.
logorrhea [ˌlɔgə'riə, lɑg-, B ˌlɔgə'rɪə] *s.* logorrea, locuacidad excesiva, incoherente o incontrolable.
logos ['lɑgɑs, 'loʊ-, B 'lɔgɔs] *s.* 1. (filos.) logos (razón universal o del hombre, principio activo del mundo). 2. (teo.) **L.**, (el) Verbo, Hijo de Dios.
logotype ['lɔgəˌtaɪp, 'lɑg-, B 'lɔg-] *s.* (tip.) logotipo.
log raft, armadía, almadía, balsa.
log reel, (mar.) carretel de la corredera.
logroll ['lɔgˌroʊl, 'lɑg-, B 'lɔg-] *v.i.* (pret. *p.p.* LOGROLLED; *p.pr.* LOGROLLING). 1. rodar, conducir o trasportar troncos por un río. 2. trocar favores, darse ayuda recíproca. —*v.t.* lograr la aprobación de un proyecto de ley prometiendo apoyar otro.
logrolling [-ɪŋ] *s.* 1. (E.U.) giro de los troncos en el agua por medio de movimientos de los pies; deporte en que los contendores tratan de derribarse mutuamente haciendo girar los troncos. 2. convenio de ayuda mutua (entre políticos, etc.).
log ship, (mar.) barquilla de la corredera, guindola.
logwood [-ˌwʊd] *s.* 1. (bot.) campeche, palo campeche (árbol y madera). 2. tinte (que se obtiene de este árbol).
logy ['loʊgɪ] *a.* 1. (E.U.) torpe, lerdo. 2. (fam.) pesado, lento, tardo.
loin [lɔɪn] *s.* 1. ijada, ijar. 2. (anat.) lomo. 3. **to gird up one's loins,** ceñirse los riñones (apercibirse para la acción).
loincloth ['lɔɪnˌklɔθ] *s.* taparrabo.
loin of beef, filete, solomillo, falda.
Loire [lwɑr, B lwɑ] *s.* Loira (río y región de Francia).
loiter ['lɔɪtər, B -ə] *v.i.* remolonear, holgazanear, vagar, haraganear. —*v.t.* **l. (time) away,** desperdiciar (tiempo) en ocio.
loiterer [-ərər, B -ərə] *s.* remolón, holgazán, vagabundo.
loll [lɑl, B lɔl] *v.i.* 1. apoyarse, recostarse. 2. pender, colgar, estar colgando (lengua de un animal). 3. reclinarse, tenderse o echarse de manera indolente, arrellanarse. —*v.t.* dejar colgar (la lengua).
lollapalooza [ˌlɑləpə'luzə, B ˌlɔl-] *s.* (jer.) persona, cosa o acontecimiento extraordinario o poco común.
Lollards ['lɑlərdz, B 'lɔlədz] *s. pl.* (hist.) lollardos.
lollipop ['lɑlɪˌpɑp, B 'lɔlɪˌpɔp] *s.* caramelo en palito, paleta, chupete (Am.).
lollop ['lɑləp, B 'lɔl-] *v.i.* 1. andar a saltos o brincos. 2. (dial., G.B.) moverse o tenderse indolentemente.
lolly ['lɑlɪ, B 'lɔlɪ] *s.* (G.B.) 1. (fam.) caramelo en palito, chupete (Am.), dulce. 2. (jer.) guita, mosca (dinero).
lollygag [-ˌgæg] *v.i.* (fam.) perder el tiempo, remolonear.
Lombard ['lɑmˌbɑrd, B 'lɔmbəd] *s.* 1. lombardo, de Lombardía. 2. prestamista, banquero.
Lombard, *s.* (hist., mil.) lombarda.
Lombardic [lɑm'bɑrdɪk, B 'lɔm'bɑd-] *a.* lombardo, lombárdico, de Lombardía, región de Italia.
Lombardy ['lɑmbərdɪ, B 'lɔmbədɪ] *s.* Lombardía, región del norte de Italia.
Lombardy poplar, (bot.) chopo lombardo.
loment ['loʊˌmɛnt] *s.* (bot.) lomento.
lomentaceous [ˌloʊmən'teɪʃəs] *a.* (bot.) lomentáceo.
lomentum [loʊ'mɛntəm] *s.* (bot.) lomento.
Lond. *abrev. de* **London,** Londres.
London ['lʌndən] *s.* Londres, capital de Gran Bretaña.
London broil, bistec asado y cortado en lascas finas.
Londoner [-dənər, B -nə] *s.* londinense.
London ivy, (G.B.) niebla londinense.
lone [loʊn] *a.* 1. solitario. 2. único, solo. 3. soltero o viudo. 4. aislado, poco frecuentado. 5. **to play a l. hand,** obrar solo, actuar por cuenta propia.
loneliness ['loʊnlɪnəs] *s.* soledad; tristeza o melancolía de estar solo.
lonely [-lɪ] *a.* (LONELIER; LONELIEST) 1. solitario, solo, señero. 2. triste; ansioso de compañía. 3. no frecuentado, aislado. —*adv.* solitariamente.
lonely hearts column, columna de corozones solitarios.
loner [-nər, B -nə] *s.* solitario, individualista; **to be a l.**, gustarle a uno estar solo.
lonesome ['loʊnsəm] *a.* 1. solitario, señero. 2. triste a causa de la soledad.
lonesomely [-lɪ] *adv.* solitariamente.
lonesomeness [-nəs] *s.* soledad.
lone wolf, *s.* (fam.) solitario, lobo solitario.
long [lɔŋ] *a.* 1. largo. 2. alto (ventana, persona, etc.). 3. alargado (rostro, cráneo, etc.). 4. de largo, ej, *the stick is four feet l.*, el bastón tiene cuatro pies de largo. 5. prolongado (grito, mirada, etc.). 6. numeroso (ej., público). 7. elevado, alto (precio). 8. de largo alcance (voz, vista, etc.). 9. remoto (fecha, conjetura, probabilidad, etc.). 10. a largo plazo (letra, deuda, etc.). 11. (com., fin.) bien abastecido. 12. (fon.) largo. 13. **at l. last,** por fin, después de mucho tiempo; **l. in the tooth,** envejecido, viejo; **of l. standing,**

de mucho tiempo; **to be in l. supply,** ser abundante; **to be (one hour, two months, three years,** etc.) **l.,** durar (una hora, dos meses, tres años, etc.); **to be l. in (doing),** tardar en (hacer), demorar mucho en (hacer); **to be l. of (cotton,** etc.), (com., fin.) tener existencias amplias de (algodón, etc.); **to be l. on,** saber mucho de; tener mucho de (algo); **to be on the l. side of the market,** (com.) tener acumuladas mercancías o valores esperando alza de precio; **to make a l. nose,** hacer morisquetas de burla (poniendo la mano extendida delante de la nariz); **to take l. views,** considerar efectos remotos. —*adv.* por mucho tiempo, durante mucho tiempo; **all night l.,** toda la noche; **as l. as,** mientras (que); siempre y cuando; **how l.,** cuánto tiempo; **l. ago,** hace mucho tiempo; **l. before,** mucho antes (que); **l. live!** ¡ viva!; **l. since,** hace mucho tiempo; **no longer,** ya no, no más; **so. l.!** (fam.) ¡hasta luego! ¡adiós!; **so l. as,** con tal que, siempre que. —*s.* 1. mucho tiempo, largo rato. 2. (*pl.*) pantalones (largos). 3. (com., fin.) especulador (que guarda mercadería con esperanza de un alza en el precio). 4. (arq.) bloque grande, (ú. gen. en: **longs and shorts,** bloques grandes y pequeños). 5. **(I shall see you,** etc.) **before l.,** (te veré, etc.) pronto; **the l. and (the) short of it,** la esencia del asunto; **to take l.,** llevar o tomar mucho tiempo, demorarse.

long [lɔŋ] *v.i.* (*pret., p.p.* LONGED; *p.pr.* LONGING) **l. for (something),** anhelar, codiciar, apetecer, añorar, desear con ansia (algo); **l. (to do),** desear mucho (hacer).

long. *abrev. de* **longitude,** longitud.

longanimity [ˌlɔŋgəˈnɪmətɪ] *s.* longanimidad, resignación; paciencia.

long bill, (orn.) becardón; becacina.

longboat [ˈlɔŋˌboʊt] *s.* (mar.) chalupa, lancha.

longbow [-ˌboʊ] *s.* arco largo (para disparar flechas); **to draw the l.,** exagerar, decir patrañas.

long butt, (billar) taco largo (de alcance mayor que el ordinario).

longcloth [-ˌkləθ] *s.* 1. tela de calicó o percal fabricada en piezas largas. 2. (*pl.*) pañal.

long-cut tobacco [-ˌkʌt-] tabaco en hebras.

long-distance [-ˈdɪstəns] *a.* 1. larga distancia, de largo alcance. 2. (dep.) de fondo (apl. a las carreras). —*s.* teléfono de larga distancia; central de teléfonos de larga distancia.

long-distance call, conferencia interurbana.

long-distance runner, (dep.) corredor de fondo, fondista.

long division, (mat.) división en que se escriben los productos parciales.

long dozen, docena de fraile, trece.

long-drawn [-ˈdrɔn] *a.* lento, pesado; prolongado.

long drink, bebida alcohólica (mezclada) con agua y servida en un vaso grande.

long drink of water, (jer., E.U.) hombre alto y delgado.

longe [lʌndʒ] *s.* 1. (equit.) cuerda larga para guiar caballos en adiestramiento. 2. (esgr.) estocada. —*v.t.* (*pret., p.p.* LONGED; *p.pr.* LONGEING) entrenar o ejercitar (un caballo) por medio de una cuerda.

long-eared bat [ˈlɔŋˈɪrd-, B -ˈɪəd-] (zool.) orejudo.

longer [ˈlɔŋgər, B -gə] *a. comp. de* **long,** más largo. —*adv. comp. de* **long,** más tiempo, más rato.

longeron [ˈlɑndʒərən, B ˈlɔn-] *s.* (aer.) larguero.

longevity [lɑnˈdʒɛvətɪ, lɔn-, B lɔn-] *s.* longevidad.

longevous [-ˈdʒivəs] *a.* longevo, de larga vida.

long face, cara larga, semblante triste.

long-faced [ˈlɔŋˌfeɪst] *a.* cariacontecido; malcontento.

long finger (dedo) índice.

long green, (jer., E.U.) billete, efectivo.

longhair [ˈlɔŋˌhɛr, B -ˌhɛə] *s.* 1. (fam.) aficionado a las artes (esp. a la música clásica). 2. artista o intelectual soñador. 3. *var. de* **hippie.**

long-haired [-ˌhɛrd, B -ˌhɛəd] *a.* de pelo largo.

longhand [-ˌhænd] *s.* escritura, caligrafía (en oposición a taquigrafía).

longhead [-ˈhɛd] *s.* cabeza alargada, cráneo ovalado.

long-headed [-əd] *a.* 1. de cabeza alargada, dolicocéfalo. 2. sagaz, previsor, perspicaz.

long-headedly [-lɪ] *adv.* sagazmente, con previsión.

long-headedness [-nəs] *s.* sagacidad, previsión, perspicacia.

longhorn [-ˌhɔrn, B -ˌhɔn] *s.* (zool.) ganado de cuernos largos (antes muy común en el sur de los Estados Unidos).

long house [-ˌhaʊs] (E.U.) agrupación indígena o vivienda comunal de los indios iroqueses.

long hundred, ciento veinte.

long hundredweight, (G.B.) unidad de medida equivalente a 112 lbs. (50,8 kg.).

longicorn [ˈlɑndʒəˌkɔrn, B ˈlɔn-ˌkɔn] *a., s.* (ento.) longicornio.

Longicornia [ˌlɑndʒəˈkɔrnɪə, B ˌlɔn-ˈkɔnɪə] *s. pl.* (zool.) longicornios.

longing [ˈlɔŋɪŋ] *s.* anhelo, deseo, añoranza. —*a.* ansioso, vehemente.

longingly [-lɪ] *adv.* anhelosamente.

longipennate [ˌlɑndʒəˈpɛnˌeɪt, B ˌlɔn-] *s., a.* (zool.) longipenne (de largas alas).

longirostral [-ˈrɑstrəl, B -ˈrɔs-] *s., a.* (pal.) longirrostro, de largo pico.

longish [ˈlɔŋɪʃ] *a.* algo largo, un poco largo.

longitude [ˈlɑndʒəˌtud, B ˈlɔn-ˌtjud] *s.* (geog.) longitud.

longitudinal [ˌlɑndʒəˈtudənəl, B ˌlɔn-ˈtjud-] *a.* longitudinal.

longitudinally [-ɪ] *adv.* longitudinalmente.

long johns, (fam.) calzón interior largo de lana.

long jump, (dep.) salto largo, salto de longitud.

longleaf pine [ˈlɔŋˌlif-] (bot.) pino amarillo, pino ponderoso.

longleaved pine [-ˌlivd-] *var. de* **longleaf pine.**

long-legged [-ˌlɛgd, -ˈlɛgəd] *a.* zanquilargo, patilargo.

long-lived [-ˈlaɪvd, -ˈlɪvd] *a.* duradero, de larga vida, ej., *l.-l. tree,* árbol de larga vida.

long measure, medida de longitud.

long memory, memorión, buena memoria, retentiva.

long moss, (bot.) tillandsia.

long-necked [-ˈnɛkt] *a.* cuellilargo.

Longobard [ˈlɑŋgəˌbɑrd, B ˈlɔŋgəˌbɑd] *s.* (*pl.* LONGOBARDS O LONGOBARDI [ˌlɑŋgəˈbɑrdaɪ, B ˈlɔŋgəˌbɑdaɪ]) longobardo.

Longobardic [ˌlɑŋgəˈbɑrdɪk, B ˌlɔŋgəˈbɑd-] *a.* longobardo.

long pig, carne humana como alimento de caníbales (traducción del término indígena).

long play, disco (fonográfico) de larga duración, microsurco, elepé.

long-playing [ˈlɔŋˈpleɪɪŋ] *a.* (disco) de larga duración.

long-playing record, disco de larga duración, elepé.

long primer, (impr.) entredós, letra de 10 puntos.

long-range [-ˈreɪndʒ] *a.* de largo alcance, de gran alcance.

long run, largo tiempo, ú. esp. en: **in the l. run,** a la larga, finalmente.

long shanked, zanquilargo.

longshanks [ˈlɔŋˌʃæŋks] *s.* (orn.) avefría de patas largas.

longshoreman [-ˈʃɔrmən, B -ˌʃɔmən] *s.* estibador, cargador.

long shot, 1. (fam.) competidor con poca probabilidad de ganar. 2. apuesta arriesgada. 3. empresa aventurada, conjetura aventurada. 4. (cinem.) escena tomada por la cámara a cierta distancia de la acción. 5. **not by a l. s.,** lejos de eso, en absoluto.

long sight, 1. buena visión. 2. (fig.) penetración, previsión.

longsighted [-ˈsaɪtəd] *a.* 1. présbite (que ve mejor de lejos que de cerca). 2. (fig.) presciente, perspicaz, previsor.

longsightedness [-nəs] *s.* 1. presbicia. 2. (fig.) previsión.

long-sleeved [ˈlɔŋˈslivd] *a.* de manga larga.

longsome [-səm] *a.* largo, extenso; tedioso, aburrido.

longspun [-ˈspʌn] *a.* prolijo, dilatado.

longspur [-ˌspɜr, B -ˌspɜ] *s.* (orn.) ave nórdica de la familia de los gorriones.

long-standing [-ˈstændɪŋ] *a.* 1. de largos años, viejo (amistad, conflicto, etc.). 2. duradero.

long staple, fibra o hebra larga.

long-suffering [-ˈsʌfərɪŋ] *s.* resignación, conformidad. —*a.* sufrido, resignado.

long suit, 1. palo fuerte (de naipes). 2. (fig.) especialidad, fuerte (de uno).

long-tailed titmouse [ˈlɔŋˌteɪld-] (orn.) chamarón.

long-term [-ˈtɜrm, B -ˈtɜm] *a.* (com.) a largo plazo.

long-time [-ˈtaɪm] *a.* antiguo, viejo.

long ton, tonelada larga, tonelada gruesa (tonelada usada en Gran Bretaña y que equivale a 2.240 libras).

long-tongued [ˈlɔŋˌtʌŋd] *a.* lenguaraz, chismoso.

long vowel, (gram.) vocal larga.

long-waisted [-ˈweɪstəd] *a.* de cintura baja o larga.

long wait, antesalazo.

long wave, (rad.) onda larga.

long-winded [-ˈwɪndəd] *a.* 1. de largo aliento. 2. verboso, prolijo; pedante.

long-windedness [-nəs] *s.* prolijidad, verbosidad.

longwise [-ˌwaɪz] **longways** [-ˌweɪz] *adv.* longitudinalmente, a lo largo, de largo a largo.

loo [lu] *s.* 1. un juego de naipes. 2. (G.B. fam.) excusado, retrete. —*v.t.* (*pret., p.p.* LOOED; *p.pr.* LOOING) multar en el juego de "loo".

looby [ˈlubɪ] *s. pl.* palurdo.

looie, looey [ˈluɪ] *s.* (jer., mil.) teniente.

look [lʊk] *v.i.* 1. mirar. 2. parecer, tener aspecto o cara de, ej., *l. ill,* parecer enfermo, *l. a fool,* tener cara de tonto. 3. dar (a), estar situado o tener el frente (hacia). 4. indicar, señalar, tender (a), ej., *it looks like an acquittal,* las pruebas parecen indicar que (el acusado) será absuelto. 5. **l. about,** estar alerta; mirar alrededor (sin fijar la vista en algo); **l. about one,** examinar el ambiente de uno; **l. about for,** estar en busca de; **l. after,** seguir con los ojos; buscar; cuidar; atender a; ocuparse de; **l. alike,** parecerse; **l. alive!** ¡apresúrate!; **l. at,** mirar; considerar, estimar, juzgar, ej., *his way of looking at events,* su manera de juzgar los acontecimientos; **l. back,** mirar atrás; reflexionar; (*ú. gen. en forma negativa*) perder ánimo, titubear, dejar de avanzar (por contemplar el pasado); volver a visitar;

l. back on, recordar, rememorar; **l. before you leap,** antes que te cases, mira lo que haces; **l. down,** mirar hacia abajo; bajar la vista; (com.) perder valor, (tender a) bajar el precio; empeorarse (negocios); **l. down on** (o **upon**) **(someone),** tener (a alguien) a menos, despreciar (a alguien); **l. down one's nose (at),** (fam.) menospreciar, despreciar (a alguien); **l. for,** buscar; **l. forward,** prever; **l. forward to,** esperar (con interés); **l. here!** ¡mira!; **l. in,** entrar al pasar, hacer una visita casual o corta; **l. in on,** visitar de paso; **l. into,** examinar, inspeccionar, investigar; **l. like,** parecerse a; **l. on,** contemplar, mirar; **l. one's best,** lucir bien, lucirse; **l. on (someone** o **something) as,** tener (a alguien o algo) por, considerar como; **l. out,** (*ú. gen. en imper.*) tener cuidado; **l. out!,** cuidado!; **l. out for,** estar atento o preparado para; **l. out of,** mirar por, asomarse a (ventana, etc.); **l. sharp,** tener mucho cuidado; obrar con cautela; (jer., E.U.) lucir elegante; **l. through,** transparentarse; penetrar (con la mirada o fig.); hojear (un libro, etc.), examinar a la ligera (documentos, etc.); **l. to,** mirar a; cuidar de, velar por; atender a; acudir a; **l. up,** mejorar(se) (precios, negocios, asuntos, etc.); **l. up to,** tener en estima, respetar; **l. upon,** considerar (como), estimar; **l. well,** tener buena cara; **l. well on,** quedar bien a, ej., *that blouse looks well on you,* esa blusa te queda bien; **l. who is talking,** mira quién habla; **l. you!** ¡oye tú!; **lovely to l. at,** de aspecto encantador; **to l. at him,** a juzgar por su apariencia; **will not l. at (it),** no quiere ni ver (lo). —*v.t.* 1. contemplar, observar, examinar. 2. expresar, mostrar, revelar (algo) la mirada. 3. aparentar, parecer (estar en cierta condición), ej., *l. his age,* aparentar su edad, *l. oneself again,* parecer repuesto (de enfermedad). 4. **l. daggers,** mirar echando chispas; **l. (one) down,** dominar, acobardar, achicar (a alguien); **l. in the face,** hacer frente a (peligro, etc.); **l. (someone) in the face,** encararse con (alguien); **l. over,** examinar, registrar; **l. through,** escudriñar, echar un vistazo escrutador; examinar (superficialmente); **l. up,** buscar, averiguar (en libro, diccionario, etc.); visitar; **l. (one) up and down,** mirar (a alguien) de arriba abajo. —*s.* 1. mirada; ojeada. 2. aspecto, apariencia. 3. aire, cara. 4. (t. *pl.*) buena apariencia (esp. **good looks**). 5. **to have a l. of,** tener un aire de; **to take a l. at,** echar una mirada a; **without a second l.,** sin mirar(lo) otra vez.

look-alike [-ə,laɪk] *s.* doble, sosia, persona que se parece a otra; (*product, machine*) imitación.

looker ['lʊkər, B -ə] *s.* 1. mirador, persona que mira. 2. (jer.) persona bien parecida, esp. una mujer.

looker-on [,lʊkər'ɔn, -'ɑn, B 'lʊkər'ɔn] *s.* (*pl.* LOOKERS-ON) espectador, observador.

look-in ['lʊk,ɪn] *s.* 1. ojeada. 2. visita corta.

looking glass [-ɪŋ-] espejo.

lookout ['lʊk,aʊt] *s.* 1. observación, vigilancia. 2. atalaya, garita, mirador. 3. (mar.) cofa para el vigía. 4. vigilante, centinela, guardia; observador. 5. (mar.) vigía. 6. perspectiva, vista, panorama. 7. cuidado, asunto, ej., *that is his l.,* eso es asunto suyo. 8. **to be on the l. for,** estar a la expectativa de, estar a la caza de.

look-see [-,si] *s.* (jer.) examen, inspección, escrutinio rápido.

loom [lum] *v.i.* 1. aparecer, asomarse (en forma vaga, indistinta o amenazadora). 2. **l. large,** cobrar mucha (o demasiada) importancia. —*s.* 1. vislumbre; sombra vaga, forma indistinta; aparición. 2. (orn.) somorgujo. 3. telar, máquina para hilar. 4. (mar.) guión (del remo). —*v.t.* hilar en un telar.

loom shuttle, lanzadera mecánica.

loon [lun] *s.* 1. (orn.) somorgujo. 2. simplón, bobo; tarambana.

loony, looney ['lunɪ] *a., s.* (jer.) loco, lunático.

loony bin, (jer.) manicomio.

loop [lup] *s.* 1. lazo, vuelta, lazada (de un cabo, cuerda, cinta, etc.). 2. recoveco (de un camino), meandro (de un río). 3. (elec.) circuito cerrado. 4. (aer.) rizo. 5. (cost.) onda, bucle; presilla (para asegurar un botón). 6. (mec.) abrazadera, anilla. 7. **to knock** (o **throw**) **for a l.,** (jer.) asombrar; exaltar; poner en desorden, descomponer; **to loop the l.,** (aer.) hacer o rizar el rizo. —*v.t.* 1. hacer una lazada en. 2. hacer una vuelta o curva en. 3. (aer.) rizar el rizo, ejecutar el rizo. 4. **l. in,** (elec.) conectar en circuito. —*v.i.* 1. enlazarse. 2. curvarse, darse la vuelta. 3. asegurarse por medio de una presilla. 4. (aer.) hacer un rizo.

loop antenna, l. aerial, (rad.) antena de cuadro, antena de lazo.

looped [lupt] *a.* 1. (jer.) bebido, intoxicado. 2. que tiene lazadas, ondas o conchas, ej., *l. fringe,* fleco de ondas.

looper ['lupər, B -ə] *s.* 1. enlazador. 2. (ento.) medidor, oruga medidora.

loophole ['lup,hoʊl] *s.* 1. (mil.) tronera, aspillera; cañonera. 2. escapatoria, excusa, pretexto para eludir (obligación, contrato, etc.). —*v.t.* hacer troneras o aberturas (en).

loop knot, nudo de vueltas.

loop stitch, (cost.) puntada de cadeneta.

loopy ['lupɪ] *a.* 1. que tiene vueltas, que tiene curvas. 2. (esco.) socarrón, taimado. 3. (jer.) loco, necio, tonto.

loose [lus] *a.* 1. suelto, sin amarrar, sin fijar. 2. suelto, flojo, holgado, ej., *with a l. rein,* con la rienda suelta, *l. clothes,* vestidos holgados. 3. vago, indeterminado, inexacto, indefinido (idea, juicio, información, etc.). 4. flojo, suelto, poco compacto, disgregado; desmenuzado, ej., *l. fabric,* tejido flojo o suelto, *l. soil,* suelo desmenuzado. 5. de moral dudosa; relajado, fácil, disoluto, ej., *l. life,* vida fácil, vida disoluta, *l. morals,* moral relajada. 6. aproximado, poco exacto (ej., traducción). 7. disperso (ej., escritura). 8. a granel (existencias, etc.). 9. **at a l. end,** sin nada en que ocuparse; sin empleo; **l. in the bowels,** flojo de vientre; **of l. build,** de figura desgarbada; **on the l.,** de parranda, de juerga; sin compromiso, desocupado; **to break l.,** desatarse, escaparse, liberarse; **to cast l.,** desatar, soltar; **to come l.,** desprenderse, desatarse, soltarse; **to cut l.,** cortar las amarras, ponerse en libertad; soltarse; **to let** (o **turn**) **l.,** soltar —*adv.* sueltamente, libremente; sin cohesión, vagamente, indefinidamente. —*v.t.* 1. desatar, desprender, desliar, aflojar. 2. libertar, poner en libertad, liberar. 3. aliviar; aflojar. 4. soltar, liberar. 5. eximir (de una obligación); absolver; remitir. 6. (mar.) soltar, dejar ir. 7. descargar, disparar (flechas, fusil). —*v.i.* (con *off*) descargar, disparar, abrir fuego con (arma de fuego), ej., *he loosed off with his gun,* abrió fuego con su fusil.

loose ends, 1. extremos o cabos sueltos. 2. (fig.) asunto pendiente, problema sin resolver. 3. **to pick up (o tie up) the l. e.,** atar cabos, acabar los últimos; **at l. e.,** en desorden; sin ocupación; desempleado.

loose-jointed ['lus'dʒɔɪntəd] *a.* 1. de articulaciones flojas; de movimientos sueltos. 2. desvencijado.

loose-leaf [-,lif] *a.* 1. de hojas sueltas (cuaderno, diario, enciclopedia, etc.). 2. (ten.) por hojas sustituibles (contabilidad).

loosely [-lɪ] *adv.* 1. sueltamente, libremente. 2. sin cohesión. 3. vagamente. 4. aproximadamente.

loosen ['lusən] *v.t.* 1. desatar, desapretar, aflojar, soltar. 2. (fig.) soltar (ej., lengua), aflojar (disciplina, etc.). 3. librar, libertar. 4. soltar, laxar (el vientre). 5. ablandar; solver. 6. **l. one's hold,** desasirse. —*v.i.* aflojarse.

looseness ['lusnəs] *s.* 1. aflojamiento, holgura. 2. relajación, licencia, libertad. 3. soltura. 4. vaguedad.

loose pulley, (mec.) polea loca.

loose-reined [-'reɪnd] *a.* a rienda suelta.

loose smut, añublo de los granos (enfermedad producida en las plantas por un hongo parásito).

loosestrife [-,straɪf] *s.* (bot.) lisimaquia; salicaria; arroyuela.

loose-tongued [-'tʌŋd] *a.* suelto de lengua, ligero de lengua.

loot [lut] *s.* 1. botín, presa. 2. saqueo, pillaje. 3. (jer.) dinero. —*v.t.* saquear, pillar (ej., una ciudad conquistada); robar. —*v.i.* andar saqueando.

looter ['lutər, B -ə] *s.* saqueador.

looting [-ɪŋ] *p.pr. de* **loot.** —*s.* saqueo, saqueamiento.

lop [lɑp, B lɔp] *v.t.* 1. desmochar, podar, escamondar (árboles, etc.). 2. (gen. con *off*) recortar, cercenar. —*s.* desmochadura, recortes; ramas podadas. —*v.i.* colgar, pender, caer flojamente. —*a.* colgante.

lope [loʊp] *v.i.* correr a medio galope; correr a paso largo. —*s.* medio galope; paso largo.

lop-eared ['lɑp,ɪrd, B 'lɔp,ɪəd] *a.* de orejas gachas o caídas.

loper ['loʊpər, B -ə] *s.* animal que galopa, que va a paso largo.

lophobranch ['loʊfə,bræŋk] (ict.) *a.* lofobranquio. —*s.* pez lofobranquio.

lophobranchiate [loʊfə'bræŋkɪət] (ict.) *a.* lofobranquiado. —*s.* pez lofobranquiado.

lopper ['lɑpər, B 'lɔpə] *s.* podador de árboles.

loppy [-ɪ] *a.* que cuelga libremente; flojo, flexible.

lopsided ['lɑp'saɪdəd, B 'lɔp-] *a.* desequilibrado, ladeado, sesgado; asimétrico; desproporcionado.

lopsidedly [-lɪ] *adv.* sesgadamente; asimétricamente, sin proporción o equilibrio.

loquacious [loʊ'kweɪʃəs] *a.* locuaz, lenguaz, gárrulo.

loquaciously [-lɪ] *adv.* locuazmente.

loquacity [-'kwæsətɪ] *s.* locuacidad, garrulidad.

loquat ['loʊ,kwɑt, B -,kwɔt] *s.* 1. (bot.) níspero. 2. níspola, níspero (fruto).

Loran ['lɔr,æn] *s.* (nav.) (de *Long Range Navigation*) lorán, sistema de navegación (marítima o aérea) para determinar la posición por medio de señales de radio.

loranthaceous [,lɔ,ræn'θeɪʃəs] *a.* (bot.) lorantáceo.

lord [lɔrd, B lɔd] *s.* 1. señor, dueño, patrón. 2. **L.,** Señor (Ser Supremo, Dios; Nuestro Señor, Jesucristo). 3. (G.B.) lord (título nobiliario). 4. (G.B.) primera palabra en el título oficial de varios dignatarios, ej., *L. Chamberlain,* camarero mayor. 5. señor (de un estado feudal). 6. (astr.) planeta dominante. 7. (poét., hum.) señor, marido, ej., *her l. and master,* su amo y señor. 8. **L.!** ¡Dios mío!; **L. bless my soul!** (exclamación de sorpresa) ¡válgame Dios!; **L. have mercy,** Señor, ten piedad; **the Lords,** cámara de los Lores; **to rest in the L.,** descansar en el Señor; **to treat like a l.,** agasajar a cuerpo de rey. —*v.i.* **l. it,** mandar; **l. it over,** tratar despóticamente. —*v.t.* conferir el título de lord.

lording ['lɔrdɪŋ, B 'lɔdɪŋ] (ant.) *s.* 1. lord. 2. señorito, pequeño lord.

Lord Lieutenant, (hist., G.B.) virrey y gobernador de Irlanda (hasta 1922).
lordliness [-lɪnəs] *s.* 1. dignidad, señorío. 2. altivez, orgullo.
lordling [-lɪŋ] *s.* (ant.) señorito, pequeño lord.
lordly [-lɪ] *a.* (LORDLIER; LORDLIEST) 1. digno de un lord, noble. 2. señorial, señoril, espléndido, magnífico. 3. altivo, despótico, imperioso, orgulloso. —*adv.* 1. noblemente. 2. señorilmente, magníficamente. 3. altivamente, imperiosamente.
Lord Mayor, (G.B.) alcalde o corregidor de Londres, York y otras ciudades importantes del reino.
lordosis [lɔr'doʊsəs, B lɔ'-] *s.* (med.) lordosis.
Lord Privy Seal, (G.B.) guardasellos, canciller.
Lord's day, día del Señor, domingo.
lordship ['lɔrd,ʃɪp, B 'lɔd-] *s.* 1. señoría, excelencia. 2. señorío (territorio). 3. señorío, dominio, poder; autoridad.
Lord's Prayer, (relig.) padrenuestro, padre nuestro.
lore ['lɔr, B lɔ] *s.* 1. ciencia popular, saber popular; erudición, ciencia, saber. 2. (ant.) enseñanza; instrucción; consejo. 3. (zool.) puente (espacio entre los ojos y la boca).
lorgnette [lɔr'njɛt, B lɔ'-] *s.* impertinentes; gemelos de teatro con manija.
lorgnon [-'njoʊn, B 'lɔnjən] *s.* impertinentes; gemelos de teatro con manija.
lorica [lə'raɪkə] *s.* 1. (hist.) loriga, peto, coraza romana. 2. (zool.) loriga (casco o cubierta protectora).
loricate ['lɔrə,keɪt, 'lɑr-, B 'lɔr-] *v.t.* enchapar, planchear; esmaltar. —*a.* (zool.) lorigado.
lorication [,lɔrə'keɪʃən, lɑr-, B ,lɔr-] *s.* enchape, esmalte.
lorikeet ['lɔrə,kit, 'lɑr-, B 'lɔr-] *s.* (orn.) perico pequeño de Australia.
loriot ['lɔrɪət] *s.* (orn.) oropéndola de Europa.
loris ['lɔrəs] *s.* (zool.) lori, loria.
lorn [lɔrn, B lɔn] *a.* 1. (poét.) abandonado, desamparado; solitario. 2. (ant.) arruinado, perdido.
Lorraine [lə'reɪn, lɔ-] *s.* Lorena (región al NE. de Francia).
Lorraine cross, cruz de Lorena.
lorry ['lɔrɪ] *s.* 1. (G.B.) autocamión. 2. (f.c.) vagoneta, carro de plataforma.
lory ['lɔrɪ] *s.* (orn.) (especie de) loro de Australia y Nueva Guinea.
losable ['luzəbəl] *a.* perdible.
lose [luz] *v.t.* (*pret., p.p.* LOST [lɔst, lɑst, B lɔst]; *p.pr.* LOSING) 1. perder (un hijo, un libro, dinero, etc.). 2. perder, arruinar. 3. hacer perder, ej., *this will l. you your job,* esto te hará perder el empleo. 4. **don't l. it,** (irón.) ¡no lo pierdas (que vale mucho)!; **l. face,** desprestigiarse; **l. ground,** (fig.) perder terreno; **l. heart,** desanimarse; **l. one's head,** (fig.) perder uno la cabeza; **l. one's heart,** enamorarse uno; **l. one's mind,** (fig.) enloquecer, cegarse de ira, etc.; **l. one's temper,** perder uno los estribos; **l. one's tongue,** quedarse uno mudo, sin palabras; **l. one's way,** perder uno el camino; **l. oneself,** perderse, desorientarse; **l. oneself in,** absorberse, concentrarse en; **l. (something) to,** perder (algo) en beneficio de; **l. sight of,** perder de vista; perder la objetividad; **l. track of,** perder la pista de. —*v.i.* sufrir una pérdida. 2. quedar vencido, perder. 3. atrasarse (reloj). 4. **l. out,** (fam.) ser derrotado.
losel ['loʊzəl] *s.* (ant.) holgazán, perdido; libertino. —*a.* despreciable, indigno, inútil.
loser ['luzər, B -zə] *s.* 1. perdedor, malapata. 2. reo que ha cumplido sentencia más de una vez, ej., *two-time l.,* convicto dos veces. 3. (bridge) (carta) perdedora.
losing [-zɪŋ] *a.* 1. perdedor (ej., naipe). 2. perdido, ej., *a l. proposition,* una causa perdida.
loss [lɔs, lɑs, B lɔs] *s.* 1. pérdida. 2. perdición; daño. 3. (seguros) muerte, lesión, accidente (como base para indemnización en una póliza). 4. (mil.) (*gen. pl.*) bajas. 5. **at a l.,** con pérdida; **to be at a l. for (words, solution,** etc.), no encontrar (palabras, solución, etc.); **to be at a l. to (do),** no saber cómo (hacer); **it's your l.,** (fam.) allá tú; **l. of face,** desprestigio, no tener cara (para algo).
loss leader, (com.) artículo de propaganda (vendido a menos del costo para atraer clientes), (artículo de) oferta (Amer.).
loss ratio, (seguros) relación entre primas y pérdidas (durante un período determinado).
lost [lɔst, lɑst, B lɔst] *pret., p.p. de* **lose.** —*a.* 1. perdido. 2. olvidado, caído en desuso, que no se practica (más). 3. arruinado. 4. perdido, extraviado, descarriado. 5. perdido, desorientado. 6. **long l.,** del que no se sabía hace mucho tiempo; **l. in thoughts,** absorto en pensamientos; **l. to,** perdido para, ej., *l. to the world,* ensimismado, en otro mundo, *l. to agriculture,* perdido para la agricultura; inaccesible para, ej., *victory was l. to them,* la victoria era inaccesible para ellos.
lost cause, causa perdida, desesperada.
lost sheep, (fig.) oveja descarriada, oveja negra.
lot [lɑt, B lɔt] *s.* 1. lote, parte, porción, cuota. 2. suerte, hado, sino. 3. solar de terreno, lote. 4. grupo (de personas). 5. (com.) lote, partida. 6. (fam.) (t. *pl.*) gran cantidad, gran número, ej., *he has lots of friends,* tiene gran cantidad de amigos. 7. (fam.) individuo, sujeto, tipo. 8. (cine) estudio y territorio colindante. 9. (ant.) impuesto, contribución; deber, obligación. 10. **a bad l.,** (fam.) mala persona, de mala calaña; **a l.,** mucho; **a l. better,** muchísimo mejor; **by l.,** al azar, por sorteo; **the l.,** la totalidad; **the l. fell upon me,** la suerte me favoreció; **to cast** (o **throw**) **one's l. with,** compartir la suerte de; **to draw lots,** echar suertes; **to fall to one's l.,** tocarle a uno en suerte. —*v.t.* (*pret., p.p.* LOTTED; *p.pr.* LOTTING) 1. formar o dividir en lotes o terrenos. 2. (gen. con *out*) asignar, repartir, distribuir. 3. escoger echando suertes, dividir echando suertes. —*v.i.* echar suertes.
lota, lotah ['loʊtə] *s.* (India) pequeña escudilla para agua (gen. fabricada de latón o cobre).
loth [loʊθ] *var. de* **loath.**
Lothario [loʊ'θærɪ,oʊ, -'θɛr-, B -'θɑr-] *s.* tenorio, galanteador, seductor.
lotic ['loʊtɪk] *a.* (biol.) lótico.
lotion ['loʊʃən] *s.* 1. loción, lavadura. 2. lavado; ablución, lavatorio.
lotophagous [loʊ'tɑfəgəs, B -'tɔf-] *s., a.* lotófago, que come lotos.
lottery ['lɑtərɪ, B 'lɔt-] *s.* 1. lotería; rifa. 2. (fig.) lotería, lance, episodio de suerte u ocasión.
lottery ticket, billete de lotería, (número de) suerte (Am.).
lotto ['lɑtoʊ, B 'lɔt-] *s.* lotería (juego casero), quina (Am.).
lotus, lotos ['loʊtəs] *s.* (bot.) loto.
lotus-eater, lotos-eater [-,itər, B -ə] *s.* 1. lotófago. 2. (fig.) soñador, persona indolente.
loud [laʊd] *a.* 1. alto (voz), fuerte (sonido). 2. recio (juramento, etc.). 3. ruidoso, ej., *l. streets,* calles ruidosas. 4. (fig.) chillón, llamativo; cursi. 5. ofensivo, apestoso (olor). 6. **l. laugh,** risotada, risa estridente; **l.-voiced,** estentóreo, de voz estentórea. —*adv.* 1. en voz alta, a gritos. 2. ruidosamente. 3. fuerte (apl. a sonidos y olores).
louden ['laʊdən] *v.i., v.t.* volver(se) más fuerte.
loudish [-ɪʃ] *a.* bastante fuerte, algo alto (sonido, voz).
loudly [-lɪ] *adv.* 1. a gritos, en voz alta. 2. ruido-amente.
loudmouth [-,maʊθ] *s.* bocón, bocona; fanfarrón, fanfarrona.
loudmouthed [-,maʊðd] *a.* bocón, fanfarrón, vocinglero.
loudness [-nəs] *s.* 1. volumen (de sonido). 2. (fam.) vulgaridad, mal gusto.
loudness level, nivel de intensidad sonora.
loudspeaker [-'spikər, B -kə] *s.* (rad., electrón.) altoparlante, altavoz, parlante; megáfono, amplificador de voz.
lough [lɑk, B lɔk] *s.* (dial.) ría, ensenada; lago; piscina; agua; mar.
louis d'or [,luɪ'dɔr, B -'dɔ] (hist.) luis (moneda de oro francesa que equivalía a 20 francos).
Louisiana [lʊ,izɪ'ænə] *s.* Luisiana, estado de los E.U.
Louisianan [lʊ,izɪ'ænən] **Louisianian** [-'ænɪən] *a.* luisianense.
lounge [laʊndʒ] *v.i.* (*pret., p.p.* LOUNGED; *p.pr.* LOUNGING) haraganear, holgazanear, callejear; pasearse perezosamente, repantigarse a sus anchas. —*v.t.* (con *away*) gastar ociosamente, malgastar (el tiempo). —*s.* 1. salón de tertulia, salón social; salón de fumar. 2. salón de entrada, antesala, vestíbulo. 3. canapé ancho y cómodo; sofá; yacija.
lounge car, (f.c.) coche salón.
lounge-lizard [-,lɪzərd, B -əd] *s.* (jer.) compañero (profesional) de baile (en hoteles y salones).
lounger ['laʊndʒər, B -ə] *s.* holgazán; callejero, paseandero (Amer.).
loup [loʊp] *v.i., v.t.* (esco.) saltar.
loupe [lup] *s.* lupa (de joyeros o relojeros).
louse [laʊs] *s.* (*pl.* LICE [laɪs]) 1. (ento.) piojo. 2. (jer.) (*pl.* LOUSES) sinvergüenza, canalla. —[laʊs, laʊz] *v.t.* 1. despiojar, espulgar. 2. **l. up,** (jer.) estropear, arruinar, echar a perder; confundir, enredar, enmarañar.
lousewort ['laʊs,wɜrt, B -,wɜt] *s.* (bot.) gallarito.
lousily ['laʊzəlɪ] *adv.* miserablemente; pésimamente.
lousiness [-zɪnəs] *s.* piojería.
lousy ['laʊzɪ] *a.* 1. piojoso, piojento. 2. (jer.) asqueroso, despreciable. 3. malo, inferior; epíteto de desaprobación. 4. **l. with (something),** (jer.) bien provisto de (algo, esp. dinero).
lout [laʊt] *v.i., v.t.* (dial., ant.) inclinar(se); hacer reverencias; doblar(se).
lout, *s.* patán, rústico, zafio. —*v.t.* mofarse de, tratar con desprecio.
loutish ['laʊtɪʃ] *a.* rústico, tosco, patán.
loutishly [-lɪ] *adv.* groseramente.
loutishness [-nəs] *s.* patanería, grosería; simpleza.
louver ['luvər, B -və] *s.* 1. (arq. medioeval) lumbrera, lucerna. 2. persiana, rejilla de ventilación, celosía de ventilación.
louver boards, louver boarding, tablas pluviales.
louvered [-vərd, B -vəd] *a.* de tablillas que pueden entornarse en forma de celosía o persiana.
Louvre ['luvrə, luv, B 'luvrə] *s.* Louvre, Luvre, famoso museo de París.
lovability [,lʌvə'bɪlətɪ] *s.* amabilidad, carácter simpático.
lovable, loveable ['lʌvəbəl] *a.* adorable, que inspira cariño.
lovableness [-nəs] *s.* calidad de lo adorable, amable o simpático.

lovably [-blɪ] *adv.* atractivamente, con amabilidad o gracia.
lovage ['lʌvɪdʒ] *s.* (bot.) 1. ligústico. 2. ligustro, alheña.
love [lʌv] *s.* 1. amor; cariño, querer. 2. amores, amorío, aventura amorosa. 3. amor (el ser amado, persona amada, persona encantadora), ej., *my l.,* mi amor; *she is an old l.,* ella es un amor. 4. amor, maravilla, preciosidad. 5. **L.,** Amor, Cupido, Eros (dios del amor); Venus. 6. (Ciencia Cristiana) (sinónimo de) Dios. 7. (tenis) cero, nada (en el marcador). 8. **for l.,** por amor; **for l. or money,** a cualquier precio, a las buenas o a las malas; (en negación) por nada del mundo; **for the l. of,** por el amor de; **in l. (with),** enamorado (de), poseído por el amor (de); **l. of learning,** amor al saber, deseos de aprender; **there is no l. lost between them,** no se gustan; **to be out of l. with,** desenamorarse; **to fall in l.,** enamorarse; **to make l.,** hacer el amor, copular; **to make l. to,** galantear, enamorar; **to play for l.,** jugar por el placer; **to send one's l. to,** mandar cariños (a). —*v.t.* (*pret., p.p.* LOVED; *p.pr.* LOVING) 1. amar, querer, tener cariño a. 2. gustar de, encantarle a uno, tener gran afición a, ej., *he simply loves to walk in the rain,* le encanta caminar bajo la lluvia. 3. acariciar. —*v.i.* amar, enamorarse, estar enamorado.
love affair, amorío, aventura amorosa.
love apple, tomate; tomatillo.
lovebird ['lʌv,bɜrd, B -,bɜd] *s.* 1. (orn.) cotorra rizada. 2. (fam.) (*pl.*) pareja de enamorados.
love child, hijo natural, hijo de ganancia.
love feast, ágape (entre los primeros cristianos).
love game (tenis) juego ganado sin pérdida de puntos.
love-in-a-mist [-ɪnə'mɪst] *s.* (bot.) ajenuz, arañuela, neguilla.
love-in-idleness [-,aɪdəlnəs] *s.* (bot.) trinitaria, pensamiento silvestre.
love knot, lazo de amor, nudo de amor.
loveless ['lʌvləs] *a.* 1. sin amor, desamorado. 2. abandonado, desamparado.
lovelessly [-lɪ] *adv.* sin amor; sin aliciente.
lovelessness [-nəs] *s.* 1. desamor. 2. abandono, desamparo.
love-lies-bleeding [-,laɪz'blidɪŋ] *s.* (bot.) moco de pavo, felpa, amaranto rojo.
loveliness [-lɪnəs] *s.* hermosura, belleza.
lovelock [-,lɑk, B -,lɔk] *s.* 1. rizo largo (de cabello en la frente o la sien que usaban los cortesanos elegantes). 2. caircl (Esp.), buscanovios (rizo que adhiere con gomina a la mejilla o la frente).
lovelorn [-,lɔrn, B -,lɔn] *a.* abandonado, olvidado por su amante; herido de amor, ansioso de amor.
lovely ['lʌvlɪ] *a.* (LOVELIER; LOVELIEST) 1. hermoso, bello, precioso; exquisito, delicioso. 2. (fam.) magnífico, encantador, ameno. 3. (ant.) amable; amado. —*adv.* (fam.) hermosamente.
love-making [-,meɪkɪŋ] *s.* 1. galanteo. 2. requerimientos de amor; técnica amorosa. 3. cópula.
love match, unión o matrimonio por amor.
love nest, nidito de amor.
love-philter [-,fɪltər, B -tə] **love-potion** [-,poʊʃən] *s.* filtro, filtro de amor, bebedizo.
lover ['lʌvər, B 'lʌvə] *s.* 1. amante, querido, novio. 2. (con *of*) amigo (de), aficionado (a), ej., *a music l.,* un aficionado a la música.
lover boy, (hum.) macho, macarra.
love seat, confidente (sofá para dos).
love set, (tenis) etapa ganada sin perder un solo juego.
lovesick [-,sɪk] *a.* enfermo de amor; herido de amor.
lovesickness [-nəs] *s.* mal de amores.
lovesome [-səm] *a.* (ant. o dial.) 1. enamorado, amoroso, tierno, apasionado. 2. amable.
love song, canción de amor, romance, balada.
lovey ['lʌvɪ] *s.* (jer., G.B.) amor, amorcito.
lovey-dovey [-'dʌvɪ] *a.* (jer.) excesivamente amoroso o sentimental.
loving ['lʌvɪŋ] *a.* 1. afectuoso, cariñoso, amoroso. 2. aficionado. 3. benigno, apacible.
loving cup, 1. copa de la amistad (copa con varias asas que pasa de mano en mano entre amigos). 2. trofeo.
lovingkindness [-'kaɪndnəs] *s.* bondad, compasión; benevolencia.
lovingly [-lɪ] *adv.* afectuosamente, cariñosamente, amorosamente.
lovingness [-nəs] *s.* afecto, cariño.
low [loʊ] *a.* 1. bajo, de poca altura, ej., *a l. hill,* una colina baja. 2. estrecho, angosto, ej., *a l. forehead,* una frente estrecha, una frente angosta. 3. bajo (situado debajo del nivel o superficie normales). 4. escotado (vestido). 5. bajo, débil, grave (voz). 6. cercano al ecuador o cerca del horizonte, ej., *l. latitudes,* latitudes cercanas al ecuador, *the moon is l.,* la luna está cerca del horizonte. 7. reciente, ej., *coin of lower date,* moneda de fecha más reciente. 8. inferior, bajo (rango; condición), ej., *the lower depths,* los bajos fondos. 9. abatido, desanimado, deprimido; débil. 10. escaso, insuficiente, ej. *l. pressure,* presión insuficiente. 11. bajo, vulgar, vil, malo, ej., *l. trick,* mala jugada. 12. insidioso, ej., *l. cunning,* astucia insidiosa, bellaquería. 13. lento, ej., *on a l. flame, in a l. oven, at a l. heat,* a fuego lento. 14. primitivo, atrasado, inferior, ej., *l. organism,* organismo primitivo. 15. (aut.) primera (velocidad), ej., *in l. gear,* en primera (velocidad). 16. (mús.) grave. 17. (fon.) abierta (vocal). 18. **high and l.,** por todas partes, todo el mundo; **to be in l. spirits,** estar abatido o deprimido; **to feel l.,** sentirse deprimido o abatido; **to have a l. opinion of,** tener a mal; **to lay l.,** abatir, echar abajo, derribar; **to lie l.,** postrarse, estar tendido; (jer.) mantenerse oculto, no hacerse conspicuo. —*adv.* 1. abajo, debajo, bajo. 2. pobremente, humildemente. 3. barato, a precio bajo. 4. en voz baja, en tono profundo; gravemente. 5. cerca del ecuador; cerca del horizonte. 6. **to aim l.,** apuntar abajo (con arma); **to bow l.,** agacharse profundamente; hacer una reverencia profunda; **to collar l.,** (fútbol) agarrar (al adversario) por o debajo de la cintura. —*s.* 1. nivel o punto bajo. 2. (meteor.) depresión. 3. (aut.) primera marcha, primera velocidad. 4. (naipes) triunfo más bajo. 5. **at the l.,** al precio más bajo.
low [loʊ] *v.i.* mugir. —*v.t.* lanzar, proferir (un mugido). —*s.* mugido.
low, lowe [loʊ] *s.* (esco.) llama; llamarada; resplandor; luz. —*v.i.* llamear; encenderse; brillar.
low-altitude bombing ['loʊ'æltə,tud-, B -,tjud-] (mil., aer.) bombardeo a poca altura.
low-altitude flying, (aer.) vuelo a poca altura.
low area, área o región de baja presión barométrica.
low beam, (aut.) luz de cruce.
low blood pressure, (med.) hipotensión arterial, tensión (o presión) arterial baja.
lowborn ['loʊ'bɔrn, B -'bɔn] *a.* de humilde cuna; plebeyo.
lowboy [-,bɔɪ] *s.* cómoda baja de patas cortas.
lowbred [-'brɛd] *a.* grosero, palurdo, malcriado, vulgar.
lowbrow [-,braʊ] *s.* ignorante, persona sin inquietudes intelectuales. —*a.* ignorante, poco intelectual, vulgar.
Low Church, iglesia no ritualista (rama no conservadora de la iglesia anglicana).
low comedy, farsa, sainete.
low-cost [-,kɔst] *a.* de bajo costo, barato.
Low Countries, Países Bajos (Holanda, Bélgica y Luxemburgo).
low-down ['loʊ'daʊn] *a.* (fam.) bajo, vil. —[-,daʊn] *s.* (jer.) informe confidencial; datos verídicos.
lower ['loʊər, B -ə] *v.t.* 1. bajar, arriar, abatir. 2. rebajar. 3. abatir, reducir, ej., *l. one's hopes,* abatir las esperanzas de uno. 4. agachar, poner más bajo; humillar. 5. aminorar, disminuir (fuerza, etc.); aminorar, reducir, ej., *l. a wall,* aminorar o reducir la altura de un muro. 6. **l. the boom,** (jer.) castigar; criticar; tratar severamente. —*v.i.* bajar, menguar, disminuir(se). —*a.* 1. más bajo, inferior. 2. baja (cámara de parlamento). 3. (geog.) meridional.
lower ['laʊər, B -ə] *v.i.* 1. fruncir el entrecejo, poner mala cara. 2. encapotarse, nublarse (el cielo). —*s.* 1. ceño, sobrecejo. 2. aspecto amenazador (del cielo).
lower berth ['loʊər-, B -ə'-] cama o litera baja (en tren o barco).
Lower California, (Méx.) Baja California.
lowercase [-,keɪs] (tip.) *s.* 1. caja baja. 2. minúscula, letra minúscula. —*a.* de caja baja, minúscula. —*v.t.* imprimir o componer con (letras) minúsculas.
lower class, (pol., econ.) clase (social) baja, clase trabajadora.
lowerclassman [-'klæsmən, B -'klɑs-] *s.* estudiante de primero o segundo año (de un colegio o Universidad).
lower criticism, (teol.) crítica textual.
lower deck, 1. (mar.) cubierta inferior. 2. **the l. d.,** (G.B.) plana menor (de la marina o de un barco).
Lower House, Cámara Baja (cámara de representantes o diputados).
lowering ['laʊərɪŋ] *a.* ceñoso, ceñudo, amenazador, encapotado (el cielo).
loweringly [-lɪ] *adv.* ceñudamente, amenazadoramente.
lower mast, (mar.) palo principal.
lower middle class, (pol., econ.) la clase media baja.
lowermost ['loʊər,moʊst, B -ə,-] *a.* más bajo que todo, ínfimo.
lower regions, (el) infierno.
lower world, 1. (la) tierra. 2. mundo subterráneo, infierno.
lowery ['laʊərɪ] *a.* encapotado, amenazador, nublado.
lowest common denominator ['loʊəst-] 1. mínimo común denominador. 2. aquello que es aceptado, comprendido y apreciado por la mayoría de la gente.
lowest common multiple, mínimo común múltiplo.
low fat, de bajo contenido graso; (*diet*) magro.
low frequency, (fís.) baja frecuencia.
low gear, (aut.) primera velocidad.
Low German, (filol.) bajo alemán.
low-grade ['loʊ,greɪd] *a.* 1. de baja o inferior calidad. 2. de grado inferior.
low-grade ore, mineral de baja ley, mineral pobre.
low-heeled [-'hild] *a.* de tacón bajo (zapato, bota).
low-key [-'ki] *a.* 1. de baja intensidad, moderado. 2. de matiz claro.
lowland ['loʊlənd] *s.* tierra baja; **the Lowlands,** Tierra Baja de Escocia. —*a.* de tierra baja; (t. L.) de la Tierra Baja (de Escocia).

lowlander [-ləndər, B -də] *s.* abajeño, llanero, natural de tierras bajas, esp. natural de la Tierra Baja de Escocia.
Low Latin, bajo latín; el que sucedió a la caída del imperio romano.
low-level [-'lɛvəl] *a.* de menor grado, subordinado (oficial, empleado, etc.); de bajo nivel (decisión, orden, etc.).
lowlife ['loʊlaɪf] *a.* de los bajos fondos, de dudosa reputación. —*s.* bajos fondos; persona ruin, perverso.
lowliness ['loʊlɪnəs] *s.* 1. humildad, condición humilde. 2. condición prosaica u ordinaria.
lowly ['loʊlɪ] *a.* (LOWLIER; LOWLIEST) 1. humilde, de baja posición, modesto. 2. inferior, secundario (en posición o desarrollo), ej., *l. organisms,* organismos inferiores. 3. prosaico, ordinario. —*adv.* 1. humildemente, modestamente. 2. bajo, ej., *a l. priced article,* un artículo de bajo precio. 3. poco, escasamente.
Low Mass, (relig.) misa rezada.
low-minded [-'maɪndəd] *a.* vil, ruin; de mentalidad vulgar.
low-mindedly [-lɪ] *adv.* vilmente, ruinmente.
low-mindedness [-nəs] *s.* ruindad, bajeza.
low-neck ['loʊˌnɛk] **low-necked** [-'nɛkt] *a.* escotado (vestido de mujer). —*s.* blusa o vestido escotado.
lowness [-nəs] *s.* 1. bajura, poca altura. 2. bajeza, vileza, ruindad. 3. bajo nivel. 4. humildad.
low-pitched [-'pɪtʃt] *a.* 1. de tono grave (sonido, voz). 2. (arq.) de techo bajo (cuarto, etc.); de poco declive, poco pendiente (techo).
low-pressure ['loʊ'prɛʃər, B -ə] *a.* de baja presión.
low pressure, baja presión.
low-priced [-'praɪst] *a.* de bajo precio, barato.
low profile, poco prominente. —*s.* conducta o acción personal deliberadamente reservada; **to keep a l.,** comportarse reservadamente.
low relief, (arte) bajo relieve.
low-speed [-'spid] *a.* de baja velocidad.
low-spirited [-'spɪrətəd] *a.* acongojado, abatido, deprimido, alicaído, desalentado.
Low Sunday, Domingo de Cuasimodo (primero después de la Pascua de Resurrección).
low-tension [-'tɛntʃən, B -'tɛnʃən] *a.* (elec.) de baja tensión, de bajo voltaje.
low-test [-'tɛst] *a.* de bajo octanaje (gasolina).
low tide, bajamar, marea baja.
low trick, perrada, mala pasada.
low-voltage ['loʊ'voʊltɪdʒ] *a.* (elec.) de bajo voltaje, de baja tensión.
low-waisted [-'weɪstəd] *a.* de talle bajo, de cintura baja.
low water, 1. marea baja. 2. (fig.) estancamiento, decadencia.
low-water mark [-'wɔtər-, -'wɑt-, B -'wɔtə-] 1. línea de bajamar. 2. línea de aguas mínimas. 3. (fig.) punto más bajo.
lox [lɑks, B lɔks] *s.* 1. (*pl.* LOX o LOXES) salmón curado o ahumado. 2. oxígeno líquido.
loxodrome ['lɑksəˌdroʊm, B 'lɔk-] *s.* (mar.) loxodromia, línea de rumbo, curva loxodrómica.
loxodromic [ˌlɑksə'drɑmɪk, B ˌlɔksə'drɔm-] *a.* (mar.) loxodrómico.
loyal ['lɔɪəl] *a.* 1. leal, fiel, constante. 2. (ant.) lícito, legítimo.
loyalism [-əˌlɪzəm] *s.* adhesión al gobierno vigente.
loyalist [-ləst] *s.* 1. partidario del gobierno. 2. (hist. E.U.) colono leal a Gran Bretaña (en la guerra de independencia). 3. (Esp.) ciudadano leal a la República (opuesto a Franco en la Guerra Civil).
loyally [-lɪ] *adv.* lealmente, fielmente.
loyalty [-əltɪ] *s.* (*pl.* LOYALTIES) lealtad, fidelidad, constancia.
lozenge [-'lɑzəndʒ, B 'lɔz-] *s.* 1. (farm.) tableta, pastilla. 2. (her.) losange. 3. (geom.) rombo.
LP ['ɛl'pi] *s. abrev. de* **long play,** elepé, disco de larga duración, microsurco.
LSD ['ɛlˌɛs'di] *s.* droga LSD, ácido lisérgico.
L.S.D. *abrev. de* **pounds, shillings and pence,** libras, chelines y peniques.
Lt. *abrev. de* **lieutenant,** teniente (tnte.).
l.t. *abrev. de* 1. **local time,** hora local. 2. **long ton,** tonelada de 2.240 libras.
Ltd. *abrev. de* **limited,** limitado (ltdo.).
Lu *símb. de* **lutetium,** lutecio (Lu).
luau ['luˌaʊ] *s.* fiesta hawaiana con banquete y diversiones al aire libre.
lubber ['lʌbər, B -ə] *s.* 1. palurdo, patán. 2. (mar.) marinero de agua dulce, marinero sin experiencia (t. **landlubber**).
lubberliness [-lɪnəs] *s.* desmaño, chabacanería, zafiedad.
lubberly ['lʌbərlɪ, B -əlɪ] *a.* palurdo, chabacano, zafio. —*adv.* chabacanamente, zafiamente, toscamente.
lubber's hole, (mar.) boca de lobo (en el cuello de un mastelero).
lubber's line, lubber line, lubber's point, (mar.) línea de fe.
lube [lub] *s. abrev. de* **lubricating oil,** aceite lubricante.
lubric ['lubrɪk] **lubrical** [-brɪkəl] *a.* (raro) lúbrico, propenso a la lujuria.
lubricant [-brɪkənt] *a.* lubricante. —*s.* substancia lubricante.
lubricate ['lubrəˌkeɪt] *v.t.* 1. lubricar, engrasar, aceitar. 2. (jer.) mojar la garganta a (alguien). 3. (jer.) untar, sobornar.
lubricating [-iŋ] *a.* lubricante.
lubrication [ˌlubrə'keɪʃən] *s.* lubricación, engrase.
lubricative ['lubrəˌkeɪtɪv] *a.* lubricativo.
lubricator [-ər, B -ə] *s.* 1. lubricador. 2. lubricante.
lubricious [lu'brɪʃəs] *var. de* **lubricous.**
lubricity [-'brɪsətɪ] *s.* 1. lubricidad (calidad o condición de resbaladizo). 2. inestabilidad, inconstancia. 3. lubricidad, lascivia, lujuria.
lubricous ['lubrɪkəs] *a.* 1. lúbrico, resbaladizo. 2. inestable; evasivo, esquivo; mañoso, falso, tramposo. 3. lúbrico, lascivo, lujurioso.
lubritorium [ˌlubrə'tɔrɪəm] **lubritory** ['lubrəˌtɔrɪ, B -tərɪ] *s.* estación de lubricación (para automotores).
lucarne [lu'kɑrn, B -'kɑn] *s.* ventanilla, buhardilla.
luce [lus] *s.* (ict.) lucio o sollo (esp. adulto).
lucency ['lusənsɪ] *s.* brillo, luminosidad.
lucent [-ənt] *a.* luciente, luminoso; claro, transparente.
lucently [-lɪ] *adv.* luminosamente.
lucerne, lucern [lu'sɜrn, B -'sɜn] *s.* (pr. G.B.) (bot.) mielga, alfalfa.
Lucerne [-'sɜrn, B -'sɜn] *s.* Lucerna (cantón y lago de Suiza Central).
lucid ['lusəd] *a.* 1. lúcido, reluciente, resplandeciente, brillante, claro, transparente. 2. lúcido, claro (razonamiento, estilo, etc.).
lucid interval, (med.) intervalo lúcido, intervalo claro.
lucidity [lu'sɪdətɪ] *s.* lucidez (de pensamiento, expresion, estilo, etc.); transparencia; brillantez.
lucidly ['lusədlɪ] *adv.* lúcidamente.
lucidness [-nəs] *s.* lucidez.
Lucifer ['lusəfər, B -fə] *s.* 1. (astr.) Lucifero (el planeta Venus como lucero del alba). 2. Lucifer, Luzbel, Satanás. 3. **l.,** (t. **l. match**) tipo antiguo de fósforo.
luciferase [lu'sɪfəˌreɪs] *s.* (bioquím.) luciferasa.
Luciferian [ˌlusə'fɪrɪən, B -'fɪər-] *a.* luciferino, endiablado, diabólico.
luciferin [lu'sɪfərən] *s.* (bioquím.) luciferina.
luciferous [-rəs] *a.* (ant.) lucífero, iluminador.
lucifugal [lu'sɪfjəgəl] **lucifugous** [-gəs] *a.* (biol.) lucífugo.
Lucite (TM) ['luˌsaɪt] *s.* lucita (una resina acrílica o transparente).
luck [lʌk] *s.* 1. suerte, fortuna, azar, acaso, casualidad. 2. buena suerte, ventura, dicha. 3. **as l. would have it,** como lo quiso la suerte; **bad l. to him,** ¡ ojalá (que) tenga mala suerte!; **best of l.!,** ¡ mucha suerte!; **better l. tomorrow,** mañana será otro dí; **for l.,** para traer buena suerte; **good l.!** ¡ buena suerte!; **hard l.,** mala suerte; **in l.,** con suerte, afortunado; **just my (your, our,** etc.) **l., mi,** (tu, nuestra) mala suerte; **no such l.!** ¡ni por pienso! ¡ ni mucho menos!; **out of l.,** sin suerte, desafortunado; **to be down on one's l.,** dar con su mala suerte; estar empobrecido, pasar apuros; **to be in l.,** estar de buena suerte; **to be out of l.,** estar de malas; **to have the l.,** tener la buena suerte o fortuna; **to try one's l.,** probar suerte uno (en el juego, empresa, etc.); **to push one's l.,** (jer.) arriesgarse innecesariamente.
luckily ['lʌkəlɪ] *adv.* afortunadamente, por suerte.
luckiness [-ɪnəs] *s.* dicha, buena fortuna o suerte, felicidad.
luckless [-ləs] *a.* desafortunado, infeliz, desdichado, desgraciado, malaventurado; sin suerte.
lucklessly [-lɪ] *adv.* desafortunadamente, desgraciadamente; sin suerte.
lucky ['lʌkɪ] *a.* 1. venturado, venturoso, afortunado, dichoso, suertudo (Am.). 2. propicio, favorable; de feliz augurio. 3. **to be l.,** tener buena suerte; **you are a l. dog,** eres un tipo de suerte (forma de felicitación, esp., al que tiene suerte en el amor).
lucky break, coyuntura favorable, oportunidad; chiripa, racha de suerte.
lucky penny, moneda de buena suerte.
lucky strike, golpe de fortuna, golpe de suerte; **to make a l. s.,** tener un golpe de suerte.
lucrative ['lukrətɪv] *a.* lucrativo, ganancioso, provechoso.
lucratively [-lɪ] *adv.* lucrativamente.
lucrativeness [-nəs] *s.* capacidad lucrativa.
lucre ['lukər, B -kə] *s.* 1. lucro, ganancia. 2. dinero. 3. **filthy l.,** vil metal.
lucubrate ['lukjəˌbreɪt] *v.i.* lucubrar.
lucubration [ˌlukjə'breɪʃən] *s.* elucubración, lucubración.
lucubrator ['lukjəˌbreɪtər, B -ə] *s.* lucubrador.
luculent ['lukjələnt] *a.* luculento, lúcido, claro, evidente.
Lucullan [lu'kʌlən] **Lucullean** [ˌlukə'liən] **Lucullian** [lu'kʌlɪən] *a.* de Lúculo; espléndido, opíparo.
ludicrous ['ludəkrəs] *a.* absurdo, ridículo, risible.
ludicrously [-lɪ] *adv.* ridículamente, de manera absurda.
ludicrousness [-nəs] *s.* ridiculez, absurdo.
lues ['luiz] *s.* (med.) lúes, lúe, sífilis.
luff [lʌf] *s.* (mar.) 1. orza. 2. orilla de proa (de una vela cangreja). —*v.i.* (mar.) orzar, barloventear, navegar de bolina; **to l. alee** o **round,** orzar a la banda; **to l. up,** tomar por avante.
luffa ['lʌfə] *s.* (bot.) estropajo.
luff tackle, (mar.) aparejo de bolinear.
Luftwaffe ['lʊftˌvɑfə] *s.* Fuerza Aérea alemana (Nazi) durante la Segunda Guerra Mundial.
lug [lʌg] *s.* 1. oreja, anillo, argolla, saliente, agarradera, asa. 2. correa de las varas (de un carruaje). 3. (jer.) patán, rústico, tonto, torpe. —*v.t., v.i.*

(*pret., p.p.* LUGGED; *p.pr.* LUGGING) 1. tirar con fuerza, halar, jalar, arrastrar (algo pesado). 2. **l. away u off,** llevarse arrastrando; **l. in** o **into,** traer de los cabellos (tema, etc. en conversación, discusión, etc.).

lug, *s.* 1. estirón. 2. (fam., E.U.) (*pl.*) afectación, aires, ej., *to put on lugs,* darse aires. 3. (mar.) vela al tercio. 4. (zool.) lombriz de cebó, gusano anélido.

Luger [ˈlugər, B -gə] *s.* marca de fábrica de una pistola automática alemana.

luggage [ˈlʌgɪdʒ] *s.* equipaje.

luggage rack, portaequipajes, estante para equipajes (en un auto, tren, etc.).

luggage van, (G.B., f.c.) furgón, vagón de equipaje.

lugger [ˈlʌgər, B -ə] *s.* (mar.) lugre.

lugsail [-ˌseɪl, -səl] *s.* (mar.) vela al tercio, vela tarquina.

lugubrious [lʊˈgubrɪəs, B lu-] *a.* lúgubre, fúnebre, triste, melancólico, lóbrego.

lugubriously [-lɪ] *adv.* lúgubremente, fúnebremente, tristemente, melancólicamente.

lugubriousness [-nəs] *s.* tristeza, melancolía.

lugworm [ˈlʌgˌwɜrm, B -ˈwɜm] *s.* (zool.) lombriz de cebo, gusano anélido.

lukewarm [ˈlukˌwɔrm, B -ˌwɔm] *a.* 1. tibio, templado. 2. (fig.) tibio, frío (ej., el interés).

lukewarmly [-lɪ] *adv.* tibiamente.

lukewarmness [-nəs] *s.* tibieza.

lull [lʌl] *v.t.* 1. arrullar, adormecer. 2. calmar, aquietar, sosegar, sedar. —*s.* 1. calma pasajera, cese temporal (de una tormenta o confusión); intervalo de silencio (en una conversación). 2. (ant.) arrullo, nana, canción de cuna.

lullaby [ˈlʌləˌbaɪ] *s.* arrullo, nana, canción de cuna. —*v.t.* (*pret., p.p.* LULLABIED; *p.pr.* LULLABYING) aquietar, calmar o arrullar con una canción de cuna.

lulu [ˈlulu] *s.* (jer.) joya, joyita (persona o cosa excelente).

lum [lʌm] *s.* (dial.) chimenea.

lumbago [lʌmˈbeɪgoʊ] *s.* (med.) lumbago.

lumbar [ˈlʌmbər, -ˌbɑr, B -bə] *a.* (anat.) lumbar.

lumber [ˈlʌmbər, B -bə] *s.* 1. madera, esp. madera aserrada, madero, tablas. 2. trastos o muebles viejos. —*a.* maderero. —*v.t.* 1. amontonar. 2. sobrecargar, llenar, obstruir (con trastos viejos, etc.). 3. desmontar (terreno). —*v.i.* 1. avanzar pesadamente, andar toscamente, pasar con estruendo. 2. retumbar.

lumber-carrier [-ˌkærɪəˌ, B -ə] *s.* barco madarero.

lumberer [-bərər, B -bərə] *s.* leñador, maderero.

lumbering [-bərɪŋ] *s.* industria maderera, negocio maderero; explotatición de bosques.

lumbering, *a.* pesado, lerdo (andar, movimiento, etc.); que anda pesadamente (persona).

lumberingly [-lɪ] *adv.* pesadamente, lerdamente.

lumberjack [ˈlʌmbərˌdʒæk, B -bəˌ-] *s.* leñador, hachero.

lumberjacket [-ˌdʒækət] *s.* chaqueta de leñador, chaquetón.

lumberman [-mən] *s.* leñador, maderero.

lumber-mill [-ˌmɪl] *s.* aserradero.

lumber room, (G.B.) trastero, cuarto depósito.

lumber-trade [-ˌtreɪd] *s.* industria maderera.

lumberyard [-ˌjɑrd, B -ˌjɑd] *s.* madereria, almacén o depósito de madera.

lumbrical [ˈlʌmbrɪkəl] **lumbricalis** [ˌlʌmbrɪˈkeɪlɪs] *a.* (anat.) lumbrical (músculo).

lumbricoid [-ˌkɔɪd] *a.* lumbricoide (de forma de lombriz).

lumbricosis [ˌlʌmbrɪˈkoʊsəs] *s.* (med.) lumbricosis.

lumen [ˈlumən] *s.* (*pl* LUMENS o LUMINA [-mənə]) 1. (fís.) lumen (unidad de flujo luminoso). 2. (anat., zool.) lumen (luz de un vaso o conducto).

luminal, lumenal [-mənəl] *a.* (fís., anat., zool.) luminal.

luminance [-nəns] *s.* (fís) luminancia.

luminary [ˈluməˌnɛrɪ, B -nərɪ] *s.* (*pl.* LUMINARIES) 1. luminar (astro). 2. luz artificial. 3. lumbrera, luminar (persona).

luminesce [ˌluməˈnɛs] *v.i.* despedir luminosidad.

luminescence [-əns] *s.* luminiscencia (emisión de luz sin incandescencia).

luminescent [-ənt] *a.* luminiscente.

luminiferous [ˌluməˈnɪfərəs] *a.* luminífero.

luminosity [-ˈnɑsətɪ, B -ˈnɔs-] *s.* luminosidad.

luminous [ˈlumənəs] *a.* 1. luminoso, brillante. 2. iluminado, lleno de luz (un cuarto, sala, etc.).

luminous energy, (fís.) energí radiante.

luminous flux, (fís.) flujo luminoso.

luminously [-lɪ] *adv.* luminosamente, brillantemente.

luminousness [-nəs] *s.* luminosidad.

luminous paint, pintura lumínica.

lummox [ˈlʌməks] *s.* (E.U.) porro, desmañado, chapucero.

lump [lʌmp] *v.t.* (fam) soportar, apechugar; aguantar; **l. it,** (vulg.) trágatelo, aguanta.

lump [lʌmp] *s* 1. terrón, borujo; grumo. 2. bulto, protuberancia, hinchazón. 3. (fig.) tronco; bodoque. 4. (ant.) racimo, hato. 5. montón; gran cantidad. 6. conjunto, totalidad. 7. **l. in the throat,** nudo en la garganta (producido por la emoción). —*v.t.* 1. echar en la masa, apelotonar. 2. agrupar, englobar, juntar. 3. aterronar. 4. abultar. —*v.i.* 1. aborujarse, aterronarse, apelotonarse; agrumarse. 2. moverse o caerse pesadamente.

lumper [ˈlʌmpər, B -pə] *s.* estibador, cargador (de muelles).

lumpish [-pɪʃ] *a.* 1. deforme. 2. lerdo, desmañado. 3. tardo, estúpido. 4. pesado, tedioso.

lumpishly [-lɪ] *adv.* 1. lerdamente, desmañadamente. 2. stúpidamente.

lumpishness [-nəs] *s.* 1. aspecto deforme. 2. pesadez, carácter tedioso. 3. estupidez, majadería.

lump sugar, azúcar de cortadillo, azúcar en terrones; azucarillo (Esp.).

lump sum, cantidad global, suma total.

lumpy [ˈlʌmpɪ] *a.* (LUMPIER; LUMPIEST) 1. cubierto o lleno de bultos, apelmazado, aterronado; grumoso (una salsa); agitado (mar). 2. deforme, desproporcionado, tosco. 3. torpe, pesado.

lumpy jaw, (vet.) actinomicosis (enfermedad del ganado).

luna [ˈlunə] *s.* (alquimia) plata.

lunacy [ˈlunəsɪ] *s.* 1. locura, demencia. 2. locura, disparate (escrito o dicho). 3. (der.) insania, locura. 4. (ant.) lunatismo (afección que se atribuía a la influencia de los cambios lunares).

lunar [ˈlunər, B -nə] *a.* 1. lunar. 2. que contiene plata, argénteo, argentino.

lunar caustic, piedra infernal; nitrato de plata.

lunar cycle, (astr.) ciclo lunar, ciclo decemnovenal o decemnovenario.

lunar eclipse, (astr.) eclipse de luna.

lunar landing, alunizaje.

lunar module, módulo lunar.

lunar month, mes lunar.

lunar observation, observación lunar.

lunar year, año lunar.

lunate [ˈluneɪt] **lunated** [-əd] *a.* lunado, en forma de media luna.

lunatic [ˈlunətɪk] *a.* 1. loco, lunático. 2. para locos, de locos (asilo, casa). —*s.* loco, orate.

lunatic asylum, manicomio, casa de locos.

lunatic fringe, extravagantes, exaltados; fanáticos, extremistas (de un partido político, movimiento social, etc.).

lunation [luˈneɪʃən] *s.* (astr.) lunación.

lunch [lʌntʃ] *s.* almuerzo; merienda, colación, refrigerio. —*v.i.* almorzar. —*v.t.* dar de almorzar a, proporcionar almuerzo a.

lunch basket, fiambrera, lonchera (Am.), cesta de merienda.

lunchbox [-bɑks] *s.* portacomidas, fiambrera, lonchera.

lunch bucket, *var. de* lunchbox, lunch pail.

lunch break, receso para almorzar.

luncheon [ˈlʌntʃən] *s.* almuerzo; merienda, colación, refrigerio.

luncheonette [ˌlʌntʃəˈnɛt] *s.* establecimiento pequeño en que se sirven comidas y bebidas no alcohólicas.

luncheon meats, (*ú. gen. pl.*) fiambres, embutidos variados.

luncher [ˈlʌntʃər, B -tʃə] *s.* persona que almuerza.

lunch pail, portacomidas, fiambrera, lonchera.

lunchroom [ˈlʌntʃˌrum, -ˌrʊm] *s.* restaurante pequeño que sirve comidas ligeras.

lunchtime [-taɪm] *s.* hora de comer.

lune [lun] *s.* 1. pihuela de halcón. 2. (geom.) lúnula.

lunes [lunz] *s. pl.* ataques de locura.

lunette [luˈnɛt] *s.* 1. (arq) luneto. 2. (fort.) luneta. 3. (mil.) argollón de contera (de cañones). 4. hueco para la cabeza en la guillotina. 5. luneta (adorno en forma de media luna).

lung [lʌŋ] *s.* 1. (anat.) pulmón; **good lungs,** voz fuerte. 2. (*pl.*) pulmones, bofes.

lunge [lʌndʒ] *s.* arremedita, acometida, embestida; estocada. —*v.t.* tirar, lanzar. —*v.i.* lanzarse, abalanzarse; arrancarse de repente (en alguna dirección); **l. at,** arremeter contra.

lungeous [ˈlʌndʒəs] *a.* (dial., G.B.) travieso, juguetón.

lunger [ˈlʌŋər, B -ə] *s.* (jer., E.U.) tísico.

lungfish [ˈlʌŋˌfɪʃ] *s.* (ict.) pez dípneo.

lungwort [-ˌwɜrt, B -ˌwɜt] *s.* (bot.) pulmonaria.

luniform [ˈlunɪˌfɔrm, B -ˌfɔm] *a.* lunado.

lunisolar [ˌlunɪˈsoʊlər, B -lə] *a.* (astr.) lunisolar.

lunitidal interval [-ˈtaɪdəl-] intervalo entre el tránsito de la luna y la pleamar siguiente.

lunkah [ˈlʌŋkə] *s.* cigarro fuerte (hecho en la India).

lunker [ˈlʌŋkər, B -kə] *s.* gigante (díc. de algo grande en su especie, esp. de un pez).

lunkhead [ˈlʌŋkˌhɛd] *s.* (fam., E.U.) tonto, estúpido, zoquete.

lunt [lʌnt] *s.* (esco.) mecha; antorcha, tea; humo. —*v.t., r.v.* (esco.) encender (se), inflamar (se), prender (se), iluminar (se). —*v.i.* humear.

lunulate [ˈlunjəˌleɪt] *a.* marcado con lunares.

lunule [ˈlunjul] *s.* (zool., anat.) lúnula, blanco de la uña.

luny, *var. de* **loony.**

Lupercalia [ˌlupərˈkeɪlɪə, B -pəˈ-] *s. pl.* (hist.) lupercales (fiestas en honor del dios Pan).

lupine [ˈlupaɪn] *a.* lupino, lobuno, voraz. —[-pən] *s.* (bot.) lupino, altramuz, atramuz.

lupulin [ˈlupjələn] *s.* (farm.) lupulino.

lupus [ˈlupəs] *s.* (med.) lupus.

lurch [lɜrtʃ, B lɜtʃ] *s.* 1. guiñada, bandazo (de un barco). 2. tambaleo, bamboleo. 3. sacudida, tumbo. —*v.i.* 1. guiñar, dar guiñadas (el buque).

2. tambalear(se), bambolear(se), andar con paso vacilante o haciendo eses. —*v.t.* acechar.

lurch, *s.* 1. abandono, deserción, defección; ú. solamente en: **to leave one in the l.,** dejar en la estacada, abandonar en dificultades. 2. (ant.) capote, victoria abrumadora (en juegos).

lurcher ['lɜrtʃər, B 'lɜtʃə] *s.* 1. (G.B.) perro cruzado de galgo con mastí, perro de caza. 2. (ant.) hurtador, ratero; estafador; cazador furtivo.

lurdane ['lɜdən, B 'lɜd-] *s.* (ant.) persona haragana y estúpida. —*a.* haragán y estúpido.

lure [lʊr, B ljʊə] *s.* 1. tentación, atractivo, aliciente. 2. cebo, señuelo, añagaza, carnada (para atraer peces y animales). —*v.t.* atraer con engaño, seducir, tentar, inducir; **l. away,**, llevarse con señuelo; **l. into,** hacer entrar o caer con añagazas; **l. (one) into (doing),** tentar (a uno) para que (haga); **l. on,** inducir a seguir adelante.

lurer ['lʊrər, B 'ljʊərə] *s.* tentador, seductor.

lurid ['lʊrəd, B 'ljʊər-] *a.* 1. sensacional, chocante; espeluznante; extravagante. 2. lívido, pálido. 3. tenue (luz). 4. **to cast a l. light (on facts),** dar aspecto sensacional (a los hechos).

lurk [lɜrk, B lɜk] *v.i.* 1. estar al acecho, esconderse, ocultarse; moverse furtivamente. 2. (fig.) estar latente (peligro, amenaza, etc.). 3. **on the l.,** en acecho.

lurker ['lɜrkər, B 'lɜkə] *s.* acechador, espí.

lurking [-ɪŋ] *a.* 1. oculto, latente. 2. furtivo.

lurkingly [-lɪ] *adv.* en acecho, ocultamente, escondidamente, furtivamente.

lurking place, 1. escondite, guarida. 2. emboscada.

Lusaka [lu'sɑkə] *s.* Lusaka, capital de Zambia.

luscious ['lʌʃəs] *a.* 1. suculento, sabroso, delicioso, exquisito, rico. 2. sensual, voluptuoso.

lusciously [-lɪ] *adv.* 1. suculentamente, sabrosamente, deliciosamente, exquisitamente. 2. sensualmente, voluptuosamente.

lusciousness [-nəs] *s.* 1. suculencia, sabor delicioso, exquisitez. 2. sensualidad, voluptuosidad.

lush [lʌʃ] *a.* 1. lujuriante, frondoso, lozano. 2. profuso, pródigo, exuberante, opulento. 3. pródigo, generoso. 4. lucrativo; próspero, floreciente. 5. delicioso, exquisito. 6. lujoso, suntuoso. 7. sensual, voluptuoso. —*s.* (jer.) 1. licor, trago. 2. borrachín, borracho, ebrio. —*v.i., v.t.* (jer.) beber o dar de beber licor.

lushness ['lʌʃnəs] *s.* 1. lozanía, frondosidad, aspecto lujuriante. 2. profusión, prodigalidad, exuberancia, opulencia. 3. prodigalidad, generosidad. 4. lujo, suntuosidad. 5. sensualidad.

Lusitanian [ˌlusə'teɪnɪən] *a.* lusitano, lusitánico. —*s.* lusitano; portugués.

Luso-Brazilian [ˌlusoʊbrə'zɪljən] *a.* lusobrasileño.

lust ['lʌst] *s.* 1. lujuria, lascivia. 2. codicia, ansia, anhelo, avidez. 3. (ant.) placer, gusto; inclinación, afición. —*v.i.* (gen. con *after* o *for*) codiciar o anhelar vehementemente; tener apetito carnal por.

luster, lustre ['lʌstər, B -tə] *s.* 1. lustre, brillo, viso. 2. fulgor, brillo, refulgencia. 3. (fig.) lustre, esplendor, gloria, distinción. 4. araña, candelabro. 5. tela lustrosa (de lana y algodón). 6. (min.) aguas, brillo, lustre. —*v.t.* lustrar, abrillantar, satinar, glasear, vidriar. —*v.i.* ser lustroso, tener lustre, brillar.

luster, lustre, *s.* lustro, quinquenio.

lusterless [-ləs] *a.* sin lustre, opaco, deslustrado, sin brillo.

lusterware, lustreware [-ˌwɛr, B -ˌwɛə] *s.* loza barnizada, loza con reflejos metálicos.

lustful ['lʌstfəl] *a.* 1. lujurioso, lascivo, carnal, voluptuoso. 2. (ant.) robusto, vigoroso.

lustfully [-fəlɪ] *adv.* lujuriosamente, lascivamente.

lustfulness [-fəlnəs] *s.* lujuria, lascivia, sensualidad.

lustily ['lʌstəlɪ] *adv.* 1. vigorosamente. 2. sensualmente. 3. poderosamente, fuertemente.

lustiness [-tɪnəs] *s.* robustez, vigor, lozanía.

lustral ['lʌstrəl] *a.* 1. lustral, lústrico, quinquenal. 2. (ant.) lústrico.

lustrate [-treɪt] *v.t.* lustrar, purificar (mediante sacrificios y ceremonias propiciatorias).

lustration [lʌs'treɪʃən] *s.* lustración, purificación.

lustring ['lʌstrɪŋ] *s.* (tej.) lustrina.

lustrous [-trəs] *a.* 1. lustroso, brillante, radiante. 2. ilustre, insigne, célebre.

lustrously [-lɪ] *adv.* 1. lustrosamente. 2. ilustremente.

lustrum ['lʌstrəm] *s.* (*pl.* LUSTRUMS O LUSTRA [-trə]) lustro, quinquenio.

lusty ['lʌstɪ] *a.* (LUSTIER; LUSTIEST) 1. robusto, vigoroso, lozano, lleno de vida. 2. sensual. 3. poderoso, fuerte. 4. (dial.) alegre, festivo.

lutanist ['lutənəst] *s.* (mús.) laudista.

lute [lut] *s.* (mús.) laúd. —*v.i.* tocar o sonar el laúd.

lute, *s.* zulaque, luten (para tapar junturas o cubrir superficies porosas); arandela de goma para cerrar tarros herméticamente. —*v.t.* zulacar, tapar o cubrir con luten.

luteal ['lutɪəl] *a.* (anat.) lúteo.

lutecium, *var. de* **lutetium.**

lutein ['lutɪən] *s.* (bioquím.) luteína.

luteinizing hormone [-ˌaɪzɪŋ-] (bioquím.) hormona luteinizante.

luteolin ['lutɪəlɪn] *s.* (quím.) luteolina.

luteous ['lutɪəs] *a.* lúteo, amarillento.

lutestring ['lutˌstrɪŋ] *s.* (tej.) lustrina.

lutetium [lu'tiʃɪəm] *s.* (quím.) lutecio.

Luther ['luθər, B -θə] *s.* (relig.) Lutero, teólogo, líder de la Reforma protestante en Alemania.

Lutheran [-θərən] *a., s.* luterano.

Lutheranism [-ˌɪzəm] *s.* luteranismo, doctrina de Lutero.

luthern ['luθərn, B 'ljuθən] *s.* (arq.) lumbrera, buharda.

luting ['lutɪŋ] *s.* zulaque, luten (para tapar junturas o cubrir superficies porosas).

lutist ['lutəst] *s.* 1. laudista. 2. fabricante de laúdes.

lutose ['lutoʊs, B 'lju-] *a.* lodoso, cenagoso.

lux [lʌks] *s.* (*pl.* LUX O LUXES) (fís.) lux (unidad internacional de intensidad luminosa).

luxate ['lʌkseɪt] *v.t.* (med.) luxar, dislocar (un hueso); descoyuntar (Amer.).

luxation [lʌk'seɪʃən] *s.* (med.) luxación, dislocación (de un hueso).

luxe [lʊks, lʌks, luks] *s.* lujo, elegancia, ú. esp. en la expresión **de l.,** de lujo, ej., *de l. edition,* edición de lujo.

Luxembourg, Luxemburg ['lʌksəmˌbɜrg, B -ˌbɜg] *s.* Luxemburgo.

luxuriance [lʌg'ʒʊrɪəns, lʌk'ʃʊr-, B lʌg'zjʊər-] **luxuriancy** [-ənsɪ] *s.* 1. exuberancia, abundancia, profusión. 2. frondosidad, lozanía.

luxuriant [-ənt] *a.* 1. lujuriante, frondoso, lozano. 2. florido, recargado, rococó. 3. prolífico, fértil, fecundo. 4. lujoso, elegante.

luxuriantly [-lɪ] *adv.* lozanamente, en abundancia.

luxuriate [-ˌeɪt] *v.i.* 1. crecer de manera exuberante. 2. regodearse, regalarse, darse buena vida. 3. deleitarse, gozarse.

luxurious [-əs] *a.* 1. lujoso, fastuoso, suntuoso. 2. sibarítico, sensual, regalón. 3. frondoso; abundante, exuberante.

luxuriously [-lɪ] *adv.* 1. lujosamente, suntuosamente. 2. sensualmente. 3. abundantemente, exuberantemente.

luxuriousness [-nəs] *s.* 1. lujo, fausto, boato. 2. sibaritismo, sensualidad. 3. frondosidad, lozanía; exuberancia.

luxury ['lʌkʃərɪ, 'lʌgʒ-, B 'lʌkʃ-] *s.* (*pl.* LUXURIES) 1. lujo, pompa, fausto, suntuosidad. 2. lujo, artículo de lujo.

lwm *abrev. de* **low-water mark,** línea de baja mar.

lycanthrope ['laɪkənˌθroʊp, laɪ'kænθroʊp] *s.* 1. (med.) licántropo. 2. hombre-lobo.

lycanthropic [ˌlaɪkən'θrɑpɪk, B -'θrɔp-] *a.* (med.) licantrópico.

lycanthropy [laɪ'kænθrəpɪ] *s.* (med.) licantropia.

lycée [li'seɪ, B 'liseɪ] *s.* liceo (colegio de segunda enseñanza en Francia).

lyceum [laɪ'siəm] *s.* liceo, ateneo; sociedad literaria.

lych-gate ['lɪtʃˌgeɪt] *s.* entrada con sotechado (de un cementerio).

lychnis ['lɪknəs] *s.* (bot.) licnis.

Lycian ['lɪʃɪən, B 'lɪs-] *a., s.* licio, de una antigua región de Asia Menor.

lycopod ['laɪkəˌpad, B -ˌpɔd] **lycopodium** [ˌlaɪkə'poʊdɪəm] *s.* (bot., farm.) licopodio.

lyddite ['lɪdaɪt] *s.* lidita (explosivo).

Lydian ['lɪdɪən] *a., s.* lidio, de Lidia, antigua región de Asia Menor.

lye [laɪ] *s.* lejía. —*v.t.* (*pret., p.p.* LYED; *p.pr.* LYING) lejiar, tratar con lejía.

lying ['laɪɪŋ] *a.* 1. mendaz, mentiroso, falso. 2. tendido, echado, yacente. —*s.* 1. mentira. 2. acción de yacer.

lying ['laɪɪŋ] *p.pr. de* lie.

lying-in ['laɪɪŋ'ɪn] *s.* (*pl.* LYINGS-IN O LYINGINS) 1. parto. 2. sobreparto, puerperio.

lying-in hospital, hospital de maternidad.

lying-in woman, parturienta.

lyingly ['laɪɪŋlɪ] *adv.* falsamente, mentirosamente.

lymph [lɪmf] *s.* 1. (anat., fisiol.) linfa. 2. (poét.) manantial; p. ext. agua. 3. (ant.) savia.

lymphadenitis [ˌlɪm''fædən'aɪtəs] *s.* (med.) linfadenitis.

lymphangitis [-fən'dʒaɪtəs] *s.* (med.) linfangitis.

lymphatic [lɪm'fæɪɪk] *a.* 1. (anat.) linfático. 2. (fig.) (de temperamento) linfático, flemático, apático. —*s.* (fisiol.) vaso linfático.

lymphatic system, (anat., fisiol.) sistema linfático.

lymphatism ['lɪmfəˌtɪzəm] *s.* (med.) linfatismo.

lymph node, (anat.) ganglio linfático.

lymphoblast ['lɪmfəˌblæst, B -ˌblast] *s.* (anat.) linfoblasto.

lymphoblastic [ˌlɪmfə'blæstɪk] *a.* (anat.) linfoblástico.

lymphocyte ['lɪmfəˌsaɪt] *s.* (anat.) linfocito.

lymphocytosis [ˌlɪmfəsɪɪ'toʊsəs] *s.* (med.) linfocitosis.

lymphocytotic [-'tɑtɪk, B -'tɔt-] *a.* (med.) linfocitósico, linfocitótico.

lymphogranulomatosis [-foʊˌgrænjə-ˌloʊmə'toʊsəs] *s.* (med.) linfogranulomatosis.

lymphoid ['lɪmfɔɪd] *a.* (anat.) linfoide, linfoideo.

lymphoid cell, (anat.) célula linfoide.

lymphoid tissue, (anat.) tejido linfoide o linfático.

lymphoma [lɪm'foʊmə] *s.* (*pl.* LYMPHOMAS O LYMPHOMATA [-tə]) (med.) linfoma.

lymphopenia [ˌlɪmfə'pinɪə] *s.* (med.) linfopenia.

lymphopoiesis [-ˌpɔɪ'isəs] *s.* (*pl.* LYMPHOPOIESES [-ˌsiz]) (fisiol.) linfopoyesis.
lyncean [lɪn'siən] *a.* linceo, de lince (vista); perspicaz.
lynch [lɪntʃ] *v.t.* linchar.
lyncher ['lɪntʃər, B -ə] *s.* linchador.
lynching [-ɪŋ] *s.* linchamiento.
lynch law, (E.U.) ley de Lynch, castigo de un reo impuesto por particulares cuando no ha sido sometido a proceso legal.
lynx [lɪŋks] *s.* (*pl.* LYNX O LYNXES) (zool.) lince.
lynx-eyed ['lɪŋksˌaɪd] *a.* de ojos linces, de ojos linceos, perspicaz, de vista muy aguda; **to be l.-e.,** tener ojos de lince, tener mirada de águila.
Lyonese [ˌlaɪə'niz, -'nis] *a., s.* (*pl.* LYONESE) lionés, de Lyon, Francia.
lyonnaise [-'neɪz] *a.* (cocina) a la lionesa. (aplíc. a papas fritas con cebollas).
lyophile ['laɪəˌfaɪl] *a.* (quím.) 1. liófilo. 2. liofilizado.
lyophilic [ˌlaɪə'fɪlɪk] *a.* (quím.) liofílico.
lyophilization [laɪ'ɑfələ'zeɪʃən, B -ˌɔfɪlaɪ-] *s.* liofilización.
lyophilize [-'afəˌlaɪz, B -'ɔf-] *v.t.* (quím.) liofilizar.
lyophobic [ˌlaɪə'foʊbɪk] *a.* (quím.) liofóbico, liófobo.

lypemania [ˌlaɪpə'meɪnɪə, B ˌlɪpi-] *s.* (med.) lipemanía.
Lyra ['laɪrə, B 'laɪərə] *s.* (astr.) Lira.
lyrate ['laɪrˌɪɪt, B 'laɪərɪt] **lyrated** [-ˌeɪtəd] *a.* 1. (bot.) lirado. 2. en forma de lira.
lyre [laɪr, B 'laɪə] *s.* 1. (mús.) lira. 2. (astr.) Lira.
lyrebird ['laɪrˌbɜrd, B -ə'bɜd] *s.* (orn.) ave lira, pájaro lira (originario de Australia).
lyric ['lɪrɪk] *a.* 1. lírico (poesía). 2. (mús.) lírico. —*s.* 1. poema o composición lírica. 2. (*pl.*) letra (de una canción).
lyrical [-ɪkəl] *a.* lírico.
lyrically [-kəlɪ] *adv.* en tono lírico, líricamente.
lyricism ['lɪrəˌsɪzəm] *s.* lirismo.
lyricist [-səst] *s.* lírico (poeta lírico).
lyric poetry, lírica; poesía lírica.
lyrism ['lɪrˌɪɪzəm] *s.* lirismo.
lyrist ['laɪrəst, B 'laɪər-] *s.* 1. (mús.) lirista. 2. ['lɪrəst] lírico (poeta).
lysate ['laɪˌsɪɪt] *s.* (med., bioquím.) lisado, producto de la lisis.
lyse [laɪs] *v.t.* (bact., fisiol.) causar lisis o disolución de (células o bacterias) por acción de las lisinas. —*v.i.* (bact., fisiol.) ser disueltas o destruidas (células o bacterias) por acción de las lisinas.

lysergic acid [lə'sɜrdʒɪk-, laɪ-, B laɪ'sɜdʒɪɪk-] (quím.) ácido lisérgico.
lysergic acid diethylamide (LSD) [-daɪ'-ɛθələˌmɪɪd] (quím.) dietilamida del ácido lisérgico.
lysine ['laɪsin] *s.* (bioquím.) lisina.
lysis ['laɪsəs] *s.* (*pl.* lyses [-ˌsiz]) (med., bioquím.) lisis.
Lysistrata [ˌlɪsə'strɑtə, B laɪ'sɪstrətə] *s.* Lisístrata, obra satírica de Aristófanes en favor de la paz.
lysogenesis [ˌlaɪsə'dʒɛnəsəs] *s.* (fisiol.) lisogénesis.
lysogenetic [-dʒə'nɛtɪk] *a.* (fisiol.) lisogénico.
lysol ['laɪsəl] *s.* marca registrada de un antiséptico líquido.
lysosome ['laɪsəˌsoʊm] *s.* lisosoma (parte de la célula viva).
lysozyme ['laɪsəˌzaɪm] *s.* (bioquím.) lisozima.
lythraceous [laɪ'θrɪɪʃəs] *a.* (bot.) litráceo, litrarieo.
lytic ['lɪtɪk] *a.* (bioquím., fisiol.) lítico.
lytta ['lɪtə] *s.* (*pl.* LYTTAE [-ˌi]) (zool.) lita, landrilla.

M

M [ɛm] *s.* m, decimotercera letra del alfabeto inglés.
m. *abrev. de* 1. **male,** hombre; **masculine,** masculino. 2. **married,** casado. 3. **mile,** milla. 4. **minute,** minuto.
ma [mɑ, mɔ, B mɑ] *s.* (fam.) mamá, mami.
M.A. *abrev. de* **Master of Arts,** (E.U.) grado académico entre la licenciatura en letras y el doctorado.
ma'am [mæm, mɑm, məm] *s.* (fam.) contr. *de* **madam,** señora.
ma-and-pa shop ['mɑən'pɑ] *s.* (fam.) tienda familiar, tienda de la esquina.
Mac [mæk] *s.* 1. (Esco., Irl.) prefijo que en los apellidos significa hijo de. 2. (jer., G.B.) tipo, sujeto, amigo, ej., *listen M.,* oiga, amigo.
macaber [mə'kɑbər, B -bə] **macabre** [-'kɑbrə] *a.* macabro; horripilante, espantoso, siniestro.
macaco [mə'kɑˌkoʊ, B -'keɪ-] *s.* (zool.) macaco.
macadam [mə'kædəm] *s.* 1. macadán, macadam. 2. piedra de macadán.
macadamia nut [ˌmækə'deɪmɪə-] fruto parecido a la avellana, propio de un árbol australiano.
macadamization [məˌkædəmə'zeɪʃən, B -maɪ-] *s.* macadamización.
macadamize [-'kædəˌmaɪz] *v.t.* macadamizar, pavimentar con macadán.
macaque [mə'kæk, -'kɑk, B -'kɑk] *s.* (zool.) macaco, macaca.
macaroni [ˌmækə'roʊnɪ] *s.* (*pl.* MACARONIS O MACARONIES) 1. macarrón, macarrones. 2. (jer., G.B.) italiano.
macaronic [-'rɑnɪk, B -'rɔn-] *a.* 1. macarrónico. 2. (ant.) mezclado, revuelto, confuso. —*s.* macarronea.
macaroon [ˌmækə'run] *s.* mostachón; macarrón; almendrado.
macassar oil, aceite de la India que antiguamente se usaba para dar brillo al pelo.
macaw [mə'kɔ] *s.* (orn.) guacamayo, ara.
Maccabean [ˌmækə'biən] *a.* (hist.) de los macabeos.
maccaboy, maccoboy ['mækəˌbɔɪ] *s.* rapé de macuba (gen. perfumado).
mace [meɪs] *s.* 1. maza, clava, porra. 2. maza ceremonial. 3. macero, ballestero. 4. antiguo taco de billar. 5. macís, macia (especia que se extrae de la corteza de la nuez moscada). 6. (E.U.) aerosol irritante gen. empleado por la policía para dispersar manifestaciones y tumultos.
mace-bearer ['meɪsˌbɛrər, B -ˌbɛərə] *s.* macero, el que porta la maza.
macedoine [ˌmæsə'dwɑn] *s.* 1. (cocina) macedonia (ensalada de frutas o legumbres). 2. (fig.) mezcolanza, mezcla confusa.
Macedonian [ˌmæsə'doʊnjən] *a.* macedón, macedonio, macedónico, de Macedonia. —*s.* macedón, macedonio (habitante o lenguaje).
macerate ['mæsəˌreɪt] *v.t.* macerar, ablandar. —*v.i.* demacrar, consumir; macerar (se).
maceration [ˌmæsə'reɪʃən] *a.* maceración.
macerator ['mæsəˌreɪtər, B -ə] *s.* macerador, machacador (Amer.).
macfarlane [mək'fɑrlən, B -'fɑlɪn] *s.* macferlán, macfarlán, gabán de estilo antiguo con esclavina.
Mach [mɑk, mæk] *s.* (aer.) *forma abreviada de* **Mach number,** número de Mach.
machete [mə'ʃɛtɪ, -'tʃɛtɪ, B -'tʃeɪtɪ] *s.* machete.
Machiavelli [ˌmækɪə'vɛlɪ] *s.* (hist.) Maquiavelo, estadista florentino.
Machiavellian [-ən] *a.* 1. maquiavelista (partidario del maquiavelismo). 2. maquiavélico (política, idea, etc.). —*s.* maquiavelista, intrigante, conspirador.
Machiavellism [-ˌɪzəm] *s.* maquiavelismo, política, mentalidad o proceder astuto, intrigante o conspirador.
machicolate [mə'tʃɪkəˌleɪt] *v.t.* (fort.) proveer de matacanes o ladroneras; aspillerar, almenar.
machicolation [-ˌtʃɪkə'leɪʃən] *s.* (fort.) matacán, ladronera; aspillera.
machinable, machineable [mə'ʃinəbəl] *a.* labrable, fresable, trabajable.
machinate ['mækəˌneɪt, 'mæʃ-, B 'mæk-] *v.t.* maquinar, urdir, tramar, complotar, conspirar.
machination [ˌmækə'neɪʃən] *s.* (*ú. gen. en el pl.*) maquinación, intriga, complot.
machinator ['mækəˌneɪtər, 'mæʃ-, B 'mæk-ə] *s.* maquinador, intrigante, conspirador.
machine [mə'ʃin] *s.* 1. máquina, aparato. 2. mecanismo, maquinaria. 3. (fam., ant.) máquina, vehículo, automóvil. 4. (fig.) maquinaria (social, política, de guerra, etc.). 5. (teat.) máquina, tramoya. —*v.t.* trabajar, labrar o terminar a máquina; fresar, tornear.
machine age, edad de la máquina, era del maquinismo.
machine bolt, perno común, perno o bulón ordinario. tornillo de máquina.
machine code, (comput.) código máquina.
machine gun, (mil.) ametralladora.
machine-gun [-ˌgʌn] *v.t.* ametrallar.
machine-gunner [-ər, B -ə] *s.* ametrallador, ametralladorista.
machine gun nest, nido de ametralladoras.
machine language, (comput.) lenguaje máquina, código en lenguaje de la máquina (sistema de caracteres, signos y simbolos que representan instrucciones e información para ser usados directamente por ordenadores).
machinelike [mə'ʃinˌlaɪk] *a.* semejante a una máquina, ej., *with m. precision,* con la precisión de una máquina.
machine-made [-ˌmeɪd] *a.* hecho a máquina.
machine operator, maquinista.
machinery [mə'ʃinərɪ] *s.* 1. maquinaria, conjunto de maquinarias. 2. (fig.) mecanismo, sistema, organización. 3. (teat.) tramoya.
machine-readable [-'ridəbəl] *a.* (comput.) legible por máquina; **in m. form,** en forma legible por el ordenador.
machine screw, tornillo, para metales.
machine shop, taller de maquinaria; taller mecánico.
machine tap, macho girado mecánicamente.
machine tool, máquina-herramienta, herramienta eléctrica.
machine translation, (comput.) traducción automática.
machine vise, tornillo de mecánico.
machine washable, lavable a máquina.
machinist [mə'ʃinəst] *s.* 1. mecánico, maquinista; ajustador. 2. (teat.) tramoyista.
machinist's mate, (mar.) maquinista subalterno, ayudante de máquinas.
machmeter ['mɑkˌmitər, 'mæk-, B -ə] *s.* machmetro (medidor del número de Mach).
Mach number, (aer.) número de Mach.
machree [mə'kri] *s.* (Irl.) mi corazón (expresión de cariño), ej., *Mother machree,* madre querida.
mack [mæk] *s.* (jer.) *forma abrev. de* **mackintosh.**
mackerel ['mækərəl, B 'mækrəl] *s.* (ict.) caballa, escombro.
mackerel sky, cielo aborregado (cubierto de cirrocúmulos).
Mackinaw blanket ['mækəˌnɔ-] manta gruesa de lana con listas de colores (que se utilizaba en el O. de E.U.).
Mackinaw boat, chalana que se usaba en los Grandes Lagos.
Mackinaw coat, especie de chamarra de lana gruesa a cuadros escoceses.
mackintosh ['mækənˌtɑʃ, B -ˌtɔʃ] *s.* 1. (G.B.) impermeable, abrigo. 2. (ant.) tela impermeabilizada.
mackle ['mækəl] *s.* 1. mácula. 2. (impr.) remosqueo, remosqueado, borrón, doble impresión. —*v.t., v.i.* 1. macular, manchar. 2. (impr.) causar remosqueo (en).
macle ['mækəl] *s.* (miner.) 1. macla. 2. mancha obscura (en un mineral).
macramé [ˌmækrə'meɪ, B mək'rɑmɪ] *s.* macramé (trabajo de pasamanería hecho a base de nudos).
macrobiotics [ˌmækroʊbaɪ'ɑtɪks, B -'ɔt-] *s. pl.* (*sing. o pl. en const.*) macrobiótica, prolongación de la vida.
macrocephalic [-sə'fælɪk, B -kə-] **macrocephalous** [-'sɛfələs, B -'kɛf-] *a.* (antrop., bot.) macrocéfalo.
macrocephaly [-'sɛfəlɪ, B -'kɛf-] *s.* (antrop., bot.) macrocefalia.
macroclimate ['mækrəˌklaɪmət] *s.* (meteor.) macroclima.
macrocosm [-ˌkɑzəm, B -ˌkɔz-] *s.* macrocosmo, la totalidad del universo.
macrocyst [-ˌsɪst] *s.* (bot., biol.) macrociste; macroquiste.
macrocyte [-ˌsaɪt] *s.* (med.) macrocito.
macrocytosis [ˌmækroʊˌsaɪ'toʊsəs] *s.* (med.) macrocitosis.
macroeconomics [-ˌikə'nɑmɪks, -ˌɛkə-, B -'nɔm-] *s.* (econ.) macroeconomía.
macrogamete [-gə'mit, -'gæmit, B -gə'mit] *s.* (biol.) macrogameto.

macrography [mæ'krɑgrəfɪ, B mə'krɔg-] *s.* 1. macrografía, examen a simple vista, sin microscopio. 2. macrografía, tendencia a escribir con letra muy grande.
macromere ['mækroʊˌmɪr, B -ˌmɪə] *s.* (biol.) macrómero.
macron ['meɪkˌrɑn, B 'mækˌrɔn] *s.* (gram.) raya que se pone sobre las vocales o sílabas para indicar su pronunciación.
macronucleus [ˌmækroʊ'nuklɪəs, B -'nju-] *s.* (biol.) macronúcleo.
macrophage ['mækrəˌfeɪdʒ] *s.* (biol.) macrófago.
macrophagic [ˌmækrə'fædʒɪk] *a.* (biol.) macrófago.
macroscopic [-'skɑpɪk, B -'skɔp-] *a.* macroscópico, visible a simple vista.
macroseismic [-'saɪzmɪk] *a.* (geof.) macrosísmico.
macrospore ['mækrəˌspɔr, B -ˌspɔ] *s.* (bot.) macróspora, macrósporo.
macrostructure [ˌmækˌroʊ'strʌktʃər, B -tʃə] *s.* (fís.) macroestructura.
Macrura [mə'krʊrə, B -'krʊərə] *a., s. pl.* (zool.) macruros.
macrural [-'krʊrəl, B -'krʊər-] *a.* (zool.) macruro.
macruroid [-ˌɔɪd] *a.* (zool.) macrúrido.
macrurous [-əs] *a.* (zool.) macruro.
macula ['mækjələ] macule [-ˌjul] *s.* (*pl.* MACULAE) [-jəˌli] mácula, mancha (solar, lunar); (med.) mácula.
maculate [-ˌleɪt] *v.t.* macular, mancillar, manchar; deshonrar. — [-lət] *a.* manchado, mancillado; maculado; deshonrado.
maculation [ˌmækjə'leɪʃən] *s.* 1. mancha, mancilla, mácula. 2. (med., zool., bot.) maculación.
macumba [mə'kʊmbə] *s.* macumba, culto religioso en Brasil (mezcla de vudú con elementos cristianos).
mad [mæd] *a.* (MADDER; MADDEST) 1. loco, demente, insano. 2. loco, tonto, insensato, descabellado. 3. furioso, enfurecido. 4. frenético, desesperado. 5. extravagante, desbordante, bullicioso. 6. rabioso (perro). 7. **like m.,** como loco, intensamente, ej, *this stings like m.,* esto pica que rabia; **m. about,** loco por (algo o alguien); **m. as a hatter,** loco de atar; **m. (at),** (fam.) molesto (con); **to drive m.,** hacer perder el juicio, volver loco, enloquecer; **to get m.,** enojarse, enfurecerse; **to go m.,** volverse loco, enloquecer; **to make m.,** enojar, enfurecer.
Madagascan [ˌmædə'gæskən] *a., s.* malgache, oriundo o perteneciente a la isla de Madagascar.
Madagascar [-kər, B -kə] *s.* Madagascar (República Malgache).
madam ['mædəm] *s.* 1. señora. 2. (*pl.* MADAMS) propietaria o encargada de un prostíbulo.
madame [mə'dɑm, B 'mædəm] *s.* (*pl.* MESDAMES [meɪ'dɑm, B 'meɪdæm]) madama, señora (apl. a damas extranjeras o distinguidas, como diplomáticas, cantantes, etc.).
madapollam [ˌmædə'pɑləm, B -'pɔl-] *s.* madapolán, tela ligera de algodón parecida al percal.
mad-brained ['mæd'breɪnd] *a.* precipitado, exaltado, irreflexivo.
madcap ['mædˌkæp] *a., s.* alocado, calavera, tarambana.
madden ['mædən] *v.t.* 1. enloquecer, volver loco. 2. enfurecer, encolerizar. —*v.i.* enloquecer, volverse loco, perder el juicio.
maddening [-ɪŋ] *a.* enloquecedor, exasperante, irritante.
maddeningly [-lɪ] *adv.* de modo enloquecedor, enloquecedoramente.
madder ['mædər, B -ə] *s.* (bot.) 1. rubia, granza. 2. rubia, alizari (raíz). 3. tinte preparado con la raíz de rubia, ej., *m. red,* color carmesí.
madding ['mædɪŋ] *a.* 1. (raro) alocado, frenético. 2. enloquecedor, exasperante, irritante.
maddish [-ɪʃ] *a.* algo loco, alocado.
made [meɪd] *pret., p.p. de* MAKE. —*a.* 1. hecho, preparado, compuesto. 2. fabricado, inventado (excusa, etc.). 3. **m.-over,** reformado, arreglado; (fam.) **you've got it made,** ¡tu éxito está asegurado! ¡qué buena vida te das!
Madeira [mə'dɪrə, B -'dɪərə] *s.* 1. Madera (isla). 2. (t. **m.**) madera, vino de Madera.
madeleine ['mædəlɪn] *s.* magdalena (bizcochuelo francés).
mademoiselle ['mædəmwə'zɛl, -mə'zɛl] *s.* señorita; joven mujer francesa; institutriz francesa.
made to measure, hecho a la medida.
made-to-order ['meɪdtə'ɔrdər, B -'ɔdə] *a.* hecho a la medida, hecho a la orden.
made-up [-'ʌp] *a.* 1. fraguado, inventado, falso. 2. artificial, ficticio. 3. maquillado.
madhouse ['mædˌhaʊs] *s.* manicomio, casa de locos; (fig.) casa de locos.
Madison Avenue ['mædəsən-] (jer., E.U.) a la manera o según los conceptos de las grandes agencias publicitarias, centradas en la avenida Madison de Nueva York.
madly ['mædlɪ] *adv.* 1. locamente. 2. alocadamente, impulsivamente. 3. furiosamente. 4. (fig.) locamente, terriblemente, ej., *m. in love,* locamente enamorado, *m. attractive,* terriblemente atractivo.
madman [-ˌmæn, -mən, B -mən] *s.* (*pl.* MADMEN [-ˌmɛn]) loco, demente, lunático.
mad money, (jer.) dinero para gastos menudos o inesperados.
madness [-nəs] *s.* 1. locura, demencia. 2. furor, furia.
Madonna [mə'dɑnə, B -'dɔnə] *s.* 1. Madona, Nuestra Señora (díc. de la Virgen María). 2. Madona (cuadro, grabado o imagen de la Virgen María). 3. sobrenombre italiano dado a una mujer (equivalente a **madam,** señora).
Madonna lily, (bot.) azucena, lirio blanco.
madras [mə'dræs, -'drɑs] *s.* (tej.) 1. madrás. 2. pañuelo grande de colores brillantes.
madrepore ['mædrəˌpɔr, B ˌmædrɪ'pɔ] *s.* (zool.) madrépora.
madreporic [ˌmædrə'pɔrɪk] *a.* (zool.) madrepórico.
Madrid [mə'drɪd] *s.* Madrid, capital de España; los Madriles (fam.).
madrigal [mædrɪgəl] *s.* (poet., mus.) madrigal, corto poema lírico y composición armonizada para varias voces.
madrigalist [-əst] *s.* madrigalista, compositor o intérprete de madrigales.
madrilène [ˌmædrə'lɛn, -'leɪn] *s.* (cocina) consomé a la madrileña (gen. en gelatina).
Madrilenian [ˌmædrə'linɪən] *a., s.* madrileño, carpetano.
madroña, madrone, madroño [mə'droʊnə] *s.* (bot.) madroño, madroñera.
maduro [mə'dʊroʊ, B mɑ-] *a.* díc. del cigarro puro confeccionado con tabaco oscuro y fuerte.
madwoman ['mædˌwʊmən] *s.* loca, alienada, demente.
madwort [-ˌwɜrt, B -ˌwɜt] *s.* (bot.) 1. raspilla. 2. camelina. 3. aliso.
Maecenas [mɪ'sinəs, B -næs] *s.* (hist.) (*pl.* MAECENASES) Mecenas; (fig.) mecenas, protector de las artes.
maelstrom ['meɪlstrəm, B -ˌstroʊm] *s.* remolino; (fig.) remolino, torbellino (de pasiones, etc.).
maenad ['minæd] *s.* (*pl.* MAENADS O MAENADES ['minəˌdiz]) 1. (hist.) ménade, bacante. 2. (fig.) ménade. 3. mujer descontrolada o frenética.
maestoso [maɪs'toʊˌsoʊ, -ˌzoʊ, B ˌmɑɛs-] *a.* (mús.) majestuoso.
maestro ['maɪsˌtroʊ, B mɑ'ɛs-] *s.* (*pl.* MAESTROS O MAESTRI [-ˌtri]) 1. maestro (esp. compositor, director de orquesta o profesor de música). 2. artista eminente en cualquiera de las bellas artes.
Mae West ['meɪ'wɛst] chaleco salvavidas.
maffick ['mæfɪk] *v.i.* (G.B., fam.) celebrar ruidosamente.
Mafia ['mɑfɪə] *s.* 1. mafia, organización clandestina de individuos al margen de la ley (pr. de origen siciliano). 2. nombre que se da en E.U. a una vasta sociedad secreta que controla internacionalmente numerosas actividades fuera de la ley. 3. crimen organizado. 4. cábala, conspiración.
Mafioso [ˌmɑfɪ'oʊˌsoʊ] *s.* (*pl.* MAFIOSI) mafioso, miembro de la mafia.
mag [mæg] *s.* (fam.) 1. revista (publicación periódica). 2. (G.B.) magneto.
magazine ['mægəˌzin, B ˌmægə'zin] *s.* 1. revista (publicación periódica). 2. (arm.) recámara, depósito o cargador (de cartuchos o balas). 3. almacén, depósito (de explosivos), polvorín. 4. (foto.) cartucho (para película). 5. (mar.) santabárbara, pañol de pólvora. 6. pertrechos, provisiones, vituallas.
magazine gun, fusil de repetición.
magazinist [-əst] *s.* escritor o redactor de una revista.
Magdalen ['mægdələn] **Magdalene** [-ˌlin] *s.* 1. (fig.) magdalena, prostituta arrepentida. 2. (G.B.) institución donde se rehabilitan las prostitutas.
magdalenian [ˌmægdə'linɪən] *a.* (arqueol.) magdaleniense.
mage [meɪdʒ] *s.* (ant.) mago.
Magellanic [ˌmædʒə'lænɪk, B ˌmæg-] *a.* (hist., geog., astr.) magallánico.
magenta [mə'dʒɛntə] *s.* color magenta, rojo purpúreo, solferino.
maggot ['mægət] *s.* 1. cresa, gusano, larva. 2. (raro) capricho, quimera, idea persistente, ej., *m. in one's head,* idea persistente en la cabeza.
maggoty [-ɪ] *a.* 1. agusanado. 2. (raro) caprichoso, quimérico.
Magi ['meɪˌdʒaɪ] *s.* (*pl. de* MAGUS) 1. los Reyes Magos. 2. sacerdotes de la relig. zoroástrica.
magic ['mædʒɪk] *s.* 1. magia, mágica. 2. (fig.) magia, encanto. 3. **as if by m.,** como por arte de magia, como por encanto. —*a.* 1. mágico, sobrenatural. 2. (fig.) mágico, misterioso; encantador, hechicero.
magical [-ɪkəl] *a.* 1. mágico, sobrenatural. 2. (fig.) mágico, misterioso; encantador, hechicero.
magically [-kəlɪ] *adv.* mágicamente.
magic carpet, alfombra mágica.
magic eye, (fam.) ojo mágico (que abre las puertas electrónicamente).
magician [mə'dʒɪʃən] *s.* 1. mago, mágico, nigromante. 2. hechicero (de una tribu primitiva, etc.).
magic lantern, linterna mágica (proyector).
magic wand, varita mágica; (fig.) solución.
Maginot line ['mæʒəˌnoʊ-] (hist.) línea Maginot, fortificaciones francesas en la frontera con Alemania antes de la Segunda Guerra Mundial.
magisterial [ˌmædʒəs'tɪrɪəl, B -'tɪər-] *a.* 1. magistral. 2. de magistrado. 3. autoritario, dominante; pomposo.

magisterially [-əlɪ] *adv.* magistralmente.
magisterium [-əm] *s.* (relig.) magisterio o autoridad de la Iglesia Católica para enseñar en materia de religión.
magistery ['mædʒəsˌtɛrɪ, B -tərɪ] *s.* 1. magisterio; maestría. 2. substancia o agente con poderes extraordinarios.
magistracy ['mædʒəstrəsɪ] *s.* 1. magistratura. 2. jurisdicción de magistrado.
magistral [-trəl, B mə'dʒɪs-] *a.* (farm., metal., fort.) magistral.
magistrate ['mædʒəˌstreɪt, -strət] *s.* (der., pol.) magistrado, ej., *chief m.*, primer magistrado (el presidente) de la nación.
magistrature [-ˌstreɪtʃər, -strəˌtʃʊr, B -strətjʊə] *s.* magistratura.
magma ['mægmə] *s.* (*pl.* MAGMATA [-tə] o MAGMAS) (geol.) 1. magma. 2. mezcla pastosa de origen mineral y orgánico. 3. magma, materia fundida de la que se forman las rocas ígneas. 4. (farm.) magma, material precipitado en una base acuosa.
Magna Charta, Magna Carta ['mægnə'kɑrtə, B -'kɑtə] (hist.) Carta Magna, p. ext. cualquier ley o constitución que garantiza los derechos civiles y políticos de un pueblo.
magnaflux ['mægnəˌflʌks] *s.* (metal.) sistema de inspección magnética.
magnanimity [ˌmægnə'nɪmətɪ] *s.* 1. magnanimidad, generosidad. 2. acto magnánimo.
magnanimous [mæg'nænəməs] *a.* magnánimo, generoso.
magnanimously [-lɪ] *adv.* magnánimamente, generosamente.
magnate ['mægˌneɪt, -nət] *s.* magnate, potentado.
magnesia [mæg'niʃə, -ʒə] *s.* (quím.) 1. magnesia. 2. magnesio.
magnesian [-ʃən, -ʒən] *a.* (quím.) magnesiano.
magnesic [-sɪk] *a.* magnésico.
magnesite ['mægnəˌsaɪt] *s.* (min.) magnesita.
magnesium [mæg'niziəm, -ʒəm, B -'nizjəm] *s.* (min.) magnesio.
magnesium flare, bengala de magnesio.
magnet ['mægnət] *s.* imán, magneto.
magnetic [mæg'nɛtɪk] *a.* 1. magnético, imantado. 2. (fig.) magnético, atractivo.
magnetically [-ɪkəlɪ] *adv.* magnéticamente.
magnetic amplifier, (rad.) amplificador magnético.
magnetic axis, (geof.) eje magnético.
magnetic bearing, (mar., aer.) rumbo magnético.
magnetic cartridge, (electrón.) pastilla o cápsula magnética, fonocaptor magnético.
magnetic clutch, (mec.) embrague electromagnético o magnético.
magnetic compass, (nav.) brújula, brújula magnética.
magnetic conductivity, (elec.) conductividad magnética, permeabilidad.
magnetic curves, (fís.) curvas de fuerza magnética.
magnetic cutout, (elec.) protector magnético.
magnetic declination, declinación, variación magnética.
magnetic deviation, (geof.) desviación magnética o de la brújula.
magnetic dip, inclinación magnética.
magnetic disturbance, (mar.) perturbaciones magnéticas.
magnetic equator, (geog.) ecuador magnético, línea aclínica.
magnetic field, (fís.) campo magnético.
magnetic flux, (fís.) flujo magnético.
magnetic force, (fís.) fuerza magnética.
magnetic induction, (fís.) inducción magnética.
magnetic leakage, *s.* dispersión magnética.
magnetic mine, (mil.) mina magnética.
magnetic moment, (fís.) momento magnético.
magnetic needle, aguja magnética, brújula.
magnetic north, (mar.) norte magnético.
magnetic parallel, (geof.) línea isóclina.
magnetic pickup, pastilla o cápsula magnética; fonocaptor magnético.
magnetic pole, 1. polo del imán. 2. (geog.) polo magnético.
magnetic recorder, magnetófono, grabadora magnética.
magnetics [mæg'nɛtɪks] *s.* (fís.) magnetismo, parte de la física que estudia los fenómenos magnéticos.
magnetic storm, borrasca magnética, tempestad magnética.
magnetic tape, cinta magnética; cinta magnetofónica.
magnetic variometer, magnetómetro.
magnetic wire, hilo magnético; hilo magnetofónico.
magnetism ['mægnəˌtɪzəm] *s.* 1. (fís.) magnetismo. 2. (fig.) magnetismo, atracción.
magnetite [-ˌtaɪt] *a.* (min.) magnetita.
magnetizable ['mægnəˌtaɪzəbəl] *a.* magnetizable.
magnetization [ˌmægnətə'zeɪʃən, B -nətaɪ-] *s.* magnetización, imantación, imanación.
magnetize ['mægnəˌtaɪz] *v.t.* 1. magnetizar, imantar, imanar. 2. (fig.) magnetizar, fascinar.
magneto [mæg'nitoʊ] *s.* (*pl.* MAGNETOS) (elec.) magneto, generador eléctrico.
magneto booster, (mec.) magneto de lanzamiento.
magnetochemistry [-'kɛməstrɪ] *s.* magnetoquímica.
magnetodynamo [-'daɪnəmoʊ] *s.* (elec.) magnetodínamo.
magnetoelectric [-ə'lɛktrɪk] *a.* (fís.) magnetoeléctrico.
magnetoelectricity [-ɪˌlɛk'trɪsətɪ] *s.* magnetoelectricidad.
magnetograph [mæg'nitoʊˌgræf, B -ˌgrɑf] *s.* (fís.) magnetómetro registrador.
magnetometer [ˌmægnə'tɑmətər, B -'tɔmɪtə] *s.* (fís.) magnetómetro.
magnetomotive force [mægˌnitoʊ'moʊtɪv-] (fís.) fuerza magnetomotriz.
magneton ['mægnəˌtɑn, B -ˌtɔn] *s.* (fís.) magnetón.
magnetophone [mæg'nitəˌfoʊn] *s.* (fís.) magnetófono, grabadora.
magnetophonic [mægˌnitə'fɑnɪk, B -'fɔn-] *a.* magnetofónico.
magnetoscope [mæg'nitəˌskoʊp] *s.* (fís.) magnetoscopio.
magnetosphere [-ˌsfɪr, B -ˌsfɪə] *s.* (astr.) magnetosfera.
magnetostriction [-ˌstrɪkʃən, B -'nitoʊ-] *s.* (fís.) magnetostricción.
magnetron ['mægnəˌtrɑn, B -ˌtrɔn] *a.* (rad.) magnetrón.
magnifiable ['mægnəˌfaɪəbəl] *a.* magnificable; apto para ser ampliado o enaltecido.
magnific [mæg'nɪfɪk] *a.* 1. (ant.) magnificente, suntuoso. 2. exaltado, sublime. 3. (ant.) grandilocuente, pomposo; laudatorio.
Magnificat [mæg'nɪfɪˌkæt] *s.* (relig.) magníficat, cántico de vísperas, p. ext. cántico de alegría y exaltación.
magnification [ˌmægnəfə'keɪʃən] *s.* 1. ampliación, aumento. 2. (ópt.) magnificación, agrandamiento. 3. alabanza, enaltecimiento. 4. (fig.) exageración.
magnificence [mæg'nɪfəsəns] *s.* magnificencia.
magnificent [-sənt] *a.* 1. magnífico (título que se daba a gobernantes famosos). 2. magnífico, espléndido.
magnificently [-lɪ] *adv.* magníficamente, espléndidamente.
magnifico [mæg'nɪfɪˌkoʊ] *s.* (*pl.* MAGNIFICOES) 1. caballero noble de Venecia. 2. personaje ilustre.
magnifier ['mægnəˌfaɪər, B -ə] *s.* 1. (ópt.) lente de aumento, lupa, amplificador. 2. panegerista, exagerador.
magnify ['mægnəˌfaɪ] *v.t.* (*pret., p.p.* MAGNIFIED; *p.pr.* MAGNIFYING) 1. (ópt.) aumentar, amplificar, agrandar. 2. exagerar, aumentar, ej., *to m. a loss,* exagerar una pérdida. 3. (ant.) magnificar, alabar, ensalzar.
magnifying glass [-ɪŋ-] lupa, lente, vidrio o lente de aumento.
magniloquence [mæg'nɪləkwəns] *s.* grandilocuencia, pomposidad.
magniloquent [-kwənt] *a.* grandilocuente, grandílocuo, rimbombante.
magniloquently [-lɪ] *adv.* de modo grandilocuente.
magnitude ['mægnəˌtud, B -ˌtjud] *s.* 1. magnitud, grandeza, excelencia. 2. magnitud, importancia. 3. magnitud, tamaño (de un cuerpo). 4. volumen (del sonido). 5. (astr., mat.) magnitud. 6. **of the first m.,** de primera magnitud, de suma importancia.
magnolia [mæg'noʊljə] *s.* (bot.) magnolia.
magnoliaceous [mægˌnoʊlɪ'eɪʃəs] *a.* (bot.) magnoliáceo.
magnum ['mægnəm] *s.* (*pl.* MAGNUMS) botella de dos litros (gen. para vino o licor).
magnum opus ['mægnəm'oʊpəs] obra maestra, la obra más importante de un artista.
magnus hitch ['mægnəs-] (mar.) ballestrinque.
magpie ['mægˌpaɪ] *s.* 1. (orn.) urraca, pega, picaza, picaraza. 2. (fig.) charlatán, hablador.
maguey [mə'geɪ, B 'mægweɪ] *s.* 1. (bot.) maguey, pita, agave mexicano. 2. pita, hilaza de maguey.
maguey worm, (zool.) tecol, gusano del maguey.
Magus ['meɪgəs] *s.* (*pl.* MAGI [-ˌdʒaɪ]) 1. Rey Mago. 2. mago (de la religión zoroástrica). 3. **m.,** mago, nigromante.
Magyar ['mægjɑr, B -jɑ] *a., s.* magiar, húngaro.
maharaja, maharajah [ˌmɑhə'rɑdʒə] *s.* maharajá, príncipe de la India.
maharani, maharanee [-'rɑni] *s.* maharani, princesa de la India.
mahatma [mə'hɑtmə, -'hætmə] *s.* (teosofía) mahatma, título que se da en la India a los sabios y los místicos del budismo.
Mahdi ['mɑdi] *s.* (relig.) caudillo, profeta, mesías (entre los musulmanes).
Mahican [mə'hikən] *s.* (*pl.* MAHICAN o MAHICANS) mahikan, mohicano (indígena de una tribu de Norteamérica).
mah-jongg ['mɑʒ'ɑŋ, -'ɔn, B 'mɑ'dʒɔn] *s.* ma-jong, juego de mesa chino.
mahlstick, *var. de* **maulstick.**
mahogany [mə'hɑgənɪ, B -'hɔg-] *s.* 1. (bot.) caoba, caobo. 2. (madera de) caoba. 3. color caoba. —*a.* de caoba; de color caoba.
Mahomet [mə'hɑmɪt, B -'hɔm-] *var. de* **Mohammed,** Mahoma.
Mahometan [-ən] *a., s.* mahometano.
mahone [mə'hoʊn] *s.* (mar.) mahona.
mahonia [mə'hoʊnɪə] *s.* (bot.) mahonia.
Mahon stock [mə'hoʊn-] (bot.) mahonesa.

Mahound [mə'haʊnd, -'hund] *s.* 1. (esco.) diablo. 2. (ant.) Mahoma.
mahout [-'haʊt] *s.* naire, cornac, el que cuida, doma y guía los elefantes.
mahratta, *var. de* **maratha.**
maid [meɪd] *s.* 1. doncella; soltera; virgen. 2. criada, moza, sirvienta, doncella, mucama (Amer.), fámula (Amer.).
maiden ['meɪdən] *s.* 1. doncella; joven soltera. 2. (dep.) caballo no ganador. 3. (hist.) especie de guillotina (usada en Escocia). —*a.* 1. virgen; célibe, soltera, ej., *m. aunt,* tía soltera. 2. virginal (inocencia, candor, belleza, etc.). 3. (fig.) virgen, primero, inicial, ej., *m. territory,* terreno virgen, *m. voyage,* viaje inaugural, primera travesía, *m. speech,* primer discurso, discurso de estreno (de nuevo diputado, etc.). 4. (fig.) virgen, intacto; no probado; no acostumbrado.
maiden flight, primer vuelo.
maidenhair [-ˌhɛr, B -ˌhɛə] *s.* (bot.) cilandrillo, culantrillo.
maidenhair fern, cabello de Venus, culantrillo.
maidenhead [-ˌhɛd] *s.* 1. (ant.) doncellez, virginidad. 2. (anat.) himen.
maidenhood [-ˌhʊd] *s.* 1. doncellez, virginidad. 2. los años célibes de la mujer.
maidenliness [-lɪnəs] *s.* modestia, pudor, recato.
maidenly [-lɪ] *a.* virginal; pudoroso, púdico; modesto. —*adv.* modestamente.
maiden name, nombre de soltera.
maid-in-waiting [ˌmeɪdən'weɪtɪŋ] *s.* (*pl.* MAIDS-IN-WAITING) dama de compañía, dama (de una reina o princesa).
maid of all work, criada para todo servicio.
maid of honor, dama de honor, menina, doncella (de una reina o princesa); dama de honor (en una boda).
Maid of Orleans, la Doncella de Orleáns, Juana de Arco.
maidservant ['meɪdˌsɜrvənt, B -ˌsɜvənt] *s.* sirvienta, criada, doncella, doméstica, mucama (Amer.).
maihem, *var. de* **mayhem.**
mail [meɪl] *s.* 1. correo. 2. correspondencia. 3. (ant., esco.) bolsa, valija. 4. **by return m.,** a vuelta de correo. —*a.* de correo, postal. —*v.t.* enviar por correo, echar al correo. —*v.i.* enviar cartas.
mail, *s.* 1. (t. **chain m.**) cota de malla. 2. armadura, cubierta protectora (de ciertos animales). —*v.t.* armar con cota de malla.
mailable ['meɪləbəl] *a.* apto para enviarse por correo.
mailbag ['meɪlˌbæg] *s.* 1. portacartas. 2. bolsa, valija o saco postal, saco de correspondencia.
mailboat [-ˌboʊt] *s.* barco correo.
mailbox [-ˌbɑks, B -ˌbɔks] *s.* buzón (de correo).
mail call, (mil.) toque para distribución del correo.
mail car, (f.c.) vagón correo, vagón postal.
mail carrier, cartero.
mail chute, buzón tubular.
mail coach, diligencia (coche); (f.c.) vagón correo, vagón postal.
mail drop, 1. buzón en la propia oficina de correos. 2. dirección usada para recibir comunicaciones en secreto.
mailed [meɪld] *a.* protegido por o cubierto con cota de malla.
mailed fist, (fig.) fuerza bruta, fuerza coercitiva (entre naciones).
mailer ['meɪlər, B -ə] *s.* 1. remitente. 2. envase especial para remitir un objeto por correo (tubo de cartón, etc.). 3. pieza de material publicitario impreso que se distribuye por correos.
mailing [-ɪŋ] *s.* (esco.) granja alquilada, renta pagada por el aparcero.
mailing list, lista de direcciones a las que se envía información o propaganda periódicamente.
mailing machine, máquina para poner sellos o imprimir direcciones (en sobres de cartas).
maillot [maɪ'oʊ] *s.* 1. traje de malla (de gimnastas y bailarines). 2. jersey. 3. traje de baño de una pieza (de mujer).
mailman ['meɪlˌmæn] *s.* cartero.
mail order, pedido postal, pedido por correo.
mail-order catalogue, catálogo de venta por correo.
mail-order house [-ˌɔrdər-, B -ˌɔdə-] casa de ventas por correo.
mail plane, avión correo.
mail pouch, mail sack, saco de lona para impresos y correspondencia.
mail train, tren correo.
maim [meɪm] *v.t.* 1. lisiar, tullir, mutilar. 2. (fig.) estropear, baldar. —*s.* (ant.) mutilación; tara o daño físico.
maimed [meɪmd] *a.* lisiado, tullido; manco, cojo.
Maimonides [maɪ'mɑnəˌdiz, B -'mɔn-] *s.* Maimónides, médico, filósofo y escritor judeo-español del siglo XII.
main [meɪn] *s.* 1. parte principal, punto esencial. 2. fuerza física; poder (*ú sólo en*) **with might and m.,** a toda fuerza; a más no poder. 3. tubo o cañería matriz; tubería maestra. 4. (elec.) conductor principal. 5. (f.c.) línea principal. 6. (mar.) palo mayor; vela mayor. 7. tierra firme; (poét.) océano. 8. jugada o tirada de dados. 9. pelea de gallos. 10. **in the m.,** en la mayor parte, en general; principalmente. —*a.* 1. fundamental, esencial. 2. principal; maestro. 3. (mar.) mayor (vela, palo, estay, etc.). 4. **the m. body (of the army),** el grueso (del ejército); **the m. point,** el punto principal; **the m. chance,** oportunidad óptima.
main bearing, cojinete principal, soporte principal.
main clause, (gram.) oración principal.
main course, 1. plato principal, plato fuerte. 2. (mar.) vela mayor.
main deck, (mar.) cubierta principal.
main dish, plato de fondo, plato principal (en una comida).
main drag, (jer.) calle principal de una ciudad o pueblo.
Maine [meɪn] *s.* Maine, estado de los E.U.
main floor, primer piso, planta baja.
mainframe ['meɪnfreɪm] *s.* (comput.) ordenador central, unidad central, elaborador central.
main highway, carretera principal de una comarca.
mainland ['meɪnˌlænd, B -lənd] *s.* tierra firme, continente, territorio continental; **m. China,** la China continental; **on the Spanish m.,** en la España penínsular, en la península.
main line, 1. (f.c.) línea principal, línea troncal, tronco (Amer.). 2. (fam.) las fuerzas vivas, la clase alta e influyente en una comunidad.
mainline [-ˌlaɪn] *v.i.* (jer.) inyectar(se) estupefacientes (esp. heroína) directamente en una vena, picarse, chutarse.
mainliner [-ˌlaɪnər, B -nə] *s.* 1. (jer.) narcómano que se inyecta por vía intravenosa. 2. miembro de la clase influyente de una comunidad.
mainly [-lɪ] *adv.* 1. mayormente, principalmente. 2. (dial., G.B.) extremadamente.
mainmast [-ˌmæst, B -ˌmɑst] *s.* (mar.) árbol o palo mayor.
main office, casa matriz, oficina central, sede social (de una empresa).
main road, camino troncal, carretera matriz.
mainsail ['meɪnˌseɪl, -səl] *s.* (mar.) vela mayor.
main shaft, 1. (mot.) árbol o eje principal. 2. (aut.) árbol de transmisión. 3. (min.) pozo maestro.
mainsheet [-ˌʃit] *s.* (mar.) escota mayor.
mainspring [-ˌsprɪŋ] *s.* 1. muelle real (en un mecanismo). 2. (fig.) causa principal, origen; móvil principal.
mainstay [-ˌsteɪ] *s.* 1. (mar.) estay mayor. 2. (fig.) sostén, apoyo, soporte principal.
main stem, vía o canal principal; (f.c.) vía troncal; (jer.) calle mayor, arteria principal (de una ciudad).
mainstream [-ˌstrim] *s.* (fig.) corriente principal; tendencia o inclinación principal de la opinión pública o de un movimiento (en arte, ciencia, etc.).
main street, calle mayor, calle principal; p. ext. costumbres, cultura y actitudes de la ciudad pequeña de E.U. (según la descripción de Sinclair Lewis en su novela de este nombre).
main switch, (elec.) interruptor principal o general.
maintain [meɪn'teɪn, mən-] *v.t.* 1. mantener (posición, actitud, correspondencia); conservar (amistad). 2. sostener, mantener (familia, persona, etc.), mantener, conservar (camino, maquinaria, etc.). 3. mantener, afirmar, asegurar.
maintainer [-ər, B -ə] *s.* mantenedor; partidario, defensor.
maintenance ['meɪntənəns] *s.* 1. mantenimiento, apoyo, defensa. 2. manutención, mantenimiento, sostenimiento. 3. sustento, pensión. 4. cuidado, limpieza, reparación, conservación (de propiedad, camino, equipo, maquinaria). 5. (der.) ayuda ilegal (a uno de los litigantes).
maintop ['meɪnˌtɑp, B -ˌtɔp] *s.* (mar.) cofa mayor o de gavia.
main-topgallant mast [-tɑp'gælənt-, B -tɔp-] (mar.) mastelerillo de mayor.
main-topgallant sail, (mar.) juanete mayor.
main-topmast [meɪn'tɑpˌmæst, -məst, B -'tɔpˌmɑst] *s.* (mar.) mastelero de mayor.
main-topsail [-ˌseɪl, -səl] *s.* (mar.) gavia.
main yard, (mar.) verga mayor.
Mainz [maɪnts] *s.* Maguncia, ciudad de Alemania.
maisonette [ˌmeɪzə'nɛt] *s.* 1. chalet, casa pequeña. 2 departamento (gen. de dos pisos).
maitre d' [ˌmeɪtər'di, B 'mɛtrə-] (fr., fam.) jefe de comedor.
maitre d'hotel [ˌmeɪtrədoʊ'tɛl, B 'mɛtrə-] 1. mayordomo; jefe de comedor. 2. salsa de mantequilla derretida con perejil picado, sal, pimienta y jugo de limón o vinagre.
maize [meɪz] *s.* maíz, panizo de las Indias.
Maj. *abrev. de* **Major,** Mayor.
majestic [mə'dʒɛstɪk] *a.* majestuoso; noble; magnífico, espléndido.
majestically [-tɪkəlɪ] *adv.* majestuosamente.
majesty ['mædʒəstɪ] *s.* (*pl.* MAJESTIES) 1. majestad, soberano. 2. **M.,** Majestad (título dado a emperadores, reyes, reinas, etc.), ej., *Your M.,* Su Majestad, *His M.,* Su Majestad. 3. majestad, esplendor, majestuosidad, grandeza.
majolica [mə'dʒɑlɪkə, -'jɑl-, B -'jɔl-] *s.* mayólica, cerámica de mayólica.
major ['meɪdʒər, B -dʒə] *a.* 1. mayor, más grande, más extenso. 2. principal, más importante. 3. mayor de edad. 4. grave (enfermedad, herida, etc.). 5. (educ.) de especialización, de la especialidad (de uno), ej., *m. field,* rama de especialización, *his m. subject,* (la) materia de su especialidad. 5. (mús.) mayor (modo, intervalo). —*s.* 1. (der.) mayor de edad. 2. (mil.) mayor, comandante. 3. (educ.) especialidad. —*v.i.* (con

in) especializarse (en una asignatura), ej., *I majored in literature,* mi especialización fue la literatura.
major axis, (geom.) eje mayor (de la elipse).
Majorca [mə'dʒɔrkə, B -'dʒɔkə] *s.* Mallorca, isla principal de las Baleares.
Majorcan [-kən] *a., s.* mallorquín, de Mallorca.
major-domo ['meɪdʒər'doʊˌmoʊ, B -dʒə'-] *s.* (*pl.* MAJOR-DOMOS) mayordomo. mo.
majorette [ˌmeɪdʒər'ɛt] *forma abrev. de* **drum majorette.**
major general, (*pl.* MAJOR GENERALS) (mil.) general de división.
major-generalship ['meɪdʒər'dʒɛnərəlˌʃɪp, B -dʒə'-] *s.* generalato de división.
majority [mə'dʒɔrətɪ, -'dʒɑr-, B -'dʒɔr-] *s.* (*pl.* MAJORITIES) 1. mayoría, mayor parte. 2. (der.) mayoría de edad. 3. mayoría, pluralidad (de votos), ej., *absolute m.,* mayoría absoluta. 4. (mil.) comandancia. 5. **the m.,** la mayoría (de la gente); **the great m.,** el grueso del pueblo; **the silent m.,** (pol., E.U.) la obediente mayoría del país que acata sin chistar la política y las decisiones de los gobernantes, la mayoría silenciosa.
majority leader, (pol.) líder o caudillo del partido mayoritario en la rama legislativa de la nación.
majority rule, (pol.) gobierno por mayoría, gobierno de la mayoría.
major key, (mús.) tono mayor.
major league, (béisbol, E.U.) liga mayor (de las principales de béisbol profesional en los E.U.).
major mode, (mús.) modo mayor.
major order, (relig.) orden mayor (en la jerarquía de los eclesiásticos).
major party, (pol.) partido mayoritario.
major premise, (lóg.) premisa mayor.
major scale, (mús.) escala mayor.
major seventh, (mús.) séptima mayor.
major sixth, (mús.) sexta mayor.
major suit, (bridge) palo mayor (espadas o corazones).
major term, (lóg.) premisa mayor.
major third, (mús.) tercera mayor.
major triad, (mús.) acorde perfecto mayor.
make [meɪk] *v.t.* (*pret., p.p.* MADE; *p.pr.* MAKING) 1. hacer, crear, construir, fabricar, confeccionar, formar, ej., *I made this dress,* yo confeccioné este vestido; *the bees m. their own wax,* las abejas fabrican su propia cera; *war makes want,* la guerra crea el hambre; *wine is made of grapes,* el vino se hace de la uva. 2. redactar, extender (testamento, documento, etc.). 3. preparar, aderezar (comida, té, etc.); arreglar, hacer (cama). 4. establecer, instituir, estatuir (regla, ley). 5. deducir, interpretar, entender, percibir, ej., *what do you m. of it?* ¿qué cosa deduces de eso? ¿cómo lo interpretas? 6. ser (igual a), importar; hacer; constituir, ser incluido, ser de, ej., *three and three m. six,* tres más tres son seis. 7. ofrecer, brindar, servir para, ej., *this book makes pleasant reading,* este libro ofrece una agradable lectura; *wool makes warm clothing,* la lana sirve para hacer ropas abrigadoras. 8. llegar a ser, volverse, ser, ej., *she will m. a good wife,* llegará a ser (o será) una buena esposa. 9. ganar (dinero, sustento); adquirir (fama, reputación, etc.). 10. dar, producir (utilidad, etc.). 11. calcular, considerar, suponer, creer, ej., *I m. it (to be) two o'clock,* calculo que son las dos, *what fish do you m. that to be?* ¿qué pescado crees que sea ése? 12. causar, inducir, compeler, obligar; encargar (de), mandar (hacer), ej., *they made him eat it,* le obligaron a comerlo, *he was made to return,* él fue obligado a regresar, *I made him buy a book for me,* le encargué (o mandé) comprar un libro para mí. 13. hacer, nombrar, ej., *they made him mayor,* le nombraron alcalde. 14. poner, hacer, ej., *it made me sad,* me puso triste. 15. recorrer, cubrir (distancia), ej., *he made fifty miles an hour,* corrió a cincuenta millas por hora. 16. cometer (error). 17. hacer prosperar, significar el éxito a, ej., *this will m. or break him,* esto le significará el éxito o la ruina. 18. conseguir un lugar o puesto en, lograr formar parte de, ej., *he made the team,* logró entrar en el equipo, le han incluido en el equipo. 19. (naipes) tomar, ganar, llevarse (baza, una carta); barajar; establecer (el triunfo). 20. (elec.) cerrar (un circuito); hacer contacto con. 21. (dep.) marcar o labrar (un tanto). 22. (mar.) divisar, avistar; tocar (tierra), llegar a, arribar a (puerto). 23. (jer.) alcanzar (tren, avión, etc.). 24. (jer.) seducir (una mujer). 25. **m. a beast of oneself,** envilecerse; **m. a bid,** ofrecer, pujar; **m. a face,** hacer una mueca; **m. a fool of,** engañar, poner en ridículo; **m. a habit of,** hacer una costumbre de; **m. a living,** ganarse la vida; **m. a mistake,** equivocarse; **m. a night of,** prolongarse (fiesta, etc.) hasta la madrugada; **m. a point of,** hacer hincapié en; **m. a start,** empezar, dar el primer paso; **m. a survey,** hacer una inspección; **m. clear,** poner en claro; **m. fast,** amarrar, asegurar; **m. friends,** hacer amistades; **m. friends with,** amistarse con; **m. into,** convertir en; **m. it,** aguantar (cierta distancia, corriendo, nadando, etc.); llegar a tiempo; salir airoso, triunfar; **m. up,** hacer las paces; **m. known,** publicar, dar a conocer; **m. little of,** sacar poco provecho de; hacer poco caso de, despreciar; **m. much of,** sacar gran provecho de; dar gran importancia a; festejar, tratar con gran deferencia (a alguien); **m. no difference,** no importar; **m. out,** llenar, redactar (documento), extender (factura, cheque, etc.); representar, hacer parecer, ej., *you m. me out a monster,* Ud. me representa como un monstruo; comprender, ej., *nobody can m. him out,* nadie puede comprenderle, *I can't m. out what he is talking about,* no puedo comprender de qué (cosa) está hablando; descifrar, ej., *I can't m. out this word,* no puedo descifrar esta palabra; divisar, vislumbrar, percibir, ej., *they made out a ship in the distance,* divisaron un barco en la distancia; **m. over (to),** ceder (posesión) (a), transferir, traspasar (a), ej., *he made over the house to his wife,* traspasó la casa a su esposa; **m. peace,** hacer las paces; concluir un tratado de paz; **m. room,** hacer sitio; **m. sail,** zarpar; **m. sense,** tener sentido; **m. the best of,** sacar el mejor partido de, aprovechar al máximo; **m. time,** ganar tiempo, avanzar; **m. it with,** (jer.) ganar los favores de (una mujer); **m. up,** completar, suplir; compensar, resarcir, indemnizar; reunir, juntar, integrar; compilar, componer; inventar, tramar, urdir; maquillar, pintar (el rostro); arreglar, concertar (matrimonio, convenio, etc.); conciliar, arreglar (disputa); (impr.) armar (página, forma); **m. up into,** hacer un atado o paquete de, ej., *she made up the linen into a bundle,* hizo un atado de la ropa; **m. up lost ground,** recobrar terreno perdido, salir del atraso; **m. up one's mind,** decidirse, resolverse; **m. war,** guerrear, hacer la guerra; **m. way,** avanzar, progresar; **m. way for,** abrir paso a (alguien). —*v.i.* 1. dirigirse, encaminarse, ir. 2. formarse, crecer; acumularse. 3. intentar, disponerse a (hacer algo), ej., *he made to go,* se dispuso a marchar(se). 4. **m. after,** perseguir, lanzarse en persecución; **m. as if one had (were),** fingir tener (ser, estar), fingir que, hacer como si hubiera; **m. as if** (o **though**) **to (do),** parecer (uno) como si estuviera a punto de (hacer); **m. at,** atacar, lanzarse contra; **m. away with,** llevarse, alzarse con; **m. believe,** fingir; **m. bold (to),** atreverse (a); tomarse la libertad (de); **m. certain,** asegurarse; **m. do with,** hacer servir (algo de calidad inferior), arreglarse con (un substituto); **m. for,** ir hacia; acometer; contribuir a, servir para; **m. of,** pensar de; entender por, interpretar; sacar de; **m. off,** partir, largarse; **m. off with,** alzarse con (cosa robada); **m. out,** salir (bien o mal); **m. ready,** prepararse, aparejarse; **make the scene,** (jer.) aparecer en un lugar; alcanzar éxito; **m. towards,** dirigirse a o hacia, encaminarse a; **m. up,** componerse (con afeites), maquillarse; **m. up for,** compensar por (pérdidas, inconveniente, etc.); **m. up to,** adular (a alguien). —*s.* 1. hechura, forma, figura, estructura, carácter, índole, genio. 2. manufactura, fabricación; producto, producción; marca, ej., *of American m.,* de fabricación americana, *what m. is your car?* ¿de qué marca es su auto? 3. (elec.) contacto, cierre (de circuito). 4. **on the m.,** (jer.) resuelto a triunfar o sacar partido; (jer.) con intención de seducir.
make and break, (elec.) distribuidor de encendido, conjuntador-disruptor, conjuntor-disyuntor.
make-believe ['meɪkbəˌliv] *s.* 1. artificio, engaño, fingimiento, simulación. 2. simulador, fingidor. —*a.* simulado, fingido, falso, de mentirijillas.
make-do [-ˌdu] *a.* improvisado, provisional, interino. —*s.* improvisación, expediente temporal, substituto provisional.
makefast [-ˌfæst, B -ˌfɑst] *s.* (mar.) amarradero; boya o poste.
make-peace [-ˌpis] *s.* pacificador, conciliador.
maker ['meɪkər, B -kə] *s.* 1. constructor, fabricante. 2. **M.,** Hacedor, Creador. 3. otorgante, expedidor, librador (de letra, pagaré, etc.). 4. (ant.) poeta.
makeready ['meɪkˌrɛdɪ] *s.* (impr.) arreglo, nivelación (del tímpano o la forma para asegurar una impresión uniforme y nítida).
makeshift [-ˌʃɪft] *s.* expediente temporal, substituto provisional. —*a.* temporal, interino, provisional.
makeup [-ˌʌp] *s.* 1. composición, constitucion, estructura. 2. cosméticos; afeite, pintura. 3. (teat.) maquillaje. 4. (impr.) compaginación, ajuste, confección. 5. (periodismo) características generales, apariencia, etc., de una publicación o periódico.
makeweight [-ˌweɪt] *s.* 1. complemento de peso (en una balanza). 2. contrapeso. 3. (fig.) relleno, suplemento. 4. tapagujeros, suplente.
making ['meɪkɪŋ] *s.* 1. hechura, fabricación, elaboracion, ej., *m. of bread,* fabricación de pan. 2. formación, preparación. 3. (*pl.*) ingredientes; (fig.) cualidades (esenciales), ej., *he has the makings of a great musician,* tiene las facultades de un gran músico. 4. (*pl.*) (esp. E.U.) papel y tabaco (para cigarrillos). 5. **to be the m. of,** causar el éxito de; **in the m.,** en formación, en preparación; en desarrollo; en marcha, ej., *history in the m.,* la historia en marcha; **of one's own m.,** debido a sus propios actos.
malacca cane [mə'lækə-] roten (bastón).
malachite ['mæləˌkaɪt] *s.* (min.) malaquita.
malacological [ˌmæləkə'lɑdʒɪkəl, B -'lɔdʒ-] *a.* (zool.) malacológico.
malacology [-'kɑlədʒɪ, B -'kɔl-] *s.* malacología, estudio de los moluscos.

malacopterygian [-ˌkɑptəˈrɪdʒɪən, B -ˌkɔp-] *a.* (ict.) malacopterigio.

malacostracan [-ˈkɑstrɪkən, B -ˈkɔs-] *s., a.* (zool.) malacóstraco, crustáceo malacostráceo.

maladaptation [ˌmælædˌæpˈteɪʃən] *s.* mala adaptación, adaptación inadecuada, inadaptación.

maladapted [-əˈdæptəd] *a.* mal adaptado, inadaptado.

maladjusted [-əˈdʒʌstəd, B ˈmæl-] *a.* mal ajustado, desajustado; mal adaptado, inadaptado, desequilibrado.

maladjustment [-ˈdʒʌstmənt] *s.* 1. ajuste defectuoso; mala adaptación, inadaptación, desequilibrio. 2. (psic.) desadaptación (al medio).

maladminister [-ədˈmɪnəstər, B -stə] *v.t.* administrar ineptamente, manejar ineficazmente; manipular fraudulentamente.

maladministration [-ˌmɪnəˈstreɪʃən] *s.* administración inepta; manejo ineficaz o fraudulento, prevaricación.

maladroit [ˌmæləˈdrɔɪt] *a.* torpe, desmañado, falto de tino, desatinado, sin tacto.

maladroitly [-lɪ] *adv.* torpemente, desmañadamente, sin tino, desatinadamente.

maladroitness [-nəs] *s.* torpeza, desmaño, falta de tino.

malady [ˈmælədɪ] *s.* (*pl.* MALADIES) 1. mal, enfermedad, dolencia. 2. trastorno (moral o mental).

mala fide [ˌmæləˈfaɪdɪ, B ˈmeɪlə-] (lat., der.) de mala fe.

Malaga [ˈmæləgə] *s.* Málaga, ciudad de España; málaga (vino y uva).

Malagasy [ˌmæləˈgæsɪ] *s.* (*pl.* MALAGASY o MALAGASIES) 1. malgache, natural de Madagascar. 2. (lengua) malgache.

Malagasy Republic, República Malgache (Madagascar).

malaguena [ˌmæləˈgeɪnjə] *s.* (mús.) malagueña, danza y copla clásicas españolas, típicas de la provincia de Málaga.

malaise [mæˈleɪz] *s.* malestar, indisposición, desazón; p. ext. intranquilidad, desazón mental o moral (de un individuo, clase social, país etc.).

malamute [ˈmæləˌmjut] *s.* perro de Alaska empleado para tirar de los trineos.

malanders [ˈmæləndərz, B -dəz] *s. pl.* (vet.) ajuagas.

malapert [ˌmæləˈpɜrt, B -ˌpɜt] *a.* (ant.) descarado, insolente, atrevido, impudente.

malapertly [-lɪ] *adv.* descaradamente, insolentemente, atrevidamente.

malaprop [ˈmæləˌprɑp, B -ˌprɔp] **malapropian** [ˌmæləˈprɑpɪən, B -ˈprɔp-] *a.* desacertado, incongruente (vocablo).

malapropism [ˈmæləˌprɑpˌɪzəm, B -ˌprɔp-] *s.* despropósito, incongruidad, palabra mal empleada.

malapropos [ˌmælæprəˈpoʊ, B ˈmælˈæprəˌpoʊ] *a.* impropio, no pertinente; inoportuno. —*adv.* fuera de propósito, impropiamente; inoportunamente.

malar [ˈmeɪlər, B -lə] *a.* 1. (anat.) malar. 2. **m. bone,** pómulo.

malaria [məˈlɛrɪə, B -ˈlɛər-] *s.* 1. (med.) malaria, paludismo. 2. (ant.) aire insalubre, esp. miasma.

malarial [-ɪəl] **malarian** [-ən] **malarious** [-əs] *a.* malárico, palúdico.

malarial fever, (med.) fiebre palúdica.

malariologist [-ˌlɛrɪˈɑlədʒəst, B -ˌlɛərɪˈɔl-] *s.* malariólogo.

malarkey [məˈlɑrkɪ, B -ˈlɑkɪ] *s.* (jer.) faramalla, hojarasca.

malate [ˈmælˌeɪt, ˈmeɪˌleɪt, B -lət] *s.* (quím.) malato.

Malawi [məˈlɑwɪ] *s.* Malawi.

Malay [məˈleɪ, ˈmeɪleɪ, B məˈleɪ] *a., s.* malayo, de Malaya.

Malaya [məˈleɪə] *s.* (geog.) Malaya, federación de Malasia.

Malayalam [ˌmæləˈjɑləm, B -ɪˈɑl-] *s.* malayalam, lenguaje drávida hablado en una región de la India.

Malayan [məˈleɪən] *a., s.* malayo.

Malay Archipelago, (geog.) Archipiélago Malayo.

Malaysia [məˈleɪʒə, -ʃə, B -zɪə] *s.* Malasia (Federación de Malasia).

Malaysian [-ʒən, B -zɪən] *a., s.* malasio.

malcontent [ˈmælkənˌtɛnt, ˌmæl-ˈtɛnt, B ˈmæl-ˌtɛnt] *a.* malcontento, descontento; esp. revoltoso, perturbador. —*s.* malcontento, revoltoso, agitador político.

male [meɪl] *a.* 1. masculino. 2. varón, ej., *m. issue,* hijo(s) varón(es). 3. varonil. 4. (bot.) masculino. 5. (zool.) macho. 6. (mec.) macho. —*s.* 1. varón, hombre. 2. macho (del animal). 3. (biol.) organismo masculino.

male alto, (mús.) contralto masculino.

maledict [ˌmæləˈdɪkt] *a.* (ant.) maldecido, maldito; abominable.

malediction [ˌmæləˈdɪkʃən] *s.* 1. maldición, imprecación. 2. calumnia.

maledictory [-ˈdɪktərɪ] *a.* maldiciente.

malefaction [ˌmæləˈfækʃən] *s.* 1. delito, crimen. 2. maldad, perversidad.

malefactor [ˈmæləˌfæktər, B -tə] *s.* malhechor, criminal; malvado.

malefactress [-trəs] *s.* malhechora, criminal (mujer); malvada.

male fern, (bot.) helecho macho.

malefic [məˈlɛfɪk] *a.* maléfico, perjudicial, dañoso, dañino.

maleficence [-əsəns] *s.* 1. maleficio, acción maléfica. 2. maleficencia, maldad.

maleficent [-sənt] *a.* maléfico, dañoso, dañino.

male gauge, calibrador macho, calibre interior.

malentendu [ˌmælɑntɑnˈdʊ] *s.* (fr.) malentendido; error.

male nurse, enfermero.

male pivot, (mec.) gorrón, muñón, quicio.

male screw, tornillo macho (que se acopla a la tuerca).

male stripper, stripteasero, striptesero.

malevolence [məˈlɛvələns] *s.* malevolencia, mala voluntad.

malevolent [-lənt] *a.* malévolo, maligno.

malevolently [-lɪ] *adv.* malignamente, con malevolencia.

malfeansance [mælˈfizəns] *s.* (der.) malversación; desaguisado, fechoría.

malformation [ˌmælfɔrˈmeɪʃən, B -fɔˈ-] *s.* (med.) malformación, deformación, deformidad.

malformed [mælˈfɔrmd, B -ˈfɔmd] *a.* malhecho, contrahecho, mal formado.

malfunction [-ˈfʌŋkʃən] *v.i.* funcionar mal o defectuosamente.

Mali [ˈmɑlɪ] *s.* Malí (República de África occidental).

malic [ˈmælɪk, ˈmeɪlɪk] *a.* 1. (quím.) málico. 2. **m. acid,** ácido málico.

malice [ˈmæləs] *s.* 1. malicia, malignidad, mala voluntad. 2. (der.) intención maliciosa. 3. **to bear m. (to),** tener inquina (a). 4. (der.) premeditación.

malice aforethought, (der.) premeditación (pr. en casos de asesinato).

malicious [məˈlɪʃəs] *a.* 1. malicioso, maligno, avieso, maléfico. 2. (der.) **m. damage,** daño doloso.

maliciously [-lɪ] *adv.* maliciosamente, malignamente.

malicious mischief, (der.) agravio doloso.

maliciousness [-nəs] *s. mala intención, malicia.*

malign [məˈlaɪn] *a.* 1. maligno, malévolo. 2. maligno, pernicioso, nocivo; (med.) maligno, ej., tumor. —*v.t.* difamar, calumniar.

malignance [məˈlɪgnəns] *s.* 1. malignidad, malevolencia. 2. (med.) malignidad (ej., de un tumor).

malignancy [-nənsɪ] *s.* (*pl.* MALIGNANCIES) 1. malignidad, malevolencia. 2. acto maligno; expresión malévola. 3. (med.) malignidad.

malignant [məˈlɪgnənt] *a.* 1. maligno, malévolo; nocivo, pernicioso. 2. (med.) maligno. 3. (ant.) malcontento, rebelde. —*s.* (ant.) malcontento, rebelde, agitador.

malignantly [-lɪ] *adv.* malignamente.

maligner [məˈlaɪnər, B -ə] *s.* detractor, difamador.

malignity [məˈlɪgnətɪ] *s.* 1. malignidad, malevolencia. 2. obra o acto malignos.

malignly [-ˈlaɪnlɪ] *adv.* malignamente.

malines [məˈlin, B mæ-] *s.* gasa fina para confeccionar vestidos.

malinger [məˈlɪŋgər, B -gə] *v.i.* hacer la encorvada, fingirse enfermo, simular una enfermedad.

malingerer [-gərər, B -ə] *s.* simulador (que finge enfermedad).

malison [ˈmæləsən, -zən] *s.* (ant.) maldición; maleficio.

malkin [ˈmɔkən] *s.* 1. (esco., G.B., dial.) liebre; gato; **M.,** gato personificado (como espectro o espíritu familiar). 2. (ant., dial.) mujer desaliñada; ramera; prostituta.

mall [mɔl, mæl] *s.* 1. pala, mallo. 2. juego de mallo, (pall mall); cancha de mallo. 3. paseo, alameda. 4. faja, isla, entre dos pistas de una carretera. 5. galería cerrada con tiendas y negocios en ambos lados, centro comercial.

mall, *var. de* **maul.**

mallard [ˈmælərd, B -əd] *s.* (orn.) pato silvestre, ánade, ánsar.

malleability [ˌmælɪəˈbɪlətɪ] *s.* maleabilidad.

malleable [ˈmælɪəbəl] *a.* 1. maleable, moldeable. 2. (fig.) maleable, adaptable, dócil.

malleable iron, hierro maleable o forjable.

mallee [ˈmæli] *s.* 1. (bot.) eucalipto (australiano) pequeño. 2. (Aust.) bosque o espesura de eucaliptos.

mallein [ˈmælɪən] *s.* (vet.) maleína.

mallemuck [ˈmælɪˌmʌk] *s.* (orn.) petrel, albatros.

malleolar [məˈlɪələr, B -lə] *a.* (anat.) maleolar.

malleolus [-ləs] *s.* (*pl.* MALLEOLI [-ˌlaɪ]) (anat.) maléolo.

mallet [ˈmælət] *s.* 1. mazo, porra, mandarria. 2. mazo, mallete (de polo o croquet).

malleus [ˈmælɪəs] *s.* (*pl.* MALLEI [-ˌaɪ]) (anat.) martillo (del oído).

mallow [ˈmæloʊ] *s.* (bot.) malva.

mallow rose, (bot.) malvarrosa, malva rósea.

malm [mɑm] *s.* 1. marga. 2. ladrillo hecho de marga. 3. mezcla de greda y arcilla (para hacer ladrillos).

malmsey [ˈmɑmzɪ] *s.* (vino de) malvasía.

malnourished [mælˈnɜrɪʃt, -ˈnʌrɪʃt, B -ˈnʌ-] *a.* desnutrido.

malnutrition [ˌmælnuˈtrɪʃən, B -nju-] *s.* (med.) desnutrición, nutrición defectuosa; alimentación deficiente.

malocclusion [-əˈkluʒən] *s.* (med.) oclusión defectuosa (esp. de la dentadura).

malodor [mæl'oʊdər, B -ə] *s.* mal olor, fetidez, hedor.

malodorous [-ərəs] *a.* 1. maloliente, hediondo, fétido, pestífero, pestilente. 2. (fig.) escandaloso.

malodorously [-lɪ] *adv.* pestilencialmente, pestíferamente, con fetidez, hediondamente.

malodorousness [-nəs] *s.* fetidez, pestilencia, hediondez, hedor.

malonic [mə'lɑnɪk, -'loʊnɪk, B -'lɔnɪk] *a.* (quím.) malónico.

Malpighiaceae [mælˌpɪgɪ'eɪsɪˌi] *s. pl.* (bot.) malpigiáceas.

malpighiaceous [-'eɪʃəs] *a.* (bot.) malpigiáceo.

Malpighian corpuscle [-'pɪgɪən-] (anat.) corpúsculo de Malpighi.

Malpighian layer, (anat.) capa de Malpighi.

Malpighian tuft, (anat.) glomérulo de Malpighi.

malposition [ˌmælpə'zɪʃən] *s.* (fisiol.) posición anormal, posición incorrecta (esp. del feto en el útero).

malpractice [mæl'præktəs] *s.* 1. acto contrario a la ética (profesional), acto impropio, conducta inmoral (de profesionales); acto de negligencia, procedimiento incompetente (profesionales), (med.) mala práctica, malpráctica médica. 2. mala conducta; fechoría.

malpractice suit, pleito por mala práctica.

malt [mɔlt] *s.* 1. malta. 2. leche malteada; cerveza de malta. —*v.t.* 1. maltear, convertir en malta, hacer germinar la cebada. 2. mezclar con malta, tratar con malta o extracto de malta. —*v.i.* convertirse en malta.

Malta fever ['mɔltə-] (med.) fiebre de Malta.

maltase ['mɔlˌteɪs] *s.* (bioquím.) maltasa.

malted ['mɔltəd] *a.* malteado.

malted milk, leche malteada; batido de leche malteada (*bebida elaborada con harina lacteada, leche y helado).*

Maltese [mɔl'tiz] *s., a.* maltés, de la isla de Malta.

Maltese cat, gato maltés.

Maltese cross, cruz de Malta (emblema y condecoración).

Maltese dog, perro maltés.

malt extract, extracto de malta.

maltha ['mælθə] *s.* malta; brea, pisasfalto.

Malthusian [mæl'θuʒən, B -'θjuzjən] *a.* maltusiano, relativo o perteneciente a las teorías demográficas de Malthus. —*s.* maltusiano, partidario de Malthus.

Malthusianism [-ˌɪzəm] *s.* maltusianismo.

malt liquor, licor de malta.

maltose ['mɔltoʊs] *s.* (quím.) maltosa.

maltreat [mæl'trit] *v.t.* maltratar.

maltreatment [-mənt] *s.* maltrato, trato rudo.

maltster ['mɔltstər, B -stə] *s.* fabricante de malta.

malty ['mɔltɪ] *a.* 1. malteado, con sabor a malta. 2. borrachín, adicto a la cerveza.

Malvaceae [mæl'veɪsɪˌi] *s. pl.* (bot.) malváceas.

malvaceous [-'veɪʃəs] *a.* (bot.) malváceo.

malvasia [ˌmælvə'siə] *s.* malvasía (uva y vino).

malvasia grape, (bot.) malvasía.

malvasian [-'siən] *a.* de la uva malvasía.

malversation [ˌmælvər'seɪʃən, B -vɜ'-] *s.* malversación; corrupción, fraude.

mama ['mɑmə, B mə'mɑ] *s.* mama, mamá.

mamba ['mɑmbə, B 'mæm-] *s.* (zool.) especie de cobra sudafricana.

mambo ['mɑmboʊ] *s.* mambo, música y baile originarios de Cuba. —*v.i.* bailar el mambo.

Mameluke ['mæməˌluk] *s.* 1. mameluco (soldado egipcio). 2. **m.,** esclavo (en países islámicos).

mamma ['mɑmə, B mə'mɑ] *s.* 1. mama, mamá. 2. (jer.) jamona; mujer madura atractiva.

mamma ['mæmə] *s.* (*pl.* MAMMAE [-ˌi]) (anat., zool.) mama, teta.

mammal ['mæməl] *s.* (zool.) mamífero.

mammalian [mə'meɪlɪən] *a., s.* (zool.) mamífero.

mammalogy [-'mælədʒɪ] *s.* (zool.) mamalogía.

mammary ['mæmərɪ] *a.* (zool.) mamario.

mammary gland, (anat.) glándula mamaria.

mamma's boy, (fam.) hombre o muchacho mimado y muy apegado a su madre.

mammee [mɑ'meɪ, -'mi, B mæ-] *s.* (bot.) mamey.

mammiferous [mæ'mɪfərəs] *a.* mamífero.

mammiform ['mæməˌfɔrm, B -ˌfɔm] *a.* mamiforme, mamilar.

mammilla [mæ'mɪlə] *s.* (*pl.* MAMMILLAE [-i]) (anat.) mamelón, pezón.

mammillary ['mæməˌlɛrɪ, B -lərɪ] *a.* 1. mamilar. 2. (bot.) mamalóneo.

mammillate [-ˌleɪt] **mammillated** [-əd] *a.* (anat.) mamelonado.

mammock ['mæmək] *s.* (dial., ant.) pedazo, piltrafa.

mammogram ['mæməgræm] *s.* mamografía.

Mammon ['mæmən] *s.* 1. (bíbl.) Mammón. 2. (fig.) riqueza; avaricia.

mammography [mə'mɑgrəfi] *s.* mamografía.

mammoth ['mæməθ] *s.* (pal.) mamut. —*a.* gigante, enorme.

mammy ['mæmɪ] *s.* (*pl.* MAMMIES) (fam.) 1. mamá, mamita, mami. 2. (E.U.) ama o niñera negra. 3. (despec.) mujer negra.

mammy wagon, pequeño ómnibus abierto (usado en África occidental).

man [mæn] *s.* (*pl.* MEN [mɛn]) 1. hombre 2. varón. 3. el hombre, la raza humana, la humanidad. 4. hombre, esposo, marido. 5. servidor, sirviente. 6. (*en vocativo*) hombre, amigo. 7. (*gen. pl.*) personal, obreros; soldados (esp. rasos). 8. pieza, trebejo (de ajedrez); ficha (de damas). 9. (antrop.) el hombre; la especie humana, el género humano. 10. (*en palabras compuestas)* barco, ej., *merchantman,* barco mercante. 11. (hist.) vasallo, siervo. 12. (ant.) hombría, masculinidad, virilidad. 13. **all to a m.,** todos sin excepción; **as one m.,** como una sola persona, unánimemente; **best m.,** padrino de boda; **he is your m.,** ahí está el que Ud. busca, él es la persona indicada; **I am your m.,** puede contar conmigo; acepto su oferta; **inner m.,** mundo interior, espíritu (del hombre); **little m.,** hombrecito (díc. a un niño en forma hum. o cariñosa); **m. alive,** ¡hombre, por Dios!; **m. and wife,** marido y mujer; **m. of his word,** hombre de palabra; **my old m.,** (fam.) mi viejo, mi padre; **no man,** nadie; **old m.,** (fam.) capitán, jefe; **old m. of the sea,** viejo lobo de mar; **rag and bone m.,** ropavejero; chatarrero; **the m.,** (jer.) el policía, polizonte, guindilla; el nombre blanco (ú. por los negros en E.U.), p. ext. cualquier persona en posición de autoridad; **the m. in the iron mask** (el hombre de) la máscara de hierro; **the m. on** (o **in**) **the street,** el hombre de la calle, el hombre común; **to be one's own m.,** tener libertad de acción, ser su propio dueño; **to play the m.,** actuar virilmente. —*v.t.* (*pret., p.p* MANNED; *p.pr.* MANNING) 1. tripular, manejar (barco, avión, etc.); armar, guarnecer, proveer de efectivos (militares) (una fortificación, etc.); dotar de personal (una fábrica, oficina, etc.). 2. atender a, manejar; servir (un cañón, etc.). 3. (mar.) disponer marineros sobre, ej., *m. the yards,* disponer marineros sobre las vergas. 4. (mar.) ocupar (puesto en el barco).

man-about-town [ˌmænəˌbaʊt'taʊn] *s.* hombre de mundo que frecuenta los lugares de moda.

manacle ['mænəkəl] *s.* manilla, grillo; (*pl.*) esposas; (fig.) freno, traba, restricción. —*v.t.* 1. maniatar, esposar, engrillar. 2. (fig.) trabar, restringir.

manage ['mænɪdʒ] *s.* 1. escuela de equitación. 2. (ant.) administración, manejo, conducción, gobierno. 3. (ant.) trote de caballo de paso. —*v.t.* 1. manejar, administrar. 2. manejar, controlar. 3. lograr, conseguir; (con *it*) lograr hacerlo. 4. manejar, entrenar (caballos). —*v.i.* 1. manejar los asuntos, dirigir una empresa. 2. (fam.) lograr su objetivo, conseguir su propósito. 3. poder con (comer), ej., *can you m. another slice?* ¿podría Ud. con una rebanada más? 4. **m. to (do),** ingeniarse para (hacer); arreglárselas para (hacer); **m. with,** arreglarse con, entenderse.

manageability [ˌmænɪdʒə'bɪlətɪ] *s.* manejabilidad, docilidad, flexibilidad.

manageable ['mænɪdʒəbəl] *a.* manejable, dócil, tratable; practicable (empresas); maniobrable.

manageableness [-nəs] *s.* manejabilidad, docilidad, flexibilidad.

manageably [-blɪ] *adv.* dócilmente, mansamente.

managed currency, moneda controlada, moneda estabilizada.

management ['mænɪdʒmənt] *s.* 1. manejo, control, dirección. 2. habilidad directiva, capacidad de manejo. 3. cuerpo directivo, junta directiva, directorio, administración, dirección, gerencia, departamento ejecutivo (de una empresa).

managerial [mænə'dʒirɪəl] *a.* empresarial.

mandarinate [-ˌeɪt] *s.* mandarinato.

mandarin duck, (orn.) pato mandarín.

mandatary ['mændəˌtɛrɪ, B -tərɪ] *s.* (der.) (*pl.* MANDATARIES) mandatario.

mandate ['mændeɪt] *s.* 1. mandato, orden, decreto. 2. mandato, encargo, comisión. 3. (der.) mandato. 4. (pol.) mandato (internacional, otorgado por la Sociedad de las Naciones o la ONU); territorio en mandato. —*v.t.* (pol.) otorgar mandato sobre; administrar por mandato.

mandator [mæn'deɪtər, B -tə] *s.* (der.) mandante.

mandatory ['mændəˌtɔrɪ, B -tərɪ] *a.* 1. forzoso, obligatorio. 2. conferido por mandato. —*s.* mandatario.

mandible ['mændəbəl] *s.* (anat., orn., ento.) mandíbula, maxilar inferior; quijada.

mandibular [mæn'dɪbjələr, B -lə] *a.* mandibular.

mandibulate [-lət] *a.* mandibulado.

Mandingo [mæn'dɪŋgoʊ] *s.* (*pl.* MANDINGO, MANDINGOS O MANDINGOES) 1. mandingo, pueblo negro del Sudán Occidental. 2. lengua mandinga. —*a.* propio de los mandingas.

mandolin [ˌmændə'lɪn, B 'mændəlɪn] *s.* (mús.) mandolina.

mandolinist [ˌmændə'lɪnəst] *s.* mandolinista.

mandragora [mæn'drægərə] *s.* (bot.) mandrágora.

mandrake ['mændreɪk] *s.* (bot.) 1. mandrágora, planta solanácea. 2. (E.U.) podofilo.

mandrel, mandril ['mændrəl] *s.* (mec.) mandril, eje de torno.

mandrill ['mændrəl] *s.* (zool.) mandril.

manager [-ər, B -ə] *s.* 1. gerente, director. 2. administrador, superintendente. 3. empresario. 4. **good m.,** hombre económico, persona ahorrativa.

manageress [-ərəs, B -'rɛs] *s.* administradora, directora.

managerial [ˌmænə'dʒɪrɪəl, B -'dʒɪər-] *a.* directivo, administrativo, ejecutivo.

managerially [-əlɪ] *adv.* a la manera de un gerente; ejecutivamente, administrativamente.
managership [-ərˌʃɪp, B -əˌ-] *s.* gerencia, dirección, gestión o gobierno (de una empresa).
Managua [mə'nɑgwə] *s.* Managua, capital de Nicaragua.
Manasseh [mə'næsə] *s.* (bibl.) Manasés.
man-at-arms ['mænət'ɑrmz, B -'ɑmz] *s.* (*pl.* MEN-AT-ARMS) (hist.) soldado, hombre de armas, esp. caballero armado, jinete armado.
manatee ['mænəˌti, B ˌmænə'ti] *s.* (zool.) manatí, vaca marina, pejebuey, pez mujer.
manchet ['mæntʃət] *s.* (ant., G.B., dial.) hogaza o panecillo de trigo candeal.
man-child ['mænˌtʃaɪld] *s.* hijo varón.
manchineel [ˌmæntʃə'nil] *s.* (bot.) manzanillo.
Manchu [mæn'tʃu, 'mæntʃu] *s.*, *a.* manchú, manchuriano, de Manchuria.
Manchurian [mæn'tʃʊrɪən, B -'tʃʊər-] *a.*, *s.* manchú.
mancipation [ˌmænsə'peɪʃən] *s.* (der. romano) mancipación.
manciple ['mænsəpəl] *s.* mayordomo, ecónomo (de un monasterio, universidad o corporación).
Mancunian [mæn'kjunɪən, B mæŋ-] *s.*, *a.* de Manchester (Ingl.).
mandamus [mæn'deɪməs] *s.* (der.) mandamiento, despacho, orden judicial.
mandarin ['mændərən] *s.* 1. mandarín (dignatario imperial chino). 2. dialecto mandarín. 3. (bot.) mandarino, mandarinero. 4. mandarina (fruta).
manducate ['mændʒʊˌkeɪt, B -djʊ-] *v.t.* (ant.) manducar, masticar, mascar.
mane [meɪn] *s.* 1. crin (del caballo), melena (del león). 2. melena, cabellera (larga).
man-eater ['mænˌitər, B -ə] *s.* 1. caníbal, antropófago. 2. (ict.) tiburón blanco. 3. tigre antropófago.
man-eating, que come carne humana.
man-eating shark (ict.) tiburón blanco.
maned [meɪnd] *a.* crinado (caballo); melenudo (león, persona).
manège [mæ'nɛʒ, -'neɪʒ, B -'neɪʒ] *s.* 1. picadero; escuela de equitación. 2. manejo, arte de la equitación.
manes ['mɑnˌeɪs, 'meɪˌniz, B 'mɑnˌeɪz] *s. pl.* manes, dioses infernales; sombras o almas de los muertos.
maneuver, manoeuvre [mə'nuvər, B -və] *s.* 1. maniobra, evolución (naval o militar); (*pl.*) maniobras, ejercicios (bélicos). 2. maniobra, manejo, tramoya. —*v.i.* 1. maniobrar, evolucionar. 2. maniobrar, intrigar. —*v.t.* 1. hacer maniobrar o evolucionar. 2. ejecutar o guiar por maniobras. 3. manipular, tramar.
maneuverability [-ˌnuvərə'bɪlətɪ, -ˌnuvrə-] *s.* maniobrabilidad.
maneuverable [-'nuvərəbəl, -'nuvrə-] *a.* maniobrable, manejable.
maneuverer [-'nuvrər, B -rə] *s.* maniobrista.
man Friday, criado fiel, hombre de confianza, mano derecha.
manful ['mænfəl] *a.* varonil, viril, valiente.
manfully [-fəlɪ] *adv.* varonilmente, virilmente, valientemente.
manfulness [-fəlnəs] *s.* virilidad, hombría, valentía.
manganate ['mæŋgəˌneɪt] *s.* (quím.) manganato.
manganblende ['mæŋgənˌblend] *s.* (mín.) alabandina.
manganese ['mæŋgəˌniz, -ˌnis, B ˌmæŋgə'niz] *s.* (quím.) manganeso.
manganese spar, espato de manganeso, rodonita, rodocrosita.
manganese steel, (metal.) acero mangánico, acero al manganeso.
manganese sulphide, sulfuro de manganeso.
manganic [mæn'gænɪk, B mæŋ-] *a.* (quím.) mangánico.
manganite ['mæŋgəˌnaɪt] *s.* 1. (min.) manganita. 2. (quím.) manganito.
manganous [-nəs] *a.* (quím.) manganoso.
mange [meɪndʒ] *s.* sarna; (vet.) sarna animal, usagre.
mangel-wurzel ['mæŋgəlˌwɜrzəl, B -'wɜzəl] *s.* (bot.) remolacha forrajera.
manger ['meɪndʒər, B -dʒə] *s.* 1. pesebre, comedero. 2. guarda-aguas de proa.
mangily ['meɪndʒəlɪ] *adv.* suciamente.
manginess [-dʒɪnəs] *s.* suciedad, condición o aspecto de sarnoso.
mangle ['mæŋgəl] *v.t.* 1. mutilar, despedazar, destrozar, lacerar. 2. (fig.) mutilar (palabras, cita); desfigurar, deformar (versión, relato, etc.).
mangle, *s.* planchadora mecánica a rodillo. —*v.t.* pasar por una planchadora mecánica.
mangler [-glər, B -glə] *s.* trituradora (máquina).
mango ['mæŋgoʊ] *s.* (*pl.* MANGOES O MANGOS) (bot.) mango (fruto y árbol).
mangonel ['mæŋgəˌnɛl] *s.* (mil.) mandrón, catapulta.
mangosteen ['mæŋgəˌstin] *s.* (bot.) mangostán (árbol y fruto).
mangrove ['mænˌgroʊv, B 'mæŋ-] *s.* (bot.) 1. mangle. 2. mangle prieto.
mangy ['meɪndʒɪ] *a.* (MANGIER; MANGIEST) 1. sarnoso, roñoso. 2. escuálido, asqueroso, sucio.
manhandle ['mænˌhændəl] *v.t.* 1. mover o manipular a mano. 2. maltratar.
manhattan [mæn'hætən] *s.* 1. **M.,** Manhattan (isla de). 2. manhattan, coctel de vermut con whiski.
manhole ['mænˌhoʊl] *s.* boca de acceso, boca de inspección, refugio, nicho (túneles).
manhole cover, tapa de registro o de acceso.
manhood [-ˌhʊd] *s.* 1. estado adulto. 2. hombría, virilidad. 3. hombres (en general).
man-hour [-ˌaʊr, B -ˌaʊə] *s.* (ind.) horahombre.
manhunt [-ˌhʌnt] *s.* caza del hombre, búsqueda sistemática de una persona (esp. de un criminal).
mania ['meɪnɪə] *s.* manía, obsesión, extravagancia; (med.) manía.
maniac ['meɪnɪˌæk] *s.*, *a.* maníaco, maniático.
maniacal [mə'naɪəkəl] *a.* maníaco, maniático.
maniacally [-kəlɪ] *adv.* locamente, de modo maniático, maniáticamente.
manic ['mænɪk] *a.* (med.) maníaco.
manic-depressive [-dɪ'prɛsɪv] *a.* (med.) maniacodepresivo, maniático-depresivo.
Manichaean, Manichean [ˌmænə'kiən] *s.*, *a.* (relig.) maniqueo.
Manichaeanism, Manicheanism [-ˌɪzəm] **Manichaeism, Manicheism** ['mænəki-] *s.* (relig.) maniqueísmo.
Manichee ['mænəˌki, B ˌmænɪ'ki] *s.* maniqueo.
manichord ['mænɪˌkɔrd, B -ˌkɔd] *s.* (mús.) manicordio o monacordio.
manicure ['mænəˌkjʊr, B -ˌkjʊə] *s.* 1. manicuro, manicura. 2. cuidado de las uñas y manos. —*v.t.* arreglar las manos y uñas a; cortar las uñas de (los dedos).
manicurist [-əst, B -ˌkjʊər-] *s.* manicuro, manicura.
manifest ['mænəˌfɛst] *a.* manifiesto, claro, patente, palpable. —*v.t.* 1. manifestar, declarar, exponer, probar (una teoría, etc.). 2. registrar en un manifiesto (de carga). —*s.* 1. (mar., aer.) manifiesto (de carga); lista de pasajeros. 2. (ant.) manifiesto, proclama, declaración.
manifestant [ˌmænə'fɛstənt] *s.* manifestante.
manifestation [-fəs'teɪʃən] *s.* 1. manifestación, declaración, exposición. 2. manifestación, demostración (pública). 3. manifestación, materialización (espiritista).
Manifest Destiny, (E.U.) doctrina del siglo XIX que propugnaba la expansión territorial de E.U.
manifestly ['mænəˌfɛstlɪ] *adv.* manifiestamente, claramente, patentemente.
manifesto [ˌmænə'fɛstoʊ] *s.* (*pl.* MANIFESTOES O MANIFESTOS) manifiesto, proclama, declaración pública. —*v.i.* (*pret.*, *p.p.* MANIFESTOED; *p.pr.* MANIFESTOING) publicar un manifiesto.
manifold ['mænəˌfoʊld] *a.* 1. múltiple, multíplice. 2. variado, vario, diverso. 3. consumado, notorio (ej., mentiroso). —*v.t.* 1. multiplicar, diversificar. 2. sacar o hacer varias copias de. —*s.* 1. multiplicidad. 2. (mat.) variedad. 3. (mec.) tubo múltiple, colector.
manifolder [-ər, B -ə] *s.* máquina multicopista.
manifoldly [-lɪ] *adv.* variadamente, de modo variado o múltiple.
manifoldness [-nəs] *s.* multiplicidad.
manikin ['mænɪkən] *s.* 1. maniquí, armazón (de sastre, escultor, etc.). 2. maniquí, modelo (la persona que exhibe ropas).
Manila, manilla [mə'nɪlə] *a.* de abacá; de Manila (papel, cáñamo). —*s.* 1. (bot.) abacá. 2. papel de Manila; cuera de cáñamo (de Manila).
Manila [mə'nɪlə] *s.* Manila, capital de las Islas Filipinas.
Manila hemp, (bot.) abacá, cáñamo de Manila.
Manila paper, papel de Manila, papel Manila.
Manila rope, cuerda de cáñamo (de Manila); cuerda de abacá.
manille [mə'nɪl] *s.* (naipes) malilla.
man in the moon, (fig., fam.) el hombre de la Luna, figura imaginaria de un hombre sobre la faz de la luna, sugerida por las manchas de ésta.
man in the street, el hombre de la calle, el hombre corriente.
manioc ['mænɪˌɑk, B -ˌɔk] *s.* (bot.) mandioca.
maniple ['mænəpəl] *s.* (relig., hist.) manípulo.
manipulable [mə'nɪpjələbəl] *a.* manejable, controlable.
manipular [-lər, B -lə] *a.* (hist.) del manípulo.
manipulatable [-ˌleɪtəbəl] *a.* manipulable, susceptible de manipuleo.
manipulate [mə'nɪpjəˌleɪt] *v.t.* 1. manipular. 2. alterar, falsificar (informe, etc.).
manipulation [-ˌnɪpjə'leɪʃən] *s.* 1. manipulación, manipuleo. 2. maquinación, intriga.
manipulative [-'nɪpjəˌleɪtɪv] *a.* de manipuleo.
manipulator [-ər, B -ə] *s.* manipulador.
manipulatory [-ləˌtɔrɪ, B -ˌleɪtərɪ] *a.* de manipuleo.
manito ['mænəˌtoʊ] **manitou, manitu** [-ˌtu] *s.* poder misterioso, ser supremo (de los indios algonquinos).
maniu [ˌmɑnɪ'u] *s.* (bot.) mañíu.
mankind ['mæn'kaɪnd] *s.* 1. humanidad, género humano. 2. ['mænˌkaɪnd] los hombres, el sexo masculino.
manlike [-ˌlaɪk] *a.* 1. parecido al hombre, de forma o aspecto humanos. 2. hombruno; masculino, varonil.
manliness [-lɪnəs] *s.* hombría, virilidad.
manly [-lɪ] *a.* (MANLIER; MANLIEST) varonil, viril; animoso, valeroso, resuelto; noble, caballeroso. —*adv.* varonilmente, virilmente; valerosamente, resueltamente.
man-made ['mæn'meɪd] *a.* 1. creado o hecho por el hombre. 2. artificial, sintético.
manna ['mænə] *s.* 1. (bíbl.) maná. 2. (bot.) maná (substancia que fluye de una especie de fresno). 3. **like m. from heaven,** como llovido del cielo.

manned [mænd] *a.* tripulado (ej., vehículo espacial).
manned space flight, vuelo espacial tripulado.
mannequin ['mænɪkən] *s.* 1. maniquí, armazón (de sastre, escultor, etc.). 2. maniquí, modelo (persona que exhibe ropas).
manner ['mænər, B -ə] *s.* 1. manera, modo, forma. 2. manera, hábito, costumbre. 3. (*pl.*) maneras, (buenos) modales; urbanidad, educación, ej., *he has no manners,* él no tiene buenos modales, no tiene buena educación. 4. porte, comportamiento. 5. género, clase. 6. **after this m.,** de esta manera; **all m. of,** todo género de, toda clase de; **by any m. of means,** de todas maneras; **comedy of manners,** comedia de costumbres; **in a m.,** en cierto sentido; hasta cierto punto; **in a m. of speaking,** por decirlo así; **in such a m. as to,** de tal suerte que; **in the m. of,** a la manera de; **the grand m.,** dignidad, elegancia; **to the m. born,** (como uno) destinado desde su nacimiento; acostumbrado desde la cuna; (fam.) hecho a la medida.
mannered [-ərd, B -əd] *a.* 1. de (ciertas) maneras o modales, ej., *a well-m. child,* un niño de buenos modales, *rough-m.,* de modales toscos. 2. amanerado, afectado.
mannerism ['mænəˌrɪzəm] *s.* 1. amaneramiento (literario o artístico). 2. hábito característico, peculiaridad; pose, afectación. 3. (pint.) manerismo.
manneristic [ˌmænə'rɪstɪk] *a.* amanerado.
mannerless ['mænərləs, B -əlɪs] *a.* malcriado, descortés, de malos modales, mal educado.
mannerliness [-lɪnəs] *s.* cortesía, urbanidad, buena educación, buenos modales.
mannerly [-lɪ] *a.* cortés, atento, (bien) educado. —*adv.* cortésmente, atentamente, educadamente.
mannish ['mænɪʃ] *a.* 1. hombruna, ahombrada (mujer). 2. masculino, varonil (ej., vestido).
mannishly [-lɪ] *adv.* varonilmente; de manera hombruna.
mannishness [-nəs] *s.* masculinidad.
mannite ['mænaɪt] *s.* (quím.) manita, manitol.
mannitol ['mænəˌtɔl, -ˌtoʊl, B -ˌtɔl] *s.* (quím.) manitol, manita.
mannitose ['mænɪˌtoʊs] *s.* (quím.) manitosa.
mannose ['mænoʊs] *s.* (quím.) manosa, manitosa.
manoeuvre, *var. de* **maneuver.**
man of distinction, hombre distinguido.
man of God, 1. hombre de iglesia, clérigo, cura. 2. santo; profeta.
man of letters, literato, hombre de letras.
man of straw, testaferro, títere.
man of the cloth, hombre de manga, religioso, clérigo.
man of the hour, hombre del momento.
man of the world, 1. hombre de mundo. 2. hombre comprensivo, amplio.
man-of-war [ˌmænəv'wɔr, B 'mæn-'wɔ] *s.* (*pl.* MEN-OF-WAR) buque de guerra.
man-of-war bird, man-of-war hawk, (orn.) rabihorcado, tijera.
manometer [mə'nɑmətər, B -'nɔmɪtə] *s.* manómetro, medidor de presión.
manometric [ˌmænə'mɛtrɪk] **manometrical** [-trɪkəl] *a.* manométrico.
manor ['mænər, B -ə] *s.* 1. finca o casa solariega, solar. 2. (E.U., hist.) terreno arrendado (a varios locatarios). 3. (G.B.) (hist.) feudo o señorío (esp. la heredad de un lord sobre la que tenía derecho de jurisdicción).
manor house, casa solariega, mansión.
manorial [mə'nɔrɪəl] *a.* señorial, solariego.
manorial court, tribunal de un señorío.
manpower ['mænˌpaʊr, B -ˌpaʊə] *s.* 1. mano de obra. 2. efectivos militares; potencial humano disponible.
manqué [mɑn'keɪ] *a.* (fr.) frustrado.
manrope ['mænˌroʊp] *a.* (mar.) guardamancebo.
mansard ['mænˌsɑrd, B -ˌsɑd] *s.* (arq.) mansarda, buhardilla, desván.
mansard roof, (arq.) techo mansarda, mansarda.
manse [mæns] *s.* rectoría, casa de un pastor protestante.
manservant ['mænˌsɜrvənt, B -ˌsɜvənt] *s.* (*pl.* MENSERVANTS) sirviente, criado, doméstico, mucamo (Amer.).
mansion ['mæntʃən, B 'mænʃən] *s.* 1. solar, casa solariega; residencia elegante. 2. (astrol.) casa del cielo. 3. (ant.) mansión, morada.
man-size ['mænˌsaɪz] **man-sized** [-ˌsaɪzd] *a.* 1. de hombre (tarea, trabajo, etc.). 2. para hombres (trago, modelo, diversión). 3. de gran tamaño.
manslaughter [-ˌslɔtər, B -ə] *s.* (der.) homicidio impremeditado.
manslayer [-ˌsleɪər, B -ə] *s.* homicida.
manstopping [-ˌstɑpɪŋ, B -ˌstɔp-] *a.* (mil.) capaz de detener el avance del enemigo (díc. de las balas dum-dum).
mansuetude ['mænswɪˌtud, B -ˌtjud] *s.* mansedumbre, docilidad; benignidad.
manta ['mæntə] *s.* 1. chal, capa de algodón rústico usada en América Latina. 2. manta (para abrigar las caballerías). 3. (ict.) manta.
manteau [mæn'toʊ] *s.* (fr.) abrigo, sobretodo; manto, capa.
mantel ['mæntəl] *s.* manto (de la chimenea); repisa de la chimenea.
mantelet [-ələt, 'mæntlət] *s.* 1. manto corto, capa, clámide. 2. (mil.) (t. **mantlet**) mantelete (refugio movible usado antiguamente por los sitiadores como protección al atacar). 3. pantalla o biombo a prueba de balas.
mantelletta [ˌmæntə'lɛtə] *s.* mantelete (de los obispos y prelados de rango).
mantelpiece ['mæntəlˌpis] **mantelshelf** [-ˌʃɛlf] *s.* repisa de la chimenea.
manteltree [-ˌtri] *s.* (arq.) dintel de la chimenea (esp. de madera).
mantic ['mæntɪk] *a.* mántico, profético; adivinatorio.
mantilla [mæn'tiə, B -'tɪlə] *s.* mantilla (tocado femenino).
mantis ['mæntəs] *s.* (*pl.* MANTISES O MANTES [-ˌtiz]) (ento.) mantis o manta religiosa, predicador, fraile rezador, mamboretá (Arg.).
mantis prawn, m. shrimp, (zool.) esquila de agua.
mantissa [mæn'tɪsə] *s.* (mat.) mantisa.
mantle ['mæntəl] *s.* 1. manto (prenda). 2. (fig.) manto, capa (de nieve, de la noche, etc.). 3. camisa (de lámpara de gas). 4. (mec.) funda o camisa exterior (de alto horno). 5. (zool.) manto (que envuelve el cuerpo de los moluscos). —*v.t.* 1. cubrir o envolver con manto. 2. (fig.) cubrir, tapar, encubrir. —*v.i.* 1. extender las alas (el halcón). 2. cubrirse de espuma (un líquido). 3. teñirse de (rubor), ruborizarse (la cara).
mantling ['mæntlɪŋ] *s.* (her.) mantelete.
mantra ['mæntrə] *s.* (relig.) mantra (versículo védico de invocación mística).
mantrap ['mænˌtræp] *s.* 1. trampa (para atrapar intrusos); (fig.) trampa, ardid, celada. 2. (fig., jer.) mujer seductora.
Mantuan ['mæntʃʊən, B -tjʊ-] *a., s.* mantuano, de Mantua, ciudad de Italia.
manual ['mænjʊəl] *a.* manual. —*s.* 1. manual, texto, compendio. 2. (hist.) manual (libro de ritos sacramentales). 3. (mil.) ejercicio de armas. 4. (mús.) teclado (de órgano o clavecín).
manual alphabet, alfabeto dactilológico, abecedario manual, letras de mano.
manual labor, trabajo manual; obra de mano.
manually [-ɪ] *adv.* manualmente, con las manos.
manual switch, (elec.) interruptor manual.
manual training, enseñanza de artes y oficios o de trabajo manual.
manubrium [mə'nubrɪəm, B -'nju-] *s.* (*pl.* MANUBRIA [-ə] O MANUBRIUMS) (anat., bot., zool.) manubrio (del esternón).
manufactory [ˌmænjə'fæktərɪ] *s.* (*pl.* MANUFACTORIES) fábrica, manufactura.
manufacture [-'fæktʃər, B -tʃə] *s.* 1. manufactura, elaboración, fabricación. 2. manufactura, artículo manufacturado. —*v.t.* 1. manufacturar, fabricar, elaborar. 2. (fig.) fabricar, inventar.
manufactured [-tʃərd, B -tʃəd] *a.* fabricado, manufacturado.
manufactured gas, gas artificial.
manufacturer [-tʃərər, B -ə] *s.* fabricante, industrial.
manufacturing [-tʃərɪŋ] *a.* industrial, fabril. —*s.* manufactura, fabricación.
manumission [ˌmænjə'mɪʃən] *s.* (der.) manumisión.
manumit [-'mɪt] *v.t.* (*pret., p.p.* MANUMITTED; *p.pr.* MANUMITTING) (der.) manumitir, conceder la libertad (a un esclavo); emancipar.
manumitter [-ər, B -ə] *s.* (der.) manumisor.
manure [mə'nʊr, B -'njʊə] *v.t.* abonar, estercolar (la tierra). —*s.* abono, estiércol, fimo, mabinga (Cuba, Méx.).
manuscript ['mænjəˌskrɪpt] *a., s.* manuscrito; (impr.) original.
manwise ['mænˌwaɪz] *adv.* a la manera de un hombre; varonilmente.
Manx [mæŋks] *a.* de (la isla británica de) Man. —*s.* 1. dialecto hablado en la isla de Man. 2. (*pl. en const.*) habitantes de (la isla de) Man.
Manx cat, gato (sin cola) de la isla de Man (G.B.).
Manxman ['mæŋksmən] *s.* nativo de la isla británica de Man.
many ['mɛnɪ] *a.* (*para formar su comp. y super. se prestan* MORE *y* MOST) muchos, numerosos, varios, diversos; **a great m.,** muchísimos; **as m.,** más, ej., *three times as m. (men),* tres veces más (hombres); **how m. (questions,** etc.), cuántas (preguntas, ect.); **in as m.,** en el mismo número de, ej., *eight mistakes in as m. lines,* ocho faltas en el mismo número de líneas; **m. a time,** (poét., ret.) más de una vez; **m. is the time,** más de una vez; **m. months,** varios meses; **m. people,** mucha gente; **m. times,** muchas veces; **one too m.,** uno de sobra, uno de más; **so m.,** tantos; **too m. cooks spoil the broth,** muchas manos descomponen la olla, muchos gatos en un plato hacen muchos garabatos. —*s.* gran número, muchos; **a great m.,** gran número, muchísimos; **as m. as,** no menos de, ej., *as m. as nine hundred,* no menos de novecientos; **how m. of,** cuántos de, ej., *how m. of these diamonds are genuine?* ¿cuántos de estos diamantes son genuinos?; **m. more,** muchos más; **m. of,** muchos de, ej., *m. of us,* muchos de nosotros. —*pron.* muchos, muchas personas; **m. knew him,** muchos lo conocieron; **m. travel,** muchos o muchas personas viajan; **the m.,** los más, la mayoría; la muchedumbre, las masas, el populacho.
many-colored [-'kʌlərd] *a.* variopinto.
manyfold [ˌmɛnɪ'foʊld] *adv.* (por) muchas veces.

manyplies ['mɛnɪˌplaɪz] *s. pl.* (*gen. sing. en const.*) (zool.) libro, omaso.
many-sided [-'saɪdəd] *a.* 1. de varios lados, multilátero. 2. de varios aspectos, con muchas habilidades. 3. versátil. 4. polifacético.
manysidedness [-nəs] *s.* versatilidad.
manzanilla [ˌmænzə'nijə, B -'nɪlə] *s.* 1. (bot.) manzanillo, olivo manzanillo (árbol o planta). 2. (vino) manzanilla (tipo de jerez seco).
manzanita [ˌmænzə'nitə] *s.* (bot.) manzanita, leño colorado.
maoism ['maʊˌɪzəm] *s.* (pol.) maoísmo, filosofía comunista predicada en China por Mao-Tse-tung.
Maori ['maʊrɪ] *s.* (*pl.* MAORI o MAORIS) maorí (pueblo y lengua de Polinesia).
map [mæp] *s.* 1. mapa, carta. 2. (fam.) cara. 3. **off the m.,** (fam.) inaccesible; sin importancia, anticuado; **on the m.,** (fam.) de importancia; **to disappear from the m.,** desaparecer del mapa; **to put on the m.,** hacer famoso, dar a conocer. —*v.t.* (*pret., p.p.* MAPPED; *p.pr.* MAPPING) 1. trazar un mapa de. 2. explorar con fines cartográficos. 3. (esp. con *out*) delinear el curso de, planear, trazar (programa, campaña, etc.).
maple ['meɪpəl] *s.* (bot.) arce, ácere.
maple sugar, azúcar de arce.
maple syrup, jarabe de arce, miel de arce (Amer.).
map maker, cartógrafo.
mapping ['mæpɪŋ] *s.* planimetría, cartografía.
maquette [mæ'kɛt] *s.* (fr.) maqueta, boceto.
maqui ['mɑkɪ] *s.* (bot.) maqui.
maquillage [ˌmækɪ'jɑʒ] *s.* maquillaje, afeite.
maquis [mæ'ki, B 'mæki] *s.* (fr.) miembro de la resistencia activa de Francia contra los nazis en la Segunda Guerra Mundial.
mar [mɑr, B mɑ] *v.t.* (*pret., p.p.* MARRED; *p.pr.* MARRING) 1. dañar, echar a perder, estropear. 2. (ant.) herir, desfigurar.
Mar. *abrev. de* **March,** marzo.
mar. *abrev. de.* 1. **marine,** marino, **maritime,** marítimo. 2. **married,** casado.
marabou, marabout ['mærəˌbu] *s.* 1. (orn.) marabú, marabú de la India, marabú de Senegal. 2. (pluma de) marabú. 3. marabú, seda marabú. 4. (relig.) morabito, morabuto (religioso mahometano).
maraca [mə'rɑkə] *s.* maraca, instrumento musical de percusión.
maracan ['mærəˌkæn] *s.* (orn.) maracaná, guacamayo.
Maragato [ˌmɑrɑ'gɑtoʊ] *s.* maragato (adorno que antiguamente usaban las mujeres en el escote).
maraschino [ˌmærə'skinoʊ, -'ʃi-, B -'ski-] *s.* marrasquino (cordial).
maraschino cherries, guindas confitadas; cerezas maceradas en marrasquino.
marasmus [mə'ræzməs] *s.* (med.) marasmo.
Maratha [mə'rɑtə] *s.* maratho (miembro de una secta de la India).
marathon ['mærəˌθɑn, B -θən] *s.* 1. maratón (carrera pedestre de los Juegos Olímpicos). 2. (fig.) maratón, cualquier competencia dura y larga. 3. **M.,** Maratón, lugar de la antigua Ática, escenario de una importante victoria de los atenienses.
maraud [mə'rɔd] *v.i.* pecorear; merodear. —*v.t.* pillar, saquear.
marauder [-ər, B -ə] *s.* merodeador; saqueador.
marauding [-ɪŋ] *a.* merodeador; saqueador. —*s.* merodeo; saqueo.
maravedi [ˌmærəvə'di, B -'veɪdɪ] *s.* maravedí, antigua moneda española.
marble ['mɑrbəl, B 'mɑbəl] *s.* 1. mármol. 2. escultura de mármol, pieza de mármol. 3. canica; (*pl.*) juego de las canicas. 4. jaspeado. —*a.* 1. marmóreo, marmoleño, de mármol. 2. (fig.) marmóreo (frío, duro, terso o blanco como el mármol). —*v.t.* jaspear, vetear, marmolear.
marble cake, (cocina) torta veteada (hecha con dos masas distintas, una de ellas coloreada, por ej., con chocolate).
marbled paper [-bəld-] papel vergé, papel jaspeado.
marblehead [-ˌhɛd] *s.* (jer., E.U.) cabeza dura, chola de piedra.
marbleize [-bəˌlaɪz] *v.t.* (E.U.) vetear; jaspear (imitando el mármol).
marble works, taller de marmolería.
marbling ['mɑrblɪŋ, B 'mɑblɪŋ] *s.* 1. marmoración (de una superficie). 2. (enc.) jaspeadura (que imita al mármol). —*a.* marmóreo, semejante al mármol.
marbly [-blɪ] *a.* marmóreo, de mármol; veteado, jaspeado.
marc [mɑrk, B mɑk] *s.* 1. (fr.) bagazo, orujo (esp. de la uva). 2. aguardiente hecho de orujo.
marcasite ['mɑrkəˌsaɪt, B 'mɑkə-] *s.* (min.) marcasita.
marcel [mɑr'sɛl, B mɑ'-] *v.t.* (*pret., p.p.* MARCELLED; *p.pr.* MARCELLING) (ant.) ondular o rizar (el pelo). —*s.* ondulación (a lo Marcel).
marcescent [mɑr'sɛsənt, B mɑ'-] *s.* (bot.) marcescente.
March [mɑrtʃ, B mɑtʃ] *s.* marzo (mes); **the Ides of M.,** (hist., lit.) los idus de marzo.
march, *s.* (hist.) frontera, lindero, marca (esp. entre Ingl. y Esco. y entre Ingl. y Gales). —*v.i.* (gen. con *with*) lindar, colindar.
march , *v.i.* 1. marchar (en fila, en orden); desfilar. 2. marchar, caminar, avanzar. 3. **m. in,** entrar; **m. on,** seguir (su) marcha, ej., *time marches on,* el tiempo sigue su marcha; **m. out, m. off,** irse, largarse; **m. past,** desfilar ante. —*v.t.* 1. hacer marchar, poner en marcha (las tropas). 2. marchar (cierta distancia). —*s.* 1. marcha, avance, adelanto, progreso. 2. (mil.) marcha, ej., *forced m.,* marcha forzada. 3. (mús.) marcha, composición de aire marcial.
marcher ['mɑrtʃər, B 'mɑtʃə] *s.* 1. habitante de la marca. 2. (dep.) caminante. 3. manifestante, el que marcha en una manifestación.
marching orders [-tʃɪŋ-] *s. pl.* (mil.) órdenes de movilización.
marchioness ['mɑrʃənəs, B 'mɑʃə-] *s.* marquesa.
marchland ['mɑrtʃˌlænd, B 'mɑtʃ-] *s.* frontera, región fronteriza.
marchpane [-ˌpeɪn] *s.* (cocina) mazapán.
march-past [-ˌpæst, B -ˌpɑst] *s.* desfile.
Marcionist ['mɑrʃənəst, B 'mɑʃə-] **Marcionite** [-ˌnaɪt] *s.* (relig.) marcionista (de una antigua secta cristiana).
Marcomannic [ˌmɑrkoʊ'mænɪk, B ˌmɑkoʊ-] *a.* marcomano, habitante de Marcomania, región de la Europa antigua.
marconigram [mɑr'koʊnɪˌgræm, B mɑ'-] *s.* (ant.) marconigrama, radiograma.
marconigraph [-ˌgræf, B -ˌgrɑf] *s.* (rad.) marconígrafo.
Marcus Aurelius ['mɑrkəsɔ'riljəs, B 'mɑk-] (hist.) Marco Aurelio, emperador romano.
Mardi gras [ˌmɑrdɪ'grɑ, B 'mɑd-] (fr.) el martes antes de cuaresma; martes de carnaval.
mare [mɛr, B mɛə] *s.* yegua; burra; hembra de la cebra.
mare ['mɛri, 'mɑri, B 'mɛərɪ] *s.* (astr.) mar, región oscura de la superficie de la luna.
mare clausum [-'klɔsəm] (lat.) mar jurisdiccional, mar territorial (de una nación).
mare liberum [-'lɪbərəm] (lat.) mar abierto a todas las naciones.
mare nostrum [-'nɑstrəm, B -'nɔs-] (lat.) mare nóstrum, nuestro mar (nombre que dieron los romanos al Mediterráneo).
mare's-nest ['mɛrzˌnɛst, B 'mɛəz-] *s.* 1. bola, embuste, engaño, ilusión. 2. olla de grillos, baraúnda; maraña, confusión.
mare's-tail [-ˌteɪl] *s.* 1. (meteor.) cirro, nube cirrosa. 2. (bot.) cola de caballo.
margaric [mɑr'gærɪk, B mɑ'-] *a.* (quím.) margárico.
margarine ['mɑrdʒərən, -əˌrin, B ˌmɑdʒə'-rin] *s.* margarina, oleomargarina.
margarita [ˌmɑrgə'ritə, B ˌmɑgə-] *s.* margarita, coctel mexicano a base de tequila.
margarite ['mɑrgəˌraɪt, B 'mɑgə-] *s.* 1. (min.) margarita. 2. (ant.) margarita, perla.
margay ['mɑrˌgeɪ, B 'mɑˌ-] *s.* (zool.) margay.
marge [mɑrdʒ, B mɑdʒ] *s.* (poét.) margen, cenefa, borde.
margin ['mɑrdʒən, B 'mɑdʒən] *s.* 1. margen (de una página, etc.). 2. borde. 3. margen, límite. 4. reserva. 5. (com.) ganancia bruta. 6. (e.p.) margen de ganancia. 7. (tip.) margen, espacio en blanco. 8. garantía (en la bolsa de valores contra pérdidas en un contrato); transacción a crédito (que el corredor financia en parte). 9. (psic.) umbral (del campo consciente). —*v.t.* 1. marginar, apostillar. 2. marginar, poner margen a. 3. (fig.) orlar, ribetear. 4. dar garantía para (compra de acciones en la bolsa de valores).
marginal [-əl] *a.* marginal; (econ.) marginal (utilidad, costo, etc.).
marginalia [ˌmɑrdʒə'neɪlɪə, B ˌmɑdʒə-] *s. pl.* apostillas, acotaciones, notas marginales.
marginally ['mɑrdʒənəlɪ, B 'mɑdʒə-] *adv.* en forma marginal, marginalmente, al margen.
marginal note, nota marginal, anotación.
marginal sensation, (psic.) sensación marginal.
marginal tribe, tribu marginal o fronteriza.
marginal utility, (e.p.) utilidad marginal.
marginate ['mɑrdʒəˌneɪt, B 'mɑdʒə-] *v.t.* marginar. —*a.* marginado.
marginated [-əd] *a.* marginado.
margin of error, posibilidad de error (en algo ya hecho).
margravate ['mɑrgrəˌveɪt, B 'mɑgrə-] **margraviate** [mɑr'greɪvɪət, B mɑ'-ˌeɪt] *s.* margraviato, dignidad y territorio de un margrave.
margrave ['mɑrˌgreɪv, B 'mɑˌ-] *s.* margrave, título de ciertos príncipes alemanes.
margravine ['mɑrgrəˌvin, B 'mɑgrə-] *s.* margravina, esposa del margrave.
marguerite [ˌmɑrgə'rit, B ˌmɑgə-] *s.* (bot.) margarita.
mariachi [ˌmɑrɪ'ɑtʃɪ] *s.* mariachi, músico y banda típicos de Jalisco, México.
Marian ['mɛrɪən, B 'mɛər-] *a.* 1. mariano, marista, de la Virgen María. 2. (G.B., hist.) de (la época de) María Tudor. —*s.* 1. devoto de la Virgen María. 2. (hist., G.B.) partidario de la reina María Estuardo.
marigold ['mærəˌgoʊld] *s.* (bot.) 1. caléndula, maravilla, virreina. 2. clavelón.
marigraph ['mærəˌgræf, B -ˌgrɑf] *s.* mareógrafo, aparato que registra la altura de las mareas.
marihuana, marijuana [ˌmærə'wɑnə, B -'hwɑnə] *s.* 1. (bot.) mariguana, marihuana, cáñamo de la India. 2. cigarrillo de marihuana.
marimba [mə'rɪmbə] *s.* (mús.) marimba.
marina [mə'rinə] *s.* dársena para embarcaciones menores, marina.

marinade [ˌmærəˈneɪd] *s.* (cocina) escabeche. —*v.t.* escabechar, marinar, macerar.
marinate [ˈmærəˌneɪt] *v.t.* (cocina) escabechar, marinar.
marine [məˈrin] *a.* 1. marino, marítimo. 2. náutico (mapa, etc.). 3. de los infantes de marina. —*s.* 1. infante de marina. 2. marina, flota mercante o naval (de un país). 3. ministerio de marina. 4. (pint.) marina. 5. **tell it to the (horse) marines,** cuéntaselo a tu abuela, a otro perro con ese hueso.
Marine Corps, (E.U.) Infantería de Marina.
marine engineer, 1. ingeniero naval o marino. 2. maquinista naval.
marine engineering, ingeniería naval o marina.
marine insurance, seguro marítimo.
marine league, legua marítima (5,56 Km).
mariner [ˈmærənər, B -nə] *s.* marinero, hombre de mar.
Mariner, *s.* (astr., E.U.) cohete teledirigido usado en la exploración interplanetaria de los planetas Marte y Venus.
mariner's compass, brújula, compás de mar.
Mariolatry [ˌmɛrɪˈɑlətrɪ, B ˌmɛərɪˈɔl-] *s.* mariolatría (culto excesivo a la Virgen María).
Mariology [-ˈɑlədʒɪ, B -ˈɔl-] *s.* mariología (estudio o doctrina relativos a la Virgen María).
marionette [ˌmærɪəˈnɛt] *s.* (fr.) títere, fantoche, marioneta.
marish [ˈmærɪʃ] *s.* (poét.) pantano.
Marist [ˈmærəst, -mɛr-, B ˈmɛər-] *s.* marista, hermano de la orden de la Sociedad de María.
marital [ˈmærətəl] *a.* marital, conyugal, matrimonial.
marital duty, obligación conyugal.
marital status, estado civil.
maritime [ˈmærəˌtaɪm] *a.* marítimo.
maritime law, código marítimo.
maritime perils, riesgos, peligros del mar.
marjoram [ˈmɑrdʒərəm, B ˈmɑdʒ-] *s.* (bot.) mejorana, amáraco, almoradux.
mark [mɑrk, B mɑk] *s.* 1. marca, señal. 2. estigma; mancha, huella. 3. fin, propósito, meta, objetivo. 4. blanco. 5. característica, rasgo, distintivo, particularidad. 6. nota, importancia, distinción. 7. norma, pauta o patrón, requisitos (de calidad, etc.). 8. marca de fábrica; etiqueta, marbete. 9. signo (gen. un aspa, con que firman los que no saben escribir). 10. signo, ej., *interrogation m.,* signo de interrogación. 11. nota, calificación, calificativo (de examen, etc.). 12. marca, punto de referencia (para orientarse, etc.); hito, señal, letrero. 13. señal o indicador de nivel, ej., *low-water m.,* señal de marea baja, *high-water m.,* señal de marea alta. 14. (mar.) nudo (de la sondaleza); línea de flotación, línea de carga máxima. 15. (dep.) boliche; (boxeo) boca del estómago; (carreras) marca, línea de partida. 16. (vet.) depresión (en los incisivos de un caballo que indica la edad). 17. (jer.) primo (persona fácil de engañar). 18. (ant., hist.) marca, límite, frontera. 19. **beyond the m.,** excesivo, fuera de (todo) límite; **near the m.,** cerca de la solución o la verdad, casi correcto o acertado; **to be beside the m.,** no venir al caso; **to come** (o **be**) **up to the m.,** llenar los requisitos; ser enteramente satisfactorio; **to get off the m.,** arrancar, partir de carrera; **to hit the m.,** acertar, dar en el blanco; **to leave one's m.,** dejar memoria de sí; **to make one's m.,** tener éxito, distinguirse; **to miss the m.,** errar el tiro; **to toe the m.,** ponerse en la raya, obrar como se debe; **wide of the m.,** completamente errado; fuera del blanco. —*v.t.* 1. marcar, señalar. 2. caracterizar, distinguir. 3. registrar, marcar, indicar. 4. advertir, notar, observar; tener presente, no olvidar, ej., *m. my words,* tenga presente lo que digo, no olvide mis palabras. 5. calificar, corregir (exámenes, etc.). 6. (com.) marcar, acotar, poner (precios). 7. (dep.) marcar, anotar (tantos en un juego). 8. **m. down,** rebajar, reducir (el precio); poner menor precio a, rebajar el precio de (artículo); tomar nota de; **m. off,** demarcar; separar o dividir con líneas; **m. out,** trazar, delinear, planear; **m. out for,** destinar or escoger para; **m. time,** marcar el paso; **m. up,** subir (el precio); poner precio más alto a, subir el precio de (artículo); (pr. G.B.) poner en (su) cuenta, apuntar (compra o consumo no pagado). —*v.i.* (dep., G.B.) marcar (un jugador a su contrario).
Mark Antony [ˈmɑrkˈæntənɪ, B ˈmɑk-] (hist.) Marco Antonio, general romano, miembro del segundo triunvirato.
markdown [ˈmɑrkˌdaʊn, B ˈmɑk-] *s.* reducción (de precio), rebaja.
marked [mɑrkt, B mɑkt] *a.* 1. marcado, con marca o señal. 2. pronunciado, notable, manifiesto, marcado, destacado. 3. (fig.) conspicuo, de fama (hombre); sospechoso (hombre); condenado, perdido (hombre).
markedly [ˈmɑrkədlɪ, B ˈmɑkəd-] *adv.* notablemente, manifiestamente, pronunciadamente, marcadamente.
marker [-kər, B -kə] *s.* 1. marcador, apuntador (en un juego). 2. marcador, señal.
marker light, (avia., mar.) farol marcador, baliza.
market [ˈmɑrkət, B ˈmɑkɪt] *s.* 1. mercado. 2. mercado, plaza o demanda (por algún producto). 3. mercado, bolsa, ej., *coffee m.,* mercado del café. 4. **at the m.,** (bolsa) al precio del mercado (del día); **to be in the m. for (something),** querer comprar (algo); (fig.) andar a la caza de algo; **to come into the m.,** salir (en venta) al mercado; **to find a ready m.,** encontrar fácil salida; **to lose one's m.,** perder uno la clientela; **to make a m. for,** crear un mercado para, crear demanda por (algún artículo); **to make a m. of** (fig.) baratear, malvender; **to play the m.,** jugar a la bolsa, especular; **to put on the m.,** poner a la venta. —*v.i.* mercadear, hacer transacciones de compra y venta en el mercado. —*v.t.* poner a la venta (en el mercado); vender; distribuir.
marketability [ˌmɑrkətəˈbɪlətɪ, B ˌmɑkɪt-] *s.* potencial de venta.
marketable [ˈmɑrkətəbəl, B ˈmɑkɪt-] *a.* 1. comerciable, vendible. 2. comercial.
marketeer [ˌmɑrkəˈtɪr, B ˌmɑkɪˈtɪə] **marketer** [ˈmɑrkətər, B ˈmɑkɪtə] *s.* vendedor; distribuidor.
market garden, huerto en que se cultivan legumbres (para el mercado).
market gardening, (el) cultivo de legumbres (como negocio).
marketing [ˈmɑrkətɪŋ, B ˈmɑkɪt-] *s.* marketing, mercadeo, técnica de venta o distribución.
market order, (bolsa) orden de compra o venta al precio corriente o del día.
marketplace [-ˌpleɪs] *s.* plaza del mercado; (fig.) el mundo mercantil.
market price, (e.p.) precio de mercado o de plaza, precio corriente.
market research, (e.p.) estudio de los mercados.
market value, (e.p.) valor en plaza; valor comercial.
marking [ˈmɑrkɪŋ, B ˈmɑk-] *s.* 1. marca, señal. 2. marcación. 3. (conjunto de) marcas. —*a.* de marcar; que marca, para marcar.
marking gauge, (carp.) gramil.
marksman [ˈmɑrksmən, B ˈmɑks-] *s.* tirador (al blanco).
marksmanship [-ˌʃɪp] *s.* puntería, buena puntería.
markup [ˈmɑrkˌʌp, B ˈmɑk-] *s.* 1. alza de precio (de un artículo). 2. (com.) margen de ganancia bruta.
marl [mɑrl, B mɑl] *s.* marga. —*v.t.* 1. margar (la tierra). 2. (mar.) trincafiar (con merlín).
marlin [ˈmɑrlən, B ˈmɑlɪn] *s.* (ict.) pez vela, aguja.
marlin, marline [ˈmɑrlən, B ˈmɑlɪn] *s.* (mar.) merlín.
marlinespike, marlinspike [-ˌspaɪk] *s.* (mar.) pasador.
marlite [ˈmɑrˌlaɪt, B ˈmɑˌ-] *s.* (min.) marlita.
marmalade [ˈmɑrməˌleɪd, B ˈmɑmə-] *s.* mermelada (esp. de frutas cítricas).
marmalade tree, (bot.) zapote.
marmoreal [mɑrˈmɔrɪəl, B mɑˈ-] **marmorean** [-ɪən] *a.* marmóreo, parecido al mármol.
marmoset [ˈmɑrməˌsɛt, B ˈmɑməˌzɛt] *s.* (zool.) tití.
marmot [ˈmɑrmət, B ˈmɑmət] *s.* (zool.) marmota.
Maronite [ˈmærəˌnaɪt] *s.* (relig.) maronita, miembro de una secta cristiana del Líbano y otros países levantinos.
maroon [məˈrun] *s.* 1. cimarrón (esclavo negro fugitivo y sus descendientes) (Amer.). 2. animal doméstico que huye al campo y se hace montaraz. 3. persona abandonada (en una isla o playa desierta). —*v.t.* 1. desembarcar y abandonar (a alguien) a su suerte. 2. abandonar, desamparar, dejar, aislar.
maroon, *s., a.* rojo obscuro, rojo con visos castaños.
marplot [ˈmɑrˌplɑt, B ˈmɑˌplɔt] *s.* aguafiestas; persona o hecho que impide la realización de un proyecto.
marque [mɑrk, B mɑk] *s.* 1. (ant.) captura por venganza. 2. patente de corso. 3. placa o emblema que identifica un automóvil.
marquee [mɑrˈki, B mɑˈki] *s.* 1. tienda de campaña grande. 2. marquesina (de metal, vidrio o lona sobre entrada de hotel, teatro, ventanales, etc.).
Marquesan [mɑrˈkeɪzən, B mɑˈkeɪs-] *s.* habitante o lenguaje de las (islas) Marquesas, archipiélago de Polinesia.
marquess, marquessate, *vars, de* **marquis, marquisate.**
marquetry, marqueterie [ˈmɑrkətrɪ, B ˈmɑkɪ-] *s.* (fr.) (*pl.* MARQUETRIES O MARQUETERIES) taracea, marquetería.
marquis [ˈmɑrkwəs, B ˈmɑkwɪs] *s.* (fr.) marqués.
marquisate [ˈmɑrkwəzət, B ˈmɑkwɪ-] *s.* marquesado.
marquise [mɑrˈkiz, B mɑˈ-] *s.* 1.marquesa 2. gran tienda de campaña; marquesina. 3. (joy.) talla elíptica (de piedras preciosas).
marquisette [ˌmɑrkwəˈzɛt, -kɪ-, B ˌmɑkɪ-] *s.* tejido fino y lustroso de algodón; tejido fino y ligero de seda, tul de agujeros cuadrados.
Marrakech, Marrakesh [məˈrɑkɛʃ, mærəˈkɛʃ, B məˈrækɛʃ] *s.* Marrakech, ciudad y antigua capital de Marruecos.
marriage [ˈmærɪdʒ] *s.* 1. matrimonio; vida de casados. 2. matrimonio, boda, casamiento, nupcias. 3. (fig.) enlace; consorcio; unión íntima.
marriageability [ˌmærɪdʒəˈbɪlətɪ] *s.* estado o condición de casadero.
marriageable [ˈmærɪdʒəbəl] *a.* casadero, núbil.
marriageableness [-nəs] *s.* estado o condición de casadero.

marriage articles, contrato matrimonial; capítulos matrimoniales.
marriage bed, (fig.) trato sexual entre casados.
marriage broker, casamentero; agente que concertaba acuerdos de matrimonio, esp. entre los judíos.
marriage by proxy, matrimonio por poder.
marriage certificate, partida de matrimonio.
marriage licence, licencia matrimonial.
marriage of convenience, matrimonio de conveniencia.
marriage portion, dote.
married ['mærɪd] *a.* 1. casado, unido en matrimonio. 2. matrimonial, conyugal, connubial.
married couple, pareja de casados, matrimonio.
married life, vida conyugal, vida matrimonial.
married state, vida o estado conyugal.
marron ['mærən, B mə'roʊn] *s.* 1. (fr.) castaña grande. 2. (*pl.*) **marrons glacés,** confite de castañas en crema espesa de vainilla.
marrow ['mæroʊ] *s.* 1. (anat.) médula o medula, meollo, tuétano. 2. (fig.) médula, meollo, substancia, esencia, lo principal o mejor (de alguna cosa), lo más íntimo y profundo (de algo). 3. **chilled to the m.,** helado hasta los tuétanos.
marrow, *s.* (esco.) compañero; consorte; semejante, igual.
marrowbone [-ˌboʊn] *s.* 1. hueso medular (comestible). 2. (*pl.*) (hum.) (las) rodillas.
marrowfat [-ˌfæt] *s.* (bot.) haba de Lima, garrofón, alubia grande y suculenta.
marry ['mærɪ] *v.t.* (*pret. p.p.* MARRIED; *p.pr.* MARRYING) 1. casar, unir en matrimonio. 2. casar, dar en matrimonio. 3. casarse con, contraer matrimonio con. 4. (fig.) casar, unir, juntar. 5. (mar.) ayustar (cabos). 6. **to get married,** casar o casarse. —*v.i.* 1. casar(se). 2. (fig.) unirse, juntarse. 3. **m. into,** emparentarse con.
Mars [mɑrz, B mɑz] *s.* 1. (mitol.) Marte, dios romano de la guerra. 2. (astr.) Marte (el planeta).
Marseillaise [ˌmɑrsə'leɪz, B ˌmɑsə-] *s.* (fr.) (la) Marsellesa (himno nacional francés).
Marseilles [mɑr'seɪlz, B mɑ'-] *s.* 1. Marsella. 2. **m.,** (tej.) tela fuerte de algodón parecida al piqué.
marsh [mɑrʃ, B mɑʃ] *s.* pantano, ciénaga, cenegal, marjal, fangal, marisma. —*a.* pantanoso, cenagoso, fangoso.
marshal ['mɑrʃəl, B 'mɑʃəl] *s.* 1. mariscal. 2. maestro de ceremonias. 3. (E.U.) ministril, alguacil; (en algunas ciudades) el jefe de policía o de bomberos. 4. (E.U.) guarda o vigilante (que mantiene el orden entre sus compañeros en una manifestación o desfile). —*v.t.* (*pret., p.p.* MARSHALED O MARSHALLED; *p.pr.* MARSHALING O MARSHALLING) 1. ordenar, poner en orden, clasificar, graduar, formar (tropas, participantes de una manifestación, etc.). 2. anunciar, introducir, acomodar; guiar, dirigir.
marshaler [-ʃələr, B -lə] *s.* el que ordena, arregla o capitanea un cuerpo de personas.
marshaling yard [-lɪŋ-] (f.c.) patio de maniobras.
Marshalsea ['mɑrʃəlˌsi, B 'mɑʃəl-] *s.* (G.B., hist.) tribunal para juzgar a la servidumbre del rey; antigua prisión de Londres para los sentenciados por deudas.
marsh cress, (bot.) (variedad de) berro.
marsh elder, (bot.) 1. (variedad de) arándano agrio. 2. (variedad de) ambrosía.
marsh gas, metano, gas de los pantanos.
marsh harrier, (orn.) arpella, borní.
marsh hen, (orn.) rey de codornices, rascón, polla de agua.
marshiness ['mɑrʃɪnəs, B 'mɑʃɪ-] *s.* estado o carácter pantanoso o cenagoso (del terreno).
marshmallow ['mɑrʃˌmɛloʊ, B 'mɑʃ-] *s.* 1. pastilla de altea (confite). 2. dulce de malvavisco. 3. (bot.) malvavisco, acalia, altea.
marsh marigold, (bot.) calta.
marsh warbler, (orn.) arandillo, saltamimbres.
marshy ['mɑrʃɪ, B 'mɑʃɪ] *a.* (MARSHIER; MARSHIEST) pantanoso, cenagoso, fangoso.
Marsi ['mɑrˌsaɪ, B 'mɑˌ-] *s. pl.* marsos, un pueblo de Italia antigua.
marsupial [mɑr'supɪəl, B mɑ'sjupjəl] *a., s.* (zool.) marsupial.
marsupium [-əm] *s.* (*pl.* MARSUPIA [-ə]) (zool.) marsupio, bolsa marsupial.
Marsyas ['mɑrsɪəs, B 'mɑsɪ-] *s.* (mitol.) Marsias, fauno tocador de flauta, vencido y desollado por Apolo.
mart [mɑrt, B mɑt] *s.* 1. mercado, plaza, emporio, centro comercial; (fig.) martillo, lugar para subastas públicas. 2. (ant.) comercio, negocio, tráfico. 3. (ant.) feria, exposición regional. 4. (esco.) res para la matanza; carne salada.
marteline ['mɑrtələn, B 'mɑtə-] *s.* martellina, martillo de cantero.
Martello tower [mɑr'tɛloʊ-, B mɑ'-] fortín circular costanero.
marten ['mɑrtən, B 'mɑt-] *s.* (zool.) marta.
martensite [-ˌzaɪt] *s.* (metal.) martensita.
martensitic [ˌmɑrtən'zɪtɪk, B ˌmɑt-] *a.* (metal.) martensítico.
martial ['mɑrʃəl, B 'mɑʃəl] *a.* marcial, bélico, guerrero; **m. music,** música militar.
martial law, ley marcial; estado de sitio.
martially [-ʃəlɪ] *adv.* marcialmente, con aire militar.
martialness [-ʃəlnəs] *s.* marcialidad, espíritu guerrero.
Martian ['mɑrʃən, B 'mɑʃjən] *a., s.* marciano (del planeta Marte).
martin ['mɑrtən, B 'mɑt-] *s.* (orn.) vencejo, avión.
martinet [ˌmɑrtən'ɛt, B ˌmɑt-] *s.* (mil.) ordenancista, persona que exige el cumplimiento riguroso de una ordenanza.
martingale ['mɑrtənˌgeɪl, B 'mɑt-] *s.* 1. gamarra, amarra. 2. (mar.) moco del bauprés. 3. martingala, sistema de apuestas.
martini [mɑr'tinɪ, B mɑ'-] *s.* martini (coctel a base de vermú y ginebra).
Martinique [ˌmɑrtə'nik, B ˌmɑtɪ-] *s.* la Martinica, isla francesa en el Caribe.
Martinmas ['mɑrtənməs, B 'mɑtɪn-] *s.* (relig.) fiesta de San Martín (11 de noviembre).
martlet ['mɑrtlət, B 'mɑt-] *s.* 1. (orn.) vencejo, avión. 2. (her.) merleta.
martyr ['mɑrtər, B 'mɑtə] *s.* mártir; **m. to,** víctima de; **to make a m. of oneself,** hacerse el mártir. —*v.t.* martirizar; atormentar, torturar.
martyrdom [-dəm] *s.* martirio.
martyrization [ˌmɑrtərə'zeɪʃən, B ˌmɑtəraɪ-] *s.* martirio.
martyrize ['mɑrtəˌraɪz, B 'mɑtə-] *v.t.* martirizar; atormentar, torturar.
martyrologist [ˌmɑrtə'rɑlədʒəst, B ˌmɑtə'rɔl-] *s.* martirologista.
martyrology [-dʒɪ] *s.* martirologio, la historia y el estudio de la vida de los mártires cristianos.
martyry ['mɑrtərɪ, B 'mɑt-] *s.* santuario o templo erigido en honor a la memoria de un mártir.
marupa [mɑ'rupɑ] *s.* (bot.) aceitero.
marvel ['mɑrvəl, B 'mɑvəl] *s.* 1. maravilla, prodigio, portento. 2. admiración, asombro. —*v.i.* (*pret., p.p.* MARVELED O MARVELLED; *p.pr.* MARVELING O MARVELLING) (gen. con *at*) maravillarse (de), admirarse, ej., *I m. at your bravery,* me admira tu valentía, me maravillo de tu valor.
marvel-of-Peru [-əvpə'ru] *s.* (bot.) maravilla, dondiego, dondiego de noche, arrebolera.
marvelous, marvellous ['mɑrvələs, B 'mɑv-] *a.* 1. maravilloso, prodigioso, portentoso. 2. milagroso. 3. (fam.) maravilloso, espléndido, magnífico.
marvelously, marvellously [-lɪ] *adv.* maravillosamente.
marvelousness, marvellousness [-nəs] *s.* carácter o aspecto maravilloso.
Marxian ['mɑrksɪən, B 'mɑk-] *a., s.* (pol.) marxista.
Marxism [-ˌsɪzəm] *s.* marxismo, doctrina económica y política desarrollada por Karl Marx.
Marxism-Leninism [-'lɛnəˌnɪzəm] *s.* marxismo-leninismo.
Marxist [-səst] *s., a.* marxista.
Maryland ['mɛrələnd, B 'mɛərɪlænd] *s.* Maryland, estado de los E.U.
marzipan ['mɑrtsəˌpɑn, 'mɑrzəˌpæn, B ˌmɑzɪ'pæn] *s.* mazapán, confite de pasta de almendras.
mascara [mæ'skærə, B -'kɑrə] *s.* rímel, cosmético para las pestañas.
mascle ['mæskəl] *s.* 1. (hist.) planchita romboidal (con que se hacían las armaduras). 2. (her.) macla.
mascot ['mæsˌkɑt, -kət, B -kət] *s.* mascota; amuleta.
masculine ['mæskjələn] *a.* 1. masculino, propio de hombre(s). 2. masculino, viril, varonil. 3. hombruna (díc. de ciertas mujeres). 4. (gram.) (del género) masculino. —*s.* 1. hombre, varón. 2. (gram.) palabra o forma masculinas; género masculino.
masculinely [-lɪ] *adv.* varonilmente, virilmente.
masculine rhyme, (poét.) rima asonantada.
masculinity [ˌmæskjə'lɪnətɪ] *s.* masculinidad.
masculinize ['mæskjələˌnaɪz] *v.t.* masculinizar, dar carácter masculino a.
maser ['meɪzər, B -zə] *s.* (fís.) maser, instrumento para convertir radiación electromagnética en microondas.
mash [mæʃ] *s.* 1. malta empastada (para hacer mosto de cerveza). 2. mezcla de granos molidos y hervidos (para alimentar el ganado). 3. amasijo, masa pulposa. 4. mezcolanza, baturrillo, batiborrillo, pepitoria. 5. (fam., G.B.) puré de patatas. 6. **mashed potatoes,** puré de patatas. —*v.t.* 1. empastar (la malta para hacer mosto de cerveza). 2. majar, machacar, reducir a pasta.
mash, *v.t.* (fam.) enamorar. —*v.i.* (fam.) coquetear, flirtear, mirar con amor. —*s.* enamoramiento.
masher ['mæʃər, B -ə] *s.* 1. moledor. 2. galanteador, enamorador.
mashie ['mæʃɪ] *s.* (*pl.* MASHIES) (golf) mashie, palo (número) cinco.
mask [mæsk, B mɑsk] *s.* 1. máscara, antifaz, careta. 2. (fig.) máscara, disfraz. 3. enmascarado, máscara (persona). 4. mascarilla, máscara (mortuoria). 5. (med., mil.) máscara (de cirujano, anestesia, de gas, etc.). 6. (arq.) mascarón. 7. (teat.) máscara. 8. **to throw off the m.,** quitarse la careta. —*v.t.* 1. enmascarar, cubrir (el rostro). 2. (fig.) embozar, encubrir, ocultar, disfrazar. 3. (mil.) camuflar, disfrazar (una posición, batería, etc.). 4. (foto.) desvanecer (parte de un negativo).
masked [mæskt, B mɑskt] *a.* 1. enmascarado. 2. (fig.) disfrazado, encubierto, oculto. 3. latente (fiebre, virus). 4. de máscaras (baile).
masker ['mæskər, B 'mɑskə] *s.* máscara, enmascarado (persona).
masking tape [-kɪŋ-] cinta adhesiva (para proteger bordes y márgenes de los brochazos de pintura).

maslin ['mæzlən] *s.* (G.B.) mixtura, mistura.
masochism ['mæsə,kɪzəm, 'mæz-, B 'mæs-] *s.* masoquismo.
masochist [-kəst] *s.* masoquista.
masochistic [,mæsə'kɪstɪk, ,mæz-, B ,mæs-] *a.* masoquista, masoquístico.
mason ['meɪsən] *s.* 1. albañil, mampostero. 2. **M.,** masón, francmasón. —*v.t.* mampostear, construir o reforzar con mampostería.
mason bee, (ento.) albañila, abeja albañila.
Mason-Dixon line [,meɪsən'dɪksən-] (hist., pol., E.U.) línea limítrofe entre los estados de Pennsylvania y Maryland, que separaba antes de la Guerra Civil a los estados del sur de los del norte.
masoned ['meɪsənd] *a.* (her.) mazonado.
Masonic [mə'sɑnɪk, B -'sɔn-] *a.* masónico.
Masonite ['meɪsən,aɪt] *s.* (marca de fábrica de) plancha de fibra de madera (usada como aislador o para paneles).
mason jar, pote de vidrio para guardar conservas.
masonry ['meɪsənrɪ] *s.* 1. albañilería (arte u oficio del albañil). 2. mampostería, (obra de) albañilería. 3. **M.,** masonería, francmasonería.
mason wasp, (ento.) avispa chibcha.
Masora, Masorah [mə'sɔrə] *s.* (relig.) masora, conjunto de tradiciones en las cuales se basa la interpretación judía del Antiguo Testamento.
Masorete ['mæsə,rit] *s.* (relig.) masoreta, intérprete judío del Antiguo Testamento.
Masoretic [,mæsə'rɛtɪk] *a.* (relig.) masorético.
masque [mæsk, B mɑsk] 1. mascarada, máscaras. 2. drama alegórico (en que los actores usan máscaras).
masquerade [,mæskə'reɪd] *s.* 1. mascarada, máscaras. 2. disfraz, traje de máscara. 3. (fig.) mascarada, fingimiento, simulación, engaño. —*v.i.* 1. enmascararse, disfrazarse; jaranear disfrazado. 2. (fig.) disfrazarse. 3. **m. as,** dárselas de, hacerse pasar por.
masquerader [-ər, B -ə] *s.* máscara, persona enmascarada.
mass [mæs] *s.* (relig.) misa; **to attend** (o **hear**) **m.,** oír misa; **to say m.,** celebrar misa.
mass, *s.* 1. masa. 2. bulto, mole. 3. montón, gran cantidad; multitud. 4. grueso, mayor parte. 5. magnitud, gran tamaño, volumen, dimensión. 6. mayoría. 7. **the m.,** populacho, plebe, vulgo. 8. (fís.) masa. 9. **in the m.,** en conjunto, en masa; **the masses,** las masas. —*v.t., v.i.* formar(se) (tropas). —*a.* 1. para las masas, popular (educación, revista, entretenimiento, etc.). 2. de las masas (psicología, reacción, etc.). 3. en masa (ataque, manifestación, etc.).
Mass. *abrev. de* **Massachusetts,** Massachusetts (E.U.).
Massachusetts [,mæsə'tʃusəts] *s.* Massachusetts, estado de los E.U.
massacre ['mæsɪkər, B -əkə] *s.* matanza, masacre, carnicería. —*v.t.* asesinar cruelmente, matar ferozmente; matar en masa, masacrar.
massacrer [-kərər, -krər, B -krə] *s.* asesino feroz (de muchas personas).
massage [mə'sɑʒ, -'sɑdʒ, B 'mæsɑʒ] *s.* masaje. —*v.t.* masajear, dar masajes a, sobar; friccionar fuertemente.
massager [-ər, B -ə] **massagist** [-əst] *s.* masajista.
massasauga [,mæsə'sɔgə] *s.* (zool.) variedad de crótalo.
mass card, tarjeta de invitación a una misa (ej., de difuntos).
mass concrete, concreto en masa.
mass cult, culto o devoción de las masas (a un ídolo creado por los medios de comunicación con fines comerciales).
mass defect, (fís., quím.) defecto de masa.
massé shot [mæ'səɪ-, B 'mæseɪ-] (billar) tacada vertical.
masseter [mæ'sitər, B -ə] *s.* (anat.) masetero.
masseteric [,mæsə'tɛrɪk] *a.* (anat.) masetérico.
masseur [mæ'sɜr, B -'sɜ] *s.* (fr.) masajista (*m.*).
masseuse [-'sɜz, -'suz, B -'sɜz] *s.* (fr.) masajista (*f.*).
mass fire, (mil.) fuego masivo, fuego en masa (de la artillería).
mass gathering, concentración masiva.
mass hysteria, histerismo colectivo, histerismo en masa.
massicot ['mæsə,kɑt, B -,kɔt] *s.* (quím.) masicote, almártaga, óxido de plomo.
massif [mæ'sif, 'mæsif] *s.* (geol.) macizo.
massive ['mæsɪv] *a.* 1. macizo, sólido; pesado, ponderoso. 2. abultado, amplio, grande, grueso. 3. tosco (díc. de las facciones). 4. impresionante, imponente, grande. 5. (fig.) monumental, colosal (simpleza, estupidez, etc.). 6. (med.) extenso, severo (díc. de las condiciones patológicas).
massively [-lɪ] *adv.* sólidamente, en forma maciza.
massiveness [-nəs] *s.* solidez, consistencia.
mass media, medios de comunicación (tales como la televisión, radio, periódicos, etc.) que influyen sobre las masas.
mass meeting, manifestación en masa, reunión popular, mitin popular.
mass murder, matanza, asesinatos múltiples; (E.U., fig.) la guerra.
mass noun, nombre no numerable, sustantivo no numerable.
mass number, (fís., quím.) número de masa.
Massorete, *var. de* **masorete.**
mass-produce ['mæsprə'dus, B -'djus] *v.t.* producir en serie o en gran escala.
mass production, producción en masa, producción en serie o en gran escala.
mass spectrograph, (fís.) espectrógrafo de masa.
mass spectrum, (fís.) espectro de masa.
mass unemployment, desempleo en masa.
massy ['mæsɪ] *a.* sólido, abultado, voluminoso; pesado.
mast [mæst, B mɑst] *s.* 1. (mar.) mástil, mastelero, palo. 2. poste. 3. hayuco, fabuco, bellota (usada como alimento para cerdos u otros animales). —*v.t.* (mar.) arbolar (una embarcación).
mastaba, mastabah ['mæstəbə] *s.* (arqueol.) mastaba, tipo de tumba de los antiguos egipcios.
mastectomy [mæs'tɛktəmɪ] *s.* (med.) mastectomía.
master ['mæstər, B 'mɑstə] *s.* 1. amo, dueño, señor; patrono, jefe. 2. señorito (título que daban los criados al amo joven). 3. triunfador, vencedor (en una disputa, reyerta o pendencia). 4. **the M.,** Jesucristo. 5. maestro, experto (de un oficio, artesanía). 6. gran maestro, artista, insigne, esp., **old m.,** pintor clásico (de los siglos XIII al XVII); obra de los grandes maestros. 7. (educ.) maestro, instructor, preceptor, profesor; director, presidente, rector. 8. (educ.) maestro (grado académico entre licenciado y doctor). 9. (mar.) capitán (de barco mercante). 10. **to be m. of,** tener a disposición; **to be one's own m.,** ser independiente; **to make oneself m. of,** adquirir dominio sobre, llegar a conocer a fondo (ciencia, arte). —*v.t.* 1. vencer, superar, domar, sojuzgar, subyugar. 2. dominar, conocer a fondo, ser maestro o perito en. 3. gobernar, regir, mandar. —*a.* 1. maestro, superior. 2. maestro, experto. 3. magistral. 4. principal, dominante.
master-at-arms [-ət'ɑrmz, B -tərət'ɑmz] *s.* (*pl.* MASTER-AT-ARMS) (mar.) sargento de marina.
master builder, 1. maestro de obras. 2. contratista de construcciones. 3. (ant.) arquitecto.
master clock, reloj de péndulo.
master cylinder, (aut.) cilindro maestro (freno hidráulico), cilindro principal.
masterdom ['mæstərdəm, B 'mɑstədəm] *s.* maestría, dominio.
masterful [-fəl] a. 1. dominante, mandón, despótico, tiránico; perentorio; imperioso, voluntarioso, absoluto. 2. magistral, hábil, diestro, perito, experto.
masterfully [-fəlɪ] *adv.* 1. despóticamente, imperiosamente. 2. magistralmente, hábilmente, diestramente.
masterfulness [-fəlnəs] *s.* 1. carácter imperioso, despotismo. 2. maestría, destreza, habilidad.
master gage, calibre maestro o patrón de comparación.
master hand, 1. experto. 2. maestría.
masterhood [-,hʊd] *s.* maestría, dominio.
master key, llave maestra.
masterless [-ləs] *a. indómito, sin amo; mostrenco.*
masterliness [-lɪnəs] *s.* maestría, destreza, habilidad, pericia.
masterly ['mæstərlɪ, B 'mɑstəlɪ] *a.* magistral, maestro; digno de un maestro. —*adv.* magistralmente, con maestría.
master mason, 1. maestro u oficial de albañilería. 2. **M. M.,** francmasón del tercer grado.
master mechanic, jefe mecánico, capataz de mecánica; maestro mecánico.
mastermind [-,maɪnd] *s.* genio creador y director; manipulador genial. —*v.t.* manipular o dirigir magistralmente.
Master of Arts, (educ.) maestro en artes o en humanidades.
master of ceremonies, maestro de ceremonias, animador que presenta un espectáculo.
Master of the Horse, caballerizo mayor del rey.
masterpiece [-,pis] *s.* obra maestra.
master plan, 1. plan maestro, plan magistral. 2. plano maestro.
master sergeant, (mil.) sargento mayor.
mastership ['mæstər,ʃɪp, B 'mɑstə,-] *s.* 1. dominio, imperio, autoridad. 2. magisterio (cargo y profesión de maestro). 3. maestría, destreza, pericia.
mastersinger [-,sɪŋər, B -ə] *var. de* **meistersinger.**
master stroke, golpe maestro, acto magistral, lance perfecto.
master switch, (elec.) conmutador de gobierno; interruptor maestro o principal.
masterwork [-,wɜrk, B -,wɜk] *s.* obra maestra.
masterwort [-,wɜrt, B -,wɜt] *s.* (bot.) imperatoria.
mastery ['mæstərɪ, B 'mɑs-] *s.* (*pl.* MASTERIES) 1. superioridad, supremacía (en una competencia); poder, gobierno. 2. maestría, destreza, habilidad.
masthead ['mæst,hɛd, B 'mɑst-] *s.* 1. (mar.) celcés, tope (de un mástil). 2. (impr.) membrete. 3. rótulo, cabecera (del periódico). —*v.t.* (mar.) 1. enviar (a un marinero como castigo) al tope del mástil. 2. izar la bandera al tope del mástil.
mastic ['mæstɪk] *s.* 1. almáciga, mástique, almástiga. 2. (bot.) alfóncigo, lentisco. 3. masilla.
masticate ['mæstəkeɪt] *v.t.* masticar, mascar.
mastication [,mæstə'keɪʃən] *s.* masticación.
masticator ['mæstə,keɪtər, B -ə] *s.* masticador.
masticatory ['mæstəkə,tɔrɪ, B -,keɪtərɪ] *a.* masticatorio. —*s.* (med.) masticatorio.

mastic tree, (bot.) 1. alfóncigo, alfónsigo, lentisco. 2. almácigo.
mastiff ['mæstəf] *s.* mastín (perro).
mastigophoran [ˌmæstə'gɑfərən, B -'gɔf-] *s.* (zool.) mastigóforo.
mastitis [mæs'taɪtəs] *s.* (med., vet.) mastitis.
mastless ['mæstləs, B 'mɑst-] *a.* 1. (mar.) desarbolado. 2. árbol que no produce castañas o bellotas.
mastodon ['mæstəˌdɑn, B -ˌdɔn] *s.* (pal.) mastodonte.
mastoid ['mæsˌtɔɪd] *a.* (anat.) mastoides (apófisis); mastoideo, mastoidal. —*s.* 1. (anat.) mastoides, apófisis mastoides. 2. (med.) mastoiditis.
mastoidectomy [ˌmæsˌtɔɪ'dɛktəmɪ] *s.* mastoidectomía.
mastoiditis [-'daɪtəs] *s.* (med.) mastoiditis.
masturbate ['mæstərˌbeɪt, B -təˌ-] *v.i.* masturbarse.
masturbation [ˌmæstər'beɪʃən, B -tə'-] *s.* masturbación.
masturbatory ['mæstərbəˌtɔrɪ, B -təˌbeɪtərɪ] *a.* masturbador.
masurium [mə'zʊrɪəm, B -'sjʊər-] *s.* (quím.) masurio.
mat [mæt] *s.* 1. estera, esterilla, petate. 2. felpudo (para limpiar las suelas de los zapatos). 3. (fig.) maraña. 4. esterilla (que se pone debajo de jarrones, vasos, platos, etc.). 5. (dep.) colchoneta (sobre la que se lucha). 6. **on the m.,** (fam.) en apuros. —*v.t.* (*pret., p.p.* MATTED; *p.pr.* MATTING) 1. esterar, cubrir con esteras. 2. enredar, enmarañar; desgreñar (cabello). —*v.i.* enredarse, enmarañarse.
mat , *a.* mate, amortiguado, apagado. —*v.t.* (*pret., p.p.* MATTED; *p.pr.* MATTING) matar, apagar (el brillo del vidrio o del metal). —*s.* 1. orla, borde de papel, marco de cartón (de un cuadro). 2. acabado mate (del metal o del vidrio). 3. (impr.) matriz, molde.
matador ['mætəˌdɔr, B -ˌdɔ] *s.* 1. (taur.) matador, diestro, primer espada. 2. (naipes) matador.
match [mætʃ] *s.* 1. igual. 2. compañero, pareja. 3. copia, imagen. 4. rival, contendor. 5. juego, conjunto. 6. apareamiento, unión, conjunción, junta. 7. matrimonio, casamiento. 8. partido (novio o novia de buena posición económica o social). 9. partido, juego, contienda. 10. **to be a m. for,** ser digno rival para; **to make a m.,** arreglar una boda; **to meet one's m.,** hallar la horma de su zapato, encontrar un rival digno de uno. —*v.t.* 1. casar, unir en matrimonio. 2. enfrentar, afrontar. 3. (con *against*) oponer (a), contraponer (a), medir (con). 4. (con *with*) competir (con), rivalizar (con). 5. equiparar, igualar; duplicar. 6. hacer juego con. 7. (con *with*) aparear (con), emparejar (con). 8. (con *with*) comparar (con). 9. (con *to*) adaptar (a), adeudar (a). 10. encajar, machihembrar. 11. (fam.) jugar a chapas con (monedas). —*v.i.* 1. hacer juego, corresponderse. 2. hermanarse, casarse, igualarse. 3. (ant.) casarse, unirse en matrimonio. 4. **m. with,** hacer juego con.
match, *s.* 1. fósforo, cerilla. 2. mecha, cuerda (combustible, para prender fuego a cañón, mina, etc.).
matchboard ['mætʃˌbɔrd, B -ˌbɔd] *s.* tabla machihembrada.
matchbook [-ˌbʊk] *s.* sobre o talonario de fósforos.
matchbox [-ˌbɑks, B -ˌbɔks] *s.* cajita de fósforos, cajetilla de cerillas, fosforera, cerillero, cerillera.
matched order [mætʃt-] (bolsa) orden para comprar y vender al mismo precio.
matchless ['mætʃləs] *a.* sin igual, sin par, incomparable.
matchlessly [-lɪ] *adv.* incomparablemente.
matchlock [-ˌlɑk, B -ˌlɔk] *s.* llave con mecha (de arcabuz antiguo); arcabuz de mecha.
matchmaker [-ˌmeɪkər, B -kə] *s.* 1. casamentero, casamentera. 2. (dep.) promotor u organizador de luchas deportivas. 3. fabricante de fósforos o cerillas.
matchmaking [-kɪŋ] *s.* 1. actividades de casamentero. 2. promoción de luchas deportivas. 3. fabricación de fósforos o cerillas.
match play, (golf) partido jugado por hoyos (y no por golpes).
match point, (dep.) tanto de la victoria, punto decisivo (para ganar un juego).
matchwood [-ˌwʊd] *s.* madera para hacer fósforos; astillas, fragmentos; **to make m. of,** hacer añicos (una cosa).
mate [meɪt] *s.* 1. camarada (*m., f.*), compañero. 2. consorte (*m., f.*), cónyuge (*m., f.*). 3. pareja (uno de un par, esp. de pájaros), compañero (de artículos de vestir). 4. asistente, ayudante. 5. (mar.) maestre. —*v.t.* 1. casar, desposar. 2. aparear (animales). 3. (fig.) hermanar, aparear, emparejar. 4. (ajedrez) dar mate a, dar jaque mate a. —*v.i.* 1. casarse. 2. aparearse (animales). 3. acoplarse. —*interj.* ¡jaque mate!
maté ['mɑteɪ, B 'mæteɪ] *s.* 1. (bot.) mate, hierba mate, hierba del Paraguay. 2. mate, té del Paraguay, té de los jesuitas.
matelote [ˌmætə'loʊt, B 'mætələt] *s.* (cocina) guiso de pescado a la marinera, servido con salsa de vino, cebollas y hongos.
mater ['meɪtər, B -ə] *s.* (fam., G.B.) madre.
material [mə'tɪrɪəl, B -'tɪər-] *a.* 1. material. 2. físico, corporal. 3. importante, substancial, esencial; adecuado, pertinente. 4. (filos.) material. —*s.* 1. material, materia. 2. ingrediente, parte constituyente, elemento (de que se compone una obra). 3. tela, género, tejido. 4. (*pl.*) materiales, útiles (necesarios para una obra); avíos (de escribir, coser, fumar, etc.).
materialism [-ˌɪzəm] *s.* (filos.) materialismo.
materialist [-əst] *s., a.* materialista.
materialistic [-ˌtɪrɪə'lɪstɪk, B -ˌtɪər-] *a.* materialista.
materiality [-ɪ'ælətɪ] *s.* 1. materialidad, corporeidad. 2. pertinencia, importancia.
materialization [-ələ'zeɪʃən, B -laɪ-] *s.* 1. materialización, encarnación (de un espíritu). 2. realización.
materialize [mə'tɪrɪəˌlaɪz, B -'tɪər-] *v.t.* 1. materializar, hacer realidad, realizar, verificar. 2. dotar de forma visible, hacer aparecer (espíritus). —*v.i.* 1. verificarse, realizarse (planes, etc.). 2. tomar forma visible, aparecer (espíritus).
materially [-lɪ] *adv.* 1. materialmente. 2. notablemente; substancialmente.
matériel, materiel [məˌtɪrɪ'ɛl, B -tɪər-] *s.* (fr., mil.) material, materiales, equipos, aparatos, suministros y pertrechos.
maternal [mə'tɜrnəl, B -'tɜn-] *a.* maternal, materno.
maternally [-ɪ] *adv.* maternalmente.
maternity [mə'tɜrnətɪ, B -'tɜnɪtɪ] *s.* 1. maternidad. 2. cariño o cuidado maternal. 3. sala de maternidad; casa de maternidad.
maternity dress, traje de maternidad.
maternity hospital, maternidad.
maternity leave, baja por maternidad.
matey ['meɪtɪ] *a.* (pr. G.B.) sociable, amistoso, compañero.
math [mæθ] (G.B.) **maths** [mæθs] *abrev. de* **mathematics.**
mathematical [ˌmæθə'mætɪkəl] *a.* matemático.
mathematical logic, lógica matemática, lógica simbólica.
mathematically [-kəlɪ] *adv.* matemáticamente.
matriculate [-ˌleɪt] *v.t., v.i.* matricular (se) (en colegio, universidad). —*s.* matriculado.
matriculation [məˌtrɪkjə'leɪʃən] *s.* matrícula, matriculación.
matrilineal [ˌmætrə'lɪnɪəl, B ˌmeɪ-] *a.* por línea materna.
matrimonial [ˌmætrə'moʊnɪəl] *a.* matrimonial; marital, conyugal, connubial, nupcial.
matrimonially [-ɪ] *adv.* matrimonialmente.
matrimony ['mætrəˌmoʊnɪ, B -mənɪ] *s.* 1. matrimonio, nupcias. 2. un juego de naipes; cualquier rey y reina en este juego.
matrimony vine, (bot.) arto, cambronera, tamujo.
matrix ['meɪtrɪks] *s.* (*pl.* MATRICES [-trəˌsiz] o MATRIXES) 1. (anat.) matriz, útero. 2. (fig.) matriz, cuna. 3. (min.) roca madre, matriz. 4. (impr.) matriz o molde de cartón, matriz estereotípica, flan, molde. 5. (anat.) matriz (de la uña). 6. (disco) matriz (de fonógrafo).
matron ['meɪtrən] *s.* 1. matrona. 2. ama de llaves (en un colegio, etc.); supervisora, dueña; carcelera.
matronage [-ɪdʒ] *s.* 1. matronas (de un país, etc.). 2. cuidado o supervisión matronal. 3. estado matronal.
matronal [-əl] *a.* matronal.
matronize [-ˌaɪz] *v.t.* 1. dar las cualidades de una matrona (a alguien). 2. actuar como una matrona o dueña (ante alguien); acompañar y cuidar (una señora a una o más señoritas).
matronliness [-lɪnəs] *s.* (aspecto de) benevolencia o dignidad (de una matrona).
matronly ['meɪtrənlɪ] *a.* matronal, (de aspecto) benévolo, venerable, digno (como una matrona).
matron of honor, madrina de boda, dama de honor.
matronymic [ˌmætrə'nɪmɪk] *s.* apellido materno.
mathematical pendulum, (fís.) péndulo simple.
mathematician [ˌmæθəmə'tɪʃən] *s.* matemático.
mathematics [ˌmæθə'mætɪks] *s. pl.* (*sing. o pl. en const.*) matemática, matemáticas.
matin ['mætən] *s.* 1. (*pl.*) (relig.) maitines; oración matinal (en la Iglesia anglicana). 2. (poét.) canto o llamada matinal.
matinal [-əl] *a.* matinal, matutino.
matinee, matinée [ˌmætə'neɪ, B 'mætɪneɪ] *s.* (teat.) función de la tarde, matinée o matiné (Amer.).
matinée idol, ídolo del público (díc. de un primer galán, cantante de moda, etc.).
mating ['meɪtɪŋ] *s.* apareamiento (en animales).
mating season, período de brama o celo en los animales.
matrass, mattrass ['mætrəs, B -ræs] *s.* (quím.) matraz.
matriarch ['meɪtrɪˌɑrk, B -ˌɑk] *s.* matriarca.
matriarchal [ˌmeɪtrɪ'ɑrkəl, B -'ɑkəl] *a.* matriarcal.
matriarchate ['meɪtrɪˌɑrkət, -ˌkeɪt, B -ˌɑkət] *s.* matriarcado, sistema de gobierno tribal dirigido por mujeres.
matriarchy [-ˌɑrkɪ, B -ˌɑkɪ] *s.* (*pl.* MATRIARCHIES) matriarcado.
matrices, *pl. de* **matrix.**
matricidal [ˌmætrə'saɪdəl, B ˌmeɪ-] *a.* de matricida, referente al matricidio.
matricide ['mætrəˌsaɪd, B 'meɪ-] *s.* 1. matricidio. 2. matricida (el que mata a su propia madre).
matriculant [mə'trɪkjələnt] *s.* estudiante que se matricula (matriculado); matriculador.

matte [mæt] *s.* (metal.) mata (mezcla de sulfuros metálicos). —*a.* mate, sin brillo (ciertas telas).
matted ['mætəd] *a.* 1. enmarañado, enredado. 2. apelotonado (pelo). 3. cubierto con esteras.
matter ['mætər, B -ə] *s.* 1. materia. 2. materia, pus; descarga purulenta. 3. asunto, cuestión. 4. (*pl.*) las cosas, las circunstancias. 5. materia, sujeto, tópico; tema, contenido. 6. material de correo; correo. 7. (lóg.) materia. 8. (fís.) materia, substancia (física). 9. (impr.) material, material periodístico; composición; tipo compuesto; impreso, lo impreso. 10. (ant.) base; razón; causa. 11. **as a m. of fact,** en realidad, de hecho; **for that m.,** en cuanto a eso; **in a m. of,** en un asunto de, ej., *in a m. of such importance,* en un asunto de tanta importancia; **on the m.,** al respecto, ej., *I want to know your views on the matter,* quiero saber tu parecer al respecto; **in the m. of,** en cuanto se refiere a; **it's a m. of,** es cosa de, es cuestión de; **no m.,** no importa; **small m.,** cosa o asunto de poca importancia; **to carry matters too far,** llevar la situación a extremos; **to go into the m.,** entrar en materia; **what is the m.? ¿qué pasa? ¿qué hay? ¿qué ocurre?; what is the m. with** (**her, him,** etc.)? ¿qué tiene (ella, él etc.)? ¿qué le ocurre a (ella, él, etc.)?; **what is the m. with** (**my singing,** etc.)? ¿qué tiene de malo (mi canto, etc.)? —*v.i.* 1. importar, tener importancia. 2. (med.) supurar. 3. **what does it m.?** ¿qué importa?
Matterhorn ['mætər,hɔrn, B -ə,hɔn] *s.* (el) Monte Cervino, en los Alpes Peninos.
matter of course, cosa rutinaria, acontecimiento esperado.
matter-of-course [-əv'kɔrs, B -ərəv'kɔs] *a.* rutinario, acostumbrado, natural.
matter of fact, (der.) cuestión de hecho.
matter-of-fact [-'fækt] *a.* prosaico, desapasionado; práctico.
matter of form, cosa de mera formalidad; (der.) punto de forma.
matter of law, (der.) cuestión de derecho.
matter of principle, cuestión de principios.
matter of state, asunto de Estado.
matting ['mætɪŋ] *s.* 1. estera, petate, esterilla. 2. materiales para esteras (cáñamo, hierba, paja, etc.).
matting, *s.* 1. superficie mate (en doradura, metalistería, vidriería, etc.). 2. passepartout, cartulina o material para enmarcar dibujos, acuarelas, etc.
mattock ['mætək] *s.* (agr.) zapapico, alcotana, piqueta, espiocha, azadón de peto o pico.
mattress ['mætrəs] *s.* 1. colchón. 2. (hidr.) defensa de ramaje con tejido de alambre (contra la erosión).
maturant ['mætʃərənt, B 'mætjʊ-] *s., a.* madurante.
maturate [-,reɪt] *v.i.* 1. madurar; sazonarse. 2. (ant.) supurar.
maturation [,mætʃə'reɪʃən] *s.* maduración.
maturative [mə'tʊrətɪv, B -'tjʊər-] *s., a.* madurativo, madurador.
mature [mə'tʊr, -'tʃʊr, B -'tjʊə] *a.* 1. maduro, sazonado. 2. completo, perfecto, preparado cuidadosamente, acabado, bien madurado, ej., *a m. plan,* un plan acabado o bien madurado. 3. maduro, juicioso (opinión, concepto, etc.). 4. maduro, adulto, plenamente desarrollado. 5. (com.) vencido, pagadero. —*v.t.* madurar; completar. —*v.i.* 1. madurarse. 2. (com.) vencer (documento, plazo), cumplirse (plazo).
maturely [-lɪ] *adv.* juiciosamente, con madurez.
matureness [-nəs] *s.* madurez.
maturity [mə'tʊrətɪ, -'tʃʊr-, B -'tjʊər-] *s.* 1. madurez; maduración; perfección; desarrollo completo. 2. (com.) vencimiento (de una letra, bono, acción, etc.).
matutinal [,mætʃʊ'taɪnəl, mə'tutənl, B ,mætju'taɪnəl] *a.* matutino, matinal, matutinal.
matutinally [-ɪ] *adv.* en las mañanas.
matweed ['mæt,wid] *s.* (bot.) albardín, barceo, esparto.
matzo ['mɑtsə, B -,soʊ] *s.* (*pl.* MATZOTH [-,soʊt] o MATZOS) pan ázimo que se come durante la pascua de los judíos.
maudlin ['mɔdlən] *a.* 1. sentimental en exceso, sensiblero. 2. borracho y lloroso. —*s.* (bot.) balsamita, agérato.
maul [mɔl] *s.* mandarria, macho, almádana, mazo, maceta, porra, combo. —*v.t.* 1. apalear, aporrear; lacerar, magullar; maltratar. 2. (E.U.) hender o partir (ej., un riel) con mandarria y calza.
maulstick ['mɔl,stɪk] *s.* (pint.) tiento.
maumet ['mɔmət] *s.* 1. (dial.) títere; muñeco; imagen. 2. (ant.) ídolo o dios falso.
maund [mɔnd] *s.* unidad de peso en la India (equivalente a 82,28 lbs).
maunder ['mɔndər, B -də] *v.i.* 1. divagar, vagar, andar a la ventura; moverse lánguidamente. 2. divagar. 3. (ant.) rezongar, quejarse.
Maundy Thursday ['mɔndɪ-] (relig.) Jueves Santo.
Mauritanian [,mɔrə'teɪnɪən] *a., s.* mauritano, lenguaje y nativo de la República de Mauritania (África).
Mauritius hemp [mɔ'rɪʃəs-, B mə-] (tej.) cabuya (fibra).
Mauser ['maʊzər, B -zə] *s.* (arm.) máuser (fusil).
mausoleum [,mɔsə'liəm, -zə-, B -sə-] *s.* (*pl.* MAUSOLEUMS o MAUSOLEA) mausoleo.
mauve [moʊv, mɔv, B moʊv] *s.* color de malva.
mauveine ['moʊ,vin] *s.* (quím.) malveína, violeta de anilina.
maverick ['mævərɪk] *s.* (E.U.) 1. animal sin marca de hierro; becerro separado de su madre. 2. (fam.) rebelde, disidente.
mavis ['meɪvəs] *s.* (orn.) malvís, malviz, zorzal.
mavournin, mavourneen [mə'vʊr,nin, B -'vʊə,-] *s.* (Irl.) vida mía, amor mío.
maw [mɔ] *s.* 1. abomaso, cuajar (de los rumiantes); buche (de las aves). 2. garganta, gola, fauces. 3. (hum.) estómago (como símbolo de un apetito voraz).
mawkin, *var. de* **malkin.**
mawkish ['mɔkɪʃ] *a.* 1. empalagoso; nauseabundo, repugnante. 2. sensiblero, sentimental.
mawkishly [-lɪ] *adv.* de modo empalagoso; con sensiblería.
mawkishness [-nəs] *s.* 1. sabor empalagoso. 2. sensiblería.
maxilla [mæk'sɪlə] *s.* (*pl.* MAXILLAE [-i] o MAXILLAS) 1. (anat.) quijada, mandíbula; (hueso) maxilar. 2. (zool.) maxilar (de los artrópodos).
maxillary ['mæksə,lɛrɪ, B mæk'sɪlərɪ] *a.* (anat., zool.) maxilar. —*s.* (*pl.* MAXILLARIES) (hueso) maxilar.
maxillary antrum, (anat.) seno maxilar.
maxilliped [mæk'sɪlə,pɛd] **maxillipede** [-,pid] *s.* (zool.) maxilipedio.
maxim ['mæksəm] *s.* máxima, axioma.
maximal ['mæksəməl] *a.* máximo.
maximalist [-əst] *s.* (pol.) maximalista, el que predica la revolución activa.
Maxim gun, (mil.) ametralladora de un solo cañón, de tiro muy rápido y enfriada por agua.
Maximilian [,mæksə'mɪljən] *s.* (hist.) Maximiliano, archiduque de Austria que fue emperador de México.
maximize ['mæksə,maɪz] *v.t.* 1. aumentar o acrecentar al máximo. 2. dar máxima importancia a, recalcar al máximo. —*v.i.* interpretar en el sentido más amplio.
maximum ['mæksəməm] *s.* (*pl.* MAXIMA [-mə] o MAXIMUMS) máximo, máximum. —*a.* máximo, mayor.
maximum security, de alta seguridad.
maxixe [mə'ʃiʃə] *s.* machicha, baile brasileño.
maxwell ['mækswɛl, -wəl] *s.* (fís.) maxwel, unidad de medida de flujo magnético.
may [meɪ] *v. aux. defec.* (*pret.* MIGHT [maɪt]) 1. poder; ser lícito o permitido, ej., *he m. go,* él puede marcharse, *if I m. say so,* si me es permitido decirlo o si puedo decirlo. 2. poder (ser contingente o posible que suceda algo), ej., *it m. not be true,* quizás no sea verdad, *come what m.,* venga lo que venga, *you might help me carry this suitcase,* usted podría ayudarme a llevar la maleta, *he might have given a larger tip,* él podría haber dado una propina mejor. 3. ojalá, ¡Dios quiera! ej., *m. you live to repent it!* ¡ojalá viva para arrepentirse de ello!, *m. you live long and happy,* Dios quiera que (u ojalá) viva usted muchos y felices años.
May [meɪ] *s.* 1. mayo (mes). 2. (fig.) primavera, flor (de la vida, de la edad, juventud). 3. fiesta del primero de mayo. 4. (ant., poét.) virgen, doncella.
Mayan ['mɑjən] *a.* maya, de los mayas. —*s.* (indio de la raza) maya.
May apple, 1. (bot.) podofilo. 2. manzana de mayo (fruta).
maybe ['meɪbɪ] *adv.* quizá, tal vez, acaso.
mayday ['meɪ,deɪ] *s.* (palabra usada como) señal de socorro (en la radiotelegrafía internacional).
May Day, primero de mayo; fiesta del primero de mayo; día del trabajo; día de las reinas de mayo.
mayflower [-,flaʊər, B -ə] *s.* (bot.) 1. (G.B.) espino, acerolo; vellorita; calta, hierba centella. 2. (E.U.) anémona; hepática; epigea rastrera. 3. **M.,** (hist.) Flor de Mayo, nombre del barco que llevó los primeros colonizadores europeos a Nueva Inglaterra (1620).
mayfly [-,flaɪ] *s.* (ento.) efímera, mosca de mayo, mosca de un día, cachipolla.
mayhap ['meɪ,hæp] **mayhappen** [,meɪ'hæpən] **mayhaps** ['meɪ,hæps] *adv.* (ant., dial.) quizá, tal vez.
mayhem ['meɪ,hɛm] *s.* 1. (der.) mutilación criminal. 2. confusión, pandemónium; pánico.
maying ['meɪɪŋ] *s.* festividad o celebración del primero de mayo.
mayn't ['meɪənt, B meɪnt] (ant.) *contr. de* **may not.**
mayo ['meɪoʊ] *abrev. de* **mayonnaise.**
mayonnaise ['meɪə,neɪz, ,meɪə'neɪz] *s.* (cocina) (salsa) mahonesa o mayonesa.
mayor ['meɪər, mɛr, B mɛə] *s.* alcalde.
mayoralty ['meɪərəltɪ, 'mɛr-, B 'mɛər-] *s.* alcaldía.
mayoress [-əs] *s.* alcaldesa.
maypole ['meɪ,poʊl] *s.* mayo (poste pintado y adornado con flores que se coloca en el centro del lugar donde se festeja las fiestas del primero de mayo).
Maypole dance, danza de cintas en las fiestas de mayo.
maypop ['meɪ,pɑp, B -,pɔp] *s.* 1. (bot.) pasionaria. 2. fruto de la pasionaria.
May queen, maya (joven que preside la fiesta de mayo).
Maytide ['meɪ,taɪd] **Maytime** [-,taɪm] *s.* mes de mayo.
mayweed [-,wid] *s.* (bot.) manzanilla bastarda, manzanilla hedionda o cimarrona, magarzuela.

May wine, 1. vino blanco (gen. alemán y aromatizado con hojas de aspérula). 2. ponche hecho con vino blanco y aromatizado con aspérula.
Mazdaism ['mæzdəˌɪzəm] *s.* mazdeísmo, religión de los antiguos persas.
maze [meɪz] *s.* 1. laberinto. 2. (pr. dial.) perplejidad, confusión; **in a maze,** perplejo. —*v.t.* 1. dejar perplejo. 2. (pr. dial.) aturdir, ofuscar.
mazel tov ['mɑzəlˌtɔv, -ˌtɔf] *s.* (fam., judío) (buena) suerte, dicha, (buena) fortuna.
mazer ['meɪzər, B -zə] *s.* escudilla grande de madera.
mazily ['meɪzəlɪ] *adv.* confusamente, intrincadamente.
mazuma [mə'zumə] *s.* (jer., E.U.) guita, mosca, plata (dinero).
mazurka [mə'zɜrkə, B -'zɜkə] *s.* mazurca (danza y música).
mazy ['meɪzɪ] *a.* (MAZIER; MAZIEST) laberíntico; sinuoso, tortuoso; intrincado, embrollado, confuso.
mazzard ['mæzərd, B -əd] *s.* (bot.) guinda silvestre.
M.B.A. *abrev. de* **Master of Business Administration,** Maestro en Administración de Empresas.
M.B.E. *abrev. de* **Member of the British Empire,** Miembro de la Orden del Imperio Británico.
mc. *abrev. de* **megacycle,** megaciclo.
M.C. *abrev. de* 1. **Master of Ceremonies,** Maestro de Ceremonias. 2. **Military Cross,** Cruz Militar.
McCoy [mə'kɔɪ] *s.* **the McC., the real McC.,** (jer., E.U.) lo auténtico, verdadero, genuino o legítimo.
Md. *abrev. de* **Maryland,** Maryland. (E.U.).
M.D. *abrev. de* **Doctor of Medicine,** Doctor en Medicina, médico.
M-day ['ɛmˌdeɪ] *s.* día de movilización (que marca el comienzo de una guerra).
mdse. *abrev. de* **merchandise,** mercancía.
me [mi] *pron.* (*acusativo* o *dativo* de *I*) 1. me, mí, a mí. 2. **for me,** para mí; **it's me,** (fam.) soy yo; **with me,** conmigo; **to me,** a mí.
Me. *abrev. de* **Maine,** Maine (E.U.).
M.E. *abrev. de* **Middle English,** inglés hablado entre los siglos XII y XVI.
M.E. *abrev. de* 1. **Master of Education,** Maestro en Educación. 2. **Mechanical Engineer,** Maestro en Ingeniería mecánica. 3. **Methodist Episcopal,** Metodista Episcopal.
mead [mid] *s.* 1. aguamiel, hidromel, aloja. 2. (poét.) prado, pradera.
meadow ['mɛdoʊ] *s.* pradera, prado, vega; henar.
meadow clary [-'klɛrɪ] (bot.) salvia de los prados.
meadow crowfoot, (bot.) francesilla.
meadow fescue [-'fɛskju] (bot.) cañuela alta.
meadow foxtail, (bot.) rabo de zorra, alopecuro, carricera.
meadowland ['mɛdoʊˌlænd] *s.* pradería, vega.
meadowlark [-ˌlɑrk B -ˌlɑk] (orn.) sabanero, triguero.
meadow mouse, (zool.) ratón del campo.
meadow mushroom, (bot.) agárico.
meadow saffron, (bot.) cólquico, quitameriendas.
meadow spear grass, (bot.) esteba.
meadowsweet [-ˌswit] *s.* (bot.) 1. ulmaria, reina de los prados. 2. filipéndula.
meager, meagre ['migər, B -gə] *a.* 1. magro, flaco, descarnado, enjuto. 2. pobre, escaso, mezquino.
meagerly, meagrely [-lɪ] *adv.* pobremente, escasamente, mezquinamente.
meagerness, meagreness [-nəs] *s.* 1. flaqueza, falta de carnes. 2. escasez, pobreza.
meal [mil] *s.* 1. grano molido; harina. 2. (E.U.) harina de maíz. 3. comida, sustento, alimento; **to make a m. of,** comer, consumir; hacer una comida de; **to make a m. of it,** atracarse bien de comida, comer a sus anchas.
mealies ['milɪz] *s. pl.* (*sing.* MEALIE O MEALY) (Sud Africa) maíz, zara (Amer.), (*sing.*) mazorca de maíz.
mealiness ['milɪnəs] *s.* calidad de harinoso, pastoso, panoso.
meal ticket, 1. cheque comida. 2. (jer.) (proveedor de la) comida diaria, sustento. 3. (jer.) fuente de ingresos.
mealtime ['milˌtaɪm] *s.* hora de comer.
mealworm [-ˌwɜrm, B -ˌwɜm] *s.* gusano de la harina.
mealy ['milɪ] *a.* (MEALIER; MEALIEST) 1. harinoso, panoso, farináceo. 2. enharinado, empolvorado. 3. mosqueado, pintado. 4. manchado (ej., un negativo fotográfico). 5. pálido. 6. meloso, hipócrita.
mealybug [-ˌbʌg] *s.* (ento.) coco.
mealymouthed [-'maʊðd, -'maʊθt, B -'maʊðd] *a.* meloso, hipócrita, falso.
mean [min] *v.t.* (*pret. p.p.* MEANT [mɛnt] *p.pr.* MEANING) 1. tener la intención de, proponerse, intentar, querer, ej., *I didn't m. to hurt you,* no tuve la intención de (o no quise) hacerte daño. 2. significar, querer decir, ej., *what does it m.?* ¿qué significa esto? *what do you m. by that?* ¿qué quiere decir con eso? 3. referirse a, ej., *whom do you m.?* ¿a quién se refiere Ud.? 4. proponer, ej., *I m. it to be used as a sword,* mi intención es que se use como espada. 5. **m. business,** estar resuelto; hablar en serio; **m. (something) for,** proponer usar (algo) como; **m. it,** decir en serio, decir de veras; **m. mischief,** proponerse o planear alguna diablura; **to be meant for,** ser su destino, nacer para; ser para; ser dirigido a, ej., *he was meant to be a sailor,* su destino fue (o nació para) ser marinero; *her remarks are meant for you,* sus observaciones están dirigidas a Ud. —*v.i.* 1. tener intenciones o propósitos (buenos o malos). 2. significar, ej., *environment means much to a child,* el medio ambiente significa mucho para un niño. 3. **m. well,** tener buenas intenciones; **m. well by (someone),** tener la intención de ayudar (a alguien), ej., *he meant well by the boy,* él tenía la intención de ayudar al muchacho.
mean [min] *a.* 1. común, cualquiera, ej., *he is no m. pianist,* (él) no es un pianista cualquiera. 2. inferior, pobre (ej., intelecto). 3. obscuro, humilde. 4. de poco valor, de pobre calidad. 5. despreciable, ruin, miserable; vulgar, bajo, golfo. 6. tacaño, miserable, mezquino. 7. vil, difícil (ej., camino para coches, etc.). 8. malo, de mal genio (ej., caballo). 9. avergonzado, indigno. 10. indispuesto. 11. (jer.) eficaz, excelente.
mean [min] *a.* 1. medio, mediano (en lugar, tiempo, orden, etc.). 2. medio, intermedio, de término medio. —*s.* 1. medio, punto medio. 2. (*pl.*) medio(s), recurso(s), instrumento(s), expediente(s). 3. (*pl.*) medios, caudal(es), recursos, fondos; posibles; riquezas. 4. (mat.) término medio (de una progresión aritmética, geométrica, etc.). 5. **a man of means,** un hombre de fortuna; **by all (manner of) means,** de todos modos; por supuesto; **by fair means,** por medios lícitos; a las buenas; **by means of,** por medio (de); **by no means,** de ninguna manera; **means to an end,** medio para conseguir un fin; **the golden m.,** el justo medio, el feliz término medio, **to live beyond one's means,** gastar más de lo que uno gana.
meander [mɪ'ændər, B -də] *a.* 1. meandro, recoveco. 2. laberinto, camino tortuoso. 3. (arq.) meandro. —*v.i.* 1. serpentear, seguir un meandro o un curso tortuoso. 2. vagar, caminar sin rumbo.
meander line, (top.) línea quebrada auxiliar, línea de meandro.
meandrous [-drəs] *a.* sinuoso, tortuoso, serpentino.
meanie ['mini] *var. de* **meany,** malo.
meaning ['minɪŋ] *s.* 1. sentido, significado, acepción, significación. 2. intención, propósito. 3. **a word full of m.,** una palabra cargada de significado; **with m.,** significativamente, en tono significativo. —*a.* 1. significativo, expresivo, ej., *a m. look,* una mirada significativa o expresiva. 2. (*en palabras compuestas*) intencionado, ej., *a well-m. man,* un hombre bien intencionado.
meaningful [-fəl] *a.* 1. significativo (modo, mirada, etc.). 2. significante, de mucho significado. 3. expresivo.
meaningless [-ləs] *a.* sin sentido; insensato, vacío.
meaningly [-lɪ] *adv.* significativamente.
meanly ['minlɪ] *adv.* 1. vilmente, bajamente. 2. pobremente, humildemente; malamente, miserablemente. 3. tacañamente, mezquinamente.
meanness ['minnəs] *s.* 1. mezquindad, tacañería. 2. bajeza, vileza, ruindad; maldad, mal genio. 3. acto indigno, ej., *to be guilty of a m.,* ser culpable de un acto indigno.
mean proportional, (mat.) media proporcional, promedio geométrico.
mean solar time, (astr.) tiempo medio solar.
means test, investigación de los ingresos de una persona.
mean sun, (astr.) sol medio.
meant [mɛnt] *pret. y p.p. de* **mean.**
mean tide, (mar.) marea media.
mean time, (astr.) tiempo medio.
meantime ['minˌtaɪm] **meanwhile** [-ˌhwaɪl, -ˌwaɪl] *adv.* entretanto, mientras tanto, por de pronto, por lo pronto. —*s.* ínterin; **in the m.,** entretanto, mientras tanto.
meany ['mini] *s.* (fam.) malo.
measled ['mizəld] *a.* infestado de cisticercos (díc. esp. de la carne de cerdo).
measles ['mizəlz] *s. pl.* (*sing. o pl. en const.*) 1. (med.) sarampión. 2. (vet.) cisticercosis.
measly ['mizlɪ] *a.* 1. enfermo de sarampión. 2. infestado de triquinas (díc. de la carne). 3. (jer.) miserable, mezquino.
measurability [ˌmɛʒərə'bɪlətɪ] *s.* mensurabilidad.
measurable ['mɛʒərəbəl] *a.* mensurable.
measurableness [-nəs] *s.* mensurabilidad.
measurably [-blɪ] *adv.* mensurablemente.
measure ['mɛʒər, B -ə] *s.* 1. medida, unidad de medida. 2. cantidad, grado. 3. medida (instrumento o artefacto para medir). 4. sistema de medidas. 5. medida, medición. 6. medida, disposición, recurso. 7. mesura, moderación. 8. (mat.) divisor, submúltiplo. 9. (geol.) (*gen. pl.*) capas, yacimientos (esp. de hulla o carbón). 10. (mús.) medida, ritmo; compás. 11. (poét.) metro, medida. 12. (ant.) baile (esp. lento y formal). 13. **beyond m.,** excesivamente, desmedidamente; **in a m.,** en parte, hasta cierto punto; **in great m.,** en gran parte; **in some m.,** hasta cierto punto; **for good m.,** para completar la cosa, por añadidura, de yapa (Amer.); **made to m.,** hecho a la medida, hecho sobre medida; **short m.,** falta de medida; **to set measures,** poner coto a; **to take measures,** tomar (las) medidas (necesarias); **to take one's m.,** tomarle a uno las medidas; (fig.) formarse una opinión de uno; **to tread a m.,**

bailar. —*v.t.* 1. medir, mensurar. 2. calibrar, graduar. 3. (t. con *off*) delimitar, marcar (los límites). 4. medir, señalar (calor, etc.). 5. (con *with* o *against*) medir (con alguien la fuerza, capacidad, etc.). 6. tantear, estimar, juzgar. 7. (ant.) recorrer, cubrir (distancia). 8. **m. arms,** medir armas; **m. one's length,** medir el suelo, caer tendido; **m. out,** repartir, distribuir, dar una porción de; **m. (someone) with one's eye,** medir (a alguien) con la vista. —*v.i.* medir, tener (una cierta) dimensión; **m. up to,** elevarse a la altura de, ser igual a.

measured [-ərd, B -əd] *a.* 1. bien proporcionado, preciso. 2. comedido, mesurado, moderado. 3. calculado, deliberado. 4. rítmico, regular. 5. métrico. 6. limitado.

measuredly [-lɪ] *adv.* 1. mesuradamente. 2. deliberadamente. 3. rítmicamente.

measureless ['mɛʒərləs, B -əlɪs] *a.* sin medida, inmensurable, inconmensurable, ilimitado, inmenso.

measurement [-mənt] *s.* 1. dimensión, medida. 2. sistema de medidas.

measurer ['mɛʒərər, B -ərə] *s.* medidor, mensurador.

measuring cup [-ərɪŋ] taza de medir (usada en cocina, laboratorio, etc. para medir ingredientes).

measuring glass, probeta graduada.

measuring pump, bomba de medición o de dosaje.

measuring tape, cinta para medir.

measuring worm, (ento.) medidor, oruga medidora, geómetra.

meat [mit] *s.* 1. carne (comestible de animales o de frutas). 2. (fig.) meollo, substancia; materia (para reflexión). 3. (ant.) comida. 4. **this was m. and drink to him,** fue un gran placer para él. 5. **one man's m. is another man's poison,** lo que a uno cura a otro mata.

meat-and-potatoes ['mitənpə'teɪˌtoʊz] *a.* (jer.) básico; rudo, sin adorno; **m.-a.-p. man,** hombre rudo.

meat ball, albóndiga, almóndiga; (jer.) estúpido.

meat chopper, máquina cortadora de carne.

meat fly, (ento.) mosca de la carne, moscarda.

meat grinder, picadora de carne.

meat hooks, *s. pl.* ganchos de carnicería; garabato, escarpia; (jer.) manos, puños.

meatless ['mitləs] *a.* sin carne; **m. Friday,** viernes de vigilia.

meat loaf, (cocina) carne mechada; carne picada y sazonada.

meatman [-ˌmæn] *s.* carnicero.

meat market, carnicería.

meat-safe [-ˌseɪf] *s.* (G.B.) fiambrera, fresquera (para guardar carne).

meat slicer, cortafiambres.

meatus [mɪ'eɪtəs] *s.* (*pl.* MEATUSES o MEATUS) (anat.) meato.

meaty ['mitɪ] *a.* (MEATIER; MEATIEST) 1. carnoso, carnudo. 2. (fig.) substancioso, substancial, que da que pensar.

Mecca ['mɛkə] *s.* la Meca (ciudad de la Arabia Saudita); (fig.) la Meca, lugar a donde se ansía llegar.

Meccan ['mɛkən] *a.* mecano, nativo de la Meca.

mechanic [mɪ'kænɪk] *s.* 1. mecánico. 2. (fig.) maquinal, mecánico. —*s.* mecánico.

mechanical [-ɪkəl] *a.* 1. mecánico. 2. (fig.) mecánico, maquinal, rutinario; automático (díc. de las acciones y personas). 3. (fís., geol.) mecánico (para diferenciarse de químico).

mechanical advantage, (mec.) ventaja o rendimiento mecánico.

mechanical drawing, (ing., mec.) dibujo mecánico (que se ejecuta con la ayuda de instrumentos).

mechanical engineer, ingeniero mecánico.

mechanical engineering, ingeniería mecánica.

mechanically [mɪ'kænɪkəlɪ] *adv.* 1. mecánicamente. 2. (fig.) maquinalmente, mecánicamente.

mechanical pencil, portaminas; lapicero.

mechanician [ˌmɛkə'nɪʃən] *s.* el que se especializa en el diseño o en la fabricación, función y teoría de la maquinaria.

mechanics [mɪ'kænɪks] *s. pl.* (*sing. o pl. en const.*) 1. mecánica. 2. mecanismo, técnica (de un arte o ciencia).

mechanism ['mɛkəˌnɪzəm] *s.* 1. mecanismo. 2. (filos., biol.) mecanicismo. 3. (psic.) mecanismo.

mechanist [-nəst] *s.* 1. (filos., biol.) mecanicista. 2. (raro) maquinista, mecánico.

mechanistic [ˌmɛkə'nɪstɪk] *a.* 1. mecánico. 2. (filos., biol.) mecanicista.

mechanization [ˌmɛkənə'zeɪʃən, B -naɪ-] *s.* mecanización.

mechanize ['mɛkəˌnaɪz] *v.t.* **mecanizar;** (mil.) mecanizar.

mechanotherapy [ˌmɛkənoʊ'θɛrəpɪ] *s.* (med.) mecanoterapia.

Mechlin ['mɛklən] *s.* 1. Malinas, ciudad de Bélgica famosa por sus encajes. 2. encaje de Malinas.

meconium [mɪ'koʊnɪəm] *s.* (fisiol.) meconio.

med [mɛd] *s.* (jer.) estudiante de medicina.

M. Ed. *abrev. de* **Master of Education,** Maestro en Pedagogía.

medal ['mɛdəl] *s.* medalla; insignia, condecoración. —*v.t.* (*pret., p.p.* MEDALED O MEDALLED; *p.pr.* MEDALING O MEDALLING) condecorar, honrar o premiar con una medalla.

medalist, medallist [-əst] *s.* 1. medallista, grabador de medallas. 2. el (que ha sido) premiado con una medalla, (el) condecorado. 3. numismático.

medallion [mə'dæljən] *s.* medallón.

Medal of Honor, (E.U.) Medalla de Honor (otorgada a militares).

medal play, (golf) partido jugado por el número de golpes (y no por hoyos).

meddle ['mɛdəl] *v.i.* (con *in* o *with*) entrometerse (en), ingerirse (en), meterse (en).

meddler ['mɛdlər, B -lə] *s.* entrometido.

meddlesome ['mɛdəlsəm] *a.* entrometido, oficioso, impertinente.

meddlesomeness [-nəs] *s.* entrometimiento, oficiosidad, impertinencia.

meddling ['mɛdlɪŋ] *a.* entremetido. —*s.* entremetimiento, intromisión.

media ['midɪə] *s.* (*pl.* MEDIAE [-ˌi]) 1. (fon.) consonante oclusiva sonora griega. 2. (anat.) media (de un vaso sanguíneo).

media, *pl. de* **medium.**

media, *s.* (*pl.* MEDIAS) medios de difusión, conjunto de medios publicitarios tales como periódicos, radio y televisión.

mediacy ['midɪəsɪ] *s.* posición intermedia.

mediaeval, mediaevalism, mediaevalist, mediaevally, *vars. de* **medieval, medievalism, medievalist, medievally.**

medial ['midɪəl] *a.* 1. de o en el centro; medianero, intermedio. 2. (fon.) medial (díc. de la consonante que se halla en el interior de una palabra). 3. (mat.) medio, medial, promedio. —*s.* (gram.) consonante medial.

medially [-əlɪ] *adv.* al medio, en el medio.

median [-ən] *a.* 1. mediano, intermedio. 2. medio (punto, valor, etc.). 3. (anat.) medial, mediano. —*s.* 1. valor medio, punto medio. 2. (geom.) mediana.

Median, *a., s.* medio, medo.

mediant [-ənt] *s.* (mús.) mediante.

mediastinal [ˌmidɪə'staɪnəl] *a.* (anat.) mediastínico.

mediastinum [-'staɪnəm] *s.* (*pl.* MEDIASTINA [-nə]) (anat.) mediastino.

mediate ['midɪət] *a.* 1. mediato, medio; interpuesto. 2. (raro) intermedio. [-ˌeɪt] *v.i.* mediar, intervenir, interceder; interponerse; actuar como mediador. —*v.t.* 1. reconciliar (diferencias, etc.); negociar como mediador (un convenio, acuerdo, etc.); dirimir, resolver, arbitrar, ajustar (controversia, etc.). 2. transmitir, comunicar (conocimientos, cultura, cualidades, etc.).

mediately [-lɪ] *adv.* mediatamente.

mediation [ˌmidɪ'eɪʃən] *s.* 1. mediación; intervención, interposición. 2. (der.) mediación, tercería.

mediative ['midɪˌeɪtɪv] *a.* mediador, mediante.

mediatization [ˌmidɪətə'zeɪʃən, B -taɪ-] *s.* (hist.) mediatización.

mediatize ['midɪəˌtaɪz] *v.t.* (hist.) mediatizar.

mediator ['midɪˌeɪtər, B -ə] *s.* mediador, intercesor, avenidor, tercero.

mediatorship [-ˌʃɪp] *s.* oficio de mediador.

mediatory ['midɪəˌtɔrɪ, B -ˌeɪtərɪ] *a.* mediador; medianero.

mediatress ['midɪˌeɪtrəs] *s.* mediadora, intercesora, avenidora.

mediatrice [ˌmidɪ'eɪtrəs, B 'midɪˌeɪ-]
mediatrix [-trɪks] *vars. de* **mediatress.**

medic ['mɛdɪk] *s.* (bot.) alfalfa, mielga.

medic, *s.* (fam.) médico; estudiante de medicina.

medicable [-ɪkəbəl] *a.* medicable, curable.

medicaid [-ˌkeɪd] *s.* (E.U.) programa de asistencia médica del gobierno para personas de pocos recursos económicos.

medical ['mɛdɪkəl] *a.* 1. médico, medicinal. 2. de medicina (estudiante, etc.).

medical attention, asistencia médica.

medical corps, servicio de sanidad.

medical examination, examen médico.

medical examiner, (der.) médico forense (que practica la autopsia).

medical insurance, seguro de enfermedad.

medical jurisprudence, medicina legal, jurisprudencia médica.

medical kit, botiquín.

medically ['mɛdɪkəlɪ] *adv.* facultativamente.

medical school, Escuela o Facultad de Medicina.

medical treatment, medicación; tratamiento médico.

medicament [mɪ'dɪkəmənt, 'mɛdɪkə-] *s.* medicamento, medicina, remedio.

Medicare ['mɛdɪˌkɛr, B -ˌkɛə] *s.* (E.U.) programa del fondo de seguro social de asistencia médica para personas mayores de 65 años.

medicaster ['mɛdəˌkæstər, B -tə] *s.* medicastro, medicucho, curandero.

medicate ['mɛdəˌkeɪt] *v.t.* 1. medicinar, medicar, medicamentar, curar. 2. impregnar con una substancia medicinal.

medication [ˌmɛdə'keɪʃən] *s.* 1. medicación; tratamiento médico. 2. medicamento, medicina, remedio.

medicative ['mɛdəˌkeɪtɪv] *a.* medicinal, curativo.

Medicean [ˌmɛdə'tʃiən, -'si-] *a.* perteneciente o relativo a los Médici.

medicinable [mɪ'dɪsnəbəl, -'dɪsənə-, B 'mɛdsə-] *a.* (ant.) medicinal.

medicinal [-'dɪsnəl, -ənəl] *a.* medicinal, curativo.

medicinally [-ɪ] *adv.* medicinalmente, de acuerdo con la medicina.

medicine ['mɛdəsən, B 'mɛdsɪn] *s.* 1. medicina, medicamento, remedio. 2. medicina, ciencias médicas. 3. ensalmo; fetiche, amuleto (de los indios norteamericanos). 4. (ant.) filtro, bebedizo. 5. **to take one's m.,** recibir (uno) resignadamente su merecido, resignarse a las consecuencias; sufrir un castigo merecido. —*v.t.* medicinar, medicamentar.
medicine ball, pelota grande y pesada usada para gimnasia.
medicine cabinet, m. chest, m. cupboard, botiquín.
medicine dance, (E.U.) baile ritual de los indios.
medicine dropper, cuentagotas.
medicine lodge, (E.U.) casilla o tienda del hechicero (de ciertos pueblos indios).
medicine man, (*of a tribe*) hechicero, hechizador; (*of a medicine show*) curandero.
medicine show, espectáculo ambulante durante el cual se venden medicamentos.
medico ['mɛdɪˌkoʊ] *s.* (*pl.* MEDICOS) (fam.) médico; cirujano; estudiante de medicina.
medieval [ˌmidɪ'ivəl, ˌmɛd-] *a.* medieval, medioeval.
medievalism [-ˌɪzəm] *s.* medievalismo, estudio de la historia medieval.
medievalist [-əst] *s.* 1. medievalista, medievista. 2. aficionado a cosas medievales; experto en cosas medievales.
medievally [-ɪ] *adv.* de modo medieval, a la manera medieval.
mediocre [ˌmidɪ'oʊkər, B -kə] *a.* mediocre, mediano, ordinario.
mediocrity [-'ɑkrətɪ, B -'ɔk-] *s.* (*pl.* MEDIOCRITIES) 1. mediocridad. 2. medianía, persona mediocre.
meditate ['mɛdəˌteɪt] *v.t.* meditar, idear, tramar, planear; (raro) considerar. —*v.i.* meditar, reflexionar, cavilar.
meditation [ˌmɛdə'teɪʃən] *s.* meditación, reflexión, cavilación.
meditative ['mɛdəˌteɪtɪv, B -tət-] *a.* meditativo, meditabundo, contemplativo.
meditatively [-lɪ] *adv.* meditativamente.
meditator [-ər, B -ə] *s.* meditador, el que medita.
mediterranean [ˌmɛdətə'reɪnɪən] *s.* **M.,** mar Mediterráneo. —*a.* 1. mediterráneo, rodeado de tierra. 2. mediterráneo, perteneciente o característico de las regiones que rodean al Mediterráneo.
Mediterranean fever, (med.) fiebre del Mediterráneo, fiebre de Malta, fiebre ondulante.
Mediterranean flour moth, (ento.) polilla de la harina.
Mediterranean fruit fly, (ento.) mosca del Mediterráneo, mosca de la fruta.
medium ['midɪəm] *s.* (*pl.* MEDIUMS O MEDIA [-ə]) 1. medio. 2. expediente, instrumento medio; intermedio. 3. medio, médium (en el espiritismo). 4. medio o método de comunicación en publicidad (en *pl.*). 5. (biol.) medio ambiente. 6. (pint.) aceite. —*a.* 1. medio, mediano, intermedio. 2. medio cocida (carne); a término medio.
medium-fine [-'faɪn] *a.* entrefino.
medium frequency, (rad.) frecuencia intermedia.
mediumistic [ˌmidɪə'mɪstɪk] *a.* perteneciente o relativo al médium (en el espiritismo).
medium of exchange, medio de cambio, medio de trueque.
medium priced, de precio medio.
medium range, de alcance medio.
medium-sized ['midɪəm'saɪzd] *a.* de tamaño mediano.
medium wave, (rad.) onda media.
medlar ['mɛdlər, B -lə] *s.* 1. (bot.) níspero. 2. níspero, níspola (fruto).
medley ['mɛdlɪ] *s.* 1. mezcla, miscelánea, mezcolanza, revoltijo, ensalada, pot-pourrí. 2. (mús.) pot-pourrí, popurrí. 3. (ant.) pelotera, alboroto. —*a.* mezclado, variado, confuso.
medulla [mə'dʌlə] *s.* (*pl.* MEDULAE [-i] O MEDULLAS) 1. (anat.) médula ósea; médula, tuétano. 2. (bot.) médula. 3. **m. spinalis** (médula espinal).
medulla oblongata [-ˌɑbˌlɔŋ'gɑtə, B -ˌɔbˌlɔŋ'geɪtə] (*pl.* MEDULLAE OBLONGATAE [-ˌi] O MEDULLA OBLONGATAS) (anat.) médula oblongada.
medullary ['mɛdəˌlɛrɪ, 'mɛdʒ-, mə'dʌlərɪ, B 'mɛdələrɪ] *a.* medular.
medullary ray, (bot.) radio medular, rayo medular.
medullary sheath, (anat., bioquín.) vaina medular, vaina de mielina.
medullated [-ˌleɪtəd] *a.* (anat., bot.) medulado.
medusa [mɪ'dusə, -zə, B -'dju-] *s.* (*pl.* MEDUSAE [-ˌsi, -ˌzi]) (zool.) medusa, aguamala, malagua (Amer.).
meed [mid] *s.* 1. (poét.) premio, galardón, recompensa. 2. (ant.) regalo, obsequio; soborno. 3. (ant.) mérito; valor, valía.
meek [mik] *a.* 1. manso, apacible, humilde; paciente, sufrido. 2. dócil, sumiso. 3. (ant.) suave, bondadoso.
meekly ['miklɪ] *adv.* 1. mansamente, humildemente; pacientemente. 2. dócilmente, sumisamente.
meekness [-nəs] *s.* 1. mansedumbre, humildad, paciencia. 2. sumisión, docilidad.
meerschaum ['mɪrʃəm, -ˌʃɔm, B 'mɪəʃəm] *s.* (min.) magnesita, espuma de mar; pipa de espuma de mar.
meet [mit] *v.t.* (*pret., p.p.* MET [mɛt]; *p.pr.* MEETING) 1. encontrarse con, encontrar. 2. topar o chocar con; tocar o rozar con. 3. ir al encuentro de, ir a recibir. 4. aceptar la opinión o condición de (uno). 5. hacer frente a, enfrentarse a; combatir, pelear o batirse con. 6. unirse a. 7. conocer, verse o entrevistarse con. 8. sufragar, correr con, hacer frente a (los gastos). 9. satisfacer, llenar (requisitos, etc.); responder a (acusación, reto, etc.); honrar, cumplir (obligaciones); pagar, saldar (letra, etc.). 10. **m. (someone) half-way,** llegar a un arreglo con (alguien); hacer una concesión a (alguien); **m. Mr. Wilson,** le presento al Sr. Wilson; **m. someone's eye,** encontrarse con la mirada de uno; sostener la mirada de uno; **m. the case,** ser adecuado o apropiado; **m. the eye,** saltar a la vista; **there's more to it than meets the eye,** aquí hay gato encerrado. —*v.i.* 1. acercarse, aproximarse; encontrarse, tocarse. 2. reunirse, congregarse, sesionar. 3. ser presentado. 4. **m. with,** encontrarse, toparse con; experimentar, sufrir (mal trato, etc.); **m. up with,** tropezar con, encontrar casualmente; **till we m. again,** hasta la vista. —*s.* 1. reunión, encuentro. 2. concurso, torneo. 3. partida de caza.
meet [mit] *a.* (ant.) apto, conveniente, apropiado, adecuado; **it is m. that,** es conveniente que.
meeting ['mitɪŋ] *s.* 1. reunión; junta, asamblea, mitin. 2. congregación (de fieles); concurrencia. 3. duelo, pelea; reunión hípica. 4. unión, intersección, confluencia (ríos, vertientes). 5. (hist.) cabildo.
meetinghouse [-ˌhaʊs] *s.* templo, iglesia o capilla protestante.
meetly ['mitlɪ] *adv.* convenientemente, apropiadamente, adecuadamente.
megabuck ['mɛgəˌbʌk] *s.* (jer., E.U.) un millón de dólares.
megacephalic [ˌmɛgəsə'fælɪk, B -kə-]
megacephalous [-'sɛfələs, B -'kɛ-] *a.* (anat.) megacéfalo, megalocéfalo, macrocéfalo.
megacephaly [-'sɛfəlɪ] *s.* megalocefalia, macrocefalia.
megacycle ['mɛgəˌsaɪkəl] *s.* (rad.) megaciclo.
megadeath [-ˌdɛθ] *s.* un millón de personas muertas, unidad empleada para calcular la cantidad de víctimas hipotéticas en una explosión nuclear.
megagamete [ˌmɛgəgə'mit] *s.* (biol.) megagameto.
megalith ['mɛgəˌlɪθ] *s.* (arqueol.) megalito.
megalithic [ˌmɛgə'lɪθɪk] *a.* megalítico.
megalocephalic [ˌmɛgəloʊsə'fælɪk, B -kə-]
megalocephalous [-'sɛfələs, B -'kɛ-] *vars. de* **megacephalic, megacephalous.**
megalomania [-'meɪnɪə] *s.* megalomanía.
megalomaniac [-ˌæk] *a., s.* megalómano.
megalomaniacal [-mə'naiəkəl] *a.* megalomaníaco, megalómano.
megalopolis [ˌmɛgə'lɑpələs, B -'lɔp-] *s.* megalópolis, región integrada por varias ciudades grandes y sus áreas adyacentes, considerada como un complejo urbano único.
megalopolitan [-loʊ'pɑlətən, B -'pɔl-] *a.* megalopolitano.
megalosaur ['mɛgələˌsɔr, B -ˌsɔ] *s.* (pal.) megalosaurio.
megaphone ['mɛgəˌfoʊn] *s.* megáfono, portavoz.
megaphonic [ˌmɛgə'fɑnɪk, B -'fɔn-] *a.* megafónico.
megapode ['mɛgəˌpoʊd] *a.* (orn.) megápodo.
megascopic [ˌmɛgə'skɑpɪk, B -'skɔp-] *a.* 1. megascópico. 2. visible (a simple vista).
megasporangium [-spə'rændʒɪəm] *s.* (*pl.* MEGASPORANGIA [-ə]) (bot.) megasporangio.
megaspore ['mɛgəˌspɔr, B -ˌspɔ] *s.* (bot.) megáspora.
megasporophyll [ˌmɛgə'spɔrəˌfɪl] *s.* (bot.) megasporofilo.
megathere ['mɛgəˌθɪr, B -ˌθɪə] *s.* (pal.) megaterio.
megaton [-ˌtʌn] *s.* megatón (unidad de fuerza explosiva de las armas termonucleares, equivalente a un millón de toneladas de T.N.T.).
megawatt [-ˌwɑt, B -ˌwɔt] *s.* (elec.) megavatio.
megohm ['mɛgˌoʊm] *s.* (elec.) megohmio.
megrim ['migrəm] *s.* (med.) 1. migraña, jaqueca, hemicránea. 2. (ant.) antojo, capricho. 3. (*pl*) melancolía, murria.
meiosis [maɪ'oʊsəs] *s.* (biol.) meiosis, meyosis.
meiotic [maɪ'ɑtɪk, B -'ɔt-] *a.* (biol.) meiótico.
Meistersinger ['maɪstərˌsɪŋər, B -stəˌsɪŋə] *s.* (*pl.* MEISTERSINGER) (hist.) maestro cantor.
Mekong ['meɪ'kɔŋ, -'kɑŋ, B -'kɔŋ] *s.* Mekong, río del Asia sudoriental.
Mekong delta, delta del Mekong, en Vietnam del Sur.
mel [mɛl] *s.* (farm.) mel, miel.
melamine ['mɛləˌmin, B -ˌmaɪn] *s.* (quím.) melamina.
melamine resin, (quím.) resina de melamina.
melancholia [ˌmɛlən'koʊlɪə] *s.* 1. (med.) lipemanía, melancolía. 2. aflicción, tristeza.
melancholiac [-ˌæk] *s.* melancólico, lipemaníaco.
melancholic [-'kɑlɪk, B -'kɔl-] *a.* melancólico, triste, deprimido.
melancholically [-ɪkəlɪ] *adv.* melancólicamente.
melancholy ['mɛlənˌkɑlɪ, B -kəlɪ] *s.* (*pl.* MELANCHOLIES) 1. melancolía, tristeza, desaliento. 2. (ant.) bilis negra, atrabilis. —*a.* 1. melancólico, triste, lúgubre. 2. entristecedor, deprimente. 3. meditativo, pensativo, meditabundo.

Melanesian [ˌmɛlə'niʒən, -ʃən, B -zjən] *a., s.* melanesio, de Melanesia, Oceanía.
mélange [meɪ'lɑndʒ, B -'lɑnʒ] *s.* mezcla, mixtura; revoltijo, mezcolanza.
melanic [mə'lænɪk] *a.* 1. (med.) melánico. 2. (zool.) melanodermo.
melanin ['mɛlənən] *s.* (bioquím.) melanina.
melanism [-ˌnɪzəm] *s.* (fisiol., zool.) melanismo.
melanite [-ˌnaɪt] *s.* (min.) melanita.
Melanochroi [ˌmɛlə'nɑkroʊˌi, B -'nɔkroʊaɪ] *s. pl.* (antrop.) melanocroicos.
Melanochroic [-noʊ'kroʊɪk] *s.* (antrop.) melanocroicos.
melanoid ['mɛlənɔɪd] *a.* melanoideo; melanoide.
melanoma [ˌmɛlə'noʊmə] *s.* (*pl.* MELANOMATA [-mətə] o MELANOMAS) (med.) melanoma (tumor pigmentario maligno).
melanosis [ˌmɛlə'noʊsəs] *s.* (med.) melanosis.
melanotic [-'nɑtɪk, B -'nɔt-] *a.* (med.) melanótico.
melanthaceous [ˌmɛlən'θeɪʃəs] *a.* (bot.) melantaceo.
melanuria [-ə'nʊrɪə, B -'njʊr-] *s.* (med.) melanuria (expulsión de pigmentos obscuros en la orina).
melaphyre ['mɛləˌfaɪr, B -ˌfaɪə] *s.* (geol.) melafiro, meláfido.
melba toast [-'mɛlbə-] tostada de pan muy delgada.
Melchior ['mɛlkɪɔr, B -kjɔ] *s.* (bíbl.) Melchor (uno de los tres Reyes Magos).
Melchite ['mɛlˌkaɪt] *s.* (hist., relig.) melquita.
Melchizedekian [mɛlˌkɪzə'dɛkɪən] *a., s.* (relig.) melquisedeciano.
meld [mɛld] *v.t., v.i.* (naipes) anunciar, declarar o tender (combinación o serie de cartas para que valgan en el puntaje). —*s.* anuncio (de una combinación o serie de cartas); combinación (serie de cartas).
meld, *v.t., v.i.* unir(se), fusionar(se), combinar(se).
melee ['meɪˌleɪ, B 'mɛ-] *s.* 1. pelotera, reyerta, refriega. 2. confusión. 3. conflicto.
melegueta pepper [ˌmɛlə'gɛtə-, B -'geɪtə-] (bot.) malagueta, pimienta de Chiapa, pimienta de Tabasco.
meliaceous [ˌmilɪ'eɪʃəs] *a.* (bot.) meliáceo.
melic ['mɛlɪk] *a.* mélico, lírico.
melilot ['mɛləˌlɑt, B -ˌlɔt] *s.* (bot.) meliloto.
melinite ['mɛləˌnaɪt] *s.* melinita (explosivo).
meliorate ['miljəˌreɪt] *v.t.* mejorar, adelantar. —*v.i.* mejorar, progresar.
melioration [ˌmiljə'reɪʃən] *s.* mejora, mejoramiento, adelanto.
meliorism ['miljəˌrɪzəm] *s.* (filos.) meliorismo.
meliorist [-rəst] *s.* partidario del meliorismo.
Melkite, *var. de* **Melchite.**
mell [mɛl] *v.t., v.i.* (ant.) mezclar(se), juntar(se); entrometer(se).
melliferous [mɛ'lɪfərəs] *a.* melífero.
mellifluence [-lʊəns] *s.* melifluencia, melifluidad.
mellifluent [-lʊənt] *a.* melifluo.
mellifluently [-lɪ] *adv.* melifluamente, dulcemente.
mellifluous [-lʊəs] *a.* melifluo, dulce, suave, tierno (díc. del lenguaje o la voz).
mellifluously [-lɪ] *adv.* melifluamente, dulcemente.
mellow ['mɛloʊ] *a.* 1. suave, tierno, maduro (frutas). 2. friable, margoso (tierras). 3. maduro; ablandado, dulcificado (por el tiempo). 4. dulce, suave (sonido, color). 5. doncel, añejo (vino). 6. ligeramente ebrio, calamocano, achispado. —*v.t., v.i.* añejar; madurar, sazonar; ablandar(se), endulzar(se).
mellowly [-lɪ] *adv.* suavemente, dulcemente.
mellowness [-nəs] *s.* 1. madurez, sazón, blandura. 2. friabilidad (de la tierra). 3. melosidad, suavidad; morbidez.
melodeon [mə'loʊdɪən] *s.* (mús.) melodión; melodina.
melodic [mə'lɑdɪk, B -'lɔd-] *a.* melódico.
melodically [-ɪkəlɪ] *adv.* melódicamente.
melodious [mə'loʊdɪəs] *a.* melodioso, armonioso, dulce, agradable.
melodiously [-lɪ] *adv.* melodiosamente.
melodiousness [-nəs] *s.* melodía.
melodist ['mɛlədəst] *s.* melodista, cantor; compositor de melodías.
melodize [-ˌdaɪz] *v.t.* ponerle música a (texto, verso); hacer melodioso. —*v.i.* componer melodías.
melodrama [-ˌdrɑmə, -ˌdræmə, B -ˌdrɑmə] *s.* melodrama.
melodramatic [-drə'mætɪk] *a.* melodramático.
melodramatically [-ɪkəlɪ] *adv.* melodramáticamente.
melodramatics [-ɪks] *s. pl.* teatralidad, conducta melodramática.
melodramatist [ˌmɛlə'dræmətəst] *s.* autor de melodramas.
melody ['mɛlədɪ] *s.* (*pl.* MELODIES) melodía.
meloid ['mɛlˌɔɪd] *s.* (ento.) meloido.
melolonthid [ˌmɛlə'lɑnθəd, B -'lɔn-] *s.* (ento.) melolóntido.
melomania [ˌmɛlə'meɪnɪə] *s.* melomanía, inclinación marcada por la música.
melomaniac [-ˌæk] *s.* melómano, melómana (persona con intensa predilección por la música).
melon ['mɛlən] *s.* 1. melón; sandía. 2. (jer., E.U.) ganancias (de una empresa), totalidad de utilidades (de un negocio); **to cut a m.,** repartir ganancias o dividendos.
melon patch, melonar.
melopoeia [ˌmɛlə'pijə] *s.* melopeya, melopea (canto rítmico).
melosa [mə'loʊsə] *s.* (bot.) **madia.**
Melpomene [mɛl'pɑməˌni, B -'pɔm-] *s.* (mitol.) Melpómene, musa de la tragedia.
melt [mɛlt] *v.i.* (*pret., p.p.* MELTED; *p.pr.* MELTING; *p.p. ant.* MOLTEN ['moʊltən]) 1. fundirse, derretirse; liquidarse, licuarse. 2. disolverse, disgregarse, desleírse. 3. (gen. con *away*) consumirse, menguar, disiparse, desvanecerse, desaparecer, esfumarse. 4. ablandarse, enternecerse, aplacarse, suavizarse. 5. **m. into,** transformarse paulatinamente en (otro color, forma, etc.), confundirse en (la distancia), mezclarse con (el fondo); **m. into tears,** deshacerse en lágrimas; **m. in one's mouth,** derretirse en la boca (de dulce, suave o rico). —*v.t.* 1. fundir, derretir, licuar. 2. desvanecer, disolver, disipar. 3. ablandar, suavizar, enternecer. 4. mezclar, combinar (colores, perfiles, sonidos). 5. **m. down,** fundir (objeto de metal). —*s.* 1. fusión, derretimiento, licuefacción. 2. fundición; (metal.) hornada, vaciada.
meltability [ˌmɛltə'bɪlətɪ] *s.* capacidad de fundirse.
meltable['mɛltəbəl] *a.* fundible.
meltdown ['mɛltdaʊn] *s.* (fís.) fusión accidental del núcleo del reactor nuclear, fundido nuclear.
melter [-ər, B -ə] *s.* fundidor, crisol.
melting [-ɪŋ] *a.* fundente. —*s.* derretimiento, fusión.
melting furnace, horno de fusión, hornillo de fundir, horno para derretir.
melting point, punto de fusión.
melting pot, 1. crisol, fusor. 2. (fig.) crisol de razas (díc. de los E.U.).
melton [-mɛltən] *s.* (tej.) tejido burdo de lana, paño melton.
meltwater ['mɛltˌwɔtər, -ˌwɑt-, B -ˌwɔtə] *s.* agua (de) nieve, aguanieve.
member ['mɛmbər, B -bə] *s.* 1. miembro, socio (de una asociación, club, etc.). 2. miembro del parlamento, diputado. 3. miembro, componente, integrante. 4. (anat.) miembro, extremidad; pene. 5. (mat.) miembro.
membered [-bərd, B -bəd] *a.* 1. provisto de miembros. 2. (her.) membrado.
membership ['mɛmbərˌʃɪp, B -bəˌ-] *s.* 1. calidad de miembro o socio. 2. número de miembros o socios (de un club, etc.).
membership dues, cuota de socio.
membership list, lista o nómina de socios.
membranaceous [ˌmɛmbrə'neɪʃəs] *a.* (bot., zool.) membranáceo, membranoso.
membrane ['mɛmbreɪn] *s.* 1. membrana. 2. hoja de pergamino (que forma parte de un rollo de escrituras antiguas). 3. (anat.) membrana, tejido que cubre o envuelve órganos.
membranous [-brənəs] *a.* membranoso, membranáceo.
memento [mɪ'mɛntoʊ] *s.* (*pl.* MEMENTOS o MEMENTOES) 1. recordatorio, advertencia. 2. recuerdo. 3. **M.,** memento (parte del canon de la misa).
Memnon ['mɛmnɑn, B -nɔn] *s.* (mitol.) Memnón, rey etiope asesinado por Aquiles.
memo ['mɛmoʊ] *abrev. de* **memorandum.**
memoir ['mɛmwɑr, B -wɑ] *s.* 1. (*pl.*) memorias, autobiografía. 2. biografía. 3. memoria, informe.
memo pad, agenda de despacio.
memorabilia [ˌmɛmərə'bɪlɪə] *s. pl.* (*sing.* MEMORABILE [-ə'ræbəlɪ]) cosas memorables.
memorability [-'bɪlətɪ] *s.* calidad de memorable.
memorable ['mɛmərəbəl] *s.* memorable, notable.
memorably [-blɪ] *adv.* memorablemente.
memorandum [ˌmɛmə'rændəm] *s.* (*pl.* MEMORANDUMS o MEMORANDA [-də]) 1. memorándum, nota, apunte; minuta, comunicación. 2. (dip.) memorándum. 3. (der.) memorándum, minuta, sumario.
memorandum clause, (seguros) cláusula de exenciones en una póliza, que exime al asegurador de ciertas obligaciones.
memorial [mə'mɔrɪəl] *a.* 1. conmemorativo, conmemoratorio, rememorativo. 2. relativo a la memoria. —*s.* 1. recuerdo. 2. monumento; reliquia. 3. memorial (en que se pide una merced o gracia). 4. (dip.) comunicación informal.
Memorial Day, (E.U.) día en que se recuerda a los soldados muertos en campaña.
memorialist [-əst] *s.* 1. memorialista. 2. escritor de memorias.
memorialize [-ˌaɪz] *v.t.* 1. dirigir un memorial a; pedir por medio de un memorial. 2. conmemorar.
memoriter [mə'mɔrəˌtɛr, -'mɑr-, B -'mɔrɪtə] *adv.* de memoria.
memorization [ˌmɛmərə'zeɪʃən, B -raɪ-] *s.* memorización.
memorize ['mɛməˌraɪz] *v.t.* aprender de memoria, memorizar.
memorizer [-ər, B -ə] *s.* aquel que aprende de memoria; que tiene buena memoria.
memory ['mɛmərɪ] *s.* (*pl.* MEMORIES) 1. memoria. 2. conmemoración. 3. recuerdo, recordación, remembranza. 4. (electrón.) memoria, componentes de una computadora, sistema de guía, etc., que suministra información o instrucciones. 5. **accommodating m.,** memoria gobernable (que

retiene solamente lo que es de interés para la persona); **from m.,** de memoria; **in m. of,** en memoria de; **of happy m.,** de feliz recordación; **to commit to m.,** confiar a la memoria; **to keep alive the m. of,** conservar la memoria de; **within living m.,** durante la vida de la presente generación; **within my m.,** que yo recuerde.

memory bank, banco de memoria.

memory book, 1. libreta de apuntes. 2. álbum de firmas.

Memphian ['mɛmfɪən] *a.* menfita, menfítico. —*s.* menfita, habitante de Menfis.

Memphis ['mɛmfəs] *s.* (hist.) Menfis, capital del antiguo Egipto.

memphite [-ˌfaɪt] *s.* (min.) menfita.

memphitic [mɛm'fɪtɪk] *a.* menfítico.

memsahib ['mɛmˌsɑˌhɪb, -ˌsɑb] *s.* título de respeto aplicado a la mujer blanca europea en la India colonial.

men [mɛn] *pl. de* **man.**

menace ['mɛnəs] *s.* 1. amenaza, amago. 2. (fam.) persona latosa; pelmazo. —*v.t., v.i.* amenazar, amagar.

menacingly [-ɪŋlɪ] *adv.* amenazadoramente.

menad, *var. de* **maenad.**

menadione [ˌmɛnə'daɪˌoʊn] *s.* (farm.) menadiona (forma de la vitamina K).

ménage [meɪ'nɑʒ] *s.* 1. casa, familia. 2. economía doméstica, manejo de la casa.

ménage à trois [-æ'trwɑ] arreglo mediante el cual una pareja de casados y el amante de uno de ellos viven juntos.

menagerie [mə'nædʒərɪ, -'næʒ-, B -'nædʒ-] *s.* 1. jardín o parque zoológico. 2. colección de animales salvajes enjaulados, esp. para exhibición.

mend [mɛnd] *v.t.* 1. enmendar, corregir, reformar, remediar. 2. reparar, componer; repasar, zurcir, remendar, emparchar. 3. mejorar, perfeccionar, adelantar. 4. curar. 5. (ant.) reparar, desagraviar. 6. **m. matters,** mejorar las cosas; **m. one's pace,** apresurar el paso; **m. one's ways,** enmendarse, reformarse; **m. or end,** o se mejora o se suprime. —*v.i.* mejorar; restablecerse (de salud); curar, sanar. —*s.* 1. mejoría; enmienda, reparación. 2. zurcido, remiendo, parche. 3. **on the m.,** mejorando (de salud, negocios, condiciones).

mendable ['mɛndəbəl] *a.* reparable, que puede componerse; reformable.

mendacious [mɛn'deɪʃəs] *a.* mendaz, mentiroso, embustero, falso.

mendaciously [-lɪ] *adv.* mentirosamente, falsamente.

mendaciousness [-nəs] *s.* mendacidad.

mendacity [mɛn'dæsətɪ] *s.* (*pl.* MENDACITIES) 1. mendacidad. 2. mentira, embuste.

mendelevium [ˌmɛndə'livɪəm] *s.* (quím.) mendelevio.

Mendelian [mɛn'dilɪən] *a.* (biol.) mendeliano.

Mendelism ['mɛndəlˌɪzəm] *s.* mendelismo.

Mendel's laws ['mɛndəlz-] (biol.) leyes de Mendel (sobre la herencia y sus características).

mender ['mɛndər, B -ə] *s.* enmendador, reparador; zurcidor, remendón.

mendicancy ['mɛndɪkənsɪ] *s.* mendicidad, mendicación, mendiguez.

mendicant [-kənt] *a.* 1. mendicante, mendigante, pordiosero. 2. mendicante (díc. de ciertas órdenes religiosas). —*s.* 1. religioso mendicante. 2. mendicante, mendigo, pordiosero.

mendicity [mɛn'dɪsətɪ] *s.* mendicidad, mendicación, mendiguez.

mending ['mɛndɪŋ] *s.* compostura, refección, zurcido; artículos por reparar, zurcir, etc.

Menelaus [ˌmɛnə'leɪəs] *s.* (mitol.) Menelao, rey de Esparta y hermano de Agamenón.

menfolk ['mɛnˌfoʊk] *s. pl.* (los) hombres (esp. de una comunidad o familia).

menhaden [mɛn'heɪdən] *s.* (ict.) especie de sábalo.

menhir ['mɛnˌhɪr, B -ˌhɪə] *s.* (arqueol.) menhir (especie de megalito).

menial ['minɪəl] *a.* 1. servil, humilde (ocupación, tarea, etc.). 2. rastrero, bajo. —*s.* criado, sirviente, lacayo, doméstico.

menially [-ɪ] *adv.* servilmente.

meningeal [mə'nɪndʒɪəl] *a.* (anat.) meníngeo.

meningitic [ˌmɛnən'dʒɪtɪk] *a.* (med.) meningítico.

meningitis [-'dʒaɪtəs] *s.* (*pl.* MENINGITIDES [-əˌdiz]) (med.) meningitis.

meningococcus [məˌnɪŋgoʊ'kɑkəs, B -'kɔk-] *s.* (*pl.* MENINGOCOCCI [-ˌsaɪ]) (bact.) meningococo.

meninx ['minɪŋks] *s.* (*pl.* MENINGES [mə'nɪndʒiz]) (anat.) meninge.

meniscus [mə'nɪskəs] *s.* (*pl.* MENISCI [-'nɪsaɪ]) (anat., ópt., fís., geom.) menisco.

menispermaceous [ˌmɛnəˌspər'meɪʃəs, B -ˌspɜ'-] *a.* (bot.) menispermáceo.

Mennonite ['mɛnəˌnaɪt] *s.* (relig.) menonita, miembro de una secta evangélica.

menology [mə'nɑlədʒɪ, B -'nɔl-] *s.* (*pl.* MENOLOGIES) (hist.) menologio.

menopausal [ˌmɛnə'pɔzəl] *a.* (fisiol.) menopáusico.

menopause ['mɛnəˌpɔz] *s.* (fisiol.) menopausia.

menorah [mə'nɔrə] *s.* menorá (candelabro ceremonial de siete brazos que se usa en los templos judíos).

menorrhagia [ˌmɛnə'reɪdʒɪə] *s.* (med.) menorragia.

mensal ['mɛnsəl] *a.* 1. relativo a la mesa. 2. mensual.

mensch [mɛnʃ] *s.* (yiddish, fam.) persona admirable (esp. por su fortaleza y firmeza).

mense [mɛns] *s.* (esco.) corrección, decoro, donaire; discreción.

menseful ['mɛnsfəl] *a.* (esco.) correcto; discreto.

menses ['mɛnsiz] *s. pl.* (fisiol.) menstruo, menstruación.

Menshevik ['mɛnʃəˌvɪk] *s.* (*pl.* MENSHEVIKI [-ˌvikɪ] o MENSHEVIKS) menchevique, partido socialista moderado que fue derrotado en Rusia por los bolcheviques.

menstrual ['mɛnstrʊəl] *a.* 1. (astr.) mensual. 2. (fisiol.) menstrual.

menstrual cycle, ciclo menstrual.

menstruate [-ˌeɪt] *v.i.* menstruar.

menstruation [ˌmɛnstrʊ'eɪʃən] *s.* menstruación.

menstruous ['mɛnstrʊəs] *a.* menstruoso, menstruo.

menstruum [-əm] *s.* (*pl.* MENSTRUUMS o MENSTRUA [-ə]) (quím.) menstruo, solvente.

mensurability [ˌmɛnsərə'bɪlətɪ, B -ʃʊr-] *s.* mensurabilidad.

mensurable [ˌmɛnsərəbəl, B -ʃʊr-] *a.* mensurable, medible.

mensural ['mɛnsərəl, 'mɛntʃ-, B 'mɛnʃ-] *a.* 1. mensural. 2. (mús.) (de notación) mensural.

mensuration [ˌmɛnsə'reɪʃən, B -sjʊ-] *s.* (mat., geom.) medición, medida, mensura; cálculo de magnitudes geométricas.

mental ['mɛntəl] *a.* 1. (anat.) mentoniano. 2. mental, intelectual. 3. (med.) mental (enfermedad, etc.).

mental age, edad mental.

mental deficiency, (med.) deficiencia mental, retraso mental.

mental derangement, enajenación mental.

mental healing, tratamiento de enfermedades por medio de concentración o sugestión hipnótica.

mental health, salud mental.

mentality [mɛn'tælətɪ] *s.* (*pl.* MENTALITIES) mentalidad, modo de pensar.

mentally ['mɛntəlɪ] *adv.* mentalmente, intelectualmente.

mental reservation, reserva mental (juicio no expresado).

mental retardation, retardo mental.

mental telepathy, telepatía, transmisión del pensamiento.

mental test, examen de capacidad mental.

menthene ['mɛnˌθin] *s.* (quím.) menteno.

menthol ['mɛnˌθɔl] *s.* (quím.) mentol.

mentholated [-θəˌleɪtəd] *a.* mentolado.

mention ['mɛntʃən, B 'mɛnʃən] *s.* mención, alusión. —*v.t.* mencionar, aludir, mentar, nombrar, referirse a; **don't m. it,** no hay de qué; **not to m.,** por no decir nada de, sin contar con; además; **to make m. of,** hacer mención de.

mentionable [-əbəl] *a.* mencionable.

mentor ['mɛntər, B -ə] *s.* mentor, tutor; consejero.

menu ['mɛnˌju, 'meɪn-, B 'mɛn-] *s.* (*pl.* MENUS) menú, minuta, carta o lista de platos (en un restaurante); comida.

meow [mɪ'aʊ] *s.* maullido (del gato). —*v.i.* maullar, mayar.

Mephistophelean, Mephistophelian [ˌmɛfəstə'filjən] *a.* mefistofélico, diabólico, perverso.

Mephistopheles [-'stɑfəˌliz, B -'stɔf-] *s.* Mefistófeles (demonio de leyendas medievales y personaje en óperas, literatura, etc.).

mephitic [mə'fɪtɪk, B mɛ-] *a.* **mefítico,** hediondo.

mephitis [-'faɪtəs] *s.* **emanación mefítica,** hediondez.

meprobamate [mɪ'proʊbəˌmeɪt] *s.* (farm.) meprobamato (tranquilizante).

merbromin [mər'broʊmən, B mə'-] *s.* (farm.) merbromina.

mercantile ['mɜrkənˌtil, B 'mɜkənˌtaɪl] *a.* 1. mercantil, mercante, comercial. 2. (e.p.) mercantil.

mercantile paper, instrumentos negociables como pagarés, letras de cambio, etc.

mercantilism [-ˌɪzəm, B -tɪl-] *s.* (e.p.) mercantilismo.

mercantilist [-əst] *s.* (e.p.) mercantilista.

mercaptan [ˌmɜr'kæpˌtæn, B mə'-] *s.* (quím.) mercaptán.

Mercator projection [ˌmɜr'keɪtər-, B mɜ'-ɔ-] (geog.) proyección de Mercator.

mercenary ['mɜrsənˌɛrɪ, B 'mɜsɪnərɪ] *a.* mercenario, venal; (mil.) mercenario. —*s.* (*pl.* MERCENARIES) (mil.) mercenario.

mercer ['mɜrsər, B 'mɜsə] *s.* (G.B.) mercero; comerciante en telas y artículos de costura.

mercerize [-səˌraɪz] *v.t.* (tej.) mercerizar.

mercery [-rɪ] *s.* (*pl.* MERCERIES) (G.B.) (artículos de) mercería; (tienda de) mercería.

merchandise ['mɜrtʃənˌdaɪz, -ˌdaɪs, B 'mɜtʃənˌdaɪz] *s.* 1. mercadería, mercancía. 2. (ant.) comercio. — [-ˌdaɪz] *v.i.* comerciar, traficar, negociar. —*v.t.* 1. comerciar con o en. 2. promover la venta de.

merchant ['mɜrtʃənt, B 'mɜtʃənt] *s.* 1. mercader, comerciante, negociante. 2. tendero, mercachifle. —*a.* 1. mercantil, mercante, comercial. 2. comercial, de tamaño corriente (barras de hierro, etc.). 3. de la marina mercante.

merchantable [-əbəl] *a.* comerciable, negociable, vendible.

merchantman [-mən] *s.* 1. barco mercante. 2. (ant.) mercader.
merchant marine, marina mercante.
merchant service, marina mercante.
merchant ship, barco mercante.
merchant vessel, buque mercante.
merciful ['mɜrsɪfəl, B 'mɜsɪ-] *a.* misericordioso, compasivo, clemente.
mercifully [-fəlɪ] *adv.* misericordiosamente, compasivamente.
mercifulness [-fəlnəs] *s.* misericordia, clemencia, compasión.
merciless ['mɜrsɪləs, B 'mɜsɪ-] *a.* despiadado, desalmado, cruel.
mercilessly [-lɪ] *adv.* despiadadamente, cruelmente.
mercilessness [-nəs] *s.* crueldad, rigor, falta de clemencia.
mercurate ['mɜrkjəˌreɪt, B 'mɜkjʊ-] *v.t.* combinar o tratar con mercurio.
mercurial [ˌmɜr'kjʊrɪəl, B ˌmɜ'kjʊər-] *a.* 1. vivaz, activo, ágil; hábil, listo. 2. veleidoso, inconstante. 3. (med.) mercurial. 4. mercurial, mercúrico, de mercurio. 5. **M.,** (astr., mitol.) mercurial. —*s.* (farm.) mercurial, preparado de mercurio.
mercurial barometer, barómetro de mercurio.
mercurialism [-ˌɪzəm] *s.* (med.) mercurialismo.
mercurialize [-ˌaɪz] *v.t.* 1. someter a un tratamiento de mercurio. 2. (foto.) revelar con mercurio.
mercurially [-əlɪ] *adv.* 1. vivazmente, ágilmente, hábilmente. 2. inconstantemente.
mercuric [ˌmɜr'kjʊrɪk, B ˌmɜ'kjʊər-] *a.* (quím.) mercúrico.
mercuric chloride, (quím.) cloruro mercúrico.
mercuric oxide, (quím.) óxido mercúrico.
mercuric sulfide, (quím.) sulfuro mercúrico.
Mercurochrome [-əˌkroʊm] *s.* (farm.) mercurocromo (marca comercial).
mercurous [ˌmɜr'kjʊrəs, 'mɜrkjər-, B 'mɜkjʊr-] *a.* (quím.) mercurioso.
mercury ['mɜrkjərɪ, B 'mɜkjʊ-] *s.* (*pl.* MERCURIES) 1. mercurio, azogue. 2. **M.,** (mitol., astr.) Mercurio. 3. (bot.) mercurial. 4. (ant.) mensajero; guía.
mercury chloride, (quím.) cloruro mercúrico (sublimado corrosivo).
mercury switch, (elec.) interruptor de mercurio.
mercury tube, (rad.) válvula a mercurio.
mercury-vapor lamp [-'veɪpər-, B -pə-] lámpara de vapor de mercurio.
mercy ['mɜrsɪ, B 'mɜsɪ] 1. misericordia, clemencia, piedad, compasión, lenidad, caridad. 2. merced, favor, perdón; gracia; bendición. 3. **for m.'s sake!** ¡por piedad!; **to be at the m. of,** estar a (la) merced de; **to have m. on,** tener piedad de, tener misericordia de; **to show m. to,** demostrar compasión hacia.
mercy killing, muerte piadosa, eutanasia.
mercy seat, 1. propiciatorio. 2. (fig.) trono de Dios.
mere [mɪr, B mɪə] *a.* (*sin comp.; super.* MEREST) 1. mero, solo, simple, puro; no más que (lo mencionado). 2. (ant.) puro, sin adulteración.
mere, *s.* 1. (poét.) laguna; el mar. 2. (ant., G.B.) confín, frontera.
merely ['mɪrlɪ, B 'mɪəlɪ] *adv.* meramente, solamente, simplemente; tan sólo.
merengue [mə'rɛŋˌgeɪ] *s.* merengue, música y baile típicos de Haití y la República Dominicana.
mere right, (der.) derecho solo (sin posesión).
meretricious [ˌmɛrə'trɪʃəs] *a.* 1. engañoso, especioso. 2. chillón; llamativo.
meretriciously [-lɪ] *adv.* engañosamente.
merganser [ˌmɜr'gænsər, B ˌmɜ'-sə] *s.* (orn.) mergo, mergánsar.
merge [mɜrdʒ, B mɜdʒ] *v.t.* 1. fusionar, combinar, fundir. 2. (ant.) hundir, sumergir. —*v.i.* 1. fusionarse, fundirse, combinarse; unirse, juntarse. 2. **m. in,** fusionarse con; ser absorbido por; **m. into,** confundirse paulatinamente con, desvanecerse gradualmente en.
mergence ['mɜrdʒəns, B 'mɜdʒəns] *s.* fusión, combinación.
merger [-dʒər, B -dʒə] *s.* 1. (der.) fusión, incorporación, unión, consolidación. 2. (com.) fusión, amalgamación (de empresas).
meridian [mə'rɪdɪən] *a.* 1. meridiano, de medio día. 2. (fig.) sumo, máximo, culminante. —*s.* 1. (astr.) meridiano superior. 2. (fig.) apogeo, cenit (de la vida). 3. (astr., geog.) meridiano, línea meridiana. 4. (ant.) medio día.
meridian circle, (astr.) círculo meridiano.
meridian instrument, meridiana, anteojo meridiano.
meridian sailing, navegación siguiendo la meridiana.
meridional [-əl] *a.* meridional, austral, perteneciente o relativo al Sur. —*s.* meridional, habitante del Sur (esp. de Francia, Italia).
meringue [mə'ræŋ] *s.* (cocina) merengue.
merino [mə'riˌnoʊ] *s.* merino, raza de oveja que produce lana fina. —*a.* de lana de merino.
meristem ['mɛrəˌstɛm] *s.* (bot.) meristema.
meristematic [ˌmɛrəstə'mætɪk] *a.* (bot.) meristemático.
meristic [mə'rɪstɪk] *a.* (bot.) merístico.
merit ['mɛrət] *s.* 1. mérito, merecimiento. 2. mérito, valor, valía, excelencia. 3. **the merits (of a case),** (der.) méritos (de un proceso); **to each according to his merits,** a cada cual de acuerdo con sus merecimientos; **to judge (an offer, proposal) on its merits,** juzgar (una oferta o propuesta) sólo a base de sus méritos. —*v.t.* merecer, ser digno de. —*v.i.* hacer méritos.
merited [-əd] *a.* merecido.
meritedly [-lɪ] *adv.* merecidamente.
meritocracy [ˌmɛrə'tɑkrəsɪ, B -'tɔk-] *s.* tipo de élite intelectual o académica.
meritorious [ˌmɛrə'tɔrɪəs] *a.* meritorio.
meritoriously [-lɪ] *adv.* meritoriamente.
meritoriousness [-nəs] *s.* merecimiento, mérito.
merkin ['mɜrkən, B 'mɜkən] *s.* peluca para el pubis de la mujer.
merl, merle [mɜrl, B mɜl] *s.* (orn.) mirlo, merla.
merlin ['mɜrlən, B 'mɜlɪn] *s.* (orn.) esmerejón, azor.
merlon ['mɜrlən, B 'mɜlən] *s.* (fort.) merlón.
mermaid ['mɜrˌmeɪd, B 'mɜˌ-] *s.* 1. (mitol.) sirena. 2. bañista, nadadora.
merman [-ˌmæn] *s.* tritón.
meroblastic [ˌmɜrə'blæstɪk] *a.* (biol.) meroblástico.
merocrine ['mɜrəkrən, B -ˌkraɪn] *a.* (fisiol.) merocrino.
Merovingian [ˌmɛrə'vɪndʒɪən] *a., s.* merovingio.
merrily ['mɛrəlɪ] *adv.* alegremente, festivamente.
merriment [-ɪmənt] *s.* 1. alegría, júbilo, gozo, regocijo, alborozo. 2. fiesta, diversión.
merriness [-nəs] *s.* (raro) alegría, regocijo, alborozo.
merry ['mɛrɪ] *a.* (MERRIER; MERRIEST) 1. alegre, feliz, alborozado. 2. gracioso, divertido. 3. festivo. 4. (ant.) agradable, delicioso (el sonido); suave, favorable (el viento); jocoso. 5. **to make m.,** divertirse; **to make m. over,** burlarse de.
merry-andrew [-'ænˌdru] *s.* bufón, payaso, persona retozona; mimo.
Merry Christmas, Feliz Navidad, Felices Pascuas.
merry-go-round [-goʊˌraʊnd] *s.* 1. tiovivo, calesitas, carrusel. 2. (fig.) giro rápido, remolino.
merrymaker [-ˌmeɪkər, B -kə] *s.* juerguista, parrandista, parrandero.
merrymaking [-kɪŋ] *a.* festivo, alegre, alborozado, regocijado. —*s.* holgorio, parranda, fiesta, jarana.
merrythought [-ˌθɔt] *s.* (pr. G.B.) espoleta (de la pechuga de las aves); hueso de la suerte.
mesa ['meɪsə] *s.* (geog.) meseta.
mésalliance [ˌmeɪˌzæl'jɑns, -zə'laɪəns, B mɛ'zælɪ-] *s.* matrimonio con una persona de rango inferior.
mescal [mɛs'kæl] *s.* 1. (bot.) mezcal. 2. (aguardiente de) mezcal, pulque.
mescaline ['mɛskəˌlin] *s.* (quím.) mescalina (droga psicodélica extraída del mezcal).
mesdames, *pl. de* **madame** o **madam.**
mesdemoiselles, *pl. de* **mademoiselle.**
meseems [mɪ'simz] *v. impers.* (ant.) me parece.
mesembryanthemum [məˌzɛmbrɪ'ænθəməm] *s.* (bot.) mesembriantemo.
mesencephalic [ˌmɛsənsə'fælɪk, B -kə-] *a.* (anat.) mesencefálico.
mesencephalon [ˌmɛzˌɛn'sɛfəˌlɑn, B ˌmɛsən'kefəˌlɔn] *s.* (anat.) mesencéfalo.
mesenchymal [məz'ɛŋkəməl, B mɛs-]
mesenchymatous [ˌmɛzən'kɪmətəs, B ˌmɛsɛŋ-] *a.* (biol.) mesenquimatoso.
mesenchyme ['mɛzənˌkaɪm, B 'mɛs-] *s.* (biol.) mesénquima.
mesenteric [ˌmɛsən'tɛrɪk] *a.* (anat., zool.) mesentérico.
mesenteritis [-tə'raɪtəs] *s.* mesenteritis.
mesenteron [ˌmɛz'ɛntəˌrɑn, B mɛs-ˌrɔn] *s.* (*pl.* MESENTERA [-tərə]) (anat.) mesenterón.
mesentery ['mɛsənˌtɛrɪ] *s.* (*pl.* MESENTERIES) (anat., zool.) mesentérico.
mesh [mɛʃ] *s.* 1. malla (de red). 2. red, tejido de malla, trama. 3. (fig.) (*gen. pl.*) red, trampa, lazo. 4. (mec.) enlace, engranaje (de los dientes). 5. **in m.,** engranado; **out of m.,** desengranado. —*v.t.* 1. enredar, coger con red. 2. (mec.) hacer engranar, endentar. 3. encajar bien, regular con precisión. —*v.i.* 1. enmallarse, enredarse. 2. (mec.) engranar. 3. encajar; concordar, armonizar.
meshuga [mə'ʃʊgə] *a.* (jer.) loco, alocado, excéntrico.
meshwork ['mɛʃˌwɜrk, B -ˌwɜk] *s.* red, retículo.
mesial ['mɛzɪəl, -sɪ-, B 'mizjəl] *a.* mediano, del medio.
mesitylene [mə'sɪtəlˌin] *s.* (quím.) mesitileno.
mesmeric [mɛz'mɛrɪk] *a.* 1. mesmeriano. 2. hipnótico, fascinante, irresistible.
mesmerism ['mɛzmərˌɪzəm] *s.* mesmerismo; hipnotismo.
mesmerize [-ˌaɪz] *v.t.* hipnotizar.
mesmerizer [-ər, B -ə] *s.* hipnotizador.
mesne [min] *a.* (der.) intermedio, intermediario.
mesne process, (der.) emplazamiento o auto interlocutorio.
mesoblast ['mɛzəˌblæst, B 'mɛs-] *s.* (fisiol.) mesoblasto.
mesoblastic [ˌmɛzə'blæstɪk, B ˌmɛs-] *a.* (fisiol.) mesoblástico.
mesocarp ['mɛzəˌkɑrp, 'mɛs-, B -ˌkɑp] *s.* (bot.) mesocarpio.

mesocephalic [ˌmɛzousəˈfælɪk, ˌmɛs-, B -kə-] *a.* (anat.) mesocéfalo, mesocefálico; (antrop.) mesocéfalo.
mesoderm [ˈmɛzəˌdɜrm, ˈmɛs-, B -ˌdɜm] *s.* (biol.) mesodermo.
mesodermal [ˌmɛzəˈdɜrməl, ˌmɛs-, B -ˈdɜməl] *a.* (biol.) mesodérmico.
mesogastric [-ˈgæstrɪk] *a.* (biol.) mesogástrico.
mesogastrium [-trɪəm] *s.* (biol.) mesogastrio.
mesoglea, mesogloea [-ˈgliə] *s.* (zool.) mesoglea.
mesognathous [məˈzɑgnəθəs, -ˈsɑg-, B -ˈsɔg-] **mesognathic** [ˌmɛsəgˈnæθɪk] *a.* (antrop.) mesognático.
Mesolithic [ˌmɛzəˈlɪθɪk, ˌmɛs-, B ˌmɛs-] *a.* (geol.) mesolítico.
mesology [məˈsɑlədʒɪ, B mɛˈsɔl-] *s.* (biol.) mesología.
mesomere [ˈmɛzəˌmɪr, ˈmɛs-, B -ˌmɪə] *s.* (biol.) mesómero.
mesomerism [məˈzɑmərˌɪzəm, B -ˈsɔm-] *s.* (quím.) mesomería.
mesomorph [ˈmɛzəˌmɔrf, ˈmɛs-, B -ˌmɔf] *s.* (antrop.) mesomorfo.
mesomorphic [ˌmɛzəˈmɔrfɪk, ˌmɛs-, B -ˈmɔfɪk] *a.* (antrop.) mesomorfo.
meson [ˈmɛzˌɑn, ˈmiz-, ˈmɛs-, ˈmis-, B ˈmizɔn] *s.* (fís., quím.) mesón.
mesonephros [ˌmɛsəˈnɛfrəs] *s.* (*pl.* MESONEPHROI [-ˌrɔɪ]) (biol.) mesonefros.
mesonic [mɛˈzɑnɪk, mi-, -ˈsɑn-, B mɛˈzɔn-] *a.* (fís.) mesónico (campo).
mesopause [ˈmɛzəˌpɔz, ˈmɛs-, B ˈmɛs-] *s.* mesopausa, región de la atmósfera, límite superior de la estratosfera.
mesophyll [-ˌfɪl] *s.* (bot.) mesófilo.
mesophyte [-ˌfaɪt] *s.* (bot.) mesófito.
mesothelial [ˌmɛzəˈθiliəl, B ˌmɛs-] *a.* (biol.) mesotélico.
mesothelium [-əm] *s.* (biol.) mesotelio.
mesothorax [-ˈθɔrˌæks] *s.* (ento.) mesotórax.
mesothorium [-ˈθɔrɪəm] *s.* (quím.) mesotorio.
mesotron [ˈmɛzəˌtrɑn, ˈmɛs-, B -ˌtrɔn] *s.* (fís.) mesotrón.
Mesozoic [ˌmɛzəˈzouɪk, ˌmɛs-, B ˌmɛs-] *a.* (geol.) mesozoico.
mesquite [məˈskit, B ˈmɛsˌkit] *s.* (bot.) mezquita.
mess [mɛs] *s.* 1. plato, ración, porción (de comida). 2. rancho (comida y conjunto de personas que toman a un tiempo esta comida). 3. lío, confusión, revoltijo, mezcolanza. 4. apariencia desaliñada; (fam.) persona de apariencia sucia o desaliñada. 5. **to get into a m.,** meterse en un lío; **to make a m. of,** desordenar, revolver; hacer un lío de; estropear. —*v.t.* 1. dar de comer a, dar rancho a. 2. (t. con *up*) ensuciar; revolver, desarreglar, desordenar; estropear; armar lío o confusión con (cosas); sobar, maltratar; desaliñar. —*v.i.* 1. tomar el rancho. 2. **m. about** (o **around**), ocuparse en fruslerías; **m. in** (o **with**), meterse en (asuntos ajenos); **m. (about) with,** chapucear, experimentar con.
message [ˈmɛsɪdʒ] *s.* 1. mensaje, recado, comunicación, noticia, aviso. 2. mensaje divino, profecía, mensaje inspirado. —*v.t.* enviar como mensaje, comunicar; **to get the m.,** captar la insinuación de una pulla o indirecta. —*v.i.* enviar mensajes.
messaline [ˌmɛsəˈlin] *s.* (tej.) raso.
mess call, (mil., mar.) toque de rancho.
messenger [ˈmɛsəndʒər, B -dʒə] *s.* 1. mensajero, mandadero, recadero, propio, correo. 2. (mar.) virador. 3. (ant.) heraldo, nuncio, precursor.
mess hall, comedor (de cuartel, colegio, institución, etc.).
Messiah [məˈsaɪə] *s.* (bíbl., fig.) Mesías.
Messiahship [-ˌʃɪp] *s.* mesiazgo.
Messianic [ˌmɛsɪˈænɪk] *a.* mesiánico.
Messianism [məˈsaɪəˌnɪzəm] *s.* mesianismo.
Messias [məˈsaɪəs] *var. de* **Messiah.**
messidor [mɛˌsiˈdɔr, B -sɪˈdɔ] *s.* (hist.) mesidor, décimo mes del calendario de la Revolución Francesa.
messieurs [məsˈjɜz, B ˈmɛsəz] *pl. de* **monsieur.**
messily [ˈmɛsəlɪ] adv. desaliñadamente, desordenadamente; chapuceramente.
messiness [ˈmɛsɪnəs] *s.* desorden, desaliño; chapucería.
mess jacket, (mil., mar.) chaqueta corta (que se usa en ocasiones de etiqueta no rigurosa).
mess kit, (mil.) juego portátil de efectos de mesa y su estuche.
messmate [ˈmɛsˌmeɪt] *s.* compañero de rancho; compañero de comidas; comensal.
Messrs. *pl. de* **M.,** Míster.
messuage [ˈmɛswɪdʒ] *s.* (der.) domicilio, casa de vivienda (con edificios anexos y tierras adyacentes).
messy [ˈmɛsɪ] *a.* (MESSIER; MESSIEST) desordenado, desaliñado; chapucero.
mestizo [mɛsˈtizou] *a., s.* (*pl.* MESTIZOS) mestizo.
met [mɛt] *pret., p.p. de* **meet.**
met. *abrev. de* 1. **metaphor,** metáfora. 2. **metaphysics,** metafísica. 3. **metropolitan,** metropolitano.
metabolic [ˌmɛtəˈbɑlɪk, B -ˈbɔl-] *a.* 1. (biol., fisiol.) metabólico. 2. (ento.) metábolo.
metabolism [məˈtæbəˌlɪzəm] *s.* (fisiol.) metabolismo.
metabolite [-ˌlaɪt] *s.* (fisiol.) metabolito.
metabolize [-ˌlaɪz] *v.t., v.i.* (fisiol.) transformar(se) por metabolismo.
metacarpal [ˌmɛtəˈkɑrpəl, B -ˈkɑpəl] *a.* (anat.) metacarpiano, metacarpeo. —*s.* (anat.) hueso metacarpiano.
metacarpus [-pəs] *s.* (anat.) metacarpo.
metacenter, metacentre [ˈmɛtəˌsɛntər, B -ə] *s.* (fís.) metacentro.
metacentric [ˌmɛtəˈsɛntrɪk] *a.* (fís.) metacéntrico.
metachromatism [-ˈkrouməˌtɪzəm] *s.* (fisiol., quím.) metacromatismo.
metachronism [məˈtækrəˌnɪzəm] *s.* metacronismo.
metagalaxy [ˌmɛtəˈgæləksɪ, B ˈmɛtəˌgæl-] *s.* (astr.) metagalaxia, el universo físico total, incluyendo las galaxias.
metagenesis [-ˈdʒɛnəsəs, B ˌmɛtə-] *s.* (biol.) metagénesis.
metagenetic [-dʒəˈnɛtɪk] *a.* (biol.) metagenético, metagenésico.
metal [ˈmɛtəl] *s.* 1. metal. 2. (fig.) carácter, temple. 3. (fig.) materia, substancia. 4. vidrio fundido. 5. (her.) metal (oro o plata). 6. (mar.) peso de la andanada (de buques de guerra). 7. (tip.) caracteres de imprenta. 8. (G.B.) macadán, grava, cascajo (de caminos y ferrocarriles). 9. (*pl.*) (G.B.) rieles. —*v.t.* (*pret., p.p.* METALED O METALLED; *p.pr.* METALING O METALLING) 1. cubrir con metal. 2. (G.B.) cubrir con grava, macadamizar (caminos).
metalanguage [ˈmɛtəˌlæŋgwɪdʒ] *s.* metalenguaje.
metal detector, detector de metales.
metalepsis [ˌmɛtəˈlɛpsəs] *s.* (*pl.* METALEPSES) (ret.) metalepsis.
metaline [ˈmɛtələn] *s.* (quím.) metalina, aleación de cobre, hierro, aluminio y cobalto.
metalization, metalize, *vars. de* **metallization, metallize.**
metallic [məˈtælɪk] *a.* 1. metálico, de metal. 2. metalífero. 3. (fig.) metálico (sonido, voz).
metallicize [-əˌsaɪz] *v.t.* (metal.) hacer completamente metálico.
metalliferous [ˌmɛtəˈlɪfərəs] *a.* metalífero.
metalline [ˈmɛtəlɪn, B -ˌlaɪn] *a.* 1. metálico. 2. cargado de sales metálicas (agua, etc.).
metallist [-ləst] *s.* 1. metalario, metalista, artesano que trabaja en metales. 2. partidario del uso de la moneda en metal, en contraposición al papel moneda.
metallization [ˌmɛtələˈzeɪʃən, B -laɪ-] *s.* metalización.
metallize [ˈmɛtəˌlaɪz] *v.t.* metalizar.
metallographer [ˌmɛtəlˈɑgrəfər, B -ˈɔgrəfə] *s.* metalógrafo.
metallographic [məˌtæləˈgræfɪk] *a.* metalográfico.
metallography [ˌmɛtəlˈɑgrəfɪ, B -ˈɔg-] *s.* metalografía.
metalloid [ˈmɛtəlɔɪd] *s.* (quím.) metaloide. —*a.* 1. semejante a un metal. 2. metalóidico, metaloideo.
metallotherapy [məˌtælouˈθɛrəpɪ] *s.* (med.) metaloterapia.
metallurgic [ˌmɛtəlˈɜrdʒɪk, B -ˈɜdʒɪk] **metallurgical** [-dʒɪkəl] *a.* metalúrgico.
metallurgist [ˈmɛtəlˌɜrdʒəst, B mɛˈtælədʒɪst] *s.* metalúrgico.
metallurgy [-dʒɪ] *s.* metalurgia.
metalware [ˈmɛtəlˌwɛr, B -ˌwɛə] *s.* trabajo de metalistería; utensilio de metal.
metalwork [-ˌwɜrk, B -ˌwɜk] *s.* trabajo de metalistería.
metalworker [-ˌwɜrkər, B -ˌwɜkə] *s.* metalario, metalista.
metalworking [-kɪŋ] *s.* elaboración de metales.
metamere [ˈmɛtəˌmɪr, B -ˌmɪə] *s.* (zool.) metámero.
metameric [ˌmɛtəˈmɛrɪk] *a.* (zool., quím.) metamérico.
metamerism [məˈtæməˌrɪzəm] *s.* (zool., quím.) metamería, metamerismo.
metamorphic [ˌmɛtəˈmɔrfɪk, B -ˈmɔfɪk] *a.* (geol.) metamórfico.
metamorphism [-ˌfɪzəm] *s.* 1. metamorfosis. 2. (geol.) metamorfismo.
metamorphose [-ˌfouz] *v.t., v.i.* metamorfosear(se), transformar(se).
metamorphosis [-fəsəs] *s.* (*pl.* METAMORPHOSES [-siz]) metamorfosis, metamórfosis.
metanephros [ˌmɛtəˈnɛfrəs, -ˌrɑs B -ˌrɔs] *s.* (*pl.* METANEPHROI [-ˌrɔɪ]) (biol.) metanefron, metanefros.
metaphase [-ˈmɛtəˌfeɪz] *s.* (biol.) metafaso.
metaphony [məˈtæfənɪ] *s.* (fon.) metafonía.
metaphor [ˈmɛtəˌfɔr, -fər, B -fə] *s.* (ret.) metáfora.
metaphoric [ˌmɛtəˈfɔrɪk, -ˈfɑr-, B -ˈfɔr-] **metaphorical** [-ɪkəl] *a.* metafórico.
metaphorically [-ɪkəlɪ] *adv.* metafóricamente.
metaphosphate [-ˈfɑsˌfeɪt, B -ˈfɔs-] *s.* (quím.) metafosfato.
metaphrase [ˈmɛtəˌfreɪz] *s.* metáfrasis; traducción literal. —*v.t.* traducir literalmente.
metaphysic [ˌmɛtəˈfɪzɪk] *a.* metafísico.
metaphysical [-ɪkəl] *a.* metafísico.
metaphysically [-kəlɪ] *adv.* metafísicamente.
metaphysician [ˌmɛtəfəˈzɪʃən] *s.* metafísico.
metaphysics [-ˈfɪzɪks] *s. pl.* (*sing. en const.*) metafísica (la ciencia).

metaplasia [-ˈpleɪʒə, B -zɪə] *s.* (biol.) taplástico.
metaplasm [ˈmɛtəˌplæzəm] *s.* 1. (biol.) metaplasma. 2. (gram.) metaplasmo.
metaplastic [ˌmɛtəˈplæstɪk] *a.* (biol.) metaplástico.
metaprotein [-ˈproʊˌtin, -ˈproʊtɪən] *s.* (bioquím.) metaproteína.
metapsychology [-saɪˈkɑlədʒɪ, B -ˈkɔl-] *s.* (*pl.* METAPSYCHOLOGIES) metapsicología.
metasomatic [-soʊˈmætɪk] *a.* (geol.) metasomático.
metasomatism [-ˈsoʊməˌtɪzəm] *s.* (geol.) metasomatismo.
metastable [-ˈsteɪbəl] *a.* (fís., quím.) metastable.
metastasis [məˈtæstəsəs] *s.* (*pl.* METASTASES [-ˌsiz]) (med.) metástasis.
metastasize [məˈtæstəˌsaɪz] *v.i.* (med.) extenderse por metástasis, diseminarse.
metastatic [ˌmɛtəˈstætɪk] *a.* (med.) metastático.
metatarsal [ˌmɛtəˈtɑrsəl, B -ˈtɑsəl] *a.* (anat.) metatárseo, metatarsiano. —*s.* hueso metatarsiano.
metatarsus [-səs] *s.* (*pl.* METATARSI [-saɪ]) (anat.) metatarso.
metathesis [məˈtæθəsəs] *s.* (*pl.* METATHESES [-ˌsiz]) 1. (gram.) metátesis. 2. (quím.) intercambio.
metathorax [ˌmɛtəˈθɔræks] *s.* (ento.) metatórax.
metazoal [-ˈzoʊəl] *a.* (zool.) metazoario.
metazoan [-ən] (zool.) *a.* metazoario. —*s.* metazoario, metazoo.
mete [mit] *v.t.* 1. (poét., ant.) mensurar, medir. 2. (gen. con *out*) repartir, distribuir, prorratear.
mete, *s.* 1. frontera; límite. 2. ámbito, mojón.
metempiric [ˌmɛtəmˈpɪrɪk] *a.* (filos.) metaempírico.
metempsychosis [məˌtɛmpsɪˈkoʊsəs, B ˌmɛtɛmp-] *s.* metempsicosis, metempsícosis, transmigración.
metencephalic [ˌmɛtˌɛnsəˈfælɪk, B -kə-] *a.* (anat.) metencefálico.
metencephalon [-ˈsɛfəˌlɑn, B -ˌlɔn] *s.* (anat.) metencéfalo.
meteor [ˈmitɪər, B -ə] *s.* 1. meteoro, metéoro. 2. (astron.) estrella fugaz; meteorito, aerolito, bólido. 3. (fig.) meteoro.
meteoric [ˌmitɪˈɔrɪk, -ˈɑr-, B -ˈɔr-] *a.* 1. meteórico, meteorológico. 2. (fig.) meteórico, rápido, deslumbrador.
meteorism [ˈmitɪəˌrɪzəm] *s.* (med.) meteorismo.
meteorite [-ˌraɪt] *s.* aerolito, meteorito; piedra meteórica.
meteoritic [ˌmitɪəˈrɪtɪk] *a.* meteorítico.
meteorograph [-ˈɔrəˌgræf, B -ˌgrɑf] *s.* meteorógrafo.
meteoroid [ˈmitɪəˌrɔɪd] *s.* meteorito, aerolito, bólido.
meteorologic [ˌmitɪərəˈlɑdʒɪk, B -ˈlɔdʒ-] **meteorological** [-ɪkəl] *s.* meteorológico.
meteorologist [-əˈrɑlədʒəst, B -ˈrɔl-] *s.* meteorólogo, meteorologista.
meteorology [-dʒɪ] *s.* meteorología.
meteor shower, meteoric shower, lluvia meteórica (de estrellas fugaces).
meter, (pr. G.B.) **metre** [ˈmitər, B -ə] *s.* 1. metro (unidad de medida). 2. medidor, contador (de gas, agua, velocidad, tiempo, etc.). 3. (poét.) metro. 4. (mús.) compás, tiempo. —*v.t.* 1. medir con medidor. 2. franquear con máquina (carta, etc.). 3. (mec.) dosificar.
meterage [-ərɪdʒ] *s.* metraje.
metering pump, (lab.) bomba contadora.
meter maid, policía femenina que controla el cumplimiento de los reglamentos de estacionamiento para el tránsito urbano.
methacrylate [ˌmɛθˈækrəˌleɪt] *s.* (quím.) metacrilato.
methacryllic acid [ˌmɛθəˈkrɪlɪk-] (quím.) ácido metacrílico.
methadone [ˈmɛθəˌdoʊn] **methadon** [-ˌdɑn, B -ˌdɔn] *s.* (farm.) metadona.
methane [ˈmɛθeɪn, B ˈmiθ-] *s.* (quím.) metano.
methanol [ˈmɛθəˌnɔl] *s.* (quím.) metanol, alcohol metílico.
metheglin [məˈθɛglən, B mɛ-] *s.* (hist.) aguamiel, hidromiel.
methemoglobin [mɛtˈhiməˌgloʊbən] *s.* (bioquím.) metahemoglobina.
methinks [mɪˈθɪŋks] *v.i.* (*pret.* METHOUGHT [-ˈθɔt]) (ant.) me parece.
methionine [məˈθaɪəˌnin] *s.* (bioquím.) metionina.
method [ˈmɛθəd] *s.* método; modo, medio, procedimiento, sistemática; vía; **there's m. in his (her,** etc.) **madness,** no es tan loco como parece.
methodic [məˈθɑdɪk, B -ˈθɔd-] **methodical** [-ɪkəl] *a.* metódico, sistemático, ordenado, regular.
methodically [-ɪkəlɪ] *adv.* metódicamente, sistemáticamente.
methodicalness [-kəlnəs] *s.* proceder metódico, naturaleza metódica.
methodics [-ɪks] *s. pl.* metodología.
Methodism [ˈmɛθəˌdɪzəm] *s.* 1. metodismo, doctrina de una secta protestante. 2. **m.,** adherencia excesiva al procedimiento sistemático.
Methodist [-dəst] *s., a.* metodista.
Methodistic [ˌmɛθəˈdɪstɪk] *a.* metodista.
methodize [ˈmɛθəˌdaɪz] *v.t.* metodizar, ordenar; sistematizar.
methodological [ˌmɛθədəˈlɑdʒɪkəl, B -ˈlɔdʒ-] *a.* metodológico.
methodology [-ˈdɑlədʒɪ, B -ˈdɔl-] *s.* metodología.
methought [mɪˈθɔt] *pret. de* **methinks.**
methoxychlor [məˈθɑksɪˌklɔr, B -ˈθɔksɪklɔ] *s.* (quím.) metoxiclor.
Methuselah [məˈθuzələ, B -ˈθju-] *s.* (bíbl.) Matusalén, patriarca hebreo.
methyl [ˈmɛθəl] *s.* (quím.) metilo.
methylal [-əˌlæl] *s.* (quím.) metilal.
methyl alcohol, (quím.) alcohol metílico.
methylamine [ˌmɛθələˈmin, B ˈmɛθɪləˌmaɪn] *s.* (quím.) metilamina.
methylate [ˈmɛθəˌleɪt] *s.* (quím.) metilato. —*v.t.* mezclar con metanol, desnaturalizar (alcohol).
methylated spirit [-əd-] (quím.) alcohol desnaturalizado, mezcla de alcoholes etílico y metílico.
methyl bromide, (quím.) bromuro de metilo.
methyl chloride, (quím.) cloruro de metilo (anestésico local).
methylene [ˈmɛθəˌlin] *s.* (quím.) metileno.
methylene blue, (quím.) azul de metileno.
methylic [məˈθɪlɪk, B mɛ-] *a.* (quím.) metílico.
meticulosity [məˌtɪkjəˈlɑsətɪ, B -ˈlɔs-] *s.* meticulosidad, minuciosidad; escrupulosidad, delicadeza excesiva.
meticulous [məˈtɪkjələs] *a.* meticuloso, minucioso, escrupuloso.
meticulously [-lɪ] *adv.* meticulosamente, minuciosamente; escrupulosamente.
meticulously clean, exquisitamente limpio.
métier [meɪˈtjeɪ, B ˈmeɪtjeɪ] *s.* oficio, profesión, ocupación.
métis [meɪˈtis] *s.* (*pl.* METIS) mestizo (esp. de indio y blanco franco-canadiense).
metol [ˈmiˌtɔl, B ˈmɛtɔl] *s.* (quím., foto.) metol.
metonic cycle [məˈtɑnɪk-, B ˌmɛˈtɔn-] (astr.) ciclo metónico.
metonym [ˈmɛtənɪm] *s.* (ret.) palabra usada en metonimia.
metonymic [ˌmɛtəˈnɪmɪk] **metonymical** [-ɪkəl] *a.* (ret.) metonímico.
metonymy [məˈtɑnəmɪ, B -ˈtɔn-] *s.* (ret.) metonimia.
metope [ˈmɛtoʊp] *s.* (arq.) métopa, metopa.
metopic [məˈtɑpɪk, B -ˈtɔp-] *a.* (anat.) metópico.
metopon (hydrochloride) [ˈmɛtəˌpɑn-, B -ˌpɔn-] metopon, droga narcótica derivada de la morfina y más potente que ésta.
metoposcopy [ˌmɛtəˈpɑskəpɪ, B -ˈpɔs-] *s.* metoposcopia.
metralgia [mɪˈtrældʒɪə] *s.* (med.) metralgia.
metre, (pr. G.B.) *var. de* **meter.**
metric [ˈmɛtrɪk] **metrical** [-trɪkəl] *a.* métrico.
metrically [-trɪkəlɪ] *adv.* métricamente.
metric horsepower, (mec.) caballo métrico.
metrician [mɛˈtrɪʃən] *s.* metrista, metrificador, versificador.
metrics [ˈmɛtrɪks] *s. pl.* (*sing. o pl. en const.*) (poét.) métrica.
metric system, sistema métrico.
metric ton, tonelada métrica (1.000 kgs).
metrifier [ˈmɛtrəˌfaɪər, B -ə] *s.* metrista, metrificador, versificador.
metrify [-ˌfaɪ] *v.t.* (*pret., p.p.* METRIFIED; *p.pr.* METRIFYING) metrificar, versificar.
metrist [-trəst] *s.* metrista, metrificador, versificador.
metritis [məˈtraɪtəs] *s.* (med.) metritis.
metro [ˈmɛtroʊ] *s.* metro (metropolitano), ferrocarril subterráneo (esp. en París y Madrid).
metrological [ˌmɛtrəˈlɑdʒɪkəl, B -ˈlɔdʒ-] *a.* metrológico.
metrologically [-kəlɪ] *adv.* metrológicamente.
metrology [mɛˈtrɑlədʒɪ, B mɪˈtrɔl-] *s.* metrología.
metronome [ˈmɛtrəˌnoʊm] *s.* (mús.) metrónomo.
metronomic [ˌmɛtrəˈnɑmɪk, B -ˈnɔm-] *a.* (mús.) metronómico.
metronymic [ˌmitrəˈnɪmɪk] *s.* appellido materno. —*a.* relativo al apellido materno.
metropolis [məˈtrɑpələs, B -ˈtrɔp-] *s.* (*pl.* METROPOLISES) metrópoli; (relig.) metrópoli.
metropolitan [ˌmɛtrəˈpɑlətən, B -ˈpɔl-] *a.* metropolitano. —*s.* 1. (relig.) metropolitano. 2. habitante de una metrópoli.
metrorrhagia [ˌmitrəˈreɪdʒɪə] *s.* (med.) metrorragia.
mettle [ˈmɛtəl] *s.* temple, fortaleza, brío, coraje, ardor, valor; **to be on one's m.,** estar lleno de bríos; estar en su elemento; **to prove one's m.,** dar pruebas de su valor.
mettled [ˈmɛtəld] *a.* lleno de ardor o de brío.
mettlesome [ˈmɛtəlsəm] *a.* brioso, vivo, fogoso, valiente.
mettlesomely [-lɪ] *adv.* vivamente, con bríos.
mettlesomeness [-nəs] *s.* brío, vivacidad.
MEV *abrev. de* **million electron volts,** millón de electronvoltios, megaelectronvoltio (MeV.).
mew [mju] *s.* 1. escondite, lugar de reclusión; guarida. 2. (*pl.*) (G.B.) fila de establos, fila de cocheras; callejón, callejuela. 3. (ant.) jaula para halcones. —*v.t.* 1. encerrar o guardar (a un halcón) en una jaula (esp. durante la muda). 2. encerrar, guardar, recluir (en jaula). —*v.i.* mudar la pluma, desplumarse (el halcón).

mew, *v.t.* maullar, miar, mayar (el gato); graznar (la gaviota). — s. 1. maullido (del gato). 2. (orn.) variedad de gaviota.

mewl [mjul] *v.i.* lloriquear, gimotear, plañir. —*s.* lloriqueo, gimoteo, plañido.

Mex. *abrev. de* **Mexico,** México, **Mexican,** mexicano.

Mexican ['mɛksɪkən] *s.* 1. mexicano. 2. (S.E. de E.U.) mestizo de sangre española e india. —*a.* mexicano.

Mexican hairless dog, perro chihuahua, originario de México, de pelaje muy corto.

Mexicanism [-kəˌnɪzəm] *s.* mexicanismo; costumbre o giro típico de México o su cultura popular.

Mexican tea, (bot.) té de México, té de España, té de Europa, hierba de Santa María del Brasil, hierba hormiguera, pasote, pazote.

Mexico ['mɛksɪˌkoʊ] *s.* México.

mezereon [mə'zɪrɪən, B -'zɪər-] *s.* (bot.) laureola hembra, mezereón.

mezzanine ['mɛzəˌnin, B 'mɛtsə-] *s.* entresuelo, entrepiso; primer balcón de butacas (en algunos teatros).

mezzo-relievo ['mɛtˌsoʊrɪ'livoʊ, B 'mɛdzoʊrɪl'jeɪ-] *s.* (*pl.* MEZZO-RELIEVOS) (arte) medio relieve.

mezzo-soprano [-sə'prænˌoʊ, -'prɑn-, B -'prɑn-] *s.* (*pl.* MEZZO-SOPRANOS) (mús.) mezzo soprano, contralto.

mezzotint [-ˌtɪnt] *s.* (arte) media tinta, grabado a buril.

mg *abrev. de* **miligram,** miligramo (mg.).

MG *abrev. de* **machine gun,** ametralladora.

Mg *símb. de* **magnesium,** magnesio (Mg).

mho [moʊ] *s.* (elec., fís.) mho (unidad de conductancia, recíproca de ohm).

mi [mi] *s.* (mús.) mi, tercera nota de la escala.

M.I. *abrev. de* **Military Intelligence,** Inteligencia Militar.

miaou, miaow, *var. de* **meow.**

miasma [maɪ'æzmə, mɪ-] *s.* (*pl.* MIASMATA [-mətə] o MIASMAS) miasma, efluvio mefítico, emanación nociva.

miasmal [-məl] **miasmic** [-mɪk] **miasmatic** [ˌmaɪəz'mætɪk] *a.* miasmático.

mib [mɪb] *s.* (dial.) canica; (*pl.*) juego de canicas.

mica ['maɪkə] *s.* (min.) mica.

micaceous [maɪ'keɪʃəs] *a.* (min.) micáceo.

mica schist, (min.) micacita, micasquisto.

Micawber [mɪ'kɔbər, B -ə] *s.* persona optimista (por un personaje de Dickens llamado así).

mice [maɪs] *pl. de* **mouse.**

micelle [mɪ'sɛl] *s.* (biol., quím.) micela.

Mich. *abrev. de* **Michigan,** Michigan (E.U.).

Michaelmas ['mɪkəlməs] *s.* (G.B.) fiesta de San Miguel, que se celebra el veintinueve de septiembre.

Michaelmas daisy, (bot.) áster silvestre (esp. uno que florece hacia la fiesta de San Miguel).

Michaelmastide [-ˌtaɪd] *s.* sanmiguelada.

miche [mɪtʃ] *v.i.* (dial.) remolonear; escabullirse; hacer novillos, hacer rabona.

Michelangelo [ˌmaɪkəl'ændʒəloʊ] *s.* Miguel Ángel, escultor, arquitecto, poeta y pintor italiano del Renacimiento.

Michigan ['mɪʃɪgən] *s.* Michigan, estado de los E.U.

mick [mɪk] *s.* (jer., E.U., despec.) inmigrante irlandés; irlandés.

Mickey Finn ['mɪkɪ'fɪn] (jer., E.U.) bebida alcohólica a la que se ha añadido subrepticiamente alguna droga.

Mickey Mouse, 1. el ratón Mickey, nombre de un dibujo animado creado por Walt Disney. —*a.* simple, fácil; infantil.

mickle ['mɪkəl] *s.* (ant., esco.) grande; mucho. —*adv.* mucho.

micro ['maɪkroʊ] *a.* 1. microscópico. 2. excesivamente pequeño. 3. agrandado o amplificado (por microscopio o micrófono). —*s.* millonésima parte de una unidad específica.

microanalysis [ˌmaɪˌkroʊə'næləsəs] *s.* (quím.) microanálisis.

microbarograph [-'bærəˌgræf, B -ˌgrɑf] *s.* (fís.) microbarógrafo.

microbe ['maɪˌkroub] *s.* microbio, microorganismo, germen.

microbial [maɪ'kroʊbɪəl] **microbic** [-bɪk] *a.* micróbico.

microbicidal [ˌmaɪkroʊbə'saɪdəl] *a.* microbicida, bactericida.

microbicide [maɪ'kroʊbəˌsaɪd] *s.* microbicida, bactericida.

microbiological [ˌmaɪkroʊˌbaɪə'lɑdʒɪkəl, B -'lɔdʒ-] **microbiologic** [-ɪk] *s.* microbiológico.

microbiologist [-baɪ'ɑlədʒəst, B -'ɔl-] *s.* microbiólogo.

microbiology [-dʒɪ] *s.* microbiología.

microbus ['maɪkrəˌbʌs] *s.* microbús.

microcephalic [-sə'fælɪk, B -kə-] **microcephalous** [-'sɛfələs, B -'kɛ-] *a.* microcéfalo, microcefálico.

microcephaly [-'sɛfəlɪ] *s.* microcefalia.

microchemistry [-'kɛməstrɪ] *s.* microquímica.

microchip [-tʃɪp] *s.* chip, microchip, pastilla de silicio.

microclimate ['maɪkroʊˌklaɪmət] *s.* (biol.) microclima.

microclimatology [ˌmaɪkroʊˌklaɪmə'tɑlədʒɪ, B -'tɔlə-] *s.* (*pl.* MICROCLIMATOLOGIES) microclimatología.

microline ['maɪkroʊˌklaɪn] *s.* (min.) microclino.

micrococcus [ˌmaɪkroʊ'kɑkəs, B -'kɔk-] *s.* (*pl.* MICROCOCCI [-'kɑksaɪ, B -'kɔk-]) (bact.) micrococo.

microcomputer [-kəmˌpjutər] *s.* microordenador, microcomputadora.

microcopy ['maɪkroʊˌkɑpɪ, B -ˌkɔpɪ] *s.* (*pl.* MICROCOPIES) (foto.) microcopia. —*v.t.* reproducir en microcopia.

microcosm ['maɪkrəˌkɑzəm, B -ˌkɔz-] *s.* microcosmo.

microcosmic [ˌmaɪkrə'kɑzmɪk, B -'kɔz-] *a.* microcósmico.

microcosmic salt, (quím.) sal microcósmica.

microcrystalline [-kroʊ'krɪstələn, B -ˌlaɪn] *a.* (geol.) microcristalino.

microcurie ['maɪkroʊˌkjʊrɪ, B -ˌkjʊərɪ] *s.* (fís.) microcurie.

microcyte ['maɪkrəˌsaɪt] *s.* (med.) microcito.

microdissection [ˌmaɪkroʊdɪ'sɛkʃən] *s.* (biol.) microdisección.

microdot [-dɑt] *s.* micropunto.

microelectronics [-ɪlɛk'trɑnɪks] *s.* microelectrónica.

microfarad [-'færˌæd] *s.* (elec.) microfaradio.

microfiche [-fiʃ] *s.* microficha.

microfilaria [ˌmaɪkroʊfə'lærɪə] *s.* (zool.) microfilaria.

microfilm ['maɪkrəˌfɪlm] *s.* microfilm, micropelícula. —*v.t., v.i.* microfilmar.

microgamete [ˌmaɪkroʊgə'mit, -'gæmˌit] *s.* (biol.) microgameto.

microgram ['maɪkrəˌgræm] *s.* (fís.) microgramo.

micrograph [-ˌgræf, B -ˌgrɑf] *s.* micrógrafo.

micrographic [ˌmaɪkrə'græfɪk] *a.* micrográfico.

micrography [maɪ'krɑgrəfɪ, B -'krɔg-] *s.* micrografia.

microgroove ['maɪkroʊˌgruv] *s.* microsurco.

microhardness [-'hɑrdnes, B -'hɑd-] *s.* (fís.) microdureza.

microhm ['maɪkroʊm] *s.* (elec.) microhmio.

microlight [-'laɪt] *s.* aeroligero.

microlite ['maɪkrəˌlaɪt] *s.* (geol.) microlito.

microlitic [ˌmaɪkrə'lɪtɪk] *a.* microlítico.

micromere ['maɪkroʊˌmɪr, B -ˌmɪə] *s.* (biol.) micrómera, micrómero.

micrometer [maɪ'krɑmətər, B -krɔmɪtə] *s.* (fís.) micrómetro.

micrometer caliper, (mec.) compás de calibre micrométrico.

micrometer screw, tornillo micrométrico, tornillo de paso muy fino.

micrometrical [ˌmaɪkroʊ'mɛtrɪkəl] *a.* micrométrico.

micrometry [maɪ'krɑmətrɪ, B -'krɔmɛ-] *s.* micrometría.

micromicron [ˌmaɪkroʊ'maɪkrɑn, B -krɔn] *s.* micromicrón, milimicrón.

micromillimeter [-'mɪləˌmitər, B -ə] *s.* micromilímetro.

micromotion ['maɪkrəˌmoʊʃən] *s.* movimiento de microorganismos u objetos pequeños, amplificado por el microscopio.

micron ['maɪkrɑn, B -krɔn] *s.* (*pl.* MICRONS o MICRA) micrón, micra (milésimo de milímetro).

Micronesian [ˌmaɪkrə'niʒən, -ʃən] *a., s.* micronesio, habitante y lenguaje de Micronesia, Oceanía.

micronucleus [-kroʊ'nuklɪəs, B -'nju-] *s.* (biol.) micronúcleo.

microorganism [-'ɔrgəˌnɪzəm, B -'ɔgə-] *s.* (biol.) microorganismo.

micropaleontology [-ˌpeɪlɪˌɑn'tɑlədʒɪ, B -ˌɔn'tɔl-] *s.* micropaleontología.

microparasite [-'pærəˌsaɪt] *s.* microparásito.

microphage ['maɪkrəˌfeɪdʒ] *s.* (fisiol.) micrófago.

microphone ['maɪkrəˌfoʊn] *s.* micrófono.

microphonic [ˌmaɪkrə'fɑnɪk, B -'fɔn-] *a.* microfónico.

microphonics [-ɪks] *s. pl.* (rad., electrón.) efectos microfónicos.

microphotograph [-'foʊtəˌgræf, B -ˌgrɑf] *s.* microfotografía.

microphotographic [-ˌfoʊtə'græfɪk] *a.* microfotográfico.

microphotography [-fə'tɑgrəfɪ, B -'tɔg-] *s.* microfotografía.

microphysics [-'fɪzɪks] *s. pl.* (*sing. en const.*) microfísica.

microphyte ['maɪkrəˌfaɪt] *s.* (bot.) micrófito.

microphytic [ˌmaɪkrə'fɪtɪk] *a.* microfítico.

microprint ['maɪkroʊˌprɪnt] *s.* impresión o reproducción de una microfotografía.

microprocessor [-'prɑsɛsər] *s.* microprocesador.

micropylar [ˌmaɪkrə'paɪlər, B -lə] *s.* (bot., zool.) micropilar.

micropyle ['maɪkrəˌpaɪl] *s.* (bot., zool.) micrópilo.

micropyrometer [ˌmaɪkroʊpaɪ'rɑmətər, B -'rɔmɪtə] *s.* (fís.) micropirómetro.

microradiograph [-'reɪdɪəˌgræf, B -ˌgrɑf] *s.* microrradiografía.

microreader ['maɪkroʊˌridər, B -ə] *s.* microlector, aparato amplificador de microrradiografías (para su lectura).

microscope ['maɪkrəˌskoʊp] *s.* microscopio.

microscopic [ˌmaɪkrə'skɑpɪk, B -'skɔp-] **microscopical** [-ɪkəl] *a.* microscópico.

microscopy [maɪ'krɑskəpɪ, B -'krɔs-] *s.* microscopía, microscopia.

microsecond [ˌmaɪkroʊˈsɛkənd] *s.* microsegundo.
microseism [ˈmaɪkrəˌsaɪzəm] *s.* (geol.) microsismo.
microseismic [ˌmaɪkrəˈsaɪzmɪk] **microseismical** [-mɪkəl] *a.* (geol.) microsísmico.
microseismograph [-məˌgræf, B -grɑf] *s.* microsismógrafo.
microsome [ˈmaɪkrəˌsoʊm] *s.* (biol.) microsoma.
microsporangium [ˌmaɪkroʊspəˈrændʒɪəm] *s.* (*pl.* MICROSPORANGIA [-ə]) (bot.) microsporangio.
microspore [ˈmaɪkrəˌspɔr, B -spɔ] *s.* (bot.) microspora.
microsporophyll [ˌmaɪkrəˈspɔrəfɪl] *s.* (bot.) microsporófilo.
microstomatous [-ˈstɑmətəs, B -ˈstɔm-] **microstomous** [maɪˈkrɑstəməs, B -ˈkrɔs-] *a.* micróstomo.
microstructure [ˈmaɪkroʊˌstrʌktʃər, B -tʃə] *s.* microestructura.
microsurgery [-ˈsɜrdʒəri] *s.* microcirugía.
microtome [-ˌtoʊm] *s.* (biol.) micrótomo.
microtomy [maɪˈkrɑtəmɪ, B -ˈkrɔt-] *s.* (*pl.* MICROTOMIES) microtomía.
microvolt [ˈmaɪkrəˌvoʊlt] *s.* (elec., rad.) microvoltio.
microwatt [-ˌwɑt, B -ˌwɔt] *s.* (elec.) microvatio.
microwave [-ˌweɪv] *s.* (electrón.) microonda. —*v.t.* calentar en horno de microondas; cocinar en horno de microondas.
microwave oven, horno de microondas.
microzoon [ˌmaɪkrəˈzoʊən] *s.* (*pl.* MICROZOA [-ˈzoʊə]) (zool.) microzoario.
micturate [ˈmɪktʃəˌreɪt, B -tjʊ-] *v.i.* orinar, mear.
micturition [ˌmɪktʃəˈrɪʃən, B -tju-] *s.* micturición, micción.
mid [mɪd] *a.* (*sin comp.; super.* MIDMOST [ˈmɪd,-moʊst]) 1. pleno, medio, ej., *in m. winter,* en pleno invierno, *in m. afternoon,* a media tarde, *in m. career,* a media carrera, *in m. ocean,* en medio del océano. 2. mediados (*ú. en palabras compuestas*), ej., *from m.-May to m.-July,* de mediados de mayo a mediados de julio. 3. (fon.) intermedio, medial (díc. de la vocal). —*s.* (ant.) medio. —*prep.* (poét.) entre, en medio de.
midair [ˈmɪdˈɛr, B -ˈɛə] *s.* punto o región en medio del aire, ej., *floating in midair,* flotando en el aire.
Midas [ˈmaɪdəs] *s.* (mitol.) Midas, rey que tornaba en oro todo lo que tocaba.
midbrain [ˈmɪdˌbreɪn] *s.* cerebro medio, mesocéfalo, mesencéfalo.
midchannel [-ˌtʃænəl] *s.* medio del estrecho o canal.
midcontinent [-ˌkɑntənənt, B -ˌkɔn-] *s.* medio del continente.
midcourse [-ˌkɔrs, B -kɔs] *s.* (astronáut.) parte del vuelo de un proyectil durante la cual se efectúan maniobras de corrección.
midday [-ˌdeɪ] *s.* mediodía. —*a.* del mediodía.
midden [ˌmɪdən] *s.* 1. estercolero. 2. basural, conchal, especialmente de origen prehistórico.
middle [ˈmɪdəl] *a.* 1. medio. 2. del medio, intermedio, mediano. 3. moderado, conciliatorio, ej., *m. course, m. way,* posición o curso moderado o conciliatorio. 4. de en medio, ej., *he chose the m. card,* escogió el naipe de en medio. —*s.* 1. medio, mitad, centro, punto medio. 2. cintura, talle. 3. **in the m. of,** a mediados de (la semana, del mes, etc.); en medio de, ej., *he stopped in the m. of his speech,* se detuvo en medio de su discurso, *the car stopped in the m. of the road,* el coche se detuvo en medio del camino. —*v.t., v.i.* 1 centrar, colocar en el centro. 2. (mar.) doblar(se) por la mitad; doblar(se) en dos. 3. (fútbol) centrar (la bola); ejecutar un centro.
middle age, edad madura.
middle-aged [ˌmɪdəlˈeɪdʒd] *a.* de edad madura, característico de la edad madura.
Middle Ages, Edad Media, medioevo.
Middle America, 1. México y la América Central. 2. (E.U.) región central de EE. UU. 3. (E.U.) clase media estadounidense.
middle bracket, de clase media (u. gen. con respecto a la situación socio-económica de una persona).
middle breaker, m. buster, (agr.) arado aporcador, arado de doble vertedera.
middlebrow [ˈmɪdəlˌbraʊ] *s., a.* (persona) de cultura mediocre.
middle C, (mús.) do mayor.
middle class, clase media; burguesía.
middle-class [ˈmɪdəlˈklæs, B -ˈklɑs] *a.* de la clase media, aburguesado, burgués.
middle distance, 1. segundo plano. 2. (dep.) (distancia de) medio fondo.
middle ear, (anat.) oído medio.
Middle East, Oriente Medio.
Middle Eastern, del Oriente Medio.
Middle English, (filol.) inglés hablado entre los siglos XII y XVI.
middle finger, dedo cordial, dedo del corazón.
middle ground, (*point of view*) punto de vista intermedio; (arte.) segundo término, segundo plano.
middle heavyweight, (boxeador de) peso medio pesado.
middleman [ˈmɪdəlˌmæn] *s.* (com.) intermediario, agente corredor.
middle management, gerencia intermedia, mandos medios, cuadros medios.
middle manager, mando intermedio.
middle name, segundo nombre.
middlemost [-ˌmoʊst] *a.* del medio; en el medio o cerca del centro.
middle-of-the-road [-əvðəˈroʊd] *a.* 1. moderado (candidato, política, gobierno, etc.). 2. que no está ni de un lado ni de otro. 3. indeciso, vacilante.
middle ordinate, (geom.) flecha, ordenada media, sagita.
middle school, (E.U.) escuela intermedia en la que se estudia desde el grado quinto al octavo (*niños de 12 a 14 años*).
middle term, término medio, término común.
middle watch, (mar.) guardia de media.
middleweight [-ˌweɪt] *s.* (boxeador de) peso medio o mediano.
Middle West, (E.U.) (los) estados centrales; el oeste medio.
middling [ˈmɪdlɪŋ] *a.* mediano, regular, mediocre, así así. —*adv.* moderadamente, bastante, ej., *m. good,* bastante bueno.
middlings [-lɪŋz] *s. pl.* 1. acemite, afrecho. 2. productos de calidad o precio medio.
middy [ˈmɪdɪ] *s.* (*pl.* MIDDIES) (fam.) guardiamarina.
middy blouse, blusa marinera.
midge [mɪdʒ] *s.* 1. (ento.) (especie de) jején. 2. (fam.) persona muy pequeña.
midget [ˈmɪdʒət] *s.* 1. persona sumamente baja pero de proporciones normales. 2. enano, enanito, gorgojo (Amer.). 3. miniatura, objeto pequeño. —*a.* diminuto, pequeñísimo.
midi [ˈmɪdɪ] *s.* midi, estilo de prenda de vestir que cae hasta media pierna.
Midianite [ˈmɪdɪəˌnaɪt] *s.* (bíbl.) medianita.
midinette [ˌmɪdəˈnɛt] *s.* joven parisina (esp. la que trabaja en una tienda de modas).
midiron [ˈmɪdˌaɪrn, B -aɪən] *s.* (golf) palo para tiros de distancia media.
midland [-lənd] *s.* región central o interior (de un país); **the Midlands,** región central de Inglaterra.
midlife [-ˈlaɪf] *s.* madurez; **in m.,** en la madurez.
midlife crisis, crisis de los 40.
midline [-ˌlaɪn] *s.* línea media, línea del medio.
midmost [-ˌmoʊst] *a.* 1. en el medio, en el mismo medio; en el centro, el más cercano al centro. 2. íntimo, recóndito. —*adv.* centralmente, en el medio.
midnight [-ˌnaɪt] *s.* medianoche; **to burn the m. oil,** (fig.) quemarse las pestañas, trabajar o estudiar hasta muy tarde en la noche. —*a.* de medianoche.
midnight mass, (relig.) misa del gallo.
midnight sun, sol de medianoche (en las regiones árticas o antárticas).
midnoon [ˈmɪdˈnun] *s.* (raro) mediodía.
midpoint [-ˌpɔɪnt] *s.* punto céntrico.
midrash [ˈmɪdˌrɑʃ] *s.* (*pl.* MIDRASHIM [mɪdˈrɑʃəm]) (relig.) midrash (exposición o comentario de la Biblia en la religión judía).
midrib [ˈmɪdˌrɪb] *s.* (bot.) nervadura central (de la hoja).
midriff [-rɪf] *s.* 1. diafragma (del cuerpo). 2. parte del vestido (femenino) que entalla el torso. 3. traje femenino de dos piezas que deja descubierta parte del torso a la altura del diafragma.
midsection [-ˌsɛkʃən] *s.* parte central, esp. región abdominal (del cuerpo).
midship [-ˌʃɪp] *a.* del medio del barco, en el medio del barco.
midship frame, (mar.) cuaderna maestra.
midshipman [-ˌʃɪpmən] *s.* (mar.) guardia marina.
midships [-ˌʃɪps] *adv.* en medio del barco.
midst [mɪdst] *s.* medio, centro; **in our (your) m.,** entre nosotros (ustedes); **in the m. of,** en medio de; **in the m. of a forest,** en el medio de un bosque; **in the m. of work,** en pleno trabajo. —*prep.* entre.
midsummer [ˈmɪdˈsʌmər, B -ə] *s.* pleno verano; solsticio de verano.
midsummer day, 24 de junio (día de San Juan).
midsummer madness, locura de atar.
midterm [ˈmɪdˌtɜrm, B -ˌtɜm] *s.* 1. tiempo en medio de un período (universitario o político). 2. examen que se rinde a mediados de un período académico, examen parcial. —*a.* en la mitad del período.
midway [-ˌweɪ] *s.* 1. avenida central (de una feria o exposición). 2. (ant.) término medio; posición intermedia. —*adv.* a medio camino, intermedio. —*a.* situado a mitad del camino; **m. between,** equidistante de.
midweek [-ˌwik] *s.* 1. medio de la semana. 2. **M.,** (relig.) mitad de la semana entre los cuáqueros. —*a.* perteneciente al medio de la semana.
midweekly [-ˌwiklɪ] *a., adv.* a mediados de cada semana.
Midwest [ˌmɪdˈwɛst] *s.* (E.U.) la región del oeste medio; los estados centrales.
midwife [ˈmɪdˌwaɪf] *s.* (*pl.* MIDWIFES o -WIVES) partera, comadrona, faculta (Ven.).
midwifery [ˈmɪdˌwaɪfərɪ, B -wɪfərɪ] *s.* obstetricia, partería.
midwinter [-ˈwɪntər, B -tə] *s.* pleno invierno; solsticio de invierno; mitad del invierno.
midyear [-ˌjɪər, B -ˌjɜ] *a.* semestral. —*s.* 1. mediados del año (calendario o académico). 2. (fam.) examen semestral; (*pl.*) período de exámenes semestrales; parciales.

mien [min] *s.* 1. aire, porte, cara, semblante. 2. aspecto, apariencia.
miff [mɪf] *s.* (fam.) riña, desavenencia; disgusto, malhumor. —*v.t.* ofender, disgustar, enfadar.
miffy ['mɪfɪ] *a.* susceptible, irritable, quisquilloso.
mig, migg [mɪg] *s.* canica, bolita.
Mig, *s.* avión de guerra de fabricación soviética.
might [maɪt] *v. aux.* (*pret. de* **may**) 1. ser posible que, tener posibilidad, ej., *he m. find out the secret,* es posible que él descubra el secreto; *you m. come earlier,* podrían venir más temprano. 2. (con inversión) ojalá, ej., *m. he live a hundred years,* ojalá viva cien años.
might, *s.* poderío, poder, fuerza; **with all one's m.,** con todas sus fuerzas; **with m. and main,** a más no poder.
mightily ['maɪtəlɪ] *adv.* 1. poderosamente. 2. extremadamente.
mightiness [-ɪnəs] *s.* poder, fuerza, poderío.
mighty ['maɪtɪ] *a.* (MIGHTIER; MIGHTIEST) 1. poderoso. 2. potente, fuerte, vigoroso. 3. eficaz. 4. extraordinario, maravilloso. —*adv.* (fam.) muy, sumamente.
mignon ['mɪnˌjɑn, B 'minjɔn] *a.* (fr.) delicado, gracioso; primoroso, menudo.
mignonette [ˌmɪnjə'nɛt] *s.* (bot.) reseda.
migraine ['maɪˌgreɪn, B 'mi-] *s.* (fr., med.) hemicránea, migraña, jaqueca, dolor de cabeza.
migrant ['maɪgrənt] *a.* migratorio. —*s.* 1. trabajador ambulante, labrador o peón migratorio (por cosecha). 2. migrante, animal migratorio.
migrate ['maɪˌgreɪt, B maɪ'greɪt] *v.i.* migrar, emigrar, transplantarse (de una región o país a otro).
migration [maɪ'greɪʃən] *s.* 1. migración o emigración. 2. (quím.) migración (de átomos o de iones).
migratory ['maɪgrəˌtɔrɪ, B -tərɪ] *a.* 1. migratorio. 2. nómada, errante, vagabundo.
mikado [mə'kɑdoʊ] *s.* (*pl.* MIKADOS) micado, título que se daba al emperador del Japón.
mike [maɪk] *s.* (jer.) micrófono, micro.
Mike, *s.* 1. Miguelito. 2. **for the love of M.,** (fam.) por amor de Dios.
mil [mɪl] *s.* 1. milipulgada, milésima de pulgada. 2. (mil.) mil (unidad angular equivalente a 1/6400 de 360).
milady [mɪ'leɪdɪ] *s.* (*pl.* MILADIES) 1. miladi (título de respeto otorgado a damas nobles inglesas). 2. mujer elegante.
Milan [mə'læn] *s.* Milán, ciudad industrial del norte de Italia.
Milanese [ˌmɪlə'niz] *a.* milanés. —*s.* (*pl.* MILANESE) 1. milanés, milanesa, natural de Milán. 2. dialecto milanés.
milch [mɪltʃ] *a.* lechero, lactífero, que da leche (animal doméstico), ej., *milch cow,* vaca lechera.
mild [maɪld] *a.* 1. apacible, dulce, blando, manso (carácter, naturaleza, persona, etc.). 2. suave, benigno, templado (clima, viento, etc.). 3. suave (cigarrillo, cerveza, queso, etc.); dulce, suave (acero). 4. leve, ligero (castigo, reproche, etc.).
milden ['maɪldən] *v.t., v.i.* suavizar(se), ablandar(se).
mildew ['mɪlˌdu, B -dju] *s.* 1. moho. 2. (agr.) mildeu, mildiú (de la vid). —*v.t., v.i.* enmohecer(se); estar atacado de mildiú.
mildewy [-ɪ] *a.* 1. mohoso. 2. (agr.) atacado de mildiú.
mildly ['maɪldlɪ] *adv.* 1. apaciblemente, suavemente, mansamente. 2. ligeramente.
mildness [-nəs] *s.* 1. suavidad, mansedumbre. 2. benignidad, indulgencia. 3. blandura. 4. ligereza, levedad.
mile [maɪl] *s.* milla.
mileage ['maɪlɪdʒ] *s.* 1. distancia en millas; gastos de viaje (pagados por millas). 2. distancia (recorrida) en millas, recorrido en millas, millaje. 3. (fam.) ventaja, rendimiento, utilidad.
mileage indicator, cuentamillas.
mileage ticket, billete kilométrico.
milepost ['maɪlˌpoʊst] *s.* poste miliar, piedra miliaria; hito, mojón.
miler [-ər, B -ə] *s.* (jer., dep.) corredor de la milla; caballo de carrera entrenado para correr una milla.
Milesian [mɪ'liʒən, B -zjən] *a., s.* milesio, habitante de Mileto, antigua ciudad de Asia Menor.
milestone ['maɪlˌstoʊn] *s.* 1. piedra miliaria, hito, mojón. 2. (fig.) acontecimiento importante; hito, algo que hace época; **to be a m.,** marcar un hito, hacer época.
Miletus [maɪ'litəs] *s.* Mileto, antigua ciudad jónica de Asia Menor.
milfoil ['mɪlˌfɔɪl] *s.* (bot.) milenrama, aquilea, altarreina, hierba meona.
miliaria [ˌmɪlɪ'ɛrɪə] *s.* (med.) erupción miliar.
miliary ['mɪlɪˌɛrɪ, B -ərɪ] *a.* (med.) miliar.
miliary tuberculosis, (med.) tuberculosis miliar.
milieu [mil'jɜ, B 'miljɜ] *s.* (fr.) medio ambiente, mundo circundante, ambiente, atmósfera, medio.
militancy ['mɪlətənsɪ] *s.* militancia, combatividad, belicosidad.
militant [-tənt] *a.* militante, luchador, combativo, agresivo. —*s.* persona militante, que lucha activamente por una causa o una creencia.
militantly [-lɪ] *adv.* activamente, enérgicamente, agresivamente.
militarily [ˌmɪlə'tɛrəlɪ, B 'mɪlɪtər-] *adv.* militarmente, marcialmente.
militarism ['mɪlətərˌɪzəm] *s.* militarismo.
militarist [-əst] *s.* 1. perito militar. 2. militarista.
militaristic [ˌmɪlətə'rɪstɪk] *a.* militarista.
militarization [ˌmɪlətərə'zeɪʃən, B -raɪ-] *s.* militarización.
militarize ['mɪlətəˌraɪz] *v.t.* militarizar.
military ['mɪləˌtɛrɪ, B -tərɪ] *a.* militar, castrense, bélico, marcial, guerrero. —*s.* (gen. **the m.**) los militares, los soldados, las fuerzas armadas.
military academy, academia militar.
military attaché, (dip.) agregado militar.
military coup, golpe militar, cuartelazo (Amer.).
military intelligence, servicio de inteligencia militar.
military law, código militar.
military police, policía militar, servicio de policía o guardas dentro de las fuerzas armadas.
militate ['mɪləˌteɪt] *v.i.* 1. (con *for* o *against*) militar (en favor o en contra); reforzar o debilitar (argumento, prueba). 2. (raro) militar, servir en filas.
militia [mə'lɪʃə] *s.* 1. milicia. 2. ejército compuesto de civiles.
militiaman [-mən] *s.* miliciano.
milk [mɪlk] *s.* leche; **m. for babes,** cuentos de niños; **m. of human kindness,** humanidad, bondad humana. —*v.t.* 1. ordeñar. 2. (fig.) explotar, aprovecharse de, chupar. 3. extraer, succionar. 4. añadir leche a. 5. **m. the ram, m. the bull,** acometer una empresa imposible. —*v.i.* dar leche.
milk adder, (zool.) serpiente de leche.
milk and honey, (fig.) toda clase de placeres; **land of m. a. h.,** (fig.) Israel.
milk-and-water ['mɪlkən'wɔtər, -'wɑt-, B -'wɔtə] *a.* débil, insípido (discurso, sentimiento).
milk bar, salón de refrescos batidos, bar lácteo (Am.).
milk can, bidón de leche.
milk diet, dieta láctea, régimen lácteo.
milk duct, (fisiol., zool.) conducto o ducto galactóforo.
milker ['mɪlkər, B -ə] *s.* 1. ordeñador. 2. vaca lechera.
milk fever, (med.) fiebre láctea, fiebre de leche; (vet.) fiebre de leche, fiebre de los avenales, fiebre del parto.
milk fish, *s.* pez comestible, esp. en Hawai.
milk-float [-ˌfloʊt] *s.* (fam., G.B.) carro de lechero (el que reparte la leche a domicilio).
milk glass, 1. ventosa para extracción de leche; pezonera. 2. vidrio opal (de un blanco opaco usado para hacer objetos decorativos).
milkiness [-ɪnəs] *s.* aspecto lechoso; consistencia lechosa.
milking [-ɪŋ] *s.* acción de ordeñar, ordeño.
milking machine, (agr.) ordeñadora mecánica.
milk leg, (med.) edema puerperal.
milk-livered ['mɪlk'lɪvərd, B -əd] *a.* cobarde, tímido, timorato.
milkmaid [-ˌmeɪd] *s.* ordeñadora, lechera, mujer que ordeña las vacas.
milkman [-ˌmæn, B -mən] *s.* 1. lechero, repartidor de leche a domicilio. 2. ordeñador de vacas.
milk of magnesia, (farm.) leche de magnesia.
milk pail, colodra, ordeñadero.
milk punch, ponche de leche.
milk run, (jer.) misión militar aérea de corta duración y poco peligrosa.
milk shake, batido de leche.
milksop ['mɪlkˌsɑp, B -sɔp] *s.* afeminado, marica.
milk sugar, lactosa, lactina.
milk thistle, (bot.) arzolla, cardo lechero o lechar, cardo de María, cardoncillo.
milk tooth, diente de leche, diente mamón.
milk vetch, (bot.) astrágalo, tragacanto.
milkweed [-ˌwid] *s.* (bot.) asclepiadea, veneetósigo, algodoncillo.
milk-white [-'hwaɪt, -'waɪt] *a.* blanco como la leche.
milkwort [-ˌwɜrt, B -ˌwɜt] *s.* (bot.) polígala, lechera amarga.
milky ['mɪlkɪ] *a.* (MILKIER; MILKIEST) 1. lechoso, lactescente. 2. blando, tierno, suave, dulce; timorato, tímido, insípido. 3. lechero, lácteo. 4. turbio, nublado (líquido).
Milky Way, (astr.) Vía Láctea, Galaxia.
mill [mɪl] *s.* 1. molino. 2. moledora (de café, pimienta, etc.). 3. fábrica de hilados o tejidos; hilandería, tejeduría; taller. 4. prensa para acuñar monedas. 5. prensa, trapiche. 6. (fig.) fábrica (de diplomas, propaganda, etc.). 7. (jer.) pugilato. 8. (esco.) tabaquera, caja de rapé. 9. (mec.) fresadora; laminadora. 10. **to go through the m.,** sufrir mucho en la vida; pasar pruebas severas, saber por experiencia; **to put through the m.,** someter a pruebas severas. —*v.t.* 1. moler, desmenuzar. 2. acuñar y acordonar (monedas). 3. dar puñetazos a, zurrar. 4. batir. 5. abatanar (paño). 6. (mec.) pulir; labrar, fresar; laminar. —*v.i.* 1. boxear, trompearse (Amer.). 2. (gen. con *about* o *around*) arremolinar(se), remolinar(se).
mill, *s.* milésima de dólar (moneda imaginaria).
millboard ['mɪlˌbɔrd, B -bɔd] *s.* cartón de encuadernar.
milldam [-ˌdæm] *s.* 1. represa, embalse, dique (para formar el cubo de un molino). 2. cubo de molino.
milled [mɪld] *a.* acordonado, cerrillado (monedas).

millenarian [ˌmɪlə'nɛrɪən] *a.* milenario. —*s.* milenario, milenarista, defensor del milenarismo.
millenarianism [-ˌɪzəm] *s.* (relig.) milenarismo.
millenary ['mɪləˌnɛrɪ, B mɪ'lɛnərɪ] *a.* milenario. —*s.* 1. milenio, milenario, mil años. 2. milenario, milenarista. 3. milenario, milésimo aniversario.
millennial [mə'lɛnɪəl] *a.* perteneciente o relativo al milenio (esp. el de la profecía cristiana).
millennium [mə'lɛnɪəm] *s.* (*pl.* MILLENNIUMS o MILLENNIA [-nɪə]) 1. milenio, milenario. 2. (fig.) período de felicidad y prosperidad.
millepede, *var. de* **millipede.**
millepore ['mɪləˌpɔr, B -pɔ] *s.* (zool.) milépora.
miller ['mɪlər, B -ə] *s.* 1. molinero, molendero, tahonero. 2. (ento.) mariposa nocturna con el cuerpo cubierto de un polvo blanquecino. 3. (mec.) fresadora.
millerite [-ərˌaɪt] *s.* (min.) milerita.
miller's-thumb ['mɪlərz'θʌm, B -əz-] *s.* (ict.) coto.
millesimal [mə'lɛsəməl] *a., s.* milésimo.
millet ['mɪlət] *s.* 1. (bot.) mijo, millo. 2. (semilla de) mijo.
mill hand, obrero textil; peón de un ingenio o un molino.
milliammeter [ˌmɪlɪ'æmˌitər, B -ɪtə] *s.* (fís.) miliamperímetro.
milliampere [-'æmpɪr, B -pɛə] *s.* (elec.) miliamperio.
milliard ['mɪlˌjɑrd, B -jɑd] *s.* (G.B.) mil millones.
milliary ['mɪlɪˌɛrɪ, B -ərɪ] *a.* miliario, miliar.
millibar ['mɪləˌbɑr, B -bɑ] *s.* (fís., meteor.) milibar.
millicurie ['mɪləˌkjʊri, B -ˌkjʊərɪ] *s.* (fís.) milicurie.
millieme [mil'jɛm] *s.* moneda equivalente a un milésimo del dinar tunecino.
millier [-'jeɪ] *s.* tonelada métrica.
millifarad ['mɪləˌfærəd] *s.* (elec.) milifaradio.
milligal ['mɪləˌgæl] *s.* (fís.) miligal.
milligram, (G.B.) **milligramme** [-ˌgræm] *s.* miligramo.
millihenry [-ˌhɛnrɪ] *s.* (elec.) milihenrio, milihenry.
millilambert [-ˌlæmbərt, B -bət] *s.* (fís.) mililambert.
milliliter (G.B.) **millilitre** [-ˌlitər, B -ə] *s.* mililitro.
millimeter, (G.B.) **millimetre** [-ˌmitər, B -ə] *s.* milímetro.
millimicron [-ˌmaɪkrɑn, B -krɔn] *s.* milimicron.
milliner ['mɪlənər, B -nə] *s.* sombrerera, sombrerero (que hace o diseña sombreros de mujer).
milline rate ['mɪl'laɪn-] (impr.) tarifa millilineal; costo por millón de una tirada de impresos publicitarios.
millinery ['mɪləˌnɛrɪ, B -nərɪ] *s.* sombrerería de damas.
milling ['mɪlɪŋ] *s.* 1. molienda, moledura. 2. acordonamiento, acuñación. 3. (metal) fresado; cordoncillo (de la moneda).
milling cutter, (mec.) cortador rotatorio de metales, fresa.
milling machine, (mec.) fresadora.
million ['mɪljən] *s.* millón.
millionaire [ˌmɪljə'nɛr, B -'nɛə] *s.* millonario.
millionfold ['mɪljənˌfoʊld] *a., adv.* un millón de veces.
millionth ['mɪljənθ] *a., s.* millonésimo.
millipede ['mɪləˌpid] *s.* (ento.) milpiés, cardador.

milliroentgen [ˌmɪlə'rɛntgən, -'rʌnt-, B -'rɔntjən] *s.* (fís.) miliroentgen.
millisecond ['mɪləˌsɛkənd] *s.* milisegundo.
millivolt [-ˌvoʊlt] *s.* (elec.) milivoltio.
milliwatt [-ˌwɑt, B -ˌwɔt] *s.* (elec.) milivatio.
millpond ['mɪlˌpɑnd, B -pɔnd] *s.* cubo, alberca del molino; **like a m.,** como un plato (díc. del mar en calma).
millrace [-ˌreɪs] *s.* saetín, caz o canal del molino; corriente de agua del saetín.
mill run, 1. madera aserrada (para la venta). 2. (fig.) el promedio, lo corriente, lo acostumbrado. 3. (min.) prueba de molino.
millstone [-ˌstoʊn] *s.* 1. muela, piedra de molino. 2. (fig.) peso agobiador, carga agobiadora.
millstream [-ˌstrim] *s.* corriente de agua del saetín.
mill train, (metal.) tren de rodillos; tren de molinos.
mill wheel, rueda del molino.
millwork [-ˌwɜrk, B -ˌwɜk] *s.* producto de un molino, taller, etc.; maquinaria de molino.
millwright [-ˌraɪt] *s.* constructor de molinos; mecánico de molino.
milo ['maɪloʊ] *s.* (*pl.* MILOS) (bot.) especie de sorgo.
milord [mɪ'lɔrd, B -'lɔd] *s.* milord (título de respeto otorgado a nobles ingleses).
milpa ['mɪlpə] *s.* milpa, maizal.
milquetoast ['mɪlkˌtoʊst] *s.* (fam., E.U.) persona de naturaleza dócil, tímida y penosa.
milreis ['mɪlˌreɪs] *s.* (*pl.* MILREIS) milreis (ant. moneda de Portugal y Brasil).
milt [mɪlt] *s.* 1. glándulas reproductoras de peces machos, esp. cuando están llenas de lecha. 2. lecha. —*v.t.* fertilizar; impregnar las huevas de los peces.
milter ['mɪltər, B -ə] *s.* pez macho.
Miltiades [mɪl'taɪəˌdiz] *s.* (hist.) Milcíades, general ateniense vencedor en la batalla de Maratón.
mim [mɪm] *a.* (dial.) melindroso, dengoso.
mime [maɪm] *s.* 1. mimo, pantomimo; bufón, payaso. 2. mímica. 3. pantomima, drama mímico. —*v.t.* imitar, remedar. —*v.i.* actuar como mimo, representar una pantomima.
mimeograph ['mɪmɪəˌgræf, B -grɑf] *s.* mimeógrafo; copia hecha con el mimeógrafo. —*v.t., v.i.* mimeografiar, reproducir copias en el mimeógrafo.
mimer ['maɪmər, B -ə] *s.* mimo, payaso, pantomimo; imitador.
mimesis [mə'misəs, B maɪ-] *s.* 1. (ret., med.) mimesis, imitación. 2. (biol.) mimetismo.
mimetic [mɪ'mɛtɪk] *a.* 1. mímico, imitativo. 2. pretendido, fingido. 3. (biol.) mimético.
mimic ['mɪmɪk] *a.* 1. mímico, imitativo. 2. fingido, simulado. —*s.* 1. mimo, pantomimo. 2. imitador, remedador. —*v.t.* (*pret., p.p.* MIMICKED; *p.pr.* MIMICKING) 1. remedar; imitar, parodiar; fingir, simular. 2. (biol.) asemejarse a (animales, plantas).
mimical [-ɪkəl] *a.* (raro) mímico.
mimicker [-ər, B -ə] *s.* mimo, imitador, remedador.
mimicry [-rɪ] *s.* (*pl.* MIMICRIES) 1. mímica, remedo, bufonería, imitación burlesca. 2. (zool., bot.) mimetismo.
mimosa [mə'moʊsə, B -zə] *s.* (bot.) mimosa, sensitiva.
mina ['maɪnə] *s.* (*pl.* MINAE [-ˌni] o MINAS) (hist.) mina (antigua unidad monetaria y de peso de Grecia).
minable, mineable ['maɪnəbəl] *a.* explotable; capaz de ser minado.

minacious [mə'neɪʃəs] *a.* amenazador, amenazante.
minaret [ˌmɪnə'rɛt, B 'mɪnərɛt] *s.* (arq.) alminar, minarete; torre de una mezquita.
minatorily ['mɪnəˌtɔrəlɪ, B -tər-] *adv.* amenazadoramente.
minatory [-ˌtɔrɪ, B -tərɪ] *a.* amenazador, amenazante.
mince [mɪns] *v.t.* 1. desmenuzar, picar (carne), hacer picadillo de, destrizar. 2. atenuar, medir (palabras). 3. actuar o decir remilgada o afectadamente. 4. **not to m. matters,** no andarse con rodeos. —*v.i.* ser afectado o melindroso en el modo de hablar, andar, etc.
mincemeat ['mɪnsˌmit] *s.* 1. carne picada. 2. mezcla de pasas, manzanas y especias finamente picadas (con o sin carne). 3. **to make m. of (someone),** hacer pedazos (a alguien).
mince pie, pastel de fruta y especias picadas.
mincer [-ər, B -ə] *s.* 1. máquina de picar, aparato para picar carne. 2. melindroso, afeminado.
mincing [-ɪŋ] *a.* melindroso, remilgado, dengoso.
mincingly [-lɪ] *adv.* a pasitos; con afectación; remilgadamente, melindrosamente.
mind [maɪnd] *s.* 1. mente. 2. entendimiento, pensamiento; inteligencia. 3. memoria, recuerdo. 4. opinión, parecer. 5. deseo, propósito, intención. 6. (fig.) cerebro, intelecto, cabeza (persona). 7. propensión, inclinación. 8. **frame of m.,** estado de ánimo; **to be in one's right m.,** estar en sus cabales, estar en su juicio; **to be in two minds about,** vacilar en cuanto a, tener dudas sobre, no poder resolverse respecto a; **to be of a m. (with),** estar de acuerdo (con); **to be of a m. to (do),** estar dispuesto a, estar inclinado a (hacer); tener ganas de (hacer); **to be of sound m., estar en sus cabales, estar en su juicio; to be on one's m.,** preocuparle a uno, tener preocupado a uno; **to be out of one's m.,** estar fuera de juicio, estar loco; **to bear in m.,** tener presente; **to bring (o call) to m.,** recordar, traer a la mente; **to change one's m.,** cambiar de idea, de opinión; **to come to m.,** venir a la mente, ocurrírsele a uno; **to cross one's m.,** pasar por las mientes; **to give (someone) a piece of one's m.,** cantárselas claras a (alguien), decir (a alguien) cuatro frescas; **to give one's m. to,** prestar atención a; **to go out of m.,** ser olvidado; **to go out of one's m.,** volverse loco, perder el juicio; **to have a (good) m. to (do),** estar en ánimo de (hacer), tener ganas de (hacer); tener la (firme) intención de (hacer); **to have in m.,** tener pensado, tener en mente; **to have on one's m.,** preocuparse de o con; **to keep in m.,** tener presente, no olvidar; **to keep one's m., on,** concentrar uno su atención sobre; **to know one's m.,** saber lo que se quiere; **to lose one's m.,** perder la razón o el juicio, volverse loco; **to make up one's m.,** decidirse; **to my (his, etc.) m.,** en mi (su, etc.) opinión, a mi (su, etc.) parecer; a mi (su, etc.) gusto; **to read one's m.,** adivinar los pensamientos de uno; **to set one's m. on (doing),** proponerse (hacer), tener firme intención de (hacer); **to set one's m. on (something),** resolverse a conseguir (algo); **to slip one's m.,** escapársele a uno de la memoria; **to speak one's m.,** hablar sin ambages, hablar con franqueza, expresar su opinión; **to take one's m. off,** distraer a uno de, hacer olvidar a uno; **with one m.,** unánimemente. —*v.t.* 1. considerar, tener presente, prestar atención a; preocuparse por, ej., *never m. the expense,* no se preocupe por el costo; **m. your manners,** preste atención a sus modales. 2. atender a, cuidar, ej., *who will m. the child?* ¿quién cuidará al niño? 3. oponerse a; sentir

desagrado por; molestarse por, tener inconveniente en, ej., *I don't m. the change,* no me opongo al cambio, *I don't m. the weather,* el clima no me desagrada, *would you m. closing the window?* ¿le molestaría cerrar la ventana? 4. recordar, no olvidar (hacer algo), ej., *m. that the door is closed,* recuerde cerrar la puerta. 5. tener cuidado con, hacer caso a; guardarse de, ej., *m. what you are doing,* tenga cuidado con lo que está haciendo, *m. the dog!* ¡cuidado con el perro! 6. (dial.) proponerse, tener la intención (de). 7. **m. one's own business,** no meterse en cosas ajenas; **m. one's P's and Q's,** tener sumo cuidado en lo que dice o hace uno. —*v.i.* 1. tener cuidado o cautela; fijarse. 2. preocuparse; importarle a uno; tener inclinación; estar dispuesto. 3. estar en contra, oponerse. 4. **never m.,** ¡no importa! ¡no se preocupe!; ¡olvídelo!

mind bending, (fam.) endiablado.

mind blowing, (fam.) alucinante, de alucine, par maravillarse.

mind boggling, (fam.) alucinante, inconcebible, que no le cabe a uno en la cabeza.

mind cure, psicoterapia.

minded ['maɪndəd] *a.* dispuesto, inclinado, propenso.

minder [-ər, B -ə] *s.* (pr. G.B.) cuidador, guardián, celador.

mind expanding, psicodélico.

mindful [-fəl] *a.* atento, cuidadoso, diligente.

mindfully [-fəlɪ] *adv.* atentamente, cuidadosamente.

mindfulness [-fəlnəs] *s.* cuidado, atención.

mindless [-ləs] *a.* 1. estúpido; insensato; sin inteligencia. 2. descuidado, negligente.

mindlessly [-ləslɪ] *adv.* 1. estúpidamente. 2. descuidadamente, negligentemente.

mind reader, adivinador del pensamiento.

mind reading, adivinación del pensamiento; lectura del pensamiento.

mind's eye, imaginación.

mine [maɪn] *pron. pos.* mío, mía, míos, mías; el mío, la mía, los míos, las mías; lo mío, ej., *vengeance is m.,* la venganza es mía, *he is a friend of m.,* es un amigo mío, *this brother of m.,* este hermano mío. —*a.* (ant., poét.) mi, mío (*ú. sólo ante vocal o h*), ej., *m. hostess,* mi patrona; *m. undoing,* mi ruina.

mine, *s.* 1. mina (de oro, carbón, etc.). 2. mina, yacimiento, filón. 3. (fig.) fuente ej., *m. of information,* fuente abundante de información. 4. (mil.) mina (explosivo). —*v.i.* 1. dedicarse a la minería; cavar, minar. 2. (mil.) sembrar minas. —*v.t.* 1. minar, socavar, abrir (una galería). 2. extraer (mineral, oro, etc.). 3. (mil.) minar, sembrar de minas.

mine detector, (mil.) detector de minas.

mine field, (mil.) campo de minas, campo minado.

minelayer ['maɪn,leɪər, B -ə] *s.* (mar.) barco plantaminas o siembraminas.

miner ['maɪnər, B -ə] *s.* 1. minero. 2. (mil.) minador, zapador.

mineral ['mɪnərəl] *s.* 1. mineral. 2. (*pl.*) (G.B.) aguas minerales. 3. (ant.) mina. —*a.* mineral.

mineralization [,mɪnərələ'zerʃən, B -laɪ-] *s.* mineralización.

mineralize ['mɪnərə,laɪz] *v.t.* 1. mineralizar. 2. convertir en mineral. 3. petrificar, fosilizar.

mineralizer [-ər, B -ə] *s.* (quím.) mineralizador.

mineral jelly, vaselina, petróleo o jalea mineral.

mineralogical [,mɪnərə'lɑdʒɪkəl, B -'lɔdʒ-] *a.* mineralógico.

mineralogist [,mɪnə'rɑlədʒəst, B -'ræl-] *s.* mineralogista.

mineralogy [-dʒɪ] *s.* mineralogía.

mineral oil, aceite mineral; petróleo.

mineral orange, albayalde anaranjado.

mineral pitch, brea mineral, asfalto.

mineral spirits, esencia mineral, espíritu de petróleo.

mineral tar, alquitrán mineral, pisasfalto, malta.

mineral water, agua mineral.

mineral wax, (min.) ozocerita, ceresina, cera fósil.

mineral wool, lana mineral o de escoria.

Minerva [mə'nɜrvə, B -'nɜvə] *s.* (mitol.) Minerva, diosa romana de la sabiduría.

mine shaft, pozo de mina, pozo de extracción.

minestrone [,mɪnəs'troʊnɪ] *s.* minestrón, sopa de legumbres.

mine surveyor, agrimensor de minas.

minesweeper ['maɪn,swipər, B -ə] *s.* (mar.) dragaminas, barreminas.

minesweeping [-,swipɪŋ] *s.* (mil., mar.) rastreo de minas.

mine thrower, (mil.) lanzaminas.

mingle ['mɪŋgəl] *v.t.* 1. mezclar; entremezclar, mixturar; unir, fusionar. 2. asociar, incorporar, juntar (personas). 3. confeccionar, preparar (mezcla, brebaje). —*v.i.* mezclarse, juntarse, asociarse, incorporarse.

miniature ['mɪnɪətʃər, B -tʃə] *s.* 1. miniatura. 2. modelo en miniatura. 3. arte de pintar miniaturas. —*a.* en miniatura; diminuto. —*v.t.* representar en miniatura.

miniaturize [-tʃər,aɪz] *v.t.* diseñar o construir en miniatura.

minicomputer ['mɪnikəm pjutər] *s.* miniordenador, minicomputadora.

Minié ball ['mɪnɪ,bəl, 'mɪnɪ,eɪ-] bala minié, bala cónica para rifles.

minify ['mɪnə,faɪ] *v.t.* (*pret., p.p.* MINIFIED; *p. pr.* MINIFYING) empequeñecer, reducir, achicar; aminorar, disminuir, minimizar.

minikin ['mɪnɪkən] *s.* (anat.) cosa o persona diminuta o delicada. —*a.* (ant.) 1. delicado; afectado; remilgado. 2. muy pequeño; menudo, diminuto.

minim ['mɪnəm] *s.* 1. (mús.) mínima. 2. pigmeo, enano; pizca, ápice, persona o cosa insignificante. 3. mínim (medida de líquidos). 4. (caligrafía) trazo (de una letra). —*a.* mínimo, pequeñísimo, diminuto minúsculo.

minimal [mɪnəməl] *a.* mínimo.

minimalist [-əlǝst] *s.* (pol.) minimalista.

minimally [-əlɪ] *adv.* como mínimo, como mínimum, en grado mínimo, apenas.

minimization [,mɪnəmə'zeɪʃən, B -maɪ-] *s.* 1. reducción al mínimo; empequeñecimiento. 2. menosprecio, desestima, desestimación.

minimize ['mɪnə,maɪz] *v.t.* 1. reducir al mínimo; disminuir, empequeñecer, minimizar. 2. menospreciar, tener en menos; subestimar, desestimar (peligro, pérdidas, riesgo, etc.).

minimum ['mɪnəməm] *s.* (*pl.* MINIMA [-mə] o MINIMUMS) mínimo, mínimum. —*a.* mínimo, muy pequeño.

minimum fare, bajada de bandera.

minimum wage, salario vital, salario de subsistencia; salario mínimo.

mining ['maɪnɪŋ] *s.* 1. minería, industria minera. 2. (mil.) siembra de minas.

mining engineer, ingeniero de minas.

minion ['mɪnjən] *s.* 1. paniaguado, valido; favorito, predilecto; esbirro, secuaz, satélite; dependiente, subordinado. 2. (impr.) miñona (tipo de letra de 7 puntos). 3. (raro) amante, querida, manceba. 4. **minions of the law,** polizontes, corchetes. —*a.* (raro) delicado, bonito, refinado.

minish ['mɪnɪʃ] *v.t., v.i.* (ant.) disminuir(se); mermar; rebajar(se).

miniskirt ['mɪnɪ,skɜrt, B -,skɜt] *s.* minifalda.

minister ['mɪnəstər, B -tə] *s.* 1. ministro, clérigo, pastor, sacerdote, cura. 2. (pol.) ministro. 3. (dip.) ministro, enviado. 4. (raro) agente, mandatario. 5. (ant.) sirviente, servidor. —*v.t.* 1. administrar, dispensar, suministrar (un sacramento, ayuda, etc.). 2. (ant.) surtir, proveer. —*v.i.* 1. (con *to*) atender, asistir; auxiliar, ayudar (a persona, causa). 2. contribuir (al éxito, resultado). 3. servir como ministro.

ministerial [,mɪnəs'tɪrɪəl] *a.* 1. ministerial. 2. administrativo. 3. sacerdotal, pastoral. 4. (con *to*) útil (para).

minister plenipotentiary, (*pl.* MINISTERS PLENIPOTENTIARY) (dip.) ministro plenipotenciario.

minister without portfolio, ministro sin cartera.

ministrant ['mɪnəstrənt] *a.* ministrante. —*s.* ministrador; oficiante (de la misa).

ministration [,mɪnəs'treɪʃən] *s.* 1. ministerio, oficio religioso. 2. servicio, socorro, ayuda. 3. agencia, mediación.

ministry ['mɪnəstrɪ] *s.* (*pl.* MINISTRIES) 1. ministerio, gabinete. 2. clero. 3. agencia, mediación, intercesión.

Ministry of Foreign Affairs, Ministerio de Relaciones Exteriores.

Ministry of Health, (G.B.) Ministerio de Salud Pública.

Ministry of Public Works, (G.B.) Ministerio de Obras Públicas.

Ministry of the Interior, Ministerio de Gobernación o del Interior.

Ministry of the Treasury, Ministerio de Hacienda.

minitrack ['mɪnɪ,træk] *s.* sistema rastreador de cohetes.

minium ['mɪnɪəm] *s.* (quím., min.) minio.

miniver ['mɪnəvər, B -və] *s.* piel blanca (en vestido ceremonial); piel de armiño.

mink [mɪŋk] *s.* 1. (zool.) visón. 2. piel de visón.

Minn. *abrev. de* **Minnesota,** Minnesota (E.U.).

minnesinger ['mɪnɪ,sɪŋər, B -ə] *s.* trovador alemán medieval.

Minnesota [,mɪnə'soʊtə] *s.* Minnesota, estado de los E.U.

minnow ['mɪnoʊ] *s.* (ict.) pez pequeño (esp. de la familia de la carpa); **Triton among the minnows,** gigante entre enanos.

Minoan [mə'noʊən] *a.* minoico, perteneciente a la cultura prehistórica de Creta.

minor ['maɪnər, B -nə] *a.* 1. menor; secundario, inferior; minoritario, de menor importancia; leve (ofensa, etc.); más chico, más pequeño. 2. menor (de edad). 3. el menor. —*s.* 1. menor (de edad). 2. (E.U., educ.) asignatura secundaria, curso menor. 3. (lóg.) menor. 4. (mús.) tono menor. —*v.i.* (con *in*) seguir una asignatura secundaria.

minor axis, (geom.) eje menor (de la elipse).

Minorca [mə'nɔrkə, B -'nɔkə] *s.* 1. (geog.) Menorca. 2. una casta de gallinas, de plumaje blanco o negro.

Minorcan [-kən] *a., s.* menorquín, natural de Menorca.

Minorite ['maɪnə,raɪt] *s.* (relig.) menor, fraile franciscano.

minority [mə'nɔrətɪ, B maɪ-] *s.* (*pl.* MINORITIES) 1. menoría, minoría, menor edad. 2. minoría (en juntas, asambleas, votación, etc.). —*a.* de la minoría.

minority leader, (pol.) jefe de la minoría parlamentaria.

minor key, (mús.) tono menor.

minor league, (dep.) liga menor, liga de clubes deportivos profesionales que compiten en segunda división.

minor mode, (mús.) modo menor.
minor orders, (relig.) órdenes menores.
minor party, (pol.) partido minoritario.
minor piece, (ajedrez) pieza menor.
minor premise, (lóg.) premisa menor.
minor scale, (mús.) escala menor.
minor sentence, (gram.) oración o cláusula subordinada.
minor seventh, (mús.) séptima menor.
minor suit, (bridge) palo menor (diamantes o tréboles).
minor surgery, cirugía menor, cirugía ministrante.
minor tenace, (naipes) tenaza menor (rey y sota).
minor term, (lóg.) término menor.
minor third, (mús.) tercera menor.
minor triad, (mús.) acorde perfecto menor.
Minos ['maɪnəs, B -nɔs] *s.* (mitol.) Minos, rey de Creta.
Minotaur ['mɪnəˌtɔr, B 'maɪnətɔ] *s.* (mitol.) Minotauro, el monstruo que habitaba el Laberinto y que mató Teseo.
minster ['mɪnstər, B -stə] *s.* 1. santuario o iglesia de monasterio. 2. basílica, catedral.
minstrel ['mɪnstrəl] *s.* 1. (hist.) trovador, cantor, juglar. 2. bardo, poeta lírico; músico. 3. cantor cómico (que se tizna la cara e imita a los negros).
minstrel show, representación teatral cómica, antiguamente popular, en la que los actores hacen papeles de negros.
minstrelsy [-sɪ] *s.* 1. arte o profesión del trovador. 2. compañía de trovadores o juglares. 3. poesía de trovadores, cancionero trovadoresco, mester de juglaría.
mint [mɪnt] *s.* 1. (bot.) menta, hierbabuena. 2. pastilla de menta.
mint, *s.* 1. casa de moneda, ceca. 2. cantidad grande (de dinero, etc.); dineral. 3. (fig.) fuente, mina (de ideas, invención, etc.). —*a.* sin usar, sin uso, no usado, en su condición original. —*v.t.* 1. acuñar, amonedar, troquelar. 2. (fig.) fabricar, inventar; forjar, fraguar. —*v.i.* (esco.) intentar, tener intención (de); insinuar.
mintage ['mɪntɪdʒ] *s.* 1. acuñación, amonedación, braceaje. 2. derechos de cuño, monedaje. 3. cuño, sello.
minter [-ər, B -ə] *s.* acuñador.
mint julep, whiski o brandy helado y sazonado con menta.
minuend ['mɪnjʊˌɛnd] *s.* (mat.) minuendo.
minuet [ˌmɪnjʊ'ɛt] *s.* minué, minuete (baile y música de compás ternario).
minus ['maɪnəs] *prep.* 1. menos, ej., *eight m. four,* ocho menos cuatro. 2. sin, des-provisto de, falto de, con (algo) de menos, ej., *he came back m. a book,* regresó con un libro de menos. —*a.* 1. menos, ej., *m. sign,* signo menos. 2. negativo, ej., *a m. quantity,* cantidad negativa. 3. (fig.) sin valor positivo. —*s.* 1. (mat.) signo menos; cantidad negativa. 2. deficiencia, pérdida.
minuscule ['mɪnəsˌkjul, mɪ'nʌs-] *s.* 1. (impr.) minúscula, letra minúscula, letra de caja baja. 2. (hist.) estilo de escritura antigua de letras simplificadas. —*a.* minúsculo, muy pequeño.
minus difference, (mat.) diferencia en menos.
minus number, (mat.) número negativo.
minus quantity, (mat.) cantidad negativa.
minus sign, (mat.) signo menos, signo negativo.
minute ['mɪnət] *s.* 1. minuto. 2. momento, instante. 3. minuta, nota, apuntamiento, memorándum; (*pl.*) minutas, actas. 4. **the m. (that),** tan pronto como; **this (very) m.,** en este instante, ahora mismo; **up to the m.,** al corriente; modernísimo; de última hora. —*v.t.* 1. minutar, levantar acta de; anotar, apuntar. 2. registrar minuto a minuto (velocidad o tiempo).
minute [maɪ'nut, B -'njut] *a.* 1. muy pequeño, menudo, diminuto, minuto. 2. insignificante, fútil. 3. minucioso, prolijo; nimio.
minute book, minutario, libro de actas o de minutas.
minute by minute, paso por paso, detallado; de un minuto al otro.
minute gun, (arm.) cañón de salvas, cañón disparado de minuto en minuto.
minute hand, minutero.
minutely ['mɪnətlɪ] *a.* (de) minuto a minuto, continuo. —*adv.* a intervalos de un minuto, a cada minuto.
minutely [maɪ'nutlɪ, B -'njut-] *adv.* minuciosamente, detalladamente.
minuteman ['mɪnətˌmæn] *s.* 1. (E.U., hist.) miliciano de la Guerra de Independencia. 2. civil armado para prestar servicio de emergencia.
minuteness [maɪ'nutnəs, B -'njut-] *s.* 1. minuciosidad, meticulosidad. 2. suma pequeñez.
minute steak, bistec al minuto, filete al minuto, bife al minuto (Amer.).
minutia [mə'nuʃɪə, B maɪ'nju-] *s.* (*pl.* MINUTIAE [-ʃɪˌi]) (*ú. gen. en pl.*) minucia, menudencia, pequeñez, nimiedad, detalle menudo o minucioso.
minx [mɪŋks] *s.* 1. coqueta, moza descarada o atrevida. 2. (ant.) ramera.
Miocene ['maɪəˌsin] *a., s.* (geol.) mioceno.
miosis [maɪ'oʊsəs] *s.* (med.) miosis, contracción de la pupila.
miotic [maɪ'ɑtɪk, B -'ɔt-] *a.* (med.) miótico.
mir [mɪr, B mɪə] *s.* mir (comunidad agrícola primitiva en Rusia).
mirabile dictu [mə'rɑbɪˌleɪ'dɪktu, B -'ræb-] (lat.) maravilloso de decir.
miracle ['mɪrɪkəl] *s.* 1. milagro. 2. maravilla, prodigio.
miracle drug, droga milagrosa, medicamento maravilloso.
miracle play, auto sacramental; drama en que se representan episodios bíblicos o vidas de santos y mártires.
miraculous [mə'rækjʊləs] *a.* 1. milagroso. 2. maravilloso, prodigioso, asombroso, pasmoso.
miraculously [-lɪ] *adv.* milagrosamente.
mirador ['mɪrəˌdɔr, B ˌmɪrə'dɔ] *s.* (arq.) mirador, corredor, galería, pabellón, terrado (para explayar la vista).
mirage [mə'rɑʒ] *s.* 1. espejismo, ilusión óptica. 2. (fig.) ilusión, sueño, ensueño, ficción.
mire [maɪr, B 'maɪə] *s.* 1. lodazal, pantano, cenagal. 2. lodo, fango, cieno. —*v.t.* 1. enlodar, encenagar. 2. enmarañar, enredar, implicar, comprometer. —*v.i.* atollarse, atascarse (en el fango).
mirity palm ['mɪrətɪ-] (bot.) moriche.
mirk, mirky, *vars. de* **murk, murky.**
mirror ['mɪrər, B -ə] *s.* 1. espejo. 2. (fig.) modelo, ejemplar, patrón. —*v.t.* 1. reflejar. 2. (fig.) reflejar, representar.
mirror image, (ópt.) imagen especular; (*direct opposite*) reflejo.
mirror-like [-ˌlaɪk] *a.* espejado.
mirth [mɜrθ, B mɜθ] *s.* alegría, regocijo, júbilo, hilaridad.
mirthful ['mɜrθfəl, B 'mɜθ-] *a.* alegre, regocijado, reidor, gozoso, jovial.
mirthfully [-fəlɪ] *adv.* alegremente, jovialmente.
mirthfulness [-fəlnəs] *s.* alegría.
mirthless [-ləs] *a.* abatido, triste, melancólico.
mirthlessly [-lɪ] *adv.* tristemente, melancólicamente.
MIRV [mɜrv, B mɜv] *abrev. de* **Multiple Independently Targetable Reentry Vehicles,** Vehículos Espaciales de Retorno y Objetivos Autónomos.
miry ['maɪrɪ, B 'maɪərɪ] *a.* cenagoso, lodoso, fangoso.
mirza ['mɪrzɑ, B 'mɜzə] *s.* mirza (título honorífico entre los persas).
misadventure [ˌmɪsəd'vɛntʃər, B -tʃə] *s.* desgracia, contratiempo, desventura, percance, revés.
misadvise [-əd'vaɪz] *v.t.* dar malos consejos, aconsejar erróneamente.
misalignment [-ə'laɪnmənt] *s.* desalineamiento.
misalliance [-ə'laɪəns] *s.* alianza desafortunada, alianza inconveniente, esp. matrimonio con una persona de rango inferior.
misally [-ə'laɪ] *v.t.* aliar o unir inconvenientemente.
misanthrope ['mɪsənˌθroʊp, B 'mɪz-] *s.* misántropo.
misanthropic [ˌmɪsən'θrɑpɪk, B ˌmɪzən'θrɔp-] **misanthropical** [-ɪkəl] *a.* misantrópico.
misanthropist [mɪs'ænθrəpəst, B mɪz-] *s.* misántropo.
misanthropy [-pɪ] *s.* misantropía.
misapplication [ˌmɪsæplə'keɪʃən, B 'mɪs-] *s.* mala aplicación, mal uso.
misapply [-ə'plaɪ] *v.t.* aplicar mal; hacer mal uso de; usar inapropiadamente.
misapprehend [-ˌæprɪ'hɛnd] *v.t.* entender mal; no comprender.
misapprehension [-ˌæprɪ'hɛnʃən] *s.* equivocación, error, concepto erróneo, mala interpretación, malentendido.
misappropriate [-ə'proʊprɪˌeɪt] *v.t.* malversar (fondos); hacer mal uso de.
misappropriation [-əˌproʊprɪ'eɪʃən] *s.* malversación, mal uso.
misarranged [-ə'reɪndʒd] *a.* desarreglado, desordenado.
misarrangement [-ə'reɪndʒmənt] *s.* desarreglo, desorden.
misbecome [ˌmɪsbɪ'kʌm, B 'mɪs-] *v.t.* no convenir a, no ser propio de, ser indigno de.
misbegotten [-bɪ'gɑtən, B -ˌgɔt-] *a.* mal habido, bastardo, espurio, ilegítimo.
misbehave [-bɪ'heɪv] *v.i.* portarse mal, conducirse mal.
misbehavior, (G.B.) **misbehaviour** [-bɪ'heɪvjər, B -jə] *s.* mala conducta, mal comportamiento.
misbelief [-bɪ'lif] *s.* creencia errónea o falsa; error, opinión errónea; herejía, heterodoxia.
misbelieve [-bɪ'liv] *v.i.* (ant.) creer equivocadamente; tener una religión falsa.
misbeliever [-ər, B -ə] *s.* hereje, incrédulo.
misbrand [mɪs'brænd] *v.t.* (com.) marcar falsamente.
miscalculate [-'kælkjəˌleɪt, B 'mɪs-] *v.t., v.i.* calcular mal.
miscalculation [ˌmɪskælkjə'leɪʃən, B 'mɪs-] *s.* cálculo errado; error.
miscall [mɪs'kɔl, B 'mɪs-] *v.t.* 1. nombrar impropiamente. 2. (ant., dial.) denostar, insultar.
miscarriage [-'kærɪdʒ, B mɪs-] *s.* 1. (med.) aborto. 2. error, acto equivocado. 3. fracaso, malogro, aborto (de un plan). 4. extravío.
miscarriage of justice, error judicial.
miscarry [mɪs'kærɪ] *v.i.* 1. abortar, malparir. 2. resultar mal, malograrse, frustrarse, fracasar (plan, proyecto, etc.). 3. extraviarse.
miscast [-'kæst, B -'kɑst] *v.t.* (teat.) dar papel inapropiado a, ej., *Jones was m. in the role of the king,* el papel del rey no era apropiado para Jones.
miscegenation [mɪsˌɛdʒə'neɪʃən, ˌmɪsədʒə-, B ˌmɪsɪ-] *s.* 1. entrecruzamiento de razas. 2. mestizaje.

miscellanea [ˌmɪsə'leɪnɪə] *s. pl.* miscelánea (esp. literaria).
miscellaneous [-əs] *a.* misceláneo, mezclado, mixto, vario, diverso; heterogéneo.
miscellaneously [-lɪ] *adv.* variadamente.
miscellanist ['mɪsəˌleɪnəst, B mɪ'sɛlə-] *s.* escritor, compilador o editor de misceláneas.
miscellany [-nɪ] *s.* (*pl.* MISCELLANIES) 1. miscelánea, mezcla, mixtura. 2. (*pl.*) miscelánea (literaria).
mischance [mɪs'tʃæns, B -'tʃɑns] *s.* desgracia, infortunio, mala suerte.
mischief ['mɪstʃəf] *s.* 1. daño, mal. 2. malicia, perversidad. 3. persona traviesa; diablillo. 4. injuria, agravio. 5. viveza, travesura, diablura. 6. **to do one a m.,** hacerle a uno una mala jugada; **to keep out of m.,** no meterse en líos; **to make m.,** crear discordia.
mischief-maker [-ˌmeɪkər, B -kə] *s.* buscapleitos, enredador.
mischievous ['mɪstʃəvəs] *a.* 1. dañino, dañoso. 2. malicioso, malévolo. 3. enredador, chismoso. 4. travieso.
mischievously [-lɪ] *adv.* maliciosamente.
mischievousness [-nəs] *s.* 1. malicia, perversidad. 2. travesura; naturaleza traviesa, picardía.
miscibility [ˌmɪsə'bɪlətɪ] *s.* (quím.) miscibilidad, calidad de lo que puede mezclarse.
miscible ['mɪsəbəl] *a.* (quím.) miscible, mezclable.
miscolor [mɪs'kʌlər, B -ə] *v.t.* (fig.) representar falsamente, falsificar, describir engañosamente (los hechos).
misconceive [ˌmɪskən'siv] *v.t.* entender mal, concebir equivocadamente, interpretar incorrectamente.
misconception [-'sɛpʃən, B 'mɪs-] *s.* mala interpretación, concepto erróneo; idea falsa; equivocación.
misconduct [-kən'dʌkt] *v.t.* administrar o manejar mal. — [mɪs'kɑndʌkt, B -'kɔn-] *s.* 1. inmoralidad; mala conducta. 2. malversación.
misconstruction [-kən'strʌkʃən] *s.* 1. mala interpretación. 2. mala construcción (esp. de oraciones o cláusulas).
misconstrue [-kən'stru] *v.t.* interpretar erróneamente, entender mal.
miscount [-'kaʊnt] *v.t.* contar mal. —*v.i.* equivocarse en la cuenta. —*s.* cuenta errónea, mal cálculo.
miscreance ['mɪskrɪəns] *s.* (ant.) descreimiento, irreligión; adhesión a una falsa fe.
miscreancy [-ənsɪ] *s.* 1. villanía, infamia, vileza. 2. (ant.) herejía.
miscreant [-ənt] *a.* 1. vil, ruin; inescrupuloso. 2. (ant.) infiel, herético; impío, mal creyente. —*s.* 1. pillo, sinvergüenza; bribón, pícaro. 2. (ant.) hereje, infiel.
miscreate [ˌmɪskrɪ'eɪt] *v.t.* dar forma inapropiada. —*a.* contrahecho, mal formado, deformado.
miscreation [-'eɪʃən] *s.* deformación.
miscue [mɪs'kju, B 'mɪs-] *s.* 1. (billar) pifia. 2. (fig.) pifia, desacierto, error; falta, descuido. —*v.i.* 1. (billar) pifiar. 2. hacer declaraciones inoportunas. 3. (teat.) entender mal el apunte, equivocarse de texto.
misdeal [-'dil] *v.t., v.i.* repartir mal (los naipes). —*s.* repartición errónea.
misdeed [-'did] *s.* malhecho, fechoría, infracción, delito.
misdeem [-'dim] *v.t., v.i.* (ant., poét.) pensar o creer equivocadamente, conceptuar o estimar erróneamente.
misdemean [ˌmɪsdə'min] *v.t., v.i.* (ant.) portarse mal; cometer una falta.
misdemeanant [-ənt] *s.* (der.) reo de delito menor; persona de mala conducta.
misdemeanor, (G.B.) **misdemeanour** [-ər, B -ə] *s.* 1. (der.) falta leve, delito menor. 2. (raro) mala conducta; fechoría.
misdirect [-də'rɛkt, B 'mɪs-] *v.t.* dar una dirección errónea a; dirigir erradamente; descaminar.
misdirection [-də'rɛkʃən] *s.* 1. mala dirección; instrucciones erradas; informe falso. 2. (der.) instrucciones erróneas (del juez al jurado sobre algún aspecto de derecho positivo).
misdo [-'du] *v.t.* errar, hacer mal. —*v.i.* faltar, delinquir.
misdoer [-'duər, B -ə] *s.* malhechor; criminal.
misdoing [-'duɪŋ] *s.* mala acción; falta; yerro.
misdoubt [-'daʊt] *v.t.* 1. dudar. 2. sospechar; recelar, desconfiar. —*s.* 1. duda. 2. sospecha; recelo, desconfianza.
mise [miz, maɪz] *s.* 1. (hist.) acuerdo, convenio. 2. (der.) tema, punto principal (en un proceso sobre un mandato de derecho).
misease [mɪs'iz] *s.* incomodidad; angustia; inquietud, desasosiego; disgusto, malestar.
mise-en-scène [mizɑn'sɛn] *s.* 1. (teat.) puesta en escena; aparato escénico, decorado. 2. (fig.) ambiente.
misemploy [ˌmɪsɪm'plɔɪ] *v.t.* emplear mal; abusar.
miser ['maɪzər, B -zə] *s.* 1. avaro, avariento, tacaño, cicatero. 2. (ant.) miserable.
miserable ['mɪzərəbəl] *a.* 1. miserable, desgraciado, desdichado, infeliz. 2. miserable, abyecto, despreciable. 3. miserable, mezquino, mísero. 4. falto de calidad, sin valor. 5. (fam.) pésimo, atroz, ej., *I feel m.,* me siento pésimo o atroz. —*s.* desgraciado.
miserableness [-nəs] *s.* estado o condición miserable.
miserably [-blɪ] *adv.* miserablemente.
Miserere [ˌmɪzə'rɛrɪ, B -'rɪərɪ] *s.* (rel., mús.) miserere.
misericord, misericorde [mɔ'zɛrɔˌkɔrd, B -kɔd] *s.* 1. misericordia (puñal medieval con que se daba el golpe de gracia). 2. misericordia (pieza en los asientos del coro para descansar disimuladamente estando de pie). 3. flexibilidad de las reglas monásticas por alguna dispensa, ej., el ayuno; lugar donde se permitía efectuar tal dispensa.
miserliness ['maɪzərlɪnəs, B -zəlɪ-] *s.* avaricia, tacanería, mezquindad, cicatería.
miserly [-lɪ] *a.* mísero, avaro, avariento, mezquino, cicatero.
misery [ˌmɪzərɪ] *s.* (*pl.* MISERIES) 1. miseria, infelicidad, desdicha, desgracia. 2. aflicción, calamidad. 3. sufrimiento, padecimiento; dolor físico prolongado.
misesteem [mɪsə'stim] *v.t.* estimar mal, estimar poco; desestimar. —*s.* pérdida de la propia estima.
misestimate [mɪs'ɛstəˌmeɪt] *v.t.* evaluar erróneamente. —*s.* evaluación errónea, estimación inapropiada.
misestimation [ˌmɪsɛstə'meɪʃən] *s.* estimación errónea.
misfeasance [mɪs'fizəns] *s.* 1. transgresión. 2. (der.) abuso de poder; ejecución ilegal de un procedimiento lícito, infidencia.
misfeature [mɪs'fitʃər, B -tʃə] *s.* (ant.) facción o rasgo deformado.
misfile [-'faɪl] *v.t.* archivar mal.
misfire [-'faɪr, B 'mɪs'faɪə] *v.i.* 1. no encender, fallar el encendido (motor). 2. fallar el tiro, fallar (arma de fuego); dar mechazo (mina). —*s.* 1. falla de encendido. 2. falla de tiro; mechazo.
misfit ['mɪsˌfɪt] *s.* 1. lo que no sienta, ajusta, entalla o encaja bien. 2. persona inadaptada. — [mɪs'fɪt, B 'mɪs-] *v.t.* desajustar. —*v.i.* desconvenir, no sentar bien, no encajar.
misfortune [mɪs'fɔrtʃən, B -'fɔtʃən] *s.* 1. desgracia, desdicha. 2. calamidad, desastre, desventura; infortunio; contratiempo, percance; revés.
misgive [-'gɪv] *v.t.* hacer dudar, hacer recelar; llenar de dudas, ej., *my mind misgives me,* mi mente me hace dudar. —*v.i.* temer, recelar; estar receloso de.
misgiving [mɪs'gɪvɪŋ] *s.* duda, recelo; presentimiento; desconfianza, temor.
misgovern [-'gʌvərn, B 'mɪs-ən] *v.t.* gobernar o administrar mal; desgobernar.
misgovernment [-'gʌvərnmənt, B -ən-] *s.* mala administración, mal manejo; desgobierno, desorden, desorganización.
misguidance [-'gaɪdəns] *s.* dirección errada; extravío, descamino, descarrío.
misguide [-'gaɪd] *v.t.* dirigir mal; aconsejar mal; descaminar, descarriar, extraviar.
misguided [-'gaɪdəd] *a.* mal aconsejado, engañado, descaminado.
mishandle [-'hændəl] *v.t.* 1. manejar mal, tratar torpemente. 2. maltratar.
mishanter [mə'ʃæntər, B -'ʃɑntə] *s.* (esco.) desgracia, desventura, percance.
mishap ['mɪshæp] *s.* 1. accidente, percance, contratiempo. 2. (ant.) desventura, mala suerte.
mishear [mɪs'hɪr, B -'hɪə] *v.t.* oír mal, entender imperfectamente.
mishit ['mɪsˌhɪt] *s.* (dep.) golpe errado.
mishmash ['mɪʃˌmæʃ, -ˌmɑʃ, B -mæʃ] *s.* revoltijo, mezcolanza, mezcla. —*v.t.* revolver, mezclar.
misinform [ˌmɪsɪn'fɔrm, B 'mɪs-'fɔm] *v.t.* informar mal, dar informes erróneos o falsos a.
misinformation [ˌmɪsˌɪnfər'meɪʃən, B -fə'-] *s.* información errónea; informes erróneos o falsos.
misinterpret [ˌmɪsən'tɜrprət, B -'tɜprɪt] *v.t.* interpretar mal; entender mal.
misinterpretation [-ˌtɜrprə'teɪʃən, B -ˌtɜprə-] *s.* mala interpretación; interpretación falsa.
misjoinder [mɪs'dʒɔɪndər, B -də] *s.* (der.) unión impropia de causas o partes diferentes en un juicio.
misjudge [-'dʒʌdʒ] *v.i.* errar (en estimación, juicio, etc.). —*v.t.* juzgar mal; juzgar injustamente; interpretar mal.
misjudgment, misjudgement [-'dʒʌdʒmənt] *s.* juicio errado, estimación equivocada, opinión errónea.
misknowledge [-'nɑlɪdʒ, B -'nɔl-] *s.* conocimiento errado o malo.
mislay [-'leɪ] *v.t.* 1. colocar mal. 2. extraviar; traspapelar.
mislead [-'lid] *v.t.* 1. extraviar, descaminar, descarriar, despistar. 2. engañar.
misleading [mɪs'lidɪŋ] *a.* engañoso, de falsas apariencias.
misleadingly [-lɪ] *adv.* engañosamente.
mislike [-'laɪk] *v.t.* 1. tener aversión a, no gustar de. 2. (ant.) desagradar, descontentar, disgustar. —*s.* aversión, antipatía.
mismade [-'meɪd] *a.* mal hecho, hecho impropiamente.
mismanage [mɪs'mænɪdʒ, B 'mɪs-] *v.t.* manejar mal, administrar mal.
mismanagement [-mənt] *s.* mal manejo, mala administración; desgobierno.
mismarriage [mɪs'mærɪdʒ] *s.* matrimonio desacertado.

mismatch [-'mætʃ] *v.t.* unir mal, emparejar mal; desigualar, deshermanar, desajustar; desemparejar; malcasar. —*s.* 1. unión mal hecha. 2. desajuste, desigualdad. 3. casamiento desacertado.
mismate [-'meɪt] *v.t.* 1. emparejar mal, hermanar mal. 2. casar mal, malcasar.
mismove [-'muv] *s.* movimiento equivocado, paso en falso.
misname [-'neɪm] *v.t.* trasnombrar; llamar por nombre equivocado.
misnomer [-'noʊmər, B 'mɪs-mə] *s.* 1. designación o nombramiento erróneo (en un instrumento legal). 2. nombre inapropiado o incorrecto; término erróneo o desacertado.
misogamic [ˌmɪsə'gæmɪk] *a.* misógamo, que aborrece el matrimonio.
misogamy [-əmɪ] *s.* misogamia, horror al matrimonio.
misogynic [ˌmɪsə'dʒɪnɪk, B maɪsə-] *a.* misógino, que aborrece a las mujeres.
misogynist [mə'sɑdʒənəst, B maɪ'sɔdʒ-] *s.* misógino, el que aborrece a las mujeres.
misogyny [-ənɪ] *s.* misoginia, odio a las mujeres.
misologist [mə'sɑlədʒəst, B maɪ'sɔl-] *s.* misólogo, el que detesta debatir, razonar o discutir.
misology [-dʒɪ] *s.* misología.
misoneism [ˌmɪsə'niˌɪzəm, B ˌmaɪsə-] *s.* misoneísmo, odio a la innovación o al cambio.
misoneist [-'niəst] *s.* misoneísta, el que detesta cualquier innovación o cambio.
mispickel ['mɪsˌpɪkəl] *s.* (min.) mispíquel.
misplace [mɪs'pleɪs, B 'mɪs-] *v.t.* 1. colocar mal o fuera de su lugar, extraviar, traspapelar. 2. equivocarse en otorgar (confianza, afectos, etc. a alguien).
misplacement [-mənt] *s.* colocación errónea (de una cosa); extravío.
misplay [mɪs'pleɪ] *s.* mala jugada; movimiento errado. —*v.t.* jugar mal.
mispleading [-'plidɪŋ] *s.* (der.) alegato erróneo.
misprint [-'prɪnt] *v.t.* (impr.) imprimir con erratas; imprimir mal. — ['mɪsˌprɪnt] *s.* errata, error de imprenta, falta tipográfica.
misprision [mɪs'prɪʒən] *s.* (der.) 1. ocultación de un crimen. 2. mala administración. 3. rebeldía, desacato. 4. delito menor.
misprize [-'praɪz] *v.t.* menospreciar, desestimar, despreciar.
mispronounce [ˌmɪsprə'naʊns, B'mɪs-] *v.t.* pronunciar mal, pronunciar incorrectamente.
mispronunciation [-prəˌnʌnsɪ'eɪʃən] *s.* pronunciación incorrecta.
misquotation [-kwoʊ'teɪʃən] *s.* cita equivocada, cita errónea.
misquote [-'kwoʊt] *v.t.* citar equivocadamente.
misread [-'rid] *v.t.* leer mal; entender o interpretar mal (la lectura).
misremember [-rɪ'membər, B -bə] *v.t.* recordar mal; no recordar correctamente; (dial.) olvidar.
misreport [-rɪ'pɔrt, B -'pɔt] *s.* informe falso o erróneo. —*v.t.* referir falsamente; informar erradamente sobre.
misrepresent [ˌmɪsˌrɛprɪ'zɛnt, B 'mɪs-] *v.t.* 1. exponer o alegar falsamente, desfigurar, pervertir, falsificar (hechos); describir engañosamente, tergiversar. 2. representar mal o fraudulentamente (a alguien).
misrepresentation [-ˌrɛprɪˌzɛn'teɪʃən] *s.* 1. exposición falsa, descripción falsa; falsificación, tergiversación. 2. representación fraudulenta.
misrule [-'rul] *v.t.* gobernar mal, desgobernar. —*s.* 1. mal gobierno, desgobierno. 2. confusión, desorden.

Miss [mɪs] *s.* (*pl.* MISSES) 1. Señorita (tratamiento de cortesía que precede al nombre o apellido de una mujer soltera). 2. muchacha, jovencita.
miss, *v.t.* 1. errar (el blanco, tiro, la pelota, etc.). 2. perder (oportunidad, función, el tren, camino, etc.), fallar, no lograr, no conseguir (un objetivo). 3. no comprender, no entender, escapársele a uno, ej., *I missed many of his words,* se me escaparon muchas de sus palabras. 4. dejar de ver, no percibir, pasar por alto. 5. no encontrar. 6. echar de menos, descubrir la falta de, ej., *when I came home I missed my gloves,* al llegar a casa eché de menos mis guantes. 7. escapar, evitar, ej., *he just missed being killed,* escapó con vida por un tris; salvó la vida por un pelo. 8. echar de menos, extrañar (Amer.). 9. omitir. 10. no concurrir, faltar a (trabajo, colegio, etc.). 11. **m. fire,** fallar la descarga (arma de fuego); **m. out,** saltar, omitir (parte de un escrito al leerse o copiarse); **m. stays,** (mar.) fallar la virada; **m. the boat,** (fam.) perder el tren, perder la oportunidad, llegar demasiado tarde; **m. the mark,** errar el tiro; **m. the point,** no comprender el verdadero sentido. —*v.i.* 1. errar el blanco. 2. fracasar, salir mal, frustrarse. 3. fallar el encendido (motor). 4. (ant.) (con *of*) fallar; no aprovechar, no lograr. —*s.* 1. tiro errado (billar), errada. 2. fiasco, fracaso, malogro; extravío. 3. (raro) pérdida; falta. 4. **near m.,** escape por un pelo; tiro apenas errado; **to give (something) a m.,** esquivar, evitar (algo); no tocar (ej., cigarrillos, bebida, etc.); no asistir a (reunión, etc.).
Miss. *abrev. de* **Mississippi,** Misisipí (E.U.).
missal ['mɪsəl] *s.* misal, libro de misa.
missay [mɪs'seɪ] *v.t., v.i.* (ant.) decir mal, decir equivocadamente; calumniar, difamar.
misseem [-'sim] *v.t.* (raro) no ser propio de; ser indigno de; no convenir a.
missend [-'sɛnd] *v.t.* enviar equivocadamente (carta, paquete, etc.).
misshape [mɪs'ʃeɪp, B 'mɪs-] *v.t.* deformar, desfigurar; afear.
misshapen [-'ʃeɪpən] *a.* deformado, desfigurado; afeado.
missile ['mɪsəl, B 'mɪsaɪl] *s.* 1. proyectil. 2. (ej., *javelin*) arma arrojadiza. 3. (*guided*) misil, cohete teledirigido.
missileer [ˌmɪsə'lɪr, B -'lɪə] **missileman** ['mɪsəlmən] *s.* diseñador o constructor de cohetes dirigidos.
missile launcher, lanzamisiles.
missilery, missilry ['mɪsəlrɪ] *s.* ciencia que estudia y proyecta el funcionamiento de cohetes teledirigidos; cohetes teledirigidos (colectivamente).
missing ['mɪsɪŋ] *a.* desaparecido; ausente; perdido; **the m.,** los desaparecidos (en una batalla); **to be missing,** faltar; haber desaparecido.
missing link. (antrop.) eslabón perdido.
mission ['mɪʃən] *s.* 1. misión (religiosa o caritativa); conjunto de misioneros; casa de la misión. 2. misión diplomática, encargo, comisión (dada a un emisario, diplomático, etc.); (E.U.) embajada. 3. profesión, vocación, tarea. 4. (mil., mar.) tarea, excursión, correría (gen. para ejecutarse en un área de combate o territorio enemigo). 5. (ant.) misión (acción de enviar). —*v.t.* 1. comisionar; nombrar. 2. trabajar como misionero en o entre. —*a.* misional, misionero (díc. esp. de las misiones españolas cerca de California).
missional [-əl] *a.* misional.
missionary [-ˌɛrɪ, B -ərɪ] *a.* misionero, misionario, misional, ej., *m. zeal,* celo misional. —*s.* misionero, misionera.

mission control, centro de control.
missioner [-ər, B -ə] *s.* misionero.
mission furniture, muebles al estilo de las misiones californianas.
missis, missus ['mɪsəz] *s.* (vulg.) dueña, señora (ama de casa); **the m.,** (vulg. o hum.) esposa, mujer.
Mississippi [ˌmɪsə'sɪpɪ] *s.* Misisipí, estado y río de E.U.
Mississippian [-ən] *a.* misisípico, misisipiense, misisipiano.
missive ['mɪsɪv] *s.* misiva, carta. —*a.* misivo, que se puede enviar o se destina a ser enviado.
Missouri [mə'zʊrɪ, B -'zʊərɪ] *s.* Misurí, estado y río de E.U.; **I'm from M.,** soy difícil de convencer, soy terco.
Missourian [-ən] *a., s.* misuriano, misuriense.
misspell [mɪs'spɛl, B 'mɪs-] *v.t., v.i.* deletrear mal, escribir con faltas de ortografía.
misspelling [-'spɛlɪŋ] *s.* falta de ortografía, deletreo erróneo.
misspend [-'spɛnd] *v.t.* malgastar, despilfarrar, malbaratar, desbaratar.
misspent [-'spɛnt] *a.* despilfarrado, malgastado, malbaratado.
misstate [-'steɪt] *v.t.* relatar mal, exponer falsamente.
misstatement [-'steɪtmənt] *s.* relato inexacto, relación equivocada; aserción errónea, falencia.
misstep [-'stɛp] *s.* paso en falso; resbalón; desliz (en conducta). —*v.t.* tropezar; dar un paso en falso.
missy ['mɪsɪ] *s.* (fam.) (*pl.* MISSIES) señorita, muchachuela.
mist [mɪst] *s.* 1. niebla, neblina; bruma, llovizna; calina. 2. oscuridad (física o mental). 3. vapor, vaho. 4. velo (de lágrimas). —*v.t., v.i.* 1. nublar(se), aneblar(se). 2. empañar(se), oscurecer. 3. velar(se).
mistakable [mə'steɪkəbəl] *a.* confundible, equívoco.
mistake [mə'steɪk] *v.t.* 1. equivocar, entender mal, interpretar mal, comprender mal. 2. confundir; tomar una cosa por otra, ej., *to m. James for John,* confundir a Santiago con Juan. 3. **there's no mistaking the fact (that),** se debe reconocer el hecho (de que). —*v.i.* errar, equivocarse. —*s.* equivocación, error, yerro, falta; errata; **and no m., make no m.,** sin duda alguna, con toda seguridad; **by m.,** por error; por descuido; **to learn from others' mistakes,** escarmentar en cabeza ajena; **to make a m.,** equivocarse, cometer un error.
mistaken [-ən] *a.* 1. errado, equivocado, incorrecto, desacertado, ej., *he is m.,* está equivocado. 2. erróneo, errado.
mistakenly [-lɪ] *adv.* por error, equivocadamente, erróneamente.
misteach ['mɪs'titʃ] *v.t.* enseñar mal, instruir mal.
mister ['mɪstər, B -tə] *s.* señor (tratamiento de cortesía que se antepone ad apellido); **hey, m.!** ¡oiga!; **got a light, m.?** ¿tiene fuego, caballero?; **watch out, m.!** ¡cuidado, socio! (no es de buena educación decir 'mister' sin el apellido).
mister big, (jer., E.U.) nombre que se aplica al que dirige una empresa, "mandamás".
misthink [mɪs'θɪŋk] *v.t., v.i.* (ant.) pensar mal o desfavorablemente (de); pensar erróneamente (de).
mistily ['mɪstəlɪ] *adv.* 1. nebulosamente. 2. confusamente, vagamente.
mistime [mɪs'taɪm] *v.t.* hacer o decir a deshora o inoportunamente; dejar pasar la ocasión favorable.

mistimed, *a.* extemporáneo, importuno; a deshora.
mistiness ['mɪstɪnəs] *s.* nebulosidad.
mistle thrush ['mɪsəl-] (orn.) charla, cagaaceite, tordo mayor.
mistletoe [-ˌtoʊ] *s.* (bot.) muérdago, liga, visco; caballera.
mistproof [-pruf] *a.* (*windshield*) antivaho.
mistral ['mɪstrəl, mɪs'trɑl] *s.* mistral, viento frío y seco.
mistreat [mɪs'trit] *v.t.* maltratar; abusar.
mistreatment [-mənt] *s.* maltrato, maltratamiento, malos tratos.
mistress ['mɪstrəs] *s.* 1. señora. 2. ama, ama de casa, dueña. 3. (fig.) dueña, ej., *you are m. of the situation,* Ud. es dueña de la situación. 4. concubina, querida; enamorada, cortejo. 5. (pr. G.B.) maestra de escuela. 6. experta, perita (en algo). 7. (ant., dial.) señora, dama, madama.
mistress of the sea, (fig.) reina de los mares (potencia naval máxima).
mistrial [mɪs'traɪəl] *s.* (der.) juicio nulo, (por error de procedimiento o por desacuerdo del jurado).
mistrust [mɪs'trʌst, B 'mɪs-] *s.* desconfianza, recelo, duda, sospecha. —*v.t.* 1. desconfiar, recelar de. 2. sospechar. 3. (raro) presentir, presagiar; conjeturar, suponer.
mistrustful [-fəl] *a.* desconfiado, receloso, sospechoso.
mistrustfully [-fəlɪ] *adv.* desconfiadamente, con desconfianza, recelosamente.
mistrustfulness [-fəlnəs] *s.* naturaleza o ánimo receloso; desconfianza, recelo.
mistrustingly [-ɪŋlɪ] *adv.* con recelo o desconfianza.
mistryst [mɪs'traɪst] *v.t.* (esco.) no poder cumplir una cita con; dejar perplejo; aturdir.
misty ['mɪstɪ] *a.* (MISTIER; MISTIEST) 1. nebuloso, brumoso. 2. vago, indistinto, confuso, ej., *a m. idea,* idea confusa o vaga. 3. velado; empañado.
misunderstand [ˌmɪsʌndər'stænd, B 'mɪs-də'-] *v.t., v.i* entender mal, no comprender; tomar en sentido erróneo.
misunderstanding [-'stændɪŋ] *s.* 1. malentendido, equivocación, error, mala inteligencia. 2. desacuerdo, desavenencia; disensión, disputa. 3. concepto erróneo.
misunderstood [-'stʊd] *a.* mal entendido, mal comprendido; insuficientemente apreciado o estimado.
misusage [mɪs'jusɪdʒ, B 'mɪs-zɪdʒ] *s.* 1. maltratamiento, maltrato, abuso, estropeo. 2. mal uso, mal empleo (de palabras, etc.).
misuse [-'juz] *v.t.* 1. emplear mal. 2. maltratar, estropear. — [-'jus] *s.* 1. mal uso, mal empleo, uso erróneo. 2. (ant.) conducta impropia.
misvalue [mɪs'vælˌju] *v.t.* valorar erradamente, estimar erróneamente; desestimar.
misventure [-'vɛntʃər, B -tʃə] *s.* desgracia, contratiempo; desventura, percance.
miswrite [-'raɪt] *v.t.* escribir incorrectamente.
MIT *abrev. de* **Massachusetts Institute of Technology,** Instituto Tecnológico de Massachusetts (E.U.).
mite [maɪt] *s.* 1. (zool.) garrapata, ácaro, arador. 2. moneda pequeña; suma ínfima de dinero, óbolo. 3. (fam.) pizca, triza, jota, ápice.
miter, mitre ['maɪtər, B -ə] *s.* 1. mitra (de los obispos, arzobispos, etc.); tiara. 2. (carp.) inglete; escuadra de inglete. —*v.t.* 1. conferir la mitra a, elevar al obispado; adornar con mitra. 2. (carp.) juntar a inglete.
miter box, (carp.) caja de ingletes.
mitered [-ərd, B -əd] *a.* mitrado (obispo).
miter gear, (máq.) engranaje de inglete.
miter plane, (carp.) cepillo de ingletes.
miter square, (carp.) falsa escuadra, escuadra de inglete.
Mithra ['mɪθrə] **Mithras** [-ræs] *s.* (mitol.) Mitra, deidad persa de la luz y la verdad.
Mithraism [-ˌɪzəm] *s.* mitraísmo, doctrina persa que se fundaba en el esclarecimiento y el estudio.
mithridate [-ˌdeɪt] *s.* (farm.) mitridato.
mithridatism [ˌmɪθrə'deɪtˌɪzəm, B 'mɪθrɪ-dət-] *s.* (med.) mitridatismo.
mithridatize [-ˌaɪz, B mɪ'θrɪdət-] *v.t.* mitridatizar.
miticide ['maɪtəˌsaɪd] *s.* insecticida contra los ácaros.
mitigable ['mɪtəgəbəl] *a.* mitigable.
mitigant [-gənt] *s.* paliativo, calmante, mitigante.
mitigate [-ˌgeɪt] *v.t.* 1. mitigar, calmar, suavizar, moderar. 2. atenuar. —*v.i.* mitigarse, aplacarse, calmarse.
mitochondrion [ˌmaɪtə'kɑndrɪən, B -'kɔn-] *s.* (*pl.* MITOCHONDRIA [-drɪə]) (biol.) mitocondrio.
mitosis [maɪ'toʊsəs, B mɪ-] *s.* (biol.) mitosis.
mitotic [-'tɑtɪk, B -'tɔt-] *a.* (biol.) mitótico.
mitrailleuse [ˌmitrə'jɜz, B ˌmɪtraɪ-] *s.* (fr., mil.) ametralladora de varios cañones.
mitral ['maɪtrəl] *a.* 1. de forma de mitra. 2. (anat.) mitral.
mitral valve, (anat.) válvula mitral.
mitt [mɪt] *s.* 1. mitón; guante deportivo, ej., de béisbol. 2. (jer.) los puños, las manos. 3. (*pl.*) (jer.) guantes de boxeo.
mitten ['mɪtən] *s.* mitón, maniquete; guante que deja los dedos al descubierto o que sólo tiene separado de la palma el pulgar.
mittimus ['mɪtəməs] *s.* 1. (der.) mandamiento de arresto, auto de prisión. 2. (G.B.) despedida (de un puesto o trabajo).
mix [mɪks] *v.t.* (*pret., p.p.* MIXED O MIXT [mɪkst]; *p.pr.* MIXING) 1. mezclar. 2. juntar, combinar. 3. hacer, confeccionar (hormigón); amasar (tortas, etc.); aderezar (ensaladas). 4. embarullar, confundir, enredar. 5. **m. up,** mezclar a fondo; (fig.) confundir (pensamientos); **to be mixed up (in** o **with),** estar mezclado o comprometido (en o con). —*v.i.* 1. mezclarse. 2. juntarse, combinarse. 3. asociarse. 4. **m. well (badly),** hacer buenas (malas) migas o ligas, llevarse, ej., *they do not m. well,* no se llevan bien; **m. with,** asociarse con; meterse con. —*s.* mezcla, mixtura.
mixable ['mɪksəbəl] *a.* miscible, mezclable.
mixed [mɪkst] *a.* 1. mezclado, mixto. 2. variado (ej., resultados). 3. (bot.) mezclado, mixto.
mixed bud, (bot.) yema mixta (que produce hojas y flores).
mixed chalice, (relig.) cáliz con vino y agua.
mixed chorus, (mús.) coro mixto (de hombres y mujeres).
mixed company, you can't say it in m. c., no puedes decirlo delante de damas.
mixed feelings, mezcla de sentimientos, sentimientos conflictivos.
mixed-flow turbine [-'floʊ-] turbina mixta.
mixed marriage, matrimonio mixto (entre personas de distintas razas o religiones).
mixed metaphor, (ret.) metáfora mixta.
mixed number, (mat.) número mixto.
mixed train, (f.c.) tren mixto, que conduce pasajeros y mercancías.
mixed-up [-'ʌp] *a.* confundido, atolondrado; revuelto.
mixer ['mɪksər, B -sə] *s.* 1. mezcladora (de cemento). 2. batidora (de cocina). 3. **bad m.,** persona insociable; **good m.,** persona sociable.
mixtilineal [ˌmɪkstɪ'lɪnɪəl] **mixtilinear** [-ər, B -ə] *a.* (geom.) mistilíneo, mixtilíneo.
mixture ['mɪkstʃər, B -tʃə] *s.* 1. mezcla, mixtura, mezcolanza. 2. (tej.) mezcla, mezclilla (tejido hecho de hilos de diferentes clases y colores).
mix-up ['mɪksˌʌp] *s.* 1. confusión, enredo, lío. 2. conflicto, pelotera, riña. 3. mezcla, mixtura.
mizzen, mizen ['mɪzən] *a.* (mar.) del palo de mesana. —*s.* (mar.) 1. mesana. 2. palo (de) mesana.
mizzenmast, mizenmast [-ˌmæst, -məst, B -mɑst] *s.* (mar.) palo de mesana.
mizzen-topgallant mast [-ˌtɑp'gælənt-, -tə-, B -tɔp-] (mar.) mastelerillo de mesana, mastelerillo de popa.
mizzen-topgallant sail, (mar.) juanete de mesana.
mizzen-topmast [-'tɑpˌmæst, -məst, B -'tɔpmɑst] *s.* mastelero de popa, mastelero de mesana.
mizzen-topsail [-seɪl, -səl] *s.* (mar.) gavia de mesana, sobremesana.
mizzle ['mɪzəl] *v.t., v.i.* llivoznar, garuar (Amer.).
mizzle, *v.i.* (jer., G.B.) irse, marcharse.
ml. *abrev. de* **milliliter,** mililitro (ml).
ml. *abrev. de* **millilambert,** mililambert.
M.L.A. *abrev. de* **Modern Language Association of America,** Asociación norteamericano para el estudio de idiomas modernos.
Mlle. *abrev. de* **Mademoiselle,** Señorita.
Mlles. *abrev. de* **Mesdemoiselles,** Señoritas.
MM. *abrev. de* **Messieurs,** Señores.
mm *abrev. de* **millimeter,** milímetro (mm).
Mme. *abrev. de* **Madame,** Señora.
Mmes. *abrev. de* **Mesdames,** Señoras.
m.m.f. *abrev. de* **magnetomotive force,** fuerza magnetomotriz.
Mn *símb. de* **manganese,** manganeso (Mn).
M.N. *abrev. de* 1. (G.B.) **Merchant Navy,** marina mercante. 2. **magnetic north,** norte magnético.
mnemonic [ni'mɑnɪk, B -'mɔn-] *a.* mnemónico, nemónico, mnemotécnico, nemotécnico.
mnemonics [-ɪks] *s. pl.* (*sing en const.*) mnemotecnia, nemotecnia, mnemónica, nemónica.
Mnemosyne [ni'mɑsəˌni, B -'mɔz-] *s.* (mitol.) Mnemosina, diosa griega de la memoria.
mo. *abrev. de* **month,** mes.
Mo. *abrev. de* **Missouri,** Misurí (E.U.). 2. (quím.) *símb. de* **molybdenum,** molibdeno (Mo).
M O *abrev. de* **medical officer,** médico (incorporado a las fuerzas armadas).
moa ['moʊə] *s.* (pal.) dinornis.
Moabite ['moʊəˌbaɪt] *s.* moabita (*m.*). —*a.* moabita, de Moab, antiguo reino de la Mesopotamia.
moan [moʊn] *s.* gemido, queja, quejido, plañido, lamento, lamentación. —*v.t.* lamentar, plañir; proferir entre gemidos. —*v.i.* gemir, quejarse, lamentarse, gimotear.
moat [moʊt] *s.* foso (de un castillo o una fortificación). —*v.t.* circuir con un foso, fosar.
mob [mɑb, B mɔb] *s.* 1. populacho, plebe, vulgo, (las) masas. 2. chusma, canalla, gentuza; turba, tumulto, multitud, tropel de gentes. 3. (jer.) pandilla (criminal). —*v.t.* (*pret., p.p.* MOBBED; *p.pr.* MOBBING) atacar, atropellar (díc. de la multitud).
mobcap ['mɑbˌkæp, B 'mɔb-] *s.* (ant.) cofia, gorra de mujer.
mobile ['moʊbəl, -ˌbil, B -baɪl] *a.* 1. móvil, movible, movedizo. 2. cambiadizo, cambiable, variable. 3. versátil, voluble. 4. (mil.) móvil, movible, ej., *m. artillery,* artillería móvil.
mobile [-ˌbil] *s.* (arte) móvil (escultura con partes movibles).

mobile home, casa rodante.
mobility [mouˈbɪlətɪ] *s.* 1. movilidad. 2. variabilidad. 3. versatilidad, volubilidad.
mobilization [ˌmoubələˈzeɪʃən, B -laɪ-] *s.* movilización.
mobilize [ˈmoubəˌlaɪz] *v.t.* 1. movilizar (fuerzas, recursos, etc.). 2. (mil.) movilizar, poner en pie de guerra.
mobocracy [mɑbˈɑkrəsɪ, B mɔbˈɔk-] *s.* (*pl.* MOBOCRACIES) oclocracia, gobierno de la plebe.
mob rule, oclocracia.
mobster [ˈmɑbstər, B ˈmɔbstə] *s.* (jer., E.U.) pandillero, gángster (que es miembro de una pandilla).
moccasin [ˈmɑkəsən, B ˈmɔk-] *s.* 1. mocasín, zapato indio. 2. (zool.) mocasín, serpiente de agua, víbora de agua.
moccasin flower, (bot.) chapín de Venus, zueco.
Mocha [ˈmoukə, B ˈmɔkə] *s.* 1. moca, moka (variedad de café). 2. especie de cuero suave y flexible para guantes.
mock [mɑk, B mɔk] *v.t.* 1. desdeñar, despreciar, no hacer caso de. 2. mofarse de, burlarse de, befar, ridiculizar. 3. defraudar, burlar. 4. desafiar. 5. imitar, remedar burlonamente. —*v.i.* (con *at*) mofarse (de), burlarse (de), reírse (de). —*s.* 1. burla, mofa, befa, escarnio. 2. objeto de burla, hazmerreír. 3. imitación, mímica. —*a.* 1. fingido, simulado. 2. imitado, falso.
mocker [ˈmɑkər, B ˈmɔkə] *s.* 1. burlador, mofador, escarnecedor. 2. (orn.) sinsonte.
mockery [-ərɪ] *s.* (*pl.* MOCKERIES) **1. burla,** mofa, escarnio. 2. objeto de burla o de risa. 3. remedo, parodia.
mock-heroic [-hɪˈrouɪk] *a.* épico-burlesco.
mocking [ˈmɑkɪŋ, B ˈmɔk-] *a.* burlón.
mockingbird [-ˌbərd, B -ˌbəd] *s.* (orn.) sinsonte.
mockingly [-lɪ] *adv.* burlonamente.
mock orange, (bot.) jeringuilla, celinda.
mock turtle soup, (cocina) sopa de carne, sazonada para que sepa como la de tortuga.
mock-up [ˈmɑkˌʌp, B ˈmɔk-] *s.* maqueta, modelo hecho a escala.
mod [mɑd, B mɔd] (E.U., G.B., jer.) *abrev. de* **modern,** moderno, de moda.
modal [ˈmoudəl] *a.* (der., mús., gram., lóg., filos.) modal, de modo.
modal auxiliary (gram. inglesa) verbo auxiliar de modo (ej., *can, might,* etc.).
modality [mouˈdælətɪ] *s.* 1. modalidad, modo de ser. 2. (lóg., med.) modalidad.
mode [moud] *s.* 1. modo, manera, método, forma. 2. (gram., filos.) modo. 3. (mús.) modo, disposición de los sonidos que forman una escala; **major m.,** modo mayor; **minor m.,** modo menor.
mode, *s.* moda, boga, estilo; costumbre.
model [ˈmɑdəl, B ˈmɔd-] *s.* 1. modelo, representación a escala. 2. modelo, dechado, pauta, norma, ejemplo. 3. modelo, molde, patrón, horma, plantilla, figurín. 4. modelo (que posa para un artista o que exhibe vestidos en los salones de moda). 5. (dial.) copia, facsímil. 6. maqueta de un edificio. —*v.t.* (*pret., p.p.* MODELED O MODELLED; *p.pr.* MODELING O MODELLING) 1. modelar, moldear. 2. (con *after, on* o *upon*) diseñar o construir según el modelo de. 3. exhibir como modelo (vestido). —*v.i.* 1. hacer figuras, modelar. 2. posar (para un artista); trabajar como modelo. —*a.* ejemplar, (de) modelo.
modeler [-ələr, B -ələ] *s.* modelista.
model home, casa modelo.
model T, el primer modelo marca Ford que se fabricó en serie.

modem [ˈmoudəm] *s.* (comput.) módem.
moderate [ˈmɑdərət, B ˈmɔd-] *a.* 1. moderado. 2. regular, mediocre. —*s.* moderado (esp. miembro de un partido moderado). — [-ˌreɪt] *v.t.* 1. moderar, mitigar. 2. bajar (la voz). 3. presidir, dirigir. —*v.i.* 1. moderarse, mitigarse. 2. actuar como presidente o director.
moderately [-lɪ] *adv.* moderadamente.
moderation [ˌmɑdəˈreɪʃən, B ˌmɔd-] *s.* moderación.
moderato [-ˈrɑtˌou] *a., adv.* (mús.) a tiempo moderado.
moderator [ˈmɑdəˌreɪtər, B ˈmɔd-ə] *s.* 1. moderador. 2. árbitro, mediador, concordador. 3. presidente (de una asamblea, junta, etc.). 4. (fís.) moderador (que sirve para frenar los neutrones en una pila atómica).
modern [ˈmɑdərn, B ˈmɔdən] *a.* moderno, nuevo, reciente, del presente. —*s.* 1. moderno. 2. (impr.) tipo moderno.
modernism [-ˌɪzəm] *s.* modernismo; **M.,** (relig.) modernismo.
modernist [-əst] *s., a.* modernista.
modernistic [ˌmɑdərˈnɪstɪk, B ˌmɔdəˈ-] *a.* modernista, de tendencias modernas.
modernity [mɑˈdərnətɪ, B mɔˈdənɪ-] *s.* (*pl.* MODERNITIES) modernismo.
modernization [ˌmɑdərnəˈzeɪʃən, B -ənaɪ-] *s.* modernización.
modernize [ˈmɑdərˌnaɪz, B ˈmɔdəˌ-] *v.t.* modernizar.
modernizer [-ər, B -ə] *s.* modernizador.
modern languages, lenguas vivas.
modernly [-lɪ] *adv.* 1. en el presente, actualmente. 2. al estilo moderno. 3. según costumbres de la época actual.
modest [ˈmɑdəst, B ˈmɔd-] *a.* 1. modesto, humilde, recatado. 2. mesurado, módico.
modestly [-lɪ] *adv.* modestamente, humildemente.
modesty [ˈmɑdəstɪ, B ˈmɔd-] *s.* modestia, humildad, recato.
modicum [ˈmɑdɪkəm, B ˈmɔd-] *s.* pequeña cantidad o porción, ápice, pizca.
modifiable [ˈmɑdəˌfaɪəbəl, B ˈmɔd-] *a.* modificable.
modification [ˌmɑdəfəˈkeɪʃən, B ˌmɔd-] *s.* 1. modificación, cambio, transformación. 2. (biol.) modificación.
modificatory [ˈmɑdəfəˌkeɪtərɪ, B ˌmɔdɪfɪˈkeɪtərɪ] *a.* modificante.
modifier [ˈmɑdəˌfaɪər, B ˈmɔd-ə] *s.* 1. modificador. 2. (gram.) modificativo, calificativo.
modify [-ˌfaɪ] *v.t.* (*pret., p.p.* MODIFIED; *p.pr.* MODIFYING) 1. modificar, cambiar, alterar. 2. moderar, templar, morigerar. 3. (gram.) calificar. —*v.i.* modificarse, sufrir una modificación.
modillion [mouˈdɪljən, B mə-] *s.* (arq.) modillón.
modiolus [mouˈdaɪələs] *s.* (*pl.* MODIOLI [-ˌlaɪ]) (anat.) modiolo.
modish [ˈmoudɪʃ] *a.* de moda, en boga.
modishly [-lɪ] *adv.* a la moda, según la moda.
modiste [mouˈdist] *s.* modista.
modular [ˈmɑdʒələr, B ˈmɔdjulə] *a.* (fís., mat.) modular, del módulo; (*furniture*) modular, a base de módulos; (educ.) dividido en módulos; (comput.) modular.
modulate [-ˌleɪt] *v.t.* 1. modular (el tono o la inflexión). 2. regular, ajustar; moderar, atemperar, templar. 3. entonar. 4. (rad.) modular (frecuencia, amplitud o fase de las ondas). —*v.i.* 1. cantar o tocar modulando el sonido. 2. (mús.) modular, cambiar la tonalidad. 3. (rad.) modular, producir modulación.
modulation [ˌmɑdʒəˈleɪʃən, B ˌmɔdju-] *s.* modulación; (rad., mús.) modulación.

modulation factor, m. index, (ing.) coeficiente de modulación.
modulator [ˈmɑdʒəˌleɪtər, B ˈmɔdju-ə] *s.* (rad.) modulador.
module [ˈmɑdʒul, B ˈmɔdjul] *s.* 1. (mat., arq., hidr., mec.) módulo. 2. (electrón.) elemento de circuito alambrado.
modulus [-ələs, B ˈmɔdju-] *s.* (mat., fís.) módulo.
modulus of elasticity, (fís.) módulo de elasticidad.
modus operandi [ˌmoudəsˌɑpəˈrændi, B ˈmɔdəsˌɔp-] (lat.) modus operandi, manera de hacer, procedimiento.
modus vivendi [-vɪˈvɛndi] (lat.) modus vivendi, manera de vivir.
mofette, moffette [mouˈfɛt] *s.* (geol.) mofeta, fumarola.
mog [mɑg, B mɔg] *v.i.* (*pret., p.p.* MOGGED; *p.pr.* MOGGING) (dial.) partir, marchar (se); moverse lentamente; andar despacio.
Mogul [ˈmouˌgʌl, B mouˈgʌl] *s.* 1. mogol, mongol. 2. **m.,** magnate, hombre de fuste.
mogul base, portalámpara de tamaño grande.
mohair [ˈmouˌhɛr, B -ˌhɛə] *s.* mohair, tela de angora.
Mohammed [mouˈhæməd] *s.* (ant.) *var. de.* **Muhammad.**
Mohammedan [-ən] **Mohameddanism** [-ˌɪzəm] (despec., ant.) *vars. de* **muhammadan, muhammadanism.**
Mohawk [ˈmouˌhɔk] *s.* (*pl.* MOHAWK O MOHAWKS) mohawk, miembro de una tribu de indios de Canadá y E.U.
Mohican [mouˈhikən, B ˈmouɪkən] *s.* mohicano, mahikan, confederación de tribus de indios algonquinos (E.U.).
mohur [ˈmouhər, B -hjuə] *s.* mohúr (antigua moneda de oro de la India y Persia).
moidore [ˈmɔɪdɔr, B -dɔ] *s.* (hist.) moneda de oro portuguesa.
moiety [ˈmɔɪətɪ] *s.* (*pl.* MOIETIES) mitad; parte, porción.
moil [mɔɪl] *v.i.* afanarse, fatigarse, trabajar arduamente. —*v.t.* (pr. dial.) humedecer, mojar, embadurnar, ensuciar. —*s.* 1. fatiga, faena. 2. confusión, tumulto, baraúnda.
moilingly [ˈmɔɪlɪŋlɪ] *adv.* afanosamente, fatigosamente, arduamente.
moiré [mwɑˈreɪ, mɔ-, B ˈmwɑreɪ] *s.* (tej.) moaré, muaré.
moist [mɔɪst] *a.* 1. húmedo, mojado. 2. lloroso (ojos); húmedo, lluvioso (clima, estación, etc.).
moisten [ˈmɔɪsən] *v.t., v.i.* humedecer(se), mojar(se).
moistener [-ənər, B -nə] *s.* 1. mojador (para sellos, sobres, etiquetas engomadas, etc.). 2. humidificador (del aire, etc.), humectador (para usos industriales).
moistness [ˈmɔɪstnəs] *s.* humedad.
moisture [ˈmɔɪstʃər, B -tʃə] *s.* humedad.
moisture index, relación de humedad.
moistureproof [-ˈpruf] *a.* a prueba de humedad.
moisture-resistant [-rɪˈzɪstənt] *a.* resistente a la humedad.
mojarra [mouˈhɑrə] *s.* (ict.) mojarra.
moke [mouk] *s.* 1. (jer., G.B.) burro, asno. 2. (jer. Aust.) jaco, rocín.
molal [ˈmouləl] *a.* (quím.) molal.
molar [ˈmoulər, B -lə] *a.* (fís., quím.) molar.
molar, *a.* 1. molar. 2. (anat.) molar (diente). —*s.* (anat.) molar, muela, diente molar.
molasses [məˈlæsəz] *s.* melaza, miel.
mold, (pr. G.B.) **mould** [mould] *s.* 1. mantillo, tierra vegetal. 2. (ant., dial.) tierra; polvo; (fig.) tumba, sepulcro.

mold, (pr. G.B.) **mould,** *s.* 1. molde, matriz; patrón, plantilla. 2. carácter, naturaleza. 3. forma, aspecto, figura; cuerpo, forma corporal. 4. (arq.) moldura, conjunto de molduras. 5. pieza fundida o vaciada. —*v.t.* 1. moldear, vaciar. 2. moldurar, adornar con molduras o entalladuras. 3. (ant.) mezclar, amasar. 4. **m. oneself on,** tomar como modelo a; **m. upon,** (lit. y fig.) amoldar a.
mold, (pr. G.B.) mould, *s.* (bot.) moho. —*v.i.* enmohecerse.
moldable [ˈmoʊldəbəl] *a.* capaz de ser moldeado, moldeable.
Moldavian [mɑlˈdeɪvɪən, B mɔl-jən] *a., s.* moldavo, de Moldavia, antiguo principado de Europa oriental.
moldboard [ˈmoʊldˌbɔrd, B -ˌbɔd] *s.* 1. (agr.) vertedera (del arado). 2. (const.) tabla del encofrado.
molder, (pr. G.B.). **moulder** [ˈmoʊldər, B -də] *s.* moldeador, vaciador.
molder, (pr. G.B.) **moulder,** *v.i.* desmoronarse, convertirse en polvo.
moldiness, (pr. G.B.) **mouldiness** [ˈmoʊldɪnəs] *s.* estado o aspecto mohoso.
molding, (pr. G.B.) **moulding** [ˈmoʊldɪŋ] *s.* 1. moldeado, moldeamiento. 2. pieza moldeada o vaciada. 3. (arq.) moldura. 4. (elec.) canal superficial.
molding knife, cuchilla de moldurar.
molding press, moldeadora.
moldy, (pr. G.B.) **mouldy** [ˈmoʊldɪ] *a.* (MOLDIER; MOLDIEST) 1. mohoso. 2. (fig.) anticuado, pasado. 3. (jer.) insulso, cansado, aburrido.
mole [moʊl] *s.* 1. lunar (de la piel). 2. (zool.) topo. 3. muelle, espigón, rompeolas. 4. (quím.) molécula gramo, mol.
mole cricket, (ento.) cortón, grillo cebollero, real o talpa.
molecular [məˈlɛkjələr, B -lə] *a.* (fís., quím.) molecular.
molecular conductivity, (fís.) conductividad molecular.
molecular weight, (fís.) peso molecular.
molecule [ˈmɑlɪˌkjul, B ˈmɔl-] *s.* (fís., quím.) 1. molécula. 2. mol, molécula gramo.
molehill [ˈmoʊlˌhɪl] *s.* topera, topinera; **to make a mountain out of a m.,** hacer de una pulga un elefante, hacer una montaña de un grano de arena.
moleskin [-ˌskɪn] *s.* 1. piel de topo. 2. (tej.) moleskín, molesquina. 3. (*pl.*) prenda de vestir, esp. pantalones de moleskín.
molest [məˈlɛst] *v.t.* 1. faltar al respeto a, importunar, molestar. 2. abusar sexualmente de.
molestation [ˌmoʊlˌɛsˈteɪʃən] *s.* 1. importunidad, vejación, acoso. 2. abusos deshonestos.
molester [məˈlɛstər, B -tə] *s.* 1. molestador. 2. persona que comete abusos deshonestos.
moline [məˈlaɪn] *a.* (her.) de áncora, ancorada (díc. de la cruz).
Molinism [ˈmoʊləˌnɪzəm, B ˈmɔl-] *s.* (relig.) molinismo.
moll [mɑl, B mɔl] *s.* (jer.) 1. golfa, ramera. 2. amante de un pandillero o bandido.
mollification [ˌmɑləfəˈkeɪʃən, B ˌmɔl-] *s.* molificación, apaciguamiento, pacificación.
mollify [ˈmɑləˌfaɪ, B ˈmɔl-] *v.t.* (*pret., p.p.* MOLLIFIED; *p.pr.* MOLLIFYING) molificar, suavizar, apaciguar, pacificar; (raro) ablandar. —*v.i.* (ant.) ablandarse.
mollusc, *var. de* **mollusk.**
molluscan [məˈlʌskən, B mɔ-] *a.* (zool.) molusco.
molluscous [-kəs] *a.* (zool.) molusco.
mollusk [ˈmɑləsk, B ˈmɔl-] *s.* (zool.) molusco.
mollycoddle [ˈmɑlɪˌkɑdəl, B ˈmɔlɪˌkɔd-] *s.* (fam.) marica; alfeñique. —*v.t.* mimar, consentir, malcriar, engreír (Amer.).
mollycoddler [-ˌkɑdlər, B -ˌkɔdlə] *s.* mimador, malcriador.
Moloch [ˈmɑlək, ˈmoʊˌlɑk, B ˈmoʊlɔk] *s.* 1. (bíbl.) Moloc. 2. **m.,** (zool.) moloc.
Molossian [məˈlɑʃən, -ˈlɑsɪən, B -ˈlɔsɪən] *a., s.* moloso, natural de Molosia, ciudad de la Grecia antigua.
Molotov cocktail [ˈmɔləˌtɔf-, B -tɔv-] (mil.) cóctel Molotov.
molt, (pr. G.B.) **moult** [moʊlt] *v.t.* mudar (la pluma, el pelo, la piel, los cuernos, etc.). —*v.i.* mudar la pluma o el pellejo. —*s.* muda (de la pluma, piel, etc.).
molten [ˈmoʊltən] *a.* fundido, derretido.
molto [ˈmoʊltoʊ, B ˈmɔl-] *adv.* (mús.) molto (muy, mucho).
moly [ˈmoʊlɪ] *s.* (*pl.* MOLIES) 1. (mitol.) moli, brebaje que protegió a Odiseo de la magia de Circe. 2. (bot.) ajo silvestre.
molybdate [məˈlɪbˌdeɪt] *s.* (quím.) molibdato.
molybdenite [-dəˌnaɪt] *s.* (min.) molibdenita.
molybdenum [-dənəm] *s.* (quím.) molibdeno.
molybdic [-dɪk] *a.* (quím.) molíbdico.
molybdous [-dəs] *a.* (quím.) molibdoso.
mom [mɑm, B mɔm] *s.* (fam.) mamá, mami, mamita.
mom-and-pop [ˈmɑmənˈpɑp] *a.* (*store, business*) (fam.) familiar.
moment [ˈmoʊmənt] *s.* 1. momento, rato, instante. 2. importancia, entidad, peso. 3. estado, grado, etapa, período. 4. (mec.) momento. 5. **at any m.,** de un momento a otro; **at the m.,** en ese momento; **for the m.,** por el momento; **in a m.,** en un momento, en un instante; **of great m.,** de mucha importancia; **of little m.,** de poca monta, de poca importancia; **(come here) this m.,** (ven aquí) al instante; **to have one's moments,** tener (uno) sus ratos.
momentarily [ˌmoʊmənˈtɛrəlɪ, B ˈmoʊməntər-] *adv.* momentáneamente.
momentariness [ˈmoʊmənˌtɛrɪnəs, B -tər-] *s.* índole efímera (de la felicidad, etc.).
momentary [ˈmoʊmənˌtɛrɪ, B -tərɪ] *a.* momentáneo, transitorio, pasajero, efímero.
momently [ˈmoʊməntlɪ] *adv.* 1. a cada momento. 2. de un momento a otro. 3. momentáneamente, por el momento, por un momento.
moment of force, (mec.) momento de una fuerza.
moment of inertia, (mec.) momento de inercia.
momentous [moʊˈmɛntəs] *a.* importante, vital, grave, trascendental, de momento.
momentously [-lɪ] *adv.* de manera trascendental, con importancia, gravemente.
momentousness [-nəs] *s.* importancia, gravedad, trascendencia, entidad, momento.
momentum [moʊˈmɛntəm] *s.* (*pl.* MOMENTA [-tə] o MOMENTUMS) 1. ímpetu, impulso. 2. (mec.) momento.
momma [ˈmɑmə] *s.* (fam.) mamá.
mommy [ˈmɑmi] *s.* (fam.) mami. mamita.
Mon. *abrev. de* **Monday,** lunes (lun.).
monachal [ˈmɑnɪkəl, B ˈmɔn-] *a.* monacal, monástico.
monachism [-ˌɪzəm] *s.* monacato.
monacid [mɑnˈæsəd, B mɔn-] *var. de* **monoacid.**
Monaco [ˈmɑnəˌkoʊ, B ˈmɔnə-] *s.* Mónaco, principado situado en la costa francesa del Mediterráneo.
monad [ˈmoʊnæd, B ˈmɔn-] *s.* (filos., biol., fís., zool.) mónada.
monadelphous [ˌmɑnəˈdɛlfəs, B ˌmɔn-] *a.* (bot.) monadelfo.
monadism [ˈmoʊnædˌɪzəm, B ˈmɔn-] *s.* (filos.) monadismo.
monadnock [məˈnædˌnɑk, B -ˌnɔk] *s.* (geol.) monadnock.
monandrous [məˈnændrəs] *a.* 1. (bot.) monandro. 2. monándrico, que tiene un solo marido.
monandry [-drɪ] *s.* monandria; (bot.) monandria.
monanthous [məˈnænθəs] *a.* (bot.) monanto.
monarch [ˈmɑnərk, -ˌɑrk, B ˈmɔnək] *s.* 1. monarca. 2. (ento.) mariposa grande de alas anaranjadas con bordes y venas negras.
monarchal [məˈnɑrkəl, B mɔˈnɑkəl] **monarchial** [-kɪəl] *a.* monárquico.
monarchianism [-kɪənˌɪzəm] *s.* (hist., teo.) monarquianismo.
monarchic [-kɪk] **monarchical** [-kɪkəl] *a.* monárquico.
monarchically [-kɪklɪ] *adv.* monárquicamente.
monarchism [ˈmɑnərˌkɪzəm, B ˈmɔnəˌ-] *s.* monarquismo, sistema monárquico.
monarchist [-kəst] *a., s.* monárquico.
monarchistic [ˌmɑnərˈkɪstɪk, B ˌmɔnəˈ-] *a.* monárquico.
monarchy [ˈmɑnərkɪ, B ˈmɔnəkɪ] *s.* (*pl.* MONARCH ES) monarquía.
monasterial [ˌmɑnəsˈtɪrɪəl, B ˌmɔn-] *a.* de monasterio.
monastery [ˈmɑnəsˌtɛrɪ, B ˈmɔnəstərɪ] *s.* (*pl.* MONASTERIES) monasterio.
monastic [məˈnæstɪk] **monastical** [-ɪkəl] *a.* monástico. —*s.* monje, religioso.
monastically [-ɪkəlɪ] *adv.* monásticamente.
monasticism [-əˌsɪzəm] *s.* monaquismo, vida monástica.
monatomic [ˌmɑnəˈtɑmɪk, B ˌmɔnəˈtɔm-] *a.* (quím.) monatómico, monoatómico.
monaural [mɑnˈɔrəl, B mɔn-] *a.* 1. monaural (sordera, etc.). 2. monofónico (sonido, radiodifusión, disco, etc.).
monaxial [-ˈæksɪəl] *a.* (bot.) monoáxico.
monazite [ˈmɑnəˌzaɪt, B ˈmɔn-] *s.* (min.) monacita.
Monday [ˈmʌndɪ] *s.* lunes.
Monday morning quarterback, persona que aconseja después de pasada la ocasión.
monecious [məˈniʃəs] *var. de* **monoecious.**
Monel metal [moʊˈnɛl-] (metal.) monel.
monetary [ˈmɑnəˌtɛrɪ, ˈmʌn-, B ˈmʌnɪtərɪ] *a.* 1. monetario. 2. pecuniario.
monetary standard, (e.p.) patrón monetario.
monetary unit, unidad monetaria.
monetization [ˌmɑnətəˈzeɪʃən, ˌmʌn-, B ˌmʌnɪtaɪ-] s. monetización, amonedación.
monetize [ˈmɑnəˌtaɪz, ˈmʌn-, B ˈmʌn-] *v.t.* 1. amonedar, monetizar (un metal). 2. monetizar, dar curso legal a (billetes, etc.).
money [ˈmʌnɪ] *s.* (*pl.* MONEYS o MONIES) 1. dinero, moneda. 2. dinero, caudal. 3. premio (de dinero). 4. **for love or m.,** (en frases negativas) por nada del mundo; **in the m.,** (jer.) acaudalado, rico; **m. in hand,** dinero contante; **m. makes m.,** dinero llama dinero; **time is m.,** el tiempo es oro; **to get one's money's worth out of,** sacar el valor de; **to make m.,** hacer dinero; **to put m. into,** invertir dinero en; **to put m. on,** apostar (dinero) a (un caballo, etc.); **your m. or your life,** la bolsa o la vida; **m. talks,** el dinero manda.
moneybag [-ˌbæg] *s.* 1. monedero, bolsa o bolsón para dinero. 2. (*pl.*) riquezas, fortuna. 3. (*pl.*) ricacho, ricachón.
money belt, faltriquera.
money box, alcancía.
money changer, cambista.
moneyed [ˈmʌnid] *a.* adinerado, rico, acaudalado.

moneyer ['mʌnɪər, B -ɪə] *s.* 1. monedero, acuñador. 2. (raro) banquero.
money exchange house, casa de cambio.
money-grubber [-ˌgrʌbər, B -ə] *s.* codicioso, avariento.
money-lender [-ˌlɛndər, B -də] *s.* prestamista.
moneymaker [-ˌmeɪkər, B -kə] *s.* 1. experto en ganar dinero. 2. éxito económico (ej., un nuevo producto, una película, etc.).
moneymaking [-ˌmeɪkɪŋ] *s.* enriquecimiento. —*a.* lucrativo, productivo, ganancioso.
money market, mercado de valores.
money of account, moneda imaginaria.
money order, giro postal, libranza postal.
moneywort ['mʌnɪˌwɜrt, B -ˌwɜt] *s.* (bot.) hierba de la moneda.
monger ['mʌŋgər, 'mɑŋ-, B 'mʌŋgə] *s.* tratante, traficante (esp. en negociaciones vergonzosas). —*v.t.* traficar en, comerciar con.
Mongol ['mɑŋgəl, -goʊl, B 'mɔŋgəl] *a., s.* mogol, mongol, de Mongolia.
Mongolia [mɑŋ'goʊlɪə, -'goʊljə, B mɔŋ-jə] *s.* Mongolia, región de Asia.
Mongolian [-ən, B -jən] *a.* 1. mogólico, mongólico, mogol, mongol. 2. (med.) mongólico, mongoloide. —*s.* mogol, mongol (natural de Mongolia, lengua mongólica).
Mongolic [-'gɑlɪk, B -'gɔl-] *a.* mogólico, mongólico. —*s.* lengua mongólica.
Mongolism ['mɑŋgəˌlɪzəm, B 'mɔŋ-] *s.* (med.) mongolismo.
Mongoloid [-ˌlɔɪd] *a., s.* mongoloide; (med.) mongoloide.
mongoose ['mɑnˌgus, B 'mɔŋ-] *s.* (*pl.* MONGOOSES) (zool.) mangosta.
mongrel ['mʌŋgrəl, 'mɑŋ-, B 'mʌŋ-] *s.* híbrido, mestizo, esp. perro cruzado. —*a.* mestizo, híbrido, cruzado, chusco (Perú); mixto.
mongst [mʌŋst] (ant.) *contr. de* **amongst.**
monies, *pl. de* **money.**
moniker, monicker ['mɑnɪkər, B 'mɔnɪkə] *s.* (jer.) nombre, apelativo, apodo.
moniliform [mə'nɪləˌfɔrm, B -ˌfɔm] *a.* (bot., zool.) moniliforme.
monish ['mɑnɪʃ, B 'mɔn-] *v.t.* amonestar, advertir.
monism ['moʊˌnɪzəm, B 'mɔn-] *s.* (filos.) monismo.
monist [-nəst] *s.* (filos.) monista.
monistic [moʊ'nɪstɪk, mɑ-, B mɔ-] *a.* (filos.) monista.
monition [moʊ'nɪʃən] *s.* 1. admonición, amonestación, prevención, consejo. 2. (der.) emplazamiento, citación, notificación, llamamiento a declarar.
monitor ['mɑnətər, B 'mɔnɪtə] *s.* 1. monitor, amonestador, admonitor. 2. monitor (alumno encargado de tareas disciplinarias). 3. (zool.) varano. 4. (mar.) monitor (barco de guerra). 5. (t.v.) monitor de imagen; (rad., t.v.) observador. —*v.t.* 1. escuchar (radiodifusiones con fines de censura o análisis); revisar, inspeccionar (telégrafo, teléfono, televisión o radio para averiguar la calidad de transmisión, fidelidad de una banda de frecuencia, señales, etc.). 2. (fís.) revisar, verificar, inspeccionar (en una superficie, rayo, destello, etc. la intensidad de radiaciones).
monitorial [ˌmɑnə'tɔrɪəl, B ˌmɔn-] *a.* 1. monitorio. 2. de monitor.
monitorship ['mɑnətərˌʃɪp, B 'mɔnɪtəˌ-] *s.* cargo de monitor.
monitory [-ˌtɔrɪ, B -tərɪ] *a.* monitorio, amonestador, admonitorio.
monk [mʌŋk] *s.* monje, fraile.
monkery ['mʌŋkərɪ] *s.* (*pl.* MONKERIES) 1. vida monástica, monaquismo; (*pl.*) usos y costumbres monásticas. 2. monasterio, frailía.
monkey ['mʌŋkɪ] *s.* (*pl.* MONKEYS) 1. (zool.) mono. 2. (fig.) mono. 3. maza; esclusa para escoria; conducto de ventilación; grapa, trinquete, fiador del martinete. 4. (jer.) (billete de) 500 libras o 500 dólares. 5. **to be made a m. of,** quedar en ridículo; **to have a m. on one's back,** (jer.) ser adicto a las drogas, ser toxicómano; (G.B.) estar resentido; **to make a m. of,** dejar hecho un mico, dejar malparado, poner en ridículo; embaucar; **to play the m.,** hacer monadas; **young m.,** niño juguetón y travieso. —*v.i.* 1. (t. con *about* o *around*) tontear, hacer payasadas, travesear, chancear. 2. **m. with,** jugar con (algo serio o peligroso); tomarse libertades con; meterse con. —*v.t.* imitar, remedar.
monkey bread, 1. fruto del baobab. 2. (bot.) baobab (árbol).
monkey business, (fam.) trampería, truco; diablura.
monkey gaff, (mar.) pico para la bandera.
monkey jacket, chaqueta corta y ajustada.
monkeynut [-ˌnʌt] *s.* maní, cacahuete, cacahuate, cacahué.
monkey puzzle, (bot.) pehuén, pino araucano (Chile).
monkeyshine [-ˌʃaɪn] *s.* (jer., E.U.) monada, diablura, payasada, monería.
monkey suit, (jer.) traje elegante (de hombre); uniforme que se usa con poca frecuencia.
monkey wrench, 1. (mec.) llave ajustable, llave inglesa. 2. **to throw a m.w. into,** obstaculizar o interferir (en planes, funcionamiento, etc.).
monkhood ['mʌŋkhʊd] *s.* 1. monacato. 2. los monjes (en común), frailería.
monkish [-ɪʃ] *a.* 1. monástico. 2. frailengo, frailesco; frailuno, ej., *m. manners,* maneras o costumbres frailunas.
monkishly [-lɪ] *adv.* de modo monástico o frailuno, frailunamente.
monk's cloth, arpillera (material de algodón grueso para hacer cortinas o sobrecamas).
monkshood ['mʌŋksˌhʊd] *s.* (bot.) napelo, acónito, anapelo, casco de Júpiter, matalobos, uva lupina o verga.
monoacid [ˌmɑnoʊ'æsəd, B ˌmɔn-] *a., s.* (quím.) monoácido.
monobasic [-'beɪsɪk] *a.* (quím.) monobásico.
monocalcic [-'kælsɪk] *a.* (quím.) monocálcico.
monocarpellary [-'kɑrpəˌlɛrɪ, B -'kɑpələrɪ] *a.* (bot.) monocarpelar.
monocarpic [-pɪk] *a.* (bot.) monocárpico.
monocarpous [-pəs] *a.* (bot.) monocarpo.
Monoceros [mə'nɑsərəs, B -'nɔsərɔs] *s.* (astr.) Monócero.
monochlamydeous [ˌmɑnəklə'mɪdɪəs, B ˌmɔnoʊ-] *a.* (bot.) monoclamídeo.
monochord ['mɑnəˌkɔrd, B 'mɔnoʊˌkɔd] *s.* (mús.) monocordio, instrumento acústico.
monochromatic [ˌmɑnəkroʊ'mætɪk, B ˌmɔn-] *a.* monocromo, monocromático.
monochromatism [-'kroʊməˌtɪzəm] *s.* (med.) monocromasia.
monochrome ['mɑnəˌkroʊm, B 'mɔn-] *s.* monocromo.
monocle ['mɑnəkəl, B 'mɔn-] *s.* monóculo.
monocled [-kəld] *a.* con monóculo, ej., *a m. gentleman,* un caballero con monóculo.
monoclinal [ˌmɑnə'klaɪnəl, B ˌmɔn-] *a.* (geol.) monoclinal —*s.* (geol.) pliegue monoclinal.
monocline ['mɑnəˌklaɪn, B 'mɔn-] *s.* (geol.) pliegue monoclinal.
monoclinic [ˌmɑnə'klɪnɪk, B ˌmɔn-] *a.* (min.) monoclínico.
monoclinous [-'klaɪnəs] *a.* (bot.) monoclino.
monocoque ['mɑnəˌkoʊk, B 'mɔnəˌkɔk] *s.* (aer.) monocasco.
monocot [-ˌkɑt, B -ˌkɔt] *s.* (bot.) monocotiledóneo.
monocotyledon [ˌmɑnəˌkɑtə'lidən, B ˌmɔnoʊˌkɔt-] *s.* (bot.) monocotiledón, monocotiledóneo.
monocotyledonous [-əs] *a.* (bot.) monocotiledón, monocotiledóneo.
monocracy [mə'nɑkrəsɪ, B -'nɔk-] *s.* autocracia.
monocular [me'nɑkjələr, B -'nɔkjʊlə] *a.* monocular.
monoculture ['mɑnəˌkʌltʃər, B 'mɔn-tʃə] *s.* (agr.) monocultivo.
monocycle [-ˌsaɪkəl] *s.* monociclo, vehículo con una sola rueda.
monocyclic [ˌmɑnə'saɪklɪk, B ˌmɔn-] *a.* (elec., quím.) monociclo.
monocyte ['mɑnəˌsaɪt, B 'mɔn-] *s.* (fisiol.) monocito.
monodactylous [ˌmɑnə'dæktələs, B ˌmɔn-] *a.* (zool.) monodáctilo.
monodic [mə'nɑdɪk, B -'nɔd-] **monodical** [-ɪkəl] *a.* (mús.) monódico (estilo de composición en la que predomina una voz sobre las otras que la apoyan).
monodist ['mɑnədəst, B 'mɔn-] *s.* compositor o cantor de monodias.
monody [-dɪ] *s.* (*pl.* MONODIES) 1. (mús.) monodia. 2. elegía, treno.
monoecious [mə'niʃəs] *a.* (biol.) monoico.
monofuel ['mɑnəˌfjuəl, B 'mɔn-] *s.* monopropulsante.
monogamic [ˌmɑnə'gæmɪk, B ˌmɔn-] *a.* monogámico, de un solo cónyuge por vida.
monogamist [mə'nɑgəməst, B -'nɔg-] *a., s.* monogamista, que cree en la monogamia.
monogamous [-məs] *a.* monógamo, que practica la monogamia.
monogamy [-mɪ] *s.* monogamia, sistema en el cual se tiene sólo un cónyuge o compañero de vida.
monogenesis [ˌmɑnə'dʒɛnəsəs, B ˌmɔn-] *s.* (biol.) monogenia, monogénesis.
monogenetic [-dʒə'nɛtɪk] *a.* (biol.) monogenésico.
monogenic [-'dʒɛnɪk] *a.* (biol.) monogénico.
monogenism [mə'nɑdʒəˌnɪzəm, B -'nɔdʒ-] *s.* (antrop., biol.) monogenismo.
monogenist [-nəst] *s.* (biol.) monogenista.
monogram ['mɑnəˌgræm, B 'mɔn-] *s.* monograma.
monograph [-ˌgræf, B -ˌgrɑf] *s.* monografía, tratado o artículo que versa sobre un solo sujeto o tema. —*v.t.* hacer una monografía de; discutir en una monografía.
monographer [mə'nɑgrəfər, B -'nɔgrəfə] *s.* monografista.
monographic [ˌmɑnə'græfɪk, B ˌmɔn-] *a.* monográfico.
monogynous [mə'nɑdʒənəs, B -'nɔdʒ-] *a.* (bot.) monógino.
monogyny [-nɪ] *s.* monogamia.
monohydrate [ˌmɑnə'haɪˌdreɪt, B ˌmɔn-] *s.* (quím.) monohidrato.
monohydric [-drɪk] *a.* (quím.) monohídrico.
monolatry [mə'nɑlətrɪ, B -'nɔl-] *s.* adoración de un solo dios, monoteísmo.
monolingual ['mɑnə'lɪŋgwəl] *a.* monolingüe.
monolith['mɑnəˌlɪθ, B 'mɔn-] *s.* monolito.
monolithic [ˌmɑnə'lɪθɪk, B ˌmɔn-] *a.* (lit., fig.) monolítico.
monologue, monolog ['mɑnəˌlɔg, -ˌlɑg, B 'mɔnəlɔg] *s.* monólogo.

monologuist [-əst] **monologist** [mə'nɑlədʒəst, B -'nɔl-] *s.* recitador de monólogos.
monomania [ˌmɑnə'meɪnɪə, B ˌmɔn-] *s.* monomanía, obsesión por algo; preocupación excesiva por un tema.
monomaniac [-'meɪnɪˌæk] *s.* monomaníaco.
monomaniacal [-mə'naɪəkəl] *a.* monomaníaco, monomaniático.
monomer ['mɑnəmər, B 'mɔnəmə] *s.* (quím.) monómero.
monomeric [ˌmɑnə'mɛrɪk, B ˌmɔn-] *a.* (quím.) monómero.
monometallic [ˌmɑnoʊmə'tælɪk, B ˌmɔn-] *a.* (metal.) 1. monometálico. 2. (e.p.) monometalista.
monometallism [-'mɛtəlˌɪzəm] *s.* (e.p.) monometalismo.
monometallist [-'mɛtələst] *s.* (e.p.) monometalista.
monomial [mɑ'noʊmɪəl, B mɔ-] *a.* (mat., biol.) que consta de un solo término. —*s.* (mat.) monomio.
monomolecular [ˌmɑnoʊmə'lɛkjələr, B ˌmɔn-lə] *a.* (fís., quím.) monomolecular.
monomorphic [-'mɔrfɪk, B -'mɔfɪk] **monomorphous** [-fəs] *a.* (biol.) monomorfo.
mononuclear [ˌmɑnoʊ'nuklɪər, B ˌmɔnoʊ'njuklɪə] *a.* mononuclear.
monopetalous [-'pɛtələs] *a.* (bot.) monopétalo.
monophagous [mə'nɑfəgəs, B -'nɔf-] *a.* monófago, que se alimenta de una sola clase de comida (díc. esp. de insectos).
monophagy [-ədʒɪ] *s.* monofagia.
monophobia [ˌmɑnə'foʊbɪə, B ˌmɔn-] *s.* (med.) monofobia.
monophonic [-'fɑnɪk, B -'foʊnɪk] *a.* 1. (mús.) monófono. 2. (electrón.) monofónico (sonido reproducido).
monophthong ['mɑnəfˌθɔŋ, B 'mɔn-] *s.* (fon.) monoptongo.
monophyletic [ˌmɑnəfaɪ'lɛtɪk, B 'mɔn-] *a.* (biol.) monofilético.
Monophysite [mə'nɑfəˌsaɪt, B -'nɔf-] *s.* (relig.) monofisita.
Monophysitic [məˌnɑfə'sɪtɪk, B -nɔf-] *a.* (relig.) monofisita.
monoplane ['mɑnəˌpleɪn, B 'mɔn-] *s.* (aer.) monoplano.
monoplegia [ˌmɑnə'plidʒɪə, B ˌmɔn-] *s.* (med.) monoplejía.
monoplegic [-'plidʒɪk] *a.* (med.) monopléjico.
monopode ['mɑnəˌpoʊd, B 'mɔn-] *s.* (bot.) monopodio.
monopodial [ˌmɑnə'poʊdɪəl, B ˌmɔn-] *a.* (bot.) monopodial.
monopolar [ˌmɑnoʊ'poʊlər, B ˌmɔn-lə] *a.* (elec.) monopolar, unipolar.
monopolist [mə'nɑpələst, B -'nɔp-] *s.* monopolista, monopolizador (que no tiene competencia).
monopolistic [məˌnɑpə'lɪstɪk, B -ˌnɔp-] *a.* monopolizador.
monopolization [-lə'zeɪʃən, B -laɪ-] *s.* monopolización.
monopolize [mə'nɑpəˌlaɪz, B -'nɔp-] *v.t.* monopolizar.
monopolizer [-ər, B -ə] *s.* monopolista, monopolizador.
monopoly [mə'nɑpəlɪ, B -'nɔp-] *s.* (*pl.* MONOPOLIES) monopolio.
monopropellant [ˌmɑnoʊprə'pɛlənt, B ˌmɔn-] *s.* monopropulsante.
monopsony [mə'nɑpsənɪ, B -'nɔp-] *s.* (*pl.* MONOPSONIES) (com.) monopsonio (cuando existe un solo comprador).
monorail ['mɑnəˌreɪl, B 'mɔn-] *s.* (f.c.) monocarril.
monosaccharide [ˌmɑnə'sækəˌraɪd, B ˌmɔn-] *s.* (quím.) monosacárido.
monosepalous [-'sɛpələs] *a.* (bot.) monosépalo.
monosodium glutamate [-'soʊdɪəm-] glutamato monosódico, substancia que se emplea para intensificar el sabor de los alimentos.
monosome ['mɑnəˌsoʊm, B 'mɔn-] *s.* (biol.) monosoma.
monospermous [ˌmɑnə'spɜrməs, B ˌmɔnə'spɜməs] **monospermal** [-məl] *a.* (bot.) monospermo.
monostele ['mɑnəˌstil, B 'mɔn-] *s.* (bot.) monostela.
monostelic [ˌmɑnə'stilɪk, B ˌmɔn-] *a.* (bot.) monostélico.
monostich ['mɑnəˌstɪk, B 'mɔn-] *s.* (poét.) poema monóstico.
monostrophe [-ˌstroʊf] *s.* (poét.) monóstrofe.
monostrophic [ˌmɑnə'strɑfɪk, B ˌmɔnə'strɔf-] *a.* monostrófico.
monostylous [-'staɪləs] *a.* (bot.) monostíleo.
monosyllabic [-sə'læbɪk] *a.* 1. (gram.) monosílabo. 2. monosilábico (respuesta, etc.).
monosyllabically [-ɪkəlɪ] *adv.* en monosílabos.
monosyllable ['mɑnəˌsɪləbəl, B 'mɔn-] *s.* monosílabo.
monosymmetric [ˌmɑnəsə'mɛtrɪk, B mɔn-] *a.* monosimétrico.
monotheism ['mɑnəθiˌɪzəm, B 'mɔn-] *s.* (relig.) monoteísmo, creencia en la existencia de un solo Dios.
monotheist [-ˌθiəst] *s.* monoteísta.
monotheistic [ˌmɑnəθi'ɪstɪk, B ˌmɔn-] **monotheistical** [-ɪkəl] *a.* monoteísta, del que cree en un solo Dios.
monotint ['mɑnəˌtɪnt, B 'mɔn-] *s.* monocromo.
monotone [-ˌtoʊn] *s.* monotonía; **in a m.,** con monotonía, monótonamente. —*a.* monótono.
monotonic [ˌmɑnə'tɑnɪk, B ˌmɔnə'tɔn-] *a.* monótono.
monotonically [-ɪkəlɪ] *adv.* monótonamente.
monotonous [mə'nɑtənəs, B -'nɔt-] *a.* monótono.
monotonously [-lɪ] *adv.* monótonamente.
monotonousness [-nəs] **monotony** [-ənɪ] *s.* monotonía.
monotrematous [ˌmɑnə'trɛmətəs, B ˌmɔn-] *a.* (zool.) monotrema, monotremado.
monotreme ['mɑnəˌtrim, B 'mɔn-] *s.* (zool.) monotrema, monotremado.
monotrichic [ˌmɑnə'trɪkɪk, B ˌmɔn-] **monotrichous** [mə'nɑtrɪkəs, B -'nɔ-] *a.* (biol.) monotrico.
monotype ['mɑnəˌtaɪp, B 'mɔn-] *s.* (impr.) monotipo.
monotypic [ˌmɑnə'tɪpɪk, B ˌmɔn-] *a.* (biol.) monotipo.
monovalent [-'veɪlənt] *a.* 1. (med.) monovalente. 2. (quím.) monovalente, univalente.
monoxide [mə'nɑkˌsaɪd, B -'nɔk-] *s.* (quím.) monóxido.
Monseigneur [ˌmoʊnˌsɛn'jɜ, B ˌmɔn-] *s.* monseñor.
monsieur [mə'sjɜ] *s.* (*pl.* MESSIEURS) 1. (fr.) (como tratamiento fr.) señor. 2. (fam.) francés (persona).
Monsignor [mɑn'sɪnjər, B mɔn-jə] *s.* (*pl.* MONSIGNORI [-ˌsin'jɔrɪ]) (relig.) monseñor (título honorífico usado por dignatarios de la iglesia católica).
monsoon [mɑn'sun, B mɔn-] *s.* monzón, viento que sopla en el Océano Índico.
monster ['mɑnstər, B 'mɔnstə] *s.* monstruo. —*a.* monstruoso; enorme; terrible; fenomenal; prodigioso.
monstrance ['mɑnstrəns, B 'mɔn-] *s.* (relig.) custodia, ostensorio.
monstrosity [mɑn'strɑsətɪ, B mɔn'strɔs-] *s.* (*pl.* MONSTROSITIES) monstruosidad.
monstrous ['mɑnstrəs, B 'mɔn-] *a.* monstruoso.
monstrously [-lɪ] *adv.* monstruosamente.
monstrousness [-nəs] *s.* monstruosidad.
Mont. *abrev. de* **Montana,** Montana (E.U.).
montage [mɑn'tɑʒ, B mɔn-] *s.* (arte, foto., cinem.) montaje. —*v.t.* combinar en un montaje, hacer un montaje de.
Montagues and Capulets ['mɑntəˌgjuzən-'kæpjələts, B 'mɔn-] cegríes y abencerrajes, Montescos y Capuletos, enemigos acérrimos.
Montana [mɑn'tænə, B mɔn-] *s.* Montana, estado de los E.U.
montane ['mɑnteɪn, B 'mɔn-] *a.* montano, montés (díc. de la flora y fauna).
Mont Blanc [ˌmoʊn'blɑn, B ˌmɔm'blɑŋ] el Monte Blanco (en los Alpes entre Francia e Italia).
monte ['mɑntɪ, B 'mɔn-] *s.* monte, monte banca (juego de naipes español e hispanoamericano).
monteith [mɑn'tiθ, B mɔn-] *s.* ponchera o aguamanil grande del siglo XVII, comúnmente de plata.
Montenegrin [ˌmɑntə'nigrən, B ˌmɔn-] *a.*, *s.* montenegrino, de un antiguo principado balcánico, hoy en Yugoslavia.
montero [mɑn'tɛrˌoʊ, B mɔn-] *s.* montera, gorra de cazador.
Montevideo [ˌmɑntəvɪ'deɪoʊ, B ˌmɔn-] *s.* Montevideo, capital de Uruguay.
montgolfier [mɑnt'gɑlfɪər, B mɔnt'gɔlfɪə] *s.* globo Montgolfier.
month [mʌnθ] *s.* mes.
monthly ['mʌnθlɪ] *a.* mensual. —*s.* (*pl.* MONTHLIES) 1. publicación mensual, revista mensual. 2. (*pl.*) mes, menstruo. — *adv.* mensualmente.
month of Sundays, (fam.) largo período, mucho tiempo.
monticule ['mɑntɪˌkjul, B 'mɔn-] *s.* 1. montículo. 2. chimenea o cono secundario (de un volcán).
montmorillonite [ˌmɑntmə'rɪləˌnaɪt, B mɔnt-] *s.* (min.) montmorillonita.
monument ['mɑnjəmənt, B 'mɔn-] *s.* 1. monumento. 2. (fig.) mojón, lindero, límite (como un río, lago, etc. que marca una línea fronteriza), hito. 3. (fig.) monumento. 4. (ant.) memorial, escrito. 5. (ant.) cripta.
monumental [ˌmɑnjə'mɛntəl, B ˌmɔn-] *a.* monumental, grandioso.
monumentalize [-ˌaɪz] *v.t.* conmemorar con un monumento, erigir un monumento en memoria de.
monumentally [-əlɪ] *adv.* de manera monumental, en forma monumental, monumentalmente.
monzonite [mɑn'zoʊˌnaɪt, 'mɑnzə-, B mɔn'zoʊ-] *s.* (min.) monzonita.
moo [mu] *v.i.* (*pret., p.p.* MOOED; *p.pr.* MOOING) mugir (la vaca). —*s.* (*pl.* MOOS) mu, mugido (de vaca).
mooch [mutʃ] (jer.) *v.i.* 1. vagar, deambular. 2. gorrear, gorronear, vivir de gorra. —*v.t.* 1. robar, ratear, birlar, sisar. 2. pedir como regalo, conseguir gratis.
moocher ['mutʃər, B -ə] *s.* (jer.) 1. vago. 2. gorrón, gorrero, gorrista. 3. ratero.
mood [mud] *s.* humor, talante, genio, disposición (de ánimo); (*pl.*) mal humor. 2. (gram.) modo (del verbo); (lóg.) modo. 3. **to be in a bad m.,**

estar de mal talante; **to be in the m. (for),** estar con ánimo (para), estar (para) ej., *he's not in the m. for jokes,* él no está para bromas.

moodily ['mudəlɪ] *adv.* 1. malhumoradamente, de modo malhumorado. 2. caprichosamente.

moodiness ['mudɪnəs] *s.* 1. malhumor, tristeza, melancolía. 2. disposición caprichosa.

moody ['mudɪ] *a.* (MOODIER; MOODIEST) 1. malhumorado, triste, taciturno. 2. caprichoso.

mool [mul] *s.* (dial., G.B.) 1. tierra, suelo, tierra vegetal. 2. (*pl.*) tumbas, sepulturas, sepulcros.

moola, moolah ['mulə] *s.* (jer.) guita, mosca, plata (dinero).

moon [mun] *s.* 1. luna. 2. (poét.) mes. 3. **once in a blue m.,** muy raramente; **to cry** (o **reach**) **for the m.,** pedir la luna, pedir peras al olmo, anhelar lo inalcanzable. —*v.i.* 1. soñar despierto, fantasear, pasar el tiempo fantaseando. 2. **m. about,** vagar sin rumbo; **m. over,** fantasear.

moonbeam ['mun,bim] *s.* rayo de luna.

moon blindness, 1. ceguera nocturna. 2. (vet.) inflamación periódica de los ojos del caballo.

mooncalf [-,kæf, B -,kɑf] *s.* 1. bobalicón, zonzo, tonto. 2. (ant.) monstruo, monstruosidad.

mooneye [-,aɪ] *s.* (vet.) ceguera nocturna.

mooneyed [-,aɪd] *a.* con los ojos desmesuradamente abiertos (por asombro, terror, pavor, etc.).

moonfaced [-,feɪst] *a.* carilleno, carirredondo, mofletudo.

moonfish ['mun,fɪʃ] *s.* (ict.) pez luna.

moonflower [-,flaʊər, B -ə] *s.* (bot.) 1. (G.B.) margarita mayor. 2. (E.U.) campanilla tropical americana.

moonish [-ɪʃ] *a.* 1. semejante a la luna. 2. caprichoso, voluntarioso.

moonlet [-lət] *s.* pequeño satélite (natural o artificial).

moonlight [-,laɪt] *s.* luz de luna, claro de luna. —*a.* iluminado por la luna. —*v.i.* (jer.) tener dos empleos a la vez.

moonlighter [-,laɪtər, B -ə] *s.* (jer.) persona que tiene dos empleos a la vez.

moonlit [-,lɪt] *a.* iluminado por la luna.

moonrise [-,raɪz] *s.* salida de la luna.

moonsail [-,seɪl] *s.* (mar.) monterilla, montera.

moonscape [-,skeɪp] *s.* paisaje lunar.

moonset ['mun,sɛt] *s.* puesta de la luna.

moonshine [-,ʃaɪn] *s.* 1. brillo o luz de la luna. 2. (jer.) tontería, disparate. 3. (jer., E.U.) licor destilado ilegalmente.

moonshiner [-,ʃaɪnər, B -nə] *s.* (jer.) el que fabrica licor ilegalmente; contrabandista de licores.

moonstone [-,stoʊn] *s.* (min.) piedra de la luna, adularia.

moonstruck [-,strʌk] *a.* 1. distraído, aturdido. 2. soñador. 3. lunático, venático.

moonwort [-,wɜrt, B -,wɜt] *s.* (bot.) lunaria menor, botriquio.

moony [-ɪ] *a.* (MOONIER; MOONIEST) 1. semejante a la luna. 2. lunado, semilunar. 3. iluminado por la luna. 4. soñador, distraído.

moor [mʊr, B mʊə] *v.t.* (mar.) amarrar, aferrar, atar con cables, afirmar con anclas. —*v.i.* (mar.) anclar, atracar, echar anclas. —*s.* (G.B.) páramo, terreno yermo; brezal, marjal.

Moor, *s.* moro, musulmán de origen berberisco y árabe.

moorage ['mʊrɪdʒ, B 'mʊərɪdʒ] *s.* (mar.) 1. amarradero. 2. amarre, amarradura. 3. amarraje.

moorfowl ['mʊr,faʊl, B 'mʊə,-] *s.* (orn.) lagópedo de Escocia.

moor hen, (orn.) 1. hembra del lagópedo de Escocia. 2. polla de agua.

mooring ['mʊrɪŋ, B 'mʊər-] *s.* (mar.) 1. (*gen. pl.*) amarra, noray, proís. 2. (*pl.*) amarradero. 3. amarre, amarradura.

mooring buoy, (mar.) boya de amarre o de anclaje.

mooring mast, m. tower, (aer.) torre de amarre de dirigibles.

Moorish ['mʊrɪʃ, B 'mʊər-] *a.* moro, morisco, moruno.

Moorish arch, (arq.) arco árabe o mudéjar.

moorland ['mʊr,lænd, B 'mʊələnd] *s.* páramo, paramera, marjal.

moose [mus] *s.* (zool.) anta, ante, alce.

moosewood ['mus,wʊd] *s.* (bot.) (variedad de) arce.

moot [mut] *s.* 1. (hist., G.B.) asamblea, grupo, junta. 2. (ant.) discusión, debate, argumento. —*v.t., v.i.* 1. someter a discusión; discutir, debatir. 2. (ant.) discutir como ejercicio o práctica (esp. estudiantes de derecho). —*a.* discutible, debatible, opinable.

moot court, tribunal ficticio (que se forma para juzgar pleitos supuestos en la enseñanza del derecho).

mop [mɑp, B mɔp] *v.i.* (*pret., p.p.*MOPPED; *p.pr.* MOPPING) hacer muecas. —*s.* 1. mueca, gesto. 2. aljofifa, estropajo, trapeador, hisopo. 3. cabellera espesa y desaliñada, greña. —*v.t.* 1. aljofifar, trapear. 2. enjugarse o secarse (lágrimas o la frente con un pañuelo). 3. **m. the floor with,** (jer.) batir o vencer de de modo aplastante, aplastar; dar una zurra tremenda a; **m. up,** enjugar, secar con estropajo o trapo; absorber, sorber, chupar; zurrar, dar una paliza a; terminar, liquidar, acabar con (los restos del enemigo), limpiar (territorio) de tropas restantes.

mopboard ['mɑp,bɔrd, B 'mɔp,bɔd] *s.* (E.U.) rodapié, friso.

mope [moʊp] *v.i.* abatirse, desanimarse; estar taciturno, abatido. —*v.t.* abatir, desanimar. —*s.* 1. (t. **moper**) persona apática o indolente. 2. (*pl.*) apatía, murria.

mopish ['moʊpɪʃ] *a.* abatido, melancólico, apático, indolente.

mopishly [-lɪ] *adv.* melancólicamente, apáticamente, abatidamente.

mopishness [-nəs] *s.* abatimiento, apatía, desaliento.

moppet ['mɑpət, B 'mɔp-] *s.* 1. (fam.) criatura, niño, niña; muñeca. 2. (ant.) querido.

moquette [moʊ'kɛt, B mə-] *s.* (tej.) moqueta.

mora ['mɔrə] *s.* (*pl.* MORAE [-,ri] o MORAS) 1. (poét.) unidad métrica, sílaba breve. 2. (fon.) mora.

moraine [mə'reɪn, B mɔ-] *s.* (geol.) morena, morrena.

moral ['mɔrəl, 'mɑr-, B 'mɔr-] *a.* 1. moral, ético, moralizador. 2. virtuoso, probo. 3. moral, virtual (certidumbre, etc.). —*s.* (*gen. pl.*) moral (*f.*), moralidad; moral sexual. 2. (*pl.*) ciencia de la moral, ética. 3. moraleja, enseñanza; máxima, proverbio. 4. (ant.) moral (*f.*), estado de ánimo, espíritu. 5. **to draw the m.**(of), sacar la moraleja (de); **to point a m.,** ilustrar una enseñanza moral.

morale [mə'ræl, B mɔ'rɑl] *s.* 1. moral (*f.*), estado de ánimo, espíritu. 2. (ant.) principios morales, ética. 3. **high m.,** buen espíritu de equipo (en tropas, conjuntos organizados, etc.).

moral hazard, (seguros) riesgo moral.

moralism ['mɔrəl,ɪzəm, 'mɑr-, B 'mɔr-] *s.* 1. moralización. 2. moralismo.

moralist [-əst] *s.* 1. moralista. 2. persona moral.

moralistic [,mɔrə'lɪstɪk, mɑr-, B ,mɔr-] *a.* moralizador.

morality [mə'rælətɪ] *s.* 1. moralidad. 2. moraleja, lección o enseñanza moral. 3. precepto moral. 4. **m. play,** (hist.) auto, moralidad (drama alegórico de las virtudes morales).

moralization [,mɔrələ,zeɪʃən, ,mɑr-, B ,mɔrəlaɪ-] *s.* moralización.

moralize ['mɔrə,laɪz, 'mɑr-, B 'mɔr-] *v.t.* 1. sacar moralejas de. 2. moralizar, reformar (malas costumbres). 3. (ant.) dar lecciones de moral. —*v.i.* moralizar, hacerse reflexiones morales.

moralizer [-ər, B -ə] *s.* moralizador.

morally ['mɔrəlɪ, 'mɑr-, B 'mɔr-] *adv.* moralmente, éticamente.

moral philosophy, filosofía de la moral, ética.

morass [mə'ræs] *s.* 1. cenagal, ciénaga, marisma. 2. (fig.) estado de confusión o embrollo.

moratorium [,mɔrə'tɔrɪəm] *s.* (*pl.* MORATORIUMS O MORATORIA [-rɪə]) moratoria.

moratory ['mɔrə,tɔrɪ, 'mɑr-, B 'mɔrətərɪ] *a.* moratorio.

Moravian [mə'reɪvɪən] *a.* moravo. —*s.* 1. moravo, nativo de Moravia, región de Checoslovaquia. 2. moravo, lengua morava. 3. (relig.) hermano moravo.

moray ['mɔreɪ, B mə'reɪ] *s.* (ict.) morena, murena.

morbid ['mɔrbəd, B 'mɔbɪd] *a.* 1. mórbido, morboso, malsano. 2. (med.) morboso, patológico; **m. anatomy,** anatomía patológica.

morbidity [mɔr'bɪdətɪ, B mɔ'-] *s.* morbosidad.

morbidly ['mɔrbədlɪ, B 'mɔbɪd-] *adv.* mórbidamente, morbosamente.

morbidness [-nəs] *s.* morbidez, morbosidad.

morbific [mɔr'bɪfɪk, B mɔ'-] morbifical [-ɪkəl] *a.* mórbido.

morbilli [mɔr'bɪlaɪ, B mɔ'-] *s. pl.* (med.) morbilli, sarampión.

mordacious [mɔr'deɪʃəs, B mɔ'-] *a.* mordaz, ácido, acre, cáustico, irónico, satírico.

mordacity [-'dæsətɪ] *s.* mordacidad, causticidad.

mordancy ['mɔrdənsɪ, B 'mɔdən-] *s.* mordacidad.

mordant [-dənt] *a.* mordaz, agudo; cáustico, sarcástico. —*s.* mordiente, mordente. —*v.t.* mordentar, aplicar mordiente a.

Mordecai ['mɔrdɪ,kaɪ, B ,mɔdɪ'keɪaɪ] *s.* (bíbl.) Mardoqueo.

mordent ['mɔrdənt, B 'mɔdənt] *s.* (mús.) mordente.

more [mɔr, B mɔ] *a.* (*ú. como comp. de* MUCH y MANY) 1. más, más grande, mayor. 2. más, adicional, otro. —*s.* más, mayor cantidad, número o suma más grande, cantidad adicional, agregado; **the m . . . the m.,** cuanto más . . . (tanto) más; **the m. the merrier,** cuantos más haya, mejor; **what is m.,** y encima de todo esto. —*adv.* 1. más, en mayor grado, en grado creciente. 2. más, además (de). 3. **any m.,** (en frase negativa) ya no; **m. and m.,** más y más, cada vez más; **m. or less,** más o menos; **m . . . than** (calificando adjetivos) más . . . que; **m. than** (con números), más de; **no m.,** ya no; **no m., no less,** ni más, ni menos; **once m.,** otra vez, una vez más; **one m.,** otro (más); **to be no m.,** dejar de existir, estar muerto.

moreen [mə'rin, B mɔ-] *s.* (tej.) filipichín; tabí.

morel [-'rɛl] *s.* (bot.) hierba mora, solano negro.

morello [-oʊ] *s.* (bot.) cerezo amargo.

moreover [mɔr'oʊvər, B -və] *adv.* además, es más, por otra parte.

mores ['mɔreɪz, -iz, B 'mɔriz] *s. pl.* costumbres, usos; costumbres establecidas; derecho consuetudinario, tradiciones con fuerza de ley.

Moresque [mə'rɛsk] *a.* moro, morisco, arábigo. —*s.* arabesco.

Morgan ['mɔrgən, B 'mɔgən] *s.* (E.U.) famosa variedad de caballos ligeros originaria de Vermont.

morganatic [,mɔrgə'nætɪk, B ,mɔgə-] *a.* morganático.

morganatically [-ɪkəlɪ] *adv.* morganáticamente.
morganite ['mɔrgə,naɪt, B 'mɔgə-] *s.* (min.) variedad de berilo.
Morgan le Fay ['mɔrgənlə'feɪ, B 'mɔgən-] (mitol.) (el hada) Morgana, hada malvada de las leyendas del Rey Arturo y la Tabla Redonda.
morgen ['mɔrgən, B mɔgən] *s.* (*pl.*MORGEN) medida de superficie holandesa y sudafricana (equivalente a 85,39 áreas).
morgue [mɔrg, B mɔg] *s.* 1. morgue, necrocomio, depósito judicial de cadáveres. 2. departamento de archivo (de un periódico).
moribund ['mɔrə,bʌnd] *a.* moribundo.
moribundity [,mɔrə'bʌndətɪ] *s.* estado moribundo.
morion ['mɔrɪ,ɑn, B -ən] *s.* (hist.) morrión, casco alto y puntiagudo de ala curvada, que se usaba en el siglo XVI.
morion, *s.* (min.) morión.
Morisco [mə'rɪskoʊ] *a.* morisco. —*s.* (*pl.* MORISCOS O MORISCOES) morisco.
Mormon ['mɔrmən, B 'mɔmən] *s.* (relig.) mormón, mormona. —*a.* mormónico.
Mormonism [-,ɪzəm] *s.* mormonismo.
morn [mɔrn, B mɔn] *s.* (poét.) mañana.
morning ['mɔrnɪŋ, B 'mɔnɪŋ] *s.* 1. mañana. 2. (fig.) aurora, principio, inicio. 3. (poét.) alba, amanecer. 4. **good m.,** buenos días; **the m. after,** la mañana siguiente (a una fiesta, reunión, etc.). —*a.* de mañana, de la mañana; matutino, matinal, mañanero.
morning coat, chaqué, levita.
morning dress, traje de mañana.
morning glory, (bot.) dondiego de día, dompedro, maravilla; enredadera de campanillas.
morning gown, bata (de levantarse), salto de cama.
Morning Prayer, (relig. anglicana) servicio matutino.
mornings ['mɔrnɪŋz, B 'mɔnɪŋz] *adv.* por las mañanas, cada mañana, matinalmente.
morning sickness, (med.) vómito de embarazo, náuseas del embarazo.
morning star, 1. lucero del alba, lucero miguero. 2. (bot.) (especie de) hierba anual californiana. 3. (arm.) mangual.
morning watch, (mil.) cuarto de la diana; (mar.) guardia del alba (de 4 a 8 a.m.).
Moro ['mɔroʊ] *s.* (*pl.* MOROS) moro (malayo filipino de religión mahometana; su idioma).
Moroccan [mə'rɑkən, B -'rɔ-] *a., s.* marroquí, marroquín, moro, de Marruecos.
Morocco [-koʊ] *s.* 1. Marruecos. 2. **m.,** marroquín, marroquí, tafilete.
moron ['mɔrɑn, B 'mɔrɔn] *s.* 1. (med.) morón, débil mental, retardado mental. 2. (fam.) imbécil, bruto.
moronic [mə'rɑnɪk, B -'rɔn-] *a.* 1. (med.) morónico. 2. (fam.) imbécil, estúpido.
moronism ['mɔrɑn,ɪzəm, B -ən-] **moronity** [mə'rɑnətɪ, B -'rɔn-] *s.* (med.) moronismo, morosis.
morose [mə'roʊs] *a.* malhumorado, arisco, adusto; displicente.
morosely [-lɪ] *adv.* con mal humor, de mal talante.
moroseness [-nəs] *s.* malhumor, acrimonia; displicencia.
morpheme ['mɔr,fim, B 'mɔ,-] *s.* (gram.) morfema.
Morpheus ['mɔrfɪəs, B 'mɔfjus] *s.* (mitol.) Morfeo, dios griego del sueño; **gone to M.,** rendido, totalmente dormido.
morphia ['mɔrfɪə, B 'mɔfjə] *s.* (quím.) morfina.
morphine ['mɔrfin, B 'mɔfin] *s.* (quím.) morfina.
morphinic [mɔr'finɪk-, B mɔ'fɪn-] *a.* morfínico.
morphinism ['mɔr,fɪn,ɪzəm, B 'mɔ,-] *s.* (med.) morfinismo, morfinomanía.
morphogenesis [,mɔrfə'dʒɛnəsəs, B ,mɔfə-] *s.* (biol.) morfogénesis, morfogenia.
morphogenic [-'dʒenɪk] *a.* (biol.) morfogénico.
morphologic [-'lɑdʒɪk, B -'lɔdʒɪk] *a.* (gram.) morfológico.
morphological [-ɪkəl] *a.* morfológico.
morphologically [-kəlɪ] *adv.* morfológicamente.
morphologist [,mɔr'fɑlədʒəst, B ,mɔ'fɔl-] *s.* experto en morfología.
morphology [-dʒɪ] *s.* (biol., geol., gram.) morfología.
morris ['mɔrəs, 'mɑr-, B 'mɔrɪs] *s.* (G.B.) antigua danza popular inglesa en que los participantes se disfrazaban al estilo de las leyendas de Robin Hood.
morris chair, poltrona con respaldo ajustable y cojines sueltos.
morrow ['mɑr,oʊ, B 'mɔr-] *s.* 1. día siguiente, mañana (*m.*). 2. (ant.) mañana (*f.*).
Morse code [mɔrs-, B mɔs-] (teleg.) código o alfabeto Morse.
morsel ['mɔrsəl, B 'mɔsəl] *s.* pequeña porción (de comida, etc.), bocado, presa; p. ext. chica joven y bonita, bocado de cardenal (fam.).
mort [mɔrt, B mɔt] *s.* 1. (caza) toque de muerte (que se da con el cuerno al morir la pieza). 2. (ant.) muerte. 3. (ict.) salmón adulto.
mortadella [,mɔrtə'dɛlə, B ,mɔtə-] *s.* mortadela, salchicha italiana muy sazonada.
mortal ['mɔrtəl, B 'mɔtəl] *a.* 1. mortal. 2. de mortales, humano (cj., anhelos, limitaciones, etc.). 3. (fam.) abrumador, tedioso, aburrido. 4. (fam.) de proporciones, enorme, terrible; extremo, sumo. 5. **every m. (thing,** etc.), (fam.) toda bendita (cosa, etc.), todas las (cosas, etc.). —*s.* 1. mortal. 2. tipo, sujeto, ej., *there's a funny m. for you,* allí tiene Ud. un tipo curioso. —*adv.* (dial.) extremadamente, terriblemente.
mortality [mɔr'tælətɪ, B mɔ'-] *s.* (*pl.* MORTALITIES) 1. mortalidad (calidad de mortal). 2. mortandad (por guerra, epidemia, etc.). 3. mortalidad (promedio de muertes sobre total de población). 4. mortales, humanidad. 5. (ant.) muerte.
mortality table, (seguros) tabla de mortalidad.
mortally ['mɔrtəlɪ, B 'mɔtəlɪ] *adv.* 1. fatalmente, mortalmente. 2. (fam.) extremadamente.
mortal sin, pecado mortal.
mortar ['mɔrtər, B 'mɔtə] *s.* 1. mortero, almirez. 2. (arm.) mortero. 3. mortero, argamasa, mezcla. —*v.t.* argamasar, enlucir.
mortarboard [-,bɔrd, B -,bɔd] *s.* 1. esparavel. 2. muceta, capirote o capelo de doctor (Amer.).
mortgage ['mɔrgɪdʒ, B 'mɔgɪdʒ] *s.* 1. hipoteca. 2. contrato de hipoteca. —*v.t.* 1. hipotecar. 2. p. ext. empeñar.
mortgage bank, banco hipotecario.
mortgagee [,mɔrgɪ'dʒi, B ,mɔgɪ-] *s.* acreedor hipotecario.
mortgagor [-'dʒɔr, B -'dʒɔ] **mortgager** ['mɔrgɪdʒər, B 'mɔgɪdʒə] *s.* deudor hipotecario.
mortice, *var. de* **mortise.**
mortician [mɔr'tɪʃən, B mɔ'-] *s.* empresario de pompas fúnebres; funerario.
mortification [,mɔrtəfə'keɪʃən, B ,mɔtɪ-] *s.* 1. mortificación, tormento, humillación. 2. (med.) mortificación, gangrena, necrosis (de tejidos u órganos).
mortify ['mɔrtə,faɪ, B 'mɔtɪ-] *v.t.* (*pret., p.p.* MORTIFIED; *p.pr.* MORTIFYING) 1. mortificar (pasiones), macerar, controlar (apetitos). 2. vejar, ofender, humillar. 3. (ant., med.) mortificar, gangrenar. —*v.i.* 1. mortificarse, torturarse. 2. (ant., med.) mortificarse, gangrenarse.
mortise, mortice ['mɔrtəs, B 'mɔtɪs] *s.* (carp.) mortaja, cotana, muesca, entalladura, gargol, escopladura. —*v.t.* 1. ensamblar, engargolar. 2. escoplear.
mortise and tenon, (carp.) caja y espiga, mortaja y espiga.
mortise gauge, (carp.) gramil doble, gramil para mortajas.
mortise gear, (mec.) engranaje de dientes postizos.
mortise lock, cerradura embutida, cerradura de embutir.
mortising chisel [-ɪŋ-] (carp.) formón, escoplo, bedano de mortaja.
mortmain ['mɔrt,meɪn, B 'mɔt-] *s.* (der.) manos muertas.
mortuary ['mɔrtʃʊ,ɛrɪ, B 'mɔtjʊərɪ] *s.* (*pl.* MORTUARIES) 1. morgue, depósito judicial de cadáveres. 2. (hist.) legado a párroco u obispo. —*a.* mortuorio, funerario.
morula ['mɔrjələ, 'mɑr-, B 'mɔrʊ-] *s.* (*pl.* MORULAE [-,li]) (biol.) mórula.
mosaic [moʊ'zeɪɪk] *s.* 1. mosaico; (fig.) mosaico, diversidad. —*v.t.* decorar con mosaicos; combinar en forma de mosaico. —*a.* mosaico.
Mosaic, *a.* mosaico, de Moisés.
mosaic gold, oro musivo.
mosaicist [-əsəst] *s.* mosaísta, fabricante de mosaicos; proveedor de mosaicos.
Mosaic Law, ley mosaica, ley de Moisés (de los antiguos hebreos).
moschatel [,mɑskə'tɛl, B ,mɔs-] *s.* (bot.) adoxa.
Moscow ['mɑskoʊ, -kaʊ, B 'mɔskoʊ] *s.* Moscú, capital de la Unión Soviética.
Moselle [moʊ'zɛl] *s.* Mosela; (vino de) Mosela.
Moses ['moʊzɔz] *s.* (bíbl.) Moisés.
mosey ['moʊzɪ] *v.i.* (jer.) 1. deambular, vagar, pasar lentamente. 2. irse, largarse.
Moslem ['mɑzləm, B 'mɔzlɛm] *var. de* **Muslim.**
Moslemism [-,ɪzəm] *var. de* **Muhammadanism.**
mosque [mɑsk, B mɔsk] *s.* mezquita.
mosquito [məs'kitoʊ] *s.* (*pl.* MOSQUITOES O MOSQUITOS) (ento.) mosquito, jején.
mosquito boat, (pr. G.B.) barco menor, lancha torpedera.
mosquito hawk, 1. (orn.) chotacabras. 2. (ento.) libélula, caballito del diablo.
mosquito net, mosquitero.
mosquito netting, gasa, tul o redecilla para mosquiteros.
moss [mɔs] *s.* (bot.) musgo, musco, moho; **a rolling stone gathers no m.,** piedra que rueda no cría moho. —*v.t.* cubrir con musgo.
moss agate, (min.) ágata musgosa, piedra de Moca.
mossback ['mɔs,bæk] *s.* (jer., E.U.) fósil; retrógrado, anticuado.
mossbunker [-,bʌŋkər, B -kə] *s.* (ict.) especie de sábalo.
moss-grown [-,groʊn] *a.* 1. musgoso. 2. (fig.) fósil, anticuado.
moss rose, (bot.) rosa musgosa.
mosstrooper [-,trupər, B -pə] *s.* (G.B., hist.) bandido, bandolero, salteador.
mosstrooping [-,trupɪŋ] *s.* (G.B., hist.) bandolerismo.
mossy ['mɔsɪ] *a.* (MOSSIER; MOSSIEST) 1. musgoso. 2. parecido al musgo, como el musgo.
most [moʊst] *a.* 1. (el) más, (el) mayor, ej., *the motor with the m. power,* el motor con más (o con la mayor) fuerza. 2. la mayor parte de, el

mayor número de, ej., *m. people believe it,* la mayor parte de la gente lo cree, *you made the m. mistakes,* Ud. cometió el mayor número de errores. 3. **for the m. part,** en su mayor parte, principalmente. —*adv.* 1. más (sirve para formar el super. de la mayoría de los adjetivos de dos o más sílabas), ej., *the m. intelligent of my sons,* el más inteligente de mis hijos. 2. muy, sumamente, ej., *this is a m. powerful motor,* éste es un motor muy (o sumamente) fuerte. 3. (fam., dial.) casi, ej., *m. everybody was there,* casi todos estaban allí. 4. **at m.,** a lo más, a lo sumo; no más de, como máximo, ej., *this is at m. a temporary solution,* esto es a lo sumo (o a lo más) una solución temporal, *few people came, twenty at m.,* poca gente vino, no más de veinte (o veinte como máximo); **m. certainly,** con toda seguridad; **m. of all,** sobre todo. —*s.* 1. la mayor parte. 2. lo más, lo máximo, ej., *the m. one can say,* lo más (o lo máximo) que se puede decir. 3. **to make the m. of it,** sacar el mayor partido de, sacar el máximo provecho de.

mostly ['moʊstlɪ] *adv.* principalmente, en su mayor parte.

Most Reverend, reverendísimo, ilustrísimo (tratamiento para arzobispo u obispo católico).

mot [moʊ] *s.* (fr.) agudeza, dicho ingenioso.

mote [moʊt] *v.i.* (*pret.* MOSTE) (ant.) poder. —*s.* mota, corpúsculo, partícula.

motel [moʊ'tɛl] *s.* motel, hotel para automovilistas.

motet [moʊ'tɛt] *s.* (mús.) motete, canto sacro de composición polifónica, gen. sin acompañamiento.

moth [mɔθ] *s.* (*pl.* MOTHS) 1. (ento.) polilla. 2. mariposa nocturna.

mothball ['mɔθˌbɔl] *s.* bola de naftalina, bola de alcanfor.

moth-eaten [-ˌitən] *a.* 1. apolillado. 2. (fig.) anticuado, viejo.

mother ['mʌðər, B -ə] *s.* 1. madre. 2. madre, causa, origen. 3. (fam.) tía, comadre (apl. a ancianas como tratamiento). 4. (ant.) amor o afecto maternal. 5. **every m.'s son,** todo hijo de vecino. —*v.t.* 1. ser madre de, dar a luz. 2. tratar con cariño maternal, cuidar de modo maternal, proteger. 3. reconocer ser madre de. 4. (fig.) concebir, inventar. 5. ser fuente u origen de. 6. atribuir. —*a.* 1. maternal, materno (ej., afecto, instinto). 2. matriz (ej., iglesia). 3. nativo (ej., idioma, suelo).

Mother Carey's chicken [-'kæriz-, B 'kɛər-] (orn.) petrel; petrel de las tormentas.

mother country, 1. madre patria (en relación a sus colonias). 2. suelo natal.

mother earth, madre tierra.

Mother Goose, La Oca Cuentista (gansa imaginaria, supuesta autora de nanas y versos infantiles).

Mother Goose's Nursery Rhymes, cuentos de Calleja.

mother hen, gallina clueca; (hum.) madraza.

motherhood [-ˌhʊd] *s.* maternidad.

motherhouse [-ˌhaʊs] *s.* casa matriz (de una orden religiosa).

Mother Hubbard, bata, ropón tropical de mujer muy suelto y ancho.

mother-in-law ['mʌðərɪnˌlɔ] *s.* 1. suegra, madre política. 2. (raro) madrastra.

motherland ['mʌðərˌlænd, B 'mʌðəˌ-] *s.* patria, país (de origen), suelo natal.

motherless [-ləs] *a.* huérfano de madre.

motherliness [-lɪnəs] *s.* disposición maternal.

mother lode, (geol.) filón principal.

motherly [-lɪ] *a.* maternal, materno. —*adv.* maternalmente.

Mother of God, (relig.) Madre de Dios.

mother-of-pearl ['mʌðərəv'pɜrl, B -'pɜl] *s.* nácar, madreperla. —*a.* nacarado; iridiscente.

Mother's Day, Día de las Madres.

mother ship, (mar.) buque escolta, barco madre.

mother superior, (relig.) superiora, madre superiora.

mother tongue, 1. lengua materna. 2. lengua madre (de la que otras se derivan).

mother wit, inteligencia natural, sentido común; chispa.

motherwort ['mʌðərˌwɜrt, B -əˌwɜt] *s.* (bot.) agripalma, cardíaca.

mothproof [-pruf] *a.* antipolilla.

mothy ['mɔθɪ] *a.* apolillado, lleno de polillas.

motif [moʊ'tif] *s.* (arte, mús.) motivo.

motile ['moʊtəl] *a.* (biol.) movible, móvil.

motility [moʊ'tɪlətɪ] *s.* (biol.) movilidad, motilidad.

motion ['moʊʃən] *s.* 1. movimiento. 2. ademán, gesto. 3. proposición, moción. 4. (der.) escrito, petición, recurso, solicitud. 5. (mús.) modulación. 6. (mec.) mecanismo (de un reloj). 7. defecación. 8. (ant.) títeres; teatro de títeres. 9. **in m.,** en movimiento; **on the m. of,** a propuesta de; **to make a m.,** presentar una moción; **to put into** (o **set in**) **m.,** poner en marcha, hacer funcionar. —*v.t.* indicar con la mano a, indicar con un gesto a (alguien), ej., *he motioned me to go,* me indicó con un gesto que me fuera. —*v.i.* hacer una señal.

motionless [-ləs] *a.* inmóvil, estático, fijo, inamovible.

motionlessly [-ləslɪ] *adv.* sin movimiento, fijamente, estáticamente.

motionlessness [-ləsnəs] *s.* inmovilidad, estatismo.

motion picture, película o cinta cinematográfica, filme.

motion sickness, náusea, mareo.

motivate ['moʊtəˌveɪt] *v.t.* motivar.

motivation [ˌmoʊtə'veɪʃən] *s.* motivación.

motive ['moʊtɪv] *s.* 1. motivo, causa, móvil. 2. (arte., mús.) tema, motivo. —*a.* 1. motor, motriz. 2. impulsor, incitador. —*v.t.* motivar, incitar, impulsar.

motive power, fuerza motriz, potencia motora.

motivity [moʊ'tɪvətɪ] *s.* potencia motriz.

mot juste [ˌmoʊ'ʒʊst] (fr.) palabra justa, palabra adecuada.

motley ['mɑtlɪ, B 'mɔt-] *a.* (MOTLEYER; MOTLEYEST) 1. multicolor, moteado, manchado, abigarrado. 2. diverso, heterogéneo, variado. —*s.* 1. mezcla caprichosa (esp. de colores). 2. (hist.) tela multicolor. 3. (hist.) botarga, traje de payaso. 4. (ant.) bufón, payaso.

motoneuron [ˌmoʊtə'nʊrɑn, B -'njʊərɔn] *s.* (fisiol.) motoneurona, neurona motora.

motor ['moʊtər, B -ə] *s.* 1. motor. 2. automóvil, vehículo automotor. 3. (mec.) motor. 4. (*pl.*) (com.) acciones de fábricas de automóviles. —*a.* 1. motor, motriz. 2. de motor, movido por motor(es). 3. (anat., fisiol.) motor. 4. para automóviles. 5. para motores (combustible). 6. para automovilistas (ej., hotel). 7. para tráfico automotor (pista, camino). —*v.i.* pasear, viajar o ir en automóvil o motocicleta.

motor-bike [-ˌbaɪk] *s.* bicicleta a motor; motocicleta liviana.

motorboat [-ˌboʊt] *s.* bote a motor, barco a motor, lancha automóvil, gasolinera.

motorbus [-ˌbʌs] *s.* autobús, ómnibus.

motorcade [-ˌkeɪd] *s.* caravana o desfile de automóviles.

motorcar [-ˌkɑr, B -ˌkɑ] *s.* automóvil, auto.

motor coach, autobús, ómnibus.

motor court, posada u hotel (en una carretera) para motoristas.

motorcycle [-ˌsaɪkəl] *s.* motocicleta. —*v.i.* pasear o viajar en motocicleta.

motorcyclist [-ˌsaɪkləst] *s.* motociclista.

motor drive, accionamiento o impulsión por motor.

motor-driven [-ˌdrɪvən] *a.* accionado o impulsado por motor.

motordrome [-ˌdroʊm] *s.* autódromo.

motored ['moʊtərd, B -əd] *a.* de motores, equipado con (cierto número de) motores (*ú. gen. en palabras compuestas*), ej., *a four-m. ship,* una nave de (o equipada con) cuatro motores.

motor generator, (elec.) motor-generador, grupo convertidor.

motoring ['moʊtərɪŋ] *s.* motorismo, automovilismo.

motorist [-əst] *s.* automovilista, motorista.

motorization [ˌmoʊtərə'zeɪʃən, B -raɪ-] *s.* motorización.

motorize ['moʊtəˌraɪz] *v.t.* motorizar.

motor launch, lancha automóvil.

motor lorry, (G.B.) autocamión.

motorman ['moʊtərmən, B -əmən] *s.* motorista, conductor (de tranvía o tren eléctrico).

motor oil, aceite para lubricar motores.

motor paralysis, (med.) parálisis motora.

motor pool, (mil.) centro común de vehículos motorizados.

motor scooter, moto pequeña, escúter, motoneta; motopatín.

motor ship, motonave.

motor torpedo boat, lancha torpedera de motor.

motor transport, transporte motorizado.

motor truck, autocamión, camión automóvil.

motor vehicle, vehículo automotor, vehículo motorizado.

motorway ['moʊtərˌweɪ, B -əˌ-] *s.* (G.B.) autopista.

motte [mɑt, B mɔt] *s.* (E.U.) pequeño grupo de árboles en una pradera o llanura.

mottle ['mɑtəl, B 'mɔt-] *v.t.* motear, jaspear, abigarrar. —*s.* 1. mancha o veta de color. 2. apariencia moteada o veteada.

mottled ['mɑtəld, B 'mɔt-] *a.* moteado, jaspeado, veteado; abigarrado.

mottler [-ələr, B -lə] *s.* pincel o brocha para motear.

motto ['mɑtoʊ, B 'mɔt-] *s.* (*pl.* MOTTOES O MOTTOS) lema, divisa, máxima.

moue [mu] *s.* mueca ligera, mohín.

mouflon, moufflon ['muflɑn, B -lɔn] *s.* (zool.) musmón, muflón.

mouillé [mu'jeɪ] *a.* (fon.) suave, palatal (díc. del sonido).

moulage [mu'lɑʒ] *s.* molde (de yeso, masilla, etc. usado como prueba en una investigación criminal).

mould, moulder, mouldy, etc., *vars. de* **mold, molder, moldy,** etc.

moulin [mu'læn] *s.* pozo casi vertical (en un ventisquero o glaciar).

moulinet [ˌmulɪ'nɛt] *s.* (esgr.) molinete.

moult, moulter, (G.B.) *vars. de* **molt, molter.**

mound [maʊnd] *s.* (her.) globo de oro (insignia real).

mound [maʊnd] *s.* 1. montón de tierra, montículo, montecillo, morón. 2. (béisbol) lomita, montículo (sobre el que se pone el lanzador). —*v.t.* 1. amontonar. 2. (ant.) atrincherar; cercar, cerrar con terraplenes.

mount [maʊnt] *s.* 1. monte, montaña. 2. (quiromancia) monte (de la palma de la mano). 3. (ant.) baluarte, terraplén.

mount [maʊnt] *v.i.* 1. montar a caballo, cabalgar. 2. subir, ascender, elevarse. 3. crecer, aumentar (una cuenta, deuda, cólera, etc.). —*v.t.* 1. montar (caballo, bicicleta, etc.). 2. ascender, subir, trepar, escalar. 3. subir a (ej., un púlpito, una plataforma, etc.). 4. poner a caballo; proveer de caballos. 5. alzar, elevar. 6. montar, engastar (una joya). 7. montar, instalar. 8. disecar (un animal). 9. preparar (una lámina portaobjetos para examen microscópico). 10. (teat.) montar, poner en escena, presentar (una obra). 11. (mil., mar.) montar, llevar (cañones); armar, artillar; montar, apostar (una guardia, etc.); disponer (tropas). 12. **to m. an offensive,** (mil.) montar una ofensiva, tomar la ofensiva. —*s.* 1. montadura, montaje. 2. montadura (de una joya); montura, montaje (de un instrumento, etc.); cureña (de un cañón): montaje, soporte, montura (de fotografías, dibujos). 3. montura, cabalgadura. 4. portaobjetos, cubreobjetos (para preparaciones microscópicas). 5. (filat.) charnela.

mountain [ˈmaʊntən] *s.* 1. montaña, monte; (*pl.*) cordillera, cadena de montañas. 2. (fig.) montón, cúmulo, sinnúmero. —*a.* montañés, montañoso, montés.

mountain artillery, artillería de montaña.

mountain ash, (bot.) serbal.

mountain cat, (zool.) puma; lince; basáride.

mountain chain, sierra, cordillera.

mountain climber, alpinista, andinista.

mountain climbing, alpinismo, andinismo, montañismo.

mountain cranberry, (bot.) arándano encarnado.

mountain damson, (bot.) aceitero.

mountain dew, (fam.) whisky de contrabando.

mountaineer [ˌmaʊntəˈnɪr, B -ˈnɪə] *s.* 1. montañés, serrano. 2. alpinista, montañero, montañista, andinista (Amer.). —*v.i.* escalar montañas, practicar el alpinismo.

mountaineering [-ˌnɪrɪŋ, B -ˈnɪər-] *s.* montañismo, alpinismo, andinismo (Amer.).

mountain goat, (zool.) cabra de las Montañas Rocosas.

mountain green, (min.) verde de montaña.

mountain laurel, (bot.) calmia.

mountain lion, (zool.) puma, león americano.

mountainous [ˈmaʊntənəs] *a.* 1. montañoso, montuoso. 2. gigantesco, inmenso, enorme.

mountainously [-lɪ] *adv.* gigantescamente, enormemente.

mountain parsley, (bot.) perejil de monte, oreoselino.

mountain pine, (bot.) pino negro.

mountain railway, ferrocarril de cremallera.

mountain range, cordillera, sierra.

mountain sheep, (zool.) musmón.

mountain sickness, (med.) mal de las montañas, mal de altura, soroche, puna (Amer.).

mountainside [ˈmaʊntənˌsaɪd] *s.* ladera, falda (de un monte).

mountaintop [-ˌtɑp, B -ˌtɔp] *s.* cumbre, cima de una montaña.

mountainy [-ɪ] *a.* montañoso.

mountebank [ˈmaʊntɪˌbaŋk] *s.* 1. saltabanco, saltabancos, charlatán de feria. 2. charlatán, farsante, embaucador.

mounted [ˈmaʊntəd] *a.* 1. montado (a caballo). 2. armado (cañones). 3. montado, engastado.

mounted police, policía montada.

mounter [-ər, B -ə] *s.* montador.

Mountie, Mounty [ˈmaʊntɪ] *s.* (fam.) miembro de la policía montada canadiense.

mounting [ˈmaʊntɪŋ] *s.* 1. monta, montadura. 2. engaste, montadura; guarnición; armadura; marco, montaje. 3. ascensión, subida.

mounting block, cabalgadero, montador.

mourn [mɔrn, B mɔn] *v.i.* 1. lamentarse, dolerse, apesadumbrarse. 2. enlutarse, vestir o llevar luto. 3. plañir, gemir. —*v.t.* llorar, deplorar, lamentar.

mourner [ˈmɔrnər, B ˈmɔnə] *s.* 1. persona que guarda luto. 2. miembro de una comitiva fúnebre, plañidera.

mournful [-fəl] *a.* 1. dolorido, triste, apenado, pesaroso, afligido. 2. penoso, lastimero, doloroso, lamentable, apesadumbrado, luctuoso.

mournfully [-fəlɪ] *adv.* tristemente.

mournfulness [-fəlnəs] *s.* pesar, tristeza.

mourning [ˈmɔrnɪŋ, B ˈmɔnɪŋ] *s.* 1. duelo, dolor, aflicción, pena. 2. luto (ropas y período); **to be in m.,** estar de luto; **to come out of (deep) m.,** aliviar el luto; **to go into m.,** ponerse (de) luto.

mourning band, brazal de luto.

mourning bride, (bot.) viuda.

mourning cloak, (ento.) mariposa de color pardo violeta con un borde ancho amarillo en las alas.

mourning dove, (orn.) (especie de) paloma torcaza.

mouse [maʊs] *s.* (*pl.* MICE [maɪs]) 1. ratón. 2. (jer.) moretón, cardenal; ojo en compota, ojo de luto. 3. pusilánime, cobarde. 4. (mar.) barrilete. — [maʊz] *v.i.* 1. cazar o coger ratones. 2. (gen. con *about*) andar husmeando, olisquear. 3. andar al acecho, andar furtivamente.

mouse-ear [ˈmaʊsˌɪr, B -ˌɪə] *s.* (bot.) 1. vellosilla, oreja de ratón, pelosilla, pelusilla. 2. nomeolvides.

mouse-ear chickweed, (bot.) cerastio.

mouse-ear hawkweed, (bot.) vellosilla, oreja de ratón, pelosilla, pelusilla.

mousehole [-ˌhoʊl] *s.* ratonera, agujero (de ratón).

mouse opossum, (zool.) marmosa.

mouser [ˈmaʊzər, B -zə] *s.* (gato) cazador, buen cazador (de ratones), ratonero.

mousetail [ˈmaʊsˌteɪl] *s.* (bot.) cola de ratón.

mousetrap [-ˌtræp] *s.* ratonera, trampa para cazar ratones, p. ext. trampa, lazo, añagaza.

mousing [ˈmaʊzɪŋ, B -sɪŋ] *s.* (mar.) barrilete.

mousquetaire [ˌmuskəˈtɛr, B -ˈtɛə] *s.* mosquetero.

mousse [mus] *s.* crema, espuma, (cocina) manjar helado de crema batida y gelatina.

mousseline [musˈlin, B ˈmuslin] *s.* (tej.) muselina.

moustache, mustache [ˈmʌsˌtæʃ, məsˈtæʃ, B -ˈtɑʃ] *s.* bigote, mostacho.

Mousterian [muˈstɪrɪən, B -ˈstɪər-] *a.* (antrop.) musteriense.

mousy [ˈmaʊsɪ] *a.* (MOUSIER; MOUSIEST) 1. quieto, silencioso, tímido, (fig.) poquita cosa. 2. plomizo, grisáceo. 3. infestado de ratones (sótano, etc.).

mouth [maʊθ] *s.* (*pl.* MOUTHS [maʊðz]) 1. boca; labios. 2. embocadura, desembocadura (de un río); boca (de una jarra, tubo, cueva, volcán, etc.). 3. mueca, gesto, mohín (hecho con los labios). 4. (fig.) portavoz, vocero. 5. impertinencia, descaro. 6. (mús.) corte (de un cañón de órgano); boquilla (de instrumento). 7. **down in the m.,** abatido, cariacontecido; **not to open one's m.,** no abrir la boca, no decir esta boca es mía; **to laugh on the wrong side of one's m.,** lamentarse, llorar; **to make one's m. water,** hacérsele a uno agua la boca; **to put words into someone's m.,** insinuarle a alguien lo que debe decir; **to shut one's m.,** cerrar la boca, callarse; **to take the words out of someone's m.,** quitarle a alguien las palabras de la boca. — [maʊð] *v.t.* 1. proferir; vocear. 2. pronunciar. 3. esbozar con los labios, recitar silenciosamente (palabras). 4. morder; tomar en la boca. 5. mascullar. —*v.i.* 1. hablar; vociferar, despotricar. 2. mover los labios; hacer muecas.

mouther [ˈmaʊðər, B -ə] *s.* 1. parlón, hablador. 2. orador afectado.

mouth-filling [ˈmaʊθˌfɪlɪŋ] *a.* altisonante, rimbombante.

mouthful [-ˌfʊl] *s.* 1. bocanada, buchada. 2. bocado. 3.(*of food*) mascada. 4. **you said a m.,** (jer.) muy bien dicho.

mouthily [ˈmaʊðəlɪ] *adv.* ampulosamente.

mouth organ, (mús.) armónica.

mouthpart [ˈmaʊθˌpɑrt, B -ˌpɑt] *s.* región bucal (de un insecto, etc.).

mouthpiece [-ˌpis] *s.* 1. boquilla (de un instrumento musical, de una herramienta, etc.); bocina (de teléfono). 2. bocado (del freno de caballos). 3. vocero, portavoz. 4. (jer.) abogado, penalista, abogado criminalista.

mouth-to-mouth method [-təˈmaʊθ-] respiración artificial de boca a boca.

mouthwash [-ˌwɔʃ, -ˌwɑʃ, B -ˌwɔʃ] *s.* enjuagatorio, enjuague (para la boca).

mouthwatering [-ˈwɔtərɪŋ, -ˈwɑt-, B -ˈwɔt-] *a.* apetitoso, que hace la boca agua.

mouthy [ˈmaʊðɪ, -θɪ, B -ðɪ] *a.* (MOUTHIER; MOUTHIEST) bombástico, rimbombante, ampuloso.

mouton [ˈmuˌtɑn, B -ˌtɔn] *s.* mutón, piel de cordero que imita la de castor.

movability, moveability [ˌmuvəˈbɪlətɪ] *s.* movilidad.

movable, moveable [ˈmuvəbəl] *a.* 1. movible, móvil, mueble. 2. movible (fiesta). —*s.* 1. (*pl.*) muebles, mobiliario, enseres, menaje. 2. (der.) (*pl.*) bienes muebles.

movableness, moveableness [-nəs] *s.* movilidad.

movable property, bienes muebles.

move [muv] *v.t.* 1. mover. 2. remover, trasladar, mudar. 3. accionar, hacer funcionar. 4. conmover, enternecer. 5. proponer, recomendar; presentar como moción (en una asamblea), mocionar (Am.). 6. (com.) vender; promover la venta de. 7. **m. heaven and earth,** mover cielo y tierra; **m. to (do),** mover, impulsar, inclinar, inducir, persuadir a (hacer); **m. to (tears, anger,** etc.), provocar (lágrimas, cólera, etc.). —*v.i.* 1. moverse. 2. girar, funcionar (una puerta, máquina, etc.). 3. ir, andar, caminar, trasladarse; progresar, avanzar; (fam.) menearse. 4. obrar, entrar en acción. 5. (gen. con *for*) presentar una moción en pro de, proponer. 6. mudarse, mudar de casa. 7. hacer una jugada (en ajedrez, damas, etc.). 8. moverse, evacuar(se) (el vientre). 9. (com.) venderse, tener salida (mercancía, etc.). 10. **m. about,** ir y venir, moverse de acá para allá; **m. along,** avanzar, seguir adelante; pasar por; **m. away,** alejarse, apartarse; **m. forward,** avanzar; **m. in,** tomar posesión de, instalarse en (una casa, etc.); instalarse; frecuentar (alta sociedad, mala compañía, etc.); **m. off,** partir, irse; **m. on,** seguir caminando, no detenerse; (fam.) largarse; **m. out,** irse, mudarse (de una casa, habitación, etc.); **m. up,** adelantar (una fecha). —*s.* 1. movimiento, moción. 2. paso, ej., *what's the next m.?* ¿cuál es el próximo paso? 3. jugada, lance, ej., *a shrewd m.,* una jugada acertada, un lance astuto. 4. jugada (en ajedrez, damas, etc.). 5. mudanza (de un lugar a otro, de casa, de habitación, etc.). 6. **it's your m.,** es su turno (de Ud.), le toca a Ud.; **on the m.,** en marcha, en movimiento; **to get a m. on,** (jer.)

moverse, darse prisa; (*en imper.*) ¡andando! muévete!; **to have the m.**, tocarle jugar a uno (en ajedrez, damas, etc.); **to make a m.**, dar un paso; tomar una medida; hacer una jugada; **don't make a m.**, no se mueva.

moveless ['muvləs] *a.* inmóvil.

movement [-mənt] *s.* 1. movimiento. 2. movimiento, tendencia; (*pl.*) movimientos, actividades (de una persona o grupo de personas). 3. (fisiol.) evacuación (del vientre). 4. (mec.) movimiento; mecanismo (de reloj, etc.). 5. (mil., mar.) movimiento, desplazamiento. 6. (mús.) movimiento; compás, tiempo. 7. (com.) movimiento, circulación; actividad (del mercado).

mover [-ər, B -ə] *s.* 1. movedor, motor, móvil. 2. promotor, promovedor, instigador, autor (de una moción). 3. empleado de una casa de mudanzas.

movie ['muvɪ] *s.* 1. película (cinematográfica), ej., *this is a good m.*, es una buena película. 2. (*pl.*) cine, sala de cine. 3. **the movies,** el cine, la industria cinematográfica; cine, función de cine, ej., *shall we go to the movies?* ¿vamos al cine?

movie camera, cámara cinematográfica.

movie film, película, cinta (de cine).

moviegoer [-ˌgoʊər, B -ə] *s.* persona que va a menudo al cine, aficionado al cine.

movie star, estrella de cine.

moving ['muvɪŋ] *a.* 1. móvil, motor, motriz. 2. patético, conmovedor. 3. de mudanza, de traslado. —*s.* mudanza, traslado.

moving coil, (elec., electrón.) bobina móvil.

moving-coil pickup [-ˌkɔɪl-] (electrón.) fonocaptor de bobina móvil.

moving picture, película (cinematográfica), cinta.

moving platform, plataforma móvil.

moving sidewalk, acera móvil, plataforma de correa sin fin, pasillo rodante.

moving staircase, m. stairway, escalera mecánica o móvil.

moving van, camión de mudanzas.

mow [maʊ, B moʊ] *s.* 1. hacina, montón de heno o de gavillas. 2. henal, henil.

mow [moʊ] *v.t.* (*pret.* MOWED; *p.p.* MOWED o MOWN [moʊn] *p.pr.* MOWING) 1. segar, guadañar, dallar. 2. (fig. con *down*) segar, abatir, ej., *the machine gun mowed them down,* la ametralladora los abatió. —*v.i.* segar, cortar; arrasar.

mow [maʊ, moʊ, B maʊ] *s.* mueca, gesto, mohín. —*v.i.* gestear, hacer muecas.

mower ['moʊər, B -ə] *s.* 1. segador, guadañador, dallador. 2. segadora mecánica, guadañadora.

mowing machine [-ɪŋ-] (agr.) segadora o guadañadora mecánica.

moxa ['mɑksə, B 'mɔk-] *s.* 1. (bot.) artemisa. 2. (med.) moxa.

moxie ['mɑksɪ, B 'mɔk-] *s.* (jer.) 1. energía, brío, fuerza. 2. coraje.

Mozarab [moʊ'zærəb] *s.* (hist.) mozárabe, cristiano adaptado durante la dominación musulmana en España.

Mozarabic [-əbɪk] *a.* (hist.) mozárabe, relativo o propio de los mozárabes.

mozzarella [ˌmɑtsə'rɛlə, B ˌmɔt-] *s.* queso fresco de origen italiano.

mozzetta [moʊ'zɛtə] *s.* (relig.) muceta.

M.P. *abrev. de* 1. **Member of Parliament,** Miembro del Parlamento, parlamentario. 2. **Military Police,** policía militar (PM). 3. **Mounted Police,** Policía Montada.

m.p. *abrev. de* **melting point,** punto de fusión.

mpg *abrev. de* **miles per gallon,** millas por galón.

mph *abrev. de* **miles per hour,** millas por hora.

Mr. ['mɪstər, B -tə] *abrev. de* **Mister,** Señor (Sr.).

Mrs. ['mɪsəz] *abrev. de* **Mistress,** Señora (Sra.).

Ms. [mɪz] nueva abreviatura que se aplica igualmente a **Miss** y **Mrs.**

MS, ms *abrev. de* **manuscript,** manuscrito.

Msgr. *abrev. de* **monseigneur, monsignor,** monseñor.

MSS *abrev. de* **manuscripts,** manuscritos.

MT *abrev. de* **mechanical** o **motor transport,** transporte motorizado.

Mt. *abrev. de* **mount** or **mountain,** monte o montaña.

much [mʌtʃ] *a.* (MORE; MOST) 1. mucho, abundante, copioso, grande. 2. (ant.) muchos (en número). 3. **as m. . . . . . . as,** tanto . . . . . . como; **too m.**, demasiado. —*s.* mucho; **as m.**, tanto; otro tanto; **I thought as m.**, ya me lo figuraba; **not m. of a,** de poca cuantía; **not m. to look at,** nada maravilloso (de mirar). —*adv.* 1. mucho, con mucho, en gran manera. 2. muy, ej., *he was m. frightened,* estaba muy asustado. 3. casi, ej., *m. the same,* casi lo mismo, poco más o menos lo mismo. 4. **as m. as,** tanto como; **how m.?** ¿cuánto?; **however m.**, por mucho que; **m. as,** por más que, a pesar de; **m. better,** mucho mejor; **m. more,** mucho más; **so m.**, tanto; **so m. the better,** tanto mejor; **too m.**, demasiado; **very m.**, muchísimo; muy.

muchness ['mʌtʃnəs] *s.* abundancia, cantidad, magnitud.

mucic ['mjusɪk] *a.* (quím.) múcico.

mucid ['mjusəd] *a.* (ant.) rancio, viscoso; mucoso, mocoso.

muciferous [mju'sɪfərəs] *a.* mucífero.

mucilage ['mjusəlɪdʒ] *s.* 1. (bot.) mucilago, mucílago. 2. mucilago, goma.

mucilaginous [ˌmjusə'lædʒənəs] *a.* mucilaginoso.

mucin ['mjusən] *s.* (bioquím.) mucina.

mucinogen [mju'sɪnədʒən] *s.* (bioquím.) mucinógeno.

mucinous ['mjusənəs] *a.* (bioquím.) mucinoso.

muck [mʌk] *s.* 1. estiércol húmedo, boñiga, bosta (Am.). 2. mantillo, humus. 3. (fam.) porquería, inmundicia, asquerosidad; basura. 4. (G.B.) pacotilla, cosa de poco valor. 5. **to make a m. of,** ensuciar; estropear. —*v.t.* 1. estercolar, abonar. 2. (fam., fig.) manchar, enlodar. 3. **m. up,** (pr. G.B.) desordenar, desbarajustar; ensuciar; estropear; enmarañar. —*v.i.* **to m. about,** (pr. G.B.) vagar, errar, andar a tontas y a locas; tontear; **m. in with** (jer., G.B.) compartir alojamiento con, vivir junto con.

mucker ['mʌkər, B -ə] *s.* (jer., G.B.) 1. patán, palurdo. 2. hombre malcriado; canalla.

muckiness [-ɪnəs] *s.* suciedad, porquería.

muckluck, *var. de* **mukluk.**

muckrake ['mʌkˌreɪk] *s.* rastrillo para estiércol o abono. —*v.i.* detraer, infamar; andar escarbando para sacar trapos sucios al sol, descubrir escándalos o corrupción (en personajes públicos).

muckraker [-ər, B -ə] *s.* (pol.) el que descubre o airea escándalos o corrupción.

mucksweat [-'swɛt] *s.* sudor abundante.

muckworm [-ˌwɜrm, B -ˌwɜm] *s.* 1. (ento.) gusano o gorgojo del estiércol. 2. avaro, avariento, tacaño.

mucky ['mʌkɪ] *a.* sucio, puerco.

mucocutaneous [ˌmjukoʊkjʊ'teɪnɪəs] *a.* (anat.) mucocutáneo.

mucoid ['mjuˌkɔɪd] (bioquím.) *s.* mucoide. —*a.* mucoideo.

mucoprotein [-koʊ'proʊtin, -'proʊtɪən] *s.* (bioquím.) mucoproteína.

mucor ['mjukər, B -kɔ] *s.* (bot.) múcor.

mucosa [mju'koʊsə] *s.* (*pl.* MUCOSAE [-ˌsi] o MUCOSAS) (anat.) mucosa, membrana mucosa.

mucoserous [ˌmjukoʊ'sɪrəs, B -'sɪər-] *a.* (fisiol.) mucoseroso.

mucosity [mju'kɑsətɪ, B -'kɔs-] *s.* (*pl.* MUCOSITIES) mucosidad.

mucous ['mjukəs] *a.* mucoso.

mucous membrane, (anat.) membrana mucosa.

mucro ['mjuˌkroʊ] *s.* (*pl.* MUCRONES [mju'kroʊniz]) (bot.) mucrón.

mucronate [-krənət, -ˌneɪt] **mucronated** [-ˌneɪtəd] *a.* (bot.) mucronato.

mucus ['mjukəs] *s.* moco, mucus, mucosidad.

mud [mʌd] *s.* 1. barro, lodo, fango, cieno. 2. (fig.) fango, vilipendio. 3. (jer.) café. 4. **(one's) name is m.**, (uno) está totalmente desacreditado; **to fling** (o **throw**) **m. at,** echar lodo (a), enlodar (a), difamar, calumniar. —*v.t.* embarrar, enfangar, enlodar; enturbiar; ensuciar.

mud bath, baño de barro (tratamiento de belleza).

mud dauber, m. wasp, (ento.) avispa del barro, avispa chibcha (Am.).

muddily ['mʌdəlɪ] *adv.* turbiamente.

muddiness [-ɪnəs] *s.* fangosidad; turbiedad, suciedad.

muddle ['mʌdəl] *v.t.* 1. confundir, turbar. 2. aturdir, atontar. 3. embriagar, embotar. 4. enredar, embrollar, revolver. 5. estropear, frangollar, chapucear. 6. revolver, mezclar. 7. enturbiar. —*v.i.* obrar confusamente; **m. on,** hacer las cosas al tuntún; **m. through,** salir del paso a duras penas, terminar algo a tontas y a locas (o a la diabla). —*s.* confusión, revoltijo, embrollo.

muddlehead [-ˌhɛd] *s.* (fam.) estúpido, tonto, persona que no hace nada a derechas.

muddleheaded [-əd] *a.* estúpido, atontado, despistado.

muddler [-ələr, B -lə] *s.* 1. persona despistada, torpe, que todo lo embrolla. 2. varilla para agitar mezclas y bebidas frías.

muddy [-ɪ] *a.* (MUDDIER; MUDDIEST) 1. lodoso, fangoso, barroso. 2. turbio, opaco; oscuro, sombrío. 3. confuso, embrollado; estúpido, tonto. —*v.t.* 1. ensuciar, embarrar, enlodar; enturbiar. 2. nublar, anublar.

mudfish ['mʌdˌfɪʃ] *s.* (ict.) locha.

mud flat, tierra baja que queda inundada con la marea alta.

mudguard [-ˌgɑrd, B -ˌgɑd] *s.* (aut.) guardabarros, guardafango (Amer.).

mud hen, (orn.) gallareta, fulica, focha; polla de agua.

mudhole ['mʌdˌhoʊl] *s.* hoyo de fango.

mudlark [-ˌlɑrk, B -ˌlɑk] *s.* (G.B.) galopín, pillete.

mudpack [-'pæk] *s.* mascarilla de caolín (usada como tratamiento cosmético).

mud pie, tortita de barro (que hacen los niños como juego).

mud puppy, (zool.) ajolote; necturo; salamandra acuática gigante.

mud scow, pontón.

mudsill ['mʌdˌsɪl] *s.* cimiento, base o soporte (que va) bajo tierra (en una construcción).

mudslinger [-ˌslɪŋər, B -ə] *s.* infamador, detractor.

mudslinging [-ɪŋ] *s.* vilipendio, detracción.

mudstone [-ˌstoʊn] *s.* (geol.) esquisto de barro.

mud turtle, (zool.) tortuga de cenagal, tortuga escorpión.

mud volcano, (geol.) salso.

mud wall, tapia.

muezzin [mu'ɛzən] *s.* (relig.) almuecín, almuédano, muecín.

muff [mʌf] *s.* 1. manguito (para las manos). 2. (béisbol) falla (al querer agarrar la bola). 3. torpeza, chapucería, error. 4. (fam.) estúpido, inútil, chambón (en el juego). —*v.t.* 1. estropear, hacer mal. 2. dejar caer, no lograr coger (ej., la pelota).
muffin ['mʌfən] *s.* mollete, (especie de) panecillo.
muffle ['mʌfəl] *v.t.* 1. embozar, arrebozar. 2. apagar, ensordecer, amortiguar (un ruido); destemplar (un tambor). —*s.* 1. amortiguador (de sonidos); sordina. 2. mufla, horno de porcelana. 3. rinario (de un animal).
muffle furnace, (cerám.) horno de mufla.
muffler ['mʌflər, B -lə] *s.* 1. bufanda, embozo. 2. mitón. 3. (mec.) sordina. 4. (aut.) silenciador, mofle (Cuba, P. Rico).
mufti ['mʌftɪ] *s.* (*pl.* MUFTIS) 1. muftí, jurisconsulto, musulmán. 2. (fam.) traje de paisano, traje de civil (esp. cuando lo usa un militar o policía).
mug [mʌg] *s.* 1. cubilete, jarra de barro o metal, pichel. 2. (jer.) jeta, hocico. 3. (jer., G.B.) incauto, primo. —*v.t., v.i.* (*pret., p.p.* MUGGED; *p.pr.* MUGGING) 1. (jer.) hacer muecas o morisquetas. 2. fotografiar (esp. a un criminal). 3. (t. con *up*) empollar, estudiar intensamente.
mug, mugg [mʌg] (jer., E.U.) *v.t., v.i.* acogotar, asaltar o atracar acogotando. —*s.* 1. tipo, tío, sujeto. 2. rufián, convicto.
mugger ['mʌgər, B -ə] *s.* tirón, asaltador, atracador, asaltante (que acogota), cogotero (Amer.).
mugger, *s.* (zool.) cocodrilo común (de la India).
mugginess ['mʌgɪnəs] *s.* bochornoso calor húmedo y sofocante.
mugging [-ɪŋ] *s.* (fam.) asalto; atracos, **robo con** violencia, gen. callejero.
muggins ['mʌgənz] *s.* 1. simplón, bobalicón. 2. un juego de dominó o de naipes.
muggy ['mʌgɪ] *a.* (MUGGIER; MUGGIEST) húmedo, bochornoso y sofocante (díc. del tiempo).
Mugilidae [mju'dʒɪlə,di, B mju-] *s. pl.* (zool.) mugílidos.
mugwort ['mʌg,wɜrt, B -,wɜt] *s.* (bot.) artemisa pegajosa, ajea, pajea.
mugwump [-,wʌmp] *s.* (E.U., pol.) 1. votante independiente (no afiliado a ningún partido político). 2. hombre importante, jefe.
Muhammad [mu'hæməd] *s.* Mahoma (*fundador del Islam*).
Muhammadan [moʊ'hæmədən, mu-] *a.,* (ant.) *s.* musulmán, islámico.
Muhamaddanism [-,ɪzəm] *s.* (ant.) el Islam, islamismo.
mujik [mu'ʒik, B 'muʒɪk] *s. var. de* **muzhik,** mujic, campesino ruso.
mukluk ['mʌk,lʌk] *s.* bota de piel de foca (que usan los esquimales).
mulatto [mjʊ'lætoʊ] *s.* (*pl.* MULATTOES) mulato.
mulberry ['mʌl,bɛrɪ, B -bərɪ] *s.* (*pl.* MULBERRIES) 1. (bot.) morera, moral. 2. mora. 3. morado (color).
mulch [mʌltʃ] *s.* (agr.) estiércol y paja (para proteger plantas). —*v.t.* cubrir (plantas) con estiércol y paja.
mulct [mʌlkt] *s.* multa. —*v.t.* 1. multar. 2. embaucar; sacar fraudulentamente (dinero); desplumar (a alguien).
mule [mjul] *s.* 1. mula, mulo, macho. 2. (biol.) híbrido estéril. 3. (tej.) selfactina, máquina de hilar intermitente. 4. (fam.) persona terca, testarudo. 5. pantufla, chinela.
mule deer, (zool.) cariacú.
mule jenny, hiladora mecánica intermitente.
mule skinner, (fam., E.U.) mulero, muletero.
muleteer [,mjulə'tɪr, B -'tɪə] *s.* mulero, muletero, arriero.
muley ['mjulɪ] *a.* (E.U.) descornada (res). —*s.* 1. res descornada. 2. vaca.
muley saw ['mjulɪ-] (mec., E.U.) sierra muley, sierra mecánica de guias.
muliebrity [,mjulɪ'ɛbrətɪ] *s.* feminidad, condición de mujer.
mulish ['mjulɪʃ] *a.* terco, obstinado, testarudo.
mulishly [-lɪ] *adv.* obstinadamente, tercamente, testarudamente.
mulishness [-nəs] *s.* terquedad, obstinación, testarudez.
mull [mʌl] *s.* 1. muselina fina y suave. 2. (agr.) mantillo, abono; humus.
mull, *v.t.* ponderar, meditar, rumiar. —*v.i.* (gen. con *over*) reflexionar, meditar sobre.
mull, *v.t.* calentar (vino) añadiendo azúcar y especias.
mullah, mulla ['mʌlə] *s.* intérprete de las leyes y dogmas del Islam.
mullein ['mʌlən] *s.* (bot.) verbasco, gordolobo, candelaria, barbasco (Amer.).
muller ['mʌlər, B -ə] *s.* moleta (para moler drogas, colores, etc.).
mullet ['mʌlət] *s.* (ict.) lisa, mújol, múgil, salmonete, barbo de mar.
mulley, *var. de* **muley.**
mulligan ['mʌlɪgən] *s.* (E.U., jer.) olla, puchero (vianda).
mulligatawny [,mʌlɪgə'tɔnɪ] *s.* (*pl.* MULLIGATAWNIES) sopa de pollo y otras carnes sazonada con cari.
mulligrubs ['mʌlɪ,grʌbz] *s. pl.* (fam.) 1. retortijón de tripas, cólico. 2. morriña, murria, mal humor.
mullion ['mʌljən] *s.* (arq.) mainel, parteluz, montante; larguero central de puerta. —*v.t.* dividir (un vano) mediante maineles o parteluces.
mullite ['mʌl,aɪt] *s.* (min.) mulita.
mullock ['mʌlək] *s.* (Aust.) escombros, roca no aurífera.
mullocky [-ɪ] *a.* (Aust.) estéril (roca).
mulse [mʌls] *s.* clarea, mezcla de vino y miel.
multiband antenna ['mʌltə,bænd-] (rad.) antena de fajas múltiples, antena multibanda.
multibreaker [-,breɪkər, B -kə] *s.* disyuntor múltiple.
multicellular [,mʌltɪ'sɛljələr, B -lə] *a.* (biol.) multicelular, pluricelular.
multichannel ['mʌltɪ'tʃænəl] *a.* con canales múltiples.
multicolored [,mʌltɪ'kʌlərd, B -əd] *a.* multicolor.
multicultural ['mʌltɪ'kʌltʃərəl] *a.* multicultural.
multiculturalism ['mʌltɪ'kʌltʃərəlɪsm] *s.* multiculturalismo.
multicylinder [-'sɪləndər, B -də] *a.* policilíndrico, de varios cilindros.
multidentate [-'dɛnteɪt] *a.* multidentado.
multidimensional [-dɪ'mɛntʃənəl, B -'mɛnʃən-] *a.* multidimensional.
multiengined [-'ɛndʒənd] *a.* multimotor.
multifarious [,mʌltə'fɛrɪəs, B -'fɛər-] *a.* 1. múltiple, variado, diverso. 2. (bot.) multifario.
multifariously [-lɪ] *adv.* variadamente, diversamente.
multifariousness [-nəs] *s.* variedad, diversidad, multiplicidad.
multifid ['mʌltɪ,fɪd] *a.* (bot.) multífido.
multiflora rose [,mʌltə'flɔrə-] (bot.) rosa multiflora, rosa de Pitiminí.
multiflorous [-'flɔrəs] *a.* (bot.) multifloro.
multiflow condenser ['mʌltɪ,floʊ-] condensador de paso múltiple.
multifold [-,foʊld] *a.* doblado muchas veces; múltiple.
multiform [-,fɔrm, B -,fɔm] *a.* multiforme.
multiformity [,mʌltɪ'fɔrmətɪ, B -'fɔmɪtɪ] *s.* variedad de formas.
multigraph ['mʌltə,græf, B -,grɑf] *s.* (impr.) multígrafo.
multilateral [,mʌltɪ'lætərəl, B 'mʌl-] *a.* 1. (geom.) multilátero. 2. multilateral (ej., un tratado).
multilaterally [-ɪ] *adv.* de manera multilateral.
multilayer glass ['mʌltɪ,leɪər, B -ə] vidrio laminado.
multilobulate [,mʌltɪ'lɑbjəleɪt, B -'lɔb-] *a.* (bot.) multilobulado.
multimillionaire [-,mɪljə'nɛr, B 'mʌl-'nɛə] *s.* multimillonario.
multinational [-'næʃənəl] *a.* multinacional.
multinominal [-'nɑmənəl, B -'nɔm-] *a.* con muchos nombres.
multinuclear [-'nuklɪər, B ,mʌltɪ'nju-ə] *a.* (fisiol.) multinuclear.
multinucleate [-klɪət] *a.* (fisiol.) multinucleado.
multioutlet [-'aʊt,lɛt] *a.* de toma múltiple.
multipara [mʌl'tɪpərə] *s.* (*pl.* MULTIPARAE [-əri]) (med.) multípara.
multiparity [,mʌltɪ'pærətɪ] *s.* multiparidad.
multiparous [mʌl'tɪpərəs] *a.* (med., zool.) multípara.
multipartite [,mʌltə'pɑr,taɪt, B -'pɑ,-] *a.* que consta de muchas partes.
multiped ['mʌltə,pɛd] *a.* de muchos pies.
multiphase [-,feɪz] *a.* (elec.) polifásico.
multiplane [-,pleɪn] *s.* (aer.) poliplano.
multiple ['mʌltəpəl] *a.* 1. múltiple, multíplice, vario. 2. (elec.) múltiple (díc. de cierta clase de circuitos). —*s.* 1. (elec.) circuito múltiple. 2. (mat.) múltiplo. 3. **in m.,** (elec.) en series múltiples.
multiple choice, con varias posibilidades; con varias respuestas (tipo de examen o prueba, en la que hay que elegir una respuesta correcta entre las varias que se proponen).
multiple factors, (biol.) factores múltiples.
multiple fruit, (bot.) fruto compuesto.
multiple neuritis, (med.) polineuritis, neuritis múltiple.
multiple sclerosis, (med.) esclerosis múltiple, esclerosis en placas.
multiple star, (astr.) estrella múltiple.
multiplet ['mʌltəplət] *s.* (fís.) multiplete.
multiple turning, (rad.) sintonización múltiple.
multiple warhead missile, cohete nodriza armado con múltiples puntas o cabezas.
multiplex [-,plɛks] *a.* 1. múltiple, multíplice. 2. (tele., teleg., rad., t.v.) multiplex (sistema de transmisión). —*v.t.* (tele., teleg., rad., t.v.) transmitir por sistema multiplex.
multipliable [-,plaɪəbəl] **multiplicable** [,mʌltə'plɪkəbəl] *a.* multiplicable.
multiplicand [,mʌltəplɪ'kænd] *s.* (mat.) multiplicando.
multiplicate ['mʌltɪplə,keɪt] *a.* múltiple, numeroso, vario.
multiplication [,mʌltəplə'keɪʃən] *s.* multiplicación.
multiplication tables, tablas de multiplicar.
multiplicative [,mʌltə'plɪkətɪv, 'mʌltəplə,keɪt-] *a.* multiplicativo.
multiplicity [,mʌltə'plɪsətɪ] *s.* multiplicidad.
multiplier ['mʌltə,plaɪər, B -ə] *s.* (mat., fís.) multiplicador.
multiply ['mʌltə,plaɪ] *v.t.* (*pret., p.p.* MULTIPLIED; *p.pr.* MULTIPLYING) multiplicar; (mat.) multiplicar. —*v.i.* multiplicarse.
multi-ply ['mʌltɪ'plaɪ] *a.* de varias capas.
multiplying [-tə,plaɪɪŋ] *a.* multiplicador, de multiplicación.

multiplying glass, espejo de imagen múltiple.
multiplying lens, lente de aumento; (foto.) lente multiplicadora.
multipolar [ˌmʌltɪˈpoʊlər, B -lə] *a.* (anat., elec.) multipolar.
multipresence [-ˈprɛzəns] *s.* ubicuidad.
multiracial [-ˈreɪʃəl] *a.* de diversas razas.
multistage [ˈmʌltɪˌsteɪdʒ] *a.* multigradual, de etapas múltiples.
multistage turbine, (mec.) turbina de expansión múltiple.
multitap [-ˌtæp] *s.* derivación múltiple.
multitube [-ˌtub, B -ˌtjub] *a.* (rad.) de varias válvulas.
multitubular boiler [-ˈtubjələr, B -ˈtjubjʊlə] caldera de tubos de humos.
multitude [ˈmʌltəˌtud, B -ˌtjud] *s.* multitud, muchedumbre; **a m. of,** una multitud de, un sinnúmero de; **the m.,** la multitud, la plebe, la masa.
multitudinous [ˌmʌltəˈtudənəs, B -ˈtjud-] *a.* 1. numeroso, innumerable. 2. (raro) de la multitud.
multitudinously [-lɪ] *adv.* numerosamente.
multitudinousness [-nəs] *s.* numerosidad.
multivalence [ˌmʌlˈtɪvələns, mʌltɪˈveɪ-, B -ˈtɪvə-] *s.* (quím., biol.) polivalencia.
multivalent [-lənt] *a.* (quím., biol.) multivalente, polivalente.
multivalve [ˈmʌltɪˌvælv] *a.* (zool.) polivalvo.
multivolume [ˌmʌltɪˈvɑljəm, B -ˈvɔl-] **multivolumed** [-jəmd] *a.* de varios tomos, en varios volúmenes.
multure [ˈmʌltʃər, B -tʃə] *s.* (pr. esco.) maquila, molienda.
mum [mʌm] *interj.* silencio, chito, chitón; **m.'s the word,** punto en boca. —*a.* silencioso, callado; **to keep m.,** guardar silencio.
mum, *v.i.* (*pret., p.p.* MUMMED; *p.pr.* MUMMING) tomar parte en una mascarada, disfrazarse, enmascararse.
mum [mʌm] *s.* 1. (fam.) mamá, mami. 2. (fam.) crisantemo. 3. cerveza fuerte.
mumble [ˈmʌmbəl] *v.t.* 1. mascullar, barbotar. 2. mascujar, mascar mal. —*s.* barboteo, refunfuño. —*v.i.* barbullar; **don't m.,** habla claro.
mumbler [-blər, B -blə] *s.* mascullador, que murmura entre dientes.
mumbletypeg [ˈmʌmbəltɪˌpɛg] *s.* juego de niños.
mumbling [ˈmʌmblɪŋ, -bəlɪŋ] *s.* acción y efecto de mascullar.
mumbo jumbo [ˈmʌmboʊˈdʒʌmboʊ] 1. fetiche, espantajo, coco. 2. abracadabra, mistificación; ritual o conjuro absurdo. 3. jerigonza, guirigay, galimatías.
mummer [ˈmʌmər, B -ə] *s.* 1. mimo, pantomimo; p. ext. actor. 2. máscara, festejador, enmascarado.
mummery [-ərɪ] *s.* 1. mascarada, momería. 2. mojiganga, ceremonia ridícula.
mummification [ˌmʌmɪfəˈkeɪʃən] *s.* momificación.
mummify [ˈmʌməˌfaɪ] *v.t.* (*pret., p.p.* MUMMIFIED; *p.pr.* MUMMIFYING) momificar. —*v.i.* momificarse, desecarse.
mummy [ˈmʌmɪ] *s.* (*pl.* MUMMIES) momia. —*v.t.* momificar.
mump [mʌmp] *v.t., v.i.* (pr. dial.) 1. mascullar, rezongar. 2. (G.B.) mendigar, trampear.
mumpish [ˈmʌmpɪʃ] *a.* malhumorado, irritable.
mumps [mʌmps] *s. pl.* (med.) paperas, parotiditis, parotitis.
mun. *abrev. de* **municipal,** municipal.
munch [mʌntʃ] *v.t., v.i.* ronzar, mascar algo quebradizo que hace ruido al partirse; comer golosamente; comer cualquier cosa entre comidas.
mundane [ˌmʌnˈdeɪn, ˈmʌnˌdeɪn, B ˈmʌn-] *a.* mundano, terrenal.
mundanely [-lɪ] *adv.* mundanamente, terrenalmente.
mungo [ˈmʌŋgoʊ] *s.* (*pl.* MUNGOS) mungo, lana de borra.
municipal [mjʊˈnɪsəpəl] *a.* municipal.
municipal council, ayuntamiento, concejo municipal, cabildo municipal.
municipal government, gobierno municipal.
municipalism [-ˌlɪzəm] *s.* gobierno municipal.
municipality [-ˌnɪsəˈpælətɪ] *s.* (*pl.* MUNICIPALITIES) municipalidad, municipio, ayuntamiento.
municipalization [-pələˈzeɪʃən, B -laɪ-] *s.* municipalización.
municipalize [-ˈnɪsəpəˌlaɪz] *v.t.* municipalizar, dar carácter municipal a.
municipal law, ley doméstica, ley municipal.
municipally [-lɪ] *adv.* municipalmente.
municipal road, camino vecinal.
municipium [ˌmjunəˈsɪpɪəm] *s.* (hist.) municipio (entre los antiguos romanos).
munificence [mjʊˈnɪfəsəns] *s.* munificencia, magnificencia, esplendidez.
munificent [-sənt] *a.* munífico, munificente.
munificently [-lɪ] *adv.* muníficamente, con gran generosidad.
muniment [ˈmjunəmənt] *s.* 1. (*pl.*) (der.) documentos de título. 2. (ant.) apoyo, defensa.
munition [mjʊˈnɪʃən] *s.* (*gen. pl.*) munición, municiones; pertrechos, equipo. —*v.t.* municionar, pertrechar.
munition ship, buque para transporte de municiones, buque arsenal.
munnion [ˈmʌnjən] *s.* (arq.) mainel, parteluz.
muntjac, muntjak [ˈmʌntdʒæk] *s.* (zool.) muntyac.
muon [ˈmjuɑn, B -ɔn] *s.* (fís.) muón.
muraena [mjʊˈrinə] *s.* (ict.) morena.
mural [ˈmjʊrəl, B ˈmjʊər-] *a.* mural, escarpado, vertical. —*s.* mural, pintura mural.
mural crown, (hist., her.) corona mural.
muralist [-əst] *s.* pintor muralista.
mural painting, pintura mural.
murder [ˈmɜrdər, B ˈmɜdə] *s.* 1. asesinato, homicidio. 2. (fig.) (fam.) cosa atroz. 3. **m. in the first degree,** (der.) homicidio premeditado; **m. in the second degree,** (der.) homicidio impremeditado; **m. will out,** un asesinato no puede ocultarse; **to cry blue m.,** berrear, protestar a gritos. —*v.t.* 1. asesinar. 2. (fig.) destruir. 3. (fig.) mutilar, estropear. 4. (fig.) deformar, ej. un idioma, chapurrear (un idioma). 5. tocar o cantar horriblemente mal. —*v.i.* cometer asesinato.
murderer [-ərər, B -ərə] *s.* asesino, homicida.
murderess [-ərəs] *s.* asesina, mujer homicida.
murderous [-ərəs] *a.* 1. asesino, sanguinario. 2. devastador, aniquilador, violento.
murderously [-lɪ] *adv.* 1. sanguinariamente. 2. violentamente.
murderousness [-nəs] *s.* intención asesina.
mure [mjʊr, B mjʊə] *s.* (ant.) muro, pared. —*v.t.* murar, cercar con muro.
murex [ˈmjʊrˌɛks, B ˈmjʊər-] *s.* (*pl.* MURICES [-əˌsiz] o MUREXES) (zool.) múrice, cañadilla, púrpura.
murexide [mjʊˈrɛkˌsaɪd, B mjʊə-] *s.* (quím.) murexida.
muriate [ˈmjʊrɪət, -ˌeɪt] *s.* (quím.) muriato.
muriatic [ˌmjʊrɪˈætɪk, B ˌmjʊər-] *a.* (quím.) muriático.
muriatic acid, (quím.) ácido muriático.
muricate [ˈmjʊrəˌkeɪt, B ˈmjʊər-] **muricated** [-əd] *a.* (bot.) muricado.
Muricidae [mjʊˈrɪsəˌdi, B mjʊə-] *s. pl.* (zool.) murícidos.
Muridae [ˈmjʊrədi, B ˈmjʊər-] *s. pl.* (zool.) múridos.
murine [-aɪn, -ən] *a., s.* (zool.) murino.
murine opossum, (zool.) marmosa.
murk [mɜrk, B mɜk] *a.* (poét., dial.) obscuro, lóbrego, sombrío. —*s.* obscuridad, lobreguez.
murkily [ˈmɜrkəlɪ, B ˈmɜkə-] *adv.* obscuramente, sombríamente.
murkiness [-kɪnəs] *s.* obscuridad, lobreguez.
murky [-kɪ] *a.* (MURKIER; MURKIEST) obscuro, sombrío, lóbrego.
murmur [ˈmɜrmər, B ˈmɜmə] *s.* 1. murmullo, susurro, murmureo. 2. (fig.) murmureo, murmullo, queja. 3. (med.) soplo cardíaco. —*v.i., v.t.* 1. murmurar, susurrar. 2. (fig.) murmurar, quejarse.
murmurer [-mərər, B -mərə] *s.* murmurador.
murmuring [ˈmɜrmərɪŋ, B ˈmɜm-] *a.* murmurante, susurrante.
murmurous [-ərəs] *a.* murmurante, susurrante.
murmurously [-lɪ] *adv.* de manera susurrante, susurrantemente.
murphy [ˈmɜrfɪ, B ˈmɜfɪ] *s.* (*pl.* MURPHIES) (hum., jer.) patata.
Murphy bed, cama empotrada o levadiza.
Murphy's Law, ley del indefectible contratiempo: si algo puede salir mal, mal seguro que saldrá.
murrain [ˈmɜrən, B ˈmʌrɪn] *s.* 1. (vet.) plaga o peste (de los animales); morriña. 2. (ant.) peste; **a m. on you!** ¡maldito seas!
murre [mɜr, B mɜ] *s.* (orn.) arán.
murrey [ˈmɜrɪ, B ˈmʌrɪ] *s.* color morado rojizo. —*a.* morado rojizo.
murrhine [ˈmɜrɪn, -aɪn, B ˈmʌrɪn] *a.* (hist.) múrrino. —*s.* (hist.) vaso múrrino.
mus. *abrev. de* 1. **museum,** museo. 2. **music,** música. 3. **musical,** musical. 4. **musician,** músico.
musaceous [mjuˈzeɪʃəs] *a.* (bot.) musáceo.
Musca [ˈmʌskə] *s.* (astr.) Mosca (constelación).
muscadel [ˌmʌskəˈdɛl] *var. de* **muscatel.**
muscadine [ˈmʌskədɪn, -ˌdaɪn] *s.* 1. (bot.) variedad de vid. 2. (hist.) vino moscatel.
muscardine [ˈmʌskərdən, B -kədɪn] *s.* muscardina, enfermedad de los gusanos de seda.
muscari [mʌsˈkærɪ, -ˈkɛrɪ, B -ˈkɛərɪ] *s.* (*pl.* MUSCARI o MUSCARIS) (bot.) almizcleña.
muscarine [ˈmʌskəˌrin] *s.* (quím.) muscarina.
muscat [ˈmʌskət, -ˌkæt, B -kət] *s.* 1. vino moscatel. 2. (bot.) vid moscatel.
muscatel [ˌmʌskəˈtɛl] *s.* 1. vino moscatel. 2. pasa moscatel.
muscid [ˈmʌsɪd] *a.* (ento.) múscido.
muscle [ˈmʌsəl] *s.* 1. músculo, tejido muscular. 2. (fig.) fuerza, vigor, robustez, desarrollo muscular. —*v.i.* (fam.) abrirse paso a la fuerza o a empujones; **m. in on,** invadir; inmiscuirse en, conseguir su participación a la fuerza en.
muscle-bound [-ˌbaʊnd] *a.* agarrotado, acalambrado, endurecido (músculo).
muscle sense, (psic., fisiol.) sentido muscular.
muscoid [ˈmʌˌskɔɪd] **muscose** [-ˌskoʊs] *a.* con musgo, musgoso.
muscovado [ˌmʌskəˈvɑdoʊ] *s.* azúcar mascabada o moscabada.
Muscovite [ˈmʌskəˌvaɪt] *s.* 1. moscovita, habitante de Moscú. 2. **m.,** (min.) muscovita, mica blanca.
Muscovy [-vɪ] *s.* (hist.) antiguo nombre de Rusia.
Muscovy duck, (orn.) pato criollo, pato almizclado.
muscular [ˈmʌskjələr, B -lə] *a.* 1. muscular (contracción, fuerza, etc.). 2. musculoso, fornido.

muscular dystrophy, (med.) distrofia muscular.
muscularity [ˌmʌskjəˈlærətɪ] *s.* musculosidad.
musculature [ˈmʌskjələtʃər, B -tʃə] *s.* musculatura.
muse [mjuz] *v.i.* (gen. con *on* o *upon*) meditar, reflexionar (sobre); contemplar. —*v.t.* decir en tono meditativo. —*s.* abstracción, meditación profunda.
Muse [mjuz] *s.* 1. (mitol.) musa. 2. **m.,** musa, numen.
museful [ˈmjuzfəl] *a.* (ant.) meditabundo, cogitabundo, pensativo.
museology [ˌmjuzɪˈɑlədʒɪ, B -ˈɔl-] *s.* museología, el estudio de la organización, dirección, etc. de un museo.
musette [mjʊˈzɛt] *s.* 1. especie de gaita o cornamusa. 2. (t. **m. bag**) mochila.
museum [mjuˈziəm, ˈmjuˌziəm, B mjuˈzi-] *s.* museo.
museum piece, 1. pieza de museo, pieza artística. 2. (fig., fam.) antigualla.
mush [mʌʃ] *s.* 1. gachas o puches de harina de maíz. 2. gacha, pasta o masa muy blanda. 3. (fam.) sensiblería, sentimentalismo exagerado. 4. (jer.) boca, cara, jeta. 5. (jer.) (rad.) interferencia. —*v.i.* (aer.) volar en estado averiado (un avión). —*v.t.* (pr. dial.) machacar, desmoronar.
mush, *s.* (E.U.) marcha a través de la nieve con un trineo tirado por perros. —*interj.* voz para apurar el paso de los perros. —*v.i.* marchar por la nieve con un trineo tirado por perros.
mushroom [ˈmʌʃrum, -rʊm] *s.* 1. seta, hongo, champiñón. 2. (ant.) advenedizo, arribista. —*a.* 1. hongoso, fungoso. 2. advenedizo. 3. de o en forma de hongo. —*v.i.* 1. tomar forma de hongo. 2. crecer o desarrollarse rápidamente, multiplicarse. 3. abrirse (punta de proyectil). 4. coger hongos. 5. **m. into,** convertirse rápidamente en.
mushroom anchor, (mar.) ancla de campana, ancla de seta.
mushroom cloud, nube-hongo, hongo atómico (Chile).
mushroom head, (mec.) cabeza de hongo.
mushroom ventilator, ventilador de campana, ventilador tipo hongo.
mushy [ˈmʌʃɪ] *a.* (MUSHIER; MUSHIEST) 1. suave, blando, mollar. 2. sensiblero, exageradamente sentimental, efusivo. 3. baboso (con las damas).
music [ˈmjuzɪk] *s.* 1. música. 2. (ant.) composición musical. 3. **to face the m.,** encararse o hacer frente a las consecuencias; **to set to m.,** poner música a (poema, letra, etc.).
musical [-zɪkəl] *a.* 1. musical, músico. 2. armonioso, melodioso. 3. aficionado a la música. 4. de músicos (organización, etc.). —*s.* 1. comedia musical. 2. (ant.) velada musical.
musical box, (G.B.) *var. de* **music box.**
musical chairs, juego de las sillas vacías.
musical clock, reloj de música.
musical comedy, comedia musical, revista.
musicale [ˌmjuzɪˈkæl] *s.* velada musical.
musicality [-ˈkælətɪ] *s.* musicalidad.
musically [ˈmjuzɪkəlɪ] *adv.* musicalmente.
musicalness [-kəlnəs] *s.* musicalidad.
musical saw, serrucho (como instrumento musical).
music book, libro de música; texto o ejercicio de instrucción musical.
music box, cajita de música.
music drama, drama musical.
music hall, 1. salón de conciertos. 2. (G.B.) teatro de variedades.
musician [mjuˈzɪʃən] *s.* músico (compositor o ejecutante).
musicianship [-ˌʃɪp] *s.* maestría musical.
music of the spheres, música, armonía de las esferas celestes (supuesta por Pitágoras).
musicographer [ˌmjuzɪˈkɑgrəfər, B -ˈkɔgrəfə] *s.* musicógrafo.
musicologist [ˌmjuzɪˈkɑlədʒəst, B -ˈkɔl-] *s.* musicólogo.
musicology [-dʒɪ] *s.* musicología.
music paper, papel pautado.
music rack, atril.
music roll, rollo para pianola.
music school, conservatorio de música.
musing [ˈmjuziŋ] *a.* meditativo, meditabundo. —*s.* meditación.
musingly [-lɪ] *adv.* meditativamente.
musk [mʌsk] *s.* 1. almizcle. 2. olor almizcleño. 3. (bot.) almizcleña. 4. (fig.) olor que se percibe en los lugares muy frondosos.
muskallonge, muskallunge, *var. de* **muskellunge.**
musk beetle, (ento.) macuba.
musk deer, (zool.) almizclero, cervatillo, portaalmizcle.
muskeg [ˈmʌsˌkɛg] *s.* (N. de E.U., Can.) pantano (esp. el poblado de musgos).
muskellunge [ˈmʌskəˌlʌndʒ] *s.* (*pl.* MUSKELLUNGE) (ict.) lucio, sollo americano.
musket [ˈmʌskət] *s.* mosquete; p. ext. fusil.
musketeer [ˌmʌskəˈtɪr, B -ˈtɪə] *s.* mosquetero.
musketry [ˈmʌskətrɪ] *s.* 1. mosquetes. 2. mosquetería. 3. mosquetazos, descarga de mosquetería, fusilería.
muskiness [ˈmʌskɪnəs] *s.* olor de almizcle; olor a selva.
muskmelon [ˈmʌskˌmɛlən] *s.* (bot.) melón, melón amarillo, melón de Castilla.
musk-ox [-ˌɑks, B -ˌɔks] *s.* (zool.) toro almizcleño.
muskrat [-ˌræt] *s.* 1. (zool.) rata almizclera, rata almizclada, desmán. 2. piel de rata almizclera.
musk rose, (bot.) rosa almizcleña.
musk turtle, (zool.) tortuga almizclada.
musky [ˈmʌskɪ] *a.* (MUSKIER; MUSKIEST) almizcleño, almizclero; díc. del olor de la selva.
Muslem [ˈmʌzləm] *var. de.* **Muslim.**
Muslim [ˈmʌzləm, ˈmʊs-] *a., s.* musulmán, muslime, islámico.
Muslim calendar, calendario islámico.
muslin [ˈmʌzlən] *s.* (tej.) muselina.
muslin kail [-keɪl] (esco.) caldo de cebada y verduras.
musquash [ˈmʌskwɑʃ, -kwɔʃ, B -kwɔʃ] *s.* (zool.) rata almizclera, rata almizclada, desmán.
muss [mʌs] *s.* 1. arrebatiña, rebatiña. 2. (jer.) riña, reyerta, disputa, pendencia, trifulca. 3. (fam.) desorden, confusión, lío, batiburrillo. —*v.t.* 1. ajar, arrugar, manchar. 2. (gen. con *up*) desarreglar, desordenar; ensuciar, desaliñar. 3. **m. up,** maltratar, zurrar; confundir, hacer caótico.
mussel [ˈmʌsəl] *s.* (zool.) mejillón, mítulo.
mussy [ˈmʌsɪ] *a.* (MUSSIER; MUSSIEST) ensuciado, desaliñado.
must [mʌst] *s.* 1. mosto. 2. olor y gusto rancios; moho.
must [mʌst, məst] *v. aux.* deber, estar obligado (a), necesitar, tener (que), deber (de), haber (de), ser preciso, ser menester, ej., *he m. be mad,* debe de estar loco, *he m. lose,* él debe perder, *I m. ask you to leave,* debo pedirle que se vaya; **m. needs,** necesariamente, sin falta. — [mʌst] *s.* 1. cosa esencial o indispensable. 2. algo que uno no debe perder (como una película, novela, etc.).
must [mʌst] *var. de* **musth.**
mustache, *var. de* **moustache.**
mustachio [məˈstæʃoʊ, -ˈstɑʃ-, B -ˈstɑʃ-] *s.* (*pl.* MUSTACHIOS) mostacho, bigote.
mustachioed [-oʊd] *a.* bigotudo, abigotado; con mostachos.
mustang [ˈmʌstæŋ] *s.* mustango, mustang, potro salvaje.
mustard [ˈmʌstərd, B -əd] *s.* 1. (bot.) mostaza. 2. mostaza (salsa, polvo).
mustard gas, (quím.) gas mostaza, sulfuro de dicloroetilo.
mustard oil, aceite de mostaza.
mustard plaster, sinapismo, cataplasma de mostaza.
mustard-seed shot [ˈmʌstərdˌsid-, B -əd-] mostacilla (munición).
mustee [mʌˈsti] *s.* mestizo ochavón; p. ext. cualquier mestizo.
Mustelidae [ˌmʌsˈtɛlədi] *s. pl.* (zool.) mustélidos.
musteline [ˈmʌstəˌlaɪn] *a.* (zool.) mustelino.
muster [ˈmʌstər, B -tə] *v.t.* 1. reunir, congregar, juntar (para pasar revista, lista, etc.). 2. tomar, mostrar (ánimo, bríos, fuerza, etc.). 3. alistar, llamar a filas, enrolar. 4. incluir, comprender. 5. **m. out.,** (mil.) dar de baja, licenciar; depurar, inhabilitar; **m. up,** tomar (resolución, ánimo, etc.); procurar. —*v.i.* reunirse, congregarse, juntarse (para pasar revista, lista, etc.). —*s.* 1. asamblea, reunión. 2. rol, lista, nómina; (mil.) revista, reseña. 3. muestra, espécimen. 4. **to pass m.,** ser aceptado, ser adecuado.
muster book, lista; rol.
muster roll, (mar.) rol, lista de dotación (de un barco); (mil.) lista de revista.
musth [mʌst] *s.* frenesí del elefante macho (durante la época de celo).
mustiness [-tɪnəs] *s.* olor a moho.
musty [ˈmʌstɪ] *a.* (MUSTIER; MUSTIEST) 1. que huele a humedad, con olor a moho; mohoso. 2. anticuado; gastado, trillado.
mutability [ˌmjutəˈbɪlətɪ] *s.* mutabilidad; inconstancia.
mutable [ˈmjutəbəl] *a.* mudable, mutable, cambiable, alterable, variable; inconstante, cambiadizo.
mutableness [-nəs] *s.* mutabilidad; inconstancia.
mutably [-blɪ] *adv.* mudablemente; inconstantemente.
mutagenic [ˌmjutəˈdʒɛnɪk] *a.* (biol.) mutagénico, mutágeno.
mutant [ˈmjutənt] *s.* (biol.) mutante.
mutate [ˈmjuˌteɪt, B mjuˈteɪt] *v.t.* mudar, alterar, transformar; (biol.) mutar. —*v.i.* cambiarse, alterarse, transformarse; (biol.) mutar.
mutation [mjuˈteɪʃən] *s.* mutación, mudanza, cambio, alteración; (biol.) mutación.
mutational [-əl] *a.* de mutación.
mutationism [-ˌɪzəm] *s.* (biol.) mutacionismo.
mutch [mʌtʃ] *s.* (dial.) gorra de lino para mujer o niño.
mute [mjut] *a.* mudo; callado, silencioso; (fon.) oclusivo. —*s.* 1. mudo. 2. (mús.) sordina. 3. (gram.) letra muda. —*v.t.* 1. disminuir la intensidad de (sonidos); apagar (colores). 2. (mús.) poner sordidina a.
mutely [ˈmjutlɪ] *adv.* mudamente.
muteness [-nəs] *s.* mudez; (fig.) mutismo, mudez.
muticate [ˈmjutəˌkeɪt] **muticous** [-ɪkəs] *a.* (bot.) mútico.
mutilate [ˈmjutəlˌeɪt] *v.t.* mutilar, truncar, lisiar.
mutilated [-əd] *a.* estropeado (libros), mocho, trunco; cancelado.
mutilation [ˌmjutəlˈeɪʃən] *s.* mutilación.
mutilator [ˈmjutəlˌeɪtər, B -ə] *s.* mutilador.
mutineer [ˌmjutənˈɪr, B -ˈɪə] *s.* amotinado, amotinador, rebelde. —*v.i.* amotinarse, rebelarse, sublevarse, alzarse.

mutinous ['mjutənəs] *a.* sedicioso, amotinador, rebelde; indócil, ingobernable.
mutinously [-lɪ] *adv.* sediciosamente, de modo rebelde.
mutinousness [-nəs] *s.* espíritu o disposición rebeldes; indocilidad.
mutiny ['mjutənɪ] *s.* (*pl.* MUTINIES) 1. motín, rebelión, sedición, insurrección, asonada, revuelta, cuartelazo (Am.). 2. (ant.) tumulto, refriega, alboroto. —*v.i.* amotinarse, rebelarse, sublevarse.
mutism ['mjut,ɪzəm] *s.* mutismo, mudez.
mutt [mʌt] *s.* (jer.) 1. tonto, zopenco, mentecato, estúpido. 2. perro de raza indefinida.
mutter ['mʌtər, B -ə] *v.i.* 1. murmurar, musitar, bisbisar. 2. refunfuñar, rezongar. —*v.t.* pronunciar (palabras) en voz baja; decir (algo) entre dientes. —*s.* 1. murmuración, bisbiseo. 2. refunfuño, refunfuñadura.
mutterer [-ərər, B -ərə] *s.* murmurador; rezongón.
muttering [-ərɪŋ] *s.* rezongo, refunfuño.
mutteringly [-lɪ] *adv.* en voz baja, bisbisando; en tono rezongón.
mutton ['mʌtən] *s.* 1. carne de carnero. 2. carnero.
mutton chop, costilla de carnero.
muttonchops [-,tʃɑps, B -,tʃɔps] *s. pl.* patillas.
muttonhead [-,hɛd] *s.* (fam.) persona estúpida, corta de luces.
muttony [-ɪ] *a.* que tiene sabor a carne de carnero.
mutual ['mjutʃʊəl, B -tju-] *a.* mutuo, mutual, recíproco.
mutual aid, apoyo, ayuda mutua.
mutual company, compañía de seguros mutuos.
mutual consent, mutuo acuerdo.
mutual fund, (com.) fondo mutualista (de inversión), mutualidad.
mutual help association, mutualidad.
mutual insurance company, compañía de seguros mutuos.
mutualism ['mjutʃʊə,lɪzəm, B -tjʊ-] *s.* mutualismo.
mutualist [-ləst] *s.* mutualista.
mutualistic [,mjutʃʊə'lɪstɪk, B -tju-] *a.* mutualista.
mutuality [-'ælətɪ] *s.* mutualidad; reciprocidad, dependencia mutua.
mutualization [-ələ'zeɪʃən, B -laɪ-] *s.* conversión en una mutualidad.
mutualize ['mjutʃʊə,laɪz, B -tjʊ-] *v.t., v.i.* 1. volver(se) mutuo. 2. organizar(se) o convertir-se(se) en una mutualidad.
mutually [-lɪ] *adv.* mutuamente, mutualmente, recíprocamente.
mutual savings bank, banco mutualista de ahorros.
mutual wall, pared intermedia.
mutuary ['mjutʃʊ,ɛrɪ, B -tjʊərɪ] *s.* (*pl.* MUTUARIES) (der.) mutuario, mutuaria, mutuatario, mutuataria.
mutuel ['mjutʃʊəl, B -tjʊ-] *s.* apuesta mutual.
mutule ['mjutʃul, B -tjul] *s.* (arq.) mútulo.
mutuum [-tʃʊəm, B -tju-] *s.* (*pl.* MUTUA [-ə]) (der.) mutuo.
muu muu ['mumu] *s.* traje suelto de tela estampada de origen hawaiano.
muzhik, muzjik [mu'ʒik, B 'muʒɪk] *s.* mujic, campesino ruso.
muzzily ['mʌzəlɪ] *adv.* aturdidamente, confusamente.
muzziness [-ɪnəs] *s.* 1. aturdimiento. 2. aspecto confuso.
muzzle ['mʌzəl] *s.* 1. hocico, morro (de los animales). 2. (hum.) jeta, boca o cara (de una persona). 3. bozal, mordaza, frenillo. 4. boca, entrada, abertura, orificio (de arma de fuego). —*v.t.* 1. abozalar, poner bozal a (un animal). 2. (fig.) amordazar, hacer callar.
muzzle-loader ['mʌzəl,loʊdər, B -ə] *s.* (arm.) pieza que se carga por la boca, pieza de avancarga.
muzzle-loading artillery [-ɪŋ-] (arm.) artillería de avancarga.
muzzle ring, anillo de la boca de un cañón.
muzzle velocity, (mil.) velocidad inicial.
muzzy ['mʌzɪ] *a.* (MUZZIER; MUZZIEST) (fam.) 1. atontado, confuso (esp. por efecto de la bebida). 2. aburrido, deprimente (ej., un día).
mv *abrev. de* **millivolt,** milivoltio.
Mv *símb. de* **mendelevium,** mendelevio (Mv).
mw *abrev. de* **milliwatt,** milivatio.
my [maɪ, mə] *pron. pos.* mi, mis. —*a.* mío, míos; (fam.) **my!** (ú. como interj.) ¡oh! ¡Dios mío!
myalgia [maɪ'ældʒɪə] *s.* (med.) mialgia.
myasis [maɪ'eɪsəs] *s.* (med.) miiasis, miasis.
myasthenia [,maɪəs'θinɪə] *s.* (med.) miastenia.
myasthenic [-'θɛnɪk] *a.* (med.) miasténico.
mycelial [maɪ'silɪəl] **mycelian** [-ən] *a.* (bot.) micelial, micélico.
mycelioid [-,ɔɪd] *a.* (bot.) micelioide.
mycelium [-əm] *s.* (*pl.* MYCELIA [-ə]) (bot.) micelio.
Mycenae [maɪ'sini] *s.* (hist.) Micenas, antigua ciudad griega.
Mycenaean [,maɪsə'niən] *a.* (arte, hist.) micénico.
mycetoma [,maɪsə'toʊmə] *s.* (med.) micetoma, enfermedad de Ballingal.
mycetophagous [-'tɑfəgəs, B -'tɔf-] *a.* (biol.) micetófago.
mycobacterium [,maɪkoʊ,bæk'tɪrɪəm, B -'tɪər-] *s.* (bact.) micobacteria.
mycoderm ['maɪkə,dɜrm, B -,dɜm] **mycoderma** [,maɪkə'dɜrmə, B -'dɜmə] *s.* (bact.) micoderma.
mycologic [,maɪkə'lɑdʒɪk, B -'lɔdʒ-] *a.* (bot.) micológico.
mycologist [maɪ'kɑlədʒəst, B -'kɔl-] *s.* micólogo.
mycology [-dʒɪ] *s.* (bot.) micología.
mycorrhiza [,maɪkə'raɪzə] *s.* (*pl.* MYCORRHIZAE [-,zi] o MYCORRHIZAS) (bot.) micorriza.
mycosis [maɪ'koʊsəs] *s.* (*pl.* MYCOSES [-siz]) (med.) micosis.
mycotic [-'kɑtɪk, B -'kɔt-] *a.* (med.) micótico.
mydriasis [mə'draɪəsəs] *s.* (med.) midríasis.
mydriatic [,mɪdrɪ'ætɪk] *a., s.* (med.) midriático.
myelencephalon [,maɪələn'sɛfə,lɑn, B -,lɔn] *s.* (anat.) mielencéfalo.
myelin, myeline ['maɪələn] *s.* (anat., bioquím.) mielina.
myelin sheath, (anat.) vaina medular.
myelitic [,maɪə'lɪtɪk] *a.* (med.) mielítico.
myelitis [-'laɪtəs] *s.* (med.) mielitis.
myelogenous [-'lɑdʒənəs, B -'lɔdʒ-] **myelogenic** [-loʊ'dʒɛnɪk] *a.* (med.) mielógeno.
myeloid ['maɪə,lɔɪd] *a.* (anat.) mieloide.
myeloma [,maɪə'loʊmə] *s.* (med.) mieloma.
myiasis ['maɪəsəs, B maɪ'eɪ-] *s.* (med.) miiasis, miasis, miiosis.
mylodont ['maɪlə,dɑnt, B -,dɔnt] *s.* (pal.) milodonte.
mylonite [-,naɪt] *s.* (geol.) minolita.
mylonitic [,maɪlə'nɪtɪk] *a.* cataclástico, minolítico.
myna, mynah ['maɪnə] *s.* (zool.) mainato.
myocardial [,maɪə'kɑrdɪəl, B -'kɑd-] *a.* (med.) miocardíaco, miocárdico.
myocardiogram [-ə,græm] *s.* (med.) miocardiograma.
myocardiograph [-,græf, B -,grɑf] *s.* miocardiógrafo.
myocarditis [-kɑr'daɪtəs, B -kɑ'-] *s.* (med.) miocarditis.
myocardium [,maɪə'kɑrdɪəm, B -'kɑd-] *s.* (anat.) miocardio.
myogenic [-'dʒɛnɪk] *a.* (med.) miogénico, miógeno.
myoglobin [-'gloʊbən] *s.* (fisiol.) mioglobina.
myogram ['maɪə,græm] *s.* miograma, representación gráfica de los fenómenos musculares.
myograph [-,græf, B -,grɑf] *s.* (fisiol.) miógrafo.
myography [maɪ'ɑgrəfɪ, B -'ɔg-] *s.* (med.) miografía.
myolemma [,maɪə'lɛmə] *s.* (anat.) miolema.
myologic [,maɪə'lɑdʒɪk, B -'lɔdʒ-] *a.* (anat.) miológico.
myology [maɪ'ɑlədʒɪ, B -'ɔl-] *s.* (anat.) miología.
myoma [-'oʊmə] *s.* (*pl.* MYOMATA [-mətə]) (med.) mioma.
myomatous [-'ɑmətəs, B -'ɔm-] *a.* (med.) miomatoso.
myoneural [,maɪə'nʊrəl, B -'njʊər-] *a.* (anat.) mioneural.
myopathy [maɪ'ɑpəθɪ, B -'ɔp-] *s.* (med.) miopatía.
myope ['maɪoʊp] *s.* (med.) miope.
myopia [maɪ'oʊpɪə] *s.* (med.) miopía.
myopic [-'ɑpɪk, B -'ɔp-] *a.* (med.) miope.
myoscope ['maɪə,skoʊp] *var. de* **myograph.**
myosin ['maɪəsən] *s.* (bioquím.) miosina.
myosis [maɪ'oʊsəs] *s.* (med.) miosis.
myosotis [,maɪə'soʊtəs] *s.* (bot.) miosota, raspilla.
myotic [maɪ'ɑtɪk, B -'ɔt-] *a.* (med.) miótico.
myotome ['maɪə,toʊm] *s.* (anat.) miotoma.
myotonia [,maɪə'toʊnɪə] *s.* (med.) miotonía.
myotonic [-'tɑnɪk, B -'tɔn-] *a.* (med.) miotónico.
myriad ['mɪrɪəd] *s.* 1. diez mil (número). 2. miríada. —*a.* innumerable, innúmero.
myriagram ['mɪrɪə,græm] *s.* miriagramo.
myrialiter [-,litər, B -ə] *s.* mirialitro.
myriameter [-,mitər, B -ə] *s.* miriámetro.
myriapod [-,pɑd, B -,pɔd] *a., s.* (zool.) miriápodo, miriópodo.
myriapodous [,mɪrɪ'æpədəs] *a.* (zool.) miriápodo.
myriawatt ['mɪrɪə,wɑt, B -,wɔt] *s.* (elec.) miriavatio.
myrica [mɪ'raɪkə] *s.* (bot.) mirica.
myriopod, *var. de* **myriapod.**
myristic acid [mə'rɪstɪk-] (quím.) ácido mirístico.
myrmecology [,mɜrmə'kɑlədʒɪ, B ,mɜmɪ'kɔl-] *s.* (ento.) mirmecología.
myrmecophagous [-'kɑfəgəs, B -'kɔf-] *a.* (zool.) mirmecófago.
myrmecophile ['mɜrmɪkə,faɪl, B 'mɜmɪ-] *s.* (zool.) mirmecófila.
myrmecophilous [,mɜrmə'kɑfələs, B ,mɜmɪ'kɔf-] *a.* (bot., zool.) mirmecófilo.
myrmecophily [-lɪ] *s.* (bot., zool.) mirmecofilia.
myrmidon ['mɜrmə,dɑn, -dən, B 'mɜmɪdən] *s.* 1. **M.,** (mitol.) Mirmidón, guerrero tesalio vasallo de Aquiles. 2. secuaz, fiel. 3. esbirro, satélite (de la ley, etc.).
myrobalan [maɪ'rɑbələn, B -'rɔb-] *s.* (bot.) mirobálano, avellana de la India, avellana índica, belérico.
myrrh [mɜr, B mɜ] *s.* mirra.
myrrhed [mɜrd, B mɜd] *a.* mirrado.
myrrhic ['mɜrɪk] *a.* mirrino, mirrado.

myrtaceous [ˌmɜr'teɪʃəs, B ˌmɜ'-] *a.* (bot.) mirtáceo.

myrtiform ['mɜrtəˌfɔrm, B 'mɜtɪˌfɔm] *a.* mirtino, parecido al mirto.

myrtle ['mɜrtəl, B 'mɜtəl] *s.* (bot.) 1. mirto, murta, arrayán. 2. laurel de California.

myrtus [-təs] *s.* (bot.) murtilla.

myself [maɪ'sɛlf, mə-] *pron.* (*pl.* OURSELVES [aʊr'sɛlvz, B aʊə'-]) 1. yo mismo, me, mí, mí mismo. 2. el mismo, ej., *I'm not m. today,* hoy no soy el mismo, no me siento muy bien hoy día. 3. **as for m.,** en cuanto a mí; **(all) by m.,** completamente solo; **with m.,** conmigo mismo.

mystagogic [ˌmɪstə'gɑdʒɪk, B -'gɔdʒ-] *a.* mistagógico, relativo a los misterios y augurios.

mystagogue ['mɪstəˌgɑg, B -ˌgɔg] *s.* mistagogo, maestro o apóstol de ideas o doctrina místicas; augur; vidente.

mysterious [mɪs'tɪrɪəs, B -'tɪər-] *a.* misterioso, enigmático, inescrutable, oculto.

mysteriously [-lɪ] *adv* misteriosamente, enigmáticamente.

mysteriousness [-nəs] *s.* aura de misterio; carácter misterioso.

mystery ['mɪstərɪ] *s.* (*pl.* MYSTERIES) 1. misterio, enigma, secreto, arcano. 2. (*pl.*) misterios (de las antiguas religiones). 3. (relig., teo.) misterio. 4. (teat.) misterio, auto sacramental. 5. novela policíaca.

mystery boat, buque trampa, buque de guerra con apariencia de buque mercante.

mystic ['mɪstɪk] *a., s.* místico.

mystical [-tɪkəl] *a.* místico.

mystically [-kəlɪ] *adv.* místicamente.

mysticism ['mɪstəˌsɪzəm] *s.* misticismo.

mystification [ˌmɪstəfə'keɪʃən] *s.* 1. mixtificación, mistificación, engaño, superchería. 2. desconcierto, perplejidad.

mystify ['mɪstəˌfaɪ] *v.t.* (*pret., p.p.* MISTIFIED; *p.pr.* MYSTIFYING) 1. envolver en el misterio, hacer obscuro; mixtificar, mistificar, engañar. 2. desconcertar, dejar perplejo, confundir.

mystique [mɪs'tik] *s.* mística, conjunto de atractivos que prestan valor y fuerza a ciertas ideas, doctrinas, o personalidades extraordinarias.

myth [mɪθ] *s.* mito, fábula, ficción, leyenda.

mythical ['mɪθɪkəl] *a.* mítico, fabuloso, imaginario, ficticio.

mythicize ['mɪθəˌsaɪz] *v.t.* convertir en mito; rodear de mitos.

mythographer [mɪ'θɑgrəfər, B -'θɔgrəfə] *s.* mitógrafo, el que escribe acerca de temas mitológicos.

mythologer [-'θɑlədʒər, B -'θɔlədʒə] *s.* mitólogo, mitologista.

mythological [ˌmɪθə'lɑdʒɪkəl, B -'lɔdʒ-] *a.* mitológico, mítico, legendario.

mythologically [-kəlɪ] *adv.* mitológicamente.

mythologist [mɪ'θɑlədʒəst, B -'θɔl-] *s.* mitologista, mitólogo.

mythologize [-ˌdʒaɪz] *v.i.* relatar, clasificar y explicar los mitos; escribir acerca de los mitos.

mythology [mɪ'θɑlədʒɪ, B -'θɔl-] *s.* (*pl.* MYTHOLOGIES) mitología.

mythomania [ˌmɪθə'meɪnɪə] *s.* (psic.) mitomanía.

mythomaniac [-ˌæk] *s., a.* (psic.) mitómano.

mythopoeic [-'piɪk] *a.* creador de mitos.

mythos ['maɪθɑs, B -θɔs] *s.* 1. mito. 2. mitología.

myxedema, myxoedema [ˌmɪksə'dimə] *s.* (med.) mixedema.

myxedematous [-'dɛmətəs] *a.* (med.) mixedematoso.

myxoma [mɪk'soʊmə] *s.* (*pl.* MYXOMAS O MYXOMATA [-mətə]) (med.) mixoma.

myxomatosis [-soʊmə'toʊsəs] *s.* (med.) mixomatosis.

myxomatous [-'sɑmətəs, B -'sɔm-] *a.* (med.) mixomatoso.

myxomycete [ˌmɪksoʊmaɪ'sit] *s.* (bot.) mixomiceto.

N

N [ɛn] *s.* 1. n, decimocuarta letra del alfabeto inglés. 2. (mat.) n (número o potencia indeterminada).
N *símb. de* **nitrogen,** nitrógeno (N).
N. *abrev. de* **north,** norte.
Na *símb. de* **sodium,** sodio (Na).
NAACP (E.U.) *abrev. de* **National Association for the Advancement of Colored People,** Asociación Nacional para promover el progreso y el bienestar de la gente de color.
nab [næb] *v.t.* (*pret., p.p.* NABBED; *p.pr.* NABBING) (jer.) 1. arrestar, detener, apresar, atrapar. 2. coger, agarrar, echar el guante a (una cosa); hurtar.
nabob ['neɪbɑb, B -bɔb] *s.* 1. nabab, nababo, europeo que se ha enriquecido en la India. 2. (fig.) nabab (hombre sumamente rico).
Nabuchodonosor [ˌnæbəkə'dɑnəsɔr, B -'dɔnəsɔ] *s.* (bíbl.) Nabucodonosor.
nacelle [nə'sɛl] *s.* (aer.) barquilla (de un aerostato o zepelín).
nacre ['neɪkər, B -kə] *s.* nácar.
nacreous [-krɪəs], **nacred** [-kərd, -kəd] *a.* nacarado, nacáreo, nacarino.
nacrite ['neɪkraɪt] *s.* (min.) nacrita.
nadir ['neɪˌdɪr, -dər, B -dɪə] *s.* (astr.) nadir; (fig.) nadir (el punto más bajo).
nae [neɪ] *a., adv.* (dial.) *var. de* **no, not.**
NAFTA ['næftə] *abrev. de* **North American Free Trade Agreement,** NAFTA (Tratado Norteamericano de Libre Comercio).
nag [næg] *v.t.* (*pret., p.p.* NAGGED; *p.pr.* NAGGING) regañar, reñir, sermonear (a alguien); encocorar, irritar, molestar con insistencia. —*v.i.* regañar, ser regañón; **n. at,** importunar, irritar, molestar. —*s.* jaca, rocín; (fam.) penco, jamelgo.
nagana [nə'gɑnə] *s.* (vet.) nagana.
nagger ['nægər, B -ə] *s.* regañón, machacón.
nagging [-ɪŋ] *a.* 1. regañón, peleón. 2. insistente (duda, miedo, etc.).
naggingly [-lɪ] *adv.* en tono regañón, porfiadamente.
Nahuatl ['nɑwɑtəl] *a., s.* nahuatl, naguatl (miembro de esta tribu de indios mexicanos; su lengua).
Nahum ['neɪhəm] *s.* (bíbl.) Nahum.
naiad ['neɪæd, B 'naɪ-] *s.* (*pl.* NAIADS O NAIADES [-əˌdiz]) 1. (mitol.) náyade, ninfa de ríos, lagos y fuentes. 2. (bot.) najas.
naif [nɑ'if] *var. de* **naive.**
nail [neɪl] *s.* 1. uña. 2. clavo. 3. antigua medida inglesa de longitud (equivalente a 2,25 pulgadas). 4. **hard as nails,** muy resistente, muy duro (persona); empedernido, empedernido, insensible; **to bite one's nails,** comerse las uñas; **to hit the n. on the head,** dar en el clavo. —*v.t.* 1. clavar, enclavar, asegurar con clavos. 2. tachonar, guarnecer o adornar con clavos. 3. fijar (la mirada en algo); cautivar, absorber (atención). 4. averiguar, descubrir (ej., origen de un mal, etc.). 5. (jer.) coger, atrapar, ej., *n. a thief,* atrapar a un ladrón. 6. (jer.) golpear. 7. **n. down,** cerrar con clavos; (fig.) establecer firmemente; exigir decisión o definición; **n. one's colors to the mast,** rehusar rendirse; perseverar, persistir; **n. up,** fijar (en una pared, etc.) con clavo; cerrar con clavos, condenar (puerta, ventana) clavándola.
nail bed, (anat.) matriz de la uña.
nail brush, cepillo para las uñas, cepillo de uñas.
nail clippers, 1. cortaclavos. 2. cortaúñas.
nailer ['neɪlər, B -ə] *s.* 1. fabricante de clavos. 2. clavadora (máquina).
nail file, lima de uñas.
nail hammer, martillo de uña, martillo de carpintero.
nailhead [-ˌhɛd] *s.* cabeza de clavo.
nail hole, clavera, agujero de clavo.
nail plate, metal en plancha para clavos.
nail polish, esmalte para las uñas, esmalte de uñas.
nail puller, sacaclavos, arrancaclavos; pata de cabra.
nail-scissors [-ˌsɪzərz, B -əz] *s. pl.* tijera(s) para las uñas, tijera(s) de uñas.
nail set, (carp.) punzón, embutidor, punzón para clavos.
nail-studded [-ˌstʌdəd] *a.* claveteado.
nail varnish, (G.B.) esmalte para las uñas, esmalte de uñas.
nainsook ['neɪnsʊk] *s.* (tej.) nansú.
Nairobi [ˌnaɪ'roʊbɪ] *s.* Nairobi, capital de Kenia.
naissant ['neɪsənt] *a.* (her.) naciente.
naïve [nɑ'iv] **naive** [nɑ'iv, B neɪv] *a.* cándido, ingenuo; crédulo; sin afectación, natural.
naïvely, naively [-lɪ] *adv.* cándidamente, ingenuamente.
naïveness, naiveness [-nɛs] *s.* candidez, ingenuidad.
naïveté, naiveté [ˌnɑˌiv'teɪ, B -'ivˌteɪ] *s.* candidez, ingenuidad, sencillez, candor.
naked ['neɪkəd] *a.* 1. desnudo, sin vestido, en cueros, calato (Perú). 2. falto, despojado, desprovisto, árido. 3. llano, puro, simple, mero, ej., *to* (o *with*) *the n. eye,* a simple vista. 4. (fig.) desnudo, patente, claro (verdad, etc.). 5. indefenso, inerme, desarmado, sin protección. 6. (der.) sin confirmación; sin título.
naked authority, (der.) autorización unilateral.
nakedly [-lɪ] *adv.* desnudamente, claramente.
nakedness [-nəs] *s.* 1. desnudez. 2. claridad, evidencia. 3. falta de defensa.
naked power, (der.) poder sin interés del apoderado.
naked trust, (der.) fideicomiso pasivo.
namaycush ['næmɪˌkʌʃ] *s.* (ict.) especie de trucha grande.
namby-pamby ['næmbɪ'pæmbɪ] *a.* melindroso; insípido, afectado. —*s.* 1. melindroso. 2. melindre, pamplina.
name [neɪm] *s.* 1. nombre, apellido. 2. título, denominación; epíteto, sobrenombre, apodo, mote. 3. reputación, fama, crédito, nombradía. 4. familia, clan. 5. (lóg.) término. 6. **by the n. of (Peter,** etc.), llamado (Pedro, etc); **in n. only,** tan sólo de nombre; **in one's n.,** en nombre de uno, como representante de uno; **in the n. of,** en el nombre de (Dios, Santos, sentido común, etc.); **my n. is (John,** etc.) me llamo (Juan, etc.); **to call (person) names,** insultar (a una persona); **to know by n.,** conocer de nombre; **to make a n. for oneself,** darse a conocer, adquirir fama; **to put one's n. down (for),** inscribirse uno (en), registrarse uno como candidato (para); **to take one's n. off the books,** renunciar, cesar como miembro; **what's your n.?** ¿cómo se llama Ud.? —*v.t.* 1. nombrar, denominar, titular, llamar, poner nombre a. 2. mencionar, mentar. 3. nombrar, designar, señalar. 4. citar, estipular (condición, precio, etc.). 5. **n. it,** (fam.) escoge, pide lo que quieras, sírvete lo que gustes; **n. the day,** designar el día, esp. para la boda.
nameable, namable ['neɪməbəl] *a.* 1. que se puede nombrar, identificable. 2. memorable, digno de mención.
name-calling [-ˌkɔlɪŋ] *s.* uso de insultos para atacar a un oponente.
name day, día del santo, día onomástico (de una persona).
name-dropper [-ˌdrɑpər, B -ˌdrɔpə] *s.* persona que espera impresionar a otras mencionando nombres de personas famosas o importantes.
nameless [-ləs] *a.* 1. anónimo, innominado, sin nombre. 2. obscuro, desconocido, humilde. 3. ilegítimo, bastardo. 4. inexpresable, indefinible, inefable, que no se puede mencionar.
namelessly [-ləslɪ] *adv.* obscuramente, anónimamente.
namelessness [-ləsnəs] *s.* obscuridad, anonimia.
namely [-lɪ] *adv.* 1. es decir, a saber, o sea. 2. (ant.) específicamente, especialmente, sobre todo, expresamente.
nameplate [-ˌpleɪt] *s.* letrero o placa con nombre (en la puerta, entrada, etc.).
namesake [-ˌseɪk] *s.* tocayo, homónimo.
nance ['nɑnseɪ] *s.* (bot.) peralejo.
nandu ['nænˌdu] *s.* (orn.) avestruz de América, ñandú.
nanism ['neɪˌnɪzəm] *s.* (med.) enanismo.
nankeen [næn'kin] **nankin** [-'kɪn] *s.* 1. (tej.) nanquín, mahón; (*pl*) pantalones de nanquín. 2. **N.,** tipo de porcelana de la China (con diseños de color azul sobre fondo blanco).
nanny ['nænɪ] *s.* (*pl.* NANNIES) (pr. G.B., fam.) nodriza, ama de cría; aya, ama, institutriz.
nanny goat, (fam.) cabra.
naos ['neɪɑs, B -ɔs] *s.* (*pl.* NAOI) (arq.) naos, cela, parte interior del templo.
nap [næp] *v.i.* (*pret., p.p.* NAPPED; *p.pr.* NAPPING) 1. dormir un rato, dormitar, adormitarse; echar o dormir la siesta, sestear. 2. (fig.) dormirse, estar desprevenido. 3. **to catch (one) napping,** encontrar dormido (a uno), coger desprevenido, coger descuidado (a uno). —*s.* 1. sueño corto o ligero, siesta. 2. **to take a n.,** dormir un rato.
nap, *s.* lanilla, pelillo (de paño); **to go against the n.,** ir a contrapelo. —*v.t., v.i.* formar(se), hacer(se) pelos o vellos en (el paño).
napalm ['neɪpɑm] *s.* (quím.) napalm, gelatina inflamable usada en bombas incendiarias. —*v.t.* bombardear, atacar con napalm.
nape [neɪp, næp, B neɪp] *s.* nuca, cogote, cerviz.

napery ['neɪpərɪ] *s.* (*pl.* NAPERIES) mantelería; ropa blanca de casa.
naphtha ['næfθə, 'næp-] *s.* (quím.) nafta.
naphthalene [-θəˌlin] *s.* (quím.) naftalina.
naphthene [-θin] *s.* (quím.) nafteno.
naphthol [-ˌθɔl] *s.* (quím.) naftol.
Napier ['neɪpɪər, B -pɪə] *s.* Neper (matemático escocés).
Napierian [nə'pɪrɪən, B -'pɪər-] *a.* (mat.) neperiano.
napiform ['neɪpəˌfɔrm, B -ˌfɔm] *a.* (bot.) napiforme.
napkin ['næpkən] *s.* 1. servilleta. 2. (pr. G.B.) pañal (de los niños). 3. sabanilla; toallita. 4. **sanitary n.,** almohadilla sanitaria.
napkin ring, servilletero, aro de servilleta.
Naples ['neɪpəlz] *s.* Nápoles, ciudad, bahía y puerto de Italia.
napoleon [nə'poʊlɪən] *s.* 1. **N.,** Napoleón. 2. napoleón (antigua moneda francesa de oro de 20 francos). 3. un juego de naipes. 4. milhojas (dulce de varias capas finas rellenas con crema).
Napoleonic [nəˌpoʊlɪ'ɑnɪk, B -'ɔn-] *a.* napoleónico.
napper ['næpər, B -ə] *s.* 1. dormilón. 2. (jer., G.B.) coco, cabeza. 3. (tej.) perchadora (máquina).
nappy ['næpɪ] *a.* 1. fuerte, embriagador (díc. de los licores). 2. velludo, lanudo. —*s.* 1. plato llano para servir comidas. 2. (G.B.) pañal (de los niños).
nappy rash, (pr. G.B.) escaldadura.
narceine ['nɑrsɪˌin, B 'nɑsɪɪn] *s.* (quím.) narceína.
narcism ['nɑrˌsɪzəm, B 'nɑˌ-] *var. de* **narcissism.**
narcissism [-səˌsɪzəm, B nɑ'sɪsɪzəm] *s.* (psic.) narcisismo.
narcissist [-səst] *s.* (psic.) narciso, narcisista.
narcissus [nɑr'sɪsəs, B nɑ'-] *s.* 1. **N.,** (mitol.) Narciso. 2. (*pl.* NARCISSUSES o NARCISSI [-'sɪsaɪ]) (bot.) narciso.
narcist ['nɑrsəst, B 'nɑsɪst] *var. de* **narcissist.**
narco ['nɑrˌkoʊ, B 'nɑˌ-] *s.* (jer., E.U.) detective o agente policíaco de la campaña contra los narcóticos.
narcoanalysis [nɑrˌkoʊə'næləsəs, B ˌnɑˌ-] *s.* (psic.) narcoanálisis.
narcolepsy ['nɑrkəˌlɛpsɪ, B 'nɑkə-] *s.* (med.) narcolepsia.
narcosis [nɑr'koʊsəs, B nɑ'-] *s.* (*pl.* NARCOSES [-ˌsiz]) narcosis.
narcosynthesis [ˌnɑrkoʊ'sɪnθəsəs, B nɑkoʊ-] *s.* (med.) narcosíntesis.
narcotic [nɑr'kɑtɪk, B nɑ'kɔt-] *a.* narcótico, somnífero, soporífero. —*s.* 1. narcótico, estupefaciente, droga somnífera. 2. (fig.) narcótico, calmante.
narcotine ['nɑrkəˌtin, B 'nɑkətɪn] *s.* (quím.) narcotina.
narcotism [-tɪzəm] *s.* narcotismo, narcomanía, narcosis.
narcotization [ˌnɑrkətə'zeɪʃən, B ˌnɑkətaɪ-] *s.* narcotización.
narcotize ['nɑrkəˌtaɪz, B 'nɑkə-] *v.t.* narcotizar; (fig.) calmar, aliviar.
nard [nɑrd, B nɑd] *s.* 1. nardo (bálsamo antiguo). 2. (bot.) nardo.
nardine ['nɑrdən, B 'nɑdɪn] *a.* (poét.) nardino, de nardo.
nares ['nɛriz, B 'nɛər-] *s. pl.* (*sing.* NARIS [-ɪs]) orificios o ventanas de la nariz.
nargileh, narghile ['nɑrgəˌli, -ˌleɪ, B 'nɑgɪlɪ] *s.* narguile, narguilé, pipa turca.
nark [nɑrk, B nɑk] *s.* 1. (jer., G.B.) soplón, espía de la policía. 2. (jer., E.U.) agente policíaco de la campaña contra los narcóticos.
narrate ['nærˌeɪt, B næ'reɪt] *v.t.* narrar, relatar, contar, referir.
narration [næ'reɪʃən] *s.* 1. narración, narrativa. 2. narración, relato, cuento.
narrative ['nærətɪv] *s.* 1. narrativa, narración. 2. narración, relato, cuento. —*a.* narrativo.
narratively [-lɪ] *adv.* a manera de narración, en forma narrativa.
narrator, narrater ['næreɪtər, -ət-, B næ'reɪtə] *s.* narrador, relator.
narrow ['næroʊ] *a.* 1. estrecho, angosto; reducido, apretado, ahogado, ajustado. 2. limitado (en extensión o número), restringido, circunscrito, ej., *in the narrowest sense,* en el sentido más restringido. 3. preciso, exacto, minucioso. 4. (fig.) estrecho, escaso, apenas suficiente, ej., *a n. majority,* una estrecha mayoría. 5. iliberal, intolerante. 6. **the n. bed,** la tumba; **to have a n. escape,** escapar por un pelo. —*s.* (*gen. pl.*) estrecho, pasaje angosto, paso estrecho. —*v.t.* 1. estrechar, angostar. 2. entrecerrar (los ojos). 3. (t. con *down*) limitar, reducir. —*v.i.* 1. estrecharse, angostarse. 2. entrecerrarse (los ojos).
narrow circumstances, pobreza, estrechez económica.
narrow-gauge [-ˌgeɪdʒ] *a.* 1. de trocha angosta, de vía estrecha o angosta (ferrocarril). 2. (fig.) intolerante, intransigente.
narrowly [-lɪ] *adv.* 1. estrechamente, angostamente. 2. por un pelo, apenas. 3. precisamente, minuciosamente. 4. con intolerancia.
narrow-minded [-'maɪndəd] *a.* iliberal, estrecho de ideas, de miras estrechas, intolerante, de mente o mentalidad estrecha.
narrow-mindedly [-lɪ] *adv.* con estrechez de ideas, con intolerancia, con mentalidad estrecha.
narrow-mindedness [-nəs] *s.* estrechez de ideas, intolerancia, mente estrecha.
narrowness ['næroʊnəs] *s.* 1. estrechura, estrechez, angostura. 2. carácter intolerante, falta de liberalidad; estrechez (de ideas).
narthex ['nɑrθɛks, B 'nɑθɛks] *s.* (arq.) nártex, atrio.
narwhal, narwal ['nɑrhwəl, -wəl, B 'nɑwəl] **narwhale** [-ˌhweɪl, -ˌweɪl] *s.* (zool.) narval.
nary ['nɛrɪ] *a.* (dial.) ninguno, ni uno solo.
NASA ['næsə] (E.U.) *abrev. de* **National Aeronautics and Space Administration,** Administración Nacional de Aeronáutica y del Espacio (la NASA).
nasal ['neɪzəl] *a.* 1. nasal, de la nariz. 2. (fon.) nasal. —*s.* 1. (anat., zool.) hueso de la nariz; narina de los animales, esp. del caballo. 2. (arm.) nasal (del casco). 3. (fon.) sonido nasal.
nasal index, (antrop.) índice nasal.
nasality [neɪ'zælətɪ] *s.* nasalidad.
nasalization [-zələ'zeɪʃən, B -laɪ-] *s.* (fon.) nasalización.
nasalize ['neɪzəˌlaɪz] *v.t.* nasalizar. —*v.i.* hablar con voz nasal, ganguear.
nasally [-əlɪ] *adv.* con voz nasal.
nasal vowel, (gram.) vocal nasal.
nasard [nə'zɑrd, B -'zɑd] *s.* (mús.) nasardo, uno de los registros del órgano.
nascence ['næsəns, 'neɪs-, B 'næs-] **nascency** [-ənsɪ] *s.* procedencia, nacimiento, principio.
nascent [-ənt] *a.* naciente, incipiente.
naseberry ['neɪzˌbɛrɪ] *s.* níspero.
nasion ['neɪzɪˌɑn, B -ɔn] *s.* (med.) nasión.
nasopharyngeal [ˌneɪzoʊfə'rɪndʒɪəl, B -ˌfærɪn'dʒɪəl] *a.* (med.) nasofaríngeo, faringonasal.
nasopharynx [-'færɪŋks] *s.* (anat.) nasofaringe.
nastic ['næstɪk] *a.* (bot.) nástico.
nastily ['næstəlɪ, B 'nɑs-] *adv.* 1. ofensivamente; maliciosamente. 2. desagradablemente, aviesamente.
nastiness [-tɪnəs] *s.* 1. carácter ofensivo o malicioso. 2. aspecto desagradable. 3. inclemencia del tiempo.
nasturtium [nə'stɜrʃəm, B -'stɜʃəm] *s.* (bot.) nastuerzo, mastuerzo, berro, capuchina.
nasty ['næstɪ, B 'nɑs-] *a.* (NASTIER; NASTIEST) 1. detestable; molesto, desagradable. 2. malicioso, avieso, malintencionado. 3. peligroso. 4. **a n. character,** un tipo repulsivo; **n. weather,** tiempo de perros; **to turn n.,** ponerse desagradable (ej., el tiempo); volverse vengativo o rencoroso.
natal ['neɪtəl] *a.* 1. natal, nativo. 2. de nacimiento.
natal grass [nə'tæl-] (bot.) hierba natal.
natality [nə'tælətɪ] *s.* natalidad (índice de).
natant ['neɪtənt] *a.* (bot.) natátil.
natation [neɪ'teɪʃən, B nə-] *s.* natación.
natatorial [ˌneɪtə'tɔrɪəl] **natatory** ['neɪtəˌtɔrɪ, B -tərɪ] *a.* natatorio.
natatorium [ˌneɪtə'tɔrɪəm] *s.* (*pl.* NATATORIUMS o NATATORIA [-rɪə]) natatorio, piscina de natación.
natch [nætʃ] *adv.* (jer.) *forma abreviada de* **naturally,** naturalmente, por supuesto, desde luego.
nates ['neɪtiz] *s. pl.* (anat.) nates, nalgas.
natheless ['neɪθləs] **nathless** ['næθ-] *adv.* (ant.) no obstante, sin embargo, empero, con todo, a pesar de todo.
nation ['neɪʃən] *s.* nación, país, estado.
national ['næʃənəl] *a.* 1. nacional. 2. patriótico. —*s.* nacional, natural, nativo, ciudadano.
national anthem, himno nacional.
national bank, banco nacional.
national debt, deuda pública.
National Endowment for the Arts, organismo del gobierno federal para el fomento de las artes.
national flag, bandera nacional.
national guard, guardia nacional.
national holiday, fiesta nacional.
national income, (e.p.) renta nacional, ingreso público.
nationalism [-ɪzəm] *s.* nacionalismo.
nationalist [-əst] *a., s.* nacionalista.
nationalistic [ˌnəʃənəl'ɪstɪk] *a.* (de tendencia) nacionalista.
nationalistically [-tɪkəlɪ] *adv.* de manera nacionalista.
nationality [ˌnæʃə'nælətɪ] *s.* (*pl.* NATIONALITIES) nacionalidad, ciudadanía.
nationalization [ˌnæʃənələ'zeɪʃən, B -laɪ-] *s.* nacionalización.
nationalize ['næʃənəˌlaɪz] *v.t.* 1. nacionalizar (industrias, banca, etc.). 2. naturalizar, nacionalizar (ciudadanos).
nationalizer [-ər, B -ə] *s.* el que nacionaliza.
National Liberation Front, Frente Nacional de Liberación, partido o movimiento revolucionario en varios países que luchan por la independencia nacional.
nationally [-əlɪ] *adv.* nacionalmente.
national park, parque nacional, área de interés turístico, histórico o científico, al cuidado del gobierno.
national product, (e.p.) producción nacional.
National Security Council, Consejo Nacional de Seguridad.
National Socialism, (pol.) nacionalsocialismo, nazismo.
National Socialist, nacionalsocialista.

NOP

nationhood ['neɪʃən,hʊd] *s.* independencia (de una nación); **to achieve n.,** alcanzar independencia (como nación).
nation-state [-'steɪt] *s.* la nación, unidad representativa de la organización política moderna.
nationwide [-,waɪd] *a.* por toda la nación, de toda la nación.
native ['neɪtɪv] *a.* 1. nativo, natural. 2. aborigen, indígena. 3. nativo, connatural, innato (cualidad, talento, etc.). 4. natal, nativo (ciudad, tierra, etc.). 5. autóctono, nacional (autor, pintor, etc.); local. 6. oriundo, originario (plantas, animales, arte, etc.). 7. natural, puro, natío (ej., oro). 8. **to go n.,** adoptar costumbres indígenas, aplatanarse (Car.). —*s.* 1. aborigen, indígena. 2. natural, nacional. 3. residente, vecino.
native-born [-,bɔrn, B -,bɔn] *a.* nacido en el país, (ciudadano) de nacimiento.
native country, n. land, patria, país de origen, tierra natal.
natively [-lɪ] *adv.* naturalmente, de naturaleza, de nacimiento.
nativeness [-nəs] *s.* condición de nativo.
native son, hijo predilecto; candidato político favorito de su ciudad o estado natal.
nativism [-ɪzəm] *s.* nacionalismo.
nativity [nə'tɪvətɪ] *s.* (*pl.* NATIVITIES) 1. natividad, nacimiento. 2. **N.,** natividad de Cristo, Natividad. 3. (astrol.) horóscopo (que corresponde a la posición de los astros al instante del nacimiento).
natl. *abrev. de* **national,** nacional.
NATO ['neɪtoʊ] *abrev. de* **North Atlantic Treaty Organization,** Organización del Tratado del Atlántico Norte (OTAN).
natrium ['neɪtrɪəm] *s.* (quím.) natrio, sodio.
natrolite ['neɪtrə,laɪt] *s.* (min.) natrolita.
natron ['neɪ,trɑn, B -trən] *s.* (min.) natrón, natronita.
nattily ['nætəlɪ] *adv.* elegantemente.
nattiness [-ɪnəs] *s.* pulcritud, elegancia.
natty ['nætɪ] *a.* (NATTIER; NATTIEST) (fam.) elegante, vestido con esmero, pulcro.
natural ['nætʃərəl] *a.* 1. natural. 2. congénito, de nacimiento (actor, etc.). 3. (mat., mús.) natural. —*s.* 1. idiota congénito, imbécil. 2. persona con talento innato; persona (más) apropiada (para un propósito). 3. (mús.) becuadro. 4. **the n.,** lo natural.
natural childbirth, (med.) parto natural.
natural domicile, (der.) domicilio de origen.
natural features, aspecto físico, geografía física.
natural gas, gas natural.
natural history, historia natural.
naturalism [-ɪzəm] *s.* naturalismo; (arte, lit., filos.) naturalismo.
naturalist [-est] *a., s.* naturalista.
naturalistic [,nætʃərə'lɪstɪk] *a.* naturalista.
naturalization [-lə'zeɪʃən, B -laɪ-] *s.* naturalización.
naturalization papers, carta de ciudadanía (de un extranjero que se nacionaliza).
naturalize ['nætʃərə,laɪz] *v.t.* 1. naturalizar. 2. volver natural, dar explicación natural a (fenómenos sobrenaturales). —*v.i.* naturalizarse.
natural law, derecho natural, ley natural.
natural logarithm, (mat.) logaritmo natural o hiperbólico.
naturally [-əlɪ] *adv.* naturalmente.
naturalness [-rəlnəs] *s.* naturalidad.
natural person, (der.) persona física, persona natural.
natural resources, fuentes naturales, recursos naturales.
natural science, ciencia natural.
natural selection, (biol.) selección natural.
natural sine, (mat.) seno natural.
natural tangent, (mat.) tangente natural.
natural theology, teología natural.
nature ['neɪtʃər, B -tʃə] *s.* 1. naturaleza, esencia; genio, temperamento. 2. carácter, clase, índole. 3. la naturaleza, natura. 4. tamaño (de cañon o bala). 5. **against n.,** contra la naturaleza, contra natura, inmoral; **against** (o **contrary to**) **n.,** innatural, milagroso; **by n.,** por naturaleza, inherente; **by** (o **in,** o **from**) **the n. of the case,** considerando la naturaleza o el origen del caso; **from n.,** del natural; **full of n.,** lleno de savia; **in n.,** en existencia; en cualquier parte; del todo, en absoluto; **in the course of n.,** en el curso natural; **in the n. of,** algo así como; **Mother N.,** la madre naturaleza; **n. is the best physician,** la naturaleza es el mejor médico; **state of n.,** estado natural (del hombre, por oposición al estado de gracia); estado primitivo; desnudez.
nature study, estudio de la naturaleza.
nature worship, culto o adoración por los elementos de la naturaleza; atracción poética por la naturaleza.
naturopath ['neɪtʃərə,pæθ] *s.* naturópata, naturista.
naturopathic [,neɪtʃərə'pæθɪk] *a.* naturópata.
naturopathy [,neɪtʃər'ɑpəθɪ, B -'ɔp-] *s.* naturopatía, naturismo.
naught [nɔt] *s.* 1. nada. 2. (mat.) cero. 3. **to bring to n.,** frustrar, desbaratar, anular; **to come to n.,** reducirse a nada, frustrarse, fracasar. —*a.* 1. sin valor, inútil. 2. (ant.) dañino. —*adv.* (ant.) nada, de ningún modo, en absoluto.
naughtily ['nɔtəlɪ] *adv.* con desobediencia, traviesamente; impropiamente, atrevidamente.
naughtiness [-ɪnəs] *s.* 1. desobediencia, picardía. 2. atrevimiento, impropiedad.
naughty ['nɔtɪ] *a.* (NAUGHTIER; NAUGHTIEST) 1. desobediente, díscolo; travieso, pícaro. 2. atrevido, licencioso, picante (ilustración, libro, cuento, etc.). 3. (ant.) perverso, malvado.
naumachia [nɔ'meɪkɪə] *s.* (*pl.* NAUMACHIAE [-,i] O NAUMACHIAS) (hist.) naumaquia, maniobras navales en la antigua Roma.
nauplius ['nɔplɪəs] *s.* 1. **N.,** (mitol.) Nauplio. 2. (*pl.* NAUPLII [-,aɪ]) (zool.) nauplio.
nausea ['nɔzɪə, -ʃə, -sɪə, -ʒə, B 'nɔsjə] *s.* 1. náusea, asco, bascas. 2. (fig.) náusea, asco, repugnancia.
nauseate [-ʒɪ,eɪt, -zɪ-, -sɪ-, -ʃɪ-, B -sɪ-] *v.t.* 1. dar náuseas a, dar bascas a. 2. (fig.) dar asco o disgusto a. —*v.i.* 1. nausear, sentir bascas. 2. (fig.) asquear.
nauseating [-ɪŋ] *a.* nauseabundo, asqueroso.
nauseous ['nɔʃəs, -zɪəs, B 'nɔsjəs] *a.* nauseoso, nauseabundo, mareado; (fig.) asqueroso, repugnante.
nauseously [-lɪ] *adv.* asquerosamente.
nauseousness [-nəs] *s.* 1. náuseas, mareos. 2. asquerosidad.
nautch [nɔtʃ] *s.* (espectáculo de) baile de las bayaderas.
nautch girl, bayadera (bailarina hindú).
nautical ['nɔtɪkəl] *a.* náutico.
nautically [-kəlɪ] *adv.* náuticamente.
nautical mile, milla marina o marítima.
nautiloid ['nɔtəlɔɪd] *a., s.* (zool.) nautilóideo.
nautilus ['nɔtələs] *s.* (*pl.* NAUTILUSES O NAUTILI [-ə,laɪ]) (zool.) nautilo.
Navaho ['nævə,hoʊ] *s.* (E.U.) navajo, miembro de la tribu de indios más grande de los E.U.; su idioma.
Navajo, *var. de* **Navaho.**
naval ['neɪvəl] *a.* naval.
naval attaché, (dip.) agregado naval.
naval base, (mar.) base naval.
naval engineer, ingeniero naval, ingeniero de la armada o de la marina.
naval intelligence, servicio de información de la armada.
naval officer, oficial de marina.
naval station, (mar.) base naval; apostadero.
Navarre [nə'vɑr, B -'vɑ] *s.* Navarra, provincia de España; antiguo reino de Francia.
Navarrese [,nævə'riz] *a., s.* navarro.
nave [neɪv] *s.* 1. cubo (de rueda). 2. nave (de las iglesias).
nave box, arandela, buje, loriga.
navel ['neɪvəl] *s.* ombligo; (fig.) ombligo, centro, medio.
navel orange, naranja umbilicada.
navel string, cordón umbilical.
navelwort [-,wɜrt, B -wɜt] *s.* (bot.) ombligo de Venus, sombrerillo.
navicert ['nævə,sɜrt, B -sɜt] *s.* (mar., mil.) pasavante.
navicula [nə'vɪkjələ] *s.* 1. (relig.) naveta, navecilla. 2. (bot.) navícula.
navicular [-lər, B -lə] *a.* navicular. —*s.* (t. **naviculare**) (anat.) hueso navicular.
navigability [,nævɪgə'bɪlətɪ] *s.* navegabilidad.
navigable ['nævɪgəbəl] *a.* 1. navegable (río, lago). 2. dirigible (globo).
navigableness [-nəs] *s.* navegabilidad.
navigate [-,geɪt] *v.i., v.t.* navegar.
navigation [,nævə'geɪʃən] *s.* navegación.
navigational [-əl] *a.* de navegación, navegacional.
navigational satellite, satélite auxiliar para la navegación.
navigation chart, (mar.) carta náutica; carta de marear; (aer.) carta aeronáutica.
navigation compass, (aer., mar.) brújula de navegación.
navigation lights, (mar., aer.) luces de situación.
navigator ['nævə,geɪtər, B -ə] *s.* 1. navegador, navegante. 2. (mar.) oficial de derrota. 3. (aer.) navegante, piloto.
navvy ['nævɪ] *s.* (*pl.* NAVVIES) (G.B.) peón, bracero, jornalero.
navy ['neɪvɪ] *s.* (*pl.* NAVIES) 1. marina (ej., mercante). 2. marina de guerra, armada. 3. (ant.) flota, escuadra.
navy bean, fríjol blanco común, judía.
navy blue, azul marino.
Navy Department, (E.U.) Ministerio de Marina.
navy yard, arsenal naval, astillero.
nawab [nə'wɑb] *var. de* **nabob.**
nay [neɪ] *adv.* 1. hasta, aun, aun más, y aun. 2. (ant.) no. —*s.* 1. negación, rechazo. 2. no, respuesta o voto negativo. 3. **will not take n.,** no acepta no como respuesta.
Nazarene [,næzə'rin] *a.* nazareno. —*s.* 1. Nazareno, Jesucristo. 2. nazareno, nazareo, habitante de Nazaret. 3. nazareno, cristiano.
Nazareth ['næzərəθ] *s.* Nazaret, pueblo de Galilea (Israel).
Nazi, nazi ['nɑtsɪ, 'næt-, B 'nɑt-] *a., s.* (pol.) nazi, nacionalsocialista.
nazify [-,faɪ] *v.t.* (*pret., p.p.* NAZIFIED; *p.pr.* NAZIFYING) volver nazi, convertir al nacionalsocialismo, nazificar.
Nazism [-sɪzəm] **Naziism** [-sɪ,ɪzəm] *s.* (pol.) nazismo, nacionalsocialismo.
Nb *símb. de* **niobium,** niobio (Nb).
N.B. *abrev. de* **nota bene,** note u observe bien.
NBA *abrev. de* 1. **National Basketball Association,** Asociación Nacional de Baloncesto. 2. **National Boxing Association,** Asociación Nacional de Boxeo.

NBC *abrev. de* **National Broadcasting Company,** Compañía Radiodifusora Nacional.
NbE *abrev. de* **north by east,** norte cuarta al noreste.
NBS *abrev. de* **National Bureau of Standards,** Oficina Nacional de Normas Industriales.
NbW *abrev. de* **north by west,** norte cuarta al noroeste.
N.C. *abrev. de* **North Carolina,** Carolina del Norte (E.U.).
NCO *abrev. de* **noncommissioned officer,** suboficial.
Nd *símb. de* **neodymium,** neodimio (Nd).
N.Dak. *abrev. de* **North Dakota,** Dakota del Norte (E.U.).
Ne *símb. de* **neon,** neón (Ne).
N.E. *abrev. de* 1. **New England,** Nueva Inglaterra. 2. **northeast,** nordeste (NE.).
Neanderthal [nɪ'ændərtɔl, B -ətɑl] *a.* (paleon.) neandertal.
Neanderthaloid [-ˌɔɪd] *a.* neandertaloide.
neap [nip] *s.* (dial., E.U.) lanza de carreta. *—a.* (díc. de la marea) de cuadratura.
Neapolitan [ˌniə'pɑlətən, B -'pɔl-] *a., s.* napolitano.
neap tide, marea muerta, marea de cuadratura, aguas muertas.
near [nɪr, B nɪə] *adv.* 1. cerca. 2. casi, cuasi, ej., *n. dead with fright,* casi muerto de miedo. 3. **far and n.,** en todas partes; **n. at hand,** a mano, próximo (en tiempo); **n. by,** cerca, a la mano; **n. upon,** cerca de; **quite n.,** muy cercano, contiguo; **to come n. (doing),** llegar casi a (hacer); **to draw n.,** aproximarse, acercarse (tiempo). *—a.* (NEARER, NEAREST) 1. cercano, allegado, íntimo, ej., *n. relation,* pariente cercano, *n. friend,* amigo íntimo. 2. cercano, próximo, inmediato, vecino; inminente. 3. izquierda (apl. a partes de animales o vehículos), ej., *n. wheel,* rueda izquierda, *n. fore leg,* pata delantera izquierda. 4. directo, corto, exacto, literal, ej., *n. translation,* traducción literal, *the nearest road,* el camino más corto. 5. tacaño, cicatero, mísero, avaro. 6. de imitación, ej., *n. silk,* imitación (de) seda. 7. **n. distance,** (teat., pint.) plano intermedio (entre fondo y primer plano); **n. escape,** escapada por un pelo; **n. miss,** yerro por poco; **n. race,** carrera reñida (ganada por estrecho margen). *—prep.* cerca de, junto a. próximo a, inmediato a; **to lie n. one's heart,** tener uno interés personal en (asunto, etc.). *—v.t., v.i.* acercar(se).
nearby ['nɪr'bɑɪ, B 'nɪəbɑɪ] *adv.* cerca, a la mano. *—a.* cercano, próximo.
Nearctic [nɪ'ɑrktɪk, B -'ɑk-] *a.* (geog.) neártico.
Near East, Cercano Oriente.
nearer ['nɪrər, B 'nɪərə] *a. comp. de* **near,** más cercano, más próximo.
nearest [-est] *a. super. de* **near,** lo más cercano o más próximo.
nearly ['nɪrlɪ, B 'nɪəlɪ] *adv.* 1. casi, aproximadamente, cerca de, estrechamente, ej., *it lasted n. a century,* duró casi un siglo. 2. (ant.) íntimamente, estrechamente. 3. **not n.,** lejos, ni con mucho.
nearness [-nəs] *s.* proximidad, cercanía.
nearsighted [-'saɪtəd] *a.* miope, corto de vista.
nearsightedly [-lɪ] *adv.* de manera miope, miopemente.
nearsightedness [-nəs] *s.* miopía, visión corta.
neat [nit] *a.* 1. puro, sin mezcla. 2. bonito, lindo, pulido, de buen gusto. 3. diestro, hábil, listo. 4. limpio, aseado, pulcro; ordenado. 5. claro, neto, nítido. 6. **as n. as a pin,** como un oro; limpio como una patena.
neaten ['nitən] *v.t.* asear, ordenar, limpiar.
'neath [niθ] *prep.* (poét.) *contr. de* **beneath.**
neat-handed ['nit'hændəd] *a.* diestro.
neatherd [-ˌhɜrd, B -ˌhɜd] *s.* (raro) vaquero.
neatly [-lɪ] *adv.* 1. diestramente, hábilmente. 2. aseadamente, pulcramente. 3. elegantemente, con buen gusto.
neatness [-nəs] *s.* 1. destreza, habilidad. 2. aseo, pulcritud, limpieza, nitidez. 3. elegancia, buen gusto.
neat's-foot oil ['nitsˌfʊt-] aceite de pata de vaca.
neb [nɛb] *s.* 1. pico; hocico, morro. 2. jeta, boca; rostro, cara. 3. punta (de la pluma de escribir).
nebbish ['nɛbɪʃ] *s.* persona inepta, tímida.
Neb., Nebr. *abrev. de* **Nebraska,** Nebraska (E.U.).
Nebraska [nə'bræskə] *s.* Nebraska, estado de los E.U.
Nebuchadnezzar [ˌnɛbjəkəd'nɛzər, ˌnɛbə-, B ˌnɛbjʊ-ə] *s.* (hist.) Nabucodonosor.
nebula ['nɛbjələ] *s.* (*pl.* NEBULAE [-ˌli] O NEBULAS) 1. (astr.) nebulosa. 2. (med.) nébula, nubécula.
nebular [-lər, B -lə] *a.* nebular.
nebular hypothesis, (astr.) hipótesis de la nebulosa primitiva, hipótesis de Laplace.
nebulization [ˌnɛbjələ'zeɪʃən, B -laɪ-] *s.* nebulización, atomización (de una droga o composición farmacéutica).
nebulize ['nɛbjəˌlaɪz] *v.t.* (farm., med.) nebulizar, atomizar.
nebulizer [-ər, B -ə] *s.* nebulizador, atomizador, pulverizador, rociador.
nebulose ['nɛbjəˌloʊs] *var. de* **nebulous.**
nebulosity [ˌnɛbjə'lɑsətɪ, B -'lɔs-] *s.* (*pl.* NEBULOSITIES) 1. nebulosidad. 2. (astr.) nebulosa.
nebulous ['nɛbjələs] *a.* 1. nebuloso, nuboso, brumoso. 2. (fig.) nebuloso, confuso, vago. 3. (astr.) nebuloso.
nebulously [-lɪ] *adv.* nebulosamente.
NEbE *abrev. de* **northeast by east,** nordeste cuarta al este.
NEbN *abrev. de* **northeast by north,** nordeste cuarta al norte.
necessaries ['nɛsəˌsɛrɪz, B -sərɪz] *s. pl.* necesidades básicas, cosas necesarias o imprescindibles.
necessarily [ˌnɛsə'sɛrəlɪ, B 'nɛsɪsər-] *adv.* necesariamente.
necessary ['nɛsəˌsɛrɪ, B -sərɪ] *a.* 1. necesario, esencial, indispensable. 2. necesario, inevitable, ineluctable; forzoso, obligatorio. *—s.* (*pl.* NECESSARIES) 1. requisito. 2. (*pl.*) (der.) menesteres, necesidades básicas. 3. (dial.) letrina, excusado, retrete.
necessitarian [nɪˌsɛsə'tɛrɪən, B -'tɛər-] *a., s.* (filos.) determinista.
necessitarianism [-ɪzəm] *s.* (filos.) determinismo.
necessitate [nɪ'sɛsəˌteɪt] *v.t.* 1. necesitar, hacer necesario. 2. necesitar, obligar.
necessitation [nɪˌsɛsə'teɪʃən] *s.* obligación.
necessities [-tɪz] *s. pl.* artículos de primera necesidad, requisitos indispensables.
necessitous [nɪ'sɛsətəs] *a.* 1. necesitado, menesteroso, indigente. 2. urgente, apremiante.
necessity [-tɪ] *s.* (*pl.* NECESSITIES) necesidad; **n. is the mother of invention,** la necesidad es la madre de la invención; **n. knows no law,** la necesidad carece de ley, la necesidad tiene cara de hereje; **of n.,** de necesidad, por necesidad; **to make a virtue of n.,** hacer de la necesidad virtud.
neck [nɛk] *s.* 1. cuello. 2. pescuezo (del animal). 3. cuello, gollete (de botellas, etc.). 4. istmo, estrecho. 5. (anat.) cuello (de un órgano). 6. (mús.) mástil, clavijero, mango. 7. (impr.) cuerpo o cabeza del ojo (del tipo de letra). 8. (cost.) escote, cuello, gola. 9. **n. and crop,** sumariamente; **n. and n.,** nariz a nariz, parejos (díc. de caballos de carrera y fig.); **n. of the woods,** rincón del bosque; (fig.) parajes, partes; **to be on someone's n.,** (fig.) molestar o perseguir con insistencia a alguien; **to break one's n.,** romperse el pescuezo, desnucarse; (fig.) trabajar o esforzarse mucho; **to get it in the n.,** (jer.) ser amonestado o castigado severamente; **to risk one's n.,** arriesgarlo todo; **to stick one's n. out,** exponerse al fracaso, al ridículo, etc. al tomar un riesgo; **to win** (o **lose**) **by a n.,** ganar (o perder) por una nariz; **to wring someone's neck,** estrangular, torcerle el cuello a alguien; **up to one's n.,** hasta las cejas. *—v.t., v.i.* 1. abrazar(se), acariciar(se), besuquear(se), manosear(se). 2. enangostar(se), estrechar(se).
neckband ['nɛkˌbænd] *s.* tirilla de camisa.
neckerchief ['nɛkərtʃəf, B -ətʃɪf] *s.* pañuelo de cuello; especie de pañoleta.
necking [-ɪŋ] *s.* 1. (arq.) collarino, garganta. 2. besuqueo, manoseo, caricias amorosas.
necklace [-ləs] *s.* collar, gargantilla.
necklet [-lət] *s.* collar.
neckline [-ˌlaɪn] *s.* 1. escote (de un vestido). 2. borde del pelo (en la nuca).
neckpiece [-ˌpis] *s.* bufanda, estola o cuello de piel(es).
necktie [-ˌtɑr] *s.* corbata, corbatín.
neckwear [-ˌwɛr, B -wɛə] *s.* prendas para usar en el cuello (corbatas, pañuelos, bufandas, chalinas, etc.).
necrobiosis [ˌnɛkroʊbaɪ'oʊsəs] *s.* (med.) necrobiosis, el proceso de descomposición de las células del cuerpo.
necrolatry [nə'krɑlətrɪ, B -'krɔl-] *s.* adoración o reverencia excesiva a los muertos.
necrological [ˌnɛkrə'lɑdʒɪkəl, B -'lɔdʒ-] *a.* necrológico.
necrologically [-kəlɪ] *adv.* necrológicamente.
necrologist [nə'krɑlədʒəst, B -'krɔl-] *s.* escritor de necrologías, registrador de defunciones.
necrology [-ədʒɪ] *s.* necrología.
necromancer ['nɛkrəˌmænsər, B -sə] *s.* nigromante, mago; brujo.
necromancy [-sɪ] *s.* necromancia, nigromancia; magia negra, brujería.
necromantic [ˌnɛkrə'mæntɪk] *a.* nigromántico.
necrophagia [ˌnɛkrə'feɪdʒɪə] *s.* necrofagia.
necrophagous [nə'krɑfəgəs, B -'krɔf-] *a.* necrófago, que se alimenta de cadáveres.
necrophilia [ˌnɛkrə'fɪlɪə] *s.* (psic.) necrofilia, atracción erótica hacia los cadáveres.
necrophobia [-'foʊbɪə] *s.* necrofobia, miedo anormal a la muerte o a los cadáveres.
necropolis [nə'krɑpələs, B -'krɔp-] *s.* (*pl.* NECROPOLEIS, NECROPOLISES, NECROPOLES O NECROPOLI) necrópolis, cementerio.
necropsy ['nɛkˌrɑpsɪ, B -rɔp-] *s.* (med.) necropsia, necroscopía, autopsia.
necroscopic [ˌnɛkrə'skɑpɪk, B -'skɔp-] **necroscopical** [-ɪkəl] *a.* necroscópico.
necrose [nə'kroʊs, 'nɛkroʊs] *v.i.* (med., bot.) gangrenarse, sufrir necrosis.
necrosis [nə'kroʊsəs] *s.* (*pl.* NECROSES [-ˌsiz]) (med., bot.) necrosis, gangrena.
necrotic [-'krɑtɪk, B -'krɔt-] *a.* (med., bot.) necrótico, gangrenoso.

necrotomic [ˌnɛkrə'tɑmɪk, B -'tɔm-] *a.* (med.) necrotómico.
necrotomy [nə'krɑtəmɪ, B -'krɔt-] *s.* (med.) necrotomía.
nectar ['nɛktər, B -tə] *s.* 1. (mitol.) néctar, la bebida de los dioses. 2. néctar, sustancia que las abejas extraen de las flores para elaborar la miel. 3. néctar, cualquier bebida deliciosa.
nectarean [ˌnɛk'tɛrɪən, B -'tɛər-] **nectareous** [-ɪəs] *a.* nectáreo, dulce como el néctar.
nectarine [ˌnɛktə'rin, B 'nɛktərɪn] *s.* griñón, melocotón, nectarino.
nectary ['nɛktərɪ] *s.* (*pl.* NECTARIES) (bot.) nectario, glándula nectaria.
née, nee [neɪ] *a. fem.* nacida (se antepone al apellido de soltera de una mujer casada), ej., *Mrs. Susan Smith, née Anthony,* la Sra. Susan Anthony de Smith.
need [nid] *s.* 1. necesidad, exigencia, urgencia, emergencia, apuro. 2. carencia, ausencia, falta. 3. pobreza, miseria. 4. (*pl.*) menesteres, necesidades. 5. **a friend in n. is a friend indeed,** en la adversidad se conocen los amigos; **if n. be,** si fuera necesario; **to be in n.,** tener necesidad, estar necesitado; **to have n. of,** necesitar, requerir (algo); **to have n. to (do),** tener necesidad de, deber (hacer). —*v.t.* necesitar, requerir, hacer falta, faltar, ej., *it needs to be painted,* necesita ser pintado; (la tercera pers. sing. es **need** en negaciones e interrogaciones cuando se omite la partícula **to** delante del infinitivo, ej., *he n. not read it again,* no tiene que volver a leerlo, *he n. not have done it,* no tenía por qué hacerlo); (ú. t. elípticamente, ej., *don't go higher than you n.,* no subas más de lo necesario).
needful ['nidfəl] *a.* necesario, requerido.
needfully [-fəlɪ] *adv.* (ant.) necesariamente; urgentemente.
needfulness [-fəlnəs] *s.* necesidad, indispensabilidad.
neediness [-ɪnəs] *s.* indigencia, pobreza, necesidad.
needle ['nidəl] *s.* 1. aguja (de coser, de tejer, de fonógrafo, etc.). 2. aguja magnética, brújula. 3. (bot.) aguja (del alerce, etc.). 4. (arm.) cabeza del percutor (de un fusil). 5. (mec.) aguja, espiga. 6. (med.) aguja. 7. (jer.) una inyección hipodérmica. 8. **on the n.,** (jer.) adicto a narcóticos; **sharp as a n.,** (fig.) muy despierto, muy listo; **to look for a n. in a haystack,** buscar una aguja en un pajar. —*v.t.* 1. coser; trabajar (algo) con aguja. 2. (fam.) reforzar (cerveza) con alcohol. 3. (fam.) fastidiar, pinchar; irritar; aguijonear, estimular.
needle bar, (cost.) barra portaagujas (en una máquina de coser).
needle-bar cam [-ˌbɑr-, B -bɑ-] (mec.) leva de barra de agujas.
needle bearing, (maq.) cojinete de agujas.
needlecase [-ˌkeɪs] *s.* alfiletero, estuche para guardar agujas.
needlefish [-ˌfɪʃ] *s.* (ict.) 1. pez aguja, espetón. 2. aguja de mar.
needleful [-ˌfʊl] *s.* hebra de hilo.
needlepoint [-ˌpɔɪnt] *s.* 1. (cost.) bordado al pasado, punto de aguja. 2. encaje punto de aguja. 3. (fig.) minuciosidad, exactitud (de un argumento, concepto, etc.).
needle-point valve, (mec.) válvula de globo tipo aguja.
needless ['nidləs] *a.* inútil, innecesario, superfluo; **n. to say,** huelga decir.
needlessly [-lɪ] *adv.* inútilmente, innecesariamente.
needlewoman ['nidəlˌwʊmən] *s.* costurera.
needlework [-ˌwɜrk, B -ˌwɜk] *s.* costura, labor; bordado.
needn't ['nidənt] *contr. de* **need not.**
needs [nidz] *adv.* necesariamente, de necesidad.
needy ['nidɪ] *a.* (NEEDIER; NEEDIEST) necesitado, menesteroso, pobre; **the n.,** los necesitados, los pobres.
ne'er [nɛr, B nɛə] *adv.* (poét.) nunca; **n. a,** ni uno solo.
ne'er-do-well ['nɛrduˌwɛl, B 'nɛədu-] *a.* haragán, holgazán, perdido. —*s.* pelafustán, holgazán, pelagatos.
nefandous [ni'fændəs] *a.* nefando, impío.
nefarious [nɪ'fɛrɪəs, B -'fɛər-] *a.* nefario, inicuo, atroz.
nefariously [-lɪ] *adv.* nefariamente, inicuamente.
negate [nɪ'geɪt] *v.t.* 1. negar. 2. anular, nulificar.
negation [nɪ'geɪʃən] *s.* 1. negación, negativa. 2. negación, nulidad.
negative ['nɛgətɪv] *a.* 1. negativo, denegatorio. 2. negativo, privativo; prohibitivo. 3. (bact., biol., elec., mat., fís., foto., lóg., psic.) negativo. —*s.* 1. negativa, negación; denegación, veto. 2. (elec.) polo negativo. 3. (mat.) cantidad negativa. 4. (foto.) negativo. 5. **in the n.,** negativamente; **to return a n.,** contestar (con) "no"; poner veto. —*v.t.* 1. negar, denegar; vetar. 2. votar en contra, rechazar. 3. refutar; contradecir. 4. neutralizar, contrarrestar.
negative acceleration, (ing.) retardación, deceleración, aceleración negativa.
negative feedback, (electrón., rad.) retroalimentación negativa.
negative lens, (ópt.) lente cóncavo.
negatively [-lɪ] *adv.* negativamente.
negativeness [-nəs] *s.* negatividad.
negative plate, (elec., quím., foto.) placa negativa.
negative pole, (elec.) polo negativo.
negative quantity, cantidad negativa; (fam. y hum.) nada.
negative sign, (mat.) signo de substracción (—) ú. para indicar cantidades negativas.
negativism [-ɪzəm] *s.* 1. escepticismo, agnosticismo. 2. (psic.) negativismo.
negativist [-əst] *a., s.* 1. escéptico. 2. negativista.
negativity [ˌnɛgə'tɪvətɪ] *s.* negatividad.
negatory ['nɛgəˌtɔrɪ, B -tərɪ] *a.* negativo.
negatron ['nɛgəˌtrɑn, B -trɔn] *s.* (fís., quím.) negatrón, negatón.
neglect [nɪ'glɛkt] *v.t.* descuidar, abandonar, desatender. —*s.* descuido, abandono, negligencia.
neglecter [-ər, B -ə] *s.* persona descuidada o negligente.
neglectful [-fəl] *a.* negligente, descuidado.
neglectfully [-fəlɪ] *adv.* negligentemente, descuidadamente.
neglectfulness [-fəlnəs] *s.* negligencia, descuido, incuria.
negligee, néglígé [ˌnɛglə'ʒeɪ, B 'nɛgliʒeɪ] *s.* neglígé; bata, batín (de mujer), salto de cama. —*a.* descuidado en el vestir.
negligence ['nɛglɪdʒəns] *s.* negligencia; (der.) negligencia.
negligent [-dʒənt] *a.* negligente, descuidado, desatento; indiferente.
negligently [-lɪ] *adv.* negligentemente.
negligibility [ˌnɛglɪdʒə'bɪlətɪ] *s.* insignificancia.
negligible ['nɛglɪdʒəbəl] *a.* despreciable, insignificante.
negotiability [nɪˌgoʊʃɪə'bɪlətɪ, B -ʃjə-] *s.* negociabilidad.
negotiable [nɪ'goʊʃɪəbəl, B -ʃjə-] *a.* negociable, transferible.
negotiant [-ʃɪənt] *s.* negociador.
negotiate [-ʃɪˌeɪt] *v.i.* negociar, tratar. —*v.t.* 1. negociar, transferir, vender; descontar (valores). 2. tramitar, gestionar. 3. (fam.) salvar, vencer, superar; llevar a cabo, lograr.
negotiation [nɪˌgoʊʃɪ'eɪʃən] *s.* negociación, conversación.
negotiator [nɪ'goʊʃɪˌeɪtər, B -ə] *s.* negociador.
Negress ['nigrəs] *s.* (despec.) negra, mujer de la raza negra.
Negrillo [nɪ'grɪlˌoʊ, B nɛ-] *s.* (*pl.* NEGRILLOS) negro enano de África.
Negrito [nə'gritoʊ, B nɛ-] *s.* (*pl.* NEGRITOS o NEGRITOES) negro enano de Oceanía o del sur de la India.
negritude ['nigrəˌtud, 'nɛg-, B -tjud] *s.* conciencia cultural del negro, esp. el africano.
Negro ['nigroʊ] *s.* (*pl.* NEGROES) (ant.) **negro.** —*a.* (ant.) negro, de raza negra.
Negroid, negroid ['nigrɔɪd] *a., s.* negroide.
negus ['nigəs] *s.* 1. carraspada, sangría. 2. N., Negus, título del emperador de Abisinia.
neigh [neɪ] *v.i.* relinchar. —*s.* relincho.
neighbor, (G.B.) **neighbour** ['neɪbər, B -bə] *s.* 1. vecino. 2. prójimo. —*a.* vecino, colindante, cercano, próximo. —*v.t.* 1. colindar, estar cercano a, estar cerca de. 2. (raro) juntar, acercar, asociar. —*v.i.* 1. avecindarse. 2. hacer visitas amistosas. 3. **n. with,** asociarse con.
neighborhood, (G.B.) **neighbourhood** [-ˌhʊd] *s.* 1. vecindad, proximidad, cercanía. 2. inmediaciones, alrededores. 3. vecindad, vecindario, vecinos, pobladores. 4. vecindad, barrio. 5. (raro) buena vecindad, sociabilidad. 6. **in the n. of,** cerca de; alrededor de, aproximadamente.
neighboring, (G.B.) **neighbouring** [-bərɪŋ] *a.* cercano, vecino, aledaño.
neighborliness, (G.B.) **neighbourliness** [-bərlɪnəs, B -bəlɪ-] *s.* buena vecindad, cortesía de vecino; sociabilidad.
neighborly, (G.B.) **neighbourly** [-lɪ] *a.* sociable, amistoso, característico del buen vecino.
neither ['niðər, 'naɪ-, B -ðə] *a.* ninguno, ninguno de los dos. —*pron.* ni (el) uno ni (el) otro, ninguno, ninguna. —*conj.* 1. ni, ej., *n. good nor bad,* ni bueno ni malo. 2. tampoco, ej., *if you did not see him, n. did I,* si Ud. no lo vio, yo tampoco. —*adv.* (bíbl., dial.) ni siquiera, ni aun.
nekton ['nɛktən, -ˌtɑn, B -tən] *s.* (zool.) necton.
nektonic [nɛk'tɑnɪk, B -'tɔn-] *a.* (zool.) nectónico.
nelson ['nɛlsən] *s.* (dep.) llave nelson (en lucha libre).
nelumbo [nɪ'lʌmboʊ] *s.* (*pl.* NELUMBOS) (bot.) nelumbio.
nemathelminth [ˌnɛmə'θɛlmɪnθ] *s.* (zool.) nematelminto.
nematocyst ['nɛmətəˌsɪst] *s.* (zool.) nematocisto.
Nematoda [ˌnɛmə'toʊdə] *s. pl.* (zool.) nemátodos.
nematode ['nɛməˌtoʊd] *a., s.* (zool.) nematodo.
nematology [ˌnɛmə'tɑlədʒɪ, B -'tɔl-] *s.* (med.) nematología.
Nemean ['nimɪən, nɪ'mi-] *a.* (hist.) nemeo, de Nemea (díc. de los juegos que se celebraban en honor a Hércules).
Nemean lion, (mitol.) león de Nemea.
nemertean [nɪ'mɜrtɪən, B -'mɜtɪ-] *s.* (zool.) nemerteo.
Nemesis ['nɛməsəs] *s.* 1. (mitol.) Némesis. 2. **n.,** (*pl.* **nemeses** [-ˌsiz]) vengador; suerte primitiva.
nenuphar ['nɛnjəˌfɑr, B -fɑ] *s.* (bot.) nenúfar.

neo- ['niou, -ə] *prefijo* neo-, nuevo, reciente.
neoarsphenamine [ˌniouars'fenəˌmin, B 'niouas-] *s.* (farm.) neoarsfenamina.
Neo-Catholic [-'kæθəlɪk] *a., s.* neocatólico.
Neo-Catholicism [-kə'θaləˌsɪzəm, B -'θɔl-] *s.* neocatolicismo.
Neo-Christianity [-ˌkrɪstʃɪ'ænətɪ, B -tɪ-] *s.* neocristianismo.
neoclassic [-'klæsɪk] *a.* neoclásico.
Neoclassicism [-əˌsɪzəm] *s.* neoclasicismo.
neoclassicist [-'klæsəsəst] *s.* neoclásico, neoclasicista.
neocolonialism [-kə'lounɪəlɪzəm] *s.* (pol.) neocolonialismo.
Neo-Darwinian [-dar'wɪnɪən, B -da'-] *a., s.* neodarwiniano.
Neo-Darwinism [-'darwənɪzəm, B -'da-wɪn-] *s.* neodarwinismo, teoría biológica.
neodymium [ˌniou'dɪmɪəm, B 'niou-] *s.* (quím.) neodimio.
neoformation [-fɔr'meɪʃən, B -fɔ'-] *s.* (med.) neoformación.
neogenesis [-'dʒɛnəsəs] *s.* (biol.) neogénesis.
neogenetic [-dʒə'nɛtɪk] *a.* (biol.) neogenético.
neo-gothic [-'gaθɪk, B -'gɔθ-] *a.* neogótico.
Neo-Hegelianism [-heɪ'geɪlɪənɪzəm, B -'giljən-] *s.* neohegelianismo.
neo-impressionism [-ɪm'prɛʃənɪzəm] *s.* (pint.) neoimpresionismo.
neo-impressionist [-ɪm'prɛʃənəst] *s., a.* (pint.) neoimpresionista.
Neo-Lamarckism [-lə'markˌɪzəm, B -'mak-] *s.* (biol.) neolamarquismo.
Neo-Latin [-'lætən] *s.* 1. latín moderno. 2. lengua(s) románica(s), lengua(s) neo-latina(s).
neolith ['niəˌlɪθ] *s.* instrumento (de piedra) del período neolítico.
neolithic [ˌniə'lɪθɪk, B ˌniou-] *a.* (geol.) neolítico.
neological [-'ladʒɪkəl, B -'lɔdʒ-] *a.* neológico.
neologism [nɪ'alədʒɪzəm, B -'ɔl-] *s.* neologismo.
neologist [-dʒəst] *s.* neólogo.
neologistic [nɪˌalə'dʒɪstɪk, B -ˌɔl-] **neologistical** [-ɪkəl] *a.* neológico.
neology [nɪ'alədʒɪ, B -'ɔl-] *s.* neologismo.
neomycin [ˌniə'maɪsən, B 'niou-] *s.* (farm.) neomicina.
neon ['nian, B -ən] *s.* (quím.) neón.
neonatal [ˌniou'neɪtəl, B 'niou-] *a.* del neonato, neonatal.
neo-nazi [-'natsɪ, -'næt-, B -'nat-] *a., s.* neo-nazi.
neon lamp, n. light, lámpara o tubo neón.
neon sign, anuncio de gas neón.
neoorthodox [-'ɔrθədaks, B -'ɔθədɔks] *a.* (teo.) neo-ortodoxo.
neophyte ['niəˌfaɪt] *s.* neófito, novato, bisoño.
neoplasia [ˌniə'pleɪʒə, B 'niou'pleɪzjə] *s.* (med.) neoplasia.
neoplasm ['niəˌplæzəm] *s.* (med.) neoplasma.
neoplastic [ˌniə'plæstɪk, B ˌniou-] *a.* (med.) neoplástico, neoplásico.
neoplasticism [-'plæstəsɪzəm] *s.* neoplasticismo.
neoplasticist [-'plæstəsəst] *s.* neoplasticista.
Neoplatonic, Neo-Platonic [-ouplə'tanɪk, B -'tɔn-] *a.* (filos.) neoplatónico.
Neoplatonism, Neo-Platonism [-'pleɪtənɪzəm] *s.* (filos.) neoplatonismo, neoplatonicismo.
Neoplatonist, Neo-Platonist [-əst] *s.* (filos.) neoplatonista.
neoprene ['niəˌprin] *s.* (quím.) neopreno.
Neosalvarsan [ˌniə'sælvərˌsæn, B 'niou-vəsən] *s.* (farm.) neosalvarsán.
neo-scholastic [-skə'læstɪk] *a.* neoescolástico.
neo-scholasticism [-skə'læstəsɪzəm] *s.* (filos.) neoescolasticismo.
neoteny ['nɪəˌtinɪ, B nɪ'ɔtɪnɪ] *s.* (zool.) neotenia.
neoteric [ˌniə'tɛrɪk] *a.* nuevo, moderno. —*s.* escritor moderno.
Neo-Thomism [ˌniou'touˌmɪzəm] *s.* (filos.) neotomismo.
neotropic [-'trapɪk, B -'trɔp-] **neotropical** [-ɪkəl] *a.* (geog., zool.) neotropical.
Neozoic [ˌniə'zouɪk] *a.* (geol.) neozoico.
Nepal [nə'pɔl, -'pal] *s.* Nepal, país situado entre la India y el Tíbet.
Nepalese [ˌnɛpə'liz, B ˌnɛpɔ-] *a.* nepalés. —*s.* (*pl.* NEPALESE) 1. nepalés, nepalesa, nepali, habitante de Nepal. 2. nepali, nepalés (díc. de la lengua).
Nepali [nɪ'pɔlɪ, -'palɪ] *s.* (*pl.* NEPALI O NEPALIS) nepali, nepalés (habitante o lengua).
nepenthe [nə'pɛnθɪ] *s.* 1. nepenta, nepente; bebida mágica. 2. (bot.) nepente.
nepheline ['nɛfəˌlin] **nephelite** [-ˌlaɪt] *s.* (min.) nefelina, nefelita.
nephelinite ['nɛfələˌnaɪt] *s.* (min.) nefelinita.
nephelometer [ˌnɛfə'lamətər, B -'lɔmɪtə] *s.* nefelómetro.
nephew ['nɛfju, B 'nɛv-] *s.* 1. sobrino. 2. (ant.) nieto; descendiente lejano.
nephology [nɪ'falədʒɪ, B -'fɔl-] *s.* (meteor.) nefiología, ciencia que estudia las nubes.
nephoscope ['nɛfəˌskoup] *s.* (meteor.) nefoscopio, instrumento que determina la dirección y velocidad de las nubes.
nephralgia [nə'frældʒə] *s.* (med.) nefralgia.
nephrectomy [nə'frɛktəmɪ] *s.* (*pl.* NEPHRECTOMIES) (med.) nefrectomía.
nephridium [nɪ'frɪdɪəm] *s.* (*pl.* NEPHRIDIA [-dɪə]) (zool.) nefridio.
nephrism ['nɛfrɪzəm] *s.* (med.) nefrismo.
nephrite ['nɛfraɪt] *s.* (min.) nefrita.
nephritic [nɪ'frɪtɪk] *a.* 1. nefrítico, renal. 2. (med.) nefrítico.
nephritis [nɪ'fraɪtəs] *s.* (med.) nefritis.
nephrogenic [ˌnɛfrə'dʒɛnɪk] *a.* (med.) nefrógeno.
nephrolith ['nɛfrəlɪθ] *s.* (med.) nefrolito.
nephron ['nɛfran, B -rɔn] *s.* (anat.) nefrón.
nephroptosis [ˌnɛfrap'tousəs, B -rɔp-] *s.* (med.) nefróptosis, riñón flotante.
nephrosis [nɪ'frousəs] *s.* (med.) nefrosis.
nephrotomy [nə'fratəmɪ, B -'frɔt-] *s.* (*pl.* NEPHROTOMIES) (med.) nefrotomía.
nepotism ['nɛpətɪzəm] *s.* nepotismo, sobrinazgo.
Neptune ['nɛpˌtun, B -tjun] *s.* (mitol., astr.) Neptuno; (poét.) Neptuno (el mar).
neptunian [nɛp'tunɪən, B -'tju-] *a.* 1. **N.,** neptúneo. 2. (geol.) neptúnico.
neptunism ['nɛpˌtunɪzəm, B -ˌtju-] *s.* (geol.) neptunismo.
neptunist [-nəst] *s.* neptunista.
neptunium [nɛp'tunɪəm, B -'tju-] *s.* (quím.) neptunio.
Nereid ['nɪrɪəd, B 'nɪər-] *s.* 1. (mitol.) Nereida, ninfa del mar. 2. (astr.) Nereo.
nereis ['nɪrɪəs, B 'nɪər-] *s.* (*pl.* NEREIDES [nə'riəˌdiz]) (zool.) nereido.
Nereus ['nɪrɪəs, B 'nɪərjus] *s.* (mitol.) Nereo, padre de las Nereidas.
nerita [nə'ritə] *s.* (zool.) nerita.
neritic [nə'rɪtɪk] *a.* (geol.) nerítico.
Nero ['nɪrou, B 'nɪərou] *s.* (hist.) Nerón, emperador romano (54-68 A.D.).
nerol ['nirəl] *s.* (quím.) nerol.
neroli oil ['nɛrəlɪ-, B 'nɪər-] esencia de nerolí.
Neronian [nɪ'rounɪən] **Neronic** [-'ranɪk, B -'rɔn-] *a.* neroniano, propio o digno de Nerón.
nerts, nertz [nɜrts, B nɜts] (jer.) *vars. de* **nuts.**
nerval ['nɜrvəl, B 'nɜvəl] *a.* nerval, nérveo.
nervate [-vəɪt] *a.* (bot.) nervado, con nervaduras.
nervation [nər'veɪʃən, B nə'-] *s.* (bot.) nervadura, venación.
nerve [nɜrv, B nɜv] *s.* 1. (anat.) nervio. 2. (fig.) nervio, fuerza, vigor. 3. (fig.) ánimo, temple. 4. (*pl.*) (fig.) nervios, nerviosismo, nerviosidad; histeria. 5. (fig.) desfachatez, descaro, tupé. 6. (bot., zool.) nervio. 7. (ant.) tendón. 8. **a fit of nerves,** ataque de nervios, acceso de nerviosidad; **to get on one's nerves,** irritar a uno, exasperar a uno; **to have nerves of steel,** tener nervios de acero; **to lose one's n.,** perder ánimo, amilanarse; **to strain every n.,** esforzarse al máximo. —*v.t.* fortalecer, dar fuerzas a, animar; **n. oneself,** tomar valor, fortalecerse.
nerve cell, (anat.) célula nerviosa.
nerve center, (anat.) centro nervioso.
nerved [nɜrvd, B nɜvd] *a.* nervudo, venoso.
nerve fiber, (anat.) fibra nerviosa.
nerve gas, gas neurotóxico.
nerve impulse, (fisiol.) impulso nervioso, impulsión nerviosa.
nerveless ['nɜrvləs, B 'nɜv-] *a.* 1. enervado, impotente, débil. 2. sin nervios, tranquilo, sereno. 3. (bot.) sin nervadura.
nervelessly [-ləslɪ] *adv.* sin nervios, tranquilamente, serenamente.
nerve-racking, n.-wracking [-ˌrækɪŋ] *a.* muy irritante, exasperante, que crispa los nervios (sonido, etc.); agudísimo (dolor); desgarrador (grito, escena, etc.).
nerve tissue, (anat.) tejido nervioso.
nerve tonic, tónico para los nervios, tónico nervioso.
nerviduct [-əˌdʌkt] *s.* (anat.) nerviducto, conducto óseo o cartilaginoso por donde pasa un nervio.
nervimotion [-ɪ'mouʃən] *s.* (fisiol.) nervimoción.
nervine [-ˌin] *a., s.* (med.) nervino.
nervous ['nɜrvəs, B 'nɜvəs] *a.* 1. nervioso, nérveo. 2. nervioso, miedoso, aprensivo; irritable; excitable. 3. inestable, movedizo (bote).
nervous breakdown, colapso nervioso, crisis nerviosa.
nervously [-lɪ] *adv.* nerviosamente.
nervous Nellie, persona tímida o indecisa.
nervousness [-nəs] *s.* nerviosidad.
nervous system, (anat.) sistema nervioso.
nervule ['nɜrˌvjul, B 'nɜˌ-] *s.* (anat.) nervezuelo, nérvulo.
nervure ['nɜrvjər, B 'nɜvjə] *s.* 1. (bot.) nervio. 2. (ento.) nervadura.
nervy ['nɜrvɪ, B 'nɜvɪ] *a.* (NERVIER; NERVIEST) 1. nervioso, excitable. 2. atrevido, osado. 3. atrevido, impertinente, descarado. 4. (ant.) fuerte, musculoso.
nescience ['nɛʃəns, B 'nɛsɪəns] *s.* 1. nesciencia, ignorancia. 2. (filos.) agnosticismo.
nescient [-ənt] *a.* 1. nesciente, ignorante. 2. (filos.) agnóstico.
ness [nɛs] *s.* promontorio; cabo.
Nesselrode ['nɛsəlˌroud] *s.* (cocina) mezcla de frutas confitadas, nueces picadas, etc. que se usa en la confección de ciertos postres.
nest [nɛst] *s.* 1. nido (de ave, de insectos); nidal (en que la gallina pone los huevos). 2. querencia, morada, nido. 3. guarida, madriguera. 4. nidada, pollada, parvada; enjambre. 5. juego (de objetos que encajan unos dentro de otros). 6. (geol.)

bolsa, depósito aislado de mineral. —*v.t.* 1. envolver, empaquetar. 2. encajar. —*v.i.* anidar, nidificar.
nest egg, 1. nidal (huevo). 2. ahorrillos, economías, reserva, hucha.
nestful ['nɛstfʊl] *s.* nidada (de huevos, aves, etc.).
nestle ['nɛsəl] *v.i.* 1. acomodarse, arrimarse, acurrucarse. 2. (raro) anidar. 3. **n. up to,** arrimarse a. —*v.t.* cobijar, abrigar.
nestler ['nɛslər, B -lə] *s.* polluelo.
nestling ['nɛstlɪŋ] *s.* polluelo, volantón.
nest of drawers, juego de gavetas o cajones.
Nestor ['nɛstər, B -tɔ] *s.* 1. (mitol.) Néstor, sabio consejero griego. 2. **n.,** (fig.) un viejo sabio.
Nestorian [nɛs'tɔrɪən] *a., s.* nestoriano.
Nestorianism [-ɪzəm] *s.* nestorianismo.
net [nɛt] *s.* 1. red, boliche (de pescar). 2. lazo, cepo, trampa. 3. malla, red; retículo, redecilla. 4. (tej.) tul. 5. (tenis) tiro a la red. —*v.t.* (*pret., p.p.* NETTED; *p.pr.* NETTING) 1. cubrir con red o malla. 2. coger con red; enredar, atrapar. 3. (tenis) tirar (la pelota) a la red.
net, *a.* neto. —*s.* 1. ganancia neta; peso neto; cantidad neta. 2. esencia, punto esencial. —*v.t.* ganar; rendir, producir (una ganancia líquida).
net balance, (com.) saldo neto o líquido.
net earnings, ganancias netas.
net embroidery, bordado reticular.
net float, (mar.) boya.
netful ['nɛtfʊl] *s.* redada.
nether ['nɛðər, B -ə] *a.* inferior, más bajo, menor.
Netherlander [-ˌlændər, B -ləndə] *a.* holandés.
Netherlandish [-dɪʃ] *a.* de los Países Bajos, holandés.
Netherlands [-ləndz] *s. pl.* **the N.,** los Países Bajos.
nether millstone, solera (de un molino).
nethermost [-ˌmoʊst] *a.* lo (el) más bajo.
nether world, 1. (el) infierno. 2. (el) otro mundo. 3. (los) bajos fondos.
netmaking ['nɛtˌmeɪkɪŋ] *s.* confección de redes.
net profit, (com.) ganancia líquida, ganancia neta, beneficio líquido, beneficio neto.
netting ['nɛtɪŋ] *s.* 1. tejedura o tejido de redes. 2. pesca con red. 3. red, malla, redecilla.
nettle ['nɛtəl] *s.* (bot.) ortiga. —*v.t.* 1. provocar, irritar, picar. 2. azotar con ortiga.
nettle rash, (med.) urticaria, onidosis, fiebre urticada.
nettlesome [-səm] *a.* irritante, molesto.
nettle tree, (bot.) almez, almezo, loto.
net ton, tonelada neta (2.000 lbs.).
net weight, peso neto.
network ['nɛtˌwɜrk, B -ˌwɜk] *s.* 1. red, malla; retículo. 2. (rad., t.v.) red, cadena, sistema.
networking [-ɪŋ] *s.* 1. (rad., t.v.) transmisión en cadena. 2. (comput.) interconexión. 3. (*finding contacts*) creación de una red de conexiones. —*v.t.* (rad., t.v.) transmitir en cadena, difundir por la red de emisores; (comput.) interconectar. —*v.i.* (*to make contacts*) creer una red de conexiones.
network television, emisiones televisivas en cadena.
neume [num, B njum] *s.* (mús.) neuma, sistema de anotación musical que se usaba en el medioevo.
neural ['nʊrəl, B 'njʊər-] *a.* (anat.) nervioso, nérveo, neural.
neural arch, (anat.) arco neural.
neural axis, (anat.) eje cerebroespinal.
neural canal, (anat.) canal neural.
neuralgia [nʊ'rældʒə, B njʊə-] *s.* (med.) neuralgia.
neuralgic [-dʒɪk] *a.* neurálgico.
neural tube, (anat.) tubo neural.
neurasthenia [ˌnʊrəs'θinɪə, B njʊər-] *s.* (med.) neurastenia, astenia nerviosa.
neurasthenic [-'θɛnɪk] *a., s.* (med.) neurasténico.
neuration [nʊ'reɪʃən, B njʊə-] *s.* (ento.) nervación, nervaduras.
neurectomy [-'rɛktəmɪ] *s.* (cir.) neurectomía.
neurilemma [ˌnʊrə'lɛmə, B ˌnjʊər-] *s.* (anat.) neurilema.
neurilemmatic [-lə'mætɪk] *a.* (anat.) neurilemático.
neurite ['nʊrˌaɪt, B 'njʊər-] *s.* (anat., fisiol.) neurita, axona, neuraxón, cilindroeje.
neuritic [nʊ'rɪtɪk, B njʊə-] *a.* (med.) neurítico.
neuritis [-'raɪtəs] *s.* (med.) neuritis.
neuroblast ['nʊrəˌblæst, B 'njʊər-] *s.* (embr.) neuroblasto.
neurocrinism [-krənˌɪzəm] *s.* (fisiol.) neurocrinia.
neurofibril [ˌnʊroʊ'faɪbrəl, B ˌnjʊəroʊ-] *s.* (fisiol.) neurofibrila, neurofibrilla.
neurofibrillary [-ˌɛrɪ, B -ərɪ] *a.* (fisiol.) neurofibrilar.
neurogenic [-'dʒɛnɪk] *a.* (fisiol.) neurógeno.
neuroglia [nʊ'rɑglɪə, B njʊə-'rɔg-] *s.* neuroglia.
neurography [-'rɑgrəfɪ, B -'rɔg-] *s.* neurografía.
neurohumor [ˌnʊroʊ'hjumər, B ˌnjʊəroʊ-mə] *s.* (fisiol.) neurohumor.
neurological [-'lɑdʒɪkəl, B -'lɔdʒ-] *a.* neurológico.
neurologist [nʊ'rɑlədʒəst, B njʊə'rɔl-] *s.* neurólogo.
neurology [-dʒɪ] *s.* neurología.
neuroma [-'roʊmə] *s.* (*pl.* NEUROMATA [-mətə] O NEUROMAS) (med.) neuroma.
neuromuscular [ˌnʊroʊ'mʌskjələr, B ˌnjʊəroʊ-lə] *a.* (fisiol.) neuromuscular.
neuron ['nʊrɑn, B 'njʊərɔn] **neurone** [-ˌoʊn] *s.* (anat.) neurona.
neuronic [nʊ'rɑnɪk, B njʊə'rɔn-] *a.* (anat.) neurónico.
neuropath ['nʊrəˌpæθ, B 'njʊəroʊ-] *s.* (med.) neurópata.
neuropathic [ˌnʊrə'pæθɪk, B ˌnjʊərə-] **neuropathical** [-ɪkəl] *a.* (med.) neuropático.
neuropathist [nʊ'rɑpəθəst, B njʊə'rɔp-] *s.* (med.) neurópata.
neuropathology [ˌnʊroʊpə'θɑlədʒɪ, B ˌnjʊə-'θɔl-] *s.* (med.) neuropatología.
neuropathy [nʊ'rɑpəθɪ, B njʊə'rɔp-] *s.* (med.) neuropatía.
neuropsychiatrist [ˌnʊroʊsə'kaɪətrəst, B ˌnjʊə-saɪ-] *s.* neuropsiquiatra.
Neuroptera [nʊ'rɑptərə, B njʊə'rɔp-] *s. pl.* (zool.) neurópteros.
neuropteran [-ən] *a., s.* (ento.) neuróptero.
neuropterous [-əs] *a.* (ento.) neuróptero.
neurosis [nʊ'roʊsəs, B njʊə-] *s.* (*pl.* NEUROSES [-'roʊˌsiz]) (med.) neurosis.
neuroskeleton [ˌnʊroʊ'skɛlətən, B ˌnjʊə-roʊ-] *s.* neuroesqueleto.
neurosurgeon [-'sɜrdʒən, B -'sɜdʒən] *s.* neurocirujano.
neurosurgery [-dʒərɪ] *s.* neurocirugía.
neurotic [nʊ'rɑtɪk, B njʊə'rɔt-] *a., s.* (med.) neurótico.
neurotomy [-əmɪ] *s.* (*pl.* NEUROTOMIES) (med.) neurotomía.
neurotoxic [ˌnʊroʊ'tɑksɪk, B ˌnjʊəroʊ'-tɔk-] *a.* (med.) neurotóxico.
neurotoxicity [-ˌtɑk'sɪsətɪ, B -ˌtɔk-] *s.* (med.) neurotoxicidad.
neurotropic [-'trɑpɪk, B -'trɔp-] *a.* (med.) neurótropo.
neuter ['nutər, B 'njutə] *a.* 1. (gram., biol.) neutro. 2. (ant.) neutral (en guerra, discusión, opinión, etc.). 3. **to stand n.,** permanecer neutral, declarar (su) neutralidad. —*s.* 1. (gram.) género, verbo o palabra neutros. 2. (ant.) persona neutral. 3. obrera (hormiga, abeja). 4. capón.
neutral ['nutrəl, B 'nju-] *a.* 1. **neutral;** indiferente, inactivo. 2. (bot., biol., elec., quím., pint.) neutro. —*s.* 1. neutral (persona, partido, nación, etc.). 2. (pint.) tono o color neutro. 3. (aut.) punto muerto, punto neutral.
neutralism [-ɪzəm] *s.* neutralidad; política de neutralidad, neutralismo.
neutralist [-əst] *s.* neutralista.
neutralistic [ˌnutrə'lɪstɪk, B ˌnjʊ-] *a.* neutralista, de tendencia neutralista.
neutrality [nu'trælətɪ, B nju-] *s.* neutralidad.
neutralization [ˌnutrələ'zeɪʃən, B ˌnju-laɪ-] *s.* neutralización.
neutralize ['nutrəˌlaɪz, B 'nju-] *v.t.* neutralizar.
neutralizer [-ər, B -ə] *s.* neutralizador.
neutral line, (fís.) línea neutra.
neutrally [-lɪ] *adv.* neutralmente.
neutral verb, (gram.) verbo neutro, verbo intransitivo.
neutrino [nu'trinoʊ, B nju-] *s.* (fís., quím.) neutrino.
neutron ['nutrɑn, B 'njutrɔn] *s.* (fís., quím.) neutrón.
neutron bomb, bomba de neutrones.
neutrophil ['nutrəˌfɪl, B 'nju-] **neutrophile** [-ˌfaɪl] *s.* (fisiol.) neutrófilo.
Nev. *abrev. de* **Nevada,** Nevada (E.U.).
Nevada [nə'vædə, -'vɑdə, B nɛ-] *s.* Nevada, estado de los E.U.
névé [neɪ'veɪ, B 'nɛveɪ] *s.* (geol.) (campo de) neviza.
never ['nɛvər, B -ə] *adv.* 1. nunca, jamás; en ningún momento. 2. de ningún modo. 3. **it is n. too late to mend,** nunca es tarde para reformarse; **n. again,** nunca más; **n. before,** nunca antes; **n. fear,** no hay cuidado, no hay temor; **n. is a long time,** ninguno puede decir, de esta agua no beberé; **n. mind,** no importa; **well I n.!** ¡no me digas!
never ending, 1. (*supply, source, devotion*) inagotable, inacabable. 2. (*dispute, argument*) interminable, eterno.
never failing, 1. (*supply, source*) inagotable, inacabable. 2. (*sympathy, interest*) permanente, constante.
nevermore [ˌnɛvər'mɔr, B -ə'mɔ] *adv.* nunca más.
never-never ['nɛvər'nɛvər, B -ə'-ə] *s.* (fam., G.B.) (sistema de) venta a plazos; **on the n.-n.,** a plazos. —*a.* irreal, imaginario, fantástico.
never-never land, (fig.) país de ensueños; mundo de ilusiones.
nevertheless [ˌnɛvərðə'lɛs, B -əðə-] *adv.* sin embargo, no obstante, con todo, a pesar de eso.
nevoid, naevoid ['nivɔɪd] *a.* (med.) nevoide.
nevus ['nivəs] *s.* (*pl.* NEVI [-ˌvaɪ]) (med.) nevo o nevus.
new [nu, B nju] *a.* 1. nuevo, reciente. 2. moderno, fresco, recién hecho. 3. novicio, novato. 4. otro, diferente, distinto. 5. **the n.,** lo nuevo; **to be n. to,** no conocer, no tener experiencia en (un trabajo, ocupación, etc.) o con (un instrumento,

herramienta, etc.); **what is n.?** ¿qué hay de nuevo? *—adv.* recién, recientemente (ú. gen. en palabras compuestas), ej., *n.-fallen snow,* nieve recién caída, *n.-found,* recién encontrado, *n.-made,* hecho recientemente.

new arrival, recién llegado o venido.

newborn ['nu'bɔrn, B 'njubɔn] *a.* 1. recién nacido. 2. (fig.) renacido, vuelto a nacer.

newcomer [-ˌkʌmər, B -ə] *s.* 1. (un) recién llegado, nuevo, ej., *he is a n. in this club,* él es nuevo en este club. 2. neófito, novato.

New Deal, (E.U., pol.) Nuevo Trato (política interna de F. D. Roosevelt).

New Delhi [-'dɛlɪ] *s.* Nueva Delhi, capital de la India.

new departure, (fig.) nueva dimensión o concepto; nuevo horizonte o camino.

newel ['nuəl, B 'njuəl] *s.* (arq.) espigón, nabo o bolo (de una escalera de caracol); poste (de una escalera).

New England, Nueva Inglaterra, los seis estados del Nordeste de los E.U.

New England aster, (bot.) áster de Nueva Inglaterra.

New Englander, (E.U.) habitante de uno de los estados de Nueva Inglaterra.

newfangled ['nu'fæŋgəld, B 'njufæŋ-] *a.* (hum., despec.) novedoso, nuevo, recién inventado.

newfashioned [-'fæʃənd] *a.* de última moda.

newfound [-'faʊnd] *a.* nuevo, de origen reciente.

Newfoundland ['nufəndlənd, -ˌlænd, B ˌnjufənd'lænd] *s.* 1. (geog.) Terranova. 2. [B nju'faʊndlənd] (zool.) terranova.

Newfoundland dog, perro de Terranova.

New Greek, neogriego.

New Hampshire [-'hæmpʃər, B -ʃɪə] *s.* Nueva Hampshire, estado de los E.U.

New Hebrew, neohebreo.

New Jersey [-'dʒɜrzɪ, B -'dʒɜzɪ] *s.* Nueva Jersey, estado de los E.U.

New Jersey tea, (bot.) ceanoto.

New Left, (pol., E.U.) (la) nueva izquierda, movimiento político izquierdista, esp. de jóvenes radicales.

new-look ['nulʊk] *a.* renovado, remodelado, de estilo nuevo.

newly ['nulɪ, B 'nju-] *adv.* 1. nuevamente, últimamente, recientemente, recién. 2. nuevamente, de nuevo, otra vez.

newlywed [-ˌwɛd] *s.* (*ú. gen. en pl.*) recién casado.

newmarket ['nuˌmɑrkət, B 'njuˌmɑkɪt] *s.* 1. (hist.) (t. **n. coat**) saco o capa larga y muy entallada. 2. un juego de naipes.

New Mexico [-'mɛksɪˌkoʊ] *s.* Nuevo México, estado de los E.U.

new moon, luna nueva, novilunio.

newness ['nunəs, B 'nju-] *s.* novedad.

news [nuz, B njuz] *s. pl.* (*sing. en const.*) 1. noticia, nuevas; novedad; actualidad. 2. **have you heard the n.?** ¿sabe Ud. la última noticia?; **no n. is good n.,** ninguna nueva, buenas nuevas; **that's no n.,** eso no es ninguna novedad, eso no es nada nuevo; **what's the n.?** ¿qué hay de nuevo? ¿qué noticias hay?

news agency, agencia noticiosa o noticiera, agencia periodística.

newsboy ['nuzˌbɔɪ, B 'njuz-] *s.* vendedor de periódicos, canillita, diariero (Amer.).

newsbreak [-ˌbreɪk] *s.* suceso de interés periodístico.

news briefs, mininoticias.

newscast [-ˌkæst, B -ˌkɑst] *s.* (rad., t.v.) noticiario.

newscaster [-ər, B -ə] *s.* (rad., t.v.) cronista de noticiarios; comentarista radiofónico.

newscasting [-ɪŋ] *s.* radiodifusión de noticias.

news conference, conferencia de prensa, rueda de periodistas.

news dealer, vendedor de periódicos y revistas.

news flash, noticia de última hora, flash informativo.

news hawk, (jer.) reportero de un periódico.

newsletter [-ˌlɛtər, B -ə] *s.* boletín de noticias, boletín interno.

newsman [-ˌmæn, B -mən] *s.* repórter, reportero, periodista.

newsmonger [-ˌmʌŋgər, -ˌmɑŋ-, B -ˌmʌŋgə] *s.* chismoso, correveidile.

newsmongering [-gərɪŋ] *s.* chismorreo, chismografía.

newspaper ['nuzˌpeɪpər, B 'njus-pə] *s.* periódico, diario.

newspaper clipping, recorte de periódico.

newspaperman [-ˌmæn, B -mən] *s.* 1. periodista, reportero, repórter. 2. editor o propietario de un periódico.

newspaperwoman [-ˌwʊmən] *s.* 1. periodista, reportera. 2. editora o propietaria de un periódico.

newsprint ['nuzˌprɪnt, B 'njuz-] *s.* papel periódico, papel de prensa.

news program, diario hablado.

newsreel [-ˌril] *s.* (cinem.) noticiario.

newsroom [-ˌrum, -ˌrʊm] *s.* 1. sala de lectura de periódicos (en una biblioteca, etc.). 2. sala de redacción, sala de noticias (de un periódico).

news service, agencia de prensa, agencia de noticias.

newsstand [-ˌstænd] *s.* puesto de periódicos, quiosco o kiosco de periódicos.

newsworthy [-ˌwɜrðɪ, B -wɜðɪ] *a.* de interés periodístico, notable.

newsy [-ɪ] *a.* (NEWSIER; NEWSIEST) (fam.) 1. lleno de noticias, noticioso (carta, publicación, etc.). 2. chismoso. 3. novedoso, llamativo.

newt [nut, B njut] *s.* (zool.) tritón, (especie de) salamandra acuática.

New Testament, Nuevo Testamento.

Newtonian [nu'toʊnɪən, B nju-] *a.* newtoniano, perteneciente a Newton, sus inventos o teorías.

New World, Nuevo Mundo (América).

new year, 1. año nuevo. 2. **N. Y.,** el día de Año Nuevo.

New Year's Day, New Year's, el día de Año Nuevo.

New Year's Eve, víspera del Año Nuevo, Nochevieja (Esp.).

New York [ˌnu'jɔrk, B 'nju'jɔk] *s.* Nueva York. *—a.* neoyorquino, de Nueva York.

New Yorker [-ər, B -ə] *s.* neoyorquino, natural de Nueva York.

New Zealand [ˌnu'zilənd, B nju-] Nueva Zelanda o Zelandia. *—a.* neocelandés, de Nueva Zelanda.

New Zealander [-ər, B -ə] *s.* neocelandés, natural de Nueva Zelanda.

next [nɛkst] *a.* 1. próximo, contiguo, adyacente, vecino; de al lado, ej., *in the n. house,* en la casa de al lado. 2. próximo, siguiente, entrante, venidero, subsiguiente, que viene. 3. **n. day,** el o al día siguiente; **n. door,** (de) al lado; **n. time,** la próxima vez; **n. week,** la semana entrante; **on Monday n.,** el próximo lunes; **to live n. door,** vivir (en la casa de) al lado. *—adv.* luego, después, ahora, inmediatamente después; en seguida; la próxima vez; **n. to,** junto a, al lado de, casi; **n. to impossible,** punto menos que imposible; **n. to nothing,** casi nada; **to come n.,** ser el que sigue, seguir, venir después; venir ahora, ej., *what comes n.?* ¿qué viene ahora?; **what n.?** ¿y luego qué? ¿y ahora qué más? *—prep.* junto a, al lado de.

next-best ['nɛkstˌbɛst] *a.* de segunda clase.

next-door [ˌnɛkst'dɔr, B -'dɔ] *a.* de al lado (vecinos, etc.).

next friend, 1. (der.) tutor de un menor de edad ante la justicia. 2. mejor amigo, amigo más íntimo.

next of kin, 1. parientes más cercanos o próximos. 2. (der.) herederos (de persona que muere intestada).

nexus ['nɛksəs] *s.* (*pl.* NEXUSES O NEXUS) nexo, vínculo, unión.

Nfld. *abrev. de* **Newfoundland,** Terranova.

N.H. *abrev. de* **New Hampshire,** New Hampshire (E.U.).

NHI *abrev. de* **National Health Insurance,** Seguro Social de Salud.

Ni *símb. de* **nickel,** níquel (Ni).

niacin ['naɪəsən] *s.* (quím.) niacina.

Niagara [naɪ'ægərə, -'ægrə] *s.* 1. (t. **n.**) catarata, torrente. 2. **N. Falls,** las cataratas del Niágara.

nib [nɪb] *s.* 1. pico (de un ave). 2. punta (de una pluma de escribir), pluma (de metal). 3. (mec.) pico, punta, púa, diente. *—v.t.* (*pret., p.p.* NIBBED; *p.pr.* NIBBING) componer la punta de (una pluma).

nibble ['nɪbəl] *v.t.* mordiscar, mordisquear, comer a bocaditos. *—v.i.* (con *at*) picar (cebo el pez); (fig.) tantear, tratar cautelosamente (un plan, idea, problema). *—a.* bocadito; mordisco.

Nibelungs ['nibəlʊŋz] *s. pl.* (mitol.) Nibelungos, epopeya germánica que sirvió de tema a varias óperas de Wagner.

niblick ['nɪblɪk] *s.* (golf) palo de cabeza de hierro.

nibs [nɪbz] *s. pl.* (jer.) (*sing. o pl. en const.*) (ú. como tratamiento irón. o despec.) **his (her) n.,** su señoría.

Nicaragua [ˌnɪkə'rɑgwə, B -'rægjʊə] *s.* Nicaragua.

Nicaraguan [-gwən, B -gjʊən] *a., s.* nicaragüeño, nicaragüense.

niccolite ['nɪkəˌlaɪt] *s.* (min.) nicolita, niquelita.

nice [naɪs] *a.* (NICER; NICEST) 1. fino, sutil. 2. delicado, difícil. 3. primoroso; decente; refinado. 4. gentil, amable. 5. preciso, exacto. 6. escrupuloso, quisquilloso. 7. placentero, agradable. 8. bonito, atractivo, bueno; lindo (t. irón.), ej., *this is a n. confusion,* linda confusión es ésta. 9. (ant.) lujurioso, lascivo. 10. **n. (and),** muy, bien, ej., *n. and dry,* bien seco, *n. and new,* nuevecito, *n. and warm,* calientito, calentito.

Nice [nis] *s.* Niza, ciudad meridional de Francia.

nice-looking ['naɪsˌlʊkɪŋ] *a.* buen mozo, bien parecido, guapo, agradable.

nicely ['naɪslɪ] *adv.* 1. exactamente, con precisión; escrupulosamente. 2. delicadamente. 3. primorosamente; decentemente; refinadamente. 4. amablemente, gentilmente. 5. muy bien.

Nicene ['naɪˌsin, ˌnaɪ'sin] *a.* (relig.) niceno (de Nicea).

Nicene Creed, (relig.) Credo o Símbolo Niceno.

nice Nelly, gazmoño, mojigato, persona que se excede en decir eufemismos.

nice-nellyism ['naɪs'nɛlɪˌɪzəm] *s.* gazmoñería, mojigatería.

niceness ['naɪsnəs] *s.* 1. refinamiento, delicadeza, primor. 2. amabilidad, gentileza.

nicety ['naɪsətɪ] *s.* 1. finura, primor, refinamiento. 2. sutileza, detalle, minucia. 3. precisión, exactitud, claridad. 4. delicadeza, ej., *a*

point of great n., asunto de gran delicadeza. 5. (ant.) elegancia excesiva; modestia, recato; remilgo. 6. **to a n.,** con precisión, hasta el último detalle.
niche [nɪtʃ] *s.* 1. (arq.) nicho, hornacina. 2. (fig.) rincón; posición conveniente. 3. (ecol.) relación funcional de un organismo con el medio ambiente. —*v.t.* colocar o poner (estatua, etc.) en un nicho.
nick [nɪk] *s.* 1. muesca, mella; corte, tajo, raja; desportilladura. 2. punto crítico, momento preciso, (ú. esp. en) **in the n. of time,** al pelo, de perilla, muy a tiempo. 3. (impr.) cran, muesca (del tipo). —*v.t.* 1. mellar, desportillar. 2. hacer muescas o cortes en. 3. cortar ligeramente, herir levemente. 4. tarjar, apuntar, anotar. 5. coger, agarrar (oportunidad, tren, etc.). 6. cobrar (un) precio(s) excesivo(s) a. 7. (jer., G.B.) sorprender, coger desprevenido; apresar. 8. (jer., G.B.) hurtar, robar. —*v.i.* **n. at,** criticar; **n. in,** (G.B.) introducirse, insinuar en (esp. lugar o posición que corresponde a otro).
nickel ['nɪkəl] *s.* 1. níquel. 2. (fam., E.U.) moneda de cinco centavos. —*v.t.* (*pret., p.p.* NICKELED O NICKELLED; *p.pr.* NICKELING O NICKELLING) niquelar.
nickel bronze, cuproníquel (aleación de cobre y níquel).
nickel-clad [-ˌklæd] *a.* revestido de níquel.
nickelic [nɪ'kɛlɪk, B 'nɪkəl-] *a.* (quím.) niquélico.
nickeliferous [ˌnɪkə'lɪfərəs] *a.* (min.) niquelífero.
nickeline ['nɪkəˌlin, B -ˌlaɪn] *s.* (min.) niquelina, niquelita.
nickelodeon [ˌnɪkə'loʊdɪən] *s.* 1. (ant., E.U.) teatro o cine donde se pagaba cinco centavos por la admisión. 2. tocadiscos o fonógrafo automático (operado por monedas).
nickelous ['nɪkələs] *a.* (quím.) niqueloso.
nickel-plate ['nɪkəl'pleɪt] *v.t.* niquelar.
nickel silver, metal blanco, plata alemana.
nickel steel, aceroníquel (aleación de acero y níquel).
nicker ['nɪkər, B -ə] *s.* 1. hin, relincho. 2. risa. —*v.i.* 1. relinchar. 2. reír, reírse.
nicker, *s.* (jer., G.B.) libra (moneda).
nicknack, *var. de* **knickknack.**
nickname ['nɪkˌneɪm] *s.* apodo, mote, sobrenombre. —*v.t.* apodar, motejar.
Nicosia [ˌnɪkə'siə] *s.* Nicosia, capital de Chipre.
nicotiana [nɪˌkoʊʃɪ'eɪnə] *s.* (bot.) nicotiana.
nicotinamide [ˌnɪkə'tinəˌmaɪd] *s.* (quím.) nicotinamida.
nicotine ['nɪkətin] *s.* (quím.) nicotina.
nicotinic [ˌnɪkə'tinɪk, -'tɪnɪk, B -'tinɪk] *a.* (quím.) nicotínico.
nicotinic acid, (quím.) ácido nicotínico.
nicotinism ['nɪkətiˌnɪzəm] *s.* (med.) nicotinismo, nicotismo.
nictitate ['nɪktəˌteɪt] *v.i.* pestañear, parpadear.
nictitating membrane ['nɪktəˌteɪtɪŋ-] (zool.) membrana nictitante.
nictitation [ˌnɪktə'teɪʃən] *s.* nictitación, nictación, pestañeo.
niddering, nidering ['nɪdərɪŋ] *s.* (ant.) cobarde. —*a.* (ant.) infame; bajo; cobarde.
nidicolous [naɪ'dɪkələs] *a.* (orn.) nidícola (díc. de las aves que al nacer no pueden salir del nido).
nidificate ['nɪdəfəˌkeɪt] *v.i.* nidificar, hacer un nido.
nidification [ˌnɪdəfə'keɪʃən] *s.* nidificación.
nidifugous [naɪ'dɪfjəgəs] *a.* (orn.) nidífugo (díc. de las aves que en cuanto nacen salen del nido).
nidify ['nɪdəˌfaɪ] *v.i.* (*pret., p.p.* NIDIFIED; *p.pr.* NIDIFYING) nidificar, hacer el nido.
nidus ['naɪdəs] *s.* (*pl.* NIDI [-daɪ] O NIDUSES) nido.
niece [nis] *s.* sobrina.
niello [nɪ'ɛloʊ] *s.* (*pl.* NIELLI [-i] O NIELLOS) 1. niel, nielado (esmalte y labor sobre metales preciosos). 2. objeto nielado. —*v.t.* (*pret., p.p.* NIELLOED; *p.pr.* NIELLOING) nielar.
Nietzschean ['nitʃɪən] *a.* (filos.) nietzscheano, de Nietzsche. —*s.* nietzscheano, seguidor de Nietzsche.
Nietzscheanism [-ˌɪzəm] **Nietzscheism** [-tʃɪˌɪzəm] *s.* nietzscheísmo, filosofía de Nietzsche, esp. su doctrina del superhombre.
nifty ['nɪftɪ] *a.* (jer.) muy bueno, excelente; elegante, majo.
Niger ['naɪdʒər, B -dʒə] *s.* Níger, república y río del África occidental.
Nigeria [naɪ'dʒɪrɪə, B -'dʒɪər-] *s.* Nigeria.
niggard ['nɪgərd, B -əd] *s.* tacaño, avaro. —*a.* tacaño, cicatero, avaro. —*v.t., v.i.* (ant.) cicatear, escasear.
niggardliness [-lɪnəs] *s.* mezquindad, tacañería, cicatería.
niggardly [-lɪ] *adv.* tacañamente, mezquinamente, cicateramente, con mezquindad o avaricia. —*a.* mezquino, miserable; tacaño, cicatero.
nigger ['nɪgər, B -ə] *s.* (despec., E.U.) negro, persona de la raza negra.
nigger heaven, (despec.) gallinero (del teatro o cine), cazuela, paraíso.
niggle ['nɪgəl] *v.i.* carecer de seriedad, ocuparse en fruslerías, ser frívolo. —*v.t.* escatimar.
niggling ['nɪglɪŋ] *a.* meticuloso, demasiado minucioso, fútil; mezquino, insignificante.
nigglingly [-lɪ] *adv.* meticulosamente; mezquinamente.
nigh [naɪ] (ant., dial.) *adv.* 1. cerca. 2. casi, cuasi. —*a.* (NIGHER; NIGHEST, NEXT) 1. cercano, próximo, vecino. 2. de la izquierda (caballo, vehículo, etc.). 3. directo; corto, breve. —*prep.* cerca de, no lejos de, junto a. —*v.t., v.i.* aproximar(se), acercar(se).
night [naɪt] *s.* 1. noche. 2. anochecer, anochecida, caída de la tarde. 3. (fig.) obscuridad, tinieblas; ocaso. 4. **all n. long,** toda la noche; **at n.,** al anochecer, por la noche; **by n.,** de noche, por la noche; **n. and day,** noche y día, siempre, sin cesar; **n. out,** noche de fiesta; noche de salida de la servidumbre; **to have a good (bad) n.,** dormir bien (mal), pasar la noche bien (mal); **to make a n. of it,** pasar la noche en una fiesta, pasar la noche divirtiéndose; **to pass** (o **spend**) **the n.,** pernoctar, pasar la noche (en). —*a.* nocturno; de noche.
night bird, 1. ave nocturna; esp. lechuza o ruiseñor. 2. (fig.) trasnochador, noctámbulo, nocherniego.
night blindness, ceguera nocturna.
night-bloomin cereus [-'blumɪŋ-] (bot.) pitahaya.
nightcap [-ˌkæp] *s.* 1. gorro de dormir. 2. (fam.) último trago, sosiega (que se toma antes de acostarse). 3. (dep.) última competencia (en una jornada deportiva).
night chair sillico, silla-retrete.
nightclothes [-ˌkloʊz, -ˌkloʊðz] *s. pl.* traje de dormir, camisa de dormir.
nightclub [-ˌklʌb] *s.* cabaret, café cantante, boite.
night crawler, (zool.) lombriz nocturna de tierra.
night dew, sereno, rocío (de la noche).
nightdress [-ˌdrɛs] *s.* camisón, camisa de dormir, camisón.
nightfall [-ˌfɔl] *s.* anochecer, crepúsculo (vespertino), término del día; **at n.,** al anochecer.
night flower, flor nocturna.
night flying, (aer.) vuelo nocturno.
nightgown ['naɪtˌgaʊn] *s.* camisa de dormir, camisón.
nighthawk [-ˌhɔk] *s.* 1. (orn.) chotacabras, tapacamino, guabairo. 2. trasnochador, nocherniego, noctámbulo.
night heron, (orn.) zumaya, capacho, garzota.
nightingale ['naɪtənˌgeɪl, -ɪŋ-, B -ɪŋ-] *s.* (orn.) ruiseñor, filomena.
nightjar ['naɪtˌdʒɑr, B -ˌdʒɑ] *s.* (orn.) chotacabras.
night latch, cerradura o pestillo de resorte.
night letter, night lettergram, telegrama nocturno, carta (telegráfica o cablegráfica) nocturna.
night life, vida nocturna.
night-light [-ˌlaɪt] *s.* lamparilla, luz de noche.
night-line [-ˌlaɪn] *s.* sedal cuyo anzuelo se deja con carnada durante la noche.
nightlong [-ˌlɔŋ] *a.* que dura toda la noche. —*adv.* por toda la noche, durante toda la noche.
nightly ['naɪtlɪ] *a.* 1. nocturno, de noche. 2. de todas las noches, de cada noche. —*adv.* todas las noches; por las noches.
nightmare [-ˌmɛr, B -ˌmɛə] *s.* 1. pesadilla. 2. (fig.) experiencia terrible; monstruosidad, objeto monstruoso. 3. (ant.) súcubo, demonio, fantasma.
nightmarish [-ɪʃ, B -ˌmɛər-] *a.* espantoso, horripilante, espeluznante, de pesadilla.
night owl, 1. (orn.) lechuza, búho mochuelo. 2. (fam.) noctámbulo, ave nocturna.
night people, 1. gente que trabaja de noche y duerme de día. 2. gente que razona o piensa mejor de noche que de día.
night piece, (pint.) escena o paisaje nocturno.
night raven, ave (de mal agüero) que canta de noche, esp. martinete.
night rest, pausa o descanso nocturno.
night rider, (E.U., hist.) jinete enmascarado (miembro de una banda nocturna que comete actos de violencia y terrorismo).
night-robe [-ˌroʊb] *s.* bata de noche.
nights [naɪts] *adv.* de noche, por la noche.
night school, escuela nocturna.
night season, (poét.) noche, las horas de la noche.
nightshade ['naɪtˌʃeɪd] *a.* (bot.) solano, hierba mora; dulcamara; belladona; beleño.
night shift, turno de noche.
nightshirt [-ˌʃɜrt, B -ˌʃɜt] *s.* camisón, camisa de dormir.
night soil, excrementos que se recogen de noche para usarlos como abono.
night spot, (fam.) lugar nocturno de pasatiempo, cabaret.
night stand, night table, mesa de noche.
nightstick [-ˌstɪk] *s.* vara de policía.
nighttide [-ˌtaɪd] *var. de* **nighttime.**
nighttime [-ˌtaɪm] *s.* noche; **in the n.,** de noche.
nightwalker ['naɪtˌwɔkər, B -kə] *s.* 1. merodeador nocturno. 2. (zool.) lombriz nocturna de tierra.
night watch, guardia nocturna; ronda nocturna.
night watchman, sereno, guarda nocturno.
nightwear [-ˌwɛr, B -ˌwɛə] *s.* lencería o ropa fina de dormir.
nightwork [-ˌwɜrk, B -ˌwɜk] *s.* trabajo nocturno.
nighty ['naɪtɪ] *s.* (fam.) camisón, bata.
nigrescent [naɪ'grɛsənt] *a.* nigrescente, negro, oscuro, ennegrecido.
nigritude ['naɪgrəˌtud, B 'nɪgrəˌtjud] *s.* negrura, negror; obscuridad profunda.
nigrosine ['naɪgrəˌsin, B 'nɪgrə-] *s.* (quím.) nigrosina.

nihilism ['naɪəˌlɪzəm] *s.* (filos., pol.) nihilismo.
nihilist [-ləst] *a., s.* nihilista.
nihilistic [ˌnaɪə'lɪstɪk] *a.* nihilista.
nihility [naɪ'hɪlətɪ] *s.* nada, la nada; inexistencia.
Nike ['naɪki] *s.* 1. (mitol.) Niké, Nika, la diosa alada de la Victoria. 2. (mil.) cohete teledirigido de las fuerzas armadas de E.U.
nil [nɪl] *s.* nada; zero.
Nile [naɪl] *s.* Nilo.
Nile green, verde Nilo (color).
nilgai ['nɪlgaɪ] *s.* (zool.) nilgó, nilgai, nilgau.
nill [nɪl] *v.t., v.i.* (ant.) negarse, rehusar; no querer; **will he n. he,** quiera o no quiera.
Nilotic [naɪ'lɑtɪk, B -'lɔt-] *a.* nilótico, perteneciente al río o al valle del Nilo.
nimble ['nɪmbəl] *a.* 1. ágil, ligero, activo. 2. listo, vivo; avispado, agudo, ingenioso.
nimbleness [-nəs] *s.* 1. agilidad, ligereza. 2. viveza; agudeza, ingeniosidad.
nimbly [-blɪ] *adv.* 1. ágilmente, ligeramente. 2. agudamente, ingeniosamente.
nimbostratus [ˌnɪmboʊ'streɪtəs] *s.* (meteor.) nimbo-estrato.
nimbus ['nɪmbəs] *s.* (*pl.* NIMBI [-baɪ] O NIMBUSES) 1. nimbo, aureola. 2. (meteor.) nimbo.
nimiety [nɪ'maɪətɪ] *s.* exceso, demasía; redundancia, prolijidad.
niminy-piminy ['nɪmənɪ'pɪmənɪ] *a.* afectado, remilgado; afeminado.
Nimrod ['nɪmˌrɑd, B -ˌrɔd] *s.* (fig.) cazador.
nincompoop ['nɪnkəmˌpup] *s.* badulaque, simplón, bobo, tonto.
nine [naɪn] *s.* 1. nueve. 2. equipo de béisbol (de nueve jugadores). 3. (golf) primer o último hoyo 4. **dressed up to the nines,** vestido de punta en blanco, vestido de veinticinco alfileres; **to the nines,** al extremo, al máximo. —*a.* nueve; **n. days' wonder,** maravilla de un día; **n. times out of ten,** generalmente; **the N.,** las nueve musas.
ninefold ['naɪnˌfoʊld] *a.* nueve veces mayor; de nueve partes. —*adv.* nueve veces.
nine hundred, novecientos.
nine hundredth, noningentésimo.
ninepence ['naɪnpəns] *s.* (G.B.) (*pl.* NINEPENCES O NINEPENCE) nueve peniques (moneda o valor).
ninepin [-ˌpɪn] *s.* bolo (uno de los palos usados en el juego de bolos).
ninepins [-ˌpɪnz] *s.* bolos, juego de bolos.
nineteen ['naɪn'tin] *a., s.* diecinueve, diez y nueve; **to talk n. to the dozen,** hablar hasta por los codos.
nineteenth [-'tinθ] *s.* 1. decimonoveno, decimonovena parte. 2. diecinueve (en fechas). —*a.* decimonono, decimonoveno.
ninetieth [-tɪəθ] *a., s.* nonagésimo, noventavo.
ninety ['naɪntɪ] *a.* noventa. —*s.* (*pl.* NINETIES) noventa; **the nineties** la década del noventa (última del siglo pasado).
ninetyfold [-ˌfoʊld] *a.* noventa veces mayor; de noventa partes. —*adv.* noventa veces.
ninny ['nɪnɪ] *s.* (*pl.* NINNIES) tonto, simplón, papanatas.
ninnyhammer [-ˌhæmər, B -ə] *s.* tonto, simplón.
ninon ['niˌnɑn, B -ˌnɔn] *s.* (fr.) ninón, tela fina y liviana; etamina.
ninth [naɪnθ] *a.* noveno, nono. —*s.* 1. noveno, nono, novena parte. 2. nueve (enfechas). 3. (mús.) novena.
ninthly ['naɪnθlɪ] *adv.* en noveno lugar, en nono lugar.
niobic [naɪ'oʊbɪk] *a.* (quím.) nióbico.
niobium [-bɪəm] *s.* (quím.) niobio.
nip [nɪp] *v.t.* (*pret., p.p.* NIPPED; *p.pr.* NIPPING) 1. pellizcar; mordiscar; apretar. 2. cortar, recortar; desmochar, podar. 3. helar, escarchar, quemar (por el frío). 4. (jer.) coger, agarrar, alzarse con. 5. lograr vencer (al rival por pequeño margen, en carrera, etc.). 6. **n. in the bud,** cortar en flor. —*v.i.* (pr. G.B.) correr, saltar, moverse ágilmente; apresurarse; **n. along!** ¡apresúrate! —*s.* 1. pellizco; mordisco. 2. sátira, dicho mordaz. 3. frío, frescura; helada. 4. gustillo, sabor picante.
nip, *s.* trago, traguito. —*v.t., v.i.* beber a traguitos.
Nip, *s., a.* (fam.) nipón, japonés.
nipa ['nipə] *s.* 1. (bot.) nipa. 2. tuba, vino de nipa. 3. techumbre de (hojas de) nipa.
nip and tuck, (E.U.) a quién ganará; muy reñida, intensamente disputada (carrera, contienda).
nipper ['nɪpər, B -ə] *s.* 1. (*gen. pl.*) pinzas, tenazas, tenacillas, alicates, cortaalambre. 2. (*pl.*) (fam.) esposas, grillos. 3. (*pl.*) quevedos, anteojos. 4. pala, incisivo (del caballo); pinza grande (de algunos crustáceos). 5. (fam., G.B.) muchachuelo, chiquillo.
nipping [-ɪŋ] *a.* 1. mordaz, picante. 2. quemante, ej., *a n. frost,* una helada quemante.
nippingly [-lɪ] *adv.* mordazmente.
nipple ['nɪpəl] *s.* 1. pezón. 2. chupón, chupador, pezón de biberón. 3. (mec.) niple, boquilla.
nipplewort [-ˌwɜrt, B -ˌwɜt] *s.* (bot.) lámpsana.
Nipponese [ˌnɪpe'niz] *s., a.* (*pl.* NIPPONESE) 1. nipón, japonés. 2. **the N.,** los japoneses.
nippy ['nɪpɪ] *a.* 1. cáustico, mordaz. 2. (G.B.) activo, ágil, listo.
nirvana [nɪr'vɑnə, B nɪə'-] *s.* 1. (filos., relig.) nirvana. 2. nirvana, estado de total serenidad de espíritu. 3. nirvana, cualquier lugar o situación que propicie dicho estado.
Nisan ['nɪsən, ni'sɑn, B 'naɪsæn] *s.* nisán (primer mes del calendario hebreo).
nisei ['niˌseɪ] *s.* (*pl.* NISEI O NISEIS) (esp. E.U. y Can.) nisei (hijo de padres japoneses nacido en el Nuevo Mundo).
nisi ['naɪˌsaɪ] (der.) a menos que.
Nissen hut ['nɪsən-] (mil.) barraca prefabricada (en forma de barril, de hierro corrugado y piso de cemento).
nisus ['naɪsəs] *s.* (*pl.* NISUS) 1. (med.) nisus, molimen. 2. (fisiol.) impulso sexual. 3. esfuerzo, impulso.
nit [nɪt] *s.* 1. liendre. 2. piojito. 3. (jer., G.B.) bobalicón, papanatas, tonto.
niter ['naɪtər, B -ə] *s.* 1. (quím.) nitro, nitrato potásico, de potasio, salitre. 2. (ant.) natrón, natronita, carbonato de sodio.
nitid ['nɪtəd] *a.* nítido, claro, puro, lustroso.
niton ['naɪtɑn, B -tɔn] *s.* (quím.) nitón, radón.
nit-pick ['nɪtˌpɪk] *v.i.* (fam.) pararse en pequeñeces, ser demasiado escrupuloso o quisquilloso.
nit-picking [-ɪŋ] *a.* criticón, quisquilloso. —*s.* critiquería.
nitrate ['naɪtreɪt, -trət] *s.* 1. (quím.) nitrato. 2. nitrato de potasio o nitrato de sodio. — [-treɪt] *v.t.* 1. nitratar, fertilizar (la tierra). 2. nitrar.
nitre, *var. de* **niter.**
nitric [-trɪk] *a.* (quím.) nítrico.
nitric acid, (quím.) ácido nítrico, agua fuerte.
nitric bacterium, (bact.) nitrobacteria, esp. bacteria nitrificante.
nitric oxide, (quím.) óxido nítrico.
nitride [-ˌtraɪd] *s.* (quím.) nitruro.
nitriding [-ɪŋ] *s.* (metal.) nitruración.
nitrification [ˌnaɪtrəfə'keɪʃən] *s.* (quím., bact.) nitrificación.
nitrify ['naɪtrəˌfaɪ] *v.t.* (*pret., p.p.* NITRIFIED; *p.pr.* NITRIFYING) (quím.) nitrificar.
nitrile ['naɪtrəl] *s.* (quím.) nitrilo.
nitrite [-ˌtraɪt] *s.* (quím.) nitrito.
nitrobacteria [ˌnaɪtroʊbæk'tɪrɪəl, B -'tɪər-] *s. pl.* (bact.) nitrobacterias.
nitrobenzene [-'bɛnˌzin, -ˌbɛn'zin] *s.* (quím.) nitrobenceno, nitrobenzol.
nitrocellulose [-'sɛljəˌloʊs] *s.* (quím.) nitrocelulosa.
nitrogen ['naɪtrədʒən] *s.* (quím.) nitrógeno, ázoe.
nitrogen balance, (fisiol., agr.) equilibrio nitrogenado o proteínico.
nitrogen cycle, (quím.) ciclo nitrogénico, ciclo del nitrógeno.
nitrogen fixation, (quím.) fijación del nitrógeno.
nitrogen-fixing [-ˌfɪksɪŋ] *a.* nitrificante (apl. a bacterias).
nitrogenization [naɪˌtrɑdʒənə'zeɪʃən ~naɪtrədʒə-, B -trɔdʒənaɪ-] *s.* nitrogenización.
nitrogenize [naɪ'trɑdʒəˌnaɪz, B -'trɔdʒ-] *v.t.* nitrogenar, azoar.
nitrogen mustard, (quím.) (especie de) gas mostaza.
nitrogenous [naɪ'trɑdʒənəs, B -'trɔdʒ-] *a.* (quím.) nitrogenado, azoado.
nitroglycerin, nitroglycerine [ˌnaɪtroʊ'glɪsərən, B -glɪsə'rin] *s.* (quím.) nitroglicerina.
nitrolic [naɪ'trɑlɪk, B -'trɔl-] *a.* (quím.) nitrólico.
nitrometer [naɪ'trɑmətər, B -'trɔmɪtə] *s.* (quím.) nitrómetro.
nitroparaffin [ˌnaɪtroʊ'pærəfən] *s.* (quím.) nitroparafina.
nitrosamine [naɪ'troʊsəˌmin] *s.* (quím.) nitrosamina.
nitrotoluene [ˌnaɪtroʊ'tɑljʊˌin, B -trə'-toʊl-] *s.* (quím.) nitrotolueno.
nitrous ['naɪtrəs] *a.* (quím.) nitroso; salitroso, salitral.
nitrous acid, (quím.) ácido nitroso.
nitrous bacteria, bacterias nitrosas.
nitrous oxide, (quím.) óxido nitroso.
nitty ['nɪtɪ] *a.* lendroso, piojoso.
nitty-gritty [-ˌgrɪtɪ] *s.* el quid (de una cuestión); la parte más substancial, real o verdadera (de una situación, acción, etc.).
nitwit ['nɪtˌwɪt] *s.* (jer.) bobalicón, papanatas, bobo.
nivôse [ni'voʊz] *s.* (hist.) nivoso, cuarto mes del calendario de la Revolución Francesa.
nix [nɪks] *s.* (jer.) nada, no (ú. para expresar desacuerdo o retención de permiso). —*v.t.* (jer.) vetar, prohibir.
nix, nixie ['nɪksɪ] *s.* ondina, ninfa de las aguas.
Nizam [nɪ'zɑm, B naɪ'zæm] *s.* 1. (hist.) Nizam (título de los soberanos de Haiderabad, India). 2. **n.,** soldado turco.
N.J. *abrev. de* **New Jersey,** Nueva Jersey (E.U.).
NLF *abrev. de* **National Liberation Front,** Frente Nacional de Liberación (en Vietnam).
N.Mex., N.M. *abrev. de* **New Mexico,** Nuevo México (E.U.).
NNE *abrev. de* **north-northeast,** nornordeste (NNE).
NNW *abrev. de* **north-northwest,** nornoroeste (NNO).
no [noʊ] *adv.* no; **no can do,** (jer.) imposible; **no good,** de ningún valor; inútil, **no longer,** ya no; **no more,** no más, ya no (vive, existe, etc.), ej., *he is no more,* él no vive más, él ha dejado de existir; *I will hear no more of it,* no quiero oír más de esto; **no more of that,** basta, no hablemos más de eso; **she is no better than she should be,** ella no es ningún dechado de virtudes. —*s.* (*pl.* NOES) 1. negación. 2. decisión o voto negativo; (*pl.*) los que votaron negativamente.

3. **the noes have it,** la moción ha sido rechazada. —*a.* ninguno; sin; **by no means,** de ninguna manera, de ningún modo; **no fooling,** sin broma, de veras; **no go,** imposible; inútil; **no man,** nadie; **no matter,** no importa; **no . . . no . . . ,** sin . . . no hay . . . , ej., *no payment, no delivery,* sin pago no hay entrega; **no one,** ninguno, nadie; **no one else,** nadie más, ningún otro; **no kidding,** (jer.) de veras, es verdad; **no smoking (parking,** etc.), se prohíbe fumar (estacionar, etc.); **no thoroughfare,** prohibido el paso; **no trump(s),** (bridge) sin triunfo; **no use,** inútil; **to no purpose,** inútilmente, en vano; **with n.,** sin, ej., *with n. qualms,* sin pena, sin reparo.

No *símb. de* **nobelium,** nobelio (No).

no-account [ˈnoʊəˌkaʊnt] *a.* (fam.) inútil, irresponsable, de poco valor (persona).

Noachian [noʊˈeɪkɪən] *a.* 1. de Noé. 2. (fig.) antiguo; anticuado.

Noah [ˈnoʊə] *s.* (bíbl.) Noé; **Noah's ark,** el arca de Noé.

nob [nɑb, B nɔb] (jer.) *s.* 1. coco, cabeza. 2. (pr. G.B.) pájaro gordo, persona de viso. —*v.t.* (*pret., p.p.* NOBBED; *p.pr.* NOBBING) golpear en la cabeza.

no ball, (criquet) pelota mal servida o tirada.

nobble [ˈnɑbəl, B ˈnɔb-] *v.t.* (jer., G.B.) 1. incapacitar, inhabilitar, drogar (un caballo de carrera). 2. sobornar, cohechar. 3. robar; estafar. 4. secuestrar.

nobbler [-ər, B -ə] *s.* (jer., G.B.) estafador; ladrón.

nobby [ˈnɑbɪ, B ˈnɔbɪ] *a.* (jer.) elegante, elegantón.

nobelium [noʊˈbilɪəm] *s.* (quím.) nobelio.

Nobel prize [ˌnoʊˈbɛl-, B ˈnoʊbɛl-] premio Nóbel.

nobiliary [noʊˈbɪlɪˌɛrɪ, B -ərɪ] *a.* nobiliario.

nobility [-ətɪ] *s.* (*pl.* NOBILITIES) 1. nobleza, hidalguía. 2. **the n.,** la nobleza.

noble [ˈnoʊbəl] *a.* 1. noble, preclaro, ilustre. 2. noble, aristocrático. 3. magnífico, imponente, majestuoso (edificio, monumento, etc.). 4. noble, magnánimo. 5. (quím.) noble, inerte. —*s.* 1. noble, hidalgo, par. 2. (hist.) noble (moneda de oro inglesa). 3. (jer.) líder de rompehuelgas.

nobleman [-mən] *s.* noble, hidalgo.

nobleness [-nəs] *s.* nobleza, hidalguía.

noble opal, (min.) ópalo noble, iris.

noblesse [noʊˈblɛs] *s.* (fr.) nobleza.

noblesse oblige [noʊˌblɛsəˈbliʒ] (fr.) comportamiento honorable que se espera de personas nobles o humanistas.

noblewoman [-ˌwʊmən] *s.* dama noble, hidalga.

nobly [ˈnoʊblɪ] *adv.* 1. noblemente. 2. magníficamente, con nobleza o hidalguía.

nobody [ˈnoʊˌbɑdɪ, -bədɪ, B -bədɪ] *pron.* nadie, ninguno; **n. but,** nadie más que; **n. else,** nadie más, ningún otro. —*s.* nadie (persona insignificante).

nocent [ˈnoʊsənt] *a.* (raro) dañoso, dañino, nocivo; perjudicial, pernicioso.

nociceptive [ˌnoʊsɪˈsɛptɪv] *a.* (fisiol.) nociceptivo, nociceptor.

nock [nɑk, B nɔk] *s.* tajadura, muesca, escotadura (al extremo de un arco para el hilo o en una flecha). —*v.t.* hacer una tajadura o escotadura en; ajustar (una flecha) en el hilo.

noctambulation [ˌnɑkˌtæmbjəˈleɪʃən, B ˌnɔk-] noctambulism [nɑkˈtæmbjəˌlɪzəm, B nɔk-] *s.* noctambulación, noctambulismo, sonambulismo, somnambulismo.

noctambulist [nɑkˈtæmbjələst, B nɔk-] *s.* noctámbulo, sonámbulo, somnámbulo.

noctiluca [ˌnɑktəˈlukə, B ˌnɔktɪˈlju-] *s.* (zool.) noctiluca.

noctule [ˈnɑktʃul, B ˈnɔk-] *s.* (zool.) (una especie de) murciélago castaño.

nocturn [ˈnɑkˌtɜrn, B ˈnɔkˌtɜn] *s.* (relig.) nocturno (parte del oficio de maitines).

nocturnal [nɑkˈtɜrnəl, B nɔkˈtɜn-] *a.* 1. nocturno, nocturnal, de la noche. 2. nocturno (animales e insectos).

nocturnal arc, (astr.) arco nocturno.

nocturnally [-ɪ] *adv.* nocturnamente.

nocturne [ˈnɑkˌtɜrn, B ˈnɔkˌtɜn] *s.* 1. (mús.) nocturno. 2. (pint.) escena nocturna.

nocuous [ˈnɑkjuəs, B ˈnɔk-] *a.* (raro) nocivo, dañoso, dañino.

nocuously [-lɪ] *adv.* (raro) nocivamente.

nod [nɑd, B nɔd] *v.i.* (*pret. p.p.* NODDED; *p.pr.* NODDING) 1. inclinar la cabeza, saludar con la cabeza. 2. cabecear. 3. estar desatento, cometer un pequeño desliz o error. 4. **nodding acquaintance,** conocimiento (entre personas) de vista. —*v.t.* 1. inclinar (la cabeza). 2. indicar con una inclinación de la cabeza, inclinar la cabeza en señal de (aprobación, consentimiento, etc.). —*s.* 1. inclinación de cabeza; seña o saludo con la cabeza. 2. cabezada, cabeceo. 3. **land of n.,** sueño; **to get the n.,** ser elegido o aprobado; **to give the n.,** consentir, aprobar.

nodal [ˈnoʊdəl] *a.* (astr.) nodal.

noddle [ˈnɑdəl, B ˈnɔd-] *s.* (fam.) coco, cabeza. —*v.i.* mover o inclinar la cabeza.

noddy [ˈnɑdɪ, B ˈnɔdɪ] *s.* 1. bobalicón, tonto, simple. 2. (orn.) golondrina de mar.

node [noʊd] *s.* 1. bulto, protuberancia. 2. nudo, enredo, trama (de una obra literaria). 3. (anat.) nudo, bulto, tumor. 4. (astr.) nodo. 5. (bot.) nudo. 6. (geom., geog.) nudo. 7. (fís.) nodo.

nodical [ˈnoʊdɪkəl, ˈnɑd-, B ˈnoʊd-] *a.* (astr.) nodal.

nodose [ˈnoʊˌdoʊs, B nəˈdoʊs] *a.* nudoso.

nodosity [noʊˈdɑsətɪ, B nəˈdɔs-] *s.* (*pl.* NODOSITIES) nudosidad.

nodous [ˈnoʊdəs] *a.* nudoso.

nodular [ˈnɑdʒələr, B ˈnɔdjʊlə] *a.* (anat., bot., astr.) nodular.

nodule [ˈnɑdʒˌul, B ˈnɔdjul] *s.* 1. nódulo, pequeño bulto. 2. (bot.) tubérculo. 3. (anat., min.) nódulo.

nodulose [-əˌloʊs, B -jʊ-] nodulous [-ləs] *a.* (med.) nodulado.

nodus [ˈnoʊdəs] *s.* (*pl.* NODI [-ˌdaɪ]) nudo, complicación, dificultad.

noël [noʊˈɛl] *s.* 1. villancico de Navidad. 2. **N.,** Navidad.

noesis [noʊˈisəs] *s.* 1. (psic.) noesis, proceso del conocimiento. 2. (filos.) noesis, conocimiento de las formas universales, conocimiento puro.

noetic [noʊˈɛtɪk] *a.* noético, intelectual, que tiende a abstraerse en temas profundos.

nog [nɑg, B nɔg] *s.* 1. (dial., G.B.) especie de cerveza fuerte. 2. (*forma abrev. de* **eggnog**) ponche de huevo. 3. bloque de madera, tarugo (empotrado en la pared para sostener clavos).

noggin [ˈnɑgən, B ˈnɔg-] *s.* 1. cubilete, pichel pequeño. 2. copita (de licor). 3. (jer.) coco, cabeza.

nogging [ˈnɑgɪŋ, B ˈnɔg-] *s.* relleno de ladrillos entre montantes de madera.

no-hit [ˈnoʊˈhɪt] *a.* (béisbol) díc. del partido en que un lanzador no permite ni tantos ni golpes al cuadro contrario.

no how [ˈnoʊˌhaʊ] *adv.* (dial.) de ninguna manera; de ningún modo; en absoluto.

noil [nɔɪl] *s.* (tej.) borra de peinadora, desperdicios de la peinadora.

noise [nɔɪz] *s.* 1. ruido. 2. bulla, gritería. 3. (ant.) rumor; difamación, calumnia. 4. **to make a n. (about),** hablar o quejarse mucho (de); **to make a n. in the world,** lograr fama, atraer la atención. —*v.t.* divulgar, propagar; **to be noised,** rumorearse; propagarse (el rumor, la noticia). —*v.i.* 1. hablar mucho. 2. hacer ruido; meter bulla.

noise filter, (rad.) filtro antiparasitario.

noise killer, (rad.) supresor de ruidos.

noiseless [ˈnɔɪzləs] *a.* sin ruido, silencioso, ej., *the n. tread of time,* el paso silencioso del tiempo.

noiselessly [-lɪ] *adv.* silenciosamente.

noiselessness [-nəs] *s.* ausencia de ruido, funcionamiento silencioso.

noise level, (rad., electrón.) nivel de ruido.

noise limiter, (rad.) limitador de ruidos.

noisemaker [ˈnɔɪzˌmeɪkər, B -kə] *s.* matraca, sonajero.

noisemaking [-kɪŋ] *s.* bullicio. —*a.* que hace ruido.

noiseproof [-ˌpruf] *a.* a prueba de ruidos, antisonoro.

noise suppression, (rad.) amortiguamiento del ruido.

noisily [ˈnɔɪzəlɪ] *adv.* ruidosamente, estrepitosamente.

noisome [ˈnɔɪsəm] *a.* 1. nocivo; dañoso, dañino. 2. apestoso, fétido, hediondo.

noisomely [-lɪ] *adv.* 1. nocivamente. 2. hediondamente, apestosamente, fétidamente.

noisomeness [-nəs] *s.* 1. nocividad. 2. fetidez, hedor.

noisy [ˈnɔɪzɪ] *a.* (NOISIER; NOISIEST) ruidoso, estrepitoso, estruendoso.

nolition [noʊˈlɪʃən] *s.* (filos.) nolición.

nolle prosequi [ˌnɑlɪˈprɑsəˌkwaɪ, B ˈnɔlɪˈprɔsɪ-] (der.) abandono de proceso.

nolo contendere [ˌnoʊˌloʊkənˈtɛndərɪ] (der.) admisión de culpabilidad como estrategia para negar las acusaciones en otro proceso.

nol-pros [ˈnɑlˈprɑs, B ˌnɔlˈprɔs] *v.t.* (*pret., p.p.* NOL-PROSSED; *p.pr.* NOL-PROSSING) abandonar (una acción judicial).

noma [ˈnoʊmə] *s.* (med.) noma.

nomad [ˈnoʊmæd, B -məd] *a., s.* nómada, nómade.

nomadic [noʊˈmædɪk] **nomadical** [-ɪkəl] *a.* nómada, nómade; errante; errabundo.

nomadism [ˈnoʊmæˌdɪzəm] *s.* nomadismo.

no-man's-land [ˈnoʊˌmænzˌlænd] *s.* 1. terreno sin reclamar; terreno sin dueño. 2. (mil.) tierra de nadie. 3. (lit. y fig.) terreno desconocido y por lo tanto peligroso.

nomarch [ˈnɑmark, B ˈnɔmɑk] *s.* (hist.) nomarca.

nomarchy [-ɑrkɪ, B -ɑkɪ] *s.* nomo, nomarquía, prefectura, subdivisión gubernamental.

nombril [ˈnɑmbrəl, B ˈnɔm-] *s.* (her.) centro de la punta (de un escudo).

nom de guerre [ˌnɑmdɪˈgɛr, B ˈnɔmdɪˈgɛə] (fr.) seudónimo adoptado en una causa polémica o controversial.

nom de plume [-ˈplum] (fr.) seudónimo de un escritor.

nome [noʊm] *s.* (hist.) nomo, nomarquía.

nomenclator [ˈnoʊmənˌkleɪtər, B -ə] *s.* 1. nomenclador, nomenclátor. 2. (ant.) anunciador de nombres de los invitados.

nomenclature [-tʃər, B noʊˈmɛnklətʃə] *s.* nomenclatura.

nominal [ˈnɑmənəl, B ˈnɔm-] *a.* nominal, sólo de nombre.

nominalism [-ˌɪzəm] *s.* (filos.) nominalismo.

nominalist [-əst] *s.* nominalista. —*a.* (t. **nominalistic**) nominalista.

nominally [-ɪ] *adv.* nominalmente.

nominal value, (com.) valor nominal.

nominal wages, salario o pago nominal.

nominate ['nɑmə,neɪt, B 'nɔm-] *v.t.* 1. nominar, nombrar; designar. 2. nombrar, nominar como candidato; proponer para candidato.

nomination [,nɑmə'neɪʃən, B ,nɔm-] *s.* nominación, nombramiento; propuesta, postulación (de un candidato); **to put** (**name,** etc.) **in n. for,** poner (nombre, etc.) entre los candidatos para (un puesto, oficio, etc.).

nominative ['nɑmə,neɪtɪv, B 'nɔmənət-] *a.* 1. asignado por nombramiento. 2. (com.) nominativo (acciones, etc.). 3. [-ənət-] (gram.) nominativo. —*s.* (gram.) nominativo, caso nominativo.

nominator ['nɑmɪ,neɪtər, B 'nɔm-ə] *s.* nominador, nombrador; proponedor, proponente.

nominee [,nɑmə'ni, B ,nɔm-] *s.* nómino, propuesto, candidato nombrado.

nomogram ['nɑmə,græm, B 'nɔm-] **nomograph** [-,græf, B -,grɑf] *s.* (mat.) nomograma.

nomography [nə'mɑgrəfɪ, B noʊ'mɔg-] *s.* (mat.) nomografía.

nomology [noʊ'mɑlədʒɪ, B -'mɔl-] *s.* nomología (formulación de las leyes de una ciencia).

nomothetic [,nɑmə'θetɪk, B ,nɔm-] *a.* nomotético.

non [nɑn, nʌn, B nɔn] *prefijo negativo* que por lo común quiere decir *no* o *a falta de.*

nonabsorbent [,nɑnəb'sɔrbənt, -'zɔr-, B 'nɔnəb'sɔbənt] *a.* no absorbente.

nonacceptance [-ək'sɛptəns] *s.* falta de aceptación.

nonage ['nɑnɪdʒ, B 'noʊnɪdʒ] *s.* 1. minoridad, minoría de edad. 2. inmadurez.

nonagenarian [,noʊnədʒə'nɛrɪən, ,nɑnə-, B ,noʊ-'nɛər-] *a., s.* nonagenario (de noventa años).

nonaggression [,nɑnə'grɛʃən, B 'nɔn-] *s.* no agresión; **n. pact,** (pol.) convenio o pacto de no agredirse (entre naciones enemigas), pacto de no agresión.

nonagon ['noʊnə,gɑn, 'nɑnə-, B 'nɔnə,-gɔn] *s.* (geom.) nonágono, eneágono.

nonalcoholic [,nɑn,ælkə'hɔlɪk, -'hɑl-, B 'nɔn-'hɔl-] *a.* no alcohólico.

nonappearance [-ə'pɪrəns, B -'pɪər-] *s.* ausencia; (der.) incomparecencia, contumacia.

nonassignable [-ə'saɪnəbəl] *a.* (der., com.) no transferible, no negociable.

nonattendance [-ə'tɛndəns] *s.* falta de asistencia, inasistencia.

nonbelligerency [-bɔ'lɪdʒərənsɪ] *s.* no beligerancia.

nonbelligerent [-ənt] *a.* no beligerante.

nonbreakable [-'breɪkəbəl] *a.* irrompible.

nonce [nɑns, B nɔns] *s.* ocasión o propósito particular, presente; (ú. pr. en) **for the n.,** por el momento, por ahora.

nonce word, palabra creada para una sola ocasión, palabra ad hoc.

nonchalance [,nɑnʃə'lɑns, B 'nɔnʃələns] *s.* indiferencia, imperturbabilidad.

nonchalant [-'lɑnt, B -lənt] *a.* indiferente, imperturbable.

nonchalantly [-lɪ] *adv.* indiferentemente, imperturbablemente.

noncollectible [,nɑnkə'lɛktəbəl, B 'nɔn-] *a.* (com.) incobrable, irrecuperable.

noncom ['nɑn,kɑm, B 'nɔn,kɔm] *s.* (fam., mil.) clase, clase de tropa, suboficial.

noncombatant [,nɑnkəm'bætənt, -'kɑmbətənt, B 'nɔn'kɔm-] *s.* (mil.) no combatiente.

noncombustible [-kəm'bʌstəbəl] *a.* no combustible, incombustible.

noncommissioned [-kə'mɪʃənd] *a.* (mil.) de clase, de clase de tropa.

noncommissioned officer, (mil.) clase, clase de tropa; suboficial (grados de cabo a sargento).

noncommittal [-kə'mɪtəl] *a.* evasivo, reservado.

noncommittally [-ɪ] *adv.* evasivamente.

noncompliance [-kəm'plaɪəns] *s.* falta de cumplimiento, incumplimiento.

non compos mentis [,nɑn,kɑmpəs'mɛntəs, B 'nɔn'kɔm-] (der.) fuera de juicio, mentalmente incapacitado.

nonconducting [-kən'dʌktɪŋ] *a.* 1. (elec.) no conductor. 2. calorífugo, antitérmico.

nonconductor [-tər, B -,dʌktə] *s.* (fís., elec.) no conductor, aislante.

nonconformance [-kən'fɔrməns, B -'fɔməns] *s.* (ú. gen. con *to*) desacato, ej., *n. to established customs,* desacato a las costumbres establecidas.

nonconformist [-məst] *s.* disidente, rebelde; excéntrico.

nonconformity [-mətɪ] *s.* disconformidad; disidencia, desacato; calidad de excéntrico.

noncontagious [-kən'teɪdʒəs] *a.* no contagioso.

noncooperation [-koʊ,ɑpə'reɪʃən, B -,ɔp-] *s.* falta de cooperación (esp. con el gobierno); resistencia pasiva.

noncooperative [-'ɑpərətɪv, -,reɪt-, B -'ɔp-ə,rət-] *a.* contrario a (toda) cooperación.

noncorrosive [,nɑnkə'roʊsɪv, B 'nɔn-] *a.* no corrosivo, anticorrosivo.

non-defining clause [-dɪ'faɪnɪŋ-] (gram.) oración relativa incidental.

nondelivery [-dɪ'lɪvərɪ] *s.* falta de entrega (de una carta, mercancía, etc.).

nondescript [-dɪ'skrɪpt, B -,skrɪpt] *a.* indescriptible, indefinido; inclasificable. —*s.* persona o cosa indescriptible.

nondirectional [-dɪ'rɛkʃənəl] *a.* (rad.) no directiva, omnidireccional (antena).

nondrip [-drɪp] *a.* (*paint*) que no chorrea.

nondurable goods [-'dʊrəbəl-, B -'djʊər-] (com.) mercancías perecederas.

nondutiable [-'dutɪəbəl, B -djut-] *a.* no imponible, franco de derechos.

none [nʌn] *pron.* 1. nadie, ninguno, ej., *n. of them came,* ninguno de ellos vino, *n. can tell,* nadie puede decir o contar. 2. nada, ej., *n. of this concerns me,* nada de esto me incumbe, *half a loaf is better than n.,* algo es algo, medio pan es mejor que nada. 3. **n. but,** solamente, ej., *n. but fools have ever believed it,* solamente los tontos creyeron eso; **to be n. of one's business,** no ser cosa que atañe o importe a uno. —*adv.* 1. nada; no, de ninguna manera, ej., *the pay is n. too high,* el salario no es muy elevado. 2. **n. the less,** sin embargo, no obstante; **to be n. the better for it,** no haberse beneficiado en nada.

none [noʊn] *s.* (relig.) nona.

noneffective [,nɑnɪ'fɛktɪv, B 'nɔn-] *a.* 1. ineficaz. 2. no vigente (ley, proyecto). 3. (mil.) inhabilitado para el servicio activo.

nonego [-'i,goʊ, B -'ɛg,oʊ] *s.* (filos.) noyo (en las doctrinas de Fichte y Schelling).

nonentity [-'ɛntətɪ] *s.* (*pl.* NONENTITIES) 1. nulidad, persona sin importancia. 2. nada, negacíon del ser. 3. cosa inexistente; ficción.

nones [noʊnz] *s.pl.* 1. (hist.) nonas (en el calendario romano). 2. (relig.) nona.

nonessential [,nɑnɪ'sɛnʃəl, B 'nɔn-] *a.* no esencial, sin importancia.

nonesuch ['nʌn,sʌtʃ] *s.* persona sin par; cosa sin igual; esp. dechado, modelo, ejemplar.

nonetheless [,nʌnðə'lɛs] *adv.* no obstante, sin embargo, con todo.

non-Euclidean, non-Euclidian [,nɑnjʊ'klɪdɪən, B 'nɔnju-] *a.* no euclidiano.

non-Euclidean geometry, geometría no euclidiana.

non-existence [-ɪg'zɪstəns] *s.* inexistencia.

nonexistent [-tənt] *a.* inexistente.

nonexplosive [-ɪk'sploʊsɪv] *a.* incapaz de hacer explosión, inerte.

nonfeasance [nɑn'fɪzəns, B 'nɔn-] *s.* (der.) omisión, negligencia, incumplimiento.

nonferrous [-'fɛrəs] *a.* (min.) no ferroso.

nonfiction [,nɑn'fɪkʃən, B 'nɔn-] *a.* dic. de libros y literatura fuera de la novelística (ensayo, biografía, historia, etc.).

nonflammable [-'flæməbəl] *a.* ininflamable, no inflamable.

nonforfeitable [-'fɔrfətəbəl, B -'fɔfɪt-] *a.* (der.) incaducable.

nonfulfillment [-fʊl'fɪlmənt] *s.* falta de cumplimiento, incumplimiento.

noninductive [-ɪn'dʌktɪv] *a.* no inductivo, ej., resistencia eléctrica.

noninflammable [-ɪn'flæməbəl] *a.* ininflamable, no inflamable.

nonintervention [-,ɪntər'vɛntʃən, B -tə'vɛnʃən] *s.* no intervención; **policy of n.,** política de no intervención.

nonintoxicating [-ɪn'tɑksə,keɪtɪŋ, B -'tɔk-] *a.* no embriagante, sin contenido alcohólico.

nonjoinder [nɑn'dʒɔɪndər, B 'nɔn-də] *s.* (der.) falta de unión, falta de asociación (de socios o codemandantes en una acción judicial).

nonjuror [-'dʒʊrər, B -'dʒʊərə] *s.* (der.) el que no presta juramento.

nonlinear [,nɑn'lɪnɪər, B 'nɔn-ə] *a.* (rad., electrón., mat.) no lineal.

nonmailable [,nɑn'meɪləbəl, B 'nɔn-] *a.* no enviable por correo, inaceptable para remisión postal.

nonmarketable [-'mɑrkətəbəl, B -'mɑkət-] *a.* no vendible.

nonmetal [nɑn'mɛtəl, B 'nɔn-] *s.* (quím.) metaloide, no metal.

nonmetallic [,nɑnmə'tælɪk, B 'nɔn-] *a.* no metálico.

nonnegotiable [-nɪ'goʊʃəbəl] *a.* inflexible; (com.) no negociable.

no-no ['noʊ'noʊ] *s.* (fam.) algo que no se hace, algo prohibido, algo inadmisible; (*faux pas*) metida de pata.

nonobjective [-əb'dʒɛktɪv] *a.* no objetivo; abstracto.

no-nonsense ['noʊ'nɑn,sɛns, B -'nɔn-] *a.* serio, importante; práctico, pragmático.

nonpareil [,nɑnpə'rɛl, B 'nɔnpərəl] *a.* sin par, incomparable, sin igual. —*s.* 1. algo sin par, cosa sin igual; persona o cosa incomparable; dechado, modelo. 2. (orn.) pinzón; calandria. 3. (impr.) nomparell.

nonparous [nɑn'pærəs, B 'nɔn-] *a.* que no ha parido, que no ha tenido prole.

nonparticipating [,nɑnpɑr'tɪsə,peɪtɪŋ, B 'nɔnpɑ'-] *a.* 1. apartado. 2. (com.) no participante (ej., acciones).

nonpartisan [nɑn'pɑrtəzən, B 'nɔn,pɑtɪ'zæn] *a.* independiente, no afiliado.

nonpasserine [-'pæsə,raɪn] *a.* (orn.) no paseriforme.

nonpayment [-'peɪmənt] *s.* falta de pago, defecto de pago.

nonperformance [,nɑnpər'fɔrməns, B 'nɔnpə'fɔməns] *s.* falta de ejecución, falta de cumplimiento, incumplimiento.

nonplus [nɑn'plʌs, B 'nɔn-] *s.* confusión, perplejidad; incertidumbre, estupefacción, (pr. en) **at a n.,** perplejo. —*v.t.* (*pret., p.p.* NONPLUSED O NONPLUSSED; *p.pr.* NONPLUSING O NONPLUSSING) confundir, desconcertar, aplastar, dejar sin palabra.
nonproductive [ˌnɑnprə'dʌktɪv, B 'nɔn-] *a.* improductivo, no productivo.
nonproductiveness [-nəs] *s.* falta de productividad, improductividad.
nonprofit organization [nɑn'prɑfət-, B nɔn'prɔf-] empresa no lucrativa; sociedad no comercial; sociedad o empresa filantrópica.
non-pros ['nɑn'prɑs, B 'nɔn'prɔs] *v.t.* (*pret., p.p.* NON-PROSSED; *p.pr.* NON-PROSSING) (der.) desechar, declarar sin lugar la demanda (cuando no se la ha fundamentado).
non prosequitur [ˌnɑnprə'sɛkwətər, B ˌnɔn-ə] (der.) sentencia contra el demandante cuando éste no aparece ante el tribunal.
nonrecognition [-ˌrɛkɪg'nɪʃən] *s.* desconocimiento, no reconocim ento.
nonrenewable [-rɪ'nuəbəl, B -'nju-] *a.* no renovable, no recambiable; (com.) no extendible, no prorrogable.
nonrepresentational [-ˌrɛprɪˌzɛn'teɪʃənəl] *a.* (arte) abstracto, no figurativo.
nonresidence [nɑn'rɛzədəns, B 'nɔn-] **nonresidency** [-ənsɪ] *s.* no residencia.
nonresident [-ənt] *a.* no residente. —*s.* persona no residente (en un lugar).
nonresistance [ˌnɑnrɪ'zɪstəns, B 'nɔn-] *s.* no resistencia, obediencia pasiva.
nonresonant [nɑn'rɛzənənt, B 'nɔn-] *a.* no resonante.
nonrestrictive [ˌnɑnrɪ'strɪktɪv, B 'nɔn-] *a.* (com.) sin restricción, ej., endoso.
nonrigid airship [nɑn'rɪdʒəd-, B 'nɔn-] (aer.) dirigible no rígido.
nonrusting [ˌnɑn'rʌstɪŋ, B 'nɔn-] *a.* inoxidable, incorrosible.
nonscheduled [ˌnɑn'skɛdʒˌʊld, B 'nɔn'-ʃɛdjuld] *a.* 1. sin itinerario fijo (línea aérea, etc.). 2. inesperado, imprevisto (acontecimiento, visita, etc.).
nonsectarian [-sɛk'tɛrɪən, B -'tɛər-] *a.* no sectario.
nonsegregated [nɑn'sɛgrɪˌgeɪtəd, B 'nɔn-] *a.* no segregado.
nonsense ['nɑnsɛns, -səns, B 'nɔn-] *s.* disparate, dislate, desatino, tontería, necedad.
nonsensical [nɑn'sɛnsɪkəl, B nɔn-] *a.* disparatado, absurdo, desatinado.
nonsensically [-kəlɪ] *adv.* disparatadadamente, tontamente, desatinadamente.
non sequitur [ˌnɑn'sɛkwətər, B 'nɔn-ə] (log.) conclusión errónea, inferencia que no puede deducirse de axiomas.
nonshattering glass [-'ʃætərɪŋ-] vidrio inastillable, cristal de seguridad.
nonsignificant [-sɪg'nɪfɪkənt] *a.* 1. no significante, sin sentido. 2. (mat.) que puede omitirse sin que el valor inicial cambie.
nonskid ['nɑn'skɪd, B 'nɔn-] *a.* antideslizante, antirresbaladizo (díc. de las llantas de los autos).
nonsmoker [-smoʊkər] *s.* no fumador, persona que no fuma.
nonsmoking [-smoʊkɪŋ] *a.* para no fumadores.
nonstandard [nɑn'stændərd, B 'nɔn-dəd] *a.* no reglamentario; extrarreglamentario.
nonstarter [ˌnɑn'stɑrtər, B 'nɔn'stɑtə] *s.* caballo retirado (de una carrera).
nonstick [ˌnɑn'stɪk] *a.* antiadherente.
nonstop [nɑn'stɑp, B 'nɔn'stɔp] *a.* directo, expreso (tren, ómnibus); sin parada, sin escalas (viaje, etc.). —*adv.* directamente, sin paradas o escalas; sin parar.
nonstop flight, (aer.) vuelo sin escalas.
nonsuch, *var. de* **nonesuch.**
nonsuit [-'sut, B -'sjut] *v.t.* (der.) desechar, desestimar (una acción por falta de pruebas o por caducidad). —*s.* fallo contra el demandante por caducidad, caducidad de la instancia.
nonsupport [ˌnɑnsə'pɔrt, B 'nɔnsə'pɔt] *s.* (der.) falta de manutención.
nontaxable [-'tæksəbəl] *a.* no imponible, exento de impuestos, libre de contribución.
nontransferable [-træns'fɜrəbəl] *a.* (com., fin.) no traspasable, intransferible, no negociable (valores, acciones, etc.).
non-U ['nɑn'ju, B 'nɔn-] *a.* (jer., G.B.) que no es propio de gente culta (esp. en la manera de hablar).
nonunion [nɑn'junjən, B 'nɔn-] *a.* no agremiado, no afiliado a gremio o sindicato alguno.
nonunion shop, taller o negocio que no está afiliado a ningún gremio o sindicato.
nonuse [-'jus] *s.* falta de uso.
nonverbal [-'vɜrbəl, B -'vɜbəl] *a.* no verbal, no oral.
nonviable [-'vaɪəbəl] *a.* no viable, incapaz de sobrevivir.
nonviolence [-'vaɪələns] *s.* abstención de la violencia; (filos.) táctica sociopolítica que rechaza la violencia para obtener un objetivo.
nonviolent [-lənt] *a.* no violento, ej., *a. n. demonstration,* una manifestación pacífica o no violenta.
nonvolatile [-'vɑlətəl, B -'vɔləˌtaɪl] *a.* no volátil.
nonwhite [ˌnɑn'hwaɪt, -'waɪt, B 'nɔn-] *s., a.* no blanco, que no pertenece a la raza blanca.
noodle ['nudəl] *s.* 1. tallarín, fideo. 2. (fam.) tonto, simplón, mentecato. 3. (jer.) coco, cabeza.
nook [nʊk] *s.* 1. rincón; rinconada, escondrijo. 2. (esco.) esquina de papel o tela.
noon [nun] *s.* 1. mediodía. 2. (fig.) culminación, apogeo, cenit. —*a.* meridional, de mediodía.
noonday ['nunˌdeɪ] *s.* mediodía, meridiano. —*a.* del mediodía, ej., *the n. meal,* el almuerzo (la comida del mediodía).
nooning ['nunɪŋ] *s.* (ant., E.U.) comida del mediodía; descanso del mediodía.
noontide ['nunˌtaɪd] **noontime** [-ˌtaɪm] *s.* mediodía.
noose [nus] *s.* 1. dogal, lazo corredizo. 2. (fig.) vínculo, lazo; trampa. —*v.t.* 1. lazar, enlazar, coger con un lazo. 2. ahorcar.
nopal [noʊ'pɑl, 'noʊpəl, B 'noʊ-] *s.* (bot.) nopal, tuna.
no-par ['noʊ'pɑr, B -ˌpɑ] *a.* (com.) sin valor nominal (acciones).
nope ['noʊp] *adv.* (jer.) no (en su forma más contundente); (fam.) nanay.
nor [nɔr, B nɔ] *conj.* 1. ni, tampoco, ej., *neither arms n. provisions,* ni armas ni provisiones, *he said he had not seen it, n. had I,* él dijo que no lo había visto, yo tampoco. 2. (poét., ant.) (con omisión de *neither*) ni . . . ni, ej., *thou n. I have made the world,* ni tú ni yo hemos creado el mundo.
nor', nor [nɔr, B nɔ] *abrev. de* **north,** norte (esp. en palabras compuestas), ej., *noreast,* noreste.
Nordic ['nɔrdɪk, B 'nɔd-] *a., s.* nórdico, escandinavo.
Norfolk Island pine ['nɔrfək-, B 'nɔfək-] (bot.) araucaria excelsa.
Norfolk jacket, chaqueta o abrigo no entallado, con cinturón flojo y una hilera de botones.
noria ['nɔrɪə] *s.* noria, antiguo molino de rueda y cubos para recoger agua.
norland ['nɔrlənd, B 'nɔlənd] *s.* (poét.) tierra o país del norte.
norm [nɔrm, B nɔm] *s.* 1. norma, regla, precepto; pauta, guía, modelo, tipo. 2. (educ.) promedio (en grupo) de aplicación.
normal ['nɔrməl, B 'nɔməl] *a.* normal. —*s.* 1. persona o cosa normal. 2. grado normal, estado normal. 3. (geom.) recta normal. 4. normal, escuela de maestros.
normalcy [-sɪ] **normality** [nɔr'mælətɪ, B nɔ'-] *s.* normalidad.
normalization [ˌnɔrmələ'zeɪʃən, B ˌnɔməlaɪ-] *s.* normalización.
normalize ['nɔrməˌlaɪz, B 'nɔmə-] *v.t.* normalizar, regularizar.
normally [-lɪ] *adv.* normalmente; naturalmente; usualmente.
normal school, escuela normal.
Norman ['nɔrmən, B 'nɔmən] *a.* normando; de Normandía, provincia de Francia. —*s.* 1. normando, natural de Normandía. 2. dialecto normando.
Normanesque [ˌnɔrmə'nɛsk, B ˌnɔmə-] *a.* (arq.) normando.
Normanize ['nɔrməˌnaɪz, B 'nɔmə-] *v.t., v.i.* dotar de caracteres normandos, adquirir caracteres normandos.
normative ['nɔrmətɪv, B 'nɔmə-] *a.* normativo, relativo a o basado en normas o reglas.
Norse [nɔrs, B nɔs] *a., s.* escandinavo; noruego.
Norseman ['nɔrsmən, B 'nɔs-] *s.* antiguo escandinavo; hombre del norte.
north [nɔrθ, B nɔθ] *s.* 1. norte. 2. **N.,** región norteña (en los E.U. aquélla en que no existió la esclavitud; en G.B. la parte al norte del río Humber). 3. (poét.) norte, bóreas, viento norte. —*a.* norteño, del norte, septentrional, situado al norte; que sopla del norte (viento). —*adv.* al norte, hacia el norte.
North America, Norteamérica, América del Norte.
North American, *a., s.* norteamericano (esp. de E.U.).
northbound ['nɔrθˌbaʊnd, B 'nɔθ-] *a.* rumbo al norte.
north by east, norte cuarta al noreste.
north by west, norte cuarta al noroeste.
North Carolina [-ˌkærə'laɪnə] *s.* Carolina del Norte, estado de los E.U.
North Dakota [-də'koʊtə] *s.* Dakota del Norte, estado de los E.U.
northeast [ˌnɔrθ'ist, B 'nɔθ-] *s.* nordeste, noreste. —*a.* nordestal. —*adv.* hacia el nordeste.
northeast by east, nordeste cuarta al este.
northeast by north, nordeste cuarta al norte.
northeaster [ˌnɔrθ'istər, B ˌnɔθ'istə] *s.* nordeste; nordestada, tempestad nordestal.
northeasterly [-lɪ] *a.* nordestal.
northeastern [-tərn, B -tən] *a.* nordestal.
Northeasterner [-tərnər, B -tənə] *s.* (E.U.) habitante de la región noreste.
northeastward [ˌnɔrθ'istwərd, B ˌnɔθ-wəd] **northeastwardly** [-lɪ] *a.* del nordeste. —*adv.* hacia el nordeste.
northeastwards [-wərdz, B -wədz] *adv.* hacia el nordeste.
norther ['nɔrðər, B 'nɔðə] *s.* bóreas, cierzo, nortada, norte.
northerly [-lɪ] *a.* que sopla del norte (viento); **in a n. direction,** con dirección al norte. —*adv.* hacia el norte. —*s.* norte, viento que sopla del norte.
northern ['nɔrðərn, B 'nɔðən] *a.* 1. norteño, nórtico, nórdico. 2. que viene o que sopla del norte. —*s.* dialecto norteño (de los E.U.).

Northern Cross, (astr.) Cruz del Cisne, constelación del Cisne.
Northern Crown, (astr.) Corona Boreal.
Northerner [-ðərnər, B -ðənə] *s.* norteño, habitante del norte.
northern lights, (meteor.) aurora boreal.
northernmost ['nɔrðərn,moʊst, B 'nɔðən-] *a.* más septentrional, más nórtico o nórdico.
Northern Rhodesia, Rodesia del Norte, antiguo nombre de Zambia.
Northern Spy, (E.U.) variedad de manzana invernal de color amarillo rojizo.
northing ['nɔrθɪŋ, -ðɪŋ, B 'nɔðɪŋ] *s.* 1. (top., mar.) progreso o deriva hacia el norte. 2. (astr.) declinación del norte.
North Korea, Corea del Norte.
northland ['nɔrθ,lænd, -lənd, B 'nɔθ-] *s.* tierras norteñas; el norte (de un país).
Northman [-mən] *s.* (*pl.* NORTHMEN) escandinavo.
north-northeast [-,nɔrθ'ist, B -,nɔθ-] *s.* nornordeste.
north-northwest [-'wɛst] *s.* nornoroeste, nornorueste.
North Pole, Polo Norte.
North Sea, Mar del Norte.
North Star, estrella polar.
Northumbrian [nɔr'θʌmbrɪən, B nɔ'θʌm-] *a.* de Northumbria; de Northumberland, condado de Inglaterra. —*s.* dialecto de Northumbria o de Northumberland.
North Vietnam, *s.* Vietnam del Norte.
northward ['nɔrθwərd, B 'nɔθwəd] *adv.* hacia el norte (t. **northwards**). —*a.* situado o dirigido hacia el norte. —*s.* dirección al norte; parte norteña.
northwardly [-lɪ] *a., adv.* hacia el norte.
northwest [,nɔrθ'wɛst, B 'nɔθ-] *s.* noroeste, norueste. —*a.* del noroeste; situado en el noroeste, dirigido hacia el noroeste; que sopla del noroeste. —*adv.* hacia o en el noroeste, del noroeste.
northwest by north, noroeste cuarta al norte.
northwest by west, noroeste cuarta al oeste.
northwester [-'wɛstər, B -tə] *s.* noroeste, cauro.
northwesterly [-lɪ] *a.* hacia el noroeste; del noroeste. —*adv.* hacia el noroeste.
northwestern [-tərn, B -tən] *a.* del noroeste.
Northwesterner [-tərnər, B -tənə] *s.* (E.U.) habitante de la región noroeste.
Northwest Passage, Paso del Noroeste, ruta del Océano Atlántico al Pacífico a través del Océano Ártico.
northwestward [,nɔrθ'wɛstwərd, B 'nɔθ-wəd] *adv., a.* hacia el noroeste; en dirección noroeste.
northwestwardly [-lɪ] *a., adv.* hacia el noroeste.
Norway ['nɔrweɪ, B 'nɔweɪ] *s.* Noruega.
Norway rat, (zool.) rata de alcantarilla.
Norwegian [nɔr'widʒən, B nɔ'wi-] *a., s.* noruego.
nose [noʊz] *s.* 1. nariz. 2. olfato, ej., *he has a good n. (for),* tiene buen olfato (para). 3. nariz, cañón (del alambique, retorta, etc.); boca (de herramientas). 4. parte prominente, resalto, saliente. 5. (aer.) nariz, proa (de un avión). 6. (mar.) proa 7. (jer., G.B.) espía, soplón (esp. para la policía). 8. **as plain as the n. in your face,** claro como el agua; **on the n.,** (jer.) exacto, correcto; exactamente, precisamente; **to bite** (o **to snap) one's n. off,** contestar mordazmente; **to blow one's n.,** sonarse, sonarse la nariz; **to count** (o **to tell) noses,** contar cabezas, contar los partidarios (de uno); decidir por mera cantidad; **to cut off one's n. to spite one's face,** vengarse con perjuicio de sí mismo; **to follow one's n.,** seguir de frente; guiarse por su instinto; **to hold one's n.,** taparse las narices; **to lead by the n.,** llevar de las narices, tener de la oreja; **to look down one's n. at,** mirar por encima del hombro, mirar con desprecio; **to pay through the n.,** pagar un ojo de la cara; **to pick one's n.,** hurgarse las narices; **to poke** (o **to thrust) one's n. (into something),** meter la cuchara (en algo); **to put one's n. out of joint,** enfadar, causar resentimiento a; desconcertar; **to see no farther than one's n.,** no ver más allá de sus narices; **to speak through the n.,** hablar por la nariz, hablar gangosamente; **to stick one's n. into,** meter las narices en; **to turn up one's n. (at),** torcer las narices; desdeñar, despreciar; **to win by a n.,** ganar por un pelo (carrera, etc.); **under the n. of,** en las barbas de. —*v.t.* 1. oler, olfatear; husmear, rastrear. 2. tocar o restregar la nariz contra (algo). 3. **n. one's way,** avanzar o abrir camino lentamente o cautelosamente (esp. barco, tren); **n. out,** descubrir, oliscar, olisquear. —*v.i.* 1. oler, husmear. 2. meterse en asuntos ajenos, cucharatear. 3. abrirse camino o avanzar cautelosamente. 4. **n. about** (o **around**), husmear, curiosear; **n. on,** (jer., G.B.) delatar.
nose ape, n. monkey, mono proboscideo.
nose bag, morral, cebadera (del caballo).
noseband ['noʊz,bænd] *s.* muserola, sobarba.
nosebleed [-,blid] *s.* hemorragia nasal.
nose cone, (aeronáut.) parte delantera de un cohete o navío espacial.
nose dive, (aer.) picada, picado de cabeza o de nariz.
nose-dive [-,daɪv] *v.i.* (aer.) picar de cabeza o de nariz.
nose flute, flauta nasal (instrumento de los habitantes de Tailandia y las Islas Fidji).
nosegay ['noʊz,geɪ] *s.* ramillete de flores, esp. el que se lleva a mano como accesorio de un conjunto de gala.
nosepiece [-,pis] *s.* 1. nasal (del yelmo). 2. lanza, boca de manguera, pitón. 3. porta-objetivo (del microscopio). 4. puente (de los lentes).
noserag [-,ræg] *s.* (jer.) pañuelo.
nosering [-,rɪŋ] *s.* nariguera, aro de nariz.
nosey, *var. de* **nosy.**
nosey Parker ['noʊzɪ'pɑrkər, B -'pɑkə] (fam., G.B.) entremetido, fisgón, metete (Amer.).
no-show ['noʊ'ʃoʊ] *s.* (E.U.) pasajero que no hace uso de su reservación ni la cancela (esp. en avión); alguien que no asiste a un espectáculo para el cual tiene entrada.
nosing ['noʊzɪŋ] *s.* (carp.) vuelo de un escalón; (arq.) saliente, salidizo.
no-smoking [-smoʊkɪn] *a.* (*section*) para no fumadores.
no smoking, (public sign) prohibido fumar.
nosogeny [noʊ'sɑdʒənɪ, B -'sɔdʒ-] *s.* (med.) nosogenia.
nosography [-'sɑgrəfɪ, B -'sɔg-] *s.* (med.) nosografía.
nosologic [,noʊsə'lɑdʒɪk, ,noʊz-, ,nɑs-, B ,nɔsə'lɔdʒ-] **nosological** [-ɪkəl] *a.* (med.) nosológico.
nosologist [noʊ'sɑlədʒəst, B nə'sɔl-] *s.* (med.) nosologista.
nosology [-dʒɪ] *s.* (med.) nosología.
nostalgia [nɑ'stældʒə, nə-, B nɔ-dʒɪə] *s.* nostalgia.
nostalgic [-dʒɪk] *a.* nostálgico.
nostologic [,nɑstə'lɑdʒɪk, B ,nɔstə'lɔdʒ-] *a.* (med.) nostológico.
nostology [nɑ'stɑlədʒɪ, B nɔ'stɔl-] *s.* (med.) nostología, gerontología.
nostril ['nɑstrəl, B 'nɔs-] *s.* ventana de la nariz; ollar (de la nariz del caballo).
nostrum ['nɑstrəm, B 'nɔs-] *s.* panacea, cúralotodo.
nosy ['noʊzɪ] *a.* curioso, entremetido, inquisitivo.
not [nɑt, B nɔt] *adv.* no, ni; **it's good, is it n.?** está bueno, ¿no es así?; **n. a little,** no poco, bastante; **n. any,** ninguno; **n. at all,** nada, de ningún modo; **n. even,** ni siquiera; **n. half,** (jer., G.B.) muy, mucho, sumamente; **n. one,** ni uno (solo); **n. so much as,** ni siquiera; **n. that,** pero es que, pero esto no quiere decir que, ej., *I don't want to do it, not that it's difficult,* no quiero hacerlo, aunque eso no significa que sea difícil; **n. yet,** todavía no; **why n.?** ¿por qué no?
notability [,noʊtə'bɪlətɪ] *s.* notabilidad (persona y cualidad).
notable ['noʊtəbəl] *a.* notable, memorable, insigne, resaltante. —*s.* notabilidad, persona notable.
notableness [-bəlnəs] *s.* notabilidad.
notably [-blɪ] *adv.* notablemente, señaladamente.
notarial [noʊ'tɛrɪəl, B -'tɛər-] *a.* notarial, notariado.
notarial certificate, acta o certificado notarial.
notarization [,noʊtərə'zeɪʃən, B -raɪ-] *s.* certificacíon notarial, atestación notarial.
notarize ['noʊtə,raɪz] *v.t.* proveer de atestación notarial, hacer certificar por notario (un documento).
notary ['noʊtərɪ] *s.* notario, escribano.
notary public, (*pl.* NOTARIES PUBLIC) escribano o notario público.
notate ['noʊ,teɪt] *v.t.* anotar, apuntar.
notation [noʊ'teɪʃən] *s.* 1. anotación; nota, apunte. 2. notación (musical, matemática, etc.).
notch [nɑtʃ, B nɔtʃ] *s.* 1. muesca, mella, corte. 2. desfiladero, paso. 3. (fam., fig.) grado, nivel, estado. —*v.t.* 1. hacer muescas en, mellar; cortar. 2. marcar, registrar. 3. lograr.
note [noʊt] *s.* 1. nota, marca, señal, característica, distintivo. 2. reputación, renombre, fama, nombradía. 3. anotación, apunte; (*gen. pl.*) minuta, apuntes. 4. nota, acotación, comentario (al margen de un escrito). 5. advertencia, atención, aviso. 6. misiva, esquela, billete, nota (diplomática). 7. pagaré, documento de crédito. 8. billete (de banco). 9. notificación, aviso. 10. tono, acento, ej., *there was a grave n. in his voice,* había un acento grave en su voz. 11. canto, trino (de ave), llamado (de animal). 12. (mús.) nota; tecla (de piano, etc.). 13. **of n.,** de nota, notable, ej., *a writer of n.,* un escritor de nota, un escritor notable; **to change one's n.,** (fig.) cambiar de tono; **to compare notes,** intercambiar ideas u opiniones; **to make a n. of,** tomar nota de, apuntar; **to strike the right n.,** hacer o decir una cosa acertada; **to take n. of,** tomar nota de, observar; **to take no n. of,** no prestar atención a; **to take notes,** tomar notas, tomar apuntes. —*v.t.* 1. anotar, reparar, advertir. 2. (t. con *down*) anotar, apuntar. 3. observar, mencionar; indicar.
notebook ['noʊt,bʊk] *s.* 1. libreta, cuaderno, memorándum, agenda. 2. (com.) registro de pagarés.
notecase [-,keɪs] *s.* (G.B.) billetero, billetera (Amer.).
noted ['noʊtəd] *a.* notable, afamado, célebre, famoso; insigne, eminente.
notedly [-lɪ] *adv.* notablemente.
notedness [-nəs] *s.* notabilidad, fama, celebridad, eminencia.
noteless ['noʊtləs] *a.* 1. desconocido, obscuro, anónimo. 2. que no es musical, inarmónico.
note of hand, (com.) vale, pagaré.

notepaper [-ˌpeɪpər, B -pə] *s.* papel de carta.

noteworthily [-ˌwɜrðəlɪ, B -ˌwɜðɪ-] *adv.* notablemente, de una manera digna de atención.

noteworthy [-ˌwɜrðɪ, B -ˌwɜðɪ] *a.* notable, digno de atencion, digno de mención.

nothing [ˈnʌθɪŋ] *s.* 1. nada. 2. nadería. 3. cero, nulidad (persona). 4. (mat.) cero, nada. 5. **for n.,** gratis; inútilmente, en vano; **in n. flat,** (fam.) en un dos por tres; **no n.,** (fam., u. incorrecto) ni nada en absoluto, ej., *there was no money, no food, no clothing, no n.,* no había ni dinero, ni comida, ni ropa, ni nada en absoluto; **n. but,** sólo, únicamente; **n. doing,** (jer.) ni en juego; **n. else,** nada más; **n. if not,** más que todo, ej., *he is n. if not stingy,* él más que todo es tacaño; **n. much,** nada del otro jueves; **n. to,** nada comparado con, ej., *this is n. to what I am going to tell you,* esto no es nada comparado con lo que voy a contarte; **n. to speak of,** poca cosa; **n. ventured n. gained,** el que no arriesga no gana; **n. yet,** todavía no; **that is n. to me,** eso nada me importa; **that is n. to you,** eso no te atañe; **there's n. for it but to (do),** no hay más remedio sino, no hay otra alternativa sino (hacer); **there's n. in it,** es falso; es sin importancia; **there's n. like,** no hay nada mejor que; **to come to n.,** resultar inútil o nulo, reducirse a nada; frustrarse, esfumarse; **to fade away to n.,** desaparecer gradualmente; **to have n. to do with,** no tener nada que ver con; **to have n. on,** no tener evidencia o pruebas; no tener nada puesto; **to make n. of,** no dar importancia a, restar importancia a, desestimar (peligro, etc.); **to make n. of (doing something),** no vacilar en (hacer algo), no importar a uno (hacer algo); **to mean n. to,** no significar nada para; no tener ninguna importancia para. —*adv.* no, nada, en nada; de ninguna manera, de ninguna forma; **n. daunted,** sin inmutarse, sin alterarse; sin temor alguno; **n. less than,** no menos que, nada menos que; **n. like,** ni con mucho, ni aproximadamente; no tan, no tanto.

nothingness [-nəs] *s.* 1. nada, la nada. 2. inexistencia; insignificancia completa. 3. nadería, nonada, bicoca.

notice [ˈnoʊtəs] *s.* 1. anuncio, aviso, proclama. 2. notificación, aviso; advertencia. 3. observación, reparo. 4. atención, consideración. 5. mención. 6. letrero, cartel, aviso. 7. **on short n.,** a la brevedad, en poco tiempo (disponible); **short n.,** corto plazo de aviso; **take n. that,** le advierto que; **to come into n.,** llamar la atención; **to escape one's n.,** pasarle inadvertido a uno, escapársele a uno; **to give n.,** dar aviso (de despedida, renuncia); **to serve n. on,** hacer saber; **to take n. of,** notar, observar, advertir; **to take no n. of,** hacer caso omiso de, dejar a un lado; **until further n.,** hasta que reciba otras instrucciones, hasta el próximo aviso. —*v.t.* 1. notar, reparar, advertir, observar; darse cuenta de; prestar atención a. 2. mencionar, hacer una observación sobre, aludir a. 3. dar aviso (de despedida, terminación de compromiso, renuncia, etc.).

noticeable [-əbəl] *a.* perceptible, sensible, conspicuo; digno de atención, notable.

noticeably [-blɪ] *adv.* perceptiblemente, notablemente.

notice board, tablero o pizarra para avisos.

notification [ˌnoʊtəfəˈkeɪʃən] *s.* 1. notificación, aviso. 2. aviso; letrero.

notify [ˈnoʊtəˌfaɪ] *v.t.* (*pret., p.p.* NOTIFIED; *p.pr.* NOTIFYING) 1. notificar, avisar. 2. participar, dar a conocer a, informar.

notion [ˈnoʊʃən] *s.* 1. noción, idea, concepto. 2. opinión; teoría, creencia. 3. disposición, intención, gana. 4. (fam.) novedad, baratija. 5. **to have a n. to (do),** tener ganas de (hacer); pensar (hacer).

notional [-əl] *a.* 1. nocional, especulativo, imaginario; irreal, fantástico. 2. (E.U.) caprichoso, chiflado, maniático.

notochord [ˈnoʊtəˌkɔrd, B -ˌkɔd] *s.* (anat., zool.) notocordio, notocorda, notocuerda.

notoriety [ˌnoʊtəˈraɪətɪ] *s.* 1. notoriedad (gen. desfavorable). 2. notabilidad (persona).

notorious [noʊˈtɔrɪəs, nə-] *a.* notorio, de mala reputación.

notoriously [-lɪ] *adv.* notoriamente (en sentido peyorativo).

notoriousness [-nəs] *s.* notoriedad, mala reputación.

no-trump [ˈnoʊˈtrʌmp] (bridge) *a.* de sin triunfo (declaración, juego); buena para sin triunfo (mano). —*s.* declaración o juego de sin triunfo.

no-trumper [-ˈtrʌmpər, B -pə] *s.* (bridge) contrato de sin triunfo; buena mano para (jugar) sin triunfo; declarante de (juego de) sin triunfo.

notwithstanding [ˌnɑtwɪθˈstændɪŋ, -wɪð-, B ˌnɔt-] *prep.* a pesar de, a despecho de. —*adv.* no obstante, sin embargo, empero. —*conj.* a pesar de que.

nougat [ˈnugət, B ˈnugɑ] *s.* nuégado, alajú (confite en pasta), turrón.

nought, *var. de* **naught.**

noughts and crosses [nɔts-] tres en raya (juego), ta-te-ti.

noumenon [ˈnuməˌnɑn, B ˈnaʊməˌnɔn] *s.* (*pl.* NOUMENA [-nə]) (filos.) nóumeno.

noun [naʊn] *s.* (gram.) nombre, sustantivo.

nounal [ˈnaʊnəl] *a.* (gram.) sustantivo.

nounally [-əlɪ] *adv.* (gram.) sustantivamente.

nourish [ˈnɜrɪʃ, B ˈnʌrɪʃ] *v.t.* 1. nutrir, alimentar; criar, mantener. 2. alentar, fomentar. 3. abrigar, sostener (esperanza, etc.).

nourisher [-ər, B -ə] *s.* 1. alimentador. 2. fomentador.

nourishing [-ɪŋ] *a.* nutritivo, alimenticio.

nourishment [-mənt] *s.* 1. nutrimento, alimento, comida; pábulo. 2. nutrición, alimentación.

nous [nus, B naʊs] *s.* (filos.) razón, inteligencia.

nouveau riche [ˌnuvoʊˈriʃ] (fr.) nuevo rico, advenedizo.

Nov. *abrev. de* **November,** noviembre (nov.).

nova [ˈnoʊvə] *s.* (*pl.* NOVAE [-vi] o NOVAS) (astr.) nova.

novaculite [noʊˈvækjəˌlaɪt] *s.* (min.) novaculita.

Nova Scotia [ˈnoʊvəˈskoʊʃə] Nueva Escocia, provincia del Canadá.

novation [noʊˈveɪʃən] *s.* 1. (der.) novación. 2. (ant.) innovación.

novel [ˈnɑvəl, B ˈnɔv-] *a.* novel, nuevo; original; reciente, moderno. —*s.* 1. novela. 2. **Novels,** (der. romano) Novelas (leyes posteriores al Código justiniano).

novelette [ˌnɑvəˈlɛt, B ˌnɔv-] *s.* novela corta.

novelist [ˈnɑvələst, B ˈnɔv-] *s.* novelista.

novelistic [ˌnɑvəˈlɪstɪk, B ˌnɔv-] *a.* novelístico.

novelization [-ləˈzeɪʃən, B -laɪ-] *s.* novelización.

novelize [ˈnɑvəˌlaɪz, B ˈnɔv-] *v.t.* novelizar (pasaje de la historia, suceso de actualidad, etc.).

novella [noʊˈvɛlə] *s.* (*pl.* NOVELLAS O NOVELLE [-i]) (ital.) novela corta; cuento corto.

novelty [ˈnɑvəltɪ, B ˈnɔv-] *s.* (*pl.* NOVELTIES) 1. novedad, innovación; originalidad. 2. (*gen. pl.*) novedades; chucherías, baratijas.

November [noʊˈvɛmbər, B -bə] *s.* noviembre.

novena [noʊˈvinə] *s.* (*pl.* NOVENAE [-ni]) (relig.) novena.

novenary [ˈnɑvəˌnɛrɪ, noʊˈvinərɪ, B ˈnɔvɪnə-] *s.* (relig.) novenario.

novice [ˈnɑvəs, B ˈnɔv-] *s.* 1. novicio, novato, aprendiz, principiante. 2. (rel.) novicio, neófito.

novicehood [-ˌhʊd] *s.* noviciado.

novitiate [noʊˈvɪʃɪət] *s.* 1. noviciado. 2. novicio; principiante.

Novocain [ˈnoʊvəˌkeɪn, B -voʊ-] *s.* (farm.) novocaína (marca de fábrica).

now [naʊ] *adv.* 1. ahora, ya, ora, en estas circunstancias; hoy (día), actualmente; al instante, inmediatamente; después de esto. 2. ahora bien, pues. 3. (en narración) entonces, luego. 4. **just. n.,** hace un momento, poco ha; **n. and again, n. and then,** de vez en cuando, de cuando en cuando; **n. . . . n.,** ora . . . ora . . . ; **n. or never,** ahora o nunca; **n. then,** ahora bien. —*conj.* (ú. gen. seguido de *that*) ya que, ahora que, puesto que. —*s.* ahora, actualidad, momento presente; **by n.,** ahora ya, ej., *by n. he must be there,* ya debe estar allí; **from n. on,** de hoy en adelante; **till n.,** hasta ahora. —*interj.* ¡vamos! ¡vaya!

nowadays [ˈnaʊəˌdeɪz] *adv.* en estos días, en estos tiempos, hoy día, hoy en día, en la actualidad, en esta época.

noway [ˈnoʊˌweɪ] **noways** [-ˌweɪz] *adv.* de ningún modo.

nowhere [-ˌhwɛr, -ˌwɛr, B -ˌwɛə, -ˌhwɛə] *s.* ninguna parte, ningún sitio; **at the back of n.,** por los quintos infiernos; **to be (to get) n.,** no haber logrado nada; haber fracasado por completo; **to have n. to turn,** no tener donde encontrar refugio, consejo, etc. —*adv.* en ninguna parte, a ninguna parte.

nowhere else, en ninguna otra parte.

nowhere near, (fam.) ni de lejos, ni con mucho.

nowheres [-ˌhwɛrz, -ˌwɛrz, B -ˌwɛəz] *adv.* (dial., E.U.) *var. de* **nowhere.**

nowhither [ˈnoʊˌhwɪðər, -ˌwɪð-, B -ə] *adv.* hacia ninguna parte.

nowise [-ˌwaɪz] *adv.* de ningún modo, de ninguna manera, en modo alguno.

noxious [ˈnɑkʃəs, B ˈnɔk-] *a.* nocivo, malsano, dañino, pernicioso.

noxiously [-lɪ] *adv.* nocivamente, dañosamente, perniciosamente.

noxiousness [-nəs] *s.* nocividad.

noyade [nwɑˈjɑd] *s.* ahogamiento; esp. **N.** (hist.) ahogamiento en masa (como en Nantes durante el Terror).

nozzle [ˈnɑzəl, B ˈnɔz-] *s.* 1. boquilla, boquerel (de regadera, soplete, pulverizador, etc.); pitón, lanza (de manga de riego). 2. (jer.) jeta, hocico, nariz.

Np *símb. de* **neptunium,** neptunio (Np).

N.P. *abrev. de* **Notary Public,** notario público.

NRA *abrev. de* **National Recovery Administration,** Agencia de Recuperación Nacional.

NSC *abrev. de* **National Security Council,** (E.U.) Consejo de Seguridad Nacional.

NSF *abrev. de* **National Science Foundation,** (E.U.) Fundación Nacional de las Ciencias.

N.S.P.C.C. *abrev. de* **National Society for the Prevention of Cruelty to Children,** Sociedad Nacional para Proteger a Niños Desamparados.

NT *abrev. de* **New Testament,** Nuevo Testamento.

nth [ɛnθ] *a.* (mat.) enésimo.

nth degree, (mat.) potencia n, potencia indefinida, enésimo grado; **to the nth degree,** elevado a la potencia n; (fig.) a un extremo, al máximo.

NTP *abrev. de* **normal temperature and pressure,** temperatura y presión normales (medio ambiente).

nu [nu, B nju] *s.* ny, decimotercera letra del alfabeto griego.

nuance ['nu,ɑns, nu'ɑns, B nju'ɑns] *s.* matiz.
nub [nʌb] *s.* 1. trozo, pedazo, trocito. 2. nudo; protuberancia. 3. quid, esencia. 4. **to a** (o **the**) **n.**, hasta no poder más, hasta quedar completamente agotado.
nubbin ['nʌbən] *s.* (E.U.) 1. mazorca de maíz imperfecta o pequeña. 2. protuberancia pequeña, pedazo saliente.
nubble ['nʌbəl] *s.* bulto pequeño, protuberancia pequeña.
nubbly [-əlɪ] *a.* nudoso, con pequeños bultos.
Nubian ['nubɪən, B 'nju-] *a., s.* nubiense, de Nubia, región del antiguo Egipto.
nubile ['nubəl, -,baɪl, B 'nju-] *a.* núbil, casadera.
nubility [nu'bɪlətɪ, B nju-] *s.* nubilidad.
nubilous ['nubələs, B 'nju-] *s.* 1. nebuloso, nublado. 2. (fig.) nebuloso, oscuro, vago.
nucellar [nu'sɛlər, B nju-ə] *a.* (bot.) nucelar.
nucellus [-əs] *s.* (*pl.* NUCELLI [-,aɪ]) (bot.) nucela.
nucha ['nukə, B 'nju-] *s.* cogote, nuca.
nuchal [-kəl] *a.* (anat.) nucal, de la nuca.
nuclear ['nuklɪər, B 'nju-ə] *a.* nuclear.
nuclear bomb, bomba nuclear o atómica.
nuclear energy, energía nuclear, energía atómica.
nuclear fallout, lluvia nuclear, lluvia radioactiva.
nuclear family, familia nuclear.
nuclear fission, (quím., fís.) fisión nuclear.
nuclear fusion, (quím., fís.) fusión nuclear.
nuclear physics, física nuclear.
nuclear power plant, central nuclear.
nuclear reaction, (fís., quím.) reacción nuclear o atómica.
nuclear reactor, reactor (dispositivo que genera reacciones atómicas).
nuclear research, investigaciones nucleares.
nuclear umbrella, sombrilla nuclear.
nuclear war, guerra nuclear.
nuclear waste, residuos nucleares.
nuclear weapon, arma nuclear.
nuclease ['nuklɪ,eɪs, B 'nju-] *s.* (bioquím.) nucleasa.
nucleate ['nuklɪət, B 'nju-] *a.* nucleado. —[-,eɪt] *v.t.* convertir en un núcleo. —*v.i.* formar un núcleo.
nucleation [,nuklɪ'eɪʃən, B ,nju-] *s.* formación de núcleos.
nucleic acid [nu'kliɪk-, B nju-] (bioquím.) ácido nucleico o nucleínico.
nuclein ['nuklɪən, B 'nju-] *s.* (bioquím.) nucleína.
nucleolar [nu'kliələr, B nju-lə] *a.* (biol.) nucleolar.
nucleolated [-,leɪtəd] **nucleolate** [-,leɪt, -lət] *a.* (biol., bot., zool.) nucleolado.
nucleole ['nuklɪ,oʊl, B 'nju-] *s.* (biol.) nucléolo.
nucleolus [nu'kliələs, B nju-] *s.* (*pl.* NUCLEOLI [-,laɪ]) (biol.) nucléolo.
nucleon ['nuklɪ,ɑn, B 'nju-,ɔn] *s.* (fís.) nucleón, partícula nuclear.
nucleonics [,nuklɪ'ɑnɪks, B ,nju-'ɔn-] *s. pl.* (*sing. en const.*) tecnología nuclear.
nucleoplasm ['nuklɪə,plæzəm, B 'nju-] *s.* (biol.) nucleoplasma.
nucleoplasmic [,nuklɪə'plæzmɪk, B ,nju-] *a.* (biol.) nucleoplásmico.
nucleoprotein [-oʊ'proʊtin, -'proʊtɪən] *s.* (bioquím.) nucleoproteína.
nucleoside ['nuklɪə,saɪd, B 'nju-] *s.* (quím.) nucleósido.
nucleotide [-,taɪd] *s.* (quím.) nucleótido.
nucleus ['nuklɪəs, B 'nju-] *s.* (*pl.* NUCLEI [-,aɪ] o NUCLEUSES) núcleo; (anat., astr., biol., fís., quím.) núcleo.
nuclide [-klaɪd] *s.* (fís.) núclido.
nude [nud, B njud] *a.* 1. desnudo. 2. (der.) sin compensación. —*s.* desnudo; **in the n.,** al desnudo.
nude contract, (der.) contrato sin causa, nudo pacto.
nudeness ['nudnəs, B 'njud-] *s.* desnudez.
nudge [nʌdʒ] *v.t.* tocar ligeramente (con el codo); dar un codazo suave a (para llamar la atención). —*s.* codazo suave.
nudibranchiate [,nudə'bræŋkɪət, B ,nju-] *a.* (zool.) nudibranquiado.
nudicaul ['nudɪ,kɔl, B 'nju-] **nudicaulous** [,nudɪ'kɔləs, B ,nju-] *a.* (bot.) nudicaule, nudicaulo.
nudism ['nu,dɪzəm, B 'nju-] *s.* nudismo.
nudist ['nudəst, B 'njud-] *s., a.* nudista.
nudity [-ətɪ] *s.* 1. desnudez. 2. desnudo.
nudnik ['nʊdnɪk] *s.* (jer.) persona importuna o molestosa, latoso, pesado.
nugatory ['nugə,tɔrɪ, B 'njugətərɪ] *a.* 1. vano, trivial; sin valor. 2. ineficaz; fútil, inútil.
nugget ['nʌgət] *s.* trozo, pedazo; pepita (de metal virgen), esp. pepita de oro, palacra.
nuisance ['nusəns, B 'nju-] *s.* 1. estorbo, molestia, fastidio. 2. (un) latoso, pesado, ej., *he's a n.,* (él) es un latoso, (él) es un pesado. 3. (der.) perjuicio, daño, acto perjudicial. 4. **to make a n. of oneself,** ponerse pesado; **what a n.!** ¡qué lata! ¡qué fastidio!
nuisance tax, impuesto menor sobre consumo.
nuisance value, capacidad para causar fastidio.
null [nʌl] *a.* 1. nulo, írrito. 2. (mat.) vacío. 3. fútil, insignificante. 4. ausente, inexistente. 5. sin expresión, indiferente. —*s.* cero.
nullah ['nʌlə] *s.* (anglo-ind.) arroyuelo.
null and void, (der.) nulo, írrito, sin efecto ni valor, nulo y de ningún efecto.
nullification [,nʌləfə'keɪʃən] *s.* 1. anulación, invalidación. 2. (hist., E.U.) negativa de un Estado a obedecer alguna ley federal.
nullificationist [-ʃənəst] *s.* (hist., E.U.) partidario de la doctrina de que un Estado tiene derecho a no obedecer alguna ley federal.
nullifidian [,nʌlə'fɪdɪən] *s.* ateo; descreído; escéptico.
nullifier ['nʌlə,faɪər, B -ə] *s.* anulador.
nullify [-,faɪ] *v.t.* (*pret., p.p.* NULLIFIED; *p.pr.* NULLIFYING) anular, invalidar, nulificar.
nullipara [nʌ'lɪpərə, B 'nʌlɪpərə] *a., s.* (*pl.* NULLIPARAE [-,ri]) (med.) nulípara.
nulliparous [nʌ'lɪpərəs] *a.* (med.) nulíparo.
nullipore ['nʌlə,pɔr, B -,pɔ] *s.* (bot.) nulípora.
nullity ['nʌlətɪ] *s.* nulidad, invalidez legal.
null sequence, (mat.) sucesión nula.
Numantian [nu'mænʃɪən, B nju'mæntɪən] *a., s.* numantino, de Numancia, antigua ciudad celtíbera.
numb [nʌm] *a.* 1. aterido, entumecido; entorpecido. 2. atontado, aturdido; pasmado. —*v.t.* 1. entumecer; entorpecer. 2. atontar, aturdir; pasmar.
number ['nʌmbər, B -bə] *s.* 1. número, cifra, guarismo. 2. número, cantidad, colección. 3. número, entrega, ejemplar (de revista, etc.). 4. (teat.) número, representación. 5. (gram.) número. 6. (*pl.*) aritmética. 7. (*pl.*) (mús., poét.) número, medida o cadencia; verso. 8. (fam.) modelo, muestra, espécimen, ej., *the saleswoman showed me a pretty n. in silk,* la vendedora me mostró un lindo modelo en seda. 9. (*pl.*) (t. **numbers game**) lotería ilegal. 10. **any n. of,** muchos; **back n.,** ejemplar atrasado o pasado; (fig.) antigualla, vejestorio (persona o cosa); **beyond n.,** muchísimos; **by the numbers,** de manera mecánica o rigurosa; (mil.) de uno en uno, en fila india; **his n. went up,** le llegó su hora, murió; **(he) is not of our n.,** no es uno de nosotros; **n. one,** uno mismo, sí mismo; el más importante (en un oficio u ocupación); **opposite n.,** contraparte; **round numbers,** cifras redondas; **to have** (o **get**) **somebody's n.,** adivinar las verdaderas intenciones de alguien; **to make up the n.,** hacer número, llenar el cupo; **to take care of n. one,** velar por sí mismo, cuidarse; **to the n. of (80,** etc.), hasta el número (80, etc.); **without n.,** sin número, incontable. —*v.t.* 1. contar, ej., *his days are numbered,* tiene sus días contados. 2. numerar. 3. computar; incluir en, contar entre, ej., *to be numbered among,* hallarse entre, contarse entre. 4. ascender a. —*v.i.* 1. (con *in*) ascender (a). 2. contar.
numberless [-ləs] *a.* innumerable, incontable.
number plate, (aut.) placa con la matrícula, chapa de número.
number pool, numbers game, (una especie de) lotería ilegal.
numbfish ['nʌm,fɪʃ] *s.* (ict.) raya eléctrica.
numbing ['nʌmɪŋ] *a.* entumecedor, entorpecedor, aturdidor.
numbles ['nʌmbəlz] *s. pl.* (ant.) asaduras, esp. de venado.
numbly ['nʌmlɪ] *adv.* 1. de manera aterida o entorpecida. 2. aturdidamente; con pasmo.
numbness [-nəs] *s.* 1. aterimiento, entumecimiento; entorpecimiento. 2. atontamiento, aturdimiento.
numbskull, *var. de* **numskull.**
numen ['numən, B 'nju-] *s.* (*pl.* NUMINA [-mənə]) (relig.) numen.
numerable ['numərəbəl, B 'nju-] *a.* numerable.
numeral [-mərəl] *a.* numeral, numérico, numerario. —*s.* 1. número, cifra, guarismo. 2. **numerals,** (E.U.) números (pertenecientes al año de estudios, escolar o universitario) usados como signo de distinción en alguna actividad, esp. deportes.
numerary [-mə,rerɪ, B -rərɪ] *a.* numerario, relativo a números.
numerate [-,reɪt] *v.t.* enumerar, contar.
numeration [,numə'reɪʃən, B ,nju-] *s.* 1. numeración; enumeración; cálculo; cuenta; censo. 2. (mat.) numeración.
numerator ['numə,reɪtər, B 'nju-ə] *s.* numerador; (mat.) numerador.
numerical [nu'merɪkəl, B nju-] *a.* numérico.
numerically [-kəlɪ] *adv.* numéricamente.
numerical value, (mat.) valor numérico.
numerology [,numə'rɑlədʒɪ, B ,njumə'rɔl-] *s.* numerología.
numerous ['numərəs, B 'nju-] *a.* numeroso, abundante.
numerously [-lɪ] *adv.* numerosamente, abundantemente.
numerousness [-nəs] *s.* numerosidad, abundancia.
Numidian [nu'mɪdɪən, B nju-] *a.* númida, numídico. —*s.* númida, miembro de un antiguo pueblo de África del Norte (hoy parte de Argelia).
numinous ['numənəs, B 'nju-] *a.* 1. sobrenatural, misterioso. 2. espiritualizado, agraciado. 3. espiritual, inmaterial.
numismatic [,numəz'mætɪk, B ,nju-] *a.* numismático.
numismatics [-ɪks] *s. pl.* (*sing. en const.*) numismática, ciencia que trata de las monedas y medallas.
numismatist [nu'mɪzmətəst, B nju-] *s.* numismático.

numismatology [-ˌmɪzmə'tɑlədʒɪ, B -'tɔl-] *s.* numismatología.
nummular ['nʌmjələr, B -lə] *a.* (med.) numular.
nummulite [-ˌlaɪt] *s.* (pal.) numulita.
nummulitic [ˌnʌmjə'lɪtɪk] *a.* (pal.) numulítico.
numskull ['nʌmˌskʌl] *s.* (fam.) tonto, bobalicón, mentecato, zopenco.
nun [nʌn] *s.* 1. monja, religiosa. 2. (orn.) paloma de toca, paloma monjil.
nun buoy, boya cónica, boya de doble cono.
nunciature ['nʌnsɪətʃər, 'nʊn-, B 'nʌn-tʃə] *s.* (relig.) nunciatura.
nuncio ['nʌnsɪˌoʊ, 'nʊn-, B 'nʌnʃɪ-] *s.* (relig.) nuncio, nuncio apostólico.
nuncle ['nʌŋkəl] *s.* (dial.) tío.
nuncupative ['nʌŋkjʊˌpeɪtɪv, nʌŋ'kjupətɪv] *a.* (der.) nuncupativo, abierto (díc. de los testamentos).
nunlike ['nʌnˌlaɪk] *a.* monjil (propio de monjas).
nunnery ['nʌnərɪ] *s.* convento de monjas.
nun's veiling, velo de monja, velo de lanilla fina.
nuptial ['nʌpʃəl] *a.* nupcial, matrimonial. —*s.* (*gen. pl.*) nupcias; matrimonio.
nurl, *var. de* **knurl.**
nurse [nɜrs, B nɜs] *s.* 1. nodriza; niñera, aya, ama. 2. enfermera. 3. (billar) carambola suave (ejecutada con el fin de mantener las bolas juntas). 4. (ento.) obrera (abeja, hormiga) que cuida a las larvas. 5. (ant.) protector, padrino, fomentador. —*v.t.* 1. criar, lactar, amamantar; alimentar. 2. cuidar, asistir (niños, enfermos, inválidos, etc.). 3. proteger, preservar, resguardar. 4. alimentar, fomentar; cultivar, abrigar (rencor, odio, etc.). 5. curar, tratar, medicamentar. 6. mimar, acariciar. 7. (billar) mantener (las bolas) juntas (durante una serie de carambolas). —*v.i.* 1. dar de mamar, lactar. 2. actuar o servir de enfermera, nodriza o niñera.
nurse-child ['nɜrsˌtʃaɪld, B 'nɜs-] *s.* niño de teta.
nurseling, *var. de* **nursling.**
nursemaid [-ˌmeɪd] *s.* niñera, aya.
nurser [-ər, B -ə] *s.* cuidador, cuidadora.
nursery ['nɜrsərɪ, B 'nɜs-] *s.* 1. cuarto de los niños. 2. guardería (de niños). 3. (fig.) cuna, semillero (de ideas, etc.). 4. (agr.) vivero, almácigo, semillero. 5. (ant.) crianza de niños ajenos.
nurserymaid [-ˌmeɪd, B 'nɜsrɪ-] *var. de* **nursemaid.**
nurseryman [-mən] *s.* (agr.) dueño o cuidador de semillero, vivero o almácigo.
nursery rhyme, versos infantiles.
nursery school, escuela de párvulos, jardín de la infancia, parvulario (Am.).
nurse-ship ['nɜrsˌʃɪp, B 'nɜs-] *s.* (**mar.**) buque nodriza.
nursing bottle [-ɪŋ-] biberón, mamadera (Amer.), tetero (Amer.).
nursing home, hogar de ancianos; (*for convalescence*) clínica de reposo.
nursling ['nɜrslɪŋ, B 'nɜs-] *s.* niño de teta, mamón.
nurture ['nɜrtʃər, B 'nɜtʃə] *s.* 1. crianza, educación. 2. nutrimiento, nutrición, alimento. —*v.t.* 1. alimentar, nutrir. 2. fomentar. 3. educar, criar, formar.
nut [nʌt] *s.* 1. nuez. 2. tuerca. 3. (mús.) ceja, cejilla (del violín). 4. (jer.) coco, cabeza; tipo, sujeto, individuo; chiflado, excéntrico, loco. 5. (*pl.*) (vulg., jer.) testículos, cocos, bolas (Amer.). 6. **a hard n. to crack,** un hueso duro de roer; persona difícil; **to be off one's n.,** (jer.) estar loco. —*v.t.* (*pret., p.p.* NUTTED; *p.pr.* NUTTING) recoger nueces.
nutant ['nutənt, B 'njut-] *a.* (bot.) nutante.
nutation [nu'teɪʃən, B nju-] *s.* (med., astr., bot.) nutación.
nut-brown ['nʌtˌbraʊn] *a.* castaño claro, marrón claro (Amer.).
nut butter, manteca o mantequilla de nueces.
nutcracker [-ˌkrækər, B -ə] *s.* 1. (t. *pl.*) cascanueces (instrumento). 2. (orn.) cascanueces.
nut-driver [-ˌdraɪvər, B -və] *s.* (mec.) aprietatuercas.
nutgall [-ˌgɔl] *s.* (bot.) cecidia, agalia.
nuthatch [-ˌhætʃ] *s.* (orn.) trepatroncos, sítido.
nut house, (jer., E.U.) manicomio.
nutlet ['nʌtlət] *s.* 1. nuececita, nuez pequeña. 2. (bot.) nuececilla.
nutmeg [-ˌmɛg] *s.* 1. nuez moscada. 2. (bot.) mirística (árbol).
nutmeg geranium, (bot.) geranio de malva.
nutmeg melon, (bot.) melón amarillo.
nut oil, aceite de nueces.
nutpick ['nʌtˌpɪk] *s.* utensilio de mesa para sacar la carne de la nuez.
nut pine, (bot.) pino doncel, pino manso, pino piñonero.
nutria ['nutrɪə, B 'nju-] *s.* 1. (zool.) coipo, nutria (Amer.) 2. piel de coipo.
nutrient ['nutrɪənt, B 'nju-] *a.* nutriente, nutricio, nutritivo. —*s.* alimento o substancia nutritiva.
nutriment [-trəmənt] *s.* nutrimento, alimento.
nutrition [nu'trɪʃən, B nju-] *s.* nutrición, alimentación, nutrimento.
nutritional [-əl] *a.* alimenticio.
nutritionist [-əst] *s.* especialista en nutrición.
nutritious [nu'trɪʃəs, B nju-] *a.* nutricio, nutritivo.
nutritiously [-lɪ] *adv.* nutritivamente.
nutritiousness [-nəs] *s.* valor nutritivo; lo nutritivo.
nutritive ['nutrətɪv, B 'nju-] *a.* nutritivo, nutricio.
nutritively [-lɪ] *adv.* nutritivamente.
nutritiveness [-nəs] *s.* valor nutritivo; lo nutritivo.
nuts [nʌts] (jer.) *a.* loco, chiflado; **to be n. (about),** estar loco o chiflado (por). —*interj.* ¡qué idiotez! ¡qué tontería! ¡naranjas!
nutshell ['nʌtˌʃɛl] *s.* 1. cáscara de nuez o avellana. 2. **in a n.,** en pocas palabras.
nutter ['nʌtər, B -ə] *s.* recolector de nueces.
nuttiness [-ɪnəs] *s.* 1. (jer.) locura, chifladura. 2. sabor a nueces.
nutting [-ɪŋ] *s.* recolección de nueces.
nutty [-ɪ] *a.* 1. abundante en nueces. 2. de sabor a nueces. 3. estimulante, picante. 4. (jer.) loco, raro, chiflado. 5. (jer., G.B.) elegante. 6. **n. as a fruitcake,** (jer.) loco de atar, loco de remate; **n. (over** o **about),** loco (por).
nut weevil, (ento.) cariedón.
nux vomica ['nʌks'vɑmɪkə, B -'vɔm-] (bot.) nuez vómica (árbol y semilla).
nuzzle ['nʌzəl] *v.t.* 1. hocicar; frotar la nariz contra. 2. (ant.) cuidar, criar. —*v.i.* hozar, hocicar; acurrucarse, arroparse; arrimarse cómodamente.
NW *abrev. de* **northwest,** noroeste (NO.).
NWbN *abrev. de* **northwest by north,** noroeste cuarta al norte.
NWbW *abrev. de* **northwest by west,** noroeste cuarta al oeste.
N.Y. *abrev. de* **New York,** estado de Nueva York (E.U.).
N.Y.C. *abrev. de* **New York City,** Ciudad de Nueva York.
nyctalopia [ˌnɪktə'loʊpɪə] *s.* (med.) nictalopía.
nyctalopic [-'lɑpɪk, B -'lɔp-] *a.* (med.) nictálope.
nylon ['naɪlɑn, B -lən] *s.* 1. nilón, nailon (Amer.). 2. (*pl.*) medias de nilón.
nymph [nɪmf] *s.* 1. (mitol., fig.) ninfa. 2. (*t.* **nympha** ['nɪmfə]) (zool.) ninfa, crisálida.
Nymphaeaceae [ˌnɪmfɪ'eɪsɪˌi] *s. pl.* (bot.) ninfeáceas.
nymphaeaceous [-'eɪʃəs] *a.* (bot.) ninfeáceo.
nymphal ['nɪmfəl] *a.* (zool.) ninfal.
nymphalid ['nɪmfələd] *s., a.* (zool.) ninfálido.
nymphet [nɪm'fɛt] *s.* muchacha adolescente, sexualmente precoz.
nympholepsy ['nɪmfəˌlɛpsɪ] *s.* entusiasmo demoníaco, frenesí por un ideal inalcanzable.
nymphomania [ˌnɪmfə'meɪnɪə] *s.* (med.) ninfomanía.
nymphomaniac [-ˌæk] (med.) *a.* ninfomaníaco. —*s.* ninfómana.
NYSE *abrev. de* **New York Stock Exchange,** Bolsa de Valores de Nueva York.
nystagmic [nɪs'tægmɪk] *a.* (med.) nistágmico.
nystagmus [-məs] *s.* (med.) nistagmo.

O

O [oʊ] *s.* 1. o, decimoquinta letra del alfabeto inglés. 2. cero. 3. nulidad.
O' [ə-] prefijo que en los apellidos irlandeses quiere decir "descendiente de", ej., *O'Reilly, O'Neil.* — **o'** *prep.* (dial.) *forma abrev. de* **of,** de; (poét.) **on,** sobre, encima, más allá.
O [oʊ] *interj., var. de* **oh.**
O. *abrev. de* **Ohio,** Ohio (E.U.).
oaf [oʊf] *s.* (*pl.* OAFS u OAVES [oʊvz]) 1. simplón, tonto, papanatas. 2. patán, zoquete, palurdo. 3. (ant.) niño contrahecho o idiota.
oafish ['oʊfɪʃ] *a.* tonto, lerdo, estúpido; zafio, tosco, grosero, simplote.
oafishly [-lɪ] *adv.* estúpidamente; toscamente.
oafishness [-nəs] *s.* torpeza, estupidez; grosería.
oak [oʊk] *s.* 1. (bot.) roble. 2. corona o guirnalda de roble. 3. (jer., G.B.) puerta (gen. de roble) esp. en: **to sport one's o.,** cerrar la puerta (para no recibir visitantes). 4. **the oaks,** (G.B.) (nombre de) carrera para yeguas de tres años (en Epsom). —*a.* de roble; **o. grove,** robledo, robledar, encinar; **o. moss,** liquen que crece en los robles.
oak apple, o. gall, bugalla, agalla del roble.
oak chestnut, roble albar.
oaken ['oʊkən] *a.* 1. de roble, hecho de roble. 2. duro, fuerte, roblizo.
oak-leaf cluster ['oʊkˌlif-] (E.U.) guirnalda de bronce o plata (que imita las hojas y bellotas de roble) que se añade a una condecoración militar.
oak leather, cuero curtido con corteza de roble.
oak spangle, agalla, bugalla del roble.
oak-tanned [-ˌtænd] *a.* curtido con corteza de roble.
oakum ['oʊkəm] *s.* (mar.) estopa, malacuenda.
oaky ['oʊkɪ] *a.* 1. duro, fuerte, roblizo. 2. abundante en robles.
oar [ɔr, B ɔ] *s.* 1. remo. 2. remero, remador. 3. **lie on your oars!** (mars.) ¡alza!; **oars! down oars!** (mar.) ¡dentro!; **he pulls a good o.,** es un buen remero; **to be chained to the o.,** (fam.) trabajar como un galeote; **to have an o. in every man's boat,** ser muy entrometido; **to put** (o **shove** o **stick**) **one's o. in,** meter la cuchara; **to rest on one's oars,** tomar un descanso, dejar de trabajar por un tiempo. —*v.i.* remar, bogar. —*v.t.* mover el remo, mover a remo.
oarage ['ɔrɪdʒ, B -ədʒ] *s.* palamenta, conjunto de remos.
oared [ɔrd, B ɔd] *a.* provisto de remos.
oarlock ['ɔrˌlɑk, B 'ɔˌlɔk] *s.* (mar.) chumacera, tolete, horquilla, escálamo.
oarsman ['ɔrzmən, B 'ɔz-] *s.* remero, remador, bogador, boga (Amer.).
oarsmanship [-ʃɪp] *s.* destreza en el manejo del remo; arte de remar.
oary ['ɔrɪ] *a.* (poét.) parecido a los remos.
OAS *abrev. de* **Organization of American States,** Organización de Estados Americanos (O.E.A.).
oasis [oʊ'eɪsəs] *s.* (*pl.* OASES [-ˌsiz]) oasis.
oast [oʊst] *s.* horno secador para lúpulo, malta o tabaco.
oat [oʊt] *s.* 1. (bot.) avena (planta y grano). 2. (ant.) avena, zampoña. 3. **off one's oats,** indispuesto, desganado; **to feel one's oats,** (fam.) estar muy pagado de sí mismo; sentirse brioso; **to sow one's wild oats,** correrla, calaverear, pasar las mocedades.
oatcake ['oʊtˌkeɪk] *s.* torta de harina de avena.
oaten [-ən] *a.* 1. aveníceo. 2. hecho de avena; hecho de harina de avena.
oatfield [-ˌfild] *s.* avenal.
oat grass, (bot.) avena loca, ballueca.
oath [oʊθ] *s.* (*pl.* OATHS [oʊðz]) 1. juramento. 2. blasfemia, voto, taco, terno. 3. **on o., upon o., under o.,** bajo juramento; **to administer an o.** o **to put upon o.,** tomar o hacer prestar juramento; **to take** (o **make** o **swear**) **an o.,** jurar, prestar juramento.
oath-breaking ['oʊθˌbreɪkɪŋ] *s.* violación de juramento; perjurio.
oath of allegiance, juramento de fidelidad.
oath of office, juramento al asumir un cargo.
oatmeal ['oʊtˌmil] *s.* 1. harina de avena. 2. gachas de avena. 3. cuáquer (Amer.).
oatmeal gruel, avenate (bebida).
obbligato [ˌɑblə'gɑtoʊ, B ˌɔb-] *s.* (*pl.* OBBLIGATOS u OBBLIGATI [-ɪ]) 1. (mús.) obligado. 2. (fig.) motivo recurrente, fondo persistente.
obconic [ɑb'kɑnɪk, B ɔb'kɔn-] *a.* (bot.) obcónico.
obcordate [-'kɔrˌdeɪt, B -'kɔˌ-] *a.* (bot.) obcordiforme.
obduracy ['ɑbdərəsɪ, B 'ɔbdjʊ-] *s.* obduración, obstinación, terquedad; impenitencia, dureza de corazón.
obdurate [-rət] *a.* 1. obstinado, inexorable, terco. 2. empedernido; endurecido. 3. insensible, duro, intratable, huraño. 4. impenitente.
obdurately [-lɪ] *adv.* obstinadamente, tercamente.
obdurateness [-nəs] *s.* obstinación, obduración, terquedad.
O.B.E. *abrev. de* **Officer of the Order of the British Empire,** Oficial de la Orden del Imperio Británico.
obedience [oʊ'bidɪəns] *s.* 1. obediencia, docilidad, sumisión. 2. (relig.) obediencia.
obedient [-ənt] *a.* obediente, sumiso, dócil.
obediently [-lɪ] *adv.* obedientemente, dócilmente.
obeisance [oʊ'beɪsəns] *s.* 1. reverencia, inclinación, zalema. 2. deferencia; homenaje; cortesía.
obeisant [-ənt] *a.* deferente; obsequioso.
obeliscal [ˌɑbə'lɪskəl, B ˌɔb-] *a.* obeliscal, de obelisco.
obelisk ['ɑbəˌlɪsk, B 'ɔb-] *s.* obelisco; (impr.) obelisco, obelo.
obelize [-ˌlaɪz] *v.t.* (impr.) señalar con un obelisco.
obelus [-ləs] *s.* (*pl.* OBELI [-ˌlaɪ]) (impr.) obelo (señal de referencia).
obese [oʊ'bis] *a.* obeso, gordo.
obesity [oʊ'bisətɪ] *s.* obesidad, gordura.
obey [oʊ'beɪ, ə-] *v.t.* obedecer, cumplir, acatar, respetar, observar. —*v.i.* ser obediente.
obeyer [-ər, B -ə] *s.* obedecedor.
obfuscate ['ɑbfəsˌkeɪt, ɑb'fʌs-, B 'ɔbfʌs-] *v.t.* 1. ofuscar, oscurecer. 2. (fig.) ofuscar, confundir (ideas, a alguien, etc.); obcecar, cegar.
obfuscation [ˌɑbfʌs'keɪʃən, B ˌɔb-] *s.* 1. ofuscación. 2. obcecación, ceguera.
obfuscatory [ɑb'fʌskəˌtɔrɪ, B ɔb-tərɪ] *a.* ofuscador.
obi ['oʊbɪ] *s.* 1. obi (cinturón ancho que los japoneses usan sobre el kimono). 2. obi, sortilegio practicado en África, las Antillas, etc. 3. obi, fetiche usado en esas ocasiones, t. llamado **obeah.**
obiism [-ˌɪzəm] *s.* tipo de fetichismo.
obit [oʊ'bɪt, 'oʊbət, B 'ɔbɪt] *s.* obituario, exequias, registro de defunciones.
obiter dictum [ˌoʊbətər'dɪktəm, B 'ɔbɪtə'-] (*pl.* OBITER DICTA [-tə]) opinión accesoria, opinión incidental.
obituary [ə'bɪtʃʊˌɛrɪ, B ə'bɪtjʊərɪ] *s.* (*pl.* OBITUARIES) necrología, obituario. —*a.* necrológico.
obituary card, esquela de defunción.
object [əb'dʒɛkt] *v.t.* 1. (gen. con *that*) objetar (que), oponer el reparo de (que). 2. (ant.) oponer, interponer, exponer; aducir —*v.i.* (gen. con *to*) oponerse (a), desaprobar, tener inconveniente (en).
object ['ɑbdʒɪkt, B 'ɔb-] *s.* 1. objeto, cosa. 2. objeto, fin, propósito. 3. objeto. materia (de ciencia, pensamiento, etc.). 4. (gram.) complemento, objeto. 5. **with the o. of,** con el objeto de.
object ball, (billar) mingo, primera bola tocada por la bola jugadora.
object glass, object lens, (ópt) objetivo.
objectify [əb'dʒɛktəˌfaɪ, B ɔb-] *v.t.* (*pret., p.p.* OBJECTIFIED; *p.pr.* OBJECTIFYING) objetivar, exteriorizar.
objection [əb'dʒɛkʃən] *s.* objeción, reparo, inconveniente; **to have no objections to (doing),** no tener inconvenientes en (hacer); **to have no objections,** no tener nada que objetar; **to raise an o.,** plantear una objeción, hacer un reparo.
objectionable [-ʃənəbəl] *a.* 1. objetable, impugnable, censurable, reprensible. 2. ofensivo, desagradable, indeseable, molesto, inconveniente.
objectivate [-'dʒɛktəˌveɪt] *v.t.* objetivar; exteriorizar.
objective [-'dʒɛktɪv] *a.* objetivo; (gram.) objetivo, complementario; (med.) objetivo. —*s.* 1. objetivo, propósito, objeto, fin, meta, blanco. 2. (filos.) lo objetivo. 3. (gram.) (caso) objetivo. 4. (ópt.) objetivo.
objectively [-lɪ] *adv.* objetivamente.
objectiveness [-nəs] *s.* objetividad.
objective plane, (mil.) plano objetivo.
objective point, meta, punto objetivo.
objective slide, cursor del objetivo.
objective zone, (mil.) zona de blanco.
objectivism [əb'dʒɛktəvˌɪzəm] *s.* (filos.) objetivismo.
objectivity [ˌɑbdʒɛk'tɪvətɪ, B ˌɔb-] *s.* objetividad.
object lesson, lección o demostración práctica.
objector [əb'dʒɛktər, B -tə] *s.* objetante, impugnador.
objet d'art [ˌɔbˌʒeɪ'dɑr, B -'dɑ] objeto de arte.
objurgate ['ɑbdʒərˌgeɪt, B 'ɔbdʒəˌ-] *v.t.* increpar, censurar, reprender, reconvenir, reprobar.

objurgation [ˌɑbdʒər'geɪʃən, B ˌɔbdʒə'-] *s.* increpación censura, reconvención, reprimenda.
objurgator ['ɑbdʒərˌgeɪtər, B 'ɔbdʒəˌ-tə] *s.* increpador, censurador, reprendedor.
objurgatory [əb'dʒɜrgəˌtɔrɪ, B ɔb'dʒɜ-gətərɪ] *a.* increpante, censurante.
oblanceolate [ɑb'lænsɪəˌleɪt, B ɔb-lɪt] *a.* (bot.) inversamente lanceolado.
oblate ['ɑbˌleɪt, B 'ɔb-] *a.* 1. (relig.) oblato. 2. (geom.) achatado (por los polos). —*s.* (relig.) oblato.
oblation [ə'bleɪʃən, oʊ-] *s.* 1. oblación. 2. (relig.) oblata (dinero que se da por razón del gasto de vino, hostias, etc.).
oblatory ['ɑbləˌtɔrɪ, B 'ɔblətərɪ] *a.* oblativo.
obligate ['ɑbləˌgeɪt, B 'ɔb-] *v.t.* obligar, constreñir, comprometer, ligar; **o. oneself to (do),** obligarse a (hacer). — [-lɪgət] *a.* 1. esencial, necesario. 2. (biol.) ligado (organismo parásito).
obligation [ˌɑblə'geɪʃən, B ˌɔb-] *s.* obligación; (der., com.) obligación; **of o.,** de precepto, obligatorio; **to be under (an) o. to (do),** estar bajo obligación de, estar obligado a (hacer); **to put** (o **place**) **under an o.,** imponer una obligación a, hacer favores.
obligator ['ɑbləˌgeɪtər, B 'ɔb-ə] *s.* obligado, deudor.
obligatorily [əˌblɪgə'tɔrəlɪ, ə'blɪgəˌtɔr-, B ɔ-tər-] *adv.* obligatoriamente, de manera obligatoria.
obligatory [ə'blɪgəˌtɔrɪ, 'ɑblɪgə-, B ɔ'blɪgətərɪ] *a.* obligatorio, compulsorio, forzoso.
oblige [ə'blaɪdʒ] *v.t.* 1. obligar, constreñir, precisar. 2. obligar, hacer un favor a, complacer. 3. (ant.) agradar. 4. **much obliged,** muy agradecido, muchas gracias; **to be obliged for,** estar agradecido por; **to be obliged to (someone),** estar o verse obligado a (alguien); **you will o. me,** me hará un gran favor, le agradeceré mucho.
obligee [ˌɑblə'dʒi, B ˌɔb-] *s.* 1. (der.) acreedor; tenedor de una obligación; aquel con quien uno está obligado, el fiador de otro. 2. (raro) persona favorecida.
obliger [ə'blaɪdʒər, B -ə] *s.* (der.) el que obliga.
obliging [-dʒɪŋ] *a.* 1. servicial, complaciente; obsequioso, cortés. 2. (ant.) obligatorio, forzoso.
obligingly [-lɪ] *adv.* servicialmente.
obligor [ˌɑblə'gɔr, B ˌɔblɪ'gɔ] *s.* (der.) obligado, deudor, el que se obliga.
oblique [oʊ'blik, ə-] *a.* 1. oblicuo, sesgado, diagonal, inclinado. 2. ambiguo, indirecto; evasivo, solapado, insincero, doloso. 3. colateral (parentesco). 4. (anat.) oblicuo (díc. de ciertos músculos). [-'blaɪk, B -'blik] *v.i.* (mil.) oblicuar, marchar o avanzar oblicuamente.
oblique angle, (geom.) ángulo oblicuo.
oblique case, (gram.) caso oblicuo.
oblique cone, (geom.) cono oblicuo.
obliquely [-lɪ] *adv.* 1. oblicuamente, sesgadamente. 2. ambiguamente, indirectamente; evasivamente, solapadamente, con rodeos.
obliqueness [-nəs] *s.* 1. oblicuidad, sesgo, inclinación. 2. ambigüedad, rodeo, falta de rectitud. 3. (arq.) aberración, esviaje.
oblique sailing, (mar.) navegación oblicua, navegación por bordadas.
oblique sphere, (astr.) esfera oblicua.
oblique triangle, (mat.) triángulo oblicuángulo.
obliquity [oʊ'blɪkwətɪ, ə-] *s.* (*pl.* OBLIQUITIES) 1. oblicuidad, sesgo, inclinación; divergencia. 2. ambages, rodeo, circunloquio. 3. (astr.) oblicuidad (de la eclíptica).
obliterate [ə'blɪtəˌreɪt, oʊ-, B ə-] *v.t.* 1. borrar, tachar; testar, matar (sello). 2. arrasar, destruir, desvanecer. 3. (med.) obliterar.
obliteration [-ˌblɪtə'reɪʃən] *s.* 1. borradura, tachadura, testadura, cancelación. 2. arrasamiento, destrucción, extinción. 3. (med.) obliteración, extirpación.
obliterator [-'blɪtəˌreɪtər, B -ə] *s.* 1. matasellos. 2. persona o cosa que arrasa o anula.
oblivion [ə'blɪvɪən] *s.* 1. olvido. 2. amnistía, perdón. 3. **to cast into o.,** echar (o relegar) al olvido.
oblivious [-əs] *a.* 1. olvidadizo, abstraído, absorto. 2. (con *of*) sin recordar, sin pensar en, ej., *o. of past offenses,* sin recordar ofensas anteriores, *o. of the crowd around him,* sin pensar en la muchedumbre que lo rodeaba. 3. que olvida o que causa olvido.
obliviously [-lɪ] *adv.* sin recordar, inconscientemente, con olvido.
obliviousness [-nəs] *s.* falta de memoria, olvido.
oblong ['ɑblɔŋ, B 'ɔb-] *a.* oblongo, apaisado; (geom.) oblongo. —*s.* figura oblonga o apaisada.
obloquy ['ɑbləkwɪ, B 'ɔb-] *s.* (*pl.* OBLOQUIES) 1. vilipendio, denigración, calumnia, difamación. 2. infamia, baldón, descrédito.
obnoxious [ɑb'nɑkʃəs, əb-, B -'nɔk-] *a.* 1. odioso, detestable, ofensivo, molesto, aborrecible. 2. expuesto o sujeto a (daño, censura, etc.). 3. (fig.) malsano, dañino.
obnoxiously [-lɪ] *adv.* odiosamente, detestablemente, ofensivamente.
obnoxiousness [-nəs] *adv.* odiosidad.
obnubilate [ɑb'nubəˌleɪt, B ɔb'nju-] *v.t.* obnubilar, obcecar.
obnubilation [ɑbˌnubə'leɪʃən, B ˌɔbnju-] *s.* obnubilación, obcecación.
oboe ['oʊˌboʊ] *s.* (mús.) oboe.
oboist ['oʊˌboʊəst] *s.* oboísta, oboe (músico).
obol ['ɑbəl, B 'ɔbɔl] *s.* (hist.) óbolo, peso y moneda de la Grecia antigua.
obovate [ɑb'oʊveɪt, B ɔb-] *a.* (bot.) obovado, trasovado.
obovoid [-ˌvɔɪd] *a.* (bot.) obovoide, trasovoide.
obreption [ɑ'brɛpʃən, B ɔ-] *s.* (der.) obrepción.
obreptitious [ˌɑbrɛp'tɪʃəs, B ˌɔ-] *a.* obrepticio.
obreptitiously [-lɪ] *adv.* obrepticiamente.
obs. *abrev. de* **obsolete,** obsoleto.
obscene [ɑb'sin, əb-, B əb-] *a.* 1. obsceno, impúdico; soez, indecente. 2. repugnante, repulsivo.
obscenely [-lɪ] *adv.* 1. obscenamente. 2. suciamente.
obsceneness [-nəs] *s.* obscenidad, indecencia.
obscenity [ɑb'sɛnətɪ, B əb'sinə-] *s.* (*pl.* OBSCENITIES) obscenidad.
obscurant [ɑb'skjʊrənt, əb-, B ɔb'skjʊər-]
obscurantic [ˌɑbskjə'ræntɪk, B ˌɔb-] *a.* obscurantista.
obscurantism [-ˌɪzəm] *s.* obscurantismo.
obscurantist [-əst] *s.* obscurantista.
obscuration [ˌɑbskjə'reɪʃən, B ˌɔb-] *s.* obscurecimiento.
obscure [ɑb'skjʊr, B əb'skjʊə] *a.* 1. obscuro, tenebroso, lóbrego. 2. obscuro, abstruso, oculto. 3. obscuro, humilde, desconocido. 4. obscuro, confuso, vago, indistinto. 5. (gram.) indistinto (vocal). —*v.t.* obscurecer, opacar, disimular, ocultar; anublar; confundir, **to o. the issue,** confundir el asunto (debate). —*s.* obscuridad, parte obscura.
obscurely [-lɪ] *adv.* obscuramente, confusamente.
obscureness [-nəs] *s.* 1. obscuridad. 2. vaguedad, confusión. 3. ambigüedad.
obscurity [-'skjʊrətɪ, B -'skjʊər-] *s.* (*pl.* OBSCURITIES) obscuridad.
obsecrate ['ɑbsəˌkreɪt, B 'ɔb-] *v.t.* (ant.) obsecrar, rogar, invocar, suplicar, implorar.
obsecration [ˌɑbsə'kreɪʃən, B ˌɔb-] *s.* obsecración, ruego, súplica, imploración.
obsequies ['ɑbsəkwɪz, B 'ɔb-] *pl. de* **obsequy.**
obsequious [əb'sikwɪəs, ɑb-, B əb-] *a.* 1. obsequioso, servil, zalamero. 2. (raro) dócil, sumiso, devoto.
obsequiously [-lɪ] *adv.* obsequiosamente; servilmente.
obsequiousness [-nəs] *s.* obsequiosidad; servilismo.
obsequy ['ɑbsəkwɪ, B 'ɔb-] *s.* (*pl.* OBSEQUIES) (*ú. sólo en pl.*) exequias, honras fúnebres.
observable [əb'zɜrvəbəl, B -'zɜvə-] *a.* observable, notable, visible, perceptible.
observably [-blɪ] *adv.* conspicuamente, notablemente, visiblemente, perceptiblemente.
observance [əb'zɜrvəns, B -'zɜvəns] *s.* 1. observancia, cumplimiento. 2. rito, ceremonia. 3. práctica, uso, costumbre. 4. observación, atención. 5. **O.,** (relig.) observancia.
observant [-vənt] *a.* (fr.) 1. observador, atento. 2. cuidadoso, mirado, atento. 3. **to be o. of,** fijarse en, prestar atención a; acatar, respetar. —*s.* 1. (relig.) **O.,** observante. 2. (ant.) servidor o criado obsequioso.
observantine [-vəntɪn] *s.* (relig.) observante.
observantly [-lɪ] *adv.* 1. con cuidado, cautelosamente. 2. con atención.
observation [ˌɑbzər'veɪʃən, B ˌɔbzə'-] *s.* 1. observación, escrutinio; examen, estudio. 2. observación, comentario. 3. (ant.) observancia. 4. **to escape o.,** evitar ser visto, no ser observado; **to keep under o.,** tener en observación, vigilar, no perder de vista; **under o.,** bajo observación (examen).
observation balloon, globo de observación.
observation car, (f.c.) coche panorámico.
observatory [əb'zɜrvəˌtɔrɪ, B -'zɜvətrɪ] *s.* 1. observatorio (astronómico, etc.). 2. atalaya, mirador, otero.
observe [əb'zɜrv, B -'zɜv] *v.t.* 1. observar, cumplir, acatar; guardar (fiestas, silencio). 2. observar, advertir, reparar, notar. 3. observar, vigilar, mirar, atisbar. —*v.i.* 1. notar, percatarse. 2. (gen. con *on, upon*) comentar, hacer comentarios (sobre).
observer [-'zɜrvər, B -'zɜvə] *s.* observador.
observing [-vɪŋ] *a.* 1. observador, atento, cuidadoso. 2. observante.
observingly [-lɪ] *adv.* atentamente, cuidadosamente.
obsess [əb'sɛs, ɑb-, B əb-] *v.t.* obsesionar, obseder, causar obsesión.
obsession [-'sɛʃən] *s.* obsesión; idea fija.
obsessive [-'sɛsɪv] *a.* obsesivo.
obsidian [əb'sɪdɪən, B ɔb-] *s.* (min.) obsidiana.
obsidional [əb'saɪdɪənəl, B -'sɪ-] *a.* (mil.) obsidional, relativo al sitio de una plaza.
obsolesce [ˌɑbsə'lɛs, B ˌɔb-] *v.i.* caer en desuso, volverse obsoleto.
obsolescence [-'lɛsəns] *s.* obsolescencia, acción de caer en desuso.
obsolescent [-ənt] *a.* obsolescente, que cae en desuso.
obsolete [ɑbsə'lit, 'ɑbsəˌlit, B 'ɔb-] *a.* 1. obsoleto, caído en desuso, fuera de uso. 2. (biol.) rudimentario, atrofiado, ausente. —*s.* (gram., ret.) voz anticuada.
obsoletely [-lɪ] *adv.* de manera o modo obsoleto.
obsoleteness [-nəs] *s.* 1. (biol.) desarrollo rudimentario o imperfecto. 2. desuso.
obstacle ['ɑbstɪkəl, B 'ɔb-] *s.* obstáculo, impedimento, obstrucción, traba, óbice, contrariedad.
obstacle course, (mil.) pista americana.
obstacle race, carrera de obstáculos.

obstetric [əb'stɛtrɪk, ɑb-, B ɔb-] **obstetrical** [-trɪkəl] *a.* obstétrico.
obstetrician [ˌɑbstə'trɪʃən, B ˌɔbstɛ-] *s.* (med.) obstétrico, tocólogo.
obstetrics [əb'stɛtrɪks, ɑb-, B ɔb-] *s. pl.* (*sing. o pl. en const.*) (med.) obstetricia, tocología.
obstinacy ['ɑbstənəsɪ, B 'ɔb-] *s.* (*pl.* OBSTINACIES) obstinación, terquedad, contumacia, testarudez, porfía, persistencia.
obstinate ['ɑbstənət, B 'ɔb-] *a.* 1. obstinado, terco, contumaz, testarudo, porfiado, pertinaz. 2. (med.) rebelde, reacio.
obstinately [-lɪ] *adv.* obstinadamente.
obstinateness [-nəs] *s.* obstinación, terquedad.
obstreperous [əb'strɛpərəs, ɑb-, B əb-] *a.* 1. estrepitoso, ruidoso. 2. turbulento, revoltoso.
obstreperously [-lɪ] *adv.* 1. turbulentamente. 2. estrepitosamente.
obstreperousness [-nəs] *s.* estrépito, bulla, alharaca.
obstruct [əb'strʌkt, ɑb-, B əb-] *v.t.* 1. obstruir, atorar, atascar, cerrar, obturar. 2. embarazar, entorpecer, dificultar, obstaculizar, impedir, estorbar; retardar.
obstructer, obstructor [-'strʌktər, B -tə] *s.* obstructor; el que impide o estorba.
obstruction [-'strʌkʃən] *s.* 1. obstrucción, obstáculo, embarazo, impedimento, estorbo. 2. obstrucción, táctica dilatoria (ej., de una minoría en una asamblea).
obstructionism [-ˌɪzəm] *s.* obstruccionismo.
obstructionist [-əst] *a., s.* obstruccionista.
obstructive [-'strʌktɪv] *a.* 1. obstructivo, obstructor. 2. (med.) opilativo.
obstruent ['ɑbstruənt, B 'ɔb-] *a.* (med.) opilativo, obstruyente.
obtain [əb'teɪn, ɑb-, B əb-] *v.t.* 1. obtener, conseguir, adquirir, poseer. 2. (ant.) lograr, alcanzar. —*v.i.* 1. estar establecido, generalizado o de moda; ser ley. 2. (ant.) prevalecer, tener éxito.
obtainable [-əbəl] *a.* obtenible, asequible.
obtainer [-ər, B -ə] *s.* 1. el que obtiene. 2. (relig.) obtentor.
obtainment [-mənt] *s.* obtención, logro, consecución.
obtected [əb'tɛktəd] *a.* (ento.) cubierto con una caparazón quitinosa (díc. de las larvas de ciertos insectos).
obtest [ɑb'tɛst, B əb-] *v.t.* 1. suplicar, implorar, rogar. 2. poner por testigo.
obtestation [ˌɑbtɛs'teɪʃən, B ˌɔb-] *s.* obtestación.
obtrude [əb'trud, ɑb-, B əb-] *v.t.* 1. extender (tentáculo, etc.). 2. exponer, ostentar (opinión, creencia, etc.). 3. introducir por la fuerza; imponer. 4. **o. oneself (into),** entrometerse o entremeterse (en), introducirse (en). —*v.i.* manifestarse.
obtruder [-ər, B -ə] *s.* entrometido, intruso.
obtrusion [-'truʒən] *s.* intrusión, entremetimiento; imposición.
obtrusive [əb'trusɪv] *a.* 1. intruso, entremetido; importuno, molesto, impertinente, atrevido; agresivo. 2. protuberante, que sobresale.
obtrusively [-lɪ] *adv.* intrusamente, impertinentemente.
obtrusiveness [-nəs] *s.* intrusión, entremetimiento, impertinencia.
obtund [ɑb'tʌnd, B əb-] *v.t.* 1. amortiguar, despuntar. 2. embotar.
obtundent [-ənt] *a., s.* obtundente, embotante.
obturate ['ɑbtəˌreɪt, B 'ɔbtjʊə-] *v.t.* obturar, tapar, cerrar.
obturation [ˌɑbtə'reɪʃən, B ˌɔbtjʊə-] *s.* obturación.
obturator ['ɑbtəˌreɪtər, B 'ɔbtjʊə-ə] *s.* obturador.
obtuse [ɑb'tus, B əb'tjus] *a.* 1. obtuso, boto, romo. 2. (fig.) obtuso, torpe, tardo (de comprensión). 3. sordo, apagado (color, ruido). 4. (geom.) obtuso.
obtuse angle, (geom.) ángulo obtuso.
obtusely [-lɪ] *adv.* obtusamente, torpemente.
obtuseness [-nəs] *s.* (fig.) obtusión; torpeza, estupidez.
obverse [ɑb'vɜrs, B 'ɔbˌvɜs] *a.* 1. obverso, vuelto de cara a, del anverso. 2. (bot.) obverso, invertido. —*s.* 1. anverso, cara (de la moneda); frente, superficie principal. 2. complemento, suplemento. 3. (lóg.) conversión.
obvert [ɑb'vɜrt, əb-, B ɔb'vɜt] *v.t.* 1. volver de frente a; dar vuelta a un objeto mostrando otra cara o superficie. 2. (lóg.) afirmar la contraparte de (una proposición).
obviate ['ɑbvɪˌeɪt, B 'ɔb-] *v.t.* obviar, contrarrestar, prevenir, evitar.
obviation [ˌɑbvɪ'eɪʃən, B ˌɔb-] *s.* prevención, contrarresto.
obvious ['ɑbvɪəs, B 'ɔb-] *a.* obvio, claro, evidente, manifiesto, patente.
obviously [-lɪ] *adv.* obviamente, claramente, evidentemente.
obviousness [-nəs] *s.* evidencia, claridad.
obvolute ['ɑbvəˌlut, B 'ɔb-] *a.* (bot.) obvoluto; sobremontado (díc. de los pétalos, hojas).
oca ['oʊkə] *s.* (bot.) oca.
ocarina [ˌɑkə'rinə, B ˌɔk-] *s.* (mús.) ocarina, instrumento de viento.
OCAS *abrev. de* **Organization of Central-American States,** Organización de Estados CentroAmericanos (O.E.C.A).
occasion [ə'keɪʒən] *s.* 1. ocasión, oportunidad, caso, circunstancia, razón, coyuntura. 2. ocasión, motivo, causa. 3. suceso, ocurrencia, experiencia. 4. (ant.) (*pl.*) necesidades, exigencias. 5. **as o. requires,** en caso necesario, cuando llegue la ocasión; **by o. of,** a consecuencia de; **I have no o. for,** no me hace falta, no necesito; **on the o. of,** con motivo de, el día de; **to be equal to the o.,** estar a la altura de las circunstancias; **to give o. to,** dar motivo o pie para; **to rise to the o.,** ponerse a la altura de las circunstancias; **on** (o **upon**) **o.,** de vez en cuando, de tiempo en tiempo. —*v.t.* ocasionar, motivar, acarrear, dar ocasión a.
occasional [-əl] *a.* 1. ocasional, fortuito, incidental; infrecuente, de ocurrencia irregular. 2. (que ocurre) de vez en cuando, una que otra vez, ej., *an o. drink won't do you any harm,* un trago de vez en cuando no le hará ningún daño, *he took an o. walk in the garden,* de vez en cuando daba un paseo por el jardín. 3. (escrito) para la ocasión. 4. improvisado.
Occasionalism [-ˌɪzəm] *s.* (filos.) ocasionalismo.
Occasionalist [-əst] *s.* (filos.) ocasionalista.
occasionally [-ɪ] *adv.* de vez en cuando, a veces, alguna que otra vez, una que otra vez.
occasioner [-ər, B -ə] *s.* 1. ocasionador, causante. 2. motivo, causa.
occident ['ɑksədənt, B 'ɔk-] *s.* 1. occidente, oeste. 2. **O.,** Occidente (conjunto de naciones del mundo occidental).
occidental [ˌɑksə'dɛntəl, B ˌɔk-] *a.* 1. occidental, del oeste. 2. **O.,** occidental, del mundo occidental.
Occidentalism [-ˌɪzəm] *s.* occidentalismo, el espíritu, cultura, costumbres, etc. del mundo occidental.
occidentalize [-ˌaɪz] *v.i., v.t.* volver occidental (en ideas o costumbres), imbuir en la cultura occidental, occidentalizar.
occidentally [-ɪ] *adv.* de manera o modo occidental.
occipital [ɑk'sɪpətəl, B ɔk-] *a.* (anat.) occipital. —*s.* (t. **o. bone**) hueso occipital.
occiput ['ɑksəˌpʌt, B 'ɔk-] *s.* (*pl.* OCCIPITA [ɑk'sɪpətə, B ɔk-]) (anat.) occipucio, colodrillo.
occlude [ə'klud, ɑ-, B ɔ-] *v.t.* 1. obstruir, cerrar, tapar. 2. (med., quím., meteor.) ocluir. —*v.i.* (odont.) ocluirse.
occluded front [-əd-] (meteor.) frente ocluído.
occlusion [ə'kluʒən, B ɔ-] *s.* (med., odont., quím., meteor., fon.) oclusión.
occlusive [-'klusɪv] *a.* oclusivo.
occult [ə'kʌlt, ɑ-, B ɔ-] *a.* 1. oculto, mágico, sobrenatural; misterioso, esotérico, ignoto. 2. (raro) escondido. —*s.* ciencias ocultas. —*v.t., v.i.* esconder(se), ocultar(se).
occultation [ˌɑkəl'teɪʃən, B ˌɔk-] *s.* 1. ocultación, escondimiento. 2. (astr.) ocultación.
occulting light [ə'kʌltɪŋ-, ɑ-, B ɔ-] luz intermitente (de faros).
occultism [ə'kʌltɪzəm, 'ɑkəl-, B 'ɔk-] *s.* ocultismo.
occultist [-təst] *s., a.* ocultista.
occupancy ['ɑkjəpənsɪ, B 'ɔk-] *s.* (*pl.* OCCUPANCIES). 1. ocupación; toma de posesión. 2. (der.) ocupación, tenencia (de bienes mostrencos).
occupant [-pənt] *s.* 1. ocupante, inquilino. 2. (der.) ocupador.
occupation [ˌɑkjə'peɪʃən, B ˌɔk-] *s.* 1. ocupación, tenencia; posesión. 2. ocupación, trabajo, tarea, quehacer, empleo, profesión, vocación.
occupational [-əl] *a.* ocupacional; de trabajo, relativo al oficio o empleo.
occupational accident, accidente de trabajo.
occupational disease, (med.) enfermedad profesional.
occupational therapist, terapeuta ocupacional.
occupational therapy, (med.) terapia ocupacional; ergoterapia.
occupied ['ɑkjəˌpaɪd, B 'ɔk-] *a.* 1. ocupado, atareado. 2. ocupado (lugar).
occupier [-ˌpaɪər, B -ə] *s.* ocupante; inquilino.
occupy ['ɑkjəˌpaɪ, B 'ɔk-] *v.t.* 1. ocupar, tomar posesión de, apoderarse de, conquistar. 2. ocupar, llenar (espacio, tiempo). 3. residir en, vivir en, habitar (casa, etc.). 4. **o. oneself with** (o **in**), ocuparse en; **to be occupied with,** estar ocupado o atareado en.
occur [ə'kɜr, B -'kɜ] *v.i.* (*pret., p.p.* OCCURRED; *p.pr.* OCCURRING) 1. ocurrir, suceder, acaecer, acontecer. 2. ocurrir, venir a la mente.
occurrence [-əns, -'kʌrəns, B -'kʌ-] *s.* ocurrencia, suceso, incidente, acontecimiento, caso, lance; **a frequent o.,** un caso frecuente.
occurrent [-ənt] *a.* 1. corriente, común. 2. casual, fortuito, incidental.
ocean ['oʊʃən] *s.* 1. océano. 2. (fig.) **mar.** 3. **oceans of,** (fig.) la mar de, infinidad de.
oceanarium [ˌoʊʃə'nɛrɪəm, B -'nɛər-] *s.* acuario grande de agua salada (para peces, plantas, etc. marinos).
ocean chart, (mar.) mapa marino, carta de navegar, carta de marear.
oceangoing ['oʊʃənˌgoʊɪŋ] *a.* de navegación oceánica, transatlántico.
Oceania [ˌoʊʃɪ'eɪnɪə] *s.* (geog.) Oceanía.
oceanic [ˌoʊʃɪ'ænɪk] *a.* oceánico.
ocean liner, transatlántico.
oceanographer [ˌoʊʃə'nɑgrəfər, B -ʃjə'nɔgrəfə] *s.* oceanógrafo.

oceanographic [-nəˈgræfɪk] **oceanographical** [-ɪkəl] *a.* oceanográfico.
oceanography [-ˈnɑgrəfɪ, B -ˈnɔg-] *s.* oceanografía.
ocellar [oʊˈsɛlər, B -ə] *a.* (zool.) ocelar.
ocellate [ˈɑsəˌleɪt, B ˈɔsəlɪt] **ocellated** [-əd] *a.* 1. (zool.) ocelado. 2. manchado, ocelado.
ocellus [oʊˈsɛləs] *s.* (*pl.* OCELLI [-aɪ]) (zool.) ocelo.
ocelot [ˈɑsəˌlɑt, B ˈoʊsɪˌlɔt] *s.* (zool.) ocelote, tigrillo.
ocher [ˈoʊkər, B -kə] *s.* 1. (min.) ocre. 2. ocre, ocre amarillo (color). —*v.t.* teñir con ocre.
ocherous [-kərəs] *a.* ocroso, que tiene ocre.
ochlocracy [ɑˈklɑkrəsɪ, B ɔˈklɔk-] *s.* (pol.) oclocracia (gobierno de la plebe).
ochlocrat [ˈɑkləˌkræt, B ˈɔk-] *a., s.* partidario de la oclocracia.
ochlocratical [ˌɑkləˈkrætɪkəl, B ˌɔk-] *a.* oclocrático.
ochlophobia [-ˈfoʊbɪə] *s.* (med., psic.) oclofobia.
ochre, *var. de.* **ocher.**
ochroid [ˈoʊkrɔɪd] *a.* ocráceo, de color ocre.
o'clock [əˈklɑk, B -ˈklɔk] *adv.* hora (completa, por el reloj); **at 7 o'clock,** a las siete.
ocotillo [ˌoʊkəˈtiˌjoʊ, B -ˈtiljoʊ] *s.* (bot., pr. E.U.) ocotillo, labarda, jarilla, tocotillo.
ocrea [ˈɑkrɪə, B ˈɔk-] *s.* (*pl.* OCREAE [-ˌi]) (bot.) ocrea.
ocreate [-ˌeɪt] *a.* (bot.) ocreado.
Ocrisia [əˈkraɪʃɪə] *s.* (mitol.) Ocrisia.
OCS *abrev. de* **Officer Candidate School,** (E.U.) Escuela de Cadetes del Ejército.
Oct. *abrev. de* **October,** octubre (oct.).
octachord [ˈɑktəˌkɔrd, B ˈɔktəˌkɔd] *s.* (mús.) octacordio (instrumento o sistema musical).
octachordal [ˌɑktəˈkɔrdəl, B ˌɔktəˈkɔd-] *a.* (mús.) octacordo.
octagon [ˈɑktəˌgɑn, B ˈɔktəgən] *s.* (geom.) octágono, octógono.
octagonal [ɑkˈtægənəl, B ɔk-] *a.* octagonal, octogonal, octágono, octógono.
octagonally [-ɪ] *adv.* en forma octagonal, octagonalmente.
octahedral [ˌɑktəˈhidrəl, B ˈɔktəˈhɛ-] *a.* octaédrico.
octahedrite [-ˌdraɪt] *s.* (min.) octaedrita.
octahedron [-drən] *s.* (*pl.* OCTAHEDRONS u OCTAHEDRA [-drə]) (geom.) octaedro.
octameter [ɑkˈtæmətər, B ɔk-ə] *a., s.* (poét.) octonario.
octandrious [ɑkˈtændrɪəs, B ɔk-] *a.* (bot.) octandro.
octane [ˈɑkteɪn, B ˈɔk-] *s.* (quím.) octano.
octane number, o. rating, índice de octano, graduación octánica, octanaje.
octangle [ˈɑktæŋgəl, B ˈɔk-] *a.* octangular. —*s.* octágono, octógono.
octangular [ɑkˈtæŋgjələr, B ɔk-lə] *a.* octangular, octogonal, octagonal.
octanol [ˈɑktəˌnɔl, B ˈɔk-] *s.* (quím.) octanol.
Octans [ˈɑktænz, B ˈɔk-] *s.* (astr.) octante.
octant [ˈɑktənt, B ˈɔk-] *s.* (geom., astr., astrol.) octante.
octastyle [ˈɑktəˌstaɪl, B ˈɔk-] *a.* (arq.) octóstilo.
Octateuch [-ˌtuk, B -ˌtjuk] *s.* (bíbl.) Octateuco.
octave [ˈɑktɪv, -ˌteɪv, B ˈɔk-] *s.* 1. (relig., mús., poét., esgr.) octava. 2. [B -tɪv] (mús.) registro de ocho pies (del órgano). —*a.* octavo.
octavo [ɑkˈteɪvoʊ, -ˈtɑvoʊ, B ɔkˈteɪvoʊ] *s.* (*pl.* OCTAVOS) libro en octavo. —*a.* en octavo.
octennial [ɑkˈtɛnɪəl, B ɔk-] *a.* que sucede cada ocho años; que dura ocho años.
octet [ɑkˈtɛt, B ɔk-] *s.* (mús.) octeto.
octillion [ɑkˈtɪljən, B ɔk-] *s.* octillón (unidad seguida por 27 ceros en E.U. y por 48 ceros en G.B.).
October [ɑkˈtoʊbər, B ɔk-bə] *s.* 1. octubre. 2. (G.B.) cerveza hecha en octubre.
octodecimo [ˌɑktoʊˈdɛsəmoʊ, B ˈɔk-] (impr.) *a.* de tamaño decimoctavo, en decimoctavo. —*s.* (*pl.* OCTODECIMOS) tamaño decimoctavo.
octogenarian [ˌɑktədʒəˈnɛrɪən, B ˌɔktoʊ-ˈ-nɛər-] *a., s.* octogenario, ochentón.
octonary [ˈɑktəˌnɛrɪ, B ˈɔktənərɪ] *s.* (*pl.* OCTONARIES) (poét.) octonario. —*a.* de ocho o en grupos de ocho.
octoploid [-ˌplɔɪd] *a.* (fisiol.) octoploide.
octopod [-ˌpɑd, B -ˌpɔd] *a., s.* (zool.) octópodo.
Octopoda [ɑkˈtɑpədə, B ɔkˈtɔp-] *s. pl.* (zool.) octópodos.
octopodan [-dən] *a., s.* (zool.) octópodo.
octopus [ˈɑktəpəs, B ˈɔk-] *s.* (*pl.* OCTOPUSES) 1. (zool.) óctopo, pulpo. 2. (fig.) organización monopolizadora poderosa con muchas sucursales.
octoroon [ˌɑktəˈrun, B ˌɔk-] *s.* ochavón; mulato claro.
octosyllabic [-səˈlæbɪk, B ˈɔktoʊ-] *a., s.* octosilábico, octosílabo.
octosyllable [ˈɑktəˌsɪləbəl, B ˈɔktoʊ-] *s.* octosílabo. —*a.* octosílabo, octosilábico.
octroi [ˈɑktrɔɪ, ɑkˈtrwɑ, B ˈɔktrwɑ] *s.* (fr., *pl.* OCTROIS) 1. derechos de puerta o de consumo. 2. fielato.
octuple [ˈɑktupəl, B ˈɔktju-] *a.* óctuple, óctuplo. —*v.t.* multiplicar por ocho.
ocular [ˈɑkjələr, B ˈɔkjʊlə] *s., a.* 1. ocular (de un instrumento óptico). 2. visual, ocular.
ocularly [-lɪ] *adv.* ocularmente, visualmente.
oculist [ˈɑkjələst, B ˈɔk-] *s.* oculista, oftalmólogo.
oculomotor [ˌɑkjələˈmoʊtər, B ˌɔk-ə] *a., s.* (fisiol.) oculomotor.
od [ɑd, B ɔd] *s.* fluido astral.
odalisk, odalisque [ˈoʊdəlˌɪsk] *s.* odalisca, esclava o concubina en un harén.
odd [ɑd, B ɔd] *a.* (ODDER; ODDEST) 1. suelto, ej., *o. volume,* libro suelto (de una colección). 2. impar, non (número); **o. or even,** juego de pares o nones. 3. de más, y pico, y tanto, ej., *forty o.,* cuarentitantos, cuarenta y pico, *sixty o. thousand,* sesentitantos mil, *ten dollars o.,* diez dólares y algunos centavos. 4. insignificante, pequeña (cantidad). 5. extra, sobrante, excedente. 6. casual, accidental, ocasional, esporádico, irregular, ej., *he picks up o. jobs,* hace trabajos ocasionales o esporádicos, trabaja irregularmente. 7. singular, original, extraordinario, extraño, curioso. 8. (fam.) excéntrico, raro. 9. que hace trabajos diversos, ej., *o. man,* hombre que hace trabajos diversos. 10. **at o. moments,** en ratos libres; **to be o. man out,** quedar fuera; **how o.!** ¡qué extraño! —*s.* (golf) golpe de más (en un hoyo, en comparación con el número de golpes hechos por el contrincante).
oddball [ˈɑdˌbɔl, B ˈɔd-] *s.* (jer.) chiflado, persona excéntrica, tipo raro. —*a.* extraño, no convencional.
odd glove, guante sin pareja.
oddity [ˈɑdətɪ, B ˈɔd-] *s.* (*pl.* ODDITIES) 1. singularidad, particularidad. 2. rareza, cosa rara, extravagancia, curiosidad. 3. fenómeno (persona). 4. **what an o.!** ¡qué cosa tan rara!
odd lot, lote suelto; (fin.) paquete pequeño (de menos de cien acciones).
oddly [-lɪ] *adv.* singularmente, extrañamente, estrambóticamente; **o. enough,** por extraño que parezca.
oddment [-mənt] *s.* retazo, retal; baratija, nadería.
oddness [-nəs] *s.* singularidad, carácter o aspecto extraño, rareza.
odd number, número impar.
odd-pinnate [-ˈpɪnˌeɪt, B -ɪt] *a.* (bot.) imparipinnado.
odds [ɑdz, B ɔdz] *s. pl.* 1. disparidad, desigualdad, diferencia (de condiciones o cosas), ej., *to make o. even,* eliminar desigualdades. 2. posibilidad, probabilidad, ej., *the o. are in our favor,* tenemos buenas posibilidades. 3. ventaja (en un juego), ej., *to give* (o *receive*) *o.,* dar (o recibir) ventaja. 4. riña, disputa, pendencia. 5. **at o. (with),** de punta (con), reñido (con), en desacuerdo (con); **to be at o.,** estar de malas; **by all o.,** sin duda; **long o.,** circunstancias o condiciones desfavorables; **over the o.,** demasiado; **the o. are (that),** lo (más) probable es (que); **to fight against o.,** luchar contra una fuerza superior, luchar en posición de desventaja; **to give o.,** dar ancas vueltas (Méx.); **to lay (o give) o. of (five to one,** etc.), ofrecer o dar (cinco a uno, etc.) en apuestas; **to play at o. or evens,** echar (o jugar) a pares y nones; **to set at o.,** enemistar, malquistar.
odds and ends, cachivaches, retazos, trozos, cosas sueltas, objetos diversos.
odds-on [ˈɑdˌɑn, -ˌɔn, B ˈɔdz-] *a.* 1. seguro (favorito, apuesta). 2. prometedor, de buen agüero; de buenos auspicios (candidato, etc.). 3. muy probable.
ode [oʊd] *s.* (poét.) oda.
odeum [oʊˈdiəm] *s.* (*pl.* ODEA [-ə]) (hist.) odeón.
Odin [ˈoʊdən] *s.* (mitol.) Odín, dios escandinavo de la sabiduría y la poesía.
odious [ˈoʊdɪəs] *a.* odioso, repugnante, execrable, abominable, aborrecible, detestable.
odiously [-lɪ] *adv.* odiosamente, detestablemente.
odiousness [-nəs] *s.* odiosidad, odio.
odium [ˈoʊdɪəm] *s.* 1. odio, rencor, aborrecimiento, encono. 2. oprobio, ignominia, afrenta, deshonra.
odograph [ˈoʊdəˌgræf, B -ˌgrɑf] *s.* odógrafo, dispositivo que registra la distancia que recorre un vehículo o un transeúnte.
odometer [oʊˈdɑmətər, B -ˈdɔmɪtə] *s.* odómetro, instrumento que mide distancias en la marcha.
odometry [-ətrɪ] *s.* odometría.
odonate [ˈoʊdəˌneɪt] *s.* (ento.) odonato.
odontalgia [ˌoʊdɑnˈtældʒɪə, B ˌɔdɔn-] *s.* odontalgia (dolor de muelas).
odontalgic [-ˈtældʒɪk] *a.* odontálgico.
odontoblast [oʊˈdɑntəˌblæst, B -ˈdɔn-] *s.* (anat.) odontoblasto.
odontoglossum [-ˌdɑntəˈglɑsəm, B -ˌdɔntəˈglɔsəm] *s.* (bot.) odontogloso.
odontograph [-ˈdɑntəˌgræf, B -ˈdɔntəˌgrɑf] *s.* (mec.) odontógrafo (instrumento para trazar dientes de engranaje).
odontoid [-ˈdɑntɔɪd, B -ˈdɔn-] *a.* (anat., zool.) odontoide, odontoideo.
odontoid process, (anat.) apófisis odontoide.
odontological [oʊˌdɑntəˈlɑdʒɪkəl, B ˌɔdɔntəˈlɔdʒ-] *a.* odontológico.
odontologist [ˌoʊdɑnˈtɑlədʒəst, B ˌɔdɔnˈtɔl-] *s.* odontólogo.
odontology [-dʒɪ] *s.* odontología.
odor, (pr. G.B.) **odour** [ˈoʊdər, B -ə] *s.* 1. olor, aroma, fragancia. 2. (fig.) olor, fama, reputación, opinión. 3. **o. of sanctity,** olor de santidad; **to be in bad o. (with),** no estar en gracia (con), tener mala fama (entre).
odoriferous [ˌoʊdəˈrɪfərəs] *a.* odorífero, odorífico, oloroso.

odorize [ˈoʊdəˌraɪz] *v.t.* olorizar, perfumar.
odorless [ˈoʊdərləs, B -əlɪs] *a.* inodoro.
odorous [-ərəs] *a.* oloroso, perfumado, fragante, aromático, odorante.
odorously [-lɪ] *adv.* con olor.
odorousness [-nəs] *s.* olor, fragancia.
odyssean [ˌɑdəˈsiən, B ˌɔdɪˈsi-] *a.* semejante a una odisea, de muchas aventuras.
Odysseus [oʊˈdɪsˌjus, -ˈdɪsɪəs, B əˈdɪsˌjus] *s.* (mitol.) Odiseo, Ulises.
odyssey [ˈɑdəsɪ, B ˈɔd-] *s.* (fig.) odisea; **the O.,** (lit.) la Odisea, poema épico de Homero.
oedema, *var. de* **edema.**
Oedipus [ˈɛdəpəs, B id-] *s.* (mitol.) Edipo, hijo de Yocasta, padre de Antígona.
Oedipus complex, (psic.) complejo de Edipo.
OEEC *abrev. de* **Organization for European Economic Cooperation,** Organización Europea de Cooperación Económica (O.E.C.E.).
oenological [ˌinəˈlɑdʒɪkəl, B -ˈlɔdʒ-] *a.* enológico (relativo al conocimiento de los vinos).
oenologist [ɪˈnɑlədʒəst, B ɪˈnɔl-] *s.* enólogo, experto en la elaboración de los vinos.
oenology [-dʒɪ] *s.* enología, ciencia que estudia la elaboración de los vinos.
oenomel [ˈinəˌmɛl] *s.* (hist.) enomel (brebaje hecho de vino y miel).
o'er [ɔr, B ˈoʊə, ɔə] *contr. de* **over.**
oersted [ˈɜrstəd, B ˈɜstɛd] *s.* (elec.) oersted.
oesophagus, *var. de* **esophagus.**
oestradiol, oestriol, oestrogen, *vars. de* **estradiol, estriol, estrogen.**
oestrin, *var. de* **estrin.**
oestrum [ˈɛstrəm, B ˈis-] *var. de* **estrus.**
oestrus, *var. de* **estrus.**
of [ɑv, əv, B ɔv, əv] *prep.* 1. de, desde (indicando derivación, separación, fuente), ej., *North of Paris,* al norte de París, *what you expect of me,* lo que esperas de mí, *within a mile of New York,* a una milla de Nueva York. 2. de, por (indicando causa, motivo o razón), ej., *the smell of flowers,* el olor de las flores, *proud of you,* orgulloso de tí, *of necessity,* por necesidad, *of oneself,* espontáneamente, naturalmente, *sick of pretense,* harto de simulaciones. 3. de, por (indicando autor), ej., *the works of Shakespeare,* las obras de Shakespeare. 4. de (indicando la composición, substancia, identidad o la materia de que está hecha una cosa), ej., *this is made of wood,* esto está hecho de madera, *a family of eight,* una familia de ocho miembros. 5. de (indicando incumbencia, referencia, dirección o condición), ej., *30 years of peace,* 30 años de paz, *he thinks well of you,* él piensa bien de ti, *of age,* mayor de edad. 6. de (indicando relación objetiva), ej., *it is characteristic of him,* es característico de él. 7. de (indicando descripción, calidad, condición), ej., *a girl of ten,* una niña de diez años, *a man of tact,* un hombre de tacto. 8. de, entre (indicando partición, clasificación, selección), ej., *ten of us,* diez de nosotros, *Song of Songs,* Cantar de los Cantares, *a friend of mine,* un amigo mío, *he of all men,* él entre todos. 9. de (indicando posesión o pertenencia), ej., *of the middle classes,* de la clase media, *a topic of conversation,* un tema de conversación, *the master of the house,* el dueño de la casa. 10. (E.U.) para, ej., *a quarter of six,* un cuarto para las seis. 11. **of late,** recientemente, últimamente.
off [ɔf] *adv.* 1. lejos, a gran distancia, ej., *it is far o.,* está muy lejos. 2. fuera de su sitio, suelto. 3. fuera de rutina, fuera de continuidad; fuera de servicio. 4. completamente, cumplidamente, por entero, ej., *to finish it o.,* terminar o acabar completamente. 5. **o. and on,** de vez en cuando, de tiempo en tiempo; **o. with his head!** ¡fuera con él!; **o. with you!** ¡lárgate!; **the gilt is o.,** se empañó, se deslució (algo); **the light is o.,** se apagó la luz; **they're o.!** ¡partieron! ¡largaron! (caballos, botes, etc. en carrera); **to be having it o. with,** (jer., G.B.) tener relaciones (sexuales) con; **to be o.,** estar partiendo; despegar (un avión); comenzar, empezar; faltar para, ej., *the examination is three weeks o.,* faltan tres semanas para el examen; **to be o. with (the old love,** etc.), haber terminado con (un antiguo amor, etc.); **to beat o. the attack,** rechazar el ataque; **to break o.,** callar súbitamente; romper relaciones; **to take a day o.,** tomar un día de asueto; **to take o. one's hat,** quitarse el sombrero; **to take one's clothes o.,** desvestirse. —*prep.* 1. de, desde; a, ej., *he got o. the horse,* él se bajó del caballo, *I bought this o. a street vendor,* compré esto a un vendedor ambulante. 2. fuera de, lejos de, ej., *o. the beaten path,* fuera del camino recorrido; (fig.) fuera de lo común. 3. a costa de, ej., *he lives o. his brother,* él vive a costa de su hermano. 4. menos que, ej., *two dollars o. the usual price,* dos dólares menos que el precio acostumbrado, *three seconds o. the world record,* tres segundos menos que la marca mundial. 5. que arranca de, ej., *a street o. Fifth Avenue,* una calle que arranca de la Quinta Avenida. 6. (mar.) frente a. a la altura de ej., *o. Salem,* frente a Salem (en el mar). 7. **o. base,** digresión, incorrección; **o. key** (mús., fig.) fuera de tono; **o. limits** (mil., fig.), prohibido; **(three miles,** etc.) **o. shore,** (tres millas, etc.) mar adentro; **o. the mark,** (fig.) fuera de foco; **o. the point,** impertinente; **o. the record,** extraoficial(mente); **to be o. duty,** no estar de servicio; **to be o. one's game,** no estar en forma, estar fuera de forma; **to go o. (smoking, drinking,** etc.) dejar de (fumar, beber, etc.), renunciar a; **to take (something) o. one's hands,** quitarle (algo) de las manos a uno. —*a.* 1. más distante, opuesto, otro, ej., *on the o. side of the building,* en el lado más distante del edificio, *on the o. side of the wall,* en el lado opuesto de la pared. 2. lateral (calle, brazo de un río, etc.). 3. desconectado, fuera de servicio. 4. cancelado, ej., *tonight's dinner is o.,* se canceló la cena de esta noche. 5. errado, equivocado (en cálculos, etc.). 6. raro, anormal (persona). 7. menos, más bajo, ej., *shares are five points o. today,* las acciones se cotizan hoy cinco puntos más bajo. 8. inferior, peor (calidad, grado). 9. libre (día, hora, etc.). 10. derecho (díc. de caballo enjaezado u otro animal de tiro, de vehículos o rueda de vehículo). 11. (criquet) derecho, opuesto al bateador (campo). 12. (bridge) falto de, ej., *for a grand slam my hand was o. an ace,* para una bola mi mano estaba falta de un as. 13. **o. days,** días en que se está indispuesto; **o. season,** fuera de la temporada; **to be badly o. for,** necesitar mucho; **to be well (comfortably,** etc.) **o.,** ser acomodado; **to be just as well o. without,** sentirse muy bien sin. —*s.* (criquet) campo derecho, campo opuesto al bateador. —*v.i.* 1. marcharse, irse. 2. (mar.) alejarse de la costa (un barco). —*v.t.* (jer.) matar.
offal [ˈɔfəl, ˈɑf-, B ˈɔf-] *s.* 1. asadura; menudos (tripa, corazón, etc.). 2. desperdicios, sobras, basura. 3. carroña.
offbeat [ˈɔfˌbit] *s.* (mús.) tiempo débil (del compás). —*a.* inusitado, extraordinario; extraño, raro, excéntrico.
offcast [-ˌkæst, B -ˌkɑst] *a.* desechado. —*s.* desecho; cosa o persona vieja y gastada.
off-center [-ˈsɛntər, B -ə] *a.* fuera de centro, descentrado.
off chance, on the o. por si acaso.
off-color, (G.B.) **off-colour** [-ˈkʌlər, B -ə] *a.* 1. que no tiene color natural, desteñido. 2. impropio, atrevido, de color subido. 3. **an o.-c. story,** un cuento colorado.
off duty, franco de servicio (S.A.).
offence, *var. de* **offense.**
offend [əˈfɛnd] *v.i.* 1. pecar. 2. ser ofensivo, causar disgusto. —*v.t.* 1. ofender, afrentar, molestar, humillar, agraviar, ultrajar, irritar, herir. 2. violar, infringir.
offender [-ər, B -ə] *s.* ofensor, agraviador, transgresor, delincuente.
offense [əˈfɛns, ˈɑfˌɛns, B əˈfɛns] *s.* 1. ofensa, insulto, afrenta, agravio, injuria. 2. pecado. 3. ataque, asalto. 4. ofensa, delito, crimen. 5. (der.) falta, infracción. 6. (ant.) tropezón, obstáculo; herida, daño. 7. **no o.,** sin ánimo de ofender; **to take o. (at),** ofenderse (de), molestarse (por), sentirse ofendido (por), picarse.
offenseless [-ləs] *a.* inofensivo, inocente, incapaz de ofender.
offensive [əˈfɛnsɪv] *a.* 1. ofensivo, agresivo. 2. odioso, detestable, repulsivo, ej., un olor. 3. insultante, agraviante, injuriante. 4. pecaminoso, delictuoso. 5. (dep.) de ataque. —*s.* ofensiva, agresión; **to take the o.,** tomar la ofensiva.
offensively [-lɪ] *adv.* ofensivamente, de manera insultante.
offensiveness [-nəs] *s.* 1. comportamiento ofensivo. 2. carácter desagradable; aspecto repulsivo. 3. nocividad.
offer [ˈɔfər, ˈɑf-, B ˈɔfə] *v.t.* 1. ofrecer, presentar, brindar, ej., *he was offered a free pardon,* le ofrecieron el indulto, *he offered no apology,* no presentó disculpa alguna. 2. ofrendar, ofrecer, sacrificar. 3. someter, proponer, sugerir, ej., *he offered an opinion,* sometió una opinión, *he offered a few remarks,* propuso ciertas observaciones. 4. ofrecer, presentar, mostrar, ej., *he offered no resistance,* no ofreció resistencia. 5. ofrecer, hacer una oferta de (cierta suma). 6. ofrecer en venta. 7. **o. to (do),** ofrecerse a; intentar, tratar de, ej., *they offered to help,* ellos se han ofrecido a ayudar. —*v.i.* 1. hacer ofrendas. 2. presentarse, ofrecerse (oportunidad, etc.). 3. declararse, proponer matrimonio. —*s.* 1. oferta. 2. propuesta, sugerencia. 3. tentativa, esfuerzo. 4. declaración, proposición de matrimonio.
offerer [-ərər, B -ərə] *s.* ofrecedor, oferente, licitador.
offering [-ərɪŋ] *s.* 1. ofrecimiento, propuesta. 2. oferta. 3. ofrenda, oblación, sacrificio. 4. don, dádiva.
offeror, *var. de* **offerer.**
offertory [-ərˌtɔrɪ, B -ətərɪ] *s.* (*pl.* OFFERTORIES) 1. (relig.) ofertorio. 2. colecta (que se hace durante la misa o servicio religioso).
offhand [ˈɔfˈhænd] *adv.* de improviso, de repente, sin pensar, sin deliberación, espontáneamente, informalmente. —*a.* 1. espontáneo, informal, natural, hecho de improviso o sin preparación. 2. **an o. remark,** una observación que no venía al caso.
offhanded [-əd] *a., var. de* **offhand.**
offhandedly [-lɪ] *adv., var. de* **offhand.**
office [ˈɔfəs, ˈɑf-, B ˈɔf-] *s.* 1. oficina, despacho, bufete, consultorio. 2. cargo, oficio, empleo; deber, función. 3. oficio, servicio, atención, favor, ej., *owing to the good offices of,* gracias a los buenos oficios de, *he did me an ill o.,* me hizo un mal servicio. 4. cocina y dependencia del servicio. 5. ministerio, ej., *War O.,* Ministerio de Guerra. 6. (relig.) rito, servicio, ceremonia, oficio; (*pl.*) exequias. 7. (jer., G.B.) signo, seña,

indirecta. 8. **the office of chief executive,** la suprema magistratura; **to be in** (o **to hold**) **o.,** estar en funciones, estar en el poder; **to resign o.,** renunciar a un cargo; **to take o.,** entrar en funciones.
office book, (relig.) oficionario.
office boy, mandadero, mensajero (de oficina).
office building, edificio de oficinas o administración.
office clerk, oficinista, escribano.
office copy, 1. copia de archivo, copia de oficina. 2. (der.) copia certificada.
office for the dead, (relig.) oficio de difuntos.
officeholder ['ɔfəsˌhouldər, 'ɑf-, B 'ɔfdə] *s.* titular (de un puesto público), funcionario, empleado público.
office hours, horario de oficina; horas de oficina, horas hábiles; horas de consulta.
office manager, jefe de oficina.
officer ['ɔfəsər, 'ɑf-, B 'ɔfɪsə] *s.* 1. oficial, funcionario, dignatario, alto empleado. 2. policía, agente, guardia. 3. (mil., mar.) oficial. 4. (ant.) oficiante, cura, sacerdote. *—v.t.* 1. dotar de oficiales. 2. mandar como oficial, ser oficial de.
officer in charge, (mil.) oficial encargado.
officer of the day, (mil.) oficial del día, oficial de servicio.
officer of the deck, (mar.) oficial de guardia (buque de guerra).
officer of the guard, (mil.) oficial de guardia.
officer of the watch, (mar.) oficial de cuarto.
officer's mess, comedor de oficiales.
office seeker, aspirante a cargo público, pretendiente; buscaempleos.
office supplies, artículos de escritorio.
office work, trabajo de oficina.
office worker, oficinista.
official [ə'fɪʃəl] *a.* 1. oficial, de oficio. 2. oficial, autorizado, autoritativo. 3. (fam.) autorizado. *—s.* funcionario, funcionario público u oficial; (G.B.) provisor o juez eclesiástico.
officialdom [-dəm] *s.* 1. oficialidad. 2. funcionarios públicos. 3. círculos oficiales.
officialism [-ˌɪzəm] *s.* oficialismo; métodos burocráticos; proceder burocrático; formalismo.
officiality [əˌfɪʃɪ'æləti] *s.* 1. cargo y oficina del provisor eclesiástico. 2. cosa oficial.
official letters, pliegos de oficio.
officially [ə'fɪʃəlɪ] *adv.* oficialmente, de oficio.
officiant [ə'fɪʃɪənt] *s.* (relig.) oficiante, celebrante.
officiary [ə'fɪʃɪˌɛrɪ, B -ɪərɪ] *a.* por oficio, debido al cargo (de uno). *—s.* 1. oficial, funcionario. 2. cuerpo de oficiales o funcionarios.
officiate [-ˌeɪt] *v.t.* 1. oficiar, celebrar (una misa o servicio religioso). 2. llevar a cabo, realizar (en forma oficial). 3. arbitrar (un partido de fútbol, etc.). *—v.i.* 1. oficiar, desempeñar un cargo. 2. (con *as*) oficiar (de), actuar (como).
officiating [-ɪŋ] *s.* oficiante.
officiation [əˌfɪʃɪ'eɪʃən] *s.* celebración, ejecución (de función oficial).
officiator [ə'fɪʃɪˌeɪtər, B -ə] *s.* oficiante.
officinal [ə'fɪsɪnəl, B ˌɔfɪ'saɪnəl] *a.* (farm.) oficinal (medicamento, planta, yerba). *—s.* (farm.) medicamento oficinal.
officious [ə'fɪʃəs] *a.* 1. oficioso, entremetido, intruso. 2. (dip.) oficioso, no oficial. 3. (ant.) amable, servicial, solícito.
officiously [-lɪ] *adv.* oficiosamente.
officiousness [-nəs] *s.* oficiosidad.
offing ['ɔfɪŋ, 'ɑf-, B 'ɔf-] *s.* alta mar, mar afuera, lejanía, lontananza; **(it) is in the o.,** está por suceder, es de esperar; está cerca, está en perspectiva.
offish ['ɔfɪʃ] *a.* (fam.) reservado, poco comunicativo, altivo, arisco, esquivo, adusto.
off key, *a.* desafinado. *—adv.* desafinando.
offlet ['ɔfˌlɛt] *s.* cañería o conducto de desagüe.
offline , (comput.) fuera de línea, desconectado.
off-load ['ɔfˌloud] *v.t.* (astronaút) (*to launch*) lanzar: (aer.) (*to unload*) descargar, desembarcar.
off-peak [-'pik] *a.* debajo del máximo; (elec.) de menos carga.
offprint [-ˌprɪnt] *s.* separata, tirada aparte (de un artículo, etc.). *—v.t.* tirar aparte (una separata, etc.).
off ramp, (aut.) vía de salida (de una autopista).
offscouring [-ˌskaurɪŋ, B -ˌskauər-] *s.* (*gen. pl.*) 1. hez, desechos, residuos, basura. 2. (fig.) hez, escoria (de la sociedad, etc.).
off season, *s.* temporada baja. *—a.* de temporada baja. *—adv.* durante *o* en la temporada baja.
offset [-ˌsɛt] *s.* 1. compensación, equivalente. 2. ramal, vástago. 3. (agr.) acodo. 4. estribo, estribación (de montaña). 5. contrapeso. 6. (ten.) contrapartida. 7. (arq.) retallo, resalto. 8. (elec.) ramal (de un conductor principal). 9. (mec.) codo. 10. (impr.) calco; offset, rotocalco. 11. (top.) línea acodada, ordenada. — [ɔf'sɛt, B ɔfˌsɛt] *v.t.* 1. hacer resaltar o sobresalir. 2. compensar, balancear; contrabalancear, contrapesar. 3. (arq.) formar un retallo o resalto en (pared, etc.). 4. (impr.) calcar (por el procedimiento offset). *—a.* 1. fuera de lugar, desalineado. 2. (mec.) no paralelo ni convergente. 3. (impr.) calcado (por el procedimiento offset).
offset lithography, fotolitografía.
offshoot [-ˌʃut] *s.* 1. retoño, vástago, renuevo. 2. ramal (de montaña, etc.). 3. rama colateral; descendiente.
offshore [ɔf'ʃɔr, B -'ʃɔ] *a.* 1. de fuera, de mar adentro (navegación, pesca, etc.). 2. terral o costanero, ej., *o. wind,* viento terral. 3. costa afuera, a corta distancia de la costa, ej., *o. island,* isla costa afuera. *—adv.* mar adentro, a distancia de la costa.
offshore drilling, perforación costa afuera.
offshore exploration, exploración costa afuera.
offshore fishing, pesca de bajura.
offshore oil, petróleo de costa afuera.
offshore oilfield, campo petrolífero submarino.
off side, (fútbol) (en) posición adelantada.
offside [-'saɪd] *a.* (fútbol) de posición adelantada.
offspring [-ˌsprɪŋ] *s.* 1. descendencia, progenie, prole, retoño. 2. resultado, fruto, consecuencia.
offstage [-'steɪdʒ] *adv., a.* 1. fuera del escenario. 2. (fig.) entre bastidores.
off-street parking[-strit] estacionamiento fuera de la vía pública, aparcamiento fuera de la vía pública.
off-the-record [-ðə'rɛkərd, B -ˌɔd] *a.* extraoficial, oficioso; confidencial.
off the wall, estrambótico, estrafalario.
off the wall remark, disparate.
off-white [-'hwaɪt, -'waɪt] *a.* blancuzco, blanquecino.
oft [ɔft] (poét.) *var. de* **often.**
often ['ɔfən, 'ɔftən] *adv.* (OFTENER; OFTENEST) frecuentemente, con frecuencia, a menudo; **as o. as,** siempre que, tan a menudo (tantas veces) como; **as o. as not,** no pocas veces; **how o.?** ¿cuántas veces?, ¿con qué frecuencia?; **not o.,** pocas veces, rara vez; **too o.,** con demasiada frecuencia. *—a.* frecuente.
oftentimes [-ˌtaɪmz] **ofttimes** ['ɔfˌtaɪmz, 'ɔftˌtaɪmz] *adv.* frecuentemente, a menudo.
ogee ['ouˌdʒi] *s.* (arq.) cimacio, gola, talón.
ogee arch, (arq.) arco conopial, arco flamígero.
ogival [ou'dʒaɪvəl] *a.* (arq.) ojival.
ogival arch, (arq.) arco ojival, arco apuntado.
ogive ['oudʒaɪv] *s.* (arq.) ojiva.
ogle ['ougəl, 'ɑg-, B 'ou-] *v.i.* coquetear con la mirada; **o. at,** mirar insinuantemente. *—v.t.* comerse con los ojos. *—s.* mirada coqueta; ojeada.
ogler ['ouglər, B -lə] *s.* el que ojea; mirón.
ogre ['ougər, B -gə] *s.* ogro, monstruo; (fam.) ogro (persona).
ogreish [-gərɪʃ] *a.* parecido a un ogro; monstruoso.
ogrish [-grɪʃ] *var. de* **ogreish.**
oh [ou] *interj.* ¡oh! ¡ah! ¡ay!; **oh how nice!** ¡oh qué bueno!; **oh what a lie!** !ay qué mentira!; **oh, yeah!** ¡no me digas! (expresión de incredulidad, sarcasmo).
Ohio [ou'haɪou] *s.* Ohio, estado de los E.U.
ohm [oum] *s.* (elec.) ohm, ohmio.
ohmage ['oumɪdʒ] *s.* (elec.) ohmiaje.
ohmic [-mɪk] *a.* (elec.) óhmico.
ohmmeter ['oumˌmitər, B -ə] *s.* ohmiómetro.
O H M S *abrev. de* **On Her o His Majesty's Service,** al servicio de Su Majestad.
oho [ou'hou] *interj.* **¡ajá!; ¡hola!**
oidium [ou'ɪdɪəm] *s.* (*pl.* OIDIUMS u OIDIA [-dɪə]) (bot.) oídio, oídium, cenicilla, ceniza, cenizo.
oil [ɔɪl] *s.* 1. aceite. 2. petróleo. 3. (pint.) óleo, pintura al óleo; color al óleo. 4. (jer.) halago, zalamería. 5. **in o.,** pintado al óleo; **to burn the midnight o.,** quemarse las pestañas; **to pour o. on troubled waters,** calmar los ánimos, aplacar las pasiones, apaciguar; **to strike o.,** encontrar petróleo; (fig.) tener éxito, enriquecerse de pronto, lograr prosperidad; **to throw** (o **to pour**) **o. on the flames,** echar leña al fuego, avivar las pasiones. *—v.t.* aceitar, lubricar; **o. one's hand,** sobornar, untar la palma; **o. one's tongue,** lisonjear, adular, halagar. *—a.* aceitoso; de óleo, al óleo.
oil-bearing ['ɔɪlˌbɛrɪŋ, B -ˌbɛər-] *a.* petrolífero, oleífero.
oil beetle, (ento.) aceitera, carraleja, cubillo.
oilbird [-ˌbɜrd, B -ˌbɜd] *s.* (orn.) guácharo.
oil brake, freno de aceite o hidráulico.
oil burner, quemador de petróleo, estufa.
oil-burning, *a.* de combustión de petróleo o aceite.
oil bush, manguito de aceite.
oil cake, torta de borujo, torta de algodón, torta de lino.
oilcan ['ɔɪlˌkæn] *s.* aceitera, alcuza; lata para aceite.
oil car, vagón tanque para petróleo.
oil change, (aut.) cambio de aceite.
oilcloth [-ˌklɔθ] *s.* encerado, hule.
oil color, color o tubo de pintura al óleo.
oil-cooled [-ˌkuld] *a.* enfriado por aceite.
oil-cooled transformer, (elec.) transformador enfriado por aceite.
oil cruet, aceitera (utensilio de mesa).
oil cup, copilla de aceite, aceitera, aceitador, taza lubricadora.
oil deposits, yacimientos de petroleo.
oil derrick, torre petrolera, torre de taladrar.
oil drum, bidón o tambor para petróleo.
oiled [ɔɪld] *a.* 1. aceitado, lubricado. 2. impregnado de aceite. 3. (jer.) ahumado, alumbrado, borracho. 4. (fig.) sobornado.
oil engine, máquina de petróleo, motor de aceite.
oiler ['ɔɪlər, B -lə] *s.* 1. aceitera, engrasador(a). 2. aceitador, engrasador (obrero). 3. pozo petrolífero. 4. buque petrolero, buque tanque. 5. (*pl.*) impermeable (de hule).
oil field, yacimiento o campo petrolífero.
oil field worker, *s.* obrero petrolero.
oil filter, (mec., aut.) filtro de aceite.

oil-fired ['ɔɪlˌfaɪrd, B -ˌfaɪəd] *a.* alimentado a petróleo.
oil furnace, horno de petróleo.
oil gas, gas de petróleo.
oil gauge, 1. indicador del nivel de aceite, manómetro del aceite. 2. oleómetro. 3. (aut.) medidor del aceite (en forma de varilla).
oil groove, (mec.) ranura de lubricación, estría de lubrificación, conducto de aceite.
oil gun, aceitera a presión.
oil heating, sistema de calefacción con petróleo.
oilhole ['ɔɪlˌhoʊl] *s.* (mec.) grasera, orificio de engrase.
oilily ['ɔɪlǝlɪ] *adv.* untuosamente.
oil industry, industria petrolífera.
oiliness [-lɪnǝs] *s.* 1. untuosidad, oleosidad. 2. modales congraciadores, zalamería.
oiling [-lɪŋ] *s.* aceitado, engrase, lubricación.
oil-insulated transformer ['ɔɪl'ɪnsǝˌleɪtǝd-, B -sjʊ-] (elec.) transformador aislado en aceite.
oil jar, zafra (de aceite).
oil lamp, lámpara de aceite.
oilless bearing ['ɔɪllǝs-] cojinete autolubricado.
oil line, (aut.) línea del aceite; tubería de aceite.
oilman [-ˌmæn, -mǝn] *s.* 1. petrolero, aceitero, tratante en aceites. 2. engrasador.
oil meal, harina de borujo.
oil mill, molino de aceite, trujal, almazara.
oil of cedar, cedreleón; (quím.) cedróleo.
oil of vitriol, aceite de vitriolo, ácido sulfúrico.
oil of wintergreen, aceite de gaulteria.
oil paint, color al óleo, pintura al óleo.
oil painting, pintura al óleo, cuadro al óleo.
oil palm, (bot.) palmera de aceite, palmera africana (pr. tropical).
oil pan, (aut.) cárter (de aceite).
oilpaper ['ɔɪlˌpeɪpǝr, B -pǝ] *s.* papel encerado.
oil pipe, tubo de engrase.
oil pipeline, oleoducto, tubería para petróleo.
oil press, molino de aceite, almazara.
oil pressure, presión de aceite.
oilproof [-ˌpruf] *a.* a prueba de aceite.
oil pump, (aut.) bomba de aceite.
oil ring, (mec.) anillo de lubricación o de engrase.
oilseed [-ˌsid] *s.* semilla oleaginosa.
oil shop, planta de lubricación; aceitera.
oilskin [-ˌskɪn] *s.* 1. tela impermeable o aceitada, hule. 2. (*pl.*) impermeable. 3. (*pl.*) traje de hule.
oil slick, mancha aceitosa en el agua.
oilstone ['ɔɪlˌstoʊn] *s.* piedra afiladora, o de aceite; asperón; piedra de asentar.
oil stove, estufa de petróleo.
oil switch, (elec.) interruptor en aceite, disyuntor de aceite.
oil tank, depósito o tanque de petróleo.
oil tanker, (mar.) buque tanque o petrolero.
oiltight [-'taɪt] *a.* (mec.) hermético o estanco al aceite.
oil well, pozo de petróleo, pozo petrolífero.
oily ['ɔɪlɪ] *a.* (OILIER; OILIEST) 1. aceitoso, oleoso. 2. grasiento, untuoso. 3. congraciador, zalamero.
oily bean, sésamo, ajonjolí.
oily calm, tranquilo como una balsa de aceite.
oink [ɔɪŋk] *s.* onomatopeya que imita el gruñido del cerdo.
ointment ['ɔɪntmǝnt] *s.* ungüento, pomada.
oiticica [ˌɔɪtǝ'sikǝ] *s.* (bot.) oiticica.
OK, okay [oʊ'keɪ] *adv.* (fam.) correcto, conforme, muy bien. —*a.* O. K., correcto, conforme, perfecto, muy bueno. —*v.t.* (*pret., p.p.* OK'D, OKAYED [oʊ'keɪd]; *p.pr.* OK'ING, OKAYING) aprobar, endosar, autorizar; poner o dar el visto bueno a. —*s.* aprobación, autorización; visto bueno.
okapi [oʊ'kɑpɪ] *s.* (*pl.* OKAPIS) (zool.) okapí.
okeh ['oʊ'keɪ] **okey-doke, okie-doke** ['oʊkɪ'doʊk] **okey-dokey, okie-dokie** [-'doʊkɪ] *vars. de* **O.K.**
Okie ['oʊkɪ] *s.* (despec.) (E.U.) trabajador agrícola migrante, esp. de Oklahoma.
Okla. *abrev. de* **Oklahoma,** Oklahoma (E.U.).
Oklahoma [ˌoʊklǝ'hoʊmǝ] *s.* Oklahoma, estado de los E.U.
okra ['oʊkrǝ] *s.* (bot.) quimbombó, quingombó, abelmosco (Méx.).
old [oʊld] *a.* (OLDER o ELDER ['ɛldǝr, B -dǝ]; OLDEST o ELDEST [-dǝst]) 1. viejo, de edad, añoso. 2. viejo, vetusto, anticuado. 3. añejo (vino, licor, etc.). 4. viejo, gastado; debilitado, agotado. 5. viejo, pasado, antiguo (mundo, cultura, etc.). 6. (fam.) bueno, ej., *the good o. times,* los buenos tiempos pasados. 7. **a man is as o. as he feels,** se tiene la edad que uno siente; **any o. time,** cuando quiera, en cualquier momento; **how o. are you (is he, etc.)?** ¿cuántos años tiene Ud. (él, etc.)?; **my o. woman,** mi vieja (esposa); **of o. standing,** que data de hace mucho tiempo; **of the o. school,** chapado a la antigua; **o. head on young shoulders,** sabiduría mayor que los años; **the o.,** la gente vieja, los ancianos; **the o. home,** la madre patria; **the o. lady** (fam.), esposa (esp. la propia), media naranja; **to be o. enough,** no ser niño, tener edad suficiente; **to become** o **grow o.,** envejecer(se), encanecer, añejarse; **to make o.,** avejentar, aviejar; **to be . . . years o.,** tener . . . años. —*s.* antigüedad, antaño; **of o.,** de antaño.
old age, ancianidad, senectud, vejez.
old bachelor, solterón.
old bag, (jer., E.U.) vieja, mujer desaliñada; (despec.) la madre.
old bean, o. egg, o. thing, o. top, (jer. G.B.) amigo, viejo, buen o fiel amigo.
old bird, (fam.) pájaro, pajarraco, persona astuta y sagaz.
old boy, (fam., G.B.) chico, viejo (expresión de afecto); (pr. G.B.) ex alumno; **O. B.,** el diablo.
old chap, (G.B.) amigo.
old-clothesman ['oʊld'kloʊðzˌmæn, -mǝn] *s.* ropavejero, trapero.
old country, madre patria, terruño.
olden ['oʊldǝn] *a.* (poét.) viejo, antiguo; **o. times,** tiempos pasados o antiguos.
Old English, 1. inglés antiguo (de los siglos VII a XII). 2. (impr.) gótico, gótico alemán.
old-established ['oʊldɪs'tæblɪʃt] *a.* establecido o reconocido desde hace mucho tiempo.
oldfangled [-'fæŋgǝld] *a.* anticuado, pasado de moda.
old-fashioned [-'fæʃǝnd] *a.* pasado de moda, anticuado, chapado a la antigua.
old fogy, old fogey, *a., s.* conservador, estirado, anticuado.
old-fogyish, old-fogeyish [-'foʊgɪɪʃ] *a.* de ideas anticuadas, engolillado, chapado a la antigua.
Old Glory, (fam., E.U.) la bandera nacional.
old goat, (jer.) 1. viejo cascarrabias. 2. viejo verde.
old gold, color oro viejo.
Old Guard, 1. (hist.) Guardia Imperial (de Napoleón). 2. **o. g.,** (fig.) guardia vieja (los elementos más conservadores de una comunidad, partido, etc.).
old hand, 1. veterano, experto, hombre experimentado. 2. (fam.) zorro viejo.
Old Harry, (fam.) Pedro Botero (el diablo).
old hat, 1. chapado a la antigua. 2. trillado. 3. anticuado.
oldish ['oʊldɪʃ] *a.* viejecito, algo viejo.
old-line ['oʊld'laɪn] *a.* 1. de mucha experiencia (persona); establecida desde hace mucho tiempo (compañía, etc.). 2. conservador, tradicionalista.
old-looking [-ˌlʊkɪŋ] *a.* viejo, de aspecto vetusto.
old maid, 1. (despec.) solterona. 2. (fig.) melindroso. 3. (naipes) (juego de) la vieja, la mona.
old-maidish [-'meɪdɪʃ] *a.* melindroso, remilgado.
old man, (fam.) 1. viejo (esposo o padre). 2. jefe, patrón, amo (de una compañía, un banco, etc.).
old master, (arte) 1. titán de la pintura. 2. obra de un gran maestro (anterior al siglo XVIII).
Old Nick [-'nɪk] (fam.) Pedro Botero (el diablo).
old people's home, hogar de ancianos.
old rose, rosa viejo (el color).
old salt, (fam.) lobo de mar.
old school, lo chapado a la antigua, conservador, de la vieja escuela.
old sledge, siete y medio (juego de cartas).
old sod, terruño natal.
old soldier, veterano, hombre experimentado.
old song, 1. canción antigua. 2. cosa fácil, bagatela.
old-squaw ['oʊld'skwɔ] *s.* pato marino.
oldster [-stǝr, B -stǝ] *s.* (fam.) anciano, viejo, otoñal.
old style, 1. estilo antiguo. 2. (impr.) romano antiguo, romano de estilo antiguo. 3. según el calendario juliano.
old-style [-ˌstaɪl] *a.* de estilo antiguo.
Old Testament, Antiguo Testamento, Viejo Testamento.
old timber, madera usada, deshecho de demolición.
old-time [-ˌtaɪm] *a.* de tiempos idos, de antaño.
old-timer [-'taɪmǝr, B -mǝ] *s.* (fam.) 1. veterano; antiguo residente, antiguo empleado. 2. anciano. 3. cosa anticuada. 4. persona chapada a la antigua.
oldwife ['oʊldˌwaɪf] *s.* 1. (ict.) cochino, pámpano, brema, escaro, sábalo. 2. (orn.) pato marino. 3. vieja (esp. chismosa).
old wine, vino añejo.
old wives' tale, cuento de viejas; remedio casero.
old woman, 1. vieja. 2. (teat.) característica.
old-womanish [-'wʊmǝnɪʃ] *a.* melindroso, remilgado; con características de vieja (hombre irritable, fastidioso).
Old World, Viejo Mundo (Europa).
old-world [-'wɜrld, B -ˌwɜld] *a.* 1. del Viejo Mundo. 2. a la antigua; pintoresco. 3. de los tiempos antiguos.
Oleaceae [ˌoʊlɪ'eɪsɪˌi] *s. pl.* (bot.) oleáceas.
oleaceous [-'eɪʃǝs] *a.* (bot.) oleáceo.
oleaginous [ˌoʊlɪ'ædʒǝnǝs] *a.* oleaginoso, aceitoso.
oleaginousness [-nǝs] *s.* oleaginosidad.
oleander ['oʊlɪˌændǝr, ˌoʊlɪ'æn-, B -dǝ] *s.* (bot.) adelfa, ojaranzo, baladre.
oleaster [ˌoʊlɪ'æstǝr, B -tǝ] *s.* (bot.) oleastro, olivastro, acebuche.
oleate ['oʊlɪˌeɪt] *s.* (quím.) oleato.
olecranon [ˌoʊlǝ'kreɪˌnɑn, B -ˌnɔn] *s.* (anat.) olécrano, olécranon.
olefin ['oʊlǝfǝn] *s.* (quím.) olefina.
oleic [oʊ'liɪk] *a.* (quím.) oleico.
oleic acid, (quím.) ácido oleico.
oleiferous [ˌoʊlɪ'ɪfǝrǝs] *a.* oleífero.
olein, oleine ['oʊlɪǝn] *s.* (quím.) oleína.
oleo ['oʊlɪˌoʊ] *s.* 1. oleomargarina. 2. oleografía.
oleograph [-ˌgræf, B -ˌgrɑf] **oleography** [ˌoʊlɪ'ɑgrǝfɪ, B -'ɔg-] *s.* oleografía.
oleomargarine [ˌoʊlɪoʊ'mɑrdʒǝrǝn, -ˌrin, B 'oʊ-ˌmɑdʒǝ'rin] *s.* oleomargarina.
oleometer [ˌoʊlɪ'ɑmǝtǝr, B -'ɔmɪtǝ] *s.* oleómetro.
oleoresin [ˌoʊlɪoʊ'rɛzǝn] *s.* oleorresina.
oleose ['oʊlɪˌoʊs] **oleous** [-lɪǝs] *a.* oleoso, aceitoso.

oleo strut, (aer.) pata oleoneumática.
olfaction [ɑl'fækʃən, oʊl-, B ɔl-] *s.* (fisiol.) 1. olfacción. 2. olfato.
olfactory [-'fæktərɪ] *a.* olfatorio, olfativo.
olfactory nerve, (ant.) nervio olfatorio.
olibanum [oʊ'lɪbənəm, B ˌɔ-] *s.* olíbano, incienso, gomorresina.
oligarch ['ɑləˌgɑrk, B 'ɔlɪˌgɑk] *s.* oligarca.
oligarchic [ˌɑlə'gɑrkɪk, B ˌɔlɪ'gɑkɪk] **oligarchical** [-kɪkəl] *a.* oligárquico.
oligarchy ['ɑləˌgɑrkɪ, B 'ɔlɪˌgɑkɪ] *s.* (*pl.* OLIGARCH ES) oligarquía.
oligist ['ɑlədʒəst, B 'ɔl-] *s.* (min.) oligisto.
Oligocene ['ɑlɪgoʊˌsin, B ɔ'lɪ-] *a., s.* (geol.) oligoceno.
oligochaete ['ɑlɪgoʊˌkit, B 'ɔl-] *a., s.* (zool.) oligoqueto.
oligochaetous [ˌɑlɪgoʊ'kitəs, B ˌɔl-] *a.* (zool.) oligoqueto.
oligoclase ['ɑlɪgoʊˌkleɪs, B 'ɔl-] *s.* (min.) oligoclasa.
oligocythemia [ˌɑlɪgoʊˌsaɪ'θimɪə, B ˌɔl-] *s.* (med.) oligocitemia.
oligophrenia [-'frinɪə] *s.* (med.) oligofrenia.
oligopoly [ˌɑlɪ'gɑpəlɪ, B ˌɔlɪ'gɔp-] *s.* (econ.) oligopolio, mercado ventajoso para el vendedor y desastroso para el comprador.
oliguresis [-gjə'risəs] *s.* (med.) oliguria.
olio ['oʊlɪˌoʊ] *s.* (*pl.* OLIOS) 1. olla podrida. 2. mezcolanza, revoltijo, miscelánea. 3. popurrí (musical).
olivaceous [ˌɑlɪ'veɪʃəs, B ˌɔl-] *a.* oliváceo, verde oliva; aceitunado.
olivary ['ɑləˌverɪ, B 'ɔlɪvərɪ] *a.* (anat.) olivar, olivario, oliviforme.
olive ['ɑlɪv, B 'ɔl-] *s.* 1. (bot.) olivo, olivera. 2. oliva, aceituna. 3. color verde olivo. —*a.* de color verde olivo.
olive bearing, olivífero (árbol).
olive branch, 1. rama de olivo (considerada como emblema de paz); (cualquier) signo de paz; **to hold out the o. b.,** hacer sondeos de paz o reconciliación.
olive dealer, aceitunero.
olive drab, color amarillo verdoso.
olive green, verde oliva, color aceitunado.
olive grove, olivar.
olive harvest, verdeo.
olivenite [oʊ'lɪvəˌnaɪt] *s.* (min.) olivenita.
olive oil, aceite de oliva, aceite de olivo.
olive press, lagar, trapiche.
olive presser, lagarero.
olive yard, olivar.
olivine ['ɑlɪˌvin, B ˌɔlɪ'vin] *s.* (min.) olivino, peridoto.
olla ['ɑlə, 'ɔljə, B 'ɔlə] *s.* (*pl.* OLLAS) (pr. S.O. de E.U.) 1. marmita, puchero, olla. 2. olla podrida.
ology ['ɑlədʒɪ, B 'ɔl-] *s.* (*pl.* OLOGIES) (hum.) ciencia, ramo del saber.
Olympiad [ə'lɪmpɪˌæd] *s.* olimpiada, olimpíada.
Olympian [-ən] *a.* 1. olímpico, de Olimpia, del Olimpo. 2. (fig.) olímpico, soberbio; celestial, divino. —*s.* 1. (mitol.) uno de los doce dioses (que habitaban en el Olimpo). 2. nativo de Olimpia. 3. participante en los juegos olímpicos.
Olympian games, (hist.) juegos olímpicos (en la Grecia antigua).
Olympic [ə'lɪmpɪk] *a.* olímpico. —*s.* (*pl.*) juegos olímpicos.
Olympic Games, *pl.* Juegos Olímpicos.
Olympus [-pəs] *s.* 1. Olimpo, residencia de los dioses. 2. (fig.) empíreo, cielo.
O.M. *abrev. de* **Order of Merit,** Orden de Mérito.
omasum [oʊ'meɪsəm] *s.* (*pl.* OMASA [-sə]) (zool.) omaso, libro (de los rumiantes).
ombre ['ɑmbər, B 'ɔmbə] *s.* hombre (juego de naipes).
ombudsman ['ɑmbədzˌmæn, B 'ɔmbʊdzmən] *s.* mediador en asuntos de interés público, protector del interés público (esp. en Suecia).
omega [oʊ'mɛgə, -'migə, B 'oʊmɪ-] *s.* 1. omega, última letra del alfabeto griego. 2. (fig.) fin, término.
omelet, omelette ['ɑmlət, 'ɑmə-, B 'ɔmlɪt] *s.* tortilla de huevos.
omen ['oʊmən, B -mɛn] *s.* augurio. agüero, presagio, predicción, pronóstico. —*v.t.* ominar, presagiar, augurar, pronosticar.
omental [oʊ'mɛntəl] *a.* (anat.) omental.
omentum [-təm] *s.* (*pl.* OMENTA [-tə] o OMENTUMS) (anat.) omento; **the great o.,** epiplón.
omer ['oʊmər, B -mə] *s.* (hist.) medida hebrea de capacidad.
omicron ['ɑməˌkrɑn, B oʊ'maɪkrən] *s.* ómicron, decimoquinta letra del alfabeto griego.
ominous ['ɑmənəs, B 'ɔm-] *a.* ominoso, siniestro, nefasto, de mal agüero, portentoso.
ominously [-lɪ] *adv.* ominosamente.
ominousness [-nəs] *s.* carácter o aspecto ominoso.
omissible [oʊ'mɪsəbəl] *a.* que se puede omitir.
omission [-'mɪʃən, ə-] *s.* omisión; olvido, descuido.
omissive [-'mɪsɪv] *a.* tendiente a omitir, que omite; omisivo.
omissively [-lɪ] *adv.* con omisión, con omisiones.
omit [oʊ'mɪt, ə-] *v.t.* (*pret., p.p.* OMITTED; *p.pr.* OMITTING) 1. omitir, excluir. 2. omitir, dejar de (hacer), prescindir de, pasar por alto.
ommatidium [ˌɑmə'tɪdɪəm, B ˌɔm-] *s.* (*pl.* OMMATIDIA [-ə]) (zool.) omatidia.
omnibus ['ɑmnɪˌbʌs, -bəs, B 'ɔm-] *s.* (*pl.* OMNIBUSES) 1. ómnibus, autobús. 2. libro que contiene varias obras (a veces de un solo autor). —*a.* colectivo, general, que comprende varios asuntos, objetos, etc.
omnibus bill, (der.) agrupación de proyectos legislativos.
omnidirectional [ˌɑmnɪdə'rɛkʃənəl, B ˌɔm-] *a.* (rad.) omnidireccional (antena, emisión, etc.).
omnifarious [-'fɛrɪəs, B -'fɛər-] *a.* de todo género, toda forma o clase, de todas variedades.
omnific [ɑm'nɪfɪk, B ɔm-] *a.* que todo lo crea.
omnificent [-əsənt] *a.* de ilimitado poder creativo.
omnipotence [ɑm'nɪpətəns, B ɔm-] *s.* omnipotencia.
omnipotency [-ənsɪ] *s.* omnipotencia.
omnipotent [-ənt] *a.* omnipotente. —*s.* **The O.,** El Todopoderoso.
omnipotently [-lɪ] *adv.* omnipotentemente.
omnipresence [ˌɑmnɪ'prɛzəns, B 'ɔm-] *s.* omnipresencia, ubicuidad.
omnipresent [-ənt] *a.* omnipresente, ubicuo.
omnirange ['ɑmnɪˌreɪndʒ, B 'ɔm-] *s.* (rad.) radiofaro omnidireccional.
omniscience [ɑm'nɪʃəns, B ɔm'nɪsɪəns] **omnisciency** *s.* omnisciencia.
omniscient [-ənt] *a.* omnisciente, omniscio.
omnisciently [-lɪ] *adv.* de modo omnisciente.
omnium ['ɑmnɪəm, B 'ɔm-] *s.* 1. (G.B.) agregado de los títulos de la deuda. 2. suma, total.
omnium-gatherum [-'gæðərəm] *s.* 1. mezcolanza, miscelánea (de personas o cosas), maremágnum. 2. reunión a la cual se invita a todo el mundo.
omnivora [ɑm'nɪvərə, B ɔm-] *s. pl.* (zool.) omnívoros.
omnivore ['ɑmnɪˌvɔr, B 'ɔmnɪˌvɔ] *s.* (zool.) omnívoro.
omnivorous [ɑm'nɪvərəs, B ɔm-] *a.* omnívoro.
omnivorously [-lɪ] *adv.* de manera omnívora.
omnivorousness [-nəs] *s.* calidad de omnívoro.
omophagous [oʊ'mɑfəgəs, B -'mɔf-] **omophagic** [ˌoʊmə'fædʒɪk] *a.* omófago.
omphalophlebitis ['ɑmfəloʊflə'baɪtəs, B 'ɔm-] *s.* (med.) onfaloflebitis.
omphalos ['ɑmfələs, B 'ɔmfəlɔs] *s.* (*pl.* OMPHALI [-ˌlaɪ]) 1. (anat.) ombligo. 2. (fig.) centro, núcleo.
on [ɑn, ɔn, B ɔn] *prep.* 1. sobre, encima de; en, a, ej., *it is on the table,* está sobre la mesa, *he goes on foot,* él va a pie, *she had a ring on her finger,* tenía un anillo en el dedo. 2. sobre, en (que tiene base, motivo, confirmación o garantía consistente en), ej., *based on facts,* basado en hechos, *swear on the Bible,* jurar sobre la Biblia, *interest on capital,* interés sobre el capital, *a tax on paper,* impuesto sobre el papel. 3. por, hacia, (con dirección) a; contra, ej., *the church is on the right,* la iglesia está por o hacia la derecha, *the ship is driving on shore,* el barco se va contra la playa. 4. (de tiempo) durante, (exactamente) a, (inmediatamente) después de; luego de, ej., *it happened on the night of* 10 *January,* ocurrió durante la noche del 10 de enero, *on my return,* a mi regreso. 5. en, sobre, concerniente a, acerca de, relacionado con, ej., *he is keen on politics,* él está interesado en la política, *a book on textiles,* un libro sobre tejidos. 6. además de, sobre, ej., *lies on lies,* mentiras sobre mentiras. 7. (fam.) a la salud de, ej., *have a drink on me,* bebe a mi salud. 8. *en locuciones adverbiales de una manera especificada por un adjetivo o sustantivo,* ej., *on the sly,* furtivamente, *on fire,* ardiendo, en llamas, *on loan,* en préstamo, *on sale,* en venta, *on strike,* en huelga. 9. (fam.) a expensas de, ej., *the joke was on me,* la broma fue a mis expensas. 10. **have you a match on you?** ¿tienes un fósforo?; **he is gone on her,** (jer.) él está enamorado de ella; **on the house,** (una copa) por cuenta de la casa; **on the instant,** inmediatamente; **on the rocks,** (jer.) en dificultades (esp. financieras); sobre hielo (esp. wisky); **on time,** puntualmente. —*adv.* 1. puesto, encendido, en funcionamiento, ej., *the light is on,* la luz está encendida, *she had her green hat on,* llevaba puesto su sombrero verde. 2. en alguna dirección, adelante, más (allá, adelante, tarde), ej., *getting on,* saliendo adelante, marchando, *later on,* más tarde, después. 3. sucesivamente (se usa para indicar continuación), ej., *and so on,* y así sucesivamente, *to march on,* seguir marchando. 4. **come on!** ¡vamos!; **from that day on,** a partir de ese día; **keep your hat on,** no te quites el sombrero; **on and off,** a intervalos, de vez en cuando; **on and on,** sin cesar, continuamente; (com.) **on account,** a cuenta; **on an average,** por término medio; **on a sudden,** de golpe, de repente; **on credit,** fiado; **on duty,** en servicio; **on guard,** alerta; **on hand,** a mano, disponible; (com.) en existencia; **on horseback,** a caballo; **on purpose,** a propósito; **on record,** que consta, registrado; **on the contrary,** al contrario; **on the cuff,** sin pagar; **on the go,** correteando, callejando; **on the road,** viajando, de viaje; **on the run,** afanándose, corriendo; **on to,** a, hacia; **on trust,** fiado; **on with your coat!** ¡ponte el abrigo!; **to be on to,** (jer.) comprender (algo), darse cuenta de, llegar a saber, estar al tanto o al corriente de; caer en la cuenta de (algo); **to send (someone) on,** mandar adelante (a alguien).

onager ['ɑnɪdʒər, B 'ɔnəgə] *s.* (*pl.* ONAGRI [-ˌgraɪ] u ONAGERS) 1. (zool.) onagro. 2. (hist.) onagro (máquina anticuada de guerra).
Onagraceae [ˌɑnə'greɪsɪˌi, B ˌɔn-] *s. pl.* (bot.) onagráceas.
onagraceous [-'greɪʃəs] *a.* (bot.) onagráceo.
onanism ['oʊnəˌnɪzəm] *s.* 1. onanismo, coito incompleto. 2. onanismo, masturbación.
once [wʌns] *adv.* 1. una vez, alguna vez, una sola vez, ej., *I have read it more than o.,* lo he leído más de una vez, *I have not seen him o.,* no lo he visto ni una sola vez. 2. anteriormente, antiguamente, en otro tiempo, otrora, otras veces, ej., *a o. famous doctrine,* una doctrina famosa antiguamente. 3. **o. and again,** una que otra vez; **o. (and) for all,** definitivamente, de una vez por todas; **o. bit twice shy,** ese perro no me muerde otra vez; **o. in a blue moon,** de Pascuas a San Juan, por jubileo, muy rara vez; **o. in a while,** de vez en cuando; **o. more,** otra vez; **o. or twice,** una o dos veces; **o. too often,** una vez más de lo prudente; **o. upon a time,** (había) una vez, érase que se era. *a.* anterior, antiguo; de ese entonces. —*s.* 1. una vez, una ocasión, ej., *o. is enough for me,* una vez es suficiente para mí. 2. **all at o.,** de súbito, de repente; **at o.,** inmediatamente, ahora mismo, en el acto, en seguida, al mismo tiempo, simultáneamente; **for o.,** una vez siquiera, esta vez; **for this o.,** por esta sola vez. —*conj.* si alguna vez; cuando; tan pronto como.
once-over ['wʌnsˌoʊvər, B -və] *s.* (jer.) ojeada, mirada; revisada o limpieza a la ligera.
oncology [ɑŋ'kɑlədʒɪ, B ɔŋ'kɔl-] *s.* (med.) oncología.
oncoming ['ɑnˌkʌmɪŋ, B 'ɔn-] *a.* 1. que viene, que se aproxima, próximo, cercano. 2. futuro, venidero.
ondograph ['ɑndəˌgræf, B 'ɔndəˌgrɑf] *s.* (elec.) ondógrafo.
ondometer [ɑn'dɑmətər, B ɔn'dɔmɪtə] *s.* (elec.) ondómetro.
one [wʌn] *a.* 1. un, uno, único, ej. *o. man in ten,* uno (hombre) entre diez, *the o. way to do it,* el único modo de hacerlo. 2. uno, un cierto, alguno, ej., *I met him o. night,* lo conocí o encontré una noche, *I will take you there o. day,* te llevaré algún día. 3. un tal, ej., *o. Jones,* un tal Jones. 4. igual, idéntico, ej., *we are of o mind,* pensamos igual. 5. **o. man o. vote,** cada hombre tiene sólo un voto, un voto por persona; **o. or two people,** poca gente. —*s.* 1. uno (número o persona), ej., *in the year o.,* en el año uno, en el año de la nana. 2. (billete) de un dólar 3. **a o.,** (fam.) un tipo único. —*pron.* 1. uno, ej., *I met o. of my friends,* me encontré con uno de mis amigos, *o. would like to know,* uno desearía saber, a uno le gustaría saber. 2. se, ej., *how can o know?* ¿cómo se sabe? 3. **all in o.,** todo junto; **a nasty o.,** un golpe severo; **I for o.,** yo por lo menos; **it is all o. to me,** me da lo mismo, eso me es indiferente; **little o.,** chiquito, niñito; **many a o.,** muchos; **of o. another,** el uno del otro; **o. after another,** uno tras otro, uno a uno; **o. and all,** todos juntos, todos; **o. and sixpence,** un chelín y seis peniques; **o. another,** se, el uno al otro, ej., *they hate o. another,* se odian mutuamente, *they told o. another,* se contaron el uno al otro; **o. by o.,** uno a uno, uno por uno; **o. for the road,** (fam.) trago o copita de despedida, la del estribo; **o. in the eye,** un golpe en el ojo; **o. night stand,** función de una sola noche, (jer.) aventura de una noche; **o. of the boys,** (fam.) camarada; **o. or two,** unos cuantos, unos pocos; **o. too many,** (fam.) un trago de más; **that o.,** aquél, ése; **the Evil O.,** el Malo; **the o. and only,** el único; **the o. that,** el o la que; **this o.,** éste; **to go o. better,** ofrecer más, arriesgar o superar por un punto o grado; **to make o.,** unir, unir en matrimonio.
one-act ['wʌn'ækt] *a.* de un acto, en un acto.
one-armed bandit [-'ɑrmd-, B -'ɑmd-] (jer.) tragamonedas (para el juego de azar).
one day, cierto día, un día de éstos.
one-dimensional [-də'mɛntʃənəl, B -'mɛnʃən-] *a.* unidimensional.
one-egg [-'ɛg] *a.* (biol.) uniovular.
one-eyed [-'aɪd] *a.* tuerto.
one-handed [-'hændəd] *a.* manco.
one-horse [-'hɔrs, B -'hɔs] *a.* 1. de un caballo (de fuerza), tirado por un solo caballo. 2. (fam.) inferior, de segunda categoría, insignificante, ej., *o.-h. town,* pueblecito rural, pueblo de mala muerte.
one hundred, cien, ciento.
oneiric [oʊ'naɪrɪk] *a.* oneírico, onírico (relativo a los sueños).
oneirocritic [-ˌnaɪrə'krɪtɪk] *s.* onirocrítico, oneirocrítico.
oneirocritical [-ɪkəl] *a.* onirocrítico, oneirocrítico.
oneiromancy [oʊ'naɪrəˌmænsɪ] *s.* oniromancia, (práctica de prever el futuro mediante la interpretación de los sueños).
one-legged ['wʌn'lɛgd, -'lɛgəd] *a.* cojo, con una sola pierna o pata.
one liner, dicho ingenioso.
one man band, hombre orquesta.
one man show, exposición de un solo artista.
oneness [-nəs] *s.* 1. unidad. 2. entereza, integridad. 3. identidad, igualdad.
one on one, uno a uno, mano a mano.
one-piece [-'pis] *a.* enterizo, de una pieza (ej., traje de baño).
onerous ['ɑnərəs, 'oʊnə-, B 'ɔnə-] *a.* 1. oneroso, molesto, cargoso. 2. (der.) oneroso.
onerous consideration, (der.) causa onerosa.
onerous title, (der.) título oneroso.
oneself [ˌwʌn'sɛlf] *pron.* uno mismo, sí, sí mismo; se; **to be o.,** tener dominio de sí mismo, conducirse con naturalidad; **to come to o.,** volver en sí; **to o.,** para sus adentros; **with o.,** consigo mismo.
one-shot ['wʌnˌʃɑt, B -ˌʃɔt] *a.* 1. de tiro (arma). 2. único, no repetido. 3. **o.-s. deal,** hecho una sola vez, asunto que no se repite.
one-sided [-'saɪdəd] *a.* 1. de un solo lado. 2. desproporcionado, desequilibrado; desigual. 3. injusto, parcial. 4. (der.) unilateral, ej., *o. contract,* contrato unilateral.
one-step [-ˌstɛp] *s.* one-step, baile de salón en compás binario; música para one-step. —*v.i.* (*pret., p.p.* ONE-STEPPED; *p.pr.* ONE-STEPPING) bailar el one-step.
one thousand, mil (unidad).
onetime [-ˌtaɪm] *a.* antiguo; de otro tiempo. —*adv.* antiguamente.
one to one, en correspondencia exacta.
one-track [-ˌtræk] *a.* 1. de carril único. 2. que se interesa por una sola cosa, ej., *he has a o -t. mind,* él se interesa por una sola cosa, es incapaz de abarcar más de un tema a la vez.
one-upmanship [ˌwʌn'ʌpmənˌʃɪp] *s.* arte de cómo superar a otros.
one-way ['wʌn'weɪ] *a.* 1. de una sola dirección; de un solo sentido (avenida, calle, tráfico, etc.). 2. unilateral. 3. (sólo) de ida (billete).
one-way street, calle de dirección única *or* sentido único *or* una vía *or* un solo sentido.
one-way ticket, billete sencillo, billete de ida.
ongoing ['ɑnˌgoʊɪŋ, 'ɔn-, B 'ɔn-] *a.* 1. en curso, actual. 2. progresivo. —*s.* 1. actividad. 2. progreso.
onion ['ʌnjən] *s.* 1. (bot.) cebolla (planta y cepa o bulbo). 2. (jer.) coco, cabeza. 3. **to know one's onions,** (fam. G.B.) ser astuto, sabérselas todas.
onion bed, cebollar.
onion-grass [-ˌgræs, B -ˌgrɑs] *s.* (bot.) (especie de) avena silvestre.
onion seed, cebollino.
onionskin [-ˌskɪn] *s.* 1. papel delgado; cuartillas para copia. 2. cáscara de cebolla.
onion-twitch [-ˌtwɪtʃ] *s.* (bot.) (especie de) avena silvestre.
on-line, (comput.) on-line, en línea (*switched on*) conectado.
onlooker ['ɑnˌlʊkər, 'ɔn-, B 'ɔnˌlʊkə] *s.* mirón, espectador.
only ['oʊnlɪ] *a.* solo, único, ej., *o. child,* hijo único. —*adv.* 1. sólo, solamente, únicamente, ej., *o you* (o *you o.*) *can guess it,* solamente Ud. puede adivinarlo, *I was only joking,* yo sólo bromeaba, *if o. for the sake of your son,* siquiera por el bien de su hijo, *he came yesterday o.,* vino sólo ayer. 2. sólo, apenas, ej., *we arrived o. today,* apenas llegamos hoy. 3. **if o.,** ojalá que, ej., *if o. someone would teach me!* ¡ojalá que alguien me enseñara!; **o. just,** con las justas; acabar de, ej., *we o. just saw her,* acabamos de verla; **not o . . . but also,** no sólo . . . sino también; **o. too,** de veras, muy, ej., *I'd be o. too glad to do it,* estaría de veras encantado de hacerlo; **o. too well,** de sobra. —*conj.* sólo que, pero, ej., *he makes good resolutions, o. he never keeps them,* toma buenas resoluciones, pero no las mantiene.
only-begotten [-bɪ'gɑtən, B -'gɔt-] *a.* unigénito.
only child, hijo único.
onomastic [ˌɑnə'mæstɪk, B ˌɔn-] *a.* 1. onomástico. 2. autógrafo.
onomastics [-tɪks] *s. pl.* (*sing. en const.*) onomástica.
onomatopoeia [ˌɑnəˌmætə'piə, B ˌɔn-] *s.* onomatopeya.
onomatopoeic [-'piɪk] **onomatopoetic** [-poʊ'ɛtɪk] *a.* onomatopéyico.
on ramp, (aut.) vía de acceso (a una autopista).
onrush ['ɑnˌrʌʃ, 'ɔn-, B 'ɔn-] *s.* arremetida; embestida; arranque; ataque, carga.
onset ['ɔnˌsɛt, 'ɑn-, B 'ɔn-] *s.* 1. ataque, asalto; arremetida. 2. principio, comienzo.
onshore [-ˌʃɔr, B -ˌʃɔ] *a.* 1. que se dirige hacia la tierra o la orilla. 2. en tierra. 3. (E.U.) del país, local. —*adv.* hacia la tierra; a tierra.
on side, (dep.) en posición correcta o permitida.
onslaught [-ˌslɔt] *s.* ataque furioso; embestida violenta; asalto.
on-stream [-'strim] *adv.* en funcionamiento.
Ont. *abrev. de* **Ontario,** Ontario.
ontic ['ɑntɪk, B 'ɔn-] *a.* (filos.) óntico.
onto ['ɔntu, 'ɑn-, B 'ɔn-] *prep.* 1. encima de, sobre, en, a. 2. (jer.) al tanto o al corriente de; en la cuenta de (algo).
ontogenesis [ˌɑntə'dʒɛnəsəs, B ˌɔn-] *var. de* **ontogeny.**
ontogenetic [-dʒə'nɛtɪk] *a.* (biol.) ontogénico.
ontogenist [ɑn'tɑdʒənəst, B ɔn'tɔdʒ-] *s.* (biol.) ontogenista.
ontogeny [-nɪ] *s.* (biol.) ontogenia, ontogénesis.
ontological [ˌɑntə'lɑdʒɪkəl, B ˌɔntə'lɔdʒ-] *a.* (filos.) ontológico.
ontologist [ɑn'tɑlədʒəst, B ɔn'tɔl-] *s.* (filos.) ontólogo.
ontology [-dʒɪ] *s.* (filos.) ontología.
onus ['oʊnəs] *s.* carga, obligación, responsabilidad; **o. probandi,** (der.) obligación de probar.
onward ['ɔnwərd, 'ɑn-, B 'ɔnwəd] **onwards** [-wərdz, B -wədz] *adv.* adelante, hacia adelante. —*a.* 1. que está delante. 2. progresivo.

onyx ['ɑnɪks, B 'ɔn-] *s.* (min.) ónice, ónix, ónique.

oocyte ['oʊəˌsaɪt] *s.* (biol.) oocito.

oodles ['udəlz] *s. pl.* (fam.) montones (de), la mar (de).

oof [uf] *s.* (jer., G.B.) mosca, guita, plata, agua (Amer.) (dinero).

oogamete [ˌoʊəgə'mit, B -'ɔgəˌmit] *s.* (biol.) oógamo.

oogamous [oʊ'ɑgəməs, B -'ɔg-] *a.* (biol.) oógamo.

oogamy [-mɪ] *s.* (biol.) oogamia.

oogenesis [ˌoʊə'dʒɛnəsəs] *s.* (biol.) oogénesis.

oogonium [-'goʊnɪəm] *s.* (*pl.* OOGONIUMS u OOGONIA [-nɪə]) (biol., bot.) oogonio.

oolite ['oʊəˌlaɪt] *s.* (geol.) oolito, oolita.

oolitic [ˌoʊə'lɪtɪk] *a.* (geol.) oolítico.

oological [-'lɑdʒɪkəl, B -'lɔdʒ-] *a.* (orn.) oológico.

oologist [oʊ'ɑlədʒəst, B -'ɔl-] *s.* (orn.) oólogo.

oology [-dʒɪ] *s.* (zool.) oología.

oolong ['uˌlɔŋ] *s.* (variedad de) té chino negro.

oomiac, oomiak, *var. de* **umiak.**

oomph [ʊmf] *s.* (jer.) 1. atractivo sexual. 2. vitalidad, brío, energía.

oophorectomy [ˌoʊəfə'rɛktəmɪ] *s.* (med.) ooforectomía, ovariotomía.

oophoritis [-'raɪtəs] *s.* (med.) ooforitis, ovaritis.

oophyte ['oʊəˌfaɪt] *s.* (bot.) oofito.

oophytic [ˌoʊə'fɪtɪk] *a.* (bot.) oofítico.

oops [ups] *interj.* ¡uf! ¡upa!

oosperm ['oʊəˌspɜrm, B -ˌspɜm] *s.* (zool.) oospermo.

oosphere [-ˌsfɪr, B -ˌsfɪə] *s.* (biol.) oosfera.

oospore [-ˌspɔr, B -ˌspɔ] *s.* (bot.) oóspora, oósporo.

ootheca [ˌoʊə'θikə] *s.* (*pl.* OOTHECAE [-ki]) (zool.) ooteca.

ootid ['oʊəˌtɪd] *s.* (biol.) oótide.

ooze [uz] *s.* 1. zumaque, catecú, cato (que se usa para curtir el cuero). 2. exudación; rezumadero, lo rezumado. —*v.i.* 1. rezumarse, manar, fluir; escurrirse; exudar; trazumarse. 2. (fig.) (con *out* o *away*) escurrirse poco a poco. 3. **o. with,** exudar. —*v.t.* manar, sudar; rezumar, supurar.

ooze, *s.* 1. fango, lama, limo, cieno. 2. pantano, ciénaga; marisma.

oozy ['uzɪ] *a.* (OOZIER; OOZIEST) lamoso, legamoso; húmedo.

op. *abrev. de* 1. **opus,** obra. 2. **operation,** operación. 3. **opposite,** opuesto. 4. **out of print,** fuera de circulación, edición agotada. 5. **opera,** ópera.

O.P. *abrev. de* 1. **observation post,** puesto de observación. 2. **Order of Preachers,** Orden de los Predicadores (O.P.), (dominicanos, dominicos).

opacity [oʊ'pæsətɪ] *s.* 1. opacidad. 2. obscuridad, falta de claridad (en lo escrito o hablado). 3. (med.) opacidad (en la córnea del ojo).

opah ['oʊpə] *s.* (zool.) pez luna.

opal ['oʊpəl] *s.* (min.) ópalo.

opalescence [ˌoʊpə'lɛsəns] *s.* opalescencia.

opalescent [-ənt] *a.* opalescente.

opaline ['oʊpəˌlaɪn, B -ˌlin] *a.* opalino.

opaque [oʊ'peɪk] *a.* 1. opaco, intransparente. 2. mate; sin brillo, amortiguado, deslucido, apagado. 3. (fig.) obscuro, ininteligible; obtuso. —*s.* (foto.) pintura opaca (para cubrir partes de un negativo).

opaquely [-lɪ] *adv.* de modo opaco.

opaqueness [-nəs] *s.* opacidad.

op art [ɑp-, B ɔp-] arte op u óptico (en que se usan formas geométricas para crear ilusiones ópticas, esp. de movimiento).

op. cit. *abrev. de* opere citato (lat.), **in the work cited,** en la obra citada.

ope [oʊp] *a.* (poét.) abierto. —*v.t.* (poét.) abrir.

open ['oʊpən] *a.* 1. abierto (no cerrado ni cubierto), ej., *o. gate,* puerta abierta, *o. passage,* pasaje abierto, libre, *o. boat,* embarcación abierta. 2. abierto, libre, sin limitación, vigente, disponible, ej., *the invitation is still o.,* la invitación aún está vigente. 3. abierto, despejado; desembarazado, llano, raso, ej., *o. field,* campo raso, descampado. 4. descubierto, destapado, ej., *o. motor,* motor destapado, o descubierto. 5. (con *to*) susceptible, expuesto (a); accesible a, ej., *o. to temptation,* expuesto a tentación, *o. to suggestions,* accesible a sugerencias. 6. público, manifiesto. 7. extendido, desplegado, desdoblado. 8. discutible, ej., *o. question,* cuestión discutible. 9. con intersticios; perforado, poroso. 10. libre, no ocupado, disponible (tiempo, hora). 11. abierto, franco, sincero, ej., *o. look,* mirada franca, *o. face,* cara franca, *I will be o. with you,* te seré sincero. 12. accesible; dócil. 13. libre de hielo (río, puerto). 14. (com.) libre (economía, mercado). 15. (mús.) de cuerdas no pisadas; natural. 16. (mil.) abierto (ciudad o pueblo). 17. (fon.) abierto, libre, ej., *o. syllable,* sílaba abierta o libre. 18. **in o. court,** tribunal en pleno; **to lay o.,** exponer, revelar, descubrir; **to throw o.,** abrir de un tirón (puerta, ventana, etc.); **with an o. hand,** con mano abierta, con generosidad; **with o. arms,** (lit., fig.) con los brazos abiertos. —*v.t.* 1. abrir. 2. exponer, descubrir, revelar, divulgar, ej., *the wonders of astronomy were opened to him,* las maravillas de la astronomía le fueron reveladas. 3. desapretar, aflojar. 4. abrir, empezar, dar comienzo a, ej., *o. the ball,* abrir el baile, dar comienzo al baile. 5. (der.) volver a poner en debate o discusión (una regla o fallo establecido). 6. **o. another's eyes,** abrirle los ojos a otro; **o. court,** abrir la sesión o la audiencia, iniciar la vista de un caso (un tribunal); **o. fire,** abrir fuego; **o. out,** desarrollar, desplegar; **o. the door to,** (fig.) abrir (la) puerta a; **o. the ground,** remover la tierra (con el arado); **o. the mind,** abrir o ampliar la mente; **o. up,** hacer accesible, dar a conocer. —*v.i.* 1. abrirse (puerta, etc.); abrir la puerta. 2. abrirse, desplegarse; destaparse. 3. abrirse, descubrirse. 4. empezar, comenzar; estrenarse. 5. (caza) echar a ladrar (perro al encontrar la pista). 6. (bridge) abrir la licitación; atacar, iniciar el juego (con cierta carta). 7. **o. into,** desembocar (en); **o. on** (u **onto**), dar a (ventana, puerta, etc.), ej., *my window opens onto a garden,* mi ventana da a un jardín; **o. out,** desplegarse, desarrollarse; acelerar a fondo (en automóvil, bote, etc.); **o. up,** abrirse, descubrirse, descubrir el pecho; (jer.) usar toda su fuerza, poner en acción todos sus recursos; atacar; empezar a disparar; **o. with,** empezar con. —*s.* 1. claro, raso, lugar abierto. 2. abertura. 3. (dep.) torneo o campeonato abierto. 4. **in the open,** al aire libre; a campo raso; en el campo; en alta mar; al descubierto.

open account, (ten.) cuenta abierta.

open admission policy, política de no reparar en credo, color o raza para facilitar el ingreso universitario (educ., E.U.).

open air, aire libre.

open-air ['oʊpənˌɛr, B -'ɛə] *a.* al aire libre, a cielo abierto.

open-and-shut [-ən'ʃʌt] *a.* (fam.) muy simple; obvio, indiscutible.

opencast [-ˌkæst, B -ˌkɑst] (pr. G.B.) *var. de* **opencut.**

open chain, (quím.) cadena abierta.

open circuit, (elec.) circuito abierto.

open city, (mil.) ciudad abierta (ej., Roma durante la Segunda Guerra Mundial).

open credit, (com.) crédito abierto, crédito en blanco.

opencut [-'kʌt] *a.* (min.) a cielo abierto, a tajo abierto.

open date, fecha por fijar.

open door, (pol.) libre acceso.

open-door ['oʊpən'dɔr, B -'dɔ] *a.* de puertas abiertas.

open-ended [-'ɛnd] *a.* (com.) abierto (sin límite fijo de vigencia o cantidad).

open-end mortgage, (com.) hipoteca indeterminada o abierta.

opener ['oʊpənər, B -ə] *s.* 1. abridor. 2. (póker) abridor; (*pl.*) cartas abridoras. 3. (dep.) primer partido de un campeonato o serie. 4. (teat.) primer acto de un espectáculo de variedades.

open-eyed [-'aɪd] *a.* 1. alerta, vigilante, receptivo. 2. con ojos asombrados; pasmado.

open-face [-'feɪs] **open-faced** [-'feɪst] *a.* 1. sin tapa (reloj). 2. de cara franca. 3. descarado.

open flank, (mil.) flanco expuesto.

open forum, asamblea, debate público.

open ground, (mil.) terreno abierto, terreno descubierto.

openhanded [-'hændəd] *a.* maniabierto, generoso, dadivoso.

openhandedly [-lɪ] *adv.* a mano abierta, dadivosamente, generosamente.

openhandedness [-nəs] *s.* generosidad, dadivosidad.

open-heart ['oʊpən'hɑrt, B -'hɑt] *a.* (med.) a corazón abierto (en cardiocirugía).

openhearted [-əd] *a.* 1. franco, sincero. 2. generoso.

openheartedly [-lɪ] *adv.* 1. francamente, sinceramente. 2. generosamente.

openheartedness [-nəs] *s.* 1. franqueza, sinceridad. 2. generosidad.

open-hearth process [-'hɑrθ-, B -'hɑθ-] (metal.) procedimiento al hogar abierto, procedimiento Siemens-Martin para elaborar el acero.

open house, casa abierta para todos; **to keep an o. h.,** tener la casa abierta para todos, recibir socialmente sin invitación específica.

opening ['oʊpənɪŋ] *a.* 1. apertura; principio, comienzo, inauguración. 2. abertura, hendidura, agujero, grieta, brecha; boquete; orificio. 3. (E.U.) claro (en un bosque). 4. oportunidad, ocasión; empleo vacante. 5. apertura (de ajedrez o damas).

opening night, noche de estreno (de una obra de teatro, ópera, etc.).

opening play, (dep.) salida, jugada de apertura.

opening price, precio de base, precio básico (en remate, subasta, etc.); precio de apertura (en la bolsa de valores).

open letter, carta abierta (gen. publicada en los periódicos).

openly ['oʊpənlɪ] *adv.* 1. abiertamente. 2. a las claras, al descubierto. 3. públicamente.

open market, mercado libre, mercado abierto.

open marks, *pl.* señales palpables.

open-minded ['oʊpən'maɪndəd] *a.* liberal, receptivo, razonable, imparcial.

open-mindedly [-lɪ] *adv.* liberalmente, razonablemente, imparcialmente, receptivamente.

open-mindedness [-nəs] *s.* liberalidad, receptividad, imparcialidad.

open mix, (const.) mezcla porosa.

openmouthed [-'maʊðd] *a.* 1. boquiabierto; embobado. 2. clamoroso, vociferante.

openness ['oʊpənnəs] *s.* 1. franqueza, sinceridad. 2. imparcialidad.

open order, (mil.) formación abierta, orden abierto.

open policy, póliza (de seguros) abierta o flotante.
open port, 1. puerto abierto (al comercio exterior). 2. puerto franco, puerto libre. 3. puerto accesible durante todo el año (no bloqueado por los hielos).
open ranks, (mil., mar.) (formación en) hileras abiertas.
open sea, altamar.
open season, temporada de caza y pesca.
open secret, secreto a voces, secreto de Anchuelo, secreto con chirimías.
open sesame, ¡ábrete sésamo! (fig.) palabras mágicas.
open shade, (foto.) sombra al descubierto.
open shame, vergüenza pública.
open shop, taller franco (que emplea obreros agremiados y no agremiados).
open sight, alza de ranura, alza entallada, mira (de un arma de fuego).
open sleeve, (cost.) manga perdida.
open spaces, espacios abiertos.
open stock, (com.) existencia de piezas de repuesto (esp. para artículos que se venden en juegos, como platos, cubiertos, etc.).
open storage, almacenaje al aire libre, almacenaje al descubierto.
open verdict, (der.) veredicto inconcluso (del jurado).
open vowel, (gram.) vocal abierta.
open warfare, (mil.) guerra declarada.
openwork ['oʊpən,wɜrk, B -,wɜk] *s.* calado.
opera ['ɑpərə, B 'ɔp-] *s.* (mús.) ópera.
operable ['ɑpərəbəl, B 'ɔp-] *a.* 1. operable, factible. 2. (med.) operable.
opéra bouffe [,ɑpərə'buf B 'ɔp-] **opera buffa** [-fɑ] (mús.) ópera bufa.
opéra comique [-kɔ'mik] (mús.) ópera cómica, zarzuela.
opera glasses, gemelos de teatro.
opera hat, clac, chistera plegable.
opera house, teatro de la ópera.
operand ['ɑpə,rænd, B 'ɔp-] *s.* (mat.) operando.
operant ['rənt] *s.* operario. *—a.* operante; (psic.) operante.
operate ['ɑpə,reɪt, B 'ɔp-] *v.i.* 1. actuar, funcionar, marchar. 2. operar, surtir efecto (medicamento, etc.). 3. especular, hacer operaciones (en la bolsa de valores). 4. (med.) (con *on* o *upon*) operar. 5. (mil., mar.) maniobrar, operar. 6. **time operates in our favor,** el tiempo nos favorece; **to o. on someone for (something),** (med.) operar a alguien de (algo). *—v.t.* 1. producir, originar. 2. manejar. 3. (med.) operar. 4. **operated by,** (mec.) accionado por.
operatic [,ɑpə'rætɪk, B ,ɔp-] *a.* operístico, de ópera.
operatically [-ɪkəlɪ] *adv.* como (en) una ópera, al estilo operístico.
operating ['ɑpə,reɪtɪŋ, B 'ɔp-] *a.* 1. en funcionamiento (motor, etc.). 2. activo (en algún negocio, etc.). 3. de operación (gasto, persona.) 4. de operaciones (sala, mesa).
operating ceiling, (aer.) techo máximo.
operating current, (elec.) corriente de régimen.
operating expenses, (com.) gastos de operación.
operating frequency, (rad.) frecuencia de funcionamiento.
operating mechanism, mecanismo de maniobra.
operating profit, (com.) utilidad de explotación.
operating range, radio de acción.
operating room, sala de operaciones, quirófano.
operating speed, régimen de crucero.
operating table, 1. (med.) mesa de operaciones. 2. mesa de control.
operating temperature, temperatura de trabajo.
operating theater, (med.) sala de operaciones, quirófano.
operation [,ɑpə'reɪʃən, B ,ɔp-] *s.* 1. operación, funcionamiento; manejo, manipulación. 2. (mil., mat.) operación. 3. (com.) operación, transacción. 4. (med.) operación, intervención quirúrgica. 5. **in o.,** en funcionamiento; en uso; **to go into o.,** entrar en función, en efecto, en acción, en vigencia.
Operation Desert Shield, Operación Escudo del Desierto.
Operation Desert Storm, Operación Tormenta del Deserto.
operational [-əl] *a.* 1. de operación, de operaciones. 2. (mat.) operacional. 3. (mil., mar.) operacional; listo para el combate.
operational flight, (aer.) vuelo de servicio.
operationalism [-,ɪzəm] *s.* (filos.) operacionalismo.
operative ['ɑpərətɪv, -,reɪt-, B 'ɔpərət-] *a.* 1. operativo, eficaz, activo. 2. operador, operante. 3. (med.) operatorio. 4. activo. *—s.* 1. operario, obrero. 2. agente secreto; detective.
operator [-,reɪtər, B -ə] *s.* 1. operador, operario. 2. operador, telefonista. 3. empresario; negociador, negociante; corredor, agente (de bolsa, de inmuebles, etc.). 4. (médico) operador. 5. (mat.) operador. 6. (jer.) ratero, ladrón, carterista; timador, estafador.
opercular [oʊ'pɜrkjələr, B -'pɜkjʊlə] *a.* (zool., bot.) opercular.
operculate [-lət] *a.* (zool., bot.) operculado.
operculum [-ləm] *s.* (*pl.* OPERCULUMS o **opercula** [-lə]) (zool., bot.) opérculo.
operetta [,ɑpə'rɛtə, B ,ɔp-] *s.* (mús.) opereta, zarzuela.
operose ['ɑpə,roʊs, B 'ɔp-] *a.* operoso, laborioso.
operosely [-lɪ] *adv.* laboriosamente.
operoseness [-nəs] *s.* laboriosidad.
ophicleide ['ɑfə,klaɪd, 'oʊ-, B 'ɔfɪ-] *s.* (mús.) oficleido, oficleide, figle.
Ophidia [oʊ'fɪdɪə, B ɔ-] *s. pl.* (zool.) ofidios.
ophidian [-ɪən] *a., s.* (zool.) ofidio.
ophiolatrous [,ɑfɪ'ɑlətrəs, B ,ɔfɪ'ɔl-] *a.* ofiolátrico, adorador de serpientes.
ophiolatry [-trɪ] *s.* ofiolatría, adoración de serpientes.
ophiological [-ə'lɑdʒɪkəl, B -'lɔdʒ-] *a.* (zool.) ofiológico.
ophiology [-ɪ'ɑlədʒɪ, B -'ɔl-] *a.* (zool.) ofiología.
ophite ['ɑf,aɪt, 'oʊ,faɪt, B 'ɔf,aɪt] *s.* (min.) ofita.
ophitic [ɑ'fɪtɪk, B oʊ-] *a.* (min.) ofítico.
Ophiuchus [,ɔfi'jukəs, B ɔ'fju-] *s.* (astr.) Ofiuco.
ophiuran [,ɑfɪ'jʊrən, B 'ɔfɪ,juər-] *a.* (zool.) ofiuro.
ophthal. *abrev. de* 1. **ophthalmologist,** oftalmólogo. 2. **ophthalmology,** oftalmología.
ophthalmia [ɑf'θælmɪə, ɑp-, B ɔf-] *s.* (med.) oftalmia.
ophthalmic [-mɪk] *a.* (med.) oftálmico.
ophthalmitis [,ɑfθəl'maɪtəs, ˏɑp-, B ,ɔfθæl-] *s.* (med.) oftalmitis.
ophthalmologic [-θælmə'lɑdʒɪk, B -'lɔdʒ-] **ophthalmological** [-ɪkəl] *a.* (med.) oftalmológico.
ophthalmologist [-'mɑlədʒəst, B -'mɔl-] *s.* (med.) oftalmólogo.
ophthalmology [-dʒɪ] *s.* (med.) oftalmología.
ophthalmometer [-'mɑmətər, B -'mɔmɪtə] *s.* (ópt.) oftalmómetro.
ophthalmometry [-trɪ] *s.* (med.) oftalmometría.
ophthalmoscope [ɑf'θælmə,skoʊp, ɑp-, B ɔf-] *s.* (ópt.) oftalmoscopio.
ophthalmoscopic [ɑf,θælmə'skɑpɪk, ɑp-, B ɔf-'skɔp-] **ophthalmoscopical** [-ɪkəl] *a.* (ópt.) oftalmoscópico.
ophthalmoscopy [,ɑf,θæl'mɑskəpɪ, ˏɑp-, B ,ɔf-'mɔs-] *s.* (med.) oftalmoscopia.
opiate ['oʊpɪət, -,eɪt] *s.* 1. opiato. 2. narcótico, hipnótico. 3. (fig.) sedativo, calmante. *—a.* 1. opiado. 2. narcótico, somnífero. — [-,eɪt] *v.t.* 1. narcotizar. 2. mezclar con opio.
opine [oʊ'paɪn, ə-] *v.i.* opinar, pensar. *—v.t.* expresar como (su) opinión, manifestar.
opinion [ə'pɪnjən] *s.* opinión; parecer, dictamen, juicio; **in my (your,** etc.) **o.,** a mi (tu, etc.) parecer; **it's a matter of o.,** es un punto discutible; **to be of the o. (that),** ser de la opinión (de que); **to have a high o. of oneself,** ser muy pagado de sí mismo; **to stick to one's o.,** aferrarse uno con su opinión.
opinionated [-,eɪtəd] *a.* pertinaz, obstinado, testarudo en sus opiniones.
opinionatedly [-lɪ] *adv.* obstinadamente, tercamente, porfiadamente.
opinionatedness [-nəs] *s.* pertinacia, obstinación, testarudez.
opinionative [-,eɪtɪv] *a.* 1. doctrinal. 2. pertinaz, obstinado, testarudo.
opinionatively [-lɪ] *adv.* pertinazmente, obstinadamente, testarudamente.
opinionativeness [-nəs] *s.* pertinacia, obstinación, testarudez.
opisthognathism [,ɑpɪs'θɑgnə,θɪzəm, B ,ɔp-'θɔg-] *s.* (med.) opistognatismo, opistognacia.
opisthognathous [-θəs] *a.* (med.) opistognato.
opium ['oʊpɪəm] *s.* opio.
opium eater, (jer.) opiómano.
opiumism [-,ɪzəm] *s.* (med.) opiomanía.
opium joint, (jer.) fumadero de opio.
opium pipe, 1. pipa para fumar opio. 2. (fig.) cualquier cosa o actividad que ayuda a soñar.
opium poppy, (bot.) adormidera, dormidera.
opobalsam [,ɑpə'bɔlsəm, B ,ɔp-] *s.* bálsamo de Judea, bálsamo de la Meca.
opoponax [ə'pɑpə,næks, B ə'pɔ-] *s.* (bot., farm.) opopónaco.
opossum [ə'pɑsəm, 'pɑsəm, B ə'pɔs-] *s.* (*pl.* OPOSSUMS u OPOSSUM) (zool.) oposum, zarigüeya.
opotherapy [,ɑpə'θɛrəpɪ, B ,ɔpə-] *s.* (med.) opoterapia.
oppidan ['ɑpədən, B 'ɔp-] *a.* (raro) lugareño, poblano, pueblerino. *—s.* ciudadano, vecino (de un pueblo).
oppilate ['ɑpə,leɪt, B 'ɔp-] *v.t.* (ant.) obstruir, ocluir.
oppilation [,ɑpə'leɪʃən, B ,ɔp-] *s.* oclusión, obstrucción.
opponency [ə'poʊnənsɪ] *s.* oposición; antagonismo.
opponent [-nənt] *a.* 1. contrario, opuesto, adverso, antagónico. 2. (anat.) antagonista, oponente (músculo). *—s.* 1. contrario, opositor, antagonista. 2. contrincante, adversario.
opportune [,ɑpər'tun, B 'ɔpə,tjun] *a.* oportuno, conveniente.
opportunely [-lɪ] *adv.* oportunamente, convenientemente.
opportuneness [-nəs] *s.* oportunidad, conveniencia.
opportunism [-'tu,nɪzəm, B -'tju-] *s.* oportunismo.
opportunist [-nəst] *s.* oportunista.

opportunistic [-tu'nɪstɪk, B -tju-] *a.* oportunista.
opportunity [ˌɑpər'tunətɪ, B ˌɔpə'tju-] *s.* oportunidad, ocasión; **to seize the o.,** aprovechar la oportunidad.
opposable [ə'poʊzəbəl] *a.* oponible.
oppose [ə'poʊz] *v.t.* 1. oponer, contraponer. 2. oponerse a, hacer frente a; resistir, combatir. —*v.i.* oponerse, resistirse.
opposed [ə'poʊzd] *a.* enemigo, opuesto, contrario; en contra de.
opposeless [ə'poʊzləs] *a.* irresistible.
opposer [-'poʊzər, B -ə] *s.* opositor, adversario, antagonista.
opposite ['ɑpəzɪt, B 'ɔp-] *a.* 1. opuesto, contrario (sentido, dirección, etc.). 2. opuesto, hostil. 3. de enfrente, ej., *the house o.,* la casa de enfrente. 4. (geom.) opuesto (lado, ángulo, etc.). 5. (bot.) opuesto. 6. **o. to, frente a.** —*s.* 1. lo opuesto, lo contrario. 2. noción opuesta, término opuesto. 3. (ant.) antagonista; opositor. —*adv.* en el lado opuesto, en la casa de enfrente. —*prep.* al otro lado de; al frente de, enfrente de, frente a.
oppositely [-lɪ] *adv.* opuestamente, enfrente.
oppositeness [-nəs] *s.* posición opuesta; calidad de opuesto; testarudez.
opposite number, colega, contraparte, contrincante (persona del mismo rango en otro gobierno, departamento, etc.).
opposition [ˌɑpə'zɪʃən, B ˌɔp-] *s.* 1. oposición. 2. resistencia, opugnación. 3. **the o.,** la oposición, el partido de oposición. 4. (astrol., lóg.) oposición.
oppositional [-əl] *a.* (pol.) de oposición, de la oposición.
oppositionist [-əst] *s.* (pol.) oposicionista.
oppress [ə'prɛs] *v.t.* 1. oprimir; agobiar, abrumar. 2. oprimir, tiranizar, despotizar (Amer.), aplastar; moler; pisotear.
oppression [-'prɛʃən] *s.* 1. opresión; tiranía. 2. opresión, angustia, ahogo.
oppressive [ə'prɛsɪv] *a.* 1. opresivo, abrumador, agobiante. 2. opresor, tiránico. 3. sofocante, bochornoso.
oppressively [-lɪ] *adv.* opresivamente.
oppressiveness [-nəs] *s.* calidad de opresivo, opresión.
oppressor [ə'prɛsər, B -ə] *s.* opresor; tirano.
opprobrious [ə'proʊbrɪəs] *a.* 1. oprobioso, abusivo, vituperioso. 2. oprobioso, ignominioso, infamante.
opprobriously [-lɪ] *adv.* oprobiosamente, ignominiosamente.
opprobriousness [-nəs] *s.* calidad de ofensivo.
opprobrium [-brɪəm] *s.* oprobio, infamia, ignominia.
oppugn [ə'pjun, B ɔ-] *v.t.* opugnar, combatir, oponerse a; controvertir, contradecir.
oppugnancy [-'pjunənsɪ] *s.* opugnación, hostilidad, antagonismo.
oppugnant [ə'pʌgnənt, B ɔ-] *a.* opugnante, hostil, antagónico.
oppugner [ə'pjunər, B ɔ-ə] *s.* opugnador.
opsonic [ɑp'sɑnɪk, B ɔp'sɔn-] *a.* (bact.) opsónico.
opsonic index, (bact.) índice opsónico.
opsonification [-ˌsɑnəfə'keɪʃən, B -ˌsɔn-] *s.* (bact.) opsonificación.
opsonin ['ɑpsənən, B 'ɔp-] *s.* (bact.) opsonina.
opt [ɑpt, B ɔpt] *v.i.* optar.
optation [ɑp'teɪʃən, B ɔp-] *s.* (ret.) optación.
optative ['ɑptətɪv, B 'ɔp-] *a.* (gram.) optativo. —*s.* (gram.) modo optativo; verbo optativo.
optic ['ɑptɪk, B 'ɔp-] *a.* óptico. —*s.* (hum.) ojo.
optical [-tɪkəl] *a.* 1. óptico. 2. visual, visorio, ocular.
optical angle, ángulo óptico.
optical fiber, fibra óptica.
optical center, centro óptico, punto principal.
optical illusion, ilusión óptica.
optically [-kəlɪ] *adv.* visualmente, por medio de la vista; mediante la óptica, ópticamente.
optical maser, (fís.) rayo láser que produce radiación visible.
optical scanner, lector óptico.
optical sight, (top.) colimador óptico.
optical telegraphy, telegrafía óptica (sistema de comunicación por medio de señales visuales).
optic axis, eje óptico.
optic disk, (anat.) disco óptico.
optician [ɑp'tɪʃən, B ɔp-] *s.* óptico.
optic nerve, (anat.) nervio óptico.
optics ['ɑptɪks, B 'ɔp-] *s. pl.* (*gen. sing. en const.*) óptica.
optic thalamus, (anat.) tálamo óptico.
optimal ['ɑptəməl, B 'ɔp-] *a.* óptimo, inmejorable.
optimally [-məlɪ] *adv.* óptimamente, inmejorablemente.
optimism ['ɑptəˌmɪzəm, B 'ɔp-] *s.* optimismo.
optimist [-məst] *s.* optimista.
optimistic [ˌɑptə'mɪstɪk, B ˌɔp-] *optimistical* [-tɪkəl] *a.* optimista, esperanzado, confiado.
optimistically [-tɪkəlɪ] *adv.* de manera optimista, confiadamente.
optimize ['ɑptəˌmaɪz, B 'ɔp-] *v.t.* perfecionar.
optimum [-məm] *s.* (*pl.* OPTIMUMS u OPTIMA) [-mə] lo óptimo, grado óptimo, cantidad óptima. —*a.* óptimo, más favorable.
option ['ɑpʃən, B 'ɔp-] *s.* 1. opción, elección, alternativa. 2. (com.) opción. 3. **to have no o. but to,** no tener otra alternativa sino; **without the o.,** (fam.) sin la posibilidad de conmutarla (una pena).
optional [-əl] *a.* opcional, facultativo, optativo.
optionally [-ɪ] *adv.* facultativamente, a voluntad.
optometer [ɑp'tɑmətər, B ɔp'tɔmitə] *s.* optómetro.
optometrist [-ətrəst] *s.* optometrista.
optometry [-trɪ] *s.* optometría.
opulence ['ɑpjələns, B 'ɔp-] **opulency** [-lənsɪ] *s.* opulencia, riqueza, abundancia, profusión.
opulent [-lənt] *a.* 1. opulento, rico. 2. exuberante, (vegetación, etc.). 3. opulento, amplio (busto).
opulently [-lɪ] *adv.* opulentamente.
opuntia [oʊ'pʌntʃɪə, B -'pʌnʃɪə] *s.* (bot.) opuncia, tuna.
opus ['oʊpəs] *s.* (*pl.* OPUSES u OPERA ['ɑpərə, B 'ɔp-]) opus, obra, composición musical o literaria.
opuscule [oʊ'pʌsˌkjul, B ɔ-] *s.* opúsculo.
opusculum [-kjələm] *s.* (*pl.* OPUSCULA [-lə]) opúsculo.
or [ɔr, B ɔ] *conj.* o, u; **this or that,** esto o lo otro; **one or the other,** uno u otro; **or else,** de otro modo, de lo contrario.
or, *s.* (her.) oro, color oro, amarillo o gualda.
orach, orache ['ɔrɪtʃ, 'ɑr-, B 'ɔr-] *s.* (bot.) orzaga, álimo, armuelle, marismo.
oracle ['ɔrəkəl, 'ɑr-, B 'ɔr-] *s.* 1. (hist.) oráculo. 2. oráculo, profeta. 3. oráculo, revelación.
oracular [ɔ'rækjələr, B -lə] *a.* 1. oracular, del oráculo. 2. profético. 3. solemne; sentencioso, dogmático. 4. ambiguo, equívoco.
oral ['ɔrəl] *a.* 1. oral, verbal, hablado. 2. (anat., fon.) oral, bucal. —*s.* (fam.) examen oral.
oral character, (psic.) carácter oral.
oral contraceptive, (med.) píldora anticonceptiva; **the Pill,** (jer.) la píldora (anticonceptiva).
orally [-əlɪ] *adv.* oralmente, verbalmente, de palabra.
orange ['ɔrɪndʒ, 'ɑr-, B 'ɔr-] *s.* 1. naranja. 2. (bot.) naranjo. 3. color naranja, anaranjado. 4. **to squeeze the o.,** sacarle el jugo (a algo). —*a.* 1. naranjero, de naranjos (jardín, etc.). 2. de naranja (zumo, jugo, cáscara, etc.). 3. anaranjado.
orangeade [ˌɔrɪn'dʒeɪd, ˌɑr-, B ˌɔr-] *s.* naranjada.
orange blossom, azahar, flor del naranjo.
orange crate, caja de naranjas, cajón de naranjas.
orange fin, (G.B.) alevino de la trucha de mar.
orange-flower water [-'flaʊər-, B -ə-] agua de azahar.
orange grove, naranjal.
orange grower, naranjero, que cultiva naranjas.
orange juice, jugo de naranja.
Orangeman ['ɔrɪndʒmən, 'ɑr-, B 'ɔr-] *s.* (hist.) orangista (miembro de una sociedad irlandesa, protestante y secreta).
orange peel, cáscara o corteza de naranja (gen. confitada).
orange pekoe, té negro de Ceilán o de la India.
orangery ['ɔrɪndʒərɪ, 'ɑr-, B 'ɔr-] *s.* invernadero de naranjos.
orange tree, (bot.) naranjo.
orange wife, (ant.) vendedora de naranjas, naranjera.
orangewood [ˌwʊd] *s.* madera de naranjo. —*a.* de madera de naranjo; **o. stick,** palito de naranjo, implemento de la manicurista.
orangutan, orangoutan [ə'ræŋətæn, B ˈɔrəŋ'u-] *s.* orangután.
orant ['oʊrənt] **orante** [oʊ'ræntɪ] *s.* (pint., esc.) figura orante.
orate [ɔ'reɪt] *v.i.* (fam.) perorar, arengar.
oration [ə'reɪʃən, ɔ-] *s.* oración, discurso ceremonial.
orator ['ɔrətər, 'ɑr-, B 'ɔrətə] *s.* 1. orador. 2. (der.) recurrente, apelante, demandante, querellante.
Oratorian [ˌɔrə'tɔrɪən, ˌɑr-, B ˌɔr-] *a., s.* (relig.) oratorio, oratoriano.
oratorical [-ɪkəl] *a.* oratorio; característico de un orador.
oratically [-kəlɪ] *adv.* oratoriamente.
oratorio [-'tɔrɪˌoʊ] *s.* (mús.) oratorio.
oratory ['ɔrəˌtɔrɪ, 'ɑr-, B -tərɪ] *s.* 1. oratoria, elocuencia. 2. (relig.) capilla, oratorio. 3. oratorio, congregación.
orb [ɔrb, B ɔb] *s.* 1. orbe, esfera, globo. 2. orbe (insignia real o papal). 3. (astr.) orbe. 4. (raro) esfera (de acción o influencia). 5. (poét.) ojo; globo del ojo. 6. (ant.) círculo, circunferencia; la tierra. —*v.t.* 1. formar en disco o globo. 2. (poét.) cercar, circundar. —*v.i.* (raro) moverse en una órbita.
orbicular [ɔr'bɪkjʊlər, B ɔ'-lə] *a.* orbicular, redondo, circular, esférico.
orbicularly [-lɪ] *adv.* orbicularmente.
orbiculate [-lət] *a.* (bot.) redondeada (hoja).
orbit ['ɔrbət, B 'ɔbɪt] *s.* 1. (anat., zool.) órbita, cavidad (del ojo). 2. (astr.) órbita. 3. (fig.) esfera (de actividad, influencia), órbita. 4. **to go into o.,** entrar en órbita. —*v.t.* 1. girar en órbita alrededor de (la tierra, planeta). 2. colocar o poner en órbita (satélite artificial). —*v.i.* 1. estar en órbita (satélite artificial). 2. dar vueltas (avión sobre campo de aterrizaje, etc.). 3. (astr., astronáut.) describir órbitas (planeta, satélite artificial).
orbital [-əl] *a.* orbital.

orbital decay, (astronáut.) decadencia orbital (producida por la atracción gravitacional de la tierra).
orbital index, (antrop.) índice orbital u orbitario.
orbital space station, estación orbital.
orbital velocity, primera velocidad cósmica, velocidad circular (de un satélite artificial, etc.).
orbiter [-ər, B -ə] *s.* orbitador (cohete espacial).
orc [ɔrk, B ɔk] *s.* (zool.) orco, orca.
orcein ['ɔrsiɪn, B 'ɔsɪ-] *s.* (quím.) orceína.
orchard ['ɔrtʃərd, B 'ɔtʃəd] *s.* huerto.
orcharding [-ɪŋ] *s.* horticultura, cultivo de los huertos y huertas.
orchardist [-əst] **orchardman** [-mən] *s.* horticultor, hortelano.
orchestra ['ɔrkəstrə, -ˌkɛs-, B 'ɔkɪ-] *s.* 1. (mús.) orquesta. 2. (hist.) orquesta (parte del teatro donde evolucionaba el coro). 3. (teat.) (lugar de la) orquesta; lunetas, platea, patio de butacas.
orchestral [ɔr'kɛstrəl, B ɔ'-] *a.* orquestral.
orchestra pit, foso de orquesta, foso orquestal.
orchestra seat, (teat.) luneta, butaca de platea.
orchestrate ['ɔrkəˌstreɪt, B 'ɔkɪ-] *v.t.* (mús.) orquestar; instrumentar para orquesta; componer (música) para orquesta.
orchestration [ˌɔrkə'streɪʃən, B ˌɔkɛ-] *s.* (mús.) orquestación, instrumentación.
orchestrion [ɔr'kɛstrɪən, B ɔ'-] **orchestrina** [ˌɔrkə'strinə, B ˌɔkɪ-] *s.* (mús.) orquestrión, orquestino.
orchid ['ɔrkəd, B 'ɔkɪd] *s.* 1. (bot.) orquídea. 2. color purpurino.
orchidaceae [ˌɔrkə'deɪsɪˌi, B ˌɔkɪ-] *s. pl.* (bot.) orquidáceas, orquídeas.
orchidaceous [-'deɪʃəs] *a.* (bot.) orquidáceo, orquídeo.
orchil ['ɔrtʃəl, B 'ɔtʃɪl] *s.* (bot.) orcina, urchilla.
orchis ['ɔrkɪs, B 'ɔkɪs] *s.* (bot.) órquide, compañón de perro.
orchitis [ɔr'kaɪtɪs, B ɔ'-] *s.* (med.) orquitis.
orcin ['ɔrsən, B 'ɔsɪn] **orcinol** ['ɔrsəˌnɔl, -ˌnoʊl, B 'ɔsɪnɔl] *s.* (quím.) orcina.
ordain [ɔr'deɪn, B ɔ'-] *v.t.* 1. ordenar, mandar, prescribir, decretar. 2. destinar, predestinar. 3. (relig.) ordenar. 4. (ant.) nombrar (para un cargo o empleo).
ordainer [-ər, B -ə] *s.* (relig.) ordenador.
ordainment [-mənt] *s.* 1. (relig.) ordenación. 2. ordenamiento.
ordeal [ɔr'diəl, 'ɔrˌdiəl, B ɔ'dil] *s.* 1. ordalía, juicio de Dios. 2. prueba severa, experiencia penosa.
order ['ɔrdər, B 'ɔdə] *s.* 1. orden (*m.*) arreglo, disposición, concierto; método, sistema. 2. orden (*m.*), paz, armonía. 3. orden (*m.*), clase, categoría; tipo, índole, ej., *considerations of a different o.,* consideraciones de otra índole. 4. orden (*f.*), hermandad, sociedad. 5. orden (*f.*), insignia, condecoración. 6. orden (*f.*) sacerdotal; (*pl.*) las sagradas órdenes. 7. orden (*f.*), coro (de los espíritus angélicos). 8. orden (*f.*), instrucción, mandato; regla, reglamento. 9. orden (*m.*), procedimiento. 10. (arq., biol., mat.) orden (*m*). 11. (com.) pedido, giro, libranza. 12. (der.) mandato judicial. 13. **a large o.,** una encomienda difícil; **at the o. of,** por orden de; **at the orders of,** a las órdenes de; **at your orders,** a sus órdenes; **by o. of,** por orden de; **in bad o.,** descompuesto; **in good o., in o.,** que está en servicio, que funciona bien; **in o. of appearance,** en orden de aparición; **in o. that,** a fin de que, para que; **in o. to,** a fin de, para; **in short o.,** pronto, enseguida; **it is on o.,** ha sido pedido, está por llegar; **made to o.,** hecho a la medida, hecho sobre pedido; **on that o.,** de esa clase; **on the o. of,** de la clase de; **out of o.,** en desorden; descompuesto, fuera de servicio; **point of o.,** cuestión de procedimiento; **to call to o.,** llamar al orden; **to give an o.,** dar una orden; hacer un pedido; **to keep o.,** mantener el orden; **to rise to o.,** interrumpir el debate para decidir una cuestión de procedimiento; **to take (holy) orders,** ordenarse; **to the o. of,** (com.) a la orden de. —*v.t.* 1. ordenar, disponer, mandar. 2. dirigir, regular. 3. (com.) pedir, hacer un pedido de. 4. (ant.) poner en orden de batalla, alistar para la batalla. 5. **o. around** (o **about**), mandar para acá y para allá, ser muy mandón con (alguien); **o. away (someone),** despedir (a alguien), decircle que se vaya; **o. in,** mandar entrar, mandar traer; **o. out,** echar, mandar salir; mandar traer; **o. to (do),** ordenar (hacer), ordenar que (se haga).
order blank, (com.) hoja de pedido.
order book, libro de pedidos, cartera de pedidos.
ordered [-ərd, B -əd] *a.* ordenado, arreglado, metódico.
orderless ['ɔrdərləs, B 'ɔdələs] *a.* desarreglado, desordenado.
orderliness [-lɪnəs] *s.* sentido de orden, proceder metódico.
orderly [-lɪ] *a.* 1. ordenado, metódico. 2. disciplinado, tranquilo, obediente. —*s.* 1. (mil.) ordenanza, asistente. 2. enfermero, barchilón (Perú). —*adv.* (raro) ordenadamente, regularmente.
orderly officer, *s.* oficial de turno.
order of arrest, (der.) orden (*f.*) de aprehensión, orden de arresto (Amer.).
order of battle, (mil.) orden (*m.*) de batalla; sequencia, progresión de instrumentos o acción.
order of the day, 1. orden del día; programa. 2. (lo que está en) moda, boga.
Order of the Garter, Orden de la Jarretera (G.B.).
Order of the Golden Fleece, Orden del Toisón de Oro (Esp.).
ordinal ['ɔrdɪnəl, B 'ɔd-] *a.* ordinal. —*s.* número ordinal.
ordinal, *s.* (relig.) ritual.
ordinal numbers, números ordinales.
ordinance ['ɔrdnəns, B 'ɔdɪnəns] *s.* 1. ordenanza, reglamento; decreto; (E.U.) ordenanza municipal. 2. (relig.) rito, ceremonia; sacramento, esp. comunión.
ordinand [ˌɔrdən'ænd, B ˌɔdɪn-] *s.* (relig.) ordenado, ordenante.
ordinarily [ˌɔrdən'ɛrəlɪ, B 'ɔdɪnər-] *adv.* ordinariamente.
ordinariness ['ɔrdənˌɛrɪnəs, B 'ɔdɪnər-] *s.* carácter o aspecto ordinario; medianía.
ordinary [-ˌɛrɪ, B -ərɪ] *a.* 1. ordinario, común, corriente; usual, normal. 2. ordinario, mediano, regular, llano. 3. (der.) ordinario (díc. de la jurisdicción procedente del foro común). —*s.* 1. ordinario (juez, obispo). 2. (relig.) ordinario (de la misa). 3. (G.B.) menú fijo, menú del día; (pr. G.B.) fonda, restaurante (que sirve menú fijo). 4. velocípedo. 5. (her.) pieza honorable de uso común. 6. **in o.,** de servicio regular, en servicio regular (ú. con títulos); (mar.) desarmado (barco); **out of the o.,** excepcional, extraordinario, fuera de lo común.
ordinary seaman, marinero, vaporino (Amer.).
ordinary shares, (com.) acciones ordinarias, acciones comunes.
ordinate ['ɔrdnət, -ənət, B 'ɔdɪn-] *s.* (mat.) ordenada. —*a.* ordenado.
ordination [ˌɔrdən'eɪʃən, B ˌɔd-] *s.* 1. (relig.) ordenación. 2. orden, arreglo; disposición.
ordnance ['ɔrdnəns, B 'ɔd-] *s.* 1. pertrechos militares. 2. cañones, artillería.
ordo ['ɔrdoʊ, B 'ɔdoʊ] *s.* (relig.) ordo.
ordonnance ['ɔrdənəns, B 'ɔd-] *s.* 1. disposición, arreglo. 2. ordenanza, decreto.
Ordovician [ˌɔrdə'vɪʃən, B ˌɔd-] *a., s.* (geol.) ordovícico, ordovicence.
ordure ['ɔrdʒər, B 'ɔdjʊə] *s.* 1. excremento; heces, estiércol. 2. (fig.) porquería, cochinería, cochinada.
ore [ɔr, B ɔ] *s.* mineral, mena, mineral metálico o metalífero.
Ore., Oreg. *abrev. de* **Oregon,** Oregón (E.U.).
oread ['ɔrɪˌæd] *s.* (mitol.) oréade, orea, oréada; ninfa.
ore deposit, (geol.) yacimiento de mineral.
ore dressing, preparación mecánica o beneficio de minerales.
oregano [ə'rɛgəˌnoʊ] *s.* (bot.) orégano, mejorana silvestre.
Oregon ['ɔrɪgən, 'ɑr-, B 'ɔr-] *s.* Oregón, estado de los E.U.
Oregon fir, O. pine, (bot.) pino oregón.
Oregon grape, (bot.) mahonia.
Oresteia [ˌoʊrɛs'tiə] *s.* (lit.) Orestíada, trilogía dramática de Esquilo.
org. *abrev. de* 1. **organic,** orgánico. 2. **organization,** organización. 3. **organized,** organizado.
organ ['ɔrgən, B 'ɔgən] *s.* 1. (mús.) órgano. 2. (mús.) organillo, órgano de manubrio. 3. (biol.) órgano. 4. (fig.) órgano (medio de comunicación o propaganda, periódico; organismo, dependencia del gobierno, organización). 5. (eufem.) órgano (pene).
organ bank, banco de órganos.
organ bench, (mús.) banco del órgano.
organdy, organdie ['ɔrgəndɪ, B 'ɔgən-] *s.* (tej.) organdí.
organelle [ˌɔrgə'nɛl, B ˌɔgə-] *s.* (biol.) organela, organelo.
organ-grinder ['ɔrgənˌgraɪndər, B 'ɔgən-də] *s.* organillero, tocador de organillo o de aristón.
organic [ɔr'gænɪk, B ɔ'-] *a.* orgánico; (biol., quím., med., der.) orgánico.
organically [-ɪkəlɪ] *adv.* orgánicamente.
organic chemistry, química orgánica.
organic disease, (med.) enfermedad orgánica.
organicism [ɔr'gænəˌsɪzəm, B ɔ'-] *s.* (filos.) organicismo.
organicist [-səst] *a., s.* organicista.
organic matter, (biol.) materia orgánica.
organism ['ɔrgəˌnɪzəm, B 'ɔgə-] *s.* organismo; (biol.) organismo.
organist ['ɔrgənəst, B 'ɔgə-] *s.* (mús.) organista.
organizable ['ɔrgəˌnaɪzəbəl, B 'ɔgə-] *a.* organizable.
organization [ˌɔrgənə'zeɪʃən, B ˌɔgənaɪ-] *s.* organización.
organizational [-əl] *a.* de organización.
organizationally [-ɪ] *adv.* a modo de organización.
organization man, fanático de la organización.
Organization of American States, *abrev.* **O A S,** Organización de Estados Americanos (O. E. A.).
organize ['ɔrgəˌnaɪz, B 'ɔgə-] *v.t.* organizar, ordenar, arreglar; establecer, constituir. —*v.i.* organizarse, constituirse.
organized [-ˌnaɪzd] *a.* organizado.
organized crime, (E.U.) crimen organizado, hampa.
organized labor, (E.U.) obreros sindicalizados.
organizer [-ˌnaɪzər, B -zə] *s.* 1. organizador. 2. (biol.) organizador, inductor.
organ loft, estrado alto en la iglesia o sala de concierto donde se encuentra el órgano.

organogenesis [ˌɔrgənoʊˈdʒɛnəsəs, B ˌɔgə-] *s.* (biol.) organogénesis, organogenia.
organographic [-ˈgræfɪk] *a.* (biol.) organográfico.
organography [-ˈnɑgrəfɪ, B -ˈnɔg-] *s.* (biol.) organografía.
organoleptic [-noʊˈlɛptɪk] *a.* (fisiol.) organoléptico.
organology [-ˈnɑlədʒɪ, B -ˈnɔl-] *s.* (biol.) organología.
organon [ˈɔrgəˌnɑn, B ˈɔgəˌnɔn] *s.* (filos.) órganon.
organotherapy [ˌɔrgənoʊˈθɛrəpɪ, B ˌɔgə-] *s.* (med.) organoterapia, opoterapia.
organotropic [-ˈtrɑpɪk, B -ˈtrɔp-] *a.* (med.) organotrópico.
organotropism [-ˈnɑtrəˌpɪzəm, B -noʊˈt-rɔ-] *s.* (med.) organotropismo.
organotropy [-ˈnɑtrəpɪ, B -ˈnɔ-] *s.* organotropía.
organ pipe, (mús.) caño del órgano.
organ stop, (mús.) registro de órgano.
organum [ˈɔrgənəm, B ˈɔgə-] *s.* (*pl.* ORGANA [-nə] u ORGANUMS) 1. (filos.) órganon. 2. (mús.) organum.
organza [ɔrˈgænzə, B ɔˈ-] *s.* (tej.) organza, organdí de seda o nylon.
organzine [ˈɔrgənˌzin, B ˈɔgən-] *s.* (tej.) organín, torzal de seda.
orgasm [ˈɔrˌgæzəm, B ˈɔˌ-] *s.* (fisiol.) orgasmo; eyaculación.
orgasmic [ɔrˈgæzmɪk, B ɔˈ-] **orgastic** [-ˈgæstɪk] *a.* (fisiol.) orgástico.
orgeat [ˈɔrˌʒɑ, B ˈɔˌ-] *s.* horchata (refresco o jarabe).
orgiastic [ˌɔrdʒɪˈæstɪk, B ˌɔdʒɪ-] *a.* orgiástico.
orgy [ˈɔrdʒɪ, B ˈɔdʒɪ] *s.* 1. orgía, bacanal. 2. (fig.) orgía, exceso.
oriel [ˈɔrɪəl] *s.* (arq.) mirador, camón.
orient [ˈɔrɪənt] *s.* 1. (poét.) oriente, este, levante. 2. **O.**, Oriente (esp. países al este del Mediterráneo; países del Asia). 3. oriente (brillo especial de las perlas). —*a.* 1. (poét.) levantino, oriental. 2. brillante, lustroso; pelúcido. 3. (ant.) naciente, saliente (sol). —*v.t.* orientar; **o. oneself,** orientarse; informarse, enterarse.
oriental [ˌɔrɪˈɛntəl] *a., s.* oriental.
Oriental carpet, pequeña alfombra oriental.
Orientalism [-ˌɪzəm] *s.* orientalismo.
Orientalist [-əst] *s.* orientalista, el que se especializa en estudios orientales.
Orientalize [-ˌaɪz] *v.t.* dar carácter oriental a, orientalizar. —*v.i.* volverse oriental, orientalizarse.
Oriental rug, alfombra oriental (grande).
orientate [ˈɔrɪənˌteɪt, -ˌɛn-] *v.t.* orientar. —*v.i.* caer o mirar hacia el este; tener orientación.
orientation [ˌɔrɪənˈteɪʃən, -ˌɛn-] *s.* orientación; (psic.) orientación.
orifice [ˈɔrəfəs, ˈɑr-, B ˈɔr-] *s.* orificio, abertura.
oriflamme [ˈɔrɪˌflæm, ˈɑr-, B ˈɔr-] *s.* oriflama, pendón, estandarte.
origami [ˌɔrəˈgɑmɪ] *s.* 1. origami (arte japonés de plegar papel para darle formas de animales o cosas). 2. objeto decorativo asi formado.
origan [ˈɔrɪgən] *s.* (fr.) (bot.) orégano, mejorana, mayorana.
origenian [ˌɔrɪˈdʒiniən, ˌɑr-, B ˌɔr-] *a.* (teol.) origenista.
origenism [ˈɔrɪdʒəˌnɪzəm, ˈɑr-, B ˈɔr-] *s.* (teo.) origenismo.
origin [ˈɔrədʒən, ˈɑr-, B ˈɔr-] *s.* 1. origen, principio. 2. origen, ascendencia; procedencia, derivación; fuente. 3. (anat.) origen.
original [əˈrɪdʒənəl] *a.* 1. original, primitivo, prístino. 2. original, no copiado, legítimo. 3. original, singular; novedoso. 4. original, inventivo, creativo. —*s.* 1. original, prototipo. 2. (arte) original (legítimo de su autor). 3. persona original o peculiar.
originality [əˌrɪdʒəˈnælətɪ] *s.* originalidad, imaginación para lo novedoso.
originally [əˈrɪdʒənəlɪ] *adv.* originalmente; al principio.
original sin, (teo.) pecado original.
originate [-ˌneɪt] *v.t.* originar, crear, inventar; ocasionar, suscitar. —*v.i.* originarse, dimanar, emanar, provenir (de); empezar, nacer.
origination [əˌrɪdʒəˈneɪʃən] *s.* 1. origen, formación, principio. 2. creación, invención.
originative [əˈrɪdʒəˌneɪtɪv] *a.* creador, inventivo.
originator [-ər, B -ə] *s.* originador, iniciador; creador, inventor.
orinasal [ˌɔrəˈneɪzəl] *a.* (fon.) oronasal, buconasal. —*s.* sonido oronasal.
oriole [ˈɔrɪˌoʊl] *s.* (orn.) oropéndola, oriol.
Orion [əˈraɪən, ɔ-] *s.* 1. (mitol.) Orión, cazador gigantesco a quien mató Artemisa. 2. (astr.) Orión (constelación).
Orion's Belt, (astr.) Cinturón de Orión, Bálteo.
Orion's Hound, (astr.) Sirio, Canícula; Can Mayor.
Orion's Sword, (astr.) espada de Orión.
orison [ˈɔrəsən, ˈɑr-, -zən, B ˈɔr-] *s.* oración, plegaria, rezo.
orle [ɔrl, B ɔl] *s.* (her.) orla; (arq.) orla, filete.
Orleanist [ˈɔrlɪənəst, ɔrˈlɪ-, B ɔˈlɪ-] *s.* (hist.) orleanista.
Orlon [ˈɔrˌlɑn, B ˈɔlɔn] *s.* (tej.) orlón (marca de fábrica).
orlop [ˈɔrˌlɑp, B ˈɔlɔp] *s.* (mar.) sollado, cubierta del sollado.
ormer [ˈɔrmər, B ˈɔmə] *s.* (zool.) abalone, oreja marina o de mar, oreja de San Pedro.
ormolu [ˈɔrməˌlu, B ˈɔmə-] *s.* similor; bronce dorado.
ornament [ˈɔrnəmənt, B ˈɔnə-] *s.* 1. ornamento, adorno. 2. (mús.) adorno, nota de adorno. 3. (*pl.*) (relig.) ornamentos (vestiduras sacerdotales). 4. persona que honra o enaltece. —[-ˌmɛnt] *v.t.* ornamentar, adornar, ornar.
ornamental [ˌɔrnəˈmɛntəl, B ˌɔnə-] *a.* ornamental, decorativo, de adorno. —*s.* planta u objeto ornamental.
ornamentation [-mɛnˈteɪʃən] *s.* 1. ornamentación. 2. ornamento, adorno.
ornamenter [ˈɔrnəˌmɛntər, B ˈɔnə-ə] *s.* adornista, decorador.
ornate [ɔrˈneɪt, B ɔˈ-] *a.* 1. ornado, ornamentado; churrigueresco, charro. 2. florido, galano (estilo).
ornately [-lɪ] *adv.* 1. ornadamente, con ornato y compostura. 2. de manera florida, floridamente, galanamente.
ornateness [-nəs] *s.* ornato, aspecto florido.
orneriness [ˈɔrnərɪnəs, ˈɑrn-, B ˈɔn-] *s.* (E.U.) intratabilidad, terquedad; vileza, villanía.
ornery [-ərɪ] *a.* (E.U.) terco, intratable, ingobernable.
ornis [ˈɔrnəs, B ˈɔnɪs] *s.* (zool.) avifauna; conjunto de aves de un país o región.
ornithologic [ɔrˌnɪθəˈlɑdʒɪk, B ˌɔnɪθəˈlɔdʒ-] **ornithological** [-ɪkəl] *a.* (zool.) ornitológico.
ornithologist [ˌɔrnəˈθɑlədʒəst, B ˌɔnɪˈθɔl-] *s.* (zool.) ornitólogo.
ornithology [-dʒɪ] *s.* (zool.) ornitología.
ornithopod [ɔrˈnɪθəˌpɑd, B ɔˈ-ˌpɔd] *a., s.* (pal.) ornitópodo.
ornithopter [ˈɔrnəˌθɑptər, B ˌɔnɪˈθɔptə] *s.* (aer.) ornitóptero.
ornithorhynchus [ɔrˌnɪθəˈrɪŋkəs, B ˌɔnɪθoʊ-] *s.* (zool.) ornitorrinco.
ornithosis [ˌɔrnəˈθoʊsəs, B ˌɔnɪ-] *s.* (*pl.* ORNITHOSES [-ˌsiz]) (med.) ornitosis.
Orobanchaceae [ˌɔroʊˌbæŋˈkeɪsɪˌi, B ˌɔrə-] *s. pl.* (bot.) orobancáceas.
orobanchaceous [-ˈkeɪʃəs] *a.* (bot.) orobancáceo.
orogenesis [ˌɔrəˈdʒɛnəsəs] *s.* (geol.) orogénesis, orogenia.
orogenic [-ɪk] *a.* (geol.) orogénico.
orogeny [ɔˈrɑdʒənɪ, B -ˈrɔdʒ-] *s.* (geol.) orogenia.
orographic [ˌɔrəˈgræfɪk] **orographical** [-ikəl] *a.* (geol.) orográfico.
orography [ɔˈrɑgrəfɪ, B -ˈrɔg-] *s.* (geol.) orografía.
oroide [ˈɔrəˌaɪd, B -ˌɪd] *s.* oro francés, aleación de metales que se emplea en la bisutería.
orological [ˌɔrəˈlɑdʒɪkəl, B -ˈlɔdʒ-] *a.* (geol.) orológico.
orologist [ɔˈrɑlədʒəst, B -ˈrɔl-] *s.* (geol.) especialista en orología, orologista.
orology [-dʒɪ] *s.* (geol.) orología.
orotund [ˈɔrəˌtʌnd, ˈɑr-, B ˈɔr-] *a.* 1. rotundo, sonoro, retumbante. 2. rimbombante, pomposo, altisonante.
orotundity [ˌɔrəˈtʌndətɪ, ˌɑr-, B ˌɔr-] *s.* 1. sonoridad, retumbancia. 2. rimbombancia, pompa.
orphan [ˈɔrfən, B ˈɔfən] *s., a.* huérfano. —*v.t.* dejar huérfano.
orphanage [-ənɪdʒ] *s.* 1. orfandad. 2. orfanato, orfelinato, hospicio, casa cuna.
orphanhood [-ˌhʊd] *s.* orfandad.
Orphean [ɔrˈfiən, B ɔˈ-] *a.* (poét.) órfico, relativo a Orfeo; melodioso, encantador.
Orpheonist [ˈɔrfɪənəst, B ˈɔfɪ-] *s.* (mús.) orfeonista, miembro de un orfeón.
Orpheus [ˈɔrfɪəs, ˈɔrˌfjus, B ˈɔˌ-] *s.* (mitol.) Orfeo, el que conmovía a las bestias con su lira, esposo de Eurídice.
Orphic [-fɪk] *a.* 1. órfico. 2. místico, esotérico; oracular. 3. fascinadora, hechicera (díc. de la música).
Orphism [-ˌfɪzəm] *s.* (hist.) orfismo.
orphrey [ˈɔrfrɪ, B ˈɔfrɪ] *s.* (ant., hist.) argentería primorosa, esp. de oro; (relig.) banda ricamente adornada de las vestiduras eclesiásticas.
orpiment [ˈɔrpəmənt, Bˈɔpə-] *s.* (min.) oropimente, oropimento.
orpin, orpine [ˈɔrpən, B ˈɔpɪn] *s.* (bot.) telefio, hierba callera.
orrery [ˈɔrərɪ, ˈɑr-, B ˈɔr-] *s.* planetario antiguo (aparato de relojería que muestra los movimientos de los planetas).
orris [ˈɔrəs, ˈɑr-, B ˈɔr-] *s.* (bot.) lirio de Florencia.
orrisroot [-ˌrut] *s.* raíz de lirio de Florencia.
ort [ɔrt, B ɔt] *s.* sobra de comida; (*pl.*) desperdicios, sobras.
orthicon [ˈɔrθɪˌkɑn, B ˈɔθɪˌkɔn] *s.* (t.v.) orticón.
ortho [ˈɔrθoʊ, B ˈɔθoʊ] *a.* (fís., foto.) ortocromático.
orthocephalic [ˌɔrθəsəˈfælɪk, B ˌɔθəkɛ-] **orthocephalous** [-ˈsɛfələs, B -ˈkɛf-] *a.* (antrop.) ortocéfalo.
orthocephaly [-ˈsɛfəlɪ] *s.* (antrop.) ortocefalia.
orthochromatic [-kroʊˈmætɪk] *a.* (fís., foto.) ortocromático.
orthochromatism [-ˈkroʊməˌtɪzəm] *s.* (fís., foto.) ortocromatismo.

orthoclase ['ɔrθəˌkleɪs, B 'ɔθə-] *s.* (min.) ortoclasa, ortosa.

orthoclastic [ˌɔrθə'klæstɪk, B ˌɔθə-] *a.* (min.) ortoclásico.

orthocymene [-'saɪˌmin] *s.* (quím.) ortocimeno, orto metil, propil benceno.

orthodontia [-'dɑntʃɪə, B -'dɔnʃɪə] *s.* (odont.) ortodoncia.

orthodontic [-'dɑntɪk, B -'dɔnt-] *a.* (odont.) ortodóntico.

orthodontics [-ɪks] *s. pl.* (odont.) (*sing. o pl. en const.*) ortodoncia.

orthodontist [-əst] *s.* (odont.) ortodontista.

orthodox ['ɔrθəˌdɑks, B 'ɔθəˌdɔks] *a.* ortodoxo.

orthodoxly [-lɪ] *adv.* convencionalmente, en forma ortodoxa.

orthodoxy [-ˌdɑksɪ, B -ˌdɔk-] *s.* 1. ortodoxia. 2. creencia ortodoxa; rito ortodoxo.

orthodromic [ˌɔrθə'drɑmɪk, B ˌɔθə'drɔm-] *a.* (mar.) ortodrómico.

orthoepic [-θoʊ'ɛpɪk] *a.* (gram.) ortológico.

orthoepist ['ɔrθoʊˌɛpəst, ɔr'θoʊə-, B 'ɔθoʊˌɛpɪst] *s.* (gram.) ortólogo.

orthoepy ['ɔrθoʊˌɛpɪ, ɔr'θoʊəpɪ, B 'ɔθoʊˌɛpɪ] *s.* (gram.) ortoepía; ortología.

orthogamous [ɔr'θɑgəməs, B ɔ'θɔg-] *a.* (bot.) ortógamo, autógamo.

orthogamy [-mɪ] *s.* (bot.) autogamia, autofecundación.

orthogenesis [ˌɔrθə'dʒɛnəsəs, B ˌɔθə-] *s.* (biol.) ortogénesis.

orthogenetic [-dʒə'nɛtɪk] *a.* (biol.) ortogenético.

orthogenic [-'dʒɛnɪk] *a.* (med.) ortogenético.

orthognathism [ɔr'θɑgnəˌθɪzəm, B ɔ'θɔg-] *s.* (antrop.) ortognatismo.

orthognathous [-θəs] *a.* (antrop.) ortognato.

orthognathy [-θɪ] *var. de* **orthognathism.**

orthogonal [ɔr'θɑgənəl, B ɔ'θɔg-] *a.* (mat.) ortogonal.

orthogonally [-'θɑgnəlɪ, B -'θɔgənə-] *adv.* (mat.) ortogonalmente.

orthograde ['ɔrθəˌgreɪd, B 'ɔθə-] *a.* (zool.) ortógrado.

orthographer [ɔr'θɑgrəfər, B ɔ'θɔgrəfə] *s.* (gram.) ortógrafo.

orthographic [ˌɔrθə'græfɪk, B ˌɔθə-] **orthographical** [-ɪkəl] *a.* (gram., geom.) ortográfico.

orthographic projection, (dib.) proyección ortográfica u ortogonal.

orthography [ɔr'θɑgrəfɪ, B ɔ'θɔg-] *s.* (gram.) ortografía.

orthopedic, orthopaedic [ˌɔrθə'pidɪk, B ˌɔθə-] *a.* (med.) ortopédico.

orthopedics, orthopaedics [-ɪks] *s.* (med.) ortopedia.

orthopedist, orthopaedist [-əst] *s.* (med.) ortopedista.

orthophosphate [ˌɔrθə'fɑsˌfeɪt, B ˌɔθə'fɔs-] *s.* (quím.) ortofosfato.

orthophosphoric [-ˌfɑs'fɔrɪk, B -ˌfɔs-] *a.* (quím.) ortofosfórico.

orthophosphoric acid, *s.* (*quím.*) ácido ortofosfórico.

orthopsychiatry [-sə'kaɪətrɪ, B -ˌsaɪ-] *s.* (med.) ortopsiquiatría, psiquiatría preventiva.

orthopteran [ɔr'θɑptərən, B ɔ'θɔp-] *a., s.* (ento.) ortóptero.

orthopteron [-ˌrɑn, B -ˌrɔn] *s.* (*pl.* ORTHOPTERA [-tərə]) (ento.) ortóptero.

orthopterous [-rəs] *a.* (ento.) ortóptero.

orthoptic [ɔr'θɑptɪk, B ɔ'θɔp-] *a.* (med.) ortóptico.

orthorhombic [ˌɔrθə'rɑmbɪk, B ˌɔθə'rɔm-] *a.* (quím.) ortorrómbico.

orthoscope ['ɔrθəˌskoʊp, B 'ɔθə-] *s.* (ópt.) ortoscopio.

orthoscopic [ˌɔrθə'skɑpɪk, B ˌɔθə'skɔp-] *a.* (ópt.) ortoscópico.

orthostatic [-'stætɪk] *a.* (med.) ortostático.

orthostichy [ɔr'θɑstɪkɪ, B ɔ'θɔs-] *s.* (bot.) ortóstico.

orthotropic [ˌɔrθə'trɑpɪk, B ˌɔθə'trɔp-] *a.* (bot.) ortótropo.

orthotropism [ɔr'θɑtrəˌpɪzəm, B ɔ'θɔ-] *s.* (bot.) ortotropismo.

orthotropous [-pəs] *a.* (bot.) ortótropo.

orthotropy [-pɪ] *s.* (bot.) ortotropía.

ortolan ['ɔrtələn, B 'ɔt-] *s.* (orn.) 1. hortelano, verdaulas. 2. porzana. 3. chambergo, charlatán.

oryx ['ɔrɪks] *s.* (zool.) orix.

Os *símb. de* **osmium,** osmio (Os).

Oscar ['ɑskər, B 'ɔskə] *s.* (E.U., cinem.) Oscar (figurilla dorada que la Academia de Artes y Ciencias Cinematográficas otorga anualmente como premio).

oscillate ['ɑsəˌleɪt, B 'ɔs-] *v.i.* 1. oscilar; variar, fluctuar. 2. (fís., mat.) oscilar.

oscillating [-ɪŋ] *a.* oscilante.

oscillation [ˌɑsə'leɪʃən, B ˌɔs-] *s.* 1. oscilación; fluctuación, variación. 2. (fís., mat.) oscilación.

oscillator ['ɑsəˌleɪtər, B 'ɔs-ə] *s.* (elec., rad.) oscilador.

oscillatory ['ɑsələˌtɔrɪ, B 'ɔs-tərɪ] *a.* oscilatorio, oscilante; vibratorio.

oscillatory circuit, (elec.) circuito oscilante.

oscillogram [ɑ'sɪləˌgræm, ə-, B ɔ-] *s.* (elec.) oscilograma.

oscillograph [-ˌgræf, B -ˌgrɑf] *s.* (elec.) oscilógrafo.

oscillographic [-ˌsɪlə'græfɪk] *a.* (elec.) oscilográfico.

oscilloscope [-'sɪləˌskoʊp] *s.* (elec.) osciloscopio.

oscilloscopic [-ˌsɪlə'skɑpɪk, B -skɔp-] *a.* (elec.) osciloscópico.

oscine ['ɑsˌaɪn, B 'ɔsɪn] *s.* (orn.) oscina.

oscitancy ['ɑsɪtənsɪ, B 'ɔs-] *s.* oscitancia; bostezo; somnolencia, soñolencia.

osculate ['ɑskjəˌleɪt, B 'ɔs-] *v.i., v.t.* 1. (ant. o hum.) besar. 2. (geom.) oscular. 3. (biol.) oscular.

osculating [-ɪŋ] *a.* (geom.) osculador, osculatriz.

osculation [ˌɑskjə'leɪʃən, B ˌɔs-] *s.* 1. (ant. o hum.) ósculo, beso. 2. (geom.) osculación.

osculatory ['ɑskjələˌtɔrɪ, B 'ɔs-tərɪ] *a.* osculatorio.

osculum [-ləm] *s.* (*pl.* OSCULA [-lə]) (bool.) ósculo (de la esponja).

osier ['oʊʒər, B -ʒə] *s.* 1. (bot.) mimbrera, mimbre; mimbre blanco. 2. (bot.) cornejo. 3. mimbre (rama usada en cestería).

Oslo ['ɑzloʊ, 'ɑs-, B 'ɔz-] *s.* Oslo, capital de Noruega.

Osmanli [ɑz'mænlɪ, B ɔz-] *a., s.* osmanlí, otomano; por ext. turco.

osmic ['ɑzmɪk, B 'ɔs-] *a.* (quím.) ósmico.

osmiridium [ˌɑzmɪ'rɪdɪəm, B ˌɔs-] *s.* (min.) osmiridio, iridosmina.

osmium ['ɑzmɪəm, B 'ɔz-] *s.* (quím.) osmio.

osmometer [ɑs'mɑmətər, ɑz-, B ɔz'mɔmɪtə] *s.* (quím., fís., fisiol.) osmómetro.

osmose ['ɑsˌmoʊs, 'ɑz-, B 'ɔs-] *v.t.* (quím., fís., fisiol.) someter a ósmosis.

osmosis [ɑs'moʊsɪs, ɑz-, B ɔz-] *s.* (quím., fís., fisiol.) ósmosis.

osmotic [-'mɑtɪk, B -'mɔt-] *a.* (quím., fís., fisiol.) osmótico.

osmotically [-ɪkəlɪ] *adv.* (quím., fís., fisiol.) por ósmosis.

osmous ['ɑzməs, B 'ɔs-] **osmious** [-mɪəs] *a.* (quím.) ósmico.

osprey ['ɑsprɪ, -ˌpreɪ, B 'ɔsprɪ] *s.* 1. (orn.) águila pescadora, halieto, aleto; águila americana. 2. airón (penacho de plumas usado como adorno).

ossein ['ɑsiɪn, B 'ɔs-] *s.* (bioquím.) oseína, osteína.

osseous [-əs] *a.* óseo, ososo, huesoso; de hueso.

Ossianic [ˌɑsɪ'ænɪk, ˌɑʃɪ-, B ˌɔsɪ-] *a.* (lit.) osiánico.

ossicle ['ɑsɪkəl, B 'ɔs-] *s.* (anat., zool.) osículo, huesecillo.

ossicular [ɑ'sɪkjələr, B ɔ-lə] **ossiculate** [-lət] *a.* (anat., zool.) osiculado.

ossiferous [ɑ'sɪfərəs, B ɔ-] *a.* osífero.

ossification [ˌɑsəfə'keɪʃən, B ˌɔs-] *s.* osificación.

ossifrage ['ɑsəfrɪdʒ, -ˌfreɪdʒ, B 'ɔsɪfrɪdʒ] *s.* (orn.) osífraga, osífrago, quebrantahuesos.

ossify ['ɑsəˌfaɪ, B 'ɔs-] *v.i., v.t.* (*pret., p.p.* OSSIFIED; *p.pr.* OSSIFYING) 1. osificar(se), convertir(se) en hueso, formar hueso. 2. (fig.) endurecer(se), tornar(se) convencional.

ossuary ['ɑʃʊˌɛrɪ, 'ɑsjʊ-, B 'ɔsjʊərɪ] *s.* osario, osar.

osteal ['ɑstɪəl, B 'ɔs-] *a.* osteico, óseo.

ostein ['ɑstɪən, B 'ɔs-] *var. de* **ossein.**

osteitis [ˌɑstɪ'aɪtəs, B ˌɔs-] *s.* (med.) osteítis.

ostensible [ɑ'stɛnsəbəl, B ɔ-] *a.* 1. aparente. 2. manifiesto, ostensible, patente, visible.

ostensibly [-blɪ] *adv.* 1. aparentemente. 2. manifiestamente, ostensiblemente, patentemente, visiblemente.

ostensive [ɑ'stɛnsɪv, B ɔ-] *a.* 1. ostensivo, demostrativo. 2. aparente.

ostensively [-lɪ] *adv.* 1. ostensivamente. 2. aparentemente.

ostensorium [ˌɑstən'sɔrɪəm, B ˌɔsˌtɛn-] **ostensory** [ɑs'tɛnsərɪ, B ɔs-] *s.* (relig.) custodia.

ostentation [ˌɑstən'teɪʃən, B ˌɔs-] *s.* ostentación, alarde.

ostentatious [-ʃəs] *a.* ostentativo, pretencioso, jactancioso; ostentoso, aparatoso.

ostentatiously [-lɪ] *adv.* ostentosamente, aparatosamente.

ostentatiousness [-nəs] *s.* ostentación, fastuosidad, pomposidad.

osteoarthritis [ˌɑstɪoʊˌɑr'θraɪtəs, B ˌɔstɪoʊˌɑ'-] *s.* (med.) osteoartritis.

osteoblast ['ɑstɪəblæst, B 'ɔstɪə-] *s.* (anat.) osteoblasto.

osteoclasis [ˌɑstɪ'ɑkləsəs, B ˌɔstɪ'ɔk-] *s.* (med.) osteoclasia, osteoclasis.

osteoclast ['ɑstɪəˌklæst, B 'ɔs-] *s.* (anat.) osteoclasto.

osteocranium [ˌɑstɪə'kreɪnɪəm, B ˌɔs-] *s.* (anat.) osteocráneo.

osteoid ['ɑstɪˌɔɪd, B 'ɔs-] *a.* (anat.) osteoide.

osteolite ['ɑstɪəˌlaɪt, B 'ɔs-] *s.* (min.) osteolita.

osteological [ˌɑstɪə'lɑdʒɪkəl, B ˌɔs-'lɔdʒ-] *a.* (anat.) osteológico.

osteologist [-'ɑlədʒəst, B -'ɔl-] *s.* (anat.) osteólogo.

osteology [-dʒɪ] *s.* 1. (anat.) osteología. 2. estructura huesosa, armazón ósea (de un organismo).

osteoma [-'oʊmə] *s.* (*pl.* OSTEOMAS u OSTEOMATA [-tə]) (med.) osteoma.

osteomalacia [-oʊmə'leɪʃə] *s.* (med.) osteomalacia.

osteomyelitis [-ˌmaɪə'laɪtəs] *s.* (med.) osteomielitis.

osteopath ['ɑstɪə,pæθ, B 'ɔs-] **osteopathist** [,ɑstɪ'ɑpəθəst, B ,ɔstɪ'ɔp-] *s.* (med.) osteópata.
osteopathic [,ɑstɪə'pæθɪk, B ,ɔs-] **osteopathical** [-ɪkəl] *a.* (med.) osteopático.
osteopathy [-'ɑpəθɪ, B -'ɔp-] *s.* 1. medicina osteopática. 2. (med.) osteopatía.
osteophyte ['ɑstɪə,faɪt, B 'ɔs-] *s.* (med.) osteófito.
osteophytic [,ɑstɪə'fɪtɪk, B ,ɔs-] *a.* (med.) osteofítico.
osteoplastic [-'plæstɪk] *a.* (med.) osteoplástico.
osteoplasty ['ɑstɪə,plæstɪ, B 'ɔs-] *s.* (med.) osteoplastia.
osteosis [,ɑstɪ'oʊsəs, B ,ɔs-] *s.* (fisiol.) osificación.
osteotome ['ɑstɪə,toʊm, B 'ɔs-] *s.* (med.) osteótomo.
osteotomy [,ɑstɪ'ɑtəmɪ, B ,ɔstɪ'ɔt-] *s.* (med.) osteotomía.
ostiary ['ɑstɪ,ɛrɪ, B 'ɔstɪərɪ] *s.* (relig.) 1. ostiario, clérigo que ha recibido el primero de los grados menores previos al sacramento de la ordenación sacerdotal. 2 (fig.) portero de templo o iglesia católica.
ostiole [-,oʊl] *s.* (biol.) ostíolo, poro.
ostler ['ɑslər, B 'ɔslə] *var. de* **hostler.**
ostmark ['ɔst,mɑrk, B -,mɑk] *s.* marco (unidad monetaria de la República Democrática Alemana).
ostracism ['ɑstrə,sɪzəm, B 'ɔs-] *s.* 1. (hist.) ostracismo (destierro político entre los atenienses). 2. ostracismo, exclusión (de una comunidad, sociedad, etc.).
ostracize [-,saɪz] *v.t.* 1. (hist.) desterrar, exilar (Amer.). 2. excluir (de una comunidad, grupo, etc.). 3. (pol.) aislar (a un país) de los demás (Amer.).
ostracod [-,kɑd, B -,kɔd] *s.* (zool.) ostrácodo.
ostrich ['ɑstrɪtʃ, 'ɔs-, B 'ɔs-] *s.* (*pl.* OSTRICH) (orn.) 1. avestruz. 2. ñandú.
Ostrogothic [,ɑstrə'gɑθɪk, B ,ɔstrə'gɔθ-] *a.* (hist.) ostrogodo.
Oswego tea [ɑs'wigoʊ-, B ɔz-] *s.* (bot.) especie de menta americana.
OT *abrev. de* **Old Testament,** Antiguo Testamento.
otacoustic [,oʊtə'kustɪk] *a.* (med., mús.) otacústico, díc. del aparato que ayuda y perfecciona el sentido del oído.
otalgia [oʊ'tældʒɪə] *s.* (med.) otalgia.
otalgic [-dʒɪk] *a.* (med.) otálgico.
Othello [ə'θɛloʊ, B oʊ-] *s.* (lit.) Otelo, personaje de la obra de Shakespeare del mismo nombre.
other ['ʌðər, B 'ʌðə] *a.* otro; **every o. day,** un día sí y otro no, en días alternos; **on the o. hand,** por otra parte; **o. from,** distinto a, ej., *a world far o. from ours,* un mundo muy distinto al nuestro; **o. ones,** otros; **o. than,** otra cosa que; menos, ej., *any person o. than yourself,* cualquier persona menos tú; **some o. time,** en otra ocasión, más tarde; **the o. day,** el otro día, hace poco; **the o. one,** el otro. *—pron.* otro; **each other,** uno al otro; **some time or o.,** cualquier día, el día menos pensado; **something or o.,** una cosa u otra. *—adv.* en otra forma, de otro modo. *—s.* otro; **of all others,** más indicado, ej., *of all others you are the man for the job,* eres el hombre más indicado para el trabajo; **the others,** los otros, los demás.
otherness [-nəs] *s.* calidad de ser otro; cosa distinta.
otherwhile [-,hwaɪl, -,waɪl] **otherwhiles** [-,hwaɪlz, -,waɪlz] *adv.* (pr. dial.) en otro tiempo, en otra oportunidad; a veces.
otherwise [-,waɪz] *adv.* 1. de otra manera, de otro modo. 2. de lo contrario; en otras circunstancias. 3. por otra parte, en otro respecto. 4. **o. called,** alias, por otro nombre. *—a.* otro, diferente.
otherworld [-,wɜrld, B -'wɜld] *s.* (el) otro mundo, (la) otra vida.
otherworldliness [-lɪnəs] *s.* espiritualidad, alejamiento de este mundo.
otherworldly [-lɪ] *a.* (fig.) ultramundano, espiritual, alejado de este mundo; fantaseador; (coll.) del otro mundo.
Othman ['ɔθmən, B ɔθ'mɑn] *s.* (ant.) *var. de* **Ottoman.**
otic ['oʊtɪk, B 'ɔt-] *a.* (med.) ótico, auricular.
otiose ['oʊʃɪ,oʊs, 'oʊtɪ-] *a.* 1. ocioso, holgazán. 2. fútil, inútil, vano.
otiosely [-lɪ] *adv.* ociosamente.
otiosity [,oʊʃɪ'ɑsətɪ, oʊtɪ-, B -ʃɪ'ɔs-] *s.* 1. ociosidad. 2. inutilidad, futilidad.
otitis [oʊ'taɪtəs] *s.* (med.) otitis.
otocyst ['oʊtə,sɪst] *s.* (zool., anat.) otocisto.
otolaryngologist [,oʊtoʊ,lærən'gɑlədʒəst, B -ɪŋ'gɔl-] *s.* (med.) otolaringólogo.
otolaryngology [-dʒɪ] *s.* (med.) otolaringología.
otolith ['oʊtə,lɪθ] *s.* (anat., zool.) otolito.
otologist [oʊ'tɑlədʒəst, B -'tɔl-] *s.* (med.) otólogo.
otology [-dʒɪ] *s.* (med.) otología.
otorhinolaryngology [,oʊtə,raɪnə,lærən'gɑlədʒɪ, B -ɪŋ'gɔl-] *s.* (med.) otorrinolaringología.
otorrhea, otorrhoea [-'riə] *s.* (med.) otorrea.
otosclerosis [,oʊtoʊsklə'roʊsəs] *s.* (med.) otosclerosis.
otoscope ['oʊtə,skoʊp] *s.* (med.) otoscopio.
otoscopy [oʊ'tɑskəpɪ, B -'tɔs-] *s.* (med.) otoscopia.
ottar ['ɑtər, B 'ɔtə] *var. de* **attar.**
ottava [oʊ'tɑvə, B ə-] *adv.* (mús.) en octava(s).
ottava rima [-'rimə] (poét.) octava real.
Ottawa ['ɑtəwə, B 'ɔt-] *s.* Ottawa, capital del Canadá.
otter ['ɑtər, B 'ɔtə] *s.* (*pl.* OTTER) 1. (zool.) nutria. 2. piel de nutria.
otto ['ɑtoʊ, B 'ɔt-] *var. de* **attar.**
Ottoman ['ɑtəmən, B 'ɔt-] *a.* otomano, turco. *—s.* 1. otomano, turco. 2. **o.,** otomana, sofá otomano. 3. (tej.) otomán.
ouabain [wɑ'beɪɪn] *s.* (quím.) ouabaína, wabaína.
oubliette [,ublɪ'ɛt] *s.* mazmorra.
ouch [aʊtʃ] *s.* (ant.) 1. joya, adorno. 2. broche; engaste, montura. *—v.t.* (ant.) adornar (con broche); enjoyar. *—interj.* ¡ay! (expresando dolor).
oud [ud] *s.* (mús.) especie de laúd del Oriente Medio y N. de África.
ought [ɔt] *v. aux.* (*ú. seguido del inf.*) deber, deber de; ser necesario, ser menester; tener la obligación de; convenir, ser conveniente, ej., *you o. to go,* debes (o deberías) irte, *it o. to be done,* es (o sería) necesario hacerlo, *you o. to help him,* debes (o tienes la obligación de) ayudarlo, *you o. to have told him,* deberías (o debías) haberle dicho. *—v.t.* (pr. esco.) adeudar; poseer. *—s.* deber, obligación.
ought, *s.* nada; (vulg.) cero. *—adv.* (ant.) de nada; al extremo.
oughtn't ['ɔtənt] *contr. de* **ought not.**
Ouija ['widʒə, B -dʒɑ] *s.* (t. **O. board**) tabla de escritura espiritista.
ounce [aʊns] *s.* 1. onza. 2. pizca. 3. (zool.) onza, leopardo de las nieves, pantera de las nieves.
our [ɑr, aʊr, B 'aʊə, ɑ] *a., pron.* nuestro, nuestra; nuestros, nuestras.
Our Father, (relig.) Padre Eterno; padrenuestro, padre nuestro (oración.).
Our Lady, (relig.) Nuestra Señora, la (Santísima) Virgen.
ours ['aʊrz, ɑrz, B 'aʊəz, ɑz] *pron. pos.* el (lo) nuestro; nuestro; los nuestros; ej., *a friend of o.,* un amigo nuestro; *nobody will use o.,* nadie usará los nuestros (o el nuestro).
ourself [ɑr'sɛlf, aʊər-, B ,aʊə'-, ɑ'-] *pron.* nos, a nosotros (ú. en estilo oficial o regio por **me, myself,** yo, yo mismo).
ourselves [-'sɛlvz] *pron.* nosotros mismos, nosotras mismas, nos, ej., *we o. will do it,* nosotros mismos lo haremos.
ousel, *var. de* **ouzel.**
oust [aʊst] *v.t.* 1. desalojar, expulsar. 2. suplir, suplantar. 3. (der.) desahuciar.
ouster ['aʊstər, B -tə] *s.* (der.) 1. desahucio, desalojamiento, desalojo. 2. desposeimiento, despojo.
out [aʊt] *adv.* 1. fuera, afuera, de fuera. 2. (béisbol, criquet) fuera de juego; (boxeo) fuera de combate; (naipes) fallo a (un palo). 3. **all o.,** (jer.) a todo dar, a todo meter; **before the week (month,** etc.) **is o.,** antes del fin de la semana (mes, etc.); antes de terminar la semana (mes, etc.); **on the voyage o.,** en el viaje de partida, de ida, de salida; **o. and about,** levantado, repuesto (díc. del que ha estado enfermo); **o. and away,** con mucho, por mucho; **o. and o.,** completamente; a fondo; **o. for, o. to do,** (fam.) empeñado (en), esforzándose (por), ej., *o. for kudos,* empeñado en conquistar honores; **o. of,** entre, de entre, ej., *he must choose o. of these,* debe escoger (de) entre éstos; fuera de, ej., *o. of the house,* fuera de casa, *o. of wedlock,* fuera del matrimonio; por, ej., *o. of charity* (*curiosity,* etc.), por caridad (curiosidad, etc.); sin, ej., *o. of work,* sin trabajo, *o. of luck,* sin suerte; más allá de, ej., *seven miles o. of New York,* siete millas más allá de Nueva York; **o. with it,** ¡dígalo!; **tired o.,** muy cansado; **to be o.,** estar fuera de casa, estar ausente, haber salido (de la casa, oficina, etc.); quedar excluido o eliminado; estar terminado, haber llegado a su fin; estar apagado (luz, fuego, incendio, etc.); estar libre, haber salido de la cárcel; haber salido a la venta (libro); estar al descubierto, haber salido a la luz o a la vista; haber sido presentada en sociedad (joven); estar reñido; estar de huelga; estar pasado de moda; no estar en el poder (partido político, etc.); estar dislocado (brazo, rodilla, etc.); **to be o. of it,** estar excluido; estar perplejo; estar mal informado; **to go o. for a walk,** salir a dar un paseo; **to have one's (Sundays,** etc.) **o.,** tener (los domingos, etc.) libres (díc. de una sirvienta, etc.); **to tell (one) right o.,** decírselo (a uno) de frente; **way o.,** trecho afuera, ej., *anchored some way o.,* anclado un trecho afuera. *—prep.* 1. por, ej., *I looked o. the window,* miré por la ventana. 2. de, ej., *from o. the house came a cry,* de la casa salió un grito. *—a.* 1. externo. 2. lejano. 3. excepcional, muy grande. 4. de salida. *—s.* (*ú. gen en pl.*) 1. empleado cesante; político fuera de oficio. 2. (impr.) omisión (de una palabra). 3. expendio, gasto, suma pagada. 4. (tenis) bola golpeada fuera de la cancha; (béisbol) jugador puesto fuera de juego. 5. (bolsa) opción de venta (de acciones) a precios estipulados. *—v.t.* echar, expulsar. *—v.i.* hacerse público, hacerse conocido. *—interj.* ¡fuera! ¡largo de aquí!
outage ['aʊtɪdʒ] *s.* 1. parada, interrupción de servicios, esp. por reparación. 2. (elec.) apagón, corte (*interrupción del servicio*). 3. (com.) parte faltante de una entrega.
out-and-out [,aʊtənd'aʊt] *a.* cabal, completo, absoluto; declarado, redomado, consumado, inveterado.
out-and-outer [-ər, B -ə] *s.* extremista.

outback ['aʊtbæk] *s.* llanura desértica, árida y abrupta del interior de un país o continente (pr. en Australia y Nueva Zelandia). *—a.* de esas llanuras.
outbacker [-ər, B -ə] *s.* habitante de las llanuras áridas del interior de un país o continente (pr. en Australia y Nueva Zelanda).
outbalance [ˌaʊt'bæləns] *v.t.* pesar más que, exceder (en peso o efecto); valer más que, importar más que.
outbid [-'bɪd] *v.t.* 1. (en subasta) sobrepujar, pujar u ofrecer más que. 2. declarar más que (en cartas).
outbidder [-ər, B -ə] *s.* pujador, postor, requintador (en subasta).
outboard ['aʊtˌbɔrd, B -ˌbɔd] *adv.* (mar.) fuera de borda. *—a.* 1. (mar.) exterior, fuera de borda. 2. (mec.) voladizo, exterior, aislado. 3. (aer.) alejado del fuselaje del avión. 4. (astronáut.) fuera de un cohete interespacial o de un satélite artificial. *—s.* (mar.) motor fuera de borda; embarcación (bote o lancha) con ese motor.
outboard motor, motor fuera de borda.
outbound [-ˌbaʊnd] *a.* por salir (buque, tren, etc.); de ida (viaje); de partida, de salida (estación, puesto).
outbrag [ˌaʊt'bræg] *v.t.* exceder en fanfarronadas.
outbrave [-'breɪv] *v.t.* 1. encarar, resistir, desafiar. 2. sobrepasar en valentía.
outbreak ['aʊtˌbreɪk] *s.* 1. erupción, brote (de epidemia, enfermedad, etc.); estallido (de guerra, hostilidades, etc.); arranque, arrebato (de cólera, etc.). 2. insurrección, levantamiento.
outbreed [-ˌbrid] *v.i.* multiplicarse por mezcla de razas.
outbreeding [-ɪŋ] *s.* (antrop., zool.) exogamia, mezcla de razas.
outbuilding [-ˌbɪldɪŋ] *s.* accesoría, dependencia, edificio anexo.
outburst [-ˌbɜrst, B -ˌbɜst] *s.* 1. arranque, explosión (de ira, cólera, etc.). 2. erupción. 3. **o. of laughter,** carcajada, risotada.
outby, outbye ['utˌbaɪ, 'aʊtˌbaɪ] *adv.* (esco.) a distancia; fuera, afuera.
outcast ['aʊtˌkæst, B -ˌkɑst] *a.* 1. desechado, inútil. 2. expulso; degradado. *—s.* 1. paria; vagabundo. 2. exilado, desterrado, expatriado. 3. desecho, sobra, desperdicio. 4. (esco.) riña.
outcaste [-ˌkæst, B -ˌkɑst] *s.* paria (en la India).
outclass [ˌaʊt'klæs, B -'klɑs] *v.t.* aventajar, descollar sobre, ser muy superior a.
outcome ['aʊtˌkʌm] *s.* resultado, consecuencia, efecto.
outcrop [-ˌkrɑp, B -ˌkrɔp] *s.* 1. (geol., min.) afloramiento (de un estrato); crestón. 2. (fig.) erupción, brote. — [-'krɑp, B -'krɔp] *v.i.* 1. (geol., min.) aflorar. 2. (fig.) manifestarse, hacerse patente.
outcropping [-ɪŋ] (geol.) *a.* aflorado. *—s.* afloramiento.
outcross [-ˌkrɔs] *v.t.* cruzar (animales) de distinto tipo, pero de la misma raza. *—s.* animal engendrado por cruce.
outcrossing [-ɪŋ] *s.* cruce de animales de distinto tipo pero de la misma raza.
outcry [-ˌkraɪ] *s.* 1. alboroto, tumulto; protesta. 2. grito, alarido. 3. subasta, venta pública. *—v.t.* gritar más que.
outcurve [-ˌkɜrv, B -ˌkɜv] *s.* (béisbol) curvatura (de la trayectoria de la bola) a la derecha (del bateador).
outdated [ˌaʊt'deɪtəd] *a.* anticuado, obsoleto; fuera de moda.
outdistance [-'dɪstəns] *v.t.* rezagar, distanciar, dejar atrás.
outdo [-'du] *v.t.* superar, vencer; **to o. oneself,** superarse.
outdoor ['aʊtˌdɔr, B -ˌdɔ] *a.* de puertas afuera, al aire libre; externo.
outdoors [-'dɔrz, B -'dɔz] *s.* aire libre, campo raso, el mundo de puertas afuera. *—adv.* fuera de casa, al aire libre, al raso, a la intemperie. *—a.* de puertas afuera, al aire libre; externo.
outer ['aʊtər, B -ə] *a.* exterior, externo; **the o. man,** apariencia personal, vestidura; **the o. world,** gente ajena. *—s.* (G.B.) círculo exterior del blanco.
outer ear, (anat.) oído externo.
outermost [-ˌmoʊst] *a.* extremo, último; más exterior. *—adv.* al extremo, al último.
outer space, 1. espacio exterior (fuera de la atmósfera terrestre). 2. espacio interplanetario, espacio interestelar.
outface [ˌaʊt'feɪs] *v.t.* 1. desconcertar, turbar (con la mirada). 2. desafiar, arrostrar.
outfall ['aʊtˌfɔl] *s.* desembocadura; despeñadero; respiradero.
outfield [-ˌfild] *s.* 1. campo abierto; (agr.) campo contiguo. 2. (béisbol) jardín, parte fuera del diamante; jardineros, jugadores de fuera del diamante. 3. (criquet) la parte del campo más lejana del bateador.
outfielder [-'fildər, B -də] *s.* (béisbol) jardinero.
outfight [ˌaʊt'faɪt] *v.t.* superar por completo (en combate, etc.), dominar, derrotar.
outfighting [-ɪŋ] *s.* (boxeo) pelea a brazo partido, combate muy reñido.
outfit ['aʊtˌfɪt] *s.* 1. equipamiento, provisión; preparación. 2. equipo, pertrechos, avíos; juego (de herramientas, etc.); (fig.) dotes, prendas, cualidades. 3. equipo, cuadrilla, tropa. 4. trajes, ropas, prendas. *—v.t., v.i.* equipar (se), pertrechar(se).
outfitter [-ər, B ə] *s.* 1. pertrechador, abastecedor, proveedor. 2. comerciante de ropa, camisero, mercero.
outflank [ˌaʊt'flæŋk] *v.t.* (mil.) desbordar o rebasar el flanco de (adversario, enemigo, etc.).
outflow ['aʊtˌfloʊ] *s.* efusión, derrame; flujo, efluvio.
outfoot [ˌaʊt'fʊt] *v.t.* 1. rezagar, dejar atrás, caminar más rápido que. 2. (mar.) (un buque) zarpar más rápido que (otro).
outfox [-'fɑks, B -'fɔks] *v.t.* ser más astuto que, superar en mañas.
outgas [-'gæs] *v.t.* purificar de gases (gen. por calentamiento).
outgeneral [-'dʒɛnərəl] *v.t.* (*pret., p.p.* OUTGENERALLED O OUTGENERALED; *p.pr.* OUTGENERALLING O OUTGENERALING) aventajar en táctica militar; ser mejor estratega que; aventajar en liderazgo.
outgo [-'goʊ] *v.t.* exceder; aventajar; sobresalir. — ['aʊtˌgoʊ] *s.* (*pl.* OUTGOES) 1. gasto, expendio. 2. flujo; efluvio.
outgoing ['aʊtˌgoʊɪŋ] *a.* 1. saliente, de salida; que parte (en un viaje). 2. comunicativo, sociable, expansivo. *—s.* 1. ida, salida, partida. 2. (*pl.*)gastos, expendios, expensas.
outgrow [ˌaʊt'groʊ] *v.t.* 1. crecer más que. 2. pasar de la edad de, ser viejo ya para. 3. quedarle chico a uno, ej., *he has outgrown his clothes,* la ropa le queda chica. 4. pasar, curar con la edad, con el tiempo, ej., *he will outgrow his thumb-sucking,* con el tiempo él dejará de chuparse el dedo.
outgrowth ['aʊtˌgroʊθ] *s.* 1. excrecencia, tumor. 2. (fig.) resultado, consecuencia, fruto.
outguard [-ˌgɑrd, B -ˌgɑd] *s.* (mil.) guardia (en puesto) de avanzada.
outguess [ˌaʊt'gɛs] *v.t.* prever, prevenir; adivinar la intención de, anticiparse a (alguien).
outgun ['aʊt'gʌn] *v.t.* sobrepasar en potencia de fuego; (*to defeat*) derrotar.
outhaul ['aʊtˌhɔl] *s.* (mar.) driza, driza de afuera.
out-Herod [ˌaʊt'hɛrəd] *v.t.* sobrepasar o exceder en maldad o violencia.
outhouse ['aʊtˌhaʊs] *s.* 1. edificio anexo, accesoria, dependencia. 2. retrete, excusado (fuera de la casa).
outing ['aʊtɪŋ] *s.* paseo, excursión.
outland ['aʊtˌlænd, -lənd] *s.* 1. el extranjero, tierra extraña. 2. (*pl.*) provincias, regiones remotas. *—a.* 1. extranjero. 2. lejano, remoto.
outlander [-'lændər, B -də] *s.* extranjero, forastero.
outlandish [ˌaʊt'lændɪʃ] *a.* 1. extravagante, estrafalario, ridículo; de apariencia extranjera o exótica. 2. tosco, rústico. 3. (ant.) extranjero.
outlandishly [-lɪ] *adv.* extravagantemente, estrafalariamente.
outlandishness [-nes] *s.* extravagancia; apariencia estrafalaria; aspecto insólito.
outlast [-'læst, B -'lɑst] *v.t.* sobrevivir a, durar más que.
outlaw ['aʊtˌlɔ] *s.* 1. proscrito, fugitivo, persona fuera de la ley. 2. (fam.) facineroso, forajido. *—v.t.* proscribir, prohibir, declarar fuera de la ley, ej., *firearms should be outlawed,* las armas de fuego deberían estar prohibidas.
outlawry [-ˌlɔrɪ] *s.* 1. proscripción. 2. estado de ilegalidad; bandidaje, bandolerismo.
outlay [-ˌleɪ, ˌaʊt'leɪ] *v.t.* gastar (dinero). — ['aʊtˌleɪ] *s.* gasto, expendio, desembolso.
outlet ['aʊtˌlɛt] *s.* 1. salida; orificio de salida; desembocadura, desagüe, desaguadero. 2. (com.) mercado; plaza; subdistribuidor, agencia, sucursal, boca de expendio. 3. (fig.) desfogue. 4. (elec.) toma (de un enchufe, etc.).
outlet box, (elec.) caja de salida o de empalme.
outlie [ˌaʊt'laɪ] *v.t.* mentir más que (otro).
outlier ['aʊtˌlaɪər, B -ə] *s.* 1. absentista, dueño ausente. 2. (geol.) macizo o roca aislada. 3. persona que reside lejos del lugar donde trabaja; persona u objeto alejado del lugar a que pertenece.
outline [-ˌlaɪn] *s.* 1. contorno, perfil. 2. boceto, esbozo. 3. compendio, reseña, resumen. 4. (*pl.*) generalidades, principios generales. 5. **in o.,** a grandes rasgos, en líneas generales. *—v.t.* 1. perfilar, trazar. 2. esbozar. 3. resumir, compendiar.
outlive [aʊt'lɪv] *v.t.* sobrevivir a; durar más que, ej., *he outlived his brother,* él sobrevivió a su hermano.
outlook ['aʊtˌlʊk] *s.* 1. perspectiva, vista, panorama. 2. punto de vista, concepto, ej., *an optimistic o.,* un punto de vista optimista. 3. perspectiva, probabilidad, porvenir. 4. vigilancia, observación, acecho.
outlying [-ˌlaɪɪŋ] *a.* distante, remoto; externo; fronterizo, de las afueras.
outmaneuver [ˌaʊtmə'nuvər, B -və] *v.t.* ser mejor estratega que; vencer por ser mejor estratega que; sobrepujar en maniobras, maniobrar mejor que.
outmarch [-'mɑrtʃ, B -'mɑtʃ] *v.t.* dejar atrás a; ir más ligero o más lejos que.
outmatch [-'mætʃ] *v.t.* prevalecer sobre, eclipsar, exceder.
outmeasure [-'mɛʒər, B -ə] *v.t.* exceder o sobrepasar en medida.
outmoded [-'moʊdəd] *a.* pasado de moda, anticuado, fuera de moda.
outmost ['aʊtˌmoʊst] *a.* extremo, último; (el) más externo o exterior.

outnumber [aʊt'nʌmbər, B -bə] *v.t.* exceder o sobrepasar en número, ser más numeroso que.
outnumbered [-bərd, B -bəd] *a.* rezagado o vencido por mayor número de contingentes.
out of breath, falto de aliento.
out of commission, 1. inservible, inutilizado, fuera de uso o servicio. 2. en reserva (buques, armamento, etc.).
out-of-date [ˌaʊtəv'deɪt] *a.* anticuado, pasado de moda.
out-of-door [-'dɔr, B -'dɔ] *a.* de puertas afuera, externo; adecuado al aire libre.
out-of-doors [-'dɔrz, B -'dɔz] *a., adv.* de puertas afuera, externo. —*s.* aire libre, campo raso, (el) mundo de puertas afuera.
out of order, no funciona (*señal*).
out-of-pocket ['aʊtəv'pɑkət, B -'pɔk-] *a.* efectivo, en efectivo (desembolsos, gastos, costo).
out-of-the-way [ˌaʊtəvðə'weɪ] *a.* 1. apartado, solitario. 2. raro, extraordinario, poco común, insólito.
out-of-towner [-'taʊnər, B -ə] *s.* visitante de otra ciudad o paraje.
outparish ['aʊtˌpærɪʃ] *s.* parroquia rural.
outpatient [-ˌpeɪʃənt] *s.* paciente externo, enfermo no hospitalizado (que recibe tratamiento en una clínica, un consultorio o un hospital).
outplay [aʊt'pleɪ] *v.t.* superar, vencer (en un juego).
outpoint [-'pɔɪnt] *v.t.* 1. (dep.) exceder en puntos a. 2. (mar.) ceñirse más al viento que (otro barco).
outpost ['aʊtˌpoʊst] *s.* 1. (mil.) avanzada. 2. (mil.) puesto de avanzada. 3. puesto o fuerte fronterizo.
outpour [-ˌpɔr, B -ˌpɔ] *s.* 1. chorreo, vertimiento. 2. chorro, flujo, efusión. — [aʊt'pɔr, B -'pɔ] *v.t.* verter; chorrear.
outpouring [-ˌpɔrɪŋ] *s.* 1. derrame, flujo. 2. (fig.) efusión; (*pl.*) palabras efusivas.
output [-ˌpʊt] *s.* 1. producción total, rendimiento. 2. (min., elec.) extracción. 3. energía suministrada; potencia generada; potencia útil. 4. (elec., electrón., rad.) potencia de salida; terminal de salida. 5. (electrón.) información de salida (de una computadora). 6. (fisiol.) rendimiento.
output factor, factor de producción.
output signal, (electrón., rad.) señal de salida.
output stage, (electrón., rad.) etapa de salida.
output tube, (electrón., rad.) tubo de potencia, válvula amplificadora.
outrage [-ˌreɪdʒ] *s.* 1. ultraje, afrenta, atropello; violación; atrocidad, desafuero. 2. indignación, cólera. —*v.t.* 1. ultrajar, injuriar, maltratar, violentar. 2. enfurecer, enconar. 3. violar, estuprar.
outrageous [aʊt'reɪdʒəs] *a.* 1. atroz. 2. extravagante, excesivo, fantástico, abusivo, ej., *you charge o. prices,* Ud. cobra precios excesivos. 3. violento. 4. ultrajante, afrentoso, injurioso, ultrajoso.
outrageously [-lɪ] *adv.* 1. atrozmente. 2. afrentosamente, injuriosamente.
outrageousness [-nəs] *s.* 1. calidad de ultrajante. 2. atrocidad; violencia.
outrange [-'reɪndʒ] *v.t.* superar en alcance.
outrank [-'ræŋk] *v.t.* exceder en rango, categoría, importancia, etc.
outré [u'treɪ, B 'utreɪ] *a.* (fr.) extremoso, extravagante; chocarrero, chocante.
outreach [aʊt'ritʃ] *v.t.* 1. tener mayor alcance que. 2. exceder, superar. 3. **o. oneself,** ir más allá de sus capacidades; propasarse. — ['aʊtˌritʃ] *s.* 1. extensión. 2. alcance.
outremer [utrə'mɛr, B -'mɛə] *s.* (fr.) ultramar, el extranjero.
outride [aʊt'raɪd] *v.t.* 1. montar mejor o más rápido que, adelantar (cabalgando). 2. (mar.) resistir bien (un temporal, díc. de un barco).
outrider ['aʊtˌraɪdər, B -ə] *s.* 1. carrerista, batidor. 2. escolta, guía.
outrigger [-ˌrɪgər, B -ə] *s.* 1. (mar.) batanga, flotador lateral. 2. (mar.) botalón; arbotante. 3. (mar.) brazo saledizo (para escalamera o chumacera); postiza. 4. (mar.) yola con chumaceras salientes. 5. (aer.) larguero de soporte del plano fijo.
outright [aʊt'raɪt] *adv.* 1. completamente, enteramente. 2. abiertamente; francamente. 3. al momento, en el instante. 4. (ant.) de frente. ['aʊtˌraɪt] *a.* 1. completo, cabal, entero. 2. directo, franco, sincero. 3. (ant.) hacia adelante.
outrival [-'raɪvəl] *v.t.* vencer, ganar.
outroot [-'rut] *v.t.* extirpar, erradicar, sacar de raíz.
outrun [-'rʌn] *v.t.* correr más aprisa que, exceder; dejar atrás, eludir.
outrunner [-ər, B -ə] *s.* (ant.) 1. volante (criado que corría al lado de un carruaje). 2. perro guía (de un trineo).
outsail [-'saɪl] *v.t.* (mar.) navegar mejor que (otro barco); dejar atrás a (otro barco).
outsell [-'sɛl] *v.t.* vender más que; vender a mejor precio que, venderse más que, ej., *magazines outsold books,* se vendieron más revistas que libros.
outset ['aʊtˌsɛt] *s.* principio, comienzo; **at the o.,** al principio; **from the o.,** desde el principio.
outshine [ˌaʊt'ʃaɪn] *v.i.* brillar, lucir, resplandecer. —*v.t.* 1. brillar más que. 2. (fig.) eclipsar, deslucir, opacar (Amer.).
outshoot [-'ʃut] *v.t.* disparar mejor que; ser mejor tirador que. —*v.i.* sobresalir, extenderse. —*s.* disparo; saliente.
outside ['aʊt'saɪd] *s.* 1. exterior, parte de afuera; sobrefaz. 2. apariencia, aspecto. 3. extremo, máximo. 4. **at the o.,** como máximo, a lo más; **on the o.,** por fuera. —*a.* 1. exterior, externo; superficial. 2. máximo, extremo, ej., *o. price,* precio máximo, *o. estimate,* cálculo extremo. 3. ajeno, ej., *o. influence,* influencia ajena. 4. no afiliado, ej., *o. broker,* corredor no afiliado (a la Bolsa). 5. independiente, ej., *o. opinion,* opinión independiente. 6. remoto (posibilidad, etc.). —*adv.* hacia afuera; afuera, fuera; **come o.!** ¡salga afuera! (esp. a pepelear). —*prep.* fuera de, más allá de; **o. of,** (E.U.) fuera de; excepto, a excepción de, ej., *no one o. of Peter would do it,* nadie excepto Pedro quiso hacerlo.
outside calipers, compás de espesores, compás de gruesos.
outside chance, (jer.) posibilidad remota.
outside diameter, diámetro exterior, diámetro máximo.
outsider [aʊt'saɪdər, B -ə] *s.* forastero, extraño; no afiliado; entremetido, intruso.
outside shutter, contraventana; persiana exterior.
out sister, (relig.) hermana portera (religiosa de claustro que se encarga del trato con el público).
outsit [-'sɪt] *v.t.* sesionar más tiempo que o pasada la hora de.
outsize ['aʊtˌsaɪz] *s.* 1. tamaño poco común, tamaño extraordinario. 2. talla extra grande. —*a.* 1. más grande que lo común, extra grande. 2. demasiado grande.
outskirt [-ˌskɜrt, B -ˌskɜt] *s.* borde, linde; (*pl.*) suburbios, arrabales; afueras.
outsmart [aʊt'smɑrt, B -'smɑt] *v.t.* (fam.) burlar, ser más astuto o listo que, ej., *he always outsmarts me,* él siempre me gana (en astucia, viveza, etc.).
outsoar [-'sɔr, B -'sɔ] *v.t.* remontarse más alto o más lejos que.
outspan [aʊt'spæn] *v.t.* (África del S.) desuncir, quitar del yugo (los bueyes). —*s.* desunción.
outspeak [-'spik] *v.t.* hablar mejor o más claro que; hablar durante más tiempo que; manifestar osada o insolentemente.
outspoken [-'spoʊkən] *a.* abierto, franco; que no tiene pelos en la lengua.
outspokenly [-lɪ] *adv.* de llano, claramente, sin ambages, con franqueza.
outspokenness [-nəs] *s.* franqueza; llaneza, sinceridad.
outspread ['aʊtˌsprɛd] *s.* extensión, despliegue, expansión. —*a.* extenso; difuso. — [aʊt'sprɛd] *v.t., v.i.* extender, desplegar.
outstand [-'stænd] *v.t.* (dial. pr. G.B.) resistir a, sufrir, aguantar, soportar. —*v.i.* 1. distinguirse, descollar. 2. (mar.) navegar mar afuera.
outstanding ['aʊtˌstændɪŋ, aʊt'stæn-] *a.* 1. distinguido, notable, destacado, descollante, destacable. 2. prominente, conspicuo. 3. existente, pendiente. 4. sobresaliente, excelente. 5. (com.) pendiente, por pagar.
outstanding bills, (com.) cuentas u obligaciones pendientes.
outstanding shares, (fin.) acciones en circulación.
outstare [ˌaʊt'stɛr, B -'stɛə] *v.t.* fijar la vista en uno sin pestañear.
outstart ['aʊtˌstɑrt, B -ˌstɑt] *s.* salida, principio. — [ˌaʊt'stɑrt, B -'stɑt] *v.i.* salir, partir. —*v.t.* comenzar antes que (otro).
outstation ['aʊtˌsteɪʃən] *s.* puesto o estación del interior; factoría.
outstay [aʊt'steɪ] *v.t.* 1. quedarse más tiempo que. 2. resistir o aguantar más que. 3. **o. one's welcome,** quedarse más tiempo de lo prudente, abusar de la hospitalidad.
outstretch [-'strɛtʃ] *v.t.* extender, desplegar, alargar.
outstretched [-'strɛtʃt] *a.* estirado, alargado, extendido, desplegado.
outstrip [-'strɪp] *v.t.* pasar, rezagar, dejar atrás; p. ext. aventajar, descollar sobre, sobrepasar.
outtalk [-'tɔk] *v.t.* hablar más que; hacer callar hablando más, vencer en discusión.
outturn ['aʊtˌtɜrn, B -ˌtɜn] *s.* 1. producción, rendimiento. 2. (com.) resultado (en la venta y entrega de mercancías).
outvalue [ˌaʊt'vælju] *v.t.* valer más, exceder en valor a.
outvie [-'vaɪ] *v.t.* sobrepujar a, sobresalir.
outvote [-'voʊt] *v.t.* vencer en la votación; **to be outvoted,** tener la mayoría de votos en contra, perder en la votación (gobierno).
outwalk [-'wɔk] *v.t.* andar más que (otro), dejar atrás a (otro).
outwall ['aʊtˌwɔl] *s.* pared exterior; parte externa.
outward ['aʊtwərd, B -wəd] *adv.* 1. fuera, afuera. 2. hacia afuera. 3. exteriormente. —*a.* 1. de fuera, exterior, externo. 2. material; corporal, corpóreo; p. ext., extrínseco; superficial. 3. **o. bound,** que sale, de ida, de salida; que parte hacia un puerto extranjero; **o. form,** apariencia; **o. man,** el cuerpo; (fam.) vestimentas; **o. things,** el mundo que nos rodea. —*s.* 1. parte externa, exterior; sobrefaz. 2. (*gen. pl.*) mundo externo, mundo material.
outward cargo, cargamento o flete de salida.
outward-flow turbine [-ˌfloʊ-] turbina centrífuga.
outward freight, cargamento o flete de ida.
outwardly [-lɪ] *adv.* exteriormente; aparentemente.

outwards [-wərdz, B -wədz] *adv. var. de* **outward.**
outwear [-'wɛr, B -'wɛə] *v.t.* 1. gastar, desgastar (con el uso), consumir. 2. durar más que, perdurar.
outweigh [-'weɪ] *v.t.* pesar más que, exceder (en peso o efecto); valer más que, importar más que.
outwit [-'wɪt] *v.t.* (*pret., p.p.* OUTWITTED; *p.pr.* OUTWITTING) 1. ser más listo que, burlar, engañar. 2. (ant.) ser más sabio que.
outwork [-'wɜrk, B -'wɜk] *v.t.* 1. trabajar más que. 2. resolver; producir.
outwork ['aʊtˌwɜrk, B -ˌwɜk] *s.* (fort.) obra exterior o accesoria.
outworn [-'wɔrn, B -'wɔn] *a.* 1. anticuado, obsoleto (juicio, ideas). 2. usado, gastado (cosas, vestimenta). 3. (fig.) ajada, exhausta (persona).
outwrite [aʊt'raɪt] *v.t.* escribir mejor que, ser mejor escritor que.
ouzel ['uzəl] *s.* (orn.) mirlo.
ouzo ['uzoʊ] *s.* licor griego con sabor a anís.
ova ['oʊvə] *pl. de* **ovum.**
oval ['oʊvəl] *a.* oval, ovalado; ovoide, aovado. —*s.* óvalo.
ovally [-vəlɪ] *adv.* en (figura de) óvalo.
ovalness [-vəlnəs] *s.* forma ovalada.
ovarian [oʊ'vɛrɪən, B -'vɛər-] **ovarial** [-əl] *a.* ovárico.
ovariectomy [oʊˌvɛrɪ'ɛktəmɪ] *s.* (*pl.* OVARIECTOMIES) (med.) ovariectomía.
ovariotomy [-'ɑtəmɪ, B -vɛərɪ'ɔt-] *s.* (*pl.* OVARIOTOMIES) (med.) ovariotomía.
ovaritis [ˌoʊvə'raɪtəs] *s.* (med.) ovaritis.
ovary ['oʊvərɪ] *s.* (*pl.* OVARIES) (anat., zool., bot.) ovario.
ovate ['oʊˌveɪt] *a.* aovado, ovado, ovalado; (bot.) aovado (hojas, pétalos, etc.).
ovation [oʊ'veɪʃən] *s.* 1. ovación, aplauso, aclamación. 2. (hist. romana) ovación (triunfo de segundo orden).
ovational [-əl] *a.* triunfante.
oven ['ʌvən] *s.* horno (casero o industrial).
ovenbird [-ˌbɜrd, B -ˌbɜd] *s.* (orn.) hornero.
oven glove, agarradera.
oven-peel [-ˌpil] *s.* pala de horno.
ovenproof ['ʌvənpruf] *a.* refractario, de horno.
oven ready, listo para el horno.
ovenware ['ʌvənwɛr] *s.* vajilla refractaria.
over ['oʊvər, B -və] *adv.* 1. al otro lado, enfrente. 2. al revés, a la vuelta. 3. de lado a lado. 4. a través. 5. encima, por encima. 6. más; de más, demasiado, de sobra, en exceso. 7. allá; más allá. 8. aparte, de lado. 9. de nuevo, otra vez. 10. de principio a fin. 11. **not o. yet,** aún sin terminar; **o. again,** otra vez, de nuevo, nuevamente; **o. against,** en frente de; en contraste o comparación con; **o. and above,** además de, en exceso de, por encima de; **o. and o.,** repetidamente, una y otra vez; **o. here,** acá, por acá; **o. there,** allá, por allá; **to ask someone o.,** pedir o invitar (a alguien) que venga; **to be all o.,** haber pasado, haberse acabado; **to be all o. with (someone),** haberse terminado todo para, ser el fin para (alguien). —*prep.* 1. sobre, encima de, por encima de. 2. más de; mejor que. 3. por todo; en todo, ej., *to wander o. the city,* vagar por toda la ciudad, *all the world o.,* en todo el mundo. 4. a lo largo de. 5. mientras, durante, ej., *keep it o. the weekend,* téngalo durante el fin de semana. 6. por, ej., *we fought o. you,* peleamos por ti. 7. a través de; al otro lado de, ej., *the church o. the road,* la iglesia al otro lado del camino. 8. **o. one's head,** sin contar con uno; sin hacer caso de uno; **o. your heads,** más allá de la comprensión de uno; **to be all o. (someone),** ser demasiado cariñoso con, ser meloso con (alguien); **to go o. the top,** (mil.) saltar de la trinchera (para atacar). —*a.* 1. (más) alto; superior. 2. excesivo. 3. sobrante. —*s.* 1. (impr.) tirada extra. 2. (mil.) largo (disparo o tiro que cae más allá del blanco). 3. (criquet) la serie de pelotas (gen. seis) boleadas alternativamente de cada meta. —*v.i., v.t.* (poét.) pasar por encima o a través de. —*interj.* 1. pase la página. 2. (rad., teleg.) escucho.
overabound [ˌoʊvərə'baʊnd] *v.i.* sobreabundar, superabundar.
overabundance [-ə'bʌndəns] *s.* sobreabundancia, superabundancia, exceso.
overabundant [-dənt] *a.* sobreabundante, superabundante.
overact [-'ækt] (teat.) *v.t.* exagerar (un papel). —*v.i.* exagerar su papel.
overactive [-'æktɪv] *a.* demasiado activo (niño, comerciante, atleta); que genera excesivamente rápido (glándula, etc.).
overage ['oʊvərɪdʒ] *s.* (com.) mercancías excedentes.
overage [ˌoʊvər'eɪdʒ] *a.* pasado de la edad requerida o debida, demasiado viejo, ej., *he is o. for this job,* tiene demasiada edad para hacer este trabajo.
overall [-'ɔl] *adv.* 1. total, en conjunto, por lo general. 2. en todas partes; de pie a cabeza. 3. (mar.) de popa a proa. — ['oʊvərˌɔl] *a.* 1. cabal, completo, total. 2. general, que lo incluye todo.
overalls ['oʊvərˌɔlz] *s., pl.* pantalones de trabajo; traje de mecánico, mono (Esp.); zahones (Esp.).
over-and-over stitch [-ənd'oʊvər-, B -və-] (cost.) punto por encima.
overanxious [-vər'æŋkʃəs] *a.* anhelante, excesivamente ansioso por lograr algo.
overanxiously [-lɪ] *adv.* con mucha ansiedad.
overarm ['oʊvərˌɑrm, B -ˌɑm] *a.* (criquet, béisbol) tirada por alto (díc. de la pelota).
overawe [ˌoʊvər'ɔ] *v.t.* intimidar, imponer respeto a; (fig.) sorprender o quitar el aliento a.
overbalance [ˌoʊvər'bæləns, B -və'-] *v.t. v.i.* 1. pesar más que. 2. (hacer) perder el equilibrio. — ['oʊvərˌbæləns, B -vəˌ-] *s.* preponderancia; exceso de peso o valor.
overbear [-'bɛr, B -'bɛə] *v.t.* 1. oprimir, abrumar, agobiar. 2. dominar, avasallar, someter. —*v.i.* producir demasiado fruto o progenie.
overbearing [-ɪŋ, B -'bɛərɪŋ] *a.* 1. altanero, arrogante; dominante, dictatorial. 2. de gran importancia o poderío.
overbearingly [-lɪ] *adv.* altaneramente, arrogantemente, altivamente.
overbid [-'bɪd] *v.i.* 1. ofrecer más que su valor, ofrecer demasiado (por). 2. (G.B.) ofrecer más, sobrepujar. 3. (bridge) sobrelicitar su mano. —*v.t.* 1. ofrecer más que, mejorar (una oferta). 2. (bridge) sobrelicitar (la mano de uno). — ['oʊvərˌbɪd, B -vəˌ-] *s.* 1. mejora (de una oferta). 2. puja en exceso.
overbidding [-ɪŋ] *s.* puja.
overblow [-'bloʊ] *v.t.* 1. dispersar, derribar (díc. del viento). 2. cubrir, recubrir, llenar (algo el viento).
overblown [-'bloʊn] *a.* 1. sobreabierto, muy maduro (flor). 2. hinchado, grueso. 3. ampuloso, pomposo.
overboard ['oʊvərˌbɔrd, B -vəˌbɔd] *adv.* al mar, al agua; **man o.!** ¡hombre al agua!; **to throw o.,** desechar, tirar por la borda; (fig.) descartar (plan, idea, etc.).
overboil [-'bɔɪl] *v.t.* hervir demasiado.
overbold [-'boʊld] *a.* temerario, muy osado.
overbridge [-ˌbrɪdʒ] *s.* (f.c.) paso superior.
overbuild [ˌoʊvər'bɪld, B -və'-] *v.t.* 1. sobreedificar, edificar encima de. 2. construir demasiado o en exceso, abigarrar con edificios (una región).
overbuilt [-'bɪlt] *a.* que tiene demasiados edificios (esp. en relación con la extensión del área).
overburden [-'bɜrdən, B -'bɜd-] *v.t.* sobrecargar, agobiar; preocupar. — ['oʊvərˌbɜrd-, B -vəˌbɜd-] *s.* sobrecarga, peso excesivo; preocupación desmesurada.
overbuy [-'baɪ] *v.t.* comprar más de lo necesario de (algo). —*v.i.* hacer compras en exceso (esp. más allá de los medios de uno).
overcall [-'kɔl] *v.t.* (bridge) declarar más que (el adversario). —*v.i.* hacer una declaración más alta. — ['oʊvərˌkɔl, B -vəˌ-] *s.* (bridge) declaración más alta (que la precedente).
overcapitalization [ˌoʊvərˌkæpətələ'zeɪʃən, B ˌoʊvəˌ-laɪ-] *s.* (com.) capitalización excesiva, exageración del capital, capitalización inflada.
overcapitalize [-'kæpətəˌlaɪz] *v.t.* (com.) 1. exagerar el valor nominal del capital de (una compañía). 2. capitalizar en exceso, sobrecapitalizar.
overcast [-'kæst, B -'kɑst] *v.t.* 1. anublar, obscurecer; eclipsar. 2. (cost.) sobrehilar. — ['oʊvərˌkæst, B -vəˌkɑst] *a.* 1. anublado, nublado, encapotado. 2. (cost.) sobrehilado. —*s.* 1. capa, cubierta, revestimiento. 2. cubierta de nubes, nublado. 3. (cost.) sobrehilado, repulgo.
overcasting [-'kæstɪŋ, B -'kɑs-] *s.* 1. enlucido. 2. (cost.) sobrehilado (puntadas que refuerzan la orilla de la tela).
overcast stitch, (cost.) sobrehilado, repulgo.
overcautious [-'kɔʃəs] *a.* excesivamente cauteloso.
overcertification [-ˌsɜrtəfə'keɪʃən, B -ˌsɜt-] *s.* (com.) certificación de un cheque sobregirado.
overcertify [-'sɜrtəˌfaɪ, B -'sɜt-] *v.t.* (com.) certificar o respaldar (un cheque sobregirado).
overcharge ['oʊvərˌtʃɑrdʒ, B -vəˌtʃɑdʒ] *s.* 1. sobrecarga, sobreprecio. 2. cargo excesivo o exorbitante, (ej., en una cuenta). 3. cargo adicional, recargo.
overcharge [ˌoʊvər'tʃɑrdʒ, B -və'tʃɑdʒ] *v.t.* 1. sobrecargar, llenar demasiado; atestar, apiñar. 2. cobrar demasiado a (alguien); cargar (cierta cantidad) de más; recargar (el precio). 3. exagerar. —*v.i.* cobrar precios excesivos.
overcheck ['oʊ-ˌtʃɛk] *s.* frontalera (de arreos).
overclothes [-ˌkloʊðz] *s. pl.* prendas (exteriores) de vestir.
overcloud [ˌoʊvər'klaʊd, B -və'-] *v.t., v.i.* nublar(se), anublar(se), cubrir(se) de nubes, cerrarse (el cielo).
overcoat ['oʊvərˌkoʊt, B -vəˌ-] *s.* sobretodo, abrigo.
overcome [ˌoʊvər'kʌm, B -və'-] *v.t.* 1. vencer, superar, salvar (obstáculo); conquistar, rendir, sujetar. 2. (raro) extender, desplegar; derramar. —*v.i.* triunfar, ganar, vencer. —*a.* vencido, agobiado; **o. with liquor,** rendido por el licor, borracho.
overcompensate [-'kɑmpənˌseɪt, B -'kɔm-] *v.i.* (psic.) sobrecompensar.
overcompensation [-ˌkɑmpən'seɪʃən, B -ˌkɔm-] *s.* (psic.) sobrecompensación.
overconfidence [-'kɑnfədəns, B -'kɔn-] *s.* confianza excesiva; presunción.
overconfident [-dənt] *a.* demasiado confiado.
overcooked [-'kʊkt] *a.* sobrecocido, quemado; excesivamente hervido.
overcrop [-'krɑp, B -'krɔp] *v.t.* agotar (un suelo) por cultivo excesivo.

overcrowd [-'kraʊd] *v.t.* atestar, apiñar (gen. personas).
overcrowded [-əd] *a.* atestado, apiñado, repleto (gen. de personas).
overcurrent ['oʊvərˌkɜrənt, -ˌkʌrənt, B -vəˌ-] *s.* (elec.) sobrecorriente.
overcurrent relay, (elec.) relai de sobrecorriente.
overdevelop [ˌoʊvərdɪ'veləp, B 'oʊvədɪ-] *v.t.* desarrollar excesivamente; (foto.) revelar (negativo) en exceso.
overdevelopment [-mənt] *s.* crecimiento excesivo; (foto.) revelado excesivo.
overdo [-'du, B ˌoʊvə'-] *v.t.* 1. excederse en, exagerar; llevar demasiado lejos. 2. asurar, requemar. 3. atarear demasiado; someter a esfuerzo excesivo. 4. **o. it,** agotarse; trabajar demasiado. —*v.i.* hacer demasiado.
overdone [-'dʌn, 'oʊ-] *a.* 1. demasiado cocido o asado. 2. exagerado, excesivo.
overdoor ['oʊvərˌdɔr, B -vəˌdɔ] *s.* panel tallado en la parte superior de una puerta.
overdose [-ˌdoʊs] *s.* dosis excesiva. — [ˌoʊvər'-doʊs, B -və'-] *v.t.* dar una dosis excesiva a.
overdraft [-ˌdræft, B -ˌdrɑft] *s.* 1. tiro, corriente de aire (que pasa sobre un fuego, horno, etc.). 2. (com.) sobregiro, giro en descubierto.
overdraft protection, crédito en cuenta corriente.
overdraw [ˌoʊvər'drɔ, B -və'-] *v.t.* 1. estirar demasiado (un arco). 2. exagerar. 3. (com.) sobregirar, girar en descubierto.
overdress [-'drɛs] *v.t.* adornar o engalanar en exceso. —*v.i.* vestirse con demasiado elegancia.
overdressed [-drɛst] *a.* con ropa demasiado elegante.
overdrink [-'drɪŋk] *v.i.* beber en exceso.
overdrive [-'draɪv] *v.t.* abrumar de trabajo; fatigar por exceso de trabajo. — ['oʊvərˌdraɪv, B -vəˌ-] *s.* (aut.) sobremarcha, sobremando.
overdue [-'du, B -'dju] *a.* 1. (com.) vencido y no pagado; retrasado. 2. demasiado, excesivo.
overdye [-'daɪ] *v.t.* teñir encima (de otro color), reteñir.
overeat [ˌoʊvər'it] *v.i.* comer en exceso, comer demasiado.
overemphasis [-'ɛmfəsɪs] *s.* énfasis exagerado.
overemphasize [-ˌsaɪz] *v.t.* acentuar demasiado, exagerar la importancia de, recalcar demasiado.
overestimate [-'ɛstɪˌmeɪt] *v.t.* sobrestimar, avaluar en exceso. — [-mət] *s.* avalúo excesivo.
overexcite [-ɪk'saɪt] *v.t.* excitar demasiado, sobreexcitar.
overexert [-ɪg'zɜrt, B -'zɜt] *v.i., v.t.* esforzar(se) en demasía.
overexpose [-ɪk'spoʊz] *v.t.* (foto.) dar exceso de exposición a, sobreexponer.
overexposure [-'spoʊʒər, B -ʒə] *s.* 1. (foto.) exceso de exposición, sobreexposición. 2. período excesivo en que una persona o cosa se expone o arriesga (ej., a los rayos del sol).
overextend [-ɪk'stɛnd] *v.t.* ensanchar o extender demasiado (economía, negocio, etc.); (mil.) extender demasiado (líneas de combate, tropas, etc.).
overfall ['oʊvərˌfɔl, B -vəˌ-] *s.* vertedero; aguas de derrame; hilero de corriente producido por los lagos.
overfamiliar [-fə'mɪljər, B -jə] *a.* confianzudo.
overfatigue [-fə'tig] *v.t.* fatigar demasiado.
overfeed [ˌoʊvər'fid, B -və'-] *v.t.* sobrealimentar. —*v.i.* atracarse, hartarse.
overfill [-'fɪl] *v.t.* sobrellenar, llenar hasta derramarse, rebosar.

overflow [-'floʊ] *v.t.* 1. inundar, anegar, desbordar por. 2. derramar de (una vasija). 3. hacer rebosar. —*v.i.* desbordarse, rebosar; **o. with,** rebosar de (alegría, felicidad, etc.). — ['oʊvərˌfloʊ, B -vəˌ-] *s.* 1. inundación, aniego. 2. rebosadura, rebosamiento, desbordamiento, derrame; exceso, sobrante. 3. desagüe, escape, rebose.
overfly [-'flaɪ] *v.t.* sobrevolar, volar por encima de.
overfrequency ['oʊvərˌfrikwənsɪ, B -vəˌ-] *s.* (elec.) sobrefrecuencia.
overgarment [-ˌgɑrmənt, B -ˌgɑmənt] *s.* vestido externo, prenda de vestir externa (chaqueta, abrigo, capa).
overgild [ˌoʊvər'gɪld, B -və'-] *v.t.* sobredorar, dorar (un objeto) excesivamente; (fig.) pintar (una situación) de manera falsamente optimista.
overglaze [-'gleɪz] *v.t.* vidriar o esmaltar. — ['oʊvərˌgleɪz, B -vəˌ-] *s.* vidriado o esmaltado (que se aplica a la porcelana, etc.).
overgrow [-'groʊ] *v.t.* 1. crecer por encima de; entapizar con plantas o hierbas. 2. pasar de la edad de, ser ya viejo para, ser ya grande para. —*v.i.* 1. sobrecrecer. 2. cundir, crecer con (demasiada) exuberancia (la yerba).
overgrown [-'groʊn] *a.* 1. crecido en exceso, ej., *he's o. for his age,* él ha crecido demasiado para su edad. 2. cubierto de hierbas.
overgrowth ['oʊvərˌgroʊθ, B -vəˌ-] *s.* 1. crecimiento excesivo. 2. vegetación exuberante.
overhand [-ˌhænd] *a.* 1. de arriba abajo (díc. de un golpe). 2. (criquet) tirada por lo alto (pelota); (tenis) ejecutado por lo alto (golpe). 3. (cost.) por encima (díc. del punto). —*adv.* 1. por lo alto; palma abajo. 2. (cost.) con puntadas por encima. —*v.t.* (cost.) recoser o repulgar un borde o una costura.
overhand knot, medio nudo.
overhand stitch, (cost.) sobrepuntada.
overhang [-ˌhæŋ] *v.t.* 1. colgar, pender; sobresalir (horizontalmente) por encima de. 2. ser inminente, amenazar. 3. adornar (con colgaduras). —*v.i.* sobresalir horizontalmente, volar. —*s.* 1. proyección, alcance (de la proyección). 2. (aer.) voladizo. 3. (arq.) saliente, voladizo, vuelo. 4. (mar.) lanzamiento de proa o popa.
overhasty [-'heɪstɪ] *a.* demasiado apresurado.
overhaul [ˌoʊvər'hɔl, B -və'-] *v.t.* 1. examinar (detenidamente); componer, reparar, reacondicionar; hacer una reparación general de. 2. descontar ventaja a, alcanzar. — ['oʊvərˌhɔl, B -vəˌ-] *s.* revisión, reparación general.
overhauling [-'hɔlɪŋ] *s.* revisión, examen; reparación general; reacondicionamiento.
overhead ['oʊvərˌhɛd, B -vəˌ-] *a.* 1. superior, de arriba; elevado. 2. (com.) general, indirecto (díc. de los gastos). —*s.* (com.) gastos generales. — [ˌoʊvər'hɛd, B -və'-] *adv.* sobre la cabeza, por encima, arriba.
overhead valve, (aut.) válvula en la culata.
overhear [ˌoʊvər'hɪr, B -və'hɪə] *v.t.* oír por casualidad, acertar o alcanzar a oír.
overheat [-'hit] *v.t.* 1. recalentar, calentar demasiado. 2. (fig.) sobreexcitar, exaltar. —*v.i.* recalentarse.
overheating [-ɪŋ] *s.* recalentamiento; (fig.) acaloramiento.
overindulge [ˌoʊvərɪn'dʌldʒ] *v.t.* ser demasiado indulgente con, consentir, mimar demasiado. —*v.i.* regalarse demasiado.
overindulgence [-'dʌldʒəns] *s.* 1. indulgencia, lenidad exagerada. 2. exceso (de comida, bebida, mimos, etc.).
overindulgent [-dʒənt] *a.* demasiado indulgente.

overissue [-'ɪʃu] (com.) *s.* emisión excesiva (ej., de bonos). —*v.t.* emitir en exceso.
overjoy [ˌoʊvər'dʒɔɪ, B -və'-] *v.t.* llenar de regocijo o júbilo, dar viva satisfacción a; **to be overjoyed (at),** rebosar de alegría (a causa de), recibir con júbilo (noticia).
overjoyed [-'dʒɔɪd] *a.* lleno de alegría.
overkill ['oʊvərˌkɪl, B -vəˌ-] *s.* 1. capacidad nuclear destructiva superior a la necesaria para arrasar varias veces la población total de un país enemigo. 2. (fig.) exceso, superabundancia.
overland [-ˌlænd, B -'lænd] *adv., a.* por tierra, por vía terrestre.
overlap [ˌoʊvər'læp, B -və'-] *v.t., v.i.* sobreponer(se), traslapar(se), solapar(se). — ['oʊvərˌlæp, B -vəˌ-] *s.* 1. solapo, traslapo; superposición. 2. (f.c.) traslapo (de los tramos). 3. (geol.) recubrimiento, solapadura.
overlay [-'leɪ] *v.t.* 1. cubrir, sobreponer, extender sobre. 2. enchapar; dorar, dar un baño (de oro, etc.) a. 3. oprimir, agobiar. 4. yacer sobre; sofocar (a un niño) echándosele encima. 5. (impr.) calzar. — ['oʊvərˌleɪ, B -vəˌ-] *s.* 1. cubierta. 2. capa, baño; enchape. 3. (impr.) alza, calzo. 4. (esco.) corbata; pañuelo para el cuello.
overlaying [-ɪŋ] *s.* (impr.) colocación del calzo; capa, cubierta.
overleap [-'lip] *v.t.* 1. saltar por encima de. 2. omitir, ignorar. 3. exceder (la meta) en un salto, pasarse (de la marca) en un salto.
overlie [-'laɪ] *v.t.* 1. descansar o yacer sobre. 2. sofocar (a una persona) echándosele encima.
overlive [-'lɪv] *v.t., v.i.* sobrevivir; durar más que.
overload [-'loʊd] *v.t.* sobrecargar, recargar. — ['oʊvərˌloʊd, B -vəˌ-] *s.* sobrecarga, recargo; (elec.) sobrecarga.
overload relay ['oʊvərˌloʊd-, B -vəˌ-] (elec.) relai de sobrecarga.
overlong [-'lɔŋ] *a.* demasiado largo.
overlook [ˌoʊvər'lʊk, B -və'-] *v.t.* 1. mirar desde lo alto; tener vista a, dar a; caer a; dominar, descollar sobre. 2. inspeccionar, examinar, reconocer. 3. supervisar, fiscalizar, controlar. 4. pasar por alto; tolerar. 5. descuidar; no notar, no fijarse en, marginar. 6. encantar, hechizar (con la mirada).
overlord ['oʊvərˌlɔrd, B -vəˌlɔd] *s.* señor; amo; jefe supremo.
overlordship [-ˌʃɪp] *s.* 1. jefatura suprema. 2. dominio absoluto.
overly ['oʊvərlɪ, B -vəlɪ] *adv.* (esco., E.U.) excesivamente, demasiado.
overman [-mən, B -ˌmæn] *s.* 1. capataz, sobrestante. 2. (der., esco.) árbitro, juez. — [ˌoʊvər'mæn, B -və'-] *v.t.* (*pret., p.p.* OVERMANNED; *p.pr.* OVERMANNING) tripular en exceso; dotar de personal demasiado numeroso.
overmantel [-ˌmæntəl] *s.* friso o adorno encima de la repisa de una chimenea.
overmaster [ˌoʊvər'mæstər, B -və'mɑstə] *v.t.* subyugar, sojuzgar; vencer.
overmastering [-tərɪŋ] *a.* subyugante, abrumador.
overmatch [-'mætʃ] *v.t.* vencer, superar; cotejar dos adversarios, uno de los cuales es obviamente más poderoso. —*s.* cotejo desigual.
overmeasure [-'mɛʒər, B -ə] *s.* colmo, medida excesiva.
overmuch [-'mʌtʃ, 'oʊvər-, B -və'-] *a.* demasiado. —*adv.* en demasía, en exceso. — ['oʊvərˌmʌtʃ, B -vəˌ-] *s.* demasía, exceso.
overnice ['oʊvər'naɪs, B -və'-] *a.* empalagoso, remilgado, excesivamente obsequioso.
overnight [-'naɪt] *s.* (la) noche anterior. —*a.* ['oʊvərˌnaɪt, B -vəˌ-] 1. de noche; de la noche anterior. 2. de una sola noche; que pasa la noche,

ej., *o. delivery,* entrega de una día para otro; ej., *o. guests,* huéspedes que pasan la noche. — [ˌouvər'naɪt, B -və'-] *adv.* 1. durante la noche, toda la noche. 2. de la noche a la mañana.
overnight bag, saco de noche, maletín.
overpass [ˌouvər'pæs, B -və'pɑs] *v.t.* 1. atravesar, salvar; pasar al otro lado o por encima de. 2. pasarse de, exceder; transgredir, infringir. 3. sobrepujar, exceder, aventajar. 4. pasar por alto, no hacer caso de. — ['ouvərˌpæs, B -vəˌpɑs] *s.* (f.c., ing.) paso superior.
overpay [-'peɪ] *v.t.* pagar demasiado por.
overpayment [-mənt] *s.* pago excesivo.
overpersuade [-pər'sweɪd, B -pə'-] *v.t.* persuadir, convencer, ganarse (a una persona venciendo su resistencia).
overpersuasion [-'sweɪʒən] *s.* persuasión (después de vencer resistencia).
overplay [-ˌpleɪ] *v.t.* 1. (teat.) sobreactuar, exagerar (un papel). 2. jugar mejor que; aventajar, vencer (en juego). 3. (golf) pasar con la pelota, lanzar la pelota más allá del (green).
overplus ['ouvərˌplʌs, B -vəˌ-] *s.* excedente, superávit.
overpopulate [ˌouvər'pɑpjəˌleɪt, B -və'pɔp-] *v.t.* poblar excesivamente.
overpopulated [-əd] *a.* superpoblado.
overpopulation [-ˌpɑpjə'leɪʃən, B -ˌpɔp-] *s.* superpoblación; exceso de población.
overpower [-'pauər, B -'pauə] *v.t.* 1. vencer; subyugar. 2. oprimir, abrumar. 3. dotar de poder o potencia excesivos.
overpowering [-ərɪŋ] *a.* 1. abrumador, opresivo. 2. irresistible.
overpoweringly [-lɪ] *adv.* 1. abrumadoramente, opresivamente. 2. irresistiblemente.
overpraise [-'preɪz] *v.t.* alabar excesivamente, elogiar con exceso o con exageración.
overprice [-'praɪs] *v.t.* fijar un precio excesivo para (artículo, mercadería, etc.).
overprint [-'prɪnt] *v.t.* (impr.) sobreimprimir; imprimir encima de. — ['ouvərˌprɪnt, B -vəˌ-] *s.* (impr., foto., filat.) sobreimpresión.
overprize [ˌouvər'praɪz, B -və'-] *v.t.* valuar o apreciar en exceso.
overproduce [-prə'dus, B -'djus] *v.t.* producir en exceso (a la demanda o al pedido original).
overproduction [-'dʌkʃən] *s.* superproducción, sobreproducción.
overproof [-'pruf] *a.* con más del 50% de alcohol (licores).
overproportion [-prə'pɔrʃən, B -'pɔʃən] *v.t.* hacer en un tamaño desproporcionadamente grande.
overproportionate [-ʃənət] *a.* muy desproporcionado.
overprotect [-prə'tɛkt] *v.t.* cuidar excesivamente (esp. a los hijos).
overprotection [-'tɛkʃən] *s.* cuidado o solicitud excesiva (de los padres con los hijos).
overprotective [-tɪv] *a.* excesivamente solícito (esp. padres con respecto a hijos).
overrate [ˌouvər'reɪt, B -və'-] *v.t.* sobrestimar.
overreach [-'ritʃ] *v.t.* 1. ir más allá de; extenderse sobre. 2. trampear, estafar, engañar. 3. (dial.) alcanzar. 4. **o. oneself,** pasarse de listo; errar por querer abarcar mucho. —*v.i.* 1. extralimitarse, pasarse, excederse. 2. exagerar. 3. (vet.) alcanzarse (rozarse los caballos la pata trasera con la delantera).
overrefinement [-rɪ'faɪnmənt] *s.* 1. exceso de refinamiento; sutileza exagerada. 2. mejora o adelanto superfluos (en un aparato, máquina, etc.).
override [-'raɪd] *v.t.* 1. pasar sobre o por encima, atropellar, pisotear. 2. fatigar, reventar (un caballo). 3. poner a un lado; abrogar, anular, hacer caso omiso de; rechazar arbitrariamente. 4. solapar, traslapar. 5. (pol., E.U.) vencer en la votación (a un veto presidencial).
overriding [-ɪŋ] *a.* dominante, avasallador.
overripe [-'raɪp] *a.* pachucho, papandujo, remaduro (Amer.) (fruta); demasiado maduro, sobremaduro.
overrule [-'rul] *v.t.* 1. decidir en contra, declarar sin lugar. 2. (der.) denegar, desechar; anular, invalidar. 3. predominar, dominar, vencer, subyugar. 4. **objection overruled,** (der.) objeción denegada.
overruling [-'rulɪŋ] *a.* invalidante; denegatorio.
overrun [-'rʌn] *v.t.* 1. inundar, cundir por. 2. invadir, infestar. 3. aplastar, destruir. 4. exceder. 5. aventajar, dejar atrás (en una carrera). 6. (impr.) repasar, recorrer (la composición). 7. (ant.) asolar; saquear. —*v.i.* 1. pasar más allá. 2. correr demasiado rápido (máquina, motor, etc.). — ['ouvəˌrʌn] *s.* 1. desbordamiento; rebosamiento. 2. (impr.) recorrido (de letras o palabras); sobrante (de ejemplares en el número completo de la tirada).
oversea [ˌouvər'si, 'ouvərˌsi, B -və'-] **overseas** ['ouvər'siz, B -və'-] *adv.* allende los mares, a ultramar. —*a.* de ultramar, extranjero.
oversee [ˌouvər'si, B -və'-] *v.t.* 1. examinar, estudiar; inspeccionar. 2. supervigilar, dirigir, fiscalizar.
overseer ['ouvərˌsiər, B -vəˌsɪə] *s.* sobrestante, capataz, inspector, mayoral; superintendente; supervisor, contramaestre (en talleres), jefe de taller; regente (de imprenta).
oversell [ˌouvər'sɛl, B -və'-] *v.t.* (com.) vender en exceso (más de aquello de que se dispone o más de lo que puede entregarse); vender en exceso a; ser demasiado entusiasta o exagerar en la presentación de un producto que no lo merece.
oversensitive [-'sɛnsətɪv] *a.* extremadamente sensitivo, sensible o quisquilloso.
overset [-'sɛt] *v.t.* 1. trastornar, perturbar. 2. volcar, voltear, tumbar. 3. hacer caer, desbaratar, frustrar, ej., *o. a plot,* frustrar un complot. 4. (impr.) poner demasiado tipo en, poner demasiado ancha (la línea); excederse en la composición (del espacio disponible). — ['ouvərˌsɛt, B -vəˌ-] *s.* trastorno, vuelco.
oversew [-'sou, 'ouvərˌsou, B -vəˌ-] *v.t.* (cost.) sobrehilar, recoser.
oversexed [ˌouvər'sɛkst, B -və'-] *a.* superdotado sexualmente; demasiado susceptible a excitarse sexualmente.
overshade [-'ʃeɪd] *v.t.* sombrear, dar sombra a, asombrar; obscurecer, ensombrecer.
overshadow [-'ʃædou] *v.t.* 1. sombrear, asombrar; obscurecer, ensombrecer. 2. (fig.) eclipsar; dominar; ser más importante que.
overshine [-'ʃaɪn] *v.t.* 1. brillar sobre o encima de; iluminar. 2. exceder en brillantez, dejar deslucido; eclipsar.
overshoe ['ouvərˌʃu, B -vəˌ-] *s.* chanclo; zapatón de goma, zapato impermeable contra la lluvia.
overshoot [ˌouvər'ʃut, B -və'-] *v.t.* 1. pasar rápidamente por encima. 2. tirar por encima del (blanco), errar por tirar demasiado lejos o muy alto. 3. superar en tiro. 4. **o. the mark,** excederse, exagerar. —*v.i.* 1. pasarse de la raya, excederse. 2. tirar largo (artillería).
overshot ['ouvərˌʃɑt, B -vəˌʃɔt] *a.* 1. que tiene saliente la mandíbula superior (como algunos perros). 2. de corriente alta, ej., *an o. (water) wheel,* (hidr.) rueda de alimentación o impulsión de corriente alta.
oversight [-ˌsaɪt] *s.* 1. vigilancia, cuidado, atención. 2. inadvertencia, descuido, olvido, omisión.
oversimplification [ˌouvərˌsɪmpləfə'keɪʃən, B -vəˌ-] *s.* simplificación exagerada.
oversimplify [-'sɪmpləˌfaɪ] *v.t.* simplificar demasiado.
oversize [-'saɪz, 'ouvərˌsaɪz, B -vəˌ-] *a.* 1. de tamaño exagerado. 2. de tamaño anormal, de un tamaño enorme.
overskirt ['ouvərˌskɜrt, B -vəˌskɜt] *s.* sobrefalda, faldellín.
oversleep [ˌouvər'slip, B -və'-] *v.i.* quedarse dormido, pegársele las sábanas a uno.
overspeed ['ouvərˌspid, B -vəˌ-] *s.* (mec.) sobre-velocidad, velocidad excesiva.
overspend [ˌouvər'spɛnd, B -və'-] *v.t.* 1. gastar o usar en exceso; agotar, consumir, disipar, dilapidar, gastar extravagantemente. 2. gastar más que. —*v.i.* disipar el dinero, gastar el dinero extravagantemente.
overspread [-'sprɛd] *v.t.* extender sobre, esparcir, regar.
overstate [-'steɪt] *v.t.* afirmar con demasiada insistencia, exagerar, ej., *he overstated his premise,* él dio demasiado énfasis a su premisa.
overstatement [-mənt] *s.* declaración muy enérgica; aseveración exagerada.
overstay [-'steɪ] *v.t.* 1. quedarse más tiempo del permitido (por licencia, hospitalidad, etc.), ej., *she overstayed her welcome,* ella abusó de la bienvenida que recibió (y se quedó demasiado tiempo). 2. (com.) dejar de vender al precio tope del (mercado).
overstep [-'stɛp] *v.t.* traspasar, transgredir, exceder, propasar.
overstitch ['ouvərˌstɪtʃ, B -vəˌ-] (cost.) *s.* sobrehilada, sobrehilo. —*v.t.* sobrehilar, repulgar, recoser.
overstock [ˌouvər'stɑk, B -və'stɔk] (com.) *v.t., v.i.* abarrotar(se) en demasía. — ['ouvərˌstɑk, B -vəˌstɔk] *s.* surtido excesivo, existencias excesivas.
overstrain [-'streɪn] *v.t.* apretar demasiado. —*v.i.* esforzarse demasiado. —*s.* tensión excesiva.
overstrew [-'stru] *v.t.* (fig.) (*ú. gen. en voz pasiva*) sembrar, salpicar, regar (calle de flores, confeti, etc.).
overstride [-'straɪd] *v.t.* 1. cruzar a grandes trancos. 2. marchar más rápido que.
overstrung [-'strʌŋ] *a.* demasiado tenso; muy sensible, demasiado impresionable, demasiado excitable.
overstuff [-'stʌf] *v.t.* atestar o llenar demasiado; henchir, rehenchir, rellenar (muebles, cojín, etc.).
oversubscribe [-səb'skraɪb] *v.t., v.i.* (com.) subscribir (bonos, acciones) en exceso de la emisión.
oversubscription [-'skrɪpʃən] *s.* (com.) subscripción en exceso de la emisión.
oversupply [-sə'plaɪ] (com.) *v.t.* abastecer o surtir en exceso. —*s.* provisión excesiva.
overt [ou'vɜrt, 'ouvɜrt, B 'ouvɜt] *a.* abierto, público, manifiesto, patente, evidente, ej., *an o. proposition,* una proposición evidente.
overtake [ˌouvər'teɪk, B -və'-] *v.t.* 1. alcanzar, dar alcance a. 2. atajar, sorprender, sobrecoger, ej., *I was overtaken by fear,* me sobrecogió el temor.
overtax [-'tæks] *v.t.* 1. agobiar con impuestos, abrumar con impuestos. 2. exigir demasiado (esfuerzo, inteligencia, capacidad, etc.).
over-the-counter [-ðə'kauntər, B -ə] *a.* *a.* (fin., com.) no inscrito, no vendido en la bolsa (díc de los valores, bonos, etc.).

overthrow [-'θroʊ] *v.t.* 1. volcar; echar abajo, tumbar, derribar; derrocar, destronar; trastornar, desbaratar. 2. subvertir, destruir, vencer. 3. lanzar más allá de. 4. (ant.) desarreglar, descomponer. — ['oʊvər,θroʊ, B -və,-] *s.* vuelco; derribo, derrocamiento; caída; derrota, ruina; subversión; destronamiento; trastorno.
overtime ['oʊvər,taɪm, B -və,-] *s.* 1. tiempo suplementario. 2. horas extra de trabajo, sobretiempo. —*adv.* fuera del tiempo estipulado; más del tiempo regular o reglamentario; **to go o.**, exceder el (límite del) tiempo reglamentario; **to work o.**, trabajar (en) horas extra. — [,oʊvər'taɪm, B -və'-] *v.t.* (foto.) dar exceso de exposición a, sobreexponer.
overtire [,oʊvər'taɪr, B -və'taɪə] *v.t.* agobiar, fatigar excesivamente.
overtly [oʊ'vɜrtlɪ, 'oʊ,vɜrt-, B -,vɜt-] *adv.* abiertamente, públicamente, manifiestamente.
overtone ['oʊvər,toʊn, B -və,-] *s.* 1. (mús.) armónico. 2. reflejo, viso, película (sobre una superficie). 3. insinuación, alusión, sugestión; significado sugerido, ej., *the speech had important overtones,* el discurso tuvo alusiones importantes.
overtop [,oʊvər'tɑp, B -və'tɔp] *v.t.* 1. superar, sobrepasar. 2. (fig.) descollar entre, sobresalir entre.
overtrade [-'treɪd] (com.) *v.i.* comerciar más allá del capital disponible, comprar más de lo que se puede vender o pagar.
overtrain [-'treɪn] *v.t., v.i.* entrenar(se) con exceso; confundir (perro, caballo, etc.) con exceso de órdenes y señales.
overtrick ['oʊvər,trɪk, B -və,-] *s.* (bridge) baza de más, sobre-baza.
overtrump [,oʊvər'trʌmp, B 'oʊvə'-] *v.t., v.i.* (naipes) contrafallar.
overture ['oʊvər,tʃʊr, -tʃər, B 'oʊvə,tjʊə] *s.* 1. insinuación, oferta, proposición; tentativa. 2. introducción, preludio. 3. (mús.) obertura. —*v.t.* hacer una oferta de, proponer, insinuar.
overturn [,oʊvər'tɜrn, B -və'tɜn] *v.t.* 1. volcar, trastornar. 2. derribar, derrocar (gobierno, etc.). —*v.i.* volcarse; (mar.) zozobrar. — ['oʊvər,tɜrn, B 'oʊvə,tɜn] *s.* 1. vuelco, trastorno. 2. derribo, derrocamiento.
overuse [-'jus] *s.* uso excesivo. — [-'juz] *v.t.* usar excesivamente.
overvalue [-'vælju] *v.t.* encarecer; estimar demasiado; exagerar el valor de una cosa.
overwatch [-'wɑtʃ, B -'wɔtʃ] *v.t.* 1. vigilar, cuidar, celar. 2. (ant.) cansar a fuerza de vigilias.
overwear [-'wɛr, B -'wɛə] *v.t.* desgastar; gastar, consumir.
overweary [-'wɪrɪ, B -'wɪərɪ] *a.* rendido, agotado, fatigado (en exceso). —*v.t.* cansar, estragar, agotar (en exceso).
overweening [-'winɪŋ] *a.* presuntuoso, arrogante, petulante, altanero, pretensioso. —*s.* presunción, arrogancia, altanería, petulancia.
overweeningly [-lɪ] *adv.* presuntuosamente, petulantemente, arrogantemente, altaneramente.
overweigh [-'weɪ] *v.t.* 1. importar más que, eclipsar. 2. oprimir, deprimir.
overweight ['oʊvər,weɪt, B -və,-] *s.* 1. exceso de peso, sobrepeso. 2. carga excesiva. —*a.* de peso anormal, obeso, pesado. — [,oʊvər'weɪt, B -və'-] *v.t.* 1. dar demasiada importancia a. 2. hacer demasiado pesado.
overwhelm [,oʊvər'hwɛlm, -'wɛlm, B -və'-] *v.t.* 1. abrumar, agobiar, abatir. 2. volcar, trastornar. 3. arrollar, aplastar. 4. sumergir, inundar. 5. **o. with,** abrumar con (preguntas, trabajo, etc.); colmar de (favores, regalos, etc.).
overwhelming [-ɪŋ] *a.* 1. abrumador, agobiante. 2. irresistible (deseo, etc.). 3. arrollador, aplastante (triunfo, mayoría, etc.).
overwhelmingly [-lɪ] *adv.* 1. abrumadoramente. 2. irresistiblemente. 3. arrolladoramente.
overwind [-'waɪnd] *v.t.* tensar con exceso la cuerda (del reloj).
overwinter [-'wɪntər, B -ə] *v.i.* sobrevivir al invierno.
overword ['oʊvər,wɜrd, B -və,wɜd] *s.* palabra repetida; (poét.) estribillo, bordón, contera.
overwork [,oʊvər'wɜrk, B -və'wɜk] *v.t.* 1. hacer trabajar en exceso, agotar, fatigar. 2. hacer demasiado uso de, trillar (palabra, frase, etc.). 3. detallar o elaborar excesivamente. 4. (*ú. sólo en p.p.*) redecorar. —*v.i.* trabajar en exceso. — ['oʊvər,wɜrk, B -və,wɜk] *s.* trabajo excesivo.
overworked [-'wɜrkt, B -'wɜkt] *a.* 1. atrabajado, agotado. 2. trillado (frase, palabra, etc.).
overworn [-'wɔrn, B -'wɔn] *a.* excesivamente gastado (por el uso, el trabajo, etc.); fatigado.
overwrite [-'raɪt] *v.t.* 1. escribir sobre (una carta, un documento, etc.). 2. redactar en estilo recargado.
overwrought [-'rɔt] *p.p. de* **overwork.** —*a.* 1. sobreexcitado, agitado. 2. labrado o adornado en exceso, recargado de ornamentos.
Ovid ['ɑvəd, B 'ɔv-] *s.* Ovidio, poeta romano, autor de delicados versos.
Ovidae ['oʊvɪ,di] *s. pl.* (zool.) óvidos.
oviduct ['oʊvə,dʌkt] *s.* (anat., zool.) oviducto.
oviferous [oʊ'vɪfərəs] *a.* (anat., zool.) ovígero, ovífero.
oviform ['oʊvɪ,fɔrm, B -,fɔm] *a.* oviforme, en forma de huevo.
ovine ['oʊ,vaɪn] *a.* 1. ovino, lanar; ovejuno. 2. (fig.) dócil; de poco carácter.
ovipara [oʊ'vɪpərə] *s. pl.* animales ovíparos.
oviparity [-vɪ'pærə,tɪ] *s.* (biol.) oviparidad.
oviparous [-'vɪpərəs] *a.* (biol., zool.) ovíparo.
oviposit ['oʊvə,pɑzət, ˌoʊvə'pɑz-, B -'pɔz-] *v.i.* (ento.) poner huevos.
oviposition [,oʊvəpə'zɪʃən] *s.* (ento.) puesta de huevos.
ovipositor ['oʊvə,pɑzətər, ˌoʊvə'pɑz-, B -'pɔzɪtə] *s.* (ento.) ovipositor.
ovisac ['oʊvə,sæk] *s.* (anat.) ovisaco.
ovoid ['oʊ,vɔɪd] *a.* ovoide, aovado, ovoideo. —*s.* cuerpo ovoide.
ovoidal [oʊ'vɔɪdəl] *a.* ovoide, aovado, ovoideo.
ovolo ['oʊvə,loʊ] *s.* (*pl.* OVOLI [-,li]) (arq.) óvolo, cuarto bocel.
ovotestis [,oʊvoʊ'tɛstəs] *s.* (biol.) ovotestis.
ovoviviparous [-vaɪ'vɪpərəs] *a.* (zool.) ovovivíparo.
ovoviviparousness [-nəs] *s.* (zool.) ovoviviparidad.
ovular ['ɑvjələr, 'oʊv-, B -lə] *a.* (bot., zool.) ovular.
ovulate [-,leɪt] *v.i.* (biol.) ovular.
ovulation [,ɑvjə'leɪʃən, ˌoʊv-, B ,oʊv-] *s.* (biol.) ovulación.
ovule ['oʊvjul] *s.* (bot., anat.) óvulo.
ovum ['oʊvəm] *s.* (*pl.* OVA [-və]) (biol.) óvulo.
owe [oʊ] *v.t.* 1. deber, adeudar (dinero u obligación moral). 2. (ant.) tener, poseer. 3. **o. (something) to,** estar adeudado por (algo) a, tener u obtener gracias a. —*v.i.* estar endeudado, tener deudas.
owing ['oʊɪŋ] *a.* 1. adeudado, debido, por pagarse. 2. (raro) endeudado; obligado (por gratitud). 3. **owing to,** debido a, por causa de.
owl [aʊl] *s.* 1. lechuza, búho. 2. (fig.) (gen. con *night*) ave nocturna, trasnochador, ej., *my brother is a night o.*, mi hermano es un trasnochador.
owlet ['aʊlət] *s.* (orn.) mochuelo; lechuza pequeña, lechucita.
owlish [-lɪʃ] *a.* 1. semejante al búho; de búho. 2. (fig.) serio, formal; sabihondo.
own [oʊn] *a.* 1. propio, ej., *in my o. house,* en mi propia casa. 2. **to be one's o. man,** ser libre, ser independiente, no depender de nadie. —*pron* 1. (*precedido del a. pos.*) (el) suyo, (la) suya, ej., *it's a small house but it's his o.,* es una casa pequeña pero es suya, *it's not my o.,* no es el mío. 2. **of one's o.,** que le pertenece (a uno), que es suyo; **on one's o.,** independientemente, por su (propia) cuenta, bajo su (propia) responsabilidad; **to be on one's o.,** estar independiente; actuar sin la ayuda de nadie; no poder contar con nadie, estar solo; **to come into one's o.,** entrar en posesión de lo suyo; lograr el éxito merecido, adquirir merecida fama; **to get one's o. back,** vengarse, cobrárselas; **to hold one's o.,** defenderse; bastárselas. —*v.t.* 1. poseer, ser dueño de, tener. 2. reconocer, admitir. —*v.i.* (con *to*) confesar, reconocer; **o. up,** (fam.) confesar sinceramente, confesar de plano.
owner ['oʊnər, B -nə] *s.* propietario, dueño; casero.
ownership [-,ʃɪp] *s.* título de propiedad; posesión, propiedad.
ox [ɑks, B ɔks] *s.* (*pl.* OXEN ['ɑksən, B 'ɔk-]) buey.
oxacid [ɑks'æsəd, B ɔks-] *s.* (quím.) oxácido.
oxalate ['ɑksə,leɪt, B 'ɔk-] *s.* (quím.) oxalato.
oxalic [ɑk'sælɪk, B ɔk-] *a.* (quím.) oxálico.
oxalic acid, (quím.) ácido oxálico.
oxalidaceous [ɑk,sælə'deɪʃəs, B ɔk-] *a.* (bot.) oxalidáceo, oxalídeo.
oxalis [ɑk'sæləs, 'ɑksə-, B 'ɔk-] *s.* (bot.) aleluya, acederilla.
oxazine ['ɑksə,zin, B 'ɔk-] *s.* (quím.) oxazina.
oxblood ['ɑks,blʌd, B 'ɔks-] *s.* (color) rojo oscuro (gen. del cuero fino y bien pulido).
oxbow [-,boʊ] *s.* 1. collera de yugo. 2. meandro, recodo (de un río, etc.).
oxcart [-,kɑrt, B -,kɑt] *s.* carreta tirada por bueyes.
oxeye [-,aɪ] *s.* (bot.) pajito; abiar, albihar, manzanilla loca, bonina.
oxeye daisy, (bot.) margarita mayor.
Oxford ['ɑksfərd, B 'ɔksfəd] *s.* zapato de estilo Oxford (estilo deportivo de tacón bajo, enlazado con cordones).
Oxford blue, azul obscuro con matiz morado.
Oxford gray, gris muy oscuro.
Oxfordian [ɑks'fɔrdɪən, B ɔks'fɔd-] *a., s.* oxoniense, natural o vecino de Oxford (ciudad inglesa).
oxheart ['ɑks,hɑrt, B 'ɔks,hɑt] *s.* (bot.) cerezo común; cerezo dulce.
oxidable ['ɑksədəbəl, B 'ɔk-] *a.* oxidable.
oxidant ['ɑksədənt, B 'ɔk-] *s.* (quím.) oxidante.
oxidase [-,deɪs, -,deɪz] *s.* (bioquím.) oxidasa.
oxidation [,ɑksə'deɪʃən, B ,ɔk-] *s.* (quím.) oxidación.
oxidation-reduction [-rɪ'dʌkʃən] *s.* (quím.) óxido-reducción.
oxidation-reduction potential, (quím.) potencial de óxido-reducción.
oxidative ['ɑksə,deɪtɪv, B 'ɔk-] *a.* (quím.) oxidante.
oxide ['ɑk,saɪd, B 'ɔk-] *s.* (quím.) óxido.
oxidizable ['ɑksə,daɪzəbəl, B 'ɔk-] *a.* oxidable.
oxidize [-,daɪz] *v.t.* (quím.) oxidar. —*v.i.* oxidarse.
oxidizer [-ər, B -ə] *s.* (quím.) oxidante.

oxime ['ɑkˌsim, B 'ɔkˌsaɪm] *s.* (quím.) oxima.
oxlip ['ɑksˌlɪp, B 'ɔks-] *s.* (bot.) primavera, hierba de San Pablo.
Oxon., *abrev. de* **of Oxford,** de Oxford (G.B.).
Oxonian [ɑk'soʊnɪən, B ɔk-] *a.* oxoniense, de Oxford. —*s.* oxoniense, nativo o residente de Oxford, Inglaterra; estudiante o ex-alumno de la Universidad de Oxford.
oxtail ['ɑksˌteɪl, B 'ɔks-] *s.* rabo de buey; **o soup,** sopa de rabo de buey (espeso y sustancioso caldo).
oxter ['ɑkstər, B 'ɔkstə] *s.* (esco.) axila, sobaco.
oxtongue ['ɑksˌtʌŋ, B 'ɔks-] *s.* (bot.) buglosa, lengua de buey, ancusa, melera; viperina, viborera.
oxyacetylene [ˌɑksɪə'sɛtələn, B 'ɔk-] *a.* (quím.) oxiacetilénico.
oxyacetylene blowpipe, o. torch, soplete oxiacetilénico.
oxyacid [-'æsəd] *a.* (quím.) oxiácido, oxácido.
oxybromide [-'broʊˌmaɪd] *s.* (quím.) oxibromuro.
oxychloride [-'klɔˌraɪd] *s.* (quím.) oxicloruro.
oxygen ['ɑksɪdʒən, B 'ɔk-] *s.* (quím.) oxígeno.
oxygen acid, (quím.) oxiácido, oxácido.
oxygenate ['ɑksɪdʒəˌneɪt, ɑk'sɪdʒə-, B ɔk-] *v.t.* (quím.) oxigenar.
oxygenation [ˌɑksɪdʒə'neɪʃən, B ˌɔk-] *s.* (quím.) oxigenación.
oxygen bag, balón.
oxygen-hydrogen welding, soldadura oxídrica.
oxygenic [ˌɑksɪ'dʒɛnɪk, B ˌɔk-] **oxygenous** [ɑk'sɪdʒənəs, B ɔk-] *a.* perteneciente al oxígeno; oxigenado.
oxygenize ['ɑksɪdʒəˌnaɪz, B 'ɔk-] *v.t.* (quím.) oxigenar.
oxygen mask, máscara de oxígeno.
oxygen ratio, (geol.) relación de oxígeno, coeficiente de acidez.
oxygen tank, balón de oxígeno.
oxygen tent, (med.) tienda de oxígeno.
oxyhemoglobin [ˌɑksɪ'himəˌgloʊbən, -'hɛmə-, B ˌɔksɪˌhimə'gloʊbɪn] *s.* (biol.) oxihemoglobina.
oxyhydrogen [-'haɪdrədʒən, B 'ɔk-] *a.* (quím.) oxídrico, oxhídrico. —*s.* (quím.) gas oxhídrico, oxihidrógeno.
oxyhydrogen blowpipe, o. torch, soplete oxídrico.
oxymel ['ɑksɪmɛl, B 'ɔk-] *s.* (farm.) oximel, oximiel.
oxymoron [ˌɑksɪ'mɔrˌɑn, B ˌɔk-ˌɔn] *s.* (*pl.* OXYMORA [-ə]) (ret.) oxímoron.
oxyphile ['ɑksɪˌfaɪl, B 'ɔk-] **oxyphil** [-ˌfɪl] **oxyphilic** [ˌɑksɪ'fɪlɪk, B ˌɔk-] **oxyphilous** [ɑk'sɪfələs, B ɔk-] *a.* (quím.) oxífilo.
oxysalt ['ɑksɪˌsɔlt, B 'ɔk-] *s.* (quím.) oxisal.
oxysulfide [ˌɑksɪ'sʌlˌfaɪd, B ˌɔk-] *s.* (quím.) oxisulfuro.
oxytetracycline [-ˌtɛtrə'saɪˌklin] *s.* (farm.) oxitetraciclina.
oxytocic [ˌɑksɪ'toʊsɪk, B ˌɔksɪ'tɔ-] *a.* (med.) oxitócico.
oxytocin [-'toʊsən] *s.* (fisiol.) oxitocina.
oxytone ['ɑksɪˌtoʊn, B 'ɔk-] *a., s.* (gram.) oxítono.
oxytone verse, (poét.) verso agudo.
oxyuriasis [ˌɑksɪjʊ'raɪəsəs, B ˌɔk-] *s.* (med.) oxiuriasis, oxiurosis.
Oxyuridae [-'jʊrɪˌdi] *s. pl.* (zool.) oxiuros.
oyer [ɔɪr, B 'ɔɪə] *s.* (der.) demanda por la presentación de un documento en poder de la parte opuesta.
oyer and terminer [ˌɔɪrən'tɜrmənər, B 'ɔɪərænd'tɜmɪnə] (der.) tribunal superior de jurisdicción criminal.
oyez [oʊ'jeɪ, -'jɛz, B -'jɛs] *interj.* (fr.) ¡oíd! (voz del oficial del tribunal para imponer silencio).
oyster ['ɔɪstər, B -stə] *s.* 1. (zool.) ostra. 2. (fig.) chiticalla, persona reticente o taciturna.
oyster bed, ostral, ostrero, parque ostrífero.
oyster catcher, (orn.) ostrero.
oyster crab, (zool.) pequeño cangrejo pinnotérido.
oyster cracker, galleta salada (que se sirve con el caldo o la sopa de ostras).
oyster farm, ostral, ostrero, vivero de ostras.
oyster farming, ostricultura.
oysterman [-mən] *s.* 1. ostricultor, ostrero (persona); recolector de ostras. 2. barco ostrero.
oyster plant, (bot.) salsifí; mertensia marítima.
oyster rake, rastrillo ostrero (para recoger ostras en aguas poco profundas).
oysterroot [-ˌrut] *s.* (bot.) salsifí.
oz. *abrev. de* **ounce,** onza (onz.).
ozokerite [ˌoʊzoʊ'kɪrˌaɪt, B -'zoʊkərɪt] *s.* (min.) ozocerita, ozoquerita.
ozonation [-'neɪʃən] *s.* (quím.) ozonización.
ozone ['oʊˌzoʊn] *s.* (quím.) ozono; (fam.) aire puro, aire fresco.
ozone hole, agujero en la capa de ozono.
ozonic [oʊ'zoʊnɪk, -'zɑn-, B -'zɔn-] *a.* (quím.) de ozono; ozonizado.
ozonic ether, (quím.) éter ozonizado.
ozonide ['oʊzoʊˌnaɪd] *s.* (quím.) ozónido, ozonuro.
ozonization [ˌoʊzoʊnə'zeɪʃən, B -naɪ-] *s.* (quím.) ozonización.
ozonize ['oʊzoʊˌnaɪz, B -zə-] *v.t., v.i.* (quím.) ozonar(se), ozonizar(se), ozonificar(se).
ozonizer [-ər, B -ə] *s.* (quím.) ozonizador.
ozonolysis [ˌoʊˌzoʊ'nɑləsəs, B -'nɔl-] *s.* (quím.) ozonólisis.
ozonometer [-'nɑmətər, B -'nɔmɪtə] *s.* ozonómetro.
ozonosphere [oʊ'zoʊnəˌsfɪr, B -ˌsfɪə] *s.* (meteor.) ozonosfera.
ozostomia [ˌoʊzə'stoʊmɪə] *s.* (med.) ozostomía.

P

P [pi] *s.* p, decimosexta letra del alfabeto inglés; **to mind one's P's and Q's,** andar con cuidado con lo que se dice, hablar cautelosamente.

P *abrev. de* 1. **pawn,** peón (en ajedrez). 2. **police,** policía.

P (quím.) *símb. de* **phosphorus,** fósforo (P).

pa [pɑ] *s.* (fam.) papá, papi.

Pa. *abrev. de* **Pennsylvania,** Pennsylvania (E.U.).

Pa (quím.) *simb. de* **protactinium,** protactinio (Pa).

P.A. *abrev. de* 1. **power amplifier,** amplificador de potencia. 2. **public address,** sistema de altavoces. 3. **Press Association,** Asociación de Prensa.

pablum ['pæbləm] *s.* 1. (fig.) escritos o ideas muy simples carentes de valor literario o intelectual. 2. nombre comercial de una marca de alimentos para niños.

pabulum ['pæbjələm] *s.* alimento, sustento, pábulo.

pac, pack [pæk] *s.* mocasín de cuero suave para proteger el pie del maltrato de la bota.

paca ['pækə, 'pɑkə, B 'pækə] *s.* (zool.) paca (mamífero roedor de América).

pace [peɪs] *s.* 1. paso; marcha; medida del paso; manera de caminar o andar. 2. paso, aire (manera de caminar el caballo); esp. portante. 3. paso, velocidad, tren, ritmo. 4. **at a slow p.,** a paso lento; **at a snail's p.,** a paso de tortuga; **to go the full p.,** ir a gran velocidad; (fig.) entregarse a los placeres; **to keep p. (with),** andar o avanzar al mismo paso (que), ir o seguir a un paso igual; **to put (someone) through his paces,** poner (a alguien) a prueba, dar (a alguien) ocasión de mostrar lo que vale; **to quicken one's p.,** alargar el paso, apretar o avivar el paso; **to set the p.,** llevar el paso, fijar el ritmo de la carrera. *—v.i.* 1. andar a pasos regulares, pasear. 2. amblar, marchar al paso (caballos). *—v.t.* 1. recorrer a pasos regulares. 2. medir a pasos. 3. controlar el paso de, regular la frecuencia de; fijar el ritmo de. 4. establecer el paso de; marcar el paso para (compañero de equipo). 5. enseñar a caminar. 6. **p. one's beat,** hacer la ronda (un policía).

paced [peɪst] *a.* 1. (*ú. en palabras compuestas*) de paso, de tren, de ritmo (lento, rápido, etc.). 2. mesurado, moderado.

pacemaker ['peɪs,meɪkər, B -kə] *s.* 1. (dep.) liebre. 2. (fig.) inspirador, promotor. 3. (anat.) nudo atrioventricular (del corazón). 4. (med.) marcapasos.

pacemaking [-kɪŋ] *s.* establecimiento del paso.

pacer ['peɪsər, B -sə] *s.* 1. caballo que marca el paso, establecedor del paso (en carreras). 2. caballo de paso portante.

pacesetter [ˌpeɪs,sɛtər] *s.* 1. líder. 2. (dep.) liebre.

pacha, pachalic, *vars. de* **pasha, pashalik.**

pachouli, *var. de* **patchouli.**

pachuco [pə'tʃu,koʊ] *s.* (ant. E.U.) pisaverde; (despec.) mexicano-americano.

pachyderm ['pækɪ,dɜrm, B -ˌdɜm] *s.* (zool.) paquidermo.

pachydermatous [ˌpækɪ'dɜrmətəs, B -'dɜmət-] **pachydermous** [-məs] *a.* 1. (zool.) paquidermo. 2. (med.) paquidérmico. 3. (fig.) encallecido, insensible.

pacifiable ['pæsə,faɪəbəl] *a.* pacificable.

pacific [pə'sɪfɪk] *a.* 1. pacífico, conciliatorio. 2. **P.,** del Pacífico (océano). *—s.* **P.,** (océano) Pacífico.

pacifical [-ɪkəl] *a.* pacífico.

pacifically [-kəlɪ] *adv.* pacíficamente.

pacification [ˌpæsəfə'keɪʃən] *s.* (pol.) pacificación, sosegamiento.

pacificator [pə'sɪfə,keɪtər, B -ə] *s.* pacificador, conciliador.

pacificatory [-kə,tɔrɪ, B -kətərɪ] *a.* conciliatorio, pacificador.

pacificism [pə'sɪfə,sɪzəm] *s.* pacifismo.

Pacific Ocean, Océano Pacífico.

Pacific time, (E.U.) hora del Pacífico (hora legal correspondiente al meridiano 120).

pacifier ['pæsə,faɪər, B -ə] *s.* 1. pacificador. 2. chupador, chupete, chupón (Amer.).

pacifism [-ˌfɪzəm] *s.* pacifismo, oposición a todas las guerras.

pacifist [-fəst] *s., a.* (pol.) pacifista, partidario de la paz.

pacifistic [ˌpæsə'fɪstɪk] *a.* pacifista, que aboga por soluciones pacíficas.

pacify ['pæsə,faɪ] *v.t.* (*pret., p.p.* PACIFIED; *p.pr.* PACIFYING) pacificar, tranquilizar, calmar, apaciguar, aplacar, conciliar.

pack [pæk] *s.* 1. paquete; lío, fardo, paca. 2. mochila, morral (de soldado, viajante, etc.). 3. cajetilla (ej., de cigarrillos). 4. (método de) envase, empaque. 5. partida, porción, lote. 6. sarta, montón (de mentiras, etc.). 7. banda, pandilla (de ladrones, etc.). 8. manada (de lobos, etc.). 9. jauría, perrada. 10. multitud; grupo. 11. banquisa de hielo (flotante). 12. (cantidad de) conservas envasadas. 13. (med.) compresa. 14. (rugby) conjunto de atacantes. 15 (naipes) baraja. *—v.t.* 1. empaquetar, empacar, embalar. 2. envasar. 3. hacer (la maleta, etc.). 4. cargar, llenar. 5. apretar, apiñar. 6. atestar, colmar. 7. (E.U.) llevar, cargar (paquete, fardo, etc.); llevar (un arma), estar armado de (pistola, etc.). 8. **p. down,** apretar, comprimir, apisonar; **p. in,** apiñar (público, gente, en un local); llenar de bote en bote (un teatro, sala, etc.); **p. off,** despedir; despachar (ej., niños al colegio, a la cama, etc.); **p. up,** liquidar; **to send packing,** despedir sumariamente. *—v.i.* 1. empacar, hacer el baúl o la maleta. 2. llenarse. 3. amontonarse, apiñarse, formar una masa compacta. 4. empacarse (fácil o difícilmente). 5. **p. off, p. away,** marcharse apresuradamente; **p. up,** amontonarse; apagarse, dejar de funcionar (motor, etc.); liar el petate, morir.

pack, *v.t.* 1. seleccionar con intento fraudulento (a un jurado complaciente, etc.). 2. (ant.) empandillar (la baraja), arreglar las cartas fraudulentamente.

package ['pækɪdʒ] *s.* 1. paquete, bulto; lío, fardo; envase. 2. (jer.) cantidad grande de dinero. 3. (jer.) mujer o joven guapa. pimpollo.

package deal, (com.) venta de artículos en conjunto; (pol.) convenio que admite intereses contrarios.

package store, (E.U.) tienda de bebibas alcohólicas.

packaging, *s.* embalaje; (com.) presentación.

pack animal, acémila, bestia de carga.

pack cloth, harpillera, halda.

pack drill, (mil.) castigo de marcha.

packed [pækt] *a.* 1. lleno, atestado; apiñado. 2. (*ú. en palabras compuestas*) lleno de, ej., *an adventure-p. novel,* una novela llena de aventuras.

packer ['pækər, B -ə] *s.* 1. empacador, embalador; envasador. 2. (E.U.) comerciante gen. al por mayor.

packet ['pækət] *s.* 1. paquete o fardo pequeño. 2. (t. **p.-boat**) (mar.) paquebote, buque correo; p. ext. buque. 3. (jer.) fortuna, suma considerable (perdida o ganada en el juego). 4. (jer., G.B.) golpe o castigo; lío, embrollo. 5. **to catch a p., to stop a p.,** (jer., G.B.) resultar gravemente herido de bala; **to make a p.,** (jer.) hacer su pacotilla, ganar una fortuna. *—v.t.* empaquetar.

packhorse ['pæk,hɔrs, B -ˌhɔs] *s.* 1. caballo de carga. 2. (fig.) trabajador asiduo.

pack ice, banquisa de hielo (flotante).

packing ['pækɪŋ] *s.* 1. embalaje; empaquetamiento, envase. 2. material para embalaje. 3. (maq.) empaque, empaquetadura, guarnición.

packing bag, sobre o bolsa acolchonada con material protector, para empacar objetos frágiles.

packing box, packing case, cajón, caja de embalaje.

packing gland, (mec.) presaestopa.

packing house, almacén de embalaje; empresa empacadora; frigorífico, empresa de productos cárnicos; lugar donde se empacan o envasan conservas.

packing paper, papel de empacar.

packing press, prensa de envasar.

packing ring, (mec.) anillo de pistón.

packing strip, cuña, cualquier objeto que sirva para ajustar o apretar un cuerpo con otro.

packman ['pækmən] *s.* buhonero, mercachifle, baratillero.

pack needle, aguja de arria o saquera; almarada.

pack rat, (zool., E.U.) neotoma; (jer.) urraca, ej. *he's a real p.,* es una urraca.

packsack ['pæk,sæk] *s.* barjuleta; bolsa de viaje, morral.

packsaddle [-ˌsædəl] *s.* basto, albarda, enjalma. *—v.t.* albardar, enalbardar, enjalmar.

packthread [-ˌθrɛd] *s.* bramante, guita, pita, piela (Amer.), piolín (Amer.).

pack train, recua, procesión de animales cargados.

pact [pækt] *s.* pacto, arreglo, compromiso, acuerdo, trato, contrato, convenio.

pad [pæd] *s.* 1. sonido sordo de pisadas o de golpes en el suelo. 2. caballo de paso suave. 3. (dial., G.B.) camino. 4. (ant.) salteador de caminos. *—v.i.* (*pret., p.p.* PADDED; *p.pr.* PADDING) 1. viajar a pie. 2. caminar con trabajo; caminar o correr pesadamente.

pad, *s.* 1. almohadilla, cojinillo, cojinete. 2. relleno, bollo (en vestido). 3. albardilla, baste. 4. taco (de calendario); cuaderno de notas, bloc. 5. tampón, almohadilla de entintar. 6. peto, plastrón (del esgrimidor, jugador de rugby, etc.). 7. pata (de ciertos animales como el zorro, lobo, liebre, nutria, etc.). 8. (E.U.) hoja de planta acuática; esp. hoja de nenúfar. 9. carnosidad en la planta de la pata (de algunos animales); pulvillo, plántula o euplántula (de los insectos). 10. (jer., E.U.) jergón o cama; por ext., cuarto o apartamento donde uno vive. —*v.t.* (*pret. p.p.* PADDED; *p.pr.* PADDING) 1. forrar, rellenar, proveer de almohadillas. 2. (fig.) aumentar con material superfluo (un escrito).

padded ['pædəd] *a.* acolchonado, rellenado, acojinado.

padded cell, celda o cuarto de paredes acolchadas (en un manicomio).

padding ['pædɪŋ] *s.* 1. relleno, atestadura (borra, algodón u otro material usado para rellenar almohadillas, cojines, colchones, etc.). 2. (fig.) paja, relleno.

paddle ['pædəl] *s.* 1. canalete, zagual, remo. 2. paleta o hélice (de agua). 3. paleta (pieza de hoja ancha usada para mezclar, batir o remover). 4. (dial., G.B., esco.) béstola, arrejada o aguijada (para limpiar el arado). —*v.i.* 1. remar con canalete. 2. remar suavemente. —*v.t.* 1. impeler o mover por medio de un canalete. 2. batir o remover con una paleta. 3. (fam., E.U.) pegar o castigar con una paleta. 4. **p. one's own canoe,** hacer de su capa un sayo, depender sólo de sí mismo, no valerse de ayudas.

paddle, *v.i.* 1. chapotear. 2. hacer pinitos o pininos (Amer.). 3. manosear, tentar, acariciar con los dedos o la mano.

paddle box, tambor de rueda de paletas (en un barco).

paddlefish [-ˌfɪʃ] *s.* (ict.) pez hoja.

paddler ['pædlər, B -lə] *s.* remero, bogador, boga (Amer.).

paddle wheel, (mar.) rueda de paletas.

paddock ['pædək] *s.* 1. dehesa, apacentadero. 2. paddock (donde se exhibe a los caballos de carrera en los hipódromos). 3. (Aust.) corral, campo cercado. —*v.t.* confinar en una dehesa.

paddy ['pædɪ] *s.* (*pl.* PADDIES) 1. palay, arroz con cáscara. 2. arrozal. 3. **P.,** (fam.) irlandés (apodo).

paddy field, sembrado de arroz, arrozal.

paddywhack [-ˌwæk] *s.* (pr. G.B.) rabieta, corajina, acceso de cólera, furia.

paddy wagon, (jer.) furgón policial, coche celular.

padishah ['pɑdəˌʃɑ, -ˌʃɔ, B -ˌʃɑ] *s.* rey, mandatario persa; Shan de Persia.

padlock ['pædˌlɑk, B -ˌlɔk] *s.* candado. —*v.t.* asegurar con candado.

padnag ['pædˌnæg] *s.* jaca que ambla, caballo de paso.

padre ['pɑdreɪ, B -rɪ] *s.* (fam.) padre, capellán, cura castrense.

padrone [pə'droʊnɪ] *s.* 1. tabernero italiano. 2. (E.U.) tramitador de empleos para inmigrantes (esp. italianos).

paduasoy ['pædʒʊəˌsɔɪ, B 'pædjʊ-] *s.* seda de Padua.

paean ['piən] *s.* 1. (mitol.) peán, himno de gracia a los dioses; peán (canto polifónico en honor de Apolo y Artemis); himno triunfal. 2. canto, himno. 3. (fig) palabras de encomio, ej. *he expected a p. of praise,* esperaba palabras de encomio.

paedogenesis [ˌpidə'dʒɛnəsəs] *s.* (biol.) paedogénesis.

paeon ['piɑn, B -ən] *s.* peón, pie de la poesía antigua compuesto de cuatro sílabas.

pagan ['peɪgən] *s.* 1. pagano, gentil, infiel. 2. (fig.) pagano, impío. —*a.* 1. pagano, gentil; idólatra, infiel. 2. (fig.) pagano, irreligioso, impío.

paganish [-gənɪʃ] *a.* propio de los paganos, de carácter pagano.

paganism [-ˌnɪzəm] *s.* paganismo, gentilismo (estado, carácter o moral).

paganize [-ˌnaɪz] *v.t., v.i.* paganizar, gentilizar, hacer o hacerse pagano.

page [peɪdʒ] *s.* 1. paje, escudero. 2. botones (en un hotel), acomodador (en teatros). 3. (E.U.) paje (en tribunales o corte). —*v.t.* 1. servir como paje, botones o acomodador. 2. llamar en voz alta o buscar a una persona en hotel, aeropuerto, etc.

page, *s.* 1. página, plana, cuartilla, carilla, cara; hoja, foja, folio. 2. (fig.) página (suceso o episodio en el curso de la historia o de una vida). 3. (impr.) plana, molde, caja (espacio que puede ocupar la composición en una página). —*v.t.* foliar, paginar; (impr.) (t. con *up*) compaginar.

pageant ['pædʒənt] *s.* 1. exhibición teatral al aire libre, celebración o espectáculo público; decorado movible (usado en estos espectáculos). 2. carro alegórico. 3. desfile espectacular, espectáculo magnífico; representación al aire libre. 4. ostentación, exhibición.

pageantry [-əntrɪ] *s.* (*pl.* PAGEANTRIES) 1. espectáculo magnífico, representación espectacular. 2. ostentación, exhíbición; boato, fausto.

page boy, paje, mensajero.

pagedom ['peɪdʒdəm] **pagehood** [-ˌhʊd] *s.* (ant.) servicio o asistencia de criados de una casa.

page proof, (imp.) prueba de páginas o planas.

pager ['peɪdʒer, B -dʒə] *s.* (impr.) compaginador; (tele.) beeper.

paginal ['pædʒənəl] *a.* 1. de páginas. 2. página por página (reproducción, etc.).

paginate [-ˌneɪt] *v.t.* paginar.

pagination [ˌpædʒe'neɪʃən] *s.* paginación.

pagoda [pə'goʊdə] *s.* pagoda, templo, estructura religiosa de carácter oriental.

pagurian [pə'gjʊrɪən] **pagurus** [-rəs] *s.* (zool.) paguro, (género de crustáceo que vive en la concha de otros mariscos).

Pahlavi ['pɑləvɪ] *s., a.* pelvi (lengua derivada del persa).

paid [peɪd] *pret., p.p. de* **pay.**

paid-up['peɪd'ʌp] *a.* desembolsado; liberado (acciones).

pail [peɪl] *s.* cubo, pozal, balde, colodra, herrada.

pailful ['peɪlˌfʊl] *s.* cantidad que cabe en una colodra, un balde, etc.

paillasse [pæl'jæs, B 'pælɪæs] *s.* colchoneta o jergón de paja.

paillette [paɪ'jɛt, B pæl'jet] *s.* lentejuela, bricho.

pain [peɪn] *s.* 1. dolor (físico). 2. (*pl.*) dolores de parto. 3. (*pr. pl.*) afán, cuidado, esmero. 4. fatiga, faena, dificultad. 5. **a p. in the neck,** (jer.) chinche, persona o cosa molesta; **on** (o **under**) **p. of,** so pena de, bajo pena de; **to go to great pains, to take pains,** afanarse, esmerarse, empeñarse; **to be in p.,** padecer, tener dolores. —*v.t.* 1. angustiar, **it pains me to (do),** me duele (hacer). —*v.i.* doler.

pained [peɪnd] *a.* apenado, adolorido, afligido.

painful [peɪnfəl] *a.* 1. doloroso (físicamente). 2. (fig.) doloroso, penoso, lamentable, deplorable, aflictivo. 3. laborioso, arduo, penoso. 4. (ant.) cuidadoso, esmerado.

painfully [-fəlɪ] *adv.* dolorosamente, penosamente.

painfulness [-fəlnəs] *s.* lo penoso, lo doloroso.

pain killer, calmante.

painless ['peɪnləs] *a.* indoloro, que no causa dolor.

painlessly [-lɪ] *adv.* sin causar o sufrir dolor.

painlessness [-nəs] *s.* 1. carencia de dolor o pena. 2. (med.) anodinia.

painstaker ['peɪnzˌteɪkər, B -kə] *s.* trabajador concienzudo o esmerado.

painstaking [-kɪŋ] *s.* esmero, cuidado. —*a.* esmerado, cuidadoso, concienzudo.

painstakingly [-lɪ] *adv.* esmeradamente, cuidadosamente, concienzudamente.

paint [peɪnt] *v.t.* 1. pintar. 2. teñir, colorar. 3. (fig.) pintar, describir, representar, ej., *the situation is not so black as you p. it,* la situación no es tan negra como tú la pintas. 4. **p. the town red,** (jer.) irse de parranda, tirar una cana al aire. —*v.i.* 1. ser pintor. 2. maquillarse, pintarse (el rostro). —*s.* 1. pintura. 2. afeite. 3. colorante.

paintbox ['peɪntˌbɑks, B -ˌbɔks] *s.* caja de colores, estuche de pinturas.

paintbrush [-ˌbrʌʃ] *s.* brocha, pincel.

painted [-ed] *a.* 1. pintado; maquillado. 2. (fig.) pintado.

painted bunting, (orn.) pinzón de bello y colorido plumaje.

painter ['peɪntər, B -ə] *s.* (pr. S. y centro de E.U.) (zool.) puma.

painter, *s.* 1. pintor (obrero y artista). 2. (mar.) boza.

painterly [-ərlɪ, B -əlɪ] *a.* 1. de pintor. 2. (fig.) pintoresco, artístico (estilo).

painter's colic, (med.) cólico de los pintores, cólico de plomo o saturnino.

Painter's Easel, (astr.) Caballete del pintor.

painting ['peɪntɪŋ] *s.* 1. pintura. 2. (arte) pintura, cuadro.

paint remover, *s.* sacapintura, quitapintura.

pair [pɛr, B pɛə] *s.* 1. par. 2. pareja. 3. parejas (de naipes o dados). 4. dos miembros de partidos opuestos que se abstienen de votar; convenio para abstenerse de votar. —*v.t.* parear, emparejar; **p. off with,** (fam.) casarse con. —*v.i.* 1. parear, emparejar; casar, convenir, adecuarse. 2. aparcarse (animales). 3. convenir en abstenerse de votar. 4. **p. off,** emparejarse, aparearse; **p. with,** emparejarse o aparearse con.

pairle [pɛrl, B pɛəl] *s.* (her.) perla.

pair-oar ['pɛrˌɔr, B 'pɛərˌɔ] *s.* par de remos, par simple, simple par (bote para dos personas en el que cada ocupante usa un solo remo).

pair of scissors, tijeras.

pair of spectacles, anteojos, gafas, lentes.

pair of suspenders, (par de) tirantes.

pair of trousers, (par de) pantalones.

pair production, (fís. nuclear) formación de pares.

paisley ['peɪzlɪ] *s.* tejido fino de algodón o lana de colores y dibujos vistosos.

Paisley shawl, chal de Paisley.

Paiute ['paɪˌjut, B paɪ'jut] *s.* (E.U.) indio de una tribu uto-azteca que radicó en los estados de Nevada y California.

pajamas [pə'dʒɑməz, -'dʒæm-, B -'dʒɑm-] *s. pl.* pijama, piyama.

Pakistan [ˌpɑkɪ'stɑn, pækɪ'stæn, B ˌpɑkɪ'stɑn] *s.* Pakistán, Paquistán. —*a.* paquistaní, pakistaní.

Pakistani [-ɪ] *a.* paquistaní, pakistaní. —*s.* (*pl.* PAKISTANIS O PAKISTANI) paquistaní, pakistaní.

pal [pæl] *s.* (fam.) compañero, camarada, amigo; amigote, compinche. —*v.i.* (*pret., p.p.* PALLED; *p.pr.* PALLING) (jer.) ser o convertirse en compañeros o compinches.

palace ['pæləs] *s.* palacio.

paladin ['pælədən] *s.* paladín; campeón.

Palaeologus [ˌpeɪlɪ'ɑləgəs, B ˌpælɪ'ɔl-] *s.* Paleólogo (familia bizantina que dio varios emperadores de Oriente).

palaeothere ['peɪlɪə,θɪr, B 'pælɪə'θɪə] *s.* (pal.) paleoterio.
palaestra [pə'lɛstrə, B -'lis-] *s.* (*pl.* PALAESTRAE [-trɪ]) (hist.) palestra, gimnasio.
palafitte ['pæləfɪt] *s.* palafito, vivienda lacustre.
palanquin, palanqueen [,pælən'kin] *s.* 1. palanquín, litera; andas. 2. mozo que lleva cargas.
palatability [pælətə'bɪlətɪ] *s.* 1. sabor agradable, sabor apetitoso. 2. aceptabilidad, admisibilidad.
palatable ['pælətəbəl] *a.* 1. sabroso, apetitoso. 2. aceptable, admisible.
palatableness [-nəs] *s.* 1. sabor agradable, sabor apetitoso. 2. aceptabilidad, admisibilidad.
palatably [-blɪ] *adv.* de manera pasable o admisible.
palatal ['pælətəl] *a.* 1. paladial, del paladar. 2. (fon.) palatal. —*s.* (fon.) sonido palatal.
palatalization [,pælətələ'zeɪʃən, B -laɪ-] *s.* (fon.) palatalización.
palatalize ['pælətəl,aɪz] *v.t.* (fon.) palatalizar.
palate ['pælət] *s.* 1. (anat.) paladar. 2. (fig.) paladar, gusto.
palatial [pə'leɪʃəl] *a.* 1. palaciego, de palacio. 2. magnífico, suntuoso.
palatially [-ɪ] *adv.* magníficamente, suntuosamente.
Palatinate [pə'lætənət] *s.* (hist.) Palatinado (título del principado alemán).
palatine ['pælə,taɪn] *a.* (anat.) palatino, paladial. —*s.* hueso palatino.
palatine, *a.* 1. palatino, palaciego. 2. palatino, del palatinado. —*s.* 1. palatino, príncipe palatino. 2. **P.,** habitante del Palatinado, una de las siete colinas de Roma. 3. palatina (adorno femenino de pieles).
palatine vault, (anat.) bóveda palatina.
palaver [pə'lævər, B -'lɑvə] *s.* 1. palabrería, palique, cháchara. 2. (fam.) labia. 3. conferencia, debate. —*v.i.* 1. palabrear, paliquear, chacharear. 2. conferenciar, debatir.
pale [peɪl] *a.* pálido, descolorido; sin brillo; apagado. —*v.i.* palidecer, descolorar. —*v.t.* poner pálido, hacer palidecer.
pale, *s.* 1. estaca. 2. recinto; límite, margen. 3. (her.) palo, bastón. 4. (ant.) estacada, palizada; barrera. 5. **beyond the p.,** fuera de los límites; reprensible; **outside** (o **out of**) **the p.,** fuera de los límites. —*v.t.* cercar, empalizar.
palea ['peɪlɪə] *s.* (*pl.* PALEAE [-,i]) (bot.) pálea, glumilla.
paleaceous [,peɪlɪ'eɪʃəs] *a.* (bot.) paleáceo.
palearctic [,peɪlɪ'ɑrktɪk, B ,pælɪ'ɑk-] *a.* paleártico (díc. de la región geográfica que comprende Eurasia y el N. de África).
paleethnologic [-,ɛθnə'lɑdʒɪk, B -'lɔdʒ-] *a.* paleoetnológico.
paleethnologist [-'nɑlədʒəst, B -'nɔl-] *s.* paleoetnólogo.
paleethnology [-dʒɪ] *s.* paleoetnología, el estudio de las razas prehistóricas del hombre.
paleface ['peɪl,feɪs] *s.* carapálida, rostropálido (Esp.) (nombre dado al hombre blanco por los indios de Norteamérica).
palely ['peɪlɪ] *adv.* pálidamente.
paleness [-nəs] *s.* palidez.
paleobotanist [,peɪlɪoʊ'bɑtənəst, B 'pælɪoʊ'bɔt-] *s.* paleobotánico.
paleobotany [-ɪ] *s.* paleobotánica (ciencia que describe los vegetales fósiles).
Paleocene ['peɪlɪə,sin, B 'pælɪ-] *a., s.* (geol.) paleoceno.
paleographer [,peɪlɪ'ɑgrəfər, B ,pælɪ'ɔgrəfə] *s.* paleógrafo, el que estudia o se especializa en descifrar las formas más primitivas de expresión gráfica.
paleographic [-ə'græfɪk] **paleographical** [-ɪkəl] *a.* paleográfico, perteneciente a las formas primitivas de expresión gráfica.
paleography [-'ɑgrəfɪ, B -'ɔg-] *s.* paleografía, primitivas formas de expresión gráfica y su estudio.
paleolith ['peɪlɪə,lɪθ, B 'pælɪ-] *s.* utensilio paleolítico (de la edad de piedra).
paleolithic [,peɪlɪə'lɪθɪk, B ,pælɪ-] *a.* paleolítico.
paleolithic man, (antrop.) hombre paleolítico.
paleontographic [-,ɑntə'græfɪk, B -,ɔn-] **paleontographical** [-ɪkəl] *a.* paleontográfico.
paleontography [-,ɑn'tɑgrəfɪ, B -,ɔn'tɔg-] *s.* paleontografía, descripción de los fósiles.
paleontologic [-tə'lɑdʒɪk, B -'lɔdʒ-] **paleontological** [-ɪkəl] *a.* paleontológico.
paleontologist [-'tɑlədʒəst, B -'tɔl-] *s.* paleontólogo, el que estudia los fósiles.
paleontology [-dʒɪ] *s.* paleontología, la ciencia que estudia y clasifica los fósiles de la prehistoria.
Paleozoic [,peɪlɪə'zoʊɪk, B ,pælɪ-] *a.* (geol.) paleozoico. —*s.* era paleozoica.
paleozoologist [-,zoʊ'ɑlədʒəst, B -'ɔl-] *s.* paleozoólogo.
paleozoology [-dʒɪ] *s.* paleozoología, ciencia que estudia los animales prehistóricos.
Palermitan [pə'lɜrmətən, B -'lɜmət-] *a., s.* palermitano, panormitano, de Palermo, ciudad de Sicilia (Italia).
Palestine [,pæləstɑɪn] *s.* Palestina.
Palestinian [,pæləs'tɪnɪən] *a., s.* palestino.
palestra, *var. de* **palaestra.**
paletot ['pælə,toʊ, B 'pæltoʊ] *s.* 1. paletó, gabán; abrigo. 2. (ant.) chaqueta entallada de mujer.
palette ['pælət] *s.* 1. (pint.) paleta. 2. gama de colores (puestos en la paleta).
palette knife, (pint.) espátula.
palfrey ['pɔlfrɪ, B 'pɔlfərɪ] *s.* (*pl.* PALFREYS) (ant.) palafrén.
Pali ['pɑlɪ] *s.* pali (antiguo dialecto de la India, el idioma religioso del budismo).
palikar ['pælə,kɑr, B -,kɑ] *s.* (hist.) palikar, antiguo miliciano de Grecia o Albania en la guerra contra Turquía.
palimpsest ['pæləmp,sɛst] *s.* palimpsesto, antiguo manuscrito que fue borrado para escribir otra cosa; (fig.) lo que se graba o escribe más de una vez.
palindrome ['pælən,droʊm] *s.* palíndromo (palabra o frase que se lee igual de derecha a izquierda que de izquierda a derecha).
paling ['peɪlɪŋ] *s.* 1. estacada, empalizada, valla, cerca. 2. estaca.
palingenesis [,pælən'dʒɛnəsəs] *s.* 1. (filos.) palingenesia, renacimiento, regeneración. 2. (biol., min.) palingénesis.
palingenetic [-dʒə'nɛtɪk] *a.* (filos.) palingenésico.
palinode ['pælə,noʊd] *s.* palinodia, retractación, recantación.
Palinurus [,pælɪ'njʊrəs] *s.* (mitol.) Palinuro, navegante de Eneas en la Eneida de Virgilio.
palisade [,pælə'seɪd] *s.* 1. palizada, palenque, estacada. 2. estaca. 3. (*gen. pl.*) acantilado. —*v.t.* cercar, empalizar.
palisade parenchyma, (bot.) parénquima clorofílico en empalizada.
palisander ['pælə,sændər, B ,pælɪ'sændə] *s.* palisandro (madera del guayabo).
palish ['peɪlɪʃ] *a.* paliducho, algo pálido.
pall [pɔl] *s.* 1. paño mortuorio. 2. ataúd, féretro. 3. (fig.) manto, nube, capa, ej., *p. of fear,* manto de terror. 4. (relig.) palio (insignia pontifical); palia, hijuela. 5. (ant.) lienzo o mantel del altar, sabanilla. —*v.t.* paliar, encubrir.
pall, *v.i.* 1. hacerse soso, tornarse aburrido; **p. of,** saciarse (de), cansarse (de); **p. on,** cansar, saciar, dejar de interesar. 2. perder sabor; dejar de ser interesante. —*v.t.* 1. volver soso, aburrido; quitar interés a. 2. saciar, empalagar.
palladic [pə'lædɪk] *a.* (quím.) paládico.
Palladium [pə'leɪdɪəm] 1. (hist.) paladión (estatua de Palas Atenea). 2. **p.** (*pl.* PALLADIA [-ə]) (fig.) paladión, salvaguardia.
palladium, *s.* (quím.) paladio.
palladous [pə'leɪdəs, 'pælədəs] *a.* (quím.) paladioso.
Pallas ['pæləs, B -æs] *s.* 1. (mitol.) Palas Atenea, diosa griega de la sabiduría. 2. (astr.) Palas (asteroide).
Pallas Athene, P. Athena, (mitol.) Palas Atena, Palas Atenea.
pallbearer ['pɔl,bɛrər, B -,bɛərə] *s.* portaféretro.
pallet ['pælət] *s.* 1. paleta o espátula de alfarero. 2. tarima, plataforma de carga. 3. paleta o cepillo plano del dorador. 4. (pint.) paleta. 5. paleta del regulador (del reloj). 6. (mec.) trinquete. 7. jergón; camastro.
palletize [-,aɪz] *v.t.* cargar (objetos) sobre una tarima.
pallette [pæ'lɛt, B 'pælət] *s.* (arm.) gocete, tarja.
pallial ['pælɪəl] *a.* (anat.) palial.
palliasse, *var. de* **paillasse.**
palliate ['pælɪ,eɪt] *v.t.* 1. paliar, mitigar, aliviar. 2. atenuar, minorar. 3. paliar, encubrir.
palliation [,pælɪ'eɪʃən] *s.* 1. paliación, mitigación, alivio. 2. atenuación, minoración. 3. paliación, encubrimiento.
palliative ['pælɪ,eɪtɪv, B -ətɪv] *a., s.* paliativo.
palliator [-,eɪtər, B -ə] *s.* mitigador, aliviador.
pallid ['pæləd] *a.* pálido, descolorido.
pallidity [pə'lɪdətɪ] **pallidness** ['pælədnəs] *s.* palidez.
pallidly [-lɪ] *adv.* pálidamente.
pallium ['pælɪəm] *s.* (*pl.* PALLIA [-ə] o PALLIUMS) 1. (anat., relig., hist.) palio. 2. (zool.) manto (de aves, moluscos, braquiópodos).
pall-mall ['pɛl'mɛl, 'pɔl'mɔl, B 'pæl'mæl] *s.* (hist.) palamallo, garito.
pallor ['pælər, B -ə] *s.* palidez, palor.
pally ['pælɪ] *a.* (fam.) amigo; amistoso.
palm [pɑm] *s.* 1. palma (de mano, guante, etc.). 2. palmo (medida). 3. pala (de remo). 4. (mar.) uña (del ancla); rempujo. 5. **to grease the p.,** (jer.) untar la palma; **to have an itching p.,** (fam.) ser pedigüeño o codicioso. —*v.t.* 1. acariciar, palmear; estrechar (las manos). 2. escamotear, esconder en la palma (de la mano). 3. **p. (something) off on (someone),** clavarle, encajarle, colarle (algo) a (alguien).
palm, *s.* 1. (bot.) palma, palmera. 2. (fig.) palma, triunfo, victoria; **to bear** (o **carry off**) **the p.,** llevarse la palma, salir victorioso; **to yield the p.,** conceder la victoria, reconocer la derrota.
Palm Sunday, Domingo de Ramos.
palmaceous [pæl'meɪʃəs, pɑ-, B pæl-] *a.* (bot.) palmáceo.
palmar ['pælmər, 'pɑ-, B 'pælmə] *a.* (anat.) palmar, de la palma (de la mano).
palmary [-mərɪ] *a.* sobresaliente, relevante, mejor, principal.
palmate [-,meɪt, B -mɪt] **palmated** [-,meɪtəd] *a.* (bot., zool.) palmeado, palmado.
palmation [pæl'meɪʃən, pɑ-, B pæl-] *s.* disposición o estructura palmeada; lóbulo palmeado; parte palmeada.

palm cabbage, (bot.) palmito del género sabal; palmito, yema comestible de algunas palmeras.

palm crab, (zool.) cangrejo de los cocoteros.

palmer ['pɑmər, 'pɑlmər, B 'pɑmə] *s.* palmero (peregrino de Tierra Santa).

palmer worm, (ento.) gusano palmero.

palmetto [pæl'mɛˌtoʊ] *s.* 1. (bot.) palmito. 2. hojas del palmito (usadas para tramar).

palmiped ['pælməˌpɛd, 'pɑmə-, B 'pælmɪ-] *a.* (zool.) palmípedo.

palmist ['pɑməst] *s.* quiromántico, palmista.

palmistry [-əstrɪ] *s.* quiromancia.

palmitate ['pælməˌteɪθ, 'pɑ-, B 'pæl-] *s.* (quím.) palmitato.

palmitic [pæl'mɪtɪk, pɑ-, B pæl-] *a.* (quím.) palmítico.

palmitic acid, (quím.) ácido palmítico.

palmitin ['pælmətən, 'pɑ-, B 'pæl-] *s.* (quím.) palmitina.

palm oil, aceite de palma.

Palm Sunday, (relig.) Domingo de Ramos.

palm wine, vino de palma.

palmy ['pɑmɪ] *a.* (PALMIER; PALMIEST) 1. lleno de palmas. 2. floreciente, próspero.

palmyra [pæl'maɪrə, B -'maɪərə] *s.* (bot.) palmera de la India.

palomino [ˌpælə'miˌnoʊ] *s.* 1. (E.U., zool.) palomilla. 2. caballo pardo con crin y rabo blancos.

palooka [pə'lukə] *s.* (jer.) 1. boxeador malo. 2. zoquete, bobalicón.

palp [pælp] *s.* (zool.) palpo.

palpability [ˌpælpə'bɪlətɪ] *s.* evidencia.

palpable ['pælpəbəl] *a.* 1. palpable, tangible. 2. (fig.) palpable, patente, manifiesto, evidente.

palpably [-blɪ] *adv.* palpablemente, evidentemente.

palpate [-ˌpeɪt] *a.* (zool.) con palpo(s). —*v.t.* palpar, examinar (esp. en medicina).

palpation [pæl'peɪʃən] *s.* palpación, palpadura, palpamiento; (med.) palpación.

palpebral ['pælpəbrəl] *a.* palpebral, relativo a los párpados.

palpi, *pl. de* **palpus.**

palpitant ['pælpətənt] *a.* palpitante.

palpitate [-ˌteɪt] *v.i.* palpitar.

palpitation [ˌpælpə'teɪʃən] *s.* palpitación.

palpus ['pælpəs] *s.* (*pl.* PALPI [-paɪ]) (zool.) palpo.

palsgrave ['pɔlzˌgreɪv] *s.* (hist., Alemania) conde palatino.

palsgravine [-grəˌvin] *s.* condesa palatina.

palsied ['pɔlzid] *a.* paralizado, paralítico.

palsy ['pɔlzɪ] *s.* (*pl.* PALSIES) (med.) perlesía, parálisis; (fig.) impotencia; ineficacia. —*v.t.* paralizar.

palsy-walsy ['pælzɪ'wælzɪ] *a.* (jer., E.U.) amigable, íntimo.

palter ['pɔltər, B -tə] *v.i.* 1. estafar, engañar. 2. (ant.) practicar engaños, obrar con falsedad.

paltrily ['pɔltrəlɪ] *adv.* 1. miserablemente, mezquinamente. 2. despreciablemente.

paltriness [-trɪnəs] *s.* 1. mezquindad. 2. vileza.

paltry ['pɔltrɪ] *a.* (PALTRIER; PALTRIEST) 1. miserable, mezquino. 2. vil, despreciable, indigno.

paludal [pə'ludəl, B -'lju-] *a.* palúdico, palustre; (med.) palúdico.

paludamentum [pəˌludə'mɛntəm, B -ˌlju-] *s.* (*pl.* PALUDAMENTA [-tə]) (hist. romana) paludamento (manto bordado de oro que usaban en campaña emperadores y caudillos).

paludism ['pæljəˌdɪzəm] *s.* (med.) paludismo.

paludous [-dəs, B pə'lju-] *a.* palúdico, que habita en los pantanos.

paly ['peɪlɪ] *a.* (PALIER; PALIEST) 1. (esp. poét.) pálido, descolorido. 2. (her.) en palo, palado.

palynology [ˌpælə'nɑlədʒɪ, B -'nɔl-] *s.* (bot.) palinología.

pam [pæm] *s.* (naipes) sota de tréboles.

pampa ['pæmpə] *s.* pampa, llanura (esp. de la Argentina).

pampas grass [-pəz-, B -pəs-] (bot.) cortadera argentina.

pampean ['pæmpɪən] *a.* pampeano, pampero. —*s.* indio pampero.

pamper ['pæmpər, B -pə] *v.t.* 1. mimar, consentir, engreír (Amer.). 2. (ant.) alimentar en exceso, hartar, saciar.

pamperer [-pərər, B -ə] *s.* mimador, consentidor, engreidor (Amer.).

Pampers (TM), pañales desechables.

pamphlet ['pæmflət] *s.* folleto, panfleto.

pamphleteer [ˌpæmflə'tɪr, B -'tɪə] *v.i.* escribir o publicar folletos. —*s.* folletista, panfletista.

pan [pæn] *s.* 1. cacerola, cazuela, sartén, perol; lebrillo, caldero. 2. platillo (de balanza). 3. crisol; mortero, almirez; batea (para lavar mineral de oro). 4. (mil.) cazoleta (en las armas de fuego antiguas). 5. substrato duro (del suelo). —*v.t.* (*pret., p.p.* PANNED; *p.pr.* PANNING) 1. lavar en batea (mineral de oro). 2. criticar severamente. —*v.i.* 1. lavar oro; encontrar oro en el proceso del lavado. 2. **p. out,** producir (la tierra, etc.), rendir (oro); resultar; salir bien, dar resultado; **p. out well,** salir bien; tener éxito.

pan, *v.i., v.t.* (*pret., p.p.* PANNED; *p.pr.* PANNING) (cinem., t.v.) girar o hacer girar (la cámara) para toma panorámica.

pan, *s.* 1. (jer.) cara, rostro, faz, fachada. 2. hoja del betel. 3. (mitol.) **P.,** Pan, dios pastoril, hijo de Hermes.

Panacea [ˌpænə'siə] *s.* 1. (mitol.) Panacea. 2. **p.,** panacea, remedio universal.

panache [pə'næʃ, -'nɑʃ] *s.* 1. penacho (esp. en un casco). 2. desenvoltura, despejo, brío.

panada [pə'nɑdə] *s.* pan cocido y sazonado (comida para enfermos).

Panama ['pænəˌmɑ, -ˌmɔ, B ˌpænə'mɑ] *s.* Panamá.

Panama Canal Zone, Zona del Canal de Panamá, administrada por los E.U.

panama hat, sombrero panamá, sombrero jipijapa.

Panamanian [ˌpænə'meɪnɪən] *a., s.* panameño.

Pan-American [ˌpænə'mɛrəkən] *a.* panamericano.

Pan-Americanism [-ɪzəm] *s.* (pol.) panamericanismo.

Pan American Union, Unión Panamericana.

Pan-Arabism ['pæn'ærəˌbɪzəm] *s.* (pol.) panarabismo.

panatela [ˌpænə'tɛlə] *s.* panatela o panetela (cigarro largo).

panbroil ['pænˌbrɔɪl] *v.i., v.t.* (*pret., p.p.* PANBROILED; *p.pr.* PANBROILING) (cocina) freír ligeramente en poca grasa.

pancake [-ˌkeɪk] *s.* hojuela, torta delgada ligeramente cocida, panqueque (Amer.); **flat as a p.,** completamente chato o aplastado. —*v.i.* (aer.) aterrizar abruptamente (en forma casi vertical).

pancake landing, (aer.) aterrizaje casi vertical.

panchromatic [ˌpænkroʊ'mætɪk] *a.* (foto.) pancromático (dícese de las películas cuya sensibilidad es casi igual para todos los colores).

panchromatism [pæn'kroʊməˌtɪzəm] *s.* (foto.) pancromatismo.

pancratist ['pænkrətəst] **pancratiast** [pæn'kreɪʃɪˌæst] *s.* (hist.) pancraciasta.

pancratium [pæn'kreɪʃɪəm] *s.* (hist.) pancracio.

pancreas ['pænkrɪəs, B 'pæŋ-] *s.* (anat.) páncreas.

pancreatic [ˌpæŋkrɪ'ætɪk] *a.* (anat.) pancreático.

pancreatic juice, (med.) jugo pancreático o pancrático.

pancreatin [pæn'kriətən, B 'pæŋkrɪ-] *s.* (farm.) pancreatina.

panda ['pændə] *s.* (zool.) 1. panda, gato ursino. 2. panda gigante.

pandanaceous [ˌpændə'neɪʃəs] *a.* (bot.) pandanáceo, pandáneo.

Pandanus [pæn'deɪnəs] *s.* (bot.) pandánea.

Pandarus ['pændərəs] *s.* (mitol.) Pándaro, troyano que intentó asesinar a Menelao.

Pandean pipes [pæn'diən-] (mús.) flauta de Pan, siringa.

Pandect ['pænˌdɛkt] *s.* 1. (*pl.*) (der.) pandectas. 2. **p.,** compendio completo.

pandemia [pæn'dimɪə] *s.* (med.) pandemia (enfermedad epidémica colectiva).

pandemic [-'dɛmɪk] *a.* (med.) pandémico. —*s.* (med.) pandemia.

Pandemonium [ˌpændə'moʊnɪəm] *s.* 1. pandemonio, pandemónium (capital imaginaria del infierno). 2. **p.,** tumulto, desenfreno, algazara, alboroto.

pander ['pændər, B -də] *s.* alcahuete; celestina. —*v.i.* alcahuetear; **p. to,** satisfacer, gratificar, complacer.

panderer [-dərər, B -ə] *s.* alcahuete.

pandora [pæn'dɔrə] *s.* (mús.) bandurria.

Pandora's Box, caja de Pandora.

pandour ['pænˌdʊr, B -ˌdʊə] *s.* (ant.) panduro (soldado húngaro).

pandowdy [pæn'daʊdɪ] *s.* (*pl.* PANDOWDIES) (E.U.) pastel de manzana hecho en vasija honda.

pandurate [pæn'dʊrət, B 'pændjʊr-] *a.* (bot.) pandurado.

pandy ['pændɪ] *s.* (*pl.* PANDIES) (dial., esco.) palmetazo, golpe en la palma de la mano. —*v.t., v.i.* dar palmetazos.

pane [peɪn] *s.* 1. hoja de vidrio, cristal (de ventana). 2. (arq.) panel, cuarterón; tablero, cuadro; entrepaño. 3. (mec.) lado de una tuerca o de la cabeza de un perno.

panegyric [ˌpænə'dʒɪrɪk] *s.* panegírico, discurso de alabanza.

panegyrical [-ɪkəl] *a.* panegírico, laudatorio, encomiástico.

panegyrist [-əst] *s.* panegirista.

panegyrize ['pænədʒəˌraɪz] *v.t.* panegirizar.

panel ['pænəl] *s.* 1. panel, tablero (de puerta o ventana). 2. (arq.) panel, entrepaño, recuadro, tramo. 3. (pint.) tabla, panel, cuadro. 4. segmento (de paracaídas). 5. (aer.) cuadro, sección, parte de las alas del avión; pieza de la envoltura de un dirigible. 6. paño (en un vestido). 7. (elec.) tablero; panel; placa; cuadro. 8. (min.) compartimiento, cámara aislada. 9. (aut.) tablero. 10. jurado; nómina del jurado. 11. grupo (de expertos, consultantes, etc.). 12. (rad., t.v.) panel, equipo. 13. lista de médicos del seguro social. 14. colección, serie (de libros). 15. **on the p.,** (G.B.) en la lista (díc. del médico del seguro social). —*v.t.* (*pret., p.p.* PANNELED O PANELLED; *p.pr.* PANELING O PANELLING). 1. (der.) elegir jurado. 2. artesonar; proveer o adornar con paneles. 3. (esco.) encausar, enjuiciar.

panel board, (elec.) tablero de cortacircuitos o de control; (mec.) cuadro de mando.

panel heating, calefacción a panel.

paneling [-ɪŋ] *s.* empanelado, entablado (de la pared).

panelist ['pænələst] *s.* (rad., t.v.) miembro de un panel o grupo de discusión.

panel lights, (aut.) luces de tablero.
panel truck, camioneta de reparto (de tipo cerrado), furgoneta.
panentheism [pæn'ɛnθɪˌɪzəm] *s.* (filos.) panenteísmo.
panetela, panetella, *vars. de* **panatela.**
pang [pæŋ] *s.* 1. dolor agudo, punzada. 2. (fig.) punzada (de remordimiento, conciencia, etc.); tormento, angustia. 3. **to have pangs of concience,** acusar (o agredir) a uno la conciencia. —*v.t.* causar dolor agudo a.
pangenesis [pæn'dʒɛnəsəs] *s.* (biol.) pangenesis.
pangenetic [-dʒə'nɛtɪk] *a.* (biol.) pangenésico.
Pan-Germanic ['pænˌdʒɜr'mænɪk, B -ˌdʒɜ'-] *a.* pangermanista.
Pan-Germanism [-'dʒɜrməˌnɪzəm, B -'dʒɜmə-] *s.* pangermanismo.
pangolin [pæn'goʊlən] *s.* (zool.) pangolín.
panhandle ['pænˌhændəl] *s.* 1. mango de caldero, sartén, etc. 2. (E.U.) brazo de un territorio que entra en otro (ej., de un estado). —*v.t. v.i.* (jer.) mendigar, pedir (esp. sin necesidad).
panhandler [-dlər, B -dlə] *s.* (jer., E.U.) mendigo, pordiosero (que mendiga sin necesidad).
Panhellenic [ˌpænhə'lɛnɪk, B -hɛ'lin-] *a.* panhelénico.
Panhellenism [ˌpæn'hɛləˌnɪzəm] *s.* panhelenismo.
Panhellenist [-nəst] *s.* panhelenista.
panic ['pænɪk] *a.* pánico, ej., *p. fear,* temor pánico. —*s.* pánico. —*v.t.* (*prét., p.p.* PANICKED; *p.pr.* PANICKING) 1. aterrar, sobrecoger de terror. 2. (jer.) asombrar, dejar pasmado, impresionar fuertemente.
panic button, *s.* botón de alarma; **to hit the p.,** (fam.) ponerso histérico.
panic grass, (bot.) mijo común; panizo.
panicky [-ɪkɪ] *a.* dominado por el pánico; aterrorizado.
panicle ['pænɪkəl] *s.* (bot.) panícula.
panicled sorghum[-kəld-] (bot.) cañota.
panic-stricken ['pænɪkˌstrɪkən] *a.* aterrorizado, despavorido, muerto de miedo, paralizado de pánico, sobrecogido de terror.
paniculate [pæ'nɪkjələt] **paniculated** [-ˌleɪtəd] *a.* (bot.) paniculado, apanojado.
Pan-Islam ['pænɪs'lɑm, B -'ɪzlɑm] **Pan-Islamism** [ˌpæn'ɪsləˌmɪzəm, B -'ɪzlə-] *s.* panislamismo.
Pan-Islamic [-ɪk, B -ɪz'læm-] *a.* panislamista.
Pan-Islamist [-əst, B -'ɪzləm-] *s.* panislamista.
Panjabi [pən'dʒɑbɪ] *s.* penjabi (natural e idioma de una región de la India).
panjandrum [pæn'dʒændrəm, B pən-] *s.* persona de campanillas, funcionario engreído.
panne [pæn] *s.* (tej.) pana.
panniculus [pə'nɪkjələs] *s.* (*pl.* PANNICULI [-laɪ]) (anat.) panículo.
pannier ['pænjər, B -ɪə] *s.* 1. cuévano, cesta, cesto, banasta, canasta. 2. tontillo, guardainfantes.
pannikin ['pænɪkən] *s.* cubilete, cazoleta, olluela.
panning ['pænɪŋ] *s.* (cinem., t.v.) toma panorámica.
panoplied ['pænəplɪd] *a.* 1. en panoplia. 2. (fig.) ataviado, engalanado.
panoply ['pænəplɪ] *s.* (*pl.* PANOPLES) 1. panoplia. 2. traje ceremonial. 3. pompa, ceremonia.
panoptic [pæn'ɑptɪk, B -'ɔp-] *a.* panóptico (dícese de un conjunto que puede verse desde un solo punto).
panorama [ˌpænə'ræmə, B -'rɑ-] *s.* panorama.
panoramic [-'ræmɪk] *a.* panorámico.
panoramic sight, (arm.) mira de periscopio (usada por los tiradores, etc.).
panpipe ['pænˌpaɪp] *s.* flauta de Pan, zampoña, siringa.
panpsychism [pæn'saɪˌkɪzəm] *s.* pampsiquismo, creencia en que toda la realidad posee una naturaleza espiritual.
Pan-Slav ['pæn'slɑv, -'slæv] *a.* paneslavista.
Pan-Slavism [-ˌɪzəm] *s.* paneslavismo.
pansophic ['pæn'sɑfɪk, B -'sɔf-] **pansophical** [-ɪkəl] *a.* pansófico, que pretende tener sabiduría universal.
pansophism [-səˌfɪzəm] *s.* pansofismo.
pansophist [-fəst] *s.* pansofista.
pansophy [-fɪ] *s.* pansofía.
panspermia [pæn'spɜrmɪə, B -'spɜmɪə] **panspermy** ['pænˌspɜrmɪ, B -ˌspɜmɪ] *s.* (biol.) panspermia.
pansy ['pænzɪ] *s.* (*pl.* PANSIES) 1. (bot.) trinitaria, pensamiento. 2. (despec., fam.) hombre afeminado; (despec., jer.) maricón, mariquita.
pant [pænt] *v.i.* 1. jadear, resollar, acezar. 2. (con *for* o *after*) suspirar (por), desear vivamente, anhelar. 3. latir, palpitar, pulsar (corazón, sangre, etc.). —*v.t.* pronunciar con sonidos entrecortados; boquear. —*s.* 1. jadeo, resuello; resoplido (de una máquina). 2. palpitación, latido, pulsación.
Pantagruelian [ˌpæntəgrʊ'ɛlɪən] *a.* pantagruélico, opíparo (díc. esp. de comidas y bebidas).
pantalets, pantalettes [ˌpæntəl'ɛts] *s. pl.* (ant.) pantalones de mujer que asomaban debajo de la falda.
pantaloon [-'un] *s.* 1. bufón, gracioso (en pantomimas). 2. (*gen. pl.*) pantalones.
pantechnicon [pæn'tɛknɪkən] *s.* (G.B.) 1. camión de mudanzas. 2. depósito de muebles.
pantheism ['pænθɪˌɪzəm] *s.* panteísmo, doctrina que identifica a Dios con el mundo.
pantheist [-əst] *s.* panteísta.
pantheistic [ˌpænθɪ'ɪstɪk] **pantheistical** [-tɪkəl] *a.* panteístico.
pantheistically [-tɪkəlɪ] *adv.* según la doctrina del panteísmo.
pantheon ['pænθɪˌɑn, B -ən] *s.* panteón (monumento funerario).
panther ['pænθər, B -θə] *s.* pantera; puma, jaguar.
panties ['pæntiz] *s. pl.* calzón (es), bombacha (Arg., Urug.).
pantile ['pænˌtaɪl] *s.* 1. teja de cimacio. 2. teja canalón, teja árabe, teja española.
panting ['pæntɪŋ] *a.* jadeante, acezante; anhelante.
pantofle ['pæntəfəl, B -ˌtɔf-] *s.* pantufla, pantuflo; zapatilla, chinela.
pantograph ['pæntəˌgræf, B -ˌgrɑf] *s.* pantógrafo; (elec.) pantógrafo, trole articulado.
pantographic [ˌpæntə'græfɪk] *a.* pantográfico.
pantometry [pæn'tɑmətrɪ, B -'tɔm-] *s.* pantometría.
pantomime ['pæntəˌmaɪm] *s.* 1. mimo, pantomimo (actor, esp. en la antigua Roma). 2. pantomima. —*v.t.* expresar o representar por gestos.
pantomimic [ˌpæntə'mɪmɪk] *a.* pantomímico, mímico.
pantomimist ['pæntəˌmaɪməst] *s.* pantomimo, mimo.
pantothenate [ˌpæntə'θɛneɪt] *s.* (quím.) pantotenato.
pantothenic acid [-'θɛnɪk-] (quím.) ácido pantoténico.
pantry ['pæntrɪ] *s.* (*pl.* PANTRIES) despensa; recodo o habitación auxiliar de la cocina.
pantryman [-mən] *s.* despensero, mayordomo.
pants [pænts] *s. pl.* 1. pantalones. 2. (G.B.) calzoncillos. 3. (jer.) hombre.
pants suit, pantsuit, traje de chaqueta y pantalon, traje pantalon, pantalon sastre.
panty ['pæntɪ] *s.* (*pl.* PANTIES) calzón(es), bombacha (Arg., Urug.).
panty girdle, *s.* faja calzón (de mujeres).
panty hose, *s.* medias panties; (Mex.) pantimedias.
pantywaist [-ˌweɪst] *s.* 1. calzones cortos (abrochados al talle). 2. (jer.) hombre afeminado. —*a.* 1. aniñado, infantil. 2. (jer.) afeminado.
panuche, *var. de* **penuche.**
panzer ['pænzər, 'pɑntsər, B 'pæntsə] *s.* carro de asalto, carro blindado, tanque.
panzer division, división blindada.
pap [pæp] *s.* 1. papilla, papas, gachas. 2. (fam.) protección o patrocinio político. 3. (ant.) pezón, teta.
papa ['pɑpə, B pə'pɑ] *s.* papá, papi, papa.
papacy ['peɪpəsɪ] *s.* (*pl.* PAPACIES) papado, pontificado.
papain [pə'peɪən] *s.* (bioquím.) papaína.
papal ['peɪpəl] *a.* papal, del papa.
Papal Chancery, Cancillería Apostólica.
papal cross, cruz papal.
papal nuncio, nuncio apostólico.
Papal States, Estados Pontificios.
papaveraceous [pəˌpævə'reɪʃəs, B -ˌpeɪ-] *a.* (bot.) papaveráceo.
papaverine [-'pævəˌrin, B -'peɪvəˌraɪn] *s.* papaverina.
papaverous [-rəs] *a.* (bot.) papaveráceo.
papaya [pə'paɪə] *s.* 1. (bot.) papayo. 2. papaya.
papelonné [ˌpæpələ'neɪ] *a.* (her.) papelonado.
paper ['peɪpər, B -pə] *s.* 1. papel; pedazo de papel. 2. hoja, pliego (que contiene cierta cantidad de un artículo, como agujas, alfileres, etc.). 3. disertación, ensayo, artículo. 4. (*pl.*) papeles, credenciales, documentos (que acreditan identidad, estado civil o condición profesional, etc.). 5. valor, vale, letra, pagaré, documento negociable. 6. periódico, diario. 7. cuestionario de examen. 8. (t. **wall-p.**) papel decorado (para empapelar paredes). 9. (jer.) papel, billete de favor, pase (para teatro, etc.). 10. **on p.,** en papel, en teoría, a juzgar por las estadísticas; **to commit to p.,** apuntar; **to put pen to p.,** empezar a escribir; **to send in one's papers,** renunciar (cargo, oficio, etc.). —*v.t.* 1. empapelar (paredes). 2. forrar o cubrir con papel; envolver. 3. (jer.) llener (teatro, etc.) regalando pases. 4. **to p. up,** cubrir con papel (pared, caja, etc.).
paperback [-ˌbæk] *s.* libro en rústica.
paper bag, bolsa de papel; cartucho (Amer.).
paperbark tree [-ˌbɑrk-, B -ˌbɑk-] (bot.) cayeputi.
paper birch, (bot.) abedul de papel.
paperboard [-ˌbɔrd, B -ˌbɔd] *s.* cartón. —*a.* de cartón.
paper-bound [-ˌbaʊnd] *a.* en rústica (edición).
paper boy, *s.* (jer.) vendedor de periódicos, canillita, diarero (Amer.).
paper chase, caza de papelitos (juego de persecución o carrera a campo traviesa en que se marca la ruta con pedazos de papel).
paper clip, *s.* clip, sujetapapeles.
paper cup, *s.* vaso de cartón.
paper cutter, cortapapeles; guillotina.
paperer ['peɪpərər, B -pərə] *s.* empapelador, papelista.
paper file, guardapapel, archivo.

paper folder, plegadera.
paper hanger, 1. empapelador, papelista. 2. (jer.) el que gira cheques sin fondos.
paper hangings, papel decorado para empapelar.
paper knife, plegadera, cortapapel(es) (Amer.).
paper money, 1. papel moneda. 2. billete de banco.
paper nautilus, (zool.) argonauta, marinero.
paper plate, *s.* plato de cartón.
paper profits, (com., ten.) ganancias por realizar.
paper pulp, pulpa (material) para fabricar papel.
paper tiger, tigre de papel (persona o institución que es débil a pesar de una demostración de fuerza).
paperweight ['peɪpər͵weɪt, B -pə͵-] *s.* pisapapeles.
paper work, trabajo rutinario de oficina, papeleo.
papery [-pərɪ] *a.* parecido al papel; delgado como el papel.
papeterie ['pæpətrɪ] *s.* juego de papel de carta y sobres.
Paphian ['peɪfɪən] *a.* 1. pafio. 2. (fig.) ilícito (amor.). —*s.* 1. pafio, natural de Pafos, antigua ciudad de Chipre. 2. cortesana.
papier-mâché [͵peɪpərmə'ʃeɪ, B ͵pæpjeɪ'mɑʃeɪ] *s.* cartón piedra. —*a.* de cartón piedra.
papilionaceous [pə͵pɪlɪə'neɪʃəs, B -'pɪljə-] *a.* (bot.) papilonáceo.
papilla [pə'pɪlə] *s.* (*pl.* PAPILLAE [-i]) (anat., bot.) papila.
papillary ['pæpə͵lɛrɪ, B pə'pɪlərɪ] *a.* (anat., bot.) papilar.
papilloma [͵pæpə'loʊmə] *s.* (*pl.* PAPILLOMATA [-mətə] o PAPILLOMAS) (med.) papiloma.
papillomatous [͵pæpə'lɑmətəs, B -'loʊ-] *a.* (med.) papilomatoso.
papillose ['pæpə͵loʊs] *a.* (anat., bot.) papiloso.
papillote [͵pɑpɪ'oʊt, B 'pæpɪ͵loʊt] *s.* 1. papelito para rizar el pelo. 2. envoltura de papel (en que se cuecen a veces ciertos filetes de pescado o carne).
papion ['peɪpɪ͵ɑn, B -͵ɔn] *s.* (zool.) papión.
papist, Papist ['peɪpəst] (despec.) *a., s.* papista.
papistry [-pəstrɪ] *s.* (despec.) papismo.
papoose [pæ'pus, B pə-] *s.* niño indio (de Norteamérica).
pappose ['pæp͵oʊs] **pappous** [-əs] *a.* (bot.) paposo.
pappus ['pæpəs] *s.* (*pl.* PAPPI [-aɪ]) (bot.) papo, vilano.
pappy ['pæpɪ] *s.* (fam.) papi, papá. —*a.* como papilla o mazamorra.
paprika [pə'prikə, 'pæ-] *s.* 1. (bot.) pimiento picante, pimiento rojo. 2. pimentón (polvo).
Pap smear, Pap test, citología, frotis, Papanicolau.
Papuan ['pæpjʊən] *s., a.* papú, natural de la Papuasia, territorio de Nueva Guinea.
papule ['pæpjul] *s.* (med.) pápula.
papuliferous [͵pæpjə'lɪfərəs] *a.* (med.) papulífero.
papulous ['pæpjələs] *a.* (med.) papuloso.
papyrus [pə'paɪrəs, B -'paɪər-] *s.* (*pl.* PAPYRI [-aɪ]) 1. (bot.) papiro. 2. (papel de) papiro. 3. (*pl.*) escritos en papiros.
par [pɑr, B pɑ] *s.* 1. paridad, equivalencia, nivel (de una unidad monetaria). 2. valor nominal. 3. igualdad, conformidad. 4. (golf) número de golpes requerido en un hoyo. 5. **above p.,** (com.) sobre la par; **at p.,** (com.) a la par; **below** (o **under**) **p.,** (com.) bajo la par, a descuento; **to be on a p. (with),** estar en conformidad, estar a la par (con); estar a nivel (de), ej., *his ability is on a p. with his rank,* su habilidad está a la par con su rango. —*a.* 1. nominal. 2. normal, regular.
parabiosis [͵pærəbaɪ'oʊsəs] *s.* (biol.) parabiosis.
parablast ['pærə͵blæst] *s.* (anat.) parablasto.
parablastic [͵pærə'blæstɪk] *a.* (anat.) parablástico.
parable ['pærəbəl] *s.* parábola, narración que revela una enseñanza moral o una verdad.
parabola [pə'ræbələ] *s.* (geom.) parábola.
parabolanus [͵pærəboʊ'leɪnəs, B -bə-] *s.* (*pl.* PARABOLANI [-͵naɪ]) (relig.) parabolano.
parabolic [͵pærə'bɑlɪk, B -'bɔl-] *a.* 1. parabólico, alegórico. 2. (geom.) parabólico.
parabolically [-ɪkəlɪ] *adv.* parabólicamente.
parabolic course, (geom.) curso o trayectoria parabólica.
parabolize [pə'ræbə͵laɪz] *v.t.* parabolizar.
paraboloid [-͵lɔɪd] *s.* (geom.) paraboloide.
paracasein [͵pærə'keɪ͵sin, B -͵siːn] *s.* (quím.) paracaseína.
parachute ['pærə͵ʃut] *s.* 1. paracaídas. 2. (zool.) membrana alar, patagio. —*v.i.* parachutar, lanzarse en paracaídas; **to p. to safety,** salvarse en paracaídas. —*v.t.* dejar caer en paracaídas (víveres, armas, etc.).
parachute flare, (mil.) bengala con paracaídas.
parachute jump, salto con paracaídas.
parachute mine, (mil.) mina lanzada en paracaídas.
parachute troops, (mil.) tropas paracaidistas.
parachutist ['pærə͵ʃutəst] *s.* paracaidista.
paracymene [͵pærə'saɪ͵min] *s.* (quím.) paracimeno.
parade [pə'reɪd] *s.* 1. ostentación, exhibición pomposa. 2. desfile, procesión; paseo. 3. paseo público. 4. (mil.) parada, desfile, revista de tropas. —*v.t.* 1. ostentar; exhibir, alardear. 2. pasear. 3. (mil.) convocar a una revista. —*v.i.* 1. desfilar. 2. (mil.) formar en parada.
paradiastole [͵pærədaɪ'æstəlɪ] *s.* (ret.) paradiástole.
paradichlorobenzene [-͵klɔrə'bɛnzin] *s.* (quím.) paradiclorobenceno.
paradigm ['pærə͵daɪm] *s.* 1. paradigma, modelo, patrón. 2. (gram.) paradigma.
paradigmatic [͵pærədɪg'mætɪk] **paradigmatical** [-ɪkəl] *a.* 1. ejemplar, típico. 2. (gram.) paradigmático.
paradisaic [͵pærə͵daɪ'seɪɪk, B -dɪ-] **paradisaical** [-əkəl] *a.* paradisíaco.
paradisal [͵pærə'daɪsəl] *a.* paradisíaco.
paradise ['pærə͵daɪs] *s.* paraíso; (fig.) paraíso.
paradisiac [͵pærə'dɪsɪ͵æk] **paradisiacal** [-də'saɪəkəl] *a.* paradisíaco.
paradox ['pærə͵dɑks, B -͵dɔks] *s.* paradoja.
paradoxical [͵pærə'dɑksɪkəl, B -'dɔk-] *a.* paradójico.
paradoxically [-kəlɪ] *adv.* paradójicamente.
paraesthesia, paraesthetic, *vars. de* **paresthesia, paresthetic.**
paraffin ['pærəfən] *s.* parafina. —*v.t.* parafinar.
paraffin oil, (G.B.) kerosén, kerosene.
paraffin series, (quím.) serie parafínica.
paraffin wax, parafina sólida, cera de parafina.
paragenesis [͵pærə'dʒɛnəsəs] *s.* (geol.) paragénesis.
paraglossa [͵pærə'glɑsə, B -'glɔsə] *s.* (*pl.* PARAGLOSSAE [-͵si]) (ento.) paraglosa.
paragoge ['pærə͵goʊdʒɪ, B ͵pærə'goʊ-] *s.* (gram.) paragoge.
paragogic [͵pærə'gɑdʒɪk, B -'gɔdʒ-] *a.* (gram.) paragógico.
paragon ['pærə͵gɑn, B -gən] *s.* 1. modelo, ejemplar, dechado, ej., *p. of beauty,* dechado de belleza. 2. diamante perfecto de 100 (o más) quilates. 3. (impr.) parangona. —*v.t.* 1 comparar con. 2. (ant.) sobrepasar, superar.
paragonite [pə'rægə͵naɪt, B 'pærəgə-] *s.* (min.) paragonita.
paragraph ['pærə͵græf, B -͵grɑf] *s.* 1. párrafo (signo tipográfico). 2. párrafo, parágrafo, acápite (Amer.) (en un discurso, capítulo o escrito). 3. suelto, gacetilla. —*v.t.* 1. escribir sueltos o gacetillas sobre. 2. dividir en párrafos.
paragrapher [-ər, B -ə] *s.* gacetillero, reportero.
paragraphia [͵pærə'græfɪə] *s.* (med.) paragrafía.
Paraguay ['pærə͵gweɪ, -͵gwaɪ] *s.* Paraguay.
Paraguayan [͵pærə'gweɪən, -'gwaɪ-] *a., s.* paraguayo, natural del Paraguay.
Paraguay tea, (bot.) té del Paraguay, hierba del Paraguay, hierba mate del Paraguay, té de los Jesuitas.
parakeet ['pærə͵kit] *s.* (orn.) perico, periquito.
paraldehyde [pə'rældə͵haɪd] *s.* (quím.) paraldehído.
paralegal [͵pærə͵ligəl] *a.* relativo a los asistentes de los abogados. —*s.* asistente de abogado.
paraleipsis [͵pærə'lipsəs, B -'laɪp-] *s.* (*pl.* PARALEIPSES [-͵siz]) (ret.) paralipsis, paralipse.
paralepsis [-'lɛp-] *s.* (*pl.* PARALEPSES [-͵siz]) *var. de* **paraleipsis.**
Paralipomena [͵pærələ'pɑmənə, B -laɪ'pɔm-] *s. pl.* 1. (bíbl.) paralipómenos. 2. suplemento de cosas omitidas (en un escrito).
paralipsis [-'lɪpsəs] *s.* (*pl.* PARALIPSES [-͵siz]) *var. de* **paraleipsis.**
parallactic [͵pærə'læktɪk] *a.* (ópt.) paraláctico.
parallax ['pærə͵læks] *s.* (ópt., astr.) paralaje.
parallel ['pærə͵lɛl] *a.* paralelo. —*s.* 1. (geom.) paralela (línea); curva paralela; plano paralelo. 2. (fig.) paralelo. 3. (elec.) circuito paralelo. 4. (fort.) paralela. 5. (geog.) paralelo. 6. (impr.) (*gen. pl.*) barras. 7. **to draw a p. between,** trazar un paralelo entre; **to run p. to,** andar paralelo a. —*v.t.* 1. comparar, cotejar. 2. igualar, conformar. 3. ser paralelo a. 4. poner en dirección paralela (con).
parallel bars, paralelas, barras paralelas (aparato de gimnasia).
parallel circuits, (elec.) circuitos en paralelo.
parallelepiped [͵pærə͵lɛlə'paɪpəd, B -lɛ'lɛpɪpɛd] *s.* (geom.) paralelepípedo.
parallel forces, (mec.) fuerzas paralelas.
parallelism ['pærəlɛl͵ɪzəm] *s.* paralelismo.
parallel of latitude, (geog.) paralelo de latitud.
parallelogram [͵pærə'lɛlə͵græm] *s.* (geom.) paralelogramo.
parallel perspective, (dib.) perspectiva paralela.
parallel postulate, (mat.) postulado de las paralelas.
parallel resonance, (rad.) resonancia en paralelo.
parallel rulers, (ing.) reglas paralelas.
parallel sailing, (mar.) navegación paralela.
parallel sphere, (astr.) esfera paralela.
paralogism [pə'rælə͵dʒɪzəm] *s.* (lóg.) paralogismo.
paralogistic [-͵rælə'dʒɪstɪk] *a.* ilógico, falaz (argumento).
paralogize [pə'rælə͵dʒaɪz] *v.i.* paralogizar.
paralysis [pə'ræləsəs] *s.* (*pl.* PARALYSES [-͵siz]) (med.) parálisis; (fig.) parálisis.
paralysis agitans [-'ædʒə͵tænz] (med.) parálisis agitante.
paralytic [͵pærə'lɪtɪk] *a., s.* paralítico.
paralyzation [-lə'zeɪʃən, B -laɪ-] *s.* paralización.
paralyze ['pærə͵laɪz] *v.t.* paralizar; (fig.) paralizar, entorpecer.
paramagnet ['pærə͵mægnət, B ͵pærə'mæg-] *s.* substancia paramagnética.
paramagnetic [͵pærə͵mæg'nɛtɪk] *a.* (fís.) paramagnético.

paramagnetism [-'mægnə,tɪzəm] *s.* (fís.) paramagnetismo.

paramatta [,pærə'mætə] *s.* tela fina parecida al bombasí, alepín, merino o fustán.

paramecium [,pærə'miʃɪəm, B -sɪəm] *s.* (*pl.* PARAMECIUMS O PARAMECIA [-əl]) (zool.) paramecio.

paramedical [,pærə'mɛdɪkəl] *a.* del personal auxiliar del médico (parteras, enfermeras, etc.).

parament ['pærəmənt] *s.* paramento, ornamento.

parameter [pə'ræmətər, B -ə] *s.* (mat.) parámetro.

parametric [,pærə'mɛtrɪk] *a.* (mat.) paramétrico.

paramilitary [-'mɪlə,tɛrɪ, B -tərɪ] *a.* paramilitar.

paramnesia [,pæræm'niʒə, B -zjə] *s.* (med.) paramnesia.

paramo ['pærə,moʊ] *s.* (*pl.* PARAMOS) páramo, puna (Amer.).

paramorphism [,pærə'mɔr,fɪzəm, B -'mɔ,-] *s.* (quím.) paramorfismo.

paramount ['pærə,maʊnt] *a.* superior, supremo, sumo, máximo, principalísimo; capital, ej., *of p. importance,* de capital importancia. —*s.* soberano; gobernador; amo supremo.

paramountcy [-sɪ] *s.* preeminencia.

paramour ['pærə,mʊr, B -,mʊə] *s.* amante, querido (esp. ilícito).

paramylum [pæ'ræmələm] *s.* (biol.) paramilo.

paranephric [,pærə'nɛfrɪk] *a.* (anat.) paranéfrico.

paranephritis [-nɪ'fraɪtəs] *s.* (med.) paranefritis.

paranephros [-'nɛfrəs, B -,frɔs] *s.* (anat.) paranefros.

parang ['pɑ,ræŋ] *s.* espada o cuchillo corto de Malaya.

paranoia [,pærə'nɔɪə] *s.* (med.) paranoia.

paranoiac [-,æk, -ɪk] *a., s.* (med.) paranoico.

paranoid ['pærə,nɔɪd] *a.* (med.) paranoide; paranoico. —*s.* paranoide.

paranoid schizophrenia, (med.) esquizofrenia paranoide.

paranormal [,pærə'nɔrməl, B -'nɔməl] *a.* paranormal, no enteramente normal; sobrenatural.

paranymph ['pærə,nɪmf] *s.* paraninfo, el padrino de bodas; el que anuncia un suceso feliz; el que pronuncia el discurso de apertura de un año escolar.

parapet ['pærəpət, -,pɛt] *s.* 1. parapeto, pretil, antepecho. 2. (fort.) parapeto.

parapeted [-əd] *a.* fortificado con parapetos, parapetado.

paraph ['pærəf] *s.* rúbrica.

paraphernalia [,pærəfər'neɪljə, B -fə'-] *s.* 1. objetos de uso personal. 2. mobiliario, conjunto de aparatos y accesorios (de un circo, casa, etc.). 3. (hist., der.) bienes parafernales.

paraphernal property [-'fɜrnəl-, B -'fɜnəl-] (der.) bienes parafernales.

paraphrase ['pærə,freɪz] *s.* paráfrasis. —*v.t., v.i.* parafrasear.

paraphraser [-ər, B -ə] **paraphrast** [-,fræst] *s.* parafraseador, parafraste.

paraphrastic [,pærə'fræstɪk] *a.* parafrástico.

paraphysis [pə'ræfəsəs] *s.* (*pl.* PARAPHYSES [-,siz]) (bot.) paráfisis.

paraplegia [,pærə'plidʒɪə, B -dʒə] *s.* (med.) paraplejía.

paraplegic [-dʒɪk] *a., s.* (med.) parapléjico.

parapsychology [-saɪ'kɑlədʒɪ, B -'kɔl-] *s.* parapsicología.

paraquet ['pærə,kɛt] *var. de* **parakeet.**

pararosaniline [,pærə,roʊ'zænələn] *s.* (quím.) pararrosanilina.

Pará rubber ['pærə-, B pæ'rɑ-] *s.* caucho natural sucamericano.

parasang ['pærə,sæŋ] *s.* parasanga, antigua medida persa.

paraselene [,pærəsə'linɪ] *s.* (*pl.* PARASELENAE [-ni]) (meteor.) paraselene.

Parashah ['pɑrə,ʃɑ, B 'pær-] *s.* Parashá, parte de una ceremonia religiosa judía.

parasite ['pærə,saɪt] *s.* 1. parásito, gorrón, vividor. 2. (biol.) parásito.

parasitic [,pærə'sɪtɪk] **parasitical** [-ɪkəl] *a.* parasítico, parasitario, parásito.

parasitically [-ɪkəlɪ] *adv.* de manera parasítica, parasitariamente.

parasiticidal [-,sɪtə'saɪdəl] *a.* parasiticida.

parasiticide [-'sɪtə,saɪd] *a., s.* parasiticida.

parasitism ['pærə,saɪt,ɪzəm] *s.* parasitismo.

parasitize ['pærəsə,taɪz, B -saɪ-] *v.t.* infestar con parásitos.

parasitologist [,pærəsə'tɑlədʒəst, B -saɪ'-tɔl-] *s.* parasitólogo.

parasitology [-dʒɪ] *s.* parasitología.

parasitosis [,pærə,saɪt'oʊsəs] *s.* (med.) parasitosis.

parasol ['pærə,sɔl, -,sɑl, B -,sɔl] *s.* parasol, quitasol, sombrilla.

parastas ['pærə,stæs, B pə'ræstəs] *s.* (*pl.* PARASTADES [pə'ræstə,diz]) (arq.) parástade.

parasympathetic [,pærə,sɪmpə'θɛtɪk] (anat.) *a.* parasimpático. —*s.* nervio parasimpático.

parasympathomimetic [-,sɪmpə,θoʊmɪ'mɛtɪk, B -maɪ'mɛt-] *a.* (fisiol.) parasimpaticomimético.

parasynapsis [-sə'næpsəs] *s.* (biol.) parasinapsis.

parasynthesis [-'sɪnθəsəs] *s.* (gram.) parasíntesis.

parataxis [-'tæksəs] *s.* (gram.) parataxis.

parathion [-'θaɪ,ɑn, B -,ɔn] *s.* (quím.) paratión.

parathyroid [-'θaɪr,ɔɪd] *s.* (anat.) paratiroides. —*a.* paratiroidea.

parathyroid gland, (anat.) glándula paratiroides.

paratrooper ['pærə,trupər, B -pə] *s.* (mil.) paracaidista.

paratroops [-,trups] *s. pl.* paracaidistas.

paratyphoid [,pærə'taɪ,fɔɪd] *a.* (med.) paratífico, paratifoide. —*s.* paratifoidea, paratifus, fiebre paratifoide.

paratyphoid fever, (med.) fiebre paratifoidea.

paravane ['pærə,veɪn] *s.* (mar.) paraván.

parboil ['pɑr,bɔɪl, B 'pɑ,-] *v.t.* 1. sancochar. 2. (fig.) calentar bien, hacer sudar.

parbuckle ['pɑr,bʌkəl, B 'pɑ,-] *s.* tiravira. —*v.t.* levantar por medio de una tiravira, tiravirar.

Parcae ['pɑr,ki, B 'pɑsi] *s. pl.* (mitol.) Parcas, las tres deidades del infierno.

parcel ['pɑrsəl, B 'pɑsəl] *s.* 1. paquete, lío, fardo. 2. lote, partida; grupo. 3. parcela, lote (de terreno). 4. parte, fragmento. —*v.t.* (*pret. p.p.* PARCELED O PARCELLED; *p.pr.* PARCELING O PARCELLING) 1. partir, dividir, fraccionar. 2. (t. con *up*) empaquetar. 3. (mar.) precintar (cabos). 4. **p. out,** repartir en lotes, dividir en porciones; parcelar (terreno). —*a.* parcial.

parceling, parcelling [-səlɪŋ] *s.* 1. repartición, repartimiento, partición, división. 2. parcelación, lotización (de terreno) (Perú). 3. (mar.) precinta.

parcel post, (servicio de) paquete postal o encomienda (Amer.); **to send by p.p.,** enviar como paquete postal o encomienda (Amer.).

parcenary ['pɑrsə,nɛrɪ, B 'pɑsɪnərɪ] *s.* (der.) herencia indivisa, copropiedad (de bienes heredados).

parcener ['pɑrsənər, B 'pɑsɪnə] *s.* (der.) coheredero de una propiedad; copropietario (de bienes heredados).

parch [pɑrtʃ, B pɑtʃ] *v.t.* 1. tostar; torrar, socarrar. 2. resecar (al fuego, por el frío o el calor). 3. agostar (las plantas por el frío o el calor). —*v.i.* 1. resecarse. 2. agostarse (plantas).

parched [pɑrtʃt, B pɑtʃt] *a.* reseco; sediento.

Parcheesi (TM) [pɑr'tʃizɪ, B pə'tʃisɪ] *s.* ludo, parchís (Esp.), parqués (Col.).

parchment ['pɑrtʃmənt, B 'pɑtʃ-] *s.* 1. pergamino, vitela. 2. papel pergamino. 3. (escrito en) pergamino.

pard [pɑrd, B pɑd] *s.* 1. (ant.) leopardo. 2. (pr. dial.) compañero, compinche, camarada.

pardie, pardi [,pɜr'di, B pɑ'di] *adv., interj.* (ant.) ciertamente, seguramente.

pardner ['pɑrdnər, B 'pɑdnə] *s.* (pr. dial.) compañero, compinche, camarada.

pardon ['pɑrdən, B 'pɑd-] *v.t.* 1. perdonar, dispensar (a alguien, una falta); eximir, excusar, disculpar, remitir (falta). 2. (der.) absolver, indultar, amnistiar. —*s.* 1. perdón, indulgencia, remisión. 2. (der.) indulto, amnistía, absolución, gracia. 3. (relig.) indulgencia. 4. **I beg your p.,** perdone; ¿cómo? ¿cómo dijo?

pardonable [-əbəl] *a.* perdonable, excusable.

pardonably [-blɪ] *adv.* de modo perdonable.

pardoner [-ər, B -ə] *s.* (hist.) perdonante.

pardy, *var. de* **pardie, pardi.**

pare [pɛr, B pɛə] *v.t.* 1. pelar (fruta, etc.), descortezar (queso, etc.). 2. mondar, recortar, quitar. 3. (fig.) cercenar, rebajar, reducir poco a poco. 4. **p. (a nail, etc.) to the quick,** (re)cortar (las uñas, etc.) hasta la carne viva.

paregoric [,pærə'gɔrɪk] *a.* paregórico, anodino, calmante. —*s.* (farm.) elixir paregórico.

parenchyma [pə'rɛŋkəmə] *s.* (bot., anat., zool.) parénquima.

parenchymatous [,pærən'kɪmətəs] *a.* (bot., anat., zool.) parenquimatoso.

parent ['pɛrənt, 'pær-, B 'pɛər-] *s.* 1. padre o madre; (*pl.*) padres. 2. autor, causa, origen. —*a.* matriz, materno, principal.

parentage [-ɪdʒ] *s.* 1. ascendencia, origen; nacimiento, extracción; alcurnia, abolengo. 2. paternidad o maternidad.

parental [pə'rɛntəl] *a.* paternal o maternal.

Parentalia [,pærən'teɪlɪə] *s. pl.* (hist. romana) parentales.

parentally [pə'rɛntəlɪ] *adv.* paternalmente o maternalmente.

parenteral [,pær'ɛntərəl] *a.* (anat., med., fisiol.) parenteral, parentérico.

parenthesis [pə'rɛnθəsəs] *s.* (*pl.* PARENTHESES [-,siz]) (gram.) paréntesis; (fig.) paréntesis, intervalo.

parenthesize [-,saɪz] *v.t.* hacer un paréntesis de, mencionar entre paréntesis; poner entre paréntesis.

parenthetic [,pærən'θɛtɪk] **parenthetical** [-ɪkəl] *a.* parentético.

parenthetically [-ɪkəlɪ] *adv.* de modo parentético.

parenthood ['pɛrənt,hʊd, 'pær-, B 'pɛər-] *s.* paternidad o maternidad.

parent house, (com.) casa principal.

parent office, oficina matriz.

parent unit, (mil.) unidad de pertenencia.

paresis [pə'risəs, B 'pærəsɪs] *s.* (*pl.* PARESES [-,siz]) (med.) paresis, parecia.

paresthesia [,pærəs'θiʒə, B -sɪə] *s.* (med., fisiol.) parestesia.

paretic [pəˈrɛtɪk] *a., s.* (med.) parético.
par excellence [ˌpɑrˌɛksəˈlɑns, B -ˈɛksəˌlɑns] por excelencia.
parfait [pɑrˈfeɪ, B pɑˈ-] *s.* postre hecho con varias clases de crema helada.
parfleche [ˈpɑrˌflɛʃ, B pɑˈflɛʃ] *s.* cuero sin curtir (que ha sido empapado en lejía, para quitarle el pelo); cajas o alforjas de cuero sin curtir.
parget [ˈpɑrdʒət, B ˈpɑdʒɪt] *v.t.* (*pret., p.p.* PARGETED O PARGETTED; *p.pr.* PARGETTING O PARGETTING) 1. enfoscar, enlucir, revocar, jaharrar. 2. ornamentar con molduras de yeso. —*s.* 1. enlucido, revoque, revoco. 2. moldura de yeso.
pargo [ˈpɑrˌgoʊ, B ˈpɑˌ-] *s.* (*pl.* PARGOS) (ict.) cubera.
parhelic [pɑrˈhilɪk, B pɑˈ-] **parheliacal** [ˌpɑrhəˈlaɪəkəl, B ˌpɑhɪ-] *a.* (meteor.) parhélico.
parhelic circle, (meteor.) círculo o anillo parhélico.
parhelion [pɑrˈhiljən, B pɑˈ-] *s.* (*pl.* PARHELIA [-jə]) (meteor.) parhelio, parhelia.
pariah [pəˈraɪə, B ˈpærɪə] *s.* paria.
Parian [ˈpærɪən, B ˈpɛər-] *s.* pario, de Paros, isla famosa por su mármol. —*s.* porcelana blanca y fina que imita al mármol de Paros.
paries [ˈpærɪˌiz, B ˈpɛər-] *s.* (*pl.* PARIETES [pəˈraɪəˌtiz]) (anat.) paries, pared.
parietal [pəˈraɪətəl] *a.* 1. (anat., bot., zool.) parietal. 2. (E.U.) de la vida interna (de una universidad). —*s.* (anat.) hueso parietal.
parietal bones, (anat.) huesos parietales.
parietal lobe, (anat.) lóbulo parietal.
pari-mutuel [ˌpærɪˈmjutʃʊəl] *s.* 1. sistema de apuestas (con totalizador). 2. totalizador.
paring [ˈpɛrɪŋ, B ˈpɛər-] *s.* peladura, mondadura, cáscara, corteza; recorte, desperdicio.
paripinnate [ˌpærɪˈpɪneɪt] *a.* (bot.) paripinnado.
Paris [ˈpærəs] *s.* 1. París, capital de Francia. 2. Paris, cuyo rapto de Helena causó la Guerra de Troya.
Paris green, (quím.) verde de Schweinfurt.
parish [ˈpærɪʃ] *s.* 1. parroquia. 2. (G.B.) subdivisión de un condado. 3. (E.U.) condado (del estado) de Luisiana. 4. **to go on the p.,** recibir ayuda pública.
parish church, iglesia parroquial.
parish council, (G.B.) cuerpo civil administrativo de parroquia rural.
parishioner [pəˈrɪʃənər, B -nə] *s.* feligrés, parroquiano.
parish register, registro parroquial.
Parisian [pəˈrɪʒən, B -ˈrɪzjən] *a., s.* parisiense, parisino.
parisyllabic [ˌpærəsəˈlæbɪk] *a.* parisilábico, parisílabo.
parity [ˈpærətɪ] *s.* (*pl.* PARTIES) paridad.
park [pɑrk, B pɑk] *s.* 1. parque (lugar arbolado). 2. (mil.) parque (de cañones, municiones, etc.). 3. parque, lugar de estacionamiento (de automóviles, etc.) 4. recinto cerrado (en estadios, arena, etc.). 5. (E.U.) valle llano. 6. (G.B., hist.) cazadero real. —*v.t.* 1. aparcar, parquear (Amer.), estacionar (Amer.) (vehículos). 2. (mil.) almacenar en parque. 3. (jer.) depositar, colocar, acomodar. —*v.i.* aparcar, estacionarse (Amer.).
parka [ˈpɑrkə, B ˈpɑkə] *s.* abrigo esquimal de piel con capucha.
parking [ˈpɑrkɪŋ, B ˈpɑk-] *s.* 1. estacionamiento, aparcamiento (de un vehículo). 2. lugar de estacionamiento, espacio para estacionar, aparcamiento. 3. **no p.,** prohibido estacionar.
parking attendant, guardacoches.
parking brake, (aut.) freno de estacionamiento.
parking garage, parking, estacionamiento, aparcamiento.
parking light, (aut.) luz de estacionamiento.
parking lot, playa de estacionamiento (Amer.), parqueadero (Amer.), parking, aparcamiento.
parking lot attendant, guardacoches.
parking meter, (aut.) parquímetro, contador de aparcamiento.
parking space, plaza o lugar de estacionamiento en una calle o un patio.
parkinsonism [ˈpɑrkənsəˌnɪzəm, B ˈpɑkɪn-] *s.* (med.) parkinsonismo.
Parkinson's disease [-sənz-] (med.) enfermedad de Parkinson, mal de Parkinson, parálisis agitante *or* temblorosa.
parkway [ˈpɑrkˌweɪ, B ˈpɑk-] *s.* avenida o carretera ajardinada; carretera principal (E.U.).
parlance [ˈpɑrləns, B ˈpɑləns] *s.* 1. dicción, lenguaje, manera de hablar o escribir. 2. (ant.) plática, parlamento.
parlay [pɑrˈleɪ, B pɑˈ-] (E.U.) *v.t.* 1. apostar (dinero) en un pároli. 2. explotar. 3. transformar. — [ˈpɑrleɪ, B ˈpɑlɪ] *s.* pároli.
parley [ˈpɑrlɪ, B ˈpɑlɪ] *s.* parlamento, plática, conferencia; esp. (mil.) parlamento. —*v.i.* 1. conversar, hablar, conferenciar. 2. (mil.) parlamentar.
parliament [ˈpɑrləmənt, B ˈpɑlə-] *s.* parlamento.
parliamentarian [ˌpɑrləˌmɛnˈtɛrɪən, B ˌpɑləˈtɛərɪən] *s.* 1. orador hábil; experto en estrategia parlamentaria. 2. (hist., G.B.) partidario del Parlamento opuesto a Carlos I.
parliamentarianism [-ˌɪzəm] *s.* parlamentarismo.
parliamentary [-ˈmɛntərɪ, -trɪ] *a.* parlamentario.
parliamentary immunity, inmunidad parlamentaria.
parliamentary law, reglamento parlamentario.
parlor, (pr. G.B.) **parlour** [ˈpɑrlər, B ˈpɑlə] *s.* 1. sala, sala de recibo. 2. **beauty p.,** salón de belleza, peluquería.
parlor car, (E.U., f.c.) coche salón.
parlor game, juego de salón.
parlormaid [-ˌmeɪd] *s.* camarera, doncella, mucama (Amer.).
parlous [ˈpɑrləs, B ˈpɑləs] *a.* 1. **riesgoso,** azaroso, peligroso. 2. (ant.) muy astuto, perspicaz. —*adv.* excesivamente, sumamente.
Parmenides [pɑrˈmɛnəˌdiz, B pɑˈ-] *s.* Parménides, filósofo griego.
Parmesan [ˈpɑrməˌzɑn, B ˌpɑmɪˈzæn] *a.* parmesano, natural de la ciudad italiana de Parma.
Parmesan cheese, queso parmesano.
Parnassian [pɑrˈnæsɪən, B pɑˈ-] *a.* parnasiano. —*s.* parnasiano (miembro de un grupo de poetas franceses que daban especial énfasis a la métrica).
Parnassus [-ˈnæsəs] *s.* 1. (geog.) **Parnaso,** monte griego consagrado a Apolo y a las musas. 2. (fig.) mundo de la poesía. 3. (fig.) peña de poetas. 4. (fig.) centro de actividades artísticas y literarias.
parochial [pəˈroʊkɪəl] *a.* 1. parroquial. 2. (fig.) (de mentalidad) provincial, estrecho de miras, intolerante.
parochialism [-ˌɪzəm] *s.* localismo, estrechez de miras, aldeanismo.
parochialist [-əst] *s.* localista, persona estrecha de miras, intolerante.
parochially [-ɪ] *adv.* 1. por parroquias. 2. con estrechez de miras, con intolerancia.
parochial school, escuela o colegio parroquial.
parodic [pəˈrɑdɪk, B -ˈrɔd-] **parodical** [-ɪkəl] *a.* paródico, burlesco, caricaturesco.
parodist [ˈpærədəst] *s.* parodista.
parodistic [ˌpærəˈdɪstɪk] *a.* paródico.
parody [ˈpærədɪ] *s.* parodía. —*v.t.* parodiar, hacer una parodia de.
paroemia [pəˈrimɪə] *s.* paremia, refrán, proverbio.
paroemiologic [-ˌrimɪəˈlɑdʒɪk, B -ˈlɔdʒ-] *a.* paremiológico, relativo a los refranes.
paroemilogist [-ˈɑlədʒəst, B -ˈɔl-] *s.* paremiólogo, especialista en refranes.
paroemiology [-dʒɪ] *s.* paremiología, tratado de refranes.
parol [pəˈrɔl, B ˈpærɔl] *s.* 1. (ant.) palabra. 2. (der.) alegato. —*a.* (der.) verbal, oral, no solemne.
parole [pəˈroʊl] *s.* 1. (der.) liberación condicional (del reo). 2. libertad provisional o condicional, libertad vigilada, libertad bajo palabra. 3. palabra dada, palabra de honor. 4. (mil.) santo y seña. 5. (**to release,** etc.) **on p.,** (poner, etc.) en libertad provisional. —*v.t.* poner en libertad condicional. —*a.* bajo palabra.
parolee [pəˌroʊˈli] *s.* convicto en libertad provisional.
paronymic [pærəˈnɪmɪk] **paronymous** [pəˈrɑnəməs, B -ˈrɔn-] *a.* (gram.) parónimo.
paronomasia [ˌpærənoʊˈmeɪʒə, B -ˈmeɪzɪə] *s.* (ret.) paronomasia.
paronomastic [-ˈmæstɪk] *a.* (ret.) paronomástico.
paronychia [ˌpærəˈnɪkɪə] *s.* (med.) paroniquia, panadizo periungueal.
paronym [ˈpærəˌnɪm] *s.* (gram.) parónimo.
paronymy [pəˈrɑnəmɪ, B -ˈrɔn-] *s.* (ret.) paronimia.
parotic [pəˈrɑtɪk, B -ˈrɔt-] *a.* 1. (zool.) parótico. 2. (anat.) de la región auricular; área parotídea.
parotid [-əd] (anat.) *a.* (glándula) parótida. —*s.* logia o región parotídea.
parotitis [ˌpærəˈtaɪtəs] *s.* (med.) parotitis, parotiditis, infección de las glándulas parótidas.
paroxysm [ˈpærəkˌsɪzəm] *s.* 1. (med.) paroxismo. 2. (fig.) paroxismo, exaltación extrema, frenesí.
paroxysmal [ˌpærəkˈsɪzməl] *a.* (med.) paroxismal.
paroxytone [pærˈɑksɪˌtoʊn, B pəˈrɔk-] *a.* (gram.) paroxítono. —*s.* palabra paroxítona.
parquet [pɑrˈkeɪ, B ˈpɑkeɪ] *s.* 1. (carp.) parqué, parquet (Amer.), entarimado. 2. (teat.) platea, esp. los asientos más cercanos a la orquesta. —*v.t.* (*pret. p.p.* PARQUETED; *p.pr.* PARQUETING) poner parquet a, entarimar (un piso). —*a.* de parquet.
parquet circle, (teat.) asientos de la platea debajo de las galerías.
parquetry [ˈpɑrkətrɪ, B ˈpɑkə-] *s.* (carp.) mosaico de madera, entarimado; parqué, parquet (Amer.).
parr [pɑr, B pɑ] *s.* (ict.) 1. esguín, murgón. 2. alevino, pez pequeño.
parral, *var. de.* **parrel.**
parramatta, *var de.* **paramatta.**
parrel [ˈpærəl] *s.* 1. (mar.) bastardo, racamento, racamenta. 2. **p. cleat,** jimelga (palo).
parrhesia [pæˈriʒɪə, B -zɪə] *s.* (ret.) parresia.
parricidal [ˌpærəˈsaɪdəl] *a.* parricida.
parricide [ˈpærəˌsaɪd] *s.* 1. parricida. 2. parricidio.
parroket, parroquet [ˈpærəˌkɛt] *vars. de* **parakeet.**

parrot ['pærət] *s.* 1. loro, papagayo, cotorra. 2. (fig.) cotorra, loro. —*v.t.* repetir como un loro; hablar sin sentido.
parrot disease, p. fever, (med.) psitacosis.
parrot fish, (ict.) (pez) papagayo; (especie de) escaro.
parry ['pærɪ] *v.t.* (*pret., pp.* PARRIED; *p.pr.* PARRYING) 1. parar, evitar (golpe). 2. evadir una respuesta directa a, replicar hábilmente a (pregunta). —*v.i.* hacer una parada, un quite; defenderse. —*s.* parada, quite, reparo; (esgr.) parada, quite.
parse [pɑrs, B pɑz] *v.t.* (gram.) analizar (oración, partes de la oración). —*v.i.* ser analizable gramaticalmente, admitir análisis gramatical.
parsec ['pɑrˌsɛk, B 'pɑˌ-] *s.* (astr.) parsec, unidad astronómica.
Parsi, Parsee ['pɑrˌsi, B pɑ'si] *s.* parsi, lenguaje o habitante (de origen persa en India).
Parsiism, Parseeism [-ˌɪzəm] *s.* parsismo, mazdeísmo, relegión de Zoroastro.
parsimonious [ˌpɑrsə'mounɪəs, B ˌpɑsɪ-] *a.* parsimonioso, cicatero, mezquino; parco, frugal en exceso.
parsimoniously [-lɪ] *adv.* parsimoniosamente.
parsimony ['pɑrsəˌmounɪ, B 'pɑsɪmənɪ] *s.* parsimonia, tacañería, mezquindad; frugalidad, parquedad.
parsley ['pɑrslɪ, B 'pɑslɪ] *s.* (bot.) perejil.
parsley butter, (cocina) salsa mayordoma.
parsnip ['pɑrsnəp, B 'pɑsnɪp] *s.* (bot.) chirivía, pastinaca.
parson ['pɑrsən, B 'pɑs-] *s.* 1. párroco o rector protestante; pastor protestante. 2. cura, clérigo.
parsonage [-ɪdʒ] *s.* casa parroquial, rectoría.
part [pɑrt, B pɑt] *s.* 1. parte, porción, pieza; pedazo, trozo, fragmento; (pieza de) repuesto. 2. parte, participación, interés. 3. (der.) parte, litigante, ej., *the other p.,* parte opositora. 4. (*pl.*) región, paraje, distrito, ej., *he is a stranger in these parts,* él es un forastero en estos parajes. 5. (teat.) papel, rol. 6. (E.U.) crencha, raya del pelo. 7. (mús.) parte (melodía para una voz o un instrumento en una partitura). 8. **for my p.,** por lo que a mí concierne, en cuanto a mí; **for the most p.,** por la mayor parte, por lo general; **in good p.,** sin ofenderse, de buen talante; **in p.,** parcialmente, en parte; **on the p. of,** de parte de; **p. and parcel,** parte esencial o integral; **to do one's p.,** cumplir con su obligación; **to look the p.,** tener los requisitos necesarios para el cargo; **to play a p.,** (fig.) actuar engañosamente; participar, tomar parte; **to play a noble p.,** portarse con hidalguía; **to take p. (in),** participar, tomar parte (en); **to take the p. (of),** respaldar (a). —*v.t.* 1. separar, desunir, apartar. 2. dividir, separar por partes; romper. 3. repartir, distribuir, ratear. 4. (ant.) abandonar, dejar. 5. **p. company (with),** separarse (de); romper relaciones (con), dejar de asociarse (con). —*v.i.* 1. separarse, dividirse; romperse. 2. partir, apartarse; despedirse, ej., *let us p. friends,* despidámonos como amigos. 3. (fam.) soltar su dinero, pagar. 4. **p. from** (o **with**), decir adiós a, despedirse de; **p. with,** desprenderse de, privarse de, deshacerse de, enajenarse de. —*a.* parcial; **in p. payment,** en parte de pago; **to meet (someone) p. way,** hacer algunas concesiones a (alguien). —*adv.* en parte, parcialmente.
part. *abrev. de* 1. **participle,** participio. 2. **particular,** particular.
partake [pɑr'teɪk, B pɑ'-] *v.i.* 1. (con *in, of* o *with*) compartir, tomar parte (en), participar (de). 2. (con *of*) consumir, comer o beber. 3. (con *of*) tener algo (de una cualidad, carácter, etc.). —*v.t.* compartir, participar de.
partaker [-ər, B -ə] *s.* participante; socio; cómplice.
partan ['pɑrtən, B pɑt-] *s.* (zool.) cangrejo grande.
parted ['pɑrtəd, B 'pɑt-] *a.* 1. separado, dividido, hendido. 2. (bot.) partido. 3. (her.) cortado, partido. 4. (ant.) fallecido, muerto.
parterre [pɑr'tɛr, B pɑ'tɛə] *s.* (fr.) 1. parterre, macizo de flores. 2. (teat.) patio de butacas, platea.
parthenocarpy ['pɑrθənouˌkɑrpɪ, B 'pɑθɪ-ˌkɑpɪ] *s.* (bot.) partenocarpia.
parthenogenesis [ˌpɑrθənou'dʒɛnəsəs, B 'pɑθɪ-] *s.* (biol.) partenogénesis.
parthenogenetic [-dʒə'nɛtɪk] *a.* (biol.) partenogenésico.
Parthenon ['pɑrθəˌnɑn, B 'pɑθɪnən] *s.* Partenón, templo de Atenas (en Grecia).
Parthian ['pɑrθɪən, B 'pɑθɪ-] *a.* parto, de Partia. —*s.* parto, natural de Partia, antiguo imperio que se extendía del mar Caspio al Éufrates.
Parthian shot, (fig.) la flecha del parto, gesto hostil al partir.
partial ['pɑrʃəl, B 'pɑʃəl] *a.* 1. parcial, sin objetividad. 2. parcial, incompleto. 3. **p. to,** que tiene predilección por, aficionado a. —*s.* 1. (mús., fís.) tono parcial. 2. (mat.) diferencial parcial.
partial fraction, (mat.) fracción parcial.
partiality [ˌpɑrʃɪ'ælətɪ, B ˌpɑʃɪ-] *s.* 1. parcialidad, partidismo, predisposición. 2. prejuicio. 3. preferencia, predilección, inclinación.
partial load, (ing.) carga fraccionada o parcial.
partially ['pɑrʃəlɪ, B 'pɑʃ-] *adv.* parcialmente, incompletamente; con prejuicio, con parcialidad.
partial tone, (mús., fís.) tono parcial.
partible ['pɑrtəbəl, B 'pɑt-] *a.* partible, divisible.
participant [pɑr'tɪsəpənt, pər-, B pɑ'-] *a.* participante, partícipe, particionero. —*s.* participante, partícipe.
participate [-ˌpeɪt] *v.i.* 1. participar. 2. **p. in,** participar en; tener algo de. —*v.t.* compartir.
participating mortgage [-ɪŋ-] (fin.) hipoteca conjunta, hipoteca de participación.
participating stock, (com.) acciones preferenciales, con participación en el beneficio sobrante.
participation [-ˌtɪsə'peɪʃən] *s.* participación.
participator [-'tɪsəˌpeɪtər, B -ə] *s.* participante, partícipe, particionero.
participial [ˌpɑrtə'sɪpɪəl, B ˌpɑt-] *a.* (gram.) participial.
participially [-əlɪ] *adv.* (gram.) con función participial.
participle ['pɑrtəˌsɪpəl, B 'pɑt-] *s.* (gram.) participio.
particle ['pɑrtɪkəl, B 'pɑt-] *s.* 1. partícula. 2. (fig.) pizca, átomo. 3. (gram., fís.) partícula. 4. (relig.) partícula (consagrada). 5. (ant.) cláusula, artículo (de una composición o documento).
parti-colored [ˌpɑrtɪ'kʌlərd, B 'pɑt-əd] *a.* multicolor, abigarrado.
particular [pər'tɪkjələr, pɑr-, B pə'-lə] *a.* 1. particular, individual, privativo. 2. particular, singular, individual; cierto, determinado. 3. particular, peculiar, especial. 4. quisquilloso, exigente; meticuloso, detallado, escrupuloso; extravagante, raro (con relación a los gustos). 5. (lóg.) particular, privativo. 6. (der.) limitado. —*s.* 1. detalle, pormenor. 2. (lóg.) particular, sujeto, individuo, especie. 3. **in p.,** en particular, particularmente, especialmente; **to go into particulars,** entrar en pormenores.
particular estate, (der.) dominio precedente, dominio de tiempo fijo.
particularism [-ləˌrɪzəm] *s.* 1. particularismo, individualismo, exclusivismo. 2. (teo.) particularismo.
particularity [pərˌtɪkjə'lærətɪ, pɑr-, B pəˌ-] *s.* 1. minuciosidad, meticulosidad; precisión. 2. particularidad, individualidad, singularidad. 3. peculiaridad, especialidad. 4. carácter quisquilloso, rareza, extravagancia. 5. particularidad, detalle.
particularization [-lərə'zeɪʃən, B -raɪ-] *s.* descripción o tratamiento individual.
particularize [-'tɪkjələˌraɪz] *v.t.* particularizar, individualizar, detallar, especificar. —*v.i.* entrar en detalles.
particularly [-lərlɪ, B -ləlɪ] *adv.* 1. particularmente, expresamente. 2. especialmente, máxime.
parting ['pɑrtɪŋ, B 'pɑt-] *a.* 1. que parte, que sale (de viaje, etc.). 2. divisorio, que separa. 3. de partida, de separación, de despedida, final. —*s.* 1. partida, división, separación, partición. 2. partida, despedida. 3. **p. of the ways,** bifurcación del camino, encrucijada; **to come to the p. of the ways,** llegar al momento de separarse.
parting strip, (arq.) listón separador.
partisan ['pɑrtəzən, -sən, B ˌpɑtɪ'zæn] *s.* 1. partidario, prosélito, secuaz, adepto, parcial. 2. (mil.) guerrillero, partisano. 3. (hist.) especie de alabarda. —*a.* 1. partidario, adepto. 2. (mil.) de guerrilla, partisano.
partisanship [-ˌʃɪp] *s.* 1. lealtad. 2. parcialidad. 3. (pol.) partidarismo (Amer.).
partite ['pɑrˌtaɪt, B 'pɑˌ-] *a.* partido, dividido en partes (ú. gen. en compuestos, ej., **bipartite, tripartite,** etc., bipartido, tripartito, etc.).
partition [pɑr'tɪʃən, B pɑ'-] *s.* 1. partición, división, separación, repartición, distribución. 2. mampara, tabique. 3. compartimiento, sección. 4. (der.) partición, división, partija, separación. 5. (lóg.) partición, división. —*v.t.* dividir; seccionar, demarcar; **p. off,** atajar, separar (por un tabique, biombo, etc.).
partitioner [-ənər, B -nə] *s.* partidor.
partitioning [-nɪŋ] *s.* (const.) tabiquería, entabicado.
partitive ['pɑrtətɪv, B 'pɑt-] *a.* partitivo; (gram.) partitivo. —*s.* palabra partitiva.
partizan, *var. de* **partisan.**
partly ['pɑrtlɪ, B 'pɑt-] *adv.* en parte, hasta cierto punto; parcialmente.
partner ['pɑrtnər, B 'pɑtnə] *s.* 1. socio, accionista, partícipe (en negocios). 2. compañero, pareja (en juegos, deportes); pareja (de baile). 3. consorte, cónyuge. 4. (der.) socio, asociado. 5. (mar.) (*pl.*) marco de fogonadura. —*v.t.* 1. asociar, unir. 2. emparejar. —*v.i.* actuar o jugar en pareja.
partnership [-ˌʃɪp] *s.* 1. asociación, consorcio, participación. 2. (com.) sociedad, compañía. 3. (der.) asociación; copropiedad o condominio (en un negocio o empresa).
part of speech, (gram.) parte de la oración.
part owner, co-propietario, condueño.
partridge ['pɑrtrɪdʒ, B 'pɑtrɪdʒ] *s.* (orn.) 1. perdiz. 2. colín, colín de Virginia.
partridgeberry [-ˌbɛrɪ] *s.* (bot.) planta rubiácea norteamericana; gaulteria del Canadá.
part-time ['pɑrt'taɪm, B 'pɑt-] *a.* por horas (trabajo, estudiante, empleado).
parturient [pɑr'turɪənt, B pɑ'tjuər-] *a.* parturienta, parturiente.
parturifacient [-ˌturɪ'feɪʃənt, B -ˌtjuər-] *s.* (med.) (substancia) parturifaciente.

parturition [ˌpɑrtʃə'rɪʃən, B ˌpɑtjʊə-] *s.* parto, alumbramiento.
partway ['pɑrt'weɪ, B 'pɑt-] *adv.* parcialmente, en parte, hasta cierto punto.
party ['pɑrtɪ, B 'pɑtɪ] *s.* 1. grupo, bando, facción. 2. partido (político). 3. destacamento (de soldados); cuadrilla (de obreros, bandidos, etc.). 4. fiesta, reunión, recepción, tertulia; partida (de paseo al campo). 5. parte (litigante, interesada, contratante, etc.). 6. (jer.) tipo, sujeto, individuo. 7. (ant.) parte o acción (de una sociedad). 8. **to be** (o **to become**) **a p. to,** tener parte en, ser partícipe de. —*a.* 1. del partido. 2. (her.) cortado, partido.
party line, 1. (tele.) línea colectiva (para varios abonados). 2. línea ideológica (de un partido político, esp. comunista). 3. linde, lindero (entre dos propiedades inmuebles).
party politics, política de partido.
party pooper, (jer.) aguafiestas.
party wall, (der.) pared medianera, pared común.
parure [pə'rʊr, B -'rʊə] *s.* aderezo, juego de joyas (del mismo estilo).
par value, (com.) valor nominal; valor a la par.
parvenu ['pɑrvəˌnu, B 'pɑvə-] (fr.) *s.* advenedizo, arribista, nuevo rico. —*a.* característico de un advenedizo.
parvis ['pɑrvəs, B 'pɑvɪs] *s.* (raro) atrio, pórtico de columnas de una iglesia.
parvolin, parvoline ['pɑrvəˌlin, B 'pɑvəlɪn] *s.* (quím.) parvolina.
pas [pɑ] *s.* 1. (danza) paso, pasos. 2. paso (baile). 3. paso, precedencia.
paschal ['pæskəl, B 'pɑs-] *a.* pascual.
paschal candle, (relig.) cirio pascual.
paschal cycle, ciclo pascual.
paschal lamb, 1. cordero pascual (sacrificado en la pascua hebrea). 2. **P.L.,** El Cordero, El Cordero de Dios (Jesucristo); Agnusdéi (oración y canto en el sacrificio de la misa).
pasch flower, *var. de* **pasqueflower.**
pas de deux [ˌpɑdə'dɜ] *s.* (fr.) variación (con dos danzarines).
pash [pæʃ] *v.t., v.i.* (dial.) romper, quebrar, destrozar.
pasha ['pɑʃə, 'pæʃə] *s.* bajá (titulo honorario en Turquia).
pashalik, pashalic, pachalic [pə'ʃɑlɪk] *s.* bajalato (jurisdicción de un bajá).
Pashto ['pʌʃtoʊ] **Pashtu** [-tu] *s.* pashtu (idioma).
pasqueflower ['pæskˌflaʊər, B -ə] *s.* (bot.) pulsatilla; anemone, anémona.
pasquil ['pæskwəl] *s.* pasquinada, pasquin.
pasquinade [ˌpæskwə'neɪd] *s.* pasquinada, pasquin. —*v.t.* pasquinar, satrizar.
pass [pæs, B pɑs] *s.* 1. paso, pasaje. 2. aprieto, situación crítica. 3. pase; permiso, licencia. 4. aprobación (en un examen); nota aprobatoria. 5. pase, finta (ej., en esgrima, boxeo, etc.). 6. pase (que hace con la mano un mago, un hipnotizador, etc.). 7. pasada (de un avión de guerra sobre el blanco). 8. tentativa. 9. (dep.) pase (de la pelota). 10. (naipes) pase. 11. desfiladero; paso, camino, trocha. 12. **to be on p.,** (mil.) estar franco, de licencia o con permiso; **to bring to p.,** llevar a cabo, realizar; **to come to p.,** realizarse, ocurrir; **to make a p. at,** tratar de acertar; hacer proposiciones amorosas a. —*v.i.* 1. pasar, ir, moverse. 2. pasar, adelantar. 3. circular, estar en circulación (dinero). 4. pasar, terminar, cesar, acabar. 5. pasar, atravesar, cruzar. 6. ocurrir, suceder; acaecer. 7. pasar, transcurrir (tiempo). 8. morir, pasar a mejor vida. 9. ser aceptable, ej., *it's not very good but it will p.,* no es muy bueno pero sí aceptable. 10. ser aceptado o aprobado (proyecto de ley); pasar, ser aprobado (en examen). 11. ser expedida, ser pronunciada o dictada (sentencia). 12. (dep.) hacer un pase. 13. (naipes) pasar. 14. pasar, no participar. 15. **p. as,** pasar por; **p. away,** llegar a su fin, morir; **p. by,** pasar por el lado, pasar cerca (de); pasar de largo; **p. for,** pasar por, ser aceptado como; **p. off,** pasar, ceder (dolor, malestar, tormento, etc.); ser llevado a cabo, realizarse; **p. on, p. upon,** decidir, llegar a una decisión sobre; dictar sentencia sobre; dar un dictamen sobre; **p. out,** (fam.) perder el conocimiento, desmayarse; morir; **p. over to,** pasarse a (enemigo, otro partido, etc.); **p. through,** pasar por, estar de paso por (ciudad, etc.); **to let (something) p.,** no hacer caso de (algo). —*v.t.* 1. pasar, dejar atrás. 2. atravesar, cruzar. 3. aventajar, superar, sobrepasar; exceder. 4. llevar, transportar, transladar. 5. hacer pasar o desfilar. 6. pasar (el tiempo, el verano, etc.). 7. aprobar (proyecto de ley, etc.); pasar (un examen). 8. poner en circulación (dinero). 9. pronunciar, dictar, expedir (sentencia). 10. (dep.) pasar (la pelota). 11. evacuar, segregar (del cuerpo). 12. **p. a dividend,** (com.) no declarar un dividendo; **p. along** (o **around**), pasar de uno a otro; **p. away,** pasar, gastar (el tiempo); **p. by,** pasar por alto, omitir; **p. each other,** cruzarse; **p. muster,** pasar sin tacha una inspección; ser aprobado; ser aceptable; **p. off,** pasar, hacer, aceptar (ej., moneda falsa); **p. off** with, disimular (ej., una observación embarazosa) con (una sonrisa, etc.); **p. on,** pasar, transmitir; entregar; **p. oneself off as,** hacerse pasar por; **p. out,** distribuir; **p. over,** omitir, no considerar, no tomar en cuenta; **p. the hat,** (jer.) pasar el cepillo, hacer una colecta; **p. up,** dejar pasar (oportunidad, etc.); **to have passed the chair,** haber sido presidente, director o alcalde.
pass. *abrev. de* 1. **passage,** pasaje; paso. 2. **passenger,** pasajero. 3. **passim,** pássim, aquí y allá. 4. **passive,** pasivo.
passable ['pæsəbəl, B 'pɑs-] *a.* 1. transitable, franqueable. 2. pasadero, pasable, aceptable, tolerable, admisible. 3. promulgable (ley). 4. corriente (moneda).
passably [-blɪ] *adv.* pasaderamente, pasablemente, medianamente, tolerablemente.
passacaglia [ˌpɑsəkɑljə, B ˌpæs-] *s.* (mús.) pasacalle.
passade [pə'seɪd] **passage** ['pæsɪdʒ] (equitación) *v.i.* andar de costado (un caballo). —*v.t.* hacer andar de costado (al caballo). —*s.* movimiento de costado (del caballo).
passado [pə'sɑdoʊ] *s.* (esgr.) estocada (que se da avanzando un pie).
passage ['pæsɪdʒ] *s.* 1. paso (de un lugar a otro). 2. transición. 3. transcurso (del tiempo). 4. pasaje, pasadizo, corredor. 5. viaje, travesía. 6. pasaje (precio de viaje, derecho a pasar). 7. aprobación, promulgación (de una ley). 8. intercambio (de observaciones, etc.); encuentro, lance (de armas, etc.). 9. pasaje, trozo, parte (de una narración, etc.). 10. (med.) evacuación, deposición. 11. (mús.) pasaje. 12. (ant.) fallecimiento, muerte; acontecimiento, episodio. —*v.i.* 1. viajar (por mar). 2. trabar combate, tener un altercado.
passageway [-ˌweɪ] *s.* pasadizo, pasaje, corredor, pasillo.
passant ['pæsənt] *a.* (her.) pasante.
passbook ['pæsˌbʊk, B 'pɑs-] *s.* 1. libreta de banco, libreta de abonos, libreta de depósitos. 2. (com.) libro de cuenta y razón.
pass degree, (G.B.) grado (universitario) que se obtiene con la mínima nota aprobatoria.
passé [pæ'seɪ, B 'pɑseɪ] *a.* (fr.) pasado, anticuado; en decadencia.
passed [pæst, B pɑst] *a.* 1. (mar.) en espera de una vacante para ascender (díc. del oficial que ha pasado el examen de promoción). 2. (com.) omitido (dividendo).
passed ball, (béisbol) bola que se le escapa al recibidor.
passel ['pæsəl] *s.* grupo (de gente), montón (de cosas).
passementerie [pæs'mɛntrɪ, B 'pæsmɛn-] *s.* (fr.) pasamanería, cordonería.
passenger ['pæsəndʒər, B -dʒə] *s.* 1. viajero, pasajero. 2. transeúnte, caminante.
passenger car, (f.c.) coche de pasajeros, vagón de pasajeros; (aut.) coche o auto.
passenger carriage, p. coach, (G.B., f.c.) coche de pasajeros, vagón de pasajeros.
passenger miles, pasajeros-kilómetro.
passenger pigeon, (orn.) paloma silvestre norteamericana.
passe-partout [ˌpæspɑr'tu, B 'pæspɑˌtu] *s.* (fr.) 1. llave maestra. 2. paspartú (papel especial para montaje de cuadros o pinturas).
passepied [pɑs'pjeɪ, B pæs-] *s.* (fr.) (mús.) paspié.
passer-by ['pæsər'baɪ, B 'pɑsə'-] *s.* (*pl.* PASSERS-BY) transeúnte.
passerine ['pæsəˌraɪn] *a.* (orn.) paserino.
pas seul [pɑ'səl, B -'sʌl] *s.* (fr.) solo de danza.
passibility [ˌpæsə'bɪlətɪ] *s.* (teo.) pasibilidad.
passible ['pæsəbəl] *a.* (teo.) pasible.
passifloraceous [ˌpæsɪfloʊ'reɪʃəs] *a.* (bot.) pasifloráceo.
passim ['pæsəm, B -ˌɪm] *adv.* pássim, aquí y allá.
passing ['pæsɪŋ, B 'pɑs-] *a.* 1. pasajero, transitorio, efímero, fugaz. 2. pasante, que pasa. 3. casual, de pasada, al paso. 4. aprobatorio, ej., *p. grade,* nota aprobatoria. 5. fúnebre, de difuntos, ej., *p. bell,* toque fúnebre o de difuntos. 6. (ant.) sobresaliente. —*adv.* sumamente, sobremanera. —*s.* 1. pasada, tránsito. 2. paso, pasaje. 3. vado. 4. aprobación obtenida en un examen). 5. fallecimiento. 6. **in p.,** de pasada; **with the p. of time,** andando el tiempo.
passing note, p. tone, (mús.) nota de transicion.
passion ['pæʃən] *s.* 1. pasión, sentimiento, emocion. 2. enardecimiento, emoción violenta; ira, cólera, furor. 3. pasión, amor. 4. (*pl.*) pasiones bajas. 5. pasión, martirio. 6. **P.,** Pasión (de Jesucristo; parte del evangelio). 7. **to have a p. for,** tener pasión por (música, arte, etc.).
passional [-əl] *s.* (relig.) martirologio (libro sobre la vida de los santos). —*a.* pasional.
passionate [-ət] *a.* 1. apasionado, arrebatado, vehemente; irascible, colérico. 2. apasionado, amoroso, ardiente.
passionately [-lɪ] *adv.* apasionadamente, vehementemente, ardientemente.
passionateness [-nəs] *s.* apasionamiento, vehemencia.
passionflower ['pæʃənˌflaʊər, B -ə] *s.* (bot.) pasionaria, granadilla.
passionless [-ləs] *a.* desapasionado, frío, impasible.
Passion play, (relig.) drama de la Pasión de Jesucristo.
Passion Week, (relig.) semana santa.
passive ['pæsɪv] *a.* 1. pasivo, no activo; inactivo, inerte. 2. pasivo, sumiso, paciente. 3. (aer.) sin motor. 4. (quím.) inerte, inactivo. 5. (gram.) pasivo. 6. (der., com.) que no devenga intereses. —*s.* (gram.) voz pasiva.
passively [-lɪ] *adv.* pasivamente.

passiveness [-nəs] *s.* pasividad.
passive resistance, resistencia pasiva, resistencia sin violencia.
passive verb, (gram.) verbo pasivo.
passive voice, (gram.) voz pasiva.
passivism ['pæsɪvˌɪzəm] *s.* pasividad.
passivity [pæ'sɪvətɪ] *s.* 1. pasividad. 2. (metal.) pasividad. 3. (quím.) inactividad.
passkey ['pæsˌki, B 'pɑs-] *s.* llave maestra.
Passover ['pæsˌoʊvər, B 'pɑsˌoʊvə] *s.* 1. (relig.) pascua de los hebreos. 2. (ant.) cordero pascual.
passport [-ˌpɔrt, B -ˌpɔt] *s.* pasaporte; (fig.) pasaporte, salvoconducto.
passport photo, foto de carnet, foto pasaporte.
passus ['pæsəs] *s.* (*pl.* PASSUS O PASSUSES) 1. (lit.) división o parte de una historia; (poét.) un canto. 2. paso romano (forma de marcha).
password ['pæsˌwɜrd, B 'pɑsˌwɜd] *s.* (mil.) santo y seña.
past [pæst, B pɑst] *a.* 1. pasado. 2. concluido, transcurrido, ej., *his prime is p.,* su mejor época ha concluido. 3. último, anterior, ex. 4. (gram.) pretérito, pasado. —*s.* 1. pasado; antecedentes, historia, ej., *he cannot undo the p.,* él no puede borrar el pasado. 2. (gram.) pretérito, pasado (tiempo o verbo). —*adv.* más allá; por el lado. —*prep.* 1. más de, más allá de, ej., *an old man p. seventy,* un anciano de más de setenta, *he ran p. the house,* corrió más allá de la casa. 2. y, ej., *quarter p. five,* (las) cinco y cuarto, *at half p. six,* a las seis y media. 3. sin (*se traduce a veces como un a. con sentido negativo*) ej., *p. belief,* increíble, *p. endurance,* intolerable, *p. recovery,* incurable. 4. **I wouldn't put it p. him to (do),** yo lo creo capaz hasta de (hacer); **to be p. (doing),** haber pasado la edad para (hacer).
pasta ['pɑstə] *s.* 1. pasta de harina de trigo, masa para hacer tallarines, etc. 2. plato de tallarines, ravioles, etc. 3. fideos, tallarines, ravioles, etc.
past absolute, (gram.) pretérito indefinido.
past anterior, (gram.) pretérito anterior.
paste [peɪst] *s.* 1. pasta, masa. 2. pasta, fideos. 3. goma, engrudo. 4. barro (para hacer cerámicas). 5. vidrio especial para imitar piedras preciosas; imitación. 6. (jer.) puñetazo, bofetón. —*v.t.* 1. pegar, empastar, engrudar. 2. (jer.) pegar, abofetear.
pasteboard ['peɪstˌbɔrd, B -ˌbɔd] *s.* 1. cartón. 2. (jer.) tarjeta (de visita); carta (de baraja), naipe; billete, boleto (Amer.). —*a.* 1. acartonado. 2. de imitación, falso.
pastedown [-ˌdaʊn] *s.* (enc.) hoja fija de la guarda.
pastel [pæs'tɛl] *s.* 1. pastel, clarioncillo. 2. pastel, pintura al pastel. 3. bosquejo o semblanza literaria. 4. color pastel. —*a.* pastel.
pastel drawing, pintura al pastel.
pastelist, pastellist [-əst] *s.* pastelista.
paster ['peɪstər, B -tə] *s.* 1. engrudador. 2. papel engomado.
pastern ['pæstərn, B -ˌtɜn] *s.* cuartilla, trabadero, cerruma (del caballo).
paste-up ['peɪstˌʌp] *s.* 1. (imp.) maqueta, modelo. 2. (imp.) emplanaje.
pasteurization [ˌpæstʃərə'zeɪʃən, B -tərai-] *s.* pasterización, pasteurización.
pasteurize ['pæstʃəˌraɪz, B -tə-] *v.t.* pasteurizar.
pasteurized milk [-ˌraɪzd-] leche pasteurizada, leche pasterizada.
past historic, (gram.) pretérito indefinido.
pasticcio [pæs'titʃoʊ] *s.* (*pl.* PASTICCI [-tʃɪ] PASTICCIOS) *var. de* **pastiche.**
pastiche [pæs'tiʃ] *s.* (teat., mús.) pastiche.
pasties ['peɪstiz] *s. pl.* (teat.) cubrepezones decorativos utilizados por bailarinas exóticas y desnudistas (Amer.).
pastille [pæs'til, B 'pæstəl] **pastil** ['pæstəl] *s.* pastilla, tableta. 2. sahumerio.
pastime ['pæsˌtaɪm, B 'pɑs-] *s.* pasatiempo.
pastiness ['peɪstɪnəs] *s.* pastosidad.
past master, 1. antiguo gran maestro (entre los masones). 2. perito, experto, conocedor.
past mistress, perita, experta, conocedora.
pastor ['pæstər, B 'pɑstə] *s.* 1. (relig.) pastor (protestante), párroco, cura. 2. (orn.) especie de estornino. 3. (raro) pastor, zagal.
pastoral ['pæstərəl, B 'pɑs-] *a.* 1. pastoral, pastoril, pastoricio. 2. pastoril, bucólico (díc. de la poesía). 3. (relig.) pastoral. —*s.* (lit., poét.) 1. pastoral, égloga, bucólica; pastorela. 2. (relig.) carta pastoral. 3. (arte) pastoral.
pastorale [ˌpæstə'rɑl, B -'rɑlɪ] *s.* (mús.) pastoral.
pastoralism ['pæstərəˌlɪzəm, B 'pɑs-] *s.* (lit., poét.) calidad o estilo pastoral o bucólico.
pastorally [-lɪ] *adv.* pastoralmente.
pastorate ['pæstərət, B 'pɑs-] *s.* 1. (relig.) parroquia, curato, rectorado. 2. casa parroquial, rectoral, rectoria. 3. clero, pastores.
pastorium [pæs'tɔrɪəm] *s.* (relig.) (S. de E.U.) parroquia protestante, esp. bautista.
pastorship ['pæstərˌʃɪp, B 'pɑstəˌ-] *s.* (relig.) curato.
pastose ['pæˌstoʊs, B pæs'toʊs] *a.* (pint.) pastoso.
pastourelle [ˌpæstə'rɛl] *s.* (fr.) (lit.) pastorela.
past participle, (gram.) participio pasado.
past perfect, (gram.) pretérito pluscuamperfecto.
pastrami [pə'strɑmɪ] *s.* brazuelo de res ahumado y sazonado (plato judío-rumano).
pastry ['peɪstrɪ] *s.* (*pl.* PASTRIES) pastelería, pasteles, pastas.
pastrycook [-ˌkʊk] *s.* pastelero, repostero.
pastry shop, pastelería, repostería.
past tense, (gram.) tiempo pasado.
pasturable ['pæstʃərəbəl, B 'pɑs-] *a.* pacedero.
pasturage [-ɪdʒ] *s.* 1. pastura, pasto, apacentadero, dehesa. 2. pastura, pasto, forraje. 3. pasto, apacentamiento. 4. (der. esco.) pasturaje (derecho).
pasture ['pæstʃər, B 'pɑstʃə] *s.* 1. pasto, apacentamiento. 2. pasto, pasturaje, apacentadero, dehesa. 3. pastura, pasto, forraje. —*v.i.* pacer (el animal). —*v.t.* pastar, apacentar, pastorear.
pasturer [-tʃərər, B -ə] *s.* pastor, apacentador.
pasty ['pæstɪ] *s.* 1. pastelillo, esp. de carne; empanada. 2. (teat.) cubrepezón decorativo. — ['peɪstɪ] *a.* (PASTIER; PASTIEST) 1. pastoso. 2. pálido, descolorido.
pat [pæt] *s.* 1. palmadita, golpecito, pasagonzalo. 2. ruido ligero (de golpecitos, pasos, etc.). 3. trocito, pedacito (de mantequilla, etc.). —*v.t.* (*pret., p.p.* PATTED; *p.pr.* PATTING) 1. golpear ligeramente, dar golpecitos a. 2. moldear o formar a golpecitos o palmaditas. 3. acariciar con palmaditas. 4. **p. (someone) on the back,** (fig.) felicitar, congratular. —*v.i.* andar o correr con pasitos ligeros. —*a.* 1. oportuno, apto; pintiparado, al pelo. 2. firme, fijo. 3. **to have (a lesson, etc.) p.,** saber al dedillo (la lección, etc.); **to stand p.,** mantenerse firme; (póquer) plantarse. —*adv.* prontamente, sin vacilar.
pat. *abrev. de* 1. **patent,** patente. 2. **patented,** patentado.
pat-a-cake ['pætəˌkeɪk] *s.* 1. verso inicial de una rima infantil. 2. juego infantil de palmaditas.
patagium [pə'teɪdʒɪəm, B ˌpætə'dʒaɪ-] *s.* (*pl.* PATAGIA [-ə]) (zool.) patagio.
Patagonian [ˌpætə'goʊnɪən] *s.* patagón, de Patagonia (Argentina y Chile). —*a.* patagón, patagónico.
patch [pætʃ] *s.* 1. parche (sobre el ojo, en una llanta, etc.); remiendo (en un pantalón, un cuadro, una pared pintada, etc.). 2. lunar artificial. 3. pedazo, trozo, fragmento, retazo, pedazo de tela; párrafo, pasaje. 4. pedazo de tierra; sembrado, mancha (conjunto de plantas en un área). 5. (med.) emplasto, parche. 6. (fam., dial.) tonto, necio, papanatas. 7. **to strike a bad p.,** atravesar un período de mala suerte. —*v.t.* 1. remendar, parchar. 2. (gen. con *together*) hacer o formar de pedazos. 3. (gen. con *up*) arreglar, componer; chapucear, frangollar, chafallar. 4. **p. it** (o **things**) **up,** hacer las paces.
patcher ['pætʃər, B -ə] *s.* remendón.
patchouli, patchouly ['pætʃəlɪ, pə'tʃu-, B 'pætʃʊ-] *s.* 1. (bot.) pachulí. 2. pachulí (perfume de esta planta).
patch pocket, bolsillo de parche o sobrepuesto.
patch test, (med.) prueba de emplasto (para determinar sensibilidad alérgica).
patchwork ['pætʃˌwɜrk, B -ˌwɜk] *s.* 1. obra de fragmentos o retacitos, ensaladilla. 2. centón (manta). 3. (fig.) baturrillo, mezela; centón (con ref. a obra lit.).
patchy ['pætʃɪ] *a.* 1. muy remendado; como de remiendos. 2. desigual, irregular.
pate [peɪt] *s.* (fam.) 1. coronilla, cabeza. 2. mollera, sesos.
pâté [pɑ'teɪ, B 'pɑteɪ] *s.* (fr.) pasta de carne o de hígado.
pâté de foie gras [-dəˌfwɑ'grɑ] pasta de hígado de ganso, paté (Amer.).
patella [pə'tɛlə] *s.* (*pl.* PATELLAE [-ˌi] O PATELLAS) 1. (anat.) rótula. 2. (zool.) patela.
patellar [-'tɛlər, B -ə] *a.* rotuliano, patelar.
patelliform [-'tɛləˌfɔrm, B -ˌfɔm] *a.* (zool.) pateliforme.
paten ['pætən] *s.* 1. (relig). patena (donde se pone la hostia durante la misa). 2. disco de metal.
patency ['pætənsɪ, B 'peɪt-] *s.* 1. evidencia. 2. (esp. med.) abertura, falta de obstrucción.
patent ['pætənt, B 'peɪt-] *a.* 1. patente, manifiesto, visible, obvio, evidente. 2. patentado, de marca registrada. 3. de patentes, ej., derecho, oficina, abogado, etc. 4. (fam.) ingenioso, bien hecho. 5. (bot., zool.) abierto, extendido. 6. (med.) abierto, no obstruído. 7. (hist.) patente (cédula); conferido por cédula patente. 8. (ant.) accesible. 9. **p. pending** (o **applied for**), patente pendiente, patente en trámite. —*s.* 1. patente (que concede un privilegio o derecho). 2. patente de invención, patente; privilegio de invención; propiedad industrial, objeto o procedimiento patentado. 3. derecho, privilegio, licencia. 4. documento de concesión de tierras; tierra bajo concesión. —*v.t.* 1. patentar. 2. privilegiar.
patentable [-əbəl] *a.* patentable.
patentee [ˌpætən'ti, B ˌpeɪt-] *s.* titular o concesionario de una patente.
patent law, derecho patentario, ley de patentes.
patent leather, charol, cuero barnizado.
patent log, (mar.) corredera en forma rotativa.
patently ['pætəntlɪ, B 'peɪt-] *adv.* patentemente, visiblemente, evidentemente.
patent medicine, medicamento de patente o patentado, específico.
Patent Office, oficina de patentes.
patentor ['pætəntər, B 'peɪtəntə] *s.* otorgante de la patente; dueño de la patente.
patent right, derecho de patente.

pater ['pɑˌtɛr, B 'peɪtə] *s.* 1. (relig.) *abrev. de* **Paternoster,** paternóster. 2. ['peɪtər, B -ə] (fam.) padre.
paterfamilias ['peɪtərfə'mɪlɪəs, B -əfə-æs] *s.* (*pl.* PATRESFAMILIAS ['peɪtrɪz-]) 1. (der. romano) paterfamilias, padre de familia. 2. jefe de la familia.
paternal [pə'tɜrnəl, B -'tɜn-] *a.* 1. paterno (lado, línea, derecho, etc.). 2. paternal (afecto, solicitud, etc.).
paternalism [-ˌɪzəm] *s.* paternalismo.
paternally [-ɪ] *adv.* paternalmente.
paternity [pə'tɜrnətɪ, B -'tɜnə-] *s.* 1. paternidad. 2. ascendencia o filiación paterna. 3. (fig.) paternidad (literaria).
paternoster ['pætərˌnɑstər, B -ə'nɔstə] *s.* 1. (relig.) padrenuestro, paternóster. 2. (fig.) hechizo, ensalmo. 3. undécima cuenta del rosario.
path [pæθ, B pɑθ] *s.* 1. senda, sendero; camino, pista. 2. ruta, curso, línea; trayectoria. 3. (fig.) senda (de la virtud, rectitud, etc.).
path. *abrev. de* 1. **pathological,** patológico. 2. **pathology,** patología.
pathetic [pə'θɛtɪk] **pathetical** [-ɪkəl] *a.* patético, conmovedor.
pathetically [-ɪkəlɪ] *adv.* patéticamente.
pathetic fallacy, falacia patética.
pathfinder ['pæθˌfaɪndər, B 'pɑθ-də] *s.* 1. descubridor, explorador; pionero. 2. (mil.) avión explorador (que marca la ruta de los bomberos).
pathless [-ləs] *a.* sin sendero o senda; desconocido, virgen (bosque, etc.).
pathogen ['pæθədʒən] *s.* (med.) agente patógeno.
pathogenesis [ˌpæθə'dʒɛnəsəs] *s.* (med.) patogénesis, patogenia.
pathogenetic [-dʒə'nɛtɪk] *a.* 1. (med.) patogénico. 2. patógeno.
pathogenic [-'dʒɛnɪk] *a.* (med.) 1. patogénico. 2. patógeno.
pathogenic bacteria, (biol.) bacterias patógenas.
pathogeny [pə'θɑdʒənɪ, B -'θɔ-] *s.* (med.) patogenia.
pathognomonic [pəˌθɑgnə'mɑnɪk, B -ˌθɔgnə'mɔn-] *a.* (med.) patognomónico.
pathol. *abrev. de* 1. **pathological,** patológico. 2. **Pathology,** patología.
pathological [ˌpæθə'lɑdʒɪkəl, B -'lɔdʒ-] **pathologic** [-ɪk] *a.* (med.) patológico; mórbido, morboso.
pathologically [-kəlɪ] *adv.* (med.) patológicamente.
pathologist [pə'θɑlədʒəst, B -'θɔl-] *s.* (med.) patólogo, médico patólogo.
pathology [-dʒɪ] *s.* (med.) patología.
pathos ['peɪθɑs, B -θɔs] *s.* pathos; expresión patética; (raro) padecimiento, aflicción.
pathway ['pæθˌweɪ, B 'pɑθ-] *s.* senda, sendero, vereda, camino.
patience ['peɪʃəns] *s.* 1. paciencia. 2. aguante; perseverancia. 3. (pr. G.B.) solitario (juego de naipes). 4. (ant.) indulgencia, conformidad, permiso. 5. **to be out of p. with,** estar enojado con, no aguantar más; **to have no p. with,** no poder aguantar, estar irritado por.
patient ['peɪʃənt] *a.* 1. paciente, indulgente, tolerante. 2. paciente; perseverante. 3. (con *of*) capaz de sufrir o aguantar; susceptible a. —*s.* paciente, enfermo.
patiently [-lɪ] *adv.* pacientemente.
patina ['pætənə] *s.* (*pl.* PATINAE [-ˌni]) (relig.) patena (plato litúrgico).
patina, *s.* pátina.
patine [pæ'tɪn, B pɑ-] *var. de* 1. **paten,** patena. 2. ['pætənə, pə'tinə, B 'pætənə] **patina,** pátina. —*v.t.* cubrir con pátina.
patinize ['pætəˌnaɪz] *v t.* (metal.) patinar.
patio ['pætɪoʊ, 'pɑt-] *s.* patio.
patisserie [pə'tɪsərɪ, B -'tis-] *s.* (fr.) pastelería francesa.
patois ['pætwɑ] *s.* (fr.) (*pl.* PATOIS) dialecto, patuá.
patriarch ['peɪtrɪˌɑrk, B -ˌɑk] *s.* 1. patriarca, anciano venerable. 2. (relig.) patriarca.
patriarchal [ˌpeɪtrɪ'ɑrkəl, B -'ɑkəl] *a.* patriarcal.
patriarchal cross, (relig.) cruz patriarcal, cruz arzobispal.
patriarchate ['peɪtrɪˌɑrkət, B -ˌɑkət] *s.* patriarcado.
patriarchy [-kɪ] *s.* patriarcado.
patrician [pə'trɪʃən] *a.* patricio; noble, aristocrático. —*s.* 1. (hist.) patricio. 2. patricio, aristócrata.
patriciate [-'trɪʃɪət] *s.* patriciado.
patricidal [ˌpætrə'saɪdəl] *a.* parricida.
patricide ['pætrəˌsaɪd] *s.* 1. parricidio. 2. parricida.
patrilineal [ˌpætrə'lɪnɪəl] *a.* patrilineal, de o por línea paterna.
patrimonial [-'moʊnɪəl] *a.* patrimonial.
patrimony ['pætrəˌmoʊnɪ, B -mənɪ] *s.* patrimonio.
patriot ['peɪtrɪət, -ˌɑt, B -ət] *s.* patriota.
patriotic [ˌpeɪtrɪ'ɑtɪk, B ˌpætrɪ'ɔt-] *a.* patriótico.
patriotically [-ɪkəlɪ] *adv.* patrióticamente.
patriotism ['peɪtrɪəˌtɪzəm, B 'pæ-] *s.* patriotismo, amor a la patria.
Patriots' Day, (E.U.) Día del Patriota (el 19 de abril, feriado en Massachusetts y Maine en conmemoración de las batallas de Lexington y Concord de la Guerra de Independencia).
patristic [pə'trɪstɪk] **patristical** [-tɪkəl] *a.* patrístico.
patristics [-tɪks] *s.* patrística.
patrol [pə'troʊl] *v.i.* (*pret., p.p.* PATROLLED; *p.pr.* PATROLLING) patrullar, rondar. —*v.t.* rondar, vigilar (las calles, la ciudad, etc.). —*s.* 1. ronda. 2. patrulla. 3. patrulla de exploradores.
patrol boat, bote patrullero.
patrol car, carro patrullero; perseguidora (Cuba).
patrol leader, jefe de patrulla, cabo de ronda.
patroller [-ər, B -ə] *s.* rondador, vigilante; miembro de una patrulla.
patrolman [-mən, B -mæn] *s.* policía, oficial o agente de policía, guardia, agente de seguridad, patrullero.
patrol wagon, (E.U.) coche o carro celular.
patron ['peɪtrən] *s.* 1. defensor, protector, amparador. 2. patrocinador, mecenas; benefactor. 3. patrón, dueño. 4. cliente, parroquiano. 5. (G.B.) patrono (que tiene derecho de presentación para beneficios eclesiásticos). 6. (der. romano) patrono (antiguo amo de un liberto). 7. (relig.) patrón, santo titular.
patronage [-ɪdʒ, B 'pætrən-] *s.* 1. patrocinio, auspicio, padrinazgo. 2. condescendencia, aire protector. 3. clientela, parroquianos. 4. (relig.) patronato, patronazgo. 5. influencia política; prebendas o favores políticos.
patronal [-əl, B pə'troʊn-] *a.* patronal.
patroness ['peɪtrənəs] *s.* patrocinadora; protectora; patrona, santa titular.
patronize ['peɪtrəˌnaɪz, B 'pæ-] *v.t.* 1. patrocinar, proteger; favorecer, amparar, ayudar. 2. tratar con aire condescendiente o protector. 3. frecuentar; ser parroquiano o cliente de; soler comprar en (una tienda, etc.).
patronizer [-ər, B -ə] *s.* 1. patrocinador. 2. frecuentador; cliente.
patronizingly [-ɪŋlɪ] *adv.* con aires de superioridad, con aire condescendiente o protector.
patron saint, (relig.) patrón, santo titular.
patronymic [ˌpætrə'nɪmɪk] *a.* patronímico. —*s.* (nombre) patronímico.
patroon [pə'trun] *s.* 1. (hist. E.U.) encomendero holandés. 2. (ant.) protector.
patsy ['pætsɪ] *s.* (E.U.), (jer.) cabeza de turco, chivo expiatorio, primo, bobo.
pattée [pə'teɪ, B pæ-] *a.* (her.) paté (díc. de la cruz cuyos extremos se ensanchan un poco).
patten ['pætən] *s.* zueco, chanclo, galocha, almadreña.
patter ['pætər, B -ə] *v.t., v.i.* musitar rápida y mecánicamente las oraciones o preces; murmurar, susurrar; charlar, parlar, parlotear. —*s.* 1. jerga (esp. de vagabundos y hampones). 2. lenguaje, habla, jerga (de médicos, abogados, etc.). 3. parloteo, palique, plática.
patter, *v.i.* 1. golpetear. 2. correr con pisadas ligeras. —*s.* golpeteo (de pisadas ligeras); chapaleteo (de las gotas de lluvia).
patterer [-ərər, B -ə] *s.* parlanchín.
pattern ['pætərn, B -ən] *s.* 1. modelo, ejemplo, dechado; norma, pauta. 2. diseño, dibujo; forma, contorno; figura o motivo (decorativo); configuración. 3. (E.U.) corte de tela. 4. (cost.) molde, patrón. 5. (metal.) molde de vaciado, modelo. 6. (arm.) rosa de dispersión de impacto, dispersión. 7. (ant.) semejanza, copia. —*v.t.* 1. (gen. con *after, on* o *upon*) modelar (según, conforme a), ajustar al molde (de). 2. decorar, adornar con diseños. 3. (dial.) imitar; compararse con.
patternmaker [-ˌmeɪkər, B -kə] *s.* carpintero modelador, modelista; plantillero.
patty ['pætɪ] *s.* (*pl.* PATTIES) 1. (cocina) pastelillo, empanada, fajardo. 2. fritura de carne o pescado. 3. **meat p.,** hamburguesa.
patty pan, molde para pastelillos, empanadas o fajardos.
patty shell, masa (para pastelillos, fajardos, etc.).
patulous ['pætʃələs] *a.* (bot.) pátulo, patente, extendido, abierto.
PAU *abrev. de* **Pan American Union,** Unión Panamericana.
paucity ['pɔsətɪ] *s.* corto número, pequeño número; insuficiencia; escasez, carestía.
paughty ['pɔtɪ] *a* (Esco., N. de Ingl.) arrogante; atrevido; picante, gracioso.
pauldron ['pɔldrən] *s.* (arm.) hombrera.
Paulianist ['pɔlɪənəst] *s.* (relig.) paulianista.
Paulician [pɔ'lɪʃən] *s.* (relig.) pauliciano.
Pauline ['pɔlɪn, B -laɪn] *a.* (relig.) paulino.
Paulist ['pɔləst] *a., s.* paulista.
paulownia [pɔ'loʊnɪə] *s.* (bot.) paulonia.
paunch [pɔntʃ] *s.* panza, barriga, vientre.
paunchy ['pɔntʃɪ] *a.* (PAUNCHIER; PAUNCHIEST) panzudo, panzón, barrigón. barrigudo.
pauper ['pɔpər, B -pə] *s.* mendigo, pobre, indigente. —*a.* pobre, paupérrimo.
pauperism [-pəˌrɪzəm] *s.* pauperismo, indigencia, mendicidad.
pauperization [ˌpɔpərə'zeɪʃən, B -raɪ-] *s.* pauperización.
pauperize ['pɔpəˌraɪz] *v.t.* depauperar, empobrecer.
pause [pɔz] *s.* 1. pausa, espera, intervalo, descanso. 2. vacilación, irresolución. 3. (gram., mús.) pausa. 4. (poét.) pausa, cesura, corte (en un verso). 5. **to give (someone) p.,** hacer vacilar (a alguien). —*v.i* 1. pausar, cesar. 2. detenerse, vacilar. 3. demorarse, espaciarse.
pavan ['pævən] **pavane** [pə'vɑn, B -'væn] *s.* pavana, antiguas danza y música cortesanas de origen español.

pave [peɪv] *v.t.* pavimentar, solar; **p. the way,** (fig.) preparar el camino o el terreno, superar dificultades iniciales.

pavé [pɑ'veɪ, B 'pæveɪ] *s.* (fr., joy.) engaste invisible.

pavement ['peɪvmənt] *s.* 1. pavimento, pavimentación. 2. (G.B.) acera.

paver [-ər, B -ə] *s.* pavimentador.

pavid ['pævəd] *a.* (raro) pávido, tímido, temeroso.

pavilion [pə'vɪljən] *s.* 1. pabellón, tienda de campaña, dosel. 2. (joy.) pabellón. 3. (anat.) pabellón (de la oreja). 4. (arq.) pabellón, cenador, glorieta; ala (de un edificio). —*v.t.* proveer o cubrir con un pabellón o pabellones.

pavin ['pævən] *var. de* **pavan.**

paving ['peɪvɪŋ] *s.* 1. pavimento; material para pavimentar. 2. pavimentación.

paving roller, (maq.) aplanadora, apisonadora, cilindro aplanador.

pavior, paviour ['peɪvjər, B -jə] *s.* pavimentador.

pavis ['pævəs] *s.* pavés.

pavonine ['pævəˌnaɪn] *s.* 1. multicolor, iridiscente. 2. relativo al pavo real.

paw [pɔ] *s.* 1. garra, zarpa, pata. 2. (fam.) mano, manota. 3. (fam.) papá, padre. —*v.t.* 1. manosear, sobar. 2. escarbar (la tierra un caballo). —*v.i.* 1. piafar. 2. **p. at,** tocar con la pata, (fig.) manosear, toquetear.

pawky ['pɔkɪ] *a.* (PAWKIER; PAWKIEST) 1. (pr. G.B.) astuto, artero, ladino. 2. (dial.) descarado, desenvuelto.

pawl [pɔl] *s.* 1. (mec.) trinquete. 2. (mar.) linguete.

pawn [pɔn] *s.* 1. (ajedrez) peón. 2. (fig.) instrumento. 3. empeño, pignoración. 4. prenda, rehén. 5. garantía, arras, señal. 6. **in** o **at p.,** en prenda. —*v.t.* 1. empeñar, pignorar, prendar. 2. aventurar, arriesgar; comprometer.

pawnage ['pɔnɪdʒ] *s.* empeño, pignoración.

pawnbroker ['pɔnˌbroʊkər, B -kə] *s.* prestamista, dueño de una casa de empeños.

Pawnee [pɔ'ni] *a., s.* (E.U.) pauni, tribu y lenguaje de los indios Algonquinos.

pawner, pawnor ['pɔnər, B -nə] *s.* (der.) afianzador, garantizador.

pawnshop ['pɔnˌʃɑp, B -ˌʃɔp] *s.* casa de empeños, monte de piedad, prendería, montepío.

pawn ticket, papeleta de empeño, papeleta de la casa de empeños.

pawpaw [pə'pɔ, 'pɔpɔ] *s.* (bot.) papaya, papayo, fruta bomba (Cuba).

pax [pæks] *s.* (relig.) paz (ceremonia o reliquia).

Pax Americana [-əˌmɛrə'kænə, B -'kɑnə] (hist.) (E.U.) paz americana (paz impuesta por razones económicas y políticas).

Pax Romana [-roʊ'mɑnɑ] 1. (hist.) paz romana (paz impuesta por los romanos en sus dominios y provincias). 2. (fig.) cualquier paz impuesta por una nación conquistadora al país o pueblo subyugado.

paxwax ['pæksˌwæks] *s.* (dial.) ligamento nucal (de los cuadrúpedos).

pay [peɪ] *v.t.* (*pret., p.p.* PAID [peɪd]; *p.pr.* PAYING) 1. pagar, remunerar; cancelar, saldar. 2. rendir, dar (provecho, utilidad). 3. rendir, prestar, ej., *p. homage to,* rendir homenaje a, *p. attention,* prestar atención. 4. hacer, ej., *p. a visit,* hacer una visita, visitar, *p. court,* cortejar, hacer la corte. 5. **p. as you go,** pagar los gastos según vayan surgiendo; **p. back,** devolver, reembolsar (cantidad); devolver el dinero a, pagar la deuda a (persona); pagar en la misma moneda; **p. (someone) back for (something),** (fig.) vengarse de (alguien) por (algo); **p. in installments,** pagar a plazos; **p. cash,** pagar al contado; **p. down,** pagar a cuenta; **p. expenses,** cubrir gastos; **p. in full,** pagar totalmente; **p. off,** pagar y despedir (a un empleado.); compensar; (mar.) filar, arriar (cabo, cable); **p. on account,** pagar a cuenta; **p. one's way,** costear (uno) sus propios gastos; **p. out,** desembolsar; (mar.) filar, arriar (cable, cabo); **p. (someone) out,** darle (a uno) su merecido; **p. the piper,** pagar por lo bailado; **p. through the nose,** pagar un dineral; **p. up,** pagar, cancelar íntegramente (deudas, cuentas, etc.). —*v.i.* 1. pagar, hacer el pago. 2. dar utilidades. 3. merecer el desembolso o el esfuerzo. 4. **p. for it,** (fig.) pagarla, pagarlas; **p. off,** (mar.) inclinarse (barco) a sotavento; (fam.) dar resultado, resultar; **p. up,** pagar una deuda (esp. después de larga demora, bajo amenaza, etc.). —*s.* 1. paga, pagamento, pago. 2. retribución. 3. salario, sueldo; honorarios; comisión. 4. pagador (bueno, malo, etc.). 5. **in the p. of,** a sueldo de, al servicio de. —*a.* 1. provechoso, de lucro. 2. de pago, de paga.

pay, *v.t.* (*pret., p.p.* PAYED; *p.pr.* PAYING) embrear, impermeabilizar (una superficie).

payable ['peɪəbəl] *a.* 1. pagadero; pagable. 2. ganancioso, lucrativo. 2. (ten.) por pagar; vencido.

pay bill, vale, póliza.

pay clerk, pagador.

payday ['peɪˌdeɪ] *s.* día de pago.

pay dirt, 1. (jer.) éxito, hallazgo, filón, ganga. 2. (min.) tierra, mineral o grava con rico contenido de oro. 3. **to strike p.d.,** (fig.) encontrar una mina de oro.

payee [peɪ'i] *s.* portador, tenedor; beneficiario.

payer ['peɪər, B -ə] *s.* pagador (esp. de un cheque, letra de cambio, etc.).

payload [-ˌloʊd] *s.* 1. carga útil. 2. (mil.) carga explosiva (en la cabeza de un cohete). 3. (aer.) pasaje o carga aérea. 4. (astronáut.) tripulación y equipo de un cohete interespacial o de un satélite artificial.

paymaster [-ˌmæstər, B -ˌmɑstə] *s.* pagador, cajero; tesorero.

paymaster's office, contaduría del ejército.

payment ['peɪmənt] *s.* 1. pago, pagamento. 2. paga, sueldo. 3. retribución; castigo; corrección.

paynim ['peɪnəm] *s.* 1. (ant.) pagano; país pagano; infiel, esp. mahometano. 2. el mundo pagano.

payoff ['peɪˌɔf] (fam.) *s.* 1. día de pago; pago. 2. utilidad, rédito; recompensa, retribución. 3. resultado final, desenlace (esp. de una narración). 4. factor decisivo. 5. (com.) ajuste de cuentas, liquidación. 6. (jer.) soborno, coima, mordida. —*a.* 1. decisivo. 2. remunerador.

payola [peɪ'oʊlə] *s.* (jer.) coima, cohecho, soborno.

payroll ['peɪˌroʊl] *s.* 1. nómina de pago, planilla de pagos (Amer.) 2. dinero para pago de sueldos y jornales.

pay station, teléfono público.

pay telephone, teléfono público.

Pb *símb. de* lead, plomo (Pb).

PBX, P.B.X. *abrev. de* **private branch exchange,** intercambio privado de sucursales (sistema de central telefónica que se intercomunica con anexos fuera del local donde funciona).

P.C. *abrev. de* 1. (G.B.) **Police Constable,** guardia, policía. 2. (G.B.) **Privy Council,** Consejo del Rey.

pct. *abrev. de* **percent,** por ciento.

pd. *abrev. de* **paid,** pagado.

Pd símb. de **palladium,** paladio (Pd).

P.D.Q. [ˌpiˌdi'kju] *adv.* (*abrev. de* **pretty damn quick**) sobre la marcha, en un dos por tres.

pea [pi] *s.* (*pl.* PEAS O PEASE [piz]) 1. (bot.) guisante, arveja, alverja (planta y semilla). 2. **as like as two peas,** parecidos como dos gotas de agua.

pea bean, (bot.) aluvia o judía pequeña.

peace [pis] *s.* 1. paz; pacto o tratado de paz. 2. paz, tranquilidad, calma; concordia, armonía. 3. **at p.,** en paz; **to hold one's p.,** guardar silencio; **to keep the p.,** mantener la paz, guardar el orden; **to make p.,** hacer las paces; **p. be with you,** la paz sea con vosotros; **p. at any price** paz a toda costa. —*interj.* ¡paz! ¡silencio!

peaceable ['pisəbəl] *a.* pacífico, apacible.

peaceableness [-nəs] *s.* carácter pacífico, apacibilidad.

peaceably [-blɪ] *adv.* pacíficamente.

Peace Corps, (E.U.) Cuerpo de Paz (organización de voluntarios para trabajar en los países subdesarrollados).

peaceful ['pisfəl] *a.* 1. apacible, pacífico. 2. sereno, sosegado, tranquilo.

peaceful coexistence, (pol.) coexistencia pacífica.

peacefully [-fəlɪ] *adv.* 1. apaciblemente, pacíficamente. 2. serenamente, sosegadadamente, tranquilamente.

peacefulness [-fəlnəs] *s.* serenidad, sosiego, tranquilidad, quietud.

peacemaker ['pisˌmeɪkər, B -kə] *s.* pacificador, conciliador, apaciguador.

peacemaking [-kɪŋ] *s.* pacificación, conciliación. —*a.* pacificador, apaciguador.

peace offering, (relig.) oferta de paz; sacrificio propiciatorio.

peace officer, agente del orden público; guardia, policía.

peace pipe, (E.U.) pipa de la paz (símbolo de acuerdo o capitulación de los jefes indios).

peacetime [-ˌtaɪm] *a.* de tiempo de paz; relativo a un período de paz. —*s.* tiempo de paz.

peach [pitʃ] *s.* 1. (bot.) melocotonero, duraznero, pérsico (árbol). 2. melocotón, durazno, pérsico (fruto). 3. (jer.) mujer guapa. 4. color del melocotón. —*a.* (de color) melocotón. —*v.t.* (jer.) soplar, delatar, traicionar. —*v.i.* (jer.) dar información; **p. on,** delatar, traicionar.

peachblow ['pitʃˌbloʊ] *s.* vidriado del color de la flor del melocotonero (apl. a la porcelana china de ese color).

peach tree, (bot.) melocotonero, duraznero, pérsico.

peachy ['pitʃɪ] *a.* (PEACHIER; PEACHIEST) 1. aterciopelado, velloso (superficie). 2. (fig.) delicado, de textura fina (tez, mejillas, etc.). 3. (fam.) excelente, perfecto.

peacock ['piˌkɑk, B -ˌkɔk] *s.* (orn.) pavo real, pavo ruán, pavón. —*v.i.* pavonearse, contonearse.

peacock blue, verde azulado opaco, azul pavo real.

peacockish [-ɪʃ] **peacocky** [-ɪ] *a.* pinturero.

peafowl [-ˌfaʊl] *s.* (orn.) pavo real; pavo real africano.

peag, peage [pig] *s.* cuentas de concha (usadas como monedas u ornamentos por los indios).

pea green, verde claro, verde guisante.

pea-green['pi'grin] *a.* (de color) verde claro.

peahead, pea-head ['piˌhɛd] *s.* (jer.) tonto, zopenco.

peahen [-ˌhɛn] *s.* (orn.) hembra del pavo real.

pea jacket, chaquetón de marinero.

peak [pik] *s.* 1. pico, promontorio; cima, cumbre; picacho. 2. visera (de gorra). 3. máximo, cumbre, tope, punto culminante. 4. (mar.) puño de la boca (en velas a cuchillo). 5. (mar.) delgado, racel, rasel. —*v.t.* 1. encumbrar, hacer culminar.

2. (mar.) embicar (verga). —*v.i.* 1. alcanzar el máximo, llegar al tope. 2. consumirse, demacrarse. —*a.* máximo; (elec.) de cresta.

peak current, (elec.) intensidad máxima de corriente.

peaked [pikt] *a.* 1. puntiagudo; picoteado, que tiene picos. 2. (fam.) consumido, emaciado, demacrado.

peak factor, (elec.) factor de amplitud.

peak hours, horas de tráfico máximo.

peak load, (elec.) carga máxima.

peak power output, (elec., rad., electrón.) potencia de salida de cresta.

peal [pil] *s.* 1. repiqueteo, repique (de campanas), carillón. 2. fragor, estruendo. —*v.i.* repiquetear, repicar; resonar, retumbar. —*v.t.* tañer, repiquetear.

peal of laughter, risotada, carcajada.

pean, *var. de* **paean.**

peanut ['piˌnʌt] *s.* 1. (bot.) cacahuete, cacahuate, maní. 2. (jer.) cosa insignificante, bagatela. 3. (*pl.*) poco dinero; nada. —*a.* mezquino, insignificante.

peanut brittle, turrón, crocante de maní.

peanut butter, mantequilla de maní, manteca de maní.

peanut gallery, (jer.) gallinero, paraíso (de teatro, etc.).

peanut oil, aceite de maní.

pear [pɛr, B pɛə] *s.* 1. pera. 2. (bot.) peral.

pearl [pɜrl, B pɜl] *s.* 1. perla, aljófar. 2. (fig.) perla. 3. madreperla, nácar. 4. (impr.) perla (tipo de 5 puntos). 5. **to cast pearls before swine,** echar margaritas a los puercos. —*v.t.* 1. perlificar, aljofarar, cubrir o adornar con perlas. 2. formar en perlas. 3. anacarar. —*v.i.* 1. formarse en perlas. 2. pescar perlas. —*a.* 1. perlero. 2. perlado, perlino.

pearl, *var. de* **purl.**

pearl ash, carbonato de potasio.

pearl barley, (bot.) cebada perlada.

pearl-colored ['pɜrlˌkʌlərd, B 'pɜl-əd] *a.* perlino.

pearl diver, p. fisher, pescador de perlas.

pearl fishery, pesca de perlas; banco de perlas.

pearl-gray ['pɜrlˌgreɪ, B 'pɜl-] *a.* gris perla, perlino.

pearlite [-ˌaɪt] *s.* (metal., geol.) perlita.

pearlitic [ˌpɜr'lɪtɪk, B ˌpɜ'-] *a.* (geol.) perlítico.

pearlized ['pɜrlˌaɪzd, B 'pɜl-] *a.* nacarado.

pearl oyster, (zool.) madreperla, ostra perlera o perlífera (Amer.).

pearl shell, madreperla, concha de perla, conchaperla (Amer.).

pearly ['pɜrlɪ, B 'pɜlɪ] *a.* 1. perlino, nacarado, nacarino, nacáreo. 2. perlero. 3. perlificado, perlado. 4. (fig.) precioso, exquisito.

pearly gates, (fig.) el cielo, las puertas del cielo.

pearly nautilus, (zool.) nautilo.

pearmain ['pɛrmeɪn, B 'pɜmeɪn] *s.* especie de manzana.

pear-shaped ['pɛrˌʃeɪpt, B 'pɛə,-] *a.* 1. piriforme. 2. suave, dulce, sonoro (voz, tono, etc.).

peart [pɪrt, B pɪət] *a.* (dial.) *var. de* **pert.**

pear tree, (bot.) peral.

peasant ['pɛzənt] *s.* 1. campesino, labriego. 2. (fig.) palurdo, patán.

peasantry [-əntrɪ] *s.* paisanaje, campesinado (Amer.).

pease [piz] *s.* (*pl.* PEASES O PEASEN ['pizən]) 1. (ant.) guisante. 2. *pl. de* **pea.**

peasecod, peascod ['pizˌkɑd, B -ˌkɔd] *s.* vaina del guisante, vaina de la arveja o alverja (Amer.).

peashooter ['piˌʃutər, B -ə] *s.* 1. bodoquera. 2. (jer.) fusil; revólver.

pea soup, 1. sopa o puré de arvejas secas. 2. (jer.) niebla espesa.

peat [pit] *s.* (agric.) turba.

peat bog, (agric.) turbal, turbera.

peat moss, 1. musgo de pantano. 2. turba, turbera.

peat tar, alquitrán de turba.

peaty ['pitɪ] *a.* (agric.) turboso, de turba.

peavey, peavy ['pivɪ] *s.* (*pl.* PEAVEYS O PEAVIES) garfio, pica o palanca de gancho (ú. en la industria forestal).

pebble ['pɛbəl] *s.* 1. guija, guijarro, canto rodado. 2. cristal de roca; lente de cristal de roca. 3. cuero abollonado. —*v.t.* 1. pavimentar con guijas. 2. arrojar guijas a. 3. granular, abollonar, agranelar (cuero). 4. **p. on the beach,** (coll.) persona que se cree única en el mundo, ej., *you aren't the only pebble on the beach,* tú no eres único en el mundo.

pebbly ['pɛblɪ] *a.* (PEBBLIER; PEBBLIEST) guijoso, guijarroso.

pecan [pɪ'kɑn, -'kæn, B -'kæn] *s.* 1. (bot.) pacana, nogal pacanero. 2. pacana, nuez lisa.

peccable ['pɛkəbəl] *a.* capaz de pecar, pecable; susceptible de caer en tentación.

peccadillo [ˌpɛkə'dɪloʊ] *s.* (*pl.* PECCADILLOES O PECCADILLOS) pecadillo, falta leve.

peccancy ['pɛkənsɪ] *s.* corrupción; vicio.

peccant [-ənt] *a.* 1. pecador, pecante. 2. corrompido, vicioso. 3. (med.) morboso, malsano, mórbido.

peccary ['pɛkərɪ] *s.* (zool.) pecarí, pécari, saíno, sajino.

peccavi [pɛ'kɑwɪ, B -vi] *s.* (relig.) confesión; **to cry p.,** confesar (haber pecado).

peck [pɛk] *v.t.* 1. picar, picotear; punzar. 2. (gen. con. *up*) recoger con el pico. 3. (fam.) besar a la ligera o apresuradamente. 4. **p. holes in,** horadar a picotazos; **p. out,** arrancar, sacar (con el pico); mordisquear. —*v.i.* 1. picar, picotear. 2. **p. at,** rezongar, regañar; (fam.) comiscar, picar, picotear. —*s.* 1. picotazo, picotada. 2. (fam.) beso ligero o apresurado. 3. picadura. 4. medida de áridos (equivalente a nueve litros); celemín. 5. (fam.) sinnúmero, montón, esp. en **a p. of troubles,** un montón de dificultades, la mar de disgustos.

pecker ['pɛkər, B -ə] *s.* 1. picoteador. 2. zapapico. 3. (fam.) rezongador. 4. persona que come melindrosamente. 5. (jer., vulg.) pájaro (pene). 6. (jer., G.B.) coraje, ánimo.

peckerwood [-ˌwʊd] *s.* 1. (orn.) pájaro carpintero. 2. (jer., E.U.) blanco pobre que vive entre negros.

pecking order [-ɪŋ-] 1. (biol.) orden en que picotean las gallinas. 2. (fig.) jerarquía (social).

Pecksniffian [pɛk'snɪfɪən] *a.* santurrón, mojigato, beato.

pectase ['pɛkteɪs] *s.* (bioquím.) pectasa.

pectate [-ˌteɪt] *s.* (quím.) pectato.

pecten ['pɛktən, B -tɛn] *s.* (zool.) pecten, peine.

pectic ['pɛktɪk] *a.* (quím.) péctico.

pectic acid, (quím.) ácido péctico.

pectin ['pɛktən] *s.* (bioquím.) pectina.

pectinate ['pɛktəˌneɪt, B -nɪt] **pectinated** [-ˌneɪtəd] *a.* (zool., anat.) pectinado.

pectineal [pɛk'tɪnɪəl] *a.* (anat.) músculo pectíneo.

pectineus [-əs] *a.* (anat.) pectíneo.

pectiniform [pɛk'tɪnəˌfɔrm, B 'pɛktɪnɪˌ-fɔm] *a.* pectiniforme.

pectoral ['pɛktərəl] *a.* 1. (anat.) pectoral, del pecho. 2. pectoral, bueno para el pecho. 3. personal, subjetivo. —*s.* 1. pectoral (del sumo sacerdote hebreo). 2. (farm.) pectoral (medicina). 3. (anat.) músculo pectoral. 4. (arm.) peto. 5. adorno para el pecho.

pectoral cross, (relig.) pectoral (de obispos).

pectoral fin, (ict.) aleta pectoral.

pectoral girdle, (zool., anat.) arco pectoral.

pectoral sandpiper, (orn.) gallineta pectoral, gallineta de Guinea.

peculate ['pɛkjəˌleɪt] *v.i., v.t.* malversar, desfalcar.

peculation [ˌpɛkjə'leɪʃən] *s.* malversación; desfalco; peculado.

peculator ['pɛkjəˌleɪtər, B -ə] *s.* malversador; desfalcador; peculador.

peculiar [pɪ'kjuljər, B -jə] *a.* 1. peculiar, particular, característico. 2. especial, singular; excéntrico, raro, extraño. —*s.* 1. (G.B.) (hist.) iglesia o parroquia que no depende de la diócesis en cuya jurisdicción se encuentra. 2. (ant.) propiedad, privilegio o interés particular.

peculiarity [pɪˌkjulɪ'ærətɪ] *s.* 1. peculiaridad, particularidad. 2. singularidad, rasgo característico. 3. excentricidad.

peculiarize [pɪ'kjuljəˌraɪz] *v.t.* hacer peculiar o distintivo; individualizar.

peculiarly [-jərlɪ, B -jəlɪ] *adv.* 1. peculiarmente, particularmente. 2. excéntricamente, extrañamente, extravagantemente.

peculium [pɪ'kjulɪəm, B -'kjuljəm] *s.* (*pl.* PECULIA [-ə, B -jə]) (der.) peculio, hacienda, caudal.

pecuniarily [pɪˌkjunɪ'ɛrəlɪ, B -'kjunjər-] *adv.* pecuniariamente.

pecuniary [-'kjunɪˌɛrɪ, B -njərɪ] *a.* pecuniario, monetario.

pedagogic [ˌpɛdə'gɑdʒɪk, -'goʊdʒ-, B -'gɔdʒ-] **pedagogical** [-ɪkəl] *a.* pedagógico.

pedagogically [-ɪkəlɪ] *adv.* pedagógicamente.

pedagogics [-ɪks] *s.* pedagogía.

pedagogue, pedagog ['pɛdəˌgɑg, B -ˌgɔg] *s.* 1. pedagogo. 2. pedante, erudito pesado.

pedagogy [-ˌgɑdʒɪ, -ˌgoʊdʒɪ, B -'gɔdʒɪ] *s.* pedagogía.

pedal ['pɛdəl] *s.* pedal; (mús.) pedal. —*v.i.* (*pret., p.p.* PEDALED O PEDALLED; *p.pr.* PEDALING O PEDALLING) pedalear. —*v.t.* impulsar pedaleando. —*a.* 1. del pie o de los pies. 2. de pedal.

pedal brake, (mec.) freno de pie, freno de pedal.

pedaling, pedalling [-ɪŋ] *s.* pedaleo.

pedal keyboard, (mús.) teclado de pedales (del órgano).

pedal point, (mús.) nota de pedal.

pedal pushers, pantalones de mujer a media pierna, pantalones pescadores (Amer.).

pedant ['pɛdənt] *s.* 1. pedante. 2. (ant.) maestro de escuela.

pedantic [pə'dæntɪk] **pedantical** [-ɪkəl] *a.* pedante, pedantesco.

pedantically [-ɪkəlɪ] *adv.* pedantescamente.

pedantry ['pɛdəntrɪ] *s.* pedantería, pedantismo.

pedate ['pɛdˌeɪt, B -ət] *a.* 1. (zool.) pedato. 2. (bot.) palmeado.

peddle ['pɛdəl] *v.i.* 1. ser buhonero, vender menudencias por las calles. 2. emplearse en bagatelas, ocuparse en fruslerías. —*v.t.* 1. vender como buhonero, ir vendiendo (baratijas) de puerta en puerta, vender al menudeo. 2. ofrecer a todo el mundo, tratar de diseminar (ideas, etc.).

peddler ['pɛdlər, B -lə] *s.* buhonero, mercachifle, pacotillero.

peddlery [-lərɪ] *s.* 1. buhonería. 2. baratijas.

peddling [-lɪŋ] *a.* baladí, insignificante.

pederast ['pɛdəˌræst] *s.* pederasta.

pederasty [-ˌræstɪ] *s.* pederastia, pedofilia.

pedestal ['pɛdəstəl] *s.* 1. (arq.) pedestal, peana. 2. (fig.) pedestal. 3. **to set on a p.,** (fig.) colocar sobre un pedestal. —*v.t.* (*pret., p.p.* PEDESTALED

O PEDESTALLED; *p.pr.* PEDESTALING O PEDESTALLING) (lit y fig.) colocar sobre un pedestal; exaltar, enaltecer.
pedestal light, (aer.) luz de pedestal, luz de pie.
pedestal pile, (const.) pilote de pedestal, pilote de pie abultado.
pedestal table, velador (mesa).
pedestrian [pə'dɛstrɪən] *a.* 1. pedestre, a pie. 2. (fig.) pedestre, ordinario, prosaico. —*s.* 1. peatón. 2. (lit., poét.) caminante.
pedestrianism [-ˌɪzəm] *s.* pedestrismo.
pedestrian traffic, tráfico de peatones.
pediatric [ˌpidɪ'ætrɪk] *a.* (med.) pediátrico.
pediatrician [ˌpidɪə'trɪʃən] *s.* (med.) pediatra.
pediatrics [ˌpidɪ'ætrɪks] *s.* (med.) pediatría.
pediatrist [-trəst] *s.* (med.) pediatra, pedíatra.
pedicab ['pɛdɪˌkæb] *s.* taxi-triciclo (en el Oriente).
pedicel ['pɛdəsəl] *s.* (anat., zool., bot.) pedicelo, pedúnculo.
pedicellate [ˌpɛdə'sɛlət, B 'pɛdɪsə-] *a.* (bot., zool.) pedicelado, pedunculado.
pedicle ['pɛdɪkəl] *s.* 1. (bot., zool.) pedículo, pedicelo, pedúnculo. 2. (med.) pedículo.
pedicular [pɪ'dɪkjələr, B -lə] *a.* 1. (med.) pedicular. 2. (jer.) piojoso.
pediculate [-lət] *a., s.* (ict.) pediculado.
pediculosis [-ˌdɪkjə'loʊsəs] *s.* (med.) pediculosis.
pediculous [-'dɪkjələs] *a.* (med.) pediculoso.
pedicure ['pɛdɪˌkjʊr, B -ˌkjʊə] *s.* 1. pedicuro, callista, quiropodista. 2. quiropodia.
pedicurist [-əst, B -ˌkjʊər-] *s.* pedicuro, callista, quiropodista.
pedigree ['pɛdəˌgri] *s.* 1. pedigree, raza pura (díc. de animales). 2. genealogía, árbol genealógico. 3. linaje, ascendencia distinguida. —*v.t.* proveer de un pedigree.
pedigreed [-ˌgrid] *a.* de pedigree, de raza pura.
pediment ['pɛdəment] *s.* (arq.) frontón.
pedipalp ['pɛdɪˌpælp] *s.* (zool.) 1. pedipalpo. 2. pedipalpio.
pedlar, pedlary, *vars. de* **peddler, peddlery.**
pedogenesis [ˌpɛdə'dʒɛnəsəs] *s.* (geol.) pedogénesis.
pedology [pɪ'dɑlədʒɪ, B -'dɔl-] *s.* 1. pedología (ciencia del niño). 2. pedología, edafología.
pedometer [pɪ'dɑmətər, B -'dɔmɪtə] *s.* podómetro, pedómetro.
pedophile ['pɛdəfaɪl] *s.* pedófilo.
pedophilia ['pɛdə'fɪlɪə] *s.* pedofilia.
peduncle ['piˌdʌŋkəl, B pɪ'dʌŋkəl] *s.* (bot., zool., anat.) pedúnculo.
peduncled [-kəld] *a.* (bot., zool.) pedunculado.
peduncular [pɪ'dʌŋkjələr, B -lə] *a.* (bot., zool.) peduncular.
pedunculate [-lət] **pedunculated** [-ˌleɪtəd] *a.* (bot., zool.) pedunculado.
pee [pi] *s.* 1. (la letra) pe. 2. (vulg.) meada, orinada. —*v.i.* (vulg.) mear, orinar.
peek [pik] *v.i.* mirar a hurtadillas, atisbar, fisgar. —*s.* atisbo, atisbadura, mirada rápida y furtiva.
peekaboo ['pikəˌbu] *s.* juego que consiste en esconderse y aparecer luego súbitamente frente al niño. —*a.* (fam.) transparente (blusas, etc.).
peel [pil] *v.t.* 1. pelar, descortezar, descascarar, mondar. 2. (jer.) desnudar, desvestir. 3. **to keep one's eyes peeled,** estar ojo avizor, avivar uno los ojos. —*v.i.* 1. pelarse, desprenderse (piel, pintura, etc.). 2. (jer.) desnudarse, desvestirse. 3. **p. off,** pelarse, desprenderse; (aer.) salirse de la formación (avión de guerra) para atacar. —*s.* 1. cáscara, mondadura (de naranja, limón u otros frutos), pellejo, hollejo. 2. pala de horno (de panadería). 3. (impr.) espito, colgador.
peeler ['pilər, B -lə] *s.* 1. peladora (utensilio). 2. tronco para hoja de madera. 3. (jer.) bailarina que se desnuda, estriptisera (Amer.), desnudista, calatista (Perú).
peeling [-lɪŋ] *s.* mondadura, peladura (ej., de patatas), hollejo.
peen [pin] *s.* peña, boca (del martillo). —*v.t.* martillar, doblar o aplanar con (la peña del) martillo.
peenge [pindʒ] *v.i.* (Esco., N. de Ingl.) quejarse, lamentarse.
peen hammer, martillo de punta.
peep [pip] *v.i.* piar, pipiar. —*s.* pío, piada; **not a p. out of you,** no digas ni pío.
peep, *v.i.* 1. mirar a hurtadillas, mirar cautelosamente (por una rendija, etc.), atisbar. 2. (t. con *out* o *through*) asomarse, mostrarse, espuntar. —*s.* 1. atisbo, atisbadura, ojeada, mirada a hurtadillas. 2. asomo, despunte.
peeper ['pipər, B -ə] *s.* 1. pollito; pajarillo piador. 2. (zool.) rubeta, rana de zarzal.
peeper, *s.* 1. atisbador, fisgón. 2. (fam.) ojo. 3. (jer.) investigador o detective privado.
peephole [-ˌhoʊl] *s.* atisbadero, mirilla.
Peeping Tom [-ɪŋ-] persona lascivamente curiosa, voyerista, mirón.
peep show, 1. mundonuevo, tutilimundi. 2. (jer.) espectáculo con bailarinas semidesnudas.
peep sight, (arm.) alza de mirilla, mira dióptica.
peer [pɪr, B pɪə] *v.i.* 1. entornar los ojos, mirar con ojos de miope, mirar curiosamente. 2. despuntar. 3. (ant.) asomar, aparecer. 4. **p. at,** fijar la vista en, escudriñar; **p. into,** fijar la mirada en el interior de; escudriñar el interior de. —*s.* 1. par, igual; semejante. 2. (G.B.) par (título), noble. 3. (ant.) camarada, compañero, socio. —*v.t.* elevar a la dignidad de par.
peerage ['pɪrɪdʒ, B 'pɪər-] *s.* 1. cuerpo de pares; rango o dignidad de par. 2. guía de la nobleza o de los pares.
peeress [-əs] *s.* (G.B.) paresa (título); mujer noble; la esposa de un par.
peer group, grupo paritario.
peerless ['pɪrləs, B 'pɪəlɪs] *a.* sin par, incomparable, sin igual.
peerlessly [-lɪ] *adv.* incomparablemente.
peerlessness [-nəs] *s.* calidad de incomparable.
peetweet ['pitˌwit] *s.* (orn.) gallineta moteada.
peeve [piv] *v.t., v.i.* (fam.) irritar (se), poner(se) de mal humor, enojar(se). —*s.* 1. rencor, resentimiento. 2. queja, quejumbre.
peevish ['pivɪʃ] *a.* 1. irritable, quisquilloso. 2. malhumorado, de malas pulgas, de mal genio. 3. obstinado, terco.
peevishly [-lɪ] *adv.* 1. quisquillosamente. 2. malhumoradamente. 3. obstinadamente, tercamente.
peevishness [-nəs] *s.* 1. quisquillosidad. 2. malhumor, mal genio. 3. obstinación, terquedad.
peewee ['piˌwi] *s.* persona o cosa pequeña.
peewit, *var. de* **pewit.**
peg [pɛg] *s.* 1. clavija, espiga, sobina. 2. estaquilla; estaca, jalón. 3. gancho, colgador; (G.B.) pinzas de ropa. 4. púa o punta; gancho o garfio. 5. (fig.) escalón o grado (ej., en estimación o en la posición social, etc.); nivel (de precio, etc.). 6. (fig.) pretexto, excusa. 7. (G.B.) trago, traguito (de licor, etc.). 8. (fam.) pie, pierna; diente. 9. (mús.) clavija (de instrumentos de cuerda). 10. **off the p.,** hecha de confección (díc. de la ropa); **to look for a p. to hang (something) on,** buscar un pretexto para (algo); **to take (someone) down a p. or two,** bajarle los humos (a alguien. —*v.t.* (*pret., p.p.* PEGGED; *p.pr.* PEGGING) 1. estaquillar, enclavijar, asegurar con clavijas. 2. estacar, jalonar. 3. fijar, estabilizar (precios). 4. calar, clasificar; reconocer, identificar. 5. (G.B.) colgar (ropa) con pinzas. 6. **p. out,** jalonar, marcar con jalones (camino, terreno, etc.). —*v.i.* 1. (gen. con *away*) trabajar con ahínco, afanarse, bregar. 2. (en ciertos juegos) marcar puntos; (croquet) chocar la pelota con una de las estacas. 3. **p. out,** (jer., G.B.) estirar la pata, morir.
Pegasus ['pɛgəsəs] *s.* 1. (astr., mitol.) Pegaso, el caballo alado. 2. (fig.) inspiración poética, musa, numen.
pegboard ['pɛgˌbɔrd, B -ˌbɔd] *s.* 1. tablero perforado para anotar puntos de juego con estaquillas. 2. tablero para muestras o herramientas. 3. juego de estaquillas (ajedrez chino).
pegbox [-ˌbɑks, B -ˌbɔks] *s.* (mús.) clavijero.
pegged [pɛgd] *a.* fijo (precio, tipo de cambio, etc.).
peg leg, 1. pata de palo. 2. (fam.) el que la lleva.
pegmatite ['pɛgməˌtaɪt] *s.* (min.) pegmatita.
peg-tooth harrow ['pɛgˌtuθ-] grada de dientes.
peg top, 1. peón, peonza. 2. (*pl.*) pantalón tubo.
peg-top trousers [-ˌtɑp-, B -ˌtɔp-] pantalón tubo.
peignoir [peɪn'wɑr, pɛn-, B 'peɪnwɑ] *s.* peinador, bata de señora, salto de cama.
pein, *var. de* **peen.**
pejoration [ˌpidʒə'reɪʃən, B -dʒɔ-] *s.* desprecio; calidad de peyorativo; (gram.), degeneración semántica.
pejorative [pɪ'dʒɔrətɪv, -'dʒɑr-, B 'pidʒərət-] *a.* peyorativo, despectivo, despreciativo. —*s.* palabra despectiva.
pejoratively [-lɪ] *adv.* en sentido peyorativo, peyorativamente.
pekan ['pɛkən] *s.* (zool.) especie de marta de N.A.
pekin ['pi'kɪn, B pi'kɪn] *s.* pequín (tela de seda).
Pekinese [ˌpikə'niz] *var. de* **Pekingese.**
Peking ['pi'kɪŋ, B pi'kɪŋ] *s.* Pekín, Pequín, capital de la República Popular China.
Peking duck, (orn.) pato de raza pequinesa.
Pekingese [ˌpikə'niz, B -kɪŋ'iz] *a.* pekinés, pequinés. —*s.* (*pl.* PEKINGESE) 1. pekinés, pequinés (habitante y dialecto). 2. (zool.) (perro) pekinés, pequinés.
pekoe ['pikoʊ] *s.* variedad fina de té negro.
pelage ['pɛlɪdʒ] *s.* pelaje (de un animal).
Pelagian [pə'leɪdʒɪən] *a., s.* (relig.) pelagiano.
Pelagianism [-ˌɪzəm] *s.* (relig.) pelagianismo.
pelagic [pə'lædʒɪk] *a.* pelágico, del piélago; oceánico.
pelargonic [ˌpɛlar'gɑnɪk, B -lə'gɔn-] *a.* (quím.) pelargónico.
pelargonium [-'goʊnɪəm] *s.* (bot.) pelargonio.
Pelasgian [pə'læzdʒɪən, B pɛ'læzgɪ-] *a., s.* (hist.) pelasgo, habitante prehistórico (Grecia, Asia menor).
Pelasgian [-dʒɪk, B -gɪk] *a.* (hist.) pelásgico, de los pelasgos.
pelerine [ˌpɛlə'rin, B 'pɛlərin] *s.* pelerina, esclavina.
pelf [pɛlf] *s.* (despec.) dinero, lucro, riquezas mal adquiridas.
pelican ['pɛlɪkən] *s.* 1. (orn.) pelícano, alcatraz. 2. (odont.) botador.
pelisse [pə'lis, B pɛ-] *s.* pelliza, pellón, pellote.
pellagra [pə'lægrə] *s.* (med.) pelagra.
pellagrin [-rən] *s.* (med.) pelagroso.
pellagrous [-rəs] **pellagrose** [-ˌroʊs] *a.* (med.) pelagroso.
pellet ['pɛlət] *s.* 1. pelotilla, pella; píldora. 2. bodoque o proyectil (gen. de piedra); bala; perdigón; bolita de papel (usada como proyectil). —*v.t.* 1. dar forma de pelotilla o bolita a. 2. tirar bolitas a.
pellicle ['pɛlɪkəl] *s.* película, piel delgada, telilla.

pellicular [pə'lɪkjələr, B -lə] *a.* pelicular.
pellitory ['pɛlə,tɔrɪ, B -tərɪ] *s.* (bot.) 1. (t. **wall p.**) parietaria, albahaquilla de río. 2. (t. **p. of Spain**) pelitre. 3. matricaria; milenrama.
pell-mell, pellmell ['pɛl'mɛl] *adv.* confusamente, desordenadamente, a trochemoche; vehementemente, atropelladamente. —*a.* confuso, tumultuoso; vehemente, atropellado. —*s.* batahola, rebujiña, pelotera (Amer.).
pellucid [pə'lusəd, B pɛ'lju-] *a.* 1. pelúcido, diáfano, transparente. 2. (fig.) claro, evidente, fácil de entender. 3. (bot.) pelúcido.
pellucidity [,pɛljʊ'sɪdətɪ, B -lju-] *s.* 1. diafanidad, transparencia. 2. (fig.) claridad.
pellucidly [pə'lusədlɪ, B pɛ'lju-] *adv.* 1. diáfanamente, de modo diáfano. 2. (fig.) claramente.
Peloponnesian [,pɛləpə'niʒən, B -ʃən] *a.* (hist.) peloponense, peloponesiaco, peloponesíaco. —*s.* peloponense.
Peloponnesian War, (hist.) guerra del Peloponeso.
Peloponnesus [-səs] *s.* Peloponeso, península al S. de Grecia.
peloria [pə'lɔrɪə] *s.* (bot.) peloria.
peloric [-ɪk] *a.* (bot.) pelórico, pelorizado.
Pelorus [pə'lɔrəs] *s.* 1. (mitol.) Peloro, piloto capitán de Aníbal. 2. (mar.) alidada de reflexión.
pelota [pə'loʊtə] *s.* (dep.) pelota vasca, jai alai.
pelt [pɛlt] *v.t.* 1. tirar, lanzar, arrojar, despedir, disparar. 2. despellejar. 3. **p. (someone) with (stones, blows, insults,** etc.), granizar (piedras, golpes, insultos, etc.) sobre (alguien); aporrear (a alguien) con (preguntas, etc.). —*v.i.* 1. correr; precipitarse. 2. **p. at,** golpear repetidamente o con fuerza. —*s.* 1. caída persistente (de lluvia, granizo, etc.). 2. golpe. 3. **(at) full p.,** a toda velocidad. 4. piel, pellejo; pelleja, zalea. 5. (hum.) pellejo, piel (de una persona).
peltast ['pɛltæst] *s.* (hist.) peltastá, peltasta (yelmo griego).
peltate [-,teɪt] *a.* (bot.) peltado.
pelting ['pɛltɪŋ] *a.* (ant.) bajo, indigno; miserable, mezquino.
peltry ['pɛltrɪ] *s.* peletería, pellejería, corambre; piel, pellejo.
pelvic ['pɛlvɪk] *a.* (anat.) pelviano, pélvico.
pelvic arch, (anat.) arco pelviano.
pelvimeter [pɛl'vɪmətər, B -ə] *s.* pelvímetro.
pelvis ['pɛlvəs] *s.* (*pl.* PELVES [-,viz]) (anat., zool.) pelvis, bacinete.
pemmican, pemican ['pɛmɪkən] *s.* 1. pemicán, especie de tasajo de los indios de N.A. 2. conserva de carne seca (usada por exploradores, etc.).
pemphigus ['pɛmfɪgəs] *s.* (med.) pénfigo.
pen [pɛn] *s.* 1. corral, redil, encerradero. 2. depósito o almacén pequeño. 3. muelle o dique para submarinos. 4. (jer.) canasta, bote, chirona, prisión. 5. (orn.) hembra del cisne, cisne hembra. —*v.t.* (*pret., p.p.* PENNED; *p.pr.* PENNING) encerrar, acorralar.
pen, *s.* 1. pluma (de escribir). 2. (fig.) cálamo, pluma (estilo de escritor). 3. (fig.) pluma, escritor. 4. (zool.) gladio (del calamar). —*v.t.* (*pret., p.p.* PENNED; *p.pr.* PENNING) escribir, redactar, componer.
PEN *abrev. de* **International Association of Poets, Playwrights, Editors, Essayists and Novelists,** Asociación Internacional de Poetas, Dramaturgos, Redactores, Ensayistas y Novelistas.
penal ['pinəl] *a.* penal.
penal code, (der.) código penal.
penal colony, colonia penal.
penalization [,pinələ'zeɪʃən, B -laɪ-] *s.* penalización.
penalize ['pinə,laɪz] *v.t.* penar, penalizar, castigar, sancionar.
penal laws, (der.) leyes penales, código penal.
penal servitude, prisión con trabajo forzado.
penalty ['pɛnəltɪ] *s.* 1. pena, castigo, penalidad, sanción. 2. multa, pena pecuniaria. 3. (dep.) sanción (por alguna falta). 4. **under p. of,** bajo pena de; **the p. of,** la desventaja de (alguna cualidad, etc.).
penalty area, (dep.) área penal.
penalty box, 1. (dep.) área de castigo (*fútbol*). 2. banquillo (de castigo) (*hockey sobre hielo*).
penalty circle, (dep.) área de castigo (*hockey*).
penalty clause, (der.) cláusula penal.
penance ['pɛnəns] *s.* (relig.) penitencia; **to do p.,** cumplir la penitencia, hacer penitencia. —*v.t.* imponer penitencia a; castigar.
pen-and-ink ['pɛnən'ɪŋk] *a.* (dibujado) a pluma.
penates [pə'neɪtiz, B pɛ'nɑteɪs] *s., pl.* (mitol. romana) (hist.) penates, dioses domésticos.
pence [pɛns] *pl. de* **penny.**
pencel ['pɛnsəl] *s.* (ant.) banderola (llevada en la lanza).
penchant ['pɛntʃənt, B 'pɑŋʃɑŋ] *s.* propensión, inclinación, afición.
pencil ['pɛnsəl] *s.* 1. lápiz (de grafito, labial, etc.). 2. pincel o brocha finos. 3. (fig.) pincel (arte, modo o estilo de pintar). 4. (ópt.) haz (de luz, de rayos, etc.). 5. (med.) lápiz, barra o barrilla (de alguna substancia medicinal). —*v.t.* (*pret., p.p.* PENCILED O PENCILLED; *p.pr.* PENCILING O PENCILLING) lapizar, dibujar a lápiz; esbozar, bosquejar a lápiz; escribir o anotar a lápiz.
pencil box, pencil case ['pɛnsəl,keɪs] *s.* estuche para lápices.
penciling, pencilling [-ɪŋ] *s.* trazado o trabajo a lápiz.
pencil sharpener, afilalápices, cortalápices, sacapuntas.
pencilwood [-,wʊd] *s.* 1. (bot.) cedro de Bermuda. 2. mordoré (color).
pend [pɛnd] *v.i.* 1. (dial.) depender. 2. estar pendiente o por resolverse.
pendant, pendent ['pɛndənt] *s.* 1. pinjante, pendiente. 2. corona y aro (de un reloj de bolsillo). 3. pandán; complemento, pareja. 4. (arq.) pinjante, dovela o clave ornamental. 5. (joy.) pendiente, medallón. 6. (elec.) enchufe, portalámpara o conmutador colgante. 7. (mar.) gallardete, brazalete. —*a.* 1. suspendido, colgante, pendiente. 2. sobresaliente. 3. (fig.) en suspenso, pendiente.
pendency [-dənsɪ] *s.* suspensión; calidad de colgante o pendiente.
pendentive [pɛn'dɛntɪv] *s.* (arq.) pechina, enjuta; albanega.
pending ['pɛndɪŋ] *a.* 1. pendiente, indeciso. 2. inminente. 3. colgante. —*prep.* durante, mientras; hasta, ej., *p. his return,* hasta su regreso.
pendragon [pɛn'drægən] *s.* 1. jefe supremo. 2. rey de los antiguos británicos.
pendular ['pɛndʒələr, B -djʊlə] *a.* pendular.
pendulous [-ləs] *a.* péndulo, colgante, pendiente; oscilante.
pendulum [-ləm] *s.* (*pl.* PENDULUMS) péndulo, péndola.
Penelope [pə'nɛləpɪ] *s.* (mitol.) Penélope, esposa de Ulises.
peneplain, peneplane ['pinɪ,pleɪn] *s.* (geol.) penillanura, peniplanicie; tierra nivelada por la erosión.
penetrability [,pɛnətrə'bɪlətɪ] *s.* penetrabilidad.
penetrable ['pɛnətrəbəl] *a.* penetrable.
penetralia [,pɛnə'treɪlɪə] *s., pl.* 1. penetrales, habitaciones interiores (esp. de un palacio o templo). 2. partes retiradas o recónditas (de una cosa); secretos; misterios.
penetrant ['pɛnətrənt] *a.* penetrante; incisivo, agudo.
penetrate [-,treɪt] *v.t.* 1. penetrar, entrar, atravesar; traspasar. 2. penetrar, calar, difundirse en, propagarse a través de. 3. afectar, conturbar, conmover. 4. comprender, entender, profundizar. —*v.i.* (con *into, to, through*) penetrar (en), adentrar (se) (en), internar (se) (en).
penetrating [-ɪŋ] *a.* 1. penetrante, incisivo, agudo. 2. (fig.) penetrante, agudo, perspicaz.
penetration [,pɛnə'treɪʃən] *s.* 1. penetración. 2. (fig.) penetración, agudeza, perspicacia, sagacidad, discernimiento.
penetrative ['pɛnə,treɪtɪv, B -trətɪv] *a.* 1. penetrativo, penetrante. 2. (fig.) penetrante, agudo, sagaz.
penetratively [-lɪ] *adv.* penetrantemente, sagazmente, agudamente.
penetrometer [,pɛnə'trɑmətər, B -'trɔmɪtə] *s.* 1. penetrómetro, instrumento con que se mide la densidad de una substancia. 2. instrumento que mide la fuerza de penetración de los rayos X.
penguin ['pɛngwən, B 'pɛŋ-] *s.* (orn.) pingüino, pájaro bobo, pájaro niño.
penholder ['pɛn,hoʊldər, B -də] *s.* portaplumas, mango de pluma.
penicillate [,pɛnə'sɪlət, B 'pɛnɪ,sɪl-] *a.* (bot., zool.) en forma de lápiz; terminado en una punta afilada.
penicillin [,pɛnə'sɪlən] *s.* (farm., med.) penicilina.
penile ['pi,naɪl] *a.* relativo al pene.
peninsula [pə'nɪnsələ, B -sjʊ-] *s.* península.
peninsular [-lər, B -lə] *a.* peninsular; **Peninsular Wars,** las guerras de Napoleón contra España y Portugal.
penis ['pinəs] *s.* (*pl.* PENES ['pi,niz] O PENISES) (anat., zool.) pene, miembro viril.
penitence ['pɛnətəns] *s.* penitencia; contrición; remordimiento.
penitent [-tənt] *a.* penitente, contrito, arrepentido, compungido. —*s.* penitente.
penitential [,pɛnə'tɛntʃəl, B -'tɛnʃəl] *a.* penitencial. —*s.* 1. (relig.) manual de penitencias. 2. penitente. 3. (*pl.*) hábito de penitente.
penitentiary [-ərɪ] *s.* 1. (relig.) penitenciario (persona); penitenciaría (tribunal). 2. penitenciaría, presidio. —*a.* 1. penitencial. 2. penitenciario, de penitencia, penal.
penitently ['pɛnətəntlɪ] *adv.* con contrición o arrepentimiento.
penknife ['pɛn,naɪf] *s.* cortaplumas, tajaplumas.
penman [-mən] *s.* 1. escritor, autor. 2. pendolista; calígrafo; maestro de escritura.
penmanship [-,ʃɪp] *s.* 1. escritura, caligrafía. 2. pluma (estilo de letra).
Penn., Penna. *abrev. de* **Pennsylvania,** Pensilvania (E.U.).
penna ['pɛnə] *s.* (*pl.* PENNAE [-i]) (orn.) pena (pluma de contorno).
pen name, seudónimo (de autor).
pennant ['pɛnənt] *s.* 1. (mar.) gallardete, pendón; insignia; banderola, bandera de señales. 2. banderín (deportivo, de decoración, colegio, etc.).
pennate [-,eɪt, B -ɪt] *a.* (bot.) pinado; (zool.) alado.
penner [-ər, B -ə] *s.* (ant.) escribiente.
penniless ['pɛnɪləs] *a.* sin dinero, sin un real; indigente, en la miseria.

Pennine Alps [ˈpɛnˌaɪn-] Alpes Peninos, en la frontera italo-suiza.
Pennine Chain, montes Peninos, cordillera del N. de Inglaterra.
pennon [ˈpɛnən] *s.* 1. grímpola, flámula. 2. bandera, estandarte. 3. (poét.) ala. 4. (mar.) pendón, gallardete; banderola (de señales).
pennoncel, pennoncelle [-ˌsɛl] *s.* pequeña banderola (que se lleva en la lanza).
Pennsylvania [ˌpɛnsəlˈveɪnjə] *s.* Pensilvania, estado de los E.U.
Pennsylvania Dutch, (E.U.) pensilvano de origen alemán; dialecto alemán de Pensilvania.
Pennsylvanian [-ˈveɪnjən] *a.* 1. pensilvano. 2. (geol.) pensilvánico. *—s.* 1. (E.U.) pensilvano, habitante de Pensilvania. 2. (pal.) período pensilvánico.
penny [ˈpɛnɪ] *s.* (*pl.* con ref. a la moneda **pennies,** con ref. a su valor **pence** [pɛns]) 1. penique. 2. (fam., E.U.) centavo. 3. dinero. 4. **a p. for your thoughts,** ¿en qué piensas?; **a pretty p.,** un dineral, un ojo de la cara; **in for a p., in for a pound,** preso por mil, preso por mil quinientos; **p. wise, pound foolish,** tacaño en lo pequeño, derrochador en lo grande; **to turn an honest p.,** ganar dinero honradamente.
penny-a-liner [-əˈlaɪnər, B -ə] *s.* gacetillero.
penny-ante [-ˈæntɪ] *a.* (jer.) insignificante, sin importancia.
penny ante, juego de póker en que la apuesta es un centavo.
penny arcade, centro de diversiones (en que los aparatos de entretenimiento funcionan cuando se les introduce una moneda).
penny dreadful, novela barata y sensacional, de crímenes o escándalos.
penny-farthing [ˈpɛnɪˈfɑrðɪŋ, B -ˈfɑðɪŋ] *s.* (G.B.) velocípedo.
penny-pinch [-ˌpɪntʃ] *v.t.* tratar con tacañería; escasear.
penny pincher, (jer.) tacaño, mezquino.
pennyroyal [ˌpɛnɪˈrɔɪəl, B ˈpɛnɪ-] *s.* (bot.) 1. poleo. 2. especie de menta de campo.
pennyweight [ˈpɛnɪˌweɪt] *s.* peso equivalente a 24 granos.
penny-wise [-ˌwaɪz] *a.* mezquinamente ahorrativo, tacaño en lo pequeño.
pennywort [-ˌwɜrt, B -ˌwɜt] *s.* (bot.) ombligo de venus.
pennyworth [-ˌwɜrθ, B ˈpɛnəθ] *s.* 1. (por el) valor de un penique, ej., *a p. of sweets,* dulces por el valor de un penique. 2. ganga. 3. pizca, poquitín.
penological [ˌpinəˈlɑdʒɪkəl, B -ˈlɔdʒ-] *a.* penológico.
penologist [piˈnɑlədʒəst, B -ˈnɔl-] *s.* criminalista, penalista.
penology [-dʒɪ] *s.* penología.
penoncel, var. de **pennoncel.**
pen pal, amigo epistolar, amigo por correspondencia.
penpusher [ˈpɛnˌpʊʃər, B -ə] *s.* (fam.) chupatintas, escritorcillo.
pensile [ˈpɛnˌsaɪl, -sɪl] *a.* 1. pensil, colgante. 2. que tiene o que construye nidos colgantes (díc. de algunos pájaros).
pension [ˈpɛntʃən, B ˈpɛnʃən] *s.* 1. pensión, retiro, jubilación. 2. [ˈpɑnsɪˌɑn, B ˈpɑŋsɪɔŋ] pensión, casa de huéspedes; pensionado, internado. *—v.t.* (t. con *off*) pensionar; jubilar.
pensionable [-əbəl] *a.* con derecho a pensión.
pensionary [-ˌɛrɪ, B -ərɪ] *a.* alquilón, alquiladizo. *—s.* 1. asalariado, mercenario, alquilón. 2. (mil.) inválido, retirado.
pensioner [-ər, B -ə] *s.* 1. pensionado, pensionista; pariente dependiente. 2. (ant.) caballero guardaespaldas del rey, mercenario; criado, sirviente.
pensive [ˈpɛnsɪv] *a.* 1. pensativo, abstraído, meditabundo. 2. melancólico.
pensively [-lɪ] *adv.* 1. pensativamente. 2. melancólicamente.
pensiveness [-nəs] *s.* melancolía; introspección.
penstock [ˈpɛnˌstɑk, B -ˌstɔk] *s.* 1. compuerta de esclusa; paradera (del caz). 2. (E.U.) canal de carga; caz (de rueda hidráulica). 3. portaplumas.
pent [pɛnt] *a.* (esp. con *in* o *up*) acorralado, encerrado, confinado; contenido.
pentachlorophenol [ˌpɛntəˌklɔrəˈfiˌnoʊl, B -nɔl] *s.* (quím.) pentaclorofenol.
pentachord [ˈpɛntəˌkɔrd, B -ˌkɔd] *s.* (mús.) pentacordio, antigua lira. *—a.* de cinco cuerdas o notas.
pentacle [-kəl] *s.* pentáculo; estrella o símbolo de cinco puntas.
pentad [ˈpɛnˌtæd] *s.* 1. grupo de cinco. 2. lustro. 3. (quím.) elemento o átomo pentavalente o quintivalente.
pentadactyl [ˌpɛntəˈdæktəl] **pentadactylate** [-tələt, -ˌleɪt] *a.* (zool.) pentadáctilo, que tiene cinco dedos en cada mano o pie.
pentadecagon [-ˈdɛkəˌgɑn, B -gən] *s.* (geom.) pentadecágono, pentedecágono; polígono de quince lados o ángulos.
pentadecagonal [-dəˈkægənəl] *a.* (geom.) pentadecágono, pentedecágono.
pentagon [ˈpɛntəˌgɑn, B -gən] *s.* (geom.) pentágono, figura plana de cinco ángulos o lados. **— the P.,** (E.U.) el Pentágono (edificio del Ministerio de Guerra).
pentagonal [pɛnˈtægənəl] *a.* pentagonal.
pentagonally [-ɪ] *adv.* en forma de pentágono.
pentagram [ˈpɛntəˌgræm] *s.* 1. pentáculo, que consta de cinco líneas. 2. *var. de* **pentacle.**
pentahedral [ˌpɛntəˈhidrəl] *a.* (geom.) pentaédrico.
pentahedron [-drən] *s.* (geom.) pentaedro, figura sólida de cinco superficies planas.
pentamerous [pɛnˈtæmərəs] *a.* (bot., ento.) pentámero.
pentameter [-ˈtæmətər, B -ə] *s.* (poét.) pentámetro.
pentane [ˈpɛnˌteɪn] *s.* (quím.) pentano.
pentangular [pɛnˈtæŋgjələr, B -lə] *a.* pentagonal, de cinco ángulos.
pentapolis [-ˈtæpələs] *s.* pentápolis.
pentaquine, pentaquin [ˈpɛntəˌkwin, -kwən] *s.* (farm.) pentaquina.
pentarchy [ˈpɛntˌɑrkɪ, B -ˌɑkɪ] *s.* (*pl.* PENTARCHIES) pentarquía, gobierno de cinco mandos con igual autoridad.
pentasyllabic [ˌpɛntəsɪˈlæbɪk] *a.* pentasílabo.
Pentateuch [ˈpɛntəˌtuk, B -ˌtjuk] *s.* (bíbl.) Pentateuco.
pentathlon [pɛnˈtæθlən, -ˌlɑn, B -lɔn] *s.* pentatlón, competición que consta de cinco pruebas atléticas.
pentatonic scale [ˌpɛntəˈtɑnɪk-, B -ˈtɔn-] (mús.) escala pentatónica, de cinco notas.
pentavalent [-ˈveɪlənt, B pɛnˈtævə-] *a.* (quím.) pentavalente.
Pentecost [ˈpɛntəˌkɔst, -ˌkɑst, B -ˌkɔst] *s.* Pentecostés.
Pentecostal [ˌpɛntəˈkɑstəl, -ˈkɔst-, B -ˈkɔst-] *a.* de Pentecostés, perteneciente a una secta fundamentalista del Protestantismo.
penthouse [ˈpɛntˌhaʊs] *s.* 1. penthouse, ático de lujo, apartamiento de azotea. 2. alpende, colgadizo, cobertizo; construcción anexa (a un edificio). 3. sobradillo, visera (de puerta o ventana).
pentlandite [ˈpɛntlənˌdaɪt] *s.* (min.) pentlandita.
pentobarbital [ˌpɛntəˈbɑrbəˌtɔl, B -ˈbɑbɪ-] *s.* (quím.) pentobarbital.
pentode [ˈpɛnˌtoʊd] *s.* (electrón.) pentodo, péntodo.
pentosan [ˈpɛntəˌsæn] *s.* (quím.) pentosano.
pentose [ˈpɛnˌtoʊs] *s.* (quím.) pentosa.
pentoside [ˈpɛntəˌsaɪd] *s.* (quím.) pentósido.
pentothal [-ˌθɔl] *s.* (quím.) pentotal.
pent-up [ˈpɛntˈʌp] *a.* contenido, reprimido (ira, emoción, etc.).
pentyl [ˈpɑntəl] *s.* (quím.) pentilo.
penuche [pəˈnutʃɪ] *s.* confitura de azúcar rubia, crema y nueces.
penuchle, penuckle [ˈpiˌnʌkəl] *vars. de* pinochle, juego de cartas.
penult [ˈpiˌnʌlt, B pɪˈnʌlt] **penultima** [pɪˈnʌltəmə] *s.* penúltimo; esp. (gram., poét.) penúltima sílaba.
penultimate [pɪˈnʌltəmət] *a.* penúltimo.
penumbra [pəˈnʌmbrə] *s.* (*pl.* PENUMBRAE [-bri] PENUMBRAS) penumbra; región sombreada o indefinida.
penurious [pəˈnʊrɪəs, B -ˈnjʊər-] *a.* 1. indigente, pobrísimo. 2. tacaño, mezquino, miserable. 3. (raro) escaso; estéril, árido, pobre, ej., *p. soil,* suelo pobre o estéril.
penuriously [-lɪ] *adv.* 1. en la miseria, miserablemente. 2. tacañamente, mezquinamente.
penuriousness [-nəs] *s.* tacañería, mezquindad, cicatería; escasez.
penury [ˈpɛnjərɪ] *s.* (*pl.* PENURIES) penuria, escasez, miseria.
penwoman [ˈpɛnˌwʊmən] *s.* escritora.
peon [ˈpiˌɑn, -ən, B pjun, ˈpiən] *s.* 1. mandadero, sirviente. 2. peón, bracero (en la América Latina).
peonage [ˈpiənɪdʒ] *s.* 1. condición de peón; uso de peones. 2. (S.E. de E.U.) sistema de contratar presos para trabajos.
peony [ˈpiənɪ, B ˈpɪ-] *s.* (*pl.* PEONIES) (bot.) peonía (planta y flor).
people [ˈpipəl] *s.* (*pl.* PEOPLE) 1. gente. 2. personas, ej., *ten p.,* diez personas. 3. (*pl.* PEOPLES) pueblo, ej., *the peoples of Europe,* los pueblos de Europa, *a warlike p.,* un pueblo guerrero. 4. humanos; raza humana. 5. habitantes (de un lugar), ej., *p. of New York,* habitantes de Nueva York. 6. parientes; familiares; antepasados, ej., *my p. were English,* mis antepasados eran ingleses, *his p. are sure to hear it,* sus parientes seguramente se enterarán; **one's p.,** la familia (de uno). 7. pueblo, plebe; **the common p.,** la plebe, el pueblo. 8. **all sorts of p.,** toda clase de gente; **p. say,** se dice; **many p.,** mucha gente; **most p.,** la mayoría, el común de la gente. *—v.t.* poblar, colonizar; habitar.
people's court, tribunal del pueblo.
people's front, frente popular.
pep [pɛp] (jer.) *s.* brío, ánimo, vigor, empuje; **full of p.,** lleno de brío. *—v.t.* (*pret., p.p* PEPPED; *p.pr.* PEPPING) (gen. con *up*) animar, estimular, vigorizar.
peplos [ˈpɛpləs] *s.* (hist.) peplo, pieza de indumentaria femenina de la Grecia antigua.
peplum [-ləm] *s.* (*pl.* PEPLUMS O PEPLA [-lə]) faldillas, haldeta, peplo.
peplus, *var. de* **peplos.**
pepo [ˈpipoʊ] *s.* (bot.) pepónide.
pepper [ˈpɛpər, B -ə] *s.* 1. pimienta (condimento, fruto). 2. pimentero, ají, pimiento. *—v.t.* 1. sazonar con pimienta. 2. acribillar (con balas, perdigones, etc.). 3. salpicar, motear.
pepper-and-salt [-ərənˈsɔlt] *a.* (tejido) mosqueteado; (pelo) entrecano.
pepperbox [-ˌbɑks, B -əˌbɔks] *s.* pimentero.

peppercorn [-ˌkɔrn, B -ˌkɔn] *s.* 1. grano de pimienta. 2. bagatela, bicoca.
pepper cress, (bot.) lepidio, mastuerzo, cardamina.
pepper family, (bot.) (familia de las) piperáceas.
peppergrass [-ˌgræs, B -ˌgrɑs] *s.* (bot.) lepidio, mastuerzo, sabelección, cardamina.
pepper mill, molinillo de pimienta.
peppermint [-ˌmɪnt] *s.* 1. menta. 2. pastilla de menta.
pepperoni [ˌpɛpəˈroʊnɪ] *s.* salchicha italiana, dura y muy sazonada.
pepper pot, 1. pimentero. 2. sopa de carne y legumbres sazonada con ají y pimienta.
pepper shaker, pimentero de mesa.
peppertree [ˈpɛpərˌtrɪ, B ˈpɛpəˌ-] *s.* (bot.) molle, lentisco del Perú, turbinto.
pepperwort [-ˌwɜrt, B -ˌwɜt] *s.* (bot.) lepidio, mastuerzo, sabelección.
peppery [ˈpɛpərɪ] *a.* 1. picante. 2. mordaz; áspero, enojado, de mal humor. 3. cáustico, punzante, hiriente (palabras).
pep pill (jer., E.U.) píldora de droga estimulante (esp. anfetamina).
peppy [ˈpɛpɪ] *a.* (PEPPIER; PEPPIEST) lleno de vida, brioso, animoso, vivaz.
pepsin [ˈpɛpsən] *s.* (bioquím.) pepsina.
pepsinogen [pɛpˈsɪnədʒən] *s.* (bioquím.) pepsinógeno.
peptalk [ˈpɛpˌtɔk] *s.* (jer.) exhortación, discurso o palabras animadoras.
peptic [ˈpɛptɪk] *a.* péptico. —*s.* substancia péptica, agente péptico.
peptidase [-təˌdeɪs] *s.* (bioquím.) peptidasa.
peptide [-ˌtaɪd] *s.* (bioquím.) péptido.
peptone [-ˌtoʊn] *s.* (bioquím.) peptona.
peptonic [pɛpˈtɑnɪk, B -ˈtɔn-] *a.* (bioquím.) peptónico.
peptonization [ˌpɛptənəˈzeɪʃən, B -naɪ-] *s.* (bioquím.) peptonización.
peptonize [ˈpɛptəˌnaɪz] *v.t.* peptonizar, peptonificar.
per [pɜr, pər, B pɜ, pə] *prep.* 1. por; según, ej., *p. yesterday's quotation,* según la cotización de ayer. 2. **as p.,** según, de acuerdo a; **p. capita,** por cabeza; **p. diem,** por día; **p. cent,** por ciento; **p. annum,** por año, anualmente.
peracid [ˈpɜrˌæsəd] *s.* (quím.) perácido.
peradventure [ˌpɜrədˈvɛntʃər, B -tʃə] *s.* posibilidad; suerte; duda, incertidumbre; **beyond** (o **without**) **p.,** sin posibilidad de duda. —*adv.* (ant.) quizá, acaso, por ventura.
perambulate [pəˈræmbjəˌleɪt] *v.t.* recorrer andando; transitar, visitar; recorrer para inspeccionar. —*v.i.* deambular, andar, pasearse, vagar, errar, vagabundear, vaguear.
perambulation [-ˌræmbjəˈleɪʃən] *s.* 1. paseo. 2. gira de inspección.
perambulator [-ˈræmbjəˌleɪtər, B ˈpræm-ə] *s.* 1. paseante. 2. (top.) podómetro. 3. cochecillo de niño.
perambulatory [pəˈræmbjələˌtɔrɪ, B -tərɪ] *a.* paseador, paseante, vagante, ambulante.
perborate [pərˈbɔrˌeɪt, B pəˈ-] *s.* (quím.) perborato.
perboric acid [-ˈbɔrɪk-] (quím.) ácido perbórico.
percale [-ˈkeɪl, B -ˈkɑl] *s.* (tej.) percal.
percaline [ˌpɜrkəˈlin, B ˌpɜkə-] *s.* percalina.
perceivable [pərˈsivəbəl, B pəˈ-] *a.* perceptible, inteligible.
perceivably [-əblɪ] *a.* perceptiblemente, inteligiblemente.
perceive [-ˈsiv] *v.t.* 1. percibir, percatarse de, advertir, observar, columbrar. 2. percibir, comprender.

percent [pərˈsɛnt, B pəˈ-] *s.* (*pl.* PERCENT) 1. (tanto) por ciento, ej., *ten p. of the population,* diez por ciento de la población, *interest at four p.,* intereses al cuatro por ciento. 2. porcentaje. 3. (*pl.* PERCENTS) (G.B.) bono de interés fijo. —*a.* de (tanto) por ciento, ej., *five p. profit,* ganancia de cinco por ciento. —*adv.* por ciento, ej., *you are a hundred p. right,* tienes razón ciento por ciento, tienes toda la razón.
percentage [-ɪdʒ] *s.* 1. porcentaje, ej., *only a small p. of horses win races,* sólo un pequeño porcentaje de caballos gana(n) carreras. 2. (jer.) ganancia, utilidad, ventaja, provecho.
percentile [-ˈsɛnˌtaɪl, -təl] *s.* percentil.
per centum [-ˈsɛntəm] por ciento.
percept [ˈpɜrˌsɛpt, B ˈpɜˌ-] *s.* (psic.) percepción, idea (representación mental de lo percibido).
perceptibility [pərˌsɛptəˈbɪlətɪ, B pəˌ-] *s.* perceptibilidad.
perceptible [-ˈsɛptəbəl] *a.* perceptible; discernible.
perceptibly [-blɪ] *adv.* perceptiblemente; de modo discernible.
perception [-ˈsɛpʃən] *s.* 1. percepción, conciencia. 2. comprensión, penetración.
perceptional [-əl] *a.* perteneciente a la percepción.
perceptive [pərˈsɛptɪv, B pəˈ-] *a.* perceptivo; observador, perspicaz.
perceptiveness [-nəs] *s.* capacidad de percepción, facultad perceptiva.
perceptivity [ˌpɜrsɛpˈtɪvətɪ, B ˌpɜsɛp-] *s.* perceptividad.
perceptual [pərˈsɛptʃʊəl, B pəˈ-] *a.* de percepción.
perceptually [-ɪ] *adv.* con percepción, de modo perceptivo.
perch [pɜrtʃ, B pɜtʃ] *s.* 1. percha, varal, cetro, alcándara; (fig.) sitio o posición elevada. 2. pértiga del coche. 3. (pr. G.B.) medida de longitud (equivale a 5,29 metros); medida de área (equivale a 24,75 pies cuadrados). 4. (ict.) perca. 5. **to knock (a person) off his p.,** vencer, aniquilar (a una persona). —*v.i.* posarse (un ave); sentarse, balancearse (en un sitio algo elevado). —*v.t.* colocar, situar (en un sitio algo elevado), ej., *town perched on a hill,* pueblo situado en la cumbre de una colina.
perchance [pərˈtʃæns, B pəˈtʃɑns] *adv.* quizá, por ventura, acaso, tal vez; posiblemente.
Percheron [ˈpɜrtʃəˌrɑn, B ˈpɜʃəˌrɔn] *s.* percherón (caballo fuerte, de tiro).
perchlorate [pərˈklɔrˌeɪt, -ət, B pəˈ-] *s.* (quím.) perclorato.
perchloric acid [-ˈklɔrɪk-] (quím.) ácido perclórico.
perchloride [-ˈklɔrˌaɪd] *s.* (quím.) percloruro.
percipience [pərˈsɪpɪəns, B pəˈ-] *s.* percepción.
percipient [-ənt] *a., s.* perceptor.
percolate [ˈpɜrkəˌleɪt, B ˈpɜkə-] *v.t., v.i.* 1. colar(se), filtrar(se). 2. (fig.) infiltrar(se).
percolation [ˌpɜrkəˈleɪʃən, B ˌpɜkə-] *s.* 1. filtración. 2. (fig.) infiltración. 3. (geol.) percolación.
percolator [ˈpɜrkəˌleɪtər, B ˈpɜkə-ə] *s.* percolador (cafetera filtradora); filtro, colador.
per contra [pərˈkɑntrə, B pəˈkɔn-] por lo contrario, por el contrario; por otra parte.
percuss [pərˈkʌs, B pəˈ-] *v.t.* (med.) percutir, golpear (suave pero firmemente, para auscultar).
percussion [-ˈkʌʃən] *s.* 1. percusión; golpe. 2. (mús.) percusión; **p. instruments,** instrumentos de percusión.

percussion cap, (arm.) cápsula o cebo fulminante.
percussion hammer, (arm.) perrillo de percusión, percusor, martillo percutor.
percussionist [-əst] *s.* músico que toca instrumentos de percusión.
percussion lock, (arm.) llave de percusión.
percussive [-ˈkʌsɪv] *a.* 1. percutiente. 2. (mec.) de percusión, por percusión.
percutaneous [ˌpɜrkjʊˈteɪnɪəs, B ˌpɜkjʊ-] *a.* (med.) percutáneo.
perdie [pərˈdi, B pəˈ-] *var. de* **pardie** (ant., interj.) ¡por Dios! ¡así es!
perdition [-ˈdɪʃən] *s.* perdición, condenación; infierno.
perdu, perdue [-ˈdu, B -ˈdju] *a.* (mil.) emboscado, perdido, escondido; **to lie p.,** estar emboscado. —*s.* (ant.) soldado o tropa encargados de una operación arriesgada.
perdurability [pərˌdʊrəˈbɪlətɪ, B pəˌdjʊər-] *s.* perdurabilidad, persistencia, permanencia.
perdurable [-ˈdʊrəbəl, B -ˈdjʊərə-] *a.* perdurable, duradero.
perdurably [-blɪ] *adv.* perdurablemente, duraderamente.
père [pɛr, B pɛə] *s.* (fr.) padre (ú. con el apellido) ej., *Alexandre Dumas, p.,* Alejandro D., padre.
peregrinate [ˈpɛrəgrəˌneɪt] *v.i.* peregrinar. —*v.t.* recorrer.
peregrination [ˌpɛrəgrəˈneɪʃən] *s.* peregrinación.
peregrinator [ˈpɛrəgrəˌneɪtər, B -tə] *s.* (ant.) peregrinante, peregrino.
peregrine [ˈpɛrəgrən, -ˌgrin] *a.* peregrino, migratorio, extranjero. —*s.* (orn.) halcón peregrino.
peremptorily [pəˈrɛmptərəlɪ] *adv.* 1. terminantemente, perentoriamente. 2. autoritariamente, dogmáticamente. 3. perentoriamente, imperiosamente.
peremptory [-ˈrɛmptərɪ] *a.* 1. terminante, perentorio. 2. autoritario, dictatorial, dogmático. 3. incontrovertible, indiscutible, irrebatible. 4. perentorio, imperioso, urgente. 5. (der.) perentorio; concluyente, decisivo.
perennate [ˈpɛrəˌneɪt] *v.i.* ser perenne, sobrevivir de año en año (como ciertas plantas).
perennial [pəˈrɛnɪəl] *a.* 1. perenne; permanente; constante, incesante; perpetuo; continuo, que se renueva. 2. (bot.) perenne.
perennial joke, chiste favorito (que se vuelve a contar cada cierto tiempo).
perennially [-ɪəlɪ] *adv.* perennemente; continuamente; constantemente.
perfect [ˈpɜrfɪkt, B ˈpɜfɪkt] *a.* 1. perfecto, entero, acabado, cumplido, completo, cabal. 2. perfecto, exacto, preciso; puro, absoluto; (fam.) redomado, ej., *p. hexagon,* hexágono perfecto; *p. red,* rojo puro, *p. fool,* tonto redomado. 3. (bot.) completo. 4. (gram.) perfecto (tiempo de verbo), ej., *future p.,* futuro perfecto. 5. (mús.) perfecto (acorde). —*s.* (gram.) tiempo perfecto. — [pərˈfɛkt, B pəˈ-] *v.t.* perfeccionar; acabar, pulir; completar, mejorar.
perfecter [pərˈfɛktər, B pəˈ-tə] *s.* perfeccionador.
perfectibility [-ˌfɛktəˈbɪlətɪ] *s.* perfectibilidad.
perfectible [-ˈfɛktəbəl] *a.* perfectible.
perfection [-ˈfɛkʃən] *s.* 1. perfección, excelencia. 2. perfeccionamiento. 3. **to do (something) to p.,** hacer (algo) a la perfección.
perfectionism [-ˈfɛkʃəˌnɪzəm] *s.* (teo.) perfeccionismo.
perfectionist [-nəst] *s.* perfeccionista; (teo.) perfeccionista.

perfective [-'fɛktɪv] *a.* (gram.) perfectivo.

perfectly ['pɜrfɪktlɪ, B 'pɜfɪkt-] *adv.* perfectamente.

perfectness [-nəs] *s.* perfección.

perfecto [pər'fɛktoʊ, B pə'-] *s.* (*pl.* PERFECTOS) tipo de cigarro puro.

perfect participle, (gram.) participio pasado.

perfect pitch (mús.) perfecta afinación o grado del diapasón.

perfect rhyme, (poét.) rima perfecta.

perfect square, (mat.) cuadrado perfecto.

perfect triad, (mús.) acorde perfecto.

perfervid [pər'fɜrvəd, B pə'fɜvɪd] *a.* muy férvido; ardiente.

perfidious [-'fɪdɪəs] *a.* pérfido, desleal, aleve, traicionero, infiel.

perfidiously [-lɪ] *adv.* pérfidamente, deslealmente, alevemente.

perfidiousness [-nəs] *s.* carácter pérfido o traicionero.

perfidy ['pɜrfədɪ, B 'pɜfɪdɪ] *s.* (*pl.* PERFIDIES) perfidia, deslealtad, alevosía, traición.

perfoliate [pər'foʊlɪət, B pə'-] *a.* (bot.) perfoliado.

perforate ['pɜrfəˌreɪt, B 'pɜfə-] *v.t., v.i.* perforar(se), agujerear(se). — [-rət] *a.* perforado.

perforation [ˌpɜrfə'reɪʃən, B ˌpɜfə-] *s.* 1. perforación, horadación, taladro, agujero. 2. trepado, perforación (en papel, etc.); (filat.) perforación.

perforce [pər'fɔrs, B pə'fɔs] *adv.* por fuerza, forzosamente, inevitablemente, necesariamente.

perform [-'fɔrm, B -'fɔm] *v.t.* 1. ejecutar, hacer, realizar, efectuar. 2. desempeñar, cumplir; practicar, ejercer. 3. **p. wonders,** hacer maravillas. —*v.i.* tocar un instrumento musical; representar, desempeñar un papel, actuar (en el teatro).

performable [-əbəl] *a.* ejecutable, realizable, factible, hacedero.

performance [-əns] *s.* 1. ejecución, realización. 2. desempeño, cumplimiento, rendimiento. 3. obra, hecho; proeza, hazaña; (dep.) performance. 4. actuación, representación (teatral, artística, etc.). 5. espectáculo, función.

performer [-ər, B -ə] *s.* ejecutante; actor; músico; bailarín, acróbata.

performing [-ɪŋ] *a.* amaestrado, preparado o entrenado para actuar; ej., *p. bear,* oso de circo o amaestrado.

perfume [pər'fjum, B pə'-] *v.t.* perfumar, perfumear, sahumar, aromatizar. — ['pɜrˌfjum, B 'pɜˌ-] *s.* perfume, fragancia; aroma, esencia.

perfumer [-'fjumər, B -ə] *s.* perfumista, perfumador.

perfumery [-ərɪ] *s.* perfumería (ciencia y arte).

perfunctorily [pər'fʌŋktərəlɪ, B pə'-] *adv.* superficialmente; indiferentemente, mecánicamente; sólo llenando las apariencias; rutinariamente.

perfunctoriness [-tərɪnəs] *s.* superficialidad; indiferencia; excesiva parquedad.

perfunctory [-tərɪ] *a.* superficial; indiferente, mecánico; rutinario.

perfuse [pər'fjuz, B pə'-] *v.t.* difundir, esparcir, hacer afluir, hacer penetrar (un líquido).

perfusion [-'fjuʒən] *s.* 1. aspersión, afusión. 2. (med.) perfusión. 3. rociada.

pergola ['pɜrgələ, B 'pɜgə-] *s.* pérgola, glorieta, cenador; quiosco de celosías enramadas.

perhaps [pər'hæps, præps, B pə'hæps] *adv.* tal vez, quizás, acaso, por ventura.

peri ['pɪrɪ, B 'pɪərɪ] *s.* 1. (mitol.) peri, hada. 2. (fig.) hurí, beldad.

perianth ['pɛrɪˌænθ] *s.* (bot.) periantio, perigonio.

periapt [-ˌæpt] *s.* periapto, amuleto, talismán.

periarteritis [ˌpɛrɪˌɑrtə'raɪtəs, B -ˌɑtə-] *s.* (med.) periarteritis.

periarthritis [-ɑr'θraɪtəs, B -ɑ'-] *s.* (med.) periartritis.

pericardial [ˌpɛrə'kɑrdɪəl, B -'kɑd-] **pericardiac** [-ɪˌæk] *a.* (anat.) pericárdico.

pericarditis [-kɑr'daɪtəs, B -kɑ'-] *s.* (med.) pericarditis.

pericardium [-'kɑrdɪəm, B -'kɑd-] *s.* (*pl.* PERICARDIA [-ɪə]) (anat.) pericardio.

pericarp ['pɛrəˌkɑrp, B -ˌkɑp] *s.* (bot.) pericarpio, folículo.

perichondrium [ˌpɛrə'kɑndrɪəm, B -'kɔn-] *s.* (*pl.* PERICHONDRIA [-drɪə]) (anat.) pericondrio.

Periclean [ˌpɛrə'kliən] *a.* de Pericles; perteneciente a la era de gran auge intelectual de la Grecia antigua.

Pericles ['pɛrəˌkliz] *s.* Pericles, estadista y general ateniense.

pericline [-ˌklaɪn] *s.* (min.) periclina.

pericope [pə'rɪkəpɪ] *s.* pequeño fragmento de un trabajo literario.

pericranial [ˌpɛrə'kreɪnɪəl] *a.* (anat.) pericraneal, del pericráneo.

pericranium [-nɪəm] *s.* (*pl.* PERICRANIA [-nɪə]) (anat.) pericráneo.

pericycle ['pɛrəˌsaɪkəl] *s.* (bot.) periciclo.

periderm [-ˌdɜrm, B -ˌdɜm] *s.* 1. (bot.) peridermis. 2. (zool.) peridermo.

peridermal [ˌpɛrə'dɜrməl, B -'dɜməl] **peridermic** [-mɪk] *a.* (bot.) peridérmico.

peridium [pə'rɪdɪəm] *s.* (*pl.* PERIDIA [-ɪə]) (bot.) peridio.

peridot ['pɛrəˌdɑt, -ˌdoʊt, B -ˌdɔt] *s.* (min.) peridoto.

peridotite [pə'rɪdəˌtaɪt, B 'pɛrɪdoʊ-] *s.* (min.) peridotita.

perigean [ˌpɛrə'dʒiən] *a.* (astr.) de perigeo.

perigee ['pɛrəˌdʒi] *s.* (astr.) perigeo.

perigonium [ˌpɛrə'goʊnɪəm] *s.* (*pl.* PERIGONIA [-iə]) (bot.) perigonio.

perigynous [pə'rɪdʒənəs] *a.* (bot.) perígino.

perihelion [ˌpɛrə'hiljən] *s.* (astr.) perihelio.

peril ['pɛrəl] *s.* peligro; riesgo. —*v.t.* (pret., *p.p.* PERILED O PERILLED; *p.pr.* PERILING O PERILLING) poner en peligro; arriesgar.

perilous [-ələs] *a.* peligroso, arriesgado, azaroso, ej., *a p. venture,* una empresa arriesgada.

perilously [-lɪ] *adv.* peligrosamente, arriesgadamente.

perilousness [-nəs] *s.* índole peligrosa, peligro, riesgo.

perimeter [pə'rɪmətər, B -ə] *s.* 1. perímetro, contorno. 2. (fig.) límite, extremo. 3. (mil.) perímetro (de defensa).

perimetric [ˌpɛrə'mɛtrɪk] *a.* perimétrico.

perimetrically [-trɪkəlɪ] *adv.* en línea perimétrica.

perimysium [-'mizɪəm] *s.* (*pl.* PERIMYSIA [-ɪə]) (anat.) perimisio.

perinephrium [-'nɛfrɪəm] *s.* (*pl.* PERINEPHRIA [-rɪə]) (anat.) perinefrio.

perineal [->'ɳɩᵊλ] *a.* (anat.) perineal.

perineum [-'niəm] *s.* (*pl.* PERINEA [-'niə]) (anat.) perineo.

perineurium [-'nʊrɪəm, B -'njʊər-] *s.* (*pl.* PERINEURIA [-ɪə]) (anat.) perineuro, perineurio.

period ['pɪrɪəd, B 'pɪər-] *s.* 1. período, fase, etapa, ciclo, espacio de tiempo. 2. hora (de clase). 3. época, ej., *after the fashion of the p.,* según la moda de esa época. 4. (geol.) período, división. 5. (mús.) frase musical completa. 6. (fisiol.) período (menstrual). 7. (gram.) punto (ortográfico). 8. (dep.) período, etapa. 9. (fís.) período (de una substancia radiactiva). 10. **to put a p. to,** poner punto o término (a). —*a.* 1. del período, de la época. 2. de estilo (muebles, joyas, etc.). 3. característico de la época (novela, pintura, etc.).

periodate [pə'raɪəˌdeɪt] *s.* (quím.) paryodato.

periodic [ˌpɪrɪ'ɑdɪk, B ˌpɪərɪ'ɔd-] *a.* periódico, regular.

periodic [ˌpɜraɪ'ɑdɪk, B pɪərˌaɪ'ɔd-] *a.* (quím.) peryódico.

periodical [ˌpɪrɪ'ɑdɪkəl, B ˌpɪərɪ'ɔd-] *a.* periódico. —*s.* periódico, publicación periódica.

periodically [-ɪkəlɪ] *adv.* periódicamente.

periodicity [-ə'dɪsətɪ] *s.* periodicidad, frecuencia.

periodic law, (quím.) ley periódica.

periodic table, (quím.) clasificación periódica de los elementos, tabla periódica (de Mendeleiev).

periodide [pə'raɪəˌdaɪd, -dɪd] *s.* (quím.) peryoduro.

periodontal [ˌpɛrɪə'dɑntəl, B -'dɔnt-] *a.* (anat.) periodontal.

periodontics [-ɪks] *s. pl.* (*sing. o pl. en const.*) (med.) periodoncia.

Perioeci [ˌpɛrɪ'isaɪ] *s. pl.* (geog.) periecos.

perioecic [-'isɪk] *a.* (geog.) perieco.

perionychium [ˌpɛrɪoʊ'nɪkɪəm] *s.* (*pl.* PERIONYCHIA [-ɪə]) (anat.) perioniquio.

periosteal [ˌpɛrɪ'ɑstɪəl, B -'ɔs-] *a.* (anat.) perióstico.

periosteum [-tɪəm] *s.* (*pl.* PERIOSTEA [-tɪə]) (anat.) periósteo, periostio.

periostitis [-ˌɑs'taɪtəs, B -ˌɔs-] *s.* (med.) periostitis, periosteítis.

periotic [ˌpɛrɪ'oʊtɪk] *a.* (anat.) periótico.

peripatetic [ˌpɛrəpə'tɛtɪk] *a.* 1. **P.,** (filos.) peripatético, aristotélico. 2. ambulante, migratorio.

Peripateticism [-'tɛtəˌsɪzəm] *s.* (filos.) peripatetismo.

Peripatetics [-'tɛtɪks] *s. pl.* (filos.) peripatéticos.

peripeteia [-'tiə, B -'taɪə] *s.* peripecia (en el drama, obra literaria, etc.).

peripety [pə'rɪpətɪ] *s.* (*pl.* PERIPETIES) *var. de* **peripeteia.**

peripheral [pə'rɪfərəl] *a.* periférico.

periphery [-ərɪ] *s.* (*pl.* PERIPHERIES) periferia.

periphrase ['pɛrəˌfreɪz] *var. de* **periphrasis.**

periphrasis [pə'rɪfrəsəs] *s.* (*pl.* PERIPHRASES [-rəˌsiz]) (ret.) perífrasis, perífrasi.

periphrastic [ˌpɛrə'fræstɪk] *a.* (gram.) perifrástico.

peripteral [pə'rɪptərəl] *a.* (arq.) períptero.

peripteros [-ˌrɑs, B -ˌrɔs] *s.* (*pl.* PERIPTEROI [-ˌrɔɪ]) (arq.) períptero.

peripterous [-rəs] *a.* (arq., bot.) períptero.

perique [pə'rik] *s.* (E.U.) tabaco de fuerte sabor de Luisiana.

perisarc ['pɛrəˌsɑrk, B -ˌsɑk] *s.* (zool.) perisarco.

periscian [pə'rɪʃɪən, B -'rɪsɪən] *a.* (geog.) periscio.

periscii [-ˌaɪ] *s., pl.* (geog.) periscios.

periscope ['pɛrəˌskoʊp] *s.* periscopio.

periscopic [ˌpɛrə'skɑpɪk, B -'skɔp-] *a.* periscópico.

perish ['pɛrɪʃ] *v.i.* perecer, morir, sucumbir, fenecer, caer. —*v.t.* **p. the thought!** ¡no lo permita Dios!

perishable [-əbəl] *a.* perecedero; breve, efímero, pasajero. —*s.* (*gen. pl.*) artículos (esp. viandas y víveres) perecederos o de fácil deterioro.

perissodactyl [pəˌrɪsə'dæktəl] *a., s.* (zool.) perisodáctilo.

perissodactylous [-tələs] *a.* (zool.) perisodáctilo.
peristalsis [ˌpɛrəˈstɔlsəs, B -ˈstæl-] *s.* (*pl.* PERISTALSES [-ˌsiz]) (fisiol.) peristalsis.
peristaltic [-tɪk] *a.* (fisiol.) peristáltico.
peristome [ˈpɛrəˌstoʊm] *s.* (bot., zool.) peristoma.
peristyle [-ˌstaɪl] *s.* (arq.) peristilo.
perithecium [ˌpɛrəˈθiʃɪəm, B -ˈθisɪ-] *s.* PERITHECIA [-ə]) (bot.) peritecio.
peritoneal, peritonaeal [ˌpɛrətəˈniəl] *a.* (anat.) peritoneal.
peritoneum, peritonaeum [-ˈniəm] *s.* (*pl.* PERITONEA, PERITONAEA [-ˈniə]) (anat.) peritoneo.
peritonitis [-ˈnaɪtəs] *s.* (med.) peritonitis.
peritrichous [pəˈrɪtrɪkəs] *a.* (bot.) perétrico.
periwig [ˈpɛrɪˌwɪg] *s.* peluca antigua (empolvada y recogida a la nuca).
periwinkle [ˈpɛrɪˌwɪŋkəl] *s.* 1. (bot.) vincapervinca, hierba doncella. 2. (zool.) bígaro, bigarro; margarita, litorina.
perjure [ˈpɜrdʒər, B ˈpɜdʒə] *v.t.* perjurar; **p. oneself,** perjurarse.
perjurer [-dʒərər, B -ə] *s.* perjuro.
perjurious [pərˈdʒʊrɪəs, B pəˈdʒʊər-] *a.* perjuro, perjurador.
perjury [ˈpɜrdʒərɪ, B ˈpɜdʒə-] *s.* perjurio; **to commit p.,** jurar en falso, perjurar.
perk [pɜrk, B pɜk] *v.i.* erguirse; pavonearse; **p. up,** animarse, avivarse, reanimarse, sentirse mejor. —*v.t.* 1. (gen. con *up*), alzar (ej., la cola); aguzar (las orejas); avivar. 2. (gen. con *up* o *out*) engalanar, adornar.
perkily [ˈpɜrkəlɪ, B ˈpɜkə-] *adv.* 1. airosamente, gallardamente. 2. viva o animadamente.
perky [-kɪ] *a.* 1. airoso, gallardo. 2. vivaz, animado.
perlèche [ˈpɜrˌlɛʃ, B ˈpɜˌ-] *s.* (med.) boquera, vaharera.
perlite [ˈpɜrˌlaɪt, B ˈpɜˌ-] *s.* (min.) perlita.
perlitic [pərˈlɪtɪk, B pəˈ-] *a.* (min.) perlítico.
permafrost [ˈpɜrməˌfrɔst, -ˌfrɑst, B ˈpɜməˌfrɔst] *s.* (geol.) permafrost, permagel.
permalloy [-ˌlɔɪ] *s.* (metal.) permalloy.
permanence [ˈpɜrmənəns, B ˈpɜm-] *s.* permanencia, estabilidad, durabilidad.
permanency [-nənsɪ] *s.* 1. permanencia, estabilidad, durabilidad. 2. cosa permanente; tenencia segura, ocupación permanente (de un oficio o cargo).
permanent [-nənt] *a.* permanente, estable, duradero, fijo, persistente; inmutable, inalterable. —*s.* permanente, ondulación permanente.
permanently [-lɪ] *adv.* permanentemente.
permanent magnet, imán permanente.
permanent magnetism, (fís.) magnetismo permanente.
permanent press, *a.* 1. de raya permanente (*pantalon*). 2. inarrugable (*falda*).
permanent wave, permanente, ondulación permanente.
permanganate [pərˈmæŋgəˌneɪt, B pəˈ-nɪt] *s.* (quím.) permanganato.
permanganic [ˌpɜrmænˈgænɪk, B ˌpɜmæn-] *a.* (quím.) permangánico.
permanganic acid, (quím.) ácido permangánico.
permeability [ˌpɜrmɪəˈbɪlətɪ, B ˌpɜmɪ-] *s.* permeabilidad.
permeable [ˈpɜrmɪəbəl, B ˈpɜmɪ-] *a.* permeable.
permeance [-əns] *s.* (elec.) permeancia.
permeate [-ˌeɪt] *v.t., v.i.* penetrar, infiltrar(se), impregnar(se), calar(se).
permeation [ˌpɜrmɪˈeɪʃən, B ˌpɜmɪ-] *s.* penetración, infiltración, impregnación.

Permian [ˈpɜrmɪən, B ˈpɜmɪ-] *a.* (geol.) pérmico.
per mill, por mil.
permillage [pərˈmɪlɪdʒ, B pəˈ-] *s.* tanto por mil.
permissibility [pərˌmɪsəˈbɪlətɪ, B pəˌ-] *s.* capacidad de ser permitido.
permissible [-ˈmɪsəbəl] *a.* permisible.
permissibly [-blɪ] *adv.* de modo permisible, lícitamente.
permission [-ˈmɪʃən] *s.* permiso, autorización, licencia.
permissive [-ˈmɪsɪv] *s.* 1. permisivo. 2. tolerante, indulgente.
permissively [-lɪ] *adv.* 1. permisivamente. 2. indulgentemente, con tolerancia, tolerantemente.
permit [pərˈmɪt, B pəˈ-] *v.t.* (*pret., p.p.* PERMITTED; *p.pr.* PERMITTING) 1. permitir, tolerar, consentir. 2. autorizar, acordar, otorgar (un permiso, una licencia, etc.). —*v.i.* admitir, prestarse a. — [ˈpɜrˌmɪt, B ˈpɜˌ-] *s.* pase, permiso, licencia, autorización.
permitter [-ˈmɪtər, B -tə] *s.* permisor, permitidor.
permittivity [ˌpɜrmɪˈtɪvətɪ, B ˌpɜmɪ-] *s.* (elec.) permitividad.
permutable [-əbəl] *a.* permutable.
permutation [-mjʊˈteɪʃən] *s.* permuta, permutación, trueque, cambio; (mat.) permutación.
permute [pərˈmjut, B pəˈ-] *v.t.* permutar, trocar, cambiar; alterar, variar; (mat.) permutar.
pernicious [pərˈnɪʃəs, B pəˈ-] *a.* pernicioso, nocivo, dañoso, dañino, perjudicial, fatal, mortal.
pernicious anaemia, (med.) anemia perniciosa.
perniciously [-lɪ] *adv.* perniciosamente.
perniciousness [-nəs] *s.* perniciosidad.
pernicketiness [-ˈnɪkətɪnəs] *s.* descontento escrupulosidad.
pernickety [-ətɪ] *a.* (fam.) descontentadizo, quisquilloso, demasiado escrupuloso; difícil, delicado.
peroneal [ˌperoʊˈniəl] *a.* (anat.) peroneo, peroneal.
peroneus [-ˈniəs] *s.* (*pl.* PERONEI [-ˈniˌaɪ]) (anat.) peroneo.
peroneus brevis [ˌpɛrəˈniəsˈbrivɪs] (anat.) peroneo lateral corto.
peroneus longus [-ˈlɔŋgəs] (anat.) peroneo lateral largo.
Peronist [pəˈroʊnəst] *a., s.* (pol., Arg.) peronista.
peroral [pərˈɔrəl] *a.* (med.) peroral.
perorate [ˈpɛrəˌreɪt] *v.i.* perorar, arengar, discursear.
peroration [ˌpɛrəˈreɪʃən] *s.* peroración.
peroxidase [pəˈrɑksəˌdeɪs, B -ˈrɔk-] *s.* (bioquím.) peroxidasa.
peroxide [-ˌsaɪd] **peroxid** [-sɪd] *s.* (quím.) peróxido; peróxido de hidrógeno. —*v.t.* teñirse el cabello con agua oxigenada.
peroxide blonde, rubia oxigenada.
peroxide of hydrogen, agua oxigenada.
perpend [ˈpɜrpənd, B ˈpɜpɛnd] *s.* (arq.) perpiaño.
perpend [pərˈpɛnd, B pəˈ-] *v.t., v.i.* (ant.) considerar, meditar, reflexionar.
perpendicular [ˌpɜrpənˈdɪkjələr, B ˌpɜpən-lə] *a.* 1. perpendicular, vertical; (geom.) perpendicular. 2. (fam.) de pie, parado (Am.). —*s.* perpendicular; posición vertical.
perpendicularity [-ˌdɪkjəˈlærətɪ] *s.* perpendicularidad.
perpendicularly [-ˈdɪkjələrlɪ, B -ləlɪ] *adv.* perpendicularmente.

perpent [ˈpɜrpənt, B ˈpɜpənt] *var. de* perpend.
perpetrate [ˈpɜrpəˌtreɪt, B ˈpɜpɪ-] *v.t.* perpetrar, cometer, consumar.
perpetration [ˌpɜrpəˈtreɪʃən, B ˌpɜpɪ-] *s.* perpetración, comisión, consumación.
perpetrator [-ər, B -ə] *s.* perpetrador.
perpetual [pərˈpɛtʃʊəl, B pəˈ-] *a.* perpetuo, eterno, imperecedero, permanente, perenne, perdurable, continuo; (bot.) perenne. —*s.* (bot.) plantas perennes.
perpetual calendar, calendario perpetuo.
perpetually [-ɪ] *adv.* perpetuamente, eternamente, perdurablemente.
perpetual motion, movimiento continuo o perpetuo.
perpetuate [-ˌeɪt] *v.t.* perpetuar, eternizar, inmortalizar.
perpetuation [pərˌpɛtʃʊˈeɪʃən, B pəˌ-] *s.* perpetuación.
perpetuator [-ˈpɛtʃʊˌeɪtər, B -ə] *s.* perpetuador.
perpetuity [ˌpɜrpəˈtuətɪ, B ˌpɜpɪˈtju-] *s.* 1. perpetuidad, eternidad. 2. (der.) perpetuidad. 3. anualidad perpetua, renta perpetua.
perplex [pərˈplɛks, B pəˈ-] *v.t.* 1. confundir, aturdir, desconcertar. 2. intrincar, embrollar, enredar.
perplexed [-ˈplɛkst] *a.* 1. perplejo, confuso, indeciso, irresoluto, vacilante. 2. intrincado, enredado.
perplexedly [-ˈplɛksədlɪ, -ˈplɛkstlɪ] *adv.* perplejamente, confusamente.
perplexing [-ˈplɛksɪŋ] *a.* que deja perplejo.
perplexingly [-lɪ] *adv.* con perplejidad o incertidumbre.
perplexity [-ˈplɛksətɪ] *s.* perplejidad, confusión, duda, irresolución, indecisión, incertidumbre, vacilación.
perquisite [ˈpɜrkwəzət, B ˈpɜkwɪ-] *s.* 1. obvención, gaje, adehala. 2. gratificación; emolumento.
perron [ˈpɛrən] *s.* (arq.) escalinata, grada al aire libre.
perry [ˈpɛrɪ] *s.* (pr. G.B.) zumo o jugo de peras.
persalt [ˈpɜrˌsɔlt, B ˈpɜˌ-] *s.* (quím.) persal.
per se [ˌpɜrˈsi, -ˈseɪ, B ˌpɜˈ-] per se, por sí, por sí mismo.
perse [pɜrs, B pɜs] *a.* azul, esp. azul oscuro.
persecute [ˈpɜrsɪˌkjut, B ˈpɜsɪ-] *v.t.* perseguir, acosar, hostigar; importunar, molestar.
persecution [ˌpɜrsɪˈkjuʃən, B ˌpɜsɪ-] *s.* persecución, perseguimiento.
persecutive [ˈpɜrsɪˌkjutɪv, B ˈpɜsɪ-] *a.* persecutorio, perseguidor.
persecutor [-ər, B -ə] *s.* perseguidor.
persecutory [-ərɪ, -kjʊˌtɔrɪ, B -ˌkjutərɪ] *a.* persecutorio, perseguidor.
Perseid [ˈpɜrsɪəd, B ˈpɜsɪ-] *s.* (astr.) Perseida.
Persephone [pərˈsɛfənɪ, B pəˈ-] *s.* (mitol.) Perséfone, hija de Zeus, identificada por los romanos como Proserpina.
Persepolis [-ˈsɛpələs] *s.* (hist.) Persépolis.
Perseus [ˈpɜrˌsus, -sɪəs, B ˈpɜˌsjus] *s.* (astr.) Perseo; (mitol.) Perseo, el que mató a Medusa y rescató a Andrómeda.
perseverance [ˌpɜrsəˈvɪrəns, B ˌpɜsɪˈvɪər-] *s.* perseverancia, persistencia, constancia, tesón, firmeza.
persevere [-ˈvɪr, B -ˈvɪə] *v.i.* perseverar, persistir; obstinarse, insistir o continuar tenazmente.
persevering [-ɪŋ, B -rɪŋ] *a.* perseverante, tenaz, persistente.
perseveringly [-lɪ] *adv.* perseverantemente, tenazmente.
Persian [ˈpɜrʒən, B ˈpɜʃən] *s.* persa (natural e idioma de Persia). —*a.* persa.

Persian blinds, persianas.
Persian lamb, 1. caracol nonato. 2. astracán (piel).
Persian wheel, noria.
persicary ['pɜrsəˌkɛrɪ, B 'pɜsɪ-] *s.* (*pl.* PERSICARIES) (bot.) persicaria, duraznillo, hierba pejiguera.
persiennes [ˌpɜrzɪ'ɛnz, B ˌpɜsɪ-] *s.* (fr.) *pl.* persiana.
persiflage ['pɜrsəˌflɑʒ, B ˌpɛəsɪ'flɑʒ] *s.* burla fina, parloteo festivo.
persimmon [pər'sɪmən, B pə'-] *s.* (bot.) placaminero, caqui.
persist [pər'sɪst, -'zɪst, B pə'sɪst] *v.i.* 1. persistir, perseverar. 2. insistir, porfiar, obstinarse. 3. **p. in (doing),** persistir en (hacer).
persistence [-'sɪstəns, -'zɪs-, B -'sɪs-] *s.* 1. persistencia, perseverancia, tenacidad. 2. insistencia.
persistency [-tənsɪ] *s.* persistencia, perseverancia, tenacidad.
persistent [-tənt] *a.* 1. persistente, tenaz. 2. permanente, durable; constante, recurrente. 3. (bot., zool.) persistente.
persistently [-lɪ] *adv.* persistentemente, tenazmente.
persnickety [pər'snɪkətɪ, B pə'-] *a.* (fam.) descontentadizo, quisquilloso, demasiado escrupuloso; difícil, delicado.
person ['pɜrsən, B 'pɜsən] *s.* 1. persona. 2. (despec.) tipo, individuo. 3. (gram.) persona. 4. (der.) persona (convencional, jurídica, etc.). 5. (ant.) personaje. 6. **in p.,** en persona.
persona [pər'soʊnə, B pə'-] *s.* (*pl.* PERSONAE [-ni]) (*ú. esp. en pl.*) personaje (de un drama, novela, etc.).
personable ['pɜrsənəbəl, B 'pɜs-] *a.* atractivo, guapo, bien parecido; agradable.
personage [-ənɪdʒ] *s.* 1. personaje, persona eminente. 2. personaje (histórico, dramático, etc.); personificación. 3. persona, individuo, tipo.
persona grata [pər'soʊnə'grætə, B pə'-'grɑtə] (*pl.* PERSONAE GRATAE O PERSONA GRATA), (dipl.) persona grata.
personal ['pɜrsənəl, B 'pɜs-] *a.* 1. personal, particular, privado. 2. personal, directo, sin mediación. 3. de carácter personal (consideración, observación, etc.). 4. (der.) personal, privado (propiedad). 5. (gram.) personal (pronombre, sufijo, etc.). 6. **to become p.,** hacer alusiones de carácter personal; **to make a p. appearance,** presentarse o aparecer en persona. —*s.* (E.U.) nota particular (en periódicos).
personal appearance, arreglo personal.
personal computer, computador personal, computadora personal, ordenador personal (Esp.).
personal effects, efectos personales, bienes de uso personal.
personal equation, factor personal; punto de vista personal.
personal file, legajo personal, dossier; archivo individual.
personal injury, (der.) lesión o daño corporal.
personalism [-ˌɪzəm] *s.* (filos.) personalismo.
personalist [-əst] *s.* (filos.) personalista.
personality [ˌpɜrsə'nælətɪ, B ˌpɜsə-] *s.* (*pl.* PERSONALITIES) 1. personalidad, características individuales. 2. personaje conocido.
personalization [-ənələ'zeɪʃən, B -laɪ-] *s.* personalización, personificación.
personalize ['pɜrsənəˌlaɪz, B 'pɜs-] *v.t.* 1. personalizar, personificar. 2. prestar carácter individual a algo.
personally [-əlɪ] *adv.* personalmente, en persona, individualmente.
personal pronoun, (gram.) pronombre personal.
personal stereo, walkman.
personal property, (der.) bienes muebles.
personalty ['pɜrsənəltɪ, B 'pɜs-] *s.* (*pl.* PERSONALITIES) (der.) bienes muebles.
persona non grata [pər'soʊnəˌnɑn'grætə, B pə'-ˌnɔn'grɑtə] (*pl.* PERSONAE NON GRATAE O PERSONA NON GRATA) (dipl.) persona no grata o no aceptable.
personate ['pɜrsənˌeɪt, B 'pɜs-] *v.t.* 1. hacer el papel de; hacerse pasar por, representar (esp. falsamente). 2. (poét.) personificar. —*a.* (bot.) personada (corola).
personation [ˌpɜrsən'eɪʃən, B ˌpɜs-] *s.* 1. representación. 2. personificación. 3. representación fraudulenta, imitación engañosa, usurpación del nombre (de otra persona).
personator ['pɜrsənˌeɪtər, B 'pɜs-ə] *s.* personificador; impostor.
personification [pərˌsɑnəfə'keɪʃən, B pəˌsɔn-] *s.* personificación, encarnación.
personifier [-'sɑnəˌfaɪər, B -'sɔnɪˌfaɪə] *s.* personificador.
personify [-ˌfaɪ] *v.t.* (*pret., p.p.* PERSONIFIED; *p.pr.* PERSONIFYING) personificar, encarnar, simbolizar.
personnel [ˌpɜrsə'nɛl, B ˌpɜsə-] *s.* personal (de una firma, casa, etc.). —*a.* del personal; **p. office,** departamento de colocación o empleo.
person-to-person, *adv.* 1. particular a particular, personalmente. 2. (tele.) — **to call somebody p.,** llamar a algn. de persona a persona.
person-to-person call, (tele.) llamada de persona a persona, conferencia persona a persona.
perspective [pər'spɛktɪv, B pə'-] *s.* 1. perspectiva. 2. (ant.) lente óptica. 3. **in p.,** en perspectiva; en su debida perspectiva. 4. (geom.) proyecto.
perspectively [-lɪ] *adv.* con arreglo a la perspectiva.
perspicacious [ˌpɜrspə'keɪʃəs, B ˌpɜrspɪ-] *a.* 1. perspicaz, sagaz, agudo. 2. (raro) de buena vista.
perspicaciously [-lɪ] *adv.* perspicazmente, sagazmente.
perspicacity [-'kæsətɪ] *s.* perspicacia, sagacidad, agudeza.
perspicuity [-'kjuətɪ] *s.* perspicuidad, claridad, lucidez.
perspicuous [pər'spɪkjuəs, B pə'-] *a.* perspicuo, claro, transparente; inteligible; lúcido.
perspicuously [-lɪ] *adv.* perspicuamente, claramente, manifiestamente.
perspicuousness [-nəs] *s.* perspicuidad, claridad, lucidez.
perspiration [ˌpɜrspə'reɪʃən, B ˌpɜspɪ-] *s.* transpiración, sudor.
perspiratory [pər'spaɪrəˌtɔrɪ B pə'-tərɪ] *a.* perspiratorio; sudoríparo (folículo, glándula).
perspire [-'spaɪr, B -'spaɪə] *v.i.* transpirar, sudar.
persuadable [-'sweɪdəbəl] *a.* fácil de convencer o persuadir.
persuade [pər'sweɪd, B pə'-] *v.t.* 1. persuadir, inducir, mover; convencer. 2. instar, urgir, rogar.
persuader [-ər, B -ə] *s.* 1. persuasor, inducidor. 2. (jer.) revólver.
persuasible [-'sweɪsəbəl, -zə-] *a* fácil de convencer o persuadir.
persuasion [pər'sweɪʒən, B pə'-] *s.* 1. persuasión, inducción. 2. persuasiva, poder de persuasión. 3. creencia, convicción, credo (esp. religioso); secta, denominación. 4. (hum.) género, clase, especie.
persuasive [-'sweɪsɪv] *a.* persuasivo, suasorio.
persuasively [-lɪ] *adv.* persuasivamente.
persuasiveness [-nəs] *s.* persuasiva.
pert [pɜrt, B pɜt] *a.* vivaz, gracioso, animado.
pertain [pər'teɪn, B pə'-] *v.i.* 1. pertenecer, corresponder. 2. ser apropriado o conveniente. 3. atañer, concernir, incumbir. 4. **pertaining to,** tocante a, perteneciente a, característico de, peculiar de; vinculado a, relacionado con; referente a, relativo a.
pertinacious [ˌpɜrtə'neɪʃəs, B ˌpɜtɪ-] *a.* pertinaz, persistente, tenaz; porfiado, terco, testarudo, obstinado.
pertinaciously [-lɪ] *adv.* pertinazmente, persistentemente, tenazmente; porfiadamente, tercamente, obstinadamente.
pertinaciousness [-nəs] *s.* pertinacia, persistencia, tenacidad; porfía, terquedad, obstinación.
pertinence ['pɜrtənəns, B 'pɜt-] *s.* pertinencia, correspondencia.
pertinency [-ənsɪ] *s. var. de* **pertinence.**
pertinent [-ənt] *a.* pertinente.
pertinently [-lɪ] *adv.* pertinentemente, a propósito.
pertly ['pɜrtlɪ, B 'pɜt-] *adv.* animadamente, vivazmente, graciosamente.
pertness [-nəs] *s.* animación, vivacidad, gracia, salero.
perturb [pər'tɜrb, B pə'tɜb] *v.t.* perturbar, turbar, alterar, trastornar; agitar; descomponer.
perturbable [-əbəl] *a.* perturbable, alterable.
perturbation [ˌpɜrtər'beɪʃən, B ˌpɜtə'-] *s.* 1. perturbación, turbación; alteración; trastorno; inquietud, agitación. 2. (astr.) perturbación.
pertussis [pər'tʌsəs, B pə'-] *s.* (med.) tos ferina o convulsiva, coqueluche.
Peru [pə'ru] *s.* el Perú.
Perugian [pə'rudʒən] *a., s.* perusino, de Perusa, Italia.
peruke [pə'ruk] *s.* peluca, peluquín.
perusal [pə'ruzəl] *s.* lectura cuidadosa; p. ext., lectura.
peruse [pə'ruz] *v.t.* 1. leer cuidadosamente; p. ext., leer. 2. (fig.) examinar, escudriñar, inspeccionar, estudiar.
peruser [-ər, B -ə] *s.* 1. lector (cuidadoso). 2. escudriñador.
Peruvian [pə'ruvɪən] *a., s.* peruano.
Peruvian bark, (bot.) quina, quinaquina, chinchona, cascarilla.
Peruvian daffodil, (bot.) amancay.
pervade [pər'veɪd, B pə'-] *v.t.* penetrar, saturar; ocupar, llenar, invadir.
pervasion [-'veɪʒən] *s.* penetración, esparcimiento, saturación; invasión.
pervasive [-'veɪsɪv] *a.* penetrante.
pervasively [-lɪ] *adv.* penetrantemente.
pervasiveness [-nəs] *s.* capacidad de penetración, fuerza penetrante.
perverse [pər'vɜrs, B pə'vɜs] *a.* 1. perverso, depravado, pervertido. 2. contumaz, refractario. 3. avieso, díscolo; petulante, malhumorado.
perversely [-lɪ] *adv.* perversamente, aviesamente.
perverseness [-nəs] *s.* 1. perversidad, maldad, corrupción, depravación. 2. contumacia.
perversion [-'vɜrʒən, -ʃən, B pə'vɜʃən] *s.* 1. perversión, corrupción, depravación. 2. perversión (sexual).
perversity [-'vɜrsətɪ, B -'vɜsɪ-] *s.* 1. perversidad; corrupción, depravación. 2. acción perversa, acto perverso.
perversive [-'vɜrsɪv, B -'vɜsɪv] *a.* pervertidor, corruptivo, corruptor.
pervert [pər'vɜrt, B pə'vɜt] *v.t.* 1. pervertir, corromper, depravar. 2. falsear, desnaturalizar, adulterar. 3. (fig.) desviar, extraviar. —

['pɜrˌvɜrt, B 'pɜˌvɜt] *s.* 1. pervertido sexual. 2. (ant.) renegado, apóstata.
perverted [-'vɜrtəd, B -'vɜt-] *a.* pervertido, corrompido; vicioso; desviado, extraviado.
pervertedly [-lɪ] *adv.* corrompidamente; con perversión o extravío.
perverter [-'vɜrtər, B -'vɜtə] *s.* pervertidor, depravador.
pervertible [-əbəl] *a.* pervertible, corrompible.
pervious ['pɜrvɪəs, B 'pɜvjəs] *a.* permeable, penetrable.
perviousness [-nəs] *s.* permeabilidad.
pesky ['pɛskɪ] *a.* (fam. E.U.) cargante, molesto, engorroso.
pessary ['pɛsərɪ] *s.* (med.) pesario.
pessimism ['pɛsəˌmɪzəm] *s.* pesimismo.
pessimist [-məst] *s.* pesimista.
pessimistic [ˌpɛsə'mɪstɪk] *a.* pesimista; abatido, triste.
pessimistically [-tɪkəlɪ] *adv.* con pesimismo; abatidamente.
pest [pɛst] *s.* 1. peste, pestilencia. 2. chinche, pelmazo, machaca, tipo pesado. 3. insecto dañino, plaga.
Pestalozzian [ˌpɛstə'lɑtsɪən, B -'lɔt-] *a.* (educ.) pestalociano.
pester ['pɛstər, B -tə] *v.t.* 1. molestar, fastidiar, importunar. 2. (ant.) llenar, atestar.
pesthole ['pɛstˌhoʊl] *s.* foco de epidemia o de infección.
pesthouse [-ˌhaʊs] *s.* (ant.) lazareto; hospital de infecciosos.
pesticide ['pɛstəˌsaɪd] *s.* (quím.) insecticida.
pestiferous [pɛs'tɪfərəs] *a.* 1. pestífero, pestilente. 2. nocivo, malsano, pernicioso. 3. (fam.) enfadoso, fastidioso; molesto.
pestilence ['pɛstələns] *s.* pestilencia, peste; esp. peste bubónica.
pestilent [-lənt] *a.* 1. mortífero, letal. 2. (fig.) pernicioso, perjudicial. 3. enfadoso, fastidioso, molesto. 4. pestilente, infeccioso, pestífero.
pestilential [ˌpɛstə'lɛntʃəl, B -'lɛnʃəl] *a.* 1. pestilencial. 2. nocivo, perjudicial. 3. enfadoso, irritante.
pestle ['pɛsəl] *s.* majadero, mano de almirez o mortero, pistadero. —*v.t.*, *v.i.* majar, triturar, pistar.
pet [pɛt] *s.* 1. mascota, animal regalón. 2. persona mimada; predilecto, favorito. 3. (fam.) amor, ej., *he's a p.*, es un amor. —*a.* 1. mimado, regalón. 2. favorito; especial, ej., *p. aversión*, fobia especial. —*v.t.* (*pret., p.p.* PETTED; *p.pr.* PETTING) mimar, acariciar. —*v.i.* acariciarse, besuquearse.
pet, *s.* fanfurriña, enojo pasajero, acceso de mal humor; **in a p.,** enojado, malhumorado; **to take p.,** ofenderse, disgustarse. —*v.i.* estar enojado, enfurruñarse.
petal ['pɛtəl] *s.* (bot.) pétalo.
petaled, petalled [-əld] *a.* que tiene pétalos, provisto de pétalos.
petaline [-əlɪn, B -əlaɪn] *a.* (bot.) petalino.
petalism [-əˌlɪzəm] *s.* (hist.) petalismo; destierro.
petaloid ['pɛtəlˌɔɪd] *a.* (bot.) petaloide, petaloideo.
petalous [-əs] *a.* (bot.) provisto de pétalos.
petard [pə'tɑrd, B -'tɑd] *s.* petardo; triquitraque.
petardeer [ˌpɛtər'dɪr, B -ə'dɪə] *s.* petardero.
petasos, petasus ['pɛtəsəs] *s.* (hist., mitol.) petaso; sombrero alado de Hermes (Mercurio).
petcock ['pɛtˌkɑk, B -ˌkɔk] *s.* (mec.) llave de purga, llave de desagüe; grifo de purga (en cilindros de vapor); (mot.) grifo de descompresión.

petechia [pə'tikɪə] *s.* (*pl.* PETECHIAE [-kɪi]) (med.) petequia.
petechial [-kɪəl] *a.* (med.) petequial.
peter ['pitər, B -ə] *v.i.* (fam.) (gen. con *out*) agotarse, acabarse; desaparecer o disminuir paulatinamente.
Peter Pan [-'pæn] (fig.) niño eterno, niño que no quiere crecer.
petersham [-ʃəm] *s.* tela gruesa de lana; abrigo grueso.
Peter's pence, dinero de San Pedro, óbolo de San Pedro.
petiolar ['pɛtɪələr, B -ˌoʊlə] *a.* (bot.) peciolar.
Petiolata [ˌpɛtɪə'lɑtə, B -'leɪtə] *s. pl.* (zool.) peciolados.
petiolate ['pɛtɪəˌleɪt] **petiolated** [-əd] *a.* (bot.) peciolado.
petiole [-ɪˌoʊl] *s.* (bot., zool.) pecíolo.
petiolule [-ɪəˌlul, B ˌpɛtɪ'ɔljul] *s.* (bot.) peciólulo.
petit ['pɛtɪ] *a.* (der.) menor; **p. jury,** jurado de juicio; jurado.
petit bourgeois, pequeño burgués.
petite [pə'tit] *a.* pequeña, chiquita, diminuta (díc. de la mujer pequeña y bien proporcionada).
petition [pə'tɪʃən] *s.* 1. petición, solicitud. 2. ruego, súplica; plegaria, oración. 3. (der.) petición, recurso, instancia, demanda. —*v.t.* rogar, suplicar; solicitar a. —*v.i.* presentar una petición o solicitud.
petitionary [-ˌɛrɪ, B -ərɪ] *a.* petitorio.
petitioner [-ər, B -ə] *s.* peticionario, suplicante, recurrente, demandante.
petit mal [pə'ti'mæl] pequeño mal, epilepsia leve.
petit point ['pɛtɪˌpɔɪnt] (cost.) petit point, punto de tapicería.
pet name, apodo cariñoso.
peto ['peɪtoʊ, B 'pi-] *s.* (ict.) peto, wahoo.
Petrarch ['piˌtrɑrk, B 'pɛtrɑk] *s.* (hist., lit.) Petrarca, poeta lírico italiano.
Petrarchism [-ˌɪzəm] *s.* petrarquismo, influencia de Petrarca.
petrel ['pɛtrəl] *s.* (orn.) petrel; petrel de las tormentas.
petri dish ['pitrɪ-, B 'pɛ-] (bact.) cápsula o caja de Petri.
petrifaction [ˌpɛtrə'fækʃən] *s.* petrificación, fosilización.
petrifactive [-'fæktɪv] *a.* petrífico, petrificante.
petrification [-fə'keɪʃən] *s.* petrificación, fosilización.
petrify ['pɛtrəˌfaɪ] *v.t.* (*pret., p.p.* PETRIFIED; *p.pr.* PETRIFYING) 1. petrificar. 2. (fig.) petrificar, paralizar, entorpecer. —*v.i.* petrificarse.
Petrinism ['pitrəˌnɪzəm] *s.* (relig.) petrinismo.
petrochemical [ˌpɛtroʊ'kɛmɪkəl] *s.* petroquímico.
petrochemistry [-'kɛməstrɪ] *s.* petroquímica.
petroglyph ['pɛtrəˌglɪf] *s.* (arqueol.) petroglifo.
petrographer [pə'trɑgrəfər, B -'trɔgrəfə] *s.* (min., geol.) petrógrafo.
petrography [-fɪ] *s.* (min., geol.) petrografía.
petrol ['pɛtrəl] *s.* (G.B.) gasolina.
petrolatum [ˌpɛtrə'leɪtəm] *s.* (farm.) petrolato, petrolado.
petroleum [pə'troʊlɪəm] *s.* petróleo; **p. industry,** industria petrolera.
petroleum jelly, petrolato, petrolado.
petrologist [pə'trɑlədʒəst, B -'trɔl-] *s.* (geol., min.) petrólogo.
petrology [-dʒɪ] *s.* (geol., min.) petrología.
petronel ['pɛtrənəl] *s.* (hist.) pistola antigua de caballería que se disparaba apoyándola en el pecho.

Petronius [pə'troʊnɪəs] *s.* (hist., lit.) Petronio, escritor y árbitro social en la Roma neroniana.
petrosal [pə'troʊsəl] *a.* (anat.) petrosal.
petrosal bone, (anat.) petrosa, peñasco del temporal.
petrous ['pɛtrəs, 'pi-] *a.* 1. pétreo, rocoso, duro. 2. (anat.) petroso.
petticoat ['pɛtɪˌkoʊt] *s.* 1. enagua, enaguas, refajo, fustán (Am.). 2. (fig., fam.) mujer, muchacha. —*a.* de mujeres (gobierno).
petticoat insulator, (elec.) aislador de campana.
pettifog [-ˌfɔg, -ˌfɑg, B -ˌfɔg] *v.i.* (*pret., p.p.* PETTIFOGGED; *p.pr.* PETTIFOGGING) trapacear, tinterillar (Amer.).
pettifogger [-ər, B -ə] *s.* rábula, tinterillo, abogado picapleitos.
pettifoggery [-ərɪ] *s.* trapacería, tinterillada; triquiñuela de abogado.
pettifogging [-ɪŋ] *a.* trapacero.
pettily ['pɛtəlɪ] *adv.* mezquinamente.
pettiness [-ɪnəs] *s.* 1. pequeñez, insignificancia, trivialidad. 2. mezquindad.
petting party [-ɪŋ-] fiesta licenciosa (gen. de jóvenes).
pettish [-ɪʃ] *a.* displicente, irritable, quisquilloso.
pettishly [-lɪ] *adv.* displicentemente, irritablemente, quisquillosamente.
pettitoes ['pɛtɪˌtoʊz] *s. pl.* 1. pezuñas del cerdo; patitas del cerdo (usadas como alimento). 2. (fam.) dedos o pies, esp. de los niños.
pettle ['pɛtəl] *v.t.* (esco.) apreciar, estimar; mimar; acariciar.
petty ['pɛtɪ] *a.* 1. insignificante, trivial, despreciable. 2. mezquino, roñoso. 3. inferior, subalterno, subordinado.
petty average, (seguros) avería menor.
petty cash, (ten.) caja chica, gastos menores de caja.
petty farmers, pequeños agricultores.
petty jury, jurado de juicio (gen. compuesto de doce personas).
petty larceny, (der.) ratería, hurto menor.
petty officer, (mar.) cabo de mar, oficial de mar.
petty thief, ladronzuelo, ratero.
petulance ['pɛtʃələns, B 'pɛtjʊ-] *s.* malhumor, mal genio.
petulant [-lənt] *a.* malhumorado, quisquilloso, irritable.
petulantly [-lɪ] *adv.* malhumoradamente.
petunia [pə'tunjə, B -'tjun-] *s.* (bot.) petunia.
petuntse, petuntze [pə'tʊntsə] *s.* (cerá.) petunsé.
pew [pju] *s.* 1. banco de iglesia. 2. (fam. G.B.) asiento. 3. (*pl.*) congregación, cofradía.
pewee ['piwi] *s.* (orn.) papamoscas norteamericano.
pewit ['piwɪt] *s.* (orn.) especie de ave fría; gaviota de capucho café; papamoscas norteamericano.
pewter ['pjutər, B -ə] *s.* peltre; utensilio de peltre. —*a.* de peltre.
pewterer [-ərər, B -ərə] *s.* peltrero.
peyote [peɪ'oʊtɪ] **peyotl** [-'oʊtəl] *s.* 1. (bot.) peyote, péyotl. 2. peyote, mezcalina, mescalina (droga).
PFC *abrev. de* **Private First Class,** soldado raso.
PG *abrev. de* **parental guidance,** (cine.) menores acompañados.
PG-13 (E.U.) mayores de 13 años o menores acompañados.
Phaedra ['fidrə] *s.* (mitol.) Fedra, esposa de Teseo.
phaeton ['feɪətən, B 'feɪtən] *s.* faetón (carruaje).
phagedena, phagedaena [ˌfædʒə'dinə] *s.* (med.) fagedeno.

phagocyte ['fægəˌsaɪt] *s.* (biol.) fagocito.
phagocytic [ˌfægə'sɪtɪk] *a.* (biol.) fagocítico; fagocitario.
phagocytic index, (biol.) índice fagocitario.
phagocytosis [-saɪ'toʊsəs] *s.* (biol.) fagocitosis.
phalange ['feɪˌlændʒ, fə'lændʒ, B 'fælændʒ] *s.* (anat.) falange.
phalangeal [fə'lændʒɪəl] *a.* (anat.) falangiano.
phalanger [-dʒər, B -dʒə] *s.* (zool.) falangero.
phalanges, *pl. de* **phalanx.**
phalangette [ˌfælən'dʒɛt] *s.* (anat.) falangeta.
phalansterian [ˌfælən'stɪrɪən, B -'stɪər-] *a., s.* (sociol.) falansteriano.
phalanstery ['fælənˌstɛrɪ, B -stərɪ] *s.* (sociol.) falansterio.
phalanx ['feɪˌlæŋks, B 'fælˌæŋks] *s.* (*pl.* PHALANXES O PHALANGES [fə'lændʒiz]) 1. (*pl.* gen. PHALANXES) falange. 2. (anat., zool.) (*pl.* PHALANGES) falange.
phalarope ['fæləˌroʊp] *s.* (orn.) falaropo, falárope.
phallic ['fælɪk] *a.* fálico.
phallicism [-əˌsɪzəm] *s.* falismo, culto al falo.
phallus ['fæləs] *s.* (*pl.* PHALLI [-ˌaɪ] O PHALLUSES) (anat.) falo, pene.
phanerogam ['fænərəˌgæm] *s.* (bot.) fanerógama.
phanerogamic [ˌfænərə'gæmɪk] **phanerogamous** [-'rɑgəməs, B -'rɔg-] *a.* (bot.) fanerógamo.
phanerophyte ['fænərəˌfaɪt] *s.* (bot.) fanerofita.
phantasm ['fænˌtæzəm] *s.* fantasma, espectro, aparición; ilusión, fantasía.
phantasmagoria [ˌfænˌtæzmə'gɔrɪə] *s.* fantasmagoría.
phantasmagoric [-'gɔrɪk] *a.* fantasmagórico; ilusorio.
phantasmagory [fæn'tæzməˌgɔrɪ, B -gərɪ] *s.* (*pl.* PHANTASMAGORIES) fantasmagoría.
phantasmal [-'tæzməl] **phantasmic** [-mɪk] *a.* fantasmal.
phantasy, *s.* (*pl.* PHANTASIES) *var. de* **fantasy.**
phantom ['fæntəm] *s.* fantasma, espectro, aparición, quimera. —*a.* 1. fantasmal, ilusorio, quimérico. 2. ficticio, inexistente.
phantom horizon, (geo.) horizonte imaginario.
phantom view, vista translúcida o fantasmagórica.
Pharaoh ['fɛroʊ, B 'fɛər-] *s.* faraón.
Pharaonic [ˌfɛreɪ'ɑnɪk, B ˌfɛərɪ'ɔn-] *a.* faraónico.
pharisaic [ˌfærə'seɪɪk] **pharisaical** [-ɪkəl] *a.* 1. farisaico, hipócrita. 2. **P.,** farisaico, de los fariseos.
pharisaically [-ɪkəlɪ] *adv.* farisaicamente, hipócritamente.
pharisaism ['færəˌseɪˌɪzəm] *s.* 1. farisaísmo, fariseísmo. 2. **P.,** farisaísmo (doctrina).
Pharisee ['færəˌsi] *s.* 1. (hist.) fariseo. 2. **p.,** fariseo, hipócrita.
Phariseeism [-ˌɪzəm] *s.* 1. (hist.) farisaísmo, fariseísmo. 2. **p.,** fariseísmo, hipocresía.
pharm., Pharm. *abrev. de* 1. **pharmaceutical,** farmacéutico. 2. **pharmacist,** farmacéutico. 3. **pharmacopeia,** farmacopea. 4. **pharmacy,** farmacia.
pharmaceutic [ˌfɑrmə'sutɪk, B ˌfɑmə-] *a.* farmacéutico.
pharmaceutical [-ɪkəl] *a.* farmacéutico.
pharmaceutically [-ɪkəlɪ] *adv.* por medios farmacéuticos.
pharmaceutics [-ɪks] *s. pl.* (*sing. en const.*) farmacia, ciencia farmacéutica.
pharmacist ['fɑrməsəst, B 'fɑmə-] *s.* farmacéutico, boticario, farmaceuta (Am.); químico farmacéutico.
pharmacodynamic [ˌfɑrməkoʊˌdaɪ'næmɪk, B ˌfɑmə-] *a.* farmacodinámico.
pharmacodynamics [-'næmɪks] *s. pl.* (*sing. en const.*) farmacodinamia.
pharmacognosy [-'kɑgnəsɪ, B -'kɔg-] *s.* farmacognosia.
pharmacological [-kə'lɑdʒɪkəl, B -'lɔdʒ-] *a.* farmacológico.
pharmacologist [-'kɑlədʒəst, B -'kɔl-] *s.* farmacólogo.
pharmacology [-ədʒɪ] *s.* farmacología.
pharmacopeia, pharmacopoeia [ˌfɑrməkə'piə, B ˌfɑmə-] *s.* farmacopea.
pharmacy ['fɑrməsɪ, B 'fɑmə-] *s.* (*pl.* PHARMACIES) farmacia, botica.
Pharos ['fɛrˌɑs, B 'fɛərɔs] *s.* 1. (hist.) Faros. 2. **p.,** faro, fanal.
Pharsalia [fɑr'seɪljə, B fɑ'-] *s.* (hist.) Farsalia.
pharyngeal [fə'rɪndʒɪəl, B ˌfærɪn'dʒiəl] *a.* (anat.) faríngeo.
pharyngitis [ˌfærən'dʒaɪtəs] *s.* (med.) faringitis.
pharyngology [-ɪŋ'gɑlədʒɪ, B -'gɔl-] *s.* (med.) faringología.
pharyngoscope [fə'rɪŋgəˌskoʊp] *s.* faringoscopio.
pharyngoscopy [ˌfærɪŋ'gɑskəpɪ, B -'gɔs-] *s.* faringoscopia.
pharynx ['færɪŋks] *s.* (*pl.* PHARYNGES [fə'rɪndʒiz] O PHARYNXES) (anat.) faringe.
phase [feɪz] *s.* fase; (astr., biol., fís., elec., electrón., quím.) fase. —*v.t.* 1. ejecutar en fases; planear por fases. 2. (con *into*) introducir por fases o etapas (en). 3. (fís., elec., electrón.) poner en fase. 4. **p. out,** eliminar por fases, excluir o discontinuar por etapas.
phase advancer, (elec.) adelantador de fases.
phase contrast microscope, microscopio de contraste de fase.
phase meter, (rad.) fasómetro.
phase modulation, (rad.) modulación de fase.
phase shift, (rad.) cambio de fase.
phasing [-ɪŋ] *s.* (t.v.) ajuste de **fase.**
phasing transformer, (elec.) transformador de fase.
phasis ['feɪsɪs] *s.* (*pl.* PHASES [-siz]) aspecto, fase.
Ph. B. *abrev. de* **Bachelor of Philosophy,** Licenciado en Filosofía.
Ph. C. *abrev. de* **Pharmaceutical Chemist,** farmacéutico.
Ph. D. *abrev. de* **Doctor of Philosophy,** Doctor en Filosofía.
pheasant ['fɛzənt] *s.* (orn.) faisán.
phelloderm ['fɛləˌdɜrm, B -ˌdɜm] *s.* (bot.) felodermo, felodermis.
phellogen [-dʒən] *s.* (bot.) felógeno.
phellogenic [ˌfɛlə'dʒɛnɪk] *a.* (bot.) felogénico, felógeno.
phenacaine ['finəˌkeɪn, 'fɛnə-] *s.* **(farm.)** fenacaína.
phenacetin [fɪ'næsətən] *s.* (farm.) fenacetina.
phenacite ['fɛnəˌsaɪt] **phenakite** [-ˌkaɪt] *s.* (min.) fenacita, fenaquita.
phenanthrene [fə'nænˌθrin] *s.* (quím.) fenantreno.
phenazine ['fɛnəˌzin] *s.* (quím.) fenazina.
phenetidine [fə'nɛtəˌdin] *s.* (quím.) fenetidina.
phenetole ['fɛnəˌtoʊl, B -tɔl] *s.* (quím.) fenetol.
phenic ['finɪk] *a.* (quím.) fénico.
phenix, *var. de* **phoenix.**
phenobarbital [ˌfinoʊ'bɑrbəˌtɔl, B -'bɑbɪ-] *s.* (farm.) fenobarbital.
phenocopy ['finəˌkɑpɪ, B -ˌkɔpɪ] *s.* (biol.) fenocopia.
phenocryst [-ˌkrɪst] *s.* (geol.) fenocristal.
phenol ['fiˌnoʊl, B -nɔl] *s.* (quím.) fenol.
phenolate ['finəlˌeɪt] *s.* (quím.) fenolato.
phenolic [fɪ'noʊlɪk, -'nɑl-, B -'nɔl-] *a.* (quím.) fenólico.
phenologist [-'nɑlədʒəst, B -'nɔl-] *s.* experto en fenología.
phenology [-ədʒɪ] *s.* (biol.) fenología.
phenolphthalein [ˌfiˌnoʊl'θælɪən, B ˌfinɔl'fθæl-] *s.* (quím.) fenolftaleína, ftaleína del fenol.
phenomena, *pl. de* **phenomenon.**
phenomenal [fɪ'nɑmənəl, B -'nɔm-] *a.* fenomenal; (fig.) fenomenal, extraordinario, excepcional.
phenomenalism [-ˌɪzəm] *s.* (filos.) fenomenalismo.
phenomenalist [-əst] *a., s.* (filos.) fenomenalista.
phenomenalistic [-ˌnɑmənəl'ɪstɪk, B -ˌnɔm-] *a.* fenomenalista.
phenomenally [-'nɑmənəlɪ, B -'nɔm-] *adv.* fenomenalmente.
phenomenological [-ˌnɑmənəl'ɑdʒɪkəl, B -ˌnɔmɪnə'lɔdʒ-] *a.* (filos.) fenomenológico.
phenomenologist [-'nɑlədʒəst, B -'nɔl-] *s.* fenomenólogo.
phenomenology [-ədʒɪ] *s.* (filos.) fenomenología.
phenomenon [fɪ'nɑməˌnɑn, B fɪ'nɔmɪnən] *s.* (*pl.* PHENOMENA [-nə] O PHENOMENONS) 1. (filos.) fenómeno. 2. (fig.) (*pl.* PHENOMENONS) fenómeno, prodigio, portento.
phenothiazine [ˌfinoʊ'θaɪəˌzin] *s.* (quím.) fenotiazina.
phenotype ['finəˌtaɪp] *s.* (biol.) fenotipo.
phenotypic [ˌfinə'tɪpɪk] *a.* (biol.) fenotipo.
phenyl ['fɛnəl] *s.* (quím.) fenilo.
phenylalanine [ˌfɛnəl'æləˌnin, 'fi-] *s.* (bioquím.) fenilalanina.
phenylamine [-ə'min] *s.* (quím.) fenilamina.
phenylene ['fɛnəlˌin] *s.* (quím.) fenileno.
phi [faɪ] *s.* phi, vigésima primera letra del alfabeto griego.
phial ['faɪəl] *s.* ampolla, ampolleta, frasco pequeño.
Phi Beta Kappa, (E.U.) 1. sociedad de estudiantes universitarios con altos méritos académicos. 2. miembro de dicha sociedad.
Phidias ['fɪdɪəs, B -æs] *s.* Fidias, escultor griego.
Phil. *abrev. de* **Phillipians,** Epístola de San Pablo a los Filipenses (Filip.).
Phila. *abrev. de* **Philadelphia,** Filadelfia (E.U.).
Philadelphia [ˌfɪlə'dɛlfɪə] *s.* (E.U.) Filadelfia.
Philadelphia lawyer, abogado astuto (hoy ú. despec.).
philadelphus [-fəs] *s.* (bot.) filadelfa; **P.,** filadelfas.
philander [fə'lændər, B -də] *v.i.* galantear, flirtear.
philanderer [-dərər, B -dərə] *s.* cupido, galanteador, tenorio.
philanthropic [ˌfɪlən'θrɑpɪk, B -'θrɔp-] **philanthropical** [-ɪkəl] *a.* filantrópico, benévolo, caritativo.
philanthropically [-ɪkəlɪ] *adv.* filantrópicamente, en forma filantrópica.
philanthropist [fə'lænθrəpəst] *s.* filántropo.
philanthropy [-pɪ] *s.* 1. filantropía. 2. obra filantrópica, obra de filantropía.

philatelic [ˌfɪlə'tɛlɪk] *a.* filatélico.
philatelist [fə'lætələst] *s.* filatelista.
philately [-əlɪ] *s.* filatelia.
philharmonic [ˌfɪlər'mɑnɪk, ˌfɪlhɑr-, B ˌfɪlɑ'mɔnɪk] *a.* filarmónico. —*s.* orquesta filarmónica; sociedad filarmónica.
philhellene [fɪl'hɛlˌin, B 'fɪlˌhɛl-] *s.* filheleno. —*a.* filheleno, helenófilo, admirador de la cultura griega.
philhellenic [ˌfɪlhə'lɛnɪk, B -'lin-] *a.* filheleno, helenófilo.
Philippian [fə'lɪpɪən] *a., s.* filipense.
Philippians [-ɪənz] *s. pl.* (*sing. en const.*) (bíbl.) Epístola a los Filipenses.
Philippic [-ɪk] *s.* 1. (hist.) Filípica (de Demóstenes). 2. **p.,** filípica; invectiva, censura acre, diatriba.
Philippine ['fɪləˌpin] *a., s.* filipino.
Philippines [-ˌpinz] *s. pl.* (las) Filipinas.
Philistine ['fɪləˌstin, fə'lɪstən, B 'fɪlɪstaɪn] *s.* 1. (hist.) filisteo. 2. filisteo, individuo inculto. —*a.* filisteo; inculto, prosaico.
philistinism [-ˌɪzəm, B -tɪn-] *s.* falta de cultura; gusto prosaico o pedestre.
philodendron [ˌfɪlə'dɛndrən] *s.* (bot.) filodendro.
philological [ˌfɪlə'lɑdʒɪkəl, B -'lɔdʒ-] *a.* filológico.
philologist [fə'lɑlədʒəst, B -'lɔl-] *s.* filólogo, filóloga.
philology [-ədʒɪ] *s.* filología.
philomel ['fɪləˌmɛl] *s.* (poét.) filomela, filomena, ruiseñor.
philoprogenitive [ˌfɪləproʊ'dʒɛnətiv] *a.* 1. prolífico. 2. que ama a su progenie o descendencia.
philoprogenitiveness [-nəs] *s.* prolificidad; amor o cariño a la progenie.
philosopher [fə'lɑsəfər, B -'lɔsəfə] *s.* filósofo.
philosopher's stone, piedra filosofal.
philosophic [ˌfɪlə'sɑfɪk, B -'sɔf-] **philosophical** [-ɪkəl] *a.* filosófico.
philosophically [-ɪkəlɪ] *adv.* filosóficamente.
philosophism [fə'lɑsəˌfɪzəm, B -'lɔs-] *s.* filosofismo, falsa filosofía; sofistería; sofisma.
philosophize [-ˌfaɪz] *v.i.* filosofar; especular. meditar.
philosophizer [-ˌfaɪzər, B -ə] *s.* filosofador.
philosophy [-fɪ] *s.* (*pl.* PHILOSOPHIES) filosofía.
philter, philtre ['fɪltər, B -tə] *s.* filtro, bebedizo, poción mágica.
phiz [fɪz] *s.* (jer.) fisonomía, facha, cara.
phlebitis [flə'baɪtəs] *s.* (med.) flebitis.
phlebotomist [-'bɑtəməst, B -'bɔt-] *s.* flebotomista, flebotomiano, sangrador.
phlebotomize [-ˌmaɪz] *v.t., v.i.* (med.) sangrar(se); hacer(se) una venesección.
phlebotomy [-mɪ] *s.* (med.) flebotomía, sangría, venesección.
phlegm [flɛm] *s.* 1. (fisiol.) flema, moco, gargajo. 2. (fig.) flema, lentitud, cachaza.
phlegmasia [flɛg'meɪʒɪə, B -zɪə] *s.* (med.) flegmasía.
phlegmatic [-'mætɪk] **phlegmatical** [-ɪkəl] *a.* flemático, flemudo, cachazudo.
phlegmatically [-ɪkəlɪ] *adv.* flemáticamente, con cachaza.
phlegmon ['flɛgˌmɑn, B -ˌmɔn] *s.* (med.) flemón.
phlegmy [-mɪ] *a.* flemoso.
phloem ['floʊˌɛm] *s.* (bot.) floema.
phlogistic [floʊ'dʒɪstɪk, B flɔ-] *a.* (quím. ant.) flogístico.
phlogiston [-tən] *s.* (quím. ant.) flogisto.
phlogopite ['flɑgəˌpaɪt, B 'flɔg-] *s.* (min.) flogopita.
phlogosis [flə'goʊsəs] *s.* (med.) flogosis.
phlomis ['floʊmɪs] *s.* (bot.) candilera.
phlorizin ['flɔrəzɪn, flə'raɪzən] **phlorhizin** [flə'raɪzən] **phloridzin** [-'rɪdzən] *s.* (quím.) florizina, floridzina.
phlox [flɑks, B flɔks] *s.* (bot.) flox.
phlyctena [flɪk'tinə] *s.* (*pl.* PHLYCTENAE [-ni]) (med.) flictena.
phlyctenule [-'tɛnjul] *s.* (med.) flicténula.
phobia ['foʊbɪə] *s.* fobia, temor o aversión morbosa.
phobic [-bɪk] *a.* fóbico, rel. a la fobia.
Phobos ['foʊbɑs, B -bɔs] *s.* (astr.) Fobos.
Phocian ['foʊʃɪən] *a., s.* (hist.) focense.
phocine ['foʊsaɪn] *a.* (zool.) focino.
phoebe ['fibɪ] *s.* (orn.) papamoscas americano, aguador.
Phoebe, *s.* (astr., mitol.) Febe.
Phoebus ['fibəs] *s.* (mitol.) Febo; (poét.) Febo (el sol personificado).
Phoenician [fə'nɪʃən] *a., s.* fenicio.
phoenix ['finɪks] *s.* 1. (mitol.) fénix, ave fénix. 2. P., (astr.) ave fénix.
phon [fɑn, B fɔn] *s.* fon, fonio (unidad de intensidad del sonido).
phonate ['foʊˌneɪt, B foʊ'neɪt] *v.i.* articular, enunciar; emitir voz, producir fonación.
phonation [foʊ'neɪʃən] *s.* fonación.
phone [foʊn] *s.* (fam.) *contr. de* **telephone,** teléfono. —*v.t., v.i.* telefonear.
phone book, guía telefónica.
phone booth (E.U.), **phone box,** (Ingl.) cabina telefónica.
phone card, tarjeta telefónica.
phone-in ['foʊnˌɪn] *s.* (rad., t.v.) colloquio por teléfono.
phoneme ['foʊˌnɪm] *s.* (fon.) fonema.
phonemic [fə'nimik, foʊ-] *a.* (fon.) fonemático, fonémico.
phonemics [-mɪks] *s. pl.* (*sing. en const.*) fonemática, fonémica.
phonetic [-'nɛtɪk] *a.* fonético.
phonetically [-ɪkəlɪ] *adv.* fonéticamente.
phonetic alphabet, alfabeto fonético.
phonetician [ˌfoʊnə'tɪʃən] *s.* fonetista.
phonetics [fə'nɛtɪks, foʊ-] *s. pl.* (*sing. en const.*) fonética.
phonetic symbol, signo fonético.
phonetist ['foʊnətəst] *s.* fonetista.
phoney, *var. de* **phony.**
phonic ['fɑnɪk, B 'foʊ-] *a.* fónico.
phonics [-nɪks] *s. pl.* (*sing. en const.*) 1. ciencia del sonido; acústica. 2. fonética, esp. sistema de fonética elemental (que se emplea para enseñar a pronunciar y a leer a los niños).
phonily ['foʊnəlɪ] *adv.* falsamente.
phoniness [-ɪnəs] *s.* falsedad.
phonogram ['foʊnəˌgræm] *s.* fonograma.
phonograph [-ˌgræf, B -ˌgrɑf] *s.* fonógrafo.
phonographic [ˌfoʊnə'græfɪk] *a.* fonográfico.
phonographically [-ɪkəlɪ] *adv.* fonográficamente.
phonography [fə'nɑgrəfɪ, foʊ-, B -'nɔg-] *s.* fonografía.
phonolite ['foʊnəˌlaɪt] *s.* (min.) fonolita.
phonologic [ˌfoʊnə'lɑdʒɪk, B -'lɔdʒ-] **phonological** [-ɪkəl] *a.* fonológico.
phonologist [fə'nɑlədʒəst, foʊ-, B -'nɔl-] *s.* fonólogo.
phonology [-dʒɪ] *s.* fonología.
phonometer [-'nɑmətər, B -'nɔmɪtə] *s.* fonómetro.
phonometry [-ətrɪ] *s.* (fís.) fonometría.
phonoscope ['foʊnəˌskoʊp] *s.* fonoscopio.
phonotype [-ˌtaɪp] *s.* (impr.) fonotipo.
phonotypic [ˌfoʊnə'tɪpɪk] **phonotypical** [-ɪkəl] *a.* fonotípico.
phonotypy ['foʊnəˌtaɪpɪ] *s.* (impr.) fonotipia, impresión con tipos que representan sonidos.
phony ['foʊnɪ] (PHONIER; PHONIEST) (jer.) *a.* falso, falsificado. —*s.* (*pl.* PHONIES) 1. cosa falsificada. 2. farsante.
phooey ['fuɪ] *interj.* ¡puf!, ¡cuentos chinos! (exclamación que expresa disgusto o desprecio).
phosgene ['fɑzˌdʒin, 'fɑs-, B 'fɔz-] *s.* (quím.) fosgeno.
phosphatase ['fɑsfəˌteɪs, B 'fɔs-] *s.* (fisiol.) fosfatasa.
phosphate [-ˌfeɪt] *s.* 1. (quím., agr.) fosfato. 2. bebida efervescente (que contiene una pequeña cantidad de ácido fosfórico).
phosphate of lime, fosfato de cal.
phosphate rock, roca fosfatada.
phosphatic [fɑs'fætɪk, B fɔs-] *a.* fosfático.
phosphatide ['fɑsfəˌtaɪd, B 'fɔs-] *s.* (bioquím.) fosfátido.
phosphatization [ˌfɑsfətə'zeɪʃən, B ˌfɔsfətaɪ-] *s.* fosfatización.
phosphatize ['fɑsfəˌtaɪz, B 'fɔs-] *v.t.* (quím.) fosfatar; reducir a fosfato.
phosphaturia [ˌfɑsfə'tʊrɪə, B ˌfɔsfə'tjʊər-] *s.* (med.) fosfaturia.
phosphene ['fɑsˌfin, B 'fɔs-] *s.* (fisiol.) fosfeno.
phosphide [-ˌfaɪd] *s.* (quím.) fosfuro.
phosphine [-ˌfin, B -ˌfaɪn] *s.* (quím.) fosfina.
phosphite [-ˌfaɪt] *s.* (quím.) fosfito.
phosphocreatine [ˌfɑsfoʊ'kriəˌtin, B ˌfɔs-] *s.* (bioquím.) fosfocreatina.
phospholipid [-'lɪpɪd] *s.* (bioquím.) fosfolípido.
phosphonium [fɑs'foʊnɪəm, B fɔs-] *s.* (quím.) fosfonio.
phosphoprotein [ˌfɑsfoʊ'proʊˌtin, B ˌfɔs-] *s.* (bioquím.) fosfoproteína.
phosphor ['fɑsfər, B 'fɔsfə] *s.* 1. (astr.) P., Fósforo (lucero del alba). 2. (t. **phosphore** [-ˌfɔr, B -ˌfɔ]) substancia fosfórica. —*a.* (raro) fosforescente, luminiscente.
phosphorated [-fəˌreɪtəd] *a.* (quím.) fosforado.
phosphor bronze, bronce fosforado.
phosphoresce [ˌfɑsfə'rɛs, B ˌfɔs-] *v.i.* fosforescer.
phosphorescence [-'rɛsəns] *s.* fosforescencia.
phosphorescent [-ənt] *a.* fosforescente, luminiscente.
phosphoreted, phosphoretted ['fɑsfəˌrɛtəd, B 'fɔs-] *a.* (quím.) fosforado.
phosphoric [fɑs'fɔrɪk, -'fɑr-, B fɔs'fɔr-] *a.* (quím.) fosfórico.
phosphoric acid, (quím.) ácido fosfórico.
phosphorism ['fɑsfəˌrɪzəm, B 'fɔs-] *s.* (med.) fosforismo.
phosphorite [-ˌraɪt] *s.* (min.) fosforita.
phosphoroscope [fɑs'fɔrəˌskoʊp, -'fɑr-, B 'fɔsfɔrə-] *s.* fosforoscopio, aparato para medir la fosforescencia.
phosphorous ['fɑsfərəs, fɑs'fɔrəs, B 'fɔsfərəs] *a.* fosforoso, fosforado, fosfórico.
phosphorous acid, (quím.) ácido fosforoso.
phosphor tin, estaño fosforado.
phosphorus ['fɑsfərəs, B 'fɔs-] *s.* (quím.) fósforo.
phosphorylase [-fərəˌleɪs] *s.* (bioquím.) fosforilasa.
phosphorylate [-ˌleɪt] *v.t.* (quím.) fosforilar.
phot [foʊt, fɑt, B fɔt] *s.* (fís.) fotio, fot, foto (unidad de iluminación).

photic ['foʊtɪk] *a.* (fís., biol.) fótico.
photo ['foʊtoʊ] *s.* (*pl.* PHOTOS) foto, fotografía. —*v.t., v.i.* (*pret., p.p.* PHOTOED; *p.pr.* PHOTOING) fotografiar, fotografiarse.
photoactinic [ˌfoʊtoʊˌæk'tɪnɪk] *a.* (foto.) fotoactínico.
photoautotrophic [-ˌɔtə'trɑfɪk, B -'trɔf-] *a.* (bot.) fotoautótrofo.
photobiotic [-baɪ'ɑtɪk, B -'ɔtɪk] *a.* (biol.) fotobiótico.
photocell ['foʊtəˌsɛl] *s.* fotocélula, célula o pila fotoeléctrica.
photochemical [ˌfoʊtoʊ'kɛmɪkəl] *a.* fotoquímico.
photochemistry [-'kɛməstrɪ] *s.* fotoquímica.
photochronograph [-'krɑnəˌgræf, B -'krɔnəˌgrɑf] *s.* fotocronógrafo.
photocomposition [-ˌkɑmpə'zɪʃən, B -ˌkɔm-] *s.* fotocomposición, fotocalcografía.
photoconductive [-kən'dʌktɪv] *a.* fotoconductivo.
photoconductivity [-ˌkɑndʌk'tɪvətɪ, B -ˌkɔn-] *s.* (elec.) fotoconductibilidad.
photocopier ['foʊtə'kɑpɪər] *s.* fotocopiadora.
photocopy ['foʊtəˌkɑpɪ, B -ˌkɔpɪ] *a.* (*pl.* PHOTOCOPIES) fotocopia. —*v.t.* fotocopiar.
photocopying [ˌ-ɪŋ] *s.* fotocopia.
photocurrent [-ˌkɜrənt, B -ˌkʌrənt] *s.* (fís.) fotocorriente.
photodisintegration [ˌfoʊtoʊdɪsˌɪntə'greɪʃən] *s.* (fís.) fotodesintegración.
photodrama ['foʊtəˌdrɑmə, -ˌdræmə, B -ˌdrɑmə] *s.* drama cinematográfico.
photoduplication [ˌfoʊtoʊˌduplə'keɪʃən, B -ˌdju-] *s.* fotoduplicación.
photodynamic [-daɪ'næmɪk] *a.* fotodinámico.
photoelectric [-ɪ'lɛktrɪk] **photoelectrical** [-əl] *a.* fotoeléctrico.
photoelectric cell, célula fotoeléctrica, fotocélula.
photoelectron [-ˌtrɑn, B -ˌtrɔn] *s.* (fís.) fotoelectrón.
photoemission [-ɪ'mɪʃən] *s.* fotoemisión.
photoemissive [-'mɪsɪv] *a.* fotoemisor.
photoengrave [-ɪn'greɪv] *v.t.* fotograbar.
photoengraver [-'greɪvər, B -ə] *s.* fotograbador.
photoengraving [-ɪŋ] *s.* fotograbado (en relieve).
photo finish, (dep.) foto-finish, fallo fotográfico.
photoflash ['foʊtəˌflæʃ] *s.* (foto.) flash, luz relámpago.
photoflood [-ˌflʌd] *s.* (foto.) lámpara de iluminación intensiva.
photofluorography [ˌfoʊtəflʊ'rɑgrəfɪ, B -'rɔg-] *s.* fotofluorografía.
photogene ['foʊtəˌdʒin] *s.* fotógeno (imagen consecutiva o accidental que persiste después del estímulo).
photogenic [ˌfoʊtə'dʒɛnɪk] *a.* 1. fotogénico (que luce bien en fotografías). 2. (bot.) fotógeno. 3. (fís.) fotogénico.
photogram ['foʊtəˌgræm] *s.* fotograma.
photogrammetric [ˌfoʊtəgrə'mɛtrɪk] *a.* fotogramétrico.
photogrammetry [-'græmətrɪ] *s.* (foto.) fotogrametría.
photograph ['foʊtəˌgræf, B -ˌgrɑf] *s.* fotografía. —*v.i., v.t.* fotografiar(se), retratar(se).
photograph axis, eje fiducial.
photographer [fə'tɑgrəfər, B -'tɔgrəfə] *s.* fotógrafo, fotógrafa.
photographic [ˌfoʊtə'græfɪk] *a.* fotográfico.
photographic studio, estudio fotográfico.
photographically [-ɪkəlɪ] *adv.* fotográficamente.
photography [fə'tɑgrəfɪ, B -'tɔg-] *s.* fotografía.
photogravure [ˌfoʊtəgrə'vjʊr, B -'vjʊə] *s.* fotograbado en hueco, huecograbado, heliograbado, fotohuecograbado.
photoheliograph [-'hilɪəˌgræf, B -ˌgrɑf] *s.* fotoheliógrafo.
photokinesis [-kə'nisəs, B -kaɪ-] *s.* (fisiol.) fotocinesis.
photokinetic [-'nɛtɪk] *a.* fotocinético.
photolith ['foʊtəˌlɪθ] *s.* fotolito.
photolithograph [ˌfoʊtə'lɪθəˌgræf, B -ˌgrɑf] *v.t.* fotolitografiar. —*s.* fotolitografía.
photolithographic [-ˌlɪθə'græfɪk] *a.* fotolitográfico.
photolithography [-lɪ'θɑgrəfɪ, B -'θɔg-] *s.* fotolitografía.
photolysis [foʊ'tɑləsəs, B -'tɔl-] *s.* (bot., fís., quím.) fotólisis.
photomap ['foʊtəˌmæp] *s.* (fotogmt.) fotomapa.
photomechanical [ˌfoʊtoʊmə'kænɪkəl] *a.* fotomecánico.
photometer [foʊ'tɑmətər, B -tɔmɪtə] *s.* fotómetro.
photometric [ˌfoʊtə'mɛtrɪk] *a.* fotométrico.
photometry [foʊ'tɑmətrɪ, B -'tɔm-] *s.* fotometría.
photomicrograph [ˌfoʊtə'maɪkrəˌgræf, B -ˌgrɑf] *s.* fotomicrografía.
photomicrography [-maɪ'krɑgrəfɪ, B -'krɔg-] *s.* fotomicrografía.
photomontage [-mɑn'tɑʒ, B -mɔn-] *s.* fotomontaje, montaje fotográfico.
photomultiplier [-'mʌltəˌplaɪər, B -ə] *s.* (fís.) fotomultiplicador.
photomural [-'mjʊrəl, B -'mjʊər-] *s.* mural fotográfico, fotomural (ampliación de gran tamaño).
photon ['foʊˌtɑn, B -ˌtɔn] *s.* (ópt., fís.) fotón, fotónico.
photo-offset [ˌfoʊtoʊ'ɔfˌsɛt] *s.* (impr.) offset, impresión indirecta, calco.
photoperiod [-'pɪrɪəd, B -'pɪər-] *s.* (bot.) fotoperíodo.
photoperiodism [-ˌɪzəm] *s.* (bot.) fotoperiodicidad.
photophilic [-'fɪlɪk] *a.* (bot.) fotófilo.
photophilous [foʊ'tɑfələs, B -'tɔf-] *a.* (biol.) fotófilo.
photophobia [ˌfoʊtə'foʊbɪə] *s.* (med.) fotofobia.
photophobic [-bɪk] *a.* fotófobo.
photopia [foʊ'toʊpɪə] *s.* (fisiol.) fotopía.
photoplay ['foʊtəˌpleɪ] *s.* drama cinematográfico; guión.
photoprint [-ˌprɪnt] *s.* (impr.) impresión fototipográfica.
photoprocessing [-'prɑˌsɛsɪŋ, B -'proʊsɪs-] *s.* tratamiento fotográfico, producción de copias fotomecánicamente.
photoreceptor [ˌfoʊtoʊrɪ'sɛptər, B -tə] *s.* fotorreceptor.
photoreconnaissance [-rɪ'kɑnəsəns, B -'kɔn-] *s.* (mil.) reconocimiento fotográfico (aéreo).
photosensitive [-'sɛnsətɪv] *a.* (fís.) fotosensible.
photosensitization [-ˌsɛnsətə'zeɪʃən, B -taɪ-] *s.* fotosensibilización.
photosensitize [-'sɛnsəˌtaɪz] *v.t.* fotosensibilizar.
photosphere ['foʊtəˌsfɪr, B -ˌsfɪə] *s.* 1. esfera luminosa. 2. (astr.) fotosfera.
photostat [-ˌstæt] *s.* fotostato, copia fotostática. —*v.i., v.t.* hacer una copia fotostática (de), fotocopiar.
photostatic [ˌfoʊtə'stætɪk] *a.* fotostático.
photosynthesis [-'sɪnθəsəs] *s.* (quím., fisiol., bot.) fotosíntesis.
photosynthetic [-sɪn'θɛtɪk] *a.* fotosintético.
phototactic [-'tæktɪk] *a.* (bot.) fototáctico.
phototaxis [-'tæksəs] **phototaxy** ['foʊtəˌtæksɪ] *s.* (bot.) fototaxis, fototactismo.
phototelegraph [ˌfoʊtə'tɛləˌgræf, B -ˌgrɑf] *s.* fototelegrafía.
phototelegraphic [-ˌtɛlə'græfɪk] *a.* fototelegráfico.
phototelegraphically [-ɪkəlɪ] *adv.* por vía fototelegráfica.
phototelegraphy [-tə'lɛgrəfɪ] *s.* fototelegrafía, telefotografía.
phototherapeutics [-ˌθɛrə'pjutɪks] *s. pl.* (*sing. o pl. en const.*) (med.) fototerapia.
phototherapy [-'θɛrəpɪ] *s.* (med.) fototerapia.
phototonus [foʊ'tɑtənəs, B -'tɔt-] *s.* (fisiol.) fototonía.
phototropic [ˌfoʊtə'trɑpɪk, B -'trɔp-] *a.* (quím., bot.) fototrópico.
phototropism [foʊ'tɑtrəˌpɪzəm, B -'tɔt-] *s.* 1. (bot.) fototropismo. 2. (quím.) fototropía.
phototube ['foʊtəˌtub, B -ˌtjub] *s.* (electrón.) válvula fotoelectrónica.
phototype [-ˌtaɪp] *s.* (impr.) fototipia.
phototypesetting [ˌfoʊtə'taɪpˌsɛtɪŋ] *s.* (impr.) fotocomposición, composición fototipográfica.
phototypic [ˌfoʊtə'tɪpɪk] *a.* (impr.) fototípico.
phototypographic [-ˌtaɪpə'græfɪk] *a.* (impr.) fototipográfico.
phototypography [-taɪ'pɑgrəfɪ, B -'pɔg-] *s.* (impr.) fototipografía.
phototypy ['foʊtəˌtaɪpɪ] *s.* (impr.) fototipia.
photovoltaic [ˌfoʊtəˌvɑl'teɪɪk, B -ˌvɔl-] *a.* (elec.) fotovoltaico.
photozincography [-ˌzɪŋ'kɑgrəfɪ, B -'kɔg-] *s.* (impr.) fotocincografía, fotozincografía.
phrase [freɪz] *s.* 1. frase, locución. 2. fraseología, lenguaje. 3. (mús.) frase. —*v.t.* 1. frasear, expresar (en palabras); formular. 2. (mús.) dividir (las notas o tonos) en frases.
phrasemonger ['freɪzˌmʌŋgər, B -gə] *s.* aficionado al cliché.
phraseogram ['freɪzɪəˌgræm] *s.* signo de frase (en taquigrafía).
phraseological [ˌfreɪzɪə'lɑdʒɪkəl, B -'lɔdʒ-] *a.* fraseológico.
phraseologist [-'ɑlədʒəst, B -'ɔl-] *s.* persona sentenciosa.
phraseology [-ədʒɪ] *s.* fraseología.
phrasing ['freɪzɪŋ] *s.* 1. manera de expresión; redacción (de un escrito); fraseología. 2. (mús.) fraseo, matiz.
phratry [freɪtrɪ] *s.* (hist.) fratría.
phreatic [frɪ'ætɪk] *a.* (geol.) freático.
phrenetic [frɪ'nɛtɪk] *var. de* **frenetic.**
phrenic ['frɛnɪk] *a.* (anat.) frénico.
phrenitis [frɪ'naɪtəs] *s.* (med.) frenitis.
phrenologic [ˌfrɛnə'lɑdʒɪk, B -'lɔdʒ-] **phrenological** [-ɪkəl] *a.* frenológico.
phrenologist [frɪ'nɑlədʒəst, B -'nɔl-] *s.* frenólogo.
phrenology [-ədʒɪ] *s.* frenología.
phrensy, *var. de* **frenzy.**
Phrygian ['frɪdʒɪən] *a., s.* (hist.) frigio.
phthalein ['θælɪən, -ˌin] *s.* (quím.) ftaleína.
phthalic ['θælɪk] *a.* (quím.) ftálico.
phthalic acid, (quím.) ácido ftálico.
phthiriasis [θə'raɪəsəs] *s.* (med.) ftiriasis.

phthisic ['tɪzɪk, B 'θaɪsɪk] *s.* (med.) tisis, consunción.
phthisical [-ɪkəl] *a.* (med.) tísico, consuntivo.
phthisis ['θaɪsəs] *s.* (*pl.* PHTHISES [-ˌsiz]) (med.) tisis, consunción.
phycology [faɪ'kɑlədʒɪ, B -'kɔl-] *s.* (bot.) ficología.
phycomycete [ˌfaɪkoʊ'maɪˌsit] *s.* (bot.) ficomiceta.
phyla ['faɪlə] *pl. de* **phylum.**
phylactery [fɪ'læktərɪ] *s.* (*pl.* PHYLACTERIES) 1. (relig.) filacteria. 2. (hist.) filacteria, amuleto, talismán.
phyletic [faɪ'lɛtɪk] *a.* (biol.) filético.
Phyllis ['fɪləs] 1. (mitol.) Filis. 2. (poét.) campesina bonita; amiga, enamorada.
phyllode ['fɪlˌoʊd] *s.* (bot.) filodio.
phylloid [-ˌɔɪd] *a.* (bot.) filoideo. —*s.* filoide.
phylloidal [fɪ'lɔɪdəl] *a.* (bot.) filoideo.
phyllome ['fɪlˌoʊm] *s.* (bot.) filoma.
phyllophagous [fɪ'lɑfəgəs, B -'lɔf-] *a.* (zool.) filófago.
phyllopod ['fɪləˌpɑd, B -ˌpɔd] *s.* (zool.) filópodo.
phyllopodan [fɪ'lɑpədən, B -'lɔp-] *s.* (zool.) filópodo.
phyllopodium [ˌfɪlə'poʊdɪəm] *s.* (biol.) filopodio.
phyllotactic [ˌfɪlə'tæktɪk] *a.* (bot.) filotáctico.
phyllotaxy ['fɪləˌtæksɪ] **phyllotaxis** [ˌfɪlə'tæksəs] *s.* (bot.) filotaxia, filotaxis.
phylloxera [ˌfɪlɑk'sɪrə, B -ɔk'sɪərə] *s.* (ento.) filoxera.
phylogenesis [ˌfaɪlə'dʒɛnəsəs] *s.* (biol.) filogénesis, filogenia.
phylogenic [-dʒə'nɛtɪk] *a.* (biol.) filogenético.
phylum ['faɪləm] *s.* (*pl.* PHYLA [-lə]) (biol.) fílum.
physiatrics [ˌfɪzɪ'ætrɪks] *s. pl.* (*sing. o pl. en const.*) fisioterapia.
physic ['fɪzɪk] *s.* 1. (raro) física, ciencias naturales. 2. remedio, medicamento, purgante. 3. (ant.) medicina (ciencia). —*v.t.* (*pret., p.p.* PHYSICKED; *p.pr.* PHYSICKING) medicinar, curar, purgar.
physical ['fɪzɪkəl] *a.* 1. físico, corporal, material. 2. físico, de la física.
physical chemistry, físicoquímica.
physical education, educación física.
physical examination, reconocimiento médico.
physical fitness, buena salud.
physicalism [-ˌɪzəm] *s.* (filos.) fisicalismo.
physicality [ˌfɪzə'kælətɪ] *s.* 1. condición o cualidad física (esp. de una persona). 2. preocupación por las necesidades o apetitos físicos.
physically ['fɪzɪkəlɪ] *adv.* físicamente, corporalmente, materialmente.
physical therapy, fisioterapia.
physician [fə'zɪʃən] *s.* médico, doctor, facultativo.
physicist ['fɪzəsəst] *s.* físico.
physic nut, (bot.) piñón criollo, piñón de Indias.
physicochemical [ˌfɪzɪkoʊ'kɛmɪkəl] *a.* fisicoquímico.
physics ['fɪzɪks] *s. pl.* (*gen. sing. en const.*) 1. física. 2. tratado de física, libro de física. 3. composición; propiedades físicas.
physiocracy [ˌfɪzɪ'ɑkrəsɪ, B -'ɔk-] *s.* (econ.) fisiocracia.
physiocrat ['fɪzɪəˌkræt] *s.* (econ.) fisiócrata.
physiognomic [ˌfɪzɪəg'nɑmɪk, B -ə'nɔm-] **physiognomical** [-ɪkəl] *a.* fisonómico.
physiognomist [-'ɑgnəməst, -'ɑnə-, B -'ɔnə-] *s.* fisonomista.
physiognomy [-mɪ] *s.* (*pl.* PHYSIOGNOMIES) 1. fisionomía, fisonomía. 2. fisiognómica, fisiognosis.
physiographer [-'ɑgrəfər, B -'ɔgrəfə] *s.* fisiógrafo.
physiographic [-ə'græfɪk] *a.* fisiográfico.
physiography [-ɑgrəfɪ, B -'ɔg-] *s.* 1. fisiografía. 2. geografía física.
physiological [-ə'lɑdʒɪkəl, B -'lɔdʒ-] **physiologic** [-ɪk] *a.* fisiológico.
physiologically [-ɪkəlɪ] *adv.* fisiológicamente.
physiologist [-'ɑlədʒəst, B -'ɔl-] *s.* fisiólogo, fisiologista.
physiology [-ədʒɪ] *s.* fisiología.
physiotherapist [ˌfɪzɪoˌθɛrəpɪst] *s.* fisioterapeuta, kinesiólogo.
physiotherapy [-pɪ] *s.* (med.) 1. kinesiología (disciplina). 2. fisioterapeuta (tratamiento).
physique [fə'zik] *s.* físico, figura; constitución, estructura corporal.
physostigmine [ˌfaɪsə'stɪgˌmin] *s.* (quím.) fisostigmina.
Phytin ['faɪtən] *s.* (farm.) fitina.
phytoflagellate [ˌfaɪtə'flædʒələt, B -ˌleɪt] *s.* (zool.) fitoflagelado.
phytogenesis [-'dʒɛnəsəs] *s.* (bot.) fitogénesis.
phytogenetic [-dʒə'nɛtɪk] *a.* (bot.) fitogenético.
phytogenic [-'dʒɛnɪk] *a.* fitógeno, de origen vegetal.
phytogeography [ˌfaɪtoʊdʒɪ'ɑgrəfɪ, B -'ɔg-] *s.* fitogeografía, geografía del reino vegetal.
phytographist [faɪ'tɑgrəfəst, B -'tɔg-] **phytographer** [-fər, B -fə] *s.* fitógrafo.
phytography [-fɪ] *s.* (bot.) fitografía.
phytohormone [faɪtə'hɔrˌmoʊn, B -'hɔˌ-] *s.* (bot., quím.) fitohormona.
phytolite ['faɪtəˌlaɪt] **phytolith** [-ˌlɪθ] *s.* (geol.) fitolita.
phytologic [ˌfaɪtə'lɑdʒɪk, B -'lɔdʒ-] **phytological** [-ɪkəl] *a.* fitológico.
phytology [faɪ'tɑlədʒɪ, B -'tɔl-] *s.* fitología, botánica.
phyton ['faɪˌtɑn, B -ˌtɔn] *s.* (bot.) fitón.
phytopathology [ˌfaɪtoʊpæ'θɑlədʒɪ, B -'θɔl-] *s.* fitopatología.
phytophagous [faɪ'tɑfəgəs, B -'tɔf-] *a.* (zool., ento.) fitófago.
phytoplankton [ˌfaɪtə'plæŋktən] *s.* (bot.) fitoplancton.
phytosociological [-ˌsoʊsɪə'lɑdʒɪkəl, -ʃɪə-, B -sjə'lɔdʒ-] *a.* fitosociológico.
phytosociologist [-'ɑlədʒəst, B -sɪ'ɔl-] *s.* fitosociólogo.
phytosociology [-ədʒɪ] *s.* (ecología) fitosociología.
phytosterol [faɪ'tɑstəˌrɔl, B -'tɔs-] *s.* (quím.) fitosterol, fitosterina.
phytotoxic [ˌfaɪtə'tɑksɪk, B -'tɔk-] *a.* fitotóxico, letal para las plantas.
pi [paɪ] *s.* 1. decimosexta letra del alfabeto griego. 2. (mat.) (número) pi (3,1416). 3. (impr.) pastel, empastelado, encaballado, empastelamiento, mezcla desordenada de tipos. —*v.t.* empastelar, mezclar, desordenar, encaballar (caracteres, renglones o planas enteras).
piacular [paɪ'ækjələr, B -lə] *a.* 1. expiatorio. 2. pecaminoso, culpable.
piaffe [pjæf] *v.i.* (equit.) piafar.
pial ['paɪəl, 'pi-] *a.* (anat.) pial.
pia mater ['paɪə'meɪtər, 'piə'mɑt-, B 'paɪə-'meɪtə] (anat.) piamadre, piamáter.
pianissimo [pɪə'nɪsəˌmoʊ, B pjæ-] *a.* (mús.) pianísimo.
pianist [pɪ'ænəst, B 'pɪən-] *s.* pianista.
piano [pɪ'ænoʊ, -'ɑnoʊ] *s.* (*pl.* PIANOS) (mús.) piano.
piano duet, dúo de piano.
pianoforte [-əˌfɔrt, -ˌfɔrtɪ, B -ˌfɔtɪ] *s.* pianoforte, piano.
Pianola (TM) [ˌpiə'noʊlə, B pɪə-] *s.* pianola, piano mecánico.
piano lesson, lección de piano.
piano stool, taburete de piano.
piano teacher, profesor de piano.
piano tuner, afinador de pianos.
piassava [ˌpiə'sɑvə] *s.* 1. (bot.) chiquichique. 2. piassava, fibra del chiquichique.
piaster, piastre [pɪ'æstər, B -tə] *s.* (numis.) piastra.
piazza [pɪ'æzə, -'ɑtsə, B -'ætsə] *s.* (italiano) (*pl.* PIAZZAS) 1. plaza. 2. pórtico, portal, galería con arcadas. 3. (dial. E.U.) veranda, porche.
pibroch ['piˌbrɑk, B -ˌbrɔk] *s.* (mús.) variaciones (gen. marciales o fúnebres) tocadas en la gaita escocesa.
pica ['paɪkə] *s.* 1. (impr.) pica. 2. (med., vet.) pica.
picarel [ˌpɪkə'rɛl] *s.* (ict.) mena.
picaresque [ˌpɪkə'rɛsk] *a.* picaresco (estilo, novela, etc.).
picaroon [-'run] *s.* 1. picarón, pícaro; bribón, pillo. 2. pirata, corsario. —*v.i.* piratear.
picayune [-ɪ'un] *s.* 1. (S. de E.U.) moneda de cinco centavos. 2. fruslería, bagatela, friolera; bicoca, comino, ej., *it's not worth a p.,* no vale un comino. —*a.* (E.U.) insignificante, mezquino.
piccalilli ['pɪkəˌlɪlɪ] *s.* picadillo de verduras y especias.
piccolo ['pɪkəˌloʊ] *s.* (*pl.* PICCOLOS) (mús.) flautín.
piccoloist [-əst] *s.* flautín (el que toca el instrumento).
piceous ['pɪsɪəs, B 'paɪ-] *a.* 1. píceo, inflamable. 2. de color de brea.
pichiciego [ˌpɪtʃəsɪ'eɪgoʊ] *s.* (zool.) pichiciego, armadillo truncado.
pick [pɪk] *s.* 1. pico, zapapico, piqueta. 2. ganzúa. 3. (mús.) plectro.
pick, *v.t.* 1. picar, perforar, agujerear; romper (con pico u otro instrumento puntiagudo). 2. mondar, escarbar, limpiar, quitar, ej., *p. one's teeth,* mondarse o escarbarse los dientes. 3. arrancar, sacar, descarnar (hueso), desplumar (ave). 4. coger, recoger (flores, fruta, etc.); escoger; seleccionar (con cuidado). 5. picar, picotear (grano, semilla). 6. deshebrar, deshilachar, ej., *p. rags,* deshilachar trapos. 7. (E.U.) (mús.) puntear, pulsar (cuerdas); tocar (instrumento de cuerdas). 8. **p. a lock,** abrir una cerradura con ganzúa; **p. a quarrel (with),** buscar camorra, provocar una pendencia (con); **p. off,** arrancar; **p. one's pocket,** hurtar del bolsillo de alguien; **p. one's steps** (o **way**), avanzar cuidadosamente, andar con tiento; **p. oneself up,** levantarse (después de haber caído); **p. out,** discernir, divisar (en el ambiente); escoger, seleccionar; comprender, extraer (el significado); tañer de oído (una melodía); destacar; **p. over,** hurgar, buscar en; **p. to pieces,** despedazar, hacer trizas; (fig.) no dejar (a uno) hueso sano, roerle (a uno) los huesos; **p. up,** romper y remover (tierra con un pico); recoger, levantar (del suelo, etc.); obtener (ganancias, información), adquirir (costumbre, hábito), ganarse (la subsistencia); lograr ver (a la luz de un reflector, antorcha, etc.) o escuchar (señal de radio, etc.); trabar amistad, entablar conversación (con persona desconocida); encontrar de nuevo (camino, sendero perdido, hilo de un relato, etc.); recobrar (ánimo o peso); **p. up speed,** adquirir velocidad, acelerarse; **to have a bone to pick with someone,** tener que vérselas con alguin. —*v.i.* 1. trabajar con un pico. 2. **p.**

and choose, escoger con (demasiado) esmero; **p. at,** picar, picotear (la comida); regañar, criticar; **p. on** (o **upon**), regañar, criticar; fastidiar, atormentar; escoger; **p. up,** recobrar la salud, restablecerse. —*s.* 1. golpe de pico. 2. lo mejor, lo más escogido. 3. cosecha. 4. **to have the p. of,** poder escoger entre; **to take one's p.,** escoger a su gusto uno, tomar lo que le guste a uno.

pick, *v.t.* 1. (tej.) lanzar (la lanzadera). 2. (dial.) tirar, aventar, arrojar; lanzar (heno). —*s.* 1. (N. de Ingl.) lanzamiento, tiro. 2. (tej.) golpe de lanzadera; hilo del tejido.

pickaback [ˈpɪkəˌbæk] *adv.* sobre los hombros, a cuestas.

pickaninny [-ˈnɪnɪ] *s.* (E.U.) (ant.) (*pl.* PICKANINNIES) negrito, negrita.

pickax, pickaxe [ˈpɪkˌæks] *s.* zapapico, azadón de peto o de pico, piqueta. —*v.t.* demoler con zapapico. —*v.i.* trabajar con zapapico.

picked [pɪkt] *a.* escogido, selecto.

picker [ˈpɪkər, B -ə] *s.* 1. (tej.) sacalanzadera, impulsor de lanzadera, recibidor. 2. colector, recogedor. 3. (tej.) desmotadora.

pickerel [ˈpɪkərəl] *s.* (ict.) lucio pequeño; sollo norteamericano.

pickerelweed [-ˌwid] *s.* (bot.) flor de la laguna, flor de agua, pontederia.

picket [ˈpɪkət] *s.* 1. estaca puntiaguda, piquete. 2. piquete de vigilancia, piquete de huelga. 3. (mil.) piquete. —*v.t.* 1. cercar con piquetas o estacas; fortificar con estacas. 2. estacar (a un animal). 3. guardar por piquetes (campamento, etc.). 4. destacar en un piquete. 5. vigilar por piquetes (lugar de trabajo).

picketer [-ər, B -ə] *s.* miembro de un piquete de huelga.

picket fence, cerca o valla de estacas puntiagudas.

picket line, piquetes (de huelguistas, manifestantes, etc.).

pickings [ˈpɪkɪŋz] *s. pl.* 1. residuos, sobras (de comida). 2. ganancias, frutos; botín, lo robado.

pickle [ˈpɪkəl] *s.* 1. salmuera, escabeche, adobo. 2. encurtido, esp. el pepino. 3. apuro, aprieto, lío, enredo, dificultad. 4. (metal.) baño químico para limpiar metales. —*v.t.* 1. encurtir, escabechar, adobar, salar, conservar en salmuera o vinagre. 2. (metal.) limpiar con baño químico.

pickled [-əld] *a.* 1. en salmuera, en vinagre. 2. (jer.) borracho, bebido.

pickler [-lər, B -lə] *s.* (metal.) tanque de ácido.

picklock [ˈpɪkˌlɑk, B -ˌlɔk] *s.* 1. ganzúa, garfio, llave falsa. 2. ladrón (nocturno), ratero.

pick-me-up [-mɪˌʌp] *s.* (fam.) 1. bebida alcohólica estimulante. 2. en gen. bebida (café, té, etc.) tomada entre horas.

pickpocket [-ˌpɑkət, B -ˌpɔk-] *s.* carterista, cortabolsas, ratero, rata, raterillo, pericote (Perú).

pickup [-ˌʌp] *s.* 1. recolección, recogida. 2. mejora, recuperación (de salud, en los negocios, etc.). 3. aceleración, pique (de un automóvil, etc.). 4. arresto, detención. 5. (jer.) conquista callejera. 6. hallazgo, cosa hallada. 7. camioneta, furgoneta, camión de reparto. 8. (elec.) fonocaptor; escobilla. 9. (rad.) dispositivo captador; captación, recuperación. 10. (rad., t.v.) transmisión. 11 (dep.) recogida (de la pelota).

pickup arm, (electrón) brazo lector.

pickup truck, camión de reparto, camioneta.

pick-up tube, (t.v.) tubo de cámara.

picky [ˈpɪkɪ] *a.* exigente, melindroso, quisquilloso.

picnic [ˈpɪknɪk] *s.* 1. picnic, jira, comida campestre. 2. (fam.) cosa fácil; rato ameno y placentero. 3. jamón curado (hecho del muslo del cerdo). —*v.i.* (*pret., p.p.* PICNICKED; *p.pr.* PICNICKING) hacer una comida campestre, merendar en el campo, ir de jira.

picnicker [-ər, B -ə] *s.* participante en una comida campestre.

picoline [ˈpɪkəˌlin, B -ˌlaɪn] *s.* (quím.) picolina.

picot [ˈpikoʊ] *s.* (*pl.* PICOTS [-koʊz]) (cost.) punto de encaje, puntilla. —*v.t.* (*pret., p.p.* PICOTED [-koʊd]; *p.pr.* PICOTING [-koʊɪŋ]) adornar con punto de encaje.

picotee [ˌpɪkəˈti] *s.* (bot.) clavel moteado.

picot stitch, (cost.) punto de encaje formando picos o borde.

picrate [ˈpɪkˌreɪt] *s.* (quím.) picrato.

picric acid [ˈpɪkrɪk-] (quím.) ácido pícrico.

picrite [-raɪt] *s.* (min.) picrita.

picrotoxin [ˌpɪkrəˈtɑksən, B -ˈtɔk-] *s.* (quím.) picrotoxina.

Pict [pɪkt] *s.* (hist., G.B.) picto.

pictograph [ˈpɪktəˌgræf, B -ˌgrɑf] *s.* pictografía.

pictographic [ˌpɪktəˈgræfɪk] *a.* pictográfico.

pictography [pɪkˈtɑgrəfɪ, B -ˈtɔg-] *s.* pictografía, escritura ideográfica.

pictorial [-ˈtɔrɪəl] *a.* 1. pictórico. 2. gráfico; ilustrado. —*s.* revista ilustrada.

pictorially [-əlɪ] *adv.* 1. con ilustraciones. 2. (fig.) gráficamente.

picture [ˈpɪktʃər, B -tʃə] *s.* 1. cuadro, pintura. 2. lámina, grabado, ilustración; retrato; fotografía. 3. (fig.) cuadro, descripción. 4. (fig.) retrato, imagen. 5. situación, circunstancias. 6. (cine) película, filme. 7. (*pl.*) (pr. G.B.) cine. 8. (t.v.) imagen. 9. **out of the p.,** fuera de lugar, no viene al caso; eliminado; **pretty as a p.,** bonito como un cuadro; **to be in the p.,** estar bien enterado, comprender la situación; conocer los hechos o las circunstancias del caso; ser importante, venir al caso; figurar en el asunto; **to come into the p.,** (fig.) aparecer en la escena; participar en el asunto; cobrar importancia; **to have one's p. taken,** hacerse sacar una fotografía; retratarse. —*v.t.* 1. representar, ilustrar. 2. pintar, dibujar. 3. (fig.) descubrir, pintar, retratar (con palabras). 4. imaginarse, representarse; concebir. 5. **p. to oneself,** representarse, formarse una imagen mental de.

picture book, libro (para niños) con láminas; libro en imágenes.

picture card, (Ingl.) carta de figura (en la baraja).

picture compression, (t.v.) compresión de la imagen.

picture frame, marco, cuadro.

picture gallery, 1. galería de pinturas. 2. (jer.) archivo fotográfico criminal.

picture hat, pamela (sombrero de ala ancha para mujer).

picture house, p. palace, p. theatre, (ant.) (sala de) cine, cine teatro.

picture postcard, tarjeta postal con fotografía (gen. de paisaje).

picturesque [ˌpɪktʃəˈrɛsk] *a.* pintoresco, vívido llamativo.

picturesquely [-lɪ] *adv.* pintorescamente, vívidamente.

picturesqueness [-nəs] *s.* carácter pintoresco, pintoresquismo.

picture tube, (t.v.) tubo de imagen, tubo de reproducción, iconoscopio.

picture white, (t.v.) señal de densidad mínima.

picture window, ventana panorámica.

picture writing, pictografía, escritura ideográfica.

piddle [ˈpɪdəl] *v.i.* 1. emplearse en bagatelas. 2. (fam.) orinar.

piddling [ˈpɪdlɪŋ] *a.* trivial, fútil, insignificante, baladí.

piddock [ˈpɪdək] *s.* (zool.) dátil de mar, uña.

pidgin [ˈpɪdʒən] *s.* 1. lengua franca. 2. (fam. G.B.) negocio; interés.

pidgin English, lengua franca formada a base de palabras inglesas.

pie [paɪ] *s.* 1. pastel, empanada; bizcocho con relleno; **easy as pie,** sumamente fácil; **to have a finger in the p.,** tener un interés en el asunto, estar metido en el asunto. 2. (orn.) picaza, urraca.

pie, *var. de* **pi** (impr.).

piebald [ˈpaɪˌbɔld] *a.* pío, picazo, de varios colores; moteado. —*s.* animal moteado o pío.

piece [pis] *s.* 1. pieza, pedazo, fragmento, trozo. 2. ejemplo, muestra. 3. pieza, porción, retazo (de tejido que se hace de una vez); tira (de papel). 4. pieza, obra, composición (literaria, dramática, musical). 5. pieza, moneda. 6. fusil, arma. 7. (mil.) pieza (de artillería), cañón. 8. (ajedrez, damas) pieza. 9. (jer.) coito. 10. (jer., despec.) mujer (como objeto sexual). 11. **a p. of advice,** un consejo; **a p. of folly,** un acto de locura; **a p. of news,** una noticia; **a p. of rubbish,** (fig.) un disparate, una tontería; **all of a p.,** de una sola pieza; **by the p.,** a destajo; **in pieces,** hecho pedazos, destrozado, roto; **of a p.,** de la misma clase, uniforme; consistente; **p. of land,** parcela, solar, terreno (Am.); **p. of furniture,** mueble; **to break to pieces,** hacer pedazos, destrozar; **to cut to pieces,** desmenuzar, destrozar; **to fall to pieces,** deshacerse en pedazos, quedar en ruinas; **to fly to pieces,** romperse en mil pedazos; **to give (someone) a p. of one's mind,** cantarle las cosas claras a (alguien); **to go to pieces,** (fig.) desmoronarse; desmoralizarse por completo; **to pick (someone) to pieces,** hablar mal de alguien; **to say one's p.,** expresar su opinión; **to take to pieces,** desarmar desmontar; refutar en todo detalle. —*v.t.* 1. reparar (con pedazos), remendar, hacer (de trozos). 2. juntar las piezas de, unir, hacer o completar de pedazos. 3. **p. on (something) to,** juntar (algo) a; **p. out,** suplir con dificultad; completar, reconstruir (relato, teoría, pruebas, etc.); **p. together,** juntar los pedazos de; (fig.) reconstruir.

pièce de résistance [ˌpjɛsdəreɪzɪsˈtɑns] (*pl.* PIÈCES DE RÉSISTANCE) (fr.) 1. plato principal, plato fuerte. 2. obra principal (en una exposición, etc.).

piece-dyed [ˈpisˌdaɪd] *a.* teñido en pieza.

piece goods, géneros de pieza, géneros que se venden por yardas (en el comercio al por menor).

piecemeal [-ˌmil] *adv.* pieza por pieza; gradualmente, poco a poco; en pedazos, en fragmentos. —*a.* gradual; fragmentario.

piecer [ˈpisər, B -ə] *s.* 1. remendón, retaceador. 2. (tej.) anudador.

piecework [-ˌwɜrk, B -ˌwɜk] *s.* trabajo a destajo.

pieceworker [-ər, B -ə] *s.* trabajador a destajo, destajero.

pie crust, pasta de pastel.

pied [paɪd] *s.* pintado, pío, de varios colores, moteado, manchado, variado.

pied-à-terre [piˌeɪdəˈtɛr, B ˈpjeɪtɑˈtɛə] *s.* (fr.) (*pl.* PIED-À-TERRE) vivienda que se utiliza esporádicamente en visitas gen. habituales a otra ciudad, país, etc.

piedmont [ˈpidˌmɑnt, B -mənt] *s.* tierras bajas (al pie de los montes).

Piedmontese [ˌpidmɑnˈtiz, B ˌpidmən-] *a.* piamontés. —*s.* (*pl.* PIEDMONTESE) piamontés, natural del Piamonte, Italia.

Pied Piper, el Flautista de Hamelín (leyenda alemana), p. ext. el que fascina a otros con promesas falsas o exageradas.
pied wagtail, (orn.) doradillo.
pie-eyed ['paɪˌaɪd] *a.* (jer.) mamado, ahumado, borracho.
pie in the sky, (fam.) 1. promesas de beneficios o ganancias en un futuro lejano. 2. ilusiones engañosas, esperanzas falsas.
pieplant [-ˌplænt, B -ˌplɑnt] *s.* (E.U.) (bot.) ruibarbo.
pier [pɪr, B pɪə] *s.* 1. pila, pilar; machón (de un puente). 2. muelle, malecón, desembarcadero; espigón, escollera. 3. (arq.) pilar, macho; entrepaño, paño de muro entre ventanas; pie derecho (del arco); pilastra.
pierce [pɪrs, B pɪəs] *v.t.* 1. agujerear, horadar, barrenar, perforar, taladrar; pinchar. 2. atravesar, traspasar (ej., el corazón una daga, etc.). 3. (fig.) penetrar. 4. abrirse paso por. 5. (fig.) afectar, conmover.
piercer ['pɪrsər, B 'pɪəsə] *s.* 1. taladrador (obrero). 2. taladro, punzón, perforadora.
piercing [-ɪŋ] *a.* 1. penetrante, agudo (frío, sarcasmo, mente, etc.). 2. penetrante, desgarrador (grito).
piercing dies, (mec.) matrices perforadoras.
piercingly [-ɪŋlɪ] *adv.* 1. agudamente. 2. de modo penetrante o inquisitorio.
pier glass, espejo de cuerpo entero, espejo grande de pared.
Pierian [paɪ'ɪrɪən, B -'ɛr-] *a.* (poét.) pierio.
pier table, consola.
pietism ['paɪəˌtɪzəm] *s.* 1. religiosidad, devoción, piedad. 2. mojigatería. 3. P., (relig.) pietismo.
pietist [-ətəst] *s.* 1. devoto. 2. beato, mojigato. 3. **P.,** pietista.
pietistic [ˌpaɪə'tɪstɪk] *a.* 1. religioso, devoto, pío. 2. beato, mojigato. 3. (relig.) pietista.
piety ['paɪətɪ] *s.* piedad, devoción, religiosidad, fervor.
piezoelectric [piˌeɪzoʊə'lɛktrɪk, B paɪ-] *a.* (fís.) piezoeléctrico.
piezoelectricity [-əˌlɛk'trɪsətɪ] *s.* (fís.) piezoelectricidad.
piezometer [ˌpiə'zɑmətər, B ˌpaɪə'zɔmɪtə] *s.* piezómetro, instrumento para medir la presión de un fluido.
piezometric [piˌeɪzə'mɛtrɪk, B paɪ-] *a.* (fís.) piezométrico.
piezometry [ˌpiə'zɑmətrɪ, B ˌpaɪə'zɔm-] *s.* (fís.) piezometría.
piffle ['pɪfəl] *s.* (fam.) disparates, dislates, despropósitos. —*v.i.* decir disparates, disparatar.
piffling [-ɪŋ] *a.* disparatado; ridículo; trivial.
pig [pɪg] *s.* 1. (zool.) cerdo, puerco, marrano, cochino, chancho (Am.). 2. carne de puerco. 3. cochino, marrano, puerco (persona). 4. (metal.) metal bruto (hierro, plomo), lingote, molde de lingote. 5. (jer., E.U., despec.) policía. 6. **to buy a p. in a poke,** comprar algo en arca cerrada, comprar a fardo cerrado, cerrar un trato a ciegas. —*v.i. (pret., p.p.* PIGGED; *p.pr.* PIGGING) 1. parir (la puerca). 2. (G.B.) (con *it*) vivir como puercos. 3. colar en lingotes.
pig bed, (metal.) moldes para hacer lingotes de hierro, era de colada.
pigboat ['pɪgˌboʊt] *s.* (jer.) submarino.
pigeon ['pɪdʒən] *s.* 1. (orn.) paloma, palomo, pichón. 2. (jer.) primo, tonto, incauto. 3. (fam.) asunto, cargo, deber.
pigeon breast, (med.) pecho de pichón.
pigeon English, *var. de* **pidgin English.**
pigeonhearted [-ˌhɑrtəd, B -ˌhɑt-] *a.* tímido, cobarde, medroso.
pigeonhole [-ˌhoʊl] *s.* 1. hornilla, casillero para nido de palomas. 2. casilla, compartimiento (de un casillero). —*v.t.* 1. archivar, encasillar. 2. arrumbar, postergar, sepultar en el olvido, dar carpetazo a (petición, proyecto de ley, etc.). 3. clasificar, ordenar.
pigeon-livered [-'lɪvərd, B -əd] *a.* manso, tímido.
pigeon-toed [-ˌtoʊd] *a.* de pies torcidos hacia adentro.
pigeonwing [-ˌwɪŋ] (E.U.) un paso de ballet; figura de fantasía en el patinaje.
pigfish ['pɪgˌfɪʃ] *s.* (ict.) ronco.
piggery ['pɪgərɪ] *s.* zahúrda, porqueriza, pocilga, chiquero.
piggin ['pɪgən] *s.* (dial.) balde pequeño; cubeta.
piggish ['pɪgɪʃ] *a.* 1. puerco, cochino, sucio. 2. codicioso, avariento; mezquino, tacaño. 3. obstinado, testarudo.
piggishly [-lɪ] *adv.* 1. puercamente, cochinamente. 2. codiciosamente, mezquinamente. 3. obstinadamente, porfiadamente.
piggishness [-nəs] *s.* 1. porquería, suciedad, inmundicia. 2. codicia, avaricia, mezquindad. 3. obstinación, testarudez.
piggy [-pɪgɪ] *s.* (*pl.* PIGGIES) 1. cerdito, cochinito, chanchito (Am.). 2. (jer.) dedo del pie.
piggyback [-ˌbæk] *adv.* 1. sobre los hombros, en hombros, a cuestas, a caballo. 2. (f.c.) en vagón plataforma.
piggy bank, alcancía, hucha, olla ciega.
pigheaded [-'hɛdəd] *a.* obstinado, terco, porfiado, testarudo.
pig iron, hierro en bruto; lingotes de hierro.
pig Latin, lenguaje secreto de niños, jerigonza de niños.
pigment ['pɪgmənt] *s.* 1. pigmento, colorante. 2. (biol.) pigmento.
pigmentary [-mənˌtɛrɪ, B -məntərɪ] *a.* pigmentario.
pigmentation [ˌpɪgmənˌteɪʃən] *s.* pigmentación.
Pigmy, *var. de* pygmy.
pignoraticious [ˌpɪgnɔrə'tɪʃəs] **pignorative** ['pɪgnəˌreɪtɪv] *a.* pignoraticio.
pignus ['pɪgnəs] *s.* (*pl.* PIGNORA [-nərəl]) (der.) prenda, caución, pignoración, empeño.
pignut ['pɪgˌnʌt] *s.* 1. (bot.) pacanero, pacana. 2. (nuez de) pacana.
pigpen [-ˌpɛn] *s.* zahúrda, pocilga, chiquero, porqueriza.
pigskin [-ˌskɪn] *s.* 1. cuero de cerdo. 2. (fam.) silla de montar. 3. pelota de fútbol.
pigstick [-ˌstɪk] *v.i.* cazar jabalíes con venablo.
pigsticker [-ər, B -ə] *s.* venablo para cazar jabalíes.
pigsticking [-ɪŋ] *s.* caza de jabalíes con venablo.
pigsty [-ˌstaɪ] *s.* (*pl.* PIGSTIES) zahúrda, pocilga, chiquero, porqueriza.
pigtail [-ˌteɪl] *s.* 1. andullo de tabaco. 2. trenza, coleta. 3. (tej.) cola de puerco. 4. (elec.) cable flexible de conexión.
pig-tailed [-ˌteɪld] *a.* con trenza(s), con coleta(s).
pigweed [-ˌwid] *s.* (bot.) cenizo, quenopodio blanco; amaranto.
pike [paɪk] *s.* 1. pica. 2. punta de lanza; pincho, aguijón. 3. camino o barrera de portazgo; peaje. 4. carretera. 5. (ict.) lucio, sollo. 6. (N. de Ingl.) cumbre o pico de montaña. —*v.t.* picar, herir o matar con la pica. —*v.i.* (fam.) ir(se), abrir(se) camino.
pikeman ['paɪkmən] *s.* (mil.) piquero.
piker ['paɪkər, B -kə] *s.* (jer.) 1. jugador o especulador en pequeña escala. 2. persona de poca monta. 3. tacaño, cicatero.
pikestaff ['paɪkˌstæf, B -ˌstɑf] *s.* 1. asta de pica o lanza. 2. (raro) báculo, cayado herrado.
pilaf, pilaff [pɪ'lɑf, 'piˌlɑf, B 'pɪlæf] *s.* plato oriental hecho de arroz con carne o pescado y especias.
pilaster [pə'læstər, B -tə] *s.* (arq.) pilastra.
Pilate ['paɪlət] *s.* (bíbl.) Pilatos.
pilau, pilaw [pɪ'lɔ, B -'laʊ] *vars. de* pilaf, pilaff.
pilchard ['pɪltʃərd, B -tʃəd] *s.* (ict.) sardina.
pile [paɪl] *s.* 1. pelo, pelaje, pelillo. 2. lanilla, pelusa, pelusilla.
pile, *s.* 1. montón, pila, rimero, cúmulo, hacina. 2. (fig.) montón, sinnúmero. 3. pira funeraria, hoguera. 4. conglomerado de edificios; masa, macizo (de edificios). 5. (fam.) fortuna, dinero. 6. (elec.) pila, batería. 7. (quím., fís.) pila atómica, reactor atómico. —*v.t.* 1. (gen. con *up*) amontonar, apilar, acumular. 2. (con *with*) cargar (de). 3. **p. it on,** exagerar; **p. on** (o **up**), intensificar. —*v.i.* 1. (gen. con *up*) acumularse, amontonarse; apiñarse. 2. **to p. in** (o **into**), entrar o salir en tropel; entrar atropelladamente.
pile, *s.* 1. (ing.) pilote, estaca. 2. (her.) pila. 3. (hist. romana) pilo (jabalina pesada de soldados). —*v.t.* estacar, empilonar; sostener con pilotes.
pile, *s.* (med.) 1. almorrana, hemorroide. 2. (*pl.*) almorranas, hemorroides.
pileate ['paɪlɪət, -ˌeɪt] pileated [-ˌeɪtəd] *a.* 1. (bot.) provisto de píleo. 2. (orn.) crestado.
piled [paɪld] *a.* con lanilla; aterciopelado.
pile driver, p. engine, malacatero de martinete; martinete.
pile dwelling, habitación sobre pilotes, habitación lacustre, palafito.
pileous ['paɪlɪəs] *a.* piloso, peludo, velloso, velludo.
pileus ['paɪlɪəs] *s.* (*pl.* PILEI [-lɪˌaɪ]) 1. (hist. romana) píleo (bonete de fieltro). 2. (bot.) píleo. 3. (relig.) píleo (de los cardenales).
pilewort ['paɪlˌwɜrt, B -ˌwɜt] *s.* (bot.) celidonia menor, ficaria, cabeza de perro.
pilfer ['pɪlfər, B -fə] *v.i., v.t.* ratear, robar, hurtar, sisar.
pilferage [-fərɪdʒ] *s.* ratería, robo, hurto, sisa.
pilferer [-fərər, B -fərə] *s.* ratero, birlador, ladrón.
pilgarlic [pɪl'gɑrlɪk, B -'gɑlɪk] *s.* (ant.) pelele, infeliz.
pilgrim ['pɪlgrəm] *s.* 1. peregrino, romero. 2. (E.U.) (hist.) **P.,** peregrino (uno de los primeros colonizadores que fundaron Plymouth). 3. (ant.) viajante, caminante.
pilgrimage [-ɪdʒ] *s.* peregrinación, peregrinaje, romería.
piling ['paɪlɪŋ] *s.* 1. recalzo con pilotes; cimentación con pilotes. 2. pilotaje, conjunto de pilotes.
pill [pɪl] *s.* 1. píldora. 2. sinsabor, disgusto, fastidio; humillación, afrenta. 3. (jer.) pelota, pelota de golf o tenis; bola de billar; bala de cañón; (*pl.*) (G.B.) billares. 4. (jer.) cigarrillo, pitillo. 5. (jer.) pelma, pelmazo, posma. 6. **the P.** o **the p.,** la píldora anticonceptiva. —*v.t.* 1. recetar píldoras a. 2. (jer.) votar en contra de, rechazar.
pillage ['pɪlɪdʒ] *s.* 1. pillaje, saqueo, rapiña. 2. botín, despojo. —*v.t., v.i.* pillar, saquear; despojar.
pillager [-ɪdʒər, B -ɪdʒə] *s.* pillador, saqueador; despojador.
pillar ['pɪlər, B -ə] *s.* 1. pilar, columna, poste; montante; pedestal; (min.) macizo. 2. **driven from p. to post,** (fig.) obligado a ir de la Ceca a la Meca. 3. (fig.) puntal, soporte principal. —*v.t.* sostener con pilares.
pillar box, (G.B.) buzón de cartas.
Pillars of Hercules, (geog.) Columnas de Hércules.

pillbox ['pɪlˌbɑks, B -bɔks] *s.* 1. cajita para píldoras. 2. sombrero redondo y pequeño sin alas (esp. de mujer). 3. (mil.) blocao pequeño, nido de ametralladoras. 4. (hum.) vehículo o edificio pequeños.
pill bug, (ento.) cochinilla de humedad.
pillion ['pɪljən] *s.* 1. asiento trasero en motocicletas. 2. silla de montar de mujer; asiento en la grupa del caballo.
pillory ['pɪlərɪ] *s.* cepo, picota. —*v.t.* (*pret., p.p* PILLORIED; *p.pr.* PILLORYING) 1. encepar, empicotar. 2. exponer al ridículo o desdén públicos, poner en la picota.
pillow ['pɪloʊ] *s.* 1. almohada, almohadón, cojín. 2. soporte. —*v.t.* descansar (algo) sobre una almohada; servir de almohada o soporte para.
pillow block, (mec.) cojinete, soporte, chumacera.
pillowcase [-ˌkeɪs] *s.* funda de almohada.
pillow lace, encaje de bolillos.
pillow sham, funda o cubierta bordada (para almohada).
pillow slip, funda de almohada, almohada.
pill-peddler ['pɪlˌpɛdlər, B -lə] *s.* (jer.) matasanos, médico; boticario o estudiante de farmacia.
pilocarpine [ˌpaɪlə'kɑrˌpin, B -kɑpɪn] *s.* (farm.) pilocarpina.
pilose ['paɪˌloʊs] *a.* piloso, peludo, velloso, velludo.
pilosity [paɪ'lɑsətɪ, B -'lɔs-] *s.* vellosidad, pilosidad.
pilot ['paɪlət] *s.* 1. (mar.) piloto, timonel. 2. practico de puerto. 3. guía, director, consejero, mentor. 4. (E.U.) quitapiedras (delante de locomotoras). 5. (aer.) piloto, aviador. 6. (mec.) pieza guía, guía de herramientas. —*a.* guiador; auxiliar. —*v.t.* pilotear, pilotar, timonear, guiar, dirigir, llevar; (aer.) pilotear, pilotar, guiar (un avión).
pilotage [-ɪdʒ] *s.* pilotaje.
pilot balloon, globo piloto.
pilot biscuit, p. bread, galleta marinera, galleta de barco.
pilot burner, mechero piloto (de una cocina de gas, etc.).
pilot engine, locomotora exploradora (que viaja delante del tren para comprobar que la vía está expedita).
pilot fish, (ict.) pez piloto, romero.
pilot house, (mar.) timonera, caseta de navegación.
piloting ['paɪlətɪŋ] *s.* pilotaje; navegación por sondeos o por señales visibles en tierra.
pilot lamp, (elec.) lámpara indicadora o testigo (que indica si un motor, horno, etc. está en funcionamiento).
pilot light, lámpara indicadora; llama piloto.
pilot plant, instalación piloto, planta de ensayo.
pilot valve, válvula piloto, válvula de mando.
pilous ['paɪləs] *a.* piloso, velludo, peludo.
pilular ['pɪljələr, B -lə] *a.* pilular, en forma de píldora.
pilule [-jul] *s.* pildorita, pildorín, píldora pequeña.
pima cotton ['pimə-] algodón pima.
pimento [pɪ'mɛntoʊ] *s.* (*pl.* PIMENTOS) (bot.) pimiento, ají; pimienta malagueta, pimienta de Jamaica.
pimiento [-'mjɛnt-, -'mɛnt-] *s.* (bot.) pimiento morrón.
pimp [pɪmp] *s.* alcahuete, proxeneta. —*v.i.* alcahuetear, tratar en blancas.
pimpernel ['pɪmpərˌnɛl, B -pəˌ-] *s.* (bot.) pimpinela, murajes, anagalis, sanguisorba.
pimping ['pɪmpɪŋ] *a.* 1. mezquino, miserable. 2. (dial.) diminuto, pequeño; enclenque.
pimple ['pɪmpəl] *s.* grano, barro (en el rostro).
pimpled [-pəld] *a.* granujiento.
pimply [-plɪ] *a.* granujiento.
pin [pɪn] *s.* 1. alfiler. 2. (mec.) pasador, espiga, clavija, clavillo. 3. broche, prendedor, prendedero. 4. gancho, pinza (para tender ropa). 5. insignia, distintivo. 6. sotrozo, rodillo de amasar, rodillo de pastelero. 7. paletón (de la llave). 8. (fam.) (*pl.*) piernas. 9. (fig.) pepino, comino. 10. (mús.) clavija. 11. (mec.) bolo. 12. (golf) asta del banderín (que marca un hoyo). 13. (mar.) cabilla (de maniobra de probado y de jarcia). —*v.t.* (*pret., p.p.* PINNED; *p.pr.* PINNING) 1. sujetar, asegurar, prender. 2. empernar, enclavijar. 3. (ajedrez) clavar. 4. **p. (someone) down,** obligar (a alguien) a manifestar su opinión o aclarar su posición; **p. (something) down,** inmovilizar (ej., tropas); **p. (something) down to,** atribuir (algo) específicamente a; **p. (something) on (someone),** (jer.) imputar (algo) a (alguien), acusar (a alguien) de (algo); **p. one's hope** (o **faith**) **on,** cifrar sus esperanzas en; **p. up,** sujetar, asegurar, prender (con alfileres, en la pared, etc.); (arq.) apuntalar, sostener, asegurar.
pinaceous [paɪ'neɪʃəs] *a* (bot.) pináceo.
pina cloth ['pinjə-] piña (tejido).
pinafore ['pɪnəˌfɔr, B -ˌfɔ] *s.* delantal, mandil.
pinaster [paɪ'næstər, B -tə] *s.* (bot.) pinastro, pino rodeno.
pinball ['pɪnˌbɔl] *s.* billar romano.
pinball machine, billar romano mecánico.
pin block, (mús.) clavijero (del piano).
pince-nez ['pænsˌneɪ, B 'pɛns-] *s.* (*pl.* PINCE-NEZ) quevedos.
pincers ['pɪnsərz, B -səz] *s. pl* 1. pinzas, tenazas de corte. 2. (zool.) pinzas (del cangrejo, alacrán, etc.). 3. **p. movement,** (mil.) movimiento de pinzas, movimiento de tenazas.
pinch [pɪntʃ] *v.t.* 1. pellizcar. 2. apretar, estrechar, comprimir, estrujar. 3. acalambrar, contraer. 4. (fig.) herir. 5. (fig.) angustiar, acongojar, afligir. 6. (fam.) afanar, robar, hurtar, birlar. 7. (jer.) arrestar, apresar, prender. 8. (mar.) navegar (un barco) ciñendo demasiado el viento, flamear la vela. 9. **p. pennies,** escatimar gastos; ser mezquino. —*v.i.* 1. comprimir, apretar. 2. economizar; ser tacaño. 3. (min.) contraerse, estrecharse (filones o vetas); **p. out,** terminar. —*s.* 1. emergencia, aprieto, apuro. 2. dolor, tormento; presión. 3. escasez. 4. pellizco. 5. pulgarada, polvo (de tabaco), polvillo (de sal). 6. (fam.) robo, hurto. 7. (jer.) prendimiento, captura, arresto. 8. **at** (o **in**) **a p.,** en caso necesario, en un apuro.
pinch bar, (mec.) palanca de pie de cabra, alzaprima.
pinchbeck ['pɪntʃˌbɛk] *s.* 1. similor. 2. falsificación. —*a.* 1. de similor. 2. falso, falsificado; fingido, de pacotilla.
pinchcock [-ˌkɑk, B -ˌkɔk] *s.* abrazadera de compresión, apretadora para tubo flexible.
pinchers ['pɪntʃərz, B -tʃəz] *s. pl.* tenacillas; pinzas.
pinch-hit ['pɪntʃ'hɪt] *v.i.* 1. (béisbol) batear de emergencia (en lugar de otro). 2. sustituir (a otro) en una emergencia.
pinch hitter, 1. (béisbol) bateador de emergencia (en lugar de otro). 2. substituto o suplente de emergencia.
pin connection, junta articulada, unión en pasador.
pin curl, rizo que se mantiene sujeto por medio de horquillas.
pincushion ['pɪnˌkʊʃən] *s.* acerico, alfiletero.
Pindar ['pɪndər, B -də] *s.* Píndaro, poeta griego.
Pindaric [pɪn'dærɪk] *a.* pindárico. —*s.* oda pindárica, oda de Píndaro.
pindling ['pɪndlɪŋ] *a.* (dial. E.U.) enteco, magro; mezquino, enfermizo.
pine [paɪn] *v.i.* languidecer; desfallecer; consumirse; **p. for** (o **after**), desear con vehemencia, suspirar por, anhelar. —*v.t.* (ant.) padecer, penar, llorar por. —*s.* (ant.) sufrimiento; dificultad; deseo; anhelo.
pine [paɪn] *s.* 1. (bot.) pino. 2. madera de pino. 3. (fam.) piña, ananá, ananás.
pineal ['pɪnɪəl, 'paɪnɪ-] *a.* 1. de figura de piña. 2. (anat.) pineal.
pineal body, p. gland, (anat.) glándula pineal.
pineapple ['paɪnˌæpəl] *s.* 1. piña, ananá, ananás. 2. (jer.) bomba de dinamita, granada de mano.
pine cone, piña (del pino).
pine marten, (zool.) marta cibelina.
pinene ['paɪˌnin] *s.* (quím.) pineno.
pine needle, pinoche, hoja del pino.
pinery ['paɪnərɪ] *s.* 1. piñal. 2. pinar.
pinesap ['paɪnˌsæp] *s.* (bot.) especie de hierba parasitaria o saprofita.
pine siskin, p. finch, (orn.) pinzón norte-americano de plumaje barrado.
pine tar, brea de pino.
pinetum [paɪ'nitəm] *s.* (*pl.* PINETA [-ə]) pinar.
pinewood ['paɪnˌwʊd] *s.* madera de pino; bosque de pinos.
pinfeather ['pɪnˌfɛðər, B -ə] *s.* (orn.) cañón (pluma naciente de ave).
pinfold ['pɪnˌfoʊld] *s.* 1. aprisco, majada, redil. 2. encierro, lugar de detención. —*v.t.* 1. redilar, apriscar, amajadar. 2. encerrar.
ping [pɪŋ] *s.* sonido agudo del impacto (de la bala). —*v.i.* hacer impacto con un sonido agudo, zumbar (balas).
ping-pong ['pɪŋˌpɑŋ, -ˌpɔŋ, B -ˌpɔŋ] *s.* ping-pong, pimpón, tenis de mesa.
pinguid ['pɪŋgwɪd] *a.* pingüe, graso; gordo, obeso; rico, fértil, feraz (suelo).
pinguidity [pɪŋ'gwɪdətɪ] *s.* graseza; gordura, obesidad.
pinhead ['pɪnˌhɛd] *s.* 1. cabeza de alfiler. 2. (fig.) pizca; cosa muy pequeña. 3. bobo, tonto. 4. (ict.) carpa pequeña.
pinheaded [-əd] *a.* bobo, bobalicón.
pinhole [-ˌhoʊl] *s.* 1. agujero minúsculo (hecho por un alfiler). 2. agujero para pasador, clavija o espiga. 3. (foto.) punto transparente (en un negativo).
pinion ['pɪnjən] *s.* 1. (orn.) extremo del ala; ala; piñón; rémige; remera. 2. (mec.) piñón; **p. drive,** transmisión por engranaje. —*v.t.* 1. atar las alas para impedir el vuelo. 2. maniatar. 3. amarrar, sujetar firmemente. — **to ride p.,** montar dos a la grupa.
pinite ['piˌnaɪt, B 'pɪ-] *s.* (min.) pinita.
pink [pɪŋk] *v.t.* 1. perforar (tela, papel); ondear, ojetear, picar. 2. picar con arma purzante. —*s.* (mar.) pingue.
pink [pɪŋk] *s.* 1. (bot.) clavel; clavelita, clavellina. 2. dechado, perfección, modelo. 3. rosa, rosado (color). 4. (despec., jer.) izquierdista, filocomunista, rojillo (Esp.). 5. **to be in the p. of health,** estar rebosante de salud. —*a.* 1. rosado. 2. de izquierdas, comunistoide. 3. muchísimo, tremendo, ej., *to be tickled p.*, tener muchísimo gusto.
pink elephants, (fam.) **to see p. e.,** tener un ataque de delírium tremens.
pinkeye ['pɪŋkˌaɪ] *s.* (med., vet.) conjuntivitis aguda.
pinkie ['pɪŋkɪ] *s.* 1. (mar.) pingue (esp. de pesca). 2. dedo meñique.

pinking [-kɪŋ] *s.* (cost.) picado, terminado en zig-zag.
pinking shears, *pl.* tijeras picafestones, tijera zigzag (Am.).
pinkish [-kɪʃ] *a.* que tira a rosado.
pink lady, un cóctel de ginebra, jugo de limón y clara de huevo.
pinko [-koʊ] *s.* (E.U.) (fam., despec.) izquierdista, comunistoide, rojillo (Esp.).
pink slip, notificación de despido.
Pinkster ['pɪŋkstər, B -stə] *s.* (E.U.) semana de Pentecostés; pascua de Pentecostés.
pinkster flower, (bot.) azalea rosada.
pink tea, (fam.) té, reunión social.
pin money, dinero para imprevistos.
pinna ['pɪnə] *s.* (*pl.* PINNAE [-ˌi] o PINNAS) 1. (bot.) pina, pinna, folíolo (de una hoja pinada). 2. (orn.) pluma; ala. 3. (ict.) aleta. 4. (anat.) pabellón de la oreja.
pinnace ['pɪnəs] *s.* (mar.) 1. pinaza. 2. bote o chalupa de motor.
pinnacle ['pɪnəkəl] *s.* 1. (arq.) pináculo. 2. (fig.) pináculo, cima, cumbre, cúspide, apogeo. —*v.t.* 1. rematar con un pináculo; proveer de pináculo. 2. elevar a la fama; hacer surgir.
pinnate ['pɪnˌeɪt, -ɪt] *a.* (bot.) pinada (hoja).
pinnately [-lɪ] *adv.* en forma pinada.
pinnatifid [pə'nætəfəd] *a.* (bot.) pinatífido, pinnatífido.
pinnatisect [-ˌsɛkt] *a.* (bot.) pinatisecto, pinatipartido.
pinner ['pɪnər, B -ə] *s.* 1. (hist.) especie de toca o toquilla. 2. (dial.) delantal.
pinniped ['pɪnəˌpɛd] *a., s.* (zool.) pinípedo, pinnípedo.
pinnule ['pɪnjul] *s.* 1. (zool.) pínula, pina. 2. (ict.) aleta pequeña.
pin oak, (bot.) roble-pino.
pinochle, pinocle ['piˌnʌkəl, -ˌnɑk-, B 'pɪˌnɔk-] *s.* un juego de naipes.
pinole [pɪ'noʊlɪ] *s.* pinole, harina de maíz tostado, máchica (Am.).
piñon ['pɪnjən] *s.* 1. (bot.) pino piñonero. 2. piñón (simiente).
pinpoint ['pɪnˌpɔɪnt] *v.t.* 1. apuntar con precisión. 2. fijar exactamente, determinar o identificar con precisión. 3. hacer resaltar, singularizar. —*a.* 1. exacto, preciso. 2. de precisión, ej., *p. bombing,* bombardeo de precisión.
pinprick [-ˌprɪk] *s.* 1. alfilerazo. 2. (fig.) pinchazo. —*v.t.* dar de pinchazos a.
pins and needles, hormigueo (en los miembros del cuerpo); **on p. a. n.,** en ascuas, ansioso.
pinstripe ['pɪnˌstraɪp] *s.* raya fina (en tela). —*a.* de rayas finas (tela).
pint [paɪnt] *s.* pinta (medida de capacidad equivalente a octavo de galón).
pinta ['pɪntə] *s.* (med.) pinta.
pintail ['pɪnˌteɪl] *s.* (orn.) 1. pato o guaco de cola larga; pato rojizo; guaco grande. 2. ganga.
pin-tailed [-ˌteɪld] *a.* 1. de cola ahusada (pájaro). 2. con cola de plumas espinosas.
pintle ['pɪntəl] *s.* (mec.) macho, clavija, cabilla, pata; perno; (mar.) pinzote (del timón).
pinto ['pɪntoʊ] *a.* pintado; de varios colores, mezclado; manchado. —*s.* (O. de E.U.) caballo pinto, caballo pío.
pinto bean, (O. de E.U.) fríjol moteado, judía pinta.
Pintsch gas ['pɪntʃ-] gas de petróleo comprimido.
pint-size ['paɪntˌsaɪz] **pint-sized** [-ˌsaɪzd] *a.* pequeño, diminuto.
pinup ['pɪnˌʌp] *a.* que se clava en la pared. —*s.* fotografía de mujer sexualmente provocativa que se pega o clava en las paredes; p. ext. chica atractiva.
pinup girl, muchacha que sirve de modelo para fotografías provocativas; p. ext. mujer sexualmente atractiva.
pinwale [-ˌweɪl] *a.* con estrías estrechas (tela de pana).
pinweed [-ˌwid] *s.* (bot.) estepa, jara.
pinwheel [-ˌhwil, -ˌwil] *s.* 1. molinete, molinillo (Esp.), rehilandera. 2. girándula, rueda giratoria (de fuegos artificiales). 3. rueda de espigas, rueda de cabillas.
pinwork [-ˌwɜrk, B -ˌwɜk] *s.* recamado bordado de realce.
pinworm [-ˌwɜrm, B -ˌwɜm] *s.* oxiuro, verme intestinal, lombriz intestinal.
pin wrench, llave de pernete o de espiga.
piolet [ˌpiə'leɪ] *s.* piqueta de los alpinistas.
pioneer [ˌpaɪə'nɪr, B -'nɪə] *s.* 1. (mil.) zapador. 2. pionero, explorador, colonizador, ej., *pioneers of the American West,* colonizadores del Oeste americano. 3. pionero, iniciador; primer promotor, ej., *p. of science,* pionero de la ciencia, científico iniciador. 4. (ant.) cavador; minero. —*a.* 1. precursor, preparatorio. 2. primero, experimental. 3. de colonización, colonizador. —*v.t.* 1. explorar, colonizar. 2. (fig.) iniciar, promover. 3. **p. a cause,** ser el primer promotor de una causa. —*v.i.* (fig.) enseñar el camino, ser el primero.
piosity [paɪ'ɑsətɪ, B -'ɔs-] *s.* gazmoñería, mojigatería.
pious ['paɪəs] *a.* 1. pío, piadoso; devoto. 2. gazmoñero, mojigato, beato, cucufato (Am.); hipócrita. 3. sagrado. 4. digno; excelente; que merece alabanza, ej., *p. effort,* esfuerzo que merece alabanza. 5. (ant.) respetuoso, leal (a los padres, familia, etc.).
piously [-lɪ] *adv.* 1. piadosamente, devotamente. 2. con gazmoñería, gazmoñamente.
piousness [-nəs] *s.* 1. piedad, devoción. 2. gazmoñería, mojigatería, cucufatería (Am.).
pip [pɪp] *s.* 1. pepita, semilla (de manzana, pera, etc.). 2. (jer.) joya, maravilla, preciosidad; persona admirable; muchacha preciosa. 3. (vet.) pepita, moquillo (de las aves). 3. (fam.) desazón, disgusto; malestar. 4. punto (de un naipe, dominó, etc.). 5. (G.B.) estrella (insignias militares). 6. (t.v.) cresta de eco. 7. (rad., t.v.) silbido corto (de señal). 8. (bot.) rizoma (esp. del lirio de los valles).
pip [pɪp] *v.i.* (*pret., p.p.* PIPPED; *p.pr.* PIPPING) 1. piar, pipiar. 2. romper el cascarón (un polluelo). 3. **p. out,** (fam. G.B.) estirar la pata, morir. —*v.t.* (G.B.) 1. suspender, catear (Esp.), aplazar (Am.) (en examen). 2. derrotar, superar.
pipage ['paɪpɪdʒ] *s.* transporte por tuberías; tuberías, caños, tubos; precio de transporte por tuberías.
pipal ['pipəl] *s.* (bot.) (especie de) higuera de la India.
pipe [paɪp] *s.* 1. tubo, caño, tubería, cañería, conducto. 2. tubo, cañón (de órgano), tubo, canuto (de gaita, etc.); (*pl.*) gaita. 3. caramillo, flauta, flautín; zampoña. 4. silbo, silbido; nota aflautada, voz atiplada. 5. pipa (de fumar). 6. pipa, tonel, barrica, casco. 7. (mar.) pito o silbato de contramaestre. 8. (dial.) canal, vaso del cuerpo. 9. (jer.) cosa fácil; éxito seguro. 10. **put that in your p. and smoke it,** ¡tómate ésa! ¡chúpate ésa! —*v.i.* 1. tocar el caramillo o la gaita. 2. hablar o cantar con voz aflautada; gritar (en voz aguda). 3. (mar.) llamar o dar órdenes por medio de pitos o señales. 4. **p. away,** dar orden de zarpada. 5. **p. down,** (mar.) dar orden para descansar; (fam.) bajar la voz, quedar callado, calmarse, aquietarse; **p. up,** comenzar a cantar o tocar; echarse a hablar; levantar la voz, hablar claramente. —*v.t.* 1. tocar (una melodía) en el caramillo. 2. llamar, guiar o conducir por el sonido de la flauta. 3. (mar.) recibir o despedir al son de flautas. 4. encañar, conducir por tuberías. 5. poner (licor) en un tonel o pipa. 6. entubar, proveer de tuberías o cañerías. 7. galonear. 8. (cost.) ribetear. 9. **pipe in,** transmitir (música o sonidos) desde un lugar remoto por medio de sistemas eléctricos o electrónicos.
pipe clay, tierras de pipas, arcilla plástica, tierra grasa, blanquizal.
pipe-clay ['paɪpˌkleɪ] *v.t.* blanquear con tierra de pipas.
pipe cleaner, limpiapipas.
pipe cutter, cortatubos, cortador de tubos, cortacaño.
pipe dream, sueño, ilusión, idea fantástica; castillos en el aire.
pipefish [-ˌfɪʃ] *s.* (ict.) aguja de mar, espetón.
pipe fitter, cañero, montador de tuberías, plomero de astilleros.
pipe fitting, accesorio para tubería, accesorio de cañería.
pipeful [-ˌfʊl] *s.* fumarada (porción de tabaco que cabe en la pipa).
pipeline [-ˌlaɪn] *s.* 1. tubería, conducto. 2. oleoducto. 3. (fig., fam.) fuente confidencial (de información, noticias). 4. línea, conducto (de transporte, etc.). 5. **in the p.,** (G.B.) en camino.
pipe of peace, pipa de la paz.
pipe organ, (mús.) órgano de cañones.
piper ['paɪpər, B -pə] *s.* 1. flautista, gaitero. 2. cañero, montador de tuberías. 3. **he who pays the p. calls the tune,** el que paga manda; **to pay the p.,** pagar el pato.
piperaceous [ˌpɪpə'reɪʃəs] *a.* (bot.) piperáceo.
piperazine [paɪ'pɛrəˌzin, B 'pɪpərəˌzaɪn] *s.* (quím.) piperacina.
piperidine [-'pɛrəˌdin, B pɪ-ˌdaɪn] *s.* (quím.) piperidina.
piperine ['pɪpəˌrin, B -ˌraɪn] *s.* (quím.) piperina.
piperonal [paɪ'pɛrəˌnæl, B pɪ-] *s.* (quím.) piperonal.
pipet, *var. de* **pipette.**
pipe tobacco, tabaco de pipa.
pipette [paɪ'pɛt, B pɪ-] *s.* pipeta, probeta.
pipe wrench, llave para tubos, llave Stillson.
piping ['paɪpɪŋ] *s.* 1. silbido, pitido, sonido agudo. 2. tubería, cañería. 3. (cocina) figura, borde trazado con azúcar. 4. (cost.) vivo, cordoncillo. —*a.* 1. pastoril; suave, tranquilo, sereno. 2. aflautado, agudo, silboso. 3. **p. hot,** muy caliente.
pipit ['pɪpət] *s.* (orn.) motacila, aguzanieves, nevatilla.
pipkin ['pɪpkən] *s.* 1. pucherito, ollita. 2. (dial.) cubeta, balde.
pippin ['pɪpən] *s.* 1. (especie de) camuesa (manzana). 2. (jer., ant.) joya, maravilla; muchacha preciosa. 3. (ant., dial.) semilla, simiente; pepita.
pippin tree, (bot.) (especie de) camueso.
pipsqueak ['pɪpˌskwik] *s.* mequetrefe, poquita cosa, nulidad.
piquancy ['pikənsɪ] *s.* (lit. y fig.) picante, sabor excitante.
piquant ['pikənt, -ˌkɑnt] *a.* 1. (lit. y fig.) picante. 2. (fig.) provocativo, seductor, cautivador. 3. (ant.) punzante; irritante.
piquantly [-lɪ] *adv.* picantemente.
pique [pik] *s.* pique, resentimiento; rencor, disgusto; despecho; inquina, ojeriza, tirria, animosidad; **in a p.,** resentido. —*v.t.* 1. enojar, molestar, desazonar, irritar. 2. despertar, excitar (curiosidad, interés, etc.). 3. estimular, acicatear.

piqué, pique [pɪ'keɪ, 'pikeɪ, B 'pikeɪ] *s.* piqué (tejido).

piquet [pɪ'keɪ, B -'kɛt] *s.* (naipes) séptimo, juego de los cientos.

piracy ['paɪrəsɪ, B 'paɪərə-] *s.* (*pl.* PIRACIES) 1. piratería. 2. plagio, edición no autorizada.

Piraeus [paɪ'riəs] *s.* el Pireo (Grecia).

piragua [pə'rɑgwə, B -'ræg-] *s.* (mar.) piragua; embarcación de dos mástiles y fondo plano.

Pirandellian [ˌpɪrən'dɛlɪən] *a.* (lit.) pirandeliano, a la manera de, o según, Pirandello (dramaturgo italiano).

piranha [pə'rænjə, -'rɑn-, B -'ræn-] *s.* (ict.) piraña, piraya, caribe, palometa, piraya.

pirarucu [pɪˌrɑrə'ku] *s.* (ict.) pirarucú, arapaima.

pirate ['paɪrət, B 'paɪər-] *s.* 1. pirata; corsario. 2. embarcación (de) pirata. —*v.t.* 1. robar, quitar. 2. plagiar, publicar sin autorización del autor. 3. ocupar o utilizar ilegalmente. —*v.i.* piratear.

piratical [pə'rætɪkəl, B paɪ-] *a.* pirático, raquero.

piratically [-kəlɪ] *adv.* de modo pirático, como un pirata.

pirn [pɜrn, B pɜn] *s.* 1. (tej.) carrete de una lanzadera. 2. (esco.) carrete de una caña de pescar.

pirogue ['piˌroʊg, B pɪ'roʊg] *var. de* **piragua.**

piroplasm ['pɪrəˌplæzəm] *s.* (zool.) piroplasma.

piroplasma [ˌpɪrə'plæzmə] *s.* (*pl.* PIROPLASMATA [-mətə] *var. de* **piroplasm.**

pirouette [ˌpɪrʊ'ɛt] *s.* (baile) pirueta; cabriola. —*v.i.* piruetar, hacer piruetas, hacer cabriolas.

Pisan ['pizən] *a., s.* pisano, de Pisa, Italia.

piscary ['pɪskərɪ] *s.* 1. (der.) privilegio de pescar en aguas ajenas. 2. pesquera, pesquería.

piscatorial [ˌpɪskə'tɔrɪəl] **piscatory** ['pɪskəˌtɔrɪ, B -tərɪ] *a.* piscatorio.

Pisces ['paɪsiz, 'pɪsˌiz] *s. pl.* (astr.) Pisces, Peces.

pisciculture ['pɪsəˌkʌltʃər, B -tʃə] *s.* piscicultura.

pisciculturist [ˌpɪsɪ'kʌltʃərəst] *s.* piscicultor.

pisciform ['pɪsəˌfɔrm, B -ˌfɔm] *a.* pisciforme.

piscina [pɪ'ʃinə, B -'si-] *s.* 1. (relig.) piscina (pila donde se echan algunas materias sacramentales). 2. vivero de peces.

piscine ['paɪˌsin, B 'pɪˌsaɪn] *a.* (zool.) de peces; pisciforme.

piscivorous [pə'sɪvərəs] *a.* (zool.) piscívoro.

pish [pɪʃ] *interj.* ¡bah!

pisiform ['paɪsəˌfɔrm, B -ˌfɔm] *a.* (bot., anat.) pisiforme.

pismire ['pɪsˌmaɪr, B -ˌmaɪə] *s.* (ento.) hormiga.

pisolite ['paɪsəˌlaɪt] *s.* (geol.) pisolita.

pisolitic [ˌpaɪsə'lɪtɪk] *a.* pisolítico.

piss [pɪs] *v.i.* orinar, mear. —*v.t.* 1. orinar, emitir. 2. orinar en (la cama, etc.). 3. **p. off!** (vulg.) ¡lárgate! —*s.* 1. (vulg.) orina. 2. (jer.) **p. and vinegar,** energía, determinación.

pissed [pɪst] *a.* 1. (jer. vulg.) enojado, desengañado. 2. (jer.) borracho. 3. **p. off,** enojado, resentido; **to be p. off at,** estar enojado con, guardar rencor a; **to get p.,** pegarse (o coger) una mona.

pissoir [pɪ'swɑr, B -'swɑ] *s.* letrina o retrete público.

pistachio [pə'stæʃɪˌoʊ, -'stɑʃ-] **pistache** [-'stæʃ] *s.* 1. (bot.) pistachero, alfóncigo, alfónsigo. 2. pistacho, alfóncigo (semilla). 3. **p. green,** color de pistacho, verde amarillento.

pistil ['pɪstəl] *s.* (bot.) pistilo.

pistillate [-tələt, -ˌleɪt] *a.* (bot.) pistilado.

pistol ['pɪstəl] *s.* pistola (arma de fuego). —*v.t.* (*pret., p.p.* PISTOLED O PISTOLLED; *p.pr.* PISTOLING O PISTOLLING) herir o matar con pistola.

pistole [pɪs'toʊl] *s.* pistola (moneda), doblón.

pistoleer [ˌpɪstə'lɪr, B -'lɪə] *s.* pistolero (soldado armado de pistola).

pistol grip, mango de pistola, cabo o empuñadura de pistola.

pistol holster, pistolera.

pistol-whip ['pɪstəlˌhwɪp, -ˌwɪp] *v.t.* golpear con una pistola.

piston ['pɪstən] *s.* 1. (mec.) pistón, émbolo. 2. (mus.) pistón, llave.

piston pin, (mec.) pasador de articulación, pasador de émbolo; bulón o eje de émbolo.

piston ring, (mec.) aro del émbolo, anillo de émbolo, aro del pistón.

piston rod, (mec.) vástago del émbolo, varilla del pistón.

piston stroke, (mec.) carrera del émbolo, pistonada, embolada.

piston travel, (mec.) recorrido del émbolo.

pit [pɪt] *s.* 1. foso, hoyo. 2. concavidad, hondura, hueco; cárcava; pozo (de mina). 3. trampa, zanja, hondón. 4. precipicio, abismo, sima. 5. depresión, hendidura. 6. boca (del estómago). 7. cicatriz, hoyo, hoyuelo, cacaraña (en el cuerpo humano), ej., *smallpox pits,* hoyos, cicatrices de viruela. 8. cancha, reñidero (para peleas de gallos, etc.). 9. (E.U.) bolsa (parte del piso en la bolsa que está dedicada a un solo producto). 10. foso de la orquesta (en un teatro). 11. (dep.) foso (lleno de arena para recibir a un saltador). 12. **the p.,** el infierno; **to dig a p. for,** tender una trampa a. —*v.t.* (*pret., p.p.* PITTED; *p.pr.* PITTING) 1. poner, enterrar o guardar en fosos, hoyos, etc. 2. marcar con hoyos, dejar hoyoso (el rostro). 3. incitar a la pelea; poner a pelear, carear. 4. **to p. (one) against (another),** oponer a (uno) contra (otro). —*v.i.* ahoyar, agujerarse.

pit [pɪt] *s.* (E.U.) hueso (de frutas como el melocotón, albaricoque, etc.). —*v.t.* deshuesar (frutas).

pita ['pitə] *s.* pita, agave, maguey (fibra y planta).

pit-a-pat ['pɪtəˌpæt] *adv.* 1. con latido rápido, ej., *his heart went p.-a-p.,* su corazón palpitaba rápidamente. 2. con un trotecito ligero. —*v.i.* 1. latir violentamente. 2. moverse con trote ligero. 3. golpetear. —*s.* 1. latido rápido. 2. sonido de un trotecito ligero; golpeteo, ej., *the p.-a-p. of little feet,* las pisadas ligeras de los niños.

pitch [pɪtʃ] *s.* 1. pez. 2. alquitrán, betún, brea. 3. resina (de ciertas coníferas). —*v.t.* alquitranar; embetunar, abetunar, embrear, brear.

pitch [pɪtʃ] *v.t.* 1. armar, montar, plantar, fijar, asentar, ej., *p. a tent,* armar una tienda de campaña. 2. echar, lanzar, tirar, arrojar, ej., *p. a quoit,* arrojar un tejo, *p. hay,* echar heno. 3. graduar o ajustar a un tono, ej. *p. the voice high,* graduar la voz a un tono alto. 4. (béisbol) lanzar o arrojar (la pelota) al bateador. 5. **to be in there pitching,** (fig., jer.) estar bregando, trabajar arduamente; defender rigurosamente sus derechos; seguir peleando. —*v.i.* 1. instalarse, establecerse; acampar. 2. precipitarse, caer hacia adelante, bajar en declive. 3. (dep.) jugar como lanzador. 4. cabecear, arfar, hocicar (barco, cohete en vuelo, etc.). 5. **p. in,** echarse a trabajar vigorosamente; contribuir, ayudar; **p. into,** abalanzarse sobre, atacar, acometer, arremeter; reprender, regañar; ponerse a comer (algo) con gusto; **p. on** (o **upon**), escoger, elegir (fortuitamente). —*s.* 1. echada, lanzada, lanzamiento, tiro. 2. grado, nivel (de excitación, regocijo, etc.). 3. cabezada (de un barco, cohete en vuelo, etc.). 4. (G.B.) puesto (de un limpiabotas, buhonero, etc.). 5. plática de propaganda; propaganda comercial. 6. declive, pendiente. 7. (arq.) inclinación, grado de inclinación (del techo, escalera, etc.). 8. (mec.) paso, avance (de rosca de tornillo, engranaje, etc.); separación, espaciado (entre remaches, surcos de un disco de gramófono, etc.); inclinación (de hélice). 9. (elec.) avance, paso (de bobinado, etc.). 10. (geol., min.) buzamiento (de un filón o yacimiento). 11. (mús., fís.) tono, altura (de sonido). 12. (mús.) diapasón, ej., *high p.,* diapasón alto, *low p.,* diapasón bajo. 13. (criquet) parte central del campo. 14. (naipes) un juego en que se debe atacar con un triunfo.

pitch apple, (bot.) copeisillo.

pitch-black ['pɪtʃ'blæk] *a.* negro como la noche.

pitchblende [-ˌblɛnd] *s.* (min.) pecblenda, pechblenda, pez blenda, pechurana, nasturano.

pitch-dark [-'dɑrk, B -'dɑk] *a.* obscuro como boca de lobo.

pitched battle [pɪtʃt-] batalla campal.

pitcher ['pɪtʃər, B -ə] *s.* 1. cántaro, jarra, jarro. 2. **little pitchers have long ears,** los niños son capaces de oír cualquier cosa, hay moros en la costa; hay ropa tendida (Esp.). 3. (bot.) hoja utricular, ascidio.

pitcher *s.* 1. lanzador (esp. en béisbol). 2. (golf.) palo liviano de hierro.

pitcher plant, (bot.) nepente; sarracenia.

pitchfork ['pɪtʃˌfɔrk, B -ˌfɔk] *s.* horca, horquilla. —*v.t.* amontonar, echar (heno, etc.) con horquilla.

pitchiness ['pɪtʃɪnəs] *s.* negrura, oscuridad, color de pez.

pitching niblick [-ɪŋ-] (golf) palo liviano de hierro.

pitchman ['pɪtʃmən] *s.* 1. buhonero, vendedor ambulante. 2. voceador o vendedor agresivo (esp. en una feria, demostración comercial, etc.).

pitchout [-ˌaʊt] *s.* 1. (béisbol) **lanzada** fuera del alcance del bateador. 2. (fútbol Am.) pase lateral hecho entre los dos zagueros fuera de la línea de defensa.

pitch pine, (bot.) pino tea.

pitch pipe, flauta o pito usado como diapasón.

pitchstone [-ˌstoʊn] *s.* vidrio volcánico.

pitchy ['pɪtʃɪ] *a.* 1. peceño; embreado. 2. (fig.) negro, oscuro.

piteous ['pɪtɪəs] *a.* 1. lastimero, lastimoso. 2. (ant.) compasivo; tierno.

piteously [-lɪ] *adv.* lastimosamente.

piteousness [-nəs] *s.* carácter o aspecto lastimoso.

pitfall ['pɪtˌfɔl] *s.* 1. trampa. 2. (fig.) escollo oculto, peligro latente.

pith [pɪθ] *s.* 1. (bot.) médula, medula. 2. médula, tuétano, meollo (de los huesos, plumas, etc.). 3. (fig.) fuerza, vigor. 4. (fig.) médula, esencia. —*v.t.* 1. matar (ganado) cortando la médula espinal, descabellar (taur.). 2. quitar la médula a (una planta).

pithecanthropus [ˌpɪθɪ'kænθrəpəs, B -kæn'θroʊpəs] *s.* (*pl.* PITHECANTHROPI [-ˌpaɪ]) (antrop.) pitecántropo.

pithily ['pɪθəlɪ] *adv.* concisamente, expresivamente, sentenciosamente.

pithiness [-ɪnəs] *s.* concisión, expresividad.

pithy [-ɪ] *a.* 1. medular; meduloso. 2. (fig.) conciso, expresivo.

pitiable ['pɪtɪəbəl] *a.* 1. lamentable, deplorable, sensible. 2. despreciable, inadecuado, miserable.

pitiably [-blɪ] *adv.* lamentablemente; despreciablemente.

pitiful ['pɪtɪfəl] *a.* 1. lastimero, triste, lastimoso; digno de compasión. 2. despreciable. 3. (ant.) compasivo.

pitifully [-fəlɪ] *adv.* lastimosamente.
pitiless [-ləs] *a.* despiadado, cruel, inhumano, duro, desalmado.
pitilessly [-lɪ] *adv.* despiadadamente; cruelmente.
pitilessness [-nəs] *s.* crueldad.
pitman ['pɪtmən] *s.* 1. (*pl.* PITMEN) peón, excavador; pocero, minero. 2. (mec.) (*pl.* PITMANS) barra de conexión, biela.
piton ['pitɑn, B pi'tɔn] *s.* pitón (utilizado en alpinismo), pico.
Pitot tube ['pitoʊ-] (hidr., aer.) tubo de Pitot.
pitpit ['pɪt,pɪt] *s.* (orn.) pitpit, pipí.
pit prop, entibo, puntal.
pit saw, sierra al aire, sierra cabrilla, sierra abrazadera, serrucho braguero.
pittance ['pɪtəns] *s.* miseria, ración o porción miserables, óbolo exiguo, jornal o sueldo de hambre.
pitted ['pɪtəd] *a.* 1. picado, cacarañado, picoso (de viruelas). 2. hoyoso, lleno de baches (camino, etc.). 3. deshuesada (fruta).
pitter ['pɪtər, B -ə] *s.* deshuesadora (de frutas).
pitter-patter [-,pætər, B -ə] *s.* golpeteo suave y continuo. —*adv.* con golpeteo suave y continuo.
pitting ['pɪtɪŋ] *s.* 1. picadura, corrosión diseminada. 2. careo (de gallos de riña).
pituitary [pə'tuə,tɛrɪ, B -'tjuɪtərɪ] *a.* (anat.) pituitario; **p. gland** o **p. body,** glándula pituitaria; cuerpo pituitario. —*s.* (med.) extracto pituitario.
pituitous [-təs] *a.* (ant.) pituitoso.
pit viper, *s.* serpiente venenosa de la familia de los crótalos, que tiene una depresión a ambos lados de la cabeza.
pity ['pɪtɪ] *s.* lástima, piedad, misericordia, compasión; **it's a p.,** es una lástima; **for p's. sake,** ¡por amor de Dios!; **more's the p.,** tanto peor; **to feel p. for,** compadecerse de, tener lástima de; **to take p. on,** tener piedad de, apiadarse de; **what a p.,** ¡qué lástima! —*v.t.* (*pret., p.p.* PITIED; *p.pr.* PITYING) compadecer, apiadarse (de); **(he) is to be pitied,** es digno de compasión, merece compasión. —*v.i.* sentir lástima.
pitying [-ɪŋ] *a* misericordioso, compasivo.
pityingly [-lɪ] *adv.* misericordiosamente, compasivamente.
pityriasis [,pɪtɪ'raɪəsəs] *s.* (med., vet.) pitiriasis.
Pius ['paɪəs] *s.* Pío, nombre que han llevado doce papas desde el siglo II.
pivot ['pɪvət] *s.* 1. pivote, gorrón, espiga, muñón, centro de giro. 2. (fig.) persona o miembro esenciales; eje, factor fundamental o crucial. —*a.* 1. de charnela, de giro. 2. (fig.) cardinal, fundamental, esencial. —*v.t.* montar en gorrón; proveer con gorrón o espiga. —*v.i.* 1. girar sobre un gorrón o espiga, girar sobre un eje. 2. rotar (jugadores de naipes). 3. **p. on,** (fig.) depender de.
pivotal [-əl] *a.* de giro, de charnela.
pivoted window [-əd-] ventana de báscula, ventana de balancín.
pix, *var. de* **pyx.**
pixie, *var. de.* **pixy.**
pixilated ['pɪksə,leɪtəd] *a.* (fam.) chiflado, destornillado, alocado, deschavetado; tonto, bobo.
pixy ['pɪksɪ] *s.* (*pl.* PIXIES) duende, hada o espíritu travieso.
pizza ['pitsə] *s.* (ital.) piza, torta de tomate y queso.
pizzazz [pə'zæz] *s.* (jer. E.U.) 1. fuerza, potencia; agresividad, brío. 2. gracia, garbo, buen tono, clase.
pizzeria [,pitsə'rɪə] *s.* (ital.) picería (Am.), tienda de despacho de pizas, restaurante donde se hacen y sirven pizas.
pizzicato [,pɪtsɪ'kɑtoʊ] *a.* (mús.) pulsada con el dedo (cuerda) pizzicato.
pizzle ['pɪzəl] *s.* 1. (vulg.) verga (del buey, toro, etc.). 2. vergajo.
pj's ['pi,djeɪz] *s. pl.* (fam.) *var. de* **pajamas.**
placability [,plækə'bɪlətɪ, ,pleɪkə-] *s.* placabilidad; clemencia.
placable ['plækəbəl, 'pleɪkə-] *a.* placable, aplacable, apacible.
placableness [-nəs] *s.* placabilidad; clemencia.
placably [-blɪ] *adv.* apaciblemente.
placard ['plæk,ɑrd, -ərd, B -,ɑd] *s.* cartel, letrero, anuncio, rótulo. —*v.t.* 1. poner carteles en, cubrir con carteles. 2. anunciar por medio de carteles.
placate ['pleɪ,keɪt, 'plæk,eɪt, B plə'keɪt] *v.t.* aplacar, conciliar, pacificar, sosegar, calmar, apaciguar.
placater [-ər, B -ə] *s.* pacificador, apaciguador.
placation [pleɪ'keɪʃən, plæ-, B plə-] *s.* aplacamiento, apaciguamiento.
placative ['pleɪ,keɪtɪv, -kət-, 'plæ-, B -kət -] *a.* placativo, capaz de aplacar.
placatory [-kə,tɔrɪ, B -tərɪ] *a.* aplacador, conciliatorio.
place [pleɪs] *s.* 1. lugar, sitio, ej., *p. of worship,* templo, *p. of amusement,* lugar de diversión. 2. espacio, cabida. 3. localidad, pueblo, región, paraje; residencia, morada. 4. local, centro; puesto, lugar. 5. punto determinado, ej., *a key p.,* un punto clave. 6. parte, pasaje (en un libro, discurso, etc.). 7. condición, rango, posición. 8. colocación, situacion, empleo; deber, ej., *it's not my p. to inquire into this matter,* no es mi deber (o no me incumbe) investigar este asunto. 9. puesto, asiento. 10. (mat.) puesto (decimal). 11. plaza (de un pueblo). 12. **P.,** (G.B.) (*ú en nombres propios*) edificio. 13. **in no p.,** en ninguna parte; **in p.,** en su lugar apropiado; **in p. of,** en lugar de; **in the first p.,** en primer término, en primer lugar; **out of p.,** fuera de lugar, inapropiado, inconveniente; **to go places,** (jer.) tener éxito; **to keep (one) in his p.,** tener a raya (a uno); **to know one's p.,** guardar su lugar, saber cuál es su sitio; **to take p.,** suceder, verificarse, tener lugar; **to take the p. of,** substituir a. —*v.t.* 1. poner, colocar, situar, ubicar, depositar, acomodar. 2. establecer, fijar, determinar. 3. dar empleo a, emplear. 4. invertir o prestar (dinero). 5. (com.) disponer (de), vender; pasar, colocar (pedidos). 6. recordar, identificar. 7. **p. before,** presentar a, someter a (comité, público, etc.). —*v.i.* llegar entre los tres primeros (esp. en carreras de caballos o de perros).
placebo [plə'siboʊ] *s.* (*pl.* PLACEBOS o PLACEBOES) 1. (relig.) primera antífona de las Vísperas para los muertos. 2. (med.) placebo. 3. palabra aplacadora.
place-kick ['pleɪs,kɪk] *s.* (fútbol Am.) tiro hecho con la pelota puesta en el suelo. —*v.t., v.i.* hacer un tiro con la pelota puesta en el suelo.
placeman [-mən] *s.* (G.B.) funcionario o empleado público.
place mat, *s.* mantelito individual.
placement [-mənt] *s.* 1. colocación, empleo. 2. (fútbol Am.) colocación de la pelota en el suelo (para patearla).
place name, topónimo, nombre geográfico.
placenta [plə'sɛntə] *s.* (*pl.* PLACENTAE [-ti]) (anat., zool., bot.) placenta.
placental [-'sɛntəl] **placentary** ['plæsən,tɛrɪ, B -tərɪ] *a.* (anat., zool., bot.) placentario.
Placentalia [,plæsən'teɪlɪə] *s. pl.* (zool.) placentarios.
placentation [-ʃən] *s.* (anat., zool., bot.) placentación.
place of business, sede de un negocio o una empresa.
placer ['plæsər, B -ə] *s.* placer (lugar donde se obtiene oro por lavado), lavadero de oro; aluvión aurífero.
placer mining, explotación de placeres (de oro), extracción de oro de lavaderos.
place setting, servicio de mesa para una sola persona.
placet ['pleɪsət] *s.* plácet, voto afirmativo.
placid ['plæsəd] *a.* plácido, tranquilo, calmo, apacible, sereno, sosegado, quieto.
placidity [plə'sɪdətɪ, plæ-] *s.* placidez, serenidad, quietud, apacibilidad, tranquilidad, sosiego, calma.
placidly ['plæsədlɪ] *adv.* plácidamente, tranquilamente, serenamente.
placidness [-nəs] *s.* placidez, serenidad, quietud, apacibilidad, tranquilidad, sosiego, calma.
placket ['plækət] *s.* 1. abertura en la cintura o el cuello de una prenda de vestir. 2. bolsillo (de una falda). 3. (ant.) enagua.
placoid ['plæk,ɔɪd] *a.* (ict.) placoideo. —*s.* pez placoideo.
plagal ['pleɪgəl] *a.* (mús.) plagal.
plagiarism ['pleɪdʒə,rɪzəm, -dʒɪə-] *s.* plagio.
plagiarist [-rəst] *s.* plagiario.
plagiaristic [,pleɪdʒə'rɪstɪk, -dʒɪə-] *a.* plagiario.
plagiarize ['pleɪdʒə,raɪz, -dʒɪə-] *v.t., v.i.* plagiar.
plagiarizer [-ər, B -ə] *s.* plagiario.
plagiary [-dʒɪ,ɛrɪ, B -dʒərɪ] *s.* (*pl.* PLAGIARIES) plagio, copia, imitación.
plagioclase ['pleɪdʒɪə,kleɪs] *s.* (min.) plagioclasa.
Plagiostomi [,pleɪdʒɪ'ɑstəmaɪ, B -'ɔs-] *s. pl.* (ict.) plagióstomos.
plagiotropic [-ɔ'trɑpɪk, B -'trɔp-] *a.* (bot.) plagiótropo.
plagiotropism [-'ɑtrə,pɪzəm, B -'ɔ-] *s.* (bot.) plagiotropismo.
plague [pleɪg] *s.* 1. plaga, peste, pestilencia, epidemia. 2. plaga, azote, calamidad. 3. (fig.) molestia, incomodidad, importunidad, engorro. 4. **p. on it!** ¡maldita sea! —*v.t.* 1. plagar, infestar, apestar. 2. (fig.) fastidiar, molestar, atormentar, importunar.
plaguer ['pleɪgər, B -ə] *s.* importuno, molestoso, fastidioso.
plaguesome [-səm] *s.* 1. fastidioso, pesado. 2. pestilente, pestilencial.
plaguily ['pleɪgəlɪ] *adv.* (pr. dial.) enfadosamente, molestamente, fastidiosamente.
plaguy, plaguey [-gɪ] *a.* (pr. dial.) molesto, enojoso, incómodo, embarazoso, fastidioso, importuno, enfadoso.
plaice [pleɪs] *s.* (*pl.* PLAICE) (ict.) platija, acedía.
plaid [plæd] *s.* 1. plaid (capa escocesa grande de lana). 2. tartán. 3. diseño de cuadros a la escocesa.
plaided ['plædəd] *a.* a cuadros.
plain [pleɪn] *a.* 1. simple, llano, sencillo, fácil, comprensible, ej., *p. words,* palabras sencillas. 2. simple, sencillo; sin adornos, sin lujo, ej., *p. living,* vida sin lujos. 3. terminante, evidente (prueba, etc.). 4. sencillo, corriente, ordinario, ej., *a p. man,* un hombre sencillo. 5. feo, carente de belleza, ej., *a p. girl,* una muchacha fea. 6. (dial.) libre, despejado, descubierto. —*s.* 1. llano, llanura, planicie. 2. (*pl.*) praderas. —*adv.* claramente, inteligiblemente.
plain chant, canto llano.

plain clothes, traje de paisano, traje de calle (que llevan policías, militares, etc.); **in p.,** de civil.
plainclothes man ['pleɪn'kloʊðz-, -'kloʊz-] detective o policía vestido de civil.
plain dealing, candor, franqueza, buena fe.
plain English, palabras claras, sin rodeos.
plain-laid ['pleɪn'leɪd] *a.* con colchado dextrógiro, de cableado corriente, de acolchado simple o de cableado cruzado (díc. de la soga o cuerda acalabrotada.).
plainly [-lɪ] *adv.* 1. visiblemente, claramente, evidentemente. 2. modestamente, humildemente, simplemente.
plainness [-nəs] *s.* 1. simpleza, sencillez, sinceridad. 2. fealdad. 3. llaneza.
plain sailing, 1. navegación en una ruta simple. 2. (fig.) cosa fácil, asunto simple.
plainsman ['pleɪnzmən] *s.* llanero.
plainsong ['pleɪn,sɔŋ] *s.* canto llano, música llana.
plain speaking, palabras francas.
plainspoken [-'spoʊkən] *a.* franco, sincero.
plaint [pleɪnt] *s.* 1. (poét.) lamento, endecha, queja. 2. querella. 3. (der.) demanda; protesta, queja, acusación.
plaintiff ['pleɪntəf] *s.* (der.) demandante, actor.
plaintive ['pleɪntɪv] *a.* quejumbroso, lastimero, melancólico, dolido, penoso.
plaintively [-lɪ] *adv.* quejumbrosamente, melancólicamente.
plaintiveness [-nəs] *s.* quejumbrosidad, melancolía.
plain weave, (tej.) ligamento tafetán, punto de tafetán.
plaister ['pleɪstər, B 'plɑstə] *var. de.* **plaster.**
plait [pleɪt, B plæt] *s.* 1. pliegue, repliegue, doblez, plisado, frunce. 2. trenza. *—v.t.* 1. plegar, doblar, plisar, fruncir. 2. trenzar, entretejer.
plaiting ['pleɪtɪŋ, B 'plæt-] *s.* plegado, plisado, fruncido.
plan [plæn] *s.* 1. plano; mapa; diseño, gráfico, bosquejo, esquema, trazo. 2. plan, proyecto, intento. 3. plan, método, manera (de pagos, ejercicios, etc.). *—v.t.* (*pret., p.p.* PLANNED; *p.pr.* PLANNING) 1. diseñar, bosquejar, trazar. 2. planear, proyectar. 3. **p. to (do),** proponerse (hacer). *—v.i.* hacer planes.
planar ['pleɪnər, B -nə] *a.* aplanado, plano.
planarian [plə'nerɪən, B -'nɛər-] *s.* (zool.) planario.
planch, planche [plæntʃ, plɑntʃ, B planʃ] *s.* (dial.) plancha, tablón, losa, laja; piso.
planchet ['plæntʃət, B 'plɑnʃət] *s.* 1. cospel, tejo para hacer monedas, tejuelo. 2. (top.) plancheta.
planchette [plæn'ʃɛt, -'tʃɛt, B plɑn'ʃɛt] *s.* 1. (top.) brújula de agrimensor. 2. tabla de escritura mesmerista.
plane [pleɪn] *a.* 1. plano, llano, igual, nivelado. 2. (geom.) plano. *—s.* 1. plano, superficie plana; llano. 2. nivel (de desarrollo, escala de valores, etc.). 3. avión, aeroplano. 4. (bot.) variedad de plátano. 5. (aer.) plano, ala. *—v.i.* 1. planear (avión). 2. (fam.) viajar en avión.
plane [pleɪn] *s.* 1. cepillo (de carpintero), garlopa. 2. llana, fratás. *—v.t.* allanar, cepillar, desbastar, alisar; **p. down,** reducir con el cepillo el espesor de; **p. off,** desbastar con el cepillo. *—v.i.* trabajar con un cepillo.
plane angle, ángulo plano o rectilíneo.
plane crash, accidente aéreo, accidente de avión.
plane geometry, geometría plana.
plane iron, cuchilla de cepillo.
plane of desfilade, (mil.) plano de desenfilada.
plane of osculation, (mat.) plano osculador.
plane of sight, (mil.) plano de tiro.
planer ['pleɪnər, B -nə] *s.* 1. cepilladora, acepilladora. 2. aplanadora, alisadora. 3. (impr.) tamborilete.
plane sailing, navegación loxodrómica.
planet ['plænət] *s.* 1. (astr.) planeta. 2. (astrol.) astro (que rige el destino de una persona).
plane table, (agrimensura) plancheta, plancheta de pinulas.
planetarium [,plænə'tɛrɪəm, B -'tɛər-] *s.* (*pl.* PLANETARIUMS O PLANETARIA [-ɪə]) planetario.
planetary ['plænə,tɛrɪ, B -tərɪ] *a.* 1. planetario. 2. errante, errabundo. 3. terrestre; mundial. 4. (mec.) planetario (engranaje). 5. (astrol.) debido a la influencia de un astro.
planetesimal [,plænə'tɛsəməl] *s.* corpúsculo del espacio.
planetoid ['plænə,tɔɪd] *s.* planetoide, asteroide.
planet-stricken ['plænət,strɪkən] **planet-struck** [-strʌk] *a.* 1. bajo influencia planetaria. 2. despavorido, aterrado.
planet wheel, (mec.) rueda planetaria, rueda satélite.
planform ['plæn,fɔrm, B -,fɔm] *s.* perfil del avión (visto de arriba).
plangency ['plændʒənsɪ] *s.* vibración, reverbero (del sonido).
plangent [-dʒənt] *a.* vibrante, reverberante (sonido).
plangently [-lɪ] *adv.* en tono vibrante o reverberante.
planimeter [plə'nɪmətər, B plæ-ə] *s.* planímetro, instrumento para medir el área de las figuras planas.
planimetric [,pleɪnə'metrɪk, B ,plænə-] *a.* planimétrico (mapa).
planimetry [plə'nɪmətrɪ] *s.* planimetría.
planish ['plænɪʃ] *v.t.* alisar, allanar, aplanar (metales).
planisher [-ər, B -ə] *s.* planador.
planisphere ['plænə,sfɪər, B -,sfɪə] *s.* planisferio.
plank [plæŋk] *s.* 1. tabla, tablón, madero. 2. tablazón, tablaje. 3. punto de programa (de partido político). 4. **to walk the p.,** andar la pasarela, pasar la plancha (pena de muerte impuesta por los piratas). *—v.t.* 1. entablar, entarimar, enmaderar; poner tablas a (piso). 2. (fam.) (gen. con **down** o **out**) pagar en el acto, poner (la plata) sobre la mesa. 3. cocer y servir sobre una tabla.
planking ['plæŋkɪŋ] *s.* tablaje, tablazón, entarimado, entablado, tablado.
plank-sheer [-,ʃɪər, B -,ʃɪə] *s.* (mar.) regala.
plankter [-tər, B -tə] *s.* organismo planctónico.
plankton ['plæŋktən] *s.* (biol.) plancton.
planktonic [plæŋk'tɑnɪk, B -'tɔn-] *a.* (biol.) planctónico, del plancton.
planner ['plænər, B -ə] *s.* 1. proyectista, diseñador, calculista. 2. trazador, tracista. 3. persona metódica o que planea las cosas.
planning [-ɪŋ] *s.* formulación de planes; planificación, planeamiento, trazado de un plano, programación.
plano-concave [,pleɪnoʊ,kɑn'keɪv, B -'kɔnkeɪv] *a.* plano-cóncavo.
plano-convex [,pleɪnoʊkɑn'vɛks, B -'kɔnvɛks] *a.* plano-convexo.
planograph ['pleɪnə,græf, B -,grɑf] *v.t.* planografiar, litografiar. *—s.* impresión planográfica o litográfica.
planographic [,pleɪnə'græfɪk] *a.* planográfico, litográfico.
planography [plə'nɑgrəfɪ, B -'nɔg-] *s.* planografía, litografía.
plant [plænt, B plɑnt] *s.* 1. planta, vegetal. 2. planta, fábrica, equipo o instalación (de maquinaria). 3. (jer.) trampa, treta fraudulenta; indicio engañoso, pista falsa, prueba falsificada. 4. **in p.,** en crecimiento. *—v.t.* 1. plantar (árbol, vástago, etc.), sembrar (semilla), cultivar (tierra). 2. plantar, fijar, colocar, sentar. 3. implantar, introducir, inculcar (una idea, etc.). 4. abastecer, proveer. 5. colonizar, establecer, fundar. 6. aclimatar, cultivar, criar (ostras, camarones, etc.). 7. abandonar, dejar plantado. 8. (jer.) plantar, asestar (un golpe). 9. (jer.) sembrar (una pista o idea falsa); colocar (objeto de prueba falsificado) para comprometer (a persona inocente).
plantaginaceous [,plæntədʒə'neɪʃəs] *a.* (bot.) plantagináceo.
plantain ['plæntən] *s.* (bot.) 1. plátano, bananero. 2. plantaina, llantén mayor, arta.
plantar ['plæntər, B -ə] *a.* (anat.) plantar, de la planta del pie.
plantation [plæn'teɪʃən] *s.* 1. plantío. 2. plantación, hacienda. 3. colonización, colonia.
planter ['plæntər, B 'plɑntə] *s.* 1. plantador, dueño de una plantación, hacendado (Am.). 2. colonizador, colono. 3. (mec.) sembradora. 4. (hor.) tiesto, maceta.
planter's punch, ponche de ron y frutas con hielo picado.
plant hormone, hormona vegetal.
plantigrade ['plæntə,greɪd] *a., s.* (zool.) plantígrado.
plant louse, áfido, brugo, pulgón, piojo de planta (Am.).
plant pathology, patología vegetal.
plant pot, (hor.) tiesto, maceta.
plantule ['plæntʃul, B -tjul] *s.* (bot.) plántula.
planula ['plænjələ] *s.* (*pl.* PLANULAE [-,li]) (zool.) plánula.
plaque [plæk, B plɑk] *s.* 1. placa o lámina (incrustada, de adorno, etc.). 2. medalla, insignia (de una hermandad, cofradía, etc.).
plaquette [plæ'kɛt] *s.* (anat.) plaqueta.
plash [plæʃ] *v.t.* (G.B.) entrelazar o entretejer (ramas o tallos de plantas, flores, etc.).
plash [plæʃ] *v.t.* salpicar, rociar, espurrear. *—v.i.* chapotear, chapalear. *—s.* 1. salpicadura, rociada. 2. chapoteo. 3. charco, poza, aguazal.
plashy ['plæʃɪ] *a.* 1. lleno de charcos. 2. pantanoso, lodoso.
plasm ['plæzəm] *var. de* **plasma.**
plasma ['plæzmə] *s.* 1. (min.) plasma, prasma. 2. (anat., fisiol.) plasma (linfático, muscular, sanguíneo, etc.). 3. (biol.) protoplasma.
plasmagene [-dʒin] *s.* (biol.) plasmagen.
plasmalemma [,plæzmə'lɛmə] *s.* (zool.) plasmalema.
plasma membrane, membrana plasmática.
plasmasol ['plæzmə,sɔl, -,sɑl, B -,sɔl] *s.* (zool.) plasmasol.
plasmatic [plæz'mætɪk] *a.* (anat., fisiol.) plasmático.
plasmodium [-'moʊdɪəm] *s.* (*pl.* PLASMODIA [-ɪə]) (biol.) plasmodio.
plasmolysis [-'mɑləsəs, B -'mɔl-] *s.* (fisiol.) plasmólisis.
plasmolyze ['plæzmə,laɪz] *v.t.* someter a plasmólisis.
plaster ['plæstər, B 'plɑstə] *s.* 1. (farm.) emplasto, parche, bizma. 2. yeso, plaste, argamasa, mortero, enlucido. *—v.t.* 1. enyesar, enlucir (con yeso), revocar. 2. pegar, fijar, adherir. 3. cubrir completamente con (anuncios, etiquetas, etc.). 4. (fig.) colmar (de elogios, favores, etc.). 5. bombardear severamente; abrumar. 6. (med.) emplastar; enyesar. 7. **p. down,** pegar (cabello);

p. over, plastecer (hueco, etc.); cubrir; extender sobre.

plasterboard [-ˌbɔrd, B -ˌbɔd] *s.* cartónyeso, cartón de yeso, plancha de yeso y fieltro. —*a.* de cartón-yeso.

plaster cast, 1. escultura vaciada en yeso blanco. 2. (med.) vendaje de yeso.

plastered [-tərd, B -təd] *a.* (jer.) hecho una cuba, mamado, borracho.

plasterer [-tərər, B -tərə] *s.* revocador, enlucidor.

plaster factory, fábrica yesera.

plastering [-tərɪŋ] *s.* 1. enlucido, jaharro, revoque, enyesado. 2. (jer.) paliza, zurra, tunda.

plaster of Paris, yeso blanco, yeso mate.

plastic ['plæstɪk] *a.* 1. plástico, formativo, creativo. 2. plástico, dúctil, maleable, flexible, adaptable. 3. plástico, modelador (arte). 4. escultural (belleza, etc.). 5. plástico, hecho de plástico. 6. (biol., med., fís.) plástico. —*s.* plástico.

plastically [-tɪkəlɪ] *adv.* 1. plásticamente, en forma plástica. 2. en cuanto a plasticidad.

plastic arts, plástica, arte de modelar (escultura, cerámica, etc.).

plastic bomb, (mil.) bomba plástica, bomba de plástico.

plasticity [plæs'tɪsətɪ] *s.* plasticidad; ductilidad, flexibilidad.

plasticize ['plæstəˌsaɪz] *v.t.* dar plasticidad a.

plasticizer [-ˌsaɪzər, B -zə] *s.* plasticizador (substancia).

plastic operation, operación plástica, corrección estética.

plastics [-tɪks] *s. pl. (sing. o pl. en const.)* plástica.

plastic surgeon, cirujano plástico, especialista en cirugía estética o cirugía plastica.

plastic surgery, cirugía plástica, cirugía estética.

plastid ['plæstəd] *s.* (biol.) plástida.

plastometer [plæs'tɑmətər, B -'tɔmɪtə] *s.* plastómetro.

plastron ['plæstrən] *s.* 1. coraza, peto. 2. (zool.) plastrón. 3. plastrón, pechera.

plat [plæt] *v.t.* (*pret., p.p.* PLATTED; *p.pr.* PLATTING) entretejer, trenzar, enlazar; plegar. —*s.* (dial.) trenza; pliegue.

plat [plæt] *s.* 1. solar, parcela, pedazo de terreno. 2. (E.U.) plano, mapa, diseño (esp. de una ciudad). —*v.t.* trazar, diseñar, hacer un plano de.

platan ['plætən] *s.* (bot.) plátano.

platanaceous [ˌplætə'neɪʃəs] *a.* (bot.) platanácco, platáneo.

plate [pleɪt] *s.* 1. plancha, placa, chapa, lámina; rótulo, letrero (metálico). 2. plato, cubierto (comida y servicio); cubiertos, orfebrería, platillo para colectas, colecta. 3. falda, matambre (Arg.) (carne de res). 4. (anat., zool.) plaqueta (de sangre); placa, lámina. 5. (dep.) copa de oro o plata (dada como premio en competencias, ej., en una carrera, etc.). 6. (béisbol) base del bateador. 7. (arq.) viga horizontal. 8. (impr.) plancha, clisé, estereotipo, estereotipia, estéreo. 9. grabado, lámina (ilustración). 10. (f.c.) riel o carril de vía. 11. (arm.) plancha de blindaje. 12. (elec.) placa de ánodo, placa; electrodo; elemento (de una pila). 13. (base de la) dentadura postiza, pieza dental. 14. (foto.) placa, placa sensible. —*v.t.* 1. platear, argentar; dorar; niquelar; platinar. 2. planchear, chapear; enchapar; blindar. 3. planchear (papel para darle brillo); satinar, glasear. 4. (impr.) hacer una plancha (o clisé) de.

plateau [plæ'toʊ, B 'plætoʊ] *s.* (*pl.* PLATEAUS o PLATEAUX [-'toʊz, B -ˌtoʊz]) meseta, mesa, altiplanicie, altiplano (Am.). —*v.i.* nivelarse, estabilizarse.

plate battery, (rad.) batería de alta tensión, batería del ánodo o placa (de una lámpara termiónica).

plate current, (elec.) corriente de placa.

plated ['pleɪtəd] *a.* 1. enchapado. 2. galvanoplastiado. 3. electroplateado. 4. blindado (buques).

plateful ['pleɪtˌfʊl] *s.* (*pl.* PLATEFULS o PLATESFUL) plato (lleno de), ej., *a p. of rice,* un plato (lleno de) arroz.

plate girder, (const.) viga de alma llena.

plate glass, vidrio cilindrado, vidrio en planchas, luna (de espejo, de escaparate).

plate holder, (foto.) bastidor de las placas.

platelet ['pleɪtlət] *s.* (fisiol.) plaqueta.

plate metal, metal en planchas o láminas.

platen ['plætən] *s.* 1. (impr.) platina; plato (de prensa). 2. cilindro o rodillo portapapel (de una máquina de escribir).

platen press, (impr.) prensa de platina, minerva.

plate printing, (impr.) impresión de grabados con planchas.

plate proof, (impr.) prueba de un grabado, prueba de clisé.

plater ['pleɪtər, B -ə] *s.* 1. plateador; dorador, niquelador. 2. caballo de carrera de calidad inferior.

plate rack, escurreplatos, escurridero, secadora de vajilla.

plate rail, 1. (pr. G.B.) riel plano. 2. repisa o anaquel para platos (en la pared).

plateresque [ˌplætə'rɛsk] *a.* (arq.) plateresco (estilo).

plate voltage, (rad.) voltaje de placa, tensión de la batería de la placa.

platform ['plætˌfɔrm, B -ˌfɔm] *s.* 1. plataforma, tablado, andamio. 2. (fig.) plataforma, programa (político), declaración formal de principios (de un partido político). 3. (f.c.) andén. 4. plataforma, estrado, tribuna. 5. (ant.) plan; propósito, designio.

platform car, (f.c.) vagón o carro de plataforma.

platform scale, báscula, romana de plataforma, balanza de plataforma.

platina [plə'tinə, B 'plætɪnə] *s.* (quím.) platino.

plating ['pleɪtɪŋ] *s.* 1. plateadura, dorado, doradura, niquelado, platinado; capa metálica. 2. blindaje.

platinic [plæ'tɪnɪk, B plə-] *a.* (quím.) platínico.

platinize ['plætənˌaɪz] *v.t.* platinar; tratar o combinar con platino.

platinocyanic [ˌplætənoʊsaɪ'ænɪk] *a.* (quím.) platinociánico.

platinocyanide [-'saɪəˌnaɪd] *s.* (quím.) platinocianuro.

platinoid ['plætənˌɔɪd] *a.* semejante al platino. —*s.* platinoide.

platinotype [-oʊˌtaɪp] *s.* (foto.) platinotipia; positivo platinotípico.

platinous [-əs] *a.* (quím.) platinoso.

platinum ['plætənəm] *s.* (quím.) platino.

platinum black, (quím.) polvo negro de platino.

platinum blonde, (fam.) rubia platinada, rubia platino.

platitude ['plætəˌtud, B -ˌtjud] *s.* lugar común, perogrullada, trivialidad.

platitudinize [ˌplætə'tudənˌaɪz, B -'tjud-] *v.i.* decir perogrulladas o trivialidades.

platitudinizer [-ər, B -ə] *s.* persona dada a decir trivialidades.

platitudinous [-ənəs] *a.* perogrullesco, trivial, insípido.

Plato ['pleɪtoʊ] *s.* Platón, filósofo griego.

Platonic [plə'tɑnɪk, pleɪ-, B -'tɔn-] *a.* 1. platónico, de Platón. 2. platónico, ideal. 3. **P. love,** amor platónico; **P. year,** (astr.) año platónico.

Platonically [-ɪkəlɪ] *adv.* platónicamente.

Platonism ['pleɪtənˌɪzəm] *s.* 1. platonismo. 2. amor platónico.

Platonist [-əst] *s.* platónico (persona).

Platonistic [ˌpleɪtə'nɪstɪk] *a.* platónico.

Platonize ['pleɪtənˌaɪz] *v.t.* dar carácter platónico a; idealizar.

platoon [plə'tun] *s.* 1. (mil.) pelotón. 2. grupo, compañía.

platoon corporal, (mil.) cabo de escuadra.

platoon sergeant, sargento de pelotón.

platter ['plætər, B -ə] *s.* 1. fuente o plato grande; bandeja, azafate (Chile). 2. disco fonográfico.

platy ['pleɪtɪ] *a.* en placas, laminado.

platycephalous [ˌplætɪ'sɛfələs] *a.* (antrop.) platicéfalo.

platyhelminth [-'hɛlmɪnθ] *s.* (zool.) platelminto.

platyhelminthic [-hɛl'mɪnθɪk] *a.* (zool.) platelminto.

platypus ['plætɪpəs] *s.* (*pl.* PLATYPUSES) (zool.) ornitorrinco.

platyrrhine [-ˌraɪn] *a., s.* (zool.) platirrino.

platyrrhinian [ˌplætɪ'rɪnɪən] *a., s.* platirrino.

plaudit ['plɔdət] *s.* aplauso, aclamación; (fig.) aprobación.

plausibility [ˌplɔzə'bɪlətɪ] *s.* admisibilidad; credibilidad aparente.

plausible ['plɔzəbəl] *a.* 1. verosímil, verisímil, creíble, posible, razonable. 2. (de personas) que usa argumentos especiosos o aparentes.

plausibleness [-nəs] *s.* admisibilidad; credibilidad aparente.

plausibly [-blɪ] *adv.* verosímilmente.

plausive ['plɔsɪv] *a.* plausivo, laudatorio.

Plautine ['plɔˌtaɪn] *a.* plautino, relativo a Plauto.

Plautus [-təs] *s.* Plauto, comediógrafo romano.

play [pleɪ] *v.i.* 1. jugar, divertirse, recrearse. 2. moverse, agitarse; revolotear, aletear; vibrar, flamear. 3. tañer, tocar; sonar (instrumento musical). 4. jugar, participar (en el juego), actuar (en equipo deportivo); jugar por dinero. 5. conducirse, comportarse, portarse, actuar, jugar (de cierta manera); hacer, fingirse, ej., *p. fair,* jugar limpio, *p. foul,* actuar desleal o falsasamente, jugar sucio, *p. sick,* fingirse enfermo, *p. dead,* fingirse muerto, hacerse el muerto. 6. actuar (en drama), desempeñar un papel (de teatro). 7. funcionar, moverse libremente, tener juego (una pieza de máquina). 8. (con *over, along,* etc.) dar (en), caer (sobre) (díc. de los rayos de luz, chorro de agua, etc.). 9. (con *on*) hacer fuego (en), disparar (sobre) (díc. de armas de fuego); (con *on* o *upon*) estimular (emociones); hacer uso de, aprovecharse de (credulidad, temor, afección, etc.). 10. **p. around,** divertirse; estar perdiendo el tiempo; **p. at,** ocuparse en, jugar a (un pasatiempo); (fig.) ocuparse en (algo) con poco empeño; **p. by ear,** tocar de oído; (jer.) actuar o proceder según lo requieran las circunstancias; **p. into the hands of (someone),** hacer (a alguien) el caldo gordo, hacer (a alguien) el juego, facilitar algo a (alguien) (gen. al opositor o enemigo); **p. on,** seguir tocando; **p. up,** esforzarse (en una contienda), darse entero (al juego, etc.); **p. up to,** (fig.) halagar, adular; **p. upon words,** usar retruécanos, hacer juego de palabras; **p. with,** juguetear; jugar con (una idea); burlarse de (afección, sentimientos). —*v.t.* 1. jugar, practicar (un deporte). 2. hacerse, simular, fingir, ej., *p. the fool,* hacerse el tonto. 3. desempeñar (papel); representar, poner en escena (drama, etc.), ej., *p. Macbeth,* representar el drama "Macbeth" (en el teatro); desempeñar el papel de Macbeth (un actor). 4. hacer, meter (broma, treta, etc.), ej., *p. a trick (on someone)* o *p. (someone) a trick,* hacer (le) una jugada, engañar (a alguien). 5. enfrentar a o contender con (alguien) en el juego; hacer jugar (a alguien en equipo). 6. apostar. 7. tocar (instrumento musical, disco, cinta, etc.); ejecutar (pieza musical). 8. manejar, manipular, menear. 9. mover (una pieza en ajedrez, damas, etc.), jugar (una carta). 10. hacer de, ej. *my sister is playing house,* mi hermana hace de casa. — **p. back,** tocar (un disco o cinta recientemente grabados); **p. (a song, etc.) by ear,** tocar (una canción, etc.) de oído; **p. (something) down,** restar importancia a (algo); **p. off,** completar el juego de (una competencia interrumpida); romper, deshacer (un empate) con un partido adicional; **p. (something) off on (someone),** (fig.) encajar (algo a alguien); **p. (a person) off against (another),** oponer (una persona) a (otra), (esp. para sacar provecho uno mismo); **p. out,** terminar (una partida de naipes, etc.). —*s.* 1. juego, jugada. 2. drama, pieza (de teatro); función, representación. 3. recreo, diversión, entretenimiento, pasatiempo. 4. broma, chanza, chiste. 5. movimiento ligero y rápido, revoloteo, aleteo; reflejo (de colores o de luces). 6. juego, apuestas. 7. juego, movimiento (de pieza en máquina, etc.); funcionamiento, operación. 8. **p. on words,** juego de palabras, retruécano; **to be at p.,** estar jugando; **to bring into p.,** hacer entrar en juego; **to come into p.,** entrar en juego; **to give full p. to,** dar rienda suelta a; dejar que ejerza toda su fuerza.

playa ['plaɪə, B 'plɑjɑ] *s.* (*pl.* PLAYAS) (geol.) playa.

playable ['pleɪəbəl] *a.* que se puede tocar (música), que se puede representar (en teatro).

playact ['pleɪˌækt] *v.t.* 1. actuar, hacer un papel (esp. como profesional). 2. fingir, hacer la comedia.

play-actor [-ˌæktər, B -tə] *s.* actor.

playback [-ˌbæk] *s.* play-back, previo, lector; reproducción (en gramófono, cine, grabadora de cinta, etc.).

playback head, (electrón.) cabeza reproductora, cabeza de lectura.

playbill [-ˌbɪl] *s.* cartel de teatro; programa (de teatro).

playboy [-ˌbɔɪ] *s.* calavera, tarambana; hombre de mundo.

play-by-play ['pleɪbaɪ'pleɪ] *a.* jugado a jugado, minuto a minuto (díc. del comentario de un evento deportivo).

playday [-ˌdeɪ] *s.* día feriado, día de asueto (esp. para la escuela).

playdown [-ˌdaʊn] *s.* (dep.) partida decisiva (para deshacer un empate).

played out [pleɪd-] exhausto, agotado, acabado.

player ['pleɪər, B -ə] *s.* 1. jugador. 2. actor, comediante. 3. (mús.) ejecutante, músico, tocador.

player piano, pianola, piano mecánico o automático, autopiano.

playfellow [-ˌfɛloʊ] *s.* compañero de juegos.

playful [-fəl] *a.* 1. juguetón, retozón, travieso. 2. humorístico, festivo.

playfully [-fəlɪ] *adv.* 1. de modo juguetón. 2. festivamente. 3. de broma.

playfulness [-fəlnəs] *s.* travesura, naturaleza juguetona.

playgoer ['pleɪˌgoʊər, B -ə] *s.* persona que frecuenta el teatro.

playground [-ˌgraʊnd] *s.* patio de recreo; campo de juegos o de deportes; parte de un parque dedicado a los niños.

playhouse [-ˌhaʊs] *s.* 1. teatro. 2. casa de muñecas.

playing card [-ɪŋ-] naipe, carta.

playing field, campo o cancha de deportes; terreno para juegos.

playland [-ˌlænd] *s.* patio de recreo; campo de juegos.

playlet [-lət] *s.* comedia corta, drama corto.

playmate [-ˌmeɪt] *s.* compañero de juegos.

play-off ['pleɪˌɔf] *s.* (dep.) partida decisiva (para deshacer un empate).

playpen [-ˌpɛn] *s.* corralito (para niños).

playroom [-ˌrum, -ˌrʊm] *s.* cuarto de juegos.

playsuit [-ˌsut, B -ˌsjut] *s.* traje de juego (para niños); traje de tenis, conjunto de playa.

plaything [-ˌθɪŋ] *s.* juguete.

playtime [-ˌtaɪm] *s.* tiempo de recreo o de juego.

playwright ['pleɪˌraɪt] *s.* dramaturgo, autor dramático, comediógrafo.

plaza ['plæzə, 'plɑzə] *s.* plaza, plazuela, plazoleta.

plea [pli] *s.* 1. argumento, razonamiento. 2. disculpa, excusa; pretexto. 3. ruego, súplica, petición, ej., *a p. for mercy,* una petición de gracia. 4. (der.) alegato, alegación; defensa. 5. (der.) acción, litigio, proceso.

plea bargaining, acuerdo con el fiscal.

pleach [plitʃ] *v.t.* entretejer; trenzar; entrelazar, trabar.

plead [plid] *v.i.* (*pret., p.p.* PLEADED o PLEAD [plɛd]; *p.pr.* PLEADING) 1. argumentar, argüir, razonar. 2. suplicar, implorar. 3. (der.) abogar. 4. **p. with (someone),** suplicar a, tratar de convencer a (alguien). —*v.t.* 1. excusarse con, presentar como excusa. 2. (der.) defender (un pleito, una causa, etc.). 3. (der.) alegar, declarar (en un alegato, ante el tribunal; **p. for,** abogar por; **p. guilty,** (der.) declararse o confesarse culpable; **p. not guilty** (der.) declararse inocente; **p. self-defense,** (der.) alegar defensa propia, alegar legítima defensa.

pleadable ['plidəbəl] *a.* (der.) alegable, abogable.

pleader [-ər, B -ə] *s.* 1. (der.) abogado, defensor. 2. intercesor, mediador, avenidor.

pleading [-ɪŋ] *s.* 1. (der.) alegato, alegación, defensa; informe; oratoria forense. 2. (*pl.*) (der.) alegatos, escritos (de defensa o demanda). 3. súplica, ruego, imploración; intercesión.

plea in abatement, (der.) instancia de nulidad.

pleasance ['plɛzəns] *s.* 1. parque; pensil, esp. jardín de una residencia. 2. (ant.) placer, delicia.

pleasant ['plɛzənt] *a.* 1. placentero, agradable, ameno, grato, gustoso, ej., *a p. breeze,* una brisa agradable. 2. simpático, afable, ej., *he is a p. man,* es un hombre simpático.

pleasantly [-lɪ] *adv.* 1. agradablemente, gratamente. 2. simpáticamente, afablemente.

pleasantness [-nəs] *s.* 1. agradabilidad, agrado, amenidad. 2. carácter simpático, afabilidad.

pleasantry [-əntrɪ] *s.* (*pl.* PLEASANTRIES) 1. occurrencia, agudeza, dicho gracioso, chanza, humorada. 2. gracia, jocosidad.

please [pliz] *v.i.* 1. agradar, gustar, placer, dar satisfacción, complacer. 2. querer, sentir deseo, estar dispuesto, ej., *do as you p.,* haga como usted quiera. 3. **if you p.,** con su permiso. 4. **p.** + *inf.,* por favor, favor de + *inf.* —*v.t.* 1. agradar a, contentar (a), satisfacer (a), complacer (a), dar gusto (a). 2. darle la gana a (uno). 3. **easy to p.,** fácil de complacer; **hard to p.,** difícil de complacer; **p. (do),** sírvase (hacer); **please oneself,** hacer uno su gusto, hacer sólo lo que se le antoja; **to be pleased (with),** complacerse (de, en o con), estar satisfecho (con o de); **to be pleased to (do),** complacerse en (hacer), tener el agrado de (hacer), tener agrado en (hacer).

pleasing ['plizɪŋ] *a.* agradable, grato, ameno, placentero, deleitable.

pleasingly [-lɪ] *adv.* agradablemente, placenteramente.

pleasurable ['plɛʒərəbəl] *a.* agradable, grato.

pleasurableness [-nəs] *s.* lo agradable.

pleasurably [-blɪ] *adv.* agradablemente, gratamente.

pleasure ['plɛʒər, B -ə] *s.* 1. placer, goce, disfrute, deleite, fruición; alegría, regocijo. 2. placer, delicia, cosa agradable. 3. gusto, voluntad, arbitrio, elección, preferencia. 4. **at p.,** a voluntad; **man of p.,** libertino, licencioso; **to take p. in (doing),** complacerse en, tener el honor de (hacer); darle placer a uno (hacer); **what is your p.?** ¿cuál es su preferencia?; **with p.,** con gusto, con placer. —*v.t.* (ant.) dar placer (a); satisfacer, complacer. —*v.i.* (ant.) 1. complacerse, deleitarse. 2. recrearse, divertirse; buscar placer.

pleasure boat, bote de excursión, bote de recreo.

pleasureless [-ləs] *a.* árido, sin placer, privado de (todo) placer.

pleasure seeker, amigo de los placeres.

pleat [plit] *s.* pliegue, doblez, repliegue, frunce, plegadura, plegado. —*v.t.* plegar, hacer pliegues en, doblar en pliegues, plisar.

pleater ['plitər, B -ə] *s.* plegador, plisador.

pleb [plɛb] *s.* (jer.) plebeyo.

plebe [plib] *s.* 1. (E.U.) (fam.) novato, estudiante de primer año en una academia naval o militar. 2. (ant.) la plebe.

plebeian [plɪ'biən] *a.* plebeyo; propio de la plebe; vulgar, común, ordinario, bajo. —*s.* uno de la plebe, plebeyo.

plesbeianism [-ˌɪzəm] *s.* plebeyismo; vulgaridad.

plebiscite ['plɛbəˌsaɪt, B -sɪt] *s.* plebiscito.

plebs [plɛbz] *s.* (*pl.* PLEBES ['plibiz]) 1. (hist.) plebe, la multitud de los ciudadanos. 2. (despec.) plebe, populacho, vulgo.

plectognath ['plɛktɑgˌnæθ, B -tɔg-] *a., s.* (ict.) plectognato.

plectognathous [plɛk'tɑgnəθəs, B -'tɔg-] *a.* (ict.) plectognato.

plectrum ['plɛktrəm] *s.* (*pl.* PLECTRA [-trə] o PLECTRUMS) (hist., mús.) plectro, púa.

pled [plɛd] (fam., dial.) *pret., p.p. de* PLEAD.

pledge [plɛdʒ] *s.* 1. prenda, señal, arras, caución, garantía, fianza. 2. pignoración, empeño. 3. brindis. 4. voto, promesa, compromiso. 5. **to take the p.,** (fam. E.U.) hacer promesa de abstenerse de bebidas alcohólicas; promesa de unirse a una fraternidad o sociedad; **as a p. of,** en señal de, en prenda de; **to keep the p.** (cumplir la promesa de) abstenerse de bebidas alcohólicas; **to put in p.,** empeñar. —*v.t.* 1. empeñar, pignorar, prendar, caucionar. 2. prometer, ofrecer, asegurar. 3. brindar por. 4. **p. one's word,** dar uno su palabra.

pledgee [plɛ'dʒi] *s.* (der.) tenedor de prenda, depositario.

pledger ['plɛdʒər, B -ə] **pledgor** [-ər, ˌplɛ'dʒɔr, B -'dʒɔ] *s.* (der.) prendador.

pledget ['plɛdʒət] *s.* (med.) tapón.

pleiad ['pliəd, B 'plaɪ-] *s.* pléyade, grupo de hombres ilustres, o intelectuales destacados.

Pleiades [-əˌdiz] *s.pl.* 1. (mitol.) Pléyades. 2. (astr.) Pléyades, Cabrillas.

Pleiocene, *var. de* **Pliocene.**

Pleistocene ['plaɪstəˌsin] *a.* (geol.) pleistoceno. —*s.* período pleistoceno.

plenarily ['plinərəlɪ] *adv.* plenariamente, plenamente.

plenary ['plinərɪ] *a.* 1. plenario, completo, perfecto (estado, inspiración, etc.). 2. plenario (asamblea, reunión, etc.).

plenary indulgence, (relig.) indulgencia plenaria.
plenipotent [plɪ'nɪpətənt] *a.* (raro) plenipotenciario.
plenipotentiary [ˌplɛnəpə'tɛntʃərɪ, B -'tɛnʃ-] *a., s.* (*pl.* PLENIPOTENTIARES) (dip.) plenipotenciario. —*a.* (dip.) plenipotenciario, investido de plenos poderes.
plenish ['plɛnɪʃ] *v.t.* (pr. G.B.) colmar, llenar, repletar; abastecer, surtir.
plenitude ['plɛnəˌtud, B -ˌtjud] *s.* 1. plenitud, totalidad, integridad. 2. abundancia, profusión.
plenitudinous [ˌplɛnə'tudənəs, B -'tjud-] *a.* 1. abundante, rico. 2. (hum.) corpulento, grueso.
plenteous ['plɛntɪəs] *a.* 1. abundante, copioso, numeroso, cuantioso. 2. fértil, fructífero, productivo.
plenteously [-lɪ] *adv.* abundantemente.
plenteousness [-nəs] *s.* abundancia.
plentiful ['plɛntɪfəl] *a.* abundante, amplio, copioso.
plentifully [-fəlɪ] *adv.* abundantemente, copiosamente.
plentifulness [-fəlnəs] *s.* abundancia, copia.
plenty ['plɛntɪ] *s.* abundancia, copia, riqueza, profusión, afluencia; copiosidad; **p. of,** bastante, mucho. —*a.* copioso, abundante; suficiente. —*adv.* (fam.) mucho, muy, bastante.
plenum ['plinəm] *s.* (*pl.* PLENUMS O PLENA [-nə]) 1. (fís.) plenum (opuesto a vacío). 2. plenitud, plétora, abundancia. 3. pleno.
pleomorphic [ˌpliə'mɔrfɪk, B -'mɔfɪk] *a.* (bot.) pleomorfo.
pleomorphism [-ˌfɪzəm] *s.* 1. (bot.) pleomorfismo. 2. polimorfismo.
pleonasm ['pliəˌnæzəm] *s.* (gram., ret.) pleonasmo.
pleonastic [ˌpliə'næstɪk] *a.* (gram.) pleonástico.
pleonastically [-tɪkəlɪ] *adv.* (gram.) pleonásticamente.
pleopod ['pliəˌpɑd, B -ˌpɔd] *s.* (zool.) pleópodo.
plesiosaur ['plisɪəˌsɔr, B -'sɔ] *s.* (pal.) plesiosaurio, plesiosauro.
plethora ['plɛθərə] *s.* 1. (med.) plétora, plenitud de sangre. 2. (fig.) plétora, exceso, hartura, abundancia, plenitud.
plethoric [plə'θɔrɪk, plɛ-] *a.* 1. (med.) pletórico. 2. (fig.) pletórico, repleto, rebosante; ampuloso, hinchado, ej., *p. phrases,* frases ampulosas.
pleura ['plʊrə, B 'plʊərə] *s.* (*pl.* PLEURAE [-ˌi] O PLEURAS) (anat., zool.) pleura.
pleural ['plʊrəl, B 'plʊər-] *a.* (anat., zool.) pleural.
pleurisy [-əsɪ] *s.* (med.) pleuresía.
pleurisy root, (bot.) vencetósigo.
pleuritic [plʊ'rɪtɪk, B plʊə-] *a.* (med.) pleurítico.
pleurodont ['plʊrəˌdɑnt, B 'plʊərəˌdɔnt] *a.* (zool.) pleurodonte. —*s.* (zool.) animal pleurodonte.
pleurodynia [ˌplʊrə'dɪnɪə, B ˌplʊər-] *s.* (med.) pleurodinia.
pleuronectid [-'nɛktəd] *a.* (ict.) pleuronecto.
pleuroperitoneum [ˌplʊroʊˌpɛrətə'niəm, B ˌplʊər-] *s.* (anat.) pleuroperitoneo.
pleuropneumonia [-nʊ'moʊnjə, B -njʊ-] *s.* (med.) pleuroneumonía.
pleurotomy [plʊ'rɑtəmɪ, B -'rɔt-] *s.* (med.) pleurotomía.
pleuston ['plustən] *s.* (bot.) pleuston.
plexiform ['plɛksəˌfɔrm, B -ˌfɔm] *a.* plexiforme, parecido al plexo.
Plexiglas (TM) [-ˌglæs, B -ˌglɑs] *s.* plexiglás, acrílico.
pleximeter [plɛk'sɪmətər, B -ə] *s.* (med.) plexímetro, plesímetro.
plexus ['plɛksəs] *s.* (*pl.* PLEXUSES *o* PLEXUS) 1. (anat.) plexo. 2. red, trabazón, entrelazamiento.
pliability [ˌplaɪə'bɪlətɪ] *s.* 1. flexibilidad. 2. docilidad.
pliable ['plaɪəbəl] *a.* 1. flexible, dúctil, plegable, doblegable. 2. dócil, manejable, tratable.
pliableness [-nəs] *s.* 1. flexibilidad. 2. docilidad.
pliably [-blɪ] *adv.* 1. flexiblemente. 2. dócilmente.
pliancy ['plaɪənsɪ] *s.* 1. flexibilidad. 2. docilidad. 3. adaptabilidad.
pliant [-ənt] *a.* 1. flexible, dúctil, plegable, doblegable. 2. dócil, manejable, tratable. 3. adaptable, acomodable.
pliantly [-lɪ] *adv.* 1. flexiblemente. 2. dócilmente.
pliantness [-nəs] *s.* 1. flexibilidad. 2. docilidad. 3. adaptabilidad.
plica ['plaɪkə] *s.* (*pl.* PLICAE [-ˌki]) 1. (anat.) plica, pliegue, doblez. 2. (med.) plica, plica polónica o polonesa.
plicate ['plaɪˌkeɪt, B -kɪt] **plicated** [-keɪtəd] *a.* (bot., zool.) plegado, doblado en forma de abanico.
plication [plaɪ'keɪʃən] *s.* 1. plegadura, doblamiento. 2. pliegue, doblez, dobladura.
pliers ['plaɪərz, B -əz] *s. pl.* pinzas, alicates, tenacillas.
plight [plaɪt] *s.* 1. apuro, aprieto, situación difícil. 2. situación, condición.
plight [plaɪt] *v.t.* empeñar, dar (la palabra); **p. one's troth,** prometer fidelidad, dar palabra de casamiento; **p. oneself (to),** celebrar esponsales (con). —*s.* (raro) promesa, compromiso solemne; esponsales.
plimsoll mark ['plɪmsəl-] (mar.) línea de carga máxima.
plimsolls ['plɪmsəlz] *s. pl.* (G.B.) zapatos de lona con suela de goma.
plink [plɪŋk] *v.i.* 1. tintinear, retiñir. 2. tirotear. —*s.* retintín, tintineo.
plinth [plɪnθ] *s.* (arq.) 1. plinto, orlo. 2. peana.
plinth course, (arq.) zócalo, embasamiento.
Pliny ['plɪnɪ] *s.* (hist.) Plinio, nombre de dos escritores romanos.
Pliocene ['plaɪəˌsin] *a., s.* (geol.) plioceno.
pliskie ['plɪskɪ] *s.* (esco.) broma pesada, chasco.
plissé, plisse [plɪ'seɪ] *s.* (tej.) plisé.
PLO *abrev. de* **Palestine Liberation Organization,** *s.* OLP.
plod [plɑd, B plɔd] *v.i.* (*pret., p.p.* PLODDED; *p.pr.* PLODDING) 1. caminar pausada y pesadamente; caminar con trabajo. 2. fatigarse, trabajar laboriosamente. 3. **p. away at,** trabajar laboriosamente en; **p. on,** seguir con su trabajo laborioso; seguir su camino con pasos pesados. —*v.t.* hacer (el recorrido) pausada y pesadamente. —*s.* trabajo o camino laborioso.
plodder ['plɑdər, B 'plɔdə] *s.* 1. el que trabaja asidua y laboriosamente; persona sin talento que trabaja con perseverancia. 2. estudiantón, empollón, chancón (Am.).
plop [plɑp, B plɔp] *v.t.* (*pret., p.p.* PLOPPED; *p.pr.* PLOPPING) dejar caer (un objeto) de golpe. —*v.i.* 1. caer con un paf, caer con ruido apagado. 2. (gen. con *down, into,* etc.) desplomarse, caer pesadamente. —*s.* paf, cataplún. —*adv.* de golpe; a plomo.
plosion ['ploʊʒən] *s.* (fon.) explosión.
plosive [-sɪv] *a., s.* (fon.) explosivo.
plot [plɑt, B plɔt] *s.* 1. lote, solar, parcela, porción pequeña de terreno. 2. (E.U.) plano, mapa de un terreno; diagrama. 3. complot, conspiración, conjura, conjuración, intriga, confabulación, maquinación. 4. argumento, trama (de un drama, novela, etc.). —*v.t.* (*pret., p.p.* PLOTTED; *p.pr.* PLOTTING) 1. delinear, trazar, marcar. 2. (gen. con *out*) diseñar o trazar el plano de (terreno, construcciones, etc.). 3. tramar, fraguar, maquinar, urdir. 4. urdir la trama de (una novela, drama, etc.). —*v.i.* conspirar.
plottage ['plɑtɪdʒ, B 'plɔt-] *s.* área de un solar.
plotter ['plɑtər, B 'plɔtə] *s.* conspirador, conjurado; maquinador, tramador.
plotting board [-ɪŋ-] 1. (mil.) mesa trenzadora; plancheta de tiro. 2. (aer.) mesa de navegación.
plough, ploughable, ploughboy, ploughhead, *var. de* **plow, plowable, plowboy, plowhead.**
plover ['plʌvər, 'ploʊ-, B 'plʌvə] *s.* (orn.) frailecillo norteamericano; chorlito.
plow [plaʊ] *s.* 1. arado. 2. (carp.) cepillo ranurador. 3. (f.c.) zapata de toma, carrillo de contacto. 4. **P.,** (astr.) Carro, Osa Mayor. —*v.t.* 1. arar, labrar, surcar. 2. surcar o cortar (las aguas un barco). 3. (carp.) acanalar, ranurar, rebajar. 4. (fam., G.B.) suspender, desaprobar (a alguien en un examen). 5. **p. back,** (fig.) reinvertir (ganancias); **p. out,** sacar con el arado; excavar, ahuecar; **p. under,** (fig.) enterrar; **p. up,** revolver (la tierra); romper (asfaltado, etc.); arrancar con el arado; (fig.) descubrir, sacar a luz. —*v.i.* 1. arar, usar o emplear un arado. 2. avanzar laboriosamente. 3. **p. through,** trabajar laboriosamente en; leer (libro) con mucha dificultad.
plowable ['plaʊəbəl] *a.* arable.
plowboy [-ˌbɔɪ] *s.* yuguero, yuntero; joven campesino.
plower [-ər, B -ə] *s.* arador, labrador.
plowhead [-ˌhɛd] *s.* abrazadera del arado.
plowman ['plaʊmən] *s.* arador, labrador, yuguero; gañán campesino.
plowshare [-ˌʃɛr, B -ˌʃɛə] *s.* reja de arado.
plowshoe ['plaʊˌʃu] *s.* portarreja (de arado).
plowstaff [-ˌstæf, B -ˌstɑf] *s.* arrejada, abéstola, aguijada.
plowtail [-ˌteɪl] *s.* esteva; **at the p.,** labrando la tierra.
ploy [plɔɪ] *s.* 1. maniobra, truco, táctica. 2. empresa, actividad. 3. travesura, aventura. 4. diversión, pasatiempo.
pluck [plʌk] *v.t.* 1. arrancar, sacar; depilar, extraer; picar. 2. pelar; desplumar (aves). 3. (con *out*) halar, tirar (de). 4. (mús.) puntear, pulsar o tocar (las cuerdas) con los dedos o el plectro. 5. (jer.) robar, estafar, desplumar. 6. (jer., G.B.) reprobar, desaprobar, suspender (en los exámenes a alguien). 7. **p. up one's spirits** o **courage,** cobrar valentía, recobrar ánimo. —*v.i.* (gen. con *at*) tirar (de), dar un tirón (a). —*s.* 1. arranque, tirón, estirón. 2. asadura (corazón, higado y bofes). 3. valor, ánimo, coraje, espíritu, resolución. 4. (mús.) plectro.
plucker ['plʌkər, B -ə] *s.* desplumador (de aves).
pluckily [-əlɪ] *adv.* animosamente, valientemente, resueltamente.
pluckiness [-ɪnəs] *s.* ánimo, valentía.
plucky [-ɪ] *a.* animoso, valiente, resuelto, denodado, intrépido, esforzado.
plug [plʌg] *s.* 1. tapón, obturador, tarugo, taco, tapador, tapadero. 2. espita, boca de agua, boca de incendio, hidrante. 3. porción o tableta de tabaco comprimido. 4. cilindro (de cerradura). 5. (elec.) clavija de contacto, enchufe, ficha, tapón de contacto, adaptador, tomacorriente. 6. (aut.) bujía. 7. (fam.) aviso o anuncio publicitario insistente. 8. (rad.) publicidad incidental (intercalada en un programa radial). 9. (jer.) rocín, penco, jamelgo. 10. (jer.) tiro, disparo (con arma). 11. (pr. G.B.) bala, proyectil. —*v.t.*

(*pret., p.p.* PLUGGED; *p.pr.* PLUGGING) 1. atarugar, taponar, tapar, obturar, entarugar, cegar. 2. (elec.) (gen. con *in*) enchufar, conectar, insertar (una clavija de conexion). 3. (odont.) orificar, empastar. 4. (mot.) parar invirtiendo la rotación. 5. (jer.) acertar (con bala); herir o matar con arma de fuego. 6. (jer.) pegar con el puño, dar de puñetazos o puñadas a. 7. (fam.) anunciar, dar publicidad insistente a. —*v.i.* (gen. con *up*) atorarse. 2. (jer.) disparar, hacer fuego.
plug fuse, tapón eléctrico o de fusión, fusible de tapón.
plug gage, (mec.) calibrador de macho, calibre cilíndrico.
plugged [plʌgd] *a.* 1. atorado, obstruido. 2. falsificado (moneda). 3. **p. end,** extremo con grifo.
plugger ['plʌgər, B -ə] *s.* 1. perforadora de percusión. 2. (odont.) orificador.
plug hat, (jer.) chistera, sombrero de copa, tarro (Am.); bombín, sombrero hongo, galerita (Am.).
plug receptacle, (elec.) toma de enchufe, caja de contacto, receptáculo o tomacorriente de clavija.
plug-ugly [-ˌʌglɪ] *s.* (jer. E.U.) matón, rufián.
plum [plʌm] *s.* 1. (bot.) ciruelo, cirolero. 2. ciruela, pruna. 3. pasa (en un bollo, etc.). 4. confite, dulce; bombón. 5. color ciruela, morado, azul rojizo. 6. breva; ganga, pichincha (Arg., Par., Urug.).
plumage ['plumɪdʒ] *s.* plumaje.
plumate ['pluˌmeɪt, -mɪt] *a.* (zool.) plumado, plúmeo.
plumb [plʌm] *s.* 1. plomada; plomo (de plomada, sonda, etc.); escandallo. 2. **in p.,** a plomo; **out of p., off p.,** fuera de plomo, desviado. —*a.* 1. vertical, recto, perpendicular. 2. (fam.) absoluto, completo, ej., *p. nonsense,* idiotez completa. —*adv.* 1. a plomo, verticalmente. 2. directamente, exactamente; inmediatamente. 3. (fam. E.U.) completamente, rematadamente, de remate, ej., *p. crazy,* loco de remate. 4. **p. in the middle,** de medio a medio. —*v.t.* 1. aplomar; verificar la verticalidad de. 2. sondear, sondar. 3. sellar con plomo. 4. instalar cañerías.
plumbaginaceous [plʌmˌbædʒə'neɪʃəs] *a.* (bot.) plumbagináceo.
plumbago [plʌm'beɪgoʊ] *s.* (*pl.* PLUMBAGOS) 1. (min.) grafito, plombagina. 2. (bot.) dentelaria, hierba del negro.
plumb bob, plomada, plomo, perpendículo.
plumbeous ['plʌmbɪəs] *a.* plúmbeo, plomizo.
plumber ['plʌmər, B -ə] *s.* plomero, cañero, fontanero, gasfitero (Am.).
plumber's helper, desatrancapilas.
plumber's snake, desatorador del plomero.
plumbery ['plʌmərɪ] *s.* plomería.
plumbic [-bɪk] *a.* (quím.) plúmbico.
plumbiferous [plʌm'bɪfərəs] *a.* (min.) plumbífero.
plumbing ['plʌmɪŋ] *s.* plomería, cañerías, fontanería.
plumbism [-ˌbɪzəm] *s.* (med.) plumbismo, saturnismo.
plumb line, 1. hilo o cuerda de plomada. 2. tranquil, línea vertical. 3. (mar.) sondaleza, cordel de sonda.
plumbous [-bəs] *a.* (quím.) plumboso.
plumb point, (top.) nadir, punto nadiral, punto.
plumb rule, nivel de albañil, nivel de perpendículo.
plumbum [-bəm] *s.* plomo.
plum duff, budín de harina con pasas, etc., cocido en una bolsa de lienzo.
plume [plum] *s.* 1. pluma (de ave). 2. plumaje. 3. plumaje, plumero, penacho (de plumas). 4. laurel, lauro, premio. 5. (zool.) apéndice plumoso. 6. (bot.) vilano. —*v.t.* 1. emplumar, adornar con plumas. 2. limpiar componer sus plumas (las aves).
plume grass, (bot.) carricera, rabo de zorra, vulpino.
plumelet ['plumlət] *s.* plumilla.
plummet [plʌmət] *s.* 1. plomo, plomada; nivel de albañil, escandallo. 2. (fig.) lastre, estorbo, peso. —*v.i.* caer a plomo, caer verticalmente.
plumose ['plumˌoʊs] *a.* plumoso, plumado.
plump [plʌmp] *a.* rollizo, rechoncho, regordete. —*v.t.* engordar, volver rollizo. —*v.i.* volverse rollizo; **p. out** o **up,** hincharse.
plump, *v.i.* caer a plomo, dejarse caer pesadamente; **p. for,** votar por, elegir; optar por. —*v.t.* soltar, dejar caer pesadamente. —*s.* (fam.) caída pesada, porrazo; ruido sordo. —*adv.* 1. directamente, derecho. 2. a plomo, verticalmente. 3. categóricamente, rotundamente. —*a.* categórico, rotundo, brusco.
plumper ['plʌmpər, B -ə] *s.* 1. porrazo, caída. 2. (ant.) golpazo, trompada.
plumpness [-nəs] *s.* gordura, corpulencia.
plum pudding, budín de ciruelas, pasas y otras frutas.
plumule ['pluˌmjul] *s.* 1. (bot.) plúmula. 2. (orn.) plumón.
plumy ['plumɪ] *a.* plumado, plumoso, plúmeo.
plunder ['plʌndər, B -də] *v.t.* pillar, saquear, rapiñar, expoliar. —*v.i.* cometer pillaje o saqueo. —*s.* 1. pillaje, saqueo, expoliación. 2. botín, despojo.
plunderage [-dərɪdʒ] *s.* pillaje (esp. a bordo de un barco); botín.
plunderer [-dərər, B -dərə] *s.* pillador, saqueador.
plunderous [-dərəs] *a.* saqueador, pillador.
plunge [plʌndʒ] *v.t.* 1. zambullir, chapuzar, sumergir. 2. meter, hundir (cuchillo, puñal, etc.). 3. arrojar, precipitar. 4. templar (aceros). —*v.i.* 1. zambullirse, sumergirse (en agua), arrojarse (a un abismo, etc.). 2. (fig.) hundirse, abismarse (en desesperación, melancolía, etc.). 3. cabecear, hocicar (un barco); corcovear (un caballo). 4. precipitarse, actuar precipitadamente. 5. jugar o apostar arriesgadamente; **to p. in headfirst,** lanzarse al agua de cabeza. —*s.* 1. zambullida, salto. 2. piscina o estanque (para zambullirse). 3. remojón, mojadura, baño ligero. 4. apuesta o especulación arriesgada. 5. **to take the p.,** aventurarse (a casarse, viajar, cambiar de casa, empleo, situación, etc.).
plunger ['plʌndʒər, B -dʒə] *s.* 1. zambullidor. 2. (jer.) especulador o apostador temerario, jugador incauto. 3. (mec.) pistón; émbolo; **brazo** móvil. 4. (aut.) émbolo buzo. 5. desatascador; chupón, desatrancador neumático (por desatascar cañería).
plunging fire [-dʒɪŋ-] (mil.) tiro fijante, tiro curvo, tiro de sumersión.
plunging neckline, (fam.) escote bajo que revela parte del busto (femenino).
plunk [plʌŋk] *v.i., v.t.* 1. arrojar, empujar o dejar caer pesadamente, sonar o caer con ruido de golpe seco. 2. puntear (guitarra), rasguear (cuerdas metálicas). 3. **p. down,** (fam.) pagar, aflojar (cierta cantidad de dinero). —*s.* 1. (fam.) golpe seco, ruido seco. 2. rasgueo, punteo (de una guitarra, etc.). 3. (jer.) dólar. —*adv.* con ruido o golpe seco.
plunker ['plʌŋkər, B -ə] *s.* especie de cebo artificial (para la pesca).
pluperfect [plu'pərfɪkt, B 'plu'pɜfɪkt] *a., s.* (gram.) pluscuamperfecto.
plural ['plʊrəl, B 'plʊər-] *a., s.* (gram.) plural.
pluralism [-ˌɪzəm] *s.* 1. pluralidad. 2. goce de más de un beneficio a un mismo tiempo (díc. de eclesiásticos). 3. (filos.) pluralismo.
pluralist [-əst] *s.* (filos.) pluralista, partidario del pluralismo.
pluralistic [ˌplʊrə'lɪstɪk, B ˌplʊərə-] *a.* pluralístico.
plurality [plʊ'rælətɪ, B plʊə-] *s.* (*pl.* PLURALITIES) mayoría, pluralidad; **by a p. of votes,** por mayoría o pluralidad de votos.
pluralize ['plʊrə, laɪz, B 'plʊərə-] *v.t.* pluralizar.
plurally [-əlɪ] *adv.* 1. pluralmente, en plural. 2. en conjunto.
pluriaxial [ˌplʊrɪ'æksɪəl, B ˌplʊərɪ-] *a.* (bot.) pluriaxial, pluriáxico.
plus [plʌs] *prep.* 1. más. 2. con el incremento de. —*a.* 1. positivo, más (díc. de cantidad, signo, etc.). 2. (bot.) plus, positivo. 3. (elec.) positivo. 4. adicional; en exceso. —*s.* 1. signo más. 2. ventaja, factor positivo. 3. excedente, sobrante.
plus fours, calzones bombachos (para golf y otros deportes).
plush [plʌʃ] *s.* (tej.) felpa. —*a.* 1. de felpa; afelpado, felposo. 2. lujoso, rico; elegante.
plushly ['plʌʃlɪ] *adv.* lujosamente.
plushy [-ɪ] *a.* 1. afelpado. 2. lujoso.
plus sign, signo más.
plus station, (top.) progresiva fraccionada.
Plutarch ['pluˌtɑrk, B -ˌtɑk] *s.* Plutarco, biógrafo griego.
Pluto ['plutoʊ] *s.* 1. (mitol.) Plutón, dios griego, rey del mundo subterráneo. 2. (astr.) Plutón.
plutocracy [plu'tɑkrəsɪ, B -'tɔk-] *s.* plutocracia, gobierno de los ricos.
plutocrat ['plutəˌkræt] *s.* plutócrata, miembro de la plutocracia.
plutocratic [ˌplutə'krætɪk] *a.* plutocrático.
plutocratically [-ɪkəlɪ] *adv.* plutocráticamente, de manera o forma plutocrática.
Plutonian [plu'toʊnɪən] *a.* (geol., mitol.) plutoniano.
plutonic [-'tɑnɪk, B -'tɔn-] *a.* (geol.) plutónico.
plutonist ['plutənəst] *s.* (geol.) plutoniano, plutonista.
plutonium [plu'toʊnɪəm] *s.* (quím.) plutonio.
Plutus ['plutəs] *s.* (mitol.) Pluto, dios de las riquezas.
pluvial ['pluvɪəl] **pluvian** [-vɪən] *a.* pluvial; (geol.) pluviátil, pluvial. —*s.* (ant.) (relig.) capa pluvial.
pluviograph [-vɪəˌgræf, B -ˌgrɑf] *s.* pluviógrafo.
pluviometer [ˌpluvɪ'ɑmətər, B -'ɔmɪtə] *s.* pluviómetro, pluvímetro.
pluviometric [-ə'mɛtrɪk] *a.* pluviométrico.
pluviometry [-'ɑmətrɪ, B -'ɔm-] *s.* pluviometría.
pluvioscope ['pluvɪəˌskoʊp] *s.* (meteor.) pluviómetro.
pluviouse ['pluvɪˌoʊs] **pluvious** [-əs] *a.* pluvioso, lluvioso.
ply [plaɪ] *v.t.* (*pret., p.p.* PLIED; *p.pr.* PLYING) doblar, plegar, curvar (seda al hilar). —*s.* (*pl.* PLIES) 1. pliegue, doblez; trenza (del hilado); capa (de tela). 2. chapa (de madera). 3. (fig.) prejuicio; propensión, inclinación.
ply, *v.t.* 1. usar, emplear, manejar (con diligencia). 2. aplicarse a, trabajar con ahínco en. 3. **p. with,** acosar con, atosigar con (preguntas, problemas, etc.); dar constantemente (comida, bebida, etc.) a. —*v.i.* 1. trabajar con diligencia, aplicarse. 2. hacer servicio regular (entre ciudades, etc.).
plywood ['plaɪˌwʊd] *s.* madera terciada; madera contrachapada, triplex (Am.).
p.m. *abrev. de* **post meridiem,** pasado el meridiano, después del mediodía.
Pm *símb. de* **promethium,** promecio (Pm).

P. M. *abrev. de* 1. **Prime Minister,** Primer Ministro. 2. **Pas Master,** persona que ejerció el cargo de maestro (corporación, logia, etc.). 3. **Pay Master,** pagador oficial, habilitado. 4. **Police Magistrate,** juez de paz, juez de instrucción. 5. **Postmaster,** administrador de correos. 6. **Provost Marshal,** capitán preboste; oficial de vigilancia.
pneuma ['numə, B 'njumə] *s.* (filos.) neuma, alma, espíritu.
pneumatic [nu'mætɪk, B nju-] *a.* 1. neumático. 2. (filos.) espiritual.
pneumatically [-ɪkəlɪ] *adv.* neumáticamente.
pneumatic brake, (f.c., aut.) freno de aire, freno neumático.
pneumatic digger, pala neumática.
pneumatics [-ɪks] *s. pl.* (*sing. en const.*) neumática.
pneumatic tire, (auto.) neumático, goma, llanta neumática.
pneumatic tool, herramienta neumática.
pneumatology [ˌnumə'tɑlədʒɪ, B ˌnjumə'tɔl-] *s.* neumatología.
pneumatolysis [-əsəs] *s.* (geol.) neumatolisis.
pneumatolytic [-tə'lɪtɪk] *a.* (geol.) neumatolítico.
pneumatometer [-'tɑmətər, B -'tɔmɪtə] *s.* (med.) neumatómetro.
pneumatophore [-'mætəˌfɔr, 'numətə-, B 'njumətəˌfɔ] *a., s.* (bot.) neumatóforo.
pneumectomy [nu'mɛktəmɪ, B nju-] *s.* (med.) neumectomía.
pneumobacillus [ˌnumoʊbə'sɪləs, B ˌnju-] *s.* (*pl.* PNEUMOBACILLI [-ˌaɪ]) (bact.) neumobacilo.
pneumococcal [-mə'kɑkəl, B -'kɔk-] **pneumococcic** [-'kɑksɪk, B -'kɔk-] *a.* (bact.) neumocócico.
pneumococcus [-'kɑkəs, B -'kɔk-] *s.* (*pl.* PNEUMOCOCCI [-'kɑksaɪ, B -'kɔk-]) (bact.) neumococo.
pneumoconiosis [-ˌkoʊnɪ'oʊsəs] *s.* (med.) neumoconiosis.
pneumodynamics [-moʊdaɪ'næmɪks] *s. pl.* (*sing. en const.*) neumodinámica.
pneumogastric [ˌnumə'gæstrɪk, B ˌnju-] *s.* (anat.) neumogástrico.
pneumograph ['numəˌgræf, B 'njuməˌgrɑf] *s.* (med.) neumógrafo.
pneumonectomy [ˌnumə'nɛktəmɪ, B ˌnju-] *s.* (med.) neumonectomía.
pneumonia [nʊ'moʊnɪə, B njʊ-] *s.* (med.) neumo ía, pulmonía.
pneumonic [-'mɑnɪk, B -'mɔn-] *a.* (anat., med.) neumónico.
pneumothorax [ˌnumə'θɔrˌæks, B ˌnju-] *s.* (med.) neumotórax.
pneumotropic [-'trɑpɪk, B -'trɔp-] *a.* (med.) neumotrópico.
Po (quím.) *símb. de* **polonium,** polonio (Po).
P.O. *abrev. de* 1. **Petty Officer,** suboficial. 2. **postal order,** giro postal. 3. **Post Office,** Dirección de Correos.
poaceous [poʊ'eɪʃəs] *a.* (bot.) poáceo.
poach [poʊtʃ] *v.t.* (cocina) escalfar, cocer a fuego lento.
poach, *v.t.* 1. entrar en (propiedad ajena) para cazar o pescar; cazar o pescar ilícitamente. 2. pisotear, hollar. —*v.i.* 1. enfangarse, encenagarse (un terreno). 2. atollarse, atascarse (en el fango).
poached egg, huevo escalfado.
poacher ['poʊtʃər, B -tʃə] *s.* cazador furtivo.
pochard ['poʊtʃərd, B -tʃəd] *s.* (orn.) pato de mar.
pock [pɑk, B pɔk] *s.* pústula, viruela; cacaraña. —*v.t.* picar de viruelas, dejar hoyoso.
pocket ['pɑkət, B 'pɔkɪt] *s.* 1. bolsillo, faltriquera. 2. bolsa, monedero, portamonedas. 3. talega, saco (para granos, etc.). 4. cavidad, receptáculo. 5. área o grupo aislado. 6. (min.) bolsa, bolsada. 7. (aer.) vacío, bolsa de aire, bache. 8. (mar.) funda de barba. 9. (mil.) foco (de resistencia). 10. (billar) tronera. 11. (dep.) cajón, posición encajonada (de un corredor, caballo, etc., al que los otros cierran el paso). 12. **empty pockets,** pelagatos, persona sin recursos; **to be out of p.,** haber perdido, ej., *I am five dollars out of p.,* he perdido cinco dólares; **to have in one's p.,** (fig.) tener uno en el bolsillo; **to put one's hand in one's p.,** (fig.) rascarse el bolsillo, gastar (dinero); **to put one's pride in one's p.,** (fig.) tragarse el orgullo. —*v.t.* 1. embolsar, guardar en la bolsa. 2. tragarse (insultos, orgullo, etc.); reprimir (emociones, etc.). 3. poner en el bolsillo, aceptar, recibir (dinero, esp. mal habido). 4. (billar) entronerar. 5. (pol.) (E.U.) retener (una ley) sin firmar (el presidente) hasta después de que el congreso se clausure. 6. (dep.) encajonar, cerrar el paso a (corredor, caballo, etc.). —*a.* 1. de bolsillo. 2. aislado.
pocket battleship, acorazado de bolsillo.
pocket billiards, billar de casín o casino.
pocketbook [-ˌbʊk] *s.* 1. cartera; billetero, billetera, monedero. 2. (fig.) recursos.
pocket book, libro de bolsillo; manual; carné de bolsillo.
pocket borough, (hist.) (G.B.) distrito municipal bajo el control de una sola persona o familia.
pocket calculator, calculador de bolsillo.
pocket diary, agenda de bolsillo.
pocket edition, 1. edición de bolsillo (de un libro). 2. (fig.) miniatura (de alguna cosa).
pocketful [-ˌfʊl] *s.* (*pl.* POCKETFULS o POCKETSFUL) (con *of*) bolsillo (lleno de).
pocketknife [-ˌnaɪf] *s.* (*pl.* POCKETKNIVES [-ˌnaɪvz]) cortaplumas.
pocket money, dinero para gastos personales; mesada; (Amer.) propina (que se da a un niño o joven).
pocket picking, *s.* ratería, robo de bolsillo.
pocket-pistol [-ˌpɪstəl] *s.* (hum.) frasco de bolsillo para licor.
pocket veto, (E.U.) veto indirecto o implícito; retención de una ley por el Presidente hasta invalidarla.
pockmark ['pɑkˌmark, B 'pɔkˌmɑk] *s.* cicatriz de viruelas; cacaraña.
pockmarked [-ˌmarkt, B -ˌmɑkt] *a.* cacarañado, picado de viruelas, borrado (Am.).
pocky [-ɪ] *a.* (med.) pustuloso, cacarañado; sifilítico.
pococurante [ˌpoʊkoʊkʊ'ræntɪ, B -kjʊ-] *a.* (italiano) indiferente; descuidado. —*s.* indiferente.
pococurantism [-ˌtɪzəm] *s.* indiferencia.
pod [pɑd, B pɔd] *s.* 1. vaina (de legumbre). 2. manada, rebaño, cardumen; bandada. 3. (mec.) portabroca (de un berbiquí). 4. ranura o canal longitudinal (de algunos taladros).
pod, *v.t.* (*pret., p.p.* PODDED; *p.pr.* PODDING) 1. producir vainas. 2. **p. up,** (jer. G.B.) abultarse, hincharse (mujer encinta).
P.O.D. *abrev. de* **pay on delivery,** pago contra entrega.
podagra [pə'dægrə] *a.* (med.) podagra, gota.
podgy ['pɑdʒɪ, B 'pɔdʒɪ] *a.* regordete, rechoncho.
podiatrist [pə'daɪətrəst] *s.* (med.) podíatra, médico podólogo.
podiatry [-ətrɪ] *s.* (med.) podiatría.
podium ['poʊdɪəm] *s.* (*pl.* PODIA [-dɪə] o PODIUMS) 1. podio. 2. estrado o plataforma (para el director de orquesta). 3. (arq.) podio.
podophyllin [ˌpɑdə'fɪlən, B ˌpɔd-] *s.* (farm.) podofilina.
podophyllotoxin [-fɪlə'tɑksən B -'tɔk-] *s.* (quím.) podofilotoxina.
podzol ['pɑdˌzɔl, B 'pɔd-] *s.* (geol.) podsol.
P.O.E. *abrev. de* **port of entry,** puerto de entrada, puerto aduanero.
poem ['poʊəm] *s.* poema; (fig.) poesía.
poesy [-əzɪ, -sɪ, B -zɪ] *s.* 1. poesía sentimental. 2. (ant.) poesía; poema.
poet ['poʊət] *s.* poeta.
poetaster [-ˌæstər, B ˌpoʊɪ'tæstə] *s.* poetastro.
poetess ['poʊətəs] *s.* poetisa, poeta (f.).
poetic [poʊ'ɛtɪk] *a.* poético.
poetical [-ɪkəl] *a.* 1. poético. 2. ficticio, idealizado.
poetically [-ɪkəlɪ] *adv.* poéticamente.
poeticize [-ˌɛtəˌsaɪz] *v.t.* poetizar, dar carácter poético.
poetic justice, la mano de Dios, justicia divina, justa retribución.
poetic license, licencia poética.
poetics [-ɪks] *s. pl.* poética, arte poética.
poetize ['poʊəˌtaɪz] *v.i., v.t.* poetizar.
poetizer [-er, B -ə] *s.* poeta.
poet laureate, (*pl.* POETS LAUREATE o POET LAUREATES) poeta laureado.
poetry ['poʊətrɪ] *s.* poesía.
poet's cassia, (bot.) guardalobo.
pogonip ['pɑgəˌnɪp, B 'pɔg-] *s.* (E.U.) niebla densa de invierno (que se forma en los valles de la Sierra Nevada).
Pogo stick ['poʊgoʊ-] sube y baja, pogo saltarín (Am.).
pogrom [poʊ'grɑm, B 'pɔgrəm] *s.* pogromo, pogrom, asesinato en masa. —*v.t.* asesinar en masa, masacrar (Am.).
pogy ['poʊgɪ] *s.* (ict.) especie de sábalo.
poi [pɔɪ] *s.* plato hawaiano hecho de taro fermentado.
poignancy ['pɔɪnjənsɪ, B -nənsɪ] *s.* 1. viveza, intensidad (de sentimientos, etc.). 2. efecto conmovedor (de un espectáculo, escena, etc.). 3. mordacidad, carácter punzante (de una sátira, etc.).
poignant [-njənt, B -nənt] *a.* 1. vivo, intenso. 2. agudo, conmovedor. 3. mordaz, punzante (sátira, etc.).
poignantly [-lɪ] *adv.* 1. vivamente, intensamente. 2. conmovedoramente. 3. mordazmente.
poikilothermism [pɔɪˌkɪlə'θɜrˌmɪzəm, B -'θɜˌ-] *s.* (zool.) poiquilotermismo.
poilu [pwɑ'lu] *s.* (fr., jer.) soldado francés.
poinciana [ˌpɔɪnsɪ'ænə] *s.* (bot.) poinciana.
poinsettia [pɔɪn'sɛtɪə, -'sɛtə] *s.* (bot.) pastora roja, flor de pascuas, flor de fuego.
point [pɔɪnt] *s.* 1. punto (ortográfico, decimal, de geometría, etc.). 2. punto, detalle (en un discurso, discusión, etc.). 3. punto, unidad (de cálculo o cuenta esp. en el racionamiento de víveres, cotización de valores, juegos deportivos, etc.). 4. punto, sitio, lugar. 5. punto, grado, ej., *boiling p.,* punto de ebullición. 6. momento decisivo, crítico o exacto, ej., *when it came to the p. he changed his mind,* llegado el momento decisivo él cambió de opinión. 7. sentido; gracia (de un chiste), agudeza, ej., *I see no p. in doing it,* para mí no tiene sentido hacerlo, *I fail to see the p.,* no veo qué gracia tiene. 8. punta (de herramienta, arma, pluma, etc.). 9. buril, punzón; herramienta puntiaguda. 10. extremo, remate. 11. promontorio, punta de tierra. 12. punta, parada (del perro ante la caza). 13. (*pl.*) puntas, encaje de punta. 14. (*pl.*) extremidades

(del caballo). 15. (elec., G.B.) conexión, toma. 16. (impr.) punto tipográfico (medida que equivale a 0,37 mm). 17. (mús.) melodía o frase cortas. 18. (*pl.*) (f.c.) aguja. 19. (her.) punta, pira. 20. (mil.) punta (de una avanzada). 21. (dep.) puesto (de jugador en equipo). 22. (mar.) punto cardinal, cuarta (de la rosa náutica). 23. (hist.) cordón de corpiño. 24. **at the p. of death,** al borde de la muerte; **beside the p.,** (que) no viene a cuento, fuera de propósito; **in p.,** apropiado, al caso, oportuno; **in p. of fact,** en realidad; **off the p.,** fuera de propósito; **on the p. of,** a punto de; **p. by p., punto por punto, a por a y b por b; possession is nine points of the law,** la posesión casi otorga derecho (sobre el objeto poseído); **(music is not his) strong p.,** (la música no es su) punto fuerte; **that's just the p.,** eso es precisamente lo que importa, allí está el detalle; **the p. is that,** la verdad es que, el asunto es que; **to a certain p.,** hasta cierto punto; **to carry one's p.,** salirse con la suya, hacer prevalecer su punto de vista, conseguir su propósito; **to catch** (o **get**) **the p.,** ver el sentido, comprender, caer en cuenta; **to come to the p.,** ir al grano, dejarse de historias (o rodeos); **to give points to,** conceder ventaja a (opositor); (fig.) ser muy superior a (alguien); **to make a p.,** comprobar o establecer una proposición; **to make a p. of,** insistir en, dar mucha importancia a; esmerarse en; **to miss the p.,** no entender; **to speak to the p.,** ir al caso; **to stretch a p.,** hacer una concesión, hacer una excepción; **to the p.,** pertinente, a propósito; **to win on points,** (dep.) ganar por puntos; **what's the p.?** ¿para qué? ¿con qué fin? —*v.t.* 1. aguzar, afilar, sacar punta a (un lápiz, herramienta, etc.). 2. apuntar (arma). 3. (const.) (gen. con *up*) rejuntar, recalcar, resanar (pared, grietas, etc.). 4. (filol.) puntar (escritura hebrea o árabe). 5. insertar pelos blancos a (una piel para mejorar su apariencia). 6. **p. out,** señalar, indicar; hacer notar u observar, recalcar; **p. up,** poner de relieve. —*v.i.* 1. parar y mostrar la caza (perro). 2. (mar.) (t. con *up*) navegar de bolina, barloventear. 3. **p. at,** indicar, señalar; señalar con el dedo; **p. to,** indicar, señalar.

point-blank ['pɔɪnt'blæŋk] *adv.* a quemarropa, a quema ropa, a boca de jarro; directamente; categóricamente, sin ambages. —*a.* directo, claro, categórico.

point duty, servicio policial que se cumple en un sitio fijo (ej., para dirigir el tráfico, guardar un edificio, etc.).

pointed [-əd] *a.* 1. puntiagudo. 2. evidente, obvio. 3. preciso, exacto. 4. directo, acentuado; significativo; mordaz.

pointed arch, (arq.) arco apuntado, arco ojival.

pointedly [-ədlɪ] *adv.* significativamente, sarcásticamente.

pointer [-ər, B -ə] *s.* 1. indicador. 2. índice; manecilla (de reloj), fiel (de balanza, etc.); puntero. 3. apuntador (artillero que apunta con un arma). 4. perro de muestra, perdiguero. 5. indicación, dato; información útil, buen consejo. 6. **Pointers,** (astr.) Guardas (de la Osa Mayor).

pointillism ['pwæntəlˌɪzəm] *s.* (pint.) puntillismo (estilo del que el francés Seurat fue el máximo exponente).

pointillist [-əst] *s.* (pint.) representante del puntillismo, pintor puntillista.

point lace, encaje en punto aguja; bordado o labor en punto aguja.

pointless ['pɔɪntləs] *a.* 1. sin punta, obtuso. 2. inútil, sin sentido. 3. sin gracia, insípido. 4. (dep.) con el marcador en cero.

pointlessly [-lɪ] *adv.* 1. inútilmente, sin sentido. 2. sin gracia, insípidamente.

pointlessness [-nəs] *s.* 1. falta de sentido, futilidad. 2. falta de gracia, insipidez.

point of departure, punto de partida.

point of distance, punto de distancia (en perspectiva).

point of honor, punto de honor, pundonor.

point of inflexion, (mat.) punto de inflexión, punto de tangencia.

point of order, cuestión de procedimiento, cuestión de orden.

point of sight, punto de (la) vista (en perspectiva).

point of view, punto de vista; **from every p. of v.,** a todas luces.

points of the compass, puntos o direcciones de la rosa náutica.

point system, 1. (tip.) sistema para medir los tipos de imprenta. 2. cualquiera de los sistemas de escritura para ciegos (Braille, etc.). 3. evaluación del trabajo académico por medio de puntos o números.

pointy ['pɔɪntɪ] *a.* (POINTIER; POINTIEST) 1. puntiagudo. 2. puntoso.

poise [pɔɪz] *v.t.* 1. equilibrar, balancear, contrapesar. 2. mantener en equilibrio o suspendido. 3. (raro) pesar. —*v.i.* 1. estar en equilibrio; estar suspendido. 2. cernerse (aves). —*s.* 1. balance, equilibrio. 2. aplomo, serenidad, donaire. 3. talante, porte sereno. 4. tranquilidad, calma.

poison ['pɔɪzən] *s.* 1. veneno. 2. (fig.) ponzoña. 3. **to hate each other like p.,** odiarse amargamente; **what's your p.? name your p.,** (fam.) ¿qué tomas? —*v.t.* 1. envenenar. 2. (fig.) emponzoñar, envenenar, corromper, pervertir. —*a.* 1. venenoso, ponzoñoso. 2. envenenado (flecha, etc.). 3. (fig.) ponzoñoso.

poison dogwood, (bot.) especie de zumaque venenoso.

poisoner [-ər, B -ə] *s.* envenenador.

poison gas, gas tóxico; gas venenoso.

poison hemlock, (bot.) cicuta.

poisoning [-ɪŋ] *s.* envenenamiento.

poison ivy, (bot.) zumaque venenoso.

poison oak, (bot.) zumaque venenoso, árbol de las pulgas.

poisonous [-əs] *a.* venenoso, ponzoñoso.

poisonously [-əslɪ] *adv.* venenosamente, ponzoñosamente.

poison parsley, (bot.) perejil de perro, cicuta menor.

poison-pen letter [-ˌpɛn-] paulina, anónimo ponzoñoso.

poison sumac, (bot.) zumaque venenoso.

poke [poʊk] *s.* 1. (dial.) bolsa, saco. 2. (esco.) barjuleta, lío de mendigo. 3. (ant., dial.) bolsillo. 4. ala abovedada (de una papalina).

poke, *v.t.* 1. picar, aguijonear. 2. atizar, ej., *p. the fire,* atizar el fuego. 3. meter, introducir, ej., *p. one's nose into,* meter las narices en (asuntos ajenos, etc.). 4. golpear; asestar (un golpe) a. 5. sacar, asomar (cabeza, etc.). 6. **p. fun at,** burlarse de, mofarse de; **p. one in the ribs,** dar (a alguien) un codazo en las costillas. —*v.i.* 1. fisgar, husmear. 2. moverse lentamente, haronear; ocuparse en fruslerías. 3. sobresalir, proyectarse. 4. **p. about** (o **around**), fisgonear, andar fisgando; andar en busca de algo; **p. at,** dirigir golpes a. —*s.* golpe; empuje, empujón; codazo; hurgonazo.

pokeberry ['poʊkˌbɛrɪ] *s.* (bot.) hierba carmín, grana (planta y baya).

poker ['poʊkər, B -kə] *s.* 1. atizador, hurgón; **as stiff as a p.,** (tan) tieso como un palo. 2. (naipes) póker, póquer.

poker face, (fam. E.U.) cara impasible o inmutable, semblante sin expresión, cara de palo (Chile).

pokeroot ['poʊkˌrut] **pokeweed** [-ˌwid] *s.* (bot.) hierba carmín, grana.

pokey ['poʊkɪ] *s.* (jer.) chirona.

poky, pokey [-kɪ] *a.* (POKIER; POKIEST) 1. apretado, ahogado; pequeño, pobre, miserable. 2. desgarbado, desgalichado. 3. mezquino, insignificante. 4. aburrido, tedioso. 5. lento, lerdo.

Pol *abrev. de* **Poland, Polish,** Polonia, polaco.

pol [pɑl, B pɔl] *s.* (jer.) político experimentado.

polacca [poʊ'lækə] *s.* 1. polonesa (danza). 2. (mar.) polacra.

Polack ['poʊˌlɑk, B -læk] *s.* (jer., despec.) polaco.

polacre [poʊ'lɑkər, B -kə] *s.* (mar.) polacra.

Poland ['poʊlənd] *s.* Polonia.

Poland China, cerdo Poland-China.

polar ['poʊlər, B -lə] *a.* polar; (quím.) polar.

polar axis, (geol.) eje polar.

polar bear, (zool.) oso polar, oso blanco.

polar body, (biol.) cuerpo o célula polar.

polar circle, (astr., geog.) círculo polar.

polar coordinate, (mat.) coordenada polar.

polar distance, (astr.) distancia polar.

polar front, (meteor.) frente polar.

polarimeter [ˌpoʊlə'rɪmətər, B -tə] *s.* (ópt.) polarímetro.

polarimetry [-ətrɪ] *s.* polarimetría.

Polaris [poʊ'lærəs] *s.* 1. (astr.) polar, estrella polar. 2. tipo de proyectil atómico que se lanza desde un submarino.

polariscope [-əˌskoʊp] *s.* (ópt.) polariscopio.

polarity [-ətɪ] *s.* (fís., fig.) polaridad.

polarizable ['poʊləˌraɪzəbəl] *a.* polarizable.

polarization [ˌpoʊlərə'zeɪʃən, B -raɪ-] *s.* polarización; (ópt., elec.) polarización.

polarize ['poʊləˌraiz] *v.t.* polarizar.

polarizer [-ər, B -ə] *s.* polarizador.

polar lights, aurora polar, aurora boreal.

polarograph [poʊ'lærəˌgræf, B -ˌgrɑf] *s.* (quím.) polarógrafo.

polarographic [poʊˌlærə'græfɪk] *a.* polarográfico.

polarography [poʊlə'rɑgrəfɪ, B -'rɔg-] *s.* polarografía.

Polaroid (TM) ['poʊləˌrɔɪd] *a., s.* (foto.) polaroid.

polar valence, (fís., quím.) electrovalencia.

polatouche [ˌpoʊlə'tuʃ] *s.* (zool.) polatuca.

polder ['poʊldər, 'pɑl-, B 'pɔldə] *s.* pólder, tierra ganada al mar por medio de diques.

pole [poʊl] *s.* 1. (geog., astr., biol., elec., fís.) polo. 2. P., polaco. 3. poste, palo; vara, pértiga. 4. lanza (de carruajes). 5. medida lineal (5,029 m.). 6. **under bare poles,** (mar.) sin vela puesta, con las velas arriadas; **up the p.,** (jer.) en líos, en dificultades. —*v.t.* empujar o sostener con palos; impeler con pértiga o botador (una embarcación).

poleax, poleaxe ['poʊlˌæks] *s.* 1. hacha de guerra; hachuela de mano. 2. hacha de matadero. —*v.t.* 1. matar o derribar con hacha. 2. (fig.) aturdir.

pole bean, (bot.) fríjol trepador, fríjol de enrame.

polecat [-ˌkæt] *s.* (zool.) veso, turón; (E.U.) mofeta.

pole horse, caballo de tronco.

pole jump, (G.B.) *var. de* **pole vault.**

polemic [pə'lɛmɪk, B pɔ-] **polemical** [-ɪkəl] *a.* polémico, controvertible. —*s.* 1. polémica, controversia. 2. polemista.

polemically [-ɪkəlɪ] *adv.* polémicamente.

polemicist [-əsəst] *s.* polemista.

polemicize [-əˌsaɪz] *v.i.* polemizar.
polemics [-ɪks] *s. pl.* (*sing. en const.*) (teo.) polémica.
polemist [-əst, 'pɑləməst, B 'pɔlə-] *s.* polemista.
polemoniaceous [ˌpɑləˌmoʊnɪ'eɪʃəs, B ˌpɔl-] *a.* (bot.) polemoniáceo.
polemonium [-'moʊnɪəm] *s.* (bot.) polemonio.
pole pitch, (elec.) paso polar, distancia entre polos.
pole plate, (arq.) carrera inferior (de una cercha).
poler ['poʊlər, B -ə] *s.* 1. caballo de tronco. 2. barquero (que impulsa una embarcación con el botador).
pole shoe, (elec.) zapata del polo.
polestar [-ˌstɑr, B -ˌstɑ] *s.* 1. estrella polar. 2. (fig.) principio orientador.
pole vault, salto con garrocha.
pole-vaulting [-ˌvɔltɪŋ] *s.* salto con garrocha.
police [pə'lis] *s.* (*pl.* POLICE) 1. policía, cuerpo de policía, ej., *the p. are on his track,* la policía está sobre su pista. 2. policía, (reglamentos del) orden público. 3. policías. 4. (E.U.) (mil.) limpieza, aseo (del campo, cuarteles, etc.). —*v.t.* 1. vigilar el orden público en, mantener bajo vigilancia policial. 2. mantener servicio de policía en. 3. supervisar, vigilar.
police action, (der. internacional) acción policial.
police car, coche de policía; coche patrullero, radiopatrulla (Am.); perseguidora (Cuba).
police constable, (G.B.) guardia, policía (*m.*).
police custody, detención preventiva.
police dog, perro policía.
police force, fuerza policial.
police headquarters, jefatura de policía, prefectura de policía.
policeman [-mən] *s.* policía (*m.*), agente, guardia.
police power, 1. facultad policial. 2. fuerza pública.
police record, antecedentes penales, antecedentes de delincuencia.
police reporter, reportero de asuntos policiales.
police state, estado policíaco.
police station, estación de policía, cuartel de policía, comisaría.
policewoman [-ˌwʊmən] *s.* mujer policía, policia, agente.
policlinic [ˌpɑlɪ'klɪnɪk, B ˌpɔl-] *s.* policlínica, policlínico (Am.).
policy ['pɑləsɪ, B 'pɔl-] *s.* (*pl.* POLICIES) 1. política, curso, costumbre, plan, sistema, plan de acción. 2. prudencia; sagacidad, astucia. 3. póliza de seguros. 4. especie de lotería. 4. **foreign p.,** política extranjera.
policyholder [-ˌhoʊldər, B -də] *s.* asegurado, tenedor de una póliza.
policy of appeasement, política de apaciguamiento.
poling board, (min.) tablestaca, tabla de blindaje, estaca de avance.
polio ['poʊlɪˌoʊ] *s.* (fam.) polio, poliomielitis.
poliomyelitis [ˌpoʊlɪoʊˌmaɪə'laɪtəs] *s.* (med.) poliomielitis.
Polish ['poʊlɪʃ] *a.* polaco. —*s.* (idioma) polaco.
polish ['pɑlɪʃ, B 'pɔl-] *s.* 1. pulimento; brillo, lustre. 2. refinamiento, urbanidad, cultura. 3. cera, bola, betún. —*v.t.* 1. pulir, bruñir, lustrar; embolar. 2. educar, civilizar, refinar. 3. **to apple-p.,** adular; **p. off,** terminar rápidamente, acabar con (esp. comida); (jer.) liquidar, matar; **p. up,** mejorar, perfeccionar. —*v.i.* recibir lustre o pulimento.
polished [-ɪʃt] *a.* 1. pulido, bruñido. 2. (fig.) pulido; acabado, consumado, perfecto.
polisher [-ɪʃər, B -ɪʃə] *s.* 1. pulidor, lustrador. 2. pulidora (máquina).
polishing lathe, torno de pulir.
polishing wax, cera para lustrar, cera encáustica.
polishing wheel, muela pulidora, rueda de bruñir.
Polish wheat, (bot.) trigo de Polonia.
Politburo ['pɑlətˌbjʊroʊ, B 'pɔlɪtˌbjʊər-] *s.* (pol.) Politburó.
polite [pə'laɪt] *a.* cortés, atento; culto, fino.
politely [-lɪ] *adv.* cortésmente, atentamente.
politeness [-nəs] *s.* cortesía, urbanidad.
polite society, la gente educada.
politesse [ˌpɑlɪ'tɛs, B ˌpɔl-] *s.* (fr.) cortesanía. cultura; decoro.
politic ['pɑləˌtɪk] *a.* 1. ingenioso; sagaz, astuto. 2. apropiado, atinado. 3. (raro) político.
political [pə'lɪtɪkəl] *a.* político.
political correctness, correción política.
political economist, experto en economía política.
political economy, economía política, crematística.
politically [-kəlɪ] *adv.* políticamente.
political prisoner, preso politico.
political science, ciencias politicas.
political scientist, experto en ciencia política.
politician [ˌpɑlə'tɪʃən, B ˌpɔl-] *s.* político; estadista.
politicize [pə'lɪtəˌsaɪz] *v.i.* politiquear. —*v.t.* llevar a la esfera política, dar carácter político a; introducir política en.
politick ['pɑləˌtɪk, B 'pɔl-] *v.i.* (fam.) politiquear.
politicker [-ər, B -ə] *s.* politiquero.
politicking [-ɪŋ] *s.* politiqueo.
politicly [-lɪ] *adv.* astutamente, sagazmente.
politico [pə'lɪtɪˌkoʊ] *s.* (gen. despec.) (*pl.* POLITICOS) politiquero, politicastro.
politics ['pɑləˌtɪks, B 'pɔl-] *s. pl.* (*sing. o pl. en const.*) política; **to enter p.,** iniciarse en la política.
polity [-ətɪ] *s.* (*pl.* POLITIES) 1. constitución política, organización política. 2. forma de gobierno, gobierno. 3. estado. 4. (*pl.*) política.
polka ['poʊlkə] *s.* polca (danza).
polka dot ['poʊkə-] (tej.) diseño formado por lunares o puntos.
poll [poʊl] *s.* 1. cabeza; nuca. 2. cotillo (de martillo). 3. votación (acción y resultado); escrutinio (de votos). 4. (*pl.*) lugar de votación, urnas electorales; votación. 5. capitación (impuesto). 6. encuesta, sondeo (de un organismo de sondaje); **to take a p.,** hacer una encuesta —*v.t.* 1. esquilar, trasquilar. 2. desmochar, podar (árbol, etc.), descornar (ganado). 3. empadronar (votantes). 4. solicitar el voto de (jurado, delegado, etc.). 5. recibir, obtener (votos). 6. encuestar, escudriñar, recoger la opinión de. —*v.i.* (con *for*) votar, emitir su voto (por).
pollack ['pɑlək, B 'pɔl-] *s.* (ict.) gado.
pollard ['pɑlərd, B 'pɔləd] *s.* 1. mocho, res descornada. 2. árbol desmochado o descopado, árbol podado. —*v.t.* desmochar, podar.
polled [poʊld] *a.* 1. descornado. 2. sin cuernos. 3. desmochado, podado (árbol, etc.).
pollee [ˌpoʊ'li] *s.* entrevistado (persona interrogada en una encuesta).
pollen ['pɑlən, B 'pɔl-] *s.* (bot.) polen.
pollenate ['pɑləˌneɪt, B 'pɔl-] *v.t.* (bot.) polinizar.
pollenation [ˌpɑlə'neɪʃən, B ˌpɔl-] *s.* (bot.) polinización.
pollen count, recuento de pólenes.
pollex ['pɑlˌɛks, -əks, B 'pɔl-] *s.* (*pl.* POLLICES [-əˌsiz]) (anat., zool.) pólice, dedo pulgar.
pollicitation [pəˌlɪsɪ'teɪʃən] *s.* (der.) policitación.
pollinate ['pɑləˌneɪt, B 'pɔl-] *v.t.* (bot.) polinizar.
pollination [ˌpɑlə'neɪʃən, B ˌpɔl-] *s.* (bot.) polinización.
pollinator ['pɑləˌneɪtər, B 'pɔl-ə] *s.* (bot.) agente polinizante.
polling ['poʊlɪŋ-] *s.* votación.
polling booth ['poʊlɪŋ-] cabina o caseta para votar.
polling clerk, escrutador (que cuenta los votos).
polliniferous [ˌpɑlə'nɪfərəs, B ˌpɔl-] *a.* (bot., zool.) polinífero.
pollinium [pɑ'lɪnɪəm, B pɔ-] *s.* (*pl.* POLLINIA [-ɪə]) (bot.) polinio).
pollinize ['pɑləˌnaɪz, B 'pɔl-] *v.t.* polinizar.
pollinosis [ˌpɑlə'noʊsəs, B ˌpɔl-] *s.* (med.) polinosis.
polliwog ['pɑlɪˌwɑg, -ˌwɔg, B ˌpɔlɪˌwɔg] *s.* (zool.) renacuajo.
pollock, *var. de* **pollack.**
pollster ['poʊlstər, B -stə] *s.* encuestador, entrevistador (que hace encuestas).
poll tax, impuesto de capitación, impuesto por persona.
pollutant [pə'lutənt] *s.* contaminante, agente contaminador.
pollute [pə'lut] *v.t.* contaminar, infectar, corromper.
polluted [-əd] *a.* contaminado, corrupto; sucio.
pollution [pə'luʃən] *s.* 1. contaminación, infección, corrupción. 2. contaminación del terreno, agua o aire por substancias nocivas.
Pollux ['pɑləks, B 'pɔl-] *s.* (astr., mitol.) Pólux.
polly ['pɑlɪ, B 'pɔlɪ] *s.* (fam.) nombre que se da comúnmente a las cotorras, p. ext. la cotorra como animal doméstico.
Pollyanna [ˌpɑlɪ'ænə, B 'pɔl-] *s.* Poliana, nombre de una heroína literaria, p. ext. persona de un excesivo optimismo.
pollywog, *var. de* **polliwog.**
polo ['poʊloʊ] *s.* (dep.) polo; polo acuático.
polo coat, abrigo cruzado con cinturón suelto, gen. de pelo de camello.
poloist [-əst] *s.* polista.
polonaise [ˌpɑlə'neɪz, ˌpoʊ-, B ˌpɔ-] *s.* 1. (hist.) polonesa (prenda de vestir). 2. (mús.) polonesa.
polonium [pə'loʊnɪəm] *s.* (quím.) polonio.
polo shirt, polo (camisa de deporte de punto), polera (Am.).
poltergeist ['poʊltərˌgaɪst, B -təˌ-] *s.* espíritu burlón, duende (al que se atribuyen ruidos inexplicables).
poltroon [pal'trun, B pɔl-] *s., a.* cobarde, pusilánime, miedoso, mandria.
poltroonery [-ərɪ] *s.* cobardía, pusilanimidad.
poltroonish [-ɪʃ] *a.* cobarde, pusilánime.
poly ['poʊlɪ] *s.* (*pl.* POLIES) (bot.) zamarrilla.
polyadelphous [ˌpɑlɪə'dɛlfəs B ˌpɔl-] *a.* (bot.) poliadelfo.
polyamide [-'æmˌaɪd] *s.* (quím.) poliamida.
polyandric [-'ændrɪk] *a.* poliándrico.
polyandrous [-drəs] *a.* 1. (bot.) poliandro. 2. poliándrico.
polyandry ['pɑlɪˌændrɪ, B 'pɔl-] *s.* poliandria; (bot.) poliandria.
polyanthus [ˌpɑlɪ'ænθəs, B ˌpɔl-] *s.* (*pl.* POLYANTHUSES O POLYANTHI [-θaɪ]) (bot.) prímula, primavera; narciso.
poliarchy ['pɑlɪˌɑrkɪ, B 'pɔlɪˌɑkɪ] *s.* (pol.) (*pl.* POLIARCHIES) poliarquía.
polybasic [ˌpɑlɪ'beɪsɪk, B ˌpɔl-] *a.* (quím.) polibásico.
polybasite [-'beɪˌsaɪt] *s.* (min.) polibasita.
polycarpellary [ˌpɑlɪ'kɑrpəˌlɛrɪ, B ˌpɔlɪ'-kɑpələrɪ] *a.* (bot.) policarpelar, policarpelario.

polycarpic [-ˈkɑrpɪk, B -ˈkɑp-] *a.* (bot.) policárpico.

polychaete [ˈpɑlɪˌkit, B ˈpɔl-] **polychaetous** [ˌpɑlɪˈkitəs, B ˌpɔl-] *a., s.* (zool.) poliqueto.

polychasium [ˌpɑlɪˈkeɪzɪəm, -ˈkɔɪʒ-, B ˌpɔl-] *s.* (*pl.* POLYCHASIA [-ə]) (bot.) policasio, pleocasio.

polychotomous [-ˈkɑtəməs, B -ˈkɔt-] *a.* (bot.) policótomo.

polychroism [ˈpɑlɪˌkroʊɪzəm, B ˈpɔlɪ-] *s.* (min.) policroísmo.

polychromatic [ˌpɑlɪkroʊˈmætɪk, B ˌpɔl-] *a.* policromo, multicolor.

polychromatophilia [-ˌmætəˈfɪlɪə] *s.* policromatofilia.

polychrome [ˈpɑlɪˌkroʊm, B ˈpɔl-] *a.* policromo, multicolor.

polychromy [-ˌkroʊmɪ] *s.* policromía.

polyclinic [ˌpɑlɪˈklɪnɪk, B ˌpɔl-] *s.* policlínica, policlínico (Am.).

polycondensation [-ˌkɑnˌdɛnˈseɪʃən, B -ˌkɔn-] *s.* (quím.) policondensación.

polyconic projection [-ˈkɑnɪk, B -ˈkɔn-] (cartografía) proyección policónica.

polycotyledon [-ˌkɑtəlˈidən, B -ˌkɔt-] *s.* (bot.) policotiledóneo.

polycotyledonous [-ənəs] *a.* policotiledóneo.

polycyclic [-ˈsaɪklɪk, -ˈsɪk-] *a.* (elec., quím.) policíclico.

polycythemia [-saɪˈθimɪə] *s.* (med.) policitemia.

polydactyl [-ˈdæktəl] *a.* (bot., zool.) polidáctilo.

polydactylism [-ˌɪzəm] *s.* (med.) polidactilia, polidactilismo.

polydactylous [-əs] *a.* (bot., zool., med.) polidáctilo.

polydipsia [-ˈdɪpsɪə] *s.* (med.) polidipsia.

polyembryonic [-ˌɛmbrɪˈɑnɪk, B -ˈɔn-] *a.* (biol.) poliembrional.

polyembryony [-ˈɛmbrɪənɪ] *s.* (biol.) poliembrionía.

polyester [ˈpɑlɪˌɛstər, B ˈpɔlɪˌɛstə] *s.* (quím.) poliéster.

polyethylene [ˌpɑlɪˈɛθəˌlin, B ˌpɔl-] *s.* (quím.) polietileno.

polygala [pəˈlɪgələ] *s.* (bot.) polígala.

polygalaceous [pəˌlɪgəˈleɪʃəs] *a.* (bot.) poligaláceo, poligáleo.

polygalactia [ˌpɑlɪgəˈlækʃɪə, B ˌpɔlɪgəˈlæktɪə] *s.* (med.) poligalia.

polygamist [pəˈlɪgəməst] *s.* polígamo.

polygamize [-ˌmaɪz] *v.i.* practicar la poligamia.

polygamous [-məs] *a.* polígamo; (bot.) polígamo.

polygamy [-mɪ] *s.* poligamia.

polygenesis [-ˈdʒɛnəsəs] *s.* poligenismo.

polygenetic [-dʒəˈnɛtɪk] *a.* (biol.) poligénico.

polygenic [ˌpɑlɪˈdʒɛnɪk, B ˌpɔl-] *a.* (biol.) polígeno.

polyglandular [-ˈglændjələr, B ˌpɔlɪ-lə] *a.* (med.) poliglandular.

polyglot [ˈpɑlɪˌglɑt, B ˈpɔlɪˌglɔt] *a.* políglota. —*s.* 1. políglota, polígloto. 2. biblia políglota.

polyglotism, polyglottism [-ˌɪzəm] *s.* poliglotía.

polygon [ˈpɑlɪˌgɑn, B ˈpɔlɪgən] *s.* (geom.) polígono.

polygonaceous [ˌpɑlɪgəˈneɪʃəs, B ˌpɔl-] *a.* (bot.) poligonáceo.

polygonal [pəˈlɪgənəl] *a.* poligonal.

polygraph [ˈpɑlɪˌgræf, B ˈpɔlɪˌgrɑf] *s.* 1. polígrafo (autor de obras de géneros diferentes). 2. (tec., med.) polígrafo (máquina).

polygraphic [ˌpɑlɪˈgræfɪk, B ˌpɔl-] *a.* poligráfico.

polygraphy [pəˈlɪgrəfɪ] *s.* poligrafía.

polygynous [-ˈlɪdʒənəs] *a.* 1. polígamo. 2. (bot.) polígino.

polygyny [-nɪ] *s.* poliginia, poligamia.

polyhedral [ˌpɑlɪˈhidrəl B ˌpɔl-] *a.* poliedro, poliédrico.

polyhedron [-drən] *s.* (geom.) poliedro.

polyhistor [-ˈhɪstər, B -tə] *s.* persona de muchos conocimientos, hombre sabio.

Polyhymnia [-ˈhɪmnɪə] *s.* (mitol.) Polimnia, musa de la oratoria.

polyisotopic [ˌpɑlɪˌaɪsəˈtɑpɪk, B ˌpɔlɪ-ˈtɔpɪk] *a.* (quím.) poli-isótopo.

polymastigote [-ˈmæstəˌgoʊt] *a.* (zool.) polimastigoto.

polymer [ˈpɑləmər, B ˈpɔlɪmə] *s.* (quím.) polímero.

polymeric [ˌpɑləˈmɛrɪk, B ˌpɔlɪˈmɛər-] *a.* (quím.) polimérico, polímero.

polymerism [pəˈlɪməˌrɪzəm] *s.* (quím., biol.) polimerismo.

polymerization [-ˌlɪmərəˈzeɪʃən, B -raɪ-] *s.* (quím.) polimerización.

polymerize [-ˈlɪməˌraɪz] *v.t., v.i.* (quím.) polimerizar(se).

polymerous [-rəs] *a.* (bot.) polímero.

polymery [-rɪ] *s.* (biol.) polimería.

Polymnia [pəˈlɪmnɪə] (mitol.) *var. de* **Polyhymnia.**

polymorph [ˈpɑlɪˌmɔrf, B ˈpɔlɪˌmɔf] *s.* (bot., zool., cristalografía) polimorfo.

polymorphic [ˌpɑlɪˈmɔrfɪk, B ˌpɔlɪˈmɔfɪk] *a.* polimorfo.

polymorphism [-ˌfɪzəm] *s.* polimorfismo.

polymorphonuclear [-ˌmɔrfəˈnuklɪər, B -ˌmɔfəˈnjuklɪə] *a.* (fisiol.) polimorfonuclear.

polymorphous [-ˈmɔrfəs, B -ˈmɔfəs] *a.* polimorfo, que toma o pasa por muchas formas o variaciones.

polymyxin [-ˈmɪksən] *s.* (quím.) polimixina.

Polynesia [ˌpɑləˈniʒə, B ˌpɔlɪˈnizjə] *s.* Polinesia.

Polynesian [-ʒən, B -zjən] *a.* polinesio. —*s.* 1. polinesio, natural de la Polinesia. 2. polinesio, lengua malayo-polinésica.

polyneuritis [-nʊˈraɪtəs, B -njʊ-] *s.* (med.) polineuritis.

polynomial [-ˈnoʊmɪəl] *s.* (mat.) polinomio.

polyp [ˈpɑləp, B ˈpɔlɪp] *s.* 1. (zool.) pólipo, pulpo. 2. (med.) pólipo.

polypary [ˈpɑləˌpɛrɪ, B ˈpɔlɪpərɪ] *s.* (zool.) polípero.

polypeptide [ˌpɑlɪˈpɛpˌtaɪd, B ˌpɔl-] *s.* (bioquím.) polipéptido.

polypetalous [-ˈpɛtələs] *a.* (bot.) polipétalo.

polyphagia [-ˈfeɪdʒɪə] *s.* (med.) polifagia.

polyphagian [-dʒiən] *a.* (med.) polífago.

polyphagous [pəˈlɪfəgəs] *a.* (med., zool.) polífago.

polyphase [ˈpɑlɪˌfeɪz, B ˈpɔl-] *a.* (elec.) polifásico, multifásico.

polyphone [-ˌfoʊn] *s.* (fon.) letra o símbolo polifónico.

polyphonic [ˌpɑlɪˈfɑnɪk, B ˌpɔlɪˈfɔnɪk] *a.* polifónico, polífono.

polyphonous [pəˈlɪfənəs] *a.* polifónico, polífono.

polyphony [-nɪ] *s.* (*pl.* POLIPHONIES) (mús.) polifonía.

polyphyletic [ˌpɑlɪfaɪˈlɛtɪk, B ˌpɔl-] *a.* (zool.) polifilético.

polypide [ˈpɑləˌpaɪd, B ˈpɔl-] *s.* (zool.) polípido.

polyploid [-ˌplɔɪd] *a., s.* (biol.) poliploide.

polyploidy [-ˌplɔɪdɪ] *s.* (biol.) poliploidia.

polypnea [ˌpɑlɪpˈniə, B ˌpɔl-] *s.* (med.) polipnea.

polypody [ˈpɑləˌpoʊdɪ, B ˈpɔlɪpədɪ] *s.* (*pl.* POLYPODIES) (bot.) polipodio común.

polypoid [-ˌpɔɪd] *a.* (zool., med.) polipoide.

polyptych [ˈpɑləpˌtɪk, B ˈpɔl-] *s.* (arte) políptico.

polypus [ˈpɑləpəs, B ˈpɔl-] *s.* (*pl.* POLYPI [-ˌpaɪ] o POLYPUSES) (med.) pólipo.

polysaccharide [ˌpɑlɪˈsækəˌraɪd, B ˌpɔl-] *s.* (quím.) polisacárido.

polysemy [ˈpɑlɪˌsɪmɪ, B ˈpɔl-] *s.* (filol.) polisemia.

polysepalous [ˌpɑlɪˈsɛpələs, B ˌpɔl-] *a.* (bot.) polisépalo.

polystyle [ˈpɑlɪˌstaɪl, B ˈpɔl-] *s.* (arq.) polistilo.

polystylous [ˌpɑlɪˈstaɪləs, B ˌpɔl-] *a.* (bot.) polistilo.

polystyrene [-ˈstaɪˌrin] *s.* (quím.) poliestireno.

polysulfide [-ˈsʌlˌfaɪd] *s.* (quím.) polisulfuro.

polysyllabic [-səˈlæbɪk] *a.* polisílabo.

polysyllable [ˈpɑlɪˌsɪləbəl, B ˈpɔl-] *s.* (gram.) polisílabo, palabra polisílaba.

polysyndeton [ˌpɑlɪˈsɪndəˌtɑn, B ˌpɔlɪ-tən] *s.* (ret.) polisíndeton.

polysynthetic [-sɪnˈθɛtɪk] *a.* polisintético (díc. de un idioma).

polytechnic [-ˈtɛknɪk] *a.* politécnico. —*s.* escuela politécnica, instituto politécnico.

polytheism [ˈpɑlɪθiˌɪzəm, B ˈpɔl-] *s.* (relig.) politeísmo.

polytheist [-ˌθiəst] *s.* (relig.) politeísta.

polytheistic [ˌpɑlɪθiˈɪstɪk, B ˌpɔl-] **polytheistical** [-ɪkəl] *a.* (relig.) politeísta.

polythene [ˈpɑlɪˌθin, B ˈpɔl-] *s.* (quím.) polietileno.

polytonal [ˌpɑlɪˈtoʊnəl, B ˌpɔl-] *a.* politono.

polytonality [-toʊˈnælətɪ] *s.* (mús.) politonalidad.

polytrophic [-ˈtrɑfɪk, B -ˈtrɔf-] *a.* (bact.) politrófico.

polytypic [-ˈtɪpɪk] *a.* politípico, que tiene o se refiere a varios tipos.

polyunsaturated [-ˌʌnˈsætʃəˌreɪtəd] *a.* (quím.) rico en enlaces no saturados (díc. de aceites o grasas).

polyurethane [-ˈjʊrəˌθeɪn, B -ˈjʊərə-] **polyurethan** [-ˌθæn] *a.* (quím.) poliuretano.

polyuria [-ˈjʊrɪə, B -ˈjʊər-] *s.* (med.) poliuria.

polyuric [-ɪk] *a.* (med.) poliúrico.

polyvalence [-ˈveɪləns] *s.* (bact., quím.) polivalencia.

polyvalent [-lənt] *a.* (bact., quím.) polivalente.

polyvinyl [-ˈvaɪnəl] *a.* (quím.) polivinílico.

polyvinyl resin, (quím.) resina polivinílica.

polyzoan [-ˈzoʊən] *a., s.* (zool.) polizoo.

polyzoarium [-zoʊˈɛrɪəm, B -ˈɛər-] *s.* (*pl.* POLYZOARIA [-ɪə]) (zool.) colonia de polizoarios o briozoos.

pomace [ˈpʌməs] *s.* pulpa de manzanas; magma.

pomaceous [poʊˈmeɪʃəs] *a.* (bot.) pomáceo.

pomade [poʊˈmeɪd, B pəˈmɑd] *s.* pomada. —*v.t.* untar con pomada.

pomander [ˈpoʊˌmændər, B pəˈmændə] *s.* pomo, bujeta, caja de perfumes.

pomatum [poʊˈmeɪtəm, pə-] *s.* pomada, ungüento perfumado.

pome [poʊm] *s.* (bot.) pomo.

pomegranate [ˈpɑmˌgrænət, ˈpʌm-, B ˈpɔm-] *s.* 1. (bot.) granado. 2. granada (fruto del granado).

pomelo [ˈpɑməˌloʊ, B ˈpɔm-] *s.* (*pl.* POMELOS) (bot.) pomelo, toronja.

Pomeranian [ˌpɑməˈreɪnɪən, B ˌpɔm-] *a.* 1. pomerano, natural de Pomerania. 2. perro de raza pomerana, perro (de) Pomerania.

pomfret ['pɑmfrət, B 'pɔm-] *s.* (ict.) castañola, japuta.
pomiculture ['poʊmə,kʌltʃər, B -tʃə] *s.* (bot.) pomicultura.
pomiferous [poʊ'mɪfərəs] *a.* pomífero.
pommel ['pʌməl, 'pɑm-, B 'pʌm-] *s.* 1. pomo (de la guarnición de la espada); culata. 2. perilla (de la montura). —*v.t.* (*pret., p.p.* POMMELED o POMMELLED; *p.pr.* POMMELING o POMMELLING) golpear con el puño o con los puños, apuñear.
pomological [,poʊmə'lɑdʒɪkəl, B -'lɔdʒ-] *a.* pomológico.
pomologist [poʊ'mɑlədʒəst, B -'mɔl-] *s.* pomólogo, especialista en frutas.
pomology [-dʒɪ] *s.* pomología, ciencia de las frutas.
pomp [pɑmp, B pɔmp] *s.* pompa; suntuosidad, magnificencia; ostentación, fausto, aparato.
pompadour ['pɑmpə,dɔr, B 'pɔmpə,dʊə] *s.* copete (díc. del peinado con copete sobre la frente).
pompano ['pɑmpə,noʊ, B 'pɔm-] *s.* (*pl.* POMPANOS) (ict.) pámpano; pampanito; salpa.
Pompeian [pɑm'peɪən, B pɔm'piən] *a., s.* pompeyano, de Pompeya.
Pompey ['pɑmpɪ, B 'pɔm-] *s.* Pompeyo, general y político romano.
pom-pom ['pɑm,pɑm, B 'pɔm,pɔm] *s.* (mil.) cañon automático ligero; cañón antiaéreo en buques de guerra.
pompon [-,pɑn, B -'pɔŋ] *s.* 1. pompón, borla, madroño. 2. (bot.) variedad de crisantemo o dalia.
pomposity [pɑm'pɑsətɪ, B pɔm'pɔs-] *s.* 1. pomposidad, ostentación. 2. gesto o hábito pomposos.
pompous ['pɑmpəs, B 'pɔm-] *a.* 1. pomposo, suntuoso. 2. pomposo, hinchado, ampuloso.
pompously [-lɪ] *adv.* 1. pomposamente, suntuosamente. 2. pomposamente, hinchadamente, ampulosamente.
pompousness [-nəs] *s.* 1. pomposidad, suntuosidad. 2. pomposidad, ampulosidad.
poncho ['pɑntʃoʊ, B 'pɔn-] *s.* (*pl.* PONCHOS) poncho, capote de monte.
pond [pɑnd, B pɔnd] *s.* charca, estanque, laguna.
ponder ['pɑndər, B 'pɔndə] *v.t.* ponderar, pesar, examinar, deliberar, considerar. —*v.i.* reflexionar, meditar; **p. on** (u **over**), meditar sobre.
ponderability [,pɑndərə'bɪlətɪ, B ,pɔn-] *s.* ponderabilidad.
ponderable ['pɑndərəbəl, B 'pɔn-] *a.* ponderable, apreciable; perceptible.
ponderosity [,pɑndə'rɑsətɪ, B ,pɔndə'rɔs-] *s.* 1. ponderosidad. 2. (fig.) pesadez.
ponderous ['pɑndərəs, B 'pɔn-] *a.* 1. ponderoso, pesado, voluminoso. 2. (fig.) pesado, tedioso, laborioso.
ponderously [-lɪ] *adv.* 1. ponderosamente. 2. pesadamente, tediosamente.
ponderousness [-nəs] *s.* 1. ponderosidad. 2. (fig.) pesadez.
pond lily, (bot.) ninfea, nenúfar.
pone [poʊn] *s.* pan de maíz, arepa (Am.) .
pong [pɑŋ, B pɔŋ] *v.i.* (jer. G.B.) apestar.
pongee [pɑn'dʒi, B pɔn-] *s.* pongís, tela muy liviana de seda japonesa.
pongid ['pɑndʒəd, B 'pɔn-] *a.* (zool.) póngido.
poniard ['pɑnjərd, B 'pɔnjəd] *s.* puñal, daga. —*v.t.* atravesar con puñal.
pons [pɑnz, B pɔnz] *s.* 1. (anat.) puente, puente de Varolio (t. **p. Varolii**) . 2. conectador, parte conectiva.
Pontederiaceae [,pɑntə,dɪrɪ'eɪsɪi, B ,pɔn-] *s. pl.* (bot.) pontederiáceas.
Pontic ['pɑntɪk, B 'pɔnt-] *s.* (hist.) póntico, del Ponto.
pontifex ['pɑntə,fɛks, B 'pɔnt-] *s.* (*pl.* PONTIFICES [pɑn'tɪfə,siz, B pɔn-]) (hist., relig.) pontífice, sumo sacerdote entre los romanos.
pontiff ['pɑntəf B 'pɔnt-] *s.* (relig.) pontífice; Sumo Pontífice, Pontífice Romano.
pontifical [pɑn'tɪfɪkəl, B pɔn-] *a.* 1. pontifical, obispal, episcopal; pontificio, papal. 2. dogmático, sentencioso. —*s.* 1. pontifical (libro de ceremonias). 2. (*pl.*) pontificales (conjunto de ornamentos)
pontificate [-,kət, -,keɪt] *s.* pontificado. — [-,keɪt] *v.i.* pontificar, dogmatizar, hablar sentenciosamente.
pontil ['pɑntɪl, B 'pɔn-] *s.* (vidriería) pontil, puntel.
Pontius Pilate ['pɑntʃəs'paɪlət, B 'pɔntjəs-] (bíbl.) Poncio Pilato.
ponton ['pɑntən, B 'pɔnt-] *var. de* **pontoon.**
pontonier [,pɑntən'ɪr, B ,pɔntə'nɪə] *s.* (mil.) pontonero.
pontoon [pɑn'tun, B pɔn-] *s.* 1. pontón. 2. (aer.) flotador. 3. (G.B.) veintiuno (juego de naipes) .
pontoon bridge, (mil.) puente de pontones, puente de barcas.
pony ['poʊnɪ] *s.* (*pl.* PONIES) 1. jaca, caballito, poni. 2. (fam.) copa o vaso pequeño, traguito (de licor). 3. (E.U.) chuleta de exámenes (clave o traducción empleada a hurtadillas). 4. (jer.) caballo de carrera. 5. (jer. G.B.) 25 libras esterlinas. —*v.t., v.i.* **p. up,** (fam.) pagar (dinero), apoquinar.
pony engine, locomotora de maniobras.
pony express, (hist.) sistema postal rápido (a través del oeste de los E.U.) por medio de remudas de caballos.
ponytail [-,teɪl] *s.* (peinado) cola de caballo.
pooch [putʃ] *s.* (jer.) perro, can.
pood [pud] *s.* pud (unidad de peso rusa equivalente a 16,38 kg) .
poodle ['pudəl] *s.* perro de lanas.
poof [puf, pʊf] *interj.* 1. exclamación que expresa un movimiento rápido e inesperado (desaparición, aparición de algo o alguien, etc.). 2. *var. de* **pooh.**
pooh [pu, pʊ] *interj.* ¡bah! ¡fu! ¡qué va!
pooh-bah ['pu,bɑ] *s.* (fam.) potentado; personaje importante.
pooh-pooh ['pu'pu, pu'pu] *v.t.* restar importancia a, desestimar, desdeñar, hacer mofa de. —*v.i.* expresar desdén, desdeñar.
pool [pul] *s.* 1. estanque, alberca, piscina, pileta, poza. 2. charco, rebalsa. 3. yacimiento petrolífero.
pool, *s.* 1. pozo (lo que se juega en cada mano de ciertos juegos de cartas). 2. (G.B.) juego de billar en el que cada jugador aporta una suma que se lleva el ganador; (E.U.) billar de casín o casino. 3. fondo, bolsa común, banca, vaca (dinero que juegan en común dos o más personas). 4. consorcio, mancomunidad, sindicato (de empresas); combinado industrial; agrupación de personal o material para uso común. —*v.t.* mancomunar, aunar, combinar, amalgamar.
poolroom ['pul,rum, -,rʊm] *s.* (E.U.) sala de apuestas (de carreras de caballos); salón de billar.
pool table, *s.* mesa de billar.
poop [pup] *s.* 1. (mar.) toldilla. 2. (jer.) pelagatos. 3. popa. —*v.t.* 1. embarcar (agua) por la popa; romper (ola, etc.) sobre la popa de (barco). 2. (jer.) dejar sin resuello; agotar, acabar. —*i.v.* (jer.) ensuciarse, hacerse caca.
poop deck, (mar.) cubierta de la bovedilla, castillo de popa.
poor [pʊr, B pʊə] *a* 1. pobre, necesitado, menesteroso, indigente. 2. pobre, deficiente, falto, escaso, inadecuado. 3. malo, inferior, insatisfactorio. 4. humilde, modesto. 5. endeble, enfermizo, delicado. 6. flaco, magro. 7. pobre, infortunado, desdichado. 8. estéril, árido, infecundo. 9. pobre, desfavorable. 10. **p. as a church mouse,** más pobre que una rata; **p. devil,** pobre diablo; **p. in,** pobre de; **p. in spirit,** pobre de espíritu; **p. old me,** pobre de mí; **p. thing,** pobrecito, pobrecita; **the p.,** los pobres.
poor box, cepo, cepillo (para recoger limosnas, esp. en iglesias) .
poorhouse ['pʊr,haʊs, B 'pʊə-] *s.* asilo, hospicio, casa de caridad o beneficencia.
poorly [-lɪ] *adv.* 1. pobremente, humildemente, indigentemente. 2. mal, insatisfactoriamente. —*a.* (fam.) indispuesto, enfermizo.
poorness [-nəs] *s.* insuficiencia; inferioridad; pobreza (de calidad) .
poor-spirited [-'spɪrətəd] *a.* cobarde, bajo, pusilánime, apocado.
poor white, (despec.) blanco (gen. del S. de E.U.) de baja condición.
pop [pɑp, B pɔp] *s.* 1. chasquido, estallido, crujido, ruido seco. 2. pistoletazo, detonación, estampido. 3. (fam.) **p. soda,** bebida gaseosa; (G.B.) champán. 4. (jer.) papá. 5. **in p.,** (jer. G.B.) empeñado, pignorado. —*v.i.* (*pret., p.p.* POPPED; *p.pr.* POPPING) 1. estallar, reventar. 2. dispararse, detonarse. 3. saltar (los ojos de las órbitas). 4. **p. in,** irrumpir, entrar de sopetón; entrar o visitar de paso; **p. off,** largarse; (jer.) morir; vociferar, clamar; **p. out,** salir por un rato; **p. out of one's head (one's eyes),** salírsele o saltársele a uno (los ojos); **p. up,** aparecer inesperadamente. —*v.t.* 1. echar, lanzar o estirar de repente. 2. hacer reventar. 3. (fam.) disparar, tirar; descerrajar, descargar. 4. (jer.) empeñar, pignorar. —*adv.* de prisa, sobre la marcha.
pop, *a.* (*forma abrev. de* **popular**) popular (música, arte, etc.) . —*s.* música popular.
pop art, arte realista que utiliza técnicas y temas populares como tiras cómicas, afiches, etc.
popcorn ['pɑp,kɔrn, B 'pɔp,kɔn] *s.* rosetas de maíz, palomitas de maíz, cancha (Perú, Col.) .
pope [poʊp] *s.* 1. papa; **the P.** el Papa. 2. pope (sacerdote ortodoxo) .
popedom [poʊpdəm] *s.* papado, papazgo.
popery [-ərɪ] *s.* (despec.) papismo.
pop-eyed ['pɑp,aɪd, B 'pɔp-] *a.* de ojos saltones.
popgun [-,gʌn] *s.* tirabala, pistola (de juguete) de aire comprimido.
popinjay ['pɑpən,dʒeɪ, B 'pɔp-] *s.* 1. farolero; petimetre; hablador, charlatán, parlanchín. 2. blanco en forma de loro. 3. (ant.) papagayo, loro.
popish ['poʊpɪʃ] *a.* (despec.) papista.
poplar ['pɑplər, B 'pɔplə] *s.* (bot.) 1. álamo blanco, álamo negro, álamo temblón. 2. (E.U.) tulipanero, tulipero.
poplin [-lən] *s.* (tej.) popelina, popelín.
popliteal [pɑp'lɪtɪəl, B pɔp-] *a.* (anat.) poplíteo.
pop music, (E.U.) música popular, música moderna bailable.
pop-off ['pɑp,ɔf, B 'pɔp-] *s.* (jer.) vocinglero.
popover [-,oʊvər, B -,oʊvə] *s.* panecillo hecho principalmente de huevos.
popper [-ər, B -ə] *s.* 1. utensilio para tostar maíz. 2. (variedad de) maíz adecuado para ser tostado.
poppet ['pɑpət, B 'pɔp-] *s.* 1. (mec.) barra, tolete, gigantón, santo (en minas), castillete. 2. (mar.) escálamo, tolete. 3. (fam. G.B.) hijito, amor. 4. (ant.) muñeca, títere, marioneta.

poppethead [-ˌhɛd] *s.* 1. (mec.) cabeza móvil del torno; contrapunto. 2. (min.) horca, caballete.
poppet valve, válvula de movimiento vertical.
poppied ['pɑpid, B 'pɔp-] *a.* 1. cubierto de amapolas (jardín, terreno). 2. somnífero, soporífico; drogado; soñoliento, amodorrado.
popping crease, (G.B., criquet) línea marcada en el suelo para indicar la posición del bateador.
popple ['pɑpəl, B 'pɔp-] *v.i.* agitarse, ondularse (esp. el agua). —*s.* chapoteo (del agua al hervir).
poppy ['pɑpɪ, B 'pɔpɪ] *s.* (*pl.* POPPIES) (bot.) 1. amapola, ababa, ababol. 2. adormidera.
poppycock [-ˌkɑk, B -ˌkɔk] *s.* (fam.) palabrería, cháchara, palique; disparate, necedad, tontería, cuento, farsa.
poppyhead [-ˌhɛd] *s.* (arq.) cúspide adornada y tallada.
Popsickle (TM) ['pɑpsɪkəl, B 'pɔp-] *s.* polo o paleta de helado.
populace ['pɑpjələs, B 'pɔp-] *s.* populacho, masas; pueblo, plebe, turba, vulgo.
popular [-lər, B -lə] *a.* 1. popular. 2. común, generalizado. 3. **popular front,** frente popular.
popularity [ˌpɑpjə'lærətɪ, B ˌpɔp-] *s.* popularidad, fama, renombre.
popularization [ˌpɑpjələrə'zeɪʃən, B ˌpɔpjʊləraɪ-] *s.* popularización.
popularize ['pɑpjələˌraɪz, B 'pɔp-] *v.t.* popularizar, difundir, divulgar, propagar, vulgarizar.
popularly ['pɑpjələrlɪ, B 'pɔpjʊləlɪ] *adv.* popularmente.
populate [-ˌleɪt] *v.t.* poblar, habitar.
population [ˌpɑpjə'leɪʃən, B ˌpɔp-] *s.* 1. población, pobladores, vecindario. 2. población (acto de poblar). 3. (biol.) colonia de organismos.
population explosion, (la) explosión demográfica, superpoblación.
Populism ['pɑpjəˌlɪzəm, B 'pɔp-] *s.* (pol.) populismo.
Populist [-ləst] *s.* (pol.) populista.
Populistic [ˌpɑpjə'lɪstɪk, B ˌpɔp-] *a.* (pol.) populista.
populous ['pɑpjələs, B 'pɔp-] *a.* populoso, muy poblado.
populousness [-nəs] *s.* densidad de población, abundancia de habitantes.
porbeagle ['pɔrˌbigəl, B 'pɔˌ-] *s.* (ict.) tiburón pequeño muy voraz.
porcelain ['pɔrsələn, B 'pɔsə-] *s.* porcelana.
porcelaneous, porcellaneous [ˌpɔrsə'leɪnɪəs, B ˌpɔsə-] *a.* frágil o delicado como la porcelana.
porcelanite ['pɔrsələˌnaɪt, B 'pɔsə-] *s.* (geol.) porcelanita.
porch [pɔrtʃ, B pɔtʃ] *s.* 1. porche, portal; terraza cubierta. 2. (ant.) pórtico.
porcine ['pɔrˌsaɪn, B 'pɔˌ-] *a.* porcino.
porcupine ['pɔrkjəˌpaɪn, B 'pɔk-] *s.* (zool.) puerco espín, puerco espino.
pore [pɔr, B pɔ] *v.i.* 1. (con *over*) escrutar, examinar; escudriñar, clavar la mirada (en), alambicar. 2. (con *over*) estudiar, leer con atención; estar absorto en la lectura (de). 3. (con *over*) meditar, reflexionar (sobre).
pore, *s.* poro.
porgy ['pɔrgɪ, B 'pɔdʒɪ] *s.* (*pl.* PORGIES) (ict.) 1. pagro, pargo, guachinango. 2. pagel, besugo, besuguete.
poriferan [pə'rɪfərən] *s.* (zool.) porífero.
poriferous [-əs] *a.* (zool.) porífero.
porism ['pɔrˌɪzəm] *s.* (geom.) porisma.
pork [pɔrk, B pɔk] *s.* 1. carne de puerco. 2. (jer. E.U.) prebenda política, coima, favores otorgados por patronazgo político.
pork barrel, (jer. E.U.) apropiación o partida del presupuesto que se usa para patronazgo político.
pork chop, chuleta o costilla de cerdo.
porker ['pɔrkər, B 'pɔkə] *s.* puerco cebado.
porkpie [-ˌpaɪ] *s.* sombrero de hombre de ala ancha y copa baja.
pork sausage, chorizo, longaniza, salchicha.
pornographer [pɔr'nɑgrəfər, B pɔ'nɔgrəfə] *s.* pornógrafo.
pornographic [ˌpɔrnə'græfɪk, B ˌpɔn-] *a.* pornográfico, obsceno.
pornography [pɔr'nɑgrəfɪ, B pɔ'nɔg-] *s.* 1. pornografía. 2. escrito pornográfico; fotografía o dibujo pornográfico; material pornográfico.
porosity [pə'rɑsətɪ, pɔ-, B pɔ'rɔs-] *s.* 1. porosidad. 2. poro.
porous ['pɔrəs] *a.* poroso.
porousness [-nəs] *s.* porosidad.
porphyria [pɔr'fɪrɪə, B pɔ'-] *s.* (med.) porfiria.
porphyrin ['pɔrfərən, B 'pɔfə-] *s.* (bioquím.) porfirina.
porphyritic [ˌpɔrfə'rɪtɪk, B ˌpɔfɪ-] *a.* (min.) 1. porfídico. 2. porfírico.
porphyroid ['pɔrfəˌrɔɪd, B 'pɔfə-] *s.* (min.) roca porfidoidea, roca porfídica.
porphyry [-rɪ] *s.* (*pl.* PORPHYRIES) (min.) pórfido, pórfiro.
porpoise ['pɔrpəs, B 'pɔpəs] *s.* (*pl.* PORPOISES) (zool.) marsopa, delfín.
porridge ['pɔrɪdʒ, 'pɑr-, B 'pɔr-] *s.* gachas, puches; plato de avena cocida con leche.
porringer [-əndʒər, B -dʒə] *s.* escudilla, plato hondo para gachas o potaje.
port [pɔrt, B pɔt] *s.* oporto, vino de Oporto.
port, *s.* 1. puerto. 2. aeropuerto. 3. (fig.) puerto, refugio, asilo. 4. **p. captain,** capitán de puerto; **p. of entry,** puerto de entrada; **to put into p.,** entrar a puerto. —*a.* portuario.
port, *s.* 1. (mar.) porta; portañola, cañonera, tronera; portilla, lumbrera. 2. (mot.) orificio, lumbrera. 3. desveno (de la embocadura del freno del caballo). 4. (pr. esco.) puerta, portal.
port, *v.t.* (mil.) llevar terciado (un fusil, etc.). —*s.* 1. porte, continente, talante. 2. (mil.) posición de fusil terciado.
port, *s.* (mar.) babor. —*v.t.* poner (en dirección) a babor. —*v.i.* virar (embarcación) a babor.
Port. *abrev. de* **Portugal, Portuguese,** Portugal, portugués.
portable ['pɔrtəbəl, B 'pɔtə-] *a.* portátil, transportable, movible, móvil. —*s.* máquina de escribir portátil.
portage ['pɔrtɪdʒ, B 'pɔtɪdʒ] *s.* 1. transporte, porteo, porte, acarreo. 2. transporte por tierra (de un río a otro). 3. (ant.) portazgo.
portal [-təl] *s.* 1. portal, portada, pórtico. 2. entrada. 3. portal (de un puente); boca, portal (de un túnel).
portal, *a.* (anat.) portal, porta (vena).
portal-to-portal pay, remuneración por el tiempo que el trabajador emplea en viajar de su casa al taller u oficina.
portal vein, (anat.) vena porta.
portance [-təns] *s.* (ant.) porte, talante.
portative [-tətɪv] *a.* portátil, transportable.
Port-au-Prince [ˌpɔrtoʊ'prɪns, B ˌpɔtoʊ-] *s.* Puerto Príncipe, capital de Haití.
port authority, 1. (E.U.) comisión gubernamental que regula y administra el sistema de comunicaciones en una ciudad portuaria. 2. dirección de puertos. 3. Junta de Obras de Puerto (Esp.).
port bar, barra del puerto, barra de porta (en buques).
portcullis [pɔrt'kʌləs, B pɔt-] *s.* 1. (fort.) rastrillo (en la entrada de castillos). 2. (her.) fretado.
Porte [pɔrt, B pɔt] *s.* (hist.) la Puerta, t. la Sublime Puerta (el gobierno del antiguo imperio turco).
porte-cochere [ˌpɔrtkoʊ'ʃɛr, B ˌpɔtkə'ʃɛə] *s.* 1. (E.U.) cobertizo para vehículos. 2. puerta cochera.
porte-monnaie ['pɔrtˌmʌnɪ, B 'pɔt-] *s.* (fr.) billetero, portamonedas.
portend [pɔr'tɛnd, B pɔ'-] *v.t.* 1. pronosticar, augurar, presagiar, anticipar. 2. significar, indicar.
portent ['pɔrtɛnt, B 'pɔtɛnt] *s.* 1. presagio, augurio, premonición. 2. carácter profético, significado siniestro. 3. portento, prodigio, maravilla, milagro.
portentous [pɔr'tɛntəs, B pɔ'-] *a.* 1. ominoso, de mal agüero, siniestro. 2. portentoso, prodigioso, maravilloso.
portentously [-lɪ] *adv.* 1. ominosamente. 2. portentosamente, prodigiosamente.
portentousness [-nəs] *s.* carácter ominoso.
porter ['pɔrtər, B 'pɔtə] *s.* 1. (pr. G.B.) portero, guardián; conserje. 2. cargador, mozo de cuerda, mozo de cordel, mandadero, changador (Amer.). 3. (E.U.) mozo, camarero (de trenes). 4. cerveza amarga y fuerte.
porterage [-tərɪdʒ] *s.* 1. portería (oficio de portero). 2. trabajo del cargador.
porterhouse [-tərˌhaʊs, B -təˌ-] *s.* 1. (**t. p. steak**) bistec, biftec. 2. (ant.) bodegón, cervecería.
porter's lodge, *s.* garita, portería.
port fire, *s.* (mil.) lanzallamas.
portfolio [pɔrt'foʊlɪˌoʊ, B pɔt-] *s.* (*pl.* PORTFOLIOS) 1. cartera, portapliegos. 2. cartera, ministerio. 3. (com.) cartera; valores en cartera. 4. (pol.) **minister without p.,** ministro sin cartera o sin despacho.
porthole ['pɔrtˌhoʊl, B 'pɔt-] *s.* 1. portañola, tronera, cañonera. 2. (mar.) porta, portilla, lumbrera.
portico ['pɔrtɪˌkoʊ, B 'pɔtɪ-] *s.* (*pl.* PORTICOES O PORTICOS) (arq.) pórtico, portal, atrio.
portière [ˌpɔrtɪ'ɛr, B pɔt'jɛə] *s.* (fr.) portier, antepuerta, cortinón.
portion ['pɔrʃən, B 'pɔʃən] *s.* 1. porción, parte, cuota. 2. destino, suerte. 3. dote. —*v.t.* 1. dividir en porciones, repartir. 2. (gen. con *out*) distribuir por cuotas. 3. legar bienes a, dotar.
portionless [-ləs] *a.* indotado, sin legado.
portland cement ['pɔrtlənd-, B 'pɔt-] cemento portland.
portliness ['pɔrtlɪnəs, B 'pɔt-] *s.* 1. presencia imponente; porte decoroso. 2. corpulencia.
portly [-lɪ] *a.* (PORTLIER; PORTLIEST) 1. corpulento, grueso. 2. solemne; decoroso.
portmanteau [pɔrt'mæntoʊ, B pɔt-] *s.* (*pl.* PORTMANTEAUS O PORTMANTEAUX [-toʊz]) portamanteo; valija, maleta grande, baúl.
portmanteau word, palabra mixta (que se forma del sonido y significado de otras dos, ej., **smog,** de **smoke** y **fog,** humo y bruma).
port of call, puerto de escala, puerto de arribada.
Port of Spain, Puerto España, capital de Trinidad y Tobago.
Porto Novo ['pɔrtoʊ'noʊvoʊ, B ˌpɔt-] *s.* Porto Novo, capital del Dahomey.
Porto Rico [-ə'rikoʊ] **Porto Rican** [-kən] *vars. de* **Puerto Rico, Puerto Rican.**
portrait ['pɔrtrət, -ˌtreɪt, B 'pɔtrɪt] *s.* 1. retrato; similitud, semejanza. 2. (fig.) retrato (descripción gráfica o verbal). 3. **to sit for a p.,** hacerse retratar.
portraitist [-əst] *s.* retratista, pintor que se especializa en retratos.

portraiture [-trətʃʊr, B -tʃə] *s.* 1. pintura de retratos; pintura del retrato (de alguien). 2. retrato. 3. (fig.) representación, descripción gráfica.
portray [pɔr'treɪ, B pɔ'-] *v.t.* 1. retratar, pintar el retrato de. 2. (fig.) retratar, describir gráficamente. 3. representar (en el teatro).
portrayal [-əl] *s.* 1. representación, descripción. 2. retrato. 3. representación (de un papel de teatro).
portrayer [-ər, B -ə] *s.* el que describe algo verbalmente o por escrito.
portress ['pɔrtrəs, B 'pɔtrɪs] **porteress** [-tərəs] *s.* portera.
Portugal ['pɔrtʃəgəl, B 'pɔtjʊ-] *s.* Portugal.
Portuguese [-ˌgiz, B ˌpɔtjʊ'giz] *a.* portugués, de Portugal. —*s.* (*pl.* PORTUGUESE) 1. portugués, de Portugal. 2. (idioma) portugués.
Portuguese man-of-war, (zool.) sifonóforo, medusa.
portulaca [ˌpɔrtʃə'lækə, B ˌpɔtjʊ'leɪkə] *s.* (bot.) verdolaga.
portulacaceous [-lə'keɪʃəs] *a.* (bot.) portulacáceo.
pose [poʊz] *v.t.* 1. dejar perplejo con una pregunta o problema; desconcertar, asombrar, confundir. 2. (ant.) preguntar, interrogar.
pose, *v.t.* 1. poner o colocar (un modelo) en cierta postura (esp. con fines artísticos). 2. proponer, plantear, formular (una pregunta); presentar (una proposición, un problema, etc.). —*v.i.* 1. posar (para pintor o fotógrafo). 2. pavonearse, tomar posturas afectadas. 3. **to p. as,** hacerse pasar por, dárselas de. —*s.* 1. posición, postura, actitud. 2. aire, apariencia. 3. afectación, amaneramiento, pose.
Poseidon [pə'saɪdən] *s.* (mitol.) Poseidón, dios griego de los mares.
poser ['poʊzər, B -zə] *s.* pregunta o problema difícil, rompecabezas, enigma.
poseur [poʊ'zɜr, B -'zɜ] *s.* (fr.) presuntuoso, persona de actitudes afectadas.
posh [pɑʃ, B pɔʃ] *a.* (fam., G.B.) elegante, a la moda; lujoso.
posit ['pɑzɪt, B 'pɔz-] *v.t.* 1. situar, colocar, poner en posición. 2. (filos.) postular, afirmar, aseverar, dar por cierto.
position [pə'zɪʃən] *s.* 1. posición. 2. colocación, empleo, puesto. 3. proposición, propuesta, aserto. 4. opinión, punto de vista. 5. **to be in a p. to (do),** estar en condiciones de (hacer); **to take the p. (that),** asumir el punto de vista (de que). —*v.t.* situar o poner en una posición conveniente o adecuada; determinar la posición (de); situar, poner, colocar; (mil.) colocar o apostar (tropas).
positional [-'zɪʃənəl] *a.* de posición.
position finder, (arm.) localizador.
position in readiness, (mil.) posición de espera, posición de apresto.
position light, (mar., aer.) luz de navegación, luz de situación.
positive ['pɑzətɪv, B 'pɔz-] *a.* 1. positivo. 2. absoluto, sumo. 3. seguro, convencido, cierto. 4. (mat., fís.) positivo. 5. (elec.) positivo; electropositivo. 6. (gram.) positivo (grado de comparación). 7. (mec.) de acción directa. 8. positivo (imagen, prueba, película, etc.). —*s.* 1. (gram.) grado positivo (de comparación). 2. (foto.) positivo. 3. **the p.,** lo positivo.
positive booster, (elec.) elevador de voltaje.
positive brush, (elec.) escobilla positiva.
positive electron, (fís.) electrón positivo, positrón.
positive feedback, (elec.) regeneración.
positive integer, (mat.) número entero positivo.
positive law, derecho positivo, ley positiva.
positive lens, (ópt.) lente convexa.
positively ['pɑzətɪvlɪ, B 'pɔz-] *adv.* 1. positivamente. 2. absolutamente, totalmente.
positive motion, (mec.) movimiento mandado.
positiveness [-nəs] *s.* seguridad, certeza; dogmatismo, porfía, terquedad.
positive offer, oferta firme.
positive order, (com.) pedido en firme.
positive pole, (elec.) polo positivo.
positive pump, bomba impelente.
positive rays, (fís.) rayos positivos.
positivism [-ˌɪzəm] *s.* (filos.) positivismo.
positivist [-əst] *a., s.* (filos.) positivista.
positivistic [ˌpɑzətɪv'ɪstɪk, B ˌpɔz-] *a.* (filos.) positivista.
positron ['pɑzəˌtrɑn, B 'pɔzɪtrɔn] *s.* (fís., quím.) positron, positón.
positronium [ˌpɑzə'troʊnɪəm, B ˌpɔz-] *s.* (fís.) positronio.
posology [pə'sɑlədʒɪ, B -'sɔl-] *s.* (med.) posología.
posse ['pɑsɪ, B 'pɔsɪ] *s.* 1. (der.) posse comitatus (grupo de civiles armados que el alguacil puede alistar para fines policiales). 2. cuerpo de alguaciles que vigila el orden público. 3. *(gang)* cuadrilla armada.
possess [pə'zɛs] *v.t.* 1. poseer, tener. 2. posesionar, poner en posesión. 3. poseer, dominar. 4. (ant.) tomar, prender.
possessed [-'zɛst] *a.* 1. poseído, poseso (de algún espíritu maligno, pasión o idea fija). 2. insano, enloquecido. 3. sereno, dueño de sí mismo. 4. **to be p. by,** ser poseído por.
possession [-zɛʃən] *s.* 1. posesión; (der.) tenencia. 2. posesión, propiedad, finca, predio; (*pl.*) posesiones, territorios. 3. posesión, apoderamiento del espíritu (por una personalidad extraña, demonio, pasión o idea). 4. serenidad, aplomo, sangre fría. 5. **in. p.,** poseído (cosa); posesor (persona); **in p. of.,** en posesión de; **in one's p.,** en su poder; **in the p. of,** poseído por; **to rejoice in the p. of,** tenner la buena suerte de poseer (algo); **to take p. of,** tomar posesión de.
possessional [-əl] *a.* posesional.
possession by entireties, (der.) posesión indivisa.
possessive [pə'zɛsɪv] *a.* 1. posesivo, posesorio, posesional. 2. dominante, egoísta (carácter, amor, etc.). 3. (gram.) posesivo. —*s.* caso posesivo; adjetivo o pronombre posesivo.
possessive adjective, (gram.) adjetivo posesivo.
possessively [-lɪ] *adv.* posesivamente, de manera posesiva, con aire dominante.
possessiveness [-nəs] *s.* carácter dominante.
possessive pronoun, (gram.) pronombre posesivo.
possessor [pə'zɛsər, B -ə] *s.* poseedor, posesor.
possessory [-ərɪ] *a* 1. posesorio, posesional. 2. poseyente, poseedor. 3. dominante.
posset ['pɑsət, B 'pɔs-] *s.* bebida caliente de leche cortada con vino o cerveza (que se usaba como remedio contra los resfriados, etc.).
possibility [ˌpɑsə'bɪlətɪ, B ˌpɔs-] *s.* (*pl.* POSSIBILITIES) 1. posibilidasd. 2. cosa posible; persona aceptable.
possible ['pɑsəbəl, B 'pɔs-] *a.* 1. posible, dable, realizable, practicable, factible, hacedero, permisible. 2. posible, eventual. 3. aceptable. 4. **as far as p.** o **as much as p.,** en lo posible; **as soon as p.,** cuanto antes; **to render p.,** posibilitar.
possibly [-blɪ] *adv.* posiblemente, con posibilidad, eventualmente; quizá, quizás.
possum ['pɑsəm, B 'pɔs-] *s.* (*forma abrev. de* **opossum**) **to play p.,** (fam.) hacerse el muerto; esconderse; proceder con suma cautela.
post [poʊst] *s.* 1. poste, pilar, columna. 2. estaca, palo. —*v.t.* 1. (t. con *up*) fijar, pegar (carteles o avisos). 2 anunciar en o divulgar por carteles. 3. anotar en una lista.
post, *s.* 1. (mil.) puesto, plaza; fuerte; guarnición. 2. (mil., G.B.) retreta, toque de clarín. 3. cargo, oficio. 4. (t. **trading p.**) factoría, establecimiento comercial (esp. en una colonia). —*v.t.* 1. apostar, situar, colocar (ej., un centinela). 2. destinar (a una plaza o mando).
post, *s.* 1. (pr. G.B.) correo (servicio y correspondencia); edificio de correos; buzón. 2. especie de papel de carta. 3. (ant.) estafeta, posta. —*v.i.* viajar por relevos; viajar de prisa. —*v.t.* 1. despachar por correo; echar al correo. 2. informar, tener al corriente. 3. (ten.) pasar (los asientos) al libro mayor; contabilizar. —*adv.* 1. por medio de postas. 2. a toda velocidad, rápidamente.
postage ['poʊstɪdʒ] *s.* franqueo, porte de correos.
postage due, franqueo a pager.
postage meter, franqueadora (de cartas, etc.).
postage stamp, sello de correo, estampilla (Amer.).
postal [-təl] *a.* postal, de correos. —*s.* (fam., E.U.) (*abrev. de* **p. card**) postal, tarjeta postal.
postal card, postal, tarjeta postal.
postal zone, zona postal.
postaxial [poʊst'æksɪəl] *a.* (anat.) postaxil.
postbellum [-'bɛləm] *a.* de postguerra, postbélico, esp. (E.U.) de después de la guerra civil.
postbox ['poʊstˌbɑks, B -ˌbɔks] *s.* buzón (de correos).
postboy [-ˌbɔɪ] *s.* postillón; correo, mensajero, propio.
postcard [-ˌkɑrd, B -kɑd] *s.* postal, tarjeta postal.
postcava [ˌpoʊst'kɑvə, B -'keɪ-] *s.* (fisiol.) postcava.
post chaise, (hist.) silla de posta, diligencia.
postdate ['poʊst'deɪt] *v.t.* poner fecha posterior a la presente, extender con fecha posterior, poner posfecha en.
postdated check, cheque a fecha.
postdiluvian [ˌpoʊstdə'luvɪən, B -daɪ-] *a.* postdiluviano. —*s.* ser postdiluviano.
posted ['poʊstəd] *a.* 1. al tanto de, enterado, al corriente. 2. (terreno) vedado, cerrado.
poster [-tər, B -tə] *s.* 1. cartel, aviso, letrero, anuncio, rótulo. 2. caballo de posta.
poste restante [ˌpoʊstɛs'tɑnt, B -'rɛstɑnt] (fr.) lista de correos.
posterior [pɑs'tɪrɪər, poʊs-, B pɔs'tɪərɪə] *a.* 1. posterior, subsiguiente. 2. posterior, trasero. 3. (bot.) superior, posterior. —*s.* nalgas, tafanario, trasero.
posteriority [-ˌtɪrɪ'ɔrətɪ, B -ˌtɪərɪ-] *s.* posterioridad.
posterity [pɑs'tɛrətɪ, B pɔs-] *s.* posteridad.
postern ['poʊstərn, 'pɑs-, B 'poʊstən] *s.* (raro) postigo, puerta trasera, entrada, particular. —*a.* posterior, trasero.
post exchange, (E.U., mil.) bazar militar, cantina.
postfix ['poʊstˌfɪks] *s.* (gram.) posfijo, postfijo, sufijo. — [poʊst'fɪks] *v.t.* agregar; (gram.) añadir (un sufijo).
post-free [-'fri] *a.* 1. con franquicia postal, libre de franqueo o porte (la correspondencia oficial, etc.). 2. (pr. G.B.) con porte pagado.
postganglionic [ˌpoʊstˌgæŋglɪ'ɑnɪk, B -'ɔn-] *a.* (med.) postganglionar.
postglacial [-'gleɪʃəl] *a.* (geol.) postglacial.
postgraduate [-'grædʒʊət, -ˌeɪt, B -'grædjʊɪt] *a., s.* postgraduado.
posthaste ['poʊst'heɪst] *s.* diligencia, prisa, rapidez. —*adv.* con diligencia, a toda prisa.

post horn, corneta de posta, clarín.
post house casa de postas, posta.
posthumous ['pɑstʃəməs, B 'pɔstjʊ-] *a.* póstumo; díc. del hijo que nace después de muerto el padre o de la obra que se publica después de muerto el autor.
posthypnotic [ˌpoʊsthɪp'nɑtɪk, B -'nɔt-] *a.* post-hipnótico.
postiche [pɔs'tiʃ] *a.* 1. postizo, artificial. 2. superfluo o recargado (en decoración).
postil ['pɑstɪl, B 'pɔs-] **postilion, postillion** [poʊs'tɪljən, pɑs-, B pəs-] *s.* postillón.
postimpressionism [ˌpoʊstɪm'prɛʃənɪzəm] *s.* (arte) postimpresionismo.
postimpressionist [-ɪm'prɛʃənəst] *s., a.* postimpresionista (artista, intérprete).
postimpressionistic [-ɪmˌprɛʃə'nɪstɪk] *a.* postimpresionista.
postliminium [-lɪ'mɪnɪəm] *s.* (der.) postliminio.
postliminy [-'lɪmənɪ] *s. var. de* **postliminium.**
postlude ['poʊstˌlud, B -ljud] *s.* (mús.) postludio, frase o movimiento que se toca al final de una composición.
postman ['poʊstmən] *s.* cartero.
postmarital [poʊst'mærətəl] *a.* posterior al matrimonio.
postmark ['poʊstˌmɑrk, B -mɑk] *s.* matasellos, sello (en cartas). —*v.t.* marcar (cartas) con matasellos, sellar.
postmaster [-ˌmæstər, B -ˌmɑstə] *s.* 1. administrador de correos. 2. (hist.) administrador de una estación para viajeros; el que suministraba caballos de posta.
postmaster general, (*pl.* POSTMASTERS GENERAL) directorgeneral de correos (en un país).
postmeridian [-mə'rɪdɪən] *a.* postmeridiano, de la tarde, después del mediodía.
post meridiem [-əm] en la tarde, después del mediodía.
postmillennial [-mə'lɛnɪəl] *a.* que sigue al milenio.
postmillennialism [-ˌɪzəm] *s.* creencia en la llegada de Cristo después del milenio.
postmistress ['poʊstˌmɪstrəs] *s.* administradora de correos.
postmortem [poʊst'mɔrtəm, B 'poʊst'-mɔtəm] *a.* postmórtem, que ocurre después de la muerte. —*s.* autopsia, necropsia.
postmortem examination, (med.) autopsia, necropsia, necroscopia.
postnasal ['poʊst'neɪzəl] *a.* (med.) postnasal.
postnasal drip, (med.) secreción crónica mucosa postnasal.
postnatal [ˌpoʊst'neɪtəl] *a.* postnatal, después del nacimiento.
postnuptial [-'nʌpʃəl] *a.* post-nupcial, postconnubial; posterior al matrimonio.
post-obit [-'oʊbət, B -'ɔb-] *a.* (gen. der.) vigente o que entra en vigencia después de la muerte.
post-obit bond, obligación pagadera después de la muerte.
post office, oficina de correos, correo, estafeta.
post office box, apartado de correos, casilla postal (Amer.).
post office order, (G.B.) orden postal, giro postal.
postoperative [ˌpoʊst'ɑpərətɪv, -əˌreɪt-, B -'ɔpərətɪv] *a.* (med.) postoperatorio.
postorbital [-'ɔrbətəl, B -'ɔb-] *a.* (anat.) postorbitario.
postpaid ['poʊst'peɪd] *a.* con porte pagado, con franqueo pagado.
postpalatal [poʊst'pælətəl] *a.* (fon.) postpalatal, pospalatal.
postpartum [-'pɑrtəm, B -'pɑtəm] *a.* (fisiol.) postparto.
postponable [-'poʊnəbəl] *a.* aplazable, diferible, dilatable.
postpone [-'poʊn] *v.t.* 1. aplazar, diferir, dilatar. 2. posponer, postergar. —*v.i.* (med.) tardar, retrasarse (fiebre, etc.).
postponement [-'poʊnmənt] *s.* 1. aplazamiento, diferimiento. 2. posposición, postergación.
postposition [ˌpoʊstpə'zɪʃən] *s.* (gram.) posposición.
postpositive [-'pɑzətɪv, B -'pɔz-] *a.* (gram.) pospositivo. —*s.* (gram.) partícula o palabra pospositiva, posposición.
postpositively [-lɪ] *adv.* (gram.) de modo pospositivo.
postprandial [poʊst'prændɪəl] *a.* de sobremesa.
postprandial speech, discurso de sobremesa.
post road, (ant.) camino por el que se llevaba el correo.
postscript ['poʊsˌskrɪpt] *s.* posdata, postdata, post scriptum.
postseason [poʊst'sizən] *a.* posterior a la temporada.
posttonic [-'tɑnɪk, B -'tɔn-] *a.* (gram.) postónica (sílaba).
posttraumatic [ˌpoʊsttrə'mætɪk, B -trɔ-] *a.* (med.) postraumático.
postulancy ['pɑstʃələnsɪ, B 'pɔstjə-] *s.* (*pl.* POSTULANCIES) (relig.) postulantado.
postulant [-lənt] *s.* (relig.) postulante, postulanta.
postulate ['pɑstʃələt, B 'pɔstjʊ-] *s.* postulado. —[-ˌleɪt] *v.t.* 1. postular, pretender, exigir, reclamar, demandar, requerir. 2. presuponer, dar por sentado.
postulation [ˌpɑstʃə'leɪʃən, B ˌpɔstjʊ-] *s.* 1. postulación. 2. postulado, suposición, supuesto.
postulator ['pɑstʃəˌleɪtər, B 'pɔstjʊ-ə] *s.* (relig.) postulador.
posture ['pɑstʃər, B 'pɔstʃə] *s.* 1. postura. 2. posición, situación. 3. condición, estado. —*v.t.* colocar en una postura. —*v.i.* 1. posar, asumir una postura. 2. pavonearse.
posturer [-tʃərər, B -tʃərə] *s.* 1. presuntuoso, fingidor. 2. acróbata, contorsionista.
postwar ['poʊst'wɔr, B -'wɔ] *a.* de postguerra.
posy ['poʊzɪ] *s.* (*pl.* POSIES) 1. mote, lema, inscripción. 2. ramillete de flores pequeñas.
pot [pɑt, B pɔt] *s.* 1. olla, caldera, puchero, marmita, pote. 2. maceta, tiesto. 3. caperuza, remate, sombrerete (de una chimenea). 4. (jer.) montón (de dinero, etc.). 5. (t. **p. shot**) tiro a mansalva. 6. puesta, pozo (en el juego). 7. (fam.) orinal, bacín, vaso de noche. 8. nasa (para coger peces, anguilas, langostas, etc.). 9. (jer.) mariguana, la yerba. 10. **to go to p.,** echarse a perder, descomponerse, desbaratarse; **to keep the p. boiling,** ganarse el sustento, mantener las cosas en pleno funcionamiento. —*v.t.* (*pret., p.p.* POTTED; *p.pr.* POTTING) 1. envasar; conservar en potes. 2. plantar en tiestos. 3. cazar para llenar la olla. 4. (billar) entronerar (una bola). 5. cocinar a fuego lento en cacerola. —*v.i.* disparar o tirar (a mansalva).
potability [ˌpoʊtə'bɪlətɪ] *s.* potabilidad.
potable ['poʊtəbəl] *a.* potable, bebedizo, bebestible. —*s.* (*pl.*) bebidas, bebestibles.
potableness [-nəs] *s.* potabilidad, calidad de bebestible.
potage [pɔ'tɑʒ] *s.* (fr.) potaje.
potash ['pɑtˌæʃ, B 'pɔt-] *s.* (quím.) 1. potasa; potasa cáustica. 2. potasio.
potassic [pə'tæsɪk] *a.* (quím.) potásico.
potassium [pə'tæsɪəm] *s.* (quím.) potasio.
potassium bromide, (quím.) bromuro potasico, bromuro de potasio.
potassium carbonate, (quím.) carbonato de potasio.
potassium chlorate, (quím.) clorato de potasio.
potassium chloride, (quím.) cloruro de potasio.
potassium cyanide, (quím.) cianuro de potasio.
potassium dichromate, (quím.) bicromato de potasio.
potassium hydroxide, (quím.) hidróxido de potasio.
potassium nitrate, (quím.) nitrato de potasio.
potassium permanganate, (quím.) permanganato de potasio.
potassium sulfate, (quím.) sulfato de potasio.
potation [poʊ'teɪʃən] *s.* 1. potación. 2. licor, bebida alcohólica.
potato [pə'teɪtoʊ] *s.* (*pl.* POTATOES) (bot.) patata, papa (Amer.) (planta y tubérculo); **a small p.,** (fam., fig.) persona o cosa de poca monta, nulidad.
potato beetle, p. bug, (ento.) chinche de la patata, dorífora.
potato blight, enfermedad de la patata.
potato chips, hojuelas de patatas fritas, patatas fritas a la inglesa, papas fritas (Amer.).
potato masher, pasapuré.
potato peeler, utensilio para mondar patatas.
potato rot, *var. de* **p. blight.**
potatory ['poʊtəˌtɔrɪ, B -tərɪ] *a.* 1. bebedor. 2. del beber.
potato slicer, cortadora de patatas.
potbellied ['pɑtˌbɛlɪd, B 'pɔt-] *a.* barrigón, barrigudo, panzón, panzudo.
potbelly [-ˌbɛlɪ] *s.* (*pl.* POTBELLIES) panza, barriga.
potboil [-ˌbɔɪl] *v.i.* escribir, componer o pintar para ganarse el sustento, prostituir uno su talento (para poder vivir).
potboiler [-ər, B -ə] *s.* (jer.) obra artística o literaria hecha únicamente para ganar dinero.
potboy [-ˌbɔɪ] *s.* (G.B., ant.) mozo, criado de posada (esp. el que sirve las bebidas).
pot cheese, requesón.
poteen [poʊ'tin] *s.* whiski irlandés destilado ilegalmente.
potence ['poʊtəns] *var. de* **potency.**
potency ['poʊtənsɪ] (*pl.* POTENCIES) *s.* 1. potencia, fuerza, fortaleza, vigor, energía. 2. potencia, potencialidad, posibilidad.
potent [-ənt] *a.* 1. potente, fuerte, poderoso. 2. potente, eficaz. 3. potente, viril, vigoroso. —*s.* (her.) potenza.
potent, *a.* (her.) potenzado.
potentate [-ənˌteɪt] *s.* potentado, soberano, monarca.
potential [pə'tɛnʃəl] *a.* 1. potencial, latente, posible. 2. (gram.) potencial. 3. (raro) potente, poderoso, influyente; eficaz. —*s.* 1. posibilidad, potencialidad. 2. (gram.) modo potencial. 3. (mat.) función potencial. 4. (fís.) potencial. 5. (elec.) potencial, voltaje, tensión.
potential barrier, (fís.) barrera de potencial.
potential energy, (fís.) energía potencial.
potential hole, (fís.) pozo de potencial.
potentiality [pəˌtɛnʃɪ'ælətɪ] *s.* (*pl.* POTENTIALITIES) potencialidad.
potentially [-'tɛnʃəlɪ] *adv.* potencialmente, virtualmente, en potencia.
potential transformer, (elec.) transformador de potencial.
potential vector, (mat.) potencial vector.
potential well, (fís.) pozo de potencial.

potentiate [pəˈtɛnʃɪˌeɪt] *v.t.* hacer potente, aumentar la potencia de (una droga, etc.).
potentilla [ˌpoʊtənˈtɪlə] *s.* (bot.) potentila, potentilla.
potentiometer [pəˌtɛnʃɪˈɑmətər, B -ˈɔmɪtə] *s.* (elec.) potenciómetro.
potently [ˈpoʊtəntlɪ] *adv.* potentemente, poderosamente.
potentness [-nəs] *s.* potencia, poder.
potful [ˈpɑtˌfʊl, B ˈpɔt-] *s.* (con *of*) una marmita u olla (llena de).
pothead [-ˌhɛd] *s.* (jer.) fumador de mariguana.
pothecary [ˈpɑθəˌkɛrɪ, B ˈpɔθɪkərɪ] *s.* (*pl.* POTHECARIES) (dial.) boticario, farmacéutico.
potheen, *var. de* **poteen.**
pother [ˈpɑðər, B ˈpɔðə] *s.* 1. nube sofocante de polvo, humo o vapor. 2. alboroto, baraúnda, bullicio. 3. alharaca, aspaviento. 4. **to make a p.,** hacer alharacas, hacer aspavientos. —*v.t.* acosar, molestar, confundir. —*v.i.* agitarse, inquietarse por pequeñeces.
potherb [ˈpɑtˌɜrb, B ˈpɔthɜb] *s.* hortalizas, hierba (usada como condimento).
potholder [-ˌhoʊldər, B -də] *s.* almohadilla, agarrador, agarradera (para pucheros, marmitas calientes, etc.).
pothole [-ˌhoʊl] *s.* 1. hoyo, hueco, poza (en los lechos rocosos de los ríos). 2. bache (en los caminos).
pothook [-ˌhʊk] *s.* 1. garabato, llares. 2. garabato (escritura mal trazada).
pothouse [-ˌhaʊs] *s.* cervecería, taberna, bodegón.
pothunter [-ˌhʌntər, B -tə] *s.* 1. cazador sin interés deportivo (que quiere sólo cobrar la pieza). 2. el que compite sólo con el objeto de ganar premios.
potion [ˈpoʊʃən] *s.* poción, brebaje, pócima, dosis.
potlatch [ˈpɑtˌlætʃ, B ˈpɔt-] *s.* 1. fiesta de invierno entre los indios de Norte América. 2. (fam.) fiesta o convite grande, a menudo con regalos; regalo, obsequio.
pot lead, *s.* (min.) grafito, plombagina, lápiz plomo. —*v.t.* **to p.-l.,** grafitar, untar o cubrir con grafito.
potlicker, potlikker [-ˈlɪkər, B -ə] *vars. de* **pot liquor.**
pot liquor, caldo, jugo de carne o verduras (esp. del que se puede hacer sopa).
potluck [ˈpɑtˈlʌk, B ˈpɔt-] *s.* comida ordinaria y sin ceremonias; **to take p.,** comer lo que haya; (fig.) aceptar lo que venga.
potman [-mən] *s.* mozo de fonda o posada, criado de taberna.
pot marigold, (bot.) caléndula, maravilla.
potpie [-ˈpaɪ] *s.* pastel de carne cocinada en olla, con una capa de pasta por encima.
potpourri [ˌpoʊpʊˈri, B poʊˈpʊrɪ] *s.* (fr.) 1. pebete (mezcla de pétalos secos y especias usada para perfumar una habitación). 2. popurrí, revoltillo, menjurje, baturrillo, mezcla confusa. 3. popurrí, miscelánea (musical).
pot roast, trozo de carne de res, perdigada y cocida a fuego lento.
potsherd [ˈpɑtˌʃɜrd, B ˈpɔtʃəd] *s.* 1. tiesto, cacharro. 2. (arqueol.) restos o residuos de cerámica.
potshot [-ˌʃɑt, B -ˈʃɔt] *s.* tiro al azar; **to take a p.** (o **potshots**) **at,** disparar al azar contra; (fig.) dirigir crítica casual contra (alguien); (fig., G.B.) intentar casualmente (empresa).
pottage [-ɪdʒ] *s.* (ant.) potaje, menestra, sopa espesa, guiso.
potted [-əd] *a.* 1. en maceta, ej., *p. palm,* palmera en maceta. 2. en conserva, ej., *p. shrimp,* camarones en conserva. 3. (fig.) condensado, muy resumido. 4. (jer.) ajumado, achispado, bebido. 5. **p. plants,** plantas en tiestos, plantas caseras; **p. meat,** carne aderezada y cocida en olla a fuego lento.
potter [-ər, B -ə] *s.* alfarero, ceramista.
potter, potterer [-ərər, B -ərə] *vars. de* **putter, putterer.**
potter's clay, p.'s earth, arcilla figulina, arcilla verde, arcilla de alfarero.
potter's field, hoyanca, fosa común.
potter's ware, alfarería, tiestos.
potter's wheel, rueda o torno de alfarero.
pottery [ˈpɑtərɪ, B ˈpɔt-] *s.* (*pl.* POTTERIES) 1. alfarería, cerámica. 2. vajilla de barro; cacharros. 3. tienda de alfarería, taller de cerámica.
pottle [ˈpɑtəl, B ˈpɔt-] *s.* 1. (ant.) azumbre (antigua medida de capacidad para líquidos equivalente a medio galón); vasija de medio galón; medio galón de vino o licor. 2. (G.B.) canastilla para frutas.
Pott's disease [pɑts-, B pɔts-] (med.) mal de Pott.
potty [ˈpɑtɪ, B ˈpɔtɪ] *a.* 1. (fam., G.B.) insignificante, trivial. 2. (jer., pr. G.B.) alocado, loco.
potty chair, *s.* silla con orinal debajo del asiento (para bebés).
pot-valiancy [-ˈvæljənsɪ] *s.* valor debido al licor, valor de borracho.
pot-valiant [-jənt] *a.* valentón o baladrón cuando está ebrio.
pouch [paʊtʃ] *s.* 1. bolsa pequeña, saquillo. 2. zurrón, morral. 3. bolsa postal, valija de correos; valija diplomática. 4. (zool.) bolsa (del canguro); abazón (de monos, murciélagos y roedores). 5. (esco.) bolsillo, faltriquera. —*v.t.* 1. formar una bolsa en. 2. poner en la valija de correos. 3. embolsar, meter en el bolsillo, embolsicar (Amer.). —*v.i.* 1. colgar como una bolsa (parte de un vestido). 2. abolsarse, formarse en una bolsa.
pouched rat [paʊtʃt-] (zool.) tuza.
pouchy [ˈpaʊtʃɪ] *a.* (POUCHIER; POUCHIEST) abolsado.
poudrette [puˈdrɛt] *s.* fertilizante compuesto.
pouf [puf] *s.* 1. rollo (de pelo). 2. puf (especie de taburete).
poularde, poulard [pʊˈlɑrd, B -ˈlɑd] *s.* (fr.) polla castrada y cebada.
poulard wheat, (bot.) trigo del milagro, trigo racimal, trigo redondillo.
poulp [pulp] *s.* (zool.) pólipo, pulpo.
poult [poʊlt] *s.* pavipollo; pollo (de gallina, faisan, etc.).
poulterer [ˈpoʊltərər, B -tərə] *s.* pollero, gallinero.
poultice [ˈpoʊltəs] *s.* cataplasma, emplasto, bizma. —*v.t.* bizmar, aplicar cataplasmas o emplastos.
poultry [ˈpoʊltrɪ] *s.* aves de corral.
poultry dealer, gallinero, recovero, pollero.
poultryman [-mən] *s.* recovero, pollero, gallinero, avicultor.
poultry manure, gallinaza (fertilizante).
poultry market, pollería.
poultry yard, corral, pollero, gallinero.
pounce [paʊns] *s.* 1. grasilla, arenilla. 2. carbón en polvo (en cisquero). —*v.t.* 1. empolvar, empolvorizar (con grasilla), estarcir (con carbón en polvo). 2. apomazar.
pounce, *v.i.* arrojarse, saltar; **p. on (upon** o **at),** calarse sobre, caer sobre (la presa un ave); abalanzarse sobre, arrojarse sobre; (fig.) coger en vuelo (oportunidad, etc.). —*s.* 1. salto súbito o inesperado (sobre algo). 2. zarpa, garra (de aves de presa).
pounce, *v.t.* 1. repujar (oro o plata). 2. (ant.) agujerear, picar, calar.
pounce bag, cisquero, muñequilla de estarcir.
pounce box, caja de grasilla.
pouncet-box [ˈpaʊnsətˌbɑks, B ˌ-ˌbɔks] *s.* (ant.) 1. bujeta, poma, cajita para perfumes. 2. caja de grasilla.
pound [paʊnd] *s.* 1. corral, redil, aprisco. 2. corral municipal (para encerrar animales errantes); depósito oficial. 3. encierro, prisión. 4. manga (red para pescar). —*v.t.* (ant.) acorralar, encerrar (ganado); llevar al depósito oficial.
pound, *s.* 1. libra (unidad de peso). 2. libra esterlina (unidad monetaria).
pound, *v.t.* 1. triturar, machacar, moler, pulverizar (con mano de mortero, etc.). 2. golpear, pegar, aporrear (con el puño, etc.); (fam.) cascar, dar una paliza a. 3. pisar el asfalto de, desempedrar (calles), hacer rondas en (la vecindad, etc. díc. de un policía). 4. **to pound the pavement,** (jer.) callejear (buscando empleo). —*v.i.* 1. (gen. con *at, away* u *on*) aporrear, pegar. 2. moverse o caerse con un ruido pesado y apagado. 3. pulsar fuertemente, latir con violencia. —*s.* choque, golpe, ruido sordo.
poundage [ˈpaʊndɪdʒ] *s.* comisión de tanto por libra esterlina; tasa de tanto por libra de peso; peso calculado en libras.
poundage, *s.* 1. embargo; retención (del ganado extraviado en un corral). 2. costo del rescate (del ganado acorralado).
poundal [-dəl] *s.* (fís.) poundal, unidad de fuerza.
pound cake, bizcocho sencillo sin más aderezo que unas pasas.
pounder [-dər, B -də] *s.* triturador, machacador.
pounder, *s.* (*ú. en palabras compuestas*) 1. algo de (cierto número de) libras, ej., *a three-p.,* un pescado de tres libras (de peso). 2. cañón de a (número de libras que pesa su proyectil), ej., *a twenty-p.,* un cañón de a veinte.
pound-foolish [ˈpaʊndˈfulɪʃ] *a.* derrochador en lo grande y ahorrativo en lo pequeño.
pound lock, corral de dos rejas.
pound net, nasa, buche (de pescar).
pound sterling, libra esterlina, unidad monetaria de Inglaterra.
pound troy, libra de 12 onzas.
pound weight, peso de una libra.
pour [pɔr, B pɔ] *v.t.* verter, vaciar; derramar; echar, escanciar (vino); **p. cold water on,** desalentar, desanimar, descorazonar; (fig.) aguar, frustrar (fiesta, reunión, etc.); **p. oil upon troubled waters,** apaciguar los ánimos; **p. out,** verter (líquido). —*v.i.* 1. fluir, manar, brotar, correr, caer copiosamente. 2. llover a cántaros, diluviar. 3. **it never rains but it pours,** cuando llueve, llueve a cántaros; lo malo se presenta a borbotones; **p. in,** llegar en abundancia (cartas, donativos, etc.); **p. into,** (fig.) entrar a montones en; **p. out** (o **forth**), salir a borbotones o a chorros, salir a montones. —*s.* 1. flujo. 2. caída copiosa (de lluvia).
pourboire [pʊrˈbwɑr, B ˈpʊəbwɑ] *s.* (fr.) propina.
pourer [ˈpɔrər, B -ə] *s.* vaciador, echador, escanciador, trasegador.
pouring [-ɪŋ] *a.* copioso, torrencial.
pourparler [pʊrpɑrˈleɪ, B pʊəˈpɑleɪ] *s.* (fr.) conferencia preliminar.
pour point, (quím.) temperatura de descongelación (de lubricantes), temperatura de fluidez crítica (de petróleos).
pourpoint [ˈpʊrˌpɔɪnt, B ˈpʊəˌ-] *s.* (fr., hist.) perpunte, jubón acolchado.
pour test, (quím., mec.) prueba de fluidez.

pousse-café [ˌpuskæ'feɪ] *s.* (fr.) (*pl.* POUSSE-CAFÉS) poscafé; copa con diversos licores dispuestos en capas separadas.
poussette [pu'sɛt] *s.* (fr.) ronda (baile).
pout [paʊt] *s.* (ict.) gado, zoarce, mustela de río, abadejo.
pout, *v.i.* hacer pucheros, enfurruñarse. —*v.t.* fruncir (los labios), hacer sobresalir (los labios). —*s.* 1. puchero. 2. (*pl.*) rabieta con pucheros.
pouter ['paʊtər, B -ə] *s.* (orn.) paloma buchona.
pouty [-ɪ] *a.* (POUTIER; POUTIEST) enfurruñado, murrio, resentido.
poverty ['pɑvərtɪ, B 'pɔvətɪ] *s.* 1. pobreza, indigencia, necesidad, privación, penuria, miseria. 2. pobreza, inopia, escasez, falta, carencia.
poverty-stricken [-strɪkən] *a.* pobretón, indigente, necesitado, de gran pobreza.
pow [paʊ] *s.* ¡paf! (sonido de un golpe o de una explosión).
P O W *abrev. de* **prisoner of war,** prisionero de guerra.
powder ['paʊdər, B -də] *s.* 1. polvo. 2. pólvora. 3. **to take a p.,** (jer.) tomar las de Villadiego, poner pies en polvorosa. —*v.t.* 1. empolvorar, empolvar, polvorear. 2. triturar, pulverizar. —*v.i.* 1. reducirse a polvo (sales). 2. usar polvo cosmético. 3. (dial.) darse prisa, precipitar el paso.
powder blue, 1. azulete. 2. color verde-azulado.
powder box, polvera, caja de polvos de tocador.
powder chest, jarra de pólvora.
powdered [-dərd, B -dəd] *a.* en polvo.
powder flask, frasco para pólvora.
powder horn, cuerno para pólvora, chifle.
powder keg, 1. cuñete de pólvora. 2. (fig.) polvorín.
powder magazine, 1. polvorín. 2. (mar.) santabárbara, pañol de la pólvora.
powder metallurgy, pulvimetalurgia.
powder mill, molino o fábrica de pólvora.
powder monkey, p. boy, (ant.) muchacho encargado de acarrear pólvora en los buques de guerra.
powder puff, borla (para empolvarse la cara).
powder room, lavabo para damas, lavabo de señoras; tocador.
powdery ['paʊdərɪ] *a.* 1. pulverulento, polvoroso, polvoriento, empolvado. 2. deleznable, friable, quebradizo.
power ['paʊər, B 'paʊə] *s.* 1. poder, poderío, fuerza, vigor, pujanza. 2. capacidad, habilidad, aptitud. 3. poder, potestad, autoridad, influencia. 4. potencia (nación). 5. (der.) poder, facultad, procura o procuración, mandato. 6. (mat.) potencia, exponente (de un número). 7. (mec., fís.) potencia, fuerza motriz, energía. 8. (ópt.) potencia (de un lente). 9. (dial., vulg.) multitud, montón. 10. (ant.) poderío naval o militar. 11. **I will do all in my p.,** haré todo lo posible (o todo lo que esté en mi poder); **in p.,** en el poder; **the powers that be,** las autoridades establecidas, los dirigentes; **to tax one's powers to the utmost,** exigir uno el máximo de sus facultades; **within one's p.,** en su poder, dentro de las posibilidades de uno.
power amplifier, (electrón.) amplificador de potencia.
powerboat [-ˌboʊt] *s.* lancha a motor, lancha de motor, motora.
power brakes, servofrenos.
power cable, (elec.) cable para transporte de fuerza, cable de transmisión.
power company, empresa de fuerza motriz.
power dive, (mil., aer.) picado con motor.
power-dive [-ˌdaɪv] *v.i.* (mil., aer.) picar (el avión) a toda marcha.
power drill, taladro, perforadora mecánica.
power driven, accionado mecánicamente, motorizado.
power factor, factor de potencia.
power failure, corte de corriente, apagón.
power feed, alimentación mecánica.
powerful ['paʊərfəl, B 'paʊəfəl] *a.* poderoso, potente, pujante, vigoroso, influyente, fuerte, eficaz, enérgico.
powerfully [-fəlɪ] *adv.* poderosamente, potentemente, fuertemente, eficazmente.
powerhouse [-ˌhaʊs] *s.* 1. estación de fuerza, central de fuerza, central eléctrica. 2. (fig.) persona de mucha energía. 3. (naipes) buena mano. 4. (dep.) un excelente equipo. 5. (fig.) fuente de talento (universidades, ciertas empresas clave, etc.).
power input, potencia alimentadora.
power lathe, torno de mecánico.
powerless [-ləs] *a.* 1. impotente, ineficaz; inepto, incapaz. 2. sin autoridad, que no tiene poder.
powerlessly [-lɪ] *adv.* impotentemente, ineficazmente.
powerlessness [-nəs] *s.* impotencia, ineficacia.
power line, línea de transmisión, línea de fuerza eléctrica.
power loading, (mec.) carga por caballo o por unidad de potencia.
power loom, telar mecánico.
power of appointment, (der.) facultad de nombrar; poder de disponer de bienes raíces.
power of attorney, (der.) poder notarial, procuración, mandato.
power output, (elec.) potencia de salida; potencia disponible.
power pack, (rad.) fuente de alimentación.
power plant, 1. planta de fuerza, central de energía; central eléctrica. 2. (aut., aer.) grupo motor.
power play, 1. (dep.) juego en que se usa la ofensiva con concentración de jugadores en un área determinada. 2. estrategia o maniobra en que se hace uso o despliegue de poder con fines coercitivos.
power politics, diplomacia respaldada por la (amenaza de) fuerza.
power press, prensa mecánica.
power rating, potencia nominal.
power saw, motosierra, sierra mecánica.
power shovel, pala mecánica, excavadora.
power station, central de fuerza motriz, central eléctrica.
power steering, (aut.) servodirección, dirección asistida.
power supply, suministro de fuerza.
power take off, (aut.) toma de fuerza.
power tool, herramienta a motor, herramienta eléctrica.
power transmission, (elec.) transmisión de energía.
power tube, (rad.) válvula generadora; (elec.) tubo de vacío generador de corriente alterna.
power unit, unidad de potencia, unidad motriz.
powwow ['paʊˌwaʊ] *s.* 1. ceremonia hechicera propia de los indios de Norte-américa 2. (fam., E.U.) conferencia. 3. (fam.) fiesta, tertulia. —*v.i.* (fam.) conferenciar.
pox [pɑks, B pɔks] *s.* 1. erupción pustulosa (de la piel). 2. (ant.) sífilis. 3. **a p. on him** ¡maldito sea!
pozzolana [ˌpɑtsə'lɑnə, B ˌpɔt-] **pozzolan** [-'lɑn] **pozzuolana** [-swə'lɑnə] *s.* (min.) puzolana, pucelana.
pozzolanic [-'lɑnɪk] *a.* puzolánico.
pp. *abrev. de* **pages,** páginas.
P.Q. *abrev. de* **Province of Quebec,** Provincia de Quebec, Canadá.
Pr *símb. de* **praseodymium,** praseodimio (Pr).
P.R. *abrev. de* **Puerto Rico,** Puerto Rico.
practic ['præktɪk] (ant.) *s.* práctica. —*a.* práctico.
practicability [ˌpræktɪkə'bɪlətɪ] *s.* viabilidad.
practicable ['præktɪkəbəl] *a.* 1. practicable, factible, posible. 2. transitable, viable. 3. (teat.) utilizable.
practicableness [-nəs] *s.* viabilidad.
practicably [-blɪ] *adv.* factiblemente, posiblemente.
practical ['præktɪkəl] *a.* 1. práctico, útil, conveniente. 2. práctico, pragmático. 3. virtual.
practicality [ˌpræktɪ'kælətɪ] *s.* 1. sentido práctico. 2. utilidad práctica, viabilidad.
practical joke, burla o broma pesada.
practically ['præktɪkəlɪ] *adv.* 1. prácticamente, útilmente. 2. virtualmente, en efecto.
practical nurse, enfermera no diplomada.
practice, practise ['præktəs] *v.t.* 1. practicar, ejercitarse en, hacer ejercicios de. 2. adiestrar, ejercitar. 3. poner en práctica, practicar. 4. emplear de costumbre (cortesía, etc.); hacer (ej., caridad). 5. practicar, ejercer (una profesión). 6. **p. what you preach,** predique con el ejemplo. —*v.i.* 1. adiestrarse, ejercitarse. 2. practicar, ejercer. 3. (ant.) tramar, intrigar, conspirar. —*s.* 1. práctica, costumbre, uso, hábito. 2. práctica, ejercicio (para aprender algo); eficiencia. 3. ejercicio (de una profesión). 4. clientela, ej., *a large p.,* una clientela numerosa. 5. estratagema, trama. 6. (der.) práctica, procedimiento. 7. **in p.,** en la práctica; **to be out of p.,** estar falto de práctica; **to keep in p.,** mantenerse en ejercicio, mantenerse bien entrenado; **to make a p. of,** hacer(una) costumbre de.
practiced, practised [-təst] *a.* experto, experimentado, diestro, hábil.
practicer, practiser [-təsər, B -tɪsə] *s.* practicante, practicador.
practitioner [præk'tɪʃənər, B -nə] *s.* profesional; esp. médico.
praedial ['pridɪəl] *a.* predial.
praemunire [ˌprimjʊ'naɪrɪ] *s.* (der., G.B.) provisión o ejecutoria para ciertas ofensas; castigo o pena que se impone por dichas ofensas.
praenomen [pri'noʊmən] *s.* (*pl.* PRAENOMINA [-'nɑmənə, B -'nɔm-] o PRAENOMENS) (hist.) prenombre.
praetor ['pritər, B -ə] *s.* (hist.) pretor, magistrado.
praetorial [prɪ'tɔrɪəl] *a.* pretorial.
praetorian [-ən] *a.* (hist.) 1. pretoriano, pretorial. 2. **P.,** pretoriano (guardia). —*s.* 1. pretor. 2. **P.,** pretoriano.
praetorship ['pritərˌʃɪp, B -əˌ-] *s.* (hist.) pretoria.
pragmatic [præg'mætɪk] *a.* 1. pragmático, práctico. 2. (ant.) dogmático. 3. oficioso, entremetido. 4. (filos.) pragmático, pragmatista. —*s.* 1. (hist.) sanción pragmática. 2. entremetido.
pragmatical [-ɪkəl] *a.* 1. pragmático, práctico. 2. oficioso, entremetido. 3. dogmático.
pragmatically [-ɪkəlɪ] *adv.* 1. de modo pragmático, prácticamente. 2. oficiosamente. 3. dogmáticamente.
pragmatics [-ɪks] *s. pl.* (*sing. o pl. en const.*) (filos.) pragmática.
pragmatic sanction, sanción pragmática (de un soberano).
pragmatism ['prægmətɪzəm] *s.* pragmatismo.
Prague [prɑg] *s.* Praga, capital de Checoslovaquia.
prairie ['prɛrɪ, B 'prɛərɪ] *s.* llanura, planicie, llano, pampa (Amer.), sabana (Amer.).

prairie chicken, (orn.) chachalaca de las praderas.
prairie dog, (especie de) marmota de las praderas.
prairie schooner, (E.U.) galera o carromato en que viajaban los colonizadores americanos.
prairie wolf, coyote.
praise [preɪz] *v.t.* alabar, loar, encomiar, ensalzar, encarecer, exaltar, elogiar. —*s.* alabanza, loa, encomio, elogio; **to sing the p.** (o **praises**) **of,** cantar las alabanzas de; **to win oneself high p.,** hacerse merecedor de grandes elogios.
praiser ['preɪzər, B -ə] *s.* alabador, loador, ensalzador, elogiador.
praiseworthily [-ˌwɜrðəlɪ, B -ˌwɜðɪ-] *adv.* laudablemente, loablemente.
praiseworthy [-ˌwɜrðɪ, B -ˌwɜðɪ] *a* laudable, loable.
Prakrit ['prɑkrɪt] *s.* pracrito, una de las antiguas lenguas de la India.
praline ['prɑlin, 'preɪ-, B 'prɑ-] *s.* almendra tostada y garapiñada; chocolate praliné.
pralltriller ['prɑlˌtrɪlər, B -ə] *s.* (mús.) trino ternario.
pram [prɑm] *s.* bote de fondo chato o plano.
pram [præm] *s. forma abrev. de* **perambulator.**
prance [præns, B prɑns] *v.i.* 1. cabriolar, corvetear, gambetear, trenzar (el caballo). 2 alardear, pavonear(se). —*v.t.* hacer cabriolar o corvetear a un caballo. —*s.* cabriola, corveta, gambeta, trenzado.
prancer ['prænsər, B 'prɑnsə] *s.* caballo que corvetea.
prandial ['prændɪəl] *a.* (hum.) prandial, relativo a una comida.
prang [præŋ] (jer., G.B.) *s.* 1. caída violenta (de avión). 2. hazaña, proeza. —*v.t.* destruir, bombardear (un blanco); derribar (un avión enemigo). —*v.i.* estrellarse (avión).
prank [præŋk] *s.* travesura, picardía, jugarreta. —*v.i.* travesear, hacer picardías.
prank, *v.t.* hermosear, engalanar, acicalar; **p. oneself,** emperejilarse, vestirse llamativamente. —*v.i.* pavonear, jactarse.
prankish ['præŋkɪʃ] *a.* travieso, pícaro, juguetón.
prankishly [-lɪ] *adv.* traviesamente, pícaramente, juguetonamente.
prankishness [-nəs] *s.* carácter travieso, disposición juguetona.
prankster [-stər, B -stə] *s.* bromista.
prase [preɪz] *s.* (min.) prasio.
praseodymium [ˌpreɪzioʊ'dimɪəm] *s.* (quím.) praseodimio.
prat [præt] *s.* (jer.) nalgas, trasero.
prate [preɪt] *v.t.* decir o expresar (algo) de modo parlero. —*v.i.* parlotear, charlar, parrafear. —*s.* cháchara.
prater ['preɪtər, B -ə] *s.* hablador, charlatán.
pratfall ['prætˌfɔl] *s.* (jer.) caída de nalgas.
pratincole ['prætɪŋkoʊl] *s.* (orn.) pratincola.
prating ['preɪtɪŋ] *a.* charlatán, gárrulo, chacharero.
pratique [præ'tik, B 'prætik] *s.* (mar.) libre platica; certificado de sanidad (que se da a buques).
prattle ['prætəl] *v.i.* parlotear, charlar, paliquear (como los niños). —*v.t.* expresar (algo) a la manera de los niños. —*s.* parloteo infantil; cháchara.
prattler ['prætlər, B -lə] *s.* charlador, parlanchín.
prau [praʊ] *s.* prao, bote malayo.
prawn [prɔn] *s.* camarón, quisquilla, esquila. —*v.i.* pescar camarones.
prawner ['prɔnər, B -ə] *s.* pescador de camarones.
praxis ['præksəs] *s.* (*pl.* PRAXES [-ˌsiz]) práctica, experiencia (en artes, ciencias o técnica).
Praxiteles [præk'sɪtəˌliz] *s.* Praxíteles, célebre escultor de la Grecia antigua.
pray [preɪ] *v.t.* (*pret., p.p.* PRAYED; *p.pr.* PRAYING) rogar, pedir, implorar, suplicar; **p. consider,** sírvase considerar; **what can we do with this, p.?** ¿qué podemos hacer con esto, por favor? —*v.i.* rezar, orar, decir sus oraciones; **p. for,** rezar por.
prayer [prɛr, B prɛə] *s.* 1. oración, rezo, plegaria (a Dios). 2. súplica, ruego, imploración. 3. **to say one's prayers,** rezar sus oraciones.
prayer beads, rosario, camándula.
prayer book, libro de oraciones, devocionanario (esp. de la iglesia anglicana).
prayer desk, reclinatorio.
prayerful ['prɛrfəl, B 'prɛəfəl] *a.* piadoso, devoto.
prayerfulness [-nəs] *s.* devoción.
prayer meeting, reunión para rezar.
prayer rug, alfombrilla oriental (para rezar arrodillado).
prayer wheel, molinillo de oraciones (de los lamaístas).
praying mantis, (ento.) mantis religiosa, rezador, predicador, mamboretá (Amer.).
preacceleration [ˌpriəkˌsɛlə'reɪʃən] *s.* (fís. nuclear) preaceleración.
preach [pritʃ] *v.i.* predicar, sermonar, sermonear. —*v.t.* 1. exhortar, aconsejar, ej., *p. patience,* aconsejar paciencia. 2. predicar (el evangelio). 3. pronunciar, decir (un sermón). 4. **p. to the winds,** (fam.) predicar en el desierto.
preacher ['pritʃər, B -tʃə] *s.* predicador (esp. sacerdote).
preachify [-tʃəˌfaɪ] *v.i.* (*pret., p.p.* PREACHIFIED; *p.pr.* PREACHIFYING) (fam.) predicar o sermonear molestamente, echar sermones; moralizar (de modo aburrido).
preaching [-tʃɪŋ] *s.* predicación, prédica, sermón. —*a.* sermoneador (tono, voz, etc.).
preachment ['pritʃmənt] *s.* 1. sermón, prédica. 2. arenga aburrida.
preachy ['pritʃɪ] *a.* (PREACHIER; PREACHIEST) sermoneador.
preadamite [pri'ædəˌmaɪt] *s.* preadamita. —*a.* preadamítico, rel. a lo que antecedió a Adán y Eva.
preamble ['priˌæmbəl, B pri'æm-] *s.* preámbulo, introducción, prefacio.
preamplifier [pri'æmpləˌfaɪər, B -ə] *s.* (rad.) preamplificador.
prearrange [ˌpriə'reɪndʒ] *v.t.* arreglar de antemano, predisponer, prever, prevenir.
prearrangement [-mənt] *s.* disposición o arreglo previo.
preassembled [-ə'sɛmbəld] *a.* prearmado, preensamblado.
preassigned [-ə'saɪnd] *a.* previamente asignado.
preatomic [-ə'tɑmɪk, B -'tɔm-] *a.* preatómico.
preaxial [-'æksɪəl] *a.* (anat.) preaxil, preaxial.
prebend ['prɛbənd] *s.* prebenda (renta eclesiástica).
prebendary [-ənˌdɛrɪ, B -dərɪ] *s.* (*pl.* PREBENDARIES) prebendado.
Pre-Cambrian [pri'kæmbrɪən] *a., s.* (geol.) precámbrico.
precancel [-'kænsəl] *v.t.* (*pret., p.p.* PRECANCELED O PRECANCELLED; *p.pr.* PRECANCELING O PRECANCELLING) cancelar de antemano (sellos postales).
precancerous [-'kænsərəs] *a.* (med.) precanceroso.
precarious [prɪ'kɛrɪəs, B -'kɛər-] *a.* 1. precario, inestable; incierto. 2. precario, inseguro.
precariously [-lɪ] *adv.* precariamente.
precariousness [-nəs] *s.* condición precaria, carácter precario.
precast [pri'kæst, B -'kɑst] *a.* (ing.) prevaciado, premoldado.
precative ['prɛkətɪv] **precatory** [-ˌtɔrɪ, B -tərɪ] *a.* suplicante, implorante.
precaution [prɪ'kɔʃən] *s.* precaución, prudencia, cautela.
precautionary [-ˌɛrɪ, B -ərɪ] **precautional** [-əl] *a.* precautorio, de precaución; preventivo.
precautious [prɪ'kɔʃəs] *a.* precavido, cauteloso, cauto.
precava [ˌpri'kɑvə, B -'keɪ-] *s.* (*pl.* PRECAVAE [-vi]) (anat.) precava.
precede [pri'sid] *v.t., v.i.* preceder, anteceder.
precedence ['prɛsədəns, B pri'sidəns] *s.* precedencia, prioridad; **to take** (o **have**) **p. over,** tener prioridad sobre.
precedency [-ənsɪ] *var. de* **precedence.**
precedent [prɪ'sidənt] *a.* precedente. — ['prɛsɪdənt] *s.* 1. precedente, antecedente. 2. (der.) precedente. 3. **without p.,** sin precedente.
preceding [prɪ'sidɪŋ] *a.* precedente, que precede, anterior.
precensor ['pri'sɛnsər, B -sə] *v.t.* censurar previamente, someter a censura previa (una publicación o película).
precentor [prɪ'sɛntər, B -tə] *s.* (relig.) chantre.
precentorial [ˌprisɛn'tɔrɪəl] *a.* de sochantre.
precentorship [prɪ'sɛntərˌʃɪp, B -təˌ-] *s.* oficio de sochantre.
precept ['prisɛpt] *s.* 1. precepto, mandamiento, regla. 2. (der.) mandato judicial.
preceptive [prɪ'sɛptɪv] *a.* preceptivo; instructivo.
preceptively [-lɪ] *adv.* preceptivamente.
preceptor [-tər, B -tə] *s.* preceptor, maestro; esp. director de colegio.
preceptorial [ˌprisɛp'tɔrɪəl] *a.* preceptoral.
preceptress [prɪ'sɛptrəs] *s.* preceptora, profesora, maestra.
precession [prɪ'sɛʃən] *s.* precesión, precedencia.
precinct ['prisɪŋkt] *s.* 1. recinto, (*pl.*) inmediaciones, alrededores. 2. límite, linde, frontera. 3. distrito, barrio.
preciosity [ˌprɛʃɪ'ɑsətɪ, B -'ɔs-] *s.* (*pl.* PRECIOSITIES) preciosismo, amaneramiento, afectación (esp. al hablar).
precious ['prɛʃəs] *a.* 1. precioso, caro, costoso. 2. precioso, preciado. 3. querido, ej., *my p.,* mi querido. 4. melindroso, amanerado, refinado. 5. consumado, insigne. 6. considerable, mucho. —*adv.* (fam.) muy.
preciously [-lɪ] *adv.* preciosamente; con remilgo; oficiosamente.
preciousness [-nəs] *s.* preciosidad.
precious stone, gema, piedra preciosa.
precipice ['prɛsəpəs] *s.* precipicio, abismo, sima.
precipitable [prɪ'sɪpətəbəl] *a.* precipitable.
precipitance [-təns] **precipitancy** [-tənsɪ] *s.* precipitación, atolondramiento, apresuramiento.
precipitant [-tənt] *a.* precipitado, atropellado, temerario. —*s.* (quím.) precipitante.
precipitantly [-lɪ] *adv.* precipitadamente.
precipitate [prɪ'sɪpətət] *a.* precipitado, temerario; apresurado, atropellado, alocado. —*s.* (quím.) precipitado. — [-ˌteɪt] *v.t.* 1. precipitar, arrojar, despeñar. 2. precipitar, apresurar, acelerar; causar, provocar. 3. (fís., meteor.) producir (rocío, lluvia, etc.). 4. (quím.) precipitar; producir (un precipitado). —*v.i.* 1. precipitarse, arrojarse, despeñarse. 2. precipitarse, apresurarse. 3. (quím.) precipitarse, depositarse.

precipitately [prɪ'sɪpətətlɪ] *adv.* precipitadamente.
precipitateness [-nəs] *s.* precipitación.
precipitation [prɪˌsɪpə'teɪʃən] *s.* 1. precipitación, atropellamiento, apresuramiento, impetuosidad. 2. (quím.) precipitación; precipitado. 3. (meteor.) precipitación (lluvia, nieve, etc.).
precipitative [prɪ'sɪpəˌteɪtɪv, B -tətɪv] *a.* precipitante.
precipitator [-ˌteɪtər, B -tə] *s.* (quím.) precipitante.
precipitin [-tən] *s.* (med.) precipitina.
precipitinogen [prɪˌsɪpə'tɪnədʒən] *s.* (med.) precipitinógeno, precipitógeno.
precipitous [prɪ'sɪpətəs] *a.* 1. precipitoso, empinado, escarpado. 2. precipitoso, precipitado, atropellado.
precipitously [-lɪ] *adv.* precipitosamente, precipitadamente.
précis [preɪ'si, B 'preɪsi] *s.* (fr.) (PRÉCIS) resumen, compendio, sumario.
precise [prɪ'saɪs] *a.* 1. preciso, inequívoco, claro. 2. preciso, exacto, estricto, justo. 3. meticuloso, puntilloso, escrupuloso.
precisely [-lɪ] *adv.* 1. precisamente, justamente, exactamente. 2. meticulosamente.
preciseness [-nəs] *s.* precisión; exactitud.
precisian [prɪ'sɪʒən] *s.* rigorista, formulista (esp. en lo religioso). —*a.* rigorista.
precisianism [-ˌɪzəm] *s.* rigorismo, formulismo.
precision [prɪ'sɪʒən] *s.* precisión, exactitud. —*a.* de precisión, exacto.
precision bombing, (mil.) bombardeo de precisión.
precision gauges, calibradores de precisión.
preclinical [pri'klɪnɪkəl] *a.* (med.) preclínico.
preclude [prɪ'klud] *v.t.* evitar, excluir; impedir, prevenir, imposibilitar.
preclusion [-'kluʒən] *s.* prevención, imposibilitación.
preclusive [-'klusɪv] *a.* impeditivo, exclusivo.
precocious [prɪ'koʊʃəs] *a.* precoz.
precociously [-lɪ] *adv.* precozmente.
precociousness [-nəs] **precocity** [-'kɑsətɪ, B -'kɔs-] *s.* precocidad.
precognition [ˌprikɑg'nɪʃən, B -kɔg-] *s.* precognición.
pre-Columbian [-kə'lʌmbɪən] *a.* precolombino.
preconceive [-kən'siv] *v.t.* preconcebir.
preconception [-kən'sɛpʃən] *s.* 1. preconcepción, idea preconcebida. 2. prejuicio; predisposición.
preconcert [-kən'sɜrt, B -'sɜt] *v.t.* concertar o acordar de antemano.
precondition [-kən'dɪʃən] *s.* condición previa. —*v.t.* condicionar de antemano.
preconization [-kənə'zeɪʃən, B -naɪ-] *s.* (relig.) preconización.
preconize ['prikəˌnaɪz] *v.t.* preconizar, encomiar públicamente; (relig.) preconizar.
preconscious [pri'kɑntʃəs, B -'kɔnʃəs] *a.* (med.) preconsciente.
precook [pri'kʊk] *v.t.* precocer, guisar previamente un alimento (para conservar o servirlo más tarde).
precritical [pri'krɪtɪkəl] *a.* (med.) precrítico.
precursive [prɪ'kɜrsɪv, B -'kɜsɪv] *a.* precursor, premonitorio.
precursor [-sər, B -sə] *s.* precursor.
precursory [-sərɪ] *a.* precursor, preliminar; premonitorio.
predacious, predaceous [prɪ'deɪʃəs] *a.* predador, de rapiña, rapaz.
predaciousness, predaceousness [-nəs] **predacity** [-'dæsətɪ] *s.* rapacidad.
predate [pri'deɪt] *v.t.* antedatar.
predation [prɪ'deɪʃən] *s.* (ecología) conducta predatoria; (raro) depredación.
predator ['prɛdətər, B -tə] *s.* (zool.) predator.
predatoriness [-ˌtɔrɪnəs, B -tərɪ-] *s.* rapacidad.
predatory [-ˌtɔrɪ, B -tərɪ] *a.* 1. predatorio. 2. predator, de rapiña, de presa, rapaz.
predecease [ˌpridɪ'sis] *v.i.* premorir. —*v.t.* morir antes que (otro).
predecesor ['prɛdəˌsɛsər, B 'pri-ə] *s.* 1. predecesor, antecesor. 2. (ant.) antepasado.
predesignate [pri'dɛzɪgˌneɪt] *v.t.* preelegir, designar o señalar de antemano.
predesignation [ˌpridɛzɪg'neɪʃən] *s.* prefijación.
predestinarian [priˌdɛstə'nɛrɪən, B -'nɛər-] *s.* creyente en la predestinación. —*a.* relativo a la predestinación.
predestinarianism [-ˌɪzəm] *s.* doctrina de la predestinación.
predestinate [pri'dɛstəˌneɪt] *a.* predestinado. —*v.t.* predestinar.
predestination [-ˌdɛstə'neɪʃən] *s.* predestinación; (teo.) predestinación.
predestine [-'dɛstən] *v.t.* predestinar.
predetermination [ˌpridɪˌtɜrmə'neɪʃən, B -ˌtɜmɪ-] *s.* predeterminación.
predeterminative [pridɪ'tɜrməˌneɪtɪv, B -'tɜmənə-] *a.* predeterminante.
predetermine [-mən] *v.t.* predeterminar.
predial, *var. de* **praedial.**
predicable ['prɛdɪkəbəl] *a.* predicable. —*s.* (lóg.) predicable.
predicament [prɪ'dɪkəmənt] *s.* 1. apuro, situación difícil. 2. (lóg.) predicamento.
predicant ['prɛdɪkənt] *a.* predicante. —*s.* predicador, orador sagrado.
predicate ['prɛdəˌkeɪt] *v.t.* 1. predicar, proclamar. 2. afirmar (un predicado). 3. (con *upon*) basar o fundar (acción, declaración, etc.) 4. implicar, denotar, significar. 5. (ant.) predecir, presagiar.[-kət] *a.* 1. predicado. 2. (gram.) que pertenece al predicado; que requiere (palabra) atributo. —*s.* (lóg., gram.) predicado.
predicate nominative, (gram.) predicado nominal.
predication [ˌprɛdə'keɪʃən] *s.* afirmación, aserción; (lóg.) predicación.
predicative ['prɛdɪˌkeɪtɪv, B prɪ'dɪkət-] *a.* predicativo.
predicatory [-kəˌtɔrɪ, B -tə-] *a.* predicador.
predict [prɪ'dɪkt] *v.t.* predecir, pronosticar, profetizar.
predictable [-əbəl] *a.* fácil de predecir; pronosticable.
prediction [-'dɪkʃən] *s.* predicción, pronóstico, profecía.
predictive [-tɪv] *a.* que predice; profético.
predictively [-lɪ] *adv.* proféticamente.
predictor [-tər, B -tə] *s.* (mil.) predictor, mecanismo de predicción (de cañón antiaéreo).
predigest [ˌpridə'dʒɛst, -daɪ-] *v.t.* (med.) digerir de antemano.
predigestion [-dʒɛstʃən] *s.* (med.) predigestión.
predilection [ˌprɛdəl'ɛkʃən, B ˌpri-] *s.* predilección; preferencia, parcialidad.
predispose [ˌpridɪs'poʊz] *v.t.* predisponer, inclinar.
predisposition [-ˌdɪspə'zɪʃən] *s.* predisposición, propensión; susceptibilidad.
predominance [prɪ'dɑmənəns, B -'dɔm-] **predominancy** [-nənsɪ] *s.* predominio, ascendiente, preponderancia.
predominant [-nənt] *a.* predominante, preponderante; prevaleciente.
predominantly [-lɪ] *adv.* predominantemente.
predominate [-ˌneɪt] *v.i.* predominar, prevalecer, preponderar.
predomination [prɪˌdɑmə'neɪʃən, B -ˌdɔm-] *s.* predominación, predominancia, ascendiente.
preeminence [pri'ɛmənəns] *s.* preeminencia; superioridad.
preeminent [-nənt] *a.* preeminente; superior, sublime.
preeminently [-lɪ] *adv.* preeminentemente.
preempt [pri'ɛmpt] *v.t.* adquirir a base de derecho de prioridad; apropiarse de (algo) en forma exclusiva. —*v.i.* (bridge) hacer una declaración o apertura preventiva.
preemption [-'ɛmpʃən] *s.* 1. prioridad; derecho de prioridad. 2. adquisición o apropiación por derecho de prioridad.
preemptive [-tɪv] *a.* 1. de prioridad. 2. (bridge) preventivo.
preemptor [-tər, B -tə] *s.* comprador por derecho de prioridad.
preen [prin] *v.t.* 1. limpiar y componer (sus plumas las aves). 2. **p. oneself,** atildarse, componerse, emperejilarse; mostrarse muy satisfecho o pagado (de sí mismo). —*v.i.* arreglarse (las plumas) con el pico; emperejilarse.
preen, *s.* (dial.) alfiler; broche.
preengage [ˌpriɪn'geɪdʒ] *v.t.* apalabrar, obligar o empeñar de antemano.
preestablish [-ə'stæblɪʃ] *v.t.* preestablecer.
preexist [-ɪg'zɪst] *v.i.* preexistir, existir antes.
preexistence [-əns] *s.* preexistencia, existencia anterior (esp. del alma).
preexistent [-ənt] *a.* preexistente.
prefab ['pri'fæb] *s.* estructura prefabricada. —[pri'fæb] *v.t.* prefabricar.
prefabricate [pri'fæbrəˌkeɪt] *v.t.* prefabricar.
prefabricated [-ˌkeɪtəd] *a.* prefabricado.
prefabrication [ˌprifæbrə'keɪʃən] *s.* prefabricación.
preface ['prɛfəs] *s.* 1. prefacio, prólogo. 2. **P.,** (relig.) prefacio (parte anterior al canon). —*v.t.* 1. prologar, poner un prólogo a. 2. introducir; anunciar, ser precursor de.
prefatorial [ˌprɛfə'tɔrɪəl] *a.* prologal, introductorio, como prefacio.
prefatorily [-əlɪ] *adv.* a modo de prefacio.
prefatory ['prɛfəˌtɔrɪ, B -tərɪ] *a.* prologal, introductorio, como prefacio.
prefect ['priˌfɛkt] *s.* prefecto.
prefectural [pri'fɛktʃərəl] *a.* prefectural.
prefecture ['prifɛktʃər, B -tjʊə] *s.* prefectura.
prefer [prɪ'fɜr, B -'fɜ] *v.t.* (*pret., p.p.* PREFERRED; *p.pr.* PREFERRING) 1. preferir. 2. (con *against*) presentar, formular contra (cargo, reclamo, etc.). 3. (der.) dar preferencia o prioridad a. 4. (ant.) preferir, ascender, promover.
preferable ['prɛfərəbəl] *a.* preferible, preferente.
preferably [-blɪ] *adv.* preferiblemente, preferentemente.
preference ['prɛfərəns] *s.* 1. preferencia. 2. promoción, ascenso. 3. (der.) prioridad o preferencia (para recibir pago de una obligación).
preference stock, (com., G.B.) acciones preferidas, acciones de preferencia.
preferent [-rənt] *a.* preferente.
preferential [ˌprɛfə'rɛntʃəl, B -'rɛnʃəl] *a.* preferente, preferencial, de preferencia.
preferential assignment, (der.) cesión con prioridades.
preferential debts, (der.) deudas privilegiadas.

preferentialism [-ˌɪzəm] *s.* (com.) política de aranceles preferenciales.
preferentially [-əlɪ] *adv.* preferentemente.
preferential shop, fábrica o establecimiento que emplea obreros sindicados.
preferential tariff, (com.) aranceles preferenciales.
preferential voting, (pol.) voto preferencial.
preferment [prɪˈfɜrmənt, B -ˈfɜmənt] *s.* 1. promoción, ascenso. 2. presentación (de acusación, cargo, etc.).
preferred [-ˈfɜrd, B -ˈfɜd] *a.* preferido.
preferred stock, (com., E.U.) acciones preferidas, acciones de preferencia.
prefiguration [priˌfɪgjəˈreɪʃən] *s.* prefiguración, prototipo.
prefigure [priˈfɪgjər, B -ˈfɪgə] *v.t.* 1. prefigurar. 2. predecir, prenunciar.
prefigurement [-mənt] *s.* prefiguración.
prefix [ˈpriˌfɪks] *s.* (gram.) prefijo. — [priˈfɪks] *v.t.* 1. anteponer; colocar al principio; poner a manera de prefijo. 2. (ant.) prefijar, fijar de antemano.
prefixal [-ˌfɪksəl] *a.* (gram.) de prefijo, prefijal.
prefixally [-əlɪ] *adv.* (gram.) como prefijo.
prefixion [ˌprifɪkˈseɪʃən] *s.* (gram.) prefijación.
prefloration [-ˌfloˈreɪ-] *s.* (bot.) prefloración.
prefoliation [-ˌfoʊlɪˈeɪ-] *s.* (bot.) prefoliación.
preform [ˈpriˈfɔrm, B -ˈfɔm] *v.t.* preformar.
preformation [ˌprifɔrˈmeɪʃən, B -fɔˈ-] *s.* preformación, formación previa.
prefrontal [priˈfrʌntəl] *a.* (anat.) prefrontal.
preganglionic [ˌprigæŋglɪˈɑnɪk, B -ˈɔn-] *a.* (med.) preganglionar.
pregnability [ˌprɛgnəˈbɪlətɪ] *s.* condición de expugnable, vulnerabilidad.
pregnable [ˈprɛgnəbəl] *a.* expugnable, vulnerable.
pregnancy [ˈprɛgnənsɪ] *s.* (*pl.* PREGNANCIES) preñez, embarazo, gravidez.
pregnant [-nənt] *a.* 1. preñada, embarazada, encinta, grávida. 2. (fig.) (gen. con *with*) preñado, prolífico, fecundo, lleno. 3. significativo, importante.
pregnantly [-lɪ] *adv.* de modo significativo, de manera alusiva; abundantemente, fecundamente.
preheat [priˈhit] *v.t.* precalentar.
prehensile [prɪˈhɛnsəl, B -saɪl] *a.* (zool.) prensil.
prehensility [priˌhɛnˈsɪlətɪ] *s.* capacidad prensil.
prehension [prɪˈhɛntʃən, B -ˈhɛnʃən] *s.* 1. (zool.) prensión. 2. comprensión, entendimiento, percepción.
prehistoric [ˌprihɪsˈtɔrɪk] **prehistorical** [-ɪkəl] *a.* prehistórico.
prehistory [priˈhɪstərɪ] *s.* prehistoria.
preignition [ˌpriɪgˈnɪʃən] *s.* (mot.) preignición, preencendido.
prejudge [priˈdʒʌdʒ] *v.t.* prejuzgar, juzgar de antemano.
prejudgment, prejudgement [-mənt] *s.* prejuicio.
prejudice [ˈprɛdʒədəs] *s.* 1. perjuicio, menoscabo, daño. 2. prejuicio, parcialidad, idea preconcebida, ej., *racial p,* prejuicio racial. 3. **without p.,** (der.) sin perjuicio, sin menoscabo, sin detrimento de derecho. —*v.t.* 1. (der.) perjudicar, menoscabar, dañar. 2. predisponer, prevenir, preocupar.
prejudicial [ˌprɛdʒəˈdɪʃəl] *a.* perjudicial, dañoso, lesivo.
prejudicially [-əlɪ] *adv.* perjudicialmente.
prejudicious [-əs] *a.* perjudicial, lesivo.
prelacy [ˈprɛləsɪ] *s.* (*pl.* PRELACIES) 1. prelacía. 2. cuerpo de prelados. 3. gobierno (de la iglesia) por prelados.
prelate [-ət] *s.* prelado.
prelatic [prɪˈlætɪk] *a.* prelaticio, de prelado.
prelature [ˈprɛləˌtʃʊr, B -tʃə] *s.* prelatura, prelacía.
prelect [prɪˈlɛkt] *v.i.* disertar públicamente, dar una conferencia.
prelection [-ˈlɛkʃən] *s.* disertación, conferencia.
prelector [-tər, B -tə] *s.* conferencista, disertante.
prelibation [ˌprilaɪˈbeɪʃən] *s.* goce anticipado.
prelim [ˈpriˌlɪm, B prɪˈlɪm] *a.,* s. (fam.) (*forma abrev. de* **preliminary**) preliminar.
preliminarily [prɪˈlɪməˌnɛrəlɪ, B -nər-] *adv.* preliminarmente, como preliminar.
preliminary [prɪˈlɪməˌnɛrɪ, B -nərɪ] *a.* preliminar, introductorio, preparatorio. —*s.* (*pl.* PRELIMINARIES) preliminar, preparativo; (*pl.*) exámenes preliminares.
preliminary design, (mercadotecnia) anteproyecto.
prelude [ˈprelˌjud, ˈpreɪˌlud, B ˈprɛljud] *s.* 1. preludio, prelusión. 2. (mús.) preludio. —*v.t.* 1. preludiar; servir de introducción a, proveer de preludio. 2. introducir, presagiar. —*v.i.* (mús.) tocar una introducción o preludio.
prelusion [prɪˈluʒən] *s.* prelusión, preludio; introducción.
prelusive [-sɪv] **prelusory** [-sərɪ] *a.* previo, introductorio, preparatorio.
prelusively [-sɪvlɪ] **prelusorily** [-sərəlɪ] *adv.* como preludio o introducción.
premarital [priˈmærətəl] *a.* premarital, prenupcial.
premature [ˌpriməˈtʊr, -ˈtʃʊr, B ˌprɛməˈtjʊə] *a.* prematuro, temprano, extemporáneo.
prematurely [-lɪ] *adv.* prematuramente.
prematureness [-nəs] **prematurity** [-ətɪ, B -ˈtjʊərɪtɪ] *s.* calidad de prematuro; precipitación.
premaxilla [ˌprimækˈsɪlə] *s.* (*pl.* PREMAXILLAE [-ˌi]) *s.* (anat., zool.) premaxilar.
premaxillary [priˈmæksəˌlɛrɪ, B -mækˈsɪlərɪ] *a., s.* (*pl.* PREMAXILLARIES) (pr. G.B.) (anat., zool.) premaxilar.
premed [ˈpriˈmɛd] *a.* (fam.) premédico.
premedical [priˈmɛdɪkəl] *a.* preparatorio para el estudio de la medicina.
premeditate [prɪˈmɛdəˌteɪt] *v.t., v.i.* premeditar.
premeditated [-əd] *a.* premeditado.
premeditatedly [-lɪ] *adv.* premeditadamente, con premeditación.
premeditative [-ɪv, B -tətɪv] *a.* premeditado, caracterizado por premeditación.
premeditation [ˌprimɛdəˈteɪʃən] *s.* premeditación.
premenstrual [priˈmɛnstrʊəl] *a.* (fisiol.) premenstrual.
premier [prɪˈmɪr, B ˈprɛmjə] *a.* primero, principal; capital. —*s.* primer ministro, presidente del consejo (de ministros).
premiere [prɪˈmjɛr, B ˈprɛmɪɛə] *s.* estreno (de una película, etc.). —*a.* sobresaliente, principal. —*v.t.* estrenar. —*v.i.* ser estrenado.
premiership [prɪˈmɪrˌʃɪp, B ˈprɛmjəˌ-] *s.* cargo del primer ministro, presidencia del consejo (de ministros).
premillennial [ˌpriməˈlɛnɪəl] *a.* anterior al milenario: que viene antes del milenario (díc. esp. del segundo advenimiento de Cristo).
premise [ˈprɛməs] *s.* 1. (lóg.) premisa. 2. (*pl.*) (der.) asertos, aserciones anteriores; observaciones preliminares (de una escritura o título de dominio). 3. (*pl.*) local, establecimiento, predio rústico o urbano. 4. off **the premises,** fuera del local o terreno. —*v.t.* sentar o establecer como premisa, exponer anticipadamente, presuponer, asumir (algo) como cierto o preexistente.
premium [ˈprimɪəm] *s.* (*pl.* PREMIUMS O PREMIA [-ə]) 1. premio, recompensa; bonificación, gratificación. 2. com.) prima, premio. 3. prima (de seguro). 4. **at a p.,** a premio, sobre la par; muy solicitado, difícil de conseguir; **to put a p. on (something),** dar mayor importancia a, apreciar más (algo). —*a.* de primera calidad.
premix [priˈmɪks] *v.t.* premezciar.
premolar [-ˈmoʊlər, B -lə] *a., s.* (anat., zool.) premolar.
premonish [-ˈmɑnɪʃ, B -ˈmɔn-] *v.t., v.i.* prevenir o advertir con anticipación.
premonition [ˌpriməˈnɪʃən] *s.* 1. premonición, presentimiento, corazonada. 2. advertencia, prevención.
premonitory [priˈmɑnəˌtɔrɪ, B -ˈmɔnɪtərɪ] *a.* premonitorio.
Premonstratensian [ˌpriˌmɑnstrəˈtɛntʃən, B -ˌmɔn-ˈtɛnʃən] *s.* premonstratense.
premorse [prɪˈmɔrs, B -ˈmɔs] *a.* (bot., ento.) premorso.
premunition [ˌprimjʊˈnɪʃən] *s.* premunición.
prenatal [priˈneɪtəl] *a.* prenatal.
prenatally [priˈneɪtəlɪ] *adv.* antes del nacimiento.
prenominate [-ˈnɑmənət, B -ˈnɔm-] *a.* (ant.) susodicho, sobredicho.
prenotion [priˈnoʊʃən] *s.* 1. prenoción, preconcepción, idea preconcebida. 2. presentimiento, premonición.
preoccupancy [-ˈɑkjəpənsɪ, B -ˈɔk-] *s.* 1. ocupación previa. 2. preocupación.
preoccupation [-ˌɑkjəˈpeɪʃən, B -ˌɔk-] *s.* preocupación.
preoccupied [-ˈɑkjəˌpaɪd, B -ˈɔk-] *a.* 1. preocupado, absorto, distraído. 2. ocupado anticipadamente.
preoccupy [-ˌpaɪ] *v.t.* (*pret., p.p.* PREOCCUPIED; *p.pr.* PREOCCUPYING) 1. preocupar, absorber, distraer. 2. preocupar, ocupar antes (que otro).
preoperative [-ˈɑpərətɪv, B -ˈɔp-] *a.* (med.) preoperatorio.
preoral [priˈɔrəl] *a.* (zool.) preoral.
preordain [ˌpriɔrˈdeɪn, B ˈpriɔˈ-] *v.t.* preordinar.
preordination [-ˌɔrdəˈneɪʃən, B -ˌɔd-] *s.* (teo.) preordinación.
prep [prɛp] *s.* 1. colegio o curso preparatorio; (G.B.) escuela primaria. 2. (G.B.) deber, tarea, trabajo escolar. —*v.i.* (*pret., p.p.* PREPPED; *p.pr.* PREPPING) seguir un curso preparatorio; (G.B.) asistir a la escuela primaria, recibir primera enseñanza.
prepackage [priˈpækɪdʒ] *v.t.* preempaquetar.
prepaid [priˈpeɪd, B ˈpri-] *a.* 1. pagado por adelantado. 2. pagado, ej. *freight p.,* flete pagado. 3. con porte pagado.
preparation [ˌprɛpəˈreɪʃən] *s.* 1. preparación. 2. (farm.) preparado, preparación.
preparative [prɪˈpærətɪv] *a.* preparativo, preparatorio. —*s.* preparativo, preparación.
preparatorily [-ˌtɔrəlɪ, B -tərɪlɪ] *adv.* preparatoriamente.
preparatory [-ˌtɔrɪ, B -tərɪ] *a.* preparatorio, preliminar; introductivo; **p. to,** antes de.
preparatory school, 1. colegio o curso preparatorio. 2. (G.B.) escuela primaria.

prepare [prɪ'pær, -'pɛr, B -'pɛə] *v.t.* 1. preparar, disponer, alistar, aprestar. 2. preparar, confeccionar (alimentos, etc.). 3. **to be prepared (to do),** estar dispuesto (a hacer). —*v.i.* hacer preparativos; prepararse, alistarse; **p. for action,** (mil.) entrar en batería (la artillería); (imper.) ¡en batería!

preparedness [-ədnəs, B -'pɛəd-] *s.* preparación, apresto; (mil.) estado de preparación.

preparer [-ər, B -'pɛərə] *s.* preparador.

prepay [pri'peɪ, B 'pri-] *v.t.* antepagar, pagar por adelantado, pagar anticipadamente.

prepayment [-mənt] *s.* pago adelantado, pago anticipado.

prepense [prɪ'pɛns] *a.* premeditado; **with malice p.,** (der.) con premeditación y alevosía.

preponderance [-'pɑndərəns, B -'pɔn-] **preponderancy** [-ənsɪ] *s.* preponderancia, predominio.

preponderant [-ənt] *a.* preponderante, predominante, prevaleciente.

preponderantly [-lɪ] *adv.* predominantemente, en su gran mayoría.

preponderate [-dəˌreɪt] *v.t.* 1. preponderar, pesar más. 2. prevalecer, predominar.

preponderating [-ɪŋ] *a.* preponderante, predominante.

preposition [ˌprɛpə'zɪʃən] *s.* (gram.) preposición.

prepositional [-əl] *a.* preposicional, prepositivo.

prepositionally [-əlɪ] *adv.* prepositivamente, de manera preposicional.

prepositive [prɪ'pɑzətɪv, B -'pɔz-] *a.* (gram.) prepositivo.

prepossess [ˌpripə'zɛs] *v.t.* 1. predisponer (esp. favorablemente). 2. preocupar, ocupar antes que otro.

prepossessing [-ɪŋ] *a.* agradable, simpático, atractivo.

prepossessingly [-lɪ] *adv.* agradablemente.

prepossession [-'zɛʃən] *s.* 1. prejuicio, predisposición, (esp. a favor de algo o alguien). 2. preocupación, concentración.

preposterous [prɪ'pɑstərəs, B -'pɔs-] *a.* absurdo, ridículo; descabellado, disparatado.

preposterously [-lɪ] *adv.* absurdamente, ridículamente.

preposterousness [-nəs] *s.* ridiculez, (lo) absurdo.

prepotency [prɪ'poʊtənsɪ] *s.* prepotencia, preponderancia.

prepotent [-ənt] *a.* prepotente, dominante, predominante.

prepotently [-lɪ] *adv.* prepotentemente.

prep school, forma abrev. de **preparatory school,** escuela preparatoria.

prepuce ['priˌpjus] *s.* (anat.) prepucio.

preputial [pri'pjuʃəl] *a.* (anat.) prepucial.

Pre-Raphaelite [pri'ræfiəˌlaɪt, -'reɪfiə-, B 'pri'ræfə-] *a., s.* (arte) prerrafaelista.

prerecord [ˌpriri'kɔrd, B -'kɔd] *v.t.* pregrabar, grabar de antemano, grabar con anterioridad.

prerecorded [-əd] *a.* pregrabado; (rad., t.v.) en diferido.

prerequisite [pri'rɛkwəzət, B 'pri-] *a.* necesario de antemano; esencial como condicion previa. —*s.* requisito previo, requisito prescrito de antemano.

prerogative [prɪ'rɑgətɪv, B -'rɔg-] *s.* prerrogativa, privilegio. —*a.* 1. privilegiado (derecho, etc.). 2. de privilegios (registro, procedimiento, etc.).

Pres. *abrev. de* 1. **President,** Presidente. 2. **Presbyterian,** presbiteriano.

presage ['prɛsɪdʒ] *s.* 1. presagio, agüero, augurio. 2. presentimiento, corazonada. 3. (ant.) predicción, profecía. — ['prɛsɪdʒ, prɪ'seɪdʒ] *v.t.* 1. presagiar, vaticinar, predecir. 2. presentir, barruntar.

presanctified [pri'sæŋktɪˌfaɪd] *a.* presantificado.

presbyope ['prɛzbɪˌoʊp] *s.* (med.) presbiope.

presbyopia [ˌprɛzbɪ'oʊpɪə] *s.* (med.) presbiopía, presbicia.

presbyopic [-'ɑpɪk, B -'ɔp-] *a.* (med.) presbiópico, présbite, présbita.

presbyter ['prɛzbətər, B -ə] *s.* (relig.) presbítero.

presbyterate [prɛz'bɪtərət] *s.* presbiterado.

presbyterial [ˌprɛzbə'tɪrɪəl, B -'tɪər-] *a.* presbiteral.

Presbyterian [-ɪən] *a., s.* presbiteriano.

Presbyterianism [-ˌɪzəm] *s.* (relig.) presbiterianismo.

presbytery ['prɛzbəˌtɛrɪ, B -tərɪ] *s.* 1. presbiterio (area del altar mayor). 2. tribunal eclesiástico de los presbiterianos. 3. parroquia, rectoría (residencia del sacerdote).

presbytic [prɛz'bɪtɪk] *a.* (med.) présbita.

preschool ['pri'skul] *a.* preescolar. — ['priˌskul] *s.* jardín de infancia, de infantes (Amer.).

prescience ['priʃɪəns, 'prɛʃ-, B 'prɛs-] *s.* presciencia.

prescient [-ɪənt] *a.* presciente.

presciently [-lɪ] *adv.* con presciencia.

prescind [prɪ'sɪnd] *v.t., v.i.* (con *from*) prescindir (de), omitir; separar, abstraer.

prescribe [prɪ'skraɪb] *v.t.* 1. prescribir, preceptuar, ordenar. 2. recetar (una medicina o un tratamiento). —*v.i.* 1. dictar, tener la dirección. 2. escribir recetas (médicas). 3. (der.) prescribir.

prescript ['priˌskrɪpt] *a.* prescrito, ordenado. —*s.* regla, ordenanza, precepto.

prescriptible [prɪ'skrɪptəbəl] *a.* prescriptible.

prescription [-'skrɪpʃən] *s.* 1. prescripción; orden, regla, precepto. 2. (med.) prescripción, receta. 3. (der.) prescripción (liberatoria adquisitiva).

prescriptive [-tɪv] *a.* 1. preceptivo. 2. (der.) de prescripción, debido a prescripción. 3. (p. ext.) acostumbrado, establecido.

prescriptive grammar, gramática normativa.

presence ['prɛzəns] *s.* 1. presencia, asistencia; interesencia. 2. presencia, porte, apariencia. 3. efecto de realismo (del sonido reproducido). 4. **in the p. of,** en presencia de.

presence chamber, (G.B.) salón de audiencia.

presence of mind, presencia de ánimo, serenidad.

present [-ənt] *a.* 1. presente, actual, corriente. 2. (gram.) presente (tiempo verbal). 3. (ant.) sereno, instantáneo, inmediato. 4. **at the p. time,** al presente, hoy, en la actualidad; **to be p.,** estar presente, asistir, concurrir. —*s.* 1. (con *the*) lo presente, la actualidad. 2. (gram.) presente. 3. (*pl.*) (der.) la(s) presente(s), ej. *by these presents,* por la presente (escritura, etc.). 4. **at p.,** ahora, al presente; **for the p.,** por lo presente, por ahora, temporalmente.

present [prɪ'zɛnt] *v.t.* 1. presentar, introducir. 2. presentar, regalar, obsequiar. 3. presentar, representar, exponer, poner, poner a consideración; exhibir, mostrar. 4. (relig.) presentar, nominar, proponer (para un beneficio). 5. (der.) denunciar, acusar. 6. (mil.) presentar (armas). 7. **p. itself,** ofrecerse, surgir (oportunidad, etc.); **p. oneself,** presentarse, apersonarse; comparecer; **p. with,** obsequiar con. — ['prɛzənt] *s.* presente, regalo, obsequio; **to make a p. of (something) to (someone),** regalar, obsequiar (algo) a (alguien).

presentability [-ˌzɛntə'bɪlətɪ] *s.* buena presencia.

presentable [-'zɛntəbəl] *a.* presentable; bien apersonado; de buena presencia.

presentableness [-nəs] *s.* buena presencia.

presentation [ˌpriˌzɛn'teɪʃən, B ˌprɛ-] *s.* presentación; (relig., filos., med., com.) presentación; **on p.,** (com.) a presentación, a la vista.

presentation copy, ejemplar de cortesía ejemplar de regalo con dedicatoria.

presentative [prɪ'zɛntətɪv] *a.* 1. presentativo. 2. (relig.) que se inviste por presentación (díc. de un beneficio). 3 (filos., psic.) perceptible, sensible; intuitivo, perceptivo.

present-day ['prɛzənt'deɪ] *a.* de hoy en día, actual.

presentee [ˌprɛzən'ti] *s.* 1. persona presentada en la corte. 2. persona recomendada (para un oficio, empleo, etc.). 3. (relig.) presentado.

presenter [prɪ'zɛntər, B -ə] *s.* presentador, presentante.

presentiment [-'zɛntəmənt] *s.* presentimiento, presagio.

presently ['prɛzəntlɪ] *adv.* 1. pronto, dentro de poco, al cabo. 2. (E.U.) presentemente, al presente; ahora, ya. 3. (ant.) en seguida, de inmediato.

presentment [prɪ'zɛntmənt] *s.* 1. exposición, manifestación. 2. (com.) presentación (de un documento). 3. (der.) acusación, denuncia. 4. (filos.) presentación o representación (de una imagen); imagen. 5. (teat.) representación. 6. retrato; semejanza, parecido.

present participle, (gram.) gerundio.

present perfect, (gram.) pretérito perfecto.

present tense, (gram.) tiempo presente.

preservable [prɪ'zɜrvəbəl, B -'zɜvə-] *a.* preservable, conservable.

preservation [ˌprɛzər'veɪʃən, B -ə'veɪ-] *s.* preservación, conservación, reservación.

preservative [prɪ'zɜrvətɪv, B -'zɜvə-] *a.* preservativo; antiséptico, de preservación, de conservación. —*s.* (agente) preservativo, profiláctico.

preserve [-'zɜrv, B -'zɜv] *v.t.* 1. preservar, resguardar, proteger. 2. guardar, mantener. 3. (cocina) conservar, curar, confitar. —*s.* 1. (*gen. pl.*) conserva (de alimentos); confitura. 2. coto, vedado, reserva. 3. (fig.) propiedad exclusiva; derechos exclusivos.

preserver [-ər, B -ə] *s.* preservador, reservador.

preset [pri'sɛt] *v.t.* prefijar, preestablecer.

preshrunk ['pri'ʃrʌŋk] *a.* (tej.) pre-encogido.

preside [prɪ'zaɪd] *v.i.* presidir, dirigir.

presidency ['prɛzədənsɪ] *s.* presidencia.

president [-dənt] *s.* presidente.

presidential [ˌprɛzə'dɛntʃəl, B -'dɛnʃəl] *a.* presidencial.

presidentship ['prɛzədəntˌʃɪp] *s.* presidencia.

presider [prɪ'zaɪdər, B -ə] *s.* presidente, dirigente.

presidial [prɪ'sɪdɪəl] **presidiary** [-ɪˌɛrɪ, B -ɪərɪ] *a.* de presidio; dotado de guarnición.

presidio [-ɪˌoʊ] *s.* (*pl.* PRESIDIOS) presidio, guarnición; fortaleza, puesto, plaza (en territorio español).

presidium [-ɪəm] *s.* (*pl.* PRESIDIA [-ɪə]) presidium, comité administrativo y gubernamental de carácter permanente, propio de los países comunistas; **P.,** presidium del Soviet Supremo en Rusia.

presignify [pri'sɪgnəˌfaɪ] *v.t.* significar o indicar con anterioridad; predecir.

pre-Socratic [ˌprisə'krætɪk] *a.* (filos.) presocrático.

press [prɛs] *v.t.* 1. apretar. 2. compeler, obligar, forzar. 3. prensar, exprimir, estrujar. 4. planchar (la ropa). 5. persuadir, instar, importunar; apresurar, apremiar, acuciar, urgir. 6. recalcar, subrayar; insistir en (punto de vista, etc.). 7. (ant.) atestar, llenar, amontonar. 8. **to be pressed for (time, funds,** etc.), estar con apuros, justo o escaso de (tiempo, fondos, etc.). —*v.i.* 1. apresurarse. 2. apretarse, apiñarse. 3. (con *on* o *upon*) pesar, abrumar. 4. importunar, ser importuno; apremiar, urgir. 5. planchar, alisar (bien o mal, una tela, ropa, etc.). 6. **p. for,** insistir en; **p. forward,** arremeter, avanzar; **p. on,** avanzar de prisa; **p. through (the crowd,** etc.), abrirse camino entre (la muchedumbre, etc.). —*s.* 1. presión, apretón, apiñamiento. 2. muchedumbre, multitud. 3. prensa, máquina impresora. 4. imprenta; impresión. 5. **the p.,** la prensa; periodismo. 6. prensa (de raqueta, etc.). 7. (dep.) levantamiento con apoyo. 8. **to go to p.,** entrar en prensa; **to have good (bad) p. reports,** tener buena (mala) prensa; **to send to (the) p.,** mandar imprimir.

press, *s.* (hist.) reclutamiento, leva, enganche. —*v.t.* levar, enganchar, reclutar; **p. into service,** poner a trabajar.

press agent, agente de prensa o de propaganda, agente de publicidad.

pressboard [ˈprɛsˌbɔrd, B -ˌbɔd] *s.* cartón prensado, cartón de Fuller.

press box, tribuna de la prensa, cabina de prensa.

press clipping, recorte de periódico.

press conference, conferencia de prensa, rueda de prensa.

presser [ˈprɛsər, B -ə] *s.* 1. prensador; satinador; planchador. 2. pisacostura, prensatela (de máquina de coser); prensa (de uña, carne, etc.).

press gallery, tribuna de prensa, galería de los periodistas.

press-gang [-ˌgæŋ] *s.* (hist.) patrulla de reclutamiento, patrulla de leva.

pressing [-ɪŋ] *a.* 1. urgente, apremiante. 2. importuno, insistente, pesado. —*s.* 1. prensadura; prensado (de un disco fonográfico). 2. planchado (de la ropa); satinaje (del papel); estampado (de chapas).

pressingly [-lɪ] *adv.* importunamente, insistentemente.

pressman [-mən] *s.* 1. prensista; impresor. 2. (G.B.) periodista, reportero.

pressmark [-ˌmɑrk, B -ˌmɑk] *s.* (G.B.) número de clasificación (de un libro en la biblioteca).

press money, (mil.) prima de enganche, prima de leva.

press of sail, p. of canvas, (mar.) máximo velamen (que un barco puede desplegar), fuerza de vela.

pressor [ˈprɛsər, B -ə] *a.* (fisiol.) presor.

press proof, prueba de imprenta.

press release, comunicado o boletín de prensa; informe a la prensa.

press roll, rodillo de presión, cilindro.

pressroom [-ˌrum, -ˌrʊm] *s.* taller de prensas.

press roundup, rueda de prensa.

pressrun [-ˌrʌn] *s.* tirada, tiraje, tiro, tirada de ejemplares.

pressure [ˈprɛʃər, B -ə] *s.* 1. presión, compresión. 2. peso, carga, opresión. 3. presión, apremio, urgencia. 4. (elec.) tensión, voltaje. 5. **to bring p. to bear upon, to exert p. on,** ejercer presión sobre. —*v.t.* ejercer presión sobre.

pressure cabin, (aer.) cabina a presión, cabina de sobrepresión, cabina anticlimática, cabina presurizada.

pressure circuit, (elec.) circuito derivado, circuito de voltaje.

pressure coil, (elec.) bobina de voltaje, bobina en derivación.

pressure-cook [-ˌkʊk] *v.t., v.i.* cocer o cocinar en olla de presión.

pressure cooker, olla de presión.

pressure gauge, indicador de presión, manómetro.

pressure group, (pol.) grupo de presión, grupo de interés.

pressure nozzle, (aer.) tobera de presión.

pressure point, (med.) punto de presión.

pressure pump, bomba de presión.

pressure regulator, (mec.) regulador de presión; (elec.) regulador de tensión.

pressure suit, (aer.) vestido presurizado.

pressure tube, (quím.) probeta de presión.

pressure valve, válvula de presión.

pressure welding, soldadura por presión, soldadura a presión.

pressure wire, (elec.) alambre de derivación.

pressurize [ˈprɛʃəˌraɪz] *v.t.* (aer.) presurizar.

pressurized cabin [-ˌraɪzd-] (aer.) cabina a presión, cabina de sobrepresión, cabina anticlimática, cabina presurizada.

presswork [ˈprɛsˌwɜrk, B -ˌwɜk] *s.* 1. (impr.) impresión, trabajo tipográfico. 2. (ebanistería) encolado de chapas.

prest [prɛst] *s.* (ant.) préstamo, adelanto de sueldo. —*a.* (ant.) presto, listo, pronto.

prester [ˈprɛstər, B -tə] *s.* (ant.) preste, sacerdote, presbítero.

presternum [priˈstɜrnəm, B -ˈstɜnəm] *s.* (anat.) presternón.

prestidigitation [ˌprɛstəˌdɪdʒəˈteɪʃən] *s.* prestidigitación, juego de manos.

prestidigitator [-ˈdɪdʒəˌteɪtər, B -ə] *s.* prestidigitador.

prestige [prɛsˈtiʒ, -ˈtidʒ, B -ˈtiʒ] *s.* prestigio, renombre, fama.

prestigious [-ˈtɪdʒəs] *a.* prestigioso; ilustre, insigne.

prestissimo [prɛsˈtɪsəˌmoʊ] *adv.* (mús.) prestissimo, en tiempo muy rápido.

presto [ˈprɛstoʊ] *adv.* 1. presto, rápidamente, prestamente. 2. (mús.) presto, en tiempo rápido. —*a.* presto, pronto. —*s.* (mús.) presto.

prestressed [priˈstrɛst] *a.* prefatigado, precomprimido (hormigón).

presumable [prɪˈzuməbəl, B -ˈzjum-] *a.* presumible.

presumably [-blɪ] *adv.* probablemente, presuntamente.

presume [prɪˈzum, B -ˈzjum] *v.t.* 1. presumir, dar por sentado, suponer. 2. atreverse. 3. asumir. —*v.i.* 1. presumir, actuar u obrar presuntuosamente. 2. **p. on** (o **upon**), abusar de.

presumedly [-ədlɪ] *adv.* probablemente, presuntamente.

presuming [-ɪŋ] *a.* presumido, presuntuoso.

presumption [-ˈzʌmpʃən] *s.* 1. presunción, conjetura, suposición. 2. presunción, engreimiento, atrevimiento, insolencia. 3. (der.) presunción.

presumptive [-tɪv] *a.* 1. presuntivo. 2. presunto, probable.

presumptively [-lɪ] *adv.* presuntivamente.

presumptuous [-ˈzʌmptʃʊəs] *a.* presuntuoso, vanidoso, presumido; insolente, atrevido.

presumptuously [-lɪ] *adv.* presuntuosamente, vanidosamente; insolentemente.

presumptuousness [-nəs] *s.* presuntuosidad, vanidad; insolencia.

presuppose [ˌprisəˈpoʊz] *v.t.* presuponer, dar por sentado, suponer previamente.

presupposition [-ˌsʌpəˈzɪʃən] *s.* presuposición.

pretence, *var. de* **pretense.**

pretend [prɪˈtɛnd] *v.t.* 1. aparentar, fingir, simular. 2. alegar, afirmar. 3. **p. to (do),** fingir (hacer); **p. to be,** fingirse, dárselas (de). —*v.i.* 1. pretender, aspirar a (trono, derecho, etc.). 2. simular. 3. **p. to,** reivindicarse (alguna cualidad); pretender en matrimonio, solicitar (la mano).

pretended [-əd] *a.* presunto, pretenso, pretendido, supuesto.

pretendedly [-lɪ] *adv.* pretendidamente, presuntamente.

pretender [-ˈtɛndər, B -də] *s.* pretendiente (esp. a un trono).

pretense [ˈpriˌtɛns, prɪˈtɛns, B -ˈtɛns] *s.* 1. pretensión, reivindicación. 2. pretensión, vanidad; jactancia, vanagloria. 3. pretexto, excusa. 4. simulación, fingimiento. 5. **devoid of all p.,** libre de toda pretension; **under false pretenses,** con apariencia engañosa; **under p. of,** so pretexto de.

pretension [prɪˈtɛntʃən, B -ˈtɛnʃən] *s.* 1. pretensión, reclamo, demanda. 2. pretexto, alegato, argumento. 3. jactancia, presunción. 4. aspiración, anhelo, ambición.

pretensionless [-ləs] *a.* sin pretensión, modesto, sencillo.

pretentious [-ˈtɛntʃəs, B -ˈtɛnʃəs] *a.* 1. pretencioso, presuntuoso, vanidoso. 2. ostentoso. 3. ambicioso, de gran alcance.

pretentiously [-lɪ] *adv.* 1. pretenciosamente, vanidosamente. 2. ostentosamente. 3. ambiciosamente.

pretentiousness [-nəs] *s.* 1. pretensión, presunción. 2. ostentación, suntuosidad.

preterit, preterite [ˈprɛtərət] *a.* 1. (gram.) pretérito indefinido (tiempo del verbo). 2. (ant.) pasado, sucedido. —*s.* (gram.) (tiempo) pretérito.

preterition [ˌprɛtəˈrɪʃən, B pri-] *s.* preterición, omisión; (der.) preterición.

pretermission [ˌpritərˈmɪʃən, B -əˈ-] *s.* pretermisión, omisión, preterición.

pretermit [-ˈmɪt] *v.t.* (*pret. p.p.* PRETERMITTED; *p.pr.* PRETERMITTING) pretermitir, omitir, preterir, pasar por alto.

preternatural [-ˈnætʃərəl] *a.* preternatural, inexplicable.

preternaturally [-ɪ] *adv.* preternaturalmente, inexplicablemente.

preternaturalness [-nəs] *s.* carácter preternatural.

pretest [ˈpriˌtɛst] *s.* prueba preliminar.

pretext [ˈpriˌtɛkst] *s.* pretexto, excusa, disculpa; **on, under** o **upon the p. of, so** pretexto de.

pretor, pretorial, pretorian, pretorship, *vars. de* **praetor, praetorial, praetorian, praetorship.**

Pretoria [prɪˈtɔrɪə] *s.* Pretoria, capital de Sudáfrica.

prettification [ˌprɪtɪfəˈkeɪʃən] *s.* acicalamiento, embellecimiento.

prettify [ˈprɪtɪˌfaɪ] *v.t.* (*pret. p.p.* PRETIFIED; *p.pr.* PRETTIFYING) acicalar, alindar, embellecer.

prettily [-əlɪ] *adv.* hermosamente, lindamente, bellamente.

prettiness [-ɪnəs] *s.* hermosura, lindeza, galanura, belleza.

pretty [ˈprɪtɪ] *a.* (PRETTIER; PRETTIEST) 1. bonito, hermoso, lindo, bello. 2. pulcro, elegante, galano. 3. bueno, excelente, fino; (irón.) bonito, grande, ej., *you are in a p. mess,* en bonito lío te has metido. 4. bastante, considerable. ej., *a p. penny,* bastante dinero, una telegada. —*adv.* (según el énfasis) moderadamente, algo, un poco; considerablemente, muy; **p. much,** bastante; **p. well,** medianamente, así así. —*s.* cosa linda; persona bonita. —*v.t.* (*pret, p.p.* PRETTIED; *p.pr.* PRETTYING) (ú. gen. con **up**) emperejilar, acicalar.

prettyish [-ɪʃ] *a.* bonitillo, algo bonito.

pretuberculous [ˌpritʊˈbɜrkjələs, B -tjʊˈbɜkjʊ-] *a.* (med.) pretuberculoso.

pretypify [priˈtɪpəˌfaɪ] *v.t.* (*pret., p.p.* PRETYPIFIED; *p.pr.* PRETYPIFYING) prefigurar; representar o simbolizar de antemano.

pretzel ['prɛtsəl] *s.* galleta o bizcocho salado en forma de lazo.
prevail [prɪ'veɪl] *v.i.* 1. prevalecer, predominar, prevaler. 2. tener éxito, ser efectivo. 3. **p. on** (o **upon** o **with**), persuadir, convencer; **p.** (**over** o **against**), triunfar (sobre).
prevailing [-ɪŋ] *a.* a. prevaleciente, predominante; corriente, común.
prevailing winds, (meteor.) vientos reinantes o predominantes.
prevalence ['prɛvələns] *s.* frecuencia, ocurrencia frecuente.
prevalent [-lənt] *a.* frecuente, generalizado, usual.
prevalently [-lɪ] *adv.* frecuentemente.
prevaricate [prɪ'værəˌkeɪt] *v.i.* 1. equivocar, sutilizar, argüir falsa o engañosamente; mentir. 2. (der.) prevaricar.
prevarication [prɪˌværə'keɪʃən] *s.* 1. equívoco, engaño, dolo. 2. (der.) prevaricación.
prevaricator [-'værəˌkeɪter, B -ə] *s.* 1. embustero; lioso. 2. (der.) prevaricador.
prevenience [prɪ'vinjəns] *s.* prevención, providencia, anticipación.
prevenient [-jənt] *a.* preveniente, precedente; preventivo; anticipante, antecedente.
prevent [prɪ'vɛnt] *v.t.* 1. impedir, obstruir, obstaculizar. 2. prevenir, precaver, evitar (daño, problema, etc.). 3. (ant.) anticipar, prever; **p. from (doing),** impedir (hacer), impedir que (haga).
preventable, preventible [-əbəl] *a.* evitable.
preventative [-ətɪv] *s.* prevención, medida preventiva. —*a.* preventivo.
preventer [-ər, B -ə] *s.* (mar.) cadena, soga o perno auxiliar.
prevention [prɪ'vɛnʃən] *s.* 1. prevención. 2. obstáculo, impedimento.
preventive [-'vɛntɪv] *a.* preventivo, impeditivo. —*s.* 1. medida preventiva. 2. (med.) profiláctico.
preventively [-lɪ] *adv.* preventivamente.
preview ['priˌvju] *s.* preestreno; (fig.) anticipo, vista anticipada; (cine.) trailer, avance, sinopsis. —*v.t.* preestrenar; (cine.) asistir al preestreno de.
previous ['privɪəs] *a.* 1. previo, anticipado, anterior, precedente. 2. (fam.) prematuro. 3. **p. to,** antes de.
previously [-lɪ] *adv.* previamente, anticipadamente, anteriormente.
previousness [-nəs] *s.* previsión, anticipación, antelación.
previous question, proposición de poner a votación inmediata la moción principal (para acelerar el procedimiento o para diferir la discusión).
previse [prɪ'vaɪz] *v.t.* (raro) prever; prevenir, advertir.
prevision [-'vɪʒən] *s.* 1. previsión. 2. presagio, pronóstico. —*v.t.* prever.
previsional [-əl] *a.* previsor.
prevue, *var. de* **preview.**
prewar ['pri'wɔr, B -'wɔ] *a.* de preguerra, de antes de la guerra.
prexy ['prɛksɪ] *s.* (*pl.* PREXIES) (jer.) presidente, director, rector (de una universidad, escuela o institución de enseñanza superior).
prey [preɪ] *s.* 1. presa, víctima. 2. (ant.) botín, despojo. 3. **to fall p. to,** caer víctima de. —*v.i.* (con *on* o *upon*) 1. rapiñar, pillar. 2. oprimir, agobiar, tener preocupado (mente, conciencia, etc.). 3. agobiar, abusar (de), hacer víctima (s) (de o entre).
Priam ['praɪəm] *s.* (mitol.) Príamo, rey de Troya.
priapic [praɪ'æpɪk] *a.* priápico, fálico.
priapism ['praɪəˌpɪzəm] *s.* (med.) priapismo.
Priapus [praɪ'eɪpəs] *s.* 1. (mitol.) Príapo, dios de la sexualidad masculina. 2. **p.,** falo.

price [praɪs] *s.* 1. precio, valor, importe. 2. precio, costo, coste. 3. recompensa, premio, precio. 4. (ant.) preciosidad. 5. **at a high p.,** (fig.) pagando un precio alto; a costa de mucho sacrificio; **at any p.,** a toda costa, a todo trance, cueste lo que cueste; **at the highest p.,** al mayor precio; **beyond** (o **without**) p., que no tiene precio, que no se puede pagar; **to set a p. on someone's head,** poner a precio (o poner precio a) la cabeza de alguien; **what p.,** para qué sirve, qué vale, ej., *what p. glory?* ¿para qué la gloria? —*v.t.* 1. valuar, avaluar, valorar, preciar, tasar. 2. poner precio a, fijar el precio de. 3. preguntar el precio de. 4. **p. out of the market,** subir de precio (un artículo) hasta que resulte invendible; **to be priced at,** tener un precio de. —*v.i.* poner precios.
price ceiling, maximo de precios.
price control, control de precios.
price-cutter ['praɪsˌkʌtər, B -ə] *s.* comerciante abaratador (esp. el que quiere eliminar la competencia).
price cutting, reducción de precios.
price fixing, fijación de precios.
price index, (e.p.) índice de precios.
priceless [-ləs] *a.* 1. inapreciable, inestimable, sin precio, que no tiene precio. 2. (*fam.*) absurdo, divertido, risible.
price list, lista de precios, tarifa.
price support, mantenimiento de precios (ej. de materias primas por acción gubernamental).
price tag, 1. etiqueta de precio (en mercancías). 2. (fig.) precio, costo.
price war, guerra de precios.
pricey, pricy ['praɪsi] *a.* caro, carito; carero (*tienda*).
prick [prɪk] *s.* 1. picadura, punzada, punzadura, pinchazo. 2. agujero, puntada. 3. instrumento punzante, espiche, aguijón, punzón. 4. escozor, resquemor. 5. remordimiento (de la conciencia). 6. (vulg.) pene, miembro viril. 7. (vulg.) pelmazo, tonto, carajo. —*v.t.* 1. agujerear, horadar, picar, pinchar, punzar. 2. remorder (la conciencia). 3. marcar, indicar o calcar con agujerillos. 4. (ant.) aguijonear, incitar. 5. **p. out** (u **off**), trasplantar (en agujeros preparados); **p. up,** erguir, enderezar, enhestar; **p. up one's ears,** aguzar o levantar las orejas, aguzar los oídos, parar las orejas. —*v.i.* 1. dar pinchazos; ser espinoso. 2. apuntar (hacia arriba), erguirse. 3. causar escozor, hacer sentir comezón. 4. galopar, espolear. 5. **p. at one's conscience,** remorderle la conciencia a uno. —*a.* enderezado, erguido, enhiesto.
prick-eared ['prɪkˌɪrd, B -ˌɪəd] *a.* 1. de orejas prominentes. 2. con las orejas erguidas.
pricker [-ər, B -ə] *s.* 1. espina, púa, aguijón. 2. soldado de caballería ligera. 3. (cost.) marcador, punzón; buril; lezna.
pricket [-ət] *s.* 1. punta aguda de candelero (la que se clava en la vela). 2. (zool.) gamo de un año.
prickle [-əl] *s.* 1. aguijón, púa, pincho, espina. 2. picazón. —*v.t.* 1. pinchar, agujerear, punzar. 2. causar picazón a. —*v.i.* sentir picazón, hacer sentir picazón.
prickly ['prɪklɪ] *a.* lleno de púas, espinoso.
prickly heat, (med.) salpullido causado por el calor.
prickly pear, 1. (bot.) nopal, tunal, higuera de Indias, higuera de tuna. 2. higo de nopal, higo de pala, (higo de) tuna, higo chumbo.
prickly poppy, (bot.) chicalote, amapola espinosa, argemone.
prick song, 1. (mús.) contrapunto. 2. antiguo sistema de anotar música.

pride [praɪd] *s.* 1. orgullo, dignidad, amor propio, altivez, arrogancia. 2. lo mejor, la flor y nata (de un grupo, clase, etc.). 3. vigor, brio, fuerza (de la juventud, etc.). 4. (lit.) pompa, esplendor. 5. manada de leones. 6. disposición o temperamento de un caballo. 7. (fam.) celo (de una hembra). 8. (ant.) adorno. —*v.t.* (gen. con *on* o *upon*) enorgullecerse, jactarse.
prideful ['praɪdfəl] *a.* 1. orgulloso, engreído. 2. jactancioso; arrogante, altivo.
pridefully [-ɪ] *adv.* 1. orgullosamente. 2. jactanciosamente; arrogantemente, altivamente.
pride of India, (bot.) acederaque.
pride of the morning, neblina o chaparrón al amanecer.
prie-dieu ['pri'djɜ, B -ˌdjɜ] *s.* (*pl.* PRIE-DIEUX [-'djɜz, B -ˌdjɜz]) reclinatorio.
prier ['praɪər, B -ə] *s.* fisgón, curioso, atisbador, husmeador.
priest [prist] *s.* 1. sacerdote, presbítero, cura. clérigo. 2. (G.B.) mazo usado para matar peces (en Irl.).
priestcraft ['pristˌkræft, B -ˌkrɑft] *s.* 1. arte y prácticas sacerdotales. 2. (despec.) intrigas clericales, maquinaciones clericales.
priestess ['pristəs] *s.* sacerdotisa.
priesthood [-ˌhʊd] *s.* sacerdocio, clero, clerecía.
priestliness [-lɪnəs] *s.* carácter sacerdotal.
priestly [-lɪ] *a.* sacerdotal, clerical.
priest-ridden [-ˌrɪdən] *a.* (despec.) dominado por clérigos.
prig [prɪg] *v.t., v.i.* (*pret., p.p.* PRIGGED; *p.pr.* PRIGGING) (esco.) regatear; rogar, suplicar.
prig *s.* persona pagada o engreída de su rectitud moral, religiosidad, formalidad, etc.; pedante, presuntuoso, melindroso, mojigato.
priggery ['prɪgərɪ] *s.* pedantería, melindre, mojigatería.
priggish [-ɪʃ] *a.* pedantesco, pedante, gazmoño.
priggishly [-lɪ] *adv.* pedantescamente, con mojigatería.
priggishness [-nəs] *s.* carácter pedantesco, pedantería, gazmoñería.
priggism ['prɪgˌɪzəm] *s.* pedantería, melindre, mojigatería.
prim [prɪm] *a.* (PRIMMER; PRIMMEST) estricto, escrupuloso; decoroso, severamente modesto; estirado, formal. —*v.i.* (*pret., p.p.* PRIMMED; *p.pr.* PRIMMING) vestir muy decorosamente, vestir con mucho recato.
prima ballerina ['primə-] (ballet) primera bailarina.
primacy ['praɪməsɪ] *s.* 1. primacía, supremacía; precedencia. 2. (relig.) primacía (empleo o dignidad de primado).
prima donna ['primə'dɑnə, B -'dɔnə] (*pl.* PRIMA DONNAS) (mús.) prima donna (cantante principal de una ópera), primera cantante.
prima-facie evidence ['praɪmə'feɪʃɪ-] (der.) prueba suficiente a prima facie, prueba suficiente a primera vista, prueba presunta.
primage ['praɪmɪdʒ] *s.* (hist.) prima (que se pagaba al capitán por los dueños de la nave); prima adicional (que se añade al flete y que pertenece al dueño).
primal [-məl] *a.* 1. primordial, fundamental, principal. 2. original, primitivo.
primarily [praɪ'mɛrəlɪ, B 'praɪmərɪlɪ] *adv.* 1. primariamente, fundamentalmente, primordialmente. 2. principalmente, originalmente, primitivamente.
primary ['praɪˌmɛrɪ, B -mərɪ] *a.* 1. primario, primero, primitivo, original. 2. primario, principal, fundamental, primordial. 3. (geol., elec., quím.) primario. —*s.* (*pl.* PRIMARIES) 1. cosa

fundamental, punto principal. 2. comicios primarios; elección preliminar. 3. (t. **p. color**) color elemental o simple. 4. (*astr.*) planeta primario. 5. (elec.) circuito primario. 6. (orn.) pluma primaria.
primary accent, p. stress, (gram.) acento primario (en una palabra de dos o más sílabas).
primary atypical pneumonia, (med.) neumonía atípica primaria.
primary cell, (elec.) pila.
primary coil, bobina primaria, bobina del circuito primario.
primary colors, colores elementales o simples.
primary current, (elec.) corriente primaria o inductora.
primary education, instrucción primaria, primera enseñanza.
primary evidence, (der.) prueba primaria.
primary school, escuela de primera enseñanza, escuela primaria.
primate [ˈpraɪˌmeɪt, -mət] *s.* 1. (relig.) primado. 2. [ˈpraɪˌmeɪt] (zool.) primate. 3. (ant.) prócer, primate.
primateship [-ʃɪp] *s.* primacía, dignidad de primado.
primatial [praɪˈmeɪʃəl] *a.* primacial.
prime [praɪm] *s.* 1. prima, primera hora del día; (relig.) prima, primera hora canónica. 2. alba, aurora, amanecer. 3. juventud, (la) flor (de la vida), plenitud (de fuerzas). 4. lo mejor, lo más escogido; flor y nata. 5. (mat.) número primero o primo. 6. (quím.) átomo sencillo. 7. (mús.) tónico, sonido fundamental. 8. (impr.) virgulilla. 9. (esgr.) primera. —*a.* 1. primo, primero, primario, original, primitivo, prístino. 2. primo, selecto, excelente, de primera clase o calidad. 3. primero, principal, primordial. 4. (mat.) primo, primario (número). —*v.t.* 1. cebar (un arma de fuego). 2. llenar; cargar. 3. imprimar, aprestar (pared, etc. para ser pintada); dar la primera mano de pintura a. 4. preparar, aleccionar, informar, alistar. —*v.i.* arrastrar agua con el vapor (en calderas).
prime cost, (com.) coste de producción, precio de fábrica; costo neto.
prime factor, (mat.) factor primo, factor esencial.
primely [ˈpraɪmlɪ] *adv.* (fam.) excelentemente.
prime meridian, primer meridiano.
prime minister, primer ministro.
prime mover, 1. (filos.) causa primera. 2. instigador, incitador, inspirador, móvil (de una acción o empresa). 3. fuerza motriz, fuente natural de energía. 4. motor primario, generador. 5. (mil.) (E.U). vehículo remolcador.
primeness [-nəs] *s.* primacía, excelencia; principalidad, importancia.
prime number, (mat.) número primo, número simple.
primer [-ər, B -ə] *s.* (arm.) cápsula fulminante, detonador; cartucho cebo, carga iniciadora.
primer [ˈprɪmər, B ˈpraɪmə] *s.* 1. silabario, cartilla (Esp.), (primer) libro de lectura. 2. manual, compendio. 3. [ˈprɪmər, B ˈprɪmə] (impr.) tipo de 10 o de 18 puntos.
primero [prɪˈmɛroʊ, B -ˈmɛər-] *s.* (hist.) primero (juego antiguo de naipes).
prime time, (rad., t.v.) período de tiempo en que los programas tienen más público.
primeval [praɪˈmivəl] *a.* primitivo, primario, prístino.
primevally [-vəlɪ] *adv.* primitivamente.
primigenial [ˌpraɪməˈdʒinɪəl] *a.* primigenio, original, inicial, primogénito.
primine [ˈpraɪmɪn] *s.* (bot.) primina.
priming [-ɪŋ] *s.* 1. (arm.) cebadura (acción de cebar), cebo. **2. p. coat,** apresto, imprimación; primera mano de pintura. 3. preparación, aleccionamiento.
priming cock, (mec.) llave de cebar, grifo de aparejamiento.
primipara [praɪˈmɪpərə] *s.* (*pl.* PRIMIPARAS O PRIMIPARAE [-əˌri]) (med.) primípara, primeriza.
primiparous [-ərəs] *a.* (med.) primeriza (mujer).
primitive [ˈprɪmətɪv] *a.* 1. primitivo. 2. (gram.) primitivo, no derivado, radical. 3. (biol.) primitivo, primordial, rudimentario. —*s.* 1. hombre primitivo. 2. idea primitiva, concepto básico. 3. (arte) primitivo.
primitively [-lɪ] *adv.* primitivamente.
primitiveness [-nəs] *s.* carácter o aspecto primitivo.
primitivism [-ˌɪzəm] *s.* primitivismo.
primitivist [-əst] *s.* partidario del primitivismo, primitivista.
primly [ˈprɪmlɪ] *adv.* estrictamente, escrupulosamente; con modestia o decoro severo.
primness [-nəs] *s.* estrictez, escrupulosidad; decoro severo, severidad.
primo [ˈprimoʊ] *s.* (mús.) primera voz.
primogenitor [ˌpraɪmoʊˈdʒɛnətər, B -ə] *s.* primogenitor, ascendiente, antepasado.
primogeniture [-ətʃər, B -ətʃə] *s.* primogenitura.
primordial [praɪˈmɔrdɪəl, B -ˈmɔd-] *a.* primordial.
primordially [-əlɪ] *adv.* primordialmente.
primordium [-ɪəm] *s.* (*pl.* PRIMORDIA [-ɪə]) (biol.) primordio.
primp [prɪmp] *v.t., v.i.* acicalar(se), emperejilar(se).
primrose [ˈprɪmˌroʊz] *s.* (bot.) primavera, prímula. —*a.* 1. de color amarillo rojizo. 2. cubierto de prímulas. 3. **p. path,** camino, posibilidad, acción, atractiva en principio pero peligrosa a la larga; vida muelle, vida de placer.
primrose peerless, (bot.) narciso.
primsie [ˈprɪmsɪ, B -zɪ] *a.* (esco.) modesto, recatado.
primula [ˈprɪmjələ] *s.* (bot.) prímula.
primulaceous [ˌprɪmjəˈleɪʃəs] *a.* (bot.) primuláceo.
prince [prɪns] *s.* príncipe.
Prince Albert [-ˈælbərt, B -bət] levita de doble botonadura.
Prince Charming, el príncipe azul.
prince consort, príncipe consorte.
princedom [ˈprɪnsdəm] *s.* principado.
Prince Edward Island [-ˈɛdwərd-, B -wəd-] (geog.) Isla Príncipe Eduardo.
princekin [-kən] *s.* pequeño príncipe, principito.
princelet [-lət] *var. de* **princeling.**
princeliness [-lɪnəs] *s.* carácter principesco; nobleza, magnificencia.
princeling [-lɪŋ] *s.* (despec.) pequeño príncipe, principillo.
princely [-lɪ] *a.* principesco; magnífico, regio, espléndido, suntuoso. —*adv.* de modo principesco, principescamente, magníficamente; noblemente.
Prince of Darkness, príncipe de las tinieblas (Satanás).
prince of the blood, príncipe de la sangre, príncipe de la casa real.
Prince of Wales, Príncipe de Gales.
prince royal, príncipe real, hijo mayor del rey.
prince's-feather [ˈprɪnsəzˈfɛðər, B -ðə] *s.* (bot.) amaranto.
princess [ˈprɪnsəs, -sɛs, B prɪnˈsɛs] *s.* princesa.
princess royal, princesa real, hija mayor del rey.
principal [-səpəl] *a.* principal, esencial, capital; máximo. —*s.* 1. jefe, principal. 2. (educ.) director, rector (de una universidad; en E.U. esp. de un colegio o academia). 3. (com.) principal, capital (en oposición al rédito o interés). 4. (arq., ing.) cercha, cimbra. 5. (der.) principal, poderdante, mandante, causante, delegante. 6. (der.) criminal, actor principal (en un delito). 7. (mús.) principal, registro de cuatro pies (del órgano); tema (de una fuga). 8. (ant.) fundamento, principio, máxima.
principal challenge, (der.) recusación por causa principal.
principality [ˌprɪnsəˈpælətɪ] *s.* (*pl.* PRINCIPALITIES) 1. principado. 2. (relig.) principado (ángel del séptimo coro). 3. (raro) principalidad.
principally [ˈprɪnsəpəlɪ] *adv.* principalmente, en la mayor parte.
principal parts, (gram.) formas principales (del verbo, las que en inglés incluyen el infinitivo, el pretérito y el participio pasado).
principal ray, (dib.) rayo principal.
principalship [-ˌʃɪp] *s.* jefatura, oficio de director.
principium [prɪnˈsɪpɪəm] *s.* (*pl.* PRINCIPIA [-ɪə]) principio; (*esp. en pl.*) principios elementales.
principle [ˈprɪnsəpəl] *s.* 1. principio, origen, raíz, causa. 2. principio, norma, máxima. 3. **a man of principles,** un hombre de principios; **a matter of p.,** una cuestión de principios; **in principle,** en principio; **on p.,** por principio.
principled [-pəld] *a.* (*ú. en palabras compuestas*) de principios, ej., *high-p.,* de elevados principios.
principle of contradiction, (lóg.) principio de contradicción.
principle of identity, (lóg.) principio de identidad.
principle of the excluded middle, (lóg.) principio del tercero excluido.
prink [prɪŋk] *v.t.* ataviar, acicalar, adornar; **p. oneself up,** acicalarse, emperejilarse.
print [prɪnt] *s.* 1. impresión, huella, marca. 2. molde, estampa, cuño, matriz. 3. (tej.) estampado. 4. impresión (de un libro, etc.). 5. (esp. E.U.) impreso; grabado, estampa; diseño, dibujo. 6. letra o texto impreso, ej., *large p.,* tipo grande de letras (de un texto, inscripción, etc.). 7. (foto.) copia; prueba positiva, positivo. 8. **in p.,** publicado, impreso; en venta (libro); **out of p.,** agotado. —*v.t.* 1. imprimir, marcar, estampar, sellar. 2. publicar, ej., *who will p. such nonsense?* ¿quién publicará tales disparates? 3. escribir con letra de imprenta. 4. (foto.) copiar, sacar una copia o un positivo, tirar (una prueba). —*v.i.* 1. ser impresor, trabajar como impresor. 2. imprimirse (bien o mal).
printable [ˈprɪntəbəl] *a.* 1. imprimible. 2. publicable.
printed circuit, (rad.) circuito impreso.
printed letter, letra de molde.
printed matter, impresos.
printer [-ər, B -ə] *s.* 1. impresor, editor; tipógrafo, gráfico. 2. (foto.) aparato copiador.
printer's devil, aprendiz de tipógrafo.
printer's dozen, (la) docena del fraile, trece.
printer's error, error de imprenta, error tipográfico.
printer's mark, (impr.) pie de imprenta.
printery [ˈprɪntərɪ] *s.* (*pl.* PRINTERIES) 1. imprenta, taller tipográfico. 2. (tej.) taller o fábrica donde se estampan telas.
printing [-ɪŋ] *s.* 1. imprenta, tipografía. 2. impresión. 3. tirada. 4. (*pl.*) papel para imprimir.
printing office, imprenta, taller tipográfico, talleres gráficos.
printing press, prensa, máquina de imprimir.

printing shop, taller tipográfico, talleres gráficos.
printless [-ləs] *a.* inmaculado, no marcado.
print maker, *s.* estampador, grabador.
printout [-ˌaut] *s.* (comput) print-out, output, impresión, listado.
print run, tirada.
print shop, estampería.
prior ['praɪər, B -ə] *s.* (relig.) prior.
prior, *a.* previo, anterior, precedente, prior. *—adv.* previamente; **p. to,** antes de.
priorate ['praɪərət] *s.* priorato, priorazgo (dignidad y comunidad).
prioress [-ərəs] *s.* (relig.) priora.
priority [praɪ'ɔrətɪ, -'ɑr-, B -'ɔr-] *s.* (*pl.* PRIORITIES) 1. prioridad, anterioridad, precedencia, antelación, prelación. 2. prioridad, superioridad (en rango, posición o privilegio).
priorship ['praɪərˌʃɪp, B -əˌ-] *s.* priorato, priorazgo (dignidad).
priory [-ərɪ] *s.* priorato.
prise, (pr. G.B.) *var. de* **prize.**
prism ['prɪzəm] *s.* (geom., ópt., min.) prisma.
prismatic [ˌprɪz'mætɪk] *a.* 1. prismático. 2. (fig.) centellante, brillante, luminoso.
prismatically [-ɪkəlɪ] *adv.* en la forma de un prisma, como por efecto de un prisma.
prismoid ['prɪzˌmɔɪd] *s.* (geom.) prismoide, prismatoide.
prismoidal [prɪz'mɔɪdəl] *a.* prismatoide, prismoide.
prison ['prɪzən] *s.* prisión, cárcel, penal. *—a.* 1. carcelario (sistema, reforma, fiebre, disciplina, etc.). 2. en prisión, en la cárcel (vida, compañeros, etc.). 3. de cárcel, de encarcelamiento (condena, término, etc.). *—v.t.* encarcelar, aprisionar.
prison camp, campamento para prisioneros (de guerra); campamento para presos.
prisoner [-ənər, B -ənə] *s.* preso, prisionero, recluso, cautivo; **to be a p. of,** estar aprisionado, en poder de, ej., *I am a p. of love,* estoy aprisionado por el amor; **to take p.,** apresar, prender.
prisoner of war, prisionero de guerra.
prisoner's base, (juego) marro, rescate.
prison fever, (med.) fiebre carcelaria.
prison system, sistema penitenciario.
prison van, coche celular.
prissily ['prɪsəlɪ] *adv.* remilgadamente, melindrosamente.
prissiness [-ɪnəs] *s.* remilgo, melindre, dengue.
prissy [-ɪ] *a.* remilgado, melindroso.
pristine ['prɪsˌtin, prɪs'tin, B 'prɪstaɪn] *a.* prístino, antiguo, primitivo.
prithee ['prɪðɪ] *interj.* (ant.) ¡por favor! ¡por Dios! ¡te ruego!
privacy ['praɪvəsɪ, B 'prɪvə-] *s.* (*pl.* PRIVACIES) 1. retiro, retraimiento, intimidad. 2. (ant.) lugar de retiro o aislamiento. 3. **in the p. of one's home,** en la intimidad del propio hogar; **to have no p.,** no tener ningún lugar donde estar solo, no poderse librar de extraños en la vida privada.
private ['praɪvət] *a.* 1. privado, particular (persona). 2. privado, no publicado; reservado, confidencial, secreto (asunto, noticia). 3. privado, personal (propiedad, etc.); íntimo, propio, personal (motivo, etc.). 4. solitario (lugar). 5. (ant.) recluido, recogido (persona). 6. **to keep p.,** tratar con reserva, ej., *the matter had to be kept p.,* era necesario tratar el asunto con reserva. *—s.* 1. (mil.) soldado raso. 2. (ant.) retiro, retraimiento, aislamiento. 3. **in p.,** en privado, privadamente, en secreto.
private detective, detective privado, investigador privado.
private enterprise, empresa particular, empresa privada.
privateer [ˌpraɪvə'tɪr, B -'tɪə] *s.* corsario, armador.
privateering [-'tɪrɪŋ, B -'tɪər-] *s.* corso, actividad del corsario.
privateersman [-'tɪrzmən, B -'tɪəz-] *s.* capitán de un barco corsario.
private eye, (jer.) detective privado.
private first class, (mil.) (E.U.) soldado de primera clase.
private law, derecho privado.
privately ['praɪvətlɪ] *adv.* en privado, privadamente, en secreto.
privateness [-nəs] *s.* carácter privado o reservado.
private parts, partes pudendas.
private person, persona particular.
private property, bienes particulares, bienes de dominio privado, propiedad privada.
private school, escuela particular, escuela privada.
privation [praɪ'veɪʃən] *s.* privación.
privative ['prɪvətɪv] *a.* privativo; (gram.) privativo (prefijo, sufijo, etc.). *—s.* (gram.) prefijo o sufijo privativo.
privatively [-lɪ] *adv.* privativamente.
privet ['prɪvət] *s.* (bot.) alheña, aligustre, ligustro.
privilege ['prɪvəlɪdʒ] *s.* privilegio, gracia, prerrogativa. *—v.t.* privilegiar, conceder privilegio a.
privileged [-əlɪdʒd] *a.* privilegiado.
privileged communication, (der.) comunicación no divulgable, comunicación de confianza.
privily ['prɪvəlɪ] *adv.* privadamente, secretamente.
privity [-ətɪ] *s.* (*pl.* PRIVITIES) 1. conocimiento particular (de secretos, designios, etc.); informe reservado o confidencial. 2. (der.) relación de partes de interés común, coparticipación. 3. (ant.) asunto privado.
privy ['prɪvɪ] *a.* 1. secreto, oculto; reservado, excusado, enterado, informado. 2. **to be p. to,** tener conocimiento particular de (algo), estar en el secreto de (algo). 3. (ant.) privado, personal. *—s.* (*pl.* PRIVIES) 1. (der.) copartícipe en un interés común. 2. retrete, excusado.
privy council, (G.B.) consejo del rey; consejo de los gobernadores.
privy purse, (G.B.) fondos para los gastos personales del rey.
privy seal, (G.B.) sello real.
prize [praɪz] *s.* 1. premio, recompensa, remuneración; (fig.) galardón, lauro, ganancia, ventaja. 2. (hist.) competencia por un premio. 3. **to take the p.,** llevarse el premio. *—a.* 1. premiado; digno de premio. 2. de premio (medalla, etc.). 3. por premios (competencia, etc.). 4. de peso (argumento, motivo, etc.). 5. tremendo, de remate (tonto, idiota, etc.). *—v.t.* 1. apreciar, estimar. 2. valuar, tasar.
prize, *s.* 1. presa, botín. 2. buque apresado (por un beligerante en uso de derecho de guerra). *—v.t.* apresar.
prize, (pr. G.B.) **prise,** *v.t.* (ú. con *up, out* u *open*) apalancar, palanquear. *—s.* palanca.
prize court, (der.) tribunal de presas.
prizefight ['praɪzˌfaɪt] *s.* (boxeo) pelea profesional, pugilato.
prizefighter [-ər, B -ə] *s.* boxeador profesional.
prizefighting [-ɪŋ] *s.* boxeo profesional.
prize money, 1. bolsa, premio de dinero. 2. (mar.) parte (individual del botín) de presa (repartido entre los oficiales y tripulación del buque apresador).
prizer ['praɪzər, B -ə] *s.* (ant.) contendor por un premio.
prize ring, cuadrilátero (de boxeo).
prizewinner ['praɪzˌwɪnər] *s.* premiado, ganador.
prizewinning ['praɪzˌwɪnɪŋ] *a.* premiado, galardonado.
pro [proʊ] *adv.* en pro, en favor. *—s.* **pro,** voto o argumento en favor; **the pros and cons,** el pro y el contra. *—a.* en pro, favorable. *—prep.* en pro de, en favor de.
pro, *s.* (*pl.* PROS) (fam.) profesional (esp. deportista); entrenador profesional (esp. de golf). *—a.* profesional.
proa ['proʊə] *s.* prao (embarcación de Malasia).
probabilism ['prɑbəbəˌlɪzəm, B 'prɔb-] *s.* (filos.) probabilismo.
probabilist [-ləst] *s., a.* probabilista.
probabilistic [ˌprɑbəbə'lɪstɪk, B ˌprɔb-] *a.* 1. basado en la probabilidad. 2. (filos.) probabilista.
probability [-'bɪlətɪ] *s.* (*pl.* PROBABILITIES) probabilidad; **in all p.,** muy probablemente.
probable ['prɑbəbəl, B 'prɔb-] *a.* probable.
probable cause, (der.) causa razonable, motivo fundado; causa presunta.
probably [-əblɪ] *adv.* probablemente.
probang ['proʊˌbæŋ] *s.* (med.) sonda esofágica.
probate ['proʊˌbeɪt, B -bɪt] *s.* (der.) validación, legalización (oficial) de un testamento. — ['proʊˌbeɪt] *v.t.* validar un testamento.
probate court, (der.) tribunal testamentario o sucesorio.
probation [proʊ'beɪʃən, B prə-] *s.* 1. prueba, probación. 2. período de prueba, tiempo de prueba. 3. (der.) libertad condicional, libertad a prueba, libertad probatoria, libertad vigilada. 4. **to put on p.,** poner a prueba; (der.) poner en libertad condicional.
probational [-əl] **probationary** [-ˌɛrɪ, B -ərɪ] *a.* probatorio.
probationer [-ər, B -ə] *s.* 1. persona (esp. enfermera) en período de prueba. 2. (der.) delincuente en libertad condicional.
probation officer, agente judicial de vigilancia (de delincuentes en libertad condicional).
probative ['proʊbətɪv] **probatory** [-ˌtɔrɪ, B -tərɪ] *a.* probatorio.
probe [proʊb] *s.* 1. (med.) sonda, algalia, cala, calador. 2. examen probatorio; indagación, interrogatorio, encuesta, investigación. *—v.t.* 1. sondar, sondear. 2. escudriñar, inquirir, indagar. *—v.i.* hacerse tanteos o sondeos; **p. for,** tratar de encontrar; **p. into,** sondear, tantear (un asunto).
probity ['proʊbətɪ] *s.* probidad, moralilidad, rectitud, honestidad, integridad.
problem ['prɑbləm, B 'prɔb-] *s.* problema. *—a.* 1. de problemas. 2. con muchos problemas; de solución o trato difícil.
problematic [ˌprɑblə'mætɪk, B ˌprɔb-] **problematical** [-ɪkəl] *a.* 1. problemático, incierto, inseguro, dudoso. 2. difícil; intrigante.
problematically [-ɪkəlɪ] *adv.* problemáticamente.
proboscidean, proboscidian [ˌproʊbə'sɪdɪən, B ˌprɔbɔ-] *a., s.* (zool.) proboscidio.
proboscis [prə'bɑsəs, proʊ-, B -'bɔs-] *s.* (*pl.* PROBOSCISES O PROBOSCIDES [-əˌdiz]) 1. (zool.) trompa prensil, probóscide. 2. (fam.) trompa, nariz.
proboscis monkey, (zool.) násico.
procaine ['proʊˌkeɪn] *s.* (farm.) procaína.
procambial [proʊ'kæmbɪəl] *a.* (bot.) procambial.
procambium [-bɪəm] *s.* (bot.) procambio, procámbium.
procarp ['proʊˌkɑrp, B -kɑp] *s.* (bot.) procarpo, procarpio.

procathedral [ˌproʊkəˈθidrəl] *s.* (relig.) parroquia usada como catedral.
procedural [prəˈsidʒərəl] *a.* (der.) procesal.
procedure [-ˈsidʒər, B -dʒə] *s.* proceder, procedimiento (judicial, legislativo, etc.).
proceed [proʊˈsid, prə-] *v.i.* 1. proceder. 2. seguir su curso, ej., *the case will now p.*, el caso seguirá ahora su curso. 3. **p. against,** (der.) proceder contra, abrir o iniciar una causa contra, entablar acción contra; **p. from,** proceder de, originarse en; **p. to,** proceder a, avanzar a, ir a (sitio); **p. to (do),** proceder a (hacer); **p. with,** proseguir con, seguir con.
proceeding [-ɪŋ] *s.* 1. proceder. 2. acto, práctica. 3. (*pl.*) acta de sesiones. 4. (*pl.*) curso de acción, acontecimientos. 5. (der.) procedimiento, proceso, trámite.
proceeds [ˈproʊˌsidz] *s. pl.* producto, ganancias, réditos, utilidades, ingresos.
proceleusmatic [ˌprɑsəlusˈmætɪk, B ˌprɔsɪljus-] *s.* (poética) proceleusmático.
procephalic [ˌproʊsəˈfælɪk, B -kɛ-] *a.* (anat.) procefálico.
procercoid [proʊˈsɜrˌkɔɪd, B -ˈsɜˌ-] *s.* (zool.) procercoide.
process [prɑsˌɛs, B ˈproʊs-] *s.* (*pl.* PROCESSES) 1. progreso, avance, proceso. 2. procedimiento, método, sistema. 3. (der.) causa, proceso, expediente; auto, citación. 4. (anat., med.) proceso. 5. (impr.) fotograbado, fotomecánica, fototipografía. 6. **in p.,** en progreso; **in the p. of time,** con el transcurso del tiempo; **to be in the p. of,** estar en, ej., *these problems are in the p. of discussion,* estos problemas están en discusión. 7. protuberancia, excrecencia. —*v.t.* 1. (der.) procesar. 2. elaborar (por un procedimiento industrial, etc.). — [prəˈsɛs] *v.i.* (pr. G.B.) andar en una procesión (religiosa, etc.). —*a.* 1. elaborado con métodos especiales. 2. de efectos especiales (película de cine). 3. (impr.) fotomecánico, fototípico, fototipográfico.
process cheese, processed c., queso preparado (mediante la mezcla de varios tipos).
processed glass, vidrio tratado.
procession [prəˈsɛʃən] *s.* 1. procesión, desfile. 2. progresión, sucesión, serie. —*v.i.* (ant.) andar en procesión.
processional [-əl] *s.* (relig.) 1. procesionario. 2. himno procesionario. —*a.* procesional.
processional moth, processionary moth [-ˌɛrɪ-, B -ərɪ-] (ento.) procesionaria.
process printing, (impr.) policromía, impresión policroma, fotocromotipografía.
process server, (der.) notificador, portador de citaciones.
pro-choice [ˈproʊˈtʃɔɪs] *a.* permitiendo el aborto con el derecho de decidir.
pro-choicer [ˈproʊˈtʃɔɪsər] *s.* persona que permite el aborto y tiene el derecho de decidir.
proclaim [proʊˈkleɪm, prə-] *v.t.* 1. proclamar, anunciar, declarar. 2. pregonar, vocear. 3. (ant.) proscribir (por una proclama), declarar.
proclamation [ˌprɑkləˈmeɪʃən, B ˌprɔk-] *s.* 1. proclamación, publicación, anuncio oficial. 2. proclama, decreto, edicto, bando.
proclitic [proʊˈklɪtɪk] *a.* (gram.) proclítico. —*s.* (gram.) palabra proclítica.
proclivity [-ˈklɪvətɪ, B prə-] *s.* (*pl.* PROCLIVITIES) proclividad, inclinación, propensión (esp. a lo malo).
proconsul [proʊˈkɑnsəl, B -ˈkɔn-] *s.* 1. (hist.) procónsul (romano). 2. (esp. G.B.) gobernador (de una colonia).
proconsular [-sələr, B -sjulə] *a.* proconsular.
proconsulate [-lət] **proconsulship** [-səlˌʃɪp] *s.* proconsulado.
procrastinate [prəˈkræstəˌneɪt, proʊ-] *v.t.* aplazar, postergar, dilatar, retrasar. —*v.i.* obrar con dilación, dilatarse, tardar.
procrastination [-ˌkræstəˈneɪʃən] *s.* dilación, retraso, retardo, dilatación.
procrastinator [-ˈkræstəˌneɪtər, B -ə] *s.* persona morosa, dilatador, que llega habitualmente tarde.
procreant [ˈproʊkrɪənt] *a.* procreador, productivo, fructífero.
procreate [-ˌeɪt] *v.t.* procrear, engendrar.
procreation [ˌproʊkvɪˈeɪʃən] *s.* procreación, engendramiento.
procreative [ˈproʊkrɪˌeɪtɪv] *a.* procreador.
procreator [-ər, B -ə] *s.* procreador.
procrustean [prəˈkrʌstɪən, proʊ-] *a.* 1. (mitol.) de Procusto. 2. (fig.) duro, inflexible; rígido (disciplina, orden, etc.).
proctodaeum [ˌprɑktəˈdiəm, B ˌprɔk-] *s.* (zool.) proctodeo, proctodeum.
proctologic [-ˈlɑdʒɪk, B -ˈlɔdʒ-] **proctological** [-ɪkəl] *a.* (med.) proctológico.
proctologist [prɑkˈtɑlədʒəst, B prɔkˈtɔl-] *s.* proctólogo.
proctology [-ədʒɪ] *s.* (med.) proctología.
proctor [ˈprɑktər, B ˈprɔktə] *s.* 1. (der.) procurador, apoderado. 2. (educ.) censor, superintendente.
proctorial [prɑkˈtɔrɪəl, B prɔk-] *a.* disciplinario, de orden; referente al procurador.
proctorship [ˈprɑktərˌʃɪp, B ˈprɔktəˌ-] *s.* (der.) procuraduría.
proctoscope [ˈprɑktəˌskoʊp, B ˈprɔk-] *s.* (med.) proctoscopio.
proctoscopy [prɑkˈtɑskəpɪ, B prɔkˈtɔs-] *s.* (med.) proctoscopia.
procumbent [proʊˈkʌmbənt] *a.* 1. boca abajo; postrado, inclinado. 2. (bot.) procumbente.
procurable [-ˈkjʊrəbəl, B prəˈkjʊər-] *a.* obtenible, asequible.
procuracy [ˈprɑkjərəsɪ, B ˈprɔk-] *s.* (ant.) procuraduría.
procurance [proʊˈkjʊrəns, B prəˈkjʊər-] *s.* obtención, consecución, adquisición.
procuration [ˌprɑkjəˈreɪʃən, B ˌprɔkjʊə-] *s.* 1. obtencion, consecución. 2. alcahuetería. 3. (der.) procuración; poder.
procurator [ˈprɑkjəˌreɪtər, B ˈprɔkjʊə-ə] *s.* (der.) procurador, apoderado.
procuratorial [ˌprɑkjərəˈtɔrɪəl, B ˌprɔk-] *a.* de procurador (capacidad, facultades, etc.).
procuratory [ˈprɑkjərəˌtɔrɪ, B ˈprɔkjʊrətərɪ] *s.* (der.) procuración, procura, poder.
procure [proʊˈkjʊr, prə-, B prəˈkjʊə] *v.t.* 1. adquirir, obtener, conseguir, lograr. 2. alcahuetear. 3. (raro) causar, ocasionar. —*v.i.* alcahuetear, servir de alcahuete.
procurement [-mənt] *s.* obtención, consecución, adquisición.
procurer [-ˈkjʊrər, B -ˈkjʊərə] *s.* alcahuete, tercero.
procuress [-ˈkjʊrəs, B -ˈkjʊər-] *s.* alcahueta, tercera, celestina.
prod [prɑd, B prɔd] *v.t.* (*pret., p.p.* PRODDED; *p.pr.* PRODDING) 1. aguijar, aguijonear, picar, pinchar, punzar. 2. (fig.) aguijar, estimular, avivar (memoria, etc.). —*s.* 1. aguijada, pincho, aguijón, espina. 2. aguijonada, aguijonazo. 3. (fig.) aguijón, estímulo.
prodigal [ˈprɑdɪgəl, B ˈprɔd-] *a.* 1. pródigo, derrochador, despilfarrador, manirroto. 2. exuberante, superabundante, profuso, lujuriante.
prodigality [ˌprɑdəˈgælətɪ, B ˌprɔd-] *s.* (*pl.* PRODIGALITIES) prodigalidad, derroche, despilfarro, exuberancia, profusión.
prodigally [ˈprɑdɪgəlɪ, B ˈprɔd-] *adv.* pródigamente.
prodigal son, hijo pródigo.
prodigious [prəˈdɪdʒəs] *a.* 1. prodigioso, maravilloso, asombroso, extraordinario. 2. enorme, inmenso, vasto, descomunal, ingente. 3. (ant.) portentoso.
prodigiously [-lɪ] *adv.* prodigiosamente.
prodigiousness [-nəs] *s.* 1. prodigiosidad. 2. enormidad, inmensidad.
prodigy [ˈprɑdədʒɪ, B ˈprɔd-] *s.* (*pl.* PRODIGIES) 1. prodigio, maravilla. 2. (ant.) portento, pasmo. 3. **a child prodigy,** un niño prodigio.
prodromal [proʊˈdroʊməl, B ˈprɔdrəməl] *a.* (med.) prodrómico.
prodrome [ˈproʊˌdroʊm, B ˈprɔdrəm] *s.* (*pl.* PRODROMATA [proʊˈdroʊmətə, B -ˈdrɔ-] o PRODROMES) (med.) pródromo.
produce [ˈprɑdus, ˈproʊd-, -jus, B ˈprɔdjus] *s.* 1. producto, producción. 2. producto, renta, rédito. 3. producto agrícola. 4. raza, cría. — [prəˈdus, B -ˈdjus] *v.t.* 1. producir, exhibir, presentar, mostrar, ej., *p. a witness in court,* presentar un testigo ante el tribunal. 2. producir, parir, dar a luz. 3. producir, manufacturar, fabricar. 4. producir, dar, rendir (interés, utilidad, etc.). 5. producir, originar, ocasionar. 6. presentar al público, poner en escena. 7. (geom.) prolongar, extender, ej., *p. a side of a triangle,* prolongar un lado del triángulo. 8. (ant.) alargar, estirar. —*v.i.* producir, dar frutos, fructificar.
producer [prəˈdusər, B -ˈdjusə] *s.* 1. productor, fabricante. 2. (teat.) director de escena; (cine) director de producción. 3. gasógeno, generador de gas pobre.
producer gas, gas pobre.
producer goods, elementos de producción.
producible [-əbəl] *a.* producible.
product [ˈprɑˌdʌkt, -dəkt, B ˈprɔ-] *s.* 1. producto, resultado, fruto. 2. (quím., mat.) producto.
production [prəˈdʌkʃən] *s.* producción.
productive [-ˈdʌktɪv] *a.* 1. productivo; creativo; fértil, fructífero, feraz. 2. productivo, beneficioso, lucrativo, fructuoso, provechoso.
productively [-lɪ] *adv.* productivamente.
productiveness [-nəs] **productivity** [ˌproʊdʌkˈtɪvətɪ, B ˌprɔ-] *s.* productividad; fertilidad, fecundidad.
proem [ˈproʊˌɛm] *s.* proemio, prólogo, prefacio; preludio.
proemial [proʊˈimɪəl] *a.* proemial, que prologa.
proenzyme [-ˈɛnˌzaɪm] *s.* (bioquím.) proenzima.
proestrus [-ˈɛstrəs] *s.* (*pl.* PROESTRUSES) (fisiol.) proestro.
prof [prɑf, B prɔf] *s.* (jer.) profesor, profe.
profanation [ˌprɑfəˈneɪʃən, B ˌprɔf-] *s.* profanación.
profanatory [prəˈfænəˌtɔrɪ, proʊ-, B prəˈfænətərɪ] *a.* profanador.
profane [proʊˈfeɪn, prə-, B prə-] *v.t.* profanar. —*a.* 1. profano, secular, seglar. 2. profano, ignorante (en una materia). 3. profano, irreverente, blasfemo.
profanely [-lɪ] *adv.* profanamente.
profaneness [-nəs] *s.* profanidad, irreverencia.
profaner [-ər, B -ə] *s.* profanador.
profanity [-ˈfænətɪ] *s.* (*pl.* PROFANITIES) 1. profanidad, irreverencia, falta de respeto. 2. blasfemia, maldición, imprecación, palabra obscena.
profert [ˈproʊfərt, B -fət] *s.* (der.) ofrecimiento de prueba (en el juzgado o tribunal).
profess [prəˈfɛs, proʊ-, B prə-] *v.t.* 1. manifestar, reconocer, admitir. 2. profesar, sentir (afecto, inclinación o interés); fingir, simular, aparentar.

3. profesar, ejercer (una ciencia, arte u oficio); practicar. 4. enseñar (una ciencia o arte). 5. (relig.) profesar. —*v.i.* hacer una declaración.
professed [-'fɛst] *a.* 1. declarado, ej., *a p. enemy,* un enemigo declarado. 2. aparente, supuesto, ej., *a p. Christian,* un supuesto cristiano, un cristiano aparente. 3. (relig.) profeso.
professedly [-'fɛsədlɪ] *adv.* 1. manifiestamente; ostensiblemente, abiertamente. 2. aparentemente, supuestamente.
profession [-'fɛʃən] *s.* 1. declaración, manifestación; admisión, confesión. 2. fe, creencia, religión. 3. profesión, carrera, oficio. 4. profesión (profesionales como grupo). 5. (relig.) profesión.
professional [-əl] *a., s.* profesional.
professionalism [-ˌɪzəm] *s.* profesionalismo.
professionalize [-ˌaɪz] *v.t.* dar carácter profesional a, profesionalizar.
professionally [-ɪ] *adv.* profesionalmente, de modo profesional.
professor [prə'fɛsər, B -ə] *s.* 1. profesor (universitario), catedrático. 2. (fam.) profesor, maestro.
professorate [-ərət] *s.* profesorado.
professorial [ˌproʊfə'sɔrɪəl, ˌprɑfə-, B ˌprɔfɛ-] *a.* 1. profesoral. 2. docto, erudito; didáctico.
professorially [-ɪəlɪ] *adv.* en tono profesoral; a la manera de un profesor.
professoriate [-ɪət] *s.* profesorado.
professorship [prə'fɛsərˌʃɪp, B -'fɛsəˌ-] *s.* profesorado, cargo de profesor.
proffer ['prɑfər, B 'prɔfə] *v.t.* ofrecer, proponer; brindar. —*s.* oferta, propuesta.
proficiency [prə'fɪʃənsɪ] *s.* pericia, destreza, habilidad; aprovechamiento.
proficient [-ənt] *s.* perito, experto. —*a.* perito, diestro, hábil.
proficiently [-lɪ] *adv.* expertamente, diestramente, hábilmente.
profile ['poʊˌfaɪl] *s.* 1. perfil, silueta. 2. contorno. 3. (arq.) perfil; (ing. civil) corte vertical. —*v.t.* perfilar.
profit ['prɑfət, B 'prɔf-] *s.* 1. provecho, ventaja; aprovechamiento. 2. (*gen. pl.*) ganancia, utilidad, lucro, beneficio. —*v.i.* 1. sacar provecho o utilidad; ganar, lucrarse. 2. (ant.) adelantar; mejorar. 3. **p. by,** sacar provecho de, beneficiarse con. —*v.t.* servir, ser de utilidad para.
profitable [-əbəl] *a.* provechoso, útil, beneficioso; fructífero, fructuoso, proficuo; ventajoso; productivo, lucrativo.
profitableness [-nəs] *s.* carácter provechoso o lucrativo.
profitably [-əblɪ] *adv.* provechosamente; lucrativamente.
profit and loss, (com.) ganancias y pérdidas.
profiteer [ˌprɑfə'tɪr, B ˌprɔfɪ'tɪə] *s.* logrero, acaparador, buitre. —*v.i.* lograr, acaparar.
profiteering [-'tɪrɪŋ, B -'tɪər-] *s.* logrería, acaparamiento.
profitless ['prɑfətləs, B 'prɔf-] *a.* infructuoso, improductivo; inútil, estéril.
profit margin, margen de beneficios, margen de utilidad.
profit sharing, participación en las utilidades.
profligacy ['prɑflɪgəsɪ, B 'prɔf-] *s.* libertinaje, disolución, licencia.
profligate [-gət] *a., s.* 1. libertino, licencioso, disoluto. 2. derrochador, despilfarrador.
profligately [-lɪ] *adv.* 1. disolutamente, licenciosamente. 2. despilfarradamente.
profluent ['prɑfluənt, B 'proʊ-] *a.* que fluye suavemente (como un arroyo).
pro forma [proʊ'fɔrmə, B -'fɔmə] 1. como mera formalidad. 2. (com.) pro forma (factura, etc.).
profound [prə'faʊnd] *a.* profundo, hondo; insondable; intenso. —*s.* (poét.) profundo (del mar, alma, futuro, etc.).
profoundly [-lɪ] *adv.* profundamente.
profoundness [-nəs] *s.* profundidad.
profundity [prə'fʌndətɪ] *s.* profundidad.
profuse [prə'fjus] *a.* 1. profuso, abundante, copioso. 2. pródigo, generoso.
profusely [-lɪ] *adv.* profusamente.
profuseness [-nəs] *s.* profusión, abundancia.
profusion [-'fjuʒən] *s.* 1. profusión, abundancia. 2. generosidad, prodigalidad.
prog [prɑg, B prɔg] *v.i.* (dial.) husmear, hurgar (con fines de robo); hurtar, robar. —*s.* (dial.) alimentos, comida (esp. la obtenida mendigando o robando).
progenitor [proʊ'dʒɛnətər, prə-, B -ə] *s.* 1. progenitor; antepasado. 2. precursor.
progeny ['prɑdʒənɪ, B 'prɔdʒ-] *s.* progenie, prole, sucesión.
progestational [ˌproʊˌdʒɛs'teɪʃənəl] *a.* (med.) progestacional.
progesterone [proʊ'dʒɛstəˌroʊn] *s.* (bioquím.) progesterona.
progestin [-'dʒɛstən] *s.* (bioquím.) progestina.
proglottid [-'glɑtəd, B -'glɔt-] *var. de* proglottis.
proglottis [-əs] *s.* (*pl.* PROGLOTTIDES [-əˌdiz]) (zool.) proglotis.
prognathic [prɑg'næθɪk, B prɔg-] *a.* (anat., zool.) prognato.
prognathism ['prɑgnəˌθɪzəm, B 'prɔg-] *s.* (anat., zool.) prognatismo.
prognathous ['prɑgnəθəs, prɑg'neɪθəs, B prɔg-] *a.* (anat., zool.) prognato.
prognosis [prɑg'noʊsəs, B prɔg-] *s.* (*pl.* PROGNOSES [-'noʊsiz]) 1. pronóstico, predicción. 2. (med.) prognosis, pronóstico.
prognostic [-'nɑstɪk, B -'nɔs-] *s.* 1. pronóstico, presagio, señal. 2. pronóstico, vaticinio, predicción. 3. (med.) pronóstico, vaticinio, predicción. 3. (med.) pronóstico, prognosis. —*a.* pronosticador.
prognosticate [-təˌkeɪt] *v.t.* pronosticar, presagiar, profetizar, predecir.
prognostication [-ˌnɑstə'keɪʃən, B -ˌnɔs-] *s.* 1. pronosticación, predicción, profecía. 2. presagio, agüero, señal. 3. (med.) prognosis.
prognosticative [-'nɑstəˌkeɪtɪv, B -'nɔs-] *a.* profético.
prognosticator [-'nɑstəˌkeɪtər, B -'nɔs-ə] *s.* pronosticador.
program, programme ['proʊˌgræm, -grəm, B -ˌgræm] *s.* programa. —*v.t.* (*pret., p.p.* PROGRAMED O PROGRAMMED; *p.pr.* PROGRAMING O PROGRAMMING) programar.
program director, (rad., t.v.) programador.
programed learning, (educ.) enseñanza programada.
programer, (E.U.) **programmer** (G.B.) [ˌproʊgræmər] *s.* (comput.) programador; (rad., t.v.) encargado de programación; (electrón) programador.
programing, (E.U.) **programming** (G.B.) [-ɪŋ] *s.* (comput., rad., t.v.) programación.
programmatic [ˌproʊgrə'mætɪk] *a.* programático, de programa.
program music, música de programa, música descriptiva.
progress ['prɑgrəs, -ˌrɛs, B 'proʊgrɛs] *s.* 1. progreso, marcha, avance. 2. progresos, mejoramiento, adelantamiento, aprovechamiento. 3. (hist.) viaje oficial. 4. **to make p.,** hacer progresos, progresar, avanzar. — [prə'grɛs] v.t. 1. progresar, adelantar, avanzar. 2. progresar, mejorar.
progression [prə'grɛʃən] *s.* 1. progresión, adelantamiento. 2. secuencia, sucesión. 3. (mat.) progresión. 4. (mús.) sucesión (de acordes); secuencia (de armonías).
progressional [-əl] *a.* progresivo.
progressionism [-ˌɪzəm] *s.* progresismo.
progressionist [-əst] *s.* (pol.) progresista; (bio.) evolucionista.
progressist ['prɑgrəsəst, B prə'grɛs-] *s.* (pol.) progresista.
progressive [prə'grɛsɪv] *a.* 1. progresivo. 2. (pol.) progresista. 3. (gram.) durativo. —*s.* progresista.
progressively [-lɪ] *adv.* progresivamente.
progressiveness [-nəs] *s.* 1. carácter progresivo. 2. (pol.) progresismo.
Progressive Party, (pol.) Partido Progresista, nombre común a varios partidos políticos aparecidos en E.U. en diversas épocas.
Progressivism [-ˌɪzəm] *s.* progresismo, ideas y doctrinas progresistas.
prohibit [proʊ'hɪbət, prə-] *v.t.* 1. prohibir, vedar, interdecir. 2. impedir, dificultar.
prohibition [ˌproʊə'bɪʃən, ˌproʊhə-] *s.* 1. prohibición, veda; interdicto, entredicho. 2. prohibicionismo. 3. **P.** (E.U.) prohibición (de fabricar y vender bebidas alcohólicas).
prohibitionist [-əst] *s.* prohibicionista.
prohibitive [proʊ'hɪbətɪv, prə-] *a.* prohibitivo.
prohibitively [-lɪ] *adv.* en grado prohibitivo.
prohibitory [-əˌtɔrɪ, B -ɪtərɪ] *a.* prohibitorio.
project [prə'dʒɛkt] *v.t.* 1. proyectar, arrojar, dirigir sobre. 2. proyectar, idear, planear. 3. hacer resaltar o sobresalir. 4. (geom.) proyectar. —*v.i.* resaltar, sobresalir, resalir. — ['prɑdʒˌɛkt, -ɪkt, B 'prɔdʒ-] *s.* proyecto; plan; diseño, plano.
projectile [-'dʒɛktəl, -ˌtaɪl, B 'prɔdʒɪkˌtaɪl] *a.* 1. proyectante, impelente, ej., *p. force,* fuerza impelente. 2. arrojadizo. —*s.* proyectil.
projecting [prə'dʒɛktɪŋ] *a.* saliente, saledizo.
projection [-ʃən] *s.* 1. proyección. 2. planeamiento. 3. saliente; (arq.) vuelo, salidizo. 4. (geol., geom.) proyección. 5. (psic.) proyección. 6. (cine) proyección.
projectional [-əl] *a.* de proyección.
projectionist [-əst] *s.* (cine) operador de cabina; (t.v.) operador de cámara.
projection room, cabina de proyección.
projective [prə'dʒɛktɪv] *a.* proyectivo.
projective geometry, geometría proyectiva.
projector [-tər, B -tə] *s.* 1. (cine., ópt.) proyector. 2. proyectista; promotor; gestor.
prolactin [proʊ'læktən] *s.* (bioquím.) prolactina.
prolamin, prolamine ['proʊləmən, -ˌmin] *s.* (bioquím.) prolamina.
prolan [-ˌlæn] *s.* (bioquím.) prolan.
prolapse ['proʊˌlæps] (med.) *s.* prolapso. — [proʊ'læps] v.i. sufrir prolapso.
prolate ['proʊˌleɪt] *a.* (bot.) prolato.
prole [proʊl] *s.* (fam.) proletario.
proleg ['proʊˌlɛg] *s.* (ento.) pata abdominal (esp. en lepidópteros).
prolegomenon [ˌproʊlɪ'gɑməˌnɑn, -nən, B -'gɔm-] *s.* (*pl.* PROLEGOMENA [-nə]) (*ú. gen. en pl.*) prolegómeno, prólogo.
prolegomenous [-nəs] *a.* introductorio, introductivo, preliminar.
prolepsis [proʊ'lɛpsəs] *s.* (*pl.* PROLEPSES [-ˌsiz]) (ret., gram.) prolepsis.

proleptic [-tɪk] *a.* (ret., gram.) proléptico.
proletarian [ˌproʊlə'tɛrɪən, B -'tɛər-] *a.*, *s.* proletario.
proletarianization [-ˌtɛrɪənə'zeɪʃən, B -ˌtɛərɪənaɪ-] *s.* proletarización.
proletarianize [-'tɛrɪəˌnaɪz, B -'tɛər-] *v.t.* volver proletario.
proletariat [-ɪət] *s.* (*pl.* PROLETARIAT) proletariado.
proliferate [prə'lɪfəˌreɪt, proʊ-] *v.i.* proliferar, multiplicarse. — [-rət, -ˌreɪt] *a.* (bot.) prolífero.
proliferation [-ˌlɪfə'reɪʃən] *s.* proliferación.
proliferous [-'lɪfərəs] *a.* (bot., zool.) prolífero.
prolific [prə'lɪfɪk, proʊ-] *a.* prolífico; fecundo, fértil, ej., *p. writer,* escritor fecundo.
prolifically [-ɪkəlɪ] *adv.* prolíficamente, fecundamente.
proline ['proʊˌlin] *s.* (bioquím.) prolina.
prolix [proʊ'lɪks, 'proʊlɪks] *a.* difuso, verboso, prolijo.
prolixity [proʊ'lɪksətɪ] *s.* verbosidad, prolijidad.
prolixly [-'lɪkslɪ] *adv.* difusamente, verbosamente, prolijamente.
prolocutor [proʊ'lɑkjətər, B -'lɔk-ə] *s.* 1. portavoz, vocero. 2. presidente (de mesa, comisión, etc.).
prologize ['proʊˌlɔgˌaɪz, B -ˌlɔdʒ-] *var. de* prologuize.
prologue ['proʊˌlɔg, -ˌlɑg, B -ˌlɔg] *s.* 1. prólogo, proemio, introducción. 2. introductor, prologuista.
prologuize [-ˌaɪz] *v.i.* prologar.
prolong [prə'lɔŋ] *v.t.* prolongar, dilatar, extender, alargar.
prolongate [-ˌgeɪt] *v.t.* prolongar, prorrogar.
prolongation [ˌproʊlɔŋ'geɪʃən] *s.* prolongación.
prolonge [proʊ'lɑndʒ, B -'lɔnʒ] *s.* (arm.) prolonga.
prolonger [prə'lɔŋər, B -ə] *s.* prolongador.
prolusion [proʊ'luʒən] *s.* prolusión, prelusión, preludio; ensayo preliminar.
prom [prɑm, B prɔm] *s.* (E.U.) baile de gala o etiqueta de los colegios o universidades (esp. al terminar el año).
promenade [ˌprɑmə'neɪd, -'nɑd, B ˌprɔm-] *s.* 1. paseo, vuelta, caminata. 2. paseo, alameda. —*v.i.* pasear, dar un paseo.
promenade concert, concierto al aire libre.
promenade deck, (mar.) cubierta de paseo.
promenader [-ər, B -ə] *s.* paseante.
Promethean [prə'miθɪən] *a.* de Prometeo, prometeico.
Prometheus [-ˌθjus, -θɪəs] *s.* (mitol.) Prometeo, titán que robó el fuego sagrado para dárselo al hombre.
promethium [-θɪəm] *s.* (quím.) prometio, prometeo, promecio.
prominence ['prɑmənəns, B 'prɔm-] *s.* 1. eminencia, distinción. 2. prominencia, protuberancia. 3. (astr.) protuberancia (solar).
prominent [-nənt] *a.* 1. prominente, protuberante; conspicuo. 2. destacado, notable, distinguido, eminente.
prominently [-lɪ] *adv.* 1. prominentemente. 2.eminentemente, notablemente.
promiscuity [ˌprɑmɪs'kjuətɪ, B ˌprɔm-] *s.* 1. promiscuidad, confusión, mezcla. 2. promiscuidad sexual.
promiscuous [prə'mɪskjuəs] *a.* 1. promiscuo, mezclado, confuso. 2. licencioso.
promiscuously [-lɪ] *adv.* promiscuamente.
promiscuousness [-nəs] *s.* promiscuidad.
promise ['prɑməs, B 'prɔm-] *s.* 1. promesa, compromiso, prometimiento. 2. (fig.) promesa, esperanza. 3. **to give p.,** prometer. —*v.t.* 1. prometer, ofrecer, comprometerse. 2. prometer, asegurar. 3. dar muestras de, presagiar. 4. **p. oneself,** prometerse. —*v.i.* 1. hacer una promesa. 2. hacer concebir esperanzas.
Promised Land [-əst-] (bíbl.) Tierra de Promisión; (fig.) tierra de promisión.
promisee [ˌprɑmə'si, B ˌprɔm-] *s.* (der.) tenedor de una promesa.
promiser ['prɑməsər, B 'prɔmɪsə] *s.* prometedor.
promising [-sɪŋ] *a.* prometedor, que promete.
promisingly [-lɪ] *adv.* de manera prometedora.
promisor [ˌprɑmə'sɔr, B 'prɔmɪsə] *s.* (der.) prometedor.
promissory ['prɑməˌsɔrɪ, B 'prɔmɪsərɪ] *a.* promisorio.
promissory note, (der.) pagaré, nota de pago.
promontory ['prɑmənˌtɔrɪ, B 'prɔməntrɪ] *s.* (*pl.* PROMONTORIES) 1. promontorio, punta. 2. (anat.) promontorio, protuberancia.
promotable [prə'moʊtəbəl] *a.* digno de promoción.
promote [-'moʊt] *v.t.* 1. promover, ascender. 2. promover, fomentar, estimular. 3. (educ.) adelantar o pasar (a alguien) de año. 4. (ajedrez) coronar.
promoter [-ər, B -ə] *s.* promotor, promovedor; gestor; agente de negocios.
promotion [-'moʊʃən] *s.* 1. promoción, ascenso. 2. (ajedrez) coronación. 3. fomento (de ventas).
promotive [-'moʊtɪv] *a.* promovedor, promotor.
prompt [prɑmpt, B prɔmpt] *a.* 1. pronto, presto, listo; dispuesto, expedito. 2. rápido, inmediato, puntual. —*s.* 1. (com.) plazo o período (para pagar mercaderías compradas al crédito); fecha de vencimiento. 2. recordatorio, aviso. —*v.t.* 1. impulsar, mover, incitar. 2. soplar, apuntar (en exámenes, etc.). (teat.) apuntar. 3. sugerir, inspirar, insinuar. 4. **p. (someone) to (do),** mover o impulsar (a alguien) a (hacer).
promptbook ['prɑmptˌbʊk, B 'prɔmpt-] *s.* (teat.) apunte, libreto del apuntador.
prompter ['prɑmptər, B 'prɔmptə] *s.* (teat.) apuntador.
prompter's box, (teat.) concha del apuntador.
promptitude [-təˌtud, B -ˌtjud] *s.* prontitud, presteza.
promptly ['prɑmptlɪ, B 'prɔmpt-] *adv.* rápidamente, prestamente, prontamente.
promptness [-nəs] *s.* prontitud, presteza; rapidez.
promulgate ['prɑməlˌgeɪt, proʊ'mʌ-, B 'prɔməl-] *v.t.* promulgar, proclamar, publicar.
promulgation [ˌprɑməl'geɪʃən, B ˌprɔm-] *s.* promulgación, proclamación, publicación.
promulgator ['prɑməlˌgeɪtər, B 'prɔm-tə] *s.* promulgador.
promulge [proʊ'mʌldʒ] *v.t.* (ant.) promulgar, publicar.
pron. *abrev. de* 1. **pronominal,** pronominal. 2. **pronoun,** pronombre. 3. **pronounced,** pronunciado. 4. **pronunciation,** pronunciación.
pronate ['proʊˌneɪt] *v.t.* causar un movimiento de pronación.
pronation [proʊ'neɪʃən] *s.* (fisiol.) pronación.
pronator ['proʊˌneɪtər, B proʊ'neɪtə] *s.* (anat.) (músculo) pronador.
prone [proʊn] *a.* 1. prono, echado boca abajo; postrado, tendido. 2. (con *to*) inclinado, propenso, prono(a); dispuesto(a). 3. en declive, pendiente.
pronely ['proʊnlɪ] *adv.* de decúbito prono.
proneness [-nəs] *s.* propensión, inclinación, tendencia.
pronephric [proʊ'nɛfrɪk] *a.* (med.) pronéfrico.
pronephros [-rəs] *s.* (anat., zool.) pronefros.
prong [prɔŋ, prɑŋ, B prɔŋ] *s.* púa, punta, diente (de tenedor, etc.); pitón (de asta). —*v.t.* pinchar, atravesar o traspasar (con diente de tenedor, punta, pica, etc.).
pronghorn ['prɔŋˌhɔrn, 'prɑŋˌhɔn] *s.* (zool.) berrendo, antilocapra, cabri, mazama.
pronominal [proʊ'nɑmənəl, B -'nɔm-] *a.* (gram.) pronominal.
pronoun ['proʊˌnaʊn] *s.* (gram.) pronombre.
pronounce [prə'naʊns] *v.t.* 1. pronunciar, articular, proferir. 2. pronunciar (un discurso, sentencia, etc.); dar (una conferencia); promulgar (un decreto). 3. afirmar, aseverar; expresar. 4. (raro) declarar públicamente. —*v.i.* (con *on, for, against, in favor of*) pronunciarse, declararse (sobre, por, en contra, a favor de).
pronounceable [-'naʊnsəbəl] *a.* pronunciable.
pronounced [-'naʊnst] *a.* pronunciado, marcado, notable.
pronouncedly [-'naʊnsədlɪ, -naʊnstlɪ] *adv.* marcadamente, notablemente.
pronouncement [-'naʊnsmənt] *s.* declaración, anuncio, proclama, manifiesto.
pronouncer [-ər, B -ə] *s.* pronunciador.
pronouncing [-ɪŋ] *a.* de pronunciación, con pronunciación (diccionario, etc.).
pronto ['prɑntoʊ, B 'prɔn-] *adv.* (fam. E.U.) pronto, presto, prontamente.
pronucleus [proʊ'nuklɪəs, B -njuk-] *s.* (*pl.* PRONUCLEI [-lɪˌaɪ]) (biol.) pronúcleo.
pronunciamento [prɔˌnʌnsɪə'mɛntoʊ] *s.* (*pl.* PRONUNCIAMENTOS O PRONUNCIAMENTOES) proclama, manifiesto (esp. el emitido durante una rebelión militar).
pronunciation [-sɪ'eɪʃən] *s.* pronunciación.
proof [pruf] *s.* 1. prueba, probación, comprobación. 2. prueba, examen. 3. graduación normal (de las bebidas alcohólicas). 4. (der., mat.) prueba. 5. (impr.) prueba, galerada. 6. (foto.) (positivo de) prueba. 7. **the p. of the pudding is in the eating,** el movimiento se demuestra andando; **to bring** (o **to put**) **to the p.,** poner a prueba; **to give p. of,** dar una prueba de. —*a.* 1. (*ú. gen. en palabras compuestas*) a prueba de, resistente a, ej., *bombproof,* a prueba de bombas. 2. de prueba (carga, esfuerzo, fuerza, etc.). 3. de grado (alcohólico, etc.). normal. —*v.t.* 1. hacer una prueba de; someter a prueba. 2. corregir las pruebas de (libro, etc.). 3. **p. against,** hacer resistente a.
proof plane, (fís.) plano de prueba.
proofread ['prufˌrid] *v.t.* (impr.) leer o corregir las pruebas o galeradas de (libro, etc.).
proofreader [-ər, B -ə] *s.* corrector de pruebas o galeradas.
proofreading [-ɪŋ] *s.* corrección de pruebas o galeradas.
proof sheet, (impr.) pliego de prensa, pliego de prueba, prueba de máquina, prueba de impresión.
prop [prɑp, B prɔp] *v.t.* (*pret., p.p.* PROPPED; *p.pr.* PROPPING) 1. (ú. t. con *up*) apuntalar, entibar. 2. (fig., ú con *up*) mantener, sustentar, sostener; afianzar, reforzar. —*s.* 1. puntal, entibo; soporte, sostén. 2. (*pl.*) (jer.) piernas.
prop, *s.* (teat.) *abrev. de* **property.**
prop, *s. contr. de* **propeller.**
propaedeutic [ˌproʊpɪ'dutɪk, B -pi'djut-] *a.* propedéutico. —*s.* propedéutica, introducción.
propaedeutical [-ɪkəl] *a.* propedéutico.
propagable ['prɑpəgəbəl, B 'prɔp-] *a.* capaz de propagarse.
propaganda [ˌprɑpə'gændə, B ˌprɔp-] *s.* propaganda.

propagandism [-ˌdɪzəm] *s.* actividad propagandística.
propagandist [-dəst] *s., a.* propagandista.
propagandize [-ˌdaɪz] *v.t.* hacer propaganda de (artículo, doctrina, etc.).
propagate ['prɑpəˌgeɪt, B 'prɔp-] *v.t., v.i.* 1. propagar(se), multiplicar(se). 2. propagar(se), extender(se), difundir(se). 3. diseminar(se).
propagation [ˌprɑpə'geɪʃən, B ˌprɔp-] *s.* 1. propagación, generación, multiplicación. 2. propagación, diseminación, difusión, divulgación.
propagative ['prɑpəˌgeɪtɪv, B 'prɔp-] *a.* propagativo.
propagator [-ər, B -ə] *s.* propagador.
propane ['proʊˌpeɪn] *s.* (quím.) propano.
proparoxytone [ˌproʊpə'rɑksɪˌtoʊn, B -'rɔk-] *s.* (gram.) palabra proparoxítona, esdrújula. —*a.* (gram.) proparoxítono. —*v.t.* esdrujulizar.
propel [prə'pɛl] *v.t.* (*pret., p.p.* PROPELLED; *p.pr.* PROPELLING) propulsar, impeler, impulsar.
propellant, propellent [-ənt] *s.* 1. propulsor, impelente. 2. (arm.) carga de proyección. 3. (aer.) propulsante (usado en los motores a chorro). —*a.* propulsor, impelente.
propeller [-ər, B -ə] *s.* hélice (de buque o avión); impulsor, propulsor.
propeller blade, (aer.) pala de hélice.
propelling force [-ɪŋ-] fuerza propulsora o impulsora.
propend [proʊ'pɛnd] *v.i.* (raro) propender, tender.
propense [-'pɛns] *a.* (ant.) propenso, inclinado.
propensity [-'pɛnsətɪ] *s.* propensión, inclinación, preferencia, parcialidad, predisposición.
proper ['prɑpər, B 'prɔpə] *a.* 1. propio, particular, característico, distintivo. 2. mismo, propio, propiamente dicho. 3. propio, apropiado, adecuado; conveniente, digno. 4. correcto, pertinente, atinado, justo, exacto. 5. decoroso, decente. 6. (gram.) propio (nombre). 7. (her.) de color natural. 8. (fam.) excelente, muy bueno. 9. (pr. G.B.) verdadero.
proper fraction, (mat.) quebrado propio, fracción propia.
properly [-lɪ] *adv.* 1. propiamente, adecuadamente, debidamente. 2. correctamente. 3. (G.B.) completamente, muchísimo.
proper noun, p. name, (gram.) nombre propio.
propertied [-tɪd] *a.* propietario; acaudalado.
property ['prɑpərtɪ, B 'prɔpətɪ] *s.* (*pl.* PROPERTIES) 1. propiedad, cualidad, atributo, característica, peculiaridad. 2. propiedad, posesión, caudal; esp. bienes raíces, inmuebles. 3. propiedad, dominio, derecho de posesión. 4. (teat.) (*pl.*) utilería (Am.), decorados. 5. **man of p.,** hombre acaudalado.
propertyless [-ləs] *a.* falto de bienes de fortuna.
property man, (teat.) encargado de los accesorios; utilero (Amer.).
property tax, impuestos sobre bienes.
prophase ['proʊˌfeɪz] *s.* (biol.) profase.
prophecy ['prɑfəsɪ, B 'prɔf-] *s.* (*pl.* PROPHECIES) 1. profecía, predicción. 2. (bíbl.) profecía.
prophesier [-ˌsaɪər, B -ə] *s.* profeta, profetizador.
prophesy [-ˌsaɪ] *v.t., v.i.* (*pret., p.p.* PROPHESIED; *p.pr.* PROPHESYING) profetizar, predecir, vaticinar.
prophet ['prɑfət, B 'prɔf-] *s.* 1. profeta, vaticinador. 2. (relig.) profeta. 3. **the P.,** el Profeta (Mahoma); **the Prophets,** (bíbl.) los Profetas.
prophetess [-əs] *s.* profetisa.
prophetic [prə'fɛtɪk] **prophetical** [-ɪkəl] *a.* profético.
prophetically [-ɪkəlɪ] *adv.* proféticamente.
prophylactic [ˌproʊfə'læktɪk, B ˌprɔf-] *a., s.* (med.) profiláctico.
prophylaxis [-'læksəs] *s.* (med.) profilaxis.
propine [prə'pin, B -'paɪn] (esco.) *v.t.* regalar, donar. —*s.* propina.
propinquity [proʊ'pɪŋkwətɪ] *s.* 1. propincuidad, cercanía, proximidad. 2. parentesco.
propionate ['proʊpɪəˌneɪt] *s.* (quím.) propionato.
propionic acid [ˌproʊpɪ'ɑnɪk-, B -'ɔn-] *s.* (quím.) ácido propiónico.
propitiate [prə'pɪʃɪˌeɪt] *v.t.* propiciar, aplacar, apaciguar; conciliar.
propitiative [-ɪv] *a.* propiciatorio.
propitiation [-ˌpɪʃɪ'eɪʃən] *s.* 1. apaciguamiento, aplacación. 2. (teo.) propiciación, sacrificio propiciatorio.
propitiator [-pɪʃɪˌeɪtər, B -ə] *s.* propiciador.
propitiatory [-'pɪʃɪəˌtɔrɪ, B -tərɪ] *a.* propiciatorio; expiatorio. —*s.* (relig.) propiciatorio.
propitious [prə'pɪʃəs] *a.* propicio, benigno, favorable, auspicioso, de buen agüero; benéfico, útil.
propitiously [-lɪ] *adv.* propiciamente, favorablemente.
prop-jet ['prɑpˌdʒɛt, B 'prɔp-] *s.* turbohélice.
propman [-ˌmæn] *s. contr. de* **property man.**
propolis ['prɑpələs, B 'prɔp] *s.* propóleos, cera aleda (apicultura).
propolization [ˌprɑpələ'zeɪʃən, B ˌprɔpəlaɪ-] *s.* engomadura (que dan las abejas a las colmenas).
propone [prə'poʊn] *v.t.* (esco.) proponer; plantear; presentar, exponer.
proponent [-'poʊnənt] *s.* proponente, proponedor; defensor, patrocinador (de una tesis); (der.) proponente.
proportion [prə'pɔrʃən, B -'pɔʃən] *s.* 1. proporción, armonía, simetría. 2. parte, porción, cuota. 3. (*pl.*) dimensiones. 4. (mat.) proporción. 5. **in p.,** en proporción; **out of (all) p.,** fuera de (toda) proporción; **to be in proportion to,** estar en proporción con. —*v.t.* 1. proporcionar, adecuar. 2. dividir, repartir.
proportionable [-əbəl] *a.* proporcionado, proporcional.
proportional [-əl] *a.* 1. proporcional. 2. (con *to*) proporcionado, en proporción (a); (mat.) proporcional. —*s.* (mat.) número o cantidad proporcional.
proportionality [-ˌpɔrʃə'nælətɪ, B -ˌpɔʃə-] *s.* proporcionalidad.
proportionally [prə'pɔrʃənəlɪ, B -'pɔʃə-] *adv.* proporcionalmente, proporcionadamente.
proportional representation, (pol.) representación proporcional del electorado.
proportionate [-nət] *a.* (gen. con *to*) proporcionado (a), en proporción (a). — [-ˌneɪt] *v.t.* proporcionar, adecuar.
proportionately [-nətlɪ] *adv.* proporcionadamente.
proposal [prə'poʊzəl] *s.* propuesta, proposición; oferta, plan; propuesta matrimonial, propuesta de matrimonio.
propose [-'poʊz] *v.t.* 1. proponer, plantear, exponer; ofrecer, someter a consideración. 2. proponerse, pensar, tener intención de (hacer algo). 3. brindar, ofrecer (un brindis). 4. proponer, recomendar (un candidato). —*v.i.* 1. proponerse. 2. ofrecer matrimonio, pedir la mano. 3. **man proposes, God disposes,** el hombre propone, Dios dispone; **p. to (do),** proponerse (hacer).
proposer [-ər, B -ə] *s.* proponente, proponedor.
proposition [ˌprɑpə'zɪʃən, B ˌprɔp-] *s.* 1. propuesta, proposición. 2. (fam.) empresa, negocio. 3. asunto, cosa, problema, ej., *this is a tough p.,* esto es un problema difícil. 4. (fam.) tipo, tío, sujeto, ej., *a queer p.,* un tipo raro. 5. (lóg.) proposición, tesis. 6. (mat.) proposición, teorema. 7. (ant.) ofrecimiento. —*v.t.* hacer una propuesta a; esp. sugerir comercio carnal a.
propositional [-əl] *a.* del carácter de una proposición, relativo a la proposición.
propound [prə'paʊnd] *v.t.* proponer, plantear, exponer.
propounder [-ər, B -ə] *s.* proponente, proponedor.
propraetor, propretor [proʊ'pritər, B -ə] *s.* (hist.) propretor.
proprietary [prə'praɪəˌtɛrɪ, B -ətərɪ] *s.* (*pl.* PROPRIETARIES) 1. propietario, dueño; (hist.) (E.U.) dueño o concesionario de una colonia. 2. conjunto de propietarios. 3. (farm.) remedio patentado o de fórmula secreta. —*a.* 1. propietario, de propiedad. 2. patentado.
proprietary colony, (hist., E.U.) colonia concedida a un individuo o grupo de individuos con plenos poderes para gobernarla.
proprietary medicine, remedio patentado.
proprietor [-ətər, B -ətə] *s.* 1. propietario, dueño, amo. 2. (hist., E.U.) dueño o concesionario de una colonia.
proprietorship [-ˌʃɪp] *s.* propiedad, derecho de propiedad.
proprietress [-ətrəs] *s.* propietaria, dueña.
propriety [-ətɪ] *s.* 1. conveniencia, idoneidad. 2. corrección, decoro. 3. **the proprieties,** los cánones sociales, las convenciones.
proprioceptor [ˌproʊprɪə'sɛptər, B -tə] *s.* (fisiol.) propioceptor.
prop root, (bot.) raíz fúlcrea.
proptosis [ˌprɑp'toʊsəs, B ˌprɔp-] *s.* (med.) proptosis.
propulsion [prə'pʌlʃən] *s.* propulsión, impulsión.
propulsive [-'pʌlsɪv] *a.* propulsor, impulsor, impelente.
propyl ['proʊpəl] *s.* (quím.) propilo.
propylaeum [ˌprɑpə'liəm, B ˌprɔp-] *s.* (*pl.* PROPYLAEA [-'liə]) (arq.) (*gen. en pl.*) propileo.
propylene ['proʊpəˌlin] *s.* (quím.) propileno.
propylite ['prɑpəˌlaɪt, B 'prɔp-] *s.* (min.) propilita.
pro rata [proʊ'reɪtə, -'rɑtə] prorrata, en proporción, proporcionalmente.
prorate [-'reɪt] *v.t.* (pr. E.U.) prorratear.
proration [-'reɪʃən] *s.* prorrateo.
prorogation [ˌproʊrə'geɪʃən] *s.* prorrogación, prórroga, (esp. de las sesiones de un cuerpo deliberante).
prosaic [proʊ'zeɪɪk] *a.* 1. prosaico. 2. en prosa.
prosaically [-ɪkəlɪ] *adv.* prosaicamente.
prosaism ['proʊzeɪˌɪzəm] *s.* 1. prosaísmo. 2. dicho prosaico.
proscenium [proʊ'siniəm] *s.* (teat.) arco proscénico; (hist.) proscenio.
proscenium arch, (teat.) arco del proscenio.
proscribe [proʊ'skraɪb] *v.t.* proscribir.
proscriber [-ər, B -ə] *s.* proscriptor.
proscription [-'skrɪpʃən] *s.* proscripción.
proscriptive [-'skrɪptɪv] *a.* proscriptor, que proscribe.
prose [proʊz] *s.* prosa. —*a.* 1. prosaico, de prosa. 2. prosaico, insulso, común. —*v.t., v.i.* escribir o poner en prosa.
prosector [proʊ'sɛktər, B -tə] *s.* (med.) prosector.
prosecutable ['prɑsɪˌkjutəbəl, B 'prɔs-] *a.* enjuiciable.

prosecute [-ˌkjut] *v.t.* 1. proseguir, continuar, llevar adelante. 2. ejercer, practicar. 3. (der.) enjuiciar, encausar, procesar. —*v.i.* entablar juicio.
prosecuting attorney [-ˌkjutɪŋ-] (der.) abogado acusador o fiscal.
prosecution [ˌprɑsɪ'kjuʃən, B ˌprɔs-] *s.* 1. prosecución, proseguimiento. 2. (der.) enjuiciamiento, procesamiento; parte acusadora.
prosecutor ['prɑsɪˌkjutər, B 'prɔs-ə] *s.* (der.) fiscal; acusador, actor, querellante, demandante.
proselyte ['prɑsəˌlaɪt, B 'prɔs-] *s.* prosélito; converso, neófito. —*v.t.* convertir (a alguien). —*v.i.* ganar prosélitos.
proselytism [-ˌɪzəm, B -lɪˌtɪzəm] *s.* proselitismo.
proselytize [-lɪˌtaɪz] *var. de* **proselyte** (*v.*).
prosencephalon [ˌprɑsˌɛn'sɛfəˌlɑn, B ˌprɔs-ˌlɔn] *s.* (anat.) prosencéfalo.
prosenchyma [prɑ'sɛŋkəmə, B prɔ-] *s.* (bot.) prosénquima.
prosenchymatous [ˌprɑsən'kɪmətəs, B ˌprɔs-] *a.* (bot.) prosenquimatoso.
prose poem, poema en prosa, prosa poética.
proser ['proʊzər, B -zə] *s.* prosista, prosador.
Proserpina [prə'sɜrpənə, B -'sɜpɪ] *s.* (mitol.) Proserpina, hija de Ceres, raptada por Plutón.
prosily ['proʊzəlɪ] *adv.* prosaicamente.
prosimian [proʊ'sɪmɪən] *a., s.* (zool.) prosimio.
prosiness ['proʊzɪnəs] *s.* carácter prosaico.
prosit ['proʊzət, B -sɪt] *interj.* ¡salud! (brindis alemán).
proslavery [proʊ'sleɪvərɪ] *a.* esclavista, partidario de la esclavitud. —*s.* defensa de la esclavitud.
prosodic [prə'sɑdɪk, B -'sɔd-] **prosodical** [-ɪkəl] *a.* métrico.
prosodist ['prɑsədəst, B 'prɔs-] *s.* persona versada en métrica o versificación.
prosody [-ədɪ] *s.* 1. versificación, métrica, arte de la versificación. 2. prosodia.
prosoma [prə'soʊmə] *s.* (zool.) prosoma.
prosopography [ˌprɑsə'pɑgrəfɪ, B ˌprɔsə'pɔg-] *s.* (ret.) prosopografía.
prosopopoeia [prəˌsoʊpə'piə, B ˌprɔsoʊ-] *s.* (ret.) prosopopeya.
prospect ['prɑsˌpɛkt, B 'prɔs-] *s.* 1. panorama, perspectiva; paisaje, vista. 2. perspectiva, expectativa; esperanza, expectación. 3. cliente en perspectiva, candidato probable. 4. (*pl.*) perspectivas, probabilidades. 5. (min.) yacimiento probable; muestra de ensayo (de mineral). 6. **in p.,** en perspectiva, a la vista, esperado. — [-ˌpɛkt, B prəs'pɛkt] *v.t., v.i.* explorar (terreno) en busca de minas, catear (Am.); **p. for,** buscar (oro, etc.).
prospective [prə'spɛktɪv] *a.* presunto, en perspectiva, esperado.
prospector ['prɑsˌpɛktər, B prəs'pɛktə] *s.* prospector, buscador de minas, cateador (Am.).
prospectus [prə'spɛktəs] *s.* prospecto, folleto.
prosper ['prɑspər, B 'prɔspə] *v.i.* prosperar, medrar; tener éxito. —*v.t.* (hacer) prosperar, hacer medrar.
prosperity [prɑ'spɛrətɪ, B prɔs'pɛr-] *s.* prosperidad, medro; éxito.
prosperous ['prɑspərəs, B 'prɔs-] *a.* próspero, venturoso, floreciente; favorable, propicio, auspicioso.
prosperously [-lɪ] *adv.* prósperamente.
prosperousness [-nəs] *s.* prosperidad.
prostate ['prɑsˌteɪt, B 'prɔs-] *a.* (anat.) prostático. —*s.* (anat.) (t. **p. gland**) próstata, glándula prostática.
prostatectomy [ˌprɑstə'tɛktəmɪ, B ˌprɔs-] *s.* (med.) prostatectomía.
prostatic [prɑ'stætɪk, B prɔ-] *a.* (anat.) prostático.
prostatism ['prɑstəˌtɪzəm, B 'prɔs-] *s.* (med.) prostatismo.
prosthesis [prɑs'θisəs, 'prɑsθəsəs, B 'prɔsθə-] *s.* 1. (méd.) prótesis. 2. (gram.) prótesis, próstesis.
prosthetic [prɑs'θɛtɪk, B prɔs-] *a.* 1. (med.) protésico. 2. (gram.) protético, prostético.
prosthetics [-ɪks] *s. pl.* (*sing. o pl. en const.*) (med.) protética.
prosthodontics [ˌprɑsθə'dɑntɪks, B ˌprɔsθə'dɔnt-] *s. pl.* (*sing. o pl. en const.*) (med.) prostodontia, prótesis dental.
prostitute ['prɑstəˌtut, B 'prɔstɪˌtjut] *v.t.* 1. prostituir (a una mujer). 2. (fig.) prostituir, deshonrar, corromper, vender (empleo, autoridad, talento, etc.). —*a.* prostituido, prostituto; corrompido, corrupto. —*s.* prostituta, ramera, meretriz.
prostitution [ˌprɑstə'tuʃən, B ˌprɔstɪ'tju-] *s.* prostitución.
prostomium [proʊ'stoʊmɪəm] *s.* (*pl.* PROSTOMIA [-mɪə]) (zool.) prostomio.
prostrate ['prɑsˌtreɪt, B 'prɔs-] *a.* 1. postrado, prosternado. 2. (fig.) postrado, humillado, rendido. 3. (bot.) procumbente. —*v.t.* 1. postrar, derribar. 2. (fig.) postrar, abatir, humillar, debilitar. 3. **p. oneself,** prosternarse, postrarse.
prostration [prɑs'treɪʃən, B prɔs-] *s.* postración.
prosy ['proʊzɪ] *a.* prosaico, inculto; tedioso.
protactinium [ˌproʊtˌæk'tɪnɪəm] *s.* (quím.) protactinio.
protagonist [proʊ'tægənəst] *s.* protagonista, personaje, héroe.
protamine ['proʊtəˌmin, B -ˌmaɪn] *s.* (bioquím.) protamina.
protasis ['prɑtəsəs, B 'prɔt-] *s.* (*pl.* PROTASES [-ˌsiz]) (gram., ret.) prótasis.
proteaceous [ˌproʊtɪ'eɪʃəs] *a.* (bot.) proteáceo.
protean ['proʊtɪən, proʊ'tiən] *a.* 1. (mitol.) de Proteo, proteico. 2. proteico, versátil.
protease ['proʊtɪˌeɪs] *s.* (bioquím.) proteasa.
protect [prə'tɛkt] *v.t.* 1. proteger, defender, amparar; guardar, custodiar. 2. (com., fin.) respaldar, afianzar el cumplimiento de (una letra, pagaré u otra obligación). 3. (e.p.) proteger, favorecer, fomentar (industria local por medio de tarifas aduaneras).
protecting [-ɪŋ] *a.* protector, de protección.
protectingly [-ɪŋlɪ] *adv.* protectoramente.
protection [-'tɛkʃən] *s.* 1. protección, amparo, resguardo, defensa. 2. salvoconducto, pasaporte. 3. (e.p.) protección. 4. (t. **p. money**) (jer.) soborno (que se paga a la policía o a los políticos para que no se ventile alguna actividad ilegal); (E.U.) dinero pagado a una organización criminal para evitar daños.
protectionism [-ˌɪzəm] *s.* (e.p.) proteccionismo, prohibicionismo.
protectionist [-əst] *s.* (e.p.) proteccionista, prohibicionista.
protective [prə'tɛktɪv] *a.* 1. protector, amparador. 2. (e.p.) proteccionista.
protective coloration, (biol.) homocromía, coloración defensiva.
protective custody, (der.) custodia preventiva.
protectively [-lɪ] *adv.* con protección o proteccionismo.
protective tariff, (e.p.) tarifa o arancel proteccionista.
protector [prə'tɛktər, B -tə] *s.* 1. protector, defensor, amparador; patrocinador. 2. defensa, dispositivo protector. 3. (hist.) (G.B.) regente.
protectoral [-tərəl] *a.* protectorio.
protectorate [-tərət] *s.* protectorado, protectoría.
protectorship [-tərˌʃɪp, B -təˌ-] *s.* protectorado, protectoría.
protectress [-trəs] *s.* protectora, protectriz.
protégé ['proʊtəˌʒeɪ] *s.* (*pl.* PROTÉGÉS) protegido; favorito.
protégée ['proʊtəˌʒeɪ] *s.* (*pl.* PROTÉGÉES) protegida; favorita.
proteid ['proʊtid, 'proʊtɪəd] *s.* (bioquím.) proteido.
protein ['proʊtin, 'proʊtɪən] *s.* (bioquím.) proteína.
proteinase ['proʊtiˌneɪs, 'proʊtɪə-] *s.* (bioquím.) proteinasa.
proteinate [-ˌneɪt] *s.* (quím.) proteinato.
proteinuria [ˌproʊti'nʊrɪə, B -'njʊr-] *s.* (med.) proteinuria.
pro tem [proʊ'tɛm] **pro tempore** [-'tɛmpərɪ] temporalmente, por el momento.
protend [ˌproʊ'tɛnd] *v.t., v.i.* alargar(se), extender(se).
protensive [-'tɛnsɪv] *s.* 1. duradero. 2. extenso, extensivo.
proteoclastic [ˌproʊtɪoʊ'klæstɪk] *a.* (quím.) proteoclástico.
proteolysis [-'ɑləsəs, B -'ɔl-] *s.* (bioquím.) proteólisis.
proteose ['proʊtɪˌoʊs] *s.* (bioquím.) proteosa.
proteranthous [ˌprɑtə'rænθəs, ˌproʊt-, B ˌprɔt-] *a.* (bot.) proterando.
Proterozoic [-ərə'zoʊɪk] *a.* (geol.) proterozoico.
protest [prə'tɛst, 'proʊˌtɛst, B prə'tɛst] *v.t.* 1. protestar de, aseverar, afirmar (inocencia, fe, etc.). 2. recusar, rechazar (a un testigo, juez, etc.); citar como testigo. 3. (com.) protestar (una letra, pagaré, etc.). —*v.i.* 1. protestar, indignarse. 2. (pr. con *about* o *against*) protestar (contra). — ['proʊˌtɛst] *s.* 1. protesta, protestación; queja; objeción, reparo. 2. (com.) protesto. 3. (der.) protesta. 4. **under p.,** bajo protesta, contra su voluntad.
Protestant ['prɑtəstənt, B 'prɔt-] *s., a.* 1. (relig.) protestante. 2. **p.,** (t. [prə'tɛs-]) protestante.
Protestantism [-ˌɪzəm] *s.* (relig.) protestantismo.
protestation [ˌprɑtəs'teɪʃən, ˌproʊˌtɛs-, B ˌproʊˌtɛs-] *s.* protestación, protesta.
protester [prə'tɛstər, B -ə] *s.* (com.) protestador.
Proteus ['proʊˌtjus, -tɪəs] *s.* (mitol.) Proteo, dios que poseía el don de tomar diversas formas.
prothalamion [ˌproʊθə'leɪmɪən] **prothalamium** [-mɪəm] *s.* (*pl.* PROTHALAMIA [-mɪə]) canción nupcial.
prothallial [proʊ'θælɪəl] **prothalline** [-'θælaɪn] *a.* (bot.) protálico, protaliano.
prothallium [-'θælɪəm] *s.* (*pl.* PROTHALLIA [-ɪə]) (bot.) protalo.
prothesis ['prɑθəsəs, B 'prɔθ-] *s.* 1. (gram.) prótesis, próstesis. 2. (med.) prótesis.
prothetic [prɑ'θɛtɪk, B prɔ-] *a.* 1. (gram.) protético, prostético. 2. (med.) protésico.
prothonotary [proʊ'θɑnəˌtɛrɪ, B -'θɔnətərɪ] *s.* (der., relig.) protonotario.
prothorax [proʊ'θɔrˌæks] *s.* (zool.) protórax.
prothrombin [-'θrɑmbən, B -'θrɔm-] *s.* (fisiol.) protrombina.
protist ['proʊtəst] *s.* (biol.) protisto.
protium [-ɪəm, 'proʊʃɪ-, B 'proʊtjəm] *s.* (quím.) protio, protonio.
protoactinium [ˌproʊtoʊˌæk'tɪnɪəm] *s.* (quím.) protoactinio, protactinio.

protochloride [-'klɔr,aɪd] *s.* (quím.) protocloruro.
protocol ['proʊtə,kɔl, -,kal, B -,kɔl] *s.* 1. protocolo, registro. 2. (dip.) protocolo. —*v.t.* protocolizar.
protohistoric [,proʊtoʊhɪs'tɔrɪk, -'tar-, B -'tɔr-] *a.* protohistórico.
protohistory [-'hɪstərɪ] *s.* protohistoria.
protohuman [-'hjumən] *s.* (antrop.) protohumano, homínido.
protolithic [-'lɪθɪk] *a.* (antrop.) protolítico, prepaleolítico.
protomartyr ['proʊtoʊ,martər, B -,matə] *s.* protomártir.
proton ['proʊ,tan, B -,tɔn] *s.* (fís., quím.) protón.
protonema [,proʊtə'nimə] *s.* (*pl.* PROTONEMATA [-mətə]) (bot.) protonema.
proton-synchrotron ['proʊ,tan'sɪŋkrə,tran, B -,tɔn-,trɔn] *s.* (fís.) protónsincrotrón.
protopathic [,proʊtə'pæθɪk] *a.* (fisiol., psic.) protopático.
protophloem [-'floʊ,ɛm] *s.* (bot.) protofloema.
protoplasm ['proʊtə,plæzəm] *s.* (biol.) protoplasma.
protoplasmic [,proʊtə'plæzmɪk] *a.* (biol.) protoplasmático.
protoplast ['proʊtə,plæst] *s.* (biol.) protoplasto.
protoplastic [,proʊtə'plæstɪk] *a.* (biol.) protoplástico.
protoporphyrin [-'pɔrfərən, B -'pɔfə-] *s.* (bioquím.) protoporfirina.
protostele ['proʊtə,stil, B -,stilɪ] *s.* (bot.) protostela.
protostelic [,proʊtə'stilɪk] *a.* (bot.) protostélico.
prototrophic [-'trafɪk, B -'trɔf-] *a.* (fisiol.) prototrófico.
prototype ['proʊtə,taɪp] *s.* prototipo.
prototypic [,proʊtə'tɪpɪk] *a.* prototípico.
protoxide [proʊ'tak,saɪd, B -'tɔk-] **protoxid** [-sɪd] *s.* (quím.) protóxido.
protoxylem [,proʊtə'zaɪləm, -,lɛm] *s.* (bot.) protoxilema.
protozoa, *pl. de* **protozoon.**
protozoan [,proʊtə'zoʊən] *s.* (zool.) protozoario, protozoo.
protozoic [-'zoʊɪk] *a.* (zool.) protozoico.
protozoologist [-zoʊ'alədʒəst, B -'ɔl-] *s.* protozoólogo.
protozoology [-dʒɪ] *s.* protozoología.
protozoon [,proʊtə'zoʊ,an, B -ən] *s.* (*pl.* PROTOZOA [-'zoʊə]) (zool.) protozoo, protozoario.
protract [proʊ'trækt, B prə-] *v.t.* 1. prolongar, dilatar, alargar; (raro) extender, estirar. 2. (top.) trazar (un plano) con escala y transportador. 3. (anat.) extender, empujar, sacar fuera (órgano, etc.).
protracted [-əd] *a.* extenso, prolijo; largo, lento.
protractedly [-ədlɪ] *adv.* prolongadamente.
protractile [-'træktəl, B -taɪl] *a.* (zool.) protráctil.
protraction [-'trækʃən] *s.* 1. prolongación, dilatación, extensión. 2. (top.) dibujo (de un plano) hecho con escala y transportador. 3. (poét.) prolongación (de una sílaba).
protractor [-tər, B -tə] *s.* 1. prolongador. 2. (dib., top.) transportador (instrumento). 3. (anat.) músculo extensor o tensor.
protrude [proʊ'trud, B prə-] *v.t.* empujar hacia afuera, sacar fuera. —*v.i.* salir fuera, resaltar, sobresalir.
protruding [-ɪŋ] *a.* saliente, sobresaliente; prominente (mentón, nariz, dientes, etc.); saltón (díc. de los ojos).
protrusion [-'truʒən] *s.* 1. condición prominente, prominencia. 2. saliente, proyección, prominencia. 3. (med.) protrusión.
protrusive [-'trusɪv] *a.* 1. saliente, protuberante. 2. entremetido, intruso.
protrusively [-lɪ] *adv.* protuberantemente, de modo protuberante.
protuberance [proʊ'tubərəns, B prə'tju-] *s.* protuberancia, prominencia.
protuberant [-bərənt] *a.* 1. protuberante, prominente, saliente. 2. saltón (ojo).
protuberate [-bə,reɪt] *v.i.* sobresalir, resaltar, descollar.
proud [praʊd] *a.* 1. orgulloso, engreído. 2. orgulloso, soberbio, altivo, desdeñoso, altanero, imperioso, ufano; satisfecho, muy contento (de). 3. glorioso, notable, memorable, imponente, ej., *it was a p. sight,* era una vista imponente. 4. pujante, brioso. 5. **p. as a peacock,** engreído como un pavo real.
proud flesh, (med.) carne viciosa, carnosidad, bezo, tejido de granulación.
proudly ['praʊdlɪ] *adv.* 1. orgullosamente. 2. soberbiamente, altivamente.
proustite ['prus,taɪt] *s.* (min.) prustita.
provable ['pruvəbəl] *a.* demostrable, comprobable.
provascular [proʊ'væskjələr, B -lə] *a.* (bot.) provascular.
prove [pruv] *v.t.* (*pret.* PROVED; *p.p.* PROVED o PROVEN ['pruvən]; *p.pr.* PROVING) 1. probar, comprobar, confirmar, demostrar. 2. comprobar, verificar (testamento, operación matemática, resultado, etc.). 3. (ant.) probar, ensayar. 4. **p. that,** comprobar que. —*v.i.* resultar, salir (bien o mal); **p. to be,** venir a ser, resultar.
proven ['pruvən] *a.* probado, comprobado.
provenance ['pravənəns, B 'prɔv-] *s.* origen, procedencia, fuente.
Provençal [,pravən'sal, B ,prɔvan-] *a.* provenzal, de la Provenza (región de Francia). —*s.* provenzal (natural de Provenza), lengua provenzal, lemosín, lengua de oc.
provender ['pravəndər, B 'prɔvɪndə] *s.* 1. forraje. 2. (hum.) comida.
provenience [prə'viniəns] *s.* procedencia, origen.
proventriculus [,proʊvɛn'trɪkjələs] *s.* (*pl.* PROVENTRICULI [-laɪ]) (zool.) proventrículo.
prover ['pruvər, B -və] *s.* probador, ensayador; tirador de pruebas (obrero de imprenta); aparato para pruebas de materiales.
proverb ['prav,ɜrb, B 'prɔvɜb] *s.* 1. proverbio. 2. **Proverbs,** (bíbl.) Proverbios, libro de los Proverbios.
proverbial [prə'vɜrbɪəl, B -'vɜbɪ-] *a.* proverbial.
proverbially [-əlɪ] *adv.* proverbialmente.
provide [prə'vaɪd] *v.t.* 1. proveer, abastecer (a alguien). 2. proveer, surtir, proporcionar, suplir, suministrar (algo). 3. estipular, disponer, fijar. 4. **p. oneself (with),** proveerse (de). —*v.i.* 1. (con *for*) prepararse (para), encargarse (de). 2. (con *against*) precaverse (de), tomar precauciones o medidas (contra). 3. (con *for*) sostener, ser sostén (de).
provided [-əd] *conj.* (t. con *that*) con tal que, a condición que, siempre que.
providence ['pravədəns, B 'prɔv-] *s.* 1. providencia. 2. **P.,** la Providencia, Dios. 3. (ant.) prevención, previsión, prudencia.
provident [-ədənt] *a.* providente; prudente.
providential [,pravə'dɛntʃəl, B prɔvɪ'dɛnʃəl] *a.* providencial.
providentially [-ɪ] *adv.* providencialmente.
providently ['pravədəntlɪ, B 'prɔv-] *adv.* con previsión; prudentemente.
provider [prə'vaɪdər, B -ə] *s.* proveedor, provisor, suministrador, abastecedor.
providing [-ɪŋ] *conj.* con tal que, a condición de que, siempre que.
province ['pravəns, B 'prɔv-] *s.* 1. provincia (de un país). 2. competencia, incumbencia; jurisdicción. 3. esfera (de acción, negocio, etc.), rama (del saber), tipo (de actividad). 4. (relig.) provincia, diócesis. 5. (*gen. pl.*) provincias, ej., *to live in the provinces,* vivir en provincias.
provincial [prə'vɪntʃəl, B -'vɪnʃəl] *a.* 1. provincial. 2. provinciano; rústico, campesino; de miras estrechas. —*s.* provinciano.
provincialism [-,ɪzəm] *s.* provincialismo.
provincialist [-əst] *s.* provinciano.
provinciality [-,vɪntʃɪ'ælətɪ, B -,vɪnʃɪ-] *s.* 1. provincialismo; carácter provinciano. 2. costumbre o usanza provinciana.
provincialize [-'vɪntʃə,laɪz, B -'vɪnʃə-] *v.t.* hacer provincial.
provincially [-lɪ] *adv.* al modo provinciano, provincianamente.
proving ground ['pruvɪŋ-] campo de pruebas, campo de ensayos; polígono de pruebas (de artillería).
provision [prə'vɪʒən] *s.* 1. provisión, aprovisionamiento, abastecimiento. 2. (*gen. pl.*) provisiones, comestibles, víveres, vituallas. 3. provisión, medida, disposición. 4. estipulación, condición, cláusula. 5. (ten.) provisión. 6. to **make p. for,** proveerse de; asegurar el porvenir de. —*v.t.* proveer, abastecer, aprovisionar.
provisional [-əl] *a.* provisional, provisorio, interino, transitorio. —*s.* (filat.) sello provisional.
provisionally [-əlɪ] *adv.* provisionalmente, provisoriamente, interinamente.
provisionary [-,ɛrɪ, B -ərɪ] *a.* (raro) provisional, transitorio.
provisioner [-ər, B -ə] *s.* abastecedor, proveedor, suministrador.
provision of funds, (com.) provisión de fondos.
proviso [prə'vaɪ,zoʊ] *s.* (*pl.* PROVISOS o PROVISOES) condición, estipulación, salvedad, cláusula.
provisory [-zərɪ] *a.* 1. provisional, provisorio. 2. condicional.
provitamin [proʊ'vaɪtəmən, B -'vɪt-] *s.* (bioquím.) provitamina.
provocation [,pravə'keɪʃən, B ,prɔv-] *s.* provocación, desafío, reto; irritación, excitación, estímulo.
provocative [prə'vakətɪv, B -'vɔk-] *a.* provocativo, provocador, desafiador; estimulante. —*s.* estimulante; incentivo.
provocatively [-lɪ] *adv.* provocativamente, provocadoramente.
provocativeness [-nəs] *s.* comportamiento o carácter provocativo.
provoke [prə'voʊk] *v.t.* 1. provocar, excitar, irritar. 2. provocar, estimular, mover, incitar, inducir (a hacer algo). 3. suscitar, causar (indignación, comentarios, etc.). 4. **p. to (do),** provocar a (hacer).
provoker [-ər, B -ə] *s.* provocador; incitador.
provoking [-'voʊkɪŋ] *a.* provocativo, provocante, irritante; incitante, estimulante.
provokingly [-lɪ] *adv.* provocativamente.
provost ['proʊ,voʊst, 'pravəst, B 'prɔvəst] *s.* 1. preboste; superintendente; funcionario jefe. 2. jefe de la corporación municipal (en Esco.). 3. (relig.) prepósito, pavorde. 4. (educ.) (E.U.) administrador de alto rango (en algunas universidades); (G.B.) director de colegio. 5. (mil.) capitán preboste. 6. guardián de prisión.

provost court, (mil.) (E.U.) tribunal de policía militar.
provost guard, (mil.) destacamento de policía militar.
provost marshal, 1. (mil.) capitán preboste. 2. jefe de policía (en algunas colonias de G.B.).
provostship [-ˌʃɪp] *s.* prebostazgo; prepositura, pavordía.
prow [praʊ] *s.* (mar., aer.) proa. —*a.* (ant.) valiente; gallardo, bizarro.
prowess ['praʊəs] *s.* 1. valentía; valor, ánimo, bravura. 2. proeza, hazaña. 3. destreza, habilidad, pericia, maña.
prowl [praʊl] *v.i., v.t.* rondar, merodear, andar al acecho; vagar. —*s.* ronda en busca de presa, merodeo.
prowl car, auto patrullero, radiopatrulla (Am.) (de la policía).
prowler ['praʊlər, B -ə] *s.* rondador, merodeador.
proximal ['prɑksəməl, B 'prɔk-] *a.* 1. próximo, contiguo. 2. (anat.) proximal.
proximate [-mət] *a.* 1. próximo, inmediato, junto, cercano. 2. próximo, inminente; siguiente.
proximately [-lɪ] *adv.* próximamente.
proximity [prɑk'sɪmətɪ, B prɔk-] *s.* proximidad, cercanía, inmediación.
proximity fuze, (arm.) espoleta de proximidad.
proximo ['prɑksəˌmoʊ, B 'prɔk-] *adv.* del mes próximo, ej., *the 10th p.*, el 10 del mes próximo.
proxy ['prɑksɪ, B 'prɔk-] *s.* (*pl.* PROXIES) 1. apoderado, delegado, mandatario, representante, poderhabiente, agente, substituto. 2. procuración, poder. 3. **by p.,** por poder, mediante mandatario o substituto.
proxy marriage, matrimonio por poder, por poderes.
prude [prud] *s.* mojigato, gazmoño; puritano.
prudence ['prudəns] *s.* prudencia, cordura, juicio, cautela, discreción; circunspección, moderación, mesura, previsión.
prudent [-ənt] *a.* prudente, juicioso, cuerdo, discreto, sagaz; cauto, moderado, cauteloso.
prudential [pru'dɛntʃəl, B -'dɛnʃəl] *a.* 1. prudencial. 2. aconsejador, asesor (junta, comité, etc.).
prudentially [-ɪ] *adv.* prudencialmente.
prudently ['prudəntlɪ] *adv.* prudentemente.
prudery ['prudərɪ] *s.* mojigatería, gazmoñería, pudibundez.
prudish [-ɪʃ] *a.* mojigato, gazmoño, pudibundo; beato, denguero, dengoso.
prudishly [-lɪ] *adv.* con mojigatería.
prudishness [-nəs] *s.* mojigatería, gazmoñería, pudibundez; puritanismo.
pruinose ['pruəˌnoʊs] *a.* (bot., zool.) cubierto de pruina.
prune [prun] *s.* 1. ciruela (pasa), pruna. 2. (jer.) papamoscas, simplainas.
prune, *v.t.* podar, escamondar, cortar, cercenar.
prunella [pru'nɛlə] *s.* (tej.) sempiterna, sarga levantina.
prunella, *s.* (quím.) prunela (sal).
prunelle [-'nɛl] *s.* 1. licor de ciruela. 2. *var. de* **prunella.**
pruner ['prunər, B -ə] *s.* podador.
pruning hook ['prunɪŋ-] podón, podadera, mácola.
prurience ['prʊrɪəns, B 'prʊər-] *s.* 1. comezón, picazón, escozor, prurito. 2. sensualidad, lascivia, deseo o pensamiento lascivo.
pruriency [-ənsɪ] *s. var. de* **prurience.**
prurient [-ənt] *a.* lascivo, sensual, libidinoso.
pruriently [-lɪ] *adv.* lascivamente, sensualmente.
pruriginous [prʊ'rɪdʒənəs] *a.* (med.) pruriginoso.
prurigo [-'raɪgoʊ] *s.* (med.) prurigo.
pruritic [-rɪtɪk] *a.* (med.) prurítico.
pruritus [-'raɪtəs] *s.* (med.) prurito, comezón, picazón.
Prussian ['prʌʃən] *a., s.* prusiano, de Prusia.
Prussian blue, azul de Prusia.
Prussianism [-ˌɪzəm] *s.* prusianismo, militarismo despótico y ambicioso.
prussiate ['prʌsɪˌeɪt, B 'prʌʃɪɪt] *s.* (quím.) prusiato.
prussic acid ['prʌsɪk-] (quím.) ácido prúsico.
pry [praɪ] *s.* (mec.) alzaprima, palanca, barra. —*v.t.* (*pret.; p.p.* PRIED; *p.pr.* PRYING) alzaprimar, palanquear; apalancar; **p. open, forzar** con alzaprima o palanca (caja, estuche, etc.); **p. out,** (fig.) arrancar (secreto, información, etc.); **p. up,** levantar o forzar con alzaprima o palanca (tapa, etc.).
pry, *v.i.* curiosear, andar atisbando, andar husmeando; **p. into,** fisgar, husmear, atisbar, meterse en.
pryer, *var. de* **prier.**
prying ['praɪɪŋ] *a.* fisgón, curioso, entremetido, inquisitivo, husmeador. —*s.* fisgoneo, husmeo, atisbadura.
P.S. *abrev. de* **postscript,** postdata (P.D.).
psalm [sɑm] *s.* salmo, cántico. —*v.t.* cantar o ensalzar en salmos.
psalmbook ['sɑmˌbʊk] *s.* salterio, libro de los salmos.
psalmist [-əst] *s.* salmista; **the P.,** (bíbl.) el Salmista (David).
psalmodist [-ədəst, B 'sælmə-] *s.* compositor de salmos.
psalmody [-dɪ] *s.* (*pl.* PSALMODIES) salmodia.
Psalms [sɑmz] *s. pl.* (bíbl.) (el libro de) los Salmos.
Psalter ['sɔltər, B -tə] *s.* 1. (bíbl.) salterio, el libro de los Salmos. 2. salmodia.
psalterium [sɔl'tɪrɪəm, B -'tɪər-] *s.* (*pl.* PSALTERIA [-ɪə]) (zool.) salterio, libro, omaso.
psaltery ['sɔltərɪ] **psaltry** [-trɪ] *s.* (*pl.* PSALTERIES; PSALTRIES) (mús.) salterio.
psammite ['sæmˌaɪt] *s.* (geol.) samita.
psephite ['siˌfaɪt] *s.* (geol.) psefita, sefita.
pseudepigrapha [ˌsudə'pɪgrəfə, B ˌsju-] *s. pl.* libros apócrifos (de carácter bíblico).
pseudo ['sudoʊ, B 'sju-] *a.* pseudo, seudo, supuesto, falso, fingido, espurio, apócrifo.
pseudocarp ['sudəˌkɑrp, B 'sjudəˌkɑp] *s.* (bot.) seudocarpo o seudocarpio.
pseudocarpous [ˌsudə'kɑrpəs, B ˌsjudə'-kɑp-] *a.* (bot.) seudocárpico.
pseudoclassic [-'kæsɪk, B 'sjud-] *a., s.* seudoclásico.
pseudomorph ['sudəˌmɔrf, B 'sjudəˌmɔf] *s.* (min.) seudomorfo.
pseudomorphic [ˌsudə'mɔrfɪk, B 'sjudə'-mɔfɪk] *a.* (min.) seudomórfico.
pseudomorphism [-ˌfɪzəm] *s.* (min.) seudomorfismo.
pseudomorphous [-fəs] *a.* (min.) seudomorfo.
pseudomycelium [ˌsudoʊˌmaɪ'silɪəm, B 'sjud-] *s.* (bot.) seudomicelio.
pseudoneuropter [-nʊˌrɑptər, B -njʊ'rɔptə] *s.* (ento.) arquíptero.
pseudoneuropteran [-tərən] *a., s.* (ento.) arquíptero.
pseudonym ['sudəˌnɪm, B 'sju-] *s.* seudónimo.
pseudonymous [su'dɑnəməs, B sju'dɔn-] *a.* seudónimo.
pseudoparenchyma [ˌsudoʊpə'rɛŋkəmə, B 'sju-] *s.* (bot.) seudoparénquima.
pseudopod ['sudəˌpɑd, B 'sjudəˌpɔd] *s.* (biol.) seudópodo.
pseudopodal [su'dɑpədəl, B sju'dɔp-] **pseudopodial** [ˌsudə'poʊdɪəl, B ˌsju-] *a.* (biol.) seudópodo.
pseudopodium [ˌsudə'poʊdɪəm, B ˌsju-] *s.* (*pl.* PSEUDOPODIA [-ɪə]) (zool.) seudópodo.
pseudoscience [ˌsudoʊ'saɪns, B 'sjudoʊ-] *s.* seudociencia, ciencia falsa.
pshaw [ʃɔ, B pʃɔ] *interj.* ¡bah! ¡fuera!
psi [saɪ, B psaɪ] *s.* psi, vigésima tercera letra del alfabeto griego.
psilomelane [saɪ'lɑməˌleɪn, B -'lɔm-] *s.* (min.) psilomelano, psilomelana.
Psittacidae [sɪ'tæsəˌdi, B psɪ-] *s. pl.* (zool.) psitácidos.
psittacosis [ˌsɪtə'koʊsəs, B ˌpsɪtə-] *s.* (med.) psitacosis.
psoas ['soʊəs, B 'psoʊæs] *s.* (anat.) psoas.
psocid ['soʊsəd, B 'sɔs-] *s.* (ento.) psócido.
psoriasis [sə'raɪəsəs] *s.* (med.) psoriasis.
PST *abrev. de* **Pacific Standard Time,** hora legal del Pacífico.
psych [saɪk] *v.t.* (jer.) 1. alterar o excitar mentalmente (gen. con *up*). 2. **p. out,** usar intuición de tipo psíquico o psicológico (esp. para controlar una persona o situación). —*v.i.* (jer.) 1. acobardarse. 2. fingirse mentalmente enfermo (para escapar de una situación).
psychasthenia [ˌsaɪkəs'θinɪə] *s.* (med.) psicastenia.
psychasthenic [-'θɛnɪk] *a.* (med.) psicasténico. —*s.* persona psicasténica.
Psyche ['saɪkɪ] *s.* 1. (mitol.) Psiquis, doncella amada por Eros. 2. p., psique, psiquis, alma.
psychedelic [ˌsaɪkə'dɛlɪk] *var. de* **psychodelic.**
Psyche knot, peinado griego.
psychiatric [-kɪ'ætrɪk] *a.* psiquiátrico, siquiátrico.
psychiatrist [sə'kaɪətrəst, saɪ-] *s.* psiquiatra, siquiatra.
psychiatry [-trɪ] *s.* psiquiatría, siquiatría.
psychic ['saɪkɪk] *a.* psíquico, síquico. —*s.* 1. persona susceptible a la influencia psíquica; médium, medio (en espiritismo). 2. (*pl.*) fenómenos psíquicos.
psychical [-kɪkəl] *a.* psíquico, síquico.
psycho ['saɪkoʊ] *s.* (jer.) 1. psicópata, sicópata. 2. alienado.
psychoanalysis [ˌsaɪkoʊə'næləsəs] *s.* psicoanálisis, sicoanálisis.
psychoanalytic [-ˌænə'lɪtɪk] **psychoanalytical** [-ɪkəl] *a.* psicoanalítico, sicoanalítico.
psychoanalytically [-ɪkəlɪ] *adv.* con medios psicoanalíticos; desde el punto de vista del psicoanálisis.
psychoanalyst [-'ænələst] *s.* psicoanalista, sicoanalista.
psychoanalyze [-ˌlaɪz] *v.t.* psicoanalizar, sicoanalizar.
psychobiology [ˌsaɪkoʊbaɪ'ɑlədʒɪ, B -'ɔl-] *s.* psicobiología.
psychodelic [ˌsaɪkə'dɛlɪk] *a.* sicodélico, psicodélico.
psychodrama ['saɪkəˌdrɑmə, -ˌdræmə, B ˌsaɪkə'drɑmə] *s.* (psic.) psicodrama.
psychodynamic [ˌsaɪkoʊdaɪ'næmɪk] *a.* psicodinámico.
psychodynamics [-ɪks] *s. pl.* (*sing. en const.*) psicodinámica.
psychogenesis [ˌsaɪkə'dʒɛnəsəs] *s.* psicogénesis.
psychogenic [-ɪk] *a.* (psic.) psicógeno.
psychognosis [ˌsaɪkəg'noʊsəs, B -kɔg-] *s.* (psic.) psicognosis.
psychological [ˌsaɪkə'lɑdʒɪkəl, B -'lɔdʒ-] **psychologic** [-ɪk] *a.* psicológico, sicológico.

psychologically [-ɪkəlɪ] *adv.* psicológicamente, sicológicamente.
psychological warfare, guerra psicológica.
psychologism [saɪ'kɑlə,dʒɪzəm, B -'kɔl-] *s.* (filos.) psicologismo, sicologismo.
psychologist [-dʒəst] *s.* psicólogo, sicólogo.
psychologize [-,dʒaɪz] *v.t.* explicar o interpretar psicológicamente.
psychology [-dʒɪ] *s.* psicología, sicología.
psychometric [,saɪkə'mɛtrɪk] *a.* psicométrico.
psychometrics [-trɪks] *s. pl.* (*sing. en const.*) psicometría.
psychometry [saɪ'kɑmətrɪ, B -'kɔm-] *s.* 1. adivinación por contacto o proximidad de un objeto. 2. psicometría.
psychomotor [,saɪkə'moʊtər, B -ə] *a.* psicomotor.
psychoneurosis [,saɪkoʊnʊ'roʊsəs, B -njʊə-] *s.* psiconeurosis.
psychoneurotic [-'rɑtɪk, B -'rɔt-] *a., s.* psiconeurótico.
psychopath ['saɪkə,pæθ] *s.* psicópata, sicópata.
psychopathic [,saɪkə'pæθɪk] *a.* psicopático, sicopático. —*s.* psicópata, sicópata.
psychopathology [-koʊpə'θɑlədʒɪ, B -'θɔl-] *s.* psicopatología.
psychopathy [saɪ'kɑpəθɪ, B -'kɔp-] *s.* psicopatía.
psychophysical [,saɪkoʊ'fɪzɪkəl] *a.* (psic.) psicofísico.
psychophysics [-'fɪzɪks] *s.* psicofísica.
psychosis [saɪ'koʊsəs] *s.* (*pl.* PSYCHOSES [-siz]) psicosis, sicosis.
psychosomatic [,saɪkəsə'mætɪk] *a.* (med.) psicosomático, sicosomático.
psychosurgery [,saɪkoʊ'sɜrdʒərɪ, B -'sɜdʒ-] *s.* psicocirugía.
psychotechnology [-tɛk'nɑlədʒɪ, B -'nɔl-] *s.* psicotecnia.
psychotherapeutic [-,θɛrə'pjutɪk] *a.* psicoterapéutico.
psychotherapeutics [-ɪks] *s. pl.* (*sing. en const.*) psicoterapéutica, psicoterapia.
psychotherapy [-'θɛrəpɪ] *s.* psicoterapia, psicoterapéutica.
psychotic [-'kɑtɪk, B -'kɔt-] *s., a.* psicópata, sicópata.
psychrometer [saɪ'krɑmətər, B -'krɔmɪtə] *s.* psicrómetro, instrumento para medir la humedad atmosférica.
psychrophilic [,saɪkroʊ'fɪlɪk] *a.* (bact.) psicrófilo.
psylla ['sɪlə] **psyllid** ['sɪləd] *s.* (ento.) psílido.
Pt *símb. de* **platinum,** platino (Pt).
P T *abrev de* 1. **Pacific Time,** hora del Pacífico. 2. **physical training,** educación física.
P. T. A. *abrev. de* **Parent-Teacher Association,** Asociación de Padres y Maestros.
ptarmigan ['tɑrmɪgən, B 'tɑmɪ-] *s.* (orn.) lagópedo, perdiz blanca.
PT boat ['pi'ti-] (mar.) (E.U.) lancha torpedera de motor.
pteridoid ['tɛrə,dɔɪd] *a.* (bot.) pteridoide.
pteridologist [,tɛrə'dɑlədʒəst, B -'dɔl-] *s.* pteridólogo.
pteridology [-dʒɪ] *s.* pteridología.
pteridophyte [tə'rɪdə,faɪt, B 'tɛrɪdoʊ-] *s.* (bot.) pteridófita.
pteridophytic [tə,rɪdə'fɪtɪk, B ,tɛrədoʊ-] **pteridophytous** [,tɛrə'dɑfətəs, B -'dɔf-] *a.* (bot.) pteridófito.
pteridosperm [-'rɪdə,spɜrm, B 'tɛrɪdoʊ,-spɜm] *s.* (pal.) pteridoesperma.
pterodactyl [,tɛrə'dæktəl] *s.* (pal.) pterodáctilo.
pteropod ['tɛrə,pɑd, B -,pɔd] *a., s.* (zool.) pterópodo.
pterosaur [-,sɔr, B -,sɔ] *s.* (pal.) pterosaurio.
pterygoid [-,gɔɪd] *a., m.* (anat.) pterigoideo.
pterygoid process, (med.) apófisis pterigoideo.
pteryla ['tɛrələ] *s.* (*pl.* PTERYLAE [-li]) (orn.) pterilio.
ptisan [tɪz'æn, 'tɪzən] *s.* tisana, ptisana.
Ptolemaic [,tɑlə'meɪɪk, B ,tɔl-] *a.* (hist.) 1. ptolemaico, relativo al sistema de Ptolomeo. 2. perteneciente a la dinastía egipcia de los Ptolomeos.
ptomaine ['toʊ,meɪn, toʊ'meɪn] *s.* (bioquím.) ptomaína, tomaína.
ptomaine poisoning, envenenamiento por tomaínas.
ptosis ['toʊsəs] *s.* (med.) ptosis.
ptyalin ['taɪələn] *s.* (bioquím.) ptialina, tialina.
ptyalism ['taɪə,lɪzəm] *s.* ptialismo, tialismo, excesiva secreción de saliva.
Pu *símb. de* **plutonium,** plutonio (Pu).
pub [pʌb] *s.* (fam.) (pr. G.B.) taberna, cantina, bar.
pub crawler, uno que va de taberna en taberna.
pubertal ['pjubərtəl, B -bət-] *a.* de la pubertad.
puberty [-bərtɪ, B -bətɪ] *s.* pubertad.
puberulent [pju'bɛrjələnt] *a.* (bot.) puberulento, pubérulo.
pubes ['pju,biz] *s.* (*pl.* PUBES) 1. (anat.) pubes, pubis. 2. vello púbico.
pubescence [pju'bɛsəns] *s.* pubescencia, pubertad.
pubescent [-ənt] *a.* pubescente; (biol.) pubescente.
pubic ['pjubɪk] *a.* (anat.) púbico, pubiano.
pubis ['pjubɪs] *s.* (*pl.* PUBES [-biz]) (anat.) pubis, hueso pubis.
public ['pʌblɪk] *a.* público. —*s.* público, gente, espectadores, concurrencia; **in p.,** en público, abiertamente; **to make p.,** publicar, divulgar.
public accountant, contador público.
public-address system [-ə'drɛs-] sistema de amplificación sonora, sistema megafónico.
publican ['pʌblɪkən] *s.* 1. (hist. romana) publicano. 2. (pr. G.B.) tabernero, cantinero.
publication [,pʌblə'keɪʃən] *s.* 1. publicación, divulgación. 2. publicación, edición, impresión.
public convenience, (pr. G.B.) tocador, lavatorio; retrete (en estaciones ferroviarias, etc.).
public conveyance, vehículo de servicio público.
public defender, (der.) defensor de oficio.
public domain, propiedad pública, dominio público.
public enemy, enemigo de la sociedad, enemigo público.
public good, 1. bienestar público. 2. interés público.
public health, salud pública, sanidad pública.
public hearing, audiencia pública.
public house, 1. posada, hostería. 2. (pr. G.B.) taberna, cantina, bar.
publicist ['pʌbləsəst] *s.* publicista.
publicity [pʌb'lɪsətɪ] *s.* 1. publicidad, notoriedad. 2. publicidad, propaganda. —*a.* de publicidad, publicitario.
publicize ['pʌblə,saɪz] *v.t.* publicar, dar publicidad a, divulgar.
public lavatory, tocador, lavatorio; retrete (en estaciones ferroviarias, etc.).
public law, derecho público.
public liability, (der.) responsabilidad civil o pública.
publicly ['pʌblɪklɪ] *adv.* públicamente.
publicness [-nəs] *s.* carácter público.
public nuisance, molestia pública, estorbo público.
public official, funcionario público.
public opinion, opinión pública.
public property, bienes públicos, bienes fiscales.
public prosecutor, fiscal.
public relations, relaciones públicas.
public revenue, (e.p.) renta fiscal.
public sale, subasta pública.
public school, 1. (G.B.) escuela particular. 2. (E.U.) escuela pública.
public servant, funcionario o empleado público, empleado del gobierno.
public service, servicio público.
public-service corporation ['pʌblɪk'sɜrvəs-, B -'sɜvɪs-] empresa de servicio público, compañía de utilidad pública.
public spirit, civismo, patriotismo.
public-spirited [-'spɪrətəd] *a.* cívico, patriótico.
public thoroughfare, vía pública.
public utility, 1. empresa de servicio público, (empresa de) utilidad pública. 2. (com.) (*gen. pl.*) acciones de empresas de utilidad pública.
public works, obras públicas.
publish ['pʌblɪʃ] *v.t.* 1. publicar, divulgar, proclamar, pregonar, revelar, anunciar. 2. publicar, editar.
publishable [-əbəl] *a.* publicable.
publisher [-ər, B -ə] *s.* editor, publicador.
publishing house [-ɪŋ-] editorial, casa editorial, empresa editora.
puccoon [pə'kun] *s.* (bot.) sanguinaria, centinodia, nevadilla.
puce [pjus] *s., a.* (de) color castaño rojizo.
puck [pʌk] *s.* 1. duende, trasgo. 2. disco de goma (en el hockey sobre hielo).
pucka, *var. de* **pukka.**
pucker ['pʌkər, B -ə] (ú. t. con *up*) *v.i.* arrugarse. —*v.t.* arrugar, fruncir, recoger, plegar. —*s.* arruga, fruncido, recogido, pliegue, rugosidad.
puckery [-ərɪ] *a.* rugoso, arrugado.
puckish [-ɪʃ] *a.* travieso, juguetón, vivaracho; malicioso.
pudding ['pʊdɪŋ] *s.* 1. budín (dulce). 2. morcilla, salchichón, relleno. 3. **the proof of the p. is in the eating,** el movimiento se demuestra andando.
pudding stone, (geol.) pudinga.
puddle ['pʌdəl] *s.* 1. charco, poza. 2. mezcla de arcilla y grava mojada, argamasa, arcilla impermeable. —*v.t.* 1. enfangar, embarrar, enlodar. 2. hacer mezcla de (arcilla y grava), convertir en argamasa; impermeabilizar con arcilla. 3. pudelar (hierro). 4. (agr.) cultivar (la tierra) cuando está mojada.
puddler ['pʌdlər, B -ələ] *s.* pudelador.
puddling [-lɪŋ, -əlɪŋ] *s.* (metal.) pudelación, pudelaje, pudelado.
puddling furnace, (metal.) horno de pudelar.
pudency ['pjudənsɪ] *s.* pudor, recato, modestia, castidad, decoro; pudibundez.
pudendal [pjʊ'dɛndəl] *a.* pudendo.
pudendum [-dəm] *s.* (*pl.* PUDENDA [-də]) (anat.) (*ú. pr. en pl.*) partes pudendas.
pudgy ['pʌdʒɪ] *a.* regordete, gordiflón, rechoncho.
pueblo [pʊ'ɛbloʊ, 'pwɛb-] *s.* 1. casa comunal, aldea de indios, pueblo. 2. **a P. Indian,** (E.U.) un indio de la tribu Pueblo.
puerile ['pjʊrəl, B 'pjʊər,aɪl] *a.* 1. pueril, infantil. 2. (fig.) pueril, fútil, trivial.
puerilely [-əlɪ, B -,aɪllɪ] *adv.* puerilmente.
puerilism [-ə,lɪzəm, B -əraɪ-] *s.* (med.) puerilismo.
puerility [pjʊ'rɪlətɪ, B ,pjʊə-] *s.* puerilidad.
puerperal [pju'ɜrpərəl, B -'ɜp-] *a.* puerperal.

puerperal fever, (med.) fiebre puerperal.

puerperium [ˌpjuər'pɪrɪəm, B ˌpjuə'pɪər-] *s.* (med.) puerperio, sobreparto.

Puerto Rican [ˌpwɛrtə'rikən, 'pɔrtə-, B 'pwɜtoʊ-] *a., s.* puertorriqueño, boricua, borinqueño.

Puerto Rico [-'rikoʊ] Puerto Rico.

puff [pʌf] *s.* 1. resoplido, soplo, soplido; bocanada (de aire o humo), fumada. 2. (cocina) bollo, buñuelo. 3. mota o borla de polvos. 4. mechón (de pelo). 5. colcha de plumón, edredón. 6. protuberancia, hinchazón. 7. (cost.) bullón, bollo. 8. bombo, elogio exagerado. —*v.i.* 1. echar bocanadas de humo o vapor. 2. soplar, resoplar, jadear. 3. (gen. con *up*) inflarse, hincharse; (fig.) hincharse, entonarse. 4. **p. away,** dar soplidos o resoplidos, lanzar bocanadas de humo. —*v.t.* 1. soplar. 2. fumar (cigarrillo, etc.). 3. (sew.) abullonar. 4. **p. out,** apagar a soplos; hinchar; pronunciar jadeando; **p. up,** inflar, hinchar; (fig.) enorgullecer; dar bombo a, alabar con exageración.

puff adder, (zool.) víbora del desierto.

puffball ['pʌfˌbɔl] *s.* (bot.) bejín; cuesco de lobo.

puffer [-ər, B -ə] *s.* 1. fumador. 2. locomotora de minas. 3. (ict.) orbe; pez globo; erizo.

puffery [-ərɪ] *s.* bombo, publicidad exagerada.

puffin ['pʌfən] *s.* (orn.) frailecillo.

puffiness ['pʌfɪnəs] *s.* condición o aspecto hinchado.

puff paste, hojaldre.

puffy [pʌfɪ] *a.* (PUFFIER; PUFFIEST) 1. hinchado, abultado. 2. jadeante.

pug [pʌg] *s.* 1. perro dogo faldero. 2. **p. nose,** nariz respingona. 3. (jer.) boxeador, púgil. 4. arcilla amasada o batida.

pug, *v.t.* (*pret., p.p.* PUGGED; *p.pr.* PUGGING) 1. batir, amasar o mezclar (arcilla, yeso, etc.). 2. tapar (un tabique), llenar con argamasa (para apagar los sonidos).

pug, *s.* (anglo-ind.) huella, pisada, rastro (de una bestia). —*v.t.* seguir las huellas (de).

pugaree, puggaree ['pʌgərɪ] **puggree** ['pʌgrɪ] *vars. de* **pugree.**

pugilism ['pjudʒəˌlɪzəm] *s.* pugilismo, boxeo.

pugilist [-dʒələst] *s.* púgil, boxeador, pugilista.

pugilistic [ˌpjudʒə'lɪstɪk] *a.* de pugilato.

pugnacious [pʌg'neɪʃəs] *a.* pugnaz, belicoso, beligerante.

pugnaciously [-lɪ] *adv.* belicosamente.

pugnaciousness [-nəs] **pugnacity** [-'næsətɪ] *s.* pugnacidad, belicosidad.

pug-nosed ['pʌgˌnoʊzd] *a.* de nariz respingona o respingada.

pugree ['pʌgrɪ] *s.* (anglo-ind.) bufanda atada alrededor de un sombrero o casco (como protección del sol).

puisne ['pjunɪ] *a.* (der.) pedáneo, de rango inferior. —*s.* juez pedáneo, alcalde pedáneo.

puissance ['pwɪsəns, 'pjuəsəns] *s.* (poét.) poder, poderío, potencia.

puissant [-ənt] *a.* (poét.) poderoso, potente, influyente.

puissantly [-lɪ] *adv.* (poét.) poderosamente, potentemente.

puke [pjuk] *v.t., v.i.* vomitar, arrojar. —*s.* vómito.

pukka ['pʌkə] *a.* (anglo-ind.) (fam.) bueno, sólido, verdadero, legítimo; genuino.

pulchritude ['pʌlkrəˌtud, B -ˌtjud] *s.* belleza, encanto.

pulchritudinous [ˌpʌlkrə'tudənəs, B -'tjud-] *a.* bello, encantador, bien parecido.

pule [pjul] *v.i.* plañir, quejarse, lloriquear, gimotear.

puling ['pjulɪŋ] *a.* plañidero, quejoso.

pulingly [-lɪ] *adv.* plañideramente, quejosamente.

pull [pʊl] *v.t.* 1. tirar, tirar de, atraer, halar. 2. sacar, extraer, arrancar. 3. sacar, desenvainar (un arma). 4. (fig.) atraer, conseguir (apoyo, clientela, etc.). 5. hacer adelantar (embarcación) al remo. 6. poner tirante, forzar (un músculo). 7. cometer, realizar o ejecutar atrevidamente. 8. sofrenar, sujetar (a un caballo, esp. en carreras para que no gane). 9. (impr.) tirar (una prueba). 10. (golf) tirar (la pelota) con efecto (que la desvía a la izquierda). 11. (dial.) pelar, desplumar (un ave). 12. **p. apart,** separar (tirando); criticar duramente, regañar; **p. down,** bajar (cortina, etc.); demoler; abatir, debilitar; (jer.) ganar, percibir (salario, dinero, etc.); **p. in,** cobrar (cordel, soga); (jer.) enjaular, arrestar; **p. off,** quitarse (medias, guantes, etc.); (jer.) lograr, llevar a cabo, conseguir (propósito); **p. on,** ponerse (las medias, los guantes, etc.); **p. one's punches,** (boxeo) dar golpes sin fuerza; (fig.) obrar con moderación; **p. oneself together,** recobrarse, dominarse; **p. out,** sacar, arrancar; **p. through,** salvar, librar de, ayudar a superar (enfermedad, peligro); **p. to pieces,** despedazar, hacer trizas de (algo); criticar duramente; **p. up,** desarraigar; detener, parar (caballo, vehículo). —*v.i.* 1. tirar (bien o mal, un caballo, etc.). 2. moverse, ser movido (embarcación) al remo. 3. sacar la pistola. 4. **p. ahead,** tomar la delantera; **p. at,** tirar de (bigote, corbata, etc.); dar chupadas o fumadas al (cigarro, pipa); beber un trago del (jarro); **p. away,** apartarse, alejarse; **p. for,** remar hacia (la playa, etc.); alentar (equipo deportivo, etc.); abogar por, apoyar; **p. in,** entrar, llegar a la estación (tren); **p. out,** salir (embarcación) a remo; partir, salir de la estación (tren); retirarse; marcharse, largarse; (aer.) salir de un picado; **p. through,** ponerse a flote, salir del apuro; **p. together,** (fig.) trabajar en armonía, hacer un esfuerzo común; **p. up,** detenerse, refrenarse; avanzar, ganar terreno (en carrera). —*s.* 1. tirón, estirón. 2. trago; bebida. 3. (fam.) ejercicio de remos, boga; esfuerzo. 4. tirador (de campanilla, etc.); aldaba. 5. (golf) tiro desviado (hacia la izquierda). 6. sofrenada (que se da al caballo para que no gane la carrera). 7. (impr.) galerada. 8. (jer.) cuña, palanca, influencia. 9. **to have p. with (someone),** tener padrino o palanca en un asunto.

pullback ['pʊlˌbæk] *s.* (mil.) retirada (de fuerzas).

pull box, (elec.) caja de paso, caja de acceso.

pull chain, (elec.) cadenilla de tiro.

pullet ['pʊlət] *s.* pollo o gallina de menos de un año.

pulley ['pʊlɪ] *s.* (*pl.* PULLEYS) polea, garrucha, trocla; roldana.

Pullman ['pʊlmən] *s.* (f.c.) coche de salón, coche-cama.

pullorum disease [pə'lɔrəm-] (vet.) diarrea blanca bacilar de los pollos; pullorum.

pullout ['pʊlˌaʊt] *s.* 1. tirador, asidero (del que se tira). 2. (aer.) restablecimiento (después de un picado). 3. (mil.) retirada ordenada, evacuación (de tropas).

pullover [-ˌoʊvər, B -və] *a.* que se pone por la cabeza. —*s.* chaqueta de lana tejida; jersey, suéter, pulóver (Am.).

pull pin, (mec.) pasador fiador, espiga enclavadora.

pullulate ['pʌljəˌleɪt] *v.i.* 1. pulular, multiplicarse. 2. (fig.) pulular, abundar, bullir.

pullulation [ˌpʌljə'leɪʃən] *s.* pululación.

pulmonary ['pʊlməˌnɛrɪ, 'pʌl-, B 'pʌlmənərɪ] *a.* pulmonar.

pulmonary artery, arteria pulmonar.

pulmonary vein, vena pulmonar.

pulmonate [-ˌneɪt] *a.* (zool.) pulmonado. —*s.* gastrópodo pulmonado.

pulmonic [pʊl'mɑnɪk, B pʌl'mɔn-] *a.* pulmonar.

pulmotor ['pʊlˌmoʊtər, B 'pʌlˌmoʊtə] *s.* pulmotor, pulmón de acero.

pulp [pʌlp] *s.* 1. pulpa (parte mollar de los vegetales o frutos). 2. pulpa (residuo de cualquier fruta o vegetal). 3. (anat.) pulpa dentaria, pulpejo. 4. (min.) producto molido mezclado con agua. 5. pasta de madera. 6. (jer. E.U.) revista vulgar o sensacionalista. —*v.t.* reducir a pulpa o pasta de madera. —*v.i.* ponerse pulposo.

pulpiness ['pʌlpɪnəs] *s.* consistencia pulposa; pastosidad.

pulpit ['pʊlpɪt, 'pʌl-, B 'pʊl-] *s.* 1. púlpito. 2. **the p.,** los predicadores (en conjunto); profesión de predicador.

pulpwood ['pʌlpˌwʊd] *s.* madera para pasta, madera de pulpa (para fabricar papel).

pulpy ['pʌlpɪ] *a.* pulposo, carnoso.

pulsant ['pʌlsənt] *a.* pulsante, bullicioso.

pulsate ['pʌlˌseɪt, B pʌl'seɪt] *v.i.* latir, palpitar, pulsar.

pulsatile ['pʌlsətəl, B -ˌtaɪl] *a.* pulsátil, pulsativo.

pulsation [pʌl'seɪʃən] *s.* pulsación, latido, pulsada.

pulsator ['pʌlˌseɪtər, ˌpʌl'seɪtər, B -ə] *s.* (mec.) pulsador.

pulsatory ['pʌlsəˌtɔrɪ, B -tərɪ] *a.* pulsativo, pulsátil, pulsatorio.

pulse [pʌls] *s.* (plantas) leguminosas; legumbres.

pulse, *s.* 1. pulso, latido. 2. cadencia, ritmo. 3. (fís., elec.) pulsación. 4. (rad.) impulso. 5. **to feel (o take) the p. of** (lit. y fig.) tomar el pulso a. —*v.t.* (rad.) modular por impulsos (ondas). —*v.i.* pulsar, latir.

pulse-jet engine, (aer.) motor pulsorreactor.

pulsimeter [ˌpʌl'sɪmətər, B -ə] *s.* pulsímetro.

pulsometer [-'sɑmətər, B -'sɔmɪtə] *s.* pulsómetro.

pulverable ['pʌlvərəbəl] *a.* pulverizable.

pulverizable [-ˌraɪzəbəl] *a.* pulverizable.

pulverization [ˌpʌlvərə'zeɪʃən, B -əraɪ-] *s.* pulverización.

pulverize ['pʌlvəˌraɪz] *v.t.* 1. pulverizar, triturar, desmenuzar, reducir a polvo. 2. (fig.) pulverizar, destrozar, demoler, desintegrar. —*v.i.* pulverizarse, reducirse a polvo.

pulverizer [-ər, B -ə] *s.* pulverizador.

pulverulent [pʌl'vɛrjələnt, B -'vɛrʊ-] *a.* 1. pulverulento, polvoriento. 2. friable, deleznable.

pulvillus [pʌl'vɪləs] *s.* (*pl.* PULVILLI [-ˌaɪ]) (zool.) pulvillo, plántula, cuplántula.

pulvinate [ˌpʌl'vaɪnət, B 'pʌlvɪˌneɪt] **pulvinated** ['pʌlvəˌneɪtəd] *a.* (bot.) pulvinular.

pulvinus [pʌl'vaɪnəs] *s.* (PULVINI [-naɪ, -ni]) (bot.) pulvínulo.

puma ['pumə, B 'pju-] *s.* (*pl.* PUMAS) (zool.) puma.

pumice ['pʌməs] *s.* pómez, piedra pómez, pumita. —*v.t.* pulir o limpiar con piedra pómez.

pumiceous [pju'mɪʃəs] *a.* (geol.) pumíceo.

pummel, *var. de.* **pommel.**

pump [pʌmp] *s.* 1. bomba. 2. inflador (de aire). 3. (jer.) el corazón. 4. escarpín, zapatilla fina, escotada y lisa. —*v.t.* 1. bombear, extraer (agua, aire, etc.). 2. achicar agua de (pozo, barco, etc.). 3. (fig.) echar, arrojar (proyectiles, balas, etc.). 4. (fig.) sonsacar (información, etc.); sondear o tantear (por información a alguien). 5. agitar, mover de arriba para abajo. 6. **p. (someone's)**

hand, estrechar efusivamente (sacudiendo) la mano (de alguien); **p. into,** (fig.) verter en; **p. out,** vaciar con bomba; (fig.) agotar; **p. up,** inflar; elevar con bomba (líquido). —*v.i.* 1. accionar una bomba; trabajar en las bombas (de un barco). 2. latir violentamente (corazón).
pump brake, amortiguador hidráulico.
pump dale, (mar.) dala, adala (de bomba).
pumper ['pʌmpər, B -pə] *s.* 1. carro de bomba (de bomberos), autobomba. 2. pozo bombeado (de petróleo). 3. el que acciona una bomba.
pumpernickel ['pʌmpərˌnɪkəl, B -pəˌ-] *s.* pan negro de centeno con semillas de alcaravea o carvi.
pump house, casa o garaje de bombas (en el cuartel de bomberos).
pump jack, guimbalete, balancín (sobre un pozo).
pumpkin ['pʌmpkən] *s.* (bot.) calabaza, zapallo (Amer.) (fruto y planta).
pump priming, (e.p.) política de inversiones estatales para fomentar la expansión económica.
pump rod, varilla de bombeo.
pun [pʌn] *s.* retruécano, juego de palabras. —*v.i.* (*pret., p.p.* PUNNED; *p.pr.* PUNNING) hacer retruécanos, hacer juegos de palabras.
punch [pʌntʃ] *v.t.* 1. punchar, picar, punzar; perforar, abrir huecos, horadar, taladrar. 2. picar, atizar; aguijonear (al ganado). 3. golpear, dar un puñetazo a. —*v.i.* 1. hacer punzadas. 2. **p. in,** marcar la (hora de) llegada en la tarjeta del reloj registrador; **p. out,** marcar la (hora de) salida. —*s.* 1. punzada, herida o picada de punta. 2. puñetazo, puñada, puñete, trompada (Amer.). 3. (fam.) fuerza, vigor, energía.
punch, *s.* 1. (mec.) punzón; botador, granete, sacabocados; ojalador. 2. ponche (bebida). 3. **P.,** Pulchinela, Polichinela; **pleased as P.,** encantado, sumamente contento.
Punch-and-Judy show [ˌpʌntʃən'dʒudɪ-] teatro de títeres.
punch bowl, ponchera, bol.
punch card, tarjeta perforada, ficha perforada.
punch-drunk ['pʌntʃˌdrʌŋk] *a.* aturdido a golpes (díc. de boxeadores); (fig.) estupefacto.
punched card [pʌntʃt-] *var. de* **punch card.**
puncheon ['pʌntʃən] *s.* 1. especie de cuño o molde (usado por los orfebres, cuchilleros, etc.). 2. (carp.) punzón; pie derecho, puntal grande de madera; puntal corto y grueso. 3. pipa, barril; (G.B.) medida de líquidos igual a 84 galones (de vino) o 72 galones (de cerveza).
puncher [-tʃər, B -tʃə] *s.* 1. perforador; punzón. 2. (E.U.) (gen. precedido de **cow**) vaquero.
punchinello [ˌpʌntʃə'nɛloʊ] *s.* (*pl.* PUNCHINELLOS O PUNCHINELLOES) pulchinela, polichinela; títere; bufón, histrión.
punching bag ['pʌntʃɪŋ-] 1. saco de arena. 2. (fig.) chivo expiatorio.
punch line, frase clave, remate, culminación ingeniosa, (de un chiste, cuento, etc.).
punch press, (mec.) prensa cortadora, prensa troqueladora.
punchy ['pʌntʃɪ] *a.* (PUNCHIER; PUNCHIEST) (jer., E.U.) aturdido (a golpes).
punctate ['pʌŋkˌteɪt] **punctated** [-əd] *a.* punteado, marcado con puntos; (bot., zool.) punteado, moteado.
punctation [ˌpʌŋk'teɪʃən] *s.* punteado.
punctilio [ˌpʌŋk'tɪlɪoʊ] *s.* (*pl.* PUNCTILIOS) 1. puntillo. 2. conducta puntillosa, meticulosidad, suma formalidad.
punctilious [-ɪəs] *a.* puntilloso, puntoso, meticuloso, minucioso.
punctiliously [-lɪ] *adv.* puntillosamente, meticulosamente, escrupulosamente.
punctiliousness [-nəs] *s.* puntillo, meticulosidad, escrupulosidad, formalidad.
punctual ['pʌŋktʃʊəl, B -tjʊ-] *a.* 1. puntual, exacto. 2. puntilloso, meticuloso, escrupuloso.
punctuality [ˌpʌŋktʃʊ'ælətɪ] *s.* puntualidad, exactitud.
punctually ['pʌŋktʃʊəlɪ, B -tjʊ-] *adv.* puntualmente, exactamente.
punctualness [-əlnəs] *s.* puntualidad, exactitud.
punctuate ['pʌŋktʃʊˌeɪt, B -tjʊ-] *v.t.* 1. puntuar, acentuar, poner puntuación en (la escritura). 2. interrumpir, intermitir (discurso con observaciones, aplausos, etc.). 3. acentuar, recalcar, realzar, marcar. —*v.i.* usar signos de puntuación, puntuar.
punctuation [ˌpʌŋktʃʊ'eɪʃən, B -tjʊ-] *s.* (gram.) punctuación.
punctuation mark, signo de puntuación.
punctuator ['pʌŋktʃʊˌeɪtər, B -tjʊ-ə] *s.* el que interrumpe para puntualizar.
puncturate [-ˌleɪt] *a.* punteado.
puncturable [-tʃərəbəl] *a.* perforable, que puede ser perforado.
puncture ['pʌŋktʃər, B -tʃə] *s.* 1. pinchadura, pinchazo; perforación. 2. (med.) punción, puntura. 3. **to have a p.,** sufrir un pinchazo (el neumático). —*v.t.* 1. punzar, perforar, agujerear; pinchar (el neumático). 2. (fig.) deshacer, demoler, desbaratar, (orgullo, amor propio, etc.). —*v.i.* agujerearse, sufrir un pinchazo (el neumático).
puncture-proof [-ˌpruf] *a.* (aut.) a prueba de pinchazos (neumático).
pundit ['pʌndət] *s.* 1. pandit (título que se da a los sabios en la India). 2. maestro; erudito. 3. corifeo, experto.
pung [pʌŋ] *s.* (E.U.) trineo de sencilla construcción en forma de caja.
pungency ['pʌndʒənsɪ] *s.* 1. picante. 2. agudeza. 3. causticidad, mordacidad.
pungent [-dʒənt] *a.* 1. picante, punzante; acre, agrio. 2. punzante, agudo. 3. mordaz, cáustico; satírico; inspirador, incitador. 4. (bot.) punzante, espinoso.
pungently [-lɪ] *adv.* 1. picantemente. 2. mordazmente, cáusticamente.
Punic ['pjunɪk] *a.* 1. púnico. 2. (fig.) pérfido, traicionero. —*s.* púnico (dialecto).
Punic Wars, Guerras Púnicas.
puniness ['pjunɪnəs] *s.* 1. tamaño diminuto. 2. pequeñez, insignificancia, minucia.
punish ['pʌnɪʃ] *v.t.* 1. castigar, penar, disciplinar, escarmentar. 2. (fam., boxeo) golpear severamente (al contrario); (dep.) agotar, agobiar (a competidor); aprovechar (débil golpe, deficiente jugada del adversario). 3. (fam.) consumir gran cantidad (de comida, etc.). —*v.i.* imponer castigo.
punishability [ˌpʌnɪʃə'bɪlətɪ] *s.* carácter de punible, punibilidad.
punishable ['pʌnɪʃəbəl] *a.* punible, penable.
punishment [-mənt] *s.* 1. castigo, corrección; represión, punición, pena, condena; disciplina. 2. maltrato. 3. (fam., boxeo) golpeadura, golpeo.
punitive ['pjunətɪv] *a.* punitivo, punitorio.
punitive damages, (der.) daños punitivos (dinero que el juez ordena se pague al demandante por daños y perjuicios; t. se dice **exemplary damages**).
punitory [-ˌtɔrɪ, B -tərɪ] *a.* punitorio, punitivo.
Punjabi [ˌpʌn'dʒɑbɪ] *s.* 1. penjabo (habitante de Punjab). 2. penjabi (lengua).
punk [pʌŋk] *s.* 1. (jer., E.U.) novicio; deportista o jugador inferior; persona o cosa inútil o inservible. 2. yesca, hupe. —*a.* inferior, miserable, malo.
punkah ['pʌŋkə] *s.* (anglo-ind.) abanico colgante (hecho de hojas de palmera).
punkie ['pʌŋkɪ] *s.* (E.U.) cierto insecto díptero.
punnet ['pʌnət] *s.* (pr. G.B.) canastilla (para frutas).
punster ['pʌnstər, B -stə] *s.* equivoquista.
punt [pʌnt] *s.* 1. (pr. G.B.) batea, chalana, barquichuelo de fondo plano. 2. (fútbol, E.U.) acción de patear la pelota dejándola caer de las manos. —*v.t.* 1. impeler (una batea) con botador. 2. (fútbol, E.U.) patear (la pelota) dejándola caer de las manos. —*v.i.* 1. ir en bote o cazar en una batea. 2. patear la pelota de fútbol.
punt, *v.i.* 1. jugar contra la banca (en algunos juegos de cartas). 2. (G.B.) apostar en las carreras de caballos.
punter ['pʌntər, B -tə] *s.* 1. excursionista o cazador que usa una batea. 2. jugador que patea la pelota en el aire. 3. (G.B.) quinielista, apostador.
punty ['pʌntɪ] *s.* (*pl.* PUNTIES) puntel, pontil, puntero (usado en la fabricación de vidrio).
puny ['pjunɪ] *a.* (PUNIER; PUNIEST) 1. pequeño, diminuto. 2. débil, insignificante. 3. (ant.) juez o alcalde.
pup [pʌp] *s.* 1. cachorro; perrito. 2. cría (de mamíferos). 3. (jer.) joven inexperto. 4. **in p.,** preñada; **to sell (someone) a p.,** estafar (a alguien, esp. vendiéndole algo con supuesto valor futuro). —*v.i.* (*pret. p.p.* PUPPED; *p.pr.* PUPPING) parir cachorros.
pupa ['pjupə] *s.* (*pl.* PUPAE [-ˌpi] O PUPAS) (ento.) ninfa, crisálida.
pupal [-pəl] *a.* pupa, de pupa, de la pupa.
pupate [-ˌpeɪt] *v.i.* convertir(se) en pupa.
pupation [pju'peɪʃən] *s.* conversión en pupa.
pupil ['pjupəl] *s.* 1. pupilo, discípulo, alumno. 2. (der.) pupilo (bajo tutela de un tutor). 3. (anat.) pupila.
pupilage, pupillage [-ɪdʒ] *s.* pupilaje, condición de pupilo.
pupillarity [ˌpjupə'lærətɪ] *s.* (der., esco.) puericia, infancia, niñez, período antes de la pubertad.
pupillary ['pjupəˌlɛrɪ, B -lərɪ] *a.* (anat.) pupilar.
Pupin system [pju'pin-] (tel.) pupinización.
puppet ['pʌpət] *s.* 1. muñeca. 2. títere. 3. (fig.) títere (persona que sirve de instrumento a otra).
puppeteer [ˌpʌpə'tɪr, B -'tɪə] *s.* titiritero, titirero, titerista.
puppet government, gobierno títere.
puppetry ['pʌpətrɪ] *s.* 1. (arte de) teatro de títeres. 2. (ant.) titeretada, mascarada.
puppet show, teatro de títeres.
puppet-valve [-ˌvælv] *s.* (mec.) válvula de contrapunto.
puppy ['pʌpɪ] *s.* (*pl.* PUPPIES) 1. cachorro, perrito. 2. pisaverde, vanidoso.
puppy love, (fam., E.U.) amor pueril, amor de adolescencia.
pup tent, pequeña tienda de campaña.
pur, *var. de* **purr.**
purblind ['pɜrˌblaɪnd, B 'pɜˌ-] *a.* 1. miope, cegatón, cegato. 2. lerdo, torpe, lento, obtuso. 3. (ant.) ciego.
purblindness [-nəs] *s.* 1. miopía, cortedad de vista. 2. torpeza, ofuscamiento.
purchasable ['pɜrtʃəsəbəl, B 'pɜtʃə-] *a.* 1. comprable, adquirible. 2. corruptible, venal.
purchase ['pɜrtʃəs, B 'pɜtʃəs] *v.t.* 1. comprar, adquirir. 2. ganar, conseguir. 3. apalancar. 4. (mar.) levar (ancla). 5. (ant.) obtener, alcanzar. —*s.* 1. compra, adquisición. 2. (mec.) apoyo, punto de apoyo; palanca, cabrestante. 3. (mar.) aparejo. 4. (ant.) obtención.

purchase tax, (G.B.) impuesto sobre la venta (que grava ciertos artículos de lujo y otros que no son indispensables).
purchasing power [-ɪŋ-] poder de adquisición, valor adquisitivo (de la moneda); capacidad de consumo.
purdah ['pɜrdə, B 'pɜdə] *s.* (anglo-ind.) velo, cortina, biombo (esp. para ocultar a las mujeres); (fig.) sistema de reclusión de las mujeres.
pure [pjʊr, B pjʊə] *a.* 1. puro, sin mezcla, castizo; simple, sencillo; mero, claro; completo, absoluto. 2. inocente, puro, casto, virtuoso. 3. puro, de pura raza. 4. puro, abstracto, teórico. 5. (bíbl.) inmaculado, ritualmente limpio, puro. 6. (filos.) puro. 7. (mús.) puro, concordante. 8. **as if it were p. gold,** como oro en paño, como oro en polvo.
pure-blood ['pjʊrˌblʌd, B 'pjʊəˌ-] *a.* de pura sangre, de pura raza. —*s.* animal de pura sangre.
pure-blooded [-əd] *a.* de pura sangre, de pura raza.
purebred [-'brɛd] *a.* de pura sangre, de raza pura. —*s.* animal de pura sangre.
purée [pjʊ'reɪ, B 'pjʊəreɪ] (cocina) *s.* puré. —*v.t.* (*pret., p.p.* PUREED; *p.pr.* PUREEING) hacer un puré de.
purely ['pjʊrlɪ, B 'pjʊəlɪ] *adv.* 1. meramente, simplemente, solamente, estrictamente. 2. puramente, sin mezcla. 3. inocentemente, castamente, virtuosamente, púdicamente. 4. completamente, absolutamente.
pure mathematics, matemáticas puras.
pureness [-nəs] *s.* 1. pureza, puridad. 2. (fig.) pureza, inocencia, castidad, virginidad.
purfle ['pɜrfəl, B 'pɜfəl] *v.t.* 1. (cost.) orlar, repulgar. 2. guarnecer, ornar, ribetear. —*s.* (cost.) orla, cenefa, orilla, borde, dobladillo, bastilla, repulgo.
purgation [ˌpɜr'geɪʃən, B pɜ'-] *s.* purgación, purgamiento.
purgative ['pɜrgətɪv, B 'pɜgət-] *a.* purgativo, purgador, catártico. —*s.* (med.) purgante, medicina purgante, purga.
purgatorial [ˌpɜrgə'tɔrɪəl, B ˌpɜgə-] *a.* 1. del purgatorio. 2. expiatorio, purificatorio.
purgatory ['pɜrgəˌtɔrɪ, B 'pɜgətərɪ] *s.* (*pl.* PURGATORIES) (teo. y fig.) purgatorio.
purge [pɜrdʒ, B pɜdʒ] *v.t.* 1. purgar, purificar, depurar; limpiar. 2. absolver, exonerar, librar de culpa. 3. (med.) purgar, evacuar. 4. (pol.) purgar, deshacerse de (elementos traidores o indeseables). 5. (der.) purgar (una sentencia), expiar (una culpa). —*v.i.* 1. purgarse. 2. librarse de impurezas, purificarse. 3. (med.) tener evacuaciones frecuentes. —*s.* 1. purgación, purgamiento. 2. (med.) purgante. 3. (pol.) purga, depuración.
purger ['pɜrdʒər, B 'pɜdʒə] *s.* purgador.
purging buckthorn [-ɪŋ-] (bot.) espino cerval.
purification [ˌpjʊrəfə'keɪʃən, B ˌpjʊər-] *s.* purificación.
purificator ['pjʊrəfəˌkeɪtər, B 'pjʊər-ə] *s.* (relig.) purificador (paño de lino con que se enjuga el cáliz).
purificatory [pjʊ'rɪfəkəˌtɔrɪ, B 'pjʊərəfəˌkeɪtərɪ] *a.* purificatorio, depuratorio.
purifier ['pjʊrəˌfaɪər, B 'pjʊərəˌfaɪə] *s.* purificador, depurador.
purify [-ˌfaɪ] *v.t., v.i.* (*pret., p.p.* PURIFIED; *p.pr.* PURIFYING) 1. purificar, acrisolar, depurar, refinar. 2. (fig.) purificar, librar de culpa.
Purim ['pʊrəm, B 'pjʊər-] *s.* (relig.) purim, festividad hebrea correspondiente al carnaval.
purine ['pjʊrˌin, B 'pjʊərˌaɪn] *s.* (quím.) purina.
purism [-ˌɪzəm] *s.* purismo, casticismo.
purist [-əst] *s.* purista, casticista.
puristic [pjʊ'rɪstɪk, B pjʊə-] *a.* purista.
Puritan ['pjʊrətən, B 'pjʊər-] *s., a.* (relig., hist.) puritano; **p.,** (fig.) puritano.
puritanical [ˌpjʊrə'tænɪkəl] *a.* 1. puritano. 2. (fig.) riguroso, severo.
puritanically [-kəlɪ] *adv.* en forma puritana, puritanamente.
Puritanism ['pjʊrətənˌɪzəm, B 'pjʊər-] *s.* 1. (relig.) puritanismo. 2. (fig.) puritanismo, austeridad, rigorismo.
purity ['pjʊrətɪ, B 'pjʊər-] *s.* 1. pureza, puridad, limpieza; casticismo; inocencia, castidad, virginidad, doncellez. 2. (pint.) saturación, pureza de color.
purl [pɜrl, B pɜl] *v.t., v.i.* 1. (cost.) orlar, guarnecer, ribetear, adornar, ornar. 2. (t. **pearl**) terminar (el encaje) con presillas pequeñas. 3. (t. **pearl**) invertir las puntadas en (el tejido). 4. bordar con presillas, adornar con fleco. —*s.* 1. orla, cenefa de oro o plata (para adornar los bordes). 2. (t. **pearl**) presilla pequeña (hecha en el borde del encaje). 3. parte de los pliegues, recogido de las golillas o gorgueras. 4. punto invertido (en el tejido).
purl, *v.i.* 1. murmurar, susurrar (los arroyos, etc.). 2. remolinar, arremolinarse; ondear, rizarse, ondular. —*s.* 1. murmullo, susurro (de un arroyo, etc.). 2. remolino, onda.
purler ['pɜrlər, B 'pɜlə] *s.* (fam., G.B.) caída de cabeza; **to come** (o **to take**) **a p.,** caer de cabeza.
purlieu ['pɜrlju, B 'pɜl-] *s.* 1. lugar frecuentado; guarida. 2. (*pl.*) alrededores, inmediaciones, afueras. 3. vecindario, suburbio; barriada. 4. (der.) lindero del bosque (esp. uno cuyo uso está regulado por las leyes forestales).
purlin ['pɜrlən, B 'pɜlɪn] *s.* (arq.) correa, parhilera.
purloin [pər'lɔɪn, B pə'-] *v.t.* hurtar, ratear.
purloiner [-ər, B -ə] *s.* ratero, ladrón.
purple ['pɜrpəl, B 'pɜpəl] *s.* 1. (color) púrpura, morado. 2. (género o manto) púrpura. 3. (fig.) púrpura, rango imperial, poder real; posición encumbrada. 4. (zool.) púrpura. —*a.* 1. purpúreo, purpurino; morado. 2. imperial, regio. 3. recargado, retórico (estilo, escritura, etc.). 4. profano, vulgar, licencioso (lenguaje, etc.). —*v.t.* purpurar, teñir de púrpura.
purple clover, (bot.) trébol encarnado.
purple gallinule, (orn.) calamón.
purple grackle, (orn.) variedad de guiscal.
Purple Heart, (E.U.) condecoración concedida a los miembros de las fuerzas armadas heridos en combate.
purple loosestrife [-'luˌstraɪf] (bot.) salicaria. arroyuela.
purple medic, (bot.) alfalfa, mielga común.
purple vetch, (bot.) almorta, tito.
purplish ['pɜrpəlɪʃ, B 'pɜpəl-] *a.* purpurino, purpúreo.
purport [pər'pɔrt, B 'pɜpət] *v.t.* significar, querer decir, implicar, dar a entender; representar, aparentar. — ['pɜrˌpɔrt, B 'pɜpət] *s.* significado, significación, tenor, sentido; substancia, quid.
purported [-əd] *a.* supuesto, reputado, pretenso, alegado.
purpose ['pɜrpəs, B 'pɜpəs] *v.t.* proponer(se), resolver, proyectar. —*s.* 1. propósito, intención, ánimo; finalidad, objectivo, mira, vista. 2. resolución, determinación, decisión, voluntad. 3. resultado, utilidad. 4. **for the p.,** para este propósito; **for what p.?** ¿con qué fin? ¿con qué objeto?; **on p.,** expresamente, de propósito, intencionalmente, adrede; **of set p.,** determinado, resuelto, de firme propósito; **to answer** (o **to serve**) **the p.,** servir para el caso; **to good p.,** con buenos resultados; **to little p.,** de poca utilidad; con poco éxito; **to no p.,** inútilmente, en vano; **to the p.,** pertinente, apropiado, a propósito.
purposeful [-fəl] *a.* que tiene propósito o fin determinado.
purposeless [-ləs] *a.* vago; sin propósito ni fin determinado.
purposely [-lɪ] *adv.* de propósito, adrede, intencionalmente, expresamente, deliberadamente.
purposive ['pɜrpəsɪv, B 'pɜpə-] *a.* 1. útil, utilizable. 2. intencional, deliberado.
purposively [-lɪ] *adv.* 1. útilmente. 2. intencionalmente, deliberadamente.
purposiveness [-nəs] *s.* 1. utilidad. 2. resolución, determinación.
purpura ['pɜrpjərə, B 'pɜpjʊərə] *s.* púrpura.
purpure [-pjʊr, B -pjʊə] *s.* (her.) púrpura.
purpuric [ˌpɜr'pjʊrɪk, B pɜ'pjʊər-] *a.* (med.) del púrpura.
purr, pur [pɜr, B pɜ] *v.i.* (*pret., p.p.* PURRED; *p.pr.* PURRING) ronronear, runrunear (el gato); zumbar (un motor). —*v.t.* expresar con ronroneos. —*s.* ronroneo (del gato); zumbido (de un motor).
purse [pɜrs, B pɜs] *s.* 1. bolso, bolsa, monedero, bolsillo. 2. caudal, fondos; bolsillo, dinero; tesoro, finanzas, ej., *common p.,* fondo común. 3. premio, bolsa (ofrecida en un concurso, competencia, etc.). —*v.t.* 1. fruncir (los labios, la frente). 2. (gen. con *up*) embolsar, embolsicar (Amer.).
purse-bearer ['pɜrsˌbɛrər, B 'pɜsˌbɛərə] *s.* tesorero.
purse crab, (zool.) cangrejo de los cocoteros.
purse-net [-ˌnɛt] *s.* red en forma de bolsa (para pescar).
purse-proud [-ˌpraʊd] *a.* envanecido por la opulencia, ufano de su riqueza.
purser ['pɜrsər, B 'pɜsə] *s.* contador, sobrecargo (esp. en buques mercantes).
purse-seine ['pɜrsˌseɪn, B 'pɜs-] *s.* red en forma de bolsa (para pescar).
purse-strings [-ˌstrɪŋz] *s. pl.* cerradero, cordones de la bolsa; **to hold the p.-s.,** guardar y disponer del dinero (en casa, familia, etc.); **to loosen (tighten) the p.-s.,** soltar (agarrar) el dinero, aflojar (apretar) la bolsa.
pursiness [-ɪnəs] *s.* dificultad en la respiración, disnea.
purslane ['pɜrslən, B 'pɜs-] *s.* (bot.) verdolaga.
pursuable [pər'suəbəl, B pə'sju-] *a.* proseguible.
pursuance [-əns] *s.* prosecución, ejecución, seguimiento, cumplimiento.
pursuant [-ənt] *a.* 1. consiguiente. 2. perseguidor. 3. p. to, conforme a, de acuerdo con, según.
pursuantly [-lɪ] *adv.* conformemente, acordemente; consecuentemente.
pursue [pər'su, B pə'sju] *v.t.* 1. perseguir, dar caza a, acosar. 2. (fig.) buscar con afán, aspirar a. 3. proseguir, seguir (un plan, etc.) 4. dedicarse a, ejercer, practicar; (der.) demandar, pleitear. —*v.i.* ir en persecución.
pursuer [-ər, B -ə] *s.* perseguidor.
pursuit [pər'sut, B pə'sjut] *s.* 1. persecución, seguimiento. 2. prosecución, búsqueda, ej., *p. of happiness,* búsqueda de la felicidad. 3. profesión, ocupación, empleo; recreación, actividad. 4. **in p. of,** en pos de, a la caza de.
pursuit plane, avión de caza o de intercepción.
pursuivant ['pɜrsɪvənt, B 'pɜsɪ-] *s.* 1. persevante. 2. (ant.) acompañante, secuaz; servidor.

pursy [ˈpɜrsɪ, B ˈpɜsɪ] *a.* (PURSIER; PURSIEST) 1. falto de aire. 2. gordo, obeso, corpulento. 3. arrogante, altivo. 4. fruncido, arrugado.
purulence [ˈpʊrələns, B ˈpjʊər-] *s.* purulencia; pus.
purulent [-lənt] *a.* (med.) purulento.
purvey [ˌpɜrˈveɪ, B pɜˈ-] *v.t.* proveer, surtir suministrar, abastecer. —*v.i.* actuar como proveedor.
purveyance [-əns] *s.* abastecimiento, abasto, suministro, provisión.
purveyor [-ər, B -ə] *s.* 1. proveedor, provisor, abastecedor. 2. (G.B., hist.) oficial que hacía requisiciones para abastecer a la casa real.
purview [ˈpɜrˌvju, B ˈpɜˌ-] *s.* 1. (der.) substancia y alcance de un estatuto o ley. 2. límite de la autoridad; competencia, incumbencia; esfera de acción. 3. campo o esfera de visión (mental o física).
pus [pʌs] *s.* pus, humores.
push [pʊʃ] *v.t.* 1. empujar, impeler, impulsar, mover. 2. (gen. con *out, forth*) echar (raíz, hojas). 3. urgir, compeler, apremiar. 4. extender (conquistas, poderío, dominio); promover (ventas), hacer propaganda de (mercadería). 5. apremiar, importunar, precisar. 6. (bíbl.) cornear, acornear. 7. **p. aside,** hacer a un lado, desalojar del camino; **p. away,** alejar, apartar; **p. back,** echar atrás, rechazar; **p. (matter) through,** llevar (asunto) a cabo; **p. (door, window) to,** juntar, emparejar (puerta, ventana). —*v.i.* 1. (gen. con *against*) ejercer presión, pujar (contra). 2. (gen. con *out*) proyectarse, extenderse. 3. esforzarse, extremarse, pugnar (para superar a otros, conseguir su fin, etc.). 4. (billar) empujar (en lugar de dar un golpe a) la bola. 5. **p. ahead,** avanzar, pujar; **p. forward,** adelantarse dando empujones; **p. off,** desatracarse; (jer.) irse, largarse; **p. on,** seguir adelante; avanzar laboriosamente. —*s.* 1. empujón, empellón. 2. impulso, estímulo. 3. apuro, aprieto, apremio, urgencia. 4. arremetida, acometida, embestida. 5. cornada. 6. empuje, brío, arranque. 7. (mil.) ofensiva. 8. (billar) empuje. 9. (jer.) pandilla, banda. 10. (jer., Aust.) gavilla, caterva (de indeseables o ladrones). 11. (jer., G.B.) despedida, destitución, ej., *to get the p.,* ser despedido. 12. **at a p.,** en un apuro, en caso de necesidad; **to make a p.,** hacer un esfuerzo.
pushball [ˈpʊʃˌbɔl] *s.* 1. (dep.) juego que se practica empujando una pelota de seis pies de diámetro. 2. balón o pelota utilizada en este juego.
push-bike [-ˌbaɪk] *s.* (G.B., fam.) bicicleta de pedales.
push button, (elec.) conmutador, pulsador; botón de contacto, botón de presión, botón de llamada.
push-button control [-ˌbʌtən-] mando accionado por botón.
push-button starter, (aut.) arrancador a botón.
push-button switch, (elec.) interruptor de botón, llave a botón.
push-button war, guerra mecánica (de cohetes y proyectiles teledirigidos).
pushcart [ˈpʊʃˌkɑrt, B -ˌkɑt] *s.* carretilla de mano.
push drill, taladro de empuje, taladro de movimiento alternativo.
pusher [-ər, B -ə] *s.* 1. empujador, impulsador. 2. (fam., E.U.) persona que vende narcóticos ilegalmente.
pusher airplane, avión con hélice detrás del motor.
pusher locomotive, locomotora de empuje, locomotora de refuerzo.
pushing [-ɪŋ] *a.* 1. emprendedor, resuelto, acometedor, enérgico, activo, diligente. 2. atrevido, agresivo, molesto.
pushover [-ˌoʊvər, B -və] *s.* 1. persona fácil de dominar; pelele, primo, incauto. 2. ganga, breva, gollería, cosa fácil, pichincha (Amer.).
pushpin [-ˌpɪn] *s.* 1. crucillo, juego de los alfileres. 2. clavo o tachuela con cabeza grande para señalar (en mapas, etc.).
push-pull [ˈpʊʃˈpʊl] (electrón.) *s.* contrafase. —*a.* en contrafase.
push-pull amplifier, (electrón.) amplificador en contrafase, amplifacador simétrico o equilibrado.
push-pull circuit, (electrón.) circuito en contrafase, circuito simétrico o equilibrado.
push-up [-ˌʌp] *s.* plancha (ejercicio gimnástico).
push wave, (fís.) onda de empuje, onda de compresión.
pushy [ˈpʊʃɪ] *a.* **(E.U., fam.) agresivo,** insistente, molestoso.
pusillanimity [ˌpjʊsələˈnɪmətɪ] *s.* pusilanimidad, cobardía, timidez, cortedad, temor, pobreza de espíritu.
pusillanimous [-ˈlænəməs] *a.* pusilánime, cobarde, apocado, tímido, corto, miedoso, timorato.
pusillanimously [-lɪ] *adv.* apocadamente, tímidamente, cobardemente.
puss [pʊs] *s.* 1. (*ú. esp. como vocativo*) minino, micho, michino, gatito. 2. (fam.) chica, moza. 3. (dial., G.B.) liebre. 4. (jer., E.U.) hocico, cara, rostro.
pussley [ˈpʌslɪ] *s.* (bot.) verdolaga.
pussy [ˈpʌsɪ] *a.* (PUSSIER; PUSSIEST) purulento, supuratorio; semejante al pus.
pussy [ˈpʊsɪ] *s.* (*pl.* PUSSIES) 1. (lenguaje infantil) (t. **p.-cat**) gatito, minino, michino, micho. 2. (fam.) amento (del avellano, sauce, etc.). 3. (vulg.) coño *(órgano sexual femenino)*, concha (S. Amer.).
pussyfoot [-ˌfʊt] *v.i.* (jer., E.U.) 1. andar cautelosamente, andar como el gato; andar con tiento. 2. andarse con rodeos.
pussyfooter [-ər, B -ə] *s.* tímido, evasivo.
pussyfooting [-ɪŋ] *s.* evasiva, subterfugio.
pussy willow, (bot.) sauce común.
pustulant [ˈpʌstʃələnt, B ˈpʌstjʊ-] *s., a.* (med.) pustulante.
pustular [-lər, B -lə] *a.* 1. pustular, pustuloso. 2. pustulado.
pustulate [-lət, B -leɪt] *a.* pustulado.
pustulation [ˌpʌstʃəˈlaɪʃən, B ˌpʌstjʊ-] *s.* 1. pustulación. 2. pústula.
pustule [ˈpʌsˌtʃul, B -tjul] *s.* (med., bot.) pústula.
put [pʊt] *v.t.* (*pret., p.p.* PUT; *p.pr.* PUTTING) 1. poner, colocar, situar. 2. lanzar, tirar, arrojar (esp. jabalina, disco, etc.). 3. echar, poner (ej., azúcar en el té, etc.). 4. expresar, decir, ej., *p. it into words,* expresarlo en palabras, *let's p. it like this,* digámoslo (o pongámoslo) así. 5. formular, hacer (preguntas). 6. presentar, exponer, ej., *p. the matter clearly before* (*someone*), presentar o exponer el asunto en forma clara a (alguien). 7. calcular, estimar, ej., *I p. the number of inhabitants at 5,000,* calculo en 5.000 el número de habitantes. 8. volver, convertir, poner (en cierto estado o condición) (*se traduce en castellano con varios verbos*) ej., *he has p. the matter in my hands,* ha puesto el asunto en mis manos, *he has p. his decision on a false assumption,* ha fundado su decisión en una presunción falsa, *he puts little value on her advice,* no aprecia mucho sus consejos, *they p. him under oath,* lo han puesto bajo juramento, *they p. the case to him,* sometieron el caso a su consideración. 9. (min.) empujar (vagonetas). 10. **I p. it to you,** recurro a Ud., apelo a Ud.; **p. about,** hacer correr (rumor, noticia, etc.); molestar, fastidiar; (mar.) cambiar de bordada, virar, voltear (el barco); **p. a bullet through,** pegar un tiro a; **p. a knife into,** acuchillar, apuñalar; **p. across,** lograr realizar, llevar a cabo con éxito; explicar bien, hacer comprender; **p. away,** guardar; acumular, ahorrar; consumir, comer, tomar; (jer.) aprisionar, poner en prisión; (jer.) empeñar, pignorar; (jer.) liquidar, matar; **p. back,** parar, retardar; retrasar, atrasar (el reloj); reponer, retornar, reintegrar; **p. by,** ahorrar, acumular, acopiar; **p. down,** suprimir, reprimir, sofocar; bajar los humos a, humillar, desairar, reprender; hacer callar; rebajar, disminuir; calcular, estimar; anotar, asentar; tragar, devorar; **p. (someone** o **something) down (as** o **for),** clasificar, considerar (a alguien o algo) como; **p. (something) down to,** atribuir, achacar (algo) a; **p. forth,** aplicar, emplear, valerse de; circular, poner en circulación; brotar, echar (hojas, renuevos); **p. forward,** exponer, proferir, sugerir; adelantar (reloj); **p. oneself forward,** adelantarse; **p. in,** meter en; instalar; presentar (reclamo, documento, etc.); interponer, intercalar, insertar; añadir; dar de adehala; (fam.) pasar, emplear (el tiempo); **p. in a word (for someone),** interceder, hablar a favor (de alguien); **p. in an appearance,** presentarse, aparecer, comparecer; **p. (someone) in the wrong,** tratar de hacer aparecer (a alguien) como culpable, tratar de hacer aparecer (a alguien) como si no tuviera razón; **p. into (French, German,** etc.), traducir al (francés, alemán, etc.); **p. it on,** (fam.) exagerar, simular; **p. off,** posponer, postergar, aplazar, diferir; desembarazarse de, despachar a (alguien, empleando excusas o disculpas); (fam.) desconcertar; disuadir (a alguien de algo); quitar, sacar, remover; **p. new life into,** dar nuevas fuerzas o revivir a; **p. on,** ponerse (ropa, etc.); asumir; simular; aumentar de peso; encender (luces); añadir; imponer, infligir (presión, etc.); engañar, tomar el pelo; (teat.) poner en escena, dar una función; **p. on airs,** darse infulas; **p. on one's thinking cap,** razonar, aguzar; **p. on steam,** (fam.) acalorarse, enojarse; **p. (someone) on to,** pasar (a alguien) el dato de, recomendar (a alguien); ayudar (a alguien) a encontrar; **p. oneself out,** esforzarse mucho; **p. oneself over,** impresionar, causar impacto; **p. out,** extender; extinguir, apagar; molestar, irritar; desconcertar, confundir; incomodar; prestar (dinero a interés), invertir; proporcionar (trabajo) fuera del local; disclocar, descoyuntar (hombro, tobillo, etc.); (criquet) poner fuera del juego, eliminar; **p. over,** mandar aceptar (idea, argumento); **p. them up!** ¡manos arriba!; **p. through,** llevar a cabo, dar curso a, realizar; (tele.) comunicar; **p. (someone) through (a book,** etc.), hacer (a alguien) leer (un libro, etc.); **p. (someone) to (do),** poner (a alguien) a (hacer); **p. to (someone),** sugerir, someter a la consideración de (alguien); **p. together,** reunir, armar; (criquet) recopilar (el puntaje); **p. up,** hospedar, alojar; (teat.) producir, financiar (una obra); postular; emplear (a alguien) como jinete de carreras; publicar (las amonestaciones); proponer como candidato; ofrecer en remate o como premio; contribuir (dinero), pagar (su parte); envolver, guardar, conservar (fruta, verduras); envainar (espada); levantar (la caza); levantar (construcción); urdir, fraguar (plan fraudulento, etc.); **p. up for sale,** poner a la venta; **p. up a good fight,** luchar con valentía; **p. (someone) up to,** informar (a alguien) de; instigar, incitar (a alguien); **to be**

p. to (do), verse obligado a (hacer); **to be p. to it (to do),** tener dificultades (para hacer), apenas poder (hacer); **to be p. upon by (someone),** sufrir abusos de (alguien). —*v.i.* dirigirse; **p. about,** cambiarse de bordada (en barcos); **p. back,** (mar.) volver (al puerto); **p. forth,** (mar.) zarpar, seguir adelante; **p. in,** aparecer, presentarse, mostrarse; (mar.) hacer escala, entrar en puerto; **p. in for,** presentarse (para candidatura), pretender (ser elegido, etc.); **p. off** (mar.) partir, soltar amarras; **p. to sea,** hacerse a la mar, salir al mar, hacerse a la vela; **p. up,** alojarse, hospedarse; **p. up with,** tolerar, aguantar, soportar (persona, molestias, insultos, etc.). —*s.* 1. puesta, tiro, lanzamiento. 2. (bolsa) opción del vendedor (para hacer entrega de acciones y valores dentro del plazo y al precio establecidos). —*a.* (fam.) puesto, fijo, en su sitio; **to stay p.,** quedar en su sitio, no moverse.

putamen [-pju'teɪmən] *s.* (*pl.* PUTAMINA [-'tæmɪnə]1. (anat.) putamen. 2. endocarpio o carozo de algunas frutas (melocotón, ciruelas).

put and take, juego de perinola con apuesta.

putative ['pjutətɪv] *a.* putativo.

putatively [-lɪ] *adv.* putativamente.

putlog ['pʊt,lɔg, -,lɑg, B 'pʌt,lɔg] *s.* (arq.) paral, almojaya.

putlog hole, (const.) mechinal.

put-off ['pʊt,ɔf] *s.* evasión; aplazamiento, postergación.

put-on [-,ɔn, -,ɑn, B -,ɔn] *s.* (jer.) 1. engaño. 2. farsa literaria (hecha intencionalmente como una broma o burla al lector o al público).

put-out [-,aʊt] *s.* (béisbol) acción de poner fuera de juego (a un jugador).

putrefaction [,pjutrə'fækʃən] *s.* putrefacción, descomposición, corrupción.

putrefactive [-tɪv] *a.* putrefactivo.

putrefiable ['pjutrə,faɪəbəl] *a.* que puede descomponerse o pudrirse.

putrefy ['pjutrə,faɪ] *v.t., v.i.* (*pret., p.p.* PUTREFIED; *p.pr.* PUTREFYING) pudrir(se), podrir(se), corromper(se), descomponer(se).

putrescence [pju'trɛsəns] *s.* putrefacción.

putrescent [-ənt] *a.* putrescente.

putrescible [-əbəl] *a.* putrescible.

putrescine [-,in, B -,aɪn] *s.* (quím.) putrescina.

putrid ['pjutrəd] *s.* 1. pútrido, podrido, putrefacto, descompuesto, corrompido. 2. (fig.) depravado, obsceno; pernicioso, malsano. 3. asqueroso.

putridity [pju'trɪdətɪ] **putridness** ['pjutrədnəs] *s.* putridez.

putrid sore throat, (med.) faringitis gangrenosa.

Putsch [pʊtʃ] *s.* (alemán) golpe de estado.

putt [pʌt] *s.* (golf) golpe suave dado a la pelota para que entre en el hoyo. —*v.t., v.i.* golpear (la pelota) suavemente para que entre en el hoyo.

puttee [,pʌ'ti, B 'pʌtɪ] (*pl.* PUTTIES; PUTTEES) *s.* polaina.

putter ['pʌtər, B -ə] *s.* (golf) palo para golpes suaves (usado en el césped circundante al hoyo). —*v.i.* ocuparse en fruslerías. —*v.t.* (con *away*) perder (el tiempo, etc.).

puttier [-ɪər, B -ɪə] *s.* vidriero.

putting green [-ɪŋ-] (golf) espacio de césped que circunda al hoyo.

putty ['pʌtɪ] *s.* (*pl.* PUTTIES) 1. masilla. 2. mástique; mástique de cal. 3. polvo para limpiar metales. —*v.t.* (*pret., p.p.* PUTTIED; *p.pr.* PUTTYING) emplastecer; enmasillar, rellenar con masilla.

putty knife, espátula para aplicar la masilla.

puttyroot [-,rut] *s.* (bot.) una orquídea americana.

put-up ['pʊt,ʌp] *a.* (fam.) planeado, tramado, urdido; arreglado de antemano; **put-up** job, trama, confabulación.

put-upon [-ə,pɔn, -,pɑn, B -,pɔn] *a.* abusado, engañado.

puzzle ['pʌzəl] *v.t.* confundir, poner perplejo, dejar en duda, enredar, embrollar, enmarañar; **p. out,** resolver, descifrar, desenredar. —*v.i.* 1. estar perplejo o desconcertado. 2. (gen. con *about* u *over*) buscar solución a (un problema). —*s.* 1. perplejidad, irresolución, vacilación. 2. enigma, misterio. 3. problema, acertijo, rompecabezas, adivinanza.

puzzleheaded [,pʌzəl'hɛdəd] *a.* confuso, de mente confusa.

puzzlement ['pʌzəlmənt] *s.* perplejidad, irresolución, enredo.

puzzler ['pʌzlər, B -lə] *s.* 1. problema complicado, enigma. 2. el o lo que confunde.

puzzling [-lɪŋ] *a.* enigmático, misterioso, abstruso, incomprensible.

P W *abrev. de* **prisoner of war,** prisionero de guerra.

PWA *abrev. de* **Public Works Administration,** Dirección de Obras Públicas (hist., E.U.).

pyaemia, *s. var. de* **pyemia,** plemia.

pycnidium [pɪk'nɪdɪəm] *s.* (*pl.* PYCNIDIA [-ə]) (bot.) picnidio.

pycnogonid [,pɪknə'gɑnəd, B -'nɔgən-] *s.* (zool.) picnogónido.

pye-dog ['paɪ,dɔg] *s.* perro errante, sin dueño (en países del Oriente).

pyelitis [,paɪə'laɪtəs] *s.* (med.) pielitis.

pyelogram ['paɪələ,græm] *s.* (med.) pielograma.

pyelography [,paɪə'lɑgrəfɪ, B -'lɔg-] *s.* (med.) pielografía.

pyelonephritis [-,loʊnə'fraɪtəs] *s.* (med.) pielonefritis.

pyemia [paɪ'imɪə] *s.* (med.) piemia.

pyemic [-mɪk] *a.* (med.) piémico.

pygidium [paɪ'dʒɪdɪəm] *s.* (*pl.* PYGIDIA [-ə]) (zool.) pigidio.

pygmaean, pygmean [pɪg'miən] *a.* pigmeo; enano, liliputiense.

Pygmalion [pɪg'meɪljən] *s.* (mitol.) Pigmalión, el escultor que se enamoró de Galatea, su estatua.

pygmoid ['pɪg,mɔɪd] *a.* (antrop.) pigmoide.

pygmy ['pɪgmɪ] *s.* (*pl.* PYGMIES) 1. pigmeo, enano, liliputiense. 2. (t. P.) (mitol.) pigmeo. 3. P., pigmeo (de raza negra que habita el Africa Central). —*a.* pigmeo.

pygmyish [-ɪʃ] *a.* enano, diminuto.

pygmy owl, (orn.) chucho.

pyic ['paɪɪk] *a.* (med.) purulento.

pyin ['paɪɪn] *s.* (bioquím.) piina.

pyjamas, (pr. G.B.) *var. de* **pajamas.**

pyknic ['pɪknɪk] *a., s.* pícnico.

pylon ['paɪ,lɑn, B -lən] *s.* 1. pilono, pilón (del templo egipcio). 2. torre metálica. 3. (aer.) poste o torre marcadora del curso de vuelo.

pyloric [paɪ'lɔrɪk] *a.* (anat., zool.) pilórico.

pylorus [-əs] *s.* (*pl.* PYLORI [-,aɪ]) (anat.) píloro.

pyoderma [,paɪə'dɜrmə, B -'dɜmə] *s.* (med.) pioderma.

pyogenesis [-'dʒɛnəsəs] *s.* (med.) piogenia.

pyogenic [-ɪk] *a.* (med.) piogénico.

pyorrhea [,paɪə'riə] *s.* (med.) piorrea.

pyorrheal, pyorrhoeal [-'riəl] *a.* (med.) piorreico.

pyosis [paɪ'oʊsəs] *s.* (med.) piosis.

pyracantha [,pɪrə'kænθə, B ,paɪər-] *s.* (bot.) piracanta, espino albar.

Pyralidae [,pɪrə'lɪdi] *s. pl.* (zool.) pirálidos.

pyralidid [pə'rælədəd] **pyralidan** [-ən] *a., s.* (zool.) pirálido.

pyramid ['pɪrəmɪd] *s.* 1. pirámide (de Egipto). 2. (geom.) pirámide. 3. (*pl.*) juego parecido al billar. —*v.t.* construir o arreglar como una pirámide; amontonar. —*v.i.* amontonarse.

pyramidal [pə'ræmədəl] *a.* piramidal.

pyramidally [-əlɪ] *adv.* piramidalmente.

pyramidic [,pɪrə'mɪdɪk] **pyramidical** [-ɪkəl] *a.* piramidal, de figura de pirámide.

pyran ['paɪr,æn, B 'paɪər-] *s.* (quím.) pirano.

pyrargyrite [paɪ'rɑrdʒə,raɪt, B -'rɑdʒə-] *s.* (min.) pirargirita.

pyre [paɪr, B 'paɪə] *s.* pira, hoguera.

pyrene ['paɪr,in] *s.* (quím.) pireno.

Pyrenean [,pɪrə'niən] *a.* pirenaico, de los Pirineos.

Pyrenees ['pɪrə,niz, B ,pɪrə'niz] *s.* Pirineos (montes).

pyrenoid [paɪ'ri,nɔɪd] *s.* (bot.) pirenoide.

pyrethrin [paɪ'rɪθrən] *s.* (quím.) piretrina.

pyrethrum [-θrəm] *s.* 1. (bot.) piretro, pelitre. 2. (farm.) piretrina (un insecticida).

pyretic [paɪ'rɛtɪk] *a.* (med.) pirético.

pyretology [,pɪrə'tɑlədʒɪ, B ,paɪərə'tɔl-] *s.* (med.) piretología.

pyretotherapy [-toʊ'θɛrəpɪ] *s.* (med.) piretoterapia.

Pyrex ['paɪr,ɛks] *s.* (E.U.) pirex, marca de fábrica de un tipo de vajilla de vidrio resistente al calor.

pyrexia [paɪ'rɛksɪə] *s.* (med.) pirexia.

pyrexic [-sɪk] *a.* (med.) pirético.

pyrheliometer ['paɪr,hilɪ'ɑmətər, B pə,-'ɔmɪtə] *s.* (fís.) pirheliómetro, pireliómetro.

pyridic [pɪ'rɪdɪk] *a.* (quím.) pirídico.

pyridine ['pɪrə,din, B 'paɪərɪdaɪn] *s.* (quím.) piridina.

pyridoxine [,pɪrə'dɑk,sin, B -'dɔksaɪn] **pyridoxin** [-sən] *s.* (quím.) piridoxina (vitamina B6).

pyriform ['pɪrə,fɔrm, B -fɔm] *a.* piriforme, de forma de pera.

pyrimidine [paɪ'rɪmə,din, B -,daɪn] *s.* (quím.) pirimidina.

pyrite ['paɪr,aɪt, B 'paɪər-] *s.* (*pl.* PYRITES [pə'raɪtiz, B paɪ-]) (min.) pirita, pirita de hierro, pirita marcial.

pyritic [pə'rɪtɪk, B paɪ-] *a.* (min.) piritoso; de pirita.

pyrocatechol [,paɪroʊ'kætə,tʃɔl] **pyrocatechin** [-tʃən] *s.* (quím.) pirocatequina.

pyrochemical [-'kɛmɪkəl] *a.* (fís., quím.) piroquímico.

pyroclastic [-'klæstɪk] *a.* (geol.) piroclástico.

pyrocondensation [-,kɑn,dɛn'seɪʃən, B -,kɔn-] *s.* (quím.) pirocondensación.

pyroconductivity [-,kɑn,dʌk'tɪvətɪ, B -,kɔn-] *s.* (elec.) piroconductibilidad.

pyroelectric [-ə'lɛktrɪk] *a.* (fís.) piroeléctrico.

pyroelectricity [-ə,lɛk'trɪsətɪ] *s.* (fís.) piroelectricidad.

pyrogallate [-'gæl,eɪt] *s.* (quím.) pirogalato.

pyrogallic acid [-ɪk-] (quím.) ácido pirogálico.

pyrogallol [-,ɔl] *s.* (quím.) pirogalol.

pyrogen ['paɪrədʒən, B 'paɪə-] *s.* (med.) pirógeno.

pyrogenic [,paɪroʊ'dʒɛnɪk] **pyrogenous** [,paɪ'rɑdʒənəs, B -'rɔdʒ-] *a.* 1. (med.) pirógeno, piretogénico. 2. (geol.) pirógeno.

pyrographer [paɪ'rɑgrəfər, B -'rɔgrəfə] *s.* (arte) pirograbador.

pyrography [-fɪ] **pyrogravure** ['paɪroʊ,grə'vjʊr, B 'paɪər-'vjʊə] *s.* pirograbado, grabado al fuego (en madera o piel).

pyroligneous [ˌpaɪroʊ'lɪgnɪəs] *a.* (quím.) piroleñoso.
pyrolignic [-nɪk] *a.* (quím.) piroleñoso.
pyrolusite [-'luˌsaɪt] *s.* (min.) pirolusita.
pyrolysis [paɪ'rɑləsəs, B -'rɔl-] *s.* (quím.) pirólisis.
pyromagnetic [ˌpaɪroʊmæg'nɛtɪk] *a.* (fís.) piromagnético.
pyromancer ['paɪrəˌmænsər, B 'paɪə-sə] *s.* piromántico, el que adivina la suerte por los símbolos del fuego.
pyromancy [-sɪ] *s.* piromancia, piromancía, adivinación por medio del fuego.
pyromania [ˌpaɪroʊ'meɪnɪə] *s.* piromanía, manía de causar incendios.
pyromaniac [-æk] *s.* piromaníaco, el que tiene la manía de causar incendios.
pyromantic [-'mæntɪk] *a.* piromántico.
pyrometallurgy [-'mɛtəlˌɜrdʒɪ, B -ˌɜdʒɪ] *s.* pirometalurgia.
pyrometer [paɪ'rɑmətər, B -'rɔmɪtə] *s.* (fís., elec.) pirómetro.
pyrometric [ˌpaɪroʊ'mɛtrɪk] **pyrometrical** [-trɪkəl] *a.* (fís.) pirométrico.
pyrometry [paɪ'rɑmətrɪ, B -'rɔm-] *s.* (fís.) pirometría.
pyromorphite [ˌpaɪrə'mɔrˌfaɪt, B -'mɔˌ-] *s.* (min.) piromorfita.
pyrone ['paɪˌroʊn] *s.* (quím.) pirona.
pyronine ['paɪrəˌnin, B 'paɪərəˌnaɪn] *s.* (quím.) pironina.
pyrope ['paɪrˌoʊp, B 'paɪər-] *s.* (min.) piropo.
pyrophobia [ˌpaɪrə'foʊbɪə] *s.* (med.) pirofobia.
pyrophoric [-'fɔrɪk, -'fɑr-, B -'fɔr-] *a.* (quím.) pirofórico.
pyrophorus [paɪ'rɑfərəs, B -'rɔf-] *s.* (*pl.* PYROPHORI [-raɪ]) (quím.) piróforo.
pyrophosphate [ˌpaɪroʊ'fɑsˌfeɪt, B -'fɔs-] *s.* (quím.) pirofosfato.
pyrophosphoric acid [-ˌfɑs'fɔrɪk-, B -fɔs-] (quím.) ácido pirofosfórico.
pyrophotometer [-foʊ'tɑmətər, B -'tɔmɪtə] *s.* (ópt., fís.) pirofotómetro.
pyrophyllyte [-'fɪlˌaɪt] *s.* (min.) pirofilita.
pyroscope ['paɪrəˌskoʊp, B 'paɪəroʊ-] *s.* (fís.) piroscopio.
pyrosis [paɪ'roʊsəs] *s.* (med.) pirosis.
pyrosphere ['paɪrəˌsfɪr, B 'paɪərəˌsfɪə] *s.* (geol.) pirosfera.
pyrostat [-ˌstæt] *s.* (fís.) piróstato.
pyrosulfate [ˌpaɪroʊ'sʌlˌfeɪt] *s.* (quím.) pirosulfato.
pyrosulfuric acid [-ˌsʌl'fjʊrɪk-] (quím.) ácido pirosulfúrico.
pyrotechnic [ˌpaɪrə'tɛknik] **pyrotechnical** [-nɪkəl] *a.* pirotécnico.
pyrotechnics [-nɪks] *s. pl.* (*sing. o pl. en const.*) 1. pirotecnia. 2. (fig.) exposición bombástica. 3. alocución con despliegue de elocuencia; ingenio y brillantez.
pyrotechnist [-nəst] *s.* pirotécnico.
pyrotechny ['paɪrəˌtɛknɪ] *s.* pirotecnia, fuegos artificiales.
pyrotoxin [ˌpaɪrə'tɑksən, B -'tɔk-] *s.* (bioquím.) pirotoxina.
pyroxene [paɪ'rɑkˌsin, B -'rɔk-] *s.* (min.) piroxeno, pirozena.
pyroxenite [-səˌnaɪt] *s.* (geol.) piroxenita.
pyroxyline, pyroxylin [-sələn] *s.* (quím.) piroxilina.
Pyrrha ['pɪrə] *s.* (mitol.) Pirra.
pyrrhic ['pɪrɪk] *s.* (poética) pirriquio. —*a.* pírrico.
Pyrrhic victory, victoria pírrica; triunfo a costa de grandes pérdidas.
Pyrrhonic [pɪ'rɑnɪk, B -'rɔn-] *a.* pirroniano, escéptico.
Pyrrhonism ['pɪrəˌnɪzəm] *s.* (filos.) pirronismo, escepticismo.
Pyrrhonist [-nəst] *s.* pirrónico, escéptico.
Pyrrhonistic [ˌpɪrə'nɪstɪk] *a.* pirrónico, escéptico.
pyrrhotite ['pɪrəˌtaɪt] *s.* (min.) pirrotita.
pyrrhuloxia [ˌpɪrə'lɑksɪə, B -'lɔk-] *s.* (orn.) pinzón, fringílido americano.
pyrrole ['pɪrˌoʊl] *s.* (quím.) pirrol.
pyruvic acid [paɪ'ruvɪk-] (quím.) ácido pirúvico.
Pythagoras [pə'θægərəs, B paɪ-æs] *s.* Pitágoras, matemático y filósofo de la Grecia antigua.
Pythagorean [-ˌθægə'riən] *a., s.* pitagórico, relativo a Pitágoras, seguidor de sus conceptos.
Pythagoreanism [-əˌnɪzəm] *s.* pitagorismo, los conceptos de Pitágoras.
Pythagorean table, tabla pitagórica.
Pythiad ['pɪθɪˌæd] *s.* (hist.) pitiada.
Pythian [-ən] *a.* (hist.) pitio, pítico.
Python ['paɪˌθɑn, B -θən] *s.* 1. (mitol.) Pitón, serpiente gigantesca que mató Apolo. 2. **p.,** (zool.) pitón.
pythoness [-θənəs] *s.* (mitol.) pitonisa.
pythonic [paɪ'θɑnɪk, B -'θɔn-] *a.* 1. pitónico, profético. 2. como un pitón; (fig). enorme, gigantesco.
pyuria [paɪ'jʊrɪə, B -'jʊər-] *s.* (med.) piuria.
pyx [pɪks] *s.* 1. (relig.) píxide, copón. 2. urna en que se guardan muestras de monedas para su ensayo (en la casa de moneda de G.B.).
pyxidium [pɪk'sɪdɪəm] *s.* (*pl.* PYXIDIA [-ə]) (bot.) pixidio.
pyxie ['pɪksɪ] *s.* (bot.) (especie de) siempreviva trepadora.
pyxis ['pɪksəs] *s.* (*pl.* PYXIDES [-səˌdiz]) (bot.) pixidio.

Q

Q [kju] *s.* q, decimoséptima letra del alfabeto inglés.
Q.E.D. *abrev de* **quod erat demonstrandum,** lo que queríamos demostrar (L Q Q D).
Q fever, (med.) fiebre Q.
Q.M. (ant.) *abrev. de* **quartermaster,** oficial del Servicio de Intendencia.
Q.M.C. (ant.) *abrev. de* **Quartermaster Corps,** Servicio de Intendencia.
q.t., on the strict q.t., en absoluto secreto, en oculto.
qua [kweɪ, kwɑ, B kweɪ] *adv.* en cuanto a; en su calidad de; como.
quack [kwæk] *v.i.* parpar, graznar (esp. el pato). —*s.* graznido.
quack, *s.* 1. curandero, matasanos, medicastro, medicucho, ensalmador. 2. charlatán, farsante. —*a.* curanderil, de charlatán. —*v.i.* hacer de curandero o charlatán. —*v.t.* curar o tratar (una enfermedad) al modo de un curandero.
quackery ['kwækərɪ] *s.* 1. curandería, curanderismo. 2. charlatanismo.
quack grass, (bot.) grama, bermuda, bermudagrass, gramilla colorada.
quackish [-ɪʃ] *a.* curanderil.
quacksalver [-ˌsælvər, B -və] *s.* curandero, charlatán.
quad [kwɑd, B kwɔd] *s.* 1. (fam.) cuadrángulo, patio cuadrangular (esp. de un colegio o universidad). 2. (impr.) cuadrado, cuadratín.
quadragenarian [ˌkwɑdrədʒə'nɛrɪən, B ˌkwɔd-'nɛərɪən] *a., s.* cuadragenario, cuarentón.
Quadragesima [-'dʒɛsɪmə] *s.* 1. (t. **Q Sunday**) primer domingo de cuaresma. 2. (relig., ant.) cuadragésima, cuaresma.
Quadragesimal [-məl] *a.* (relig.) cuadragesimal, cuaresmal.
quadragintesimal [-dʒən'tɛsəməl] *a.* cuadringentésimo.
quadrangle ['kwɑdˌræŋgəl, B'kwɔd-] *s.* 1. (geom.) cuadrángulo, cuadrilátero, tetrágono. 2. plaza; patio (esp. de un colegio o universidad).
quadrangular [kwɑ'dræŋgjələr, B kwɔ-lə] *a.* cuadrangular, cuadrilateral.
quadrant ['kwɑdrənt, B 'kwɔd-] *s.* 1. (astr.) cuadrante (instrumento para medir las altitudes). 2. (geom.) cuadrante, cualquiera de las cuatro partes en que se divide un plano. 3. (mec.) sector oscilante, codo de palanca; balancín de escuadra (de bombas de mina); lira (del torno de roscar).
quadrantal [kwɑ'dræntəl, B kwɔ-] *a.* del cuadrante. —*s.* (hist.) cuadrantal.
quadrant compass, compás de arco; compás de cuadrante.
quadrat ['kwɑdrət, B 'kwɔd-] *s.* (impr.) cuadratín, cuadrado.
quadrate ['kwɑdˌreɪt, B 'kwɔdrət] *a.* 1. cuadrado. 2. (her.) con cuadrado en la juntura (cruz). —*s.* 1. cuadrado, rectángulo. 2. (anat.) hueso y músculo cuadrado. — [B kwɔ'dreɪt] *v.t.* cuadrar, conformar, ajustar (una cosa con otra). —*v.i* (con *with*) acordar, convenir, cuadrar (con).
quadratic [kwɑ'drætɪk, B kwə-] *a.* (mat.) cuadrático. —*s.* ecuación o expresión cuadrática.
quadratic equation, (mat.) ecuación cuadrática, ecuación de segundo grado.
quadratics [-ɪks] *s. pl.* (*sing. o pl. en const.*) (mat.) álgebra de las ecuaciones cuadráticas.
quadrature ['kwɑdrətʃər, B 'kwɔdrətʃə] *s.* (mat., elec., astr.) cuadratura.
quadrature of the circle, (mat.) cuadratura del círculo.
quadrennial [kwɑ'drɛnɪəl, B kwə-] *a.* cuadrienal.
quadrennially [-əlɪ] *adv.* cada cuatro años.
quadrennium [-ɪəm] *s.* (*pl.* QUADRENNIUMS o QUADRENNIA [-ə]) cuadrienio, cuatrienio.
quadric ['kwɑdrɪk, B 'kwɔd-] *s.* (mat.) cuádrica.
quadricentennial [ˌkwɑdrɪsɛn'tɛnɪəl, B ˌkwɔd-] *s.* cuarto centenario. —*a.* de cada cuatro siglos.
quadriceps ['kwɑdrəˌsɛps, B 'kwɔd-] *s.* (anat.) cuadríceps.
quadricycle [-ˌsaɪkəl] *s.* cuadriciclo.
quadrifid [-ˌfɪd] *a.* (bot.) cuadrífido.
quadrifoliate [ˌkwɑdrɪ'foʊlɪət, B ˌkwɔ-] *a.* (bot.) cuadrifolio, cuadrifoliado.
quadrifoliolate [-əˌleɪt] *a.* (bot.) cuadrifoliolado.
quadriform ['kwɑdrəˌfɔrm, B 'kwɔ-ˌfɔm] *a.* cuadriforme.
quadriga [kwɑ'drigə, B kwə-] *s.* (*pl.* QUADRIGAE [-ˌgaɪ]) (hist.) cuadriga.
quadrigeminal [ˌkwɑdrə'dʒɛmənəl, B ˌkwɔd-] *a.* cuadrigémino.
quadrilateral [-'lætərəl] *a.* cuadrilátero, cuadrangular. —*s.* (geom., mil.) cuadrilátero.
quadrilingual [-'lɪŋgwəl] *a.* cuatrilingüe.
quadrille [kwɑ'drɪl, B kwə-] *s.* 1. (fr.) cuadrilla (baile). 2. cuatrillo, cuatrino, cascarela (juego de naipes). 3. cuadrícula. —*a.* cuadricular.
quadrillion [kwɑ'drɪljən, B kwɔ-] *s.* (E.U.) mil billones; (G.B.) cuatrillón.
quadrinomial [ˌkwɑdrə'noʊmɪəl, B ˌkwɔd-] *s.* (mat.) cuadrinomio.
quadripartite [-'pɑrˌtaɪt, B -'pɑˌ-] *a.* 1. cuadripartido. 2. de cuatro partes (contrato, tratado, etc.).
quadriplegia [-'plidʒɪə] *s.* (med.) cuadriplegia, parálisis total del cuerpo.
quadriplegic [-dʒɪk, B -'plɛdʒɪk] *s., a.* (med.) cuadripléjico.
quadrisyllabic [-sɪ'læbɪk] *a.* cuatrisílabo.
quadrisyllable ['kwɑdrəˌsɪləbəl, B'kwɔd-] *s.* cuatrisílabo.
quadrivalent [ˌkwɑdrə'veɪlənt, B ˌkwɔd-] *a.* (quím.) cuadrivalente, tetravalente.
quadrivium [kwɑ'drɪvɪəm, B kwɔ-] *s.* (hist.) cuadrivio, la más alta división de las artes liberales de la Edad Media: aritmética, geometría, astronomía y música.
quadroon [-'drun] *s.* mulato, cuarterón.
quadrumane ['kwɑdrʊˌmeɪn, B 'kwɔd-] *s.* (zool.) cuadrúmano, cuadrumano.
quadrumanous [kwɑ'drumənəs, B kwɔ-] *a.* (zool.) cuadrúmano, cuadrumano.
quadruped ['kwɑdrəˌpɛd, B 'kwɔdrʊ-] *s., a.* (zool.) cuadrúpedo.
quadrupedal [kwɑ'drupədəl, B kwɔ-] *a.* cuadrupedal.
quadruple [-'drupəl, -'drʌp-, B 'kwɔdrʊp-] *v.t., v.i.* cuadruplicar(se), cuadriplicar(se), cuatrodoblar(se). —*a.* cuádruple, cuádruplo. —*s.* cuatrotanto, cuádruplo.
quadruple measure, q. time, (mús.) compás de dos por cuatro.
quadruplet [-drʌplət, -'drup-, B 'kwɔdrʊp-] *s.* 1. cuadrupleto (gemelo de un parto cuádruple). 2. juego o conjunto de cuatro.
quadruplicate [kwɑ'drupləˌkeɪt, B kwɔ-] *v.t.* cuadruplicar, cuadriplicar, cuatrodoblar. —[-ˌplɪkət] *a.* (mat.) cuádruplo. —*s.* cuadruplicado.
quadruplication [-ˌdruplə'keɪʃən] *s.* cuadruplicación.
quadruply ['kwɑdrʊplɪ, B 'kwɔd-] *adv.* al cuádruplo.
quadrupole [-ˌpoʊl] *s.* (fís.) cuadrípolo.
quaestor, quaestorial, quaestorship, *vars. de* **questor, questorial, questorship.**
quaff [kwɑf, kwæf, B kwɑf] *v.i., v.t.* beber a tragantadas, continuamente. —*s.* tragantada.
quaffer ['kwɑfər, 'kwæf-, B 'kwɑfə] *s.* bebedor a tragantadas.
quag [kwɑg, kwæg, B kwæg] *s.* marjal, pantano, ciénaga.
quagga ['kwægə] *s.* cuaga (mamífero africano extinto).
quaggy ['kwægɪ, 'kwɑgɪ, B 'kwægɪ] *a.* (QUAGGIER; QUAGGIEST) 1. pantanoso, cenagoso, fangoso. 2. fofo, blando, flojo.
quagmire [-ˌmaɪr, B -ˌmaɪə] *s.* 1. ciénaga, lodazal, pantano, cenagal, fangal; tremedal, tembladal, tolladar. 2. (fig.) posición o situación personal difícil o confusa, atolladero.
quahog, quahaug ['kwɔˌhɔg, -ˌhɑg, B kwə'hɔg] *s.* (zool.) almeja, chirla.
quail [kweɪl] *v.i.* acobardarse, amedrentarse, amilanarse, encogerse, descorazonarse. —*s.* (orn.) codorniz.
quaint [kweɪnt] *a.* 1. raro, extraño, peregrino, peculiar, pintoresco, exótico, original. 2. (ant.) de curioso o exquisito primor; bonito; fino.
quaintly ['kweɪntlɪ] *adv.* 1. extravagantemente, pintorescamente. 2. (ant.) exquisitamente.
quaintness [-nəs] *s.* 1. rareza, peculiaridad, extravagancia. 2. (ant.) exquisitez.
quake [kweɪk] *v.i.* temblar, estremecerse. —*s.* 1. estremecimiento; temblor. 2. terremoto.
Quaker ['kweɪkər, B -kə] *s.* cuáquero, cuákero, miembro de una secta laica cristiana que se opone a la guerra y la violencia.
Quaker gun, (E.U.) cañón de madera (forma simbólica de oposición cuáquera a la guerra y al militarismo).
Quaker-ladies [ˌkweɪkər'leɪdɪz, B -kə'-] *s. pl.* (bot., E.U.) (especie de) aciano.
Quaker meeting, 1. congregación de cuáqueros. 2. (fig., fam.) reunión silenciosa, reunión de personas faltas de conversación.
quaking bog ['kweɪkɪŋ-] tremendal, lugar cenagoso que retiembla.

quaking grass, (bot.) tembladera, briza, cedacillo, zarcillitos.
quaky [ˈkweɪkɪ] *a.* tembloroso, inseguro (lugar u objeto).
qualification [ˌkwaləfəˈkeɪʃən, B ˌkwɔl-] *s.* 1. calificación. 2. idoneidad, capacidad, habilidad; requisito, condición. 3. limitación, salvedad, modificación.
qualified [ˈkwaləˌfaɪd, B ˈkwɔl-] *a.* 1. calificado; competente, apto, idóneo, hábil, capacitado. 2. limitado, restringido.
qualifiedly [-lɪ] *adv.* idóneamente, competentemente.
qualified voter, elector capacitado o habilitado para votar.
qualifier [-ˌfaɪər, B -ˌfaɪə] *s.* 1. calificador. 2. (gram.) calificativo.
qualify [ˈkwaləˌfaɪ, B ˈkwɔl-] *v.t.* (*pret., p.p.* QUALIFIED; *p.pr.* QUALIFYING) 1. calificar, capacitar, habilitar. 2. restringir, modificar, limitar. 3. suavizar, mitigar, templar, moderar. 4. suavizar o diluir (un licor). 5. (gram.) calificar, modificar. —*v.i.* 1. ser apto o idóneo (para un empleo), ser aprobado (en un examen), llenar los requisitos. 2. (dep.) clasificarse (en competencia eliminatoria para participar en la prueba final). 3. (E.U.) ser apto para prestar juramento antes de comenzar una función pública.
qualitative [ˈkwaləˌteɪtɪv, B ˈkwɔlɪtət-] *a.* cualitativo.
qualitative analysis, (quím.) análisis cualitativo.
quality [ˈkwalətɪ, B ˈkwɔl-] *s.* (*pl.* QUALLITIES) 1. cualidad, característica. 2. calidad, clase, categoría, grado, tipo. 3. capacidad, virtud, cualidad o rasgo distintivo. 4. (fon.) timbre (de una vocal). 5. (raro) naturaleza, genio. 6. **in (the) q. of,** en calidad de.
quality control, control de la calidad, sistema metódico, realizado con el fin de mantener el nivel requerido de producción.
qualm [kwam] *s.* 1. escrúpulo, remordimiento de conciencia, desasosiego, duda, incertidumbre. 2. hastío, fastidio.
qualmish [ˈkwamɪʃ] *a.* escrupuloso; titubeante, incierto.
qualmishly [-lɪ] *adv.* con inseguridad o duda.
qualmishness [-nəs] *s.* escrupulosidad; inseguridad.
quandary [ˈkwandərɪ, B ˈkwɔn-] *s.* (*pl.* QUANDARIES) dilema, apuro, aprieto.
quanta, *pl. de* **quantum.**
quantic [ˈkwantɪk, B ˈkwɔnt-] *s., a.* (mat.) quántico, cuántico.
quantification [ˌkwantəfəˈkeɪʃən, B ˌkwɔnt-] *s.* (lóg.) cuantificación.
quantify [ˈkwantəˌfaɪ, B ˈkwɔnt-] *v.t.* (*pret., p.p.* QUANTIFIED; *p.pr.* QUANTIFYING) 1. medir o determinar la cantidad de. 2. (lóg.) cuantificar.
quantitative [ˈkwantəˌteɪtɪv, B ˈkwɔntɪtət-] *a.* cuantitativo.
quantitative analysis, (quím.) análisis cuantitativo.
quantitatively [-lɪ] *adv.* cuantitativamente, en cuanto a cantidad, según la cantidad.
quantity [ˈkwantətɪ, B ˈkwɔnt-] *s.* (*pl.* QUANTITIES) cantidad, cuantía; dosis (determinada o indeterminada).
quantity production, fabricación en masa, producción en masa.
quantity surveying, cálculo y medida de los materiales en las construcciones.
quantization [ˌkwantəˈzeɪʃən, B ˌkwɔntaɪ-] *s.* (fís.) cuantificación.
quantize [ˈkwanˌtaɪz, B ˈkwɔn-] *v.t.* 1. (fís.) cuantificar, subdividir (energía) en quanta. 2. expresar en términos de la mecánica cuántica.
quantum [ˈkwantəm, B ˈkwɔnt-] *s.* (*pl.* QUANTA [-ə]) 1. tanto, cantidad; suma. 2. (fís.) cuanto, quantum.
quantum mechanics (fís.) mecánica cuántica.
quantum number, (fís.) número cuántico.
quantum theory, (fís.) teoría cuántica, teoría de los cuantos o quanta.
quarantine [ˈkwɔrənˌtin, ˈkwar-, B ˈkwɔr-] *s.* 1. cuarentena, período de cuarenta días. 2. cuarentena, aislamiento. 3. estación de cuarentena. —*v.t.* poner en cuarentena, aislar.
quarrel [ˈkwɔrəl, ˈkwar-, B ˈkwɔr-] *s.* 1. reyerta, pendencia, riña, disputa, altercado, querella, camorra. 2. **to have no q. with,** no tener queja contra; no desaprobar, no estar en desacuerdo con; **to pick a q.,** buscar pleito. —*v.i.* (*pret., p.p.* QUARRELED O QUARRELLED; *p.pr.* QUARRELING O QUARRELLING) 1. pelear, reñir, pendenciar, altercar. 2. (con *with*) criticar, quejarse (de).
quarrel, *s.* 1. (hist.) flecha o dardo de punta cuadrada (esp. para ballesta). 2. vidrio cuadrangular (de vidriera, etc.).
quarreler, quarreller [-ər, B -ə] *s.* pendenciero, peleador, camorrista, pleitista.
quarrelsome [-səm] *a.* pendenciero, peleador, reñidor, camorrista, pleitista.
quarrelsomely [-lɪ] *adv.* pendencieramente.
quarrelsomeness [-nəs] *s.* pugnacidad, carácter pendenciero.
quarrier [ˈkwɔrɪər, ˈkwar-, B ˈkwɔrɪə] *s.* cantero, picapedrero.
quarry [ˈkwɔrɪ, ˈkwarɪ, B ˈkwɔrɪ] *s.* (*pl.* QUARRIES) 1. cuadrado de vidrio, loseta o teja. 2. presa; caza. 3. (ant.) montón de piezas cobradas.
quarry, *s.* (*pl.* QUARRIES) cantera, pedrera. —*v.t.* (*pret., p.p.* QUARRIED; *p.pr.* QUARRYING) minar, excavar, sacar (piedra, mármol, etc. de una cantera); (fig.) sacar (datos, información, etc. de libros o documentos).
quarrying [-ɪŋ] *s.* excavación, minería (de piedra, mármol, etc.).
quarryman [-mən] *s.* picapedrero.
quart [kwɔrt, B kwɔt] *s.* 1. cuarto de galón. 2. botella o jarro de un cuarto de galón.
quart [kart, B kat] *s.* (esgr., naipes) cuarto.
quartan [ˈkwɔrtən, B ˈkwɔt-] (med.) *a.* cuartanal (fiebre). —*s.* cuartana, fiebre cuartanal (que recidiva cada cuatro días).
quarte [kart, B kat] *s.* (esgr.) cuarta.
quarter [ˈkwɔrtər, B ˈkwɔtə] *s.* 1. cuarto, cuarta, cuarta parte. 2. arroba (un cuarto de quintal); un cuarto de libra. 3. cuarto de milla. 4. trimestre. 5. cuarto (de hora), ej., *a q. to three,* falta un cuarto para las tres. 6. (E.U., Can.) veinticinco centavos (moneda y suma). 7. cuarto (cada una de las partes en que se considera dividido el cuerpo de los cuadrúpedos y aves). 8. (*pl.*) cuartos, miembros descuartizados de un animal. 9. (*gen. pl.*) (t. **hind quarters**) caderas (de hombre y animal). 10. punto cardinal, dirección, lugar, punto, región; origen, fuente (de información, ayuda, noticia, etc.). 11. distrito, barrio o sección de una ciudad. 12. (*pl.*) postas, apostaderos, puestos (militares o navales). 13 (*pl.*) cuartel, morada, habitación; (S. de E.U.) (hist.) cabañas de esclavos o barracones (en las plantaciones). 14. cuartel, clemencia. 15. (astr.) cuarto (fase de la luna). 16. muralla (del casco del caballo). 17. (her.) cuartel. 18. (mar.) aleta (parte del casco de una nave). 19. (mar.) (un) cuarto de braza. 20. parte lateral del zapato (desde la empella al talón). 21. (dep.) carrera de un cuarto de milla. 22. (fútbol, E.U.) (*forma abrev. de* **q.-back**) mariscal de campo; jugador de defensa. 23. **and a q. five,** (mar.) cinco brazas y (un) cuarto; **a q. less five,** (mar.) cinco brazas menos un cuarto; **at close quarters,** de cerca; cuerpo a cuerpo; **from all quarters,** de todas partes; **on the q.,** (mar.) por la aleta, entre la popa y la manga; **to ask for** (o **to cry**) **q.,** pedir tregua o clemencia; **to beat** (o **call**) **to quarters,** (mar.) mandar a la tripulación a ocupar los puestos de servicio (en preparación para la batalla, etc.); **to give no q.,** no dar cuartel; **to take up one's quarters (at, in** o **with),** alojarse (en o con); **what q. is the wind in?** ¿de dónde sopla el viento?; (fig.) ¿cómo andan las cosas?; **winter quarters,** cuartel invernal, cuarteles de invierno (para tropas). —*v.t.* 1. cuartear. 2. descuartizar, hacer cuartos, desmembrar. 3. acuartelar, acomodar, hospedar, alojar. 4. cuartear, recorrer (terreno) en todas direcciones (díc. de los perros de caza). 5. (her.) cuartelar; añadir (blasón) al escudo de armas. 6. (mec.) calar en ángulo recto. —*v.i.* 1. alojarse, hospedarse. 2. correr en todas direcciones venteando (perros de caza). 3. (mar.) soplar (viento) por la aleta. —*a.* cuarto.
quarterage [ˈkwɔrtərɪdʒ, B ˈkwɔt-] *s.* 1. sueldo o salario trimestral; asignación, pensión. 2. cuartel, alojamiento.
quarterback [ˈkwɔrtərˌbæk, B ˈkwɔtəˌ-] *s.* (fútbol, E.U.) mariscal de campo, corebac. —*v.t.* ser el mariscal de campo de, ser el corebac de.
quarter-bell [-ˌbɛl] *s.* (mar.) campana que toca cada cuarto de hora.
quarter binding, (enc.) empaste con cuero sólo en el lomo del libro.
quarter butt, (billar) taco de billar corto.
quarter day, primer día de un trimestre, esp. día de pagos trimestrales.
quarter-deck [-ˌdɛk] *s.* (mar.) alcázar.
quarter-deck ladder, escala de alcázar.
quartered [ˈkwɔrtərd, B ˈkwɔtəd] *a.* 1. cuarteado. 2. que tiene habitación, alojado. 3. aserrado a lo largo en cuartos (tronco de madera). 4. (her.) acuartelado, cantonado.
quarterfinal [-ərˈfaɪnəl, B -əˈ-] (dep.) *a.* del cuarto de final. —*s.* cuarto de final.
quarterfinalist [-əst] *s.* cuartofinalista.
quarter gallery, (mar.) espacio para paseo u observación, esp. en barcos veleros.
quarter-hour [-ərˈaʊr, B -ˈaʊə] *s.* cuarto de hora.
quarter-inch [-ˈɪntʃ] *s.* cuarto de pulgada.
quartering [-ɪŋ] *a.* 1. (mec.) puesto o montado en ángulo recto. 2. (mar.) de aleta (díc. del viento, olas, etc.). —*s.* 1. cuarteo, división en cuatro partes; división. 2. cuarteo, serpenteo, zigzagueo. 3. acuartelamiento (de tropas). 4. (her.) cuartel (de un escudo).
quarter left, (mil.) media vuelta a la izquierda.
quarterly [ˈkwɔrtərlɪ, B ˈkwɔtəlɪ] *adv.* 1. por cuartos; trimestralmente. 2. (her.) en forma acuartelada. —*a.* 1. trimestral. 2. (her.) acuartelado. —*s.* (*pl.* QUARTERLIES) periódico trimestral; publicación trimestral.
quartermaster [-ˌmæstər, B -ˌmastə] *s.* 1. (mil.) comisario ordenador, oficial del servicio de intendencia. 2. (mar.) cabo de mar.
Quartermaster Corps, (mil.) servicio de intendencia.
quartermaster depot, (mil.) depósito de intendencia.
quartermaster general, (mil.) intendente general.
quartermaster stores, (mil.) depósito de intendencia.
quarter-miler [ˈkwɔrtərˈmaɪlər, B ˈkwɔtəˈ-lə] *s.* corredor en carreras de un cuarto de milla.

quartern [-ərn, B -ən] *s.* 1. cuarto, cuarta parte. 2. (G.B.) pan de cuatro libras.
quarter note, (mús.) semínima, negra.
quarter of honor, (her.) cantón de honor.
quarter-phase [-ər'feɪz, B -ə'-] *a.* (elec.) bifásico.
quarter plate, (foto.) placa de tres por cuatro pulgadas.
quarter point, rumbo de la brújula.
quarter right, (mil.) media vuelta a la derecha.
quarter round, (arq.) óvolo, cuarto bocel.
quartersaw [-ˌsɔ] *v.t.* aserrar por cuartos (tronco).
quarter section, 1. cuarta, cuarto. 2. (E.U., Can.) área de un cuarto de milla cuadrada (160 acres).
quarter sessions, *pl.* (der.) tribunal que sesiona trimestralmente para juzgar delitos menores.
quarterstaff [-ˌstæf, B -ˌstɑf] *s.* (ant., arm.) (*pl.* QUARTERSTAVES [-ˌsteɪvz]) pica (lanza larga).
quarter step, q. tone, (mús.) cuarto de tono.
quarter turn, cuarto de vuelta.
quarter-wave [-ˌweɪv] *a.* (rad.) de un cuarto de onda.
quarter wheel, (esgr.) cuarto de conversión.
quartet, quartette [kwɔr'tɛt, B kwɔ'-] *s.* 1. cuaternidad, conjunto de cuatro personas o cosas. 2. (mús.) cuarteto.
quartic ['kwɔrtɪk, B 'kwɔt-] (mat.) *a.* cuártico. —*s.* ecuación cuártica.
quartile ['kwɔrˌtaɪl, -təl, B 'kwɔˌtaɪl] *s.* 1. (astr.) cuartil; cuadro, cuadrado. 2. (estadística) distrito (en que se suelen dividir las grandes poblaciones).
quarto ['kwɔrtˌoʊ, B 'kwɔt-] *a.* (impr.) en cuarto. —*s.* libro en cuarto; cuaderno.
quartz [kwɔrts, B kwɔts] *s.* (min.) cuarzo.
quartz battery, (min.) bocarte, molino de mazos, batería de mazos.
quartz crystal, cristal de cuarzo.
quartz glass, vidrio de cuarzo, cuarzo fusionado.
quartziferous [kwɔrt'sɪfərəs, B kwɔt-] *a.* (min.) cuarcífero.
quartzite ['kwɔrtˌsaɪt, B 'kwɔt-] *s.* (min.) cuarcita.
quartz lamp, lámpara de cuarzo.
quartzose ['kwɔrtsoʊs, B 'kwɔts-] *a.* cuarzoso.
quartz plate, (elec.) placa de cuarzo.
quasar ['kweɪzɑr] *s.* fuente cuasiestelar de radio.
quash [kwɑʃ, B kwɔʃ] *v.t.* (der.) anular, invalidar, derogar.
quash, *v.t.* sofocar, reprimir, dominar (rebelión, levantamiento, etc.).
quasi ['kweɪˌzaɪ, -ˌsaɪ, B 'kwɑzɪ] *adv.* cuasi, casi; al parecer. —*a.* aparente, cuasi.
quasi contract, (der.) cuasicontrato, casicontrato.
quasi corporation, (der.) cuasicorporación.
quasi delict, (der.) cuasidelito.
quasi-judicial [-dʒu'dɪʃəl] *a.* cuasijudicial.
Quasimodo [ˌkwɑsɪ'moʊdoʊ, ˌkwɑz-, B ˌkweɪsaɪ-] *s.* (relig.) Cuasimodo, domingo de Cuasimodo.
quasi-public [-'pʌblɪk] *a.* cuasipúblico, semipúblico.
quasi-stellar radio source ['kwɑzi'stɛlər] *s.* fuente cuasiestelar de radio.
quasi usufruct, (der.) usufructo imperfecto.
quass, *var. de* **kvass,** bebida rusa.
quassia ['kwɑʃə, B 'kwɔʃə] *s.* (bot.) cuasia.
quatern ['kweɪtərn, B kwə'tɜn] *s.* cuaterna; cuarta, cuarta parte.
quaternary ['kwɑtərˌnɛrɪ, B kwə'tɜnə-] *a.* 1. (quím.) cuaternario. 2. **Q.,** (geol.) cuaternario. —*s.* 1. cuaternidad, grupo de a cuatro. 2. **Q.,** (geol.) período cuaternario.
quaternary ammonium compound, (quím.) compuesto cuaternario de amonio.
quaternion [kwə'tɜrnɪən, B -'tɜnjən] *s.* 1. grupo de cuatro; cuarteto, cuaternidad. 2. (mat.) cuaternio, cuaternión. 3. (*pl.*) (mat.) cálculos del cuaternio.
quatrain ['kwɑˌtreɪn, B 'kwɔˌtreɪn] *s.* (fr.) (poét.) cuarteto, cuarteta, redondilla, estrofa de cuatro versos.
quatrefoil ['kætərˌfɔɪl, B 'kætrə-] *s.* 1. (bot.) flor cuadrifolia o cuadrifoliada; hoja con cuatro hojuelas. 2. (arq.) cuatrifolia (cuatro arcos convergentes).
quattrocentist [ˌkwɑtroʊ'tʃɛntəst] *s.* cuatrocentista, artista, esp. italiano, del siglo XV.
quattrocento [-toʊ] *s.* período cuatrocentista, esp. italiano.
quattuordecillion [ˌkwɑtʊɔrdɪ'sɪljən, B ˌkwɔtʊɔdɪ-] *s.* (E.U.) mil septillones; (G.B.) cuatrodecillón.
quatuorvir [ˌkwɑtu'ɔrvɪr, B ˌkweɪtju'ɔvɪə] *s.* (hist.) cuatorviro.
quatuorvirate [-'ɔrvərət, B -'ɔvɪrɪt] *s.* (hist.) cuatorvirato.
quaver ['kweɪvər, B -və] *v.i.* 1. temblar, estremecerse, vibrar. 2. hablar en tono trémulo. 3. (mús.) trinar (con la voz o con un instrumento). —*v.t.* (gen. con *out*) decir o pronunciar trémulamente. —*s.* 1. tono trémulo o vibrante. 2. (mús.) trino. 3. (mús.) corchea.
quavering ['kweɪvərɪŋ] *a.* trémulo, vibrante. —*s.* gorjeo; (fam.) gorgorito.
quavery [-ərɪ] *a.* tembloroso, trémulo, vibrante.
quay [ki, kweɪ, B ki] *s.* muelle, desembarcadero.
quayage ['kiɪɑʒ, 'kweɪ-, B 'kɪ-] *s.* 1. muellaje. 2. (sistema de) muelles. 3. espacio en un muelle.
quayside [-ˌsaɪd] *s.* tierra al costado de un muelle.
Que. *abrev. de* **Quebec,** Quebec.
quean [kwin] *s.* 1. mujerzuela, mujercilla; ramera, prostituta. 2. (esco.) moza, muchacha; mujer soltera. 3. (jer.) maricón, afeminado.
queasily ['kwizəlɪ] *adv.* remilgadamente, fastidiosamente.
queasy ['kwizɪ] *a.* (QUEASIER; QUEASIEST) 1. delicado, débil (estómago). 2. remilgado, fastidioso. 3. difícil, complicado, arduo, peligroso, arriesgado. 4. intranquilo, incómodo. 5. nauseabundo. 6. bascoso.
quebracho [keɪ'brɑtʃoʊ] *s.* (bot.) quebracho.
Quechua ['kɛtʃʊə] *a., s.* (*pl.* QUECHUA O QUECHUAS) quechua, quichua, indígena (y su idioma).
Quechuan [-ʊən] *a.* quechua, quichua.
queen [kwin] *s.* 1. reina. 2. **Q.,** (como título) la Reina, ej., *Q. Elizabeth,* la reina Isabel. 3. (fig.) diosa, ej., *q. of heaven,* diosa del cielo (Juno), *q. of love,* diosa del amor (Venus), *q. of night,* diosa de la noche (Diana). 4. (fig.) reina (de algún evento u ocasión), ej., *q. of (the) May,* reina de mayo o de la primavera. 5. (fig.) reina, emperatriz (lugar o país de cierta eminencia), ej., *q. of the Adriatic,* reina del Adriático (Venecia), *q. of the seas,* emperatriz de los mares (Inglaterra). 6. (ento.) reina (de abejas, hormigas, etc.). 7. (ajedrez) reina, dama. 8. (naipes) reina. 9. (despec, jer.) maricón, homosexual muy afeminado. —*v.t.* 1. convertir en reina, hacer una reina de. 2. (ajedrez) coronar (un peón). —*v.i.* 1. (ajedrez) coronarse, convertirse en reina (un peón). 2. **q. it,** hacerse la reina, darse aires de reina.
Queen Anne's lace, (bot.) dauco, zanahoria silvestre.
Queen Anne style, estilo reina Ana (en muebles y decoración).
queen bee, 1. abeja reina, abeja machiega, abeja maesa o maestra. 2. (fig.) persona que lleva la voz cantante en un lugar o situación.
queen conch, (zool.) casis.
queen consort, (*pl.* QUEENS CONSORT) esposa del rey.
queendom ['kwindəm] *s.* 1. reino (gobernado por una reina). 2. dignidad de reina.
queen dowager, reina viuda, reina madre.
queenliness [-lɪnəs] *s.* realeza, majestad (de una reina).
queenly [-lɪ] *a.* (QUEENLIER; QUEENLIEST) real, majestuoso, propio de una reina, digno de una reina, apropiado para una reina.
queen mother, reina madre.
queen of the meadows, (bot.) ulmaria, barba de cabra, reina de los prados.
queen olive, (bot.) aceituna de la reina.
queen post, (arq.) péndola.
queen regent, reina regente.
queen regnant, (*pl.* QUEENS REGNANT) reina reinante.
queen's bishop, (ajedrez) alfil de la reina.
Queen's English, la lengua inglesa refinadamente escrita y hablada (t. **King's English**).
queen's gambit, (ajedrez) gambito de la reina.
queen's knight, (ajedrez) caballo de la reina.
queen's rook, (ajedrez) torre de la reina.
Queen's weather, (G.B.) luz del sol, luz del día, claridad.
queen truss, (arq.) armadura de dos péndolas.
queer [kwɪr, B kwɪə] *a.* 1. singular, peculiar, raro, curioso, extraño. 2. (jer.) espurio, falsificado; falso. 3. sospechoso, misterioso, dudoso. 4. (fam.) raro, excéntrico, estrafalario; tocado, chiflado. 5. indispuesto, bascoso; lánguido, abatido, aturdido. 6. (despec., jer.) afeminado, amanerado, marica, maricón. 7. **a q. fish,** un tipo raro; **q. in the head,** (fam.) chiflado, deschavetado. —*v.t.* 1. estropear, echar a perder. 2. malquistar, desprestigiar. 3. **q. oneself,** malquistarse, desprestigiarse; **q. the pitch for someone,** (jer., G.B.) estropearle de antemano la oportunidad a alguien. —*s.* (jer.) 1. moneda falsa. 2. homosexual, maricón.
queerly ['kwɪrlɪ, B 'kwɪəlɪ] *adv.* extrañamente; estrafalariamente.
queerness [-nəs] *s.* rareza, extrañeza.
quell [kwɛl] *v.t.* 1. sofocar, reprimir, sojuzgar (rebelión); domar, someter (a rebeldes); dominar, controlar (temor); destruir, suprimir. 2. calmar, mitigar (un dolor).
queller ['kwɛlər, B -ə] *s.* opresor, domador, sojuzgador.
quench [kwɛntʃ] *v.t.* 1. apagar, extinguir (fuego); mitigar, reprimir, dominar, suprimir (pasiones). 2. aplacar, calmar (sed). 3. enfriar, refrescar, esp. con agua; ahogar; templar, sumergir (metales incandescentes). 4. (jer.) callar (a un opositor). —*v.i.* extinguirse, acabarse (algo que se quema); ir a menos, apaciguarse, calmarse (pasiones, etc.); enfriarse.
quenchable ['kwɛntʃəbəl] *a.* apagable, extinguible, aplacable.
quencher [-ər, B -ə] *s.* 1. apagador. 2. (jer.) bebida.
quenchless [-ləs] *a.* inapagable, inextinguible.
quercetic [kwər'sɛtɪk, B kwɜ'-] *a.* (quím.) quercético.
quercetin ['kwɜrsətən, B 'kwɜsɪt-] *s.* (quím.) quercetina.
quercitron ['kwɜrsətrən, B 'kwɜsɪ-] *s.* 1. (bot.) quercitrón, roble negro. 2. quercitrón (corteza y colorante).
querist ['kwɪrəst, B 'kwɪər-] *s.* inquiridor, inquisidor, averiguador; preguntante, preguntador.
quern [kwɜrn, B kwɜn] *s.* molinillo de mano.

querulous ['kwɛrʊləs] *a.* 1. quejumbroso, quejicoso. 2. irritable, displicente.
querulously [-lɪ] *adv.* quejumbrosamente; displicentemente.
querulousness [-nəs] *s.* temperamento quejicoso.
query ['kwɪrɪ, B 'kwɪərɪ] *s.* (*pl.* QUERIES) 1. pregunta, averiguación. 2. duda, cuestión, interrogante. 3. signo de interrogación. —*v.t.* (*pret., p.p.* QUERIED; *p.pr.* QUERYING) 1. inquirir, preguntar, averiguar. 2. poner en duda. 3. marcar con signo de interrogación.
quest [kwɛst] *s.* 1. búsqueda, busca. 2. averiguación, indagación. 3. (raro) jurado indagatorio. —*v.i., v.t.* 1. rastrear. 2. buscar, ir en búsqueda de.
quester ['kwɛstər, B -ə] *s.* buscador, el que busca o indaga.
question ['kwɛstʃən] *s.* 1. pregunta. 2. interrogación, interrogante. 3. objeción. 4. duda. 5. cuestión, problema, tema. 6. posibilidad (*ú. esp. en frases negativas*), ej., *there is no q. of avoiding disaster,* no hay posibilidad de evitar el desastre. 7. **beside the q.,** que no viene al caso; **beyond q.,** fuera de duda; **in q.,** en cuestión, de referencia; **in the q. of,** en punto de; **out of the q.,** imposible, inaceptable; **to be a q. of** (**time,** etc.), ser cuestión de (tiempo, etc.); **to come in q.,** merecer consideración, cobrar importancia; **to make no q. of,** no dudar de; **to put a q. to (someone),** formular una pregunta a (alguien); **to put** (**a motion,** etc.) **to the q.,** poner (moción, etc.) al voto; **to raise the q. of,** plantear el problema de; **what is the q.?** ¿de qué se trata?; **without q.,** sin duda, sin discusión. —*v.t.* 1. interrogar, preguntar a, interpelar. 2. cuestionar, dudar, poner en duda. 3. objetar a, oponerse a, recusar. —*v.i.* inquirir.
questionable [-əbəl] *a.* 1. cuestionable, controvertible, discutible; dudoso, sospechoso. 2. (ant.) que invita a ser preguntado; que admite ser preguntado.
questionableness [-nəs] *s.* carácter discutible.
questionably [-blɪ] *adv.* cuestionablemente.
questionary [-ˌɛrɪ, B -ərɪ] *s.* cuestionario. —*a.* en forma de pregunta.
questioner ['kwɛstʃənər, B -ə] *s.* interrogador, preguntador, inquiridor.
questioning [-ɪŋ] *a.* 1. inquisitivo. 2. interrogativo. —*s.* interrogatorio.
questioningly [-lɪ] *adv.* interrogativamente.
questionless [-ləs] *a.* incuestionable, indubitable, indudable.
question mark, signo de interrogación; (fig.) interrogante.
questionnaire [ˌkwɛstʃə'nɛr, B -tɪə'nɛə] *s.* 1. cuestionario. 2. encuesta.
question time, (G.B.) período de preguntas (que se puede hacer a los ministros durante una sesión del parlamento).
questor ['kwɛstər, B -tə] *s.* (hist.) cuestor (magistrado romano).
questorial [kwɛs'tɔrɪəl] *a.* (hist.) de los cuestores.
questorship ['kwɛstərˌʃɪp, B -təˌ-] *s.* (hist.) cuestura.
quetzal [kɛt'sɑl, B 'kɛtsəl] *s.* (*pl.* QUETZALS o QUETZALES) 1. (orn.) quetzal. 2. quetzal, unidad monetaria de Guatemala.
queue [kju] *s.* (fr.) 1. coleta, trenza. 2. hilera, fila, cola (de personas). —*v.i.* (*pret., p.p.* QUEUED; *p.pr.* QUEUING o QUEUEING) (t. con *up*) formar fila o hilera, hacer cola. —*v.t.* trenzar, formar trenza o coleta del (pelo).
quibble ['kwɪbəl] *s.* 1. evasiva, subterfugio; equívoco, sofisma. 2. (raro) retruécano, juego de palabras. —*v.i.* usar evasivas o subterfugios; hacer uso de equívocos o sofismas.
quibbler ['kwɪblər, B -lə] *s.* sofista, equivoquista.
Quiché [ˌki'tʃəɪ] *a., s.* quiché (indígena y lenguaje maya).
quick [kwɪk] *a.* 1. rápido, veloz, ligero, presto, pronto; listo, ágil. 2. vivo, despierto; agudo, penetrante; sensitivo, perceptivo. 3. movedizo. 4. (ant.) vivo, animado. 5. **q. with,** (fig.) preñado de; **q. with child,** embarazada; **the q. and the dead,** los vivos y los muertos; **to be q.,** darse prisa; **to have a q. temper,** perder fácilmente la calma, encolerizarse rápidamente, tener mal genio, ser irascible; **too q.,** impaciente, precipitado. —*s.* 1. carne viva, lo vivo. 2. (fig.) lo más hondo, lo más íntimo (del alma). 3. **to cut (to hurt** o **to sting) (one) to the q.,** herir (a uno) en lo vivo; **to the q.,** hasta el tuétano, ej., *he is Tory to the q.,* es conservador hasta el tuétano. —*adv.* rápido, rápidamente. —*v.t.* (ant.) animar, avivar.
quick-acting valve ['kwɪkˌæktɪŋ-] válvula de acción rápida, válvula de cierre rápido.
quick assets, (com.) activo disponible, bienes negociables.
quick-break switch [-ˌbreɪk-] (elec.) interruptor de ruptura brusca, interruptor instantáneo.
quick-change ['kwɪkˌtʃeɪndʒ] *a.* de cambio rápido.
quick-change artist, (teat.) transformista.
quicken [-ən] *v.t.* 1. avivar, estimular, dar vida a. 2. acelerar, apurar (Amer.). 3. **q. one's pace,** apretar o avivar el paso. —*v.i.* 1. avivarse, estimularse, animarse. 2. acelerarse. 3. clarear (el alba). 4. llegar al estado del embarazo en que se siente el movimiento del feto.
quick-fire [-ˌfaɪr, B -ˌfaɪə] **quick-firing** [-ɪŋ, B -rɪŋ] *a.* (arm.) de tiro rápido.
quick-freeze [-'friz] *v.t.* congelar, liofilizar.
quick-freezing [-ɪŋ] *s.* congelación rápida de alimentos, liofilización.
quick grass, (bot.) agropiro.
quick hedge, (pr. G.B.) seto vivo.
quickie ['kwɪkɪ] *s.* 1. uno rápido, una rápido. 2. una preguntita, una pregunta relámpago. 3. un trago corto. 4. — **let's have a q.,** echémonos un polvito (jer.) (a brief sexual encounter).
quickie divorce, divorcio rápido.
quicklime [-ˌlaɪm] *s.* cal viva.
quickly [-lɪ] *adv.* rápidamente, prontamente.
quick march, (mil.) (marcha a) paso ordinario, (marcha a) paso largo o redoblado.
quickness [-nəs] *s.* 1. rapidez, presteza, celeridad. 2. sagacidad, viveza.
quick one, (fam.) trago corto.
quicksand [-ˌsænd] *s.* arena movediza.
quickset [-ˌsɛt] *s.* (pr. G.B.) seto vivo. —*a.* de arbustos vivos.
quick-setting [-'sɛtɪŋ] *a.* de fraguado o endurecimiento rápido.
quick-sighted ['kwɪk'saɪtəd] *a.* de vista aguda; alerto.
quick-sightedness [-nəs] *s.* agudeza de vista, penetración.
quicksilver [-ˌsɪlvər, B -və] *s.* mercurio, azogue. —*v.t.* azogar.
quickstep [-ˌstɛp] *s.* 1. (mil.) paso ordinario, paso redoblado. 2. marcha militar de ritmo rápido. 3. (mús.) fox trot de compás vivo.
quick-tempered [-'tɛmpərd, B -pəd] *a.* irascible, irritable.
quick time, (mil.) paso ordinario, paso largo o redoblado.
quick-witted [-'wɪtəd] *a.* listo, agudo, vivo de ingenio, perspicaz.
quick-wittedly [-lɪ] *adv.* agudamente, de manera lista.
quick-wittedness [-nəs] *s.* agudeza, viveza de ingenio.
quid [kwɪd] *s.* 1. mascada (de tabaco). 2. (jer., G.B.) libra esterlina.
quiddity ['kwɪdətɪ] *s.* (*pl.* QUIDDITIES) 1. quid, busilis, esencia. 2. sutileza, equívoco. 3. extravagancia, excentricidad.
quidnunc [-ˌnʌŋk] *s.* fisgón; chismoso, cuentero, correveidile.
quiescence [kwaɪ'ɛsəns] *s.* estado de reposo; inmovilidad.
quiescent [-ənt] *a.* 1. en reposo; inmóvil, tranquilo. 2. (med.) quiescente.
quiescently [-lɪ] *adv.* en reposo; inmóvilmente, tranquilamente.
quiet ['kwaɪət] *a.* 1. quieto, quedo; sosegado, tranquilo, calmado. 2. callado, silencioso. 3. sencillo, modesto. 4. discreto (color). 5. apartado, retirado (sitio). 6. privado, oculto. 7. (com.) inactivo (díc. del mercado). 8. **on the q.,** en oculto, de callada; **q. as a graveyard,** que ni habla ni parla. —*s.* 1. quietud, tranquilidad, sosiego, calma. 2. silencio. —*v.t.* aquietar, calmar, sosegar; acallar, hacer callar. —*v.i.* (gen. con *down*) aquietarse, sosegarse, calmarse. —*adv.* quietamente, sosegadamente, calmadamente; silenciosamente, calladamente.
quieten [-ən] *v.t., v.i.* (esp. G.B.) aquietar(se), acallar(se), callar(se).
quieter [-ər, B -ə] *s.* apaciguador, tranquilizador.
quietism ['kwaɪətˌɪzəm] *s.* 1. (filos.) quietismo. 2. quietismo, quietud, sosiego.
quietist [-əst] *a., s.* quietista, partidario del quietismo.
quietly [-lɪ] *adv.* 1. quietamente, calmadamente, sosegadamente. 2. silenciosamente, calladamente.
quietness [-nəs] *s.* 1. quietud, sosiego, calma. 2. silencio.
quietude ['kwaɪəˌtud, B -ˌtjud] *s.* (fr.) quietud, tranquilidad, sosiego.
quietus [kwaɪ'itəs] *s.* 1. quitanza, finiquito; relevación (de empleo o cargo). 2. tiro de gracia, muerte. 3. inactividad, estancamiento.
quiff [kwɪf] *s.* (G.B.) mechón, copete (de pelo).
quill [kwɪl] *s.* 1. pluma de ave; cañón de pluma. 2. púa (del erizo, puercoespín, etc.). 3. pluma, cálamo. 4. (tej.) canilla, carretillo (de la lanzadera). 5. (farm.) rollo de corteza seca (de canela o quina). 6. (mús.) cañón (de instrumento); plectro, púa. —*v.t.* 1. encanillar (un hilo). 2. (cost.) rizar, hacer un encarrujado en (tela, etc.).
quillai [kɪ'laɪ, B ki'jaɪ] *s.* (bot.) quillay, lava cabeza, palo de jabón, tarsana.
quill driver, (despec.) cagatintas.
quill embroidery, bordado a canutillo.
quillon [kɪ'joʊn] *s.* (arm.) arriaz, gavilán de espada.
quillwort ['kwɪlˌwɜrt, B -ˌwɜt] *s.* (bot.) algodoncillo de los pantanos.
quilt [kwɪlt] *s.* edredón, cobertor acolchado, colcha. —*v.t.* acolchar, acojinar, estofar. —*v.i.* hacer acolchados.
quilter ['kwɪltər, B -ə] *s.* colchero, acolchador (oficio).
quilting [-ɪŋ] *s.* 1. colchadura. 2. material para colchas o edredones.
quilting bee [-'bi] *s.* (E.U.) reunión social de mujeres que cosen edredones como distracción o para fines benéficos.
quilting needle, aguja colchonera.
quina ['kinə] *s.* (bot.) quina.
quinacrine ['kwɪnəˌkrin, B -ˌkraɪn] *s.* (quím.) quinacrina.

quinary ['kwaɪnərɪ] *a.* quinario, quíntuple.
quinate ['kwaɪˌneɪt] *a.* (bot.) quinoi.
quinazoline [kwɪ'næzəˌlin, B -ˌlaɪn] *s.* (quím.) quinazolina.
quince [kwɪns] *s.* 1. (bot.) membrillero, membrillo (árbol). 2. membrillo (fruto).
quince jelly, jalea de membrillo.
quincuncial [kwɪn'kʌntʃəl, B -'kʌnʃəl] *a.* (bot.) quincuncial.
quincunx ['kwɪnˌkʌŋks] *s.* (*pl.* QUINCUNXES) 1. (bot.) disposición quincuncial (esp. de las partes de una flor). 2. quincunce, tresbolillo.
quindecagon [kwɪn'dɛkəˌgɑn, B -gən] *s.* (geom.) pentadecágono.
quindecennial [ˌkwɪndɪ'sɛnɪəl] *a.* quindenial. —*s.* quindenio.
quinic acid ['kwɪnɪk-] (quím.) ácido quínico.
quinidine ['kwɪnəˌdin, B -ˌdaɪn] *s.* (quím.) quinidina.
quinine ['kwaɪˌnaɪn, B kwɪn'in] *s.* (quím., farm.) quinina.
quinine water, gaseosa de quina (t. **tonic**).
quinoa [kɪ'noʊə, B kwɪ-] *s.* (bot.) quinua.
quinoidine [kwə'nɔɪdən, B -ˌdaɪn] *s.* (quím.) quinoidina.
quinoline ['kwɪnəlˌin, B -əˌlaɪn] *s.* (quím.) quinoleína, quinolina.
quinone [kwɪn'oʊn] *s.* (quím.) quinona.
quinoxaline [kwɪ'nɑksəˌlin, B -'nɔksəˌlaɪn] *s.* (quím.) quinoxalina.
quinquagenarian [ˌkwɪŋkwədʒə'nɛrɪən, B -'nɛər-] *a.* quincuagenario, de cincuenta años. —*s.* quincuagenario, cincuentón.
Quinquagesima [-'dʒɛsəmə] *s.* (t. **Q. Sunday**) quincuagésima.
quinquefoliate [-kwɪ'foʊlɪət] *a.* (bot.) quinquefoliado.
quinquefoliolate [-əˌleɪt] *a.* (bot.) quinquefoliolado.
quinquenniad [kwɪŋ'kwɛnɪˌæd] *s.* quinquenio, lustro, cinco años.
quinquennial [-'kwɛnɪəl] *a.* quinquenal. —*s.* quinquenio.
quinquennially [-əlɪ] *adv.* cada cinco años, quinquenalmente.
quinquennium [-ɪəm] *s.* (*pl.* QUINQUENNIA [-ə] o QUINQUENNIUMS) quinquenio.
quinquevalent [ˌkwɪŋkwɪ'veɪlənt, B kwɪn'kwɛvə-] *a.* (quím.) quinquevalente.
quinsy ['kwɪnzɪ] *s.* 1. (med.) amigdalitis supurativa, angina. 2. (vet.) ahoguijo.
quint [kɪnt, kwɪnt] *s.* (fam., E.U.) quintillizo, quíntuple (Chile, Ven.).
quintain ['kwɪntən] *s.* (hist.) armazón de tablas usadas como blanco para ser alanceado por los caballeros en las justas o torneos.
quintal ['kwɪntəl] *s.* quintal (medida de peso).
quintan ['kwɪntən] *a.* (med.) quintana (fiebre).
quintant ['kwɪntənt] *s.* (astr.) quintante.
quinte [kænt] *s.* (esgr.) quinta.
quintessence [kwɪn'tɛsəns] *s.* quintaesencia.
quintessential [ˌkwɪntə'sɛntʃəl, B -'sɛnʃəl] *a.* más esencial, depuradísimo.
quintet, quintette [kwɪn'tɛt] *s.* 1. (mús.) quinteto. 2. grupo de cinco.
quintile ['kwɪnˌtaɪl] *s.* (astrol.) aspecto quintil.
Quintilian [kwɪn'tɪljən] *s.* Quintiliano, retórico latino nacido en España.
quintillion [kwɪn'tɪljən] *s.* (E.U.) un millón de billones; (G.B.) quintillón.
quintuple [-'tupəl, -'tʌp-, B 'kwɪntjʊp-] *a.* quíntuple. —*v.t., v.i.* quintuplicar(se).
quintuplet [-'tʌplɪt, -'tup-, B 'kwɪntjʊp-] *s.* quintillizo, quíntuple (Chile, Ven.).
quintuplicate [-'tuplɪkət, B -'tju-] *v.t.* quintuplicar. —*a.* quíntuplo. —*s.* quinta copia.
quip [kwɪp] *s.* 1. agudeza, ocurrencia, gracia, salida, sutileza; sarcasmo, pulla. 2. subterfugio, pretexto, efugio, escapatoria. 3. rareza, cosa extravagante. —*v.i.* (*pret., p.p.* QUIPPED; *p.pr.* QUIPPING) echar pullas; decir agudezas o gracias; mofarse.
quipster ['kwɪpstər, B -stə] *s.* bromista, chancero, pullista.
quipu ['kipu] *s.* (quechua) quipo, quipu, forma de escritura y contabilidad a base de cuerdas con nudos usado por los incas.
quire [kwaɪr, B 'kwaɪə] *s.* mano de papel (24 ó 25 hojas).
Quirinal ['kwɪrɪnəl] *s.* Quirinal, palacio de Roma, antigua residencia de los monarcas italianos.
Quirinus [kwɪ'raɪnəs] *s.* (mitol.) Quirino, uno de los dioses de la guerra.
quiritarian [ˌkwɪrɪ'tɛrɪən, B -'tɛər-] *a.* (der. romano) quiritario.
Quirites [kwɪ'raɪtiz] *s. pl.* (der. romano) quirites, ciudadanos civiles.
quirk [kwɜrk, B kwɜk] *s.* 1. plumada, ringorrango. 2. subterfugio, argucia, efugio, escapatoria. 3. peculiaridad, singularidad. 4. (arq.) caveto, esgucio. 5. (ant.) sutileza, gracia, salida, arranque. —*v.t.* 1. curvar, encorvar. 2. acanalar, estriar. 3. golpear con un látigo.
quirt [kwɜrt, B kwɜt] *s.* látigo corto para las caballerías, cuarta. —*v.t.* golpear con un látigo, cuartear.
quisling ['kwɪzlɪŋ] *s.* traidor (a su patria).
quit [kwɪt] *v.t.* (*pret., p.p.* QUITTED o QUIT; *p.pr.* QUITTING) 1. dejar, salir de, abandonar. 2. descontinuar, dejar de (trabajar, etc.). 3. librar (de); libertar (de). 4. pagar, reembolsar, compensar. 5. **q. hold of,** soltar; **q. it!** (jer.) ¡basta ya! —*v.i.* 1. desistir, cesar; abandonar el esfuerzo; renunciar. 2. (fam.) dejar de trabajar. 3. irse, marcharse. —*a.* libre, descargado, absuelto.
quitch [kwɪtʃ] *s.* (t. **q. grass**) (bot.) agropiro, grama.
quitclaim ['kwɪtˌkleɪm] (der.) *s.* renuncia, finiquito, quitación. —*v.t.* renunciar, ceder.
quitclaim deed, (der.) escritura de traspaso de finiquito, escritura de traspaso de quitación.
quite [kwaɪt] *adv.* 1. completamente, enteramente, totalmente, íntegramente. 2. absolutamente, realmente, verdaderamente, efectivamente, justamente. 3. bastante, muy, más bien. 4. **he is q. a hero,** es un verdadero héroe; **it is q. the thing,** está en boga; **q. a bit,** considerable(mente), bastante; **q. near,** muy cerca; **q. so** (o **q.**), ¡correcto! ¡de acuerdo!
Quito ['kitoʊ] *s.* Quito, capital del Ecuador.
quitrent ['kwɪtˌrɛnt] *s.* (hist., der.) censo que se pagaba por conmutación de ciertos servicios feudales; renta fija pagada sobre propiedad inmueble.
quits [kwɪts] *a.* igual, a la par; **to be q.,** estar parejos, estar a la par, estar desquitados; **to cry q., to call it q.,** dar por terminado (riña, discusión, etc.), dejar de seguir (peleando, discutiendo, etc.).
quittance ['kwɪtəns] *s.* 1. quitanza, descargo, finiquito, liberación, pago. 2. recompensa, compensación, retorno.
quitter [-ər, B -ə] *s.* 1. el que fácilmente deja lo empezado o se da por vencido; cobarde; desertor. 2. (metal.) escorias.
quittor ['kwɪtər, B -ə] *s.* (vet.) llaga supurante (en las patas de los caballos, asnos, etc.).
quiver ['kwɪvər, B -ə] *s.* 1. aljaba, carcaj. 2. flechas, dardos, saetas en un carcaj. 3. **q. full of children,** (fig.) familia numerosa; **to have an arrow left in one's q.,** tener recursos, no haberse quedado sin recursos.
quiver, *v.i.* temblar, retemblar, estremecerse; trepidar, vibrar. —*s.* temblor, estremecimiento, trepidación, vibración.
qui vive [ki'viv] (mil.) ¿quién vive?; **to be on the q.v.,** estar ojo avizor, estar sobre aviso.
Quixote ['kwɪksət] *s.* 1. Quijote. 2. **q.,** (fig.) quijote, persona demasiado idealista o impráctica; romántico, visionario.
quixotic [kwɪk'sɑtɪk, B -'sɔt-] **quixotical** [-ɪkəl] *a.* quijotesco.
quixotically [-ɪkəlɪ] *adv.* quijotescamente.
quixotism ['kwɪksəˌtɪzəm] *s.* quijotismo; quijotería, quijotada.
quiz [kwɪz] *s.* (*pl.* QUIZZES) 1. bromista, chancero. 2. chanza, burla, broma pesada. 3. examen, serie de preguntas; (rad., t.v.) programa de preguntas. 4. (raro) excéntrico, extravagante. —*v.t.* (*pret., p.p.* QUIZZED; *p.pr* QUIZZING) 1. burlarse de; mirar con aire burlón. 2. examinar, interrogar.
quizmaster [-ˌmæstər, B -ˌmɑstə] *s.* (rad., t.v.) presentator, moderador.
quizzer ['kwɪzər, B -ə] *s.* 1. examinador, interrogador. 2. (rad., t.v.) programa de preguntas al público.
quizzical ['kwɪzɪkəl] *a.* 1. raro, original, excéntrico, extravagante. 2. burlón, irónico. 3. curioso, inquisitivo.
quizzically [-kəlɪ] *adv.* 1. excéntricamente. 2. burlonamente, irónicamente. 3. curiosamente.
quizz show, concurso de conocimientos generales.
quod [kwɑd, B kwɔd] *s.* (jer., G.B.) chirona, cárcel.
quodlibet ['kwɑdləˌbɛt, B 'kwɔd-] *s.* 1. cuodlibeto, discusión o debate académico. 2. (mús.) fantasía, improvisación.
quohog, *var. de* **quahog.**
quoin [kɔɪn] *s.* 1. (arq.) piedra angular, clave. 2. esquina, ángulo. 3. (impr.) cuña, cabecera. —*v.t.* 1. acuñar. 2. asegurar o edificar con piedras angulares.
quoiner ['kɔɪnər, B -ə] *s.* acuñador.
quoin post, (arq.) poste de quicio, quicial.
quoit [kwɔɪt, kɔɪt] *s.* 1. herrón, tejo. 2. (*pl.*) hito, juego de tejos. —*v.t.* lanzar o tirar como un tejo; jugar al tejo.
quondam ['kwɑndəm, B 'kwɔn-] *a.* de otro tiempo, que fue, ej., *a q. friend of mine,* uno que fue amigo mío.
Quonset ['kwɑnsət, B 'kwɔn-] *s.* (E.U.) marca de fábrica de una cabaña prefabricada, de planchas corrugadas con techo semicilíndrico.
quorum ['kwɔrəm] *s.* 1. quórum. 2. (G.B., hist.) grupo selecto de jueces de paz; jueces de paz. 3. cuerpo selecto.
quota ['kwoʊtə] *s.* (*pl.* QUOTAS) 1. cuota, cupo, contingente. 2. contribución.
quotable ['kwoʊtəbəl] *a.* citable.
quotation [kwoʊ'teɪʃən] *s.* 1. cita, citación, referencia. 2. (com.) cotización.
quotation mark, (impr.) comillas.
quote [kwoʊt] *v.t.* 1. citar (un texto, etc.), ej., *to q. Shakespeare,* citar a Shakespeare. 2. aducir, alegar, ej., *q. an instance,* aducir una instancia. 3. (com.) cotizar. 4. poner entre comillas. —*s.* 1. cita, citación. 2. comillas.
quoter ['kwoʊtər, B -ə] *s.* 1. (com.) cotizador. 2. citador.
quoth [kwoʊθ] *v.t.* (ant.) (*primera y tercera personas del sing. en pret.*) dije, dijo.
quotidian [kwoʊ'tɪdɪən, B kwɔ-] *a.* cotidiano, cuotidiano. —*s.* (med.) fiebre cotidiana.
quotient ['kwoʊʃənt] *s.* (mat.) cociente, cuociente.

R

R [ɑr, B ɑ] *s.* r, decimoctava letra del alfabeto inglés; **the three R's,** lectura, escritura y aritmética (reading, (w)riting, (a)rithmetic, consideradas como la base de enseñanza elemental).
Ra [rɑ] *s.* (mitol.) Ra, divinidad egipcia símbolo del sol.
Ra *símb. de* **radium,** radio (Ra).
RA *abrev. de* 1. **regular army,** ejército regular. 2. **Royal Artillery,** Real Artillería.
Rabat [rə'bɑt] *s.* Rabat, capital de Marruecos.
rabato [rə'bɑtoʊ] *s.* (hist.) cuello duro sobresaliente.
rabbet ['ræbət] *s.* (carp.) rebajo, encaje, muesca, barbilla, ranura, alefriz. —*v.t.* (*pret., p.p.* RABBETED; *p.pr.* RABBETING) (carp.) 1. rebajar, ranurar. 2. juntar o ensamblar a rebajo. —*v.i.* ensamblarse.
rabbet joint, (carp.) junta a media madera, junta a rebajo.
rabbet plane, (carp.) guillame, garlopín.
rabbi ['ræbˌaɪ] *s.* (*pl.* RABBIS O RABBIES) rabí, rabino.
rabbin [-ən] *s.* (ant.) rabino, rabí.
rabbinate [-ənət, -ˌneɪt] *s.* 1. oficio o cargo de rabí. 2. grupo de rabíes.
Rabbinic [ræ'bɪnɪk, rə-] **rabbinical** [-ɪkəl] *a.* rabínico.
rabbinism ['ræbəˌnɪzəm] *s.* rabinismo.
rabbinist [-nəst] *s.* rabinista.
rabbit ['ræbət] *s.* 1. (zool.) conejo. 2. (E.U.) liebre. 3. piel de conejo. 4. (*forma abrev. de* **welsh r.**) plato de queso derretido (a veces mezclado con cerveza) en tostadas. —*v.i.* cazar conejos.
rabbit ears, (fam.) antena en forma de V, antena de conejo, antena interior de televisión.
rabbiter ['ræbətər, B -ə] *s.* perro lebrero.
rabbit fever, (med.) tularemia.
rabbit food, (fam.) cualquier tipo de verdura esp. cruda en ensalada.
rabbit-foot clover [-ˌfʊt-] (bot.) pie de liebre.
rabbit punch, (boxeo) golpe corto a la nuca o a la base del cráneo.
rabbitry [-ətrɪ] *s.* (*pl.* RABBITRIES) conejera, conejar, conejal.
rabbit's foot, pata trasera de un conejo usada como amuleto.
rabble ['ræbəl] *s.* 1. canalla, populacho, plebe, chusma (Am.). 2. multitud turbulenta.
rabble, (metal.) *s.* hurgón. —*v.t.* rablear.
rabblement [-mənt] *s.* disturbio, conmoción, tumulto, desorden, alboroto.
rabble-rouser [-ˌraʊzər, B -zə] *s.* agitador, demagogo.
Rabelaisian [ˌræbə'leɪʒən, B -ʒɪən] *a.* rabelesiano, característico de Rabelais; de imaginación exuberante y humor grosero. —*s.* estudiante o imitador de Rabelais.
rabic ['reɪbɪk, B 'ræ-] *a.* (med., vet.) rábico.
rabid ['ræbəd] *a.* 1. rabioso, rábido, furioso. 2. rabioso, que padece rabia.
rabidity [rə'bɪdətɪ] *s.* rabia; fanatismo.
rabidly ['ræbədlɪ] *adv.* rabiosamente.
rabidness [-nəs] *s.* rabia; fanatismo.
rabies ['reɪbiz] *s.* (med., vet.) rabia, hidrofobia.
raccoon [ræ'kun, B rə-] *s.* (*pl.* RACCOON O RACCOONS) 1. (zool.) mapache, oso lavador. 2. piel de mapache.
race [reɪs] *s.* 1. corriente de agua. 2. caz, canaleta. 3. carrera, certamen, competencia, concurso. 4. (*pl.*) carreras de caballos. 5. curso, trayecto, recorrido, carrera. 6. (aer.) corriente de aire de la hélice. 7. (mec.) anillo-guía, anillo de voladura (en cojinete de bolas). 8. raíz de jengibre. —*v.i.* 1. correr de prisa. 2. correr o competir en una carrera. 3. desbocarse, embalarse, dispararse (un motor, etc.). —*v.t.* 1. competir (con alguien). 2. hacer correr de prisa; acelerar (un motor) al máximo.
race, *s.* 1. raza, estirpe, casta. 2. sabor (del vino); (raro) viveza, sabor (de una conversación). 3. (ant.) manada (de caballos). 4. grupo, clase (de personas). 5. (tej.) paso, carrera de lanzadera.
racecourse ['reɪsˌkɔrs, B -ˌkɔs] *s.* 1. hipódromo. 2. pista de carreras. 3. autódromo.
race horse, caballo de carreras.
racemate [reɪ'siˌmeɪt, B 'ræsɪ-] *s.* (quím.) racemato.
raceme [reɪ'sim, B rə-] *s.* (bot.) racimo.
racemic [-'simɪk] *a.* (quím.) acémico.
racemic acid, (quím.) ácido racémico.
racemiform [-məˌfɔrm, B -ˌfɔm] *a.* (bot.) raciniforme.
racemization [reɪˌsimə'zeɪʃn, B ˌræsɪmaɪ-] *s.* (quím.) racemización.
racemose ['ræsəˌmoʊs] *a.* (bot.) racimoso, racimado.
race problem, problema racial o de razas.
racer ['reɪsər, B -sə] *s.* 1. corredor. 2. caballo de carreras. 3. bicicleta o auto de carreras. 4. culebra negra americana. 5. (mil.) plataforma giratoria. 6. (tej.) devanadera. 7. (carp.) legra.
race relations, relaciones raciales.
race riot, disturbio provocado por antagonismo racial.
race pride, orgullo de raza.
race suicide, reducción voluntaria de la población; suicidio de la raza.
racetrack ['reɪsˌtræk] *s.* carrera, pista de carreras; hipódromo.
raceway [-ˌweɪ] *s.* 1. caz, saetín. 2. (mec.) caja, canal; anillo de rodadura (en cojinete de bolas). 3. (elec.) canal para alambres, conducto eléctrico.
rachialgia [ˌreɪkɪ'ældʒɪə] *s.* (med.) raquialgia.
rachidian [rə'kɪdɪən] *a.* (anat., bot.) raquídeo.
rachis ['reɪkɪs] *s.* (*pl.* RACHISES O RACHIDES [-kəˌdiz]) 1. (anat., bot.) raquis. 2. cañón de pluma.
rachitic [rə'kɪtɪk] *a.* raquítico.
rachitis [-'kaɪtəs] *s.* (med.) raquitis, raquitismo.
rachitome ['reɪkɪˌtoʊm] *s.* (med.) raquítomo.
racial ['reɪʃəl] *a.* racial.
racial discrimination, discriminación racial.
racial integration, integración racial.
racialism [-ˌɪzəm] *s.* prejuicios raciales; racismo.
racialist [-əst] *s.* racista.
racially ['reɪʃəlɪ] *adv.* racialmente.
racing ['reɪsɪŋ] *s.* deporte hípico, hipismo, carreras de caballos. —*a.* frecuente (pulso); embalado (motores).
racing driver, corredor de coches.
racing form, programa de carreras de caballos.
racism ['reɪˌsɪzəm] *s.* racismo.
racist [-səst] *s.* racista.
rack [ræk] *s.* 1. costillar de la parte delantera de un cordero; parte delantera de la res (vacuna). 2. (ant.) cuello y espinazo del cuarto delantero de la ternera, cerdo, y esp. carnero. 3. destrucción. 4. portante, entrepaso, paso de andadura, trote cochinero (del caballo). —*v.i.* caminar a paso de andadura, caminar con paso portante (caballo).
rack, *s.* 1. nubes cirrosas arrastradas por el viento. 2. (dial.) curso, recorrido de una tempestad; vestigio, huella. —*v.i.* volar, ser llevado por el viento, moverse a favor del viento (bruma, niebla, nube).
rack [ræk] *s.* 1. pesebre, comedero. 2. potro de tormento. 3. percha, perchero (para ropa); astillero, armero; rejilla, enrejado. 4. estirón, arranque, efecto tirante. 5. (mec.) cremallera, escalerilla. 6. (impr.) chibalete, burro (para cajas tipográficas). 7. **r. and pinion,** engranaje de cremallera y piñón; **on the r.,** en tormento. —*v.t.* 1. torturar en el potro. 2. atormentar, agobiar. 3. estirar, forzar. 4. subir excesivamente (alquileres). 5. **r. one's brains,** devanarse los sesos.
rack, *v.t.* 1. **r. up,** (dep.) acumular (tantos). 2. (gen. con *off*) decantar, trasegar (vino). 3. despedazar, rasgar; extorsionar; atormentar.
racket ['rækət] *s.* 1. raqueta (de tenis, etc.). 2. (*pl.*) (*gen.* **racquets**) juego parecido al tenis que se practica en una cancha rectangular rodeada de paredes. 3. raqueta (para caminar sobre la nieve).
racket, *s.* 1. alboroto, baraúnda, vocerío, bullicio, gritería. 2. parranda, juerga, jarana. 3. prueba severa, tensión, esfuerzo. 4. (jer.) fraude organizado; supercheria, estafa, engaño, latrocinio. 5. (jer.) oficio, ocupación. —*v.i.* 1. armar una parranda, estar de juerga. 2. hacer ruido; moverse con ruido.
racketeer [ˌrækə'tɪr, B -'tɪə] *s.* extorsionista, chantajista, socaliñero, estafador. —*v.i.* cometer estafas, vivir de fraudes o chantajes.
racketeering [-ɪŋ, B -'tɪər-] *s.* fraude organizado, latrocinio.
rackety ['rækətɪ] *a.* 1. ruidoso. 2. alegre, festivo; disipado, disoluto.
racking ['rækɪŋ] *s.* 1. trasiego (de licores). 2. tortura.
rackle ['rækəl] *a.* (dial.) cabezudo, terco, testarudo; atolondrado.
rack railway, r. railroad, ferrocarril de cremallera.
rack rent, arriendo o alquiler exorbitante.
rack-rent ['ræk'rɛnt] *v.t.* exigir alquiler o arriendo usurario a; arrendar a un precio exorbitante.
rack-renter [-ər, B -ə] *s.* arrendatario que paga precios exorbitantes; arrendador que exige precios exorbitantes.

rackwork [-ˌwɜrk, B -ˌwɜk] *s.* mecanismo de cremallera.
racon [ˈreɪˌkɑn, B -ˌkɔn] *s.* radiofaro de respuesta; radiofaro con un receptoremisor.
raconteur [ˌrækɑnˈtɜr, B -ɔnˈtɜ] *s.* (fr.) cuentista, narrador; anecdotista.
racoon, *var. de* **raccoon.**
racquet, *var. de* **racket** (raqueta).
racy [ˈreɪsɪ] *a.* (RACIER; RACIEST) 1. animoso, vivo, vigoroso. 2. picante, aromático. 3. chispeante. 4. atrevido, picante (cuento, etc.).
radar [ˈreɪˌdɑr, B -də] *s.* radar.
radar beacon, faro radar.
radar dish, antena de radar.
radar fence, *s.* barrera de radar.
radarman [-mən] *s.* operador de radar.
radarscope [-ˌskoʊp] *s.* radariscopio.
radar screen, pantalla de radar.
raddle [ˈrædəl] *v.t.* (G.B.) entrelazar, entretejer, enlazar, trabar.
raddle, *s.* almagre, ocre rojo. —*v.t.* 1. pintar con ocre rojo. 2. arrebolar (la cara) excesivamente.
radial [ˈreɪdɪəl] *a.* 1. radial. 2. (anat.) radial. 3. (zool.) radiado. —*s.* radial (neumático).
radial drill, (maq.) taladradora radial.
radial engine, (mec.) motor radial, motor en estrella.
radially [-əlɪ] *adv.* radialmente.
radian [ˈreɪdɪən] *s.* (mat.) radián.
radiance [ˈreɪdɪəns] *s.* radiación, brillo, resplandor, refulgencia.
radiancy [-ənsɪ] *s. var. de* **radiance.**
radian frequency, (ing.) frecuencia angular.
radiant [-ənt] *a.* 1. radiante, refulgente, resplandeciente, brillante. 2. (fig.) radiante (rostro, ojo, mirada). 3. (fís.) radiante. —*s.* 1. (astr., ópt.) radiante. 2. (geom.) foco irradiador; línea radial; objeto radiante.
radiant energy, (fís.) energía radiante.
radiant flux, (fís.) densidad de radiación.
radiant heating, calefacción a panel radiante.
radiantly [-lɪ] *adv.* brillantemente, radiantemente.
radiate [ˈreɪdɪˌeɪt] *v.i.* resplandecer, centellear, rutilar, brillar. —*v.t.* radiar, emitir, irradiar (calor, simpatía, etc.); emitir; difundir. — [-ət, -ˌeɪt] *a.* 1. radiado, radial. 2. (zool.) radiado.
radiation [ˌreɪdɪˈeɪʃən] *s.* 1. radiación; irradiación. 2. arreglo radial.
radiation field, (fís.) campo de radiación.
radiation shield, blindaje contra la radiación.
radiator [ˈreɪdɪˌeɪtər, B -ə] *s.* 1. radiador, aparato de calefacción. 2. (aut., mec.) radiador. 3. (fís. nuclear) emisor de radiaciones.
radiator cap, (aut.) tapón de radiador.
radiator grille, (aut.) rejilla del radiador, parrilla del radiador.
radical [ˈrædɪkəl] *a.* 1. radical, de la raíz. 2. radical, original, fundamental. 3. radical, extremo, extremado, drástico. 4. (pol., bot., mat.) radical. —*s.* 1. radical, raíz; fundamento. 2. (pol., mat.) radical. 3. (filol.) radical. 4. (gram.) radical (de una palabra).
radical expression, (mat.) expresión radical.
radicalism [-ˌɪzəm] *s.* radicalismo.
radicality [rædɪˈkælətɪ] **radicalness** [ˈrædɪkəlnəs] *s.* naturaleza radical o fundamental.
radically [ˈrædɪkəlɪ] *adv.* radicalmente.
radical sign, (mat.) signo radical, signo de radicación.
radicand [ˈrædəˌkænd] *s.* (mat.) radicando.
radicate [-ˌkeɪt] *v.t.* radicar, arraigar.
radicel [-ˌsɛl] *s.* (bot.) raicilla, radícula.
radices, *pl. de* **radix.**
radicicolous [ˌrædəˈsɪkələs] *a.* (zool.) radicícola.
radicle [ˈrædɪkəl] *s.* (bot.) radícula.
radicolous [rəˈdɪkələs] *var. de* **radicicolous.**
radicular [ræˈdɪkjələr, B -lə] *a.* (bot.) radicoso.
radii, *pl. de* radius.
radio [ˈreɪdɪˌoʊ] *s.* (*pl.* RADIOS) 1. radio (emisión radiofónica o radiorreceptor). 2. (fam.) radiograma. —*a.* de radio. —*v.t.* (*pret., p.p.* RADIOED; *p.pr.* RADIOING) comunicar o transmitir por radio. —*v.i.* radiar, radiodifundir, perifonear.
radioactinium [ˌreɪdɪoʊækˈtɪnɪəm] *s.* (quím.) radioactinio.
radioactive [-ˈæktɪv] *a.* radioactivo, radioactivo.
radioactive waste, residuos radioactivos.
radioactivity [-ˌækˈtɪvətɪ] *s.* radioactividad, radioactividad.
radio amateur, radioaficionado.
radio astronomy, radioastronomía.
radio balloon, globo radiosonda.
radio beacon, radiofaro.
radio beam, enlace herziano, haz radioeléctrico.
radio bearing, (avia.) marcación por radiofaro, rumbo radiogoniométrico.
radiobiology [ˌreɪdɪoʊbaɪˈɑlədʒɪ, B -ˈɔl-] *s.* radiobiología.
radiobroadcast [-ˈbrɔdˌkæst, B -ˌkɑst] *v.t.* radiar, radiodifundir, perifonear.
radiobroadcaster [-ər, B -ə] *s.* radiodifusor, perifoneador.
radiobroadcasting [-ɪŋ] *s.* radioemisión, radiodifusión.
radiocarbon [-ˈkɑrbən, B -ˈkɑbən] *s.* (quím.) radiocarbón.
radiocarbon dating, (fís.) método del carbono 14, determinación de la antigüedad por radiocarbono.
radiocast [ˈreɪdɪoʊˈkæst, B -ˌkɑst] *v.t.* radiar, radiodifundir, perifonear.
radiocaster [-ər, B -ə] *s.* radiodifusor, perifoneador.
radio channel, (rad.) faja de frecuencia, canal de radio, radiocanal.
radiochemistry [ˌreɪdɪoʊˈkɛməstrɪ] *s.* radioquímica.
radio colloid [-ˈkɑlˌɔɪd, B -ˈkɔl-] *s.* (quím.) radiocoloide.
radio compass, radiobrújula, radiocompás.
radioconductor [-kənˈdʌktər, B -tə] *s.* (elec.) radioconductor.
radio control, gobierno o mando (de un mecanismo) por ondas hertzianas, control remoto.
radio-controlled, de control remoto, con radiomando, teledirigido.
radio-controlled taxi, radio taxi.
radiodetector [-dɪˈtɛktər, B -tə] *s.* radio detector, detector de ondas radiales.
radio direction finder, radiogoniómetro, radiorientador.
radioelectronics [-ɪˌlɛkˈtrɑnɪks, B -ˈtrɔn-] *s.* radioelectrónica.
radioelement [ˌreɪdɪoʊˈɛləmənt] *s.* (quím.) radioelemento.
radio engineering, radiotécnica, ingeniería de radio.
radio frequency, radiofrecuencia.
radiogenic [-ˈdʒɛnɪk] *a.* radiógeno.
radiogoniometer [-ˌgoʊnɪˈɑmətər, B -ˈɔmɪtə] *s.* (rad.) radiogoniómetro.
radiogoniometry [-trɪ] *s.* (rad.) radiogoniometría.
radiogram [ˈreɪdɪoʊˌgræm] *s.* 1. radiografía. 2. radiograma. 3. (G.B.) radiogramófono, radiogramola.
radiograph [-ˌgræf, B -ˌgrɑf] *s.* radiografía. —*v.t.* radiografiar.
radiographer [ˌreɪdɪˈɑgrəfər, B -ˈɔgrəfə] *s.* radiógrafo.
radiographic [-oʊˈgræfɪk] *a.* radiográfico.
radiography [-ˈɑgrəfɪ, B -ˈɔg-] *s.* radiografía.
radio hookup, *s.* circuito de radio.
radioisotope [-oʊˈaɪsəˌtoʊp] *s.* (fís., quím.) radioisótopo.
radio jamming, interferencia radial (de propósito).
radiolarian [-oʊˈlɛrɪən, B -əˈlær-] *a., s.* (zool.) radiolario.
radio link, circuito radiotelefónico intercalado en otro.
radio listener, radioescucha, radioyente.
radiolocation [-oʊˌloʊˈkeɪʃən] *s.* radiolocalización.
radiolocator [ˈreɪdɪoʊˈloʊˌkeɪtər, B -ə] *s.* radiodetector.
radiological [ˌreɪdɪəˈlɑdʒɪkəl, B -ˈlɔdʒ-] *a.* radiológico.
radiologist [-ˈɑlədʒəst, B -ˈɔl-] *s.* radiólogo.
radiology [-dʒɪ] *s.* radiología.
radio loop, antena de cuadro.
radiolucent [-oʊˈlusənt] *a.* (med.) radiolúcido.
radioluminescence [-ˌluməˈnɛsəns] *s.* (fís. nuclear) radioluminiscencia.
radiolysis [-ˈɑləsəs, B -ˈɔl-] *s.* (quím.) radiolisis.
radioman [ˈreɪdɪoʊˌmæn] *s.* 1. radiotelegrafista. 2. radiotécnico.
radiometer [ˌreɪdɪˈɑmətər, B -ˈɔmɪtə] *s.* radiómetro.
radiometric [-oʊˈmɛtrɪk] *a.* radiométrico.
radiometry [-ˈɑmətrɪ, B -ˈɔm-] *s.* radiometría.
radiomimetic [-oʊməˈmɛtɪk] *a.* radiomimético.
radio network, red o cadena de emisoras.
radionics [-ˈɑnɪks, B -ˈɔn-] *s. pl.* (*sing. en const.*) electrónica.
radionuclide [-oʊˈnuklaɪd, B -ˈnju-] *s.* (fís. nuclear) radionúclido.
radio operator, *s.* operador de radio.
radiophare [ˈreɪdɪoʊˌfɛr, B -ˌfɛə] *s.* radiofaro.
radiophone [-ˌfoʊn] *s.* 1. (fís.) radiófono. 2. radioteléfono.
radiophonic [ˌreɪdɪəˈfɑnɪk, B -ˈfɔn-] *s.* 1. radiofónico. 2. radiotelefónico.
radiophony [-ˈɑfənɪ, B -ˈɔf-] *s.* (fís., rad.) radiofonía.
radiophoto [-oʊˈfoʊtoʊ] **radiophotograph** [-təˌgræf, B -ˌgrɑf] *s.* radiofoto.
radiophotography [-fəˈtɑgrəfɪ, B -ˈtɔg-] *s.* radiofotografía.
radio range, (aer.) radiofaro direccional, radioguía.
radio receiver, radiorreceptor.
radioresistance [-rɪˈzɪstəns] *s.* (med., fís.) radioresistencia.
radioscopic [-əˈskɑpɪk, B -ˈskɔp-] *a.* radioscópico.
radioscopy [-ˈɑskəpɪ, B -ˈɔs-] *s.* radioscopia.
radiosensitive [-oʊˈsɛnsətɪv] *a.* (med.) radiosensible.
radiosensitivity [-ˌsɛnsəˈtɪvətɪ] *s.* (med.) radiosensibilidad.
radio set, aparato de radio.
radiosonde [ˈreɪdɪoʊˌsɑnd, B -ˌsɔnd] *s.* (meteor.) radiosonda.
radiosonic [ˌreɪdɪoʊˈsɑnɪk, B -ˈsɔn-] *a.* radiosónico.
radio spectrum, (rad.) radioespectro.
radio station, estación de radio, radioestación.
radiostrontium [-ˈstrɑntʃɪəm, B -ˈstrɔnʃɪ-] *s.* (quím.) estroncio radiactivo.

radiosymmetrical [-sə'mɛtrɪkəl] *a.* (bot.) radiosimétrico.
radiotechnology [-tɛk'nɑlədʒɪ, B -'nɔl-] *s.* radiotecnia.
radiotelegram [-'tɛlə,græm] *s.* radiotelegrama.
radiotelegraph [-,græf, B -,grɑf] *s.* radiotelégrafo. —*v.t.* radiotelegrafiar.
radiotelegraphic [-,tɛlə'græfɪk] *a.* radiotelegráfico.
radiotelegraphy [-tə'lɛgrəfɪ] *s.* radiotelegrafía.
radiotelephone [-'tɛlə,foʊn] *s.* radioteléfono.
radiotelephonic [-,tɛlə'fɑnɪk, B -'fɔn-] *a.* radiotelefónico.
radiotelephony [-tə'lɛfənɪ] *s.* radiotelelefonía.
radio telescope, radiotelescopio.
radiotherapy [-'θɛrəpɪ] *s.* radioterapia; radiumterapia, raditerapia.
radiothermy ['reɪdɪoʊ,θɜrmɪ, B -,θɜmɪ] *s.* radiotermia.
radiothorium [,reɪdɪoʊ'θɔrɪəm] *s.* (quím.) radiotorio.
radio tracking, localización por radio.
radio transmission, radiotransmisión.
radio transmitter, radiotransmisor.
radio tube, tubo electrónico, tubo o válvula de radio, lámpara de radio.
radiovision [-'vɪʒən] *s.* radiovisión, transmisión de fotografías cinematográficas por radio.
radio wave, onda radioeléctrica, onda hertziana.
radish ['rædɪʃ] *s.* (bot.) rábano.
radium ['reɪdɪəm] *s.* (quím.) radio, rádium.
radium therapy, (med.) radiumterapia, raditerapia; radioterapia.
radius ['reɪdɪəs] *s.* (*pl.* RADII [-,aɪ] O RADIUSES) 1. (geom., anat., zool.) radio. 2. (mec.) curva de unión, curva de acuerdo. 3. **r. of curvature,** radio de curvatura; **r. of gyration,** radio de giro.
radius gage, plantilla de curvas de unión.
radius vector, (*pl.* RADII VECTORES O RADIUS VECTORS) (geom., astr.) radiovector.
radix ['reɪdɪks] *s.* (*pl.* RADICES ['rædə,siz] O RADIXES) 1. (bot.) raíz. 2. (mat.) base (de un sistema de numeración). 3. (filol.) raíz; radical.
radome ['reɪdoʊm] *s.* radomo, cúpula de antena de radar (esp. en una aeronave).
radon ['reɪ,dɑn, B -,dɔn] *s.* (quím.) radón.
radula ['rædʒələ] *s.* (*pl.* RADULAE [-,li] radulas) (zool.) rádula.
R A F *abrev. de* **Royal Air Force,** Real Fuerza Aérea.
raff [ræf] *s.* gentuza, canalla, plebe, chusma (Am.).
raffia ['ræfɪə] *s.* 1. (bot.) rafia (palmera). 2. fibra de rafia.
raffia palm, (bot.) palmera rafia.
raffinose ['ræfə,noʊs] *s.* (quím.) rafinosa.
raffish ['ræfɪʃ] *a.* 1. pícaro, pillo, bajo, ruin. 2. vulgar, ordinario.
raffishly [-lɪ] *adv.* 1. pícaramente. 2. vulgarmente, ordinariamente.
raffishness [-nəs] *s.* 1. bajeza, ruindad. 2. vulgaridad.
raffle ['ræfəl] *s.* rifa, sorteo, lotería. —*v.i.* (con *for*) participar, entrar en una rifa. —*v.t.* rifar, sortear.
raffle, *s.* desecho, restos, residuos, desperdicios.
raffler ['ræflər, B -lə] *s.* rifador, sorteador.
raft [ræft, B rɑft] *s.* 1. balsa, almadía, armadía, zatara, jangada. 2. masa flotante (de hielo, etc.). 3. (fam.) montón, sinnúmero, gran cantidad. —*v.t.* 1. transportar en balsa, transportar como balsa. 2. cruzar (río, lago, etc.) en balsa. 3. juntar (maderos) en una balsa. —*v.i.* viajar en balsa, manejar una balsa.
rafter ['ræftər, B 'rɑftə] *s.* 1. maderero (que conduce las maderadas por los ríos), almadiero. 2. (arq.) par, alfarda; cabio, cabrio (de una armadura).
raftsman ['ræftsmən, B 'rɑfts-] *s.* 1. viajero en balsa. 2. maderero (que conduce las maderadas por los ríos).
rag [ræg] *s.* 1. trapo, jirón. 2. (*gen. pl.*) andrajos, harapos, trapos (prendas de vestir). 3. (desp. o irón.) pañuelo; cortina; vela; bandera. 4. periodicucho. 5. (*pl.*) restos, fragmentos. 6. película interior blanca (de las naranjas, limones). 7. **from rags to riches,** (llegar) de la pobreza a la riqueza; **in rags,** cubierto de andrajos; **to chew the r.,** (jer.) parlar, chacharear; refunfuñar.
rag, *v.t.* (*pret., p.p.* RAGGED; *p.pr.* RAGGING) (jer.) 1. regañar, sermonear, fastidiar. 2. embromar. —*v.i.* (pr. G.B.) travesear, hacer payasadas. —*s.* (pr. G.B.) 1. travesura, payasada, chacota. 2. chanza, broma pesada. 3. pizarra para techar; laja de piedra.
ragamuffin ['rægə,mʌfən] *s.* zarrapastrón, pelagatos; golfo, galopín, pelafustán.
ragbag ['ræg,bæg] *s.* 1. bolsa para retazos, bolsa para trapos. 2. (fig.) mezcolanza.
rag bolt, perno arponado, perno de anclaje, perno para empotrar.
rag doll, muñeca de trapo.
rage [reɪdʒ] *s.* 1. rabia, ira, furor, enojo, cólera. 2. braveza, furia (del mar, fuego, tempestad, etc.). 3. frenesí, vehemencia, encarnizamiento. 4. exaltación, pasión, excitación, fervor. 5. ansia, anhelo, deseo. 6. (ant.) insania. 7. **to be the r.,** hacer furor, estar de moda, estar en boga; to **fly into a r.,** montar en cólera, ponerse furioso, enfurecerse. —*v.i.* 1. rabiar, arrebatarse, encolerizarse, enfurecerse. 2. bramar, rugir (la tempestad, el viento, etc.).
ragged ['rægəd] *a.* 1. roto, rasgado; gastado, raído; andrajoso, harapiento, ej., *a r. coat,* un saco (Am.) o chaqueta raído, *a r. beggar,* un mendigo harapiento. 2. mellado, dentado, serrado. 3. irregular, desigual. 4. áspero, escabroso. 5. discordante, disonante. 6. **on the r. edge,** en situación precaria (económica, de salud, nervios, etc.).
raggedly [-lɪ] *adv.* 1. andrajosamente. 2. irregularmente. 3. escabrosamente.
raggedness [-nəs] *s.* 1. estado andrajoso. 2. irregularidad. 3. aspereza, escabrosidad.
raggedy [-ɪ] *a.* un poco rasgado o roto.
raggle ['rægəl] *s.* (arq.) ranura.
raggle-taggle [-,tægəl] *a.* mezclado, mixto, variado; abigarrado.
raging ['reɪdʒɪŋ] *a.* 1. violento, incontenible, feroz (pasión, ira, etc.). 2. extraordinario, tremendo (belleza, éxito, etc.).
raglan ['ræglən] *s.* (cost.) raglán, ranglán.
raglan sleeve, manga raglán, manga ranglán.
ragman ['ræg,mæn] *s.* trapero.
ragout [ræ'gu, B 'rægu] *s.* (cocina) ragú.
rag paper, papel de hilo.
ragpicker ['ræg,pɪkər, B -ə] *s.* trapero.
ragtag ['ræg,tæg] *s.* muchedumbre heterogénea.
ragtag and bobtail, morralla, canalla, gentuza, chusma (Am.).
ragtime [-,taɪm] *s.* (mús.) tiempo sincopado, ragtime; **in r.,** sincopado.
ragweed ['ræg,wid] *s.* (bot.) ambrosia, ambrosía.
rag wheel, rueda dentada, rueda de ferrocarril.
ragwort ['ræg,wɜrt, B -,wɜt] *s.* (bot.) zuzón, hierba cana.
rah [rɑ] *interj.* ¡hurra! ¡viva!
raid [reɪd] *s.* 1. correría, irrupción, incursión, ataque inesperado. 2. allanamiento (de un establecimiento, etc.), batida (de la policía). 3. (bolsa) tentativa (de corredores) para bajar los precios. —*v.t.* 1. atacar por sorpresa; invadir. 2. allanar (establecimiento, etc.). —*v.i.* dirigir ataques sorpresivos contra, depredar.
raider ['reɪdər, B -ə] *s.* 1. buque corsario. 2. (E.U., mil.) soldado entrenado para la lucha cuerpo a cuerpo. 3. avión incursor.
rail [reɪl] *s.* (orn.) rey de codornices, polla de agua, rascón. —*v.i.* (con *at* o *against*) denostar, vituperar, insultar, reñir; mofarse o burlarse (de).
rail [reɪl] *s.* 1. carril, riel, raíl, rail. 2. baranda, barandal, barandilla; parapeto (de puentes); balaustrada; barra de apoyo. 3. cerca, cerco, valla, vallado, defensa; reja, verja, enrejado. 4. (*abrev. de* **railroad**) ferrocarril (como medio de transporte), ej., *send by r.,* enviar por ferrocarril. 5. (arq.) carrera, peinazo; travesaño (de puertas o ventanas). 6. (mar.) barandilla, pasamanos. 7. (impr.) (*pl.*) bandas. 8. (billar) baranda. 9. **off the rails,** desorganizado, en desorden, que no está funcionando bien; equivocado, errado; **on the rails,** en marcha, en camino, en progreso; en el camino recto. —*v.t.* 1. poner barandilla o enrejado a, cercar, vallar. 2. (pr. G.B.) transportar por ferrocarril. 3. r. **off.** separar con barandilla.
railcar ['reɪl,kɑr, B -,kɑ] *s.* (f.c.) automotor, automotriz, autorriel.
rail chair, (f.c.) cojinete de riel, cojinete del carril.
railer [-ər, B -ə] *s.* maldiciente, vituperador, insultador.
rail guard, (f.c.) limpiavía, rastrillo.
railhead [-,hɛd] *s.* 1. (mil.) cabeza de etapa ferroviaria. 2. término de la vía (de un ferrocarril en construcción).
rail head, (f.c.) cabeza de carril, hongo de riel.
railing ['reɪlɪŋ] *s.* 1. barrera, baranda, barandal, barandilla; balaustrada; cerca, cercado, valla, verja. 2. (f.c.) carriles, rieles; material para rieles.
raillery [-ərɪ] *s.* zumba, burla, fisga, tomadura de pelo, chirigota, cuchufleta.
rail-motor [-,moʊtər, B -ə] *s.* (f.c.) coche o vagón automotor.
railroad ['reɪl,roʊd] *s.* ferrocarril, vía férrea. —*v.t* (E.U.) 1. transportar por ferrocarril, enviar por ferrocarril. 2. (fam.) apresurar, obligar a hacer rápidamente; hacer aprobar con precipitación (ej., una ley, etc.). 3. (jer.) hacer encarcelar (a alguien) bajo cargos falsos (para librarse de él).
railroad car, vagón o coche ferroviario.
railroad crossing, cruce ferroviario, cruce de ferrocarril.
railroad depot, (E.U.) estación de ferrocarril.
railroad flat, apartamento sin pasillo con las habitaciones dispuestas como los vagones en un **ferrocarril.**
railroading [-ɪŋ] *s.* construcción u operación de un ferrocarril; ocupación o empleo en un ferrocarril; administración de un ferocarril.
railroad junction, (f.c.) entronque.
railroad siding, r. switch, desviadero, apartadero.
railway [-,weɪ] *s.* 1. ferrocarril para tráfico ligero, esp. tranvía. 2. (G.B.) ferrocarril.
railway line, línea férrea.
railway spine, (med.) conmoción medular.
raiment ['reɪmənt] *s.* vestimenta, indumentaria, atavío.
rain [reɪn] *s.* 1. lluvia. 2. (fig.) lluvia, copia, ej., *a r. of sparks,* una lluvia de chispas. 3. **the rains,** la estación de lluvias; **r. or shine,** llueva o no, con buen o mal tiempo. —*v.i.* llover; **it is raining,** llueve; **it never rains but it pours,** las

desgracias nunca vienen solas; **r. or shine,** llueva o truene, de todas maneras. —*v.t.* llover, derramar copiosamente; dejar caer profusamente; **r. cats and dogs,** llover a cántaros, llover a chorros; **r. (flowers, presents,** etc.) **on,** colmar de (flores, regalos, etc.); **r. out,** interrumpirse o anularse a causa de la lluvia (un espectáculo, ceremonia, etc.).
rainbow ['reɪnˌboʊ] *s.* arco iris.
rainbow trout, (ict.) trucha arco iris.
rain check, 1. billete (que se da a los espectadores de un espectáculo al aire libre) válido para otra ocasión en caso de lluvia. 2. seguridad, promesa (de poder volver, continuar, etc.).
raincoat [-ˌkoʊt] *s.* impermeable.
rain doctor, brujo propiciador de la lluvia.
raindrop [-ˌdrɑp, B -ˌdrɔp] *s.* gota de lluvia.
rainfall [-ˌfɔl] *s.* 1. lluvia, chaparrón, aguacero. 2. precipitación (cantidad de lluvia que cae durante un tiempo determinado).
rain forest, bosque tropical muy denso donde llueve todo el año.
rain gauge, pluviómetro.
rainmaker [-ˌmeɪkər, B -kə] *s.* (entre los indios americanos) brujo con poderes mágicos para atraer la lluvia.
rainproof ['reɪnˌpruf] *a.* impermeable, a prueba de lluvia. —*v.t.* hacer impermeable.
rainsquall [-ˌskwɔl] *s.* chubasco.
rainstorm ['reɪnˌstɔrm, B -ˌstɔm] *s.* tempestad de lluvia, temporal.
raintight [-ˌtaɪt] *a.* a prueba de lluvia, estanco a la lluvia.
rain water, agua llovediza, agua lluvia o de lluvia, aguas vertientes, aguas pluviales.
rainwear [-ˌwɛr, B -ˌwɛə] *s.* vestido o ropa impermeable.
rainy ['reɪnɪ] *a.* (RAINIER; RAINIEST) lluvioso, pluvioso.
rainy day, día lluvioso; (fig.) tiempos de apremio o necesidad, ej., *to provide for a r. day,* ahorrar para tiempos de apremio o necesidad.
rainy season, estación de las lluvias.
raise [reɪz] *v.t.* 1. levantar, alzar; poner en pie. 2. mover, excitar; suscitar (interés, duda, etc.). 3. levantar, sublevar, amotinar. 4. levantar, erigir, elevar, erguir. 5. reclutar, alistar. 6. reunir, recoger, juntar (fondos, dinero, etc.). 7. criar, educar (niños). 8. criar, cultivar. 9. evocar (espíritus, etc.). 10. provocar, dar lugar a. 11. plantear, presentar, formular (objeción, etc.). 12. aumentar, subir (precio, sueldo, apuesta). 13. promover, ascender. 14. fermentar, subir (pan, masa, etc.). 15. levantar, revocar, hacer cesar (una prohibición, etc.). 16. levantar (la caza). 17. abandonar (sitio, bloqueo, etc.). 18. (mat.) elevar (a potencia). 19. (com.) falsificar, aumentar el valor de (efectos negociables cambiando fraudulentamente las cifras). 20. (mar.) divisar (tierra, barco, etc.). 21. **raise an eyebrow,** (fam.) alzar, arquear la ceja; **raise an objection,** poner una objeción; **raise a point,** hacer una observación; **r. Cain (hell, the devil),** armar un alboroto, causar gran conmoción, armar un lío; **r. one's glass to,** brindar por; **r. (someone) from the dead,** resucitar, volver a la vida (a alguien). —*v.i.* (dial.) levantarse, ascender, subir. —*s.* 1. aumento (de salario, apuesta, etc.). 2. cuesta. 3. (min.) contracielo, tiro, chimenea.
raised [reɪzd] *a.* 1. en relieve, saliente, que sobresale, que resalta, de realce. 2. leudo, fermentado (pan, pastel, etc.). 3. peraltado (arcos).
raiser ['reɪzər, B -ə] *s.* cultivador, productor; ganadero; educador, fundador.
raisin ['reɪzən] *s.* pasa (uva seca).
raising ['reɪzɪŋ] *s.* acción de levantar, erigir; levantamiento; elevación; cría.
raison d'être ['reɪzoʊn'dɛtrə, B -ˌzɔn'd-eɪt-] (fr.) razón de ser.
raj [rɑdʒ] *s.* (anglo-ind.) reinado, soberanía.
raja, rajah ['rɑdʒə] *s.* rajá.
rake [reɪk] *v.i.* inclinarse (ej., mástil, chimenea, proa, etc.). —*s.* 1. inclinación, desviación de la vertical. 2. (aer.) corte diagonal (de las alas de un avión para darles forma de trapecio). 3. ángulo de inclinación del cuchillo (en máquinas cortadoras).
rake [reɪk] *s.* rastro, rastra, rastrillo, mielga, bieldo, bielgo. —*v.t.* 1. rastrillar, barrer; revolver, remover; atizar (el fuego). 2. barrer; raspar, rascar, raer. 3. explorar, escudriñar, registrar a fondo. 4. enfilar, barrer a lo largo de (barco, columna de tropas, etc.) con fuego de artillería. 5. **r. in,** recoger con el rastrillo (apuestas, dinero, etc.); (fig.) ganar en abundancia (dinero, utilidades, etc.); **r. over the coals,** censurar ásperamente; **r. together,** juntar, acumular; **r. up,** (fig.) desentrañar, descubrir (escándalo, secreto, etc.); **to r. out,** ahondar raspando.
rake, *s.* calavera, libertino, perdido, licencioso, calvatrueno, juerguista. —*v.i.* 1. (caza) lanzarse o precipitarse (el halcón) sobre la caza. 2. (dial.) rastrear, husmear, correr (un perro) con la nariz pegada al suelo.
rakee, raki [rɑ'ki, 'rækɪ] *s.* arack, arac.
rakehell ['reɪkˌhɛl] *s.* (ant.) lascivo, lujurioso, libertino, perdido, calaverón.
rake-off [-ˌɔf] *s.* (jer.) comisión ilícita, lucro ilegal, tajada.
raker ['reɪkər, B -ə] *s.* 1. rastrillador (hombre). 2. rastrilladora (mecánica). 3. puntal.
raking fire ['reɪkɪŋ-] (mil.) tiro de rastrilleo, tiro de enfilada.
rakish [-ɪʃ] *a.* 1. libertino, lascivo, disoluto. 2. (mar.) de mástiles inclinados. 3. gallardo.
rakishly [-lɪ] *adv.* gallardamente.
rakishness [-nəs] *s.* 1. libertinaje, disolución. 2. caída, inclinación de los palos.
rale [ræl, B rɑl] *s.* (med.) estertor (que se produce en ciertas enfermedades del aparato respiratorio).
ralliform ['rælәˌfɔrm, B -ˌfɔm] *a.* (orn.) raliforme.
rally ['rælɪ] *v.t.* (*pret., p.p.* RALLIED; *p.pr.* RALLYING) reunir y reanimar (tropas), rehacer (regimiento, etc.); recobrar (la fuerza, la salud, etc.). —*v.i.* 1. reunirse, rehacerse, reagruparse (tropas dispersas). 2. reanimarse, recobrar las fuerzas, revivir. 3. unirse (para apoyo activo). 4. (tenis) intercambiar tiros (para ganar un punto). 5. (com.) recobrarse (los precios en la bolsa, etc.). 6. **r. round** (o **to**), acudir a, dar apoyo a. —*s.* (*pl.* RALLIES) 1. reunión popular, reunión política; unión o reunión (de tropas dispersas). 2. recuperación, recobro (ej., de los precios en la bolsa). 3. (tenis) intercambio de tiros (antes de ganar un punto).
rally *v.t.* (*pret., p.p.* RALLIED; *p.pr.* RALLYING) burlarse de, ridiculizar, zumbar.
ram [ræm] *s.* 1. (zool.) carnero, morueco. 2. (mar.) espolón; buque con espolón; (mil.) ariete. 3. (mec.) ariete hidráulico; émbolo de percusión (de una bomba, etc.); martinete, pisón. 4. **R.,** (astr.) Aries. —*v.t.* (*pret., p.p.* RAMMED; *p.pr.* RAMMING) 1. apisonar, pisonar; golpear con un espolón o ariete. 2. (con *down, in* o *into*) meter por la fuerza, apretar, apretujar (en). 3. atacar (un arma de fuego). 4. (con *with*) atestar, rellenar, henchir (de o con). 5. (con *against*) golpear (algo) violentamente (contra). 6. embestir.
RAM *abrev. de* **random access memory,** (comput.) memoria de acceso aleatorio.
Ramadan ['ræməˌdɑn B ˌræmə'dɑn] *s.* ramadán (noveno mes de los mahometanos); retiro y vigilia que hace el musulmán en dicha época.
ramal ['reɪməl] *a.* (bot.) rámeo.
ramble ['ræmbəl] *v.i.* 1. errar, vagar, callejear, vagabundear, caminar a la ventura. 2. divagar, ir(se) por las ramas. 3. dar vueltas, serpentear (camino, río); extenderse o crecer serpenteando (las enredaderas, etc.). —*s.* paseo, caminata, vagabundeo.
rambler [-blər, B -blə] *s.* 1. vagabundo, callejero, paseador; divagador. 2. (bot.) rosa trepadora.
rambling [-blɪŋ] *a.* 1. divagador, digresivo. 2. irregularmente construído (casa, etc.); de formación irregular. 3. vagante, vagueante. 4. trepador, rastrero (plantas, etc.).
Rambouillet [ˌræmbə'leɪ, B 'ræmbuˌleɪ] *s.* (zool.) rambouillet (tipo de oveja merino francesa).
rambunctious [ræm'bʌŋkʃəs] *a.* (fam.) revoltoso, enredador, travieso, inmanejable, ingobernable; alborotador, turbulento.
rambutan [-'butən] *s.* (bot.) rambután (fruto y árbol).
ramekin ['ræmɪkən, B 'ræmkɪn] *s.* 1. quesadilla. 2. pequeña cazuela para quesadillas; cacharro pequeño sin tapa y poco hondo.
ramentum [rə'mɛntəm] *s.* (*pl.* RAMENTA [-ə]) (bot.) ramento.
ramequin, *var. de* **ramekin.**
ramie ['ræmɪ] *s.* 1. (bot.) ramio. 2. ramina (fibra).
ramification [ˌræməfə'keɪʃən] *s.* ramificación.
ramiform ['ræməˌfɔrm, B -ˌfɔm] *a.* ramiforme.
ramify [-ˌfaɪ] *v.t., v.i.* (*pret., p.p.* RAMIFIED; *p.pr.* RAMIFYING) ramificar(se).
ramjet engine ['ræmˌdʒɛt-] (aer.) estatorreactor.
rammer ['ræmər, B -ə] *s.* 1. pisón, apisonador, machota. 2. baqueta de fusil. 3. (mar.) espolón.
rammish [-ɪʃ] *s.* 1. carneruno. 2. maloliente, que huele a carnero.
ramose ['reɪˌmoʊs, B rə'moʊs] *a.* **ramoso.**
ramous ['reɪməs] *a.* ramoso; ramiforme.
ramp [ræmp] *v.i.* 1. erguirse sobre las patas traseras con las garras extendidas (león). 2. rabiar, agitarse. 3. saltar, brincar. 4. trepar (plantas). 5. (her.) ser rampante. —*s.* 1. brinco, salto; avance o postura amenazadora. 2. (jer. G.B.) fraude, estafa.
ramp, *s.* 1. rampa, repecho, pendiente. 2. rampa (para subir al avión). 3. (arq.) curva de enlace o de transición (ej., de una escalera, etc.). 4. (fort.) rampa.
rampage [ˌræm'peɪdʒ] *v.t.* andar rabioso, alborotarse. — ['ræmˌpeɪdʒ, B ræm'peɪdʒ] *s.* comportamiento violento; alboroto, tumulto; **to be on a r.,** andar rabioso, alborotarse.
rampageous [-'peɪdʒəs] *a.* revoltoso, alborotador, turbulento, indócil, inmanejable.
rampancy ['ræmpənsɪ] *s.* exuberancia, extravagancia, desenfreno.
rampant [-pənt] *a.* 1. imperioso, agresivo, feroz; desenfrenado. 3. exuberante, lozano, frondoso, lujuriante. 3. difundido por todas partes (rumor, idea, etc.). 4. (her.) rampante; aculado (caballo). 5. (arq.) por tranquil, cojo (arco).
rampant arch, (arq.) arco cojo, arco por tranquil; bóveda rampante.
rampantly [-lɪ] *adv.* 1. imperiosamente, agresivamente. 2. lozanamente.

rampart ['ræm,pɑrt, -pərt, B -,pɑt] *s.* 1. (fort.) terraplén, bastión, baluarte; muro, muralla. 2. (fig.) defensa, amparo; resguardo, abrigo. —*v.t.* abaluartar, murar, abastionar.
rampike [-,paɪk] *s.* árbol quebrado o muerto (en pie).
rampion ['ræmpɪən] *s.* (bot.) rapónchigo, ruiponce.
ramrod ['ræm,rɑd, B -,rɔd] *s.* 1. cargador, baqueta de fusil; atacador. 2. escobillón (para armas portátiles). —*a.* muy rígido; de suma severidad o dureza.
ramshackle ['ræm,ʃækəl] *a.* desvencijado, destartalado, ruinoso.
ramshorn ['ræmz,hɔrn, B -,hɔn] *s.* (zool.) especie de caracol (que se usa en acuarios para limpiarlos).
ramulose ['ræmjə,loʊs] *a.* (bot.) con muchos rámulos.
ramus ['reɪməs] *s.* (bot., anat.) ramal, ramificación.
ran [ræn] *pret. de* **run.**
rance [ræns] *s.* mármol belga rojo con rayas azules y blancas.
ranch [ræntʃ, B rɑntʃ] *s.* finca de ganado, estancia (Am.); rancho, hacienda. —*v i.* vivir o trabajar en una finca de ganado o hacienda; ser hacendado.
rancher ['ræntʃər, B 'rɑntʃə] *s.* ganadero, estanciero (Am.), ranchero; hacendado.
ranch house, 1. casa hacienda; casa de campo. 2. casa grande particular de un solo piso.
ranchman ['ræntʃmən] *s.* ganadero, estanciero (Am.), ranchero; hacendado.
rancid ['rænsəd] *a.* 1. rancio, rancioso. 2. repugnante, desagradable.
rancidity [ræn'sɪdətɪ] **rancidness** ['rænsədnəs] *s.* ranciedad, rancidez.
rancor, (G.B.) **rancour** ['ræŋkər, B -kə] *s.* rencor, aborrecimiento, resentimiento, encono, inquina.
rancorous [-kərəs] *a.* rencoroso, vengativo.
rancorously [-lɪ] *adv.* rencorosamente.
rancorousness [-nəs] *s.* calidad de rencoroso.
rand [rænd] *s.* 1. (dial.) borde o margen; tira, faja, lista. 2. (Sudáfrica) altiplanicie al lado de la cuenca de un río. 3. calzo del zapato. 4. rand, unidad monetaria (de varios países sudafricanos).
random ['rændəm] *s.* (raro) azar, casualidad; **at r.,** a la ventura, al azar. —*a.* casual, fortuito, impensado, accidental, aleatorio.
random access, (comput.) acceso aleatorio, acceso directo.
random access memory, memoria de acceso aleatorio *or.* directo.
randomized ['rændəmɑɪzd] *a.* aleatorio.
randomly [-lɪ] *adv.* al azar.
random number, número aleatorio.
R and R, (jer.) *abrev. de* **Rest and Recuperation,** descanso y recuperación (licencia a los soldados en el frente de guerra).
randy ['rændɪ] *a.* (RANDIER; RANDIEST) (fam., G.B.) 1. cachondo, rijoso, lujurioso, sensual. 2. (esco.) brusco, vulgar. —*s.* (esco.) mujer licenciosa, verdulera.
ranee, *var. de* **rani.**
rang [ræŋ] *pret. de* **ring.**
range [reɪndʒ] *v.t.* 1. enfilar, alinear, ordenar, disponer, arreglar, clasificar. 2. recorrer; batir (campo, monte). 3. pastar, llevar al pasto (ganado). 4. (mar.) navegar a lo largo de (la costa). 5. enfocar (telescopio); reglar (el tiro); apuntar (cañón) ajustando su alcance. —*v.i.* 1. corretear, vagar, deambular, errar. 2. extenderse; variar, fluctuar (entre límites). 3. (arm.) tener alcance (un cañón), ej., *it ranges over a mile,* tiene un alcance de más de una milla. 4. determinar la distancia de tiro (disparando alternadamente más alto y más bajo). 5. (bot., zool.) habitar (en), ser originario (de cierta región). 6. **r. with,** estar clasificado (en grado, rango, posición, etc.) con, estar en la misma altura o el mismo nivel que, ej., *he ranges with the great writers,* él reza entre los grandes escritores. —*s.* 1. fila, hilera, línea. 2. cordillera, cadena de montañas, sierra. 3. pradera, pasto o cazadero extenso. 4. escala, gama, serie (de velocidades, precios, etc.). 5. orden, clase. 6. recorrido, extensión, límites; campo o esfera de acción. 7. extensión (de la voz). 8. (aer.) radio de acción (total). 9. (arm.) línea de dirección, línea de tiro; alcance. 10. campo de tiro. 11. hornillo, cocina económica. 12. (bot., zool.) habitación (región donde naturalmente se cría una especie vegetal o animal). 13. **at close r.,** a quema ropa, a quemarropa; **to be out of r.,** estar fuera del alcance de tiro; **within r.,** a tiro; **within r. of,** al alcance de (los cañones, etc.).
range adjustment, (arm.) reglaje en alcance, reglaje del alza (artillería).
range finder, (arm., foto.) telémetro.
range light, (avia.) luz de balizamiento.
ranger ['reɪndʒər, B -dʒə] *s.* 1. guardabosque. 2. (G.B.) guardián del bosque real. 3. vigilante, guardia montado. 4. (mil.) comando, soldado de tropa de asalto. 5. (ant.) vagabundo, andorrero.
range rate, velocidad de trayectoria (de un cohete), variación en alcance por unidad de tiempo.
Rangoon [ræŋ'gun] *s.* Rangún, capital de Birmania.
rangy ['reɪndʒɪ] *a.* (RANGIER; RANGIEST) 1. ancho, espacioso. 2. montañoso. 3. de patas largas y cuerpo delgado (animal). 4. larguirucho y esbelto.
rani [rɑ'ni] *s.* rani, princesa o esposa de un príncipe de la India.
ranid ['rænəd] *s.* (zool.) ránido.
ranine vein ['reɪ,naɪn-] (anat.) vena ranina, vena leónica.
rank [ræŋk] *a.* 1. lozano, frondoso, espeso, exuberante, fértil. 2. grosero, indecente, vulgar. 3. rancio; fétido, maloliente. 4. acabado, consumado, completo, total (cobardía, traición, disparate, etc.). 5. (ant.) (ú. sólo en der.) excesivo, extremado.
rank [ræŋk] *s.* 1. fila, hilera, línea; serie; ringlera. 2. orden, arreglo, disposición. 3. condición, posición, rango (social, etc.). 4. jerarquía, distinción, eminencia; cuantía, calidad. 5. (mil.) grado, graduación, categoría. 6. (ajedrez) línea. 7. **the ranks,** (mil.) las filas de tropa, los soldados rasos; (fig.) el pueblo, las clases bajas; **to break ranks,** (mil.) romper filas; **to fall in r.,** (mil. y fig.) ponerse en fila; **to rise from the ranks,** ascender a la clase de oficial desde las filas; (fig.) alcanzar eminencia por experiencia o méritos. —*v.t.* 1. enfilar, alinear (esp. tropa). 2. clasificar, colocar por grados. 3. (mil., mar.) tener un grado superior a; superar en rango a. —*v.i.* 1. tener (tal o cual) grado o clasificación, ocupar una posición, ej., *r. below the average,* ocupar una posición por debajo del promedio. 2. ocupar (primer, segundo, etc.) lugar. 3. figurar, contarse entre; ser el más antiguo. 4. **r. high,** sobresalir; gozar de mucha estima; tener alto rango; **r. with,** estar al nivel de, tener el mismo grado que; ser de la misma calidad que.
rank and file, 1. (la) tropa, (los) soldados rasos. 2. (las) masas, (el) pueblo. 3. (el) cuerpo, (los) miembros ordinarios (de un partido, asociación, nación, etc.).
ranker ['ræŋkər, B -kə] *s.* (fam.) patatero, chusquero (Esp.), oficial en el ejército que comenzó de soldado raso.
ranking [-kɪŋ] *a.* de rango; de más alto rango, principal.
rankle [-kəl] *v.i.* 1. enconarse, inflamarse, ulcerarse, supurar. 2. causar encono o resentimiento.
rankness ['ræŋknəs] *s.* 1. exuberancia, frondosidad. 2. rancidez, fetidez.
ransack ['rænsæk] *v.t.* 1. registrar a fondo, escudriñar, explorar. 2. saquear, pillar, robar.
ransacker [-ər, B -ə] *s.* 1. registrador, escudriñador. 2. saqueador.
ransom ['rænsəm] *s.* rescate. —*v.t.* 1. rescatar; recobrar; librar, liberar. 2. redimir (ej., del pecado). 3. exigir rescate a o por. 4. **to be worth a king's r.,** valer un Potosí; **to hold (one) for r.,** exigir rescate por la liberación de (uno).
ransomer [-ər, B -ə] *s.* 1. rescatador. 2. prenda (que se da para rescatar buque capturado).
rant [rænt] *v.i.* 1. despotricar, desbarrar, desvariar, delirar. 2. regañar vehementemente. 3. (dial., ant.) deleitarse; jaranear, parrandear; alborotarse. —*s.* 1. lenguaje campanudo y retumbante. 2. (dial.) parranda bulliciosa.
ranter ['ræntər, B -ə] *s.* vociferador, energúmeno.
ranting [-ɪŋ] *a.* ampuloso, campanudo, altisonante.
rantingly [-lɪ] *adv.* ampulosamente, en tono ampuloso o altisonante.
ranula ['rænjələ] *s.* (med.) ránula; (vet.) sapillo, barba, barbilla.
ranunculaceous [rə,nʌŋkjə'leɪʃəs] *a.* (bot.) ranunculáceo.
ranunculus [-'nʌŋkjələs] *s.* (*pl.* RANUNCULUSES O RANUNCULI [-,laɪ]) (bot.) ranúnculo, botón de oro.
rap [ræp] *v.t., v.i.* (*pret., p.p.* RAPPED; *p.pr.* RAPPING) 1. golpear, tocar, dar un golpe corto y seco (a). 2. reprender severamente. 3. **r. out,** comunicar por golpes (mensaje, etc.); decir bruscamente; **r. over the knuckles,** (fig.) reprender. 4. (jer.) hablar, charlar. —*s.* 1. golpe corto y seco, taque. 2. reprimenda, regaño; crítica mordaz. 3. (jer.) cargo, acusación. 4. **to beat the r.,** (jer.) defenderse con éxito de una acusación; **to take the r. for,** (jer.) sufrir la pena o las consecuencias (gen. de un crimen o delito cometido por otro).
rap, *s.* (fam.) bledo, ardite, ej., *I don't care a r.,* no me importa un bledo, nada me importa.
rap, *v.t.* (*pret., p.p.* RAPPED O RAPT; *p.pr.* RAPPING) 1. arrebatar. 2. transportar con éxtasis; embelesar, arrobar, extasiar.
rapacious [rə'peɪʃəs] *a.* 1. rapaz. 2. de presa, de rapiña (ave). 3. voraz, devorador.
rapaciously [-lɪ] *adv.* rapazmente, con rapacidad; vorazmente.
rapacity [rə'pæsətɪ] **rapaciousness** [-'peɪʃəsnəs] *s.* rapacidad, rapacería; voracidad.
rape [reɪp] *v.t.* 1. violar, estuprar, ultrajar, deshonrar. 2. (ant.) hurtar, robar (con violencia); saquear. —*s.* 1. violación, estupro, ultraje. 2. (ant.) robo, saqueo, hurto.
rape, *s.* (bot.) 1. naba, nabo gallego. 2. colza. 3. bagazo de uva.
rape oil, rapeseed oil, aceite de colza.
rapeseed ['reɪp,sid] *s.* nabina, semilla de naba; semilla de colza.
Raphaelesque [,ræfɪə'lɛsk] *a.* rafaelesco, a la manera del pintor renacentista Rafael.
raphania [rə'feɪnɪə] *s.* (med.) rafania.
raphe ['reɪfɪ] *s.* (anat., bot.) rafe.
raphia ['reɪfɪə] *s.* (bot.) rafia.

raphide ['reɪfəd, 'ræfəd, B 'reɪfaɪd] *s.* (*pl.* RAPHIDES ['ræfədiz, 'reɪ-]) (bot.) rafidio.
rapid ['ræpəd] *a.* 1. rápido, veloz, ligero, raudo, presto, pronto. 2. (foto.) de exposición rápida. —*s.* (*gen. pl.*) rápido, rabión, raudal, recial.
rapid-fire [-'faɪr, B -ə] **rapid-firing** [-ɪŋ, B -rɪŋ] *a.* de tiro rápido (arma).
rapidity [rə'pɪdətɪ] *s.* rapidez, velocidad, prontitud, ligereza, agilidad.
rapidly ['ræpədlɪ] *adv.* rápidamente, velozmente.
rapier ['reɪpɪər, B -ə] *s.* espadín, estoque, espetón.
rapine ['ræpən, B -aɪn] *s.* rapiña, pillaje.
rapist ['reɪpəst] *s.* violador, raptor.
rapparee [ˌræpə'ri] *s.* (hist.) filibustero irlandés; saqueador, ladrón; vagabundo.
rappee [ræ'pi] *s.* rapé.
rappel [ræ'pɛl, rə-] *s.* rappel, descenso a soga doble (en alpinismo). —*v.i.* (*pret., p.p.* RAPPELLED; *p.pr.* RAPPELLING) descender a soga doble, descender con cuerda (alpinista).
rapper ['ræpər, B -ə] *s.* aldaba, aldabón.
rapport [ræ'pɔr, B -'pɔ] *s.* armonía, afinidad, simpatía, concordia, concordancia.
rapprochement [ˌræpˌroʊʃ'mɑnt, B -'prɔʃmɑŋ] *s.* (fr.) acercamiento, reconciliación.
rapscallion [ræp'skæljən] *s.* pícaro, bribón, pillo, tunante.
rapt [ræpt] *a.* 1. transportado, elevado (en espíritu). 2. arrobado, arrebatado, extasiado. 3. absorto.
raptorial [ræp'tɔrɪəl] *a.* (zool.) de rapiña, de presa, rapaz.
rapture ['ræptʃər, B -tʃə] *s.* 1. arrobamiento, embeleso, éxtasis, rapto, arrebato. 2. **to go into raptures,** entusiasmarse, extasiarse, dar muestras de entusiasmo. —*v.t.* (poét.) transportar, arrebatar, arrobar.
rapturous [-tʃərəs] *a.* extasiado, extático.
rapturously [-lɪ] *adv.* con arrobamiento, en éxtasis, arrobadamente, extáticamente.
rara avis ['rɛrə'eɪvəs, B 'rɑrə'æ-] rara avis, mirlo blanco.
rare [rɛr, B rɛə] *a.* 1. raro, enrarecido, tenue (gas, atmósfera). 2. raro, extraordinario, excepcional. 3. poco asado, casi crudo (la carne); **not too r.,** a medio asar.
rarebit ['rɛrbət, B 'rɛəbɪt] *s.* plato de queso derretido (a veces mezclado con cerveza) en tostadas.
rare earth, (quím.) tierra rara.
raree-show ['rɛrɪˌʃoʊ, B 'rɛərɪ-] *a.* mundonuevo, tutilimundi, mundonovi; p. ext., espectáculo callejero.
rarefaction [ˌrɛrə'fækʃən, B ˌrɛər-] *s.* rarefacción, enrarecimiento.
rarefactive [-'fæktɪv] *a.* rarificativo.
rarefiable [-'faɪəbəl] *a.* capaz de rarefacción.
rarefied ['rɛrəˌfaɪd, B 'rɛər-] *a.* 1. (fig.) enrarecido, delicado, sutil, esotérico (atmósfera, ambiente). 2. (fig.) muy elevado, altísimo (rango, etc.).
rarefy [-ˌfaɪ] *v.t.* (*pret., p.p.* RAREFIED; *p.pr.* RAREFYING) 1. enrarecer, rarificar, rarefacer. 2. (fig.) refinar, purificar, espiritualizar. —*v.i.* enrarecerse, rarificarse, rarefacerse.
rarely ['rɛrlɪ, B 'rɛəlɪ] *adv.* 1. raramente, rara vez. 2. extraordinariamente. 3. excelentemente, maravillosamente.
rareness [-nəs] *s.* rareza, raridad.
rareripe ['rɛrˌraɪp, B 'rɛəˌ-] *a.* de crecimiento o madurez precoz (fruta). —*s.* fruta o legumbre de crecimiento o madurez precoces.
raring ['rɛrɪŋ, B 'rɛər-] *a.* deseoso, ansioso, impaciente, entusiasta (por hacer algo), ej., *r. to go,* deseoso de luchar, de comenzar.
rarity [-ətɪ] *s.* 1. raridad, rareza, tenuidad; escasez, infrecuencia. 2. rareza, cosa rara, preciosidad, curiosidad.
rascal ['ræskəl, B 'rɑs-] *s.* 1. pícaro, bribón, pillo, truhán, tunante, bellaco, villano, maleante. 2. (fam.) pilluelo, mozalbete. —*a.* (ant.) de baja ralea, malo, vil.
rascality [ræs'kælətɪ, B rɑs-] *s.* picardía, bribonada, pillada, truhanería tunantada, bellaquería, vileza.
rascally ['ræskəlɪ, B 'rɑs-] *a.* pícaro, bribón, bajo, rastrero, vil. —*adv.* ruinmente, vilmente, pícaramente.
rase [reɪz] *v.t.* 1. rasar, arrasar, allanar; demoler, destruir. 2. (raro) borrar.
rash [ræʃ] *s.* 1. salpullido, sarpullido, roncha, erupción, eflorescencia, exantema. 2. (fig.) proliferación.
rash, *a.* imprudente, temerario, arriesgado, arrojado; apresurado, atropellado, precipitado; irreflexivo, atolondrado, desconsiderado.
rasher ['ræʃər, B -ə] *s.* lonja de tocino, torrezno, magra.
rashly [-lɪ] *adv.* imprudentemente, temerariamente; apresuradamente, precipitadamente; irreflexivamente, atolondradamente.
rashness [-nəs] *s.* imprudencia, temeridad; arrebato, precipitación; irreflexión, atolondramiento.
rasorial [rə'sɔrɪəl] *a.* (orn.) de los rasores, gallináceo.
rasp [ræsp, B rɑsp] *v.t.* 1. raspar, raer; restregar, frotar, refregar. 2. irritar, molestar, exacerbar. 3. pronunciar con voz áspera. —*v.i.* rozar, chirriar. —*s.* 1. escofina, raspador, lima. 2. chirrido; sonido estridente, voz áspera. 3. (carp., esc.) escarpelo.
raspberry ['ræzˌbɛrɪ, -bərɪ, B 'rɑzbərɪ] *s.* 1. (bot.) frambuesa, sangüesa, frambueso, sangüeso. 2. (jer.) sonido de desprecio, trompetilla (producido por la vibración de la lengua entre los labios). 3. (jer. G.B.) despedida. 4. (jer. G.B.) pedo. 5. **to give (someone) the r.,** abuchear, silbar, chiflar (a alguien).
rasped [ræspt, B rɑspt] *a.* de barbas (díc. del borde de las páginas de los libros hecho desigualmente).
rasper ['ræspər, B 'rɑspə] *s.* raspador, rallo, rallador.
rasping [-pɪŋ] *a.* 1. chirriador, chirreador, irritante. 2. raspante, áspero.
raspy [-pɪ] *a.* (RASPIER; RASPIEST) 1. chirriador, chirreador, chillón, irritante (voz, etc.). 2. áspero, basto. 3. irascible, irritable.
raster ['ræstər, B -tə] *s.* (t.v.) cuadro, red, trama, fondo sobre el que se construye la imagen.
rasure ['reɪʃər, B -ʒə] *s.* borradura, raspadura.
rat [ræt] *s.* 1. (zool.) rata. 2. (fam., E.U.) postizo para el pelo. 3. (jer.) vil, cobarde, canalla. 4. (jer.) desertor, renegado. 5. (jer.) esquirol. 6. soplón, delator. 7. **like a drowned r.,** como un pollo mojado; **rats!** (jer.) ¡tonterías!; **to smell a r.,** tener sospechas, haber gato encerrado. —*v.i.* (*pret., p.p.* RATTED; *p.pr.* RATTING) 1. desertar; actuar con cobardía o vileza. 2. cazar ratas (esp. con un perro). 3. (con *on*) (jer.) soplar, delatar a (alguien, esp. un cómplice), dar información de (alguien).
ratable ['reɪtəbəl] *a.* 1. tasable, valorable, valuable. 2. proporcional. 3. (G.B.) imponible.
ratably [-blɪ] *adv.* a prorrata, proporcionalmente.
ratafia [ˌrætə'fiə, B -'fɪə] *s.* 1. ratafía, rosoli (licor). 2. galleta de almendras.
ratan, *s., var. de* **rattan.**
ratany ['rætənɪ] *s.* (bot.) rotania.
rataplan [ˌrætə'plæn] *s.* rataplán.
rat-a-tat ['rætəˌtæt] **rat-a-tat-tat** [ˌrætəˌtæ'tæt] *s.* matraqueo; tras, tras (imitación del tableteo de la ametralladora).
rat-catcher ['rætˌkætʃər, B -ə] *s.* 1. cazador de ratas. 2. (G.B.) vestido de caza (informal).
ratch [rætʃ] *s.* rueda dentada con trinquete; cremallera.
ratchet ['rætʃət] *s.* 1. (mec.) trinquete, carraca, catraca, chicharra. 2. retén, uña (de trinquete).
ratchet brace, berbiquí de trinquete.
ratchet drill, taladro de trinquete, de carraca.
ratchet feed, (maq.) avance por trinquete.
ratchet jack, gato a crique o de cremallera; cric de cremallera.
ratchet screwdriver, destornillador de chicharra.
ratchet wheel, rueda de trinquete, rueda de estrella o de gatillo.
ratchet wrench, llave de trinquete o a crique o de chicharra.
rate [reɪt] *v.t.* reprender, reconvenir, amonestar. —*v.i.* regañar, reñir.
rate, *s.* 1. valor, precio, coste. 2. porcentaje, tanto por ciento, proporción. 3. tipo, cuota, tasa. 4. velocidad, ej., *at the r. of four miles an hour,* a la velocidad de cuatro millas por hora. 5. rango, clase. 6. tarifa de consumo (luz, gas, agua, etc.). 7. (e.p.) (*gen. pl.*) contribución, impuesto; (G.B.) impuesto municipal. 8. prima (de seguro), porcentaje (de una prima). 9. (ant.) cantidad, suma. 10. error o variación diaria de un reloj. 11. **at any r.,** en todo caso, sea como fuere, de todos modos; **at that r.,** a ese ritmo; de ese modo, si eso es verdad; **at the r. of,** a razón de, a una tasa de. —*v.t.* 1. considerar, tener por, dar por. 2. estimar, evaluar, fijar (precio); tasar, valuar, justipreciar. 3. clasificar (un buque mercante; un alumno); imponer (rango o clase). 4. (jer.) merecer (algo). —*v.i.* ser considerado como, ser tenido por, estar o ser clasificado como; **r. with (someone),** (jer.) gozar de la estima de (alguien), imponer simpatía o confianza en (alguien).
rateable, rateably, *vars. de* **ratable, ratably.**
rated capacity ['reɪtəd] potencia nominal (capacidad nominal).
rated power, (ing.) potencia nominal.
rated speed, (maq.) velocidad de régimen.
ratel ['reɪtəl] *s.* (zool.) ratel.
rate of climb, (aer.) régimen ascensional.
rate of exchange, tipo de cambio, cambio.
rate of speed, velocidad unitaria, índice de velocidad.
ratepayer ['reɪtˌpeɪər, B -ə] *s.* (G.B.) contribuyente.
ratepaying [-ɪŋ] *a.* (G.B.) contribuyente. —*s.* pago de impuestos.
rater ['reɪtər, B -ə] *s.* tasador; clasificador.
rathe [reɪð] *adv.* 1. (dial., poét.) temprano (en el día), al principio (de la estación). 2. (ant.) pronto, rápidamente. —*a.* 1. (poét.) matinal; que pertenece al principio de la estación. 2. (dial., poét.) que sucede temprano (en el día) o al comenzar una estación. 3. (ant.) presto; veloz; ansioso.
rather ['ræðər, B 'rɑðə] *adv.* 1. de preferencia, preferentemente, preferiblemente. 2. mejor dicho. 3. más bien, antes, antes bien. 4. un poco, algo; bastante. 5. **r.!** (fam.) ¡sí! ¡cómo no! ¡por supuesto!; **r. than,** antes que, más bien que; **(I, he,** etc.) **would** or **had r.,** preferiría; **(I, he,** etc.) **would r. have,** (yo, él) hubiera preferido.

rathskeller [ˈrɑtˌskɛlər, ˈræθ-, B ˈrɑt-ə] *s.* (alemán) restaurante o cantina en un sótano.
raticide [ˈrætəˌsaɪd] *s.* raticida.
ratification [ˌrætəfəˈkeɪʃən] *s.* ratificación, confirmación; aprobación, sanción.
ratifier [ˈrætəˌfaɪər, B -ə] *s.* ratificador.
ratify [-ˌfaɪ] *v.t.* (*pret., p.p.* RATIFIED; *p.pr.* RATIFYING) ratificar, confirmar; aprobar, sancionar.
ratihabition [ˌrætɪhəˈbɪʃən] *s.* (der.) ratihabición, ratificación, sanción.
ratiné, ratine [ˌrætəˈnəɪ] *s.* (tej.) ratina.
rating [ˈreɪtɪŋ] *s.* reprimenda, represión, regaño, amonestación, sermón.
rating, *s.* 1. clasificación (de acuerdo con el grado, rango, clase). 2. avalúo o imposición (de un impuesto o contribución). 3. (com.) renombre, reputación, crédito. 4. (mar.) clase, categoría (de un buque mercante o de un marinero). 5. (G.B.) (*pl.*) marinero (s) en la armada británica.
ratio [ˈreɪʃoʊ, -ʃɪˌoʊ, B -ʃɪˌoʊ] *s.* 1. relación, proporción; porcentaje. 2. (mat.) razón. 3. (raro) porción, ración.
ratiocinate [ˌrætɪˈoʊsəˌneɪt, ræʃɪ-, -ˈɑs-, B ˌrætɪˈɔs-] *v.i.* raciocinar, razonar.
ratiocination [-ˌoʊsəˈneɪʃən, -ˌɑs-, B -ˌɔs-] *s.* raciocinación, razonamiento, raciocinio, argumento.
ratiocinator [-ˈoʊsəˌneɪtər, -ˈɑs-, B -ˈɔs-ə] *s.* razonador.
ration [ˈræʃən, ˈreɪʃən, B ˈræʃən] *s.* 1. ración, porción (esp. de provisiones o alimentos). 2. cuota. 3. (mil.) ración; (*pl.*) raciones, provisiones. —*v.t.* racionar.
rational [ˈræʃənəl] *a.* 1. racional, inteligente. 2. (mat.) racional.
rationale [ˌræʃəˈnæl, B -ˈnɑl] *s.* 1. razón fundamental; motivo principal, razón de ser. 2. exposición razonada.
rationalism [ˈræʃənəlˌɪzəm] *s.* (filos.) racionalismo.
rationalist [-əst] *a., s.* racionalista.
rationalistic [ˌræʃənəlˈɪstɪk] *a.* racionalista.
rationalistically [-tɪkəlɪ] *adv.* de manera racionalista.
rationality [-əˈnælətɪ] *s.* 1. racionalidad. 2. opinión o acto racional. 3. racionalismo.
rationalization [-ənələˈzeɪʃən, B -əlaɪ-] *s.* 1. racionalización, reorganización racional (de industria, producción.) 2. explicación racional.
rationalize [ˈræʃənəlˌaɪz] *v.t.* 1. dar explicación racional a, explicar racionalmente; buscar explicación racional a. 2. reorganizar (industria, producción, etc.) en forma racional.
rationally [-ɪ] *adv.* racionalmente, inteligentemente.
ratite [ˈræˌtaɪt] *a., s.* (orn.) rátida.
ratlike [ˈrætˌlaɪk] *a.* ratonesco, ratonil.
ratlin, ratline [ˈrætlən] *s.* (mar.) (*ú. gen. en pl.*) flechaste, flechadura.
ratoon [ræˈtun, B rə-] *s.* (bot.) retoño, brote de una raíz cortada; soca, retoño de caña de azúcar. —*v.i.* crecer o brotar (un retoño o de un retoño).
rat race, (jer.) competencia inexorable (para el progreso profesional, social o económico).
ratsbane [ˈrætsˌbeɪn] *s.* raticida, esp. arsénico blanco.
rattail file [ˈrætˌteɪl-] lima de cola de rata.
rattan [ræˈtæn, rə-] *s.* 1. (bot.) roten, rota, junco de Indias, caña de Indias, caña de Bengala, palasan. 2. roten (bastón).
ratteen [ræˈtin] *s.* (tej.) ratina, bayeta, droguete, frisa.
ratter [ˈrætər, B -ə] *s.* 1. desertor, renegado, esquirol. 2. cazador de ratas; perro cazador de ratas.
rattle [ˈrætəl] *v.i.* 1. matraquear, guachapear (una herradura o chapa de hierro). 2. (fam.) (gen. con *on, away, along*) charlatanear, parlotear, hablar por los codos. 3. (gen. con *down, along, past,* etc.) ir o pasar traqueteando, traquetear (vehículo). —*v.t.* 1. batir o sacudir con ruido de matraca, hacer resonar, castañetear. 2. (gen. con *off, out, away,* etc.) decir o recitar (verso, cuento, juramento) con precipitación. 3. batir (huidero) para levantar la caza; perseguir con empeño. 4. (fam.) consternar, desconcertar, confundir; inquietar, azorar, alarmar. 5. (mar.) (ú. gen. con *down*) poner rebengues o flechaduras(a). 6. **r. the saber,** blandir la espada, amenazar con guerra. —*s.* 1. cascabeleo, matraque, traqueteo. 2. cascabel, matraca, carraca. 3. sonajero (de niño). 4. cascabel (del crótalo). 5. ruido, bulla, baraúnda. 6. (t. **death-r.**) estertor (de muerte).
rattlebox [-ˌbɑks, B -ˌbɔks] *s.* 1. cascabel (juguete). 2. charlador.
rattlebrain [-ˌbreɪn] **rattlehead** [-ˌhɛd] **rattlepate** [-ˌpeɪt] *s.* cabeza de chorlito, persona casquivana.
rattlebrained [-ˈbreɪnd] **rattleheaded** [-ˈhɛdəd] **rattlepated** [-ˈpeɪtəd] *a.* casquivano, atolondrado, alegre de cascos, ligero de cascos.
rattler [ˈrætlər, B -lə] *s.* 1. (zool.) (serpiente de) cascabel. 2. matraca. 3. (fam., E.U.) tren de carga. 4. (jer.) algo extraordinario.
rattlesnake [-əlˌsneɪk] *s.* (zool.) (serpiente de) cascabel, culebra de cascabel, crótalo.
rattlesnake plantain, (bot.) (variedad de) orquídea de hojas jaspeadas.
rattlesnake root, (bot.) lechera, amaya.
rattlesnake weed, (bot.) vellosilla, oreja de raton.
rattletrap [ˈrætəlˌtræp] *s.* 1. carricoche. 2. trasto, cosa destartalada. 3. (jer. G.B.) parlanchín, hablador, charlatán.
rattling [ˈrætlɪŋ] *a.* 1. estrepitoso. 2. vivaz, vivo, animado, vigoroso. 3. (fam.) excelente, espléndido. —*adv.* (fam.) muy, en sumo grado.
rattly [-lɪ] *a.* que matraquea o traquetea, ruidoso.
ratton [ˈrætən] *s.* (dial.) rata, ratón.
rattrap [ˈrætˌtræp] *s.* 1. ratonera, trampa para cazar ratas. 2. casa destartalada. 3. (fig.) callejón sin salida, situación desesperante.
ratty [ˈrætɪ] *a.* (RATTIER; RATTIEST) 1. ratonero, ratonil, ratonesco. 2. (jer.) desaseado, andrajoso, zarrapastroso.
raucity [ˈrɔsətɪ] *s.* ronquera, bronquedad.
raucous [ˈrɔkəs] *a.* ronco, bronco, áspero, agrio, estridente (voz, sonido, etc.).
raucously [-lɪ] *adv.* roncamente, ásperamente.
raucousness [-nəs] *s.* ronquera, bronquedad, aspereza, carraspera.
raunchy [ˈrɔntʃɪ, ˈrɑn-, B ˈrɔn-] *a.* (jer.) desaseado, destartalado.
rauwolfia [rəˈwʊlfɪə] *s.* (bot.) rauwolfia.
ravage [ˈrævɪdʒ] *s.* asolamiento, devastación, estrago, destrucción. —*v.t.* asolar, devastar, arruinar, destruir.
ravager [-ər, B -ə] *s.* devastador.
rave [reɪv] *v.i.* 1. delirar, desvariar, devanear, disparatar, desbarrar. 2. bramar, enfurecerse; rabiar. 3. **r. about,** hablar con excesivo entusiasmo de, deshacerse en elogios de, hacerse lenguas de. —*v.t.* pronunciar o expresar con desvarío (disparates, dolor, sentimientos). —*s.* 1. desvarío, delirio, disparate, devaneo. 2. (jer.) apasionamiento, enamoramiento. 3. (jer.) alabanza extravagante o exagerada.
ravehook [ˈreɪvˌhʊk] *s.* (mar.) descalcador, magujo.
ravel [ˈrævəl] *v.t.* (*pret., p.p.* RAVELED O RAVELLED; *p.pr.* RAVELLING O RAVELLING) (ú. gen. con *out*) 1. deshilar, destorcer, deshilachar, destejer, deshebrar, deshacer, desmoronarse en el borde (carreteras). 2. desenredar, desenmarañar, desembrollar; hacer simple o llano. —*v.i.* 1. (gen. con *out*) deshilacharse, deshilarse, deshacerse. 2. (ant.) enredarse, confundirse. —*s.* 1. enredo, embrollo, lío, maraña, confusión. 2. hilacha, deshiladura.
ravelin [ˈrævlɪn] *s.* (fort.) ravellín.
raveling, ravelling [ˈrævəlɪŋ] *s.* deshiladura, hilacha.
ravelment [-mənt] *s.* embrollo, maraña, enredo, confusión, lío.
raven [ˈrævən] *v.t.* 1. devorar, engullir, tragar. 2. (ant.) apresar, prender, apoderarse de algo por fuerza, rapiñar. —*v.i.* comer con avidez.
raven [ˈreɪvən] *s.* (orn.) cuervo. —*a.* negro y brillante.
ravening [ˈrævənɪŋ] *a.* 1. rapaz, voraz. 2. hambriento, famélico. —*s.* rapacidad, rapiña.
ravenous [-nəs] *a.* 1. rapaz, voraz. 2. famélico, hambriento. 3. **to be r. for,** estar ansioso de.
ravenously [-lɪ] *adv.* vorazmente, con rapacidad.
ravenousness [-nəs] *s.* rapacidad, voracidad.
ravin [ˈrævən] *s.* 1. rapacidad, rapiña. 2. presa; botín.
ravine [rəˈvin] *s.* barranca, barranco, cañada, hondonada.
raving [ˈreɪvɪŋ] *s.* desvarío, delirio, devaneo. —*a.* 1. desvariado, que delira, de atar, ej., *r. mad,* loco de atar. 2. extraordinario, soberbio (belleza, etc.).
ravioli [ˌrævɪˈoʊlɪ] *s. pl.* (cocina) ravioles.
ravish [ˈrævɪʃ] *v.t.* 1. arrebatar, llevar por fuerza, raptar, secuestrar. 2. arrebatar, encantar, atraer, cautivar, apasionar. 3. violar, estuprar.
ravisher [-ər, B -ə] *s.* 1. arrebatador, cautivador, 2. violador, estuprador.
ravishing [-ɪŋ] *a.* arrebatador, encantador, cautivador, arrobador.
ravishingly [-lɪ] *adv.* de manera arrebatadora o encantadora, arrebatadoramente, encantadoramente.
ravishment [-mənt] *s.* 1. arrebato, éxtasis, arrobamiento, embeleso, rapto, transporte. 2. estupro, violación.
raw [rɔ] *a.* 1. crudo, sin cocer. 2. en bruto, no elaborado o manufacturado; en rama (textiles); sin cocer (ladrillos); crudo, sin curtir (cuero); sin depurar (licores). 3. inconcluso; inexperto, novato, bisoño, nuevo. 4. rudo, tosco, vulgar. 5. en carne viva, despellejado, pelado. 6. húmedo, descapacible, frío, destemplado, frígido. 7. (jer.) desnudo. —*s.* 1. herida en carne viva, despellejadura. 2. punto sensible (de sentimientos, etc.). 3. persona sin cultura. 4. **in the r.,** en pelota, en cueros, desnudo.
Rawalpindi [ˌrɑwəlˈpɪndɪ, B ˈrɑ-ˌpɪn-] *s.* Rawalpindi, capital de Pakistán (1960-66).
rawboned [ˈrɔˈboʊnd] *a.* huesudo, enjuto, magro.
raw cotton, algodón en rama.
raw deal, mala pasada; tratamiento severo o injusto; **to give one a r. d.,** jugarle a uno una mala pasada; tratar a uno con severidad o injusticia.
raw flesh, carne viva.
raw hand, novato, novicio.
rawhide [-ˌhaɪd] *s.* cuero al pelo, cuero verde o crudo, cuero sin curtir. —*v.t.* azotar (con látigo de cuero crudo).
rawish [-ɪʃ] *a.* algo crudo, un tanto crudo.
rawly [ˈrɔlɪ] *adv.* crudamente, rudamente, toscamente.
raw material, materia prima, materia bruta.
rawness [-nəs] *s.* 1. crudeza. 2. inexperiencia. 3. rudeza, tosquedad, vulgaridad.

raw silk, seda en bruto o en rama, seda cruda.
raw spirits, licores puros o sin mezcla.
raw tallow, sebo puro o en rama.
raw umber, ocre natural, siena natural (pintura), pardo de manganeso.
raw weather, tiempo crudo.
ray [reɪ] *s.* 1. rayo, línea de luz; resplandor, brillo. 2. (fig.) vislumbre, indicio (que ilumina el entendimiento). 3. raya, línea delgada; trayectoria. 4. (bot.) radio (pedicelo en las umbelíferas). 5. (fís.) rayo (de energía radiante). 6. (zool.) espina (de la aleta de los peces); brazo (de una estrella de mar). 7. (ant.) mirada, vista, percepción, visión. 8. (ict.) raya, manta. —*v.i.* brillar, irradiar, radiar. —*v.t.* 1. irradiar o radiar (un mensaje, rayos, etc.). 2. exponer a radiación (de rayos X, luz ultravioleta, etc.). 3. (fam.) radiografiar, fotografiar con rayos X.
ray filter, pantalla fotocrómica.
ray grass, (bot.) vallico.
rayless ['reɪləs] *a.* sin rayos, obscuro.
ray of light, (ópt.) rayo de luz; (fig.) rayo de luz.
rayon ['reɪˌɑn, B -ˌɔn] *s.* (tej.) rayón, rayona (tejido, fibra).
raze [reɪz] *v.t.* 1. raspar, rasar, cortar. 2. arrasar, demoler, destruir. 3. (raro) herir ligeramente. 4. (ant.) borrar.
razee [reɪ'zi, B rə'zi] *s.* (mar.) buque rebajado (a menor porte).
razor ['reɪzər, B -zə] *s.* navaja de afeitar.
razorback [-ˌbæk] *s.* (zool.) 1. rorcual. 2. cerdo cimarrón. —*a.* de lomo angosto y filudo (caballo, etc.).
razor-backed [ˌreɪzər'bækt, B -zə'-] *a.* de lomo angosto y filudo (caballo, etc.).
razor-bill ['reɪzərˌbɪl, B -zəˌ-] *s.* (orn.) (variedad de) alca.
razor blade, hoja de afeitar.
razor clam, (zool.) muergo, muérgano, macha, mango de cuchillo, navaja (marisco).
razor strop, suavizador, asentador.
razz [ræz] *s.* (jer.) sonido de desprecio (producido por la vibración de la lengua entre los labios). —*v.t., v.i* tomar el pelo a, hacer zumba de, burlarse de.
razzle-dazzle ['ræzəl'dæzəl] *s.* 1. alboroto, confusión, excitación. 2. abigarramiento de colores; deslumbramiento. 3. tiovivo ondulante.
razzmatazz [ˌræzmə'tæz] *s.* 1. alboroto, confusión. 2. parloteo confuso, cháchara engañosa. 3. fuerza, brío, vigor.
Rb *símbolo de* **rubidium,** rubidio (Rb).
R. C. *abrev. de* 1. **Roman Catholic,** Católico Romano. 2. **Red Cross,** Cruz Roja.
RCAF *abrev. de* **Royal Canadian Air Force,** Real Fuerza Aérea del Canadá.
Rd. *abrev. de* **road,** calle; camino.
re [reɪ] *s.* (mús.) re.
re [ri, reɪ, B ri] *prep.* (der., com.) (t. **in re**) con referencia a, acerca de.
Re *símb. de* **rhenium,** renio (Re).
reabsorb [ˌriəb'sɔrb, -'zɔrb, B -'sɔb, -'zɔb] *v.t.* resorber, reabsorber.
reabsorption [-'sɔrpʃən, -'zɔrp-, B -'sɔp-, -'zɔp-] *s.* resorción, reabsorción.
reach [ritʃ] *v.t.* 1. (gen. con *out*) extender, alargar, estirar. 2. tocar; dar en (con un proyectil). 3. entregar, alargar. 4. llegar a, alcanzar. 5. afectar, impresionar. 6. comunicarse con (alguien), notificar a (alguien). 7. **r. one's heart,** tocar al corazón de uno. —*v.i.* 1. extender o estirar el brazo o la mano. 2. extenderse, estirarse. 3. llegar, alcanzar (la voz, vista, tiro de un arma, etc.). 4. (mar.) navegar de bolina, ceñir el viento. 5. **r. for (o after),** esforzarse por coger; aspirar a, anhelar; **r. into,** meter la mano en. —*s.* 1. extensión, expansión. 2. alcance. 3. poder, facultad, capacidad (mental). 4. tramo, trecho, parte recta entre dos curvas (del río, canal). 5. barra de extensión. 6. (mar.) bordada. 7. **beyond r. of, out of r. of,** fuera del alcance de; **within r.,** al alcance de la mano, a tiro; **within r. of,** al alcance de; a corta distancia de.
reachable ['ritʃəbəl] *a.* asequible.
reach-me-down ['ritʃmɪˌdaʊn] *s.* (fam. G.B.) ropa barata o de segunda mano.
react [rɪ'ækt] *v.i.* 1. reaccionar, responder. 2. (con *upon*) producir efecto (en). 3. actuar, comportarse. 4. (mil.) contraatacar.
reactance [-'æktəns] *s.* (elec.) reactancia, reacción de autoinducción.
reaction [-'ækʃən] *s.* 1. reacción (a un estímulo). 2. (la) reacción, tendencia retrógrada (esp. en política). 3. respuesta, contestación. 4. (med., quím., psic., fisiol., mec.) reacción. 5. (mil.) contraataque.
reactionary [-ʃəˌnɛrɪ, B -nərɪ] *a.* reaccionario. —*s.* (*pl.* REACTIONARIES) retrógrado, reaccionario (esp. en política).
reaction engine, motor de reacción.
reaction motor, motor de reacción.
reaction turbine, turbina de reacción.
reactivate [ri'æktəˌveɪt] *v.t.* activar de nuevo, reponer en servicio, reactivar.
reactivation [-ˌæktə'veɪʃən] *s.* reactivación.
reactive [-'æktɪv] *a.* reactivo.
reactivity [-ˌæk'tɪvətɪ] *s.* reactividad.
reactor [-'æktər, B -tə] *s.* 1. (quím.) reactivo. 2. (elec.) reactor, bobina de reación. 3. (fís.) reactor (nuclear).
read [rid] *v.t.* (*pret., p.p.* READ [rɛd]; *p.pr.* READING) 1. leer. 2. (pr. con *aloud, out u off*) leer en voz alta. 3. interpretar, descifrar. 4. estudiar (una materia, especialidad). 5. marcar, registrar, indicar (díc. de instrumentos medidores). 6. **r. into,** atribuir (sentido distinto, no expresado, etc.) a (texto); **r. one a lesson,** (fig.) leerle a uno la cartilla, reprender a uno; **r. oneself hoarse,** seguir leyendo hasta enronquecer; **r. oneself stupid,** aturdirse con (mucha) lectura; **r. someone's hand,** leer la palma de la mano a alguien; **r. (right) through,** leer de cabo a rabo; **r. someone out (of),** expulsar a alguien (de una organización). —*v.i.* 1. leer, saber leer. 2. rezar, leerse (texto, inscripción, etc.). 3. sonar al leer (bien, mal, etc.). 4. ofrecer lectura (amena, desagradable, etc.) 5. r. **between the lines,** leer entre líneas; **r. of** (o about), leer acerca de, informarse, enterarse (por lectura). — [rɛd] *a.* leído, instruido, informado (por medio de lecturas).
readability [ˌridə'bɪlətɪ] *s.* interés, amenidad de estilo.
readable ['ridəbəl] *a.* 1. legible (díc. de la escritura). 2. interesante, que vale la pena leerse; de lectura fácil y amena.
readableness [-nəs] *s.* interés, amenidad de estilo.
readably [-blɪ] *adv.* legiblemente, en forma legible.
reader ['rɪdər, B -ə] *s.* 1. lector. 2. elocucionista, declamador, recitador profesional. 3. empleado que lee medidas o índices. 4. corrector de pruebas. 5. lector (de casa editorial). 6. libro de lectura; antología, selección de lecturas. 7. (relig.) (t. **lay r.**) lector (que lee enseñanzas u oraciones sagradas). 8. (educ.) conferencista. 9. (*pl.*) (jer.) naipes marcados (con el fin de enfullar).
readership [-ˌʃɪp] *s.* 1. lectoría. 2. (número de) lectores (de un periódico, semanario, revista, etc.).
readily ['rɛdəlɪ] *adv.* 1. prontamente, sin demora; servicialmente. 2. sin dificultad, fácilmente.
readiness [-ɪnəs] *s.* 1. prontitud, celeridad. 2. habilidad, aptitud, destreza. 3. disposición favorable. 4. estado de alerta, estado de preparación. 5. **to be in r. (for),** estar listo o preparado (para).
reading ['ridɪŋ] *s.* 1. lectura. 2. recital, conferencia, lectura en público (de una obra, etc.). 3. material de lectura; contexto, contenido (de un escrito). 4. medida, indicación, cantidad (que marca o señala un instrumento). 5. interpretación (de un papel); versión. —*a.* 1. lector, estudioso, que lee o estudia. 2. de lectura, para leer.
reading matter, (material de) lectura.
reading room, sala de lectura.
readjust [ˌriə'dʒʌst] *v.t.* reajustar, readaptar, ajustar de nuevo.
readjuster [-'dʒʌstər, B -tə] *s.* reajustador, readaptador.
readjustment [-'dʒʌstmənt] *s.* readaptación, reajuste.
readmission [ˌriəd'mɪʃən] *s.* readmisión.
readmission ticket, contraseña de salida (en teatro, etc.).
readmit [-'mɪt] *v.t.* readmitir.
readmittance [-əns] *s.* readmisión.
ready ['rɛdɪ] *a.* 1. listo, preparado, dispuesto. 2. pronto. fácil (respuesta, sonrisa, etc.). 3. diestro, hábil, capaz. 4. vivo, ágil. 5. a la mano, disponible. 6. (ant.) inmediato (pago). 7. (ant.) presente, aquí (como respuesta a un llamado). 8. **r. to,** dispuesto a; propenso a, inclinado a; a punto de; **to get r.,** alistar(se), preparar(se); to **make r.,** preparar, alistar. —*v.t.* (*pret., p.p.* READIED; *p.pr.* READYING) preparar, alistar. —*s.* (mil.) posición de apresto.
ready box, (mar.) caja de munición lista.
ready-made ['rɛdɪ'meɪd] *a.* 1. (ya) hecho; confeccionado, hecho (para venta), ej., *r.-made clothing,* ropa hecha. 2. preconcebido, ej., *r.-made beliefs,* ideas preconcebidas, prejuicios.
ready-mix [-ˌmɪks] *s.* 1. mezcla preparada. 2. pintura hecha o preparada. 3. cemento premezclado, hormigón de fábrica.
ready money, dinero efectivo, dinero contante; dinero disponible.
readyprint [-ˌprɪnt] *s.* (impr.) pliegos semiimpresos; suplemento ya impreso.
ready-to-wear [-tə'wɛr, B -'wɛə] *a.* hecho, ya hecho, hecho de antemano (díc. esp. de la ropa), listo para llevar.
ready-witted [-'wɪtəd] *a.* de ingenio vivo.
reaffirm [ˌriə'fɛrm, B -'fɜm] *v.t.* reafirmar, reforzar, confirmar.
reaffirmation [-ˌæfər'meɪʃən, B -ˌæfə'-] *s.* reafirmación, confirmación.
reagent [rɪ'eɪdʒənt] *s.* (quím.) reactivo.
reagin [-dʒən] *s.* (fisiol.) reagina.
real ['riəl] *a.* 1. real, verdadero, genuino, legítimo, auténtico. 2. (mat., filos., der.) real. 3. **he is a r. man,** es todo un hombre, es un hombre de verdad; **this is the r. thing,** esto es genuino, esto es legítimo; **for r.,** (jer.) de veras. —*adv.* (jer.) muy, de veras, sumamente. —*s.* (con *the*) la realidad, lo real.
real ['riəl, B reɪ'ɑl] *s.* real (moneda de plata de España).
real estate, r. property, bienes raíces o inmuebles; arraigo; propiedad inmueble.
real estate agency, agencia inmobiliaria.
real estate agent, agente de propriedad inmobiliaria, agente inmobiliario.
realgar [rɪ'ælgər, B -gə] *s.* (min.) rejalgar.
realign [ˌriə'laɪn] *v.t.* realinear.
realignment [-mənt] *s.* realinación.

real image, (ópt.) imagen real.
realism [ˈriəˌlɪzəm] *s.* realismo.
realist [-ləst] *a., s.* realista.
realistic [ˌriəˈlɪstɪk] *a.* realista.
realistically [-tɪkəlɪ] *adv.* de manera realista, con realismo.
reality [rɪˈæləti] *s.* 1. realidad. 2. realismo, ej., *reproduced with startling r.,* reproducido con un realismo asombroso. 3. **in r.,** en verdad, en realidad, efectivamente.
realizable [ˈriəˌlaɪzəbəl, B ˈrɪə-] *a.* 1. realizable, factible. 2. imaginable.
realization [ˌriələˈzeɪʃən, B ˌrɪəlaɪ-] *s.* 1. comprensión, accion de darse cuenta. 2. realización; conversión (en dinero).
realize [ˈriəˌlaɪz, B ˈrɪə-] *v.t.* 1. comprender, darse cuenta de, hacerse cargo de. 2. realizar, efectuar, ejecutar. 3. dar verosimilitud o realismo a. 4. (com.) realizar, vender, convertir en dinero o en efectivo, ej., *r. assets,* convertir en dinero el haber. 5. obtener, ganar; producir, rendir, ej., *r. large profits,* obtener grandes beneficios.
realizer [-ər, B -ə] *s.* ejecutor, creador.
real-life, de la vida real, en la vida real, auténtico.
reallocate [riˈæləˌkeɪt] *v.t.* volver a asignar o destinar, señalar o distribuir de nuevo, reasignar.
reallocation [-ˌæləˈkeɪʃən] *s.* nueva colocación, nueva asignación o distribución, reasignación.
really [ˈriəlɪ, B ˈrɪə-] *adv.* 1. realmente, verdaderamente; efectivamente. 2. positivamente, de veras, en realidad. 3. **r.?** ¿es verdad? ¿es posible?; **r. and truly,** real y verdaderamente.
realm [rɛlm] *s.* 1. (lit. y fig.) reino, ej., *the laws of the r.,* las leyes del reino, *the r. of fantasy,* el reino de la fantasía. 2. (zool.) extension de una fauna.
real McCoy [ˈriəlməˈkɔɪ, B ˈrɪ-] **the r. M.,** el auténtico, el legítimo (cosa, producto, etc.); **this is the r. M.,** (fam.) esto es excelente.
realness [ˈriəlnəs, B ˈrɪəl-] *s.* realidad.
real number, (mat.) cantidad real.
real time, (comput.) tiempo real.
realtor [-tər, B -tə] *s.* (E.U.) corredor de bienes raíces, corredor de fincas, agente de propiedad inmobiliaria, agente inmobiliario.
realty [-tɪ] *s.* (*pl.* REALTIES) bienes raíces, bienes inmuebles.
ream [rim] *s.* 1. resma (de papel) 2. (*pl.*) (fam.) montones (de algo escrito, impreso o hablado). —*v.t.* 1. agrandar, dar más cabida. 2. escariar, abocardar. 3. extraer el jugo de (limón, naranja, etc.). 4. (mar.) alisar.
reamer [ˈrimər, B -ə] *s.* 1. (mec.) escariador, ensanchador; fresador. 2. exprimidor (de jugo de fruta). 3. (mar.) alegra.
reanimate [riˈænəˌmeɪt] *v.t.* reanimar, revivir, resucitar, vivificar, alentar.
reanimation [-ˌænəˈmeɪʃən] *s.* reanimación.
reap [rip] *v.t.* 1. segar, cortar, cercenar. 2. cosechar; recoger, recolectar. —*v.i.* cosechar; obtener el fruto del trabajo propio; hacer agosto.
reaper [ˈripər, B -pə] *s.* 1. segador, máquina segadora. 2. **the R., the Grim R.,** la Muerte, la Parca.
reaping hook [-pɪŋ-] hoz, segadera.
reaping machine, máquina segadora.
reaping time, siega.
reappear [ˌriəˈpɪr, B ˈriəˈpɪə] *v.i.* reaparecer, resurgir.
reappearance [-əns, B -rəns] *s.* reaparición, resurgimiento.
reappoint [-ˈpɔɪnt] *v.t.* volver a nombrar (en un cargo, etc.), designar de nuevo.
reappointment [ˌriəˈpɔɪntmənt] *s.* nuevo nombramiento (en el mismo cargo).
reapportion [-ˈpɔrʃən, B -ˈpɔʃən] *v.t.* proporcionar o repartir de nuevo.
reappraisal [-ˈpreɪzəl] *s.* revaluación, retasa, reconsideración.
rear [rɪr, B rɪə] *s.* 1. (mil.) retaguardia. 2. zaga, espalda; fondo; cola, parte de atrás. 3. (t. **r. end**) nalgas. 4. **at the r. of,** detrás de; **in the r.,** de atrás; en el fondo, a la zaga; **to bring** (o **to close**) **up the r.,** cerrar la marcha. —*a.* 1. posterior, trasero, de atrás. 2. de retaguardia.
rear, *v.t.* 1. levantar, alzar, elevar. 2. edificar, erigir, construir. 3. criar, fomentar, cultivar; cuidar, educar. —*v.i.* encabritarse, empinarse (un caballo).
rear admiral, contraalmirante.
rear axle, eje trasero; (aut.) puente trasero, eje trasero.
rear drive, (aut.) tracción trasera, tracción posterior.
rear echelon, (mil.) escalón de retaguardia.
rear end, (fam.) trasero.
rear-engined, con motor trasero.
rear guard, (mil.) retaguardia.
rearhorse [ˈrɪrˌhɔrs, B ˈrɪəˌhɔs] *s.* (ento.) mantis religiosa, predicador, mamboretá (Am.).
rearm [riˈɑrm, B ˈriˈɑm] *v.t.* (mil.) rearmar.
rearmament [-ˈɑrməmənt, B -ˈɑmə-] *s.* rearme.
rearmost [ˈrɪrˌmoʊst, B ˈrɪəˌ-] *a.* último de atrás, último de todos; de más atrás.
rearrange [ˌriəˈreɪndʒ, B ˈriə-] *v.t.* volver a arreglar o disponer; cambiar de orden.
rearrangement [ˌriəˈreɪndʒmənt] *s.* nuevo arreglo, nueva disposición, reordenamiento.
rear sight, (arm.) alza (de armas de fuego).
rearview mirror [ˈrɪrˌvju-, B ˈrɪəˌ-] (aut.) espejo **retrovisor.**
rearward [-wərd, B -wəd] *a.* postrero, último. —*adv.* hacia atrás. —*s.* retaguardia, cola.
rear window, (aut.) ventanilla trasera.
reason [ˈrizən] *s.* 1. razón, motivo, causa; argumento; justificación, explicación. 2. razón, intelecto, ej., *he has lost his r.,* ha perdido la razón. 3. sensatez, moderación, prudencia. 4. (ant.) cuenta, relación; justicia; corrección. 5. **by r. of,** a causa de, en virtud de; **in** (o **within**) **r.,** dentro de lo razonable; **to bring to r.,** hacer entrar en razón; **to listen to r.,** dejarse convencer; **to stand to r.,** ser lógico, estar claro; **with r.,** con razón. —*v.i.* 1. discutir, ej., *we reasoned with him for an hour,* discutimos con él durante una hora. 2. raciocinar. —*v.t.* 1. razonar, ej., *a reasoned exposition,* una exposición razonada. 2 debatir, argüir. 3. **r. (someone) into,** persuadir (a alguien); **r. (someone) out of,** persuadir (a alguien) de la irracionalidad de, ej., *r. him out of his fears,* persuadirle de la irracionalidad de sus temores; **r. (something) out,** analizar, resolver por lógica (algo).
reasonable [-əbəl] *a.* 1. racional, dotado de razón. 2. razonable, justo; sensato. 3. razonable, módico, moderado, mediano, regular.
reasonableness [-nəs] *s.* racionalidad, moderación, sensatez.
reasonably [-əblɪ] *adv.* razonablemente.
reasoner [-ər, B -ə] *s.* razonador; argumentador.
reasoning [-ɪŋ] *s.* 1. razonamiento. 2. raciocinio.
reasonless [-ləs] *a.* sin razón; que no tiene sentido.
reassemble [ˌriəˈsɛmbəl, B ˈriə-] *v.t., v.i.* volver a reunir(se); volver a armar(se) o juntar(se).
reassert [-ˈsɜrt, B -ˈsɜt] *v.t.* reafirmar.
reassign [-ˈsaɪn] *v.t.* volver a asignar, destinar o repartir de nuevo.
reassignment [-mənt] *s.* nuevo destino; nueva repartición, reinstalación.
reassociate [-ˈsoʊʃɪˌeɪt] *v.t., v.i.* volver a asociar(se).
reassume [-ˈsum, B -ˈsjum] *v.t.* reasumir.
reassurance [ˌriəˈʃʊrəns, B -ˈʃʊər-] *s.* 1. seguridad, confianza, garantía o afirmación repetidas; circunstancia tranquilizadora o satisfactoria. 2. (com.) reaseguro.
reassure [-ˈʃʊr, B -ˈʃʊə] *v.t.* 1. tranquilizar, aquietar, satisfacer, dar seguridades a. 2. (com.) reasegurar, volver a asegurar.
reassuring [-ɪŋ, B -rɪŋ] *a.* tranquilizador, apaciguante.
reassuringly [-lɪ] *adv.* de modo tranquilizador, tranquilizadoramente.
reawaken [-ˈweɪkən] *v.t., v.i.* volver a despertar(se); reanimar (la atención, el interés, etc.).
reb [rɛb] *s.* (fam., E.U.) *abrev. de* **rebel,** soldado de la Confederación en la Guerra de Secesión.
rebaptize [ˌriˈbæpˌtaɪz] *v.t.* **rebautizar;** volver a dar nombre.
rebarbative [rɪˈbɑrbətɪv, B -ˈbɑbə-] *a.* repulsivo, repugnante, repelente; molesto.
rebate [ˈriˌbeɪt] *s.* rebaja, descuento, deducción; disminución, reducción; reembolso, ej., *a r. to a shipper,* reembolso a un embarcador. —[ˈriˌbeɪt, rɪˈbeɪt] *v.t.* rebajar, descontar, reembolsar.
rebate [ˈriˌbeɪt, ˈræbət, B ˈræb-] *var. de* rabbet.
rebato, *var. de* **rabato.**
rebec, rebeck [ˈriˌbɛk] *s.* (mús.) **rabel** (antiguo instrumento de cuerdas, precursor del violín).
rebel [ˈrɛbəl] *a., s.* rebelde, faccioso, insurrecto, insurgente. — [rɪˈbɛl] *v.i.* (*pret., p.p.* REBELLED; *p.pr.* REBELLING) rebelarse, insurreccionarse, sublevarse, insubordinarse; levantarse, alzarse.
rebellion [rɪˈbɛljən] *s.* 1. rebelión, insurrección, levantamiento, alzamiento, sublevación, revuelta, amotinamiento. 2. resistencia, desafío, oposición (a las autoridades).
rebellious [-jəs] *a.* rebelde, faccioso, insurrecto; refractario.
rebelliously [-lɪ] *adv.* rebeldemente, con rebeldía, refractariamente.
rebelliousness [-nəs] *s.* rebeldía, insubordinación.
rebirth [riˈbɜrθ, B ˈribɜθ] *s.* 1. renacimiento. 2. reencarnación.
reboant [ˈrɛboʊənt] *a.* (poét.) resonante.
rebore [riˈbɔr, B ˈriˈbɔ] *v.t.* (mec.) rectificar (un cilindro).
reborn [riˈbɔrn, B ˈriˈbɔn] *a.* 1. renacido. 2. **to be r.,** volver a nacer.
rebound [rɪˈbaʊnd] *v.i.* 1. rebotar. 2. repercutir, resonar. —*v.t.* rebotar (eco, sonido). —[ˈriˌbaʊnd] *s.* 1. rebote, repercusión. 2. reacción (emocional), despecho, ej., *to marry on the r.,* casarse por despecho.
rebroadcast [riˈbrɔdˌkæst, B -ˌkɑst] (rad.) *v.t.* retransmitir, volver a transmitir (un programa anteriormente difundido). —*s.* retransmisión.
rebuff [rɪˈbʌf] *s.* 1. rechazo, desaire. 2. repulsa, denegación. —*v.t.* rechazar, desairar.
rebuild [riˈbɪld, B ˈri-] *v.t.* reconstruir, reedificar.
rebuke [rɪˈbjuk] *v.t.* reprender, censurar, increpar, regañar. —*s.* repulsa; reproche, reprimenda.
rebuker [-ər, B -ə] *s.* criticón, censurador, reprobador.
rebus [ˈribəs] *s.* 1. acertijo, jeroglífico, hieroglífico, logogrifo. 2. (her.) armas parlantes.
rebut [rɪˈbʌt] *v.t.* (*pret., pp.* REBUTTED; *p.pr.* REBUTTING) 1. refutar, contradecir, impugnar. 2. (ant.) repeler, rebatir (fuerza, violencia).

rebuttal [-əl] *s.* (der.) refutación, contradicción, impugnación (esp. de la prueba presentada por la parte contraria).
rebutter [-ər, B -ə] *s.* (der.) refutación, contrarréplica.
recalcitrance [rɪ'kælsətrəns] **recalcitrancy** [-trənsɪ] *s.* obstinación, terquedad, porfía.
recalcitrant [-trənt] *a.* recalcitrante, obstinado, terco, reacio. —*s.* persona recalcitrante.
recalcitrate [-ˌtreɪt] *v.i.* (con *against* o *at*) recalcitrar, oponerse obstinadamente a.
recalcitration [rɪˌkælsɪ'treɪʃən] *s.* oposición porfiada.
recalculate [ri'kælkjəˌleɪt] *v.t.* volver a calcular (esp. para descubrir un error).
recalescence [ˌrikə'lɛsəns] *s.* (metal.) recalescencia.
recall [rɪ'kɔl] *v.t.* 1. hacer volver, mandar retornar. 2. recordar, rememorar. 3. revocar, anular; deponer, retirar. —*s.* 1. llamada (para hacer volver). 2. revocación, anulación. 3. retirada (de un diplomático). 4. recordación, remembranza. 5. (mil.) toque de llamada. 6. **beyond r.,** irrevocable; echado al olvido, enterrado en el olvido. 7. (pol., E.U.) facultad de destituir funcionarios o anular sus decisiones por votación popular.
recallable [-əbəl] *a.* revocable, anulable.
recant [rɪ'kænt] *v.t.* retractar; revocar, retirar públicamente (opiniones); desmentir. —*v.i.* retractarse, desdecirse, desmentirse.
recantation [ˌrikæn'teɪʃən] *s.* retractación.
recanter [rɪ'kæntər, B -ə] *s.* el que se retracta o desmiente.
recap [ri'kæp] *v.t.* recubrir, recauchutar, reencauchar (neumático).
recap ['riˌkæp] *s., abrev. de* **recapitulation,** recapitulación. —*v.t., abrev. de* **recapitulate,** recapitular.
recapitalization [riˌkæpətələ'zeɪʃən, B -əlaɪ-] *s.* (com.) recapitalización.
recapitalize [-'kæpətəlˌaɪz] *v.t.* (com.) volver a capitalizar.
recapitulate [ˌrikə'pɪtʃəˌleɪt, B -'pɪtjʊ-] *v.t., v.i.* recapitular; resumir, sintetizar.
recapitulation [-ˌpɪtʃə'leɪʃən, B -ˌpɪtjʊ-] *s.* recapitulación.
recapitulatory [-'pɪtʃələˌtɔrɪ, B -'pɪtjʊlətərɪ] *a.* que recapitula.
recapping [ri'kæpɪŋ] *s.* (aut.) reencauchaje (de un neumático).
recapture [-'kæptʃər, B -tʃə] *s.* 1. recobro, recuperación. 2. represa. —*v.t.* 1. recobrar, volver a tomar. 2. recordar; volver a experimentar. 3. (der.) recobrar. 4. (mar.) represar.
recast [ri'kæst, B 'ri'kɑst] *v.t.* 1. refundir. 2. (fig.) refundir, reconstruir, dar nueva forma a (obra literaria); (teat.) repartir de nuevo los papeles. — ['riˌkæst, B -'kɑst] *s.* 1. refundición. 2. (fig.) refundición, reconstrucción.
recd. rec'd. *abrev. de* **received,** recibido.
recede [rɪ'sid] *v.i.* 1. retroceder, retirarse, desandar, recular. 2. contraerse, encogerse. 3. apartarse, separarse, alejarse, desistir. —*v.t.* volver a ceder.
receipt [rɪ'sit] *s.* 1. recibo, carta de pago, descargo, cobranza. 2. recibo, recepción. 3. (*pl.*) entradas, ingresos, recaudación. 4. receta, fórmula. 5. **on r. of,** al recibo de; **r. in full,** (com.) recibo de finiquito, recibo por saldo; **to acknowledge r.,** acusar recibo; **to be in r. of,** obrar en poder de uno (carta, etc.), ej., *we are in r. of your letter,* obra en nuestro poder su carta. —*v.t.* dar o extender recibo por; poner el recibí a (cuentas).
receipt book, 1. recetario, registro de recetas. 2. (com.) libro de recibos.
receiptor [-ər, B -ə] *s.* (der.) depositario de propiedades embargadas.
receivable [rɪ'sivəbəl] *a.* 1. recibidero admisible, ej., *r. certificates,* certificados admisibles. 2. (ten.) por cobrar, ej., *accounts r.,* cuentas por cobrar.
receivables [-bəlz] *s. pl.* (ten., com.) activo, corriente, activo exigible; efectos a cobrar.
receive [rɪ'siv] *v.t.* 1. recibir, tomar; percibir, cobrar. 2. aceptar, admitir, dar cabida a, contener. 3. hospedar, agasajar; acoger. 4. **r. a person's confession,** confesar a una persona, oír la confesión de una persona; **r. a petition,** acoger una petición; **r. stolen goods,** recibir, ocultar cosas robadas; **r. the sacraments,** comulgar. —*v.i.* 1. recibir, ser el que recibe. 2. estar de recibo, recibir visitas. 3. comulgar. 4. (rad., t.v.) recibir, captar (una estación de radio).
receiver [-'sivər, B -və] *s.* 1. recibidor, receptor, recipiente. 2. tesorero. 3. perista, comprador de cosas robadas, reducidor (Am.). 4. (quím.) recipiente (en alambiques); tubo de condensación. 5. (elec.) auricular, receptor, receptriz. 6. (der.) síndico, síndico provisional, administrador judicial, receptor; (E.U.) liquidador, administrador judicial. 7. (rad., t.v.) radiorreceptor, receptor.
receiver general, (der.) recaudador general.
receivership [-ˌʃɪp] *s.* (der.) sindicatura; receptoria; administración judicial.
receiving [-vɪŋ] *a.* receptor, de recibir.
receiving line, comisión de honor, fila de recepción.
receiving set, radiorreceptor, equipo receptor.
receiving station, (rad.) estación receptora.
receiving teller, recibidor (de banco).
recency ['risənsɪ] *s.* (ant.) novedad.
recension [rɪ'sɛntʃən, B -'sɛnʃən] *s.* 1. recensión. 2. texto revisado, revisión crítica.
recent ['risənt] *a.* 1. reciente, novedoso, nuevo. 2. (geol.) reciente, holocénico.
recently [-lɪ] *adv.* recientemente.
recentness [-nəs] *s.* novedad.
receptacle [rɪ'sɛptəkəl] *s.* 1. receptáculo, recipiente, vasija. 2. (bot.) receptáculo.
reception [-'sɛpʃən] *s.* 1. recepción, recibimiento, recibidor, sala de recibo. 2. recepción, admisión (de un académico, etc.). 3. recepción, recibimiento (social), fiesta, reunión. 4. acogida, ej., *a cold r.,* una acogida fría. 5. (rad., t.v.) recepción.
receptionist [-əst] *s.* recibidor, recibidora (que recibe a los visitantes), recepcionista (Am.).
receptive [rɪ'sɛptɪv] *a.* receptivo.
receptively [-lɪ] *adv.* con receptividad, receptivamente.
receptiveness [-nəs] **receptivity** [riˌsɛp'tɪvətɪ] *s.* receptividad.
receptor [rɪ'sɛptər, B -tə] *s.* 1. receptor. 2. (fisiol.) receptor, órgano sensorio.
recess ['riˌsɛs, rɪ'sɛs] *s.* 1. hueco, nicho; depresión, cavidad, entrada. 2. retiro, escondrijo; lugar apartado, ej., *in the inmost recesses of the Alps,* en los lugares más apartados de los Alpes. 3. receso, suspensión, cesación, tregua. 4. recreo, tiempo de recreo. —*v.t.* 1. separar, apartar. 2. ahuecar; rebajar; hacer un nicho en, ej., *r. a wall,* hacer un nicho en una pared. —*v.i.* suspenderse temporalmente, entrar en receso, levantar la sesión.
recession [rɪ'sɛʃən] *s.* 1. retroceso, reculada, retirada. 2. procesión que vuelve a la sacristía. 3. (e.p.) recesión, depresión económica. 4. [ˌrɪ-] (der.) retrocesión.
recessional [-əl] *a.* de retirada. —*s.* (t. **r. hymn**) himno, música final (esp. de un servicio religioso).
recessive [-'sɛsɪv] *a.* 1. regresivo. 2. (biol.) recesivo. —*s.* (biol.) carácter o factor recesivo.
recessive character, *s.* (biol.) carácter recesivo.
recharge [ri'tʃɑrdʒ, B -'tʃɑdʒ] *vt., v.i.* cargar, alimentar, reforzar.
rechargeable [ri'tʃɑrdʒəbəl] *a.* recargable.
recharter [-'tʃɑrtər, B -'tʃɑtə] *v.t.* fletar o alquilar de nuevo.
réchauffé [ˌreɪʃoʊ'feɪ, B -'ʃoʊfeɪ] *s.* (fr.) comida recalentada; (fig.) refundición, refrito.
recherché [rəˌʃɛr'ʃeɪ, B -'ʃɛəʃeɪ] *a.* (fr.) 1. rebuscado, estudiado. 2. esmerado, exquisito.
recidivism [rɪ'sɪdəˌvɪzəm] *s.* reincidencia; recaída; (der.) reincidencia (en el delito).
recidivist [-vəst] *s.* (criminal) reincidente.
recipe ['rɛsəpɪ] *s.* 1. receta, fórmula (de médico). 2. receta de cocina. 3. pauta, plan, modelo.
recipience [rɪ'sɪpɪəns] *var. de* **recipiency.**
recipiency [-ənsɪ] *s.* receptividad.
recipient [-ənt] *a., s.* recibidor, recipiente.
reciprocal [rɪ'sɪprəkəl] *a.* recíproco; mutuo; permutable; (gram., mat.) recíproco. —*s.* 1. lo recíproco. 2. (mat.) número recíproco.
reciprocality [-ˌsɪprə'kælətɪ] *s.* reciprocidad, correspondencia mutua.
reciprocally [-'sɪprəkəlɪ] *adv.* recíprocamente, mutuamente.
reciprocal pronoun, (gram.) pronombre recíproco.
reciprocal verb, (gram.) verbo recíproco.
reciprocate [-ˌkeɪt] *v.i.* 1. corresponder, hacer o dar en recompensa. 2. reciprocarse. 3. (mec.) alternar, oscilar, tener movimiento alternativo o de vaivén. —*v.t.* 1. intercambiar. 2. reciprocar. 3. (mec.) dar movimiento alternativo o de vaivén a.
reciprocating engine [-ɪŋ-] máquina alternativa, motor de pistones.
reciprocating saw, sierra alternativa.
reciprocation [rɪˌsɪprə'keɪʃən] *s.* 1. intercambio. 2. reciprocación; correspondencia. 3. alternación.
reciprocity [ˌrɛsə'prɑsətɪ, B -'prɔs-] *s.* 1. reciprocidad; correspondencia mutua. 2. (der.) reciprocidad (entre naciones).
recision [rɪ'sɪʒən] *s.* rescisión; cancelación.
recital [rɪ'saɪtəl] *s.* 1. recitación, declamación. 2. narración, relato, exposición. 3. (mús.) recital, concierto (gen. de solista).
recitation [ˌrɛsə'teɪʃən] *s.* 1. recitación, declamación. 2. narración.
recitative [-tə'tiv] *a.* 1. narrativo, expositivo. 2. (mús.) recitativo. —*s.* (mús.) recitado.
recite [rɪ'saɪt] *v.t., v.i.* 1. recitar, declamar. 2. narrar, relatar, contar; citar. 3. decir la lección.
reciter [-ər, B -ə] *s.* recitador, declamador.
reck [rɛk] *v.i.* (ant.) 1. preocuparse, inquietarse, desvelarse. 2. hacer caso, importar. —*v.t.* 1. preocupar, importar a (uno). 2. atender a, hacer caso de, considerar.
reckless ['rɛkləs] *a.* imprudente, precipitado, atolondrado, temerario.
recklessly [-lɪ] *adv.* imprudentemente, precipitadamente, temerariamente.
recklessness [-nəs] *s.* imprudencia, atolondramiento, temeridad.
reckon ['rɛkən] *v.t.* 1. calcular, contar, computar. 2. considerar, estimar, ej., *r. him prosperous,* considerarle próspero. 3. concluir, inferir, deducir, colegir; (fam.) pensar, suponer. —*v.i.* 1. hacer un cálculo. 2. arreglar o ajustar cuentas. 3. (dial.) pensar, suponer, creer. 4. **r. with,** tener o tomar en cuenta, habérselas con.
reckoner [-ər, B -ə] *s.* contador, calculador.
reckoning [-ɪŋ] *s.* 1. cálculo, cómputo, computación; cuenta. 2. (mar.) cálculo de posición, estima. 3. (ant.) arreglo de cuentas.

reclaim [rɪ'kleɪm] *v.t.* 1. reformar o corregir (a los que hacen mala vida); enmendar. 2. hacer utilizable, hacer labrantío, ganar terreno (al mar), recobrar (tierras), ej., *r. overflowed lands,* recobrar tierras inundadas. 3. recuperar, obtener (algún material antes desechado). 4. (ant.) amansar, domesticar; entrenar (esp. halcones). —*s.* restitución, recuperación; **beyond r.,** perdido irremisiblemente, irrecuperable, incorregible.

re-claim [ri'kleɪm] *v.t.* reclamar; exigir la restitución de algo, intentar recuperar.

reclaimable [rɪ'kleɪməbəl] *a.* recuperable.

reclaimant [-ənt] *s.* reclamante.

reclaimer [-ər, B -ə] *s.* recuperador; el que recobra.

reclamation [ˌrɛklə'meɪʃən] *s.* 1. reclamación, reclamo. 2. recuperación (de materiales). 3. restauración, mejoramiento.

reclinate ['rɛkləˌneɪt] *a.* (bot.) reclinado.

recline [rɪ'klaɪn] *v.t., v.i.* reclinar(se), recostar(se), inclinar(se); **r. upon,** descansar sobre, apoyarse sobre.

recluse ['rɛkˌlus, rɪ'klus, B rɪ-] *a.* solitario, retirado, apartado, aislado. —*s.* ermitaño, anacoreta, cenobita, solitario.

reclusion [rɪ'kluʒən] *a.* reclusión, retiro, aislamiento.

recognition [ˌrɛkəg'nɪʃən] *s.* 1. reconocimiento, aceptación, admisión; agradecimiento. 2. (dip.) reconocimiento (de un gobierno o estado).

recognizable ['rɛkəgˌnaɪzəbəl] *a.* reconocible.

recognizably [-blɪ] *adv.* visiblemente.

recognizance [rɪ'kɑgnəzəns, B -'kɔg-] *s.* 1. (der.) obligación contraída; suma en garantía de una obligación. 2. (ant.) señal, distintivo, símbolo.

recognize ['rɛkəgˌnaɪz] *v.t.* 1. reconocer, admitir, conceder. 2. reconocer, distinguir. 3. (dip.) reconocer (a un gobierno, estado, etc.).

recognizer [-ər, B -ə] *s.* reconocedor.

recoil [rɪ'kɔɪl] *v.i.* 1. retirarse, recular, echarse atrás, retroceder; volver al origen. 2. espantarse; disgustarse. 3. (mil.) replegarse. —*s.* 1. reculada, rechazo, retroceso. 2. repugnancia, disgusto, espanto. 3. (arm.) retroceso, culatazo.

recoilless [-ləs] *a.* de retroceso amortiguado; sin retroceso (fusil).

recoil mechanism, (arm.) mecanismo de retroceso.

recoil spring, muelle de retroceso.

recoin [ri'kɔɪn] *v.t.* volver a acuñar.

recoinage [-ɪdʒ] *s.* nueva acuñación.

re-collect [ˌrikə'lɛkt] *v.t.* volver a colectar, recuperar; congregar, reunir.

recollect [ˌrɛkə'lɛkt] *v.t.* 1. recordar, rememorar. 2. **r. (oneself),** componerse, calmarse, tranquilizarse. —*v.i.* acordarse.

recollected [-'lɛktəd] *a.* 1. tranquilo, pausado, quieto, sosegado. 2. recordado, traído a la memoria.

recollectedness [-nəs] *s.* calma, tranquilidad.

recollection [-'lɛkʃən] *s.* recuerdo, remembranza, reminiscencia, memoria, evocación.

recollective [-tɪv] *a.* recordativo, recordatorio.

recombination [riˌkɑmbə'neɪʃən, B -ˌkɔm-] *s.* (biol.) recombinación.

recommence [ˌrikə'mɛns, B 'ri-] *v.t., v.i.* recomenzar, empezar de nuevo.

recommend [ˌrɛkə'mɛnd] *v.t.* 1. recomendar, encargar, encomendar. 2. recomendar, alabar, elogiar, acreditar. 3. proponer, sugerir, aconsejar.

recommendable [-əbəl] *a.* recomendable.

recommendation [-mən'deɪʃən] *s.* 1. recomendación, presentación. 2. consejo, sugerencia.

recommendatory [-'mɛndəˌtɔrɪ, B -dətərɪ] *a.* recomendatorio.

recommender [-'mɛndər, B -ə] *s.* recomendante, el que presenta, acredita o sugiere.

recommit [ˌrikə'mɪt] *v.t.* 1. volver a cometer. 2. arrestar de nuevo, volver a enviar o mandar (a prisión, etc.). 3. volver a presentar (proyecto, plan, ley, etc.).

recommitment [-mənt] **recommittal** [-əl] *s.* 1. reincidencia (de un delito, etc.). 2. nueva presentación (de un proyecto, etc.).

recompense ['rɛkəmˌpɛns] *v.t.* recompensar, compensar; remunerar. —*s.* recompensa, compensación; remuneración.

recompose [ˌrikəm'poʊz, B 'ri-] *v.t.* 1. recomponer, rehacer, arreglar de nuevo. 2. tranquilizar.

recomposition [riˌkɑmpə'zɪʃən, B -ˌkɔm-] *s.* recomposición, rearreglo.

recon ['riˌkɑn, B rɪ'kɔn] *s.* (fam.) *abrev. de* **reconnaissance,** reconocimiento.

reconcilable [ˌrɛkən'saɪləbəl, B 'rɛkənˌ-saɪ-] *a.* reconciliable, conciliable, compatible.

reconcilableness [-nəs] *s.* compatibilidad.

reconcile ['rɛkənˌsaɪl] *v.t.* reconciliar, amistar; conciliar, ajustar, avenir, adaptar; **r. oneself (to),** resignarse (a), conformarse (con); **to become reconciled,** reconciliarse.

reconciliation [ˌrɛkənˌsɪlɪ'eɪʃən] **reconcilement** ['rɛkənˌsaɪlmənt] *s.* reconciliación, conciliación; ajuste.

reconciliatory [ˌrɛkən'sɪljəˌtɔrɪ, B -tərɪ] *a.* reconciliador.

recondite ['rɛkənˌdaɪt, rɪ'kɑn-, B -'kɔn-] *a.* recóndito, oculto, reservado, escondido, guardado; abstruso, intrincado.

recondition [ˌrikən'dɪʃən] *v.t.* renovar, restaurar; rehabilitar, reformar.

reconnaissance, reconnoissance [rɪ'kɑnəzəns, -səns, B -'kɔn-] *s.* (ing., geol., mil.) reconocimiento, exploración.

reconnaissance flight, (aer.) vuelo de reconocimiento.

reconnoiter, reconnoitre [ˌrikə'nɔɪtər, -ˌrɛkə-, B ˌrɛk-ə] *v.t.* reconocer, explorar, inspeccionar, registrar. —*v.i.* practicar un reconocimiento.

reconnoiterer [-ərər, B -ərə] **reconnoitrer** [-'nɔɪtrər, B -'nɔɪtərə] *s.* explorador, inspector.

reconsider [ˌrikən'sɪdər, B 'ri-ə] *v.t.* volver a considerar, reconsiderar, examinar nuevamente (proyecto o moción).

reconsideration [-ˌsɪdə'reɪʃən] *s.* nueva consideración o discusión, reconsideración.

reconsignment [-'saɪnmənt] *s.* 1. nueva consignación. 2. cambio en la disposición de un embarque en tránsito.

reconstitute [-'kɑnstəˌtut, B -'kɔnstɪˌtjut] *v.t.* 1. reconstituir; reorganizar. 2. reconvertir a su consistencia original (alimentos deshidratados, añadiéndoseles líquido).

reconstitution [-ˌkɑnstə'tuʃən, B -ˌkɔnstɪ'tju-] *s.* reconstitución; reorganización.

reconstruct [ˌrikən'strʌkt, B 'ri-] *v.t.* 1. reedificar, reconstruir. 2. reconstituir.

reconstruction [-'strʌkʃən] *s.* 1. reconstrucción, reedificación. 2. (E.U.) (hist.) **R.** reorganización gubernamental de los estados secesionistas después de la Guerra Civil.

reconstructive [-tɪv] *a.* reconstructivo.

reconvene [ˌrikən'vin, B 'ri-] *v.i., v.t.* convocar, juntar(se) o reunir(se) de nuevo, reanudar la sesión.

reconvention [-'vɛntʃən, B -'vɛnʃən] *s.* (der.) reconvención.

reconvert [-'vɜrt, B -'vɜt] *v.t., v.i.* 1. volver(se) a su estado original, devolver a su uso antiguo (fábrica, máquina, etc.). 2. reconvertir(se) a una idea, religión, etc. que se había abandonado.

reconvey [-'veɪ] *v.t.* devolver, reponer, restituir (a su sitio o propietario).

reconveyance [-əns] *s.* reposición, restitución.

record ['rɛkərd, B 'rɛkɔd] *s.* 1. registro, inscripción, anotación. 2. acta, documento, partida. 3. relación, crónica, historia. 4. hoja de servicios, antecedentes, historia personal, historial; (educ.) expediente académico. 5. disco fonográfico. 6. memoria, recuerdo, recordatorio. 7. archivo; protocolo (de un notario); padrón, matrícula. 8. (der.) memorial, informe, expediente. 9. (dep.) récord, registro, marca, plusmarca. 10. (ant.) testimonio, prueba. 11. **matter of r.,** hecho establecido; **off the r.,** extraoficialmente, en confianza, reservadamente; **to be on r.,** estar inscrito (oficial o legalmente); constar; **to break** (o **beat) the r.,** batir el récord; mejorar la marca; (fig.) superar lo mejor; **to go on r.,** dejar constancia, declarar públicamente; **to keep to the r.,** atenerse a los hechos (establecidos). —*a.* récord, ej., *r. time,* tiempo récord, *r. crop,* cosecha récord; (electrón.) discográfico, disquero. [rɪ'kɔrd, B -'kɔd] *v.t.* 1. registrar, inscribir; asentar; protocolizar (documentos); anotar, marcar, indicar. 2. grabar (en disco fonográfico o cinta magnetofónica).

record cabinet, discoteca.

record changer, cambiadiscos automático.

record collection, discoteca.

recorder [rɪ'kɔrdər, B -'kɔdə] *s.* 1. registrador, archivero. 2. (máquina) grabadora (de sonidos). 3. (der.) (G.B.) juez municipal superior que conoce de causas criminales. 4. (mec.) indicador, contador. 5. (mús.) flauta dulce.

recorder of deeds, (der.) registrador de la propiedad.

recordership [-ˌʃɪp] *s.* cargo de archivero o registrador.

recording [-ɪŋ] *s.* grabación; disco fonográfico, cinta magnetofónica en la que algo se ha grabado.

recording head, (electrón.) cabeza de grabación (de un magnetófono).

recording secretary, *s.* escribiente, secretario de actas.

recording studio, estudio de grabación.

recording tape, cinta magnetofónica.

record player, tocadiscos, fonógrafo, gramófono.

record shop, discoteca, disquería.

recount [rɪ'kaʊnt] *v.t.* narrar, detallar, referir por partes.

recount [ri'kaʊnt] *v.t.* 1. recontar, volver a contar. 2. narrar, detallar, referir por partes. —['riˌkaʊnt] *s.* recuento.

recountal [rɪ'kaʊntəl] *s.* narración, recitación, relato.

recoup [rɪ'kup] *v.t.* 1. recobrar, recuperar (pérdidas, fuerzas, etc.). 2. reembolsar, indemnizar, resarcir.

recoupment [-mənt] *s.* recuperación, resarcimiento, reembolso; desquite.

recourse ['riˌkɔrs, rɪ'kɔrs, B rɪ'kɔs] *s.* recurso; expediente, ayuda; **to have r. to,** recurrir a, valerse de; **without r.,** (der., com.) sin recurso.

re-cover ['ri'kʌvər, B -ə] *v.t.* recubrir, volver a cubrir, poner cubierta(s) nueva(s).

recover [rɪ'kʌvər, B -ə] *v.t.* 1. recobrar, recuperar; rescatar; reconquistar. 2. (der.) reivindicar, cobrar. 3. **r. one's legs,** ponerse de pie (después

de caída). —*v.i.* 1. recobrar la salud o el conocimiento, mejorarse, convalecer. 2. (der.) obtener sentencia favorable, ganar un pleito.
recoverable [-ərəbəl] *a.* recuperable, recobrable.
recovery [-ərɪ] *s.* 1. recobro, cobranza, recuperación; rescate, reconquista. 2. restablecimiento; mejoría, convalecencia. 3. (astronáut.) recuperación de una cápsula o cámara, después de un viaje espacial.
recovery room, sala de recuperación o restablecimiento (en hospital, etc.).
recreancy ['rɛkrɪənsɪ] *s.* 1. cobardía. 2. deslealtad.
recreant [-ənt] *a.* 1. cobarde. 2. falso, desleal. —*s.* 1. cobarde. 2. apóstata, desleal.
recreate [-ˌeɪt] *v.t.* recrear, divertir, deleitar; refrescar, reanimar. —*v.i.* recrearse, divertirse; distraerse (en algo ameno).
re-create [ˌrikrɪ'eɪt] *v.t.* recrear, crear de nuevo, reconstruir.
recreation [ˌrɛkrɪ'eɪʃən] *s.* recreación, recreo; esparcimiento; pasatiempo, diversión, entretenimiento.
re-creation [ˌrikrɪ'eɪʃən] *s.* cosa recreada; nueva creación, reconstrucción.
recreational [ˌrɛkrɪ'eɪʃənəl] *a.* 1. recreativo. 2. de recreación, de recreo.
recreative ['rɛkrɪˌeɪtɪv] *a.* recreativo.
recrement ['rɛkrəmənt] *s.* (fisiol.) recremento; hez, escoria.
recremental [ˌrɛkrə'mɛntəl] *a.* recrementicio.
recriminate [rɪ'krɪməˌneɪt] *v.t.* reprochar, recriminar.
recrimination [rɪˌkrɪmə'neɪʃən] *s.* recriminación, reproche.
recriminatory [rɪ'krɪmənəˌtɔrɪ, B -ˌneɪtərɪ] *a.* recriminatorio.
recross [ri'krɔs, B 'ri-] *v.t., v.i.* volver a cruzar; pasar de nuevo (calle, etc.).
recrudesce [ˌrikru'dɛs] *v.i.* recrudecer; (fig.) empeorar.
recrudescence [-əns] *s.* recrudecimiento.
recrudescent [-ənt] *a.* recrudescente.
recruit [rɪ'krut] *v.t.* 1. (mil.) reclutar, alistar, enganchar. 2. contratar. 3. abastecer. —*v.i.* alistar, reclutar. —*s.* 1. (mil.) recluta (*m.*); novicio. 2. (ant.) renuevo, suministro.
recruiter [-ər, B -ə] *s.* reclutador.
recruitment [-mənt] *s.* reclutamiento, alistamiento, conscripción (Am.).
recrystallize [ri'krɪstəˌlaɪz] *v.t., v.i.* volver a cristalizar; cristalizar repetidamente.
rectal ['rɛktəl] *a.* (anat.) rectal, del recto.
rectangle ['rɛkˌtæŋgəl] *s.* (geom.) rectángulo.
rectangular [rɛk'tæŋgjələr, B -lə] *a.* rectangular.
rectangular coordinate, (geom.) coordenada cartesiana.
rectangularity [-ˌtæŋgjə'lærətɪ] *s.* forma rectangular.
rectangularly [-'tæŋgjələrlɪ, B -ləlɪ] *adv.* en forma rectangular.
rectangularness [-nəs] *s.* calidad de rectangular.
rectifiable ['rɛktəˌfaɪəbəl] *a.* rectificable.
rectification [ˌrɛktəfə'keɪʃən] *s.* rectificación, corrección, enmienda; (quím., elec., geom.) rectificación.
rectifier ['rɛktəˌfaɪər, B -ə] *s.* (mec., elec., rad.) rectificador; refinador.
rectify [-ˌfaɪ] *v.t.* (*pret., p.p.* RECTIFIED; *p.pr.* RECTIFYING) 1. rectificar, corregir, enderezar, enmendar. 2. (quím.) rectificar, refinar, depurar. 3. (elec.) rectificar (corriente alterna). 4. (geom.) rectificar.
rectilineal [ˌrɛktə'lɪnɪəl] **rectilinear** [-ɪər, B -ɪə] *a.* rectilíneo.
rectitude ['rɛktəˌtud, B -'tjud] *s.* rectitud, corrección, probidad.
recto ['rɛktou] *s.* (*pl.* RECTOS) (impr.) página impar, folio recto.
rector ['rɛktər, B -tə] *s.* rector (de una universidad); prior, superior, cura párroco.
rectorate [-tərət] *s.* rectorado, rectoría.
rectorial [rɛk'tɔrɪəl] *a.* rectoral.
rectory ['rɛktərɪ] *s.* rectoría.
rectrix ['rɛktrɪks] *s.* (*pl.* RECTRICES [-trəˌsiz]) (orn.) (pluma) rectriz.
rectum ['rɛktəm] *s.* (*pl.* RECTUMS O RECTA [-tə]) (anat.) recto.
rectus [-təs] *s.* (*pl.* RECTI [-taɪ]) (anat.) músculo recto.
recumbency [rɪ'kʌmbənsɪ] *s.* reclinación, inclinación.
recumbent [-bənt] *a.* reclinado, recostado, reposado, echado.
recumbently [-lɪ] *adv.* en posición reclinada, en postura de reposo.
recuperate [rɪ'kupəˌreɪt, B -'kju-] *v.t.* recuperar, recobrar, rescatar; reconquistar. —*v.i.* recuperarse, restablecerse, recobrarse, reponerse, convalecer.
recuperation [-ˌkupə'reɪʃən, B -ˌkju-] *s.* recuperación, rehacimiento.
recuperative [-'kupəˌreɪtɪv, B -'kjupərə-] *a.* recuperativo.
recuperator [-ˌreɪtər, B -ə] *s.* 1. recuperador, regenerador. 2. (arm.) mecanismo de recuperación.
recur [rɪ'kɜr, B -'kɜ] *v.i.* (*pret., p.p.* RECURRED; *p.pr.* RECURRING) 1. repetirse, reiterarse; presentarse nuevamente. 2. (med.) volver (la misma dolencia o enfermedad). 3. (raro) acudir, recurrir.
recurrence [-əns, -'kʌrəns, B -'kʌ-] *s.* 1. repetición, reaparición. 2. (med.) recidiva.
recurrent [-'kɜrənt, -'kʌrənt, B -'kʌ-] *a.* 1. periódico, reiterativo, cíclico. 2. (anat.) recurrente (nervio). 3. (mat.) recurrente.
recurrently [-lɪ] *adv.* periódicamente, reiteradamente, repetidamente.
recurring decimal, número decimal periódico.
recurvate [rɪ'kɜrˌveɪt, B -'kɜveɪt] *a.* (bot.) recurvado.
recurve [-'kɜrv, B ri'kɜv] *v.t.* doblarse hacia atrás; reclinarse hacia atrás; torcerse en sentido opuesto.
recusancy ['rɛkjəzənsɪ] *s.* recusación, rechazo, repudio (esp. de prácticas o reglas religiosas).
recusant [-ənt] *a., s.* recusante.
recusation [ˌrɛkjə'zeɪʃən] *s.* (for.) recusación.
recuse [rɪ'kjuz] *v.t.* (der.) recusar.
recycle [ri'saɪkəl] *v.t.* (fís.) recircular.
red [rɛd] *a.* (REDDER; REDDEST) 1. rojo; encarnado, escarlata, punzó, colorado. 2. ruboroso, enrojecido (rostro), inyectado (ojo). 3. tinto (vino). 4. rojo, comunista; revolucionario. —*s.* 1. color rojo. 2. indio piel roja. 3. rojo, comunista; revolucionario. 4. **the r.,** el debe (de una cuenta); (billar) el mingo; **to be in the r.,** estar endeudado; **to see r.,** enfurecerse, ponerse furioso.
red, *v.t.* (dial.) *var. de* **redd.**
redact [rɪ'dækt] *v.t.* redactar, escribir, componer.
redaction [-'dækʃən] *s.* redacción; revisión (de un escrito).
redactor [-tər, B -tə] *s.* redactor, escritor, revisor.
redan [rɪ'dæn] *s.* (fort.) rediente.
red ant, (ento.) hormiga roja, hormiga colorada.
redbait ['rɛdˌbeɪt] *v.i.* acusar de comunista a una persona o grupo.
red bark, (bot.) especie fina de quino.
red-berried mistletoe [-ˌbɛrid-] (bot.) agraz.
redbird [-ˌbɜrd, B -ˌbɜd] *s.* (orn.) cardenal, cardenal de cresta roja.
red blood cell, glóbulo rojo de la sangre.
red-blooded [-'blʌdəd] *a.* valiente, valeroso, enérgico, animoso.
redbreast [-ˌbrɛst] *s.* (orn.) pechirrojo, pechicolorado.
redbrick [-ˌbrɪk] *a.* (G.B.) recién fundada, recién establecida (universidad).
redbud [-ˌbʌd] *s.* (bot.) ciclamor, árbol del amor, árbol de Judea.
redcap [-ˌkæp] *s.* 1. (E.U.) portero, maletero, mozo de cuerda. 2. (fam. G.B.) policía militar. 3. (orn.) jilguero, cardelina, pintacilgo.
red-carpet ['rɛd'kɑrpət, B -'kɑpɪt] *a.* 1. (fam.) preferencial (trato), de lujo (recepción). 2. a **red-carpet affair, una** fiesta suntuosa.
red cedar, (bot.) cedro colorado.
red cent, centavo (de cobre); **I don't have a r. c.,** no tengo un cobre.
red chickweed, (bot.) murajes, anagalis.
Red China, (fam.) la China Roja, la República Popular de China.
red clover, (bot.) trébol rojo, morado, pratense o trébol de los prados.
redcoat ['rɛdˌkout] *s.* (hist.) soldado inglés (durante la guerra de Independencia de E.U.).
red corpuscle, (fisiol.) corpúsculo o glóbulo rojo.
Red Cross, Cruz Roja.
redd [rɛd] *v.t.* (dial.) limpiar, cavardenar.
red deer, (zool.) venado, ciervo.
redden ['rɛdən] *v.t.* teñir de rojo. —*v.i.* enrojecer(se), ponerse colorado, ruborizarse.
reddish [-ɪʃ] *a.* rojizo, bermejizo (pelo).
reddle ['rɛdəl] *var. de* **ruddle.**
redecorate [ri'dɛkəˌreɪt] *v.t.* poner nueva decoración. —*v.i.* cambiar el docorado.
redeem [rɪ'dim] *v.t.* 1. redimir rescatar; (gen. con *from*) librar, salvar (de). 2. recuperar. 3. cumplir (promesa). 4. compensar, contrapesar, subsanar, ej., *it has one redeeming feature,* tiene un aspecto compensador.
redeemable [-əbəl] *a.* redimible, rescatable.
redeemer [-ər, B -ə] *s.* redentor; **R.,** Redentor, Jesucristo.
redeeming [-ɪŋ] *a.* redentor, rescatador; compensante.
redemand [ˌridɪ'mænd, B -'mɑnd] *v.t.* volver a demandar o pedir.
redemption [rɪ'dɛmpʃən] *s.* 1. redención; rescate; salvación. 2. reembolso, amortización (de una deuda).
redemptioner [-ʃənər, B -nə] *s.* (hist.) emigrante que pagaba su pasaje a América con servicio personal.
redemptive [-'dɛmptɪv] *a.* redentor.
Redemptorist [-tərəst] *a., s.* (relig.) redentorista.
redemptory [-tərɪ] *a.* redentor.
redeploy [ˌridɪ'plɔɪ, B 'ri-] *v.t.* (mil.) cambiar o transferir el despliegue de (tropas a material bélico), cambiar de frente.
redesign [ˌridɪ'zaɪn] *v.t.* cambiar el diseño de, cambiar la forma o apariencia de, dar nueva forma a.
redetermination [-ˌtɜrmə'neɪʃən, B -ˌtɜmɪ-] *s.* determinación o fijación nueva.
redetermine [-'tɜrmən, B -'tɜmɪn] *v.t.* volver a determinar, determinar de nuevo.
redevelopment [-'vɛləpmənt] *s.* reurbanización.
redeye ['rɛdˌaɪ] *s.* (ict.) (especie de) perca.
red-eye, *s.* (jer., E.U.) whiski barato.

red-eyed [-ˌaɪd] *a.* 1. de ojos enrojecidos. 2. con los ojos inyectados. 3. (jer.) furioso.
red fir, (bot.) 1. abeto del norte, abeto rojo. 2. pino albar, pino Oregón.
redfish [-ˌfɪʃ] *s.* (nombre comercial del) salmón y otros pescados de aspecto rojizo.
red fox, 1. (zool.) zorro rojo. 2. piel de zorra roja.
red guenon [-gəˈnoʊn, B -ˈnɔn] (zool.) cefo.
red gum, (bot.) eucalipto australiano.
red-handed [ˈrɛdˈhændəd] *a., adv.* 1. en flagrante, con las manos en la masa. 2. **to be caught r.-h.,** ser cogido con las manos en la masa.
redhead [-ˌhɛd] *s.* 1. pelirrojo. 2. (E.U.) pato americano.
red heat, calor rojo.
red herring, 1. arenque ahumado. 2. despiste, pista falsa, indicio falso. 3. **to draw a r. h. across the track** (o **path**), distraer la atención, despistar.
redhibition [ˌrɛdəˈbɪʃən, B -həˈbɪʃ-] *s.* (der.) redhibición.
redhibitory [rɛdˈhɪbəˌtɔrɪ, B -tərɪ] *a.* (der.) redhibitorio.
red-hot [ˈrɛdˈhɑt, B -ˈhɔt] *a.* 1. calentado al rojo, de un calor ardiente, candente. 2. fervoroso, vehemente (pasión, discurso, etc.). 3. muy reciente, fresquísimo (dato, noticia, etc.). 4. sensacional (periódico, orquesta de jazz, etc.). 5. muy cotizado (favorito).
red Indian, (fam., E.U.) piel roja.
redingote [ˈrɛdɪŋˌgoʊt] *s.* redingote, abrigo largo, cruzado, levitón.
redintegrate [rɪˈdɪntəˌgreɪt, rɛ-, B rɛ-] *v.t.* (ant.) reintegrar; restituir, restablecer.
redintegration [-ˌdɪntəˈgreɪʃən] *s.* (ant.) reintegración, reintegro; restitución, restauración, restablecimiento.
redirect [ˌridəˈrɛkt, -daɪ-, B ˈri-] *v.t.* 1. cambiar la dirección de. 2. enviar a nueva dirección (carta, etc.). 3. señalar o mostrar otro camino a (uno).
redirect examination, (E.U.) (der.) segundo interrogatorio directo (de un testigo).
rediscount [riˈdɪsˌkaunt] *v.t.* (com.) redescontar, volver a descontar. —*s.* redescuento.
rediscover [ˌridɪsˈkʌvər, B ˈri-ə] *v.t.* volver a descubrir, redescubrir.
rediscovery [-ərɪ] *s.* nuevo descubrimiento, redescubrimiento.
redistribute [ˌridɪsˈtrɪbjʊt] *v.t.* distribuir o repartir de nuevo, redistribuir.
redistribution [ˌridɪstrəˈbjuʃən] *s.* segunda o nueva distribución, redistribución.
redistrict [riˈdɪstrɪkt] *v.t.* (E.U.) volver a dividir en distritos (esp. distritos electorales para el Congreso).
redivivus [ˌrɛdəˈvaɪvəs] *a.* redivivo, resucitado.
red jasmine, r. jessamine, (bot.) frangipani, jazmín mango.
red lead, (quím.) minio, minio de plomo.
red-legged falcon [ˈrɛdˌlɛgəd-, -ˌlɛgd-] (orn.) baharí.
red-legged partridge, (orn.) perdiz real, perdiz roja.
red-letter [ˈrɛdˈlɛtər, B -ə] *a.* feriado, de fiesta; memorable (díc. de los días).
red light, luz roja, señal de detenerse o de peligro; **to see the r. l.,** darse cuenta del peligro inminente.
red light district [-ˈlaɪt-] distrito rojo, barrio que tácitamente se reserva para las prostitutas; zona de tolerancia.
red linnet, orn. jilguero, colorín.
red man, (fam., E.U.) piel roja.
red meat, carne de res (vacuna) o de carnero (en contraste con la de ternera, puerco o pollo).
red mullet, (ict.) salmonete, mullo, trigla, trilla.
red-neck [ˈrɛdˌnɛk] *s.* (despec., E.U.) blanco inculto de las áreas rurales de los estados del sur (gen. enemigo de los negros).
redness [-nəs] *s.* rojez, calidad de rojo o rojizo.
redo [riˈdu, B ˈri-] *v.t.* 1. rehacer, hacer de nuevo. 2. decorar de nuevo.
red oak, (bot.) roble colorado.
red ocher, (min.) ocre rojo, almagre, almazarrón.
redolence [ˈrɛdələns] *s.* 1. fragancia, perfume, aroma. 2. (fig.) súbita remembranza de algo placentero.
redolent [-ənt] *a.* 1. oloroso, fragante, aromático, perfumado. 2. (fig.) (con *of*) sugestivo (de), recordatorio (de). 3. (con *with*) impregnado o saturado de.
redolently [-lɪ] *adv.* con fragancia, fragantemente.
red osier, (bot.) 1. mimbre rojo. 2. variedad de cornejo.
redouble [riˈdʌbəl] *v.t.* 1. redoblar, aumentar, intensificar. 2. (ant.) repetir. —*v.i.* 1. redoblarse, aumentarse, intensificarse. 2. (bridge) decir recontra, redoblar. —*s.* (bridge) recontra, redoble.
redoubt [rɪˈdaʊt] *s.* (fort.) reducto.
redoubtable [-əbəl] *a.* formidable, temible.
redound [rɪˈdaʊnd] *v.i.* (gen. con *to* o *upon*) redundar (en), resultar (en), contribuir (a), conducir (a).
redowa [ˈrɛdəwə, B -və] *s.* (mús.) redova (danza eslava).
red-pencil [ˈrɛdˈpɛnsəl] *v.t.* 1. marcar con rojo. 2. (fig.) censurar; corregir, tachar.
red pepper, 1. (bot.) pimiento. 2. pimentón (polvo).
redpoll [-ˌpoʊl] *s.* (orn.) pajarel, pardillo.
redraft [ˈriˌdræft, B -ˌdrɑft] *s.* 1. (com.) resaca. 2. nuevo dibujo, copia o borrador; nueva redacción.
red rattle, (bot.) hierba piojera, estafisagria.
redraw [riˈdrɔ, B ˈri-] *v.t., v.i.* volver a dibujar o trazar.
redress [rɪˈdrɛs] *v.t.* 1. remediar, reparar; resarcir, compensar, desagraviar. 2. enmendar, rectificar, corregir. 3. reajustar, restablecer, ej., *r. the balance,* restablecer el equilibrio o la igualdad. 4. (aer.) enderezar. — [ˈriˌdrɛs, B rɪˈdrɛs] *s.* 1. remedio, reparación; compensación, desagravio. 2. enmienda, corrección.
redroot [ˈrɛdˌrut] *s.* (bot.) sanguinaria.
red sandalwood, (bot.) sándalo rojo, narra.
Red Sea, Mar Rojo.
redshank [-ˌʃæŋk] *s.* (orn.) agachadiza.
redshirt [-ˌʃɜrt, B -ˌʃɜt] *s.* (pol.) camisa roja, comunista.
redskin [-ˌskɪn] *s.* (despec.) piel roja, indio de E.U.
red spider, (ento.) ácaro rojo, cresa roja.
red spruce, (bot.) abeto falso, abeto rojo.
red squill, (bot.) escila.
red squirrel, (zool.) ardilla norteamericana.
redstart [ˈrɛdˌstɑrt, B -ˌstɑt] *s.* (orn.) colirrojo, candelita.
red tape, papeleo, expedienteo, trámites burocráticos.
redtop [-ˌtɑp, B -ˌtɔp] *s.* (bot.) agrostis alba.
reduce [rɪˈdus, B -ˈdjus] *v.t.* 1. reducir, disminuir, aminorar, rebajar, mermar, bajar. 2. debilitar, ej., *to be in a very reduced state,* estar muy débil. 3. contraer, abreviar, acortar. 4. sujetar, someter, sojuzgar, subyugar. 5. convertir, transformar, cambiar. 6. ordenar, metodizar, clasificar. 7. diluir. 8. (arit., biol., quím., metal.) reducir. 9. (med.) reducir, enderezar, corregir. 10. (mil.) degradar, ej., *the sergeant was reduced to the ranks,* el sargento fue degradado a soldado raso. 11. (foto.) debilitar (la densidad del negativo). 12. (raro) obligar, forzar. 13. **in reduced circumstances,** empobrecido. —*v.i.* 1. adelgazar, estar a dieta. 2. reducirse, encogerse, mermarse, diluirse.
reducer [-ər, B -ə] *s.* 1. (quím., mec., elec.) reductor. 2. (foto.) debilitador.
reductase [rɪˈdʌkˌteɪs] *s.* (biol.) reductasa.
reduction [-ˈdʌkʃən] *s.* reducción; rebaja, disminución; **r. to absurdity,** reducción al absurdo.
redundancy [rɪˈdʌndənsɪ] *s.* 1. redundancia, superabundancia, superfluencia, superfluidad. 2. (gram.) redundancia, pleonasmo.
redundant [-dənt] *a.* 1. superabundante, profuso, superfluo; innecesario. 2. (gram.) redundante, pleonástico.
redundantly [-lɪ] *adv.* 1. profusamente, superfluamente, innecesariamente. 2. (gram.) redundantemente, pleonásticamente.
reduplicate [rɪˈduplɪkət, B -ˈdju-] *a.* 1. repetido, reiterado. 2. (bot.) reduplicado. — [-ˌkeɪt] *v.t.* 1. redoblar, reduplicar, reiterar. 2. (gram.) repetir (sílaba en una palabra).
reduplication [-ˌduplɪˈkeɪʃən, B -ˌdju-] *s.* 1. reduplicación, reiteración; duplicado. 2. (gram.) repetición (de una sílaba en la palabra).
reduviid [rɪˈduvɪəd, B -ˈdju-] *a.* (ento.) redúvido.
red valerian, (bot.) milamores.
red vitriol, (quím.) caparrosa roja.
red wine, vino tinto.
redwing [ˈrɛdˌwɪŋ] *s.* (orn.) 1. tordo alirrojo, malvís, malviz. 2. mirlo negro americano.
redwing blackbird, red-winged blackbird, (orn.) mirlo negro americano.
redwood [-ˌwʊd] *s.* 1. (bot.) secoya. 2. madera de secoya.
reecho [riˈɛkoʊ] *v.i.* resonar, repercutir, hacer eco, responder el eco; repetirse el eco. —*v.t.* hacer resonar.
reed [rid] *s.* 1. (bot.) caña; carrizo. 2. tallo de caña. 3. cañaveral, cañal. 4. caramillo, flautilla de caña. 5. (arq.) baqueta, junquillo, moldura de junquillos. 6. (mús.) lengüeta; (*pl.*) (ciertos) instrumentos de viento (en conjunto). 7. (bíbl.) antigua medida judía de longitud equivalente a seis codos. 8. (tej.) peine de telar. 9. (poét.) flecha, saeta. —*v.t.* 1. techar con cañas o barda. 2. (arq.) ornamentar con baquetas o junquillos.
reedbird [ˈridˌbɜrd, B -ˌbɜd] *s.* (orn.) (S. de E.U.) chambergo.
reedbuck [-ˌbʌk] *s.* (zool.) un antílope africano.
reediness [ˈridɪnəs] *s.* tono chillón o agudo.
reeding [-ɪŋ] *s.* 1. (arq.) baqueta, junquillo. 2. (carp.) decoración con baquetas (esp. en muebles).
reedling [-lɪŋ] *s.* (orn.) especie de paro.
reed mace, (bot.) espadaña, nea, anea.
reed organ, (mús.) órgano de lengüetas, armonio.
reed pipe, (mús.) 1. caramillo. 2. cañón de lengua, cañón de lengüeta (del órgano).
reed stop, (mús.) grupo de cañones de lengüeta del órgano (controlados por un solo registro).
reeducate [riˈɛdʒəˌkeɪt, B ˈriˈɛdjʊ-] *v.t.* reeducar, rehabilitar (esp. por medio de la instrucción); acondicionar (a un nuevo ambiente, situación, etc.).
reeducation [riˌɛdʒəˈkeɪʃən, B ˈriˌɛdjʊ-] *s.* reeducación.
reedwork [ˈridˌwɜrk, B -ˌwɜk] *s.* (mús.) lengüetería (de un órgano).
reedy [ˈridɪ] *a.* 1. cubierto de cañas. 2. hecho de caña. 3. largo y delgado (como la caña), larguirucho. 4. chillón, agudo (tono).

reef [rif] *s.* 1. escollo, arrecife; bajo, bajío; banco de arena. 2. (fig.) escollo. 3. (min.) veta, vena, venero; filón. 4. (mar.) rizo (de vela de buques); **to let out** (o **shake out) the r.,** zafar los rizos; **to take in the r.,** tomar rizos. —*v.t.* (mar.) arrizar (las velas) de un buque, tomar (rizos), recoger (las velas).
reefer ['rifər, B -fə] *s.* 1. (mar.) guardia marina. 2. chaquetón de tela gruesa, gen. cruzado. 3. (jer.) cigarrillo de mariguana. 4. (jer.) refrigerador, cámara frigorífica; carro o barco frigorífico.
reef knot, (mar.) nudo cruzado.
reek [rik] *s.* 1. vaho, vapor, emanación. 2. tufo, aire fétido. 3. (dial.) humo. —*v.i.* vahar, vahear; humear; **r. of,** oler a, apestar a. —*v.t.* 1. ahumar. 2. exhalar, exudar.
reeky ['rikɪ] *a.* 1. vaporoso, lleno de exhalaciones, miasmático. 2. hediondo, maloliente.
reel [ril] *s.* 1. carrete, bobina. 2. carrete de la caña de pescar. 3. (pr. G.B.) canilla (de máquina de coser). 4. rollo de película (cinematográfica). 5. ovillo (enrollado en un carrete). 6. danza muy viva, de origen escocés. 7. **off the r.,** sin cesar; directamente, sin preparación. —*v.t.* 1. devanar, enrollar en un carrete. 2. **r. in** (o **up),** cobrar (cuerda, soga, etc.); tirar de (pez, corredera) enrollando el cordel en un carrete; **r. off,** desenrollar, (la seda de un capullo, cuerda del carrete, etc.); (fig.) narrar fácil y prestamente.
reel, *v.i.* 1. remolinar, dar vueltas (los ojos, la mente o la cabeza); estar aturdido, tener vértigo. 2. flaquear, tambalear, bambolear, caminar o moverse con paso vacilante, hacer eses. —*v.t.* remolinear, hacer girar. —*s.* tambaleo, bamboleo.
reelect [ˌriə'lɛkt, B 'ri-] *v.t.* reelegir, elegir de nuevo (a un cargo, puesto, etc.).
reelection [-'lɛkʃən] *s.* (pol.) reelección.
reembark [-ɪm'bɑrk, B -'bɑk] *v.t., v.i.* 1. embarcar(se) de nuevo; (fig.) volver a emprender.
reemerge [-ɪ'mɜrdʒ, B -'mɜdʒ] *v.i.* reaparecer, resurgir.
reemergence [-əns] *s.* reaparición, resurgimiento.
reemphasize [ri'ɛmfəˌsaɪz] *v.t.* volver a recalcar o acentuar.
reemploy [-ɪm'plɔɪ] *v.t.* volver a emplear.
reenact [-ɪn'ækt, B 'ri-] *v.t.* 1. promulgar o estatuir de nuevo, revalidar (una ley). 2. volver a realizar, representar (una escena de teatro o un suceso verídico).
reenactment [-mənt] *s.* 1. restablecimiento, revalidación (de una ley). 2. nueva realización o representación (de escena, incidente, suceso).
reenforce, *var. de* **reinforce.**
reenforcement, *var. de* **reinforcement.**
reengage [-ɪn'geɪdʒ] *v.t.* emplear de nuevo; volver a contratar.
reengagement [-mənt] *s.* 1. nueva contratación, nuevo trato. 2. (mil.) nuevo ataque o encuentro.
reenlist [-ɪn'lɪst] *v.t., v.i.* reenganchar(se); volver a sentar plaza (en la milicia), volver a alistarse.
reenlistment [-mənt] *s.* reenganche (en un cuerpo militar).
reenter [ri'ɛntər, B -tə] *v.i.* reingresar, volver a entrar. —*v.t.* registrar de nuevo, volver a anotar.
reentrance [-trəns] *s.* reingreso; segunda entrada.
reentrant [-trənt] *a.* entrante. —*s.* mocheta, ángulo entrante.
reentrant angle, (arq.) mocheta, ángulo entrante.
reentry [-trɪ] *s.* 1. reingreso; segunda entrada. 2. (der.) reposesión, recuperación de una posesión. 3. (bridge) nueva entrada. 4. (aeroesp.) reentrada.

reestablish [ˌriɪs'tæblɪʃ, B 'ri-] *v.t.* restablecer, restaurar (la paz, normas, relaciones, etc.).
reestablishment [-mənt] *s.* restablecimiento, restauración.
reeve [riv] *v.t.* (*pret., p.p.* ROVE [roʊv] o REEVED; *p.pr.* REEVING) (mar.) pasar (una cuerda) por una polea, pasar (un cabo, etc.) por un ojal o jareta; **r. in** (o **to),** atar, amarrar (en o a). —*v.i.* (mar.) laborear. —*s.* 1. (orn.) hembra del pavo marino. 2. (hist., G.B.) magistrado principal de un pueblo o distrito.
reexamination [ˌriɪgˌzæmə'neɪʃən, B 'ri-] *s.* nuevo examen; revisión, repaso; (der.) reexaminación (hecha después de un interrogatorio).
reexamine [-'zæmən] *v.t.* reexaminar, revisar, repasar.
reexport [ˌriɛks'pɔrt, B 'ri-'pɔt] *v.t.* reexportar. — [-'ɛksˌpɔrt, B -ˌpɔt] *s.* reexportación.
reexportation [-ˌɛkspɔr'teɪʃən, B -pɔ'-] *s.* reexportación.
ref. *abrev. de* 1. **referee,** árbitro, juez de campo. 2. **reference,** referencia. 3. **referred,** mencionado. 4. **reformation,** corrección, reforma. 5. **reformed,** reformado. 6. **refund,** reembolso.
reface [-'feɪs] *v.t.* renovar la fachada o frontis de (un edificio, tela, pieza de vestir).
refashion [-'fæʃən] *v.t.* rehacer, formar de nuevo, refaccionar (Am.).
refection [rɪ'fɛkʃən] *s.* refacción, refresco, refrigerio, colación.
refectory [-tərɪ] *s.* refectorio, comedor (en conventos, colegios, etc.).
refectory table, mesa de comedor larga y angosta (esp. la usada antiguamente en monasterios).
refer [rɪ'fɜr, B -'fɜ] *v.t.* (*pret., p.p.* REFERRED; *p.pr.* REFERRING) 1. atribuir, asignar, imputar. 2. referir, remitir; someter (a examen o decisión). —*v.i.* (ú. gen. con *to*) 1. referirse (a), aludir (a). 2. relacionarse (con). 3. consultar, ej., *during his speech he often referred to his notes,* durante su discurso él consultaba a menudo sus apuntes.
referable ['rɛfərəbəl, B rɪ'fɜr-] *a.* atribuible, asignable.
referee [ˌrɛfə'ri] *s.* juez, dirimente; (dep.) árbitro, juez de campo; (for.) arbitrador. —*v.t., v.i.* (*pret., p.p.* REFEREED; *p.pr.* REFEREEING) arbitrar, servir de árbitro o juez.
reference ['rɛfərəns] *s.* 1. referencia, remisión; alusión, mención. 2. respecto, relación. 3. signo de referencia, nota (en un libro o escrito). 4. libro de consulta; fuente de información (persona). 5. informe, recomendación, referencia, certificado de trabajo. 6. **in** (o **with) r. to,** con respecto a, respecto a; **to make r. to,** referirse a, hacer alusión a; **without r. to,** sin consideración a. —*v.t.* proveer de referencias (obra literaria, etc.).
reference mark, (impr.) llamada, llamada marginal.
reference work, obra de consulta.
referendum [ˌrɛfə'rɛndəm] *s.* (*pl.* REFERENDUMS o REFERENDA [-də]) (pol.) referéndum, plebiscito.
referent ['rɛfərənt] *s.* 1. informador. 2. palabra o término de remisión (en texto).
referential [ˌrɛfə'rɛntʃəl, B -'rɛnʃəl] *a.* de referencia, como referencia.
referral [rɪ'fɜrəl] *s.* referencia.
referrible [-əbəl] *a.* atribuible, asignable.
refill ['riˌfɪl] *s.* 1. carga de recambio, recambio (para bolígrafo, etc.). 2. segunda preparación (de una receta médica). — [ri'fɪl] *v.t., v.i.* rellenar(se), reenvasar.
refinance [ˌrifə'næns, ri'faɪˌnæns] *v.t.* financiar de nuevo, volver a capitalizar.
refine [rɪ'faɪn] *v.t.* 1. refinar, purificar, clarificar, depurar, acrisolar. 2. (fig.) refinar, mejorar; perfeccionar, alisar. 3. (fig.) refinar, educar, pulir (a una persona). —*v.i.* refinarse, purificarse.

refined [-'faɪnd] *a.* 1. refinado, purificado. 2. (fig.) fino, cortés; culto, bien educado.
refinement [-'faɪnmənt] *s.* 1. refinación, refinadura, purificación, mejoramiento. 2. refinamiento, esmero; exquisitez, finura, urbanidad, cortesía; ingeniosidad, sutileza; filigrana.
refiner [-ər, B -ə] *s.* refinador.
refinery [-ərɪ] *s.* (*pl.* REFINERIES) refinería (industrial).
refining [-ɪŋ] *s.* refinación, purificación.
refinish [ri'fɪnɪʃ] *v.t.* dar un acabado nuevo; barnizar (muebles, etc.).
refit [ri'fɪt, B 'ri-] *v.t.* (*pret., p.p.* REFITTED; *p.pr.* REFITTING) 1. rehabilitar, reparar, renovar, rehacer. 2. volver a equipar o pertrechar. —*v.i.* obtener provisiones frescas o equipo nuevo. —*s.* rehabilitación, reparación, renovación, restauración.
reflation [ri'fleɪʃən] *s.* (e.p.) reflación.
reflect [rɪ'flɛkt] *v.t.* 1. reflejar (luz, imagen, etc.). 2. (fig.) reflejar, revelar (emoción, verdad, intención, etc.). 3. hacer recaer o redundar (prestigio, deshonra, etc.). 4. (ant.) desviar, apartar. —*v.i.* 1. reflejar, reflectar, reverberar (la luz, el calor, el sonido, etc.). 2. reflexionar, meditar, contemplar. 3. **r. on** (o **upon),** reflexionar sobre (algo); desprestigiar, desacreditar (a alguien).
reflectance [-'flɛktəns] *s.* (fís.) reflectancia.
reflected ray [-təd-] (ópt.) rayo reflejo, rayo reflejado.
reflecting circle [-tɪŋ-] (astr., mar.) círculo de reflexión.
reflecting telescope, telescopio de espejo, telescopio de reflexión.
reflection, (pr. G.B.) **reflexion** [-'flɛkʃən] *s.* 1. reflexión, reverbero, reverberación. 2. reflejo (luz, calor o imagen reflejados). 3. reproche, censura, crítica, tacha, imputación. 4. reflexión, meditación, deliberación, contemplación. 5. (*pl.*) reflexiones, comentarios, acotaciones. 6. (anat.) repliegue. 7. **on r.,** deliberándolo, si uno piensa bien.
reflectional [-əl] *a.* propio de la reflexión.
reflective [rɪ'flɛktɪv] *a.* 1. que refleja, reflexivo (superficie, etc.). 2. (fig.) reflexivo, pensativo, ponderado. 3. (gram.) reflexivo.
reflectively [-lɪ] *adv.* reflexivamente.
reflectiveness [-nəs] *s.* 1. poder de reflexión, índice de reflexión. 2. (fig.) naturaleza o carácter reflexivo.
reflectivity [ˌriˌflɛk'tɪvətɪ] *s.* poder de reflexión.
reflectometer [-'tɑmətər, B -'tɔmɪtə] *s.* (fís.) reflectómetro.
reflector [rɪ'flɛktər, B -tə] *s.* (ópt.) reflector; telescopio de reflexión.
reflex ['riˌflɛks] *a.* 1. reflejo, reflejado. 2. (fisiol.) reflejo. 3. (rad.) de reflexión. —*s.* 1. reflejo, reflexión, imagen reflejada; semejanza; parecido, reproducción. 2. (fisiol.) reflejo.
reflex action, (fisiol.) acción refleja, acto reflejo.
reflex amplification, (rad.) amplificación reflejada.
reflex angle, (geóm.) ángulo reflejo, ángulo cóncavo.
reflex arc, (fisiol.) arco reflejo.
reflex camera, (foto.) cámara reflex.
reflex circuit, (rad.) circuito de reflexión.
reflexive [rɪ'flɛksɪv] *a.* 1. reflexivo. 2. (fisiol.) reflejo. 3. (gram.) reflexivo. —*s.* pronombre o verbo reflexivos.
reflexively [-lɪ] *adv.* reflexivamente.
reflexiveness [-nəs] *s.* poder de reflexión, reflexividad; índice de reflexión.
reflexive pronoun, (gram.) pronombre reflexivo.

reflexive verb, (gram.) verbo reflejo o reflexivo.
reflexivity [ˌriflɛk'sɪvətɪ] *s.* poder de reflexión, reflexividad; índice de reflexión.
refloat [ri'floʊt, B 'ri-] *v.t.* poner otra vez a flote, reflotar.
reflow [ri'floʊ] *v.i.* refluir.
refluence ['rɛfluəns] *s.* reflujo.
refluent [-ənt] *a.* refluente, menguante (marea).
reflux ['riˌflʌks] *s.* reflujo, menguante (de la marea).
reforest [ri'fɔrəst, -'fɑr-, B -'fɔr-] *v.t.* repoblar de árboles, reforestar.
reforestation [-ˌfɔrəs'teɪʃən, -ˌfɑr-, B -ˌfɔr-] *s.* repoblación forestal, reforestación.
reforge [ri'fɔrdʒ, B -'fɔdʒ] *v.t.* forjar de nuevo; rehacer.
reform [rɪ'fɔrm, B -'fɔm] *v.t.* 1. reformar. 2. abolir, suprimir (abusos, inmoralidad, etc.). —*v.i.* reformarse. —*s.* reforma, reformación.
re-form [ri'fɔrm, B 'ri'fɔm] *v.t., v.i.* formar(se) de nuevo, rehacer(se).
reformable [rɪ'fɔrməbəl, B -'fɔmə-] *a.* reformable.
reformation [ˌrɛfər'meɪʃən, B -fə'-] *s.* 1. reformación, reforma, corrección. 2. **R.,** (hist.) la Reforma.
re-formation [ˌrifɔr'meɪʃən, B -fɔ'-] *s.* nueva formación.
reformational [ˌrɛfər'meɪʃənəl, B -fə'-] *a.* de la Reforma.
reformative [rɪ'fɔrmətɪv, B -'fɔmə-] *a.* reformativo.
reformatory [-ˌtɔrɪ, B -tərɪ] *a.* reformatorio. —*s.* (*pl.* REFORMATORIES) reformatorio.
reformed [-'fɔrmd, B -'fɔmd] *a.* 1. reformado, corregido, enmendado. 2. **R.,** (relig.) reformado, protestante.
Reformed churches, iglesias protestantes.
reformer [-'fɔrmər, B -'fɔmə] *s.* reformador.
reformism [-ˌmɪzəm] *s.* reformismo (doctrina).
reformist [-məst] *s.* 1. reformista. 2. (relig.) protestante.
reform school, reformatorio (para menores).
reformulate [ri'fɔrmjəˌleɪt, B -'fɔmjʊ-] *v.t.* formular de nuevo.
refract [rɪ'frækt] *v.t.* 1. (fís.) refractar. 2. (med., ópt.) medir el índice de refracción de (un lente o de un ojo).
refracted ray [-əd-] (ópt.) rayo refracto, rayo refractado.
refractile [-'fræktəl, -ˌaɪl] *a.* refractivo.
refracting telescope [-ɪŋ-] telescopio de refracción.
refraction [rɪ'frækʃən] *s.* (fís.) refracción.
refractive [-tɪv] *a.* refractivo, refringente.
refractive index, índice de refracción.
refractively [-lɪ] *adv.* con refracción.
refractiveness [-nəs] **refractivity** [ˌrifræk'tɪvətɪ] *s.* refractividad.
refractometer [ˌrifræk'tɑmətər, B -'tɔmɪtə] *s.* refractómetro.
refractometry [-trɪ] *s.* refractometría.
refractor [rɪ'fræktər, B -tə] *a.* refractor. —*s.* medio refringente.
refractoriness [-tərɪnəs] *s.* 1. contumacia, indocilidad. 2. (med.) resistencia al tratamiento. 3. (fís.) resistencia al calor, poder refractario.
refractory [-tərɪ] *a.* 1. refractario, recalcitrante, indócil, intratable. 2. (fís., quím.) poco fusible (minerales), refractario. —*s.* material refractario.
refrain [rɪ'freɪn] *v.i.* **r. from,** refrenarse de, abstenerse de. —*v.t.* (ant.) refrenar, reprimir, contener.
refrain, *s.* 1. estribillo, bordón, contera (de verso). 2. (fig.) bordón, muletilla.
refrangibility [rɪˌfrændʒə'bɪlətɪ] *s.* (fís.) refrangibilidad.
refrangible [rɪ'frændʒəbəl] *a.* (fís.) refrangible.
refrangibleness [-nəs] *s.* refrangibilidad.
refresh [rɪ'frɛʃ] *v.t.* 1. refrescar, enfriar. 2. (fig.) refrescar (memoria, conocimiento, etc.); reavivar, reponer las fuerzas a. 3. llenar o surtir de nuevo. 4. refrescar, renovar. —*v.i.* refrescarse, reanimarse.
refreshen [-ən] *var. de* **refresh.**
refresher [-ər, B -ə] *s.* 1. refresco, refrigerio, refrescamiento; 2. recordatorio, advertencia; curso de repaso. 3. (der.) adehala (que se da al abogado en las causas que se prolongan demasiado).
refresher course, curso de repaso.
refreshing [-ɪŋ] *a.* refrescador, refrescante; alentador, placentero.
refreshingly [-ɪŋlɪ] *adv.* de manera refrescante, refrescantemente.
refreshment [-mənt] *s.* 1. refrescadura. 2. refresco, refrescamiento; (*pl.*) refrigerio, colación, refacción ligera.
refrigerant [rɪ'frɪdʒərənt] *a.* refrigerante, refrescador, refrescante. —*s.* 1. (med.) refrigerante. 2. (quím.) mezcla refrigerante, mezcla frigorífica.
refrigerate [-ˌreɪt] *v.t.* refrigerar, enfriar, (los alimentos).
refrigeration [rɪˌfrɪdʒə'reɪʃən] *s.* refrigeración.
refrigerative [-'frɪdʒəˌreɪtɪv, B -rətɪv] *s.* refrigerante. —*a.* refrigerativo.
refrigerator [-ˌreɪtər, B -ə] *s.* nevera, refrigerador, refrigeradora.
refrigerator car, (f.c.) vagón frigorífico.
refrigeratory [-'frɪdʒərəˌtɔrɪ, B -tərɪ] *a.* refrigerante.
refringent [rɪ'frɪndʒənt] *a.* refringente.
refuel [ri'fjuəl] *v.t., v.i.* reabastecer(se) de combustible, repostar.
refuge ['rɛfjudʒ] *s.* refugio, amparo; asilo, retiro; **to take r. in,** refugiarse en. —*v.t., v.i.* refugiar(se).
refugee [ˌrɛfjʊ'dʒi] *s.* refugiado.
refulgence [rɪ'fʌldʒəns] *s.* refulgencia, resplandor, esplendor, brillo, brillantez.
refulgent [-dʒənt] *a.* refulgente, brillante.
refund [ri'fʌnd] *v.t.* consolidar (una deuda).
refund [rɪ'fʌnd] *v.t.* reembolsar, devolver (el dinero). — ['riˌfʌnd] *s.* 1. reembolso, devolución de dinero. 2. cantidad reembolsada.
refurbish [ri'fɜrbɪʃ, B 'ri'fɜbɪʃ] *v.t.* renovar, restaurar, retocar, pulir.
refurnish [-'fɜrnɪʃ, B -'fɜnɪʃ] *v.t.* amueblar de nuevo, reamoblar.
refusal [rɪ'fjuzəl] *s.* 1. negativa, denegación, repulsa. 2. opción.
refuse [-'fjuz] *v.t.* 1. rehusar, rechazar, recusar, no aceptar. 2. denegar, negarse (a). 3. rehusar saltar (obstáculo, díc. del caballo). 4. (mil.) contener. 5. (naipes) no servir en (cierto palo). 6. (ant.) renunciar, descartar. 7. **r. (someone),** denegar (a uno) su pedido, ej., *I have never been refused,* nunca me han denegado un pedido; **r. to (do),** negarse a (hacer).
refuse ['rɛfˌjus] *a.* desechado, inservible, inútil, sin valor. —*s.* desperdicios, desecho, barreduras; basura.
refutable [rɪ'fjutəbəl, 'rɛfjətə-] *a.* refutable.
refutation [ˌrɛfjʊ'teɪʃən] *s.* refutación, rebatimiento, confutación, impugnación.
refute [rɪ'fjut] *v.t.* refutar, confutar, rebatir, impugnar (opinión, argumento, declaración, etc.).
regain [rɪ'geɪn] *v.t.* 1. recobrar, recuperar. 2. reconquistar, ganar o alcanzar de nuevo (una posición o lugar).
regal ['rigəl] *a.* real, regio; magnífico, suntuoso, majestuoso.
regale [rɪ'geɪl] *v.t., v.i.* regalar(se), banquetear(se), agasajar, festejar(se), recrear(se), deleitar(se). —*s.* 1. banquete, festín. 2. golosina, bocado exquisito; refresco, refacción ligera.
regalement [-mənt] *s.* agasajo, regalo, regalamiento.
regalia [-jə] *s. pl.* 1. galas reales, emblemas o insignias reales. 2. galas, adornos, atavío especial. 3. **in full r.,** de punta en blanco.
regalist ['rigələst] *s.* regalista.
regality [rɪ'gælətɪ] *s.* 1. realeza, soberanía. 2. jurisdicción soberana.
regally ['rigəlɪ] *adv.* regiamente, suntuosamente.
regard [rɪ'gɑrd, B -'gɑd] *v.t.* 1. mirar, observar, contemplar, mirar con atención. 2. respetar, estimar. 3. tomar en consideración, tener en cuenta, hacer caso de. 4. considerar, juzgar. 5. tocar, concernir, atañer, respectar, referirse a. 6. (ant.) cuidar, interesarse por. 7. **as regards, regarding,** en cuanto a, en lo que respecta a. —*v.i.* fijar(se) (en algo), contemplar, mirar con fijeza o atención. —*s.* 1. mirada. 2. atención, consideración, cuidado, interés. 3. respecto, relación, referencia. 4. respeto, estimación; (*pl.*) saludos, memorias, recuerdos (que se envían como expresiones de amistad a un ausente). 5. (ant.) aspecto, apariencia, semblante. 6. **in r. to, with r. to,** con respecto o referencia a, en cuanto a, con relación a; **to have no r. for,** no estimar, no respetar; **to pay r. to,** respetar, hacer caso de; **with due r. to,** sin menoscabo de; **without r. to,** sin hacer caso de, sin tomar en consideración; sin miramientos por.
regardant [-ənt] *a.* (her.) contornado.
regardful [-fəl] *a.* 1. atento, cuidadoso. 2. respetuoso.
regardfully [-fəlɪ] *adv.* atentamente.
regardfulness [-fəlnəs] *s.* atención; respeto.
regarding [-ɪŋ] *prep.* con respecto o referencia a, sobre, en cuanto a.
regardless [-ləs] *a.* despreocupado, desconsiderado, indiferente. —*adv.* sin consideración alguna; a pesar de todo; **r. of,** sin considerar, a pesar de.
regardlessly [-lɪ] *adv.* desconsideradamente, sin hacer caso (de advertencia, etc.).
regatta [rɪ'gɑtə, -'gætə, B -'gætə] *s.* (*pl.* REGATTAS) (dep.) regata.
regelate ['ridʒəˌleɪt] *v.i.* (fís.) volver a helarse.
regelation [ˌridʒə'leɪʃən] *s.* (fís.) regelación.
regency ['ridʒənsɪ] *s.* regencia.
regeneracy [rɪ'dʒɛnərəsɪ] *s.* regeneración.
regenerate [-ˌreɪt] *v.t.* 1. regenerar, reformar. 2. regenerar, reproducir, renovar. 3. (elec., mec.) regenerar. —*v.i.* regenerarse. — [-rət] *a.* regenerado.
regenerated cellulose [-ˌreɪtəd-] (quím.) celulosa regenerada.
regeneration [rɪˌdʒɛnə'reɪʃən] *s.* regeneración.
regenerative [-'dʒɛnəˌreɪtɪv, -rətɪv, B -rətɪv] *a.* regenerador, regenerativo.
regenerative amplifier, (rad., electrón.) amplificador de reacción positiva.
regenerative braking, frenaje de regeneración, frenaje de recuperación, frenado reostático.
regenerative detector, (rad.) detector de reacción.
regenerative furnace, horno de regeneración, de recuperación.

regenerator [-ˌreɪtər, B -ə] *s.* regenerador; (mec.) regenerador, recuperador.
regent ['ridʒənt] *a.* regente. —*s.* 1. regente. 2. (raro) gobernante, gobernador. 2. (E.U.) miembro del directorio, de la junta de gobierno (de una universidad).
regentship [-ˌʃɪp] *s.* regencia, cargo de regente.
regicidal [ˌrɛdʒə'saɪdəl] *a.* regicida.
regicide ['rɛdʒəˌsaɪd] *s.* 1. regicida. 2. regicidio.
regild [ri'gɪld] *v.t.* redorar.
regime, régime [rə'ʒim, reɪ-, B reɪ-] *s.* régimen, sistema social o de gobierno.
regimen ['rɛdʒəmən] *s.* 1. régimen, gobierno. 2. (med.) régimen, dieta, cura, tratamiento. 3. (gram.) régimen.
regiment [-mənt] *s.* 1. (mil.) regimiento. 2. (raro) regimiento, gobierno, mando. —*v.t.* 1. (mil.) regimentar, formar en regimiento o regimientos; destinar a un regimiento. 2. (fig.) regimentar, reglamentar, uniformar, ordenar estrictamente.
regimental [ˌrɛdʒə'mɛntəl] *a.* de regimiento, del regimiento.
regimentals [-əlz] *s.* (*pl.*) uniforme de regimiento; uniforme militar.
regimentation [ˌrɛdʒəmən'teɪʃən] *s.* regimentación.
region ['ridʒən] *s.* 1. región, zona, lugar, espacio, territorio; comarca, distrito (esp. administrativo). 2. (anat., zool.) región, zona, parte (del cuerpo). 3. **in the r. of,** alrededor de (cierta suma).
regional [-əl] *a.* regional.
regionalism [-əˌlɪzəm] *s.* regionalismo.
regionally [-əlɪ] *adv.* en forma regional, regionalmente.
regisseur [ˌreɪʒɪ'sɜ] *s.* (teat., fr.) régisseur, director escénico.
register ['rɛdʒəstər, B -tə] *s.* 1. registro, padrón, matrícula; lista, archivo, escalafón, protocolo. 2. registro, inscripción, asiento. 3. registro, regulador (de la entrada de aire en un horno, estufa, etc.). 4. registrador (aparato). 5. (mús.) registro (de la voz o de un instrumento). 6. (impr.) registro (de las dos caras del pliego impreso). 7. (mar.) abanderar. —*v.t.* 1. registrar, inscribir, asentar, anotar, matricular, empadronar. 2. registrar, indicar (temperatura, presión de aire, humedad, etc. díc. de un instrumento). 3. hacer corresponder (exactamente). 4. certificar (carta, paquete, etc.). 5. denotar (emoción en el rostro). —*v.i.* 1. registrarse, inscribirse, matricularse. 2. corresponder exactamente. 3. (impr.) estar en registro.
register, *s.* registrador; archivero, archivador, archivista.
registered [-tərd, B -təd] *a.* 1. registrado, inscrito. 2. matriculado. 3. nominativo (bonos, acciones, etc.). 4. de pedigree (ganado). 5. certificado, autenticado.
registered letter, carta certificada.
registered mail, correo certificado.
registered nurse, enfermera diplomada, Ayudante Técnico Sanitario.
registerer [-tərər, B -tərə] *s.* registrador.
register tonnage, tonelaje de registro.
registrar ['rɛdʒəˌstrɑr, B ˌrɛdʒɪs'trɑ] *s.* jefe de registros civiles; registrador (de propiedades); archivero, archivista, archivador.
registrate [-ˌstreɪt, B 'rɛdʒɪ-] *v.i.* (mús.) seleccionar y graduar los registros del órgano.
registration [ˌrɛdʒə'streɪʃən] *s.* 1. registro, matrícula, encabezamiento, empadronamiento. 2. asiento, inscripción, registro. 3. matrícula, (número de) personas registradas o empadronadas. 4. (mús.) selección y graduación de los registros (del órgano); combinación de los registros (del órgano).
registration fee, derecho de matrícula.
registry ['rɛdʒəstrɪ] *s.* 1. registro, empadronamiento, inscripción, matriculación; padrón, matrícula. 2. registro, oficina de registro; archivo. 3. registro, protocolo.
regius professor ['ridʒɪəs-] profesor que ocupa una cátedra instituida por dádiva real en las universidades de Oxford o Cambridge.
reglet ['rɛglət] *s.* 1. (arq.) filete. 2. (impr.) regleta, corondel.
regnal ['rɛgnəl] *a.* de un reino o reinado, real.
regnancy [-nənsɪ] *s.* predominio; soberanía, dominio.
regnant [-nənt] *a.* reinante, predominante, prevaleciente.
regolith ['rɛgəˌlɪθ] *s.* (geol.) regolito.
regorge [ri'gɔrdʒ, B -'gɔdʒ] *v.t.* vomitar, arrojar, devolver. —*v.i.* brotar o manar de nuevo.
regrant [ri'grænt] *v.t.* volver a conceder u otorgar; renovar (una concesión). —*s.* nueva concesión.
regress ['riˌgrɛs] *s.* 1. regreso, retiro, retirada; salida. 2. retroceso, regresión; retrogradación; retrogresión; decadencia — [rɪ'grɛs] *v.i.* 1. regresar, retroceder. 2. (astr.) **retrogradar.**
regression [rɪ'grɛʃən] *s.* regresión, retroceso, retroceso.
regressive [-'grɛsɪv] *a.* 1. regresivo. 2. decreciente.
regret [rɪ'grɛt] *v.t.* (*pret., p.p.* REGRETTED; *p.pr.* REGRETTING) 1. lamentar, deplorar. 2. sentir, dolerse, arrepentirse de, ej., *to r. one's past mistakes,* apprepentirse de los errores cometidos. —*s.* 1. pena, pesar, sentimiento. 2. pesadumbre, compunción, remordimiento, arrepentimiento. 3. (*pl.*) excusas (que se envían rechazando una invitación).
regretful [rɪ'grɛtfəl] *a.* pesaroso, arrepentido.
regretfully [-fəlɪ] *adv.* con pesar, tristemente, sentidamente.
regretfulness [-fəlnəs] *s.* arrepentimiento, pesar.
regrettable [-əbəl] *a.* lamentable, sensible; deplorable.
regrettably [rɪ'grɛtəblɪ] *adv.* lamentablemente, sensiblemente.
regroup [ˌri'grup] *v.t., v.i.* distribuir(se) en grupos nuevos, formar(se) un grupo nuevo, reagrupar(se).
regular ['rɛgjələr, B -lə] *a.* 1. regular, arreglado; uniforme, simétrico. 2. constante, continuo. 3. regular, ordinario; corriente; metódico, sistemático, ej., *a. r. life,* una vida metódica (sin excesos). 4. (relig.) regular (díc. de órdenes religiosas). 5. (bot.) regular, simétrico (los miembros de cada verticilio). 6. (gram., geom.) regular. 7. (mil.) regular, de línea, ej., *r. army,* (mil.) ejército permanente. 8. (fam.) cabal, completo, verdadero, típico. 9. (jer.) amable, simpático, decente, ej., *he is a r. guy,* es un buen chico. —*s.* 1. parroquiano regular. 2. (fam.) empleado permanente. 3. (relig.) regular. 4. (mil.) soldado regular o de línea; (*pl.*) tropa de línea, tropas regulares.
regular clergy, clero regular (que no es secular).
regularity [ˌrɛgjə'lærətɪ] *s.* regularidad; simetría, igualdad; uniformidad, método, orden, constancia, continuidad.
regularization [-lərɪ'zeɪʃən, B -raɪ-] *s.* regularización.
regularize ['rɛgjələˌraɪz] *v.t.* regularizar, regular, normalizar, metodizar, ordenar.
regularly [-lərlɪ, B -ləlɪ] *adv.* regularmente; comúnmente, ordinariamente.
regular member, académico de número.
regular verb, (gram.) verbo regular.
regular year, año regular (del calendario judío).
regulate [-ˌleɪt] *v.t.* 1. regular, reglar, normar, regir, regularizar. 2. reglamentar, sujetar a reglamento; ajustar (a la ley, orden, etc.), ej., *r. industries,* reglamentar las industrias. 3. ordenar, metodizar (costumbre, hábito, etc.).
regulating valve [-ɪŋ-] (mec.) válvula reguladora.
regulation [ˌrɛgjə'leɪʃən] *s.* 1. regulación, ordenamiento. 2. regla, ordenanza, orden (*f.*), reglamento.
regulative ['rɛgjəˌleɪtɪv, B -lət-] *a.* regulativo, regulador, normativo. —*s.* regulador.
regulator [-ˌleɪtər, B -ə] *s.* regulador, (tec., mec., elec.) regulador (de una máquina, turbina, etc.); registro (de reloj); cronómetro regulador.
regulatory [-ləˌtɔrɪ, B -lətərɪ] *a.* 1. regulador. 2. reglamentario.
regulus ['rɛgjələs] *s.* (*pl.* REGULUSES) 1. (quím., metal.) régulo. 2. **R.,** (astr.) Régulo. 3. (orn.) reyezuelo.
regurgitate [rɪ'gɜrdʒəˌteɪt, B -'gɜdʒɪ-] *v.i.* regurgitar. —*v.t.* volver a la boca, devolver sin esfuerzo (alimento, bebida).
regurgitation [-ˌgɜrdʒə'teɪʃən, B -ˌgɜdʒɪ-] *s.* regurgitación.
rehabilitate [ˌrihə'bɪləˌteɪt, ˌriə-] *v.t.* rehabilitar; restablecer; restituir, reincorporar.
rehabilitation [-ˌbɪlə'teɪʃən] *s.* 1. rehabilitación, restablecimiento; reincorporación. 2. (der.) reivindicación.
rehash [ˌri'hæʃ] *v.t.* volver a presentar, repetir una y otra vez, reargüir (el mismo tema, argumento, etc.) — ['riˌhæʃ] *s.* 1. refrito (esp. de una obra literaria o dramática). 2. repetición (de viejos argumentos, etc.). 3. refundición.
rehearing [-'hɪrɪŋ, B -'hɪər-] *s.* (der.) nueva audiencia, revista, revisión de la causa (por el mismo tribunal); reconsideración.
rehearsal [rɪ'hɜrsəl, B -'hɜsəl] *s.* ensayo (esp. de teatro); prueba.
rehearse [-'hɜrs, B -'hɜs] *v.t.* 1. ensayar, probar. 2. repetir. 3. recitar, recontar; enumerar. 4. (ant.) referir, relatar, contar. —*v.i.* ensayarse; ocuparse en un ensayo.
reheat [ri'hit] *v.t.* recalentar; recocer.
reheater [-ər, B -ə] *s.* (mec.) recalentador.
reheating [-ɪŋ] *s.* recalentamiento; recocido.
rehydrate [ri'haɪˌdreɪt] *v.t.* rehidratar, volver a hidratar.
reification [ˌriəfə'keɪʃən] *s.* materialización, objetivación.
reify ['riəˌfaɪ] *v.t.* (*pret., p.p.* REIFIED; *p.pr.* REIFYING) convertir (una abstracción) en una cosa; materializar; objetivar, atribuir existencia real a.
reign [reɪn] *s.* 1. reinado, imperio; soberanía. 2. dominio, predominio. —*v.i.* 1. reinar, imperar, regir. 2. dominar, predominar, prevalecer, estar en boga.
reign of terror, 1. régimen de terror. 2. **the R. of T.,** el Terror (en la Revolución Francesa).
reimbursable [ˌriɪm'bɜrsəbəl, B -'bɜsə-] *a.* reembolsable, pagable, reintegrable.
reimburse [-'bɜrs, B -'bɜs] *v.t.* 1. reembolsar; reintegrar. 2. restituir, indemnizar.
reimbursement [-mənt] *s.* 1. reembolso; reintegración. 2. indemnización.
reimport [ˌriɪm'pɔrt, B -'pɔt] *v.t.* reimportar. —*s.* mercancía reimportada.
reimportation [-pɔr'teɪʃən, B -pɔ'-] *s.* reimportación.
reimposition [ˌriɪmpə'zɪʃən] *s.* nueva imposición.

reimpression [-ˈprɛʃən] *s.* (impr.) reimpresión.

rein [reɪn] *s.* 1. (*gen. pl.*) rienda. 2. (fig.) freno, refrenamiento, moderación. 3. **to assume the reins of government,** tomar las riendas del gobierno; **to draw r.,** tener las riendas; (lit. y fig.) tirar la(s) rienda(s); **to give the horse the r.,** soltar las riendas al caballo; **to give (free) r. to,** dar rienda suelta a, dar libre curso a; **to take the reins,** tomar las riendas. —*v.t.* 1. poner riendas a. 2. **r. in,** refrenar, parar (al caballo); (fig.) contener, refrenar (imaginación, impaciencia, etc.). —*v.i.* **r. in** o **up,** tirar de las riendas del caballo, frenar al caballo; detener el paso.

reincarnate [ˌriɪnˈkɑrˌneɪt, B -ˈɪnkɑˌ-] *v.t.* reencarnar, encarnar nuevamente.

reincarnation [-ɪnkɑrˈneɪʃən, B -kɑˈ-] *s.* reencarnación.

reincarnationist [-ʃənəst] *s.* creyente en la reencarnación.

reindeer [ˈreɪnˌdɪr, B -ˌdɪə] *s.* (*pl.* REINDEER o REINDEERS) (zool.) reno, rangífero, rengífero, tarando.

reindeer moss, (bot.) liquen de los renos.

reinfection [ˌriɪnˈfɛkʃən] *s.* (med.) reinfección.

reinflate [-ˈfleɪt] *v.t., v.i.* inflar(se) nuevamente.

reinflation [-ˈfleɪʃən] *s.* nueva inflación, nuevo inflamiento.

reinforce [-ˈfɔrs, B -ˈfɔs] *v.t.* reforzar, fortalecer, robustecer; esp. (mil.) reforzar con tropas o barcos adicionales. —*s.* (arm.) camisa zunchada, refuerzo (de un cañón).

reinforced concrete [-ˈfɔrst-, B -ˈfɔst-] hormigón o cemento armado, concreto reforzado.

reinforcement [-ˈfɔrsmənt, B -ˈfɔs-] *s.* 1. refuerzo; ayuda, socorro. 2. (arq.) armazón (del hormigón armado). 3. (*pl.*) (mil.) refuerzos, fuerzas de auxilio.

reins [reɪnz] *s. pl.* 1. (anat.) riñones, región renal. 2. (fig.) entrañas (donde radican los afectos, las pasiones, etc.).

reinsert [ˌriɪnˈsɜrt, B -ˈsɜt] *v.t.* insertar de nuevo, reinsertar.

reinstall [-ˈstɔl] *v.t.* reinstalar, restablecer.

reinstallment, reinstalment [-mənt] *s.* reinstalación, restablecimiento; rehabilitación.

reinstate [-ˈsteɪt] *v.t.* (con *in*) reinstalar, reponer (en), reintegrar (en posesión, etc.); volver a investir (de privilegios, cargos, etc.); rehabilitar, restablecer; reparar lo dañado (seguros).

reinstatement [-mənt] *s.* reinstalación; rehabilitación.

reinsurance [ˌriɪnˈʃʊrəns, B -ˈʃʊər-] *s.* (com.) reaseguro.

reinsure [-ˈʃʊr, B -ˈʃʊə] *v.t.* reasegurar, cubrir con reaseguro (riesgo).

reinsurer [-ˈʃʊrər, B -ˈʃʊərə] *s.* compañía de reaseguros, reasegurador.

reintegrate [riˈɪntəˌgreɪt] *v.t.* reintegrar.

reintegration [-ˌɪntəˈgreɪʃən] *s.* reintegro, reintegración.

reinter [ˌriɪnˈtɜr, B -ˈtɜ] *v.t.* enterrar de nuevo; enterrar en otra tumba.

reinterpret [-ˈtɜrprət, B -ˈtɜprɪt] *v.t.* dar una interpretación nueva o diferente a, reinterpretar.

reintroduce [ˌriˌɪntrəˈdus, B -ˈdjus] *v.t.* introducir de nuevo, reintroducir.

reintroduction [-ˈdʌkʃən] *s.* nueva introducción, reintroducción.

reinvest [ˌriɪnˈvɛst] *v.t., v.i.* reinvertir, invertir de nuevo (esp. dinero adquirido en antiguas inversiones).

reinvestment [-mənt] *s.* reinversión.

reinvigorate [-ˈvɪgəˌreɪt] *v.t.* vigorizar o vigorar de nuevo, revigorizar.

reissue [riˈɪʃu] *s.* 1. nueva publicación o edición; reimpresión. 2. (filat.) nueva emisión (de sellos postales de un mismo diseño). —*v.t.* 1. volver a publicar; reimprimir. 2. volver a emitir.

reiterate [riˈɪtəˌreɪt] *v.t.* reiterar, repetir continuamente.

reiteratedly [-ədlɪ] *adv.* reiteradamente; repetidamente.

reiteration [riˌɪtəˈreɪʃən] *s.* reiteración, repetición continua.

reiterative [riˈɪtəˌrətɪv, B -rət-] *a.* reiterativo.

reject [rɪˈdʒɛkt] *v.t.* 1. rechazar, repeler, rehusar; descartar, desechar. 2. arrojar, vomitar. 3. (ant.) abandonar, desamparar. — [ˈriˌdʒɛkt] *s.* 1. producto defectuoso. 2. recluta excluído del servicio militar.

rejection [-ˈdʒɛkʃən] *s.* rechazo, repudio.

rejoice [rɪˈdʒɔɪs] *v.t.* regocijar, alegrar, alborozar. —*v.i.* regocijarse, alegrarse, gozar(se).

rejoicer [-ˈdʒɔɪsər, B -sə] *s.* regocijador, alborozador.

rejoicing [-sɪŋ] *s.* 1. regocijo, alegría, alborozo, gozo. 2. festividad.

rejoin [rɪˈdʒɔɪn] *v.i.* 1. replicar. 2. (der.) duplicar, responder (el demandado a la réplica del actor). —*v.t.* (der.) contestar en dúplica.

rejoin [ˈri-] *v.t.* 1. volver a unir o juntar. 2. volver a juntarse con. 3. reincorporarse a (partido, club, etc.).

rejoinder [rɪˈdʒɔɪndər, B -də] *s.* 1. respuesta, réplica. 2. (der.) contrarréplica, dúplica.

rejuvenate [-ˈdʒuvəˌneɪt] *v.t.* rejuvenecer, remozar.

rejuvenation [-ˌdʒuvəˈneɪʃən] *s.* rejuvenecimiento, remozamiento, remozadura.

rejuvenator [-ˈdʒuvəˌneɪtər, B -ə] *s.* rejuvenecedor.

rejuvenescence [-ˌdʒuvəˈnɛsəns] *s.* rejuvenecimiento, remozamiento, remozadura.

rejuvenescent [-ənt] *a.* rejuvenecedor.

rejuvenize [-ˈdʒuvəˌnaɪz] *v.t.* rejuvenecer, remozar.

rekindle [riˈkɪndəl] *v.t.* 1. volver a encender, reencender, encender de nuevo. 2. (fig.) reavivar (esperanza, entusiasmo, etc.).

rel [rɛl] *s.* (elec.) rel, unidad de reluctancia.

relapse [rɪˈlæps] *v.i.* 1. recaer (enfermo). 2. **to r. into,** hundirse en, sumirse en, ej., *r. into a stupor,* sumirse en un estupor. 3. (relig.) renegar. —*s.* 1. recaída, reincidencia. 2. (med.) recidiva.

relapsing fever [-ɪŋ-] (med.) fiebre recurrente.

relatable [rɪˈleɪtəbəl] *a.* narrable.

relate [-ˈleɪt] *v.t.* 1. relatar, referir, contar, narrar. 2. relacionar; emparentar. —*v.i.* (gen. con *to*) relacionarse (con); pertenecer (a), concernir (a), tocar (a), referirse (a).

related [-əd] *a.* 1. relacionado; conexo, afín. 2. emparentado. 3. (mús.) de una conexión melódica o armónica (díc. de tonos, cuerdas o tonalidades).

relater [-ər, B -ə] *s.* relator, relatador, narrador.

relation [rɪˈleɪʃən] *s.* 1. relación, relato, narración, cuento. 2. pariente, familiar, allegado. 3. parentesco. 4. relación, referencia, alusión. 5. relación, conexión, correspondencia. 6. (*pl.*) relaciones, tratos, asuntos. 7. (*pl.*) relaciones sexuales. 8. **in r. to,** con relación a; **to bear (no) r. to,** (no) estar relacionado con, (no) tener que ver con.

relational [-əl] *a.* 1. de parentesco. 2. correlativo. 3. (gram.) de relación (sintáctica).

relationship [-ˌʃɪp] *s.* 1. correspondencia, relación, vínculo, allegamiento. 2. parentesco.

relative [ˈrɛlətɪv] *a.* 1. relativo. 2. pertinente. 3. (gram.) relativo. —*s.* 1. pariente, deudo, allegado. 2. (gram.) término relativo.

relative clause, (gram.) oración relativa.

relative humidity, (meteor.) humedad relativa.

relatively [-lɪ] *adv.* relativamente.

relativeness [-nəs] *s.* relatividad.

relative pronoun, (gram.) pronombre relativo.

relativism [-ˌɪzəm] *s.* (filos., fís.) relativismo.

relativist [-əst] *s.* relativista.

relativistic [ˌrɛlətɪˈvɪstɪk] *a.* relativista.

relativity [-ˈtɪvətɪ] *s.* relatividad.

relativity of knowledge, (filos.) relatividad del conocimiento.

relator [rɪˈleɪtər, B -ə] *s.* 1. relator, relatador, narrador. 2. (der.) denunciante.

relax [rɪˈlæks] *v.t.* 1. relajar, aflojar. 2. rebajar, mitigar, suavizar, ablandar. 3. laxar (el vientre). —*v.i.* 1. relajarse, aflojarse. 2. relajarse, mitigarse, moderarse, ceder. 3. descansar, reposar, esparcirse.

relaxant [-ənt] *a., s.* (med.) relajante.

relaxation [ˌrilækˈseɪʃən] *s.* 1. relajación, aflojamiento. 2. relajación, mitigación, moderación. 3. descanso, reposo, esparcimiento.

relaxed [rɪˈlækst] *a.* 1. relajado. 2. sosegado, reposado, calmado. 3. informal, libre.

relaxin [rɪˈlæksən] *s.* (bioquím.) relaxina.

relaxing [rɪˈlæksɪŋ] *a.* 1. calmante, sosegante. 2. agradable; apacible.

relay [ˈriˌleɪ, B rɪˈleɪ] *s.* 1. relevo, reemplazo, remuda. 2. posta, parada (de caballos, etc.). 3. (dep.) carrera de relevos, carrera de postas; tramo (en una carrera de relevos). 4. [ˈrileɪ] (elec.) relevador, contactor, disyuntor, relé; (tele.) relevador; (teleg.) repetidor. 5. máquina auxiliar reguladora; servomotor. — [ˈriˌler, rɪˈleɪ] *v.t.* (*pret., p.p.* RELAYED; *p.pr.* RELAYING) 1. transmitir, pasar (noticia, información, mensaje, etc.). 2. (rad.) transmitir por repetidor; retransmitir, enviar por posta. 3. (elec.) regular (la corriente, etc.) por relevador o relé.

re-lay [ˈriˈleɪ] *v.t.* (*pret., p.p.* RE-LAID; *p.pr.* RE-LAYING) volver a colocar, colocar de nuevo; reponer (vía).

relay broadcast, (rad.) redifusión, difusión por una radioemisora de programas recibidos de otra.

relay race [ˈriˌleɪ-] (dep.) carrera de relevos, carrera de postas.

re-lease [ˈriˈlis] *v.t.* arrendar o alquilar de nuevo.

release [rɪˈlis] *v.t.* 1. soltar, desatar, desceñir. 2. soltar (el freno, embrague de automóvil, etc.). 3. soltar, libertar, poner en libertad. 4. relevar, exonerar; aligerar, aliviar, eximir (de dolor, dificultad, castigo). 5. permitir, lanzar, iniciar la publicación o estreno de; poner en circulación, dar al público, emitir. 6. (der.) librar, liberar, relevar, descargar (de una obligación, etc.). 7. (ant.) renunciar a, abandonar. 8. (mil.) lanzar (bombas desde un avión). 9. (mec.) desenganchar, soltar, disparar. —*s.* 1. liberación, alivio (de dolor, dificultad, etc.). 2. exoneración, exención (de una obligación); renuncia, cesión (de un derecho, etc.). 3. permiso de publicación. 4. publicación, divulgación, representación. 5. comunicado (de prensa). 6. (der.) descargo, liberación, finiquito, contenta, quita. 7. (ing.) disparador, relevador; escape, trinquete. 8. (máq.) escape. 9. (mec.) disparador, relevador; disparo. 10. (elec.) interruptor.

releaser [-ˈlisər, B -sə] *s.* dispositivo de puesta en marcha, separador; desenganchador; desconectador.

release spring, (mec.) resorte antagonista.

releasing [-sɪŋ] *s.* disparo, desenganche, desprendimiento.

releasing gear, mecanismo de desenganche, órgano de desprendimiento.

releasing mechanism, dispositivo de lanzamiento o desenganche.

relegate ['rɛlə,geɪt] *v.t.* 1. relegar, desterrar. 2. (fig.) relegar, trasladar, remover (a otra posición, clase o esfera gen. inferior); posponer, detraer. 3. (con *to*) someter a la decisión (de); referir (a).

relegation [,rɛlə'geɪʃən] *s.* 1. relegación; exilio. 2. relegación, traspaso de un asunto a una posición inferior.

relent [rɪ'lɛnt] *v.t.* 1. aplacarse, desenojarse; ablandarse, enternecerse, ceder. 2. (ant.) liquidarse, derretirse; reblandecerse. —*v.t.* (ant.) ablandar; molificar.

relentless [-ləs] *a.* implacable, inexorable, inflexible, severo.

relentlessly [-lɪ] *adv.* implacablemente, inexorablemente, inflexiblemente, sin piedad.

relentlessness [-nəs] *s.* inexorabilidad, inclemencia.

relevance ['rɛləvəns] **relevancy** [-vənsɪ] *s.* pertinencia, oportunidad; aplicabilidad.

relevant ['rɛləvənt] *a.* pertinente, a propósito, que hace o viene al caso.

relevantly [-lɪ] *adv.* pertinentemente, a propósito.

reliability [rɪ,laɪə'bɪlətɪ] *s.* calidad de ser confiable, integridad, formalidad; seguridad de funcionamiento, fiabilidad.

reliable [-'laɪəbəl] *a.* 1. confiable, digno de confianza, seguro, acreditado, veraz, fidedigno. 2. de funcionamiento seguro (máquina, etc.); de efecto seguro (medicamento, etc.).

reliableness [-nəs] *s.* carácter de seguro, confiable o responsable.

reliably [-blɪ] *adv.* con seguridad, con confianza.

reliance [rɪ'laɪəns] *s.* (gen. con *upon, on, in*) confianza; seguridad, resguardo, ej., *my r. is upon God,* mi seguridad está en Dios.

reliant [-ənt] *a.* confiado; seguro.

relic ['rɛlɪk] *s.* 1. reliquia. 2. (*pl.*) ruinas; restos, residuos. 3. (*pl.*) despojos, restos mortales. 4. vestigio; recuerdo, recordatorio; monumento (del pasado).

relict ['rɛlɪkt] *s.* 1. (ant.) viuda. 2. (*pl.*) restos mortales. 3. (geol.) residuo.

relief [rɪ'lif] *s.* 1. ayuda, auxilio, socorro, asistencia, alivio, consuelo, confortación. 2. limosna, caridad; beneficencia pública. 3. relevo. 4. relevación, aligeramiento. 5. solaz, descanso. 6. (der.) desagravio, reparación, compensación, satisfacción. 7. (arq., pint.) relieve, realce, resalte, resalto. 8. (mot.) descompresión, refajo, franqueo. 9. (mec.) relieve; (hombres) relevo; (presión) alivio, desahogo. 10. **in r.,** en relieve; **to give r.,** dar alivio a; **to live on r.,** vivir del socorro estatal.

relief agencies, servicios o agencias de socorro o auxilio.

relief angle, (mec.) ángulo de rebajo o de relieve, ángulo de juego.

relief map, mapa en relieve.

relief pitcher, (béisbol) lanzador suplente.

relief port, (ing.) lumbrera de escape.

relief train, tren de socorro.

relief valve, válvula de seguridad.

relievable [rɪ'livəbəl] *a.* aliviable, remediable.

relieve [rɪ'liv] *v.t.* 1. relevar, remediar, socorrer. 2. aligerar, aliviar, mitigar, suavizar (el dolor, la pena, etc.). 3. relevar (tropas, etc.). 4. destituir; reemplazar, mudar, substituir (en un empleo). 5. relevar, descargar, exonerar (de un cargo u obligación); reparar, desagraviar. 6. quitar la monotonía a, variar, vivificar. 7. poner de relieve, realzar. 8. **r. oneself,** orinar; evacuar; **r. (someone) of,** quitarle, aliviar, aligerar (el peso, etc.) a (alguien); (hum.) despojar (a alguien) de, pelar (a alguien su reloj, dinero, etc.); **r. one's feelings,** desahogar (uno) sus sentimientos.

relieving arch [-ɪŋ-] (arq.) arco de descarga, sobrearco.

relieving tackle, 1. (mar.) pluma de chata de carena. 2. aparejos de la caña del timón.

relievo [rɪ'livoʊ] *s.* (*pl.* RELIEVOS) (arq., pint.) relieve.

relievo-work [-,wɜrk, B -,wɜk] *s.* obra de relieve; mazonería.

relight [ri'laɪt] *v.t.* reencender, encender de nuevo.

religion [rɪ'lɪdʒən] *s.* religión; **to get r.,** (vulg. o hum.) tornarse religioso; **to make a r. of (doing),** hacer un ritual de (hacer), ej., *he made a r. of taking a walk each morning,* hizo un ritual de dar un paseo todas las mañanas.

religionism [-,ɪzəm] *s.* fanatismo religioso, religiosidad excesiva; fariseísmo.

religionist [-əst] *s.* devoto fanático.

religiose [rɪ'lɪdʒɪ,oʊs] *a.* religioso.

religiosity [-,lɪdʒɪ'ɑsətɪ, B -'ɔs-] *s.* religiosidad excesiva, devoción exagerada.

religious [rɪ'lɪdʒəs] *a.* 1. religioso, devoto, pío, piadoso. 2. religioso, fiel, exacto, concienzudo, puntual. —*s.* religioso; monje, fraile; monja.

religiously [-lɪ] *adv.* religiosamente.

religiousness [-nəs] *s.* religiosidad, devoción, piedad.

reline ['ri'laɪn] *v.t.* forrar de nuevo, revestir; reforrar (frenos); reguarnecer (cojinetes).

relinquish [ri'lɪŋkwɪʃ] *v.t.* 1. abandonar (esperanza, fe, costumbre, plan, estudio, etc.). 2. renunciar a, despojarse de, ceder (derecho, propiedad, etc.).

relinquishment [-mənt] *s.* abandono, renuncia.

reliquary ['rɛlə,kwɛrɪ, B -kwərɪ] *s.* (*pl.* RELIQUARIES) relicario.

relique [rɪ'lik, 'rɛlɪk] *var. de* **relic.**

reliquiae [rɪ'lɪkwɪ,i] *s. pl.* 1. restos del pasado (edificios, ruinas). 2. restos mortales (fósiles, etc.).

relish ['rɛlɪʃ] *s.* 1. gusto, sabor característico, dejo (esp. grato). 2. un toque, una pizca (de sazonador, etc.). 3. gusto, deleite, placer, goce, fruición. 4. (fig.) apetito, apetencia, inclinación. 5. condimento, salsa. 6. **to have no r. for,** no ser del especial agrado (de uno); **with r.,** con deleite, con fruición. —*v.t.* 1. sazonar, condimentar, aderezar (los manjares). 2. comer o beber con fruición; saborear, paladear. 3. gustar de; gozar de, gozarse en. —*v.i.* (con *of*) saber (a), tener sabor (a).

relishable [-əbəl] *a.* gustoso, sabroso, apetitoso.

relive ['ri'lɪv] *v.t.* recordar (un tiempo pasado); experimentar de nuevo (una vivencia); **r. one's life,** volver a vivir uno su vida. —*v.i.* volver a la vida.

reload [-'loʊd] *v.t., v.i.* recargar(se), volver a cargar(se); transbordar (mercancías).

relocate [-'loʊ,keɪt] *v.t.* trasladar, volver a establecer, situar de nuevo (residencia, negocio); establecer en un nuevo lugar. —*v.i.* trasladarse.

relocation ['riloʊ'keɪʃən] *s.* traslado, situación o colocación nueva.

relucent [rɪ'lusənt] *a.* reluciente, refulgente, radiante.

reluct [-'lʌkt] *v.i.* (raro) (con *at, against*) sentir repulsión, mostrar repugnancia (hacia); rebelarse (contra).

reluctance [-'lʌktəns] *s.* 1. renuencia, desgana, disgusto; renuencia. 2. (elec.) reluctancia. 3. **with r.,** de mala gana, con renuencia, a regañadientes.

reluctancy [-tənsɪ] *s. var. de* **reluctance.**

reluctant [-tənt] *a.* reacio; renuente, mal dispuesto, contrario.

reluctantly [-lɪ] *adv.* de mala gana, con renuencia, a regañadientes.

reluctivity [rɪ,lʌk'tɪvətɪ] *s.* (elec.) reluctividad.

relume [rɪ'lum] **relumine** [-'lumən] *v.t.* (poét.) volver a encender, reencender.

rely [rɪ'laɪ] *v.i.* (*pret., p.p.* RELIED; *p.pr.* RELYING) (con *on, upon*) depender (de), confiar (en), contar (con), fiar o fiarse (de), atenerse (a).

remain [-'meɪn] *v.i.* 1. quedar, restar; sobrar, estar de más. 2. permanecer, estarse; quedarse, demorarse. 3. continuar; seguir siendo, durar, perdurar. 4. **I r. yours truly,** quedo atentamente suyo (forma de concluir una carta); **r. behind,** rezagarse, quedarse atrás, retrasarse; **r. to be (done),** estar por (hacer), ej., *the letter remains to be written,* la carta está por escribirse; **r. with,** quedar en manos de; **to let it r. as it is,** dejarlo como es o como está; **r. silent,** guardar silencio. —*s.* 1. (*gen. en pl.*) resto, residuo, remanente, sobra, sobrante, rezago. 2. (*pl.*) obras póstumas (esp. obras literarias). 3. (*pl.*) despojos, restos mortales. 4. (ant.) estada.

remainder [-dər, B -də] *s.* 1. residuo. resto, remanente, saldo, sobrante. 2. saldo de ejemplares (de un libro que ya no tiene salida). 3. (der.) restante, resto. 4. (mat.) resta, resto, residuo. —*a.* restante, sobrante.

remainder estate, (der.) nuda propriedad.

remaining [-ɪŋ] *a.* restante, sobrante.

remake ['ri'meɪk] *v.t.* rehacer, hacer de nuevo.

reman [-'mæn] *v.t.* 1. volver a tripular, volver a dotar o guarnecer. 2. alentar de nuevo; infundir nuevo valor a.

remand [rɪ'mænd, B -'mɑnd] *v.t.* (esp. der.) 1. volver a poner bajo custodia (a un acusado); volver a encarcelar (temporalmente). 2. devolver (los autos) al tribunal inferior. —*s.* reenvío (del acusado) a prisión; (mandato de) devolución (de los autos) al tribunal inferior.

remanence ['rɛmənəns] *s.* (fís.) remanencia.

remanent [-nənt] *a.* 1. sobrante, sobrado. 2. (fís.) remanente, residual.

remanent magnetism, (fís.) magnetismo remanente.

remark [rɪ'mɑrk, B -'mɑk] *v.t.* 1. advertir, notar, reparar, observar, percibir, percatarse de. 2. observar, expresar, comentar. —*v.i.* (con *on, upon*) aludir (a), hacer comentarios (sobre). —*s.* observación, comentario, nota; reparo; **worthy of r.,** notable.

remarkable [-əbəl] *a.* notable, extraordinario, no común; considerable; conspicuo, admirable.

remarkableness [-nəs] *s.* notabilidad.

remarkably [-blɪ] *adv.* notablemente, extraordinariamente.

remarriage ['ri'mærɪdʒ] *s.* segundo matrimonio, segundas nupcias.

remarry [-'mærɪ] *v.t., v.i.* volver a casar o casarse; contraer segundas nupcias.

rematch [-'mætʃ, B 'ri,mætʃ] *s.* (dep.) partido de desquite, partido de revancha.

remediable [rɪ'midɪəbəl] *a.* remediable, reparable.

remediably [-blɪ] *adv.* de modo remediable.

remedial [-əl] *a.* remediador; reparador; terapéutico.

remediless ['rɛmədɪləs] *a.* irremediable, irreparable; sin cura posible.

remedy ['rɛmədɪ] *s.* (*pl.* REMEDIES) 1. remedio, medicamento. 2. remedio, correctivo, cura. 3. (der.) recurso, ej., *r. of appeal,* recurso de apelación. —*v.t.* (*pret., p.p.* REMEDIED; *p.pr.* REMEDYING) remediar, curar, sanar; corregir, reparar.

remember [rɪ'mɛmbər, B -bə] *v.t.* 1. recordar, remembrar, rememorar, acordarse de. 2. retener, conservar, guardar en la memoria. 3. conmemorar. 4. tener presente, tener en cuenta. 5. premiar, recompensar, dar propina a, ej., *to r. the waiter,* dar propina al camarero. 6. dar recuerdos o saludos a, ej., *r. me to him,* déle recuerdos míos, déle mis saludos. —*v.i.* 1. acordarse. 2. hacer memoria.

remembrance [-brəns] *s.* 1. remembranza, recuerdo, memoria, recordación, reminiscencia. 2. recordativo, recordatorio, prenda de recuerdo. 3. (*pl.*) recuerdos, saludos.

remembrancer [-brənsər, B -sə] *s.* 1. recordatorio, recordativo. 2. (G.B.) oficial de Hacienda.

remex ['reɪˌmɛks, B 'ri-] *s.* (*pl.* REMIGES ['rɛməˌdʒiz]) (orn.) rémige, remera.

remigrate ['ri'maɪˌgreɪt] *v.i.* retornar de la migración (aves o peces); volver de la emigración; emigrar de nuevo. —*s.* retorno de la migración o emigración.

remilitarization [riˌmɪlətərə'zeɪʃən, B -raɪ-] *s.* remilitarización, reinstalación de tropas o fortificaciones.

remilitarize [ri'mɪlətəˌraɪz] *v.t.* remilitarizar, fortificar de nuevo.

remind [rɪ'maɪnd] *v.t.* recordar, acordar, traer a la memoria; **r. (someone) of (something),** recordar o hacer acordar de (algo) a (alguien); **r. (someone) to (do),** recordar (a alguien) que (haga).

reminder [-ər, B -ə] *s.* recordatorio, recordativo; señal, advertencia.

remindful [-fəl] *a.* 1. atento. 2. (con *of*) recordativo (de). 3. rememorativo.

reminisce [ˌrɛmə'nɪs] *v.i.* tener reminiscencias, narrar reminiscencias; refrescar recuerdos, sumirse en recuerdos.

reminiscence [-əns] *s.* 1. reminiscencia, recuerdo, remembranza. 2. (*pl.*) memorias (biográficas). 3. (filos.) reminiscencia.

reminiscent [-ənt] *a.* recordativo, evocativo, evocador.

reminiscential [-nɪs'ɛntʃəl, B -'ɛnʃəl] *a.* recordativo, rememorativo.

remise [rɪ'maɪz] *v.t.* (der.) desistir de, ceder por escritura (un derecho, etc.).

remiss [rɪ'mɪs] *a.* 1. negligente, descuidado, desidioso. 2. remiso, flojo. 3. deficiente (servicio, etc.).

remissibility [ˌrɪmɪsə'bɪlətɪ] *s.* carácter remisible, venialidad.

remissible [rɪ'mɪsəbəl] *a.* remisible, perdonable.

remission [-'mɪʃən] *s.* 1. remisión, perdón, absolución. 2. disminución (en intensidad). 3. (com.) remesa, remisión, envío. 4. (der.) dejación, desistimiento, abandono, cancelación. 5. (ant.) relajamiento, laxitud. 6. (med.) remisión.

remissness [-'mɪsnəs] *s.* negligencia, descuido, desidia, dejadez.

remissory [-ərɪ] *a.* remisivo, remisorio.

remit [rɪ'mɪt] *v.t.* (*pret., p.p.* REMITTED; *p.pr.* REMITTING) 1. remitir, perdonar. 2. remitir de, eximir de, libertad de (una obligación), exonerar. 3. remitir, mitigar, disminuir, menguar. 4. remitir, someter, referir (un asunto). 5. remitir, diferir, aplazar. 6. (com.) remesar, remitir (dinero). 7. (der.) devolver a una corte inferior. 8. (raro) devolver. —*v.i.* 1. remitir(se), menguar, moderarse. 2. (com.) hacer una remesa, girar. —*s.* (der.) devolución de una causa legal.

remittable [-əbəl] *a.* remisible.

remittal [-əl] *s.* perdón; remisión (de una pena).

remittance [-əns] *s.* remesa (de dinero), giro, envío, letra de cambio.

remittent [-ənt] *a.* (med.) remitente (fiebre).

remittent fever, (med.) fiebre remitente.

remittently [-lɪ] *adv.* (med.) con remitencia.

remitter [-ər, B -ə] *s.* remitente, el que envía o remite.

remnant ['rɛmnənt] *s.* 1. remanente, residuo, saldo, resto. 2. fragmento, trozo, retazo. 3. (fig.) vestigio, rastro, indicio. —*a.* remanente, restante.

remnant sale, venta de saldos o retazos.

remodel [ri'mɑdəl, B -'mɔd-] *v.t.* remodelar, modelar de nuevo; reconstruir; refaccionar.

remold [ri'moʊld] *v.t.* moldear de nuevo.

remonetization [riˌmɑnətə'zeɪʃən, -'mʌn-, B -taɪ-] *s.* restablecimiento en el curso legal (de un metal), remonetización.

remonetize [-'mɑnəˌtaɪz, -'mʌn-, B -'mʌn-] *v.t.* restablecer en el curso legal (un metal), remonetizar.

remonstrance [rɪ'mɑnstrəns, B -'mɔn-] *s.* 1. reconvención, protesta. 2. (hist.) memorial de reivindicaciones públicas.

remonstrant [-strənt] *a., s.* protestante (el que protesta); peticionario, exponente.

remonstrate [-ˌstreɪt, B 'rɛmən-] *v.i.* 1. (gen. con *against, on* o *upon*) protestar (contra), objetar (a). 2. **r. with,** reconvenir. —*v.t.* urgir, instar; reclamar.

remonstration [-ˌmɑn'streɪʃən, B ˌrɛmən-] *s.* protesta.

remonstrator [rɪ'mɑnˌstreɪtər, B 'rɛmən-ə] *s.* protestante, reclamante.

remontant [rɪ'mɑntənt, B -'mɔn-] *a., s.* (bot.) remontante.

remora ['rɛmərə] *s.* 1. (ict.) rémora, pez reverso. 2. obstrucción, impedimento, detenimiento.

remorse [rɪ'mɔrs, B -'mɔs] *s.* 1. remordimiento, compunción. 2. (ant.) compasión, misericordia. 3. **without r.,** sin piedad, despiadadamente; despiadado.

remorseful [-fəl] *a.* lleno de remordimiento, compungido, arrepentido, contrito.

remorsefully [-fəlɪ] *adv.* arrepentidamente, con arrepentimiento, con remordimiento.

remorseless [-ləs] *a.* despiadado, desalmado.

remorselessly [-lɪ] *adv.* despiadadamente, desalmadamente.

remorselessness [-nəs] *s.* falta de compasión, falta de piedad, inclemencia.

remote [rɪ'moʊt] *a.* 1. remoto, distante, lejano; alejado, apartado, retirado. 2. divergente, desligado. 3. (*ú. pr. el super.*) ligero, leve, ej., *not the remotest idea,* ni la más leve idea. 4. remoto, inverosímil, improbable. 5. **r. from,** (fig.) extraño a, ajeno a.

remote control, control remoto, mando a distancia, telemando, telecontrol.

remote-controlled, con mando a distancia, con control remoto, teledirigido.

remote-control TV, televisor con mando a distancia *or* con control remoto.

remotely [-lɪ] *adv.* remotamente.

remoteness [-nəs] *s.* 1. lejanía. 2. inverosimilitud, improbabilidad.

remotion [rɪ'moʊʃən] *s.* 1. remoción. 2. (ant.) partida, salida.

remould, *var. de* **remold.**

remount [ri'maʊnt] *v.t.* 1. remontar; volver a subir; volver a engastar (piedras preciosas). 2. remontar (a la tropa, etc.). —*v.i.* remontarse. —['riˌmaʊnt] *s.* caballo de relevo.

removability [riˌmuvə'bɪlətɪ] *s.* calidad de movible o trasladable, amovilidad.

removable [-'muvəbəl] *a.* 1. movible, transportable, móvil. 2. amovible (funcionario). 3. extirpable.

removal [-'muvəl] *s.* 1. remoción, removimiento; destitución, deposición, despedida. 2. transferencia, traslado, traslación, mudanza, cambio de domicilio. 3. eliminación, extirpación.

remove [rɪ'muv] *v.t.* 1. remover, transferir; trasladar, mudar. 2. quitar, alzar, levantar; desarrimar, apartar. 3. despedir, destituir, remover, deponer, separar. 4. deshacerse de, quitar de en medio. 5. sacar; extirpar, erradicar. 6. eliminar, matar. —*v.i.* irse, alejarse; mudarse, cambiar de domicilio. —*s.* 1. mudanza, translado, cambio de domicilio. 2. distancia. 3. grado, paso, intervalo; esp. grado de parentesco. 4. (G.B.) cambio de platos (durante la comida).

removed [-'muvd] *a.* apartado, retirado, distante, remoto; **my first cousin twice r.,** mi primo segundo, primo lejano.

remover [-'muvər, B -ə] *s.* 1. quitador, apartador; cargador (de muebles, mercancías, etc.). 2. sustancia que deslíe o quita otra, ej., *nail polish r.,* acetona quita-esmalte (de las uñas).

remunerate [rɪ'mjunəˌreɪt] *v.t.* remunerar, pagar; gratificar, recompensar, premiar.

remuneration [rɪˌmjunə'reɪʃən] *s.* remuneración, pago; gratificación, recompensa, premio.

remunerative [rɪ'mjunəˌreɪtɪv, B -rət-] *a.* remunerativo, lucrativo; remunerador, ventajoso, provechoso.

remuneratively [-lɪ] *adv.* ventajosamente, provechosamente.

remunerator [-ˌreɪtər, B -ə] *s.* remunerador.

Remus ['riməs] *s.* (mitol.) Remo, hermano de Rómulo, fundador de Roma.

renaissance [ˌrɛnə'sɑnts, B rə'neɪsəns] *s.* (fr.) renacimiento; **the R.,** el Renacimiento.

renal ['rinəl] *a.* (anat.) renal.

rename [ri'neɪm] *v.t.* nombrar de nuevo; poner un nuevo nombre a.

renascence [rɪ'næsəns] *s.* renacimiento; **the R.,** el Renacimiento.

renascent [-ənt] *a.* renaciente.

rencontre [rɛn'kɑntər, B -'kɔntə] *s.* (fr.) 1. encuentro casual. 2. debate; combate, lance.

rencounter [-'kaʊntər, B -ə] *v.t.* (raro) encontrar por casualidad. —*s.* 1. encuentro casual. 2. debate; combate, lance.

rend [rɛnd] *v.t.* (*pret., p.p.* RENT [rɛnt]; *p.pr.* RENDING) 1. arrancar, arrebatar. 2. (fig.) hender, rasgar, ej., *shouts rent the still of the night,* gritos hendieron o rasgaron la quietud de la noche. 3. desgarrar, rasgar, ej., *r. one's clothes,* desgarrar o rasgar uno sus ropas. —*v.i.* henderse; partirse, dividirse.

render ['rɛndər, B -də] *v.t.* 1. rendir (homenaje, honores), dar (gracias, etc.); dar, prestar (ayuda, dignidad, etc.); hacer (servicio). 2. dar, pronunciar, emitir (sentencia, veredicto, etc.). 3. presentar, someter (informe, cuentas, etc.). 4. rendir, reditual, producir (interés, etc.). 5. volver, convertir, cambiar. 6. traducir, verter. 7. presentar, producir (versión, copia, etc.). 8. representar, interpretar (concepto, obra musical, etc.); desempeñar (papel). 9. hacer (justicia). 10. hacer (inútil, superfluo, etc., algo), ej., *the new bridge rendered the road superfluous,* el nuevo puente hizo superfluo el camino. 11. entregar. 12. devolver, restituir. 13. derretir, disolver. 14. extraer la grasa de. 15. aplicar la primera capa de (enlucido, cemento, etc.) a (pared). —*v.i.* dar recompensa. —*s.* 1. tributo, contribución. 2. primera capa de enlucido o cemento.

rendezvous ['rɑndɪˌvu, -deɪ-, B 'rɔndɪ-] *s.* (*pl.* RENDEZVOUS [-ˌvuz]) 1. lugar de reunión; (mil.) punto de reunión (de tropas, barcos, etc.). 2. cita, reunión. 3. (ant.) refugio, retiro. —*v.i., v.t.* reunirse, tener una cita, encontrarse (con).

rendition [rɛn'dɪʃən] *s.* 1. rendición, capitulación, entrega. 2. versión o traducción. 3. (mús., teat.) representación, interpretación, ejecución.

rendzina [rɛn'dʒinə] *s.* (geol.) renzina.
renegade ['rɛnɪˌgeɪd] *s., a.* renegado, apóstata; traidor, desertor. —*v.i.* volverse renegado, renegar.
renege [rɪ'nɪg, B -'nig] *v.t.* renegar, negar, rehusar. —*v.i.* 1. (naipes) renunciar; 2. (fam.) echarse atrás en una promesa; **r. on,** no cumplir (lo prometido, la palabra). —*s.* (naipes) renuncio.
renegotiable [ˌrinɪ'goʊʃɪəbəl] *a.* (com.) renegociable.
renegotiate [-'goʊʃɪˌeɪt] *v.t.* 1. (com.) renegociar, negociar de nuevo. 2. (E.U.) negociar nuevo contrato para (suministros de guerra, etc. a fin de eliminar ganancias excesivas).
renegotiation [-ˌgoʊʃɪ'eɪʃən] *s.* nueva negociación.
renew [rɪ'nu, B -'nju] *v.t.* 1. renovar, restaurar; regenerar; restablecer, reconstruir. 2. reavivar, revivificar; (fig.) recrear. 3. renovar, reiterar. 4. reanudar. recomenzar. 5. renovar, reponer; reemplazar. 6. (com.) renovar, extender. —*v.i.* 1. renovarse, cobrar nueva fuerza. 2. reanudarse, empezar de nuevo. 3. hacer una renovación o extensión (de un contrato, alquiler, etc.).
renewable [-əbəl] *a.* renovable.
renewal [-əl] *s.* renovación.
renewedly [-ədlɪ] *a.* nuevamente, repetidamente.
reniform ['rɛnəˌfɔrm, B 'riniˌfɔm] *a.* reniforme, con forma de riñón.
renig [rɪ'nɪg] *v.i.* (*pret., p.p.* RENIGGED; *p.pr.* RENIGGING) *var. de* **renege.**
renin ['rinən] *s.* (bioquím.) renina.
renitency ['rɛnətənsɪ, rɪ'naɪt-] *s.* renitencia, obstinación.
renitent ['rɛnətənt, rɪ'naɪtənt] *a.* renitente, obstinado.
rennet ['rɛnət] *s.* cuajo; sustancia que cuaja la leche.
rennet bag, r. stomach, (zool.) cuajar, abomaso, cuajo.
rennin ['rɛnən] *s.* (biol.) renina.
renominate [ri'nɑməˌneɪt, B -'nɔm-] *v.t.* nominar o nombrar de nuevo (esp. como candidato).
renomination [-ˌnɑmə'neɪʃən, B -ˌnɔm-] *s.* nueva nominación.
renounce [rɪ'naʊns] *v.t.* 1. renunciar, dimitir, abdicar, abjurar. 2. repudiar, desconocer. 3. renunciar a, abandonar, ej., *r. the world,* renunciar al mundo, abandonar los asuntos mundanos. 4. (naipes) renunciar. —*v.i.* (naipes) cometer renuncio. —*s.* (naipes) renuncio.
renouncement [-mənt] *s.* renuncia, renunciamiento, abdicación.
renovate ['rɛnəˌveɪt] *v.t.* renovar, restaurar, rehacer. —*v.i.* renovarse.
renovation [ˌrɛnə'veɪʃən] *s.* renovación, restauración.
renovator ['rɛnəˌveɪtər, B -ə] *s.* renovador, restaurador.
renown [rɪ'naʊn] *s.* 1. renombre, fama, celebridad, reputación, lustre. 2. (ant.) rumor, noticia.
renowned [-'naʊnd] *a.* renombrado, afamado, célebre, reputado, famoso, connotado (Amer.).
rent [rɛnt] *s.* 1. desgarro, rotura, rasgón, rasgadura, raja, grieta. 2. cisma, división, escisión. 3. desgarramiento, rompimiento.
rent, *s.* 1. alquiler, arrendamiento. 2. (e.p.) renta, rédito. 3. **for r.,** se alquila, por alquilar. —*v.t.* alquilar, arrendar; (Mex.) rentar. —*v.i.* alquilarse, arrendarse.
rent [rɛnt] *pret., p.p. de* **rend.**
rentable ['rɛntəbəl] *a.* alquilable, arrendable.
rental [-əl] *s.* 1. alquiler (precio). 2. alquiler, arrendamiento, arriendo, alquilamiento. 3. propiedad alquilada. —*a.* 1. de alquiler. 2. por alquilar (automóviles, casas, etc.).
rent day, día señalado para pagar el alquiler.
renter [-ər, B -ə] *s.* arrendatario, inquilino.
rent-roll [-roʊl] *s.* registro de alquileres (de tierras).
renumber [ri'nʌmbər, B -bə] *v.t.* volver a numerar, numerar de nuevo.
renunciation [rɪˌnʌnsɪ'eɪʃən] *a.* 1. renunciación, renuncia, renunciamiento; desistimiento. 2. abnegación.
renunciative [-'nʌnsɪˌeɪtɪv, B -ətɪv] **renunciatory** [-əˌtɔrɪ, B -tərɪ] *a.* renunciante; abnegado.
reoccupation [riˌɑkjə'peɪʃən, B -ˌɔk-] *s.* reocupación, nueva ocupación.
reoccupy [-'ɑkjəˌpaɪ, B -'ɔk-] *v.t.* reocupar, volver a ocupar, ocupar de nuevo.
reopen [ri'oʊpən] *v.t.* 1. reabrir, volver a abrir, abrir de nuevo. 2. reanudar, volver a empezar. —*v.i.* reabrirse.
reopening [-ɪŋ] *s.* reapertura.
reorder [ri'ɔrdər, B -'ɔdə] *s.* (com.) nuevo pedido, nueva orden (de mercancía). —*v.t.* 1. rearreglar, reorganizar. 2. (com.) ordenar de nuevo, pedir de nuevo. —*v.i.* hacer un nuevo pedido.
reorganization [riˌɔrgənə'zeɪʃən, B -ˌɔgənaɪ-] *s.* reorganización, nueva organización.
reorganize [-'ɔrgəˌnaɪz, B -'ɔgə-] *v.t.* reorganizar, organizar de nuevo, volver a organizar.
reorganizer [-ər, B -ə] *s.* reorganizador.
reorient [ri'ɔrɪənt] *v.t.* reorientar, dar nueva orientación a.
reorientation [-ˌɔrɪən'teɪʃən] *s.* reorientación, nueva orientación.
rep [rɛp] *s.* 1. (tej.) reps, teletón. 2. (jer.) reputación, renombre. 3. (fam.) representante.
repackage [ri'pækɪdʒ] *v.t.* empaquetar de nuevo (esp. en forma más atractiva o mejor).
repaid [ri'peɪd] *pret., pp. de repay.*
repaint [ri'peɪnt] *v.t.* repintar, volver a pintar, pintar de nuevo. —*s.* repinte.
repair [rɪ'pɛr, B -'pɛə] *v.i.* (ú. con *to*) 1. ir (a), dirigirse (a), concurrir (a), acudir (a). 2. recurrir (a), acogerse (a). —*s.* 1. punto de reunión, guarida. 2. (esco.) concurso, concurrencia.
repair, *v.t.* 1. reparar, restaurar, componer, enmendar, arreglar. 2. curar, sanar, remediar, restablecer la salud. 3. (raro) indemnizar, resarcir, restituir. —*s.* 1. reparación, restauración, enmienda, arreglo; refacción, compostura, remiendo. 2. (buena) condición, (buen) estado, ej., *in bad r.,* en mal estado, *in good r.,* en buen estado, *it is out of r.,* está en mal estado, no se puede componer.
repairable [-'pɛrəbəl, B -'pɛər-] *a.* reparable, enmendable, subsanable.
repairer [-ər, B -ə] *s.* reparador, restaurador.
repairing [-ɪŋ] *s.* reparación, restauración; compostura.
repairman [-'pɛrmən, -ˌmæn, B -'pɛəmən] *s.* reparador, mecánico (de reparaciones).
repair parts, (mec.) repuestos, piezas de reparación o de recambio.
repair ship, buque taller.
repair shop, taller de reparaciones.
repair squad, equipo de reparación.
repair truck, camión de reparaciones.
repand [rɪ'pænd] *a.* (bot.) repando (díc. de la hoja con bordes ondulados).
reparable ['rɛpərəbəl] *a.* reparable, remediable, resarcible.
reparation [ˌrɛpə'reɪʃən] *s.* 1. reparación, restauración, compostura, arreglo. 2. compensación, satisfacción, reparación, resarcimiento. 3. (*ú, pr. en pl.*) indemnización, resitución.
reparative [rɪ'pærətɪv] *a.* reparativo, restaurador; compensativo, compensatorio.
repartee [ˌrɛpər'ti, B -pɑ'ti] *s.* respuesta o réplica aguda, agudeza.
repartition [ˌripɑr'tɪʃən, B -pɑ'-] *s.* 1. repartición, repartimiento, reparto. 2. nuevo reparto, nueva partición.
repass [ri'pæs, B -'pɑs] *v.t., v.i.* repasar, pasar de nuevo.
repassage [-'pæsɪdʒ] *s.* repaso, regreso.
repast [rɪ'pæst, B -'pɑst] *s.* comida. —*v.i.* alimentarse, comer. —*v.t.* (ant.) alimentar.
repatriate [ri'peɪtrɪˌeɪt, B -'pæ-] *v.t., v.i.* repatriar(se).
repatriation [riˌpeɪtrɪ'eɪʃən, B -ˌpæ-] *s.* repatriación.
repave [ri'peɪv] *v.t.* pavimentar de nuevo, volver a pavimentar; adoquinar.
repay [ri'peɪ] *v.t.* 1. reembolsar, reintegrar. 2. compensar (esfuerzo, labor, etc.). 3. reciprocar, recompensar por (amabilidad, favor, etc.). 4. desquitarse de, vengarse de, pagar con la misma moneda. —*v.i.* pagar, efectuar los pagos de reembolso.
repayable [-əbəl] *a.* pagadero, reembolsable, reintegrable.
repayment [-mənt] *s.* reembolso, reintegro, pago.
repeal [rɪ'pil] *v.t.* 1. revocar. rescindir; anular, abolir; derogar, abrogar. 2. (raro) renunciar, retractar. 3. (ant.) hacer volver, llamar. —*s.* 1. revocación, rescisión; anulación, abolición; derogación. 2. (hist., E.U.) **R.,** enmienda constitucional que terminó con la prohibición de bebidas alcohólicas.
repealable [-əbəl] *a.* revocable, anulable, derogable.
repealer [-ər, B -ə] *s.* revocador, anulador, derogador.
repealing [-ɪŋ] *a.* derogatorio.
repeat [rɪ'pit] *v.t.* 1. repetir, reiterar. 2. repetir, reproducir. 3. **r. oneself,** repetirse. —*v.i.* 1. repetirse, que repite (la comida). 2. reiterar; volver a hacer; volver a actuar; (E.U.) votar varias veces (en una misma elección). —*s.* 1. repetición. 2. dos puntos (signo ortográfico). 3. (mús.) repetición. 4. (com.) pedido duplicado.
repeatable [-əbəl] *a.* repetible, iterable.
repeated [-əd] *a.* repetido, reiterado.
repeatedly [-lɪ] *adv.* repetidamente, reiteradamente.
repeater [-ər, B -ə] *s.* 1. reloj de repetición. 2. arma de repetición. 3. (educ.) repetidor (alumno matriculado por segunda vez en el mismo grado). 4. (teleg.) repetidor. 5. (E.U.) elector que vota varias veces (en una misma elección). 6. reincidente. 7. (mat.) fracción periódica.
repeating [-ɪŋ] *a.* repetidor; de repetición.
repeating circle, (top., astrol.) círculo repetidor.
repeating coil, (elec.) bobina aclopada de inducción.
repeating decimal, (mat.) fracción decimal periódica.
repeating firearm, arma de repetición.
repeating watch, reloj de repetición.
repel [rɪ'pɛl] *v.t.* (*pret., p.p.* REPELLED, *p.pr.* REPELLING) 1. repeler, rechazar. 2. ahuyentar, alejar. 3. repugnar, aborrecer. 4. (fís.) repeler. —*v.i.* causar repulsión o aversión.
repellency [-ənsɪ] *s.* fuerza repelente, carácter de repelente.
repellent [-ənt] *a.* repelente, repugnante, repulsivo. —*s.* (med.) substancia repelente; (tej.) tela impermeable.
repent ['ripənt] *a.* (bot., zool.) repente, rastrero.

repent [rɪ'pɛnt] *v.t.* arrepentirse de. *—v.i.* arrepentirse; **r. of,** arrepentirse de.
repentance [-əns] *s.* arrepentimiento, contrición, pesar, compunción.
repentant [-ənt] *a.* arrepentido, contrito, pesaroso, compungido; penitente.
repentantly [-lɪ] *adv.* arrepentidamente, contritamente.
repenter [-ər, B -ə] *s.* el que se arrepiente; penitente.
repeople [ri'pipəl] *v.t.* repoblar.
repercussion [ˌripər'kʌʃən, ˌrɛpər-, B ripə'-] *s.* 1. repercusión, resonancia, reverberación, eco, retumbo. 2. repercusión, trascendencia, consecuencia.
repercussive [-'kʌsɪv] *a.* reverberante, retumbante, resonante.
repertoire ['rɛpərˌtwɑr, B -ətwɑ] *s.* (fr.) repertorio (de obras de teatro, música, etc., de una compañía, actor o músico).
repertory [-ərˌtɔrɪ, B -ətərɪ] *s.* (*pl.* REPERTORIES) 1. tesorería; depósito, almacén; inventario, lista; colección. 2. repertorio.
repertory theater, teatro de repertorio (en el que una compañía presenta obras diversas en una temporada).
repetend ['rɛpəˌtɛnd] *s.* 1. estribillo, cantinela, cantilena. 2. (mat.) dígitos infinitos (fracción decimal).
repetition [ˌrɛpə'tɪʃən] *s.* 1. repetición, reiteración. 2. recitación. 3. réplica, copia. 4. (mús.) capacidad de repetición (de un instrumento musical).
repetition rate, (electrón.) régimen de repetición.
repetitious [-əs] *a.* redundante, que repite (palabras, frases, etc.).
repetitiously [-lɪ] *adv.* con repetición monótona, redundantemente.
repetitive [rɪ'pɛtətɪv] *a.* 1. repetidor. 2. reiterativo, redundante.
rephrase [ri'freɪz] *v.t.* expresar en otra forma, volver a expresar cambiando la frase.
repine [rɪ'paɪn] *v.i.* afligirse, apenarse, desconsolarse, quejarse, lamentarse.
repiner [-ər, B -ə] *s.* el que se queja.
repining [-ɪŋ] *s.* queja, descontento.
repiningly [-lɪ] *adv.* quejosamente, desconsoladamente.
replace [rɪ'pleɪs] *v.t.* 1. reponer, poner de nuevo, volver a poner. 2. reemplazar, substituir; suplir, suplantar. 3. restituir, reembolsar, devolver.
replaceable [-əbəl] *a.* reemplazable, substituible.
replacement [-mənt] *s.* 1. reemplazo, substitución. 2. reposición, restitución, devolución. 3. (pieza de) repuesto. 4. (mil.) reemplazo (de un contingente), relevo.
replacer [-ər, B -ə] *s.* reemplazante, substituto, suplente.
replant [ri'plænt, B -'plɑnt] *v.t.* 1. replantar, plantar de nuevo. 2. poblar de plantas nuevas.
replay [ri'pleɪ] *v.t.* volver a jugar, volver a tocar o presentar. — ['riˌpleɪ] *s.* (dep.) repetición de un encuentro (de fútbol, etc.).
repleader [ri'plidər, B -ə] *s.* (der.) nuevo alegato; derecho a presentar nuevos alegatos.
replenish [rɪ'plɛnɪʃ] *v.t.* 1. llenar, rellenar, henchir. 2. llenar de nuevo, volver a llenar. 3. (ant.) surtir o abastecer con creces.
replenishment [-mənt] *s.* acción de volver a llenar o colmar.
replete [rɪ'plit] *a.* repleto, lleno, colmado; atiborrado, saciado; **r. with,** repleto de; (fig.) lleno de.
repleteness [-nəs] *s.* plenitud, repleción.
repletion [-'pliʃən] *s.* 1. repleción; saciedad, ahíto, hartazgo. 2. satisfacción.
repleviable [rɪ'plɛvɪəbəl] *var. de* **replevisable.**
replevin [-'plɛvən] *s.* (der.) reivindicación; auto de reivindicación. *—v.t.* reivindicar, desembargar.
replevisable [-əsəbəl] *a.* (der.) reivindicable.
replevy [-ɪ] (der.) *v.t.* (*pret., p.p.* REPLEVIED; *p.pr.* REPLEVYING) reivindicar; apresar bajo auto de reivindicación. *—s.* reivindicación.
replica ['rɛplɪkə] *s.* réplica, reproducción; copia, duplicado.
replicate [-ləˌkeɪt] *v.t.* 1. duplicar, repetir. 2. (bot.) replegar. — [-lɪkət] *a.* (bot.) replegado.
replicated [-əd] *a.* (bot.) replegado.
replication [ˌrɛplə'keɪʃən] *s.* 1. réplica, respuesta, contestación. 2. repercusión, eco, reverberación. 3. réplica, reproducción, copia. 4. (der.) réplica, replicato. 5. (raro) pliegue, repliegue.
reply [rɪ'plaɪ] *v.i.* (*pret, p.p.* REPLIED; *p.pr.* REPLYING) contestar, responder, replicar. *—v.t.* decir en contestación, contestar. *—s.* (*pl.* REPLIES) réplica, contestación, respuesta.
reply coupon, cupón-respuesta (postal).
report [rɪ'pɔrt, B -'pɔt] *v.t.* 1. relatar, contar, narrar, referir. 2. dar parte de, presentar informe sobre; comunicar, informar, enterar de. 3. anunciar, divulgar. 4. denunciar, delatar. 5. (rad., t.v.) narrar. 6. **it is reported,** se dice, corre la voz. *—v.i.* 1. presentar un informe o dictamen. 2. comunicarse. 3. presentarse, comparecer, personarse. 4. trabajar como corresponsal (de un periódico). *—s.* 1. información, relato; narración, reporte, parte. 2. rumor, voz, habladuría. 3. informe, dictamen, comunicado. 4. fama, reputación. 5. estampido, estallido, trueno. 6. denuncia, acusación. 7. (*pl.*) (der.) recopilación de decisiones. 8. **r. of a gun,** pistoletazo, cañonazo, escopetazo.
reportable [-əbəl] *a.* narrable, referible, comunicable.
reportage [-ɪdʒ, B ˌrɛpɔ'tɑʒ] *s.* reportaje.
report card, libreta de calificaciones, carnet de notas.
reportedly [rɪ'pɔrtədlɪ, B -'pɔt-] *adv.* según se informa; según se dice.
reporter [-ər, B -ə] *s.* 1. repórter, reportero, noticiero. 2. (der.) relator (en tribunales).
reportorial [ˌrɛpər'tɔrɪəl, B ˌrɛpɔ'-] *a.* reporteril.
reposal [rɪ'poʊzəl] *s.* (ant.) reposo, descanso.
repose [rɪ'poʊz] *v.t.* 1. (ú. con *in*) tener o depositar (confianza, esperanza, etc. en). 2. (ant.) depositar.
repose, *v.t.* reposar, descansar. *—v.i.* 1. descansar. 2. (gen. con *on* o *upon*) descansar (sobre); apoyarse (en), basarse (en). 3. **r. in state,** estar de cuerpo presente. *—s.* 1. reposo, descanso. 2. paz, calma, tranquilidad, sosiego, quietud. 3. compostura, serenidad.
reposeful [-fəl] *a.* reposado, sosegado; tranquilo, sereno.
reposit [rɪ'pɑzət, B -'pɔz-] *v.t.* depositar, almacenar, guardar.
reposition [ˌripə'zɪʃən] *s.* 1. depósito, almacenamiento. 2. (ant., esco.) reposición, restauración, restablecimiento.
repositor [rɪ'pɑzətər, B -'pɔzɪtə] *s.* reponedor.
repository [-ˌtɔrɪ, B -tərɪ] *s.* (*pl.* REPOSITORIES) 1. depositario, recipiente. 2. depósito, almacén, repositorio. 3. (fig.) mina (de información). 4. fosa (de sepultura).
repossess [ˌripə'zɛs] *v.t.* 1. poseer de nuevo, volver a poseer; recuperar. 2. volver a dar posesión (de algo) a (alguien), devolver (a). 3. (esco.) reinstalar, restablecer.
repossession [-'zɛʃən] *s.* recuperación, recobro de la posesión.
repoussé [rəˌpu'seɪ, B -'puˌseɪ] *a.* (fr.) repujado.
repp, *var. de* rep, reps, telebón.
reprehend [ˌrɛprɪ'hɛnd] *v.t.* reprender, regañar, reñir, increpar.
reprehensibility [-ˌhɛnsə'bɪlətɪ] *s.* carácter reprensible.
reprehensible [-'hɛnsəbəl] *a.* reprensible, censurable, reprobable.
reprehensibleness [-nəs] *s.* carácter reprensible.
reprehensibly [-blɪ] *adv.* culpablemente, reprensiblemente, censurablemente.
reprehension [-'hɛntʃən, B -'hɛnʃən] *s.* reprensión, reprimenda, reprobación.
represent [ˌrɛprɪ'zɛnt] *v.t.* 1. representar; figurar, simbolizar, ej., *he will r. me at the conference,* él me representará en la conferencia. 2. (teat.) representar (un papel). 3. equivaler o corresponder a, ej., *that represents an insult,* eso equivale a un insulto.
re-present [ˌriprɪ-] *v.t.* (esp. com.) volver a presentar (cheque, documento, etc.).
representation [ˌrɛprɪˌzɛn'teɪʃən] *s.* 1. representación. 2. exposición, manifestación. 3. protesta. 4. representación parlamentaria, delegación. 5. (teat.) representación.
representational [-əl] *a.* realista (arte o escuela), figurativo.
representative [-'zɛntətɪv] *s.* 1. representativo, ej., *a r. government,* gobierno representativo. 2. (con *of*) representador (de), que representa. 3. típico, característico. *—s.* 1. representante, representador. 2. (E.U.) representante (al Congreso).
representatively [-lɪ] *adv.* de modo representativo.
repress [rɪ'prɛs] *v.t.* 1. reprimir, refrenar, represar, contener. 2. reprimir, oprimir, dominar.
repressed [-'prɛst] *a.* 1. comedido, moderado. 2. (psic.) reprimido.
represser [-'prɛsər, B -e] *s.* represor.
repression [-'prɛʃən] *s.* represión; (psic.) represión.
repressive [-'prɛsɪv] *a.* represivo.
repressively [-lɪ] *adv.* represivamente.
repressiveness [-nəs] *s.* capacidad o carácter represivo.
repressuring [ri'prɛʃərɪŋ] *s.* (ing.) aumento de presión, renovación de la presión natural.
reprieve [rɪ'priv] *v.t.* 1. retrasar, diferir, posponer, postergar, aplazar. 2. suspender la ejecución de (un criminal condenado a muerte). 3. aliviar temporalmente. *—s.* 1. respiro o descanso momentáneo, alivio temporal. 2. suspensión de la ejecución, suspensión temporal de la pena capital.
reprimand ['rɛprəˌmænd, B -ˌmɑnd] *s.* reprimenda, reprensión, regaño. *—v.t.* 1. reprender, regañar. 2. (fam.) sermonear.
reprint ['riˌprɪnt] *s.* 1. reimpresión. 2. (E.U.) tirada aparte, separada. 3. (filat.) reimpresión. — [ri'prɪnt] *v.t.* reimprimir, imprimir de nuevo.
reprinter [ri'prɪntər, B -ə] *s.* editor de reimpresiones.
reprisal [rɪ'praɪzəl] *s.* represalia, retorsión, desquite, venganza (esp. en guerra); (der.) represalia.
reprise [rɪ'priz, B -'praɪz] *s.* 1. (der.) deducción o gravamen anual (sobre bienes raíces). 2. [-'priz] (mús.) repetición, bis.
repro ['riproʊ] *s.* (impr.) repro (prueba para reproducir o de reproducción en fotomecánica).
reproach [rɪ'proʊtʃ] *v.t.* 1. reprochar. 2. censurar, criticar. 3. (ant.) desacreditar, deshonrar. *—s.* 1. reproche. 2. censura, crítica, ej., *a term of*

r., una palabra de censura. 3. oprobio, deshonra, ignominia; descrédito. 4. **above r.,** sin tacha.
reproachable [-əbəl] *a.* reprochable; censurable, reprensible.
reproachableness [-nəs] *s.* reprensibilidad.
reproachful [-fəl] *a.* 1. reprobador, lleno de reproche, increpador. 2. (ant.) vergonzoso.
reproachfully [-fəlɪ] *adv.* con reproche, de modo reprobatorio.
reprobate ['rɛprəˌbeɪt] *a.* 1. vicioso, malvado; corrompido, depravado. 2. (teo.) réprobo. —*s.* 1. malvado, depravado, bribón. 2. (teo.) réprobo. —*v.t.* 1. reprobar, desaprobar, condenar. 2. rechazar, denegar. 3. (teo.) condenar.
reprobation [ˌrɛprə'beɪʃən] *s.* 1. reprobación, desaprobación; censura, condena. 2. (teo.) condena.
reprobative ['rɛprəˌbeɪtɪv] *a.* reprobador, reprobatorio.
reprocessing [ri'prɑsəsɪŋ, B -'proʊs-] *s.* reacondicionamiento, reprocesamiento.
reproduce [ˌriprə'dus, B -'djus] *v.t.* reproducir, duplicar, copiar. —*v.i.* reproducirse; multiplicarse.
reproducer [-ər, B -ə] *s.* reproductor.
reproducible [-əbəl] *a.* reproductible.
reproduction [-'dʌkʃən] *s.* 1. reproducción, copia, duplicado. 2. reproducción, procreación.
reproductive [-'dʌktɪv] *a.* reproductivo, reproductor.
reproductiveness [-nəs] *s.* reproductividad.
reproductory [-tərɪ] *a.* reproductor, reproductivo.
reproof [rɪ'pruf] *s.* 1. reprobación, reproche, reprimenda, reprensión. 2. (ant.) deshonra, ignominia.
reprovable [-'pruvəbəl] *a.* reprobable; censurable.
reprove [rɪ'pruv] *v.t.* 1. reprobar, increpar, reprender; censurar, desaprobar, criticar. 2. (ant.) condenar; refutar.
reprover [-ər, B -ə] *s.* reprensor, reprobador, censurador.
reproving [-ɪŋ] *a.* reprobatorio.
reptant ['rɛptənt] *a.* 1. (zool.) reptante. 2. (bot.) rastrero.
reptile [-təl, B -ˌtaɪl] *s.* 1. (zool.) reptil. 2. (fig.) reptil, rastrero, vil. —*a.* 1. reptil. 2. rastrero, bajo, despreciable.
Reptile Age, (geol.) época mesozoica.
reptilian [rɛp'tɪlɪən] *a., s.* reptil (de reptil, de los reptiles).
republic [rɪ'pʌblɪk] *s.* república.
republican [-lɪkən] *a., s.* 1. republicano. 2. (E.U.) **R. Party,** Partido Republicano (uno de los dos partidos del sistema político).
republicanism [-ˌɪzəm] *s.* republicanismo.
republicanize [-ˌaɪz] *v.t., v.i.* republicanizar(se), hacer(se) o volver(se) republicano.
republication [ˌripʌblə'keɪʃən] *s.* nueva publicación; reimpresión.
republic of letters, república de las letras, república literaria.
republish [-'pʌblɪʃ] *v.t.* volver a publicar; reimprimir.
repudiate [rɪ'pjudɪˌeɪt] *v.t.* 1. repudiar, rechazar (insinuación, acusación, etc.). 2. desconocer, negar (a hijos). 3. negar (una deuda, reclamo, etc.). 4. repudiar, desechar (a esposa).
repudiation [-ˌpjudɪ'eɪʃən] *s.* repudiación, repudio; rechazo, desconocimiento (de una deuda, reclamo, etc.).
repugn [rɪ'pjun] *v.i.* (ant.) esforzarse o luchar contra algo. —*v.t.* (raro) oponerse a, resistir; repugnar.
repugnance [-'pʌgnəns] *s.* 1. repugnancia, aversión, antipatía; mala gana. 2. repugnancia, inconsistencia, incompatibilidad, incongruencia.
repugnancy [-nənsɪ] *s.* (*pl.* REPUGNANCIES) repugnancia.
repugnant [-nənt] *a.* 1. repugnante, repulsivo. 2. contradictorio, incompatible, irreconciliable. 3. (ant.) hostil. 4. **r. to,** incompatible con; repugnante a.
repugnantly [-lɪ] *adv.* repugnantemente.
repulse [rɪ'pʌls] *v.t.* 1. repeler, rechazar (un asalto, al enemigo, etc.). 2. desairar, rechazar. —*s.* 1. repulsión, repulsa, rechazo. 2. negación, rechazo, desaire.
repulsion [-'pʌlʃən] *s.* 1. repulsa, repulsión. 2. repugnancia, aversión, antipatía. 3. (fís.) repulsión.
repulsion motor, motor de repulsión.
repulsive [-'pʌlsɪv] *a.* 1. repulsivo, repelente. 2. (fig.) repulsivo, repugnante.
repulsively [-lɪ] *adv.* repulsivamente, repugnantemente.
repulsiveness [-nəs] *s.* 1. carácter repulsivo o repugnante. 2. (fís.) fuerza repulsiva.
repurchase [ri'pɜrtʃəs, B -'pɜtʃəs] *v.t.* comprar o adquirir de nuevo. —*s.* nueva adquisición o compra.
reputability [ˌrɛpjətə'bɪlətɪ] *s.* buena reputación.
reputable ['rɛpjʊtəbəl] *a.* 1. de buena fuente; honorable, respetable, estimable, intachable. 2. puro, castizo (vocablo).
reputably [-blɪ] *adv.* honorablemente; en buena lid.
reputation [ˌrɛpjʊ'teɪʃən] *s.* reputación; fama, renombre.
repute [rɪ'pjut] *v.t.* (*ú. gen. en pasivo*) reputar, estimar, considerar; **to be reputed as,** tener la reputación de. —*s.* reputación, fama.
reputed [-ed] *a.* 1. reputado, estimado, considerado. 2. putativo, supuesto. 3. **highly r.,** de muy buena reputación.
reputedly [-lɪ] *adv.* según opinión común; según se cree.
req. *abrev. de* 1. **request,** petición, solicitud. 2. **required,** requerido. 3. **requisition,** requisición, demanda.
request [rɪ'kwɛst] *s.* 1. ruego, súplica, instancia, solicitud, petición. 2. demanda, pedido. 3. **at (by** u **on** o **upon) r. (of),** a petición (de), a solicitud (de); **to be in r.,** tener demanda. —*v.t.* pedir, rogar, suplicar; solicitar, demandar; **r. from,** pedir a; **r. (someone) to (do),** pedir (a alguien) que (haga).
requiem ['rɛkwɪəm] *s.* (relig., mús.) réquiem; misa de réquiem.
requiescat [ˌrɛkwɪ'ɛsˌkɑt, B -ˌkæt] *s.* oración fúnebre.
require [rɪ'kwaɪr, B -ə] *v.t.* 1. requerir, exigir. 2. requerir, demandar, necesitar, precisar. 3. ordenar, obligar, compeler. 4. (ant.) pedir. 5. (G.B.) desear, ej., *will you r. tea at five?* ¿desea el té a las cinco? —*v.i.* exigir, imponer una obligación, e.j., *to do as the law r.,* hacer lo que manda la ley.
requirement [-mənt] *s.* 1. requerimiento, exigencia, demanda. 2. requisito, condición, necesidad; formalidad.
requirer [-'kwaɪrər, B -ə] *s.* requeridor.
requisite ['rɛkwəzət] *a.* necesario, indispensable, forzoso. —*s.* requisito.
requisiteness [-nəs] *s.* necesidad, indispensabilidad.
requisition [ˌrɛkwə'zɪʃən] *s.* 1. requisición, requisa. 2. pedido, demanda. 3. requisito, condición. 4. (der.) requisitoria, requerimiento. 5. **to be in r.,** estar en servicio o uso. —*v.t.* requisar.
requisitory [rɪ'kwɪzəˌtɔrɪ, B -tərɪ] *a.* (der.) requisitorio. —*s.* requisitoria.
requital [rɪ'kwaɪtəl] *s.* compensación, paga, retribución; desquite, venganza.
requite [-'kwaɪt] *v.t.* 1. corresponder a, pagar (gentileza, amor, etc.). 2. recompensar, premiar. 3. vengarse de, desquitarse de.
reradiation [riˌreɪdɪ'eɪʃən] *s.* (fís.) rerradiación.
reread [ri'rid] *v.t.* releer, volver a leer.
rerebrace ['rɪrˌbreɪs, B 'rɪəˌ-] *s.* (arm.) brafonera.
reredos ['rɛrəˌdɑs, B 'riədɔs] *s.* 1. (arq.) retablo. 2. (ant.) parte de atrás de la chimenea. 3. biombo ornamental o pared falsa que sirve de fondo a los altares.
reremouse ['rɪrˌmaʊs, B 'rɪəˌ-] *s.* (dial.) murciélago.
reroll [ri'roʊl] *v.t.* 1. volver a arrollar, enrollar de nuevo. 2. (tec.) remandrilar (tubo de caldera). 3. relaminar.
rerolled steel [-'roʊld-] acero relaminado, acero de rieles.
reroute [ri'rut, -'raʊt] *v.t.* desviar (tráfico, vehículo, nave, etc.).
rerun ['riˌrʌn] *s.* (cinem., t.v.) reestreno, segunda presentación (de una película). — [ri'rʌn] *v.t.* reestrenar, volver a presentar (una película).
resail [ri'seɪl] *v.i.* volver a zarpar, volver a hacerse a la vela.
resalable [-'seɪləbəl] *a.* que se puede revender, revendible.
resale ['riˌseɪl, B rɪ'seɪl] *s.* reventa.
rescale [ri'skeɪl] *v.t.* reajustar, readaptar.
rescind [rɪ'sɪnd] *v.t.* rescindir, abrogar; anular, cancelar.
rescission [-'sɪʒən] *s.* rescisión, abrogación; anulación, cancelación.
rescissory [-'sɪsərɪ] *a.* (der.) rescisorio.
rescript ['riˌskrɪpt] *s.* 1. rescripto. 2. edicto, decreto. 3. nuevo artículo, nuevo escrito.
rescue ['rɛskju] *v.t.* 1. salvar; librar. 2. rescatar, redimir. 3. (der.) recobrar por la fuerza; libertar por fuerza e ilegalmente (de la custodia legal). —*s.* 1. salvamento, salvación; liberación. 2. rescate. 3. (der.) recuperación o liberación ilegal. 4. **to come** (o **go**) **to the r. (of),** acudir al socorro (de).
rescue boat, bote de salvamento.
rescue party, partida de salvamento, partida de socorro.
rescuer [-ər, B -ə] *s.* salvador, rescatador.
reseal [ri'sil] *v.t.* resellar, sellar de nuevo.
research [rɪ'sɜrtʃ, 'riˌsɜrtʃ, B rɪ'sɜtʃ] *s.* 1. investigación, experimentación (esp. científica). 2. búsqueda minuciosa, rebusca. —*v.i.* investigar, experimentar.
research and development, investigación y desarrollo.
researcher [-ər, B -ə] *s.* (científico) investigador.
researchist [-əst] *s.* (científico) investigador.
research station, estación experimental.
reseat [ri'sit] *v.t.* 1. volver a sentar. 2. renovar el asiento de (una silla, etc.). 3. instalar nuevos asientos en (un teatro, etc.). 4. (mec.) rectificar (válvula). 5. volver a herrar (caballo).
resect [rɪ'sɛkt] *v.t.* (med.) resecar.
resection [-'sɛkʃən] *s.* (med.) resección.
reseda [rɪ'sidə, B 'rɛsɪdə] *s.* 1. (bot.) reseda, gualda. 2. ['reɪzəˌdɑ, B 'rɛsɪdə] color de reseda.
resedaceous [ˌrɛsə'deɪʃəs] *a.* (bot.) resedáceo.
reseed [ri'sid] *v.t.* replantar, volver a plantar.
resell [ri'sɛl] *v.t.* revender.
reseller [-ər, B -ə] *s.* revendedor.

resemblance [rɪ'zɛmbləns] *s.* parecido, semejanza, similitud, aire.
resemblant [-blənt] *a.* 1. similar. parecido. 2. representativo (arte).
resemble [-bəl] *v.t.* 1. asemejar, asemejarse a, semejar(se) a, parecerse a. 2. (ant.) comparar, parangonar.
resend [ri'sɛnd] *v.t.* volver a mandar; reenviar.
resent [rɪ'zɛnt] *v.t.* resentirse por, ofenderse por; sentirse agraviado por, tomar a mal.
resentful [-fəl] *a.* resentido, ofendido.
resentfully [-fəlɪ] *adv.* con resentimiento, resentidamente.
resentfulness [-fəlnəs] *s.* resentimiento.
resentment [-mənt] *s.* resentimiento, pique, enojo, enfado.
reserpine [rɪ'sɜrpən, B -'sɜpɪn] *s.* **(farm.)** reserpina.
reservation [ˌrɛzər'veɪʃən, B ˌrɛzə'-] *s.* 1. reservación. 2. reserva, restricción, salvedad, cautela. 3. (E.U.) reservación, tierra o territorio reservado (por el estado para los indios). 4. **mental r.,** restricción mental.
reserve [rɪ'zɜrv, B -'zɜv] *v.t.* reservar, guardar, retener, conservar. *—s.* 1. reserva, provisión, abasto. 2. reserva, reticencia, recato. 3. reserva, restricción, salvedad, cautela; **without r.,** sin restricción, sin reserva. 4. base mínima (en un remate). 5. tierra reservada (por el estado para un uso especial). 6. (fin.) reserva. 7. (mil.) reserva; retén. *—a.* de reserva, de la reserva, reservista.
reserve bank, banco de reserva.
reserved [-'zɜrvd, B -'zɜvd] *a.* 1. reservado, guardado. 2. reservado, circunspecto, cauteloso; callado, discreto.
reservedly [-'zɜrvədlɪ, B -'zɜv-] *adv.* reservadamente.
reservedness [-nəs] *s.* reserva, cautela; reticencia.
reserve officer, (mil.) oficial del servicio de reserva.
reserve supply, provisión de reserva.
reserve troops, (mil.) tropas de reserva.
reservist [rɪ'zɜrvəst, B -'zɜv-] *s.* (mil.) reservista, miembro del cuerpo o servicio de reserva.
reservoir ['rɛzərvˌwɑr, -ˌwɔr, B -əvˌwɑ] *s.* (fr.) 1. represa, embalse. 2. depósito, tanque (de agua, gas, petróleo, etc.). 3. (provisión de) reserva.
reset [ri'sɛt] *v.t.* 1. (joy.) volver a engastar; volver a montar, volver a encajar. 2. (med.) emplazar.
resettle [-əl] *v.t.* repoblar, volver a colonizar (territorio); establecer de nuevo (a refugiados, exiliados, etc.). *—v.i.* volver a radicarse.
resettlement [-mənt] *s.* 1. nueva colonización. 2. restablecimiento.
reshape [ri'ʃeɪp] *v.t.* moldear de nuevo, rehacer, volver a formar.
reship [ri'ʃɪp] *v.t.* reembarcar; reenviar; reexpedir. *—v.i.* reembarcarse.
reshipment [-mənt] *s.* reembarque; reenvío.
reshuffle [ri'ʃʌfəl] *v.t.* 1. volver a barajar. 2. reorganizar (gen. distribuyendo de nuevo los elementos existentes).
reside [rɪ'zaɪd] *v.i.* 1. residir, vivir, habitar, morar, domiciliarse. 2. **r. in,** (fig.) residir en, radicar en, ser inherente a.
residence ['rɛzədəns] *s.* 1. residencia, estada, permanencia. 2. residencia, morada, domicilio; casa, mansión. 3. **to take up one's r.,** fijar (o establecer) su residencia o domicilio; **in r.,** díc. del que reside en un sitio (universidad, hospital, etc.).
residence hall, dormitorio para estudiantes.
residency [-ənsɪ] *s.* 1. residencia oficial (de un embajador, gobernador, etc.). 2. (E.U.) período de residencia hospitalaria para médicos postgraduados.
resident ['rɛzədənt] *a.* 1. residente. 2. permanente. 3. (orn.) no migratorio. *—s.* 1. residente (en un país, ciudad, etc.). 2. médico residente. 3. (dipl.) ministro residente.
resident commissioner, 1. (E.U.) representante de una dependencia (en la Cámara de Diputados). 2. (G.B.) administrador residente (de una colonia o posesión).
residential [ˌrɛzə'dənʃəl, B -'dɛnʃəl] *a.* 1. residencial (barrio, etc.). 2. para alumnos internos (colegio, etc.).
residentiary [-'dɛnʃɪˌɛrɪ, B -'dɛnʃərɪ] *a.* residencial (empleo, beneficio, etc.).
residual [rɪ'zɪdʒʊəl, B -'zɪdjʊ-] *a.* residual. *—s.* 1. (mat.) residuo, cantidad residual. 2. subproducto.
residual estate, (der.) heredad residual, heredad residuaria.
residual magnetism, (elec.) magnetismo remanente.
residuary [-'zɪdʒʊˌɛrɪ, B -'zɪdjʊərɪ] *a.* residual.
residuary clause, (der.) cláusula sobre disposición de la heredad residuaria.
residuary legatee, heredero universal.
residue ['rɛzəˌdu, B -ˌdju] *s.* (fr.) 1. residuo, remanente, resto, restante, sobrante. 2. (mat.) resto, residuo, diferencia. 3. (der.) bienes residuales (de una herencia).
residuum [rɪ'zɪdʒʊəm, B -'zɪdjʊ-] *s.* (*pl.* RESIDUA [-ə]) 1. residuo, remanente, resto. 2. (der.) bienes residuales (de una herencia).
resign [rɪ'zaɪn] *v.t.* 1. dimitir, renunciar; abdicar. 2. ceder, dimitir (el mando). 3. **r. oneself** (*to*), resignarse (a), conformarse (con), someterse (a). *—v.i.* 1. renunciar, retirarse; presentar renuncia. 2. (ajedrez) abandonar.
resignation [ˌrɛzɪg'neɪʃən] *s.* 1. renuncia, dimisión, renunciamiento. 2. resignación, sumisión.
resigned [rɪ'zaɪnd] *a.* resignado, sumiso.
resignedly [-'zaɪnədlɪ] *adv.* resignadamente, sumisamente.
resignedness [-nəs] *s.* resignación, sumisión.
resile [rɪ'zaɪl] *v.t.* rebotar; volver a tomar su forma (cuerpos elásticos).
resilience [rɪ'zɪljəns] **resiliency** [-jənsɪ] *s.* 1. (lit. y fig.) elasticidad. 2. (mec.) resiliencia.
resilient [-jənt] *a.* 1. (lit. y fig.) elástico, flexible, adaptable. 2. (mec.) resiliente.
resin ['rɛzən] *s.* resina; colofonia. *—v.t.* tratar con resina; aplicar una capa de resina a.
resinate [-ˌeɪt] *v.t.* impregnar de resina.
resin canal, (bot.) canal resinífero.
resin cerate, ungüento amarillo.
resiniferous [ˌrɛzə'nɪfərəs] *a.* resinífero.
resinoid ['rɛzənˌɔɪd] *a.* resinoideo. *—s.* resina sintética; gomorresina.
resinous [-əs] *a.* resinoso; (elec.) resinoso.
resist [rɪ'zɪst] *v.t.* 1. resistir, aguantar, tolerar, soportar. 2. resistir a, combatir, contrarrestar; frustrar; hacer frente a, repeler, impedir. *—v.i.* resistir, defenderse, oponerse. *—s.* capa protectora o repelente.
resistance [-'zɪstəns] *s.* resistencia; (elec.) resistencia; **line of r.,** dirección de la resistencia; **to offer** (o **put up**) **r.,** oponer resistencia; **to take the line of least r.,** adoptar la solución más fácil.
resistance box, (elec.) caja de resistencias.
resistance braking, (elec.) frenaje reostático.
resistance coil, (elec.) carrete o bobina de resistencia.
resistance drop, (elec.) caída de tensión por resistencia.
resistance frame, (elec.) cuadro de resistencia, reóstato de cuadro.
resistance thermometer, termómetro de resistencia.
resistance welding, soldadura por resistencia.
resistant [-tənt] *a.* resistente.
resister [-tər, B -tə] *s.* resistor, el que o lo que resiste.
resistibility [rɪˌzɪstə'bɪlətɪ] *s.* capacidad resistiva.
resistible [-'zɪstəbəl] *a.* resistible.
resistive [-tɪv] *a.* resistivo.
resistivity [rɪˌzɪs'tɪvətɪ, ˌri-] *s.* capacidad resistiva; (elec.) resistividad.
resistless [rɪ'zɪstləs] *a.* 1. irresistible. 2. incapaz de resistir, indefenso.
resistlessly [-lɪ] *adv.* 1. irresistiblemente. 2. sin resistencia u oposición.
resistlessness [-nəs] *s.* calidad de irresistible.
resistor [rɪ'zɪstər, B -tə] *s.* (elec.) resistencia, reóstato, resistor.
resnatron ['rɛznəˌtrɑn, B -ˌtrɔn] *s.* (electrón.) resnatrón.
resole [ri'soʊl] *v.t.* sobresolar, remontar (zapatos).
resolubility [rɪˌzɑljə'bɪlətɪ, B -ˌzɔl-] *s.* solubilidad.
resoluble [-'zɑljəbəl, B -'zɔl-] *a.* resoluble, soluble.
resolubleness [-nəs] *s.* solubilidad.
resolute ['rɛzəˌlut] *a.* resuelto, determinado; firme.
resolutely [-lɪ] *adv.* resueltamente, determinadamente; firmemente.
resoluteness [-nəs] *s.* resolución, determinación; firmeza.
resolution [rɛzə'luʃən] *s.* 1. resolución, tesón, firmeza, constancia. 2. resolución, acuerdo, decisión (de una asamblea, etc.). 3. resolución, solución, respuesta. 4. (mús.) resolución (de un acorde disonante a otro consonante). 5. (med.) resolución (de una enfermedad, fiebre, etc.). 6. (mat.) descomposición, resolución. 7. (quím.) separación. 8. (ópt.) análisis.
resolutory condition [rə'zɑljəˌtɔrɪ-, B 'rɛzəljʊtərɪ-] (der.) condición resolutoria.
resolvable [rɪ'zɑlvəbəl, B -'zɔl-] *a.* resoluble, soluble.
resolve [rɪ'zɑlv, B -'zɔlv] *v.t.* 1. resolver, determinar, decidir. 2. acordar, tomar el acuerdo de, tomar la resolución de. 3. resolver, descomponer. 4. resolver, solucionar, solventar. 5. (mús.) resolver (un acorde disonante a uno consonante). 6. (ópt.) resolver, descomponer. 7. **r. into,** (fig.) transformar en, convertir en. *—v.i.* 1. resolverse, determinarse. 2. resolverse; reducirse (por análisis). 3. (mús.) resolverse. 4. **r. on** (o **upon**), resolverse por; **r. to (do),** resolverse a (hacer). *—s.* 1. resolución, determinación, propósito. 2. resolución, firmeza, intrepidez.
resolved [-'zɑlvd, B -'zɔlvd] *a.* resuelto, determinado, firme.
resolvedly [-'zɑlvədlɪ, B -'zɔl-] *adv.* resueltamente, decididamente.
resolvent [-vənt] *a., s.* 1. (med.) resolutivo. 2. (quím.) solvente.
resolver [-vər, B -və] *s.* resolvente, disolvente.
resolving power [-vɪŋ-] (ópt., foto.) poder resolvente o separador, poder de resolución.
resonance ['rɛzənəns] *s.* (quím., elec., med., mús., fís.) resonancia.
resonant [-ənt] *a.* resonante, resonador; sonoro.
resonantly [-lɪ] *adv.* resonantemente, con resonancia; sonoramente.

resonate [-ˌeɪt] *v.i.* (fís., quím.) resonar.
resonator [-ər, B -ə] *s.* resonador.
resorb [rɪ'sɔrb, -'zɔrb, B -'sɔb] *v.t.* resorber.
resorcin [rə'zɔrsən, B -'zɔs-] **resorcinol** [-ˌɔl] *s.* (quím.) resorcinol, resorcina.
resorption [ri'sɔrpʃən, -'zɔrp-, B -'sɔp-] *s.* resorción.
resorptive [-tɪv] *a.* reabsorbedor.
resort [rɪ'zɔrt, B -'zɔt] *v.i.* (ú. con *to*) 1. frecuentar, concurrir (a). 2. recurrir (a), acudir (a), apelar (a), valerse (de), hacer uso (de). —*s.* 1. recurso, expediente, medio; refugio. 2. recreo, lugar de temporada, lugar frecuentado; punto de reunión. 3. frecuentación, concurrencia, concurso. 4. **as a last r.,** como último recurso; **to have r. to,** recurrir a; **without r. to,** sin recurrir a.
resorter [-ər, B -ə] *s.* veraneante (que frecuenta lugares de temporada).
re-sound [ri'saʊnd] *v.t., v.i.* volver a (hacer) sonar; repetir(se) el sonido(de).
resound [rɪ'zaʊnd] *v.i.* 1. resonar, repercutir, retumbar. 2. producir o hacer eco; tener resonancia. 3. (fig.) resonar, hacer eco; ser celebrado. —*v.t.* 1. hacer resonar o repercutir (el sonido); repetir (el eco), repetir (algo) como el eco. 2. (fig.) cantar, celebrar.
resounding [-ɪŋ] *a.* resonante (victoria, triunfo, etc.); rimbombante.
resource ['riˌsɔrs, B rɪ'sɔs] *s.* 1. recurso, medio. 2. (*pl.*) recursos, medios, fondos; bienes, riquezas. 3. recurso, expediente, procedimiento, arbitrio. 4. habilidad, destreza, ingeniosidad, inventiva.
resourceful [rɪ'sɔrsfəl, B -'sɔs-] *a.* listo, ingenioso, diestro, inventivo, hábil.
resourcefulness [-nəs] *s.* ingenio, habilidad.
respect [rɪ'spɛkt] *v.t.* 1. respetar, venerar, honrar; estimar, acatar. 2. respectar, atañer, corresponder a, tocar a; concernir, referir(se) a. 3. (ant.) pensar, considerar. —*s.* 1. respeto, estima, estimación, deferencia; veneración, consideración; honra, decoro. 2. respecto, relación, referencia. 3. punto de vista, aspecto, detalle, particular. 4. (*pl.*) recuerdos, respetos; saludos. 5. (ant.) motivo causal. 6. **in every r.,** en todo concepto; **in other r.,** por lo demás, por otra parte; **in r. of,** respecto a, respecto de; **in that r.,** respecto a eso, bajo ese respecto, en cuanto a eso; **out of r. for,** por consideración a; **to hold in r.,** hacer estima de, respetar; **to pay r. to,** prestar atención a, tomar en cuenta o consideración; **to pay (one's) respects (to),** presentar sus respetos (a); **with r. to,** con respecto a, tocante a; en cuanto a.
respectability [-ˌspɛktə'bɪlətɪ] *s.* 1. respetabilidad. 2. personas respetables, gente respetable. 3. decoro, cortesía.
respectable [rɪ'spɛktəbəl] *a.* 1. respetable, honorable, estimable. 2. respetable, decoroso, decente. 3. respetable, considerable, apreciable.
respectably [-blɪ] *adv.* respetablemente, decorosamente, decentemente.
respectful [-fəl] *a.* respetuoso, considerado, deferente.
respectfully [-fəlɪ] *adv.* respetuosamente, deferentemente.
respectfulness [-fəlnəs] *s.* respetuosidad, respeto.
respecting [-'spɛktɪŋ] *prep.* (con) respecto a, en cuanto a, por lo que toca a, (en lo) tocante a.
respective [-tɪv] *a.* 1. respectivo, particular, individual. 2. (raro) atento, cuidadoso. 3. (ant.) parcial.
respectively [-lɪ] *adv.* respectivamente.
respell [ri'spɛl] *v.t.* volver a deletrear; escribir de modo fonético (una palabra).
respirable ['rɛspərəbəl, rɪ'spaɪr-] *a.* respirable.
respiration [ˌrɛspə'reɪʃən] *s.* respiración, respiro.
respirator ['rɛspəˌreɪtər, B -ə] *s.* 1. respirador; aparato filtrante para mejorar la inhalación de aire. 2. aparato para administrar respiración artificial.
respiratory ['rɛspərəˌtɔrɪ, rɪ'spaɪr-, B -'spaɪərətərɪ] *a.* respiratorio.
respiratory system, (fisiol.) sistema respiratorio.
respire [rɪ'spaɪr, B -ə] *v.i., v.t.* respirar.
respite ['rɛspət, B -ˌpaɪt] *s.* 1. pausa, respiro, descanso, alivio, sosiego. 2. (der.) suspensión temporal (de la pena de muerte o de una condena). 3. **without r.,** sin respirar, sin tregua. —*v.t.* 1. pensar, posponer, aplazar. 2. (der.) suspender (una ejecución o una condena).
resplendence [rɪ'splɛndəns] **resplendency** [-dənsɪ] *s.* resplandor, esplendor, fulgor, brillo, lucimiento, lustre.
resplendent [-dənt] *a.* resplandeciente, reluciente, refulgente, luminoso, esplendoroso, brillante, lustroso.
resplendently [-lɪ] *adv.* esplendorosamente, brillantemente.
respond [rɪ'spɑnd, B -'spɔnd] *v.i.* 1. responder, contestar. 2. (gen. con *to*) responder (a tratamiento, estímulo, etc.). —*s.* (arq.) pilar empotrado (que sirve de apoyo para un arco de bóveda).
respondence [-'spɑndəns, B -'spɔn-] *s.* 1. respuesta. 2. correspondencia; acuerdo.
respondent [-dənt] *a.* 1. respondedor. 2. (ant.) correspondiente. —*s.* 1. persona respondiente; respondedor. 2. (der.) demandado (esp. en juicios de divorcio).
responder [-dər, B -də] *a.* radiofaro de respuesta.
response [rɪ'spɑns, B -'spɔns] *s.* 1. respuesta, contestación, réplica. 2. reacción. 3. (relig.) responso, responsorio. 4. (rad.) respuesta. 5. rendimiento, retardo, inercia (de motores).
responsibility [-ˌspɑnsə'bɪlətɪ, B -ˌspɔn-] *s.* (*pl.* RESPONSIBILITIES) responsabilidad; **on one's own r.,** bajo su propia responsabilidad.
responsible [-'spɑnsəbəl, B -'spɔn-] *a.* 1. responsable. 2. de responsabilidad (cargo, posición, persona). 3. **to be r. for,** ser responsable de; ser causa de.
responsibleness [-nəs] *s.* responsabilidad.
responsibly [-blɪ] *adv.* responsablemente, con responsabilidad.
responsions [rɪ'spɑntʃənz, B -'spɔnʃənz] *s. pl.* (el) primer examen para el grado de Bachiller en Artes (en la Universidad de Oxford).
responsive [-spɑnsɪv, B -'spɔn-] *a.* 1. que sirve como respuesta o réplica. 2. impresionable, sensible a, fácil de conmover (público, audiencia). 3. respondedor, respondiente, responsivo. 4. (mec.) sensible (anaratos mecánicos).
responsively [-lɪ] *adv.* con simpatía, responsivamente.
responsiveness [-nəs] *s.* 1. simpatía; impresionabilidad, sensibilidad, comprensión. 2. (mec.) sensibilidad.
responsory [-sərɪ] *s.* (*pl.* RESPONSORIES) (relig.) responsorio.
rest [rɛst] *s.* 1. descanso, reposo, inacción, holganza; quietud, tranquilidad. 2. descanso, apoyo, base, soporte; estribo (para el pie). 3. descansadero (para cocheros, marineros, etc.); parador, posada. 4. (mús.) pausa. 5. (poét.) pausa, cesura. 6. (billar) violín, diablo, soporte. 7. **at r.,** en reposo; tranquilo, quieto; en paz (díc. de los muertos); **to come to r.,** detenerse finalmente; **to give (person, horse, machine,** etc.) **a r.,** dejar descansar (a persona, caballo, máquina, etc.); **to lay to r.,** enterrar; **to set someone's mind at r.,** apaciguar el ánimo de alguien, tranquilizar a alguien; **to take a short r.,** darse un corto descanso, tomar un rato de descanso. —*v.i.* 1. descansar, reposar, echarse, yacer. 2. quedar, permanecer. 3. (der.) concluir la presentación de alegatos. 4. **r. assured,** pierda cuidado, no se preocupe; esté seguro (que); tenga la seguridad (de que); **r. from,** descansar de (trabajo, etc.); **r. on** (o **upon**), posarse en; estribar en, descansar sobre, apoyarse en; gravitar sobre, cargar sobre; **r. with,** tocar a alguien (respuesta, decisión, etc.), recaer sobre alguien (responsabilidad, etc.). —*v.t.* 1. dejar descansar. 2. apoyar, asentar. 3. poner (esperanzas, etc.). 4. (der.) concluir (presentación de alegatos).
rest, *s.* 1. **the r.,** los demás, los otros; lo demás, el resto, lo restante, el residuo. 2. **as for the r.,** por lo demás.
rest, *s.* (arm.) cuja, ristre (de lanza).
restart [ri'stɑrt, B -'stɑt] *v.i.* recomenzar, comenzar de nuevo. —*v.t.* 1. volver a poner en marcha. 2. recomenzar.
restate [ri'steɪt] *v.t.* exponer o declarar de nuevo; exponer en forma modificada.
restatement [-mənt] *s.* nueva exposición o declaración.
restaurant ['rɛstərənt, -ˌrɑnt, B -ˌrɔŋ] *s.* restaurante, restorán.
restaurateur [ˌrɛstərə'tɜr, B -tɔrə'tɜ] *s.* (fr.) dueño de un restaurante.
rest-balk ['rɛstˌbɔk] *s.* (agr.) caballón, lomo.
rest cure, cura de reposo.
rest day, día de descanso.
restful ['rɛstfəl] *a.* descansado, reposado, sosegado, quieto, tranquilo.
restfully [-fəlɪ] *adv.* descansadamente, tranquilamente.
restfulness [-fəlnəs] *s.* tranquilidad, quietud, calma.
restharrow [-ˌhæroʊ] *s.* (bot.) detienebuey, gatuña, arnacho, asnacho, asnallo, aznallo.
rest home, sanatorio (de recuperación).
restiform ['rɛstəˌfɔrm, B -ˌfɔm] *a.* (anat.) restiforme.
resting ['rɛstɪŋ] *a.* (biol., bot.) latente.
resting-place [-ˌpleɪs] *s.* 1. sitio para descansar; lugar de descanso. 2. última morada.
restitute ['rɛstəˌtut, B -ˌtjut] *v.t.* restituir.
restitution [ˌrɛstə'tuʃən, B -'tju-] *s.* restitución, restauración, restablecimiento; reparación, indemnización.
restive ['rɛstɪv] *a.* inquieto, intranquilo, ingobernable, inmanejable.
restively [-lɪ] *adv.* inquietamente, intranquilamente.
restiveness [-nəs] *s.* inquietud, intranquilidad.
restless ['rɛstləs] *a.* inquieto, desasosegado, intranquilo.
restless cavy, (zool.) corí, curiel.
restlessly [-lɪ] *adv.* inquietamente, nerviosamente.
restlessness [-nəs] *s.* inquietud, desasosiego, desazón.
restock [ri'stɑk, B -'stɔk] *v.t.* volver a surtir; renovar. —*v.i.* hacer nuevas provisiones.
restorable [rɪ'stɔrəbəl] *a.* susceptible de rehabilitación (reo, prisionero, etc.).
restoration [ˌrɛstə'reɪʃən] *s.* 1. restauración, renovación, rehabilitación, restablecimiento. 2. reintegración, restitución. 3. **R.,** (G.B., hist.) (la) Restauración de la Monarquía (con Carlos II).
restorative [rɪ'stɔrətɪv] *a., s.* restaurativo.

restore [rɪ'stɔr, B -'stɔ] *v.t.* 1. restaurar, rehacer, reparar, renovar. 2. reconstruir. 3. restituir, devolver (energías, salud, etc.). 4. restaurar (casa real, etc.). 5. curar, reponer.
restorer [-'stɔrər, B -ə] *s.* restaurador.
restrain [rɪ'streɪn] *v.t.* 1. refrenar, reprimir, represar; sujetar, contener. 2. restringir, limitar. 3. (der.) prohibir, vedar. 4. recluir, encerrar. 5. (ing.) sujeción, fijación.
restrainable [-əbəl] *a.* restringible, refrenable.
restrainedly [-ədlɪ] *adv.* moderadamente, comedidamente.
restrainer [-ər, B -ə] *s.* (foto.) agente retardador (del desarrollo).
restrain index, (ing.) índice de fijación.
restraining [-ɪŋ] *a.* coercitivo; restringente.
restraint [rɪs'treɪnt] *s.* 1. limitación, restricción. 2. refrenamiento, cohibición. 3. coerción, prohibición. 4. moderación, comedimiento, reserva. 5. reclusión, encierro. 6. **to be under r.,** tener libertad limitada (para); **without r.,** sin restricción, sin tasa.
restraint of trade, (com.) restricción de comercio.
restrict [rɪ'strɪkt] *v.t.* restringir, limitar, circunscribir, reducir; coartar, prohibir.
restricted [-əd] *a.* limitado, restringido, no abierto al público.
restricted area, zona prohibida.
restrictedly [-lɪ] *adv.* limitadamente, con restricción, restringidamente.
restriction [rɪ'strɪkʃən] *s.* restricción, limitación.
restrictive [-tɪv] *a.* restrictivo.
restrictively [-lɪ] *adv.* restrictivamente.
restrictor [-tər, B -tə] *a.* (mec.) limitador.
restring [ri'strɪŋ] *v.t.* 1. encordar de nuevo (instrumento de música, raqueta, etc.). 2. enhebrar o ensartar de nuevo (perlas, etc.).
rest room, tocador, baño; retrete.
result [rɪ'zʌlt] *v.i.* resultar; **r. from,** resultar de; **r. in,** resultar en; dar por resultado. *—s.* resultado, resulta, consecuencia, efecto; **as a r. of,** a causa de; **without r.,** sin resultado, sin éxito.
resultant [-ənt] *a.* resultante. *—s.* (fís.) resultante.
resulting [-iŋ] *a.* 1. emergente, consecutivo a, resultante. 2. **r. use,** (der.) usufructo reversible.
resume [rɪ'zum, B -'zjum] *v.t.* 1. reasumir, recobrar, recuperar. 2. volver a ocupar, volver a tomar (asiento). 3. reanudar, continuar (lectura, viaje, trabajo, etc.). 4. resumir, extractar, compendiar. *—v.i.* 1. recomenzar a hablar. 2. reanudar actividad.
résumé, resume ['rɛzə,meɪ, B 'rɛzjʊ-] *s.* 1. resumen, compendio, extracto, epítome, sumario. 2. (E.U.) historial personal, hoja de vida, currículum vitae.
resummon [rɪ'sʌmən] *v.t.* volver a citar o convocar a.
resumption [rɪ'zʌmʃən] *s.* reasunción, reanudación, continuación.
resupinate [rɪ'supənət, B -'sju-] *a.* (bot.) resupinado.
resupine [,rɛsə'paɪnm, B ,risju-] *a.* supino, tendido sobre el dorso.
resurface [ri'sɜrfəs, B -'sɜfɪs] *v.t.* volver a alisar o a igualar.
resurge [rɪ'sɜrdʒ, B -'sɜdʒ] *v.i.* resurgir, resucitar, renacer.
resurgence [-'sɜrdʒəns, B -'sɜdʒəns] *s.* resurgimiento, resurrección, renacimiento, reaparición.
resurgent [-dʒənt] *a.* resurgente, renaciente.
resurrect [,rɛzə'rɛkt] *v.t.* resucitar, revivir.
resurrection [-'rɛkʃən] *s.* resurrección; renovación, restablecimiento; **The R.,** la Resurrección (de Jesucristo).
resurrectionist [-əst] *s.* 1. resurreccionista. 2. resucitador (de una doctrina, etc.).
resurvey [,risər'veɪ, B -sɜ'-] *v.t.* reexaminar, rever; (top.) volver a medir. — [rɪ'sɜr,veɪ, B -'sɜ,-] *s.* nuevo examen o estudio.
resuscitable [rɪ'sʌsətəbəl] *a.* resucitable.
resuscitate [-,teɪt] *v.t., v.i.* resucitar.
resuscitator [-ər, B -ə] *s.* resucitador.
resuscitation [-,sʌsə'teɪʃən] *s.* 1. (med.) resucitación. 2. renacimiento.
resynthesis [ri'sɪnθəsəs] *s.* (quím.) resíntesis.
ret [rɛt] *v.t.* (*pret., p.p.* RETTED; *p.pr.* RETTING) enriar (cáñamo, lino o maderas).
retable [rɪ'teɪbəl] *s.* (relig.) retablo.
retail ['ri,teɪl] *s.* menudeo, venta al por menor; **at r.,** al por menor. *—a.* minorista; al por menor, al menudeo. *—adv.* al por menor, al menudeo. — [rɪ'teɪl] *v.t.* vender al menudeo, vender al por menor. *—v.i.* venderse al por menor.
retailer [-ər, B -ə] *s.* minorista, detallista, comerciante al por menor.
retail market, (com.) mercado minorista.
retain [rɪ'teɪn] *v.t.* 1. retener, guardar, conservar, reservar, quedarse con. 2. detener, contener, represar. 3. contratar (esp. a un abogado). 4. retener, recordar, rememorar.
retained income [-'teɪnd-] (ten., com.) utilidades incorporadas.
retainer [-'teɪnər, B -nə] *s.* 1. (der.) contrato para servicios de abogado; iguala, señal, anticipo (dado al abogado para asegurar sus servicios). 2. dependiente, servidor, criado. 3. adherente, partidario.
retaining fee [-nɪŋ-] 1. anticipo, adelanto. 2. suma fija que se paga a un experto, abogado, etc.
retaining wall, muro de contención, muro de sostenimiento.
retake [,ri'teɪk] *v.t.* 1. volver a tomar, reasumir; recoger. 2. recapturar. 3. (cinem.) volver a fotografiar o filmar. — ['ri,teɪk] *s.* (cinem.) segundo rodaje, nueva toma (de una escena).
retaliate [rɪ'tæli,eɪt] *v.i.* vengarse, desquitarse, ejercer represalias; **r. upon,** desquitarse con.
retaliation [-,tæli'eɪʃən] *s.* 1. represalia, venganza, desquite. 2. desagravio.
retaliative [-'tæli,eɪtɪv] *a.* vengativo, vengador.
retaliatory [-ə,tɔrɪ, B -ətərɪ] *a.* vengador, de carácter vengativo.
retard [rɪ'tɑrd, B -'tɑd] *v.t.* retardar, retrasar, atrasar, demorar. *—v.i.* retardarse, atrasarse. *—s.* retardo, demora, retraso, atraso, dilación.
retardation [,ri,tɑr'deɪʃən, B -,tɑ'-] *s.* 1. retardo, atraso, retraso. 2. (med.) atraso mental.
retardation coil, (elec.) bobina de reacción.
retardative [rɪ'tɑrdətɪv, B -'tɑd-] *a.* retardativo.
retardatory [-,tɔrɪ, B -tərɪ] *a.* retardatario, dilatorio.
retarded [-əd] *a.* atrasado (mentalmente).
retarder [-ər, B -ə] *s.* 1. (foto.) agente retardador. 2. (f.c.) retardador, freno automático.
retch [rɛtʃ] *v.i.* arquear, basquear, nausear. *—s.* bascas, náuseas.
retell [ri'tɛl] *v.i.* relatar o contar de nuevo.
retem [rə'tɛm, B 'ritɛm] *s.* (bot.) retama blanca.
retene ['ri,tin, B rɛ'tin] *s.* (quím.) reteno.
retention [rɪ'tɛntʃən, B -'tɛnʃən] *s.* 1. retención, conservación; (med.) retención. 2. retentiva, memoria.
retentive [-'tɛntɪv] *a.* retentivo; dotado de buena memoria.
retentiveness [-nəs] *s.* retentiva.
retentivity [,ri,tɛn'tɪvətɪ] *s.* (fís.) retentividad.
retiarius [,reɪtɪ'ɑrɪəs, B ,riʃɪ'ɛər-] *s.* (hist.) (*pl.* RETIARII [-i]) reciario, gladiador armado de una red en la que envolvía al adversario.
reticence ['rɛtəsəns] *s.* 1. reserva, discreción. 2. silencio discreto.
reticency [-sənsɪ] *s., var. de* **reticence.**
reticent [-sənt] *a.* reservado, callado, discreto.
reticently [-lɪ] *adv.* reservadamente, calladamente.
reticle ['rɛtɪkəl] *s.* (ópt.) retículo, retícula.
reticular [rɪ'tɪkjələr, B -lə] *a.* reticular, reticulado; intrincado.
reticulate [-lət, -,leɪt] *a.* (bot.) reticulado; (biol., anat.) reticular. — [-,leɪt] *v.t., v.i.* dividir(se) en forma reticular, formar(se) o trazar cuadrículas.
reticulation [-,tɪkjə'leɪʃən] *s.* disposición o trazado reticular.
reticule ['rɛtɪ,kjul] *s.* 1. (ópt.) retículo. 2. ridículo (bolso de mujer).
reticulocyte [rɪ'tɪkjəloʊ,saɪt] *s.* (fisiol.) reticulocito.
reticuloendothelial [-,ɛndə'θiliəl] *a.* (fisiol.) reticuloendotelial.
reticulum [rɪ'tɪkjələm] *s.* (*pl.* RETICULA [-lə]) 1. (zool.) retículo, redecilla, bonete. 2. (anat.) retículo (tejido en forma de red).
retiform ['ritə,fɔrm, B -,fɔm] *a.* retiforme.
retina ['rɛtənə] *s.* (*pl.* RETINAS O RETINAE [-,i]) (anat.) retina.
retinaculum [,rɛtən'ækjələm] *s.* (*pl.* RETINACULA [-lə]) (anat.) retináculo.
retinal ['rɛtənəl] *a.* (anat.) retinal.
retinene ['rɛtən,in] *s.* (quím.) retineno.
retinitis [,rɛtə'naɪtəs] *s.* (med.) retinitis.
retinol ['rɛtən,ɑl, B -,ɔl] *s.* (quím.) retinol.
retinoscopy [,rɛtən'ɑskəpɪ, B -'ɔs-] *s.* (fisiol., med.) retinoscopia.
retinue ['rɛtən,u, B -,ju] *s.* tren, comitiva, séquito, acompañamiento, corte.
retire [rɪ'taɪr, B -'taɪə] *v.i.* 1. retirarse, retroceder. 2. retirarse, recluirse, recogerse, retraerse. 3. jubilarse. 4. irse a dormir. *—v.t.* 1. (mil.) retirar. 2. recoger, retirar de la circulación. 3. jubilar. 4. (dep.) retirar (a un jugador).
retired [-'taɪrd, B -'taɪəd] *a.* 1. retirado, distante, apartado; solitario, aislado. 2. retraído. 3. jubilado.
retired life, 1. vida jubilada. 2. vida solitaria o inactiva.
retired pay, pensión (de jubilación).
retirement [-'taɪrmənt, B -'taɪəmənt] *s.* 1. retirada, retiro, retiramiento. 2. recogimiento, recogida. 3. retiro, jubilación. 4. retiro, refugio.
retirement years, tercera edad.
retiring [-'taɪrɪŋ, B -'taɪər-] *a.* reservado, retraído, tímido.
retonation wave [rɪ,toʊ'neɪʃən-] onda de retroceso.
retool [ri'tul] *v.t., v.i.* 1. equipar con herramientas nuevas. 2. (fig.) reorganizar.
retorsion, *var. de* **retortion.**
retort [rɪ'tɔrt, B -'tɔt] *v.t.* 1. devolver (un insulto, crítica, ofensa, etc.). 2. retorcer, redargüir (argumento). 3. replicar a; decir en réplica, replicar. *—s.* 1. réplica. 2. (quím.) retorta.
retortion [-'tɔrʃən, B -'tɔʃən] *s.* retorsión.
retouch [ri'tʌtʃ] *v.t.* 1. retocar, perfeccionar, mejorar, pulir, limar. 2. (foto.) retocar. *—s.* retoque, última mano.
retoucher [-ər, B -ə] *s.* (foto.) retocador.
retrace [ri'treɪs] *v.t.* 1. seguir (el paso, huellas); buscar el origen de; repasar (en la memoria). 2. desandar, retroceder, volver atrás. 3. trazar de

nuevo; repasar el trazado de (letras, dibujo, etc.). 4. **r. one's way** (o **steps**), volver sobre sus pasos.

retract [ri'trækt] *v.t.* 1. retractar, revocar, retirar (palabras, promesa, etc.). 2. retraer, contraer (garras, uñas, etc.). —*v.i.* 1. retractarse, desdecirse. 2. retraerse, contraerse (uñas del gato, etc.).

retractable [-'træktəbəl] *a.* 1. retractable. 2. retráctil.

retractable undercarriage, (avia.) tren de aterrizaje retractable.

retractile [-təl, B -ˌtaɪl] *a.* retráctil.

retractility [ˌritræk'tɪlətɪ] *s.* retractilidad.

retracting mechanism [rɪ'træktɪŋ-] mecanismo de repliegue.

retraction [-'trækʃən] *s.* 1. retractación. 2. retracción, contracción.

retractor [-'træktər, B -tə] *s.* (med.) retractor (instrumento y músculo).

retral ['ritrəl] *a.* trasero, posterior.

retransfer [ri'trænsfər, B -fə] *v.t.* volver a transferir, transferir de nuevo.

retransmission [ˌritræns'mɪʃən, -trænz-] *s.* (rad.) retransmisión.

re-tread [ri'trɛd] *v.t.* repisar, pisar o andar de nuevo, repasar por.

retread *v.t.* recauchutar, reencauchar (Amer.) (neumáticos). — ['riˌtrɛd] *s.* 1. recauchado, reencauche (Am.). 2. llanta recauchutada.

retreat [rɪ'trit] *s.* 1. retirada, retiro. 2. retiro, asilo, refugio, abrigo. 3. recogimiento, retraimiento. 4. sanatorio u hospital de convalecientes. 5. (mil.) retirada; retreta (toque). 6. **to be in full r.,** estar en plena retirada; **to beat a r.,** emprender la retirada, huir; **to intercept the r. of,** cortar la retirada de. —*v.i.* 1. retirarse, replegarse, retroceder; cejar. 2. retraerse; refugiarse. —*v.t.* 1. hacer retirar o retroceder. 2. (ajedrez) mover hacia atrás, hacer retroceder (una pieza).

retrench [rɪ'trɛntʃ] *v.t.* 1. aminorar, reducir, disminuir (salario, gastos, etc.). 2. acortar, abreviar (discurso, etc.). 3. quitar, omitir (párrafo, etc.). 4. recortar, podar. —*v.i.* hacer economías o ahorros.

retrenchment [-mənt] *s.* 1. reducción, disminución; economía, ahorro. 2. (mil.) trinchera; atrincheramiento.

retrial [ri'traɪəl] *s.* (der.) prueba o examen nuevo; nuevo juicio.

retribution [ˌrɛtrə'bjuʃən] *s.* 1. justo castigo, punición. 2. retribución, recompensa.

retributive [rɪ'trɪbjətɪv] **retributory** [-ˌtɔrɪ, B -tərɪ] *a.* 1. castigador. 2. retributivo.

retrievable [rɪ'trivəbəl] *a.* recobrable, recuperable.

retrieval [-vəl] *s.* 1. recobro, recuperación. 2. (caza) cobra, cobranza.

retrieve [rɪ'triv] *v.t.* 1. cobrar, recoger (la caza). 2. desenterrar (un recuerdo, algo olvidado). 3. recuperar, recobrar. 4. (dep.) lograr devolver (pelota, etc.). 5. **r. from,** salvar de, rescatar de. —*s.* 1. recobro, recuperación. 2. (dep.) devolución (de la pelota).

retriever [-'trivər, B -və] *s.* perro cobrador, perdiguero.

retroaction [ˌrɛtroʊ'ækʃən] *s.* 1. efecto retroactivo, retroactividad (de la ley, etc.). 2. reacción, acción recíproca.

retroactive [-'æktɪv] *a.* retroactivo.

retroactively [-lɪ] *adv.* retroactivamente.

retroactivity [-ˌæk'tɪvətɪ] *s.* retroactividad.

retrocede [-'sid] *v.i.* retroceder, recular, cejar.

retrocession [-'sɛʃən] *s.* retroceso, retrocesión; contramarcha.

retrochoir ['rɛtrəˌkwaɪr, B -ˌkwaɪə] *s.* (arq.) girola, espacio detrás del coro o del altar (que se usa a veces como capilla).

retroflex ['rɛtrəˌflɛks] *v.t., v.i.* doblar(se) hacia atrás. —*a.* doblado hacia atrás; (med.) retroflejo; (bot.) retroflexo.

retroflexion, retroflection [ˌrɛtrə'flɛkʃən] *s.* 1. flexión hacia atrás, repliegue. 2. (med.) retroflexión.

retrogradation [ˌretroʊgreɪ'deɪʃən] *s.* retrogradación, retroceso, deterioro.

retrograde ['rɛtrəˌgreɪd] *a.* 1. retrógrado, de retroceso. 2. inverso, invertido. 3. retrógrado, declinante, decadente. 4. (astr., biol.) retrógrado. —*v.i.* 1. retroceder, recular. 2. degenerar, deteriorarse.

retrogress [ˌrɛtrə'grɛs] *v.i.* retroceder; degenerar.

retrogression [-'grɛʃən] *s.* 1. retroceso, retrocesión, regresión. 2. (astron.) retrogradación. 3. (biol.) retrogresión.

retrogressive [-'grɛsɪv] *a.* retrógrado, regresivo.

retrogressively [-lɪ] *adv.* regresivamente.

retrolental [ˌrɛtroʊ'lɛntəl] *a.* (anat.) retrolental.

retrorocket ['rɛtroʊˌrɑkət, B -ˌrɔk-] *s.* retrocohete, cohete de retropropulsión (para disminuir la velocidad de un avión o vehículo espacial).

retrorse [rɪ'trɔrs, B -'trɔs] *a.* (biol.) retrorso.

retrospect ['rɛtrəˌspɛkt] *v.i.* hacer recuerdos o memorias. —*v.t.* recapacitar (el pasado, memorias). —*s.* retrospección; **in r.,** en retrospección.

retrospection [ˌrɛtrə'spɛkʃən] *s.* retrospección; meditación sobre el pasado, repaso de sucesos antiguos.

retrospective [-'spɛktɪv] *a.* retrospectivo.

retrospectively [-lɪ] *adv.* retrospectivamente.

retroussé [rəˌtru'seɪ, B -'truseɪ] *a.* arremangada, respingona, respingada (díc. de la nariz).

retroversion [ˌrɛtroʊ'vɜrʒən, B -'vɜʃən] *s.* 1. inclinación o movimiento hacia atrás. 2. (med.) retroversión.

retry [ri'traɪ] *v.t.* (der.) rever (un caso); volver a procesar (a alguien).

return [rɪ'tɜrn, B -'tɜn] *v.i.* 1. regresar, volver, tornar, retornar; revertir. 2. responder, replicar. 3. **r. to,** regresar a; volver a. —*v.t.* 1. dar (informe, fallo, gracias, etc.), rendir (cuentas, veredicto, etc.). 2. elegir, designar (alguien al parlamento, consejo administrativo, etc.). 3. devolver, restituir, reintegrar (objeto). 4. devolver, reciprocar (visita, favor, cumplido, golpe, etc.). 5. producir, rentar, redituar. 6. (const.) doblar (la pared) en ángulo. 7. (naipes) servir, devolver (el palo). 8. (dep.) devolver (la pelota). 9. **r. like for like,** pagar en la misma moneda. —*s.* 1. retorno, devolución, restitución. 2. vuelta, regreso; reaparición. 3. recompensa, retribución. 4. (*gen. pl.*) rédito, rendimiento, ganancia, utilidad. 5. (*pl.*) informe oficial, parte (*m.*). 6. (*pl.*) resultados, cifras (de elecciones, censo, etc.). 7. (pr. G.B.) elección (de un candidato). 8. réplica, respuesta. 9. (*pl.*) (com.) respuestas recibidas (a aviso). 10. (*pl.*) declaración (de impuestos). 11. (pr. G.B.) billete de ida y vuelta. 12. curva, vuelta (de río, galería en minas, trinchera, etc.). 13. (arq.) ala (de pared), vuelta (de moldura). 14. (der.) retorno (de un documento). 15. (*pl.*) (com.) devoluciones, mercaderías devueltas o por devolver. 16. (dep.) devolución (de la pelota). 17. **by r. mail,** a vuelta de correo; **in r. (for),** a cambio (de), en recompensa (por); **many happy returns,** feliz cumpleaños. —*a.* 1. de regreso (camino, viaje, etc.). 2. de recompensa (favor, etc.). 3. contra (golpe). 4. en devolución (mercadería, carga, etc.). 5. recurrente, repetido (fase, etc.). 6. (arq.) en ángulo (pared, fachada, etc.). 7. (mec., elec.) de retorno. 8. (dep.) de vuelta, de revancha, de desquite.

returnable [rɪ'tɜrnəbəl, B -'tɜnə-] *a.* 1. restituíble, reintegrable. 2. (der.) devolutivo, contestable. 3. (com.) con derecho de devolución.

return address, señas o dirección del remitente.

return circuit, (f.c., elec.) corriente de retorno.

returned empties, (com.) cajas o envases (vacíos) devueltos.

return game, r. match, juego o partido de desquite.

return stroke, (mec.) carrera de regreso, carrera de retroceso.

return ticket, 1. (E.U.) billete de vuelta. 2. (G.B.) billete de ida y vuelta.

retuse [rɪ'tus, B -'tjus] *a.* (bot.) retuso.

retype [ri'taɪp] *v.t.* mecanografiar de nuevo, volver a mecanografiar, volver a pasar a máquina, volver a escribir a máquina.

reunification [ˌriˌjunəfə'keɪʃən] *s.* reunificación.

reunify [ri'junəˌfaɪ] *v.t.* reunificar, restablecer la unidad de.

reunion [-'junjən] *s.* reunión, congregación.

reunionist [-əst] *s.* partidario de la reunificación de las Iglesias Católica y Anglicana.

reunite [ˌrijʊ'naɪt] *v.t., v.i.* reunir(se), juntar(se).

re-up [ri'ʌp] *v.i.* (jer., mil.) reengancharse, volver a alistarse.

reusable [ri'juzəbəl] *a.* para uso repetido.

reuse [ri'juz] *v.t.* volver a usar. — [-'jus] *s.* uso repetido.

rev [rɛv] *s. forma abrev. de* **revolution,** revolución (de un motor). —*v.t., v.i.* (*pret., p.p.* REVVED; *p.pr.* REVVING) (gen. con *up*) acelerar, (hacer) funcionar de prisa (el motor).

Rev. *abrev. de* 1. **Revelations,** libro de la Revelación. 2. **Reverend,** Reverendo (Rdo., Rev.).

revaluate [ri'væljʊˌeɪt] *v.t.* revalorizar, volver a valorar.

revaluation [ˌrivæljʊ'eɪʃən] *s.* nueva evaluación, revaluación, valorización.

revalue [ri'vælju] *v.t.* 1. valorizar (moneda). 2. revalorizar, volver a valorar.

revamp [ri'væmp] *v.t.* (fam.) 1. remendar, reformar (empleando el mismo material). 2. renovar.

revanche [rə'vɑnʃ] *s.* revancha, desquite, venganza.

reveal [rɪ'vil] *v.t.* revelar; divulgar, descubrir, publicar, dar a conocer. —*s.* (arq.) mocheta, costado de vano (de puerta o ventana); jamba.

revealable [-'viləbəl] *a.* revelable; comunicable, divulgable.

revealer [-ər, B -ə] *s.* revelador; divulgador.

revealment [-mənt] *s.* revelación; divulgación, descubrimiento.

revehent ['rɛvəhənt] *a.* (anat.) revehente.

reveille ['rɛvəlɪ, B rɪ'vælɪ] *s.* (mil.) diana, toque de alborada.

revel ['rɛvəl] *v.i.* (*pret., p.p.* REVELED O REVELLED; *p.pr.* REVELING O REVELLING) jaranear, ir de parranda; **r. in,** deleitarse en; recrearse con. —*s.* algazara, jarana, parranda; francachela.

revelation [ˌrɛvə'leɪʃən] *s.* revelación, divulgación; (relig.) revelación divina; **the R., Revelations,** (bíbl.) (libro de la) Revelación, el Apocalipsis.

revelationist [-əst] *s.* 1. (teo.) autor de la Revelación (San Juan). 2. creyente de la versión bíblica de la creación del mundo.

revelator ['rɛvəˌleɪtər, B -ə] *s.* revelador, divulgador.

revelatory ['rɛvələˌtɔrɪ, B -tərɪ] *a.* revelador.

reveler, reveller ['rɛvələr, B -lə] *s.* parrandista, jaranero.
revelry [-əlrɪ] *s.* (*pl.* REVELRIES) parranda, jarana, juerga.
revenant ['rɛvənənt, B -nɑn] *s.* aparecido; fantasma.
revenge [rɪ'vɛndʒ] *v.t.* vengar, vindicar; **r. oneself,** vengarse; desquitarse. —*v.i.* (ant.) vengarse, tomar revancha. —*s.* venganza, vindicta, vindicación; desquite, revancha.
revengeful [-fəl] *a.* vengativo, vindicativo.
revengefully [-fəlɪ] *adv.* vindicativamente, vengativamente.
revengefulness [-fəlnəs] *s.* carácter vengativo; sed de venganza.
revenger [rɪ'vɛndʒər, B -ə] *s.* vengador, vindicador.
revenue ['rɛvə,nu, B -,nju] *s.* 1. renta, entrada, ingreso. 2. fuente de ingresos. 3. rentas públicas, ingresos del erario. 4. oficina fiscal (encargada del cobro de las rentas públicas).
revenue cutter, escampavía, guardacostas.
revenue officer, aduanero, empleado de aduana, resguardo; agente fiscal.
revenuer [-ər, B -ə] *s.* 1. aduanero, resguardo. 2. escampavía, guardacostas.
revenue stamp, timbre fiscal o de impuesto; sello fiscal; sello de rentas internas.
reverberant [rɪ'vɜrbərənt, B -'vɜbə-] *a.* reverberante; resonante, retumbante.
reverberate [-bə,reɪt] *v.t.* 1. hacer reverberar o reflejar (luz, calor); hacer repercutir, hacer reflejar o retumbar (sonido). 2. rebotar, rechazar. —*v.i.* 1. reverberar, reflejarse (luz, calor); repercutir, reflejarse, retumbar (sonido). 2. rebotar.
reverberation [rɪ,vɜrbə'reɪʃən, B -,vɜbə-] *s.* reverberación, reverbero (de luz, calor); eco, repercusión (de sonido).
reverberative [-'vɜrbə,reɪtɪv, B -'vɜbə-] *a.* reverberante, reflexivo.
reverberator [-ər, B -ə] *s.* reverberador, reflector, reverbero.
reverberatory [-rə,tɔrɪ, B -tərɪ] *a.* de reverbero, reverberatorio. —*s.* horno de reverbero.
revere [rɪ'vɪr, B -'vɪə] *v.t.* reverenciar, respetar, venerar, honrar.
reverence ['rɛvərəns] *s.* 1. reverencia, veneración, deferencia, respeto. 2. reverencia, zalema, inclinación del cuerpo. 3. dignidad, rango elevado. 4. (vulg., hum.) reverendo, reverencia (como tratamiento a clérigos). 5. **to hold in r.,** tener respeto por, estimar; **to pay r.,** rendir homenaje. —*v.t.* reverenciar, respetar, venerar, acatar.
reverend [-ənd] *a.* reverendo. —*s.* (fam.) clérigo, religioso, sacerdote; **reverends and right reverends,** clérigos y obispos.
reverent [-ənt] *a.* reverente; reverencial, respetuoso.
reverential [,rɛvə'rɛntʃəl, B -'rɛnʃəl] *a.* reverencial, respetuoso, reverente.
reverentially [-'rɛntʃəlɪ, B -'rɛnʃ-] *adv.* de modo reverencial, reverentemente.
reverently ['rɛvərəntlɪ] *adv.* reverentemente.
reverie ['rɛvərɪ] *s.* ensueño, meditación, contemplación, arrobamiento, fantasía, ilusión.
revers [rɪ'vɪr, B -'vɪə] *s.* (*pl.* REVERS [-'vɪrz, B -'ᵛ əž]) (cost.) solapa; caída; vuelta.
reversal [rɪ'vɜrsəl, B -'vɜsəl] *s.* 1. inversión, trastorno, volteo, trastrocamiento. 2. (der.) revocación, anulación (de una sentencia, etc.).
reverse [rɪ'vɜrs, B -'vɜs] *a.* 1. volteado, trastornado, invertido. 2. contrario, opuesto; contradictorio, contrapuesto. 3. de contramarcha, de marcha atrás. —*s.* 1. (con *the*) lo opuesto, lo contrario, lo inverso. 2. revés, desgracia, infortunio, percance, contratiempo. 3. reverso, inverso, dorso, respaldo, revés, envés. 4. (mec.) contramarcha, marcha atrás. 5. **in r.,** en marcha atrás; **quite the r.,** lo contrario; **to put in r.,** poner en marcha atrás. —*v.t.* 1. invertir, trastornar, poner de cabeza, volver al revés; **r. arms,** (mil.) invertir las armas. 2. voltear, transponer, cambiar. 3. (der.) revocar, anular (una sentencia, etc.). 4. (mec.) dar marcha atrás a, dar contramarcha a (máquina, motor, etc.). 5. **r. oneself,** cambiar de opinión, contradecirse. —*v.i.* 1. voltearse. 2. empezar a girar en sentido inverso (al bailar). 3. (mec.) poner marcha atrás o contramarcha.
reverse contact, (elec.) contacto de inversión.
reverse current, (elec.) corriente inversa, contracorriente.
reverse curve, (f.c.) curva inversa, contracurva.
reverse-flow valve [rɪ'vɜrs,floʊ-, B -'vɜs-] válvula de contraflujo.
reverse gear, (aut.) (engranaje de) marcha atrás, (engranaje de) contramarcha.
reversely [-lɪ] *adv.* al revés, al contrario.
reverser [-ər, -ə] *s.* (elec.) inversor.
reverse speed, velocidad de retroceso.
reversi [-ɪ] *s.* (naipes) revesino.
reversibility [rɪ,vɜrsə'bɪlətɪ, B -,vɜsə-] *s.* reversibilidad.
reversible [-'vɜrsəbəl, B -'vɜsə-] *a.* 1. reversible, transformable, cambiable. 2. (quím., mec.) reversible. 3. (der.) reponible. 4. (tej.) reversible.
reversible booster, (elec.) elevador-reductor.
reversibly [-blɪ] *adv.* de modo reversible.
reversion [rɪ'vɜrʒən, B -'vɜʃən] *s.* 1. reversión. 2. (biol.) reversión, regresión, retrogradación. 3. (der.) reversión; derecho de sucesión.
reversional [-əl] **reversionary** [-,ɛrɪ, B -ərɪ] *a.* (der.) de reversión.
reversioner [-ər, B -ə] *s.* (der.) tenedor de reversión.
revert [rɪ'vɜrt, B -'vɜt] *v.i.* 1. recudir, resurtir. 2. (der.) revertir, volver (cosa, derecho, etc.). 3. (biol.) revertir, volver a su estado primitivo. 4. **r. to,** volver sobre (tema, tópico, etc.); recaer en, volver a. —*s.* el que revierte a su fe.
reverter [-ər, B -ə] *s.* (der.) reversión.
revertible [-əbəl] *a.* reversible.
revery, *s.* (*pl.* REVERIES) *var. de* **reverie.**
revest [ri'vɛst] *v.t.* reponer, restablecer, reinstalar. —*v.i.* reinstalarse, revestirse.
revet [rɪ'vɛt] *v.t.* (*pret., p.p.* REVETTED; *p.pr.* REVETTING) (mil., ing.) revestir, cubrir con revestimiento.
revetment [-mənt] *s.* (mil., ing.) revestimiento; muro de contención.
revictual [ri'vɪtəl] *v.t., v.i.* reabastecer(se) abastecer(se) de nuevo, volver a abastecer(se).
review [rɪ'vju] *v.t.* 1. reexaminar, remirar, repasar. 2. mirar retrospectivamente, reflexionar sobre. 3. reseñar, criticar, analizar. 4. (der.) revisar (sentencias, etc.). 5. (mil.) revistar, pasar revista a. 6. (ant.) rever, ver de nuevo, volver a ver. —*v.i.* 1. hacer un repaso. 2. escribir reseñas o críticas. —*s.* 1. reexaminación, nueva inspección, repaso, revista. 2. retrospección, reflexión. 3. reseña, crítica, recensión. 4. revista (publicación periódica). 5. (teat.) revista. 6. (educ.) repaso. 7. (der.) revisión (de procedimientos, fallos, etc.). 8. (mil., mar.) revista, parada, reseña. 9. **to pass in r.,** pasar revista (a).
reviewal [-əl] *s.* 1. revisión, inspección, examen. 2. revista, crítica, reseña.
reviewer [-ər, B -ə] *s.* 1. revisor, inspector, examinador. 2. revistero, crítico.
revile [rɪ'vaɪl] *v.t.* vilipendiar, injuriar, denigrar, oprobiar, denostar, insultar. —*v.i.* echar denuestos, proferir injurias.
revilement [-mənt] *s.* vilipendio, injuria, oprobio, denuesto, insulto.
reviler [-ər, B -ə] *s.* vilipendiador, injuriador, denigrador, denostador, insultador.
revilingly [-ɪŋlɪ] *adv.* injuriosamente, denigrativamente.
revisal [rɪ'vaɪzəl] *s.* revisión, inspección.
revise [rɪ'vaɪz] *v.t.* 1. releer, repasar. 2. revisar, reexaminar, reconsiderar. 3. corregir, enmendar. —*s.* 1. revisión. 2. ['ri,vaɪz, B rɪ'vaɪz] (impr.) segunda prueba.
Revised Standard Version [-'vaɪzd-] Versión Normal Revisada (de la Biblia).
Revised Version, Versión Revisada (de la Biblia).
reviser, revisor [-'vaɪzər, B -zə] *s.* 1. revisor. 2. (impr.) corrector de pruebas.
revision [-'vɪʒən] *s.* 1. revisión, revista, repaso. 2. corrección, enmienda, modificación. 3. (impr.) segunda prueba (con correcciones).
revisional [-əl] **revisionary** [-,ɛrɪ, B -ərɪ] *a.* de revisión.
revisionism [-ɪzəm] *s.* revisionismo.
revisionist [-əst] *a., s.* revisionista.
revisit [ri'vɪzət] *v.t.* volver a visitar, visitar de nuevo. —*s.* segunda o nueva visita.
revisory [rɪ'vaɪzərɪ] *a.* revisor.
revitalization [ri,vaɪtələ'zeɪʃən, B -əlaɪ-] *s.* revitalización, revivificación.
revitalize [-'vaɪtəl,aɪz] *v.t.* revitalizar, revivir, revivificar.
revival [rɪ'vaɪvəl] *s.* 1. renacimiento, restauración; restablecimiento, renovación. 2. (teat.) reposición, reestreno. 3. (impr.) reedición (de libros). 4. (relig.) reunión o serie de reuniones de evangelistas. 5. (der.) restablecimiento o restauración de vigencia (de una deuda, obligación, etc.).
revivalism [-,ɪzəm] *s.* (relig.) movimiento renovador de la fe.
revivalist [-əst] *s.* predicador, renovador (de la fe).
revive [rɪ'vaɪv] *v.t.* 1. revivir, resucitar. 2. (fig.) reanimar, reavivar, refrescar; restaurar, restablecer. 3. (quím.) reactivar. —*v.i.* 1. volver en sí, recobrarse. 2. (fig.) reanimarse, reavivarse.
reviver [-ər, B -ə] *s.* vivificador, resucitador, reanimador.
revivification [ri,vɪvəfə'keɪʃən] *s.* revivificación, reanimación.
revivify [-'vɪvə,faɪ] *v.t. v.i.* volver en sí, revivir, revivificar, reanimar.
reviviscence [rɪ,vaɪ'vɪsəns, B ,rɛvɪ-] *s.* 1. restablecimiento, renacimiento. 2. (biol.) reviviscencia.
reviviscency [-ənsɪ] *s.* (*pl.* REVIVISCENCIES) *var. de* **reviviscence.**
reviviscent [-ənt] *a.* (biol.) reviviscente.
revocability [,rɛvəkə'bɪlətɪ] *s.* revocabilidad.
revocable ['rɛvəkəbəl] *a.* revocable, derogable, anulable.
revocably [-blɪ] *adv.* revocablemente.
revocation [,rɛvə'keɪʃən] *s.* revocación, anulación, abrogación, abolición, derogación.
revocatory ['rɛvəkə,tɔrɪ, B -tərɪ] *a.* revocatorio, derogatorio.
revokable [rɪ'voʊkəbəl] *var. de* **revocable.**
revoke [rɪ'voʊk] *v.t.* 1. revocar, derogar, rescindir, abrogar, abolir, cancelar. 2. (raro) recordar, traer a la memoria. —*v.i.* (naipes) renunciar. —*s.* 1. (naipes) renuncio. 2. (raro) revocación, anulación.
revoker [-ər, B -ə] *s.* revocador, derogador, anulador.

revolt [rɪ'voʊlt] *s.* 1. revuelta, rebelión, insurrección, sublevación, alzamiento, revolución, sedición. 2. repugnancia, aversión; repulsión, repelo, rechazo. 3. **in r.,** en rebelión. —*v.i.* 1. rebelarse, sublevarse. 2. **r. at** (o **against**), sentir repugnancia o repulsión hacia; rebelarse o alzarse contra. —*v.t.* 1. repugnar, repeler, dar asco. 2. incitar a rebelión, hacer sublevar, insurreccionar.
revolting [-'voʊltɪŋ] *a.* repugnante, nauseabundo; chocante, ofensivo, escandaloso.
revoltingly [-lɪ] *adv.* repugnantemente; ofensivamente, escandalosamente.
revolute ['rɛvə,lut] *a.* (bot.) revoluto, revolutado.
revolution [,rɛvə'luʃən] *s.* 1. revolución, rotación; giro, vuelta. 2. revolución, insurrección, rebelión, sublevación. 3. (astr.) revolución (de los astros en su órbita); rotación (de un astro sobre su eje).
revolutionary [-ʃə,nɛrɪ, B -nərɪ] *a.* revolucionario. —*s.* (*pl.* REVOLUTIONARIES) revolucionario.
revolution counter, (mec.) cuentarrevoluciones, contador de vueltas, tacómetro.
revolutionist [-nəst] *s.* revolucionario, sedicioso.
revolutionize [-,naɪz] *v.t.* 1. revolucionar, sublevar, soliviantar. 2. (fig.) revolucionar, cambiar totalmente, alterar radicalmente.
revolvable [rɪ'vɑlvəbəl, B -'vɔl-] *a.* giratorio, rotatorio.
revolve [-'vɑlv, B -'vɔlv] *v.t.* 1. revolver, hacer girar o rodar. 2. revolver, considerar, meditar (problema, idea). —*v.i.* 1. girar. 2. dar vueltas (una idea, etc., en la cabeza). 3. (astr.) revolverse (astro en su órbita). 4. **r. about,** (fig.) girar en torno a (tema, punto de interés, etc.); **r. upon,** meditar sobre, reflexionar sobre.
revolver [rɪ'vɑlvər, B -'vɔlvə] *s.* (arm.) revólver.
revolving [-ɪŋ] *a.* 1. giratorio, rotatorio. 2. (fig.) rotativo.
revolving chair, silla giratoria.
revolving credit, (com.) crédito global, crédito rotativo.
revolving door, puerta giratoria.
revolving fund, fondo rotativo.
revolving light, (avia., mar.) luz giratoria, fanal giratorio.
revolving stage, (teat.) escenario giratorio.
revue [rɪ'vju] *s.* (teat.) revista.
revulsion [rɪ'vʌlʃən] *s.* 1. asco, repugnancia, aversión repentina. 2. cambio brusco. 3. (med.) revulsión.
revulsive [-sɪv] *a.* (med.) revulsivo (díc. del medicamento).
rewake [ri'weɪk] **rewaken** [-'weɪkən] *v.t., v.i.* volver a despertar(se).
reward [rɪ'wɔrd, B -'wɔd] *v.t.* premiar, recompensar, retribuir, gratificar, remunerar. —*s.* premio, recompensa, retribución, remuneración.
rewarder [-ər, B -ə] *s.* premiador, remunerador, gratificador.
rewarding [-ɪŋ] *a.* 1. provechoso, útil (experiencia, pasatiempo, reunión, etc.). 2. gratificador, remunerador.
rewind [ri'waɪnd] *v.t.* volver a dar cuerda; (mec.) rebobinar.
rewire [-'waɪr, B -ə] *v.t.* 1. alambrar de nuevo, volver a alambrar. 2. volver a telegrafiar.
reword [-'wɜrd, B -'wɜd] *v.t.* 1. volver a pronunciar, repetir con las mismas palabras. 2. expresar con otras palabras, parafrasear.
rework [ri'wɜrk, B -'wɜk] *v.t.* 1. volver a explotar (ej., una mina). 2. refundir, adaptar (una obra, un tema, etc.). 3. elaborar de nuevo (un producto echado a perder).
rewrite [ri'raɪt] *v.t.* 1. reescribir, volver a escribir, describir de nuevo; redactar de nuevo. 2. (E.U.) redactar, refundir. ['ri,raɪt] *s.* (E.U.) artículo que utiliza material proporcionado por un reportero.
Reykjavik ['reɪkjə,vik] *s.* Reykjavik, capital de Islandia.
Reynard ['reɪnərd, B 'rɛnəd] *s.* el Zorro (personificado en fábulas y folklore).
rezone [ri'zoʊn] *v.t.* dividir en zonas nuevas, fijar zonas nuevas para, rezonificar (Amer.).
Rh *símb. de* **rhodium,** rodio (Rh).
R. H. *abrev. de* **Royal Highness,** Su Alteza (S.A.).
rhabdocoele ['ræbdə,sil] *s.* (zool.) rabdocelo.
rhabdomancy [-,mænsɪ] *s.* rabdomancia.
rhabdomantist [-təst] *s.* rabdomante.
rhadamanthine [,rædə'mænθən, B -θaɪn] *a.* riguroso, muy justo.
Rhadamanthus [-θəs] *s.* (mitol.) Radamanto, juez de los muertos.
Rhaetian ['riʃɪən] **Rhaetic** ['ritɪk] *a.* rético, de una antigua provincia romana.
Rhaeto-Romanic [,ritoʊroʊ'mænɪk] *s.* retorromano.
rhamnaceous [ræm'neɪʃəs] *a.* (bot.) ramnáceo, rámneo.
rhamnose ['ræm,noʊs] *s.* (quím.) ramnosa.
rhamnus [-nəs] *s.* (bot.) ramnea, ramnácea.
rhapsodical [ræp'sɑdɪkəl, B -'sɔd-] **rhapsodic** [-ɪk] *a.* 1. semejante a una rapsodia. 2. extático.
rhapsodically [-kəlɪ] *adv.* con éxtasis, con entusiasmo inusitado.
rhapsodist ['ræpsədəst] *s.* 1. (hist.) rapsoda. 2. el que recita poemas épicos.
rhapsodize [-,daɪz] *v.i.* 1. cantar, recitar o escribir con exaltación o extravagancia. 2. extasiarse.
rhapsody [-dɪ] *s.* (*pl.* RHAPSODIES) 1. (lit., mús.) rapsodia. 2. (fig.) elogio extático.
rhatany ['rætənɪ] *s.* (*pl.* RHATANIES) (bot.) ratania.
rhea ['riə, B 'rɪə] *s.* 1. (orn.) ñandú, ñandu, avestruz de América. 2. **R.,** (astr.) Rea.
Rhenish ['rɛnɪʃ, B 'rin-] *a.* renano, del Rin. —*s.* vino del Rin.
rhenium ['rinɪəm] *s.* (quím.) renio.
rheology [ri'ɑlədʒɪ, B -'ɔl-] *s.* reología, el estudio de los cambios y las formas de los elementos fluidos.
rheometer [-'ɑmətər, B -'ɔmɪtə] *s.* reómetro, dispositivo que mide la velocidad con que fluye un elemento líquido.
rheophile ['riə,faɪl] *a.* (biol.) reófilo.
rheoscope [-,skoʊp] *s.* reoscopio.
rheostat [-,stæt] *s.* (elec.) reóstato.
rheotaxis [,riə'tæksəs] *s.* (biol.) reotaxis.
rheotron ['riə,trɑn, B -,trɔn] *s.* (rad.) reotrón, betatrón.
rheotrope [-,troʊp] *s.* (elec.) reótropo.
rheotropism [ri'ɑtrə,pɪzəm, B -'ɔt-] *s.* (biol.) reotropismo.
Rhesus ['risəs] *s.* (zool.) rhesus.
Rhesus factor, (med.) factor rhesus.
rhetor ['ri,tɔr, B 'ritə] *s.* rétor, profesor de retórica; orador.
rhetoric ['rɛtərɪk] *s.* 1. retórica. 2. (fig.) retóricas.
rhetorical [rɪ'tɔrɪkəl] *a.* retórico.
rhetorically [-kəlɪ] *adv.* retóricamente.
rhetorical question, (ret.) interrogación retórica.
rhetorician [,rɛtə'rɪʃən] *s.* 1. retórico, profesor de retórica. 2. orador elocuente.
rheum [rum] *s.* 1. (med.) reuma, fluxión. 2. (poét.) lágrimas.
rheumatic [rʊ'mætɪk] *a.* reumático. —*s.* 1. reumático, persona reumática. 2. (*pl.*) (dial.) reumatismo.
rheumatic fever, (med.) fiebre reumática.
rheumatism ['rumə,tɪzəm] *s.* (med.) reumatismo.
rheumatoid [-,tɔɪd] *a.* (med.) reumatoideo.
rheumatoid arthritis, (med.) artritis reumatoidea.
rheumy ['rumɪ] *a.* (RHEUMIER; RHEUMIEST) 1. (med.) reumático. 2. frío y húmedo (aire, neblina, etc.).
Rh factor ['ɑr'eɪtʃ-] (bioquím.) factor Rh.
rhinal ['raɪnəl] *a.* (anat.) rinal, nasal.
rhinalgia [raɪ'nældʒɪə] *s.* (med.) rinalgia.
Rhine [raɪn] *s.* Rin (río).
Rhinegold ['raɪn,goʊld] *s.* (mitol., mús.) el oro del Rin.
rhinencephalon [,raɪnɛn'sɛfə,lɑn, B -,lɔn] *s.* (*pl.* RHINENCEPHALA [-lə]) (anat.) rinencéfalo.
rhinestone ['raɪn,stoʊn] *s.* piedra falsa, imitación de diamante (hecha gen. de vidrio).
rhinitis [raɪ'naɪtəs] *s.* (med.) rinitis.
rhino ['raɪnoʊ] *s.* (jer., G.B.) guita, mosca, monises (dinero).
rhino, *s.* (*pl.* RHINOS) (*forma abrev. de* rhinoceros) rinoceronte.
rhinoceros [raɪ'nɑsərəs, B -'nɔs-] *s.* (*pl.* RHINOCEROS, RHINOCEROSES O RHINOCERI [-,raɪ]) rinoceronte.
rhinolaryngology [,raɪnoʊ,lærən'gɑlədʒɪ, B -'gɔl-] *s.* (med.) rinolaringología.
rhinologist [raɪ'nɑlədʒəst, B -'nɔl-] *s.* (med.) rinólogo.
rhinology [-dʒɪ] *s.* (med.) rinología.
rhinopharyngitis [,raɪnoʊ,færən'dʒaɪtəs] *s.* (med.) rinofaringitis.
rhinoplasty ['raɪnə,plæstɪ] *s.* (med.) rinoplastia.
rhinoscope [-,skoʊp] *s.* (med.) rinoscopio.
rhinoscopy [raɪ'nɑskəpɪ, B -'nɔs-] *s.* (med.) rinoscopia.
rhizocarpous [,raɪzə'kɑrpəs, B -'kɑpəs] *a.* (bot.) rizocárpico.
rhizocephalan [-zoʊ'sɛfələn] *s.* (crustáceo) rizocéfalo.
rhizocephalous [-ləs] *a.* (zool.) rizocéfalo.
rhizogenic [-zə'dʒɛnɪk] **rhizogenous** [-'zɑdʒənəs, B -'zɔdʒ-] *a.* (bot.) rizógeno.
rhizoid ['raɪ,zɔɪd] *a., s.* (bot.) rizoide.
rhizoidal [raɪ'zɔɪdəl] *a.* (bot.) rizoidal.
rhizomatous [-'zoʊmətəs] *a.* (bot.) rizomatoso.
rhizome ['raɪ,zoʊm] *s.* (bot.) rizoma.
rhizomorphous [,raɪzə'mɔrfəs, B -'mɔfəs] *a.* (bot.) rizomorfo.
rhizophagous [raɪ'zɑfəgəs, B -'zɔf-] *a.* (zool.) rizófago.
rhizophoraceous [-,zɑfə'reɪʃəs, B-,zɔf-] *a.* (bot.) rizoforáceo, rizofóreo.
rhizopod ['raɪzə,pɑd, B -,pɔd] *s.* (zool.) rizópodo.
rhizotomy [raɪ'zɑtəmɪ, B -'zɔt-] *s.* (med.) rizotomía.
rho [roʊ] *s.* ro, decimoséptima letra del alfabeto griego.
rhodamine ['roʊdə,min] *s.* (quím.) rodamina.
Rhode Island [roʊd'aɪlənd] *s.* Rhode Island, estado de los E.U.
Rhodes [roʊdz] *s.* Rodas, isla griega donde estuvo emplazada en la antigüedad la estatua gigantesca de Apolo, el coloso de Rodas.
Rhodesia [roʊ'diʒə, B -ʒjə] *s.* Rodesia.
Rhodian ['roʊdɪən] *a., s.* rodio, de la isla de Rodas.

rhodium [-ɪəm] *s.* (quím., metal.) rodio.
rhodochrosite [ˌroʊdə'kroʊˌsaɪt] *s.* (min.) rodocrosita.
rhododendron [-'dɛndrən] *s.* (bot.) rododendro.
rhodolite ['roʊdəˌlaɪt] *s.* (min.) rodolita.
rhodonite [-ənˌaɪt] *s.* (min.) rodonita.
Rhodophyceae [ˌroʊdə'faɪsɪˌi] *s. pl.* (bot.) rodofíceas.
rhodoplast ['roʊdəˌplæst] *s.* (bot.) rodoplasto.
rhodopsin [roʊ'dɑpsən, B -'dɔp-] *s.* (fisiol.) rodopsina.
rhomb [rɑmb, B rɔm] *s.* (geom.) rombo.
rhombencephalon [ˌrɑmbɛn'sɛfəˌlɑn, B ˌrɔm-ˌlɔn] *s.* (anat.) rombencéfalo.
rhombic ['rɑmbɪk, B 'rɔm-] *a.* 1. rombal. 2. (quím.) ortorrómbico.
rhombohedral [ˌrɑmboʊ'hidrəl, B ˌrɔm-] *a.* (geom.) romboédrico.
rhombohedron [-drən] *s.* (*pl.* RHOMBOHEDRONS O RHOMBOHEDRA [-drə]) (geom.) romboedro.
rhomboid ['rɑmˌbɔɪd, B 'rɔm-] *s.* (geom.) romboide. —*a.* romboidal.
rhomboidal [rɑm'bɔɪdəl, B rɔm-] *a.* (geom.) romboidal.
rhombus ['rɑmbəs, B 'rɔm-] *s.* (*pl.* RHOMBUSES O RHOMBI [-ˌbaɪ]) (geom.) rombo.
Rhône [roʊn] *s.* Ródano (río).
rhopalic [roʊ'pælɪk] *a.* (poét.) ropálico.
rhotacism ['roʊtəˌsizəm] *s.* (fon.) rotacismo.
rhubarb ['ruˌbarb, B -ˌbɑb] *s.* 1. (bot.) ruibarbo, raíz de ruibarbo usada como laxativo; pecíolos de ruibarbo usados como alimento. 2. (jer.) alboroto, lío, riña (ej., de jugadores durante un partido de béisbol).
rhumb [rʌm] *s.* (mar.) rumbo, cuarta (de la rosa náutica).
rhumb line, (mar.) línea de rumbo, línea loxodrómica.
rhyme [raɪm] *s.* 1. rima, verso, poesía. 2. rima, consonancia. 3. **without r. or reason,** sin ton ni son. —*v.i.* 1. rimar, versificar. 2. rimar, consonar, armonizarse. —*v.t.* 1. rimar, versificar, poner en verso. 2. hacer rimar.
rhymer ['raɪmər, B -ə] *s.* rimador, versificador.
rhyme scheme, distribución de rima (en una estrofa o un poema).
rhymester [-stər, B -stə] *s.* coplero, poetastro, rimador.
rhynchocephalian [ˌrɪŋkoʊsə'feɪljən] *a., s.* (zool.) rincocéfalo.
rhynchophorous [rɪŋ'kɑfərəs, B -'kɔf-] *a.* (zool.) que tiene pico.
rhyodacite [ˌraɪə'deɪˌsaɪt] *s.* (min.) riodacita.
rhyolite ['raɪəˌlaɪt] *s.* (min.) riolita.
rhythm ['rɪðəm] *s.* 1. ritmo. 2. (med.) periodicidad.
rhythmic ['rɪðmɪk] **rhythmical** [-mɪkəl] *a.* rítmico, acompasado, cadencioso.
rhythmically [-mɪkəlɪ] *adv.* rítmicamente.
rhythmics [-mɪks] *s. pl.* (*gen. sing. en const.*) rítmica.
rhythmize ['rɪðəˌmaɪz] *v.t.* dar ritmo a, componer en forma rítmica.
rhythm method, (fisiol.) método rítmico, método de Ogino-Knaus.
rhytidome ['rɪtəˌdoʊm] *s.* (bot.) ritidoma.
rhyton ['raɪtɑn, B -tɔn] *s.* (*pl.* RHYTA [-tə]) ritón, antigua copa griega de forma de cuerno o de la cabeza de un animal.
R. I. *abrev. de* **Rhode Island,** Rhode Island.
rialto [rɪ'æltoʊ] *s.* 1. mercado, lonja. 2. distrito de teatros (esp. en Nueva York).
riant ['raɪənt] *a.* risueño, placentero, gracioso.
riantly [-lɪ] *adv.* risueñamente, placenteramente.
riata [ri'ætə, B -'ɑtə] *s.* reata, lazo, mangana.
rib [rɪb] *s.* 1. (anat.) costilla. 2. (bot.) costilla, nervadura, nervio. 3. cañón (de la pluma). 4. varilla (del paraguas). 5. (arq.) nervio (de arco), arista (de bóveda). 6. (tej.) cordoncillo; bordón. 7. (aer.) costilla. 8. (cocina) costilla (de vaca, cerdo, etc.). 9. (mar.) costilla, cuaderna. 10. (enc.) (*pl.*) nervura, nervios. 11. (hum.) costilla, esposa. 12. **to poke one in the ribs,** darle un codazo a uno en las costillas. —*v.t.* (*pret., p.p.* RIBBED; *p.pr.* RIBBING) 1. reforzar con cuadernas o costillas. 2. acanalar. 3. (jer.) tomar el pelo a, burlarse de.
ribald ['rɪbəld] *s., a.* impúdico, lúbrico; burlón, atrevido, procaz.
ribaldry [-əldrɪ] *s.* (*pl.* RIBALDRIES) obscenidad, procacidad; lujuria.
riband ['rɪbənd] *s.* cinta, listón, banda (esp. la que se usa como adorno).
ribat [rə'bɑt] *s.* morabito, marabuto (ermita mahometana).
ribband ['rɪbˌbænd, B 'rɪbənd] *s.* maestra de construcción (de buques).
ribbed [rɪbd] *a.* 1. acanalado. 2. (tej.) de cordoncillo, a bordones.
ribbing ['rɪbɪŋ] *s.* 1. (bot.) nervadura. 2. (tej.) acanalado. 3. superficie ondulada (de la madera). 4. (enc.) nervura.
ribbon ['rɪbən] *s.* 1. cinta, banda, listón, faja. 2. tira; (*pl.*) tiras, jirones, desgarrones. 3. (*pl.*) riendas. 4. (mil.) cordón (de una orden), galón, pasador (de una condecoración). 5. maestra de construccion (de buques). 6. **to take** (o **to handle**) **the ribbons,** tomar las riendas. —*v.t.* 1. encintar, adornar (con cintas). 2. hacer jirones.
ribbon building, (G.B.) construcciones a lo largo de una carretera.
ribbon development, urbanización que alinea las casas a lo largo de las carreteras que salen de las ciudades.
ribbonfish [-ˌfɪʃ] *s.* (ict.) cinta, anguileta del mar, látigo, pez llama.
ribbon grass, (bot.) cinta.
ribby ['rɪbɪ] *a.* (RIBBIER; RIBBIEST) (tej.) a bordones.
rib cage, (anat.) caja torácica.
ribgrass [-ˌgræs, B -ˌgrɑs] *s.* (bot.) llantén menor, lancéola.
riboflavin [ˌraɪbə'fleɪvən] *s.* (bioquím.) riboflavina.
ribose ['raɪˌboʊs] *s.* (quím.) ribosa.
ribwort ['rɪbˌwɜrt, B -ˌwɜt] *s.* (bot.) llantén menor, lancéola, quinquenervia.
rice [raɪs] *s.* arroz.
ricebird ['raɪsˌbɜrd, B -ˌbɜd] *s.* (orn.) chambergo, charlatán.
rice field, arrozal.
rice mill, molino arrocero.
rice paper, 1. papel de arroz. 2. papel de China.
rice pudding, arroz con leche.
ricer ['raɪsər, B -sə] *s.* prensador (utensilio de cocina).
rice rat, rata de campo.
rich [rɪtʃ] *a.* 1. rico, adinerado, opulento, pudiente, acomodado, acaudalado. 2. rico, suntuoso, lujoso, soberbio, espléndido, exquisito, magnífico, precioso, costoso, valioso. 3. grasoso, suculento, condimentado (comida, alimentos). 4. intenso, fuerte, subido (color). 5. modulada, sonora (voz). 6. significativo (díc. de las palabras). 7. rico, de alta combustibilidad (díc. de la mezcla de aire y gas). 8. rico, abundante, copioso, exuberante (cosecha). 9. rico, fructífero, fértil, fecundo (terreno). 10. (fam.) gracioso, divertido, humorístico. 11. absurdo, risible. 12. (jer., G.B.) indecente, verde (cuento, chiste, etc.). 13. **the r.,** los ricos.
Richard Roe ['rɪtʃərd'roʊ, B -əd-] (der., G.B.) Fulano de Tal (ú. en documentos, como nombre ficticio cuando se desconoce el verdadero).
richen ['rɪtʃən] *v.t.* enriquecer, volver más rico.
riches [-əz] *s. pl.* riqueza, riquezas.
richly [-lɪ] *adv.* 1. ricamente, opulentamente, exquisitamente. 2. abundantemente.
richness [-nəs] *s.* 1. riqueza, opulencia, suntuosidad. 2. abundancia; delicia.
ricin ['raɪsən] *s.* (quím.) ricina.
ricinoleic [ˌraɪsənoʊ'liɪk] *a.* (quím.) ricinoleico.
ricinus ['rɪsənəs] *s.* (bot.) ricino.
rick [rɪk] *s.* niara, almiar, hacina, fajina. —*v.t.* hacer niaras o hacinas de.
rick, *s.* (pr. G.B.) torcedura, esguince.
rickets ['rɪkəts] *s.* (med.) raquitis, raquitismo.
rickettsia [rɪk'ɛtsɪə] *s.* (*pl.* RICKETTSIAS O RICKETTSIAE [-ˌi]) (bact.) ricketsia, rickettsia.
rickety ['rɪkətɪ] *a.* 1. raquítico. 2. (fig.) desvencijado, destartalado, tambaleante, inseguro.
rickey ['rɪkɪ] *s.* bebida preparada con licor, jugo de limón, azúcar y agua gaseosa.
rickrack ['rɪkˌræk] *s.* (cost.) fleco; borde o entredós serpenteado, cinta zig-zag.
ricksha, rickshaw ['rɪkˌʃɔ] *formas abrev. de* **jinrikisha.**
ricochet ['rɪkəˌʃeɪ] *s.* rebote (esp. de un proyectil). —*v.i.* (*pret., p.p.* RICOCHETED O RICOCHETTED; *p.pr.* RICOCHETING O RICOCHETTING) rebotar (un proyectil).
ricochet fire, (mil.) tiro de rebote.
ricrac, *var. de* **rickrack.**
rictus ['rɪktəs] *s.* 1. ensanche de la boca (en las aves). 2. rictus, mueca, gesto (de dolor, asombro, etc.).
rid [rɪd] *v.t.* (*pret., p.p.* RID O RIDDED; *p.pr.* RIDDING) 1. librar, desembarazar, quitar de encima, zafar. 2. (ant.) rescatar, salvar. 3. **r. oneself of,** deshacerse de, librarse de; **to be r. of,** estar libre de; **to get r. of,** librarse de, desembarazarse de.
ridable ['raɪdəbəl] *a.* 1. que se puede montar, de silla (ej., un caballo). 2. viable, transitable (un camino).
riddance ['rɪdəns] *s.* liberación, libramiento; **good r.,** ¡al fin salí de eso! ¡en buena hora me libré!
ridden ['rɪdən] *p.p. de* **ride.** —*a.* dominado o acosado, ej., *fear-r.,* agobiado por el miedo.
riddle ['rɪdəl] *s.* acertijo, enigma, adivinanza; misterio. —*v.t.* resolver (acertijo, etc.), adivinar. —*v.i.* hablar enigmáticamente.
riddle, *s.* criba, cedazo, harnero, zaranda. —*v.t.* 1. cribar, cerner, cernir. 2. acribillar. 3. **r. with bullets,** acribillar a balazos; **to be riddled with disease, estar** flagelado por enfermedades.
ride [raɪd] *v.i.* (*pret.* RODE [roʊd]; *p.p.* RIDDEN; *p.pr.* RIDING) 1. montar, cabalgar. 2. ir o viajar, dejarse llevar (en vehículo). 3. flotar, surcar las aguas (del mar, etc.). 4. ir, moverse, andar, correr; funcionar (bien, mal, etc.). 5. pasear en coche. 6. **let it r.,** déjalo (pasar), no le prestes atención; **r. at anchor,** estar fondeado (barco); **r. for a fall,** cabalgar atolondradamente; (fig.) actuar precipitadamente; **r. hard,** cabalgar aprisa; **r. in,** viajar en (vehículo); **r. on,** montar (caballo, bicicleta, etc.); dejarse llevar por (viento, olas, etc.); estar sentado sobre (rodillas, hombros, etc. de alguien); (E.U.) depender de; **r. to hounds,** ir de caza, cazar; **r. up,** subirse (pantalones, camisa, etc.). —*v.t.* 1. montar; guiar, conducir, dirigir, manejar (caballo, bicicleta, etc.). 2. recorrer (a caballo, en vehículo),

ej., *we rode about a hundred miles,* recorrimos alrededor de cien millas (a caballo, en vehículo). 3. llevar montado, llevar a horcajadas. 4. flotar sobre; surcar (las olas). 5. tener monta en (carrera). 6. ceder al impacto del (golpe) para amortiguar su efecto. 7. oprimir, dominar, tiranizar, acosar. 8. burlarse de, ridiculizar. 9. **r. a ford,** vadear a caballo; **r. herd,** arrear al rebaño (a caballo); **r. down,** dar alcance a uno (a caballo); pisotear, derribar y hollar a uno (a caballo); **r. one's horse,** (fig.) discurrir sobre su tema favorito; entregarse a su pasatiempo predilecto; hacer su broma favorita; **r. out,** aguantar, soportar, pasar por; **r. out the storm,** salvar o vencer una tormenta (barco); **r. to death,** causar la muerte de (un caballo) por agotamiento; (fig.) exagerar, repetir hasta la saciedad; **to be ridden by,** estar acosado o agobiado por. —*s.* 1. viaje a caballo; paseo a caballo o en algún vehículo. 2. camino de herradura. 3. (mil.) grupo de reclutas montados. 4. **to take (someone) for a r.,** (jer.) secuestrar y asesinar (a alguien); embaucar, estafar.

rideable, *var. de* **ridable.**

rident ['raɪdənt] *a.* (raro) risueño, alegre, gracioso.

rider ['raɪdər, B -ə] *s.* 1. jinete, caballero, cabalgador; ciclista. 2. (der.) cláusula adicional, anexo, añadidura, aditamento (a un documento o proyecto de ley). 3. (mar.) vuelta de cabo (alrededor de algo). 4. (mar.) (*pl.*) bulárcamas, sobreplanes, cochinatas.

riderless [-ləs] *a.* sin jinete.

ridge [rɪdʒ] *s.* 1. lomo, grupa. 2. loma; cerro, colina; cordillera. 3. cresta; reborde; escollo, arrecife; saliente; camellón; arista; onda (de arena). 4. (arq.) arista, caballete (de tejado). —*v.t.* formar en lomos o camellones, alomar, acanalar, arrugar. —*v.i.* formarse en crestas (olas), formarse en ondas (arena).

ridgeband ['rɪdʒˌbænd] *s.* sufra (de los arreos).

ridgepole [-ˌpoʊl] **ridgepiece** [-ˌpis] **ridgeplate** [-ˌpleɪt] *s.* (arq.) parhilera, hilera, cumbrera, caballete, lomera.

ridge roof, tejado a dos aguas.

ridge tile, teja lomada, teja de cumbrera.

ridgy ['rɪdʒɪ] *a.* (RIDGIER; RIDGIEST) acanalado, aristoso.

ridicule ['rɪdəˌkjul] *s.* irrisión, mofa, rechifla, burla, ridículo; **to expose to r.,** poner en ridículo. —*v.t.* ridiculizar, mofarse o burlarse de.

ridiculer [-ər, B -ə] *s.* mofador.

ridiculous [rə'dɪkjələs] *a.* ridículo, absurdo, risible, grotesco.

ridiculously [-lɪ] *adv.* ridículamente, grotescamente, absurdamente.

ridiculousness [-nəs] *s.* carácter o aspecto ridículo, ridiculez.

riding ['raɪdɪŋ] *s.* 1. equitación, cabalgata, paseo a caballo, bicicleta, etc. 2. camino de herradura (esp. en bosques). —*a.* 1. de montar; de silla (díc. de un caballo). 2. de equitación; de montar.

riding academy, escuela de equitación.

riding boots, botas de montar.

riding breeches, pantalones de equitación, pantalones de montar.

riding crop, látigo de jinete, fusta.

riding habit, traje de montar.

riding light, (mar.) luz de anclaje, luz de fondeo.

riding master, maestro de equitación.

riding school, escuela de equitación, picadero.

riding whip, fusta, látigo de jinete.

ridotto [rɪ'dɑtoʊ, B -'dɔt-] *s.* (*pl.* RIDOTTOS) (G.B., hist.) mascarada, especie de fiesta carnavalesca.

Riesling ['rizlɪŋ] *s.* riesling (vino blanco).

rife [raɪf] *a.* corriente, dominante; **r. with,** lleno de, repleto de.

Rife [rɪf] *s.* rifeño, miembro de una tribu beréber de la región montañosa del Rif en Africa del Norte.

Riffian ['rɪfɪən] *s., a.* rifeño, de las montañas del Rif.

riffle ['rɪfəl] *s.* 1. rápido de poca altura; rabión. 2. peinado (de la baraja). —*v.t.* 1. hojear (libro), dejar pasar (hojas de un libro, etc.). 2. peinar (la baraja). —*v.i.* 1. formarse un bajío o un rabión. 2. **r. through (a book,** etc.), hojear rápidamente (un libro, etc.).

riffle, *s.* (min.) ranura o canal en el fondo de una gamella; separador de mineral.

riffraff ['rɪfˌræf] *s.* 1. gentuza, morralla, canalla, populacho, chusma (Am.). 2. desperdicio, desecho, basura.

rifle ['raɪfəl] *v.t.* pillar, saquear, desvalijar, robar.

rifle, *s.* 1. rifle, fusil. 2. (mil.) (*pl.*) fusileros, rifleros. —*v.t.* rayar (un arma).

riflebird [-ˌbɜrd, B -ˌbɜd] *s.* (orn.) ave del paraíso.

rifleman [-mən] *s.* fusilero.

rifle pit, (mil.) pozo de tirador o fusilero.

rifle practice, ejercicio de tiro.

rifler ['raɪflər, B -lə] *s.* saqueador, ladrón.

rifle range, 1. campo de tiro. 2. tiro de rifle.

riflery ['raɪfəlrɪ] *s.* tiro al blanco (con rifle).

riflescope [-ˌskoʊp] *s.* mira telescópica (para rifle).

rifle shot, tiro o disparo de fusil o rifle.

rifling ['raɪflɪŋ] *s.* rayado en espiral (de un fusil), estriado.

rift [rɪft] *s.* 1. hendidura, raja, grieta, fisura, rendija. 2. (fig.) desunión, discusión, desavenencia, enajenamiento. —*v.t.* hender, agrietar, rajar. —*v.i.* agrietarse, henderse, partirse.

rift saw, sierra de hender, sierra de rajar.

rig [rɪg] *v.t.* (*pret., p.p.* RIGGED; *p.pr.* RIGGING) 1. aparejar, enjarciar (buques). 2. armar, montar, equipar. 3. (gen. con *out*) equipar, guarnecer, guarnir; ataviar, adornar, vestir (esp. con extravagancia). 4. arreglar, manipular fraudulentamente; amarrar (juego, carreras, etc.). 5. **r. up,** erigir o construir en forma provisional. —*s.* 1. aparejo (distintivo de los varios tipos de buques). 2. (fam.) perifollos, traje, vestimenta (esp. extravagantes). 3. instalación, equipo (mecánicos); avíos, carruaje o coche (con sus caballos). 4. manipuleo (de precios en la bolsa). 5. (pr. G.B.) engañifa, artimaña, chanchullo.

rigadoon [ˌrigə'dun] *s.* (mús.) rigodón.

rigamarole ['rɪgəməˌroʊl] *var. de* **rigmarole.**

rigger ['rɪgər, B -ə] *s.* 1. (mar.) aparejador. 2. (aer.) montador. 3. andamiaje (para protección de los peatones). 4. pincel fino. 5. manipulador (en la bolsa).

rigging [-ɪŋ] *s.* 1. (mar.) obencadura, obenques, jarcia muerta, aparejo, cordaje. 2. avíos, equipo. 3. (fam.) atavío, vestidura.

Riggs' disease [rɪgz-] (med.) piorrea alveolar.

right [raɪt] *a.* 1. derecho, recto. 2. correcto, cierto. 3. bueno, debido, correcto. 4. justo, exacto. 5. legítimo, genuino. 6. apropiado, idóneo. 7. sano, cuerdo. 8. derecho (cara de la tela, etc.; lado, mano, bolsillo, etc.). 9. justo, recto (hombre, causa, etc.). 10. recto (ángulo, triángulo, etc.). 11. **all r.,** bien; a salvo; **¡all r.!** ¡muy bien! ¡de acuerdo! ¡bueno!; **all rights reserved** (señal) reservados todos los derechos; **in one's r. mind,** en su sano juicio, en sus cabales; **r. you are!** tienes razón, estás en lo cierto; **r. about!** (mil.) ¡derecha! ¡media vuelta a la derecha!; **r. or wrong,** tenga o no razón; **that's r.,** eso es; **the r. people,** la gente que cuenta; gente con influencia; the **r. thing,** lo correcto, lo debido; **the r. word,** la palabra justa; **to be all r.,** estar bien; **to be on the r. side of** (forty, etc.), no llegar a los (cuarenta, etc. años de edad); **to be r.,** tener razón; **to come** (o **turn**) **out r.,** salir (o resultar) bien; **to get on the r. side of,** ganar el favor de; **to get up on the r. side of the bed,** levantarse con el pie derecho; **to prove one r.,** dar la razón a uno; **to put oneself r. with,** justificarse ante (alguien); **to put r.,** enmendar, componer; arreglar, poner en orden; curar, devolver la salud a; **to set r.,** poner en orden, arreglar. —*adv.* 1. directamente, en derechura. 2. immediatamente. 3. bien, debidamente. 4. correctamente. 5. mismo, ej., *r. there,* allí mismo; *r. from the heart,* del corazón mismo. 6. exactamente, precisamente. 7. extremadamente, muy; mucho, ej., *I know r. well,* conozco (o sé) muy bien. 8. a la derecha, hacia la derecha. 9. all **r.,** muy bien; correctamente; **go r. on!** ¡sigue adelante! ¡sigue derecho!; **r. afterwards,** acto seguido; **r. along,** sin cesar, sin interrupción; **r. and left,** a diestra y siniestra; **r. away, r. off,** ahora mismo; inmediatamente; **r. now, ahora** mismo, en este momento, ej., *r. now it would be difficult,* en este momento sería difícil; **r. off the bat,** (jer.) inmediatamente; desde el comienzo; **to get it r.,** entender bien; hacer bien. —*s.* 1. justicia. 2. derecho. 3. derecho (lado); derecha (mano). 4. (pol.) derecha, conservadurismo. 5. (com.) opción de suscripción (de accionistas para comprar nuevas emisiones). 6. (*pl.*) condición verdadera, hechos (de un caso, etc.). 7. **by rights,** por derecho; propiamente; **in one's own r.,** por derecho propio de uno; **on the r.,** a la derecha; **r. and wrong,** el bien y el mal; **the r.,** el caso justo; **to assert** (o **to stand on**) **one's rights,** insistir en sus derechos; **to be in the r.,** tener razón; estar justificado; **to do one r.,** ser justo con uno; **to have r. on one's** side, tener la justicia de su lado; **to put to rights,** poner en orden. —*v.t.* 1. enderezar, volver a la posición inicial. 2. corregir, rectificar. 3. poner en orden, ordenar. 4. hacer justicia (a), vindicar, rehabilitar (a). 5. **r. oneself,** recobrar el balance; adrizarse (nave). —*v.i.* enderezarse.

right-about ['raɪtəˌbaʊt] *s.* vuelta atrás, media vuelta. —*adv.* en dirección opuesta (a la anterior).

right-about-face [-'feɪs] *s.* (fig.) cambio completo (de linea política, etc.). —*v.i.* 1. dar vuelta a la derecha. 2. (fig.) hacer un cambio completo.

right-and-left screw ['raɪtən'lɛft-] tornillo de pasos contrarios, tornillo de rosca a derechas y a izquierdas.

right angle, ángulo recto.

right-angled [-'æŋgəld] *a.* rectangular, rectángulo.

right arm, (fig.) brazo derecho.

right ascension, (astr.) ascensión recta.

right cone, (geom.) cono recto.

right-down ['raɪtˌdaʊn] *a.* cabal, completo, absoluto. —*adv.* completamente, muy.

righteous ['raɪtʃəs] *a.* 1. recto, probo, virtuoso, honrado. 2. justo.

righteously [-lɪ] *adv.* rectamente, honradamente, virtuosamente.

righteousness [-nəs] *s.* 1. rectitud, probidad. 2. justicia.

righter ['raɪtər, B -ə] *s.* enderezador de entuertos; el que hace justicia, vindicador.

right field, (béisbol) jardín derecho.

right fielder, (béisbol) jardinero derecho.

rightful [-fəl] *a.* 1. equitativo, justo. 2. legal, lícito. 3. legítimo (propietario, sucesor, etc.). 4. correcto, propio, apropiado.
rightfully [-fəlɪ] *adv.* 1. legalmente, legítimamente. 2. correctamente, propiamente.
rightfulness [-fəlnəs] *s.* justicia, legalidad.
right hand, 1. mano derecha. 2. (fig.) brazo derecho, ayuda o ayudante indispensable.
right-hand [-ˌhænd] *a.* 1. de la mano derecha, diestro. 2. que usa la mano derecha. 3. de izquierda a derecha (movimiento).
right-handed [-'hændəd] *a.* 1. que usa la mano derecha habitualmente. 2. que se hace con la diestra o que está adaptado para ser usado con ella, ej., *r.-h. tool,* herramienta que se usa sólo con la derecha. 3. dextrógiro.
right-hand man, brazo derecho.
right-hand rope, soga de hebras torcidas de izquierda a derecha.
rightism ['raɪtˌɪzəm] *s.* (pol.) derechismo.
rightist [-əst] *a., s.* (pol.) derechista, conservador.
right line, línea recta.
right-lined [-'laɪnd] *a.* hecho en línea recta.
rightly [-lɪ] *adv.* 1. rectamente, justamente. 2. debidamente, apropiadamente, adecuadamente, aptamente. 3. correctamente, exactamente, precisamente. 4. **r. so,** con toda razón, con toda justicia.
right-minded [-'maɪndəd] *a.* justo, recto, honrado.
rightness [-nəs] *s.* 1. rectitud, derechura, justicia; virtud, corrección. 2. exactitud, precisión. 3. aptitud, propiedad.
right of assembly, derecho de reunión.
right of asylum, (pol., der.) derecho de asilo.
right of property, derecho de propiedad.
right of search, (der., mar.) derecho de inspección.
right-of-way [ˌraɪtəv'weɪ] *s.* 1. derecho de paso o de vía. 2. prioridad de paso (en el tránsito). 3. pasaje autorizado, pista con derecho de paso. 4. (der.) servidumbre de paso. 5. (f.c.) servidumbre de vía.
right on, (E.U.) ¡adelante! consigna de los Panteras Negras, adoptada hoy por otros movimientos.
Right Reverend, reverendísimo.
right sphere, (astr.) esfera recta.
right-to-life (movement) *a.* derecho a la vida (antiabortista).
right triangle, (geom.) triángulo recto.
right whale, (zool.) ballena franca, ballena verdadera, ballena del sur.
right wing, ala derecha (de un ejército, partido político, etc.).
right-wing ['raɪtˌwɪŋ] *a.* (pol.) de la derecha, derechista.
right-winger [-ər, B -ə] *s.* derechista.
rigid ['rɪdʒəd] *a.* 1. rígido, tieso. 2. (fig.) rígido, firme, inflexible; riguroso, estricto, severo. 3. preciso, exacto (razonamiento). 4. (aer.) rígido.
rigidify [rə'dʒɪdəˌfaɪ] *v.t., v.i.* (*pret., p.p.* RIGIDIFIED; *p.pr.* RIGIDIFYING) volver(se) rígido.
rigidly ['rɪdʒədlɪ] *adv.* 1. rígidamente, tiesamente, firmemente. 2. (fig.) rígidamente, inflexiblemente; rigurosamente, estrictamente, severamente.
rigidness ['rɪdʒədnəs] **rigidity** [rə'dʒɪdətɪ] *s.* 1. rigidez, tiesura. 2. (fig.) rigidez, firmeza, inflexibilidad; rigurosidad, estrictez, severidad.
rigmarole ['rɪgməˌroʊl] *s.* jerigonza, monserga, galimatías.
rigol ['rɪgəl] *s.* (ant.) anillo, círculo.
rigor, (pr. G.B.) **rigour** ['rɪgər, B -ə] *s.* 1. rigor, rigurosidad, severidad; aspereza; austeridad. 2. rigor, exactitud. 3. (fisiol.) rigor. 4. (ant.) rigidez, tiesura.
rigorism, (pr. G.B.) **rigourism** [-ərˌɪzəm] *s.* rigorismo, rigidez, severidad, austeridad (de principios, modo de vida, etc.).
rigorist, (pr. G.B.) **rigourist** [-əst] *s., a.* rigorista.
rigorous ['rɪgərəs] *a.* riguroso, estricto, inflexible, inclemente, severo, duro.
rigorously [-lɪ] *adv.* rigurosamente, inflexiblemente, inclementemente, severamente.
rigorousness [-nəs] *s.* rigurosidad, inflexibilidad, inclemencia, severidad.
rigwiddie ['rɪgˌwɪdɪ] **rigwoodie** [-ˌwʊdɪ] *a.* (esco.) enjuto y desgarbado, flacucho.
rile [raɪl] *v.t.* enojar, enfurecer, ponerse furioso, irritar.
riley ['raɪlɪ] *a.* (fam. E.U.) 1. turbio, lodoso, fangoso. 2. irritado, enojado, enfurecido.
rill [rɪl] *s.* riachuelo, arroyuelo.
rill, rille, *s.* (astr.) fisura o dique lunar.
rillet ['rɪlət] *s.* arroyuelo pequeño.
rim [rɪm] *s.* 1. borde, orilla; canto, contorno, margen (esp. de un objeto circular). 2. llanta, aro. 3. (mec.) reborde, pestaña. 4. (aut.) corona (de la rueda de engranajes). 5. (mar.) superficie (del agua). —*v.t.* (*pret. p.p.* RIMMED; *p.pr.* RIMMING) 1. poner canto o margen a. 2. bordear. —*v.i.* formar un contorno.
rime [raɪm] *s.* escarcha, helada. —*v.t.* cubrir de escarcha.
rime, rimer, rimester, *vars. de* **rhyme, rhymer, rhymester.**
rimland ['rɪmˌlænd] *s.* región periférica.
rimose ['raɪˌmoʊs] **rimous** [-məs] *a.* resquebrajado, hendido, rajado, agrietado.
rimy ['raɪmɪ] *a.* (RIMIER; RIMIEST) escarchado.
rind [raɪnd] *s.* 1. corteza (del queso, de la naranja), pellejo (del tocino, etc.). 2. (fig.) corteza, superficie.
rinderpest ['rɪndərˌpɛst, B -dəˌpɛst] *s.* (vet.) fiebre biliosa hematúrica, ictericia hematúrica; morriña, comalia.
ring [rɪŋ] *s.* 1. anillo, sortija. 2. aro, argolla. 3. anilla (de colgaduras, de gimnasia). 4. anillo (de humo, de sedimentos, etc.). 5. rizo (de cabello). 6. corte anular (en corteza de árboles). 7. corrillo, corro, círculo (de gente). 8. argolla, camarilla. 9. arena (en el circo). 10. cuadrilátero (de boxeo). 11. arena, redondel (de toros). 12. (fig.) arena, campo de competencia. 13. (bot.) anillo (anular de árboles). 14. (quím.) cadena (atómica). 15. (mar.) arganeo (del ancla). 16. **r. under the eyes,** ojera; **the r.,** el boxeo; recinto de apostadores; corredores de apuestas; **to dance (o run) rings round,** dar vueltas a, superar o aventajar fácilmente; hacer las cosas con más rapidez que. —*v.t.* 1. rodear, circundar, cercar. 2. anillar, ensortijar, poner anilla a (animales). 3. hacer un corte anular en la corteza de (árboles); cortar en rodajas. 4. tirar anillos al (hito). —*v.i.* 1. moverse en círculo. 2. formarse en círculo. 3. subir en espiral (ej., el halcón). 4. tomar la forma de anillos (humo).
ring [rɪŋ] *v.i.* (*pret.* RANG [ræŋ]; *p.p.* RUNG [rʌŋ]; *p.pr.* RINGING) 1. sonar (timbre, teléfono, campana, palabras, etc.). 2. campanillear, campanear. 3. retumbar, resonar. 4. zumbar (oído). 5. llenarse (de rumores o comentarios). 6. tocar la campana, tocar el timbre. 7. **r. at the door,** tocar (el timbre) a la puerta; **r. for,** llamar; **r. off,** terminar una llamada telefónica; **r. out,** resonar. —*v.t.* 1. tocar, sonar, tañer (campanas, timbre, etc.). 2. (gen. con *in, out*) anunciar, proclamar (con repique de timbre o campanas). 3. **r. an alarm,** dar la alarma; **r. a bell,** (fam.) sonar, hacer recordar (por asociación); **r. the bell,** tocar el timbre; (fig.) tener éxito; **r. the curtain down,** hacer bajar el telón; **r. the curtain down on,** (fig.) terminar con, poner coto a; **r. the knell of,** (fig.) anunciar o presagiar el fin de; **r. up,** (pr. G.B.) llamar por teléfono. —*s.* 1. compañada, toque de campana; toque de timbre; tañido, repique (de campanas, etc.). 2. campaneo, campanilleo. 3. tintín, retintín, tintineo. 4. llamada por teléfono, ej., *give me a r.,* llámeme por teléfono. 5. (fig.) son, tono, timbre (de voz), ej., *a ring of defiance,* un tono de desafío. 6. juego de campanas.
ring-around-a-rosy ['rɪŋəˌraʊndə'roʊzɪ] *s.* corro, ronda (juego de niños).
ring auger, barrena de ojo.
ringbark ['rɪŋˌbɑrk, B -ˌbɑk] *v.t.* quitar (a un árbol) un anillo de corteza.
ringbolt [-ˌboʊlt] *s.* perno de aro o de argolla, cáncamo de argolla.
ring chuck, (mec.) boquilla de collar.
ringdove [-ˌdʌv] *s.* (orn.) paloma torcaz o torcaza; tórtola.
ringed [rɪŋd] *a.* 1. (zool.) anillado; de collar. 2. que lleva anillo de matrimonio; casado.
ringent ['rɪndʒənt] *a.* (bot.) ringente.
ringer ['rɪŋər, B -ə] *s.* 1. herrón que da en el clavo (en los juegos de herrón, hito y similares). 2. juego de canicas.
ringer, *s.* 1. campanero; dispositivo de llamada. 2. caballo inscrito fraudulentamente (en carrera). 3. (jer.) (con *for*) imagen viva (de otra persona).
ring finger, (dedo) anular.
ring girder, viga circular.
ring-goal [-ˌgoʊl] *s.* juego parecido al hito.
ringing [-ɪŋ] *s.* sonido (del timbre); tañido (de campanas); zumbido, silbido (en el oído). —*a.* resonante, sonoro.
ringleader [-'lidər, B -ə] *s.* cabecilla, jefe, caudillo (de huelguistas, revoltosos o de una pandilla).
ringlet [-lət] *s.* 1. anillejo, anillete, arillo, arete, círculo pequeño. 2. sortija, bucle, rizo, crespo.
ring-man [-ˌmæn] *s.* (G.B.) corredor de apuestas.
ringmaster ['rɪŋˌmæstər, B -'mɑstə] *s.* maestro de ceremonias (de un circo, arena, cuadrilátero, etc.).
ringneck [-ˌnɛk] *s.* pájaro que tiene un anillo de color al cuello.
ringnecked [-ˌnɛkt] *a.* de collar, con collar de plumas (faisán, paloma, etc.).
Ring of the Nibelung [-'nibəˌlʊŋ] (mitol., mús.) (el) Anillo de los Nibelungos.
ringsail [-ˌseɪl] *s.* (mar.) vela de baticulo.
ringside [-ˌsaɪd] *s.* 1. lugar inmediato al cuadrilátero de boxeo, liza o arena. 2. (fig.) primera fila. —*a.* (lit., fig.) de primera fila.
ring snake, (zool.) tropidonoto de collar.
ring stand, estante de probetas (de laboratorio).
ringster [-stər, B -stə] *s.* (fam.) miembro de una camarilla, (esp. política); pandillero, pandillista.
ringtail [-ˌteɪl] *s.* (zool.) 1. cacomixtle, basáride. 2. mapache, oso lavador. 3. capuchino, mono sapajú.
ringtail boom, (mar.) mástil de baticulo.
ring-tailed ['rɪŋˌteɪld] *a.* de cola (marcada) con franjas anulares (mono, zarigüeya, etc.).
ringtail sail, (mar.) vela de baticulo.
ringtaw [-ˌtɔ] *s.* canica (que se juega en un círculo).
ring winding, (elec.) devanado de anillo, arrollamiento anular.
ringworm [-ˌwɜrm, B -ˌwɜm] *s.* (med., vet.) tiña, empeine, culebrilla, serpigo.
rink [rɪŋk] *s.* 1. patinadero; sala o pista de patinar. 2. campo de juego de una bolera. 3. equipo o cuadro (en el juego de tejo, bolos, etc.).

rinse [rɪns] *v.t.* enjuagar, lavar ligeramente, deslavar, limpiar, aclarar. —*s.* 1. enjuague, enjuagadura, enjuagatorio, lavado, lavadura, lavamiento. 2. enjuague de color, tintura (temporal) para el cabello.
rinser ['rɪnsər, B -ə] *s.* 1. lavandero. 2. recipiente para enjuagar.
rinsing [-ɪŋ] *s.* 1. enjuague, enjuagadura, enjuagatorio. 2. (*gen. pl.*) últimas gotas, heces.
riot ['raɪət] *s.* 1. alboroto, disturbio, desorden, tumulto, gresca. 2. (fig.) bullanga, desbordamiento, aluvión (de colores, sonidos, etc.). 3. licencia, exceso, disipación. 4. (der.) motín, sedición, asonada. 5. (jer.) algo fenomenal, fenómeno; cosa muy divertida; persona muy chistosa. 6. **to run r.,** desenfrenarse. —*v.i.* 1. amotinarse, alborotarse. 2. entregarse a vicios; parrandear. —*v.t.* pasar o emplear (el tiempo) en jaranas, disipar (tiempo, dinero, etc.).
Riot Act, (G.B.) ley de sedición; **to read the r. a.,** (t. hum.) advertir (a niños) que cese el alboroto.
rioter [-ər, B -ə] *s.* amotinador, sedicioso.
riot gun, escopeta recortada.
riotous [-əs] *a.* 1. tumultuoso, bullicioso; sedicioso. 2. libertino, licencioso, jaranero.
riot policeman, guardia de asalto.
rip [rɪp] *v.t.* (*pret., p.p.* RIPPED; *p.pr.* RIPPING) 1. rasgar, desgarrar, romper. 2. (carp.) partir al hilo, serrar a lo largo (madera). 3. descoser (vestido, dobladillo, etc.). 4. **let it r.,** (fam., G.B.) dale todo, déjalo correr (motor, máquina, etc.); **r. off,** quitar rasgando, quitar violentamente; (E.U., jer.) robar, hurtar; **r. open,** abrir desgarrando; abrir violentamente; **r. out,** arrancar, sacar de un tirón; **r. up,** rasgar, desgarrar; romper (pavimento, etc.). —*v.i.* 1. rasgarse, henderse, romperse, rajarse, desgarrarse. 2. (fam.) ir a todo vapor, precipitarse. 3. **r. into,** abalanzarse sobre, acometer. —*s.* rasgadura, rasgón.
rip, *s.* 1. (fam.) calavera, licencioso, libertino. 2. agua revuelta (por la confluencia de corrientes o mareas). 3. (dial.) parva pequeña o montoncillo de heno o de grano en tallo.
riparian [rə'pɛrɪən, B raɪ'pɛər-] *a.* ribereño.
riparian rights, derechos ribereños.
rip cord, (aer.) 1. cordón de apertura (del paracaídas). 2. cabo de desgarre (que permite el escape de gas de un globo aerostático).
rip current, rip tide, corriente de resaca.
ripe [raɪp] *a.* 1. maduro, en sazón; tierno, blando. 2. rosado y carnoso (labio). 3. maduro, avanzado (edad), ej., *to die at a r. old age,* morir a edad avanzada. 4. consumado, acabado. 5. listo, pronto, preparado, dispuesto. 6. (med.) maduro (díc. de diviesos, tumores, etc.). 7. **time (moment) is r.,** ha llegado el tiempo (momento).
ripe, *v.t., v.i.* (esco.) buscar, explorar; pillar, saquear.
ripely ['raɪplɪ] *adv.* maduramente.
ripen ['raɪpən] *v.i., v.t.* madurar, sazonar(se); perfeccionar(se), completar(se) (para uso, etc.).
ripeness ['raɪpnəs] *s.* madurez, sazón.
Ripley's Believe It or Not, Aunque Ud. Lo Crea de Ripley.
riposte [rɪ'poʊst] *s.* 1. (esgr.) estocada de contragolpe. 2. réplica pronta y aguda. —*v.i.* 1. (esgr.) reparar y dar la estocada de contragolpe. 2. replicar con agudeza.
rip panel, (aer.) banda de desgarre.
ripper ['rɪpər, B -ə] *s.* 1. desgarradora (máquina). 2. (const.) rompedor de caminos. 3. (jer.) persona o cosa muy notable.
ripping [-ɪŋ] *a.* (fam., G.B.) excelente, magnífico.
ripple ['rɪpəl] *s.* carda o peine para desgargolar.
ripple, *v.i.* 1. agitarse, rizarse, correr con rizos u olas pequeñas (la superficie del agua). 2. murmurar (el agua). —*v.t.* rizar, ondear (la superficie del agua). —*s.* 1. escarceo, onda, rizo (del agua). 2. murmullo.
ripple mark, óndula.
ripplet ['rɪplət] *s.* onda o rizo pequeños.
ripple voltage, (elec.) componente alternado de voltaje unidireccional.
ripply [-lɪ] *a.* (RIPPLIER; RIPPLIEST) rizado, ondulado.
riprap ['rɪp,ræp] *s.* (const.) 1. escolladero, escollera de defensa, enrajonado, enrocamiento. 2. ripio, losas de defensa, rocalla, cascajo. —*v.t.* (*pret., p.p.* RIPRAPPED; *p.pr.* RIPRAPPING) (const.) 1. enrajonar, enrocar, defender con piedra grande. 2. revestir de piedra; construir con ripio.
rip-roaring [-,rɔrɪŋ] *a.* (jer.) alborozado, bullicioso, alegre.
ripsaw [-,sɔ] *s.* sierra de hender o de cortar a lo largo. —*v.t.* aserrar al hilo o a lo largo.
ripsnorter [-,snɔrtər, B -,snɔtə] *s.* (fam.) fenómeno (cosa o persona extraordinaria o excelente).
riptide [-,taɪd] *s.* corriente de resaca.
rise [raɪz] *v.i.* (*pret.* ROSE [roʊz] *p.p.* RISEN ['rɪzən] *p.pr.* RISING) 1. levantarse, ascender, subir, elevarse. 2. surgir, emerger, sobresalir. 3. salir (un astro). 4. levantarse, ponerse de pie, ej., *the audience rose,* el público se puso de pie. 5. levantarse (de la cama), ej., *he rose at six thirty,* se levantó a las seis y treinta. 6. levantarse, resucitar. 7. extenderse, alcanzar, alzarse, ej., *the Pyrenees r. on the north of Spain,* los Pirineos se alzan al norte de España, *the tree rose thirty feet,* el árbol alcanzó una altura de treinta pies. 8. medrar, mejorar de posición. 9. levantarse, rebelarse; (fig.) indignarse, rebelarse. 10. aumentar de fuerza (viento); subir de precio (artículo, acciones, etc.); intensificarse (aplauso, indignación, etc.). 11. subir a la superficie (del agua, ej., un pez o cadáver). 12. inflarse, hincharse; levantarse (masa). 13. **r. above,** alzarse por encima de; mostrarse superior a; **r. from,** brotar en; originarse en, provenir de; **r. in the world,** lograr mejor posición social; **r. to,** mostrarse capaz de enfrentar, sentirse con fuerza para; **r. to one's feet,** ponerse de pie; **r. to the occasion,** ponerse a la altura de las circunstancias; **rising ground,** terreno en pendiente. —*v.t.* levantar, ver levantarse (la caza, un pájaro, etc.). —*s.* 1. ascensión, elevación. 2. salida, aparición (de un astro). 3. resurrección. 4. salto (de un pez a la superficie del agua). 5. altura, eminencia, elevación (de terreno); cuesta, subida. 6. subida, crecimiento (de un río, marea, etc.). 7. ascenso (en un empleo, rango, posición, etc.). 8. subida, alza (de precios). 9. adelantamiento, medro. 10. (gen. con *in*) aumento (de fama, valor, etc.). 11. (G.B.) aumento (de jornales o salarios). 12. fuente, origen, nacimiento, principio, causa. 13. (mús.) cambio de llave (hacia arriba). 14. (jer.) respuesta (a una provocación), réplica mordaz. 15. **r. in prices,** aumento de precios; **to be on the r.,** estar subiendo (río, costo de vida, precios, etc.); **to get a r. out of (someone)** (fig.) provocar una explosión (de ira, indignación, etc.), hacer perder los estribos (a alguien); **to give r. to,** dar origen (a), causar, motivar, ocasionar.
rise and fall, (mar.) pleamar y bajamar; (fig.) subida y caída, ascenso y descenso.
riser ['raɪzər, B -zə] *s.* 1. *ú. en las frases compuestas:* **early r.,** madrugador; **late r.,** persona que se levanta tarde. 2. (arq.) contrahuella, contraescalón. 3. (elec.) conductor vertical. 4. tubería vertical o de elevación, tubo ascendente o montante, caño de subida.
risibility [,rɪzə'bɪlətɪ] *s.* risibilidad, facultad de reír.
risible ['rɪzəbəl] *a.* risible.
rising ['raɪzɪŋ] *a.* 1. ascendente; que se levanta. 2. prometedor (cantante, científico, autor, hombre de negocios, etc.). 3. naciente, saliente (sol). 4. creciente. 5. actual, ej., *the r. generation,* la juventud actual. —*s.* 1. ascenso, subida, levantada. 2. levantamiento, insurrección, alzamiento. 3. salida (de un astro). 4. resurrección, renacimiento. 5. prominencia, protuberancia. 6. (med.) tumor, divieso, furúnculo.
risk [rɪsk] *s.* riesgo; **to run risks,** correr riesgos; **to run the r. of (doing),** correr el riesgo de (hacer); **to take a r.,** arriesgarse. —*v.t.* arriesgar, aventurar, exponer; **r. (doing),** exponerse al riesgo de (hacer).
risk capital, (com.) capital empresario o aventurado.
riskiness ['rɪskɪnəs] *s.* riesgo, carácter arriesgado (de un experimento, aventura, etc.).
risky [-kɪ] *a.* (RISKIER; RISKIEST) arriesgado, peligroso, aventurado.
risqué [rɪs'keɪ] *a.* (fr.) 1. arriesgado. 2. (fig.) escabroso, subido de color, ej., *a r. story,* un cuento subido de color.
rite [raɪt] *s.* 1. rito, ceremonias; acto u observancia ceremonial. 2. (relig.) rito, liturgia.
ritornello [,rɪtər'nɛloʊ, B -ə'-] *s.* (mús.) ritornelo.
ritual ['rɪtʃʊəl] *a.* ritual, ceremonial. —*s.* 1. ritual; ceremonial religioso. 2. código de ceremonias, libro de fórmulas ceremoniales.
ritualism [-,ɪzəm] *s.* 1. ritualidad. 2. ritualismo.
ritualist [-əst] *s.* ritualista.
ritualistic [,rɪtʃʊə'lɪstɪk] *a.* ritualista, ceremonioso, ceremonial.
ritualistically [-tɪkəlɪ] *adv.* con ritualismo, ceremoniosamente, ceremonialmente.
ritualize ['rɪtʃʊəl,aɪz] *v.i.* adherirse a rituales. —*v.t.* convertir en ritual, someter a rituales.
ritually [-ɪ] *adv.* ritualmente, según el ritual, conforme a los ritos.
ritz [rɪts] *s.* (jer.) opulencia, ostentación.
ritzy ['rɪtsɪ] *a.* elegante, lujoso, opulento.
rivage ['rɪvɪdʒ, B 'raɪvɪdʒ] *s.* (ant.) orilla, ribera, costa, playa.
rival ['raɪvəl] *s.* rival, competidor. —*a.* rival, competidor, émulo, opuesto. —*v.t.* (*pret., p.p.* RIVALED O RIVALLED; *p.pr.* RIVALING O RIVALLING) 1. competir con, rivalizar con; emular. 2. poder rivalizar con, igualar a. —*v.i.* rivalizar, competir, contender.
rivalry [-rɪ] *s.* (*pl.* RIVALRIES) rivalidad, competencia, emulación.
rive [raɪv] *v.t., v.i.* (*pret.* RIVED; *p.p.* RIVED [raɪvd] O RIVEN ['rɪvən]; *p.pr.* RIVING) rasgar(se), rajar(se), hender(se), partir(se).
river ['rɪvər, B -ə] *s.* 1. río. 2. (fig.) río, ej., *rivers of oil,* ríos de petróleo. 3. **down r.,** río abajo; **to sell down the r.,** (jer.) traicionar; **up r.,** río arriba; **up the r.,** en la cárcel.
river basin, cuenca de río, cuenca fluvial.
riverbed [-,bɛd] *s.* lecho, madre de río.
riverboat [-,boʊt] *s.* bote, canoa (fluvial).
river crossing, paso o cruce de ríos.
riverfront [-,frʌnt] *s.* áreas ribereñas; barrio ribereño (de una ciudad).
riverhead [-,hɛd] *s.* fuente o nacimiento de un río.
river horse, (zool.) hipopótamo.
riverine ['rɪvər,aɪn] *a.* fluvial.
river lamprey, (ict.) lampreílla.
River Plate, Río de la Plata.
riverside ['rɪvər,saɪd, B -ə,-] *s.* ribera, orilla o margen del río.

riverward [-wərd, B -wəd] *a., adv.* hacia el río.
rivet ['rɪvət] *s.* remache, roblón. —*v.t.* 1. remachar, roblonar, roblar. 2. asegurar con firmeza, afianzar. 3. clavar o fijar los ojos en (algo); cautivar (la atención).
riveter [-ər, B -ə] *s.* remachador, roblonador (persona); remachadora (máquina).
riveting [-ɪŋ] *s.* remachadura, remachado, roblonado, roblonadura.
riveting hammer, martillo remachador, martillo neumático de remachar.
rivet set, (mec.) embutidera, uñeta (remachado).
Riviera [ˌrɪvɪ'ɛrə, B -'ɛərə] *s.* la Riviera, costa mediterránea, la de Francia e Italia.
riviere [-'ɛr, B -'ɛə] *s.* (fr.) collar de piedras preciosas.
rivulet ['rɪvjələt] *s.* riachuelo, arroyo.
rix-dollar ['rɪksˌdɑlər, B -ˌdɔlə] *s.* (numis.) rixdal.
Riyadh [rɪ'jɑd] *s.* El Riad, capital de Arabia Saudita.
rm. (*pl.* **rms.**) *abrev. de* **room,** habitación.
Rn *símb. de* **radon,** radón (Rn).
RN *abrev. de* 1. **Royal Navy,** Armada Real. 2. **registered nurse,** enfermera diplomada.
RNA *abrev. de* **ribonucleic acid,** ácido ribonucleico.
roach [roʊtʃ] *s.* 1. (ento.) cucaracha. 2. (jer.) colilla, pucho (Amer.) de cigarrillo esp. de marihuana. 3. (mar.) alunamiento del pujamen (de las velas). 4. lámina de agua que se levanta por detrás del flotador (de un hidroavión). 5. (ict.) especie de carpa pequeña.
road [roʊd] *s.* 1. camino, vía, carretera. 2. (fig.) senda, sendero; rumbo, curso, dirección, ej., *the r. to ruin,* la senda a la ruina. 3. (*gen. pl.*) (mar.) rada; fondeadero. 4. vía férrea, ferrocarril. 5. **for the r.,** (fig.) de despedida (trago, etc.); **on the r. to,** en el camino de, camino de; **over the r.,** (jer.) a la cárcel; **rule of the r.,** reglas del tráfico (terrestre o marítimo); **the royal r. (to),** la vía fácil (para lograr algo); **to be on the r.,** estar viajando; **to hit the r.,** (jer.) emprender viaje; volver a viajar; trabajar como vendedor viajero.
road agent, (fam.) salteador de caminos.
roadbed ['roʊdˌbɛd] *s.* 1. (f.c.) lecho de la vía, explanación, plataforma, asiento de los durmientes. 2. (Am.) firme, piso de camino o carretera.
roadblock [-ˌblɑk, B -ˌblɔk] *s.* 1. (mil.) barricada (obstrucción en la carretera); valla, parapeto o barrera (esp. policial). 2. (fig.) impedimento, obstáculo.
road engineering, ingeniería vial o de caminos.
road hog, motorista o conductor inconsiderado.
roadhouse [-ˌhaʊs] *s.* parador, posada u hostería en el camino.
road machinery, maquinaria caminera, equipo para construcción de caminos.
road map, mapa de carreteras, mapa de rutas o de caminos.
road metal, escoria, piedra triturada (para caminos), grava para carreteras.
road roller, apisonadora, cilindradora, rodillo aplanador de caminos.
roadrunner ['roʊdˌrʌnər, B -ə] *s.* (orn.) caminera, correcaminos.
roadshow [-ˌʃoʊ] *s.* espectáculo teatral presentado por una compañía ambulante.
roadside [-ˌsaɪd] *s.* orilla o borde del camino. —*a.* (que está) a la orilla del camino, ej., *r. inn,* posada a la orilla del camino.
roadstead [-ˌstɛd] *s.* (mar.) rada, fondeadero.
roadster [-stər, B -stə] *s.* 1. automóvil de dos asientos, coche de turismo, coche de deporte. 2. caballo de silla.
roadway ['roʊdˌweɪ] *s.* 1. carretera, calzada. 2. (f.c.) lecho de la vía.
road worker, peón caminero.
roam [roʊm] *v.i.* vagar, vagabundear, andar errante, andorrear. —*v.t.* vagar por, andar o recorrer a la ventura. —*s.* vagabundeo, correteo.
roamer ['roʊmər, B -ə] *s.* vago, vagabundo.
roan [roʊn] *a.* 1. roano, ruano, rosillo, sabino (díc. de caballos). 2. hecho de badana de color roano. —*s.* 1. color roano. 2. caballo roano o ruano. 3. badana de color roano.
roar [rɔr, B rɔ] *v.i.* 1. rugir, bramar (leon, tempestad, mar, etc.). 2. reírse estrepitosamente. 3. pasar o correr con estruendo (locomotora, etc.). 4. (vet.) roncar (caballos). —*v.t.* decir a gritos. —*s.* 1. rugido, bramido. 2. estruendo, estrépito.
roarer ['rɔrər, B -ə] *s.* 1. bramador. 2. (vet.) (caballo) roncador.
roaring [-ɪŋ] *a.* 1. tormentoso, estrepitoso, ruidoso, ej., *a r. night,* una noche tormentosa o ruidosa; (fig.) una noche de francachela. 2. (fam.) colosal, formidable, superlativo, inmenso, ej., *we did a r. business,* hicimos un negocio colosal. —*s.* 1. rugido, bramido (de ciertas bestias). 2. (vet.) ronquido (de caballos).
roaring twenties, — the r., los locos años veinte.
roast [roʊst] *v.t.* 1. asar, soasar, cocer o cocinar al fuego. 2. tostar (café, maní, etc.). 3. (fam.) ridiculizar, burlarse o mofarse de, criticar o censurar severamente. 4. (metal.) calcinar. —*v.i.* 1. asarse (carne, pescado, etc.). 2. tostarse (café, maní, etc.). —*s.* 1. asado; carne para asar. 2. (fam.) burla, mofa; crítica o represión severas. 3. (fam.) fiesta al aire libre (en que se comen manjares asados), asado (Am.), pachamanca (Am.). —*a.* asado; tostado.
roast beef, rosbif, carne de res asada.
roaster ['roʊstər, B -stə] *s.* 1. asador, tostador. 2. lechón o pollo para asar.
rob [rɑb, B rɔb] *v.t.* (*pret., p.p.* ROBBED; *p.pr.* ROBBING) 1. robar, pillar, hurtar. 2. (con *of*) usurpar, defraudar, desvalijar, despojar (de algo). 3. **r. Peter to pay Paul,** desnudar a un santo para vestir a otro; **r. the cradle,** tener amores o casarse con una persona mucho más joven que uno. —*v.i.* cometer robo, robar.
robalo ['roʊbəloʊ] *s.* (*pl.* ROBALOS O ROBALO) (ict.) róbalo, robalo, lubina.
roband ['roʊˌbænd, B -bənd] *s.* (mar.) envergue.
robber ['rɑbər, B 'rɔbə] *s.* ladrón, ratero, hurtador; salteador, bandido.
robber baron, 1. señor feudal que robaba a los viajeros que pasaban a través de sus dominios. 2. capitalistas de E.U. que a fines del siglo XIX adquirieron inmensas riquezas por medio de la explotación, el cohecho, etc.
robber fly, (ento.) asilo.
robbery [-ərɪ] *s.* (*pl.* ROBBERIES) robo, hurto, latrocinio, substracción.
robbin ['rɑbɪn, B 'rɔb-] *var. de* **roband.**
robe [roʊb] *s.* 1. manto, manteo; túnica, túnico; ropón, abrigo, toga, traje talar. 2. (*pl.*) indumentaria, ropaje, vestiduras. 3. traje de ceremonia. 4. (E.U.) manta (de coche, para abrigo). 5. **gentlemen of the r.,** la curia, juristas, abogados; **the long r.,** vestidura del abogado o del sacerdote. —*v.t., v.i.* vestir(se), ataviar(se); cubrir(se).
robin ['rɑbən, B 'rɔb-] *s.* (orn.) 1. pechicolorado, petirrojo. 2. (E.U.) tordo norteamericano.
Robin Hood, Robin Hood, legendario héroe inglés del siglo XII.
robin redbreast, (orn.) pechicolorado, petirrojo.
robin's-egg blue[-ənzˌɛg-] color azul verdoso; color aguamarina.
roble ['roʊbleɪ] *s.* (bot.) roble blanco de California.
roborant ['rɑbərənt, B 'rɔ-] *a.* (med.) roborante, roborativo, fortificante. —*s.* (droga) roborante, tónico.
robot ['roʊˌbɑt, -bət, B -ˌbɔt] *s.* 1. robot, autómata, mecanismo automático; figura o muñeca automática, maniquí mecánico. 2. (fig.) autómata, persona insensible.
robot bomb, (mil.) bomba voladora, avion cohete, proyectil teledirigido.
robotism [-ɪˌzəm] *s.* automatismo.
robotization [ˌroʊˌbɑtə'zeɪʃən, -bət-, B -aɪ'zeɪ-] *s.* 1. conversión en robot (del hombre). 2. automatización (de un proceso, fábrica, etc.).
robotize ['roʊbəˌtaɪz] *v.t.* automatizar.
robust [roʊ'bʌst] *a.* 1. robusto, fuerte, vigoroso. 2. robustecedor, vigorizador (ejercicio, régimen). 3. sano, sensato, sólido (intelecto, mente, etc.).
robustious [-'bʌstʃəs] *a.* 1. (hum.) robusto. 2. bullicioso, alborotado, ruidoso.
robustly [-'bʌstlɪ] *adv.* robustamente.
robustness [-nəs] *s.* robustez, robusteza, fuerza, vigor.
roc [rɑk, B rɔk] *s.* rocho, ruc (ave fabulosa de las leyendas árabes).
rocaille [roʊ'kaɪ] *s.* (arte) rocalla.
rocambole ['rɑkəmˌboʊl, B 'rɔk-] *s.* (bot.) rocambola.
Rochelle powder [roʊ'ʃɛl-, B rə-] (farm.) polvo de la Rochela, polvos de Seidlitz.
Rochelle salt, (farm.) sal de la Rochela.
rochet ['rɑtʃət, B 'rɔtʃ-] *s.* (relig.) roquete.
rock [rɑk, B rɔk] *s.* 1. roca, peña, peñasco, peñón. 2. piedra. 3. (*gen. pl.*) escollo, estorbo, impedimento. 4. (fig.) sostén, soporte, base. 5. (G.B.) (fam.) dulce o caramelo duro en forma de barra. 6. (jer.) diamante. 7. mecedura, oscilación, tambaleo. 8. **built on r.,** (fig.) seguro; **on the rocks,** (fam.) arruinado, quebrado; bebida (esp. alcohólica) servida pura con cubitos de hielo; **the R.,** **el** Peñón (de Gibraltar); **to go on the rocks,** irse a la ruina, (ej., negocio).
rock, *v.t.* 1. mecer; acunar, cunear. 2. estremecer, sacudir, hacer temblar o tambalear. 3. aturdir, dejar estupefacto. 4. (min.) lavar (arena aurífera) en artesa oscilante. 5. **r. the boat,** hacer mover peligrosamente el barco; (fig.) romper la calma, perturbar la armonía. —*v.i.* 1. mecerse. 2. estremecerse, temblar, tambalear. 3. oscilar, vibrar. 4. aturdirse, quedar estupefacto. 5. **r. with laughter,** desternillarse de risa.
rock-and-roll [rɑkən'roʊl, B ˌrɔk-] o **rock'n-'roll** *s.* rocanrol, rock and roll, baile y música, popular en la década del cincuenta.
rockaway ['rɑkəˌweɪ, B 'rɔk-] *s.* carruaje liviano y bajo de cuatro ruedas, con techo pero abierto a los costados.
rock bottom, el fondo, lo más profundo.
rock-bottom [-'bɑtəm, B -'bɔt-] *a.* mínimo, bajísimo, ej., *r.-b. prices,* precios bajísimos.
rockbound [-ˌbaʊnd] *a.* 1. cercado o rodeado de rocas. 2. rocoso, roqueño.
rock brake, (bot.) (especie de) helecho.
rock candy, azúcar cande o candi, azúcar de candil.
rock cork, (min.) amianto ligniforme.
rock crystal, (min.) cristal de roca.
rock dove, (orn.) paloma zorita, paloma zurana.
rock drill, perforadora, barrena, taladro.
rocker ['rɑkər, B 'rɔkə] *s.* 1. arco (de mecedora o cuna). 2. mecedora (silla); cuna; caballito mecedor (juguete). 3. (mec.) oscilador, balanceador. 4. (min.) artesa oscilante. 5. figura de patinaje artístico. 6. **to be off one's r.,** (jer.) estar loco; **to go off one's r.,** (jer.) perder la chaveta.

rocker arm, (mec.) brazo o palanca oscilantes, balancín, palanca de vaivén, basculador.
rocket [ˈrɑkət, B ˈrɔk-] *s.* 1. cohete, volador, petardo. 2. cohete (militar o espacial). 3. (bot.) oruga, ruqueta. —*v.i.* 1. ascender o volar como un cohete, lanzarse como una exhalación; subir verticalmente (díc. esp. de los faisanes). 2. (fig.) subir vertiginosamente (precios). —*v.t.* 1. atacar con cohetes. 2. elevar por cohete. 3. (fig.) elevar, exaltar.
rocket bomb, (mil.) cohete, proyectil cohete.
rocket drive, propulsión por reacción pirotécnica.
rocketeer [rɑkəˈtɪr, B ˌrɔkəˈtɪə] *s.* especialista en cohetería, cohetero.
rocket launcher, (mil.) lanzacohetes.
rocket-propelled [ˈrɑkətprəˈpɛld, B ˈrɔk-] *a.* propulsado por cohete(s).
rocket propulsion. propulsión por cohete.
rocketry [-ətrɪ] *s.* cohetería, técnica de los cohetes.
rocket ship, nave espacial (propulsada por cohetes).
rocketsonde [ˈrɑkətˌsɑnd, B ˈrɔkɪtˌsɔnd] *s.* cohete-sonda, cohete meteorológico.
Rock fever, (med.) fiebre ondulante, fiebre de Malta o mediterránea.
rockfish [ˈrɑkˌfɪʃ, B ˈrɔk-] *s.* (ict.) 1. escorpina, escorpena, diablo de mar, rescaza; rescacio de roca. 2. lobina, róbalo; perca, raño.
rock garden, jardín entre rocas, jardín con adornos de piedras.
Rockies [ˈrɑkɪz, B ˈrɔk-] *s. pl. forma abrev. de* **Rocky Mountains.**
rocking chair [ˈrɑkɪŋ-, B ˈrɔk-] mecedora (silla), mecedor, sillón.
rocking horse, caballito mecedor, caballo de balancín.
rock jasmine, (bot.) cantarillo.
rock music, música popular juvenil, originaria de los E.U.
rock'n'roll [ˌrɑkənˈroʊl, B ˌrɔk-] *contr. de* **rock-and-roll.**
Rock of Gibraltar, el Peñón de Gibraltar.
rock oil, petróleo.
rock pigeon, (orn.) paloma zorita, paloma zurana.
rock ptarmigan, (orn.) perdiz blanca.
rock-ribbed [ˈrɑkˈrɪbd, B ˈrɔk-] *a.* 1. con filones de roca (tierra, playa, etc.). 2. (fig.) fuerte, firme; inflexible.
rockrose [-ˈroʊz] *s.* (bot.) jara, lada, ladón; jara estepa, jaguarzo blanco, estepilla.
rock salt, sal de piedra, sal gema, sal de compás, sal pedrés.
rockshaft [-ˌʃæft, B -ˌʃɑft] *s.* (mec.) eje oscilante.
rockskipper [-ˌskɪpər, B -ə] *s.* (ict.) blenia.
rock wallaby, (zool.) canguro de las rocas, wallabi de las rocas.
rockweed [-ˌwid] *s.* (bot.) fuco.
rock wool, lana de roca, lana mineral, asbestos.
rocky [ˈrɑkɪ, B ˈrɔkɪ] *a.* (ROCKIER; ROCKIEST) 1. roqueño, rocoso, peñascoso. 2. duro (como la roca), pétreo; (fig.) obstinado, inflexible, despiadado.
rocky, *a.* (jer.) tambaleante, inestable, débil.
Rocky Mountains, (E.U., Can.) Montañas Rocosas.
rococo [rəˈkoʊkoʊ] *a., s.* (arte) rococó, barroco.
rod [rɑd, B rɔd] *s.* 1. vara, varilla. 2. disciplina(s), azote; (fig.) castigo, corrección. 3. cetro; bastón de mando; (fig.) autoridad; tiranía; opresión. 4. caña de pescar. 5. medida de longitud (equivalente a 5,029 metros); vara o regla de medir. 6. (anat.) bastoncillo (de la retina). 7. (bact.) bastoncito. 8. (jer.) pistola, revólver.
rode [roʊd] *pret. de* **ride.**
rodent [ˈroʊdənt] *a., s.* (zool.) roedor.
rodenticide [roʊˈdɛntəˌsaɪd] *s.* veneno para matar roedores.
rodeo [ˈroʊdɪˌoʊ, rəˈdeɪ-] *s.* rodeo (reunión del ganado y fiesta de los vaqueros).
rodman [ˈrɑdmən, B ˈrɔd-] *s.* (top.) jalonero, portamira.
rodomontade [ˌrɑdəmənˈteɪd, B ˌrɔdəmɔn-] *s.* bravata, fanfarronada, baladronada. —*a.* fanfarrón, jactancioso. —*v.i.* fanfarronear, jactarse, baladronear, bravear.
roe [roʊ] *s.* 1. (zool.) corzo. 2. hueva (de pescado). 3. freza, ovas de crustáceos.
roebuck [ˈroʊˌbʌk] *s.* (*pl.* ROEBUCK o ROEBUCKS) (zool.) corzo (macho).
roe deer, (zool.) corzo.
roentgen [ˈrɛntgən, B ˈrɔntjən] (fís.) *s.* roentgen. —*a.* roentgénico, de rayos X.
roentgenize [-ˌaɪz] *v.t.* (med.) exponer a los rayos X.
roentgenogram [-əˌgræm, B rɔntˈgɛnə-] *s.* roentgenograma, roentgenografía, radiografía.
roentgenograph [-ˌgræf, B -ˌgrɑf] *s.* roentgenografía, radiografía.
roentgenographic [ˌrɛntgənəˈgræfɪk, B ˌrɔnt-] *a.* roentgenográfico.
roentgenography [-ˈɑgrəfɪ, B -ˈɔg-] *s.* roentgenografía, radiografía.
roentgenologist [-ˈɑlədʒəst, B -ˈɔl-] *s.* roentgenólogo, radiólogo.
roentgenology [-dʒɪ] *s.* roentgenología, radiología.
roentgenoscope [ˈrɛntgənəˌskoʊp, B ˈrɔnt-] *s.* (med.) roentgenoscopio, fluoroscopio.
roentgenotherapy [ˌrɛntgənəˈθɛrəpɪ, B ˌrɔnt-] *s.* (med.) roentgenoterapia, radioterapia.
Roentgen ray, rayo Roentgen, rayo X.
rogation [roʊˈgeɪʃən] *s.* (relig.) rogativa; letanía; (*pl.*) rogaciones.
Rogation days, (relig.) rogativas (tres días antes de la Ascensión).
rogatory [ˈrɑgəˌtorɪ, B ˈrɔgətərɪ] *a.* (der.) rogatorio.
Roger [ˈrɑdʒər, B ˈrɔdʒə] *s.* 1. (rad.) (contestación que significa que) se ha recibido el mensaje; está bien; conforme. 2. (fam.) ¡bien! ¡correcto!
rogue [roʊg] *s.* 1. bribón, pícaro, bellaco, pillo. 2. pilluelo, tunantuelo (díc. de niños). 3. vagabundo, holgazán, vago. 4. elefante que vive separado del rebaño. 5. (biol.) variación casual (apl. a las plantas inferiores).
rogue elephant, elefante bravo (que vive separado del rebaño).
roguery [ˈroʊgərɪ] *s.* (*pl.* ROGUERIES) 1. picardía, bellaquería; engaño, truco. 2. travesura, tunantada.
rogues' gallery, álbum policial de retratos de malhechores, archivo policial fotográfico.
rogues' march, (hist.) música burlona (que se tocaba al degradar a un soldado).
roguish [ˈroʊgɪʃ] *a.* 1. bribón, pícaro, bellaco, socarrón. 2. travieso, juguetón.
roguishly [-lɪ] *adv.* pícaramente.
roguishness [-nəs] *s.* 1. bribonería, picardía. 2. travesura.
roil [rɔɪl] *v.t.* 1. enturbiar. 2. irritar, enojar, molestar.
roily [ˈrɔɪlɪ] *a.* (ROILIER; ROILIEST) 1. turbio, fangoso (agua, etc.). 2. turbulento.
roister [ˈrɔɪstər, B -stə] *v.i.* 1. jaranear. 2. (pr. G.B.) fanfarronear, bravear.
roisterer [-stərər, B -ə] *s.* 1. jaranero, jaranista (Am.). 2. (pr. G.B.) fanfarrón, baladrón.
rok [rɑk, B rɔk] *s.* 1. (jer.) soldado perteneciente al ejército de la República de Corea. 2. **R.**, *abrev. de* **Republic of South Korea,** República de Corea del Sur.
Roland [ˈroʊlənd] *s.* (hist.) Rolando, Roldán, Orlando (personaje legendario, héroe de cantares del tiempo de Carlomagno).
role, rôle [roʊl] *s.* papel (del actor); **to play the r. of,** actuar en el papel de, desempeñar el papel de, hacer el papel de.
roll [roʊl] *v.t.* 1. volver, revolver, girar, hacer rodar. 2. arrollar, enrollar. 3. envolver, fajar; liar (un cigarrillo). 4. impeler, propulsar, llevar adelante o consigo. 5. enunciar (palabras) sonoramente, declamar. 6. (hacer) vibrar (la erre). 7. apisonar, allanar, cilindrar. 8. tocar redobles en (el tambor). 9. balancear, bambolear (el cuerpo). 10. (impr.) entintar con rodillo. 11. (metal.) laminar. 12. (cine, t.v.) hacer girar, poner en funcionamiento (las cámaras). 13. (jer.) desplumar, despojar de todo (a persona ebria o que duerme). 14. **r. back,** hacer retroceder, echar atrás; bajar (precios) a su nivel anterior; **r. off,** imprimir (en rotativa); **r. one's own,** liar sus propios cigarrillos; **r. oneself up,** envolverse en, ej., *he rolled himself up in a blanket,* se envolvió en una manta; **r. out,** desenrollar (un mapa, etc.); tender (una alfombra); **r. over,** (fin.) refinanciar mediante nuevo crédito (una obligación vencida); **r. (someone) over,** derribar, echar a rodar (a alguien); **r. up** envolver; arrollar; arremangar; acumular (votos, etc.), (mil.) hacer retroceder (esp. los flancos de la línea enemiga). —*v.i.* 1. rodar, dar vueltas. 2. moverse o avanzar rodando. 3. ondular, extenderse en ondulaciones (terreno); ondear (el agua). 4. girar, revolverse. 5. bambolearse, ir bamboleándose. 6. balancearse, ej., *the ship rolled heavily,* el barco se balanceaba mucho. 7. voltearse patas arriba (caballo, etc.), revolcarse, ej., *the horse tried to r. over,* el caballo trató de revolcarse (para derribar a su jinete). 8. retumbar, reverberar; resonar, vibrar (eco, voz, etc.); redoblar (tambor). 9. extenderse, desparramarse (bajo la presión de un rodillo), ej., *the ink rolls well,* la tinta se extiende bien. 10. trinar (los pájaros). 11. **r. in,** (fam.) acostarse; entrar a raudales (dinero); **r. on (o by),** seguir pasando (tiempo), pasar uno tras otro, ej., *the years r. on,* los años pasan (uno tras otro); **r. out,** (fam.) levantarse; **r. up,** enrollarse, hacerse una bola; crecer, acumularse; llegar en coche; (fam.) hacer su aparición, presentarse; **to be rolling in** (money, etc.), nadar (o bañarse) en (dinero, etc.); **to be rolling in it,** (fam.) nadar en riquezas, estar podrido en plata. —*s.* 1. rollo (de papel, tejido, etc.). 2. bobina, rodillo, cilindro. 3. bamboleo, balanceo, ej., *the r. of a ship,* el balanceo de un barco. 4. rodadura, revuelco. 5. echada, tiro (de dados). 6. rol, registro, lista, nómina, catálogo, ej., *a long r. of heroes,* una larga lista de héroes, *in the r. of saints,* en la nómina de los santos. 7. ondulación, undulación (de terrenos). 8. retumbo, resonancia; redoble (de tambor). 9. cadencia (rítmica), ej., *the fine r. of the best verse,* la delicada cadencia del mejor verso. 10. bollo, panecillo. 11. (aer.) tonel (revolución completa del eje longitudinal). 12. (fam.) fajo (de dinero). 13. (jer.) plata en el banco, dinero en cuenta bancaria. 14. **to call the r.,** pasar lista; **to strike off the rolls,** inhabilitar; expulsar (de un club, etc.); (G.B.) tachar de la nómina de abogados.
rollaway [ˈroʊləˌweɪ] *a.* montado sobre ruedas para facilitar su desplazamiento (díc. de muebles o aparatos domésticos).

rollback [-ˌbæk] *s.* reducción de precios a su nivel original por orden gubernamental.
roll call, 1. lista, acto de pasar lista (a soldados, escolares, etc.). 2. toque o señal para llamar a lista.
rolled [roʊld] *p.p. de* **roll.** —*a.* 1. enrollado, alisado, emparejado. 2. (metal.) laminado. 3. **r. oats,** avena desmenuzada.
rolled bridge, puente corredizo.
roller ['roʊlər, B -lə] *s.* 1. rodillo, rollete; tambor, cilindro. 2. ruedecilla (de mueble o patín). 3. aplanadora. 4. venda arrollada, faja en rollo. 5. (orn.) pichón volteador. 6. (orn.) canario flauta. 7. (mar.) onda u ola grande. 8. **hair r.,** rulo (Am.), rizador de pelo, bigudí.
roller bearing, (mec.) cojinete o rodamiento de rodillos, cojinete de rulemán, apoyo de rodillos.
roller coaster, montaña rusa.
roller conveyor, transportador de rodillos.
roller derby, (E.U.) carrera de patinaje (sobre ruedas).
roller rink, pista de patinaje (sobre ruedas).
roller gate, (hidr.) compuerta rodante, compuerta de rodillos.
roller mill, molino o trituradora de cilindros.
roller skate, patín de ruedas.
roller-skate ['roʊlərˌskeɪt, B -ləˌ-] *v.i.* patinar con patines de ruedas.
roller skating, patinaje sobre ruedas.
roller towel, toalla sin fin, toalla continua.
roll film, (foto.) película en carrete.
rollick ['rɑlɪk, B 'rɔl-] *v.i.* juguetear, retozar; travesear; alborozar.
rollicking [-ɪŋ] **rollicksome** [-səm] *a.* juguetón, travieso, retozón; jovial; alegre, alborozador.
rolling ['roʊlɪŋ] *s.* 1. rodadura, rodamiento. 2. tamboleo, balanceo. 3. ondulación, undulación. 4. redoble (de tambor). —*a.* 1. rodador, giratorio. 2. rodante. 3. ondulado, ondeado (terreno). 4. vibrante; ondulante (sonidos). 5. doblegado o plegado sobre sí mismo. 6. que se bambolea, oscilante; que avanza (niebla, etc.).
rolling hitch, (mar.) nudo de vuelta redonda y dos cotes.
rolling kitchen, (mil.) cocina rodante, cocina de campaña.
rolling mill, taller de laminación, laminador, tren de laminar.
rolling pin, rodillo, rollo de pastelero, rulo para pastas, fruslero.
rolling press, laminador, calandria.
rolling stock, (f.c.) tren rodante, equipo rodante, material móvil o rodante.
rolling stone, (geol.) canto rodado, galga.
roll of honor, cuadro de mérito, cuadro de honor.
rolltop desk ['roʊlˌtɑp-, B -ˌtɔp-] escritorio americano, escritorio de tapa corrediza, escritorio de cortina.
rollway [-ˌweɪ] *s.* plataforma inclinada para cargar troncos; vertedero sin compuertas (en presas).
roly-poly ['roʊlɪ'poʊlɪ] *s.* 1. budín en forma de rollo. 2. persona gordiflona; cosa redonda y gruesa. —*a.* regordete, rechoncho, gordiflón.
Rom. *abrev. de* **Romans,** Epístola de San Pablo a los Romanos (Rom.).
Romaic [roʊ'meɪɪk] *a., s.* romaico, perteneciente a la Grecia moderna.
romaine lettuce [roʊ'meɪn-] lechuga romana.
Roman ['roʊmən] *a.* 1. romano. 2. (impr.) romano (tipo, letra). —*a.* 1. romano. 2. (impr.) letra romana, redonda. 3. católico.
roman-à-clef [rɔˌmɑnˌɑ'kleɪ] (fr.) novela en clave (sobre personajes reales que aparecen con nombres ficticios).
Roman arch, (arq.) arco de medio punto.
Roman calendar, calendario romano.
Roman candle, vela romana, candela romana.
Roman Catholic, católico romano.
Roman Catholic Church, Iglesia Católica Romana.
Roman Catholicism, catolicismo.
romance [roʊ'mæns, 'roʊˌmæns, B roʊ'mæns] *s.* 1. aventura romántica. 2. lo atractivo, romántico, o novelesco; el encanto legendario, ej., *the r. of history,* lo novelesco de la historia. 3. novela romántica. 4. romance (cantar de gesta, libro de caballería). 5. ideas románticas, ej., *a girl full of r.,* una muchacha llena de ideas románticas. 6. fantasía, invención, fábula. 7. (filol.) lenguas romances. 8. (mús.) romanza. —*v.i.* 1. contar o escribir romances. 2. entregarse a fantasías, ilusionarse; exagerar, falsear la verdad. —*v.t.* 1. exagerar en forma romántica, idealizar. 2. galantear.
Romance, *a.* romance, románico.
Romance language, lengua romance o neolatina.
romancer [-ər, B -ə] *s.* 1. romancero. 2. fantaseador, hombre de ilusiones.
Roman collar, cuello clerical.
Roman Empire, Imperio Romano.
Romanesque [ˌroʊmə'nɛsk] *a.* 1. (arte, arq.) románico. 2. romance (lengua). —*s.* 1. estilo románico. 2. lengua romance.
Roman holiday, 1. espectáculo público de caracter bárbaro o escandaloso. 2. placeres o ventajas adquiridos a costa del sufrimiento de otros. 3. vacaciones extraordinarias.
Romanian [roʊ'meɪnɪən] *var. de* **Rumanian.**
Romanic [roʊ'mænɪk] *a.* (filol.) románico, romance.
Romanism ['roʊˌməˌnɪzəm] *s.* (t. despec.) catolicismo.
Romanist [-nəst] *s.* 1. (filol.) romanista. 2. (t. despec.) católico. —*a.* romanista.
Romanization [ˌroʊmənə'zeɪʃən, B -naɪ-] *s.* 1. romanización. 2. conversión al catolicismo.
Romanize ['roʊməˌnaɪz] *v.t.* 1. romanizar; latinizar. 2. convertir al catolicismo. —*v.i.* romanizarse, convertirse al catolicismo.
Roman law, derecho romano.
Roman letter, (impr.) letra romana o redonda.
Roman nose, nariz aguileña, perfil romano.
Roman numeral, número romano.
Romans ['roʊmənz] *s. pl.* (*con sentido de sing.*) (bíbl.) Epístola a los romanos.
Romansh, Romansch [roʊ'mɑntʃ, B -'mænʃ] *s.* romanche, rético (uno de los cuatro idiomas oficiales de Suiza).
romantic [-'mæntɪk, rə-] *a.* 1. romántico. 2. pintoresco, encantador (lugar). —*s.* 1. (lit.) romántico. 2. persona romántica. 3. (*pl.*) ideas quijotescas, plática romántica.
romantically [-ɪkəlɪ] *adv.* románticamente, de modo romántico.
romanticism [-əˌsɪzəm] *s.* (lit.) romanticismo.
romanticist [-səst] *s.* (lit.) romántico.
romanticize [-ˌsaɪz] *v.t.* romantizar, hacer romántico, dar carácter romántico a. —*v.i.* tener ideas románticas; fantasear.
Roman vitriol, (quím.) caparrosa azul.
Romany ['rɑmənɪ, B 'rɔm-] *s.* (*pl.* ROMANIES) gitano; lengua gitana, caló.
romaunt [roʊ'mɔnt, -'mɑnt, B -'mɔnt] *s.* (ant.) romance (esp. en verso).
Rome [roʊm] *s.* Roma, capital de Italia.
Romeo ['roʊmɪˌoʊ] *s.* (fig.) galán, joven amante.
Romish ['roʊmɪʃ] *a.* (gen. despec.) (católico) romano.
Romishness [-nəs] *s.* (gen. despec.) catolicismo rígido.
romp [rɑmp, B rɔmp] *s.* 1. saltabardales, muchacha retozona, joven traviesa. 2. retozo, brinco, salto; juego, travesura. 3. (jer.) galope. 4. **to win in a r.,** ganar al galope (en carrera de caballos). —*v.i.* 1. retozar, corretear, juguetear, triscar. 2. tener relaciones amorosas. 3. (jer.) galopar, correr fácilmente (delante del pelotón). 4. **r. home,** ganar al galope; **r. through,** tocar (música) con brío.
romper ['rɑmpər, B 'rɔmpə] *s.* 1. sartabardales. 2. (*pl.*) mameluco, traje holgado de una pieza (para niños).
Romulus ['rɑmjələs, B 'rɔm-] *s.* (mitol.) Rómulo, fundador y primer rey de Roma.
rondeau ['rɑndoʊ, B 'rɔn-] *s.* (*pl.* RONDEAUX [-doʊz]) (poét.) rondó.
rondel [-dəl] **rondelle** [rɑn'dɛl, B rɔn-] *s.* (poét.) rondel.
rondo ['rɑndoʊ, B 'rɔn-] *s.* (*pl.* RONDOS) (mús.) rondó, gen. el último movimiento de una sonata.
rondure ['rɑndʒər, B 'rɔndjʊə] *s.* redondela, redondel; círculo; curva.
röntgen, *var. de* **roentgen.**
rood [rʊd] *s.* 1. cruz, crucifijo. 2. medida inglesa de longitud (7 u 8 yardas) o de superficie (cuarto de un acre); parcela.
roof [ruf, rʊf, B ruf] *s.* 1. techo, techumbre; cubierta; azotea. 2. (fig.) techo, casa, hogar, ej., *under one's r.,* debajo de su propio techo, en su casa. 3. **r. of the mouth,** paladar; **r. of the world,** techo del mundo, montaña altísima; **to raise the r.,** (fam.) poner el grito en el cielo, armar una bronca, causar un alboroto (esp. en protesta o al enfurecerse). —*v.t.* techar, entechar; tejar.
roofer ['rufər, 'rʊf-, B 'rufə] *s.* techador; constructor de techos.
roof garden, jardín en la azotea, restaurante o local de diversión en la azotea de un edificio.
roofing [-ɪŋ] *s.* (arq.) techado; material para techos. —*s.* de tejado, usado para techar.
roofless [-ləs] *a.* 1. sin techo, destechado. 2. sin hogar; mostrenco.
rooftop [-ˌtɑp, B -ˌtɔp] *s.* tejado (esp. de una casa); azotea, cumbrera.
rooftree [-ˌtri] *s.* (arq.) cumbrera, parhilera, hilera, caballete, lomera.
rook [rʊk] *s.* 1. (orn.) grajo, cuervo europeo. 2. tahúr, timador, embustero, fullero. 3. (ajedrez) torre, roque. —*v.t.* trampear, enfullar.
rookery ['rʊkərɪ] *s.* 1. grajera. 2. banda de grajos. 3. criadero de pingüinos o de focas. 4. casa de vecindad destartalada.
rookie ['rʊkɪ] *s.* (jer.) 1. recluta. 2. bisoño, novato.
rooky ['rʊkɪ] *a.* grajero; lleno de grajos.
room [rum, rʊm] *s.* 1. lugar, espacio, sitio. 2. cuarto, pieza, aposento, habitación, sala. 3. (*pl.*) departamento, morada. 4. los presentes, gente, compañía (en un cuarto, sala, etc.). 5. ocasión, posibilidad, oportunidad; causa, motivo, ej., *there is r. for improvement,* hay posibilidad de mejoramiento. 6. (ant.) rango, posición. 7. **there is plenty of r.,** hay mucho lugar; **there's no r. for,** no cabe (más gente, duda, disputa, etc.); **to make r. for,** hacer lado, hacer campo, hacer sitio (para); **to make r. for oneself,** hacerse lugar; **to take up (much) r.,** ocupar (mucho) sitio. —*v.i.* (E.U.) alojarse, hospedarse. —*v.t.* (E.U.) alojar, hospedar.
roomer ['rumər, 'rʊ-, B -mə] *s.* (E.U.) inquilino; huésped (de una pensión).
roomette [ru'mɛt, rʊ-] *s.* cabina de una cama (en vagones del f.c.).
roomful ['rumˌfʊl, 'rʊm-] *s.* 1. gente que cabe en un cuarto; todos los del cuarto, todo el cuarto. 2. (con *of*) (un) cuarto lleno de (gente, muebles, etc.).

roomily [-əlɪ] *adv.* espaciosamente, ampliamente.
roominess [-ɪnəs] *s.* espaciosidad, anchura, amplitud.
rooming house [-ɪŋ-] casa de huéspedes, pensión para huéspedes.
roommate [-ˌmeɪt] *s.* compañero de cuarto.
room service, servicio (de restorán) en la habitación (en hoteles, etc.).
roomy [-ɪ] *a.* (ROOMIER; ROOMIEST) amplio, espacioso, ancho, holgado.
roorback, roorbach [ˈrʊrˌbæk, B ˈrʊə,-] *s.* (E.U.) acusación falsa (hecha con fines políticos).
roose [ˈruz] *v.t.* (dial.) alabar, elogiar.
roost [rust] *s.* 1. percha o varal (esp. de gallinero). 2. lugar de descanso. 3. **curses come home to r.,** las maldiciones recaen sobre quien las pronuncia; **to rule the r.,** (fam.) mandar, ser el que mueve las cuerdas, ser el gallo del corral. —*v.i.* 1. descansar (las aves) en la percha. 2. pasar la noche (en cierto lugar). —*v.t.* alojar (por la noche), dar cama a.
rooster [ˈrustər, B -tə] *s.* 1. gallo. 2. (jer.) persona activa o arrogante.
root [rut, rʊt, B rut] *v.t.* 1. (E.U.) (ú. con *for*) aplaudir, alentar a gritos, vitorear (a competidores). 2. apoyar, patrocinar. 3. hocicar, hozar (ej., el cerdo). 4. **r. about,** andar buscando, hurgar. —*v.t.* **r. out,** (fig.) descubrir, desenterrar; **r. up,** revolver, hocicar (la tierra); (fig.) descubrir, desenterrar.
root, *s.* 1. (bot.) raíz. 2. (fig.) raíz, causa, origen, principio. 3. base (de una colina, montaña, etc.). 4. (fig.) base, fundamento. 5. (anat.) raíz (de la uña, de la lengua, de los dientes, etc.); raigón (de los dientes). 6. (mat., filol.) raíz. 7. (mús.) nota o sonido principal o fundamental de un acorde. 8. **to be at the r. of,** ser la raíz de (problema, mal, etc.); **to get to the r. of,** ir a la raíz, atacar en las raíces (problema, mal, etc.); **to pull up by the roots,** (fig.) extirpar, cortar o arrancar de raíz; **to take** (o **to strike**) **r.,** echar raíces. —*v.i.* 1. arraigar, echar raíces. 2. radicar, establecerse. —*v.t.* 1. implantar; establecer. 2. **r. out,** erradicar, extirpar; **r. up,** desarraigar, arrancar. —*a.* radical, fundamental, perteneciente a la raíz.
rootage [ˈrutɪdʒ, ˈrʊt-, B ˈrut-] *s.* 1. (conjunto de) raíces. 2. (fig.) causa, origen, principio.
root beer, bebida no alcohólica hecha de extractos de varias raíces y hierbas.
root cap, (bot.) cofia, caliptra.
root climber, (bot.) planta trepadora (que sube por medio de raíces).
rooter [ˈrutər, B -ə] *s.* 1. (jer., E.U.) hincha (que aplaude y alienta ruidosamente a un equipo, competidor, etc.). 2. (zool.) animal hozador.
root hair, (bot.) pelos absorbentes o radicales.
rootless [-ləs] *a.* sin raíces; (fig.) desarraigado.
rootlet [-lət] *s.* raicilla, raicita, radícula.
rootstalk [-ˌstɔk] *s.* (bot.) rizoma.
rootstock [-ˌstɑk, B -ˌstɔk] *s.* (bot.) rizoma.
rooty [-ɪ] *a.* (ROOTIER; ROOTIEST) lleno de raíces; radicoso.
rope [roʊp] *s.* 1. cuerda, soga, cable, cordel. 2. ristra; sarta, hilo, hilera, ej., *r. of pearls,* hilo de perlas. 3. filamento fibroso y viscoso (que se forma en líquidos). 4. **on the r.,** atados por una cuerda (montañeros, alpinistas); **on the ropes,** (fig.) en situación precaria; **r. of sand,** (fig.) seguridad ilusoria; **the ropes,** las sogas o cuerdas (de un cuadrilátero de boxeo); (fig.) los trucos, las reglas; **to give one plenty of r.,** aflojarle la cuerda a uno; **to give someone r. enough to hang himself,** aflojarle la cuerda a uno con la esperanza de que se arruine; **to know the ropes,** conocer todos los trucos, tener experiencia. —*v.t.* 1. atar, amarrar con una cuerda. 2. enlazar (caballos, etc.). 3. (jer., E.U.) atraer, tentar; embaucar, engañar. 4. **r. in,** (fam.) agarrar (a alguien) (para un trabajo, juego, etc.); **r. off,** separar o cercar con soga (ej., una calle). —*v.i.* 1. formar hilos. 2. **r. up,** atarse con soga.
ropedancer [ˈroʊpˌdænsər, B -ˌdɑnsə] *s.* bailarín o bailarina de la cuerda floja, volatinero, volatinera, funámbulo, funámbula.
ropedancing [-sɪŋ] *s.* baile en la cuerda floja.
rope ladder, escala de cuerdas.
ropemaker [-ˌmeɪkər, B -ə] *s.* soguero, cordelero.
ropery [ˈroʊpərɪ] *s.* 1. cordelería, soguería. 2. (ant.) bribonería, picardía.
ropewalk [ˈroʊpˌwɔk] *s.* cordelería; soguería.
ropewalker [-ər, B -ə] *s.* bailarín o bailarina de la cuerda floja, volatinero, volatinera, funámbulo, funámbula.
ropeway [-ˌweɪ] *s.* cablevía, andarivel, vía aérea de cable, funicular aéreo, teleférico.
rope yarn, filástica, cabo de cordelero.
ropiness [ˈroʊpɪnəs] *s.* 1. viscosidad. 2. fibrosidad.
ropy [-pɪ] *a.* 1. viscoso, glutinoso, ej., *r. sirup,* jarabe viscoso. 2. correoso, fibroso.
roque [roʊk] *s.* juego semejante a la argolla o al croquet.
Roquefort cheese [ˈroʊkfərt-, B ˈrɔkfɔ-] *s.* queso de Roquefort.
roquelaure [ˈroʊkəˌlɔr, B ˈrɔkəˌlɔ] *s.* (hist.) capa hasta la rodilla abotonada adelante que se usó alrededor de 1700.
roquet [roʊˈkeɪ, B ˈroʊkɪ] *v.t., v.i.* (croquet) hacer chocar la bola del que juega con otra.
rorqual [ˈrɔrkwəl, B ˈrɔkwəl] *s.* (zool.) rorcual.
rosaceous [roʊˈzeɪʃəs, B rə-] *a.* (bot.) rosáceo.
rosaniline [roʊˈzænələn, B -laɪn] *s.* (quím.) rosanilina.
rosarian [-ˈzɛrɪən, B rəˈzɛər-] *s.* cultivador de rosas.
rosary [ˈroʊzərɪ] *s.* (*pl.* ROSARIES) 1. rosaleda, rosalera, jardín de rosales; macizo de rosales. 2. (relig.) rosario.
roscoe [ˈrɑskoʊ, B ˈrɔs-] *s.* (jer.) pistola, revólver.
rose [roʊz] *s.* 1. rosa. 2. (bot.) rosal. 3. roseta (de regadera, ducha, etc.). 4. rosa, color rosado. 5. rosa, escarapela (en zapato, en sombrero de clérigo). 6. (joy.) talla de rosa (de diamantes, etc.); diamante rosa. 7. (mar.) rosa náutica, rosa de los vientos. 8. **bed of roses,** lecho de rosas; **it's not all roses,** no es puro placer; **r. without a thorn,** (fig.) felicidad imposible. —*v.t.* sonrosar; sonrojar. —*a.* 1. de color de rosa, rosado, rosáceo. 2. de rosas; para rosas.
rose [roʊz] *pret. de* **rise.**
rosé [roʊˈzeɪ] *s.* vino rosé, vino rosado, clarete.
rose acacia, (bot.) acacia rosa.
rose apple, (bot.) pomarrosa.
roseate [ˈroʊzɪət] *a.* 1. rosáceo, rosado, róseo. 2. (fig.) optimista, ej., *r. views,* opiniones optimistas.
roseately [-lɪ] *adv.* 1. con color rosáceo. 2. (fig.) con optimismo.
rosebay [ˈroʊzˌbeɪ] *s.* (bot.) 1. adelfa, baladre. 2. rododendro.
rose box, 1. (bot.) griñolera. 2. filtro de admisión (de bombas).
rosebud [-ˌbʌd] *s.* 1. pimpollo, capullo, botón de rosa. 2. (fig.) pimpollo, adolescente bonita.
rosebush [-ˌbʊʃ] *s.* rosal.
rose campion, (bot.) 1. colleja. 2. neguilla, neguillón.
rose chafer, (ento.) cetonia dorada.
rose color, (color) rosado.
rose-colored [-ˌkʌlərd, B -əd] *a.* 1. rosado, róseo, de color de rosa. 2. atractivo, placentero; optimista. 3. **to view the world through r.-c. glasses,** verlo todo de color de rosa.
rose daphne, (bot.) laurel rosa, adelfa.
rose geranium, (bot.) geranio de rosa.
rose mallow, (bot.) malva rósea; malva arbórea, malva loca o real.
rosemary [ˈroʊzˌmɛrɪ, B -mərɪ] *s.* (*pl.* ROSEMARIES) (bot.) romero, rosmarino.
rose moss, (bot.) verdolaga de jardín.
rose of China, (bot.) rosa de la China, tulipán rojo, sangre de Cristo.
rose of Jericho, (bot.) rosa de Jericó.
rose of Sharon, (bot.) rosa de Siria.
roseola [roʊˈziələ, ˌroʊzɪˈoʊ-, B -ˈziə-] *s.* (med.) roseola; esp. rubéola.
rosery [ˈroʊzərɪ] *s.* (*pl.* ROSERIES) rosaleda, rosalera, rosedal (Am.).
rose sash, (med.) **roséola.**
roset [ˈrɑzət, B ˈrɔz-] *s.* (esco.) resina.
Rosetta stone [roʊˈzɛtə-] (arqueol.) piedra de Rosetta o Roseta.
rosette [roʊˈzɛt] *s.* 1. rosa (lazo de cintas), moña; escarapela. 2. (arq.) rosetón, florón. 3. (bot.) rosetón, roseta.
rose water, 1. agua de rosas. 2. (fig.) trato suave o delicado; cumplidos.
rose-water [ˈroʊzˌwɔtər, -ˌwɑt-, B -ˌwɔtə] *a.* 1. de agua de rosas. 2. (fig.) delicado, afectado, repipi.
rose window, (arq.) rosetón (ventana).
rosewood [-ˌwʊd] *s.* (bot.) 1. palo de rosa. 2. palisandro.
Rosicrucian [ˌroʊzəˈkruʃən, ˌrɑzə-, B ˌroʊzɪ-] *a., s.* (filos.) rosacruz.
Rosicrucianism [-ˌɪzəm] *s.* doctrinas y teorías de los rosacruces.
rosily [ˈroʊzəlɪ] *adv.* 1. con color de rosa. 2. alegremente, agradablemente.
rosin [ˈrɑzən, B ˈrɔz-] *s.* resina de trementina, colofonia, pez rubia; resina, abetinote, pez griega. —*v.t.* frotar con colofonia (arco de violín, etc.).
rosiness [ˈroʊzɪnəs] *s.* 1. color o aspecto rosado. 2. carácter prometedor, aspecto favorable (del porvenir, etc.); aspecto alegre.
rosinous [ˈrɑzənəs, B ˈrɔz-] *a.* resinoso.
rosinweed [-ˌwid] *s.* (bot.) planta magnética.
rosolio [rəˈzoʊlɪoʊ] *s.* rosoli (licor).
rostellum [rɑˈstɛləm, B rɔ-] *s.* (bot., zool.) rostelo.
roster [ˈrɑstər, B ˈroʊstə] *s.* 1. (mil.) lista, rol, orden del día. 2. registro, nómina, matrícula.
rostra, *pl. de* **rostrum.**
rostral [ˈrɑstrəl, B ˈrɔs-] *a.* (zool.) rostral, rostrado.
rostral column, (arq.) columna rostrada.
rostrate [-ˌtreɪt, B -trɪt] *a.* (zool., arq.) rostrado.
rostrum [-trəm] *s.* (*pl.* ROSTRUMS O ROSTRA [-trə]) 1. (*pl.*) (hist.) tribuna. 2. púlpito, plataforma, tribuna. 3. (anat., zool.) rostro; pico, hocico. 4. (mar.) rostro, espolón (de la nave).
rosy [ˈroʊzɪ] *a.* (ROSIER; ROSIEST) 1. róseo, rosado; ruboroso, sonrojado. 2. (fig.) prometedor, favorable; alegre, optimista.
rot [rɑt, B rɔt] *v.i.* (*pret., p.p.* ROTTED; *p.pr.* ROTTING) 1. podrirse, pudrirse, descomponerse, echarse a perder. 2. (fig.) languidecer, consumirse. 3. (fig.) corromperse, depravarse, degenerar. 4. (jer., G.B.) burlarse, hablar irónicamente.

—*v.t.* 1. podrir, pudrir, descomponer, echar a perder. 2. enriar (cáñamo o lino). 3. (jer., G.B.) chasquear; ironizar, burlar; embromar, tomar el pelo a. —*s.* 1. pudrimiento, putrefacción, descomposición, corrupción. 2. (vet.) morriña (de los ovinos), comalia. 3. (jer.) tontería, disparate, sandez, estupidez. —*interj.* ¡qué tontería! ¡qué estupidez!

rota ['roʊtə] *s.* 1. (pr. G.B.) rol, nómina, lista rotatoria. 2. (relig.) Rota (tribunal supremo de la Iglesia Católica).

rotameter [-ˌmitər, B -ə] *s.* (fís.) rotámetro, tacómetro.

Rotarian [roʊ'tɛriən, B rə'tɛər-] *s.* rotario, miembro del Club Rotario.

Rotarianism [-ˌɪzəm] *s.* rotarismo.

rotary ['roʊtərɪ] *a.* rotatorio, giratorio, rotativo. —*s.* (*pl.* ROTARIES) 1. máquina rotativa. 2. óvalo, glorieta, círculo de tráfico.

rotary beam antenna, (rad.) antena de haz giratorio.

Rotary Club, Club Rotario, organización internacional de hombres de negocio y profesionales.

rotary condenser, (elec.) condensador rotatorio, condensador sincrónico.

rotary drill, perforadora giratoria.

rotary engine, 1. motor en estrella. 2. máquina alternativa, máquina rotativa.

rotary field, (elec.) campo o inductor giratorio.

rotary motion, (mec.) movimiento angular, giratorio o rotativo.

rotary plow, 1. arado de nieve, quitanieves giratorio. 2. arado rotatorio.

rotary press, prensa rotativa.

rotary pump, bomba rotatoria o rotativa.

rotary transformer, (elec.) transformador rotativo o rotatorio.

rotary-wing aircraft ['roʊtərɪ'wɪŋ-] (aer.) rotaplano, aerodino de alas giratorias.

rotatable ['roʊˌteɪtəbel, B roʊ'teɪt-] *a.* 1. girable. 2. cultivable en rotación.

rotate ['roʊˌteɪt, B roʊ'teɪt] *v.i.* 1. girar, dar vueltas, rotar. 2. turnar, alternar. —*v.t.* 1. hacer girar, revolver. 2. hacer turnar, hacer alternar. 3. (agr.) sembrar o cultivar en rotación, rotar.

rotating [-ɪŋ] *s.* giratorio, rotativo.

rotation [roʊ'teɪʃən] *s.* 1. rotación, giro, revolución. 2. alternación, uso o empleo por turnos. 3. (agr.) rotación (de cultivos). 4. **by r., in r.,** por turnos, alternadamente, alternativamente.

rotational [-əl] *a.* rotatorio, giratorio.

rotative [-'roʊˌteɪtɪv, B -tə-] *a.* rotativo; rotatorio, giratorio.

rotator [-ər, B roʊ'teɪtə] *s.* 1. parte o pieza rotatoria (en máquina, etc.); aparato rotativo. 2. (anat.) músculo rotatorio.

rotatory ['roʊtəˌtɔrɪ, B -tərɪ] *a.* 1. rotatorio, giratorio. 2. alternado, alternativo.

ROTC *abrev. de* **Reserve Officers Training Corps,** Centro de Entrenamiento de Oficiales de la Reserva (E.U.).

rotche, rotch [rɑtʃ, B rɔtʃ] *s.* (orn.) alca.

rote [roʊt] *s.* 1. ruido de las olas al romper en la playa. 2. (mús.) antiguo instrumento celta de cuerdas. 3. rutina, hábito, costumbre; repetición mecánica. 4. **by r.,** de memoria, a coro.

rotenone ['roʊtənˌoʊn] *s.* (quím.) rotenona.

rotgut ['rɑtˌgʌt, B 'rɔt-] *s.* (jer.) balarrasa, matarratas (licor de pésima calidad).

rotifer ['roʊtəfər, B -fə] *s.* (zool.) rotífero.

rotiferous [roʊ'tɪfərəs, B rə-] *a.* (bot.) rotífero.

rotiform ['roʊtəˌfɔrm, B -ˌfɔm] *a.* (bot., zool.) rotiforme, estrellado; radiado.

rotisserie [roʊ'tɪsərɪ] *s.* 1. rotisería. 2. asador.

rotogravure [ˌroʊtəgrə'vjʊr, B -'vjʊə] *s.* rotograbado.

rotometer ['roʊtəˌmitər, B -ə] *s.* (fís.) rotámetro.

rotor ['roʊtər, B -ə] *s.* (aer., elec., hidr.) rotor, pieza giratoria.

rotorcraft [-ˌkræft, B -ˌkrɑft] *s.* (aer.) rotoplano, aerodino de alas giratorias.

rotor ship, buque de rotores, buque de propulsión por rotores.

roto section ['roʊtoʊ-] sección (de un diario) dedicada a ilustraciones en rotograbado.

rototill ['roʊtəˌtɪl] *v.t.* cultivar con arado rotatorio.

rotten ['rɑtən, B 'rɔt-] *a.* 1. podrido, putrefacto, carroño. 2. deteriorado, descompuesto; quebradizo (piedra, hielo, etc.). 3. corrompido, envilecido. 4. (vet.) que padece de morriña (ovinos). 5. (fam.) pésimo, muy malo, de mala calidad. 6. (fam.) bestial, brutal, desagradable, abominable.

rottenly [-lɪ] *adv.* (fam.) 1. pésimamente, muy mal. 2. desagradablemente, abominablemente.

rottenness [-nəs] *s.* podredumbre, putrefacción; corrupción.

rottenstone [-ˌstoʊn] *s.* trípoli, trípol.

rotter ['rɑtər, B 'rɔtə] *s.* (jer.) canalla, sinvergüenza.

rotund [roʊ'tʌnd] *a.* 1. rotundo, redondo. 2. rotundo, lleno, sonoro (lenguaje, estilo, etc.). 3. regordete, gordiflón.

rotunda [roʊ'tʌndə] *s.* rotonda, rotunda.

rotundity [-dətɪ] *s.* 1. rotundidad, redondez. 2. rotundidad, sonoridad. 3. superficie rotunda. 4. frase sonora.

rotundly [-dlɪ] *adv.* sonoramente.

roturier [roʊ'tʊrɪˌeɪ, B -'tjʊrjeɪ] *s.* (fr.) plebeyo.

rouble, *var. de* **ruble.**

roué [ru'eɪ] *s.* libertino, depravado.

Rouen [ru'ɑn, B 'ruɑŋ] *s.* Ruán, ciudad en el N. de Francia.

rouge [ruʒ] *s.* 1. colorete, arrebol. 2. (joy.) colcótar. 3. lápiz de labios. —*v.t.* 1. colorear, arrebolar, pintar (las mejillas, los labios). 2. (fig.) enrojecer. —*v.i.* 1. usar colorete o lápiz de labios. 2. (fig.) enrojecerse.

rouge et noir [ˌruʒeɪ'nwɑr, B -'nwɑ] treinta y cuarenta (juego de naipes).

rough [rʌf] *a.* 1. áspero, desigual, escabroso, quebrado, rugoso, accidentado, abrupto. 2. peludo, velludo, hirsuto. 3. agitado, intranquilo, turbulento, alborotado, ej., *r. sea,* mar agitado o turbulento. 4. borrascoso, tempestuoso. 5. tosco, basto, crudo, chapucero (trabajo, etc.). 6. rudo, inculto, descortés, grosero. 7. rudo, malo, ej., *r. luck,* mala suerte. 8. áspero, agrio, acídulo (vino, etc.). 9. bronco, disonante (voz, instrumento, etc.). 10. aproximado, aproximativo. 11. preparatorio, preliminar, primitivo (plano, esquema, etc.). 12. (fon.) aspirado. 13. (jer.) peligroso, difícil, penoso. 14. **to be r. on,** maltratar, jugar una mala pasada a; **to have a r. time,** pasar un mal rato, sufrir privaciones o maltrato; **to have a r. tongue,** ser grosero. —*s.* 1. rufián, matón; alborotador. 2. terreno escabroso, terreno accidentado o quebrado. 3. lo áspero, lo tosco o mal acabado. 4. penalidad, privación. 5. (golf) maleza, obstáculos (en el campo). 6. **in the r.,** en bruto, sin pulimento. —*v.t.* 1. encrudecer, endurecer. 2. insertar clavos o ramplones en (la herradura de un caballo). 3. domar (caballos). 4. dar los primeros cortes a (diamantes, gemas). 5. (mús.) (gen. con *up*) afinar chapuceramente. 6. **r. in** (o **out**), bosquejar; **r. it,** vivir sin comodidades, pasar trabajos; **r. out,** moldear en bruto; **r. up,** erizar, levantar (plumas, cabello, etc.); (jer.) moler a golpes, dar una pateadura a, dar una zurra a (esp. para amedrentar). —*adv.* rudamente, rufianescamente; **to play r. (with),** emplear violencia (con), tratar rudamente (a).

roughage ['rʌfɪdʒ] *s.* 1. substancia áspera y ordinaria. 2. (E.U.) alimento o forraje indigestible o indigesto.

rough-and-ready [-ən'rɛdɪ] *a.* 1. rudimentario pero efectivo (cosa). 2. inculto pero eficiente (persona). 3. aproximado, no detallado.

rough-and-tumble [-'tʌmbəl] *a.* desordenado, desenfrenado, violento. —*s.* lucha violenta, pelea atolondrada.

rough breathing, (gram. griega) marca de aspiración, aspiración, aspiración.

roughcast ['rʌfˌkæst, B -ˌkɑst] *s.* 1. bosquejo, modelo tosco, obra sin acabar. 2. revoco, basto, enforscado. —*v.t.* 1. bosquejar, revocar o enfoscar, con mezcla de cal y piedras. 2. colar en basto.

rough copy, borrador, minuta.

rough diamond, (lit., fig.) diamante en bruto.

rough draft, borrador; boceto, bosquejo.

roughdry [-'draɪ] *v.t.* secar (la ropa) sin plancharla. —*a.* secado sin plancha.

roughen ['rʌfən] *v.t., v.i.* endurecer(se); enrudecer(se); poner(se) tosco o áspero.

rough file, lima basta.

rough-hew, roughew ['rʌf'hju] *v.t.* desbastar; labrar toscamente; modelar en bruto.

roughhouse [-ˌhaʊʃ] (jer.) *s.* pelea, pelotera, camorra, trifulca. —*v.t.* tratar con rudeza jocosa. —*v.i.* armar una camorra o pelea.

roughing lathe ['rʌfɪŋ-] (maq.) torno desbastador.

rough-legged hawk ['rʌfˌlɛgəd-, -'lɛgd-] (orn.) peuco.

roughly [-lɪ] *adv.* 1. ásperamente. 2. rudamente, brutalmente; groseramente. 3. aproximadamente. 4. toscamente, bastamente.

roughneck [-ˌnɛk] *s.* (fam.) maleante; patán, rufián; palurdo, rústico; alborotador.

roughness [-nəs] *s.* 1. aspereza (de una superficie), escabrosidad (del camino, terreno, etc.). 2. rudeza, brutalidad; grosería. 3. agitación (del mar). 4. severidad, dureza, inclemencia (del tiempo). 5. carácter aproximado (de una valuación, etc.).

roughrider [-'raɪdər, B -ə] *s.* 1. domador de caballos. 2. **R.,** (hist.) soldado de caballería (esp. del regimiento organizado y comandado por Teodoro Roosevelt en la guerra contra España de 1898).

roughshod [-'ʃɑd, B -ˌʃɔd] *a.* herrado con clavos o ramplones (caballo); **to ride r. over,** (fig.) obrar sin hacer caso de dificultades; tiranizar, atropellar, tratar sin miramiento.

rough sketch, boceto, bosquejo.

rough stuff, (jer.) violencia, matanza, tortura.

roulade [ru'lɑd] *s.* (mús.) gorjeo.

rouleau [ru'loʊ] *s.* (*pl.* ROULEAX, ROULEAUS [-'loʊz]) cucurucho; rollito; cartucho, lío cilíndrico de monedas.

roulette [ru'lɛt] *s.* 1. ruleta (juego). 2. roleta de grabador, ruedecilla con púas. 3. (filat.) perforación hecha con roleta. —*v.t.* (*pret., p.p.* ROULETTED; *p.pr.* ROULETTING) perforar con la roleta.

Roumanian, *var. de* Rumanian.

round [raʊnd] *a.* 1. redondo; circular; cilíndrico. 2. entero, completo, cabal; redondo, global, ej., *r. dozen,* docena completa, *r. numbers,* cifras redondas o globales, *r. score,* puntaje completo. 3. redondo, rechoncho. 4. rotundo (afirmación, palabras, reniego, etc.). 5. suave, sonoro (tono, voz). 6. fuerte, severo (castigo, golpe, etc.). 7. completo, cabal, acabado. —*s.* 1. redondo;

esfera, disco, orbe. 2. curva, curvatura (de un objeto). 3. revolución, giro, vuelta. 4. ronda, ruta, recorrido; paseo, rodeo. 5. ciclo, período. 6. rutina. 7. (*pl.*) visitas de rutina. 8. conjunto, círculo (de personas). 9. vuelta, tiempo, serie, tanda (en una competencia o juego); asalto (de boxeo); ronda, partida, tanda (de billar, naipes, etc.). 10. ronda (de copas de licor); ración, asignación. 11. rueda, tajada (de carne de res). 12. porción, tajada (de pan, tostada, etc.). 13. salva (de tiros, aplausos, etc.); andanada, descarga (de armas de fuego). 14. cartucho con bala. 15. peldaño, travesaño (de escala). 16. ronda (danza rural que se baila en círculo). 17. (esco.) bulto redondo. 18. **in r.,** (enc.) redondeado; **in the r.,** en su totalidad, completamente; sentados en círculo, en redondo; alrededor (audiencia, etc.); **to make the rounds,** hacer visitas sucesivas; patrullar, hacer una ronda de inspección; ir de boca en boca (noticia, rumor, etc.); **to make** (o **to go**) **one's rounds,** hacer uno su recorrido (de inspección, vigilancia, etc.). —*v.t.* 1. redondear. 2. cercar, circundar, rodear. 3. ir alrededor de, dar vueltas a; doblar (esquina, etc.). 4. (mar.) voltear, ej., *r. the boat,* voltear el barco contra la marea. 5. (fon.) labializar (sonido). 6. **r. off** (o **out**), completar, acabar, rematar; **r. up,** rodear, encerrar, reunir (el ganado); reunir, juntar, recoger (a personas rezagadas, etc.). —*v.i.* redondearse, llenarse. 2. dar vueltas, hacer círculos. 3. (mar.) orzar, voltearse. 4. **r. into,** completar su desarrollo llegando a (ser); completar; entrar en; **r. to,** (mar.) ponerse al pairo (el barco). —*prep.* 1. alrededor de, a la vuelta de, en torno de (o a). 2. durante, por todo, ej., *the year r.,* durante o por todo el año. —*adv.* 1. alrededor, al derredor, en derredor, en circuito, en torno, a la redonda. 2. a todos, a cada uno, en todas direcciones. 3. (pr. E.U.) acá y allá, de acá para acullá. 4. **all r.,** para todos, ej., *Home Rule all r.,* autonomía para todos (los pueblos); **r. and r.,** dando vueltas.

roundabout ['raʊndəˌbaʊt] *s.* 1. ruta tortuosa. 2. circunlocución, rodeo de palabras. 3. (G.B.) tiovivo. 4. (hist.) chaqueta, casaca. 5. (ant.) pista circular. —*a.* 1. tortuoso, indirecto. 2. rechoncho, gordiflón.

round angle, (mat.) ángulo de una vuelta.

round arch, (arq.) arco de círculo, arco de medio punto, bóveda de cañón.

round clam, (zool.) almeja.

round dance, 1. danza bailada en redondo. 2. baile de salón que se ejecuta alrededor de la sala.

rounded ['raʊndəd] *a.* 1. redondeado, esférico, cilíndrico. 2. pulido, refinado; cabal, terminado, acabado. 3. (fon.) labializado.

roundel ['raʊndəl] *s.* 1. panel, ventana o nicho circular. 2. (poét.) rondel, rondó. 3. (her.) tortillo.

roundelay ['raʊndəˌleɪ] *s.* 1. canción simple, tonada, tonadilla. 2. baile rural que se baila en círculo; vals. 3. (poét.) especie de rondel.

rounder ['raʊndər, B -də] *s.* 1. libertino, calavera. 2. (boxeo) encuentro de (cierto número de) asaltos, ej., *a ten-r.,* un encuentro de diez asaltos. 3. (*pl.*) (G.B.) juego de pelota parecido al béisbol. 4. (G.B.) predicador metodista.

round file, lima cilíndrica.

round hand, letra (escritura) redonda.

Roundhead ['raʊndˌhed] *s.* (G.B., hist.) cabeza redonda (sobrenombre burlón aplicado a los puritanos).

round-head screw, tornillo de cabeza redonda.

roundheel [-ˌhil] *s.* (jer.) mujer fácil.

roundhouse [-ˌhaʊs] *s.* 1. (f.c.) depósito de locomotoras, casa de máquinas. 2. (mar.) chupeta, tumbadillo, toldilla. 3. (boxeo) gancho largo.

roundish ['raʊndɪʃ] *a.* redondeado, casi o medio redondo.

roundishness [-nəs] *s.* forma redondeada.

roundlet ['raʊndlət] *s.* disco pequeño, aro o anillo pequeños.

roundly [-lɪ] *adv.* 1. completamente. 2. abiertamente, lisa y llanamente. 3. rotundamente, categóricamente, terminantemente. 4. redondamente, circularmente.

roundness [-nəs] *s.* redondez.

round numbers, cifras globales (sin fracciones), cifras redondas.

round robin, 1. memorial firmado en círculo (para ocultar el orden en que van las firmas). 2. carta enviada en cadena (de una persona a otra para que cada una contribuya con un mensaje adicional). 3. torneo (de tenis, ajedrez, etc. en que todos los participantes se enfrentan uno a otro).

round shot, bala del cañón sin estrías, bala rasa.

round-shouldered [-'ʃoʊldərd, B -dəd] *a.* cargado de espaldas, de hombros caídos.

roundsman ['raʊndzmən] *s.* 1. (E.U.) cabo de policía, cabo de ronda. 2. (G.B.) mandadero (de lechería, panadería, etc.) que hace entregas a domicilio.

round steak, bistec de rueda, bistec de tapa.

round table, 1. mesa redonda (lugar de reunión o de conferencia). 2. R. T., (G.B., hist.) Tabla Redonda (alrededor de la cual se reunían el rey Arturo y sus caballeros).

round-the-clock ['raʊndðə'klɑk, B -'klɔk] *a., adv.* día y noche, constantemente.

round timber, madera en troncos.

round top, (mar.) cofa; gavia de vigía.

round trip, viaje de ida y vuelta, viaje redondo.

round turn and half hitch, (mar.) nudo de vuelta redonda y cote.

roundup ['raʊndˌʌp] *s.* 1. rodeo, reunión del ganado mayor (para contarlo o marcarlo); vaqueros que toman parte en el rodeo. 2. (fam.) redada, apresamiento, batida (de la policía), detención en masa. 3. resumen, sumario.

roundworm [-wɜrm, B -ˌwɜm] *s.* (zool.) ascáride.

roup [rup] *s.* (vet.) moquillo simple, coriza contagiosa, coriza infecciosa.

roupet ['roʊpət, B 'rup-] *a.* (esco.) ronco.

roupy ['rupɪ] *a.* 1. (esco.) ronco. 2. (vet.) enfermo con moquillo simple.

rouse [raʊz] *v.t.* 1. despertar. 2. animar, estimular. 3. excitar, suscitar, provocar; conmover. 4. agitar, revolver (líquido. esp. cerveza al elaborarla). 5. levantar (caza). 6. (mar.) (gen. con *in, out* o *up*) halar, tirar fuertemente. 7. **r. oneself,** animarse. —*v.i.* 1. despertarse. 2. crecer, cobrar fuerza. —*s.* 1. alboroto. 2. (mil., G.B.) diana. 3. (ant.) trago de licor; brindis; festín, jolgorio, parranda.

rouser ['raʊzər, B -zə] *s.* 1. utensilio para agitar la cerveza. 2. (jer., G.B.) mentira descarada.

rousing [-zɪŋ] *a.* 1. vehemente, conmovedor. 2. estimulante, vigorizador, provocador. 3. extraordinario, espléndido.

roust [raʊst] *v.t.* (gen. con *out* o *up*) 1. despertar, suscitar, provocar. 2. (gen. con *up*) (fig.) desenterrar, descubrir, lograr encontrar.

roustabout ['raʊstəˌbaʊt] *s.* 1. (E.U.) peón, gañán, estibador, trabajador portuario. 2. (E.U.) vaquero vagabundo.

rouster [-stər, B -stə] *s.* (E.U.) peón, gañán, estibador, trabajador portuario.

rout [raʊt] *s.* 1. derrota, huida o fuga desordenada. 2. tumulto, confusión, alboroto. 3. multitud, muchedumbre. 4. populacho, chusma. 5. recepción, fiesta, sarao. 6. (der.) disturbio, complot. 7. (ant.) rugido, bramido, rebuzno. 8. **to put to r.,** poner en huida. —*v.i.* 1. escarbar, hozar, hocicar. 2. buscar, registrar. 3. (dial.) hozar, rugir, bramar, rebuznar. —*v.t.* 1. desarraigar. 2. (gen. con *out*) echar fuera, hacer salir, sacar. 3. (gen. con *out* o *up*) (fig.) desenterrar, descubrir, lograr encontrar. 4. (impr.) fresar, rautear.

route [rut, raʊt] *s.* 1. ruta, derrotero, rumbo; vía, camino; itinerario. 2. (mil.) ruta, vía; itinerario. 3. (med.) vía. 4. **on r.,** en camino. —*v.t.* (*pret., p.p.* ROUTED; *p.pr.* ROUTING) encaminar, enviar, dirigir.

routeman ['rutmən, 'raʊt-] *s.* vendedor viajero (con una ruta asignada).

route march, (mil.) marcha de viaje.

route order, (mil.) orden de marcha.

router ['raʊtər, B -ə] *s.* 1. guimbarda, ranurador. 2. contorneador, buriladora, máquina para fresar, fresa de acanalar, recanteadora de chapa.

routh [ruθ, B raʊθ] *s.* (esco.) abundancia, exuberancia, afluencia.

routine [ru'tin] *s.* rutina; costumbre, hábito. —*a.* rutinario; habitual.

routing plane ['raʊtɪŋ-] guimbarda, ranurador, cepillo ranurador.

routinist [ru'tinəst] *s.* rutinero, rutinario.

routinize [-ˌnaɪz] *v.t.* acostumbrar, habituar; convertir en rutina, hacer rutinario.

rove [roʊv] *v.i.* vagar, vagabundear; errar; dar vueltas, serpentear. —*v.t.* 1. vagar o andar vagando por. 2. (tej.) torcer el hilo antes de encanillarlo. —*s.* 1. vagancia, vagabundeo; paseo. 2. arandela de remache. 3. (tej.) mecha, torzal.

rove [roʊv] *pret., p.p. de* **reeve.**

rove beetle, (ento.) aleócaro.

rover ['roʊvər, B -və] *s.* 1. pirata, corsario; barco pirata. 2. vagabundo, errante, vagamundo. 3. jefe de grupo de (niños) exploradores. 4. (ballestería) blanco ocasional; blanco fijo a larga distancia. 5. (croquet) (t. **r. ball**) pelota que ha pasado por todos los arcos pero que todavía no ha tocado la estaca.

roving [-vɪŋ] *a.* ambulante, vagante. —*s.* (tej.) primera torsión; hebra, hilado.

roving frame, (tej.) mechera.

row [raʊ] *s.* 1. (fam.) barahúnda, bochinche, camorra, trifulca, disputa, pendencia. 2. (jer., pr. G.B.) estruendo, ruido. 3. (jer., pr. G.B.) boca. 4. **to kick up a r.,** armar un alboroto; protestar vivamente. —*v.t.* (pr. G.B.) regañar. —*v.i.* pelearse, trabarse en una camorra o trifulca.

row [roʊ] *v.t.* 1. impeler (bote) al remo; navegar a remo. 2. conducir o llevar en un bote a remo. 3. estar equipado con (cierta cantidad de remos). 4. remar en, participar en (regata); competir con (otro en una regata). 5. alinear, poner en fila. 6. **r. down,** sobrepasar (otro bote) en una regata. —*v.i.* remar, bogar. —*s.* 1. excursión en bote de remos. 2. hilera, fila, línea, ristra; columna de números. 3. fila (de asientos). 4. calle, calleja, callejón. 5. **in a r., in rows,** en fila; **in a r.,** seguidos, ej., *she won three games in a r.,* ganó tres juegos seguidos.

rowan ['raʊən] *s.* 1. (bot.) serbal, serbo, amargoso. 2. (t. **r. berry**) serba.

rowboat ['roʊˌboʊt] *s.* bote de remos.

rowdily ['raʊdəlɪ] *adv.* de modo pendenciero, bulliciosamente, alborotadamente.

rowdiness [-ɪnəs] *s.* carácter camorrista o bochinchero, disposición pendenciera, comportamiento alborotador.

rowdy ['raʊdɪ] *s.* camorrero, camorrista, bochinchero. —*a.* pendenciero, camorrero, camorrista, bochinchero.

rowdyish [-ɪʃ] *a.* pendenciero, alborotador; ruidoso.
rowdyism [-ˌɪzəm] *s.* matonismo.
rowel ['raʊəl] *s.* 1. rodaja (de la espuela). 2. (vet.) sedal. —*v.t.* (*pret., p.p.* ROWELED O ROWELLED; *p.pr.* ROWELING O ROWELLING) espolear, picar con la espuela.
rowen ['raʊən] *s.* segunda cosecha; segunda siega.
rower ['roʊər, B -ə] *s.* remero, remador, bogador, boga.
rowlock ['rɑlək, B 'rɔl-] *s.* 1. (mar.) tolete, escálamo. 2. (arq.) sardinel.
rowlocked [-əkt] *a.* (const.) asardinado.
royal ['rɔɪəl] *a.* 1. real, regio. 2. (fig.) magnífico, majestuoso, grandioso, suntuoso, espléndido; extraordinario, primoroso; superior; de tamaño grande. 3. **blood r.,** la familia real; **to have a r. time,** divertirse en grande. —*s.* 1. (t. **r. paper**) (impr.) papel de escribir (de 19 por 24 pulgadas) o de imprimir (de 20 por 25 pulgadas). 2. (t. **r. sail**) (mar.) sobrejuanete. 3. (t. **r. stag**) (fam.) ciervo con cornamenta de 12 o más puntas. 4. (fam., G.B.) miembro de la familia real.
royal antler, tercer mogote (en la cornamenta de los ciervos).
royal blue, (color) esmalte de cobalto.
royal coachman, mosca artificial empleada en la pesca del salmón.
royal fern, (bot.) helecho real.
royal flush, (naipes) escalera real.
royalism ['rɔɪəˌlɪzəm] *s.* realismo, monarquismo.
royalist [-ləst] *a., s.* realista, monárquico.
royalistic [rɔɪə'lɪstɪk] *a.* realista, monárquico.
royal jelly, jalea real (obtenida de las abejas).
royally ['rɔɪəlɪ] *adv.* regiamente, a cuerpo de rey, magníficamente, majestuosamente, suntuosamente, espléndidamente, excelentemente, superiormente.
royal mast, (mar.) sobrejuanete.
royal palm, (bot.) palma real, palmiche.
royal poinciana, (bot.) poinciana real.
royalty ['rɔɪəltɪ] *s.* (*pl.* ROYALTIES) 1. realeza, dignidad o soberanía real. 2. la persona del rey; (*gen. pl.*) miembro de la familia real. 3. majestad real, magnificencia, pompa. 4. privilegio real. 5. (*gen. pl.*) regalías; derechos de autor, derechos de inventor o de patente.
royal water lily, (bot.) irupé.
rozelle, *var. de* **roselle.**
r.p.m. *abrev. de* **revolutions per minute,** revoluciones por minuto (R.P.M., r.p.m.).
r.p.m. indicator, (mec.) tacómetro, indicador de r.p.m.
r.p.s. *abrev. de* **revolutions per second,** revoluciones por segundo.
R.R., rr *abrev. de* **railroad,** ferrocarril.
rsvp (fr.) *abrev. de* **the favor of a reply is requested,** se ruega la respuesta.
Rt. Hon. *abrev. de* **Right Honorable,** Muy Honorable.
Rt. Rev. *abrev. de* **Right Reverend,** Muy Reverendo.
Ru *símb. de* **ruthenium,** rutenio (Ru).
rub [rʌb] *v.t.* (*pret., p.p.* RUBBED; *p.pr.* RUBBING) 1. frotar, friccionar; ludir, luir. 2. fregar, estregar, restregar; pulir o bruñir frotando. 3. calcar, copiar. 4. **r. against** (u **on** u **over**), rozar, pasar sobre, frotar contra; **r. down,** desgastar restregando; almohazar (un caballo, etc.); **r. elbows** (o **shoulders**) **with,** codearse (con); **r. oneself down,** frotarse el cuerpo; **r. in** (o **into**), hacer penetrar frotando; (fig.) reiterar (cosa desagradable) porfiadamente; **r. off** (o **away**), quitar (brillo, etc.) fregando; limpiar estregando; **r. one's hands,** frotarse las manos (esp. con satisfacción o complacencia); **r. out,** borrar; (jer.) asesinar, matar; **r. the right way,** halagar hábilmente, tratar con tino, adivinar el gusto de; **r. the wrong way,** irritar, molestar, fastidiar. —*v.i.* 1. rozarse, frotarse. 2. desgastarse, raerse. 3. borrarse. 4. dar cólera, ser irritante. 5. **r. against,** rozarse contra, raspar; **r. off** (o **away**), desgastarse (lanilla, brillo); (fig.) desvanecer (timidez, etc.). —*s.* 1. roce, frotación. 2. (fig.) roce, fricción, desacuerdo. 3. obstáculo, dificultad, busilis. 4. desaire, insulto. 5. desigualdad (de superficie, terreno, etc.). 6. **there's the r.!** ¡allí está el busilis!
rub-a-dub ['rʌbəˌdʌb] *s.* rataplán, tamborileo. —*v.i.* redoblar, tamborilear.
rubasse [ru'bæs] *s.* cuarzo rojo.
rubber ['rʌbər, B -ə] *s.* 1. masajista, friccionador, frotador. 2. caucho, goma, goma elástica, jebe (Am.). 3. goma de borrar, borrador. 4. (*pl.*) chanclo de goma. 5. (vulg.) preservativo, goma, condón.
rubber *s.* (naipes) partida, esp. la partida impar que define ciertos juegos; (bridge) rubber.
rubber band, liga elástica, cinta de goma, elástico.
rubber-base paint [-ˌbeɪs-] pintura con base de caucho.
rubber cement, cemento de goma, pasta de caucho o de hule, pegamento a base de caucho.
rubber check, (jer.) cheque sin fondos.
rubber heel, tacón de goma, taco de jebe (Am.).
rubber hose, manguera de goma.
rubberize ['rʌbəˌraɪz] *v.t.* encauchar, cauchutar, impermeabilizar (con caucho).
rubberized [-raɪzd] *a.* ahulado.
rubberlike [-ərˌlaɪk, B -əˌ-] *a.* semejante al caucho, elástico, resistente.
rubberneck [-ˌnɛk] (jer.) *s.* 1. inquisidor, curioso, fisgón. 2. turista. —*v.i.* 1. estirar el cuello para curiosear o fisgonear, meter las narices. 2. hacer turismo.
rubber plant, (bot.) árbol del caucho.
rubber stamp, sello de caucho, estampilla, tampón. 2. (fig.) visto bueno. 3. aprobación rutinaria.
rubber-stamp [ˌrʌbər'stæmp, B -ə'-] *v.t.* 1. sellar. 2. (fam.) aprobar maquinalement; autorizar, aprobar con carácter oficial.
rubber tire, goma neumática, llanta de caucho.
rubbery ['rʌbərɪ] *a.* semejante al caucho, elástico.
rubbing ['rʌbɪŋ] *s.* 1. calco. 2. frote, fricción, roce.
rubbish ['rʌbɪʃ] *s.* 1. desperdicio, basura, desecho; cachivache, trasto. 2. disparate, tontera, necedad, hojarasca.
rubbishy [-ɪʃɪ] *a.* 1. lleno de basura. 2. lleno de disparates (libro, discurso, etc.).
rubble [-'ʌbəl] *s.* 1. grava, morrillo, canto rodado; mampuesto, escollera. 2. ripio, escombros, cascajo, cascote.
rubble masonry, albañilería de piedra bruta, mampostería concertada.
rubblework [-ˌwɜrk, B -ˌwɜk] *s.* albañilería de piedra bruta, mampostería concertada.
rubbly ['rʌblɪ] *a.* ripioso, cascajoso; en bloques.
rubdown ['rʌbˌdaʊn] *s.* masaje, fricción (esp. de todo el cuerpo después de un baño).
rube [rub] *s.* (jer.) aldeano, campesino, rústico, patán.
rubefacient [ˌrubə'feɪʃənt, B -ʃjənt] *s.* (med.) rubefaciente.
rubefaction [-'fækʃən] *s.* (med.) rubefacción.
rubella [ru'bɛlə] *s.* (med.) rubéola.
rubellite [-'bɛlˌaɪt, B 'rubəˌlaɪt] *s.* (min.) ruberita, cuprita.
rubeola [-'biələ, B ru-] *s.* (med.) 1. sarampión. 2. rubéola.
rubescence [ru'bɛsəns] *s.* rubescencia; sonrojo, rubor.
rubescent [-ənt] *a.* rubescente; sonrojado, enrojado; ruborizado.
rubiaceous [ˌrubɪ'eɪʃəs] *a.* (bot.) rubiáceo.
rubicelle ['rubɪˌsel] *s.* (min.) espinela.
Rubicon ['rubɪˌkɑn, B -kən] *s.* Rubicón, río de Italia, el cual cruzó César camino a Roma; **to cross the R.,** pasar el Rubicón, dar un paso decisivo.
rubicund ['rubɪkʌnd] *a.* rubicundo.
rubicundity [ˌrubɪ'kʌndətɪ] *s.* rubicundez.
rubidium [ru'bɪdɪəm] *s.* (quím.) rubidio.
rubiginous [-'bɪdʒənəs] *a.* (bot., zool.) rubiginoso.
rubious ['rubɪəs] *a.* (raro) rojo, de color rubí.
ruble ['rubəl] *s.* (numis.) rublo.
rubric ['rubrɪk] *s.* 1. rúbrica, rótulo, epígrafe. 2. título, encabezamiento (de un capítulo o de una ley); letra inicial. 3. (relig.) rúbrica. 4. precepto, regla.
rubrical [-brɪkəl] *a.* 1. de rúbrica. 2. escrito o impreso en rojo.
rubricate [-ˌkeɪt] *v.t.* 1. marcar o distinguir con rojo. 2. poner como rúbrica o epígrafe. 3. proveer de rúbricas. 4. ordenar en rúbricas.
rubus ['rubəs] *s.* (bot.) rubo.
ruby ['rubɪ] *s.* (*pl.* RUBIES) 1. rubí. 2. color de rubí. 3. (impr., G.B.) tipo ágata. —*a.* de color de rubí. —*v.t.* enrojecer, rubificar; arreglar.
ruby grass, (bot.) hierba natal, ilusión.
ruby silver ore, (min.) 1. plata roja oscura, pirargirita. 2. plata roja clara, prustita.
ruby spinel, (min.) rubí espinela.
ruche [ruʃ] *s.* (cost.) ruche, volante rizado; golilla, lechuguilla.
ruching ['ruʃɪŋ] *s.* tejido adecuado para hacer ruches o volantes.
ruck [rʌk] *s.* 1. multitud, muchedumbre; masa, aglomeración; pelotón (esp. de competidores o caballos fuera de carrera). 2. arruga; fruncido, pliegue. —*v.t., v.i.* arrugar(se), fruncir(se), plegar(se).
rucksack ['rʌkˌsæk, B 'rʊk-] *s.* mochila, morral.
ruckus ['rʌkəs] *s.* (jer.) tumulto, alboroto, zacapela, tole tole.
ruction ['rʌkʃən] *s.* (fam.) alboroto, vocerío, estrépito, bullicio; trifulca.
rudder ['rʌdər, B -ə] *s.* 1. timón (de buques); timón de dirección (de aviones). 2. (fig.) norma, guía.
rudderfish [-ˌfɪʃ] *s.* (ict.) chopa.
rudder pedals, (avia.) pedales del timón, pedales de mando del timón.
rudderpost [-ˌpoʊst] *s.* (mar.) 1. vástago del timón, mecha del timón. 2. contracodaste; falso codaste; codaste de popa o popel.
rudderstock [-ˌstɑk, B -ˌstɔk] *s.* (mar.) vástago del timón, mecha del timón.
rudder trunk, (mar.) rancho de Santa Bárbara.
ruddle ['rʌdəl] *s.* rojo, ocre rojo, almagre. —*v.t.* teñir de rojo.
ruddock ['rʌdək] *s.* (orn.) petirrojo, pechicolorado europeo.
ruddy ['rʌdɪ] *a.* (RUDDIER; RUDDIEST) 1. rojizo (díc. de la luz, fuego, cielo, etc.). 2. rosada, rubicunda (la cara); vigoroso (salud, juventud, etc.). 3. (jer., G.B.) maldito, infame; cabal, completo (mentira, error, etc.).

rude [rud] *a.* 1. rudo, crudo, tosco, primitivo. 2. rudo, grosero, descortés, ofensivo. 3. riguroso, crudo (el tiempo, clima, etc.). 4. vigoroso, fuerte. 5. aproximado, aproximativo (cálculo, evaluación, etc.). 6. **to be r. to,** tratar con descortesía.

rudely [ˈrudlɪ] *adv.* 1. rudamente, groseramente. 2. crudamente, toscamente.

rudeness [-nəs] *s.* 1. rudeza, crudeza, tosquedad. 2. rudeza, rigor (del tiempo, clima, etc.). 3. rudeza, descortesía.

rudesby [ˈrudzbɪ] *s.* (ant.) hombre rudo; tosco.

rudiment [ˈrudəmənt] *s.* 1. (*pl.*) rudimentos (de una ciencia o arte). 2. (biol.) rudimento, embrión.

rudimental [ˌrudəˈmɛntəl] *a.* rudimental, rudimentario.

rudimentarily [-ərəlɪ] *adv.* rudimentariamente.

rudimentary [-ərɪ] *a.* 1. rudimentario, elemental. 2. (biol.) rudimentario, embrionario.

rue [ru] *v.t.* lamentar, sentir; arrepentirse, sentir, deplorar. —*s.* 1. desilusión, desengaño; arrepentimiento, pesar. 2. (esco.) compasión.

rueful [ˈrufəl] *a.* 1. arrepentido, apesarado, desconsolado, triste. 2. lamentable, deplorable, lastimoso.

ruefully [-fəlɪ] *adv.* con pesar, desconsoladamente, tristemente, apesaradamente.

ruefulness [-fəlnəs] *s.* pesar, desconsuelo, tristeza.

rufescence [ruˈfɛsəns] *s.* rojez, rojura.

rufescent [-ənt] *a.* (zool.) rojizo.

ruff [rʌf] *s.* 1. (cost.) gorguera, gola, golilla, escarola. 2. (zool.) collarín de plumas o de pelo. 3. (orn.) gallineta de collar, pavo marino. 4. (orn.) paloma de moño, paloma moñuda. 5. (bridge) fallada. 6. (ant.) juego de naipes similar al whist. —*v.t., v.i.* (bridge) fallar.

ruffed [rʌft] *a.* de collar, que tiene gorguera o collarín.

ruffed grouse, (orn.) bonasa americana.

ruffian [ˈrʌfɪən] *s.* bellaco, rufián. —*a.* brutal, cruel.

ruffianism [-ˌɪzəm] *s.* bellaquería, rufianería, brutalidad.

ruffianly [-lɪ] *a.* bellaco, rufianesco, arrufianado, malvado.

ruffle [ˈrʌfəl] *v.t.* 1. (cost.) fruncir (un volante), plegar, doblar, alechugar. 2. encrespar, erizar (pluma, cabello, etc.). 3. ajar, arrugar. 4. descomponer, desordenar, revolver. 5. (fig.) encrespar, irritar, enfadar. 6. barajar (naipes). 7. dejar pasar, pasar rápidamente (páginas de un libro, etc.). —*v.t.* 1. encresparse (olas, etc.). 2. irritarse, enfadarse; descomponerse (buena disposición, etc.). 3. rizarse, ondular (banderas, etc.). 4. baladronear, fanfarronear, darse aires (de). —*s.* 1. (cost.) volante plegado o fruncido. 2. encrespamiento; escarceo, rizo (del agua). 3. desorden, turbación. 4. desazón, enfado, enojo. 5. (mil.) tamborileo apagado y vibrante.

ruffler [ˈrʌflər, B -lə] *s.* 1. baladrón, fanfarrón. 2. turbador, alborotador. 3. (cost.) fruncidor (en máquina de coser).

ruffly [-lɪ] *a.* fruncido, rizado.

ruff pigeon, (orn.) paloma de moño, paloma moñuda.

rufous [ˈrufəs] *a.* rufo, bermejo, leonado.

rug [rʌg] *s.* 1. alfombra, tapiz; tapete. 2. manta.

ruga [ˈrugə] *s.* (*pl.* RUGAE [-ˌgaɪ]) (*ú. esp. en pl.*) arruga, pliegue, repliegue (de la piel).

rugate [-ˌgeɪt] *a.* arrugado, rugoso.

Rugby [ˈrʌgbɪ] *s.* (dep.) rugby.

rugged [ˈrʌgəd] *a.* 1. áspero, escarpado, escabroso, abrupto. 2. duro, austero, severo; desapacible; malhumorado, arisco. 3. tosco, basto; rudo, crudo. 4. robusto, vigoroso, fuerte, resistente.

ruggedly [-lɪ] *adv.* rudamente, ásperamente.

ruggedness [-nəs] *s.* 1. aspereza, escabrosidad. 2. robustez, fuerza, resistencia.

rugger [ˈrʌgər, B -ə] *s.* (fam., G.B.) rugby.

rugose [ˈruˌgoʊs] *a.* 1. arrugado. 2. (bot.) rugoso.

rugosely [-lɪ] *adv.* 1. con arrugas. 2. (bot.) rugosamente, en forma rugosa.

rugosity [ruˈgɑsətɪ, B -ˈgɔs-] *s.* rugosidad.

Ruhmkorff coil [ˈrumˌkɔrf-, B -ˌkɔf-] (fís.) carrete de Ruhmkorff, bobina o carrete de inducción.

ruin [ˈruən, B ˈrʊ-] *s.* 1. ruina. 2. (*gen. pl.*) ruinas, escombros; restos, vestigios. 3. edificio, casa ruinosa. 4. **to bring to r.,** arruinar; **to be the r. of,** causar la ruina de; **to lie in ruins,** estar en ruinas. —*v.t.* arruinar; **r. oneself,** arruinarse, perder (el buen nombre, la reputación). —*v.i.* 1. convertirse en una ruina. 2. arruinarse. 3. precipitarse, derrumbarse.

ruinate [-əˌneɪt] *v.t.* arruinar, demoler, destruir. —*a.* arruinado, demolido, destruido.

ruination [ˌruəˈneɪʃən, B ˌrʊ-] *s.* arruinamiento, ruina; perdición.

ruined [ˈruənd, B ˈrʊ-] *a.* arruinado (esp. económica o moralmente).

ruinous [-ənəs] *a.* 1. ruinoso, destructivo, desastroso, fatal, funesto. 2. ruinoso, en ruinas.

ruinously [-lɪ] *adv.* ruinosamente.

ruinousness [-nəs] *s.* 1. estado ruinoso. 2. efecto ruinoso.

rule [rul] *s.* 1. regla, norma, pauta, precepto, guía. 2. costumbre, rutina. 3. gobierno, autoridad, dominio; régimen, reinado, imperio. 4. regla (para trazar), metro recto; línea recta. 5. reglas, código de disciplina (observado por órdenes religiosas). 6. (der.) resolución, disposición; precepto, dirección, dispositivo, reglamento. 7. (impr.) raya, filete. 8. (ant.) conducta, comportamiento. 9. **as a r.,** por regla general, de costumbre, por lo general; **by r.,** en regla; **hard and fast rule,** fórmula rígida; **standing r.,** regla establecida (de procedimiento); **to be the r.,** ser la regla; **to make a r. of (doing), to make it a r. to (do),** hacerse una regla de. —*v.t.* 1. gobernar, mandar, regir, dominar. 2. dirigir, guiar. 3. (der.) fallar, determinar, decidir, disponer. 4. rayar, cubrir de líneas o rayas. 5. **r. out,** excluir, descartar, desechar; eliminar; hacer imposible, hacer evitar, impedir; **r. over,** gobernar, regir. —*v.i.* 1. gobernar, mandar. 2. prevalecer, estar en boga. 3. (der.) establecer una regla, pronunciar o dictar un fallo, emitir una resolución o una sentencia.

rule of false position, (mat.) regla de falsa posición.

rule of law, (el) imperio de la ley.

rule of three, (mat.) regla de tres, regla de oro o de proporción.

rule of thumb, cálculo primitivo; método práctico, regla empírica.

ruler [ˈrulər, B -lə] *s.* 1. soberano, gobernador, mandatario. 2. regla (para trazar líneas).

rulership [-ˌʃɪp] *s.* oficio o función de un gobernante o mandatario; soberanía; gobierno, reinado; imperio.

ruling [ˈrulɪŋ] *s.* 1. (der.) resolución, decisión. 2. rayado. —*a.* 1. predominante, prevaleciente, imperante, corriente. 2. predilecto, predominante (interés, ocupación, etc.).

rum [rʌm] *s.* 1. ron. 2. (E.U.) licor, bebida alcohólica. —*a.* (fam., pr. G.B.) raro, extraño, singular, ej., *r. customer,* tipo raro.

Rumania [ruˈmeɪnjə] *s.* Rumania.

Rumanian [-njən] *a.* rumano. —*s.* 1. rumano, natural de Rumania. 2. (idioma) rumano.

rumba [ˈrʌmbə, ˈrum-, B ˈrʌm-] *s.* rumba (baile de origen cubano).

rumble [ˈrʌmbəl] *v.i.* 1. retumbar. 2. rugir, sonar (las tripas). 3. hablar en voz grave, gruñir, murmullar. 4. (con *along, by, past,* etc.) avanzar o pasar con estruendo. —*v.t.* 1. (t. con *out, forth,* etc.), decir en voz grave. 2. (jer.) descubrir, darse cuenta de, percatarse de. —*s.* 1. ruido sordo, retumbo. 2. rugido (de las tripas). 3. (aut.) asiento trasero descubierto. 4. (jer.) rumor, runrún. 5. (jer.) pelea callejera. 6. (mec.) tambor de limpieza, tambor de rotación. 7. (aut.) picado de la biela.

rumbler [-blər, B -blə] *s.* (mec.) tambor de limpieza, tambor de rotación.

rumble seat, (aut.) asiento trasero descubierto.

rumbling [-blɪŋ] *a.* retumbante. —*s.* retumbo, ruido sordo.

rumen [ˈrumən, B -mɛn] *s.* (*pl.* RUMINA [-mənə]) (zool.) rumen.

ruminant [-mənənt] *a.* 1. (zool.) rumiante. 2. (fig.) meditabundo, pensativo. —*s.* (zool.) rumiante.

ruminate [ˈruməˌneɪt] *v.t., v.i.* (lit., fig.) rumiar.

rumination [ˌruməˈneɪʃən] *s.* 1. rumia, rumiación, rumiadura. 2. (fig.) meditación, reflexión.

ruminative [ˈruməˌneɪtɪv, B -nət-] *a.* 1. rumiador, rumiante. 2. (fig.) meditador, meditativo, meditabundo.

rummage [ˈrʌmɪdʒ] *s.* 1. búsqueda desordenada, revuelta, trastorno. 2. mescolanza. 3. venta de artículos donados con fines caritativos. —*v.t.* 1. registrar, buscar en, examinar, revolver. 2. (t. con *out* o *up*) hallar, desenterrar. —*v.i.* hacer una búsqueda; **r. through,** explorar, escudriñar, examinar.

rummager [-ər, B -ə] *s.* inspector, registrador (esp. de aduana).

rummage sale, venta de prendas usadas (a veces, con fines benéficos).

rummer [ˈrʌmər, B -ə] *s.* copa o vaso altos.

rummy [ˈrʌmɪ] *a.* (fam.) (RUMMIER; RUMMIEST) raro, extraño. —*s.* 1. borracho. 2. un juego de naipes.

rumor, (pr. G.B.) **rumour** [ˈrumər, B -mə] *s.* rumor, runrún, chisme. —*v.t.* divulgar, propalar; **it is rumored,** se dice, se rumorea.

rumormonger [-ˌmʌŋgər, -ˌmɑŋ-, B -ˌmʌŋgə] *s.* chismoso.

rump [rʌmp] *s.* 1. rabadilla, obispillo (de ave); anca o grupa (de caballo); cuarto trasero, nalgas, cadera (de vaca). 2. resto, retazo.

rumple [ˈrʌmpəl] *v.t.* 1. arrugar, ajar, chafar (la ropa). 2. desgreñar (los cabellos). —*s.* arruga, pliegue, doblez.

rumply [-plɪ] *a* (RUMPLIER; RUMPLIEST) 1. arrugado, ajado, chafado (ropa). 2. desgreñado (cabellos).

rumpot [ˈrʌmˌpɑt, B -ˌpɔt] *s.* (jer.) borrachón.

rumpus [ˈrʌmpəs] *s.* (fam.) bataola, tole tole; alboroto, tumulto; **to raise a r.,** armarla, armar la de San Quintín.

rumpus room, sala de juegos, sala de recreo, cuarto de juegos (en una casa).

rumrunner [ˈrʌmˌrʌnər, B -ə] *s.* contrabandista de licor.

rumrunning [-ɪŋ] *s.* contrabando de licor.

run [rʌn] *v.i.* (*pret.* RAN [ræn]; *p.p.* RUN; *p.pr.* RUNNING) 1. correr. 2. galopar (caballo). 3. escapar, fugarse, huir. 4. andar de prisa, apresurarse. 5. correr, competir, participar (en carreras); ocupar (cierto) lugar, llegar, ej., *r. second,* ocupar el segundo lugar (en carrera); llegar segundo. 6. (gen. con *for*) contender, disputar, postular, presentarse (para oficio, candidatura, etc.). 7.

moverse, pasar; transcurrir, correr; deslizar; rodar, girar; dar vueltas; marchar, andar, funcionar. 8. (teat.) estar en escena; ser representado continuamente, ej., *the play ran fifty nights,* la obra se ha representado continuamente durante cincuenta noches. 9. extenderse, alcanzar, llegar (la vista) hasta; remontarse (memoria). 10. (con *from, to* o *between*) ir y venir, transitar. 11. derretirse, liquidarse. 12. manar, brotar, fluir, correr. 13. correrse, emborracharse (color, vela, etc.). 14. soltarse, deshacerse, correrse los puntos (en mallas, medias, etc.). 15. correr, ir, extenderse (en cierta dirección); continuarse, seguir siendo. 16. rezar, decir (un texto, pasaje en libro, etc.). 17. circular, estar en vigencia, tener curso. 18. migrar, andar en cardúmenes (peces). 19. **r. about,** deambular, andar de una a otra parte; retozar (niños); **r. across,** atravesar corriendo; dar o tropezar con; **r. after,** ir tras de, perseguir; rondar; **r. against,** tropezar con; competir como contrario u oponente de otro esp. en elecciones; desfavorecer; ser contrario a; **r. aground,** (mar.) encallar, zabordar, embarrancarse, varar; **r. along,** ¡vete!; **r. around with,** asociarse con; **r. at,** arremeter, acometer; **r. at the nose,** destilarle la nariz a uno; **r. away,** huir, escapar, fugarse; zafarse; desbocarse (caballo); ganar fácilmente (en carrera); **r. away with,** fugarse con (persona, botín, etc.); arrebatar; dejarse arrastrar por, adoptar precipitadamente (idea, noción, etc.); **r. back,** regresar corriendo; **r. back over,** recapitular (el pasado, etc.); **r. by,** ser conocido por, pasar por (cierto nombre); **r. cold,** (fig.) helarse (la sangre); **r. down,** quedarse sin cuerda (reloj), dejar de funcionar (máquina); debilitarse, desgastarse; **r. dry,** secarse, desecarse; **r. for,** correr en busca de; presentar su candidatura para, postular; **r. for it,** (jer.) darse a la fuga, correr para librarse; **r. high,** exaltarse (ánimos), intensificarse (las pasiones); **r. in,** entrar al pasar (para corta visita); trabarse en combate cuerpo a cuerpo; **r. in the family,** venir de familia; **r. into,** ir a parar en, topar, chocar contra; encontrarse con, tropezar con; llegar a, alcanzar (suma, ediciones, etc.); continuarse con; **r. low,** escasear, estar escaso; **r. off,** irse de prisa, escaparse; derramarse, salirse, descorrer (un líquido); **r. off at the mouth,** (jer.) hablar demasiado (esp. indiscretamente); **r. on,** versar sobre; hablar sin cesar; pasar (el tiempo); seguir funcionando; ligarse (caligrafía); (impr.) ir seguido (nueva oración en la misma línea en que termina otra); **r. out,** salir corriendo; agotarse, acabarse (existencias); llegar a su término, expirar (periodo, plaza, etc.); escurrirse, derramarse (líquido); ir largándose, ir soltándose (cordel, cable, etc.); salir, sobresalir; **r. out on,** dejar plantado, desertar; **r. out** (o **short**) of, quedarse sin, acabársele a uno; **r. over,** pasar por encima de, atropellar; rebosar, derramarse; **r. round,** rodear; **r. through,** pasar por; examinar por encima, leer a la ligera, dar una ojeada, repasar (un escrito); disipar, desperdiciar (en corto tiempo); **r. to,** acudir a; ascender a (importe, número, etc.); alcanzar, bastar para; inclinarse a, propender a; **r. to help,** acudir en ayuda (de); **r. together,** confluir, unirse; **r. up,** crecer rápidamente; aumentar, subir (precio, deuda, etc.); llegar segundo (en carrera); **r. up against,** tropezar con (dificultad, obstáculo, etc.); **r. up and down,** correr de una parte a otra; **to cut and r.,** (jer.) huir al instante, fugarse precipitadamente. —*v.t.* 1. correr, hacer correr; mover, accionar; manejar, dirigir, gobernar, ej., *r. a steamer,* gobernar un buque a vapor, *r. a business,* manejar un negocio. 2. recorrer, cubrir (camino, distancia); seguir (línea, curso, ruta); pasar por, pasar encima de. 3. correr en, participar en; inscribir en (carrera, competencia), ej., *r. a race,* correr o participar en una carrera, *r. a horse,* correr un caballo (en carrera), *r. a candidate,* inscribir a un candidato. 4. trazar, marcar. 5. llevar, transportar, ej., *r. messages,* llevar recados. 6. publicar (noticia, novela por entregas, etc. en un periódico). 7. introducir, conducir, meter, ej., *he ran the firm into debt,* metió la firma en deudas. 8. exponerse a, correr (riesgo, peligro, etc.). 9. exhibir (película en cine, etc.). 10. hilvanar, bastear (tela). 11. fundir, moldear (balas, etc.). 12. marcar una serie de (tantos, puntos). 13. **r. a blockade,** burlar un bloqueo; **r. a chance of being,** tener posibilidad de ser (elegido, nombrado, etc.); **r. a temperature,** tener fiebre; **r. cattle,** pastar el ganado; **r. down,** atropellar (automóviles); dar caza a, dar alcance a; alcanzar, encontrar (al cabo de una búsqueda); rajar de, poner lengua en, desprestigiar, difamar, vilipendiar; gastar (la salud), debilitar (el cuerpo); (mar.) embestir y echar a pique; **r. errands,** hacer mandados; **r. in,** hacer funcionar (máquina o motor nuevos) para que se asiente, rodar; (fam.) detener, meter en la cárcel; (impr.) insertar, poner de seguido (en texto); **r. its course,** seguir su curso; **r. off,** recitar o tocar sueltamente (verso, pieza musical, etc.); escurrir, sacar (líquido); (dep.) resolver (empate) en carrera decisiva; (impr.) tirar (copias, ejemplares); **r. on,** (impr.) poner de seguido (inserción); **r. out,** dar carrete a, largar (cordel, cable, etc.); sacar (cañón) por la tronera; (fam.) expulsar, echar (de un club, comunidad, etc.); **r. over,** repasar, revisar, recapitular; atropellar (con vehículo); **r. the rapids,** salvar los rabiones, bajar los rápidos; **r. the gantlet,** correr baquetas, pasar por baquetas; (fig.) soportar severas críticas; **r. the show,** (jer.) llevar la voz cantante (en alguna empresa); **r. the streets,** golfear, callejear (como pilluelo); **r. through,** pasar por; leer por encima, examinar a la ligera (un escrito); atravesar (con arma blanca); tachar, tildar (palabra, escrito, etc.); **r. up,** acumular rápidamente (suma, deuda); subir (precio); obligar a mejorar; **r. whisky (rum,** etc.), comerciar en whiski (ron, etc.) de contrabando. —*s.* 1. corrida, carrera; viaje, (corta) excursión, vuelta, paseo; visita; ej., *we had a good r.,* tuvimos una buena corrida (en caza de zorros); tuvimos un viaje (o travesía) agradable, *a r. to Boston,* una corta excursión o visita a Boston. 2. curso, rumbo, dirección; tendencia, marcha (regular), ej., *the r. of the market was favorable,* la tendencia (o marcha del mercado) fue favorable. 3. serie, periodo, racha; tramo (continuo), cadena, continuación, ej., *a r. of luck,* una racha de suerte. 4. demanda general e insistente, ej., *there was a r. on the banks,* los clientes asediaron a los bancos, *a r. on gold,* una gran demanda de oro. 5. tipo, clase, grupo. 6. carrera, rotura (en medias, etc.). 7. cardumen, arribazón. 8. pasto, corral, ej., *poultry-r.,* corral de aves, gallinero, *sheep-r.,* pasto de ovejas. 9. libre uso, libre acceso. 10. caz o saetín de madera (para conducir agua). 11. (mús.) carrerilla, pasaje rápido (en escala). 12. (mar.) racel, delgado (de un buque). 13. (dep.) serie (de puntos); carrera (en béisbol). 14. at a r., corriendo; **in the long r.,** a la larga; **the common r. of men,** el común de las gentes; **to be on the r.,** estar de fuga; ajetrearse; **to have a r. for one's money,** obtener alguna satisfacción por el dinero o esfuerzo gastados; divertirse en proporción al gasto. —*a.* 1. derretido (miel, mantequilla, etc.). 2. desteñido. 3. agotado, jadeante. 4. de contrabando.

runabout [ˈrʌnəˌbaʊt] *s.* 1. vagabundo. 2. carrera descubierta. 3. (aut.) coche liviano; torpedo de dos plazas. 4. lancha pequeña de motor.

runagate [-əˌgeɪt] *s.* (ant.) fugitivo, prófugo; vagabundo.

runaround [-əˌraʊnd] *s.* (jer.) evasiva maliciosa, medios evasivos; **to give (someone) the r.,** hacer falsas promesas a (alguien para eludir una obligación, etc.).

runaway [-əˌweɪ] *s.* 1. fugitivo, prófugo. 2. caballo desbocado. 3. desbocamiento. —*a.* 1. fugitivo, huidizo, huidor. 2. decisivo, amplio, abrumador, holgado, ej., *a r. victory,* un triunfo holgado. 3. (com.) incontrolable, galopante, ej, *r. inflation,* inflación galopante.

runcible spoon [ˈrʌnsəbəl-] tenedor pequeño (para entremés, postre, etc.).

runcinate [ˈrʌnsəˌneɪt, B -nɪt] *a.* (bot.) runcinado.

rundle [ˈrʌndəl] *s.* 1. peldaño, escalón, grada. 2. (mar.) campana (de cabrestante).

rundlet [-dlət] *s.* 1. (G.B.) pequeño barril (de diferentes medidas). 2. medida antigua de 68 litros.

run-down [ˈrʌnˈdaʊn] *a.* 1. agotado, debilitado. 2. ruinoso, maltrecho. 3. parado, sin cuerda (díc. de un reloj).

rundown [-ˌdaʊn] *s.* informe detallado; resumen, sumario, gen. oral.

rune [run] *s.* 1. runa. 2. antigua poesía finlandesa o nórdica. 3. magia, misterio.

rung [rʌŋ] *s.* 1. peldaño, travesaño (de escalera); rayo (de rueda); travesaño (de silla). 2. (ant., esco.) garrote, estaca, porra.

rung [rʌŋ] *pret., p.p. de* **ring.**

runic [ˈrunɪk] *a.* 1. rúnico, runo. 2. misterioso, mágico.

run-in [ˈrʌnˌɪn] *s.* 1. (impr.) inserción; intercaladura (en un texto). 2. (jer., E.U.) reyerta, encuentro.

runlet [-lət] *s.* arroyuelo.

runlet [-lət] *var. de* **rundlet.**

runnel [-əl] *s.* arroyuelo, riachuelo, riacho.

runner [ˈrʌnər, B -ə] *s.* 1. corredor. 2. mensajero, recadero. 3. caballo de carreras. 4. contrabandista. 5. patín (del trineo); cuchilla (del patín). 6. pasacaminos, alfombra continua. 7. camino (de mesa). 8. carrera, punto o hilo corrido (en medias). 9. (bot.) rastrera, trepadora. 10. (ict.) especie de jurel. 11. (mec.) roldana (de tractor de oruga). 12. (impr.) carril guía (de prensa). 13. (G.B., hist.) alguacil, oficial de policía.

runner bean, (pr. G.B., bot.) judía de España, judía escarlata.

runner-up [-əˌrʌp] *s.* (dep.) corredor, jugador o equipo que llega en segundo lugar; subcampeón.

running [ˈrʌnɪŋ] *s.* 1. dirección, manejo, administración, conducción. 2. corrida. 3. funcionamiento. 4. contrabando. 5. **in the r.,** en carrera (con posibilidades de ganar); **out of the r.,** fuera de carrera (sin posibilidades de ganar). —*a.* 1. corredor (caballo). 2. corriente, continuo (comentario, ritmo, etc.). 3. corredizo, movedizo (terreno, etc.). 4. corrido, linear (medida). 5. de carrera. 6. cursivo, corrido (escritura, lectura). 7. corredizo (lazo, nudo). 8. (med.) supurante. 9. (com.) abierto, flotante (póliza de seguro); a plazo indeterminado, de vencimiento indefinido (contrato, arriendo, etc.). —*adv.* consecutivamente, continuamente, seguido, ej., *she had headaches for five days r.,* tuvo dolores de cabeza por cinco días seguidos.

running board, estribo (de un coche o automóvil), larguero.
running bowline, (mar.) nudo de ahorcaperros.
running expenses, gastos corrientes.
running fight, (mar.) combate en retirada.
running fire, (G.B.) fuego graneado, fuego a discreción.
running gate, bebedero de orificio alimentador (de un molde).
running gear, tren de rodaje, tren rodante.
running hand, letra (escritura) corrida.
running head, r. headline, (impr.) título de página, título corrido, titulillo.
running knot, nudo corredizo.
running light, luz de situación, luz de marcha, luz de navegación (de un barco o avión).
running mate, 1. pareja (caballo que corre sólo para ayudar al otro en una carrera). 2. (pol.) compañero, candidato de fórmula (para un puesto subalterno), esp. (E.U.) candidato para la vicepresidencia. 3. (fam.) compañero constante.
running rail, riel de recorrido, carril maestro.
running rigging, (mar.) jarcias de labor.
running title, (impr.) título de página, titulillo.
running track, 1. (f.c.) vía principal, vía de corrido. 2. (dep.) pista de recorrido.
running water, agua corriente.
runny ['rʌnɪ] *a.* 1. que gotea, que chorrea o destila (ej., díc. de la nariz). 2. corredizo, movedizo (terreno, pantano, etc.).
runoff ['rʌnˌɔf] *s.* 1. escurrimiento; afluencia, aflujo (de aguas de superficie que se vierten en corrientes). 2. carrera final.
runoff election, votación de desempate.
run-of-the-mill [ˌrʌnəvðə'mɪl] *a.* (fam.) corriente, común, mediocre.
run-on ['rʌnˌɔn, -ˌɑn, B -ˌɔn] *s.* (impr.) texto seguido, texto puesto de seguido. —*a.* (impr.) seguido, puesto de seguido (a un texto).
run-over [-'oʊvər, B -və] *a.* (impr.) de pase, de traslado.
runover [-ˌoʊvər, B -və] *s.* (impr.) paso, continuación, salto, alcance.
runt [rʌnt] *s.* 1. animal diminuto (más pequeño que los de su especie). 2. (fig.) gorgojo, redrojo, enano. 3. tocón; tallo (de una planta).
run-through ['rʌnˌθru] *s.* (fam.) 1. ensayo, práctica. 2. lectura rápida, lectura superficial.
runtiness ['rʌntɪnəs] *s.* falta de desarrollo, pequeñez.
runty [-ɪ] *a.* falto de desarrollo, enano, pequeño.
runway ['rʌnˌweɪ] *s.* 1. lecho, madre, cauce. 2. senda, sendero; vía, camino. 3. (aer.) pista de despegue y aterrizaje.
runway light, farol de pista, baliza.
rupee [ru'pi] *s.* rupia, unidad monetaria de la India, Pakistán, etc.
rupestrian [ru'pɛstrɪən] *a.* rupestre, relativo a las rocas.
rupestrine [-trən] *a.* (biol.) rupícola, que vive en las rocas.
rupiah [ru'piə] *s.* rupia, unidad monetaria de Indonesia.
rupicolous [ru'pɪkələs] *a.* (biol.) rupícola.
rupture ['rʌptʃər, B -tʃə] *s.* 1. rompimiento, ruptura, rotura, desgarradura. 2. (fig.) ruptura (de relaciones amistosas, etc.). 3. (med.) hernia, quebradura. —*v.t., v.i.* romper(se), quebrar(se), rajar(se), desgarrar(se); **r. oneself,** (med.) quebrarse, hacerse una hernia.
ruptured [-tʃərd, B -tʃəd] *a.* 1. fracturado, roto; quebrado. 2. (med.) quebrado, herniado (ej., apéndice).
rural ['rʊrəl, B 'rʊər-] *a.* rural, rústico, campesino, campestre, agrícola.
rural free delivery, distribución gratuita del correo en regiones rurales.
ruralism [-ˌɪzəm] *s.* 1. rusticidad, rustiquez, rustiqueza. 2. palabra o frase rústica.
ruralist [-əst] *s.* 1. granjero, campesino. 2. partidario de la vida rural.
rurality [rʊr'æləti, B rʊər-] *s.* (*pl.* RURALITIES) 1. rusticidad, rustiquez, rustiqueza. 2. característica rural; cosa o escena rústica.
ruralization [ˌrʊrələ'zeɪʃən, B ˌrʊərəlaɪ-] *s.* adaptación a la vida rural.
ruralize ['rʊrəˌlaɪz, B 'rʊər-] *v.t., v.i.* volver(se) rural.
rurally [-əlɪ] *adv.* ruralmente.
ruse [rus, B ruz] *s.* artificio, truco, ardid, astucia, artimaña.
rush [rʌʃ] *s.* 1. prisa, precipitación, apuro (Am.), ej., *there's no r. about it,* no corre prisa, no hay ningún apuro para eso. 2. embestida, acometida, arremetida, embate. 3. ajetreo. 4. (con *on, for*) demanda, requerimiento (del consumidor). 5. torrente (de agua); aflujo (de sangre, etc.); afluencia (de compradores, etc.). 6. agolpamiento (de gente). 7. (cine) primera copia (de un film) que se hace después de filmada una escena (para la inspección del director, etc.). 8. (rugby) corrida, carrera, avance (con el balón en la mano). 9. (bot.) junco, junquera. 10. **in a r.,** apresuradamente, con urgencia; **with a r.,** a chorros, ej., *the water came out with a r.,* el agua salió a chorros. —*v.i.* 1. correr, correr de prisa, precipitarse. 2. correr o afluir rápidamente (agua, sangre, etc.). 3. **r. about,** correr por todas partes, dar vueltas de un lado a otro; **r. back,** regresar corriendo; **r. forward,** lanzarse adelante, precipitarse; **r. in (out),** entrar (salir) precipitadamente; **r. through,** hacer o leer de prisa, ejecutar apresuradamente. —*v.t.* 1. embestir, acometer, arremeter. 2. apremiar, apurar (Am.). 3. acelerar, precipitar. 4. tomar de asalto, capturar de golpe. 5. (fam.) cortejar, galantear insistentemente (a una mujer). 6. (rugby) llevar (el balón) en corridas. 7. **r. through,** impulsar, hacer ejecutar apresuradamente; **to be rushed,** que debe ser apremiado o apurado (Am.).
rush-bottomed chair ['rʌʃ'bɑtəmd-, B -'bɔt-] silla con asiento de junco o de enea.
rush candle, vela hecha de junco y sebo.
rushee [ˌrʌʃ'i] *s.* estudiante universitario popular (solicitado y buscado por una fraternidad estudiantil universitaria).
rush hour, hora de máxima o mayor afluencia (de tránsito y habitantes) de una ciudad.
rushlight ['rʌʃˌlaɪt] *s.* 1. vela de junco. 2. (fig.) luz débil, luz trémula.
rush mat, estera de junco o esparto.
rushy ['rʌʃɪ] *a.* 1. juncino. 2. juncoso (terreno).
rusk [rʌsk] *s.* bizcocho, tostada; galleta dulce.
russet ['rʌsət] *s.* 1. (hist.) paño rústico gen. de color bermejo. 2. color bermejo. 3. (bot.) variedad de manzana. —*a.* bermejo, castaño.
Russia ['rʌʃə] *s.* Rusia.
Russia leather, cuero de Rusia (usado para encuadernaciones).
Russian ['rʌʃən] *a., s.* ruso.
Russian dressing, salsa rusa, aderezo para ensaladas.
Russianize [-ˌaɪz] *v.t.* rusificar.
Russian olive, (bot.) acebuche, olivastro.
Russian thistle, (bot.) barrilla de borde.
Russian wolfhound, galgo ruso, borzoi.
russify ['rʌsəˌfaɪ] *v.t.* (*pret., p.p.* RUSSIFIED; *p.pr.* RUSSIFYING) rusificar.
Russophile [-ˌfaɪl] *a., s.* rusófilo.
Russophobe [-ˌfoʊb] *a., s.* rusófobo.
Russophobia [ˌrʌsə'foʊbɪə] *s.* rusofobia.
rust [rʌst] *s.* 1. orín, moho, herrumbre. 2. color rojizo (del orín). 3. (bot.) roya, tizón. 4. (fig. ant.) ociosidad, inacción. —*v.t., v.i.* 1. oxidar(se), enmohecer(se), aherrumbrar(se). 2. volver(se) rojizo. 3. (fig.) deteriorar(se), corromper(se), echarse a perder por el ocio o la indolencia.
rustic ['rʌstɪk] *a.* 1. rústico, campesino, pastoril, rural. 2. simple, sencillo; tosco, ordinario, zafio, rudo; burdo, inculto, palurdo. 3. (const.) de juntas rebajadas, de aristas biseladas (junta). —*s.* 1. rústico, campesino; persona sencilla. 2. tosco, palurdo, patán.
rustical [-tɪkəl] *a., s.* rústico.
rustically [-kəlɪ] *adv.* rústicamente.
rusticate [-tɪˌkeɪt] *v.i.* 1. rusticar; volverse rústico. —*v.t.* (G.B.) 1. suspender (en una universidad). 2. volver rústico. 3. (const.) construir con juntas de aristas biseladas, biselar con juntas rebajadas.
rustication [ˌrʌstɪ'keɪʃən] *s.* rusticación.
rusticity [-'tɪsətɪ] *s.* rusticidad, rustiquez; desmaña, torpeza.
rustic joint, (const.) junta de aristas biseladas.
rustic work, 1. mampostería de aristas biseladas o de juntas rebajadas. 2. objetos hechos de madera al natural.
rustily ['rʌstəlɪ] *adv.* con herrumbre.
rustiness [-tɪnəs] *s.* 1. oxidación, estado oxidado. 2. rojura, color rojizo. 3. ronquedad, bronquedad. 4. (fig.) carácter anticuado.
rustle ['rʌsəl] *v.i.* 1. susurrar, murmurar (las hojas, etc.), crujir (seda, etc.). 2. moverse con energía o rapidez, trafagar. 3. (E.U.) robar ganado. —*v.t.* 1. hacer susurrar o crujir. 2. forrajear. 3. (E.U.) robar o hurtar (ganado). 4. **r. up,** (fam.) lograr conseguir, reunir apresuradamente. —*s.* susurro, crujido.
rustler ['rʌslər, B -lə] *s.* 1. trafagón, buscavidas. 2. (E.U.) abigeo, ladrón de ganado, cuatrero. 3. hombre emprendedor y activo.
rustproof ['rʌstˌpruf] *a.* inoxidable, a prueba de orín o de herrumbre.
rusty ['rʌstɪ] *a.* (RUSTIER; RUSTIEST) 1. oxidado, herrumbrado, herrumbroso, mohoso. 2. rojizo. 3. ronco, bronco (sonido, voz). 4. (fig.) anticuado. 5. (fig.) falto de práctica. 6. deslustrado (esp. traje negro). 7. (pr. dial.) terco, testarudo, tozudo, obstinado; rebelde.
rut [rʌt] *s.* 1. rodada, carrilada, surco, rodera, releje. 2. (fig.) rutina, costumbre; sendero trillado, camino de siempre. 3. brama, celo (de animales). —*v.t.* 1. hacer rodadas o surcos en. 2. cubrir a la hembra (animal en celo). —*v.i.* estar en celo (animales).
rutabaga [ˌrutə'beɪgə] *s.* (bot.) rutabaga, nabo de Suecia.
rutaceous [ru'teɪʃəs] *a.* (bot.) rutácea.
ruth [ruθ] *s.* 1. piedad; compasión, conmiseración, misericordia. 2. dolor, tristeza; pesadumbre, aflicción; arrepentimiento.
ruthenic [ru'θɛnɪk] *a.* (quím.) ruténico.
ruthenious [-'θiniəs] *a.* (quím.) rutenioso.
ruthenium [-əm] *s.* (quím.) rutenio.
rutherford ['rʌðərfərd, B -əfəd] *s.* (fís. nuclear) rutherford (unidad de radioactividad).
ruthful ['ruθfəl] *a.* 1. piadoso, compasivo. 2. lastimero, lastimoso, lamentable.
ruthless [-ləs] *a.* cruel, despiadado, inhumano, insensible.
ruthlessly [-lɪ] *adv.* cruelmente, despiadadamente.

ruthlessness [-nəs] *s.* crueldad.
rutilant ['rutələnt] *a.* rutilante, brillante.
rutile ['ru,til, B -tɪl] *s.* (min.) rutilo.
ruttish ['rʌtɪʃ] *a.* toriondo, verriondo, salido en celo.
rutty ['rʌtɪ] *a.* lleno de rodadas.
R.V. *abrev. de* **Revised Version,** Versión Revisada (de la Biblia).
Ry. *abrev. de* **railway,** ferrocarril (f.c.).
rye [raɪ] *s.* 1. (bot.) centeno. 2. whiski de centeno. 3. (dial.) caballero (entre los gitanos).
rye bread, pan de centeno.
rye grass, (bot.) ballico.
rye whiskey, whiski de centeno.
ryot ['raɪət] *s.* campesino, agricultor, labrador, labriego (en la India).

S

S [ɛs] *s.* s, decimonovena letra del alfabeto inglés.
S *símb. de* **sulfur,** azufre (S).
S *abrev. de* **South,** sur (S.).
S.A. *abrev. de* 1. **South Africa,** África del Sur. 2. **South America,** Sudamérica.
Saba ['seɪbə, B 'sɑ-] *s.* (bíbl.) Saba, Sabá.
sabadilla [ˌsæbə'dɪlə] *s.* (bot.) cebadilla.
Sabaean [sə'biən] *a., s.* sabeo, de saba.
Sabbatarian [ˌsæbə'tɛrɪən, B -ˌtɛər-] *a., s.* sabatario, que guarda el sábado.
Sabbatarianism [-ˌɪzəm] *s.* sabatismo.
Sabbath ['sæbəθ] *s.* (bíbl.) 1. sabat. 2. día de descanso.
Sabbath school, escuela parroquial dominical (para educación religiosa).
sabbatic [sə'bætɪk] *a.* 1. sabático, sabatino. 2. de descanso.
sabbatical [-ɪkəl] *a.* sabático, sabatino. *—s.* 1. año sabático (de los profesores). 2. (*pl.*) traje dominguero.
sabbatical year, (relig., fig.) año sabático.
sabellian [sə'bɛlɪən] *a.* 1. sabélico (pueblo). 2. (teo.) sabeliano. *—s.* 1. (idioma) sabélico. 2. (teo.) sabeliano, sabeliana.
saber ['seɪbər, B -bə] *s.* 1. sable. 2. (*pl.*) compañía de caballería. 3. **the s.,** (fig.) la espada, la bota, fuerza o régimen militar. *—v.t.* (*pret., p.p.* SABERED O SABRED; *p.pr.* SABERING O SABRING) cortar o herir con sable, matar con sable.
saber rattling, (fig.) blandimiento de la espada, alardeo amenazador del poder militar.
saber-toothed ['seɪbərˌtuθt, B -bəˌ-] *a.* de colmillos largos y afilados.
saber-toothed tiger, (pal.) macairodo, tigre de dientes de sable.
sabin ['seɪbən] *s.* (son.) sabín, sabine, sabinio (unidad de absorción acústica).
Sabine ['seɪˌbaɪn, B 'sæbˌaɪn] *a., s.* (hist.) sabino.
sable ['seɪbəl] *s.* 1. (zool.) marta cibelina, marta cebellina. 2. (piel de la) marta cebellina. 3. (*gen. en pl.*) vestimenta de luto. 4. (her.) sable. 5. (pint.) pincel de pelo de cebellina. *—a.* (poét.) negro, obscuro.
sable antelope, (zool.) antílope negro.
sabot [sæ'boʊ, B 'sæboʊ] *s.* 1. zueco, almadreña. 2. (arm.) casquillo para el tiro con proyectiles de calibre reducido.
sabotage ['sæbəˌtɑʒ] *s.* sabotaje. *—v.t.* sabotear.
saboteur [ˌsæbə'tɜr, B -'tɜ] *s.* saboteador.
sabra ['sɑbrə] *s.* sabra, israelí de nacimiento.
sabre, *var. de* **saber.**
sabulous ['sæbjələs] *a.* arenoso, arenisco; (med.) sabuloso.
sac [sæk] *s.* (anat., bot., zool., orn.) saco.
SAC *abrev. de* **Strategic Air Command,** Mando Estratégico de las Fuerzas Aéreas.
sacaton ['sækəˌtoʊn] *s.* (bot.) zacatón.
saccate ['sækˌeɪt] *a.* (bot., zool.) saculiforme, en forma de saco o bolsa.
saccharase ['sækəˌreɪs] *s.* (quím.) sacarasa.
saccharate [-ˌreɪt, B -rɪt] *s.* (quím.) sacarato.
saccharic [sə'kærɪk] *a.* (quím.) sacárico.
saccharide ['sækəˌraɪd] *s.* (quím.) sacárido.
sacchariferous [ˌsækə'rɪfərəs] *a.* (quím.) sacarífero.
saccharification [səˌkærəfə'keɪʃən] *s.* sacarificación.
saccharify [-'kærəˌfaɪ] *v.t.* (*pret., p.p.* SACCHARIFIED; *p.pr.* SACCHARIFYING) sacarificar.
saccharimeter [ˌsækə'rɪmətər, B -ə] *s.* sacarímetro, sacarómetro.
saccharimetry [-trɪ] *s.* (quím.) sacarimetría.
saccharin ['sækərən] *s.* (quím.) sacarina.
saccharine [-rən, B -ˌraɪn] *a.* 1. sacarino. 2. (fig.) azucarado; meloso, empalagoso.
saccharinity [ˌsækə'rɪnətɪ] *s.* sabor sacarino.
saccharoid ['sækəˌrɔɪd] *a.* sacaroide.
saccharoidal [ˌsækə'rɔɪdəl] *a.* sacaroideo.
saccharomycete [-roʊ'maɪˌsit] *s.* (bot.) sacaromicetácea.
saccharomycetic [-maɪ'sitɪk, B -'set-] *a.* (bot.) sacaromicético.
saccharose ['sækəˌroʊs] *s.* sacarosa.
saccharous ['sækərəs] *a.* sacarino, azucarado.
saccular ['sækjələr, B -lə] *a.* sacular, en forma de saco.
sacculated [-leɪtəd] *a.* saculado.
sacculation [ˌsækjə'leɪʃən] *s.* saculación.
saccule ['sækjul] *s.* (med.) sáculo.
sacerdotal [ˌsæsər'doʊtəl, B -ə'-] *a.* sacerdotal, clerical.
sacerdotally [-əlɪ] *adv.* clericalmente, sacerdotalmente.
sacerdotalism [-əlˌɪzəm] *s.* 1. normas o prácticas sacerdotales. 2. clericalismo.
sachem ['seɪtʃəm] *s.* (E.U.) 1. cacique (de las tribus algonquinas). 2. síndico o gobernador de la sociedad política de Tammany.
sachet [sæ'ʃeɪ, B 'sæʃeɪ] *s.* sachet, perfumador, saco perfumado.
sack [sæk] *s.* 1. saco, costal, talega. 2. bolsa (de papel, etc.). 3. (t. **sacque**) saco; chaqueta. 4. (jer.) despedida, despido. 5. (jer.) cama. 6. **to get the s.,** (jer.) ser despedido; **to give (someone) the s.,** (jer.) despedir (a alguien); **to hit the s.,** (jer.) tumbarse, echarse en la cama; **s. time,** (jer.) hora de acostarse. *—v.t.* 1. ensacar, encostalar, empacar. 2. embolsar (dinero, ganancias). 3. (jer.) despedir, echar (empleado, etc.).
sack, *s.* 1. saqueo, saqueamiento, pillaje (de un pueblo). 2. (hist.) vino blanco y seco (importado a Inglaterra del S. de Europa). *—v.t.* saquear o pillar (un pueblo).
sackbut ['sækˌbʌt] *s.* (mús., hist.) 1. sacabuche medieval. 2. sambuca.
sackcloth [-ˌklɔθ] *s.* 1. arpillera, harpillera, rázago. 2. (hist.) cilicio. 3. **in s. and ashes,** (relig.) en túnica de penitente.
sack coat, chaqueta, americana, saco (Am.).
sacker [-ər, B -ə] *s.* saqueador.
sackful [-ˌfʊl] *s.* (*pl.* SACKFULS O SACKSFUL) (un) saco (lleno de) ej., *a s. of flour,* un saco (lleno de), harina.
sacking [-ɪŋ] *s.* tela para costales, harpillera, arpillera.
sack race, carrera de encostalados, carrera de sacos.
sacque [sæk] *s.* 1. (ant.) saco, abrigo holgado (de mujer). 2. ropón (para nene).
sacral ['seɪkrəl] *a.* 1. sacro, sagrado (precepto, ley, etc.); religioso, eclesiástico (autoridades, etc.). 2. ['sækrəl, B 'seɪ-] (anat.) sacro.
sacrament ['sækrəmənt] *s.* 1. sacramento. 2. **the S.,** (relig.) el sacramento eucarístico, el sacramento del altar. 3. **to take the s. upon,** (ant.) prometer bajo juramento (algo o hacer algo).
sacramental [ˌsækrə'mɛntəl] *s.* (relig.) sacramental. *—a.* sacramental.
sacramentally [-əlɪ] *adv.* sacramentalmente.
Sacramentarian [-ˌmɛn'tɛrɪən, B -'tɛər-] *a., s.* (relig.) sacramentario.
sacramentary [-'mɛntərɪ] *a.* sacramental. *—s.* (relig.) sacramentario.
sacrarium [sə'krɛrɪəm, B -'krɛər-] *s.* (*pl.* SACRARIA [-ɪə]) 1. (relig.) sagrario. 2. (hist.) santuario. 3. (arqueol.) capillita.
sacred ['seɪkrɔd] *a.* sagrado, sacro, santo.
sacred baboon, papión sagrado (venerado antiguamente por los egipcios).
sacred bean, (bot.) nelumbio.
sacred college, (relig.) Colegio de cardenales.
sacred cow, (fig.) vaca sagrada, persona, asociación o creencia por encima de toda crítica y prácticamente intocable.
sacredly [-lɪ] *adv.* sagradamente, santamente.
sacredness [-nəs] *s.* carácter sagrado, santidad.
sacred weed, (bot.) hierba sagrada.
sacrifice ['sækrəˌfaɪs] *s.* sacrificio; **at a s.,** con pérdida, por debajo del precio de coste; **at the s.** of, sacrificando. *—v.t.* 1. sacrificar, inmolar. 2. vender con pérdida (mercadería). *—v.i.* hacer sacrificios.
sacrificer [-ər, B -ə] *s.* sacrificador.
sacrificial [ˌsækrə'fɪʃəl] *a.* sacrificatorio, sacrificante, de sacrificio.
sacrificially [-əlɪ] *adv.* como (un) sacrificio.
sacrilege ['sækrəlɪdʒ] *s.* sacrilegio, profanación.
sacrilegious [ˌsækrə'lɪdʒəs] *a.* sacrílego.
sacrilegiously [-lɪ] *adv.* sacrílegamente.
sacrilegiousness [-nəs] *s.* carácter sacrílego.
sacring ['seɪkrɪŋ] *s.* (ant.) consagración (esp. de elementos sacramentales).
sacring bell, campanilla cuyo tañido anuncia la elevación en misa.
sacristan ['sækrəstən] *s.* (relig.) sacristán.
sacristy [-stɪ] *s.* sacristía.
sacroiliac [ˌsækroʊ'ɪlɪˌæk, ˌseɪkroʊ-, B ˌseɪkroʊ-] (anat.) *a.* sacroilíaco. *—s.* región sacroilíaca.
sacrosanct ['sækroʊˌsæŋkt] *a.* (gen. irón.) sacrosanto; sacratísimo; inviolable.
sacrosanctity [ˌsækroʊ'sæŋktətɪ] *s.* carácter sacrosanto.
sacrum ['sækrəm, 'seɪ-] *s.* (*pl.* SACRA [-krə]) (anat., zool.) sacro.
sad [sæd] *a.* (SADDER; SADDEST) 1. triste; melancólico, pesaroso. 2. lamentable, lastimoso. 3. bajo, apagado (colores). 4. (fam.) pésimo; detestable, abominable. 5. **s. to say,** desgraciadamente, la triste verdad es que.

sadden ['sædən] *v.t.* entristecer, acongojar, apenar, afligir. —*v.i.* entristecerse, acongojarse.
saddle ['sædəl] *s.* 1. silla de montar, montura; sillín (de bicicleta, motoneta, etc.). 2. asiento, soporte. 3. (mec.) silleta, caballete, silla, albardón. 4. (cocina) lomo, cuarto trasero (de una res). 5. soporte del muñón (en la cureña de los cañones). 6. depresión, garganta, paso, puerto (entre dos cimas). 7. parte posterior del espinazo (de las aves). 8. **in the s.,** en la silla; (fig.) en posición de mando. —*v.t.* 1. ensillar. 2. **s. with,** (fig.) cargar con, gravar con (responsabilidades, obligaciones, etc.).
saddleback [-ˌbæk] *s.* ensillada (en el lomo de una montaña).
saddlebag [-ˌbæg] *s.* alforja, bizaza, jaque, maletín de grupa.
saddlebow [-ˌboʊ] *s.* arzón delantero, fuste de la silla.
saddlecloth [-ˌklɔθ] *s.* sudadero (debajo de la silla de montar), mantilla de silla.
saddle horse, caballo de silla.
saddler ['sædlər, B -lə] *s.* sillero, talabartero.
saddle roof, tejado de dos gabletes, cubierta de dos aguas.
saddlery ['sædlərɪ] *s.* talabartería.
saddle soap, jabón para limpiar y acondicionar las pieles.
saddle sore, llaga causada por la fricción de la silla, en el jinete o la montura.
saddletree ['sædəlˌtri] *s.* 1. arzón, fuste de silla. 2. (bot.) tulipanero.
Sadduccan [ˌsædʒə'siən, B ˌsædjʊ-] *a.* (bíbl.) saduceo.
Sadducee ['sædʒəˌsi, B 'sædjʊ-] *s.* saduceo, saducea.
sadiron ['sædˌaɪərn, B -ˌaɪən] *s.* plancha maciza de hierro colado (para ropa).
sadism ['seɪˌdɪzəm, 'sæ-] *s.* sadismo.
sadist [-dəst] *a., s.* sádico.
sadistic [sə'dɪstɪk] *a.* sádico.
sadistically [-tɪkəlɪ] *adv.* sádicamente, con sadismo.
sadly ['sædlɪ] *adv.* 1. tristemente, melancólicamente. 2. lamentablemente.
sadness [-nəs] *s.* tristeza, melancolía.
sadomasochism [ˌseɪdoʊ'mæsəˌkɪzəm, ˌsæd-] *s.* (psic.) sadomasoquismo.
sad sack, simplón, desgraciado, esp. recluta inepto.
safari [sə'fɑrɪ] *s.* safari (expedición o caravana de caza esp. en el África Oriental). —*v.i.* participar en un safari.
safe [seɪf] *a.* 1. seguro, salvo; ileso, indemne, incólume; intacto. 2. fiel, leal, digno de confianza. 3. prudente, cauteloso; moderado (persona), ej., *a s. estimate,* un cálculo prudente. 4. inocuo, inofensivo. 5. **it is s. to say,** se puede decir sin temor a equivocarse; **is it s. to (do)?** ¿no es peligroso (hacer)?; **s. and sound,** sano y salvo; **s. from,** a salvo de; **to be on the s. side,** obrar sin riesgos, irse por lo seguro, tomar un márgen de seguridad; para mayor seguridad; **to be s.,** estar a salvo, estar en seguro; estar en un lugar seguro. —*s.* 1. caja fuerte, caja de caudales, caja de fierro (Am.). 2. condón, preservativo.
safeblower ['seɪfˌbloʊər, B -ə] *s.* ladrón que abre las cajas fuertes por medio de explosivos.
safe-conduct [-'kɑndʌkt, B -'kɔn-] *s.* 1. salvoconducto. 2. escolta de protección.
safecracker [-ˌkrækər, B -ə] *s.* ladrón de cajas fuertes.
safe-deposit [-dɪ'pɑzət, B -'pɔz-] *s.* cámara acorazada.
safe-deposit box, caja de seguridad.
safeguard ['seɪfˌgɑrd, B -ˌgɑd] *s.* 1. salvaguarda, guarda; amparo, escolta. 2. salvoconducto, carta de seguridad, garantía. 3. dispositivo de seguridad (para prevenir accidentes). —*v.t.* proteger, defender, poner a salvo, guardar, salvaguardar.
safekeeping [-'kipɪŋ] *s.* custodia, guarda, depósito.
safelight [-ˌlaɪt] *s.* (foto.) luz velada, luz para revelar.
safe load, (ing.) carga límite o admisible o de seguridad.
safely [-lɪ] *adv.* 1. sin peligro, sin riesgo, con seguridad. 2. sin accidentes, sin contratiempos, ej., *they s. reached the shore,* llegaron a la playa sin accidentes (o contratiempos). 3. tranquilamente, sin arriesgarse, sin lugar a dudas, sin exagerar, ej., *we can s. say that,* podemos decir sin lugar a dudas (o sin exagerar) que.
safe stress, (ing.) esfuerzo de trabajo, fatiga de seguridad.
safety ['seɪftɪ] *s.* 1. seguridad; inocuidad, indemnidad. 2. dispositivo de seguridad; seguro (en armas de fuego). 3. **s. first!** ¡seguridad ante todo!; **to reach s.,** ponerse a salvo. —*a.* de seguridad.
safety arch, (const.) arco de descarga.
safety belt, 1. (mar.) cinturón salvavidas. 2. cinturón de seguridad (en automóviles, aviones, etc.).
safety bolt, 1. cerrojo de seguridad. 2. pasador de seguridad (en cerraduras).
safety catch, 1. fiador, retén de seguridad. 2. seguro (en armas de fuego). 3. (joy.) pasador de seguridad.
safety chain, cadena de seguridad.
safety curtain, (teat.) telón de protección.
safety deposit box, caja de seguridad.
safety device, dispositivo de seguridad, aparato de seguridad.
safety factor, coeficiente de seguridad, factor de seguridad.
safety film, (foto.) película de seguridad.
safety fuse, mecha lenta, mecha de seguridad.
safety glass, cristal de seguridad, vidrio inastillable.
safety island, burladero, refugio (para peatones); isla o plataforma de peatones.
safety lamp, (min.) lámpara de seguridad.
safety lock, 1. cerradura de seguridad. 2. (arm.) seguro.
safety match, fósforo de seguridad; fósforo sueco.
safety outlet, (elec.) tomacorriente a tierra.
safety pin, imperdible, alfiler de gancho; (Col.) gancho; (Mex.) seguro.
safety rail, guardarriel.
safety razor, máquina de afeitar.
safety stop, mecanismo de parada o detención.
safety switch, (elec.) interruptor de seguridad.
safety valve, (mec.) válvula de seguridad.
safety zone, zona de seguridad, zona de peatones.
safflower ['sæfˌlaʊər, B -ə] *s.* 1. (bot.) alazor, cártamo, cártama, azafrán bastardo. 2. tinte de alazor.
saffron [-rən] *s.* 1. (bot.) azafrán, croco. 2. colorante o sazonador de azafrán. 3. color azafrán. —*a.* azafranado, de color de azafrán.
safranine [-rəˌnin, B -nən] *s.* (quím.) safranina.
safrole ['sæfˌroʊl] *s.* (quím.) safrol.
sag [sæg] *s.* 1. hundimiento; flexión (del techo), depresión (en la tierra), comba (de cables); pandeo (de muros). 2. (mar.) deriva. 3. baja (en la bolsa de valores). —*v.t.* (*pret., p.p.* SAGGED; *p.pr.* SAGGING) 1. hundirse; combarse (un cable). 2. (fig.) aflojarse, debilitarse, decaer (espíritu, salud o físico); ablandarse, colgar (los músculos, la carne). 3. (mar.) ir a la deriva, (esp. en) **s. to leeward,** derivar o abatir a sotavento. —*v.t.* hundir, deprimir.
saga ['sɑgə] *s.* saga, leyenda.
sagacious [sə'geɪʃəs] *a.* sagaz, perspicaz; ladino, astuto, sutil; agudo.
sagaciously [-lɪ] *adv.* sagazmente, perspicazmente; astutamente.
sagaciousness [-nəs] *s.* sagacidad, perspicacia, penetración; astucia.
sagacity [sə'gæsətɪ] *s.* sagacidad, perspicacia, penetración; astucia.
sagamore ['sægəˌmɔr, B -ˌmɔ] *s.* (E.U.) cacique inferior entre ciertas tribus de los indios de E.U.
sagapenum [ˌsægə'pinəm] *s.* sagapeno.
sage [seɪdʒ] *a.* 1. sabio. 2. cuerdo, juicioso (consejo, etc.). 3. (ant.) grave, solemne. —*s.* 1. sabio. 2. (bot.) salvia. 3. (bot.) artemisa.
sagebrush ['seɪdʒˌbrʌʃ] *s.* (bot.) artemisa, artemisia.
sage grouse, (orn.) especie de chachalaca (oriunda de los campos de artemisa del O. de E.U.).
sagely ['seɪdʒlɪ] *adv.* 1. sabiamente. 2. cuerdamente, juiciosamente, sensatamente.
sageness [-nəs] *s.* 1. sabiduría. 2. cordura, sensatez.
saggar, sagger ['sægər, B -ə] *s.* (cerá.) gaceta (caja refractaria para cocer la loza).
sagittal ['sædʒətəl] *a.* (anat.) sagital.
sagittaria [ˌsædʒə'tɛrɪə, B -'tɛər-] *s.* (bot.) saetilla, sagitaria.
Sagittarius [-ɪəs] *s.* (astr.) Sagitario.
sagittate ['sædʒəˌteɪt] *a.* (bot.) sagitado.
sago ['seɪgoʊ] *s.* (bot.) sagú.
sago palm, (bot.) palmera sagú.
sag rod, (const.) barra atiesadora, tensor.
Sahara [sə'hærə, -'hɛrə, B -'hɑrə] *s.* Sahara.
Sahib ['sɑˌɪb, 'sɑhɪb] *s.* 1. sahib (título honorario en la India). 2. señor (tratamiento que se daba en el Oriente a los europeos).
said [sɛd] *pret., p.p. de* **say** . —*a.* (der.) antes mencionado, citado, antedicho.
Saigon [saɪ'gɑn, B -'gɔn] *s.* Saigón, capital de Vietnam del Sur.
sail [seɪl] *s.* 1. vela. 2. velas, velamen; veleros, velero. 3. aspa o vela (de molino). 4. viaje o paseo en velero; travesía. 5. aleta dorsal (de un pez vela); lámina (de un nautilo). 6. (poét.) ala. 7. **full s.,** a toda vela; **s. ho!** (mar.) ¡buque a la vista!; **to make s.,** alzar velas, desplegar las velas; **to set s.,** hacerse a la vela; **to shorten s.,** apocar las velas; **to strike s.,** arriar las velas; **to take in s.,** apocar las velas; (fig.) recoger velas; **under s.,** con las velas alzadas; navegando. —*v.i.* 1. viajar, navegar (en velero o buque). 2. darse a la vela; ir a la vela; zarpar, partir (buque). 3. deslizarse, flotar, planear (como un ave). 4. **s. in,** (fig.) entrar majestuosamente, hacer una entrada aparatosa (esp. mujeres); **s. into,** (jer.) regañar; caer encima de. —*v.t.* 1. dirigir o hacer navegar (un buque); maniobrar (un velero). 2. surcar (los mares, etc.).
sailboat ['seɪlˌboʊt] *s.* velero, buque de vela.
sailcloth [-ˌklɔθ] *s.* lona (para confeccionar velas, toldos, etc.).
sailer ['seɪlər, B -ə] *s.* velero (de cierto andar) ej., *she is a light s.,* un velero de andar ligero.
sailfish [-ˌfɪʃ] *s.* (ict.) pez vela, agujas, ojón.
sail flying, (avia.) vuelo de planeador, vuelo sin motor.
sailing ['seɪlɪŋ] *s.* 1. náutica, navegación. 2. zarpa, salida (de un barco). 3. (deporte de) la vela. 4. **clear s.,** (fig.) camino o curso fácil, cosa

fácil. —*a.* de vela; de o relativo a la navegación; **s. directions,** avisos o noticias marítimas; **sailing master,** piloto; **s. orders,** últimas instrucciones que se dan al capitán de un barco; **s. regatta,** regata de veleros.

sailing ship, s. vessel, buque velero.

sail locker, (mar.) pañol de velas.

sailmaker [-ˌmeɪkər, B -ə] *s.* velero (persona), fabricante de velas.

sailor [ˈseɪlər, B -ə] *s.* 1. marinero, marino. 2. canotier, canotié (sombrero de paja de copa plana). 3. **bad s.,** persona susceptible a mareos, que se marea en el mar.

sailor hat, canotier, canotié (sombrero de paja de copa plana).

sailoring [-ərɪŋ] *s.* marinería (el oficio y la afición).

sailor's-choice [ˈseɪlərzˈtʃɔɪs, B -əz-] *s.* (ict.) pagro o pargo pequeño; papel, besugo; ronco.

sailor's-knot [-ˌnɑt, B -ˌnɔt] *s.* 1. nudo en cruz. 2. (bot.) geranio silvestre.

sailor suit, traje de marinero (para niños).

sailplane [ˈseɪlˌpleɪn] *s.* (aer.) planeador, avión velero.

sail yard, (mar.) verga.

sain [seɪn] *v.t.* (dial. G.B., ant.) 1. persignar. 2. bendecir.

sainfoin [ˈseɪnˌfɔɪn, B ˈsæn-] *s.* (bot.) pipirigallo, esparceta.

saint [seɪnt] *s.* 1. (relig.) santo, santo canonizado. 2. (fig.) santo (persona buena, caritativa, sacrificada, etc.). —*a.* santo. —*v.t.* santificar, canonizar.

Saint Andrew's cross [-ˈændruz-, B sənt-] cruz en aspa, cruz de San Andrés.

Saint Anthony's cross [-ˈæntəniz-] (pr. G.B.) cruz de San Antonio, cruz en forma de T.

Saint Anthony's fire, (med.) fuego sacro, erisipela; ergotismo.

Saint Bernard [-bərˈnɑrd, B -bəˈnɑd] perro San Bernardo.

saintdom [ˈseɪntdəm] *s.* santidad.

sainted [-əd] *a.* 1. santo; santificado, canonizado, bendito; sagrado. 2. virtuoso, piadoso. 3. (raro) que está en el cielo (díc. de recién fallecidos).

Saint Elmo's fire, S.E.'s light [ˈɛlmoʊz-, B sənt-] fuego de Santelmo, santelmo.

Saint George's cross [-ˈdʒɔrdʒəz-, B -ˈdʒɔdʒɪz-] (her.) cruz griega.

sainthood [ˈseɪntˌhʊd] *s.* 1. santidad. 2. los santos (en conjunto), el coro de los santos.

Saint-John's-wort [-ˈdʒɑnzˌwɜrt, B -ˈdʒɔnzˌwɜt] *s.* (bot.) hierba de San Juan, hipérico; castellar, todabuena.

Saint John the Baptist, San Juan Bautista.

saintliness [ˈseɪntlɪnəs] *s.* santidad, santimonia.

saintly [-lɪ] *a.* (SAINTLIER; SAINTLIEST) santo; virtuoso, piadoso.

Saint Patrick's day [-ˈpætrɪks-, B sənt-] Día de San Patricio (el 17 de marzo, fiesta oficial de los irlandeses y de los descendientes de irlandeses en honor de San Patricio, patrón de Irlanda).

Saint-Peter's-wort [-ˈpitərzˌwɜrt, — B sənt-əzˌwɜt] *s.* (bot.) ásciro.

saintship [ˈseɪntˌʃɪp] *s.* santidad.

Saint-Simonian [-saɪˈmoʊnɪən, B sənt-] *a., s.* (hist., sociol.) sansimoniano.

Saint Valentine's Day, día de San Valentín, día de los enamorados (14 de febrero).

Saint Vitus' dance [ˈseɪntˈvaɪtəs-, -əsəz-, B sənt-] (med.) baile de San Vito, corea.

saith [sɛθ, ˈseɪəθ, B sɛθ] (ant.) *tercera per. sing. de* **say.**

saithe [seɪθ] *s.* (ict.) gado.

sake [seɪk] *s.* 1. motivo, razón, causa. 2. respeto, bien, amor. 3. **for art's s.,** por amor al arte; **for God's s.,** por Dios; **for my own s. as well as yours,** por mi propio bien tanto como por el de Ud.; **for my s.,** por mí; **for the s. of,** por el bien de, por consideración a, por respeto a; **for the s. of arguing, for argument's s.,** por el puro placer de discutir; **for the s. of argument,** para esclarecer el tema (de la discusión); **for your (his, etc.) s.,** por su bien, por consideración a Ud. (él, etc.).

sake, saki [ˈsɑkɪ] *s.* sake (bebida alcohólica japonesa).

saker [ˈseɪkər, B -kə] *s.* (orn.) sacre.

Sakhalin [ˈsækəˌlin, B ˌsækəˈlin] *s.* (geografía) Sajalín.

sal [sæl] *s.* (quím., farm.) sal.

salaam [səˈlɑm] *s.* zalema. —*v.i., v.t.* saludar con una zalema, hacer una zalema a.

salability [ˌseɪləˈbɪlətɪ] *s.* posibilidad de venta (de un artículo).

salable [ˈseɪləbəl] *a.* vendible, de venta fácil; comerciable, realizable.

salacious [səˈleɪʃəs] *a.* salaz, lujurioso, lascivo.

salaciously [-lɪ] *adv.* salazmente, lujuriosamente, lascivamente.

salaciousness [-nəs] *s.* salacidad, lascivia, lujuria.

salacity [-ˈlæsətɪ] *s.* salacidad, lujuria, lascivia.

salad [ˈsæləd] *s.* 1. ensalada. 2. verdura, hortaliza; esp. (E.U., dial.) lechuga.

salad bowl, ensaladera.

salad burnet, (bot.) pimpinela, sanguisorba.

salad days, (período de) juventud inexperta; días o época de pujanza.

salad dressing, aderezo, aliño o adobo para ensalada.

Saladin [ˈsælədən] *s.* (hist.) Saladino, héroe musulmán.

salamander [ˈsæləˌmændər, B -də] *s.* 1. (mitol., zool.) salamandra. 2. salamandra (hornillo portátil).

salamandrine [ˌsæləˈmændrən] *a.* salamandrino.

salami [səˈlɑmɪ] *s.* salame, salchichón de tipo italiano.

sal ammoniac, sal amoníaco, sal amoniaco.

salaried [ˈsælərɪd] *s.* 1. asalariado (personal, clase, etc.) 2. a sueldo, retribuido (empleo).

salary [-rɪ] *s.* (*pl.* SALARIES) sueldo, salario, estipendio, paga.

sale [seɪl] *s.* venta; **on s.,** en liquidación, a la venta a precios especiales; **for s.,** de venta, en venta; **to put up for s.,** ofrecer en venta.

saleable, *var. de* **salable.**

salep [ˈsæləp] *s.* salep, droga y alimento que se obtiene de ciertas orquídeas.

saleratus [ˌsæləˈreɪtəs] *s.* bicarbonato de soda, bicarbonato de potasa, bicarbonato sódico, potásico.

sales check, comprobante de venta, boleta, recibo de venta.

salesclerk [ˈseɪlzˌklərk, B -ˌklɑk] *s.* vendedor, dependiente de tienda.

salesgirl [-ˌgɜrl, B -ˌgɜl] *s.* vendedora, dependienta (de tienda).

Salesian [səˈliʒən] *a., s.* (relig.) 1. salesiano. 2. salesa.

saleslady [ˈseɪlzˌleɪdɪ] *s.* vendedora, dependienta (de tienda).

salesman [-mən] *s.* vendedor; corredor de comercio, viajante (de ventas); agente comercial; dependiente (de tienda).

salesmanship [-ˌʃɪp] *s.* arte y maña de vender.

sales promotion, (com.) promoción de ventas.

sales resistance, aversión a la propaganda (esp. comercial); resistencia del público a la publicidad.

salesroom [ˈseɪlzˌrum, -ˌrʊm] *s.* salón de ventas; salón de exhibición.

sales slip, talón de venta.

sales talk, arenga del vendedor, promoción de ventas, propaganda por parte del vendedor; (fig.) argumentos persuasivos.

sales tax, impuesto sobre la venta; impuesto de compraventa.

saleswoman [-ˌwʊmən] *s.* vendedora; dependienta (de tienda).

Salian [ˈseɪlɪən] *a.* 1. (hist.) salio, sálico. 2. (mitol.) salio (de un antiguo pueblo franco). —*s.* 1. salio (franco). 2. (mitol.) salio (de los sacerdotes de Marte).

Salic [ˈsælɪk] *a.* (hist.) sálico.

Salicaceae [ˌsælɪˈkeɪsɪi] *s. pl.* (bot.) salicáceas.

salicin [ˈsæləsən] *s.* (quím.) salicina.

Salic law, (hist.) ley sálica.

salicylate [səˈlɪsəˌleɪt] *s.* (quím.) salicilato.

salicylic [ˌsæləˈsɪlɪk] *a.* (quím.) salicílico.

salience [ˈseɪljəns] *s.* 1. prominencia. 2. rasgo, característica o punto sobresaliente.

saliency [-jənsɪ] *s., var. de* **salience.**

salient [-jənt] *a.* 1. saliente, saledizo, ej., *s. angle,* ángulo saliente. 2. prominente, sobresaliente, conspicuo; dominante, ej., *one's s. traits,* rasgos dominantes de uno. 3. saltarín, brincador. —*s.* (mil., fort.) saliente.

salientian [ˌseɪlɪˈɛntʃən, B -ˈɛnʃən] *a., s.* (zool.) anuro.

saliferous [səˈlɪfərəs] *a.* salífero.

salify [ˈsæləˌfaɪ] *v.t.* (*pret., p.p.* SALIFIED; *p.pr.* SALIFYING) (quím.) salificar; impregnar de sal o combinar con sal (una substancia).

salimeter [səˈlɪmətər, B -ə] *s.* salinómetro, pesasales.

salina [səˈlaɪnə] *s.* 1. marisma; saladar; charco artificial de agua de mar. 2. salina.

saline [ˈseɪˌlin, -ˌlaɪn, B -ˌlaɪn] *a.* salino. —[səˈlin, ˈseɪˌlin, B səˈlaɪn] *s.* 1. salina. 2. substancia salina; sal metálica. 3. (fisiol.) solución salina.

salinity [səˈlɪnətɪ] *s.* salinidad.

salinometer [ˌsæləˈnɑmətər, B -ˈnɔmɪtə] *s.* salinómetro, pesasal.

salipyrin [-ˌpaɪrən, B -ˈpaɪə-] **salipyrine** [-ˌrin] *s.* (med., quím.) salipirina.

Salisbury [ˈsɔlzˌbɛrɪ, B -bərɪ] *s.* Salisbury, capital de Rhodesia.

Salisbury steak, (cocina) albondigón, especie de bistec preparado con carne picada.

saliva [səˈlaɪvə] *s.* saliva.

salivary [ˈsæləˌvɛrɪ, B -vərɪ] *a.* (fisiol.) salival.

salivary glands, (anat.) glándulas salivales.

salivate [-ˌveɪt] *v.t.* hacer salivar. —*v.i.* salivar.

salivation [ˌsæləˈveɪʃən] *s.* salivación; (med.) salivación, tialismo.

sallet [ˈsælət] *s.* (arm.) celada.

sallow [ˈsæloʊ] *s.* (bot.) sauce europeo.

sallow, *a.* cetrino, pálido, amarillento. —*v.t.* poner cetrino.

sallowish [-ɪʃ] *a.* que tira a cetrino, aceitunado.

sallowness [-nəs] *s.* palidez, lividez.

sally [ˈsælɪ] *s.* (*pl.* SALLIES) 1. (mil.) salida, surtida. 2. paseo, excursión; caminata. 3. ímpetu, arranque. 4. salida, ocurrencia, humorada. 5. (arq.) saliente, saledizo. —*v.i.* (gen. con *out* o *forth*) 1. (mil.) hacer una salida. 2. salir con ímpetu; tener un arranque.

Sally Lunn [ˈsælɪˈlʌn] (G.B.) variedad de bollo dulce.

sally port, (fort.) surtida; poterna.
salmagundi [ˌsælmə'gʌndɪ] *s.* 1. salpicón, picadillo. 2. mezcolanza, revoltijo.
salmi ['sælmɪ] *s.* (fr.) guisado de caza asado y estofado en una salsa.
salmon ['sæmən] *s.* (*pl.* SALMON O SALMONS) salmón. —*a.* 1. de salmón. 2. salmonado; de color de salmón.
salmonberry [-ˌbɛrɪ] *s.* (bot.) especie de frambueso de flores rojas.
salmonella [ˌsælmə'nɛlə] *s.* salmonela (tipo de bacterias que producen varias clases de enfermedades en el hombre y en los animales).
salmonellosis [-ˌnɛl'oʊsəs] *s.* (med.) salmonelosis.
salmon pink, color salmonado, rosa salmón.
salmon trout, (ict.) trucha salmonada.
Salome [sə'loʊmɪ] *s.* (bíbl.) Salomé.
salon [sə'lɑn, B 'sælɔŋ] *s.* salón.
saloon [sə'lun] *s.* 1. salón, gran sala. 2. salón (literario, de artistas, etc.). 3. (E.U.) bar, taberna. 4. salón, galería. 5. (G.B.) (f.c.) coche salón; (aut.) sedán.
saloonkeeper [-ˌkipər, B -ə] *s.* (E.U.) tabernero, cantinero.
saloop [sə'lup] *s.* 1. salep. 2. bebida caliente hecha de salep o de sasafrás.
salp [sælp] **salpa** ['sælpə] *s.* (zool.) salpa, pámpano.
salpingian [sæl'pɪndʒɪən] *a.* (anat.) salpingiano.
salpingitis [ˌsælpən'dʒaɪtəs] *s.* (med.) salpingitis.
salpinx ['sælpɪŋks] *s.* (*pl.* SALPINGES [sæl'pɪndʒiz]) (anat.) salpinge.
salse [sæls] *s.* (geol.) salso, volcán de cieno.
salsify ['sælsəfɪ, -ˌfaɪ, B -fɪ] *s.* (bot.) salsifí.
sal soda, sal de sosa, carbonato de sosa, sal de barrillas.
salt [sɔlt] *s.* 1. sal. 2. (fig.) sal, agudeza, ingenio. 3. (fam.) marinero. 4. (quím.) sal. 5. (*pl.*) (med.) sal mineral; sal purgante; sales olorosas. 6. **not to be worth one's s.,** no valer uno el pan, ser deficiente; **old s.,** (fam.) marinero de gran experiencia; **the s. of the earth,** la sal de la tierra; (fig.) la gente mejor del mundo; **to take with a grain** (o **pinch**) **of s.,** aceptar o creer con reservas. —*a.* 1. salado (alimentos, agua, tierra). 2. curado en sal. 3. de sal (estatua, columna, etc.). —*v.t.* 1. salar, acecinar, curar con sal (carnes). 2. salar, sazonar o espolvorear con sal. 3. dar sal (al ganado). 4. poner mineral en (una mina) para aparentar yacimientos. 5. **s. away** (o **down**), conservar en sal (carnes); (fam.) reservar para uso futuro, ahorrar (dinero); **s. out,** precipitar (una substancia disuelta en una solución) añadiéndole sal; **smelling salts,** sales aromáticas.
SALT *abrev. de* **Strategic Arms Limitations Talks,** *s.* SALT.
saltant ['sæltənt] *a.* saltante, saltador, danzador.
saltarello [ˌsæltə'rɛloʊ] *s.* saltarelo, saltarel (danza italiana).
saltation [sæl'teɪʃən] *s.* 1. salto. 2. variación brusca, transición. 3. (biol.) mutación.
saltatorial [ˌsæltə'tɔrɪəl] *a.* de salto (s), para salto(s).
saltatory ['sæltəˌtɔrɪ, B -tətərɪ] *a.* 1. de saltar, de saltos. 2. saltador, saltarín (por ej. insecto). 3. (fig.) irregular, intermitente.
saltbush ['sɔltˌbʊʃ] *s.* (bot.) salado, barrilla, caramillo.
salt cedar, (S.O. de E.U., bot.) tamarisco.
saltcellar [-ˌsɛlər, B -ə] *s.* salero (de mesa).
salt content, salobridad.
salted ['sɔltəd] *a.* 1. salado. 2. (vet.) inmune (debido a enfermedad previa).
salter [-ər, B -ə] *s.* 1. salinero, fabricante de sal; negociante en salazones. 2. salador (de carne, pescado).
saltern [-ərn, B -ən] *s.* salina.
salt horse, (jer., mar.) cecina, tasajo.
saltier, *var.* **de saltire.**
saltigrade ['sæltəˌgreɪd] *a.* (zool.) saltígrado.
saltine [sɔl'tin] *s.* galleta salada.
saltiness ['sɔltɪnəs] *s.* salsedumbre, salobridad.
salting [-tɪŋ] *s.* 1. salazón, saladura. 2. (pr. G.B.) marisma.
saltire ['sɔlˌtaɪr, 'sæl-, B -ˌtaɪə] *s.* (her.) sotuer, sautor, aspa.
saltish ['sɔltɪʃ] *a.* un poco salobre, un poco salado, saladillo.
salt lick, salegar, salero, lamedero (lugar donde se reúnen los animales para lamer la sal de depósitos naturales).
salt marsh, saladar, salina.
salt of Saturn, sal de Saturno, sal de plomo.
salt pan, salina, recipiente para evaporar agua salada.
saltpeter, saltpetre ['sɔlt'pitər, B -ə] *s.* 1. nitro, salitre. 2. nitrato sódico, nitro de Chile, caliche.
saltpetrous [ˌsɔlt'pitrəs] *a.* salitroso, salitral; salitrado.
salt pit, saladar, hoyo de saladar.
salt pork, pella salada.
salt rheum, (med.) eczema.
salt shaker, salero.
salt spring, fuente de agua salada.
salt water, agua salada, agua salobre, agua de mar.
saltwater ['sɔltˌwɔtər, -ˌwɑt-, B -ˌwɔtə] *a.* de agua salada; marino.
saltworks [-ˌwɜrks, B -ˌwɜks] *s. pl.* salinas; refinerías de sal.
saltwort [-ˌwɜrt, B -ˌwɜt] *s.* (bot.) 1. almajo, almarjo, barrilla, salado, salicor, sosa, sapina. 2. caramillo, jijallo, sisallo; barreleta.
salty ['sɔltɪ] *a.* (SALTIER; SALTIEST) 1. salado; salobre. 2. (fig.) saleroso, ingenioso, picante, agudo (conversación, carácter, etc.).
salubrious [sə'lubrɪəs] *a.* salubre, saludable, sano.
salubriously [-lɪ] *adv.* saludablemente.
salubriousness [-nəs] *s.* salubridad, sanidad.
salubrity [-brətɪ] *s.* salubridad.
salutarily [ˌsæljə'tɛrəlɪ, B 'sæljʊtər-] *adv.* saludablemente.
salutariness ['sæljəˌtɛrɪnəs, B -tər-] *s.* carácter o efecto saludable.
salutary [-ˌtɛrɪ, B -tərɪ] *a.* 1. saludable, curativo, salutífero, ej., *s. exercise,* ejercicio saludable. 2. saludable, benéfico, útil, ej., *s. warning,* advertencia útil.
salutation [ˌsæljə'teɪʃən] *s.* salutación, saludación, saludo.
salutatorian [səˌlutə'tɔrɪən] *s.* (E.U.) estudiante que pronuncia el discurso de salutación (en las ceremonias de entrega de diplomas).
salutatory [-'lutəˌtɔrɪ, B -tərɪ] (E.U.) *s.* discurso de salutación (esp. en las universidades). —*a.* de salutación, de bienvenida; saludador.
salute [sə'lut] *v.t.* 1. saludar, dar la bienvenida a. 2. (mil., mar.) saludar. —*v.i.* hacer un saludo. —*s.* 1. saludo, salutación. 2. (mil., mar.) saludo, salva, ej., *a s. of seven guns,* una salva de siete cañonazos. 3. postura de saludo (de un soldado, policía, etc.). 4. triquitraque (cohete).
saluter [-ər, B -ə] *s.* saludador.
salvability [ˌsælvə'bɪlətɪ] **salvableness** ['sælvəbəlnəs] *s.* posibilidad de ser salvado o redimido.
salvable ['sælvəbəl] *a.* salvable, redimible.
Salvador ['sælvəˌdɔr, B -ˌdɔ] *s.* República de El Salvador.
Salvadoran [ˌsælvə'dɔrən] **Salvadorian** [-ɪən] *a., s.* salvadoreño.
salvage ['sælvɪdʒ] *s.* 1. salvamento (en el mar); derechos de salvamento, prima de salvamento. 2. mercaderías aseguradas rescatadas. —*v.t.* salvar, recuperar, recobrar (del mar, incendio, etc.).
salvation [sæl'veɪʃən] *s.* salvación.
salvational [-əl] *a.* de salvación, salvador.
Salvation Army, Ejército de Salvación (sociedad benéfica).
salve [sæv, sɑv, B sɑv] *s.* 1. ungüento, bálsamo; emplasto, bizma. 2. (fig.) bálsamo, remedio, alivio, consuelo. 3. (fig.) adulación, lisonja, halago. —*v.t.* 1. aquietar, calmar; aliviar, atemperar (conciencia, orgullo, etc.). 2. (ant.) ungir, untar.
salve [sælv] *v.t.* salvar, recuperar.
salve ['sælvɪ] *interj.* ¡salve! ¡salud!
salver [-vər, B -və] *s.* bandeja, salvilla.
salvia [-vɪə] *s.* (bot.) salvia.
salvo [-voʊ] *s.* 1. (*pl.* SALVOS) salvedad, reservación, excusa, pretexto, excepción, descargo. 2. (mil., mar.) salva, andanada, descarga simultánea (de varios cañones, etc.). 3. salva (de aplausos o aclamaciones).
Salzburg ['sɔlzˌbɜrg, 'sɑlz-, B 'sæltsˌbɜg] *s.* Salzburgo, ciudad de Austria, cuna de Mozart.
SAM *abrev. de* **surface-to-air missile,** misil tierra-aire.
samara ['sæmərə] *s.* (bot.) sámara.
Samaritan [sə'mærətən] *s., a.* (hist. y fig.) samaritano; **the good S.,** el buen Samaritano.
samarium [sə'mɛrɪəm, B -'mɛər-] *s.* (quím.) samario.
samarskite [-'mɑrˌskaɪt, B -'mɑˌ-] *s.* (min.) samarsquita.
samba ['sæmbə, 'sɑm-, B 'sæm-] *s.* samba (danza brasileña). —*v.i.* bailar samba.
sambar ['sɑmbər, 'sæm-, B 'sæmbə] *s.* (zool.) sambar (especie de ciervo asiático con cuello crinado).
sambo ['sæmboʊ] *s.* (despec. S. de E.U.) zambo; negro o mulato.
Sam Browne belt ['sæm'braʊn-] (mil.) cinturón de cuero sostenido por una correa que pasa sobre el hombro derecho.
sambuke ['sæmbjuk] *s.* (mús.) sambuca, instrumento antiguo.
sambur, *var. de* **sambar.**
same [seɪm] *a.* mismo, idéntico, igual; uniforme, semejante, monótono; **all the s.,** a pesar de todo; **at the s. time,** al mismo tiempo; **if it is the s. to you,** si le es a Ud. igual; **it is all the s. to me,** a mí me da lo mismo, me da igual, para mí es igual; **just the s.,** lo mismo, sin embargo; **much the s.,** casi lo mismo; **s. here,** (jer.) yo también; a mí también, para mí también; lo mismo para mí; **the s. as,** lo mismo que, igual que; **the s. old story,** el cuento eterno, lo de siempre. —*adv.* del mismo modo; igualmente. —*pron.* 1. el mismo, la misma persona. 2. (com.) la cosa o persona antes mencionada.
sameness ['seɪmnəs] *s.* 1. igualdad, identidad. 2. uniformidad, regularidad, monotonía.
samiel [səm'jɛl, B 'seɪmjəl] *s.* simún, viento del desierto.
samisen ['sæməˌsɛn] *s.* (mús.) samisén, instrumento japonés.
samite ['sæmˌaɪt] *s.* (tej.) jamete, tela suntuosa.
samlet [-lət] *s.* (ict.) esguín, murgón.
Samnite [-ˌnaɪt] *a., s.* (hist.) samnita, samnite.
Samoan [sə'moʊən] *a., s.* samoano.

Samothrace ['sæmə,θreɪs] *s.* (hist., geog.) Samotracia.
Samothracian [,sæmə'θreɪʃən] *a., s.* (hist.) samotracio.
samovar ['sæmə,vɑr, ˌsæmə'vɑr, B -'vɑ] *s.* samovar, recipiente de origen ruso para preparar el té.
Samoyed, Samoyede ['sæmə,jɛd, B ,sæmɔɪ'ɛd] *a.* samoyedo. —*s.* 1. samoyedo. 2. perro samoyedo.
Samoyedic [,sæmə'jɛdɪk, B -mɔɪ'ɛd-] *a.* samoyedo.
samp [sæmp] *s.* (E.U.) maíz molido grueso; potaje del mismo.
sampan ['sæm,pæn] *s.* (mar.) sampán, champán, tipo de barca oriental.
samphire [-,faɪr, B -,faɪə] *s.* (bot.) 1. perejil de mar, perejil marino, hinojo marino, empetro. 2. almajo, almarjo, almajo salado, alacranera.
sample ['sæmpəl, B 'sɑm-] *s.* muestra, modelo; espécimen. —*v.t.* 1. gustar, probar, catar (vinos, manjares, etc.). 2. sacar o tomar una muestra de. 3. hojear (libros), leer a la ligera (literatura, etc.).
sample book, muestrario.
sample copy, ejemplar de muestra (de un libro, etc.).
sampler [-plər, B -plə] *s.* 1. probador, catador (persona). 2. sacamuestras, muestradora. 3. muestrario.
sampler, *s.* modelo de bordado, dechado, marcador.
sample room, salón de muestras, salón de exhibición.
sampling [-plɪŋ] *s.* 1. muestra, pedazo o ejemplar de muestra. 2. cateo, catadura; escandallo, cata, cala.
Samson ['sæmsən] *s.* (bíbl.) Sansón.
samurai ['sæmə,raɪ] *s.* (*pl.* SAMURAI) samurai, antiguo guerrero japonés.
sanatarium [,sænə'tɛrɪəm, B -'tɛər-] *var. de* **sanatorium.**
sanative ['sænətɪv] *a.* sanativo, curativo.
sanatorium [,sænə'tɔrɪəm] *s.* (*pl.* SANATORIUMS O SANATORIA [-ɪə]) sanatorio.
sanatory ['sænə,tɔrɪ, B -tərɪ] *a.* sanador, curativo, curador.
sanbenito [,sænbə'nitoʊ] *s.* (hist.) sambenito.
sanctification [,sæŋktɪfə'keɪʃən] *s.* santificación.
sanctified ['sæŋktɪ,faɪd] *a.* 1. santo, sin pecado. 2. santurrón, beato, mojigato, cucufato (Am.).
sanctifier [-,faɪər, B -ə] *s.* santificador.
sanctify [-,faɪ] *v.t.* (*pret., p.p.* SANCTIFIED; *p.pr.* SANCTIFYING) 1. sanctificar, consagrar. 2. justificar, sancionar.
sanctimonious [,sæŋktə'moʊnɪəs] *a.* santurrón, beato, mojigato, gazmoño, santón.
sanctimoniously [-lɪ] *adv.* con mojigatería, santurronamente.
sanctimoniousness [-nəs] *s.* santurronería, beatería, mojigatería.
sanctimony ['sæŋktə,moʊnɪ, B -mə-] *s.* 1. santurronería, mojigatería. 2. (ant.) santidad.
sanction ['sæŋkʃən] *s.* 1. sanción, ratificación, confirmación, aprobación, autorización. 2. sanción, pena, castigo. 3. (ant.) decreto, mandato. —*v.t.* sancionar.
sanctity [-tətɪ] *s.* 1. santidad, santimonia. 2. inviolabilidad. 3. (*pl.*) obligaciones u objetos sagrados.
sanctuary [-tʃʊ,ɛrɪ, B -tjʊərɪ] *s.* (*pl.* SANCTUARIES) 1. santuario (en iglesias). 2. (fig.) santuario, asilo, refugio. 3. **to seek s.,** buscar asilo; **to take s.,** acogerse a sagrado; **to violate the s.,** violar el asilo.
sanctum [-təm] *s.* (*pl.* SANCTUMS O SANCTA [-tə]) 1. lugar sagrado. 2. (gen. hum.) cuarto privado o favorito.
sanctum sanctorum [-,sæŋk'tɔrəm] (bíbl.) sanctasanctórum.
Sanctus ['sæŋktəs] *s.* (relig., mús.) sanctus.
sand [sænd] *s.* 1. arena. 2. (*pl.*) arenales; playas, bajío. 3. (jer.) valentía, resolución, valor. 4. **the sands are running out,** los momentos de gracia se están acabando; **to build on s.,** edificar sobre arena. —*v.t.* 1. enarenar, arenar. 2. mezclar con arena. 3. enjugar con arenilla (escrito). 4. polvorear. 5. enarenar, rellenar con arena (puertos). 6. lijar.
sandal ['sændəl] *s.* 1. sandalia, zapatilla. 2. cinta para sujetar pantuflas o zapatillas. 3. abarca.
sandaled, sandalled [-dəld] *a.* calzando sandalias.
sandalwood [-dəl,wʊd] *s.* (bot.) sándalo (árbol y madera).
sandarac [-də,ræk] *s.* 1. (min.) sandáraca, rejalgar. 2. (quím.) sandáraca (resina).
sandarac tree, (bot.) tuya articulada, arar, alerce africano.
sandbag ['sænd,bæg] *s.* 1. saco de arena; saco terrero. 2. cachiporra (llena) de arena. —*v.t.* (*pret., p.p.* SANDBAGGED; *p.pr.* SANDBAGGING) 1. proteger con sacos de arena; reforzar con sacos de arena (refugio, dique, etc.). 2. atacar o golpear con cachiporra de arena. 3. (fig.) obligar, inducir (contra la voluntad). 4. (jer., E.U.) engañar, e.g. *he was sandbagging me,* no estaba jugando a tope, para engañarme. —*v.i.* no jugar a tope para engañar.
sandbagger [-ər, B -ə] *s.* salteador (que ataca a sus víctimas con una cachiporra llena de arena).
sandbank [-,bæŋk] *s.* banco de arena, encalladero, bancal.
sandbar [-,bɑr, B -,bɑ] *s.* banco de arena.
sandblast [-,blæst, B -,blɑst] *s.* 1. chorro de arena. 2. chorreadora de arena. —*v.t.* pavonar o limpiar con un chorro de arena.
sand-blind [-,blaɪnd] *a.* (ant.) cegato, miope, débil de vista.
sandbox [-,bɑks, B -,bɔks] *s.* 1. cajón de arena (en que juegan los niños). 2. (f.c.) arenero. 3. salvadera.
sandbox tree, (bot.) jabillo, árbol del diablo.
sandbur, sandburr [-,bɜr, B -,bɜ] *s.* (bot.) hierba mora, solano negro.
sand-cast [-,kæst, B -,kɑst] *v.t.* (metal.) fundir en molde de arena.
sand casting, pieza fundida en arena.
sand crack, (vet.) fisura en el casco (del caballo).
sand dollar, (zool.) erizo de mar aplanado.
sand dredger, draga aspirante.
sand dune, médano, duna.
sander ['sændər, B -də] *s.* 1. chorreadora de arena. 2. (f.c.) arenero. 3. lijadora.
sanderling [-lɪŋ] *s.* (orn.) chorlito blanco.
sand flea, (ento.) nigua, pique (Am.).
sand fly, (ento.) mosquito simúlido.
sandglass ['sænd,glæs, B -,glɑs] *s.* reloj de arena, ampolleta.
sandhi ['sændɪ, 'sɑn-, B 'sæn-] *s.* (fon.) sandhi.
sandhog ['sænd,hɔg, -,hɑg, B -,hɔg] *s.* (jer.) trabajador en cajón hidráulico.
sandiness ['sændɪnəs] *s.* estado arenoso.
sanding machine [-dɪŋ-] máquina lijadora, máquina pulidora.
sandlot ['sænd,lɑt, B -,lɔt] *s.* solar (terreno entre edificios).
sandman [-,mæn] *s.* personaje de un cuento que hace dormir a los niños con su arena mágica.
sandpaper [-,peɪpər, B -pə] *s.* papel de lija, papel abrasivo. —*v.t.* lijar.
sand pile, (const.) pilote de arena.
sandpile [-,paɪl] *s.* montón de arena.
sandpiper [-,paɪpər, B -pə] *s.* (orn.) lavandera, aguzanieves.
sandpit ['sænd,pɪt] *s.* mina de arena, cantera de arena.
sand pump, bomba desarenadora o para arena; cubeta sacalodo.
sandsoap [-,soʊp] *s.* jabón arenoso (para limpieza).
sandstone [-,stoʊn] *s.* (min.) arenisca.
sandstorm [-,stɔrm, B -,stɔm] *s.* tempestad de arena.
sand trap, (golf.) hoyo de arena (como obstáculo).
sandwich ['sænd,wɪtʃ, B 'sænwɪdʒ] *s.* emparedado, sandwich. —*v.t.* intercalar, insertar (entre cosas diferentes).
sandwich board, cartelones de anuncios (que se cuelgan del pecho y espalda de un hombre).
sandwich man, hombre sandwich, hombre-anuncio.
sandwort ['sænd,wɜrt, B -,wɜt] *s.* (bot.) arenaria.
sandy ['sændɪ] *a.* 1. arenoso, arenisco. 2. del color de la arena (cabellos).
sane [seɪn] *a.* cuerdo, sensato; razonable, en sus cabales.
sanely ['seɪnlɪ] *adv.* cuerdamente, sensatamente.
saneness [-nəs] *s.* cordura, sensatez.
Sanforized (TM) ['sænfə,raɪzd] *a.* sanforizado (díc. de un proceso industrial a que se somete la fibra de algodón).
sang [sæŋ] *pret. de* **sing.**
sangaree ['sæŋgə'ri] *s.* sangría, bebida hecha con vino y frutas.
sangfroid [,sæŋ'frwɑ, B 'sɑŋ-] *s.* (fr.) sangre fría, ecuanimidad.
sanguinaria [,sæŋgwə'nɛrɪə, B -'nɛər-] *s.* (bot., farm.) sanguinaria.
sanguinarily [-'nɛrəlɪ, B 'sæŋgwɪnər-] *adv.* sanguinariamente, cruelmente.
sanguinariness [-ɪnəs] *s.* carácter sanguinario.
sanguinary ['sæŋgwə,nɛrɪ, B -nərɪ] *a.* 1. sanguinario. 2. sanguíneo.
sanguine ['sæŋgwən] *a.* 1. sanguíneo, sanguinoso. 2. confiado, esperanzado, optimista. 3. sanguino, sanguíneo (complexión, color). 4. sanguinario, sangriento. —*s.* 1. color sanguíneo. 2. (med.) plétora.
sanguinely [-lɪ] *adv.* 1. confiadamente, con mucho optimismo. 2. sanguinariamente, sangrientamente.
sanguineness [-nəs] *s.* gran optimismo.
sanguineous [sæn'gwɪnɪəs, B sæŋ-] *a.* 1. sanguino, sanguíneo, rojo, bermejo. 2. sangriento, sanguinario. 3. (med.) sanguíneo; pletórico.
sanguinity [-ətɪ] *s.* (fig.) gran optimismo.
sanguinolent [-ələnt] *a.* sanguinolento, sangriento.
Sanhedrin [sæn'hidrən, B 'sænɪd-] *s.* (bíbl.) sanedrín.
sanicle ['sænɪkəl] *s.* (bot.) sanícula.
sanidine ['sænə,din] *s.* (min.) sanidina.
sanies ['seɪnɪ,iz] *s.* (*pl.* SANIES) (med.) sanies, sanie.
sanious [-əs] *a.* (med.) sanioso, icoroso.
sanitarian [,sænə'tɛrɪən, B -'tɛər-] *a., s.* sanitario.
sanitarily [-'tɛrəlɪ, B 'sænɪtər-] *adv.* de modo sanitario, sanitariamente, higiénicamente.
sanitarium [-ɪəm, B ,sænɪ'tɛər-] *s.* (*pl.* SANITARIUMS O SANITARIA [-ɪə]) *var. de* **sanatorium.**

sanitary ['sænə,terɪ, B -tərɪ] *a.* sanitario, higiénico.
sanitary belt, cinturón higiénico femenino.
sanitary cordon, (mil.) cordón sanitario.
sanitary corps, (mil.) cuerpo de saneamiento.
sanitary engineer, ingeniero sanitario.
sanitary engineering, ingeniería sanitaria.
sanitary napkin, paño higiénico, compresa higiénica.
sanitary towel, (G.B.) toalla higiénica, compresa higiénica, paño higiénico.
sanitate ['sænə,teɪt] *v.t.* proveer de instalaciones sanitarias, sanitizar.
sanitation [,sænə'teɪʃən] *s.* saneamiento, medidas sanitarias; higiene pública.
sanitize ['sænə,taɪz] *v.t.* hacer sanitario.
sanity ['sænətɪ] *s.* cordura, sensatez, juicio; **to lose one's s.,** perder el juicio.
San José [,sænə'zeɪ, B -'hoʊ-] *s.* San José, capital de Costa Rica.
San Jose scale [B 'sænhoʊ,zeɪ-] (ento.) cochinilla de San José.
sank [sæŋk] *pret. de* **sink.**
sans [sænz] *prep.* sin.
San Salvador [sæn'sælvə,dɔr, B -,dɔ] *s.* San Salvador, capital de El Salvador.
Sanscrit, *var. de* **Sanskrit.**
sans-culotte [,sænskjʊ'lɑt, B -'lɔt] *s.* (fig.) revolucionario, extremista.
Sanskrit ['sæn,skrɪt] *s., a.* sánscrito.
sans serif, (impr.) tipo grotesco, tipo abastonado, tipo antiguo, tipo gótico.
Santa Claus ['sæntə'klɔz] San Nicolás, Papá Noel (Am.) (que trae regalos a los niños).
Santa Maria tree ['sæntəmə'riə-, B 'sɑn-] (bot.) calaba, calambuco.
Santiago [,sæntɪ'ɑgoʊ] *s.* Santiago, capital de Chile.
Santo Domingo [,sæntədə'mɪŋgoʊ] *s.* Santo Domingo, capital de la República Dominicana.
santonica [sæn'tɑnɪkə, B -'tɔn-] *s.* (bot., farm.) santónico, semencontra.
santonin ['sæntənən] *s.* (quím., farm.) santonina.
sap [sæp] *s.* 1. savia. 2. (fig.) savia, vigor; vitalidad. 3. cachiporra. 4. (jer.) pelele, lelo, bobo; **you s.!,** ¡bobo!. —*v.t.,* (*pret., p.p.* SAPPED; *p.pr.* SAPPING) 1. desecar (madera). 2. derribar de un cachiporrazo, dar un cachiporrazo a.
sap, *s.* (mil.) zapa. —*v.i.* (mil.) hacer trabajos de zapa, minar, zapar. —*v.t.* 1. socavar. 2. (fig.) agotar, debilitar, destruir.
sapajou ['sæpə,dʒu] *s.* (zool.) (mono) sapajú, sajú.
sapanwood, *var. de* **sappanwood.**
sap chafer, (ento.) cetonia.
saphead ['sæp,hɛd] *s.* (fam.) pelele, lelo.
sapheaded [-əd] *a.* lelo, zonzo.
saphena [sə'finə] **saphenous** [-nəs] *a.* (anat.) safena (vena).
sapid ['sæpəd] *a.* sápido, sabroso.
sapidity [sə'pɪdətɪ] *s.* sapidez, sabor, gusto.
sapience ['seɪpɪəns] *s.* sapiencia, sabiduría, sagacidad.
sapient [-ənt] *a.* sabio, sagaz.
sapiential [,seɪpɪ'ɛntʃəl, B -'ɛnʃəl] *a.* sapiencial.
sapiently ['seɪpɪəntlɪ] *adv.* sabiamente, sagazmente.
Sapindaceae [,sæpɪn'deɪsiɪ] *s. pl.* (bot.) sapindáceo.
sapless ['sæpləs] *a.* 1. sin savia, sin jugo, seco. 2. falto de vigor, débil.
sapling [-lɪŋ] *s.* 1. árbol joven. 2. galgo joven. 3. jovenzuelo, mozalbete.
sapodilla [,sæpə'dɪlə] *s.* (bot.) chico zapote, zapotillo, níspero americano.
saponaceous [-'neɪʃəs] *a.* 1. saponáceo, como jabón. 2. (fig.) escurridizo, elusivo.
saponated ['sæpə,neɪtəd] *a.* saponado.
saponifiable [sə'pɑnə,faɪəbəl, B -'pɔn-] *a.* saponificable.
saponification [-,pɑnəfə'keɪʃən, B -,pɔn-] *s.* saponificación.
saponify [-'pɑnə,faɪ, B -'pɔn-] *v.t., v.i.* (*pret., p.p.* SAPONIFIED; *p.pr.* SAPONIFYING) saponificar(se).
saponin ['sæpənən] *s.* (quím.) saponina.
saponite [-,naɪt] *s.* (min.) saponita, piedra de jabón.
sapor ['seɪpər, -,pɔr, B -,pɔ] *s.* sabor, gusto.
saporific [,seɪpə'rɪfɪk] *a.* saporífero.
saporous ['seɪpərəs] *a.* sabroso.
sapota [sə'poʊtə] *s.* (bot.) chicozapote, níspero americano.
sapotaceous [,sæpə'teɪʃəs] *s.* (bot.) sapotáceo.
sappanwood [sə'pæn,wʊd, B 'sæpən-] *s.* (bot.) sapán, sibucao.
sapper ['sæpər, B -ə] *s.* (mil.) zapador, gastador.
Sapphic ['sæfɪk] *a.* 1. sáfico (verso). 2. de Safo. 3. lesbiano, lesbio. —*s.* verso sáfico.
sapphire ['sæf,aɪr, B -,aɪə] *s.* 1. zafiro. 2. color del zafiro. —*a.* zafirino.
sapphirine [-ə,raɪn] *a.* 1. zafirino. 2. (hecho de) zafiro. — [-,aɪr,in, B -,aɪər-] *s.* (min.) zafirina.
sapphirine gurnard, (ict.) golondrina, golondrino.
sapphism [-,ɪzəm] *s.* (poét.) safismo, homosexualidad en la mujer.
Sappho ['sæfoʊ] *s.* (lit.) Safo, poetisa griega de la isla de Lesbos.
sappiness ['sæpɪnəs] *s.* 1. jugosidad. 2. simpleza, necedad.
sappy [-ɪ] *a.* 1. lleno de savia. 2. sensiblero, sentimental. 3. (jer.) zonzo, tonto. 4. (dial.) jugoso.
sapremia [sæ'primɪə] *s.* (med.) sapremia.
saprobe ['sæp,roʊb] *s.* (biol.) saprobio.
saprobic [sæ'proʊbɪk] *a.* (biol.) sapróbico. saprobio.
saprogenic [,sæprə'dʒɛnɪk] *a.* (med.) saprógeno.
saprolite ['sæprə,laɪt] *s.* (geol.) saprolita.
sapropelic [,sæprə'pɛlɪk] *a.* (bot.) sapropélico.
saprophagous [sæ'prɑfəgəs, B -'prɔf-] *a.* (biol.) saprófago.
saprophyte ['sæprə,faɪt] *s.* (biol.) saprófito.
saprophytic [,sæprə'fɪtɪk] *a.* (biol.) saprofítico.
saprozoic [-'zoʊɪk] *a.* (biol.) saprozoico.
sapsago [sæp'seɪgoʊ] *s.* queso suizo fermentado mezclado con meliloto.
sapsucker ['sæp,sʌkər, B -ə] *s.* (orn.) variedad de carpintero (que destruye la albura de los árboles).
sapwood [-,wʊd] *s.* (bot.) albura, alburno, sámago.
saraband, sarabande ['særə,bænd] *s.* zarabanda (danza).
Saracen ['særəsən] *s., a.* sarraceno.
Saragossa [,særə'gɑsə, B -'gɔsə] *s.* Zaragoza (España).
Sarah ['sɛrə, 'særə, B 'sɛərə] *s.* (bíbl.) Sara, esposa de Abraham.
saran [sə'ræn] *s.* sarán; nombre genérico de un material plástico empleado para empaquetar.
SaranWrap (TM) [sə'ræn,wræp] *s.* film transparente.
Saratoga trunk [,særə'toʊgə-] baúl mundo.
sarcasm ['sɑr,kæzəm, B 'sɑ,-] *s.* sarcasmo.
sarcastic [sɑr'kæstɪk, B sɑ'-] *a.* sarcástico, mordaz.
sarcastically [-tɪkəlɪ] *adv.* sarcásticamente, mordazmente.
sarcenet ['sɑrsnət, B 'sɑs-] *s.* (tej.) zangalete.
sarcocarp ['sɑrkə,kɑrp, B 'sɑkə,kɑp] *s.* (bot.) sarcocarpio, sarcocarpo.
sarcocele [-,sil] *s.* (med.) sarcocele.
sarcocolla [,sɑrkə'kɑlə, B ,sɑkə'kɔlə] *s.* sarcocola (goma).
sarcoid ['sɑr,kɔɪd, B 'sɑ,-] *a.* (biol.) sarcoideo.
sarcoma [sɑr'koʊmə, B sɑ'-] *s.* (*pl.* SARCOMATA [-tə] o SARCOMAS) (med.) sarcoma.
sarcomatoid [-,tɔɪd] *a.* (med.) sarcomatoideo.
sarcomatosis [-,koʊmə'toʊsɪs, B -,kə-] *s.* (med.) sarcomatosis.
sarcomatous [-'kɑmətəs, B -'koʊm-] *a.* sarcomatoso.
sarcophagous [-'kɑfəgəs, B -'kɔf-] **sarcophagic** [,sɑrkə'fædʒɪk, B ,sɑkə-] *a.* (ento.) sarcófago.
sarcophagus [-gəs] *s.* (*pl.* SARCOPHAGI [-,gaɪ], SARCOPHAGUSES), 1. sarcófago, lucillo. 2. (ant.) variedad de piedra caliza.
sarcous ['sɑrkəs, B 'sɑkəs] *a.* (anat.) sarcoso.
sard [sɑrd, B sɑd] *s.* (min.) sarda, sardoína.
Sardanapalus [,sɑrdən'æpələs, B ,sɑd-] *s.* (hist.) Sardanápalo.
sardar, *var. de* **sirdar.**
sardine ['sɑr,daɪn, B 'sɑ,-] *s.* (min.) sardoína, sarda.
sardine [sɑr'din, B sɑ'-] *s.* (ict.) sardina; **like sardines in a tin,** como sardinas en lata.
Sardinia [-'dɪnɪə] *s.* Cerdeña, isla de Italia.
Sardinian [-ɪən] *s.* sardo (natural o lengua de Cerdeña). —*a.* sardo.
sardius ['sɑrdɪəs, B 'sɑd-] *s.* (joy., min.) sarda, sardoína.
sardonic [sɑr'dɑnɪk, B sɑ'dɔn-] *a.* sardónico, sarcástico, irónico, burlón.
sardonically [-ɪkəlɪ] *adv.* burlonamente, irónicamente.
sardonyx [-'dɑnɪks, B 'sɑdən-] *s.* (min., joy.) sardónica, sardónice, sardonio.
saree, *var. de* **sari.**
sargasso [sɑr'gæsoʊ, B sɑ'-] *s.* (bot.) sargazo.
Sargasso Sea, Mar de los Sargazos.
sarge [sɑrdʒ, B sɑdʒ] *s.* (jer.) sargento.
sari ['sɑrɪ] *s.* sari (vestido de mujer en la India).
sark [sɑrk, B sɑk] *s.* (dial. G.B.) camisa.
sarmentose [sɑr'mɛn,toʊs, B sɑ'-] *a.* (bot.) sarmentoso.
sarong [sə'rɔŋ, -'rɑŋ, B -'rɔŋ] *s.* sarong (vestido para ambos sexos del archipiélago malayo y algunas partes de la India).
sarraceniaceous [,særə,sinɪ'eɪʃəs] *a.* (bot.) sarraceniáceo.
sarsaparilla [,sæspə'rɪlə, B ,sɑsə-] *s.* (bot.) zarzaparrilla.
sarsenet, *var. de* **sarcenet.**
sartor ['sɑrtər, B 'sɑtɔ] *s.* (esp. hum.) sastre.
sartorial [sɑr'tɔrɪəl, B sɑ'-] *a.* sastre; de sastrería.
sartorius [-əs] *s.* (anat.) (músculo) sartorio.
sash [sæʃ] *s.* 1. (*pl.* SASH o SASHES) bastidor o marco de ventana. 2. (*pl.* SASHES) faja, banda; cinturón, ceñidor, cinto, cinta.
sashay [sæ'ʃeɪ] *v.i.* (*pret., p.p.* SASHAYED; *p.pr.* SASHAYING) 1. ejecutar pasos de patinaje (al bailar). 2. (jer., E.U.) caminar con pasitos cortos o con afectación; caminar, andar. —*s.* 1. paso de patinaje. 2. paseo, excursión.
sash bar, parteluz, montante.
sash cord, cadena para contrapeso de ventana.
sash window, ventana de guillotina.
sasin ['seɪsɪn, B 'sæ-] *s.* (zool.) sasí, sasín, antílope indio.

saskatoon [ˌsæskə'tun] *s.* (E.U., bot.) (especie de) guillomo de fruto morado.
sass [sæs] *s.* (E.U.) réplica insolente, insolencia. —*v.t.* replicar en forma insolente a, ponerse insolente con.
sassafras ['sæsəˌfræs] *s.* (bot., farm.) sasafrás.
Sassanian, Sasanian [sə'seɪnɪən, B sæ-] *vars. de* **sassanid.**
Sassanid [-'sɑnəd, B 'sæsən-] *s., a.* sasánida.
Sassenach ['sæsəˌnæk] *s.* (esco., Irl.) Sajón, inglés.
sassy ['sæsɪ] *a.* (SASSIER; SASSIEST) (E.U.) respondón, insolente.
sat [sæt] *pret., p.p. de* **sit.**
Sat. *abrev. de* **Saturday,** sábado (sáb.).
S. A. T. *abrev. de* **Scholastic Aptitude Test,** examen de aptitud escolar.
Satan ['seɪtən] *s.* Satán, Satanás.
satanic [sə'tænɪk] *a.* satánico.
satanically [-ɪkəlɪ] *adv.* satánicamente, de modo satánico.
Satanism ['seɪtənˌɪzəm] *s.* satanismo.
satchel ['sætʃəl] *s.* cartapacio (de escolares); bolso, taleguilla.
sate [seɪt] *v.t.* saciar, satisfacer, hartar, hastiar.
sateen [sæ'tin] *s.* (tej.) satén.
satellite ['sætəlˌaɪt] *s.* 1. (astr.) satélite, planeta secundario. 2. (fig.) satélite. 3. (aeroesp.) satélite (artificial); **to broadcast by s.,** retransmitir via satélite.
satellite dish, antena parabólica.
satellite orbit, (astronáut.) órbita satelitaria.
satellite state, estado o país satélite.
sati, *var. de* **suttee.**
satiability [ˌseɪʃɪə'bɪlətɪ] *s.* capacidad de saciarse.
satiable ['seɪʃəbəl] *a.* saciable.
satiableness [-nəs] *s.* capacidad de saciarse.
satiate [-ʃɪət] *a.* saciado, harto, repleto, lleno. — [-ˌeɪt] *v.t.* saciar, hartar, repletar.
satiation [ˌseɪʃɪ'eɪʃən] *s.* saciedad, hartura, hartazgo.
satiety [sə'taɪətɪ] *s.* saciedad, hartura, hartazgo.
satin ['sætən] *s.* (tej.) raso, satén (de seda). —*a.* satinado.
satinet [ˌsætən'ɛt] *s.* (tej.) rasete, raso corriente, raso de algodón, satén de algodón; imitación raso.
satin finish, acabado lustroso (de metales).
satinflower ['sætənˌflaʊər, B -ə] **satinpod** [-ˌpɑd, B -ˌpɔd] *s.* (bot.) lunaria.
satin stitch, (cost.) punto relleno.
satin weave, ligamento o tejido raso.
satinwood [-ˌwʊd] *s.* 1. (bot.) especie de caoba. 2. satín.
satiny ['sætənɪ] *a.* satinado, lustroso.
satire ['sæˌtaɪr, B -ˌtaɪə] *s.* 1. sátira. 2. ironía, sarcasmo.
satiric [sə'tɪrɪk] **satirical** [-ɪkəl] *a.* satírico.
satirically [-ɪkəlɪ] *adv.* satíricamente.
satirist ['sætərəst] *s.* satírico.
satirize [-ˌraɪz] *v.t., v.i.* satirizar.
satirizer [-ər, B -ə] *s.* persona satírica.
satisfaction [ˌsætəs'fækʃən] *s.* 1. satisfacción. 2. **to demand s.,** exigir satisfacción; **to the s. of,** a satisfacción de.
satisfactorily [-'fæktərəlɪ] *adv.* satisfactoriamente.
satisfactory [-'fæktərɪ] *a.* satisfactorio, satisfaciente.
satisfy ['sætəsˌfaɪ] *v.t.* (*pret., p.p.* SATISFIED; *p.pr.* SATISFYING) satisfacer; **s. oneself,** satisfacerse, convencerse. —*v.i.* 1. dar o causar satisfacción. 2. ser satisfactório.
satisfyingly [-ɪŋlɪ] *adv.* satisfactoriamente.
satrap ['seɪtræp, B 'sæ-] *s.* sátrapa.
satrapy [-trəpɪ] *s.* satrapía.
saturable ['sætʃərəbəl] *a.* saturable.
saturant [-ərənt] (quím.) *a.* saturante, saturativo. —*s.* substancia saturativa.
saturate ['sætʃəˌreɪt] *v.t.* saturar. — [-rət] *a.* saturado.
saturated [-əd] *a.* saturado.
saturation [ˌsætʃə'reɪʃən] *s.* saturación.
saturation bombing, (mil.) bombardeo de saturación.
saturation current, (elec., rad.) corriente de saturación.
saturation curve, (ing.) curva de saturación magnética.
saturation factor, (ing.) factor de saturación.
saturation point, punto de saturación.
saturation rate, (electrón.) régimen de saturación.
saturator ['sætʃəˌreɪtər, B -ə] *s.* saturador (aparato).
Saturday ['sætərdɪ, B -ədɪ] *s.* sábado.
Saturn ['sætərn, B -ən] *s.* (mitol., astr.) Saturno.
Saturnalia [ˌsætər'neɪljə, B -ə'-] *s. pl.* 1. (*sing. o pl. en const.*) (hist.) saturnales. 2. (*pl.* SATURNALIAS *o* SATURNALIA) saturnal, orgía.
Saturnalian [-jən] *a.* saturnal.
Saturnian [sæ'tɜrnɪən, B -'tɜnjən] *a.* (hist., astr.) saturnio, saturnal.
Saturnian age, (fig.) edad de oro.
saturnic [-nɪk] *a.* (med.) saturnino.
saturniid [-niɪd] *s. pl.* (ento.) satúrnidos.
saturnine ['sætərˌnaɪn, B -əˌ-] *a.* 1. saturnino, triste, taciturno, melancólico. 2. (med.) saturnino.
saturnine poisoning, (med.) intoxicación saturnina.
saturnism [-ˌnɪzəm] *s.* (med.) saturnismo.
satyr ['seɪtər, B 'sætə] *s.* 1. (mitol.) sátiro. 2. (fig.) sátiro, hombre lascivo. 3. (ento.) mariposa de color marrón y gris.
satyriasis [ˌseɪtə'raɪəsəs, B ˌsæt-] *s.* (med.) satiriasis.
satyric [sə'tɪrɪk] *a.* satírico.
sauce [sɔs] *s.* 1. salsa. 2. (E.U.) compota, puré (de frutas). 3. (fig.) sainete, gracia. 4. (fam.) insolencia, atrevimiento; réplica insolente. 5. (jer.) trago, licor. —*v.t.* 1. aderezar, aliñar; condimentar, sazonar; dar sabor picante a. 2. insolentarse con; responder insolentemente a, atreverse con.
sauceboat ['sɔsˌboʊt] *s.* salsera.
saucebox [-ˌbɑks, B -ˌbɔks] *s.* (fam.) atrevido, insolente; niño respondón.
saucedish [-ˌdɪʃ] *s.* plato dulcero; salsera.
saucepan [-ˌpæn, B -pən] *s.* cacerola, cazuela, perol.
saucer ['sɔsər, B -sə] *s.* platillo (esp. para taza); **flying s.,** platillo volador.
saucily ['sɔsəlɪ] *adv.* impertinentemente, atrevidamente, insolentemente, descaradamente.
sauciness [-ɪnəs] *s.* impertinencia, atrevimiento, insolencia, descaro, impudencia, desvergüenza.
saucy [-ɪ] *a.* (SAUCIER; SAUCIEST) impertinente, atrevido, insolente, descarado, impudente, desvergonzado.
Saudi Arabia [sɑ'udɪə'reɪbɪə, B 'saʊdɪ-] Arabia Saudita.
sauerbraten ['saʊrˌbrɑtən, B -əˌ-] *s.* (alemán) carne de res macerada en vinagre con cebollas, condimentos, etc.
sauerkraut [-ˌkraʊt] *s.* (cocina) chucrut, chucruta, col picada en salmuera.
sauger ['sɔgər, B -gə] *s.* (ict.) variedad de perca.
saugh, sauch [saʊk] *s.* (esco., bot.) sarga, sauce.
sauna ['saʊnə, 'sɔ-] *s.* sauna.
saunter ['sɔntər, B -ə] *v.i.* ambular, deambular, pasearse.
saunterer [-ərər, B -ə] *s.* paseante, paseador.
saurel [sɔ'rɛl] *s.* (ict.) saurel, jurel.
saurian ['sɔrɪən] *s., a.* (zool.) saurio.
sauropod ['sɔrəˌpɑd, B -ˌpɔd] *s., a.* saurópodo.
sausage ['sɔsɪdʒ] *s.* salchicha, embutido, chorizo, longaniza, salchichón.
sausage maker, salchichero.
sausage shop, salsamentaria, salchichería.
sauté [sɔ'teɪ, B 'soʊteɪ] (cocina) *a.* salteado. —*v.t.* (*pret., p.p.* SAUTÉED O SAUTÉD; *p.pr.* SAUTÉING) saltear (un manjar).
savable, *var. de* **saveable.**
savage ['sævɪdʒ] *a.* 1. salvaje, indomado, indómito, cerril, chúcaro. 2. salvaje, incivilizado, bárbaro. 3. salvaje, feroz, fiero, cruel, brutal. 4. furioso, rabioso. —*s.* salvaje. —*v.t.* 1. atacar furiosamente. 2. magullar, lastimar, lacerar. 3. embrutecer.
savagely [-lɪ] *adv.* ferozmente, fieramente, cruelmente, brutalmente.
savageness [-nəs] *s.* 1. salvajez, estado salvaje. 2. ferocidad, crueldad, brutalidad, salvajismo.
savagery [-rɪ] *s.* 1. salvajez. 2. salvajismo; acto salvaje o brutal. 3. ferocidad, crueldad, brutalidad, salvajismo.
savanna, savannah [sə'vænə] *s.* sabana.
savant [sæ'vɑnt, B 'sævənt] *s.* sabio, científico, erudito, docto.
save [seɪv] *v.t.* 1. salvar, rescatar; libertar, librar. 2. resguardar, proteger, guardar. 3. guardar, reservar (asiento, etc.). 4. cuidar, cuidarse (los ojos, la voz, etc.). 5. salvar, redimir (de la vida pecaminosa, vicios, etc.). 6. ahorrar (dinero, provisiones, tiempo, etc.). 7. evitar, ahorrar (la necesidad, el gasto, etc.). 8. (fútbol) salvar (la portería) de un tanto. 9. **a stitch in time saves nine,** no dejes para mañana lo que puedes hacer hoy; **God s. me from my friends,** líbreme Dios de los buenos consejos (que de los malos me libro yo); **God s. the Queen!** ¡Dios guarde a la Reina!; **s. appearances,** salvar las apariencias; **s. it! (jer.)** ¡cállate! ¡basta!; **s. one's skin,** (fam.) salvar el pellejo; **s. one's breath,** callarse, guardarse sus opiniones; **s. oneself the trouble,** ahorrarse el trabajo o molestia; **s. the situation,** evitar el desastre, encontrar la solución de una dificultad; **s. the tide,** hacer uso de la marea (para zarpar o entrar en el puerto). —*v.i.* 1. hacer ahorros, ahorrar, economizar, vivir económicamente. 2. conservarse. 3. **s. up,** ahorrar, hacer ahorros.
save, *prep.* excepto, salvo, sino, menos. —*conj.* a no ser que; con excepción de; **s. that,** a menos que, si no fuera porque; **s. for,** excepto por, salvo por.
saveable ['seɪvəbəl] *a.* salvable, redimible.
save-all ['seɪvˌɔl] *s.* 1. apuracabos. 2. recogedor de aceite (en máquina, etc.). 3. (mar.) vela suplementaria. 4. (dial.) mono, traje de mecánico. 5. (pr. dial.) alcancía.
saveloy ['sævəˌlɔɪ] *s.* embutido de puerco muy sazonado.
saver ['seɪvər, B -və] *s.* 1. ahorrador; perseverador. 2. (jer.) apuesta compensadora.
savin, savine ['sævən] *s.* (bot.) 1. sabina. 2. cedro colorado, cedro Virginia, enebro de Virginia, cedro de España.
saving ['seɪvɪŋ] *a.* 1. salvador, rescatador; redentor; atenuante, ej., *s. grace,* rasgo atenuante. 2. ahorrativo; frugal, económico. 3. reservativo, de reserva. —*s.* 1. economía. 2. (*gen. pl.*) ahorros. 3. (der.) excepción, reserva.

saving, *prep., conj.* salvo, excepto.
saving clause, (der.) cláusula de salvedad (en documento).
savingly [-lɪ] *adv.* económicamente, parcamente, frugalmente.
savings account, cuenta de ahorros.
savings and loan association o **company,** sociedad de ahorro y préstamos.
savings bank, banco o caja de ahorros.
savings bonds, bonos de ahorro.
savior, saviour ['seɪvjər, B -jə] *s.* salvador; **the S.,** el Salvador, el Redentor (Jesucristo).
savoir faire [ˌsæv,wɑr'fɛr, B 'sævwɑ'fɛə] (fr.) don de gente; tino, roce.
savor ['seɪvər, B -və] *s.* 1. sabor, dejo, gusto, gustillo, sainete, sazón. 2. (raro) olor, perfume. —*v.i.* (con *of*) tener sabor (de), oler (a); tener la cualidad (de). —*v.t.* 1. sazonar, dar sabor a, saborear; perfumar. 2. saborear, percibir con deleite, gozar; apreciar.
savorer [-vərər, B -ə] *s.* saboreador.
savoriness [-vərɪnəs] *s.* 1. buen sabor, gusto agradable. 2. fragancia.
savorless [-vərləs, B -vəlɪs] *a.* insípido, insulso, desabrido, soso.
savorous ['seɪvərəs] *a.* sabroso, gustoso, apetitoso, delicioso.
savory [-vərɪ] *a.* (SAVORIER; SAVORIEST) 1. sabroso, apetitoso. 2. picante, salado. 3. fragante. —*s.* (*pl.* SAVORIES) 1. (bot.) ajedrea. 2. (G.B.) entrada o postre (no dulce), digestivo.
savour, savourer, savouriness, etc. *vars. de* **savor, savorer, savoriness,** etc.
Savoy [sə'vɔɪ] *s.* 1. Saboya. 2. **s.,** (bot.) repollo de Milán, repollo de hojas rizadas.
Savoyard [sə'vɔɪˌɑrd, B -ɑd] *s.* 1. saboyano, natural de Saboya. 2. admirador, actor o productor de las operetas de Gilbert y Sullivan. —*a.* saboyano.
savvy ['sævɪ] (jer.) *v.i.* captar, comprender, saber. —*s.* sentido común, comprensión, astucia.
saw [sɔ] *s.* dicho, decir; refrán, proverbio; máxima, adagio, aforismo.
saw [sɔ] *s.* serrucho, sierra. —*v.t.* (*pret.* SAWED; *p.p.* SAWN [sɔn] o SAWED) aserrar, serrar, cortar con la sierra; **s. out,** (fig.) producir (tono, música) rasgando (en el violín, violoncello, etc.); **s. wood,** (jer.) roncar, dormir. —*v.i.* 1. usar una sierra. 2. cortar con la sierra.
saw [sɔ] *pret. de* **see.**
sawbones ['sɔˌbounz] *s.* (jer.) matasanos, galeno.
sawbuck [-ˌbʌk] *s.* 1. caballete de aserrar. 2. (jer.) billete de 10 dólares.
saw cut, corte o trazo de sierra, aserradora.
sawdust [-ˌdʌst] *s.* aserrín, serrín.
saw-edged [-'ɛdʒd] *a.* de filo dentado, de borde mellado.
sawed-off ['sɔdˌɔf] *a.* 1. acortado (fusil, etc.). 2. (fig.) de talla reducida, diminuto.
sawer ['sɔər, B 'sɔə] *s.* aserradero, serrador.
saw file, lima para sierra; limadora.
sawfish ['sɔˌfɪʃ] *s.* (ict.) pez sierra, priste.
sawfly [-ˌflaɪ] *s.* (ento.) mosca de sierra.
saw grass, (bot.) variedad de juncia.
saw grinder, rectificador de sierras.
sawhorse [-ˌhɔrs, B -ˌhɔs] *s.* caballete de aserrar, cabrilla, burro, asnilla.
sawlog [-ˌlɔg, -ˌlɑg, B -ˌlɔg] *s.* tronco serradizo o por aserrar.
sawmill [-ˌmɪl] *s.* aserradero; sierra de agua.
sawn [sɔn] *p.p. de* **saw.**
saw set, triscador, tenazas de triscar.
sawtooth ['sɔˌtuθ] *a.* serrado.
saw-toothed [-ˌtuθt] *a.* serrado.
sawwort [-ˌwɜrt, B -ˌwɜt] *s.* (bot.) serrátula.
sawyer ['sɔjər, B -jə] *s.* 1. aserrador, serrador. 2. (ento.) termes, comején, anay.
sax [sæks] *s.* (jer.) saxófono.
saxatile ['sæksətəl] *a.* (bot., zool.) sexátil.
Saxe [sæks] *s.* 1. Sajonia, antiguos condados de Alemania. 2. azul de Sajonia.
saxhorn ['sæksˌhɔrn, B -ˌhɔn] *s.* (mús.) bombardino.
saxicoline [sæk'sɪkəˌlaɪn] **saxicolous** [-ləs] *a.* (bot., zool.) saxicola.
saxifragaceous [ˌsæksəfrə'geɪʃəs] *a.* saxifragáceo.
saxifrage ['sæksəfrɪdʒ] *s.* (bot.) saxífraga, saxifragia.
Saxon ['sæksən] *s., a.* 1. sajón. 2. anglosajón.
Saxony [-sənɪ] *s.* 1. Sajonia, región de Alemania. 2. (tej.) tejido fino de lana.
saxophone ['sæksəˌfoun] *s.* (mús.) saxofón, saxófono.
saxophonist [-əst, B sæk'sɔfən-] *s.* saxofonista.
saxtuba ['sæksˌtubə, B -ˌtjubə] *s.* (mús.) bombardón.
say [seɪ] *v.t.* (*pret., p.p.* SAID [sɛd]; *p.pr.* SAYING; *tercera pers. sing.* SAYS [sɛz]) 1. decir; pronunciar, manifestar, expresar, formular. 2. recitar (la lección, oraciones, etc.). 3. indicar, marcar (reloj la hora, etc.). 4. **he has had his s.,** ha terminado su peroración; ha acabado con lo que quiso decir; **have you nothing to s. for yourself?** ¿no tiene nada que aducir de su parte?; **I cannot s.,** no sé; **I should s. so!** ¡ya lo creo!; **I s.,** ¡caracoles!; de veras, ej., *I s., what a beautiful girl!* ¡caracoles! qué muchacha tan linda; **it goes without saying,** huelga decir, es obvio; **it is said,** se dice, se rumorea; **it says,** se dice, ej., *it says in this book that there's life on Mars,* se dice en este libro que hay vida en Marte; **let us s.,** digamos; **no sooner said than done,** dicho y hecho; **not to s.,** por no decir, ej., *her clothes are somewhat striking, not to s. vulgar,* su vestido es algo llamativo, por no decir vulgar; **s.!** ¡oiga!; **s. a good word for,** recomendar; excusar; **s. no more!** ¡ni una palabra más!; **s. over again,** repetir, volver a decir; **s. the word,** dar la orden; **s. to oneself,** decir para si; **s. yes,** consentir; aceptar; confirmar; **says I,** (fam.) digo yo; **saying and doing,** decir y hacer; **so to s.,** por decirlo así; **that is to s.,** es decir, o sea; en otras palabras; o al menos; **there's no saying,** no hay modo de saber, es imposible decir, ej., *there's no saying what he'll do,* es imposible decir (o no hay modo de saber) qué hará él; **they s.,** se dice, dicen; **to s. the least,** por lo menos, si no algo peor; **to s. nothing of,** sin mencionar; **you don't s.!** ¡no me diga! ¡no es posible!; **you may well s. so,** con razón puede decirlo. —*v.i.* hablar, expresarse. —*s.* 1. voz, ej., *he has no s. in the matter,* él no tiene voz en el asunto. 2. opinión, ej., *to have one's s.,* expresar uno su opinión. 3. **to have the s.,** (E.U.) tener la última palabra, tener derecho a decidir.
sayable ['seɪəbəl] *a.* 1. decible, pronunciable. 2. de efecto oratorio, elocuente.
saying [-ɪŋ] *s.* dicho, decir; frase, refrán, adagio, proverbio, máxima; **as the s. is (goes),** como reza el refrán.
say-so [-ˌsou] *s.* 1. mera palabra, aserción infundada. 2. voz, autoridad. 3. última palabra, derecho a decidir. 4. orden (*f.*).
Sb *simb. de* **stibium** (antimony), antimonio (Sb).
S.B. *abrev. de* **Bachelor of Science,** Licenciado en Ciencias.
S by E *abrev. de* **South by East,** sur cuarta al sudeste.
S by W *abrev. de* **South by West,** sur cuarta al suroeste.
Sc *símb. de* **scandium,** escandio (Sc).
S.C. *abrev. de* 1. **South Carolina,** Carolina del Sur (E.U.). 2. **Supreme Court,** Corte Suprema, Tribunal Supremo.
scab [skæb] *s.* 1. costra, postilla, escara. 2. (vet.) roña, escabro (de ganado lanar). 3. (jer.) obrero no agremiado; rompehuelgas, esquirol. 4. (jer.) canalla, sinvergüenza, bribón, truhán. —*v.i.* (*pret., p.p.* SCABBED; *p.pr.* SCABBING) 1. volverse costroso, cubrirse de postilla. 2. trabajar como obrero no agremiado.
scabbard ['skæbərd, B -əd] *s.* vaina de espada, cuchillera, funda. —*v.t.* envainar, enfundar.
scabbily ['skæbəlɪ] *adv.* sórdidamente, mezquinamente, vilmente.
scabbiness [-ɪnəs] *s.* 1. estado costroso o sarnoso. 2. sordidez, mezquindad.
scabble ['skæbəl] *v.t.* desbastar, labrar (sillares).
scabby [-ɪ] *a.* 1. costroso. 2. (vet.) **roñoso. 3. (fam.) sórdido, mezquino, vil, despreciable, desdeñable.**
scabies ['skeɪbiz, B -bɪiz] *s.* (*pl.* SCABIES) (med.) escabies, sarna.
scabietic [ˌskeɪbɪ'ɛtɪk] *a.* (med.) escabioso, sarnoso.
scabiosa [-'ousə] *s.* (bot.) escabiosa.
scabious ['skeɪbɪəs] *a.* escabioso, sarnoso. —*s.* (bot.) escabiosa, esp. escabiosa común, escabiosa viuda.
scabrous ['skæbrəs, B 'skeɪb-] *a.* 1. escabroso, áspero. 2. escamoso, casposo. 3. dificultoso, arduo, difícil. 4. escabroso, salaz, licencioso; escandaloso.
scabrously [-lɪ] *adv.* escabrosamente, licenciosamente; escandalosamente.
scabrousness [-nəs] *s.* 1. escabrosidad, aspereza. 2. estado escamoso. 3. escabrosidad, licencia.
scads [skædz] *s. pl.* (jer., E.U.) montones (de dinero, etc.).
scaffold ['skæfəld] *s.* 1. andamio, andamiaje, andamiada. 2. cadalso, patíbulo. 3. (dial., E.U.) henil, granero. 4. (hist.) escenario, tabla (al aire libre). —*v.t.* proveer (construcción) de andamiaje.
scaffolding [-ɪŋ] *s.* andamiaje, andamiado, entablado.
scagliola [skæl'joulə] *s.* escayola.
scagliolist [-ləst] *s.* escayolista.
scalable ['skeɪləbəl] *a.* escalable.
scalage ['skeɪlɪdʒ] *s.* 1. porcentaje de merma. 2. graduación, clasificación (según peso, cantidad o dimensión).
scalar ['skeɪlər, B -lə] *a.* 1. escalonado. 2. (mat.) escalar. —*s.* (mat.) magnitud o cantidad escalar.
scalare [skə'lɛrɪ, B -'lɛərɪ] *s.* (ict.) angelote.
scalation [skeɪ'leɪʃən] *s.* (zool.) estructura de escamas; escamado.
scalawag ['skæləˌwæg] *s.* 1. pícaro, bribón, pillete, pilluelo. 2. animal flaco. 3. (E.U., hist.) (despec.) republicano del Sur (después de la Guerra de Secesión).
scald [skɔld] *v.t.* 1. escaldar. 2. calentar sin llegar al punto de ebullición. 3. cocer en agua hirviendo. —*v.i.* 1. escaldarse. 2. quemar. —*s.* 1. escaldadura, quemadura. 2. (bot.) escaldadura.
scald, *var. de* **skald.**
scalding ['skɔldɪŋ] *s.* 1. abrasador. 2. (fig.) ardiente (sol, rayos, etc.). 3. hirviente, que hierve. 4. mordaz, acerbo (crítica, editorial, etc.).
scale [skeɪl] *s.* 1. (*gen. pl.*) balanza, báscula. 2. platillo de balanza. 3. **Scales,** (astr.) Libra, Balanza. 4. **to tip the scales,** inclinar la balanza;

to turn the s. (o **scales**), (fig.) inclinar la balanza, ser decisivo (factor, circunstancia, etc.). —*v.t.* pesar. —*v.i.* tener (cierto) peso.
scale, *s.* 1. escama. 2. (fig.) escama, lámina, hoja. 3. (bot.) escama. 4. capa de óxido (en metales). —*v.t.* 1. escamar. 2. pelar, mondar, descortezar, descascarar. 3. cubrir con escamas. 4. tirar horizontalmente (sombrero, piedra chata, etc.). 5. (esco.) dispersar. —*v.i.* 1. incrustarse de escamas (cutis, calderas, etc.). 2. descamarse (epidermis); (t. con *off*) perder las escamas, pelarse.
scale [skeɪl] *s.* 1. escala, graduación, división. 2. escala, regla de medida. 3. escala, proporción. 4. (mús.) escala. 5. (ant.) escala, escalera de mano. 6. **in s.,** en proporción; **on** (o **to**) **a s. of,** a escala de; **on a small (large) s.,** en pequeña (gran) escala; **out of s.,** fuera de proporción; **to run over one's scales,** tocar o cantar escalas (como ejercicio). —*v.t.* 1. escalar; subir (escaleras); ascender, trepar. 2. graduar; clasificar. 3. (gen. con *down*) reducir en escala o proporción; (con *up*) ampliar o agrandar en proporción. 4. medir la cantidad de pies de tabla que hay en (un tronco). —*v.i.* 1. ser escalable (fácil o difícilmente). 2. ascender gradualmente (terreno, montaña). 3. escalar. —*a.* a escala (mapa, dibujo, modelo, etc.).
scale armour, armadura de escamas imbricadas.
scaleboard ['skeɪlˌbɔrd, B -ˌbɔd] *s.* tabla delgada; tabla para enchapar.
scaled [skeɪld] *a.* escamoso.
scale-down ['skeɪlˌdaʊn] *s.* reducción progresiva.
scale drawing, (dib.) dibujo a escala.
scale fern, (bot.) doradilla.
scale fraction, (ing.) relación de escala.
scale insect, (ento.) coco.
scale leaf, (bot.) hoja escamosa.
scale model, (ing., arq.) modelo a escala, maqueta a escala.
scale moss, (bot.) hepática frondosa.
scalene ['skeɪˌlin, B skə'lin] *a.* (geom.) escaleno.
scalepan ['skeɪlˌpæn] *s.* platillo de balanza.
scale paper, (ing., dib.) papel milimetrado.
scale protractor, (dib.) transportador de escala.
scaler [-ər, B -ə] *s.* 1. escalador. 2. registrador electrónico.
scale-up [-ˌʌp] *s.* aumento progresivo.
scale-winged [-ˌwɪŋd] *a.* (ento.) lepidóptero.
scale-work [-ˌwɜrk, B -ˌwɜk] *s.* escamado.
scaliness ['skeɪlɪnəs] *s.* escamosidad.
scall [skɔl] *s.* caspa, costra (de la piel).
scallawag, *var. de* **scalawag.**
scallion ['skæljən] *s.* (bot.) escalonia, escaloña, ascalonia, chacota.
scallop ['skɑləp, 'skæl-, B 'skɔl-] *s.* 1. concha, venera. 2. valva de concha (usada como plato). 3. (cost.) festón, onda. 4. (hist.) pechina, venera (distintivo de los peregrinos). 5. (cocina) escalope. —*v.t.* 1. (cost.) bordar con festones, festonear, ondular. 2. cubrir de pan rallado y hornear en salsa (ej., papas).
scalloped potatoes, (cul.) papas gratinadas or al gratén, patatas (Esp.) gratinadas or al gratén.
scalloper [-ər, B -ə] *s.* pescador de conchas.
scallopine, scallopini [ˌskɑlə'pini, ˌskæl-, B ˌskɔl-] *s.* (cocina italiana) carne de ternera en lonjas delgadas salteadas en vino con condimentos.
scallywag ['skælɪˌwæg] *var. de* **scalawag.**
scalp [skælp] *s.* 1. cuero cabelludo. 2. (fig.) trofeo. 3. pequeña ganancia (de un especulador). 4. (pr. esco.) cerrejón árido. 5. **to clamor for someone's s.,** pedir la cabeza de alguien, exigir la destitución o el castigo de alguien; **out for scalps,** en pie de guerra; con ánimo agresivo, buscando víctimas. —*v.t.* 1. escalpar, quitar el cuero cabelludo a. 2. (fig.) ridiculizar, humillar. 3. aplastar, liquidar, triunfar sobre (rival). 4. comprar y vender por pequeñas ganancias, revender (boletos, etc.).
scalpel ['skælpəl] *s.* (med.) escalpelo.
scalper ['skælpər, B -ə] *s.* especulador; revendedor (de billetes de teatro, etc.).
scalp lock, mechón de cabello (que se dejaban los indios en la cabeza afeitada).
scaly ['skeɪlɪ] *a.* 1. escamoso. 2. de escamas imbricadas (armadura, brote, etc.). 3. infestado de insectos (fruta). 4. laminoso (piedra, etc.). 5. (jer.) despreciable, vil: miserable, pésimo.
scaly anteater, (zool.) pangolín.
scammony ['skæmənɪ] *s.* (bot., farm.) escamonea.
scamp [skæmp] *s.* bribón, pícaro; pilluelo, bribonzuelo. —*v.t.* frangollar, ejecutar con descuido.
scamper ['skæmpər, B -pə] *v.i.* 1. retozar, corretear. 2. **s. away** (u **off**), escaparse. —*s.* retozo, correteo (de niños, animales pequeños, etc.).
scamping [-pɪŋ] *s.* mala ejecución del trabajo para perjudicar a la empresa; acción capciosa dirigida a los obreros de una fábrica rival.
scan [skæn] *v.t.* (*pret., p.p.* SCANNED; *p.pr.* SCANNING) 1. examinar, escudriñar, escrutar, registrar, recorrer (un escrito). 2. (poét.) escandir, recitar métricamente. 3. (t.v.) explorar. 4. (radar) registrar. 5. (med.) hacer un escáner de, hacer un scanner de; hacer una ecografía de. 6. (astr., comput., mil.) explorar. —*v.i.* (poét.) tener forma métrica; prestarse a recitación métrica. —*s.* 1. escudriñamiento. 2. radio de visión. 3. (med.) escáner, scanner, escanograma; ecografía. 4. (astr., comput., mil.) exploración.
scandal ['skændəl] *s.* 1. escándalo. 2. ignominia, deshonra. 3. **to bring s. to,** deshonrar; **to give rise to s.,** causar escándalo.
scandalization [ˌskændələ'zeɪʃən, B -laɪ-] *s.* consternación.
scandalize ['skændəˌlɑɪz] *v.t.* escandalizar, indignar.
scandalizer [-ər, B -ə] *s.* escandalizador.
scandalmonger [-dəlˌmʌŋgər, -ˌmɑŋ-, B -ˌmʌŋgə] *s.* murmurador, propagador de escándalos.
scandalous [-əs] *a.* 1. escandaloso, escandalizativo. 2. vergonzoso; ignominioso, oprobioso. 3. difamatorio, injuriante.
scandalously [-lɪ] *adv.* 1. escandalosamente. 2. vergonzosamente; ignominiosamente.
scandal sheet, periódico sensacionalista, pasquín.
scandent ['skændənt] *a.* (bot.) escandente.
scandia ['skændɪə] *s.* (quím.) óxido de escandio.
Scandian ['skændɪən] *a., s.* escandinavo.
scandic ['skændɪk] *a.* (quím.) escándico.
Scandinavian [ˌskændə'neɪvɪən] *a., s.* escandinavo.
scandium ['skændɪəm] *s.* (quím.) escandio.
scan form, ficha de scanner.
scannable ['skænəbəl] *a.* escudriñable.
scanner [-ər, B -ə] *s.* 1. (electrón., t.v., radar) explorador, unidad exploradora; (ing.) analizador. 2. (med.) escáner, scanner, escanógrafo; ecógrafo. 3. (comput.) analizador de léxico, explorador.
scanning [-ɪŋ] *s.* (t.v.) exploración, escudriñamiento; (ing.) analización.
scanning beam, (rad.) haz explorador.
scanning disk, (electrón.) disco analizador; (t.v.) disco explorador.
scanning line, (top.) línea de exploración.
scansion ['skæntʃən, B 'skænʃən] *s.* (poét.) escansión.
scant [skænt] *a.* 1. escaso, magro, insuficiente; limitado. 2. (con *of*) deficiente (en), corto (de). —*v.t.* limitar, escatimar, escasear; (fig.) reducir, contraer. —*adv.* (dial.) escasamente.
scanties ['skæntiz] *s. pl.* ropa interior muy breve, de mujer.
scantily [-əlɪ] *adv.* 1. escasamente, estrechamente. 2. escasamente, a la ligera, muy ligeramente.
scantiness [-ɪnəs] *s.* 1. escasez, estrechez. 2. escasez, insuficiencia (de ropa).
scantling ['skæntlɪŋ] *s.* 1. porción pequeña. 2. escuadría, marco; tirantillo, alfarda. 3. poste de tabique; cuartón de madera. 4. (*pl.*) dimensiones, escantillones.
scantly [-lɪ] *adv.* escasamente, insuficientemente; deficientemente.
scantness [-nəs] *s.* escasez, insuficiencia.
scanty ['skæntɪ] *a.* (SCANTIER; SCANTIEST) 1. escaso, corto, reducido, estrecho. 2. escaso, muy ligero (díc. de vestidura).
scape [skeɪp] *s.* 1. (bot.) escapo, bohordo. 2. (ento.) escapo (primer artejo diferenciado de las antenas). 3. (zool.) cañón (de una pluma). 4. (arq.) escapo.
scape, *s.* 1. (dial.) escape, escapada, escapatoria. 2. (ant.) tropiezo, falta. —*v.i.* (ant.) escapar, huir.
scapegoat ['skeɪpˌgoʊt] *s.* chivo expiatorio; cabeza de turco.
scapegrace [-ˌgreɪs] *s.* pícaro, empecatado, bribón, incorregible.
scape wheel, rueda dentada, rueda de trinquete (de los relojes).
scaphoid ['skæfɔɪd] *a., s.* (anat.) escafoides.
scapiform ['skeɪpəˌfɔrm, B -ˌfɔm] *a.* (bot.) escapiforme.
scapolite ['skæpəˌlaɪt] *s.* (min.) escapolita.
scapula ['skæpjələ] *s.* (*pl.* SCAPULAE [-ˌli] o SCAPULAS) (anat., zool.) escápula.
scapular [-lər, B -lə] *a.* (anat.) escapular. —*s.* 1. (relig.) escapulario. 2. (anat., zool.) escápula. 3. (orn.) pluma escapular.
scapulary [-ˌlɛrɪ, B -lərɪ] *s.* (relig.) escapulario.
scar [skɑr, B skɑ] *s.* 1. cicatriz, señal, chirlo, costurón. 2. (fig.) cicatriz. —*v.t.* (*pret., p.p.* SCARRED; *p.pr.* SCARRING) 1. marcar con una cicatriz; dejar una cicatriz. 2. (fig.) herir profundamente. —*v.i.* cicatrizar(se).
scar, *s.* peñasco, peñón, farallón.
scarab ['skærəb] *s.* (ento., hist.) escarabajo.
scarabaean [ˌskærə'biən] *a., s.* (ento.) escarabeino.
scarabaeid [-əd] *a., s.* (ento.) escarabeido.
scarabaeus [-əs] *s.* (*pl.* SCARABAEUSES O SCARABAEI [-ˌaɪ]) (ento., hist.) escarabajo.
Scaramouch ['skærəˌmuʃ, B -maʊtʃ] *s.* 1. fanfarrón, cobarde; pícaro, bribón. 2. **s.,** botarga, bufón.
scarce [skɛrs, B skɛəs] *a.* escaso, insuficiente; raro, poco común; **to make oneself s.,** hacerse escaso, brillar por su ausencia. —*adv.* apenas.
scarcely ['skɛrslɪ, B 'skɛəs-] *adv.* 1. apenas. 2. casi no. 3. difícilmente. 4. ciertamente no, probablemente no, ej., *you will s. believe that,* probablemente no creerá eso. 5. **s. anything,** casi nada; **s. ever,** casi nunca.
scarcement [-mənt] *s.* (arq.) resalto, saliente (en la pared, en la roca); zarpa (de cimiento).
scarceness [-nəs] *s.* escasez, insuficiencia; carestía.
scarcity ['skɛrsətɪ, B 'skɛəsə-] *s.* escasez, falta, insuficiencia; rareza.
scare [skɛr, B skɛə] *v.t.* 1. asustar, espantar; amedrentar; atemorizar, intimidar, alarmar. 2. **s. away,** ahuyentar; **s. the pants off (someone),**

aterrorizar, aterrar (a alguien); **s. up,** (fam.) lograr reunir (a duras penas); **scared stiff,** (fam.) muerto de miedo. —*v.i.* asustarse; alarmarse, inquietarse. —*s.* susto, miedo, espanto; sobresalto, alarma.
scarecrow ['skɛr,kroʊ, B 'skɛə,-] *s.* 1. espantapájaros, espantajo. 2. (fig.) espantajo (persona mal arreglada o andrajosa).
scarehead [-,hɛd] *s.* (E.U.) título sensacional, gran titular (ej., en un diario).
scaremonger [-,mʌŋgər, -,mɑŋ-, B -,mʌŋgə] *s.* alarmista.
scarf [skɑrf, B skɑf] *s.* (*pl.* SCARVES [skɑrvz, B skɑvz] o SCARFS) 1. bufanda, chal, chalina (Amer.). 2. pañuelo para el cuello. 3. camino (de mesa), tapete. —*v.t.* envolver en una bufanda, cubrir o adornar con un chal.
scarf [skɑrf, B skɑf] *v.t.* 1. (carp.) empalmar, ensamblar, empotrar, encabezar; biselar, rebajar (madera, etc. para empalme). 2. descuartizar (ballenas) en fajas, quitándoles la grasa. —*s.* (*pl.* SCARFS) 1. (carp.) rebajo, espera. 2. corte en ranura o canal (a lo largo de una ballena).
scarfer ['skɑrfər, B 'skɑfə] *s.* ensamblador; biselador.
scarf joint, (carp.) junta biselada; junta a diente de sierra; empalme a media madera, empalme endentado.
scarfpin ['skɑrf,pɪn, B 'skɑf-] *s.* alfiler de corbata.
scarfskin [-,skɪn] *s.* (anat.) epidermis.
scarification [,skærəfə'keɪʃən] *s.* (med.) 1. escarificación. 2. sajadura, saja.
scarificator ['skærəfə,keɪtər, B -ə] *s.* (med.) escarificador.
scarifier [-,faɪər, B -ə] *s.* (med., agr.) escarificador.
scarify [-,faɪ] *v.t.* (*pret., p.p.* SCARIFIED; *p.pr.* SCARIFYING) 1. (med.) escarificar, sajar. 2. (fig.) lacerar, desgarrar (sentimientos); criticar severamente. 3. (agr.) escarificar.
scarious ['skɛrɪəs, B 'skɛər-] *a.* (bot.) escarioso.
scarlatina [,skɑrlə'tinə, B ,skɑlə-] *s.* (med.) escarlatina.
scarlatinoid [-,nɔɪd] *a.* (med.) escarlatinoide.
scarlet ['skɑrlət, B 'skɑlɪt] *s.* 1. escarlata, carmesí, grana (color). 2. tela o ropas escarlatas. —*a.* 1. de color escarlata. 2. lascivo, pecaminoso.
scarlet fever, (med.) escarlatina.
scarlet letter, (hist., E.U.) letra escarlata (estigma que estaban condenadas a llevar sobre el vestido las mujeres adúlteras).
scarlet lychnis [-'lɪknɪs] (bot.) cruz de Jerusalén.
scarlet pimpernel, (bot.) anagalis, murajes.
scarlet runner, s. runner bean, (bot.) judía de España, judía escarlata.
scarlet sage, (bot.) salvia.
scarp [skɑrp, B skɑp] *s.* 1. escarpa, declive, pendiente, acantilado. 2. (fort.) escarpa. —*v.t.* escarpar, cortar en declive, hacer escarpa en.
scarper ['skɑrpər, B 'skɑpə] *v.i.* (jer., G.B.) (ú. gen. con *off* o en *imper*) escaparse, marcharse.
scarry ['skɑrɪ] *a.* cubierto de cicatrices; cicatrizado.
scar tissue, tejido cicatrizal.
scarus ['skærəs, B 'skeɪr-] *s.* (ict.) escaro.
scarves, *pl. de* **scarf,** bufanda.
scary ['skɛrɪ, B 'skɛərɪ] *a.* (SCARIER; SCARIEST) (fam.) 1. pavoroso, temeroso. 2. asustadizo, espantadizo, miedoso. 3. alarmante.
scat [skæt] *v.i.* (*pret., p.p.* SCATTED; *p.pr.* SCATTING) 1. largarse, irse precipitadamente. 2. correr rápidamente. 3. improvisar letra disparatada, cantar una letra improvisada. —*s.* canción de jazz con letra disparatada.
scathe [skeɪð] *s.* (ant., dial.) daño, perjuicio, mal; lesión, herida, desgracia, desdicha. —*v.t.* 1. lastimar, lesionar; chamuscar, abrasar. 2. (fig.) criticar acerbamente.
scatheless ['skeɪðləs] *a.* ileso.
scathing ['skeɪðɪŋ] *a.* acerbo, mordaz, severísimo, ej., *a s. rebuke,* un reproche severísimo.
scathingly [-lɪ] *adv.* acerbamente, mordazmente, con severidad.
scatological [,skætə'lɑdʒɪkəl, B -'lɔdʒ-] *a.* escatológico.
scatology [skə'tɑlədʒɪ, B -'tɔl-] *s.* escatología.
scatophagous [skæ'tɑfəgəs, B skə'tɔf-] *a.* (biol.) escatófago.
scatter ['skætər, B -ə] *v.t.* 1. esparcir, diseminar, desparramar. 2. disipar. 3. dispersar, poner en fuga. 4. (fís.) dispersar (luz, rayo de radiación, etc.). —*v.i.* 1. esparcirse. 2. dispersarse. —*s.* 1. esparcimiento. 2. dispersión; disipación. 3. puñado; pizca.
scatterbrain [-,breɪn] *s.* (fam.) cabeza de chorlito.
scatterbrained [-,breɪnd] *a.* (fam.) atolondrado, casquivano, ligero de cascos.
scattered showers, lluvias aisladas.
scattergood [-,gʊd] *s.* derrochador, pródigo, manirroto, malgastador, despilfarrador.
scattering ['skætərɪŋ] *s.* 1. dispersión, esparcimiento, desparramamiento, desperdigamiento. 2. puñado; pizca, pequeña cantidad. —*a.* disperso; dividido entre varios (ej., votos entre candidatos).
scatter rug, alfombra pequeña (que se usa para llenar espacios entre alfombras grandes, muebles, etc.).
scavenge ['skævəndʒ] *v.t.* 1. limpiar, barrer (calles, patios, etc.), recoger (la basura). 2. encontrar entre la basura, rescatar de entre los desechos (alimento, cosas utilizables, etc.). 3. (mot.) barrer, expulsar (los gases de los cilindros de un motor de combustión interna). 4. (metal.) lavar, purificar. —*v.i.* trabajar de basurero.
scavenger [-əndʒər, B -dʒə] *s.* 1. basurero. 2. trapero. 3. (pr. G.B.) barrendero. 4. animal que se alimenta de carroña.
scavenging stroke [-dʒɪŋ-] (mec.) carrera de expulsión.
Sc. D. *abrev. de* **Doctor of Science,** Doctor en Ciencias.
scedastic [sə'dæstɪk] *a.* (estadística) sedástico.
scenario [sə'nɛrɪ,oʊ, B -'nɑr-] *s.* (*pl.* SCENARIOS) 1. trama, argumento (de una obra de teatro, libreto de una ópera, etc.). 2. (cinem.) guión, argumento.
scenarist [-əst] *s.* (cinem.) guionista.
scend [sɛnd] (mar.) *v.i.* arfar, cabecear (buque). —*s.* arfada, cabeceo.
scene [sin] *s.* 1. escena, cuadro (en obra teatral, de t.v., etc.). 2. escena, paraje, lugar (de un acontecimiento o acción). 3. escena, vista, panorama; paisaje, ej., *a desolate s.,* un paisaje desolado. 4. (*gen. pl.*) (teat.) decoracion, decorado, bastidor. 5. (fig.) escena, escándalo, ej., *now don't make a s.,* no vayas a armar un escándalo. 6. (hist.) escenario, teatro. 7. **behind the scenes,** (teat. fig.) entre bastidores; **on the s.,** presente.
scenery ['sinərɪ] *s.* (*pl.* SCENERIES) 1. (teat.) decoraciones, decorado. 2. paisaje, vista, panorama.
sceneshifter ['sin,ʃɪftər, B -tə] *s.* (teat.) tramoyista.
scenic ['sinɪk] **scenical** [-ɪkəl] *a.* 1. escénico, dramático, teatral, ej., *s. effects,* efectos escénicos. 2. pintoresco, ej., *the s. beauty of the landscape,* la belleza pictórica del paisaje. 3. gráfico, vivido.
scenic railway, tren en miniatura (en ferias y parques de diversiones).
scenographer [si'nɑgrəfər, B -'nɔgrəfə] *s.* escenógrafo.
scenographic [,sinə'græfɪk] *a.* escenográfico.
scenographically [-ɪkəlɪ] *adv.* escenográficamente.
scenography [si'nɑgrəfɪ, B -nɔg-] *s.* escenografía.
scent [sɛnt] *v.t.* 1. oler. 2. olfatear, husmear, ventear; (fig.) sospechar, ej., *s. a plot,* sospechar una conspiración. 3. perfumar. —*v.i.* 1. olfatear, husmear. 2. **s. of,** oler a. —*s.* 1. olor, aroma, fragancia. 2. (fig.) indicio, huella; esp. rastro, pista, ej., *the dogs found* (o *picked up*) *the s.,* los perros encontraron el rastro (o hallaron la pista). 3. perfume. 4. olfato. 5. trozos de papel (que se arrojan en el juego de la caza de las liebres). 6. **false s.,** pista falsa; **on the s.,** sobre (o en) la pista; **to follow the s.,** ponerse a la pista; **to throw** (o **put**) **off the s.,** despistar, engañar con falsos indicios.
scented ['sɛntəd] *a.* perfumado.
scepsis, sceptic, sceptical, sceptically, scepticalness, scepticism, *vars. de* **skepsis, skeptic, skeptical, skeptically, skepticalness, skepticism.**
scepter, sceptre ['sɛptər, B -tə] *s.* cetro. —*v.t.* dotar o proveer de cetro; investir de autoridad real.
sceptered, sceptred [-tərd, B -təd] *a.* 1. dotado de cetro. 2. real, imperial, soberano.
schedule ['skɛdʒʊl, -əl, B 'ʃɛdjul] *s.* lista, cuadro, catálogo; inventario; programa, plan, horario, ej., *behind s.,* atrasado (tren, proyecto, tarea, etc.). —*v.t.* catalogar; inventariar; proyectar; fijar la hora de.
scheelite ['ʃeɪl,aɪt, B 'ʃil-] *s.* (min.) scheelita.
Scheherezade [ʃə,hɛrə'zɑd, B -,hɪərə'zɑdə] *s.* Sherezada, personaje central de *Las Mil y una Noches.*
schema ['skimə] *s.* (*pl.* SCHEMATA [-mətə]) esquema; plan, proyecto, programa o diagrama; sumario, sinopsis, cuadro; (lóg.) figura silogística.
schematic [skɪ'mætɪk] *a.* esquemático, gráfico.
schematically [-ɪkəlɪ] *adv.* esquemáticamente.
schematism ['skimə,tɪzəm] *s.* esquematismo.
schematize [-,taɪz] *v.t.* esquematizar.
scheme [skim] *s.* 1. esquema; plan, programa, proyecto. 2. ardid, treta, artificio, intriga; designio. 3. plan sistemático; sistema, arreglo, disposición. 4. (astrol.) horóscopo. 5. (ant.) diagrama. —*v.t.* proyectar, idear, concebir; fraguar, tramar, urdir. —*v.i.* formar proyectos; urdir o maquinar una intriga; tramar una treta.
schemer ['skimər, B -ə] *s.* intrigante, maquinador; tracista.
scheming [-ɪŋ] *a.* intrigante, maquinador; astuto, mañoso.
scherzo ['skɛrt,soʊ, B 'skɛət-] *s.* (*pl.* SCHERZOS) (mús.) scherzo, trozo vivo y alegre.
Schick test [ʃɪk-] (med.) prueba de Schick.
schilling ['ʃɪlɪŋ] *s.* schilling (unidad monetaria de Austria).
schipperke ['skɪpərkɪ, B 'ʃɪpəkɪ] *s.* perro faldero oriundo de Bélgica.
schism ['sɪzəm, 'skɪz-] *s.* 1. cisma; escisión, separación, división. 2. (relig.) pecado del cisma. 3. secta o facción cismáticas.
schismatic [sɪz'mætɪk] *a., s.* cismático.
schismatical [-ɪkəl] *a.* cismático.
schismatically [-kəlɪ] *adv.* cismáticamente.
schismatist ['sɪzmətəst] *s.* cismático.
schismatize [-mə,taɪz] *v.i.* volverse cismático. —*v.t.* provocar cisma, dividir.

schist [ʃɪst] *s.* (geol.) esquisto.
schistose ['ʃɪstoʊs] **schistous** [-təs] *a.* (geol.) esquistoso.
schistosomiasis [ˌʃɪstəsoʊ'maɪəsəs] *s.* (med., vet.) esquistosomiasis.
schizo ['skɪtsoʊ] *s.* (fam.) esquizofrénico.
schizocarp ['skɪzəˌkɑrp, B 'skaɪzəˌkɑp] *s.* (bot.) esquizocarpo.
schizocarpic [ˌskɪzə'kɑrpɪk, B ˌskaɪzə'kɑpɪk] *a.* (bot.) esquizocárpico.
schizogenesis [-'dʒɛnəsəs] *s.* (biol.) esquizogénesis.
schizogony [skɪ'zɑgənɪ, B skaɪ'zɔ-] *s.* (biol.) esquizogonia.
schizoid ['skɪtˌsɔɪd] (psic.) *a., s.* esquizoide.
schizomycete [ˌskɪzə'maɪˌsit, B ˌskaɪzə-] *s.* (bot.) esquizomiceta.
schizomycosis [-oʊmaɪ'koʊsəs] *s.* (med.) esquizomicosis.
schizophrene ['skɪtsəˌfrin] *s.* (med.) esquizofrénico.
schizophrenia [ˌskɪtsə'frinɪə] *s.* (med.) esquizofrenia.
schizophrenic [-'frɛnɪk] *a., s.* (med.) esquizofrénico.
schizophyte ['skɪzəˌfaɪt, B 'skaɪzə-] *s.* (bot.) esquizófita.
schizopod [-ˌpɑd, B -ˌpɔd] *s.* (zool.) esquizópodo.
schizothymia [ˌskɪtsə'θaɪmɪə] *s.* esquizotimia.
schizothymic [-mɪk] *a.* (psic.) esquizotímico.
schlemiel [ʃlə'mil] *s.* (jer.) bobo, zoquete, memo, simplón.
schmaltz, schmalz [ʃmɔlts, ʃmɑlts, B ʃmɔlts] *s.* (jer.) sensiblería, sentimentalismo (en la expresión del arte); música exageradamente sentimental.
schmo, schmoe [ʃmoʊ] *s.* (*pl.* SCHMOES) (jer.) pelmazo servil.
schmuck [ʃmʌk] *s.* (yiddish, jer., E.U.) persona muy necia.
schnapper ['ʃnæpər, B -pə] *s.* (ict.) pagro dorado de Australia y Nueva Zelandia.
schnapps [ʃnæps] *s.* aguardiente, esp. ginebra de Holanda.
schnauzer ['ʃnaʊzər, B 'ʃnaʊtsə] *s.* (zool.) grifón alemán.
schnitzel ['ʃnɪtsəl] *s.* (cocina austríaca) chuleta de ternera.
schnook [ʃnʊk] *s.* (jer.) bobalicón; nulidad.
schnorrer ['ʃnɔrər, B -ə] *s.* (jer., E.U.) gorrón, gorrista, sablista.
schnozzle ['ʃnɑzəl, B 'ʃnɔz-] *s.* (jer.) nariz.
scholar ['skɑlər, B 'skɔlə] *s.* 1. escolar, colegial; alumno, pupilo. 2. becario. 3. erudito, docto, sabio, hombre de letras. 4. (dial.) persona instruida, esp. uno que sabe leer y escribir.
scholarch ['skɑlɑrk, B 'skoʊlɑk] *s.* (hist.) director o principal de una escuela (esp. de una escuela ateniense de filosofía).
scholarism [-əˌrɪzəm, B 'skɔl-] *s.* saber escolástico; pedantería.
scholarly ['skɑlərlɪ, B 'skɔləlɪ] *a.* erudito, ilustrado, docto, letrado. —*adv.* (raro) eruditamente, doctamente, sabiamente.
scholarship [-ˌʃɪp] *s.* 1. erudición, saber. 2. beca, plaza pensionada, colegiatura, bolsa (de estudios); **athletic s.,** (E.U.) beca deportivo.
scholastic [skə'læstɪk] *a.* 1. escolástico, escolar; académico, ej., *s. rank,* jerarquía académica. 2. (filos.) escolástico. 3. pedante, formal. —*s.* 1. (filos.) (gen. **S.**) escolástico. 2. (despec.) pedante, formalista.
scholastical [-tɪkəl] *a., s.* escolástico.
scholastically [-kəlɪ] *adv.* escolásticamente.
scholasticate [skə'læstəˌkeɪt] *s.* (relig.) instituto de enseñanza para jesuitas o estudiantes de escolástica.
scholasticism [-ˌsɪzəm] *s.* 1. (filos.) escolasticismo, escolástica. 2. escolasticismo (apego a los métodos o enseñanzas tradicionales).
scholiast ['skoʊlɪˌæst] *s.* escoliador, escoliasta; comentador; anotador.
scholiastic [ˌskoʊlɪ'æstɪk] *a.* de los escoliastas.
scholium ['skoʊlɪəm] *s.* (*pl.* SCHOLIA [-ə] o SCHOLIUMS) escolio; glosa, anotación.
school [skul] *s.* 1. escuela, colegio. 2. escuela, alumnado. 3. enseñanza, instrucción; clase, curso. 4. escuela (de un maestro, doctrina, estilo, etc.), ej., *the Socratic s.,* la escuela de Sócrates, *Venetian, Flemish,* etc. *s.,* escuela veneciana, flamenca, etc. (de pintura). 5. (mús.) manual (de violín, contrapunto, etc.). 6. (hist.) aula, cátedra, (esp. en la Edad Media, para clases de lógica, metafísica y teología). 7. **a gentleman of the old s.,** un caballero a la antigua; **in s.,** en la escuela; (fig.) lealtad excesiva a clase o grupo (al que pertenece uno); **to go to s.,** ir al colegio; estudiar, hacer sus estudios; matricularse (por primera vez) en la escuela. —*v.t.* 1. educar, instruir, enseñar. 2. aleccionar, adiestrar, disciplinar; ejercitar, entrenar. 3. **s. oneself in,** ejercitarse en. —*a.* escolar, escolástico; de escuela.
school, *s.* cardumen, cardume, banco (de peces). —*v.i.* nadar (los peces) en cardúmenes o bancos.
school age, edad escolar.
schoolbag ['skulˌbæg] *s.* cartapacio, maleta o maletín escolar.
school board, junta de educación.
schoolbook [-ˌbʊk] *s.* texto escolar, libro de colegio.
schoolboy [-ˌbɔɪ] *s.* colegial, escolar, alumno de escuela.
school bus, ómnibus escolar.
schoolchild [-ˌtʃaɪld] *s.* colegial, escolar.
school day, día lectivo.
schooldays [-ˌdeɪz] *s. pl.* años de colegio (ú. esp. al recordarse de ellos).
school divine, teólogo escolástico.
school edition, edición escolar (de un texto).
schoolfellow ['skulˌfɛloʊ] *s.* condiscípulo, compañero de escuela.
schoolgirl [-ˌgɜrl, B -ˌgɜl] *s.* colegiala, alumna de escuela, estudiante.
schoolhouse [-ˌhaʊs] *s.* (edificio de) escuela, colegio.
schooling [-ɪŋ] *s.* 1. instrucción, educación, enseñanza; experiencia. 2. precio o costo de la instrucción escolar. 3. entrenamiento (de caballos y jinetes, esp. en una escuela de equitación). 4. (ant.) castigo; reprobación.
schoolman [-mən] *s.* 1. polemista, docto. 2. maestro o director de escuela. 3. teólogo, escolástico.
schoolma'am ['skulˌmɑm] **schoolmarm** [-ˌmɑrm, B -ˌmɑm] *s.* maestra (de escuela).
schoolmaster [-ˌmæstər, B -ˌmɑstə] *s.* 1. maestro de escuela, profesor; pedagogo. 2. (ict.) especie de pargo.
schoolmate [-ˌmeɪt] *s.* compañero o compañera de colegio.
schoolmistress [-ˌmɪstrəs] *s.* maestra de escuela, profesora.
schoolroom [-ˌrum, -ˌrʊm] *s.* aula, sala de clase.
school ship, buque escuela, barco de entrenamiento.
schoolteacher ['skulˌtitʃər, B -tʃə] *s.* maestro o maestra de escuela (esp. de escuela primaria).
schooltime [-ˌtaɪm] *s.* 1. comienzo del año escolar. 2. años escolares. 3. período de entrenamiento.
schoolwork [-ˌwɜrk, B -ˌwɜk] *s.* tarea(s) o trabajo(s) escolar(es).
schoolyard [-ˌjɑrd, B -ˌjɑd] *s.* patio de recreo (de una escuela).
school year, año escolar, año lectivo.
schooner ['skunər, B -nə] *s.* 1. (mar.) goleta. 2. vaso grande de cerveza.
schooner rig, (mar.) aparejo de goleta.
schooner-rigged [-ˌrɪgd] *a.* (mar.) de velas cangrejas.
schorl [ʃɔrl, B ʃɔl] *s.* (min.) chorlo, turmalina negra.
schottische ['ʃɑtɪʃ, B ʃɔ'tiʃ] *s.* chotis (baile y música).
schuss [ʃʊs, ʃus] *s.* (esquí) deslizamiento veloz en línea recta; recorrido en línea recta. —*v.i.* deslizar en línea recta.
schwa [ʃwɑ] *s.* (fon.) (símbolo de) vocal inacentuada de sonido indeterminado.
sciamachy [saɪ'æməkɪ] *s.* lucha contra una sombra; combate imaginario o fútil.
sciatic [saɪ'ætɪk] *a.* 1. ciático. 2. enfermo de ciática.
sciatica [-ɪkə] *s.* (med.) ciática.
science ['saɪəns] *s.* 1. ciencia. 2. ciencias naturales. 3. arte, destreza, habilidad, pericia.
science fiction, ciencia ficción.
scient ['saɪənt] *a.* entendido, hábil, diestro, ducho.
sciential [saɪ'ɛntʃəl, B -'ɛnʃəl] *a.* 1. del conocimiento. 2. con conocimientos útiles, capaz, competente.
scientific [ˌsaɪən'tɪfɪk] *a.* científico.
scientifically [-ɪkəlɪ] *adv.* científicamente.
scientist ['saɪəntəst] *s.* científico, hombre de ciencia, sabio.
scilicet ['sɪləˌsɛt, B 'saɪ-] *adv.* a saber, o sea, es decir.
scimitar, scimiter ['sɪmətər, B -ə] *s.* cimitarra, alfanje.
scincoid ['sɪŋkɔɪd] (zool.) *a., s.* escíncido.
scintilla [sɪn'tɪlə] *s.* centella, chispa; vestigio, huella.
scintillant ['sɪntələnt] *a.* centelleante, centellante, chispeante, titilador, titilante.
scintillate [-ˌeɪt] *v.i.* chispear, chisporrotear; centellear, escintilar; titilar. —*v.t.* echar chispazos de (ingenio, etc.).
scintillating [-ɪŋ] *a.* centelleante; chispeante, ej., *s. wit,* ingenio chispeante.
scintillation [ˌsɪntə'leɪʃən] *s.* 1. centelleo, chispeo. 2. chispazo, destello, resplandor. 3. (astr.) titilación (de estrellas o del planeta Mercurio).
scintillation counter, (fís.) contador de centelleo.
scintillometer [ˌsɪntəl'ɑmətər, B -'ɔmɪtə] *s.* (fís.) contador de centelleo.
sciolism ['saɪəˌlɪzəm] *s.* conocimientos superficiales.
sciolist [-ləst] *s.* erudito a la violeta.
sciomancy ['saɪəˌmænsɪ] *s.* adivinación por consulta a los espíritus o sombras de los muertos.
scion ['saɪən] *s.* 1. púa, acodo, plantón, vástago, retoño, renuevo, verdugo. 2. vástago, hijo, hija, descendiente.
scirocco [ʃɪ'rɑkoʊ, B -'rɔk-] *var. de* **sirocco.**
scirrhoid ['skɪrˌɔɪd, B 'sɪr-] *a.* (med.) escirroide.
scirrhous [-əs] *a.* (med.) escirroso, cirroso.
scirrhus [-əs] *s.* (*pl.* SCIRRHI [-aɪ] o SCIRRHUSES) (med.) escirro.

scissel ['sɪsəl] *s.* desperdicios de metal.
scissile ['sɪsəl, B -ˌaɪl] *a.* hendible.
scission ['sɪʒən] *s.* escisión.
scissor ['sɪzər, B -ə] *v.t.* cortar con tijeras, tijeretear.
scissors [-ərz, B -əz] *s. pl.* 1. (t. **pair of s.**) tijeras. 2. (gimnasia) salto de tijera. 3. (lucha libre) toma de tijera.
scissors kick, (natación) golpe de tijera.
scissors truss, (arq.) cuchillo de armadura.
scissortail [-ərˌteɪl, B -əˌ-] *s.* (orn.) tijereta.
scissure ['sɪʒər, B -ʃjuə] *s.* cortada, cisura; ruptura.
sciurine ['saɪjərən, B -ˌraɪn] *a.* (zool.) esciurino.
sciuroid [-ˌrɔɪd] *a.* 1. (zool.) esciúrido. 2. como una cola de ardilla (espiga, cebada, etc.).
sclaff [sklæf] *s.* 1. (esco.) golpe leve; chasquido ligero. 2. (golf) golpe errado (que da en la tierra detrás de la pelota). —*v.i.* (golf) golpear la tierra detrás de la pelota. —*v.t.* (golf) rozar (la tierra) en golpe mal ejecutado.
SCLC *abrev. de* **Southern Christian Leadership Conference,** Concilio de Líderes Cristianos Sureños, organización pro derechos civiles de los negros de los E.U.
sclera ['sklɪrə, B 'sklɪərə] *s.* (anat.) esclerótica.
sclerenchyma [sklə'reŋkəmə] *s.* (bot.) esclerénquima (tejido).
sclerenchymatous [ˌsklɪrən'kɪmətəs, B ˌsklɪər-] *a.* (bot.) esclerenquimático.
scleriasis [sklɪ'raɪəsəs] *s.* (med.) escleriasis.
sclerite ['sklɪraɪt, B 'sklɪər-] *s.* (zool.) placa quitinosa (de artrópodos).
scleritis [sklɪ'raɪtəs] *s.* (med.) escleritis.
scleroderma [ˌsklɪrə'dɜrmə, B ˌsklɪərə'dɜmə] *s.* (med.) esclerodermia.
scleroid ['sklɪrˌɔɪd, B 'sklɪər-] *a.* (bot. zool.) escleroide.
scleroma [sklɪ'roʊmə] *s.* (*pl.* SCLEROMATA [-mətə]) (med.) escleroma.
sclerometer [-'rɑmətər, B -'rɔmɪtə] *s.* esclerómetro.
scleroprotein [ˌsklɪrə'proʊtin, -'proʊtɪən, B ˌsklɪər-] *s.* (quím.) escleroproteína.
sclerose [sklə'roʊs, B sklɪə-] *v.t., v.i.* volver(se) escleroso, endurecer(se).
sclerosed [-'roʊst] *a.* escleroso, esclorósico.
sclerosis [-'roʊsəs] *s.* (*pl.* SCLEROSES) (med., bot.) esclerosis.
sclerotic [-'rɑtɪk, B -'rɔt-] *a.* esclerótico. —*s.* esclerótica.
sclerotitis [ˌsklɪrə'taɪtəs, B ˌsklɪər-] *s.* (med.) esclerotitis.
sclerotomy [sklə'rɑtəmɪ, B -'rɔt-] *s.* (*pl.* SCLEROTOMIES) esclerotomía.
sclerous ['sklɪrəs, B 'sklɪər-] *a.* (anat., bot.) escleroso.
scoff [skɔf, skɑf, B skɔf] *s.* 1. mofa, burla, escarnio, befa, ludibrio. 2. adefesio; cosa ridícula. —*v.i.* mofarse, burlarse, befar; **s. at,** burlarse de, mofarse de. —*v.t.* ridiculizar, escarnecer, mofarse de.
scoffer ['skɔfər, 'skɑf-, B 'skɔfə] *s.* mofador, burlador, burlón.
scoffingly [-ɪŋlɪ] *adv.* con mofa y escarnio.
scofflaw [-ˌlɔ] *s.* persona que burla la ley.
scold [skoʊld] *s.* 1. regañón, reñidor, abusador. 2. regaño, reprensión. —*v.i., v.t.* 1. regañar, increpar, reñir, reprender, sermonear, reconvenir, amonestar. 2. (ant.) alborotar, vilipendiar.
scolder ['skoʊldər, B -ə] *s.* regañón, reñidor.
scolding [-ɪŋ] *a.* regañón. —*s.* regaño, reprensión.
scoldingly [-lɪ] *adv.* con regaños, en tono regañón.
scolecite ['skɑləˌsaɪt, B 'skɔl-] *s.* (min.) escolecita.
scolex ['skoʊlɛks] *s.* (*pl.* SCOLECES [-ləˌsiz]) (zool.) escólex.
scoliosis [ˌskoʊlɪ'oʊsəs, B ˌskɔlɪ-] *s.* (med.) escoliosis.
scollop, scolloper, *vars. de* **scallop, scalloper.**
scolopendrid ['skɑlə'pɛndrəd, B ˌskɔl-] *s., a.* (zool.) escolopéndrido.
scombroid ['skɑmˌbrɔɪd, B 'skɔm-] *s., a.* (ict.) escombroideo.
sconce [skɑns, B skɔns] *s.* brazo de luz, candelabro de pared.
sconce, *s.* 1. fortín, baluarte, fuerte destacado. 2. (ant.) refugio, abrigo. —*v.t.* (ant.) fortificar, atrincherar, escudar, proteger.
sconcheon ['skɑntʃən, B 'skɔnʃən] *s.* (arq.) mocheta.
scone [skoʊn, B skɔn] *s.* panecillo que gen. se toma con el té.
scoop [skup] *s.* 1. cuchara, cucharón, cazo. 2. pala de mano, paleta. 3. cangilón (de draga). 4. (mar.) achicador. 5. cucharada, paletada, palada. 6. cavidad, hueco, hoyo. 7. primicia, noticia sensacional exclusiva (en un periódico). 8. (fam., G.B.) ganancia inesperada; fortunón. —*v.t.* 1. (t. con *up*) sacar con cuchara o pala. 2. (mar.) achicar, vaciar (agua). 3. (gen. con *out*) cavar, excavar, ahuecar. 4. adelantar en dar noticia sensacional (al periódico o periodista rival). 5. adueñarse de, acaparar. 6. **s. in,** recaudar (ganancias); **s. up,** recoger; levantar.
scooper ['skupər, B -ə] *s.* 1. gubia, buril. 2. (orn.) avoceta.
scoopful [-ˌfʊl] *s.* cucharada o palada (como medida de capacidad).
scoop net, red barredera.
scoot [skut] *s.* (fam.) pasada veloz. —*v.i.* (fam.) 1. pasar o correr rápidamente. 2. largarse, poner pies en polvorosa. —*interj.* (fam.) ¡largo! ¡lárgate! ¡vete!
scooter ['skutər, B -ə] *s.* 1. patineta, patinete (de niño). 2. (t. **motor s.**) motoneta.
scop [skɑp, B skɔp] *s.* (hist.) bardo, poeta.
scope [skoʊp] *s.* 1. campo o esfera de acción; oportunidad (para talento, etc.). 2. alcance, ej., *of wide s.,* de gran alcance. 3. propósito, intención. 4. *forma abrev. de* **telescope,** telescopio, **microscope,** microscopio, etc.
scopolamine [skoʊ'pɑləˌmin, B skə'pɔl-] *s.* (quím.) escopolamina.
scops owl ['skɑps-, B 'skɔps-] (orn.) buharro.
scopula ['skɑpjələ, B 'skɔp-] *s.* (zool.) escópula.
scorbutic [skɔr'bjutɪk, B skɔ'-] *a.* (med.) escorbútico.
scorch [skɔrtʃ, B skɔtʃ] *v.t.* 1. chamuscar, tostar, socarrar; abrasar (plantas, etc.). 2. (fig., fam.) herir, agravar, afectar con sarcasmo o crítica acerba. 3. (mil.) devastar por completo, arrasar. —*v.i.* 1. quemarse, tostarse (al sol). 2. (fam.) ir a gran velocidad (en coche o bicicleta).
scorched earth [skɔrtʃt-, B skɔtʃt-] (mil.) tierra abrasada.
scorcher ['skɔrtʃər, B 'skɔtʃə] *s.* 1. respuesta sarcástica, crítica acerba. 2. día excesivamente caluroso. 3. (fam.) automovilista o ciclista que corre a velocidad excesiva. 4. (jer.) lo mejor (dentro de su clase); bomba, sorpresa grande.
scorching [-tʃɪŋ] *a.* 1. ardiente, caluroso, bochornoso. 2. mordaz, acerbo, cruel, hiriente (crítica, ingenio, etc.).
score [skɔr, B skɔ] *s.* 1. muesca, incisión, raya (esp. la hecha para llevar cuentas o como registro). 2. línea, raya, marca (de partida o meta). 3. cuenta, cuentas. 4. resultado, nota (en competencia o examen). 5. tantos, tanteo (en juegos y deportes). 6. razón, motivo. 7. veintena; (*pl.*) cantidad grande, multitud; gran número de gente. 8. (mús.) partitura. 9. (fam.) acierto, lance, jugada afortunada. 10. **on that s.,** en cuanto a eso, a ese respecto; **to keep s.,** tantear, apuntar los tantos; **to know the s.,** conocer la situación (verdadera); saber cuántas son cinco; **to pay off old scores,** saldar cuentas, vengarse de ofensas pasadas; **to settle a s.,** ajustar cuentas. —*v.t.* 1. marcar, rayar, delinear. 2. registrar, marcar con cortes o muescas; apuntar, anotar. 3. asentar, poner en cuenta, cargar. 4. (juegos) marcar o ganar (tantos, puntos); apuntar (tantos). 5. alcanzar, lograr, conseguir, ej., *he has scored a success,* él ha logrado un triunfo. 6. clasificar (ganado, fruta, etc.); calificar (candidatos); graduar (exámenes). 7. reprender, castigar. 8. (cocina) estriar, hacer cortes en (carne, etc.). 9. (mús.) instrumentar, orquestar. 10. **s. out** (**words,** etc.), tachar (palabras, etc. en un escrito). —*v.i.* 1. tantear, actuar como registrador de tantos (en el juego). 2. marcar un tanto; apuntarse un tanto. 3. tener ventaja, ser superior. 4. **s. over (someone),** superar, sobrepujar (a alguien).
scoreboard ['skɔrˌbɔrd, B 'skɔˌbɔd] *s.* marcador, tanteador, pizarra o tablero de resultados.
scorecard [-ˌkɑrd, B -ˌkɑd] *s.* (dep.) anotador (tarjeta).
scorekeeper [-ˌkipər, B -pə] *s.* (dep.) marcador o tanteador (persona).
scoreless [-ləs] *a.* (dep.) sin abrir el marcador, con el marcador en cero, ej., *the match ended in a s. draw,* el partido terminó empatado a cero.
scorer ['skɔrə] *s.* 1. marcador, registrador, computador. 2. jugador que hace tantos o gana puntos para su equipo; (fútbol) goleador.
scoria ['skɔrɪə] *s.* (*pl.* SCORIAE [-ˌi]) escoria.
scorification [ˌskɔrəfə'keɪʃən] *s.* escorificación.
scorify ['skɔrəˌfaɪ] *v.t.* (*pret., p.p.* SCORIFIED; *p.pr.* SCORIFYING) escorificar.
scorn [skɔrn, B skɔn] *s.* 1. desdén, desprecio, menosprecio. 2. objeto de desdén o desprecio. —*v.t.* desdeñar, despreciar, desestimar, menospreciar; **s. to (do),** no dignarse, rehusar (hacer). —*v.i.* mofarse, burlarse.
scorner ['skɔrnər, B 'skɔnə] *s.* desdeñador, desestimador.
scornful [-fəl] *a.* desdeñoso, despreciativo, despectivo.
scornfully [-fəlɪ] *adv.* desdeñosamente, despectivamente.
scornfulness [-fəlnəs] *s.* desdén inherente, carácter despectivo (de voz, palabras, mirada, etc.).
scorpaenid [skɔr'pinəd, B skɔ'-] *s., a.* (ict.) escorpénido.
scorpene ['skɔrpin, B 'skɔpin] *s.* (ict.) peje diablo, rascacio, rescaza.
Scorpio ['skɔrpɪˌoʊ, B 'skɔpɪ-] *s.* (astr., astrol.) Escorpión.
scorpioid [-ˌɔɪd] *a.* 1. (zool.) escorpiónido, escorpionideo. 2. (bot.) escorpioide.
scorpion ['skɔrpɪən, B 'skɔpjən] *s.* 1. escorpión, alacrán. 2. (bíbl., hist.) escorpión (azote; ballesta). 3. **S.,** (astr.) Escorpión.
scorpion broom, (bot.) especie de retama.
scorpion fish, (ict.) escorpina, escorpión, baila, raño.
scorpion grass, (bot.) raspilla, miosota.
scorpion senna, (bot.) alacranera.
scot [skɑt, B skɔt] *s.* (hist.) escote; tasa, impuesto, contribución.
Scot, *s.* escocés, natural de Escocia.

Scot. *abrev. de* **Scotland, Scottish, Escocia,** escocés.
scot and lot, 1. (G.B., hist.) derechos parroquiales. 2. (fig.) obligaciones en conjunto.
scotch [skɑtʃ, B skɔtʃ] *v.t.* 1. cortar, herir ligeramente. 2. erradicar, suprimir. 3. calzar, engalgar (una rueda o ruedas). 4. (fig.) detener, frustrar. —*s.* 1. corte, cortadura, herida superficial; incisión. 2. galga, cuña (para ruedas).
Scotch, *a.* escocés. —*s.* 1. (dialecto) escocés. 2. whiski escocés. 3. **the S.,** los escoceses. 4. (marca de fábrica) cinta adhesiva transparente.
Scotch broth, sopa de cebada y verduras.
Scotch fir, (bot.) pino albar, pino manso.
Scotch-Irish ['skɑtʃ,aɪrɪʃ, B 'skɔtʃ-] *a.* (de familia o ascendencia) escocesa e irlandesa.
Scotch kale, (bot.) col.
Scotchman [-mən] *s.* escocés.
Scotch mist, llovizna (muy común en las colinas escocesas).
Scotch pebble, (min.) cuarzo amarillo, topacio ahumado.
Scotch pine, (bot.) pino albar, pino de Valsaín.
Scotch tape, (TM), cinta durex *or* pegante *or* scotch, cinta adhesiva transparente.
Scotch terrier, *var. de* **Scottish terrier.**
Scotch thistle, (bot.) 1. cardo borriquero o borriqueño, cardo yesquero. 2. cardo.
Scotch woodcock, tostada con huevo y crema de anchoa.
scoter ['skoʊtər, B -ə] *s.* (*pl.* SCOTER O SCOTERS) (orn.) foja, fúlica, negreta, pato negro.
scot-free ['skɑt'fri, B 'skɔt-] *a.* 1. impune. 2. incólume, ileso. 3. libre de pago; sin haber pagado nada.
scotia ['skoʊʃə] *s.* (arq.) escocia, nacela.
Scotia, *s.* (poét.) Escocia.
Scotism ['skoʊt,ɪzəm] *s.* (filos.) escotismo.
Scotist [-əst] *s.* (filos.) escotista.
Scotland ['skɑtlənd, B 'skɔt-] *s.* Escocia.
Scotland Yard, 1. cuerpo de investigación criminal de la policía londinense. 2. pequeña calle sede original de este organismo.
scotoma [skə'toʊmə] *s.* (*pl.* SCOTOMATA [-mətə] O SCOTOMAS) (med.) escotoma.
Scots [skɑts, B skɔts] *a.* escocés.
Scotsman ['skɑtsmən, B 'skɔts-] *s.* escocés.
Scotticism ['skɑtə,sɪzəm, B 'skɔt-] *s.* modismo o localismo escoceses.
Scottie ['skɑtɪ, B 'skɔtɪ] *s.* 1. (fam.) escocés. 2. **s., terrier** escocés.
Scottish [-ɪʃ] *a.* escocés. —*s.* (dialecto) escocés; **the S.,** los escoceses.
Scottish terrier, (zool.) terrier escocés.
scoundrel ['skaʊndrəl] *s., a.* pícaro, bribón, bergante, truhán, pillo, villano.
scoundrelly [-drəlɪ] *a.* bribonesco.
scour [skaʊr, B 'skaʊə] *v.i.* correr velozmente, esp. en persecución o búsqueda. —*v.t.* batir (el campo, monte); registrar, recorrer, explorar.
scour, *v.t.* 1. fregar, restregar, estregar, frotar, pulir. 2. purgar. 3. depurar; limpiar, desengrasar, quitar manchas a; baldear, lavar con un chorro de agua. 4. (ant.) barrer, expulsar (al enemigo). —*v.i.* lavarse, limpiarse. —*s.* 1. fregado, fricción, frotación, lavado. 2. (substancia) detergente. 3. (*gen. pl.*) diarrea (en los animales).
scourer ['skaʊrər, B 'skaʊərə] *s.* 1. (ant.) azotacalles; ladrón nocturno. 2. polvo abrasivo para fines de limpieza y pulimento.
scourge [skɜrdʒ, B skɜdʒ] *v.t.* 1. azotar, flagelar, fustigar. 2. castigar severamente, mortificar, acosar, hostigar, atormentar. —*s.* 1. azote, flagelo, látigo. 2. (fig.) flagelo, azote; calamidad, plaga (esp. como castigo divino).
scourger ['skɜrdʒər, B -ə] *s.* azotador, flagelador, fustigador, castigador.
scouring ['skaʊrɪŋ, B 'skaʊər-] *s.* 1. barredura, basura. 2. (fig.) (*gen. pl.*) canalla, escoria.
scouring rush, (bot.) cola de caballo, rabo de mula.
scouse [skaʊs] *s.* (mar.) porción al horno del rancho del marinero.
scout [skaʊt] *v.i.* 1. (mil.) hacer reconocimiento; (raro) montar guardia. 2. **s. for,** buscar. —*v.t.* 1. explorar, registrar. 2. (mil.) reconocer, explorar. —*s.* 1. exploración, reconocimiento. 2. explorador. 3. niño explorador. 4. (fam.) sujeto, tipo, compañero. 5. (G.B.) criado, sirviente (en la Universidad de Oxford). 6. avión de reconocimiento. 7. (mil.) explorador. 8. (dep.) informador (que obtiene datos en cuanto a habilidad, forma de juego, etc. del rival).
scout, *v.t.* rechazar, despreciar, desdeñar (idea, sugerencia, etc.). —*v.i.* (gen. con *at*) burlarse, mofarse (de).
scout car, (mil.) carro de exploración.
scoutcraft ['skaʊt,kræft, B -,krɑft] *s.* habilidad en exploración.
scouter [-ər, B -ə] *s.* 1. explorador. 2. (E.U.) muchacho explorador veterano (mayor de 18 años).
scouth [skuθ] *s.* (esco.) abundancia.
scouting ['skaʊtɪŋ] *s.* 1. exploración, reconocimiento. 2. actividades de los niños exploradores.
scoutmaster [-,mæstər, B -,mɑstə] *s.* jefe de tropa de niños exploradores.
scow [skaʊ] *s.* chalana, lanchón.
scowl [skaʊl] *v.i.* 1. fruncir el entrecejo, mirar ceñudamente, mirar con severidad o mal humor. 2. presentar un aspecto amenazador (ej., una montaña). —*v.t.* expresar con ceño. —*s.* ceño, sobrecejo, aspecto ceñudo.
scowlingly ['skaʊlɪŋlɪ] *adv.* ceñudamente, severamente.
scowman ['skaʊmən] *s.* lanchero.
scrabble ['skræbəl] *v.i.* 1. rascar, raspar, escarbar, piafar. 2. arrastrarse; trepar. 3. garrapatear, garabatear, escarabajear. —*v.t.* 1. escarbar (tierra, etc.). 2. rascar con (uñas, etc.). 3. garrapatear. —*s.* 1. arrebatiña, trepa. 2. garabato, garrapato. 3. rascadura repetida. 4. un juego de salón (en que se colocan letras formando palabras sobre un tablero).
scrabbly ['skræblɪ] *a.* (SCRABBLIER; SCRABBLIEST) 1. ronco, áspero (sonido, voz). 2. achaparrado; miserable.
scrag [skræg] *s.* 1. persona o animal flaco y pellejudo. 2. pescuezo (de ovejas o carneros). 3. (G.B.) pescuezo, cuello (de personas). —*v.t.* (*pret., p.p.* SCRAGGED; *p.pr.* SCRAGGING) 1. ahorcar, agarrotar. 2. estrangular. 3. torcer el pescuezo a. 4. (G.B.) agarrar por el cuello.
scragginess ['skrægɪnəs] *s.* 1. aspereza, escabrosidad. 2. flaqueza, flacura.
scraggly ['skræglɪ] *a.* (SCRAGGLIER; SCRAGGLIEST) 1. irregular, tortuoso (pista, etc.). 2. ralo (barba, bigote, etc.).
scraggy ['skrægɪ] *a.* (SCRAGGIER; SCRAGGIEST) 1. áspero, escabroso. 2. flaco, descarnado, enjuto, huesudo.
scram [skræm] *v.i.* (*pret., p.p.* SCRAMMED; *p.pr.* SCRAMMING) (jer.) largarse. —*s.* (imper.) ¡lárgate! ¡vete! ¡largo!
scramble ['skræmbəl] *v.i.* 1. gatear, escarebajear. 2. (gen. con *for*) andar a la rebatiña (por), bregar, reñir (por). 3. extenderse desigualmente (ej., un pueblo). —*v.t.* 1. arrebañar; hacinar, amontonar. 2. mezclar desordenada o confusamente; embrollar. 3. (cocina) hacer un revoltillo de (huevos). 4. (tel., teleg., rad.) desmodular. —*s.* rebatiña, arrebatiña; brega, riña, pelea confusa (por conseguir algo).
scrambled eggs, (cocina) huevos revueltos.
scrambler [-blər, B -blə] *s.* (tele., teleg.) criptógrafo, desmodulador.
scrannel ['skrænəl] *a.* 1. chirriador, discorde (voz, sonido). 2. (dial.) escaso, pobre (cosecha, etc.).
scrap [skræp] *s.* 1. pedazo, trozo (de papel, etc.); fragmento (de algo escrito). 2. (*pl.*) restos, sobras (de comida). 3. desperdicios, desechos, chatarra. 4. (*pl.*) chicharrones. 5. (fig.) vestigio, pizca, ápice, ej., *not a s. of,* ni un vestigio o ápice, ni una pizca de (pruebas, etc.). —*v.t.* (*pret, p.p.* SCRAPPED; *p.pr.* SCRAPPING) 1. arrumbar, desmontar (maquinaria, fábrica, etc.); desguazar (buques). 2. desechar, descartar, abandonar (ideas, métodos, etc.). —*a.* hecho de sobrantes o restos (ej., comidas).
scrap, *s.* (jer.) trifulca, riña, camorra. —*v.i.* reñir, disputar, pelear.
scrapbook ['skræp,bʊk] *s.* álbum de recortes.
scrape [skreɪp] *v.t.* 1. raspar, rascar, raer. 2. raspar, arañar, rascar (violín, etc.). 3. (gen. con *up* o *together*) arañar, juntar a duras penas (dinero, etc.). 4. **s. a living,** vivir de milagro; **s. off** (o **out** o **away),** remover raspando; **s. one's chin,** afeitarse; **s. one's plate,** dejar el plato limpio. —*v.i.* 1. (restregar el pie al) hacer reverencia. 2. ahorrar, economizar. 3. (gen. con *away*) rasgar, raspar (produciendo un chirrido). 4. **s. against,** rasar; **s. along,** ganarse la vida a duras penas; ir tirando; **s. through,** componérselas; pasar a duras penas (examen). —*s.* 1. rasguño, arañazo, roedura, raspadura. 2. ruido de raspar, ruido de arrastrar (los pies). 3. reverencia hecha llevando un pie atrás. 4. embrollo, enredo, apuro, apremio.
scraper ['skreɪpər, B -ə] *s.* 1. ahorrador, avaro, mísero. 2. rascador, raspador, escarbador, descarnador (cuchilla). 3. rascatripas. 4. desuellacaras.
scrap heap, 1. montón de chatarra. 2. montón de desechos; basurero. 3. **to throw on the s. h.,** desechar.
scrap iron, chatarra, hierro viejo.
scrapman ['skræpmən, -,mæn] *s.* chatarrero.
scrap merchant, (G.B.) chatarrero.
scrap paper, papel de desecho, papel para apuntes y notas (de inferior calidad).
scrapper ['skræpər, B -ə] *s.* (jer.) camorrista, pendenciero, buscapleitos, pleitista.
scrappily ['skræpəlɪ] *adv.* agresivamente, de modo belicoso.
scrapple ['skræpəl] *s.* pasta frita de carne de cerdo picada con harina y especias.
scrappy ['skræpɪ] *a.* (SCRAPPIER; SCRAPPIEST) 1. fragmentario, deshilvanado, incoherente. 2. (fam.) camorrista, pendenciero, agresivo, belicoso.
scratch [skrætʃ] *v.t.* 1. arañar, rasguñar; raspar. 2. rascar (la cabeza, picadura, etc.). 3. retirar (caballo, atleta, etc. de una competencia o carrera). 4. garabatear, garrapatear. 5. **s. my back and I will s. yours,** favor con favor se paga; **s. one's head,** (fig.) quedarse perplejo; **s. out,** cancelar, tachar, borrar; sacar (ojos) con las uñas; **s. the surface of,** (fig.) no profundizar mucho en (un asunto, etc.); **s. together,** arañar, juntar a duras penas (dinero). —*v.i.* 1. arañar (el gato, una pluma de escribir, etc.). 2. economizar. 3. (billar) chiripear, hacer una jugada de chiripa. 4. **s. along,** (jer.) ingeniárselas (para vivir); **s. for, s. around for,** buscar afanosamente. —*s.* 1.

arañazo, araño, rasguño. 2. garrapato, garabato. 3. rascadura, ruido de rascar, ruido de rozadura. 4. línea de partida (en carreras). 5. retiro, competidor retirado (de una carrera). 6. (billar) chiripa, barbarría. 7. (*pl.*) (vet.) grietas en las cuartillas. 8. (jer.) cuartos, guita, plata. 9. **a s. of the pen,** un rasgo de la pluma; **from s.,** desde el principio; de la nada, sin nada; **to come up to s.,** resultar tan bueno como se esperaba; alcanzar el nivel o grado requerido; **to start from s.,** empezar desde el principio; empezar sin nada. —*a.* 1. en borrador, de prueba. 2. para apuntes, de apuntes. 3. compuesto a la ventura, heterogéneo. 4. de chiripa; casual, venturoso. 5. (dep.) que no recibe ventaja.

scratch awl, lesna de marca.

scratcher ['skrætʃər, B -ə] *s.* raspador.

scratch filter, (rad.) filtro contra el rascado (de la aguja del gramófono).

scratch hardness, (metal.) dureza esclerométrica.

scratch hit, (béisbol) golpe logrado por chiripa.

scratch line, (dep.) línea de partida, línea de salida.

scratch pad, bloc para apuntes.

scratch paper, papel para apuntes, papel para borrador.

scratch wig, peluquín, bisoñé.

scratchy ['skrætʃɪ] *a.* (SCRATCHIER; SCRATCHIEST) 1. chirriante, estridente (sonido). 2. garrapatoso. 3. punzante; irritante.

scrawl [skrɔl] *v.t., v.i.* garrapatear, garabatear, escarabajear. —*s.* garrapato, garabato.

scrawly ['skrɔlɪ] *a.* garabateado.

scrawny ['skrɔnɪ] *a.* (E.U.) flacucho, huesudo, larguirucho.

screak [skrik] *v.i.* chirriar, rechinar, chillar. —*s.* chirrido, rechinamiento, chillido.

scream [skrim] *v.i.* 1. chillar, gritar, vociferar. 2. **s. with laughter,** reírse a gritos. —*v.t.* proferir a gritos, vocear gritando. —*s.* 1. grito, chillido. 2. (jer.) persona o cosa muy chistosa.

screamer ['skrimər, B -mə] *s.* 1. chillón, gritón, vociferador. 2. (orn.) palamedea; chajá. 3. (jer.) joya, perla (persona). 4. (jer.) comedia hilarante; tipo muy chistoso. 5. (jer., impr.) signo de exclamación. 6. (jer.) titular escandaloso (de periódico).

screaming [-mɪŋ] *a.* 1. estridente, chirriante. 2. bramante (viento, tormenta). 3. chillón (colores, diseño, etc.). 4. llamativo, sensacional (titulares, etc.). 5. divertidísimo, graciosísimo, chistosísimo. 6. **the s. meemies,** (jer.) delírium tremens; locura, ataque histérico.

screamingly [-lɪ] *adv.* extremadamente (chistoso, cómico, etc.).

scree [skri] *s.* piedrecilla, guijarro; ladera cubierta de guijarros y piedras.

screech [skritʃ] *v.i.* chillar, gritar. —*v.t.* hablar a gritos. —*s.* chillido, grito.

screecher ['skritʃər, B -ə] *s.* chillador, gritador.

screech owl, (orn.) lechuza blanca.

screed [skrid] *s.* 1. lista o discurso largo; perorotas, retahíla; andanada; diatriba. 2. (t. **floating s.**) maestra, listón-guía (para enlucir). 3. (dial.) fragmento, pedazo; tira, retazo; banda. 4. (esco.) rasgadura, rasgón; bebida; borrachera. —*v.t., v.i.* (esco.) rasgar(se); desgarrar(se).

screen [skrin] *s.* 1. biombo, mampara, antipara; pantalla; alambrado, alambrera, miriñaque (Mex.) (de ventanas); reja. 2. criba, harnero, zaranda. 3. (arq.) tabique, partición, pared protectora. 4. (mil., mar.) fuerzas de cobertura o de protección. 5. (cinem.) pantalla; **the s.,** el cine; el celuloide. 6. (impr.) retícula, trama (de fotograbado). 7. (fís., t.v.) pantalla. 8. (criquet) biombo de fondo (de color blanco, que se pone al extremo de la cancha para que el bateador tenga más visión). —*v.t.* 1. escudar, defender, proteger. 2. ocultar, encubrir (por medio de un biombo, partición, etc.). 3. cribar, cerner, tamizar. 4. (cinem.) proyectar (película); filmar, adaptar (una historia, un drama, etc.) para el cine. 5. examinar, investigar; seleccionar (a personas). —*v.i.* (cinem.) prestarse (bien o mal) a ser filmado o proyectado.

screenable ['skrinəbəl] *a.* (cinem.) que puede ser filmado o proyectado.

screen battery, (rad.) batería de pantalla.

screen classifier, (quím.) clasificador de cedazo.

screened cable, (elec., rad.) cable blindado.

screener ['skrinər, B -ə] *s.* 1. cribador, tamizador, cernedor. 2. seleccionador.

screengrid [-ˌgrɪd] *s.* (rad., electrón.) rejilla-pantalla.

screening [-ɪŋ] *s.* 1. (*pl.*) desperdicios del cribado, cerniduras, granzas. 2. (*pl.*) malla (metálica o de plástico). 3. (rad.) blindaje. 4. (cinem.) proyección privada.

screening cage, (electrón.) jaula de Faraday.

screening plant, planta cribadora o clasificadora, equipo clasificador, instalación cribadora.

screenland [-ˌlænd] *s.* el mundo del cine; la industria cinematográfica.

screenplay ['skrinˌpleɪ] *s.* (cinem.) argumento, libreto.

screen set, (cinem.) plató, foro.

screen test, (cinem.) prueba cinematográfica.

screen-test [-ˌtɛst] *v.t.* tomar prueba cinematográfica de.

screenwriter [-ˌraɪtər, B -ə] *s.* (cinem.) libretista, guionista, argumentista.

screw [skru] *s.* 1. tornillo; husillo. 2. vuelta de tornillo. 3. rosca, filete (de tornillo). 4. sacacorchos. 5. hélice. 6. empulgueras (instrumento de tortura). 7. avaro, tacaño. 8. penco, rocín. 9. (G.B.) pequeño paquete (de tabaco, pimienta, etc.). 10. (jer., pr. G.B.) salario, paga. 11. (billar, G.B.) efecto. 12. (jer.) carcelero. 13. (jer., vulg.) coito. 14. **to have a s. loose,** (fam., fig.) faltarle a uno un tornillo; **to put the screw(s) on (someone),** (jer.) apretarle las clavijas (a alguien). —*v.t.* 1. atornillar. 2. enroscar. 3. torcer, retorcer. 4. extorsionar. 5. (jer.) estafar, embaucar. 6. (jer., vulg.) joder, tener relaciones sexuales con. 7. **s. on,** enroscar; **s. open,** desenroscar; **s. out of,** sonsacar a; **s. someone,** fastidiar o perjudicar a alguien; **s. up,** torcer (el rostro, etc.); ajustar las clavijas a; (fig.) intensificar, intensar; (jer.) confundir, enredar, enmarañar; **s. up one's courage,** hacer de tripas corazón, cobrar valor; **to have one's head screwed on the right way,** tener la cabeza bien puesta (o en su sitio). —*v.i.* 1. enroscarse. 2. torcerse, retorcerse.

screw auger, barrena salomónica o helicoidal.

screwball ['skruˌbɔl] *s.* 1. (béisbol) lance de bola con trayectoria caprichosa. 2. (jer.) pájaro raro, tipo alocado, estrafalario. —*a.* loco, alocado, estrafalario.

screw bean, (bot.) tornillo.

screw bolt, perno roscado.

screw cap, tapón de tuerca, tapa roscada.

screw chaser, plantilla de filetear, peine de roscar, engastador de tornillo.

screw conveyor, transportador de tornillo sin fin, conductor de gusano.

screw coupling, manguito roscado.

screw-cutting lathe ['skruˌkʌtɪŋ-] torno de roscar, roscadora.

screwdriver [-ˌdraɪvər, B -və] *s.* 1. destornillador, atornillador, desentornillador. 2. mezcla de vodka y zumo de naranja.

screwed [skrud] *a.* 1. atornillado, roscado. 2. torcido, retorcido, contorsionado. 3. (jer., E.U.) jodido, fastidiado.

screwed-up ['skrud'ʌp] *a.* (jer., vulg.) 1. confuso, enmarañado; arruinado, estropeado. 2. desafortunado; confuso; neurótico.

screw eye, armella roscada, pitón.

screw feeder, alimentador sin fin.

screw gear, (mec.) engranaje de tornillo sin fin.

screwhead ['skruˌhɛd] *s.* cabeza de tornillo.

screw hook, gancho de tornillo.

screw jack, gato de husillo, gato de tornillo, gato de rosca o de gusano.

screw joint, junta roscada.

screw machine, máquina de fabricar tornillos; torno de roscar.

screw nail, clavo de rosca, clavo-tornillo.

screw nut, tuerca.

screw pile, pilote de rosca.

screw pine, (bot.) (especie de) pandánea.

screw pitch, paso de rosca.

screw plate, terraja, cojinete de roscar.

screw plug, tapón roscado.

screw post, (enc.) piquete de tornillo, piquete sujetador.

screw press, prensa de husillo.

screw propeller, hélice.

screw pump, bomba espiral.

screw steamer, vapor a hélice.

screw tap, macho de aterrajar.

screw-top ['skrutɑp] *a.* con tapón de rosca; con tapa de rosca.

screw top, tapón de rosca; tapa de rosca.

screw thread, filete o rosca de tornillo.

screw valve, válvula de paso o de cierre.

screw wheel, rueda helicoidal.

screw wrench, llave de tuercas.

screwy ['skruɪ] *a.* (SCREWIER; SCREWIEST) (jer.) chiflado, descabellado, loco, absurdo.

scribal ['skraɪbəl] *a.* de escribiente (error, etc.).

scribble ['skrɪbəl] *v.t.* 1. emborronar, escribir de prisa (unas líneas o palabras). 2. llenar de garrapatos o escarabajos (papel, etc.). —*v.i.* garrapatear, garabatear, escarabajear, borrajear. —*s.* garrapatos, garabatos.

scribbler ['skrɪblər, B -lə] *s.* escritorzuelo, escribidor, mal escritor.

scribe [skraɪb] *s.* 1. amanuense, escribiente. 2. calígrafo, pendolista; copiante (de manuscritos antiguos). 3. (hum.) autor, escritor, periodista. 4. (relig.) escriba. 5. (t. **s.-awl**) punta de trazar, gramil. —*v.i.* actuar como escribiente, escribir. —*v.t.* marcar, rayar, contornear, trazar (sobre madera o metal).

scriber ['skraɪbər, B -bə] *s.* punta o punzón de trazar, aguja de marcar, gramil, broca de tres puntas.

scrieve [skriv] (esco.) *v.i.* deslizarse. —*v.t.* narrar o cantar con facilidad (una historia o canción).

scrim [skrɪm] *s.* lienzo o cañamazo ligero.

scrimmage ['skrɪmɪdʒ] *s.* 1. escaramuza, refriega, riña, pelea, trifulca. 2. (fútbol, E.U.) líneas cerradas de los delanteros de ambos equipos que se enfrentan. —*v.i.* escaramuzar, pelear.

scrimp [skrɪmp] *v.t.* escatimar, cercenar, escasear. —*v.i.* ser tacaño.

scrimpily ['skrɪmpəlɪ] *adv.* tacañamente.

scrimpiness [-pɪnəs] *s.* tacañería.

scrimpy [-pɪ] *a.* (SCRIMPIER; SCRIMPIEST) escaso, reducido, miserable, mezquino.

scrimshaw ['skrɪmˌʃɔ] *v.i., v.t.* (mar.) pintar, tallar o grabar (conchas, madera, etc.). —*s.* (mar.) concha pintada, figura tallada (de madera o marfil).

scrip [skrɪp] *s.* 1. certificado, cédula, póliza, vale (dado por otro documento de valor). 2. esquela, apunte; pedazo de papel. 3. (E.U.) papel moneda de poco valor. 4. (jer.) plata (dinero).

scrip dividend, (com.) certificado de dividendo diferido.
scrip holder, tenedor de certificados provisionales.
script [skrɪpt] *s.* 1. caligrafía, escritura (a mano). 2. (der.) documento original; escritura. 3. (impr.) plumilla, plumilla inglesa. 4. (teat., cinem., rad., t.v.) manuscrito; libreto, guión. 5. (raro) escrito.
scriptorium [skrɪp'tɔrɪəm] *s.* (*pl.* SCRIPTORIA [-ə]) (hist.) aposento de los calígrafos o copiantes (en los monasterios).
scriptural ['skrɪptʃərəl] *a.* bíblico, de la Escritura.
scripturally [-ɪ] *adv.* según la Escritura, conforme a la Biblia.
scripture ['skrɪptʃər, B -tʃə] *s.* 1. **S.,** la Biblia, (*pl.*) las Sagradas Escrituras. 2. (cualquier) escrito religioso. 3. **S.,** pasaje o capítulo de la Biblia. 4. texto, escrito, manuscrito.
scriptwriter ['skrɪpt'raɪtər, B -ə] *s.* (cine, rad., t.v.) libretista, guionista, argumentista.
scrivener ['skrɪvnər, B -nə] *s.* (hist.) 1. escribano; amanuense. 2. notario.
scrobiculate [skroʊ'bɪkjələt] *a.* (zool., bot.) escrobiculado.
scrod [skrɑd, B skrɔd] *s.* (ict.) cría (de una variedad) de bacalao.
scrofula ['skrɑfjələ, B 'skrɔf-] *s.* (med.) escrófula, lamparones.
scrofulism [-ˌlɪzəm] *s.* (med.) escrofulismo.
scrofulous [-ləs] *a.* 1. (med.) escrofuloso. 2. (fig.) gastado, destartalado. 3. (fig.) inmoral.
scroll [skroʊl] *s.* 1. rollo de pergamino, rollo de papiro o papel; rollo de escritura. 2. lista, programa. 3. (arq.) voluta. 4. voluta o concha (que remata el mástil del violín, la viola, etc.). 5. rasgo, arabesco, rúbrica (escritura). 6. (hidr.) caja de turbina con conducto de caracol. —*a.* en espiral, de caracol. —*v.t.* adornar con volutas.
scroll saw, sierra de marquetería, sierra de arco, sierra de calar o para contornear.
scrollwork ['skroʊlˌwɜrk, B -ˌwɜk] *s.* ornamentación con volutas; obra de calado (esp. en madera).
Scrooge [skrudʒ] *s.* t. **s.** avaro, tacaño (nombre de un personaje de Dickens, notable por su avaricia).
scroop [skrup] (dial.) *v.i.* crujir, rechinar, chirriar. —*s.* crujido, rechinamiento, chirrido.
scrophularia [ˌskrɑfjə'lærɪə, B ˌskrɔfjʊ'lɛər-] *s.* (bot.) escrofularia.
scrophulariaceous [-ˌlærɪ'eɪʃəs, B -ˌlɛər-] *a.* (bot.) escrofulariáceo.
scrotal ['skroʊtəl] *a.* (anat.) escrotal.
scrotum [-əm] *s.* (*pl.* SCROTA [-ə] o SCROTUMS) (anat.) escroto.
scrouge [skraʊdʒ] *v.t.* (pr. dial.) apretar, estrujar, comprimir.
scrounge [skraʊndʒ] *v.t.* 1. sacar con halagos, obtener con maña (dinero, etc.). 2. petardear. —*v.i.* sablear, gorrear; **s. around,** (jer.) vagar, deambular; **s. for,** ir en busca de.
scrounger ['skraʊndʒər, B -ə] *s.* sablista, gorrón.
scrounging [-ɪŋ] *s.* gorronería, modo de vivir a costa ajena.
scrub [skrʌb] *s.* 1. matorral, maleza, maraña; árbol achaparrado y deforme; monte bajo. 2. (fig.) gorgojo, redrojo. 3. (dep.) jugador suplente. 4. animal cruzado. 5. escobilla de cerdas cortas. 6. bigote de pelos cortos. —*a.* 1. achaparrado, esmirriado. 2. inferior, despreciable, mezquino. 3. (dep.) formado por suplentes (equipo).
scrub, *v.t.* (*pret., p.p.* SCRUBBED; *p.pr.* SCRUBBING) 1. fregar, estregar, restregar, frotar limpiando. 2. separar o extraer impurezas de (un gas). 3. (jer.) cancelar, suprimir. —*s.* fregamiento, estregadura, restregadura, fricción.
scrubber ['skrʌbər, B -ə] *s.* lavador, limpiador; depurador (de gases).
scrub brush, cepillo de fregar, estregadera, cepillo limpiasuelos.
scrubby [-ɪ] *a.* (SCRUBBIER; SCRUBBIEST) 1. pequeño, chico, bajo. 2. cubierto de malezas o matorrales. 3. (fam.) miserable, mezquino.
scrub typhus, (med.) enfermedad de tsutsugamushi, fiebre fluvial japonesa.
scrubwoman [-ˌwʊmən] *s.* fregona, fregandera (Amer.).
scruff [skrʌf] *s.* nuca, cerviz, cogote (ú. sólo en) **by the s. of the neck,** por el cogote.
scruffy ['skrʌfɪ] *a.* 1. zaparrastroso. 2. despreciable, desdeñable.
scrum [skrʌm] *forma abrev. de* **scrummage.**
scrummage ['skrʌmɪdʒ] (fútbol, E.U.) *s.* líneas cerradas de los delanteros de los equipos que se enfrentan. —*v.i.* enfrentarse en líneas cerradas los delanteros (de ambos equipos).
scrumptious ['skrʌmpʃəs] *a.* (fam.) de rechupete, delicioso, excelente, magnífico, elegante.
scrunch [skrʌntʃ] *v.i.* ronzar, ronchar, tascar. —*v.t.* triturar, cascar, estrujar, apretar, aplastar. —*s.* crujido, chasquido.
scruple ['skrupəl] *s.* 1. escrúpulo, duda, recelo, aprensión. 2. migaja, pizca, cantidad ínfima. 3. (farm.) escrúpulo (medida de peso equivalente a 1,198 gramos). 4. **without scruples,** sin escrúpulos; **to have scruples about (doing),** tener escrúpulos para (hacer). —*v.t., v.i.* escrupulizar, tener escrúpulos.
scrupulosity [ˌskrupjə'lɑsətɪ, B -'lɔs-] *s.* escrupulosidad.
scrupulous ['skrupjələs] *a.* escrupuloso.
scrupulously [-lɪ] *adv.* escrupulosamente.
scrupulousness [-nəs] *s.* escrupulosidad.
scrutable ['skrutəbəl] *a.* escudriñable, comprensible.
scrutator ['skruˌteɪtər, B skru'teɪtə] *s.* escudriñador, escrutiñador, escrutador.
scrutineer [ˌskrutən'ɪr, B -'ɪə] *s.* (G.B.) escrutador, escrutiñador (esp. de votos en elecciones).
scrutinize ['skrutənˌaɪz] *v.t.* escudriñar, escrutar. —*v.i.* hacer un escrutinio.
scrutinizer [-ər, B -ə] *s.* escudriñador, escrutador, escrutiñador.
scrutinizingly [-ɪŋlɪ] *adv.* con mirada escrutadora.
scrutiny ['skrutənɪ] *s.* (*pl.* SCRUTINIES) 1. escudriñamiento, escrutinio, inspección minuciosa. 2. mirada escrutadora. 3. escrutinio, recuento (de votos).
scuba ['skubə, B 'skju-] *s.* escafandra autónoma.
scud [skʌd] *v.i.* (*pret., p.p.* SCUDDED; *p.pr.* SCUDDING) 1. moverse, correr o volar rápidamente y en línea recta; deslizarse. 2. (mar.) correr viento en popa (una embarcación). —*s.* 1. carrera rápida, movimiento escurridizo. 2. nubes vaporosas impulsadas rápidamente por el viento. 3. ráfaga de viento; neblina impulsada por el viento. 4. (Esco., Irl.) bofetada, cachetada; palmada, nalgada.
scudo ['skudoʊ] *s.* (*pl.* SCUDI [-di]) (hist.) escudo, antigua moneda italiana de plata o de oro.
scuff [skʌf] *v.i.* 1. caminar arrastrando los pies. 2. rasguñarse, arañarse. 3 **s. at,** tocar con el pie, frotar con el pie. —*v.t.* 1. golpear. 2. arrastrar (pie). 3. rasguñar, arañar. —*s.* 1. arrastre de los pies, chancleteo. 2. chancleta. 3. rasguño, arañazo.
scuffle ['skʌfəl] *v.i.* 1. luchar, forcejear. 2. caminar arrastrando los pies. —*s.* refriega, forcejeo, sarracina.
scuffle hoe, azada de jardín con ambos bordes afilados.
sculduddery [skʌl'dʌdərɪ] *s.* (G.B.) grosería, ordinariez; indecencia.
scull [skʌl] *s.* 1. espadilla (para cinglar una embarcación). 2. remo corto. 3. bote de remos cortos. —*v.t.* 1. cinglar. 2. impeler (bote) con remos cortos. —*v.i.* remar, bogar.
sculler ['skʌlər, B -ə] *s.* bote de remos cortos.
scullery ['skʌlərɪ] *s.* (*pl.* SCULLERIES) fregadero, trascocina; repostería (buques).
scullion ['skʌljən] *s.* marmitón, sollastre, pinche de cocina.
sculpin ['skʌlpən] *s.* (ict.) (especie de) escorpina, pez escorpión.
sculpt [skʌlpt] *v.t., v.i.* esculpir, entallar, modelar.
sculptor ['skʌlptər, B -tə] *s.* escultor, esculpidor; tallador.
sculptress [-trəs] *s.* escultora.
sculptural ['skʌlptʃərəl] *a.* escultural, escultórico.
sculpture ['skʌlptʃər, B -tʃə] *s.* escultura. —*v.t., v.i.* esculpir; entallar, cincelar, modelar.
sculpturesque [ˌskʌlptʃə'rɛsk] *a.* escultural, escultórico.
sculpturesquely [-lɪ] *adv.* esculturalmente, en forma escultural.
scum [skʌm] *s.* 1. espuma, telilla, tela, capa de impurezas (en la superficie de algunos líquidos). 2. escoria, horrura. 3. desecho, desperdicio, basura. 4. (fig.) escoria, hez (de la humanidad, etc.). —*v.t., v.i.* (*pret., p.p.* SCUMMED; *p.pr.* SCUMMING) espumar, cubrirse de telilla.
scumble ['skʌmbəl] *v.t.* (dib.) esfuminar, esfumar; (pint.) suavizar, cubrir de un color opaco (un cuadro). —*s.* 1. (dib.) esfumino; esfuminación. 2. (pint.) suavidad (de los colores de un cuadro).
scummy ['skʌmɪ] *a.* 1. espumoso, espumajoso, cubierto de escoria o impurezas. 2. despreciable, vil, bajo, ruin.
scunner ['skʌnər, B -ə] *s.* aversión, abominación, detestación. —*v.i.* (G.B.) sentir disgusto o aversión.
scup [skʌp] *s.* (ict.) (especie de) pagel.
scupper ['skʌpər, B -ə] *s.* (mar.) imbornal, embornal. —*v.t.* (jer., G.B.) echar a pique, hundir; (fig.) arruinar, frustrar (planes, proyecto, etc.).
scuppernong [-ˌnɔŋ, -ˌnɑŋ, B -ˌnɔŋ] *s.* tipo de uva norteamericana.
scurf [skɜrf, B skɜf] *s.* 1. caspa. 2. costra. 3. (fig.) hez, escoria (de la sociedad).
scurfy ['skɜrfɪ, B 'skɜfɪ] *a.* 1. casposo. 2. costroso.
scurrile, scurril ['skɜrəl, B 'skʌrɪl] (ant.) *vars. de* **scurrilous.**
scurrility [skə'rɪlətɪ] *s.* procacidad, grosería, insolencia; improperio, denuesto.
scurrilous ['skɜrələs, B 'skʌrɪ-] *a.* procaz, grosero, insolente, soez; difamatorio.
scurrilously [-lɪ] *adv.* procazmente, groseramente, insolentemente, soezmente.
scurrilousness [-nəs] *s.* procacidad, insolencia.
scurry ['skɜrɪ, B 'skʌrɪ] *v.i.* (*pret., p.p.* SCURRIED; *p.pr.* SCURRYING) correr, escurrirse, escabullirse. —*s.* 1. fuga precipitada, huida. 2. carrera corta (esp. para caballos).
scurvily ['skɜrvəlɪ, B 'skɜvɪ-] *adv.* vilmente, ruinmente, ignominiosamente.
scurviness [-vɪnəs] *s.* vileza, ruindad.
scurvy [-vɪ] *a.* 1. vil, despreciable, ruin. 2. (ant.) casposo; cubierto de costras. —*s.* (med.) escorbuto.

scurvy grass, (bot.) coclearia.
scut [skʌt] *s.* rabillo (esp. de conejo, liebre o ciervo).
scutage ['skutɪdʒ, B 'skjut-] *s.* (hist.) pago que hacía un terrateniente feudal en lugar del servicio militar.
Scutari ['skutərɪ] *s.* Escutari, barrio de Estambul en la parte asiática del Bósforo.
scutate ['skuˌteɪt, B 'skjuteɪt] *a.* (bot.) escutiforme.
scutch [skʌtʃ] *v.t.* agramar, espadar, espadillar, tascar. —*s.* 1. agramadera, agramador. 2. martillo cortador de ladrillos.
scutcheon ['skʌtʃən] *s., var. de* **escutcheon.**
scutcher ['skʌtʃər, B -ə] *s.* agramadera, agramador, cuchilla desbastadora; batidera; aventador.
scute [skjut] *s.* (zool.) escudo.
scutellate ['skjutəˌleɪt] *a.* (bot., zool.) escuteliforme.
scutellum [skju'tɛləm] *s.* 1. (bot.) órgano escutiforme. 2. (ict., ento.) escutelo.
scutiform ['skjutəˌfɔrm, B -ˌfɔm] *a.* escutiforme.
scutter ['skʌtər, B -ə] *v.i.* (G.B.) correr aprisa, escurrirse, escabullirse.
scuttle ['skʌtəl] *s.* (G.B.) 1. canasta de poco fondo. 2. (t. **coal s.**) cubo o balde (para carbón). 3. fuga precipitada, huida. —*v.i.* correr aprisa, escurrirse, escabullirse.
scuttle, *s.* 1. escotillón, trampa cerradiza. 2. (mar.) escotilla. —*v.t.* 1. (mar.) barrenar, dar barreno a, echar a pique (una embarcación). 2. (fig.) frustrar, arruinar; anular.
scuttlebutt [-ˌbʌt] *s.* 1. (mar.) pipa o tonel de agua para beber; fuente para beber (en los buques). 2. (jer.) rumor, runrún; chisme, hablilla.
scutum ['skjutəm] *s.* (*pl.* SCUTA [-ə]) 1. (hist.) escudo oblongo. 2. (zool.) escudete. 3. (anat.) escudo, rótula.
Scylla ['sɪlə] *s.* (mitol., geog.) Escila; **between S. and Charybdis,** entre Escila y Caribdis, (fig.) entre dos fuegos, sin salida.
scyllarian [sɪ'lɛrɪən, B -'lɛər-] *s.* (zool.) cigala.
scyphistoma [saɪ'fɪstəmə, B ˌsaɪfɪs'toʊ-] *s.* (zool.) escifistoma.
scyphozoan [-fə'zoʊən] *s.* (zool.) escifozoario.
scyphus ['saɪfəs] *s.* 1. (hist.) escudilla griega. 2. (bot.) escifo.
scythe [saɪð] *s.* guadaña, dalle. —*v.t.* guadañar, dallar; segar.
Scythia ['sɪθɪə, B 'sɪð-] *s.* (hist., geog.) Escitia, antigua región en la costa N. del Mar Negro.
Scythian [-ɪən] *a.* escita, escítico. —*s.* escita (habitante e idioma de la Escitia).
S. Dak., S.D. *abrev. de* **South Dakota,** Dakota del Sur (E.U.).
SDS *abrev. de* **Students for a Democratic Society,** Estudiantes por una Sociedad Democrática (E.U.).
Se *símb. de* **selenium,** selenio (Se).
SE *abrev. de* **southeast,** sudeste (SE).
sea [si] *s.* 1. mar. 2. mar, marejada, olaje, oleaje, oleada. 3. (fig.) mar (de dificultades, preocupaciones, lágrimas, etc.); infinidad, multitud. 4. **at s.,** en el mar; (fig.) perdido, desorientado, confuso, perplejo; **beyond (the) s.** (o **seas**), allende el mar; **by s.,** por mar; por vía marítima; **by s. mail,** por correo marítimo; **by the s.,** en la playa, a la orilla del mar; **in** (o **into**) **the s.,** en el mar; **heavy s.,** mar bravo, mar gruesa; **on the s.,** en el mar; **short s.,** mar picado, mar agitado; **the high seas,** alta mar; **to follow the s.,** ser marinero; **to go to s.,** hacerse marinero; **to put to s.,** hacerse a la mar; **when the s. gives up its dead,** (al llegar) el día de la resurrección. —*a.* 1. del mar, de mar, marino (animal, planta, vida, etc.). 2. marítimo, náutico (mapa, término, etc.). 3. marítimo, naval (ruta, tráfico, etc.).
sea acorn, (zool.) lapa, broma.
sea anchor, (mar., aer.) ancla flotante.
sea anemone, (zool.) anémona de mar, ortiga de mar.
sea-bag ['siˌbæg] *s.* saco o talega de marinero.
sea bass, (ict.) perca de mar, róbalo.
seabed [-ˌbɛd] *s.* lecho del mar u océano.
Seabee [-ˌbi] *s.* (jer., mil.) miembro del Cuerpo de Ingenieros de la Infantería de Marina (E.U.).
seabird [-ˌbɜrd, B -ˌbɜd] *s.* ave de mar, ave marina.
sea biscuit, bizcocho de mar, galleta de barco, sequete.
sea blite, (bot.) sargadilla.
seaboard [-ˌbɔrd, B -ˌbɔd] *s.* costa, playa, litoral, ribera.
sea-born ['siˌbɔrn, B -ˌbɔn] *a.* nacido del mar.
seaborne [-ˌbɔrn, B -ˌbɔn] *a.* transportado por mar.
sea bream, (ict.) besugo, pagel.
sea breeze, brisa de mar, virazón.
sea calf, (zool.) foca común, becerro marino.
sea canary, (zool.) ballena blanca.
sea captain, capitán de marina mercante.
sea card, rosa náutica.
sea carriage, transporte por mar, transporte marítimo.
sea chart, carta de marear, carta de derrota.
sea chest, baúl de marinero; toma de agua de mar (de un buque).
seacoast ['siˌkoʊst] *s.* litoral, costa marítima, orilla del mar.
sea cow, (zool.) 1. vaca marina, manatí. 2. morsa. 3. (raro) hipopótamo.
seacraft [-ˌkræft, B -ˌkrɑft] *s.* 1. arte de navegar. 2. embarcaciones marineras.
sea crawfish, sea crayfish, (zool.) cigarra de mar.
sea crow, (orn.) especie de gaviota.
sea cucumber, (zool.) cohombro de mar, pepino de mar, holoturia.
sea daffodil, (bot.) amormío.
sea devil, (ict.) raya, manta.
sea dog, 1. (ict.) perro marino, cazón, tollo. 2. (zool.) foca común. 3. (fam.) lobo de mar, marinero veterano. 4. (hist.) pirata, corsario, filibustero.
seadog ['siˌdɔg] *s.* punto luminoso que se ve a veces en la niebla cerca del horizonte.
seadrome [-ˌdroʊm] *s.* (aer.) aeródromo flotante.
sea duck, (zool.) pato de agua salada.
sea eagle, (orn.) 1. halieto, águila pescadora, águila marina, pigargo. 2. osífrago, quebrantahuesos.
sea-ear ['siˌɪr, B -ˌɪə] *s.* (zool.) oreja marina, oreja de mar.
sea elephant, (zool.) elefante marino.
seafarer [-ˌfɛrər, B -ˌfɛərə] *s.* marino, navegante, marinero, nauta.
seafaring [-ɪŋ] *s.* 1. navegación. 2. vida del marino; marinería. —*a.* marino, marinero, navegante, nauta.
sea fight, combate naval.
seaflower ['siˌflaʊər, B -ə] *s.* (zool.) anemone de mar.
sea foam, 1. espuma del agua de mar. 2. (min.) espuma de mar, magnesita.
seafolk [-ˌfoʊk] *s.* (fam.) marinos, navegantes, marineros, nautas.
sea food, marisco y pescado de mar comestibles.
seafood cocktail, salpicón de mariscos.
seafowl [-ˌfaʊl] *s.* ave marina, ave de mar.
sea fox, (ict.) zorra de mar.
seafront [-ˌfrʌnt] *s.* ribera, costa, orilla del mar.
sea gate, paso o canal de salida al mar; playa de salida al mar.
sea-gauge ['siˌgeɪdʒ] *s.* (mar.) 1. calado. 2. instrumento de sondeo.
seagirt [-ˌgɜrt, B -ˌgɜt] *a.* rodeado por el mar.
seagoer [-ˌgoʊər, B -ə] *s.* 1. marino, navegante, nauta. 2. viajero por mar.
seagoing [-ɪŋ] *a.* 1. de alta mar, propio para la navegación de altura. 2. marino, navegante de mar. —*s.* marinería, navegación.
sea grape, 1. (bot.) uvero; uva de playa. 2. (ict.) (*pl.*) huevos de jibia.
sea green, verdemar, glauco.
sea gull, (orn.) gaviota.
sea hare, (zool.) liebre marina, liebre de mar.
sea hedgehog, (zool.) erizo de mar, erizo marino.
sea hog, (zool.) puerco de mar, marsopa.
sea holly, (bot.) eringe, cardo corredor.
sea horse, 1. (mitol.) criatura con cuerpo de caballo y cola de pez. 2. (zool.) morsa. 3. (ict.) hipocampo, caballo marino. 4. (mar.) cresta (de una ola).
sea kale, (bot.) col marina.
sea king, jefe pirata escandinavo (de la Edad Media).
seal [sil] *s.* 1. sello, timbre; precinto. 2. (hidr.) obturación; substancia o artefacto de cierre. 3. **under my hand and s.,** firmado y sellado por mí; **s. of love,** (fig.) beso; **to set one's s. to,** (fig.) autorizar, confirmar. —*v.t.* 1. sellar, poner el sello a. 2. sellar, cerrar. 3. lacrar (sobre, etc.). 4. marcar con sello (en garantía de exactitud, medida o calidad). 5. (fig.) sellar, ratificar, concluir (contrato, documento, etc.). 6. (fig.) determinar, decidir irrevocablemente. 7. **s. off** (o **in** o **up**), cerrar (herméticamente), encerrar (firmemente).
seal, *s.* 1. (zool.) foca, becerro marino. 2. piel o cuero de foca. —*v.i.* cazar focas.
sealable ['siləbəl] *a.* capaz de ser sellado, precintable.
sea ladder, escala de soga, escala de gato (para subir a bordo).
sea-lane ['siˌleɪn] *s.* ruta marina (establecida).
sealant ['silənt] *s.* sellador, tapador.
sea lavender, (bot.) acelga silvestre.
sea lawyer, (mar.) marino argumentador y capcioso.
seal cap, (mec.) casquete sellador.
sealed will [sild-] (der.) testamento cerrado.
sea legs, (fam.) pie de marino, habilidad en conservar el equilibrio a bordo de un barco; **to get one's s. l.,** acostumbrarse al balanceo de un barco.
sealer ['silər, B -ə] *s.* 1. sellador (esp. funcionario que prueba y certifica pesos, medidas, etc.). 2. cazador de focas. 3. barco para la caza de focas.
sealery [-ərɪ] *s.* caza o cazadero de focas.
sea-letter ['siˌlɛtər, B -ə] *s.* pasavante (permiso de navegación a un buque neutral en tiempo de guerra).
sea level, nivel del mar.
sea light, faro, luz de puerto, baliza.
sea lily, (zool.) lirio del mar.
sea line, 1. horizonte del mar. 2. tubería marítima; oleoducto submarino.
sealing wax ['silɪŋ-] lacre.
sea lion, (zool.) león marino, lobo marino.
seal ring, sortija de sello.
sealskin ['silˌskɪn] *s.* piel de foca.
sea lungwort, (bot.) especie de borraja.
Sealyham terrier [ˌsilɪˌhæm-, B 'silɪəm-] terrier galés blanco.

seam [sim] *s.* 1. costura, cosedura. 2. juntura, junta; grieta, hendedura, intersticio. 3. cicatriz, costurón, chirlo. 4. arruga (en la piel). 5. (med.) sutura. 6. (geol.) estrato, filón, veta, venero. 7. (mar.) costura (de los tablones). 8. (esco.) costura, labor; material de costura. —*v.t.* 1. rayar, marcar con cicatrices. 2. hacer arrugas en, arrugar (la piel). 3. (cost.) pespuntar, pespuntear, orlar. 4. (raro) coser. —*v.i.* 1. rajarse, resquebrajarse, agrietarse. 2. (cost.) aplicar pespuntes.
sea-maid ['si,meɪd] **sea-maiden** [-ən] *s.* (poét.) sirena; diosa del mar; nereida.
seaman ['simən] *s.* 1. marinero, marino, nauta. 2. marinero, esp. de cubierta. 3. (E.U.) marinero raso.
seaman apprentice, aprendiz de marinero.
seamanlike [-,laɪk] *a.* marinero, marinesco, propio de un buen marino. —*adv.* como un buen marino, a la marinesca.
seamanly [-lɪ] *a.* marinero, marinesco, propio de un buen marino.
seaman recruit, marinero raso.
seamanship [-,ʃɪp] *s.* náutica, mareaje, pericia de la navegación.
seamark ['si,mark, B -,mɑk] *s.* 1. línea que marca el límite de las mareas (en la costa). 2. baliza, boya, marca, faro.
seamer ['simər, B -ə] *s.* (mec.) engatilladora.
sea mew, (orn.) gaviota.
sea mile, milla marina.
seamless ['simləs] *a.* sin costura, inconsútil.
sea monster, monstruo marino (leyenda).
sea moss, (bot.) ceiba.
seamount [-,maʊnt] *s.* montaña submarina.
sea mouse, (zool.) gusano marino.
seamstress [-strəs, B 'sɛm-] *s.* costurera, modistilla.
seam welding, soldadura de costura.
seamy ['simɪ] *a.* (SEAMIER; SEAMIEST) 1. (fig.) peor, menos agradable o presentable. 2. (fig.) despreciable, bajo, degradado. 3. (ant.) con costuras o costurones. 4. **the s. side,** el revés (de un vestido, etc.); (fig.) el lado peor o malo, el aspecto menos presentable o atractivo.
séance ['seɪ,ɑns] *s.* 1. sesión, reunión. 2. sesión espiritista.
sea needle, (ict.) pez aguja.
sea nettle, (zool.) ortiga de mar, acalefo.
sea-nymph ['si,nɪmf] *s.* nereida, ninfa marina.
sea oak, (bot.) especie de fuco.
Sea of Galilee [-'gælə,li] Mar de Galilea.
Sea of Japan, Mar del Japón.
Sea of Tiberias [-taɪ'bɪrɪəs, B -'bɪər-] Lago de Tiberíades.
sea onion, (bot.) escila, albarra o cebolla albarra.
sea ooze, cieno de mar.
sea orange, (zool.) holoturia globosa de color anaranjado.
sea-orb ['si,ɔrb, B -,ɔb] *s.* (ict.) orbe.
sea otter, (zool.) nutria marina.
sea-ox [-,ɑks, B -,ɔks] *s.* (zool.) morsa.
sea-pad [-,pæd] *s.* (zool.) estrella de mar.
sea pass, (mar.) pasavante (permiso de navegación a un buque neutral en tiempo de guerra).
sea pay, (mar.) paga por servicio activo en el mar.
sea pen, (zool.) pluma de mar.
sea pig, (zool.) 1. puerco de mar, marsopa. 2. dugongo.
sea pike, (ict.) pez aguja, róbalo; merluza.
sea pink, (bot.) clavel silvestre.
seaplane [-,pleɪn] *s.* (aer.) hidroavión, hidroplano.
seaport [-,pɔrt, B -pɔt] *s.* puerto marítimo, puerto de mar.
sea power, 1. potencia naval (país). 2. poderío naval.
sea purse, (ict.) bolsa de huevos de la raya.
seaquake ['si,kweɪk] *s.* maremoto, terremoto submarino.
sear [sɪr, B sɪə] *v.t.* 1. secar, marchitar, agostar. 2. tostar, chamuscar, socarrar; cauterizar; estigmatizar. 3. (fig.) endurecer, hacer calloso o insensible (conciencia, alma, etc.). —*v.i.* 1. marchitar, agostar. 2. (ant.) secarse, marchitarse, mustiarse. —*s.* quemadura, socarra, chamusquina. —*a. var. de* **sere.**
sea raven, (ict.) especie de coto.
search [sɜrtʃ, B sɜtʃ] *v.t.* 1. buscar. 2. explorar, examinar. 3. inquirir, escudriñar. 4. registrar, inspeccionar. 5. (med.) tentar, reconocer con la tienta (cavidad de una herida, etc.). 6. **s. me!,** (fam.) a mí que me registren, no tengo la menor idea; **s. out,** encontrar o descubrir (algo o alguien) en su escondrijo. —*v.i.* buscar; **s. for** o **after,** ir en busca de; **s. into,** indagar, investigar. —*s.* 1. búsqueda, busca, buscada. 2. registro, inspección. 3. escudriñamiento, reconocimiento; investigación, indagación. 4. (mar.) visita. 5. **in s. of,** en busca de.
searchable ['sɜrtʃəbəl, B 'sɜtʃ-] *a.* investigable, escudriñable.
searcher [-ər, B -ə] *s.* 1. buscador, explorador, escudriñador. 2. registrador; vista de aduanas. 3. (med.) tienta (instrumento quirúrgico). 4. (ópt.) buscador. 5. (ento.) variedad de escarabajo.
searching [-ɪŋ] *a.* escrutador, penetrante (mirada).
searchingly [-lɪ] *adv.* penetrantemente, de modo escrutador.
searchlight [-,laɪt] *s.* faro, reflector, proyector de luz.
search warrant, (der.) orden de registro o de allanamiento, mandamiento de registro.
sea risk, riesgo o peligro de mar.
sea robin, (ict.) rubio colorado, ganeo, testolín.
sea room, (mar.) espacio para maniobrar (en el mar).
sea rover, pirata; barco pirata.
seascape ['si,skeɪp] *s.* 1. vista o panorama marino. 2. (pint.) marina (cuadro o pintura que representa el mar).
seascapist [-əst] *s.* (pint.) marinista (pintor).
sea scorpion, (ict.) coto.
sea serpent, serpiente marina (animal fabuloso).
sea shanty, saloma, canción de marinero.
seashell ['si,ʃɛl] *s.* concha marina, caracol.
seashore [-,ʃɔr, B -'ʃɔ] *s.* costa, litoral, playa, ribera u orilla del mar. —*a.* costero, costanero, costeño, ribereño.
seasick [-,sɪk] *a.* mareado.
seasickness [-nəs] *s.* mareo.
seaside ['si,saɪd] *s.* costa, litoral.
sea snail, (zool.) caracolillo marino.
sea snake, 1. (zool.) hidra, culebra marina (venenosa). 2. serpiente marina (animal fabuloso).
season ['sizən] *s.* 1. sazón, tiempo oportuno, coyuntura. 2. estación (del año). 3. tiempo, momento. 4. temporada, época. 5. (ant.) condimento, aliño, aderezo. 6. **for a s.,** durante una temporada; por cierto tiempo; **in and out of s.,** en tiempo y a destiempo; **in s.,** a su tiempo; oportunamente; en sazón; en celo (animal); **out of s.,** fuera de sazón. —*v.t.* 1. sazonar, condimentar, aliñar, aderezar, dar gusto o sabor a. 2. madurar, curar (vino, tabaco, etc.). 3. secar (madera). 4. habituar, acostumbrar, aclimatar, avezar. 5. (ant.) templar, moderar. —*v.i.* 1. sazonarse; secarse, curarse, madurarse. 2. habituarse, acostumbrarse, aclimatarse, avezarse.
seasonable [-əbəl] *a.* oportuno, estacional, propio de la estación vigente.
seasonableness [-nəs] *s.* oportunidad, tempestividad.
seasonably [-blɪ] *adv.* oportunamente, tempestivamente, a tiempo.
seasonal [-zənəl] *a.* 1. estacional. 2. de temporada (industrias, deporte, empleo, etc.).
seasonally [-ɪ] *adv.* 1. en cada estación. 2. de temporada a temporada.
seasoned lumber ['sizənd-] madera desecada, curada, sazonada o estacionada.
seasoner ['sizənər, B -ə] *s.* 1. sazonador (persona). 2. condimento, aliño.
seasoning [-ɪŋ] *s.* 1. condimento, aderezo, aliño. 2. punto, madurez. 3. aclimatación. 4. desecación, cura (de la madera).
season ticket, billete de abono; (teat.) abono (de temporada).
season ticket holder, abonado.
sea spider, (zool.) araña de mar.
sea spray, rocío de mar, rocío de las olas.
sea squirt, (zool.) ascidia.
sea stores, *pl.* provisiones de viaje (de un barco).
seastrand ['si,strænd] *s.* costa, litoral, orilla del mar.
sea swallow, (orn.) golondrina de mar.
seat [sit] *s.* 1. asiento. 2. escaño, curul (en parlamento, concejo, etc.). 3. (teat.) localidad. 4. morada, residencia, domicilio. 5. sitio, teatro (como lugar o escenario de un acontecimiento). 6. centro (de manufactura, cultura, erudición, etc.); sede (de un gobierno, saber, etc.). 7. foco (del dolor, dolencia, etc.). 8. asentaderas, posaderas. 9. fondillos (de los pantalones). 10. postura o manera de sentarse. 11. (mec.) asiento. 12. **by the s. of one's pants,** (jer.) por los pelos, a la fuerza; **to take a s.,** tomar asiento, sentarse. —*v.t.* 1. sentar, asentar, colocar en asientos. 2. instalar, fijar, afianzar. 3. ajustar (maquinaria, válvula, etc.) en su asiento. 4. establecer, arraigar, ej., *a deep-seated disease,* una enfermedad (profundamente) arraigada. 5. tener asientos para (cierto número de personas); proveer de asientos. 6. poner asiento a; reparar asiento de (una silla); remendar los fondillos de (pantalones). 7. **pray be seated,** siéntese por favor; **s. a candidate,** elegir un diputado; **s. oneself,** sentarse.
seat belt, (aut., aer.) cinturón de seguridad.
seating ['sitɪŋ] *s.* 1. disposición, arreglo de asientos (alrededor de una mesa, etc.). 2. tapiz para asientos. 3. (mec.) asiento, lecho, base.
seating capacity, cabida, número de asientos.
seat mile, costos operacionales por milla de pasajeros.
SEATO ['sitoʊ] *abrev. de* **Southeast Asia Treaty Organization,** Organización del Tratado del Sudeste Asiático.
seatrain ['si,treɪn] *s.* 1. buque para transportar vagones de carga. 2. convoy de buques de carga.
sea trout, (ict.) trucha de mar, trucha marina.
sea urchin, (zool.) erizo marino, erizo de mar, equino.
sea wall [-,wɔl] rompeolas, muralla o dique de mar.
seaward [-wərd, B -wəd] *s.* dirección o lado hacia el mar. —*a.* que da al mar, del lado del mar. —*adv.* hacia el mar, mar adentro.
seawards [-wərdz, B -wədz] *adv.* hacia el mar, mar adentro.
seaware [-,wɛr, B -,wɛə] *s.* algas marinas usadas como abono.
seaway [-,weɪ] *s.* (mar.) 1. mar gruesa o alborotada. 2. marcha o avance de un buque; estela. 3. ruta marítima, vía o canal para barcos de gran calado (tierra adentro).
seaweed [-,wid] *s.* (bot.) alga marina.
sea-whip ['si,hwɪp, -,wɪp] *s.* coral en forma de látigo.

seawolf [-ˌwʊlf] *s.* 1. (ict.) lobo de mar. 2. pirata; vikingo.
seaworn [-ˌwɔrn, B -ˌwɔn] *a.* 1. gastado por las olas, corroído por el mar. 2. agotado por el viaje marítimo.
seaworthiness [-ˌwɜrðɪnəs, B -ˌwɜðɪ-] *s.* navegabilidad, estado apropiado (de un buque) para hacerse a la mar.
seaworthy [-ˌwɜrðɪ, B -ˌwɜðɪ] *a.* apropiado para navegación marítima, marinero (díc. de buques en buen estado).
sea wrack, algas acumuladas en la playa.
sebaceous [sɪ'beɪʃəs] *a.* (fisiol.) sebáceo.
sebaceous glands, (fisiol.) glándulas sebáceas.
sebacic [sɪ'bæsɪk] *a.* (quím.) sebácico.
Sebastopol [sə'bæstəˌpoʊl, B -pəl] *s.* Sebastopol, ciudad y puerto de Ucrania, en la península de Crimea.
seborrhea [ˌsɛbə'riə] *s.* (med.) seborrea.
sebum ['sibəm] *s.* (fisiol.) secreción sebácea.
sec [sɛk] *a.* seco (díc. de champaña o de vinos espumantes). —*s.* (fam.) momento, ratito, ej.,*wait a s.,* espere un momento (o un ratito).
sec. *abrev. de* 1. **secretary,** secretario. 2. **second,** segundo. 3. **secant,** secante.
SEC *abrev. de* **Securities and Exchange Commission,** Comisión Controladora de Acciones y Valores.
secant ['siˌkænt, B -kənt] *a., s.* (geom., mat.) secante.
secateurs ['sɛkətərz, B ˌsɛkə'tɜz] *s.* (G.B.) (*ú. en pl.*) podaderas, tijeras de podar.
secede [sɪ'sid] *v.i.* separarse (de una organización, congregación o federación).
seceder [-ər, B -ə] *s.* separatista.
secern [sɪ'sɜrn, B -'sɜn] *v.t.* 1. separar, discriminar, distinguir. 2. (fisiol.) secretar, segregar.
secernment [-mənt] *s.* secreción.
secession [sɪ'sɛʃən] *s.* secesión, separación; **War of S.,** (hist., E.U.) la guerra civil.
secessionism [sɪ'sɛʃəˌnɪzəm] *s.* (E.U.) (hist.) separatismo.
seclude [sɪ'klud] *v.t.* 1. recluir, aislar; retraer, apartar, ej.,*s. oneself from society,* aislarse de la sociedad. 2. (ant.) excluir, prohibir; expulsar.
secluded [-əd] *a.* 1. apartado, retirado, aislado (lugar). 2. recogido, solitario (persona); recoleto (monje).
secludedly [-lɪ] *adv.* en recogimiento, solitariamente.
seclusion [-'kluʒən] *s.* reclusión, soledad, retiro, recogimiento; aislamiento, retraimiento.
seclusive [-'klusɪv] *a.* retraído, solitario.
seclusiveness [-nəs] *s.* retraimiento, carácter de lo retraído.
second ['sɛkənd] *s.* 1. segundo. 2. ayudante; brazo derecho. 3. padrino (en desafío a duelo). 4. (*pl.*) artículos de segunda calidad. 5. dos (en fechas). 6. (*pl.*) segunda porción (que se toma de un plato). 7. (mús.) segunda. 8. (aut.) segunda (velocidad). 9. **a good s.,** segundo a poca distancia (en carrera). —*a.* 1. segundo. 2. segundo, otro (seguidor), ej.,*a s. Picasso,* otro Picasso. 3. (mús.) segundo; de tono bajo. 4. **every s.,** uno de cada dos; **in the s. place,** en segundo lugar; **on s. thought,** después de pensarlo bien; **s. to none,** sin comparación, sin par; **to come in** (o **to finish**) **s.,** llegar segundo (en carrera); **to marry for the s. time,** casarse en segundas nupcias; **to play s. fiddle (to someone),** desempeñar un papel secundario (al lado de alguien). —*adv.* en segundo lugar. —*v.t.* 1. secundar, asistir, ayudar, auxiliar. 2. secundar, promover, patrocinar, favorecer, apoyar (moción, propuesta, etc.).
second, *s.* 1. segundo (de tiempo). 2. (fam.) momento, ratito.
Second Advent, (teo.) segundo advenimiento, segunda venida de Cristo.
Second Adventist, creyente en la doctrina del segundo advenimiento.
secondarily [ˌsɛkən'dɛrəlɪ, B 'sɛkəndər-] *adv.* secundariamente, segundariamente.
secondary ['sɛkənˌdɛrɪ, B -dərɪ] *a.* 1. secundario, subsecuente, subsiguiente, resultante. 2. secundario, subsidiario, auxiliar, accesorio, suplementario. 3. (quím., elec.) secundario. 4. (geol.) secundaria (formación); mesozoico. 5. (zool.) posterior (ala de insectos); segunda (articulación), secundario (rémige del ala de las aves). —*s.* 1. lugarteniente, subalterno. 2. (elec.) circuito secundario. 3. (zool.) ala posterior (de insectos); rémige secundaria (en el ala de aves).
secondary accent, (fon.) acento secundario.
secondary cause, (filos.) causa segunda.
secondary cell, (elec.) elemento secundario, elemento de acumulador; acumulador.
secondary education, segunda enseñanza; enseñanza media (Esp.); bachillerato (liceo en Francia, gimnasio en Alemania, escuela superior en E.U.).
secondary emission, (rad.) emisión secundaria, desprendimiento secundario.
secondary energy, energía secundaria o provisoria.
secondary fever, (med.) fiebre secundaria.
secondary power, (mec.) potencia secundaria, fuerza provisoria; energía secundaria; (mat.) segunda potencia.
secondary road, camino secundario; ramal tributario.
secondary winding, (elec.) bobinado secundario, arrollamiento secundario.
second best, el mejor después del primero.
second-best ['sɛkənd'bɛst] *a.* (el) mejor después del primero, que sigue al mejor; **to come off s.-b.,** llevar la peor parte.
second childhood, segunda infancia, senilidad, chochez.
second-class [-'klæs, B -'klɑs] *a.* 1. de segunda clase. 2. de clase inferior; mediano, mediocre.
second class, segunda clase (viajera); clase de turista.
second cousin, primo segundo.
second-degree burn [ˌsɛkəndɪˌgri'bɜrn, B -'bɜn] (med.) quemadura de segundo grado.
second dog watch, (mar.) segundo cuartillo.
seconde [sə'kɑnd, B -'kɔnd] *s.* (esgr.) segunda.
seconder ['sɛkəndər, B -ə] *s.* patrocinador (de una proposición, etc.).
second growth, (agr.) bosque renacido.
second-guess ['sɛkənd'gɛs] *v.t.* 1. inventar explicaciones justificativas después del (suceso). 2. ser más listo que.
second hand, 1. intermediario (persona o cosa). 2. segundero (del reloj). 3. **at s. h.,** indirectamente; por medio de un intermediario.
secondhand [-'hænd] *a.* 1. derivado. 2. de segunda mano; usado.
second-in-command [ˌsɛkəndɪnkə'mænd, B -'mɑnd] (mil.) segundo jefe, subjefe; segundo en mando.
second lieutenant, (mil.) segundo teniente, subteniente, alférez; (mar.) alférez de fragata.
secondly ['sɛkəndlɪ] *adv.* en segundo término.
second mate, (mar.) el segundo de a bordo.
second mortgage, segunda hipoteca.
second nature, segunda naturaleza; instinto, naturaleza arraigada (en la persona).
second offender, (der.) reincidente.
second offense, (der.) reincidencia.
second papers, (E.U.) segunda y última solicitud que hace un extranjero para naturalizarse como ciudadano norte-americano.
second-rate ['sɛkənd'reɪt] *a.* de segundo orden, de calidad inferior, de menor cuantía.
second self, (psic.) alterego.
second sight, segunda vista, doble vista, clarividencia.
second-story man [-'stɔrɪ-] (fam.) ladrón que entra por una ventana del piso alto.
second-string [-'strɪŋ] *a.* inferior en calidad o rango.
second teeth, segunda dentición.
second wind, fuerzas que se recuperan después de un arduo esfuerzo físico; **he got his s. w.,** recobró nuevo aliento.
secrecy ['sikrəsɪ] *s.* 1. secreto, reserva, silencio, sigilo, ej., *I can rely on his s.,* puedo confiar en su silencio. 2. encubrimiento, ocultación; **there can be no s. about it,** no se puede ocultar. 3. **in s.,** en secreto, en confianza.
secret ['sikrət] *a.* 1. secreto, escondido, oculto, recóndito, ej., *a s. drawer,* un cajón secreto. 2. secreto, confidencial, ej., *a s. agent,* un agente secreto. 3. callado, reservado, discreto. 4. secreto, inescrutable; esotérico. 5. solitario, retraído; retirado. —*s.* 1. secreto, misterio, ej., *a trade s.,* secreto de fábrica, *the s. of his success,* el secreto de su éxito. 2. (relig.) secreta (oración antes del Prefacio). 3. **in s.,** en secreto; **to keep a s.,** guardar un secreto; **to keep (something) s.,** tener (un asunto) en secreto; **to meet in s.,** encontrarse en secreto.
secretarial [ˌsɛkrə'tɛrɪəl, B -'tɛər-] *a.* de secretario, de secretaria.
secretariat [-'tɛrɪət, B -'tɛər-] *s.* 1. secretaría, secretariado; ministerio. 2. cuerpo de secretarios.
secretary ['sɛkrəˌtɛrɪ, B -trɪ] *s.* 1. secretario, secretaria. 2. ministro, ej., *S. of War,* Ministro de Guerra. 3. escritorio, secreter. 4. (ant.) confidente.
secretary bird, (orn.) serpentario, secretario, mensajero.
Secretary-General [-'dʒɛnərəl] *s.* Secretario General.
Secretary of State, (E.U.) Ministro de Relaciones Exteriores.
Secretary of the Interior, (E.U.) Ministro de Gobernación, Ministro del Interior.
Secretary of the Navy, (E.U.) Ministro de Marina.
Secretary of the Treasury, (E.U.) Ministro de Hacienda.
secretaryship [-ˌʃɪp] *s.* 1. secretaría, secretariado. 2. ministerio.
secret code, código secreto (de comunicaciones).
secrete [sɪ'krit] *v.t.* 1. esconder, ocultar, encubrir; disimular. 2. (fisiol., biol.) secretar, segregar (humor, etc.).
secretin [-ən] *s.* (bioquím.) secretina.
secretion [-'kriʃən] *s.* 1. ocultación, escondimiento; encubrimiento. 2. (fisiol., biol.) secreción, segregación.
secretionary [-ʃəˌnɛrɪ, B -nərɪ] *a.* (fisiol., biol.) de la secreción, formado por la secreción.
secretive ['sikrətɪv, sɪ'krit-] *a.* 1. callado, sigiloso, reservado. 2. [sɪ'krit-] (fisiol., biol.) secretorio.
secretively [-lɪ] *adv.* calladamente, sigilosamente, reservadamente.
secretiveness [-nəs] *s.* disimulo, sigilio, reserva.
secretly ['sikrətlɪ] *adv.* secretamente, calladamente, escondidamente, ocultamente.
secretory [sɪ'kritərɪ] *a.* (fisiol.) secretorio. —*s.* glándula secretoria, órgano secretorio.
secret service, policía secreta; (E.U.) servicio secreto.

sect [sɛkt] *s.* 1. secta, partido, facción. 2. (relig.) secta. 3. (ant.) clase, orden (de gente).
sectarian [sɛk'tɛrɪən, B -'tɛər-] *a.* sectario. —*s.* sectario, sectador, disidente, secuaz fanático.
sectarianism [-ˌɪzəm] *s.* sectarismo, fanatismo.
sectarianize [-ˌaɪz] *v.t.* convertir en sectario; someter al control de sectas. —*v.i.* obrar como sectarios.
sectary ['sɛktərɪ] *s.* (hist.) sectario; disidente (esp. protestante).
sectile ['sɛktəl, B -taɪl] *a.* 1. (med.) sectil. 2. (bot.) seccionado, secto.
sectility [sɛk'tɪlətɪ] *s.* (med.) sectilidad.
section ['sɛkʃən] *s.* 1. sección, división. 2. segmento, parte, porción, tajada (de una fruta). 3. sección, párrafo; inciso, artículo (de leyes, contratos, etc.). 4. (geom.) sección, corte (*m.*), ej., *longitudinal s.,* sección o corte longitudinal. 5. (fig.) sección, clase, comunidad, grupo, ej., *popular with all sections and classes,* popular en todos los grupos y clases. 6. (E.U.) medida agraria (640 acres). 7. (biol.) sección. 8. (impr.) párrafo (signo de referencia). 9. barrio, parte (de una ciudad). 10. (mil., mar.) sección, grupo de combate. 11. (f.c.) tramo, trayecto. —*v.t.* 1. cortar, seccionar, dividir en trozos. 2. representar en secciones. —*v.i.* seccionarse, fraccionarse.
sectional [-əl] *a.* 1. en secciones, por secciones; desmontable; hecho de compartimentos. 2. divisional, parcial, regional, local. 3. dividido en secciones, seccionado, ej., *a s. bookcase,* armario seccionado para libros.
sectional elevation, (dib.) alzada en corte.
sectionalism [-ˌɪzəm] *s.* (E.U.) regionalismo, localismo.
sectionalize [-ˌaɪz] *v.t.* 1. seccionar. 2. (E.U.) dividir por regiones geográficas o según intereses locales.
sectionally [-ɪ] *adv.* parcialmente, regionalmente, en secciones.
sectional view, (dib.) vista seccional.
section gang, (f.c.) cuadrilla de tramo.
section hand, peón ferrocarrilero, el que trabaja en la cuadrilla de tramo.
sector ['sɛktər, B -ə] *s.* 1. sector, grupo. 2. (geom., mil.) sector. 3. compás de proporciones. —*v.t.* dividir en sectores.
secular ['sɛkjələr, B -lə] *a.* 1. secular, seglar; civil. 2. (relig.) seglar, lego, sin órdenes clericales, ej., *s. clergy,* clero seglar. 3. secular, centenario. —*s.* seglar, lego, profano.
secularism [-lərɪzəm] *s.* secularismo, laicismo.
secularist [-əst] *s.* partidario de la educación secular, librepensador.
secularistic [ˌsɛkjələ'rɪstɪk] *a.* de carácter secular.
secularity [-'lærətɪ] *s.* seglaridad, mundanalidad.
secularization [-lərə'zeɪʃən, B -raɪ-] *s.* secularización, laicización.
secularize ['sɛkjələˌraɪz] *v.t.* secularizar.
secularly [-lərlɪ, B -ləlɪ] *adv.* seglarmente; civilmente.
secundines ['sɛkənˌdaɪnz] *s. pl.* (anat.) secundinas, placenta.
securance [sɪ'kjʊrəns, B -'kjʊər-] *s.* 1. aseguramiento, fijación. 2. seguridad, garantía.
secure [sɪ'kjʊr, B -'kjʊə] *a.* 1. seguro, a salvo; impenetrable, inexpugnable; bien asegurado; firme, ej., *a s. retreat,* un retiro impenetrable, *a s. foundation,* cimiento firme, *are you sure it is s.?* ¿está Ud. seguro de que eso está bien asegurado? 2. seguro, cierto. 3. libre de temores; tranquilo. —*v.t.* 1. asegurar, resguardar; proteger. 2. asegurar, afirmar, cerrar, ej., *s. a door,* asegurar una puerta. 3. asegurar, garantizar, ej., *s. a loan,* garantizar un préstamo, *how can I s. myself against the consequences?* ¿cómo puedo asegurarme contra las consecuencias? 4. obtener, conseguir, procurar, ej., *I have secured front seats,* he conseguido asientos de primera fila. —*v.i.* (mar.) atracar (barco); suspender el trabajo, dejar de estar de servicio (marinero, tripulación).
securely [-lɪ] *adv.* 1. seguramente, firmemente. 2. tranquilamente, sin riesgo.
secureness [-nəs] *s.* seguridad, certeza.
security [-ətɪ, B -'kjʊər-] *s.* (*pl.* SECURITIES) 1. seguridad. 2. firmeza; estabilidad, solidez. 3. certeza, certidumbre. 4. protección, defensa. 5. razones de seguridad (nacional), ej., *s. does not permit me to say more,* razones de seguridad no me permiten decir más. 6. (der.) seguridad, garantía, prenda, fianza, caución. 7. (*pl.*) valores, obligaciones, títulos, efectos, ej., *securities in hand,* valores en cartera, *public securities,* efectos públicos. 8. **in s. for,** en prenda por.
Security Council, Consejo de Seguridad (de la ONU).
security guard, guarda jurado.
sedan [sɪ'dæn] *s.* 1. (t. **s. chair**) silla de manos, litera. 2. (aut.) sedán.
sedate [sɪ'deɪt] *a.* 1. sosegado, sereno, reposado. 2. serio, formal.
sedately [-lɪ] *adv.* 1. sosegadamente, serenamente, reposadamente. 2. seriamente, formalmente.
sedateness [-nəs] *s.* 1. serenidad, compostura. 2. seriedad, formalidad.
sedation [sɪ'deɪʃən] *s.* (med.) sedación.
sedative ['sɛdətɪv] *a., s.* (med.) sedativo, sedante, calmante.
sedentary ['sɛdənˌtɛrɪ, B -tərɪ] *a.* 1. sedentario (vida, ocupación, etc.). 2. inactivo (persona). 3. (zool.) sedentario (pájaros, etc.).
sedge [sɛdʒ] *s.* (bot.) juncia.
sedge bird, s. warbler, s. wren, (orn.) saltamimbres, curruca de los pantanos.
sedgy ['sɛdʒɪ] *a.* 1. júnceo. 2. poblado de juncias, lleno de juncias.
sedilia [sə'dɪlɪə, B sɛ'daɪljə] *s. pl.* (*sing.* SEDILE [-'daɪlɪ]) (relig.) asientos en el entrecoro (para el clero oficiante durante los intervalos del servicio).
sediment ['sɛdəmənt] *s.* 1. sedimento, poso, borra, hez, concho (Am.). 2. (geol.) sedimento. —*v.i.* sedimentarse.
sedimentary [ˌsɛdə'mɛntərɪ] *a.* sedimentario; (geol.) sedimentario.
sedimentary basin, (geol.) cuenca de sedimentación.
sedimentation [-mən'teɪʃən] *s.* sedimentación.
sedition [sɪ'dɪʃən] *s.* sedición, insurrección, rebelión, insurgencia.
seditionary [-'ɛrɪ, B -ərɪ] *a., s.* sedicioso, rebelde.
seditious [sɪ'dɪʃəs] *a.* sedicioso, rebelde, insurrecto, insurgente.
seditiously [-lɪ] *adv.* sediciosamente.
seditiousness [-nəs] *s.* rebeldía, naturaleza rebelde.
seduce [sɪ'dus, B -'djus] *v.t.* 1. seducir. 2. tentar, inducir. 3. atraer (interés, etc.).
seduceable, seducible [-əbəl] *a.* capaz de ser seducido.
seducement [-mənt] *s.* 1. seducción. 2. tentación.
seducer [-ər, B -ə] *s.* seductor.
seduction [sɪ'dʌkʃən] *s.* 1. seducción. 2. tentación, ej., *the seductions of the city,* las tentaciones de la ciudad.
seductive [-'dʌktɪv] *a.* seductivo; seductor, tentador.
seductively [-lɪ] *adv.* seductoramente.
seductiveness [-nəs] *s.* atracción seductiva, gracia tentadora.
seductress [-'dʌktrəs] *s.* seductora.
sedulity [sɪ'dulətɪ, B -'djul-] *s.* diligencia, ahínco, empeño.
sedulous ['sɛdʒələs, B 'sɛdjʊ-] *a.* diligente, asiduo, cuidadoso.
sedulously [-lɪ] *adv.* diligentemente, asiduamente.
sedulousness [-nəs] *s.* diligencia, asiduidad.
sedum ['sidəm] *s.* (bot.) uva de gato, siempreviva menor; hierba callera, crásula mayor.
see [si] *v.t.* (*pret.,* SAW [sɔ]; *p.p.* SEEN [sin]; *p.pr.* SEEING) 1. ver, divisar, avistar. 2. ver, comprender, entender, reconocer, ej., *I cannot s. the joke,* no veo qué hay de chistoso (en eso). 3. cumplir, ej., *he will never s. 60 again,* jamás volverá a cumplir los 60. 4. ver, visitar; recibir (la visita de), ej., *he refused to s. me,* se negó a verme, *can I s. you for a minute?* ¿puedo verle por un minuto? *I'll s. him in my office,* le recibiré en mi oficina. 5. imaginar, presumir, ej., *I cannot s. myself doing it,* no puedo imaginarme haciéndolo. 6. acompañar, escoltar, ej., *may I s. you home?* ¿puedo acompañarla a su casa? 7. considerar, advertir. 8. atender, ver, encargarse de; no olvidar, tener cuidado de, ej., *s. that you do what is necessary,* ocúpese de hacer lo necesario, *s. that you don't catch cold,* tenga cuidado de no coger un resfrío. 9. aceptar (apuesta, reto); hacer frente a, aceptar la apuesta de (alguien). 10. **(it) has seen better days,** ha conocido mejores tiempos; **s.,** véase (ú. como referencia en libros, etc.); **s. (something) done,** ver o supervisar la ejecución de (algo); **s. eye to eye,** estar de completo acuerdo; **s. (someone) off,** ir a despedir (a alguien); **s. one's way to (do o doing),** encontrar el modo de (hacer), ver la posibilidad de (hacer); **s. out,** acompañar hasta la puerta; **s. red,** (jer.) echar chispas, ponerse furioso; **s. stars,** (fig.) ver las estrellas; **s. the light,** ver la luz, llegar a comprender, despertar; **s. things,** tener visiones, alucinarse; **s. (someone) through a difficulty,** ayudar (a alguien) a salir de un apuro; **s. you! (fam.)** ¡hasta la vista! ¡hasta pronto!; **seeing is believing,** ver para creer; **I have to s. a man about a dog,** (hum.) perdón, tengo que irme (gen. al baño), disculpe, tengo que salir. —*v.i.* 1. poder ver. 2. llegar a comprender, darse cuenta, ej., *I see,* ¡ya veo! comprendo, *as far as I can s.,* por lo que veo, por lo que comprendo. 3. mirar, **s. here!** ¡mire Ud! 4. **let me s.,** deje que lo piense, déme tiempo de reflexionar; **let's s.,** a ver, veamos; **see?** (fam.) ¿comprendido?; **s. about,** atender a, ocuparse de; **s. after,** cuidar, cuidar de; **s. into,** investigar, estudiar; **s. through,** conocer el juego de, entrever (intención, etc.); **s. to,** atender a, ocuparse de o en; **s. to it that,** ver que se haga (algo); **s. to one's business,** ocuparse de o en sus (propios) asuntos; **we will s. about it,** ya veremos (más tarde).
see, *s.* 1. sede. 2. (ant.) silla, esp. trono.
seeable ['siəbəl] *a.* visible.
seed [sid] *s.* (*pl.* SEED O SEEDS) 1. semilla. 2. (bíbl.) descendencia, progenie, prole, ej., *the s. of David,* la progenie de David. 3. (fig.) semilla. 4. (biol., fisiol.) semen. 5. (bot.) simiente, pepita, pepa (Am.) 6. **in s.,** germinando; **to go (o to run) to s.,** granar; (fig.) deteriorarse, envejecerse, gastarse, echarse a perder; **to sow the seeds of,** (fig.) sembrar, dar principio a. —*v.t.* 1. sembrar; sementar. 2. despepitar. 3.

impregnar (nube) de partículas sólidas. 4. (dep.) destacar (a los mejores) en grupos distintos (para evitar que se encuentren en los primeros partidos). —*v.i.* 1. sembrar, arrojar la semilla, hacer la siembra. 2. granar (plantas); madurarse; dejar en barbecho.
seedbed ['sid,bɛd] *s.* plantío, plantel.
seed bud, botón, germen.
seedcake [-,keɪk] *s.* torta de semillas aromáticas (como el anís, el sésamo, etc.).
seed capsule, (bot.) cápsula que contiene semillas.
seedcase [-,keɪs] *s.* (bot.) pericarpio.
seed coat, (bot.) tegumento, testa externa (de la semilla).
seed coral, pequeñas cuentas de coral (usadas como adorno).
seed corn, maíz para sembrar, maíz para semilla.
seed drill, sembradera, máquina de sembrar.
seeded ['sidəd] *a.* sembrado; despepitado.
seeder [-ər, B -ə] *s.* 1. sembrador, sembradora, sembradera. 2. máquina de despepitar, despepitadora.
seedily [-əlɪ] *adv.* andrajosamente, miserablemente.
seediness [-ɪnəs] *s.* 1. aspecto andrajoso o miserable. 2. carácter desdoroso o inmoral (de entretenimiento, diversión, etc.).
seeding [-ɪŋ] *s.* 1. siembra, caída de semillas. 2. (meteor.) acto de sembrar en las nubes (para producir lluvia).
seed lac, laca de grano.
seed leaf, (bot.) cotiledón.
seedless [-ləs] *a.* sin semillas, sin pepitas, sin pepas (Amer.).
seedlike [-,laɪk] *a.* semejante a una semilla (cuentas o abalorios).
seedling [-lɪŋ] *s.* 1. árbol de pie. 2. planta que ha crecido de semilla, planta de semillero. 3. plantón, pimpollo, plántula, planta de vivero.
seed oyster, ostra joven (apta para ser transplantada).
seed pearl, perlita, aljófar, rostrillo.
seed plant, planta de semilla; planta o árbol que echa semillas.
seed plot, semillero.
seedpod [-,pɑd, B -,pɔd] *s.* (bot.) vaina (de legumbre), cápsula (de una planta).
seedsman ['sidzmən] *s.* 1. sembrador. 2. comerciante en semillas.
seed sowing, siembra.
seed stock, provisión de semillas (para sembrar); reserva (de peces, animales, etc.) para crianza.
seedtime ['sid,taɪm] *s.* siembra, sementera, tiempo de sembrar.
seed vessel, (bot.) pericarpio.
seed weevil, (ento.) gorgojo, calapatillo.
seedy ['sidɪ] *a.* (SEEDIER; SEEDIEST) 1. lleno de semillas, con muchas semillas. 2. raído, gastado, andrajoso, zarrapastroso. 3. destartalado, miserable. 4. desdoroso, algo inmoral, degradado (entretenimiento, diversión, etc.). 5. indispuesto, enclenque, enfermizo.
seeing ['siɪŋ] *s.* vista, visión. —*a.* que ve, vidente.
seeing, *conj.* visto que, siendo así, puesto que, considerando que.
Seeing Eye dog, perro lazarillo, perro guía.
seek [sik] *v.t.* (*pret., p.p.* SOUGHT [sɔt]; *p.pr.* SEEKING) 1. buscar. 2. aspirar a, anhelar. 3. tratar de obtener, procurar. 4. **s. (something) from,** solicitar (algo) a, requerir (algo) a; **s. out,** seleccionar, singularizar, escoger después de una búsqueda; **s. someone's life,** atentar contra la vida de alguien, tratar de matar a alguien; **s. to (do),** tratar de, intentar (hacer); **sought after,** en mucha demanda. —*v.i.* ir buscando, buscar; **s. after,** tratar de conseguir o adquirir; **s. for,** buscar, andar en busca de.
seeker ['sikər, B -ə] *s.* 1. buscador; investigador. 2. aparato guiador (en cohetes). 3. sonda delgada.
seel [sil] *v.t.* 1. coser los párpados del (halcón). 2. (ant.) cegar; cerrar (los ojos).
seem [sim] *v.i.* 1. parecer, ej., *he seems to be tired,* parece cansado, *I s. to be sleepy,* parece que tengo sueño. 2. **I do not s. to like him,** él no acaba de gustarme; **so it seems, so it would s.,** parece que es así.
seeming ['simɪŋ] *a.* aparente, supuesto, ej., *a s. friend,* un supuesto amigo. —*s.* apariencia.
seemingly [-lɪ] *adv.* aparentemente.
seemingness [-nəs] *s.* apariencia; exterioridad.
seemliness ['simlɪnəs] *s.* 1. bien parecer. 2. decoro, decencia, propiedad.
seemly [-lɪ] *a.* 1. bien parecido, agradable. 2. decente, decoroso, correcto. 3. (ant.) conveniente, apropiado.
seen [sin] *p.p. de* **see.**
seep [sip] *v.i.* filtrarse, rezumarse, escurrirse; **s. in,** colar, recalarse, penetrar. —*s.* rezumadero.
seepage ['sipɪdʒ] *s.* 1. filtración, infiltración, rezumamiento. 2. rezumadero, lo que rezuma.
seer ['siər, B -ə] *s.* 1. el que ve. 2. [sɪr, B sɪə] vidente, profeta, adivinador, adivino.
seeress ['sɪrəs, B 'sɪər-] *s.* vidente, profetisa.
seersucker ['sɪr,sʌkər, B 'sɪə,-ə] *s.* tejido de lino o algodón (generalmente) rayado en relieve (vichy).
seesaw ['si,sɔ] *s.* 1. balancín, columpio de tabla, sube y baja (juguete de niños). 2. vaivén, balance, vaivén de balance. —*a.* de vaivén, balance. —*v.i.* 1. columpiarse, balancear (se). 2. oscilar, vacilar, alternar. —*v.t.* columpiar.
seethe [sið] *v.i.* 1. bullir. 2. (fig.) hervir. 3. **s. with,** arder de (ira, pasión, descontento, etc.). —*v.t.* 1. hervir, cocer. 2. empapar, remojar. —*s.* (esp. fig.) hervor, ebullición.
seething ['siðɪŋ] *a.* 1. hirviente, herviente. 2. (fig.) agitado, desbordante.
segment ['sɛgmənt] *s.* 1. segmento, sección, división, gajo (de naranja). 2. (geom.) segmento. — [-,mɛnt, B -'mɛnt] *v.t., v.i.* segmentar(se), dividir(se) en segmentos.
segmental [sɛg'mɛntəl] *a.* 1. (compuesto) de segmentos. 2. parcial, fragmentario (dato, información, etc.). 3. (zool.) segmentado.
segmental arch, (arq.) arco rebajado, arco circular rebajado.
segmentary ['sɛgmən,tɛrɪ, B sɛg'mɛntərɪ] *a.* segmentario.
segmentation [,sɛgmən'teɪʃən] *s.* segmentación, división en segmentos, fragmentación; (biol.) segmentación.
segmentation cavity, (biol.) cavidad de segmentación.
segregate ['sɛgrə,geɪt] *v.t.* segregar, separar; aislar, recluir. —*v.i.* segregarse, separarse; (biol.) segregarse. — [-gət] *a.* segregado, separado.
segregated [-əd] *a.* 1. segregado, separado. 2. segregacionista (educación, estado, escuela, etc.).
segregated school, (E.U.) escuela de estudiantes negros.
segregation [,sɛgrə'geɪʃən] *s.* 1. segregación, separación. 2. segregación (racial).
segregationist [-əst] *s.* segregacionista, partidario de la segregación de las razas.
segregative ['sɛgrə,geɪtɪv] *a.* segregativo.
segue ['sɛgweɪ] *v.i.* (*pret., p.p.* SEGUED; *p.pr.* SEGUEING) hacer una transición suave (en música).
seidel ['saɪdəl] *s.* (alemán) vaso grande para cerveza.
Seidlitz powders ['sɛdləts-] (farm.) polvos o sal de Seidlitz.
seigneur [seɪn'jɛr, B -'jɜ] *s.* (hist.) señor (de un feudo y título de honor).
seigneurial [-ɪəl, B -'jɔr-] *a.* señorial, señoril.
seignior [seɪn'jɔr, B 'seɪnjə] *s.* 1. señor (antiguo título de respeto). 2. señor de un señorío; dueño de una casa solariega.
seigniorage ['seɪnjərɪdʒ] *s.* señoreaje, monedaje; derecho de braceaje.
seigniory [-ɪ] *s.* (hist.) señoría, señorío.
seignorial [seɪn'jɔrɪəl] *a.* señoril.
seignory, *var. de* **seigniory.**
seine [seɪn] *s.* red barredera, jábega, traína. —*v.t., v.i.* pescar con red barredera.
Seine [seɪn, sɛn] *s.* Sena, río de Francia.
seise [siz] *v.t.* (ant., der.) (gen. con *of*) posesionarse (de), tomar posesión (de).
seisin, *var. de* **seizin.**
seism ['saɪzəm] *s.* sismo, seísmo, terremoto, temblor.
seismic ['saɪzmɪk] *a.* sísmico.
seismicity [saɪz'mɪsətɪ] *s.* propensión a sismos (de una región), sismicidad.
seismic ray, onda sísmica.
seismic survey, (geof.) estudio sísmico.
seismism ['saɪz,mɪzəm] *s.* fenómenos sísmicos.
seismogram [-mə,græm] *s.* sismogramo, sismograma.
seismograph [-,græf, B -,grɑf] *s.* sismógrafo, sismómetro.
seismographer [saɪz'mɑgrəfər, B -'mɔgrəfə] *s.* sismólogo.
seismographic [,saɪzmə'græfɪk] *a.* sismográfico.
seismography [saɪz'mɑgrəfɪ, B -'mɔg-] *s.* (geof.) sismografía.
seismological [,saɪzmə'lɑdʒɪkəl, B -'lɔdʒ-] *a.* sismológico.
seismologically [-kəlɪ] *adv.* de modo sismológico.
seismologist [saɪz'mɑlədʒəst, B -'mɔl-] *s.* sismólogo.
seismology [-dʒɪ] *s.* sismología, seismología.
seismometer [-'mɑmətər, B -'mɔmɪtə] *s.* sismómetro.
seismometric [,saɪzmə'mɛtrɪk] **seismometrical** [-trɪkəl] *a.* del sismómetro, sismométrico.
seismophone ['saɪzmə,foʊn] *s.* sismófono, geófono.
seismoscope [-,skoʊp] *s.* sismoscopio.
seizable ['sizəbəl] *a.* 1. agarrable, que se puede asir o coger. 2. (der.) embargable.
seize [siz] *v.t.* 1. asir, tomar, coger, agarrar. 2. capturar, arrestar, apresar, aprehender. 3. embargar, secuestrar; confiscar, decomisar, incautarse de. 4. comprender, penetrar, darse cuenta de. 5. (mar.) trincar. 6. **to be seized with (dizziness, s.,** etc.), sufrir un ataque de (mareo, etc.). —*v.i.* **s. on** (o **upon**), apoderarse de, apropiarse de; agarrar, apresurarse a adoptar o aceptar (un plan, excusa, ayuda, etc.); **s. up,** (pr. G.B.) atorarse, atascarse; agarrotar (partes de maquinaria).
seizer ['sizər, B -ə] *s.* 1. agarrador. 2. (der.) secuestrador.
seizin ['sizɪn] *s.* (der.) posesión, toma de posesión (de tierras por quien tiene título).
seizing [-ɪŋ] *s.* 1. asimiento, agarro; captura, apresamiento. 2. (mar.) trinca, traba; ligadura.
seizor [-ər, B -ə] *s.* (der.) embargador, secuestrador.
seizure ['siʒər, B -ə] *s.* 1. embargo, comiso, confiscación, secuestro, incautación, decomiso. 2. ataque, acceso (de una enfermedad); ataque de apoplejía, ataque apoplético.

sejant, sejeant ['sidʒənt] *a.* (her.) sentado (león u otra bestia).
selachian [sɪ'leɪkɪən] *a., s.* (ict.) selacio.
seladang [sə'lɑ,dɑŋ, B -,dæŋ] *s.* buey o tapir de Malaya.
seldom ['sɛldəm] *adv.* raramente, rara vez, pocas veces. —*a.* raro, infrecuente.
seldomness [-nəs] *s.* infrecuencia, rareza.
select [sə'lɛkt] *a.* 1. selecto, escogido, la flor y nata. 2. exclusivo (club, sociedad, etc.). —*v.t., v.i.* seleccionar, escoger, elegir.
selectee [-,lɛk'ti] *s.* (E.U.) recluta.
selection [-'lɛkʃən] *s.* 1. selección, eleción. 2. cosa escogida. 3. colección de cosas escogidas; surtido.
selective [-'lɛktɪv] *a.* 1. selectivo, escogedor. 2. (rad.) selectivo.
selective service, (E.U.) servicio militar obligatorio; reclutamiento obligatorio.
selective tuning, (rad.) sintonización selectiva.
selectivity [-,lɛk'tɪvətɪ] *s.* (rad.) selectividad.
selectman [sə'lɛkt,mæn, B -mən] *s.* (E.U.) administrador municipal.
selectness [-nəs] *s.* calidad de selecto o escogido.
selector [sə'lɛktər, B -ə] *s.* 1. seleccionador. 2. (aut., mec., rad., t.v.) selector.
selector switch, (elec.) conmutador selector, selector.
selenate ['sɛlə,neɪt, B -nət] *s.* (quím.) seleniato.
selenic [sə'linɪk, B -'lɛn-] *a.* (quím.) selénico.
selenic acid, (quím.) ácido selénico.
selenide ['sɛlə,naɪd] *s.* (quím.) seleniuro.
seleniferous [,sɛlə'nɪfərəs] *a.* (quím.) selenífero.
selenious [sə'liniəs] *a.* (quím.) selenioso.
selenite ['sɛlə,naɪt] *s.* (min.) selenita.
selenium [sə'liniəm] *s.* (quím.) selenio.
selenium cell, (elec.) pila de selenio.
selenium rectifier, (rad.) rectificador de selenio.
selenographer [,sɛlə'nɑgrəfər, B -'nɔgrəfə] *s.* (astr.) selenógrafo.
selenographic [sə,linə'græfɪk] *a.* selenográfico.
selenography [,sɛlə'nɑgrəfɪ, B -'nɔg-] *s.* (astr.) selenografía.
selenosis [-'noʊsəs] *s.* (vet.) selenosis.
Seleucid [sə'lusɪd, B -'ljusɪd] *s.* (*pl.* SELEUCIDAE [-sɪ,di]) (hist.) Seléucida, miembro de una dinastía del Asia Menor.
self [sɛlf] *a.* 1. propio; puro, no mezclado, igual, uniforme (color). 2. (ant.) mismo; idéntico. —*pron.* uno mismo, sí mismo. —*s.* (*pl.* SELVES) 1. personalidad o identidad propia, naturaleza. 2. interés o ventaja propia; egoísmo. 3. **one's other s.,** el otro yo de uno; **second s.,** amigo íntimo; brazo derecho; **the s.,** el yo, el propio yo.
self-abandonment [,sɛlfə'bændənmənt] *s.* inmoderación, incontinencia.
self-abasement ['sɛlfə'beɪsmənt] *s.* humillación de sí mismo.
self-abhorrence [-əb'hɔrəns] *s.* aborrecimiento o repugnancia de sí mismo.
self-abnegating [-'æbnə,geɪtɪŋ] *a.* abnegado, sacrificado, desinteresado.
self-abnegation [-,æbnə'geɪʃən] *s.* abnegación, renunciamiento.
self-absorbed [-əb'sɔrbd, -'zɔrbd, B -'sɔbd] *a.* ensimismado, pensativo, abstraído en sí mismo.
self-absorption [-'sɔrpʃən, -'zɔrp-, B -'sɔp-] *s.* ensimismamiento, abstracción.
self-abuse ['sɛlfə'bjus] *s.* 1. autocrítica. 2. masturbación.
self-accusation [-,ækjə'zeɪʃən] *s.* autoacusación.
self-accusatory [-ə'kjuzə,tɔrɪ, B -tərɪ] *a.* que se acusa a sí mismo.
self-accusing ['sɛlfə'kjuzɪŋ] *a.* que se acusa a sí mismo.
self-acquired [-ə'kwaɪrd, B -'kwaɪəd] *a.* adquirido por o para sí mismo.
self-acting [-'æktɪŋ] *a.* automático; autoactuador, de acción automática; que actúa por sí mismo.
self-action [-'ækʃən] *s.* acción independiente.
self-activity [-æk'tɪvətɪ] *s.* acción independiente.
self-addressed ['sɛlfə'drɛst] *a.* 1. con la dirección del remitente (díc. de los sobres incluidos en cartas comerciales, circulares, etc.). 2. dirigido a sí mismo.
self-adjusting [-ə'dʒʌstɪŋ] *a.* autoajustador, de ajuste propio.
self-adjustment [-'dʒʌstmənt] *s.* adaptación de sí mismo (al ambiente, etc.).
self-administered [-əd'mɪnəstərd, B -stəd] *a.* aplicado o administrado por uno mismo.
self-admiration [-ædmə'reɪʃən] *s.* vanidad, engreimiento, presunción.
self-advancement [-əd'vænsmənt, B -'vɑns-] *s.* progreso por esfuerzo propio.
self-affected [-ə'fɛktəd] *a.* presumido, arrogante, presuntuoso, vanidoso.
self-aggrandizement [-ə'grændəzmənt] *s.* exaltación propia.
self-aligning [-ə'laɪnɪŋ] *a.* autoalineador, de alineación propia.
self-analysis ['sɛlfə'næləsəs] *s.* autoanálisis.
self-analytical [-,ænə'lɪtɪkəl] *a.* analítico o analizador de sí mismo.
self-applauding [-ə'plɔdɪŋ] *a.* que se alaba o felicita a sí mismo, complacido consigo mismo.
self-appointed [-ə'pɔɪntəd] *a.* nombrado por sí mismo, autoelegido.
self-approbation [-,æprə'beɪʃən] *s.* complacencia, aprobación de sí mismo, autocomplacencia.
self-asserting [-ə'sɜrtɪŋ, B -'sɜt-] *a.* 1. enérgico, vigoroso. 2. confiado, inmodesto, presumido.
self-assertion [-ə'sɜrʃən, B -'sɜʃən] *s.* 1. energía, vigor. 2. conducta agresiva, agresividad.
self-assertive [-'sɜrtɪv, B -'sɜt-] *a.* agresivo, arrogante.
self-assumption [-ə'sʌmpʃən] *s.* vanidad, pretensión, engreimiento, presunción.
self-assurance ['sɛlfə'ʃʊrəns, B -'ʃʊər-] *s.* seguridad o confianza en sí mismo.
self-assured [-ə'ʃʊrd, B -'ʃʊəd] *a.* seguro de sí mismo.
self-awareness [-ə'wɛrnəs, B -'wɛənəs] *s.* conocimiento de sí mismo.
self-balancing [-'bælənsɪŋ] *a.* (elec.) autoequilibrador.
self-binder [-'baɪndər, B -'baɪndə] *s.* (agr.) segadora agavilladora.
self-capacitance [-kə'pæsətəns] *s.* (rad.) capacitancia propia, autocapacitad.
self-care [-'kɛr, B -'kɛə] *s.* cuidado de sí mismo; automanutención.
self-castigation [-,kæstə'geɪʃən] *s.* autocastigo, autoflagelación.
self-centered ['sɛlf'sɛntərd, B -təd] *a.* egocéntrico, egoísta, ególatra.
self-centering [-tərɪŋ] *a.* (mec.) autocentrador, de centraje propio.
self-charging [-'tʃɑrdʒɪŋ, B -'tʃɑdʒɪŋ] *a.* autocargador (fusil, etc.).
self-cleaning [-'klinɪŋ] *a.* autolimpiador, autolimpiante.
self-collected [-kə'lɛktəd] *a.* sereno, dueño de sí mismo.
self-colored [-'kʌlərd, B -əd] *a.* de un solo color, de color natural o propio.
self-command [-kə'mænd, B -'mɑnd] *s.* dominio de sí mismo, aplomo.
self-complacency [-kəm'pleɪsənsɪ] *s.* satisfacción de sí mismo, complacencia consigo mismo.
self-complacent [-ənt] *a.* pagado de sí mismo, creído (Am.), sobrado (Am.).
self-composed ['sɛlfkəm'poʊzd] *a.* calmado, sereno.
self-composedly [-'poʊzədlɪ] *adv.* con aplomo, serenamente.
self-conceit [-kən'sit] *s.* engreimiento, presunción, arrogancia.
self-conceited [-əd] *a.* presumido, presuntuoso, arrogante.
self-concern [-kən'sɜrn, B -'sɜn] *s.* egolatría, mórbido interés por sí mismo.
self-concerned [-'sɜrnd, B -'sɜnd] *a.* egoísta, ególatra.
self-condemned [-kən'dɛmd] *a.* condenado por sus propias palabras, condenado por sí mismo.
self-confessed [-kən'fɛst] *a.* abiertamente reconocido, confeso.
self-confession [-'fɛʃən] *s.* confesión o admisión espontánea, franco reconocimiento.
self-confidence ['sɛlf'kɑnfədəns, B -'kɔn-] *s.* confianza en sí mismo.
self-confident [-dənt] *a.* confiado en sí mismo o en sus propios recursos.
self-confidently [-lɪ] *adv.* confiadamente, con confianza en sí mismo.
self-congratulation [-kən,grætʃə'leɪʃən] *s.* la propia alabanza.
self-conscious [-'kɑnʃəs, B -'kɔnʃəs] *a.* cohibido, falto de naturalidad, tímido.
self-consciously [-lɪ] *adv.* tímidamente, en forma o manera cohibida.
self-consciousness [-nəs] *s.* cohibición, falta de naturalidad, timidez.
self-consecration [-,kɑnsə'kreɪʃən, B -,kɔn-] *s.* auto-consagración.
self-consequence [-'kɑnsə,kwɛns, B -'kɔnsɪkwəns] *s.* sentido de la propia importancia, engreimiento, vanidad, pomposidad.
self-consistency [-kən'sɪstənsɪ] *s.* coherencia intrínseca.
self-consistent [-tənt] *a.* de coherencia intrínseca, intrínsecamente coherente.
self-constituted [-'kɑnstə,tutəd, B -'kɔnstɪtjut-] *a.* constituido o establecido por sí mismo (oficio, autoridad, etc.).
self-contained ['sɛlfkən'teɪnd] *a.* 1. autónomo, independiente. 2. callado, reservado, poco comunicativo. 3. (mec.) completo, independiente, enterizo, autocontenido.
self-contamination [-kən,tæmə'neɪʃən] *s.* auto-contaminación.
self-contemplation [-,kɑntəm'pleɪʃən, B -,kɔn-] *s.* contemplación de sí mismo.
self-contempt [-kən'tɛmpt] *s.* desprecio de sí mismo.
self-content [-kən'tɛnt] *s.* satisfacción vanidosa, presunción.
self-contented [-əd] *a.* complacido con sí mismo.
self-contradiction [-,kɑntrə'dɪkʃən, B -,kɔn-] *s.* contradicción inherente.
self-contradictory [-'dɪktərɪ] *a.* contradictorio en sí mismo, que se refuta a sí mismo.
self-control ['sɛlfkən'troʊl] *s.* dominio de sí mismo.
self-controlled [-'troʊld] *a.* 1. continente, con dominio de sí mismo. 2. autorregulado.

self-cooled [-'kuld] *a.* enfriado automáticamente.
self-cooling [-'kulɪŋ] *a.* de enfriamiento automático.
self-critical [-'krɪtɪkəl] *a.* auto-crítico, crítico de sí mismo.
self-criticism [-'krɪtə,sɪzəm] *s.* autocrítica.
self-deceit [-dɪ'sit] *s.* engaño de sí mismo.
self-deceived [-'sivd] *a.* engañado por sí mismo, iluso.
self-deceiver [-dɪ'sivər, B -ə] *s.* iluso, soñador.
self-deceiving [-ɪŋ] *a.* entregado a ilusiones, soñador.
self-deception [-'sɛpʃən] *s.* engaño de sí mismo.
self-dedication [ˌsɛlfˌdɛdɪ'keɪʃən] *s.* dedicación íntegra (a una causa o ideal).
self-defeating [-dɪ'fitɪŋ] *a.* contraproducente.
self-defense [-dɪ'fɛns] *s.* defensa propia, legítima defensa; **in s.-d.,** en defensa propia.
self-deluded [-dɪ'ludəd] *a.* engañado por sí mismo, guiado por ilusiones.
self-delusion [-'luʒən] *s.* engaño de sí mismo.
self-denial [-dɪ'naɪəl] *s.* abnegación, sacrificio, renunciamiento.
self-denying [-'naɪɪŋ] *a.* abnegado, sacrificado, desinteresado.
self-dependence [-dɪ'pɛndəns] *s.* confianza en sí mismo, independencia.
self-deprecating ['sɛlf'dɛprɪˌkeɪtɪŋ] *a.* humilde, modesto.
self-destroying ['sɛlfdɪ'strɔɪɪŋ] *a.* que se destruye a sí mismo, suicida.
self-destruction [-'strʌkʃən] *s.* suicidio, autodestrucción.
self-destructive [-'strʌktɪv] *a.* suicida.
self-determination [-dɪˌtɜrmə'neɪʃən, B -ˌtɜmɪ-] *s.* autodeterminación, libre determinación.
self-determining [-'tɜrmənɪŋ, B -'tɜm-] *a.* de libre determinación, autónomo (persona, nación, etc.).
self-development [-dɪ'vɛləpmənt] *s.* desarrollo propio.
self-directed [-də'rɛktəd, -daɪ-] *a.* guiado por voluntad propia, independiente.
self-directing [-tɪŋ] *a.* auto-dirigido.
self-direction [-'rɛkʃən] *s.* guía o dirección automáticas.
self-discharging [ˌsɛlfdɪs'tʃɑrdʒɪŋ, B -'tʃɑdʒiŋ] *a.* (mec.) de descarga automática.
self-discipline ['sɛlf'dɪsəplən] *s.* autodisciplina, dominio de sí mismo.
self-disciplined [-plənd] *a.* disciplinado en su propia persona, autodisciplinado.
self-discovery [ˌsɛlfdɪs'kʌvərɪ] *s.* conocimiento de sí mismo.
self-distrust [-dɪs'trʌst] *s.* falta de confianza en sí mismo; timidez, apocamiento.
selfdom ['sɛlfdəm] *s.* esencia del propio yo; individualidad.
self-doubt [-'daʊt] *s.* duda de su propia capacidad, desconfianza de sí mismo.
self-doubting [-ɪŋ] *a.* falto de fe en sí mismo; vacilante.
self-dramatizing ['sɛlf'dræməˌtaɪzɪŋ] *a.* lleno de teatralidad (conducta propia, etc.).
self-driven [-'drɪvən] *a.* automático, automóvil, con accionamiento propio.
self-educated [-'ɛdʒəˌkeɪtəd, B -'ɛdju-] *a.* autodidacta.
self-education [ˌsɛlfˌɛdʒə'keɪʃən, B -ˌɛdju-] *s.* autodidáctica, aprendizaje por sí mismo.
self-effacement [-ə'feɪsmənt] *s.* retraimiento, humildad, modestia.
self-effacing [-ɪŋ] *a.* retraído, modesto.
self-elected [-ə'lɛktəd] *a.* nombrado por sí mismo, autoelegido.

self-employed [-ɪm'plɔɪd] *a.* que trabaja por cuenta propia.
self-emplyed person, empresa unipersonal.
self-energizing ['sɛlf'ɛnərˌdʒaɪzɪŋ, B -'ɛnəˌ-] *a.* (mot.) de fuerza automultiplicadora.
self-enrichment [ˌsɛlfɪn'rɪtʃmənt] *s.* enriquecimiento del espíritu propio.
self-esteem [-əs'tim] *s.* dignidad, pundonor; amor propio.
self-evidence ['sɛlf'ɛvədəns] *s.* evidencia, certeza manifiesta.
self-evident [-ədənt] *a.* patente, manifiesto, evidente por sí mismo.
self-exalting [ˌsɛlfˌɪg'zɔltɪŋ] *a.* vanaglorioso, jactancioso.
self-examination [-ɪgˌzæmə'neɪʃən] *s.* examen de conciencia, introspección.
self-excited [-ɪk'saɪtəd] *a.* (elec.) autoexcitado.
self-executing ['sɛlf'ɛksəˌkjutɪŋ] *a.* (der.) de efecto inmediato.
self-exiled [-'ɛgˌzaɪld, -'ɛkˌsaɪld] *a.* exiliado por voluntad propia.
self-existence [ˌsɛlfɪg'zɪstəns] *s.* existencia independiente.
self-existent [-tənt] *a.* que existe por sí mismo.
self-explaining [-ɪk'spleɪnɪŋ] **self-explanatory** [-'splænəˌtɔrɪ, B -tərɪ] *a.* que se explica por sí mismo.
self-expression [-ɪk'sprɛʃən] *s.* expresión o manifestación de la personalidad o carácter propios; estilo propio.
self-faced ['sɛlf'feɪst] *a.* en bruto, sin labrar (piedra); (piedra) en laja.
self-feeder [-'fidər, B -ə] **self-feeding** [-ɪŋ] *a.* de alimentación automática (caldera, máquina, etc.).
self-fertility [ˌsɛlfˌfər'tɪlətɪ, B -ˌfɜ-] *s.* (bot.) autofertilidad.
self-fertilization [-tələ'zeɪʃən, B -aɪ'zeɪ-] *s.* autofertilización.
self-filling [-'fɪlɪŋ] *a.* autorrellenador.
self-flattery ['sɛlf'flætərɪ] *s.* adulación de sí mismo.
self-focusing [-'foʊkəsɪŋ] *a.* (foto., ópt.) de foco automático (objetivo, lente, etc.).
self-fulfillment [ˌsɛlf fʊl'fɪlmənt] *s.* realización de los propios deseos o ambiciones por esfuerzo propio.
self-giving ['sɛlf'gɪvɪŋ] *a.* abnegado, altruista, desinteresado.
self-glorification [ˌsɛlfˌglɔrəfə'keɪʃən] *s.* glorificación de sí mismo, vanagloria, egolatría.
self-glorifying ['sɛlf'glɔrəˌfaɪɪŋ] *a.* jactancioso, fanfarrón, sobrado (Amer.).
self-governed [-'gʌvərnd, B -ənd] *a.* autónomo, independiente.
self-governing [-ərnɪŋ, B -ənɪŋ] *a.* autónomo (que se gobierna a sí mismo).
self-government [-'gʌvərnmənt, -əmənt, B -'gʌvənmənt] *s.* 1. autonomía, gobierno propio. 2. dominio de sí mismo.
self-gratification [ˌsɛlfˌgrætəfə'keɪʃən] *s.* satisfacción de los deseos propios.
self-hardened ['sɛlf'hɑrdənd, B -'hɑd-] *a.* (metal.) autotemplado, autoendurecido.
self-hardening [-ənɪŋ] *a.* (metal.) autotemplable, autoendurecible.
self-hate [-'heɪt] **self-hatred** [-'heɪtrəd] *s.* aborrecimiento de sí mismo, odio a sí mismo.
selfheal [-ˌhil] *s.* (bot.) sanícula, hierba de San Lorenzo.
self-help [-'hɛlp] *s.* esfuerzo propio, ayuda que se da uno a sí mismo.
selfhood [-ˌhud] *s.* 1. individualidad, personalidad. 2. egoísmo.

self-humiliation [ˌsɛlfhjuˌmɪlɪ'eɪʃən] *s.* humillación de sí mismo.
self-hypnosis [-hɪp'noʊsəs] *s.* autohipnosis.
self-identification [-aɪˌdɛntəfə'keɪʃən] *s.* identificación de uno mismo (con otra persona o cosa ajena).
self-ignite [-ɪg'naɪt] *v.i.* encenderse espontáneamente (ej., bajo alta compresión).
self-ignition [-'nɪʃən] *s.* autoencendido, autoignición, encendido espontáneo.
self-immolation [-ˌɪmə'leɪʃən] *s.* autoinmolación, auto-sacrificio.
self-importance [-əm'pɔrtəns, B -'pɔt-] *s.* importancia propia, engreimiento, vanidad, pomposidad.
self-important [-ənt] *a.* engreído, vanidoso, pomposo.
self-imposed [-əm'poʊzd] *a.* impuesto a sí mismo, asumido por sí mismo, autoimpuesto (tarea, responsabilidad, etc.).
self-improvement [-əm'pruvmənt] *s.* autosuperación, mejoramiento de uno mismo mediante el esfuerzo propio.
self-inclusive [ˌsɛlfɪn'klusɪv] *a.* completo en sí mismo.
self-incriminating [-ɪn'krɪməˌneɪtɪŋ] *a.* (der.) que incrimina a uno mismo (prueba, testimonio, etc.).
self-incrimination [-ˌkrɪmə'neɪʃən] *s.* (der.) autoincriminación, que va contra uno mismo (acto, testimonio, etc.).
self-induced [-ɪn'dust, B -'djust] *a.* (elec.) auto-inducido.
self-inductance [-'dʌktəns] *s.* (elec.) autoinductancia.
self-induction [-'dʌkʃən] *s.* (elec.) autoinducción.
self-indulgence [-ɪn'dʌldʒəns] *s.* indulgencia o complacencia para consigo mismo, falta de sobriedad; desenfreno.
self-indulgent [-dʒənt] *a.* indulgente consigo mismo; desenfrenado.
self-indulgently [-lɪ] *adv.* con indulgencia o complacencia consigo mismo; desenfrenadamente.
self-inflicted [ˌsɛlfɪn'flɪktəd] *a.* infligido o causado a sí mismo (pena, herida).
self-instructed [-ɪn'strʌktəd] *a.* autodidacta, instruido por sí mismo.
self-instruction [-'strʌkʃən] *s.* autoeducación.
self-insurance [-ɪn'ʃurəns, B -'ʃʊər-] *s.* autoseguro.
self-insurer [-ər, B -ə] *s.* autoasegurador.
self-interest ['sɛlf'ɪntərəst, -tərəst] *s.* interés propio, egoísmo.
selfish ['sɛlfɪʃ] *a.* egoísta, interesado.
selfishly [-lɪ] *adv.* con egoísmo, egoístamente.
selfishness [-nəs] *s.* egoísmo.
self-justification [ˌsɛlfˌdʒʌstəfə'keɪʃən] *s.* auto-justificación.
self-knowing ['sɛlf'noʊɪŋ] *a.* conocedor de sí mismo.
self-knowledge [-'nɑlɪdʒ, B -'nɔl-] *s.* conocimiento de sí mismo.
selfless ['sɛlfləs] *a.* desinteresado, desprendido; abnegado.
selflessly [-lɪ] *adv.* desinteresadamente; abnegadamente.
selflessness [-nəs] *s.* desprendimiento; abnegación.
self-limitation [ˌsɛlfˌlɪmə'teɪʃən] *s.* autolimitación.
self-liquidating ['sɛlf'lɪkwəˌdeɪtɪŋ] *a.* autoamortizable.
self-loader [-'loʊdər, B -ə] *s.* arma de autocarga, fusil o revólver semiautomáticos.

self-loading [-ɪŋ] *a.* (mec., elec.) autocargador, de autocarga.
self-locking [-'lɑkɪŋ, B -'lɔk-] *a.* de cierre automático.
self-love [-'lʌv] *s.* 1. egoísmo. 2. egolatría.
self-loving [-ɪŋ] *a.* 1. egoísta. 2. ególatra.
self-lubricating [-'lubrəˌkeɪtɪŋ] *a.* autolubricador, autoengrasador.
self-luminous ['sɛlf'lumənəs] *a.* autoluminoso.
self-made [-'meɪd] *a.* hecho por uno mismo; logrado por esfuerzo propio.
self-made man, hombre humilde que triunfa en la vida por esfuerzo propio.
self-mastery [-'mæstərɪ, B -'mɑs-] *s.* dominio de sí mismo.
self-mortification [ˌsɛlfˌmɔrtəfə'keɪʃən, B -ˌmɔtə-] *s.* mortificación de sí mismo, automortificación.
self-moving ['sɛlf'muvɪŋ] *a.* automotor, autopropulsor, locomotor.
selfness ['sɛlfnəs] *s.* 1. egoísmo, egotismo, egolatría. 2. personalidad consciente, individualidad; mismidad.
self-observation [ˌsɛlfˌɑbsər'veɪʃən, -zər-, B -ˌɔbzə'-] *s.* introspección, observación de sí mismo.
self-operating ['sɛlf'ɑpəˌreɪtɪŋ, B -'ɔp-] **self-operative** [-rətɪv, -ˌreɪt-, B -rət-] *a.* automático.
self-opinionated [ˌsɛlfə'pɪnjəˌneɪtəd] **self-opinioned** [-'pɪnjənd] *a.* 1. presuntuoso, engreído. 2. obstinado, terco.
self-ordained [-ɔr'deɪnd, B -ɔ'-] *a.* decretado o nombrado por sí mismo.
self-originated [-ə'rɪdʒəˌneɪtəd] *a.* originado por sí mismo, auto-originado.
self-perpetuation [-pərˌpɛtʃʊ'eɪʃən, B -pəˌ-] *s.* proceso por el cual un individuo se mantiene (en un cargo, posición, etc.) indefinidamente.
self-pity ['sɛlf'pɪtɪ] *s.* compasión de sí mismo (esp. la de tipo quejumbroso y llorón).
self-pleased [-'plizd] *a.* satisfecho de sí mismo.
self-pollinated [-'pɑləneɪtəd, B -'pɔl-] *a.* (bot.) autofecundado, autopolinado.
self-pollination [ˌsɛlfˌpɑlə'neɪʃən, B -ˌpɔl-] *s.* (bot.) autopolinización.
self-pollution [-pə'luʃən] *s.* masturbación.
self-portrait ['sɛlf'pɔrtrət, B -'pɔtrɪt] *s.* autorretrato.
self-possessed [ˌsɛlfpə'zɛst] *a.* sereno, dueño de sí mismo.
self-possession [-'zɛʃən] *s.* sangre fría, serenidad, aplomo.
self-praise ['sɛlf'preɪz] *s.* alabanza o elogio de sí mismo, autobombo.
self-preservation [ˌsɛlfˌprɛzər'veɪʃən, B -ə'veɪ-] *s.* 1. conservación propia. 2. instinto de conservación.
self-pride ['sɛlf'praɪd] *s.* orgullo de uno mismo, orgullo de lo propio.
self-priming [-'praɪmɪŋ] (mec.) *s.* cebado automático. —*a.* autocebador.
self-proclaimed [ˌsɛlfproʊ'kleɪmd, -prə-] *a.* titulado por sí mismo, autotitulado.
self-produced [ˌsɛlfprə'dust, B -'djust] *a.* creado por sí mismo o por poderes propios.
self-pronouncing ['sɛlfprə'naʊnsɪŋ] *a.* (fon.) con la pronunciación correcta mostrada por signos diacríticos.
self-propelled [ˌsɛlfprə'pɛld] **self-propelling** [-'pɛlɪŋ] *a.* automotor, automóvil.
self-propulsion [-'pʌlʃən] *s.* autopropulsión.
self-protection [-prə'tɛkʃən] *s.* protección de uno mismo, auto-protección; defensa propia.
self-punishment ['sɛlf'pʌnɪʃmənt] *s.* castigo de uno mismo.
self-questioning [-'kwɛstʃənɪŋ] *s.* examen de conciencia.
self-radiation [-ˌreɪdɪ'eɪʃən] *s.* (fís.) autorradiación.
self-raising [-'reɪzɪŋ] (G.B.) *var. de* **self-rising.**
self-realization [ˌsɛlfˌriələ'zeɪʃən, B -ˌrɪəlaɪ-] *s.* desarrollo y expresión de la personalidad propia.
self-recording [-rɪ'kɔrdɪŋ, B -'kɔd-] *a.* autorregistrador.
self-rectifying ['sɛlf'rɛktəˌfaɪɪŋ] *a.* (rad.) autorrectificador.
self-reducing [-rɪ'dusɪŋ, B -'djus-] *a.* (mec.) autorreductor.
self-reflection [ˌsɛlfrɪ'flɛkʃən] *s.* introspección.
self-reflective [-'flɛktɪv] *a.* introspectivo.
self-regard [-rɪ'gɑrd, B -'gɑd] *s.* 1. interés o consideración por sí mismo, amor propio. 2. dignidad o respeto de sí mismo.
self-registering ['sɛlf'rɛdʒəstərɪŋ] *a.* autorregistrador.
self-regulating [-'rɛgjəˌleɪtɪŋ] *a.* autorregulador, de regulación automática.
self-regulation [ˌsɛlfˌrɛgjə'leɪʃən] *s.* autorregulación.
self-reliance [-rɪ'laɪəns] *s.* confianza en sí mismo.
self-reliant [-ənt] *a.* confiado en sí mismo.
self-renouncing [-rɪ'naʊnsɪŋ] *a.* abnegado, sacrificado; altruista.
self-renunciation [-ˌnʌnsɪ'eɪʃən] *s.* abnegación, altruismo.
self-repression [-rɪ'prɛʃən] *s.* represión de las inclinaciones naturales, represión de la personalidad propia.
self-reproach [-rɪ'proʊtʃ] *s.* reproche a sí mismo.
self-reproachful [-fəl] *a.* que se culpa a sí mismo.
self-reproof [ˌsɛlfrɪ'pruf] *s.* censura de sí mismo o del comportamiento propio.
self-reproving [-'pruvɪŋ] *a.* que se censura a sí mismo.
self-respect [-rɪ'spɛkt] *s.* dignidad, pundonor, respeto de sí mismo.
self-respecting [-'spɛktɪŋ] *a.* digno, pundonoroso.
self-restraint [-rɪ'streɪnt] *s.* moderación, continencia; refrenamiento de sí mismo.
self-revelation [-ˌrɛvə'leɪʃən] *s.* revelación o descubrimiento (gen. no intencionado) de los sentimientos, pensamientos, etc. de uno mismo.
self-rewarding [-rɪ'wɔrdɪŋ, B -'wɔd-] *a.* 1. que se recompensa (a sí mismo). 2. que lleva en sí mismo la recompensa (trabajo, actividad, etc.).
self-righteous ['sɛlf'raɪtʃəs] *a.* que se cree muy justo y bueno, farisaico, santurrón.
self-righteously [-lɪ] *adv.* como un fariseo o santurrón.
self-righting [-'raɪtɪŋ] *a.* que se endereza por sí mismo (díc. de un bote), autoadrizante.
self-rising [-'raɪzɪŋ] *a.* (cocina) que no necesita levadura (díc. de harinas).
self-rule [-'rul] *s.* gobierno autónomo, autonomía.
self-ruling [-'rulɪŋ] *a.* autónomo.
self-sacrifice [-'sækrəˌfaɪs] *s.* abnegación, altruismo, renunciamiento.
self-sacrificing [-ɪŋ] *a.* abnegado, altruísta.
selfsame [-ˌseɪm] *a.* igual, idéntico.
selfsameness [-nəs] *s.* igualdad.
self-satisfaction [ˌsɛlfˌsætəs'fækʃən] *s.* satisfacción vanidosa, presunción.
self-satisfied ['sɛlf'sætəsˌfaɪd] *a.* complaciente, presumido.
self-scrutiny [-'skrutənɪ] *s.* instrospección.
self-sealing [-'silɪŋ] *a.* autosellador, de cierre propio, de cierre automático.
self-searching [-'sɜrtʃɪŋ, B 'sɜtʃɪŋ] *s.* examen de conciencia.
self-seeker [-'sikər, B -kə] *s.* egoísta.
self-seeking [-kɪŋ] *s.* egoísmo, egotismo. —*a.* egoísta.
self-service [-'sɜrvəs, B -'sɜvɪs] *s.* auto-servicio.
self-sown [-'soʊn] *a.* sembrado sin intervención humana.
self-starter [-'stɑrtər, B -'stɑtə] *s.* 1. autoarrancador. 2. (fam.) persona llena de resolución e iniciativa.
self-starting [-ɪŋ] *a.* de arranque automático.
self-styled [-'staɪld] *a.* 1. nombrado o designado por sí mismo. 2. supuesto.
self-sufficiency [ˌsɛlfsə'fɪʃənsɪ] *s.* 1. autosuficiencia, autarquía. 2. insociabilidad.
self-sufficient [-ənt] **self-sufficing** [-'faɪsɪŋ] *a.* 1. auto-suficiente, independiente. 2. altanero, arrogante.
self-suggestion [-səg'dʒɛstʃən, B -sə'dʒɛs-] *s.* (psic.) autosugestión.
self-support [-sə'pɔrt, B -'pɔt] *s.* 1. mantenimiento económico propio. 2. auto-estabilidad.
self-supported [-əd] *a.* 1. autoestable. 2. que se sostiene por sí mismo.
self-supporting [-ɪŋ] *a.* que se mantiene por sus propios esfuerzos, que se gana la vida sin ayuda; independiente; que no necesita subvención.
self-surrender [-sə'rɛndər, B -də] *s.* rendición de sí mismo, abandono (a vicio, influencia, etc.), abandono de la propia voluntad.
self-sustaining [-sə'steɪnɪŋ] *a.* 1. que se sostiene o mantiene por sus propios esfuerzos o recursos. 2. de automantenimiento.
self-taught ['sɛlf'tɔt] *a.* autodidacta.
self-tightening [-'taɪtənɪŋ] *a.* de apretamiento automático; autotensante.
self-timer ['sɛlf'taɪmər] *s.* autodisparador.
self-treatment [-'tritmənt] *s.* (med.) cura de sí mismo, automedicación.
self-understanding [ˌsɛlfˌʌndər'stændɪŋ, B -də'-] *s.* comprensión o conocimiento de sí mismo.
self-unloading [-ʌn'loʊdɪŋ] *a.* de descarga automática; de autodescarga.
self-willed ['sɛlf'wɪld] *a.* terco, porfiado, obstinado.
self-winding [-'waɪndɪŋ] *a.* de cuerda automática (relojes o maquinaria); de arrollamiento automático.
self-worship [-'wɜrʃɪp, B -'wɜʃɪp] *s.* egolatría, culto de sí mismo.
self-worshipper [-ər, B -ə] *s.* ególatra.
sell [sɛl] *v.t.* (*pret., p.p.* SOLD [soʊld] *p.pr.* SELLING) 1. vender. 2. hacer aceptar o reconocer, convertir, convencer. 3. traicionar, vender (a la patria, compañeros, etc.). 4. (jer.) burlar; engañar; timar, embaucar. 5. **s. down the river,** (fam.) traicionar; **s. for a song,** vender muy barato; **s. off,** rematar, liquidar (mercadería, existencias); **s. one's life dearly,** vender cara la vida; **s. oneself,** venderse, prostituirse; **s. out,** realizar, liquidar, agotar; traicionar; **s. up,** (G.B.) vender (las pertenencias del deudor) por vía judicial; **to be sold on,** estar convencido (de), entusiasmarse (por.) —*v.i.* venderse; estar en venta; encontrar compradores; **s. like hot cakes,** venderse como pan caliente; **s. out,** liquidar las existencias, vender todo el stock; hacer traición, obrar a traición.

—*s.* 1. decepción. 2. engaño, estafa, fraude. 3. venta.

seller ['sɛlər, B -ə] *s.* vendedor, vendedora.

seller's market, mercado del vendedor (en que los bienes de consumo son escasos y los precios relativamente altos).

selling [-ɪŋ] *a.* 1. de venta, relativo a la venta. 2. de venta (rápida, lenta, etc.).

selling price, precio de venta.

sell-off ['sɛl,ɔf] *s.* baja de valores (en la bolsa). —*v.i.* vender a precios reducidos para liquidar las existencias.

sellout [-,aʊt] *s.* 1. (fam.) liquidación total, venta completa. 2. (fam.) éxito de taquilla (obra de teatro, evento deportivo, etc. para el que se venden todas las entradas). 3. (fam.) traición.

Seltzer ['sɛltsər, B -sə] *s.* agua de Seltz, agua mineral.

selvage, selvedge ['sɛlvɪdʒ] *s.* 1. hirma, crillo (del paño). 2. cabecera, placa de frente (de cerraduras). 3. (min.) salbanda.

selves [sɛlvz] *pl. de* **self.**

semanteme [sə'mæn,tim] *s.* (filol.) semantema.

semantic [sɪ'mæntɪk] *a.* (filol.) semántico.

semantical [-ɪkəl] *a.* (filol.) semántico.

semanticist [-əsəst] *s.* especialista o experto en semántica, semasiólogo.

semantics [-ɪks] *s. pl.* (*sing. en const.*) (filol.) semántica, semasiología.

semaphore ['sɛmə,fɔr, B -,fɔ] *s.* 1. semáforo, telégrafo óptico. 2. comunicación por banderines. —*v.t., v.i.* comunicar o comunicarse por señales, banderines, etc.; emitir luces o señales.

semaphore blade, (f.c.) aleta de semáforo.

semasiological [sɪ,meɪsɪə'lɑdʒɪkəl, B -'lɔdʒ-] *a.* (filol.) semasiológico, semántico.

semasiologist [-'ɑlədʒəst, B -'ɔl-] *s.* experto en semasiología, semasiólogo.

semasiology [-dʒɪ] *s.* (filol.) semasiología, semántica.

semblance ['sɛmbləns] *s.* 1. apariencia, aspecto exterior. 2. parecido, similitud, semejanza.

semeiology [,simaɪ'ɑlədʒɪ, B -'ɔl-] *s.* (med.) semilogía, semiología.

semeiotics [,simaɪ'ɑtɪks, B -'ɔt-] *s. pl.* (*sing. o pl. en const.*) (med.) semiótica.

semen ['simən, B -mɛn] *s.* (*pl.* SEMINA ['sɛmənə] o SEMENS) (fisiol.) semen, esperma.

semester [sə'mɛstər, B -tə] *s.* semestre.

semestral [-trəl] **semestrial** [-trɪəl] *a.* semestral.

semi- ['sɛmɪ, -aɪ, B -ɪ] *prefijo* semi, medio.

semi, (aut) camión articulado.

semi-abstraction [,sɛmɪæb'strækʃən] *s.* composición semi-abstracta (ej., una pintura o escultura).

semiadjustable [-ə'dʒʌstəbəl] *a.* semiajustable.

semiangle ['sɛmɪ'æŋgəl] *s.* (geom.) semiángulo.

semiannual [,sɛmɪ'ænjʊəl] *a.* semestral.

semiarch ['sɛmɪ'ɑrtʃ, B -'ɑtʃ] *s.* (arq.) semiarco, semibóveda.

semiarid [,sɛmɪ'ærəd] *a.* semiárido.

semiautomatic [-,ɔtə'mætɪk] *a.* semiautomático.

semibreve ['sɛmɪ,briv] *s.* (mús. G.B.) semibreve.

semibreve rest, aspiración de semibreve.

semicentennial [,sɛmɪsɛn'tɛnɪəl] *a., s.* cincuentenario.

semichromatic [-kroʊ'mætɪk] *a.* (mús.) semicromático.

semicircle ['sɛmɪ,sɜrkəl, B -,sɜkəl] *s.* (geom.) semicírculo.

semicircular [,sɛmɪ'sɜrkjələr, B -'sɜkjʊlə] *a.* semicircular.

semicircular arch, (arq.) arco de medio punto o de centro pleno; bóveda de medio cañón.

semicircular canal, (anat.) canal semicircular (del oído).

semicircumference [-sər'kʌmfərəns, B -sə'-] *s.* (geom.) semicircunferencia.

semicivilized [-'sɪvə,laɪzd] *a.* semicivilizado; inculto.

semicolon ['sɛmɪ,koʊlən] *s.* (gram.) punto y coma.

semiconductive [,sɛmɪkən'dʌktɪv] semiconducting [-tɪŋ] *a.* (electrón.) semiconductor.

semiconductor [-tər, B -tə] *s.* (electrón.) semiconductor.

semiconscious [-'kɑntʃəs, B -'kɔnʃəs] *a.* semiconsciente.

semiconsonant [-'kɑnsənənt, B -'kɔn-] *s.* (gram.) semiconsonante.

semidarkness [-'dɑrknəs, B -'dɑk-] *s.* penumbra, media luz.

semidetached [-dɪ'tætʃt] *a.* semiseparado, separado por una pared medianera (díc. de casas de familia colindantes).

semideveloped [-dɪ'vɛləpt] *a.* parcialmente desarrollado.

semidiameter [-daɪ'æmətər, B -ə] *s.* (geom.) semidiámetro.

semidiurnal [-daɪ'ɜrnəl, B -'ɜn-] *a.* que ocurre dos veces al día.

semidivine [-də'vaɪn] *a.* medio divino, semidivino.

semidome ['sɛmɪ,doʊm] *s.* (arq.) cúpula o bóveda semicircular.

semidomesticated [,sɛmɪdə'mɛstɪ,keɪtəd] *a.* domesticado a medias.

semidouble [-'dʌbəl] *a.* (bot.) semidoble.

semiellipse [-ə'lɪps] *s.* semielipse.

semielliptic [-ə'lɪptɪk] semielliptical [-tɪkəl] *a.* semielíptico.

semifinal [-'faɪnəl, B 'sɛmɪ-] *a., s.* (dep.) semifinal.

semifinalist [,sɛmɪ-əst] *s.* (dep.) semifinalista.

semifinished [-fɪnɪʃt] *a.* semiacabado, semielaborado.

semifluid [-'fluəd] *a.* semifluido, medio fluido.

semiglobular [-'glɑbjələr, B -'glɔbjʊlə] *a.* semiesférico.

semiliquid [-'lɪkwəd] *a.* semilíquido.

semiliterate [-'lɪtərət] *a.* semianalfabeto.

semilunar [,sɛmɪ'lunər, B -nə] *a.* semilunar; de o en forma de media luna.

semilunar valve, (anat.) válvula semilunar.

semimanufactures [-,mænjə'fæktʃərz, B tʃəz] *s. pl.* productos a medio acabar, semielaborados.

semimat, semimatt, semimatte [-'mæt] *a.* semimate.

semimonastic [-mə'næstɪk] *a.* casi monástico, semimonástico.

semimonthly [-'mʌnθlɪ] *a.* bimensual, quincenal, quincenario; de cada quince días. —*adv.* cada quince días, dos veces al mes. —*s.* publicación bimensual, publicación quincenal.

seminal ['sɛmənəl, B 'sim-] *a.* 1. seminal, espermático. 2. (fig.) germinativo, originario, primordial. 3. original y de gran influencia en la evolución de nuevas ideas (obra literaria, teoría filosófica, etc.).

seminar ['sɛmə,nɑr, B -,nɑ] *s.* seminario.

seminarian [sɛmə'nɛrɪən, B -'nɛər-] *s.* seminarista.

seminary ['sɛmə,nɛrɪ, B -nərɪ] *s.* (*pl.* SEMINARIES) 1. colegio secundario particular, academia. 2. seminario conciliar.

semination [,sɛmə'neɪʃən] *s.* propagación, diseminación; fecundación.

seminiferous [,sɛmə'nɪfərəs] *a.* (biol.) seminífero.

seminific [-'nɪfɪk] *a.* sementino; seminífero, seminal.

seminivorous [-'nɪvərəs] *a.* (biol.) seminívoro, gramívoro.

Seminole ['sɛmə,noʊl] *s.* (*pl.* SEMINOLE O SEMINOLES) seminola (tribu de indios; indios norteamericanos).

semiofficial [,sɛmɪə'fɪʃəl] *a.* semioficial.

semiofficially [-əlɪ] *adv.* semioficialmente.

semiology [,simɪ'ɑlədʒɪ, B ,sɛmɪ'ɔl-] *s. var. de* **semeiology.**

semiopaque [,sɛmɪoʊ'peɪk] *a.* semiopaco.

semiotic [,sɛmɪ'ɑtɪk, B -'ɔt-] *s.* (filos., filol., med.) semiótica, teoría de signos y símbolos, esp. del análisis de la naturaleza y relación de los signos.

semipalmate [,sɛmɪ'pæl,meɪt] **semipalmated** [-əd] *a.* (orn.) semipalmado.

semiparasite [-'pærə,saɪt] *s.* (bot.) semiparásito, hemiparásito.

semiparasitic [-,pærə'sɪtɪk] *a.* semiparásito.

semipermeable [-'pɜrmɪəbəl, B 'pɜmjə-] *a.* semipermeable.

semipostal [-'poʊstəl] *a., s.* (filat.) (sello) semipostal (con recargo sobre su valor de franqueo).

semiprecious [-'prɛʃəs] *a.* semi-preciosa (piedra).

semipro ['sɛmɪ,proʊ] *a.* (fam.) semiprofesional.

semiprofessional [,sɛmɪprə'fɛʃənəl] *a.* semiprofesional.

semiquaver ['sɛmɪ,kweɪvər, B -və] *s.* (mús.) semicorchea.

Semiramis [sɪ'mɪrəmɪs, B sɛ-] *s.* Semíramis, reina legendaria de Asiria, esposa de Nino.

semiskilled [,sɛmɪ'skɪld] *a.* semidiestro, no especializado.

semisweet [-'swit] *a.* medio dulce, semidulce, semiamargo (chocolate).

semisynthetic [-sɪn'θɛtɪk] *a.* semisintético.

Semite ['sɛmaɪt, B 'si-] *s.* semita.

Semitic [sə'mɪtɪk] *a.* semítico.

Semitism ['sɛmə,tɪzəm] *s.* semitismo.

Semitist [-ətəst] *s.* semitista.

semitone ['sɛmɪ,toʊn] *s.* (mús.) semitono.

semitrailer ['sɛmɪ,treɪlər, B -lə] *s.* camión articulado.

semitransparent [,sɛmɪtræns'pærənt, -'pɛr-, B -'pɛər-] *a.* semitransparente.

semitropic [-'trɑpɪk, B -'trɔp-] **semitropical** [-ɪkəl] *a.* semitropical (país, región, clima).

semivocalic [-voʊ'kælɪk] *a.* semivocal.

semivowel ['sɛmɪ,vaʊəl] *s.* (fon.) semivocal.

semiweekly [,sɛmɪ'wiklɪ] *a.* bisemanal. —*adv.* dos veces por semana. —*s.* publicación bisemanal.

semiyearly [-'jɪrlɪ, B -'jɜlɪ] *a.* semestral.

semolina [,sɛmə'linə] *s.* sémola.

sempervivum [,sɛmpər'vaɪvəm, B -pə'-] *s.* (bot.) siempreviva, perpetua.

sempiternal [-pɪ'tɜrnəl, B -'tɜn-] *a.* sempiterno, eterno.

sempiternity [-'tɜrnətɪ, B -'tɜnətɪ] *s.* eternidad.

sempstress ['sɛmpstrəs] *var. de* **seamstress.**

sen [sɛn] *s.* (*pl.* SEN) sen (moneda japonesa).

Sen. *abrev. de* 1. **Senior,** padre. 2. **Senator,** senador.

senary ['sɛnərɪ, B 'sin-] *a.* senario.

senate ['sɛnət] *s.* 1. senado. 2. junta directiva o administrativa (de algunas universidades).

senate house, senado (sala).

senator ['sɛnətər, B -ə] *s.* senador.

senatorial [ˌsɛnəˈtɔrɪəl] *a.* senatorial.
senatorian [-ən] *a.* senatorial, senatorio.
senatorship [ˈsɛnətərˌʃɪp, B -əˌ-] *s.* senaduría.
senatus consultum, senadoconsulto.
send [sɛnd] *v.t.* (*pret., p.p.* SENT [sɛnt]; *p.pr.* SENDING) 1. enviar, mandar; remitir, despachar, expedir. 2. mover, propulsar; lanzar (golpe, bola, flecha, proyectil, cohete, etc.). 3. disponer, decretar, querer. 4. hacer, ej., *the blow sent him reeling,* el golpe le hizo tambalear. 5. emitir, transmitir, difundir (díc. de la radio). 6. (jer.) deleitar, excitar. 7. **s. (someone) about his business,** echar o enviar (a alguien) a pasear; **s. away,** despedir, poner en la calle, echar de casa; despachar, enviar (carta); **s. back,** devolver, reenviar; **s. down,** (G.B.) expulsar de la universidad; **s. in** (o **up**), hacer entrar; mandar inscribir, someter (nombre, obra, etc. de alguien en un concurso, competencia, etc.); **s. in one's papers,** renunciar; **s. off,** poner en el correo; ir a despedir; **s. on,** mandar adelante (equipaje, etc.); reexpedir (carta, etc.); **s. out** (o **forth**), echar (humo, retoños, etc.), despedir (olor, rayos de luz, etc.), exhalar; dar (un grito); **s. packing,** despedir con cajas destempladas; **s. round,** hacer circular; **s. up,** condenar a prisión, meter en la cárcel; **s. word (to),** mandar recado (a), avisar (a). —*v.i.* 1. emitir, transmitir (la radio). 2. (mar.) precipitarse (barco por impulso de una ola); arfar, cabecear. 3. **s. for,** enviar a buscar, enviar por. —*s.* impulso, ímpetu (de una ola).
sendal [ˈsɛndəl] *s.* (tej.) cendal.
sender [ˈsɛndər, B -ə] *s.* 1. remitente. 2. (rad.) transmisor, emisor.
sending [-ɪŋ] *s.* (rad.) transmisión.
send-off [-ˌɔf] *s.* (fam.) despedida ceremonial o halagüeña; crítica encomiástica (de obra literaria, teatral, etc.).
Seneca [ˈsɛnɪkə] *s.* Séneca, filósofo y escritor romano nacido en España.
Senecan [-kən] *a.* senequiano, senequista.
senega [ˈsɛnɪgə] *s.* (bot.) senega, polígala de Virginia.
Senegal [ˌsɛnɪˈgɔl] *s.* Senegal.
Senegalese [-gəˈliz] *a.* senegalés. —*s.* (*pl.* SENEGALESE) senegalés, senegalesa.
senescence [sɪˈnɛsəns] *s.* senectud.
senescent [-ənt] *a.* senescente, que envejece.
seneschal [ˈsɛnəʃəl] *s.* senescal, mayordomo.
senile [ˈsinˌaɪl] *a.* senil.
senility [sɪˈnɪlətɪ, sɛ-] *s.* senilidad, senectud, caduquez.
senior [ˈsinjər, B -njə] *a.* 1. mayor, de mayor edad. 2. más antiguo, de más alto rango. 3. **the s. partner,** socio mayoritario; **the s. service,** (G.B.) la armada. —*s.* 1. persona mayor (que otra). 2. oficial o funcionario más antiguo. 3. (E.U.) escolar del último año. 4. (G.B.) profesor universitario de mayor antigüedad.
senior citizen, (E.U.) persona anciana; jubilado.
senior high school, (E.U.) los tres últimos años de la escuela secundaria.
seniority [sinˈjɔrətɪ, -ˈjɑr-, B ˌsinɪˈɔr-] *s.* (*pl.* SENIOR TIES) antigüedad; prioridad, precedencia.
senior officer, oficial superior.
senna [ˈsɛnə] *s.* (bot.) sen, sena.
sennet [ˈsɛnət] *s.* (hist., G.B.) toque de trompetas que, en el teatro isabelino, anunciaba la entrada de ciertos personajes.
sennit [ˈsɛnət] *s.* (mar.) cajeta.
sensate [ˈsɛnˌseɪt] *a.* percibido por los sentidos.
sensation [sɛnˈseɪʃən] *s.* sensación, sentimiento, percepción.
sensational [-əl] *a.* sensacional.
sensationalism [-ˌɪzəm] *s.* sensacionalismo; (filos.) sensacionalismo.
sensationalist [-əst] *s.* sensacionalista.
sensationalistic [-ˌseɪʃənəlˈɪstɪk] *a.* sensacionalista.
sensationally [-ˈseɪʃənəlɪ] *adv.* sensacionalmente, notablemente.
sense [sɛns] *s.* 1. sentido (facultad). 2. sentido, sensación, sentimiento. 3. sentido, juicio, ej., *a man of s.,* un hombre de juicio. 4. (*pl.*) razón, (sano) juicio, ej., *I was frightened out of my senses,* el susto me hizo perder el juicio. 5. sentido, significado, significación, acepción. 6. sentir o parecer general, opinión común. 7. sentido, apreciación (de humor, belleza, gratitud, etc.). 8. **in a s.,** en cierto sentido, hasta cierto punto; **in all senses of the word,** en toda la extensión de la palabra; **in no s.,** de ninguna manera; **the five senses,** los cinco sentidos; **to be in one's senses,** estar uno en su juicio; **to be out of one's senses,** haber perdido la razón; **to come to one's senses,** volver a sus cabales; **to have the s. to (do),** ser lo suficientemente cuerdo como para (hacer); **to make s.,** tener sentido; **to make s. (out) of,** comprender, explicarse; sacar (algún) sentido de; **to take leave of one's senses,** perder la razón, volverse loco; **to talk s.,** hablar con razón o sentido; hablar razonablemente o cuerdamente; **to talk s. into,** meter (a uno) en razón. —*v.t.* 1. sentir, percibir por medio de los sentidos. 2. intuir, inferir, comprender.
senseless [ˈsɛnsləs] *a.* 1. desmayado, inconsciente, sin conocimiento, insensible. 2. insensato, necio. 3. sin sentido, absurdo.
senselessly [-lɪ] *adv.* insensatamente, sin sentido.
senselessness [-nəs] *s.* insensatez, tontería.
sense of humor, sentido del humor.
sense organ, (fisiol.) órgano sensorio.
sense perception, percepción sensoria.
sensibility [ˌsɛnsəˈbɪlətɪ] *s.* 1. sensibilidad. 2. receptividad mental; discernimiento. 3. precisión (de un instrumento). 4. (*gen. pl.*) susceptibilidad, delicadez.
sensible [ˈsɛnsəbəl] *a.* 1. sensible, perceptible; apreciable, manifiesto. 2. sensitivo, capaz de sentir. 3. sabedor, consciente. 4. razonable, sensato, inteligente.
sensible horizon, (geog.) horizonte sensible.
sensibleness [-nəs] *s.* cordura, sensatez.
sensibly [-blɪ] *adv.* 1. sensiblemente, perceptiblemente. 2. sensatamente, razonablemente.
sensitive [ˈsɛnsətɪv] *a.* 1. sensitivo, sensorial, sensorio. 2. sensible, impresionable; sentido. 3. susceptible. 4. (quím., foto.) sensibilizado (superficie, etc.). 5. (foto.) sensible (película, etc.). 6. (fís., mec.) sensible, delicado (instrumento, etc.). 7. (rad.) de alta sensibilidad.
sensitively [-lɪ] *adv.* sensiblemente.
sensitiveness [-nəs] *s.* 1. sensibilidad (de una persona). 2. susceptibilidad; finura, delicadeza. 3. (fís., mec., foto., rad.) sensibilidad.
sensitive plant, (bot.) sensitiva, mimosa vergonzosa, mimosa púdica.
sensitivity [ˌsɛnsəˈtɪvətɪ] *s.* sensibilidad; (fís., mec., foto., rad.) sensibilidad.
sensitization [ˌsɛnsətəˈzeɪʃən, B -taɪ-] *s.* sensibilización, sensitización; (t.v.) activación.
sensitize [ˈsɛnsəˌtaɪz] *v.t.* 1. (quím., foto.) sensibilizar, sensitizar. 2. (med.) sensibilizar.
sensitizer [-ər, B -ə] *s.* sensibilizador.
sensitometer [ˌsɛnsəˈtɑmətər, B -ˈtɔmɪtə] *s.* (ópt.) sensitómetro.
sensor [ˈsənsər, -ˌsɔr, B -sə] *s.* sensor, detector.
sensorial [sɛnˈsɔrɪəl] *a.* sensorio, sensitivo, sensual.
sensorimotor [ˌsɛnsərɪˈmoʊtər, B -ə] *a.* (anat.) sensorimotor.
sensorium [sɛnˈsɔrɪəm] *s.* (*pl.* SENSORIUMS O SENSORIA [-əl]) (fisiol., psic.) sensorio.
sensory [ˈsɛnsərɪ] *a.* sensorio, sensitivo, sensual.
sensory panel, grupo que aprecia el olor y sabor de un producto.
sensual [ˈsɛntʃʊəl, B ˈsɛnsjʊ-] *a.* 1. sensual; carnal; voluptuoso, lascivo, lujurioso. 2. (ant.) sensorio o sensitivo.
sensualism [-ˌɪzəm] *s.* 1. sensualismo; sensualidad. 2. (filos.) sensualismo.
sensualist [-əst] *s.* sensualista; (filos.) sensualista.
sensuality [ˌsɛntʃʊˈælətɪ, B ˌsɛnsjʊ-] *s.* sensualidad; voluptuosidad, lascivia.
sensualization [-ələˈzeɪʃən, B -əlaɪ-] *s.* acción o efecto de volver sensual.
sensualize [ˈsɛntʃʊəˌlaɪz, B ˈsɛnsjʊ-] *v.t.* hacer sensual; volver sensual.
sensually [-lɪ] *adv.* sensualmente, voluptuosamente.
sensuous [ˈsɛntʃʊəs, B ˈsɛnsjʊ-] *a.* 1. sensorial, sensorio, sensitivo. 2. sensual. 3. placentero, agradable.
sensuously [-lɪ] *adv.* de modo sensual, sensualmente.
sensuousness [-nəs] *s.* 1. sensibilidad. 2. sensualidad.
sent [sɛnt] *pret., p.p. de* **send.**
sentence [ˈsɛntəns] *s.* 1. (gram.) oración, cláusula, período. 2. (der.) sentencia, fallo, condena. 3. (mús.) frase. 4. máxima, aforismo, axioma. 5. (ant.) sentencia, decisión, opinión. —*v.t.* condenar, sentenciar.
sentential [sɛnˈtɛntʃəl, B -ˈtɛnʃəl] *a.* 1. de sentencias, de máximas (libro, colección, etc.). 2. proverbial (frase, dicho). 3. oracional.
sententious [-ˈtɛntʃəs, B -ˈtɛnʃəs] *a.* 1. sentencioso, conceptuoso, aforístico, axiomático. 2. sentencioso, ampuloso (lenguaje).
sententiously [-lɪ] *adv.* sentenciosamente.
sententiousness [-nəs] *s.* carácter o estilo sentenciosos.
sentience [ˈsɛntʃəns, B ˈsɛnʃəns] *s.* 1. estado consciente, percepción. 2. receptividad de los sentidos, capacidad de sentir.
sentient [-tʃənt, B -ʃənt] *a.* 1. consciente. 2. sensitivo, sensible. 3. emotivo, emocional.
sentiment [ˈsɛntəmənt] *s.* 1. sentimiento. 2. sentimentalismo, sensibilidad, susceptibilidad. 3. sentir, modo de pensar, juicio, opinión, concepto. 4. (*pl.*) afectos, simpatías, emociones.
sentimental [ˌsɛntəˈmɛntəl] *a.* sentimental; romántico, impresionable.
sentimentalism [-ˌɪzəm] *s.* sentimentalismo.
sentimentalist [-əst] *s.* persona sentimental.
sentimentality [-mɛnˈtælətɪ] *s.* 1. sentimentalismo. 2. idea o frase sentimental.
sentimentalize [-ˈmɛntəlˌaɪz] *v.t.* imbuir de sentimiento. —*v.i.* pensar u obrar sentimentalmente.
sentimentally [-ɪ] *adv.* sentimentalmente.
sentinel [ˈsɛntənəl] *s.* centinela; vigilante, guardia. —*v.t.* (*pret., p.p.* SENTINELED O SENTINELLED; *p.pr.* SENTINELING O SENTINELLING) 1. vigilar como centinela. 2. poner un centinela a. 3. apostar como centinela.
sentry [ˈsɛntrɪ] *s.* (*pl.* SENTRIES) 1. guardia, sereno, guarda, vigilante. 2. (mil.) centinela.
sentry box, garita de centinela.
Seoul [soʊl] *s.* Seúl, capital de Corea del Sur.
sepal [ˈsipəl, B ˈsɛp-] *s.* (bot.) sépalo.
sepaled, sepalled [-əld] *a.* (bot.) dotado de sépalos.

sepaloid [-ə,lɔɪd] *a.* (bot.) sepaloideo.
separability [,sɛpərə'bɪlətɪ] *s.* calidad de separable.
separable ['sɛpərəbəl] *a.* separable, partible, disgregable.
separableness [-nəs] *s.* calidad de separable.
separably [-blɪ] *adv.* separablemente; en forma separable.
separate ['sɛpə,reɪt] *v.t.* separar. —*v.i.* separarse. — [-rət] *a.* 1. separado, suelto, desunido, segregado. 2. separado, que pertenece sólo a uno; propio, privado, particular, personal, ej., *s. rooms,* cuartos privados. —*s.* separata, reimpresión (de un artículo, etc.).
separately [-rətlɪ] *adv.* separadamente, por separado, uno a uno, aparte, de por sí.
separateness [-nəs] *s.* estado de separación; carácter separado.
separates [-rəts] *s. pl.* diferentes piezas de ropa que coordinan entre sí.
separation [,sɛpə'reɪʃən] *s.* separación; (der.) separación, separación de cuerpos.
separation center, (mil.) centro de desmovilización, centro de licenciamiento.
separatism ['sɛpərət,ɪzəm] *s.* (pol.) separatismo.
separatist [-əst] *s.* 1. separatista. 2. (relig.) cismático, disidente. 3. (E.U., hist.) separatista, secesionista.
separative ['sɛpə,reɪtɪv, B -ərət-] *a.* separativo.
separator ['sɛpə,reɪtər, B -ə] *s.* 1. separador, divisor, partidor. 2. separador, centrífuga (para desnatar leche). 3. (min.) escogedor, separador. 4. (elec.) separador.
Sephardi [sə'fɑrdɪ, B -'fɑdɪ] *s.* (*pl.* SEPHARDIM [-dəm]) sefardí.
Sephardic [-dɪk] *a.* sefardí, sefardita.
sepia ['sɪpɪə, B -pjə] *s.* 1. sepia (pigmento, tinta); color sepia. 2. (ict.) sepia, jibia. 3. (foto.) copia de color sepia. —*a.* de sepia.
sepiolite ['sipɪə,laɪt] *s.* (min.) sepiolita.
sepoy ['si,pɔɪ] *s.* cipayo, soldado indio.
sepsis ['sɛpsəs] *s.* (*pl.* SEPSES [-,siz]) (med.) sepsis.
sept [sɛpt] *s.* (Irl., hist.) clan, tribu.
Sept. *abrev. de* **September,** septiembre (sept., set.).
septa, *pl. de* **septum.**
septal ['sɛptəl] *a.* (anat., bot., zool.) septal.
septangle ['sɛp,tæŋgəl] *s.* (geom.) heptágono.
septarium [sɛp'tɛrɪəm, B -'tɛər-] *s.* (min.) septario.
septate ['sɛpteɪt] *a.* (bot.) septado.
septectomy [sɛp'tɛktəmɪ] *s.* (*pl.* SEPTECTOMIES) (med.) septectomía.
September [sɛp'tɛmbər, B -bə] *s.* septiembre, setiembre.
Septembrist [-brəst] *s.* (hist.) septembrista.
septenary ['səptə,nɛrɪ, B -nərɪ] *a.* 1. septenario. 2. séptuplo. —*s.* 1. (poética) septenario. 2. (ant.) septena; septenio.
septendecillion [,sɛp,tɛndɪ'sɪljən] *s.* (E.U.) unidad seguida de 54 ceros; (G.B.) unidad seguida de 102 ceros.
septennial [sɛp'tɛnɪəl] *a.* sieteñal.
septennially [-əlɪ] *adv.* a intervalos sieteñales.
septennium [-'tɛnɪəm] *s.* (*pl.* SEPTENNIUMS O SEPTENNIA [-ə]) septenio.
septentrional [-'tɛntrɪənəl] *a.* septentrional.
septet, septette [sɛp'tɛt] *s.* (mús.) septeto.
septfoil ['sɛpt,fɔɪl] *s.* (bot.) sieteenrama, tormentila.
septic ['sɛptɪk] *a.* séptico. —*s.* substancia séptica.
septicemia [,sɛptə'simɪə] *s.* (med.) septicemia.
septicemic [-mɪk] *a.* (med.) septicémico.
septicidal [-'saɪdəl] *a.* (bot.) septicida.
septicity [sɛp'tɪsətɪ] *s.* septicidad.
septic tank, tanque o pozo séptico, cámara o fosa séptica.
septifragal [-'tɪfrɪgəl] *a.* (bot.) septífrago.
septillion [-'tɪljən] *s.* septillón (unidad seguida de 24 ceros en E.U. y de 42 en G.B.).
septime ['sɛptim] *s.* (esgr.) séptima.
septimole ['sɛptə,moʊl] *s.* (mús.) septillo.
septuagenarian [,sɛptuədʒə'nɛrɪən, B -tj-ʊ-'nɛər-] *a., s.* septuagenario.
septuagenary [-'dʒɛnərɪ, B -'dʒin-] *a.* septuagenario, setentón.
Septuagesima [-tʊə'dʒɛsəmə, B -tjʊ-] *s.* (relig.) septuagésima.
Septuagint [sɛp'tuədʒənt, B 'səptjʊ-] *s.* (bíbl.) Septuaginta, versión griega de los Setenta.
septum ['sɛptəm] *s.* (*pl.* SEPTA [-tə]) (anat., bot., zool.) septum, septo, tabique.
septuor ['sɛptʊər, B -tjʊə] *s.* (mús.) septeto.
septuple [sɛp'tupəl, B 'sɛptjʊpəl] *a.* séptuplo. —*v.t.* septuplicar.
septuplet [-'tʌplət, B 'sɛptjʊplət] *s.* (mús.) septillo.
septuplicate [-'tuplə,keɪt, B sɛp'tju-] *v.t.* septuplicar.
sepulcher, sepulchre ['sɛpəlkər, B -kə] *s.* sepulcro; **the Holy S.,** el Santo Sepulcro. —*v.t.* (*pret., p.p.* SEPULCHERED O SEPULCHRED; *p.pr.* SEPULCHERING O SEPULCHRING) sepultar.
sepulchral [sə'pʌlkrəl] *a.* sepulcral; lúgubre, tétrico, fúnebre, funesto.
sepulchrally [-krəlɪ] *adv.* lúgubremente.
sepulture ['sɛpəltʃər, B -tʃə] *s.* 1. sepultura, entierro, inhumación. 2. sepulcro.
sequacious [sɪ'kweɪʃəs] *a.* 1. imitativo. 2. (ant.) servil, obsecuente.
sequacity [-'kwæsətɪ] *s.* 1. carácter imitativo. 2. (ant.) servilismo.
sequel ['sikwəl] *s.* 1. secuela, consecuencia, corolario. 2. resultado, efecto final. 3. continuación (de un artículo, novela, etc.).
sequela [sɪ'kwɛlə, B -kwilə] *s.* (*pl.* SEQUELAE [-i, B -li]) (med.) secuela.
sequence ['sikwəns] *s.* 1. sucesión; orden de sucesión. 2. cadena, sarta, serie. 3. resultado, consecuencia, efecto. 4. (relig., mús., cinem.) secuencia. 5. (naipes) secansa, escalera, runfla. —*v.t.* ordenar en serie.
sequency [-kwənsɪ] *var. de* **sequence.**
sequent ['sikwənt] *a.* siguiente, consecutivo. —*s.* consecuencia, secuela.
sequential [sɪ'kwɛntʃəl, B -'kwɛnʃəl] *a.* consecutivo; consiguiente.
sequentially [-tʃəlɪ, B -ʃə-] *adv.* consecutivamente; consiguientemente.
sequester [sɪ'kwɛstər, B -tə] *v.t.* 1. separar, segregar, apartar, alejar. 2. (der.) secuestrar, embargar; confiscar; apropiarse de. 3. (ant.) recluir o encerrar; retirar.
sequestered [-tərd, B -təd] *a.* retirado, solitario; alejado o apartado.
sequestrable [-trəbəl] *a.* secuestrable.
sequestrate [-,treɪt] *v.t.* 1. confiscar, decomisar, incautarse de. 2. (ant.) separar, apartar, alejar.
sequestration [,sikwəs'treɪʃən, B -kwes-] *s.* 1. retiro, reclusión, apartamiento, separación. 2. (der.) secuestro, secuestración, embargo.
sequestrator [sɪ'kwɛs,treɪtər, B 'sikwɛs-ə] *s.* (der.) secuestrador.
sequestrum [sɪ'kwɛstrəm] *s.* (*pl.* SEQUESTRUMS O SEQUESTRA [-trə]) (med.) secuestro.
sequin ['sikwən] *s.* 1. cequí o sequí (moneda antigua de oro de Italia y Turquía). 2. lentejuela (para adornar vestidos).
sequoia [sɪ'kwɔɪə] *s.* (bot.) secoya, abeto gigante de California.
sera, *pl. de* **serum.**
seraglio [sə'ræljoʊ, B sɛ'rɑlɪoʊ] *s.* (*pl.* SERAGLIOS O SERAGLI) 1. serrallo. 2. (hist.) palacio del sultán (en Turquía).
serai [-'raɪ] *s.* caravasar, caravansera, posada de caravanas.
serail [seɪ'rɑjə, B sə'reɪl] *var. de* **seraglio.**
serape [sə'rɑpɪ, B sɛ'rɑpeɪ] *s.* serape; capote de monte, poncho (Amer.).
seraph ['sɛrəf] *s.* (*pl.* SERAPHIM [-ə,fɪm] O SERAPHS) serafín.
seraphic [sə'ræfɪk] *a.* seráfico; angélico.
seraphically [-ɪkəlɪ] *adv.* seráficamente; angelicalmente.
seraphim, *pl. de* **seraph.**
Serbian ['sɜrbɪən, B 'sɜbjən] *a., s.* servio, de Servia.
Serbo-Croatian [,sɜrboʊkroʊ'eɪʃən, B ,sɜboʊ-] *s., a.* servocroata.
sere [sɪr, B sɪə] *a.* seco, marchito, agostado.
serenade [,sɛrə'neɪd] *s.* (mús.) serenata. —*v.t.* dar serenata a. —*v.i.* dar serenata(s).
serenader [-ər, B -ə] *s.* el que da serenatas.
serendipity [,sɛrən'dɪpətɪ] *s.* (buena) suerte para hallar cosas valiosas por casualidad.
serene [sə'rin] *a.* 1. sereno, claro, despejado (cielo, etc.). 2. sereno, plácido, apacible (persona). 3. serenísimo, ej., *His S Highness,* Su Serenísima Alteza. —*s.* extensión o espacios serenos del cielo, mar o luz.
serenely [-lɪ] *adv.* serenamente.
serenity [sə'rɛnətɪ] *s.* 1. serenidad, sosiego, calma. 2. Serenidad (título del emperador romano, del papa, obispos, etc.).
serf [sɜrf, B sɜf] *s.* siervo.
serfdom ['sɜrfdəm, B 'sɜf-] **serfhood** [-,hʊd] *s.* servidumbre, esclavitud.
serge [sɜrdʒ, B sɜdʒ] *s.* (tej.) sarga, estameña, anascote.
sergeancy ['sɑrdʒənsɪ, B 'sɑdʒən-] *s.* sargentía.
sergeant ['sɑrdʒənt, B 'sɑdʒənt] *s.* 1. (mil.) sargento. 2. oficial de orden (en un cuerpo legislativo).
sergeant at arms, oficial de orden (en un cuerpo legislativo).
sergeant first class, (mil.) sargento de brigada.
sergeant fish, (zool.) (especie de) róbalo.
sergeantship [-,ʃɪp] *s.* sargentía, grado de sargento.
Sergt. *abrev. de* **Sergeant,** sargento.
serial ['sɪrɪəl, B 'sɪər-] *a.* de serie, consecutivo, sucesivo, formando serie; gradual. —*s.* obra publicada por entregas; (rad., t.v.) serial.
serial bonds, (fin.) bonos de vencimiento escalonado.
serialization [,sɪrɪələ'zeɪʃən, B ,sɪərɪəlaɪ-] *s.* publicación por entregas.
serialize ['sɪrɪə,laɪz, B 'sɪər-] *v.t.* publicar por entregas.
serially [-lɪ] *adv.* 1. en serie. 2. por entregas o episodios.
serial number, número de serie.
seriate ['sɪrɪ,eɪt, B 'sɪərɪət] *a.* arreglado u ordenado en serie.
seriatim [,sɪrɪ'eɪtəm, B ,sɪər-] *adv.* en serie; consecutivamente, punto por punto, sucesivamente.
sericate ['sɛrəkeɪt] *a.* sedoso; velludo.
sericeous [sə'rɪʃəs] *a.* 1. sérico, seroso, sedeño. 2. (bot.) seríceo.
sericin ['sɛrəsən] *s.* (quím.) sericina.
sericultural [,sɛrə'kʌltʃərəl] *a.* sericícola.

sericulture ['sɛrəˌkʌltʃər, B -tʃə] *s.* sericicultura, sericultura.
sericulturist [ˌsɛrə'kʌltʃərəst] *s.* sericicultor, sericultor.
seriema [ˌsɛri'imə] *s.* (orn.) chuña, chuña real o saraí.
series ['sɪriz, B 'sɪər-] *s.* (*pl.* SERIES) 1. serie; sucesión; progresión; cadena, sarta, retahíla. 2. serie, colección (de volúmenes, números de un periódico, artículos, etc.). 3. (elec.) serie, ciclo; (geol.) formación. 4. (mat.) serie. 5. **in s.,** (elec.) en serie. —*a.* (elec.) en serie.
series motor, (elec.) motor devanado en serie; motorserie.
series winding, (elec.) devanado en serie.
series-wound [-'waʊnd] *a.* (elec.) devanado o arrollado en serie.
serif ['sɛrəf] *s.* (impr.) línea de pie, trazo de pie, bigotillo, trazo terminal.
serigraph ['sɛrəˌgræf, B -ˌgrɑf] *s.* grabado mediante serigrafía.
serigraphy [sə'rɪgrəfɪ] *s.* serigrafía.
serin [sə'ræn, B 'sɛrɪn] *s.* (orn.) variedad de pinzón, verderón.
serine ['sɛrˌin, B -ˌaɪn] *s.* (quím.) serina.
seringa [sə'rɪŋgə] *s.* (bot.) siringa.
seriocomic [ˌsɪrɪoʊ'kɑmɪk, B 'sɪər-'kɔm-] *a.* jocoserio.
serious ['sɪrɪəs, B 'sɪər-] *a.* 1. serio, formal; verdadero, sincero. 2. **and now to be s.,** y ahora (hablemos) en serio; **are you s.?** ¿lo dice en serio? 3. grave (enfermedad, heridas).
seriously [-lɪ] *adv.* seriamente, en serio, con seriedad.
serious-minded [-'maɪndəd] *a.* de mentalidad seria, formal.
seriousness [-nəs] *s.* seriedad; severidad; gravedad (heridas).
serjeant, serjeantship, *vars. de* **sergeant, sergeantship.**
sermon ['sɜrmən, B 'sɜmən] *s.* 1. sermón; prédica, homilía. 2. (fig.) sermón, sermoneo, reprimenda.
sermonize [-məˌnaɪz] *v.i.* 1. sermonar, predicar. 2. sermonear. —*v.t.* 1. dirigir (largos) discursos a, arengar. 2. convertir en un discurso largo.
sermonizer [-ər, B -ə] *s.* predicador; regañón.
Sermon on the Mount, (bíbl.) Sermón de la Montaña.
serologic [ˌsɪrə'lɑdʒɪk, B ˌsɪərə'lɔdʒ-] *a.* (fisiol.) serológico.
serologist [sə'rɑlədʒəst, B ˌsɪə'rɔl-] *s.* serólogo.
serology [-dʒɪ] *s.* serología.
seron [sə'roʊn, B 'sɪərən] *s.* 1. sera, serón. 2. **s. of cinnamon,** churla de canela; **s. of indigo,** zurrón de añil.
serosa [sə'roʊsə] *s.* (zool.) (membrana) serosa.
serosity [sə'rɑsətɪ, B -'rɔs-] *s.* (*pl.* SEROSITIES) serosidad.
serotherapy [ˌsɪroʊ'θɛrəpɪ, B ˌsɪərə-] *s.* (med.) sueroterapia, seroterapia.
serotinous [sə'rɑtənəs, B -'rɔt-] *a.* (bot.) serondo, serótino.
serotonin [ˌsɪrə'toʊnən, B ˌsɪər-] *s.* (bioquím.) serotonina.
serous ['sɪrəs, B 'sɪər-] *a.* seroso; icoroso.
serous fluid, (fisiol.) líquido seroso.
serous membrane, (anat.) membrana serosa.
serow [sə'roʊ, B 'sɛroʊ] *s.* (zool.) cabra del Tibet.
serpent ['sɜrpənt, B 'sɜpənt] *s.* 1. serpiente, sierpe, culebra. 2. (fig.) serpiente (persona astuta, traicionera y maliciosa). 3. buscapiés, carretilla. 4. (mús.) serpentón. 5. **the S.,** (astr.) Serpiente, Serpentario; (bíbl.) el Serpiente, Satanás.
serpentarium [ˌsɜrpən'tɛrɪəm, B ˌsɜpən'tɜər-] *s.* (*pl.* SERPENTARIUMS O SERPENTARIA [-ə]) serpentario.
serpentine ['sɜrpənˌtin, B 'sɜpənˌtaɪn] *a.* 1. serpentino. 2. astuto; marrullero, diabólico, traicionero. 3. sinuoso, tortuoso, torcido.
serpentine, *s.* (min.) serpentina.
serpentine marble, mármol serpentino.
serpiginous [sər'pɪdʒənəs, B sə'-] *a.* (med.) serpiginoso.
serpigo [-'paɪgoʊ] *s.* (med.) serpigo, culebrilla.
serranid [sə'reɪnəd, B -'rænəd] *a., s.* (ict.) (pez) serránido.
serrate ['sɛrˌeɪt, -ət] **serrated** [sə'reɪtəd] *a.* serrado; (bot.) serrado, aserrado; (mec.) dentado, estriado.
serrate leaf, (bot.) hoja aserrada.
serration [sə'reɪʃən] **serrature** ['sɛrətʃər, B -tʃə] *s.* endentadura, serie de recortaduras.
serried ['sɛrɪd] *a.* apretado, apiñado, atestado; **in s. ranks,** (mil.) en filas o hileras apretadas.
serriform ['sɛrəˌfɔrm, B -ˌfɔm] *a.* serrado, dentado.
serrulate ['sɛrələt, -ˌleɪt] **serrulated** [-ˌleɪtəd] *a.* serrulado.
serrulation [ˌsɛrə'leɪʃən] *s.* endentadura fina.
serry ['sɛrɪ] *v.i., v.t.* (*pret., p.p.* SERRIED; *p.pr.* SERRYING) (ant.) apretar(se), juntar(se), esp. en filas o hileras.
serum ['sɪrəm, B 'sɪər-] *s.* (*pl.* SERUMS O SERA [-ə]) 1. (med., biol.) suero. 2. suero suero de la leche.
serum albumin, seroalbúmina.
serum globulin, seroglobulina.
serum therapy, (med.) sueroterapia, seroterapia.
servable ['sɜrvəbəl, B 'sɜvə-] *a.* servible.
serval ['sɜrvəl, B 'sɜvəl] *s.* (zool.) serval.
servant ['sɜrvənt, B 'sɜvənt] *s.* 1. criado, sirviente, doméstico. 2. funcionario, empleado público, ej., *civil s.,* empleado o funcionario público. 3. **your humble s.,** su servidor, su seguro servidor.
serve [sɜrv, B sɜv] *v.i.* 1. servir, ser criado, trabajar de criado. 2. prestar servicio (esp. militar), ej., *he has served in Vietnam,* ha prestado servicio en Vietnam. 3. servir, atender, asistir (a la mesa). 4. servir, ser útil; bastar, ser suficiente o adecuado, ej., *it will s.,* bastará, será adecuado. 5. (dep.) servir la pelota, efectuar el saque. 6. **as memory serves,** cada vez que recuerde; **as occasion serves,** cuando se presente la oportunidad; **s. as,** servir de; **s. for,** servir de, hacer oficio de; **s. on,** ser miembro de (un jurado, comisión, etc.). —*v.t.* 1. servir, estar al servicio de, trabajar para. 2. servir de, ser útil para; ser suficiente para, satisfacer. 3. desempeñar, cumplir, ej., *s. an office,* desempeñar un cargo, *s. a sentence,* cumplir una condena. 4. (t. con *up*) servir (comida, plato, etc.), servir, escanciar (vino, etc.); abastecer, suplir. 5. tratar, ej., *he served me shamefully,* me ha tratado vergonzosamente. 6. asistir, servir, rendir un servicio a. 7. cubrir, pisar (el macho a la hembra). 8. atender a, manejar, hacer funcionar. 9. (der.) entregar a, hacer entrega a, ej., *s. with a writ,* hacer entrega de una notificación o decreto a (alguien). 10. (mar.) aforrar, abarbetar. 11. (dep.) servir, sacar (la pelota). 12. **s. a purpose,** servir para un propósito; **s. notice on (someone),** notificar, dar aviso a (alguien); **s. one right,** merecerlo bien, ej., *it serves you right!* ¡bien te lo mereces! ¡bien hecho!; **s. one's time,** cumplir un período (de un cargo, oficio, etc.); cumplir una condena; **s. one's turn,** bastar para uno, ser adecuado para uno; **s. the purpose of,** usarse como, usarse en vez de; **s. the time** (o **the hour**), actuar de modo oportunista, adoptar una política oportunista; **s. time,** estar en prisión. —*s.* (tenis) servicio, saque.
server ['sɜrvər, B 'sɜvə] *s.* 1. servidor, criado de mesa; mozo de café; mensajero, portador. 2. bandeja, salvilla. 3. (relig.) acólito. 4. (dep.) sacador, servidor, saque (en el tenis, etc.).
Servia ['sɜrvɪə, B 'sɜvɪə] **Servian** [-vɪən] (ant.) *vars. de* **Serbia, Serbian.**
service ['sɜrvəs, B 'sɜvɪs] *s.* 1. servicio, servidumbre; empleo. 2. servicio, obsequio, favor, ej., *will you do me a s.,* ¿me hará Ud. un favor? 3. cargo, deber, función; funcionamiento. 4. ayuda, asistencia, uso, utilidad. 5. vajilla, servicio de mesa, juego de cubiertos. 6. ramo de servicio (público o estatal). 7. oficios religiosos; rito, ceremonia, culto; canto litúrgico. 8. cubrición (de animal macho a la hembra). 9. (com.) servicio (de mantenimiento). 10. (dep.) saque, servicio (en tenis, etc.). 11. (der.) entrega (de un expediente, despacho, citación, etc.). 12. (mar.) barbeta. 13. (hist.) atención amorosa (del galán a su dama). 14. **at the s. of,** a las órdenes de; **at your s.,** a sus órdenes, a los pies de Ud.; **in s.,** funcionando, en funcionamiento; **the services,** las fuerzas armadas; **to be of s. (to),** servir (a); ser útil, ser de ayuda (a); **to have seen s.,** haber estado en uso por mucho tiempo, estar gastado o usado; **to see s.,** prestar servicio militar o de marinero; **to take into one's s.,** emplear. —*a.* 1. de servicio. 2. de uso diario. 3. de las fuerzas armadas. —*v.t.* 1. atender a. 2. mantener, reparar. 3. cubrir (macho a la hembra).
service, *s.* (bot.) serbal, serbo; serbal silvestre.
serviceability [ˌsɜrvəsə'bɪlətɪ, B ˌsɜvə-] *s.* utilidad.
serviceable ['sɜrvəsəbəl, B 'sɜvə-] *a.* 1. servible, útil; utilizable, beneficioso, ventajoso. 2. duradero, durable.
serviceableness [-nəs] *s.* utilidad.
service area, 1. (rad.) área de recepción. 2. (mil.) zona de los servicios. 3. lugar para descansar y repostar (en las autopistas).
serviceberry [-ˌbɛrɪ] *s.* (bot.) 1. serba. 2. guillomo.
service book, (relig.) misal; libro litúrgico.
service brake, (aut.) freno de pedal, freno de servicio.
service capacity, capacidad útil, capacidad en servicio.
service ceiling, (ear.) techo práctico.
service charge, sobrecargo por servicios, porcentaje de servicio.
service club, 1. club militar, hogar del soldado. 2. organización o asociación dedicada al servicio de la comunidad.
service connection, conexión domiciliaria, derivación particular, conexión de entrada; acometida (de agua), toma particular.
service dress, (mil.) uniforme corriente o diario.
service elevator, (E.U.) montacargas. ascensor de cargo.
service entrance, entrada de servicio (servidumbre, etc.).
service industry, industria terciaria.
service lift, (G.B.) montacargas, ascensor de cargo.
service line, (tenis) línea de saque, línea de servicio, línea de ataque; línea central de servicio; línea de mitad de campo.
serviceman ['sɜrvəsmən, B 'sɜvɪs-] *s.* 1. militar. 2. mecánico, reparador.

service medal, (mil.) medalla por servicios en campaña.
service pipe, tubería de servicio, tubería de toma, acometida; tubo de alimentación.
service record, (mil.) hoja de servicios.
service station, (aut.) estación de servicio, taller de reparaciones.
service stripe, (mil.) galón de servicio.
service tree, (bot.) serbal, serbo, acafresna, acerollo.
service workshop, taller de reparaciones.
servicing ['sɜrvəsɪŋ, B 'sɜvɪs-] *s.* servicio.
servient tenement ['sɜrvɪənt-, B 'sɜvɪ-] (der.) predio sirviente.
serviette [ˌsɜrvɪ'ɛt, B ˌsɜvɪ-] *s.* (pr. G.B.) servilleta.
servile ['sɜrvəl, B 'sɜvaɪl] *a.* 1. servil, de los siervos. 2. servil, abyecto, bajo, rastrero.
servilely [-lɪ] *adv.* servilmente.
servility [sər'vɪlətɪ, B sɜ'-] *s.* servilismo, carácter servil.
serving ['sɜrvɪŋ, B 'sɜvɪŋ] *s.* porción (de comida). —*a.* para servir, de servir (cubierto, etc.).
servitor ['sɜrvətər, B 'sɜvətə] *s.* servidor; (hist.) seguidor, secuaz.
servitude [-ˌtud, B -ˌtjud] *s.* 1. esclavitud, servidumbre; vasallaje; sujeción. 2. (der.) servidumbre.
servo brake ['sɜrvoʊ-, B 'sɜvoʊ-] (aut.) servofreno.
servo control, (aer.) servocontrol, aleta de servomando.
Servo-Croatian [ˌsɜrvoʊkroʊ'eɪʃən, B ˌsɜvoʊ-] (ant.) *var. de* **Serbo-Croatian.**
servomechanism ['sɜrvoʊˌmɛkəˌnɪzəm, B 'sɜvoʊ-] *s.* servomecanismo.
servomotor [-ˌmoʊtər, B -ə] *s.* servomotor.
sesame ['sɛsəmɪ] *s.* 1. (bot.) sésamo, alegría, ajonjolí. 2. **open s.!** ¡ábrete sésamo!
sesamoid [-ˌmɔɪd] (anat.) *a.* sesamoide, sesamoideo. —*s.* sesamoide.
sesquicentennial [ˌsɛskwɪsɛn'tɛnɪəl] *a., s.* sesquicentenario, aniversario de siglo y medio.
sesquioxide [-'ɑksaɪd, B -'ɔk-] *s.* (quím.) sesquióxido.
sesquipedalian [-kwəpə'deɪlɪən] **sesquipedal** [sɛs'kwɪpədəl] *a.* 1. sesquipedal. 2. excesivamente larga (palabra); (fig.) pesado, engorroso (estilo).
sessile ['sɛsəl, B -ˌaɪl] *a.* (bot., zool.) sesil, sésil, sentado.
session ['sɛʃən] *s.* 1. sesión, junta. 2. (E.U.) período escolar. 3. (*pl.*) (der.) audiencias (en un tribunal de jurisdicción limitada).
sessional [-əl] *a.* de la sesión (agenda, programa, etc.).
sesterce ['sɛstərs, B -tɜs] *s.* (hist.) sestercio.
sestertium [sɛs'tɜrʃɪəm, B -'tɜtjəm] *s.* (*pl.* SESTERTIA [-ʃɪə, B -tjə]) (hist.) mil sestercios.
sestet [sɛs'tɛt] *s.* 1. (mús.) sexteto. 2. (poética) los dos últimos tercetos de un soneto; sextilla.
sestina [-'tinə] *s.* (*pl.* SESTINE [-nɪ] o SESTINAS) (poética) sextina, sexta rima (poema de seis estrofas y de seis versos).
set [sɛt] *v.t.* (*pret., p.p.* SET; *p.pr.* SETTING) 1. poner, colocar, acomodar. 2. poner, meter, aplicar, adaptar (a). 3. ajustar, regular, armar. 4. poner, situar, asentar, afirmar, fijar. 5. engastar (un diamante, rubí, perla, etc.). 6. poner (en cierto estado o condición); alistar, arreglar. 7. indicar, asignar, dar, establecer, ej., *s.* (*someone*) *an example,* dar ejemplo (a alguien), *s.* (*someone*) *a task,* asignar un deber (a alguien). 8. guarnecer, adornar, salpicar, ej., *s. a ring with diamonds,* guarnecer una sortija con diamantes. 9. endurecer, atiesar; (raro) cuajar. 10. **s. a bone (joint, leg, fracture),** reducir o ensalmar un hueso (articulación, pierna, fractura); **s. a price on,** fijar el precio de; **s. a price on one's head,** ofrecer recompensa por la captura de uno; **s. (someone) a problem,** confrontar (a alguien) con un problema; **s. a trap,** armar una trampa; **s. a watch, s. the watch,** (mar.) rendir la guardia, poner centinela(s); **s. (one person) against (another),** indisponer (a una persona) con (otra); **s. (one thing) against (another),** contraponer, cotejar (una cosa) con (otra); **s. apart,** poner aparte, reservar; **s. aside,** reservar, ahorrar; desechar, descartar; **s. at liberty,** poner en libertad, libertar; **s. at loggerheads with,** malquistar con, meter (a alguien) en pendencia con; **s. at odds,** desunir, malquistar; **s. back,** echar atrás, hacer retroceder; atrasar, retrasar (reloj, etc.); (jer.) costar (cierta suma a uno); **s. close,** (impr.) componer apretado; **s. down,** sentar; poner en tierra; hacer aterrizar (avión); poner por escrito; establecer, fijar (regla, procedimiento, etc.); (dep., juegos) derrotar, suspender (a un jugador); **s. (something) down to,** atribuir (algo) a, achacar (algo) a; **s. (something) down as,** explicarse (algo) como, tener (algo) por, considerar (algo) como; **s. eyes on,** avistar; **s. fire to,** prender fuego a, encender, incendiar; **s. foot on,** pisar, poner el pie sobre; **s. forth,** divulgar, declarar, exponer; **s. free,** poner en libertad, libertar; **s. (motor, etc.) going,** poner (motor, etc.) en marcha; **s. (one's) mind at ease,** tranquilizar, apaciguar el ánimo de (alguien); **s. (one's) house in order,** (fig.) arreglar sus negocios; **s. in,** insertar; **s. off,** hacer resaltar, poner de relieve; adornar, embellecer; hacer estallar; compensar, contrapesar; **s. (someone) off (doing),** inducir, provocar, mover (a alguien) a (hacer); **s. on** (o **upon**), instigar, incitar contra; azuzar (perro) contra; **s. on edge,** dar dentera a; poner en vilo; sacar de quicio; **s. on fire** (o **afire**), encender, incendiar; **s. (movement,** etc.) **on foot,** dar el primer impulso a, iniciar (un movimiento, etc.); **s. oneself against,** oponerse firmemente a; desaprobar resueltamente; **s. one's hair,** peinar, arreglar, ondular el pelo a uno; **s. one's hand** (o **seal) to,** poner su firma (o sello) **a; s. one's heart** (o **mind** o **hopes) on,** anhelar o esperar tenazmente, confiar en conseguir, aspirar a; **s. one's wits to (a question, a problem),** aplicarse a, concentrarse en (una cuestión, un problema); **s. oneself to (do),** ponerse a (hacer); **s. oneself up as,** meterse a, ej., *he sets himself up as a judge,* él se mete a juez; **s. out,** aderezar, adornar; demostrar, exhibir; declarar, manifestar, exponer; trazar, delinear; **s. (someone) over (others),** poner (a alguien) por encima de (otros); **s. a question at rest, resolver** o poner fin a una cuestión; **s. right,** poner en orden; corregir, enmendar; **s. sail,** alzar velas; hacer(se) a la vela, largar las velas; **s. great store** (o **much) by,** apreciar mucho, dar mucha importancia a; **s. the alarm,** poner el despertador (en una hora); **s. the fashion,** dictar la moda; **s. the pace,** imprimir el ritmo o velocidad; **s. the table,** poner la mesa; **s. (someone) to (do),** mandar, ordenar (a alguien hacer o que haga), ej., *they s. him to dig,* le mandaron excavar, le ordenaron que excavara; **s. (lyrics) to music,** poner música a (poema, letra), adaptar música a (poema, letra); **s.** (o **s. up) type,** (impr.) componer (tipos); **s. up,** erigir, levantar; poner a la vista; emprender, abrir (negocio); establecer, fundar (institución, escuela, etc.); instituir, poner en marcha (campaña, etc.); establecer, financiar (a una persona en negocio, carrera, profesión, etc.); reponer, devolver la salud a, restaurar; desarrollar el cuerpo de (alguien); causar, originar (tirantez, resentimiento, etc.); exponer, propugnar (teoría); planear, hacer planes para; soltar, pegar (grito, protesta, etc.); convidar (a alguien), convidarle a uno (alguna cosa); (impr.) poner en tipo (un manuscrito); **s. up the drinks,** convidar a beber; **s. (someone) up with,** proveer ampliamente (a alguien) de; **s. (one's) watch,** poner (uno) su reloj en la hora; **s. wide** (o **out**), (impr.) componer flojo; **to be hard s. for,** estar apurado de (dinero, etc.); **to be (dead) s. on (doing),** estar muy metido en, estar resuelto a (hacer); **to be s. to (do),** estar listo o determinado a (hacer). —*v.i.* 1. endurecerse, solidificarse, cuajarse, trabarse, fraguarse. 2. tomar forma, desarrollarse por completo, consolidarse. 3. ponerse (astro). 4. moverse, fluir (marea, corriente, etc.). 5. (fig.) inclinarse, cobrar fuerza, crecer (sentimiento, costumbre, etc.), tender a definirse. 6. parar (perro de caza). 7. caer (bien o mal), ajustarse, sentar (vestido, prenda, etc.). 8. enclocar, encloquecer, empollarse (aves). 9. producir fruto (árbol, flor). 10. **s. about,** empezar, emprender; **s. forth,** ponerse en marcha, salir; **s. in,** sobrevenir, llegar; establecerse, volver constante; ponerse a; empezar a subir (marea); **s. off,** emprender viaje, partir; **s. on** (o **upon**), acometer, embestir, atacar; **s. out,** emprender viaje, partir; **s. out for,** partir para, salir para; **s. out to (do),** empezar a (hacer); **s. to,** aplicarse con vigor a, afanarse en; ponerse a (pelear, discutir, etc.); **s. to (do),** empezar a (hacer), echarse a (hacer); **s. up,** establecerse (como profesional, comerciante, etc.). —*a.* 1. establecido, determinado, prescrito, señalado. 2. meditado, estudiado, deliberado, ej., *in s. terms,* en términos meditados. 3. inmóvil, rígido, yerto; persistente; fijo, invariable, ej., *s. price,* precio fijo. 4. acabado, desarrollado. 5. (mec.) armado. 6. (joy.) engastado, montado. 7. (dial.) obstinado, terco. —*s.* 1. juego, colección, conjunto, surtido, serie, grupo, clase, ej., *s. of chairs,* juego de sillas, *s. of poems,* colección de poemas. 2. compañía, camarilla, cuadrilla, banda, hato, pandilla, ej., *the political s.,* la camarilla política. 3. endurecimiento (de una substancia); fraguado (del cemento, etc.). 4. forma, porte, postura, apariencia, conformación, configuración, ej., *the s. of one's shoulders,* la configuración de los hombros de uno. 5. dirección, curso, movimiento, tendencia (de corriente, viento, opinión, etc.) 6. punta (de perro de muestra). 7. nidada (de huevos). 8. puesta (de un astro), ocaso. 9. caida, ajuste (de una prenda de vestir), ej., *the s. of a coat,* la caída de un saco. 10. figura básica (en el baile de cuadrillas). 11. (teat., cinem.) plató, decorado, decoración (para una escena). 12. (rad.) aparato (receptor). 13. (filat.) serie (de sellos o estampillas). 14. (tenis) set (cada una de las etapas de que se compone un partido). 15. (mec.) encorvadura, torcedura, deformación permanente; triscamiento (de los dientes de una sierra); triscador (herramienta). 16. (min.) marco (de galería de una mina de carbón). 17. (impr.) grosor, grueso, espesor, ancho, prosa, ojo (del tipo). 18. (agr.) planta de transplantar, bulbo, pie de árbol; fruto en estado rudimentario. 19. (const.) última capa de enlucido (de una pared). 20. **on the s.,** (teat., cinem.) en el foro, en el escenario; **s. of teeth,** dentadura (artificial o natural).
setaceous [sɪ'teɪʃəs] *a.* setáceo, cerdoso, cerdudo.
setback ['sɛtˌbæk] *a.* s. 1. retraso, parada, demora. 2. revés, derrota. 3. baja, caída (de precios). 4. (arq.) retallo.

setbolt [-ˌboʊlt] *s.* (mar.) botador, perno de trabante.
set chisel, cortafrío de herrero.
setdown [-ˌdaʊn] *s.* desaire, repulsa.
set expression, frase hecha.
Seth [sɛθ] *s.* (bíbl.) Set.
setiform [ˈsitəˌfɔrm, B -ˌfɔm] *a.* de forma de cerda.
set-in [ˈsɛtˌɪn] *a.* empotrado (estante de libros, etc.).
setoff [-ˌɔf] *s.* 1. compensación; contrapeso. 2. relieve, realce, adorno. 3. (der.) contrarreclamación, compensación, neutralización. 4. (arq.) saliente, vuelo, nervadura.
seton [ˈsitən] *s.* (med., vet.) sedal.
setose [ˈsiˌtoʊs] *a.* cerdoso, cerdudo; setáceo.
setout [ˈsɛtˌaʊt] *s.* 1. arreglo, disposición. 2. exhibición, presentación. 3. comienzo. 4. reunión, evento social.
set piece, 1. pieza realista de escenario. 2. composición en estilo florido o elaborado (ej., en literatura).
setscrew [-ˌskru] *s.* tornillo prisionero, tornillo de presión o de aprieto.
settee [sɛˈti] *s.* canapé, sofá.
setter [ˈsɛtər, B -ə] *s.* 1. (*ú. en palabras compuestas*) el que pone, coloca o fija, ej., *typesetter,* compositor, cajista, *bricksetter,* albañil. 2. sétter, perro de muestra o de ojeo, perdiguero.
set theory, (mat.) la teoría de los conjuntos.
setting [ˈsɛtɪŋ] *s.* 1. colocación, montadura, fijación. 2. medio, ambiente (de una narración o relato). 3. armadura, marco, guarnición. 4. (fig.) marco, fondo (musical, etc.). 5. música de fondo. 6. nidada (de huevos). 7. (astr.) puesta, ocaso (de un astro). 8. (teat.) decorado, decoración, escena, puesta en escena. 9. (joy.) engaste, montadura. —*a.* poniente (sol).
setting angle, (mec.) ángulo de decalaje.
setting-board [-ˌbɔrd, B -ˌbɔd] *s.* tablilla para montar (muestras entomológicas).
setting point, (quím.) punto de solidificación.
setting-rule [-ˌrul] *s.* (impr.) sacalíneas.
settle [ˈsɛtəl] *s.* banco largo (con respaldar alto y brazos, gen. con una especie de arca o baúl debajo del asiento).
settle, *v.t.* 1. colocar; asentar, establecer, acomodar. 2. asentar, consolidar, afirmar. 3. arreglar, poner en orden, ej., *s. one's affairs,* poner en orden sus asuntos. 4. acordar, resolver, determinar, fijar, ej., *s. one's doubts,* resolver sus dudas uno, *s. the succession,* determinar la sucesión (esp. de herederos). 5. depurar; clarificar, ej., *s. the soup with the white of an egg,* clarificar la sopa con la clara de un huevo. 6. asentar, matar (el polvo). 7. componer, conciliar (diferencias, etc.), poner fin a (una reyerta, disputa, etc.). 8. poblar, colonizar (región, país, etc.); colonizar con, establecer (personas en una región). 9. liquidar, pagar, saldar, cancelar. 10. acabar con, liquidar. 11. **s. accounts,** (lit., fig.) saldar cuentas; **s. on,** legar a; dar en dote a; **s. oneself,** ubicarse; acomodarse; **s. up,** arreglar definitivamente. —*v.i.* 1. posarse, reposarse, asentarse (pájaro, mariposa, etc.). 2. caer, venir (la noche). 3. arraigar, establecerse, radicarse, domiciliarse, fijar su residencia. 4. asentarse, depositarse, irse al fondo (hez, impureza, etc.). 5. hacerse compacto, solidificarse. 6. asentarse (el polvo). 7. empezar a hundirse (barco). 8. asentarse, clarificarse (por sedimentación, ej., vino). 9. apaciguarse, calmarse, sosegarse. 10. establecerse o fluir en una dirección (viento, corriente, etc.). 11. (t. con **up**) saldar cuentas, hacer pago; pagar la cuenta, ej., *will you s. for me?* ¿quiere pagar la cuenta por mí? 12. **s. down,** calmarse, serenarse; formalizarse, entrar en juicio; echar raíces, radicarse; acostumbrarse; **s. down to (work, reading, bridge,** etc.), ponerse a (trabajar, leer, jugar bridge, etc.); **s. for,** contentarse con, conformarse con, aceptar; **s. in,** ocupar, establecerse en (nueva casa, etc.); **s. on,** decidirse a, resolverse a; **s. with,** pagar uno su deuda a; ponerse de acuerdo con, llegar a un acuerdo con, arreglarse con; **s. with creditors** llegar a un acuerdo con los acreedores.
settled [-əld] *a.* 1. arraigado. 2. estable, firme. 3. pagado (factura, cuenta, etc.).
settlement [-əlmənt] *s.* 1. instalación, establecimiento. 2. colonización. 3. colonia. 4. poblado, pueblo. 5. caserío (esp. de esclavos). 6. arreglo, ajuste, conciliación (de diferencias, disputas, etc.); convenio. 7. (com.) pago, cancelación (de deudas, una cuenta, etc.). 8. (der.) donación; dote. 9. (der.) domicilio, residencia. 10. (arq.) hundimiento, descenso, asiento (de una pared, edificio, etc.); (*pl.*) rajaduras, dislocaduras (causadas por hundimiento).
settler [-lər, B -lə] *s.* 1. árbitro, conciliador (de disputas). 2. colonizador, colono, poblador.
settling [-lɪŋ] *s.* 1. instalación. 2. colonización. 3. arreglo, conciliación. 4. (*pl.*) zurrapas, heces; sedimiento, poso. 5. (arq.) hundimiento, asiento, sentamiento.
settlor [-lər, B -lə] *s.* (der.) fundador, fideicomitente.
set-to [-ˌtu] *s.* (*pl.* SET-TOS) (fam.) lucha, combate, disputa.
setup [-ˌʌp] *s.* 1. organización, estructura. 2. arreglo, disposición (de instrumentos, equipo, partes de maquinaria, etc.). 3. presencia, porte; constitución (de una persona). 4. plan, proyecto. 5. situación. 6. cubierto, servicio de mesa. 7. tarea fácil; posición fácil (en billar). 8. contienda arreglada (hecha fácil a propósito). 9. (jer.) local, oficina, establecimiento.
seven [ˈsɛvən] *s.* siete, ej., *the s. of clubs,* el siete de tréboles, *s. of them,* siete de ellos. —*a.* siete; **the s. wise men,** los siete sabios (de Grecia); **the s. deadly sins,** los siete pecados capitales; **the s. seas,** los siete mares.
sevenfold [-ˌfoʊld] *a.* séptuplo. —*adv.* siete veces.
Seven Hills of Rome, Las siete colinas de Roma.
seven hundred, setecientos.
seven hundredth, septingentésimo.
sevenscore [-ˌskɔr, B -skɔ] *a., s.* siete veintenas.
seventeen [ˌsɛvənˈtin] *s., a.* diecisiete, diez y siete.
seventeenth [-ˈtinθ] *s.* 1. decimoséptimo; diecisieteavo. 2. diecisiete (en fechas). —*a.* decimoséptimo; diecisieteavo.
seventeen-year locust [-tinˈjɪr-, B -ˈjɜ-] (ento.) cigarra americana (cuya larva vive hasta diecisiete años en el N. y trece en el S. de los E.U.).
seventh [ˈsɛvənθ] *s.* 1. séptimo. 2. siete (en fechas). 3. (mús.) séptima. —*a.* séptimo.
seventh-day [-ˌdeɪ] *a.* sabatario.
Seventh-Day Adventist, (relig.) adventista del séptimo día.
seventh heaven, 1. séptimo cielo (el cielo último y más alto en el mahometismo). 2. (fig.) éxtasis, arrobamiento, extrema felicidad.
seventhly [-lɪ] *adv.* en séptimo lugar.
seventieth [ˈsɛvəntɪəθ] *s.* setentavo (fracción). —*a.* septuagésimo.
seventy [ˈsɛvəntɪ] *s.* (*pl.* SEVENTIES) setenta. —*a.* setenta.
seventy-five [ˌsɛvəntɪˈfaɪv] *s.* (mil.) cañon de 75 mm.
seventy-four [-ˈfɔr, B -ˈfɔ] *s.* (hist.) buque de guerra con 74 cañones.
seven-up [-ˈʌp] *s.* un juego de naipes (en que siete puntos constituyen una partida).
seven-year itch [ˈsɛvənˌjɪr-, B -jɜr-] 1. (med.) sarna. 2. (hum.) comezón del séptimo año (tedio o inquietud de los esposos que se presenta al cumplir siete años de casados).
Seven Years' War, Guerra de los Siete Años.
sever [ˈsɛvər, B -ə] *v.t.* 1. separar, desunir; dividir; partir, romper (cuerda, etc.), cortar (cabeza, etc.). 2. (fig.) romper, cortar (relaciones diplomáticas). —*v.i.* partirse, romperse (cuerda, cable, etc.).
severable [-ərəbəl] *a.* 1. separable. 2. (der.) divisible (díc. de derechos y obligaciones).
several [ˈsɛvərəl, B ˈsɛvrəl] *a.* 1. varios, diversos, algunos. 2. individual, particular, respectivo. 3. distinto, diferente.
severalfold [-foʊld] *a.* 1. de varias partes; multiforme. 2. múltiple.
severally [-ɪ] *adv.* separadamente, individualmente; respectivamente.
severalty [-tɪ] *s.* posesión exclusiva; **in s.,** (der.) en posesión exclusiva.
severance [ˈsɛvərəns] *s.* 1. separación, división, partición. 2. cesantía. 3. (der.) separación de la defensa de varios demandados. 4. (dip.) ruptura, rompimiento (de relaciones).
severance benefit, regalía por cese de empleo o servicio.
severance pay, indemnización por cese de empleo.
severe [səˈvɪr, B -ˈvɪə] *a.* 1. severo (persona, crítico, ley, prueba, mirada, etc.). 2. estricto, exacto, riguroso (lógica, etc.). 3. inclemente, riguroso (clima, tiempo, invierno). 4. grave, serio (herida, depresión económica, etc.). 5. duro (golpe, pena, etc.). 6. **to be s. with,** tratar severamente; poner a prueba.
severely [-lɪ] *adv.* severamente.
severeness [-nəs] *s. var. de* **severity.**
severity [səˈvɛrətɪ] *s.* 1. severidad. 2. exactitud, estrictez. 3. inclemencia, rigor (del clima, etc.). 4. gravedad (de una herida, etc.).
Seville orange [səˈvɪl-] naranja sanguínea, naranja de jugo.
Sevillian [səˈvɪljən] *a., s.* sevillano.
sew [soʊ] *v.t.* (*pret.* SEWED [soʊd]; *p.p.* SEWED o SEWN [soʊn]; *p.pr.* SEWING) coser; **s. up,** cerrar con costura (hueco, rasgadura, herida, etc.); asegurarse, monopolizar; contratar en forma exclusiva; finiquitar, concluir, completar. —*v.i.* trabajar como costurera, ser costurera.
sewage [ˈsuɪdʒ, B ˈsju-] *s.* aguas cloacales, aguas negras, aguas de alcantarilla, aguas de albañal o fecales, aguas servidas, aguas residuales.
sewer [ˈsuər, B ˈsjuə] *s.* (hist.) camarero de categoría que atendía la mesa; mayordomo de comedor.
sewer, *s.* cloaca, albañal, alcantarilla.
sewerage [-ərɪdʒ] *s.* 1. desagüe, alcantarillado (sistema). 2. aguas de albañal, aguas cloacales, aguas de alcantarilla, aguas servidas.
sewer rat, rata de alcantarilla.
sewing [ˈsoʊɪŋ] *s.* costura, labor.
sewing basket, cesta de costura.
sewing circle, grupo de mujeres que se reúnen periódicamente para coser (gen. con fines benéficos).
sewing machine, máquina de coser.
sewing silk, hilo de seda.

sewing thread, hilo de coser.
sewn [soʊn] *p.p. de* **sew.**
sex [sɛks] *s.* 1. sexo. 2. acto sexual. 3. **the fair s., the gentle s.,** el bello sexo. —*a.* sexual, ej., *s. instinct,* instinto sexual.
sexagenarian [ˌsɛksədʒə'nɛrɪən] *s.* sexagenario; sesentón. —*a.* sexagenario.
sexagenarian cycle, ciclo sexagesimal (período de 60 años usados por los chinos para calcular el tiempo).
sexagenary [ˌsɛk'sædʒəˌnɛrɪ, B -nərɪ] *a.* 1. de sesenta; sexagesimal. 2. sexagenario. —*s.* (*pl.* SEXAGENARIES) sexagenario.
sexagesimal [-sə'dʒɛsəmel] *a.* sexagesimal. —*s.* fracción sexagesimal.
Sexagesima Sunday [ˌsɛksə'dʒɛsəmə-] (relig.) domingo de sexagésima.
sex appeal, atracción sexual, sexapil, sexy.
sexcentenary [ˌsɛk'sɛntəˌnɛrɪ, B -sɛn'tɛnərɪ] *a., s.* sexcentésimo.
sex change, cambio de sexo.
sex change operation, operación de cambio de sexo.
sex chromosome, (biol.) cromosoma sexual.
sex-crazed, obsesionado por el sexo.
sex crime, crimen sexual.
sexed [sɛkst] *a.* 1. con deseos sexuales. 2. de carácter sexual.
sexennial [sɛk'sɛnɪəl] *a.* sexenal. —*s.* sexenio, acontecimiento sexenal.
sexennially [-əlɪ] *adv* cada seis años.
sex hormone, (bioquím.) hormona sexual.
sexiness ['sɛksɪnəs] *s.* atracción sexual, erotismo.
sexism [-ɪzm] *s.* sexismo, prejuicio o discriminación sexual (esp. en contra de la mujer).
sexist ['sksst] *a., s.* sexista.
sexless [-ləs] *a.* asexual, asexuado, sin sexo, neutro.
sexlessness [-ləsnəs] *s.* carácter asexual; falta de sexualidad, asexualidad.
sex life, vida sexual.
sex-mad, obsesionado por el sexo.
sex offender, delincuente sexual.
sexologist [ˌsɛk'sɑlədʒəst, B -'sɔl-] *s.* especialista o experto en sexología, sexólogo.
sexology [-dʒɪ] *s.* sexología.
sexpartite [sɛks'pɑrˌtaɪt, B -'pɑˌ-] *a.* dividido en seis partes; de seis partes.
sexpot ['sɛksˌpɑt, B -ˌpɔt] *s.* (jer.) chica muy sexy, cachonda.
sex shop, sexería, sex-shop.
sex-starved, hambriento de contacto sexual.
sex symbol, sex-símbol.
sext [sɛkst] *s.* (relig.) sexta.
Sextans ['sɛkˌstænz, B -stənz] *s.* (astr.) Sextante.
sextant ['sɛkstənt] *s.* sextante (instrumento).
sextet, sextette [sɛks'tɛt] *s.* (mús.) sexteto.
sextile ['sɛkˌstaɪl] *a.* (astr.) aspecto sextil (de los astros).
sextillion [sɛks'tɪljən] *s.* (E.U.) unidad seguida de 21 ceros; (G.B.) unidad seguida de 36 ceros.
sextodecimo [ˌsɛkstə'dɛsəmoʊ] *s.* (*pl.* SEXTODECIMOS) tamaño de dieciseisavo (de un libro).
sexton ['sɛkstən] *s.* sacristán.
sexton beetle, (ento.) enterrador.
sextuple [sɛks'tupəl, B 'sɛkstjʊ-] *a.* 1. séxtuplo. 2. (mús.) en forma de sextillo o seisillo. —*v.t., v.i.* sextuplicar(se).
sextuplet [sɛks'tʌplət, B 'sɛkstjʊ-] *s.* 1. séxtuplo. 2. (mús.) seisillo, sextillo.
sextuplicate [-'tupləkət, B -'tju-] *a.* sextuplicado. — [-pləˌkeɪt] *v.t.* sextuplicar.
sexual ['sɛkʃʊəl, B -sjʊ-] *a.* sexual.
sexual abuse, abusos deshonestos.
sexual-appetite, apetito sexual.
sexual harassment, acoso sexual, importunación sexual, hostigamiento sexual.
sexual intercourse, coito, cópula, relaciones sexuales.
sexuality [ˌsɛkʃʊ'ælətɪ, B ˌsɛksjʊ-] *s.* 1. sexualidad. 2. preocupación sexual. 3. vida sexual.
sexually ['sɛkʃʊəlɪ, B 'sɛksjʊ-] *adv.* sexualmente, en cuanto al sexo, en (su) carácter o aspecto sexual.
sexually transmitted disease, enfermadad de transmisión sexual.
sexual organs, órganos genitales.
sexual relations, relaciones sexuales.
sexy ['sɛksɪ] *a.* (SEXIER; SEXIEST) erótico, excitante.
sferics ['sfɪrɪks, B 'sfɛrɪks] *s. pl.* 1. (rad.) atmosféricos, parásitos. 2. radiogoniómetro de estáticos.
sfumato [sfu'mɑˌtoʊ] *a.* (pint.) esfumado.
sgraffito [zgræ'fitoʊ] *s.* (*pl.* SGRAFFITI [-ti]) esgrafiado, estofado, estofo; **to do s. work on,** esgrafiar, estofar.
Sgt. *abrev. de* **Sergeant,** sargento.
sh [ʃ] *interj.* ¡chitón!
shabbily ['ʃæbəlɪ] *adv.* 1. andrajosamente, zarrapastrosamente. 2. vilmente, despreciablemente, miserablemente, mezquinamente.
shabbiness [-ɪnəs] *s.* 1. estado andrajoso o zarrapastroso; estado ruinoso, ruina. 2. ruindad, vileza; mezquindad.
shabby [-ɪ] *a.* (SHABBIER; SHABBIEST) 1. gastado, raído, muy usado; andrajoso, zarrapastroso, harapiento. 2. vil, ruin, despreciable; miserable, mezquino.
shabby-genteel [-dʒɛn'til] *a.* que ha visto mejores tiempos; que cubre las apariencias.
shabby-gentility [-'tɪlətɪ] *s.* pobreza en que se guarda las apariencias.
shack [ʃæk] *s.* choza, cabaña. —*v.i.* (jer.) (gen. con *up*) morar, vivir; tomar albergue, alojarse; **s. up with,** (jer.) vivir con, ir a vivir con, cohabitar con (amante, mujer).
shackle ['ʃækəl] *s.* 1. grillete, abrazadera, argolla. 2. (*pl.*) esposas, grillos; arropea, trabón (para animales). 3. (fig.) impedimentos, trabas. —*v.t.* 1. esposar, aherrojar, encadenar, engrilletar. 2. (fig.) trabar, impedir, obstruir, estorbar, obstaculizar.
shackle bar, alzaprima con grillete para arrancar clavos.
shackle bolt, pasador de grillete; perno de horquilla; gancho de candado.
shacklebone [-ˌboʊn] *s.* (esco.) muñeca, carpo.
shackler ['jæklər, B -lə] *s.* 1. encadenador. 2. estorbador, obstaculizador.
shad [ʃæd] *s.* (ict.) sábalo, saboga, alosa.
shadberry ['ʃædˌbɛrɪ] *s.* (*pl.* SHADBERRIES) (bot.) guillomo (fruto).
shadblow [-ˌbloʊ] **shadbush** [-ˌbʊʃ] *s.* (bot.) guillomo (arbusto).
shaddock ['ʃædək] *s.* (bot.) (variedad de) pomelo o pampelmusa.
shade [ʃeɪd] *s.* 1. sombra. 2. umbráculo, umbría, sombría. 3. (*gen. en pl.*) atardecer, sombras. 4. celosía, persiana. 5. toldo. 6. pantalla (de lámpara). 7. matiz. 8. (fig.) ligera diferencia, cantidad pequeña, vestigio; poco, algo. 9. sombra, fantasma, espectro, alma. 10. (*pl.*) candiotera, bodega. 11. (*pl.*) (jer.) gafas de sol. 12. **the shades,** averno, infierno. —*v.t.* 1. sombrar, asombrar. 2. esconder (en las sombras); resguardar (de la luz). 3. ocultar, encubrir, proteger, amparar. 4. (fig.) ensombrecer, entristecer. 5. (pint.) sombrear, matizar. 6. (com.) rebajar un poco (precios). —*v.i.* obscurecerse; **s. off** (o **into**), cambiarse gradualmente (un color en otro).
shadeless ['ʃeɪdləs] *a.* privado de sombra.
shadily [-əlɪ] *adv.* 1. de modo sombrío o umbrío. 2. (fam.) vergonzosamente, deshonrosamente.
shadiness [-ɪnəs] *s.* 1. abundancia de sombras (en un lugar). 2. (fam.) carácter desdoroso o deshonrado.
shading [-ɪŋ] *s.* (pint.) sombreado; matizado.
shadoof [ʃɑ'duf, B ʃə-] *s.* cigoñal (usado en Egipto para sacar agua).
shadow ['ʃædoʊ] *s.* 1. sombra. 2. (*pl.*) obscuridad, lobreguez, tenebrosidad. 3. sombrajo, sombraje. 4. vestigio, pizca, indicio, huella. 5. sombra, espectro, aparición. 6. sombra, apéndice (compañero inseparable). 7. (pint.) sombra, sombreado. 8. **(not) to be a s. of one's former self, (not) to be a s. of what one was,** no ser uno ni sombra de lo que era; **to be reduced to a s.,** estar convertido en un espectro; **to cast a s.,** hacer sombra; **without a s. of doubt,** sin lugar a dudas. —*v.t.* 1. sombrear, sombrar. 2. anublar; obscurecer. 3. seguir en forma secreta, espiar, perseguir. 4. (pint.) sombrear, matizar, esbatimentar. 5. (ant.) guarecer del sol; proteger, amparar.
shadowbox [-ˌbɑks, B -ˌbɔks] *v.t.* (dep.) boxear con un adversario imaginario.
shadowboxing [-ˌbɑksɪŋ, B -ˌbɔk-] *s.* (dep.) boxeo con un adversario imaginario; (fig.) disputa con un adversario imaginario.
shadow cabinet, (pol.) gabinete fantasma.
shadower [-ər, B -ə] *s.* perseguidor.
shadowgraph [-ˌgræf, B -ˌgrɑf] *s.* 1. sombras chinescas. 2. (fotgmt.) radiografía, sombrógrafo.
shadowless [-ləs] *a.* sin sombra.
shadow play, sombras chinescas.
shadowy [-ɪ] *a.* 1. insubstancial, inconsistente, incorpóreo, impalpable, intangible. 2. sombroso, sombrío, umbrío, umbroso; tenebroso, lóbrego, obscuro. 3. vago, impreciso, dudoso. 4. (ant.) simbólico, emblemático.
shady ['ʃeɪdɪ] *a.* (SHADIER; SHADIEST) 1. sombreado, sombroso, sombrío, umbroso, umbrío. 2. (fam.) desdoroso, deshonroso, vergonzoso, sospechoso, dudoso. 3. **on the s. side of forty,** más allá de los cuarenta años.
shaft [ʃæft, B ʃɑft] *s.* 1. lanza, venablo, arpón. 2. flecha, dardo, saeta. 3. rayo (de relámpago); haz (de luz). 4. (fig.) dardo (de ironía, burla, etc.). 5. pértiga, vara larga. 6. palo, caña, vara. 7. tallo (de planta, árbol, etc.). 8. limonera, lanza (de un carruaje). 9. mango, puño, asa. 10. fuste, asta (de una lanza, flecha, etc.). 11. pozo (de ascensor, luz, ventilación, etc. en edificios). 12. (arq.) caña, fuste (de la columna). 13. (mec.) eje, árbol. 14. (min.) pozo de chimenea. 15. (orn.) cañon (de pluma). —*v.t.* (jer.) aprovecharse de; martirizarse; engañar.
shaft drive, (aut.) junta de cardán.
shaft furnace, horno de cuba, horno de cubilote.
shaft governor, (mec.) regulador axial (en el eje).
shaft horse, caballo uncido.
shaft horsepower, caballos al eje.
shaft house, (min.) edificio que encierra la boca del pozo.
shafting ['ʃæftɪŋ, B 'ʃɑf-] *s.* sistema de ejes.
shaft pump, bomba de pozo.
shaft tunnel, (const. naval) callejón o túnel del eje.
shag [ʃæg] *s.* 1. pelo áspero, pelo hirsuto o desgreñado; lana enredada. 2. borra o lanilla gruesas. 3. tabaco desmenuzado y grueso. 4. (ant.)

felpa tripe; jergón. —*v.t.* (*pret., p.p.* SHAGGED; *p.pr.* SHAGGING) 1. hacer peludo o difícil. 2. poner áspero.
shag *v.t.* (fam., G.B.) 1. perseguir. 2. ahuyentar. —*v.i.* bailar cierta danza de E.U. —*s.* (E.U.) danza que consiste en saltar en uno y otro pie.
shagbark [ˈʃæɡˌbɑrk, B -ˌbɑk] *s.* (bot.) variedad de nogal.
shagginess [-ɪnəs] *s.* calidad de peludo o afelpado.
shaggy [-ɪ] *a.* (SHAGGIER; SHAGGIEST) 1. hirsuto, híspido, velludo. 2. despeinado, desgreñado. 3. áspero, escabroso. 4. tosco, rudo.
shaggy dog story, chiste de desenlace absurdo.
shagreen [ʃæˈɡrin] *s.* 1. chagrén, zapa. 2. piel áspera (de ciertos tiburones).
shah [ʃɑ] *s.* cha, sha (soberano de Persia).
shaitan [ʃeɪˈtɑn] *s.* satán, satanás; espíritu maligno; demonio.
shake [ʃeɪk] *v.t.* (*pret.* SHOOK [ʃʊk] *p.p.* SHAKEN [ˈʃeɪkən] *p.pr.* SHAKING) 1. sacudir. 2. estremecer, hacer temblar. 3. agitar, blandir, menear. 4. (fig.) agitar, chocar, disturbar, conmover. 5. (fig.) debilitar, disminuir (fe, convicción, etc.). 6. librarse de (hábito, etc.). 7. trinar (una nota). 8. **s. a leg,** (fam.) menearse, darse prisa, apurarse (Amer.); bailar; **s. down,** hacer caer por sacudidas (fruta del árbol, etc.); echar al suelo, extender en el suelo (frazada, cama improvisada); registrar minuciosamente; (fam.) dar un sablazo a (alguien); extorsionar a (alguien); **s. hands,** estrecharse las manos; **s. off,** arrojar o desprender con sacudidas; sacudirse de, librarse de, quitarse de encima, zafarse de; **s. someone's hand,** estrechar la mano a alguien; **s. one's composure,** desconcertarle a uno, escandalizarle a uno; **s. one's fist at (person),** amenazar (a una persona) con el puño; **s. one's head,** menear la cabeza, negar, rehusar; **s. one's head over** (o **at**), desaprobar, dar muestras de displicencia hacia (algo); **s. out,** vaciar o desempolvar sacudiendo; desplegar (velas, bandera, etc.); **s. to pieces,** desmoronar sacudiendo; **s. up,** remover, mezclar sacudiendo; agitar, estimular; trastornar, perturbar; reorganizar. —*v.i.* 1. temblar (mano, etc.); trepidar (suelo, etc.); estremecerse (voz). 2. sacudirse, agitarse. 3. (fig.) agitarse, perturbarse. 4. estrecharse las manos. 5. **s.!** ¡venga esa mano!; **s. down,** hacerse una cama (improvisada); (fam.) acostarse; **s. in one's boots,** temblar de miedo, estar aterrorizado; **s. with,** temblar de (ira, miedo, etc.); tiritar de (frío). —*s.* 1. sacudida, sacudimiento 2. estremecimiento, vibración. 3. meneo (de la cabeza). 4. apretón de manos. 5. batido (de leche, chocolate, etc.). 6. fisura, grieta, rajadura (en tierra, roca, tronco de árbol, etc.). 7. temblor (de tierra). 8. momento, instante, rato, periquete. 9. despido, despedida. 10. (mús.) trino. 11. **in two shakes (of a donkey's tail),** en un dos por tres; en un abrir y cerrar de ojos; **the shakes,** tiritón; escalofrío (de fiebre); estremecimiento (de miedo); (fam.) delírium tremens; **to be no great shakes,** (fam.) no ser nada del otro mundo, no valer mucho; no importar mucho (persona).
shakedown [ˈʃeɪkˌdaʊn] *s.* 1. cama improvisada; lecho de paja. 2. extorsión, exacción. 3. registro minucioso. 4. ajuste, acomodación. 5. baile bullicioso. —*a.* de prueba.
shakedown cruise, (mar.) viaje de pruebas (para habituar la tripulación al buque).
shakefork [-ˌfɔrk, B -ˌfɔk] *s.* (her.) perla.
shake-out [-ˌaʊt] *s.* (com.) recesión moderada (en la bolsa de valores, etc.).
shakeproof [-ˌpruf] *a.* a prueba de vibración, antivibrante.
shaker [-ər, B -ə] *s.* 1. coctelera. 2. (mec.) transportador, sacudidor, criba vibradora, zaranda vibratoria.
Shakespearean, Shakespearian [ʃeɪkˈspɪrɪən, B -ˈspɪər-] *a.* shakesperiano, de Shakespeare. —*s.* erudito conocedor de las obras de Shakespeare.
shake-up [ˈʃeɪkˌʌp] *s.* 1. sacudida, sacudimiento, agitación. 2. reorganización completa (de una empresa, fábrica, etc.).
shakily [ˈʃeɪkəlɪ] *adv.* 1. temblorosamente, trémulamente. 2. inconstantemente, inciertamente. 3. de modo tambaleante, vacilantemente.
shakiness [-ɪnəs] *s.* 1. inestabilidad, tambaleo. 2. debilidad, inconstancia.
shaking [-ɪŋ] *s.* sacudida, sacudimiento; agitación; traqueteo, meneo; vibración.
shaking palsy, (med.) perlesía, parálisis agitante.
shako [ˈʃækˌoʊ] *s.* (*pl.* SHAKOS O SHAKOES) (mil.) chacó, morrión.
shaky [ˈʃeɪkɪ] (SHAKIER; SHAKIEST) 1. tembloroso, trémulo, tremulante, tremulento. 2. movedizo, tambaleante, bamboleante. 3. inconstante, vacilante, variable, incierto 4. (fam.) indigno de confianza; discutible, dudoso.
shale [ʃeɪl] *s.* esquisto, pizarra.
shall [ʃæl, ʃəl] *v. aux.* (*pret. y condicional* SHOULD [ʃʊd, ʃəd]; *carece de inf., participio e imper.*) se usa: 1. en primera pers. para formar un futuro simple, declaración condicional o pregunta, ej., *we s. hear about it tomorrow,* mañana tendremos noticias de eso, *s. I hear from you soon?* ¿sabré de Ud. pronto? 2. en segunda y tercera pers. para formar una declaración futura y condicional expresando intención o deseo, ej., *you s. not catch me again,* no volverá a agarrarme. 3. en preguntas de la segunda pers. correspondientes al tipo 1, indicando la respuesta esperada, ej., *s. you be going to church?* ¿vas a ir a la iglesia? 4. en cualquier pers. para formar declaraciones o preguntas que implican la noción de mando o deberes, obligaciones, etc. futuros y condicionales, ej., *you s. not do it,* no lo harás, *he should have been more careful,* él debió haber sido más cuidadoso, *s. I open the door?* ¿quiere que (yo) abra la puerta? 5. en todas las personas para formar prótasis condicional o cláusulas indefinidas, ej., *if we should be defeated,* si fuéramos derrotados.
shalloon [ʃəˈlun] *s.* (tej.) tela de lana asargada.
shallop [ˈʃæləp] *s.* (mar.) chalupa.
shallot [ʃəˈlɑt, B ˈlɔt] *s.* (bot.) chalote, escalona, escaloña, cebolla escalonia.
shallow [ˈʃæloʊ] *a.* 1. bajo, somero, poco profundo. 2. somero, superficial, trivial. —*s.* bajo, bajío. —*v.t., v.i.* tornar(se) poco profundo.
shallow-brained [-ˌbreɪnd] *a.* ligero de cascos, bobo.
shallow dish, plato llano, plato tendido, plato playo (Amer.).
shallow-draft [-ˌdræft, B -ˌdrɑft] *a.* (mar.) de poco calado.
shallowly [-lɪ] *adv.* superficialmente, trivialmente.
shallowness [-nəs] *s.* 1. poca profundidad. 2. superficialidad, trivialidad.
shalom [ʃɑˈloʊm] *s.* (hebreo) paz (ú. como saludo y despedida).
shalt [ʃælt, ʃəlt] (ant.) *segunda pers. sing. de* **shall.**
sham [ʃæm] *s.* 1. substituto, imitación, copia. 2. falsificación, impostura, farsa; truco, engaño. 3. hipocresía. 4. farsante, impostor. —*a.* 1. falso, supuesto, postizo. 2. disimulado, fingido. 3. imitado; imitación, ej., *s. diamond,* imitación de diamante. 4. falsificado, adulterado (víveres). —*v.t.* (*pret., p.p.* SHAMMED; *p.pr.* SHAMMING) 1. simular, fingir, pretender, aparentar. 2. (ant.) engañar, burlar. —*v.i.* hacer fingimientos, disimular.
shaman [ˈʃɑmən, B ˈʃæ-] *s.* chamán, shamán.
shamanism [-ˌɪzəm] *s.* chamanismo, shamanismo.
sham attack, (mil.) ataque falso, simulacro de ataque.
sham battle, (mil.) simulacro de combate.
shamble [ˈʃæmbəl] *v.i.* arrastrar los pies, andar con dejadez, caminar lerdamente. —*s.* paso lerdo, arrastre de los pies.
shambles [-bəlz] *s. pl.* (*gen. sing. en const.*) 1. matadero, degolladero, desolladero; (fig.) lugar de carnicería o matanza. 2. confusión, revoltijo.
shame [ʃeɪm] *s.* 1. vergüenza, pudor, ej., *red with s.,* rojo de vergüenza. 2. vergüenza, ignominia, deshonra, deshonor, desdoro. 3. **for s.! s. on you!** ¡qué vergüenza!; **it is a s.,** es una lástima; **to bring s. upon,** deshonrar; **to put to s.,** avergonzar, humillar; **what a s.!** ¡qué lástima! —*v.t.* 1. avergonzar, humillar. 2. deshonrar. 3. **s. into,** inducir (a alguien) a que haga algo, haciéndole sentir vergüenza; **s. out of,** inducir (a alguien) a que desista de algo, haciéndole sentir vergüenza.
shamefaced [ˈʃeɪmˌfeɪst] *a.* 1. modesto, pudoroso, tímido, vergonzoso. 2. avergonzado, abochornado.
shamefacedly [-feɪsədlɪ, B -ˈfeɪstlɪ] *adv.* 1. modestamente, pudorosamente, tímidamente, vergonzosamente. 2. avergonzadamente; confusamente.
shamefacedness [-nəs] *s.* 1. pudor, timidez, vergüenza. 2. bochorno.
shameful [ˈʃeɪmfəl] *a.* vergonzoso, oprobioso; escandaloso, indecoroso.
shamefully [-fəlɪ] *adv.* vergonzosamente, oprobiosamente; escandalosamente, indecorosamente.
shamefulness [-fəlnəs] *s.* vergüenza, oprobio; indecencia.
shameless [-ləs] *a.* 1. desvergonzado, inmodesto; impudente, impúdico. 2. descarado, desfachatado, insolente, atrevido, sinvergüenza.
shamelessly [-ləslɪ] *adv.* 1. desvergonzadamente, impúdicamente. 2. insolentemente, atrevidamente.
shamelessness [-ləsnəs] *s.* 1. desvergüenza, inmodestia; impudicia, impudencia. 2. descaro, desfachatez, atrevimiento.
sham fight, (mil.) maniobras, simulacro.
shammer [ˈʃæmər, B -ə] *s.* impostor, fingidor, simulador.
shammes [ˈʃɑməs] *s.* (*pl.* SHAMMOSIM O SHAMMASHIM [ʃɑˈmɔsəm]) sacristán de sinagoga.
shammy, shamoy [ˈʃæmɪ] *vars. de* **chamois.**
sham plea, (der.) alegato ficticio.
shampoo [ʃæmˈpu] *v.t.* (*pret., p.p.* SHAMPOOED; *p.pr.* SHAMPOOING) 1. lavar la cabeza, dar champú a. 2. (ant.) dar masaje a. —*s.* lavado de cabeza, champú.
shamrock [ˈʃæmˌrɑk, B -rɔk] *s.* (bot.) 1. (variedad de) trébol. 2. acetosilla, acederilla. 3. lupulina. 4. trébol (como emblema de Irlanda).
shamus [ˈʃɑməs, ˈʃeɪ-] *s.* (jer.) 1. policía, agente. 2. detective privado.
shandrydan [ˈʃændrɪˌdæn] *s.* 1. tipo de calesa. 2. vehículo destartalado o desvencijado.
shandy [ˈʃændɪ] *var. de* **shandygaff.**
shandygaff [-ˌɡæf] *s.* bebida de cerveza mezclada con jengibre.
shanghai [ʃæŋˈhaɪ] *v.t.* (*pret., p.p.* SHANGHAIED; *p.pr.* SHANGHAIING) 1. narcotizar (o emborrachar) y embarcar (a marinero); reclutar por

fuerza. 2. llevar (a uno) con engaño o por fuerza, raptar (a alguien).
Shangri-La [ˌʃæŋgrɪ'lɑ] *s.* lugar utópico o imaginario; paraíso idílico o secreto.
shank [ʃæŋk] *s.* 1. espinilla, canilla (de la pierna). 2. pierna. 3. zanca (de las aves). 4. pedúnculo (de la flor). 5. astil, mango. 6. enfranque (de la suela del zapato). 7. presilla (de botón). 8. (fam.) término, parte final. 9. (mar.) caña (del ancla o del anzuelo). 10. (impr.) cuerpo (del tipo). —*v.i.* 1. marchitarse o caerse (hoja o flor, debido a enfermedad del tallo). 2. (esco.) (t. **s. it**) viajar a pie, recorrer.
shankpiece ['ʃæŋkˌpis] *s.* enfranque (de la suela del zapato).
shanny ['ʃænɪ] *s.* (*pl.* SHANNIES) (ict.) blénido europeo.
shan't [ʃænt, B ʃɑnt] *contr. de* **shall not.**
shantey, *var. de* **chantey.**
shantung ['ʃæn'tʌŋ] *s.* (tej.) shantung.
shanty, *var. de* **chantey.**
shanty ['ʃæntɪ] *s.* (*pl.* SHANTIES) casucha, choza, chabola, cabaña, bohío (Amer.).
shantytown [-ˌtaʊn] *s.* el suburbio, las chabolas, la villa miseria (Arg.), la población (Chile).
shape [ʃeɪp] *s.* 1. forma, configuración. 2. aspecto, apariencia. 3. contorno, figura, imagen, cuerpo, perfil. 4. fantasma, aparición, espectro. 5. condición, estado; orden. 6. molde, horma. 7. **in bad** (o **poor**) **s.,** en mal estado, deteriorado; enfermo; **in s.,** en buen estado; **out of s.,** deformado; **to get** (o **put**) **into s.,** poner en orden, ordenar, arreglar; **to keep in s.,** conservar su estado, mantenerse en forma; **to take s.,** tomar forma. —*v.t.* 1. formar, moldear, hormar. 2. diseñar, planear, idear; definir (curso, acción, etc.). 3. formular, dar cuerpo a (ideas, palabras). 4. (ant.) ordenar, decretar. 5. **s. to,** adaptar o acomodar a, modelar sobre, ajustar a. —*v.i.* 1. tomar forma, formarse. 2. acontecer, acaecer, resultar. 3. (fam.) prometer, dar o concebir esperanzas; mostrar progreso.
SHAPE, *abrev. de* **Supreme Headquarters Allied Powers in Europe,** Cuartel General de las Fuerzas Aliadas en Europa.
shapeless ['ʃeɪpləs] *a.* deforme, informe, disforme.
shapelessly [-lɪ] *adv.* sin forma.
shapelessness [-nəs] *s.* deformidad.
shapeliness ['ʃeɪplɪnəs] *s.* belleza de forma, proporción.
shapely [-lɪ] *a.* (SHAPELIER; SHAPELIEST) bien formado, bien proporcionado; de buena figura, de forma agradable.
shaper [-ər, B -ə] *s.* formador; hormador.
shard [ʃɑrd, B ʃɑd] *s.* 1. tiesto, casco. 2. fragmento. 3. escama; (ento.) élitro.
share [ʃɛr, B ʃɛə] *s.* 1. porción, ración, cuota, cupo, escote. 2. parte, contribución, participación. 3. (com.) acción. 4. **s. and s. alike,** por partes iguales, por igual; **the lion's s.,** la mejor parte; **to do one's s.,** hacer de su parte; **to go shares,** ir a medias. —*v.t.* 1. partir, dividir. 2. compartir, participar en. 3. **s. out,** repartir, distribuir, prorratear. —*v.i.* **s. in,** participar en, tener parte en.
share, *s.* reja (del arado).
sharecrop ['ʃɛrˌkrɑp, B 'ʃɛəˌkrɔp] *v.i.* trabajar como aparcero. —*v.t.* cultivar (tierra) como aparcero.
sharecropper [-ər, B -ə] *s.* aparcero.
shareholder ['ʃɛrˌhoʊldər, B 'ʃɛəˌhoʊldə] *s.* (com.) accionista.
share-list [-ˌlɪst] *s.* (com., G.B.) lista de cotizaciones (de acciones).
sharepusher [-ˌpʊʃər, B -ˌpʊʃə] *s.* (G.B.) corredor de bolsa (gen. el que mercadea con acciones sin valor).
sharer ['ʃɛrər, B -ə] *s.* partícipe, copartícipe; compartidor.
sharif, *var. de* **sherif.**
shark [ʃɑrk, B ʃɑk] *s.* 1. (ict.) tiburón. 2. estafador, petardista. 3. (jer., E.U.) estudiante brillante; experto. —*v.i.* cometer estafas, vivir como petardista, dar sablazos. —*v.t.* (ant.) acaparar fraudulentamente.
shark oil, aceite de tiburón.
sharkskin [-ˌskɪn] *s.* 1. piel de tiburón. 2. (tej.) tela de lana asargada; cierta tela de rayón.
shark's mouth, (mar.) abertura del mástil en la toldilla.
sharp [ʃɑrp, B ʃɑp] *a.* 1. agudo, puntiagudo, aguzado. 2. afilado, cortante. 3. áspero. 4. anguloso, angular, ej., *s. face,* rostro anguloso, *s. features,* facciones enjutas. 5. distinto, claro, definido; nítido (imagen, fotografía, etc.). 6. picante, pungente, acre, acerbo, agrio, ej., *s. flavor,* sabor picante, *s. taste,* sabor acre. 7. penetrante, agudo, estridente (voz, detonación, ruido). 8. penetrante, cortante (aire, viento, etc.). 9. agudo, incisivo, hiriente, mordaz, ej., *s. pain,* dolor agudo, *s. remark,* observación mordaz. 10. agudo, fino (oído, olfato), agudo (vista), penetrante (ojos). 11. agudo, penetrante, perspicaz (intelecto, etc.); sagaz, astuto, vivo. 12. severo, riguroso, estricto. 13. áspero, vehemente, impaciente, impetuoso, ej., *s. temper,* genio áspero. 14. feroz (lucha), intenso, disputado (certamen). 15. activo, animado, enérgico. 16. estrecho, intenso (atención, vigilancia, etc.); atento. 17. (mús.) sostenido. 18. (fon.) sordo; mudo. 19. **as s. as a needle,** muy perspicaz, muy inteligente. —*v.t.* (mús.) elevar (una nota) medio tono; marcar con un sostenido. —*v.i.* (mús.) dar un agudo, tocar más alto (que el tono debido). —*adv.* 1. agudamente, aguzadamente. 2. vivamente, rápidamente. 3. (fam.) exactamente, puntualmente, en punto, ej., *at six o'clock s.,* a las seis en punto. —*s.* 1. (cost.) (*gen. pl.*) aguja muy delgada. 2. (mús.) sostenido. 3. fullero, tahúr. 4. (jer.) experto, perito.
sharp curve, curva cerrada o estrecha, curva brusca.
sharp edge, canto o filo vivo.
sharp-edged ['ʃɑrp'ɛdʒd, B 'ʃɑp-] *a.* afilado, aguzado.
sharpen [-ən] *v.t.* 1. afilar, aguzar, sacar punta a. 2. hacer más severo (una ley, la voz, etc.), intenso (contienda) o agudo (dolor, etc.). —*v.i.* afilarse (facciones, rostro, etc.).
sharpener [-ənər, B -ə] *s.* 1. afilador, amolador, aguzador. 2. tajador, sacapuntas, afilalápices.
sharper [-ər, B -ə] *s.* fullero, tahúr; petardista, estafador.
sharp-eyed [-'aɪd] *a.* (jer.) lince, de ojos penetrantes; observador.
sharp-fanged [-'fæŋd] *a.* que tiene colmillos afilados; sarcástico, mordaz.
sharp-freeze [-'friz] *v.t.* congelar (rápidamente).
sharp-freezer [-ər, B -ə] *s.* congelador, frigorífico congelador.
sharpie ['ʃɑrpɪ, B 'ʃɑpɪ] *s.* 1. (mar., E.U.) velero de poco calado con uno o dos mástiles y velas triangulares. 2. fullero, tahúr; petardista, estafador; vivo.
sharply [-lɪ] *adv.* 1. agudamente. 2. precisamente, exactamente. 3. vivamente, activamente. 4. abruptamente, pronunciadamente, escarpadamente. 5. claramente, distintamente. 6. incisivamente. 7. severamente, rigurosamente.
sharpness [-nəs] *s.* 1. agudeza, filo. 2. nitidez. 3. acritud. 4. agudeza, perspicacia; astucia, viveza. 5. severidad.
sharp-nosed [-'noʊzd] *a.* 1. de nariz afilada. 2. (fig.) de finísimo olfato.
sharp-pointed pliers, alicates de punta.
sharp practice, método dudoso; prácticas ilícitas.
sharp-set ['ʃɑrp'sɛt, B 'ʃɑp-] *a.* 1. colocado en ángulo agudo. 2. ávido, vehemente.
sharpshooter [-ˌʃutər, B -ə] *s.* tirador de primera, tirador certero; (mil.) tirador apostado.
sharpshooting [-ˌʃutɪŋ] *s.* puntería certera.
sharp-sighted [-'saɪtəd] *a.* lince, de vista aguda; perspicaz, penetrante.
sharp-sightedness [-nəs] *s.* visión aguda; perspicacia.
sharp-tongued [-'tʌŋd] *a.* de lenguaje sarcástico, severo o crítico.
sharp tuning, (rad.) sintonización exacta.
sharp turn, viraje súbito, vuelta repentina (que da un automóvil, etc.).
sharp-witted [-'wɪtəd] *a.* agudo, ingenioso, perspicaz; discernidor.
sharp-wittedness [-nəs] *s.* agudeza, ingenio, perspicacia; discernimiento.
sharp words, palabras mayores.
shastra ['ʃɑstrə] *s.* colección de escritos filosóficos y sagrados de la India.
shatter ['ʃætər, B -ə] *v.t.* 1. destrozar, despedazar, astillar, hacer añicos; estrellar, romper. 2. (fig.) quebrantar, arruinar; aniquilar, frustrar; destrozar, ej., *shattered hopes,* esperanzas frustradas, *shattered nerves,* nervios destrozados. 3. (ant.) dispersar, esparcir, diseminar. —*v.i.* destrozarse, hacerse añicos. —*s.* fragmento, pedazo; **in shatters,** hecho añicos.
shatterproof [-'pruf] *a.* a prueba de fractura; inastillable.
shatterproof glass, vidrio o cristal inastillable, vidrio de seguridad.
shave [ʃeɪv] *v.t.* (*pret.* SHAVED; *p.p.* SHAVED or SHAVEN ['ʃeɪvən]; *p.pr.* SHAVING) 1. afeitar (la cara); rasurar, rapar (las barbas). 2. (carp.) desbastar, acepillar. 3. rebanar, cortar en tajadas finas. 4. rozar, pasar rozando, rasar. 5. (com.) descontar (una letra, etc.) a un tipo de interés exorbitante. —*v.i.* afeitarse; rasurarse, raparse. —*s.* 1. afeitada; rasuración. 2. rebanada, tajada fina. 3. cuchillo para desbastar o rebanar. 4. (fam.) salida difícil, escapada venturosa (de una situación crítica). 5. **to have a close s.,** salvarse por un pelo.
shave hook, raspador de plomero, rasqueta.
shaveling ['ʃeɪvlɪŋ] *s.* 1. mozalbete, jovenzuelo. 2. (despec.) cura, fraile.
shaver [-ər, B -ə] *s.* 1. barbero, rapabarbas. 2. máquina de afeitar, afeitadora; 3. (fam.) mozalbete, jovencito, muchacho.
shavetail ['ʃeɪvˌteɪl] *s.* (jer.) alférez.
Shavian ['ʃeɪvɪən] *s.* admirador de (G.B.) Shaw. —*a.* del estilo literario de Shaw.
shavie ['ʃeɪvɪ] *s.* (esco.) treta, ardid, jugarreta; burla.
shaving ['ʃeɪvɪŋ] *s.* 1. afeitada, rasuración. 2. acepilladura, desbaste. 3. acepilladura, viruta.
shaving brush, brocha de afeitar.
shaving cream, crema de afeitar.
shaving horse, mesa de carpintero.
shaw [ʃɔ] *s.* (ant., dial.) soto, matorral; bosquecillo.
shawl [ʃɔl] *s.* mantón, manta, pañolón, chal. —*v.t.* enmantar, envolver en un chal.
shawm [ʃɔm] *s.* (mús.) chirimía.
shay [ʃeɪ] *s.* (dial.) calesín, calesa.
she [ʃi] *pron.* ella. —*s.* mujer; hembra.
sheaf [ʃif] *s.* (*pl.* SHEAVES [ʃivz]) 1. gavilla, haz, mostela. 2. atado, paquete, fajo; manojo. —*v.t.* agavillar, formar gavillas.

shear [ʃɪr, B ʃɪə] *v.t.* (*pret.* SHEARED, *ant.* SHORE [ʃɔr, B ʃɔ] *p.p.* SHEARED o SHORN [ʃɔrn, B ʃɔn]; *p.pr.* SHEARING) 1. cortar con tijeras, cizallar. 2. rapar, cortar de raíz, tonsurar, cortar el pelo a. 3. (tej.) tundir (pelo de paños). 4. esquilar, trasquilar. 5. podar. 6. (fig.) despojar, privar. 7. (fam.) pelar, desplumar. 8. (esco., dial.) segar, cosechar. —*v.i.* 1. abrirse camino (por). 2. (mec.) dividirse, partirse (por fuerza cortante). 3. (esco.) segar la cosecha. —*s.* 1. (*pl.*) cizallas, tijeras grandes (de jardinero, etc.). 2. esquila, trasquila, esquileo. 3. (mec.) cizalla, tijera mecánica. 4. (mec.) esfuerzo cortante; deslizamiento o deformación debida al esfuerzo cortante. 5. (*pl.*) (const.) grúa de tijeras o de tijera, cabría de tres patas. 6. (tej.) tundidora. 7. (*gen. pl.*) (mec.) bancada, banco (de torno, fresadora, cepilladora, etc.). 8. (ant.) ala.
sheared, sheared plate, plancha recortada o cizallada.
shearer [ˈʃɪrər, B ˈʃɪərə] *s.* 1. esquilador, trasquilador. 2. cizallador.
shearing strength [-ɪŋ-] (mec.) resistencia al corte o al cizallamiento.
shear legs, machina, grúa de tijera(s).
shear pattern, (geof.) diagrama de corte, contorno de deslizamiento.
shear steel, acero de paquete.
sheartail [ˈʃɪrˌteɪl, B ʃɪə,-] *s.* (orn.) (variedad de) colibrí.
shearwater [-ˌwɔtər, -ˌwɑt-, B -ˌwɔtə] *s.* (orn.) meauca.
she-ass [ˈʃiˌæs] *s.* borrica, burra, jumenta.
sheatfish [ˈʃitˌfɪʃ] *s.* (ict.) siluro.
sheath [ʃiθ] *s.* (*pl.* SHEATHES [ʃiðz]) 1. estuche, vaina, funda; envoltura, cubierta. 2. (bot.) vaina. 3. (zool.) élitro.
sheathe [ʃið] *v.t.* 1. envainar, enfundar. 2. meter o hundir en la carne (espada, colmillo, etc.). 3. retraer (las garras). 4. forrar, cubrir, poner vaina a. 5. (carp.) entablar, entarimar, encofrar. 6. (mar.) aforrar, acorazar (cables); embonar (el casco).
sheathing [ˈʃiðɪŋ] *s.* 1. forro, revestimiento, resguardo; enfundadura; cubierta. 2. (carp.) entablado, tablazón, entarimado. 3. (mar.) forro, revestimiento (de cables); embono (del casco). *a.* de revestimiento, de forro.
sheathing board, (const.) tabla de tabicar.
sheathing nail, puntilla o clavo de entablar.
sheathing paper, papel de revestimiento.
sheath knife, cuchillo con vaina, cuchillo, puñal.
sheave [ʃiv] *v.t.* agavillar.
sheave [ʃɪv, ʃiv] *s.* roldana, polea acanalada o de garganta.
sheave factor, (ing.) relación del diámetro de la garrucha al diámetro del cable.
sheaves, *pl. de* **sheaf, sheave.**
Sheba [ˈʃibə] *s.* (bíbl.) Saba, Sabá.
shebang [ʃɪˈbæŋ] *s.* (jer.) 1. choza, cabaña. 2. asunto, cosa; **the whole s.,** el asunto entero, todo el asunto, toda la cosa.
shed [ʃɛd] *s.* cobertizo, tinglado, tejavana, sombraje, sombrajo, cabaña, barraca. —*v.t.* (*pret., p.p.* SHEDDED; *p.pr.* SHEDDING) poner o guardar en un cobertizo.
shed, *v.t.* (*pret., p.p.* SHED; *p.pr.* SHEDDING) 1. verter, derramar (sangre, lágrimas, etc.). 2. difundir, impartir, esparcir (luz, amor, perfume, etc.). 3. echar de sí, quitarse (ropa, etc.), dejar caer (hojas). 4. mudar, cambiar (caparazón, pelo, etc.). 5. **s. light on,** (esp. fig.) iluminar. —*v.i.* pelechar.
she'd [ʃid] *contr. de* **she had, she would.**
shedder [ˈʃɛdər, B -ə] *s.* (E.U.) cangrejo o langosta que comienza o que acaba de mudar de caparazón.
shed dormer, buhardilla (con techo plano paralelo al de la casa o edificio).
sheen [ʃin] *s.* lustre, brillo, resplandor, viso; apariencia brillosa. —*v.i.* brillar, resplandecer. —*a.* (ant.) respliandeciente; hermoso.
sheeny [ˈʃini] *a.* (SHEENIER; SHEENIEST) lustroso, brillante, radiante.
sheeny, sheenie, *s.* (*pl.* SHEENIES) (jer., despec.) judío.
sheep [ʃip] *s.*(*pl.* SHEEP) 1. carnero; oveja. 2. pusilánime; papanatas. 3. piel o cuero de carnero. 4. **black s. (of the family),** oveja negra (de la familia).
sheepberry [ˈʃipˌbɛri] *s.* (*pl.* SHEEPBERRIES) (bot.) (variedad de) viburno o lantana norteamericanos.
sheep bot [-bɑt, B -bɔt] (ento.) rezno.
sheepcote [-ˌkoʊt] *s.* (pr. G.B.) redil, corral, aprisco.
sheep dog, perro ovejero, perro pastor.
sheepfold [-ˌfoʊld] *s.* redil, corral, aprisco, majada (de carneros).
sheepherder [-ˌhɜrdər, B -ˌhɜdə] *s.* (E.U.) pastor.
sheepherding [-ɪŋ] (E.U.) *s.* pastoreo. —*a.* pastoril, pastoral.
sheephook [-ˌhʊk] *s.* cayado, cayada.
sheepish [ˈʃipɪʃ] *a.* 1. tímido, pusilánime, manso. 2. avergonzado.
sheepishly [-lɪ] *adv.* 1. tímidamente, de modo pusilánime. 2. con vergüenza.
sheepishness [-nəs] *s.* 1. timidez, pusilanimidad. 2. vergüenza.
sheep laurel, (bot.) laurel enano norteamericano.
sheepman [-ˌmæn, -mən] *s.* 1. ganadero, criador de ganado lanar. 2. (ant.) carnerero.
sheep ranch, finca de ovejas.
sheep run, establo de ovejas.
sheep's eyes, mirada de carnero degollado; **to cast** (o **make**) **s.'s eyes at,** mirar como un carnero degollado, echar una mirada amorosa a.
sheepshank [ˈʃipˌʃæŋk] *s.* 1. pierna de carnero. 2. (mar.) margarita (nudo).
sheepshead [ˈʃipsˌhɛd] *s.* 1. (ict.) (variedad de) salema. 2. (ant.) simplón, cabezota.
sheepshearer [ˈʃipˌʃɪrər, B -ˌʃɪərə] *s.* 1. esquilador. 2.esquiladora (máquina).
sheepshearing [-ˌʃɪrɪŋ, B -ˌʃɪər-] *s.* 1. esquileo, trasquila o trasquiladura de carneros. 2. fiesta con motivo de la trasquila de los carneros.
sheepskin [-ˌskɪn] *s.* 1. piel de oveja; badana. 2. pergamino. 3. (fam.) pergamino, diploma.
sheep sorrel, (bot.) acetosa, acedrilla, acedra.
sheep tick, (ento.) variedad de garrapata.
sheepwalk [-ˌwɔk] *s.* (pr. G.B.) pasto de ovejas, dehesa carneril.
sheer [ʃɪr, B ʃɪə] *a.* 1. delgado, transparente, diáfano, claro, ligero, fino. 2. perpendicular; abrupto, escarpado. 3. puro, mero. 4. verdadero; cabal, completo, absoluto. 5. (ant.) brillante, reluciente. —*adv.* 1. completamente; de un golpe, directamente. 2. perpendicularmente; abruptamente, en cuesta.
sheer, *v.i.* (mar.) desviarse; torcerse, doblarse; mudar de dirección (para evitar a alguien). —*v.t.* (mar.) desviar; torcer, doblar. —*s.* (mar.) 1. arrufo, arrufadura. 2. desviación del rumbo o derrota.
sheer legs, machina; cabria (improvisada mediante vigas).
sheerly [ˈʃɪrlɪ, B ˈʃɪəlɪ] *adv.* 1. meramente, solamente. 2. directamente. 3. perpendicularmente; abruptamente, en cuesta.
sheer plan, (ing.) sección longitudinal.
sheet [ʃit] *s.* 1. sábana. 2. pliego; hoja; lámina, plancha (de metal). 3. periodicucho. 4. extensión o capa (de agua, hielo, etc.). 5. cortina (de niebla, humo, lluvia, etc.). 6. (geol.) banco, capa, intercalación. 7. (filat.) pliego (de sellos o estampillas). 8. **between the sheets,** en cama; **in sheets,** en rama (díc de un libro sin encuadernar). —*v.t.* envolver en sábanas, cubrir con sábanas o láminas; amortajar; extender en láminas u hojas.
sheet, *s.* (mar.) 1. escota, escotín. 2. (*pl.*) espacio abierto a proa o a popa del bote. 3. **three sheets in the wind,** (jer.) borracho. —*v.t.* (*gen.* **s. home**) (mar.) cazar.
sheet anchor, 1. (mar.) ancla de la esperanza. 2. (fig.) áncora, último recurso.
sheet bend, (mar.) vuelta sencilla de escota, nudo de tejedor.
sheet brass, hoja o chapa de latón, chapa metálica.
sheet copper, hoja o chapa de cobre.
sheet glass, vidrio plano, vidrio laminado.
sheeting [ˈʃitɪŋ] *s.* 1. lienzos o lencería para sábanas. 2. encofrado; cobertura de placas; forro de zanja, estacadas.
sheet iron, chapa de hierro; palastro.
sheet lightning, relámpago difuso, fucilazo.
sheet metal, lámina metálica, metal en lámina, palastro.
sheet music, música (escrita en hojas).
sheet pile, (const.) tablestaca.
sheet piling, (const.) tablestacado.
sheet rubber, hoja de caucho, lámina de goma.
sheet shop, hojalatería, cinguería.
sheik, sheikh [ʃik, B ʃeɪk] *s.* 1. jeque. 2. (jer.) hombre mujeriego.
sheikdom, sheikhdom [ˈʃikdəm, B ˈʃeɪk-] *s.* dominio del jeque.
sheitan, *var. de* **shaitan.**
shekel [ˈʃɛkəl] *s.* 1. (hist.) siclo (moneda hebrea). 2. (*pl.*) (jer.) dinero, riqueza, caudal.
sheldrake [ˈʃɛlˌdreɪk] *s.* (orn.) 1. tadorna. 2. mergansar, mergo, cuervo marino.
shelf [ʃɛlf] *s.* (*pl.* SHELVES) [ʃɛlvz] 1. anaquel, estante, repisa. 2. bajío, banco de arena. 3. plataforma submarina, zócalo (continental, etc.). 4. (geol.) cama de roca. 5. **on the s.** arrinconado, desechado, olvidado.
shelf ice, capa de hielo que comienza en la tierra y continúa sobre el agua del mar.
shelf life, tiempo de durabilidad antes de la venta.
shelfpiece [ˈʃɛlfˌpis] *s.* (mar.) durmiente.
shell [ʃɛl] *s.* 1. cáscara (de nuez, huevo, etc.). 2. concha, carapacho, caparazón (de moluscos, crustáceos, etc.). 3. vaina (de guisantes, etc.). 4. corteza, envoltura. 5. armazón, esqueleto. 6. casco (de barco). 7. molusco, marisco. 8. granada; proyectil de mortero. 9. (quím.) capa (en el átomo). 10. (arm.) cápsula; casco, casquillo (de proyectil, cohete, etc.). 11. (cocina) cáscara (comestible) para rellenar. 12. (dep.) lancha remera, canoa remera. 13. (poét.) lira. 14. **to come out of one's s.,** (fig.) salir de su concha, volverse comunicativo, perder la reserva o timidez; **to retire into one's s.,** meterse en su concha, volverse taciturno. —*v.t.* 1. descascarar, descortezar, desvainar, deshollejar, mondar, pelar; desgranar. 2. bombardear, cañonear. 3. **s. out,** (jer.) soltar, aflojar, desembolsar (el dinero). —*v.i.* 1. descascararse; desconcharse. 2. recoger conchas. 3. **s. out,** (jer.) dar plata, entregar dinero.
she'll [ʃil, ʃɪl] *contr. de* **she will, she shall.**
shellac, shellack [ʃəˈlæk] *s.* laca, goma laca, barniz de laca. —*v.t.* (*pret., p.p.* SHELLACKED; *p.pr.* SHELLACKING) 1. barnizar con goma laca; laquear. 2. (E.U., jer.) zurrar, castigar; derrotar.
shellacking [-ˈlækɪŋ] *s.* (jer., E.U.) paliza, tunda; derrota aplastante; **to take a s.,** recibir una paliza; sufrir una derrota aplastante.

shellback [ˈʃɛlˌbæk] *s.* (jer.) marinero viejo, lobo de mar.
shellbark [-ˌbɑrk, B -ˌbɑk] *s.* (bot.) (variedad de) nogal.
shell case, (arm.) envuelta de granada.
sheller [-ər, B -ə] *s.* desgranador, descascarador.
shellfire [-ˌfaɪr, B -ˌfaɪə] *s.* (mil.) cañoneo, bombardeo.
shellfish [-ˌfɪʃ] *s.* molusco, crustáceo, marisco; mariscos, conchas.
shell game, fullería hecha con tres cáscaras de nuez y una bolita o guisante.
shell hole, (mil.) embudo de explosión, cráter de explosión.
shelling [ˈʃɛlɪŋ] *s.* descascaramiento; desgrane, desgranamiento; bombardeo.
shell jacket, chaqueta entallada.
shell marble, mármol lumaquela.
shellproof [ˈʃɛlˌpruf] *a.* a prueba de bombas.
shell shock, (med.) neurosis de guerra (causada por bombardeo).
shell transformer, (elec.) transformador acorazado.
shell work, trabajo u obra de concha.
shelly [-ɪ] *a.* (SHELLIER; SHELLIEST) conchado, conchudo.
shelter [ˈʃɛltər, B -tə] *s.* refugio, asilo; santuario; protección, resguardo, amparo; **to take s.,** refugiarse, abrigarse. —*v.t.* refugiar, asilar; proteger, resguardar. amparar; **s. oneself,** refugiarse, abrigarse. —*v.i.* refugiarse, asilarse®sguardarse, ampararse.
shelterer [-ər, B -tərə] *s.* amparador, protector.
shelterless [-ləs, B -təlɪs] *s.* desamparado, sin abrigo.
shelter tent, (mil.) tienda abrigo, tienda de campaña.
shelty, sheltie [ˈʃɛltɪ] *s.* (*pl.* SHELTIES) 1. shetlandia (caballo). 2. perro ovejero de Shetlandia.
shelve [ʃɛlv] *v.i.* inclinarse, estar en declive. —*v.t.* 1. proveer de estantes o anaqueles. 2. poner sobre un estante o anaquel. 3. arrinconar, desechar; postergar indefinidamente. 4. deponer, despedir.
shelving [ˈʃɛlvɪŋ] *s.* 1. postergación, abandono (de un proyecto, etc.). 2. estantería, anaquelería; material para anaqueles o estantes.
shelvy [-vɪ] *a.* inclinado, en declive.
Shem [ʃɛm] *s.* (bíbl.) Sem.
Shemite [ˈʃɛmˌaɪt] *s.* semita.
Shemitic [ʃəˈmɪtɪk] *a.* semítico.
shenanigan [ʃəˈnænɪgən] *s.* (fam.) artificio, embuste; jugarreta.
she-oak [ˈʃiˈoʊk] *s.* (bot.) casuarina.
Sheol [ˈʃioʊl] *s.* infierno, baratro.
shepherd [ˈʃɛpərd, B -əd] *s.* pastor; **The Good S.,** (bíbl.) El Buen Pastor. —*v.t.* pastorear.
shepherd dog, perro ovejero, perro pastor.
shepherdess [-əs] *s.* 1. pastora. 2. muchacha del campo, zagala.
shepherd's hut, tugurio, refugio de pastores.
shepherd's pie, guisado de carnero, tomate y cebollas, cubierto de puré de papas y dorado al horno.
shepherd's pipe, zampoña, flauta de pastor.
shepherd's purse, (bot.) bolsa de pastor, zurrón de pastor, pan y quesillo.
sherardize [ˈʃɛrərˌdaɪz, B ˈʃɛrəˌ-] *v.t.* galvanizar.
sherbet [ˈʃɜrbət, B ˈʃɜbət] *s.* sorbete, helado.
sherd [ʃɜrd, B ʃɜd] *var. de* **shard.**
sherif [ʃəˈrif] *s.* jerife.
sheriff [ˈʃɛrəf] *s.* (E.U., G.B.) alguacil de policía.
sherlock [ˈʃɜrˌlɑk, B ˈʃɜlɔk] *s.* (fam.) detective.
sherry [ˈʃɛrɪ] *s.* jerez, vino de Jerez.
she's [ʃiz] *contr. de* **she is, she has.**
Shetland [ˈʃɛtlənd] *s.* 1. Shetlandia, islas escocesas en el Atlántico. 2. **S. pony,** caballo de Shetlandia. 3. **S. wool,** lana fina de las ovejas de Shetlandia.
shew [ʃoʊ] *s.* (ant.) *var. de* **show.**
shewbread [ˈʃoʊˌbrɛd] *s.* (bíbl.) pan de proposición.
shibboleth [ˈʃɪbələθ] *s.* 1. lema, consigna, causa. 2. ceremonia o costumbre distintivas.
shied, *pret., p.p. de* **shy.**
shield [ʃild] *s.* 1. escudo; rodela, broquel. 2. (fig.) escudo, amparo, defensa, resguardo. 3. refuerzo, forro protector (en vestidos, etc.). 4. placa (de policía). 5. (her.) escudo (de armas). 6. (arm.) blindaje (de cañón, etc.). 7. (elec.) pantalla, blindaje. 8. (zool.) caparazón. —*v.t.* 1. escudar; amparar, defender, resguardar, proteger. 2. (ant.) desviar; prohibir.
shield bearer, escudero.
shielded [ˈʃildəd] *a.* protegido, acorazado; (elec.) blindado.
shield fern, (bot.) helecho macho.
shield-shaped [ˈʃildˌʃeɪpt] *a.* escutiforme.
shier, shyer[ˈʃaɪər, B -ə] *s.* caballo asustadizo.
shift [ʃɪft] *v.t.* 1. cambiar, mudar, substituir. 2. desplazar, trasladar, transportar. 3. (filol.) transmutar (una consonante en otra). 4. **s. about,** mover de un lado a otro; **s. gears,** cambiar de marcha (en automóvil); **s. one's ground,** cambiar de argumento (en discusión); **s. the blame (to),** echar la culpa (a); **s. the cargo,** volver a estibar, mover la carga (a otra parte del barco); **s. the scene,** cambiar de escena, cambiar de panorama. —*v.i.*1. moverse, cambiar (de sitio o rumbo), ej., *the wind shifted to the North,* el viento cambió hacia el norte. 2. deslizarse, desarreglarse, ej., *the cargo shifted,* se desarregló la estiba. 3. ayudarse, ingeniárselas, componérselas, ej., *from now on he must s. for himself,* desde ahora en adelante tiene que ingeniárselas solo. 4. cambiar de velocidad, cambiar de marcha (en automóvil). 5. tergiversar, usar equívocos. 6. (filol.) transmutarse (una consonante en otra). —*s.* 1. cambio, substitución, alternación. 2. tanda, turno (de obreros, centinelas, guardias, etc.). 3. esfuerzo, medio, recurso (para un fin). 4. maña, ardid, subterfugio, artificio; evasión, excusa. 5. cambio (de rumbo, dirección, etc.); desviación, viraje. 6. (geol.) deslizamiento (de capas de roca, tierra, etc.). 7. (mús.) cambio de posición (de la mano en un instrumento). 8. (fútbol) desplazamiento lateral (de jugadores). 9. **to work in shifts,** trabajar en turnos.
shifter [-ər, B -ə] *s.* 1. tergiversador. 2. dispositivo transportador. 3. (elec.) decalador.
shift fault, (geof.) falla horizontal.
shiftily [-əlɪ] *adv.* 1. mañosamente. 2. evasivamente, furtivamente. 3. ingeniosamente.
shiftiness [-ɪnəs] *s.* 1. astucia. 2. carácter evasivo o furtivo.
shift key, tecla de mayúsculas (en máquina de escribir).
shiftless [-ləs] *a.* inútil, incapaz, inepto, ineficaz; ocioso, perezoso.
shiftlessness [-ləsnəs] *s.* inutilidad, incapacidad, ineptitud, ineficacia; pereza.
shift pedal, (mús.) pedal suave, pedal de sordina (del piano).
shifty [-ɪ] *a.* (SHIFTIER; SHIFTIEST) 1. mañoso, astuto. 2. evasivo, furtivo, ej., *s. eyes,* ojos de mirada furtiva. 3. ingenioso.
Shiism [ˈʃiˌɪzəm] *s.* (relig.) shiísmo.
Shiite [ˈʃiˌaɪt] *s.* creyente en el shiísmo.
shikar [ʃɪˈkɑr, B -ˈkɑ] *s.* (anglo-ind.) caza. —*v.t.* cazar.
shikari, shikaree [-ˈkɑrɪ] *s.* (anglo-ind.) guía o cazador nativo.
shill [ʃɪl] *s.* (jer.) señuelo, cómplice (que actúa para un tahúr).
shill, *a.* (dial.) chillón, estridente, agudo.
shillelagh, shillalah [ʃəˈleɪlɪ] *s.* garrote de roble; cachiporra.
shilling [ˈʃɪlɪŋ] *s.* chelín (moneda inglesa).
shilly-shally [ˈʃɪlɪˌʃælɪ] *v.i.* titubear, vacilar, estar irresoluto. —*s.* titubeo, vacilación, irresolución. —*a* titubeante, vacilante, irresoluto.
shily, *var. de* **shyly.**
shim [ʃɪm] (mec.) *s.* calza, cuña, zoquete, plancha o tira de relleno. —*v.t.* (*pret., p.p.* SHIMMED; *p.pr.* SHIMMING) acuñar, calzar.
shimmer [ˈʃɪmər, B -ə] *v.i.* rielar, brillar tenuemente. —*s.* vislumbre, luz trémula, débil resplandor.
shimmy, shimmey [ˈʃɪmɪ] *s.* 1. (fam.) camisa (de mujer o niña). 2. shimmy (baile con música de jazz). 3. (mec.) vibración (por defecto); bamboleo, abaniqueo (de las ruedas del auto). —*v.i.* 1. bailar el shimmy. 2. oscilar, bambolear (ruedas, etc.); vibrar excesivamente.
shim stock, (mec.) material para cuñas o relleno.
shin [ʃɪn] *s.* (anat.) espinilla, canilla. —*v.i.* (*pret., p.p.* SHINNED; *p.pr.* SHINNING) **s. down,** bajar a gatas; **s. up,** trepar (por), encaramarse (a, en). —*v.t.* 1. trepar. 2. patear o golpear en las canillas.
shinbone [ˈʃɪnˌboʊn] *s.* (anat.) tibia.
shindig [ˈʃɪnˌdɪg] *s.* (jer., E.U.) 1. baile, fiesta, jarana. 2. alboroto, algazara.
shindy [ˈʃɪndɪ] *s.* (*pl.* SHINDIES) 1. (jer.) alharaca, alboroto. 2. (jer., E.U.) fiesta, baile, jarana. 3. **to kick up a s.,** meter cisco, armar un lío o escándalo, causar un alboroto.
shine [ʃaɪn] *v.i.* (*pret., p.p.* SHONE [ʃoʊn, B ʃɔn]; *p.p. ant.* SHINED; *p.pr.* SHINING) 1. brillar, resplandecer, lucir, relumbrar, relucir. 2. (fig.) brillar, sobresalir, destacarse, distinguirse. 3. **s. up to,** tratar de conquistar la amistad de, congraciarse con (esp. miembros del otro sexo). —*v.t.* 1. hacer brillar, relucir o resplandecer; distinguir. 2. dirigir el rayo de luz de (reflector, linterna, etc.). 3. lustrar (zapatos, etc.). —*s.* 1. brillo, resplandor, lustre, iluminación, esplendor. 2. buen tiempo. 3. (jer., E.U.) afición, inclinación. 4. (*gen. pl.*) travesura, jugarreta. 5. (fam.) brillo o lustre de zapatos. 6. **rain or s.,** llueva o truene; **to put a good s. on,** dar un buen lustre a (zapatos); **to take a s. to,** aficionarse a, tomar simpatía por; **to take the s. out of,** quitar el brillo a.
shiner [ˈʃaɪnər, B -ə] *s.* 1. (ict.) carpa plateada. 2. (jer.) diamante, brillante. 3. (jer.) ojo amoratado.
shingle [ˈʃɪŋgəl] *s.* 1. guijo, guijarro, cascajo. 2. guijarral.
shingle, *s.* 1. (arq.) ripia, teja de madera, tejamaní. 2. letrero (de consultorio). 3. corte de cabello a ras. 4. **to hang out one's s.,** abrir uno su consultorio u oficina. —*v.t.* 1. (arq.) cubrir con ripia, entejar. 2. cortar en forma escalonada (cabello).
shingle, *v.t.* (metal.) cinglar (el hierro).
shingler [-glər, B -glə] *s.* tejador de ripias.
shingles [ˈʃɪŋgəlz] *s.* (med.) herpes, zoster, zona.
shingly [-glɪ] *a.* guijarroso, cascajoso.
shin guard, (dep.) espinillera, canillera.
shininess [ˈʃaɪnɪnəs] *s.* brillantez, resplandor.
shining [ˈʃaɪnɪŋ] *a.* 1. brillante, radiante, resplandeciente, reluciente, lúcido. 2. (fig.) brillante, ilustre, destacado, distinguido.
shinleaf [ˈʃɪnˌlif] *s.* (*pl.* SHINLEAFS) (bot.) pirola.

shinny, shinney ['ʃɪnɪ] *s.* forma sencilla de hockey (jugado por escolares).
shinny, *v.i.* (fam., E.U.) (ú. pr. con *up*) trepar, encaramarse.
shinplaster [-ˌplæstər, B -ˌplɑstə] *s.* 1. ungüento para lesiones en las canillas. 2. (E.U., Can.) (hist.) billete o moneda de poco valor.
Shinto ['ʃɪnˌtoʊ] *s.* sintoísmo, religión que predomina en el Japón.
Shintoist [-əst] *a., s.* sintoísta, del sintoísmo.
shiny ['ʃaɪnɪ] *a.* (SHINIER; SHINIEST) brillante, lustroso; radiante.
ship [ʃɪp] *s.* 1. buque, barco, nave, navío, embarcación, bajel. 2. nave aérea, aeroplano; dirigible. 3. (hum.) bote, lancha (esp. de regata). 4. tripulación. 5. **when my s. comes home,** cuando me saque el gordo, cuando mis esperanzas se realicen. —*v.t.* (*pret., p.p.* SHIPPED [ʃɪpt]; *p.pr.* SHIPPING) 1. embarcar, enviar, despachar. 2. (fam.) (gen. con*off*) despedir, deshacerse de (una persona). 3. traer a bordo. 4. armar, montar (mástil, timón, etc.) a bordo. 5. enganchar, alistar (a marinero). 6. **s. oars,** desarmar los remos (sacándolos de las chumaceras). —*v.i.* 1. embarcarse, embarcar, ir a bordo. 2. engancharse como marinero.
ship biscuit, s. bread, galleta dura, pan de marinero.
shipboard ['ʃɪpˌbɔrd, B -ˌbɔd] *s.* bordo; **on s.,** a bordo.
shipboy [-ˌbɔɪ] *s.* (mar.) grumete.
shipbreaker [-ˌbreɪkər, B -ə] *s.* (mar.) desguazador.
ship broker, corredor marítimo, agente de una línea de navegación; agente de seguros marítimos.
shipbuilder [-ˌbɪldər, B -də] *s.* constructor naval, constructor de buques.
shipbuilding [-dɪŋ] *s.* construcción naval.
ship canal, canal navegable para buques de gran calado.
ship carpenter, carpintero de ribera, carpintero de buque.
ship chandler, (mar.) proveedor de buques, proveedor de efectos navales.
ship chandlery, (mar.) tienda de artículos navales.
ship fever, tifus, tifo.
shiplap ['ʃɪpˌlæp] *s.* (carp.) rebajo (a media madera); traslapo.
shipload [-ˌloʊd] *s.* cargamento entero (esp. de un solo género).
shipman [-mən] *s.* 1. capitán o patrón de buque. 2. (ant.) marinero, hombre de mar.
shipmaster [-ˌmæstər, B -ˌmɑstə] *s.* capitán de buque, capitán mercante, patrón (de embarcación).
shipmate [-ˌmeɪt] *s.* camarada de a bordo, compañero de tripulación.
shipment [-mənt] *s.* 1. embarque, despacho, consignación. 2. cargamento, cargo, envío, remesa.
ship money, (G.B., hist.) impuesto para construcción de buques de guerra.
ship of the desert, nave del desierto (camello).
ship of the line, (mar.) navío de línea, navío de alto bordo.
shipowner [-ˌoʊnər, B -nə] *s.* naviero, armador.
shippable [-əbəl] *a.* que puede ser embarcado, enviado o despachado.
shipper ['ʃɪpər, B -ə] *s.* 1. embarcador, cargador, fletador. 2. expedidor, remitente.
shipping [-ɪŋ] *s.* 1. embarque, envío, remesa. 2. barcos, flota.
shipping agency, agencia de embarques (pasajeros o carga).
shipping agent, embarcador, transportista.
shipping articles, contrato de la tripulación.
shipping charges, gastos de envío o embarque.
shipping clerk, dependiente encargado del envío o embarque de mercaderías.
shipping company, empresa naviera.
shipping notice, aviso de embarque.
shipping room, sala o cuarto de despachos (en donde se preparan los envíos).
shipping ton, (mar.) cuarenta pies cúbicos.
shippon ['ʃɪpən] *s.* (esco.) establo cerrado.
ship railway, vía de carena.
ship-rigged ['ʃɪp'rɪgd] *a.* (mar.) aparejado con velas cuadradas y tres mástiles.
ship's articles, contrato de la tripulación.
ship's company, tripulación.
ship's corporal, (mar., G.B.) asistente al cabo de mar.
shipshape ['ʃɪpˌʃeɪp] *a.* muy limpio y ordenado, en buen orden, bien arreglado; **to have everything s.,** tener todo en perfecto orden.
ship's husband, armador gerente; consignatario del buque; capitán de armamento.
shipside ['ʃɪpˌsaɪd] *s.* dársena; desembarcadero, muelle.
ship's log, (mar.) diario de navegación, cuaderno o libro de bitácora.
ship's papers, (mar.) documentación del buque o de a bordo.
ship's stores, provisiones para la marina.
ship's time, hora local del barco.
ship surveyor, (mar.) arqueador.
ship timber, madera para construcción naval.
shipway ['ʃɪpˌweɪ] *s.* (mar.) 1. grada (de astillero). 2. canal navegable.
shipworm [-ˌwɜrm, B -ˌwɜm] *s.* (zool.) broma, tiñuela, taladro, taraza.
shipwreck [-ˌrɛk] *s.* 1. naufragio. 2. (fig.) naufragio, ruina. 3. restos de buque náufrago. —*v.t.* 1. hacer naufragar, zozobrar. 2. (fig.) arruinar, desgraciar, acabar con.
shipwrecked [-ˌrɛkt] *a.* naufragado.
shipwright [-ˌraɪt] *s.* carpintero de ribera o de buque, carpintero de navío.
shipyard [-ˌjɑrd, B -ˌjɑd] *s.* astillero, arsenal, varadero, carenero.
shirk [ʃɜrk, B ʃɜk] *v.t.* evitar, eludir, evadir, esquivar, rehuir (un trabajo, deber, etc.). —*v.i.* evadirse, desentenderse (de), faltar.
shirr [ʃɜr, B ʃɜ] *s.* (cost.) frunce. —*v.t.* 1. (cost.) fruncir. 2. (cocina) poner al fuego (huevos) con leche o con migajas.
shirred eggs, (cocina) huevos escalfados en crema.
shirring ['ʃɜrɪŋ] *s.* (cost.) frunce, fruncidos.
shirt [ʃɜrt, B ʃɜt] *s.* 1. camisa. 2. camiseta. 3. blusa. 4. **in s. sleeves,** en mangas de camisa; **to keep one's s. on,** (fam.) no enojarse, quedarse sereno; **to lose one's s.,** (fam.) perder hasta la camisa.
shirtband ['ʃɜrtˌbænd, B 'ʃɜt-] *s.* cabezón (de camisa).
shirtfront [-ˌfrʌnt] *s.* pechera (de camisa).
shirting [-ɪŋ] *s.* tela para camisas.
shirtless [-ləs] *a.* descamisado.
shirtmaker [-ˌmeɪkər, B -ə] *s.* camisero.
shirt-sleeves [-ˌslivz] *a.* 1. en mangas de camisa. 2. para quitarse la chaqueta (clima, tiempo, calor). 3. duro (trabajo). 4. informal. 5. elemental (hecho, conocimiento, etc.).
shirttail [-ˌteɪl] *s.* faldón de camisa.
shirtwaist [-ˌweɪst] *s.* blusa camisera, vestido camisero.
shirty [-ɪ] *a.* (SHIRTIER; SHIRTIEST) enojado, molesto, irritado.
shit [ʃɪt] (vulg.) *s.* 1. mierda. 2. imbecilidades; **he's full of s.,** es un mentiroso de mierda. 3. **shits,** cagalera; **to have the s.,** tener el vientre descompuesto. —*v.i.* (*pret., p.p.* SHITTED; *p.pr.* SHITTING) cagarse.
shitty [ˌʃɪtɪ] *a.* (vulg.) de mierda.
shiv [ʃɪv] *s.* (jer.) cuchilla de hoja angosta.
Shiva ['ʃivə, B 'ʃɪvə] **Shivaism** [-ˌɪzəm] *vars. de* **Siva, Sivaism.**
shivaree [ˌʃɪvə'ri] *var. de* **charivari.**
shiver ['ʃɪvər, B -ə] *s.* astilla. —*v.t., v.i.* hacer(se) astillas, estrellar(se).
shiver, *v.i.* tiritar, estremecerse, temblar. —*v.t.* (mar.) hacer flamear (la vela al viento). —*s.* tiritón, estremecimiento, temblor; escalofríos.
shivery [-ərɪ] *a.* 1. trémulo, tembloroso. 2. friolero, friolento. 3. estremecedor, amedrentador. 4. astilloso, quebradizo.
shnook, schnook[ʃnʊk] *s.* (jer.) persona tonta o ridícula.
shoal [ʃoʊl] *s.* 1. cardumen, banco (de peces). 2. concurrencia, multitud, muchedumbre; cantidad, montón. —*v.i.* formarse cardumen (de peces) o multitud (de gente).
shoal, *s.* bajo, bajío, alfaque. —*v.i.* disminuir(se) en profundidad, perder profundidad. —*v.t.* 1. hacer menos profundo. 2. llegar a (aguas) menos profundas.
shoaliness ['ʃoʊlɪnəs] *s.* falta de profundidad; abundancia de bajos; calidad de somero.
shoaly [-lɪ] *a.* lleno de bajos; vadoso; somero.
shoat [ʃoʊt] *s.* (zool.) cochinillo, gorrino, lechón, cerdo pequeño.
shock [ʃɑk, B ʃɔk] *s.* 1. choque, golpe, impacto, sacudida, ej., *three shocks of the earthquake were felt,* se sintieron tres sacudidas en el terremoto. 2. choque, colisión. 3. susto, sobresalto, emoción, conmoción, ej., *the news gave me a s.,* las noticias me causaron conmoción. 4. (med.) choque, conmoción, parálisis, ej., *died of s.,* murió de conmoción. —*v.t.* 1. chocar a, sobresaltar; conmover; escandalizar, disgustar, ofender. 2. (ant.) sacudir. 3. **to be shocked at,** escandalizarse por. —*v.i.* chocar.
shock, *s.* fajina, hacina, montón (de trigo, mieses, etc.). —*v.t.* amontonar (trigo, etc.).
shock, *s.* greñas, masa (de pelo tupido). —*a.* lanudo; desgreñado.
shock absorber, 1. (mec.) amortiguador de choque. 2. (hidr.) amortiguador de ariete.
shocker ['ʃɑkər, B 'ʃɔkə] *s.* cuento o suceso horripilante.
shock-head [-ˌhɛd] **shockheaded** [-ˌhɛdəd] *a.* cabello greñudo, cabello chascón o chascudo.
shocking [-ɪŋ] *a.* 1. espantoso, horrible, horroroso. 2. chocante, escandalizador; ofensivo, repugnante.
shockingly [-ɪŋlɪ] *adv.* 1. espantosamente, horriblemente, horrorosamente. 2. de modo chocante, ofensivamente.
shockproof [-ˌpruf] *a.* a prueba de choque o de golpe.
shock tactics, (mil.) táctica del ataque en masa; (fig.) táctica de coger de sorpresa a uno.
shock test, (ing.) ensayo de golpe.
shock therapy, (med.) tratamiento por electroshock; terapia por choques insulínicos.
shocktrooper [-ˌtrupər, B -ə] *s.* guardia de asalto.
shock troops, (mil.) tropas de choque.
shock wave, (mil.) onda de choque, onda de presíon y depresíon (de una bomba, etc.).
shod [ʃɑd, B ʃɔd] *pret., p.p. de* **shoe.**
shoddy ['ʃɑdɪ, B 'ʃɔdɪ] *s.* 1. (tej.) shoddy, lana regenerada. 2. paño burdo de lana. 3. imitación. 4. ostentación vulgar. —*a.* (SHODDIER; SHODDIEST) 1. (tej.) de shoddy, de lana regenerada. 2. falso, de imitación. 3. de mala calidad.

shoe [ʃu] *s.* 1. zapato, calzado; bota. 2. herradura. 3. zapata, calzo (de un freno mecánico); galga de carro. 4. regatón (en bastón, lanza, etc.); azuche (en pilotes). 5. (aut.) llanta, cubierta (de neumático). 6. (elec.) patín, zapata. 7. (mec.) calzo, calce. 8. **in another's shoes,** en el pellejo de; **to know where the s. pinches,** saber donde aprieta el zapato; **to put the s. on the right foot,** poner las cosas en su lugar. —*v.t.* (*pret., p.p.* SHOD [ʃɑd, B ʃɔd]; *p.pr.* SHOEING) 1. calzar. 2. herrar (caballos). 3. poner regatón a; azuchar (pilotes). 4. poner llantas o neumáticos a (ruedas).
shoeblack [ˈʃuˌblæk] *s.* limpiabotas, lustrabotas (Amer.).
shoe brush, cepillo para embetunar o lustrar calzado.
shoe buckle, hebilla de zapato.
shoehorn [-ˌhɔrn, B -ˌhɔn] *s.* calzador. —*v.t.* 1. apretujar, apretar. 2. forzar, obligar.
shoelace [-ˌleɪs] *s.* cordón de zapato, pasador.
shoe leather, *s.* cuero para zapatos; correjel.
shoemaker [-ˌmeɪkər, B -ə] *s.* zapatero.
shoe polish, bola, betún.
shoer [-ər, B -ə] *s.* herrador.
shoeshine [ˈʃuˌʃaɪn] *s.* lustrada, betunada.
shoeshine boy, limpiabotas, betunero, lustrabotas (Amer.).
shoestring [-ˌstrɪŋ] *s.* 1. cordón de zapato. 2. **on a s.,** (fam.) con muy poco dinero, con escasos recursos.
shoe tree, horma (de zapato).
shofar, *var. de* **shophar.**
shogun [ˈʃoʊgən, B -gun] *s.* shogún (título antiguo de los gobernadores militares del Japón).
shogunate [-gənət, B -ˌgu-] *s.* shogunado (período de gobierno o dignidad del shogún).
shone, *pret., p.p. de* **shine.**
shoo [ʃu] *interj.* ¡fuera! ¡vete! —*v.t., v.i.* (*pret., p.p.* SHOOED [ʃud] *p.pr.* SHOOING) oxear.
shoofly [ˈʃuˌflaɪ] *s.* 1. mecedora en forma de animal (para niños). 2. planta que repele a las moscas (según creencia popular). 3. **s. pie,** pastel de crema y azúcar morena (sur de E.U.).
shoo-in [-ˌɪn] *s.* (fam.) seguro y fácil ganador (entre candidatos para un puesto público o en una competencia).
shook [ʃʊk] *s.* juego de duelas (para formar un tonel o barril); juego de tablas para hacer cajas; montón de gavillas.
shook, *pret. de* **shake.**
shool [ʃul] (dial.) *v.i., v.t.* traspalar. —*s.* pala.
shoot [ʃut] *v.t.* (*pret., p.p.* SHOT [ʃɑt, B ʃɔt], *p.pr.* SHOOTING) 1. tirar, lanzar, arrojar; proyectar, emitir, hacer salir, echar; descargar o vaciar de golpe, verter violentamente. 2. descargar (un proyectil), disparar (un arma de tiro); tirar (bien o mal). 3. herir o matar a tiros; fusilar, ej., *he was shot as a spy,* fue fusilado por espía. 4. cazar (con armas de fuego). 5. pasar en bote rápidamente por debajo de (un puente); bajar por (un rápido). 6. (foto., cinem.) fotografiar; rodar, filmar (una escena, etc.). 7. (dep.) disparar (la bola) al gol; anotar de tiro (un gol). 8. (carp.) cepillar (el canto de una tabla, etc) en línea recta. 9. detonar (barreno, carga explosiva), volar. 10. (*ú. sólo en p.p.*) jaspear, matizar (tela, seda, etc.), ej., *silk shot with silver,* seda matizada con plata. 11. **s. a match,** competir en certamen de tiradores; **s. craps,** jugar a los dados; **s. down,** matar a tiros; derribar (avión); **s. off,** disparar (arma de fuego); **s. off one's mouth,** hablar demasiado o fuera de turno; **s. one's bolt,** quemar su último cartucho; **s. the bolt,** echar el cerrojo (de una puerta); **s. the bull,** (jer.) charlar, chacharear; chismear; **s. the sun,** (mar.) medir la altura del sol (con sextante); **s. the works,** apostar todo lo que tiene uno; jugarse el todo por el todo; esforzarse al máximo; **s. to death,** matar a tiros; **s. up,** sembrar el terror disparando armas indistintamente en (una población, distrito, etc.). —*v.i.* 1. (u. gen. con *out, forth, along, up, across,* etc.) lanzarse, precipitarse, moverse o correr rápidamente. 2. correrse (cerrojo, etc.). 3. punzar (dolor). 4. tirar, dispararse, tener alcance, ej., *this gun shoots four miles,* este fusil tiene un alcance de cuatro millas. 5. nacer, brotar, germinar. 6. (foto., cinem.) fotografiar. 7. (dep.) tirar la pelota, lanzar bolas. 8. (jer.) inyectar una droga o estupefaciente. 9. **s.!** (jer.) ¡dígalo!; **s. ahead,** tomar rápidamente la delantera (en carrera, competencia, etc.) **s. at,** tirar a, disparar un arma contra; (fig.) tener por objeto, aspirar a, esforzarse por; **s. off,** largarse o salir precipitadamente; **s. up,** crecer o aumentar rápidamente; subir de repente precios, cotizaciones, etc.). —*s.* 1. partida de caza, certamen de tiradores. 2. disparo, tiro. 3. lanzamiento (de un cohete, etc.) 4. vástago; brote, yema, retoño, renuevo. 5. conducto inclinado; canaleta inclinada; tolva (para aguas, etc.); artesa inclinada. 6. rabión, raudal. 7. punzada (de dolor). 8. movimiento repentino, ademán o gesto rápidos.
shooter [ˈʃutər, B -ə] *s.* 1. disparador, tirador. 2. (*en palabras compuestas*) revólver, pistola o fusil de (tantos) tiros, ej., *five-s.,* pistola de cinco tiros. 3. estrella fugaz. 4. (impr.) botador.
shooting box, (pr. G.B.) pabellón de caza.
shooting brake, (G.B.) furgoneta, automóvil rural, coche de estación, rubia (fam.).
shooting gallery, galería de tiro.
shooting iron, (jer., E.U.) arma de fuego.
shooting lodge, (pr. G.B.) pabellón de caza.
shooting pains, dolores punzantes.
shooting script, 1. (cinem.) guión técnico, guión de rodaje. 2. (t.v.) libreto.
shooting star, 1. estrella fugaz. 2. (bot.) (variedad americana de) primavera.
shooting stick, (impr.) botador.
shooting war, guerra abierta, guerra declarada.
shop [ʃap, B ʃɔp] *s.* 1. tienda, almacén. 2. taller, obrador. 3. ocupación, oficio (de una persona). 4. **to set up s.,** abrir una tienda; **to shut up s.,** (fig.) dejar de ejercer un oficio, abandonar una ocupación o trabajo; **to talk s.,** hablar de su oficio, hablar de su propio trabajo. —*v.i.* (*pret., p.p.* SHOPPED; *p.pr.* SHOPPING) ir de compras, ir de tiendas; hacer compras; **s. around (for),** ir de tienda en tienda (en busca de); **to go shopping,** ir de compras. —*v.t.* 1. delatar, traicionar. 2. comprar.
shop assistant, (G.B.) dependiente, vendedor (en una tienda).
shopgirl [ˈʃɑpˌgɜrl, B ˈʃɔpˌgɜl] *s.* dependienta, vendedora.
shophar [ˈʃoʊfər, B -fə] *s.* (relig.) trompeta de cuerno (usada por los judíos).
shopkeeper [ˈʃɑpˌkipər, B ˈʃɔpˌkipə] *s.* tendero; almacenista.
shoplift [-ˌlɪft] *v.t.* hurtar (mercadería en una tienda). —*v.i.* hurtar en tiendas.
shoplifter [-ˌlɪftər, B -tə] *s.* ratero de tiendas, mechera.
shoplifting [-ˌlɪftɪŋ] *s.* ratería de tiendas.
shopman [-mən] *s.* (G.B.) tendero, mercader.
shopper [ˈʃɑpər, B ˈʃɔpə] *s.* comprador.
shopping [-ɪŋ] *s.* compras; **to do one's s.,** hacer uno sus compras.
shopping center, centro comercial.
shopping district, sector comercial.
shopping mall, galería comercial.
shopping spree, to go on (o **to have**) **a s.s.,** hacer una serie de compras (extravagantes).
shop steward, dirigente obrero (en una fábrica, taller, etc.).
shoptalk [ˈʃɑpˌtɔk, B ˈʃɔp-] *s.* discusión de la profesión propia.
shopwalker [-ˌwɔkər, B -ə] *s.* (G.B.) vigilante de tienda, vigilante de taller.
shopwindow [-ˈwɪndoʊ] *s.* escaparate, vidriera, vitrina (Amer.).
shopworn [-ˌwɔrn, B -ˌwɔn] *a.* 1. gastado, deteriorado con el trajín de la tienda. 2. (fig.) trillado, gastado. 3. (fig.) carcomido.
shoran [ˈʃɔrˌæn] *s.* (aer.) sistema radar shoran.
shore [ʃɔr, B ʃɔ] *s.* 1. puntal, codal. 2. (mar.) escora. 3. (min.) edema, ademe. —*v.t.* (*t.* con *up*) 1. apuntalar, acodalar. 2. (mar.) escorar. 3. (min.) ademar, entibar.
shore, *s.* costa, ribera, playa; orilla; **off s.,** a lo largo de la costa; **on s.,** en tierra; **on the shores of,** a orillas de.
shore, *v.t.* (esco.) ofrecer; amenazar; regañar.
shore, (ant., dial.) *prep., p.p. de* **shear.**
shore battery, (mil.) batería costera.
shore crab, (zool.) cangrejo de mar.
shore duty, servicio en tierra (para marineros).
shore leave, permiso para ir a tierra (para marineros).
shoreless [ˈʃɔrləs, B ˈʃɔlɪs] *a.* 1. sin costa ni playa. 2. ilimitado (aguas, mar).
shoreline [-ˌlaɪn] *s.* borde de la playa.
shore patrol, (E.U.) policía militar de la Marina, guardacostas.
shoring [ˈʃɔrɪŋ] *a.* apuntalamiento, acomodamiento, entibación; maderas para apeos.
shorl, *var. de* **schorl.**
shorn, *p.p. de* **shear.**
short [ʃɔrt, B ʃɔt] *a.* 1. corto, pequeño, reducido. 2. corto, breve, de poca duración. 3. bajo (de estatura). 4. breve, conciso. 5. brusco, seco, ej., *a s. answer,* una respuesta brusca, *he was very s. with me,* fue muy seco conmigo. 6. insuficiente, poco. 7. quebradizo, friable (metal). 8. (com.) corto (crédito, plazo, venta, etc.); escaso (dinero, etc.). 9. (fon., poética) breve. 10. **a s. five miles,** unas cinco millas escasas; **a s. time (ago),** (hace) poco tiempo; **a. s. way off,** cerca, a corta distancia; **a. s. while (ago),** (hace) un ratito; **for s.,** para abreviar; **in a s. time,** en breve, en poco tiempo, dentro de poco; **in s. order,** prontamente, sin demora; **in s. supply,** escaso; **nothing s. of,** nada menos que, **ej.,** *nothing s. of a kingdom,* nada menos que un reino; **on s. notice,** con poco tiempo de aviso; **s. of,** escaso de, falto de, corto de, ej., *s. of money,* escaso de dinero, *s. of breath,* falto (o corto) de aliento; **s. on,** desprovisto de, careciente de; deficiente en; ser bajo (de estatura); faltar, no alcanzar (el dinero, etc.); (com.) haber escasez de, ser escaso (dinero); **to be s. of,** faltarle a uno (algo); **to get the s. end of the stick,** llevar la peor parte; ser estafado o engañado; **to make s. work of,** despachar sumariamente; consumir rápidamente. —*s.* 1. película de corta duración. 2. (*pl.*) calzones cortos, calzoncillos (esp. para deportes). 3. (*pl.*) resto, retal. 4. (dial.) suma, resultado; resumen, compendio. 5. (fam., béisbol) jugador que está entre la segunda y tercera base. 6. (elec.) corto circuito. 7. (bolsa) déficit; venta al descubierto, venta a plazos; el que vende al descubierto. 8. (mil.) disparo corto. 9. mezcla de salvado y harina basta. 10. (fon., poética)

sonido breve; sílaba breve. 11. **in s.,** en suma, en resumen; **the long and the s. of it,** el total, el todo; el resumen. —*adv.* 1. brevemente; sucintamente, lacónicamente, cortamente, bruscamente; abruptamente. 2. (bolsa, com.) al descubierto, corto. 3. **s. of,** excepto, dejando de lado; **to pull up s.,** parar o detenerse abruptamente; **to fall s. of,** ser insuficiente para, no alcanzar; (fig.) no llegar a, quedar atrás de; **to cut s.,** interrumpir o terminar bruscamente; **to fall** (o **drop**) **s.,** caer corto (tiro, flechazo, etc.); **to run s.,** menguar, estar acabándose; **to run s. of (gas, money, patience,** etc.), escasear o estar agotándosele a uno (gasolina, dinero, paciencia, etc.); **to sell s.,** vender al descubierto, vender corto; **to stop s.,** quedar parado, pararse bruscamente. —*v.t.* 1. (elec.) poner en corto-circuito. 2. (fam.) estafar, engañar. —*v.i.* (elec.) ponerse en cortocircuito.

short account, (ten.) cuenta al descubierto.

shortage [ˈʃɔrtɪdʒ, B ˈʃɔt-] *s.* 1. déficit. 2. merma, falta. 3. escasez, insuficiencia.

short allowance, ración insuficiente.

shortbread [-ˌbrɛd] *s.* torta dulce hecha con abundante mantequilla.

shortcake [-ˌkeɪk] *s.* pequeña torta o galleta dulce elaborada con abundante mantequilla.

shortchange [-ˌtʃeɪndʒ] *v.t.* (fam.) 1. dar de menos en vuelta o vuelto, no dar el cambio o vuelta debida. 2. estafar, engañar.

shortchanger [-ˌtʃeɪndʒər, B -ə] *s.* estafador, engañador.

short chord, (top.) subcuerda.

short circuit, (elec.) cortocircuito.

short-circuit [ˈʃɔrtˈsɜrkət, B ˈʃɔtˈsɜkɪt] *v.t.* 1. poner en cortocircuito. 2. pasar por alto (trámite, etc.); evitar, evadir. 3. frustrar, poner trabas a.

shortcoming [-ˈkʌmɪŋ] *s.* defecto, deficiencia, imperfección, falla, falta, mengua.

short-commons [-ˈkɑmənz, B -ˈkɔm-] *s. pl.* ración escasa de comida.

shortcut [-ˌkʌt] *s.* atajo.

short-cut, *v.i.* atajar.

short date, (com.) corto plazo.

short division, (mat.) división aproximada.

shorten [ˈʃɔrtən, B ˈʃɔt-] *v.t.* 1. acortar, abreviar; reducir. 2. (mar.) arrizar (vela). 3. (cocina) hacer friable (pastelería). —*v.i.* acortarse, abreviarse; reducirse.

shortening [-ɪŋ] *s.* 1. acortamiento, abreviación; reducción; disminución. 2. manteca para mezclar con la masa; grasa para hacer la pastelería más friable.

shortfall [ˈʃɔrtˌfɔl, B ˈʃɔt-] *s.* déficit.

shorthand [-ˌhænd] *s.* taquigrafía, estenografía; **to take s.,** tomar dictado. —*a.* 1. taquigráfico (signo, sistema, etc.). 2. que usa taquigrafía (persona). 3. taquigrafiado (informe, relato, etc.). —*v.t.* taquigrafiar.

shorthanded [-ˈhændəd] *a.* escaso de mano de obra; escaso de ayudantes.

shorthorn [-ˌhɔrn, B -ˌhɔn] *s.* (raza de) vacuno de cuernos cortos.

shortish [-ɪʃ] *a.* algo corto, algo pequeño.

short line, (poét.) pie quebrado.

short-lived [-ˈlaɪvd, B -ˈlɪvd] *a.* de breve vida, de breve duración, efímero.

shortly [ˈʃɔrtlɪ, B ˈʃɔtlɪ] *adv.* 1. luego, en breve; al instante. 2. en pocas palabras; brevemente. 3. descortésmente, bruscamente. 4. **s. before (after),** poco antes (después).

shortness [-nəs] *s.* 1. cortedad, brevedad. 2. pequeñez. 3. escasez, insuficiencia; deficiencia. 4. brusquedad.

short order, plato de rápida preparación (en restaurante).

short-range [-ˈreɪndʒ] *a.* de corto alcance.

short rib, (anat.) costilla flotante.

short sale, (bolsa) venta corta; venta al descubierto.

short score, (mús.) partitura corta (para música coral, con las voces femeninas reunidas en un pentagrama y las masculinas en otro).

short seller, vendedor corto, vendedor al descubierto.

short selling, venta corta; venta al descubierto.

short-sheet [-ˌʃit] *v.t.* **s.-s. beds,** hacer (o jugar a) cama corta.

short shrift, tiempo breve para confesarse antes de morir; breve tregua o respiro; **to make s. s. of,** despachar sumariamento, acabar rápido con.

short sight, 1. vista corta, miopía. 2. (fig.) falta de perspicacia o previsión.

shorts [ʃɔrts] *s. pl.* shorts; **a pair of s.,** unos shorts.

shortsighted [ˈʃɔrtˈsaɪtəd, B ˈʃɔt-] *a.* 1. miope, corto de vista. 2. (fig.) miope, falto de perspicacia, falto de previsión.

shortsightedly [-lɪ] *adv.* 1. con miopía. 2. con falta de perspicacia o previsión.

shortsightedness [-nəs] *s.* 1. miopía, cortedad de vista. 2. falta de perspicacia o previsión.

short-sleeved [-ˈslivd] *a.* de manga corta.

short-spoken [-ˈspoʊkən] *a.* brusco, áspero; lacónico.

shortstop [-ˌstɑp, B -ˌstɔp] *s.* 1. (béisbol) juga dor situado entre la segunda y tercera bases. 2. (foto.) baño o solución que detiene el revelado.

short story, cuento, relato, narración.

short subjects, (cinem.) películas cortas (noticieros, documentales, etc.).

short suit, (naipes) palo corto (de menos de cuatro cartas).

short-tempered [-ˈtɛmpərd, B -pəd] *a.* de mal genio, colérico.

short-term [ˈʃɔrtˈtɜrm, B ˈʃɔtˈtɜm] *a.* (com.) a corto plazo.

short ton, tonelada corta (equivalente a 1031 kilos en G.B. y 920 kilos en E.U.).

short turn, vuelta cerrada, curva cerrada.

short vowel, (fon.) vocal breve.

short waist, (cost.) talle alto.

shortwave [-ˈweɪv] (rad.) *s.* onda corta. —*a.* de onda corta; en onda corta.

short-winded [-ˈwɪndəd] *a.* corto de resuello; de respiración rápida o difícil.

shorty [-ɪ] *a.* (jer.) de corta estatura.

Shoshoni, Shoshone [ʃəˈʃoʊnɪ, B ʃoʊ-] *s.* (*pl.* SHOSHONI, SHOSHONIS, SHOSHONE O SHOSHONES) indio shoshón.

shot [ʃɑt, B ʃɔt] *s.* 1. tiro, disparo, escopetazo; ej., *several shots were fired,* se hicieron varios disparos. 2. proyectil, bala. 3. (*pl.* SHOT) perdigón, balín. 4. jugada, golpe, tirada (de billar, etc.). 5. (fig.) conjetura, suposición; tentativa. 6. tiro, alcance. 7. inyección. 8. tiro, tirador. 9. oportunidad, chance. 10. trago (de licor). 11. dosis. 12. (foto., cinem.) toma. 13. **exchange of shots,** tiroteo; **like a s.,** como una bala; con sumo placer; **long s.,** probabilidad remota; conjetura arriesgada; **not by a long s.,** ni con mucho, ni por asomo; **out of s.,** fuera de alcance; **s. in the arm,** (fig.) estímulo, dosis vivificante; **s. in the dark,** (fig.) conjetura al azar; **to be a good s.,** tener buena puntería; **to have a s. at (something),** probar (algo); **to have a s. at (doing),** tratar de (hacer); **to put the s.,** (dep.) lanzar la bala, tirar la pesa; **within cannon s.,** a tiro de cañón.

shot, *pret., p.p. de* **shoot.** —*a.* 1. que ha sido disparado. 2. tornasolado (telas); jaspeado. 3. agotado; gastado. 4. (jer.) embriagado, borracho. 5. **s. through with,** saturado de, cargado de; **s. with** (G.B.). mezclado con, abigarrado con.

shot cartridge, cartucho de perdigones.

shote [ʃoʊt] *s.* cochinillo, gorrino, cerdo pequeño.

shotgun [ˈʃɑtˌgʌn, B ˈʃɔt-] *s.* escopeta; **to ride s.,** viajar como guardia armado.

shotgun marriage, matrimonio a la fuerza.

shot hole, pozo de explosión, hoyo de disparo.

shot of lightning, golpe de rayo.

shot pattern, (arm.) rosa de tiro.

shot put, (dep.) lanzamiento de bala, tiro de la pesa.

shot-putter [ˈʃɑtˌpʊtər, B ˈʃɔt-ə] *s.* lanzador de bala o pesa.

shot silk, seda tornasolada.

should, *pret. y condicional de* **shall.** — equivalente de **ought to** que se usa como defectivo con la significación de deber o haber de, ej., *you should cable them immediately,* debes cablegrafiarles en seguida, *you should have seen her!* ¡deberías haberla visto! *I should be leaving right now,* debiera irme ahora mismo.

shoulder [ˈʃoʊldər, B -də] *s.* 1. hombro. 2. (*pl.*) hombros, espaldas, lomos. 3. brazuelo, cuarto delantero (de res, etc.). 4. borde (del camino o carretera), hombrillo. 5. (mec., carp.) hombro, resalto, espaldón. 6. (impr.) hombro, rebaba, quijada. 7. (fort.) saliente (de un bastión). 8. **s. to s.,** hombro a hombro; **straight from the s.,** con toda franqueza; **to cry on someone's s.,** aquejarse en busca de consuelo; **to give the cold s. to,** volver la espalda a; desairar; **to have broad shoulders,** tener buenas espaldas; **to put one's s. to the wheel,** arrimar el hombro; **to rub shoulders with,** tener contacto con; **to square one's shoulders,** enderezar los hombros. —*v.t.* 1. empujar con los hombros, empellar. 2. llevar en hombros, cargar sobre los hombros; tomar sobre sí, asumir, cargar con; hacerse responsable de, ej., **s.** *a debt,* hacerse responsable de una deuda. 3. (mil.) cargar con (fusil). 4. **s. arms!** (mil.) ¡armas al hombro! —*v.i.* empujar con los hombros.

shoulder bag, bolsa debandolera.

shoulder belt, bandolera.

shoulder blade, escápula, omóplato.

shoulder eyebolt, (mec.) cáncamo de cuello, armella de resalto.

shoulder holster, pistolera.

shoulder knot, (mil.) dragona, charretera.

shoulder-of-mutton sail, (mar.) vela triangular.

shoulder screw, tornillo de tope, tornillo limitador, tornillo de resalto.

shoulder strap, 1. tirante. 2. correa o tira para llevar objetos suspendidos del hombro; correón (de aguadores). 3. (mil.) dragona.

shouldn't [ˈʃʊdənt] *contr. de* **should not.**

shout [ʃaʊt] *v.i.* gritar, dar voces; **s. at,** gritar a (persona); **s. down,** hacer callar a gritos; **s. with laughter,** reír a carcajadas, soltar una risotada. —*v.t.* vocear, gritar; vociferar. —*s.* grito, clamor, alarido, voz; alboroto, aclamación.

shouter [ˈʃaʊtər, B -ə] *s.* gritador; aclamador, vociferador.

shouting [-ɪŋ] *s.* 1. vocería, gritería; aclamación. —*a.* que vocea, vociferador.

shove [ʃʌv] *v.t.* 1. empujar, empellar; impeler; dar empujones a. 2. (fam.) poner. 3. **s. along,** empujar, hacer avanzar por empujones; **s. out,** empujar hacia afuera. —*v.i.* dar un empujón; avanzar a empujones; **s. off,** desatracarse (bote de muelle u orilla con un empellón); (jer.) largarse. —*s.* empujón, empellón; **to give one a s.,**

dar un empujón a uno; (fig.) poner en marcha, ayudar a empezar (negocio, empresa, etc.).
shovel ['ʃʌvəl] *s.* 1. pala, palana (Am.). 2. palada, ej., *a s. of coal,* una palada de carbón. —*v.t.* (*pret., p.p.* SHOVELED O SHOVELLED; *p.pr.* SHOVELING O SHOVELLING) 1. traspalar, traspalear; echar con pala. 2. cavar o excavar con pala, palanear (Am.). 3. (fig.) echar en grandes cantidades.
shovelbill [-ˌbɪl] *s.* (orn.) espátula común; pato cuchareta, ánade cucharetero.
shovelboard [-ˌbɔrd, B -ˌbɔd] *var. de* **shuffleboard.**
shoveler, shoveller [-ər, B -ə] *s.* 1. paleador. 2. (orn.) espátula común; pato cuchareta, ánade cucharetero.
shovelful [-ˌfʊl] *s.* (*pl.* SHOVELFULS O SHOVELSFUL) palada, lo que abarca una pala (de carbón, arena, etc.).
shovel hat, sombrero de teja, de ala plana y volteada a los lados, que usan con frecuencia los clérigos anglicanos.
shovelhead [-ˌhɛd] *s.* (ict.) tiburón parecido al pez martillo.
shovel nose, animal de hocico aplanado; pez de cabeza ancha y plana.
shovel-nosed [-ˌnoʊzd] *a.* de o con hocico aplanado (animal); de cabeza ancha y plana (pez).
show [ʃoʊ] *v.t.* (*pret.* SHOWED; *p.p.* SHOWN O SHOWED; *p.pr.* SHOWING) 1. mostrar, enseñar; exhibir, exponer; lucir, ostentar. 2. descubrir, mostrar, revelar; hacer saber (a). 3. otorgar, conferir. 4. dirigir, guiar, conducir, ej., *he showed us around the house,* nos guió por la casa para mostrárnosla. 5. demostrar, probar, ej., *s. the truth of a statement,* demostrar la verdad de una declaración. 6. marcar, indicar, ej., *the sign shows the way,* el letrero indica el camino. 7. (der.) alegar; defender (una causa). 8. (G.B.) **on your own showing,** según tus propias palabras; tú mismo has reconocido (que); **s. cause,** (der.) alegar una causa; **s. (someone) in,** hacer entrar (a alguien); **s. off,** sacar a relucir, destacar; **s. one's hand,** (fig.) revelar sus designios; **s. oneself,** aparecer, dejarse ver; **s. (someone) out,** acompañar a la puerta (a alguien); **s. signs of wear,** mostrar señales de uso; **s. the door to,** echar (de la casa); despedir; **s. (someone) the way,** guiar (a alguien); **s. up,** sacar a luz, revelar, desenmascarar; presentarse, apersonarse; **to have nothing to s. for it,** no sacar ningún beneficio (de algo). —*v.i.* 1. mostrarse, aparecer; verse, notarse, ej., *does the spot s.?* ¿se nota la mancha? 2. parecer. 3. llegar en tercer puesto (en carrera). 4. (teat.) dar una representación; (cine) exhibirse (una película). 5. **s. off,** farolear, alardear; **s. up,** aparecer; destacarse. —*s.* 1. exhibición, exposición, ej., *a fine s. of sculpture,* buena exposición de escultura. 2. demostración, ej., *a s. of force,* demostración de fuerza. 3. apariencia; exterioridad; pretensión, fingimiento. 4. indicación, señal; indicio, huella, ej., *some s. of reason,* alguna señal de razón. 5. ostentación, pompa; boato. 6. vista. 7. espectáculo, función, exhibición. 8. ocasión, oportunidad, suerte, ej., *give him a fair s.,* denle una buena oportunidad. 9. (jer.) empresa, negocio, asunto. 10. (jer.) tercer puesto en una carrera. 11. **to give the s. away,** revelar planes; **to make a s. of,** hacer gala de; **to steal the s.,** llevarse todos los aplausos.
show bill, cartel; cartelón.
show biz [-bɪz] (jer., E.U.) la farándula, el teatro, la industria y profesión del teatro.
showboat ['ʃoʊˌboʊt] *s.* buque teatro. —*v.i.* (jer.) alardear, farolear.
showbread, *var. de* **shewbread.**
show business, la farándula, el mundo del espectáculo.
show card, letrero (gen. de anuncio).
showcase [-ˌkeɪs] *s.* vitrina, escaparate (de exposición).
showdown [-ˌdaʊn] *s.* 1. confrontación decisiva, arreglo de cuentas, prueba definitiva de fuerzas. 2. (naipes) revelación de las manos (en póker).
shower ['ʃoʊər, B -ə] *s.* mostrador (persona); exhibidor.
shower ['ʃaʊ-] *s.* 1. aguacero, chubasco, chaparrón. 2. (fig.) rociada, lluvia (de cartas, regalos, etc.). 3. fiesta de regalos que se da a las novias; fiesta de regalos previa al nacimiento de un niño. 4. ducha. —*v.t.* 1. regar, mojar. 2. derramar con abundancia. 3. **s. with,** (fig.) colmar de. —*v.i.* 1. llover, caer en abundancia. 2. ducharse.
shower bath, baño de ducha, baño de regadera, ducha.
shower cap, gorro de ducha.
shower curtain, cortina de ducha.
showery [-ərɪ] *a.* lluvioso.
show girl, corista (en revistas musicales).
showily ['ʃoʊəlɪ] *adv.* con aparato, ostentosamente, aparatosamente.
showiness [-ɪnəs] *s.* ostentación.
showing [-ɪŋ] *s.* 1. exhibición, exposición, ej., *a s. of millinery,* una exposición de sombreros de señora. 2. presentación (de un hecho, condición, etc.). 3. actuación. 4. resultado (s), ej., *a bad financial s.,* malos resultados financieros. 5. **to make a good (poor) s.,** tener una buena (o mala) actuación o ejecutoria; quedar bien (o mal).
showman [-mən] *s.* 1. director de teatro; empresario de espectáculos, productor. 2. persona con dotes teatrales.
showmanship [-mənˌʃɪp] *s.* 1. habilidad para presentar espectáculos. 2. (fig.) habilidad para hacer apreciar sus cualidades (de uno), teatralidad.
show-me [-mɪ] *a.* (fam.) escéptico, incrédulo.
shown [ʃoʊn] *p.p. de* **show.**
show-off ['ʃoʊˌɔf] *s.* 1. ostentación. 2. (fam.) pinturero, farolero, ostentador.
show of hands, votación por medio de manos levantadas.
showpiece ['ʃoʊˌpis] *s.* obra sobresaliente, pieza de resistencia (en una exhibición, etc.), ejemplo relevante (de la habilidad, arte, etc. de alguien).
showplace [-ˌpleɪs] *s.* espectáculo, lugar digno de verse, atracción turística.
showroom [-ˌrum, -ˌrʊm] *s.* sala de muestras, sala de exhibición.
showy [-ɪ] *a.* (SHOWIER; SHOWIEST) 1. vistoso, llamativo. 2. ostentoso, aparatoso.
SHP *abrev. de* **shaft horsepower,** caballos al eje.
shrank, *pret. de* **shrink.**
shrapnel ['ʃræpnəl] *s.* (mil.) granada fragmentaria, metralla, granada de metralla.
shrapnel mine, (mil.) mina de metralla.
shred [ʃrɛd] *s.* 1. filamento; jirón. 2. fragmento, pedazo, retazo; pizca, ej., *without a s. of clothing,* sin pizca de ropa. 3. **in shreds,** hecho pedazos, desgarrado; **to tear to shreds,** desgarrar, hacer pedazos, hacer jirones; **without a s. of evidence,** sin prueba alguna. —*v.t.* (*pret., p.p.,* SHREDDED; *p.pr.* SHREDDING) picar, desmenuzar, triturar; hacer pedazos.
shredded ['ʃrɛdəd] *a.* desmenuzado, hecho trizas.
shredder [-dər, B -də] *s.* trituradora, desmenuzadora, desfibradora.
shrew [ʃru] *s.* 1. mujer bravía y regañona, arpia, fierecilla. 2. (zool.) musaraña, musgaño.
shrewd [ʃrud] *a.* 1. astuto, sagaz, listo, despierto; perspicaz, ej., *a s. guess,* una conjetura astuta, *a s. observer,* un observador perspicaz. 2. (ant.) penetrante, agudo, cortante. 3. (ant.) malo, dañoso, malicioso; mañoso.
shrewdly ['ʃrudlɪ] *adv.* astutamente, sagazmente.
shrewdness [-nəs] *s.* astucia, sagacidad.
shrewish ['ʃruɪʃ] *a.* regañón, de mal genio.
shrewishness [-nəs] *s.* mal genio, carácter regañón.
shrewmouse ['ʃruˌmaʊs] *s.* (zool.) musaraña, musgaño.
shriek [ʃrik] *v.i.* chillar, gritar, dar alaridos; **s. with laughter,** reír a carcajadas. —*v.t.* (gen. con *out*) decir o proferir gritando. —*s.* chillido, alarido, grito agudo; risotada chillona.
shrieker ['ʃrikər, B -ə] *s.* chillador, chillón, gritador.
shrieval ['ʃrivəl] *a.* de (l) alguacil.
shrievalty [-tɪ] *s.* alguacilazgo.
shrift [ʃrɪft] *s.* (ant.) confesión (de los pecados).
shrike [ʃraɪk] *s.* (orn.) alcaudón, galdón, picagrega, pega reborda, picaza chillona o manchada.
shrill [ʃrɪl] *a.* chillón; agudo, penetrante, estridente. —*s.* chillido. —*v.t., v.i.* chillar; sonar con tono agudo.
shrillness [-nəs] *s.* agudez (de voz, tono, luz, etc.).
shrilly ['ʃrɪllɪ] *adv.* en voz chillona, con ruido agudo y penetrante.
shrimp [ʃrɪmp] *s.* 1. (zool.) camarón, gamba, langostino. 2. (fig.) gorgojo, renacuajo (hombrecillo). —*v.i.* pescar camarones.
shrimpfish ['ʃrɪmpˌfɪʃ] *s.* (ict.) chocha de mar.
shrine [ʃraɪn] *s.* 1. relicario (esp. de cosas sagradas). 2. sepulcro de un santo. 3. santuario, templo. 4. lugar sagrado. —*v.t.* (poét.) guardar en un relicario, poner en un altar.
shrink [ʃrɪŋk] *v.i.* (*pret.,* SHRANK [ʃræŋk] O SHRUNK [ʃrʌŋk]; *p.p.* SHRUNK O SHRUNKEN ['ʃrʌŋkən]; *p.pr.* SHRINKING) 1. encoger, contraerse, acortarse. 2. encogerse, acobardarse, rehuirse, retirarse. 3. **s. back,** retraerse, rehuirse; **s. from,** evadir, huir de; aborrecer; **s. into oneself,** abstraerse, volverse taciturno. —*v.t.* contraer, hacer encoger; **s. on,** (mec.) montar o zunchar en caliente. —*s.* 1. contracción, encogimiento; reculada. 2. (jer.) psiquiatra.
shrinkable ['ʃrɪŋkəbəl] *a.* encogible.
shrinkage [-ɪdʒ] *s.* 1. contracción, encogimiento; reducción, disminución. 2. merma, pérdida, depreciación (de valores). 3. pérdida de peso (en el ganado durante su embarque).
shrinkage factor, (ing.) coeficiente de contracción.
shrink fit, (ing.) ajuste por contracción, ajuste en caliente.
shrinking violet, (fig., fam.) persona tímida y vergonzosa.
shrive [ʃraɪv] *v.t.* (*pret.* SHROVE [ʃroʊv] O SHRIVED; *p.p.* SHRIVEN ['ʃrɪvən]; *p.pr.* SHRIVING) (ant.) 1. confesar, oír en confesión. 2. dar la absolución a; perdonar, aliviar. —*v.i.* confesarse.
shrivel ['ʃrɪvəl] *v.i.* (*pret., p.p.* SHRIVELED O SHRIVELLED; *p.pr.* SHRIVELING O SHRIVELLING) 1. arrugarse; avellanarse. 2. marchitarse, secarse, resecarse. 3. **s. up,** marchitarse; consumirse. —*v.t.* 1. arrugar. 2. marchitar; consumir.
shriven, *p.p. de* **shrive.**
shroff [ʃrɑf, B ʃrɔf] *s.* banquero, cambista (en el oriente).
shroud [ʃraʊd] *s.* 1. mortaja, sudario. 2. cubierta, recubrimiento. 3. (fig.) velo, ej., *wrapped in a s. of mystery,* envuelto en un velo de misterio. 4.

(mar.) obenque. 5. (*pl.*) cuerdas (del paracaídas). —*v.t.* 1. amortajar. 2. cubrir, ocultar. 3. (fig.) velar, ej., *shrouded in mystery,* velado en el misterio. 4. (ant.) proteger; amparar. —*v.i.* (ant.) buscar refugio; refugiarse.

shroud-laid [ˈʃraʊdˌleɪd] *a.* (mar.) de cuatro torones con alma (díc. de la soga).

shrove [ʃroʊv] *pret. de* **shrive.**

Shrovetide [ˈʃroʊvˌtaɪd] *s.* (relig.) carnestolendas.

Shrove Tuesday, martes de carnaval.

shrub [ʃrʌb] *s.* 1. cordial o cóctel hecho de jugo de frutas y alguna bebida alcohólica. 2. arbusto.

shrubbery [ˈʃrʌbərɪ] *s.* arbustos (colectivamente), maleza.

shrubby [-ɪ] *a.* 1. cubierto o lleno de arbustos. 2. (bot.) arbustivo.

shrug [ʃrʌg] *v.i.* (*pret., p.p.* SHRUGGED; *p.pr.* SHRUGGING) alzarse o encogerse de hombros. —*v.t.* **s. off,** echar de lado con una sacudida; (fig.) quitar importancia a, no hacer caso de; **s. one's shoulders,** encogerse de hombros. —*s.* encogimiento de hombros; **with a s.,** encogiéndose de hombros, con indiferencia.

shrunk [ʃrʌŋk] *pret., p.p. de* **shrink.**

shrunken [ˈʃrʌŋkən] *p.p. de* **shrink.** —*a.* encogido, contraído, disminuido, mermado.

shuck [ʃʌk] *s.* 1. cáscara (de nuez, huevo, etc.); corteza, vaina, hollejo. 2. (E.U.) valva, desbulla, concha de marisco. 3. (fam., E.U.) insignificancia, nadería, tontería, cosa de poca monta. —*v.t.* 1. descascarar, pelar, deshollejar. 2. desbullar.

shucks [ʃʌks] *interj.* (E.U.) ¡caramba! (ú. gen. para expresar disgusto o desilusión).

shudder [ˈʃʌdər, B -ə] *v.i.* temblar, estremecerse, escalofriarse. —*s.* temblor, estremecimiento, escalofrío.

shudderingly [-ɪŋlɪ, B -dərɪŋ-] *adv.* temblorosamente, con estremecimientos.

shuffle [ˈʃʌfəl] *v.t.* 1. entremezclar. 2. revolver, desordenar. 3. barajar (naipes). 4. arrastrar (los pies). 5. **s. off,** despojarse de (vestiduras, etc.) desmañadamente; (fig.) librarse de (responsabilidades, etc.); **s. the cards,** (fig.) cambiar de táctica. —*v.i.* 1. barajar los naipes. 2. moverse con torpeza, proceder con dificultad. 3. caminar o bailar arrastrando los pies; taconear al bailar. 5. tergiversar, andar con rodeos, hablar en forma evasiva. 6. **s. along,** ir pasándola; ir arrastrando los pies; **s. in** (o **into**), ponerse (prenda, etc.) desmañadamente; meterse en, colarse en; **s. off,** marcharse de un sitio, irse arrastrando los pies; **s. out** (o **out of**), salirse a duras penas (de una dificultad, aprieto, etc.); **s. through,** hacer sin cuidado, atender algo en forma desordenada. —*s.* 1. turno de barajar (los naipes); barajadura, barajada (de naipes). 2. triquiñuela, evasiva, tergiversación. 3. arrastre o arrastramiento de pies (al caminar o en el baile).

shuffleboard [-ˌbɔrd, B -bɔd] *s.* 1. mesa o juego de tejo. 2. tejo de cubierta (en barcos).

shuffler [ˈʃʌflər, B -flə] *s.* 1. el que baraja (los naipes). 2. (orn.) pato marino.

shuffling [-flɪŋ] *a.* 1. lerdo, pesado. 2. evasivo.

shun [ʃʌn] *v.t.* (*pret., p.p.* SHUNNED; *p.pr.* SHUNNING) evitar, esquivar, huir de, rehuir.

shunpike [ˈʃʌnˌpaɪk] *a.* que utiliza caminos secundarios (para evitar una carretera de portazgo o peaje), ej., *a s. tour,* una gira por caminos secundarios o libres de peaje.

shunt [ʃʌnt] *v.t.* 1. desviar, apartar. 2. (f.c.) hacer cambiar de vía (tren, vagones, etc.). 3. (elec.) poner o conectar en derivación, derivar. —*v.i.* 1. desviarse, apartarse. 2. (f.c.) cambiar de vía. —*s.* 1. desviación. 2. (f.c.) desvío. 3. (elec.) derivación, resistencia en derivación.

shunt circuit, (elec.) circuito derivado.

shunt coil, (elec.) bobina o carrete de derivación.

shunter [ˈʃʌntər, B -ə] *s.* 1. locomotora de maniobras. 2. guardagujas; enganchador de vagones (obrero).

shunt field, (elec.) campo de derivación.

shunting engine, locomotora de maniobras.

shunt winding, (elec.) devanado o enrollamiento en derivación.

shunt-wound [ˈʃʌntˈwaʊnd] *a.* (elec.) devanado en derivación.

shush [ʃʌʃ] *interj.* ¡chito! ¡chitón! —*v.t.* hacer callar.

shut [ʃʌt] *v.t.* (*pret., p.p.* SHUT; *p.pr.* SHUTTING) 1. cerrar, encerrar. 2. cerrar (hojas de una navaja, cuchillo, etc.); doblar, plegar (abanico, etc.). 3. dejar aprisionado o atrapado (la mano, ropa, dedo, etc.) en. 4 **s. away,** guardar bajo llave, encerrar; **s. down,** bajar (ventana, cortina, etc.); cerrar (una fábrica, etc.); **s. in,** encerrar; rodear (enemigo, tropas, etc.); **s. into,** encerrar, confinar; **s. off,** aislar; cerrar, cortar (agua, gas, etc.); **s. one's eyes** (o **ears**) **to,** negarse a ver (o escuchar); fingir no ver (u oír); **s. out,** cerrar la puerta a (uno); no dejar entrar o penetrar; tapar, ocultar (de la vista); tapar (la vista); excluir, desechar (la posibilidad, etc.); **s. (someone) out of (his room,** etc.), echar (a alguien) fuera de (su cuarto, etc.); **s. the door upon,** (fig.) cerrar la puerta a (acuerdo, negociaciones, etc.); **s. up (a house),** cerrar (una casa, esp. todas sus puertas y ventanas); **s. (someone) up,** hacer callar (a alguien); encerrar, recluir, aprisionar, encarcelar (a alguien); **s. up shop,** cerrar el negocio, levantar tienda (al fin del día o permanentemente). —*v.i.* cerrarse, encerrarse; **s. down,** cerrar la tienda; **s. up,** (fam.) (*ú. esp. en imper.*) callarse la boca. *a.* 1. cerrado, asegurado. 2. (fon.) oclusivo. —*s.* 1. cierre, término. 2. juntura, costura de unión (en soldadura).

shutdown [ˈʃʌtˌdaʊn] *s.* paro o suspensión del trabajo (en una fábrica, mina, etc.).

shut-eye [-ˌaɪ] *s.* (jer.) sueño; **to get some s.,** echar un sueño corto; pegar el ojo.

shut-in [-ˌɪn] *a.* 1. confinado (en casa) (díc. de los inválidos). 2. (psic.) introvertido. —*s.* inválido o enfermo confinado en hospital.

shutoff [-ˌɔf] *s.* 1. válvula, interruptor, interceptor, oclusor. 2. cierre, corte, interrupción, oclusión.

shutoff valve, válvula de cierre.

shutout [-ˌaʊt] *s.* 1. cierre de fábrica (impuesto por los patronos). 2. (dep.) triunfo o partido en que el equipo perdedor no marca tantos.

shut-out bid, (bridge) declaración exclusiva.

shutter [ˈʃʌtər, B -ə] *s.* 1. cerradura, cerrador, cierre. 2. postigo de ventana, contraventana, puertaventana; persiana, sobrevidriera. 3. (foto.) obturador. 4. **to put up the shutters,** levantar tienda, cerrar el negocio. —*v.t.* cerrar o cubrir con contraventana o persianas.

shutterbug [-ˌbʌg] *s.* (jer.) fotógrafo aficionado.

shuttle [ˈʃʌtəl] *s.* 1. lanzadera (del telar). 2. lanzadera, jugadera (de máquinas de coser). 3. (E.U.) tren lanzadera, tren de enlace. 4. (avia.) puente aéreo. 5. (aeroesp.) transbordador espacial, lanzadera espacial. —*v.t., v.i.* mover o moverse como lanzadera; ir y venir (entre dos puntos).

shuttlecock [-ˌkɑk, B -ˌkɔk] *s.* volante, rehilete. —*v.t.* pelotear; pasar de uno a otro.

shuttle flight, puente aéreo.

shuttle saw, sierra de vaivén.

shuttle service, servicio de enlace.

shy [ʃaɪ] *a.* (SHYER O SHIER; SHYEST O SHIEST) 1. tímido, asustadizo, temeroso; corto, apocado, vergonzoso. 2. cauteloso, prudente; desconfiado, receloso. 3. recatado, reservado. 4. escondido, apartado. 5. improductivo. 6. **s. of,** falto de; **to be s. of (doing),** hesitar, vacilar en (hacer); estar maldispuesto a, estar reacio a (hacer); **to be s. of (something),** desconfiar de, estar receloso de (algo); faltarle a uno (dinero, etc.); **to fight s. of,** (tratar de) eludir; evitar el trato con; evitar ir a. —*v.i.* (*pret., p.p.* SHIED; *p.pr.* SHYING) 1. respingar (caballo). 2. sobresaltarse, asustarse, sobrecogerse, apocarse. 3. **s. at** (o **from**), respingar al ver (díc. del caballo); retroceder ante; rehusar hacer; **s. away,** huir o escapar asustado. —*s.* (*pl.* SHIES) respingo (de un caballo).

shy *v.t.* lanzar, arrojar, tirar. —*s.* (*pl.* SHIES) 1. echada, lanzamiento, tiro. 2. (jer.) sarcasmo, mofa.

shyer [ˈʃaɪər, B -ə] *s.* caballo asustadizo, caballo pajarero (Amer.).

Shylock [-ˌlɑk, B -lɔk] *s.* usurero, avaro (del personaje central de la obra de Shakespeare *El Mercader de Venecia*).

shyly [-lɪ] *adv.* 1. tímidamente, temerosamente. 2. cautelosamente.

shyness [-nəs] *s.* 1. timidez; cortedad, apocamiento. 2. cautela. 3. recato.

shyster [ˈʃaɪstər, B -stə] *s.* (E.U.) leguleyo, picapleitos, tinterillo (Amer.).

si [si] *s.* (mús.) si.

Si *símb. de* **silicon,** silicio (Si).

sialagogic [saɪˌæləˈgɑdʒɪk, B -ˈgɔdʒ-] *a.* (med.) sialagogo, sialógeno, tialagogo, que provoca secreción de saliva.

sialagogue [saɪˈæləˌgɑg, B ˈsaɪələgoʊg] *s.* (med.) sialagogo.

sialid [ˈsaɪəlɪd] **sialidan** [saɪˈælɪdən] *a., s.* (ento.) siálido.

Sialidae [saɪˈælɪˌdi] *s. pl.* (ento.) siálidos.

Siam [saɪˈæm] *s.* Siam, antiguo nombre de Tailandia.

siamang [ˈsiəˌmæŋ, B ˈsaɪ-] *s.* (zool.) siamang, siamanga.

Siamese [ˌsaɪəˈmiz] *s.* (*pl.* SIAMESE) 1. siamés, natural de Siam. 2. (idioma) siamés. —*a.* siamés.

Siamese cat, gato siamés.

Siamese twins, hermanos siameses.

sib [sɪb] *s.* 1. parentesco, parientes. 2. pariente consaguíneo. —*a.* pariente, allegado, consanguíneo.

Siberian [saɪˈbɪrɪən] *a., s.* siberiano.

Siberian husky, perro siberiano.

Siberian squirrel, (zool.) gris.

sibilance [ˈsɪbələns] **sibilancy** [-ɪ] *s.* 1. carácter sibilante. 2. tono sibilante.

sibilant [ˈsɪbələnt] *a.* (esp. fon.) sibilante. —*s.* sibilante (*f.*), sonido sibilante.

sibilantly [-lɪ] *adv.* de modo sibilante.

sibilate [ˈsɪbəˌleɪt] *v.t.* articular con sibilante (inicial). —*v.i.* 1. pronunciar una sibilante. 2. silbar, sisear.

sibilation [ˌsɪbəˈleɪʃən] *s.* articulación sibilante.

sibling [ˈsɪblɪŋ] *s.* 1. hermano, hermana. 2. medio hermano, media hermana. —*a.* fraternal.

sibyl [ˈsɪbəl] *s.* (mitol.) sibila; pitonisa, adivina, profetisa.

sibylic, sibyllic [səˈbɪlɪk] **sibylline** [ˈsɪbəˌlaɪn, B sɪˈbɪlaɪn] *a.* sibilino, sibilítico.

Sibylline books, (hist.) libros sibilinos.

sic [sɪk] *v.t* 1. atacar. 2. (con *on*) incitar (a un perro) a atacar. —*adv* (lat.) sic, así dice (el texto). —*a.* (Esco.) *var. de* **such.**

Sicani [sɪˈkeɪnaɪ] *s. pl.* sicanos, sicilianos.

Sicanian [sɪˈkeɪnɪən] *a.* sicano, siciliano.

siccative [ˈsɪkətɪv] *a., s.* secante, desecante.

Sicilian [sɪˈsɪljən] *a., s.* siciliano.

Sicily ['sɪsəlɪ] *s.* Sicilia, isla de Italia.
sick [sɪk] *a.* 1. enfermo. 2. pálido, demacrado, descolorido. 3. mórbido, morboso (humor, mente, ideas, etc.). 4. doliente, triste (gesto, sonrisa, etc.). 5. pobre, agotada (tierras), ej., *clover s.,* agotada para producir tréboles. 6. (com.) estancado, inactivo (mercado, economía, etc.). 7. **the s.,** los enfermos; **to be s.,** estar enfermo; arrojar, vomitar; **to be s. and tired of,** estar hasta la coronilla con, estar harto por demás de (algún asunto, etc.); **to be s. at heart,** estar afligido, estar angustiado; **to be s. to one's stomach,** sentir náuseas; **to be s. for,** tener ansias de, anhelar; **to be s. of,** estar aburrido de, estar harto de; **to be s. with (fear, anxiety,** etc.), estar enfermo de (miedo, ansiedad, etc.); **to fall s.,** caer enfermo; **to feel s.,** sentir náuseas; **to look s.,** tener aspecto enfermizo; (fig.) parecer inferior, presentar un aspecto pobre; **to make s.,** hacer vomitar, provocar náuseas; (fig.) poner enfermo, dar asco; **to take s.,** caer enfermo. —*v.t.* **s. up,** (G.B., jer.) vomitar.
sick, *v.t.* 1. (*u. gen. en imper.*) atacar, agarrar (díc. a los perros). 2. (gen. con *on*) azuzar, incitar (al perro).
sick bay, (mar.) enfermería, dispensario.
sickbed ['sɪkˌbɛd] *s.* lecho de enfermo.
sick book, (mil.) libro de reconocimiento (médico), libro de registro de enfermos.
sick call, (mil.) (toque de) visita médica.
sick day, (E.U.) día de permiso.
sicken ['sɪkən] *v.t.* 1. enfermar; marear. 2. hartar, hastiar, dar asco. —*v.i.* 1. enfermarse; nausear, marearse. 2. **s. of,** hartarse de, cansarse de.
sickener [-ər, B -ə] *s.* cosa que da asco; golpe contundente; dosis excesiva.
sickening [-ɪŋ] *a.* 1. nauseabundo, asqueroso, repugnante. 2. deprimente, desagradable, lamentable.
sickeningly [-ɪŋlɪ] *adv.* asquerosamente, repugnantemente.
sicker ['sɪkər, B -ə] *a.* (esco.) seguro, firme, leal, fiel, responsable.
sick flag, bandera amarilla (que indica que un barco está en cuarentena).
sick headache, migraña, jaqueca.
sickish ['sɪkɪʃ] *a.* enfermizo, enclenque, propenso a sentir náuseas.
sickishly [-lɪ] *adv.* provocando náuseas.
sickishness [-nəs] *s.* efecto nauseabundo.
sickle ['sɪkəl] *s.* hoz, segadera, falco.
sick leave, permiso por enfermedad, baja, licencia por enfermedad.
sickle cell, (med.) célula falciforme.
sickle-cell anemia, anemia drepanocítica, drepanocitosis.
sick list, lista de enfermos.
sickly ['sɪklɪ] *a.* (SICKLIER; SICKLIEST) 1. enfermizo, achacoso; enclenque, endeble, lánguido. 2. insalubre, malsano. 3. pálido, demacrado, macilento. 4. desdichado, infeliz (sonrisa, mirada, etc.). 5. nauseabundo, nauseoso. —*adv.* lánguidamente. —*v.t.* (*pret., p.p.* SICKLIED; *p.pr* SICKLYING) hacer enfermizo, endeble.
sickness [-nəs] *s.* 1. enfermedad; dolencia. 2. náusea.
sick pay, subsidio por enfermedad.
sickroom [-ˌrum, -ˌrʊm] *s.* cuarto de enfermo.
sick ward, pabellón de enfermos.
siddur [sɪ'dʊr, B 'sɪdə] *s.* (relig.) siddur (libro de plegarias de los judíos).
side [saɪd] *s.* 1. lado; costado, flanco. 2. lado, cara, faz, ej., *a cube has six sides,* el cubo tiene seis caras. 3. ladera, declive, falda (de una montaña, colina, etc.). 4. bando, facción, parte. 5. lado, margen, orilla. 6. lado, aspecto, fase, ej., *he studied all sides of the problem,* estudió el problema en todos sus aspectos. 7. lado, línea (genealógica). 8. (G.B.) equipo, ej., *Oxford has a strong s.,* Oxford tiene un buen equipo (de fútbol, etc.). 9. (mat., geom.) lado. 10. (teat.) papel, parte (de un actor). 11. (mar.) bordo, costado, banda (del buque). 12. (billar) efecto lateral. 13. (jer., G.B.) jactancia, engreimiento, aire. 14. **at my (his,** etc.) **s.,** a mi (su, etc.) lado; **by the s. of,** al lado de; **from all sides,** de todos lados; **on all sides,** por todas partes, por todos lados; **on both sides,** por ambas partes; **on every s.,** por todas partes, por todos lados; **on one s.,** a un lado, aparte; **on one's mother's** (o **father's**) **s.,** por parte de madre (o padre), por el lado materno (o paterno); **on the high s.,** bastante elevado (precio, etc.); **on the s.,** como negocio extra, aparte de su ocupación principal; **on the wrong s. of the tracks,** en el barrio pobre del pueblo, en circunstancias humildes; **on this s. (of) the grave,** con vida, vivo todavía; **s. by s.,** codo a codo; **s. of bacon,** lonja de tocino; **s. of mutton,** costado de carnero; **to be on someone's s.,** estar de parte de alguien; **to be on the right** (o **wrong**) **s. of fifty,** etc., tener menos (o más) de cincuenta (etc.) años; **to have on one's s.,** tener de su parte; **to take sides,** tomar partido; **to take someone's s., to take sides with someone,** ponerse de parte de alguien, ponerse al lado de alguien. —*a.* 1. lateral, ladero, colateral. 2. incidental, secundario; incidente, indirecto. 3. adicional. —*v.t.* 1. soportar, ayudar. 2. estar al lado de. 3. proveer de lados o caras. 4. (dial.) poner o desplazar a un lado, desechar, dejar de lado. —*v.i.* **s.with,** dar la razón a; aliarse con, ponerse de parte de.
side arm, arma portátil (que se lleva en el cinturón).
sidearm ['saɪdˌɑrm, B -ˌɑm] *a.* (béisbol) de lanzamiento lateral.
side armor, (mar.) coraza de costado (de un buque de guerra).
side band, (rad.) faja o banda lateral.
side bet, apuesta colateral, envite.
sideboard [-ˌbɔrd, B -bɔd] *s.* 1. aparador, bufete. 2. (*pl.*) (jer.) patillas.
sideburns [-ˌbɜrnz, B -ˌbɜnz] *s. pl.* patillas.
sidecar [-ˌkɑr, B -kɑ] *s.* 1. cochecito lateral (de una motocicleta). 2. cóctel de brandy, licor de naranja y zumo de limón.
side chapel, capilla o altar lateral.
sidecheck [-ˌtʃɛk] *s.* engallador (que va del bocado al cuello del caballo).
side clearance, 1. (maq.) juego o huelgo lateral. 2. (f.c.) franqueo lateral, espacio libre lateral.
side cutter, (mec.) fresa de disco, fresa reflenadora.
side dish, guarnición, plato adicional que acompaña al principal de una comida.
side door, puerta lateral, puerta accesoria; puerta falsa.
side effect, efecto secundario (gen. adverso de una droga, medicamento, etc.).
side-glance ['saɪdˌglæns, B -ˌglɑns] *s.* mirada de soslayo, mirada de través.
side grafting, (agr.) injerto de escudete.
sidehead [-ˌhɛd] *s.* título marginal, subtítulo, ladillo.
sidehill [-ˌhɪl] *s.* (E.U.) ladera, falda (de montañas). —*a.* a media ladera (camino, casa, etc.).
side issue, cuestión secundaria, asunto incidental.
sidekick [-ˌkɪk] *s.* 1. ayudante; socio. 2. (fam.) amigo íntimo; compinche.
sidelight [-ˌlaɪt] *s.* 1. luz lateral. 2. (fig.) información incidental; aspecto secundario. 3. (mar.) luz de situación (en buques).
sideline [-ˌlaɪn] 1. (fig.) negocio adicional, actividad suplementaria. 2. (f.c.) línea secundaria. 3. (dep.) línea de toque, línea lateral. 4. (*pl.*) (dep.) sitio fuera del campo (donde se colocan los jugadores suplentes). 5. **on the sidelines,** sin intervenir, sin tomar parte, desde la barrera.
sideling, sidling ['saɪdlɪŋ] *adv.* lateralmente, oblicuamente. —*a.* 1. inclinado. 2. oblicuo.
sidelong [-ˌlɔŋ] *adv.* lateralmente, oblicuamente. —*a.* 1. lateral, inclinado. 2. de soslayo, indirecto (mirada, etc.).
sideman [-ˌmæn] *s.* miembro de orquesta (esp. de baile).
sidenote [-ˌnoʊt] *s.* nota marginal.
sidepiece [-ˌpis] *s.* pieza o parte lateral.
side play, (mec.) juego lateral, holgura abierta.
side post, (arq.) jamba.
sidereal [saɪ'dɪrɪəl, B -'dɪərɪ-] *a.* (astr.) sideral, sidéreo, astral, estelar.
sidereal day, día sideral, día estelar, día sidéreo.
sidereal hour, hora sideral.
sidereal year, año sideral, año sidéreo.
siderite ['sɪdəˌraɪt, B 'saɪdə-] *s.* (min.) siderita, siderosa.
siderolite ['sɪdərəˌlaɪt] *s.* (geol.) siderolito.
siderosis [sɪdə'roʊsɪs] *s.* (med.) siderosis.
siderurgical [-'rɜrdʒɪkəl, B -'rɜdʒɪ-] *a.* (metal.) siderúrgico.
siderurgy ['sɪdəˌrɜrdʒɪ, B -ˌrɜdʒɪ] *s.* (metal.) siderurgia.
sidesaddle ['saɪdˌsædəl] *s.* jamuga, jamugas, silla de amazona; **to ride s.,** ir en jamugas, montar a mujeriegas, montar a asentadillas o sentadillas.
sideshow [-ˌʃoʊ] *s.* espectáculo secundario, exhibición secundaria; acción o actividad secundaria; (mil.) diversión.
sideslip [-ˌslɪp] *v.i.* 1. patinar, derrapar (un automóvil). 2. (aer.) resbalar (de ala). 3. (esgr.) deslizarse hacia un lado patinando. —*s.* 1. (mil.) rebasamiento. 2. (aer.) resbalamiento. 3. patinazo (de un automóvil).
sidespin [-ˌspɪn] *s.* efecto lateral, rotación horizontal (de una pelota, bola, etc.).
sidesplitting [-ˌsplɪtɪŋ] *a.* para desternillarse de risa. ej., *a s. joke,* un chiste para desternillarse de risa.
side step, 1. paso lateral. 2. (dep.) esguince, regate, quiebro, quite.
sidestep [-ˌstɛp] *v.i.* 1. dar un paso lateral. 2. regatear, hacer un movimiento evasivo, hacer un quite. 3. eludir responsabilidades, evadir decisiones, dejar a un lado, no tocar (un asunto). —*v.t.* 1. esquivar, evitar (un golpe, etc.). 2. evadir (una decisión).
sidestroke [-ˌstroʊk] *s.* brazada de costado (en natación).
sideswipe ['saɪdˌswaɪp] *v.t.* (fam.) golpear de refilón en un costado. —*s.* golpe de refilón.
sidetrack [-ˌtræk] *v.t.* 1. (f.c.) desviar, apartar. 2. (fam.) desviar, apartar, hacer cambiar (de tema, propósito, etc.), echar a un lado. —*s.* 1. (f.c.) apartadero, desvío, vía apartadera, vía derivada o lateral. 2. (fam.) desvío.
side view, 1. vista de costado o lateral. 2. (vista de) perfil.
sidewalk [-ˌwɔk] *s.* acera, vereda (Am.).
sidewalk superintendent, (hum.) mirón, espectador (en un trabajo de construcción o de demolición).
sidewall [-ˌwɔl] *s.* 1. pared lateral. 2. (aut.) costado, flanco (de neumático).
sideward ['saɪdwərd, B -wəd] **sidewards** [-wərdz, B -wədz] *a.* de lado, de costado; lateral. —*adv.* hacia un lado o costado.

sideway [-ˌweɪ] **sideways** [-ˌweɪz] *adv.* 1. de lado, de costado, de soslayo. 2. al través. 3. lateralmente, oblicuamente. —*a.* lateral, ladero.
side-wheel [-ˌhwil, -ˌwil] *a.* de ruedas laterales (díc. de un vapor).
side-wheeler [-ər, B -ə] *s.* vapor de ruedas laterales.
side whiskers, *s. pl.* patillas.
sidewinder [-ˌwaɪndər, B -ˌwaɪndə] *s.* 1. crótalo, serpiente de cascabel. 2. (jer.) golpe de costado.
sidewise [-ˌwaɪz] *adv.* 1. de lado, de costado, de soslayo. 2. al través. 3. lateralmente, oblicuamente. —*a.* lateral, ladero.
siding ['saɪdɪŋ] *s.* 1. (f.c.) desvío, apartadero, desviadero. 2. (E.U.) tablas de forro, tablas de chilla.
sidle ['saɪdəl] *v.i.* moverse furtivamente, andar tímida o rastreramente; **s. up to,** acercarse furtivamente a (alguien). —*s.* movimiento furtivo, andar tímido y rastrero.
siege [sidʒ] *s.* 1. sitio, cerco; bloqueo, asedio. 2. largo período (de enfermedad, etc.). 3. temporada de disgustos y molestias. 4. (fam.) (con *of*) montón, serie (de enfermedades, sinsabores, etc.). 5. (ant.) lugar, sitio. 6. (ant.) trono, sitial. 7. **to lay s. to,** poner sitio a; **to raise the s. of,** levantar el sitio de (una plaza). —*v.t.* sitiar; asediar, bloquear.
siege artillery, artillería de plaza, artillería de sitio.
siege basket, (fort.) gavión.
Siegfried ['sigfrid] *s.* Sigfrido, héroe de la épica germánica.
sienna [sɪ'ɛnə] *s.* tierra de siena.
sierra [sɪ'ɛrə] *s.* 1. sierra, cordillera. 2. (ict.) pez sierra, priste.
Sierra Leone [-lɪ'oʊn] República de Sierra Leona.
sierran [-'ɛrən] *s.* 1. serrano. 2. S., (E.U.) de la Sierra Nevada.
siesta [sɪ'ɛstə] *s.* siesta.
sieve [sɪv] *s.* 1. cedazo, tamiz, criba, cernidor, harnero, zaranda, coladera. 2. (fam.) persona incapaz de guardar un secreto. —*v.t.* cerner, tamizar, cribar, colar. —*v.i.* pasar por un cedazo o tamiz.
sieve tube, (bot.) tubo criboso.
sift [sɪft] *v.t.* 1. cerner, cernir, tamizar, cribar, zarandar, colar. 2. (fig.) separar, seleccionar, entresacar. 3. (fig.) examinar, escudriñar. 4. esparcir, regar con (usando cernidor, etc.). —*v.i.* 1. filtrarse, pasarse. 2. seleccionar, hacer distinciones.
sifter ['sɪftər, B -ə] *s.* 1. tamiz fino, cedazo (de harina). 2. escudriñador.
sifting [-ɪŋ] *s.* 1. cernido. 2. (*pl.*) (material) cernido, granzas.
sigh [saɪ] *v.i.* 1. suspirar, dar un quejido. 2. **s. for,** suspirar por, desear con ansia, añorar. —*v.t.* 1. decir suspirando. 2. lamentar con suspiros. —*s.* suspiro; **to breathe a s. of (relief, weariness,** etc.), dar un suspiro de (alivio, cansancio, etc.).
sigher ['saɪər, B -ə] *s.* el que suspira.
sighingly [-ɪŋlɪ] *adv.* con suspiros.
sight [saɪt] *s.* 1. vista, visión. 2. vista, vistazo, mirada, observación. 3. percepción, perspicacia. 4. vista, perspectiva, campo visual. 5. espectáculo, algo digno de verse; (*gen.pl.*) lugar de interés, ej., *they went to see the sights,* fueron a ver los lugares de interés (de la ciudad, etc.). 6. espectáculo ridículo; visión, espantajo, facha (persona). 7. mira (de armas, instrumentos ópticos, etc.). 8. (fam.) gran cantidad, montón, ej., *it is a long s. worse,* es mucho peor. 9. **a s. for sore eyes,** una vista deleitable; persona grata (cuya vista da placer a uno); **at (u on) s.,** a primera vista; **at first s.,** a primera vista; a la vista; **by s.,** de vista; **can not stand the s. of (someone),** no poder ver (a alguien) ni pintado; **in s.,** visible; **out of my s.!** ¡ retírese de mi presencia!; **out of s.,** fuera de la vista; **out of s., out of mind,** ojos que no ven corazón que no siente; **payable at s.,** (com.) pagadero a la vista; to **be in s.** of, estar al alcance de la vista de; **to catch s. of,** avistar; **to come in s.,** aparecer, divisarse, asomar; **to get s.** of, divisar; avistar; **to keep s. of,** no perder de vista; **to know by s.,** conocer de vista; **to lose s. of,** perder de vista; no haber visto hace tiempo, ej., *I have lost s. of him,* no lo he visto hace tiempo; **to make a s. of oneself,** ir hecho una facha (Esp.), vestirse de manera extravagante; **to play music at s.,** repentizar (música); **to put out of s.,** esconder; no tomar en cuenta, pasar por alto; **sight unseen,** sin examinar, sin ver (algo). —*v.t.* 1. (mar.) avistar, divisar, ver, descubrir con la vista. 2. apuntar (con mira); ajustar la mira de (rifles). 3. equipar con miras. —*v.i.* 1. (con *down, along,* etc.) mirar detenidamente (por, a lo largo de, etc.). 2. apuntar hacia.
sight draft, (com.) letra a la vista, documento a la vista.
sighted ['saɪtəd] *a.* 1. *ú. en palabras compuestas,* ej., *clear-s.,* perspicaz, *quick-s.,* de vista aguda. 2. con sentido de la vista, con visión. 3. provisto de mira (armas, etc.).
sight glass, vidrio de nivel, tubo indicador.
sighthole [-ˌhoul] *s.* atisbadero, mirilla, ventanilla.
sighting [-ɪŋ] *s.* (top.) puntería.
sighting shot, tiro de prueba (para poder ajustar la mira).
sightless [-ləs] *a.* 1. ciego. 2. (poét.) invisible.
sightliness [-lɪnəs] *s.* vistosidad.
sightly [-lɪ] *a.* (SIGHTLIER; SIGHTLIEST) 1. agradable a la vista, de aspecto agradable, vistoso, hermoso. 2. (E.U.) con vista amena (casa, etc.).
sight-read [-ˌrid] *v.t.* leer (una lengua extranjera, etc.) a primera vista; (mús.) repentizar.
sight reticle, (top.) retículo del colimar.
sight rhyme, rima falsa, rima imperfecta (de coincidencia ortográfica pero no fonética).
sight rod, (top.) jalón, vara de agrimensor.
sight-seeing [-ˌsiɪŋ] *a.* que visita lugares de interés. —*s.* visita a lugares de interés.
sight-seer [-ˌsiər, B -ˌsiə] *s.* visitante de lugares de interés; turista.
sigil ['sɪdʒəl] *s.* 1. sello, sigilo. 2. (astrol.) palabra mágica, signo cabalístico.
Sigismund ['sɪgɪsmənd] *s.* Segismundo, emperador del Sacro Imperio Romano-Germánico.
sigma ['sɪgmə] *s.* sigma, decimoctava letra del alfabeto griego.
sigmate ['sɪgˌmeɪt, B -mət] *a.* en forma de sigma o de S.
sigmoid [-ˌmɔɪd] **sigmoidal** [sɪg'mɔɪdəl] *a.* (anat.) sigmoide, sigmoideo.
sigmoid flexure, (anat.) flexura sigmoidea, colon sigmoide.
Sigmund ['sɪgmənd] *s.* Segismundo, padre de Sigfrido en la épica germánica.
sign [saɪn] *s.* 1. signo, símbolo. 2. gesto, seña, señal, ademán, indicación. 3. letrero, rótulo, aviso. 4. muestra, prueba. 5. signo, señal, portento, indicio, augurio. 6. vestigio, huella, rastro, traza. 7. (astr.) signo (del zodíaco). 8. (caza) (E.U.) huella, rastro. 9. (mat.) signo. 10. (med.) síntoma, signo, señal. 11. (mús.) signo. 12. **s. and countersign,** santo y seña, contraseña; **signs of the times,** señales de los tiempos; **to make no s.,** no dar señales; **to show signs of,** dar muestras de; **to use s. language,** hablar por señas. —*v.t.* 1. firmar; rubricar, suscribir, señalar, marcar. 2. indicar, señalar, dar señal de. 3. persignar, signar, santiguar. 4. proveer de señales de tráfico. 5. **s. away,** ceder (gen. con prodigalidad); **s. on,** emplear bajo firma o contrato; **s. over,** traspasar, ceder; **s. up,** cerrar el contrato con (cliente); contratar; **s. up with,** (fam.) fichar por. —*v.i.* 1. firmar, poner firma. 2. hacer señas. 3. **s. on,** trabajar o emplearse bajo contrato; **s. off,** (rad.) cortar la transmisión, finalizar el programa, anunciar el fin del programa; **s. up,** firmar el contrato; aceptar el empleo; **s. up for,** firmar un contrato por.
signal ['sɪgnəl] *s.* 1. señal, seña, contraseña. 2. aviso, indicación. 3. (elec.) señal (de telegrafía, etc.). —*a.* notable, memorable, insigne, señalado; de proporciones, ej., *a s. defeat,* una derrota de proporciones. —*v.t., v.i.* (*pret., p.p.* SIGNALED O SIGNALLED; *p.pr.* SIGNALING O SIGNALLING) comunicar, indicar, avisar u ordenar por señales.
signal board, cuadro de señales.
signal book, código de señales.
signal box, (f.c., G.B.) cabina de cambio de agujas, garita de señales, torre de señales.
signal code, código de señales.
signal corps, (mil., E.U.) servicio de transmisiones, cuerpo de transmisiones.
signaler, signaller [-ər, B -ə] *s.* 1. señalador, aparato o mecanismo de señales. 2. (mil.) señaladero. 3. (f.c.) guardabarreras, semaforista.
signal flag, bandera de señales.
signal flare, bengala de señales.
signal generator, (rad.) generador de señales, oscilador de toda onda, heterodina.
signaling, signalling [-ɪŋ] *s.* 1. señalización. 2. ademanes para llamar la atención. 3. (mil.) transmisión de señales.
signalization [ˌsɪgnələ'zeɪʃən, B -aɪ'zeɪ-] *s.* 1. señalamiento. 2. instalación de señales (de tránsito, etc.).
signalize ['sɪgnəlˌaɪz] *v.t.* 1. señalar, marcar. 2. indicar, destacar, singularizar. 3. hacer señales a, indicar por señales a. 4. poner señales de tránsito en (una calle, intersección, etc.).
signally [-ɪ] *adv.* notablemente, señaladamente, en forma insigne.
signalman [-mən, -ˌmæn] *s.* 1. (mil.) señaladero. 2. (f.c.) guardabarreras, guardavía, semaforista. 3. escotillero (en descarga de buques).
signalment [-mənt] *s.* marca, descripción por marcas características (de identificación, esp. de los criminales).
signal meter, (rad.) medidor de la intensidad de señal.
signal noise ratio, (rad.) relación de señal a ruido.
signal officer, (mil.) oficial de transmisiones.
signal panel, (mil.) cuadro de señales.
signal rocket, cohete de señales.
signal strength, (rad.) intensidad de señal.
signal tower, (f.c.) garita de señales, torre de señales, cabina de cambio de agujas.
signatory ['sɪgnəˌtɔrɪ, B -tərɪ] *a.* firmante, signatario. —*s.* (*pl.* SIGNATORIES) firmante, signatario.
signature [-tʃər, B -tʃə] *s.* 1. firma, rúbrica. 2. (mús., impr.) signatura. 3. (farm.) indicaciones (para el paciente) en una receta. 4. (rad., t.v.) señal (musical) de identificación. 5. (ant.) marca.
signboard ['saɪnˌbɔrd, B -bɔd] *s.* letrero; tablero de anuncios.

signer [-ər, B -ə] *s.* firmante, signatario, infrascripto.
signet ['sɪgnət] *s.* 1. sello, signáculo, timbre (esp. en documentos oficiales). 2. sello, impresión (que deja un sello). —*v.t.* sellar.
signet ring, sortija con sello, anillo de sello.
significance [sɪg'nɪfɪkəns] *s.* 1. significación, significado. 2. significación, importancia.
significancy [-kənsɪ] *s.* (*pl.* SIGNIFICANCIES) *var. de* **significance.**
significant [-kənt] *a.* 1. significativo, sugestivo. 2. significante, significativo, importante.
significant figures, (mat.) cifras significativas.
significantly [-kəntlɪ] *adv.* significativamente.
signification [ˌsɪgnəfə'keɪʃən] *s.* 1. significación. 2. notificación (de un decreto judicial, etc.). 3. significado, sentido.
significative [sɪg'nɪfəˌkeɪtɪv, B -kət-] *a.* significativo.
significatively [-lɪ] *adv.* significativamente.
signifier ['sɪgnəˌfaɪər, B -ˌfaɪə] *s.* significado, signo.
signify ['sɪgnəˌfaɪ] *v.t.* (*pret., p.p.* SIGNIFIED; *p.pr.* SIGNIFYING) significar. —*v.i.* significar, tener importancia.
signing [saɪnɪŋ] *s.* 1. firma. rúbrica. 2. lenguaje de gestos.
sign language, lenguaje mímico de gestos, lenguaje gestual; **to talk in s.,** hablar por señas.
sign manual, (*pl.* SIGNS MANUAL) rúbrica, firma (esp. la del soberano en un documento real).
sign of the cross, señal de la cruz.
signory ['sinjərɪ] *var. de* **seigniory.**
signpost ['saɪnˌpoʊst] *s.* hito, pilar de guía, poste de dirección, poste indicador; (fig.) guía, faro.
sike [saɪk] *s.* (dial., G.B.) arroyuelo, riachuelo.
Sikh [sik] *s.* sikh, miembro de una secta religiosa de la India.
Sikhism ['sikˌɪzəm] *s.* sikhismo, religión de una secta de la India.
silage ['saɪlɪdʒ] (agr.) *s.* ensilaje. —*v.t.* ensilar.
silence ['saɪləns] *s.* silencio; **in s.,** en silencio; **s. is golden,** el silencio es oro; **to keep s.,** guardar silencio. —*v.t.* 1. callar, pasar en silencio. 2. silenciar, acallar, imponer silencio a. 3. aquietar, calmar, tranquilizar. 4. (mil.) silenciar (la artillería enemiga, etc.), apagar (el fuego enemigo). —*interj.* ¡silencio!
silencer [-lənsər, B -sə] *s.* silenciador.
silent ['saɪlənt] *a.* 1. callado, silencioso, taciturno. 2. silencioso, quieto. 3. inactivo (por ej. un volcán). 4. muda (película de cine). 5. (fon.) muda (letra). 6. **to be s.,** callar.
silent butler, recogedor de colillas (receptáculo con tapa en el que se vacía el contenido de los ceniceros en el transcurso de una reunión).
silent chain, (mec.) cadena silenciosa, cadena sorda.
silent majority, mayoria silenciosa.
silent partner, (com.) socio comanditario, socio capitalista.
silent picture, (cine) película muda.
silent service, (ú. con *the*) (fam.) la marina; (esp. en E.U.) el servicio de submarinos.
Silenus [saɪ'linəs] *s.* (mitol.) Sileno, dios de los bosques.
silesia [saɪ'liʃə, B -'lizjə] *s.* (tej.) linón de algodón.
Silesian [-ʃən, B -zjən] *a., s.* silesiano, silesio, de una región de Polonia.
silex ['saɪˌlɛks] *s.* (quím.) sílice; silex, pedernal.
silhouette [ˌsɪlʊ'ɛt] *s.* silueta, perfil. —*v.t.* (ú. gen. en voz pasiva) dibujar la silueta de, perfilar; proyectar en silueta, destacar sobre el horizonte.
silica ['sɪlɪkə] *s.* (min.) sílice.
silica gel, (quím.) sílice gelatinosa.
silicate ['sɪləˌkeɪt, B -ɪkət] *s.* (quím.) silicato.
silicate cotton, lana mineral.
siliceous [sə'lɪʃəs] **silicious** [sə'lɪʃəs] *a.* silíceo.
silicic [-'lɪsɪk] *a.* (quím.) silícico.
silicic acid, (quím.) ácido silícico.
silicicolous [ˌsɪlə'sɪkələs] *a.* (bot.) silicícolo.
silicide ['sɪləˌsaɪd] *s.* (quím.) siliciuro.
siliciferous [ˌsɪlə'sɪfərəs] *a.* silíceo.
silicification [səˌlɪsəfə'keɪʃən] *s.* silicificación.
silicify [sə'lɪsəˌfaɪ] *v.t., v.i.* (*pret., p.p.* SILICIFIED; *p.pr.* SILICIFYING) silicificar, convertir(se) en sílice, impregnar(se) con sílice.
silicle ['sɪlɪkəl] *s.* (bot.) silícula.
silicon ['sɪlɪkən] *s.* (quím.) silicio.
silicon chip, (comput.) pastilla de silicio.
silicon wafer, (comput.) lámina de silicio.
silicone ['sɪləˌkoʊn] *s.* (quím.) silicón, silicona.
silicosis [sɪlə'koʊsəs] *s.* (med.) silicosis.
siliculose [sə'lɪkjəˌloʊs] **siliculous** [-ləs] *a.* (bot.) siliculiforme, siliculoso.
silique [sə'lik] *s.* (bot.) silicua.
siliquose ['sɪləˌkwoʊs] **siliquous** [-kwəs] *a.* (bot.) silicuiforme; silicuoso.
silk [sɪlk] *s.* 1. seda. 2. (ú. esp. en *pl.*) sedería. 3. (G.B.) toga de seda (usada por abogados de la más alta jerarquía). 4. **all s.,** pura seda. —*a.* de seda; **to make a s. purse out of a sow's ear,** producir una cosa fina de material burdo o por medios inadecuados. —*v.i.* (E.U.) madurar (maíz).
silkaline, silkoline [ˌsɪlkə'lin] *s.* (tej.) sedalina.
silk cotton, (tej.) lana vegetal.
silk-cotton tree, (bot.) ceiba de lana, árbol de algodón.
silk culture, sericultura.
silken ['sɪlkən] *a.* 1. sedoso, sedeño, sedero. 2. lustroso, suave, delicado. 3. vestido de seda.
silk floss, kapok, capoc.
silk goods, géneros de seda.
silk hat, sombrero de copa, chistera.
silkily [-kəlɪ] *adv.* suavemente.
silk industry, industria sedera.
silkiness [-kɪnəs] *s.* 1. aspecto sedoso. 2. suavidad.
silk-screen print, serigrafía, impresión con estarcido de seda.
silk serge, sarga.
silk stocking, 1. media de seda. 2. persona encopetada; persona aristocrática. 3. (E.U., hist.) federalista.
silk-stocking ['sɪlk'stɑkɪŋ, B -'stɔk-] *a.* 1. elegante; lujoso. 2. aristocrático; adinerado, rico. 3. (E.U., hist.) del partido federalista.
silkweed [-ˌwid] *s.* (bot.) algodoncillo.
silkworm [-ˌwɜrm, B -wɜm] *s.* (ento.) gusano de seda.
silky ['sɪlkɪ] *a.* (SILKIER; SILKIEST) 1. sedoso, sedeño. 2. suave (sonido, voz).
sill [sɪl] *s.* 1. antepecho, alféizar (de ventana), umbral (de puerta). 2. (arq.) solera; durmiente. 3. (mar.) batiporte (de la porta de una batería).
sillabub ['sɪləˌbʌb] *s.* 1. manjar de leche, crema o nata dulces y vino o sidra. 2. (fig.) lenguaje florido.
sillily ['sɪləlɪ] *adv.* tontamente, disparatadamente.
sillimanite ['sɪləməˌnaɪt] *s.* (min.) silimanita.
silliness [-ɪnəs] *s.* tontera, simpleza, bobada.
silly ['sɪlɪ] *a.* (SILLIER; SILLIEST) 1. necio, tonto, bobo; absurdo, ridículo. 2. rústico, simple; cándido, inocente. 3. (esco., N. de G.B.) débil, enfermizo. 4. (ant.) humilde, desamparado. —*s.* (fam.) tonto, bobo.
silo ['saɪloʊ] (agr.) *s.* (*pl.* SILOS) silo, granero, silero. —*v.t.* ensilar.
silt [sɪlt] *s.* cieno, légamo, limo, sedimento del lodo —*v.t., v.i.* obstruir(se) con cieno o légamo, entarquinarse.
silty ['sɪltɪ] *a.* (SILTIER; SILTIEST) cenagoso, legamoso, lodoso.
silundum [sɪ'lʌndəm] *s.* (min.) silundo.
Silurian [sɪ'lʊrɪən, B saɪ'ljʊər-] *a., s.* (geol.) silúrico, siluriano.
silurid [-əd] *a.* (ict.) silúrido.
siluroid ['sɪljəˌrɔɪd] *s., a.* (ict.) siluroideo.
silva ['sɪlvə] *s.* (*pl.* SILVAS O SILVAE [-ˌvi]) 1. árboles silvestres (de una región o un país en conjunto). 2. tratado sobre los árboles (de una región o un país).
silvan, *var. de* **sylvan.**
Silvanus [sɪl'veɪnəs] *s.* (mitol.) Silvano, dios de los bosques y los prados.
silver ['sɪlvər, B -və] *s.* 1. plata. 2. plata, moneda o monedas de plata; suelto, sencillo (Am.). 3. servicio o vajilla de plata, plata labrada. 4. color plateado. 5. **speech is s. but silence is golden,** bueno es hablar pero mejor es callar. —*a.* 1. de plata. 2. argentado, argentino. 3. (fig.) argentino (voz, etc.) 4. blanco, cano (pelo, cabellera). 5. argentífero (mineral). —*v.t.* 1. platear, argentar. 2. azogar (espejo). 3. blanquear, volver cano.
silver age, 1. (mitol.) edad de plata, una de las cuatro edades mitológicas del hombre. 2. (lit.) **S. A.,** edad de plata, siglo de plata de la lit. latina.
silver anniversary, vigésimo quinto aniversario; bodas de plata.
silver bath, (foto.) baño de (nitrato de) plata.
silver-bearing [-'bɛrɪŋ, B -'bɛər-] *a.* (geol.) argentífero.
silver bromide, 1. (quím.) bromuro de plata. 2. (min.) bromirita.
silver bullion, plata en barras o lingotes.
silver certificate, (com.) certificado de plata.
silver chloride, (quím.) cloruro de plata.
silver doctor, (pesca) mosca artificial.
silver dollar, dólar de plata.
silverer ['sɪlvərər, B -ə] *s.* plateador.
silver fir, (bot.) abeto blanco.
silverfish ['sɪlvərˌfɪʃ, B 'sɪlvəˌ-] *s.* 1. (ict.) pez plateado. 2. (ento.) lepisma, pescadito de plata.
silver foil, hoja de plata, pan de plata.
silver fox, (zool.) zorro plateado.
silveriness ['sɪlvərɪnəs] *s.* 1. viso o aspecto plateado, brillo argentino. 2. (fig.) suavidad (de tono, voz, etc.).
silvering [-ɪŋ] *s.* capa o baño de plata; plateadura; plateado.
silver iodide, 1. (quím.) yoduro de plata. 2. (min.) yodirita.
silver jubilee, vigésimo quinto aniversario.
silver lining, 1. borde blanco (de una nube). 2. (fig.) perspectiva consoladora. 3. **every cloud has a s. l.,** no hay mal que por bien no venga.
silver litharge, (quím.) litargirio de plata.
silverly ['sɪlvərlɪ, B -vəlɪ] *adv.* 1. con viso plateado, plateado, argentado. 2. con sonido argentino.
silvern [-vərn, B -vən] *a.* (ant.) de plata, plateado.
silver nitrate, (quím.) nitrato de plata.
silver paper, papel plateado, hoja o papel de estaño, platina (Amer.).
silver perch, (ict.) perca blanca (del E. de los E.U.).
silver plate, 1. plaqué, plateado, revestimiento de plata. 2. vajilla de plata, platería (Am.).
silver-plate, *v.t* platear.
silver-plating, *s.* plateado, plateadura, plaqué.

silver screen, the s. s., (fig.) la pantalla cinematográfica.
silversmith [-vər,smɪθ, B -və,-] *s.* platero, orfebre de plata.
silver standard, patrón de plata (en sistema monetario).
silver-tongued [-'tʌŋd] *a.* elocuente, fácil de palabra, de pico de oro.
silverware [-,wɛr, B -wɛə] *s.* servicio de mesa, plata labrada, vajilla de plata, plateria (Amer.).
silver wedding, bodas de plata.
silverweed [-,wid] *s.* (bot.) argentina; potentila, pontentilla.
silvery ['sɪlvərɪ] *a.* 1. argénteo, argentino (brillo, viso, etc.). 2. argentoso, argentífero. 3. argénteo, de plata. 4. (fig.) argentino, suave (voz, tono, etc.).
silviculture ['sɪlvə,kʌltʃər, B -tʃə] *s.* silvicultura, cultivo de bosques.
silviculturist [,sɪlvə'kʌltʃərəst] *s.* silvicultor.
simarouba [,sɪmə'rubə] *s.* (bot.) simaruba.
simaroubaceous [,sɪməru'beɪʃəs] *a.* (bot.) simarubáceo.
Simeon Stylites ['sɪmɪənstaɪ'laɪtiz] Simeón Estilita, anacoreta y estilita sirio.
simian ['sɪmɪən] *a.* símico, simiesco. —*s.* simio, mono.
similar ['sɪmələr, B -lə] *a.* similar, semejante, parecido.
similarity [,sɪmə'lærətɪ] *s.* (*pl.* SIMILARITIES) similitud, semejanza, parecido.
similarly ['sɪmələrlɪ, B -ləlɪ] *adv.* 1. similarmente, de igual manera, semejantemente. 2. asimismo.
simile ['sɪməlɪ] *s.* (ret.) símil.
similitude [sə'mɪlətud, B -tjud] *s.* 1. similitud, parecido, semejanza. 2. símil, comparación. 3. sosia, sosias, alter-ego. 4. semejante, imagen.
simious ['sɪmɪəs] *a.* simiesco, símico.
simmer ['sɪmər, B -ə] *v.i., v.t.* cocer o hervir a fuego lento; **s. down,** calmarse gradualmente, sosegarse lentamente; **s. with rage,** hervir de rabia contenida.
simnel ['sɪmnəl] *s.* (G.B.) 1. especie de bizcocho o pan hecho con harina fina. 2. torta de frutas (para Navidad o Pascua Florida).
simoleon [sɪ'moʊlɪən] *s.* (jer., E.U.) dólar.
simoniac [saɪ'moʊnɪ,æk] *s., a.* simoníaco, simoniático.
simoniacal [,saɪmə'naɪəkəl] *a.* simoníaco, simoniático.
simonist ['saɪmənəst] *s.* simoníaco, simoniático.
simonize ['saɪmə,naɪz] *v.t.* abrillantar, lustrar con cera (esp. un automóvil).
Simon Legree [,saɪmənlə'gri] (fig.) negrero (del personaje del libro La Cabaña del Tío Tom).
simon-pure [-'pjʊr, B -'pjʊə] *a.* genuino, auténtico, puro.
simony ['saɪmənɪ] *s.* (*pl.* SIMONIES) simonía.
simoom [sə'mum] **simoon** [sə'mun] *s.* simún, viento abrasador del desierto.
simp [sɪmp] *s.* (jer.) bobo, zonzo (Amer.), mentecato.
simper ['sɪmpər, B -pə] *v.i.* sonreír tontamente. —*v.t.* decir sonriendo tontamente. —*s.* sonrisa tonta.
simperingly ['sɪmpərɪŋlɪ] *adv.* con una sonrisa tonta.
simple ['sɪmpəl] *a.* (SIMPLER; SIMPLEST) 1. simple, solo, mero. 2. sencillo, llano. 3. simple, natural, sin afectación. 4. humilde, sencillo, ej., *the s. life,* la vida sencilla. 5. simple, inocente, ingenuo. 6. ignorante, cándido; necio, zonzo (Amer.). 7. (mús., bot., quím.) simple. —*s.* 1. persona de humilde condición o alcurnia. 2. simple, simplón. 3. (farm.) simple.
simple beauty, belleza natural.
simple contract, (der.) contrato simple, contrato informal.
simple engine, máquina de simple expansión.
simple equation, (mat.) ecuación de primer grado.
simple eye, (zool.) ojo simple.
simple fraction, (mat.) quebrado o fracción común.
simple fracture, (med.) fractura simple.
simple interest, (fin.) interés simple.
simple larceny, (der.) hurto sencillo.
simple machine, máquina simple, mecanismo elemental.
simple-minded [-'maɪndəd] *a.* cándido, candoroso; ingenuo, confiado; zonzo (Amer.), tonto.
simple-mindedly [-lɪ] *adv.* cándidamente, candorosamente; ingenuamente; zonzamente, tontamente.
simple-mindedness [-nəs] *s.* candidez, candor; ingenuidad; simpleza, zoncería, tontería.
simple motion, (mec.) movimiento simple.
simpleness ['sɪmpəlnəs] *s.* sencillez, simpleza.
simple ore, mineral de un solo metal.
simple pendulum, (fís.) péndulo simple.
simple quantity, (mat.) número simple.
simple radical, (quím.) radical simple.
simple sentence, (gram.) oración simple.
Simple Simon, 1. bobo, simplón, bobalicón. 2. el tonto Simón (personaje de una canción infantil).
simpleton ['sɪmpəltən] *s.* simplón, bobalicón, papanatas.
simplex ['sɪm,plɛks] *a.* 1. simple, sencillo. 2. simplex, unidireccional (telegrafía).
simplicidentate [,sɪmplɪsə'dɛnteɪt] *a.* (zool.) simplicidentado.
simplicity [sɪm'plɪsətɪ] *s.* (*pl.* SIMPLICITIES) 1. simplicidad, sencillez, llaneza. 2. sencillez, rusticidad. 3. simpleza, tontería.
simplification [,sɪmpləfə'keɪʃən] *s.* simplificación.
simplifier ['sɪmplə,faɪər, B -faɪə] *s.* simplificador.
simplify [-,faɪ] *v.t.* (*pret., p.p.* SIMPLIFIED; *p.pr.* SIMPLIFYING) simplificar.
simplism ['sɪm,plɪzəm] *s.* 1. simplismo. 2. idea simplista, simplificación exagerada.
simplistic [sɪm'plɪstɪk] *a.* simplista.
simply ['sɪmplɪ] *adv.* 1. simplemente, sencillamente. 2. meramente, solamente. 3. (fam.) de veras, de verdad, realmente, verdaderamente, absolutamente. 4. tontamente.
simulacrum [,sɪmjʊ'leɪkrəm] *s.* (*pl.* SIMULACRA [-krə] o SIMULACRUMS) 1. simulacro, imagen. 2. imitación, farsa, apariencia.
simulant ['sɪmjʊlənt] *a., s.* simulador.
simulate ['sɪmjə,leɪt] *v.t.* simular, fingir.
simulation [,sɪmjə'leɪʃən] *s.* 1. simulación, fingimiento. 2. imitación.
simulator ['sɪmjə,leɪtər, B -,leɪtə] *s.* simulador.
simulcast ['saɪməl,kæst, B 'sɪm-,kɑst] *v.t., v.i.* transmitir simultáneamente (por radio y televisión). —*s.* transmisión simultánea (de un programa por radio y televisión).
simultaneity [,saɪməltə'niətɪ, B ,sɪməl-] *s.* simultaneidad.
simultaneous [-'teɪnɪəs] *a.* simultáneo.
simultaneous equations, (mat.) ecuaciones simultáneas.
simultaneously [-'teɪnɪəslɪ] *adv.* simultáneamente.
simultaneousness [-nəs] *s.* simultaneidad.
sin [sɪn] *s.* pecado, vicio, culpa, transgresión; **for my sins,** (hum.) para expiar mis pecados; **mortal s.,** pecado mortal; **the seven deadly sins,** los siete pecados capitales. —*v.i.* (*pret., p.p.* SINNED; *p.pr.* SINNING) pecar. —*v.t.* cometer (pecados).
sinalbin [sə'nælbən] *s.* (quím.) sinalbina.
sinapine ['sɪnəpaɪn, B -pɪn] *s.* (quím.) sinapina.
sinapism ['sɪnə,pɪzəm] *s.* (med.) sinapismo.
since [sɪns] *adv.* desde entonces, hace; **long s.,** desde hace mucho tiempo. —*prep.* desde, después de, a contar de, a partir de. —*conj.* 1. desde que, después (de) que. 2. ya que, puesto que, en vista (de que). 3. **ever s.,** desde que . . . siempre.
sincere [sɪn'sɪr, B -'sɪə] *a.* 1. sincero, franco. 2. sincero, veraz, genuino. 3. (ant.) puro, sin diluir.
sincerely [-lɪ] *adv.* sinceramente.
sincereness [-nəs] *s.* sinceridad.
sincerity [-'sɛrətɪ] *s.* sinceridad, franqueza.
sincipital [sɪn'sɪpətəl] *a.* (anat.) sincipital.
sinciput ['sɪnsə,pʌt] *s.* (anat.) sincipucio.
sine [saɪn] *s.* (mat.) seno. — ['saɪnɪ] *prep.* (lat.) sin.
sine bar, (mec.) regla de senos.
sinecure ['saɪnɪ,kjʊr, B -kjʊə] *s.* 1. canonjía (beneficio eclesiástico). 2. sinecura, prebenda, canonjía.
sine curve, (mat.) sinusoide, curva sinusoide, curva sinusoidal.
sine law, (mat.) ley senoidal.
sinew ['sɪnju] *s.* 1. tendón. 2. (fig.) fibra, vigor. 3. (fig.) (*gen. pl.*) sostén. 4. (fig.) (*pl.*) recursos, elementos, ej., *sinews of war,* elementos para la guerra. 5. (ant.) nervio. —*v.t.* reforzar, fortalecer.
sine wave, (mat., rad., electrón.) onda sinusoidal.
sinewy [-ɪ] *a.* 1. tendinoso, nervudo. 2. fibroso, estropajoso (carne, etc.). 3. (fig.) fuerte, vigoroso.
sinfonia [,sɪnfə'niə] *s.* (*pl.* SINFONIE [-'ni,eɪ]) (mús.) sinfonía, obertura (de óperas italianas primitivas).
sinfonietta [,sɪnfən'jɛtə] *s.* (mús.) pequeña orquesta sinfónica de cuerdas; sinfonía corta para orquesta pequeña.
sinful ['sɪnfəl] *a.* pecaminoso.
sinfully [-fəlɪ] *adv* pecaminosamente.
sinfulness [-fəlnəs] *s.* carácter pecaminoso, maldad.
sing [sɪŋ] *v.i.* (*pret.* SANG [sæŋ] *o* SUNG [sʌŋ] *p.p.* SUNG; *p.pr.* SINGING) 1. cantar. 2. murmurar (el agua); silbar (proyectiles, aves); zumbar (oídos). 3. (jer.) soplar, dar información. 4. **s. out,** dar un grito. —*v.t.* cantar; **s. a different tune,** cambiar de tono, cambiar de actitud; **s. one's praises,** colmar de alabanzas a uno; **s. out,** pregonar, anunciar en voz alta; despedir (ej., año viejo) cantando; **s. (a child) to sleep,** arrullar (a un niño). —*s.* 1. (fam.) canto; cantata. 2. zumbido, silbido (de balas).
sing. *abrev. de* **singular,** singular.
singable ['sɪŋəbəl] *a.* cantable.
Singapore ['sɪŋgə,pɔr, B ,sɪŋgə'pɔ] *s.* Singapur, isla y ciudad al S. de la península de Malaya.
singe [sɪndʒ] *v.t.* chamuscar, socarrar, sollamar, quemar las puntas de (pelo, plumas, etc.). —*s.* chamusquina, socarra, quemadura leve.
singer ['sɪŋər, B -ə] *s.* cantante, cantor (hombre); cantante, cantatriz, cantora (mujer).
Singhalese [,sɪŋgə'liz] *a., s.* cingalés, de Ceilán.
singing ['sɪŋɪŋ] *s.* 1. canto. 2. reunión de canto. 3. silbido (de balas, etc.). 4. zumbido (en el oído). —*a.* 1. cantante. 2. (orn.) cantor.
singing arc, (elec.) arco cantante.

singing bird, ave cantora o canora.
singing school, escuela de canto.
single ['sɪŋgəl] *a.* 1. único. 2. individual, particular. 3. singular, solo, aislado. 4. individual, personal, cuerpo a cuerpo (lucha, combate, etc.). 5. soltero, célibe. 6. honesto, sincero, recto. 7. simple, sencillo. 8. singular, extraordinario. 9. (electrón.) disco sencillo. —*v.t.* **s. out,** escoger, elegir, separar; singularizar, particularizar. —*v.i.* 1. caminar (un caballo) a paso fino. 2. (béisbol) pasar a primera base. —*s.* 1. individuo; persona; cosa, objeto. 2. (béisbol) primera base. 3. (criquet) golpe para un tanto. 4. (*pl.*) (tenis) juego de simples; (golf) juego entre dos jugadores. 5. (fam., E.U.) billete de un dólar.
single-acting [-'æktɪŋ] *a.* de simple efecto, de acción simple, de efecto único.
single-action [-'ækʃən] *a.* 1. de simple efecto, de acción simple, de efecto único. 2. (arm.) de tiro a tiro.
single-barreled [-'bærəld] *a.* de un (solo) cañon (escopeta, etc.).
single bed, cama de una plaza.
single block, (mar.) motón sencillo.
single bowknot, (mar.) vuelta o nudo de escota.
single-breasted [-'brɛstəd] *a.* (cost.) de una sola hilera de botones, recto (abrigos, chalecos, etc.).
single-case turbine, turbina de envoltura simple.
single-cut file, lima de talla simple, lima de picadura sencilla.
single cycle, (mec.) monocíclico.
single entry, (ten.) partida simple o sencilia.
single file, fila india; (mil.) columna de a uno; en fila india, uno tras otro.
single-flow condenser, condensador de un paso.
single-flow turbine, (mec.) turbina de efecto simple.
single-foot ['sɪŋgəlˌfʊt] *s.* (*pl.* SINGLE-FOOTS) paso fino (de un caballo). —*v.i.* caminar a paso fino (un caballo).
single game, partido simple (entre dos jugadores).
single-handed [-'hændəd] *a.* 1. solo, hecho a solas, hecho sin ayuda; que trabaja sin ayuda, que trabaja solo. 2. para una mano; manejable con una mano. —*adv.* sin ayuda, solo.
single-handedly [-lɪ] *adv.* a solas; sin ayuda; por una sola persona; con una mano.
single-hearted [-'hɑrtɪd, B -'hɑtɪd] *a.* 1. sincero, franco, sin doblez. 2. constante, firme, leal (devoción, propósito, etc.).
single-heartedly [-lɪ] *adv.* 1. sinceramente, francamente, sin doblez. 2. constantemente, firmemente, lealmente.
single knot, (mar.) nudo ahorcaperros.
single life, vida de soltero o de soltera.
single-loader [-'loʊdər, B -'loʊdə] *s.* arma de tiro a tiro.
single-minded [-'maɪndɪd] *a.* 1. con un solo propósito, testarudo. 2. sincero, franco, sin doblez.
single-mindedly [-lɪ] *adv.* 1. con un solo propósito. 2. sinceramente, sin doblez.
single-mindedness [-nəs] *s.* 1. perseverancia, tenacidad, constancia. 2. sinceridad, franqueza.
singleness [-nəs] *s.* 1. unidad. 2. singularidad, individualidad. 3. sinceridad, honradez. 4. soltería, celibato.
single-parent family, familia monoparental.
single-phase ['sɪŋgəl'feɪz] *a.* (elec.) monofásico.
single-pole [-'poʊl] *a.* (elec.) unipolar, monopolar.
single-seater [-'sitər, B -ə] *s.* avión monoplaza.
single shift, jornada simple, turno único.
single-shot [-'ʃɑt, B -'ʃɔt] *a.* de tiro a tiro (escopeta).
single-space [-'speɪs] *v.t.* escribir o imprimir a un solo espacio.
single-speed [-'spid] *a.* de velocidad única.
single-stage [-'steɪdʒ] *a.* de grado único (turbina); de una (sola) etapa (cohete), de un escalón.
singlestick [-ˌstɪk] *s.* (esgr.) bastón; esgrima de bastón.
singlesticker [-ər, B -ə] *s.* (fam.) balandra, balandro.
singlet ['sɪŋglət] *s.* (G.B.) camiseta.
single tax, (fin.) impuesto único.
single track, (f.c.) vía única o sencilla.
single-throw switch, interruptor de vía única.
singleton [-gəltən] *s.* (naipes) única carta de un palo (en la mano); (bridge) semifallo.
single-track [-'træk] *a.* 1. de vía única, de una sola vía. 2. (fig.) dedicado a un solo propósito; de alcance (intelectual) limitado, sin ideas.
singletree [-ˌtri] *s.* balancín, volea.
single wicket, (G.B.) criquet rudimentario.
single-wire [-'waɪr, B -'waɪə] *a.* monofilar.
singly ['sɪŋglɪ] *adv.* 1. singularmente, individualmente. 2. a solas, sin ayuda.
singsong ['sɪŋˌsɔŋ] *s.* 1. verso con cadencia uniforme. 2. sonsonete, tonillo, melodía o ritmo monótono. 3. (G.B.) reunión social para cantar. —*a.* de cadencia uniforme o monótona.
singular ['sɪŋgjələr, B -lə] *a.* 1. singular, extraordinario; peculiar, extraño, raro. 2. singular, único, solo, impar. 3. (gram., mat.) singular. 4. (der.) individual. 5. (lóg.) singular. 6. (filos.) individual. —*s.* 1. (gram.) singular, número singular. 2. (lóg.) particular, término, proposición, punto.
singularity [ˌsɪŋgjə'lærətɪ] *s.* 1. singularidad, individualidad. 2. singularidad, peculiaridad, rareza.
singularize ['sɪŋgjələˌraɪz] *v.t.* singularizar, particularizar; individualizar.
singularly [-gjələrlɪ, B -ləlɪ] *adv.* 1. singularmente, particularmente. 2. peculiarmente, extrañamente.
singularness [-nəs] *s.* 1. singularidad, individualidad. 2. singularidad, peculiaridad, rareza.
singultus [sɪŋ'gʌltəs] *s.* (med.) singulto, hipo.
Sinhalese, *var. de* **Singhalese.**
Sinic ['sɪnɪk] *a.* sínico, chinesco, chino.
Sinicism ['sɪnəˌsɪzəm] *s.* cosa china, costumbre sínica; (gram.) modismo o idiotismo chino.
Sinicize [-ˌsaɪz] *v.t.* dar carácter chino a.
Sinify [-ˌfaɪ] *v.t.* (*pret., p.p.* SINIFIED; *p.pr.* SINIFYING) dar carácter chino a.
sinigrin ['sɪnəgrən] *s.* (quím.) sinigrina.
sinister ['sɪnəstər, B -tə] *a.* 1. siniestro, malo, avieso, maligno. 2. (her.) siniestrado. 3. aciago, ominoso. 4. (ant.) fraudulento.
sinisterly [-lɪ] *adv.* siniestramente.
sinisterness [-nəs] *s.* 1. malignidad. 2. carácter aciago u ominoso.
sinistral ['sɪnəstrəl] *a.* siniestro; zurdo, izquierdo.
sinistrorse ['sɪnəˌstrɔrs, B -ˌstrɔs] **sinistrorsal** [ˌsɪnə'strɔrsəl, B -'strɔs-] *a.* (bot.) sinistrorse.
sinistrorsely [-lɪ] *adv.* (bot.) sinistrórsum.
sinistrous ['sɪnəstrəs] *a.* 1. desafortunado, desventurado, malhadado. 2. siniestro, maligno, funesto.
Sinitic [sɪ'nɪtɪk] *a.* sínico, chino.
sink [sɪŋk] *v.i.* (*pret.* SANK [sæŋk] (raro) SUNK [sʌŋk]; *p.p.* SUNK, SUNKEN ['sʌŋkən]; *p.pr.* SINKING) 1. hundirse, sumergirse; afondar, irse a pique (barco). 2. bajar, descender, declinarse, hundirse, ej., *the ground sinks,* el suelo está hundiéndose, el terreno está en declive. 3. ponerse, ocultarse (astro), ej., *the sun sunk on the horizon,* el sol se ocultó detrás del horizonte. 4. (fig.) caer, descender, ej., *darkness sank upon the countryside,* la oscuridad descendió sobre el campo. 5. sumirse, ej., *his cheeks have sunk (o sunk in),* se le han sumido las mejillas. 6. abatirse, moderarse, calmarse, menguar, minorarse, disminuirse; reducirse; bajar, ej., *her voice sank to a whisper,* su voz se redujo a un susurro, *s. in one's estimation,* bajar en la estima de uno. 7. decaer, declinar, bajar; desmejorarse, debilitarse, morirse, ej., *the wounded man sank rapidly,* el (hombre) herido desmejoraba rápidamente. 8. (con *in* o *into*) introducirse, hundirse; penetrar, calar, arraigarse, ej., *his sword sank in to the hilt,* su espada se hundió hasta la empuñadura, *the lesson sank into his mind,* la lección se arraigó en su memoria, *dye sinks in,* el tinte cala (a fondo). 9. **he waited for his words to s. in,** esperaba para dejar caer sus palabras; s. **or swim, (we have to do it)**, (fig.) fracasemos o no (tenemos que hacerlo). —*v.t.* 1. hundir, sumergir; echar a pique, ej., *the French would sooner s. the ship than surrender,* los franceses preferirian hundir el barco antes que rendirse. 2. bajar, dejar caer. 3. (fig.) hundir, arruinar, abrumar. 4. introducir, meter, ahondar, ej., *he sank his hands in the bag,* metió las manos en la bolsa. 5. clavar, ej., *s. a post,* clavar un poste (en la tierra). 6 abrir, cavar, excavar, perforar (hoyo, pozo, etc.). 7. grabar en hueco (ej., un cuño). 8. **s. money (into),** invertir dinero (esp. sin provecho), perder dinero, malbaratar (en inversiones arriesgadas, etc.). —*s.* 1. sumidero, desaguadero. 2. vertedero, fregadero, pileta. 3. (fig.) antro (de vicio, etc.). 4. (geol.) depresión (esp. con lago salino).
sinkable ['sɪŋkəbəl] *a.* hundible, sumergible.
sinkage ['sɪŋkɪdʒ] *s.* 1. hundimiento, depresión; asiento (en minas, terrenos, cimentación). 2. (impr.) cortesía.
sinker [-ər, B -ə] *s.* 1. plomo, plomada (en sedal o redes de pesca). 2. perforador, excavador. 3. (jer., E.U.) rosca, buñuelo, bollo redondo.
sinkhole [-ˌhoʊl] *s.* sumidero, agujero de desagüe; hoyo de aguas sucias.
sinking [-ɪŋ] *s.* hundimiento; (sensación de) amilanamiento o aprensión.
sinking fund, fondo de amortización, fondo amortizante.
sinking pump, (mec.) bomba colgante, bomba suspendida.
sinking speed, (avia.) velocidad de descenso, velocidad de pérdida.
sinless ['sɪnləs] *a.* inmaculado, exento de pecado, impecable.
sinlessly [-lɪ] *adv.* sin pecar, sin pecado.
sinlessness [-nəs] *s.* impecabilidad.
sinner ['sɪnər, B -ə] *s.* 1. pecador. 2. (fam.) bribón, pícaro.
Sino-Japanese [ˌsaɪnoʊˌdʒæpə'niz, B ˌsɪn-] *a.* sinojaponés, chino-japonés.
Sinological [ˌsaɪnə'lɑdʒɪkəl, B ˌsɪnə'lɔdʒ-] *a.* sinológico.
Sinologist [saɪ'nɑlədʒəst, B -'nɔl-] **Sinologue** ['saɪnəˌlɔg, B 'sɪ-] *s.* sinólogo.
Sinology [-'nɑlədʒɪ, B -'nɔl-] *s.* sinología, el estudio del arte y la civilización de la China.
sinter ['sɪntər, B -tə] *s.* (geol.) sinter, toba, concreción. —*v.t.* sinterizar, aglutinar; aglomerar.
sinuate ['sɪnjuət, -ˌeɪt] *a.* (bot.) 1. sinuoso, ondeado, ondulado. 2. sinuado (díc. de las hojas).

sinuately [-lɪ] *adv.* en forma sinuosa; (bot.) en forma sinuada, con borde sinuado.
sinuosity [ˌsɪnjʊ'ɑsətɪ, B -'ɔs-] *s.* sinuosidad, ondulación.
sinuous ['sɪnjʊəs] *a.* 1. sinuoso, ondulado. 2. tortuoso, intrincado. 3. (bot.) sinuado (díc. de las hojas).
sinuously [-lɪ] *adv.* 1. tortuosamente. 2. en forma sinuosa, sinuosamente.
sinuousness [-nəs] *s.* 1. sinuosidad. 2. tortuosidad, intrincación.
sinus ['saɪnəs] *s.* (*pl.* SINUS, SINUSES) (anat., zool., bot., med.) seno.
sinusitis [ˌsaɪnə'saɪtəs] *s.* (med.) sinusitis.
sinusoid ['saɪnəˌsɔɪd] *s.* (mat.) sinusoide.
sinusoidal [ˌsaɪnə'sɔɪdəl] *a.* sinusoidal.
sinusoidal projection, (cartografía) proyección sinusoidal.
Sion ['saɪən] *var. de* **Zion.**
Siouan ['suən] *a.* siux, sioux.
Sioux [su] *s.* (*pl.* SIOUX [su, suz]) indio americano de la tribu siux o sioux.
Sioux State, (E.U.) Estado Siux (apodo del Estado de Dakota del N.).
sip [sɪp] *v.t.* (*pret., p.p.* SIPPED; *p.pr.* SIPPING) 1. sorber, beber a tragos, ej., *s. tea,* sorber té. 2. (p. ext.) gustar, probar. —*v.i.* sorber. —*s.* 1. sorbo, trago. 2. (p. ext.) gustación, prueba.
siphon ['saɪfən] *s.* 1. sifón (para trasegar líquidos). 2. sifón, botella de sifón. 3. (zool.) sifón, tubo chupador (en algunos moluscos, gastrópodos, etc.). —*v.t.* sacar con sifón, trasegar con sifón. —*v.i.* pasar a través de un sifón.
siphon bottle, sifón, botella de sifón.
siphoning [-ɪŋ] *s.* sifonaje.
siphonophore [saɪ'fɑnəˌfɔr, B 'saɪfənəˌfɔ] *s.* (zool.) sifonóforo.
siphonostele [-ˌstil, B -'stili] *s.* (bot.) sifonostela.
sippet ['sɪpət] *s.* 1. sopa (pedazo de pan que se moja en líquido). 2. fragmento, pizca.
sir [sɜr, B sɜ] *s.* 1. (*ú. en vocativo*) señor, caballero, don. 2. **S.,** sir (tratamiento honorífico, título de caballero de una orden). 3. (ant.) amo, dueño.
sirdar ['sɜrˌdɑr, B 'sɜdɑ] *s.* 1. sirdar, jefe militar (en la India). 2. (hist.) comandante en jefe (en Egipto esp. del ejército anglo-egipcio). 3. portador de palanquín (en la India).
sire [saɪr, B 'saɪə] *s.* 1. Sire, Majestad (tratamiento propio del rey). 2. (poét.) progenitor, padre. 3. caballo padre. 4. (ant.) señor, amo, dueño. —*v.t.* 1. engendrar; procrear. 2. (fig.) ser el padre o creador de (proyecto, plan, etc.).
siree, *var. de* **sirree.**
siren ['saɪrən] *s.* 1. (mitol.) sirena. 2. tentadora, mujer peligrosa. 3. sirena (pito eléctrico o de vapor). 4. (fís.) sirena. 5. (zool.) sirenio. —*a.* de sirena; hechicera, encantadora, seductora.
sirenian [saɪ'riniən] *s.* (zool.) sirenio.
Sirius ['sɪriəs] *s.* (astr.) Sirio.
sirloin ['sɜrˌlɔɪn, B 'sɜlɔɪn] *s.* lomo; (E.U.) solomillo.
sirocco [sə'rɑkoʊ, B -'rɔk-] *s.* siroco; sudeste.
sirrah, sirra ['sɪrə] *s.* (ant.) señoritongo.
sirree [sə'ri] *s.* señor mío, ej., *yes, s.!* ¡sí, señor mío!
sirup, sirupy, *vars. de* **syrup, syrupy.**
sirvente [sɪr'vɑnt, B 'sɪəˌvɑnt] *s.* (*pl.* SIRVENTES) (hist., lit.) serventesio, sirventés.
sis [sɪs] *s. forma abrev. de* **sister,** (fam.) hermana.
sisal ['saɪsəl] *s.* 1. (bot.) sisal, henequén, agave. 2. sisal, sisol, hilo sisal, cabuya, pita.
sisal rope, cable de henequén, soga de sisal.
siskin ['sɪskən] *s.* (orn.) variedad de pinzón.
sissified ['sɪsɪˌfaɪd] *a.* afeminado; tímido, apocado.
sissy ['sɪsɪ] (despec.) *a.* (SISSIER; SISSIEST) afeminado. —*s.* (*pl.* SISSIES) 1. (despec.) afeminado. 2. (jer.) persona tímida o cobarde.
sissyish [-ɪʃ] *a.* (fam.) afeminado; tímido.
sister ['sɪstər, B -tə] *s.* 1. hermana. 2. hermana, monja; sor. 3. (pr. G.B.) jefa de enfermeras; enfermera. 4. (jer.) (*ú. en vocativo*) joven (*f.*), mujer. —*a.* hermano, gemelo, ej., *s. nation,* nación hermana, *s. ships,* buques gemelos.
sisterhood [-ˌhʊd] *s.* hermandad; confradía de mujeres; conjunto de hermanas o religiosas.
sister-in-law ['sɪstərɪnˌlɔ] *s.* (*pl.* SISTERS-IN-LAW) cuñada, hermana política.
sisterly ['sɪstərlɪ, B -təlɪ] *adv.* como una hermana, propio de una hermana.
Sistine ['sɪstin, B -taɪn] *a.* sixtino, rel. a cualquiera de los papas llamados Sixto.
Sistine Chapel, Capilla Sixtina.
sistrum ['sɪstrəm] *s.* (*pl.* SISTRUMS O SISTRA [-trə]) (mús., hist.) sistro.
sisymbrium [sə'sɪmbrɪəm] *s.* (bot.) sisimbrio.
Sisyphean [ˌsɪsɪ'fiən] **Sisyphian** [sɪ'sɪfɪən] *a.* (mitol.) de Sísifo.
Sisyphus ['sɪsɪfəs] *s.* (mitol.) Sísifo, rey de Corinto condenado en los Infiernos a empujar cuesta arriba una gran piedra sin cesar.
sit [sɪt] *v.i.* (*pret., p.p.* SAT [sæt]; *p.pr.* SITTING) 1. tomar asiento, ocupar un asiento, estar sentado. 2. posarse o descansar (las aves en una percha). 3. reunirse, celebrar junta o sesión, ej., *the courts are sitting,* los tribunales están celebrando sesión. 4. empollar, encobar, incubar, ej., *the hen is sitting,* la gallina está empollando. 5. posar (como modelo), ej., *s. for a painter,* posar para un pintor. 6. descansar, apoyarsc. 7. cstar situado. 8. sentar, caer (bien o mal), ej., *the coat sits well on you,* el abrigo le sienta (o cae) bien. 9. cuidar niños ocasionalmente (en ausencia de sus padres o guardianes). 10. **s. at ease,** arrellanarse; **s. at home,** quedarse en casa, estar inactivo; **s. at table,** sentarse a la mesa; estar sentado en la mesa; **s. back,** sentarse cómodo, acomodarse (en la silla); (fig.) relajarse, descansar; **s. down,** sentarse; **s. for,** representar, ser diputado por (distrito electoral); presentarse a (examen); **s. for one's portrait,** posar para un retrato, hacerse retratar; **s. in Congress,** (E.U.) ocupar un escaño parlamentario; **s. in for,** reemplazar temporalmente; **s. in judgement,** asumir el derecho de juzgar a otros; censurar sentenciosamente; **s. in on,** asistir a; **s. on,** formar parte de, ser miembro de (comité, junta, etc.); celebrar sesión para tratar sobre (un tema, asunto, etc.); suprimir; retener, dilatar, retrasar; **s. pretty,** estar en posición ventajosa, estar en buena posición; **s. still,** quedarse en su sitio, no moverse; **s. tight,** no moverse, no hacer nada (en espera de que suceda algo); no arriesgarse; **s. up,** velar, quedarse en vela; enderezarse (en el asiento); incorporarse; prestar atención; **s. up and take notice,** despabilarse, darse cuenta de las cosas; **s. upon,** celebrar sesión para tratar sobre (un tema, asunto, etc.). —*v.t.* 1. sentar, ubicar, poner en posición. 2. mandar sentarse. 3. montar, cabalgar (un caballo, etc.), ej., *he could not s. his mule,* no pudo montar su mula. 4. tener asientos o sitio para. 5. **sit out,** aguantar hasta el fin, quedarse hasta el fin (de la función); quedarse más tiempo que (otros invitados); quedarse sentado durante, no participar en (esp. un baile). —*s.* tiempo que se pasa sentado, espera.
sitar [sə'tɑr, B sɪtɑ] *s.* sitar (instrumento músico de la India).
sit-down strike, huelga sentada, huelga de brazos cruzados o de brazos caídos (con ocupación del lugar de trabajo).
site [saɪt] *s.* sitio, paraje, local; lugar; situación, ubicación, emplazamiento (de una obra). —*v.t.* colocar, ubicar.
sit-in ['sɪtˌɪn] *s.* huelga de brazos caídos, manifestación de protesta gen, caracterizada por la ocupación pacífica de un establecimiento, institución, oficina, etc.; (educ.) huelga de brazos caídos de estudiantes.
sitology [saɪ'tɑlədʒɪ, B -'tɔl-] *s.* sitiología, sitología.
sitosterol [saɪ'tɑstəˌrol, B -'tɔs-] *s.* (quím.) sitosterol.
sitter ['sɪtər, B -ə] *s.* 1. persona que posa (para un pintor). 2. niñera, persona para cuidar niños en ausencia de sus padres. 3. clueca, ave que empolla. 4. (jer.) blanco fácil (de acertar); cosa segura o fácil.
sitter-in [ˌsɪtə'rɪn] *s.* (*pl.* SITTERS-IN) (G.B.) niñera (empleada por horas).
sitting ['sɪtɪŋ] *s.* 1. asentada, sentada, ej., *he wrote the song at (in) one s.,* escribió la canción de una sentada. 2. echadura, incubación; pollazón, nidada (huevos). 3. sesión, junta, ej., *a s. of a court,* sesión de una corte. 4. asiento (de teatro, iglesia, etc.). —*a.* 1. sentado. 2. clueca (gallina). 3. fácil (blanco, juego, etc.).
sitting duck, (fig.) blanco muy fácil (de ataques, o críticas); primo, víctima fácil (de estafadores, etc.).
sitting room, sala, sala dc cstar, salón.
situate ['sɪtʃʊˌeɪt] *v.t.* situar, ubicar.
situated [-əd] *a.* 1. situado, ubicado. 2. de (cierta) situación económica. **ej.,** *well s.,* de buena situación económica.
situation [ˌsɪtʃʊ'eɪʃən] *s.* 1. situación, ubicación, posición, colocación. 2. situación, condición, trance, ej., *he found himself in a difficult s.,* se encontró en un trance difícil. 3. puesto, colocación; ej., *he could not find a s.,* no pudo encontrar un puesto.
situs ['saɪtəs] *s.* 1. lugar, localidad; lugar de origen. 2. (der.) domicilio. 3. (med.) situs, posición, colocación.
sitz bath ['sɪts-] baño de asiento, semicupio.
sitzkrieg ['sɪtsˌkrig] *s.* (alemán) guerra estática.
sitzmark [-ˌmɑrk, B -ˌmɑk] *s.* (esquí) depresión dejada por un esquiador al caer hacia atrás.
six [sɪks] *a.* seis; **it is s. of one and half-a-dozen of the other,** da lo mismo, es igual uno que otro; **s. o'clock,** las seis; **s. to one,** (cotización de) seis a uno (en apuestas); (fig.) probabilidad remota. —*s.* seis; **at sixes and sevens, en** confusión, en desorden; en desacuerdo.
sixfold ['sɪksˌfoʊld] *a.* séxtuplo; de seis clases. —*adv.* seis veces.
six hundred, seiscientos.
six hundredth, sexcentésimo.
six-pack [-ˌpæk] *s.* caja o conjunto de seis botellas (de gaseosas, cervezas, etc.).
sixpence [-ˌpɛns, B -pəns] *s.* (G.B.) seis peniques; moneda de seis peniques.
sixpenny [-ˌpɛnɪ, B -pənɪ] *a.* 1. de seis peniques. 2. (fig.) mezquino, insignificante; barato, común.
sixpenny nail, clavo de dos pulgadas.
sixscore [-ˌskɔr, B -skɔ] *a., s.* seis veintenas.
six-shooter [-ˌʃutər, B -ə] *s.* revólver de seis tiros.
sixte [sɪkst] *s.* (esgr.) parada en sexta.
sixteen ['sɪks'tin] *s., a.* dieciséis, diez y seis.
sixteenmo [sɪks'tinˌmoʊ] *s.* (impr.) libro en dieciseisavo.

sixteenth ['sɪks'tinθ] *s.* 1. decimosexto, dieciseisavo. 2. dieciséis (en fechas). 3. (mús.) semicorchea. —*a.* decimosexto, dieciseisavo.
sixteenth note, (mús.) semicorchea.
sixth [sɪksθ] *s.* 1. sexto. 2. seis (en fechas). 3. (mús.) sexta. —*a.* sexto.
sixth chord, (mús.) acorde en sexta.
sixthly ['sɪksθlɪ] *adv.* en sexto lugar.
sixth sense, (fig.) sexto sentido (agudo poder intuitivo).
sixtieth [-tɪəθ] *s., a.* sexagésimo, sesentavo.
Sixtine ['sɪks,tin, B -taɪn] *var. de* **Sistine.**
sixty ['sɪkstɪ] *s.* (*pl.* SIXTIES) sesenta. —*a.* sesenta.
sixty-fourth note [,sɪkstɪ'fɔrθ-, B -'fɔθ-] (mús.) semifusa.
sizable ['saɪzəbəl] *a.* considerable, grande, cuantioso.
sizableness [-nəs] *s.* tamaño considerable.
sizably [-blɪ] *adv.* considerablemente.
sizar ['saɪzər, B -zə] *s.* estudiante de las universidades de Cambridge y Dublín que recibe ayuda económica.
size [saɪz] *s.* 1. tamaño, dimensión, magnitud. 2 importancia, magnitud; fuste, prestigio. 3. talla, medida, número, ej., *I take s. six in shoes,* yo tengo el número seis en zapatos. 4. (fam.) situación, condición (verdadera), ej., *that's about the s. of it,* ésta es la situación actual, así es el asunto. 5. (instrumento) clasificador de perlas. 6. **of a s.,** del mismo tamaño. —*v.t.* 1. clasificar según el tamaño. 2. medir el tamaño de. 3. (ant.) ajustar, arreglar; fijar. 4. **s. up,** (fam.) juzgar, valuar, justipreciar; enfocar (problema, etc.). —*v.i.* **s. up to,** dejarse comparar (bien, mal, etc.).
size, *s.* sisa (de doradores); cola, goma, apresto (para papel, telas, etc.); cola de retal (para colores al temple). —*v.t.* sisar; plastecer, encolar, aprestar (papel, telas).
sizeable, *var. de* **sizable.**
sizer, *var. de* **sizar.**
sizer ['saɪzər, B -zə] *s.* 1. medidor, calibrador. 2. clasificador. 3. (carp.) igualador.
size stick, cartabón.
sizing [-zɪŋ] *s.* encolado, aparejo, encolaje, barniz de apresto, plaste (para telas, pinturas, etc.).
sizzle ['sɪzəl] *v.i.* chisporrotear, chirriar, sisear; (fig.) hervir (de furia o indignación). —*s.* chirrido, siseo.
sizzler ['sɪzlər, B -lə] *s.* (fam.) día excesivamente caluroso.
sizzling [-lɪŋ] *a.* chiriador, que sisea; muy caliente.
S.J. *abrev. de* **Society of Jesus,** Sociedad de Jesús.
skald [skɔld] *s.* bardo escandinavo, escaldo.
skat [skɑt] *s.* (cierto) juego de naipes (entre tres personas).
skate [skeɪt] *s.* 1. patín (de hielo o de ruedas). 2. (ict.) raya. 3. (jer., E.U.) jamelgo, matalón, mancarrón (Amer.). —*v.i.* patinar; **s. on thin ice,** (fig.) estar en situación precaria.
skateboard ['skeɪtbɔrd] *s.* monopatín.
skateboarder ['skeɪtbɔrdər] *s.* persona que va en monopatín.
skater ['skeɪtər, B -ə] *s.* 1. patinador. 2. (ento.) tejedor, chinche de agua, zapatero.
skating rink, pista de patinaje.
skatole ['skæt,oʊl, B -ɔl] *s.* (quím.) escatol.
skean ['skin, B 'skiən] *s.* daga, puñal (usados en Irl. y en las montañas de Esco.).
skedaddle [skɪ'dædəl] *v.i.* (fam.) tomar las de Villadiego, huir precipitadamente, fugarse. —*s.* largada, fuga, huída precipitada.
skee, *var. de* **ski.**
skeet [skit] *s.* tiro al platillo.
skeeter ['skitər, B -ə] *s.* 1. (dial., E.U.) mosquito. 2. tirador al platillo.
skeg [skɛg] *s.* (mar.) solera del codaste.
skein [skeɪn] *s.* 1. madeja, cadejo. 2. bandada (de aves silvestres, etc.). 3. (fig.) enredo, maraña. —*v.t.* devanar en madejas.
skeletal ['skɛlətəl] *a.* esquelético.
skeleton [-ən] *s.* 1. esqueleto, osamenta, **s. in the closet** (o **family s.**), secreto vergonzoso (de familia). 2. (fig.) esqueleto (persona o animal muy flacos). 3. (fig.) esqueleto, armazón, armadura. 4. (fig.) esquema (de una obra literaria).
skeleton crew, tripulación mínima, dotación básica.
skeletonize [-,aɪz] *v.t.* 1. preparar el esqueleto o armadura de. 2. reducir a partes esenciales; bosquejar. 3. (mil.) reducir (un regimiento) a su tripulación mínima, reducir a su dotación básica.
skeleton key, ganzúa, llave maestra.
skellum ['skɛləm] *s.* (pr. esco.) bribón, pícaro, truhán.
skelp [skɛlp] (dial., G.B.) s. 1. bofetada, manotada. 2. (mec.) plancha para tubos. —*v.t.* golpear, dar una bofetada a, pegar. —*v.i.* andar a prisa, caminar vivamente.
skene, *var. de* **skean.**
skep [skɛp] *s.* 1. escriño, cesta de paja. 2. colmena de paja o mimbre.
skeptic ['skɛptɪk] *a., s.* escéptico.
skeptical [-tɪkəl] *a.* escéptico.
skeptically [-kəlɪ] *adv.* con escepticismo, escépticamente, de modo escéptico.
skepticism ['skɛptə,sɪzəm] *s.* escepticismo; (filos.) escepticismo.
skerry ['skɛrɪ] *s.* (esco.) arrecife, escollo.
sketch [skɛtʃ] *s.* 1. esbozo, bosquejo, boceto, croquis. 2. bosquejo, esquema (ej., de una obra literaria). 3. ensayo o cuento breves. 4. (teat.) pieza corta (esp. en teatro frívolo). —*v.t.* esbozar, trazar; bosquejar; delinear, hacer el croquis de; reseñar. —*v.i.* hacer un boceto o bocetos, dibujar.
sketchbook ['skɛtʃ,bʊk] *s.* cuaderno de bocetos; libro de bosquejos.
sketcher [-ər, B -ə] *s.* dibujante de bocetos.
sketchily [-əlɪ] *adv.* a grandes rasgos, superficialmente, incompletamente.
sketchiness [-ɪnəs] *a.* superficialidad, insuficiencia.
sketchy [-ɪ] *a.* (SKETCHIER; SKETCHIEST) superficial, incompleto, deficiente.
skew [skju] *v.i.* 1. torcerse, ponerse al sesgo. 2. (dial.) torcer la vista, mirar de soslayo. —*v.t.* 1. sesgar, oblicuar. 2. falsear, tergiversar. —*a.* 1. oblicuo, sesgado; inclinado. 2. asimétrico. 3. (geom.) alabeado. —*s.* oblicuidad, sesgo, sesgadura; (arq.) esviaje.
skew arch, (arq.) arco en esviaje, arco sesgado u oblicuo.
skewback ['skju,bæk] *s.* (arq.) sotabanco, imposta, salmer, sillar de arranque; (min.) rafa.
skewbald [-,bɔld] *a.* pintado (caballo).
skewer ['skjuər, B -ə] *s.* 1. brocheta, broqueta, espetón (de cocina). 2. aguja, palillo, pincho. 3. (hum.) espada, daga. —*v.t.* espetar.
skewness [-nəs] *s.* 1. oblicuidad; torcimiento, deformación, distorsión. 2. (estadística) desigualdad, asimetría (de distribución o frecuencia).
skew polygon, (geom.) polígono alabeado.
ski [ski] *s.* (*pl.* SKI, SKIS o SKIIS) esquí. —*v.i.* esquiar.
skiagram ['skaɪə,græm] **skiagraph** [-,græf, B -grɑf] *s.* radiografía.
skiagraphy [skaɪ'ægrəfɪ] *s.* esquiagrafía, radiografía.
skiascope ['skaɪə,skoʊp] *s.* (med.) oftalmoscopio.
skiascopy [skaɪ'æskəpɪ] *s.* (med.) esquiascopía.
skid [skɪd] *s.* 1. larguero, corredera, viga de asiento (para deslizar barriles, bultos, etc.). 2. calzo, rastra (de ruedas). 3. resbalón, patinazo, deslizamiento. 4. (aer.) patín. 5. (mar.) varadera. 6. **to be on the skids,** ir a la ruina, vivir en abandono; **to put the skids on** o **under,** hacer caer o fracasar. —*v.t.* (*pret., p.p.* SKIDDED; *p.pr.* SKIDDING) 1. poner calzo a, calzar (rueda). 2. hacer deslizar sobre rodillos. 3. (mar.) proveer de varaderas. —*v.i.* patinar, resbalar (rueda, bicicleta, automóvil, etc.).
skiddoo, skidoo [skɪ'du] *v.i.* (jer., ant.) largarse, marcharse.
skid hoist, malacate de patines, malacate sobre largueros.
skid road, 1. camino de arrastre (para troncos de madera). 2. barrio bajo, bajos fondos.
skid row, barrio bajo, bajos fondos.
skier ['skiər, B -ə] *s.* esquiador.
skiff [skɪf] *s.* (mar.) esquife, caique, botecillo.
skiing ['skiɪŋ] *s.* el esquí, deporte de esquiar.
ski jump, salto con esquís; pista de salto (con esquís).
skilful, skilfully, *vars. de* **skillful, skillfully.**
skill [skɪl] *s.* 1. destreza, habilidad. 2. pericia, experiencia, arte, habilidad adquirida. 3. (ant.) entendimiento, juicio. —*v.i. (ant.) importar, ser de utilidad.*
skilled [skɪld] *a.* 1. diestro, hábil. 2. perito, experto, experimentado, ej., *s. mechanic,* mecánico experto.
skilled labor, mano de obra calificada.
skilled work, trabajo calificado, trabajo de experto, trabajo especializado.
skillet ['skɪlət] *s.* (pr. G.B.) caldereta; (E.U.) sartén.
skillful ['skɪlfəl] *a.* hábil, diestro, experto.
skillfully [-fəlɪ] *adv.* hábilmente, expertamente, diestramente.
skillfulness [-fəlnəs] *s.* habilidad, destreza, pericia.
skim [skɪm] *v.t.* (*pret., p.p.* SKIMMED; *p.pr.* SKIMMING) 1. desnatar, espumar, despumar. 2. hojear, leer o examinar superficialmente. 3. rasar, rozar, tocar ligeramente. 4. jugar cabrillas con (piedras); arrojar (sombrero, etc.). —*v.i.* 1. deslizar, rozar, pasar rasando. 2. **s. over,** cubrirse de una película o espuma; **s. through,** repasar a la ligera, examinar a la ligera. —*s.* 1. despumación. 2. leche desnatada. 3. capa delgada, película. —*a.* 1. desnatado. 2. de leche desnatada o descremada.
skimble-skamble ['skɪmbəl,skæmbəl] *a.* (ant.) inconexo, desconectado, sin sentido.
skimmer ['skɪmər, B -ə] *s.* 1. espumadera, desnatadora. 2. (orn.) rayador, picotijera.
skim milk, leche desnatada o descremada.
skimming [-ɪŋ] *s.* espuma; escoria.
skimp [skɪmp] *v.t.* escatimar. —*v.i.* economizar. —*a.* escaso, limitado.
skimpily ['skɪmpəlɪ] *adv.* escasamente.
skimpiness [-ɪnəs] *s.* escasez, deficiencia.
skimpy [-ɪ] *a.* (SKIMPIER; SKIMPIEST) (fam.) escaso, limitado, deficiente.
skin [skɪn] *s.* 1. piel, cutis. 2. odre, pellejo (para líquidos). 3. (fig.) pellejo, vida (de uno mismo). 4. piel, corteza, cáscara (de fruta, etc.); pellejo (de salchicha, etc.). 5. capa exterior de nácar (que recubre a la perla). 6. (ind.) cuero, piel. 7. (mar.) forro (de una nave). 8. (jer.) avaro, tacaño;

pillo, tramposo. 9. **thick s.,** corteza o cáscara gruesa; desfachatez; desparpajo; insensibilidad; **thin s.,** corteza o cáscara delgada; susceptibilidad, carácter quisquilloso; **to be no s. off one's nose** (o **back**), no ser asunto de uno; **to escape by the s. of one's teeth,** escapar con las justas; **to get under one's s.,** exasperar, irritar a uno; **to save one's s.,** salvar el pellejo; **under the s.,** en el fondo. —*v.t.* (*pret., p.p.* SKINNED; *p.pr.* SKINNING) 1. cubrir con piel. 2. desollar, despellejar, pelar. 3. (jer.) pelar, sacar dinero o propiedades a. 4. **s. alive,** desollar vivo; torturar, martirizar; escarmentar, regañar severamente. —*v.i.* 1. (gen. con *over*) cubrirse de piel, cubrirse de pellejo; cicatrizar(se). 2. **s. up,** encaramarse, trepar.

skin-deep [ˈskɪnˈdip] *a.* superficial. —*adv.* superficialmente.

skin disease, (med.) dermatosis.

skin diver, buceador sin escafandra, cazador submarino.

skin diving, submarinismo, buceo sin escafandra.

skin effect, (elec.) efecto superficial, efecto pelicular, efecto Kelvin (en corrientes de alta frecuencia).

skin flick, (jer.) película pornográfica.

skinflint [ˈskɪnˌflɪnt] *s.* cicatero, cochino, tacaño, amarrete (Amer.).

skinful [-ˌfʊl] *s.* 1. (contenido de) un odre o pellejo. 2. tragantada (esp. de licor).

skin game, (jer.) estafa.

skin graft, (med.) injerto cutáneo, injerto de piel.

skink [skɪŋk] *s.* (zool.) estinco, esquinco.

skinless [ˈskɪnləs] *a.* sin pellejo (salchicha, sardinas, etc.).

skinner [-ər, B -ə] *s.* 1. desollador; peletero. 2. tronquista; carretero. 3. (jer.) tahúr, fullero, petardista.

skinniness [ˈskɪnɪnəs] *s.* flacura, magrura, magrez.

skinny [ˈskɪnɪ] *a.* (SKINNIER; SKINNIEST) 1. como la piel. 2. flaco, magro, enjuto.

skin test, (med.) prueba cutánea, cutirreacción.

skintight [-ˈtaɪt] *a.* ajustado al cuerpo, pegado a la piel.

skip [skɪp] *v.i.* (*pret., p.p.* SKIPPED; *p.pr.* SKIPPING) 1. saltar, brincar, cabriolar, chozpar. 2. rebotar. 3. saltar, pasar por alto. 4. (educ., E.U.) saltar un grado. 5. (fam.) escapar, huir, desaparecer. —*v.t.* 1. saltar (algo). 2. (fig.) saltar, omitir. 3. (fam.) hacer rebotar. 4. dejar de ir a, no participar en (reunión, etc.). 5. (dep.) capitanear, dirigir un equipo. —*s.* 1. brinco, salto, cabriola. 2. rebote. 3. (fig.) salto, omisión. 4. (dep.) capitán de equipo (esp. en juego de bolos).

ski pants, pantalones de esquiar (cogidos al pie con una tirilla).

skip-bomb [ˈskɪpˌbɑm, B -bɔm] *v.t.* (mil.) bombardear de rebote.

skipjack [-ˌdʒæk] *s.* 1. (ict.) bonito, barrilete, cachurreta. 2. (ento.) escarabajo de resorte; baticabeza.

ski pole, bastón de esquiar.

skipper [ˈskɪpər, B -ə] *s.* 1. saltador, brincador. 2. (ict.) pez saltador. 3. (ento.) insecto saltador. 4. (mar.) capitán, patrón. 5. (aer.) capitán del avión, piloto.

skipping rope [-ɪŋ-] cuerda para saltar, soga de saltar, comba.

skirl [skɜrl, B skɜl] (esco., dial.) *v.t., v.i.* gritar, chillar; sonar con estridencia (como la gaita). —*s.* sonido estridente (como el de la gaita).

skirmish [ˈskɜrmɪʃ, B ˈskɜmɪʃ] *v.i.* escaramuzar, trabar escaramuza, escaramucear. —*s.* (mil.) escaramuza, refriega, tiroteo.

skirmisher [-ər, B -ə] *s.* (mil.) tirador; escaramuzador.

skirr [skɜr, B skɜ] *v.i.* correr o volar precipitadamente (esp. causando zumbido). —*s.* zumbido, aleteo.

skirt [skɜrt, B skɜt] *s.* 1. falda, saya. 2. (*pl.*) faldones (de la montura). 3. borde, orilla, margen; reborde, pestaña. 4. (*pl.*) alrededores, contornos, afueras (de una ciudad). 5. (jer.) muchacha, mujer. —*v.t.* 1. bordear, ir o correr por el borde o la orilla de. 2. ribetear, guarnecer. 3. rodear, dar un rodeo a. —*v.i.* (gen. con *along*) moverse o caminar por el borde o la orilla (de).

skirting [ˈskɜrtɪŋ, B ˈskɜt-] *s.* 1. orilla, borde, filo; (G.B.) friso inferior (de madera), zócalo. 2. material para faldas.

skirting board, (G.B.) friso inferior, zócalo.

skit [skɪt] *s.* 1. befa, mofa, burla, escarnio. 2. sátira, historia humorística. 3. (teat.) cuadro suelto; escena cómica (incluida en una representación dramática). 4. (esco.) engaño, mentira; chanza, broma.

skite [skaɪt] *s.* (esco., dial.) chaparrón, chubasco; bofetada, golpe desviado; chisguete, chorro, jeringazo.

skitter [ˈskɪtər, B -ə] *v.i.* 1. resbalarse o deslizarse con saltitos rápidos (esp. sobre agua las aves al posarse o levantarse). 2. pescar arrastrando el anzuelo en la superficie. 3. **s. off,** escabullirse dando saltitos (ej., una ardilla). —*v.t.* lanzar (piedrecitas) haciéndolas rebotar en el agua.

skittish [-ɪʃ] *a.* 1. caprichoso, vivaracho, juguetón. 2. asustadizo, espantadizo, inquieto (díc. esp. de caballos). 3. tímido, recatado.

skittishly [-lɪ] *adv.* 1. caprichosamente, juguetonamente. 2. inquietamente. 3. tímidamente, recatadamente.

skittishness [-nəs] *s.* vivacidad; frivolidad; inconstancia.

skittle [ˈskɪtəl] *s.* 1. (*pl.*) juego de bolos. 2. bolo, palo (en el juego de bolo). 3. (fig.) (*pl.*) diversión, entretenimiento, ú. pr. en: **life is not all beer and skittles,** la vida no es pura diversión.

skive [skaɪv] *v.t.* chiflar, adelgazar (las pieles); cortar en capas o pedazos; pelar, raspar, rasurar; pulir (gemas).

skiver [ˈskaɪvər, B -və] *s.* 1. cuero ordinario hecho de la piel de carnero. 2. chifla (cuchilla ancha para adelgazar cueros).

skivvies [ˈskɪvɪz] *s. pl.* ropa interior.

skivvy [ˈskɪvɪ] *s.* (fam., G.B.) (gen. despec.) criada.

skoal [skoʊl] *interj.* (neol.) ¡salud!

skua [ˈskjuə] *s.* (orn.) skúa; gaviota parda.

skulduggery [ˌskʌlˈdʌgərɪ] *s.* tretas, artimañas.

skulk [skʌlk] *v.i.* 1. salir furtivamente o a hurtadillas. 2. esconderse, emboscarse. 3. (G.B.) esquivar, eludir (deber, etc.); fingirse enfermo, simular. —*s.* 1. bandada de zorros. 2. (G.B.) remolón, holgazán.

skulker [ˈskʌlkər, B -ə] *s.* (G.B.) remolón, holgazán.

skull [skʌl] *s.* 1. cráneo, sesera, calavera. 2. (fig.) cabeza, mente, inteligencia.

skull and crossbones, 1. bandera pirata (con calavera y dos huesos cruzados) 2. etiqueta con calavera y dos huesos cruzados.

skullcap [ˈskʌlˌkæp] *s.* 1. casquete, gorro casero. 2. (bot.) escutelaria.

skull practice, (jer.) clase de estrategia (para un equipo deportivo).

skunk [skʌŋk] *s.* 1. (zool.) mofeta, zorrino (Am.), zorrillo (Am.) 2. piel de zorrino. 3. (fig.) canalla, pillo. —*v.t.* 1. (jer., E.U.) ganar (a alguien en un juego) adjudicándose todos los puntos. 2. estafar.

sky [skaɪ] *s.* (*pl.* SKIES) 1. cielo, firmamento. 2. (fig.) (t. en *pl.*) cielo, cielos, gloria, paraíso. 3. (*gen. pl.*) clima, tiempo. 4. (ant.) nube. 5. **out of a clear blue s.,** de repente, inesperadamente; **the s. is the limit,** (fam.) no hay límite; **to praise to the skies** (o **to the s.**), poner por las nubes, poner por los cielos; **under the open s.,** a cielo abierto, a campo raso. —*v.t.* 1. (pr. G.B.) aventar, echar al viento o al cielo. 2. (fam.) colgar (un cuadro) cerca del techo (en una exhibición).

sky blue, (color) celeste, azul celeste.

sky-blue [ˈskaɪˈblu] *a.* (de color) celeste, azul celeste.

skyborne [-ˌbɔrn, B -ˌbɔn] *a.* transportado por avión (tropas, etc.).

skycap [-ˌkæp] *s.* mozo de cuerda o de cordel, changador (Amer.) (en un aeropuerto).

Skye terrier [ˈskaɪ-] (zool.) variedad escocesa de perro terrier.

skyey [ˈskaɪɪ] *a.* (poét.) celestial, etéreo, célico.

sky-high [-ˈhaɪ] *a.* tan alto como el cielo. —*adv.* por las nubes.

skyjack [-ˌdʒæk] *v.t.* secuestrar en vuelo (un avión).

Skylab [ˈskaɪˌlæb] *s.* laboratorio espacial.

skylark [-ˌlɑrk, B -lɑk] *s.* (orn.) alondra, copetuda, calandria. —*v.i.* travesear, retozar, juguetear.

skylight [-ˌlaɪt] *s.* tragaluz, claraboya, lumbrera, lucera, lucerina; luz cenital.

skyline [-ˌlaɪn] *s.* línea del horizonte; silueta, contorno (de uno o varios objetos) en el horizonte.

sky pilot, (jer.) capellán; misionero; sacerdote.

skyrocket [ˈskaɪˌrɑkət, B -ˌrɔkɪt] *s.* cohete, fuegos artificales. —*v.i.* (fam.) subir como cohete; subir hasta las nubes (precios). —*v.t.* elevar o alzar súbitamente.

skysail [-ˌseɪl, -səl] *s.* (mar.) sosobre.

sky-scape [-ˌskeɪp] *s.* fotografía o paisaje del cielo.

skyscraper [-skreɪpər, B -pə] *s.* rascacielos.

skyward [-wərd, B -wəd] **skywards** [-wərdz, B -wədz] *adv.* hacia el cielo. —*a.* que se dirige al cielo.

sky wave, (rad.) onda ionosférica, onda reflejada, onda indirecta, onda de cielo.

skyway [-ˌweɪ] *s.* 1. ruta aérea. 2. carretera en terraplén.

skywrite [-ˌraɪt] *v.t., v.i.* escribir con humo lanzado por un avión.

skywriting [-ɪŋ] *s.* palabras formadas con humo lanzado por avión.

slab [slæb] *s.* 1. rebanada gruesa; plancha o lámina gruesa; losa, placa. 2. costero (de madera). 3. (jer.) (béisbol) base del lanzador. —*v.t.* (*pret., p.p.* SLABBED; *p.pr.* SLABBING) 1. aserrar en costeros, quitar los costeros a. 2. cortar láminas o planchas gruesas; cubrir con planchas o losas. 3. poner una gruesa capa de (mantequilla, crema, etc.). —*a.* (pr. dial. G.B.) espeso, viscoso, pegajoso.

slabber [ˈslæbər, B -ə] *v.i., v.t. var. de* **slobber.**

slab-sided [-ˈsaɪdəd] *a.* (fam.) plano, chato, largo y delgado.

slabstone [-ˌstoʊn] *s.* piedra (apropiada) para lajas.

slack [slæk] *a.* 1. flojo, laxo, suelto, relajado; de poca tensión, ej., *s. rope,* soga de poca tensión. 2. negligente, descuidado; remiso. 3. lento, despacioso; pesado, calmoso, ej., *s. weather,* tiempo pesado o calmoso. 4. que fluye o sopla lentamente. 5. flojo, inactivo, ej., *s. market,* mercado flojo o inactivo. 6. inadecuado, imperfecto. 7.

to keep a s. hand (o **rein**), cabalgar a rienda suelta; (fig.) gobernar con indulgencia. —*v.t.* 1. aflojar, relajar, desapretar. 2. (fig.) aflojar, disminuir. 3. (fig.) moderar, aplacar. 4. apagar (cal). —*v.i.* 1. aflojarse, relajarse. 2. (fig.) aflojarse, disminuirse. 3. holgazanear. 4. apagarse (la cal). 5. **s. off,** disminuir(se), reducirse; **s. up,** aflojar el paso, reducir la velocidad (antes de parar). —*s.* 1. flojedad, flojera, languidez, relajamiento. 2. inactividad, inercia. 3. período de poca actividad, estación muerta, estación de calma. 4. parte floja (de cable, cordel, etc.). 5. (*pl.*) pantalones. 6. (poét.) sílaba átona. 7. (dial. G.B.) paso entre montañas; cañada, vallejo. 8. cisco.

slack-baked ['slæk'beɪkt] *a.* soasado, a medio asar; cocido a medias; (fig.) retardado (mental y físicamente).

slacken [-ən] *v.i.* 1. aflojar, relajarse; volverse negligente. 2. reducirse, disminuirse (velocidad); amainarse (viento, etc.). —*v.t.* 1. retardar, atrasar, retrasar. 2. disminuir, reducir (velocidad, interés, etc.). 3. moderar, calmar, amainar. 4. aflojar, desapretar, relajar.

slacker [-ər, B -ə] *s.* 1. haragán, holgazán. 2. (mil.) prófugo.

slack lime, cal muerta, cal apagada.

slackly [-lɪ] *adv.* 1. flojamente; negligentemente. 2. lentamente, calmadamente; inactivamente.

slackness [-nəs] *s.* 1. flojedad, estado flojo. 2. (fig.) negligencia, descuido. 3. languidez; relajamiento, inactividad; inercia.

slack suit, vestido cómodo (de pantalones sueltos y saco o camisa deportiva).

slack water, agua muerta; marea muerta.

slag [slæg] *s.* 1. escoria, cagafierro. 2. escoria, lava esponjosa (de los volcanes).

slag wool, lana mineral, lana de escorias.

slain, *p.p. de* **slay.**

slake [sleɪk] *v.t.* 1. satisfacer, saciar; aplacar, apagar (la sed). 2. calmar, mitigar, aminorar, disminuir, reducir (fuerza, vehemencia, etc.). 3. apagar (la cal). —*v.i.* apagarse (cal); desintegrarse, desmoronarse, desmenuzarse (carbón, etc.).

slaked lime, cal apagada, cal muerta.

slalom ['slɑləm, B 'sleɪ-] *s.* (esquí) slalom.

slam [slæm] *v.t.* (*pret., p.p.* SLAMMED; *p.pr.* SLAMMING) 1. cerrar golpeando; golpear con estrépito. 2. (fam.) criticar severamente. 3. **s. down,** colgar bruscamente (auricular); cerrar o bajar de golpe (ventana, etc.); dejar caer con estrépito (puño sobre la mesa, etc.); **s. one's fist down on (table,** etc.), golpear (la mesa, etc.) con el puño; **s. the door,** tirar la puerta, dar un portazo; **s. the door on,** (fig.) cerrar la puerta a (arreglo, posibilidad, etc.). —*v.i.* **s. into,** embestir; empezar vigorosamente. —*s.* 1. golpe fuerte, impacto pesado. 2. portazo. 3. crítica severa. 4. (naipes) capote (suerte en que un jugador hace todas las bazas); (bridge) slam, bola o semibola (Esp.).

slam-bang ['slæm'bæŋ] *adv.* precipitadamente, de cabeza.

slander ['slændər, B 'slɑndə] *s.* calumnia, difamación; (der.) libelo infamatorio. —*v.t.* difamar, calumniar, desacreditar, infamar.

slanderer [-dərər, B -ə] *s.* difamador, calumniador, infamador.

slanderous [-əs] *a.* calumnioso, difamatorio, difamador, infamatorio.

slang [slæŋ] *s.* jerga, jerigonza. —*a.* jergal, de jerga. —*v.t.* (pr. G.B.) tildar (a alguien) con palabras de jerga; insultar. —*v.i.* usar lenguaje insultante o de jerga.

slangily ['slæŋəlt] *adv.* en jerga.

slanginess [-ɪnəs] *s.* carácter jergal (del lenguaje).

slangy [-ɪ] *a.* que emplea jerga; lleno de palabras de jerga, jergal.

slant [slænt, B slɑnt] *a.* (pr. poét.) inclinado, oblicuo, soslayo, sesgo. —*s.* 1. inclinación, oblicuidad, sesgo, declive, pendiente. 2. vistazo, mirada. 3. punto de vista, parecer. 4. **a s. of wind,** (mar.) brisa favorable; **on the s.,** al sesgo, de soslayo. —*v.t.* 1. inclinar, sesgar, oblicuar. 2. interpretar con prejuicio, presentar con parcialidad. —*v.i.* inclinarse, sesgarse.

slanting ['slæntɪŋ, B 'slɑnt-] *a.* inclinado, oblicuo, diagonal; en declive, al sesgo, sesgado.

slantingly [-lɪ] *adv.* con inclinación, oblicuamente, diagonalmente; al sesgo, en declive.

slantly [-lɪ] *adv.* al sesgo, en declive.

slantways [-ˌweɪz] *adv.* con inclinación, oblicuamente, al soslayo.

slantwise [-ˌwaɪz] *a.* inclinado, oblicuo. —*adv.* con inclinación, oblicuamente, de soslayo.

slap [slæp] *s.* palmetazo, palmada; bofetada, bofetón, lapo, cachetada, sopapo; **s. on the back,** espaldarazo; **s. in the face,** (fig.) desaire, descortesía, insulto. —*adv.* súbito, de repente, repentinamente, instantáneamente; directamente. —*v.t.* (*pret., p.p.* SLAPPED; *p.pr.* SLAPPING) 1. dar un palmetazo o palmada a; abofetear, acachetear, sopapear. 2. poner o tirar violenta y descuidadamente. 3. **s. down,** prohibir abruptamente, reprimir bruscamente.

slapdash ['slæpˌdæʃ] *adv.* impetuosamente, de repente, violentamente; precipitadamente. —*a.* impetuoso, repentino, descuidado; chapucero; **in a s. manner,** chapuceramente.

slap-happy [-ˌhæpɪ] *a.* (jer.) aturdido (a golpes); estupefacto, atolondrado.

slapjack [-ˌdʒæk] *s.* 1. (E.U.) tortilla o panqueque (Amer.) hecho a la parrilla. 2. juego de cartas de niños.

slapstick [-'stɪk] *s.* 1. palmeta de payaso. 2. comedia burda, comedia chocarrera, payasada. —*a.* bufonesco, chocarrero.

slap-up [-ˌʌp] *a.* (jer., pr. G.B.) fino, excelente; elegante, al último grito de la moda.

slash [slæʃ] *v.t.* 1. acuchillar, dar cuchilladas a; hacer corte(s) largo(s) en. 2. (cost.) acuchillar (un vestido). 3. azotar, flagelar. 4. censurar sin piedad, criticar acerbamente. 5. reducir radicalmente (precios, gastos, etc.). —*v.i.* tirar o dar tajos y reveses. —*s.* 1. cuchillada, tajo, corte largo, cortadura. 2. tala (del bosque). 3. (cost.) cuchillada. 4. (E.U.) tierra baja pantanosa.

slasher ['slæʃər, B -ə] *s.* 1. acuchillador. 2. espada; cuchilla; navaja.

slashing [-ɪŋ] *s.* 1. cuchillada, tajo, corte, cortadura. 2. latigazo, azote, flagelo. 3. (cost.) rasgada, corte, cuchillada (a la tela). —*a.* 1. despiadado, desalmado. 2. arrojado; vigoroso, brioso, animoso. 3. inmenso, enorme, vasto (suceso).

slash pine, (bot.) pino del incienso.

slat [slæt] *s.* 1. tablilla, tableta, listón. 2. bofetada o golpe sonoro. —*v.t.* (*pret., p.p.* SLATTED; *p.pr.* SLATTING) 1. cubrir de tablillas, proveer de listones. 2. (dial.) arrojar, tirar, lanzar; golpear, pegar. —*v.i.* (mar.) gualdrapear (las velas).

slate [sleɪt] *s.* 1. pizarra, esquisto. 2. pizarra. teja. 3. pizarra o pizarrón (de escuela). 4. (E.U.) lista de candidatos elegibles. 5. (color) pizarra. 6. **to clean the s.,** empezar de nuevo, borrar los antecedentes; liquidar obligaciones; **to have a clean s.,** tener las manos limpias, no tener antecedentes. —*v.t.* 1. empizarrar. 2. registrar, inscribir; nominar, nombrar. 3. (pr. G.B., fam.) azotar, zurrar, apalear; castigar, corregir. 4. reprender, regañar; criticar, censurar.

slate blue, azul pizarra.

slate-colored ['sleɪtˌkʌlərd, B -əd] *a.* apizarrado, (de) color (de) pizarra.

slate pencil, pizarrín.

slate quarry, pizarral, pizarrería, cantera de pizarra.

slater [-ər, B -ə] *s.* 1. pizarrero. 2. (ento.) cochinilla de tierra. 3. (pr. G.B.) crítico severo; censor violento.

slate roof, empizarrado, techo o techumbre de pizarra.

slather ['slæðər, B -ə] *v.t.* (fam.) untar con una capa gruesa; gastar o usar en cantidad.

slating ['sleɪtɪŋ] *s.* empizarrado.

slatted ['slætəd] *a.* de rejilla, hecho de tablillos o listones.

slattern ['slætərn, B -ən] *s.* mujer sucia y desaliñada.

slatternly [-lɪ] *a.* sucia, desaliñada. —*adv.* suciamente, desaliñadamente.

slaty ['sleɪtɪ] *a.* pizarroso, pizarreño; esquistoso (contextura); de color pizarroso.

slaughter ['slɔtər, B -ə] *s.* 1. matanza de reses. 2. matanza, carnicería, masacre, degollina. —*v.t.* 1. matar o sacrificar (las reses). 2. matar en masa, matar despiadadamente, masacrar.

slaughterer [-ərər, B -ə] *s.* 1. jifero, matachín, matarife. 2. matador, asesino, verdugo.

slaughterhouse [-ərˌhaʊs, B -əˌ-] *s.* matadero, desolladero.

slaughterous [-ərəs] *a.* destructivo, sanguinario, cruel.

Slav [slɑv, slæv] *s.* eslavo.

slave [sleɪv] *s.* esclavo, siervo. —*v.i* trabajar como esclavo; afanarse, fatigarse, atrafagar. —*v.t.* (raro) esclavizar. —*a.* esclavo.

slave ant, (ento.) hormiga obrera.

slave-born ['sleɪvˌbɔrn, B -ˌbɔn] *a.* nacido en la esclavitud.

slave driver, capataz de esclavos; (fam.) negrero, jefe despótico.

slaveholder [-ˌhoʊldər, B -də] *s.* dueño de esclavos.

slaveholding [-dɪŋ] *s.* posesión de esclavos. —*a.* poseedor de esclavos.

slave labor, 1. trabajo de esclavos. 2. trabajadores explotados; explotación del trabajador.

slaver ['slævər, 'slɑv-, B 'slævə] *v.i.* babear, echar la baba. —*v.t.* (ant.) babosear, llenar de baba. —*s.* babeo, baboseo.

slaver ['sleɪvər, B -və] *s.* 1. negrero, esclavista. 2. barco negrero. 3. tratante de blancas.

slavery [-vərɪ] *s.* 1. esclavitud; cautiverio, servidumbre. 2. tráfago, trajín.

slave ship, barco negrero.

Slave States, (E.U., hist.) estados esclavistas, pr. los estados del Sur, en los cuales la esclavitud era legal antes de la Guerra Civil.

slave trade, tráfico de esclavos, trata de esclavos.

slavey ['sleɪvɪ, B 'slæ-] *s.* (*pl.* SLAVEYS) (fam.) sirvienta, criada, mucama (Amer.).

Slavic ['slævɪk, 'slɑvɪk] *a., s.* eslavo.

slavish ['sleɪvɪʃ] *a.* 1. servil, abyecto. 2. (ant.) esclavista; tiránico. 3. servil (imitación), literal, textual (tradución).

slavishly [-lɪ] *adv.* servilmente.

slavishness [-nəs] *s.* servilismo.

slavocracy [ˌsleɪ'vɑkrəsɪ, B -'vɔk-] *s.* (E.U., hist.) facción esclavista.

Slavonian [slə'voʊnɪən] *a., s.* eslavonio, eslavón, de una región de Yugoslavia.

Slavonic [-'vɑnɪk, B -'vɔn-] *a., s.* eslavo.

Slavophile ['slævəˌfaɪl, 'slɑ-] **Slavophil** [-ˌfɪl] *s.* eslavófilo.

Slavophobe [-ˌfoʊb] *s.* eslavófobo.
slaw [slɔ] *s. forma abrev. de* **coleslaw,** ensalada de col.
slay [sleɪ] *v.t.* (*pret.* SLEW [slu]; *p.p.* SLAIN [sleɪn]; *p.pr.* SLAYING) 1. matar, asesinar. 2. (ant.) herir, golpear, aporrear.
slayer ['sleɪər, B -ə] *s.* matador, asesino.
sleave [sliv] *v.t.* (ant.) desenredar, desenmarañar. —*v.i.* deshilacharse. —*s.* madeja.
sleaziness ['slizɪnəs] *s.* 1. mala calidad (textura). 2. vileza, ruindad, mezquindad.
sleazy ['slizɪ] *a.* 1. de mala calidad, mal hecho, débil; usado, raído. 2. vil, ruin, mezquino. 3. baladí, cursi, barato.
sled [slɛd] *s.* trineo. —*v.t.* (*pret., p.p.* SLEDDED; *p.pr.* SLEDDING) llevar o transportar en trineo. —*v.i.* viajar o ir en trineo.
sledder ['slɛdər, B -ə] *s.* 1. viajante en trineo. 2. caballo (u otro animal) para tirar de trineos.
sledding [-ɪŋ] *s.* 1. transporte por trineo. 2. estado de la nieve que permite el uso de trineos. 3. (fig.) estado, condiciones, circunstancias, estado (de negocios, empresa etc.). 4. **it was hard s. all the way,** fue dificultosa (la empresa) de principio a fin.
sledge [slɛdʒ] *s.* 1. (G.B.) trineo. 2. trineo de carga. 3. almádena, almádana, marra, acotillo. —*v.i.* (G.B.) viajar o ir en trineo. —*v.t.* llevar o transportar en trineo.
sledgehammer ['slɛdʒˌhæmər, B -ə] *s.* almádena, almádana, marra, acotillo, martillo macho. —*v.t.* 1. batir con almádena. 2. (fig.) machacar en.
sledge handle, mango de marra, cabo de combo.
sleek [slik] *v.t.* 1. pulir, alisar, bruñir. 2. (fig.) acicalar. —*a.* 1. alisado, bruñido; liso y brillante (pelo). 2. suave, blando, zalamero. 3. elegante. 4. (de aspecto) próspero.
sleeken ['slikən] *v.t.* suavizar, alisar.
sleekly [-lɪ] *adv.* 1. suavemente, blandamente. 2. elegantemente.
sleekness [-nəs] *s.* 1. suavidad, blandura. 2. elegancia.
sleep [slip] *s.* 1. sueño, dormida. 2. (fig.) descanso, reposo; sopor, entorpecimiento. 3. **broken s.,** sueño sobresaltado; **in one's s.,** durante el sueño (de uno); **overcome with s.,** vencido por el sueño; **the s. of the just,** el sueño de los justos, sueño profundo; **to get to s.,** dormirse, conciliar el sueño; **to go to s.,** dormirse; (fig.) morir; **to put to s.,** adormecer, hacer dormir; **to read oneself to s.,** leer hasta quedarse dormido. —*v.i.* (*pret., p.p* SLEPT [slɛpt]; *p.pr.* SLEEPING) 1. dormir, estar dormido. 2. dormir, adormecerse. 3. (fig.) dormir, descansar, reposar; estar inactivo o muerto. 4. dormir (el trompo). 5. **s. at,** pernoctar en, pasar la noche en; **s. in,** pernoctar en, pasar la noche en; dormir en el lugar de trabajo; **s. like a log,** dormir como un tronco (o un lirón); **s. on** (o **upon** u **over**) **(a question,** etc.), dejar (un problema, etc.) para mañana, pensar (un asunto, etc.) hasta el día siguiente; **s. on it,** consultar con la almohada; **s. out,** dormir al aire libre; dormir fuera de casa; ir a su casa de noche (criada, cocinera, etc.); **s. the clock round,** (fig.) dormir por veinticuatro horas; **s. with,** dormir con, tener trato sexual con; **to let sleeping dogs lie,** (fig.) dejar las cosas tranquilas; no remover un asunto. —*v.t.* 1. pasar (la noche, tarde, etc.) durmiendo. 2. tener o proporcionar alojamiento a, ej., (*it*) *sleeps 600 persons,* tiene alojamiento para 600 personas. 3. **s. away,** pasar durmiendo, desperdiciar en sueño (tiempo, etc.); **s. it off,** dormir (borrachera), dormir hasta que pase (dolor de cabeza, enfado, etc.).
sleeper ['slipər, B -pə] *s.* 1. durmiente (persona que duerme). 2. (G.B.) (const., f.c.) traviesa, durmiente (Amer.). 3. (f.c.) coche dormitorio, coche cama. 4. ganador inesperado (caballo de carrera que gana sin haber tenido posibilidades); artículo de valor insospechado.
sleepily [-pəlɪ] *adv.* soñolientamente.
sleepiness [-pɪnəs] *s.* somnolencia, soñolencia.
sleeping bag, saco o talego para dormir (a la intemperie).
sleeping beauty, (la) bella durmiente.
sleeping car, coche dormitorio, coche cama.
sleeping partner, socio secreto, socio comanditario.
sleeping pill, píldora somnífera o soporífera, píldora para dormir.
sleeping sickness, 1. (med.) enfermedad del sueño, tripanosomiasis. 2. (med.) encefalitis letárgica.
sleepless ['slipləs] *a.* desvelado, insomne.
sleeplessly [-lɪ] *adv.* desveladamente, con insomnio.
sleeplessness [-nəs] *s.* insomnio, desvelo.
sleepwalk ['slipˌwɔk] *v.i.* caminar dormido.
sleepwalker [-ər, B -ə] *s.* sonámbulo, somnámbulo.
sleepwalking [-ɪŋ] *s.* somnambulismo, sonambulismo.
sleepy ['slipɪ] *a.* (SLEEPIER; SLEEPIEST) 1. soñoliento. 2. soporífero, soporoso.
sleepyhead [-ˌhɛd] *s.* dormilón, lirón.
sleet [slit] *s.* helada en el suelo, aguanieve, cellisca. —*v.i.* cellisquear, caer cellisca.
sleety ['slitɪ] *a.* (SLEETIER; SLEETIEST) de cellisca, con aguanieve, helada, cubierto de helada.
sleeve [sliv] *s.* 1. manga. 2. (mec.) manguito, camisa, manga, casquillo. 3. **to have (something) up one's s.,** tener (algo) en reserva u oculto (pero listo para su uso); **to laugh in one's s.,** reírse disimuladamente; **to turn** (o **roll**) **up one's s.,** arremangarse; (fig.) prepararse para pelear o trabajar.
sleeve coupling, (mec.) acoplamiento de manguito.
sleeveless ['slivləs] *a.* 1. (cost.) sin mangas. 2. (mec.) sin camisa.
sleevelet [-lət] *s.* mangote, manguito (para proteger las mangas de la chaqueta).
sleeve target, (aer.) blanco de manga remolcada.
sleigh [sleɪ] *s.* trineo. —*v.i.* ir en trineo.
sleigh bell, cascabel.
sleigh ride, paseo en trineo.
sleight [slaɪt] *s.* 1. artificio, artimaña, ardid, treta. 2. destreza, habilidad, maña, pericia. 3. (raro) arte (manual).
sleight of hand, juego de manos, prestidigitación.
slender ['slɛndər, B -də] *a.* 1. delgado, cenceño, esbelto. 2. débil, ligero, leve, escaso, pobre, inadecuado, poco, ej., *s. hopes,* escasas o pocas esperanzas, *s. means,* medios inadecuados. 3. ligero, limitado, frugal (dieta, comida, etc.).
slenderize [-dəˌraɪz] *v.t.* adelgazar, reducir el peso de, enflaquecer.
slenderly ['slɛndərlɪ, B -dəlɪ] *adv.* 1. esbeltamente, con una silueta delgada. 2. débilmente, ligeramente, levemente, escasamente, pobremente. 3. frugalmente.
slenderness [-nəs] *s.* 1. delgadez, esbeltez. 2. ligereza, levedad; insuficiencia, escasez, pobreza.
slept, *pret., p.p. de* **sleep.**
sleuth [sluθ] *s.* (fam.) sabueso, detective, investigador. —*v.i.* hacer de detective; **s. after,** investigar, seguir la pista de (algo o alguien).
sleuthhound ['sluθˌhaʊnd] *s.* 1. perro sabueso, perro rastrero. 2. (fam.) sabueso, detective, investigador.
slew [slu] *s.* 1. pantano; terreno pantanoso; estuario de río, ría. 2. (fam.) montón, la mar (de). 3. *var. de* **slue** (*v.*). —*pret. de* **slay.**
slice [slaɪs] *s.* 1. rebanada, tajada, lonja, raja. 2. espátula, paleta pequeña. 3. (cocina) cuchillo romo; cuchillo de pescado; paleta. 4. (golf) golpe con efecto (que desvía la pelota de su trayectoria recta). 5. (jer.) tajada, ganancia. —*v.t.* 1. rebanar, cortar en tajadas o lonjas, tajar. 2. dividir, partir (gen. en pequeñas porciones). 3. (golf) golpear con efecto (la pelota desviándola de su trayectoria recta). 4. **s. off,** quitar con una tajadura. —*v.i.* (golf) dar efecto a la pelota, desviar la pelota (de su trayectoria recta).
slice bar, hurgón, atizador, atizadero, limpiaparrilla.
slicer ['slaɪsər, B -ə] *s.* cuchillo tajador; máquina de rebanar.
slick [slɪk] *v.t.* pulir, suavizar; alisar; **s. up.** refinar, dar apariencia vistosa a; emperejilar, acicalar. —*a.* 1. listo, hábil, ingenioso; tramposo, embaucador. 2. liso, bruñido, resbaladizo. —*s.* capa aceitosa, película oleosa. —*adv.* ingeniosamente, hábilmente.
slickenside ['slɪkənˌsaɪd] *s.* (geol.) espejo de falla, plano de resbalamiento.
slicker ['slɪkər, B -ə] *s.* 1. gabán de lona encerada, impermeable. 2. (fam.) embaucador, farsante.
slick magazine, (jer., E.U.) revista impresa en papel satinado; revista elegante o de buen tono.
slide [slaɪd] *v.i.* (*pret., p.p.* SLID [slɪd]; *p.pr.* SLIDING) 1. resbalar, deslizarse. 2. deslizarse, patinar (sobre el hielo), resbalarse (sobre la nieve). 3. caer, escurrirse. 4. pasar suave o imperceptiblemente, ej., *s. from one tone to another,* pasar suavemente de un tono a otro (en música, canto, etc.). 5. **s. over,** saltar, pasar en blanco, ej., *s. over a painful subject,* pasar en blanco un tema penoso; **to let things s.,** dejar pasar las cosas sin tomar ninguna accíon. —*v.t.* hacer resbalar o deslizar. —*s.* 1. resbalón, resbaladura, desliz. 2. alud, deslizamiento, derrumbe. 3. deslizadero, resbaladero; tobogán, plano inclinado. 4. corredera, bomba (de trombón). 5. tapa corrediza. 6. platina, portaobjeto (para microscopio). 7. (foto.) diapositivo. 8. (mec.) (t. **s. valve**) válvula corrediza.
slide bar, guía de la corredera, barra corrediza.
slide box, (elec.) caja del distribuidor, caja de resistencias con cursor.
slide calipers, calibre corredizo de espesor, calibre a colisa, cartabón corredizo, calibrador a cursor.
slide fastener, cierre de cremallera, cierre relámpago (Amer.).
slide knot, (mar.) nudo de corbata.
slider ['slaɪdər, B -ə] *s.* (mec.) cursor, resbalador, deslizador; guía de deslizamiento, corredera de máquinas.
slide rest, (mec.) soporte del carro, soporte de corredera (del torno).
slide rod, (mec.) resbaladera de la cruceta; biela del distribuidor; barra del distribuidor; vástago del distribuidor.
slide rule, regla de cálculo.
slide trombone, (mús.) trombón de varas.
slide valve, (mot.) corredera, distribuidor, distribuidor de concha, válvula corrediza.
sliding ['slaɪdɪŋ] *a.* corredizo, deslizante, resbaladizo.
sliding board, deslizadero (en campo de juego para niños).
sliding bolts, cerrojos movibles.
sliding door, puerta corrediza, puerta de corredera.

sliding gate, 1. (hidr.) compuerta deslizante, compuerta de guillotina. 2. (f.c.) barrera corrediza.
sliding gear, (aut.) tren desplazable; cambio de velocidades con tren corredizo.
sliding way, (const. naval) cuna de botadura.
sliding window, ventana corrediza, ventana de corredera.
slight [slaɪt] *a.* 1. delgado, flaco; delicado, sutil, tenue. 2. ligero, leve; escaso, insuficiente; superficial; magro, pobre. 3. insignificante, trivial. —*v.t.* 1. menospreciar, despreciar. 2. desdeñar, tener en poco, desairar. 3. descuidar, desatender. —*s.* 1. menosprecio, desprecio. 2. desdén, desaire, feo, acto de descortesía, desatención.
slighting ['slaɪtɪŋ] *a.* despreciador, menospreciador, que desaira, desdeñador.
slightingly [-lɪ] *adv.* desdeñosamente, desatentamente, con menosprecio.
slightly ['slaɪtlɪ] *adv.* 1. delicadamente, ej., *s. built,* delicadamente formado, de talle delicado. 2. ligeramente; un poco, ej., *this is s. better,* esto es un poco mejor.
slightness [-nəs] *s.* 1. delgadez, flaqueza. 2. pequeñez, insignificancia.
slily, *var. de* **slyly.**
slim [slɪm] *a.* (SLIMMER; SLIMMEST) 1. delgado, cenceño, flaco. 2. (fig.) escaso, poco (público, concurrencia, etc.). 3. (fig.) leve, débil (esperanza, oportunidad, etc.). 4. astuto, artero. —*v.t.* (*pret., pp.* SLIMMED; *p.pr.* SLIMMING) hacer más delgado, poner delgado, adelgazar; **s. down,** reducir. —*v.i.* bajar de peso, adelgazar.
slime [slaɪm] *s.* 1. légamo, cieno, limo, lama, fango, pecina. 2. babaza, baba (de caracoles, peces, etc.). —*v.t.* 1. enfangar, enlodar, ensuciar con lama o cieno. 2. limpiar de la babaza. —*v.i.* cubrirse de lama o babaza.
sliminess ['slaɪmɪnəs] *s.* 1. estado o aspecto legamoso o baboso. 2. viscosidad, glutinosidad.
slimjim ['slɪm'dʒɪm] *s.* (fam.) tipo flaquito, alfeñique.
slimly [-lɪ] *adv.* escasamente.
slimming [-ɪŋ] *a.* adelgazador (ej., un traje).
slimness [-nəs] *s.* 1. delgadez, flacura. 2. (fig.) escasez, insuficiencia. 3. (fig.) debilidad.
slimy ['slaɪmɪ] *a.* 1. legamoso, pecinoso. 2. baboso, viscoso, glutinoso. 3. (fig.) asqueroso, vil.
sling [slɪŋ] *s.* 1. honda. 2. tiragomas, tirador. 3. lanzamiento, hondazo. 4. cabestrillo. 5. eslinga, braga. 6. charpa, portafusil. 7. (mar.) balso; (*pl.*) grátil o gratil (parte central de la verga). 8. (fam., E.U.) bebida alcohólica hecha de ginebra con agua, azúcar y limón, ponche de ginebra. —*v.t.* (*pret., p.p.* SLUNG [slʌŋ]; *p.pr.* SLINGING) 1. tirar con honda. 2. arrojar, despedir, tirar. 3. poner en cabestrillo, poner en una eslinga. 4. **s. hash,** (jer.) trabajar de mozo o moza (en un restaurante, etc.).
slinger ['slɪŋər, B -ə] *s.* 1. (hist.) hondero. 2. (mec.) dispositivo lubricador (de cojinetes).
slingshot [-ˌʃɑt, B -ʃɔt] *s.* 1. tiragomas, tirador. 2. honda.
slink [slɪŋk] *v.i.* (*pret., p.p.* SLUNK [slʌŋk]; *p.pr.* SLINKING) (gen. con *off, away, by*) escurrirse, escaparse, escabullirse, salir furtivamente. —*v.t.* (vet.) parir prematuramente; malparir (díc. de la hembra de un animal). —*s.* animal (esp. becerro) nacido prematuramente; abortón. —*a.* prematuro.
slinkingly ['slɪŋkɪŋlɪ] *adv.* furtivamente.
slip [slɪp] *v.i* (*pret., p.p.* SLIPPED; *p.pr.* SLIPPING) 1. escabullirse, escaparse, escurrirse. 2. deslizarse; resbalar. 3. pasar suave o rápidamente. 4. írsele (a uno la mano). 5. errar, equivocarse, descarriarse. 6. soltarse, zafarse, desprenderse. 7. declinar, decaer, deteriorarse. 8. **s. away,** escabullirse, huir; s. by, correr, pasar rápido (ej., tiempo); **s. down,** dejarse caer, descolgarse; **s. in,** introducirse o meterse secretamente; **s. into,** introducirse, entrometerse, insinuarse; ponerse (vestidos) rápidamente; (jer., G.B.) aporrear, apalear; devorar; **s. off,** escabullirse; **s. out,** salir inadvertido; **s. through one's fingers,** caérsele; escapársele o escabullírsele de las manos; **s. up,** (fam.) equivocarse; salir mal; **to be slipping,** perder la habilidad acostumbrada, volverse inseguro (en su profesión, etc.); **to let s.,** revelar, dejar escapar (secreto, palabras). —*v.t.* 1. omitir, dejar escapar. 2. eludir, escapar de (perseguidores, etc.). 3. desprenderse de, zafarse de, librarse de (traba, etc.). 4. hacer o dejar deslizar; insertar o colocar suavemente, pasar rápidamente. 5. deslizar en la mano (billete, moneda, pedazo de papel, etc.), ej., *I slipped him a fiver,* le deslicé en la mano (un billete de) cinco dólares. 6. dislocar (hombro, rodilla, etc.). 7. malparir, parir prematuramente (animal). 8. **s. anchor,** (mar.) levantar anclas; **s. its skin,** cambiar de piel (serpiente); **s. off,** quitarse rápidamente (vestido, prenda, etc.); **s. on,** ponerse rápidamente (vestido, prenda, etc.); **s. one over on,** (jer.) pegársela, hacer una mala pasada (a alguien); **s. one's mind,** olvidársele a uno, irsele de la memoria a uno; **s. the cable,** (mar.) soltar el cable. —*s.* 1. resbalón, deslizamiento, paso en falso. 2. desliz, falta; lapso, lapsus, equivocación, error. 3. evasión, escape, huida. 4. enaguas, fustán (Am.); delantal de niño; funda de almohada. 5. traílla (de perro). 6. muelle, embarcadero, arrimadero; plataforma flotante para embarcar o desembarcar; varadero, grada de construcción. 7. baja (de precios). 8. pérdida de velocidad teórica (de un barco o avión). 9. (especie de) piedra de afilar. 10. (geol.) deslizamiento, desplazamiento, desprendimiento (de tierras); falla, grieta. 11. (mot.) deslizamiento; pérdida o escape de fuerza (en bombas). 12. (béisbol, criquet) jugador fuera del cuadrado; terreno fuera del cuadrado. 13. (cerám.) barbotina. 14. **there's many a s. twixt the cup and the lip,** de la mano a la boca se pierde la sopa; **to give (one) the s.,** dar esquinazo a (uno), eludir (a uno). —*a.* escurridizo, deslizante, corredizo, resbaladizo.
slip, *s.* 1. vástago, renuevo, retoño, sarmiento (de una planta). 2. tira, faja, listón, pedazo (de cualquier material). 3. cédula, papeleta, ficha. 4. (E.U.) banco de iglesia largo y angosto. 5. **s. of a boy,** mozuelo, rapaz, mozalbete; **s. of a girl,** mozuela. —*v.t.* cortar o sacar vástagos de (plantas).
slipcase ['slɪpˌkeɪs] *s.* estuche, funda (para proteger libros).
slipcover [-ˌkʌvər, B -ə] *s.* 1. funda (de muebles, etc.). 2. estuche, funda (para proteger libros).
slip gallery, (impr.) galería para la composición de una columna.
slip hook, gancho de deslizamiento, gancho de escape.
slipknot ['slɪpˌnɑt, B -nɔt] *s.* nudo corredizo.
slip noose, lazo con nudo corredizo.
slip of the pen, error de pluma, lapsus cálami.
slip of the tongue, error de lengua, lapsus linguae.
slip-on ['slɪpˌɔn, -ˌɑn, B -ˌɔn] **slipover** [-ˌoʊvər, B -və] *s.* prenda de vestir fácil de poner y de quitar (por ej. suéter).
slippage [-ɪdʒ] *s.* 1. desprendimiento, resbalamiento (de correa, ruedas, etc.). 2. (mec.) pérdida de fuerza de transmisión; gasto no medido.
slipped disk, (med.) disco intervertebral luxado.
slipper ['slɪpər, B -ə] *s.* 1. zapatilla, babucha, pantufla, pantuflo, chinela, chancleta. 2. (mec.) zapata, patín (de ruedas). —*a.* (dial.) resbaladizo, escurridizo.
slippered [-ərd, B -əd] *a.* 1. que calza zapatillas (díc. de los pies). 2. (fig.) confortable, relajado.
slippery [-ərɪ] *a.* 1. resbaladizo, resbaloso. 2. escurridizo, deslizadizo. 3. (fig.) evasivo, astuto, mañoso, marrullero.
slippery elm, (bot.) variedad norteamericana de olmo.
slip plane, (ing.) plano de deslizamiento.
slippy ['slɪpɪ] *a.* (SLIPPIER; SLIPPIEST) 1. resbaladizo, resbaloso. 2. escurridizo, deslizadizo. 3. (fig.) evasivo, falso, marrullero.
slip ring, (elec.) anillo colector, anillo rozante o de frotamiento.
slip rope, (mar.) cabo pasado por seno.
slipsheet [-ˌʃit] *s.* hoja de papel protectora (entre hojas recién impresas). —*v.t.* interfoliar (hojas impresas).
slipshod [-ˌʃɑd, B -ʃɔd] *a.* 1. en chancleta, gastado (zapato). 2. desaliñado, descuidado, desaseado. 3. desordenado, indiferente, remiso, negligente.
slipslop [-ˌslɑp, B -slɔp] *s.* 1. (fig.) aguachirle, despropósito, disparate, cotorreo. 2. (ant.) aguachirle, aguapié.
slipsole [-ˌsoʊl] *s.* plantilla.
slipstick [-ˌstɪk] *s.* (jer.) regla de cálculo.
slip stitch, (cost.) puntada invisible (esp. para dobladillos).
slipstream [-ˌstrim] *s.* torbellino, estela (de una hélice).
slip switch, (f.c.) cruzamiento de agujas, cruzamiento con cambiavía, cambio de cruzamiento.
slip-up ['slɪpˌʌp] *s.* (fam.) error, descuido, equivocación; contratiempo.
slipway [-ˌweɪ] *s.* grada (en astillero).
slit [slɪt] *v.t.* (*pret., p.p.* SLIT; *p.pr.* SLITTING) 1. hender, cortar, rajar, ranurar; dividir, partir. 2. cortar en tiras; rasgar. —*s.* rajadura, hendidura, hendimiento, grieta, ranura, rendija, raja.
slit-eyed ['slɪt'aɪd] *a.* de ojos rasgados.
slither ['sliðər, B -ə] *v.i.* 1. rodar, resbalarse, deslizarse. 2. culebrear, escurrirse por el suelo. —*v.t.* hacer deslizar; hacer resbalar o rodar.
slithery [-ərɪ] *a.* resbaladizo, resbaloso.
slitter ['slɪtər, B -ə] *s.* 1. ruedecilla cortadora (de piedras preciosas), tajadera. 2. disco cortador (de papel, película, etc.).
slitting file, lima-cuchillo, lima de hender, lima achaflanada.
slitting shears, cortador mecánico para hojalata, cizalla para chapa metálica.
slit trench, (mil.) trinchera abrigo.
sliver ['slɪvər, -ə] *s.* 1. astilla. 2. (tej.) torzal, mecha (de fibras textiles). —*v.t.* cortar en tiras, reducir a astillas. —*v.i.* astillarse, dividirse en astillas.
slob [slɑb, B slɔb] *s.* 1. nieve blanda o pulposa. 2. (despec.) sujeto desaliñado; mollejón; palurdo, patán. 3. (Irl.) fango, cieno, limo, légamo.
slobber ['slɑbər, B 'slɔbə] *v.i.* 1. babear, babosear. 2. (fig.) hablar con efusión o sensiblería. —*v.t.* babosear, cubrir de baba. —*s.* 1. babeo, baboseo. 2. efusión, sensiblería; aguachirle.
slobbery [-ərɪ] *a.* 1. baboso. 2. efusivo, sentimental. 3. desordenado, desaliñado.
sloe [sloʊ] *s.* 1. (bot.) endrino, andrino, asarero, ciruelo silvestre, acacia bastarda. 2. endrina, andrina, amargaleja, abruñeiro.
sloe-eyed ['sloʊ'aɪd] *a.* de ojos endrinos, ojinegro.
sloe gin, ginebra de endrinas.
slog [slɑg, B slɔg] *v.t.* (*pret., p.p.* SLOGGED; *p.pr.* SLOGGING) golpear, aporrear, pegar con violencia. —*v.i.* 1. andar pesadamente. 2. trabajar tenazmente, atrafagar, fatigarse. —*s.* golpetazo, golpazo.

slogan ['sloʊgən] *s.* 1. consigna, lema. 2. (Esco., Irl., hist.) grito de combate. 3. lema, refrán (publicitario o político).

sloganeer [ˌsloʊgə'nɪər, B -'nɪə] *s.* inventor de lemas (publicitarios). —*v.i.* usar lemas.

sloganize ['sloʊgəˌnaɪz] *v.t.* convertir en lema o refrán (publicitarios).

slogger ['slɑgər, B 'slɔgə] *s.* 1. boxeador de golpes fuertes. 2. trafagón.

sloop [slup] *s.* (mar.) balandra, balandro, chalupa.

sloop of war, (mar.) corbeta.

slop [slɑp, B slɔp] *s.* 1. cieno, fango, limo, lodo blando. 2. (*gen. pl.*) aguachirle, aguapié, zupia. 3. (*pl.*) líquido derramado; mojadura. 4. (*pl.*) lavazas, agua sucia. 5. (*pl.*) desperdicios, desechos, sobras, restos, residuos. 6. (*pl.*) lías, heces. 7. obra empalagosa, escrito disparatado. 8. mono holgado, traje de faena; blusa o delantal de obrero. 9. (*pl.*) ropa barata. 10. (*pl.*) (mar.) pacotilla. 11. (*pl.*) (hist.) pantalones holgados, pantalón bombacho. —*v.t.* (*pret., p.p.* SLOPPED; *p.pr.* SLOPPING) 1. derramar, verter. 2. mojar; ensuciar, enlodar. 3. cebar (con desperdicios). —*v.i.* 1. derramarse, verterse. 2. (fam.) (gen. con *over*) ponerse muy sentimental. 3. caminar pesadamente (en el fango). 4. chacolotear.

slop basin, (G.B.) taza para residuos.

slop chute, conducto para arrojar desperdicios (en la popa de los barcos).

slope [sloʊp] *v.i.* 1. ir oblicuamente, ir sesgadamente, desviarse. 2. inclinarse, declinar, estar en declive. —*v.t.* sesgar, inclinar, colocar en declive, oblicuar. —*s.* 1. inclinación, declive. 2. talud, falda, ladera, cuesta, recuesto. 3. vertiente (de un continente). 4. (rad.) atenuación gradual. —*a.* (poét.) sesgado; inclinado, oblicuo.

slope level, (top.) clinómetro, nivel de pendiente.

sloping ['sloʊpɪŋ] *a.* inclinado, oblicuo.

slopingly [-lɪ] *adv.* sesgadamente, oblícuamente.

sloppily ['slɑpəlɪ, B 'slɔp-] *adv.* 1. descuidadamente, desordenadamente. 2. efusivamente, empalagosamente.

sloppiness [-ɪnəs] *s.* desaliño, desgarbo; descuido.

sloppy [-ɪ] *a.* (SLOPPIER; SLOPPIEST) 1. muy mojado; lodoso, lleno de charcos (camino, vía, etc.). 2. desaliñado, descuidado, desgarbado, desgalichado. 3. desordenado; chapucero. 4. (fam.) meloso, empalagoso, sentimental.

slopwork [-ˌwɜrk, B -ˌwɜk] *s.* 1. manufactura de ropa barata y mal hecha. 2. chapucería, trabajo mal hecho.

slopworker [-ər, B -ə] *s.* chapucero.

slosh [slɑʃ, B slɔʃ] *v.i.* chapotear, chapalear. —*v.t.* 1. (esp. con *around*) remolinear (líquido en una vasija, etc.). 2. derramar; salpicar. 3. (jer., G.B.) golpear, asestar un golpe a, dar una bofetada a. —*s.* lodo blanco, aguanieve barrosa.

sloshed [slɑʃt, B slɔʃt] *a.* (jer., pr. G.B.) hecho una cuba, muy borracho; **to get s.,** emborracharse, pegarse una mona.

slot [slɑt, B slɔt] *s.* 1. abertura, hendija, ranura, muesca, canal. 2. (aer.) tobera divergente. 3. pista, rastro, huella (esp. de venado, ciervo). —*v.t.* (*pret., p.p.* SLOTTED; *p.pr.* SLOTTING) ranurar, acanalar, enmuescar.

slot cutter, (maq.) cortadora de ranuras.

sloth [slɔθ, B sloʊθ] *s.* (*pl.* SLOTHS) 1. pereza, holgazanería, haraganería, indolencia, inercia, flojera (Am.). 2. (zool.) perezoso, perico ligero, calípedes.

sloth bear, (zool.) oso bezudo.

slothful ['slɔθfəl, B 'sloʊθ-] *a.* perezoso, haragán, holgazán, indolente, poltrón, flojo (Amer.).

slothfully [-fəlɪ] *adv.* perezosamente, indolentemente.

slothfulness [-fəlnəs] *s.* pereza, haraganería, holgazanería, flojera (Amer.).

slot machine, tragamonedas, tragaperras, máquina de frutas; **to play a s.,** jugar a las máquinas (tragamonedas *or* tragaperras).

slotted nut, (mec.) tuerca encastillada.

slotted screw, (mec.) tornillo de cabeza ranurada.

slotting machine, máquina de ranurar.

slouch [slaʊtʃ] *s.* 1. postura floja o desgarbada, andar indolente. 2. haragán, holgazán, gandul. 3. **to walk with a s.,** caminar con pasos indolentes. —*v.i.* 1. moverse con indolencia, estar en postura desgarbada; repantigarse (en un asiento). 2. colgar fláccidamente (como el ala de un sombrero). —*v.t.* poner gacho.

slouch hat, sombrero gacho de ala flexible.

slouchily ['slaʊtʃəlɪ] *adv.* flojamente; con desgarbo (vestido, etc.).

slouchy [-ɪ] *a.* (SLOUCHIER; SLOUCHIEST) relajado, flojo (en postura); desgarbado.

slough [slu, B slaʊ] *s.* 1. lodazal, fangal, cenagal; pantano; entrada de un río; ría; (E.U.) estero. 2. estado de abatimiento, estado de desánimo; degradación moral.

slough [slʌf] *s.* 1. camisa (de culebra). 2. (med.) escara. —*v.i.* 1. (gen. con *off*) caerse (piel); desprenderse (costra o escara). —*v.t.* 1. mudar (piel). 2. desechar, echar de sí, descartar; (fig.) deshacerse de, abandonar (un hábito, etc.). 3. (bridge) descartar. 4. **s. over,** quitar importancia a, tratar superficialmente.

sloughy ['sluɪ, B 'slaʊɪ] *a.* (SLOUGHIER; SLOUGHIEST) cenagoso, pantanoso, fangoso.

Slovak ['sloʊvɑk, -vækm, B -væk] *s., a.* eslovaco, de Eslovaquia, parte oriental de Checoslovaquia.

Slovakian [sloʊ'vɑkɪən, -'væk-, B -'væk-] *a.* eslovaco, de Eslovaquia. —*s.* eslovaco, eslovaca.

sloven ['slʌvən] *s.* persona desaseada o desaliñada. —*a.* 1. desaseado, desaliñado. 2. no desarrollado, inculto.

Slovene ['sloʊˌvin] *s., a.* esloveno, de Eslovenia, una de las repúblicas yugoslavas.

Slovenian [sloʊ'vinɪən] *s., a.* esloveno, de Eslovenia.

slovenliness ['slʌvənlɪnəs] *s.* desaliño, desaseo; descuido, dejadez; pereza.

slovenly [-lɪ] *a.* (SLOVENLIER; SLOVENLIEST) desaliñado, desaseado, descuidado, dejado; perezoso, flojo. —*adv.* desaliñadamente, desaseadamente, descuidadamente; perezosamente.

slow [sloʊ] *a.* 1. lento, despacioso, pausado. 2. lento, tardo, torpe, lerdo, estúpido. 3. lento, aburrido. 4. retrasado, atrasado, retardado. 5. lento, gradual, paulatino. 6. (foto.) de diafragma reducido (díc. de la lente). —*adv.* despacio, lentamente. —*v.t.* retardar, demorar, retrasar. —*v.i.* (gen. con *down o up*) disminuir la velocidad, aflojar el paso; ir o trabajar más despacio (que antes).

slow burn, (jer.) acción de acumular indignación contra algo o alguien.

slow-burning powder, pólvora de combustión lenta.

slowcoach [-koʊtʃ] *s.* (G.B.) tardón, demorón (Amér.).

slowdown [-ˌdaʊn] *s.* (fam.) retraso, retardo; dilación, retardación.

slow fire, fuego lento.

slow-footed [-fʊtəd] *a.* lento, despacioso; que camina con dificultad.

slowish [-ɪʃ] *a.* un poco lento, algo lento.

slowly [-lɪ] *adv.* lentamente, despacio, de modo calmoso, pausadamente, gradualmente; **s. but surely,** despacio pero seguro.

slow match, mecha lenta, mecha tardía, mecha de seguridad.

slow motion, in s. m., (cine) en retardado, a cámara lenta.

slow-motion picture, película a cámara lenta.

slowness [-nəs] *s.* 1. lentitud. tardanza, retraso, dilación. 2. torpeza.

slowpoke ['sloʊˌpoʊk] *s.* (fam.) tardón, demorón (Am.).

slow roll, (aer.) tonel lento.

slow-witted [-'wɪtəd] *a.* lerdo, estúpido.

slowworm [-ˌwɜrm, B -wɜm] *s.* (zool.) lución.

slub [slʌb] *v.t.* (*pret., p.p.* SLUBBED; *p.pr.* SLUBBING) (tej.) sacar y torcer ligeramente (como la lana). —*s.* mechón, botón, gata (en hilos).

sludge [slʌdʒ] *s.* 1. lodo, cieno, fango. 2. fango de alcantarillas, cieno de cloaca; barro (de barreno), lodo de perforación (en sondeos); sedimento, grasa (en calderas). 3. capa de hielo de formación reciente (en el mar).

sludgy ['slʌdʒɪ] *a.* (SLUDGIER; SLUDGIEST) lodoso, fangoso.

slue [slu] *v.t.* hacer girar, volver. —*v.i.* girar, volverse, dar una vuelta. —*s.* 1. sesgo, inclinación (de una verga). 2. giro, vuelta.

slue, *var. de* **slew** (montón), **slough** (lodazal).

slug [slʌg] *s.* 1. (zool.) babosa, babaza. 2. haragán, holgazán. 3. (fam.) golpe fuerte; puñetazo. —*v.t.* (*pret., p.p.* SLUGGED; *p.pr.* SLUGGING) golpear con fuerza.

slug, *s.* 1. balín, posta. 2. pedazo (deforme) de metal. 3. proyectil, bala. 4. trago. 5. unidad de masa (equivalente a 32,2 lbs). 6. (impr.) lingote, plomada (para separar las líneas); línea de linotipia. —*v.i.* deformarse (como las balas al pasar por el ánima de un rifle).

slugabed ['slʌgəˌbɛd] *s.* perezoso (que se queda en la cama).

slugfest [-ˌfɛst] *s.* (jer.) golpeteo, pelea a golpazos.

sluggard ['slʌgərd, B -əd] *s.* haragán, holgazán. —*a.* flojo, perezoso.

sluggardly [-lɪ] *a.* de naturaleza ociosa, indolente.

sluggardness [-nəs] *s.* pereza, indolencia.

slugger ['slʌgər, B -ə] *s.* (jer.) boxeador agresivo.

sluggish [-ɪʃ] *a.* 1. ocioso, perezoso, tardo, indolente. 2. lento (en actividad, ej., el hígado). 3. lento, despacioso (flujo, río, aguas). 4. (com.) flojo, inactivo, estancado (mercado, bolsa, etc.).

sluggishly [-lɪ] *adv.* perezosamente, lentamente, indolentemente.

sluggishness [-nəs] *s.* pereza, lentitud, indolencia, inactividad, ociosidad; pachorra, cachaza (fam.).

sluice [slus] *s.* 1. compuerta, paradera, esclusa. 2. saetín, cauce, canal; agua represada, conducto (de agua). —*v.t.* 1. avenar, encañar. 2. anegar, mojar, regar; lavar con corriente de agua. 3. transportar por corriente de agua (troncos, etc.). —*v.i.* verterse, prorrumpir (en agua de un canal).

sluice box, (min.) mesa de lavar.

sluice gate, compuerta de esclusa, llave de descarga.

sluiceway ['slusˌweɪ] *s.* canal, conducto de evacuación, esclusa, aliviadero de fondo (de presas).

sluit [slut] *s.* (Sudáfrica) quebrada, cañada, hondonada, zanja honda (formada por las lluvias torrenciales).

slum [slʌm] *s.* barrio pobre y superpoblado; (*pl.*) barrios pobres, barriadas (Am.). —*v.i.* (*pret., p.p.* SLUMMED; *p.pr.* SLUMMING) visitar los barrios bajos; **to go slumming,** ir a divertirse en los barrios bajos.

slumber ['slʌmbər, B -bə] *v.i.* 1. dormitar. 2. (fig.) estar inactivo, flojear. —*s.* sueño, sueño ligero, adormecimiento, sopor.
slumberous [-bərəs] **slumbrous** [-brəs] **slumbery** [-bərɪ] *a.* 1. soñoliento, soñador. 2. adormecedor, soporífero.
slum clearance, demolición de barrios pobres.
slumgullion ['slʌm,gʌljən, B slʌm'gʌl-] *s.* cierto guiso de carne.
slumlord ['slʌm,lɔrd, B -lɔd] *s.* (jer.) casero, dueño de viviendas pobres de alquileres excesivamente altos.
slump [slʌmp] *v.i.* 1. hundirse o caerse súbitamente, desplomarse. 2. repantigarse. 3. (com.) bajar súbitamente (precios, ventas, etc.). —*s.* (com.) baja repentina (de precios, valores, demanda, etc.); depresión.
slung, *pret., p.p. de* **sling.**
slungshot ['slʌŋ,ʃɑt, B -ʃɔt] *s.* rompecabezas, mangual.
slunk, *pret., p.p. de* **slink.**
slur [slɜr, B slɜ] *v.t.* (*pret., p.p.* SLURRED; *p.pr.* SLURRING) 1. manchar, empañar. 2. (fig.) difamar, calumniar, mancillar (una reputación). 3. (impr.) hacer remosquearse, macular. 4. (gen. con *over*) pasar por alto, pasar por encima, hacer poco caso de, encubrir (defecto, falla, etc.). 5. (mús.) ligar (dos o más notas), marcar con ligaduras. 6. farfullar, pronunciar indistintamente. —*s.* 1. mancha, mácula, descoloramiento. 2. (fig.) reparo, desdoro, estigma (en reputación); difamación, calumnia. 3. (impr.) remosqueo, remosqueamiento. 4. (mús.) ligadura, ligado. 5. farfulla.
slurp [slɜrp, B slɜp] *v.t.* sorber (con ruido); comer (haciendo ruido).
slurry ['slɜrɪ, B 'slʌrɪ] *s.* (*pl.* SLURRIES) pasta aguada, lechada.
slush [slʌʃ] *s.* 1. aguanieve. 2. fango, lodo, barro. 3. (fig.) sensiblería, sentimentalismo tonto. 4. compuesto antiherrumbroso (para máquinas). 5. residuos de grasa y gordos (esp. en la cocina de los barcos). 6. pulpa de papel en suspensión acuosa. 7. (const.) mortero blando. —*v.t.* 1. enlodar, enfangar. 2. rellenar con mortero blando. —*v.i.* 1. chapalear. 2. **s. through,** vadear.
slush fund, 1. (mar.) fondo obtenido de la venta de desechos. 2. (jer., E.U.) fondos para sobornos políticos o propaganda corruptiva.
slushiness ['slʌʃɪnəs] *s.* fangosidad.
slushy [-ɪ] *a.* (SLUSHIER; SLUSHIEST) 1. fangoso, lodoso. 2. sensiblero, tontamente sentimental.
slut [slʌt] *s.* 1. mujer sucia y desaliñada. 2. suripanta, prostituta, meretriz. 3. perra.
sluttish ['slʌtɪʃ] *a.* 1. puerco, sucio, desaliñado. 2. meretricio.
sluttishly [-lɪ] *adv.* 1. asquerosamente. 2. de modo inmoral, inmoralmente.
sluttishness [-nəs] *s.* 1. desaliño, suciedad. 2. inclinación inmoral, inmoralidad.
sly [slaɪ] *a.* (SLIER o SLYER; SLIEST o SLYEST) 1. mañoso, marrullero, socarrón, solapado, taimado. 2. secreto, furtivo, artificioso, disimulado. 3. travieso, enredador. 4. (dial.) hábil, ducho, diestro, sagaz. 5. **on the s.,** (fam.) a escondidas.
slyly ['slaɪlɪ] *adv.* 1. astutamente, solapadamente. 2. disimuladamente, furtivamente.
slyness [-nəs] *s.* 1. astucia, sagacidad. 2. disimulo.
Sm *símb. de* **samarium,** samario (Sm).
smack [smæk] *s.* 1. dejo, gustillo, sabor característico. 2. pizca, pequeña cantidad; (fig.) indicio, huella, traza. 3. chasquido. 4. palmada o manotada resonante. 5. beso sonoro. 6. (jer.) dólar. 7. (mar.) queche. 8. **to have a s. at,** (G.B., fam.) tentar, ensayar. —*v.t.* 1. producir un chasquido con (los labios). 2. besar sonoramente. 3. hacer un chasquido con (látigo, mano, etc.); dar una palmada sonora a. 4. **s. down,** (jer.) reprimir (a uno que se propasa). —*v.i.* 1. chasquear. 2. **s. of,** saber a, oler a; (fig.) oler a. —*adv.* de golpe, directamente, derecho.
smack-dab ['smæk'dæb] *adv.* (fam.) exactamente directamente.
smacker [-ər, B -ə] *s.* (jer.) dólar.
smacking [-ɪŋ] *a.* vigorizador, cortante, fresco (viento, brisa, etc.).
small [smɔl] *a.* 1. pequeño; menudo, diminuto. 2. poco; corto, reducido. 3. insignificante, trivial, banal. 4. menor, inferior. 5. pequeño, en pequeña escala. 6. miserable, mezquino. 7. sumiso, humilde, modesto. 8. suave, tierno, blando; débil, flojo (licores). 9. **in a s. way,** en pequeña escala; en forma modesta; **to feel s.,** sentirse insignificante; sentir vergüenza. —*adv.* 1. en trocitos (cortado, etc.); finamente (molido, etc.). 2. con desdén, con desprecio (tratar, mirar, etc.). 3. débilmente, tímidamente, desmayadamente. —*s.* 1. parte estrecha, parte espigada (de algo). 2. (*pl.*) artículos menudos. 3. (*pl.*) (G.B.) ropa interior. 4. (*pl.*) (G.B., hist.) calzones. 5. **the s. of the back,** la región lumbar.
smallage ['smɔlɪdʒ] *s.* (bot.) apio caballar, apio equino, perejil macedonio, esmirnio.
small arms, armas portátiles, armas ligeras, armas de mano.
small beer, 1. (G.B.) cerveza floja, cerveza débil. 2. bagatela; persona o cosa insignificante.
small calorie, caloría pequeña, caloríagramo, gramocaloría.
small capital, letra mayúscula pequeña; (impr.) versalilla, versalita.
small change, cambio, suelto, sencillo (Am.) (monedas).
small craft, embarcación menor; botes.
small fry, 1. alevinos, pececillos. 2. morralla, gente sin importancia. 3. criaturas, niños, bebés.
small game, caza menor.
small gross, diez docenas.
small holding, (G.B.) pequeña propiedad de tierra.
small hours, primeras horas de la madrugada.
small intestine, (anat.) intestino delgado.
smallish ['smɔlɪʃ] *a.* pequeñito, bastante pequeño.
small letters, (letras) minúsculas.
small-minded [-'maɪndəd] *a.* de miras estrechas, intolerante; mezquino.
small-mindedness [-nəs] *s.* estrechez de miras, intolerancia; mezquindad.
smallness ['smɔlnəs] *s.* pequeñez.
small potatoes, (fig.) 1. bagatela, cosa trivial. 2. nulidad, don nadie, persona de poca monta.
smallpox [-,pɑks, B -pɔks] *s.* (med.) viruela.
small print, letras menudas.
small-scale ['smɔl'skeɪl] *a.* en pequeña escala.
small stores, (mar.) artículos de uso personal, en venta para la tripulación.
small stuff, 1. (mar.) cabos de mena reducida. 2. fruslerías, menudencias.
smallsword [-,sɔrd, B -,sɔd] *s.* (esgr.) espada corta.
small talk, palique, charla, conversación trivial.
small-time [-'taɪm] *a.* insignificante, sin importancia; de poca monta (esp. estafador, ladrón, etc.).
small-town [-'taʊn] *a.* provinciano, pueblerino.
smalt [smɔlt] *s.* esmalte, esmaltín.
smaltite ['smɔl,taɪt] *s.* (min.) esmaltita, cobalto blanco.
smalto ['smɑl,toʊ, B 'smɔl-] *s.* (pedazo de) vidrio de color, vidrio de esmalte (usado en mosaicos).
smaragd [smə'rægd, B 'smærægd] *s.* (raro) *var. de* **emerald,** esmeralda.
smaragdine [smə'rægdən] *a.* esmeraldino.
smaragdite [smə'ræg,daɪt] *s.* (min.) anfibolita.
smart [smɑrt, B smɑt] *v.i.* 1. escocer, resquemar, punzar, picar. 2. (fig.) sufrir, dolerse, sentir irritación. 3. (fig.) costar mucho, ej., *you shall s. for this,* te costará mucho esto (como amenaza). 4. **s. under,** afligirse con (o de o por), sufrir con. —*a.* 1. sagaz, inteligente, listo. 2. astuto, vivo, listo. 3. vigoroso, brioso, animoso, alerto. 4. ingenioso, agudo. 5. elegante, de buen tono, a la moda. 6. (ant.) punzante, picante, mordicante. —*s.* 1. dolor punzante; escozor, resquemor. 2. remordimiento; aflicción.
smart aleck, s. alec, (fam.) sabelotodo, sabidillo, sabihondo.
smarten ['smɑrtən, B 'smɑt-] *v.t., v.i.* (gen. con *up*) hermosear(se), aderezar(se); acicalar(se), emperejilar(se), emperifollar(se).
smartly [-lɪ] *adv.* 1. sagazmente, inteligentemente. 2. astutamente. 3. vigorosamente, briosamente, con brío. 4. ingeniosamente, agudamente. 5. elegantemente, a la moda.
smart money, 1. (G.B.) bonificación (que se da a soldados y marineros) por heridas o accidentes sufridos en el servicio. 2. bonificación por accidente de trabajo. 3. (der.) daños punitivos.
smartness [-nəs] *s.* 1. sagacidad, inteligencia. 2. astucia, viveza, ingenio. 3. vigor, brío. 4. ingeniosidad, agudeza. 5. elegancia, buen tono.
smart set, gente de buen tono, gente de sociedad.
smartweed [-,wid] *s.* (bot.) pimienta de agua.
smarty, smartie [-ɪ] *s.* (*pl.* SMARTIES) (fam.) sabelotodo, sabidillo; sabidilla, marisabidilla.
smarty-pants [-,pænts] *s. pl.* (*sing. en const.*) (fam.) sabelotodo, sabidillo, sabihondo; sabidilla, marisabidilla.
smash [smæʃ] *v.t.* 1. destrozar, hacer añicos, deshacer, romper. 2. golpear violentamente. 3. destruir, aplastar, arruinar, estropear. 4. (tenis) enviar (la pelota) con un smash. 5. **s. up,** aniquilar, destruir. —*v.i.* 1. hacerse pedazos. 2. (t. con *up*) arruinarse, quebrar. 3. (tenis) ejecutar un smash. 4. **s. into,** embestir contra; **s. through,** abrirse paso por la fuerza, romper y atravesar. —*s.* 1. destrozo, rotura. 2. golpe violento. 3. ruina; quiebra, bancarrota. 4. choque o colisión violenta. 5. bebida alcohólica con hielo, agua, azúcar, menta o jugos de fruta. 6. (tenis) smash, golpe rápido y fuerte dado por encima de la cabeza. —*a.* descomunal, extraordinario, sensacional (éxito, obra, etc.).
smasher ['smæʃər, B -ə] *s.* 1. (fig.) maravilla, persona muy atractiva o interesante. 2. golpe aplastante. 3. destructor, destrozador. 4. **to be a s.,** dar la hora (una mujer), estar muy atractiva.
smash hit, gran éxito popular, esp. obra teatral o disco fonográfico.
smashing [-ɪŋ] *a.* 1. aplastante (golpe, etc.). 2. devastador, extraordinario, impresionante, estupendo.
smashup [-,ʌp] *s.* 1. colisión violenta. 2. derrumbe, ruina. 3. (med.) colapso. 4. (com.) quiebra, ruina.
smatter ['smætər, B -ə] *v.t.* 1. chapurrear (un idioma extranjero). 2. conocer o estudiar fragmentos de (un tema). —*s.* noción superficial, conocimiento fragmentario, tintura (fig.).
smatterer [-ərər, B -ə] *s.* persona de conocimientos fragmentarios.
smattering [-ɪŋ] *s.* noción superficial, conocimiento fragmentario, tintura (fig.), ej., *he has a s. of history,* tiene algunas nociones de historia.

smaze [smeɪz] *s.* mezcla de niebla y humo.
smear [smɪr, B smɪə] *s.* 1. substancia grasosa, ungüento. 2. embarradura, mancha (hecha por una substancia grasosa). 3. (fig.) vilipendio, difamación, calumnia, mancha (en la reputación). 4. (bact.) frotis. —*v.t.* 1. manchar, untar, tiznar, embadurnar, embarrar. 2. (fig.) vilipendiar, difamar, manchar.
smearcase ['smɪrˌkeɪs, B 'smɪəˌ-] *s.* (E.U.) requesón, neterón, názula.
smear test, (med.) análisis citológico.
smear word, epíteto injurioso.
smeary ['smɪrɪ, B 'smɪərɪ] *a.* (SMEARIER; SMEARIEST) 1. manchado. 2. graso, grasoso, grasiento.
smectic ['smɛktɪk] *a.* esméctico.
smeddum ['smɛdəm] *s.* (esco.) 1. harina de malta; polvo, harina. 2. espíritu, vigor.
smeek [smik] *s.* (esco.) humo.
smell [smɛl] *v.t.* (*pret., p.p.* SMELLED [smɛld] o SMELT [smɛlt]; *p.pr.* SMELLING) 1. oler. 2. (fig.) oler, percibir. 3. olfatear, oliscar. 4. **s. out,** husmear, fisgar, descubrir. —*v.i.* 1. tener (sentido de) olfato, percibir olores, ej., *can fishes s.?* ¿tienen los peces olfato? 2. oler, despedir (buen, mal, etc.) olor. 3. husmear, heder, apestar, despedir mal olor. 4. **s. at** (o **about**), ir husmeando o venteando; **s. of,** (fig.) oler a, tener señas de. —*s.* 1. olfato, sentido del olfato. 2. olor (bueno o malo), fragancia, aroma, perfume, hedor, hediondez. 3. (fig.) sospecha; indicio, barrunto. 4. olfacción, olfateo.
smeller ['smɛlər, B -ə] *s.* 1. oledor, husmeador. 2. (jer.) trompa, hocico, nariz. 3. (jer.) golpe en la nariz.
smelling bottle, frasco de sales aromáticas.
smelling salts, sales aromáticas.
smelly [-ɪ] *a.* (SMELLIER; SMELLIEST) hediondo, maloliente.
smelt [smɛlt] *s.* (*pl.* SMELTS o SMELT) (ict.) pez esperinque, eperlano. —*v.t.* 1. fundir, beneficiar (metales). 2. reducir, refinar, purificar. —*pret., p.p. de* **smell.**
smelter ['smɛltər, B -tə] *s.* 1. fundidor (operario). 2. fundición, fundería (fábrica).
smelting furnace, horno de fundición, horno de beneficio.
S meter, *var. de* **signal meter.**
smew [smju] *s.* (orn.) variedad de mergo o mergánsar.
smidgen, smidgeon, smidgin ['smɪdʒən] *s.* pizca, ápice.
smilacaceous [ˌsmaɪlə'keɪʃəs] *a.* (bot.) esmiláceo.
smilax ['smaɪˌlæks] *s.* (bot.) zarzaparrilla.
smile [smaɪl] *v.i.* sonreír, sonreírse; **s. at, on** o **upon,** sonreír (a). —*v.t.* 1. expresar o demostrar con una sonrisa. 2. **s. away,** olvidar (pena, dolor, etc.) con sonrisas. — **s.** sonrisa.
smiling ['smaɪlɪŋ] *a.* sonriente, risueño; (fig.) risueño.
smilingly [-lɪ] *adv.* con una sonrisa, sonriendo, sonrientemente.
smirch [smɜrtʃ, B smɜtʃ] *v.t.* 1. tiznar, ensuciar, manchar. 2. (fig.) tiznar, desdorar, mancillar (la reputación). —*s.* 1. tiznón, mancha. 2. (fig.) tiznadura, desdoro, baldón.
smirk [smɜrk, B smɜk] *v.i.* sonreír(se) con afectación, o presunción. —*s.* sonrisa afectada, vana o presuntuosa.
smite [smaɪt] *v.t.* (*pret.* SMOTE [smoʊt]; *p.p.* SMITTEN ['smɪtən] o SMOTE; *p.pr.* SMITING) 1. golpear, pegar, batir. 2. castigar, penar. 3. derribar. 4. destruir, aniquilar. 5. **to be smitten by** (o **with**), ser afectado por; estar impresionado con; estar prendado de. —*v.i.* (raro, lit.) golpear o dar con fuerza repentina.
smith [smɪθ] *s.* herrero, forjador.
smithereens [ˌsmɪðə'rinz] *s. pl.* trizas, añicos, átomos, fragmentos.
smithery ['smɪθərɪ] *s.* herrería.
smithsonite ['smɪθsəˌnaɪt] *s.* (min.) esmitsonita.
smithy ['smɪθɪ, B 'smɪðɪ] *s.* 1. herrería. 2. herrero.
smitten, *p.p. de* **smite.**
smock [smɑk, B smɔk] *s.* 1. bata corta, camisa de mujer. 2. guardapolvo. —*v.t.* (cost.) fruncir.
smocking ['smɑkɪŋ, B 'smɔk-] *s.* frunce decorativo (en vestidos).
smog [smɑg, smɔg, B smɔg] *s.* humo mezclado con niebla; smog.
smoggy ['smɑgɪ, 'smɔgɪ, B 'smɔgɪ] *a.* lleno de humo mezclado con niebla.
smokable ['smoʊkəbəl] *a.* fumable, bueno para fumar.
smoke [smoʊk] *s.* 1. humo. 2. fumarada, fumada. 3. (jer.) pito, cigarrillo, cigarro. 4. **there is no s. without fire,** cuando el río suena agua lleva, cuando el río suena piedras trae; **to go up in s.,** hacerse humo, reducirse a nada; **to have a s.,** echar un cigarrillo o cigarro. —*v.i.* 1. ahumar, echar humo o vaho. 2. fumar. 3. moverse rápidamente; levantar polvo (al correr, con un vehículo, etc.). —*v.t.* 1. fumigar. 2. ahumar, sahumar, curar con humo. 3. fumar (un cigarrillo, pipa, etc.); 4. (jer.) fumar marihuana. 5. **s. out,** ahogar o echar fuera por medio de humo, hacer salir por medio de humo (insectos, el enemigo, etc.); hacer salir a la vista, hacer revelar, descubrir (secreto, etc.).
smoke bomb, bomba fumígena, bomba de humo.
smokebox ['smoʊkˌbɑks, B -bɔks] *s.* caja de humos (en locomotora).
smoke detector, detector de humo, detector de incendios.
smoked glass, vidrio ahumado; espejo ahumado o veteado, espejo veneciano.
smoke-dried ['smoʊkˌdraɪd] *a.* curado, ahumado.
smoke-filled room [-ˌfɪld-] (E.U., fig.) cuarto de reunión (ej., en un hotel) en que principalmente los políticos conferencian y formulan planes.
smokehouse [-ˌhaʊs] *s.* ahumadero.
smokejack [-ˌdʒæk] *s.* 1. asador movido por el aire caliente en la chimenea. 2. (f.c.) tragante, humero (en depósito de locomotoras).
smokeless [-ləs] *a.* sin humo.
smokeless powder, pólvora sin humo.
smoke meter, medidor de humo, fumímetro.
smoke pipe, conducto de humo, chimenea.
smokeproof ['smoʊkˌpruf] *a.* a prueba de humo.
smoker [-ər, B -ə] *s.* 1. fumador. 2. tertulia de hombres. 3. (f.c.) coche de fumadores.
smoke rocket, 1. inyector de humo (usado para revelar huecos o roturas en una cañería). 2. (mil) cohete fumígeno.
smoke sail, (mar.) guardahumo.
smoke screen, cortina o pantalla de humo.
smokestack ['smoʊkˌstæk] *s.* 1. chimenea. 2. conducto de humo, tubo de escape.
smoke tree, (bot.) fustete, árbol de las pelucas.
smokiness [-ɪnəs] *s.* fumosidad.
smoking [-ɪŋ] *a.* humeante. —*s.* el fumar; **no s.,** prohibido fumar.
smoking car, (f.c.) coche de fumadores.
smoking jacket, 1. chaqueta cómoda, batín. 2. chaqueta de media gala, con solapas de raso pero sin faldones.
smoking room, salón de fumar.
smoking-room ['smoʊkɪŋˌrum, -ˌrʊm] *a.* (fig.) de color subido, atrevido, indecente, ej., *s.-r. joke,* chiste o cuento de color subido.
smoky [-ɪ] *a.* (SMOKIER; SMOKIEST) 1. humeante, humoso, fumoso. 2. ahumado (color, techo, etc.).
smoky quartz, (min.) cuarzo ahumado.
smolder ['smoʊldər, B -də] *s.* fuego lento humeante y sin llama. —*v.i.* 1. arder o humear sin llama, arder en rescoldo. 2. (fig.) estar latente, estar oculto o escondido; arder (una pasión); llamear (ojos de ira, odio, etc.).
smolt [smoʊlt] *s.* (ict.) esguín, murgón.
smooch [smutʃ] *v.t.* (E.U.) tiznar, manchar. —*v.i.* (jer.) abrazarse, besuquearse. —*s.* 1. tizne, mancha. 2. (jer.) beso.
smooth [smuð] *a.* 1. liso, parejo, pulido. 2. plano, llano. 3. sin pelo, calvo, lampiño, afeitado. 4. fluido, continuo, uniforme, ininterrumpido. 5. sereno, manso, tranquilo. 6. afable, halagüeño, congraciador. 7. lisonjero, halagador. 8. suave, grato (al paladar, oído, sentimientos, etc.). 9. alisado, emparejado, nivelado. 10. (mec.) liso, llano; suave. 11. (gram. griega) no aspirado. 12. **as s. as silk,** como una seda; **to be in s. water,** estar a salvo, haber salvado los obstáculos. —*adv.* lisamente, suavemente, llanamente. —*v.t.* 1. alisar, bruñir, igualar, pulimentar. 2. (fig.) pulir, corregir. 3. (t. con *down*) allanar, aplanar. 4. (fig.) (gen. con *over* o *away*) suavizar, calmar; mitigar, paliar. —*s.* 1. terreno llano, superficie (del mar, etc.) en calma. 2. alisadura.
smoothbore ['smuð'bɔr, B -'bɔ] *a.* (arm.) de ánima lisa (cañón).
smooth breathing, (gram. griega) vocal no aspirada.
smooth dogfish, (ict.) nioto, cazón.
smoothen [-ən] *v.t., v.i.* pulir(se), suavizar(se), emparejar(se).
smoother [-ər, B -ə] *s.* alisador; pulidor.
smooth-faced [-'feɪst] *a.* 1. lampiño; afeitado. 2. liso, de superficie suave. 3. (fig.) blando, congraciador; hipócrita.
smooth hound, (ict.) cazón, pique, tollo.
smoothie, *var. de* **smoothy.**
smoothing [-ɪŋ] *a.* de emparejar, de allanar. —*s.* alisadura.
smoothing iron, alisador, plancha.
smoothly [-lɪ] *adv.* 1. lisamente, suavemente, llanamente. 2. halagüeñamente, con aire congraciador.
smoothness [-nəs] *s.* 1. llanura, suavidad, uniformidad, tersura. 2. serenidad, tranquilidad. 3. afabilidad, blandura.
smooth-shaven [-'ʃeɪvən] *a.* bien afeitado; sin barba ni bigote.
smooth-spoken [-'spoʊkən] *a.* de hablar agradable y placentero.
smooth-tongued [-'tʌŋd] *a.* 1. de hablar agradable. 2. meloso; lisonjero, adulador.
smoothy [-ɪ] *s.* (*pl.* SMOOTHIES) 1. persona de modales refinados. 2. meloso; lisonjero.
smorgasbord ['smɔrgəsˌbɔrd, B 'smɔgəsˌbɔd] *s.* 1. variedad de manjares como quesos, pescado, carne, ensaladas, etc. para que cada cual se sirva. 2. cena o comida compuesta de estos platos variados. 3. restaurante que sirve esta clase de comidas.
smote [smoʊt] *pret. de* **smite.**
smother ['smʌðər, B -ə] *s.* 1. sofoco, sofocación, asfixia. 2. confusión, conmoción. —*v.t.* 1. ahogar, asfixiar, sofocar. 2. apagar. 3. suprimir, encubrir, reprimir. 4. colmar, abrumar (con). 5. (cocina) estofar. —*v.i.* 1. ahogarse, asfixiarse. 2. apagarse.

smothered mate [-ərd-, B -əd-] (ajedrez) mate ahogado.
smothering ['smʌðərɪŋ] *a.* asfixiante, sofocante.
smothery [-ərɪ] *a.* sofocador, sofocante; polvoriento, humoso.
smoulder, (G.B.) *var. de* **smolder.**
smudge [smʌdʒ] *s.* 1. tiznajo, tiznón, borrón, mancha, mácula, tacha. 2. hoguera (para fumigación). 3. humo denso y sofocante. —*v.t.* 1. tiznar, manchar, ensuciar. 2. ahumar, fumigar (jardín, huerta, etc.). —*v.i.* tiznarse, ensuciarse.
smudgily ['smʌdʒəlɪ] *adv.* con manchas o tiznajos, suciamente.
smudginess [-ɪnəs] *s.* tiznadura, suciedad, aspecto manchado o borroso.
smudgy [-ɪ] *a.* (SMUDGIER; SMUDGIEST) manchado, sucio, borroso, tiznado.
smug [smʌg] *a.* (SMUGGER; SMUGGEST) 1. apuesto, pulcro, limpio, pulido, acicalado. 2. relamido, presumido, pagado de sí; complacido de sí.
smuggle ['smʌgəl] *v.i.* contrabandear. —*v.t.* pasar de contrabando; **s. in,** meter o pasar de contrabando; **s. out,** sacar de contrabando.
smuggler ['smʌglər, B -lə] *s.* contrabandista.
smugly ['smʌglɪ] *adv.* 1. limpiamente, pulcramente. 2. presumidamente, relamidamente.
smugness [-nəs] *s.* 1. pulcritud, limpieza. 2. presunción; satisfacción vanidosa.
smut [smʌt] *s.* 1. mancha de hollín, tizne; suciedad. 2. obscenidad, lenguaje grosero o indecente. 3. (agr.) roya negra; tizón. —*v.t.* (*pret., p.p.* SMUTTED; *p pr.* SMUTTING) tiznar, ensuciar, manchar. —*v.i.* 1. tiznarse. 2. (agr.) contraer la roya.
smutch [smʌtʃ] *s.* tizne, mancha, tiznón. —*v.t.* tiznar, embarrar, manchar.
smutchy ['smʌtʃɪ] *a.* tiznado, manchado.
smuttily ['smʌtəlɪ] *adv.* 1. suciamente. 2. obscenamente, indecentemente.
smuttiness [-ɪnəs] *s.* 1. suciedad. 2. obscenidad, indecencia.
smutty [-ɪ] *a.* (SMUTTIER; SMUTTIEST) 1. manchado, sucio. 2. obsceno, indecente. 3. ahumado, negruzco, pardo (color). 4. (agr.) que tiene roya.
Sn *símb. de* **stannum** (tin), estaño (Sn).
snack [snæk] *s.* 1. tentempié, refrigerio, bocadillo. 2. (ant.) parte, porción.
snack bar, merendero; cantina o mostrador donde se sirven comidas ligeras y refrescos.
snack table, mesita plegable portátil (para una persona).
snaffle ['snæfəl] *s.* (t. s. bit) (equit.) freno acodado. —*v.t.* 1. dirigir (caballo) mediante el freno acodado. 2. (fig.) controlar, manejar. 3. obtener o conseguir con maña.
snafu [snæ'fu] *abrev. de* **Situation Normal, All Fouled Up,** (jer., mil.) situación normal, todo enredado. —*a.* (jer.) caótico, enmarañado. —*s.* confusión, caos. —*v.t.* (*pret., p.p.* SNAFUED; *p.pr.* SNAFUING) confundir, enredar.
snag [snæg] *s.* 1. tocón, gancho (de una rama rota o desgajada). 2. protuberancia, púa; raigón (de un diente). 3. tronco o rama sumergidos (en el agua). 4. (fig.) dificultad inesperada, tropiezo, obstáculo, ej., *to strike a s.,* tropezar con un obstáculo inesperado. 5. pitón del asta de un ciervo. —*v.t.* (*pret., p.p.* SNAGGED; *p.pr.* SNAGGING) 1. impedir, obstruir, enredar. 2. obstaculizar, estorbar. 3. rasgar o dañar con un gancho, clavo o tronco sumergido. 4. librar de impedimentos u obstáculos. 5. (fam.) agarrarse, cogerse.
snaggletooth ['snægəlˌtuθ] *s.* (odont.) diente roto; diente prominente o fuera de lugar.
snaggy [-ɪ] *a.* 1. ganchoso, nudoso; lleno de troncos sumergidos. 2. difícil, lleno de obstáculos.
snail [sneɪl] *s.* 1. (zool.) caracol. 2. (zool.) babosa. 3. (fig.) cachazudo, posma. 4. **at a s.'s pace,** a paso de tortuga.
snail-paced ['sneɪl'peɪst] *a.* lento, pesado, cachazudo.
snake [sneɪk] *s.* 1. serpiente, sierpe, culebra. 2. (fig.) traidor. 3. **s. in the grass,** persona desleal, enemigo oculto; peligro latente. —*v.i.* culebrear, serpentear, moverse sinuosamente. —*v.t.* 1. mover sinuosamente, hacer culebrear o serpentear. 2. (E.U.) halar (troncos).
snakebird ['sneɪkˌbɜrd, B -ˌbɜd] *s.* (orn.) marbella.
snakebite [-ˌbaɪt] *s.* mordedura de serpiente (esp. venenosa).
snake buzzard, (orn.) águila culebrera.
snake charmer, encantador de serpientes.
snake dance, baile ceremonial de ciertas tribus de indios norteamericanos en el que se imita el manejo y los movimientos de las serpientes.
snake eyes, (jer.) tiro de dos unos en juego de dados.
snake fence, (E.U.) cerca o valla en zigzag (hecha de troncos colocados horizontalmente).
snakelike ['sneɪkˌlaɪk] *a.* parecido a una serpiente.
snake pit, 1. nido de serpientes. 2. (fig.) manicomio, pandemónium.
snakeroot [-ˌrut] *s.* (bot.) dragontea, serpentaria.
snakeskin [-ˌskɪn] *s.* piel de culebra.
snakeweed [-ˌwid] *s.* (bot.) 1. historia. 2. dragontea, serpentaria.
snakily ['sneɪkəlɪ] *adv.* sinuosamente, serpenteando, culebreando.
snaky [-kɪ] *a.* (SNAKIER; SNAKIEST) 1. que tiene o lleva serpientes, ej., 8. *hair,* cabello coronado de serpientes (de las furias). 2. serpenteado, tortuoso; serpentino. 3. (fig.) astuto, solapado; traidor, maligno, malévolo.
snap [snæp] *v.i.* (*pret., p.p.* SNAPPED; *p.pr.* SNAPPING) 1. mordiscar o dentellar sin hacer presa. 2. hablar con irritación, decir bruscamente. 3. romperse con un chasquido; partirse en dos; crujir. 4. chasquear, dar un chasquido, crepitar; dar un estampido, ej., *the rifle snapped,* el fusil dio un estampido (al disparar); el fusil falló el tiro. 5. **s. at,** tratar de morder (a); replicar, contestar bruscamente (a); **s. into it,** (jer.) despabilarse, menearse, echarse rápidamente a trabajar o hacer algo; **s. out of it,** (jer.) dejar un hábito, abandonar una rutina; dejar de mortificarse, desechar una preocupación, cambiar de humor (malo). —*v.t.* 1. morder, mordisquear. 2. romper en dos con un chasquido. 3. hacer crujir, chasquear o estallar; cerrar o abrir de golpe. 4. (foto.) tomar (una instantánea), tomar una instantánea de (alguien). 5. (fútbol) poner (la bola) en juego rápidamente. 6. **s. one's fingers,** chasquear los dedos; **s. one's fingers at (someone),** (fig.) desdeñar, burlarse de (alguien); **s. someone's head off,** hablar airadamente a, tratar groseramente (a alguien); **s. out,** pronunciar en forma brusca; **s. (something) up,** echar la zarpa a, asir, agarrar, arrebatar (algo); (fig.) comprar o llevar con avidez (un artículo, una ganga, etc.). —*s.* 1. estallido, chasquido. 2. mordisco, tarascada. 3. crujido, crepitación. 4. corto período (esp. de frío). 5. broche de presión, cierre de resorte. 6. galletita, galletica. 7. (fam.) vigor, energía, brío. 8. (fig.) tarascada, réplica áspera. 9. (foto.) instantánea. 10. (jer.) mamandurria, ganga, cosa fácil. 11. **not to care a s.,** no importarle un comino. —*a.* rápido, instantáneo, hecho de repente, hecho de golpe. —*adv.* con un chasquido.
snapback ['snæpˌbæk] *s.* 1. (fútbol) pase (de la bola) hacia atrás (con las manos). 2. restablecimiento rápido.
snap bean, judía o habichuela verde, vainita (Amer.).
snapdragon [-ˌdrægən] *s.* 1. (bot.) dragón, boca de dragón, dragoncillo, conejito. 2. juego en que se sacan pasas de aguardiente o coñac en llamas.
snap fastener, corchete de presión.
snap judgment, opinión o decisión impremeditada.
snapper [-ər, B -ə] *s.* 1. (*pl.*) castañuelas. 2. tralla (de látigo). 3. habichuela verde, vainita (Amer.). 4. corchete de presión. 5. (ento.) insecto saltador. 6. (zool.) tortuga mordedora. 7. (ict.) cubera.
snapper-back [-ˌbæk] *s.* (fútbol) centro delantero.
snappily [-əlɪ] *adv.* 1. mordazmente. 2. enérgicamente, vigorosamente.
snappiness [-ɪnəs] *s.* 1. mordacidad. 2. vigor, vivacidad.
snapping beetle [-ɪŋ-] (ento.) escarabajo de resorte; baticabeza.
snapping turtle, (zool.) tortuga mordedora.
snappish [-ɪʃ] *a.* 1. arisco, mordaz; respondón, irritable, regañón, agrio. 2. propenso a morder.
snappishly [-lɪ] *adv.* mordazmente, de manera irritable.
snappishness [-nəs] *s.* mordacidad, acritud.
snappy ['snæpɪ] *a.* (SNAPPIER; SNAPPIEST) 1. arisco, mordaz; respondón, irritable. 2. vivo, enérgico, vigoroso. 3. fresco, vigorizante (el frío). 4. crujiente, crepitante. 5. garboso, elegante. 6. **make it s.,** (fam.) hazlo rápido, no pierdas tiempo.
snap roll, (aer.) tonel rápido, tonel horizontal.
snap-roll ['snæpˌroʊl] *v.t.* (aer.) hacer un tonel rápido.
snapshot [-ˌʃɑt, B -ʃɔt] *s.* (foto.) instantánea; foto informal. —*v.t.* (foto.) tomar una instantánea de.
snare [snɛr, B snɛə] *s.* 1. lazo, trampa, cepo; celada, asechanza, artimaña, red. 2. señuelo, reclamo. 3. bordón, tirante (de un tambor). 4. (med.) cordón metálico para extraer tumores. —*v.t.* tender lazos a, coger con trampa; (fig.) hacer caer en el lazo.
snare drum, tambor militar pequeño.
snarer ['snɛrər, B 'snɛərə] *s.* trampero, cazador con trampas; perseguidor.
snarl [snɑrl, B snɑl] *s.* 1. greña, mota de pelo enmarañado; maraña. 2. lío, maraña, complicación. —*v.t., v.i.* enredar(se), enmarañar(se); (fig.) enmarañar(se).
snarl, *v.i.* gruñir; regañar, rezongar; refunfuñar. —*v.t.* decir con un gruñido. —*s.* gruñido, gruñimiento; refunfuño, refunfuñadura.
snarler ['snɑrlər, B 'snɑlə] *s.* regañón, gruñón.
snarly [-ɪ] *a.* (SNARLIER; SNARLIEST) 1. enmarañado (ovillo, hilos, etc.); enredado. 2. hosco, huraño, irritable.
snatch [snætʃ] *v.i.* **s. at,** tratar de agarrar o arrebatar. —*v.t.* 1. agarrar, arrebatar. 2. (jer.) raptar, secuestrar. 3. **s. from,** arrebatar a. —*s.* 1. arrebato, arrebatamiento, arranque. 2. pedacito; trocito; ratito, momento. 3. (jer.) rapto, secuestro. 4. (dep.) levantamiento con arranque (de pesas).
snatch block, (tec.) pasteca.
snatcher ['snætʃər, B -ə] *s.* 1. arrebatador. 2. (jer.) raptor, secuestrador.
snatchy [-ɪ] *a.* (SNATCHIER; SNATCHIEST) irregular, intermitente.

snath [snæθ] **snathe** [sneɪð] *s.* mango de la hoz.
snazzy ['snæzɪ] *a.* (SNAZZIER; SNAZZIEST) (jer.) llamativo, demasiado vistoso, cursi.
sneak [snik] *v.i.* 1. escabullirse, escurrirse, andar a hurtadillas. 2. cobardear, arrastrarse. 3. **s. in,** entrar a hurtadillas; **s. out,** salirse a hurtadillas. —*v.t.* 1. mover o hacer a hurtadillas, ej., *s. a smoke,* fumar un cigarrillo a hurtadillas. 2. (jer.) birlar, hurtar. 3. **s. in** (o **into**), introducir a hurtadillas. —*s.* 1. salida furtiva. 2. sujeto solapado; ladrón de guante blanco, descuidero. 3. (*pl.*) zapatos o zapatillas de gimnasia. 4. **on the s.,** (jer.) clandestinamente.
sneaker ['snikər, B -kə] *s.* 1. tipo solapado. 2. (*pl.*) zapatos o zapatillas de gimnasia, zapatos de lona con suela de caucho.
sneakily [-kəlɪ] *adv.* solapadamente, furtivamente.
sneakiness [-kinəs] *s.* carácter furtivo.
sneaking [-kiŋ] *a.* 1. furtivo, solapado, cobarde. 2. latente, oculto. 3. indefinido, vago, ej., *s. suspicion,* ligera sospecha.
sneakingly [-lɪ] *adv.* furtivamente, solapadamente.
sneak preview, (cinem.) estreno preliminar de sorpresa (de una película para saber como la recibe el público).
sneak thief, ladrón de guante blanco.
sneaky [-kɪ] *a.* (SNEAKIER; SNEAKIEST) solapado, furtivo, oculto.
sneer [snɪr, B snɪə] *v.i.* (t. con *at*) hablar o reír despectivamente (de), hacerle un ademán despectivo o despreciativo (a), mofarse (de). —*v.t.* decir despectivamente, expresar burlonamente. —*s.* mofa, befa, escarnio.
sneerer ['snɪrər, B 'snɪərə] *s.* escarnecedor, burlón.
sneering [-ɪŋ] *a.* burlón, despreciativo, despectivo.
sneeringly [-lɪ] *adv.* burlonamente, despectivamente, con mofa.
sneeze [sniz] *v.i.* estornudar; **not to be sneezed at,** no ser cualquier cosa, tener mérito; **s. at,** despreciar. —*s.* estornudo.
sneezeweed ['sniz,wid] *s.* (bot.) variedad de helenio.
sneezewort [-,wɜrt, B -,wɜt] *s.* (bot.) variedad de milenrama.
sneezing powder [-ɪŋ-] polvo estornutatorio.
snell [snɛl] *a.* 1. agudo, penetrante, severo. 2. (dial.) rápido, veloz; agudo. —*s.* hilo con que se ata el anzuelo al sedal.
snick [snɪk] *v.t.* 1. cortar ligeramente; mellar, hacer muescas en. 2. (criquet) golpear levemente (la pelota) para desviarla. —*s.* 1. corte pequeño o leve. 2. (criquet) golpe leve a la pelota.
snicker ['snɪkər, B -ə] *v.i.* reír disimuladamente. —*s.* risita, risa tonta.
snickersnee [-,sni] *s.* cuchillo de monte, puñal de cazador.
snide [snaɪd] *a.* 1. deshonroso, fraudulento. 2. insinuador, sarcástico. 3. vil, bajo, mezquino. 4. falso, falsificado. —*s.* tipo sarcástico.
sniff [snɪf] *v.t.* 1. oler, olfatear. 2. **s. out** (**trouble, secret,** etc.), husmear, olfatear, oliscar, descubrir (dificultad, secreto, etc.). —*v.i.* 1. aspirar por la nariz, sorber el aire. 2. **s. at,** oliscar; (fig.) tratar con desdén, despreciar. —*s.* 1. aspiración (de aire). 2. expresión de desdén, muestra de desprecio.
sniffily ['snɪfəlɪ] *adv.* (fam.) altivamente, despreciativamente, desdeñosamente.
sniffiness [-ɪnəs] *s.* altivez, aire desdeñoso.
sniffish [-ɪʃ] *a.* desdeñoso, altivo.
sniffle [-əl] *v.i.* resollar fuerte y repetidamente; lloriquear. —*s.* resuello fuerte y repetido; lloriqueo.
sniffy [-ɪ] *a.* (SNIFFIER; SNIFFIEST) (fam.) altivo, despreciativo, desdeñoso.
snifter [-tər, B -tə] *s.* 1. (jer.) trago (de licor). 2. copa ancha de boca estrecha (para aspirar el aroma del licor).
snigger ['snɪgər, B -ə] *var. de* **snicker.**
sniggle ['snɪgəl] *v.t., v.i.* pescar anguilas.
snip [snɪp] *v.t.* (*pret., p.p.* SNIPPED; *p.pr.* SNIPPING) (gen. con *off*) tijeretear, recortar, cortar de un tijeretazo. —*s.* 1. tijeretazo, tijeretada. 2. recorte, retazo, pedacito. 3. (*gen. pl.*) tijeras de hojalatero. 4. (jer.) mozuelo, joven insolente. 5. (fam., G.B.) sastre. 6. (jer., G.B.) cucaña, cosa o apuesta segura. 7. (jer., G.B.) ganga, cosa barata.
snipe [snaɪp] *s.* 1. (orn.) agachadiza, rayuelo. 2. (mil.) tiro de emboscada. 3. (jer., E.U.) pucho, colilla (de cigarrillo). —*v.i.* 1. (orn.) cazar agachadizas. 2. (mil.) tirar emboscado, francotirotear. 3. **s. at,** tirar desde un escondite contra.
sniper ['snaɪpər, B -ə] *s.* 1. francotirador. 2. paco, tirador emboscado.
sniperscope [-,skoʊp] *s.* telescopio de infrarrojo (en fusil, etc.).
snippersnapper ['snɪpər,snæpər, B -ə,-ə] *s.* títere, mequetrefe, pelele.
snippet ['snɪpət] *s.* 1. recorte, retazo. 2. persona o cosa pequeña e insignificante.
snippety [-ətɪ] *a.* insignificante, menudo, pequeño.
snippiness [-ɪnəs] *s.* 1. aire irritable, mordacidad. 2. brusquedad, descortesía. 3. arrogancia, desprecio.
snippy [-ɪ] *a.* (SNIPPIER; SNIPPIEST) 1. irritable, mordaz. 2. brusco, descortés. 3. arrogante, desdeñoso, despreciativo.
snip-snap [-,snæp] *s.* réplica pronta y aguda.
snit [snɪt] *s.* (jer.) arranque de furia, pica (gen. con *in* o *into*).
snitch [snɪtʃ] *v.t.* (jer.) ratear, escamotear. —*v.i.* (jer.) soplonear, traicionar. —*s.* (jer.) soplón.
snivel ['snɪvəl] *v.t.* (*pret., p.p.* SNIVELED o SNIVELLED; *p.pr.* SNIVELING o SNIVELLING) 1. moquear, moquetear. 2. gimotear, lloriquear. —*s.* 1. mocos, moqueo, moquita. 2. gimoteo, lloriqueo, puchero.
sniveler [-ələr, B -lə] *s.* mocoso, llorón, lloraduelos.
snob [snɑb, B snɔb] *s.* esnob, persona presuntuosa.
snobbery ['snɑbərɪ, B 'snɔb-] *s.* fachenda, esnobismo, pretensiones sociales.
snobbish [-ɪʃ] *a.* propio de un esnob.
snobbishly [-lɪ] *adv.* con esnobismo.
snobbishness [-nəs] *s.* esnobismo.
snobby [-ɪ] *a.* (SNOBBIER; SNOBBIEST) propio de un esnob.
snood [snud] *s.* 1. bolsera, redecilla (para cabellos). 2. (esco.) banda o cinta para el cabello. —*v.t.* asegurar (el cabello) con una bolsera o redecilla, recoger (el cabello) con una red.
snook [snʊk, B snuk] *s.* 1. (ict.) róbalo, robalo. 2. (pr. G.B.) higa (gesto burlón); **to cock a s. at,** dar una higa a.
snooker ['snʊkər, B 'snukə] *s.* snooker (variedad del juego de billar).
snoop [snup] *v.i.* curiosear, husmear. —*s.* buscavidas, husmeador, entremetido.
snooper ['snupər, B -pə] *s.* buscavidas, husmeador.
snooperscope [-,skoʊp] *s.* telescopio de infrarrojo (en fusil, etc.).
snoopy ['snupɪ] *a.* (SNOOPIER; SNOOPIEST) (fam., E.U.) curioso, husmeador, entremetido, intruso.
snoot [snut] *s.* (jer.) 1. hocico, trompa, nariz. 2. mueca desdeñosa.
snootily ['snutəlɪ] *a.* altaneramente, altivamente, desdeñosamente.
snootiness [-ɪnəs] *s.* altanería, altivez, desdén.
snooty [-ɪ] *a.* (SNOOTIER; SNOOTIEST) altanero, altivo, desdeñoso.
snooze [snuz] *s.* siesta, sueño ligero. —*v.i.* dormitar, cabecear; hacer siesta.
snore [snɔr, B snɔ] *v.i.* roncar. —*s.* ronquido.
snorer ['snɔrər, B -ə] *s.* roncador.
snorkel ['snɔrkəl, B 'snɔkəl] *s.* esnórquel, tubo de respiración (de submarinos y nadadores). —*v.i.* nadar bajo el agua con tubo de respiración.
snort [snɔrt, B snɔt] *v.i.* 1. bufar, resoplar. 2. reírse fuertemente, soltar risotadas (de desprecio o indignación). —*v.t.* decir o expresar con un bufido o resoplido. —*s.* 1. bufido, resoplido. 2. (jer.) trago de licor.
snorter ['snɔrtər, B 'snɔtə] *s.* 1. cosa extraordinaria, algo colosal, fenómeno, prodigio. 2. (jer.) trago de licor.
snot [snɑt, B snɔt] *s.* 1. moco. 2. mocoso, mocosa.
snotty ['snɑtɪ, B 'snɔtɪ] *a.* (SNOTTIER; SNOTTIEST) 1. (vulg.) mocoso. 2. (jer.) iracundo, irritable.
snout [snaʊt] *s.* 1. hocico, trompa (de animal). 2. (fam.) hocico, trompa, nariz. 3. pico (de tetera, manguera, caño); embocadura (de un cañón).
snout beetle, (ento.) gorgojo.
snow [snoʊ] *s.* 1. nieve; (*pl.*) nevada, nevasca. 2. (poét.) canas; extensión blanca (de pétalos, etc.). 3. (t.v.) nieve. 4. (jer.) cocaína. —*v.i.* nevar. —*v.t.* (fig.) nevar, derramar; **s. under,** (*ú pr. en voz pasiva*) cubrir con nieve; (fig.) cubrir completamente, sepultar; abrumar, aplastar, derrotar abrumadoramente; **snowed in,** sitiado, detenido o encerrado por una nevada.
snowball ['snoʊ,bɔl] *s.* 1. bola de nieve. 2. (bot.) mundillo, sauquillo, viburno. —*v.i.* 1. jugar con bolas de nieve. 2. (fig.) acrecerse o acumularse rápidamente. —*v.t.* 1. tirar bolas de nieve a (una persona). 2. acrecer o acumular rápidamente.
snowbank [-,bæŋk] *s.* banco de nieve.
snowbell [-,bɛl] *s.* (bot.) estoraque americano.
snowberry [-,bɛrɪ] *s.* (bot.) bolita de nieve.
snowbird [-,bɜrd, B -,bɜd] *s.* 1. (zool.) pinzón de las nieves. 2. (jer.) adicto a las drogas.
snow-blind [-,blaɪnd] *a.* deslumbrado por la nieve.
snow blindness, deslumbramiento debido a la nieve.
snow boot, bota para nieve.
snow-bound [-,baʊnd] *a.* detenido por la nieve; inmovilizado o paralizado por la nevada (tráfico, etc.).
snow-broth [-,brɔθ] *s.* nieve derretida.
snow bunting, (zool.) pinzón de las nieves.
snowcap ['snoʊ,kæp] *s.* corona o capa de nieve (ej., en una montaña o pico).
snowcapped [-,kæpt] *a.* coronado de nieve.
snowdrift [-,drɪft] *s.* ventisquero, lomo de nieve, banco de nieve.
snowdrop [-,drɑp, B -drɔp] *s.* (bot.) 1. campanilla de invierno. 2. amarilis.
snowfall [-,fɔl] *s.* nevada, nevasca.
snow fence, palizada para nieve, paranieve, valla paranieves.
snowfield [-,fild] *s.* campo nevado; zona de nevado.
snowflake [-,fleɪk] *s.* 1. copo de nieve, ampo. 2. (orn.) pinzón de las nieves. 3. (bot.) campanilla (de otoño, invierno, etc.).
snow gage, medidor de nevada, nivómetro.

snow-grouse [-ˌgraʊs] *s.* (orn.) perdiz blanca.
snowiness [ˈsnoʊɪnəs] *s.* aspecto nevoso; albura.
snow leopard, (zool.) onza.
snow lily, (bot.) violeta americana de flores blancas.
snow line, límite de las nieves perpetuas.
snowman [-ˌmæn] *s.* figura o muñeco de nieve, hombre de nieve.
snowmobile [-moʊˌbil] *s.* vehículo automotor para viajar sobre la nieve.
snow-on-the-mountain [ˌsnoʊɑnðəˈmaʊntən, -ɔn, B -ɔn-] *s.* (bot.) (especie de) euforbio.
snowplow [ˈsnoʊˌplaʊ] *s.* 1. quitanieve, limpianieve. 2. (esquí) frenado ejecutado con ambos esquís.
snow pudding, (cocina) budín hecho con claras de huevo y dulce de limón.
snowshed [-ˌʃɛd] *s.* cobertizo contra aludes.
snowshoe [-ˌʃu] *s.* raqueta (para caminar sobre la nieve). —*v.i.* andar en la nieve con raquetas.
snowslide [-ˌslaɪd] *s.* avalancha de nieve, alud.
snowstorm [-ˌstɔrm, B -ˌstɔm] *s.* tormenta de nieve, nevasca, ventisca.
snowsuit [-ˌsut] *s.* traje muy abrigado para la nieve.
snow tire, neumático para nieve.
Snow White, Blanca Nieve, Blancanieves.
snow-white [-ˌhwaɪt, -ˌwaɪt, B -ˈwaɪt] *a.* nevado, blanco como la nieve.
snowy [-ɪ] *a.* (SNOWIER; SNOWIEST) 1. nevoso, nevado, cubierto de nieve. 2. níveo (blancura, etc.). 3. (fig.) nevado, puro, sin mancha.
snub [snʌb] *v.t.* (*pret., p.p.* SNUBBED; *p.pr.* SNUBBING) 1. repulsar, rechazar. 2. desairar, tratar con arrogancia, humillar. 3. detener o parar bruscamente. 4. **s. out,** extinguir (cigarrillo). —*s.* 1. repulsa, rechazo. 2. desaire, humillación. —*a.* romo, chato.
snubber [ˈsnʌbər, B -ə] *s.* 1. persona arrogante. 2. (mec.) tambor de frenaje; empaquetadura de fricción. 3. (aut.) amortiguador.
snubby [-ɪ] *a.* (SNUBBIER; SNUBBIEST) 1. romo. 2. que tiende a rechazar o a humillar.
snub nose, nariz respingona.
snub-nosed [-ˈnoʊzd] *a.* romo, de nariz chata, de nariz respingona.
snuff [snʌf] *v.t.* 1. aspirar, inspirar. 2. oler, husmear, olfatear, oliscar. 3. despabilar. 4. **s. out,** apagar, extinguir. —*v.i.* 1. oliscar, husmear. 2. tomar rapé. —*s.* 1. olfateo, husmeo. 2. tabaco en polvo, (tabaco) rapé. 3. pabilo (carbonizado), moco, costra (de una vela). 4. **up to s.,** despierto, avisado, listo; en buen estado; satisfactorio.
snuffbox [ˈsnʌfˌbɑks, B -bɔks] *s.* caja de rapé. 5. (zool.) marsopa.
snuffer [-ər, B -ə] *s.* 1. apagador, apagavelas, matacandelas. 2. (*pl.*) despabiladeras. 3. resollador. 4. adicto a tomar rapé, tabaquera.
snuffle [-əl] *v.i.* 1. husmear, ventear. 2. resollar, ganguear. —*s.* 1. husmeo. 2. resuello, gangueo. 3. (*pl.*) (med.) romadizo.
snuffy [-ɪ] *a.* (SNUFFIER; SNUFFIEST) 1. semejante al rapé; tabacoso. 2. adicto a tomar rapé. 3. desagradable, molesto, fastidioso.
snug [snʌg] *a.* (SNUGGER; SNUGGEST) 1. cómodo, acomodado; abrigado. 2. cómodo, confortable (renta, ingresos, etc.). 3. ordenado, aseado. 4. ajustado, amoldado, ceñido. 5. bien dispuesto, bien aparejado (buque o sus partes). 6. escondido, encubierto, secreto. 7. **s. as a bug in a rug,** sumamente cómodo. —*v.i.* (*pret., p.p.* SNUGGED; *p.pr.* SNUGGING) (dial.) arrimarse, apretarse. —*v.t.* 1. acomodar, abrigar. 2. ajustar, amoldar. 3. esconder, encubrir. 4. (mar.) (gen. con *down*) reducir el velamen de (barco antes de una tormenta).
snuggery [ˈsnʌgərɪ] *s.* (*pl.* SNUGGERIES) (pr. G.B.) aposento cómodo, cuarto acogedor; querencia.
snuggle [-əl] *v.i.* apretarse, arrimarse, arrellanarse; **s. up to,** arrimarse a. —*v.t.* apretar, arrimar.
snugly [-lɪ] *adv.* 1. cómodamente. 2. ordenadamente. 3. ajustadamente, de modo ceñido, ceñidamente.
snugness [-nəs] *s.* comodidad; buen ajuste.
so [soʊ] *adv.* 1. así, de este modo, de esa manera. 2. tan, tanto, de tal manera, de igual manera. 3. igualmente, también, ej., *so am I,* yo también lo soy o estoy. 4. por consiguiente, por eso. 5. **and so on,** y así sucesivamente; **and so to,** (y) después (fui, fuimos, etc.) a, ej., *and so to bed,* (y) después fui a la cama (o fui a acostarme); **how so?** (fam.) ¿cómo es eso? ¿cómo así?; **I told you so!** ¡te lo dije! ¡te lo advertí!; **if so,** si así es, si lo fuere, en tal caso; **in so far as,** hasta, hasta donde; **is that so?** ¿ah sí? ¿de veras? ¡no me diga!; **just so,** ni más ni menos; **not so,** no es así, eso no es verdad; **not so much as,** menos que, ni siquiera; (**it is,** etc.) **only so much** (**rubbish,** etc.), es pura (tontería, etc.); **or so,** más o menos; **so as to,** para, a fin de; **so be it,** así sea, amén; **so forth,** etcétera; **so far as,** tan lejos como; hasta, hasta donde; **so far as I know,** hasta donde yo sé; **so far so good,** hasta aquí (ahí) muy bien; **so forth and so on,** y así sucesivamente; **so long,** hasta luego, adiós; **so long as,** mientras que, hasta que; **so many,** tantos; **so much,** tanto; **so much for,** eso en cuanto a, eso basta en cuanto a; **so much so that,** hasta tal grado que, tanto que; **so so,** tal cual; así, así; **so that,** de suerte que, de modo que; para que, a fin de que; **so that's that,** (fam.) así son las cosas, así están las cosas; **so then,** así pues, conque, por tanto; **so what?** (jer.) ¿y qué?; **so to say, so to speak,** por decirlo así; **very much so,** mucho, en extremo; **you don't say so!** ¡no me diga! —*conj.* 1. así que, conque, con tal que. 2. pues; por lo tanto. 3. para que, ej., *leave me now, so that I can read,* déjeme solo ahora, para que pueda leer. —*interj.* ¡bien! ¿verdad? ¡así sea! ¡que así se haga! —*pron.* tanto, lo mismo, igual; **or so,** (ú. después de números y cantidades) poco más o menos. —*s.* (mús.) sol (nota musical).
So. *abrev. de* **South,** sur.
soak [soʊk] *v.i.* 1. empaparse, remojarse, calarse, estar en remojo. 2. beber, empinar el codo. 3. **s. into** (o **through**), penetrarse, infiltrarse; infundirse. —*v.t.* 1. empapar, remojar, calar. 2. beber (licor) con exceso. 3. (jer.) hacer pagar (precios, impuestos exorbitantes). 4. (jer.) asestar golpe a, apuñear. 5. **soaked to the skin,** calado hasta los huesos; **s. oneself,** ajumarse, emborracharse; **s. up** (o **in**), absorber, embeber. —*s.* 1. remojo, remojón, empapamiento; mojada, mojadura. 2. líquido para empapar. 3. (jer.) puñete, puñetazo; bofetón. 4. (fam.) ebrio, borracho, borrachín; borrachera.
soakage [ˈsoʊkɪdʒ] *s.* 1. remojo, remojón, empapamiento, mojada, mojadura. 2. cantidad absorbida.
soaker [-ər, B -ə] *s.* 1. chaparrón. 2. (fam.) borrachín.
soaking [-ɪŋ] *a.* hasta los huesos, completamente, ej., *s. wet,* calado hasta los huesos. —*s.* empapada, ensopada, mojadura.
soaking furnace, (metal.) horno de recalentar.
so-and-so [ˈsoʊənˌsoʊ] *s.* fulano, fulano de tal; **as so-a.-so once said,** como dijera fulano.
soap [soʊp] *s.* 1. jabón. 2. (jer., E.U.) dinero, esp. (dinero para) soborno. 3. **no s.,** (jer.) ni de riesgo, ni en sueños. —*v.t.* 1. jabonar, enjabonar. 2. (fig.) dar jabón a, enjabonar.
soapbark [ˈsoʊpˌbɑrk, B -ˌbɑk] *s.* (bot.) quillay, palo de jabón.
soapberry [-ˌbɛrɪ] *s.* (bot.) jaboncillo.
soapbox [-ˌbɑks, B -ˌbɔks] *s.* 1. caja de jabón. 2. (fig.) plataforma improvisada (para orador callejero).
soap bubble, burbuja de jabón, pompa de jabón.
soap dish, jabonera.
soap earth, jaboncillo de sastre, esteatita.
soap flakes, escamas de jabón, jabón desmenuzado.
soapiness [ˈsoʊpɪnəs] *s.* consistencia jabonosa o saponácea.
soapmaker [ˈsoʊpˌmeɪkər, B -ə] *s.* jabonero.
soapmaking [-ɪŋ] *s.* fabricación de jabón, industria jabonera.
soap opera, (jer.) (rad., t.v.) serial lacrimógeno, melodrama.
soap plant, (bot.) jabonera.
soapstone [-ˌstoʊn] *s.* (min.) esteatita, creta hispánica, jaboncillo de sastre, saponita.
soapsuds [-ˌsʌdz] *s. pl.* jabonaduras, burbujas o espuma de jabón.
soapwort [-ˌwɜrt, B -wɜt] *s.* (bot.) saponaria, jabonera, herbada, hierba jabonera, lanaria.
soapy [ˈsoʊpɪ] *a.* (SOAPIER; SOAPIEST) jabonoso, saponáceo.
soar [sɔr, B sɔ] *v.i.* 1. remontarse, encumbrarse, cernerse. 2. (fig.) elevarse (ideas, ideales, etc.). 3. subir desmesuradamente (precios, etc.). 4. (aer.) planear. —*s.* 1. vuelo alto, remonte. 2. (fig.) alcance.
sob [sɑb, B sɔb] *v.i.* (*pret., p.p.* SOBBED; *p.pr.* SOBBING) sollozar. —*v.t.* decir sollozando, expresar con sollozos. —*s.* sollozo.
S.O.B. *abrev. de* **son of a bitch,** (vulg.) hijo de puta, hijo de perra.
sobbingly [ˈsɑbɪŋlɪ, B ˈsɔb-] *adv.* con voz sollozante, con sollozos, sollozando.
sobeit [soʊˈbiɪt] *conj.* (ant.) si así fuese.
sober [ˈsoʊbər, B -bə] *a.* 1. sobrio. 2. serio, solemne, grave; **in s. fact,** en realidad, de verdad. 3. sensato, cuerdo. 4. sobrio (estilo). 5. sobrio, decente (color). —*v.t.* 1. poner sobrio, desembriagar. 2. (t. con *down*) calmar, serenar. —*v.i.* **s. down,** calmarse, serenarse; **s. up,** desembriagarse, pasarle (a uno) la embriaguez.
soberly [-lɪ] *adv.* 1. sobriamente, serenamente, tranquilamente. 2. seriamente, solemnemente. 3. sensatamente, cuerdamente.
sober-minded [-ˌmaɪndəd] *a.* desapasionado, sereno.
soberness [-nəs] *s.* 1. sobriedad. 2. serenidad, tranquilidad, calma. 3. seriedad, solemnidad. 4. sensatez, cordura.
sobersided [-ˌsaɪdəd] *a.* solemne, serio, formal.
sobersides [-ˌsaɪdz] *s. pl.* (*sing. o pl. en const.*) (fam.) tragavirotes.
sobriety [səˈbraɪətɪ] *s.* 1. sobriedad. 2. serenidad. 3. seriedad, solemnidad. 4. sensatez, cordura.
sobriquet [ˈsoʊbrɪˌkeɪ] *s.* apodo, sobrenombre, apelativo.
sob sister, (jer., E.U.) 1. mujer periodista que escribe artículos sentimentales. 2. persona sentimental.
sob story, (jer.) historia sentimental o lacrimosa.
socage [ˈsɑkɪdʒ, B ˈsɔk-] *s.* (hist.) tenencia feudal de la tierra que requería pago de renta (en dinero o en especie) pero sin la obligación de prestar servicio militar.

so-called ['soʊ'kɔld] *a.* así llamado, llamado.
soccer ['sɑkər, B 'sɔkə] *s.* (dep.) fútbol.
sociability [ˌsoʊʃə'bɪlətɪ] *s.* sociabilidad, cordialidad, amabilidad.
sociable ['soʊʃəbəl] *a.* sociable, amigable, amistoso. —*s.* (E.U.) tertulia, velada, reunión informal.
sociableness [-nəs] *s.* sociabilidad, amistosidad.
sociably [-blɪ] *adv.* sociablemente, amigablemente.
social ['soʊʃəl] *a.* 1. social. 2. sociable, ej., *man is a s. being,* el hombre es un ser sociable, el hombre es esencialmente sociable. 3. socialista. 4. (zool.) gregario. 5. (hist.) aliado, confederado. —*s.* tertulia, velada, reunión informal.
social climber, advenedizo, persona con ambiciones sociales.
Social Democracy, doctrina social-demócrata.
Social Democrat, social-demócrata.
Social Democratic, social-demócrata.
social disease, 1. enfermedad social, enfermedad venérea. 2. enfermedad causada por factores socio-económicos (ej., tuberculosis).
social insurance, seguro social.
socialism [-ʃəˌlɪzəm] *s.* socialismo.
socialist [-ləst] *s., a.* socialista.
socialistic [ˌsoʊʃə'lɪstɪk] *a.* socialista.
socialistically [-tɪkəlɪ] *adv.* conforme al socialismo.
socialite ['soʊʃəˌlaɪt] *s.* persona de alta sociedad.
sociality [ˌsoʊʃɪ'ælətɪ] *s.* sociabilidad.
socialization [ˌsoʊʃələ'zeɪʃən, B -laɪ-] *s.* 1. adaptación al medio social. 2. socialización.
socialize ['soʊʃəˌlaɪz] *v.t.* 1. volver sociable, adaptar al medio social. 2. socializar.
socialized medicine, medicina estatal, sistema que provee servicios médicos a una comunidad por medio de fondos públicos.
socially [-lɪ] *adv.* 1. en la sociedad (popular, inferior, etc.). 2. por la sociedad (aceptado, condenado, etc.).
social-minded [ˌsoʊʃəl'maɪndəd] *a.* interesado en el bienestar social.
social register, guía social, registro de personas de prominencia social.
social science, 1. sociología. 2. ciencia social (economía, política, etc.).
social scientist, 1. sociólogo. 2. especialista en ciencias sociales.
social security, 1. seguridad social. 2. seguro social, previsión social.
social service, programa o servicio de bienestar, programa de asistencia social.
social settlement, centro de asistencia o servicio social (en una ciudad populosa).
social welfare, asistencia social, auxilio social, bienestar social.
social work, asistencia social, auxilio social, servicio social.
social worker, asistente social, trabajador social.
societal [sə'saɪətəl] *a.* social, perteneciente a la sociedad.
society [-ɪ] *s.* (*pl.* SOCIETIES) 1. sociedad; comunidad. 2. sociedad, vida elegante. 3. compañía (de otra persona). 4. asociación, gremio; consorcio. 5. **to be in s.,** estar en sociedad.
Society of Friends, (relig.) Sociedad de los Amigos (los cuáqueros).
Society of Jesus, (relig.) Compañía de Jesús.
Socinianism [se'sɪnɪəˌnɪzəm] *s.* (teo.) socinianismo.
socioeconomic [ˌsoʊsɪˌoʊˌɛkə'nɑmɪk, -ʃɪ-, B -ˌikə'nɔm-] *a.* socio-económico.
sociologic [-ə'lɑdʒɪk, B -'lɔdʒ-] **sociological** [-ɪkəl] *a.* sociológico.
sociologically [-ɪkəlɪ] *adv.* sociológicamente.
sociologist [ˌsoʊsɪ'ɑlədʒəst, -ʃɪ-, B ˌsoʊsɪ'ɔl-] *s.* sociólogo.
sociology [-dʒɪ] *s.* sociología.
sociopolitical [ˌsoʊsɪˌoʊpə'lɪtɪkəl, -ʃɪ-] *a.* socio-político.
sock [sɑk, B sɔk] *s.* 1. (*pl.* t. sox [sɑks, B sɔks]) calcetín, media corta. 2. coturno (de los actores griegos); p. ext. comedia.
sock, *v.t.* pegar, golpear, apuñear; (jer., E.U.) **s. it to (him, her,** etc.), alentar (a él, ella, etc.) enérgica y vigorosamente; (ú. t. como exclamación). —*s.* puñete, puñada; golpe fuerte.
socket ['sɑkət, B 'sɔk-] *v.t.* 1. enchufar. 2. proveer de un enchufe. —*s.* 1. cuenca (del ojo); alvéolo (del diente); cavidad. 2. (mec.) manguito, casquillo, boquilla, quicionera, rangua, tejuelo macho. 3. (elec.) portalámpara, tomacorriente, enchufe hembra. 4. (rad.) portaválvula, portatubo. 5. (mar.) bocabarra.
socket gage, calibrador de cubo, calibre de copa.
socket punch, sacabocado, sacabocado a golpe.
socket wrench, llave de casquillo, llave de cubo.
sockeye [-ˌaɪ] *s.* (ict.) salmón de Alaska.
socko [-oʊ] *a.* (jer.) muy popular, de mucho éxito.
socle ['sɑkəl, B 'sɔk-] *s.* (arq.) zócalo.
Socrates ['sɑkrəˌtiz, B 'sɔk-] *s.* Sócrates, filósofo y maestro ateniense.
Socratic [sə'krætɪk, B sɔ-] *a., s.* socrático, de Sócrates.
Socratically [-ɪkəlɪ] *adv.* de modo socrático, socráticamente.
sod [sɑd, B sɔd] *s.* 1. césped, tierra herbosa; terrón herboso, tepe. 2. (vulg.) sodomita. 3. (jer.) estúpido, desgraciado. 4. **under the s.,** (fig.) en la tumba. —*v.t.* (*pret., p.p.* SODDED; *p.pr.* SODDING) cubrir de césped (un terreno).
soda ['soʊdə] *s.* 1. (quím.) sosa, soda. 2. (**t. s. water**) agua de soda, soda, gaseosa. 3. (naipes) la carta que se muestra antes de tallar (en el juego de faro).
soda alum, alumbre sódico.
soda ash, ceniza de soda, sosa comercial.
soda biscuit, s. cracker, galleta de soda.
soda fountain, fuente de soda (tienda o mostrador donde se despachan helados y bebidas).
soda jerk, s. jerker, (jer.) dependiente en una fuente de soda.
sodalite ['soʊdəˌlaɪt] *s.* (min.) sodalita.
sodality [soʊ'dælətɪ] *s.* (*pl.* SODALITIES) asociación, confraternidad; cofradía, hermandad.
soda pop, (bebida) gaseosa.
soda water, agua de soda; (bebida) gaseosa.
sodden ['sɑdən, B 'sɔd-] *a.* 1. empapado, saturado; húmedo. 2. pastoso, mal cocido. 3. fláccido, entorpecido (cara, facciones). —*v.t., v.i.* empapar(se), saturar(se); impregnar(se).
sodium ['soʊdɪəm] *s.* (quím.) sodio.
sodium benzoate, (quím.) benzoato de sodio.
sodium bicarbonate, (quím.) bicarbonato de sodio, carbonato ácido de sodio.
sodium bromide, (quím.) bromuro de sodio.
sodium carbonate, (quím.) carbonato sódico.
sodium chlorate, (quím.) clorato de sodio.
sodium chloride, (quím.) cloruro de sodio.
sodium cyanide, (quím.) cianuro de sodio.
sodium dichromate, (quím.) dicromato sódico, bicromato sódico.
sodium hydroxide, (quím.) hidróxido de sodio.
sodium hyposulfite, (quím.) hiposulfito de sodio, tiosulfato de sodio.
sodium nitrate, (quím.) nitrato de sodio.
sodium pentothal, (med.) pentotal (sódico) (marca de fábrica).
sodium peroxide, (quím.) peróxido de sodio.
sodium phosphate, (quím.) fosfato de sodio.
sodium sulfate, (quím.) sulfato de sodio.
sodium thiosulfate, (quím.) tiosulfato de sodio, hiposulfito de sodio.
sodium-vapor lamp [-'veɪpər-, B -pə-] (elec.) lámpara de vapor de sodio.
Sodom ['sɑdəm, B 'sɔd-] *s.* Sodoma; (fig.) antro de pecado.
sodomite [-ˌaɪt] *s.* sodomita; **S.,** sodomita.
sodomitical [ˌsɑdə'mɪtɪkəl, B ˌsɔd-] *a.* sodomítico.
sodomy ['sɑdəmɪ, B 'sɔd-] *s.* sodomía.
soever [soʊ'ɛvər, B -ə] *adv.* 1. por más; por mucho. 2. de cualquier clase.
sofa ['soʊfə] *s.* sofá.
sofa bed, sofá cama.
soffit ['sɑfət, B 'sɔf-] *s.* (arq.) sofito, plafón, intradós.
Sofia ['soʊfɪə, soʊ'fiə] *s.* Sofía, capital de Bulgaria.
soft [sɔft] *a.* 1. blando, tierno, muelle, mole (materia, material, etc.). 2. blando, suave, liso (superficie), ej., *s. skin,* cutis suave. 3. blando, blandengue; moderado, conciliador; apacible, tranquilo; sentimental, emotivo. 4. suave, gradual (pendiente, declive, etc.). 5. blando, templado (clima, aire, etc.). 6. blando, suave (agua). 7. no alcohólico (bebida). 8. indistinto, confuso; de contorno suave, de trazo borroso. 9. tonto, bobo, estúpido. 10. (fam.) fácil. 11. (fís.) blando, poco penetrante (ciertos rayos, esp. rayos X). 12. (fon.) suave (pronunciación). 13. **s. in the head,** estúpido, tonto; **to be s. on,** ser condescendiente con. —*adv.* blandamente, suavemente. —*s.* 1. parte blanda o suave. 2. tonto, necio. —*interj.* (ant.) ¡poco a poco! ¡despacio! ¡chist! ¡chito!
softball ['sɔftˌbɔl] *s.* (dep.) variedad de béisbol (jugada con una pelota blanda).
soft-boiled [-'bɔɪld] *a.* pasado por agua (huevo).
soft chancre, (med.) chancro blando, chancroide.
soft coal, hulla, grasa, carbón bituminoso o graso.
soft drink, bebida no alcohólica.
soften ['sɔfən] *v.t.* 1. ablandar, reblandecer, enmollecer, molificar; atenuar (un pedido); 2. (mil.) (ú. t. con *up*) ablandar (las posiciones enemigas por medio de bombardeos aéreos, cañones, etc.). —*v.i.* ablandarse, reblandecerse.
softened [-əd] *a.* atenuado.
softener [-ər, B -ə] *s.* ablandador (de metales, etc.); suavizador, ablandador (de agua).
softening of the brain, (med.) reblandecimiento cerebral.
soft-finned ['sɔft'fɪnd] *a.* (zool.) de aletas cartilaginosas.
softhead [-ˌhɛd] *s.* gaznápiro, papanatas, simplón, zonzo.
softheaded [-'hɛdəd] *a.* falto de juicio, de pocas luces, simple.
softhearted [-'hɑrtəd, B -'hɑt-] *a.* blando de corazón, bondadoso, compasivo, tierno.
softie, *var. de* **softy.**
soft iron, hierro dulce, hierro blando.
softly ['sɔftlɪ] *adv.* blandamente, suavemente.
softness [-nəs] *s.* 1. blandura, suavidad, morbidez. 2. dulzura, ternura, afabilidad. 3. debilidad de carácter; afeminación.
soft palate, velo del paladar.
soft pedal, 1. (mús.) sordina, pedal de sordina (del piano). 2. (jer., fig.) freno, limitación, restricción; esp. prohibición de hablar.
soft-pedal [-'pɛdəl] *v.t.* 1. tocar con sordina (piano). 2. (jer.) suavizar, moderar.
soft sell, arte de vender por medio de persuasión sutil.

soft-shell [-ˌʃɛl] **soft-shelled** [-ˈʃɛld] *a.* de concha o carapacho blando.

soft-shell clam, almeja de forma ovalada (*Mya arenaria*).

soft-shell crab, cangrejo después de la muda.

soft-shell turtle, (zool.) triónix espinífero.

soft soap, 1. jabón blando. 2. (fam.) jabón, adulación, halago, lisonja.

soft-soap[-ˈsoʊp] *v.t., v.i.* 1. frotar(se) o untar(se) con jabón blando. 2. (fam.) dar jabón a, adular, lisonjear.

soft-soaper [-ˈsoʊpər, B -pə] *s.* lisonjero, zalamero, adulador.

soft solder, soldadura blanda, soldadura de estaño.

soft-spoken [ˈsɔftˈspoʊkən] *a.* 1. de voz baja, de voz suave o dulce. 2. suave, afable.

soft steel, acero dulce, acero suave.

soft tack, (mar.) pan.

soft touch, (jer.) persona que se deja persuadir fácilmente, esp. para prestar dinero.

soft water, agua delgada, agua blanda.

soft wheat, trigo blando.

softwood [-ˌwʊd] *s.* 1. madera blanda, madera tierna. 2. árbol de madera blanda.

soft-wooded [-əd] *a.* de madera blanda.

softy [-ɪ] *s.* (*pl.* SOFTIES) (fam.) alfeñique, hombre sentimental; mentecato.

soggy [ˈsɑgɪ, ˈsɔgɪ, B ˈsɔgɪ] *a.* (SOGGIER; SOGGIEST) 1. empapado, saturado de humedad. 2. pastoso (pan, etc.). 3. pesado, aburrido (estilo, prosa, etc.).

soil [sɔɪl] *v.t.* 1. ensuciar, manchar, empañar, emporcar. 2. (fig.) corromper, viciar, deshonrar, infamar, mancillar (el honor). 3. alimentar (ganado) con alcacer o verduras; purgar con alcacer o verduras. —*v.i.* ensuciarse, mancharse, emporcarse. —*s.* 1. mancha, mácula, tiznadura, ensuciamiento. 2. inmundicia, mugre, porquería, suciedad. 3. abono, estiércol, fimo. 4. suelo, tierra. 5. tierra negra, tierra vegetal. 6. tierra, país.

soilage [ˈsɔɪlɪdʒ] *s.* (agr.) alcacer, verdes (para alimentar ganado encerrado).

soil conservation, conservación de la tierra cultivable contra la erosión.

soil mechanics, (geof.) mecánica de los suelos.

soil physics, física de suelos, geofísica.

soil pipe, cañería de desagüe de cloacas, cañería de fundición liviana.

soil survey, estudio de suelos, investigación geofísica.

soiree, soirée [swɑˈreɪ, B ˈswɑreɪ] *s.* (fr.) sarao, velada.

soja bean [ˈsoʊdʒə-] (bot.) soya, soja.

sojourn [ˈsoʊˌdʒɜrn, soʊˈdʒɜrn, B ˈsɔˌdʒɜn] *v.i.* residir, morar, hacer mansión (temporal). —*s.* residencia temporal, estada.

sojourner [-ər, B -ə] *s.* morador o residente temporal, transeúnte.

soke [soʊk] *s.* (G.B., hist.) derecho de administrar justicia y cobrar los honorarios y multas correspondientes.

sol [soʊl, B sɔl] *s.* (mús.) sol.

sol [sɑl, sɔl, B sɔl] *s.* 1. (*pl.* SOLS o SOLES [ˈsoʊleɪs]) sol (unidad monetaria del Perú). 2. (quím.) sol (solución coloidal). 3. sol, oro (de los alquimistas). 4. (hist.) sueldo (moneda de cobre de Francia). 5. **S.,** (mitol.) el dios sol; (hum.) el sol.

solace [ˈsɑləs, B ˈsɔl-] *s.* solaz, desahogo; confortación, consuelo. —*v.t.* 1. consolar, confortar (al afligido). 2. aliviar, aquietar, apaciguar. 3. distraer, divertir, solazar.

solacement [-mənt] *s.* solaz, consuelo, esparcimiento, recreo.

solacer [-ər, B -ə] *s.* consolador, confortador.

solanaceous [ˌsɑləˈneɪʃəs, B ˌsɔl-] *a.* (bot.) solanáceo.

solan goose [ˈsoʊlən-] (orn.) planga, clanga, alcatraz, bubía, onocrótalo.

solanine, solanin [ˈsoʊləˌnin, B -nɪn] *s.* (quím.) solanina.

solanum [səˈleɪnəm, -ˈlɑn-] *s.* (bot.) solanácea.

solar [ˈsoʊlər, B -lə] *a.* 1. solar (año, sistema, rayos, etc.). 2. de energía solar, ej., *s. engine,* máquina de energía solar.

solar battery, batería solar.

solar compass, (top.) brújula de anteojo solar.

solar constant, (astr.) constante solar.

solar cycle, (astr.) ciclo solar.

solar energy, energía solar.

solar home, casa solar.

solarium [soʊˈlærɪəm, B -ˈlɛər-] *s.* (*pl.* SOLARIA [-ə] o SOLARIUMS) solana, carasol.

solarization [ˌsoʊlərəˈzeɪʃən, B -raɪ-] *s.* 1. asoleo. 2. (foto.) solarización.

solarize [ˈsoʊləˌraiz] *v.t.* 1. asolear, exponer a los rayos del sol. 2. (foto.) solarizar.

solar microscope, microscopio solar.

solar plexus, (anat.) plexo solar.

solar system, (astr.) sistema solar.

solar time, (astr.) tiempo solar, aparente o verdadero.

solatium [soʊˈleɪʃɪəm] *s.* (*pl.* SOLATIA [-ə]) compensación, desagravio.

sold [soʊld] *pret., p.p. de* **sell.**

soldan [ˈsɑldən, B ˈsɔl-] *s.* (hist.) soldán, sultán (esp. de Egipto).

solder [ˈsɑdər, ˈsɔd-, B ˈsɔldə] *s.* soldadura. —*v.t.* soldar. —*v.i.* soldarse, pegarse.

solderer [-ərər, B -ə] *s.* soldador.

soldering [-ərɪŋ] *s.* soldadura.

soldering flux, fundente para soldar.

soldering iron, hierro para soldar, soldador, cautín.

soldering paste, pasta para soldar, compuesto de soldar.

soldier [ˈsoʊldʒər, B -dʒə] *s.* 1. soldado, militar. 2. soldado raso. 3. militante, partidario (de alguna causa). 4. (ento.) soldado (clase de termita); obrera (clase de hormiga). —*v.i.* 1. (*ú. gen. en p.pr.*) militar, servir como soldado. 2. fingir trabajar; fingirse enfermo.

soldiering [ˈsoʊldʒərɪŋ] *s.* servicio militar, vida militar.

soldierly [-dʒərlɪ, B -dʒəlɪ] *a.* soldadesco; marcial, militar.

soldier of fortune, 1. (soldado) mercenario, condotiero. 2. aventurero.

soldiership [-ˌʃɪp] *s.* 1. soldadesca, milicia. 2. profesión de soldado. 3. pericia militar.

soldier's wind, (mar.) viento favorable para ida y retorno.

soldiery [ˈsoʊldʒərɪ] *s.* 1. soldadesca, soldados en conjunto; tropa. 2. carrera militar. 3. artes militares.

soldo [ˈsɔldoʊ] *s.* (*pl.* SOLDI [-di]) sueldo (moneda italiana).

sole [soʊl] *s.* 1. planta (del pie); suela (del zapato, etc.). 2. base (de la cabeza de un palo de golf). 3. cama (de carro, carreta, arado). 4. (ict.) lenguado, suela. —*v.t.* solar, echar suela (al calzado). —*a.* 1. único, solo, exclusivo. 2. (der.) célibe, soltero. 3. (ant.) solitario, aislado.

sole agent, agente exclusivo.

solecism [ˈsɑləˌsɪzəm, B ˈsɔl-] *s.* 1. (gram.) solecismo. 2. desacierto, despropósito.

solecistic [ˈsɑləˈsɪstɪk, B ˌsɔl-] *a.* propio del solecismo; incorrecto, impropio.

sole leather, *s.* vaqueta.

solely [ˈsoʊlɪ] *adv.* 1. solamente, únicamente, exclusivamente. 2. a solas.

solemn [ˈsɑləm, B ˈsɔl-] *a.* 1. solemne; grave, serio. 2. pomposo, afectado. 3. (der.) solemne. 4. (ant.) importante, de peso; suntuoso, espléndido.

solemnify [səˈlɛmnəˌfaɪ] *v.t.* (*pret., p.p.* SOLEMNIFIED; *p.pr.* SOLEMNIFYING) solemnizar.

solemnity [-nətɪ] *s.* (*pl.* SOLEMNITIES) 1. solemnidad, formalidad, celebración, pompa. 2. acto solemne, ceremonia. 3. dignidad, seriedad, gravedad.

solemnization [ˌsɑləmnəˈzeɪʃən, B ˈsɔl-naɪ-] *s.* solemnización, celebración.

solemnize [ˈsɑləmˌnaɪz, B ˈsɔl-] *v.t.* 1. solemnizar. 2. celebrar, formalizar (matrimonio).

solemnizer [-ˌnaɪzər, B -ə] *s.* solemnizador.

solemnly [-lɪ] *adv.* solemnemente.

solemn mass, misa solemne.

solemnness [-nəs] *s.* solemnidad.

solemn vow, (relig.) voto solemne.

solenodon [soʊˈlinəˌdɑn, B -dən] *s.* (zool.) aire.

solenoglyph [-ˌglɪf] *s.* (zool.) solenoglifo.

solenoid [ˈsoʊləˌnɔɪd] *s.* (elec.) solenoide.

solenoidal [ˌsoʊləˈnɔɪdəl] *a.* (elec.) solenoidal.

soleplate [ˈsoʊlˌpleɪt] *s.* 1. cara interior de una plancha. 2. (const.) placa de asiento. 3. (carp.) solera inferior. 4. (maq.) bancada, bancaza.

soleus [ˈsoʊlɪəs, B soʊˈliəs] *s.* (anat.) sóleo.

sol-fa [ˈsoʊlˈfɑ, B sɔl-] *v.t., v.i.* (*pret., p.p.* SOL-FAED; *p.pr.* SOL-FAING) (mús.) solfear. —*s.* (mús.) solfa, solfeo; gama o escala musical.

sol-faist [-əst] *s.* (mús.) solfista, solfeador.

sol-fa syllables, (mús.) voces de la escala musical.

solfatara [ˌsoʊlfəˈtɑrə, B ˌsɔl-] *s.* (geol.) solfatara.

solfege [sɑlˈfɛʒ, -ˈfeɪʒ, B sɔl-] *s.* (mús.) solfeo.

solfeggio [-ˈfɛdʒoʊ, B -ɪoʊ] *s.* (*pl.* SOLFEGGI [-i] o SOLFEGGIOS) (mús.) solfeo.

solicit [səˈlɪsət] *v.t.* 1. demandar, reclamar; instar, importunar; pedir, requerir, solicitar, peticionar. 2. tentar, incitar, inducir, atraer. 3. abordar, solicitar (prostituta callejera). —*v.i.* dedicarse a la prostitución callejera.

solicitant [-ətənt] *s.* solicitante.

solicitation [səˌlɪsəˈteɪʃən] *s.* 1. requerimiento, instancia, ruego, solicitación; importunación, porfía. 2. incitación, tentación.

solicitor [səˈlɪsətər, B -ə] *s.* 1. solicitador, diligenciero, agente (esp. el que solicita contribuciones para un fondo, etc.). 2. (der., G.B.) abogado; procurador.

solicitor general, *s.* (*pl.* SOLICITORS GENERAL) (der., G.B.) procurador, subfiscal de la corona; (E.U.) subsecretario de justicia; procurador general (de un Estado).

solicitorship [-ˌʃɪp] *s.* abogacía; procuraduría.

solicitous [-əs] *a.* 1. solícito, deseoso, gustoso. 2. aprensivo, receloso, ansioso. 3. circunspecto, esmerado.

solicitously [-lɪ] *adv.* solícitamente.

solicitousness [-nəs] *s.* solicitud.

solicitude [səˈlɪsəˌtud, B -tjud] *s.* 1. solicitud, afán, ansiedad. 2. cuidado o interés excesivo.

solid [ˈsɑləd, B ˈsɔl-] *a.* 1. sólido, consistente. 2. sólido, macizo, compacto. 3. tri-dimensional, cúbico, ej., *s. foot,* pie cúbico. 4. firme, estable, fuerte, fornido, ej., *a man of s. build,* un hombre de constitución fornida. 5. continuo, entero, solo, ej., *s. color,* color entero o liso, un solo color. 6. unánime, firme, ej., *s. vote,* votación unánime, *the s. South,* los estados firmes del Sur (de los E.U., que han votado siempre por el Partido Demócrata). 7. seguido, continuado, ininterrumpido, entero (período de tiempo). 8. (fig.) sólido, sano, bien fundado (argumento, opinión, consideración, etc.). 9. constante, estable; completo, serio, de confianza, solvente. 10. (impr.) desinterlineado, sin interlíneas; mazorral. 11. **to go (o to be) s. for,** estar unánimemente en favor de. —*s.* 1. sólido, materia o substancias sólidas. 2. (geom.) sólido, cuerpo.

solid angle, (geom.) ángulo sólido.
solidarity [ˌsɑlə'dærətɪ, B ˌsɔl-] *s.* solidaridad.
solidary ['sɑlɪˌdɛrɪ, B 'sɔlɪdərɪ] *a.* solidario.
solid ashlar, (const.) sillar lleno.
solid fuel, combustible pirotécnico.
solid geometry, geometría del espacio, geometría tridimensional.
solidification [səˌlɪdəfə'keɪʃən] *s.* solidificación; consolidación.
solidify [sə'lɪdəˌfaɪ] *v.t., v.i.* (*pret., p.p.* SOLIDIFIED; *p.pr.* SOLIDIFYING) solidificar (se), volver(se) sólido (un cuerpo líquido o gaseoso); cristalizar(se).
solidity [-tɪ] *s.* 1. solidez, consistencia, firmeza. 2. (fig.) solidez, firmeza mental, estabilidad moral o económica. 3. (fig.) solidez (de un argumento, tesis, etc.). 4. (geom.) solidez, volumen.
solid line, (dib.) línea llena.
solidly ['sɑlədlɪ, B 'sɔl-] *adv.* sólidamente, firmemente.
solid measure, medida para sólidos.
solidness [-nəs] *s.* 1. solidez, consistencia, densidad, dureza. 2. firmeza, estabilidad.
solid square, (mil.) formación cuadrada.
solid state, (fís.) estado sólido.
solid-state [-'steɪt] *a.* (electrón.) de estado sólido, transistorizado.
solid tire, (aut.) llanta maciza, bandaje macizo.
solidungulate [ˌsɑlə'dʌŋgjələt, -ˌleɪt, B ˌsɔl-lət] *a., s.* (zool.) solípedo.
solidus [ˌsɑlədəs, B 'sɔl-] *s.* (*pl.* SOLIDI [-daɪ]) 1. (impr.) guión oblicuo. 2. (hist.) sólido (antigua moneda de oro romana).
soliloquist [sə'lɪləkwəst] *s.* 1. recitador de soliloquios. 2. el que habla a solas.
soliloquize [-ˌkwaɪz] *v.i.* soliloquiar, monologar.
soliloquy [-kwɪ] *s.* (*pl.* SOLILOQUIES) soliloquio, monólogo.
soliped ['sɑləˌpɛd, B 'sɔl-] *s.* (zool.) solípedo.
solipsism ['sɑləpˌsɪzəm, B 'soʊləp-] *s.* (filos.) solipsismo.
solitaire ['sɑləˌtɛr, B ˌsɔlɪ'tɛə] *s.* 1. solitario, anacoreta. 2. (joy.) solitario. 3. (naipes) solitario. 4. (orn.) pájaro solitario, tordo loco.
solitarily [ˌsɑlə'tɛrəlɪ, B 'sɔlɪtər-] *adv.* solitariamente.
solitariness ['sɑləˌtɛrɪnəs, B 'sɔlɪtər-] *s.* soledad, retiro.
solitary [-ˌtɛrɪ, B -tərɪ] *a.* 1. solitario, señero, solo. 2. despoblado, deshabitado, apartado (sitio o paraje). 3. solo, único. 4. (bot., zool.) solitario. *s.* (*pl.* SOLITARIES) 1. solitario, anacoreta. 2. (fam.) aislamiento penal.
solitary confinement, aislamiento penal.
solitary sandpiper, (orn.) zarapico.
solitude [-ˌtud, B -tjud] *s.* 1. soledad, aislamiento, apartamiento, retiro, reclusión. 2. soledad, lugar desierto o solitario.
solleret [ˌsɑlə'rɛt, B 'sɔlərɛt] *s.* (arm.) escarpe.
solmization [ˌsɑlmə'zeɪʃən, B ˌsɔl-] *s.* (mús.) solfeo.
solo ['soʊloʊ] *s.* (*pl.* SOLOS) 1. (mús.) (*pl. t.* SOLI) solo. 2. (naipes) solo, solitario. 3. (aer.) vuelo de un aviador solo. *—a.* 1. solo, sin compañía. 2. (mús.) (arreglado) para un solo, ej., *s. composition,* composición para un solo. *—adv.* a solas.
solo flight, (aer.) vuelo solo.
soloist [-əst] *s.* (mús.) solista.
Solomon ['sɑləmən, B 'sɔl-] *s.* (bíbl.) Salomón, sabio rey de Israel, hijo y sucesor de David.
Solomonic [ˌsɑlə'mɑnɪk, B ˌsɔlə'mɔn-] *a.* salomónico.
Solomon's seal, 1. sello de Salomón (amuleto antiguo). 2. (bot.) sello de Salomón, sello de Santa María.
solon ['soʊlən, -ˌlɑn, B -lɔn] *s.* 1. **S.,** (hist.) Solón, legislador ateniense. 2. (fig.) legislador, legislador sabio.
solstice ['sɑlstəs, 'soʊl-, B 'sɔl-] *s.* (astr.) solsticio.
solstitial [sɑl'stɪʃəl, soʊl-, B sɔl-] *a.* (astr.) solsticial.
solubility [ˌsɑljə'bɪlətɪ, B ˌsɔl-] *s.* solubilidad.
solubilize ['sɑljəbəlaɪz, B 'sɔl-] *v.t.* (quím.) solubilizar.
soluble ['sɑljəbəl, B 'sɔl-] *a.* soluble.
soluble glass, vidrio soluble.
solubleness [-nəs] *s.* solubilidad.
solubly [-blɪ] *adv.* de modo soluble.
solus ['soʊləs] *adv, a.* (teat.) solo.
solute ['sɑlˌjut, 'soʊˌlut, B ˌsɔl'jut] *s.* (quím.) soluto, substancia disuelta. *—a.* disuelto.
solution [sə'luʃən] *s.* 1. solución (de un misterio, problema, etc.). 2. (fís., quím.) solución. 3. (mat.) solución, resolución. 4. (med.) solución, interrupción, desgarro.
Solutrean, Solutrian [sə'lutrɪən] *a.* (geol.) solutrense.
solvability [ˌsɑlvə'bɪlətɪ, B ˌsɔl-] *s.* solubilidad.
solvable ['sɑlvəbəl, B 'sɔl-] *a.* 1. soluble, disoluble. 2. soluble, resoluble.
solvate [-ˌveɪt] *s.* (quím.) solvatación, solvato. *—v.t.* solvatar.
solve [sɑlv, B sɔlv] *v.t.* 1. resolver, solucionar, solventar, aclarar. 2. saldar, cancelar (deudas).
solvency ['sɑlvənsɪ, B 'sɔl-] *s.* solvencia.
solvent [-vənt] *a.* 1. solvente (capaz de satisfacer deudas). 2. soluble, disoluble; disolvente, disolutivo. *—s.* solvente, disolvente.
solvolysis [sɑl'vɑləsəs, B sɔl'vɔl-] *s.* (quím.) solvolisis.
soma ['soʊmə] *s.* (biol.) soma.
Somaliland [soʊ'mɑlɪlænd] *s.* Somalía, región del África Oriental.
somatic [soʊ'mætɪk] *a.* somático.
somatic cell, (biol.) célula somática.
somatogenic [ˌsoʊmətə'dʒɛnɪk] *a.* (biol.) somatogenético.
somatological [-'lɑdʒɪkəl, B -'lɔdʒ-] *a.* somatológico.
somatology [-'tɑlədʒɪ, B -'tɔl-] *s.* somatología.
somatoplasm ['soʊmətəˌplæzəm] *s.* somatoplasma.
somatoplastic [ˌsoʊmətə'plæstɪk] *a.* somatoplástico.
somatopleure ['soʊmətəˌplur, B -ˌpluə] *s.* (biol.) somatopleura.
somatotype [-ˌtaɪp] *s.* somatotipo.
somber, sombre ['sɑmbər, B 'sɔmbə] *a.* 1. sombrío, lóbrego, lúgubre, oscuro, tétrico. 2. sombrío, melancólico; grave, triste, ej., *man of s. character,* hombre de carácter melancólico.
somberly, sombrely [-lɪ] *adv.* 1. lúgubremente. 2. melancólicamente.
somberness, sombreness [-nəs] *s.* 1. lobreguez, aspecto sombrío. 2. carácter melancólico.
sombrero [sɑm'brɛroʊ, B sɔm'brɛər-] *s.* sombrero de ala ancha.
some [sʌm, səm] *a.* 1. alguno, algún, cierto, ej., *s. fool has locked the door,* algún tonto ha cerrado la puerta. 2. un poco de, unos cuantos, algunos, varios, ej., *s. years ago,* hace unos cuantos años. 3. cerca de, (algo) como, más o menos, ej., *s. twenty minutes,* cerca de veinte minutos. 4. (jer.) de calidad extraordinaria; grande, todo uno, vaya, ej., *that was s. fight!* ¡fue toda una pelea! *s. acting!* ¡vaya una actuación! *—pron.* 1. algunos. 2. algo, parte, una parte, un poco. 3. **and then s.,** y algunos más. *—adv.* 1. algo, un poco. 2. (jer.) bastante, mucho.
somebody ['sʌmˌbɑdɪ, -bədɪ, B -bədɪ] *s.* (*pl.* SOMEBODIES) personaje, alguien, ej., *he thought himself a s.,* se creyó un personaje. *—pron.* alguien, alguno, alguna persona; **s. else,** algún otro, otra persona.
someday [-ˌdeɪ] *adv.* algún día.
somehow [-ˌhaʊ] *adv.* de algún modo, de alguna manera, por alguna razón; (con énfasis) de una u otra manera.
someone [-ˌwʌn] *pron.* alguien, alguno, alguna persona; **as s. once said,** como alguien dijera. *—s.* personaje.
someplace [-ˌpleɪs] *adv.* en alguna parte, a alguna parte.
somersault ['sʌmərˌsɔlt, B -əˌ-] **somerset** [-ˌsɛt] *s.* salto mortal, voltereta; (fig.) cambio completo de actitud u opinión. *—v.i.* dar un salto mortal o saltos mortales.
something ['sʌmˌθɪŋ] *s.* 1. algo, alguna cosa, ej., *I have s. to do tonight,* tengo algo que hacer esta noche. 2. **or s.,** o algo por el estilo, ej., *he broke his foot or s.,* se rompió el pie o algo por el estilo; **s. else,** otra cosa, algo más; (jer.) alguien o algo extraordinario; **s. like,** algo como cerca de; **s. of a,** medio, ej., *he is s. of a rascal,* es medio sinvergüenza; **s. or. other,** una cosa u otra, algo, alguna cosa; **to be s.,** ser de alguna importancia, ser alguien; **to make s. of,** hallarle utilidad (a); atribuir importancia (a). *—adv.* 1. algo, un poco, algún tanto. 2. (jer.) muy, sumamente. 3. **s. like** (**thirty miles,** etc.), cosa de (treinta millas, etc.).
sometime [-ˌtaɪm] *adv.* 1. algún día, alguna vez, un día de estos, uno de estos días. 2. a veces, ocasionalmente. 3. en otro tiempo, antiguamente. 4. **s. soon,** pronto, en breve, sin tardar mucho. *—a.* antiguo, pasado, de otro tiempo; ex, ej., *a s. professor,* un ex profesor.
sometimes [-ˌtaɪmz] *adv.* 1. a veces, unas veces, algunas veces, ej., *s. black and s. white,* unas veces negro y otras veces blanco. 2. ocasionalmente, de vez en cuando. 3. (ant.) en otros tiempos, antiguamente.
someway [-ˌweɪ] **someways** [-ˌweɪz] *adv.* (fam.) de algún modo, de un modo u otro, de alguna manera.
somewhat ['sʌmˌhwɑt, -ˌwɑt, B -wɔt] *s.* 1. algo, un poco, en cierto modo, ej., *it was s. of a surprise to him,* en cierto modo fue una sorpresa para él. 2. algo, alguna cosa. 3. sujeto o cosa importante. *—adv.* algo, algún tanto, un poco, ej., *it is s. old,* es un poco antiguo.
somewhere [-ˌhwɛr, -ˌwɛr, B -wɛə] *adv.* en alguna parte, a alguna parte; **s. else,** en otra parte, a otra parte. *—s.* lugar (indeterminado).
somewhither [-ˌhwɪðər, -ˌwɪð-ʙ-ə] *adv.* (ant.) hacia alguna parte, en una u otra dirección.
somite ['soʊˌmaɪt] *s.* (anat., zool.) somito.
sommelier [ˌsɔməl'jeɪ] *s.* (fr.) camarero (en un restaurante) encargado de servir los vinos.
somnambulant [sɑm'næmbjələnt, B sɔm-] *a.* sonámbulo, somnámbulo.
somnambulate [-ˌleɪt] *v.i., v.t.* levantarse y andar dormido.
somnambulation [sɑmˌnæmbjə'leɪʃən, B sɔm-] *s.* sonambulismo, somnambulismo.
somnambulator [sɑm'næmbjəˌleɪtər, B sɔm-ə] *s.* sonámbulo, somnámbulo.
somnambulism [-ˌlɪzəm] *s.* sonambulismo, somnambulismo.
somnambulist [-ləst] *s.* sonámbulo, somnámbulo.
somnambulistic [sɑmˌnæmbjə'lɪstɪk, B sɔm-] *a.* sonámbulo, somnámbulo.

somniferous [-'nɪfərəs] *a.* somnífero, hipnótico, soporífero, soporoso.
somnific [-'nɪfɪk] *a.* somnífero, narcótico.
somniloquence [-'nɪləkwəns] *s.* somnilocuencia.
somniloquist [-kwəst] *s.* somnílocuo.
somniloquy [-kwɪ] *s.* somniloquia, el hábito de hablar dormido.
somnolence ['sɑmnələns, B 'sɔm-] **somnolency** [-lənsɪ] *s.* somnolencia, soñolencia; sopor, modorra.
somnolent [-lənt] *a.* 1. soñoliento. 2. soporífico.
son [sʌn] *s.* 1. hijo. 2. (*pl.*) hijos, descendientes. 3. **the S.,** el Hijo (Jesucristo).
sonance ['soʊnəns] *s.* 1. sonido. 2. sonoridad.
sonant [-nənt] *a.* 1. sonante, sonoro. 2. (fon.) sonoro, entonado. —*s.* (fon.) sonora.
sonar ['soʊnɑr, B -nɑ] *s.* sonar, sonda de ultrasonidos.
sonarman [-mæn] *s.* (mar.) operador de sonar.
sonata [sə'nɑtə] *s.* (mús.) sonata.
sonatina [ˌsɑnə'tinə, B ˌsɔn-] *s.* (mús.) sonatina.
sonde [sɑnd, B sɔnd] *s.* (meteor.) sonda.
song [sɔŋ] *s.* 1. canto, canción, cantar. 2. (p. ext.) poesía, verso. 3. (mús.) canción. 4. bagatela, nimiedad, poca cosa. 5. (fig., fam.) alharaca, batahola. 6. **for a s.,** por cuatro cuartos, por una nimiedad; **nothing to make a s. (and dance) about,** nada como para poner el grito en el cielo; **(to sing) the same old s.,** (volver a) la misma cantaleta.
songbird ['sɔŋˌbɜrd, B 'sɔŋbɜd] *s.* 1. ave cantora, pájaro cantor. 2. (fig.) cantora, cantatriz.
song book, cancionero.
songfest [-ˌfɛst] *s.* reunión para cantar (en grupo).
songful [-fəl] *a.* 1. inclinado al canto. 2. melodioso.
song hit, canción de moda, canción popular del momento.
songless [-ləs] *a.* sin canto, incapaz de cantar.
Song of Songs, (bíbl.) Cantar de los Cantares.
songsmith [-ˌsmɪθ] *s.* compositor de canciones.
song sparrow, (orn.) (variedad americana de) gorrión cantor.
songster [-stər, B -stə] *s.* 1. cantor, cantante, cancionista; poeta. 2. ave cantora, pájaro cantor.
songstress [-strəs] *s.* cantante, cantora, cantatriz, cancionista, cantarina; poetisa.
song thrush, (orn.) malvis, zorzal, tordo alirrojo.
songwriter [-ˌraɪtər, B -ə] *s.* compositor de canciones; compositor de letra para canciones.
sonic ['sɑnɪk, B 'sɔn-] *a.* sónico.
sonic barrier, barrera sónica, barrera del sonido.
sonic boom, (aer.) estampido sónico, estruendo.
sonic depth finder, sonda acústica.
sonic mine, (arm.) mina acústica.
son-in-law ['sʌnənˌlɔ] *s.* (*pl.* SONS-IN-LAW) yerno, hijo político.
sonnet ['sɑnət, B 'sɔn-] *s.* soneto. —*v.t., v.i.* sonetizar, componer sonetos (sobre o acerca de).
sonneteer [ˌsɑnə'tɪr, B ˌsɔnɪ'tɪə] (gen. despec.) *s.* sonetista, autor de sonetos. —*v.t., v.i.* sonetizar, componer sonetos (sobre o acerca de).
sonnetize ['sɑnəˌtaɪz, B 'sɔn-] *v.i.* sonetizar. —*v.t.* componer sonetos sobre (o acerca de).
sonny ['sʌnɪ] *s.* (fam.) hijito.
sonobuoy ['soʊnəˌbuɪ, -ˌbɔɪ, B 'sɔnə-] *s.* (mar.) boya o baliza sonora.
son of a bitch, (vulg.) hijo de puta, hijo de perra (expresión de fastidio, desprecio, etc.).
son of a gun, (fam.) alteración eufemística de **son of a bitch** que implica indulgencia, familiaridad, etc.
sonometer [soʊ'nɑmətər, B -'nɔmɪtə] *s.* sonómetro, monocordio.
sonority [sə'nɔrətɪ, -'nɑr-, B -'nɔr-] *s.* sonoridad, resonancia.
sonorous [sə'nɔrəs, 'sɑnərəs, B sə'nɔr-] *a.* 1. sonoro. 2. resonante, impresionante.
sonorously [-lɪ] *adv.* sonoramente.
sonorousness [-nəs] *s.* sonoridad, resonancia.
sonsy, sonsie ['sɑnsɪ, B 'sɔn-] *a.* (pr. dial.) gracioso, atractivo; afable.
soon [sun] *adv.* (SOONER, SONNEST) 1. pronto, en breve, luego, próximamente, dentro de poco. 2. temprano, ej., *what made you come so s.?* ¿qué le hizo venir tan pronto? 3. **as s.,** de preferencia, más bien, ej., *I would (just) as s. stay at home,* de preferencia (o más bien) me quedaría en casa; **as s. as,** tan pronto como, luego que, así que; **as s. (do) as,** (es) mejor que (haga) en vez de, (resulta) preferible que (haga) en vez de; **had sooner,** preferiría; **how s.?** ¿cuándo? ¿ cuándo a más tardar?; **no sooner,** no antes; apenas, ej., *the words were no sooner out of his mouth than he collapsed,* apenas hubo pronunciado estas palabras cuando se desplomó; **no sooner said than done,** dicho y hecho; **s. after,** poco después; **the sooner the better,** cuanto más pronto, mejor; **sooner or later,** tarde o temprano; **sooner than,** antes que, ej., *they would sooner die than tolerate tyranny,* preferirían morir antes que tolerar una tiranía.
sooner ['sunər, B -nə] *s.* 1. (E.U., hist.) primer colono (que se estableció en tierras del Oeste para gozar la prioridad que la ley le otorgaba). 2. **S.** (E.U.) (apodo de un) nativo o habitante de Oklahoma.
soot [sʊt, sut, B sʊt] *s.* hollín, tizne. —*v.t.* tiznar, manchar, ensuciar con o cubrir de hollín.
sooth [suθ] *a.* 1. (poét.) consolador; dulce, amable; blando, suave. 2. (ant.) verdadero, roal. —*s.* (ant.) verdad, realidad.
soothe [suð] *v.t.* 1. calmar, sosegar, mitigar, sedar. 2. halagar, complacer. 3. (ant.) acceder, satisfacer.
soother ['suðər, B -ə] *s.* consolador, aliviador, apaciguador.
soothing ['suðɪŋ] *a.* calmante, sedante.
soothingly [-lɪ] *adv.* en tono conciliador; de modo calmante.
soothsay ['suθˌseɪ] *v.i.* predecir, adivinar.
soothsayer [-ər, B -ə] *s.* adivino, augur.
soothsaying [-ɪŋ] *s.* 1. adivinación. 2. profecía, predicción.
sootiness ['sʊtɪnəs, 'sut-, B 'sut-] *s.* fuliginosidad.
sooty [-ɪ] *a.* tiznado; ennegrecido, lleno de hollín.
sop [sɑp, B sɔp] *v.t.* (*pret., p.p.* SOPPED; *p.pr.* SOPPING) ensopar, empapar, remojar, mojar; **s. up,** absorber. —*v.i.* remojarse, estar empapado. —*s.* 1. (dial.) sopa (pan, etc. empapado en un líquido). 2. (fig.) regalo, soborno (dado para sosegar, aquietar, etc.).
sophism ['sɑfˌizəm, B 'sɔf-] *s.* sofisma, paralogismo; sofistería.
Sophist [-əst] *s.* 1. sofista. 2. pensador, filósofo. —*a.* sofista.
sophister [-əstər, B -tə] *s.* (G.B.) estudiante de segundo o tercer año (en las universidades de Oxford y Cambridge).
sophistic [sə'fɪstɪk] **sophistical** [-tɪkəl] *a.* 1. sofista. 2. sofístico.
sophistically [-tɪkəlɪ] *adv.* sofísticamente.
sophisticate [-təˌkeɪt] *v.t.* 1. sofisticar, adulterar, falsificar. 2. hacer mundano, desilusionar. 3. complicar. — [-təkət] *s.* mundano, hombre mundano, persona corrida.
sophisticated [-əd] *a.* 1. sofisticado, mundano, corrido, falto de simplicidad. 2. complicado, complejo. 3. sutil, refinado.
sophistication [səˌfɪstə'keɪʃən] *s.* 1. sofistería. 2. sofisticación, mundanería, falta de simplicidad.
sophistry ['sɑfəstrɪ, B 'sɔf-] *s.* (*pl.* SOPHISTRIES) sofistería, sofismo.
Sophocles ['sɑfəˌkliz, B 'sɔf-] *s.* Sófocles, uno de los más grandes dramaturgos de la antigua Grecia.
sophomore ['sɑfəˌmɔr, B 'sɔfəˌmɔ] *s.* (E.U.) estudiante de segundo año (de universidad o de secundaria).
sophomoric [ˌsɑfə'mɔrɪk, B ˌsɔf-] *a.* 1. (propio de los estudiantes) de segundo año. 2. (fig.) inmaturo; ampuloso, superficial.
sopor ['soʊpər, B -pə] *a.* sopor, modorra, adormecimiento.
soporiferous [ˌsɑpə'rɪfərəs, B ˌsɔp-] *a.* soporífero, adormecedor.
soporific [-ɪk] *a.* soporífero, soporífico, adormecedor, narcótico. —*s.* soporífico, narcótico (droga).
sopping ['sɑpɪŋ, B 'sɔp-] *a.* empapado, mojado.
soppy [-ɪ] *a.* (SOPPIER; SOPPIEST) 1. empapado, mojado. 2. (jer., G.B.) muy sentimental, empalagoso. 3. (jer., G.B.) estúpido, zonzo.
soprano [sə'prænoʊ, -'prɑn-, B -'prɑn-] *s.* (mús.) soprano, tiple. —*a.* de soprano, para soprano.
sora rail ['sɔrə-] (orn.) (variedad norteamericana del) rascón o ralo acuático.
sorb [sɔrb, B sɔb] *s.* 1. (bot.) serbal, serbo, acapesma, amargoso. 2. serba.
sorb apple, serba.
sorbent ['sɔrbənt, B 'sɔbənt] *s.* absorbente; adsorbente.
sorbic acid ['sɔrbɪk-, B 'sɔbɪk] (quím.) ácido sórbico.
Sorbonne [sɔr'bɑn, B sɔ'bɔn] *s.* Sorbona, sede de las facultades de Ciencias y Letras de la universidad de Paris.
sorbose ['sɔrˌboʊs, B 'sɔˌ-] *s.* (quím.) sorbosa.
sorcerer ['sɔrsərər, B 'sɔsərə] *s.* hechicero, brujo, mago.
sorceress [-sərəs] *s.* hechicera, bruja.
sorcerous [-əs] *a.* hechiceresco, brujesco, mágico.
sorcery [-ɪ] *s.* (*pl.* SORCERIES) hechiceriá, brujería, magia; nigromancia.
sordid ['sɔrdəd, B 'sɔdɪd] *a.* 1. sórdido, sucio, inmundo. 2. sórdido, vil, bajo; despreciable. 3. mezquino, tacaño, avariento. 4. (bot., zool.) de color lodoso.
sordidly [-lɪ] *adv.* sórdidamente, vilmente.
sordidness [-nəs] *s.* 1. sordidez, suciedad. 2. sordidez, vileza. 3. avaricia.
sordino [sɔr'dinoʊ, B sɔ'-] *s.* (*pl.* SORDINI [-ni]) (mús.) sordina.
sore [sɔr, B sɔ] *a.* 1. sensitivo, adolorido, ej., *she has a s. leg,* tiene una pierna adolorida. 2. inflamado. 3. penoso, doloroso, lastimoso, ej., *a s. sight,* un espectáculo doloroso. 4. arduo, dificultoso (trabajo, situación, etc.). 5. disgustado, enfadado, picado. 6. **a sight for s. eyes,** una vista agradable; **to be s. at,** estar enconado con. —*s.* 1. llaga, úlcera. 2. (fig.) dolor, disgusto, aflicción. 3. **to reopen old sores,** abrir viejas heridas. —*adv.* penosamente, dolorosamente.
sore eyes, ojos irritados y cansados.
sorehead ['sɔrˌhɛd, B 'sɔˌ-] *s.* (fam.) cascarrabias, descontentadizo.
sorely [-lɪ] *adv.* 1. penosamente, dolorosamente; urgentemente. 2. severamente. 3. extremadamente, sumamente.
soreness [-nəs] *s.* 1. estado dolorido. 2. amargura, angustia. 3. severidad, rigor. 4. punto sensitivo, parte dolorida.

sore point, (fig.) punto neurálgico, asunto espinoso.
sore throat, dolor de garganta.
sorghum ['sɔrgəm, B 'sɔgəm] *s.* 1. (bot.) alcandía, zahína, adaza, sorgo. 2. melaza o jarabe de sorgo.
sorgo [-goʊ] *s.* (bot.) sorgo azucarado.
sori ['sɔr,aɪ] *pl. de* **sorus.**
soricine ['sɔrə,saɪn, 'sɑr-, B 'sɔrəsɪn] *a.* sorícido.
sorites [sə'raɪtiz] *s.* (*pl.* SORITES) (lóg.) sorites, polisilogismo.
sororal [-'rɔrəl] *a.* de hermana (s), entre hermanas, hermanal.
sororate [-ət] *s.* segundo matrimonio de un hombre con la hermana de su esposa (divorciada o muerta).
sororicide [-ə,saɪd] *s.* 1. sororicidio. 2. sororicida.
sorority [-ətɪ] *s.* (*pl.* SORORITIES) club o asociación femenina estudiantil.
sorose ['sɔr,oʊs] *a.* (bot.) soróforo.
sorosis [sə'roʊsəs] *s.* (bot.) sorosis.
sorption ['sɔrpʃən, B 'sɔp-] *s.* (fís., quím.) absorción; adsorción.
sorrel ['sɔrəl, 'sɑr-, B 'sɔr-] *s.* (bot.) acedera, vinagrera, acetosa.
sorrel, *s.* 1. alazán, alazano (color). 2. (caballo) alazán. —*a.* alazán, alazano.
sorrily ['sɑrəlɪ, 'sɔr-, B 'sɔr-] *adv.* 1. dolorosamente, penosamente. 2. con pesar, con arrepentimiento. 3. tristemente, melancólicamente.
sorriness [-ɪnəs] *s.* 1. pesar. 2. tristeza, melancolía.
sorrow ['sɑroʊ, 'sɔr-, B 'sɔr-] *s.* 1. dolor, pesar, pena. 2. arrepentimiento, lamento, pesadumbre, penitencia. —*v.i.* 1. dolerse, apenarse, sentir pena. 2. arrepentirse. 3. **s. for,** añorar, extrañar (Am.).
sorrowful [-fəl] *a.* 1. pesaroso, acongojado, desconsolado, triste. 2. doloroso, deplorable (espectáculo, escena, etc.). 3. arrepentido.
sorrowfully [-fəlɪ] *adv.* con pena, tristemente.
sorrowfulness [-fəlnəs] *s.* 1. pesar, tristeza. 2. arrepentimiento.
sorrow-stricken [-,strɪkən] *a.* afligido.
sorry ['sɑrɪ, 'sɔrɪ, B 'sɔrɪ] *a.* (SORRIER; SORRIEST) 1. doloroso, penoso, lastimoso, miserable. 2. pesaroso, afligido, apesadumbrado, apenado; arrepentido. 3. triste, melancólico. 4. **a s. fellow,** un desgraciado; **s.!** ¡perdón! ¡disculpe! ¡lo siento!; **to be** (o **to feel**) **s.,** sentir; arrepentirse; **to be s. for (something),** arrepentirse de (algo), ej., *you will be s. for this,* Ud. se arrepentirá de esto; **to feel** (o **to be**) **s. for (someone),** compadecerse de (alguien); **to feel s. for oneself,** sentir conmiseración o piedad por sí mismo; **to be s. to (do),** sentir (hacer).
sort [sɔrt, B sɔt] *s.* 1. clase, especie, tipo, orden, variedad, ej., *a new s. of car,* un automóvil de tipo nuevo. 2. modo, manera, forma. 3. carácter, índole, naturaleza. 4. (impr.) tipo, suerte. 5. **after a s.,** de cierto modo; **a good s.,** (fam.) persona simpática o buena; un buen tipo; **nothing of the s.,** nada de eso; **of a s., of sorts,** una especie de, algo parecido a; (despec.) de mala calidad; **out of sorts,** indispuesto, de mal humor; **s. of,** (fam.) en cierta medida, en cierto modo, un poco, ej., *I was s. of glad to help him,* en cierto modo me gustó ayudarle. —*v.t.* 1. (gen. con *out*) clasificar, ordenar, arreglar, dividir en grupos; separar, escoger, seleccionar. 2. (dial.) ajustar, arreglar, corregir. 3. (esco.) castigar. (ant.).
sort, *s.* (ant.) suerte, hado, destino; adivinación por suertes.
sortable ['sɔrtəbəl, B 'sɔt-] *a.* clasificable, separable.
sorter [-ər, B -ə] *s.* distribuidor, clasificador.
sortie ['sɔrtɪ, ʃɔr'ti, B 'sɔti] *s.* 1. (mil.) salida. 2. (mil.) misión o ataque a cargo de un solo avión.
sortilege ['sɔrtɪlɪdʒ, B 'sɔt-] *s.* sortilegio; hechicería, encantamiento.
sorting ['sɔrtɪŋ, B 'sɔt-] *s.* distribución, clasificación.
sortition [sɔr'tɪʃən, B sɔ'-] *s.* sorteamiento, sorteo.
sorus ['sɔrəs] *s.* (*pl.* SORI [-,aɪ]) (bot.) soro.
SOS [,ɛsoʊ'ɛs] 1. (rad.) s.o.s. (señal internacional para pedir auxilio). 2. (fig.) llamada de auxilio.
Sosigenes [sə'sɪdʒəniz] *s.* Sosígenes, cráter de la luna.
so-so ['soʊ,soʊ] *a.* (fam.) regular, pasable; mediano, mediocre. —*adv.* regularmente; medianamente, mediocremente.
sostenuto [,soʊstə'nutoʊ, B ,sɔs-] (mús.) —*a.* sostenido. —*s.* movimiento o pasaje sostenido.
sot [sɑt, B sɔt] *s.* borracho, borrachín.
soteriology [soʊ,tɪrɪ'ɑlədʒɪ, B -,tɪərɪ'ɔl-] *s.* (teo.) soteriología.
Sothic ['soʊθɪk, 'sɑθ-, B 'soʊ-] *a.* (astr.) sotíaco.
Sothic ['soʊθɪk] *a.* (astr.) sotíaco.
sotol [soʊ'tɔl, B 'soʊtɔl] *s.* (bot.) sotol.
sotted ['sɑtəd, B 'sɔt-] *var. de* **besotted.**
sottish [-ɪʃ] *a.* embrutecido por la bebida; como una cuba, borracho; embotado, estúpido.
sottishly [-lɪ] *adv.* (como) embrutecido por la bebida; estúpidamente.
sotto voce [,sɑtoʊ'voʊtʃɪ, B 'sɔt-] (a) sovoz. en voz baja.
sou [su] *s.* sueldo (moneda francesa de bronce); **he hasn't a s.,** (G.B.) está sin un centavo.
soubise [su'biz] *s.* (**t. s. sauce**) salsa blanca de cebollas.
soubrette [su'brɛt] *s.* 1. (teat.) camarera o confidenta, doncella coqueta. 2. actriz especializada en esta clase de papeles.
soubriquet, *var. de* **sobriquet.**
soucar [soʊ'kɑr, B 'saʊkɑ] *s.* (anglo-ind.) banquero indio.
Souchong ['su,tʃɔŋ, -,ʃɔŋ] *s.* variedad de té negro de la China.
Soudan, *var. de* **Sudan.**
souffle ['sufəl] *s.* (med.) soplo.
soufflé [su'fleɪ, B 'sufleɪ] *s.* (cocina) soufflé.
sough [saʊ, sʌf, B saʊ] *s.* 1. susurro, suspiro (del viento). 2. (esco., Irl.) rumor vago; zumbido, silbido. —*v.i.* 1. susurrar, suspirar, ej., *the wind soughing through the trees,* el viento susurrando entre los árboles. 2. (esco.) predicar u orar con sonsonete.
sought [sɔt] *pret., p.p. de* **seek.**
soul [soʊl] *s.* 1. alma, espíritu. 2. (fig.) alma, ánimo, corazón, vitalidad, ej., *he is the s. of the enterprise,* él es el alma de la empresa. 3. personificación, imagen, ej., *he is the s. of honor,* es la honradez personificada. 4. alma, persona, individuo, ej., *not a s.,* ni un alma. 5. ánima, alma, espíritu (de los muertos). 6. **a simple s.,** un alma de Dios; **to be unable to call one's s. one's own,** estar completamente sometido (a otro); **upon my s.!** ¡por vida mía! 7. (jer., E.U.) entre los negros, conjunto de características raciales, culturales, etc., propias de su grupo étnico. —*a.* (jer.) propio y característico de la cultura de los negros de E.U.
soul food, (E.U.) comida tradicional de los negros del Sur.
soulful ['soʊlfəl] *a.* espiritual, sentimental, conmovedor.
soulfully [-fəlɪ] *adv.* sentimentalmente; con sentimiento.
soulless [-ləs] *a.* 1. desalmado, sin conciencia. 2. sin ánimo ni entusiasmo.
soullessly [-lɪ] *adv.* desalmadamente.
soul mate, 1. compañero espiritual. espíritu afín, amigo del alma. 2. amante.
soul music, (mús.) música de estilo **"blue"** con influencia de canciones religiosas de los negros de E.U.
soul-searching [-,sɜrtʃɪŋ, B -,sɜtʃɪŋ] *s.* examen de conciencia.
sound [saʊnd] *a.* 1. sano, saludable, robusto. 2. sano, ileso, incólume, entero, íntegro. 3. firme, fuerte, sólido; estable, (com.) solvente. 4. seguro, fidedigno. 5. correcto, exacto, acertado (razonamiento, etc.). 6. profundo (ej., sueño). 7. **of s. mind, s. of mind,** en su sano juicio; **s. as a bell,** en perfecto estado de salud. —*adv.* profundamente, ej., *s. asleep,* profundamente dormido.
sound, *s.* 1. sonido. 2. ruido, ej., *s. of rejoicing,* ruido (o gritos) de júbilo. 3. son, tañido, ej., *at the s. of the trumpet,* al son de la trompeta, *the s. of bells,* el tañido de las campanas. 4. **within (out) of s.,** al (fuera del) alcance del oído. —*v.i.* 1. sonar, resonar; parecer, ej., *his story sounds incredible,* su relato parece increíble. 2. **s. off,** declamar, arengar. —*v.t.* 1. sonar, tocar, tañer. 2. expresar, proferir, formular. 3. auscultar, ej., *s. the chest,* auscultar el pecho. —*a.* 1. sonoro, acústico. 2. (rad.) de sonido (transmisión, etc.).
sound, *v.t.* 1. sondar, sondear. 2. (fig.) (gen. con *out*) sondear, tantear, inquirir, indagar. 3. desentrañar, destripar (peces). 4. (med.) sondar, explorar con sonda. —*v.i.* 1. hacer sondeos. 2. sumergirse precipitadamente (peces). —*s.* (med.) sonda, tienta.
sound, *s.* 1. canal, brazo de mar. 2. vejiga natatoria (de peces).
soundable ['saʊndəbəl] *a.* que se puede tocar (instrumento musical).
sound absorber, amortiguador del sonido.
sound barrier, barrera sónica, barrera del sonido; **to break the s. b.,** pasar la barrera sónica (avión).
soundboard [-,bɔrd, B -bɔd] *s.* 1. secreto, tabla de armonía, caja armónica (de un instrumento musical). 2. tornavoz.
sound bow, pata de la campana (donde golpea el badajo).
sound box, 1. cabeza resonadora, captador acústico (del gramófono antiguo). 2. secreto, caja acústica, caja de resonancia.
sound effects, (cinem., rad., t.v.) efectos sonoros.
sounder ['saʊndər, B -də] *s.* resonador, sonador; receptor acústico (de telegrafía).
sound film, película sonora, película parlante.
sound head, (cinem.) cabeza sonora.
sounding [-dɪŋ] *a.* sonante, sonoro; resonante, retumbante.
sounding, *s.* (mar.) 1. sondaje, sondeo, braceaje, escandallada. 2. (*pl.*) fondo de mar o de río (que pueda ser alcanzado con la sonda).
sounding balloon, (meteor.) globo sonda.
sounding board, 1. (mús.) secreto, tabla de armonía, caja armónica. 2. tornavoz.
sounding lead, (mar.) escandallo.
sounding line, (mar.) sondaleza; bolina, sonda.
soundingly [-lɪ] *adv.* sonoramente.
sounding machine, máquina sondadora.
sounding rocket, cohete sonda.
soundings [-dɪŋz] *s. pl.* (geol.) sondajes, sondeos.

soundless ['saʊndləs] *a.* 1. insondable. 2. silencioso, silente; mudo.
soundlessly [-lɪ] *adv.* sin sonido, sin ruido, silenciosamente; mudamente.
soundly ['saʊndlɪ] *adv.* 1. firmemente, seguramente. 2. correctamente. 3. profundamente.
soundness [-nəs] *s.* 1. sanidad; entereza. 2. solidez; firmeza. 3. corrección, exactitud.
sound pressure, presión acústica.
soundproof [-ˌpruf] *a.* a prueba de ruidos o sonidos, antisonoro, insonoro. —*v.t.* insonorizar, tornar insonoro.
soundproofing [-ɪŋ] *s.* 1. aislamiento acústico, insonorización. 2. revestimiento sordo.
sound track, (cinem.) banda de sonido, pista sonora.
sound velocity, (son., aer.) velocidad del sonido.
sound wave, onda sonora, onda acústica.
soup [sup] *s.* 1. sopa, caldo. 2. (jer.) fuerza o potencia adicional. 3. (jer.) nitroglicerina o dinamita. 4. (jer.) revelador fotográfico. 5. (jer.) niebla espesa. 6. **in the s.,** (jer.) en apuros. —*v.t.* **s. up,** (jer.) reforzar, aumentar la potencia de (automóvil, motor, bomba, etc.).
soupçon [sup'soʊn, 'supˌsɑn, B 'supsɔŋ] *s.* traza, huella.
souped-up ['supt'ʌp] *a.* (jer.) 1. de potencia aumentada (motor, etc.). 2. mejorado, embellecido, engalanado.
soup kitchen, 1. comedor de beneficencia (para los pobres). 2. (G.B., mil.) cocina de campaña.
soupy ['supɪ] *a.* (SOUPIER; SOUPIEST) 1. espeso como una sopa. 2. (fam.) empalagoso, sentimental. 3. nebuloso, nublado, denso (niebla).
sour [saʊr, B 'saʊə] *a.* 1. agrio, ácido, acedo, acidulo; avinagrado, picado; ej., *s. apples,* manzanas agrias, *s. milk,* leche agria. 2. rancio, fermentado, ej., *s. bread,* pan rancio. 3. acre, de olor acre; picante, irritante. 4. (fig.) acre, áspero, desabrido, avinagrado. 5. agrio, sulfuroso (petróleo). —*s.* 1. substancia agria o ácida. 2. coctel de sabor agrio. —*v.i., v t.* agriar(se), avinagrar(se), acedar(se); ranciar(se).
source [sɔrs, B sɔs] *s.* 1. fuente, manantial, venero, venera. 2. (fig.) fuente, origen, fundamento, principio.
source book, libro de consulta.
source language, lengua de origen, lenguaje original, lengua de base.
sour cherry, 1. (bot.) guindo 2. guinda.
sour cream, crema agria, nata agria.
sourdine [sʊr'din, B sʊə'-] *s.* (mús.) sordino.
sour dock, (bot.) acedera.
sourdough ['saʊrˌdoʊ, B 'saʊəˌ-] *s.* 1. masa fermentada para pan (que llevaban los cateadores consigo). 2. cateador experimentado del Canadá, Alaska, y del oeste de los E.U.
sour grapes, (fig.) las uvas verdes.
sourish ['saʊrɪʃ, B 'saʊər-] *a.* agrete, algo ácido; un poco rancio.
sourly [-lɪ, B -əlɪ] *adv.* agriamente, ácidamente, amargamente.
sourness [-nəs] *s.* 1. agrura, acedía, acidez. 2. (fig.) acrimonia, acritud, desabrimiento.
sourpuss [-ˌpʊs] *s.* (fam.) aguafiestas, cara de acelga.
sour salt, (quím.) ácido cítrico.
soursop [-ˌsɑp, B -sɔp] *s.* 1. (bot.) guanábano. 2. jirasal, guanábana (fruta).
sousaphone ['suzəˌfoʊn] *s.* (especie de) tuba (inventada por J.P. Sousa).
souse [saʊs] *s.* 1. encurtido, esp. adobo de cabeza, orejas y patas de cerdo, queso de cerdo, chicharrones (Esp.). 2. escabeche, salsa, adobo. 3. empapamiento, mojada. 4. (jer., E.U.) borrachín; borrachera, parranda. —*v.t.* 1. escabechar, adobar, encurtir. 2. empapar, remojar, saturar de agua. 3. sumir, sumergir. 4. (jer., E.U.) emborrachar. 5. **s. oneself in,** (fig.) embeberse en, empaparse en. —*v.i.* 1. sumergirse, bañarse. 2. (jer., E.U.) emborracharse.
souse, *s.* (ant.) ataque repentino del halcón. —*v.i., v.t.* (ant.) arrojarse con violencia, atacar repentinamente. —*adv.* de cabeza, precipitadamente.
soutache [su'tæʃ, B 'sutɑʃ] *s.* (fr.) trencilla, galoncillo.
soutane [su'tɑn] *s.* sotana.
souter ['sutər, B -ə] *s.* (esco.) zapatero.
south [saʊθ] *s.* sur, sud, mediodía; **the S.,** (E.U.) los Estados del Sur. —*a.* meridional, austral, del sur. —*adv.* hacia el sur, en el sur, desde el sur. — [B saʊð] *v.i.* girar o dirigirse hacia el sur.
South Africa, Sudáfrica.
South African, sudafricano.
South America, Sudamérica, América del Sur, Suramérica.
South American, sudamericano, suramericano.
South Australia, Australia Meridional.
southbound ['saʊθˌbaʊnd] *a.* con rumbo al sur.
south by east, (mar.) sur cuarta al sudeste.
south by west, (mar.) sur cuarta al suroeste.
South Carolina [-ˌkærə'laɪnə] *s.* Carolina del Sur, estado de los E.U.
South Dakota [-də'koʊtə] *s.* Dakota del Sur, estado de los E.U.
southeast [saʊθ'ist, B 'saʊθ'ist] *s.* sudeste. —*a.* al sudeste, del sudeste. —*adv.* hacia el sudeste, desde el sudeste.
southeast by east, (mar.) sudeste cuarta al este.
southeaster [saʊθ'istər, B -tə] *s.* sudeste (viento o vendaval).
southeasterly [-lɪ] *a.* que lleva rumbo al sudeste; desde el sudeste. —*adv.* hacia el sudeste, al sudeste.
southeastern [-tərn, B -tən] *a.* del sudeste.
southeasternmost [-ˌmoʊst] *a.* del extremo sudeste.
southeastward [saʊθ'istwərd, B -wəd] **southeastwards** [-wərdz, B -wədz] *adv.* con rumbo al sudeste.
souther ['saʊðər, B -ðə] *s.* austro, sur, ábrego.
southerly ['sʌðərlɪ, B -əlɪ] *a.* meridional, austral, del sur; antártico. —*adv.* hacia el sur; desde el sur.
southern [-ərn, B -ən] *a.* meridional, austral, del sur, situado al sur; (E.U.) (de los Estados) del Sur. —*s.* (E.U.) dialecto del Sur.
Southern Cross, (astr.) Cruz del Sur.
Southern Crown, (astr.) Corona Austral.
Southerner [-ərnər, B -ənə] *s.* habitante del sur, sureño, sureña; (E.U.) sudista, habitante de los Estados del Sur.
Southern Fish, (astr.) Pez austral.
Southern Hemisphere, hemisferio meridional o austral.
southernism [-ˌnɪzəm] *s.* (E.U.) 1. modismo o frase idiomática del Sur; pronunciación característica del Sur. 2. costumbre o comportamiento característico del Sur.
southern lights, (astr.) aurora austral.
southernly ['sʌðərnlɪ, B -ənlɪ] *a.* meridional, austral, del sur.
southernmost [-ˌmoʊst] *a.* del extremo sur.
Southern Rhodesia, Rodesia del Sur.
southernwood [-ˌwʊd] *s.* (bot.) abrótano, brótano, boja, guardarropa.
southing ['saʊθɪŋ, B -ðɪŋ] *s.* 1. derrota o curso hacia el sur. 2. (astr.) desviación al sur. 3. (mar.) diferencia de latitud hacia el sur.
South Korea, Corea del Sur.
South Korean, surcoreano.
southland [-ˌlænd, -lənd] *s.* tierra meridional, región del sur.
southpaw [-ˌpɔ] *a.* (dep. jer.) zurdo. —*s.* (dep.) zurdo; (béisbol) jugador zurdo.
South Pole, 1. (geog.) Polo Sur. 2. **s. p.** (fís.) polo sur (del imán).
Southron ['sʌðrən] *s.* 1. (esp. S. de E.U.) anteriormente, habitante del sur. 2. (esco.) inglés. —*a.* (pr. esco.) inglés.
South Sea Islands, islas de los mares del Sur.
south-southeast ['saʊθˌsaʊθ'ist] *s.* sursudeste. —*adv.* hacia o desde el sursudeste.
south-southwest [-'wɛst] *s.* sur-sudoeste. —*adv.* hacia o desde el sur-sudoeste.
South Vietnam, Vietnam del Sur.
southward ['saʊθwərd, B -wəd] *a.* situado en el sur, que va hacia el sur. —*adv.* hacia el sur. —*s.* dirección del sur.
southwardly [-lɪ] *adv.* con dirección al sur, con ubicación hacia el sur.
southwards [-wərdz, B -wədz] *adv.* hacia el sur.
southwest [saʊθ'wɛst] *s.* sudoeste, suroeste; región del suroeste. —*a.* del sudoeste. —*adv.* hacia el sudoeste, en el sudoeste, desde el sudoeste.
southwest by south, (mar.) suroeste cuarta al sur.
southwest by west, (mar.) suroeste cuarta al oeste.
southwester [-'wɛstər, B -tə] **sou'wester** [saʊ'wɛstər, B -tə] *s.* 1. vendaval del sudoeste. 2. (raro) sueste (sombrero de lona encerada de los marinos).
southwesterly [-lɪ] *a.* hacia el sudoeste, del sudoeste.
southwestern [-tərn, B -tən] *a.* del sudoeste.
southwestward [-'wɛstwərd, B -wəd] *a.* situado hacia el sudoeste, dirigido al sudoeste. —*adv.* (con dirección) al sudoeste, con ubicación hacia el sudoeste. —*s.* dirección del sudoeste.
southwestwards [-wərdz, B -wədz] *adv.* (con dirección) al sudoeste.
souvenir ['suvənɪr, ˌsuvə'nɪr, B 'suvənɪə] *s.* recuerdo, recordatorio, prenda de recuerdo.
souvenir sheet, (filat.) hoja conmemorativa.
sovereign ['sɑvrən, -ərn, B 'sɔvrɪn] *a.* 1. supremo, sumo (bien, importancia, virtud, etc.). 2. soberano, independiente, ej., *s. state,* estado soberano. 3. soberano, excelente, regio. 4. eficaz, eficiente, ej., *s. remedy,* remedio eficaz. 5. supremo, máximo (desdén, orgullo, etc.). 6. de remate (loco, etc.). —*s.* 1. soberano, monarca. 2. (G.B.) libra esterlina de oro.
sovereignly [-lɪ] *adv.* soberanamente, independientemente.
sovereignty [-tɪ] *s.* 1. soberanía. 2. estado soberano.
soviet ['soʊvɪˌɛt] *s.* 1. soviet (consejo gubernamental comunista). 2. **S.,** (*pl.*) oficiales del gobierno o del pueblo de la Unión Soviética. —*a.* soviético.
sovietization [ˌsoʊvɪˌɛtə'zeɪʃən, B -ətaɪ-] *s.* sovietización.
sovietize ['soʊvɪˌɛtˌaɪz] *v.t* sovietizar.
Soviet Russia, la Rusia Soviética.
Soviet Union, Unión Soviética, Unión de Repúblicas Socialistas Soviéticas.
sovkhoz [sɑf'kɔz, -'kɔs, B sɔf-] *s.* (*pl.* SOVKHOZY o SOVKHOZES) (ruso) granja estatal.
sow [saʊ] *s.* 1. (zool.) cerda, puerca, cochina, marrana. 2. (metal.) reguera, fosa, goa, galápago.
sow [soʊ] *v.t.* (*pret.* SOWED; *p.p.* SOWN [soʊn], SOWED; *p.pr.* SOWING) 1. sembrar (semillas, la tierra). 2. (fig.) sembrar, esparcir, diseminar, dispersar, desparramar. 3. **s. one's wild oats,** hacer

travesuras juveniles, correrla de joven; **s. on stony ground,** sembrar en la arena; **he who sows the wind reaps the whirlwind,** quien siembra viento(s) cosecha tempestades. —*v.i.* sembrar, espartir las semillas.

sowar [soʊ'wɑr, B sʌ'wɑ] *s.* soldado de caballería (en la India).

sowbelly ['saʊˌbɛlɪ] *s.* (E.U.) pella salada, carne de puerco salada.

sowbread [-ˌbrɛd] *s.* (bot.) pamporcino, pan porcino.

sow bug, (ento.) cochinilla de la humedad, bicho munición.

sowcar, *var. de* **soucar.**

sowens ['suənz, 'soʊ-] *s. pl.* (dial.) potaje hecho del hollejo de la avena.

sower ['soʊər, B -ə] *s.* 1.sembrador, diseminador, desparramador. 2. sembradora (máquina).

sown, *p.p. de* **sow.**

sow thistle, (bot.) cerraja.

sox[sɑks, B sɔks] *pl. de* **sock.**

soy [sɔɪ] **soya** ['sɔɪə] *s.* 1. (bot.) soja, soya. 2. salsa de soya.

soybean ['sɔɪ'bin] *s.* 1. (bot.) soja. 2. semilla de soja, de soya.

sozin ['soʊzɪn] *s.* (bioquím.) socina, sozina, sozalbumina.

sozolic acid [soʊ'zɑlɪk-, B -'zɔl-] (quím.) ácido sozoyodólico.

sozzled ['sɑzəld, B 'sɔz-] *a.* (jer.) hecho una cuba, muy borracho; **to get s.,** pegarse una mona.

Sp. *abrev. de* **Spain, Spanish,** España, español.

sp. *abrev de* 1. **spelling,** deletreo. 2. **specific,** específico.

s.p. *abrev. de* **sine prole** (Lat.), **without issue,** sin sucesión (der.).

spa [spɑ] *s.* 1. manantial de agua mineral. 2. balneario de aguas minerales.

space [speɪs] *s.* 1. espacio (cósmico). 2. espacio, lugar, cabida; área. 3. espacio, duración, intervalo, período (de tiempo). 4. espacio, intervalo, distancia (entre cuerpos). 5. (mús.) espacio (entre las rayas del pentagrama). 6. (mat., impr.) espacio, blanco. 7. (ant.) rato. —*v.t.* 1. espaciar. 2. (impr.) (ú. gen. con *out*) dar blancos a (composición); interlinear, regletear. 3. **s. closely,** espaciar estrechamente; (impr.) componer cerrado.

space age, era espacial, era de exploración espacial.

space band, (impr.) espaciador, espacio de cuña.

space bar, espaciador, barra espaciadora (de la máquina de escribir).

space capsule, cápsula espacial.

space center, centro espacial.

space charge, (elec.) carga espacial, carga de espacio.

spacecraft ['speɪsˌkræft, B -krɑft] *s.* astronave, nave espacial.

space flight, vuelo espacial.

space heater, calentador unitario, calentador de espacio.

space heating, calentamiento unitario, calentamiento de espacio.

space lattice, (quím., fís.) conjunto reticular (en cristales); red cristalina.

spaceless [-ləs] *a.* 1. ilimitado, sin límites. 2. inextenso.

space line, (impr.) interlínea.

spaceman [-ˌmæn, -mən] *s.* 1. piloto espacial, astronauta. 2. visitante del espacio (a la tierra).

space platform, plataforma espacial.

spaceport [-ˌpɔrt, B -pɔt] *s.* estación de lanzamiento (de cohetes, satélites artificiales, etc.).

space probe, sonda espacial.

space program, programa de exploración espacial.

spacer ['speɪsər, B -sə] *s.* espaciador, separador.

spaceship ['speɪsˌʃɪp] *s.* astronave, nave espacial.

space shuttle, transbordador espacial, lanzadera espacial.

space station, estación espacial.

space suit, vestido o traje espacial, escafandra espacial.

space telescope, telescopia espacial.

space-time [-'taɪm] *s.* espacio-tiempo.

space travel, viaje(s) espacial(es), navegación espacial.

space vehicle, vehículo interplanetario.

space walk, paseo espacial.

space-walk, pasear por el espacio.

spaceward [-wərd, B -wəd] *adv.* hacia el espacio.

space writer, reportero pagado según la extensión de su artículo.

spacial, *var. de* **spatial.**

spacing ['speɪsɪŋ] *a.* espaciamiento, espacio, intervalo (entre dos objetos, líneas, etc.).

spacing wave, (rad.) onda separadora o de reposo, onda espaciadora.

spacious [-ʃəs] *a.* espacioso, extenso, amplio, dilatado.

spaciously [-lɪ] *adv.* espaciosamente, extensamente, ampliamente.

spaciousness [-nəs] *s.* espaciosidad, amplitud.

spade [speɪd] *s.* pala, laya, azada; **to call a s. a s.,** llamar al pan pan y al vino vino. —*v.t., v.i.* layar, revolver con pala (la tierra).

spade, *s.* 1. (naipes) espada; (*pl.*) palo de espadas. 2. (jer., despec.) persona de color, negro.

spadeful [-ˌfʊl] *s.* palada.

spade guinea, (hist.) guinea con escudo en forma de espada de naipe.

spader [-ər, B -ə] *s.* paletador; pala neumática.

spadework [-ˌwɜrk, B -wɜk] *s.* (fig.) trabajos preparatorios.

spadiceous [speɪ'dɪʃəs] *a.* (bot.) espadíceo.

spadix ['speɪdɪks] *s.* (*pl.* SPADICES [-dəˌsiz, B speɪ'daɪsiz]) (bot.) espádice.

spaghetti [spə'gɛtɪ] *s.* 1. fideos largos, macarrón delgado; tallarín. 2. (elec.) tubo de algodón tejido.

spagyric [spə'dʒɪrɪk] *a.* (hist.) espagírico, relativo a la alquimia.

spahi ['spɑˌhi] *s.* (mil.) espahí, soldado de caballería (en Turquía y Argelia).

spail, *var. de* **spale.**

Spain [speɪn] *s.* España.

spake [speɪk] (ant.) *pret. de* **speak.**

spale [speɪl] *s.* (dial.) lata, listón, latilla, astilla.

spall [spɔl] *s.* astilla, fragmento; laja, lasca de piedra. —*v.t., v.i.* (min.) astillar(se), descantillar(se), desconchar (se), desgajar(se); labrar la piedra, desbastar.

spalpeen [spæl'pin] *s.* (pr. Irl.) bribón, pícaro.

span [spæn] *s.* 1. cuarta, palmo. 2. trecho, distancia, tramo, trayecto. 3. lapso, espacio, transcurso, duración, período, intervalo. 4. pareja, yunta (de caballos, bueyes, etc.) 5. (arq.) tramo, luz (de puente). 6. (aer.) envergadura. —*v.t.* (*pret., p.p.* SPANNED, *p.pr.* SPANNING) 1. medir por cuartas o palmos; medir. 2. extender sobre, echar sobre, tenderse sobre, conectar, cubrir, llegar de un lado al otro de. 3. (ant.) abarcar.

span, (ant.) *pret. de* **spin.**

Span. *abrev. de* **Spanish,** español.

spandrel ['spændrəl] *s.* (arq.) seno, enjuta, sobaco, tímpano de los arcos.

spanemia [spə'nimɪə] *s.* (med.) anemia, isquemia.

spanemic [-mɪk] *a.* (med.) anémico.

spang [spæŋ] *adv.* 1. (fam.) completamente. 2. justamente, directamente, de frente.

spangle ['spæŋgəl] *s.* lentejuela, bricho; adorno brillante. —*v.t.* adornar con lentejuelas. —*v.i.* brillar con lentejuelas; centellear, rutilar.

Spanglish ['spæglɪʃ] *s.* (hum.) espanglés.

Spaniard ['spænjərd, B -jəd] *s.* español.

spaniel [-jəl] *s.* 1. (zool.) perro de aguas. 2. (fig.) adulador servil.

Spanish [-ɪʃ] *a.* español, hispano, hispánico, ibérico. —*s.* español, castellano (idioma).

Spanish-American [-ə'mɛrəkən] *a., s.* hispanoamericano.

Spanish Armada, (hist.) (la) Armada Invencible.

Spanish bayonet, (bot.) variedad de yuca.

Spanish broom, (bot.) piorno, gayomba.

Spanish cedar, (bot.) cabima.

Spanish-English, español-inglés.

Spanish fir, (bot.) pinsapo.

Spanish fly, (ento.) abadejo, cantárida.

Spanish grass, (bot.) esparto.

Spanish jasmine, (bot.) jazmín de España, jazmín real.

Spanish leather, cordobán; piel de cabra curtida.

Spanish mackerel, (ict.) escombro, caballa.

Spanish Main, (hist.) 1. (el) mar Caribe. 2. Tierra Firme.

Spanish moss, (bot.) barbón, barba de monte, barba española, musgo negro o de Florida.

Spanish needles, 1. (bot.) bidente. 2. aquenio del bidente.

Spanish oak, (bot.) roble colorado.

Spanish omelet, (cocina) tortilla de huevos, cebolla, pimientos y tomate.

Spanish onion, (bot.) cebolla grande de sabor suave, muy usada en ensalada.

Spanish paprika, (bot.) (variedad de) pimiento dulce de España; pimentón.

Spanish puff, buñuelo.

Spanish shawl, mantón de Manila.

Spanish sheep, (zool.) oveja merina.

Spanish soap, jabón de Castilla.

Spanish speaker, hispanohablante, hispanoparlante.

Spanish-speaking ['spænɪʃˌspikɪŋ] *a.* de habla española, de habla castellana, hispanohablante, hispanoparlante.

Spanish tile, teja lomuda, teja árabe.

Spanish white, (quím.) blanco de España, yeso mate.

Spanish windlass, palo tortor, molinete, palo para atortorar, palo del torniquete.

spank [spæŋk] *v.i.* caminar rápidamente, moverse garbosamente.

spank, *v.t.* dar palmadas o nalgadas a, zurrar, dar una zurra a, azotar. —*s.* nalgada, zurra, tunda, azotaina.

spanker ['spæŋkər, B -kə] *s.* 1. (mar.) cangreja de popa. 2. caballo veloz. 3. azotador, el que da una azotaina.

spanker boom, (mar.) botavara.

spanking [-kɪŋ] *a.* (fam.) 1. asombroso, extraordinario, maravilloso. 2. fuerte, fresco (viento, brisa).

spanking, *s.* zurra, tunda.

spanner ['spænər, B -ə] *s.* 1. (pr. G.B.) llave de tuercas, llave de manguera, llave de gancho o de horquilla. 2. (ento.) oruga geómetra.

span-new ['spæn'nu, B -'nju] *a.* flamante, novísimo.

span roof, cubierta o techo a dos aguas.

spanworm [-ˌwɜrm, B -wɜm] *s.* (ento.) medidor, oruga medidora.

spar [spɑr, B spɑ] *s.* (min.) espato.
spar, *s.* 1. (mar.) palo, pértiga, berlinga, mástil, verga. 2. (aer.) larguero, viga mayor. —*v.t.* (*pret., p.p.* SPARRED; *p.pr.* SPARRING) equipar con mástiles, vergas o palos.
spar, *v.i.* 1. pelear o golpear con espolones (gallos). 2. hacer práctica de boxeo. 3. altercar. —*s.* 1. pelea con espolones (de gallos). 2. amago, finta, ademán de ataque o defensa. 3. boxeo de práctica.
sparable ['spærəbəl] *s.* puntilla (clavo pequeño de los zapateros).
spar buoy, (mar.) baliza, boya de pértiga o de asta.
spar deck, (mar.) cubierta superior, cubierta de guindaste.
spare [spɛr, B spɛə] *v.t.* 1. escatimar, no usar, prescindir de. 2. ahorrar (a uno trabajo, dificultades, etc.). 3. privarse de, pasar sin. 4. exceptuar, excepcionar. 5. perdonar, compadecerse de. 6. preocuparse de, ej., *don't s. the horses, let's go as fast as we can,* no te preocupes de los caballos, vamos rápido, a toda máquina. 7. **and to s.,** y (mucho) más; **s. (someone's) feelings,** no herir los sentimientos (de alguien); **s. me,** no me mates; **s. me a dime,** regálame diez centavos; **s. oneself,** cuidarse, ahorrarse trabajos; **to have (something) to s.,** tener (algo) de sobra; **to s.,** de sobra; **with minutes to s.,** faltando algunos minutos. —*v.i.* 1. ser frugal, ser parsimonioso. 2. desistir de hacer daño; tener piedad o misericordia. —*a.* 1. de repuesto, de reserva, suplementario, adicional. 2. disponible, sobrante, excedente. 3. libre, de ocio, ej., *s. hours,* horas libres, *s. time,* ratos de ocio, ratos perdidos. 4. enjuto, descarnado. 5. parsimonioso, mezquino, cicatero, agarrado (Am.). 6. frugal, parco, ej., *s. diet,* dieta frugal, *s. of speech,* parco de palabras. —*s.* 1. reserva. 2. (pr. G.B.) repuesto. 3. neumático de recambio, llanta de repuesto (Am.). 4. (dep.) jugador de reserva. 5. (dep.) sobrante (jugada en bowling).
spareable ['spɛrəbəl, B 'spɛər-] *a.* disponible, sobrante.
sparely ['spɛrlɪ, B 'spɛəlɪ] *adv.* 1. moderadamente, frugalmente. 2. escasamente, apenas. 3. delgadamente.
spareness [-nəs] *s.* 1. escasez. 2. frugalidad. 3. delgadez, flacura.
spare part, repuesto, pieza de repuesto, pieza de recambio o de refacción.
spareribs [-ˌrɪbz] *s. pl.* el extremo descarnado de la costilla de cerdo.
spare stores, (mar.) cordaje de repuesto, pertrechos de repuesto.
spare tire, (aut.) neumático de repuesto, goma de recambio, llanta de refacción.
sparge [spɑrdʒ, B spɑdʒ] *v.t., v.i.* regar, rociar, salpicar. —*s.* rocío, riego, salpicadura.
sparger ['spɑrdʒər, B 'spɑdʒə] *s.* tubo rociador (esp. el usado en la fabricación de cerveza).
sparid ['spærɪd] *a.* (ict.) espárido. —*s.* pez espárido.
sparing ['spɛrɪŋ, B 'spɛər-] *a.* 1. económico, parco, frugal. 2. escaso.
sparingly [-lɪ] *adv.* 1. económicamente, parcamente, frugalmente. 2. escasamente, apenas.
spark [spɑrk, B spɑk] *s.* 1. chispa, centella, morcella. 2. (fig.) centelleo, destello, resplandor. 3. (fig.) chispa, pizca, ej., *not a s. of life remained,* no ha quedado ni una chispa de vida. 4. (elec.) chispa, chispa de descarga. 5. (*pl.*) (fam.) radiotelegrafista (en barcos). 6. (mot.) encendido de bujías. —*v.i.* 1. chispear, echar chispas. 2. (mot.) dar chispa (encendido). —*v.t.* 1. excitar, animar, incitar. 2. **s. off,** encender por chispa; (fig.) desatar, causar.
spark, *s.* 1. petimetre, pisaverde. 2. hombre galante, galán, enamorado. —*v.i., v.t.* (fam.) galantear, enamorar, hacer la corte.
spark arrester, 1. parachispas (en chimeneas, ante el portillo del horno, etc.). 2. (elec.) parachispas, apagachispas, amortiguador de chispas.
spark coil, (elec.) bobina de inducción, bobina de chispas o de encendido.
spark condenser, (elec.) supresor de chispas.
sparker ['spɑrkər, B 'spɑkə] *s.* 1. cohete chispero. 2. (fam. G.B.) radiotelegrafista (en barcos). 3. objeto que chispea.
spark gap, (elec.) distancia explosiva, distancia disruptiva, entrehierro, explosor.
spark ignition, (mot.) encendido de chispa o por chispa.
sparking plug, (mot.) bujía de encendido.
sparking points, (mot.) puntos de chispa.
sparkish [-kɪʃ] *a.* 1. galante, galanteador. 2. garboso, elegante.
sparkle [-kəl] *s.* 1. destello, centelleo, chispa. 2. (fig.) animación, vivacidad, viveza. —*v.i.* 1. centellar, centellear, rutilar, chispear, relumbrar. 2. burbujear, ser efervescente. 3. (fig.) volverse animado, tornarse vivaz. 4. (fig.) brillar (en la ejecución de algo).
sparkler [-klər, B -klə] *s.* 1. cohete chispero. 2. diamante, brillante.
sparkling [-klɪŋ] *a.* 1. centellante, centelleante, chispeante, rutilante, resplandeciente, brillante, ej., *s. eyes,* ojos brillantes o chispeantes. 2. (fig.) chispeante, animado, vivaz (conversación, escrito, etc.). 3. espumoso, espumante, efervescente, ej., *s. wine,* vino espumante.
sparklingly [-lɪ] *adv.* 1. resplandecientemente, en forma resplandeciente, con resplandor, brillantemente. 2. (fig.) animadamente.
spark plug, 1. (mot.) bujía, bujía de encendido. 2. (fam. E.U.) persona emprendedora y activa.
sparkproof ['spɑrkˌpruf, B 'spɑk-] *a.* a prueba de chispas.
spark transmitter, (rad.) transmisor de chispas, radio transmisor a chispas.
sparling ['spɑrlɪŋ, B 'spɑlɪŋ] *s.* (ict.) esperlano.
sparoid ['spærɔɪd, 'spɛr-] *a.* (ict.) espárido. —*s.* pez espárido.
sparring partner ['spɑrɪŋ-] (boxeo) pareja de entrenamiento.
sparrow ['spæroʊ] *s.* (orn.) gorrión, pardal.
sparrowgrass [-ˌgræs, B -grɑs] *s.* (pr. dial.) (bot.) espárrago.
sparrow hawk, (orn.) gavilán; esparaván; halcón canela, halconcito, cernícalo, mochete.
sparry ['spɑrɪ] *a.* (min.) espático.
sparse [spɑrs, B spɑs] *a.* esparcido, disperso, desparramado; escaso, ralo; (bot., zool.) esparcido.
sparsely ['spɑrslɪ, B 'spɑs-] *adv.* aquí y allá, escasamente, en forma rala, ralamente.
sparseness [-nəs] **sparsity** ['spɑrsətɪ, B 'spɑsə-] *s.* dispersión, escasez; raleza.
Sparta ['spɑrtə, B 'spɑtə] *s.* Esparta, antigua ciudad de Grecia.
Spartacist [-səst] *s.* (hist.) espartaquista.
Spartacus ['spɑrtəkəs, B 'spɑtə-] *s.* Espartaco, gladiador de origen tracio y caudillo de una rebelión de esclavos contra Roma.
Spartan ['spɑrtən, B 'spɑtən] *a., s.* espartano.
Spartanism [-ˌɪzəm] *s.* carácter espartano; severidad, austeridad; intrepidez.
sparteine, spartein ['spɑrtɪən, B 'spɑtɪ-] *s.* (quím.) esparteína.
spar varnish, barniz marino, barniz resistente a la intemperie.
spasm ['spæzəm] *s.* 1. (med.) espasmo, contracción muscular. 2. (fig.) convulsión, arrebato, acceso (de temor, nerviosidad, indignación, ira, etc.).
spasmodic [spæz'mɑdɪk, B -'mɔd-] *a.* espasmódico, irregular, intermitente; (med.) espasmódico.
spasmodically [-ɪkəlɪ] *adv.* 1. espasmódicamente, convulsivamente. 2. (fig.) irregularmente, intermitentemente.
spasmodic asthma, (med.) asma espasmódica, asma bronquial.
spastic ['spæstɪk] *a.* (med.) espástico, espasmódico. —*s.* (med.) víctima de parálisis espástica.
spastic paralysis, (med.) parálisis espástica o espasmódica.
spat [spæt] *s.* (*pl.* SPAT O SPATS) (ict.) ostra joven. —*v.i.* desovar, frezar (las ostras).
spat, *s.* botín, polaina corta.
spat, *v.i.* (*pret., p.p.* SPATTED; *p.pr.* SPATTING) 1. abofetear, dar una bofetada o palmada a. 2. disputar, reñir (por cosas de poca importancia). —*s.* 1. bofetada, sopapo, palmada. 2. riña, disputa.
spat, *pret., p.p. de* **spit.**
spate [speɪt] *s.* (G.B.) 1. avenida, crecida, creciente. 2. demasía, exceso; torrente, tropel (de palabras).
spathaceous [speɪ'ðeɪʃəs] *a.* (bot.) espatáceo.
spathe [speɪð] *s.* (bot.) espata.
spathic ['spæθɪk] *a.* (min.) espático.
spathulate ['spæθjələt] (bot.) *var. de* spatulate.
spatial ['speɪʃəl] *a.* espacial, relativo al espacio.
spatially [-əlɪ] *adv.* en el aspecto espacial.
spatiotemporal [ˌspeɪʃɪoʊ'tɛmpərəl] *a.* espaciotemporal.
spatter ['spætər, B -ə] *v.t.* 1. salpicar, manchar, rociar, esparcir. 2. (fig.) manchar, deslustrar (con calumnia, etc.). 3. **s. with,** salpicar de. —*v.i.* salpicar, gotear. —*s.* salpicadura, rociada; **s. of applause,** unos cuantos aplausos; **s. of fire,** fuego intermitente (de armas); **s. of rain,** unas gotas de lluvia.
spatterdash [-ˌdæʃ] *s.* (*ú. gen. en pl.*) polainas, botines.
spatterdock [-ˌdɑk, B -ˌdɔk] *s.* (bot.) nenúfar amarillo.
spatteringly ['spætərɪŋlɪ] *adv.* salpicando, con efecto de salpicaduras.
spattle ['spætəl] *s.* (ceram.) instrumento para motear la vajilla de loza.
spatula ['spætʃələ, B 'spætjʊ-] *s.* espátula, paleta.
spatulate [-lət] *a.* 1. (bot.) espatulado. 2. ancho y chato (dedo, mano, pie).
spavin ['spævən] *s.* (vet.) esparaván.
spavined [-ənd] *a.* (bot.) que padece esparaván.
spawn [spɔn] *v.t.* 1. depositar (huevos). 2. producir, generar (en abundancia). 3. (bot.) sembrar con micelios de hongos. —*v.i.* 1. desovar, mugar, frezar. 2. reproducirse en abundancia, multiplicarse en masa. —*s.* 1. freza, hueva. 2. (despec.) engendro, ej., *s. of the devil,* engendro del diablo. 3. producto, resultado. 4. vástago. 5. (fig.) semilla, germen. 6. (bot.) micelio del hongo.
spawner ['spɔnər, B -ə] *s.* (ict.) pez hembra.
spawning [-ɪŋ] *s.* desove, muga.
spay [speɪ] *v.t.* (vet.) quitar los ovarios.
spay, spayard ['speɪərd, B -əd] *s.* (zool.) enodio.
S.P.C.A. *abrev. de* **Society for the Prevention of Cruelty to Animals,** Sociedad Protectora de Animales.
S.P.C.C. *abrev. de* **Society for the Prevention of Cruelty to Children,** Sociedad para la Protección del Niño.

speak [spik] *v.i.* (*pret.*, SPOKE [spoʊk] *p.p.* SPOKEN, ['spoʊkən] *p.pr.* SPEAKING) 1. hablar. 2. (fig.) estar hablando, ej., *the portrait speaks,* el retrato está hablando. 3. hablar, perorar, discursear, pronunciar un discurso. 4. sonar (un instrumento). 5. **not to s. to,** no hablar con; **nothing to s. of,** nada digno de mención, prácticamente nada; **roughly speaking,** aproximadamente, hablando en términos generales; **so to s.,** como si dijéramos, como quien dice; **s. about,** hablar o tratar de; **s. behind someone's back,** hablar a espaldas de (alguien); murmurar; **s. for,** hablar en favor de, hablar en nombre de; ser señal de, ser recomendación para; **speak for itself,** hablar por sí mismo, ser evidente por sí mismo; **s. ill of,** hablar mal de; **s. of,** hablar de, mencionar, citar (esp. en un escrito); **s. out,** hablar claro, dar su opinión; **s. to (someone),** dirigirse a (alguien); reprender (a alguien); **s. to (fact, matter,** etc.), aseverar, confirmar, referirse a (hecho, asunto, etc.); **s. to the point,** ir al grano, dejarse de rodeos; **s. up,** hablar en alta voz, levantar la voz; hablar claro; interponer; **s. well of,** hablar bien de; **s. well for,** decir mucho en favor de, ser un indicio favorable de; **s. with** (o **to**), hablar, conversar (con). —*v.t.* 1. articular, pronunciar, expresar, decir. 2. hablar de, revelar. 3. hablar, usar, emplear (un idioma). 4. (mar.) ponerse al habla con (barco). 5. (ant.) mostrar, demostrar, evidenciar. 6. **s. daggers,** desatarse en improperios, echar chispas; **s. one's mind,** decir uno lo que piensa; hablar en plata; **s. volumes for,** exaltar, alabar enormemente a. —**English spoken,** (señal) se habla inglés.

speakable ['spikəbəl] *a.* decible, pronunciable.

speakeasy ['spɪˌkizɪ] *s.* (jer., E.U.) taberna clandestina (del tiempo del prohibicionismo).

speaker [-kər, B -kə] *s.* 1. orador, conferenciante, disertante. 2. portavoz. 3. presidente (de una asamblea legislativa). 4. altavoz, altoparlante. 5. **S. of the House,** el presidente de la Cámara de Representantes en E.U.

speakership [-ˌʃɪp] *s.* presidencia (de una asamblea legislativa).

speaking [-kiŋ] *a.* 1. parlante, hablante. 2. de habla, ej., *English-s.,* de habla inglesa. 3. viviente, expresivo (cara, etc.). 4. (fig.) elocuente (testigo, prueba, etc.). 5. fiel, vivo (retrato, etc.). 6. **not to be on s. terms,** estar peleado, no hablarse con (alguien). —*s.* 1. habla, oratoria. 2. discurso. 3. mitin.

speaking acquaintance, conocido superficial (con quien se habla ocasionalmente).

speaking trumpet, bocina, megáfono.

speaking tube, tubo acústico.

spean [spin] *v.t.* (esco.) destetar, ablactar.

spear [spɪr, B spɪə] *s.* 1. lanza, pica, asta, venablo. 2. arpón. 3. lancero. 4. (bot.) hoja (de hierba), brote (de raíz). —*v.t.* lancear, alancear. —*v.i.* (bot.) **brotar.**

spearfish ['spɪrˌfɪʃ, B 'spɪəˌ-] *s.* (ict.) (especie de) pez vela o pez aguja. —*v.t.* pescar con arpón.

spear grass, (bot.) espiguilla, hierba de punta, hierba de los prados.

spearhead [-ˌhɛd] *s.* 1. punta de lanza. 2. (fig.) punta de lanza, cabeza de ataque, fuerzas avanzadas de choque, tropa de asalto. —*v.t.* encabezar (ataque, campaña, etc.), iniciar un ataque.

spearman [-mən] *s.* lancero.

spearmint [-ˌmɪnt] *s.* (bot.) menta verde.

spear side, lado paterno, línea paterna, lado masculino.

spearwort [-ˌwɜrt, B -wɜt] *s.* (bot.) (variedad de) ranúnculo.

spec. *abrev. de* 1. **special,** especial. 2. **specially,** especialmente.

special ['spɛʃəl] *a.* 1. especial. 2. específico, detallado. 3. caro, íntimo (amigo, etc.). —*s.* 1. cosa o persona especial. 2. edición especial (de diario). 3. tren especial. 4. carta de entrega inmediata.

special act, ley o resolución legislativa especial.

special assessment, (com.) tasación para mejoras.

special delivery, entrega inmediata; correspondencia urgente, correo urgente.

special-delivery letter, carta urgente.

special education, educación especial.

special interests, intereses particulares.

specialism ['spɛʃəˌlɪzəm] *s.* especialización.

specialist [-ləst] *a., s.* especialista.

speciality [ˌspɛʃɪ'ælətɪ] *s.* (*pl.* SPECIALITIES) especialidad.

specialization [-ələ'zeɪʃən, B -laɪ-] *s.* especialización.

specialize ['spɛʃəˌlaɪz] *v.t.* 1. especializar, particularizar, diferenciar, individualizar. 2. canalizar, encauzar, encaminar (esfuerzo, talento, etc.). 3. (biol.) especializar, adaptar. —*v.i.* especializarse.

special jury, (der.) jurado especial.

specially [-lɪ] *adv.* especialmente.

special pleading, 1. (der.) nuevo alegato en réplica. 2. (fam.) argumento tendencioso y parcial.

specialty ['spɛʃəltɪ] *s.* (*pl.* SPECIALTIES) 1. especialidad. 2. (der.) contrato bajo sello, instrumento sellado, obligación firmada formalmente.

speciation [ˌspiʃɪ'eɪʃən, B -sɪ-] *s.* (biol.) (proceso de) evolución de las especies.

specie ['spiʃɪ] *s.* metálico, numerario; **in s.,** en numerario; (fig.) en la misma moneda.

species ['spiʃiz] *s.* (*pl.* SPECIES) 1. especie, clase, variedad, género. 2. (lóg.) especie, imagen mental. 3. (relig.) especies sacramentales. 4. (biol., lóg.) especie, clase. 5. (ant.) metálico.

specifiable ['spɛsəˌfaɪəbəl] *a.* especificable.

specific [spɪ'sɪfɪk] *a.* 1. específico, determinado. 2. específico, preciso, explícito. 3. (med., fís.) específico. —*s.* 1. cosa específica. 2. (*pl.*) datos específicos, detalles. 3. (med.) específico.

specific absorptive index, absorbencia específica.

specifically [-ɪkəlɪ] *adv.* especificadamente, específicamente.

specification [ˌspɛsəfə'keɪʃən] *s.* 1. especificación. 2. (*pl.*) datos específicos, descripción detallada (de un plan, invento, etc.); presupuesto detallado; especificaciones, normas.

specific capacity, (ing.) capacidad específica; rendimiento específico.

specific character, (biol.) carácter específico.

specific energy, (ing.) energía específica.

specific gravity, (fís.) gravedad específica, peso específico.

specific heat, (fís.) calor específico.

specific humidity, (meteor.) relación de humedad específica.

specificity [ˌspɛsə'fɪsətɪ] *s.* especificidad, carácter específico.

specific performance, (der.) 1. cumplimiento específico (por sentencia). 2. recurso de equidad (que acarrea un cumplimiento específico).

specific resistance, (elec.) resistividad, resistencia específica.

specific weight, (fís.) peso específico.

specify ['spɛsəˌfaɪ] *v.t.* (*pret., p.p.* SPECIFIED; *p.pr.* SPECIFYING) 1. especificar, detallar, precisar. 2. estipular, indicar, prescribir.

specimen ['spɛsəmən] *s.* 1. espécimen, muestra, modelo. 2. (fam.) individuo, tipo, ejemplar.

speciosity [ˌspiʃɪ'ɑsətɪ, B -'ɔs-] *s.* especiosidad, perfección aparente.

specious ['spiʃəs] *a.* 1. especioso, aparente, engañoso. 2. (ant.) ostentoso, vistoso.

speciously [-lɪ] *adv.* especiosamente.

speciousness [-nəs] *s.* especiosidad, apariencia engañosa, carácter especioso.

speck [spɛk] *s.* 1. manchita, mácula, motita. 2. pizca, partícula. —*v.t.* manchar, motear, jaspear.

speckle ['spɛkəl] *s.* manchita, puntito. —*v.t.* manchar, motear, salpicar.

specs [spɛks] 1. (fam.) anteojos, gafas. 2. (fam.) especificaciones.

spectacle ['spɛktɪkəl] *s.* 1. espectáculo, vista. 2. espectáculo, exposición, exhibición. 3. (*pl.*) anteojos, espejuelos, lentes, gafas. 4. **to see life through rose-colored spectacles,** ver la vida color de rosa.

spectacled [-kəld] *a.* que lleva anteojos; con anteojos, con gafas.

spectacular [spɛk'tækjələr, B -lə] *a.* espectacular, grandioso, admirable. —*s.* vista espectacular, función o exhibición grandiosa.

spectacularly [-lɪ] *adv.* espectacularmente, grandiosamente, admirablemente.

spectator ['spɛkˌteɪtər, B spɛk'teɪtə] *s.* espectador.

specter, spectre ['spɛktər, B -tə] *s.* 1. espectro, aparición, fantasma. 2. (meteor.) espectro.

spectra, *pl. de* **spectrum.**

spectral [-trəl] *a.* 1. fantasmal, espectral, de aparecidos. 2. (fís.) espectral.

spectrality [spɛk'trælətɪ] *s.* carácter fantasmal.

spectral line, (fís.) raya del espectro.

spectrally ['spɛktrəlɪ] *adv.* 1. de modo fantasmal. 2. (fís.) de modo espectral.

spectrogram [-ˌgræm] *s.* (fís.) espectrograma.

spectrograph [-ˌgræf, B -grɑf] *s.* (fís.) espectrógrafo.

spectroheliogram [ˌspɛktroʊ'hilɪəˌgræm] *s.* (astr.) espectroheliograma.

spectroheliograph [-ˌgræf, B -ˌgrɑf] *s.* (astr.) espectroheliógrafo.

spectrohelioscope [-ˌskoʊp] *s.* (astr.) espectrohelioscopio.

spectrometer [spɛk'trɑmətər, B -'trɔmɪtə] *s.* (fís.) espectrómetro.

spectrometry [-trɪ] *s.* espectrometría.

spectrophotometer [ˌspɛktroʊfə'tɑmətər, B -'tɔmɪtə] *s.* (ópt.) espectrofotómetro.

spectrophotometry [-trɪ] *s.* (ópt.) espectrofotometría.

spectroscope ['spɛktrəˌskoʊp] *s.* (fís.) espectroscopio.

spectroscopic [ˌspɛktrə'skɑpɪk, B -'skɔp-] *a.* (fís.) espectroscópico.

spectroscopy [spɛk'trɑskəpɪ, B -'trɔs-] *s.* (fís.) espectroscopia.

spectrum ['spɛktrəm] *s.* (*pl.* SPECTRA [-trə] o SPECTRUMS) (fís., elec.) espectro.

spectrum analysis, (fís.) análisis espectroscópico.

specula, *pl. de* **speculum.**

specular ['spɛkjələr, B -lə] *a.* 1. especular. 2. (med.) (que se efectúa) con espéculo.

speculate ['spɛkjəˌleɪt] *v.i.* 1. especular, meditar, reflexionar. 2. (com.) especular.

speculation [ˌspɛkjə'leɪʃən] *s.* 1. especulación, meditación. 2. (com.) especulación.

speculative ['spɛkjəˌleɪtɪv, B -lətɪv] *a.* especulativo, contemplativo; teórico; (com.) especulativo, arriesgado, aventurado.

speculatively [-lɪ] *adv.* teóricamente; (com.) especulativamente, arriesgadamente.

speculator ['spɛkjəˌleɪtər, B -ə] *s.* especulador (esp. en la bolsa).

speculatory [-lə,tɔrɪ, B -lətərɪ] *a.* especulador, especulativo.
speculum ['spɛkjələm] *s.* (*pl.* SPECULA [-lə] o SPECULUMS) 1. (med.) espéculo. 2. (orn.) espéculo, espejo. 3. (hist.) espejo de bronce o plata.
sped, *pret., p.p. de* **speed.**
speech [spitʃ] *s.* 1. habla, palabra; conversación. 2. habla, discurso, alocución, oración, conferencia. 3. habla, idioma, lenguaje, lengua, dialecto. 4. (ant.) rumor; informe. 5. **a set s.,** un discurso preparado; **to make a s.,** pronunciar un discurso.
speech area, área lingüística.
speech clinic, centro de foniatría.
speech correction, foniatría, logopedía.
speech form, forma lingüística.
speechify ['spitʃə,faɪ] *v.i.* (*pret., p.p.* SPEECHIFIED; *p.pr.* SPEECHIFYING) pronunciar un discurso; arengar, perorar.
speechless [-ləs] *a.* sin habla, mudo, callado; estupefacto; **to be left s.,** quedarse sin habla, quedarse mudo.
speechlessly [-lɪ] *adv.* sin habla, mudamente, calladamente.
speechlessness [-nəs] *s.* mudez, silencio; estupefacción.
speech writer, escritor de discursos.
speed [spid] *s.* 1. velocidad, rapidez, ligereza, prontitud, presteza, celeridad, prisa. 2. (foto.) rapidez, sensibilidad (de la placa, etc.); luminosidad (del objetivo); tiempo de exposición, velocidad de obturación. 3. (ant.) progreso, éxito, prosperidad. 4. (jer., E.U.) drogas estimulantes. 5. **at full s.,** a toda velocidad; **to make s.,** ir velozmente; **to put on s.,** acelerar. —*v.i.* (*pret., p.p.* SPED [spɛd] O SPEEDED; *p.pr.* SPEEDING) 1. apresurarse, apurarse (Am.); ir o correr rápido. 2. (ant.) progresar, prosperar. 3. **s. up,** acelerarse; ir más rápido; trabajar más rápido; **to be speeding,** (aut.) correr mucho, correr con exceso de velocidad. —*v.t.* 1. despedir, despachar, expedir. 2. adelantar. 3. (gen. con *up*) hacer acelerar o apresurar. 4. (ant.) promover, ayudar.
speedboat ['spid,bout] *s.* lancha automóvil veloz, lancha de carreras.
speeder ['spidər, B -ə] *s.* 1. regulador de velocidad. 2. automovilista que corre a gran velocidad.
speedily [-əlɪ] *adv.* velozmente.
speed indicator, indicador de velocidad; contador de vueltas, tacómetro.
speediness [-ɪnəs] *s.* velocidad, rapidez, celeridad, prisa, prontitud.
speeding [-ɪŋ] *s.* (aut.) exceso de velocidad.
speedlight [-,laɪt] *s.* (rad.) estrobotrón.
speed limit, velocidad máxima permitida, límite de velocidad.
speed merchant, (jer., G.B.) automovilista que corre a velocidad excesiva.
speedometer [spɪ'dɑmətər, B -'dɔmɪtə] *s.* velocímetro, indicador de velocidad; contador kilométrico, cuentamillas, cuentakilómetros, espidómetro.
speed reading, lectura rápida, lectura veloz.
speed skating, patinaje de velocidad.
speedster ['spidstər, B -stə] *s.* automovilista que corre a gran velocidad.
speed trap, (aut.) trecho de carretera en el que la policía de tráfico atrapa a los automovilistas que llevan exceso de velocidad.
speedup [-,ʌp] *s.* (com.) aumento de producción (sin aumento de salarios).
speedway [-,weɪ] *s.* 1. vía de tráfico rápido. 2. pista de carreras, autopista de carreras.
speedwell [-,wɛl] *s.* (bot.) verónica, becabunga.
speedy [-ɪ] *a.* (SPEEDIER; SPEEDIEST) veloz, rápido; pronto, presto.
speer, speir [spɪr, B spɪə] (esco.) *v.i.* hacer indagaciones o preguntas. —*v.t.* preguntar, indagar, inquirir por.
speleologist [,spilɪ'ɑlədʒəst, B -'ɔl-] *s.* espeleólogo.
speleology [-dʒɪ] *s.* espeleología, estudio y exploración de cavernas.
spell [spɛl] *v.t.* (*pret., p.p.* SPELLED O SPELT [spɛlt]; *p.pr.* SPELLING) 1. deletrear (una palabra). 2. escribir (correcta o incorrectamente). 3. formar, componer (letras una palabra). 4. significar. 5. **s. backward,** escribir o decir (letras de una palabra) al revés; **s. (someone) down,** derrotar (a alguien) en un concurso de ortografía; **s. it out to (someone),** (fam.) explicar detalladamente (a alguien); **s. out,** leer con dificultad, leer deletreando, leer letra por letra; explicar en forma clara; comprender, captar (sentido, etc.); entrever, divisar, descubrir. —*v.i.* 1. deletrear. 2. tener (buena o mala) ortografía, ej., *she can't s.,* tiene mala ortografía.
spell, *v.t.* (*pret., p.p.* SPELLED; *p.pr.* SPELLING) relevar, reemplazar; hacer descansar. —*v.i.* 1. tomar su turno, trabajar en turnos. 2. descansar un rato. —*s.* 1. relevo, revezo. 2. turno, tanda. 3. (pr. Aust.) descanso corto, intervalo, receso (Am.). 4. rato. 5. temporada (de mal tiempo, etc.). 6. ataque, acceso (de enfermedad, mal humor, etc.).
spell, *s.* conjuro, hechizo, encanto, encantamiento, fascinación; **to cast a s. on,** encantar, hechizar; **under a s.,** hechizado, fascinado. —*v.t.* hechizar, encantar, fascinar.
spellbind ['spɛl,baɪnd] *v.t.* hechizar, encantar, fascinar, embelesar, cautivar por hechizo o encanto.
spellbinder [-'baɪndər, B -də] *s.* 1. orador arrebatador, orador persuasivo. 2. algo que encanta y fascina.
spellbound [-,baund] *a.* encantado, hechizado, fascinado, embelesado, arrebatado.
speller [-ər, B -ə] *s.* 1. deletreador (persona). 2. (E.U.) silabario, abecedario. 3. **to be a good (poor) s.,** tener buena (mala) ortografía.
spelling [-ɪŋ] *s.* deletreo; ortografía.
spelling bee, concurso de deletreo, concurso de ortografía.
spelling book, silabario, abecedario.
spelt [spɛlt] (pr. G.B.) *pret., p.p. de* **spell.** —*s.* (bot.) espelta, escanda.
spelter ['spɛltər, B -tə] *s.* peltre, zinc.
spelt wheat, (bot.) escanda, escandia.
spelunker [spɪ'lʌŋkər, B -kə] *s.* espeleólogo aficionado.
spelunking [-kɪŋ] *s.* exploración de cuevas (como deporte).
spence [spɛns] *s.* (dial. G.B.) despensa, repostería.
spencer ['spɛnsər, B -sə] *s.* (mar.) vela cangreja.
spencer, *s.* chaqueta corta.
Spencerian [spɛn'sɪrɪən, B -'sɪər-] *a.* (filos.) de (Herbert) Spencer, spenceriano.
Spencerianism [-ə,nɪzəm] *s.* filosofía de (Herbert) Spencer.
spend [spɛnd] *v.t.* (*pret., p.p.* SPENT [spɛnt]; *p.pr.* SPENDING) 1. gastar, expender (dinero, etc.). 2. gastar, consumir; extinguir. 3. pasar (tiempo), emplear, usar (conocimientos, etc.). 4. (mar.) perder (el mástil, un palo). 5. **s. itself,** perder fuerza. —*v.i.* 1. gastar el dinero, ser gastador. 2. gastarse.
spendable ['spɛndəbəl] *a.* gastable, agotable.
spender [-ər, B -ə] *s.* gastador, derrochador, pródigo.
spending [-ɪŋ] *s.* gasto, desembolso; dispendio, derroche.
spending money, dinero para gastos personales.
spendthrift [-,θrɪft] *s., a.* pródigo, gastador, disipador, manirroto, derrochador, despilfarrador.
spent [spɛnt] *a.* exhausto, agotado, rendido, consumido; viciado (aire).
spent bullet, bala fría, bala muerta.
spent herring, arenque desovado.
sperm [spɜrm, B spɜm] *s.* (*pl.* SPERM O SPERMS) 1. (biol.) esperma, semen. 2. espermaceti, esperma de ballena.
spermaceti [,spɜrmə'sitɪ, -'sɛtɪ, B ,spɜmə-] *s.* espermaceti, cetina, esperma o blanco de ballena.
spermagonium [-'gounɪəm] *s.* (*pl.* SPERMAGONIA) (bot.) espermagonio, espermatogonio.
spermary ['spɜrmərɪ, B 'spɜmə-] *s.* (*pl.* SPERMARIES) (zool., anat.) glándula espermática.
spermatic [spɜr'mætɪk, B spɜ'-] *a.* espermático, seminal.
spermatic cord, (anat.) cordón espermático.
spermatid ['spɜrmətɪd, B 'spɜmə-] *s.* (biol.) espermátide.
spermatium [spɜr'meɪʃɪəm, B spɜ'-] *s.* (*pl.* SPERMATIA [-ə]) (bot.) espermacio.
spermatocidal [-,mætə'saɪdəl, B -mətə-] *a.* espermatocida.
spermatocyte [-'mætə,saɪt, B 'spɜmətə-] *s.* (biol.) espermatocito.
spermatogenesis [,spɜrmətə'dʒɛnəsəs, B ,spɜmə-] *s.* (biol.) espermatogénesis.
spermatogonium [-'gounɪəm] *s.* (*pl.* SPERMATOGONIA) 1. (zool.) espermatogonio. 2. (bot.) espermogonia.
spermatophore [spɜr'mætə,fɔr, 'spɜrmət-, B 'spɜmətə,fɔ] *s.* (zool.) espermatóforo.
spermatophyte [-,faɪt] *s.* (bot.) espermatófita.
spermatorrhea [spɜr,mætə'rɪə, B spɜmət-] *s.* (med.) espermatorrea.
spermatozoid [-'zouəd] *s.* (bot.) espermatozoide.
spermicidal [,spɜrmə'saɪdəl, B 'spɜmɪ,saɪ-] *a.* espermaticida.
spermine ['spɜr,min, B 'spɜmɪn] *s.* (bioquím.) espermina.
spermiogenesis [,spɜrmɪou'dʒɛnəsəs, B ,spɜmɪ-] *s.* (med.) espermiogénesis.
spermogonium [-mə'gounɪəm] *s.* (*pl.* SPERMOGONIA [-ə]) (bot.) espermogonia.
sperm oil, aceite de esperma, cetina, aceite de ballena.
spermophile ['spɜrmə,faɪl, B 'spɜmə-] *s.* (zool.) espermófilo.
sperm sac, (anat.) vesícula seminal.
sperm whale, (zool.) cachalote, catodonte.
sperrylite ['spɛrɪ,laɪt] *s.* (min.) esperrilita.
spessartite ['spɛsər,taɪt, B -ə,-] *s.* (min.) espesartina.
spew [spju] *v.t., v.i.* vomitar, arrojar. —*s.* vómito.
spewer ['spjuər, B -ə] *s.* el que vomita.
sphacelate ['sfæsə,leɪt] *v.i.* (med.) esfacelarse, gangrenarse.
sphacelation [,sfæsə'leɪʃən] *s.* (med.) esfacelación, mortificación, gangrena húmeda.
sphacelus ['sfæsələs] *s.* (med.) esfacelo.
sphagnous ['sfægnəs] *a.* (bot.) esfagnáceo, esfagnal.
sphagnum [-nəm] *s.* (bot.) musgo esfagnáceo o esfagnal.
sphalerite ['sfælə,raɪt] *s.* (min.) esfalerita.
sphene [sfin] *s.* (min.) esfena, esfeno.
sphenoid ['sfi,nɔɪd] *s.* (anat.) esfenoides.
sphenoidal [sfɪ'nɔɪdəl] *a.* (anat.) esfenoidal.
spheral ['sfɪrəl, B 'sfɪər-] *a.* esferal, esférico.
sphere [sfɪr, B sfɪə] *s.* 1. (geom.) esfera. 2. (astr.) globo, orbe. 3. esfera celeste, esfera ideal. 4. esfera, ambiente; círculo de acción; esfera de

influencia. 5. esfera, clase, posición (social). 6. (poét.) esfera, los cielos. 7. (ant.) órbita. —*v.t.* 1. colocar en una esfera. 2. redondear. 3. rodear, abarcar.
sphere of influence, (pol.) esfera de influencia.
spheric ['sfɪrɪk, B 'sfɛr-] *a.* esférico.
spherical [-ɪkəl] *a.* esférico.
spherical aberration, (fís.) aberración esférica, aberración de esfericidad.
spherical angle, (mat.) ángulo esférico.
spherical coordinate, (geom.) coordenada esférica.
spherical excess, (mat.) exceso esférico.
spherical geometry, geometría esférica.
spherical polygon, (geom.) polígono esférico.
spherical sailing, (mar.) navegación esférica (que toma en cuenta la curvatura esférica).
spherical segment, (geom.) zona esférica.
spherical surface, (geom.) superficie esférica.
spherical triangle, (mat.) triángulo esférico.
spherical trigonometry, trigonometría esférica.
spherical zone, (geom.) zona esférica.
sphericity [sfɪr'ɪsətɪ, B sfɛr-] *s.* esfericidad, redondez.
spherics ['sfɪrɪks, B 'sfɛr-] *s. pl.* (*sing. en const.*) trigonometría esférica; geometría esférica.
spheroid ['sfɪrˌɔɪd, B 'sfɪər-] *s.* esferoide. —*a.* esferoidal.
spheroidal [ˌsfɪr'ɔɪdəl, B ˌsfɪər-] *a.* esferoidal.
spherometer [-'ɑmətər, B -'ɔmɪtə] *s.* esferómetro.
spherule ['sfɪrˌul, B 'sfɛrjul] *s.* esférula, esfera pequeña.
sphery ['sfɪrɪ, B 'sfɪərɪ] *a.* esférico, orbicular, como una esfera.
sphincter ['sfɪŋktər, B -tə] *s.* (anat., zool.) esfínter.
sphingid ['sfɪndʒəd] *s.* (ento.) esfíngido.
Sphingidae ['sfɪndʒədi] *s. pl.* (ento.) esfíngidos.
sphinx [sfɪŋks] *s.* (*pl.* SPHINXES o SPHINGES ['sfɪndʒiz]) 1. (mitol.) esfinge. 2. (ento.) esfinge, calavera. 3. (fig.) esfinge, persona inescrutable.
sphragistics [sfrə'dʒɪstɪks] *s. pl.* (*sing.* o *pl. en const.*) estudio de los sellos con que se estampan documentos.
sphygmic ['sfɪgmɪk] *a.* (fisiol.) esfígmico; pulsátil.
sphygmograph [-məˌgræf, B -ˌgrɑf] *s.* (fisiol.) esfigmógrafo.
sphygmographic [ˌsfɪgmə'græfɪk] *a.* (fisiol.) esfigmográfico.
sphygmoid ['sfɪgmɔɪd] *a.* (fisiol., med.) esfigmoideo, parecido al pulso.
sphygmomanometer [ˌsfɪgmoʊmə'nɑmətər, B -'nɔmɪtə] *s.* (fisiol.) esfigmomanómetro.
sphygmometer [sfɪg'mɑmətər, B -'mɔmɪtə] *s.* (fisiol.) esfigmómetro.
sphygmus ['sfɪgməs] *s.* (fisiol.) pulso.
spic [spɪk] *s.* (jer., despec., E.U.) persona de habla española, o de origen hispano.
spica ['spaɪkə] *s.* (*pl.* SPICAE [-si]) 1. (bot.) espiga, espiga de trigo. 2. **S.,** (astr.) Espiga, Espiga de la Virgen. 3. (med.) espica, espiga, vendaje en espica.
spic-and-span, *var. de* **spick-and-span.**
spicate ['spaɪˌkeɪt, B -kət] *a.* (bot., zool.) espigado.
spice [spaɪs] *s.* 1. especia. 2. aroma, fragancia. 3. (fig.) sazón, sabor, sainete, sabor picante, interés. 4. (ant.) espécimen, cantidad módica, pequeña porción. —*v.t.* sazonar (con especias).
spiceberry ['spaɪsˌbɛrɪ] *s.* (bot.) gaulteria.
spice box, especiero, caja para especias.
spicebush [-ˌbʊʃ] *s.* (bot.) calicanto.
spice of life, (fig.) lo bueno o sabroso de la vida; la sal de la vida.
spicery [-ərɪ] *s.* (*pl.* SPICERIES) 1. especiería, especería. 2. especias, conjunto de especias. 3. sabor picante o aromático.
spiciform ['spaɪkəˌfɔrm, B 'spaɪsɪˌfɔm] *a.* espiciforme.
spicily ['spaɪsəlɪ] *adv.* de modo picante, sabrosamente.
spiciness [-ɪnəs] *s.* sabor picante o aromático.
spick-and-span [ˌspɪkən'spæn] *a.* 1. flamante, novísimo. 2. inmaculado, reluciente, limpísimo.
spicula ['spɪkjələ] *s.* (*pl.* SPICULAE [-ˌli]) (zool.) espícula.
spiculate ['spɪkjələt, -ˌleɪt, B -lət] *a.* 1. (zool.) cubierto de espículas. 2. (bot.) espicúleo, compuesto de espiguillas.
spicule ['spɪkjul, B 'spaɪk-] *s.* (zool.) espícula.
spiculum ['spɪkjələm] *s.* (*pl.* SPICULA [-lə]) (zool.) espícula.
spicy ['spaɪsɪ] *a.* (SPICIER; SPICIEST) 1. aromático, picante, que sabe a especias. 2. (fig.) picante, salado, atrevido, ej., *s. story,* cuento colorado, chiste picante.
spider ['spaɪdər, B -ə] *s.* 1. (zool.) araña. 2. trébodes. 3. (mec.) araña, estrella.
spider crab, (zool.) centolla, araña de mar.
spider line, hilo de tela de araña (en el retículo de un instrumento).
spider mite, (zool.) ácaro rojo, cresa roja.
spider monkey, (zool.) mono araña, ateles.
spider web, spider's web, tela de araña, telaraña.
spidery [-ərɪ] *a.* 1. semejante a una araña. 2. largo y delgado (pierna, rayo de rueda, etc.); muy fina (línea, letra, etc.).
spiegeleisen ['spigəlˌaɪzən] *s.* (metal.) hierro especular, fundición especular.
spiegel iron, (metal.) hierro especular, fundición especular.
spiel [spil] (jer., E.U.) *s.* habla, palabrería, perorata, charla típica (de un vendedor, político, etc.). —*v.i.* perorar, discursear (de un modo verboso o extravagante). —*v.t.* expresar.
spieler ['spilər, B -ə] *s.* 1. (fam., pr. Aust.) fullero, tahúr. 2. voceador; pregonero (de circo, exhibición, etc.). 3. (jer., E.U.) anunciador de la radio o televisión.
spiffing ['spɪfɪŋ] (jer.) *var. de* **spiffy.**
spiffy [-ɪ] *a.* (SPIFFIER; SPIFFIEST) (jer.) 1. elegante, a la moda. 2. excelente, espléndido.
spigot ['spɪgət] *s.* 1. espiche (para tapar un agujero). 2. espita, canilla, tapón de llave, grifo.
spike [spaɪk] *s.* (bot.) espiga.
spike, *s.* 1. púa. 2. clavo largo, escarpia, alcayata, chillón real. 3. asta (no ramificada de un ciervo joven). 4. (*pl.*) zapatillas con clavos o refuerzos metálicos (de corredor, etc.). 5. (ict.) caballa joven. —*v.t.* 1. clavar, empernar, escarpiar. 2. perforar; espetar, empalar. 3. clavar (un cañón). 4. (fig.) impedir, frustrar, inutilizar. 5. **s. the guns (of),** clavar la artillería; (fig.) frustrar los designios (de alguien), poner fuera de acción (a alguien), anular.
spiked [spaɪkt] *a.* 1. (bot.) con inflorescencia de espigas. 2. con púas.
spike heel, tacón de aguja, taco de aguja (Am.).
spike lavender, (bot.) espliego, alhucema.
spikelet ['spaɪklət] *s.* (bot.) espiguita, espiguilla.
spikelike [-ˌlaɪk] *a.* espigado, semejante a una espiga.
spikenard ['spaɪkˌnɑrd, B -nɑd] *s.* (bot.) nardo, espicanardo, espicanardi, nardo índico, azúmbar; (variedad de) aralia.
spiky ['spaɪkɪ] *a.* espigado; puntiagudo, erizado.
spile [spaɪl] *s.* 1. tarugo, clavija, espiche, cuña. 2. pilote de madera. 3. gotera de sangría (de árboles). 4. estaca de avance (túneles). —*v.t.* 1. tapar con espiche, poner espiche a, cerrar con tarugo. 2. afirmar con pilote(s). 3. sangrar (árbol) mediante gotera.
spiling ['spaɪlɪŋ] *s.* (estructura de) pilotes.
spilite ['spaɪlaɪt] *s.* (min.) espilita.
spill [spɪl] *s.* 1. astilla, esquirla. 2. espiche, clavija, tarugo. 3. varilla, alfiler metálico.
spill, *v.t.* (*pret., p.p.* SPILLED o SPILT [spɪlt] *p.pr.* SPILLING) 1. derramar, verter, desparramar. 2. revelar, divulgar. 3. volcar, tumbar; arrojar, hacer caer (caballo al jinete). 4. (mar.) quitar el viento a (la vela). 5. **no use crying over spilt milk,** a mal que no tiene remedio ponerle buena cara; **s. the beans,** (jer.) revelar el secreto, cometer una indiscreción; **s. the blood of,** derramar la sangre (de), matar. —*v.i.* 1. derramarse, verterse. 2. tumbar, caer. —*s.* 1. derramamiento. 2. derrame (porción derramada). 3. vertedero, derramadero. 4. vuelco, caída, tumbo (de un caballo, vehículo, etc.). 5. (fam.) chaparrón, aguacero. 6. **to take a s.,** dar un tumbo.
spillage ['spɪlɪdʒ] *s.* 1. derramamiento, derramadura. 2. derrame (porción derramada).
spillikin ['spɪlɪkən] *s.* 1. pajita, astilla, palito (que se usan en ciertos juegos). 2. (*pl.*) juego de la pajita; palitos chinos, palito chino.
spilling line, (mar.) trapa.
spillway ['spɪlˌweɪ] *s.* vertedero, (canal) aliviadero, derramadero.
spilth [spɪlθ] *s.* 1. derramamiento, derramadura. 2. derrame (porción derramada). 3. basura, desecho.
spin [spɪn] *v.t.* (*pret.* SPUN [spʌn]; ant. SPAN [spæn]; *p.p.* SPUN; *p.pr.* SPINNING) 1. hilar. 2. retorcer, revolver, hacer girar, hacer dar vueltas. 3. hacer bailar (trompo, peón). 4. (gen. con *out*) prolongar, alargar, redactar extensamente (relato, narración). 5. dar efecto a (una bola, pelota). 6. **s. a yarn,** narrar una aventura, contar un cuento increíble. —*v.i.* 1. girar, revolver(se); dar vueltas, rodar, ej., *the blow sent him spinning,* el golpe lo hizo rodar. 2. formar un tejido, hilar una tela. 3. bailar (trompo, etc.). 4. rodar velozmente (un vehículo). 5. pescar con anzuelo de cuchara. 6. (aer.) descender en barrena. —*s.* 1. vuelta, giro muy rápido, rotación. 2. paseo corto (en vehículo), paseíto, vueltecita. 3. (aer.) barrena. 4. rotación lateral, efecto (de bola de tenis, billar, etc.). 5. **to be in a s.,** estar aturdido; **to give (something) a s.,** revolver, hacer girar (algo); **to go for a s.,** dar un paseíto, dar una vueltecita (en vehículo de ruedas); **to go into a s.,** (aer.) entrar en barrena.
spinach ['spɪnɪʃ, B -ɪdʒ] *s.* (bot.) espinaca.
spinach dock, (bot.) hierba de la paciencia.
spinal ['spaɪnəl] (anat.) *a.* espinal.
spinal canal, (anat.) conducto vertebral.
spinal column, (anat.) espina dorsal, columna vertebral.
spinal cord, (anat.) médula espinal.
spindle ['spɪndəl] *s.* 1. huso, broca. 2. perno; aguja. 3. (mec.) husillo, árbol, mandril, eje. —*v.i.* 1. espigarse, crecer en espiga. 2. crecer muy alto y delgado.
spindle-legged [-ˌlɛgd, -ˌlɛgəd] **splindle-shanked** [-ˌʃæŋkt] *a.* zanquivano, zanquilargo.
spindlelegs [-ˌlɛgz] **spindleshanks** [-ˌʃæŋks] *s. pl.* (*sing. en const.*) (fam.) zanquivano, zanquilargo, zancudo.
spindle tree, (bot.) bonetero, evónimo, husera.

spindling [ˈspɪndlɪŋ] *var. de* **spindly.**
spindly [-dlɪ] *a.* larguirucho, cenceño.
spindrift [ˈspɪnˌdrɪft] *s.* rociada (del mar).
spine [spaɪn] *s.* 1. (anat.) espinazo, espina dorsal; raquis. 2. (fig.) espíritu, temple. 3. (bot.) espina, púa. 4. (zool.) espina espícula, aguijón. 5. (enc.) lomo (de libros).
spinel, spinelle [spəˈnɛl] *s.* (min.) espinel, espinela.
spineless [ˈspaɪnləs] *a.* 1. sin espinazo; invertebrado. 2. (fig.) débil de carácter, sumiso; sin energía, sin nervio. 3. sin espinas.
spinelessly [-lɪ] *adv.* 1. de modo invertebrado. 2. (fig.) sumisamente, sin ánimo, sin decisión.
spinelessness [-nəs] *s.* (fig.) sumisión, debilidad de carácter.
spinel ruby, (min.) espinela-rubí (de un rojo claro).
spinescent [spaɪˈnɛsənt] *a.* (bot.) espinoso; puntiagudo.
spinet [ˈspɪnət, B spɪˈnɛt] *s.* (mús.) espineta.
spinnaker [ˈspɪnəkər, B -kə] *s.* (mar.) balón, spinnaker.
spinner [ˈspɪnər, B -ə] *s.* 1. hilador, hilandero. 2. cebo artificial giratorio (de pesca). 3. aguja giratoria (en juegos de suerte). 4. (aer.) ojiva, cono de la hélice; carenado del cubo de la hélice. 5. (criquet) bola con efecto.
spinneret [ˌspɪnəˈrɛt, B ˈspɪnərɛt] *s.* 1. (zool.) hilera (órgano hilandero de arañas y gusanos de seda). 2. hilera (usada en la fabricación de rayón).
spinney [ˈspɪnɪ] *s.* (G.B.) soto, matorral, maleza, maraña.
spinning [ˈspɪnɪŋ] *s.* 1. hila, hilado, hilanza. 2. hilandería (arte de hilar). —*a.* de hilar, de hilandería.
spinning frame, máquina de hilar, hiladora continua de anillos.
spinning jenny, (mec.) hiladora con varios husos.
spinning lathe, torno de chapista, torno de conformar.
spinning machine, máquina de hilar.
spinning wheel, torno de hilar a mano.
spinny, *s.* (*pl.* SPINNIES) *var. de* **spinney.**
spinose [ˈspaɪˌnoʊs] *a.* espinoso.
spinosely [-lɪ] *adv.* con espinas.
spinosity [spaɪˈnɑsətɪ, B -ˈnɔs-] *s.* 1. calidad de espinoso. 2. (fig.) problema difícil, asunto irritante.
spinous [ˈspaɪnəs] *a.* espinoso; puntiagudo.
spinous process, (anat.) apófisis espinosa.
Spinozism [spɪˈnoʊˌzɪzəm] *s.* (filos.) espinosismo, doctrina del filósofo holandés Benito Espinosa.
Spinozist [-zəst] *s.* espinosista.
spinster [ˈspɪnstər, B -stə] *s.* 1. hilandera. 2. solterona.
spinsterhood [-ˌhʊd] *s.* soltería (de mujer).
spinsterish [ˈspɪnstərɪʃ] *a.* remilgado, característico de una solterona.
spinthariscope [spɪnˈθærəˌskoʊp] *s.* espintariscopio.
spinule [ˈspaɪnjul] *s.* espínula, espinilla.
spinulose [-njəˌloʊs] *a.* espinuloso.
spiny [-nɪ] *a.* (SPINIER; SPINIEST) 1. espinoso; puntiagudo. 2. (fig.) espinoso, arduo.
spiny anteater, (zool.) equidno, equidna.
spiny dogfish, (ict.) mielga, escualo.
spiny lobster, (zool.) langosta marina.
spiracle [ˈspaɪrɪkəl, B ˈspaɪər-] *s.* (zool.) espiráculo.
spiraea [spaɪˈriə] *s.* (bot.) espirea.
spiral [ˈspaɪrəl, B ˈspaɪə-] *a.* espiral, helicoidal; acaracolado. —*s.* 1. espiral. 2. (fútbol) patada o pase con efecto. 3. (aer.) vuelo en espiral. —*v.i.* (*pret., p.p.* SPIRALED O SPIRALLED; *p.pr.* SPIRALING O SPIRALLING) 1. seguir un curso espiral, moverse en espiral, dar vueltas; volar en espiral. —*v.t.* formar o torcer en espiral.
spiral column, (arq.) columna entorchada, columna salamónica.
spiral curve, (ing.) curva o espiral de transición.
spirally [-rəlɪ] *adv.* en espiral, espiralmente.
spiral nebula, (astr.) nebulosa espiral.
spiral spring, resorte o muelle en espiral, muelle helicoidal.
spiral staircase, escalera de caracol, escalera de husillo.
spirant [ˈspaɪrənt, B ˈspaɪə-] *s.* (fon.) consonante fricativa.
spire [spaɪr, B ˈspaɪə] *s.* 1. espiral, espira; vuelta, rosca. 2. cúspide, cima, ápice (de una concha en forma de espiral).
spire, *s.* 1. brizna (de hierba). 2. (arq.) aguja, chapitel; torrecilla. 3. cima, cúspide, ápice. 4. vuelta espiral. —*v.i.* 1. crecer en forma de espiral; rematar en punta. 2. (bot.) germinar.
spirea, *var. de* **spiraea.**
spired [spaɪrd, B ˈspaɪəd] *a.* 1. con chapitel. 2. que remata en un ápice. 3. espiral.
spireme [ˈspaɪrˌim, B ˈspaɪər-] *s.* (biol.) espirema.
spirillum [spaɪˈrɪləm] *s.* (*pl.* SPIRILLA [-ə]) (bact.) espirilo.
spirit [ˈspɪrət] *s.* 1. espíritu, alma. 2. espíritu, espectro, aparecido. 3. individuo, persona, ej., *a humble s.,* persona humilde. 4. (*pl.*) humor, temple. 5. espíritu, ánimo, valor, vivacidad, brío. 6. espíritu, principio, tendencia. 7. espíritu, intención, sentido, ej., *we must consider the s. of the law,* debemos considerar el espíritu de la ley. 8. (*pl.*) licor fuerte (aguardiente, ron, ginebra o whiski). 9. (farm.) alcohol; tintura alcohólica. 10. **high (o good) spirits,** (de) buen humor, animado; **in a friendly s.,** de (una) manera amistosa; **in s.,** en sus adentros; **poor (o low) spirits,** depresión, abatimiento; **the poor in s.,** los pobres de espíritu; **the S.,** el Espíritu Santo; **to be in good spirits,** estar de buen humor; **to break one's s.,** quebrar la voluntad o resistencia de uno; **to keep up one's s.,** no desalentarse, no perder ánimo. —*v.t.* 1. alentar, animar. 2. **s. away (u off),** llevarse en secreto. —*a.* 1. del espíritu. 2. de alcohol, ej., *s. lamp,* lámpara de alcohol, infernillo, infiernillo.
spirited [-əd] *a.* espiritoso, animoso, fogoso, vivo, brioso, ej., *a s. attack,* un ataque fogoso.
spiritedly [-lɪ] *adv.* espiritosamente, animosamente, briosamente.
spiritism [-ˌɪzəm] *s.* espiritismo.
spiritist [-əst] *s.* espiritista.
spiritistic [ˈspɪrəˈtɪstɪk] *a.* espiritista.
spiritless [ˈspɪrətləs] *a.* apocado, timorato; insípido.
spiritlessly [-lɪ] *adv.* sin vigor, sin espíritu.
spirit level, nivel de burbuja, nivel de aire.
spirit rapping, comunicación con los espíritus por medio de golpes sobre la mesa.
spirits of hartshorn, agua amoniacal.
spirits of wine, espíritu de vino.
spirits of turpentine, esencia o aceite de trementina.
spiritual [ˈspɪrɪtʃʊəl, B -tjʊəl] *a.* 1. espiritual, incorpóreo. 2. espiritual, intelectual; mental. 3. religioso, eclesiástico. 4. espiritual, místico, santo. —*s.* 1. (*pl.*) asuntos eclesiásticos. 2. espiritual (tonada religiosa de los negros de E.U.).
spiritual advisor, consejero espiritual, capellán.
spiritualism [-ˌɪzəm] *s.* 1. (filos.) espiritualismo. 2. espiritismo.
spiritualist [-əst] *s.* 1. (filos.) espiritualista. 2. espiritista.
spiritualistic [ˌspɪrɪtʃʊəˈlɪstɪk, B -tjʊə-] *a.* 1. (filos.) espiritualista. 2. espiritista.
spiritualist séance, sesión espiritista.
spirituality [-tʃʊˈælətɪ, B -tjʊ-] *s.* 1. espiritualidad. 2. clero, clerecía. 3. (relig.) pertenencias espirituales (de la iglesia).
spiritualization [-tʃʊələˈzeɪʃən, B -tjʊəlaɪ-] *s.* espiritualización, acto de espiritualizar.
spiritualize [ˈspɪrɪtʃʊəˌlaɪz, B -tjʊə-] *v.t.* 1. espiritualizar. 2. (fig.) purificar, refinar.
spiritually [-əlɪ] *adv.* espiritualmente.
spiritualness [-əlnəs] *s.* espiritualidad.
spiritualty [-əltɪ] *s.* 1. clero, clerecía. 2. (relig.) pertenencias espirituales (de la iglesia).
spirituel, spirituelle [ˌspɪrɪtʃʊˈɛl, B -tjʊ-] *a.* 1. ingenioso, agudo. 2. refinado, delicado, sutil.
spirituous [ˈspɪrɪtʃʊəs, B -tjʊəs] *a.* 1. espiritoso, espirituoso (licores). 2. destilado, fermentado, de contenido alcohólico.
spirochaete, spirochaetosis, *vars. de* **spirochete, spirochetosis.**
spirochetal [ˈspaɪrəˈkitəl, B ˈspaɪə-] *a.* (med.) causado por espiroquetas.
spirochete [ˈspaɪrəˌkit, B ˈspaɪə-] *s.* (bact.) espiroqueta, espiroqueto.
spirochetosis [ˌspaɪrəˌkitˈoʊsəs, B ˌspaɪə-] *s.* (med.) espiroquetosis.
spirograph [ˈspaɪrəˌgræf, B ˈspaɪərəˌgrɑf] *s.* espirógrafo, instrumento para medir el movimiento respiratorio.
spirogyra [ˌspaɪrəˈdʒaɪrə, B ˌspaɪə-ˈdʒaɪə-] *s.* (bot.) espirogira.
spiroid [ˈspaɪrɔid, B ˈspaɪə-] *a.* espiroidal.
spirometer [spaɪˈrɑmətər, B -ˈrɔmɪtə] *s.* espirómetro, instrumento para determinar la capacidad pulmonar.
spirt, *var. de* **spurt.**
spirula [ˈspɪrʊlə, B ˈspaɪərjʊlə] *s.* (zool.) espírula.
spiry [ˈspaɪrɪ, B ˈspaɪərɪ] *a.* 1. espiral, espiriforme. 2. acaracolado, enrollado, serpentino. 3. con muchos chapiteles; torreado. 4. piramidal, puntiagudo, terminado en punta.
spit [spɪt] *v.t.* (*pret., p.p.* SPAT [spæt] O SPIT; *p.pr.* SPITTING) 1. escupir; esputar, expectorar. 2. (fig.) escupir, despedir, arrojar, echar. 3. encender (una mecha, espoleta, etc.). 4. **s. it out,** (jer.) ¡dígalo! —*v.i.* 1. escupir, arrojar saliva. 2. caer blandamente y por ratos, rociar (la lluvia). 3. chisporrotear (huevo en la sartén, mecha de una mina, etc.). 4. **s. on (o upon o at),** (fig.) mostrar desprecio a. —*s.* 1. salivazo, escupitajo, esputo, saliva. 2. rocío (de lluvia). 3. (fig.) copia, imagen, ej., **he is the very s. and image of his father,** es la imagen viva de su padre.
spit, *s.* 1. espetón, asador. 2. (geog.) punta de tierra, lengua de tierra, banco de arena. —*v.t.* (*pret., p.p.* SPITTED; *p. pr.* SPITTING) espetar, atravesar, clavar, ensartar.
spital [ˈspɪtəl] *s.* (ant.) lazareto; hospital que trata especialmente las enfermedades contagiosas.
spit and polish, acicaladura, atavío, compostura.
spitball [-ˌbɔl] *s.* 1. pelotilla de papel mascado (que se usa como proyectil). 2. (béisbol) lanzamiento ilegal con pelota mojada (con saliva o sudor).
spitballer [-ər, B -ə] *s.* (béisbol) jugador que lanza pelotas mojadas (con saliva o sudor).
spitchcock [ˈspɪtʃˌkɑk, B -kɔk] *s.* anguila frita en tajadas. —*v.t.* preparar (anguila) para freír en tajadas.
spit curl, caracol buscanovio (rizo aplastado de cabello).
spite [spaɪt] *s.* 1. despecho, rencor, inquina, ojeriza, mala voluntad. 2. (raro) vejación, mortificación. 3. **in s. of,** a pesar de, no obstante;

out of s., por despecho; **to have a s. against (someone),** tener inquina a (alguien). *—v.t.* 1. despechar; molestar, fastidiar, dar pique, mostrar resentimiento, ej., *he does it to s. me,* lo hace para fastidiarme. 2. **to cut off one's nose to s. one's face,** (fig.) vengarse uno con perjuicio de sí mismo, vengarse a su propia costa.

spiteful ['spaɪtfəl] *a.* resentido; rencoroso, malicioso, malévolo.

spitefully [-fəlɪ] *adv.* por despecho, con rencor, con tirria.

spitefulness [-fəlnəs] *s.* despecho, malevolencia, malicia, rencor.

spitfire ['spɪtˌfaɪr, B -ˌfaɪə] *s.* cascarrabias, generalmente en referencia a la mujer colérica.

spitter ['spɪtər, B -ə] *s.* 1. (zool.) ciervo joven (cuyas astas empiezan a despuntar). 2. el que espeta; escupidor.

spittle [-əl] *s.* 1. saliva; salivazo, esputo, escupida. 2. secreción de un insecto.

spittle, *var. de* **spital.**

spittoon [spɪ'tun] *s.* escupidera, escupidero.

spitz [spɪts] *s.* perro de Pomerania, perro lulú.

spiv [spɪv] *s.* (jer., G.B.) 1. traficante en el mercado negro. 2. gandul, haragán.

splanchnic ['splæŋknɪk] *a.* (anat.) esplácnico; visceral.

splanchnology [ˌsplæŋk'nɑlədʒɪ, B -'nɔl-] *s.* (anat.) esplacnología.

splash [splæʃ] *v.t.* 1. (con *with*) salpicar, mojar, manchar (algo o alguien con agua, lodo, etc.). 2. (con *about, on, over*) arrojar, esparcir, rociar (agua, lodo, etc. sobre algo o alguien). 3. (con *with*) (fig.) salpicar, motear (de), ej., *sky splashed with stars,* cielo salpicado de estrellas. 4. **s. one's way (across, along, through),** ir, moverse o abrirse paso chapoteando. 5. exhibir llamativamente (mercaderías); publicar con grandes titulares (noticias). *—v.i.* 1. chapotear, chapalear. 2. caer o moverse con chapoteo. 3. esparcirse. *—s.* 1. salpicadura, rociada. 2. manchón. 3. chapaleo, chapoteo. 4. exhibición llamativa (de mercaderías); grandes titulares (que recibe una noticia). 5. **to make a s.,** (fig.) hacer una fuerte impresión, causar sensación.

splashboard ['splæʃˌbɔrd, B -bɔd] *s.* 1. guardabarros, alero, guardafango (de carruajes). 2. alza (de una presa).

splash dam, dique de un río para contener el agua y empujar madera río abajo.

splashdown [-ˌdaʊn] *s.* (astronáut.) 1. descenso en el mar de una cápsula espacial. 2. lugar exacto donde ocurre el descenso. 3. hora del descenso.

splasher ['splæʃər, B -ə] *s.* 1. persona que salpica. 2. cobertura o protección contra salpicaduras.

splash erosion, erosión causada por la caída de la lluvia.

splash guard, (aut.) salpicadero, guardafango.

splashily [-əlɪ] *adv.* ostentosamente, llamativamente, vulgarmente.

splashing [-ɪŋ] *s.* salpicadura, mojadura.

splash lubrication, lubricación por barboteo o salpicadura, lubricación a salpique.

splashy [-ɪ] *a.* (SPLASHIER; SPLASHIEST) 1. ostentoso, llamativo, vulgar. 2. cenagoso, lodoso, sucio; salpicado.

splat [splæt] *s.* 1. listón de respaldo (de una silla). 2. ruido sordo, chapoteo.

splatter ['splætər, B -ə] *v.t., v.i.* salpicar, manchar. *—s.* salpicadura, rociada.

splay [spleɪ] *v.t.* 1. extender. 2. dislocar (huesos, esp. del caballo). 3. biselar, achaflanar, descantar. *—v.i.* 1. extenderse. 2. inclinarse, sesgarse. *—s.* 1. extensión, expansión. 2. chaflán, bisel. 3. (arq.) alféizar, derrame (de ventanas o puertas). *—a.* 1. extendido, desplegado, ancho. 2. desmañado, torpe.

splayed arch, (arq.) arco abocelado, arco abocinado, arco aboquillado.

splayfoot ['spleɪˌfʊt] *s.* (med.) pie aplastado. *—a.* zancajoso.

splayfooted [-əd] *a.* zancajoso.

splaymouth [-ˌmaʊθ] *a.* boquiancho.

spleen [splin] *s.* 1. (anat.) bazo. 2. (fig.) esplín; malicia; mal humor. 3. (ant.) capricho, antojo; melancolía. 4. **to vent one's s.,** descargar la bilis.

spleenful ['splinfəl] *a.* bilioso, irritable, irascible, enfadadizo.

spleenwort [-ˌwɜrt, B -wɜt] *s.* (bot.) escolopendra, lengua de ciervo, doradilla.

spleeny [-ɪ] *a.* bilioso, irritable, irascible.

splendent ['splɛndənt] *a.* 1. (min.) brillante, lustroso, esplendente. 2. (fig.) brillante, ilustre.

splendid ['splɛndəd] *a.* 1. espléndido, esplendente, resplandeciente, brillante. 2. (fig.) espléndido, vistoso, magnífico; ilustre, grande, glorioso. 3. excelente, muy bueno.

splendidly [-lɪ] *adv.* 1. espléndidamente, esplendorosamente. 2. excelentemente, brillantemente.

splendidness [-nəs] *s.* vistosidad; excelencia.

splendiferous [splɛn'dɪfərəs] *a.* (hum.) espléndido, magnífico, regio.

splendor, (pr. G.B.) **splendour** ['splɛndər, B -də] *s.* 1. esplendor, resplandor, brillantez, brillo. 2. (fig.) esplendor, magnificencia, pompa.

splendorous [-dərəs] **splendrous** [-drəs] *a.* esplendoroso, brillante.

splenectomy [splɪ'nɛktəmɪ] *s.* (med.) esplenectomía.

splenetic [splɪ'nɛtɪk] *a.* 1. (med.) esplénico. 2. irritable, malhumorado, displicente. *—s.* 1. persona irritable. 2. medicamento para enfermedad del bazo.

splenetically [-ɪkəlɪ] *adv.* con mal humor, malhumoradamente.

splenial ['splinɪəl] *a.* (anat.) del esplenio.

splenic ['splinɪk, B 'splɛn-] *a.* (med.) esplénico, del bazo.

splenic fever, (med.) fiebre esplénica, ántrax maligno.

splenitis [splɪ'naɪtəs] *s.* (med.) esplinitis, inflamación del bazo.

splenius ['splinɪəs] *s.* (anat.) esplenio, músculo esplénico.

splenomegaly [ˌsplinoʊ'mɛgəlɪ] *s.* (med.) esplenomegalia.

splenotomy [splɪ'nɑtəmɪ, B -'nɔt-] *s.* (med.) esplenotomía.

spleuchan ['splukən] *s.* (esco., Irl.) petaca (esp. para tabaco o dinero).

splice [splaɪs] *v.t.* 1. ayustar, empalmar. 2. (fig.) unir, juntar; (fam.) casar, unir en matrimonio. *—s.* 1. ayuste, empalme. 2. (fam.) matrimonio, bodas.

splice box, (elec.) caja de empalme.

splice grafting, (agr.) injerto de cópula.

splicer ['splaɪsər, B -ə] *s.* 1. (mar.) ayustador; pasador. 2. (mec., cinem., elec.) empalmador.

spline [splaɪn] *s.* 1. lengüeta postiza, lengüeta paralela. 2. regla flexible (para dibujar líneas curvas). 3. ranura para una junta de cuña. *—v.t.* ranurar; proveer de cuña.

spline machine, (maq.) fresadora ranuradora.

splint [splɪnt] *s.* 1. astilla, tablilla, esquirla. 2. varilla (que sirve de armazón en tejidos de paja, juncos, etc.). 3. (med.) tablilla. 4. (vet.) sobrehueso (de los caballos). 5. (arm.) launa. 6. **in a s.,** (med.) entablillado. *—v.t.* (med.) entablillar (hueso roto, etc.).

splint bone, (vet.) estilete.

splinter ['splɪntər, B -ə] *s.* astilla (de madera, pedernal, vidrio, etc.), esquirla (de hueso). *—v.t.* astillar, hacer astillas. *—v.i.* hacerse astillas.

splinter bar, balancín, volea (de carruajes).

splinter group, organización o grupo que se ha separado de una facción política mayor.

splinterproof [-ərˌpruf, B -əˌ-] *a.* inastillable.

splintery [-ərɪ] *a.* astilloso, que puede astillarse.

splintwood [-ˌwʊd] *s.* alburno (madera).

split [splɪt] *v.t.* (*pret., p.p.* SPLIT; *p.pr.* SPLITTING) 1. hender, rajar, partir. 2. cuartear, resquebrajar. 3. (dep.) ganar la mitad de los partidos, ej., *the team s. the series,* el cuadro ganó la mitad de los partidos en la serie. 4. **s. hairs (o straws),** pararse en pelillos, pesar humos, andarse con quisquillas; **s. one's sides (with laughter),** desternillarse de risa; **s. one's vote,** votar por candidatos de diferentes partidos; **s. up,** repartir, dividir, fraccionar, disociar, separar; separarse, romper (relaciones amorosas); **s. the difference,** dividir la diferencia (en partes iguales). *—v.i.* 1. abrir, partirse o dividirse longitudinalmente; cuartearse, quebrarse, henderse. 2. dividirse, fraccionarse. 3. estallar, reventar. 4. (jer.) revelar secretos, soplar. 5. (jer.) largarse, irse. 6. **my head is splitting,** tengo un terrible dolor de cabeza; **s. on,** (jer. pr. G.B.) delatar (a alguien); **s. up,** disgregarse; (fig.) dividirse (en fracciones). *—s.* 1. hendidura, grieta, raja, cuarteadura, fisura, rendija. 2. cisma, división (en grupos, partidos políticos, etc.). 3. astilla, esquirla, fragmento. 4. tiras de mimbre (para determinados trabajos de cestería). 5. despatarrada (figura de gimnasia o baile que consiste en abrir las piernas en línea recta). 6. (curtiduría), capa delgada (en que se divide la piel). 7. (bolos) posición de los bolos en que es imposible derribarlos de un solo tiro. 8. (jer.) porción del botín; media botella, medio vaso, media porción. 9. **banana s.,** postre de banana con helado, almíbar y nueces. *—a.* hendido, partido, dividido, rajado, cuarteado; fraccionado.

split ballot, split ticket, papeleta de voto dividida, en que no se vota por todos los candidatos de un mismo partido.

split bearing, (mec.) cojinete seccional.

split bushing, (mec.) casquillo partido.

split decision, (boxeo) decisión dividida.

split flap, (aer.) freno aerodinámico intrado y extrado.

split infinitive, (gram.) infinitivo con una o más palabras interpuestas entre **to** y el verbo (gen. para evitar ambigüedad), ej., *to really learn,* aprender realmente, *to clearly see,* ver claramente.

split-level ['splɪt'lɛvəl] *a.* de pisos a desnivel (díc. de casas en que el piso de unos cuartos está a nivel intermedio entre los pisos de los demás cuartos).

split nut, (mec.) tuerca hendida o partida.

split page, (periodismo) página (de periódico) que reemplaza a otra de una edición anterior, conteniendo más o menos la misma información en formato distinto.

split peas, arvejas secas (divididas en mitades).

split personality, (med.) personalidad alternante, personalidad dual, doble personalidad.

split phase, (elec.) fase partida, fase dividida.

split run, tiraje de un periódico o revista interrumpido para permitir la sustitución de ciertas páginas de anuncios o texto.

splitsaw ['splɪtˌsɔ] *s.* sierra para cortar madera longitudinalmente.

split screen, proceso fotográfico por el cual dos o más tomas se yuxtaponen y se proyectan simultáneamente en la pantalla.

split second, fracción de segundo, abrir y cerrar de ojos, instante.
split shift, jornada de trabajo dividida en dos turnos.
splitter [ˈsplɪtər, B -ə] *s.* 1. (mec.) partidor. 2. quisquilloso. 3. (fís.) **atom s.,** ciclotrón.
splitting [-ɪŋ] *s.* 1. hendimiento. 2. (fig.) partición, división. 3. (fís.) fisión (del átomo). 4. (quím.) desdoblamiento, hidrólisis. *—a.* fuerte, violento, agudo, penetrante (dolor).
splore [splɔr, B splɔ] *s.* (esco.) 1. juego, retozo, travesura. 2. conmoción, tumulto.
splotch [splɑtʃ, B splɔtʃ] *s.* mancha, manchón, borrón. *—v.t.* manchar, cubrir de manchones.
splotchy [ˈsplɑtʃɪ, B ˈsplɔtʃɪ] *a.* moteado, cubierto de manchas, salpicado, emborronado.
splurge [splɜrdʒ, B splɜdʒ] *s.* (fam.) fachenda, ostentación; boato, lujo. *—v.i.* (fam.) fachendear, hacer ostentación. *—v.t.* gastar de modo extravagante.
splurger [ˈsplɜrdʒər, B ˈsplɜdʒə] *s.* manirroto, botarata.
splutter [ˈsplʌtər, B -ə] *v.i.* 1. farfullar, tartajear. 2. chisporrotear. *—v.t.* farfullar. *—s.* 1. farfulla, tartajeo. 2. chisporroteo.
splutterer [-ərər, B -ərə] *s.* farfullador, barullero.
spluttery [-ərɪ] *a.* farfullador.
Spode [spoʊd] *s.* (cerám.) tipo de fina porcelana inglesa.
spoil [spɔɪl] *v.t.* (*pret., p.p.* SPOILED, SPOILT [spɔɪlt]; *p.pr.* SPOILING) 1. averiar, deteriorar, estropear, estragar, echar a perder, viciar, malograr. 2. mimar, malcriar, consentir (niños), ej., *he is the spoilt child of fortune,* es el niño mimado de la fortuna. 3. despojar, desposeer. 4. (jer. G.B.) mutilar, lisiar; matar. 5. (ant.) pillar, saquear. 6. **s. one's fun,** aguar a uno la fiesta. *—v.i.* 1. averiarse, deteriorarse, inutilizarse, dañarse; echarse a perder, pudrirse, ej., *it will not s. with keeping,* no se echará a perder si se guarda. 2. **to be spoiling for,** tener afán por. *—s.* 1. (*gen. pl.*) botín, despojo; (fig.) breva, sinecura, prebenda, canonjía. 2. dragado. 3. producto defectuoso, pieza con defecto. 4. (impr.) pliego perdido. 5. (raro) rapiña. 6. (ant.) deterioro, menoscabo.
spoilage [ˈspɔɪlɪdʒ] *s.* 1. corrupción. 2. desperdicio, desecho.
spoiled sheet, (impr.) pliego perdido.
spoiler [ˈspɔɪlər, B -lə] *s.* 1. aguafiestas. 2. despojador. 3. corruptor. 4. (aer.) freno aerodinámico. 5. (jer., dep.) persona o equipo que triunfa inesperadamente.
spoilsman [ˈspɔɪlzmən] *s.* (pol., E.U.) oportunista que sirve a un partido para obtener un cargo público como recompensa.
spoilsport [ˈspɔɪlˌspɔrt, B -ˌspɔt] *s.* aguafiestas.
spoils system, (pol., E.U.) práctica de dar sinecuras como recompensa política.
spoke [spoʊk] *s.* 1. radio, rayo (de rueda). 2. (mar.) cabilla (de la rueda del timón). 3. peldaño, escalón (de escalera). 4. **to put a s. in someone's wheel,** (fig.) frustrar los propósitos de alguien; poner trabas a alguien. *—v.t.* enrayar.
spoke, *pret. de* **speak.**
spoken [ˈspoʊkən] *p.p. de* **speak.** *—a.* hablado, oral.
spokeshave [ˈspoʊkˌʃeɪv] *s.* (carp.) cepillo o cuchillo raspador.
spokesman [ˈspoʊksmən] *s.* vocero, portavoz.
spokesperson [ˈspoʊkspɜrsən] *s.* vocero, portavoz.
spoliate [ˈspoʊlɪˌeɪt] *v.t.* despojar de.
spoliation [ˌspoʊlɪˈeɪʃən] *s.* 1. despojo; rapiña, saqueo; expoliación (esp. de barcos neutrales, autorizada en guerra). 2. (der.) alteración o daño de un documento por un tercero.
spoliator [ˈspoʊlɪˌeɪtər, B -ə] *s.* expoliador.
spondaic [spɑnˈdeɪɪk, B spɔn-] *a.* (poét.) espondaico.
spondaic hexameter, (poét.) verso espondaico.
spondee [ˈspɑnˌdi, B ˈspɔn-] *s.* (poét.) espondeo.
spondyl, spondyle [ˈspɑndəl, B ˈspɔn-] *s.* (anat.) espóndil, espóndilo, vértebra.
spondylitis [ˌspɑndəˈlaɪtəs, B ˌspɔn-] *s.* (med.) espondilitis.
spondylosis [-ˈloʊsəs] *s.* (med.) espondilosis.
sponge [spʌndʒ] *s.* 1. esponja. 2. (fam.) gorrero, parásito. 3. (metal.) esponja, metal esponjoso. 4. (fam.) persona glotona o bebedora. 5. **to throw** (o **toss**) **in the s.,** (fam.) abandonar la lucha, darse por vencido. *—v.t.* 1. limpiar o mojar con una esponja. 2. **s. down,** frotar o lavar con esponja; **s. up,** absorber; (fam.) conseguir de gorra, conseguir a costa ajena. *—v.i.* 1. ser absorbente. 2. (fam.) gorrear, andar de gorra, vivir a costa de otro. 3. pescar o recoger esponjas. 4. **s. on,** vivir a costa de (otro).
sponge bath, lavado del cuerpo con una esponja, sin tomar baño de inmersión.
sponge cake, bizcochuelo; pastel esponjoso de harina, huevos batidos y azúcar.
sponge cloth, ratina, tela de lana entrefina, delgada y con granillo.
sponge iron, (quím.) hierro reducido, hierro fino poroso.
sponge lead, (metal.) plomo esponjoso.
sponger [ˈspʌndʒər, B -ə] *s.* (fam.) gorrista, sablista, pegote, sanguijuela, chupasangre (Amer.).
sponge rubber, goma o caucho esponjoso.
spongin [ˈspʌndʒən] *s.* (bioquím.) espongina.
sponginess [ˈspʌndʒɪnəs] *s.* esponjosidad, porosidad.
sponging [-ɪŋ] *s.* 1. acción de limpiar o enjuagar con esponja. 2. acción de gorrear o de aprovecharse de lo ajeno.
sponging house, (G.B., hist.) cárcel de deudores (para darles la oportunidad de llegar a un arreglo con sus acreedores)
spongioblast [ˈspʌndʒɪoʊˌblæst] *s.* (embr.) espongioblasto, una de las células primordiales del cerebro.
spongy [ˈspʌndʒɪ] *a.* (SPONGIER; SPONGIEST) esponjoso, poroso, absorbente.
sponsion [ˈspɑnʃən, B ˈspɔn-] *s.* 1. (der.) acto o compromiso en nombre de un estado por quien no está autorizado especialmente para ello. 2. (com.) afianzamiento, garantía.
sponson [ˈspɑnsən, B ˈspɔn-] *s.* 1. (mar.) plataforma lateral saliente para cañones; compartimiento del casco (en buques de guerra). 2. cámara de aire (en el casco de un hidroavión para estabilizarlo).
sponsor [ˈspɑnsər, B ˈspɔnsə] *s.* 1. fiador, garante, avalista. 2. (rad., t.v.) auspiciador, patrocinador, promotor. 3. (relig.) padrino, madrina. 4. patrocinador, persona o instituto que auspicia programas de intercambio cultural o educacional. *—v.t.* 1. fiar, garantizar, responsabilizarse por; apadrinar. 2. (rad., t.v.) patrocinar, costear (un programa). 3. patrocinar o auspiciar programas culturales o educacionales.
sponsorial [spɑnˈsɔrɪəl, B spɔn-] *a.* propio del fiador; patrocinador.
sponsorship [ˈspɑnsərˌʃɪp, B ˈspɔnsəˌ-] *s.* padrinazgo, patronazgo, patrocinio.
spontaneity [ˌspɑntəˈniɪtɪ, B ˌspɔn-] *s.* 1. espontaneidad. 2. acto o gesto espontáneo.
spontaneous [spɑnˈteɪnɪəs, B spɔn-] *a.* 1. espontáneo, voluntario. 2. espontáneo, de propio movimiento, instintivo. 3. (biol.) espontáneo.
spontaneous combustion, combustión espontánea, autoinflamación.
spontaneous generation, (biol.) generación espontánea, abiogénesis, autogénesis.
spontaneous ignition, (mot.) inflamacion espontánea, encendido espontáneo.
spontaneously [-lɪ] *adv.* espontáneamente, instintivamente, naturalmente.
spontaneousness [-nəs] *s.* espontaneidad.
spontoon [spɑnˈtun, B spɔn-] *s.* (arm.) espontón.
spoof [spuf] *s.* (fam.) engaño, impostura, superchería, burla, tomadura de pelo, broma. *—v.t.* engañar, hacer burla de, embromar. *—v.i.* burlarse, chancear.
spook [spuk] *s.* espectro, fantasma, aparición. *—v.t.* 1. frecuentar, penar en (casa, etc. como fantasma). 2. asustar, espantar. *—v.i.* (con *at*) asustarse, espantarse (de).
spooky [ˈspukɪ] *a.* (SPOOKIER; SPOOKIEST) 1. fantasmal; espantoso. 2. nervioso, inquieto (caballo).
spool [spul] *s.* carrete, canilla, bobina. *—v.t.* ovillar, encanillar, devanar.
spoon [spun] *s.* 1. cuchara. 2. anzuelo de cuchara, cebo o carnada artificial (de pesca). 3. (golf) un palo de golf (para dar elevación a la pelota). 4. (jer.) simplón, bobalicón, enamorado tonto o acaramelado. 5. **to be born with a silver s. in one's mouth,** rico desde la cuna. *—v.t.* 1. cucharear, sacar con cuchara. 2. ahuecar en forma de cuchara. 3. galantear, cortejar. 4. (croquet, golf) golpear (la pelota) dando elevación. *—v.i.* 1. pescar con carnada artificial. 2. (fam.) besuquearse. 3. (croquet, golf) ejecutar un golpe que levanta la pelota.
spoonbill [ˈspunˌbɪl] *s.* (orn.) cuchareta, ave de cuchara, espátula.
spoon bread, pan de maíz, ligero como un budín.
spoondrift [-ˌdrɪft] *s.* rocíon, rocío del mar.
spoonerism [ˈspunəˌrɪzəm] *s.* trastrocamiento accidental de las sonidos iniciales de dos o más palabras, ej., *let me sew you to your sheet* en lugar de *let me show you to your seat.*
spoon-fed [ˈspunˌfɛd] *a.* 1. mimado; consentido; desprovisto de oportunidad (para actuar solo). 2. alimentado con una cuchara (bebé, anciano, etc.).
spoon-feed [-ˌfid] *v.t.* alimentar con cuchara (a bebé, enfermo, etc.).
spoonful [-ˌfʊl] *s.* (*pl.* SPOONFULS o SPOONSFUL) cucharada.
spoon hook, anzuelo de cuchara.
spoon meat, alimento líquido o semisólido (esp. para bebés).
spoony [ˈspunɪ] *a.* (SPOONIER; SPOONIEST) 1. sensiblero, tontamente sentimental. 2. (fam.) amartelado, acaramelado. 3. (fam.) besador, besuqueador. 4. **to become s.,** acaramelarse.
spoor [spʊr, B spʊə] *s.* rastro, pista, huella (de animal salvaje). *—v.i.* seguir un rastro o pista. *—v.t.* rastrear.
sporadic [spəˈrædɪk] *a.* 1. esporádico, ocasional. 2. aislado.
sporadically [-ɪkəlɪ] *adv.* de modo esporádico, esporádicamente.
sporadic reflection, (rad.) reflexión esporádica o anormal.
sporangial [spəˈrændʒɪəl] *a.* (bot.) espórico.
sporangiophore [-dʒɪəˌfɔr, B -ˌfɔ] *s.* (bot.) esporangióforo.

sporangium [-dʒɪəm] *s.* (bot.) esporangio.

spore [spɔr, B spɔ] *s.* (biol.) espora, esporo. —*v.i.* formar o desarrollar esporas (una planta).

spore case, (bot.) esporangio.

spore fruit, (bot.) fruto esporígeno.

sporidium [spə'rɪdɪəm] *s.* (bot.) esporidio.

sporiferous [spə'rɪfərəs] *a.* (bot.) esporífero.

sporocarp ['spɔrəˌkɑrp, B -kɑp] *s.* (bot.) esporocarpo.

sporocyst [-ˌsɪst] *s.* 1. (zool.) esporocisto. 2. (bot.) esporocito.

sporocyte [-ˌsaɪt] *s.* (biol.) célula madre de las esporas.

sporogenesis [ˌspɔrə'dʒɛnəsəs] *s.* (biol.) esporogénesis, esporogenia.

sporogenous [spə'rɑdʒənəs, B -'rɔdʒ-] *a.* (biol.)esporógeno.

sporogeny [-ənɪ] *s.* (biol.) esporogenia, esporogénesis.

sporogonium [ˌspɔrə'goʊˌnɪəm, B 'spɔrəˌ-goʊ-] *s.* (bot.) esporogonio.

sporogony [spə'rɑgənɪ, B -'rɔg-] *s.* (biol.) esporogonia.

sporont ['spɔrɑnt, B -ɔnt] *s.* (biol.) esporonto.

sporophore ['spɔrəˌfɔr, B -fɔ] *s.* (bot.) esporóforo.

sporophyll [-ˌfɪl] *s.* (bot.) esporófilo.

sporophyte [-ˌfaɪt] *s.* (bot.) esporófito.

sporozoan [ˌspɔrə'zoʊən] *a., s.* (zool.) esporozoario, esporozoo.

sporozoite [-'zoʊˌaɪt] *s.* (zool.) esporozoito.

sporran ['spɑrən, B 'spɔr-] *s.* morral de los montañeses de Escocia.

sport [spɔrt, B spɔt] *s.* 1. deporte; juego. 2. recreación, entretenimiento, pasatiempo, diversión, placer. 3. broma, chanza, chacota, burla. 4. juguete. 5. (fam.) persona alegre o despreocupada. 6. buen perdedor. 7. (biol., bot.) mutación. 8. (ant.) coqueteo amoroso. 9. **in s.,** bromeando, en broma; **to make s. of,** burlarse (de). —*v.t.* (fam.) lucir o vestir con ostentación, hacer alarde de. —*v.i.* 1. jugar, juguetear, retozar. 2. practicar deportes. 3. bromear, burlarse. 4. (biol., bot.) mudar, cambiar, variar. —*a.* deportivo.

sport clothes, ropas deportivas, ropa de sport.

sportful ['spɔrtfəl, B 'spɔt-] *a.* juguetón, divertido, alegre.

sportfully [-fəlɪ] *adv.* juguetonamente.

sportfulness [-fəlnəs] *s.* carácter juguetón, naturaleza alegre.

sporting ['spɔrtɪŋ, B 'spɔt-] *a.* 1. deportivo. 2. justo, equitativo, decente (oferta, etc.). 3. jugador, de apuestas.

sporting chance, buena probabilidad.

sporting house, 1. (fam.) burdel. 2. (ant.) taverna, casa de juego.

sporting lady, s. woman, 1. (fam.) prostituta. 2. deportista.

sportive [-ɪv] *a.* 1. juguetón, bromista, alegre, festivo. 2. deportivo.

sportively [-lɪ] *adv.* juguetonamente; deportivamente.

sportiveness [-nəs] *s.* carácter juguetón, naturaleza alegre.

sports [spɔrts, B spɔts] *a.* deportivo.

sports car, sport car, automóvil deportivo, carro de tipo deportivo.

sportscast ['spɔrtsˌkæst, B 'spɔtskɑst] *s.* transmisión deportiva (de un evento por radio o televisión).

sports complex, complejo deportivo.

sports facilities, instalaciones deportivas.

sport shirt, sports shirt, camisa deportiva, camisa sport.

sports jacket, chaqueta deportiva, chaqueta sport (Amer.).

sportsman [-mən] *s.* 1. deportista. 2. buen perdedor.

sportsmanlike [-ˌlaɪk] *a.* justo, leal, honrado, noble, caballeroso.

sportsmanly [-lɪ] *a.* deportivo.

sportsmanship [-ˌʃɪp] *s.* ética deportiva, deportividad; **bad s.,** falta de deportividad; **good s.,** deportividad.

sportswear ['spɔrtsˌwɛr, B 'spɔtswɛə] *s.* ropa de deporte, ropa de sport.

sportswoman [-ˌwʊmən] *s.* deportista (*f.*).

sportswriter [-ˌraɪtər, B -ə] *s.* reportero o cronista deportivo.

sporty ['spɔrtɪ, B 'spɔtɪ] *a.* 1. aficionado a deportes. 2. vestido casual o informal. 3. divertido, vistoso; alegre. 4. (fam.) ostentoso.

sporulate ['spɔrjəˌleɪt] *v.i.* (biol.) esporular.

sporulation [ˌspɔrjə'leɪʃən] *s.* (biol.) esporulación.

sporule ['spɔrjul] *s.* (biol.) espórula.

spot [spɑt, B spɔt] *s.* 1. mancha. 2. (fig.) mancilla, tacha, baldón (en reputación); defecto, falta (de carácter). 3. mofa, lunar, mancha. 4. punto (de naipe). 5. sitio, lugar, paraje, plaza, punto. 6. puesto, situación; empleo. 7. (*pl.*) mercancías para entrega inmediata. 8. (fam.) pequeña cantidad, poquito; corto tiempo, rato; trago (de licor). 9. **to hit the s.** (fam.) hacer (o decir) exactamente lo necesario, satisfacer una necesidad, ej., *iced tea hits the s. during the summer months,* el té frío es lo más apropiado durante los meses de verano. 10. **in a (bad) s.,** en apuros; **in spots,** en forma dispersa, aquí y allí; en algunos respectos; **on the s.,** en el acto, inmediatamente; sobre el terreno, allí mismo; (jer.) en situación precaria, en peligro; **tender s.,** (fig.) punto débil; talón de Aquiles (de una persona); **to put (someone) on the s.,** (jer.) abochornar a alguien. —*v.t.* (*pret., p.p.* SPOTTED; *p.pr.* SPOTTING) 1. manchar. 2. (fig.) manchar, macular, mancillar, desdorar (la reputación). 3. motear, puntear. 4. situar, colocar (en determinado lugar). 5. (fam.) reconocer, descubrir, notar, avistar. 6. (mil.) localizar, emplazar; concentrar con precisión (fuego de artillería). —*v.i.* 1. mancharse, cubrirse de manchas. 2. dejar una mancha. 3. (mil.) observar el tiro. —*a.* 1. (com.) (que hay) en existencia, para entrega inmediata, contra pago inmediato (mercancías); con pago al contado (operación, venta, etc.). 2. (seleccionado) al azar.

spot ball, (billar) bola con punto.

spot cash, (com.) dinero contante y sonante, pago al contado.

spot check, verificación a la ventura, comprobación hecha al azar.

spot-check ['spɑt'tʃɛk, B 'spɔt-] *v.t.* verificar a la ventura, probar al azar.

spot elevation, (top.) elevación acotada.

spot landing, (aer.) aterrizaje de precisión.

spotless [-ləs] *a.* 1. inmaculado, sin mancha, puro. 2. intachable (reputación).

spotlessly [-lɪ] *adv.* inmaculadamente.

spotlessness [-nəs] *s.* aspecto o estado inmaculado.

spotlight [-ˌlaɪt] *s.* 1. luz concentrada. 2. proyector orientable. 3. proyector de teatro. 4. (aut.) luz de estribo. 5. (fig.) notoriedad. 6. (fig.) luz repentina. 7. **to be in the s.,** estar en una posición conspicua, a vista del público. —*v.t.* 1. iluminar con un proyector de luz. 2. (fig.) poner de relieve, destacar.

spot map, (top.) mapa estadístico o llave.

spot news, 1. últimas noticias, dadas apenas ocurrido el incidente. 2. noticias que ocurren inesperadamente.

spot price, (com.) precio al contado.

spot-remover [ˌspɑtrɪ'muvər, B 'spɔt-ə] *s.* quitamanchas (substancia o persona).

spotted [-əd] *a.* 1. moteado, pintado, de lunares. 2. manchado, deslustrado.

spotted cavy, (zool.) paca.

spotted crake, (orn.) porzana.

spotted crane's-bill, (bot.) geranio silvestre.

spotted fever, (med.) 1. tifus (exantemático), fiebre tifus. 2. fiebre cerebral, meningitis cerebroespinal. 3. fiebre purpúrea americana, fiebre de las Montañas Rocosas.

spotted flycatcher, (orn.) moscareta, muscaria.

spotted hyena, (zool.) hiena manchada.

spotted woodpecker, (orn.) picapuerco.

spotter ['spɑtər, B 'spɔtə] 1. (mil.) marcador de puntería, observador de tiro. 2. (mec.) situador. 3. (fam.) persona empleada para descubrir actos deshonestos (en un banco, etc.). 4. (radio, t.v.) locutor que identifica a los jugadores en el campo. 5. operario en una tintorería cuya labor consiste en quitar manchas.

spot test, 1. prueba rápida (que da resultados inmediatos). 2. prueba selectiva. 3. (quím.) test por el cual se identifica elementos, ya sea por cambio de color o precipitación de los mismos.

spottily [-əlɪ] *adv.* irregularmente, desigualmente.

spottiness [-ɪnəs] *s.* 1. aspecto o estado manchado. 2. irregularidad, desigualdad.

spotty [-ɪ] *a.* (SPOTTIER, SPOTTIEST) 1. manchado. 2. cubierto de pintas o lunares. 3. irregular, desigual.

spot-weld [-ˌwɛld] *v.t.* soldar por puntos.

spot welding, (maq.) soldadura por puntos.

spousal ['spaʊzəl] *s.* (*gen. pl.*) esponsales, nupcias, bodas. —*a.* nupcial.

spouse [spaʊs, B spaʊz] *s.* 1. esposo, esposa, cónyuge, consorte. 2. (fam.) media naranja, cara mitad. — [spaʊz] *v.t.* (ant.) desposar; casar.

spouseless ['spaʊsləs] *a.* soltero o viudo; sin cónyuge.

spout [spaʊt] *v.t.* 1. arrojar, echar a borbotones (o borbollones) (un líquido). 2. (fig.) declamar, recitar pomposamente (versos, etc.). 3. (jer., G.B.) empeñar, dar en prenda. —*v.i.* 1. borbotar, borbollar, salir a chorro, brotar. 2. (fam.) declamar. —*s.* 1. pico (de vasijas); caño, canilla, espita; tubo de descarga. 2. surtidor, chorro (de un líquido). 3. (ant.) casa de empeño.

spouter ['spaʊtər, B -ə] *s.* 1. pozo surgente o brotante (de petróleo). 2. orador, recitador (pomposo).

sprag [spræg] *s.* 1. calza, cuña de madera (para frenar las ruedas de vehículos). 2. (E.U.) abadejo o bacalao pequeño. —*v.t.* calzar las ruedas de los vehículos.

sprain [spreɪn] *v.t.* dislocarse, torcer (muñeca, tobillo, etc.), relajar (un músculo). —*s.* dislocación, luxación, torcedura, esguince; relajamiento.

sprang [spræŋ] *pret. de* **spring.**

sprat [spræt] *s.* (ict.) arenque pequeño; sardineta.

sprawl [sprɔl] *v.i.* 1. arrellanarse, repantigarse. 2. tenderse, caer a lo largo, ej., *the blow sent him sprawling,* el golpe lo dejó tendido. 3. desparramarse (una planta). —*v.t.* tender (por el suelo) en forma irregular. —*s.* postura desgarbada.

sprawling ['sprɔlɪŋ] *a.* irregular y grande (díc. de letras o escritura).

spray [spreɪ] *s.* 1. rocío (de las olas del mar), rociada, ducha. 2. vaporizador, pulverizador, atomizador. 3. ramita, ramaje. 4. diseño o adorno en forma de ramita. —*v.t.* 1. rociar. 2. pintar o cubrir (con barniz o pintura pulverizadas), pasar (barniz pulverizado, etc.) sobre. —*v.i.* esparcirse, disiparse (un líquido pulverizado).

spray can, aerosol.

spray carburator, (mot.) carburador pulverizador o de chorro, carburador de surtidor.

spray cooling, enfriamiento por rocío.

spray deodorant, desodorante en aerosol.

sprayer [ˈspreɪər, B -ə] *s.* 1. rociador, pulverizador. 2. pistola pulverizadora.

spray gun, pistola pulverizadora, pistola de pintar.

spray nozzle, 1. boquilla de regar, pico regador. 2. pitón atomizador, boquilla pulverizadora.

spread [sprɛd] *v.t.* (*pret., p.p.* SPREAD; *p.pr.* SPREADING) 1. (t. con *out*) tender, desencoger, desenvolver, extender, estirar; expandir, dilatar; desplegar (velas, bandera, alas, etc.). 2. exhibir. 3. apartar, abrir, extender (piernas, brazos, etc.). 4. esparcir (mantequilla, grasa, etc.), desparramar, extender (pintura, estiércol, etc.). 5. (fig.) diseminar, esparcir, difundir (noticias, fama, etc.). 6. untar (pan, etc. con mantequilla, grasa, etc.). 7. cubrir (con mantel, alfombras, etc.); poner (la mesa). 8. (imp.) espaciar. 9. **to s. abroad,** esparcir, divulgar, propalar; **s. across the page,** (impr.) a todo despliegue; **s. oneself,** (jer.) fachendear, alardear; no escatimar el dinero, no escatimar gastos; **s. oneself thin,** tratar de hacer muchas cosas a la vez. —*v.i.* 1. extenderse, desencogerse, desplegarse, estirarse. 2. (fig.) esparcirse, diseminarse, difundirse, cundir. 3. apartarse, separarse. —*s.* 1. extensión, amplitud, anchura. 2. envergadura (de las alas); expansión (del ramaje de un árbol, etc.). 3. dilatación. 4. (fig.) difusión, propagación, diseminación. 5. cubrecama, cobertor, colcha; sobremesa, tapete. 6. mermelada o queso (u otro alimento) para untar. 7. (fam.) comilona. 8. (impr.) despliegue a toda página; doble página, doble; anuncio a doble página, anuncio a página doble (en periódicos).

spread eagle, 1. figura de un águila con las alas extendidas. 2. (dep.) águila grande, luna (figura de patinaje).

spread-eagle [ˈsprɛdˌigəl] *a.* (fam., E.U.) pretensioso, fanfarrón, ampuloso; patriotero. —*v.t.* 1. extenderse sobre, abarcar. 2. (mar.) flagelar (a un hombre atado a las jarcias con los brazos y piernas extendidos). —*v.i.* 1. yacer o caer con los brazos y piernas extendidos. 2. (dep.) ejecutar (la figura de) un águila grande, trazar una luna (con los patines).

spread-eagleism [-ˌɪzəm] *s.* (fam., E.U.) oratoria patriotera.

spreader [ˈsprɛdər, B -ə] *s.* 1. propagador, divulgador (de noticias, etc.). 2. untador. 3. separador. 4. viga cepo, viga de separación, travesaño, balancín.

spreadsheet [ˈsprɛdˌʃit] s. (contabilidad) hoja de cálculo.

spree [spri] *s.* 1. jolgorio, fiesta, parranda, jarana; borrachera. 2. período de actividad extraordinaria; gasto extraordinario, ej., *to go on a shopping s.,* hacer muchas compras. 3. **to go on a s.,** andar de parranda, ir de francachela, darse una escapada.

sprig [sprɪg] *s.* 1. (bot.) ramito, vástago, retoño (de planta). 2. diseño o adorno en forma de ramito. 3. (hum., fig.) vástago, retoño, jovenzuelo. 3. puntilla, clavo sin cabeza; clavo remachado, tachuela. —*v.t.* (*pret., p.p.* SPRIGGED; *p.pr.* SPRIGGING) 1. adornar o bordar con diseño de ramitos. 2. clavar, asegurar (con puntillas o tachuelas).

sprigged [sprɪgd] *a.* bordada o adornada con ramitas (tela, muselina, etc.).

spriggy [ˈsprɪgɪ] *a.* lleno de ramitas.

sprightliness [ˈspraɪtlɪnəs] *s.* vivacidad, viveza, animosidad, desenvoltura.

sprightly [-lɪ] *a.* (SPRIGHTLIER; SPRIGHTLIEST) vivaz, alegre, animado.

spring [sprɪŋ] *v.i.* (*pret.* SPRANG [spræŋ] o SPRUNG [sprʌŋ]; *p.p.* SPRUNG; *p.pr.* SPRINGING) 1. saltar, brincar. 2. rebotar. 3. alabearse, torcerse, combarse (madera). 4. rajarse, resquebrarse (madera). 5. explotar, estallar (una mina). 6. (arq.) arrancar desde la imposta (arco o bóveda). 7. **s. at,** abalanzarse sobre; **s. back,** saltar hacia atrás; **s. forth,** brotar; **s. forward,** saltar adelante, lanzarse adelante; **s. to one's feet,** levantarse de un salto; **s. up,** nacer, brotar, surgir, manar (líquido, creencia, convicción, etc.); levantarse, elevarse (edificio, muro, obstáculo, etc.); levantarse de repente (viento); **s. upon,** abalanzarse sobre. —*v.t.* 1. hacer saltar, salir, surgir o brotar (líquidos). 2. soltar (un muelle o resorte). 3. (fig.) revelar (inesperadamente). 4. torcer, combar, encorvar (madera). 5. rajar, hender, partir (madera). 6. hacer estallar, volar (una mina). 7. (arg.) arrancar o vaciar (un arca). 8. levantar (caza). 9. doblar por fuerza; insertar o meter doblando o forzando. 10. saltar por encima de, pasar saltando. 11. armar con resortes. 12. (jer.) soltar (a un preso de la cárcel); conseguir que se ponga en libertad (a un detenido). 13. **s. a surprise,** dar una sorpresa; **s. a surprise on (someone),** coger de sorpresa (a alguien); **s. a leak,** empezar a salirse o a hacer agua (un buque, una vasija). —*s.* 1. muelle, resorte. 2. rebote, elasticidad. 3. (fig.) elasticidad, vigor, energía. 4. fuente, manantial. 5. (fig.) fuente, principio, origen. 6. salto, brinco, corcovo. 7. primavera. 8. ballesta (del carruaje). 9. (arq.) arranque (desde la imposta de arcos); curvatura (de una viga). 10. (mar.) fenda, grieta (en la madera). 11. (*pl.*) período de marea viva. 12. (esco.) danza o tonada vivaz. —*a.* 1. elástico, amortiguador. 2. provisto de resortes; de resorte, de muelle. 3. primaveral, vernal.

springald [ˈsprɪŋəld] **springal** [-əl] *s.* 1. (ant.) máquina militar para arrojar piedras y proyectiles, catapulta. 2. (ant.) jovenzuelo, mozalbete.

spring back, (enc.) lomo plegado (de un libro de cuentas, etc.).

spring balance, balanza de resorte, balanza de tensión.

spring beam, (arq.) viga de aire.

spring beauty, (bot.) claytonia.

spring bed, colchón de muelles, colchón de resortes.

springboard [ˈsprɪŋˌbɔrd, B -bɔd] *s.* trampolín; (fig.) ayuda, palanca.

springbok [-ˌbɑk, B -bɔk] *s.* (zool.) gacela del África del Sur.

spring bolt, cerrojo de resorte, pestillo de golpe.

springbuck [-ˌbʌk] *var. de* **springbok.**

spring carriage, s. cart, carruaje montado sobre ballestas.

spring chicken, 1. polluelo. 2. (fig.) persona joven e inexperta, esp. una mujer.

spring-cleaning [-ˈklinɪŋ] *s.* limpieza anual o primaveral; (fig.) limpieza completa (de un lugar).

spring coil, resorte espiral.

spring contact, (elec.) contacto de resorte.

springe [sprɪndʒ] *s.* lazo, trampa (para atrapar caza menuda).

springer [ˈsprɪŋər, B -ə] *s.* 1. saltador, brincador. 2. perro ojeador. 3. (zool.) orca. 4. (zool.) gacela del África del Sur. 5. (arq.) almohadón. 6. (O. de E.U.) vaca preñada.

springer spaniel, perro ojeador.

spring fever, 1. (hum.) modorra o pereza primaveral. 2. sensación de rejuvenecimiento que afecta a las personas con el advenimiento de la primavera.

spring gun, escopeta o revólver de trampa (que dispara al accionarse un mecanismo).

springhalt [-ˌhɔlt] *var. de* **stringhalt.**

springhead [-ˌhɛd] *s.* fuente, manantial.

springily [ˈsprɪŋəlɪ] *adv.* elásticamente, con elasticidad.

springiness [-ɪnəs] *s.* elasticidad, fuerza elástica.

springing [ˈsprɪŋɪŋ] *s.* 1. (arq.) arranque, (línea de) imposta (de arcos). 2. (bot.) retoño, tallo.

spring latch, picaporte de resbalón.

spring leaf, (mec.) hoja de ballesta, lámina de ballesta.

springlet [-lət] *s.* manantial pequeño; arroyuelo, riachuelo.

spring lock, cerradura de golpe, cerradura de golpe y porrazo.

spring mattress, colchón de muelles, colchón de resortes.

spring snowflake, (bot.) campanilla de primavera.

spring steel, acero para ballesta.

springtail [-ˌteɪl] *s.* (ento.) tisanuro.

springtide [ˈsprɪŋˌtaɪd] *s.* primavera, época primaveral.

spring tide, marea viva; (fig.) inundación, torrente.

springtime [-ˌtaɪm] *s.* primavera, época primaveral.

spring-tooth harrow [ˈsprɪŋˌtuθ-] (agr.) grada de dientes flexibles.

spring valve, válvula de resorte.

spring vetch, (bot.) ervilla.

spring washer, arandela elástica o de resorte.

springwater [-ˌwɔtər, -ˌwɑt-, B -ˈwɔtə] *s.* agua de manantial.

spring wheat, trigo de primavera, trigo marzal, trigo de marzo, trigo tremés.

springwood [-ˌwʊd] *s.* (bot.) albura de primavera.

springy [-ɪ] *a.* (SPRINGIER; SPRINGIEST) 1. elástico, flexible. 2. de muchos manantiales.

sprinkle [ˈsprɪŋkəl] *v.t.* rociar, asperjar, salpicar, polvorear (suelo, objeto); espolvorear, esparcir (líquido, cenizas, etc.); regar, desparramar. —*v.i.* 1. rociar. 2. lloviznar, chispear. —*s.* 1. rociada, llovizna. 2. una pizca, un poco.

sprinkler [-klər, B -klə] *s.* 1. rociador, regadera, irrigador. 2. regadera rotativa (para césped). 3. aspersorio.

sprinkler head, boquilla de regadera.

sprinkler system, instalación para la extinción de incendios por rociadura automática.

sprinkler trunk, camión regador o de riego.

sprinkling [-klɪŋ] *s.* 1. rociada, rociadura, aspersión. 2. (fig.) poco, pizca; pequeño número. —*a.* de rociar, de riego.

sprint [sprɪnt] *v.i.* correr a toda velocidad. —*s.* 1. carrera a toda velocidad, período corto de trabajo intenso. 2. (dep.) carrera corta (de gran velocidad).

sprinter [ˈsprɪntər, B -ə] *s.* (dep.) corredor de carreras cortas.

sprit [sprɪt] *s.* (mar.) botavara, verga de abanico.

sprite [spraɪt] *s.* 1. duende, trasgo, gnomo; hada. 2. sombra, fantasma, aparición. 3. (zool.) especie de cangrejo.

spritsail [ˈsprɪtˌseɪl, -səl] *s.* (mar.) cabadera, vela de abanico.

sprocket [ˈsprɑkət, B ˈsprɔk-] *s.* (mec.) rueda de cadena.

sprocket gear, (mec.) engranaje de rueda y cadena.
sprocket wheel, (mec.) rueda de cadena, piñón, rueda catalina (Esp.).
sprout [spraʊt] *v.i.* (bot.) brotar, retoñar, germinar. —*v.t.* 1. brotar, echar (retoños, hojas, etc.). 2. hacer crecer (bigote, cuerno, etc.). 3. hacer brotar o germinar. 4. (fig.) brotar. —*s.* 1. (bot.) brote, retoño. 2. (fig.) retoño, vástago. 3. (*pl.*) (bot.) bretones.
spruce [sprus] *s.* (bot.) abeto, picea. —*a.* pulido, pulcro, galano, elegante. —*v.t., v.i.* (gen. con *up*) vestir(se) con esmero; emperifollar(se), engalanar(se), emperejilar(se).
spruce beer, cerveza de abeto.
sprucely ['sprusli] *adv.* elegantemente, pulcramente, garbosamente.
spruceness [-nəs] *s.* elegancia, galanura, pulcritud, garbo.
sprue [spru] *s.* (metal.) 1. bebedero (de un molde). 2. mazarota. 3. (med.) esprue, estomatitis tropical, psilosis.
sprung [sprʌŋ] *pret., p.p. de* **spring.** —*a.* 1. armado con resortes. 2. (fam., G.B.) achispado.
sprung mast, (mar.) palo (mástil) rendido.
sprung rhythm, (poét.) ritmo salteado.
spry [spraɪ] *a.* (SPRIER O SPRYER; SPRIEST O SPRYEST) vivaz, ágil, activo, enérgico, listo.
spryly ['spraɪlɪ] *adv.* vivazmente, ágilmente, enérgicamente.
spryness [-nəs] *s.* viveza, agilidad, energía.
spud [spʌd] *s.* 1. escarda (para arrancar malas hierbas). 2. (fam.) patata, papa. 3. escoplo, laya (para descortezar madera). 4. (mec.) copa, lomo. —*v.t.* (*pret., p.p.* SPUDDED; *p.pr.* SPUDDING) escardar, entresacar (malas hierbas).
spudder ['spʌdər, B -ə] *s.* descortezador, máquina descortezadora.
spue, *var. de* **spew.**
spume [spjum] *s.* espuma. —*v.i.* espumar, hacer espuma.
spumous ['spjuməs] *a.* espumoso.
spumy [-ɪ] *a.* (SPUMIER; SPUMIEST) espumoso.
spun [spʌn] *pret., p.p. de* **spin.**
spun glass, vidrio o cristal hilado, lana de vidrio.
spunk [spʌŋk] *s.* 1. hupe, yesca. 2. (fig.) ánimo, coraje, arrojo, corazón, valor. 3. (dial., G.B.) chispa; fogata; fósforo. —*v.i.* (dial.) prender, arder; inflamarse.
spunkie ['spʌŋkɪ] *s.* (esco.) 1. fuego fatuo. 2. licor, alcohol.
spunkily [-kəlɪ] *adv.* valientemente, animosamente, valerosamente.
spunkiness [-kɪnəs] *s.* valor, valentía.
spunky ['spʌŋkɪ] *a.* (SPUNKIER; SPUNKIEST) valiente, animoso, valeroso.
spun lining, (mec.) forro centrifugado, revestimiento por rotación.
spun rayon, hilado de rayón.
spun silk, seda azache.
spun sugar, algodón de azúcar.
spun yarn, (mar.) meollar.
spur [spɜr, B spɜ] *s.* 1. espuela. 2. (fig.) espuela, acicate, estímulo. 3. ramal (de plantas); cornezuelo (de centeno). 4. navaja (para gallo de pelea). 5. trepadera, pincho o garfio (para trepar árboles, postes, etc.). 6. estribación, espolón (ramal corto de una montaña). 7. (bot., zool.) espolón. 8. (arq.) puntal, codal, jabalcón; grifo, garra. 9. (carp.) riostra, tornapunta. 10. (fort.) botaral, contrafuerte, machón. 11. (f.c.) (t. **s. track**) vía muerta, apartadero. 12. **on the s.** of the **moment,** impulsivamente, sin pensarlo; **to win one's spurs,** (fig.) hacerse de fama, distinguirse. —*v.t.* (*pret., p.p.* SPURRED; *p.pr.* SPURRING) 1. espolear. 2. poner espuelas en (botas, etc.). 3. (fig.) (t. con *on*) espolear, estimular. —*v.i.* espolear uno su caballo; cabalgar velozmente; apretar el paso, ir de prisa.
spurgall ['spɜr,gɔl, B 'spɜ,-] *s.* espoleadura. —*v.t.* herir con la espuela.
spurge [spɜrdʒ, B spɜdʒ] *s.* (bot.) lechetrezna, titímalo, tártago.
spur gear, s. gearing, (mec.) engranaje recto, engranaje cilíndrico.
spurge flax, (bot.) torvisco.
spurge laurel, (bot.) adelfillo, lauréola macho, lauréola hembra.
spurious ['spjʊrɪəs, B 'spjʊər-] *a.* 1. espurio, bastardo, ilegítimo. 2. (fig.) espurio, falso, falsificado, adulterado. 3. (bot.) similar en apariencia pero diferente en estructura o función.
spuriously [-lɪ] *adv.* de modo espurio, falsamente.
spuriousness [-nəs] *s.* carácter espurio, falsedad.
spurious radiation, (rad.) emisión a frecuencia falsa, radiación espuria.
spurn [spɜrn, B spɜn] *v.t.* 1. desdeñar, rechazar con desdén. 2. (ant.) pisar, pisotear, dar patadas a. —*v.i.* 1. (gen. con *at*) menospreciar. 2. (ant.) cocear. —*s.* 1. desdén, menosprecio, desprecio. 2. (ant.) coz, puntapié.
spurner ['spɜrnər, B 'spɜnə] *s.* menospreciador.
spur-of-the-moment ['spɜrəvðə'moʊmənt] *a.* instantáneo, espontáneo, impensado.
spur pinion, (mec.) piñón recto.
spurred [spɜrd, B spɜd] *a.* 1. que lleva espuelas. 2. (bot., zool.) espolonado.
spurrey, *var. de* **spurry.**
spurrier ['spɜrɪər, B -ə] *s.* el que forja espuelas.
spurry ['spɜrɪ, B 'spʌrɪ] *s.* (*pl.* SPURRIES) (bot.) maleza arvense.
spurt [spɜrt, B spɜt] *s.* 1. esfuerzo extraordinario y breve; arranque, arrebato (de ira, etc.); aumento repentino (en actividad, negocios, etc.). 2. momento, rato. 3. chorro repentino. —*v.i.* 1. ir o subir velozmente; experimentar un aumento repentino (precios, valor de acciones, etc.). 2. salir en chorro. —*v.t.* arrojar en chorro.
spurtle ['spɜrtəl, B 'spɜt-] *s.* (esco.) palo para batir gachas o puches.
spur track, (f.c.) desvío muerto, ramal corto.
spurt wheel, (mec.) engranaje recto, engranaje cilíndrico.
sputnik ['spʊtnɪk, 'spʌt-] *s.* sputnik, satélite artificial lanzado por la Unión Soviética en 1957.
sputter ['spʌtər, B -ə] *v.i.* 1. hablar echando saliva, barbotar. 2. chisporrotear. 3. farfullar. —*v.t.* 1. espurrear, espurriar. 2. farfullar, tartajear. —*s.* 1. farfulla, balbuceo. 2. chisporroteo, chispeo de saliva.
sputterer [-ərər, B -ərə] *s.* farfullador.
sputtering [-ərɪŋ] *s.* (metal.) deposición electrónica, chisporroteo, peterreo.
sputum ['spjutəm] *s.* 1. saliva; 2. (med.) esputo.
spy [spaɪ] *v.t.* 1. divisar, avistar, columbrar. 2. espiar, atisbar, acechar, aguaitar (Amer.). 3. **s. out,** escrutar, escudriñar. —*v.i.* 1. ser espía, andar espiando. 2. **s. on** (o **upon**), atalayar. —*s.* 1. espía, espión. 2. escudriñamiento.
spy boat, *s.* barco explorador, barco espía.
spyglass ['spaɪ,glæs, B -glɑs] *s.* catalejo, anteojo de larga vista.
spy satellite, satélite espía.
sq. abrev. de 1. **square,** plaza (de una ciudad). 2. **squadron,** escuadrón.
sq. ft. *abrev. de* **square foot,** pie cuadrado.
sq. in. *abrev. de* **square inch,** pulgada cuadrada.
sq. mi. *abrev. de* **square mile,** milla cuadrada.
squab [skwɑb, B skwɔb] *s.* 1. (orn.) pichón, pollo, polluelo. 2. persona regordeta. 3. cojín, almohada; sofá, otomana. —*a.* 1. regordete, rechoncho. 2. implume.
squabble ['skwɑbəl, B 'skwɔb-] *v.i.* reñir, disputar, pendenciar, altercar. —*v.t.* (impr.) encaballar, desarreglar (tipos y líneas). —*s.* riña, pendencia, reyerta, disputa, contienda, trifulca.
squabbler [-ələr, B -lə] *s.* buscapleitos, buscarruidos, pleitista.
squad [skwɑd, B skwɔd] *s.* 1. cuadrilla, partida, escuadra, grupo, equipo. 2. (mil.) escuadra, patrulla, pelotón. —*v.t.* ordenar en escuadras, agrupar.
squad car, (auto) patrullero, carro de policía, radiopatrulla (Amer.). (de la policía).
squadron ['skwɑdrən, B 'skwɔd-] *s.* (mil.) escuadrón; (aer.) escuadrilla; (mar.) escuadra, armada, flota. —*v.t.* escuadronar.
squadron leader, (aer.) guión de escuadrilla, jefe.
squad room, 1. (mil.) dormitorio. 2. cuarto de reunión (en cuartel de policía).
squalid ['skwɑləd, B 'skwɔl-] *a.* 1. escuálido, sucio. 2. (fig.) sórdido.
squalidly [-lɪ] *adv.* 1. suciamente. 2. (fig.) sórdidamente.
squalidness [-nəs] *s.* 1. escualidez, escualor, suciedad. 2. (fig.) sordidez.
squall [skwɔl] *s.* 1. ráfaga, racha (de viento); ventolera, borrasca; grupada, chubasco, turbonada. 2. (fam.) disturbio, reyerta. 3. (meteor.) turbonada, chubasco. 4. chillido, berrido. —*v.i., v.t.* chillar, berrear, gritar.
squaller ['skwɔlər, B -ə] *s.* chillador, chillón.
squall line, (meteor.) zona de ráfaga y cambios violentos en el clima de una región.
squally ['skwɔlɪ] *a.* chubascoso, borrascoso, tempestuoso.
squaloid ['skweɪ,lɔɪd] *a.* (ict.) escualoideo.
squalor ['skwɑlər, B 'skwɔlə] *s.* escualor, escualidez, suciedad, mugre.
squalus ['skweɪləs] *s.* (ict.) escualo.
squama ['skweɪmə] *s.* (biol.) escama, estructura escamosa; laminilla delgada de hueso.
squamate [-,meɪt, B -mət] *a.* escamoso.
squamation [skwə'meɪʃən] *s.* estructura de escamas (en un animal).
squamosal [-'moʊsəl] (anat., zool.) *a.* escamoso. —*s.* escama.
squamose ['skweɪ,moʊs] **squamous** [-məs] *a.* escamoso.
squamosely, squamously [-lɪ] *adv.* con escamas, en forma escamosa.
squamulose [-mjə,loʊs] *a.* de pequeña escamas.
squander ['skwɑndər, B 'skwɔndə] *v.t., v.i.* 1. malgastar, derrochar, malbaratar, despilfarrar, malrotar, dilapidar, disipar. 2. (ant.) desparramar, dispersar. —*s.* derroche, despilfarro.
squanderer [-dərər, B -dərə] *s.* derrochador, manirroto, malgastador, disipador, malbaratador, botarate (Amer.).
square [skwɛr, B skwɛə] *s.* 1. cuadrado, cuadro. 2. plaza, parque (cuadrilátero). 3. manzana, cuadra (de casas). 4. casilla, escaque (del tablero de ajedrez, etc.). 5. (mat.) cuadrado, segunda potencia. 6. (geom.) cuadrado. 7. (dib.) escuadra, cartabón; (carp.) escuadra, codal. 8. (mil.) cuadro (formación cuadrilátera de la infantería). 9. (jer. despec.) persona conservadora, chapada a la antigua. 10. (ant.) norma, principio, patrón. 11. **on the s.,** en ángulo recto, a escuadra; (fam.) honradamente, de buena fe, con honestidad; **out of s.,** fuera de escuadra, no en ángulo recto; irregular; oblicuamente, incorrectamente; **to be on the s.,** (fam.) obrar de buena fe. —*v.t.* 1. cuadrar. 2. escuadrar, acodar. 3. igualar; ajustar, arreglar, saldar (cuentas, etc.); pasar (balance). 4. poner en ángulo recto. 5. cuadricular. 6. (mat.) cuadrar, elevar al cuadrado; medir (una superficie) en metros, pies, etc. cuadrados. 7. (mar.)

orientar, colocar (en posición, rumbo, etc. correctos). 8. (dep.) igualar (tantos, marcador); empatar (el juego). 9. (fam.) arreglar, satisfacer; ej., *can you s. the porter?* ¿puede usted arreglarse (dar propina) con el portero? 9. **s. a debt,** arreglar (resolver) una deuda; liquidar una cuenta (fig.); **s. accounts with,** (fig.) saldar cuentas con, vengarse de; **s. one's shoulders,** sacar el pecho; **s. the circle,** cuadrar el círculo; hacer o tratar de hacer algo imposible; **s. with,** conformar con, conciliar con, ajustar a; adaptar a. —*v.i.* 1. (ú. t. con *with*) cuadrar, estar de acuerdo, armonizar, convenir, concordarse (con), encajar (en), ajustarse (a), conformarse, ponerse de acuerdo (con). 2. (ú. esp. con *up*) (fam.) saldar cuentas; liquidar con acreedores. 3. (golf) quedar en empate. 4. **s. away,** prepararse, disponerse, dejar todo en orden (para); alistarse a pelear; (mar.) bracear en cuadro; **s. off,** alistarse para pelear; **s. up to,** ponerse en guardia contra (alguien, esp. para boxear); enfrentar con coraje; considerar de manera realista. —*a.* 1. rectángulo, rectangular, ej., *a s. frame,* un marco rectangular. 2. cuadrado (superficie), ej., *a s. foot,* un pie cuadrado. 3. (fig.) cuadrado, perfecto, exacto, justo, cabal; ordenado. 4. directo; honesto, ej., *a s. answer,* una respuesta honesta (directa). 5. justo, equitativo, razonable, íntegro, recto. 6. saldado. 7. (fam.) abundante, amplio, satisfactorio (una comida). 8. recto, derecho; rotundo, inequívoco, intransigente, ej., *a s. denial,* una negativa rotunda. 9. (jer.) tradicional, conservador, anticuado. 10. (geom.) cuadrado, escuadrado. 11. (mat.) elevado al cuadrado. 12. (dib.) cuadriculado (papel). 13. (mar.) cuadrado, de cruz (vela, aparejo). 14. (dep.) igualado, empatado (marcador, etc.). 15. **a man of s. frame,** (un) hombre fornido; **to get s. with,** vengarse o desquitarse de; hacérselas pagar a; **to get a s. deal,** hacer un trato justo; **to make a s. meal,** constituir una comida completa. —*adv.* 1. honestamente, honradamente, de buena fe. 2. de frente, cara a cara. 3. directamente. 4. firmemente, fijamente; sólidamente. 5. en cuadro; en ángulo recto.

square bracket, (impr.) corchete, paréntesis angular, paréntesis rectangular o cuadrado.

square column, (arq.) columna cuadrada, columna ática.

square-cut diamond, diamante tabla.

square dance, contradanza, baile de figuras.

squared circle, (fam.) cuadrilátero de boxear.

square deal, (fam.) trato o juego de buena fe; trato recto o justo; juego limpio.

squared paper, papel cuadriculado.

square edge, canto vivo o escuadra.

square-faceted ['skwɛr'fæsətəd, B 'skwɛə'-] *a.* (joy.) jaquelado.

squarehead [-ˌhɛd] *s.* (despec., E.U.) alemán, germano, nórdico.

square jaw, maxilar cuadrado, mandíbula cuadrada.

square knot, nudo llano, nudo derecho.

squarely [-lɪ] *adv.* 1. en cuadro; a escuadra. 2. de frente, cara a cara. 3. honradamente, con toda equidad. 4. firmemente.

square measure, medida de superficie.

squareness [-nəs] *s.* 1. forma cuadrada. 2. honradez, equidad, justicia.

square peg, (jer.) persona que no se adapta, que no encaja en ningún sitio.

squarer ['skwɛrər, B 'skwɛərə] *s.* trabajador que escuadra madera, piedra, etc.

square-rigged [-'rɪgd] *a.* (mar.) que lleva velas cuadradas, con velas de cruz (buque).

square-rigger [-'rɪgər, B -ə] *s.* (mar.) buque de cruz.

square root, (mat.) raíz cuadrada.

square sail, (mar.) vela de cruz.

square shooter, (fam.) persona honrada; hombre justo, hombre correcto.

square-shouldered [-'ʃoʊldərd, B -dəd] *a.* de hombros cuadrados.

square-toed [-'toʊd] *a.* 1. de puntera cuadrada (zapato). 2. (fig.) anticuado; conservador; estricto; estirado.

squaring ['skwɛrɪŋ B 'skwɛər-] *s.* (carp.) acodadura; cuadratura, escuadreo, cuadriculación.

squaring the circle, cuadratura del círculo.

squarish [-ɪʃ] *a.* más o menos cuadrado.

squarrose ['skwærˌoʊs] *a.* 1. (bot.) escuarroso. 2. (biol.) áspero.

squash [skwɑʃ, B skwɔʃ] *v.t.* 1. despachurrar, machacar; (fig.) chafar, aplastar, apabullar. 2. aplastar, suprimir, sofocar, reprimir (revuelta, levantamiento, etc.). —*v.i.* 1. aplastarse, aplanarse. 2. apretarse, apretujarse. 3. (fam.) caminar chapoteando (con zapatos empapados, sobre suelo mojado, etc.). 4. **s. into,** entrar o caber apiñado en. —*s.* 1. pulpa, masa blanda. 2. caída pesada (de un cuerpo blando). 3. aplastamiento, despachurramiento; apretón, apiñamiento. 4. chapoteo (al caminar sobre suelo mojado). 5. (t. **s. tennis**) juego de pelota contra una pared y con raquetas. 6. (G.B.) (refresco de) jugo de fruta (limonada, naranjada, etc.). 7. calabaza, chayote, cidra, cidra cayote. —*adv.* con chapoteo.

squash beetle, s. borer, s. bug, insectos norteamericanos que atacan la calabaza.

squash hat, (G.B.) sombrero flexible.

squashily ['skwɑʃəlɪ, B 'skwɔʃ-] *adv.* blandamente.

squashiness [-ɪnəs] *s.* blandura, esponjosidad, contextura fofa.

squash racquets, juego parecido al tenis, que se juega con raquetas más cortas, pelotas de goma y en un campo más pequeño rodeado de paredes altas.

squashy [-ɪ] *a.* (SQUASHER; SQUASHIEST) blando, esponjoso, fofo y mojado o lodoso; papandujo (fruta).

squat [skwɑt, B skwɔt] *v.t.* hacer acuclillarse, hacer ponerse en cuclillas. —*v.i.* 1. acuclillarse, ponerse en cuclillas. 2. agazaparse, acurrucarse; agacharse (pájaro, liebre, etc.). 3. **s. on,** ocupar (un terreno ajeno) sin derecho o (un terreno público) para crear un derecho. —*a.* 1. puesto en cuclillas; agachado, agazapado. 2. regordete, cachigordo. —*s.* 1. postura de uno que está en cuclillas o agachado. 2. lugar de retiro, guarida (de liebres, ardillas, etc.).

squatter ['skwɑtər, B 'skwɔtə] *s.* 1. intruso, ocupante ilegal (que se establece en casas o terrenos no ocupados). 2. persona o animal que se acuclilla.

squatty [-ɪ] *a.* rechoncho, regordete y de baja estatura.

squaw [skwɔ] *s.* 1. (despec.) india norteamericana; mujer, muchacha (entre los indios). 2. (fig., hum., despec.) mujer; esposa.

squawk [skwɔk] *v.i.* 1. graznar, crascitar. 2. (fam.) chillar, quejarse en voz bronca, protestar. —*v.t.* decir en voz chillona o broncamente. —*s.* 1. graznido. 2. (fam.) queja (en voz chillona o bronca). —*s.* (orn.) garzota de cabeza negra.

squawk box, (fam.) altavoz (de intercomunicación).

squawker ['skwɔkər, B -ə] *s.* 1. graznador, chillador. 2. (fam.) altavoz. 3. (jer.) informante, soplón, delator.

squaw man, (despec.) hombre blanco casado con india.

squawroot ['skwɔˌrut] *s.* (bot.) (variedad de) orobanca o hierba tora.

squeak [skwik] *v.i.* 1. chirriar, rechinar, chillar. 2. (jer.) confesar; delatar, soplar. 3. **s. by,** ingeniárselas, componérselas; **s. through,** pasar a duras penas. —*v.t.* pronunciar en voz chillona. —*s.* 1. chillido, chirrido. 2. oportunidad, chance (Am.). 3. (jer.) ayudante, asistente. 4. **a narrow s.,** (fam.) escapada por un pelo, escapada angustiosa; **I do not want to hear a s. out of you,** no quiero oírles decir ni pío.

squeaker ['skwikər, B -ə] *s.* 1. juguete chirriador. 2. (G.B.) lechón. 3. (jer. G.B.) delator, soplón.

squeakily [-əlɪ] *adv.* con un chirrido; en voz chillona.

squeaky ['skwikɪ] *a.* chirriador, chirriante (puerta, ruedas, etc.); chillón (voz).

squeal [skwil] *v.i.* 1. chillar, dar chillidos. 2. (fam.) quejarse, protestar. 3. (jer.) delatar, soplar. —*v.t.* decir entre chillidos. —*s.* 1. chillido, alarido. 2. (jer.) delación, denuncia.

squeamish ['skwimɪʃ] *a.* 1. delicado, fastidioso, remilgado, quisquilloso, melindroso, escrupuloso. 2. propenso a la náusea; nauseabundo.

squeamishly [-lɪ] *adv.* remilgadamente; fastidiosamente.

squeamishness [-nəs] *s.* remilgo, melindre.

squeegee ['skwiˌdʒi] *s.* 1. escobilla de goma, barredora o rodillo de goma (para secar y restregar superficies mojadas). 2. (foto.) escurridor (para estregar las copias y ampliaciones y darles brillo). —*v.t.* limpiar con escobilla, estregar con rodillo de goma o escurridor.

squeeze [skwiz] *v.t.* 1. apretar, estrechar, comprimir. 2. (ú. t. con *out*) estrujar, prensar, exprimir. 3. (ú. t. con *from*) forzar, meter o hacer por presión. 4. (fig.) oprimir, acosar, agobiar (con cargas, impuestos, etc.). 5. (fam.) extorsionar, sacar u obtener por fuerza; exigir (dinero, favor, por influencia o presión.). 6. (bridge) forzar (a un adversario) a descartar. 7. **s. in,** hacer entrar apretando; **s. out,** exprimir; hacer salir. —*v.i.* 1. dejarse estrujar (fácil o difícilmente). 2. **s. in (o into),** entrar apretadamente en; apiñarse en; agolparse en; **s. out,** salir con dificultad; **s. through,** pasar apretadamente a través de, forzar paso por. —*s.* 1. apretadura, apretón, estrujón; presión. 2. apretón; abrazo fuerte. 3. apiñamiento, agolpamiento (de gente, etc.). 4. (fam.) ganancia ilícita; extorsión. 5. (bridge) (juego de) aprieto. 6. **to give (one) a s.,** darle un apretón (a uno); **to put the s. on (someone),** (fam.) apretarle las clavijas a (alguien), poner a (alguien) las peras a cuarto.

squeeze play, 1. (bridge) juego de aprieto. 2. presión ejercida con el fin de obtener concesiones u objetivos. 3. (béisbol) jugada en la cual el bateador golpea ligeramente la pelota para que ruede muy poco.

squeezer ['skwizər, B -ə] *s.* 1. exprimidera. 2. prensa de moldear (ej., ladrillos). 3. (metal.) cinglador.

squeeze riveter, (mec.) remachadora de presión.

squelch [skwɛltʃ] *s.* (fam.) 1. chapaleo, chapoteo (sonido producido al caminar sobre lodo). 2. (fam.) despachurro, réplica desconcertante. —*v.t.* 1. aplastar, suprimir. 2. apabullar, despachurrar, desconcertar. —*v.i.* chapotear, chapalear.

squelcher ['skwɛltʃər, B -ə] *s.* (fam.) despachurro, réplica desconcertante.

squelch voltage, (rad.) voltaje silenciador.

squib [skwɪb] *s.* 1. buscapiés, carretilla; cohete roto cuya pólvora arde pero no explota. 2. detonador; cebo eléctrico. 3. suelto, escrito satírico, pasquín, pulla. —*v.i.* (*pret., p.p.* SQUIBBED; *p.pr.* SQUIBBING) 1. escribir pasquines o pullas. 2. prender buscapiés o carretillas. —*v.t.* 1. pasquinar, lanzar pasquines o libelos contra (alguien). 2. hacer detonar o estallar.
squid [skwɪd] *s.* (zool.) calamar.
squiffy ['skwɪfɪ] *a.* (jer., pr. G.B.) ajumado, achispado, borracho.
squiggle ['skwɪgəl] *v.i.* 1. retorcerse, culebrear. 2. garrapatear, garabatear, escarabajear. —*v.t.* emborronar, borrajear. —*s.* 1. rasgo ondulante. 2. garrapato, garabato, escarabajo.
squilgee, squillgee ['skwɪlˌdʒi] *vars. de* **squeegee.**
squill [skwɪl] *s.* 1. (bot.) escila, esquila, cebolla albarrana, albarranilla. 2. (zool.) esquila.
squilla ['skwɪlə] *s.* (zool.) esquila, camarón.
squinch [skwɪntʃ] *s.* (arq.) pechina. —*v.t.* torcer (la vista, el semblante, etc.). —*v.i.* bizquear.
squinny ['skwɪnɪ] (ant.) *s.* bizquera, mirada bizca, estrabismo. —*v.i.* bizquear.
squint [skwɪnt] *a.* 1. desviado (ojo). 2. que mira de soslayo, torcido, avieso. —*v.i.* 1. mirar de soslayo. 2. bizquear; ser bizco o estrábico. 3. (gen. con *towards*) aludirse indirectamente; inclinarse hacia, tender a. —*v.t.* bizcar, torcer (los ojos); entrecerrar (los ojos). —*s.* 1. mirada bizca; mirada furtiva o de soslayo; (fam.) ojeada, mirada, ej., *let's have a s. at it,* echemos una ojeada a esto. 2. ojo desviado; bizquera, estrabismo. 3. propensión, inclinación, tendencia. 4. (arq.) hagioscopio.
squinter ['skwɪntər, B -ə] *s.* bizco, estrábico.
squint-eyed [-ˌaɪd] *a.* 1. bizco, bisojo, estrábico. 2. de soslayo (mirada). 3. (fig.) avieso, maligno.
squirarchy, *var. de* **squirearchy.**
squire [skwaɪr, B 'skwaɪə] *s.* 1. escudero. 2. (G.B.) hacendado, esp. principal terrateniente (de un distrito). 3. (título dado al) alcalde, juez de paz, juez local. 4. asistente (de un gran personaje). 5. (fam.) acompañante (de una dama), galán. —*v.t.* asistir servir como asistente; acompañar, escoltar (a una dama).
squirearchy ['skwaɪrˌɑrkɪ, B -ərˌɑkɪ] *s.* 1. clase terrateniente. 2. gobierno de la clase terrateniente.
squirm [skwɜrm, B skwɜm] *v.i.* 1. retorcerse, serpear, serpentear, culebrear. 2. **s. out,** salir con dificultad (de un aprieto). —*s.* retorcimiento, serpenteo, culebreo, contorsión.
squirmy ['skwɜrmɪ, B 'skwɜmɪ] *a.* retorcido, serpenteado (movimiento); intranquilo, intratable (niño).
squirrel ['skwɜrəl, B 'skwɪr-] *s.* (zool.) ardilla.
squirrel-cage motor, motor de jaula de ardilla o de inducido de barras.
squirrel monkey, (zool.) tití.
squirrel shrew, (zool.) tupaya.
squirrel winding, (elec.) devanado en jaula.
squirrely ['skwɜrlɪ, B 'skwɪrəlɪ] *a.* (fig., fam.) rarísimo, extrañísimo, alocado.
squirt [skwɜrt, B skwɜt] *v.t.* arrojar a chorros, hacer salir a chorros; espurrear; jeringar. —*s.* 1. jeringa, chisguete. 2. chorro, jeringazo; chorretada. 3. (fam.) joven insignificante pero presumido e insolente.
squirt gun, pistola de agua.
squirting cucumber, (bot.) cohombrillo amargo, pepino del diablo, pepino purgante, pepino silvestre, calabacilla.
squish [skwɪʃ] *v.i.* chapolear, chapotear. —*s.* 1. lodo blando. 2. (jer., G.B.) mermelada.
squishy ['skwɪʃɪ] *a.* blando y húmedo (lodo, fango, nieve derretida, etc.).
Sr *símb. de* **strontium,** estroncio (Sr).
Sr. *abrev. de* 1. **Senior,** padre. 2. **Sister,** hermana.
SRBM, *abrev. de* **short range ballistic missile,** proyectil balístico de corto alcance.
S.R.O. *abrev. de* **standing room only,** (teat.) solamente hay localidades de pie (entrada general, sin asiento).
SS *abrev. de* **steamship,** buque de vapor.
SSE *abrev. de* **South-southeast,** sur-sudeste (SSE).
SSM *abrev. de* **surface-to-surface missile,** proyectil (teledirigido) del suelo al suelo, cohete suelo-suelo.
SST *abrev. de* **supersonic transport,** avión supersónico de transporte, avión de línea supersónico.
SSW *abrev. de* **South-southwest,** sur-sudoeste.
St. *abrev. de* 1. **Saint,** San (S., Sto., Sta.). 2. **street,** calle. 3. **statute,** (der.) estatuto.
sta. *abrev. de* 1. **station,** estación. 2. **stationary,** estacionario.
stab [stæb] *v.t.* (*pret., p.p.* STABBED; *p.pr.* STABBING)apuñalar, apuñalear; traspasar, atravesar o herir (con arma blanca); **s. to death,** matar a puñaladas, matar de una puñalada; **to be stabbed to death,** morir apuñalado. —*v.i.* apuñalar, dar de puñaladas. —*s.* 1. puñalada, cuchillada, estocada. 2. esfuerzo, tentativa, prueba. 3. **s. in the back,** puñalada por la espalda, traición; **to make a s. at,** esforzarse por hacer; tratar de aprender o adivinar.
Stabat Mater ['stɑbɑtmɑtər, B -bɑɛt-ə] (relig., mús.) Stábat Máter, Stábat.
stabber ['stæbər, B -ə] *s.* acuchillador, apuñalador, heridor (con arma blanca).
stabile ['steɪˌbɪl] *a.* 1. fijo, estable, estacionario. 2. (med.) estable, resistente al calor moderado. — [-ˌbil] *s.* escultura abstracta estacionaria.
stability [stə'bɪlətɪ] *s.* 1. estabilidad, permanencia, firmeza. 2. (fig.) firmeza, constancia, resolución, entereza. 3. (relig.) voto que une por vida (a un religioso) a un mismo monasterio. 4. (mec., aer.) estabilidad. 5. (ant.) coherencia, solidez, consistencia.
stability factor, (ing.) factor de estabilidad.
stability limit, (aer.) límite de estabilidad.
stabilization [ˌsteɪbələ'zeɪʃən, B -laɪ-] *s.* estabilización.
stabilize ['steɪbəˌlaɪz] *v.t.* estabilizar.
stabilizer [-ər, B -ə] *s.* 1. (mec., quím.) estabilizador. 2. (aer.) plano estabilizador. 3. (auto.) amortiguador.
stabilizing speed, (avia.) velocidad mínima de sustentación.
stable ['steɪbəl] *s.* 1. establo, cuadra, caballeriza. 2. caballeriza, caballos de carrera de un establo; personal de un establo (de caballos de carrera). 3. (fam.) grupo (de artistas, atletas, etc.) bajo la administración de una persona. —*v.t.* poner, guardar en un establo. —*v.i.* albergarse (caballo) en un establo. —*a.* 1. estable, firme, fijo; duradero, permanente. 2. (fig.) estable, constante. 3. (quím., fís.) estable.
stableboy [-ˌbɔɪ] *s.* establero, caballerizo, mozo de cuadra, mozo de caballerías.
stable companion, caballo del mismo establo; (fam.) miembro del mismo colegio, club, etc.
stableman [-mən, -mæn] *s.* caballerizo, mozo de cuadra.
stableness [-nəs] *s.* estabilidad.
stabling ['steɪblɪŋ] *s.* estabulación, cría y mantenimiento de los ganados en establo.
stably [-blɪ] *adv.* establemente.
staccato [stə'kɑtoʊ] *a.* 1. (mús.) staccato. 2. entrecortado (ruido, etc.).
stack [stæk] *s.* 1. niara, hacina, almiar. 2. rimero, pila (de libros, leña, etc.). 3. cañón, humero (de chimenea); chimenea (de buque). 4. tubo de escape (de motor de combustión). 5. (*gen. pl.*) estante, estantería (para libros). 6. (fig.) (t. *pl.*) montón, gran número, ej., *we have stacks of work to get through,* tenemos un montón de trabajo por acabar. 7. (G.B.) unidad de medida para carbón y madera como combustible (108 pies cúbicos). 8. (arq.) grupo de humeros. 9. (mil.) pabellón de fusiles. 10. (póker) pila de fichas (de un jugador). 11. **to blow one's s.,** (jer.) perder los estribos. —*v.t.* 1. hacinar, apilar, amontonar, entongar (Amer.). 2. (mil.) poner (las armas) en pabellón. 3. arreglar o componer fraudulentamente. 4. **the cards are stacked against (one),** las circunstancias son desfavorables para (uno); **s. the cards,** amarrar (los naipes); (jer.) asegurarse (con mañas) del resultado favorable; **well stacked,** (jer.) de formas curvilíneas, de figura escultural (mujer). —*v.i.* apilarse, acumularse; **s. up,** resultar en suma; **s. up against,** comparse con.
stacker ['stækər, B -ə] *s.* apiladora, amontonadora (máquina).
stacte ['stæktɪ] *s.* estacte, especia usada por los antiguos hebreos para hacer incienso.
staddle ['stædəl] *s.* 1. parte baja de una niara. 2. armazón o estructura de soporte.
stade [steɪd] *s.* (hist.) estadio (medida griega).
stadia ['steɪdɪə] *s.* (top.) 1. estadia; mira taquimétrica. 2. estadímetro, estadiómetro.
stadia arc, arco taquimétrico.
stadia constant, constante taquimétrica.
stadia hairs, (top.) hilos taquimétricos, pelos de la estadia.
stadia rod, (top.) estadia; mira taquimétrica.
stadia survey, (top.) levantamiento taquimétrico, levantamiento estadimétrico.
stadiometer [ˌsteɪdɪ'ɑmətər, B -'ɔmɪtə] *s.* estadiómetro, estadímetro.
stadium ['steɪdɪəm] *s.* (*pl.* STADIA [-ə] o STADIUMS) 1. (hist.) estadio (medida griega o romana); pista de carreras. 2. (*pl. gen.* STADIUMS) estadio; anfiteatro, coliseo. 3. fase, período, etapa.
stadtholder ['stætˌhoʊldər, B -də] *s.* (hist.) estatúder.
stadtholderate [-dərət] **stadtholdership** [-dərˌʃɪp, B -dəˌ-] *s.* (hist.) estatuderato.
staff [stæf, B stɑf] *s.* (*pl.* STAFFS o STAVES [steɪvz]) 1. palo, estaca, varilla; bastón. 2. (fig.) soporte, apoyo, sostén. 3. palo, asta (de lanza, pica, bandera, etc.). 4. garrote, cachiporra, maza. 5. vara o bastón de mando; vara de medir; (top.) jalón de mira. 6. personal, cuerpo (de administración). 7. escalón, peldaño (de escala de mano); travesaño (de una silla). 8. (relig.) báculo pastoral, cayado. 9. (mil.) plana, estado mayor. 10. (mil.) oficiales de escolta. 11. (mil.) cuerpo de oficiales administrativos (sin comando). 12. (med.) sonda acanalada. 13. (mús.) pentagrama. 14. (const.) mezcla de yeso y fibra (usada en construcciones temporales). —*a.* del estado mayor (militar); del cuerpo administrativo (de una empresa). —*v.t.* proveer de personal, dotar de funcionarios u oficiales.
staffer ['stæfər, B 'stɑfə] *s.* funcionario, empleado (de una empresa); reportero estable, miembro de la redacción, redactor (de un periódico).
staff gage, (meteor.) escala hidrométrica, limnímetro.
staff officer, (mil.) oficial de estado mayor.
staff of life, (fig.) alimento principal, alimento básico (gen. pan).

staff tree, (bot.) celastro.
stag [stæg] *s.* 1. ciervo, venado. 2. (animal) castrado. 3. varón sin compañera (en una reunión social). 4. (pr. esco.) potro, potrillo. —*a.* 1. sólo para hombres (filme, reunión, comida, etc.). 2. sin compañera, sin compañero. —*v.i.* (*pret., p.p.* STAGGED; *p.pr.* STAGGING) asistir sin compañera, ir solo (hombre a un baile, reunión social, etc.) —*v.t.* (jer., G.B.) espiar, observar; seguir muy de cerca.
stag beetle, (ento.) ciervo volante.
stage [steɪdʒ] *s.* 1. escenario, escena (de teatro); tablas (fig.). 2. plataforma, estrado, tablado. 3. andamio. 4. (fig.) teatro, arte dramático; la carrera de las tablas. 5. campo (de acción); escenario, teatro (de un suceso). 6. parada, posta, descansadero; estación. 7. etapa, jornada, ej., *by easy stages,* en etapas cómodas. 8. diligencia, coche. 9. (biol.) período (en el desarrollo y crecimiento de animales y plantas). 10. (e. p., sociol.) estado, etapa, fase (del desarrollo material del hombre, de una raza o de un país). 11. portaobjeto, platina de microscopio. 12. (rad.) etapa, paso. 13. (aer.) etapa (de un cohete). 14. **on the s.,** en el escenario; en el teatro; **to be in its early stages,** estar en pañales; **to go on the s.,** subir a las tablas, hacerse actor. —*v.t.* 1. poner en escena, montar, escenificar, representar (en el teatro). 2. preparar, organizar, presentar (en forma llamativa).
stagecoach ['steɪdʒˌkoʊtʃ] *s.* diligencia (coche).
stagecraft [-ˌkræft, B -krɑft] *s.* arte teatral.
stage direction, indicación escénica (en obra teatral).
stage director, (teat.) director (de una obra).
stage door, (teat.) entrada de artistas.
stage effect, (teat.) efecto escénico.
stage fright, miedo al público, trac (Esp.).
stagehand ['steɪdʒˌhænd] *s.* (teat.) tramoyista, metesillas y sacamuertos, metemuertos.
stage-manage [-ˌmænɪdʒ] *v.t.* 1. dirigir (obra de teatro). 2. preparar o exhibir (con mucho efecto). 3. (pol.) manipular, preparar entre bastidores.
stage manager, (teat.) director de escena.
stage name, nombre de teatro, nombre adoptado por un actor en su profesión.
stager [-ər, B -ə] *s.* (gen. **old s.**) veterano, persona de gran experiencia.
stage set, s. setting, (teat.) decorado.
stagestruck [-ˌstrʌk] *a.* fascinado por el teatro, ansioso por hacerse actor o actriz.
stage whisper, 1. (teat.) cuchicheo de un actor destinado al oído de los espectadores. 2. cuchicheo dirigido a los presentes.
stagey, *var. de* **stagy.**
staggard ['stægərd, B -əd] *s.* (zool.) enodio.
stagger ['stægər, B -ə] *v.i.* hacer eses, bambolear, tambalear, vacilar, titubear. —*v.t.* 1. hacer tambalear o titubear; (fig.) dejar perplejo, asombrar. 2. escalonar, espaciar (horas de trabajo, etc.); arreglar en intervalos. 3. (aer.) escalonar (las alas de un biplano). —*s.* 1. tambaleo, bamboleo, vacilación. 2. (aer.) decalaje (de los planos de un avión). 3. *pl.* (*sing. en const.*) (vet.) modorra, torneo.
staggerer [-ərər, B -ərə] *s.* argumento o suceso desconcertantes.
staggering [-ərɪŋ] *a.* asombroso; tambaleante.
staggie [-ɪ] *s.* (esco.) potre.
staghound [-ˌhaʊnd] *s.* (zool.) sabueso (grande para cazar ciervos).
stagily ['steɪdʒəlɪ] *adv.* teatralmente.
staging ['steɪdʒɪŋ] *s.* 1. andamio, tablado; andamiaje, cadalso. 2. (teat.) puesta en escena, escenificación, representación. 3. servicio de diligencias (coches). 4. viaje en diligencias. 5. (mil.) estacionamiento (de tropas o efectos).
staging area, (mil.) zona de estacionamiento (de tropas).
stagnancy ['stægnənsɪ] *s.* estancamiento, estancación; paralización.
stagnant [-nənt] *a.* estancado, estático; inactivo, paralizado.
stagnate [-ˌneɪt, B stæg'neɪt] *v.i.* estancarse; vegetar.
stagnation [stæg'neɪʃən] *s.* estancamiento, estancación; inactividad, paralización.
stag party, tertulia para hombres solos.
stagy ['steɪdʒɪ] *a.* teatral, teátrico.
staid [steɪd] *a.* formal, sobrio, serio, sentado, juicioso.
staid, *p.p. de* **stay.**
staidly ['steɪdlɪ] *adv.* juiciosamente, sobriamente, seriamente.
staidness [-nəs] *s.* sobriedad, seriedad, formalidad.
stain [steɪn] *v.t.* 1. manchar; ensuciar, emporcar, macular. 2. colocar, teñir; tiznar. 3. (fig.) manchar, mancillar, desdorar; corromper. —*v.i.* 1. mancharse. 2. manchar, hacer manchas. —*s.* 1. mancha, mácula; descoloramiento; descoloración. 2. (fig.) mancha, borrón, estigma. 3. tinte, tintura; solución colorante (usada en microscopía).
stainable ['steɪnəbəl] *a.* teñible.
stained glass, vidrio de color.
stained-glass window, vitral.
stainer ['steɪnər, B -ə] *s.* 1. tintorero. 2. tintura, tinte, color.
stainless [-ləs] *a.* 1. inmaculado, limpio, acendrado, sin estigma. 2. inoxidable, inmanchable.
stainlessly [-lɪ] *adv.* limpiamente.
stainless steel, acero inoxidable.
stair [stɛr, B stɛə] *s.* 1. escalón, peldaño. 2. (*gen. pl.*) escaleras, escalinata. 3. **below stairs,** en el cuartel de los sirvientes; **flight of stairs,** tramo de escalera.
staircase ['stɛrˌkeɪs, B 'stɛəˌ-] *s.* escalera (con su armazón), escalinata.
stairhead [-ˌhɛd] *s.* rellano o meseta de escalera.
stair landing, rellano, descansillo, descanso (Amer.).
stair rail, pasamano de escalera.
stairway [-ˌweɪ] *s.* escalera.
stairwell [-ˌwɛl] *s.* caja de escalera, pozo o cañón de escalera.
stake [steɪk] *s.* 1. estaca, palo, hito. 2. poste de la hoguera; (fig.) suplicio de la hoguera. 3. telero, varal de carros. 4. apuesta, posta, puesta. 5. aporte, contribución, interés (en empresa, etc.). 6. (*pl.*) premio (de una carrera, esp. de caballos). 7. (relig.) división territorial de la iglesia mormona bajo un obispo. 8. **at s.,** envuelto, implicado; en juego; comprometido; **to die at the s.,** morir en la hoguera; **to have a s. in,** tener dinero invertido en, tener intereses (económicos) en; **to have at s.,** arriesgar, ej., *I have my whole fortune at s. in this venture,* arriesgo toda mi fortuna en esta empresa; **to pull up stakes,** (fam.) irse, mudarse. —*v.t.* 1. marcar con estacas (límites, camino, etc.). 2. estacar, atar a una estaca, asegurar con estacas. 3. (gen. con *on*) arriesgar, aventurar; apostar. 4. abastecer (a un buscador de minas); dar o prestar dinero o capital a (persona). 5. **s. all,** jugarse el todo por el todo; apostar el resto; aventurarlo todo; **s. out,** estacar, estaquillar; delimitar (una mina).
stake boat, bote anclado (que sirve de hito para señalar el curso de una regata).
stake body, (aut.) chasis de plataforma con teleros (de autocamión).
stake driver, (orn.) avetoro.
stakeholder ['steɪkˌhoʊldər, B -də] *s.* depositario de una apuesta.
stake truck, autocamión de plataforma con teleros.
stakhanovism [stə'kɑnəˌvɪzəm] *s.* (de Aleksei Stakhanov, minero soviético) estajanovismo, sistema en la Unión Soviética por el cual se retribuye a los trabajadores por su celo y diligencia.
stalactite [stə'læktaɪt, B 'stælək-] *s.* (geol.) estalactita.
stalactitic [ˌstælˌæk'tɪtɪk] *a.* estalactítico.
stalag ['stɑlˌɑg, B 'stælæg-] *s.* campo de prisioneros (en Alemania).
stalagmite [stə'lægmaɪt, B 'stæləg-] *s.* (geol.) estalagmita.
stalagmitic [ˌstælˌæg'mɪtɪk] *a.* estalagmítico.
stalagmometer [-'mɑmətər, B -'mɔmɪtə] *s.* estalagmómetro.
stale [steɪl] *a.* 1. añejo, viejo, rancio, pasado. ej., *s. bread,* pan viejo, *s. air,* aire viciado. 2. (fig.) gastado, trillado; añejo, anticuado, ej., *s. joke,* chiste trillado, *s. news,* noticia añeja. 3. pasado de entrenamiento (atleta); decaído, menoscabado. 4. (der., com.) caducado, atrasado. —*v.t.* añejar, enranciar. —*v.i.* 1. volverse añejo o rancio. 2. (fig.) perder su novedad. 3. orinar (el ganado). —*s.* orina del ganado.
stalely ['steɪllɪ] *adv.* (raro) con olor o sabor añejo o rancio.
stalemate [-ˌmeɪt] *s.* 1. (ajedrez) ahogado, ahogo del rey. 2. estancamiento, estancación; punto muerto. —*v.t.* 1. (ajedrez) ahogar (al rey). 2. estancar, paralizar.
staleness [-nəs] *s.* 1. ranciedad, rancidez, vejez. 2. antigüedad. 3. calidad de vencido, caducidad (de un documento, etc.).
Stalinism ['stɑləˌnɪzəm] *s.* estalinismo.
stalk [stɔk] *v.i.* 1. acercarse cautelosamente a una presa. 2. caminar airosamente; andar majestuosamente, taconear. 3. (fig.) rondar, merodear (enfermedad, peste, etc.). 4. (ant.) pasar o caminar furtivamente. —*v.t.* cazar al acecho; acechar (una presa), registrar (terreno, bosque, etc.) en busca de caza. —*s.* 1. tallo, troncho. 2. (zool.) cañón de pluma. 3. (bot.) pecíolo, pedúnculo, cabillo, pedículo. 4. caza al acecho. 5. paso airoso, andar majestuoso, taconeo.
stalked [stɔkt] *a.* talludo, tronchudo.
stalker ['stɔkər, B -ə] *s.* cazador al acecho.
stalking-horse [-ɪŋˌhɔrs, B -hɔs] *s.* 1. buey de cabestrillo. 2. (fig.) pretexto, disfraz. 3. (pol.) candidato falso (que se divide la oposición o que oculta la candidatura real de alguien).
stalkless [-ləs] *a.* sin tallo, sin troncho.
stall [stɔl] *s.* 1. establo, cuadra, caballeriza; pesebre, casilla de establo. 2. puesto; parada, tabanco; mostrador. 3. banca con brazos; banco, sitial de coro (en iglesia). 4. (fig.) dignidad, oficio (eclesiástico). 5. (teat., G.B.) luneta, butaca; (*pl.*) lunetas (fila de butacas situadas frente a la orquesta). 6. lugar de estacionamiento de un automóvil. 7. pérdida de velocidad. —*v.t.* 1. poner o guardar en establo, estabular. 2. atollar, atascar. 3. parar, ahogar (motor). 4. (ant.) engordar o cebar en el pesebre. —*v.i.* 1. atollarse, atascarse. 2. pararse, ahogarse (motor). 3. (fam.) no esforzarse. 4. (aer.) perder velocidad bruscamente, entrar en pérdida (el avión).
stall, *v.t.* (fam.) (ú. gen. con *off*) evitar, rehuir, esquivar, obstruir, traer en palabras (a uno); despachar de (alguien). —*v.i.* dar largas al asunto, andar con rodeos, ganar tiempo. —*s.* excusa, disculpa, pretexto.

stall-fed ['stɔl,fɛd] *a.* engordado en pesebre (ganado).

stall-feed [-,fid] *v.t.* cebar en un pesebre.

stalling speed, (avia.) velocidad crítica.

stallion ['stæljən] *s.* caballo padre, semental, garañón, padrillo (Am.).

stall landing, (avia.) aterrizaje con velocidad crítica, desplome.

stalwart ['stɔlwərt, B -wət] *a.* 1. fornido, forzudo, robusto, fuerte. 2. bravo, valiente, denodado. 3. resuelto, determinado, firme, ej., *s. supporters,* partidarios resueltos. —*s.* 1. persona fuerte o corpulenta. 2. partidario fiel y leal.

stalwartly [-lɪ] *adv.* firmemente, resueltamente.

stalwartness [-nəs] *s.* 1. fortaleza, corpulencia. 2. resolución, determinación, firmeza.

stamen ['steɪmən] *s.* (bot.) estambre.

stamina ['stæmənə] *s.* vigor, fibra, nervio, aguante.

staminal ['stæmənəl] *a.* (bot.) estamíneo, estaminal.

staminate ['stæmənət] *a.* (bot.) estaminado, provisto de estambres; estaminífero.

staminiferous [,stæmə'nɪfərəs] *a.* (bot.) estaminífero.

staminode ['stæmə,noʊd] **staminodium** [,stæmə'noʊdɪəm] *s.* (bot.) estaminodio.

staminody ['stæmə,noʊdɪ] *s.* (bot.) metamorfosis en estambre (de un órgano de la flor).

stammel ['stæməl] *s.* 1. (ant.) ropa interior de lana burda (roja) usada por monjes medievales. 2. color rojo parecido al que se usaba para teñir estas ropas.

stammer ['stæmər, B -ə] *v.t., v.i.* tartamudear, balbucear. —*s.* tartamudeo, balbuceo.

stammerer [-ərər, B -ərə] *s.* tartamudo.

stammeringly [-ərɪŋlɪ] *adv.* con tartamudeo, balbuceando.

stamp [stæmp] *v.t.* 1. patear, pisotear, hollar. 2. estampar, cortar con molde, moldear, troquelar, acuñar. 3. imprimir, sellar, estampar. 4. marcar, signar; (fig). marcar, caracterizar, señalar; estigmatizar. 5. (fig.) grabar (en la memoria, etc.). 6. estampillar, sellar; timbrar. 7. triturar, bocartear, pulverizar (minerales). 8. **s. out,** apagar pisoteando (fuego); extirpar, erradicar, acabar, destruir. —*v.i.* 1. patear, patalear. 2. (ant.) golpear, aplastar. 3. caminar con pasos pesados. —*s.* 1. estampado, estampación. 2. troquel, molde, cuña; mano, majadero (para triturar minerales). 3. estampado, marca, impresión. 4. sello (de correo), estampilla (Amer.); timbre (fiscal, etc.). 5. (fig.) estampa, carácter, calaña, laya.

stamp collector, coleccionista de sellos de correo, coleccionista de estampillas (Amer.).

stampede [stæm'pid] *s.* 1. desbocamiento, estampida (Amer.) (de animales). 2. fuga precipitada, pánico. —*v.i.* dispersarse en desorden, huir por pánico; salir de estampía. —*v.t.* 1. hacer huir por pánico. 2. (fig.) ahuyentar, precipitar.

stamped envelope, sobre con sello, listo para ser enviado por correo.

stamper ['stæmpər, B -pə] *s.* 1. estampador; impresor. 2. mano de almirez, mazo, martillo, pilón, pisón. 3. máquina trituradora. 4. máquina de estampar.

stamping ground, (fam.) territorio personal, lugar predilecto, guarida.

stamping machine, (maq.) estampadora, troqueladora.

stamping mill, stamp mill, (min.) bocarte, molino de pisones o de bocarte; batería de mazos.

stamping press, (maq.) prensa de estampar o de troquelar.

stamp pad, almohadilla entintada.

stance [stæns] *s.* 1. postura, posición (esp. en golf, criquet, etc.). 2. actitud o posición moral o intelectual. 3. (esco.) solar, sitio, situación.

stanch [stɔntʃ, B stɑntʃ] *var. de* **staunch.** —*v.t.* restañar (la sangre); taponar (una herida). —*v.i.* restañarse. —*a.* 1. hermético (juntura, etc.), a prueba de agua (estanco, barco). 2. sólido, firme, constante, leal, fiel (amigo, partidario, etc.).

stanchion ['stæntʃən, B 'stɑnʃən] *s.* 1. montante, puntal, asnilla, poste. 2. par de puntales en forma de yugo (al que se unce el ganado en su pesebre). 3. (mar.) puntal candelero. 4. (min.) pie derecho, ademe, estemple. —*v.t.* 1. apuntalar, asegurar con pilares o columnas. 2. encerrar (el ganado) en su pesebre con un par de puntales.

stand [stænd] *v.i.* (*pret., p.p.* STOOD [stud]; *p.pr.* STANDING) 1. estar de pie, quedarse en pie. tenerse derecho, ej., *he was too tired to s.,* estaba demasiado cansado para quedarse en pie. 2. ponerse de pie; enderezarse, pararse (Amer.) 3. erguirse, levantarse; tener (cierta) altura, ej., *an old tree stands in the garden,* un árbol viejo se yergue en el jardín. *he stands six feet,* tiene seis pies de altura. 4. estar (en cierta posición o situación); hallarse, ej., *how does the matter s now?* ¿cómo está el asunto ahora? 5. cotizarse, ej., *cotton stands higher than ever,* el algodón se cotiza (a un precio) más alto que nunca. 6. detenerse, pararse, quedarse, pausar, ej., *don't s. there arguing,* no te quedes ahí discutiendo. 7. durar, perdurar, permanecer, subsistir; quedar, ej., *the passage must s.,* el pasaje debe quedar (en libro, documento, etc.). 8. mantenerse, no ceder; persistir, perseverar. 9. estancarse, juntarse (agua en un charco, lágrimas en los ojos, etc.). 10. (mar.) mantener o poner cierto rumbo. 11. (caza) apuntar, señalar (el perro). 12. (gen. G.B.) ser candidato a funcionario público. 13. all **standing,** (mar.) sin tiempo para arriar las velas; (fig.) tomado por sorpresa; **how do you s. in the matter of (fuel,** etc.)? ¿cómo andan ustedes de (combustible, etc.); **s. about,** estar parado en un sitio, remolonear; **s. aloof,** aislarse, retraerse, apartarse; **s. aside,** hacerse a un lado; **s. against,** oponerse, combatir, estar en contra; **s. at attention,** (mil.) cuadrarse; **s. at ease,** (mil.) descansar; **s. back,** cejar, dar un paso hacia atrás; ceder el paso; **s. by,** estar cerca, ser espectador pasivo; estar alerta, mantenerse preparado, alistarse (para actuar, prestar ayuda, etc.); (rad.) estar listo para recibir o transmitir señales; **s. by (person, promise, terms),** (fig.) tomar partido por, apoyar, sostener, ayudar a (persona); cumplir con, acatar (promesa, condiciones); **s. clear (of),** no mezclarse en (asuntos); **s. convicted (of murder,** etc.), ser convicto (de homicidio, etc.); **s. corrected,** reconocer su error, aceptar la corrección; **s. down,** retirarse; (der.) abandonar el estrado de testigos; (mil.) salir de la guardia; **s. fast,** no cejar, no ceder; **s. for,** representar, significar, simbolizar; postular, ser candidato para (oficio, diputado, etc.); defender, abogar por; (fam.) soportar, tolerar; consentir (algo); **s. in good stead,** servir, ser útil; **s. in for,** reemplazar; **s. in line,** hacer cola, ponerse en línea; **s. in one's light,** taparle a uno la luz; **s. in the way,** ser un obstáculo o impedimento; **s. in with,** gozar del favor de; **s. off,** apartarse, mantenerse a distancia; (mar.) retirarse (barco) de la costa; **s. off and on,** (mar.) navegar alternando el curso (para no perder de vista una marca); **s. on** (o **upon**), insistir en, cumplir u observar a la letra (esp. ceremonia, etiqueta, etc.); depender de; **s. on,** (mar.) seguir el mismo curso; estar sostenido por, ej., *the table stands on four legs,* la mesa está sostenida por cuatro patas; **s. on end (hair),** ponérsele de punta (los pelos) a uno; **s. on one's own feet** (o **legs**), valerse por sí mismo; **s. out,** destacarse, resaltar, perdurar, persistir, mantenerse firme; **s. over,** vigilar, supervisar; **s. pat,** (fam.) estarse o mantenerse en sus trece, oponerse a cambios; **s. still,** no moverse, permanecer quieto; estancarse; **s. to,** (mil.) ocupar puesto de alerta, estar listo para entrar en acción; **s. to reason,** ser lógico, ser justo; **s. to sea,** (mar.) poner rumbo al mar, llevar la proa al mar; **s. to win** (o **lose**), esperar ganar (o perder); **s. together,** mantenerse unidos; **s. up,** ponerse de pie, quedarse en pie; (fig.) mantenerse (argumento, prueba, etc.); **s. up for,** ponerse al lado de, apoyar, sacar la cara por, defender (persona, causa); **s. up to,** hacer frente a, enfrentar resueltamente (oponente, peligro, etc.); no gastarse (por uso), resistir (uso); **s. well with (one's superiors,** etc.), estar bien considerado uno por (sus jefes, etc.); **s. with,** estar por, apoyar; aliarse con; **where do we s.?** ¿en qué quedamos? —*v.t.* 1. hacer pararse, poner derecho, poner de pie; colocar, poner (en cierta posición), ej., *s. (something) on the table,* colocar algo sobre la mesa. 2. soportar, sufrir, tolerar, aguantar, ej., *I could never s. him,* nunca le pude aguantar, *he will s. no nonsense,* no suele tolerar tonterías. 3. sostener, soportar, aguantar, resistir, ej., *s. fire,* aguantar el fuego (del enemigo). 4. someterse a, pasar por, enfrentar, afrontar, ej., *s. the test,* pasar (por) la prueba. 5. invitar (a brindar), pagar por (bebida, comida, etc.). 6. encontrarse; librar o trabar, ej., *s. battle,* librar batalla. 7. **s. a chance (of),** tener una posibilidad (de); **s. (someone) in good stead,** ser útil, servir a (alguien); **s. (someone) off,** tener (a alguien) a raya; repeler, rechazar (a alguien); **s. (something) off,** aplazar, dejar para más tarde (algo); **s. one's ground,** no ceder, resistir, mantenerse firme (en lucha, discusión, etc.); **s. (someone) up,** dar esquinazo a, faltar a una cita con, dejar plantado a (alguien). —*s.* 1. parada, alto, detención. 2. posición, postura; actitud, opinión. 3. puesto, sitio, posición, situación. 4. estrado, plataforma, tribuna; (E.U.) estrado de testigos. 5. mostrador, puesto (en mercado, exposición, feria, etc.). 6. pedestal, descanso, atril. 7. lugar de estacionamiento (para vehículos). 8. (teat.) parada (durante la gira de una compañía en las ciudades donde dan función). 9. herbaje, cosecha (de trigo, centeno, etc.) de pie. 10. (*gen. pl.*) (E.U.) graderías (estadio, etc.). 11. (Aust.) (madera obtenible de un) bosque (en su aspecto comercial). 12. **to come to a s.,** detenerse; **to make a s.,** detenerse y hacer resistencia; **to take one's s.,** decidirse, pronunciarse, ej., *I'll take my s. when I've heard your arguments,* me pronunciaré cuando haya escuchado sus argumentos; **to take the s.,** subir al estrado de testigos.

standard ['stændərd, B dəd] *s.* 1. bandera, estandarte, pabellón, pendón, enseña. 2. patrón (de medida o peso). 3. nivel; norma, regla fija. 4. tipo, modelo, ejemplo. 5. criterio, pauta. 6. soporte, pie, base; columna, posta, pilar. 7. (tec.) pie derecho; montante; caballete. 8. ley del oro o de la plata (en las monedas); peso legal (de las monedas). 9. (bot.) planta erecta. 10. (G.B.) clase, año (de escuela). —*a.* 1. de ley, de patrón. 2. normal, corriente (precio, tamaño, etc.). 3. de autoridad, de autoridad reconocida (obra, libro, etc.). 4. corriente, regular (equipo, etc.). 5. reglamentario, de reglamento (abastecimientos, etc.). 6. oficial (tiempo, inglés, etc.). 7. (impr.) normal.

standard atmosphere, (meteor.) atmósfera tipo o patrón.
standard-bearer [-ˌbɛrər, B -ˌbɛərə] *s.* 1. (mil.) abanderado, portaestandarte. 2. (fig.) (pol.) abanderado, jefe (de una organización o movimiento).
standardbred [-ˌbrɛd] *s.* caballo ligero, de trote y de paso, criado en los E.U.
standard candle, bujía (unidad lumínica).
standard cell, (elec.) pila patrón.
standard deviation, (estadística) medida de dispersión en una distribución.
standard error, error tabular (en balística, estadística).
standard frequency, (rad.) frecuencia patrón, frecuencia normal.
standard gauge, 1. (mec.) calibre, plantilla. 2. (f.c.) trocha normal, vía normal.
standardization [ˌstændərdə'zerʃən, B -dədaɪ-] *s.* uniformación, normalización.
standardize ['stændərˌdaɪz, B -dəˌ-] *v.t.* uniformar, normalizar.
standardizer [-ər, B -ə] *s.* uniformador, normalizador.
standard of living, nivel de vida, norma de vida.
standard pitch, 1. (aer.) paso nominal. 2. (mús.) diapasón normal.
standard rigging, (mar.) jarcia firme.
standard solution, (quím.) solución normal, solución valorada o volumétrica.
standard specification, especificación modelo o normal.
standard time, hora legal, hora oficial.
standby ['stændˌbaɪ] *s.* 1. partidario fiel, persona de confianza, paño de lágrimas. 2. reserva, sustituto. 3. persona que espera lugar disponible para viajar (gen. en avión).
standee [stæn'di] *s.* (fam.) espectador de pie (en una función).
stand-in ['stændˌɪn] *s.* substituto; doble (esp. de un actor de cine).
standing ['stændɪŋ] *a.* 1. de pie, en pie; derecho, vertical, recto, enhiesto, erguido, parado (Amer.). 2. parado, inactivo; estancado, ej., *s. water,* agua estancada. 3. duradero, permanente, establecido; estable; constante, ej., *s. committee,* comisión permanente. 4. de pedestal, de pie. 5. que se hace de pie o en pie. —*s.* 1. postura, posición. 2. puesto, paraje. 3. posición, reputación, categoría. 4. duración, antigüedad. 5. **of good s.,** de importancia, de consecuencia; **of long s.,** de larga duración, de hace mucho tiempo; **with official s.,** de posición oficial, de categoría oficial.
standing army, ejército permanente.
standing committee, (pol., der.) comisión o comité permanente.
standing order, 1. reglamento vigente (en el parlamento). 2. (com.) orden o pedido permanente.
standing rigging, (mar.) jarcias muertas, obencadura, jarcia firme.
standing room, (teat.) entrada general (sin asiento ni numeración), espacio para estar de pie durante la función.
standing wave, 1. (fís.) onda estacionaria. 2. (hidr., opt.) marejada de reflexión, de fija o estacionaria.
standish ['stændɪʃ] *s.* (ant.) tintero.
stand of arms, (mil.) armamento, pertrechos (completos de un soldado).
stand of colours, (mil.) juego de banderas (de un regimiento).
standoff ['stændˌɔf] *s.* 1. alejamiento, retraimiento, apartamiento, retiro. 2. empate, tablas.
standoff insulator, aislador de pie.
standoffish [ˌstænd'ɔfɪʃ] *a.* reservado, frío, inamistoso; estirado, entonado (en el trato).
stand oil, aceite de linaza hervido (usado en pintura, barnices, etc.).
standout ['stændˌaʊt] *s.* 1. persona destacada o descollante. 2. (fam.) individualista, solitario. 3. opositor.
standpat [-ˌpæt] *a.* (fam.) inflexible, inmovible; opuesto a cambios; conservador; (que está) plantado en sus trece.
standpatter [-ər, B -ə] *s.* (E.U.) político inflexible (que se atiene estrictamente al programa de su partido).
standpipe [-ˌpaɪp] *s.* tubo vertical, torre depósito, depósito regulador o columna reguladora (de agua).
standpoint [-ˌpɔɪnt] *s.* punto de vista.
standstill [-ˌstɪl] *s.* parada, detención, alto; at a s., parado, atascado, paralizado; **to come to a s.,** detenerse, pararse, cesar. —*a.* parado, estático.
stand-up [-ˌʌp] *a.* 1. recto, derecho, vertical, enhiesto, erguido. 2. (fam.) (que se hace o toma) de pie.
stanhope ['stænəp] *s.* cabriolé ligero.
stank, *pret. de* **stink.**
stannary ['stænərɪ] *s.* (G.B.) mina de estaño; fundición de estaño.
stannate [-ˌeɪt, B -ət] *s.* (quím.) estannato.
stannic [-ɪk] *a.* (quím.) estánnico.
stannite [-ˌaɪt] *s.* (min.) estannita.
stannous [-əs] (quím.) estañoso, estannoso.
stannum [-əm] *s.* (min.) estaño.
stanza ['stænzə] *s.* (poét.) estancia, estrofa.
stapedial [stə'pidɪəl] *a.* (anat.) del estribo.
stapedius [stə'pidɪəs] *s.* (*pl.* STAPEDII [-aɪ]) (anat.) estapedio.
stapelia [stə'pilɪə] *s.* (bot.) variedad africana del algodoncillo.
stapes ['steɪpiz] *s.* (*pl.* STAPES o STAPEDES [-pədiz]) (anat.) estribo.
staphylococcal [ˌstæfəloʊ'kakəl, B -lə'kɔk-] **staphylococcic** [-'kaksɪk, B 'kɔk-] *a.* causado por el estafilococo, estafilocócico.
staphylococcia [-'kaksɪə, B -'kɔk-] *s.* (med.) estafilococia.
staphylococcus [-'kakəs, B -'kɔk-] *s.* (*pl.* STAPHYLOCOCCI [-'kaksaɪ, B -'kɔk-]) (bact.) estafilococo.
staphyloma [ˌstæfə'loʊmə] *s.* (med.) estafiloma.
staphylorrhaphy [-'lɔrəfɪ] *s.* (med.) estafilorrafia.
staphylotomy [-'latəmɪ, B -'lɔt-] *s.* (*pl.* STAPHYLOTOMIES) (med.) estafilotomía.
staple ['steɪpəl] *s.* 1. grapa, grampa (Amer.) (para juntar papeles, sujetar alambres, etc.). 2. armella (de candado). —*v.t.* engrapar, engrampar (Amer.) (papeles, etc.); fijar con grapa(s).
staple, *s.* 1. renglón principal de comercio; producto o artículo principal. 2. (fig.) elemento principal, tema central. 3. materia prima, materia bruta. 4. emporio, mercado, almacén. 5. fibra, hebra (de algodón, lana, etc., que indica su calidad). —*a.* 1. principal, prominente, ej., *s. food,* alimento principal o básico. 2. establecido, reconocido. —*v.t.* clasificar (hebras textiles) según la longitud.
stapler [-plər, B -plə] *s.* 1. negociante en artículos principales de consumo. 2. clasificador (de lana, algodón, etc.). 3. engrapador, abrochador, engrampador (Amer.).
staple ring, (mec.) argolla con espiga.
star [star, B sta] *s.* 1. estrella, astro. 2. (figura de) estrella. 3. condecoración, medalla, insignia (en forma de estrella). 4. estrella (de teatro, cine); astro (de un deporte). 5. (fig.) estrella, suerte, hado. 6. **to be born under a lucky s.,** nacer con buena estrella; **to see stars,** (fig.) ver las (lucky) estrellas; **to thank one's (lucky) stars,** estar agradecido por su buena estrella. —*v.t.* (*pret., p.p.* STARRED; *p.pr.* STARRING) 1. estrellar, adornar con estrellas; adornar con lentejuelas o brichos. 2. marcar con estrellas; marcar con asterisco. 3. (teat., cinem.) presentar como estrella. —*v.i.* 1. brillar como estrella; brillar, ser prominente. 2. (teat., cinem.) desempeñarse o figurar como estrella. —*a.* 1. estrellado, estrellar. 2. (fig.) excelente, sobresaliente, preeminente.
star apple, (bot.) caimito (árbol y fruta).
star bit, broca estrellada.
starboard ['starbərd, B 'stabəd] (mar.) *s.* estribor. —*a.* de estribor. —*adv.* a estribor. —*v.t., v.i.* poner (timón) o moverse (barco) hacia estribor.
starch [startʃ, B statʃ] *s.* 1. almidón, fécula. 2. (fig.) manera estirada y formal, rigidez, inflexibilidad, tiesura. 3. (jer., E.U.) energía, vigor, ánimo. —*v.t.* almidonar.
Star Chamber, (G.B., hist.) antiguo tribunal británico de inquisición, aborrecido por la injusticia y crueldad de sus sentencias.
star-chamber ['star'tʃeɪmbər, B 'sta'-bə] *a.* clandestino, arbitrario, despiadado.
starchiness ['startʃɪnəs, B 'statʃɪ-] *s.* (fig.) rigidez.
starchy ['startʃɪ, B 'statʃɪ] *a.* (STARCHIER; STARCHIEST) 1. almidonado. 2. (fig.) tieso, estirado, rígido.
star connection, (elec.) conexión en estrella.
star-crossed ['starˌkrɔst, B 'staˌ-] *a.* con el santo de espaldas, con mala suerte, de mala estrella, ej., *the s-c. lovers,* Romeo y Julieta.
stardom ['stardəm, B 'stadəm] *s.* 1. estrellato, condición de estrella (de cine, etc.). 2. grupo de estrellas.
star drill, barrena de cruz, barrena de filo de cruz.
star dust, 1. nebulosa. 2. polvo cósmico.
stardust [-ˌdʌst] *s.* (fig.) embeleso, encanto.
stare [stɛr, B stɛə] *v.i.* 1. fijar la vista. 2. saltar a la vista, llamar la atención. 3. erizarse (el pelo). 4. **s. at,** mirar con fijeza, mirar con asombro; **s. into,** fijar la vista en, dirigir una mirada fija a. —*v.t.* 1. mirar fijamente, clavar la vista en, fijar la vista en, encararse con; mirar de hito en hito, mirar descaradamente. 2. **s. down,** hacer bajar la vista con la mirada; amedrentar con la mirada; **s. (one) in the face,** saltar (a uno) a la cara; ser inminente para (uno). —*s.* mirada fija.
star facet, faceta de la corona (del brillante).
starfish ['starˌfɪʃ, B 'staˌ-] *s.* (zool.) estrellamar, estrella de mar, asteria.
starflower [-ˌflaʊər, B -ə] *s.* (bot.) leche de gallina.
stargaze [-ˌgeɪz] *v.i.* 1. observar las estrellas. 2. soñar despierto, fantasear.
stargazer [-ˌgeɪzər, B -zə] *s.* 1. (hum.) astrólogo; astrónomo. 2. (ict.) uranoscópido.
stargazing [-zɪŋ] *s.* 1. observación de las estrellas. 2. (fig.) distracción, distraimiento, abstracción.
staring ['stɛrɪŋ, B 'stɛər-] *a.* 1. que mira fijamente. 2. conspicuo, llamativo, chillón.
stark [stark, B stak] *a.* 1. tieso, rígido. 2. (fig.) rígido, riguroso, duro; estricto. 3. (fig.) severo (clima). 4. (fig.) árido, desolado (paraje, escena, etc.). 5. simple, sin adorno, pelado, austero. 6. completo, absoluto, total, ej., *s. folly,* locura completa. 7. (dial., poét.) intratable, obstinado, tereo. 8. (ant.) fuerte, fornido. —*adv.* 1. rígidamente. 2. severamente, rigurosamente. 3.

absolutamente; completamente. 4. **s. raving mad,** loco de atar; **s. naked,** en cueros (vivos), en pelota.

starkly ['stɑrklɪ, B 'stɑk-] *adv.* 1. rigurosamente, severamente. 2. áridamente.

starless ['stɑrləs, B 'stɑlɪs] *a.* sin estrellas.

starlet [-lət] *s.* 1. estrellita, estrella pequeña. 2. (teat., cinem.) estrella joven, estrella en cierne.

starlight [-ˌlaɪt] *s.* luz de las estrellas.

starlike [-ˌlaɪk] *a.* 1. estrellado, como una estrella. 2. brillante, rutilante.

starling ['stɑrlɪŋ, B 'stɑlɪŋ] *s.* 1. (orn.) estornino. 2. (arq.) tajamar, espolón, estancada de protección (de los pilares en los puentes).

starlit ['stɑrˌlɪt, B 'stɑˌ-] *a.* iluminado por las estrellas, bajo la luz de las estrellas.

Star of Bethlehem, estrella de Belén.

star-of-Bethlehem['stɑrəv'beθlɪˌhem] *s.* (bot.) leche de gallina, leche de pájaro, matacandiles.

Star of David [-'deɪvəd] estrella de David, emblema del Estado de Israel.

star polygon, (geom.) polígono estrellado.

starred [stɑrd, B stɑd] *a.* 1. estrellado (cielo). 2. marcado con una estrella. 3. (teat.) presentado como estrella.

starred angles, columna de dos ángulos formando cruz, ángulos en cruz.

starry ['stɑrɪ] *a.* (STARRIER; STARRIEST) 1. estrellar, de las estrellas (luz, etc.). 2. estrellado, tachonado de estrellas (cielo, noche, etc.). 3. brillante, rutilante, centelleante, titilante. 4. (fig.) estelar, etéreo (altura, aspiración, etc.).

starry-eyed [-ˌaɪd] *a.* (fam.) visionario, soñador.

Stars and Bars, (E.U., hist.) barras y estrellas (primera bandera de la Confederación de los Estados del Sur).

Stars and Stripes, estrellas y listas, franjas y estrellas (nombre popular de la bandera de los E.U.).

star sapphire, (min.) zafiro estrellado.

starshake ['stɑrˌʃeɪk, B 'stɑˌ-] *s.* cuadranura, pata de gallina.

star shell, (mil.) bengala de estrella.

star shower, lluvia de estrellas; caída de meteoritos.

star-spangled [-ˌspæŋgəld] *a.* estrellado, tachonado de estrellas.

Star-Spangled Banner, estrellas y listas (nombre popular de la bandera de E.U. y del poema adoptado como letra del himno nacional de E.U.).

star switch, (elec.) interruptor de estrella.

start [stɑrt, B stɑt] *v.i.* 1. sobresaltarse, dar un brinco, asustarse. 2. sobresalir, salir fuera, desorbitarse. 3. comenzar, empezar. 4. partir, salir. 5. aflojarse, descoyuntarse. 6. **s. after,** salir en busca de; **s. back,** dar un respingo; emprender el viaje de regreso; **s. for,** ponerse en camino hacia; **s. from,** salir fuera de, saltar de; brotar, manar; **s. in (to do),** (fam.) principiar, empezar, comenzar (a hacer); **s. in one's sleep,** despertarse sobresaltado; **s. off,** partir, ponerse en marcha; **s. out (to do),** (fam.) ponerse a (hacer algo); **to s. with,** en primer término; al principio. —*v.t.* 1. poner en marcha, poner en movimiento, hacer mover o funcionar; (mec.) hacer arrancar. 2. principiar, comenzar, empezar; iniciar, originar. 3. inscribir, hacer participar (en carrera, competencia, etc.). 4. levantar, hacer salir (caza). 5. fundar, establecer (empresa, etc.). 6. aflojar, dislocar. 7. verter, vaciar. 8. emplear, ej., *the company started him as an office boy,* la compañía le empleó primero como mensajero. 9. (esco.) espantar, asustar. 10. **s. (doing** o **to do),** empezar a (hacer), ej., *he started reading,* empezó a leer, *it started to rain,* empezó a llover; **s. something,** armar un lío. —*s.* 1. principio, comienzo. 2. sobresalto, respingo, susto. 3. impulso, ímpetu, arranque, pronto. 4. salida, partida. 5. lugar de partida; fuente de origen o procedencia. 6. ventaja, delantera (en una competencia). 7. **at the s.,** al principio, al primer paso; **by fits and starts,** a saltos y a corcovos; **to give a s.,** tener un sobresalto, sobresaltarse; **to give (someone) a s.,** dar su primer trabajo a, iniciar en el trabajo (a alguien), ayudar a establecerse (a alguien); car ventaja a (alguien); **to give (something) a s.,** poner en marcha (algo); **to make a s.,** empezar; **to make a fresh s.,** empezar de nuevo, volver a empezar, recomenzar.

starter ['stɑrtər, B 'stɑtə] *s.* 1. iniciador. 2. despachador (de un vehículo). 3. (aut., elec.) arrancador, auto-arrancador, arranque, mecanismo de arranque. 4. (dep.) juez de salida o partida. 5. (dep.) competidor (inscrito en una carrera, etc.). 6. **as a s.,** para comenzar, para empezar, como aperitivo.

star thistle, (bot.) (variedad de) cardo estrellado, tríbudo, abrojo, calcitrapa.

starting box [-ɪŋ-] (elec.) arrancador, reóstato o caja de arranque.

starting button, (elec., aut.) botón de arranque.

starting crank, (aut.) manivela de arranque.

starting motor, motor de arranque.

starting point, punto de partida.

starting post, (dep.) poste de partida.

starting price, cotización de ventaje al empezar la carrera, precio inicial.

starting torque, momento de torsión de arranque.

startle ['stɑrtəl, B 'stɑt-] *v.i.* sobresaltarse, asustarse, sorprenderse. —*v.t.* sobresaltar, asustar, dar un susto a, alarmar. —*s.* sobresalto, susto, alarma; respingo.

startling ['stɑrtlɪŋ, B 'stɑt-] *a.* pasmoso, alarmante; sorprendente, asombroso.

startlingly [-lɪ] *adv.* en forma alarmante, alarmantemente.

start-up ['stɑrtˌʌp, B 'stɑt-] *s.* arranque, puesta en marcha.

star turn, (pr. G.B.) número principal (en teatro).

starvation [stɑr'veɪʃən, B stɑ'-] *s.* 1. hambre, inanición. 2. (med.) síndrome clínico de hombre.

starvation wages, salarios inhumanamente bajos.

starve [stɑrv, B stɑv] *v.i* 1. hambrear, padecer hambre, morir de hambre. 2. (fig.) estar hambriento, estar famélico. 3. (ant.) morir o sufrir de frío. 4. **s. for,** sufrir, sufrir por la falta de; morir por la falta de. —*v.t.* 1. matar de hambre. 2. despojar; exponer a privación. 3. (ant.) congelar, matar por medio del frío. 4. **s. into submission,** someter por hambre; **s. out,** hacer rendirse por hambre.

starveling ['stɑrvlɪŋ, B 'stɑv-] *s.* persona famélica o demacrada. —*a.* hambriento, famélico.

star wheel, rueda con dientes triangulares; rueda catalina de reloj.

starwort ['stɑrˌwɜrt, B 'stɑˌwɜt] *s.* (bot.) estrellada, amelo.

stash [stæʃ] *v.t.* 1. (jer., E.U.) esconder (para uso futuro), almacenar (en un lugar secreto). 2. (jer., pr. G.B.) (*ú. gen. en imper.*) dejar, desistir de. —*s.* escondite, escondrijo. 2. cosa oculta o escondida.

stasis ['steɪsəs, B ˌstæ-] *s.* (*pl.* STASES [-ˌsiz]) (fisiol.) estasis, estancamiento (esp. de la sangre venosa); coprostasia, coprostasis, estasis intestinal.

statable ['steɪtəbəl] *a.* declarable, que se puede afirmar.

state [steɪt] *s.* 1. estado, condición; naturaleza. 2. estado de ánimo; humor, genio (esp. anormal). 3. estado social, clase económica; rango (elevado), eminencia. 4. majestad, dignidad; pompa, suntuosidad, ceremonia. 5. (*pl.*) estados (eclesiástico, plebeyo, etc.). 6. estado, cuerpo político. 7. estado, provincia, cantón. 8. **in s.,** con gran pompa, de gran ceremonia; **to be in (quite) a s. about,** (fam.) inquietarse (mucho) por; **to lie in s.,** yacer en capilla ardiente o cámara mortuoria, estar de cuerpo presente; **what a s. you are in!** (fam.) ¡qué desaliñado (o sucio) estás! —*a.* 1. de estado; del estado; estatal; político, público. 2. de lujo, de gala; ceremonial. —*v.t.* 1. manifestar, declarar, expresar, exponer; afirmar; enunciar, formular (un principio, ley, etc.); plantear (un problema). 2. establecer, fijar.

State bank, (E.U.) banco estatal.

state call, (fam.) visita ceremonial.

state capitalism, (pol.) capitalismo de estado.

statecraft ['steɪtˌkræft, B -ˌkrɑft] *s.* política, arte de gobernar; habilidad de estadista.

stated ['steɪtəd] *a.* 1. fijo, establecido, regular. 2. reconocido, admitido; dicho, formulado, expresado.

State Department, (E.U.) Ministerio de Estado o de Relaciones Exteriores.

statedly [-lɪ] *adv.* de modo fijo, en forma establecida.

Statehood ['steɪtˌhʊd] *s.* (E.U.) condición de estado (de la Unión).

Statehouse [-ˌhaʊs] *s.* (E.U.) edificio de la cámara legislativa de un estado de la Unión.

stateless [-ləs] *a.* apátrida, desplazado; persona que no tiene nacionalidad.

stateliness ['steɪtlɪnəs] *s.* majestad, grandeza, dignidad, señorío.

stately [-lɪ] *a.* majestuoso, augusto, solemne, sublime; imponente, ej., *with a s. air,* con aire imponente. —*adv.* majestuosamente.

state medicine, medicina socializada; servicios médicos proporcionados por el estado.

statement ['steɪtmənt] *s.* 1. declaración, exposición, relación, informe, presentación (oral o escrita); afirmación, aserto, aseveración, manifestación, enunciación. 2. (com.) estado de cuenta.

state of alert, estado de prevención.

state of emergency, estado de alarma o emergencia.

state of grace, (teo.) estado de gracia.

state of innocence, (relig.) justicia original.

state of war, estado de guerra.

State prison, (E.U.) penitenciaría del estado, prisión del estado.

stater ['steɪtər, B -ə] *s.* (hist.) estatera (antigua moneda griega).

state rights, states' rights, (E.U.) soberanía o derechos de los estados (con respecto a la Unión).

stateroom ['steɪtˌrum, -ˌrʊm] *s.* 1. (mar.) camarote. 2. (f.c.) compartimiento privado.

State's attorney, (E.U.) procurador del estado.

state secret, secreto de estado.

state's evidence, (E.U., der.) testimonio en contra del reo, prueba de cargo; **to turn s.'s e.,** dar testimonio en contra de sus cómplices (reo para asegurarse impunidad).

stateside ['steɪtˌsaɪd] *a.* (fam.) de los Estados Unidos, que está hecho o que ocurre en los Estados Unidos; estadounidense. —*adv.* (fam.) en los Estados Unidos, a los Estados Unidos.

statesman ['steɪtsmən] *s.* estadista, gobernante, hombre de estado.

statesmanlike [-ˌlaɪk] *a.* propio de un estadista.

statesmanly [-lɪ] *a.* de un estadista, digno de un estadista.
statesmanship [-ˌʃɪp] *s.* habilidad de estadista; calidad de estadista.
State university, (E.U.) universidad del estado.
state-wide ['steɪt'waɪd] *a.* por todo el estado, en toda la extensión del estado.
static ['stætɪk] *a.* 1. estático; estacionario, inactivo. 2. (fís., elec.) estático. —*s.* (rad.) descarga atmosférica que interfiere con la recepción.
statically [-ɪkəlɪ] *adv.* de modo estático, estáticamente.
statically indeterminate, (ing.) estáticamente indeterminado, hiperestático.
static balance, (ing.) equilibrio estático.
static defense, (mil.) defensa pasiva.
static electricity, electricidad estática.
static head, (hidr.) carga estática.
static induction, (elec.) inducción eletrostática.
static line, (aer.) cuerda de apertura automática (del paracaídas).
staticproof ['stætɪkˌpruf] *a.* (rad.) a prueba de interferencia atmosférica.
statics ['stætɪks] *s. pl.* (*sing o pl. en const.*) (mec.) estática, rama de la mecánica que trata sobre masas en reposo o en equilibrio.
static torque, (ing.) momento de torsión de arranque.
static transformer, (elec.) transformador estático.
station ['steɪʃən] *s.* 1. estación (de ferrocarril, ómnibus, etc.). 2. puesto, sitio; posición, ubicación, colocación. 3. (*pl.*) (mar.) puestos de servicio (en batalla). 4. estado, rango, condición o posición (social), ej., *of humble s.*, de condición humilde. 5. (relig.) estación (de la cruz). 6. (rad.) estación (transmisora o receptora). 7. (Aust.) dehesa de ovejas; granja. 8. (raro) porte, postura. —*v.t.* estacionar; apostar, colocar, situar; alojar.
stationary ['steɪʃəˌnɛrɪ, B -nərɪ] *a.* estacionario; parado, inmóvil, fijo; inalterado.
stationary engine, máquina estacionaria, motor fijo.
stationary target, (mil.) blanco fijo.
stationary transformer, (elec.) transformador estático.
stationary wave, (fís.) onda estacionaria.
station break, corta interrupción del programa para identificar la estación emisora, dar la hora, o transmitir anuncios o boletines informativos.
stationer ['steɪʃənər, B -nə] *s.* 1. papelero, papelista. 2. (ant.) librero, estacionario. 3. **s.'s,** papelería, ej., *I bought this pencil at the s.'s on the corner,* compré este lápiz en la papelería de la esquina.
stationery ['steɪʃəˌnɛrɪ, B -nərɪ] *s.* 1. artículos o útiles de escritorio. 2. papel y sobre de cartas (esp. particulares de una persona, un hotel, etc.).
station house, comisaría, cuartel de policía; cuartel de bomberos; estación de ferrocarril (gen. rural).
stationmaster ['steɪʃənˌmæstər, B -ˌmɑstə] *s.* (f.c.) jefe de estación.
station porter, mozo de estación.
stations of the cross, (relig.) estaciones, estaciones de la cruz.
station wagon, camioneta, automóvil rural, rubia, ranchera, coche familiar.
statism ['steɪtˌɪzəm] *s.* (pol.) estatismo.
statist [-əst] *s.* partidario del estatismo.
statistic [stə'tɪstɪk] *a.* estadístico. —*s.* dato estadístico.
statistical [-tɪkəl] *a.* estadístico.
statistically [-kəlɪ] *adv.* según la estadística.
statistician [ˌstætəs'tɪʃən] *s.* estadístico, perito en estadística.
statistics [stə'tɪstɪks] *s. pl.* 1. (*sing. o pl. en const.*) estadística (ciencia). 2. (*pl. en const.*) datos estadísticos, estadísticas.
statocyst ['stætəˌsɪst] *s.* (zool.) estatocisto.
statolith [-ˌlɪθ] *s.* (zool.) estatolito.
stator ['steɪtər, B -ə] *s.* (mec., elec.) estator, parte fija de un motor o dínamo.
statoscope ['stætəˌskoʊp] *s.* (fís., aer.) estatoscopio, barómetro aneroide.
statuary ['stætʃʊˌɛrɪ, B 'stætjʊərɪ] *s.* (*pl.* STATUARIES) 1. estatuario, escultor. 2. estatuaria. 3. colección de estatuas. —*a.* estatuario.
statue ['stætʃu] *s.* estatua, escultura.
Statue of Liberty, (E.U.) Estatua de la Libertad (en el puerto de Nueva York).
statuesque [ˌstætʃʊ'ɛsk, B ˌstætjʊ-] *a.* escultural, estatuario.
statuesquely [-lɪ] *adv.* en forma escultural, esculturalmente.
statuesqueness [-nəs] *s.* aspecto escultural.
statuette [ˌstætʃʊ'ɛt, B ˌstætjʊ-] *s.* (fr.) figurilla, estatuita.
stature ['stætʃər, B -ə] *s.* 1. estatura, talla, tamaño. 2. (fig.) situación (social), importancia.
status ['steɪtəs] *s.* 1. estado, condición. 2. estado legal; estado civil. 3. condición social, nivel social.
status quo [-'kwoʊ] statu quo (estado de las cosas en un momento dado).
statutable ['stætʃətəbəl, B 'stætjʊtə-] *a.* estatutario, conforme a los estatutos.
statute ['stætʃut B 'stætjut] *s.* estatuto, decreto, reglamento; ley.
statute law, derecho escrito, derecho estatutario.
statute mile, milla ordinaria o terrestre.
statute of limitations, (der.) ley de prescripción.
statutory ['stætʃəˌtɔrɪ, B 'stætjʊtərɪ] *a.* estatutario, estatuido, establecido por la ley.
statutory offense, (der.) crimen establecido por ley.
statutory rape, (der.) violación de menores.
staunch [stɔntʃ, stɑntʃ] **staunchly** ['stɔntʃlɪ, 'stɑntʃ-] **staunchness** [-nəs] *vars. de* **stanch, stanchly, stanchness.**
staurolite ['stɔrəˌlaɪt] *s.* (min.) estaurolita, piedra de cruz.
stauroscope [-ˌskoʊp] *s.* (min.) estauroscopio.
stave ['steɪv] *s.* 1. estaca, palo, garrote, tranca, bastón. 2. duela (de barril). 3. escalón, peldaño (de escala). 4. (poét.) estrofa, estancia. 5. (mús.) pentagrama. —*v.t.* (*pret., p.p.* STAVED O STOVE [stoʊv]; *p.pr.* STAVING) 1. romper las duelas de (barril). 2. poner duelas a. 3. **s. in,** abrir un boquete en; romper (ej., costillas); (mar.) desfondar (barco); **s. off,** parar, detener, impedir; evitar, prevenir; diferir, retardar. —*v.i.* 1. (gen. con *in*) romperse, hacerse pedazos (barril, etc.); (mar.) desfondarse (barco, etc.). 2. caminar o moverse rápidamente.
staves, *s. pl. de* **staff** o **stave.**
stavesacre ['steɪvzˌeɪkər, B -kə] *s.* (bot.) hierba piojera o piojenta, uva taminea o taminia, estafisagria, albarraz.
stay [steɪ] *v.t.* (*pret., p.p.* STAYED; *ant.* STAID [steɪd]; *p.pr.* STAYING) 1. (gen. con *up*) sostener; apuntalar, afianzar, apoyar; asentar, cimentar, fundamentar. 2. calmar, apaciguar, aplacar. 3. durar por, permanecer por (cierto tiempo). 4. impedir, poner freno a, obstaculizar; retardar, diferir. 5. (der.) aplazar, posponer (un fallo); demorar. 6. (dep.) soportar, aguantar (ritmo de carrera, etc.). 7. **s. one's appetite,** matar el hambre (temporalmente). —*v.i.* 1. detenerse, parar; tardar, demorarse (Amer.), quedarse, permanecer. 2. morar, alojarse, hospedarse. 3. aguantar, resistir, no ceder. 4. (póker) quedarse (en el juego). 5. (raro, ú. con *on*) ser criado o sirviente (de). 6. **it has come to s., is here to s.,** se ha establecido (costumbre, moda, etc.); **s. away,** ausentarse, quedar ausente; quedarse apartado; no volver, dejar de venir o visitar; **s. in,** quedarse en casa, no salir; **s. on,** permanecer, quedarse; **s. out,** quedarse fuera, no entrar; **s. put,** estarse quieto, ej., *he will not s. put,* no quiere estarse quieto; **s. up,** quedarse levantado, no acostarse, velar. —*s.* 1. sostén, apoyo, soporte, sustentáculo, puntal; báculo. 2. (*pl.*) corsé. 3. freno, impedimento, obstáculo. 4. detención, suspensión; (der.) diferimiento (de un fallo judicial). 5. estancia, estada, permanencia, quedada. 6. (fam.) resistencia, aguante, fibra (fig.). 7. (ant.) moderación.
stay, *s.* 1. (mar.) estay. 2. tirante, riostra, cuerda o cabo de retén. 3. **in stays,** en la virada. —*v.t.* 1. asegurar, sujetar con tirantes o cuerdas; arriostrar, riostrar. 2. (mar.) inclinar (un mástil hacia adelante, hacia la popa o a un lado) con los estays. —*v.i.* (mar.) virar, cambiar de bordada, voltajear.
stay-at-home ['steɪətˌhoʊm] *a.* hogareño, casero. —*s.* persona hogareña, casera o retraída.
stay bolt, perno de puntal; (carp.) virotillo.
stayer ['steɪər, B -ə] *s.* competidor con aguante (en carrera, lucha, etc.); caballo resistente.
staying power [-ɪŋ-] aguante, garra, fuerza para resistir.
stay-in strike ['steɪˌɪn-] (G.B.) huelga sentada, huelga de brazos caídos.
staysail ['steɪˌseɪl, 'steɪsəl] *s.* (mar.) vela de estay, vela de cuchillo.
stead [stɛd] *s.* 1. ventaja, provecho, utilidad. 2. (ant.) lugar, sitio. 3. **in (someone's) s.,** en lugar de (alguien); **to stand (someone) in good s.,** ser útil, servir a (alguien). —*v.t.* ser de provecho a; ayudar; beneficiar, aprovechar.
steadfast ['stɛdˌfæst, B -fəst] *a.* 1. constante, inmutable, estable; resuelto, firme. 2. establecido, inmovible, fijo.
steadfastly [-lɪ] *adv.* constantemente, resueltamente.
steadfastness [-nəs] *s.* constancia, inmutabilidad; resolución.
steadier ['stɛdɪər, B -ə] *s.* el que afirma o asegura.
steadily [-əlɪ] *adv.* firmemente, fijamente, seguramente.
steadiness [-ɪnəs] *s.* firmeza, solidez, estabilidad.
steading ['stɛdɪŋ] *s.* (esco.) alquería, pequeña granja.
steady ['stɛdɪ] *a.* (STEADIER; STEADIEST) 1. firme, fijo, seguro, estable. 2. (fig.) asentado, juicioso; formal, sereno. 3. constante, confiable; resuelto, determinado. 4. regular, uniforme, ininterrumpido, continuo. 5. sobrio, serio. 6. (mar.) estable (díc. del rumbo de un barco). 7. **s. on!** ¡alto!; **to go s. with,** estar siempre en la compañía de, ser compañero (o compañera) constante de (persona del otro sexo, antes de comprometerse); **to keep (her) s.,** (mar.) conservar el rumbo (del barco). —*v.t., v.i.* (*pret., p.p.* STEADIED; *p.pr.* STEADYING) estabilizar(se); reforzar(se), calmar(se); volver(se) firme. —*interj.* 1. ¡calma! ¡tranquilo! 2. (mar.) ¡vía! (voz de mando para que el piloto mantenga el curso). —*s.* (fam.) enamorada (a la que se corteja con propósitos serios).
steady rest, (mec.) centrador fijo, soporte fijo, luneta fija.
steak [steɪk] *s.* 1. bistec, filete, lonja o tajada (de carne o pescado). 2. carne molida (para asar).
steak house, restaurante que se especializa en bistecs.

steak knife, cuchillo muy afilado, a veces con el filo aserrado, para cortar carne.
steal [stil] *v.t.* (*pret.* STOLE [stoʊl]; *p.p.* STOLEN ['stoʊlən]; *p.pr.* STEALING) 1. robar, hurtar, ratear. 2. (fig.) cautivar, ganar (afección, etc.). 3. (gen. con *in, into,* etc.) mover clandestinamente, conducir o introducir a hurtadillas; pasar o meter de contrabando. 4. (béisbol) ganar (una base) sin la ayuda de un batazo o de un error. 5. **s. a look at,** echar una mirada furtiva a, mirar a hurtadillas; **s. a march on,** anticiparse o adelantarse a; ganar por la mano a (uno); **s. the show,** llevarse los aplausos. —*v.i.* 1. robar, hurtar, ratear. 2. **s. away,** escabullirse, colarse; **s. by,** pasar furtivamente; **s. down,** bajar a hurtadillas por (la escalera, etc.); **s. in** (o **into**), entrar a hurtadillas en o a, entrar clandestinamente en o a; **s. out of,** salir a escondidas de, salir sin ser visto de (un cuarto, etc.); **s. up,** subir a hurtadillas por (la escalera, etc.); **s. upon,** acercarse furtivamente o a hurtadillas a. —*s.* 1. hurto, robo. 2. ganga (compra ventajosa).
stealer ['stilər, B -ə] *s.* ladrón, ratero, hurtador.
stealing [-ɪŋ] *s.* hurto, ratería, robo. —*a.* ladrón, hurtador.
stealth [stɛlθ] *s.* 1. subrepción, recato. 2. (ant.) robo; botín. 3. **by s.,** a hurtadillas, furtivamente.
stealth airplane, avion antiradar.
stealthily ['stɛlθəlɪ] *adv.* clandestinamente, furtivamente.
stealthiness [-θinəs] *s.* clandestinidad.
stealthy [-θɪ] *a.* (STEALTHIER; STEALTHIEST) furtivo, subrepticio, secreto, clandestino.
steam [stim] *s.* 1. vapor; vaho. 2. (fig.) vigor, fuerza, energía; **full s. ahead,** avante a toda máquina. 3. **on one's own s.,** por sus propios recursos, sin ayuda; **to get up s.,** dar presión (de vapor); (fig., fam.) reunir energías (para hacer algo); **to let off s.,** descargar vapor; (fig., fam.) desahogarse. —*a.* de vapor, para vapor, por vapor. —*v.i.* 1. emitir o exhalar vapor o vaho, vaporear, humear, vahear. 2. evaporarse, emanar (como vapor). 3. navegar a vapor. 4. (fam.) encolerizarse. 5. **s. up,** empañarse (vidrio, etc.). —*v.t.* 1. ablandar con vapor; cocer al vapor, dar baño de vapor a. 2. **s. open (envelope,** etc.), abrir (un sobre, etc.) por vapor; **s. up,** empañar (vidrio, espejo, etc.); encolerizar, enfadar; excitar; dar ímpetu a, vitalizar (empresa, economía, etc.).
steam bath, baño de vapor.
steamboat ['stim,boʊt] *s.* vapor, buque de vapor.
steam boiler, caldera de vapor.
steam box, s. chest, cámara o caja de vapor.
steam coil, serpentín de vapor.
steam dome, cúpula de vapor, domo de vapor (de locomotora); cúpula de caldera.
steam-driven [-,drɪvən] *a.* de vapor, a vapor, accionado por vapor.
steam engine, máquina de vapor, máquina a vapor.
steamer ['stimər, B -mə] *s.* 1. máquina o vehículo de vapor; bomba de incendios. 2. vapor, buque de vapor. 3. marmita al vacío (para cocinar, esterilizar, etc. con vapor). 4. vaporario.
steamer rug, manta de viaje.
steamer trunk, baúl de camarote.
steam fitter, tubero, cañero; montador de calderas de vapor.
steam fitting, montaje de calderas y tuberías de vapor.
steam gage, manómetro.
steam gas, vapor altamente recalentado.
steam hammer, martillo a vapor.
steam heating, calefacción de vapor.
steamily ['stiməlɪ] *adv.* humeando.
steaminess [-mɪnəs] *s.* atmósfera llena de vapor.
steam iron, plancha de vapor, plancha a vapor.
steam launch, lancha de vapor, lancha a vapor.
steam locomotive, (f.c.) locomotora de vapor.
steam pipe, tubería de vapor.
steam plant, instalación de calderas, planta generadora de vapor, planta eléctrica a vapor.
steam pressure, presión de vapor.
steamproof ['stim,pruf] *a.* a prueba de vapor.
steamroller [-,roʊlər, B -ə] *s.* 1. apisonadora de vapor, rodillo de vapor. 2. (fig.) fuerza arrolladora, fuerza incontrastable. —*v.t.* 1. apisonar, aplanar con apisonadora o rodillo de vapor. 2. (fig.) aplastar, abrumar, agobiar (empleando fuerza irresistible).
steamship [-,ʃɪp] *s.* vapor, buque de vapor.
steam shovel, pala mecánica.
steam table, mesa calentada a vapor (para conservar caliente la comida).
steam trap, trampa de vapor, interceptor, separador de agua, colector de condensado.
steam turbine, turbina de vapor, turbina a vapor.
steamy ['stimɪ] *a.* (STEAMIER; STEAMIEST) vaporoso, humeante, humoso.
steapsin [stɪ'æpsən] *s.* (bioquím.) esteapsina.
stearate ['stiə,reɪt] *s.* (quím.) estearato.
stearic [stɪ'ærɪk] *a.* (quím.) esteárico.
stearic acid, (quím.) ácido esteárico.
stearin ['stiərən, B 'stɪər-] *s.* 1. (quím.) estearina. 2. (t. **stearine**) triestearina. 3. (gen. **stearine**) estearina (ácido esteárico en uso comercial).
stearoptene [,stiə'rɑptɪn, B -'rɔptin] *s.* (quím.) estearopteno.
steatite ['stiə,taɪt, B 'stɪə-] *s.* (min.) esteatita.
steatolysis [,stiə'tɑləsəs, B ,stɪə'tɔl-] *s.* (med.) esteatólisis.
steatoma [-'toʊmə] *s.* (*pl.* STEATOMAS O STEATOMATA [-mətə]) (med.) esteatoma.
steatopygia [-toʊ'pɪdʒɪə, B -'paɪdʒɪə] *s.* esteatopigia.
steatorrhea [-tə'riə] *s.* (med.) esteatorrea.
stedfast, stedfastly, stedfastness, *vars. de* **steadfast, steadfastly, steadfastness.**
steed [stid] *s.* (lit., poét., hum.) corcel, caballo.
steel [stil] *s.* 1. acero. 2. acero, arma (blanca), espada, puñal. 3. afilón, chaira (de afilar cuchillos, etc.); eslabón (para sacar fuego de un pedernal). 4. (fig.) acero, ánimo, brío, resolución, aplomo. 5. industria de acero; (*pl.*) acciones en fábricas de acero. —*a.* 1. de acero. 2. acerado. 3. (fig.) férreo, duro, frío. —*v.t.* 1. acerar, cubrir o armar de acero. 2. (fig.) acerar, fortalecer. 3. endurecer. 4. **s. oneself,** acerarse, fortificarse; hacerse insensible.
steel band, banda de percusión originaria del Caribe, de tambores hechos de tanques de petróleo.
steel blue, azul acerado, azul acero.
steel-blue ['stil'blu] *a.* de color azul acerado.
stell casting, fundición de acero.
steel-clad ['stil'klæd] *a.* cubierto o revestido de acero, acorazado.
steel engraving, grabado de acero; impresión de un grabado en acero.
steel foundry, fundición de acero.
steel gray, color gris acero.
steel guitar, guitarra hawaiana.
steelhead ['stil,hɛd] *s.* (ict.) trucha arco iris.
steeliness ['stilɪnəs] *s.* (fig.) severidad, dureza.
steel-jacketed bullet [-'dʒækətəd-] bala con envuelta de acero.
steel mill, fábrica de acero, acería.
steel plate, plancha o palastro de acero.
steel wool, virutas de acero, estopa de acero.
steelwork [-,wɜrk, B -,wɜk] *s.* 1. artículos de acero. 2. estructura de acero; montaje de acero estructural. 3. (*pl.*) (*sing. o pl. en const.*) fábrica de acero, acería, usina siderúrgica.
steelworker [-,wɜrkər, B -,wɜkə] *s.* obrero en una fábrica de acero; herrero de obra; erector, montador.
steely ['stilɪ] *a.* (STEELIER; STEELIEST) 1. acerado, de acero. 2. (fig.) fuerte, firme, inflexible, severo, duro.
steelyard ['stil,jɑrd, 'stɪljərd, B 'stɪl,jɑd] *s.* romana.
steenbok ['stin,bɑk, B -,bɔk] *var. de* **steinbok.**
steep [stip] *a.* 1. empinado, pendiente, pino, escarpado, precipitoso. 2. embravecido, bravo (mar). 3. (fam.) alto, excesivo, exorbitante (precio, cuenta, etc.); exagerado (cuento, relato, etc.). 4. **it's a bit s.!** ¡es un poco caro! —*s.* cuesta empinada, precipicio, despeñadero, derrumbadero.
steep, *v.t.* 1. empapar, remojar, impregnar, poner en infusión; extraer (la esencia) remojando o empapando. 2. **to be steeped in,** versarse en, empaparse en, ej., *steeped in anthropology,* versado en antropología. —*v.i.* (fam.) estar en infusión; empaparse. —*s.* infusión (estado o proceso); remojo, baño de infusión; vasija para infusiones.
steepen ['stipən] *v.t., v.i.* hacer(se) o volver(se) más empinado o pendiente.
steeple ['stipəl] *s.* aguja, chapitel; campanario, torre (de iglesia).
steeplechase [-,tʃeɪs] *s.* carrera de obstáculos, carrera de vallas (a caballo); carrera a campo traviesa.
steeplechaser [-,tʃeɪsər, B -sə] *s.* corredor de carrera de obstáculos (persona o animal).
steeplejack [-,dʒæk] *s.* escalatorres, reparador de campanarios o chimeneas altas.
steeply ['stiplɪ] *adv.* de modo empinado, de modo escarpado.
steepness [-nəs] *s.* escarpa, escarpadura.
steer [stɪr, B stɪə] *v.t.* 1. gobernar (un barco); guiar, conducir, dirigir (automóvil, etc.). 2. encaminar, encauzar. 3. (fam.) seguir (un rumbo o dirección). —*v.i.* 1. navegar, timonear. 2. seguir un curso, dirigirse. 3. obedecer al timón (barco). 4. **s. clear of,** evitar, ponerse a resguardo de; **s. for,** encaminarse a, tomar un camino hacia. —*s.* 1. res, novillo. 2. (jer., E.U.) información, consejo, recomendación (confidencial), ej., *a bum s.,* una pista falsa.
steerable ['stɪrəbəl, B 'stɪər-] *a.* gobernable, conducible.
steerage ['stɪrɪdʒ, B 'stɪər-] *s.* 1. gobierno, dirección (de un barco o vehículo). 2. (mar.) efecto del timón o gobernalle (en un barco). 3. (mar.) entrepuente; tercera clase.
steerage passenger, pasajero de tercera clase (en barco).
steerageway [-,weɪ] *s.* (mar.) velocidad suficiente para poder gobernar (una nave) por medio del timón.
steerer [-ər, B -ə] *s.* conductor, timonel, guiador.
steering assembly [-ɪŋ-] (aut.) mecanismo de dirección.
steering column, (aut.) columna de dirección.
steering committee, (pol.) comité directivo de un cuerpo legislativo (encargado de señalar la prioridad de los asuntos en debate); comisión de iniciativas.
steering gear, 1. (mar.) aparato de gobierno. 2. (aut.) mecanismo de dirección.
steering wheel, 1. (mar.) rueda del timón. 2. (aut.) volante (de dirección), timón (Amer.).

steersman ['stɪrzmən, B 'stɪəz-] *s.* (mar.) piloto, timonel, timonero.

steeve [stiv] *v.t.* (mar.) estibar, colocar (la carga) en un barco; llenar; almacenar. —*s.* grúa usada para estibar.

steeve, (const. naval) *v.i., v.t.* elevar(se) en ángulo (el bauprés). —*s.* lanzamiento, elevación angular (del bauprés).

stegomyia [ˌstɛgə'maɪə] *s.* (ento.) estegomía.

stegosaurus [-'sɔrəs] *s.* (pal.) estegosauro.

stein [staɪn] *s.* pichel para cerveza.

steinbok ['staɪnˌbɑk, B -ˌbɔk] *s.* (zool.) antílope sudafricano.

stela ['stilə] *s.* (*pl.* STELAE [-li]) (arq.) estela.

stele ['stilɪ] *s.* 1. (arq.) estela. 2. (bot.) cilindro central (en los tallos y raíces de las plantas vasculares).

stellar ['stɛlər, B -ə] *a.* 1. estelar, astral. 2. con estrellas (decoración). 3. (fig.) estelar, principal, capital; sobresaliente, superlativo. 4. de una estrella (de cine o de teatro).

stellate ['stɛlət, -ˌeɪt] **stellated** [-ˌeɪtəd] *a.* estrellado, estrellar; radiado.

stellately [-lɪ] *adv.* en forma estrellada o estrellar.

stelliferous [stɛ'lɪfərəs] *a.* estelífero.

stelliform ['stɛləˌform, B -ˌfɔm] *a.* esteliforme, de forma de estrella.

stellionate ['stɛljənət, -ˌneɪt] *s.* (der.) estelionato.

stellite ['stɛˌlaɪt] *s.* (metal.) estelita.

stellular ['stɛljələr, B -lə] *a.* estrellado; radiado.

stem [stɛm] *s.* 1. tallo, tronco, caña, vástago. 2. estirpe, linaje. 3. cañón (de una pipa; de una pluma); caña, tronco, tija, espiga (de una llave); grueso (trazo más ancho de la letra); pie (de copa). 4. (mús.) rabo, rabito (de una nota). 5. (mec.) vástago, varilla, caña, cabilla. 6. (mar.) roda, roa, branque, tajamar. 7. (bot.) rabillo, pecíolo, pedúnculo; cabeza (de plátanos). 8. (filol.) raíz. 9. **from s. to stern,** de proa a popa, de punta a cabo. —*v.t.* (*pret., p.p.* STEMMED; *p.pr.* STEMMING) despalillar; quitar los pedúnculos a. —*v.i.* **s. from,** provenir, descender, emanar (de); derivar, dimanar (de); nacer, originarse.

stem, *v.t.* (*pret., p.p.* STEMMED; *p.pr.* STEMMING) 1. estancar, represar; detener, contener; restañar. 2. (esquí) inclinar (el esquí) para retardarse. 3. **s. the torrent** (**of words,** etc.), detener el torrente (de palabras, etc.); **s. the tide** (**of public opinion,** etc.), hacer frente a la corriente (de opinión pública, etc.). —*v.i.* 1. contenerse, reprimirse; ser contenido o detenido. 2. (esquí) retardarse volviendo el talón del esquí hacia afuera. —*s.* (esquí) vuelta de los esquíes a fin de retardarse.

stemhead ['stɛmˌhɛd] *s.* (mar.) caperol.

stemless [-ləs] *a.* (bot.) sin tallo.

stemmed [stɛmd] *a.* 1. (*ú. gen. en palabras compuestas*) de (cierto) tallo, ej., *short s.,* de tallo corto. 2. despalillado.

stemmer ['stɛmər, B -ə] *s.* 1. máquina despalilladora. 2. (min.) atacadera. 3. persona que despalilla.

stemple, stempel ['stɛmpəl] *s.* (min.) estemple, ademe; montante, travesaño.

stemson ['stɛmsən] *s.* (mar.) contrabranque, contrarroda (en buques de madera).

stemware ['stɛmˌwɛr, B -ˌwɛə] *s.* copas, vasos de cristalería con pie o tallo.

stem-winder ['stɛmˌwaɪndər, B -də] *s.* remontuar (reloj).

stem-winding [-dɪŋ] *a.* de remontuar.

stench [stɛntʃ] *s.* hedor, hediondez.

stenchful ['stɛntʃfəl] *a.* apestoso, maloliente.

stencil ['stɛnsəl] *s.* 1. esténcil, patrón picado. 2. estarcido. —*v.t.* (*pret., p.p.* STENCILED O STENCILLED; *p.pr.* STENCILING O STENCILLING) estarcir.

stenciler, stenciller ['stɛnsələr, B -lə] *s.* estarcidor.

stencil paper, papel esténcil.

steno ['stɛnoʊ] *s.* (fam.) 1. *forma abrev. de* **stenographer,** estenógrafo, estenógrafa, taquígrafa, taquígrafo. 2. **stenography,** estenografía, taquigrafía.

stenocardia [ˌstɛnə'kɑrdɪə, B -'kɑdɪə] *s.* (med.) estenocardia.

stenograph ['stɛnəˌgræf, B -ˌgrɑf] *v.t.* estenografiar, taquigrafiar. —*s.* escritura taquigráfica, máquina para taquigrafiar.

stenographer [stə'nɑgrəfər, B -'nɔgrəfə] *s.* estenógrafo, taquígrafo; estenógrafa, taquígrafa.

stenographic [ˌstɛnə'græfɪk] *a.* estenográfico, taquigráfico.

stenographically [-ɪkəlɪ] *adv.* estenográficamente, taquigráficamente.

stenography [stə'nɑgrəfɪ, B -'nɔg-] *s.* estenografía, taquigrafía.

stenophagous [-'nɑfəgəs, B -'nɔf-] *a.* (zool.) estenófago.

stenosed [-'noʊst, -'noʊzd] *a.* (med.) afectado por estenosis.

stenosis [stə'noʊsəs] *s.* (med.) estenosis.

stenothermal [ˌstɛnə'θɜrməl, B -'θɜməl] *a.* (med.) estenotérmico, estenotermo.

stenotype ['stɛnəˌtaɪp] *s.* estenotipo (máquina).

stenotypy [-ˌtaɪpɪ] *s.* estenotipia (escritura).

stentor ['stɛntɔr, B -tɔ] *s.* 1. **S.,** (hist.) Esténtor, heraldo griego de la Ilíada. 2. persona de voz estentórea.

stentorian [stɛn'tɔrɪən] *a.* estentóreo.

step [stɛp] *s.* 1. paso. 2. pisada, huella. 3. paso, manera de andar. 4. paso, escalón, peldaño, grada; (*pl.*) escalera de tijera, escalera de mano. 5. grado, categoría, etapa. 6. paso, medida, gestión. 7. (baile) paso. 8. (mús.) intervalo (entre dos grados). 9. (mar.) carlinga. 10. (rad.) etapa. 11. **at every s.,** a cada paso; **in s.,** llevando el paso; conforme, de acuerdo, acorde; **out of s.,** no llevando el paso; disconforme, en desacuerdo, discorde; **s. by s.,** paso a paso, por partes; **to be out of s. with,** (fig.) no estar a tono con; **to break s.,** perder el paso (en marcha); **to change s.,** cambiar el paso; **to follow in his steps,** seguirle los pasos; **to keep (in) s.,** llevar el paso; **to retrace one's steps,** volver sobre sus pasos; **to take steps to (do),** tomar medidas para (hacer); **watch** (o **mind**) **your s.,** ¡fíjese donde pisa! ¡tenga cuidado! —*v.i.* 1. dar un paso, dar pasos. 2. andar, caminar; pasar. 3. **s. aside,** hacerse a un lado; **s. after,** seguir o ir detrás; (fig.) retirarse; **s. back,** retroceder; dar un paso atrás; **s. down,** bajarse; apearse; **s. forth,** avanzar; **s. in,** entrar, hacer una visita corta; meterse; **s. off,** bajarse, apearse (del tren, etc.); **s. on,** pisar, ej., *s. on the starter,* pisar el arrancador; **s. on it,** (jer.) acelerar; apresurarse; **s. on the gas,** (fig., fam.) darse prisa; **s. out,** alargar el paso; salir; andar de parranda; **s. over,** pasar por encima de; **s. short,** dar pasos cortos; **s. up,** ascender, ser promovido; subir. —*v.t.* 1. poner, plantar (el pie). 2. escalonar, colocar de trecho en trecho; medir a pasos (distancia). 3. escalonar; modificar (algo) por etapas. 4. (mar.) plantar (un mástil); colocar (la cubierta). 5. **s. down,** disminuir, reducir; **s. off,** medir a pasos; **s. up,** elevar, aumentar.

stepbrother ['stɛpˌbrʌðər, B -ə] *s.* hermanastro, medio hermano.

step-by-step [-baɪ'stɛp] *a.* gradual, paulatino; escalonado; (elec.) por grados.

stepchild [-ˌtʃaɪld] *s.* hijastro, entenado, alnado; hijastra, entenada, alnada.

step chuck, (mec.) mandril escalonado.

stepdaughter [-ˌdɔtər, B -ə] *s.* hijastra, entenada, alnada.

step-down [-ˌdaʊn] *a.* (elec.) reductor. —*s.* reducción, disminución.

step-down ratio, (mec.) relación reductora.

step-down transformer, (elec.) transformador reductor.

stepfather [-ˌfɑðər, B -ə] *s.* padrastro.

step fault, (geol.) falla escalonada, fractura en gradas.

stephanite ['stɛfəˌnaɪt] *s.* (min.) estefanita.

stephanotis [ˌstɛfə'noʊtəs] *s.* (bot.) estefanote.

step-in ['stɛpˌɪn] *a.* sostenido por elástico (díc. de ciertas prendas de vestir). —*s.* prenda de vestir (sostenida por elástico que se pone comenzando por los pies); (*pl.*) pantalón interior de mujer.

stepladder [-ˌlædər, B -ə] *s.* escalera doble, escalera de tijera, escalera de mano.

stepmother [-ˌmʌðər, B -ə] *s.* madrastra.

stepparent [-ˌpærənt, -ˌpɛr- B -ˌpɛər-] *s.* padrastro; madrastra.

steppe [stɛp] *s.* (geog.) estepa.

stepped [stɛpt] *a.* escalonado.

stepped arch, (arq.) arco de trasdós escalonado.

stepped-up ['stɛptˌʌp] *a.* intensificado, aumentado, acelerado.

stepper ['stɛpər, B -ə] *s.* 1. caballo veloz. 2. bailador.

stepping-off place [ˌstɛpɪŋ'ɔf-] 1. final de una línea de transporte. 2. punto de partida hacia territorio desconocido.

stepping-stone ['stɛpɪŋˌstoʊn] *s.* 1. pasadera, estriberón. 2. (fig.) escalón (para avanzar o progresar).

step rocket, cohete de etapas, cohete de secciones.

stepsister ['stɛpˌsɪstər, B -tə] *s.* media hermana, hermanastra.

stepson [-ˌsʌn] *s.* hijastro, entenado, alnado.

step turn, (esquí) vuelta ejecutada al bajar una ladera, levantando un esquí del suelo y colocándolo en la dirección deseada y luego poniendo el otro esquí paralelo.

step-up [-ˌʌp] *a.* (mec.) multiplicador (ej., engranaje); (elec.) elevador.

step-up transformer, (elec.) transformador elevador.

stepwise [-ˌwaɪz] *a.* escalonado; gradual.

stercoraceous [ˌstɜrkə'reɪʃəs, B ˌstɜkə-] *a.* estercóreo, estercolizo.

sterculiaceous [stɜrˌkjulɪ'eɪʃəs, B stɜˌ-] *a.* (bot.) esterculiáceo.

stere [stɪr, B stɪə] *s.* estéreo, metro cúbico.

stereo ['stɛrɪˌoʊ, B 'stɪər-] *s.* 1. aparato estereofónico (tocadiscos, radio, etc.). 2. *abrev. de* **stereotype,** estereotipo. 3. *abrev. de* **stereoscopy,** estereoscopia, método o efecto estereoscópico; fotografía estereoscópica. 3. estereofonía, reproducción estereofónica (del sonido); sistema de sonido estereofónico. —*a.* 1. (impr.) estereotipado. 2. estereoscópico. 3. estereofónico.

stereobate [-ˌbeɪt] *s.* (arq.) estereóbato.

stereocamera [-ˌkæmərə] *s.* (fotgmt.) cámara estereofotogramétrica.

stereocartograph [ˌstɛrɪoʊ'kɑrtəˌgræf, B ˌstɪərɪoʊ'kɑtəˌgrɑf] *s.* (fotgmt.) estereocartógrafo.

stereochemistry [-'kɛməstrɪ] *s.* estereoquímica.

stereochromic [-ə'kroʊmɪk] *a.* estereocrómico.

stereochromy ['stɛrɪəˌkroʊmɪ, B 'stɪər-] *s.* estereocromía.

stereogoniometer [ˌstɛrɪoʊˌgoʊnɪ'ɑmətər, B ˌstɪər-'ɔmɪtə] *s.* (fotgmt.) estereogoniómetro, goniómetro estereoscópico.

stereogram ['stɛrɪə,græm, B 'stɪər-] *s.* estereograma; estereografía.
stereograph [-,græf, B -,grɑf] *s.* estereografía. —*v.t., v.i.* hacer una estereografía (de).
stereographic [,stɛrɪə'græfɪk, B ,stɪər-] *a.* estereográfico.
stereography [-'ɑgrəfɪ, B -'ɔg-] *s.* estereografía.
stereoisomer [-oʊ'aɪsəmər, B -mə] *s.* estereoisómero.
stereoisomeric [-,aɪsə'mɛrɪk] *a.* estereoisómero.
stereoisomerism [-aɪ'sɑmə,rɪzəm, B -'sɔm-] *s.* (quím.) estereoisomería, isomería espacial.
stereometric [,stɛrɪə'mɛtrɪk, B ,stɪər-] *a.* estereométrico.
stereometry [-'ɑmətrɪ, B -'ɔm-] *s.* estereometría.
stereomicroscope [-oʊ'maɪkrə,skoʊp] *s.* microscopio estereoscópico.
stereophonic [-ə'fɑnɪk, B -'fɔn-] *a.* estereofónico.
stereophotography [-oʊfə'tɑgrəfɪ, B -'tɔg-] *s.* fotografía estereoscópica, estereofotografía.
stereopsis [-'ɑpsəs, B -'ɔp-] *s.* visión estereoscópica.
stereoradian [,stɛrɪoʊ'reɪdɪən] *s.* (geom.) estereorradián.
stereoscope ['stɛrɪə,skoʊp, B 'stɪər-] *s.* estereoscopio.
stereoscopic [,stɛrɪə'skɑpɪk, B ,stɪərɪə's-kɔp-] *a.* estereoscópico.
stereoscopy [-'ɑskəpɪ, B -'ɔs-] *s.* estereoscopia.
stereostatic [-ə'stætɪk] *a.* geostático, estereostático.
stereotaxis [-'tæksəs] *s.* (biol.) estereotaxis.
stereotelemeter [-'tɛlə,mitər, B -ə] *s.* (fotgmt.) estereotelémetro.
stereotomy [-'ɑtəmɪ, B -'ɔt-] *s.* estereotomía.
stereotropism [-'ɑtrə,pɪzəm, B -'ɔtrə-] *s.* (biol.) estereotropismo.
stereotype ['stɛrɪə,taɪp, B 'stɪər-] *s.* 1. (impr.) estereotipo, plancha estereotípica. 2. (fig.) estereotipo. —*v.t.* 1. (impr.) estereotipar. 2. (fig.) estereotipar, uniformizar.
stereotyped [-,taɪpt] *a.* estereotipado, uniformizado.
stereotyper [-,taɪpər, B -pə] *s.* (impr.) estereotipador.
stereotypic [,stɛrɪə'tɪpɪk, B ,stɪər-] *a.* estereotípico.
stereotypy ['stɛrɪə,taɪpɪ, B 'stɪər-] *s.* estereotipia.
stèric ['stɛrɪk] *a.* (fís.) espacial (disposición de los átomos).
sterile ['stɛrɪl, B -,aɪl] *a.* 1. estéril, infecundo, impotente, improductivo, infructuoso, árido. 2. (bact.) estéril. 3. (bot.) infructífero.
sterility [stə'rɪlətɪ, B stɛ-] *s.* esterilidad, infecundidad, aridez.
sterilization [,stɛrələ'zeɪʃən, B -laɪ-] *s.* esterilización.
sterilize ['stɛrə,laɪz] *v.t.* esterilizar.
sterilizer [-ər, B -ə] *s.* 1. substancia esterilizadora. 2. esterilizador (aparato).
sterilizing [-ɪŋ] *a.* esterilizador.
sterlet ['stɜrlət, B 'stɜlɪt] *s.* (ict.) (variedad pequeña de) esturión.
sterling ['stɜrlɪŋ, B 'stɜlɪŋ] *s.* 1. libra esterlina (moneda inglesa). 2. plata fina, plata de ley. —*a.* 1. de libra esterlina. 2. fina, de ley (plata). 3. genuino, puro, verdadero, legítimo; legal. 4. de excelentes cualidades, ej., *he is a s. fellow,* es una persona de excelentes cualidades.
sterling silver, plata fina (de 0,925).
stern [stɜrn, B stɜn] *a.* 1. severo, estricto, riguroso, austero. 2. firme, decidido, inflexible. —*s.* 1. popa. 2. ancas; nalgas.
sternal ['stɜrnəl, B 'stɜn-] *a.* (anat.) esternal.
stern chase, (mar.) persecución en que una nave sigue la estela de otra.
stern chaser, (mar.) guardatimón.
stern fast, s. line, (mar.) codera.
sternforemost ['stɜrn'fɔr,moʊst, B ,stɜn'fɔ,-] *adv.* 1. con la popa hacia adelante. 2. al revés; en una posición difícil; embarazosamente.
stern gallery, (mar.) galería de popa.
sternly ['stɜrnlɪ, B 'stɜn-] *adv.* 1. severamente, rigurosamente. 2. firmemente.
sternmost ['stɜrn,moʊst, B 'stɜn-] *a.* (mar.) popel.
sternness ['stɜrnnəs, B 'stɜn-] *s.* 1. severidad, austeridad. 2. firmeza.
Sterno ['stɜrnoʊ, B 'stɜnoʊ] *s.* (marca de fábrica) gelatina de alcohol metílico que se vende en latas para usarse como combustible de hornillas pequeñas y escalfetas.
sternocostal [,stɜrnoʊ'kɑstəl, B -'kɔst-] *a.* (anat.) esternocostal.
sternpost ['stɜrn,poʊst, B 'stɜn-] *s.* (mar.) codaste.
stern sheets, cámara (de un bote).
sternson [-sən] *s.* (mar.) estrave, talón de quilla.
sternum ['stɜrnəm, B 'stɜnəm] *s.* (*pl.* STERNA [-nə] o STERNUMS) (anat.) esternón.
sternutation [,stɜrnjə'teɪʃən, B ,stɜnjʊ-] *s.* estornudo.
sternutative [-'nutətɪv, B -'njut-] **sternutatory** [-ə,tɔrɪ, B -ətərɪ] *a.* estornutatorio.
sternward ['stɜrnwərd, B 'stɜnwəd] **sternwards** [-wərdz, B -wədz] *adv. a.* hacia la popa, por la popa.
sternway [-,weɪ] *s.* (mar.) retroceso, movimiento hacia atrás.
stern-wheeler [-'hwilər, -'wilər, B -lə] *s.* (E.U.) bote de ruedas a popa.
steroid ['stɪrɔɪd, 'stɛr-, B 'stɪər-] *s.* (quím.) esteroide.
sterol [-,ɔl] *s.* esterol.
stertor ['stɜrtər, B 'stɜtə] *s.* (med.) estertor.
stertorous [-ərəs] *a.* estertoroso.
stertorously [-lɪ] *adv.* de modo estertoroso.
stet [stɛt] *s.* (impr.) vale, deje como está (indicación de no suprimir lo ya cancelado). —*v.t.* (*pret., p.p.* STETTED; *p.pr.* STETTING) (impr.) desvirtuar (una cancelación), marcar para que no se suprima; dejar como está, no cambiar.
stethoscope ['stɛθə,skoʊp] *s.* (med.) estetoscopio.
stethoscopic [,stɛθə'skɑpɪk, B -'skɔp-] **stethoscopical** [-ɪkəl] *a.* estetoscópico.
stethoscopically [-ɪkəlɪ] *adv.* de modo estetoscópico.
stethoscopy [stɛ'θɑskəpɪ, B -'θɔs-] *s.* estetoscopia.
stevedore ['stivə,dɔr, B -,dɔ] *s.* estibador, arrumador. —*v.t., v.i.* estibar, arrumar.
stevedore's knot, nudo (parecido al) de vuelta de braza.
stew [stu, B stju] *v.t.* guisar, estofar, cocer a fuego lento. —*v.i.* 1. cocer a fuego lento. 2. sudar, abochornarse. 3. (fam.) inquietarse, preocuparse, agitarse. 4. empollar (estudiar con ahínco). 5. **s. in one's own juice,** (fig.) carcomerse, cocerse en su propia salsa. —*s.* 1. guisado, puchero (Amer.); estofado. 2. (fig.) mezcolanza. 3. (fam.) ansiedad, agitación mental. 4. burdel, lupanar; (*pl.*) barrio de los lupanares. 5. (ant.) cazuela, cacerola. 6. **to be in a s.,** estar agitado o ansioso, estar perplejo.
steward ['stuərd, B 'stjuəd] *s.* 1. mayordomo; senescal. 2. administrador, gerente, director, dirigente. 3. camarero, mozo (de buque o avión).
stewardess [-əs] *s.* camarera (de buque); aeromoza, azafata, asistenta (en aviones).
stewardship [-,ʃɪp] *s.* 1. mayordomía. 2. administración, gerencia.
stewed [stud, B stjud] *p.p. de* **stew.** —*a.* (jer.) achispado, ajumado, ahumado, borracho; **s. to the gills,** hecho una cuba.
stewpan ['stu,pæn, B 'stju-] *s.* cazuela, cacerola, olla.
sthene [sθin] *s.* (fís.) estenio.
sthenia ['sθinɪə, B sθə'naɪə] *s.* (med.) estenia.
sthenic ['sθɛnɪk] *a.* (med., psic.) esténico.
stibine ['stɪb,in, B -,aɪn] *s.* (quím.) estibina.
stibium [-ɪəm] *s.* (quím.) estibio.
stibnite [-,naɪt] *s.* (min.) estibinita.
stich [stɪk] *s.* (poét.) verso; línea.
stichometry [stɪ'kɑmətrɪ, B -'kɔm-] *s.* (poét.) esticometría.
stichomythia [,stɪkə'mɪθɪə] *s.* esticomitia.
stick [stɪk] *s.* 1. palo, estaca. 2. vara, varilla, pértiga, bastón. 3. garrote, porra, tranca. 4. palillo, barra (de chocolate, jabón, etc.); cartucho (de dinamita). 5. tallo (leñoso). 6. bombas en serie (para ser lanzadas sobre un blanco desde un bombardero). 7. (jer.) cigarrillo de mariguana. 8. estocada, pinchazo; puñalada. 9. pegajosidad, adhesividad; adhesión, pegadura. 10. impedimento; parada, demora, retraso. 11. (fam.) bodoque (persona pesada o aburrida). 12. (aer.) palanca de mando. 13. (mar., fam.) mástil, verga, palo. 14. (impr.) componedor; texto contenido en el componedor. 15. (dep.) palo, raqueta. —*v.t.* (*pret., p.p.* STUCK [stʌk]; *p.pr.* STICKING) 1. clavar, hincar, picar, punzar, apuñalar, ej., *he will pull out a knife and s. you,* sacará un cuchillo y te lo clavará. 2. meter, introducir; (fam.) poner, ej., *s. a few commas in,* ponga unas cuantas comas. 3. empalar, espetar, clavar; fijar (con tachuelas). 4. pegar, adherir, ej., *s. photographs* (*in a book, an album,* etc.), pegar fotografías (en libro, álbum, etc.). 5. (fam.) confundir, dejar perplejo. 6. (jer.) obligar a pagar; cobrar (cierto precio); trampear, timar, defraudar. 7. **s. (someone) for,** dar un sablazo (a alguien) de (cierta suma); hacer pagar (a alguien) por (almuerzo, bebidas, etc.); **s. it out,** (jer.) aguantarlo, soportarlo; **s. it on,** cobrar mucho; exagerar; **s. one's neck out,** arriesgarse; **s. out,** extender; sacar (la lengua, mano, etc.); **s. out one's chest,** sacar uno el pecho; **s. up,** pegar (cartel, anuncio); (jer.) asaltar, atracar; **s. up a bank,** atracar un banco; **to be stuck on,** (jer.) estar enamorado de; **to be stuck with,** no poder deshacerse de; **to get stuck on,** (jer.) acaramelarse con. —*v.i.* 1. estar hincado, estar clavado. 2. pegarse, adherirse. 3. permanecer; permanecer fijo; quedarse; perseverar. 4. atascarse; quedarse, estar cerca, quedarse parado. 5. **s. around,** quedarse, estar cerca, no irse; **s. at,** tener dificultades con; **s. at (doing),** vacilar en (hacer); **s. fast,** quedarse inmovilizado; **s. fast to,** adherirse o pegarse fuertemente a; **s. in one's gut,** (fig.) no poder digerir, no poder aceptar (algo); **s. (something) in one's throat,** atascársele (algo) en la garganta a uno; **s. in the mud,** atascarse en el fango; (fig.) quedarse relegado o atrasado (en ideas, modo de vivir, etc.); **s. indoors (all day),** permanecer en casa (todo el día); **s. out,** salir; sobresalir, proyectarse; (fig.)

resaltar; aguantar, soportar; **s. out a mile,** (jer.) ser obvio; **s. out for (better terms, prices,** etc.), porfiar por, perseverar para lograr (mejores condiciones, precios, etc.); **s. to (someone),** seguir de cerca (a alguien); **s. to business,** hablar sin ambages, dejarse de rodeos; concentrarse en el asunto; **s. to it,** perseverar en algo, no abandonarlo; **s. to one's guns,** plantarse en sus opiniones; **s. to someone's heels,** seguirle los pasos a alguien; **s. to the point,** concretarse a lo tratado, no irse por las ramas, no divagar; **s. together,** mantenerse unidos, no separarse; **s. up,** erguirse, erizarse; **s. up for,** defender.

stick ball, juego de niños, parecido al béisbol, que se juega en las calles con equipo improvisado.

sticker ['stɪkər, B -ə] *s.* 1. punta, espina. 2. etiqueta engomada, marbete engomado. 3. persona perseverante. 4. (filat.) charnela (de papel engomado). 5. (jer.) navaja usada como arma.

stickful [-ˌfʊl] *s.* (impr.) trozo de composición; paquete (trozo indeterminado de composición).

stickily [-əlɪ] *adv.* 1. pegajosamente, de modo pegajoso. 2. desagradablemente. 3. de manera húmeda, húmedamente.

stickiness [-ɪnəs] *s.* 1. pegajosidad; viscosidad. 2. humedad.

sticking plaster [-ɪŋ-] esparadrapo, tafetán inglés.

stick-in-the-mud ['stɪkənðəˌmʌd] *s.* (fam.) persona de ideas atrasadas, conservador extremista; chapado a la antigua.

stickit ['stɪkət] *a.* (esco.) 1. inconcluso, inacabado. 2. fracasado, frustrado (esp. en una profesión).

stickle ['stɪkəl] *v.i.* 1. contender, porfiar, disputar por menudencias. 2. tener escrúpulos acerca de; objetar.

stickleback ['stɪkəlˌbæk] *s.* (ict.) pez espinoso.

stickler ['stɪklər, B -lə] *s.* 1. (ú. gen. con *for*) rigorista. 2. problema peliagudo.

stickman ['stɪkˌmæn] *s.* empleado en un garito que se encarga de recoger dados y fichas con una vara.

stickpin [-ˌpɪn] *s.* alfiler de corbata.

sticktight [-ˌtaɪt] *s.* (bot.) (variedad de) maravilla, flamenquilla.

stick-to-itive [stɪk'tuətɪv] *a.* tenaz, terco, obstinado, pertinaz, constante.

stick-to-itively [-lɪ] *adv.* tenazmente, obstinadamente.

stick-to-itiveness [-nəs] *s.* tenacidad, obstinación.

stickum ['stɪkəm] *s.* (fam.) cualquier substancia pegajosa o adhesiva.

stickup [-ˌʌp] *s.* (jer.) atraco, asalto.

stickweed [-ˌwid] *s.* (bot.) 1. zuzón, hierba cana. 2. ambrosia. 3. agrimonia.

sticky [-ɪ] *a.* (STICKIER; STICKIEST) 1. pegajoso, pegadizo, viscoso. 2. difícil, ej., *a s. subject,* un tema escabroso. 3. húmedo y caluroso, bochornoso. 4. (jer.) desagradable, penoso.

sticky fingers, (jer.) inclinación a robar o ratear.

stiff [stɪf] *a.* 1. rígido, inflexible, ej., *he has a s. leg,* tiene una pierna rígida. 2. tieso, duro, firme, ej., *s. collar,* cuello duro (muy almidonado). 3. tieso, tenso, tirante, ej., *s. rein,* rienda tirante. 4. espeso; viscoso; craso (arcilla, pasta). 5. denso, compacto, consistente. 6. (fig.) tieso, estirado, ceremonioso, afectado (modales, comportamiento, etc.). 7. fuerte (viento, corriente, etc.). 8. fuerte, cargado (bebidas alcohólicas), ej., *a s. glass of whisky,* un vaso de whiski fuerte. 9. (fig.) severo, duro, ej., *a s. sentence,* una condena severa. 10. (fig.) difícil, arduo, ej., *a s. subject,* una materia difícil. 11. (fam.) subido, excesivo (precio, etc.); firme (mercado, precio). 12. (jer.) borracho. 13. (fam.) a más no poder, ej., *bored s.,* aburrido como una ostra, *scared s.,* muerto de miedo. 14. (mar.) de aguante; que no se inclina mucho (velero). 15. **to be as s. as a board,** estar duro o tieso como un palo; **to keep a s. upper lip,** no amilanarse, mostrar tesón (en adversidad). —*s.* (jer.) 1. cadáver. 2. estúpido, desmañado, patán. 3. vago, vagabundo. 4. gañán.

stiff-arm ['stɪfˌɑrm, B -ˌɑm] *v.t.* (fútbol E.U.) desviar (al contrario) con el brazo estirado.

stiff collar, cuello duro (de la camisa).

stiffen ['stɪfən] *v.t., v.i.* 1. entiesar(se), atiesar(se); poner(se) rígido; endurecer(se), espesar(se). 2. obstinar(se).

stiffener [-ənər, B -nə] *s.* atiesador, montante de refuerzo, ángulo atiesador.

stiffening [-nɪŋ] *s.* refuerzo; atirantamiento.

stiffening beam, (const.) viga refuerzo o de rigidez.

stiffly ['stɪflɪ] *adv.* 1. tiesamente. 2. (fig.) estiradamente, rígidamente, ceremoniosamente.

stiff neck, 1. tortícolis. 2. (fig.) cabeza dura, cabezón.

stiff-necked [-'nɛkt] *a.* terco, obstinado, testarudo, tozudo.

stiffness [-nəs] *s.* 1. tiesura, inflexibilidad. 2. (fig.) estiramiento, rigidez. 3. rigor; obstinación.

stifle ['staɪfəl] *v.t.* 1. sofocar, ahogar, asfixiar. 2. ahogar, apagar, extinguir (fuego, brasas, etc.). 3. ahogar, reprimir, suprimir (sollozo, bostezo, etc.). —*v.i.* ahogarse, asfixiarse, sofocarse. —*s.* (vet.) babada, babilla (articulación de la pata trasera de un cuadrúpedo que corresponde a la rodilla).

stifling ['staɪflɪŋ] *a.* sofocante, asfixiante.

stiflingly [-lɪ] *adv.* sofocantemente.

stigma ['stɪgmə] *s.* (*pl.* STIGMATA [-mətə] o STIGMAS) 1. estigma, lacra. 2. (fig.) estigma, desdoro, afrenta, baldón. 3. (teo.) (*pl.* STIGMATA) estigmas (huellas sobre-naturales en el cuerpo de algunos santos). 4. (anat., zool., bot., med.) estigma. 5. (ant.) estigma (marca de esclavo o de criminal).

stigmasterol [stɪg'mæstəˌrɔl] *s.* (quím.) estigmasterol.

stigmatic [stɪg'mætɪk] **stigmatical** [-ɪkəl] *a.* 1. (bot.) estigmático. 2. (ópt.) anastigmático. 3. estigmatizador, infamante. —*s.* estigmatizado, estigmatizada.

stigmatism ['stɪgməˌtɪzəm] *s.* (ópt.) estigmatismo.

stigmatist [-mətəst] *s.* estigmatizado, estigmatizada.

stigmatization [ˌstɪgmətə'zeɪʃən, B -mətaɪ-] *s.* estigmatización.

stigmatize ['stɪgməˌtaɪz] *v.t.* 1. estigmatizar, marcar con estigmas. 2. (fig.) estigmatizar, infamar, afrentar.

stigmatizer [-ər, B -ə] *s.* estigmatizador, estigmatizadora.

stilbene ['stɪlbin] *s.* (quím.) estilbeno.

stilbestrol [stɪl'bɛsˌtrɔl] *s.* (bioquím.) estilbestrol.

stile [staɪl] *s.* 1. peldaños para pasar sobre una valla, tapia o muro, portillo con escalones. 2. torniquete. 3. (arq.) larguero, montante.

stiletto [stə'lɛtoʊ] *s.* (*pl.* STILETTOS o STILETTOES) 1. estilete, puñal. 2. estilete, púa, punzón. 3. tacón puntiagudo. —*v.t.* apuñalar con un estilete.

still [stɪl] *a.* 1. inmóvil, fijo, inactivo; tranquilo, ej., *s. lake,* lago tranquilo. 2. apacible, sosegado. 3. quieto; silencioso, callado, ej., *s. as the grave,* silencioso como una tumba. 4. quedo, bajo, suave (voz); sordo (ruido). 5. no espumoso (vino). 6. (foto.) fijo (que no muestra movimiento). 7. **to keep s.,** quedarse inmóvil o quieto. —*s.* 1. silencio, quietud, ej., *in the s. of the night,* en la quietud de la noche. 2. (foto.) vista fija, fotografía de lo inmóvil. 3. (cine) fotografía de escenas (para fines de propaganda). 4. alambique, destiladera, destilador. 5. destilería, destilatorio. —*v.t.* 1. aquietar, calmar, apaciguar. 2. apagar (sed); aliviar, mitigar (hambre). 3. acallar, hacer callar, silenciar. 4. destilar. —*v.i.* 1. callar, calmarse, ej., *when the wind stills,* cuando se calme el viento. 2. destilar(se).

still [stɪl] *adv.* 1. todavía, aún. 2. (poét.) continuamente, constantemente, habitualmente. 3. **s. do,** seguir con la costumbre, ej., *although he's eighty, he s. takes a stroll in the garden every night,* aunque cumplió ochenta años, él sigue con la costumbre de dar un paseo en el jardín todas las noche; **s. more,** aun más; **to be s. doing,** seguir con la intención de hacer, siempre hacer (Amer.), ej., *are you s. going to this evening's performance?* ¿por fin vas a la función de esta tarde? —*conj.* sin embargo; con todo; no obstante.

still air, (meteor.) aire tranquilo, aire quieto.

still alarm, alarma de fuego dada sin hacer sonar la sirena (como por ejemplo con una llamada telefónica).

stillbirth ['stɪlˌbɜrθ, B -ˌbɜθ] *s.* parto de un feto muerto.

stillborn [-ˌbɔrn, B -ˌbɔn] *a.* nacido muerto.

still hunt, (E.U.) cacería al acecho.

still-hunt [-ˌhʌnt] *v.t., v.i.* cazar al acecho.

still life, (pint.) bodegón, naturaleza muerta.

stillman ['stɪlmən] *s.* destilador; alambiquero.

stillness ['stɪlnəs] *s.* 1. inmovilidad. 2. tranquilidad, calma. 3. silencio, quietud.

Stillson wrench ['stɪlsən-] (mec.) llave Stillson, llave de tubos.

stilly ['stɪlɪ] *a.* (STILLIER; STILLIEST) (poét.) quieto, silencioso, quedo, calmo, tranquilo.

stilly ['stɪllɪ] *adv.* (raro) tranquilamente, quietamente, silenciosamente.

stilt [stɪlt] *s.* 1. zanco. 2. soporte, pilote. 3. (orn.) cigoñuela. 4. **on stilts,** (fig.) formal, pomposo, ampuloso. —*v.t.* poner en zancos o en soportes.

stilted ['stɪltəd] *a.* tieso, formal, pomposo, ampuloso.

stilted arch, (arq.) arco realzado, arco peraltado, arco remontado.

stime [staɪm] *s.* (pr. Esco. e Irl.) ojeada, vistazo, vislumbre.

stimulant ['stɪmjələnt] *s.* 1. estimulante. 2. bebida alcohólica. 3. (fisiol.) estimulante, agente que produce actividad vital. —*a.* (raro) estimulante.

stimulate [-ˌleɪt] *v.t.* estimular, aguijonear, aguijar, animar, incitar; avivar, excitar. —*v.i.* servir de estímulo o aguijón; ser estimulante.

stimulating [-ɪŋ] *a.* estimulante; excitante.

stimulation [ˌstɪmjə'leɪʃən] *s.* 1. estímulo, incentivo, aguijón; avivamiento. 2. (fisiol.) estímulo, excitación.

stimulative ['stɪmjəˌleɪtɪv, B -lət-] *a.* estimulador, estimulante.

stimulator [-ˌleɪtər, B -ə] *s.* estimulador; excitador.

stimulus ['stɪmjələs] *s.* (*pl.* STIMULI [-ˌlaɪ]) 1. estímulo, incentivo. 2. (psic., fisiol.) estímulo, estimulante.

stimy, *var. de* **stymie.**

sting [stɪŋ] *v.t.* (*pret., p.p.* STUNG [stʌŋ]; *p.pr.* STINGING) 1. picar, pinchar, punzar; herir. 2. (fig.) (*ú. pr. en p.p.* con *with*) atormentar, afligir (por). 3. estimular, incitar, espolear, aguijonear.

4. (jer.) cobrar exorbitantemente; estafar; hacer gastar (dinero). —*v.i.* picar. —*s.* 1. aguijón. 2. picadura, picada. 3. picazón, dolor agudo (del hambre, etc.). 4. (fig.) picante. 5. (fig.) fuerza, vigor, ej., *it has no s. in it,* no tiene fuerza, carece de vigor. 6. sarcasmo, alusión sarcástica (en un chiste). 7. (bot., zool.) aguijón.

sitingaree ['stɪŋəˌri] *s.* (ict.) raya con púa, raya vaca; pastinaca.

stingbull [-ˌbʊl] *s.* (ict.) peje araña.

stinger [-ər, B -ə] *s.* 1. aguijón, púa (de animal o planta), aguijón (de insecto). 2. dicho mordaz. 3. (E.U.) cóctel de crema de menta y brandy.

stingily ['stɪndʒəlɪ] *adv.* miseramente, mezquinamente; escasamente.

stinginess [-dʒɪnəs] *s.* miseria, mezquindad; insuficiencia.

stinging hair ['stɪŋɪŋ-] (bot.) pelo urticante.

stingless [-ləs] *a.* sin aguijón.

stingray [-ˌreɪ] *s.* (ict.) raya con púa, raya vaca; pastinaca.

stingy ['stɪndʒɪ] *a.* (STINGIER; STINGIEST) 1. mísero, avariento, cicatero, tacaño. 2. escaso, poco, insuficiente.

stingy ['stɪŋɪ] *a.* (STINGIER; STINGIEST) punzante; urticante.

stink [stɪŋk] *v.i.* (*pret.* STANK [stæŋk] o STUNK [stʌŋk]; *p.p.* STUNK; *p.pr.* STINKING) 1. apestar, heder. 2. (fig.) tener mala fama o reputación. 3. (jer.) ser muy malo o de mala calidad (actuación, novela, film, etc.). 4. **s. of money,** (jer.) estar podrido en plata. —*v.t.* 1. (gen. con *up*) dar mal olor a, hacer oler mal. 2. (jer.) oler. 3. **s. (one) out,** ahuyentar con humos o vapores hediondos (a uno). —*s.* 1. hedor, hediondez, mal olor. 2. (*pl.*) (jer., G.B.) química (como materia o clase en colegio, etc.). 3. **to raise a s.,** armar un escándalo.

stinkard ['stɪŋkərd, B -kəd] *s.* 1. persona o animal pestilente. 2. (zool.) teledu, tejón malayo. 3. (jer.) tipo vil, canalla.

stink bomb, bomba apestosa, bomba fétida.

stinkbug ['stɪŋkˌbʌg] *s.* (ento.) chinche del bosque; chinche de la madera.

stinker [-ər, B -ə] *s.* 1. tipo maloliente, persona apestosa. 2. (orn.) petrel grande. 3. (jer.) canalla. 4. (jer.) cosa de pésima calidad. 5. (jer.) algo muy difícil (examen, pregunta, etc.).

stinkhorn [-ˌhɔrn, B -ˌhɔn] *s.* (especie de) hongo pestilente.

stinking [-ɪŋ] *a.* 1. hediondo, apestoso, pestilente. 2. (jer.) repugnante, desagradable; (jer.) pésimo, inaceptable.

stinking camomile, (bot.) manzanilla bastarda, manzanilla cimarrona, manzanilla hedionda, magarzuela.

stinking iris, (bot.) lirio hediondo, jíride.

stinkingly [-lɪ] *adv.* hediondamente, con hedor.

stinking nightshade, (bot.) beleño, beleño negro.

stinking smut, (bot.) tizón.

stinko ['stɪŋkoʊ] *a.* (jer.) borracho, ebrio.

stinkpot [-ˌpɑt, B -ˌpɔt] *s.* 1. (hist., mil.) jarro lleno de materiales hediondos y asfixiantes que antiguamente se arrojaba a la cubierta de los barcos enemigos. 2. (jer.) lancha de motor.

stinkstone [-ˌstoʊn] *s.* piedra caliza que al ser frotada o golpeada despide mal olor, esp. antraconita.

stinkweed [-ˌwid] *s.* (bot.) ailanto; higuera loca, estramonio, chamico (Amer.).

stinkwood [-ˌwʊd] *s.* árbol hediondo.

stint [stɪnt] *v.t.* 1. coartar, limitar, restringir. 2. escatimar. 3. (ant.) parar, poner fin a. —*v.i.* 1. cicatear, ser económico o frugal. 2. (ant.) desistir, parar. —*s.* 1. limitación, restricción, límite. 2. tarea, tajo, cuota (de trabajo, etc.). 3. (ant.) cese, cesación, paro. 4. (orn.) tringa.

stinter ['stɪntər, B -ə] *s.* el que restringe o limita; cicatero.

stipe [staɪp] *s.* (bot.) estípite, estipe.

stipel ['staɪpəl] *s.* (bot.) estípula.

stipellate [staɪ'pɛlət, B stɪ-] *a.* (bot.) estipulado.

stipend ['staɪpɛnd, -pənd] *s.* estipendio; remuneración, salario.

stipendiary [staɪ'pɛndɪˌɛrɪ, B -'pɛndjərɪ] *a.* estipendiario, asalariado. —*s.* (*pl.* STIPENDIARIES) 1. estipendiario, asalariado. 2. (hist.) tributario, pechero.

stipes ['staɪpiz] *s.* (*pl.* STIPITES ['stɪpəˌtiz]) 1. (zool.) pedúnculo. 2. (zool., ento.) estípite.

stipitate ['stɪpəˌteɪt] *a.* (bot.) estipitado.

stipitiform [-təˌfɔrm, B -ˌfɔm] *a.* (zool., ento.) estipitiforme.

stipple ['stɪpəl] *v.t.* granear, puntear. —*s.* graneo, (trabajo) punteado, picado.

stippler ['stɪplər, B -lə] *s.* graneador.

stippling [-lɪŋ] *s.* graneo, (trabajo) punteado, picado.

stipular ['stɪpjələr, B -lə] *a.* (bot.) estipular.

stipulate ['stɪpjəˌleɪt] *v.i.* **s. for,** estipular, requerir. —*v.t.* estipular, fijar como condición; condicionar.

stipulate [-lət] **stipulated** [-ˌleɪtəd] *a.* (bot.) estipulado.

stipulation [ˌstɪpjə'leɪʃən] *s.* estipulación, cláusula, condición.

stipulator ['stɪpjəˌleɪtər, B -ə] *s.* estipulante.

stipulatory [-ləˌtɔrɪ, B -tərɪ] *a.* estipulante.

stipule ['stɪpjul] *s.* (bot.) estípula.

stir [stɜr, B stɜ] *v.t.* (*pret., p.p.* STIRRED; *p.pr.* STIRRING) 1. agitar, revolver. 2. mover, remover. 3. atizar, avivar (la lumbre). 4. (fig.) agitar, disturbar (agua, silencio, conciencia, etc.). 5. mover, incitar. 6. despertar, provocar (sentimiento, controversia, etc.). 7. **s. one's bile,** enfadar, molestar a uno; **s. one's blood,** entusiasmar, exaltar, hacerle bullir a uno la sangre; **s. oneself,** esforzarse, hacer un esfuerzo; **s. the pulse,** hacer bullir la sangre; **s. up,** agitar, incitar, inflamar; estimular, fomentar; **s. up discontent,** fomentar el descontento. —*v.i.* 1. moverse, cambiar de posición. 2. agitarse, menearse, estar ocupado. 3. levantarse (de la cama), ej., *he is not stirring yet,* todavía no se ha levantado. 4. (ant.) excitarse, inflamarse. 5. revolver un líquido. —*s.* 1. impresión, sensación, ej., *the news of his death made a great s.,* la noticia de su muerte causó honda impresión. 2. conmoción, alboroto, tumulto, disturbio. 3. movimiento corto o ligero, meneo. 4. hurgonazo; aguijonada, aguijonazo; (fig.) acicate, estímulo. 5. (jer.) chirona, gayola, cana (Amer.). 6. **to create a s.,** hacer (o meter) ruido; **to make a s.,** dejar una impresión.

stirabout ['stɜrəˌbaʊt] *s.* gachas de harina de avena o maíz hervida en agua o leche.

stir-crazy ['stɜrˌkreɪzɪ, B 'stɜˌ-] *a.* (jer.) neuróticamente afectado por un prolongado encierro, particularmente en una prisión.

stirk [stɜrk, B stɜk] *s.* (G.B.) eral.

stirp [stɜrp, B stɜp] *s.* estirpe, linaje.

stirpiculture ['stɜrpɪˌkʌltʃər, B 'stɜp-tʃə] *s.* estirpicultura.

stirps [stɜrps, B stɜps] *s.* (*pl.* STIRPES ['stɜrpiz, B 'stɜpiz]) 1. estirpe, linaje. 2. raza, casta (de animales). 3. (der.) estirpe.

stirrer ['stɜrər, B 'stɜrə] *s.* agitador (instrumento); varilla agitadora.

stirring [-ɪŋ] *a.* incitador, incitante, excitador; conmovedor. —*s.* 1. ligero movimiento. 2. (*gen. pl.*) remordimientos (de la conciencia).

stirringly [-lɪ] *adv.* en tono incitante o conmovedor.

stirrup ['stɜrəp, B 'stɪr-] *s.* 1. estribo, estribera. 2. (mar.) estribo de marchapié.

stirrup bone, (anat.) estribo.

stirrup cup, trago o copa de despedida, copa del estribo.

stirrup leather, s. strap, ación.

stirrup pump, bomba de estribo.

stitch [stɪtʃ] *s.* 1. puntada (de costura), punto (de costura o tejido); sutura. 2. punzada, punto de costado. 3. (fam.) el mínimo (esp. de ropa). 4. (dial.) espacio recorrido; distancia; jornada, lapso (de tiempo). 5. **to be in stitches,** desternillarse de risa; **to drop a s.,** dejar escapar un punto (de tejido); **to have not a dry s. on (oneself),** empaparse por completo. —*v.t.* 1. coser; hilvanar, embastar, bastear. 2. engrapar, unir con grapas. 3. **s. up,** remendar. —*v.i.* hacer labores o costuras.

stitch welding, soldadura por puntos.

stitchwort ['stɪtʃˌwɜrt, B -ˌwɜt] *s.* (bot.) álsine.

stithy ['stɪðɪ] *s.* (*pl.* STITHIES) (ant., poét.) 1. yunque, bigornia. 2. herrería; fragua, forja.

stive [staɪv] *s.* harija.

stiver ['staɪvər, B -və] *s.* 1. moneda holandesa. 2. (fig.) pito, comino, ej., *it's not worth a s.,* no vale un pito, no vale un comino. 3. (fig.) blanca, centavo, ej., *I haven't a s.,* estoy sin blanca, no tengo ni un centavo.

stoa ['stoʊə] *s.* (*pl.* STOAE [-i] o STOAS) (hist.) estilóbato, pórtico (en la antigua Grecia).

stoat [stoʊt] *s.* (zool.) armiño europeo; comadreja o armiño de cola negra.

stob [stɑb, B stɔb] *s.* (dial.) estaca, poste, garrote.

stoccado [stə'kɑdoʊ] *a.* (ant.) estocada, puñalada.

stochastic [stoʊ'kæstɪk, B stɔ-] *a.* fortuito, casual.

stock [stɑk, B stɔk] *s.* 1. tronco, tocón. 2. madero, palo, poste. 3. (fig.) zoquete, tronco, tonto. 4. base, soporte, puntal. 5. caja (del fusil, del cepillo); cepo (del ancla, del cañon); portacojinetes. 6. cepa, tallo. 7. patrón (en que se hace un injerto). 8. cepa, linaje, estirpe, raza; p. ext. fuente, origen. 9. mango (de látigo, caña de pescar, etc.). 10. berbiquí, manubrio de taladro; terraja. 11. (*pl.*) cepo chino. 12. (*pl.*) potro (en que se sujeta a un animal para marcarlo o herrarlo). 13. materia prima. 14. extracto, base concentrada, esencia (de sopa, carne, etc.). 15. abasto, existencias, surtido, provisión (de mercaderías). 16. (com.) capital comercial, acciones; valores. 17. ganado; ganado y equipo (de una granja), ej., *fat s.,* ganado cebado. 18. alzacuello, corbatín. 19. baceta (de naipes); monte (de dominó). 20. (bot.) (variedad de) alhelí. 21. (teat.) repertorio. 22. (*pl.*) (mar.) basada (de construcción). 23. **in s.,** en existencia (mercancía, etc.); **laughing s.,** hazmerreír; **lock s. and barrel,** por completo; **off the stocks,** (mar.) lanzado, botado (buque); (fig.) terminado, completado; **on the stocks,** (mar.) en construcción; (fig.) en preparación; **out of s.,** agotado; **to have (something) in s.,** tener existencias de (algo); **to take s.,** inventariar, hacer inventario; **to take s. in,** (fig.) interesarse por; **to take s. of,** (fig.) evaluar, estimar (carácter, situación, etc.). —*v.t.* 1. abastecer, proveer, surtir. 2. llevar en existencia; almacenar, aprovisionar. 3. apacentar, pacer. 4. encepar (armas de fuego, anclas, etc.). —*v.i.* 1. brotar, salir (hojas o renuevos). 2. **s. up on,** proveerse de (bastimentos), abastecerse de. —*a.* 1. constante, usual. 2. muy usado o repetido, estereotipado, trillado, banal. 3. semental (animal macho); dedicado a la reproducción, reproductor. 4. ganadero, para ganado. 5. bursátil, de la bolsa (de valores); (teat.) de repertorio. 6. (com.) existente, de surtido (mercancías); 7. (com.) accionario (mercado).

stockade [stɑ'keɪd, B stɔ-] *s.* 1. palenque, empalizada, valla, vallado, estacada. 2. cercado, corral (de empalizadas). 3. prisión militar. —*v.t.* empalizar; fortificar o proteger con empalizadas.

stock book, 1. (com., ten.) libro de existencias, libro de almacén. 2. (filat.) libro para sellos (de correo) sueltos (en venta o para canje).

stockbreeder ['stɑkˌbridər, B 'stɔk-ə] *s.* criador de ganado.

stockbroker [-ˌbroʊkər, B -kə] *s.* (bolsa) bolsista, corredor de bolsa.

stockbrokerage [-kərɪdʒ] *s.* correduría de bolsa; corredores de bolsa (en conjunto).

stockbroking [-kɪŋ] *s.* corretaje de bolsa.

stock car, 1. (f.c.) vagón jaula (para transportar ganado). 2. automóvil corriente modificado para carreras.

stock certificate, certificado o título de acciones.

stock clerk, empleado de almacén.

stock company, 1. (fin.) sociedad anónima, sociedad o compañía por acciones. 2. (teat.) compañía de repertorio.

stock dividend, (com.) dividendo en acciones.

stock dove, (orn.) paloma brava, paloma silvestre.

stock exchange, 1. (com.) bolsa (de valores), lonja (de acciones). 2. asociación de corredores de bolsa.

stock farm, granja o hacienda ganadera.

stock farmer, ganadero.

stock farming, ganadería.

stockfish ['stɑkˌfɪʃ, B 'stɔk-] *s.* pescado secado al aire libre y sin sal (como bacalao, merluza, etc.).

stockholder [-ˌhoʊldər, B -də] *s.* accionista, tenedor de títulos o acciones.

Stockholm ['stɑkˌhoʊm, B 'stɔk-] *s.* Estocolmo, capital de Suecia.

Stockholm tar, alquitrán de leña.

stockily ['stɑkəlɪ, B 'stɔk-] *adv.* robustamente.

stockiness [-ɪnəs] *s.* robustez, fortaleza.

stockinette, stockinet [ˌstɑkə'nɛt, B ˌstɔk-] *s.* (tej.) tricot, tejido elástico de punto (usado para medias, ropa interior, etc.).

stocking ['stɑkɪŋ, B 'stɔk-] *s.* media, calceta; **in one's s. feet,** sólo con las medias puestas (sin zapatos).

stocking cap, gorro tejido en forma de cono con una borla en el extremo (usado para ciertos deportes o por los niños).

stockingless [-ləs] *a.* sin medias.

stock in hand, (com., ten.) existencias disponibles.

stock-in-trade ['stɑkən'treɪd, B 'stɔk-] *s.* 1. existencias de una tienda (para la venta). 2. equipo indispensable (para ejercer un oficio), útiles (de un artesano). 3. (fig.) recursos o expedientes usuales.

stockish ['stɑkɪʃ, B 'stɔk-] *a.* como un tronco, insensible; estúpido, necio, tonto.

stockjobber [-ˌdʒɑbər, B -ˌdʒɔbə] *s.* (E.U.) corredor de bolsa; agiotista; especulador de bolsa; (G.B.) agente de corredores de bolsa.

stockjobbing [-ɪŋ] *s.* corretaje de bolsa; agio, especulación.

stockman [-mən, -ˌmæn] *s.* 1. ganadero, ranchero; vaquero. 2. (E.U.) almacenero.

stock market, (com.) mercado o bolsa de valores, lonja (de acciones); **to play the s. m.,** jugar a la bolsa de valores.

stock option, opción que concede al tenedor el privilegio de comprar acciones de una empresa antes de una fecha específica a determinado precio.

stockpile [-ˌpaɪl] *s.* reservas, acumulación, acopio (de materias primas, alimentos, etc.). —*v.t., v.i.* acumular, almacenar, acopiar, apilar.

stockpot [-ˌpɑt, B -ˌpɔt] *s.* 1. olla para preparar extracto (de sopa, etc.). 2. vasija de zarandajas.

stock power, carta poder sobre acciones.

stock raiser, criador de ganado, ganadero.

stock raising, ganadería, cría de ganado.

stockroom ['stɑkˌrum, -ˌrʊm, B 'stɔk-] almacén, depósito (de mercaderías).

stocks and stones, cosas exánimes; gente aletargada.

stock split, (com.) reparto de acciones gratis.

stock-still ['stɑk'stɪl, B 'stɔk-] *a.* inmóvil, enteramente quieto (como un poste).

stocky [-ɪ] *a.* (STOCKIER; STOCKIEST) rechoncho, recoquín, regordete; robusto.

stockyard ['stɑkˌjɑrd, B 'stɔkˌjɑd] *s.* corral de ganado (esp. temporal).

stodge [stɑdʒ, B stɔdʒ] *v.t.* atiborrar, atracar, hartar, ahitar (de comida). —*v.i.* tragar.

stodgily ['stɑdʒəlɪ, B 'stɔdʒ-] *adv.* torpemente; con pedantería; insípidamente, aburridamente, pesadamente.

stodginess [-ɪnəs] *s.* torpeza; pesadez; insipidez.

stodgy ['stɑdʒɪ, B 'stɔdʒɪ] *a.* (STODGIER; STODGIEST) 1. pesado, indigestible, que sacia o harta (comida). 2. atestado, colmado, henchido, relleno. 3. rechoncho. 4. pesado, aburrido, torpe, soso, pedante, insípido.

stoechiology [ˌstikɪ'ɑlədʒɪ, B -'ɔl-] **stoechiometry** [-'ɑmətrɪ, B -'ɔm-] *vars. de* **stoichiology, stoichiometry.**

stogie, stogy ['stoʊgɪ] *s.* (*pl.* STOGIES) 1. tagarnina, cigarro barato. 2. bota o zapato fuerte y burdo.

stoic ['stoʊɪk] *s.* 1. **S.,** (filos.) estoico. 2. persona estoica. —*a.* 1. **S.,** (filos.) estoico, de los estoicos. 2. estoico, impasible.

stoically [-ɪkəlɪ] *adv.* estoicamente, impasiblemente.

stoicalness [-ɪkəlnəs] *s.* estoicismo, impasibilidad.

stoichiology [ˌstɔɪkɪ'ɑlədʒɪ, B -'ɔl-] *s.* (fisiol.) estequiología.

stoichiometric [-ə'mɛtrɪk] *a.* estequiométrico.

stoichiometry [-'ɑmətrɪ, B -'ɔm-] *s.* estequiometría.

stoicism ['stoʊəˌsɪzəm] *s.* 1. **S.,** (filos.) estoicismo. 2. estoicismo, impasibilidad.

stoke [stoʊk] *v.t.* 1. atizar, avivar (el fuego); cebar, alimentar (horno, etc.); cargar (caldera). 2. llenar (de comida). —*v.i.* 1. atizar el fuego; alimentar el fuego; cebar el horno, cargar la caldera. 2. llenarse (de comida).

stokehold ['stoʊkˌhoʊld] *s.* (mar.) cuarto de calderas, puesto del fogonero.

stokehole [-ˌhoʊl] *s.* 1. boca del horno. 2. puesto del fogonero.

stoker ['stoʊkər, B -kə] *s.* 1. fogonero, cargador. 2. (mec.) alimentador cargador (aparato).

stokesia [stoʊ'kiʒɪə, B 'stoʊksɪə] *s.* (bot.) áster de Stokes.

stole [stoʊl] *s.* estola.

stole [stoʊl] *pret. de* **steal.**

stolen ['stoʊlən] *p.p. de* **steal.**

stolid ['stɑləd, B 'stɔl-] *a.* impasible, insensible, imperturbable.

stolidity [stɑ'lɪdətɪ, stə-, B stə-] *s.* impasibilidad.

stolidly ['stɑlədlɪ, B 'stɔl-] *adv.* impasiblemente.

stollen ['stoʊlən, B 'stɔ-] *s.* (*pl.* STOLLEN o STOLLENS) pan dulce con frutas y nueces.

stolon ['stoʊlən] *s.* (bot., zool.) estolón.

stoloniferous [ˌstoʊlə'nɪfərəs] *a.* (bot., zool.) estolonífero.

stoma ['stoʊmə] *s.* (*pl.* STOMATA [-mətə] o STOMAS) (bot., fisiol.) estoma.

stomach ['stʌmək] *s.* 1. estómago. 2. (fig.) apetito; deseo, inclinación, gana. 3. (fam.) abdomen, vientre, barriga. 4. (ant.) disposición, humor, temple; orgullo, arrogancia. 5. **pit of the s.,** boca del estómago; **to have a strong s.,** tener mucho estómago; **to turn one's s.,** revolver el estómago a uno. —*v.t.* (*pret., p.p.* STOMACHED; *p.pr.* STOMACHING) 1. (fig.) tragar, aguantar, sufrir. 2. (ant.) resentirse de.

stomachache [-ˌeɪk] *s.* dolor de estómago.

stomacher [-ər, B -ə] *s.* (hist.) peto (antigua prenda de vestir).

stomachic [stə'mækɪk] *a.* estomacal, estomatical; (med.) digestivo. —*s.* (med.) digestivo, medicamento estomacal.

stomach pump, bomba estomacal.

stomach tooth, (anat.) canino inferior (de leche).

stomachy ['stʌməkɪ] *a.* 1. barrigudo, panzudo, ventrudo. 2. (dial. G.B.) irritable; porfiado.

stomata, *pl. de* **stoma.**

stomatal ['stoʊmətəl, B 'stɔm-] *a.* (bot., zool.) estomático.

stomatic [stoʊ'mætɪk] *a.* (bot., zool.) estomático.

stomatitis [ˌstoʊmə'taɪtəs, B ˌstɔmə-] *s.* (med.) estomatitis.

stomatology [-'tɑlədʒɪ, B -'tɔl-] *s.* (med.) estomatología.

stomatopod [-'mætəˌpɑd, B -ˌpɔd] *s.* (zool.) estomatópodo.

stomodaeum, stomodeum [-mə'diəm] *s.* (*pl.* STOMODAEA, STOMODEA) (anat.) estomodeo.

stomp [stɑmp, B stɔmp] *s.* baile con música de jazz y zapateo.

stone [stoʊn] *s.* 1. piedra. 2. canto, guijarro. 3. lápida sepulcral; pedernal, muela; piedra amoladera o afiladera. 4. piedra (preciosa), gema. 5. hueso, cuesco (de las frutas). 6. (*pl.* STONE) (G.B.) 14 libras (medida de peso). 7. piedra litográfica. 8. (med.) cálculo, piedra. 9. (impr.) piedra o mesa de imponer. 10. **those who live in glass houses should not throw stones,** quien tiene rabo de paja no debe acercarse al fuego; **to cast the first s.,** arrojar la primera piedra; **to leave no s. unturned,** no dejar piedra por mover. —*v.t.* 1. apedrear, lapidar, matar a pedradas. 2. deshuesar, despepitar. 3. empedrar, revestir de piedras; fortificar con piedras. 4. (ant.) endurecer, petrificar. 5. **s. to death,** matar a pedradas. —*a.* pétreo, de piedra.

Stone Age, Edad de Piedra.

stone ax, 1. martillo para desbastar piedra. 2. hacha de piedra (prehistórico).

stone-blind ['stoʊnˌblaɪnd] *a.* ciego como un topo, completamente ciego.

stone-blindness [-nəs] *s.* ceguera absoluta.

stone-broke ['stoʊn'broʊk] *a.* (jer.) arrancado (Amer.), arruinado, sin un centavo.

stonechat [-ˌtʃæt] *s.* (orn.) culiblanco; sacristán.

stone coal, antracita, carbón de piedra.

stone-cold [-'koʊld] *a.* completamente frío.

stonecrop [-ˌkrɑp, B -ˌkrɔp] *s.* (bot.) uva cana, uva canilla, uva de gato.

stone crusher, (maq.) chancadora de piedra, quebradora de roca, trituradora.

stone curlew, (orn.) alcaraván, charadrio.

stonecutter [-ˌkʌtər, B -ˌkʌtə] *s.* 1. picapedrero, cantero, cincelador, pedrero, tallista de piedra. 2. máquina para labrar piedra.

stonecutting [-ˌkʌtɪŋ] *s.* cantería, labrado de la piedra, aserrado de la piedra.
stoned [stoʊnd] *a.* 1. (jer.) ajumado, borracho; intoxicado o delirante (por efecto de las drogas). 2. deshuesado (frutas).
stone-deaf ['stoʊn'dɛf] *a.* sordo como una tapia.
stone-deafness [-nəs] *s.* sordera total.
stone fruit, (bot.) fruta de hueso.
stone-ground ['stoʊn'graʊnd] *a.* molido por piedra (de molino).
stoneman [-mən] *s.* (impr.) platinero, impositor, imponedor.
stone marten, s. martin, (zool.) garduña, garduño, fuina.
stonemason [-ˌmeɪsən] *s.* albañil, mampostero, asentador.
stonemasonry [-ˌmeɪsənrɪ] *s.* albañilería o mampostería de piedra.
stone parsley, (bot.) (variedad de) amomo.
stone pit, cantera, pedrera.
stoner ['stoʊnər, B -ə] *s.* 1. apedreador. 2. empedrador. 3. despepitador, deshuesador (de frutas).
stone saw, sierra de cantero, sierra de piedra.
stone's throw, tiro de piedra; **a s.'s t. from,** a tiro de piedra de, a dos (o pocos) pasos de.
stonewall ['stoʊn'wɔl] *v.i.* 1. (criquet) jugar sólo a la defensiva (el bateador). 2. (pr. G.B.) practicar obstruccionismo (parlamentario), emplear tácticas obstruccionistas (para ganar tiempo).
stonewaller [-ər, B -ə] *s.* obstruccionista.
stoneware [-ˌwɛr, B -wɛə] *s.* vasijas de gres, cacharros de barro.
stonework [-ˌwɜrk, B -wɜk] *s.* 1. cantería, albañilería de piedra, obra de mampostería o de sillería. 2. tallado y engaste de piedras preciosas.
stonewort ['stoʊnˌwɜrt, B -wɜt] *s.* (bot.) (especie de) alga carácea.
stonily ['stoʊnəlɪ] *adv.* rígidamente, inflexiblemente, sin compasión, despiadadamente.
stoniness [-ɪnəs] *s.* rigidez, inflexibilidad, insensibilidad.
stony [-ɪ] *a.* (STONIER; STONIEST) 1. pedregoso, cascajoso, guijoso, lleno o cubierto de piedras. 2. pétreo, lapídeo, lapidoso. 3. (fig.) rígido, duro, inflexible, insensible, despiadado. 4. (fig.) paralizador (miedo, pena, etc.). 5. (ant., poét.) hecho de piedra.
stony-broke ['stoʊnɪ'broʊk] *a.* (jer., G.B.) arrancado (Amer.), arruinado, sin un centavo.
stonyhearted [-'hartəd, B -ˌhɑt-] *a.* de corazón de piedra, insensible, cruel, despiadado.
stood, *pret., p.p. de* **stand.**
stooge [studʒ] *s.* 1. (jer.) actor que hace preguntas preparadas a un comediante que las contesta chistosamente. 2. (jer.) lugarteniente, secuaz servil, paniaguado. 3. (jer.) soplón, delator, espía.
stook [stuk, stʊk] *s.* (G.B.) fajina de maíz. —*v.i.* atresnalar.
stool [stul] *s.* 1. taburete, banqueta (para sentarse). 2. escañuelo, escabel, banqueta (para los pies). 3. bacín, inodoro, sillico. 4. evacuación del vientre; deposiciones, cámara. 5. (bot.) tocón, cepa, planta madre. —*v.i.* 1. echar tallos o retoños. 2. defecar, evacuar el vientre. 3. (jer.) dar el soplo, hacer el papel de soplón.
stoolie ['stulɪ] *s.* (fam.) soplón, delator, espía (al servicio de la policía).
stool pigeon, 1. cimbel (paloma que sirve de señuelo). 2. (fig., fam.) soplón, delator, espía (al servicio de la policía).
stoop [stup] *v.i.* 1. agacharse, encorvarse. 2. (fig.) condescender, dignarse. 3. (fig.) rebajarse, degradarse. 4. ceder, flaquear, doblegarse, someterse. 5. abatirse, arrojarse sobre la presa (halcón, etc.). —*v.t.* 1. inclinar hacia adelante, encorvar. 2. (fig.) rebajar, degradar. —*s.* 1. inclinación (hacia adelante), encorvada. 2. condescendencia; concesión. 3. abatimiento (de un ave de rapiña). 4. (E.U.) corredor o galería (a la entrada de una casa), pórtico, porche, veranda. 5. (dial.) poste, columna, pilar.
stoop, *var. de* **stoup.**
stop [stɑp, B stɔp] *v.t.* (*pret., p.p* STOPPED; *p.pr.* STOPPING) 1. parar, detener. 2. atajar, parar, interceptar. 3. interrumpir. 4. suspender, cortar, suprimir. 5. paralizar. 6. (t. con *up*) cerrar, tapar o cubrir (agujero o abertura); obturar, taponar, rellenar; obstruir, atascar; contener, estancar, represar; restañar. 7. (mús.) pisar (cuerda de violín, guitarra, etc.); tapar (agujeros de clarinete, trompeta, etc.). 8. (gram., ret.) puntuar. 9. (dep.) derribar (púgil), p. ext. derrotar, vencer. 10. (mar.) amarrar. 11. (bridge) bloquear (un palo). 12. **s. (doing),** dejar de (hacer); **s. a blow,** parar un golpe; **s. a bullet,** recibir un balazo; **s. a tooth,** (pr. G.B.) empastar un diente; **s. down,** (foto.) diafragmar (cámara, objetivo); **s. from,** impedir, disuadir (a alguien); retener (una suma, etc.) de (sueldo, etc.); **s. off,** apelmazar con arena (parte del molde de fundición); **s. one,** (jer.) recibir un balazo; **s. one's breath,** asfixiar, sofocar, matar a uno; **s. one's ears,** taparse los oídos; **s. one's mouth,** (fig.) tapar la boca a uno; **s. out,** (impr.) enmascarar (parte de un negativo); **s. payment (of a check,** etc.), mandar suspender el pago (de un cheque, etc.); **s. the gas (water,** etc.), cortar el (suministro de) gas (agua, etc.). —*v.i.* 1. detenerse, hacer alto, pararse. 2. acabarse, terminar. 3. cesar, desistir, parar. 4. (pr. G.B.) quedarse, permanecer; demorarse, tardar. 5. **s. at,** alojarse en, hospedarse en; **s. at nothing,** no reparar en nada; **s. by,** hacer una visita corta; **s. dead** (o **short**), pararse de sopetón, pararse en seco; **s. off (at),** apearse (en); quedarse un rato (en); **s. over,** pasar la noche, pernoctar; quedarse un poco; **s. up,** atascarse, atorarse, obstruirse; no acostarse, velar; **s. with,** alojarse en la casa de (alguien). —*s.* 1. alto, detención, parada. 2. cesación, interrupción, suspensión, paro. 3. pausa. 4. fin, término. 5. estada, estancia, permanencia, quedada. 6. apeadero, parada (de autobús, etc.), paradero. 7. obstáculo, obstrucción. 8. taco, tapón, tarugo. 9. (mec.) fiador, leva, linguete, retén, tope, limitador, parador; trinquete, seguro. 10. (mús.) agujero (de flauta, clarinete, etc.); tecla, llave; traste (de guitarra); registro (del órgano). 11. punto (en cablegramas, telegramas, etc.). 12. (gram.) (pr. G.B.) signo de puntuación. 13. (fon.) cierre; consonante oclusiva. 14. (mar.) baderna, barbeta, boza. 15. (ópt., foto.) abertura (del objetivo); diafragma. 16. **to bring to a s.,** parar, detener; **to come to a (full) s.,** cesar o parar (completamente); **to pull out all the stops,** echar todos los registros (de un órgano); (fig.) hacer todo lo que uno puede.
stop bath, (foto.) baño de corte.
stopcock ['stɑpˌkɑk, B 'stɔpˌkɔk] *s.* robinete, llave de cierre, llave de paso, grifo.
stop collar, (mec.) collar de tope.
stope [stoʊp] *s.* (min.) bancada, labor escalonada, labor vertical. —*v.i., v.t.* (min.) excavar en escalones.
stopgap ['stɑpˌgæp, B 'stɔp-] *s.* 1. tapón, relleno. 2. recurso momentáneo, substituto temporal.
stop knob, (mús.) llave de registro (del órgano).
stoplight [-ˌlaɪt] *s.* 1. semáforo (para dirigir el tránsito). 2. lámpara de alto, luz de parada, farolito señalero.
stop nut, (mec.) tuerca limitadora, contra tuerca.
stop order, stop-loss order, (bolsa) orden de compra (o venta) a precio determinado.
stopover [-ˌoʊvər, B -oʊvə] *s.* escala, parada temporal, apeadero.
stoppage [-ɪdʒ] *s.* 1. parada, detención, alto. 2. cesación, interrupción. 3. obstrucción, impedimento. 4. obturación, oclusión. 5. paralización, suspensión; entorpecimiento, cese, paro, huelga. 6. (med.) estrangulación.
stop payment, suspensión del pago (de un cheque por el girador).
stopped [stɑpt, B stɔpt] *a.* 1. cerrado, tapado. 2. obstruído, atorado, bloqueado. 3. refrenado, reprimido, contenido.
stopper ['stɑpər, B 'stɔpə] *s.* 1. tapón, taco, tarugo, tapador, tapadero, obturador, detenedor; retén, fiador. 2. (mar.) baderna, barbeta, boza. 3. (fam.) persona o cosa que atrae la atención. 4. **to put a s. on (something),** hacer cesar, poner coto a (algo). —*v.t.* 1. taponar. 2. (mar.) abozar, abarbetar.
stopper knot, nudo en una cuerda que le impide pasar por una abertura.
stopple [-əl] *s.* tapón, taco. —*v.t.* taponar.
stop screw, tornillo limitador, tornillo de tope.
stop street, calle en una intersección donde todo el tráfico debe hacer una pausa antes de continuar.
stop valve, válvula de cierre.
stopwatch [-ˌwɑtʃ, B -wɔtʃ] *s.* cronómetro, cronógrafo.
storable ['stɔrəbəl] *s.* que se puede guardar o almacenar (mercancías, víveres, etc.).
storage ['stɔrɪdʒ] *s.* 1. almacenamiento, acopio. 2. depósito, almacén. 3. almacenaje. 4. (elec.) acumulación.
storage battery, (elec.) acumulador, batería de acumuladores.
storage cell, (elec.) acumulador, elemento de acumulador.
storage reservoir, embalse de almacenamiento, embalse de reserva, depósito de acumulación.
storax ['stɔræks] *s.* (bot.) estoraque (árbol y bálsamo), azúmbar (bálsamo).
store [stɔr, B stɔ] *v.t.* 1. almacenar, guardar. 2. dar cabida a, contener. 3. abastecer, proveer; municionar, pertrechar. 4. **s. away,** acumular, reservar. —*s.* 1. tienda, almacén. 2. almacen, depósito. 3. provisión, surtido. 4. (fig.) reservas, abundancia, acopio. 5. (*pl.*) pertrechos, equipo (militares, navales, etc.). 6. **to be in s. for one,** esperarle a uno (una sorpresa); **to have in s.,** tener guardado, tener reservado; **to have in s. for,** guardar para; **to set s. by,** dar importancia a, apreciar. —*a.* 1. (t. **stores**) de almacenamiento. 2. de almacén, confeccionado, de confección.
storefront ['stɔrˌfrʌnt, B 'stɔˌ-] *s.* la parte frontal de una tienda o almacén; las vidrieras o escaparates frontales. —*a.* alojado o situado en un espacio originalmente destinado para una tienda.
storehouse [-ˌhaʊs] *s.* 1. almacén, depósito 2. (fig.) mina (de conocimientos, noticias, etc.), fuente inagotable (de energías, etc.).
storekeeper [-ˌkipər, B -ˌkipə] *s.* 1. guardalmacén, almacenero. 2. tendero. 3. (mar.) pañolero.
storeroom [-ˌrum, -ˌrʊm] *s.* 1. cuarto de almacenar, bodega, despensa. 2. (mar.) pañol.
storewide [-ˌwaɪd] *a.* en toda la tienda, por todo el almacén, ej., *s. sale,* venta general, realización de todos los artículos.
storey ['stɔrɪ] **storeyed** [-ɪd] *vars. de* **story** (piso), **storied** (de pisos).

storied [-ɪd] *a.* 1. historiado. 2. legendario; celebrado por la historia. 3. (*ú. en palabras compuestas*) de (tantos) pisos (edificio), ej., *three-s. house,* casa de tres pisos.
stork [stɔrk, B stɔk] *s.* (orn.) cigüeña.
stork's-bill ['stɔrks,bɪl, B 'stɔks-] *s.* (bot.) geranio.
storm [stɔrm, B stɔm] *s.* 1. tempestad, temporal, tormenta, borrasca. 2. (fig.) tempestad, tormenta, confusión, tumulto; arrebato; frenesí. 3. (mil.) ataque, asalto. 4. (mar.) vendaval, huracán. 5. **to take by s.,** tomar por asalto. —*v.i.* 1. haber tormenta, descargar la tempestad. 2. (fig.) tempestear, bramar o estallar de cólera. —*v.t.* asaltar, tomar por asalto.
stormbound ['stɔrm,baʊnd, B 'stɔm-] *a.* demorado o paralizado por la tormenta.
storm cellar, sótano que sirve de refugio durante las tormentas.
storm center, 1. centro de una tormenta o ciclón. 2. (fig.) centro o foco de un problema, tumulto o disturbio.
storm door, guardapuerta, contrapuerta, cancel.
stormily [-əlɪ] *adv.* tempestuosamente, violentamente.
storm in a teacup, tempestad en un vaso de agua.
storminess [-ɪnəs] *s.* 1. estado tempestuoso. 2. ambiente acalorado, atmósfera caldeada (de una sesión, debate, etc.).
storm jib, (mar.) trinquetilla de capa.
storm lantern, (pr. G.B.) farol de seguridad.
storm trooper, miliciano nazi.
storm window, contraventana, contravidriera, sobrevidriera.
stormy [-ɪ] *a.* (STORMIER; STORMIEST) tempestuoso, borrascoso, violento, turbulento.
stormy petrel, 1. (orn.) petrel de las tormentas. 2. (fig.) pendenciero; persona de mal agüero.
story ['stɔrɪ] *s.* (*pl.* STORIES) 1. historia, cuento; fábula, anécdota. 2. trama, argumento. 3. narración, relato, versión. 4. (fam.) mentira, embuste. 5. (E.U.) artículo (noticioso). 6. piso, planta. 7. **it is quite another s. now,** ésta es una versión distinta: eso es harina de otro costal; **the s. goes,** se dice, corre el rumor; to make a long s. short, en resumidas cuentas. —*v.t.* (*pret., p.p.* STORIED; *p.pr.* STORYING) 1. embellecer con historias. 2. (ant.) historiar; narrar.
storybook [-,bʊk] *s.* libro de cuentos (gen. de historietas para niños).
storyteller [-,tɛlər, B -,tɛlə] *s.* 1. narrador. 2. (fam.) cuentista, mentiroso, chismoso.
storytelling [-,tɛlɪŋ] *s.* 1. narración. 2. chismorreo. —*a.* 1. narrador. 2. cuentista, chismoso.
stoup [stup] *s.* 1. copa, vaso. 2. (relig.) pila (de agua bendita). 3. (esco.) balde, cubo.
stour [stʊr, B stʊə] *s.* 1. (dial., G.B.) tumulto, alboroto. 2. (esco.) polvo, barcia. 3. (ant.) lucha, conflicto.
stout [staʊt] *a.* 1. bravo, valiente, intrépido. 2. firme, determinado; obstinado, terco. 3. fuerte, vigoroso, enérgico, violento. 4. sólido, duradero, substancial. 5. grueso, robusto, corpulento, gordo. 6. **a s. heart,** (fig.) coraje. —*s.* 1. persona gorda o corpulenta. 2. tamaño extra grande (de ropa). 3. cerveza (fuerte) de malta.
stouthearted ['staʊt'hɑrtəd, B -'hɑt-] *a.* bravo, valiente, intrépido.
stoutheartedly [-lɪ] *adv.* bravamente, valientemente.
stoutish ['staʊtɪʃ] *a.* algo robusto, bastante gordo o corpulento, tirando a gordo.
stoutly [-lɪ] *adv.* 1. resueltamente, valientemente; con vigor. 2. firmemente, sólidamente; obstinadamente.
stoutness [-nəs] *s.* 1. fuerza, solidez. 2. resolución, determinación, firmeza, fortaleza. 3. grosor, robustez; corpulencia, gordura.
stove [stoʊv] *s.* 1. estufa, hornillo, cocina. 2. horno. 3. (pr. G.B.) invernáculo, invernadero.
stove [stoʊv] *pret., p.p de* **stave.**
stovepipe ['stoʊv,paɪp] *s.* 1. tubo de la chimenea, tubo de la estufa. 2. (fam., E.U.) chistera, sombrero de copa (alta), tarro (de unto) (Amer.).
stover ['stoʊvər, B -və] *s.* (dial., G.B.) forraje (para animales).
stow [stoʊ] *v.t.* 1. guardar, almacenar. 2. alojar, acomodar, dar cabida a. 3. abarrotar, atestar. 4. (mar.) estibar, arrumar. 5. (jer.) dejar de lado, cesar. 6. **s. it!** ¡cállate! —*v.i.* **s. away,** viajar de polizón, viajar de pavo (Amer.) (a bordo de un vehículo).
stowage ['stoʊɪdʒ] *s.* 1. almacenamiento, almacenaje. 2. estiba, arrumaje. 3. bodega. 4. depósito.
stowaway [-ə,weɪ] *s.* polizón, pavo (Amer.).
stower [-ər, B -ə] *s.* estibador.
stownlins ['stoʊnlɪnz] *adv.* (esco.) cautelosamente, a hurtadillas.
strabismic [strə'bɪzmɪk] *a.* (med.) estrábico.
strabismus [-məs] *s.* (med.) estrabismo.
strabotomy [strə'bɑtəmɪ, B -'bɔt-] *s.* (med.) estrabotomía.
straddle ['strædəl] *v.i.* 1. ponerse o sentarse a horcajadas, esparrancarse. 2. arrellanarse, repantigarse. 3. estar por ambas partes, nadar entre dos aguas. —*v.t.* 1. montar a horcajadas (un caballo, etc.). 2. (fig.) no tomar partido en (un debate, asunto, etc.). 3. (mil.) encuadrar (el blanco). —*s.* 1. posición (del que está) a horcajadas. 2. (fig.) posición equívoca o ambigua. 3. (fin.) arbitraje. 4. (mil.) encuadramiento. 5. (bolsa) opciones (combinadas) de compra y venta (a precios estipulados).
straddler [-ələr, B -lə] *s.* (fam.) el que no se decide, el que está entre dos aguas.
Stradivarius [,strædə'vaɛrɪəs] *s.* estradivario, violín u otro instrumento de cuerdas hecho por Antonio Stradivarius o sus descendientes.
strafe [streɪf, B strɑf] *v.t.* castigar, ametrallar, bombardear (esp. desde un avión). —*s.* castigo, bombardeo (desde un avión en vuelo bajo).
straggle ['strægəl] *v.i.* 1. rezagarse; separarse, extraviarse. 2. estar disperso, caminar dispersado, ej., *the army straggled along,* el ejército caminaba dispersado.
straggler [-ələr, B -lə] *s.* rezagado, disperso.
straggly [-lɪ] *a.* (STRAGGLIER; STRAGGLIEST) disperso, diseminado; desordenado.
straight [streɪt] *a.* 1. derecho, recto. 2. derecho, seguido, directo, ininterrumpido, continuo, consecutivo. 3. en orden, arreglado. 4. recto, honesto, correcto; franco, candoroso, ej., *a s. race,* una carrera correcta (sin fraude); *s. speaking,* lenguaje franco. 5. correcto, exacto. 6. severo, rígido. 7. puro, genuino, sin mezcla, ej., *to drink whisky s.,* beber whiski puro (sin añadir agua). 8. de confianza, confiable, fidedigno, de buena fuente (información, consejo, etc.). 9. (E.U.) fijo, uniforme, igual (precios). 10. (pol., E.U.) absoluto, incondicional (partidario, secuaz, etc.). 11. (jer.) convencional, conservador; puritano. 12. (naipes) de valor correlativo, en escalera. 13. (mot.) lineal, en línea recta (disposición de cilindros). 14. **the accounts are s.,** las cuentas están llevadas debidamente. —*adv.* 1. directamente, rectamente; en derechura, derechamente, derecho. 2. francamente. 3. correctamente. 4. **let me get it s.,** pongamos las cosas en orden; **s. ahead,** en frente; **s. from the shoulder,** desde el hombro (golpe asestado en boxeo); (fig.) sin ambages, a las claras; **s. off,** sin vacilar, de inmediato; **to go s.,** (fig.) ir por el camino recto, enmendarse; **to go s. to,** ir directamente a; **to keep s. on,** seguir derecho; **to live s.,** vivir rectamente, vivir honestamente, llevar una vida honrada; **to put s.,** ordenar, poner en orden; **to put things s.,** poner las cosas en su lugar; **to set (one) s.,** explicar bien las cosas a, enseñar la situación verdadera a (uno), mostrar el camino a (uno); **to tell (one) s.,** decirle sin ambages a (uno); **to think s.,** pensar correctamente; **to walk s.,** caminar derecho. —*s.* 1. línea recta; alineación recta. 2. (juegos, dep.) serie (de tantos o puntos que llevan al triunfo). 3. (dep.) recta, (el) derecho (tramo final de la pista). 4. ganador (como apuesta). 5. (póker) escalera. 6. (jer.) la verdad, declaración verídica. —*v.t.* (esco.) alinear, poner derecho.
straight angle, (geom.) ángulo llano.
straight arch, (arq.) arco a nivel, arco adintelado.
straight-arm ['streɪt,ɑrm, B -,ɑm] *v.t.* (fútbol) desviar (al contrario con el brazo estirado).
straightaway [-ə,weɪ] *a.* (G.B.) derecho, recto, directo, seguido. —*adv.* enseguida, inmediatamente. —*s.* tramo recto (del camino).
straight chain, (quím.) cadena abierta recta (de átomos).
straightedge [-,ɛdʒ] *s.* escantillón, renglon, regla recta, formaleta.
straighten [-ən] *v.t., v.i.* enderezar(se); **s. out,** arreglar(se), desenmarañar(se); ordenar(se); **s. up,** erguir el busto, enderezar(se).
straight face, cara inexpresiva o seria, cara de palo.
straight-faced [-'feɪst] *a.* de cara inexpresiva o seria, de cara de palo.
straight flush, (póquer) escalera de color.
straight-flute [-,flut] *a.* (mec.) de estrías rectas, de labios rectos.
straightforward [,streɪt'fɔrwərd, B -'fɔwəd] *a.* directo, recto, franco, sincero; honrado, honesto.
straightforwardly [-lɪ] *adv.* directamente, francamente, sinceramente; honestamente.
straightforwardness [-nəs] *s.* rectitud, franqueza, sinceridad; honradez, honestidad.
straightforwards [-'fɔrwərdz, B -'fɔwədz] *adv.* directamente, francamente, sinceramente.
straightjacket, *var. de* **straitjacket.**
straight-laced [-'leɪst] *a.* excesivamente estricto en conducta o moralidad; mojigato, remilgado.
straight line, (geom.) línea recta, recta.
straight-line ['streɪt,laɪn] *a.* (mec.) lineal, de variación lineal; en línea recta.
straight-line amortization, amortización constante.
straight-line depreciation, (fin.) depreciación de línea simplista, depreciación de línea recta.
straight-line motion, (mec.) movimiento rectilíneo.
straight man, actor que representa el papel serio (en un número cómico) dando pie al gracioso para sus chistes.
straightness [-nəs] *s.* 1. derechura, rectitud. 2. (fig.) rectitud; franqueza, sinceridad.
straight-out [-,aʊt] *a.* (fam., E.U.) 1. sincero, franco, abierto. 2. cabal, completo.
straight razor, navaja barbera, verduguillo.
straight ticket, (pol., E.U.) 1. balota o papeleta de votación para la elección de una lista completa (de un partido). 2. programa cabal (de un partido).
strain [streɪn] *s.* 1. raza, casta, cepa, ascendencia (esp. de animales). 2. rasgo, característica, nota, traza. 3. tono, tonada, aire, acorde, melodía. 4.

modo, manera, tono, estilo, sentido (empleado en poema, discurso, etc.). 5. humor, disposición. 6. (raro) especie, clase.

strain, *v.t.* 1. entiesar, atiesar, tender, poner tirante; extremar, ejercitar al máximo, forzar, violentar. 2. propasarse, excederse en, ej., *s. one's powers, rights,* etc., excederse en sus poderes, derechos, etc. 3. distender, causar relajamiento de (un músculo); aflojar. 4. fatigar, agotar, sobreexcitar (corazón, etc.). 5. filtrar, colar; tamizar. 6. (mec.) estirar, deformar. 7. **s. a point,** propasarse, hacer una concesión; **s. every nerve,** esforzarse al máximo; **s. one's eyes,** forzar uno la vista. —*v.i.* 1. esforzarse, hacer esfuerzo intenso; tenderse, estirarse. 2. filtrarse, colarse. 3. **s. at,** tirar de (traílla, ancla, etc.); objetar a, resistir; **s. under,** obrar con dificultad; soportar con gran esfuerzo. —*s.* 1. tensión, fatiga, cansancio. 2. distensión; esfuerzo violento. 3. relajación, torcedura. 4. (mec.) deformación.

strain aging, (metal.) envejecimiento por deformación.

strained [streɪnd] *a.* 1. forzado (ej., hospitalidad, risa, etc.). 2. tirante (ej., relaciones).

strainer ['streinər, B 'streɪnə] *s.* colador, coladera; filtro; cedazo, tamiz.

strain gage, (ing.) detector de deformación.

straining piece, s. beam, (const.) tirante (armadura).

strait [streɪt] *a.* 1. limitado, restringido. 2. (ant.) estrecho, angosto; ajustado, apretado; estricto, riguroso. —*s.* 1. (*gen. pl.*) estrecho. 2. (*gen. pl.*) apuro, aprieto. 3. (raro) istmo. 4. (ant.) garganta, desfiladero, callejón.

straiten ['streɪtən] *v.t.* 1. confinar, reducir, estrechar, constreñir, contraer. 2. (raro) apremiar, restringir. 3. **in straitened circumstances,** alcanzado, apurado, falto de dinero, necesitado.

straitjacket [-ˌdʒækət] *s.* camisa de fuerza. —*v.t.* sujetar con (una) camisa de fuerza, poner camisa de fuerza a (alguien).

strait-laced [-'leɪst] *a.* 1. ajustado, ceñido. 2. escrupuloso, remilgado; puritano; mojigato, gazmoño.

straitly [-lɪ] *adv.* limitadamente, estrechamente, rigurosamente.

straitness [-nəs] *s.* limitación; estrechez, angostura; apuro; penuria.

Strait of Gibraltar, Estrecho de Gibraltar.

strake [streɪk] *s.* 1. (mar.) traca, hilada. 2. raya, lista. 3. batea (minas).

stramash ['stræmɪʃ, B -mæʃ] *s.* (pr. esco.) 1. disturbio, barullo. 2. choque, colisión.

stramineous [strə'mɪnɪəs] (ant.) *a.* 1. pajizo, de color paja. 2. sin valor, insignificante.

stramonium [strə'moʊnɪəm] *s.* (bot., farm.) estramonio, chamico (Am.).

strand [strænd] *s.* playa, ribera; costa. —*v.t.* 1. varar, hacer encallar. 2. dejar perdido, abandonar. —*v.i.* varar(se), encallar.

strand, *s.* 1. hebra, filamento, hilo, cabo. 2. ramal (de cables, cuerdas, etc.). 3. soga, cable, cordón. 4. sarta (de perlas, etc.). —*v.t.* 1. romper uno de los cabos de (una cuerda). 2. trenzar (cuerda, etc.) de ramales. 3. retorcer (hilos, etc.).

stranded ['strændəd] *a.* 1. (mar.) varado. 2. (fig.) desamparado, sin recursos.

strander [-ər, B -ə] *s.* máquina trenzadora (de cables, sogas, etc.); máquina torcedora.

strandline [-ˌlaɪn] *s.* borde de la playa.

strange [streɪndʒ] *a.* (STRANGER; STRANGEST) 1. extraño, ajeno, desconocido. 2. extraño, raro; peculiar, excéntrico; extraordinario, singular. 3. desafecto, indiferente. 4. desacostumbrado, nuevo. 5. (ant.) extranjero. 6. **it feels s.,** causa una sensación extraña; **to feel s.,** sentirse extraño (esp. mareado); sentirse desorientado.

strangely ['streɪndʒlɪ] *adv.* extrañamente, raramente; peculiarmente, excéntricamente; extraordinariamente, singularmente.

strangeness [-nəs] *s.* 1. extrañeza, rareza; peculiaridad. 2. indiferencia, desafección.

stranger [-ər, B -ə] *s.* 1. forastero, extraño, desconocido; extranjero. 2. (der.) tercero sin interés legítimo. 3. **to be a s. to,** desconocer, ser inexperto en; ser desconocido (para); **to make a s. of,** tratar con frialdad (a alguien); **you are quite a s.,** has estado perdido; ¿qué es de tu vida?

strangle ['stræŋgəl] *v.t.* 1. estrangular; sofocar, ahogar, asfixiar. 2. (fig.) sofocar, suprimir, reprimir. —*v.i.* estrangularse; sofocarse, asfixiarse.

stranglehold [-ˌhoʊld] *s.* 1. (lucha) toma por la garganta, llave estranguladora. 2. (fig.) opresión, dominio absoluto. 3. **to have a s. on,** (fig.) tener asido por la garganta.

strangler [-glər, B -glə] *s.* estrangulador.

strangles [-gəlz] *s.* (vet.) adivas.

strangulate [-gjəˌleɪt] *v.t.* estrangular. —*v.i.* (med.) estrangularse, ocluirse.

strangulation [ˌstræŋgjʊ'leɪʃən] *s.* estrangulación.

strangullion [ˌstræŋ'gʌljən] *s.* (vet.) estrangol, adivas.

strangury ['stræŋgjərɪ] *s.* (med.) estranguria.

strap [stræp] *s.* 1. correa, tira, faja, banda. 2. asentador (para afilar); hombrera (de uniformes); trabilla (de pantalón); tirilla (de botas, borcequíes, etc.). 3. barra chata, solera, llanta (de acero). 4. (bolsa) opciones (combinadas) para (dos) compras y (una) venta (a precios estipulados). 5. **the s.,** castigo o pena de azotes. —*v.t.* (*pret., p.p.* STRAPPED; *p.pr.* STRAPPING) 1. (t. con *up* o *down*) atar o sujetar con correas. 2. azotar con una correa. 3. asentar (una navaja). 4. (med.) cubrir (herida); fajar, vendar con esparadrapo.

straphang ['stræpˌhæŋ] *v.i.* (pr. G.B.) viajar de pie (cogido del pasamano).

straphanger [-ər, B -ə] *s.* (fam.) pasajero de pie (cogido del pasamano, correa, etc. en un ómnibus, tranvía, etc.), p. ext. persona que diariamente utiliza los servicios del transporte público urbano.

strap hinge, bisagra de paleta, bisagra de ramal.

strap iron, fleje (de hierro), cinta de hierro.

strapless ['stræpləs] *a.* sin tirantes (esp. vestido de mujer).

strappado [strə'peɪdoʊ, -'pɑdoʊ] *s.* (*pl.* STRAPPADOES) (hist.) estrapada, trato de cuerda.

strapped [stræpt] *a.* (fam.) necesitado, sin fondos.

strapper ['stræpər, B -ə] *s.* 1. persona grande y robusta. 2. persona o máquina que lía, ata, cincha, etc.

strapping [-ɪŋ] *a.* fornido, robusto, corpulento.

strap weld, soldadura reforzada, soldadura con cubrejunta.

strap wrench, llave de correa.

strass [stræs] *s.* estrás (cristal que imita al diamante).

strata, *pl. de* **stratum.**

stratagem ['strætədʒəm] *s.* estratagema, ardid, treta, artimaña.

stratameter [ˌstrə'tæmətər, B -ə] *s.* (geol.) estratómetro.

strategic [strə'tidʒɪk] **strategical** [-dʒɪkəl] *a.* estratégico.

strategically [-dʒɪkəlɪ] *adv.* estratégicamente.

strategist ['strætədʒəst] *s.* estratega.

strategy [-dʒɪ] *s.* (*pl.* STRATEGIES) 1. (mil.) estrategia. 2. (fig.) estrategia, artimaña, artificio, intriga.

strath [stræθ] *s.* (Esco.) valle llano y extenso.

strathspey [stræθ'speɪ] *s.* danza escocesa.

stratification [ˌstrætəfə'keɪʃən] *s.* estratificación.

stratiform ['strætəˌfɔrm, B -ˌfɔm] *a.* (anat., geol.) estratiforme.

stratify [-ˌfaɪ] *v.t.* (*pret., p.p.* STRATIFIED; *p.pr.* STRATIFYING) 1. estratificar. 2. conservar (semillas de árboles) entre capas de tierra. —*v.i.* estratificarse.

stratigrapher [strə'tɪgrəfər, B -fə] *s.* experto en estratigrafía.

stratigraphic [ˌstrætə'græfɪk] *a.* estratigráfico.

stratigraphy [strə'tɪgrəfɪ] *s.* (geol., min.) estratigrafía.

stratocracy [strə'tɑkrəsɪ, B -'tɔk-] *s.* (*pl.* STRATOCRACIES) gobierno de los militares.

stratocumulus [ˌstreɪtoʊ'kjumjələs] *s.* (meteor.) estratocúmulo.

stratosphere ['strætəˌsfɪr, B -sfɪə] *s.* (meteor.) estratósfera.

stratospheric [ˌstrætə'sfɪrɪk, B -'sfɛr-] *a.* estratosférico.

stratum ['streɪtəm, 'stræt-, B 'strɑt-] *s.* (*pl.* STRATA [-ə] o STRATUMS) (biol., meteor., geol.) estrato; (fig.) estrato, capa, ej., *the upper strata of society,* los estratos superiores de la sociedad.

stratus ['streɪtəs, 'stræt-, B 'streɪt-] *s.* (*pl.* STRATI) (meteor.) estrato.

stravage, stravaig [strə'veɪg] *v.i.* (esco.) vagar, andar errante.

straw [strɔ] *s.* 1. paja. 2. (fig.) paja, insignificancia, bagatela, ej., *not to care a s.* (*about*), no importar una paja a uno, no dar un comino (por). 3. **a s. in the wind,** un indicio de algo; **the last s.,** el colmo, la última gota; **to grasp, clutch,** o **catch at a s.,** agarrarse de un pelo, agarrarse de un clavo ardiendo; **to draw straws,** echar pajas; **to make bricks without s.,** trabajar con medios inadecuados. —*a.* 1. pajizo, de color paja. 2. insignificante, sin valor. 3. pajizo, hecho de paja.

strawberry ['strɔˌbɛrɪ, B -bərɪ] *s.* (*pl.* STRAWBERRIES) (bot.) fresa (planta y fruta), frutilla (Amer.).

strawberry blonde, (E.U.) mujer de cabello rubio rojizo.

strawberry bush, (bot.) bonetero americano.

strawberry mark, antojo, mancha vinosa (marca rosácea de nacimiento).

strawberry patch, fresal.

strawberry shrub, (bot.) calicanto.

strawberry tomato, (bot.) alquequenje, capulí.

strawberry tree, (bot.) madroño, aborio, alborto, albecho.

strawboard ['strɔˌbɔrd, B -ˌbɔd] *s.* cartón de paja.

straw boss, 1. (fam.) capataz interino. 2. cabo de cuadrilla, subcapataz.

straw color, color pajizo.

straw-colored ['strɔˌkʌlərd, B -ˌkʌləd] *a.* pajizo, de color de paja.

strawflower [-ˌflaʊər, B -ˌflaʊə] *s.* (bot.) siempreviva, perpetua.

straw hat, sombrero de paja.

straw-hat circuit ['strɔ'hæt-] región semiurbana donde se presenta teatro variado en el verano.

straw man, 1. figura de paja, nulidad, persona de poca monta. 2. testaferro, títere, hombre de paja.

straw vote, votación extraoficial, encuesta preelectoral.

straw wine, vino de pasas.
strawworm ['strɔˌwɜrm, B -ˌwɜm] *s.* (ento.) especie de gorgojo.
strawy ['strɔˌi] *a.* 1. pajoso, de paja (aspecto, contextura). 2. pajizo (color).
stray [streɪ] *v.i.* 1. perderse, extraviarse, descarriarse, desviarse, desmandarse. 2. vagar, deambular. —*s.* 1. animal (doméstico) perdido o extraviado. 2. niño vagabundo, niño abandonado. 3. (rad.) parásito, interferencia. 4. (elec.) fuga, vagabundo. —*a.* 1. descarriado, perdido, extraviado, abandonado. 2. disperso, aislado, suelto.
stray current, (elec.) corriente desviada o vagabunda.
streak [strik] *s.* 1. línea, lista, raya, vena (de color); faja, rayo (de luz). 2. veta, filón, vena. 3. vena (de humor); capa, rasgo (de carácter). 4. (fam.) racha (de fortuna). 5. (min.) huella, raspadura. 6. **like a s.,** como un rayo, velozmente; **to talk a blue s.,** hablar hasta por los codos. —*v.t.* marcar o trazar con rayas, vetear. —*v.i.* moverse o pasar muy velozmente.
streaked [strikt] *a.* 1. rayado, veteado, listado, jaspeado. 2. (jer.) alterado, contrariado; enclenque, miserable.
streakiness ['strikɪnəs] *s.* aspecto rayado, superficie veteada o listada.
streak of lightning, relámpago.
streaky [-kɪ] *a.* (STREAKIER; STREAKIEST) 1. rayado, veteado, listado. 2. inconstante, inestable, variable. 3. (G.B.) entreverado (tocino).
stream [strim] *s.* 1. corriente, arroyo, río. 2. flujo, curso, chorro (de líquido); rayo, haz (de luz); procesión, desfile, sucesión (de autos, etc.). 3. (fig.) corriente, curso. 4. **against the s.,** contra la corriente; **down s.,** aguas abajo; **to go with the s.,** irse con la corriente; **up s.,** aguas arriba. —*v.i.* 1. correr, fluir, brotar, manar. 2. fluir a torrentes; derramar con abundancia. 3. ondear, flamear, tremolar. 4. **s. out,** salir a torrentes. —*v.t.* 1. hacer fluir o manar. 2. hacer ondear (bandera, etc.).
stream bed, madre, lecho, álveo, cauce (de un río o arroyo).
streamer ['strimər, B -mə] *s.* 1. gallardete, banderola, grímpola. 2. rayo o faja de luz (en el horizonte). 3. (impr.) título a toda plana.
streamer fly, (pesca) (una clase de) mosca artificial.
stream gage, escala hidrométrica, escala fluviométrica, limnímetro.
streamlet ['strimlət] *s.* arroyuelo, riachuelo.
streamline [-ˌlaɪn] *s.* perfil aerodinámico; trayectoria de flujo, curso o línea de corriente. —*v.t.* 1. hacer aerodinámico. 2. (fig.) modernizar.
streamlined [-ˌlaɪnd] *a.* 1. aerodinámico, perfilado, fusiforme. 2. (hidr.) hidrodinámico, correntilíneo. 3. (fig.) modernizado.
streamline flow, flujo laminar, (aer.) correntilíneo o viscoso.
streamliner [-ˌlaɪnər, B -ˌlaɪnə] *s.* vehículo de perfil aerodinámico; tren lujoso.
streamy [-ɪ] *a.* surcado de arroyos; que mana a chorros.
streek [strik] *v.t.* (esco.) estirar, extender.
street [strit] *s.* 1. calle. 2. **of the streets,** de la vida airada, que vive de la prostitución; **on the s.,** en la calle; **the s.,** calle principal de una localidad; **to live in the s.,** callejear, vivir en la calle; **up one's s.,** del interés de uno; de la especialidad o competencia de uno. —*a.* de calle (vestido, etc.).
streetcar ['stritˌkɑr, B -ˌkɑ] *s.* tranvía.
street cleaner, basurero, barredor de calles.
street cleaning, limpieza de calles, aseo urbano.
street clothes, traje de calle.
street door, puerta de la calle, puerta principal.
street fighting, riñas callejeras.
street floor, primer piso, planta baja.
streetlamp ['stritˌlæmp] *s.* farol de pie (para el alumbrado público).
street patrol, patrulla de calles (de la policía urbana).
street price, precio en el mercado negro.
street sprinkler, carricuba, regadora de calles.
street sweeper, 1. barredor de calles. 2. barredera (máquina).
streetwalker ['stritˌwɔkər, B -ˌwɔkə] *s.* prostituta callejera.
streetwalking [-ˌwɔkɪŋ] *s.* 1. callejeo. 2. prostitución callejera.
streetwise ['stritwaɪz] *a.* experimentado en la vida callejera.
strength [strɛŋkθ, strɛŋθ] *s.* (*pl.* STRENGTHS) 1. fuerza, vigor, fortaleza. 2. solidez, dureza, firmeza, resistencia. 3. fuerza, intensidad; poder, potencia. 4. fuerza numérica (esp. de un cuerpo militar), número (de soldados). 5. (com.). estabilidad (de precios). 6. **on the s. of,** en virtud de, a base de; confiado en, fundándose en.
strengthen ['strɛŋkθən, 'strɛŋθ-] *v.t, v.i.* fortalecer(se), vigorizar(se), robustecer(se).
strengthener [-ər, B -ə] *s.* refuerzo; respaldo, apoyo.
strengthening [-ɪŋ] *s.* fortalecimiento, consolidación. —*a.* fortificante, tónico.
strengthless [-ləs] *a.* débil, sin fuerzas.
strenuous ['strɛŋjʊəs] *a.* 1. estrenuo, vigoroso, enérgico; tenaz, persistente. 2. arduo, difícil, penoso (trabajo, tarea, etc.).
strenuously [-lɪ] *adv.* 1. vigorosamente; tenazmente. 2. arduamente, con mucha dificultad, penosamente.
strenuousness [-nəs] *s.* 1. vigorosidad; tenacidad. 2. arduidad, suma dificultad.
strep [strɛp] *a.* (med.) *contr. de* **streptococcal,** estreptocóccico.
strepitous ['strɛpətəs] **strepitant** [-ənt] *a.* estrepitoso, ruidoso; bullanguero, bullicioso.
strep throat, (med.) inflamación séptica de la garganta.
streptobacillus [ˌstrɛptoʊbə'sɪləs] *s.* (med.) estreptobacilo.
streptococcal [ˌstrɛptə'kɑkəl, B -'kɔk-] **streptococcic** [-sɪk] *a.* (bact.) estreptocócico.
streptococcus [-əs] *s.* (*pl.* STREPTOCOCCI [-saɪ]) (bact.) estreptococo.
streptokinase [ˌstrɛptə'kaɪnˌeɪs] *s.* (bioquím.) estreptoquinasa.
streptolysin [strɛp'tɑləsən, B -'tɔl-] *s.* (bioquím.) estreptolisina.
streptomycin [ˌstrɛptə'maɪsən] *s.* (farm.) estreptomicina.
streptothricin [-'θraɪsɪn] *s.* (farm.) estreptotricina.
stress [strɛs] *v.t.* 1. acentuar, subrayar, relevar, dar énfasis a. 2. (mec.) someter a un esfuerzo, fatigar, sobrecargar. —*s.* 1. tensión, opresión, carga. 2. apremio, apuro, compulsión. 3. esfuerzo intenso. 4. acento, énfasis. 5. (mús., fon., poét.) acento. 6. (mec.) esfuerzo, fatiga. 7. **to lay s. on,** hacer hincapié en, dar importancia a.
stress accent, acento prosódico, acento de intensidad.
stress distribution, (ing.) repartición de esfuerzos.
stressful ['strɛsfəl] *a.* lleno de tensiones, inquieto, agitado (días, tiempo, época, etc.).
stressless [-ləs] *a.* 1. inacentuado. 2. fácil, sin esfuerzo.
stress relief (metal.) alivio de esfuerzos, desfatigamiento.
stretch [strɛtʃ] *v.t.* 1. alargar, extender. 2. estirar, alongar, expandir, dilatar. 3. tensar, tender, atiesar, hacer tirante. 4. forzar, exagerar. llevar al extremo, violentar (la verdad, principios, etc.). 5. **s. it,** exagerar, mentir; **s. one's legs,** estirar las piernas; **s. oneself,** desperezarse; **s. out (hand, foot),** extender (la mano, la pierna). —*v.i.* 1. tenderse, extenderse. 2. estirarse, alargarse, dar de sí. 3. desperezarse, estirarse. 4. **s. out,** extenderse, echarse; extender la mano; alargar el paso. —*s.* 1. alargamiento, estiramiento. 2. trecho, tramo, tracto; intervalo, rato. 3. alcance. 4. vuelta (de paseo, caminata). 5. (fam.) pena, condena (de prisión). 6. recta de la pista, esp. recta final (en carreras de caballos). 7. (mar.) bordada. —*a.* elástico (nilón, géneros de punto, etc.).
stretcher ['strɛtʃər, B -ə] *s.* 1. estirador, dilatador, atesador, ensanchador. 2. viga, madero largo; tirante. 3. camilla, parihuelas. 4. (mec.) tensor, atesador. 5. (const.) soga, ladrillos al hilo (en una pared).
stretcher-bearer [-ˌbɛrər, B -ˌbɛərə] *s.* camillero, el que carga la camilla.
stretching [-ɪŋ] *s.* 1. estiraje, alargamiento, tensión. 2. desperezo.
stretching press, (ing.) prensa de tensión.
stretch-out ['strɛtʃˌaʊt] *s.* (fam., E.U.) sistema laboral de fábricas en que los obreros deben hacer trabajos extra por muy poca o sin ninguna paga adicional.
stretchy [-ɪ] *a.* 1. estirable, extendible; elástico. 2. que se despereza.
strew [stru] *v.t.* (*pret.,* STREWED; *p.p.* STREWED O STREWN [strun]; *p.pr.* STREWING) 1. esparcir, echar, derramar, rociar (flores, arena, etc.). 2. salpicar (superficie u objeto con flores, arena, etc.). 3. diseminar, divulgar.
stria ['straɪə] *s.* (*pl.* STRIAE [-i]) estría; acanaladura, raya; cuerdas.
striate [-ˌeɪt] *v.t.* estriar. —*a.* estriado.
striated [-əd] *a.* estriado.
striation [straɪ'eɪʃən] *s.* 1. formación de estrías, estado estriado. 2. estría.
strick [strɪk] *s.* manojo o puñado de lino, yute o cáñamo.
stricken ['strɪkən] *p.p. de* **strike** . —*a.* 1. herido. 2. afligido, apenado. 3. (con *with*) afectado, agobiado (por enfermedad); atacado de (locura). 4. agotado, debilitado, ej., *s. in years,* debilitado por la vejez, entrado en años.
strickle ['strɪkəl] *s.* 1. rasero. 2. herramienta para afilar guadañas. 3. (metal.) terraja. —*v.t.* 1. rasar. 2. (metal.) aterrasar.
strict [strɪkt] *a.* 1. estricto, severo, riguroso, ej., *s. morals,* moralidad severa, costumbres puritanas. 2. estricto, exacto, preciso, ej., *in the s. sense,* en (el) sentido estricto. 3. (bot.) erguido, derecho. 4. (ant.) apretado; tieso.
striction ['strɪkʃən] *s.* constricción, encogimiento.
strictly ['strɪktlɪ] *adv.* estrictamente, exactamente; rigurosamente, severamente.
strictness [-nəs] *s.* exactitud; rigor, severidad.
stricture [-tʃər, B -tʃə] *s.* 1. contracción. 2. crítica severa, censura. 3. (med.) estrictura, estrechez. 4. (fon.) grado de abertura (en la articulación de un sonido).
stride [straɪd] *v.i.* (*pret.* STRODE [stroʊd]; *p.p.* STRIDDEN ['strɪdən]; *p.pr.* STRIDING) 1. caminar a zancadas, andar a trancos largos. 2. (raro)

ponerse a horcajadas. —*v.t.* 1. pasar a zancadas, cruzar de un tranco. 2. montar a horcajadas. —*s.* 1. zancada, tranco, trancada. 2. (fig.) adelanto, avance. 3. **to get into one's s.,** (fig.) entrar en el juego, asentarse en (una ocupación), empezar a funcionar bien; **to make great strides,** progresar a grandes pasos; **to take (an obstacle) in one's s.,** salvar (un obstáculo) de paso; (fig.) vencer (obstáculo) sin esfuerzo; tomar nota (de algo) sin alterarse; **to throw (someone) off his s.,** sacar de su paso a (alguien); hacer perder el hilo a (alguien que habla).

stridence ['straɪdəns] **stridency** [-ənsɪ] *s.* estridencia.

strident [-ənt] *a.* estridente, chirriante.

stridently [-əntlɪ] *adv.* con voz estridente, con sonido chirriante.

stridor ['straɪdər, B -ə] *s.* (med.) estridor.

stridulate ['strɪdʒəˌleɪt] *v.i.* estridular, chirriar (insectos).

stridulation [ˌstrɪdʒə'leɪʃən] *s.* chirrido.

stridulatory ['strɪdʒələˌtɔrɪ, B -tərɪ] *a.* capaz de estridular; chirriador; (med.) estriduloso.

stridulous [-ləs] *a.* chirriador; (med.) estriduloso.

stridulously [-ləslɪ] *adv.* chirriante, rechinante.

strife [straɪf] *s.* 1. rivalidad, emulación, competencia. 2. contienda, refriega, lucha; conflicto. 3. (ant.) esfuerzo, empeño.

strigil ['strɪdʒəl] *s.* (hist.) estrigila, raedora.

strigose ['straɪˌgoʊs] *a.* (bot.) estrigoso.

strike [straɪk] *v.t.* (*pret.* STRUCK [strʌk]; *p.p.* STRUCK o STRICKEN ['strɪkən]; *p.pr.* STRIKING) 1. golpear, pegar; asestar (un golpe). 2. chocar con o contra, dar o estrellar contra, ej., *s. an obstacle,* chocar contra un obstáculo. 3. atacar, morder (díc. de una serpiente). 4. herir (díc. de una bala, proyectil; luz, sonido; mala noticia, etc.). 5. caer sobre, ej., *lightning struck the house,* un rayo cayó sobre la casa. 6. descubrir, hallar, encontrar, ej., *s. oil,* descubrir petróleo, (fig.) hacerse rico. 7. indicar o señalar (por golpes); dar (la hora), ej., *the clock strikes six,* el reloj da las seis. 8. tocar, tañer. 9. brotar en, atacar, ej., *an epidemic struck the village,* una epidemia brotó en el pueblo. 10. impresionar, afectar; ocurrírse(le) a; parecer(le) a, ej., *how does it s. you?* ¿qué le parece?, *it strikes me he may have changed his mind,* se me ocurre que quizás él haya cambiado de idea. 11. afectar, gravar. 12. bajar, arriar (bandera, vela, etc.). 13. tachar, quitar, ej., *s. a word through,* tachar una palabra de un plumazo. 14. asumir (una postura). 15. declararse en huelga, parar (el trabajo). 16. nivelar, igualar; rasar. 17. enganchar (pez) en el anzuelo; arponear (una ballena). 18. **s. a balance,** (com.) hacer balance; encontrar el promedio o equilibrio (entre cosas); **s. a bargain,** cerrar un trato; **s. a discordant note,** dar una nota discordante; desentonar; **s. a light,** encender (un fósforo); **s. an arc,** (elec.) formar un arco; **s. an average,** sacar el promedio, tomar el término medio; **s. (one) blind,** cegar (a uno); **s. camp,** levantar el campo; **s. (one) dead,** dar muerte a (uno); **s. (one) deaf,** ensordecer (a uno); **s. down,** derribar; (fig.) abatir; desviar (la mano, un arma, etc.) hacia abajo con un golpe; **s. dumb,** dejar mudo; **s. (knife, dagger, etc.) from one's hand,** hacer soltar (cuchillo, puñal, etc.) de un golpe; **s. it rich,** encontrar un buen filón; tener un golpe de fortuna; **s. me dead!** ¡que me caiga muerto!; **s. off,** quitar de golpe; tachar; deducir, descontar; (impr.) tirar; **s. one's attention,** cautivar la atención de uno; **s. one's fancy,** agradarle a uno, gustarle a uno; **s. one's flag,** (mar.) arriar (la) bandera (para rendirse); batir banderas (en saludo); **s. out,** tachar, suprimir; **s. out (a plan,** etc.), forjar o idear (un plan, etc.); **s. out a line for oneself,** ser independiente, actuar conforme a las propias ideas (de uno); **s. roots,** echar raíces; **s. tents, (mil.) batir tiendas; s. the target,** hacer blanco; **s. up (a tune,** etc.), empezar a cantar o tocar (una tonada, etc.); **s. up a friendship,** trabar amistad (rápida o casualmente); **s. with terror,** sobrecoger de terror. —*v.i.* 1. dar golpes, descargar un golpe; chocar. 2. morder (serpiente). 3. sonar, dar la hora, ej., *the hour has struck,* (lit., fig) sonó la hora. 4. parar, ir a la huelga. 5. penetrar, entrar, atravesar, ej., *the cold struck through his light overcoat,* el frío atravesó su ligero sobretodo. 6. echar raíces. 7. dirigirse, avanzar (en cierta dirección). 8. arriar la bandera; (fig.) rendirse. 9. morder la carnada (pez). 10. **s. against (on** o **upon),** chocar con, estrellarse contra; **s. at,** dirigir un golpe a, acometer; **s. at the root of,** tratar de cortar de raíz; amenazar con destrucción; **s. back,** devolver un golpe, dar golpe por golpe; **s. for,** dirigirse hacia; **s. home,** hacer blanco, dar en lo vivo (golpe, crítica, etc.); **s. in with (idea, suggestion),** intervenir (en conversación, debate, etc.) con (una idea, sugerencia); **s. into,** empezar con ímpetu; **s. into a gallop,** echarse a galopar; **s. out,** lanzar un golpe fuerte; mover los miembros vigorosamente (al nadar, patinar, caminar); **s. out for,** ponerse en marcha hacia; echarse a nadar hacia; **s. to (the right, left,** etc.), volver hacia (la derecha, izquierda, etc.); **s. up,** entonar, empezar a cantar o tocar; **s. upon (an idea, plan,** etc.), ocurrírsele a uno (una idea, un plan, etc.); caer sobre (luz, rayo, etc.). —*s.* 1. golpe. 2. rasero. 3. huelga, paro. 4. encuentro, hallazgo, descubrimiento (de petróleo, etc.). 5. ganga, buen éxito, golpe de fortuna. 6. mordedura (con que el pez traga el anzuelo). 7. sonería (de reloj). 8. (béisbol) lanzamiento de pelota, pasada (que el bateador no contesta). 9. (bolos) golpe (que derriba los diez bolos a la vez). 10. (mil.) acometida, ataque (esp. de aviones). 11. (geol., min.) rumbo, arrumbamiento (de una capa mineral, etc.). 12. (fam.) **have two strikes against one,** estar en posición desfavorable; **a lucky s.,** un golpe de suerte; **on s.,** de paro, en huelga; **to go on s.,** declararse en huelga.

strikebound ['straɪkˌbaʊnd] *a.* paralizado por la huelga.

strikebreaker [-ˌbreɪkər, B -kə] *s.* esquirol, rompehuelgas, amarillo (Amer.).

strikebreaking [-ˌbreɪkɪŋ] *s.* medidas para romper huelgas.

striker ['straɪkər, B -kə] *s.* 1. huelguista. 2. aprendiz de herrero. 3. percutor; macillo (de sonería de reloj). 4. (E.U.) ordenanza. 5. bateador (en criquet).

striking [-kɪŋ] *s.* impresionante, llamativo; sorprendente.

strikingly [-kɪŋlɪ] *adv.* de modo impresionante, impresionantemente.

string [strɪŋ] *s.* 1. cuerda, cordel, bramante. 2. hilera, fila, sarta, ristra. 3. (fig.) retahíla. 4. (mús.) cuerda; (*pl.*) instrumentos de cuerda; sección de instrumentos de cuerda (de la orquesta). 5. (fig.) recurso, expediente. 6. fibra (de plantas). 7. (*pl.*) (fam.) condiciones, estipulaciones. 8. caballeriza (de un establo o dueño). 9. (arq.) carrera, larguero, montante; gualdera, zanca (de escaleras). 10. (min.) galápago. 11. (billar, billas) línea de arranque (para las bolas al comenzar el juego); tiro inicial (que decide el turno de los jugadores). 12. (ant.) nervio, tendón, cordón. 13. **(a) s. of pearls,** hilo, sarta de perlas; **for strings,** (mús.) para instrumentos de cuerdas; **to harp on one s.,** porfiar sobre un solo tema; **to have (someone) on a s.,** tener bajo su férula (a alguien), tener (a alguien) en un puño; **to have two strings to one's bow,** tener dos alternativas, tener dos posibilidades; **to pull strings,** hacer uso de su influencia, **to pull the strings,** manipular disimuladamente; **to touch a s.,** (fig.) tocar las fibras del corazón. —*v.t.* (*pret., p.p.* STRUNG [strʌŋ]; *p.pr.* STRINGING) 1. encordar. 2. estirar, atiesar. 3. templar (un instrumento). 4. ensartar, enhilar, encordelar. 5. atar, amarrar con bramante o cuerda. 6. quitar las fibras a (judías). 7. extender en línea, colocar en serie. 8. (jer.) engañar, burlar. 9. **high strung,** muy sensitivo; neurótico; **s. (someone) along,** traer (a uno) al retortero; engañar, embaucar; **s. up** (fam.) ahorcar; (fig.) (*ú. pr. en p.p.*) volver tenso o determinado, excitar, arrebatar. —*v.i.* 1. extenderse, moverse o avanzar en línea. 2. (billar, billas) hacer el tiro inicial (para decidir el turno de los jugadores). 3. **s. along (with),** acompañar, seguir (a); **s. out** (jer.) tomar drogas, estar bajo la influencia de las drogas.

string bean, (*pl.* STRING BEANS) (bot.) judía, alubia, vainita (Amer.).

stringboard ['strɪŋˌbɔrd, B -ˌbɔd] *s.* (arq.) mamperlán, mampirlán.

stringcourse [-ˌkɔrs, B -ˌkɔs] *s.* (arq.) cordón saliente.

stringed [strɪŋd] *a.* 1. encordado, encordelado. 2. atado con cuerdas. 3. ensartado, enhebrado. 4. (mús.) de cuerda (instrumento).

stringed instrument, (mús.) instrumento de cuerda.

stringency ['strɪndʒənsɪ] *s.* 1. rigor, severidad, exactitud. 2. fuerza de persuasión (de un argumento tesis, etc.). 3. (fin.) estrechez, escasez.

stringent [-dʒənt] *a.* 1. severo, estricto, riguroso. 2. convincente, fuerte. 3. (fin.) estrecho, escaso.

stringently [-dʒəntlɪ] *adv.* estrictamente, severamente, convincentemente.

stringer ['strɪŋər, B -ə] *s.* 1. encordador, ensartador. 2. (arq., carp.) larguero, viga longitudinal; riostra. 3. (f.c.) traviesa longitudinal, durmiente; carrera (en puente). 4. (periodismo) corresponsal local. 5. (fig.) (*ú. en palabras compuestas*) fila, ej., *second s.,* (hombre) de segunda fila.

string galvanometer, galvanómetro de cuerda, galvanómetro de hilo metálico.

stringhalt [-ˌhɔlt] *s.* (vet.) ancado, cujera (del caballo).

stringiness [-ɪnəs] *s.* fibrosidad, viscosidad.

stringing [-ɪŋ] *s.* cordería (ej., de una raqueta de tenis).

string insulator, aislador de cadena.

string line, (billar, billas) línea de arranque (que marca el límite en que deben situarse las bolas al comenzar el juego).

string orchestra, orquesta de cuerdas.

stringpiece ['strɪŋˌpis] *s.* (arq.) carrera, larguero, riostra.

string quartet, (mús.) cuarteto de cuerdas.

string tie, corbatín angosto.

stringy [-ɪ] *a.* (STRINGIER; STRINGIEST) 1. fibroso, filamentoso. 2. correoso, viscoso; pegajoso (líquido). 3. largo y delgado pero fuerte.

strip [strɪp] *v.t.* (*pret., p.p.* STRIPPED; raro STRIPT [strɪpt]; *p.pr.* STRIPPING) 1. descortezar (árbol); despellejar, desollar (animal); pelar (fruta). 2. desnudar. 3. desarmar, desmontar, desmantelar (fábrica, barco, etc.). 4. (mec.) estropear, desgarrar, pasarse (rosca de un tornillo, etc.). 5. **s.**

down, desguarnecer; **s. of,** despojar de, privar de; **s. off** (o **from**), quitar, sacar (cubierta, envoltura, ropa, etc.); **s. tobacco,** desvenar o despalillar el tabaco. —*v.i.* desvestirse, despojarse, desnudarse. —*s.* 1. franja, faja (de tierra), tira, lista (de material), tira, fleje (de metal). 2. (filat.) fila de (tres o más) sellos. 3. (t. **air s., landing s.**) pista de aterrizaje.

strip-crop ['strɪpˌkrɑp, B -ˌkrɔp] *v.t., v.i.* cultivar (plantas) en fajas alternadas.

strip-cropping [-ɪŋ] *s.* cultivo de mieses en fajas alternadas.

stripe [straɪp] *s.* 1. lista, raya, banda, franja, gaya. 2. (fig.) índole, calaña, tipo, carácter. 3. (mil.) (*gen. pl.*) galón, divisa, ej., *sergeant's stripes,* galón de sargento. 4. (tej.) tela o diseño a rayas. 5. azote, azotazo. 6. **to get one's stripes,** (mil.) ser ascendido; **to lose one's stripes,** (mil.) ser degradado. —*v.t.* rayar, listar, gayar.

striped [straɪpt] *a.* rayado, listado, a rayas.

striped hyena, (zool.) hiena rayada.

striped mullet, (ict.) céfalo, lisa, múgil, mújol, capitón, matajudío.

striper ['straɪpər, B -ə] *s.* (jer.) militar que tiene galones.

strip fuse, (elec.) fusible de cinta, tira fusible.

striping ['straɪpɪŋ] *s.* listas, franjas (pintadas o aplicadas sobre una superficie).

stripling ['strɪplɪŋ] *s.* mozuelo, muchacho, mozalbete.

strip mill. (metal.) laminador de tiras, tren de laminación de fleje.

strip mining, (min.) explotación a cielo abierto por excavadora.

stripped [strɪpt] *a.* desnudo; despojado; desplumado.

stripped gasoline, gasolina estabilizada.

stripper ['strɪpər, B -ə] *s.* 1. (mec.) desmoldador, separador; raspador, enjugador. 2. (teat., fam.) desnudista, bailarina que se desnuda en un número de teatro, variedades, cabaret, etc.; (*female stripper*) striptisera, stripteasera, encueratriz (fam., Méx.); (*male stripper*) striptisero, stripteasero.

stripping, *s.* 1. despalillación (tabaco). 2. desencofrado; remoción (barniz, pintura). 3. corte en tiras.

striptease [-ˌtiz] *s.* número de cabaret o teatro de variedades, en el que la bailarina se desnuda lentamente al son de la música.

stripteaser [-ˌtizər, B -ˌtizə] *s.* (teat.) desnudista, artista de cabaret o teatro que se desnuda lentamente al son de la música.

stripy ['straɪpɪ] *a.* (STRIPIER; STRIPIEST) listado, listeado.

strive [straɪv] *v.i.* (*pret.* STROVE [stroʊv] o STRIVED; *p.p.* STRIVEN ['strɪvən] o STRIVED; *p.pr.* STRIVING) 1. (gen. con *for* o *after*) esforzarse (por), porfiar (en), procurar. 2. (gen. con *with* o *against*) luchar, batallar, pugnar, disputar (con). 3. (ant.) competir, rivalizar.

striver ['straɪvər, B -ə] *s.* luchador, porfiador.

strobe [stroʊb] *s.* 1. *contr. de* **stroboscope,** estroboscopio. 2. *contr. de* **strobotron,** estrobotrón.

strobe lights, luces estroboscópicas (usadas en fotografía, discotecas, teatros, etc.).

strobila [stroʊ'baɪlə] *s.* (*pl.* STROBILAE [-'baɪli]) (zool.) estróbilo.

strobilaceous [ˌstroʊbə'leɪʃəs] *a.* (bot.) estrobiláceo.

strobile ['stroʊbaɪl, -bɪl] *s.* (bot.) estróbilo.

stroboscope ['stroʊbəˌskoʊp] *s.* (ing.) estroboscopio.

stroboscopic [ˌstroʊbə'skɑpɪk, B -'skɔp-] *a.* estroboscópico.

strobotron ['stroʊbəˌtrɑn, B -ˌtrɔn] *s.* (electrón.) estrobotrón.

strode, *pret. de* **stride.**

stroke [stroʊk] *s.* 1. golpe. 2. apoplejía; ataque apoplético; ataque de parálisis. 3. lance, jugada (hábil). 4. campanada (del reloj), tañido (de la campana). 5. latido, pulsación (del corazón). 6. caricia (con la mano). 7. palada, remada. 8. brazada (de natación). 9. toque, rasgo, plumada, trazo (de una letra). 10. pincelada, brochada. 11. (mec.) carrera (del pistón, émbolo, etc.). 12. (dep.) golpe, jugada, ej., *he did the hole in ten strokes,* completó el hoyo (de golf) en diez jugadas. 13. (dep.) primer remero, bogavante. 14. **at one s.,** de un solo golpe; **at the s. of (nine,** etc.), al dar las, a golpe de las (nueve, etc.); **finishing s.,** golpe de gracia; **finishing strokes,** toques finales; **I have not done a s. of work,** no he dado golpe, no he hecho absolutamente nada; **it was on the s. of (nine,** etc.), estaba a punto de dar (las nueve); **on the s. of (nine,** etc.), a las (nueve, etc.) en punto; **s. of fortune** (o **luck**), golpe de fortuna; **s. of genius,** rasgo de ingenio; **s. of lightning,** rayo; **s. of wit,** dicho agudo, gracia; **to keep s.,** remar al compás; **to row a fast s.,** tener una remada rápida; **with one s.,** de un plumazo. —*v.t.* 1. acariciar, frotar suavemente, pasar la mano (sobre). 2. fijar el ritmo de la remada para (la tripulación, el barco).

stroll [stroʊl] *v.i.* pasear, vagar, corretear. —*v.t.* pasearse por (un lugar, calles, etc.). —*s.* paseo; vuelta; **to go for a s.,** dar un paseo.

stroller ['stroʊlər, B -ə] *s.* 1. paseante. 2. vagabundo. 3. cómico de la legua. 4. cochecillo de niño, sillita de ruedas para niño (Esp.).

strolling company, compañía ambulante (de cómicos, músicos, etc.).

strolling player, músico ambulante.

stroma ['stroʊmə] *s.* (*pl.* STROMATA [-mətə]) (anat.) estroma.

stromatic [stroʊ'mætɪk] *a.* (anat.) estromático.

stromeyerite ['stroʊmaɪəˌraɪt] *s.* (min.) estromeyerita.

strong [strɔŋ] *a.* 1. fuerte, robusto, recio, resistente. 2. fuerte, potente, ej., *s. beer,* cerveza fuerte. 3. bueno (memoria, ojos, etc.). 4. fuerte, versado (en una materia, ciencia, etc.). 5 grande, numeroso, ej., *a s. army,* un ejército grande. 6. de cierto número (*gen. no se traduce en castellano*), ej., *an army ten thousand s.,* un ejército de diez mil hombres. 7. intenso, marcado, pronunciado. 8. ardiente, violento, ej., *a s. advocate of peace,* un partidario ardiente de la paz, *s. language,* lenguaje violento. 9. firme, bien establecido, arraigado, ej., *a s. habit,* un hábito arraigado. 10. (teat.) conmovedor, dramático (situación, escena, etc.). 11. (com.) firme, en alza (mercado). 12. (gram.) fuerte, irregular (verbo, conjugación). 13. (fam.) rancio, pasado; maloliente. 14. **are you quite s. again?** ¿ha recobrado Ud. completamente la salud?; **with a s. arm,** con mano de hierro, por la fuerza; **the s.,** la gente sana; la gente poderosa; **to be going s.,** (jer.) marchar bien, no aflojarse; seguir gozando de buena salud; **to come on strong,** (jer.) con énfasis, fuertemente, con todas sus fuerzas. —*adv.* fuertemente, vigorosamente, enérgicamente; con entusiasmo.

strong-arm ['strɔŋˌɑrm, B -ˌɑm] *a.* (fam.) violento, opresivo, ej., *s.-a. methods,* métodos violentos. —*v.t.* 1. violentar, aporrear. 2. intimidar.

strong-arm man, guardaespaldas.

strongbox [-ˌbɑks, B -ˌbɔks] *s.* caja fuerte; cofre de caudales; **s. with time-delay mechanism,** (señal) caja fuerte con apertura retardada.

strong breeze, (mar.) viento fresco.

strong drink, bebida fuerte (alcohólica).

strong gale, (mar.) viento muy fuerte.

stronghold [-ˌhoʊld] *s.* fuerte, fortaleza, plaza fuerte, ciudadela.

strongly [-lɪ] *adv.* fuertemente, vigorosamente, enérgicamente; enfáticamente.

strong-minded ['strɔŋ'maɪndəd] *a.* resuelto, decidido, determinado.

strong-mindedly [-lɪ] *adv.* resueltamente, decididamente, determinadamente.

strong-mindedness [-nəs] *s.* resolución, decisión, determinación.

strongpoint ['strɔŋˌpɔɪnt] *s.* (mil.) punto de resistencia, punto de apoyo.

strong room, (G.B.) bóveda de seguridad.

strong-willed [-'wɪld] *a.* de voluntad o carácter fuerte, tesonero, resuelto; obstinado.

strongyle, strongyl ['strɑnˌdʒaɪl, B 'strɔndʒɪl] *s.* 1. (zool.) estróngilo. 2. estrongiloide.

strongylosis [ˌstrɑndʒə'loʊsəs, B ˌstrɔn-] *s.* (vet.) estrongiloidosis.

strontia ['strɑntʃɪə, B 'strɔnʃɪə] *s.* (quím.) estronciana.

strontian [-ɪən] *s.* (quím.) estroncio.

strontianite [-əˌnaɪt] *s.* (min.) estroncianita.

strontic ['strɑntɪk, B 'strɔn-] *a.* del estroncio.

strontium [-tʃəm, B -ʃɪəm] *s.* (quím.) estroncio.

strop [strɑp, B strɔp] *s.* suavizador, asentador (de navajas). —*v.t.* (*pret., p.p.* STROPPED; *p.pr.* STROPPING) suavizar, asentar (navajas).

strophanthin [stroʊ'fænθən] *s.* (farm.) estrofantina.

strophe ['stroʊfɪ] *s.* estrofa.

strophic ['strɑfɪk, B 'strɔ-] *a.* estrófico.

strophulus ['strɑfjələs, B 'strɔf-] *s.* (med.) estrófulo.

stroud [straʊd] *s.* manta de lana (que se usaba como artículo de trueque con los indios de Norteamérica).

strove, *pret. de* **strive.**

struck, *pret. de* **strike.**

struck [strʌk] *a.* cerrado o afectado por una huelga.

struck jury, (der.) jurado especial escogido (de 12 miembros aceptados por las dos partes).

structural ['strʌktʃərəl] *a.* 1. estructural. 2. debido a la estructuración social (ej., desempleo). 3. (biol., geol.) estructural.

structural engineer, ingeniero de estructuras.

structural formula, (fís.) fórmula de estructura.

structuralization [ˌstrʌktʃərələ'zeɪʃən, B -laɪ-] *s.* estructuración, incorporación dentro de una estructura.

structuralize ['strʌktʃərəˌlaɪz] *v.t.* estructurar.

structurally [-lɪ] *adv.* en (cuanto a la) estructura, estructuralmente.

structural shape, perfilado, hierro perfilado, perfil estructural.

structural steel, acero estructural o de construcción.

structural worker, herrero de obra, montador.

structure ['strʌktʃər, B 'strʌktʃə] *s.* 1. estructura. 2. construcción. 3. (fig.) textura, hechura. —*v.t.* 1. estructurar. 2. construir.

structure contours, (geol.) curvas de nivel.

structureless [-ləs] *a.* sin estructura, esp. (anat.) sin estructura celular (membrana).

strudel ['strudəl] *s.* (alemán) pastel de hoja relleno de fruta o queso.

struggle ['strʌgəl] *v.i.* 1. luchar; forcejear, esforzarse. 2. (con *through, up, along, in,* etc.) abrirse paso, avanzar o moverse con dificultad, esforzarse para pasar. 3. bregar; vivir difícilmente.

4. **s. against,** luchar contra; **s. to (do),** luchar por (hacer), ej., *he struggled to control his feelings,* luchó por dominar sus sentimientos. —*s.* 1. lucha, pugna; contienda. 2. esfuerzo, forcejeo.
struggle for survival, la lucha por la existencia, la lucha por la vida.
struggler ['strʌglər, B -lə] *s.* luchador.
strugglingly [-lɪŋlɪ] *adv.* a duras penas, con mucho esfuerzo.
strum [strʌm] *v.i., v.t.* (*pret., p.p.* STRUMMED; *p.pr.* STRUMMING) rasguear (guitarra, etc.); cencerrear. —*s.* rasgueo; cencerreo.
struma ['strumə] *s.* (*pl.* STRUMAE [-mi]) 1. (med.) estruma, bocio. 2. (bot.) apófisis. 3. (ant.) escrófula.
strummer ['strʌmər, B -ə] *s.* el que rasguea un instrumento de cuerdas.
strumming [-ɪŋ] *s.* rasgueo, rasgueado.
strumose ['strumoʊs] **strumous** [-məs] *a.* (med.) estrumoso.
strumpet ['strʌmpət] *s.* prostituta, ramera, meretriz.
strung, *pret., p.p. de* **string.**
strut [strʌt] *v.i.* (*pret., p.p.* STRUTTED; *p.pr.* STRUTTING) pavonearse, inflarse, farolear. —*v.t.* apuntalar, acodar, acodalar. —*s.* 1. pavoneo. 2. puntal, codal, apoyador, poste, jabalcón, asnilla.
struthious ['struθɪəs] *a.* (orn.) estrucióniido, estrutiónido.
strychnia ['strɪknɪə] *s.* (quím.) estricnina.
strychnic [-nɪk] *a.* de estricnina, causado por la estricnina.
strychnine ['strɪknaɪn, -nən, B -ˌnin] *s.* (quím.) estricnina.
strychninism [-ˌɪzəm] *s.* (med.) estricnismo.
Stuart ['stuərt, B 'stjʊət] *s.* (hist.) Estuardo, dinastía de Escocia e Inglaterra.
stub [stʌb] *s.* 1. tocón, cepa (de árboles). 2. fragmento, resto, trozo, zoquete. 3. colilla (de cigarrillo), pucho (Amer.). 4. rabillo. 5. pluma (de escribir) de punta roma; cacho (de lápiz). 6. talón, matriz (de cheque). 7. guarda (de cerradura). —*v.t.* (*pret., p.p.* STUBBED; *p.pr.* STUBBING) 1. extirpar, arrancar, desarraigar (tocones, maleza). 2. rozar, desherbar, escardar (un terreno). 3. (gen. con *out*) apagar (cigarro, cigarrillo) aplastándolo. 4. **s. one's toe (against),** tropezar (con piedra u otro objeto).
stubble ['stʌbəl] *s.* 1. rastrojo. 2. barba cerdosa.
stubbly [-əlɪ] *a.* (STUBBLIER; STUBBLIEST) 1. cubierto de rastrojo. 2. cerdoso (ej., barba).
stubborn ['stʌbərn, B -ən] *a.* 1. obstinado, terco, testarudo, porfiado, pertinaz. 2. refractario, intratable. 3. (ant.) firme, robusto.
stubbornly [-lɪ] *adv.* obstinadamente, tercamente.
stubbornness [-nəs] *s.* obstinación, terquedad, testarudez, pertinacia.
stubby ['stʌbɪ] *a.* (STUBBIER; STUBBIEST) 1. corto, grueso y romo. 2. rechoncho, regordete, recoquín, cachigordo. 3. lleno de troncos o de tocones.
stub iron, hierro de clavos viejos.
stub mortise, mortaja ciega.
stub nail, clavo de herrar viejo, puntilla.
stub switch, (f.c.) cambio de tope.
stub track, (f.c.) desvío muerto.
stucco ['stʌkˌoʊ] *s.* (*pl.* STUCCOES o STUCCOS) estuco. —*v.t.* (*pret., p.p.* STUCCOED; *p.pr.* STUCCOING) estucar.
stuccowork [-ˌwɜrk, B -ˌwɜk] *s.* estuco, obra de estuco, estucado.
stuck [stʌk] *pret., p.p. de* STICK. =*Ma.* (jer.) **s. on,** enamorado, encantado con (algo o alguien).
stuck-up ['stʌk'ʌp] *a.* (fam.) presumido, tieso, estirado, orgulloso, engreído.
stud [stʌd] *s.* 1. yeguada, caballada. 2. acaballadero. 3. caballeriza (de un solo dueño). 4. (t. **studhorse**) caballo semental, caballo padre; garañón, padrillo, padrote (Amer.). 5. (jer.) hombre conocido por llevar una vida sexual muy activa. 6. **to stand at s.,** servir de semental; **to send to s.,** poner de semental.
stud, *s.* 1. clavo de adorno, tachón. 2. botón de cuello; gemelo de puño. 3. contrete, travesaño (en los eslabones de cadenas). 4. (t. **s. poker**) póker que se juega con una carta cubierta y cuatro descubiertas. 5. (const.) pie derecho, montante, alfarda. 6. (mec.) husillo; perno prisionero. —*v.t.* (*pret., p.p.* STUDDED; *p.pr.* STUDDING) 1. tachonar. 2. clavetear, enclavijar; fijar con pernos prisioneros. 3. (fig.) tachonar, salpicar. 4. (const.) armar con pies derechos.
stud bolt, tornillo opresor, perno prisionero.
studbook ['stʌdˌbʊk] *s.* registro genealógico de caballos de pura sangre.
studding [-ɪŋ] *s.* (const.) entramado.
studding sail, (mar.) ala, arrastradera, rastrera.
student ['studənt, B 'stjud-] *s.* 1. estudiante; escolar, educando; alumno. 2. observador, investigador.
student body, estudiantado.
student lamp, lámpara ajustable de lectura.
studentship [-ˌʃɪp] *s.* 1. condición de estudiante. 2. (G.B.) beca; pensión (universitaria).
student union, 1. club de estudiantes universitarios. 2. centro estudiantil (edificio en el campus).
stud farm, acaballadero.
studhorse ['stʌdˌhɔrs, B -ˌhɔs] *s.* caballo semental, caballo padre; garañón, padrillo, padrote (Amer.).
studied ['stʌdɪd] *a.* 1. premeditado, intencional, planeado. 2. artificioso, afectado. 3. (raro) docto, erudito.
studiedly [-lɪ] *adv.* adrede, deliberadamente.
studiedness [-nəs] *s.* manera artificial, deliberación afectada.
studio ['studɪoʊ, B 'stju-] *s.* 1. estudio, gabinete, atelier, taller (de artista). 2. (rad., cinem., t.v.) estudio.
studio couch, diván, gen. convertible en cama doble.
studious ['studɪəs, B 'stju-] *a.* 1. estudioso. 2. diligente, afanoso, asiduo. 3. solícito, ej., *with s. politeness,* con cortesía solícita. 4. (poét.) propicio para el estudio. 5. planeado, pensado, intencional.
studiously [-lɪ] *adv.* 1. estudiosamente. 2. solícitamente.
studiousness [-nəs] *s.* estudiosidad, inclinación al estudio.
stud poker, (naipes) póker abierto.
studwork ['stʌdˌwɜrk, B -ˌwɜk] *s.* (const.) entramado.
study ['stʌdɪ] *s.* 1. estudio; examen, análisis. 2. asignatura, materia (que se estudia), curso (Am.). 3. diligencia, atención, solicitud, cuidado. 4. ensimismamiento, meditación. 5. estudio, gabinete, despacho. 6. (arte) ensayo; boceto; bosquejo; estudio. 7. (mús.) estudio, ejercicio. —*v.i.* (*pret., p.p.* STUDIED; *p.pr.* STUDYING) 1. cursar estudios. 2. **s. for the bar,** estudiar derecho, prepararse para la abogacía; **s. to (do),** esforzarse por (hacer). —*v.t.* 1. estudiar; aprender. 2. estudiar, investigar, examinar, analizar. 3. (teat.) **s. one's part,** aprender su papel.
study hall, salón de estudios (en una escuela).
stuff [stʌf] *s.* 1. materia, material, substancia; elemento, parte componente, ingrediente. 2. género, tejido, paño (esp. de lana). 3. cosas, objetos, materias, bienes, efectos, asuntos (en general). 4. cualidades, habilidades, ej., *he has good s. in him,* tiene grandes cualidades, tiene buena madera. 5. fruslerías, basura. 6. tontería, disparate. 7. (jer.) cualquier droga. 8. (fam.) habilidad especial de un jugador en un dep.; efecto especial dado a la pelota. 9. **do your s.!** ¡haz tu deber! ¡muéstranos lo que sabes!; **s. and nonsense,** ¡tonterías! ¡necedades! —*v.t.* (*pret., p.p.* STUFFED; *p.pr.* STUFFING) 1. henchir, llenar, atestar, rellenar (pollo, pavo, etc.). 2. (fig.) hartar, embutir, atiborrar (de conocimientos). 3. (gen. con *up*) obstruir, obturar, atorar (nariz, etc.). 4. apiñar, apretar, empacar, empaquetar. 5. disecar (animales para preservarlos), ej., *stuffed bird,* pájaro disecado. 6. (E.U.) poner votos fraudulentos en (las urnas electorales). 7. impregnar (cueros) con aceite. —*v.i.* engullir la comida, tupirse, rellenarse.
stuffed shirt [stʌɪt-] (jer., E.U.) persona estirada o excesivamente formal y pretensiosa.
stuffily ['stʌfəlɪ] *adv.* 1. sosamente, obstinadamente. 2. pésadamente. 3. de manera pomposa.
stuffiness [-ɪnəs] *s.* 1. mala ventilación. 2. pesadez, pomposidad, exceso de formalidad. 3. obstinación.
stuffing ['stʌfɪŋ] *s.* atestamiento, relleno; (cocina) relleno; **to knock the s. out of,** (fam.) quitar los humos a.
stuffing box, (mec.) caja de estopas o de empaquetaduras, prensaestopas.
stuffing nut, (mec.) tuerca del prensaestopas.
stuffless [-ləs] *a.* falto de materia, insubstancial.
stuffy [-ɪ] *a.* (STUFFIER; STUFFIEST) 1. mal ventilado, sofocante. 2. obstruido, tupido. 3. soso, aburrido, pesado; pomposo; chapado a la antigua. 4. obstinado; colérico, malhumorado.
stull [stʌl] *s.* (min.) andamio de protección, estemple, puntal.
stultification [ˌstʌltəfə'keɪʃən] *s.* 1. estupefacción, atontamiento, embrutecimiento. 2. frustración, invalidación. 3. (der.) alegato de locura.
stultify ['stʌltəfaɪ] *v.t.* (*pret., p.p.* STULTIFIED; *p.pr.* STULTIFYING) 1. estupidizar, atontar, embobecer, idiotizar, embrutecer. 2. ridiculizar. 3. frustrar, hacer ineficaz, neutralizar; invalidar, inutilizar. 4. (der.) probar o alegar locura de (alguien).
stum [stʌm] *s.* mosto.
stumble ['stʌmbəl] *v.i.* 1. tropezar, dar un traspié. 2. tambalearse, vacilar. 3. desatinar, disparatar. 4. pecar. 5. **s. along,** caminar haciendo eses; **s. across (on, onto o upon),** encontrar de casualidad, tropezar accidentalmente con. —*v.t.* 1. hacer tropezar, trompicar. 2. dejar perplejo, confundir, turbar. —*s.* 1. tropiezo, traspié, paso en falso. 2. (fig.) tropezón, desliz.
stumblebum [-ˌbʌm] *s.* pugilista chabacano; pugilista aturdido (por los golpes).
stumbling block, obstáculo, impedimento, tropiezo, estorbo, embarazo.
stumblingly [-blɪŋlɪ] *adv.* a tropezones, con traspiés; desatinadamente.
stumer ['stumər, B 'stjumə] *s.* (jer., G.B.) 1. cheque sin fondos. 2. moneda falsa. 3. cosa sin valor; fracasado. 4. bancarrota, fracaso.
stump [stʌmp] *s.* 1. tocón, cepa, toza. 2. fragmento, resto; raigón (de diente); muñón (de un miembro); colilla (de cigarro); cabo de vela. 3. (*pl.*) (fam.) piernas. 4. tribuna o plataforma política. 5. (pint.) esfumino, difumino. 6. (criquet) estaca. 7. (fam.) reto, desafío. 8. **on the s.,** (fam.) pronunciando una arenga política, enfrascado en agitación política; **to get one up a s.,** dejar perplejo a uno; **to go on the s., to take the**

s., pronunciar discursos (en campaña política). —*v.t.* 1. reducir a un tocón, cercenar. 2. limpiar de tocones, rozar (un campo); desarraigar (tocones). 3. caminar con pasos pesados por. 4. confundir, dejar sin palabra. 5. hacer giras políticas por (distritos electorales, etc.). 6. desafiar, retar. 7. (pint.) esfumar, difuminar, difumar. 8. (criquet) eliminar (a un bateador) derribando las estacas con la pelota. 9. **to be stumped,** estar perplejo, no saber qué hacer o qué decir. —*v.i.* 1. renquear, cojear, caminar pesadamente, andar torpemente. 2. pronunciar discursos políticos (durante una gira electoral).

stumpage ['stʌmpɪdʒ] *s.* precio de madera viva, derecho de bosque; madera en pie.

stump oratory, oratoria política.

stumpy ['stʌmpɪ] *a.* (STUMPIER; STUMPIEST) 1. lleno de tocones. 2. cachigordo, pequeño y gordo; grueso.

stun [stʌn] *v.t.* (*pret., p.p.* STUNNED; *p.pr.* STUNNING) 1. aturdir, atontar; pasmar, privar. 2. atolondrar, aturullar. —*s.* choque, impacto, sacudida.

stung [stʌŋ] *pret., p.p. de* **sting.** —*a.* timado, chasqueado.

stunk [stʌŋk] *pret., p.p. de* **stink.**

stunner ['stʌnər, B -ə] *s.* golpe aturdidor; (jer.) cosa extraordinaria; persona muy atractiva, persona guapa.

stunning [-ɪŋ] *a.* 1. asombroso, sorprendente. 2. (fam.) magnífico, excelente, muy hermoso, elegantísimo.

stunningly [-ɪŋlɪ] *adv.* 1. asombrosamente. 2. (fam.) magníficamente.

stunsail, stunsle ['stʌnsəl] (mar.) *contr. de* **studding sail.**

stunt [stʌnt] *s.* (fam.) 1. acto de habilidad; despliegue de destreza. 2. truco, malabarismo; ardid públicitario. 3. (aer.) acrobacia. 4. atrofia (de plantas). 5. planta enana. —*v.i.* hacer malabarismos; (aer.) hacer acrobacias. —*v.t.* impedir el crecimiento o desarrollo de; empequeñecer, achicar.

stunt flying, vuelo acrobático.

stupa ['stupə] *s.* (arq.) estupa.

stupe [stup, B stjup] *s.* 1. (med.) fomento, compresa, cataplasma, apósito. 2. (**jer.**) estúpido (persona).

stupefacient [ˌstupə'feɪʃənt, B ˌstjupɪ-] *a.* estupefaciente, estupefactivo, soporífero. —*s.* estupefaciente, narcótico.

stupefaction [-'fækʃən] *s.* estupefacción, pasmo, estupor.

stupefactive [-'fæktɪv] *a.* estupefactivo, estupefaciente.

stupefy ['stupəˌfaɪ, B 'stju-] *v.t.* (*pret., p.p.* STUPEFIED; *p.pr.* STUPEFYING) 1. estupefacer; estupidizar, entontecer, embotar. 2. dejar estupefacto, asombrar.

stupendous [stu'pɛndəs, B stjʊ-] *a.* estupendo, asombroso, prodigioso, maravilloso.

stupendously [-lɪ] *adv.* estupendamente, asombrosamente, maravillosamente.

stupendousness [-nəs] *s.* apariencia estupenda, presentación maravillosa.

stupid ['stupəd, B 'stju-] *a.* 1. estúpido. 2. estupefacto, turulato. —*s.* estúpido.

stupidity [stu'pɪdətɪ, B stjʊ-] *s.* estupidez.

stupidly ['stupədlɪ, B 'stju-] *adv.* estúpidamente.

stupidness [-nəs] *s.* 1. estupidez. 2. estupor.

stupor ['stupər, B 'stjupə] *s.* estupor, atontamiento, letargo.

stuporous [-pərəs] *a.* pasmoso, asombroso.

sturdily ['stɜrdəlɪ, B 'stɜdɪlɪ] *adv.* 1. firmemente, tenazmente. 2. fuertemente, robustamente.

sturdiness [-ɪnəs] *s.* 1. firmeza, tenacidad. 2. fortaleza, robustez.

sturdy [-ɪ] *a.* (STURDIER; STURDIEST) 1. firme, resuelto, determinado, tenaz, porfiado. 2. fuerte, robusto, lozano. —*s.* (vet.) modorra.

sturgeon ['stɜrdʒən, B 'stɜdʒən] *s.* (ict.) esturion, marón, sollo.

sturt [stɜrt, B stʌt] *s.* (esco.) disturbio, alteración.

stutter ['stʌtər, B -ə] *v.i., v.t.* tartamudear, tartajear. —*s.* tartamudeo.

stutterer [-ər, B -ərə] *s.* tartamudo, tartajoso.

stutteringly [-ɪŋlɪ] *adv.* con tartamudeo, tartamudeando.

sty [staɪ] *s.* (*pl.* STIES) 1. zahúrda, pocilga, porqueriza. 2. (med.) orzuelo. —*v.t., v.i.* (*pret., p.p.* STIED; *p.pr.* STYING) vivir o alojarse en una pocilga.

Stygian ['stɪdʒɪən] *a.* 1. estigio, de la Estigia. 2. (fig.) estigio, infernal, tenebroso. 3. inviolable (juramento).

stylar ['staɪlər, B -ə] *a.* estilístico; con la forma de un estilo.

stylate ['staɪlˌeɪt] *a.* (ento.) estilopoide.

style [staɪl] *s.* 1. estilo (para escribir). 2. cincel; buril. 3. estilo, gnomon, varilla (del reloj de sol). 4. aguja (de fonógrafo). 5. (med.) estilete; sonda, cánula. 6. (poét.) pluma. 7. estilo (de escribir o hablar, de arquitectura, literario, etc.). 8. estilo, uso, práctica, costumbre, moda. 9. distinción, calidad, ej., *there's no s. about her,* no es una dama distinguida. 10. diseño, modelo, forma (de artículos de vestir, manufacturas, etc.). 11. tratamiento, designación; título. 12. estilo, calendario. 13. (bot.) estilo. 14. (zool.) púa, pincho. 15. (impr.) estilo (conjunto de reglas que se emplean en la redacción). 16. **in s.,** en la debida forma; elegantemente, lujosamente; **in the s. of,** al estilo de; **of s.,** elegante, distinguido, de moda. —*v.t.* 1. intitular, titular; nombrar, llamar. 2. diseñar (ropa, etc.). 3. poner a la moda.

styleless ['staɪlləs] *a.* falto de estilo, sin estilo.

styler [-ər, B -ə] *s.* diseñador, modista.

stylet ['staɪlət] *s.* 1. estilete, puñal, punzón. 2. (med.) estilete, sonda, tienta. 3. (zool.) púa, pincho.

styliform ['staɪləˌfɔrm, B -ˌfɔm] *a.* estiliforme, estiloide, estiloideo.

stylish ['staɪlɪʃ] *a.* elegante, de moda.

stylishly [-lɪ] *adv.* elegantemente, a la moda.

stylishness [-nəs] *s.* elegancia.

stylist ['staɪləst] *s.* 1. estilista. 2. diseñador (de modas).

stylistic [staɪ'lɪstɪk] **stylistical** [-tɪkəl] *a.* estilístico.

stylistically [-tɪkəlɪ] *adv.* en cuanto al estilo.

stylistics [-tɪks] *s. pl.* (*sing. o pl. en const.*) estilística, estudio del estilo (literario).

stylite ['staɪˌlaɪt] *s.* (hist., relig.) estilita.

stylitic [staɪ'lɪtɪk] *a.* (hist.) estilita.

stylization [ˌstaɪlə'zeɪʃən, B -laɪ-] *s.* estilización.

stylize ['staɪˌlaɪz] *v.t.* estilizar.

stylobate ['staɪləˌbeɪt] *s.* (arq.) estilóbato.

stylograph [-ˌgræf, B -grɑf] *s.* estilográfica, estilógrafo.

stylographic [ˌstaɪlə'græfɪk] *a.* 1. estilográfico. 2. escrito con un estilo.

stylography [staɪ'lɑgrəfɪ, B -'lɔg-] *s.* escritura o trazado mediante un estilo.

styloid ['staɪˌlɔɪd] *a.* (med.) estiloide, estiloideo.

stylolite ['staɪləˌlaɪt] *s.* (geol.) estilolito.

stylopodium [ˌstaɪlə'poʊdɪəm] *s.* (*pl.* STYLIPODIA [-dɪə]) (bot.) estilopodio.

stylus ['staɪləs] *s.* (*pl.* STYLI [-laɪ] o STYLUSES) 1. estilo, punzón. 2. aguja (de fonógrafo).

stymie ['staɪmɪ] *s.* 1. (golf) situación en que una bola obstruye a otra la entrada en el hoyo. 2. (fig.) situación embarazosa, callejón sin salida. —*v.t.* 1. (golf) obstruir con la bola. 2. (fig.) obstaculizar, bloquear, impedir.

stymy, *s.* (*pl.* STYMIES), *v.t.* (*pret., p.p.* STYMIED; *p.pr.* STYMYING) *var. de* **stymie.**

stypsis ['stɪpsəs] *s.* (med.) aplicación de estípticos.

styptic [-tɪk] *a.* (med.) estíptico, hemostático, astringente. —*s.* estíptico, substancia astringente.

stypticity [stɪp'tɪsətɪ] *s.* (med.) estipticidad, astringencia, astricción.

styptic pencil, lápiz hemostático.

Styracaceae [ˌstaɪrə'keɪsɪˌi] *s. pl.* (bot.) estiracáceas.

styracaceous [-'keɪʃəs] *a.* (bot.) estiracáceo.

styrax ['staɪrˌæks] *var. de* storax.

styrene ['staɪrˌin] *s.* (quím.) estireno.

stythe [staɪθ, B staɪð] *s.* mofeta, grisú (en minas).

Styx [stɪks] *s.* (mitol.) Estige, Estigia, laguna del mundo inferior que atravesaban las almas de los muertos.

suable ['suəbəl, B 'sjʊ-] *a.* (der.) procesable, justiciable, acusable, demandable.

suasion ['sweɪʒən] *s.* persuasión.

suasive ['sweɪsɪv] *a.* persuasivo, suasorio.

suave [swɑv] *a.* suave, afable; agradable, pulido; cortés, atento; urbano.

suavely ['swɑvlɪ] *adv.* suavemente, afablemente; agradablemente; cortésmente, atentamente.

suaveness [-nəs] **suavity** [-ətɪ] *s.* suavidad, afabilidad; cortesía, urbanidad.

sub [sʌb] *s.* (fam.) 1. submarino. 2. subterráneo. 3. subordinado, subalterno, subteniente. 4. substituto. 5. subscripción. 6. (foto.) *abrev. de* **substratum,** base de gelatina (que facilita la adhesión de la emulsión sensitiva). —*a.* auxiliar, subordinado; secundario. —*v.i.* (*pret., p.p.* SUBBED; *p.pr.* SUBBING) **s. for,** substituir a, hacer las veces de. —*v.t.* (foto.) aplicar una base de gelatina a (la película).

subacetate [ˌsʌb'æsəˌteɪt] *s.* (quím.) subacetato, acetato básico.

subacid [-'æsəd] *a.* 1. (quím.) subácido, un poco ácido. 2. un tanto mordaz (estilo, prosa, etc.).

subacute [-ə'kjut] *a.* 1. semiagudo (ángulo), poco agudo. 2. (med.) subagudo.

subaerial [-'ɛrɪəl] *a.* subaéreo.

subagency [sʌb'eɪdʒənsɪ] *s.* subagencia.

subagent ['sʌbˌeɪdʒənt] *s.* subagente.

subalpine [ˌsʌb'ælpaɪn] *a.* subalpino.

subaltern [səb'ɔltərn, B 'sʌbəltən] *a.* 1. subalterno, subordinado; dependiente. 2. (lóg.) particular (proposición). —*s.* 1. subordinado, subalterno. 2. (lóg.) proposición particular. 3. (G.B.) (mil.) subalterno.

subalternation [-ˌɔltərneɪʃən, B -tə'-] *s.* subordinación.

subaquatic [ˌsʌbə'kwætɪk] *a.* semi-acuático; submarino, subacuático.

subaqueous [-'eɪkwɪəs, -'æk-] *a.* 1. submarino, subacuático. 2. (geol.) subacuático (díc. esp. de la lapidificación bajo el agua).

subarctic [-'ɑrktɪk, B -'ɑk-] *a.* subpolar, subártico.

subassembly [ˌsʌbə'sɛmblɪ] *s.* subconjunto, subgrupo.

subatmospheric [ˌsʌbˌætməs'fɪrɪk, B -'fɛr-] *a.* subatmosférico.

subatom [-'ætəm] *s.* (quím., fís.) partícula subatómica.

subatomic [-ə'tɑmɪk, B -'tɔm-] *a.* (quím., fís.) subatómico.

subaverage [-'ævərɪdʒ] *a.* debajo del promedio.
subbasement ['sʌbˌbeɪsmənt] *s.* subsótano.
subbass [-'beɪs] *s.* (mús.) registro grave del pedal del órgano.
subbing ['sʌbɪŋ] *s.* 1. (fam.) reemplazo, substitución. 2. (foto.) base de gelatina (que facilita la adhesión de la emulsión sensitiva).
subcaliber [ˌsʌb'kæləbər, B -bə] *a.* (arm.) 1. subcalibrado (proyectil). 2. de calibre reducido (tiro).
subcartilaginous [-ˌkɑrtə'lædʒənəs, B -kɑtɪ-] *a.* (anat., zool.) subcartilaginoso.
subcelestial [-sə'lɛstʃəl, B -tjəl] *a.* terrenal, mundano.
subcellar ['sʌbˌsɛlər, B -ˌsɛlə] *s.* subsótano.
subchanter [-'tʃæntər, B -'tʃɑntə] *s.* (relig.) sochantre.
subchaser [-ˌtʃeɪsər, B -ə] *s.* (mar.) cazasubmarino.
subchloride [ˌsʌb'klɔraɪd] *s.* (quím.) subcloruro.
subclass ['sʌbˌklæs, B -ˌklɑs] *s.* (biol.) subclase.
subclavian [ˌsʌb'kleɪvɪən] *a.* (anat.) subclavio, subclavicular.
subclavian artery, (anat.) arteria subclavia.
subclinical [-'klɪnɪkəl] *a.* (med.) subclínico.
subcommittee ['sʌbkəˌmɪtɪ] *s.* subcomisión, subcomité.
subconscious [ˌsʌb'kɑnʃəs, B -'kɔn-] *a.* subconsciente. —*s.* subconsciencia.
subconsciously [-lɪ] *adv.* de modo subconsciente, en la subconsciencia, subconscientemente.
subconsciousness [-nəs] *s.* subconsciencia.
subcontinent ['sʌb'kɑntənənt, B -'kɔn-] *s.* subcontinente.
subcontract [-'kɑnˌtrækt, B 'kɔn-] *s.* subcontrato. — [-ˌsʌbkən'trækt] *v.t.* subcontratar.
subcontrariety [-ˌkɑntrə'raɪətɪ, B -kɔn-] *s.* (lóg.) relación entre proposiciones sub-contrarias.
subcontrary [-ˌsʌb'kɑnˌtrɛrɪ, B -'kɔntrərɪ] *a.* (lóg.) subcontrario.
subcool [-'kul] *v.t.* (quím.) subenfriar.
subcortex [-'kɔrtɛks, B -'kɔtɛks] *s.* (anat.) subcórtex.
subcortical [-'kɔrtɪkəl, B -'kɔtɪ-] *a.* (anat.) subcortical.
subcostal [-'kɑstəl, B -'kɔs-] *a.* (anat., zool.) subcostal.
subcritical [-'krɪtɪkəl] *a.* (fís., quím.) subcrítico (materia fisionable, reactor atómico).
subculture ['sʌbˌkʌltʃər, B -tʃə] *s.* (bact.) subcultivo.
subcutaneous [ˌsʌbkjʊ'teɪnɪəs] *a.* (anat.) subcutáneo.
subcutaneously [-lɪ] *adv.* de modo subcutáneo, por vía subcutánea, subcutáneamente.
subcutis [-'kjutəs] *s.* (anat.) subcutis, tejido subcutáneo.
subdeacon ['sʌb'dikən] *s.* (relig.) subdiácono.
subdeaconry [-rɪ] *s.* subdiaconado, subdiaconato.
subdeb ['sʌbˌdɛb] **subdebutante** [ˌsʌb'dɛbjʊˌtɑnt] *s.* (E.U.) tobillera, jovencita que aún no ha sido presentada en sociedad.
subdelegate ['sʌb'dɛlɪgət] *s.* subdelegado. — [sʌb'dɛlɪˌgeɪt] *v.t.* subdelegar.
subdelegation [-ˌdɛlə'geɪʃən] *s.* subdelegación.
subdelirium [ˌsʌbdɪ'lɪrɪəm] *s.* (med.) subdelirio.
subdentate ['sʌb'dɛnˌteɪt] *a.* (bot.) imperfectamente dentada (hoja).
subdepot [-'dɛpoʊ] *s.* (mil.) depósito secundario.
subdiaconate [ˌsʌbdaɪ'ækənət] *s.* (relig.) subdiaconato, subdiaconado.
subdirector [-də'rɛktər, B -tə] *s.* subdirector.
subdirectorship [-ʃɪp] *s.* subdirección.
subdividable [-də'vaɪdəbəl] *a.* subdivisible.
subdivide ['sʌbdə'vaɪd] *v.t., v.i.* subdividir(se) (esp. un terreno grande).
subdivision [-də'vɪʒən] *s.* subdivisión.
subdominant [-'dɑmənənt, B -'dɔm-] *s.* (mús.) subdominante.
subdouble [-'dʌbəl] *s.* (mat.) subduplo.
subdual [-'duəl, B -'dju-] *s.* subyugación, conquista; dominación.
subduct [səb'dʌkt] *v.t., v.i.* substraer, quitar, sacar, restar.
subdue [səb'du, B -'dju] *v.t.* 1. someter, sojuzgar, subyugar, avasallar, conquistar. 2. reprimir, dominar, domar, amansar. 3. suavizar, apaciguar, amortiguar, mitigar. 4. ganar para el cultivo (tierra).
subdued [-'dud, B 'djud] *a.* 1. deprimido, alicaído. 2. amortiguado, discreto (color); bajo, suave (tono, voz).
subdued light, media luz.
subduer [-'duər, B -'djuə] *s.* subyugador, conquistador; dominador.
suber ['subər, B 'sjubə] *s.* (bot.) súber.
suberic [su'bɛrɪk, B sju-] *a.* (quím.) subérico.
suberic acid, (quím.) ácido subérico.
suberin ['subərən, B 'sju-] *s.* (quím.) suberina.
suberization [ˌsubərə'zeɪʃən, B ˌsjubəraɪ-] *s.* (bot.) suberización.
suberize ['subəˌraɪz, B 'sjubə-] *v.t.* (bot.) convertir en súber.
suberose [-ˌroʊs] **subereous** [-rəs] *a.* (bot.) suberoso.
subessential [ˌsʌbə'sɛnʃəl] *a.* menos esencial.
subfamily ['sʌbˌfæməlɪ] *s.* (biol.) subfamilia.
subfebrile [-'fɛbrəl, B -'fibraɪl] *a.* (med.) subfebril.
subfossil [-ˌfɑsəl, B -fɔs-] *a.* (pal.) subfósil.
subfreezing [-'frizɪŋ] *a.* debajo del punto de congelación.
subfusc [sʌb'fʌsk, B 'sʌbfʌsk] *a.* incoloro, opaco, monótono.
subgenus ['sʌbˌdʒinəs] *s.* (biol.) subgénero, subdivisión del género.
subgrade [-ˌgreɪd] *s.* rasante, explanación, plantilla, plataforma de la vía.
subgroup [-ˌgrup] *s.* (biol., quím.) subgrupo, división de un grupo.
subhead ['sʌbˌhɛd] **subheading** [-ɪŋ] *s.* 1. subtítulo, título secundario. 2. subdirector (de un colegio o escuela, etc.).
subhuman [ˌsʌb'hjumən] *a.* infrahumano; casi humano.
subindex [ˌsʌb'ɪndɛks] *s.* (*pl.* SUBINDICES [-dɪˌsiz]) (mat.) subíndice.
subinterval [ˌsʌb'ɪntərvəl, B -'ɪntəvəl] *s.* (mús., mat.) subintervalo.
subirrigate [sʌb'ɪrɪˌgeɪt] *v.t.* irrigar bajo tierra (por medio de tubería porosa).
subirrigation [ˌsʌbɪrɪ'geɪʃən] *s.* irrigación subterránea, subirrigación, subregadío.
subj. *abrev. de* 1. **subjunctive,** subjuntivo. 2. **subject, materia, asignatura.**
subjacent [sʌb'dʒeɪsənt] *a.* subyacente.
subject ['sʌbdʒɪkt] *a.* 1. súbdito, sometido, supeditado, dominado. 2. (con *to*) expuesto, propenso, dispuesto (a). 3. (con *to*) dependiente (de), sujeto (a), pasible (de) (condición, circunstancia, etc.). 4. **to hold s.,** mantener en servidumbre. —*s.* 1. súbdito. 2. individuo, sujeto. 3. materia, tópico, asunto, tema. 4. asignatura, materia, curso (Amer.) (de estudios). 5. (gram., lóg., filos.) sujeto. 6. (mús.) tema, frase melódica. 7. **on the s. of,** sobre el tema o asunto de; **to change the s.,** cambiar de tema, hablar de otro asunto. — [səb'dʒɛkt] *v.t.* 1. sojuzgar, subyugar, avasallar, dominar. 2. **s. to,** someter a, sujetar a; supeditar a, subordinar a (condición, etc.); exponer a (calor, crítica, etc.).
subjection [səb'dʒɛkʃən] *s.* 1. sujeción, subyugación, sometimiento, supeditación, vasallaje, dependencia. 2. (gram.) subordinación.
subjective [-tɪv] *a.* subjetivo.
subjectively [-tɪvlɪ] *adv.* subjetivamente.
subjectiveness [-tɪvnəs] *s.* subjetividad.
subjectivism [-tɪˌvɪzəm] *s.* (filos.) subjetivismo.
subjectivist [-tɪvəst] *s.* (filos.) subjetivista.
subjectivity [ˌsʌbdʒɛk'tɪvətɪ] *s.* subjetividad.
subject matter, materia, asunto, tema (de que se trata).
subjoin [ˌsʌb'dʒɔɪn] *v.t.* añadir, anexar, adjuntar, agregar.
subjugate ['sʌbdʒɪˌgeɪt] *v.t.* subyugar, someter, avasallar, dominar, sojuzgar.
subjugation [ˌsʌbdʒɪ'geɪʃən] *s.* subyugación, dominación.
subjugator ['sʌbdʒɪˌgeɪtər, B -tə] *s.* subyugador, dominador.
subjunction [səb'dʒʌŋkʃən] *s.* añadidura, anexión, adjunción.
subjunctive [səb'dʒʌŋktɪv] *a.* (gram.) subjuntivo.
subjunctive mood, (gram.) modo subjuntivo.
subkingdom ['sʌbˌkɪŋdəm] *s.* (biol.) subreino, subdivisión.
sublate [səb'leɪt] *v.t.* negar, denegar; cancelar, eliminar.
sublease ['sʌbˌlis] *s.* subarriendo, subarrendamiento. — [səb'lis] *v.t.* subarrendar, subalquilar (Amer.).
sublessee [ˌsʌblɛ'si] *s.* subarrendatario.
sublessor [ˌsʌblɛ'sɔr, B -'sɔ] *s.* subarrendador, sublocador.
sublet ['sʌb'lɛt] *v.t.* subarrendar.
subletter [-'lɛtər, B -tə] *s.* subarrendador.
subletting [-tɪŋ] *s.* subarrendamiento.
sublevel [-'lɛvəl] *s.* subnivel.
sublieutenant [ˌsʌblu'tɛnənt, B -lɛ-] *s.* (mil.) subteniente, alférez.
sublimate ['sʌbləˌmeɪt] *v.t.* sublimar. — ['sʌblɪmət] *a.* sublimado. —*s.* (quím.) sublimado.
sublimation [ˌsʌblə'meɪʃən] *s.* 1. sublimación. 2. refinamiento.
sublimatory ['sʌbləməˌtɔrɪ, B -tərɪ] *a.* (quím.) sublimatorio. —*s.* (quím.) recipiente para sublimar.
sublime [sə'blaɪm] *a.* 1. sublime, exaltado; grandioso, majestuoso. 2. (fig.) sobresaliente, eminente, incomparable. 3. (ant.) elevado, encumbrado. —*s.* (gen. con *the*) lo sublime, sublimidad. —*v.t.* 1. (quím.) sublimar. 2. (fig.) sublimar, exaltar.
sublimely [-lɪ] *adv.* sublimemente.
sublimeness [-nəs] *s.* sublimidad.
subliminal [ˌsʌb'lɪmənəl] (psic.) *a.* subliminal. —*s.* subconsciencia, conciencia subliminal.
sublimity [sə'blɪmətɪ] *s.* 1. sublimidad. 2. cosa sublime.
sublingual [ˌsʌb'lɪŋgwəl] *a.* (anat.) sublingual.
sublunar [-'lunər, B -'lunə] **sublunary** [-'lunərɪ] *a.* 1. sublunar. 2. (poét.) terrenal, mundano.
submachine gun [-mə'ʃinˌgʌn] (mil.) pistola ametralladora, ametralladora ligera, metralleta.
submarginal [-'mɑrdʒənəl, B -'mɑdʒ-] *a.* 1. (e.p.) submarginal. 2. (biol.) cerca del margen.

submarine [ˌsʌbmə'rin] *a.* submarino. — ['sʌbməˌrin] *s.* submarino, sumergible. —*v.t.* atacar o hundir con un submarino.
submarine chaser, cazasubmarinos.
submariner [ˌsʌbmə'rinər, B səb'mærɪnə] *s.* tripulante de un submarino.
submaxilla [ˌsʌbmæk'sɪlə] *s.* (*pl.* SUBMAXILLAE [-'sɪli]) (anat.) maxilar inferior; mandíbula inferior.
submaxillary [-'mæksəˌlɛrɪ, B -mæk'sɪlərɪ] (anat.) *a.* submaxilar. —*s.* (*pl.* SUBMAXILLIARIES) hueso o arteria submaxilar.
submaxillary gland, (anat.) glándula submaxilar.
submediant [-'midɪənt] *s.* (mús.) superdominante.
submerge [səb'mɜrdʒ, B -'mɜdʒ] *v.i., v.t.* 1. sumergir(se), hundir(se), sumir(se). 2. empantanar, inundar (ej., una ciudad).
submerged [-'mɜrdʒd, B -'mɜdʒd] *a.* 1. (bot.) sumergido, que crece debajo del agua. 2. arruinado, sumido en la miseria. 3. oculto, no aparente.
submergence [-'mɜrdʒəns, B -'mɜdʒəns] *s.* sumersión, sumergimiento, hundimiento.
submergibility [səbˌmɜrdʒə'bɪlətɪ, B -ˌmɜdʒə-] *a.* capacidad de sumersión.
submergible [-'mɜrdʒəbəl, B -'mɜdʒə-] *a.* sumergible.
submerse [-'mɜrs, B -m'ɜs] *v.t.* sumergir, hundir, sumir.
submersed [-'mɜrst, B -'mɜst] *a.* (bot.) sumergido, que crece debajo del agua.
submersible [-'mɜrsəbəl, B -'mɜsə-] *s.* sumergible, submarino. —*a.* sumergible, hundible.
submersion [-'mɜrʒən, B -'mɜʃən] *s.* sumersión, sumergimiento.
submicroscopic [ˌsʌbmaɪkrə'skɑpɪk, B -'skɔp-] *a.* ultramicroscópico.
subminiature [ˌsʌb'mɪnɪətʃər, B -tʃə] *a.* (rad.) subminiatura (tubo electrónico).
submiss [səb'mɪs] *a.* (ant.) sumiso, obsequioso.
submission [səb'mɪʃən] *s.* 1. sumisión, rendimiento. 2. sumisión, obsequiosidad, obediencia. 3. sometimiento, presentación (a examen, inspección, etc.). 4. proposición, parecer, teoría. 5. (der.) sometimiento a arbitraje.
submissive [səb'mɪsɪv] *a.* 1. dócil, sumiso, obediente. 2. rendido, obsequioso.
submissively [-lɪ] *adv.* 1. dócilmente, obedientemente. 2. obsequiosamente.
submissiveness [-nəs] *s.* 1. docilidad, sumisión, obediencia. 2. obsequiosidad.
submit [səb'mɪt] *v.t.* (*pret., p.p.* SUBMITTED; *p.pr.* SUBMITTING) 1. someter, referir. 2. presentar, exponer, proponer; ofrecer (una teoría, tesis, etc.). —*v.i.* someterse, rendirse; conformarse.
submittal [səb'mɪtəl] *s.* sumisión.
submontane [ˌsʌb'mɑnteɪn, B -'mɔn-] *a.* situado al pie de una montaña.
submontanely [-lɪ] *adv.* al pie de una montaña.
submultiple [ˌsʌb'mʌltɪpəl] *s.* (mat.) submúltiplo.
subnormal [-'nɔrməl, B -'nɔməl] *a.* subnormal, deficiente esp. mental. —*s.* persona subnormal.
subocular [-'ɑkjələr, B -'ɔkjʊlə] *a.* (anat.) subóptico, suborbitario.
subopposite [-'ɑpəsət, B -'ɔp-] *a.* (bot.) casi opuesta (hoja).
suborbital [-'ɔrbətəl, B -'ɔbɪt-] *a.* suborbital, por debajo de la órbita ocular.
suborder ['sʌbˌɔrdər, B -ˌɔdə] *s.* suborden.
subordinacy [sə'bɔrdənəsɪ, B -'bɔdə-] *s.* sujeción, subordinación, dependencia.
subordinate [sə'bɔrdənət, B -'bɔdɪnɪt] *a.* 1. subalterno, subordinado, inferior. 2. (gram.) subordinado. —*s.* subalterno, subordinado. — [sə'bɔrdɪˌneɪt, B -'bɔdɪ-] *v.t.* subordinar, someter, sujetar.
subordinate clause, (gram.) oración subordinada.
subordinate conjunction, conjunción subordinada.
subordinately [-lɪ] *adv.* subordinadamente.
subordination [səˌbɔrdə'neɪʃən, B -ˌbɔdɪ-] *s.* subordinación, dependencia.
suborn [sə'bɔrn, B -'bɔn] *v.t.* (der.) sobornar, cohechar.
subornation [ˌsʌbɔr'neɪʃən, B -ɔ'-] *s.* 1. soborno, cohecho. 2. (der.) **s. of perjury,** soborno de testigo.
suborner [sə'bɔrnər, B -'bɔnə] *s.* sobornador, cohechador.
subovate [ˌsʌb'oʊveɪt] *a.* aproximadamente aovado.
suboxide [sʌb'ɑksaɪd, B -'ɔk-] *s.* (quím.) subóxido.
subplot ['sʌbˌplɑt, B -ˌplɔt] *s.* trama o argumento secundario (en novelas, dramas, etc.).
subpoena, subpena [sə'pinə] (der.) *s.* citación, comparendo. —*v.t.* (*pret., p.p.* SUBPOENAED; *p.pr.* SUBPOENAING) citar, emplazar.
subprefect [ˌsʌb'priˌfɛkt] *s.* subprefecto.
subprefecture [-fɛktʃər, B -tʃə] *s.* subprefectura.
subprincipal [-'prɪnsəpəl] *s.* 1. subdirector (ej., de un colegio). 2. (mús.) registro de octava grave (del órgano). 3. (carp.) cabio secundario.
subreption [səb'rɛpʃən] *s.* (der.) subrepción.
subreptitious [ˌsʌbrɛp'tɪʃəs] *a.* subrepticio.
subrogate ['sʌbroʊˌgeɪt] *v.t.* (der.) subrogar, substituir.
subrogation [ˌsʌbrə'geɪʃən] *s.* (der.) subrogación, substitución.
sub rosa [-'roʊzə] (lat.) secretamente, confidencialmente, en confianza.
subsaturated [sʌb'sætʃəˌreɪtəd] *a.* casi saturado.
subscapular [ˌsʌb'skæpjələr, B -jʊlə] *a.* (anat.) subescapular, subscapular.
subscribe [səb'skraɪb] *v.t.* 1. subscribir, firmar (carta, documento, etc.). 2. subscribir, convenir con, estar de acuerdo con. —*v.i.* 1. subscribir, firmar. 2. **s. for (stock, a book,** etc.), subscribirse a (acciones antes de su emisión, un libro antes de su publicación, etc.); **s. to,** subscribirse a (periódico, revista, etc.); subscribir, convenir con, estar de acuerdo con.
subscriber [-ər, B -ə] *s.* 1. subscriptor, firmante, el que subscribe. 2. abonado (a servicio de teléfonos). 3. subscriptor (a un periódico, revista, etc.).
subscript ['sʌbskrɪpt] *a.* (gram. griega) subscrito. —*s.* (mat., quím.) subíndice.
subscription [səb'skrɪpʃən] *s.* 1. subscripción, firma. 2. subscripción, abono.
subsection ['sʌb'sɛkʃən] *s.* 1. subdivisión. 2. apartado (de un artículo de ley).
subsequence ['sʌbsəˌkwɛns] *s.* 1. posterioridad. 2. suceso subsiguiente.
subsequent [-kwənt] *a.* subsecuente, subsiguiente, consecutivo.
subsequently [-ˌkwɛntlɪ] *adv.* posteriormente, consecutivamente, seguido, con posterioridad.
subserve [səb'sɜrv, B -'sɜv] *v.t.* servir, ayudar, promover (plan, propósito, etc.).
subservience [-'sɜrvɪəns, B -'sɜvɪ-] **subserviency** [-vɪənsɪ] *s.* 1. subordinación. 2. servilismo, obsequiosidad.
subservient [-vɪənt] *a.* 1. subordinado. 2. servil, obsequioso. 3. (con *to*) útil, de ayuda (a, para).
subserviently [-vɪəntlɪ] *adv.* subordinadamente, servilmente, obsequiosamente.
subside [səb'saɪd] *v.i.* 1. hundirse, sumirse, asentarse, irse al fondo; descender, bajar. 2. amainarse, aquietarse, serenarse, calmarse. 3. (fam.) dejarse caer, desplomarse (en una silla).
subsidence [-əns, 'sʌbsədəns] **subsidency** [-ənsɪ] *s.* 1. hundimiento, descenso; (geol.) subsidencia. 2. sedimento. 3. amaine, aquietamiento, disminución.
subsidiarily [ˌsʌbˌsɪdɪ'ɛrəlɪ, B -'sɪdjər-] *adv.* subsidiariamente.
subsidiary [səb'sɪdɪˌɛrɪ, B -'sɪdjərɪ] *a.* subsidiario, auxiliar, incidental, secundario. —*s.* (*pl.* SUBSIDIARIES) 1. auxiliar, contribuidor, accesorio. 2. (com.) subsidiaria, compañía subsidiaria, compañía filial, sucursal. 3. (mús.) tema o motivo subordinado.
subsidization [ˌsʌbsədə'zeɪʃən, B -daɪ-] *s.* otorgamiento de subvención.
subsidize ['sʌbsəˌdaɪz] *v.t.* subvencionar, dar subsidio a.
subsidizer [-ər, B -ə] *s.* el que subvenciona.
subsidy ['sʌbsədɪ] *s.* (*pl.* SUBSIDIES) subsidio, subvención.
subsist [səb'sɪst] *v.i.* subsistir, existir, perdurar; conservarse, permanecer, sustentarse, mantenerse. —*v.t.* alimentar, mantener.
subsistence [-əns] *s.* 1. subsistencia, existencia. 2. subsistencias, víveres. 3. (filos.) subsistencia (complemento último de la substancia). 4. (ant.) persistencia, continuidad.
subsistent [-ənt] *a.* 1. subsistente, existente. 2. (con *in*) inherente (en).
subsoil ['sʌbˌsɔɪl] *s.* subsuelo. —*v.t.* trabajar o labrar el subsuelo de.
subsolar [ˌsʌb'soʊlər, B -lə] *a.* 1. situado bajo el sol, subsolar. 2. intertropical.
subsonic [ˌsʌb'sɑnɪk, B -'sɔnɪk] *a.* (fís.) subsónico.
subsonic speed, velocidad subsónica.
subspace ['sʌbˌspeɪs] *s.* (mat.) subespacio.
subspecies [-ˌspiʃiz] *s.* (*pl.* SUBSPECIES) (biol., bot.) subespecie.
substage [-ˌsteɪdʒ] *s.* 1. (geol.) subestratificación. 2. disposición de accesorios debajo de la platina del microscopio.
substance ['sʌbstəns] *s.* 1. substancia, ser, naturaleza. 2. esencia, principio. 3. substancia, solidez, ej., *there is no s to it,* eso no tiene solidez. 4. caudal, bienes, ej., *man of s.,* hombre acaudalado, *to waste one's s.,* despilfarrar sus bienes. 5. (quím.) substancia. 6. **in s.,** en substancia, en lo esencial.
substandard [ˌsʌb'stændərd, B -dəd] *a.* 1. (E.U.) de calidad inferior a lo establecido (alimentos, drogas). 2. (filol.) (de uso) vulgar.
substantial [səb'stænʃəl] *a.* 1. substancial, considerable, cuantioso, importante. 2. real, verdadero, existente. 3. substancioso, substancial (sopa, alimento, etc.); copioso, abundante (comida, almuerzo, etc.). 4. sólido, firme, fuerte. 5. material. 6. acomodado, hacendado, acaudalado. —*s.* 1. realidad. 2. parte esencial.
substantiality [-ˌstænʃɪ'ælətɪ] *s.* realidad; materialidad.
substantially [-'stænʃəlɪ] *adv.* sólidamente, substancialmente.
substantialness [-ʃəlnəs] *s.* fuerza, firmeza; solidez.
substantiate [-ʃɪˌeɪt] *v.t.* justificar, probar, verificar, comprobar.
substantiation [səbˌstænʃɪ'eɪʃən] *s.* justificación, verificación, comprobación.

substantiative [səb'stænʃɪˌeɪtɪv] *a.* probador, justificativo, tendiente a comprobar.
substantival [ˌsʌbstən'taɪvəl] *a.* (gram.) substantivo.
substantive ['sʌbstəntɪv] *a.* 1. substantivo. 2. real, positivo. 3. permanente, duradero. 4. importante. 5. esencial. 6. independiente. —*s.* (gram.) substantivo.
substantively [-lɪ] *adv.* 1. substantivamente. 2. (gram.) substantivamente, en forma substantivada.
substantiveness [-nəs] *s.* substantividad.
substantive right, derecho primario, derecho substantivo.
substantivity [ˌsʌbstən'tɪvətɪ] *s.* substantividad, sustantividad.
substantivize ['sʌbstəntɪvˌaɪz] **substantize** [-ˌtaɪz] *v.t.* (gram.) substantivizar.
substation ['sʌbˌsteɪʃən] *s.* 1. (elec.) subcentral. 2. sucursal de correos.
substituent [sʌb'stɪtʃʊənt] *s.* (quím.) átomo sustituyente.
substitutable ['sʌbstəˌtutəbəl, B -ˌtju-] *a.* substituible.
substitute ['sʌbstəˌtut, B -ˌtjut] *s.* substituto, substituidor, suplente, reemplazo. —*v.t., v.i.* substituir, reemplazar, remplazar, suplir.
substitution [ˌsʌbstə'tuʃən, B -'tju-] *s.* substitución, reemplazo.
substitutional [-ʃənəl] *a.* de substitución o sustitución; substituidor, suplente.
substitutionally [-ʃənəlɪ] *adv.* en reemplazo; como substituto o suplente.
substitutionary [-ʃəˌnɛrɪ, B -ʃənərɪ] *a.* de substitución o sustitución; substituidor, suplente.
substitutive ['sʌbstəˌtutɪv, B -ˌtju-] *a.* substitutivo.
substrate ['sʌbˌstreɪt] *s.* 1. (quím.) substrato. 2. (biol., bact.) medio.
substratosphere [ˌsʌb'strætəˌsfɪr, B -ˌsfɪə] *s.* (meteor.) subestrastosfera.
substratum ['sʌbˌstreɪtəm, -ˌstræt-, B -'st-rɑt-] *s.* (*pl.* SUBSTRATA [-ə]) 1. (geol., agr.) substrato, subsuelo. 2. (biol.) substrato. 3. (foto.) substrato, base de gelatina (que fija la emulsión a la película, papel, etc.).
substructure [-ˌstrʌktʃər, B -tʃə] *s.* 1. (arq.) subestructura, infraestructura, estructura inferior; cimientos. 2. (f.c.) vía.
subsume [səb'sum, B -'sjum] *v.t.* subsumir, incluir (en una clase, categoría, etc.).
subsumption [-'sʌmpʃən] *s.* 1. subsunción, inclusión (en una categoría, etc.). 2. (lóg.) premisa menor.
subsurface ['sʌbˌsɜrfəs, B -ˌsɜfəs] *s.* subterráneo, subálveo. —*a.* subterráneo, que está bajo una superficie esp. la terrestre.
subsurface flow, (hidr.) corriente freática.
subtangent ['sʌb'tændʒənt] *s.* subtangente.
subteen ['sʌb'tin] *s.* niño o niña menor de trece años.
subtemperate [ˌsʌb'tɛmpərət] *a.* (meteor.) semitemplado (clima).
subtenancy [-'tɛnənsɪ] *s.* subarriendo.
subtenant [-'tɛnənt] *s.* subarrendatario.
subtend [səb'tɛnd] *v.t.* 1. (geom.) subtender. 2. (bot.) abrazar.
subtense ['sʌbˌtɛns] *s.* (geom.) subtensa.
subterfuge ['sʌbtərˌfjudʒ, B 'sʌbtəˌ-] *s.* subterfugio, efugio, escapatoria, evasiva.
subterranean [ˌsʌbtə'reɪnɪən] **subterraneous** [-nɪəs] *a.* subterráneo.
subtile ['sʌtəl] *a.* (*forma ant. de* **subtle**) 1. sutil, tenue, etéreo, delicado. 2. astuto, artificioso. 3. penetrante.
subtileness ['sʌtəlnəs] *s.* (*forma ant. de* **subtleness**) 1. sutilidad. 2. astucia.
subtility [sʌb'tɪlətɪ] *s.* (*pl.* SUBTILITIES) 1. sutileza, sutilidad. 2. perspicacia, argucia, agudeza, ingenio.
subtilization [ˌsʌtələ'zeɪʃən, B -əlaɪ-] *s.* sutilización.
subtilize ['sʌtəˌlaɪz] *v.t., v.i.* sutilizar, hacer distinciones sutiles.
subtitle ['sʌbˌtaɪtəl] *s.* subtítulo; (cinem.) leyenda (en películas). —*v.t.* subtitular, poner subtítulo a; (cinem.) poner leyendas a (película).
subtle ['sʌtəl] *a.* 1. sutil, tenue, etéreo (vapor, perfume, etc.). 2. impalpable, místico (poder, arte, magia, etc.). 3. sutil, agudo, perspicaz, penetrante (sentido, observador, intelecto, etc.). 4. ingenioso. 5. insidioso, taimado.
subtleness [-nəs] *s.* sutilidad, agudeza, perspicacia, penetración.
subtlety [-tɪ] *s.* (*pl.* SUBTLETIES) 1. sutileza, sutilidad, astucia. 2. sutileza, distinción sutil.
subtly ['sʌtlɪ] *adv.* 1. sutilmente, ingeniosamente. 2. insidiosamente; imperceptiblemente.
subtonic [ˌsʌb'tɑnɪk, B -'tɔn-] *s.* (mús.) sensible, séptima nota (en la escala mayor y menor).
subtract [səb'trækt] *v.t., v.i.* substraer, sustraer, restar; deducir.
subtraction [-'trækʃən] *s.* substracción, deducción; (mat.) resta, substracción.
subtractive [-tɪv] *a.* 1. (foto.) sustractivo (procedimiento). 2. que tiende a substraer, a disminuir. 3. (mat.) que tiene el signo menos (—).
subtrahend ['sʌbtrəˌhɛnd] *s.* (mat.) substraendo, sustraendo.
subtreasurer [-ˌtrɛʒərər, B -ə] *s.* subtesorero, vicetesorero.
subtreasury [-ˌtrɛʒərɪ] *s.* subtesorería, vicetesorería.
subtropic [ˌsʌb'trɑpɪk, B -'trɔp-] **subtropical** [-ɪkəl] *a.* subtropical.
subtropics [-ɪks] *s. pl.* subtrópicos.
subulate ['subjələt] *a.* (bot.) subulado.
subumbrella [ˌsʌbʌm'brɛlə] *s.* (zool.) subumbrela (de la medusa).
suburb ['sʌbɜrb, B -ɜb] *s.* 1. suburbio, arrabal, barrio periférico. 2. (*pl.*) afueras, inmediaciones, alrededores; periferia.
suburban [sə'bɜrbən, B -'bɜbən] *a., s.* suburbano, de las afueras de un centro urbano.
suburbanite [-bəˌnaɪt] *s.* suburbano, habitante de las afueras.
suburbia [-bɪə] *s.* 1. alrededores, inmediaciones, afueras. 2. habitantes de un suburbio (colectivamente).
suburbicarian [səˌbɜrbə'kɛrɪən, B -ˌbɜbə-] *a.* suburbicario.
subvene [səb'vin] *v.i.* 1. subvenir. 2. proveer.
subvention [səb'vɛnʃən] *s.* subvención, subsidio, ayuda.
subversion [səb'vɜrʒən, B -'vɜʃən] *s.* 1. subversión. 2. trastorno; alteración de un orden o modo.
subversive [-sɪv] *a.* subversivo.
subversiveness [-sɪvnəs] *s.* tendencia subversiva.
subvert [səb'vɜrt, B -'vɜt] *v.t.* 1. subvertir, trastrocar. 2. derruir, demoler, arruinar.
subverter [-ər, B -ə] *s.* subversor, destructor.
subvertible [-əbəl] *a.* 1. subvertible. 2. destruible.
subway ['sʌbˌweɪ] *s.* 1. ferrocarril subterráneo, metropolitano, metro, subte (Amer.). 2. galería o conducto subterráneo. 3. paso a desnivel.
succedaneous [ˌsʌksə'deɪnɪəs] *a.* sucedáneo, sustituto.
succedaneum [-nɪəm] *s.* (*pl.* SUCCEDANEA [-nɪə]) sucedáneo, sustituto.
succedent [sək'sidənt] *a.* sucediente, subsiguiente, subsecuente.
succeed [sək'sid] *v.i.* 1. subseguir, suceder. 2. tener éxito, conseguir su propósito. 3. suceder, seguir en el puesto, ocupar el puesto (después de otra persona). 4. **s. in,** triunfar en, salir bien en, tener éxito en; **s. in (doing),** conseguir, lograr (hacer); **s. to,** seguir a, reemplazar; asumir (título, oficio), subir al (trono). —*v.t.* 1. seguir, subseguir; seguir a, ej., *night succeeds day,* la noche sigue al día. 2. suceder (a otro). 3. **day succeeded day,** pasaron los días.
succeeder [-ər, B -ə] *s.* sucesor.
succentor [sək'sɛntər, B -ə] *s.* (relig.) sochantre.
success [sək'sɛs] *s.* 1. triunfo, (buen) éxito. 2. (ant.) resultado, consecuencia. 3. **nothing succeeds like s.,** de un éxito nacen otros; **to be a s.,** ser un éxito (cosa); tener éxito (persona); **to make a s. of (life,** etc.), tener éxito en (la vida, etc.).
successful [-fəl] *a.* 1. exitoso (experimento, campaña, etc.). 2. de éxito (escritor, etc.); próspero (banquero, etc.). 3. **to be s. in,** tener éxito en.
successfully [-fəlɪ] *adv.* con buen resultado, con (buen) éxito, con ventura.
succession [sək'sɛʃən] *s.* 1. sucesión, secuencia, serie. 2. (der.) sucesión, herencia. 3. (der.) herederos (en conjunto). 4. **in s.,** en serie, sucesivamente; **in s.** to, (der.) como sucesor a, como heredero de.
successional [-əl] *a.* sucesorio.
successionally [-əlɪ] *adv.* en serie, a continuación, en sucesión.
succession duty, (pr. G.B.) impuesto de sucesión, impuesto a la herencia.
successive [sək'sɛsɪv] *a.* sucesivo, siguiente, consecutivo.
successively [-lɪ] *adv.* sucesivamente, consiguientemente.
successiveness [-nəs] *s.* continuidad.
successor [sək'sɛsər, B -ə] *s.* sucesor.
succinate ['sʌksəˌneɪt] *s.* (quím.) succinato.
succinct [ˌsʌk'sɪŋkt] *a.* sucinto, compendioso, breve, conciso.
succinctly [-lɪ] *adv.* sucintamente, brevemente.
succinctness [-nəs] *s.* brevedad, concisión.
succinic [ˌsʌk'sɪnɪk] *a.* (quím.) succínico.
succinic acid, (quím.) ácido succínico.
succor, (G.B.) **succour** ['sʌkər, B 'sʌkə] *s.* 1. ayuda, socorro, auxilio. 2. (*pl.*) (ant.) socorro, refuerzos (militares). —*v.t.* ayudar, socorrer, auxiliar.
succorer, (G.B.) **succourer** [-ər, B -ərə] *s.* socorredor, auxiliador.
succory ['sʌkərɪ] *s.* (*pl.* SUCCORIES) (bot.) achicoria.
succotash ['sʌkəˌtæʃ] *s.* guiso de maíz y habas.
succuba ['sʌkjəbə] *s.* (*pl.* SUCCUBAE [-ˌbi]) súcubo.
succubus ['sʌkjəbəs] *s.* (*pl.* SUCCUBI [-ˌbaɪ]) súcubo.
succulence ['sʌkjələns] **succulency** [-lənsɪ] *s.* suculencia, jugosidad.
succulent [-lənt] *a.* suculento, jugoso.
succulently ['sʌkjʊləntlɪ] *adv.* suculentamente.
succumb [sə'kʌm] *v.i.* sucumbir, morir; rendirse.
succursal [sə'kɜrsəl, B -'kɜsəl] *a.* sucursal, subsidiaria.
succusatory [sə'kʌsəˌtɔrɪ, B -tərɪ] *a.* sacudidor (díc. del movimiento sísmico vertical).
succuss ['sʌkəs] *v.t.* (med.) realizar la sucusión.
succussion [sə'kʌʃən] *s.* (med.) sucusión.

such [sʌtʃ] *a.* 1. tal, ej., *there's no s. thing,* no hay tal cosa. 2. qué tal, ej., *he is s. a fool!* ¡qué tal tonto es él! 3. **one s.,** un tal; **s. as it is,** tal cual es. —*pron.* 1. tal. 2. los mismos; cosas tales, cosas por el estilo. 3. **all s.,** todos los semejantes; **as s.,** como tal, en sí, en cuanto tal; **s. as,** (ret., poét.) los que, aquellos que; **s. is life,** tal (así) es la vida; **s. like,** cosas por el estilo, gente por el estilo. —*adv.* tan, ej., *I don't need s. a big car,* no necesito un auto tan grande.
such and such, tal(es) y tal(es), cierto(s), cierta(s); tal(es) o cual(es).
suchlike ['sʌtʃˌlaɪk] *a.* tal, semejante, similar, por el estilo. —*pron.* cosas o personas semejantes, gente por el estilo.
suck [sʌk] *v.t.* 1. mamar. 2. chupar, libar. 3. aspirar (aire, gas, etc.). 4. **s. (one) dry,** (fig.) sacar(le) la última gota (a uno); **s. in,** sumir, succionar (remolino al nadador); (fig.) absorber; **s. out,** chupar, sacar, chupando; **s. up,** (fig.) absorber. —*v.i.* 1. mamar. 2. chupar algo, dar chupadas. 3. rebajarse, comportarse servilmente. 4. **s. up to,** (jer.) lisonjear, enjabonar. —*s.* 1. succión. 2. (fam.) mamada, chupada; **s. off,** (vulg.) succión de órganos genitales. 3. (jer., G.B.) decepción, fiasco, fracaso.
sucker ['sʌkər, B 'sʌkə] *s.* 1. succionador, chupador. 2. mamantón, mamón. 3. (fam.) caramelo con palito. 4. (fam.) primo, incauto. 5. (zool.) ventosa. 6. (bot.) chupón, haustorio; retoño, serpollo. 7. (ict.) pez catostómido. 8. (mec.) pistón, tubo de aspiración; chupón, émbolo; succionador. —*v.i.* (bot.) echar chupones. —*v.t.* (bot.) podar (chupones).
suckfish [-ˌfɪʃ] *s.* (ict.) rémora, pequeño pez del Pacífico.
sucking [-ɪŋ] *a.* 1. mamador, mamantón. 2. principiante. 3. lechal (animal).
sucking pig, lechón.
suckle [-əl] *v.t.* lactar, amamantar; dar de mamar a.
suckling [-lɪŋ] *s.* lactante, mamón (díc. de niños); mamantón (díc. de animales).
sucrate ['suˌkreɪt] *s.* (quím.) sucrato, saccarato.
sucrose ['suˌkroʊs] *s.* (quím.) sacarosa, sucrosa.
suction ['sʌkʃən] *s.* 1. succión; aspiración. 2. dispositivo de succión, tubo aspirante.
suction chamber, (ing.) cámara de aspiración.
suction cup, copa de succión.
suction head, (hidr.) carga de aspiración, altura de succión.
suction nozzle, tobera de aspiración.
suction pump, bomba aspirante, bomba chupadora; bomba de succión.
suction stroke, (mot.) carrera de aspiración.
suction valve, válvula de aspiración, válvula de succión.
suctorial [ˌsʌk'tɔrɪəl] *a.* suctorio.
Sudan [su'dæn, B su'dɑn] *s.* República del Sudán.
Sudanese [ˌsudə'niz] *a.* sudanés. —*s.* (*pl.* SUDANESE) sudanés, del Sudán.
Sudan grass, (bot.) hierba del Sudán, sorgo del Sudán.
Sudanic [ˌsu'dænɪk] *a., s.* sudanés (idioma).
sudatorium [ˌsudə'tɔrɪəm] *s.* (*pl.* SUDATORIA [-rɪə]) sudadero.
sudatory ['sudəˌtɔrɪ, B -tərɪ] *s.* (*pl.* SUDATORIES) sudadero.
sudden ['sʌdən] *a.* 1. repentino, súbito. 2. precipitado. —*s.* (ant.) suceso súbito o inesperado; **(all) of a s.,** de repente.
sudden death, 1. (med.) muerte súbita. 2. (dep.) tiempo suplementario (para desempatar con la primera anotación).
suddenly [-lɪ] *adv.* 1. repentinamente, de repente, súbitamente. 2. precipitadamente.
sudenness [-nəs] *s.* 1. carácter repentino. 2. premura, precipitación.
Sudetenland [su'deɪtənˌlænd] *s.* territorio de los Sudetes (Checoslovaquia).
Sudetes [su'ditˌiz] *s. pl.* Montes Sudetes, entre Checoslovaquia y Polonia.
sudoriferous [ˌsudə'rɪfərəs] *a.* sudorífero.
sudorific [-'rɪfɪk] *a.* sudorífico. —*s.* (med.) sudorífico.
Sudra ['sudrə] *s.* sudra, miembro de la cuarta casta inferior de la India.
suds [sʌdz] *s. pl.* (*sing.* o *pl. en const.*) 1. jabonaduras, espuma. 2. (jer.) cerveza. —*v.t.* lavar en jabonaduras. —*v.i.* formarse jabonaduras o espuma.
sudsy ['sʌdzɪ] *a.* (SUDSIER; SUDSIEST) jabonoso, espumoso.
sue [su, B sju] *v.i.* 1. hacer la corte, cortejar. 2. entablar demanda, iniciar juicio. 3. **s. for,** rogar, suplicar (por algo); pedir, ej., *s. for an armistice,* pedir un armisticio, *s. for her hand,* pedirle la mano, *s. for peace,* pedir la paz; **s. to,** solicitar, pedir (a alguien). —*v.t.* 1. cortejar, enamorar. 2. demandar, procesar. 3. (der.) **s. for damages,** demandar por daños y perjuicios; **s. for divorce,** solicitar el divorcio.
suede, suède [sweɪd] *s.* 1. gamuza, ante, gamuzón. 2. (t. **s. cloth**) tela agamuzada.
suer ['suər, B 'sjuə] *s.* solicitante, demandante.
suet ['suət, B 'sjuɪt] *s.* sebo.
suety [-ɪ] *a.* seboso.
Suez Canal [su'ɛz kə'næl, B 'suɪz-] canal de Suez.
suffer ['sʌfər, B 'sʌfə] *v.t.* 1. sufrir, experimentar. 2. sufrir, tolerar, soportar, aguantar. 3. dejar, permitir. —*v.i.* 1. sufrir dolor. 2. ser dañado, sufrir daño, perjudicarse. 3. **s. from,** padecer de, adolecer de.
sufferable ['sʌfərəbəl] *a.* sufrible, tolerable.
sufferably [-əblɪ] *adv.* tolerablemente, soportablemente.
sufferance [-əns] *s.* 1. consentimiento o permiso tácito. 2. indulgencia, tolerancia. 3. (raro) paciencia, resignación. 4. **beyond s.,** más allá del límite de tolerancia; **on s.,** por indulgencia, por tolerancia.
sufferer [-ər, B -ə] *s.* 1. víctima. 2. perjudicado, damnificado.
suffering [-ɪŋ] *s.* sufrimiento, dolor, dolencia. —*a.* 1. adolorido, doliente. 2. sufrido, ej., *her s. husband,* su sufrido marido.
sufferingly ['sʌfərɪŋlɪ] *adv.* con dolor, dolorosamente.
suffice [sə'faɪs] *v.i.* bastar, ser suficiente; **s. it to say,** basta decir. —*v.t.* bastar para, alcanzar para; satisfacer.
sufficiency [sə'fɪʃənsɪ] *s.* 1. cantidad suficiente, lo bastante. 2. (ant.) suficiencia, competencia.
sufficient [-ənt] *a.* 1. suficiente, bastante, adecuado. 2. (ant.) competente.
sufficiently [-əntlɪ] *adv.* suficientemente.
suffix ['sʌfɪks] *s.* 1. (gram.) sufijo, afijo, postfijo. 2. (mat.) subíndice. — ['sʌfɪks, sə'fɪks] *v.t.* (gram.) añadir como sufijo.
suffixal ['sʌfɪksəl] *a.* sufijo, sufijal.
suffixion [sə'fɪkʃən] *s.* (gram.) terminación o flexión (de una voz).
suffocate ['sʌfəˌkeɪt] *v.t., v.i.* sofocar(se), asfixiar(se), ahogar(se).
suffocating [-ɪŋ] *a.* sofocante, sofocador, asfixiante.
suffocation [ˌsʌfə'keɪʃən] *s.* sofocación, asfixia, ahogo.
suffocative ['sʌfəˌkeɪtɪv] *a.* sofocante, sofocador.
suffragan ['sʌfrəgən] *a.* sufragáneo. —*s.* (t. **s. bishop**) obispo sufragáneo.
suffrage ['sʌfrɪdʒ] *s.* 1. sufragio, voto; aprobación, asentimiento. 2. derecho de sufragio, derecho al voto. 3. oración de intercesión, súplica, preces, rogativa.
suffragette [ˌsʌfrə'dʒɛt] *s.* sufragista (mujer).
suffragist ['sʌfrɪdʒəst] *s.* sufragista.
suffrutescent [ˌsʌfru'tɛsənt] *a.* (bot.) sufrutescente.
suffruticose [səf'rutɪˌkoʊs] *a.* (bot.) sufruticoso.
suffumigation [səˌfjumə'geɪʃən] *s.* (med.) sufumigación, fumigación.
suffuse [sə'fjuz] *v.t.* afluir a, bañar, llenar, cubrir, ej., *blood suffused his cheeks,* la sangre afluyó a sus mejillas, *tears suffused her eyes,* sus ojos se bañaron en lágrimas.
suffusion [-'fjuʒən] *s.* 1. afluencia. 2. (med.) sufusión, aflujo (esp. sanguíneo). 3. difusión.
suffusive [sə'fjusɪv] *a.* difusivo.
Sufi ['suˌfi] *s.* sufí (místico musulmán).
Sufism [-ˌfɪzəm] *s.* (relig., filos.) sufismo.
sugar ['ʃʊgər, B -ə] *s.* 1. azúcar. 2. terrón de azúcar, cucharadita de azúcar, ej., *do you take your coffee with one or two sugars?* ¿Ud. toma su café con uno o dos terrones de azúcar (o cucharaditas de azúcar)? 3. (fig.) lindura, ricura. 4. (en vocativo) amorcito. —*v.t.* 1. azucarar; garapiñar, almibarar, mezclar azúcar con. 2. poner o echar azúcar en (té, etc.). 3. (fig.) endulzar, suavizar, mitigar (lo desagradable). 4. **s. the pill,** dorar la píldora. —*v.i.* 1. formar azúcar, tornarse cristalino. 2. granularse. 3. **s. off,** hacer el azúcar de arce.
sugar almonds, almendras garapiñadas, almendras confitadas.
sugar apple, (bot.) anona, chirimoya.
sugar basin, (G.B.) azucarero, azucarera (Amer.).
sugar beet, (bot.) remolacha, betarraga, betarrata, betabel (Amer.).
sugarberry [-ˌbɛrɪ] *s.* (bot.) almez.
sugar bowl, azucarero, azucarera (Amer.).
sugar bush, (E.U.) arboleda de arces de azúcar.
sugar candy, azúcar cande o candi.
sugarcane [-ˌkeɪn] *s.* (bot.) caña de azúcar, cañamiel, caña dulce, caña melar.
sugarcane grinding, molienda de caña de azúcar.
sugarcoat [-'koʊt] *v.t.* 1. confitar, garapiñar. 2. (fig.) dorar (la píldora), endulzar (la verdad).
sugarcoated [-əd] *a.* confitado, azucarado.
sugarcoating [-ɪŋ] *s.* 1. capa de azúcar, garapiña. 2. (fig.) dorado (de lo desagradable).
sugar crop, zafra.
sugar daddy, (jer.) amante viejo y rico (esp. de una mujer joven), gavilán (Amer.).
sugared ['ʃʊgərd, B 'ʃʊgəd] *a.* azucarado, dulce, garapiñado.
sugarhouse [-ərˌhaʊs, B -əˌ-] *s.* fábrica o refinería de azúcar.
sugar icing, alcorza.
sugaring off, proceso de convertir la savia de arce en azúcar.
sugarloaf [-ˌloʊf] *s.* pan de azúcar; cono de azúcar. —*a.* en forma de pan de azúcar (colina, montaña, etc.).
sugar lump, terrón de azúcar.
sugar maple, (bot.) arce sacarino, arce de azúcar.
sugar mill, ingenio o trapiche azucarero, central azucarera.
sugar of lead, (quím.) azúcar de plomo, sal de plomo, sal de Saturno.
sugar of milk, lactina, lactosa.
sugar orchard, arboleda de arces de azúcar.
sugar palm, (bot.) barú; nipa.

sugar plantation, cañaveral; plantación de azúcar.
sugarplum ['ʃʊgərˌplʌm, B 'ʃʊgəˌplʌm] *s.* confite, dulce, bombón.
sugar refinery, refinería de azúcar.
sugar squirrel, (zool.) ardilla del azúcar.
sugar syrup, melado.
sugar tongs, tenacillas (para azúcar).
sugary ['ʃʊgərɪ] *a.* 1. azucarado, dulce. 2. (fig.) azucarado; dulzarrón, dulzón, sacarino.
suggest [sə'dʒɛst] *v.t.* 1. sugerir, insinuar, inspirar. 2. indicar, intimar, proponer. 3. evocar, traer a la memoria. 4. **s. itself,** venir a la mente, ej., *an idea suggested itself,* una idea vino a la mente.
suggestibility [səˌdʒɛstə'bɪlətɪ] *s.* sugestibilidad.
suggestible [sə'dʒɛstəbəl] *a.* sugestionable.
suggestion [-tʃən] *s.* 1. sugerencia, insinuación, inspiración. 2. indicación, traza, sombra. 3. (psic.) sugestión.
suggestive [-tɪv] *a.* 1. sugerente, significante. 2. sugestivo; insinuante, insinuativo. 3. **s. of,** indicativo de.
suggestively [-lɪ] *adv.* sugestivamente.
suggestiveness [-tɪvnəs] *s.* aspecto sugestivo; poder sugestivo.
suicidal [ˌsuə'saɪdəl, B sjʊɪ-] *a.* suicida.
suicidally [-ɪ] *adv.* de manera suicida.
suicide ['suəsaɪd, B 'sjuɪ-] *s.* 1. suicidio. 2. suicida. 3. **to commit s.,** suicidarse. —*v.i.* (fam.) suicidarse.
Suidae ['suədi] *s. pl.* (zool.) suidos.
suing ['suɪŋ, B 'sju-] *s.* 1. (der.) procesamiento, presentación de pleito o demanda. 2. corte, galanteo.
suint ['suənt] *s.* juarda, suarda, churre.
suit [sut, B sjut] *s.* 1. juego (de velas, fichas, armas). 2. traje, terno; traje sastre (de mujer). 3. (naipes) palo (de la baraja). 4. petición, demanda, súplica. 5. galanteo, cortejo. 6. (der.) pleito, litigio, juicio. 7. (ant.) librea, uniforme. 8. **to bring suit,** entablar juicio; **to follow suit,** servir de palo; jugar el mismo palo, (fig.) seguir el ejemplo, hacer lo mismo. —*v.t.* 1. vestir, ataviar. 2. sentar, ir o venir bien a, favorecer. 3. convenir, satisfacer, agradar. 4. **s. oneself,** hacer como guste; **s. to,** cuadrar con, adaptar a, acomodar a, ir con; **to be suited to** (o **for**), ser propio para, ser digno de. —*v.i.* **s. (one) to a T,** quedar perfecto a (uno), caer al pelo a (uno); (ant.) **s. with,** convenir, adaptarse a; armonizar con; corresponder a; ir con.
suitability [ˌsutə'bɪlətɪ, B ˌsju-] **suitableness** ['sutəbəlnəs, B 'sju-] *s.* conveniencia, adaptabilidad.
suitable ['sutəbəl, B 'sju-] *a.* adecuado, apropiado, conveniente, satisfactorio.
suitably ['sutəblɪ, B 'sju-] *adv.* convenientemente, adecuadamente.
suitcase ['sutˌkeɪs] *s.* maleta, valija.
suite [swit] *s.* 1. séquito, comitiva, tren, acompañamiento. 2. serie de habitaciones, piso, departamento. 3. serie, colección; juego, ej., *a bedroom s.,* un juego de dormitorio. 4. (mús.) suite.
suiting ['sutɪŋ, B 'sju-] *s.* tela para trajes.
suit of armor, armadura, arnés.
suit of clothes, traje, vestido completo.
suitor ['sutər, B 'sjutə] *s.* 1. suplicante, aspirante, peticionario. 2. galán, pretendiente, enamorado, novio. 3. (der.) demandante, parte actora, actor.
sukiyaki [sʊki'jɑki] *s.* (cocina) plato japonés de tajadas delgadas de carne frita con cebollas y salsa de soja, sakí y azúcar.
sulcate ['sʌlkeɪt] **sulcated** [-əd] *a.* (bot., anat.) sulcado, asurcado, acanalado.
sulcus ['sʌlkəs] *s.* (*pl.* SULCI [-ˌsaɪ]) (anat.) sulcus, surco, cisura, canal.
sulfa ['sʌlfə] *s.* (*pl.* SULFAS) (farm., quím.) sulfa (medicamento).
sulfadiazine [ˌsʌlfə'daɪəˌzin] *s.* (farm.) sulfadiazina.
sulfa drug, medicamento a base de sulfa.
sulfamide [-'fæˌmaɪd] *s.* (farm.) sulfamida.
sulfanilamide [-fə'nɪləˌmaɪd] *s.* (quím., farm.) sulfanilamida.
sulfanilic acid [-'nɪlɪk-] (quím.) ácido sulfanílico.
sulfapyridine [-'pɪrəˌdin, B -'paɪrɪˌdaɪn] *s.* (farm.) sulfapiridina.
sulfarsenide [sʌl'fɑrsəˌnaɪd, B -'fɑsə-] *s.* sulfarsénico, sulfoarsénico, sulfarseniuro.
sulfate ['sʌlˌfeɪt] *s.* (quím.) sulfato. —*v.t.* 1. sulfatar, convertir en sulfato. 2. (elec.) sulfatar. —*v.i.* convertirse en sulfato.
sulfathiazole [ˌsʌlfə'θaɪəˌzoʊl] *s.* (farm.) sulfatiazol.
sulfation [ˌsʌl'feɪʃən] *s.* (quím., elec.) sulfatación.
sulfide ['sʌlˌfaɪd] *s.* (med.) sulfuro.
sulfite [-ˌfaɪt] *s.* (quím.) sulfito.
sulfite paper, papel sulfito.
sulfonamide [ˌsʌl'fɑnəˌmaɪd, B -'fɒnə-] *s.* (quím.) sulfonamida.
sulfonate ['sʌlfəˌneɪt] *s.* (quím.) sulfonato. —*v.t.* sulfonar.
sulfone [-ˌfoʊn] *s.* (quím.) sulfona.
sulfonic [ˌsʌl'fɑnɪk, B -'fɒnɪk] *a.* (quím.) sulfónico.
sulfonic acid, (quím.) ácido sulfónico.
sulfonium [-'foʊnɪəm] *s.* (quím.) sulfonio.
sulfonmethane [-ˌfoʊn'mɛθeɪn] *s.* (farm.) sulfonmetano.
sulfonyl ['sʌlfəˌnɪl] *s.* (quím.) sulfurilo, sulfonilo.
sulfosalt [-ˌsɔlt] *s.* (quím.) sulfosal.
sulfur ['sʌlfər, B 'sʌlfə] *s.* azufre. —*v.t.* azufrar (tratar o impregnar con azufre); (quím.) sulfurar (combinar con azufre, ej., el cobre).
sulfurate ['sʌlfərɪt] *a.* (quím.) sulfurado. — ['sʌlfəˌreɪt] *v.t., var. de* **sulfur.**
sulfuration [ˌsʌlfə'reɪʃən] *s.* 1. azuframiento (tratamiento o impregnación con azufre). 2. (quím.) sulfuración (combinación con azufre). 3. (agr.) sulfuración.
sulfur dioxide, (quím.) dióxido de azufre, anhídrido sulfuroso.
sulfureous [ˌsʌl'fjʊrɪəs] *a.* sulfúreo, sulfuroso, azufroso.
sulfuret ['sʌlfjəˌrɪt] *s.* sulfuro. — [-ˌrɛt] *v.t.* (*pret., p.p.* SULFURETED O SULFURETTED; *p.pr.* SULFURETING O SULFURETTING) (quím.) sulfurar.
sulfuric [ˌsʌl'fjʊrɪk] *a.* sulfúrico.
sulfuric acid, (quím.) ácido sulfúrico.
sulfurize ['sʌlfjəˌraɪz] *v.t., var. de* **sulfur.**
sulfurous ['sʌlfərəs] *a.* 1. (quím.) sulfuroso, sulfúreo. 2. (fig.) infernal. 3. (fig.) virulento, vehemente (lenguaje), enardecido, acalorado (discusión).
sulfurous acid, (quím.) ácido sulfuroso.
sulfurously [-lɪ] *adv.* (fig.) con vehemencia, vehementemente, acaloradamente.
sulfur trioxide, (quím.) trióxide de azufre, anhídrido sulfúrico.
sulfuryl ['sʌlfjəˌrɪl] *s.* sulfurilo.
sulk [sʌlk] *v.i.* enfurruñarse, malhumorarse, estar resentido o malhumorado. —*s.* (*ú. gen. en pl.*) enfurruñamiento, murria, malhumor, resentimiento.
sulkily ['sʌlkəlɪ] *adv.* con malhumor o resentimiento.
sulkiness ['sʌlkɪnəs] *s.* enfurruñamiento, resentimiento.
sulky [-kɪ] *a.* (SULKIER; SULKIEST) 1. enfurruñado, malhumorado, mohíno, resentido. 2. con ruedas y un asiento para el conductor (ej., un arado). —*s.* (*pl.* SULKIES) sulky (especie de cabriolé para una sola persona).
sulla clover ['sʌlə-] (bot.) zulla, sulla.
sullage ['sʌlɪdʒ] *s.* 1. desecho, basura, desperdicio; aguas de alcantarilla; suciedad, inmundicia, mugre. 2. cieno (depositado por las crecidas de ríos). 3. escoria, nata (de fundición de metales).
sullen ['sʌlən] *a.* 1. malhumorado, insociable; hosco, murrio, taciturno, adusto. 2. lóbrego, tenebroso, sombrío, tétrico (lugar). 3. indolente, perezoso, lento (río).
sullenly [-lɪ] *adv.* 1. con malhumor. 2. tétricamente.
sullenness [-nəs] *s.* malhumor, murria.
sully ['sʌlɪ] *v.t., v.i.* (*pret., p.p.* SULLIED; *p.pr.* SULLYING) (pr. fig.) manchar(se), mancillar(se), ensuciar(se), desdorar(se). —*s.* (ant.) mancha, mancilla, mácula, desdoro.
sulphide, sulphite, *vars. de* **sulfide, sulfite.**
sulpho sal ['sʌlfoʊ-] (quím.) sulfonato.
sulphur, *var. de* **sulfur.**
sulphur-bottom ['sʌlfərˌbɑtəm, B 'sʌlfəˌbɒt-] *s.* (zool.) ballena azul.
sulphur butterfly, (ento.) mariposa anaranjada.
sulphuric, sulphurous, *vars. de* **sulfuric, sulfurous.**
sulphuric anhydride, (quím.) anhídrido sulfúrico, trióxido de azufre.
sulphur ore, (geol.) pirita.
sulphur yellow, (color) amarillo azufre.
Sulpician [ˌsʌl'pɪʃən] *s.* (relig.) sulpiciano (clérigo).
sultan ['sʌltən] *s.* 1. sultán, soldán. 2. **S.,** (orn.) polla sultana.
sultana [ˌsʌl'tænə, B -'tɑn-] *s.* 1. sultana. 2. (orn.) calamón. 3. uva o pasa de Esmirna.
sultanate ['sʌltəneɪt] *s.* sultanía, sultanato.
sultrily ['sʌltrəlɪ] *adv.* 1. de modo bochornoso o sofocante. 2. (fig.) sensualmente, voluptuosamente.
sultriness [-trɪnəs] *s.* 1. bochorno. 2. (fig.) sensualidad, voluptuosidad.
sultry [-trɪ] *a.* (SULTRIER; SULTRIEST) 1. bochornoso, sofocante, caluroso y húmedo. 2. tórrido, abrasador. 3. (fig.) sensual, voluptuoso.
Sulu ['suˌlu] *s.* sulú, joló, joloano (especie de saya usada por los melanesios).
sum [sʌm] *s.* 1. suma, cantidad, monto (de dinero). 2. total, suma, agregado (de varias cosas). 3. sumario, compendio, epítome. 4. (fig.) colmo, lo sumo (de locura, felicidad, etc.). 5. (*pl.*) aritmética, cálculo. 6. **in s.,** en suma, en resumen; **to do a s.,** hacer un cálculo. —*v.t.* (*pret., p.p.* SUMMED; *p.pr.* SUMMING) 1. sumar, totalizar. 2. **sum up,** resumir, compendiar; recapitular. —*v.i.* **s. to** (o **into**), ascender a.
sumac, sumach ['suˌmæk] *s.* 1. (bot.) zumaque. 2. hojas del zumaque (usadas para teñir).
sum and substance, esencia o substancia; lo más importante.
Sumerian [sʊ'merɪən, B -'mɪr-] *s.* 1. sumerio, súmero, natural de Sumeria, antiguo pueblo semita. 2. súmero (lengua). —*a.* sumerio, súmero.
summa ['sumə] *s.* tratado, suma.
summarily [ˌsʌ'merəlɪ, B 'sʌmə-] *adv.* sumariamente, brevemente.
summariness ['sʌmərɪnəs] *s.* carácter sumario, brevedad.
summarization [ˌsʌmərə'zeɪʃən, B -raɪ-] *s.* 1. resumen, recapitulación. 2. sumario.

summarize [ˈsʌməˌraɪz] *v.t.* resumir, epitomar, compendiar, abreviar. —*v.i.* hacer un resumen.
summary [-rɪ] *a.* 1. sumario, conciso, breve, sucinto. 2. (der.) sumario. —*s.* (*pl.* SUMMARIES) sumario, resumen, compendio.
summary proceedings, (der.) vía sumaria.
summation [ˌsʌˈmeɪʃən] *s.* 1. suma, adición. 2. total, agregado (esp. uno formado por acumulación). 3. recapitulación.
summer [ˈsʌmər, B ˈsʌmə] *s.* 1. verano, estío. 2. (fig.) abril (año de vida), ej., *a girl of fourteen summers,* una niña de catorce abriles. —*v.i.* (con *at* o *in*) veranear en (alguna parte). —*v.t.* preservar o pastar durante el verano (esp. ganado). —*a.* veraniego, estival.
summer, *s.* (arq.) viga maestra; imposta, sotabanco; dintel.
summer boarder, veraneante.
summer camp, campamento de veraneo.
summer cholera, (med.) cólera esporádico.
summer coat, abrigo de verano.
summerhouse [-ˌhaʊs] *s.* glorieta, cenador.
summer house, casa de verano, casa de campo.
summer lightning, fucilazo.
summer resort, lugar de veraneo.
summersault, *var. de* **sumersault.**
summer school, escuela de verano; curso de verano (esp. en universidades).
summer solstice, (astr., meteor.) solsticio vernal, solsticio de verano.
summertime [-ˌtaɪm] *s.* verano, estío.
summer time, (pr. G.B.) hora de verano.
summerwood [-ˌwʊd] *s.* albura de verano, madera de estío.
summery [ˈsʌmərɪ] *a.* veraniego, estival.
summing-up [ˈsʌmɪŋˈʌp] *s.* recapitulación, resumen (esp. de las pruebas por el juez).
summit [ˈsʌmət] *s.* 1. ápice, cumbre, cima, cúspide. 2. (fig.) cumbre, ej., *meeting at the s.,* reunión en la cumbre, *he reached the s. of fame,* llegó a la cumbre de la fama.
summit meeting, reunión en la cumbre.
summon [ˈsʌmən] *v.t.* 1. convocar, llamar, invitar. 2. mandar llamar (al médico, etc.). 3. requerir, demandar. 4. evocar, recordar. 5. (der.) citar, emplazar, notificar. 6. **s. up,** reunir (coraje, valor, etc.).
summoner [-ər, B -ə] *s.* (der.) emplazador.
summons [ˈsʌmənz] *s.* (*pl.* SUMMONSES) 1. orden, llamamiento, invitación. 2. (der.) emplazamiento, citación, notificación, comparendo, requerimiento, auto de comparecencia. —*v.t.* entregar una citación.
sump [sʌmp] *s.* 1. sumidero, resumidero, poceta, pozo negro, letrina. 2. (mot.) colector de aceite. 3. (mín.) pileta, colector de aguas; socavón del frente de arranque.
sump pump, bomba de sumidero, bomba de sentina.
sumpter [ˈsʌmptər, B -tə] *s.* bestia de carga, acémila.
sumptuary [ˈsʌmptʃʊˌerɪ, B -tjʊərɪ] *a.* suntuario.
sumptuary law, ley suntuaria (que grava el lujo con impuestos).
sumptuous [ˈsʌmptʃʊəs] *a.* suntuoso, costoso, lujoso, regio, espléndido.
sumptuously [-lɪ] *adv.* suntuosamente.
sumptuousness [-nəs] *s.* suntuosidad.
sum total, 1. total, monto total. 2. (fig.) totalidad.
sun [sʌn] *s.* 1. sol. 2. (p. ext.) astro. 3. **a place in the s.,** situación o condición favorable; (ant.) **from s. to s.,** de sol a sol; **his s. is set,** (ya) está en el ocaso de su vida; **to hold a candle to the s.,** actuar superfluamente; **to make hay while the s. shines,** aprovechar la ocasión; **to rise with the s.,** madrugar, levantarse temprano; **to shoot the s.,** (mar.) tomar el sol; **to take the s.,** tomar el sol; **under the s.** en el mundo; **with the s.,** (moviendo) de izquierda a derecha. —*v.t.* (*pret., p.p.* SUNNED; *p.pr.* SUNNING) solear, asolear. —*v.i.* asolearse.
Sun. *abrev. de* **Sunday,** domingo (dom.).
sun and planet, engranaje planetario.
sunbaked [ˈsʌnˌbeɪkt] *a.* 1. secado al aire (adobe, ladrillo). 2. desecado o tostado por el sol.
sunbath [-ˌbæθ, B -ˌbɑθ] *s.* baño de sol.
sunbathe [-ˌbeɪð] *v.i.* tomar un baño de sol, tomar sol.
sunbathed [-ˌbeɪðd] *a.* asoleado.
sunbathing [-ˌbeɪðɪŋ] *s.* baño de sol.
sunbeam [-ˌbim] *s.* rayo solar, rayo de sol.
sun-blind [-ˌblaɪnd] *s.* persiana; toldo.
sunbonnet [-ˌbɑnət, B -ˌbɔn-] *s.* cofia, papalina (para protegerse del sol).
sunbow [-ˌboʊ] *s.* (poét.) arco iris.
sunburn [-ˌbɜrn, B -ˌbɜn] *s.* quemadura de sol, solanera, eritema solar. —*v.t.* tostar al sol. —*v.i.* asolarse, tostarse al sol.
sunburst [-ˌbɜrst, B -ˌbɜst] *s.* 1. rayo o resplandor repentino de sol (entre las nubes). 2. broche en forma de sol.
sundae [ˈsʌndɪ, B -deɪ] *s.* helado con crema, frutas, almíbar y nueces.
sun dance, danza ritual del sol (entre los indios de las praderas de los E.U.).
Sunda Strait [ˈsʌndə-] Estrecho de la Sonda, situado entre Java y Sumatra.
Sunday [ˈsʌndɪ] *s.* domingo. —*a.* 1. dominical (misa, descanso, etc.). 2. dominguero (traje, fumador, pintor, etc.). —*v.i.* pasar el domingo (en alguna parte).
Sunday best, traje dominguero; **to put on one's S. b.,** endomingarse.
Sunday-go-to-meeting [-ˌgoʊtəˈmitɪŋ] *a.* (hum.) dominguero, dominical; apropiado para ir a la iglesia los domingos.
Sunday punch, (boxeo) golpe de gracia (para poner fuera de combate a un oponente).
Sunday school, escuela dominical.
sun deck, 1. cubierta superior (de un barco). 2. techo o terraza (de una casa) para tomar baños de sol.
sunder [ˈsʌndər, B -də] *v.t.* separar, partir, dividir, romper. —*s.* separación.
sun dog, parhelio, parhelia, nimbo.
sundown [-ˌdaʊn] *s.* puesta del sol, ocaso del sol.
sundowner [-ˌdaʊnər, B -ə] *s.* 1. (Aust.) vago, vagabundo. 2. (fam.) trago que se toma al ponerse el sol.
sun-dried [ˈsʌnˌdraɪd] *a.* secado al sol.
sundries [ˈsʌndrɪz] *s. pl.* artículos varios.
sundry [-drɪ] *a.* varios, diversos, misceláneos. —*s.* (*pl. en const.*) miscelánea.
sunfast [ˈsʌnˌfæst, B -ˌfɑst] *a.* resistente al sol (ej., un color).
sunfish [-ˌfɪʃ] *s.* (ict.) pez luna, mola, pez roda, peje-sol, rueda, rodador.
sunflower [-ˌflaʊər, B -ə] *s.* (bot.) girasol, mirasol.
sung [sʌŋ] *pret., p.p. de* **sing.**
sun gear, (mec.) engranaje planetario.
sunglasses [ˈsʌnˌglæsəz, B -ˌglɑsɪz] *s. pl.* gafas contra el sol, anteojos de sol, anteojos oscuros.
sunglow [-ˌgloʊ] *s.* arrebol, aurora.
sung mass, misa cantada.
sun god, dios del sol, dios Sol.
sun helmet, casco tropical.
sunk [sʌŋk] *pret., p.p. de* **sink.**
sunken [ˈsʌŋkən] *a.* sumido, hundido.
sunk fence, zanja con un muro de retención (para separar tierras).
sunlamp [ˈsʌnˌlæmp] *s.* lámpara de rayos ultravioletas.
sunless [-ləs] *a.* sin sol, sombrío, umbrío, nublado.
sunlight [-ˌlaɪt] *s.* luz solar, luz del sol.
sunlike [-ˌlaɪk] *a.* 1. parecido al sol. 2. resplandeciente.
sunlit [-ˌlɪt] *a.* iluminado por el sol.
sunn [sʌn] **sunn hemp** *s.* (bot.) cáñamo de Bengala.
Sunna, Sunnah [ˈsʊnə, B ˈsʌnə] *s.* (relig.) sunna, zuna, reglamento y leyes prácticas impartidas por Mahoma.
sunnily [ˈsʌnəlɪ] *adv.* alegremente.
Sunnism [ˈsʊˌnɪzəm, B ˈsʌ-] *s.* (relig.) sunnismo.
Sunnite [-ˌnaɪt] *s.* zunita, sunnita, sunní, miembro de una secta mahometana.
sunny [ˈsʌnɪ] *a.* (SUNNIER; SUNNIEST) 1. soleado, bañado por el sol. 2. de sol (horas, clima, etc.). 3. (fig.) alegre, risueño (carácter). 4. **to be s.,** hacer sol.
sunny side, (fig.) lado bueno o favorable (de algo).
sunny-side up [-ˌsaɪd-] frito por un solo lado (díc. de un huevo).
sun parlor, s. porch, solana, mirador, solario.
sun print, heliografía, copia heliográfica.
sunproof [-ˌprʊf] *a.* a prueba de sol.
sunray [ˈsʌnˌreɪ] *s.* rayo de sol.
sunrise [ˈsʌnˌraɪz] *s.* salida del sol, orto del sol; **from s. to sunset,** de sol a sol.
sunscald [-ˌskɔld] **sunscorch** [-ˌskɔrtʃ, B -ˌskɔtʃ] *s.* (bot.) enfermedad originada por exceso de sol.
sunset [-ˌset] *s.* 1. puesta del sol, ocaso del sol. 2. (fig.) ocaso (de la vida).
sunshade [-ˌʃeɪd] *s.* 1. parasol, sombrilla, quitasol. 2. toldo, marquesina. 3. visera. 4. (foto.) parasol.
sunshine [-ˌʃaɪn] *s.* 1. luz, rayos o calor del sol. 2. sol, soleamiento, solana, ej., *this side of the house has five hours of s. daily,* este lado de la casa tiene cinco horas de sol al día. 3. (fig.) alegría, contento. 4. **in the s.,** al sol.
sunshiny [-ˌʃaɪnɪ] *a.* 1. iluminado por el sol. 2. alegre, risueño.
sunspot [-ˌspɑt, B -ˌspɔt] *s.* (astr.) 1. mancha solar, mácula del sol. 2. peca.
sun spurge, (bot.) lechetrezna, ésula, titímalo.
sunstroke [-ˌstroʊk] *s.* (med.) insolación, asoleada (Amer.).
sunstruck [ˈsʌnˌstrʌk] *a.* que sufre de insolación.
sunsuit [ˈsʌnˌsut, B -ˌsjut] *s.* traje para tomar baños de sol.
suntan [-ˌtæn] *s.* bronceado (de la piel por exposición al sol).
suntan lotion, crema bronceadora.
sunup [-ˌʌp] *s.* salida del sol.
sunward [-wərd, B -wəd] *a.* que mira hacia el sol. —*adv.* hacia el sol.
sunwards [-wərdz, B -wədz] *adv.* hacia el sol.
sunwise [-ˌwaɪz] *adv.* 1. en el mismo sentido de las manecillas del reloj. 2. en el sentido del movimiento aparente del sol; como el sol.
sup [sʌp] *v.i.* (fam.) cenar. —*v.t.* (*pret., p.p.* SUPPED; *p.pr.* SUPPING) (pr. dial.) sorber. —*v.i.* beber a sorbos. —*s.* sorbo, trago (de licor).
super [ˈsupər, B ˈsjupə] *s.* 1. (fam.) superintendente. 2. alza (parte superior movible de una colmena). 3. (enc.) capricho (tela para reforzar libros). 4. (jer., teat.) figurante, suplente, comparsa. 5. (jer., com.) calidad excelente; talla

extra grande. —*a.* 1. (fam.) superfino, excelente, de primera calidad. 2. (irón.) en exceso, en demasía (ej., leal, patriota, etc.). —*v.t.* (enc.) reforzar con capricho (un libro).
superable ['supərəbəl] *a.* superable, vencible.
superabound [ˌsupərə'baʊnd] *v.i.* superabundar, sobreabundar.
superabundance [ˌsupərə'bʌndəns] *s.* superabundancia, sobreabundancia, plétora, redundancia.
superabundant [-dənt] *a.* superabundante.
superabundantly [-dəntlɪ] *adv.* superabundantemente, sobreabundantemente.
superadd [-'æd] *v.t.* sobreañadir.
superaddition [-ə'dɪʃən] *s.* sobreañadidura.
superannuate [-'ænjʊˌeɪt] *v.t.* 1. jubilar, pensionar, hacer cesar (por vejez, incapacidad, etc.). 2. hacer anticuado; poner fuera de uso. —*v.i.* volverse anticuado.
superannuated [-'ænjʊˌeɪtəd] *a.* 1. cesante, jubilado. 2. anticuado, desusado, fuera de moda.
superannuation [ˌsupərˌænjʊ'eɪʃən] *s.* jubilación, cesación.
superb [sʊ'pɜrb, B sʊ'pɜb] *a.* magnífico, excelente, espléndido; majestuoso, soberbio.
superbly [-lɪ] *adv.* espléndidamente; soberbiamente.
superbness [-nəs] *s.* esplendidez; soberbia.
supercalender ['supərˌkæləndər, B -pəˌkæləndə] *s.* calandria. —*v.t.* dar lustre a (papel) con la calandria.
supercargo [-ˌkɑrgoʊ, B -ˌkɑgoʊ] *s.* (*pl.* SUPERCARGOES O SUPERCARGOS) (mar.) sobrecargo.
supercelestial [-sə'lɛstʃəl, B -tjəl] *a.* sobrecelestial.
supercharge [-tʃɑrdʒ, B -ˌtʃɑdʒ] *v.t.* 1. (mot.) sobrealimentar, sobrecargar. 2. (aer.) presurizar (una cabina).
supercharger [-ər, B -ə] *s.* (mot.) sobrealimentador, compresor de sobrealimentación.
superciliary [ˌsupər'sɪlɪˌɛrɪ, B -pə'-ərɪ] *a.* (anat.) superciliar.
supercilious [-'sɪlɪəs] *a.* altanero, desdeñoso, arrogante.
superciliously [-'sɪlɪəslɪ] *adv.* altaneramente, desdeñosamente, arrogantemente.
superciliousness [-'sɪlɪəsnəs] *s.* altanería, arrogancia.
superclass ['supərˌklæs, B 'sjupəˌklɑs] *s.* (bot.) clase superior.
superconductive [ˌsupərkən'dʌktɪv, B -pəkən-] *a.* (elec.) superconductor, supraconductor.
superconductivity [-ˌdʌk'tɪvətɪ] *s.* (elec.) superconductividad, supraconductividad.
supercool [-'kul] *v.t.* (quím., fís.) sobreenfriar.
supercooled [-'kuld] *a.* (quím.) sobreenfriado, en sobrefusión.
supercritical [-'krɪtɪkəl] *a.* (fís.) supercrítico.
superdominant [-'dɑmənənt, B -'dɔm-] *s.* (mús.) superdominante.
super-duper ['supər'dupər, B -pə'-pə] *a.* (jer.) colosal, magnífico.
superego [ˌsupər'igoʊ, B -'ɛgoʊ] *s.* (psic.) superego.
superelevate [ˌsupə'rɛləˌveɪt] *v.t.* peraltar (curva de un camino o vía férrea).
superelevation [-ˌrɛlə'veɪʃən] *s.* peralte (de la curva de un camino o vía férrea).
supereminence [-'rɛmənəns] *s.* supereminencia (en rango, posición, etc.).
supereminent [-'rɛmənənt] *a.* supereminente.
supereminently [-lɪ] *adv.* de modo supereminente.
superempirical [ˌsupərɪm'pɪrəkəl] *a.* (filos.) trascendente, transcendental.
supererogate [-'ɛrəˌgeɪt] *v.t.* hacer más de lo obligatorio o debido.
supererogation [-ˌɛrə'geɪʃən] *s.* supererogación.
supererogatory [-ɪ'rɑgətɔrɪ, B -'rɔgətərɪ] *a* 1. supererogatorio. 2. superfluo, innecesario.
superexcellent [-'ɛksələnt] *a.* muy excelente, óptimo.
superfamily ['supərˌfæməlɪ, B -pəˌ-] *s.* (zool., bot.) superfamilia.
superfecundation [ˌsupərˌfɛkən'deɪʃən, B -pəˌ-] *s.* (fisiol.) superfecundación.
superfetation [-fɪ'teɪʃən] *s.* (biol.) superfetación.
superficial [-'fɪʃəl] *a.* superficial, somero.
superficiality [-ˌfɪʃɪ'ælətɪ] *s.* superficialidad.
superficially [-'fɪʃəlɪ] *adv.* superficialmente.
superficialness [-'fɪʃəlnəs] *s.* superficiallidad.
superficies [-'fɪʃˌiz] *s.* (*pl.* SUPERFICIES) superficie.
superfine [-'faɪn] *a.* 1. superfino (mercancía). 2. refinado, delicado; melindroso.
superfinish [-'fɪnɪʃ] *v.t.* superacabar.
superfluidity [-flu'ɪdətɪ] *s.* (fís.) superfluidez.
superfluity [-'fluətɪ] *s.* (*pl.* SUPERFLUITIES) 1. superabundancia, demasía. 2. superfluidad.
superfluous [sʊ'pɜrfluəs, B -'pɜfluəs] *a.* superfluo, demasiado, sobrante, excedente.
superfluously [-lɪ] *adv.* superfluamente.
superfluousness [-nəs] *s.* superfluidad, demasía.
superfortress ['supərˌfɔrtrəs, B 'sjupəˌfɔtrəs] *s.* (mil.) superfortaleza volante.
supergalaxy [-ˌgæləksɪ] *s.* (astr.) cúmulo de galaxias.
superheat [-ˌhit] *s.* supercalor. — [ˌsupər'hit, B -pə'-] *v.t.* recalentar, sobrecalentar.
superheated steam, vapor recalentado.
superheater [ˌsupər'hitər, B -pə'-ə] *s.* recalentador, supercalentador, sobrecalentador.
superheterodyne [-'hɛtərəˌdaɪn] *a.*, *s.* (rad.) superheterodino.
superhigh frequency, (rad.) frecuencia superelevada.
superhighway [-'haɪˌweɪ] *s.* supercarretera.
superhuman [-'hjumən] *a.* sobrehumano.
superhumanity [-ˌhju'mænətɪ] *s.* lo sobrehumano.
superhumanly [-'hjumənlɪ] *adv.* en forma sobrehumana, sobrehumanamente.
superhumeral [-'hjumərəl] *s.* (relig.) superhumeral.
superimpose [ˌsupərɪm'poʊz] *v.t.* superponer, sobreponer.
superimposition [-ˌɪmpə'zɪʃən] *s.* superposición.
superincumbent [-ɪn'kʌmbənt] *a.* superyacente, sobrepuesto.
superindividual [-ɪndə'vɪdʒʊəl] *a.* superindividual, supra-individual.
superinduce [-ɪn'dus, B -'djus] *v.t.* sobreañadir; promover.
superinduction [-ɪn'dʌkʃən] *s.* sobreañadidura.
superintend [-ɪn'tɛnd] *v.t.* superentender, vigilar, inspeccionar.
superintendence [ˌsupərɪn'tɛndəns] *s.* superintendencia, supervisión (función).
superintendency [-dənsɪ] *s.* superintendencia.
superintendent [-dənt] *s.* superintendente, inspector; capataz.
superior [sʊ'pɪrɪər, B -'pɪərɪə] *a.* 1. superior, de arriba. 2. superior (de posición, dignidad, importancia, grado, etc.). 3. (fig.) superior, mejor (calidad, etc.). 4. sereno, impasible. 5. altanero, altivo, orgulloso. 6. (bot.) súpero. 7. **s. to,** superior a; **s. to (doing something),** incapaz de, indiferente a (hacer algo). —*s.* 1. superior, principal, jefe. 2. superiora, priora; superior, prior (de un convento).
superior conjunction, (astr.) conjunción superior.
superior court, (der.) tribunal superior, corte superior.
superior general, (*pl.* SUPERIORS GENERAL) (relig.) superior (de una orden religiosa).
superiority [sʊˌpɪrɪ'ɔrɪtɪ] *s.* superioridad, supremacía, preeminencia.
superiority complex, complejo de superioridad.
superiorly [sʊ'pɪrɪərlɪ, B -əlɪ] *adv.* 1. superiormente. 2. altaneramente, altivamente.
superior numbers, superioridad numérica, fuerza más numerosa.
superior officer, (mil.) oficial de mayor graduación.
superior planet, (astr.) planeta superior, planeta exterior.
superlative [sʊ'pɜrlətɪv, B -'pɜlə-] *a.* 1. superlativo, supremo. 2. exagerado, inmoderado, excesivo. 3. (gram.) superlativo. —*s.* 1. (gram.) el grado superlativo. 2. exageración, expresión exagerada de elogio, ej., *talk in superlatives,* proferir exageraciones, emplear expresiones exageradas de elogio.
superlatively [-lɪ] *adv.* superlativamente; extremadamente.
superlativeness [-nəs] *s.* superlación.
superliner ['supərˌlaɪnər, B -pəˌ-ə] *s.* trasatlántico de lujo, supertransatlántico.
superlunar [ˌsupər'lunər, B -pə'-nə]
superlunary [-'lunərɪ] *a.* 1. (fig.) celestial. 2. de más allá de la luna.
superman ['supərˌmæn, B -pəˌ-] *s.* superhombre.
supermarket [-ˌmɑrkət, B -ˌmɑkət] *s.* supermercado; **large s.,** gran superficie.
supernal [sʊ'pɜrnəl, B -'pɜnəl] *a.* (poét., ret.) superno, excelso; celestial, celeste, célico.
supernatant [ˌsupər'neɪtənt, B -pə'-] *a.* sobrenadante, flotante.
supernatural [-'nætʃərəl] *a.* sobrenatural.
supernaturalism [-'nætʃərəlˌɪzəm] *s.* 1. carácter sobrenatural. 2. sobrenaturalismo.
supernaturally [-'nætʃərəlɪ] *adv.* sobrenaturalmente.
supernaturalness [-'nætʃərəlnəs] *s.* índole sobrenatural, carácter sobrenatural.
supernormal [-'nɔrməl, B -'nɔməl] *a.* 1. superior a lo normal. 2. sobrehumano.
supernova [-'noʊvə] *s.* (astr.) supernova.
supernumerary [-'numəˌrɛrɪ, B -'njumərərɪ] *a.* 1. supernumerario; extra; supletorio, suplementario. 2. excesivo, superfluo. —*s.* (*pl.* SUPERNUMERARIES) 1. supernumerario. 2. (teat.) figurante, comparsa; (cinem.) extra.
superordinate [ˌsupər'ɔrdənət, B -'ɔd-] *a.* de rango o clase superior.
superphosphate [-'fɑsˌfeɪt, B -'fɔs-] *s.* (quím.) superfosfato.
superphysical [-'fɪzɪkəl] *a.* inmaterial, incorpóreo.
superpose [-'poʊz] *v.t.* sobreponer, superponer.
superposition [-pə'zɪʃən] *s.* sobreposición, superposición.
superpower ['supərˌpaʊər, B 'supəˌpaʊə] *s.* superpotencia.
supersaturate [ˌsupər'sætʃəˌreɪt, B -pə'-] *v.t.* (quím.) sobresaturar.

supersaturation [-ˌsætʃə'reɪʃən] *s.* (quím.) sobresaturación.
superscribe ['supərˌskraɪb, B -pəˌ-] *v.t.* sobrescribir.
superscript [-ˌskrɪpt] *a.* sobrescrito. —*s.* (mat.) índice sobrescrito.
superscription [ˌsupər'skrɪpʃən, B -pə'-] *s.* sobrescrito.
supersede [-'sid] *v.t.* 1. reemplazar, substituir. 2. desalojar, suplantar; invalidar. 3. (der.) sobreseer.
supersedeas [-'sidɪəs] *s.* (*pl.* SUPERSEDEAS) (der.) auto de suspensión del juicio; auto de sobreseimiento.
superseder [-'sidər, B -ə] *s.* reemplazo, substituto.
supersedure [-'sidʒər, B -'sidʒə] *s.* substitución de una nueva reina (en la colmena de abejas).
supersensible [-'sɛnsəbəl] *a.* suprasensible.
supersensitive [-'sɛnsətɪv] *a.* supersensible (película fotográfica, etc.).
supersensory [-'sɛnsərɪ] *a.* suprasensorial (percepción).
superserviceable [-'sɜrvəsəbəl, B -'sɜvəs-] *a.* demasiado servicial, obsequioso, casi servil.
supersonic [-'sɑnɪk, B -'sɔn-] *a.* 1. supersónico (velocidad). 2. (fís.) ultrasonoro (frecuencia, onda). —*s.* (fís.) onda ultrasonora; frecuencia ultrasonora.
supersonics [-'sɑnɪks, B -'sɔn-] *s. pl.* (*sing. en const.*) supersónica.
superstate ['supərˌsteɪt, B -pəˌ-] *s.* (pol.) superestado (un estado o sistema de gobierno que tiene poder sobre otros estados subordinados).
superstition [ˌsupər'stɪʃən, B -pə'-] *s.* superstición.
superstitious [-'stɪʃəs] *a.* supersticioso.
superstitiously [-lɪ] *adv.* supersticiosamente.
superstitiousness [-nəs] *s.* naturaleza supersticiosa.
superstratum ['supərˌstreɪtəm, B -pəˌstrɑt-] *s.* estrato superior.
superstructure [-ˌstrʌktʃər, B -tʃə] *s.* (arq., mar., const.) superestructura.
supersubtle [ˌsupər'sʌtəl, B -pə'-] *a.* muy sutil, muy astuto.
supersubtlety [-tɪ] *s.* sutileza extraordinaria.
supertanker ['supərˌtæŋkər, B -pəˌ-ə] *s.* barco tanque de gran capacidad.
supertax [-ˌtæks] *s.* 1. sobretasa. 2. impuesto complementario (de tasa progresiva).
supertonic [ˌsupər'tɑnɪk, B -pə'tɔn-] *s.* (mús.) supertónica.
supervene [-'vin] *v.t.* sobrevenir, supervenir, seguir.
supervenience [-'vinjəns] *s.* superveniencia.
supervenient [-'vinjənt] *a.* superveniente.
supervention [-'vɛnʃən] *s.* sobrevenida, superveniencia; (der.) supervención.
supervise ['supərˌvaɪz, B -pəˌ-] *v.t.* superentender, supervisar, inspeccionar, vigilar.
supervision [ˌsupər'vɪʒən, B -pə'-] *s.* superintendencia, supervisión, inspección.
supervisor ['supərˌvaɪzər, B -pəˌ-zə] *s.* superintendente, supervisor, sobrestante, inspector.
supervisory [ˌsupər'vaɪzərɪ, B 'sjupəvaɪ-] *a.* 1. supervisor, inspector. 2. de inspección, ej., *s. duties,* funciones de inspección. 3. de superintendente, ej., *in a s. capacity,* en capacidad de superintendente.
supervoltage ['supərˌvoultɪdʒ, B -pəˌ-] *s.* (elec.) sobretensión, supertensión.
supinate ['supəˌneɪt] *v.t., v.i.* volver(se) con la palma hacia arriba (la mano).
supination [ˌsupə'neɪʃən] *s.* (fisiol.) supinación.
supinator ['supəˌneɪtər, B -ˌneɪtə] *a.* (anat.) supinador (músculo).
supine [su'paɪn] *a.* 1. supino. 2. (poét.) pendiente. 3. indolente, desidioso.
supine ['suˌpaɪn] *s.* (gram.) supino.
supinely [su'paɪnlɪ] *adv.* 1. boca arriba, en posición supina. 2. sin energías, indolentemente, sumisamente.
supineness [-nəs] *s.* letargo, indolencia, sumisión.
supper ['sʌpər, B 'sʌpə] *s.* cena.
supperless [-ləs] *a.* sin cenar.
supper time, hora de cenar.
supplant [sə'plænt, B sə'plɑnt] *v.t.* 1. suplantar (con malas artes). 2. reemplazar, substituir. 3. (ant.) desarraigar, erradicar, desalojar.
supplantation [səˌplæn'teɪʃən] *s.* 1. suplantación. 2. reemplazo, substitución.
supplanter [sə'plæntər, B sə'plɑntə] *s.* 1. suplantador. 2. reemplazante, substituto.
supple ['sʌpəl] *a.* 1. flexible. 2. (fig.) flexible, adaptable, elástico (idea, etc.). 3. manejable, doblegable, dúctil; sumiso, obsequioso. —*v.t.* 1. volver flexible. 2. volver dócil o sumiso; amansar (caballo). 3. aliviar, calmar (con un ungüento). —*v.i.* volverse flexible.
supplejack [-ˌdʒæk] *s.* (bot.) guaraná, paulinia.
supplely [-əlɪ] *adv.* flexiblemente, dócilmente.
supplement ['sʌpləmənt] *s.* 1. suplemento, complemento. 2. suplemento (de diario o revista). 3. (mat.) suplemento. — ['sʌpləˌmɛnt] *v.t.* suplir, complementar.
supplemental [ˌsʌplə'mɛntəl] *a.* suplemental, supletorio.
supplementary [-'mɛntərɪ] *a.* suplementario, supletorio.
supplementary angle, (mat.) ángulo suplementario.
supplementary evidence, (der.) prueba suplementaria.
suppleness ['sʌpəlnəs] *s.* flexibilidad, elasticidad.
suppletory [sə'plitərɪ, B 'sʌplɪtərɪ] *a.* supletorio, suplementario.
suppliance ['sʌplɪəns] *s.* (raro) suplicación, ruego.
suppliant [-lɪənt] *a., s.* suplicante.
suppliantly ['sʌplɪəntlɪ] *adv.* de modo suplicante, suplicantemente.
supplicant [-ləkənt] *a., s.* suplicante.
supplicate [-ləˌkeɪt] *v.i.* (gen. con *to*) hacer súplicas (esp. a Dios). —*v.t.* suplicar, implorar, impetrar.
supplicating ['sʌpləˌkeɪtɪŋ] *a.* suplicante, deprecatorio.
supplication [ˌsʌplə'keɪʃən] *s.* súplica, suplicación.
supplicatory ['sʌplɪkəˌtɔrɪ, B -tərɪ] *a.* suplicante, rogativo.
supplier [sə'plaɪər, B -'plaɪə] *s.* proveedor, abastecedor, suministrador.
supply [sə'plaɪ] *v.t.* (*pret., p.p.* SUPPLIED; *p.pr.* SUPPLYING) 1. proporcionar, suministrar (mercadería, energía, etc.). 2. aprovisionar con, abastecer de (víveres, etc.). 3. abastecer, aprovisionar, proveer (ciudad, fábrica, etc. de algo). 4. suplir (falta), llenar, satisfacer (una necesidad). 5. proporcionar, dar (respuesta). 6. suplir, reemplazar; tomar el lugar de. —*v.i.* servir como substituto; actuar como suplente. —*s.* 1. aprovisionamiento, provisión. 2. (*gen. pl.*) suministros, abastecimiento; pertrechos (de armas); provisiones, víveres. 3. (econ.) oferta; producción, cantidades producidas. 4. (com.) existencias, surtido. 5. suplente, esp. cura suplente. 6. (ant.) asistencia, ayuda. 7. **in short s.,** escaso.
supply ['sʌplɪ] *var. de* **supplely.**
supply and demand, (econ.) oferta y demanda.
supply depot, (mil.) depósito de suministros.
supply line, (mil.) vía de abastecimiento.
supply pipe, surtidor, caño de alimentación, tubo abastecedor.
supply route, (mil.) camino de abastecimiento.
supply-side economics, economía de la oferta.
supply train, (mil.) tren de abastecimientos, tren de campaña, tren de combate.
support [sə'pɔrt, B -'pɔt] *v.t.* 1. apoyar, soportar, sostener (peso, construcción, etc.). 2. aguantar, tolerar, sufrir, soportar, ej., *he could not s. her taunts,* no pudo tolerar sus mofas, *I cannot s. his insolence any longer,* no puedo aguantar más su insolencia. 3. respaldar, apoyar (a persona, partido, etc.), sustentar (idea, tesis, causa, etc.); reforzar, corroborar (acusación, declaración, etc.). 4. mantener (a su familia, institución, etc.). 5. asistir, confortar; dar fuerzas a, ej., *what supported him was a glass of brandy,* lo que le dio fuerzas fue un vaso de aguardiente. 6. (teat.) acompañar (a un actor principal). —*s.* 1. sustentación, sostenimiento. 2. soporte, sostén, apoyo; ayuda, protección, respaldo. 3. mantenimiento (de la familia, una institución, etc.). 4. **to give s. to,** dar apoyo a; **to speak in s. of,** hablar en defensa de.
supportable [-əbəl] *a.* soportable, sufrible.
supportably [-əblɪ] *adv.* soportablemente.
supporter [-ər, B -ə] *s.* 1. defensor, mantenedor, partidario, sostenedor. 2. liga (para medias). 3. suspensorio. 4. (her.) tenante (del escudo). 5. (dep.) hincha (Amer.).
supporting distance [-ɪŋ-] (mil.) distancia de apoyo recíproco.
supporting fire, (mil.) fuego de apoyo.
supportive [sə'pɔrtɪv, B -'pɔtɪv] *a.* sustentador.
support mission, (mil.) misión de apoyo, incursión de apoyo.
supposable [sə'pouzəbəl] *a.* presumible, concebible, imaginable.
supposal [sə'pouzəl] *s.* suposición, hipótesis, creencia.
suppose [sə'pouz] *v.t.* 1. suponer, poner como hipótesis. 2. presumir, creer, imaginar. 3. presuponer, dar por sentado o existente; poner por caso. 4. **I s. so,** así lo creo; **to be supposed,** tener por deber; corresponder (a alguien), ej., *he is not supposed to do that,* a él no le corresponde hacer eso. —*v.i.* conjeturar; opinar, pensar.
supposed [-'pouzd] *a.* supuesto, presunto, hipotético, pretendido; imaginado.
supposedly [-'pouzədlɪ] *adv.* de modo supuesto; presuntamente, según lo que se cree.
supposition [ˌsʌpə'zɪʃən] *s.* suposición.
suppositional [-əl] *a.* supositivo, hipotético.
suppositionally [-əlɪ] *adv.* a modo de suposición, como hipótesis.
supposititious [səˌpɑzə'tɪʃəs, B -ˌpɔz-] *a.* 1. supositicio, espurio, falsificado, falso, fingido. 2. supuesto, hipotético.
supposititiously [-lɪ] *adv.* 1. de modo supositicio. 2. hipotéticamente.
suppositive [sə'pɑzətɪv, B -'pɔz-] *a.* supositivo; supuesto.
suppository [-ˌtɔrɪ, B -tərɪ] *s.* (med.) supositorio.
suppress [sə'prɛs] *v.t.* 1. suprimir (partido, costumbre, impuesto, etc.). 2. reprimir, sofocar, extinguir, aplastar, dominar (rebelión, agitación,

etc.). 3. ocultar (información, pruebas, etc.); prohibir (publicación). 4. reprimir, contener, ocultar, inhibir (sentimientos). 5. parar, contener (flujo, hemorragia, enfermedad). 6. (rad., t.v.) suprimir (parásitos). 7. (psiquiatría) desterrar de la mente (ideas inaceptables, impulsos, etc.).
suppression [-ˈprɛʃən] *s.* 1. supresión (de un partido, costumbres, impuestos, etc.). 2. represión (de una rebelión, agitación, etc.). 3. ocultación (de noticias, pruebas, etc.). 4. (psic.) represión, inhibición.
suppressive [-ˈprɛsɪv] *a.* supresor; represivo.
suppressor [-ˈprɛsər, B -ə] *s.* 1. represor. 2. supresor, amortiguador. 3. (rad., t.v.) dispositivo antiparásito.
suppurate [ˈsʌpjəˌreɪt] *v.i.* supurar.
suppuration [ˌsʌpjəˈreɪʃən] *s.* supuración.
suppurative [ˈsʌpjəˌreɪtɪv] *a.* supurativo; supurante.
supraliminal [ˌsuprəˈlɪmənəl, B ˈsjuprə-] *a.* (psic.) supraliminal.
supranational [-ˈnæʃənəl] *a.* supranacional.
supraorbital [-ˈɔrbətəl, B -ˈɔbɪt-] *a.* (anat.) supraorbital.
supraorganism [-ˈɔrgəˌnɪzəm, B -ˈɔgə-] *s.* unidad social orgánica (ej., de ciertos insectos).
supraprotest [-ˈproʊˌtɛst] *s.* (der.) supraprotesto, intervención bajo protesto.
suprarenal [-ˈrinəl] (anat.) *a.* suprarrenal. —*s.* glándula suprarrenal.
suprarenal gland, (anat.) glándula suprarrenal.
supraspinous [-ˈspaɪnəs] *a.* (anat.) supraspinoso.
supremacist [sʊˈprɛməsəst, B sju-] *s.* sostenedor de la supremacía (de un grupo, nación, raza, etc.).
supremacy [sʊˈprɛməsɪ, B sjʊ-] *s.* supremacía, predominio, superioridad, hegemonía.
supreme [sʊˈprim, B sjʊ-] *a.* 1. supremo, sumo. 2. supremo, último, final. 3. máximo, extremo.
Supreme Being, Ser Supremo.
supreme commander, (mil.) generalísimo, jefe supremo.
supreme court, (der.) tribunal supremo, corte suprema.
supreme folly, (el) colmo de la locura.
supremely [-lɪ] *adv.* supremamente, sumamente.
supreme moment, momento supremo.
supremeness [-nəs] *s.* supremacía, preeminencia.
supreme sacrifice, sacrificio de la propia vida.
Supreme Soviet, Soviet Supremo, parlamento de la Unión Soviética.
supreme work, trabajo óptimo, obra cumbre.
supt. *abrev. de* **superintendent,** portero (de un edificio de vivienda).
sura [ˈsʊrə, B ˈsʊərə] *s.* (relig.) sura (lección o capítulo en el Alcorán).
surah [ˈsʊrə, B ˈsjʊərə] *s.* (tej.) surá, surah.
sural [-əl] *a.* (anat.) sural.
surbase [ˈsɜrˌbeɪs, B ˈsɜ,-] *s.* (arq.) cornisa de pedestal; astrágalo, espira (de la columna).
surbased [-ˌbeɪst] *a.* (arq.) provisto de cornisa de pedestal; con astrágalo o espira (columna); rebajado (arco).
surcease [sɜrˈsis, B sɜˈsis] (ant.) *v.t., v.i.* suspender, poner fin a; cesar. — [ˈsɜrˌsis, B sɜˈsis] *s.* suspensión, cesación; fin.
surcharge [ˈsɜrˌtʃɑrdʒ, B ˈsɜtʃɑdʒ] *s.* 1. recargo, sobretasa, sobreprecio. 2. resello (en billetes de banco). 3. (filat.) sobrecarga. 4. sobrepeso, sobrecarga. — [B sɜˈtʃɑdʒ] *v.t.* 1. recargar. 2. resellar (billetes de banco). 3. (filat.) sobrecargar, proveer de sobrecarga (sellos postales). 4. sobrecargar, cargar demasiado.
surcingle [-ˌsɪŋgəl] *s.* 1. sobrecincha. 2. (raro) cíngulo, ceñidor (de una sotana).
surcoat [-ˌkoʊt] *s.* (hist.) gabán, sobretodo; sobrevesta, sobreveste (sobre la armadura).
surculose [ˈsɜrkjəˌloʊs, B ˈsɜkjə-] *a.* (bot.) surculado, surculoso.
surd [sɜrd, B sɜd] *a.* 1. (mat.) irracional sordo. 2. (fon.) sordo. —*s.* 1. (mat.) número sordo o irracional. 2. (fon.) sonido o consonante sordos.
sure [ʃʊr, B ʃʊə] *a.* 1. seguro, firme, estable, constante; certero, infalible, ej., *he did it with a s. hand,* lo hizo con mano firme, *a s. shot,* un tirador certero, *s. faith,* fe firme. 2. seguro, cierto, ej., *are you s.?* ¿ está Ud. seguro? 3. seguro, confiable, indudable, indubitable. 4. (ant.) salvo. 5. **a s. card,** (fig.) una carta de triunfo; **be s. to (do),** no deje de, no olvide (hacer), ej., *be s. to close the door,* no deje de (o no olvide) cerrar la puerta; **be s. not to (do),** guárdese de, ponga cuidada en no (hacer), ej., *be s. not to touch the needle,* guárdese de (o ponga cuidado en no) tocar la aguja; **for s.,** seguramente; **to be s.,** sin duda, seguramente; de veras; **to be s. of** (o **that**), estar seguro, tener la certeza de (o de que), ej., *I am s. of success,* estoy seguro de tener éxito; **to be s. to (do),** ser seguro que (hará), (hará) con seguridad, ej., *the plan is s. to fail,* es seguro que el plan fracasará, *he is s. to come,* vendrá, con seguridad; **to make s. (that),** cerciorarse, convencerse (de que); **to make s. of,** asegurarse de; asegurar que. —*adv.* 1. seguramente, realmente, ej., *it s. was cold,* (fam.) realmente hacía frío. 2. por supuesto, ej., *will you come with us? s. I will come!* ¿vendrás con nosotros? ¡por supuesto que voy! 3. **s. enough,** efectivamente; **s. thing,** (*ú. como interj.*) ¡sin falta! ¡cierto!
surefire [ˈʃʊrˈfaɪr, B ˈʃʊəˈfaɪə] *a.* seguro, de éxito seguro.
surefooted [-ˌfʊtəd] *a.* 1. de pie firme, seguro. 2. (fig.) infalible, certero.
surely [-lɪ] *adv.* seguramente, ciertamente, sin duda, indudablemente, ej., *s. I have met you before,* seguramente lo he conocido antes.
sureness [-nəs] *s.* seguridad, certeza.
surety [ˈʃʊrətɪ, B ˈʃʊər-] *s.* (*pl.* SURETIES) 1. seguridad, certeza. 2. seguridad, garantía, fianza, dita. 3. (der.) fiador, garante. 4. **to stand s. for,** ser fiador de, salir de garante de.
surety bond, (com.) fianza, fianza de caución, fianza de seguridad.
suretyship [-ˌʃɪp] *s.* afianzamiento, garantía.
surf [sɜrf, B sɜf] *s.* oleaje, resaca. —*v.i.* practicar (deporte de) tabla hawaiana.
surface [ˈsɜrfəs, B ˈsɜfɪs] *s.* 1. superficie, sobrefaz, cara. 2. aspecto superficial, ej., *he looks only at the s. of things,* él mira sólo el aspecto superficial de las cosas. 3. (geom., aer.) superficie. —*a.* superficial, de (la) superficie, externo, exterior. —*v.t.* 1. allanar, alisar. 2. cepillar, pulir (madera). 3. emplastecer (pared, etc.). 4. (f.c.) emparejar, nivelar. 5. hacer volver a la superficie (submarino). —*v.i.* 1. trabajar en la superficie. 2. salir o volver a la superficie, emerger (submarino, pez, etc.).
surface gauge, calibre de altura.
surface generator, (elec.) generador de ondas o de sobrecorriente.
surface grinder, (maq.) esmeriladora o amoladora de superficie.
surface hardening, (metal.) endurecimiento de superficie.
surface mail, correo de superficie; **by s.,** por vía terrestre, por vía marítima.
surface noise, ruido producido por la fricción de la aguja de un tocadiscos al moverse en los surcos del disco.
surface plate, (mec.) placa para probar superficies planas.
surfacer [-ər, B -ə] *s.* alisadora; cepilladora.
surface tension, (fís.) tensión superficial.
surface-to-air [ˈsɜrfəstʊˈɛr, B ˈsɜfɪstʊˈɜə] *a.* del suelo al aire (díc. de cohetes, proyectiles, etc.).
surface-to-air missile, misil tierra-aire.
surface-to-surface [-tə-] *a.* del suelo al suelo (díc. de cohetes, proyectiles, etc.).
surface velocity, velocidad superficial, velocidad de (la) superficie.
surface water, agua superficial (de la superficie).
surfacing [-ɪŋ] *s.* 1. acabado; revestimiento, arreglo de la superficie. 2. afirmado (de un camino). 3. (f.c.) nivelación.
surfboard [ˈsɜrfˌbɔrd, B ˈsɜfˌbɔd] *s.* (dep.) acuaplano, tabla hawaiana.
surfboat [-ˌboʊt] *s.* bote para navegar en marejadas fuertes.
surfeit [ˈsɜrfət, B ˈsɜfɪt] *s.* 1. exceso, demasía. 2. empacho, indigestión, ahíto. 3. (fig.) empalago, empalagamiento, hartura, saciedad, hastío. —*v.t.* hartar, saciar, ahitar. —*v.i.* (ant.) hartarse, atracarse, ahitarse.
surficial [sərˈfɪʃəl, B səˈ-] *a.* superficial, de la superficie.
surfing [ˈsɜrfɪŋ, B ˈsɜf-] *s.* (deporte de) acuaplano, (deporte de) tabla hawaiana.
surge [sɜrdʒ, B sɜdʒ] *s.* 1. oleada, oleaje, marejada, mareta. 2. (fig.) ola, onda (de indignación, emoción, etc.). 3. (elec.) onda de impulso, onda errante o irruptiva; sobrevoltaje. 4. (mar.) mecha (del cabrestante). —*v.i.* 1. undular, olear; bullir, agitarse. 2. (elec.) producirse sobrevoltaje o exceso de corriente. 3. (mar.) lascarse, aflojarse (cable). —*v.t.* (mar.) lascar, aflojar poco a poco (cable).
surge generator, (elec.) generador de ondas o de corrientes.
surgeon [ˈsɜrdʒən, B ˈsɜdʒən] *s.* cirujano, quirurgo.
surgeoncy [-sɪ] *s.* (G.B.) oficio o posición de cirujano.
surgeon general, (*pl.* SURGEONS GENERAL) inspector general de sanidad.
surgeon's knot, nudo de cirujano.
surgery [ˈsɜrdʒərɪ, B ˈsɜdʒər-] *s.* 1. cirugía. 2. intervención quirúrgica, operación. 3. gabinete de cirujano; sala de operaciones, quirófano.
surge tank, (hidr.) tanque igualador o de oleaje o de oscilación, chimenea de equilibrio.
surgical [-dʒɪkəl] *a.* quirúrgico.
surgical area, (med.) campo operatorio.
surgical gloves, gantes de cirujano.
surgically [-kəlɪ] *adv.* (fig.) extremadamente (exacto, limpio, aseado, etc.).
surging [ˈsɜrdʒɪŋ, B ˈsɜdʒ-] *s.* (elec.) pulsación.
suricate [ˈsʊrəˌkeɪt, B ˈsɜr-] *s.* (zool.) suricate.
surlily [ˈsɜrləlɪ, B ˈsɜlə-] *adv.* ásperamente, con mal humor, desabridamente.
surliness [-lɪnəs] *s.* mal genio, mal humor, displicencia, desabrimiento.
surly [-lɪ] *a.* (SURLIER; SURLIEST) 1. áspero, rudo, hosco, arisco, desabrido. 2. (raro) arrogante.
surmise [sərˈmaɪz, B səˈ-] *v.t.* conjeturar, suponer, presumir. — [B ˈsɛmaɪz] *s.* conjetura, suposición, presunción.
surmount [-ˈmaʊnt] *v.t.* 1. superar, salvar, vencer (obstáculo, dificultad, etc.). 2. levantarse (sobre); coronar, ej., *peaks surmounted with snow,* picos coronados de nieve. 3. escalar, trepar a. 4. (ant.) sobrepasar, exceder, trascender.
surmountable [-əbəl] *a.* superable, vencible.

surmullet [ˌsɜr'mʌlət, B sɜ'-] *s.* (ict.) mullo, salmonete, barbadilla, barbo de mar.
surname ['sɜrˌneɪm, B 'sɜˌ-] *s.* 1. apellido, nombre de familia. 2. sobrenombre, apodo. —*v.t.* 1. apellidar. 2. apodar, poner un sobrenombre a.
surpass [sər'pæs, B sə'pɑs] *v.t.* sobrepasar, exceder, superar, sobrepujar, aventajar.
surpassable [-əbəl] *a.* superable.
surpassing [-ɪŋ] *a.* sobresaliente, excelente, superior.
surpassingly [-lɪ] *adv.* de modo sobresaliente; excelentemente, sobresalientemente.
surplice ['sɜrpləs, B 'sɜplɪs] *s.* (relig.) sobrepelliz.
surplus ['sɜrplʌs, B 'sɜpləs] *s.* 1. sobrante, excedente, demasía. 2. (com.) superávit, excedente. —*a.* sobrante, excedente.
surplusage [-ɪdʒ] *s.* 1. sobrante, excedente, exceso, demasía. 2. (der.) materia inconexa, impertinencia (en un alegato).
surplus reserves, (com., ten.) superávit reservado, reservas del excedente.
surplus stock, (com., ten.) existencias en demasía.
surplus value, (e.p.) plusvalía (en la doctrina marxista).
surprint ['sɜrˌprɪnt, B 'sɜˌ-] *v.t.* sobreimprimir. —*s.* sobreimpresión.
surprisal [sər'praɪzəl, B sə'-] *s.* (raro) sorpresa.
surprise [sər'praɪz, B sə'-] *v.t.* sorprender; **I'm surprised at you,** me sorprende su conducta; **s. someone,** sorprender a alguien; **to be surprised at (something),** sorprenderse de o con (algo), ej., *he was surprised at the news,* le sorprendió la noticia, se sorprendió con la noticia. —*s.* sorpresa; **to one's (great,** etc.) **s.,** para su (gran, etc.) sorpresa; **to take by s.,** coger de sorpresa, tomar por sorpresa.
surprising [-ɪŋ] *a.* sorprendente, inesperado.
surprisingly [-lɪ] *adv.* de modo sorprendente, inesperadamente, sorprendentemente.
surra ['sʊrə] *s.* (vet.) surra.
surrealism [sə'riəˌlɪzəm] *s.* surrealismo, superrealismo.
surrealist [-ləst] *s., a.* surrealista, superrealista.
surrealistic [səˌriə'lɪstɪk] *a.* surrealista, superrealista.
surrealistically [-tɪkəlɪ] *adv.* al estilo surrealista o superrealista.
surrebutter [ˌsɜrɪ'bʌtər, B ˌsʌr-ə] **surrebuttal** [-əl] *s.* (der.) tríplica.
surrejoinder [-'dʒɔɪndər, B -də] *s.* (der.) contrarréplica.
surrender [sə'rɛndər, B -də] *v.t.* rendir, entregar, ceder, renunciar a; **s. oneself,** rendirse; (fig.) abandonarse, entregarse (a vicio, placer, etc.). —*v.i.* rendirse, entregarse, capitular. —*s.* 1. rendición, capitulación, entrega. 2. renuncia, dejación, abandono. 3. (com.) rescate.
surrender value, valor de rescate (de un seguro).
surreptitious [ˌsɜrəp'tɪʃəs, B ˌsʌr-] *a.* subrepticio, clandestino, furtivo.
surreptitiously [-lɪ] *adv.* clandestinamente, furtivamente, subrepticiamente.
surreptitiousness [-nəs] *s.* subrepción, clandestinidad.
surrey ['sɜrɪ, B sʌrɪ] *s.* birlocho, coche de tiro abierto con toldo.
surrogate ['sɜrəˌgeɪt, B 'sʌrə-] *v.t.* (der.) subrogar. — [-gət] *s.* 1. substituto. 2. (relig., G.B.) vicario. 3. (der., E.U.) juez del tribunal testamentario; juez de testamentarías.
surrogate mother, madre de alquiler, madre suplente.
surround [sə'raʊnd] *v.t.* 1. cercar, encerrar, circuir, rodear, circundar, circunvalar, ceñir. 2. (mil.) sitiar, asediar, acorralar. —*s.* (rad.) anillo, suspensión del cono (en altoparlantes).
surrounding [-ɪŋ] *s.* 1. circunvalación, rodeo; sitio. 2. (*pl.*) ambiente, medio, alrededores, cercanías, contornos. —*a.* circundante, circunvecino.
surroyal ['sɜˌrɔɪəl] *s.* corona de la cornamenta (de un ciervo).
surtax ['sɜrˌtæks, B 'sɜˌ-] *s.* sobretasa, recargo tributario, impuesto complementario. —*v.t.* recargar (con un impuesto), imponer un impuesto adicional a.
surtout [sər'tu, B 'sɜtu] *s.* sobretodo, gabán.
surveillance [-'veɪləns] *s.* vigilancia, observación (continua).
surveillant [-lənt] *s.* vigilante, guardián.
survey [sər'vəɪ, B sə'-] *v.t.* 1. examinar, estudiar. 2. inspeccionar, reconocer. 3. medir, deslindar, apear (terrenos). 4. (mar.) arquear. — ['sɜrˌveɪ, B 'sɜˌ-] *s.* 1. examen, inspección. 2. estudio, reconocimiento, peritación. 3. encuesta (ej., de la opinión pública). 4. visión panorámica o general (de una materia). 5. agrimensura; levantamiento de planos, planimetría; apeo, deslinde, medición.
surveying [sər'veɪɪŋ, B sə'-] *s.* agrimensura; levantamiento de planos; peritación.
surveying aneroide barometer, aneroide de topógrafo.
surveyor [-ər, B -ə] *s.* 1. inspector, investigador, examinador. 2. agrimensor, topógrafo; apeador, deslindador. 3. (E.U.) vista (de aduanas). 4. (mar.) arqueador.
surveyor's chain, cadena de agrimensor.
surveyorship [sər'veɪərˌʃɪp, B sə'-əˌ-] *s.* oficio de agrimensor.
surveyor's level, nivel de anteojo.
surveyor's measure, sistema de medida en agrimensura (que tiene como unidad la cadena de agrimensor).
survival [sər'vaɪvəl, B sə'-] *s.* 1. supervivencia. 2. reliquia.
survival of the fittest, (biol.) (la) supervivencia del más apto.
survival value, (biol.) utilidad (de las propiedades de un organismo) en la lucha por la existencia.
survivance [-vəns] *s.* supervivencia.
survive [sər'vaɪv, B sə'-] *v.i.* sobrevivir, subsistir, perdurar; salir o quedar con vida. —*v.t.* sobrevivir a, durar más que.
surviving [-'vaɪvɪŋ] *a.* sobreviviente.
survivor [-vər, B -və] *s.* sobreviviente, superviviente.
survivorship [-ˌʃɪp] *s.* (der.) supervivencia; presunción de supervivencia.
susceptibility [səˌsɛptə'bɪlətɪ] *s.* (*pl.* SUSCEPTIBILITIES) 1. susceptibilidad, impresionabilidad, sensibilidad, delicadez. 2. (*pl.*) puntos sensitivos (en los sentimientos o naturaleza de una persona). 3. (fís., elec.) susceptibilidad.
susceptible [sə'sɛptəbəl] *a.* 1. susceptible, sensitivo. 2. (con *to*) susceptible (a), susceptivo (a), impresionable (por). 3. (con *of* o *to*) expuesto (a).
susceptibleness [-bəlnəs] *s.* susceptibilidad.
susceptibly [-blɪ] *adv.* de modo susceptible, susceptiblemente.
susceptive [sə'sɛptɪv] *a.* 1. susceptivo, receptivo. 2. susceptible, delicado.
susceptivity [səˌsɛp'tɪvətɪ] *s.* susceptibilidad.
suspect ['sʌsˌpɛkt] *a.* sospechoso, sospechable. —*s.* sospechoso. — [sə'spɛkt] *v.t.* 1. sospechar. 2. sospechar de, recelar de. —*v.i.* figurarse, imaginarse, tener sospechas.
suspend [sə'spɛnd] *v.t.* suspender. —*v.i.* 1. cesar o dejar de funcionar temporalmente. 2. colgar. 3. (quím.) dispersarse.
suspended animation, muerte aparente.
suspended cadence, (mús.) cadencia suspendida.
suspended sentence, condena condicional.
suspender [-'spɛndər, B -də] *s.* 1. suspendedor. 2. (*pl.*) (E.U.) tirantes (del pantalón). 3. (*pl.*) (G.B.) ligas (de las medias).
suspense [səs'pɛns] *s.* 1. suspensión, interrupción. 2. suspenso; ansiedad. 3. (der.) suspensión. 4. **in s.,** en suspenso.
suspense account, (ten.) cuenta transitoria, cuenta de puente, cuenta de suspensión.
suspension [-'pɛnʃən] *s.* suspensión; (mús., fís., quím., ret.) suspensión.
suspension bridge, puente colgante, puente suspendido.
suspension cable, cable portante.
suspension of arms, suspensión de armas.
suspension points, (E.U.) puntos suspensivos.
suspensive [səs'pɛnsɪv] *a.* 1. suspensivo. 2. indeciso, irresoluto; incierto.
suspensoid [-ˌsɔɪd] *s.* (quím.) suspensoide.
suspensor [-sər, B -sə] *s.* (bot.) suspensor.
suspensory [-sərɪ] *a.* 1. suspensorio. 2. suspensivo. —*s.* (med.) suspensorio.
suspensory ligament, (anat.) 1. ligamento suspensorio, zónula de Zinn (del ojo). 2. ligamento falciforme (del hígado).
suspicion [sə'spɪʃən] *s.* 1. sospecha, recelo, desconfianza. 2. sospecha, barrunto, conjetura. 3. (con *of*) traza, pizca, sombra. 4. **above s.,** fuera de sospecha; **on s.,** como sospechoso, ej., *he was arrested on s.,* lo arrestaron como sospechoso; **to come under the s. of,** ser sospechado de. —*v.t.* (dial.) sospechar, recelar.
suspicious [-əs] *a.* 1. sospechoso, dudoso. 2. sospechoso, receloso, suspicaz.
suspiciously [-lɪ] *adv.* sospechosamente, suspicazmente.
suspiciousness [-nəs] *s.* suspicacia, naturaleza sospechosa; recelo, desconfianza.
suspiration [ˌsʌspə'reɪʃən] *s.* (poét.) suspiro.
suspire [sə'spaɪr, B -'spaɪə] *v.i.* (poét.) suspirar.
sustain [sə'steɪn] *v.t.* 1. mantener, sustentar, alimentar, nutrir. 2. sostener, llevar, cargar, soportar (peso, construcción, etc.); sufrir, aguantar. 3. mantener, continuar (discusión, esfuerzo, etc.). 4. (fig.) mantener (el espíritu) en alto; animar, confortar, alentar. 5. sufrir, soportar, experimentar (derrota, pérdida, etc.). 6. (der.) declarar fundada (demanda, objeción, moción, etc.). 7. probar, corroborar, confirmar (teoría, afirmación, etc.). 8. (mús.) sostener. 9. (raro) apoyar, respaldar (esp. con tropas, pertrechos militares, etc.).
sustainable [-əbəl] *a.* sustentable, sostenible.
sustainer [-ər, B -ə] *s.* sustentador, sostenedor; defensor; protector.
sustaining program, programa de radio o televisión sin patrocinador comercial.
sustenance ['sʌstənəns] *s.* 1. sustento, alimento, comida. 2. subsistencia, mantenimiento, sostenimiento. 3. apoyo, respaldo.
sustentacular [ˌsʌstən'tækjələr, B -lə] *a.* (anat.) sustentacular.
sustentation [-'teɪʃən] *s.* 1. mantenimiento, sostenimiento, sustentamiento, sustentación. 2. preservación. 3. alimentación. 4. respaldo, apoyo.
sustentative ['sʌstənˌteɪtɪv, sə'stɛntətɪv] *a.* sustentante.
sustention [sə'stɛntʃən, B -'stɛnʃən] *var. de* **sustentation.**

susurrant [sʊ'sɜrənt, B sjʊ'sʌr-] *a.* susurrante, susurrador, murmurante.
susurration [ˌsusə'reɪʃən, B ˌsju-] *s.* surración, murmuración.
susurrous [sʊ'sɜrəs, B sjʊ'sʌr-] *a.* susurrador, susurrante, murmurador.
sutler ['sʌtlər, B -lə] *s.* vivandero, el que va con las tropas para venderles comida, tabaco, etc.
suttee [sə'ti, B 'sʌtɪ] *s.* viuda hindú que se inmola en la pira funeraria del marido; costumbre de inmolarse en la pira (practicada por la viuda hindú).
sutural ['sutʃərəl] *a.* (bot.) sutural.
suture ['sutʃər, B -tʃə] *s.* (anat., bot., med.) sutura. —*v.t.* (med.) suturar (labios de una herida).
suzerain ['suzərən, B -reɪn] *s.* 1. señor feudal. 2. (der.) estado protector. —*a.* 1. suzerano, soberano. 2. superior, supremo, principalísimo.
suzerainty [-tɪ] *s.* (der.) suzeranía, protectorado.
svelte [sfɛlt, B svɛlt] *a.* 1. esbelto, delgado. 2. suave, refinado.
SW *abrev. de* **southwest,** sudoeste (SO).
swab [swɑb, B swɔb] *v.t.* (*pret., p.p.* SWABBED; *p.pr.* SWABBING) 1. limpiar, fregar (con estropajo, etc.). 2. (mar.) lampacear. 3. (med.) limpiar con torunda o tapón. —*s.* 1. aljofifa, fregajo, estropajo. 2. (mar.) lampazo. 3. (med.) torunda, tapón. 4. (arm.) escobillón. 5. (jer.) marinero. 6. (jer.) maleta, tosco, patán.
swabber ['swɑbər, B 'swɔbə] *s.* aljofifa, fregajo, estropajo; escobillón.
Swabia ['sweɪbɪə] *s.* Suabia, Suevia, región de Alemania.
Swabian [-bɪən] *a., s.* suevo, suabo, de Suabia o Suevia.
swaddle ['swɑdəl, B 'swɔd-] *v.t.* 1. fajar, vendar, empañar. 2. enrollar, envolver. 3. (fig.) trabar, embarazar. —*s.* faja, pañal.
swaddling clothes, s. bands, s. clouts['swɑdlɪŋ-, B 'swɔd-] 1. envueltas, envoltura, mantillas, pañales, fajas. 2. (fig.) trabas, embarazos, limitaciones, restricciones.
swag [swæg] *s.* 1. festón, guirnalda. 2. fardel, maleta, atado (de equipaje). 3. bamboleo. 4. (Aust.) lío de ropa (de un vagabundo). 5. (jer.) botín, presa. —*v.i.* (*pret., p.p.* SWAGGED, *p.pr.* SWAGGING) 1. tambalear(se), bambolearse, ladearse. 2. hundirse (por su propio peso). 3. (Aust.) vagar, vagabundear (con el atado al hombro).
swage [sweɪdʒ] *s.* estampa, tas, macho de estampar. —*v.t.* forjar en estampa, estampar (con una matriz).
swage block, bloque de estampar, tas de estampar, placa sufridera, yunque estampador.
swagger ['swægər, B -ə] *v.i.* 1. contonearse, caminar dándose aires. 2. baladronear, fanfarronear, jactarse. —*s.* 1. contoneo. 2. baladronada, fanfarronada, jactancia. —*a.* lujoso, elegante.
swaggerer [-ərər, B -ərə] *s.* fanfarrón, baladrón.
swaggeringly [-ərɪŋlɪ] *adv.* fanfarroneando.
swagger stick, (mil.) bastón ligero.
swagging machine, máquina de estampar.
swagman ['swægmən] *s.* (pr. Austr.) vago, vagabundo (esp. el que lleva un atado o fardel).
swain [sweɪn] *s.* 1. zagal, chaval. 2. enamorado, amante.
swainish ['sweɪnɪʃ] *a.* rústico, agreste; grosero.
swale [sweɪl] *s.* terreno pantanoso, bajío (Amer.).
swallow ['swɑloʊ, B 'swɔl-] *s.* (orn.) golondrina.
swallow, *v.t.* 1. tragar, ingerir. 2. tragar, retractar (lo dicho, etc.); tragarse (el orgullo). 3. (fig.) tragar, tragarse, creer a ciegas. 4. (fig.) tragar, soportar, aguantar (persona, insulto); contener, reprimir (ira, resentimiento, etc.). 5. **s. one's words,** comerse sus palabras. 6. **s. up,** tragar, devorar; (fig.) devorar. —*v.i.* tragar, deglutir. —*s.* 1. tragadero, gaznate, esófago. 2. deglución. 3. trago; bocado. 4. apetito; tragonería. 5. (mar.) garganta (de poleas); abertura de paso (en cuadernal).
swallower [-ər, B -ə] *s.* tragón, glotón.
swallow fish, (ict.) golondrina.
swallowtail [-ˌteɪl] *s.* 1. cola de golondrina. 2. mariposa con alas posteriores bifurcadas. 3. frac. 4. (carp.) cola de milano.
swallow-tailed coat, frac, chaqueta masculina de gala.
swallowwort [-ˌwɜrt, B -wɜt] *s.* (bot.) celidonia, golondrinera, hierba de las golondrinas; vencetósigo.
swam [swæm] *pret. de* **swim.**
swami ['swɑmɪ] *s.* 1. maestro (en la India). 2. erudito, sabio.
swamp [swɑmp, swɔmp, B swɔmp] *s.* ciénaga, pantano. —*a.* de pantano. —*v.t.* 1. empantanar, enaguazar, enaguachar. 2. sumergir, hundir. 3. (fig.) inundar, abrumar (con trabajo, cartas, etc.). 4. (mar.) hacer zozobrar. —*v.i.* empantanarse; hundirse, sumergirse.
swamp buggy, 1. tractor anfibio. 2. bote de fondo plano (para cruzar pantanos).
swamper ['swɑmpər, 'swɔmp-, B 'swɔmpə] *s.* 1. habitante de un pantano. 2. asistente, ayudante (para todo trabajo).
swamp fever, fiebre de los pantanos, malaria, paludismo.
swampland [-ˌlænd] *s.* ciénaga, pantano, marisma.
swamp milkweed, (bot.) algodoncillo.
swamp white oak, (bot.) roble blanco de California, roble de los pantanos.
swampy [-ɪ] *a.* (SWAMPIER; SWAMPIEST) pantanoso, cenagoso.
swan [swɑn, B swɔn] *s.* 1. (orn.) cisne. 2. (fig.) cisne (poeta). 3. **S.,** (astr.) Cisne.
swan dive, (natación) salto del ángel, salto del cisne.
swanherd ['swɑnˌhɜrd, B 'swɔnhɜd] *s.* cuidador de cisnes.
swank [swæŋk] *a.* 1. (esco.) activo, enérgico, vivaz. 2. (jer.) ostentoso, lujoso, elegante. —*s.* boato, lujo, ostentación. —*v.i.* fanfarronear, ser ostentoso.
swankily ['swæŋkəlɪ] *adv.* ostentosamente.
swankiness [-kɪnəs] *s.* elegancia ostentosa, ostentación.
swanky [-kɪ] *a.* (SWANKIER; SWANKIEST) (jer.) ostentoso, lujoso, elegante.
swan-like ['swɑnˌlaɪk, B 'swɔn-] *a.* semejante al cisne; de cisne.
swannery [-ərɪ] *s.* criadero de cisnes.
swansdown ['swɑnzˌdaʊn, B 'swɔnz-] *s.* 1. plumones del cisne (usados como adorno). 2. fustán, muletón.
swanskin ['swɑnˌskɪn, B 'swɔn-] *s.* 1. piel del cisne con los plumones y plumas. 2. muletón.
swan song, 1. (poét.) canto del cisne. 2. (fig.) la última obra de un escritor o un artista.
swap [swɑp, B swɔp] *v.t., v.i.* (*pret., p.p.* SWAPPED; *p.pr.* SWAPPING) (fam.) cambalachear, trocar. —*s.* (fam.) cambalache, trueque.
swaraj [swə'rɑdʒ] *s.* (India) autonomía, independencia.
sward [swɔrd, B swɔd] *s.* césped.
swarf [swɔrf, B swɔf] *s.* virutas (de taladro, aguja cortadora, etc.).
swarm [swɔrm, B swɔm] *s.* 1. jabardo, enjambre. 2. (fig.) enjambre, jabardillo, multitud, gentío. —*v.i.* 1. enjambrar, jabardear, desahijar (las abejas). 2. pulular, hervir, bullir, hormiguear (una multitud, gentío o enjambre). 3. (gen. con *with*) abundar (en), estar lleno (de). 4. (biol.) escapar o salir en masa (como los zoosporos de un esporangio). —*v.t.* 1. enjambrar (abejas). 2. atestar (de gente).
swarm, *v.i., v.t.* (gen. con *up*) trepar, subir, escalar.
swarmer ['swɔrmər, B -ə] *s.* enjambradera (abeja que está por salir de la colmena).
swart [swɔrt, B swɔt] *a.* 1. moreno, atezado, aceitunado. 2. pernicioso, maligno.
swarth [swɔrθ, B swɔθ] (dial.) *var. de* **sward.**
swarthiness ['swɔrðɪnəs, B 'swɔðɪ-] *s.* tez morena.
swarthy [-ðɪ, -θɪ] *a.* (SWARTHIER; SWARTHIEST) moreno, obscuro, aceitunado, atezado, prieto.
swash [swɑʃ, swɔʃ, B swɔʃ] *v.i.* 1. chapotear. 2. fanfarronear, baladronear; pavonearse. —*v.t.* echar (mucha agua) sobre, inundar. —*s.* 1. bulla, baladronada, fanfarronería; pavoneo. 2. fanfarrón, bravucón. 3. chorretada. 4. canalizo; banco de arena (que lamen las olas). 5. reventazón de las olas (contra algo).
swashbuckle ['swɑʃˌbʌkəl, 'swɔʃ-, B 'swɔʃ-] *v.i.* fanfarronear, hacerse el valentón, baladronear.
swashbuckler [-ˌbʌklər, B -lə] *s.* valentón, bravucón, baladrón, espadachín.
swashbuckling [-lɪŋ] *s.* valentonada, fanfarronería. —*a.* valentón, bravucón, baladrón.
swash bulkhead (const. naval) mamparo amortiguador o de obstrucción.
swasher [-ər, B -ə] *s.* valentón, bravucón, matasiete, baladrón.
swastika ['swɑstɪkə, B 'swɔs-] *s.* svástica, esvástica, cruz gamada, símbolo del Nazismo.
swat [swɑt, B swɔt] *v.t.* (*pret., p.p.* SWATTED; *p.pr.* SWATTING) (E.U.) dar un golpe repentino a, aporrear; aplastar, matar con golpe (insectos, etc.). —*s.* golpe violento, aporreadura.
swatch [swɑtʃ, B swɔtʃ] *s.* muestra (de tela, cuero, etc.); pequeño muestrario.
swath [swɑθ, B swɔθ] **swathe** [swɑð, B sweɪð] *s.* 1. golpe de guadaña. 2. campo despejado en una pasada de guadaña; ringlera de hierba o mies acabada de cortar. 3. fila, hilera, faja, tira. 4. **to cut a s.,** (fig.) hacer viso, hacer un gran papel.
swathe [swɑð, B sweɪð] *v.t.* 1. fajar, vendar. 2. envolver, cubrir. —*s.* faja, venda.
swather ['swɑðər, B 'sweɪðə] *s.* agavilladora, mecanismo agavillador (en segadora).
swatter ['swɑtər, B 'swɔtə] *s.* matamoscas.
sway [sweɪ] *v.i.* 1. ladearse, inclinarse; oscilar, balancearse; virar, rolar (el viento). 2. desviarse. 3. gobernar, regir. —*v.t.* 1. cimbrar, vibrar, hacer oscilar. 2. torcer, apartar, desviar. 3. (fig.) hacer vacilar. 4. inducir, influir en el ánimo de. 5. ganar (votos, simpatía, etc.). 6. (ant.) blandir (cetro, espada, etc.). 7. gobernar, dirigir, regir, mandar. 8. (mar.) guindar, izar, enarbolar, drizar. —*s.* 1. oscilación, balanceo, ladeo, vaivén. 2. dominio, imperio, gobierno. 3. predominio, preponderancia. 4. **to hold s. over,** dominar.
swayback ['sweɪˌbæk] *s.* 1. lomo hundido (de los caballos). 2. lordosis.
sway-backed [-ˌbækt] *a.* de lomo hundido (caballo).
SW by S *abrev. de* **southwest by south,** suroeste cuarta al sur.
SW by W *abrev. de* **southwest by west,** suroeste cuarta al oeste.
swear [swɛr, B swɛə] *v.i.* (*pret.* SWORE [swɔr, B swɔ]; *p.p.* SWORN [swɔrn, B swɔn]; *p.pr.* SWEARING) 1. jurar, votar. 2. blasfemar, jurar, renegar, echar ternos, maldecir. 3. **s. at,** renegar

contra (alguien); **s. by,** afirmar bajo juramento; jurar por; (fam.) tener fe absoluta en (algo); **s. to,** afirmar bajo juramento; **s. to (do),** jurar (hacer). —*v.t.* 1. pronunciar, prestar (juramento). 2. obligar (a alguien) bajo juramento, hacer jurar, ej., *s. (someone) to secrecy,* hacer jurar (a alguien) para que guarde secreto. 3. juramentar. 4. denunciar (un delito), acusar de (un crimen, etc.) bajo juramento. 5. **s. in,** investir de un cargo o dignidad bajo juramento; **s. off,** jurar abandonar, jurar renunciar a (vicio, práctica, etc.); **s. out (a warrant,** etc.), obtener (una orden de detención, etc.) mediante denuncia juramentada. —*s.* reniego, blasfemia.

swearer [ˈswɛrər, B ˈswɛərə] *s.* blasfemo, maldiciente.

swearword [-ˌwɜrd, B ˈswɛəwɜd] *s.* terno, maldición, grosería.

sweat [swɛt] *v.i.* (*pret., p.p.* SWEAT O SWEATED; *p.pr.* SWEATING) 1. sudar, transpirar. 2. resudar, sudar, exudar (plantas); fermentar (el tabaco); transpirar (las piedras, etc.); sudar, rezumar (la pared). 3. (fam.) sudar, afanarse, fatigarse. 4. sufrir explotación (obreros). —*v.t.* 1. sudar, exudar, trasudar (sangre, resina, etc.). 2. empapar de sudor (camisa, ropas, etc.). 3. hacer transpirar. 4. hacer fermentar (el tabaco). 5. fundir (la soldadura); unir por soldadura indirecta; soldar. 6. (fig.) desplumar, pelar, despojar. 7. explotar (obreros). 8. (jer.) torturar; someter a un interrogatorio minucioso (con tortura). 9. **s. off,** perder (ej., peso) sudando; **s. blood,** (fig.) sudar sangre; **s. it out,** aguantarlo; **s. out,** producir a duras penas, producir laboriosamente. —*s.* 1. sudor, transpiración. 2. sudor, trabajo penoso. 3. sudor, exudación (de una planta, superficie, etc.). 4. ejercicio preparatorio (de un caballo antes de una carrera). 5. sudación, sudores. 6. **by the s. of his brow,** con el sudor de su frente; **old s.,** (jer., G.B.) viejo soldado; **to be in a s.,** (fam.) estar angustiado, estar preso de ansiedad.

sweatband [ˈswɛtˌbænd] *s.* (tira de) tafilete o badana (en el interior de los sombreros).

sweatbox [-ˌbɑks, B -bɔks] *s.* 1. sudadero (en el baño). 2. tina de apelambrar.

sweat cloth, sudadero (manto que se pone a los caballos).

sweated [-əd] *a.* explotado (obrero); que se basa en la explotación (industria).

sweater [-ər, B -ə] *s.* 1. explotador (de obreros). 2. sudorífero, sudatorio, sudorífico. 3. suéter, jersey, chompa (Amer.).

sweater girl, mujer de busto bien formado.

sweat gland, (anat.) glándula sudorípara.

sweatily [ˈswɛtəlɪ] *adv.* sudorosamente.

sweatiness [-ɪnəs] *s.* estado sudoso.

sweating [-ɪŋ] *s.* transpiración, exudación; sudante.

sweating room, sudadero, cuarto de sudar.

sweating sickness, (hist.) fiebre epidémica que asoló Inglaterra en los siglos XV y XVI.

sweating system, sistema opresivo de explotación que obliga a trabajar en pésimas condiciones por sueldo mínimo.

sweat pants, (dep.) pantalones de entrenamiento.

sweat shirt, (dep.) camisa de entrenamiento, sudadera, camiseta gruesa.

sweatshop [-ˌʃɑp, B -ʃɔp] *s.* fábrica donde se explota a los obreros.

sweaty [-ɪ] *a.* (SWEATIER; SWEATIEST) sudoroso, sudoso, sudado.

Swede [swid] *s.* 1. sueco, sueca. 2. **s.,** (bot.) rutabaga, nabo de Suecia, col de Laponia.

Sweden [ˈswidən] *s.* Suecia.

Swedish [-dɪʃ] *a.* sueco. —*s.* 1. **the S.,** el pueblo sueco, los suecos. 2. sueco (idioma).

Swedish turnip, (bot.) rutabaga, nabo de Suecia, col de Laponia.

sweeny [ˈswinɪ] *s.* atrofia muscular de los caballos (esp. en la espalda).

sweep [swip] *v.t.* (*pret., p.p.* SWEPT [swɛpt]; *p.pr.* SWEEPING) 1. barrer, escobar, deshollinar. 2. despejar, limpiar. 3. (gen. con *up*) barrer; recoger, recolectar (de un solo golpe). 4. (gen. con *along, away, down* u *off*) llevar, llevarse, arrebatar. 5. arrasar con, barrer con. 6. cubrir, abarcar; recorrer, pasar sobre; pasar la vista por, escudriñar. 7. **s. a constituency,** llevarse la mayoría de los votos; **s. off one's feet,** (fig.) arrebatar a uno (de amor, pasión, emoción, etc.); hacer perder la cabeza; **s. the board,** barrer con todos los premios; **s. the bottom,** (mar.) dragar; **s. the seas,** ser dueño de los mares, dominar sobre el mar. —*v.i.* 1. barrer, hacer barridos. 2. pasar rápidamente, precipitarse. 3. (gen. con *along, from, out of,* etc.) caminar o moverse majestuosamente. 4. (t. con *away, off,* etc.) extenderse, dilatarse. —*s.* 1. barrido, barredura, escobada, despejo. 2. recorrido, vuelo, vuelta. 3. envergadura, alcance, extensión. 4. curva, corvadura (de un camino, río, etc.); desviación vertical de laminación; curvadura transversal (de carriles, vigas laminadas). 5. (*pl.*) barreduras; basura. 6. barrendero; deshollinador. 7. cigoñal (de pozos someros); guimbalete (de bomba); brazo (de molino de viento). 8. carrera de caballos en que una sola persona es el ganador del monto de las apuestas. 9. (naipes) recogida de todas las cartas que están en la mesa (en el juego de casino); ganancia de todas las bases en una mano (en whist). 10. (mar.) remo de espadilla, remo largo para gobernar (barcazas). 11. **to make a clean s. of,** limpiar por completo de; hacer mesa gallega de, ganar o conquistar todos los (premios, etc.).

sweepback [ˈswipˌbæk] *s.* (aer.) flecha (ángulo de inclinación de las alas).

sweeper [-ər, B -ə] *s.* 1. barrendero, barredor. 2. escoba mecánica, barredora.

sweep hand, secundario concéntrico (de reloj).

sweeping [-ɪŋ] *s.* 1. barrido. 2. (*pl.*) barreduras; basura. —*a.* 1. barredor, arrollador. 2. extenso, vasto; completo. 3. comprensivo, general, generalizado.

sweepingly [-lɪ] *adv.* 1. extensamente; completamente. 2. de modo generalizador, sin discriminar.

sweepingness [-nəs] *s.* 1. amplitud; vastedad. 2. tendencia o carácter generalizador.

sweep net, 1. jábega. 2. red para atrapar insectos (usada por los entomólogos).

sweep seine, jábega.

sweepstake [ˈswipˌsteɪk] *var. de* **sweepstakes.**

sweepstakes [-ˌsteɪks] *s. pl.* (*sing. o pl. en const.*) monto total de apuestas en una carrera de caballos que se entrega al ganador; carrera en que una sola persona es el ganador del monto total de apuestas.

sweepy [-ɪ] *a.* (SWEEPIER; SWEEPIEST) (poét.) arrebatador, arrollador.

sweet [swit] *a.* 1. dulce. 2. (fig.) dulce, grato, agradable; placentero. 3. bonito, lindo, encantador. 4. querido, bienamado. 5. fragante, delicioso (olor). 6. suave, melodioso (voz). 7. romántico, sentimental, dulzón (música, canción, etc.). 8. generoso, fértil (tierra). 9. (fam.) de funcionamiento suave, silencioso (motor, máquina). 10. **at one's own s. will,** según le da la gana a uno; arbitrariamente; **s. one,** querido; **to be s. on,** (fam.) estar enamorado (de); **to have a s. tooth,** ser goloso o dulcero. —*adv.* dulcemente, agradablemente, amablemente. —*s.* 1. (*gen. pl.*) dulces, golosinas. 2. (G.B.) bombón 3. (G.B.) postre. 4. (*gen. pl.*) deleites, placeres. 5. amor, querido, persona querida. 6. (ant.) dulzura; fragancia.

sweet alyssum, (bot.) alhelicillo.

sweet-and-sour [ˈswitənˈsaʊər, B -ə] *a.* agridulce, sazonado con azúcar y vinagre o limón.

sweet apple, anona, chirimoya.

sweet balm, (bot.) melisa, toronjil, toronjina, abejera.

sweet basil, (bot.) albahaca, alábega, alfábega.

sweet bay, (bot.) 1. laurel. 2. (variedad de) magnolia americana.

sweetbread [ˈswitˌbrɛd] *s.* lechecillas, mollejas.

sweetbrier, sweetbriar [-ˌbraɪr, B -ə] *s.* (bot.) eglantina; escaramujo cloroso.

sweet cherry, (bot.) ciruelo dulce.

sweet cicely, (bot.) perifollo cloroso.

sweet clover, (bot.) trébol cloroso, trébol de olor, meliloto.

sweet corn, (bot.) maíz dulce, maíz azucarado amarillo.

sweeten [-ən] *v.t.* 1. endulzar, dulcificar, dulzonar. 2. (fig.) endulzar, dulcificar, almibarar, suavizar. 3. (com.) ofrecer más garantías para (un préstamo). 4. (jer., póker) aumentar (la apuesta), poner más fichas en (el pozo). —*v.i.* endulzarse.

sweetener [-ər, B -ə] *s.* 1. (substancia) dulcificante. 2. consuelo.

sweetening [-ɪŋ] *s.* 1. dulcificación, endulzadura. 2. (substancia) dulcificante.

sweet fern, (bot.) polipodio, helecho macho.

sweet flag, (bot.) ácoro.

sweet flag root, cálamo aromático, cálanis.

sweet gum, (bot.) liquidámbar, ocozol.

sweetheart [ˈswitˌhɑrt, B -hɑt] *s.* enamorado, enamorada, amante, galán; (*en vocativo*) amor, querido, querida.

sweetie [-ɪ] *s.* (fam.) 1. (*pl.*) (G.B.) dulces. 2. amor, querido, querida.

sweetie pie, (fam.) amor, querido, querida.

sweeting [-ɪŋ] *s.* camuesa.

sweeting apple tree, (bot.) camueso.

sweetish [-ɪʃ] *a.* algo dulce; dulzarrón.

sweetly [-lɪ] *adv.* dulcemente, con dulzura, con suavidad.

sweet marjoram, (bot.) mejorana, amáraco.

sweetmeat [-ˌmit] *s.* confitura, fruta garapiñada, confite, dulce.

sweet myrtle, (bot.) mirto oloroso.

sweetness [ˈswitnəs] *s.* dulzura; dulcedumbre, suavidad, apacibilidad.

sweet oil, (cocina) aceite comestible; aceite de oliva.

sweet pea, (bot.) guisante de olor, haba de las Indias, arvejilla (Amer.).

sweet pepper, (bot.) pimiento dulce, pimiento morrón.

sweet potato, (bot.) batata, camote, boniato, buniato, moniato.

sweetroot [-ˌrut] *s.* (bot.) regaliz, arozuz.

sweet rush, 1. (bot.) ácoro. 2. esquenanto.

sweet scabious, (bot.) viuda.

sweet-scented [-ˌsɛntəd] *a.* perfumado.

sweet seventeen, la dulce edad de diecisiete años (díc. en referencia a la belleza juvenil femenina).

sweetshop [-ˌʃɑp, B -ʃɔp] *s.* dulcería, confitería, tienda de dulces.

sweet sixteen, los dieciséis abriles (díc. en referencia a la belleza juvenil femenina).

sweet-smelling [-ˌsmɛlɪŋ] *a.* odorífero.

sweetsop [-ˌsɑp, B -sɔp] *s.* 1. (bot.) anona, anón, chirimoyo. 2. chirimoya.

sweet sorghum, (bot.) sorgo azucarado.
sweet-spoken [-ˌspoʊkən] *a.* melifluo.
sweet-talk ['switˌtɔk] *v.t.* (fam.) engatusar, acariciar, halagar, lisonjear. —*v.i.* usar de lisonjas.
sweet-tempered [-ˌtɛmpərd, B -pəd] *a.* de carácter suave, complaciente.
sweet tooth, gusto por los dulces.
sweet-toothed [-ˌtuθt, -ˌtuðd] *a.* goloso, laminero.
sweet william, (bot.) minutisa, manutisa, clavel del Japón, ramillete de Constantinopla.
swell [swɛl] *v.i.* (*pret.* SWELLED; *p.p.* SWELLED o SWOLLEN ['swoʊlən]; *p.pr.* SWELLING) 1. hincharse; entumecerse, engrosarse, dilatarse, expandirse. 2. (fig.) hincharse, engreírse, ensoberbecerse, ej., *s. with pride,* hincharse de orgullo. 3. (gen. con *up*) abultarse; sobresalir. 4. intensificarse, crecer, cobrar fuerza (voz, ruido), amontonarse, aumentar(se) (gastos, etc.). —*v.t.* 1. hinchar, inflar; abultar, engrosar; dilatar, expandir. 2. (fig.) inflar, engreír, llenar (de orgullo, etc.). 3. intensificar, acrecentar, aumentar. 4. (mús.) aumentar gradualmente (el sonido). —*s.* 1. hinchazón, chichón, bulto, protuberancia, prominencia. 2. oleada, marejada; mar tendida. 3. ondulación (del terreno). 4. intensificación, crecimiento. 5. (fam.) petimetre, currutaco; pájaro gordo, hombre influyente, personaje (en la sociedad). 6. (mús.) unión de crescendo y diminuendo; regulador, registro de sonoridad (en el órgano). —*a.* 1. (fam.) elegante, a la moda, de buen tono; distinguido. 2. (jer.) de primera, excelente, magnífico, regio, de órdago.
swell box, (mús.) caja de expresión (de un órgano).
swell-butted ['swɛl'bʌtəd] *a.* muy grande en la base (díc. de un árbol).
swell chick, s. doll, (jer.) real moza.
swelled head, presunción, humos, ínfulas; **to get** (o **have**) **a s. h.,** tener muchos humos, darse ínfulas, estar muy pagado de sí mismo.
swellfish ['swɛlˌfɪʃ] *s.* (ict.) pez globo.
swellhead [-ˌhɛd] *s.* presumido, presumida.
swellheaded [-əd] *a.* hinchado, presumido, soberbio, arrogante.
swellheadedness [-nəs] *s.* presunción, soberbia, arrogancia.
swelling ['swɛlɪŋ] *s.* 1. hinchazón, hinchamiento, inflación. 2. chichón, protuberancia, bulto. 3. (med., vet.) tumefacción, entumescencia, turgencia, abotagamiento. —*a.* 1. hinchado, inflado. 2. turgente. 3. exaltado (emoción, etc.). 4. ampuloso, rimbombante (discurso, etc.).
swelling sea, mar agitado.
swell pedal, (mús.) rodillera (de un órgano).
swelter ['swɛltər, B -tə] *v.i.* sofocarse de calor, abochornarse, sudar la gota gorda. —*v.t.* 1. abochornar, sofocar o abrumar de calor. 2. (ant.) exudar, rezumar. —*s.* 1. bochorno, calor sofocante. 2. (fig.) confusión, excitación; **in a s.,** aturdido, excitado.
sweltering [-tərɪŋ] *a.* bochornoso, sudoroso, sofocante.
swept [swɛpt] *pret., p.p. de* **sweep.**
swept-back ['swɛpt'bæk] *a.* en flecha, de forma aerodinámica.
swerve [swɜrv, B swɜv] *v.i.* desviarse, torcerse, virar bruscamente, hacerse a un lado. —*v.t.* desviar. —*s.* desviación, viraje brusco.
SWG *abrev. de* **standard wire gauge,** calibre patrón de alambre.
swift [swɪft] *a.* 1. rápido, veloz, ligero, raudo. 2. repentino, súbito. 3. vivo, listo, pronto, presto. —*adv.* (poét.) rápidamente. —*s.* 1. (mec.) tambor de carda; devanadera. 2. (orn.) vencejo, arrejaque, avión. 3. (zool.) variedad de lagartija.
swifter ['swɪftər, B -tə] *s.* (mar.) 1. guirnalda. 2. andarivel de cabrestante. —*v.t.* (mar.) tesar (las jarcias).
swift-footed ['swɪft'fʊtəd] *a.* de paso ligero, alípedo.
swiftly [-lɪ] *adv.* 1. rápidamente, velozmente. 2. repentinamente.
swiftness [-nəs] *s.* 1. rapidez, velocidad, ligereza. 2. prontitud.
swig [swɪg] *s.* (fam.) tragantada. —*v.t., v.i.* (*pret., p.p.* SWIGGED; *p.pr.* SWIGGING) (fam.) beber a tragantadas; tragar.
swigger ['swɪgər, B -ə] *s.* tragón (esp. de licor).
swill [swɪl] *v.t., v.i.* 1. lavar (con abundante agua), enjuagar, empapar. 2. beber a grandes tragos. —*s.* 1. bazofia. 2. inmundicia, basura. 3. trago de licor.
swim [swɪm] *v.i.* (*pret.,* SWAM [swæm]; *p.p.* SWUM [swʌm]; *p.pr.* SWIMMING) 1. nadar. 2. flotar, sobrenadar, boyar. 3. resbalar o deslizarse suavemente. 4. hacerse borroso (delante de los ojos). 5. dar vueltas (la cabeza). 6. **s. across,** atravesar a nado; **s. in** (o **with**), estar inundado o sumergido, nadar en; **s. with the tide,** (fig.) seguir la corriente, ir con la corriente. —*v.t.* 1. pasar o cruzar a nado; cubrir (distancia) a nado. 2. hacer nadar (ej., caballo); hacer flotar. —*s.* 1. natación. 2. (fig.) corriente de la moda, influencia o simpatía popular. 3. vértigo, vahído, desvanecimiento. 4. (ict.) vejiga natatoria. 5. **to be in the s.,** estar al corriente; estar al día; **to go for a s., to take a s.,** ir a nadar, meterse al agua.
swim bladder, (ict.) vejiga natatoria.
swim fin, aleta de caucho (en el pie para bucear sin escafandra).
swimmable ['swɪməbəl] *a.* que se puede atravesar a nado.
swimmer [-ər, B -ə] *s.* nadador, nadadora.
swimmeret, swimmerette [ˌswɪmə'rɛt, B 'swɪmərɛt] *s.* (zool.) pleópodo.
swimmer's itch, (med.) urticaria marítima.
swimming ['swɪmɪŋ] *s.* 1. natación. 2. vértigo, vahído, desvanecimiento. —*a.* 1. nadador, natatorio, nadante. 2. de natación. 3. lleno de lágrimas (ojos).
swimming bath, (G.B.) piscina (natatoria), pileta (Amer.).
swimming bell, (zool.) nectóforo, órgano natatorio.
swimming crab, (zool.) cangrejo nadador.
swimmingly [-lɪ] *adv.* espléndidamente, como una seda.
swimming pool, piscina, alberca, pileta.
swimming trunks, traje de baño, pantalon de baño, bañador (Esp.).
swimmy ['swɪmɪ] *a.* 1. mareado. 2. borrosa (visión, vista).
swimsuit ['swɪmˌsut, B -sjut] *s.* traje de baño.
swindle ['swɪndəl] *v.i.* trampear, petardear; usar de engaños. —*v.t.* petardear, estafar, timar, trampear, engañar. —*s.* estafa, timo, petardo, trampa, engaño.
swindler [-dlər, B -dlə] *s.* estafador, timador, petardista, trampeador.
swindle sheet, (jer.) cuenta de gastos.
swindling [-dlɪŋ] *s.* estafa, timo, petardo, trampa, engaño.
swine [swaɪn] *s.* (*pl.* SWINE) 1. marrano, puerco, cerdo, cochino, chancho (Amer.). 2. (fig.) puerco, marrano, canalla.
swineherd ['swaɪnˌhɜrd, B -hɜd] *s.* porquerizo, porquero.
swine's-snout ['swaɪnzˌsnaʊt] *s.* (bot.) diente de león.
swing [swɪŋ] *v.t.* (*pret., p.p.* SWUNG [swʌŋ]; *p.pr.* SWINGING) 1. columpiar, mecer, cunear, balancear; hacer oscilar. 2. colgar, suspender (por un extremo); tender, ej., *s. a hammock,* tender una hamaca. 3. blandir, florear, menear (espada, garrote, palo, etc.). 4. hacer girar, hacer dar media vuelta (sobre un pivote). 5. (E.U.) manejar con éxito, llevar a cabo, lograr. 6. (mús.) tocar o dirigir (música) en tiempo (sincopado) de swing. 7. **s. the lead,** (jer., G.B.) evadirse de ejercicios (militares); evitar trabajar, holgazanear. —*v.i.* 1. colgar, pender. 2. oscilar, balancearse, columpiarse, mecerse. 3. ser ahorcado. 4. girar, dar medias vueltas, virar. 5. (con *along, past, by,* etc.) marchar o caminar airosamente, andar con movimientos briosos. 6. (mús.) tocar o ejecutar en movimiento de swing. 7. (jer.) estar al día en modas; dedicarse a placeres mundanos. 8. **s. at,** dirigir un golpe a, tratar de golpear; **s. clear,** hacer un viraje para evitar un choque; **s. open,** abrirse (de par en par); **s. to,** cerrarse (puerta). —*s.* 1. oscilación, vaivén, balanceo, balance. 2. arco de oscilación. 3. impulso, ímpetu, brío. 4. libertad de acción, libre curso; marcha. 5. vuelta, turno, período. 6. swing, golpe lateral (en boxeo). 7. columpio, péndulo. 8. (mús.) swing, música sincopada de baile. 9. (poét., mús.) ritmo o compás uniformes. 10. **at full s.,** a toda velocidad; **in full s.,** en plena marcha. —*a.* giratorio, engoznado.
swing bolt, perno de charnela.
swing bridge, puente giratorio.
swing door, puerta giratoria.
swinge [swɪndʒ] *v.t.* (pr. dial.) aporrear, vapulear.
swinge, (dial.) *var. de.* **singe.**
swingeing ['swɪndʒɪŋ] (pr. G.B.) *a.* enorme, ingente, colosal; magnífico, estupendo, de primera. —*adv.* sumamente, extremadamente.
swinger ['swɪŋər, B -ə] *s.* 1. oscilador, mecedor. 2. (jer.) persona de mucho mundo, moderna y recorrida, sin inhibiciones en cuanto a placeres mundanos.
swinging [-ɪŋ] *s.* oscilación, balanceo. —*a.* 1. oscilante, mecedor. 2. (jer.) (persona) de mundo, sin inhibiciones; ultramoderno.
swinging door, puerta giratoria.
swingingly [-lɪ] *adv.* con movimientos briosos.
swing joint, unión giratoria (de tubos).
swing lamp, lámpara colgante.
swingle ['swɪŋgəl] *v.t.* espadar, espadillar.
swingletree [-ˌtri] *s.* balancín, volea (de los carruajes).
swing music, música popular rítmica.
swing saw, sierra colgante, sierra de columpio, sierra de péndulo.
swing shift, turno de tarde (de obreros).
swingy ['swɪŋɪ] *a.* (SWINGIER; SWINGIEST) brioso, vivaz.
swinish ['swaɪnɪʃ] *s.* porcuno, porcino; cochino, bestial.
swinishly [-lɪ] *adv.* cochinamente, bestialmente.
swinishness [-nəs] *s.* bestialidad, vileza, marranada.
swipe [swaɪp] *s.* 1. bofetada, manotazo o manotada fuertes. 2. (mec.) palanca de bomba, palanca de arranque, palanca de disparo. —*v.t.* 1. manotear, abofetear. 2. (jer.) hurtar, birlar, ratear.
swipes [swaɪps] *s.* (G.B.) cerveza mala.
swiple, swipple ['swɪpəl] *s.* brazo corto del mayal.
swirl [swɜrl, B swɜl] *v.i.* remolinar, hacer remolinos o torbellinos. —*v.t.* remolinear. —*s.* remolino, torbellino.
swirling ['swɜrlɪŋ, B 'swɜlɪŋ] *a.* turbulento, revuelto.

swish [swɪʃ] *v.t., v.i.* golpear o azotar produciendo silbido; silbar al cortar el aire (bastón, látigo, azote, etc.). —*s.* silbido (del látigo o bastón); ruido silbante; crujido (de la seda).
swish, *a.* 1. (de moda) elegante. 2. (jer.) propio de homosexuales afeminados.
swishy ['swɪʃɪ] *a.* (SWISHIER; SWISHIEST) 1. silbante (ruido de un latigazo, etc.). 2. crujidero, crujiente (telas de seda al frotarse). 3. (jer.) propio de homosexuales afeminados.
Swiss [swɪs] *a.* suizo. —*s.* (*pl.* SWISS) 1. suizo, nativo de Suiza. 2. (tej.) organdí suizo, muselina moteada.
Swiss chard, (bot.) acelga.
Swiss cheese, queso suizo, queso de Emmenthal.
Swiss mountain pine, (bot.) pino negro.
Swiss roll, (cocina) enrollado.
Swiss steak, biftec machacado cocido lentamente en salsa de tomate, cebolla y otros condimentos.
switch [swɪtʃ] *s.* 1. fusta, latiguillo, varilla flexible, bastoncillo. 2. punta de la cola (del buey, caballo, etc.). 3. añadido, postizo, trenza postiza. 4. latigazo, varillazo. 5. cambio, substitución, transferencia. 6. (elec.) interruptor, conmutador, toma de corriente; seccionador. 7. (f.c.) agujas, cambio de vía, cambio. 8. (bridge) cambio de palo (durante las declaraciones). —*v.t.* 1. varear, azotar, dar latigazos a, fustigar. 2. blandir (látigo, vara, etc.). 3. cambiar. 4. (f.c.) desviar. 5. (elec.) conmutar; interrumpir, desconectar; conectar. 6. (bridge) cambiar de (palo). 7. **s. off,** desconectar, cortar (la corriente); apagar (las luces); **s. on,** conectar (la corriente); encender (las luces). —*v.i.* 1. desviarse, apartarse, cambiarse. 2. hacer un cambio. 3. (bridge) cambiar de palo.
switchback ['swɪtʃ,bæk] *s.* 1. (f.c.) vía en zigzag, pendiente de vaivén. 2. (G.B.) montaña rusa.
switchblade knife [-,bleɪd-] navaja de resorte, cuchillo de resorte.
switchboard [-,bɔrd, B -bɔd] *s.* 1. (elec.) tablero de distribución, cuadro de distribución. 2. (teleg.) cuadro de conmutadores. 3. (tele.) cuadro de conexión manual.
switched outlet [swɪtʃt-] (elec.) tomacorriente con interruptor.
switcher ['swɪtʃər, B -ə] *s.* 1. (elec.) interruptor. 2. (f.c.) locomotora para servício de línea, locomotora de maniobras. 3. (f.c.) guardagujas.
switcheroo [,swɪtʃə'ru] *s.* (jer., E.U.) cambio inesperado.
switchgear ['swɪtʃ,gɪr, B -gɪə] *s.* (elec., mec.) mecanismo de control, dispositivos de distribución.
switch-hitter [-'hɪtər, B -ə] *s.* (béisbol) bateador ambidextro.
switching engine, (f.c.) locomotora de maniobras.
switching yard, (f.c.) patio de maniobras, playa de distribución (Amer.).
switch knife, navaja de resorte, cuchillo de resorte.
switch lever, 1. (elec.) palanca del interruptor. 2. (f.c.) palanca de maniobras de agujas.
switch line, (mil.) sistema de trincheras de comunicación.
switchman ['swɪtʃmən] *s.* (f.c.) guardagujas, cambiador.
switch plate, (elec.) placa de interruptor, chapa de pared.
switch rail, (f.c.) carril de cambio, carril de aguja.
switch signal, (f.c.) señal de cambio.
switch stand, (f.c.) plataforma de maniobra (de las agujas).
switch tie, (f.c.) traviesa de cambio, durmiente de aguja (Amer.).
switch tower, (f.c.) torre de maniobra de cambios.
switchyard ['swɪtʃ,jɑrd, B -jɑd] *s.* (f.c.) patio de maniobras, playa de distribución (Amer.).
swith [swɪθ] *adv.* (dial.) instantáneamente, en el acto.
Switzer ['swɪtsər, B -sə] *s.* suizo, suiza.
Switzerland [-lənd] *s.* Suiza.
swivel ['swɪvəl] *s.* eslabón giratorio; placa giratoria; alacrán; eje (*pivoto*). —*v.t., v.i.* (*pret., p.p.* SWIVELED o SWIVELLED; *p.pr.* SWIVELING o SWIVELLING) (hacer) girar (sobre un eje).
swivel block, (mar.) motón giratorio.
swivel chair, silla giratoria.
swivel gun, colisa.
swivel vise, morsa giratoria, tornillo giratorio.
swivet ['swɪvət] *s.* (fam.) arrebato, agitación extrema, éxtasis, irritación.
swizzle ['swɪzəl] *s.* cóctel de ron o cualquier otro licor con hielo picado, azúcar y amargo de angostura.
swizzle stick, palillo para remover cocteles.
swob, *var. de* **swab.**
swollen ['swoʊlən] *p.p. de* **swell.**
swoon [swun] *v.i.* desmayarse, desvanecerse, desfallecer. —*s.* desmayo, desvanecimiento, deliquio, desfallecimiento.
swoop [swup] *v.i.* bajar en picada; arremeter; **s. (down) upon,** abalanzarse, abatirse o calarse sobre. —*v.t.* agarrar, arrebatar, llevarse. —*s.* calada, descenso rápido; arremetida; **at one fell s.,** de un solo golpe muy fuerte.
swoosh [swuʃ] *v.i.* hacer ruido silbante; pasar como una exhalación (automóvil, tren, etc.); salir en chorros.
swop, *var. de* **swap.**
sword [sɔrd, B sɔd] *s.* espada; **by fire and s.,** a sangre y fuego; **the s.,** (fig.) la guerra; el poder militar; **to be at swords' point,** estar a matarse, estar como perros y gatos; **to cross** (o **to measure**) **swords,** cruzar espadas; **to draw the s.,** desenvainar la espada; **to fight with swords,** batirse a espada; **to put to the s.,** pasar a cuchillo; **to throw one's s. into the scale,** respaldar una pretensión con la fuerza; **with a s. at one's throat,** con la soga al cuello.
sword bean, (bot.) canavalia.
sword-bearer ['sɔrd,bɛrər, B 'sɔd,bɛərə] *s.* (hist.) portador del estoque real.
sword belt, cinturón, talabarte, biricú.
swordbill [-,bɪl] *s.* (orn.) colibrí de pico largo.
sword cane, bastón de estoque.
sword dance, danza de las espadas.
sword fern, (bot.) helecho de frondos ensiformes.
swordfish [-,fɪʃ] *s.* 1. (ict.) pez espada, jifia, alfanje. 2. **the S.,** (astr.) Pez Espada, Pez Dorado, Dorado.
sword grass, (bot.) espadaña.
sword hilt, empuñadura, mango, puño.
sword knot, 1. borla de espada. 2. (hist.) tira de cuero del puño de la espada (para sujetarla a la muñeca).
sword law, dominación militar.
sword lily, (bot.) estoque.
Sword of Damocles [-'dæmə,kliz] espada de Damocles (peligro inminente).
swordplay [-,pleɪ] *s.* 1. esgrima. 2. (fig.) intercambio de réplicas agudas.
sword-shaped [-,ʃeɪpt] *a.* ensiforme.
swordsman ['sɔrdzmən, B 'sɔdz-] *s.* 1. esgrimidor, esgrimista, espada. 2. (ant.) soldado.
swordsmanship [-,ʃɪp] *s.* arte de espadachín.
sword stick, bastón de estoque.
sword-swallower ['sɔrd,swɑloʊər, B 'sɔd,swɔloʊə] *s.* tragasables.
swore [swɔr, B swɔ] *pret. de* **swear.**
sworn [swɔrn, B swɔn] *p.p. de* **swear.**
sworn enemy, enemigo jurado, enemigo implacable.
sworn evidence, testimonio dado bajo juramento.
sworn friends, amigos íntimos.
swot [swɑt, B swɔt] *v.t.* (*pret., p.p.* SWOTTED; *p.pr.* SWOTTING) (fam., G.B.) empollar, estudiar con ahínco. —*s.* empollón.
swum [swʌm] *p.p. de* **swim.**
swung [swʌŋ] *pret., p.p. de* **swing.**
Sybaris ['sɪbərəs] *s.* Síbaris, Sibari, antigua ciudad de Grecia.
Sybarite ['sɪbə,raɪt] *s.* sibarita, de Síbaris; (fig.) sibarita, persona que gusta de los placeres mundanos.
Sybaritic [,sɪbə'rɪtɪk] *a.* sibarítico, sibarita.
sybaritically [-ɪkəlɪ] *adv.* sibaríticamente.
Sybaritism ['sɪbə,raɪ,tɪzəm] *s.* sibaritismo, afición a los placeres mundanos.
sycamine ['sɪkə,maɪn, -mən] *s.* (bíbl.) morera, negra, moral.
sycamore ['sɪkə,mɔr, B -mɔ] *s.* (bot.) sicomoro, sicómoro; plátano falso; (E.U.) plátano.
sycamore fig, (bot.) higuera loca, higuera moral, higuera silvestre.
syce [saɪs] *s.* mozo, lacayo, camarero (en la India).
sycee ['saɪ,si, B saɪ'si] *s.* (hist.) lingotes de plata sellados que se usaban como medio de intercambio en la China.
sycon ['saɪkɑn, B -kɔn] *s.* (zool.) sicón.
syconium [saɪ'koʊnɪəm] *s.* (*pl.* SYCONIA [-ə]) (bot.) siconio, sicono.
sycophancy ['sɪkəfənsɪ] *s.* adulación, servilismo.
sycophant [-fənt] *s.* adulador, servil, parásito.
sycophantic [,sɪkə'fæntɪk] *a.* adulatorio, lisonjero.
sycophantish [-ɪʃ] *var. de* **sycophantic.**
sycosis [saɪ'koʊsəs] *s.* (med.) sicosis, impétigo piloso.
syenite ['saɪə,naɪt] *s.* (min.) sienita.
syenitic [,saɪə'nɪtɪk] *a.* (min.) sienítico.
syenodiorite ['saɪənoʊ'daɪə,raɪt] *s.* (geol.) sienodiorita.
syllabarium [,sɪlə'bɛrɪəm, B -'bɛər-] *s.* (*pl.* SYLLABARIA [-ə]) silabario.
syllabary ['sɪlə,bɛrɪ, B -bərɪ] *s.* (*pl.* SYLLABARIES) silabario.
syllabic [sə'læbɪk] *a.* silábico. —*s.* signo o sonido silábicos.
syllabically [-ɪkəlɪ] *adv.* por sílabas.
syllabication [sə,læbə'keɪʃən] **syllabification** [sɪ,læbəfə'keɪʃən] *s.* silabeo.
syllabify [sə'læbə,faɪ] *v.t.* (*pret., p.p.* SYLLABIFIED; *p.pr.* SYLLABIFYING) silabear.
syllabism ['sɪlə,bɪzəm] *s.* silabismo.
syllable [-bəl] *s.* sílaba; **not a s.!** ¡ni una palabra! —*v.t., v.i.* 1. silabar, silabear, articular. 2. (poét.) pronunciar.
syllabub ['sɪlə,bʌb] *s.* bebida hecha con leche, vino y azúcar.
syllabus ['sɪləbəs] *s.* (*pl.* SYLLABUSES o SYLLABI [-,baɪ]) 1. programa de estudios. 2. extracto (de un discurso, tratado, etc.). 3. (der.) compendio, resumen, sumario del dictamen. 4. (relig.) sílabo.
syllepsis [sə'lɛpsəs] *s.* (*pl.* SYLLEPSES [-,siz]) (gram.) silepsis.
syllogism ['sɪlə,dʒɪzəm] *s.* silogismo.
syllogist [-dʒəst] *s.* experto en razonamiento silogístico; silogizante.
syllogistic [,sɪlə'dʒɪstɪk] **syllogistical** [-tɪkəl] *a.* silogístico.
syllogistically [-tɪkəlɪ] *adv.* silogísticamente.

syllogize ['sɪlə,dʒaɪz] *v.i.* silogizar. —*v.t.* deducir por silogismos.
sylph [sɪlf] *s.* 1. silfo. 2. (fig.) sílfide (mujer delgada y graciosa).
sylphid ['sɪlfəd] *s.* (mitol.) sílfide pequeña.
sylva, *var. de* silva.
sylvan ['sɪlvən] *a.* 1. selvático, silvático, silvestre. 2. boscoso, arbolado. —*s.* habitante del bosque; rústico.
sylvanite ['sɪlvə,naɪt] *s.* (min.) silvanita.
sylvatic [sɪl'vætɪk] *a.* silvático, selvático.
sylviculture, *var. de* **silviculture.**
sylvite ['sɪl,vaɪt] **sylvine** ['sɪlvɪn] *s.* (min.) silvita.
symbiont ['sɪm,baɪ,ɑnt, -bɪ-, B -ɔnt] *s.* (biol.) simbión, simbiota, simbionte.
symbiosis [,sɪm,baɪ'oʊsəs, -bɪ-, B -bɪ-] *s.* (biol.) simbiosis.
symbiotic [-'ɑtɪk, B -'ɔt-] *a.* simbiótico.
symbol ['sɪmbəl] *s.* símbolo. —*v.i., v.t.* (*pret., p.p.* SYMBOLED O SYMBOLLED; *p.pr.* SYMBOLING O SYMBOLLING) simbolizar.
symbolic [sɪm'bɑlɪk, B -'bɔl-] **simbolical** [-ɪkəl] *a.* simbólico.
symbolically [-ɪkəlɪ] *adv.* simbólicamente.
symbolic logic, lógica simbólica.
symbolism ['sɪmbə,lɪzəm] *s.* simbolismo.
symbolist [-ləst] *s.* simbolista.
symbolistic [,sɪmbə'lɪstɪk] *a.* 1. de los simbolistas. 2. simbólico.
symbolization [,sɪmbələ'zeɪʃən, B -laɪ-] *s.* simbolización.
symbolize ['sɪmbə,laɪz] *v.i.* usar símbolos. —*v.t.* simbolizar.
symbology [sɪm'bɑlədʒɪ, B -'bɔl-] *s.* simbología.
symmetalism ['sɪm'mɛtə,lɪzəm] *s.* (e.p.) sistema de acuñación basado en una unidad monetaria hecha de dos o más metales.
symmetrical [sɪ'mɛtrɪkəl] **symmetric** [-trɪk] *a.* simétrico.
symmetrically [-kəlɪ] *adv.* simétricamente.
symmetricalness [-kəlnəs] *s.* proporciones simétricas, aspecto simétrico.
symmetrize ['sɪmə,traɪz] *v.t.* simetrizar.
symmetry ['sɪmətrɪ] *s.* simetría.
sympathectomy [,sɪmpə'θɛktəmɪ] *s.* (med.) simpatectomía.
sympathetic [,sɪmpə'θɛtɪk] *a.* 1. compasivo, ej., *a s. soul,* un alma compasiva. 2. (anat., fisiol., fís., mús.) simpático. 3. **s. to** (o **toward**), favorablemente dispuesto a (o hacia), simpatizante (con).
sympathetically [-ɪkəlɪ] *adv.* 1. compasivamente. 2. con simpatía, con agrado, con complacencia.
sympathetic ink, tinta invisible.
sympathetic nervous system, (anat.) sistema nervioso simpático, sistema nervioso del gran simpático, gran simpático.
sympathetic sound, resonancia, vibración.
sympathetic strike, huelga de apoyo moral.
sympathetic vibration, vibración simpática.
sympathin ['sɪmpəθən] *s.* (bioquím.) simpatina.
sympathize ['sɪmpə,θaɪz] *v.i.* 1. simpatizar. 2. armonizar, convenir, congeniar. 3. condolerse, compadecerse, expresar simpatía. 4. **s. with,** compadecer a, compadecerse de.
sympathizer [-ər, B -ə] *s.* 1. simpatizante; partidario, aficionado. 2. condoliente.
sympatholytic [,sɪmpəθoʊ'lɪtɪk] *a.* (farm.) simpaticolítico.
sympathomimetic [-mɪ'mɛtɪk] *a.* (farm.) simpatomimético, simpaticomimético.
sympathy ['sɪmpəθɪ] *s.* 1. compasión, conmiseración, lástima. 2. armonía, compatibilidad. 3. condolencia, pésame, ej., *I offer you my sympathies,* le presento mis condolencias. 4. simpatía, interés, afinidad. 5. (med.) simpatía. 6. **to be in s. with,** simpatizar con; estar en armonía con; **to have s. for,** mirar con compasión (a alguien); simpatizar con (causa, idea, etc.).
sympathy strike, huelga de apoyo moral.
sympatric [sɪm'pætrɪk] *a.* (ecol.) simpátrico.
sympetalous [sɪm'pɛtələs] *a.* (bot.) simpétalo.
symphonic [sɪm'fɑnɪk, B -'fɔn-] *a.* sinfónico.
symphonic poem, (mús.) poema sinfónico.
symphonious [sɪm'foʊnɪəs] *a.* armonioso.
symphoniously [-lɪ] *adv.* armoniosamente.
symphonist ['sɪmfənəst] *s.* sinfonista.
symphony ['sɪmfənɪ] *s.* (*pl.* SYMPHONIES) 1. sinfonía. 2. (ant.) armonía, consonancia.
symphony orchestra, (mús.) orquesta sinfónica.
symphysis ['sɪmfəsəs] *s.* (*pl.* SYMPHYSES [-,siz]) (anat., bot.) sínfisis.
sympodial [sɪm'poʊdɪəl] *a.* (bot.) simpodial, simpódico.
sympodium [-dɪəm] *s.* (*pl.* SYMPODIA [-ə]) (bot.) simpodio.
symposiarch [sɪm'poʊzɪ,ɑrk, B -ɑk] *s.* (hist.) simposiarca.
symposium [-əm] *s.* (*pl.* SYMPOSIA [-ə] O SYMPOSIUMS) 1. simposio, conferencia; discusión. 2. colección, recopilación (de artículos, comentarios, etc.). 3. (hist.) simposio (banquete o fiesta en la antigua Grecia).
symptom ['sɪmptəm] *s.* 1. (med.) síntoma. 2. síntoma, indicio, seña, señal.
symptomatic [,sɪmptə'mætɪk] *a.* 1. (med.) sintomático. 2. sintomático, característico, indicativo.
symptomatically [-ɪkəlɪ] *adv.* sintomáticamente, de modo sintomático, característicamente.
symptomatic anthrax, (vet.) morriña negra.
symptomatology [,sɪmptəmə'tɑlədʒɪ, B -'tɔl-] *s.* sintomatología.
synaeresis, *var. de* **syneresis.**
synaesthesia, *var. de* **synesthesia.**
synagogal [,sɪnɪ'gɑgəl, B -'gɔg-] *a.* de sinagoga (música, canto, rito, etc.); en la sinagoga (adoración).
synagogue, synagog ['sɪnɪ,gɑg, B -gɔg] *s.* sinagoga.
synalepha, *var. de* **synaloepha.**
synallagmatic [,sɪnə,læg'mætɪk] *a.* (der.) sinalagmático.
synaloepha [,sɪnə'lifə] *s.* (gram.) sinalefa.
synapse ['sɪn,æps, sə'næps, B 'saɪnæps] *s.* (fisiol.) sinapsis.
synapsis [sə'næpsəs] *s.* (*pl.* SYNAPSES [-,siz]) (fisiol., biol.) sinapsis.
synaptic [-tɪk] *a.* (fisiol., biol.) sináptico.
synarthrosis [,sɪnɑr'θroʊsəs, B -ɑ'-] *s.* (anat.) sinartrosis.
sync [sɪŋk] *forma abrev. de* **synchronization,** sincronización, **synchronism,** sincronismo y **synchronize,** sincronizar.
syncarp ['sɪnkɑrp, B -kɑp] *s.* (bot.) sincarpo.
syncarpous [sɪn'kɑrpəs, B -'kɑpəs] *a.* (bot.) sincárpico.
synchro-cyclotron [,sɪŋkroʊ'saɪklə,trɑn, B -trɔn] *s.* (fís.) sincrociclotrón.
synchroflash ['sɪŋkroʊ,flæʃ] *a.* (foto.) con flash sincronizado (con el obturador).
synchromesh [-,mɛʃ] (aut.) *a.* sincronizado, de sincronización. —*s.* cambio sincronizado de velocidades, dispositivo de cambio sincronizado.
synchronal ['sɪŋkrənəl] *var. de* **synchronous.**
synchronic [sɪn'krɑnɪk, sɪŋ-, B -'krɔn-] *a.* sincrónico.
synchronism ['sɪŋkrə,nɪzəm] *s.* sincronismo.
synchronization [,sɪŋkrənə'zeɪʃən, B -naɪ-] *s.* sincronización.
synchronize ['sɪŋkrə,naɪz] *v.i.* ser sincrónico, coincidir. —*v.t.* sincronizar.
synchronizer [-ər, B -ə] *s.* sincronizador.
synchronous [-nəs] *a.* sincrónico, sincrono, sincronizado.
synchronous condenser, (elec.) condensador sincrónico, condensador rotatorio.
synchronous converter, (elec.) convertidor rotativo, convertidor sincrónico.
synchronously [-lɪ] *adv.* sincrónicamente, en forma sincrónica o sincronizada.
synchronous motor, motor sincrónico.
synchronousness [-nəs] *s.* sincronismo.
synchronous speed, velocidad de sincronismo.
synchroscope ['sɪŋkrə,skoʊp] *s.* sincronoscopio.
synchrotron [-,trɑn, B -trɔn] *s.* (fís.) sincrotrón.
synclastic [sɪn'klæstɪk] *a.* (mat., fís.) sinclástico.
synclinal [-'klaɪnəl] *a.* (geol.) sinclinal.
syncline ['sɪn,klaɪn] *s.* (geol.) sinclinal, pliegue sinclinal.
syncopal ['sɪŋkəpəl] *a.* (med.) sincopal.
syncopate [-,peɪt] *v.t.* (mús., gram.) sincopar.
syncopated [-əd] *a.* 1. (mús.) sincopado. 2. abreviado.
syncopation [,sɪŋkə'peɪʃən] *s.* (mús., gram.) síncopa.
syncope ['sɪŋkəpɪ] *s.* 1. (med.) síncope. 2. (mús., gram.) síncopa.
syncretic [sɪn'krɛtɪk, B sɪŋ'krit-] **syncretistic** [,sɪŋkrə'tɪstɪk] *a.* sincrético.
syncretism ['sɪŋkrə,tɪzəm] *s.* sincretismo.
syncytial [sɪn'sɪʃəl] *a.* (fisiol.) sincitial.
syncytium [sɪn'sɪʃɪəm, B -'sɪtɪ-] *s.* (*pl.* SYNCYTIA [-ə]) sincitio.
syndactyl, syndactile [sɪn'dæktəl] *a., s.* (zool.) sindáctilo.
syndesis ['sɪndəsəs] *s.* (biol.) síndesis.
syndesmosis [,sɪn,dɛz'moʊsəs] *s.* (*pl.* SYNDESMOSES [-,siz]) (anat.) sindesmosis.
syndetic [sɪn'dɛtɪk] *a.* (gram.) conjuntivo.
syndic ['sɪndɪk] *s.* síndico.
syndical [-dɪkəl] *a.* sindical.
syndicalism [-kə,lɪzəm] *s.* sindicalismo.
syndicalist [-kələst] *a., s.* sindicalista.
syndicalistic [,sɪndɪkə'lɪstɪk] *a.* sindicalista.
syndicate ['sɪndəkət] *s.* 1. sindicato. 2. agencia periodística; agencia distribuidora de material periodístico. — ['sɪndə,keɪt] *v.t.* 1. sindicar (personas de una profesión, etc.). 2. vender (artículos periodísticos, dibujos, etc.) para publicación simultánea. —*v.i.* sindicarse.
syndrome ['sɪn,droʊm] *s.* (med.) síndrome.
syne [saɪn] *adv.* (pr. esco.) hace tiempo.
synecdoche [sə'nɛkdəkɪ] *s.* (ret.) sinécdoque.
synecology [,sɪnɪ'kɑlədʒɪ, B -'kɔl-] *s.* (med.) sinecología.
syneresis [sɪ'nɛrəsəs, B -'nɪər-] *s.* (gram., bioquím.) sinéresis.
synergetic [,sɪnər'dʒɛtɪk, B -ə'-] *a.* sinergético.
synergic [sə'nɜrdʒɪk, B -'nɜdʒɪk] *a.* sinergético.
synergically [-dʒɪkəlɪ] *adv.* sinérgicamente, sinergéticamente.
synergid [sə'nɜrdʒəd, B -'nɜdʒɪd] *s.* (bot.) sinérgida.
synergism ['sɪnər,dʒɪzəm, B -ə,-] *s.* sinergismo.
synergist [-dʒəst] *s.* (teol.) sinergista.
synergy [-dʒɪ] *s.* (med., fisiol.) sinergia, sinergismo.

synesthesia [ˌsɪnəs'θiʒɪə, B -zɪə] *s.* (fisiol.) sinestesia.
syngamic [sɪn'gæmɪk] *a.* (biol.) singámico.
syngamy ['sɪŋgəmɪ] *s.* (biol.) singamia.
syngenesis [sɪn'dʒɛnəsəs] *s.* (biol.) singénesis.
syngenetic [ˌsɪndʒə'nɛtɪk] *a.* (geol.) singenético, singenésico.
synizesis [ˌsɪnə'zisəs] *s.* (biol., gram.) sinícesis, sinizesis.
synkaryon [sɪn'kærɪˌɑn, B -ɔn] *s.* (biol.) sincario, sincarion.
synochal ['sɪnəkəl] *a.* (med.) sinocal, sínoco (díc. de la fiebre).
synochus ['sɪnəkəs] *s.* (med.) fiebre sínoca, fiebre sinocal.
synod ['sɪnəd] *s.* (relig.) sínodo.
synodal [-əl] *a.* (astr.) sinodal.
synodical [sə'nɑdɪkəl, B -'nɔd-] *a.* sinódico.
synoecious [sə'niʃəs] *a.* (bot.) sinoico.
synoecy [sə'nisɪ] *s.* (bot.) sinecia.
synonym ['sɪnəˌnɪm] *s.* sinónimo.
synonymic [ˌsɪnə'nɪmɪk] **synonymical** [-ɪkəl] *a.* sinónimo.
synonymist [sə'nɑnəməst, B -'nɔn-] *s.* sinonimista.
synonymity [ˌsɪnə'nɪmətɪ] *s.* sinonimia.
synonymize [sə'nɑnəˌmaɪz, B -'nɔn-] *v.t.* dar el sinónimo (o los sinónimos) de (una palabra); proveer de sinónimos (un diccionario, etc.).
synonymous [-məs] *a.* sinónimo.
synonymously [-lɪ] *adv.* con el mismo significado.
synonymy [-mɪ] *s.* (*pl.* SYNONYMIES) 1. sinonimia. 2. estudio de los sinónimos; lista de sinónimos.
synopsis [sə'nɑpsəs, B -'nɔp-] *s.* (*pl.* SYNOPSES [-ˌsiz]) sinopsis, resumen.
synopsize [-ˌsaɪz] *v.t.* condensar en sinopsis; epitomar.
synoptic [-tɪk] **synoptical** [-tɪkəl] *a.* sinóptico.
synoptically [-tɪkəlɪ] *adv.* de manera sinóptica, sinópticamente.
synoptic gospels, evangelios sinópticos (de San Mateo, San Marcos y San Lucas).
synostosis [ˌsɪnɑs'toʊsəs, B -ɔs-] *s.* (anat.) sinostosis.
synovia [sə'noʊvɪə] *s.* (anat.) sinovia.
synovial [-vɪəl] *a.* (anat.) sinovial.
synovitis [ˌsɪnə'vaɪtəs] *s.* (med.) sinovitis.
synsepalous [sɪn'sɛpələs] *a.* (bot.) sinsépalo.
syntactic [sɪn'tæktɪk] **syntactical** [-tɪkəl] *a.* (gram.) sintáctico.
syntactically [-tɪkəlɪ] *adv.* (gram.) de acuerdo a la sintaxis.
syntactic construction, (gram.) construcción sintáctica.
syntax ['sɪnˌtæks] *s.* (gram.) sintaxis.
synthesis ['sɪnθəsəs] *s.* (*pl.* SYNTHESES [-ˌsiz]) síntesis, suma, resumen; (quím.) síntesis.
synthesize [-ˌsaɪz] *v.t.* sintetizar.
synthetic [sɪn'θɛtɪk] **synthetical** [-ɪkəl] *a.* sintético.
synthetically [-ɪkəlɪ] *adv.* sintéticamente.
synthetic resin, resina sintética.
synthetic rubber, caucho sintético.
synthetize ['sɪnθəˌtaɪz] *v.t.* sintetizar.
syntonic [sɪn'tɑnɪk, B -'tɔn-] *a.* (rad.) sintónico.
syntonin ['sɪntənɪn] *s.* (bioquím.) sintonina.
syntonization [ˌsɪntənə'zeɪʃən, B -naɪ-] *s.* sintonia.
syntonize ['sɪntəˌnaɪz] *v.t.* sintonizar.
syphilis ['sɪfələs] *s.* (med.) sífilis.
syphilitic [ˌsɪfə'lɪtɪk] *a., s.* (med.) sifilítico.
syphilologist [-'lɑlədʒəst, B -'lɔl-] *s.* sifilólogo.
syphilology [-dʒɪ] *s.* sifilología.
syphiloma [-'loʊmə] *s.* (med.) sifiloma.
syphon, *var. de* **siphon.**
syren, (pr. G.B.) *var. de* **siren.**
Syria ['sɪrɪə] *s.* Siria.
Syriac [-ˌæk] *a., s.* siríaco.
Syrian [-ən] *a., s.* sirio, de Siria.
syringa [sə'rɪŋgə] *s.* (bot.) jeringuilla, celinda.
syringe [sə'rɪndʒ, B 'sɪrɪndʒ] *s.* (med.) jeringa, jeringuilla; lavativa. —*v.t.* jeringar.
syringeal [sə'rɪŋgɪəl, B sə'rɪndʒɪəl] *a.* (orn.) de la siringe.
syringomyelia [səˌrɪŋgoʊˌmaɪ'ilɪə] *s.* (med.) siringomielia.
syrinx ['sɪrɪŋks] *s.* (*pl.* SYRINGES [sɪ'rɪndʒiz] o SYRINXES) 1. (orn.) siringe. 2. (mús.) siringa, flauta de Pan, flauta pagana.
syrup ['sɜrəp, B 'sɪr-] *s.* jarabe, almíbar.
syrupy [-ɪ] *a.* (lit., fig.) almibarado.
syssarcosis [ˌsɪsˌɑr'koʊsəs, B -ɑ'-] *s.* (anat.) sisarcosis.
systaltic [sɪs'tɔltɪk, B -'tæl-] *a.* (fisiol.) sistáltico.
system ['sɪstəm] *s.* sistema.
systematic [ˌsɪstə'mætɪk] **systematical** [-ɪkəl] *a.* sistemático.
systematically [-ɪkəlɪ] *adv.* sistemáticamente.
systematics [-ɪks] *s. pl.* (*sing. en const.*) sistemática.
systematic theology, teología sistemática.
systematism ['sɪstəməˌtɪzəm] *s.* sistematismo.
systematization [ˌsɪstəmətə'zeɪʃən, B -taɪ-] *s.* sistematización.
systematize ['sɪstəməˌtaɪz] *v.t.* sistematizar.
systemization [ˌsɪstəmə'zeɪʃən, B -maɪ-] *s.* sistematización.
systemize ['sɪstəˌmaɪz] *v.t.* sistematizar.
systole ['sɪstəlɪ] *s.* (fisiol., biol.) sístole.
systolic [sɪs'tɑlɪk, B -'tɔl-] *a.* (biol., fisiol.) sistólico.
systyle ['sɪˌstaɪl] *s.* (arq.) sístilo.
syzygy ['sɪzədʒɪ] *s.* (*pl.* SYZYGIES) (astr.) sicigia.

T

T [ti] *s.* 1. **t,** vigésima letra del alfabeto inglés. 2. **to a t,** a la perfección.
Ta *símb. de* **tantalum,** tantalio (Ta).
tab [tæb] *s.* 1. lengüeta, tira pequeña (de papel, cuero, tela, etc.); oreja (de zapato); orejera (de gorra). 2. (fam.) cuenta, factura. 3. (aer.) aleta (de aviones). 4. indicador (en una tarjeta de catálogo). 5. etiqueta, marbete. 6. **to keep a t.** (o **tabs) on,** observar, seguir con atención; vigilar; controlar. *—v.t.* (*pret., p.p.* TABBED; *p.pr.* TABBING) 1. proveer de indicadores (a las tarjetas de un fichero o catálogo). 2. designar, destinar, señalar. 3. denominar.
tabanid [tə'beɪnəd, B 'tæbənɪd] (ento.) *s.* mosca tabánida. *—a.* tabánido.
tabard ['tæbərd, B -əd] *s.* (hist.) 1. tabardo. 2. (hist.) cota.
Tabasco (TM) [tə'bæskoʊ] *s.* salsa picante.
tabby ['tæbɪ] *s.* (*pl.* TABBIES)1. gato atigrado. 2. gata. 3. (tej.) tabí, moaré. 4. chismosa, comadre. 5. (pr. G.B.) solterona. 6. (ant.) tafetán. *—a.* 1. hecho de tabí. 2. con bandas o aguas como el moaré. 3. atigrado.
tabernacle ['tæbər,nækəl, B -ə,-] *s.* 1. (relig.) tabernáculo. 2. santuario, templo, lugar de adoración. 3. (ant.) refugio temporal; el cuerpo (como refugio del alma). *—v.i.* residir temporalmente, tener cobijo.
tabernacular [,tæbər'nækjələr, B -ə'nækjʊlə] *s.* (arq.) tabernacular (estilo).
tabernaemontana [tə,bɜrnɪmɑn'teɪnə, B -,bɜnɪmən'tɑnə] *s.* (bot.) muermera.
tabes ['teɪbiz] *s.* (*pl.* TABES) (med.) tabes, consunción.
tabetic [tə'bɛtɪk] **tabid** ['tæbɪd] *a.* (med.) tabético.
tabinet ['tæbə,nɛt] *s.* (tej.) tabinete.
tablature ['tæblətʃər, B -tʃə] *s.* 1. (mús.) tabladura. 2. (ant.) superficie (lápida, etc.) con inscripciones.
table ['teɪbəl] *s.* 1. mesa. 2. tabla, plancha; tablero. 3. comida, manjares, viandas. 4. comensales, compañeros de mesa (grupo de personas sentadas a la mesa para discutir, jugar, etc.). 5. tabla, lista, catálogo, índice. 6. cuadro sinóptico, diagrama. 7. tabla o cuadro de números. 8. mesa, meseta, altiplanicie. 9. (*pl.*) tablas reales, chaquete. 10. (mec.) banco. 11. (joy.) faceta superior (de un diamante, etc.). 12. palma de la mano (en quiromancia). 13. **at t.,** al comer, durante la comida; **the two tables,** (bíbl.) las tablas; **to clear the t.,** quitar o levantar la mesa; **to help at t.,** servir la mesa; **to keep a good t.,** servir buena comida; **to rise from t.,** levantarse de la mesa; **to set the t.,** poner la mesa; **to sit down to t.,** sentarse a la mesa; **to turn the tables (on person),** volver las tornas, voltear posiciones; **under the t.,** completamente borracho. *—v.t.* 1. tabular. 2. poner sobre la mesa, extender sobre la mesa. 3. (E.U.) postergar, dilatar indefinidamente (esp. proyecto de ley). 4. (G.B.) poner en la lista, poner sobre el tapete.
tableau ['tæb,loʊ] *s.* (*pl.* TABLEAUX [-,loʊz] o TABLEAUS) 1. cuadro. 2. arreglo; agrupación, grupo. 3. escena.
tableau vivant [tæ'bloʊvi'vɑn, B 'tæbloʊ'-vivɑn] (teat., fr.) cuadro vivo.
table boarder, pupilo, pensionista.
tablecloth ['teɪbəl,klɔθ] *s.* mantel.
table d'hote ['tɑbəl'doʊt] (*pl.* TABLES D'HOTE ['tɑbəlz-, B 'tɑbəl-]) 1. (fr.) comida a precio fijo. 2. menú (del día), comida corrida (Méx.).
table-hop ['teɪbəl,hɑp, B -,hɔp] *v.i.* (fam.) ir de mesa en mesa (saludando amigos en un restaurante).
table lamp, lámpara de mesa.
tableland [-,lænd] *a.* mesa, meseta, altiplanicie.
table linen, mantelería.
table manners, modales en la mesa.
table of contents, índice de materias.
table salt, sal de mesa.
table service, vajilla.
tables of the law, (bíbl.) tablas de la ley.
tablespoon ['teɪbəl,spun] *s.* cuchara de sopa, cuchara grande.
tablespoonful [-,fʊl] *s.* (*pl.* TABLESPOONFULS O TABLESPOONSFUL) cucharada.
tablet ['tæblət] *s.* 1. lápida, placa, plancha. 2. tableta, tablilla; bloc de papel, libreta de apuntes, memorándum. 3. tableta, comprimido, pastilla.
table talk, conversación de sobremesa.
table tennis, tenis de mesa, ping-pong.
tabletop ['teɪbəl,tɑp, B -,tɔp] *s.* 1. tabla de la mesa. 2. fotografía de escenas en miniatura.
tableware [-,wɛr, B -,wɛə] *s.* servicio de mesa, vajilla.
table water, agua mineral (embotellada para consumo).
table wine, vino de mesa.
tabloid ['tæb,lɔɪd] *a.* 1. condensado, conciso, breve, comprimido. 2. sensacionalista, vulgar (díc. de la prensa). *—s.* tabloide.
taboo, tabu [tə'bu, tæ-, B tə-] *a.* tabú. *—s.* tabú, prohibición, veda, interdicción (sagrada). *—v.t.* 1. declarar tabú. 2. prohibir, vedar; proscribir.
tabor, tabour ['teɪbər, B -bə] *s.* (mús.) tamboril, tamborín, tamborino. *—v.i.* tamborilear; tamborear, tabalear.
taborer, tabourer [-bərər, B -ə] *s.* tamborilero.
taboret, tabouret [,tæbə'rɛt, B 'tæbərɪt] *s.* 1. taburete, banquillo, banqueta. 2. bastidor de bordar. 3. pequeño tamboril o tamborín.
taborin ['tæbərən] **taborine** [,tæbə'rin] *s.* tamboril, tamborilete.
tabret ['tæbrət] *s.* tamborilete.
tabular ['tæbjələr, B -lə] *a.* tabular.
tabula rasa [-lə'rɑsə, B -'reɪ-] (lat.) página en blanco, tabla rasa (díc. de la mente humana antes de las primeras percepciones o experiencias).
tabularly [-lərlɪ, B -ləlɪ] *adv.* en forma tabular.
tabulate ['tæbjə,leɪt] *a.* (zool.) tabulado. *—v.t.* tabular, poner en tabla o sinopsis.
tabulation [,tæbjə'leɪʃən] *s.* tabulación.
tabulator ['tæbjə,leɪtər, B -ə] *s.* tabulador (esp. de una máquina de escribir); tabuladora (máquina).
tacamahac ['tækəmə,hæk] *s.* (bot.) tacamaca, tacamacha, tacamahaca.
tace, *var. de* **tasse.**
tachistoscope [tə'kɪstə,skoʊp] *s.* (psic.) taquistoscopio.
tachograph ['tækə,græf, B -,grɑf] *s.* tacógrafo, registrador de velocidad.
tachometer [tæ'kɑmətər, B -'kɔmɪtə] *s.* taquímetro, tacómetro, contador de velocidad.
tachoscope ['tækə,skoʊp] *s.* (ing.) tacóscopo.
tachycardia [,tækɪ'kɑrdɪə, B -'kɑd-] *s.* (med.) taquicardia.
tachygrapher [tæ'kɪgrəfər, B -fə] **tachygraphist** [-fəst] *s.* taquígrafo, taquígrafa.
tachygraphic [,tækɪ'græfɪk] **tachygraphical** [-ɪkəl] *a.* taquigráfico.
tachygraphy [tæ'kɪgrəfɪ] *s.* taquigrafía, estenografía (esp. la de los griegos y romanos de la antigüedad).
tachylyte, tachylite ['tækə,laɪt] *s.* (min.) taquilita.
tachymeter [tæ'kɪmətər, B -ə] *s.* (top.) taquímetro, taqueómetro.
tachymetric [,tækɪ'mɛtrɪk] *a.* taquimétrico.
tachymetry [tæ'kɪmətrɪ] *s.* (top.) taquimetría.
tachysterol [tæ'kɪstə,roʊl, B -,rɔl] *s.* (bioquím.) taquisterol.
tacit ['tæsət] *a.* tácito, implícito, ej., *t. understanding,* entendimiento tácito.
tacitly [-lɪ] *adv.* tácitamente, implícitamente.
tacitness [-nəs] *s.* carácter tácito o implícito (de una condición, etc.).
taciturn ['tæsə,tɜrn, B -,tɜn] *a.* taciturno, callado, silencioso.
taciturnity [,tæsə'tɜrnətɪ, B -'tɜnɪ-] *s.* taciturnidad.
Tacitus ['tæsətəs] *s.* (hist.) Tácito, historiador romano.
tack [tæk] *s.* 1. tachuela, puntilla, clavete, clavito. 2. (mar.) amura (del puño de la vela); puño de la vela. 3. (mar.) virada por avante; bordada; rumbo (con relación a la orientación de las velas). 4. (fig.) cambio de política o línea de conducta, nuevo plan de acción, ej., *try another t.,* pruebe otro plan de acción. 5. (*gen. pl.*) hilván, basta, embaste. 6. adhesión, pegajosidad, viscosidad. *—v.t.* 1. clavetear; clavar con tachuela. 2. hilvanar, embastar. 3. añadir, anexar. 4. (mar.) virar por avante. 5. **t. on (u on to),** dejar prendido ligeramente en, fijar en forma insegura en; (fig.) agregar (esp. a un proyecto de ley). *—v.i.* 1. (mar.) voltejear, virar, cambiar de bordada. 2. (fig.) cambiar de política, cambiar de línea de conducta.
tack board, tablilla para anuncios.
tack claw, sacatachuelas.
tack hammer, martillo para clavar tachuelas.
tackiness ['tækɪnəs] *s.* viscosidad, pegajosidad.
tackle ['tækəl] *s.* 1. avíos, aparejo, enseres, equipo. 2. (mar.) aparejo, jarcias. 3. (mar.) polea, garrucha, cuadernal; poleame. 4. (dep.) atajo, agarrada. 5. (fútbol Am.) atajador. *—v.t.* 1. enjaezar (caballo). 2. agarrar, asir. 3. emprender, abordar (a alguien, un problema, asunto, etc.). 4. (dep.) atajar (al adversario). *—v.i.* (dep.) atajar al adversario.

tackle block, (mar.) motón de aparejo.
tackle fall, tira de aparejo.
tackle hooks, ganchos de aparejo.
tackler ['tæklər, B -lə] *s.* (dep.) atajador (fútbol Am.).
tackling [-lɪŋ] *s.* 1. (mar.) aparejo, jarcias. 2. aparejo, enseres (para determinada actividad). 3. arnés (de caballo de tiro). 4. (fútbol, Am.) atajo; habilidad de atajar.
tack-weld ['tæk,wɛld] *v.t.* soldar por puntos o provisionalmente.
tacky ['tækɪ] *a.* (TACKIER; TACKIEST) viscoso, pegajoso (pintura, barniz, etc.).
tacky, *a.* (TACKIER; TACKIEST) 1. vulgar, común, chillón. 2. descuidado, raído, mal vestido; de mala calidad, de apariencia pobretona. 3. cursi, pasado de moda.
tacky party, (fam., E.U.) fiesta de disfraces chillones (en que se otorgan premios a los más estrafalarios).
tacmahack ['tækmə,hæk] *var. de* **tacamahac.**
tact [tækt] *s.* 1. acierto, tacto, discreción. 2. (raro) (sentido del) tacto.
tactful ['tæktfəl] *a.* discreto, político, atinado.
tactfully [-fəlɪ] *adv.* discretamente, políticamente.
tactfulness [-fəlnəs] *s.* discreción, tacto.
tactic ['tæktɪk] *a.* 1. táctico. 2. (biol.) del taxismo.
tactical [-tɪkəl] *a.* táctico.
tactically [-kəlɪ] *adv.* tácticamente.
tactician [tæk'tɪʃən] *s.* táctico (persona).
tactics ['tæktɪks] *s. pl.* (*sing.* o *pl. en const.*) táctica, tácticas, métodos; (mil.) táctica.
tactile ['tæktəl, B -,taɪl] *a.* táctil, tangible, palpable.
tactile corpuscle, (anat.) corpúsculo táctil.
tactile organ, órgano táctil.
tactility [tæk'tɪlətɪ] *s.* cualidad de tangible.
taction ['tækʃən] *s.* toque, contacto.
tactless ['tæktləs] *a.* indiscreto, falto de tacto, impolítico, imprudente.
tactlessly [-lɪ] *adv.* indiscretamente, sin tacto.
tactlessness [-nəs] *s.* indiscreción, falta de tacto.
tactual ['tæktʃʊəl, B -tjʊ-] *a.* táctil, tactivo; del tacto.
tactually [-əlɪ] *adv.* al tacto, por medio del tacto.
tad [tæd] *s.* (E.U., fam.) niño pequeño.
tadpole ['tæd,poʊl] *s.* (zool.) renacuajo.
tael [teɪl] *s.* tael (medida de peso y antigua moneda).
taenia, tenia ['tinɪə] *s.* (*pl.* TAENIAE [-,i] o TAENIAS) (anat., zool., arq.) tenia.
taeniacide [-,saɪd] *s.* (med.) tenicida.
taeniafuge [-,fjudʒ] *s.* (med.) tenífugo.
taeniasis [ti'naɪəsəs] *s.* (med.) teniasis.
taffeta ['tæfətə] *s.* (tej.) tafetán.
taffeta weave, (tej.) ligamento tafetán, punto de tafetán.
taffrail ['tæf,reɪl] *s.* (mar.) 1. pasamano de la borda a popa. 2. coronamiento (de un navío de madera).
taffy ['tæfɪ] *s.* 1. melcocha, arropía. 2. (fam.) lisonja, halago. 3. **T.,** (fam., G.B.) (*ú. gen. como vocativo*) galés.
tafia ['tæfɪə] *s.* tafia (aguardiente de caña de las Antillas).
tag [tæg] *s.* 1. arrapiezo, pingajo. 2. borlita, vedija, fleco. 3. cola, rabito, extremo (del rabo). 4. marbete, etiqueta, rótulo, cartela. 5. herrete. 6. tirador (de botas). 7. palabra o frase de efecto; epíteto. 8. cliché, perogrullada. 9. residuo, fragmento, vestigio. 10. (pesca) pedacito de oropel (usado como señuelo). 11. (jer.) nombre. —*v.t.* (*pret., p.p.* TAGGED; *p.pr.* TAGGING) 1. clavetear, poner herretes a. 2. pegar un marbete a, marcar con marbete o etiqueta; proveer de etiqueta. 3. llamar, denominar; identificar. 4. denominar, apodar. 5. multar (a motorista por infracción). 6. (fam.) perseguir, seguir los pasos de. 7. **t. to** (o **on to**), agregar, añadir; **t. together,** juntar, acoplar (esp. textos). —*v.i.* (fam.) (ú. t. con *at, onto, behind, after,* etc.) quedar cerca.
tag, *s.* (juego de niños) peste (Esp.), mancha (Arg.), pillarse (Chile), la pega (Perú), pesca (Bolivia). —*v.t.* alcanzar y tocar.
Tagalog [tə'gɑləg, -,ɔg, B -,ɔg] *s.* (*pl.* TAGALOG o TAGALOGS) 1. tagalo (persona). 2. tagalo (idioma principal de las Islas Filipinas).
tagboard ['tæg,bɔrd, B -,bɔd] *s.* etiqueta de cartón.
tag day, (E.U.) día de colecta pública (con fines caritativos, etc.) en los que cada donante recibe una etiqueta o marca identificadora.
tag end, 1. fin, final, término. 2. (*pl.*) fragmentos misceláneos, retales, restos.
tagged atom ['tægd-] *s.* (fís.) átomo marcado.
taguan ['tɑ,gwɑn] *s.* (zool.) taguán.
Tagus ['teɪgəs] *s.* el Tajo, río de España y Portugal.
Tahitian [tə'hiʃən, B tɑ-] *a., s.* tahitiano, de la isla polinesia de Tahití.
Tai, *var. de* **Thai.**
taiga [taɪ'gɑ, B 'taɪgɑ] *s.* taiga (selva de árboles coníferos de Siberia).
tail [teɪl] *s.* 1. cola, rabo. 2. extremidad, apéndice; cola (de cometa, ropa, vestido, etc.); cabo, fin, parte trasera. 3. trasera (de una carreta); cola, entrega (de un ladrillo); parte salida (de una teja en el techo). 4. rabo, ángulo (del ojo). 5. (*pl.*) cruz, reverso (de una moneda). 6. escolta, comitiva, séquito; fila de gente. 7. (*pl.*) (fam.) frac; chaqué. 8. (aer.) cola, planos de cola. 9. (impr., enc.) pie de página; margen inferior. 10. (poét.) estrambote; coda. 11. (jer.) rastro, pista (de un fugitivo). 12. (jer.) perseguidor. 13. (jer.) (t. *pl.*) culo, nalgas. 14. **to turn t.,** poner pies en polvorosa; **with his t. between his legs,** con el rabo entre las piernas, sin ánimo, decaído. —*v.t.* 1. proveer de cola. 2. ser arrastrado (como una cola). 3. añadir (al fin). 4. atar (por el extremo). 5. (jer.) espiar, seguir o vigilar muy de cerca. 6. (arq.) (gen. con *in*) fijar o empotrar por un extremo (en una pared o soporte). —*v.i.* 1. formar cola; extenderse (como cola). 2. (fam.) (gen. con *after*) quedar cerca (de), andar atrás (de), pisar los talones (a). 3. (arq.) sostenerse por un extremo. 4. (mar.) oscilar o balancearse con la marea (díc. de un buque en áncora). 5. **t. after,** seguir de cerca (a), pisar los talones a; **t. off** (o **away**), quedarse atrás, estar quedándose; disminuir poco a poco, desvanecerse, apagarse, ej., *her words tailed off into a murmur,* sus palabras se desvanecieron en un murmullo. —*a.* postrero, último; final, terminal, posterior.
tail, *a.* (der.) limitado; abreviado; reducido, acortado. —*s.* (der.) limitación de propiedad; abreviación, vínculo, vinculación.
tailboard ['teɪl,bɔrd, B -,bɔd] *s.* compuerta de cola (de un carro o camión, que se puede bajar o quitar).
tailbone [-,boʊn] *s.* (anat.) vértebra caudal, hueso caudal.
tail boom, (aer.) fuselaje secundario.
tailcoat [-'koʊt] *s.* frac.
tail end, 1. extremo trasero. 2. nalgas, trasero. 3. fase final.
tailer ['teɪlər, B -lə] *s.* perseguidor, perseguidora.
tail fin, 1. (oct.) aleta caudal. 2. (aer.) estabilizador vertical, plano de deriva.
tailgate ['teɪl,geɪt] *v.t.* seguir demasiado de cerca (a otro vehículo), ir pisándole los talones a. —*v.i.* manejar pegado al vehículo de delante.
tail gate, tailgate puerta trasera, puerta de atrás.
tailgate party, *s.* (fam., E.U.) picnic al lado del coche.
tail gust, (avia.) racha de cola.
tailing ['teɪlɪŋ] *s.* 1. (*pl.*) (min.) desechos, restos, residuos; deslave, relaves, colas. 2. (arq.) cola, entrega.
tail lamp, (G.B.) luz trasera, piloto.
tailless [-ləs] *a.* sin cola; desrabado.
taillight [-,laɪt] *s.* luz trasera, piloto.
tailor ['teɪlər, B -lə] *s.* sastre. —*v.i.* trabajar de sastre. —*v.t.* 1. cortar y coser (un vestido el sastre). 2. vestir, proveer de ropa (a una persona). 3. (fig.) ajustar, acomodar, encuadrar, adaptar.
tailorbird [-,bɜrd, B -,bɜd] *s.* (orn.) pájaro sastre.
tailored [-lərd, B -ləd] *a.* 1. cortado por sastre. 2. hecho a la medida. 3. de corte sobrio (ropa).
tailoring ['teɪlərɪŋ] *s.* 1. (arte, obra de) sastrería. 2. corte y confección (de trajes sobrios).
tailor-made [-lər'meɪd, B -lə'-] *a.* 1. hecho por sastre, hecho con corte de sastre. 2. hecho a la medida; hecho de encargo.
tailor's chalk, tiza de sastre, jaboncillo de sastre.
tailpiece ['teɪl,pis] *s.* 1. apéndice; cabo. 2. cola (de violín o guitarra). 3. (arq.) viga apoyada en el cabecero. 4. (impr.) marmosete, viñeta (al final de un capítulo o página).
tail pipe, *s.* 1. (aut.) tubo de escape. 2. (aer.) tobera (de un motor a reacción).
tail plane, (aer.) plano de cola.
tailrace [-,reɪs] *s.* 1. saetín de salida (que sigue a la rueda del molino). 2. socaz, canal o caz de descarga, canal de fuga o desagüe, cauce de escape.
tail skid, (avia.) patín de cola, esquilla, bequilla.
tail slide, (aer.) resbalamiento de cola.
tailspin [-,spɪn] *s.* (aer.) barrena picada; **to go into a t.,** (fig.) caer en picada.
tailstock [-,stɑk, B -,stɔk] *s.* (mec.) muñeca corrediza, cabeza móvil, contrapunta.
tail unit, (aer.) conjunto de cola.
tail wheel, (aer.) rueda de cola.
tail wind, (aer.) viento de cola, viento trasero.
tain [teɪn] *s.* hojuela de estaño (para espejos); lámina de estaño.
Taino ['taɪnoʊ] *s.* taino, tribu hoy desaparecida originaria de las Antillas.
taint [teɪnt] *v.t.* contaminar, corromper, inficionar, envenenar. —*v.i.* (ant.) corromperse, viciarse. —*s.* 1. mancha, mácula, corrupción, infición. 2. (ant.) tintura, tinte.
taintless ['teɪntləs] *a.* incorrupto, inmaculado.
Taipei ['taɪ'peɪ] *s.* Taipeh, capital de Formosa o Taiwán.
take [teɪk] *v.t.* (*pret.* TOOK [tʊk]; *p.p.* TAKEN ['teɪkən]; *p.pr.* TAKING) 1. tomar, coger, asir, ej., *he took me by the hand,* me cogió de la mano. 2. tomar, ocupar; apresar, capturar. 3. prender, agarrar, sorprender, ej., *they took him at a disadvantage,* le sorprendieron en una situación desventajosa. 4. (fig.) cautivar, encantar, ej., *he takes his audience with him,* él cautiva la atención de su público. 5. tomar, obtener, ej., *I'll t. your advice,* tomaré tu consejo. 6. ganar, percibir, cobrar. 7. comprar; estar suscrito a, ej., *do you t. Time magazine?* ¿está Ud. suscrito a la revista Time? 8. tomar, alquilar, contratar. 9. tomar, comer, beber, ej., *what will you t. at noon?* ¿qué cosa tomará (o comerá) Ud. a mediodía? 10. tomar, requerir, necesitar; costar, ej., *this work takes time,* este trabajo toma tiempo, *t.*

your time, no se dé prisa, *it takes a lot of doing,* esto requiere mucho esfuerzo, *it took much time and money,* costó mucho tiempo y dinero. 11. llevar (consigo), llevarse; conducir, acompañar, ej., *shall I t. you home?* ¿quiere que le acompañe a casa? *the deuce t it!* ¡que lo lleve el diablo! 12. coger, contraer (enfermedad), ej., *t. cold,* coger un resfrío. 13. tomar, entender, tener entendido, interpretar; juzgar, considerar, dar por, suponer, ej., *I t. this to be directed against me,* entiendo que eso está dirigido contra mí, *I t. it that we are not wanted here,* supongo que no somos bien recibidos aquí. 14. tomar, aceptar, recibir, ej., *you must t. things as they are,* hay que tomar (o aceptar) las cosas tal como son. 15. admitir, tolerar, aguantar, ej., *I will t. no nonsense,* no toleraré tonterías, *don't worry, I can t. it,* no te preocupes, yo lo aguantaré. 16. deducir, restar. 17. fotografiar, ej., *I took him in his uniform,* lo fotografié en su uniforme. 18. (ajedrez, damas) comer, capturar. 19. (jer.) engañar, embaucar. 20. **not to be taking any,** (jer.) no querer nada de eso; **t. a back seat,** asumir un papel pasivo; **t. a bath,** tomar un baño, bañarse; **t. a bet, aceptar una apuesta; t. a bite,** comer algo; **t. about,** escoltar (en público); **t. a bow,** agradecer el aplauso (actor); recibir reconocimiento; **t. account of,** tener en cuenta, tener presente; **t. a chance** (**on** o **with**), arriesgarse (con); **t. a copy,** sacar (uno) copia; **t. action (against),** actuar, tomar medidas (contra); **t. a dislike (to),** cobrar antipatía (por); **t. (one's) advice,** seguir el consejo de (uno); **t. a fancy to,** prendarse, antojarse (de); **t. a hint,** hacer caso de indirectas; **t. aim (at),** apuntar (a); **t. a joke,** aguantar una broma (a expensas de uno mismo); **t. alarm,** advertir el peligro; alarmarse; **t. a leap,** dar un salto; **t. a letter,** tomar dictado, escribir una carta al dictado; **t. a liking to,** tomar o cobrar cariño a; **t. along,** llevar consigo (a alguien); **t. a look (glance,** etc.) **at,** echar una mirada (ojeada, etc.) a; **t. an examination,** examinarse, tener un examen; **t. apart,** desarmar, descomponer (mecanismo, etc.); hacer pedazos, despedazar; **t. a short cut,** ir por el atajo, atajar; **t. a step,** dar un paso; tomar una medida; **t. (someone) at his word,** tomar la palabra de (uno), aceptar lo dicho por (uno); **t. a trip,** hacer un viaje; **t. a turn (in),** dar un paseo, dar una vuelta (en); **t. a (different, optimistic,** etc.) **view,** adoptar una opinión (diferente, optimista, etc.); **t. a walk,** dar un paseo; **t. away,** quitar; separar; llevar, llevarse; **t. back,** recibir devuelto; devolver; volver a emplear; retractar, desdecirse de; llevar a tiempos pasados, evocar el pasado a (uno); **t. breakfast,** tomar desayuno, desayunar; **t. care,** tener cuidado; **t. care not to,** tener cuidado de que no; **t. care of,** cuidar de, tener a su cuidado; **t. chances,** correr riesgos, dejar a la suerte; **t. charge (of),** encargarse (de), hacerse cargo (de); **t. counsel (of, with),** entrar en cuentas (con), consultar; **t. dinner,** cenar, comer; **t. down,** bajar, descolgar; llevar o conducir abajo; anotar, poner por escrito; humillar, bajar los humos a; postrar; desmontar, desarmar; tragar; **t. effect,** surtir efecto; entrar en vigencia (ley, decreto, etc.); **t. flight,** huir, darse a la fuga; **t. for a fool,** tomar por un tonto; **t. (something) for granted,** dar (algo) por sentado o sabido; **t. fright,** atemorizarse, sobresaltarse; **t. from,** sacar de, quitar a; copiar; **t. heart,** animarse, cobrar aliento; **t. hold,** agarrarse; asumir el mando; surtir efecto; **t. hold of,** agarrar, asir, coger; apoderarse de; encargarse de; **t. in,** tomar, aceptar (trabajo para hacer en casa); recibir, admitir, acoger (en la casa, etc. de uno); estar suscrito a; acompañar (dama) al comedor; (fam.) arrestar, tomar en custodia; cobrar, recibir o ganar (dinero); observar, percatarse de; comprender, asimilar; abarcar, incluir; encoger, contraer, acortar; (cost.) embeber, meter; sisar (vestido); aferrar (velas); (jer.) visitar (lugares de interés), ir a ver (cine, espectáculo, etc.); (fam.) tragar (mentira, etc.); estafar, engañar, embaucar; **t. in hand,** emprender, hacerse cargo de (un asunto); manejar; disciplinar, someter a disciplina (a niños, etc.); **t. into one's confidence,** depositar confianza en, iniciar (a una persona) en asuntos confidenciales de uno; **t. it into one's head,** metérsele a uno en la cabeza; **t. it big,** (jer.) impresionarse mucho; **t. it easy,** no afanarse, descansar; ir despacio o con cuidado; hacer con cautela; **t. it badly,** tomarlo a mal; **t. it on the chin,** (fam.) sufrir derrota completa; aguantar sufrimiento o fracaso; **t. it or leave it!** ¡tómelo o déjelo!; **t. it out of (one),** fatigar (a uno); **t. it out on,** desquitarse a costa de, hacer pagar el pato a; **t. it that,** suponer que; **t. it upon oneself to (do),** meterse a (hacer); **t. leave,** despedirse, marcharse; **t. (someone's) life,** quitar la vida (a alguien); **t. lunch,** almorzar; **t. no notice (of),** hacer caso omiso (de); **t. note (of),** tomar nota (de), apuntar; **t. notes,** hacer apuntes; **t. notice (of),** hacer caso (de), prestar atención (a); **t. (an) oath,** prestar juramento; **t. off,** quitar; quitarse (prendas); retirar (de servicio, del programa), descontinuar; llevarse, recoger; sacar (copias, retrato); imitar, remedar, parodiar; descontar, rebajar (parte del precio); levantar (restricciones, impuestos, etc.); tomarse (tiempo para vacaciones, descanso, etc.); beber de un trago; **t. office,** asumir el poder, entrar en funciones; **t. off one's hat to,** quitarse uno el sombrero ante; **t. one's chance,** correr el riesgo; **t. one's life into one's hands,** arriesgar uno su vida; **t. one's medicine,** (fig.) tragar la píldora, tomar su merecido, aguantar castigo merecido; **t. on,** cargar con, encargarse de (trabajo, tarea, etc.); asumir (responsabilidad, postura, carácter, etc.); adoptar (costumbres, idioma, etc.); cubrirse de; contratar, emplear; aceptar (como cliente o paciente); enfrentarse a, aceptar el reto de; **t. or leave,** añádele o quítale (tanto) más o (tanto) menos; **t. out,** llevar fuera, poner fuera; pasear; sacar (licencia, patente, etc.); quitar (mancha, etc.), extraer, eliminar; salir con, escoltar, cortejar, galantear; tomar (seguro); (bridge) sacar (al compañero) de la declaración; **t. (the nonsense,** etc.) **out of,** acabar con (las tonterías, etc.) de, quitar (las tonterías, etc.) de la cabeza; **t. out on,** satisfacer por o mediante; **t. over,** hacerse cargo de, asumir la dirección de; apoderarse de, adoptar; **t. place,** tener lugar, ocurrir; **t. precedence over,** tener precedencia sobre; **t. (one) prisoner,** hacer prisionero (a uno); **t. shape,** formarse, desarrollarse; hacerse realidad; **t. sides,** tomar partido; **t. supper,** cenar; **t. the fence (obstacle,** etc.), salvar la cerca (obstáculo, etc.) (un caballo); **t. the field,** entrar en el campo, salir al campo (equipo deportivo); salir a campaña (militar); **t. the oath,** renunciar a la bebida; **t. the road,** emprender camino; ir de pueblo en pueblo (esp. compañía viajera de teatro); **t. the wind out of one's sails,** apagarle los fuegos a uno, desalentar a uno; **t. (up) the word,** tomar o coger la palabra; **t. to heart,** tomar a pecho; **t. up,** llevar arriba; levantar, alzar; coger, recoger, prender; absorber; asumir; ocupar, llenar (tiempo, espacio); instalar, establecer (residencia, etc.); tomar preso; admitir, tomar (pasajeros); patrocinar, tomar bajo su protección; interrumpir (al que habla); empezar, comenzar; reanudar; dedicarse a (una carrera, profesión, etc.); abordar, tratar sobre (un tema, una materia, etc.); escoger para estudio; proseguir (investigación, etc.); aceptar (apuesta, reto, etc.); (com.) tomar (un préstamo); pagar, reembolsar (préstamo, letra, etc.); **t. (it) upon oneself (to),** encargarse de, asumir; **t. up with,** asociarse con (alguien); **t. water,** (mar.) hacer agua (el barco); **to be taken ill,** caer enfermo; **to be taken with** (o **by**), estar prendado de (belleza, etc.); encontrar simpático (a alguien); **you may t. it from me,** puede Ud. creerme. —*v.i.* 1. arraigar, afirmarse. 2. adherirse, pegar (bien). 3. tener efecto, prender. 4. tener éxito, ganar popularidad, difundirse. 5. (con **across, after, down,** etc.) dirigirse, irse (a través de, en pos de, a lo largo de, etc.). 6. ponerse, volverse. 7. picar (pez). 8. (der.) entrar en posesión (como heredera). 9. (ajedrez, damas) capturar, comer (díc. de una pieza). 10. salir (bien, mal, etc.) en fotografía. 11. **t. after,** parecerse a, salir a; **t. away,** levantar la mesa; **t. down,** desarmar; **t. down with,** caer víctima de (esp. enfermedad); **t. from,** disminuir, mermar; t. ill (o **sick**), caer enfermo; **t. kindly to,** tener simpatía a; dar buena acogida a; **t. off,** saltar, comenzar a saltar; (aer.) despegar; alzar el vuelo (pájaro); marcharse; cambiar de rumbo; amainar, aflojar (viento), bajar (marea); tomar vacaciones; **t. off from,** (fig.) desviarse de, apartarse de; **t. out (for),** ponerse en camino (a), emprenderla (para); **t. over,** hacerse cargo, asumir la autoridad; ocupar el puesto de uno; prevalecer, sobreponerse; **t. to,** ponerse a; acoger (idea, etc.); tomar el hábito de; adaptarse a; dedicarse a, aficionarse a; prendarse de (una persona); dirigirse a; entrar a; internarse en (el bosque, etc.); **t. up,** empezar, emprender; **t. up for,** prestar apoyo a, salir en defensa de; **t. up with,** interesarse por (cosas, ideas, etc.); asociarse con; adoptar, hacer suya (proposición, idea, etc.). —*s.* 1. presa, pesca; redada. 2. entrada, producto, ingresos (de una función, etc.). 3. participación (del estado, etc. en ingresos); parte, porción. 4. botín (de un criminal). 5. reacción. 6. (ajederez, damas), captura, toma. 7. (cinem.) toma (de una escena). 8. (impr.) toma.

takedown ['teɪk daʊn] *a.* desmontable, desarmable. —*s.* 1. desmontadura, desarmadura. 2. mecanismo desmontable. 3. humillación.

take-home pay [-ˌhoʊm-] salario neto (descontados los impuestos y cuotas obligatorias).

take-in [-ˌɪn] *s.* (fam.) engaño, estafa.

takeoff [-ˌɔf] *s.* 1. imitación, remedo; parodia. 2. arranque, (comienzo del) salto. 3. línea de arranque (para saltos); punto de salida, punto de partida. 4. cantidad estimada (necesaria de un material). 5. (aer.) despegue. 6. (mec.) toma de fuerza.

take-off run, (avia.) recorrido de despegue.

take-off speed, (avia.) velocidad de despegue.

takeout [-ˌaʊt] *a.* díc. de alimentos preparados para ser consumidos fuera del restaurant.

takeout double, (bridge) contra informativa.

takeover, take-over ['teɪkˌoʊvər, B -və] *s.* 1. toma del mando, toma del poder. 2. (com.) adquisición (de una compañía por otra).

taker ['teɪkər, B -ə] *s.* 1. tomador; ocupador, conquistador. 2. colector. 3. comprador, cliente. 4. apostador.

take-up [-ˌʌp] *s.* 1. toma; absorción; encogimiento, contracción (fibras). 2. (mec.) compensación.

taking [-ɪŋ] *s.* 1. toma, captura; ocupación. 2. (*pl.*) ganancias, ingresos. 3. presa; pesca. 4. (ant.) agitación, arrebato, trance. —*a.* 1. atractivo, encantador. 2. (fam.) contagioso, infeccioso.

talapoin [ˈtæləˌpɔɪn] *s.* 1. bonzo (en Indochina y Ceilán). 2. (zool.) mono pequeño de África Occidental.
talaria [təˈlɛrɪə, B -ˈlɛər-] *s. pl.* (mitol.) talares (sandalias aladas de Mercurio).
talayot [təˈlɑˌjoʊt] *s.* (arqueol.) talayote.
talc [tælk] *s.* (min.) talco.
talcky [ˈtælkɪ] *a.* talcoso.
talcose [-ˌkoʊs] **talcous** [-kəs] *a.* talcoso.
talcum powder [ˈtælkəm-] 1. talco en polvo. 2. (polvos de) talco (de tocador).
tale [teɪl] *s.* 1. cuento, relato. 2. cuento, fábula, rumor, chisme. 3. (ant., poét.) cuenta, recuento, cómputo. 4. (ant.) discurso, habla. 5. **it tells its own t.,** habla por sí mismo; **old wives' tales,** cuentos de viejas; **to tell tales,** contar chismes.
talebearer [ˈteɪlˌbɛrər, B -ˌbɛərə] *s.* chismoso, chismero, cuentista, correveidile.
talebearing [-ɪŋ] *a.* chismero, chismoso, cuentista. —*s.* chismografía, chismorreo.
talent [ˈtælənt] *s.* 1. talento, capacidad, ingenio. 2. talento, hombre talentoso; gente de talento. 3. talento (moneda y peso antiguos). 4. (ant.) disposición (esp. maliciosa).
talented [-əntəd] *s.* talentoso, de talento.
talent scout, persona cuya ocupación es descubrir gente con aptitudes especiales (para el cine, etc.), buscatalentos.
taler [ˈtɑlər, B -ə] *s.* (numis.) tálero.
tales [ˈteɪliz] *s.* (der.) lista de jurados suplentes.
talesman [ˈteɪlzmən, B ˈteɪliz-] *s.* (der.) jurado suplente.
taleteller [ˈteɪlˌtɛlər, B -ə] *s.* cuentista; chismoso, chismosa.
taletelling [-ɪŋ] *s.* chismería, chismografía, chismorreo.
talion [ˈtælɪən] *s.* (ley del) talión.
taliped [ˈtæləˌpɛd] *a.* (med.) talipédico.
talipes [-ˌpiz] *s.* (med.) talipes.
talipot [ˈtæləˌpɑt, B -ˌpɔt] *s.* (bot.) palmera de sombrilla.
talisman [ˈtæləsmən, B -ɪz-] *s.* (*pl.* TALISMANS) talismán, amuleto, dije, mascota.
talismanic [ˌtæləsˈmænɪk, B -ɪz-] *a.* talismánico.
talk [tɔk] *v.i.* 1. hablar, conversar, departir. 2. parlar; parlotear, chismear. 3. **look who's talking!** ¡mira quién habla! **now you are talking,** (jer.) ¡eso es hablar! ¡buena idea!; **t. about,** hablar de (algo); **t. away,** hablar sin parar, seguir hablando; **t. back,** replicar con insolencia; **t. behind (someone's) back,** cortar un sayo a (alguien), murmurar de (alguien) en su ausencia; **t. big,** jactarse, fanfarronear; **t. down to,** hablar con altivez a; **t. for the sake of talking,** hablar por hablar; **t. of,** mencionar; discutir sobre, hablar de (algo); **t. on,** hablar sin parar, seguir hablando; hablar sobre o acerca de (un tema, etc.); **t. through one's hat,** (jer.) decir disparates, hablar sin fundamento; **t. to,** hablar con o a (alguien); (fam.) reprender (a alguien); **t. to each other,** hablarse; **t. to no purpose,** hablar en vano; **t. up,** elevar la voz, hablar alto, hablar claro. —*v.t.* 1. decir, expresar. 2. hablar de (un tema o asunto). 3. **t. a blue streak,** (fam.) hablar hasta por los codos; **t. away (time),** gastar (tiempo) con palabras; **t. (someone) down** apabullar, abrumar con palabras (a alguien); **t. (something) down,** menospreciar, achicar, quitar importancia a (una cosa); **t. (somcone) into,** persuadir, inducir (a alguien); **t. nonsense,** decir tonterías; **t. oneself hoarse,** hablar hasta quedarse ronco; **t. (someone) out of,** disuadir (a alguien); **t. (something) over,** discutir, debatir (algo); **t. (someone) over** (o **round**), persuadir (a alguien); **t. sense,** hablar de modo sensato, hablar inteligentemente; (imper.) ¡no digas tonterías!; **t. (cold) turkey,** (fam.) decir la verdad, hablar sin rodeos; **t. (something) up,** alabar, ensalzar (algo); **to be talked about,** andar en boca de la gente. —*s.* 1. charla, plática; conversación, discusión; habla. 2. conferencia, discurso. 3. mención, rumor; chisme, comidilla. 4. tema (de conversación). 5. cháchara, palabrería. 6. dialecto, lengua, estilo de habla. 7. **to be the t. of the town,** andar de boca en boca, ser la comidilla del pueblo; **to have a t. with,** hablar con, sostener una conversación con; **to keep the t. going,** hacer conversación.
talkative [ˈtɔkətɪv] *a.* hablador, locuaz, facundo.
talkatively [-lɪ] *adv.* locuazmente.
talkativeness [-nəs] *s.* locuacidad, facundia.
talker [ˈtɔkər, B -ə] *s.* hablador, conversador, charlador.
talkie [ˈtɔkɪ] *s.* (ant.) cine sonora.
talking [-ɪŋ] *a.* parlante, hablante; hablador. —*s.* habla; conversación. 2. habladuría, palabrería.
talking book, libro sonoro (disco fonográfico para ciegos con la lectura de un libro o revista).
talking doll, muñeca parlante, muñeca que habla.
talking picture, (ant.) cine sonora.
talking point, 1. tema de conversación. 2. argumento de peso.
talking-to [ˈtɔkɪŋˌtu] *s.* (fam.) reprensión, regaño, rapapolvo.
talk show, programa de entrevistas.
talky [ˈtɔkɪ] *a.* (TALKIER; TALKIEST) 1. hablador, parlanchín, locuaz. 2. con diálogo superfluo o excesivo (película de cine, obra de teatro, libro).
tall [tɔl] *a.* 1. alto, espigado (persona); alto, elevado (árbol, edificio, etc.). 2. de (cierta) estatura, ej., *six feet t.,* de seis pies de estatura. 3. (jer.) excesivo, exorbitante, irrazonable; exagerado; increíble. 4. (ant.) gracioso; bravo, valiente. —*adv.* exageradamente; **to talk t.,** baladronear, jactarse.
tallage [ˈtælɪdʒ] *s.* (hist.) tributo pagado por un vasallo a su amo; impuesto feudal.
tallboy [ˈtɔlˌbɔɪ] *s.* 1. cómoda alta; cajonería. 2. (G.B.) guardaropa, ropero, armario para ropa.
tallcase clock [ˈtɔlˌkeɪs] *s.* reloj de pie, reloj de caja, reloj de péndulo.
tallish [-ɪʃ] *a.* bastante alto.
tallith [ˈtɑləs, B ˈtælɪθ] *s.* (relig.) taled, talet (ornamento judío).
tallness [ˈtɔlnəs] *s.* altura, estatura alta, talla espigada.
tall oil, subproducto de la producción de pulpa química de madera.
tall order, (fam.) pretensión exagerada, poco razonable; tarea difícil.
tallow [ˈtæloʊ] *s.* sebo. —*v.t.* ensebar. —*a.* seboso, sebáceo; de sebo.
tallowy [-ɪ] *a.* seboso, sebáceo.
tally [ˈtælɪ] *s.* (*pl.* TALLIES) 1. tarja, tara. 2. cuenta en tarjas. 3. marca, muesca (en una tarja). 4. unidad, lote, grupo, ej., *to buy goods by the t.,* comprar mercaderías por lotes (docenas, gruesas, etc.). 5. tarja, contraseña, tarjeta de identidad; etiqueta, rótulo. 6. talón, resguardo, contraparte; duplicado (de una factura, guía, etc.). —*v.t.* (*pret., p.p.* TALLIED; *p.pr.* TALLYING) 1. tarjar. 2. contar, contramarcar. 3. hacer cuadrar o concordar. —*v.i.* (con *with*) cuadrar, concordar, ajustarse (con).
tallyho [ˌtælɪˈhoʊ] *s.* 1. (G.B.) señal del cazador (al avistar al zorro). 2. (G.B.) coche de paseo de cuatro caballos.
tallyman [ˈtælɪmən] *s.* 1. tarjador. 2. (G.B.) vendedor al crédito o al fiado.
tally sheet, t. card, hoja de cuentas, hoja de apuntes.
Talmud [ˈtɑlˌmʊd, B ˈtæl-] *s.* (relig.) Talmud.
Talmudic [tælˈmudɪk, B -ˈmʊd-] **Talmudical** [-ɪkəl] *a.* talmúdico.
Talmudist [ˈtælmʊdəst] *s.* talmudista.
talon [ˈtælən] *s.* 1. garra. 2. (arq.) talón, cimacio, cima reversa (de molduras). 3. baceta, monte (de naipes). 4. proyección del pestillo (en cerraduras).
taloned [-ənd] *a.* 1. en forma de garra. 2. agarrotados (dedos).
talus [ˈteɪləs] *s.* 1. talud. 2. (geol.) talud detrítico.
talus [ˈteɪləs] *s.* (*pl.* TALI [-ˌlaɪ]) (anat.) astrágalo, talus.
tam [tæm] *s.* boina escocesa.
tamable [ˈteɪməbəl] *a.* domable, domesticable.
tamale [təˈlmɑlɪ] *s.* tamal.
tamandua [təˌmændəˈwɑ, B -ˈmændjʊə] *s.* (zool.) tamanduá o tamandúa mirim.
tamarack [ˈtæməˌræk] *s.* (bot.) alerce americano.
tamarau [ˌtæməˈraʊ] *s.* (zool.) tamarao.
tamaricaceous [ˌtæmərəˈkeɪʃəs] *a.* (bot.) tamaricáceo, tamariscíneo.
tamarin [ˈtæmərən] *s.* (zool.) variedad de mono tití.
tamarind [ˈtæmərənd] *s.* (bot.) tamarindo.
tamarisk [ˈtæməˌrɪsk] *s.* (bot.) tamarisco, taray, taraje, tamariz.
tambac [ˈtæmbæk] *var. de* **tombac.**
tambour [ˈtæmˌbʊr, B -ˌbʊə] *s.* 1. (mús.) tambor. 2. (cost.) tambor, bastidor; bordado hecho en bastidor. —*v.t., v.i.* bordar sobre un bastidor.
tambourine [ˌtæmbəˈrin] *s.* (mús.) pandero, pandereta.
Tamburlaine [ˈtæmbərˌleɪn, B -bəˌ-] *s.* (hist.) *var. de* **Tamerlane.**
tame [teɪm] *a.* 1. domesticado, domado, manso. 2. sumiso, dócil, tratable, innocuo, gentil. 3. insubstancial, insípido; aburrido, tedioso. —*v.t.* 1. domesticar, domar, desbravar, amansar. 2. (fig.) avasallar. 3. suavizar. —*v.i.* domesticarse, amansarse.
tameable, *var. de* **tamable.**
tameless [ˈteɪmləs] *a.* salvaje, indomesticable, indomable.
tamely [-lɪ] *adv.* dócilmente; desanimadamente, débilmente, sumisamente.
tameness [-nəs] *s.* sumisión, docilidad, mansedumbre.
tamer [-ər, B -ə] *s.* domador, amansador.
Tamerlane [ˈtæmərˌleɪn, B -əˌ-] *s.* (hist.) Tamerlán, guerrero y conquistador tártaro que fundó el segundo imperio mogol.
Tamil [ˈtæməl] *s.* tamil, grupo de pueblos de la raza drávida en la India.
taming [ˈteɪmɪŋ] *s.* doma, amansamiento.
tamis [ˈtæmɪ, B -mɪs] *s.* tamiz, colador.
tam-o-shanter [ˌtæməˈʃæntər, B -ə] *s.* gorra o boina escocesa.
tamp [tæmp] *v.t.* 1. atacar (un barreno). 2. apisonar, pisonear, pisonar.
tamper [ˈtæmpər, B -ə] *s.* pisón.
tamper, *v.i.* **t. with,** manosear, tocar o manipular indebidamente; alterar (un texto, pruebas, etc.); cohechar, corromper (testigos, etc.); sobornar. —*v.t.* alterar, falsificar.
tamper bar, pisón metálico.
tamping [-ɪŋ] *s.* apisonamiento.
tampion [ˈtæmpɪən] *s.* 1. (mús.) tapón dc cañon (de órganos). 2. tapabocas (de cañones).
tampon [ˈtæmˌpɑn, B -pən] *s.* (med.) tapón, tampón. —*v.t.* taponar.
tamponade [ˌtæmpəˈneɪd] **tamponage** [ˈtæmpəˌnɪdʒ] *s.* (med.) taponamiento.

tam-tam ['tæm,tæm] *s.* tam-tam, batintín.
tan [tæn] *v.t.* (*pret., p.p.* TANNED; *p.pr.* TANNING) 1. curtir, adobar, zurrar (pieles). 2. curtir, quemar, tostar (al sol). 3. (fam.) zurrar, azotar, tundir. —*v.i.* tostarse, quemarse. —*s.* 1. casca, curtido. 2. tanino, curtiente (astringente para curtir). 3. color tostado; color de canela. —*a.* tostado, bronceado, requemado, de color canela; de color tostado o quemado.
tanager ['tænɪdʒər, B -dʒə] *s.* (orn.) tanagra.
Tanagra ['tænəgrə] *s.* 1. Tanagra, antigua ciudad en Beocia. 2. tanagra, (figuritas de barro cocido halladas en esta ciudad).
Tananarive [tə'nænə,riv] *s.* Tananarive, capital de Malgache.
tanbark ['tæn,bɑrk, B -,bɑk] *s.* casca, cortesa curtiente.
Tancred ['tæŋkrəd, B -krɛd] *s.* (hist.) Tancredo, jefe normando de la primera cruzada.
tandem ['tændəm] *adv.* uno tras otro; doble. —*s.* 1. coche tirado por dos caballos (uno detrás del otro). 2. tándem (bicicleta de dos asientos). —*a.* con asientos uno tras otro.
tandem bicycle, tándem, bicicleta para dos ciclistas.
tandem engines, (mec.) motores en tándem, motores en líneas interconectadas.
tang [tæŋ] *s.* 1. espiga, cola, rabo (de formón, lima, cuchillo, etc.). 2. dejo, gustillo; sabor u olor penetrante. —*v.t.* **t. with,** impregnar con sabor u olor de.
tang, *s.* tañido. —*v.t., v.i.* tañer, tocar; tantanear.
Tanganyika [,tæŋgæn'jikə, B -gən-] *s.* Tanganica, región africana que forma parte de Tanzania.
tangency['tændʒənsɪ] *s.* tangencia.
tangent [-dʒənt] *a.* tangente, tangencial. —*s.* 1. (geom.) tangente. 2. (mús.) tangente (alfiler que golpea la cuerda del clavicordio). 3. **to fly** (o **to go) off at a t.,** (fig.) cambiar bruscamente de tema o actitud, salir por la tangente.
tangential [tæn'dʒɛntʃəl, B -'dʒɛnʃəl] *a.* 1. tangencial. 2. digresivo, inconexo, impertinente.
tangentially [-'dʒɛntʃəlɪ, B -'dʒɛnʃ-] *adv.* 1. tangencialmente, de modo tangencial. 2. en forma digresiva o inconexa.
Tangerine ['tændʒə,rin, B ,tændʒə'rin] *a.* tangerino. —*s.* 1. tangerino, tangerina, natural de Tánger. 2. **t.,** naranja mandarina. 3. **t.,** color de mandarina.
tangibility[,tændʒə'bɪlətɪ] *s.* tangibilidad.
tangible ['tændʒəbəl] *a.* tangible, perceptible, palpable; substancial, apreciable. —*s.* (ten.) (partida del) activo tangible.
tangible assets, (ten.) activo tangible, activo físico.
tangibleness [-nəs] *s.* tangibilidad.
tangibly [-blɪ] *adv.* perceptiblemente, palpablemente; substancialmente, apreciablemente.
Tangier [tæn'dʒɪr, B -'dʒɪə] *s.* Tánger, ciudad y puerto en Marruecos, antigua capital de la zona internacional de Tánger.
tangle ['tæŋgəl] *s.* alga marina grande.
tangle, *v.t., v.i.* enredar(se), enmarañar(se), embrollar(se), confundir(se). —*s.* enredo, maraña, embrollo, laberinto, confusión.
tangled [-gəld] *a.* enmarañado, enredado.
tanglement [-gəlmənt] *s.* enmarañamiento, enredo.
tangly ['tæŋglɪ] *a.* (TANGLIER; TANGLIEST) enredado, nudoso, intrincado.
tango ['tæŋgoʊ] *s.* (*pl.* TANGOS) (baile, mús.) tango. —*v.i.* bailar tango.
tangy ['tæŋɪ] *a.* (TANGIER; TANGIEST) penetrante, fuerte (olor, sabor, etc.).
tank [tæŋk] *s.* 1. tanque, aljibe, depósito (de agua, combustible, gas, etc.). 2. (mil.) tanque, carro de combate. 3. (dial.) estanque, laguna. 4. (jer.) celda en una comisaría. —*v.t.* almacenar o guardar en un tanque o depósito. —*v.i.* **t. up,** (jer.) tomar tragos, beber mucho.
tankage ['tæŋkɪdʒ] *s.* 1. almacenamiento; gasto o precio de almacenamiento. 2. capacidad, cabida (de un tanque). 3. (agr.) residuos grasos usados como fertilizante, fertilizante orgánico.
tankard ['tæŋkərd, B -kəd] *s.* pichel, bock, jarra (de cerveza).
tank barrier, (mil.) barrera antitanque.
tank battallion, (mil.) batallón de tanques.
tank car, (f.c.) carro tanque, vagón cisterna.
tank circuit, (rad.) circuito de absorción.
tank commander, (mil.) jefe de tanque.
tank destroyer, (mil.) cañon automóvil antitanque; destructor de tanques.
tank engine, (f.c.) locomotora-ténder.
tanker ['tæŋkər, B -kə] *s.* 1. buque cisterna, buque tanque; buque petrolero. 2. (mil.) tanquista. 3. (aer.) avión cisterna, avión nodriza.
tank farm, patio de tanques (de petróleo).
tank locomotive, (f.c.) locomotora ténder.
tank test, (hidr.) ensayo en canal hidrodinámico.
tank town, pueblo insignificante, villorrio (donde los trenes se detienen sólo para tomar agua).
tank trailer, tanque remolcador, tanque de remolque, remolque tanque.
tank trap, (mil.) trampa antitanque.
tank truck, camión tanque, camión cisterna.
tannage ['tænɪdʒ] *s.* curtimiento, curtido (de cueros).
tannate ['tæn,eɪt, B -ɪt] *s.* (quím.) tanato.
tanner ['tænər, B -ə] *s.* 1. curtidor, zurrador. 2. (fam. G.B.) moneda de seis peniques.
tannery [-ərɪ] *s.* (*pl.* TANNERIES) tenería, curtiduría.
tannic ['tænɪk] *a.* (quím.) tánico.
tannic acid, (quím.) ácido tánico.
tannin [-ən] *s.* (quím.) tanino.
tanning ['tænɪŋ] *s.* 1. curtimiento, curtido. 2. tostadura, bronceado (de la piel por los rayos del sol). 3. zurra, tunda.
tannish [-ɪʃ] *a.* que tira a color canela, acanelado.
Tanoan ['tɑnoʊən] *s.* tano, uno de los lenguajes de los indios norteamericanos.
tanrec ['tænrɛk] *var. de* **tenrec.**
tansy ['tænzɪ] *s.* (*pl.* TANSIES) (bot.) tanaceto, hierba lombriguera.
tantalate ['tæntə,leɪt, B -lɪt] *s.* (quím.) tantalato.
tantalic [tæn'tælɪk] *a.* (quím.) tantálico.
tantalite ['tæntə,laɪt] *s.* (min.) tantalita.
tantalization [,tæntəlɪ'zeɪʃən, B -laɪ-] *s.* exasperación, tentación sin satisfacción posible.
tantalize ['tæntə,laɪz] *v.t., v.i.* tentar, provocar, exasperar.
tantalizing [-ɪŋ] *a.* tentador, provocador, exasperante, incitador.
tantalizingly [-lɪ] *adv.* tentadoramente, provocadoramente, exasperantemente.
tantalum ['tæntələm] *s.* (quím.) tantalio.
tantalus ['tæntələs] *s.* 1. **T.,** (mitol.) Tántalo. 2. (orn.) tántalo. 3. (pr. G.B.) frasquera (en que se guardan las botellas bajo llave).
tantamount ['tæntə,maʊnt] *a.* equivalente; **to be t. to,** ser equivalente a.
tantara [tæn'tærə, B 'tæntərə] *s.* tarará (sonido).
tantivy [tæn'tɪvɪ] *adv.* (ant.) rápidamente, velozmente. —*a.* rápido, veloz. —*s.* 1. carrera, corrida, galope. 2. (caza) grito de caza; grito al avistar la presa.
Tantra ['tʌntrə, B 'tɑntrɑ] *s.* (relig.) tantra, uno de los libros de la religión hindú.
Tantrism ['tæn,trɪzəm] *s.* (relig.) tantrismo, doctrina contenida en los libros del tantra.
tantrum ['tæntrəm] *s.* (fam.) berrinche, pataleta, rabieta.
Tanzania [,tænzə'niə, B -'nɪə] *s.* la República Unida de Tanzania.
Tanzanian [-'niən, B -'nɪ-] *s., a.* tanzaniano.
Taoism ['taʊ,ɪzəm, B 'tɑoʊ-] *s.* (relig.) taoísmo.
Taoist [-əst] *a., s.* taoísta.
tap [tæp] *v.t.* (*pret., p.p.* TAPPED; *p.pr.* TAPPING) 1. tocar, golpear, dar palmadas a (ligeramente). 2. tabalear. 3. remendar con tapa, poner tapas o suelas a (calzado). 4. designar, proponer (para oficio, etc.). —*s.* 1. golpecito, golpe ligero, palmadita. 2. (*pl.*) (mil.) toque de silencio. 3. tapa, media suela (de calzado).
tap, *s.* 1. canilla, espita (para sacar vino de un barril). 2. tapón, tarugo. 3. cerveza (sacada) del barril. 4. (fam.) bar, mostrador de taberna. 5. grifo, llave de agua. 6. (mec.) macho, macho de terraja, macho de roscar. 7. (elec.) derivación, toma de corriente. 8. (med.) drenaje (de un abceso, etc.) 9. (jer.) sablazo (pedido de préstamo). 10. (ant.) calidad, clase (de vino o cerveza). 11. **on t.,** espitado (barril); sacado del barril (cerveza); (fig.) a mano, listo. —*v.t.* 1. agujerear, horadar, perforar; espitar (barril, etc.). 2. sacar con espita (líquido). 3. hacer sangrar (un árbol). 4. (elec.) derivar, tomar derivación dc (línca principal, etc.); hacer una derivación en (transformadores). 5. intervenir, interceptar (teléfonos, telégrafos). 6. hacer una conexión en (cañerías, luz, etc.) para suministro local. 7. (mec.) aterrajar, terrajar, roscar (tornillo o tuerca). 8. (fig.) utilizar, aprovechar (fuente nueva de energía, etc.). 9. (med.) drenar. 10. (jer.) dar un sablazo a.
tap circuit, (elec.) derivación.
tap dance, (baile) zapateado.
tap-dance ['tæp,dæns, B -,dɑns] *v.i.* bailar con zapateo.
tap dancer, bailarín (a) de zapateado.
tap drill, taladro para rosca.
tape [teɪp] *s.* 1. cinta, galón, trencilla. 2. (dep.) cinta tendida para marcar la meta. 3. **to breast the t.,** ganar la carrera. —*v.t.* 1. asegurar o atar con cinta. 2. medir con cinta (métrica). 3. grabar (en cinta) —*v.i.* medir.
tape deck, platina, pletina.
tape machine, (audio) grabadora; (video) video, vídeo; (G.B.) teleimpresor.
tape measure, cinta métrica.
taper ['teɪpər, B -pə] *s.* 1. cerilla, velita (larga y delgada); cirio. 2. ahusamiento. —*a.* 1. ahusado; cónico, piramidal. 2. graduado, escalonado. —*v.t.* ahusar. —*v.i.* ahusarse, afilarse, ir disminuyendo; **t. off,** ahusarse; ir disminuyendo, dejar de funcionar gradualmente.
taper attachement, (mec.) accesorio para torneado cónico, dispositivo de ahusar.
tape-record [,teɪprɪ'kɔrd, B -'kɔd] *v.t.* grabar en cinta.
tape recorder, grabadora, grabador de cinta, grabadora de cinta, magnetófono.
tape recording, grabación en cinta.
tapered wing ['teɪpərd-, B -pəd-] (aer.) ala de perfil trapezoidal.
taper gager, (mec.) calibrador de ahusamiento o conocidal.
taper key, (mec.) cuña.
taper thread, rosca cónica.
tapestried ['tæpəstrɪd] *a.* 1. cubierto o decorado con tapicería. 2. representado en tapicería.

tapestry [-trɪ] *s.* (*pl.* TAPESTRIES) tapiz, tapicería. —*v.t.* cubrir o adornar con tapicería.
tapestry maker, tapicero; el que hace tapices.
tapetum [tə'pitəm] *s.* (*pl.* TAPETA [-ə]) 1. (bot.) tapete. 2. (anat.) tapetum, tapete.
tapeworm ['teɪpˌwɜrm, B -ˌwɜm] *s.* tenia, solitaria.
tap holder, (mec.) portamachos.
taphole ['tæpˌhoʊl] *s.* (metal.) bigotera (en alto horno para la salida de escorias); piquera (para vaciar la fundición o el arrabio).
taphouse [-ˌhaʊs] *s.* (G.B.) taberna, bar.
tapioca [ˌtæpɪ'oʊkə] *s.* tapioca.
tapir ['teɪpər, B -pə] *s.* (*pl.* TAPIR O TAPIRS) (zool.) tapir, danta.
tapis [tæ'pi, B 'tæpi] *s.* (ant.) tapiz, tapete; **on the t.,** (fig.) sobre el tapete.
tapper ['tæpər, B -ə] *s.* 1. manipulador o tecla de telégrafo; transmisor. 2. (mec.) aterrajadora.
tappet ['tæpət] *s.* (mec.) botador, impulsor, varilla de levantamiento; alzaválvulas.
tapping [-ɪŋ] *s.* 1. golpes ligeros. 2. sangría (de árboles). 3. (elec.) toma, derivación. 4. (med.) punción.
taproom ['tæpˌrum, -ˌrʊm] *s.* taberna, bar.
taproot [-ˌrut, -ˌrʊt, B -ˌrut] *s.* (bot.) raíz primaria.
taps [tæps] *s. pl.* (mil.) toque de silencio.
tapsal-teerie [ˌtæpsəl'tɪrɪ, B -'tɪərɪ] *adv.* (esco.) patas arriba, en desorden.
tapster ['tæpstər, B -stə] *s.* cantinero, mozo de taberna.
tar [tɑr, B tɑ] *s.* 1. brea, alquitrán. 2. marinero, hombre de mar. —*v.t.* (*pret., p.p.* TARRED; *p.pr.* TARRING) alquitranar, embrear; **tarred and feathered,** embreado y emplumado (como castigo); **to be tarred with the same brush,** ser lobo(s) de la misma camada.
tar, *v.t.* (ú. gen. con *on*) incitar, aguijonear, provocar.
taradiddle [ˌtærə'dɪdəl, B 'tærəˌdɪd-] *s.* (fam.) 1. mentirilla, embuste. 2. disparates, insensateces.
tarantara [ˌtærən'tærə] *var. de* **tantara.**
tarantella [ˌtærən'tɛlə] *s.* (danza, mús.) tarantela.
tarantism ['tærənˌtɪzəm] *s.* (med.) tarantismo.
tarantula [tə'ræntʃələ, B -tjʊ-] *s.* (*pl.* TARANTULA O TARANTULAE [-ˌli]) (ento.) tarántula.
taraxacum [tə'ræksɪkəm] *s.* (farm.) taraxacina.
tarboosh [tɑr'buʃ, B tɑ'-] *s.* tarbuch, fez, sombrero cónico de fieltro rojo.
tarbrush ['tɑrˌbrʌʃ, B 'tɑˌ-] *s.* brocha para alquitranar; **to have a touch of the t.,** (jer.) tener algún ascendiente negro, tener un poco de sangre negra en las venas.
Tardigrada [ˌtɑrdə'greɪdə, B ˌtɑdɪ-] *s. pl.* (zool.) tardígrados.
tardigrade ['tɑrdəˌgreɪd, B 'tɑd-] (zool.) *a., s.* tardígrado.
tardily ['tɑrdəlɪ, B 'tɑd-] *adv.* tardíamente, morosamente, lentamente.
tardiness [-ɪnəs] *s.* tardanza, demora, dilación, morosidad, lentitud.
tardy ['tɑrdɪ, B 'tɑdɪ] *a.* (TARDIER; TARDIEST) tardo, tardío, dilatorio, lento, moroso, demorón (Amer.).
tare ['tɛr, B 'tɛə] *s.* 1. (bot.) vicia, veza, algarroba. 2. (bíbl.) cizaña, mala semilla.
tare, *s.* tara. —*v.t.* destarar, restar la tara al pesar.
target ['tɑrgət, B 'tɑgɪt] *s.* 1. blanco, diana. 2. (fig.) blanco, objeto, objetivo. 3. (f.c.) placa de señal, banderola. 4. (mil.) objetivo. 5. (top.) mirilla.
target area, (mil.) zona-objetivo, zona a batir.
target date, fecha fijada (para un acontecimiento, suceso, objetivo, etc.).
target leveling rod, mira de tablilla (nivelación).
target map, (mil.) plano de objetivos.
target practice, prácticas de tiro (al blanco).
Targum ['tɑrˌgʊm, B 'tɑgəm] *s.* (relig.) Targum, interpretación de los antiguos textos hebreos.
tariff ['tærəf] *s.* 1. tarifa. 2. arancel, derecho arancelario. —*v.t.* tarifar; fijar los aranceles de (mercaderías).
tarlatan ['tɑrlətən, B 'tɑlət-] *s.* (tej.) tarlatán, tarlatana.
tarmac ['tɑrˌmæk, B 'tɑˌ-] *s.* superficie asfaltada (de un camino o pista); (aer.) pista de aterrizaje asfaltada.
tarmacadam [ˌtɑrmə'kædəm, B ˌtɑmə-] *s.* macadam, macadán.
tarn [tɑrn, B tɑn] *s.* lago pequeño entre montañas.
tarnish ['tɑrnɪʃ, B 'tɑnɪʃ] *v.t., v.i.* empañar(se), deslucir(se), deslustrar(se), descolorar(se), manchar(se), perder el brillo, exidar(se). —*s.* deslustre, descoloramiento, mancha, mácula.
tarnishable [-əbəl] *a.* que puede ser empañado o deslucido, empañable.
taro ['tɑroʊ, B 'tær-] *s.* (*pl.* TAROS) (bot.) taro, colocasia, chonque, malanga isleña, malangay.
tar paper, papel alquitranado, cartón embetunado.
tarpaulin [tɑr'pɔlən, B tɑ'-] *s.* 1. encerado, alquitranado. 2. (raro) marinero.
Tarpeia [tɑr'piə, B tɑ'-] *s.* (mitol.) Tarpeya, vestal que traicionó a los romanos.
Tarpeian rock [-'piən] (hist.) Roca Tarpeya (en Roma).
tarpon ['tɑrpən, B 'tɑpɔn] *s.* (*pl.* TARPON O TARPONS) (ict.) tarpón.
Tarquin ['tɑrkwɪn, B 'tɑkwɪn] *s.* (hist.) Tarquino, nombre de una antigua familia romana; dos reyes romanos de esta familia.
tarradiddle, *var. de* **taradiddle.**
tarragon ['tærəgɑn, B -gən] *s.* (bot.) artemisa, tanago, salvia, estragón, dragoncillo.
tarred [tɑrd, B tɑd] *a.* embreado, alquitranado.
tarriance ['tærɪəns] *s.* (ant.) tardanza, dilación, demora.
tarry ['tɑrɪ] *a.* (TARRIER; TARRIEST) alquitranado, embreado, píceo.
tarry, *v.t.* (*pret., p.p.* TARRIED; *p.pr.* TARRYING) (ant.) esperar, aguardar. —*v.i.* 1. tardar, demorarse. 2. quedarse. —*s.* espera, detención, parada, demora.
tarsal ['tɑrsəl, B 'tɑsəl] *a.* (anat., zool.) tarsal, tarsiano. —*s.* tarso.
tarsier ['tɑrsɪər, B 'tɑsɪə] *s.* (zool.) tarsero.
tarsometatarsus [ˌtɑrsoʊˌmɛtə'tɑrsəs, B ˌtɑsoʊ-'tɑsəs] *s.* (orn.) tarsometatarso.
tarsus ['tɑrsəs, B 'tɑsəs] *s.* (*pl.* TARSI [-saɪ]) 1. (anat., zool.) tarso. 2. (orn.) tarsometatarso. 3. (anat.) tarso palpebral.
Tarsus *s.* Tarso, ciudad en Turquía, cuna de San Pablo apóstol.
tart [tɑrt, B tɑt] *a.* 1. acerbo, acre, agrio, acídulo. 2. (fig.) acre, áspero, cáustico.
tart, *s.* 1. torta, pastel de frutas, pastelillo. 2. (jer.) prostituta, buscona.
tartan ['tɑrtən, B 'tɑt-] *s.* (tej.) tartán, lana con dibujo escocés. —*a.* de tartán, con cuadros escoceses.
tartan, *s.* (mar.) tartana.
tartar ['tɑrtər, B 'tɑtə] *s.* 1. tártaro (del vino). 2. tártaro, sarro dental.
Tartar, *s.* 1. tártaro. 2. **t.,** persona salvaje o intratable. 3. **to catch a t.,** encontrar un contrario duro.
Tartarean [tɑr'tɛrɪən, -'tær-, B tɑ'tɛər-] *a.* (mitol.) tartáreo, infernal.
tartar emetic, (quím.) tártaro emético.
Tartarian [tɑr'tɛrɪən, B tɑ'tɛər-] *a.* tártaro, propio de o relativo a los tártaros.
tartaric [-'tærɪk] *a.* tártrico, tartárico.
tartaric acid, (quím.) ácido tartárico.
tartarin ['tɑrtərən, B 'tɑt-] *s.* (zool.) tartarín, papión.
tartarine ['tɑrtərən, B 'tɑt-] *s.* (tej.) tartarí.
tartarize ['tɑrtəˌraɪz, B 'tɑtə-] *v.t.* (quím.) tartarizar.
tartarous [-rəs] *a.* (quím.) tartaroso, tartarado.
tartar sauce, (cocina) salsa tártara, mayonesa a la que se añaden diversos ingredientes (mostaza, alcaparras, etc.).
Tartarus ['tɑrtərəs, B 'tɑt-] *s.* (mitol.) Tártaro, abismo donde yacían los Titanes; infierno; reino de los muertos en general.
Tartary ['tɑrtərɪ, B 'tɑtərɪ] *s.* (hist.) Tartaria, nombre con que se conocía la región dominada por los tártaros.
tartlet ['tɑrtlət, B 'tɑt-] *s.* tarta o pastel pequeño.
tartly ['tɑrtlɪ, B 'tɑt-] *adv.* acremente, agriamente, ásperamente.
tartness [-nəs] *s.* acidez, acedía, agrura; acrimonia.
tartrate ['tɑrtreɪt, B 'tɑtrɪt] *s.* (quím.) tartrato.
tartrated [-əd] *a.* (farm., quím.) tártrico, tartaroso.
Tartuffe [tɑr'tʊf, B tɑ'-] *s.* (fr.) Tartufo (personaje de una comedia de Moliére, p. ext. hipócrita santurrón).
tarweed ['tɑrˌwid, B 'tɑˌ-] *s.* (bot.) madia.
tasco ['tæskoʊ] *s.* talque (tierra talcosa usada para hacer crisoles).
tasimeter [tə'sɪmətər, B -tə] *s.* tasímetro, termómetro de presión.
task [tæsk, B tɑsk] *s.* 1. tarea, faena, deber, labor; misión. 2. **to take (o call) to t.,** censurar, regañar (a alguien). 3. (ant.) impuesto, tributo. —*v.t.* 1. dar una tarea a, encargar de. 2. atarear, abrumar, exigir demasiado de, someter a esfuerzo; poner a prueba. 3. (ant.) (con *with*) acusar o tachar (de error, etc.).
task force, (mil.) agrupación de fuerzas para una misión especial, fuerza operante.
taskmaster ['tæskˌmæstər, B 'tɑskˌmɑstə] *s.* 1. capataz, supervisor que señala tareas a otros. 2. supervisor exigente y riguroso.
taskwork [-ˌwɜrk, B -ˌwɜk] *s.* 1. destajo, trabajo a destajo. 2. trabajo duro.
Tasmanian [tæz'meɪnɪən] *a., s.* tasmaniano, de la isla australiana de Tasmania.
Tasmanian devil, *s.* (zool.) dasiuro.
Tasmanian tiger, T. wolf, (zool.) yabi, lobo de Tasmania.
tasmanite ['tæzməˌnaɪt] (geol.) tasmanita.
tasse ['tæs] *s.* (arm.) faldar, pancera, escarcela.
tassel ['tæsəl] *s.* 1. borla. 2. (bot.) espiguilla (esp. del maíz). —*v.t.* (*pret., p.p.* TASSELED O TASSELLED; *p.pr.* TASSELING O TASSELLING) adornar con borlas. —*v.i.* echar espiguillas.
tassel, *var. de* **tercel.**
taste [teɪst] *v.t.* 1. gustar, saborear, paladear. 2. catar, probar. 3. (fig.) percibir, experimentar, gustar. 4. (ant.) palpar, gozar, apreciar. —*v.i.* 1. tener sabor o gusto. 2. sentir sabor, saborear. 3. **t. of,** saber a; (fig.) saborear. —*s.* 1. sabor, gusto. 2. (sentido del) gusto, paladar. 3. cata, gustación, paladeo. 4. pizca, un poco. 5. (fig.) gusto, preferencia, afición, inclinación, goce. 6. gusto, discernimiento, apreciación. 7. (ant.) ensayo,

prueba. 8. **a t. of the whip,** azotaína, zurra; **in bad t.,** de mal gusto; **to have a t. for,** gustar de; **to lose one's t. for,** perder el gusto por.

taste bud, (anat.) papila del gusto, papila gustativa.

tasteful ['teɪstfəl] *a.* 1. elegante, de buen gusto. 2. (raro) sabroso, apetitoso, gustoso.

tastefully [-fəlɪ] *adv.* elegantemente, con gusto.

tastefulness [-fəlnəs] *s.* gusto, discernimiento; gracia, elegancia, buen gusto.

tasteless [-ləs] *a.* 1. insípido, insulso, soso. 2. de mal gusto, vulgar, de mal tono. 3. desabrido, falto de gracia.

tastelessly [-lɪ] *adv.* insípidamente, sin gusto; de mal gusto, sin elegancia, sin arte, sin gracia.

tastelessness [-nəs] *s.* insipidez, insulsez, desabor, falta de gusto o gracia, sosera, sosería, vulgaridad.

taster ['teɪstər, B -tə] *s.* 1. catador, catavinos, probador. 2. catavino (taza).

tastily [-təlɪ] *adv.* 1. sabrosamente, gustosamente, apetitosamente. 2. con gusto.

tastiness [-tɪnəs] *s.* 1. sabrosura, calidad de gustoso. 2. buen gusto, gracia.

tasty [-tɪ] *a.* (TASTIER; TASTIEST) 1. sabroso, gustoso, apetitoso, apetitivo. 2. de buen gusto.

tat [tæt] *v.t.* (*pret., p.p.* TATTED; *p.pr.* TATTING) hacer encaje de frivolité. —*v.t.* tejer (un encaje de frivolité).

ta-ta [tɑ'tɑ, B 'tæ-] *interj.* (fam., G.B.) hasta luego.

Tatar ['tɑtər, B -ə] *var. de* **Tartar.**

Tatary [-ərɪ] *var. de* **Tartary.**

tater ['teɪtər, B -ə] *s.* (dial.) patata, papa (Am.).

tatouay ['tætuˌeɪ, B ˌtɑtu'aɪ] *s.* (zool.) tabú iba, cabasu de orejas largas.

tatter ['tætər, B -ə] *s.* andrajo, harapo, guiñapo, pingajo, arrapiezo. —*v.t.* hacer tiras (de una tela); convertir o transformar en harapos. —*v.r.* deshilacharse.

tatterdemalion [ˌtætərdɪ'meɪljən, B ˌtætədə-] *s.* zarrapastroso, andrajoso.

tattered ['tætərd, B -əd] *a.* 1. andrajoso, harapiento, trapajoso. 2. hecho tiras, gastado, raído. 3. roto, destrozado, desmoronado. 4. destartalado.

tatting ['tætɪŋ] *s.* (cost.) encaje de hilo, frivolité.

tattle ['tætəl] *v.i.* 1. charlar, parlotear, cotorrear, hablar por los codos. 2. chismear, comadrear, chismorrear. —*v.t.* divulgar secretos, contar chismes. —*s.* 1. cháchara, charla. 2. chisme, chismografía, comadreo.

tattler ['tætlər, B -lə] *s.* 1. charlador, charladora, cotorra, chacharero, chacharera. 2. chismoso, chismosa. 3. (orn.) zarapito, zarapico.

tattletale [-əlˌteɪl] *s.* chismoso, chismosa, cuentista, correveidile; acusón, acusica (esp. entre niños). —*a.* revelador, acusador.

tattletale gray, blanco grisáceo, blanco perla, blanco humo.

tattoo [tæ'tu, B tə-] *s.* 1. tamboreo, tabaleo. 2. (mil.) retreta, toque de retreta. 3. **to beat the devil's t.,** tabalear. —*v.i.* tabalear, tamborear.

tattoo, *v.t.* (*pret., p.p.* TATTOOED; *p.pr.* TATTOOING) tatuar. —*s.* tatuaje.

tau [taʊ] *s.* tau, decimonona letra del alfabeto griego.

tau cross, tao, cruz de San Antonio, cruz en forma de T.

taught [tɔt] *pret., p.p. de* **teach.**

taunt [tɔnt, tɑnt, B tɔnt] *a.* (mar.) de mucha guinda, muy alto (díc. del mástil).

taunt, *v.t.* befar, mofar, burlar, ridiculizar; **t. a person into (doing something),** incitar o provocar con burlas a una persona para que (haga algo). —*s.* dicterio, befa, mofa, burla; reto o provocación sarcástica.

taunter ['tɔntər, 'tɑnt-, B 'tɔntə] *s.* mofador, burlón.

tauntingly [-ɪŋlɪ] *adv.* en tono insolente o de mofa, burlonamente.

taupe [toʊp] *s.* gris oscuro con un ligero tinte pardo.

Taurid ['tɔrɪd] *s.* (astr.) Taurida.

tauriform ['tɔrəˌfɔrm, B -ˌfɔm] *a.* con forma de toro, tauriforme.

taurine ['tɔrˌaɪn] *a.* taurino.

taurine [-ˌin, B -ˌaɪn] *s.* (bioquím.) taurina.

taurobolium [ˌtɔrə'boʊlɪəm] *s.* (*pl.* TAUROBOLIA [-ə]) (hist.) tauróbolo.

taurocholic [-'koʊlɪk, B -'kɔlɪk] *a.* (bioquím.) taurocólico.

tauromachian [-'meɪkɪən] **tauromachic** [-'mækɪk] *a.* tauromáquico.

tauromachy [tɔ'rɑməkɪ, B -'rɔm-] *s.* tauromaquia.

Taurus ['tɔrəs] *s.* (astr.) Tauro.

taut [tɔt] *a.* 1. tirante, tieso, teso, estirado, ajustado. 2. tenso, en tensión (nervios, etc.). 3. aseado, arreglado, en buen orden (barco).

tauten ['tɔtən] *v.t.* entesar, atiesar; (mar.) tesar (las velas). —*v.i.* atiesarse, entiesarse.

tautly ['tɔtlɪ] *adv.* tensamente, tiesamente, con tirantez.

tautness [-nəs] *s.* tirantez, tensión, tiesura.

tautochrone ['tɔtəˌkroʊn] *s.* (mat.) curva tautócrona.

tautog ['tɔˌtɔg, -ˌtɑg, B -ˌtɔg] *s.* (ict.) tautoga.

tautological [ˌtɔtə'lɑdʒɪkəl, B -'lɔdʒ-] *a.* tautológico, redundante.

tautologically [-kəlɪ] *adv.* tautológicamente, de manera tautológica, con redundancia.

tautologize [tɔ'tɑləˌdʒaɪz, B -'tɔl-] *v.i.,* repetir, emplear redundancias.

tautologous [-gəs] *a.* tautológico.

tautology [-dʒɪ] *s.* (ret.) tautología, redundancia.

tautomer ['tɔtəmər, B -mə] *s.* (quím.) tautómero.

tautomeric [ˌtɔtə'mɛrɪk] *a.* (quím.) tautómero.

tautomerism [tɔ'tɑməˌrɪzəm, B -'tɔm-] *s.* (quím.) tautomería.

tautonym ['tɔtəˌnɪm] *s.* (zool.) tautónimo.

tautonymic [ˌtɔtə'nɪmɪk] *a.* (bot., zool.) tautónimo.

tavern ['tævərn, B -ən] *s.* 1. taberna, bodega, cantina, bar. 2. mesón, posada, hostería.

taverner [-ərnər, B -ənə] *s.* (ant.) tabernero; parroquiano de taberna.

tavern keeper, tabernero, posadero.

taw [tɔ] *s.* 1. canicas; canica (juego de muchachos o la bolita para este juego). 2. línea de lanzamiento (en el juego de canica). —*v.i.* jugar con canicas.

taw, *v.t.* 1. curtir en blanco (piel). 2. (dial.) agramar (el cáñamo).

tawdrily ['tɔdrəlɪ] *adv.* charramente.

tawdriness [-rɪnəs] *s.* charrería.

tawdry [-rɪ] *a.* (TAWDRIER; TAWDRIEST) charro, chillón y poco elegante; (fig.) deslucido.

tawer ['tɔər, B -ə] *s.* 1. curtidor (de pieles). 2. (dial.) agramador (de cáñamo).

tawniness ['tɔnɪnəs] *s.* color tostado.

tawny ['tɔnɪ] *a.* (TAWNIER; TAWNIEST) atezado, tostado, leonado.

tawny owl, (zool.) oto, autillo, alucón, cárabo, úlula.

tawpie ['tɔpɪ] *s.* (esco.) simplón o bobarrón joven.

tax [tæks] *v.t.* 1. imponer (contribuciones), gravar, exigir impuestos a. 2. cargar, abrumar. 3. (gen. seguido de *with*) acusar (de), censurar (por). 4. (der.) tasar, avaluar, fijar (costas), gravar. 5. poner a prueba (la paciencia de alguien). —*s.* 1. impuesto, contribución, gabela. 2. (con *on* o *upon*) demanda, carga, exacción. —*a.* tributario; de impuestos.

taxability [ˌtæksə'bɪlətɪ] *s.* imponibilidad.

taxable ['tæksəbəl] *a.* imponible, gravable, sujeto a impuestos.

taxable income, renta imponible, renta gravable.

taxable profits, (ten.) utilidades impositivas.

taxable value, (ten.) valor impositivo.

taxaceous [tæk'seɪʃəs] *a.* (bot.) taxáceo.

taxation [tæk'seɪʃən] *s.* 1. tributación, fijación de impuestos, sistema tributario. 2. impuestos, contribución de impuestos.

tax base, base imponible, base impositiva.

tax collector, recaudador de impuestos.

tax-deductible *a.* desgravable.

tax deduction, gasto deducible.

tax evasion, evasión fiscal, evasión de impuestos.

tax-exempt ['tæksɪg'zɛmpt] *a.* exento de impuestos, no gravable.

tax exemption, (E.U.) desgravación fiscal, deducción impositiva.

tax-free [-'fri] *a.* libre de impuestos.

taxgatherer [-ˌgæðərər, B -ə] *s.* recaudador de contribuciones, exactor.

tax haven, paraíso fiscal.

taxi ['tæksɪ] *s.* (*pl.* TAXIS) taxi. —*v.i.* (*pret., p.p.* TAXIED; *p.pr.* TAXIING O TAXYING) 1. ir en taxi. 2. (aer.) carretear, rodar, deslizar (un avión). —*v.t.* 1. llevar en taxi. 2. (aer.) carretear, hacer rodar por tierra (un avión).

taxicab [-ˌkæb] *s.* taxi, carro de alquiler, coche o auto de alquiler (Am.).

taxi dancer, pareja de baile pagada.

taxidermal [ˌtæksə'dɜrməl, B -'dɜməl] *a.* de taxidermia.

taxidermist ['tæksəˌdɜrməst, B -ˌdɜmɪst] *s.* taxidermista, disecador.

taxidermy [-mɪ] *s.* taxidermia (disecación de animales).

taxi driver, taxista, chofer de taxi (Am.).

taximan ['tæksɪmən] *s.* (pr. G.B.) taxista.

taximeter [-ˌmitər, B -ə] *s.* taxímetro.

taxing ['tæksɪŋ] *a.* oneroso, gravoso, agotador, fatigoso.

taxis ['tæksəs] *s.* 1. (biol.) taxismo, taxia. 2. (med.) taxis.

taxi stand, parada de coches, parada de taxis, estación de taxis (Amer.).

taxite ['tækˌsaɪt] *s.* (min.) taxita.

taxiway ['tæksɪˌweɪ] *s.* (aer.) pista de rodaje, pista de maniobras, antepista.

tax list, lista de contribuyentes.

taxon ['tækˌsɑn, B -ˌsɔn] *s.* (*pl.* TAXA [-sə] o TAXONS) grupo o entidad taxonómica.

taxonomic [ˌtæksə'nɑmɪk, B -'nɔm-] *a.* taxonómico, propio o relativo a la clasificación.

taxonomist [tæk'sɑnəməst, B -'sɔn-] *s.* especializado en taxonomía.

taxonomy [-mɪ] *s.* (biol.) taxonomía, taxinomía.

taxpayer ['tæksˌpeɪər, B -ə] *s.* contribuyente.

tax rate, tasa tributaria o impositiva.

tax stamp, timbre fiscal.

tax system, sistema tributario.

taxus ['tæksəs] *s.* (bot.) tejo.

Taylorism ['teɪləˌrɪzəm] *s.* (relig.) taylorismo, doctrina que sigue la tendencia calvinista con algunas modificaciones.

Tb *símb. de* **terbium,** terbio (Tb).

TB *abrev. de* **tuberculosis,** tuberculosis.

T-bar ['tiˌbɑr, B -ˌbɑ] (const.) barra T, perfil T.

t bevel, falsa escuadra en T.

T bolt, perno de cabeza en T.

Tc *símb. de* **technetium,** tecnecio (Tc).
T connector, conector en T.
Te *símb. de* **tellurium,** telurio (Te).
tea [ti] *s.* 1. té (planta, hoja, bebida). 2. infusión; caldo, ej., *beef t.*, caldo concentrado de carne. 3. (jer.) marihuana. 4. té, reunión o acontecimiento social en el que se sirve té.
tea bag, bolsita de té.
tea ball, huevo del té, esfera metálica perforada para hacer té.
teaberry ['tiˌbɛrɪ] *s.* (bot.) gaulteria.
tea biscuit, (G.B.) galleta, pastelito.
tea cake, (G.B.) bizcocho chato; pastelito.
tea canister, lata para guardar té.
teacart ['tiˌkɑrt, B -ˌkɑt] mesa rodante, carrito del té.
teach [titʃ] *v.t.* (*pret., p.p.* TAUGHT [tɔt]; *p.pr.* TEACHING) enseñar, instruir; educar; **t. (someone) a lesson,** dar a (alguien) una lección. —*v.i.* dar instrucción, ser maestro, ejercer el magisterio.
teachability [ˌtitʃə'bɪlətɪ] *s.* 1. docilidad, capacidad o habilidad para ser enseñado. 2. utilidad para la enseñanza (díc. de un libro, texto, etc.).
teachable ['titʃəbəl] *a.* enseñable, instruible, educable; dócil.
teacher ['titʃər, B -tʃə] *s.* maestro, maestra, profesor, instructor, preceptor.
teachers college, (ant.) escuela normal.
teachers institute, instituto pedagógico.
teach-in ['titʃˌɪn] *s.* asamblea o reunión especial, en una escuela o universidad, con debates, conferencias, etc. sobre temas específicos, fuera del plan de estudios.
teaching ['titʃɪŋ] *s.* 1. enseñanza, instrucción. 2. enseñanza, doctrina. 3. magisterio.
teaching method, método de enseñanza, método pedagógico.
teaching staff, personal docente, cuadro de profesores.
tea cozy, abrigo de tetera, cubretetera.
teacup ['tiˌkʌp] *s.* taza de té; **a storm in a t.,** una tempestad en un vaso de agua.
teacupful [-ˌfʊl] *s.* (*pl.* TEACUPFULS) (medida de una) taza de té, taza (llena de té).
tea dance, té bailable.
teahouse [-ˌhaʊs] *s.* salón de té.
teak [tik] *s.* (bot.) teca.
teakettle ['tiˌkɛtəl] *s.* tetera.
teakwood ['tikˌwʊd] *s.* madera de teca.
teal [til] *s.* (*pl.* TEAL O TEALS) (orn.) cerceta, trullo.
tea leaf, 1. hoja de té. 2. (*pl.*) (G.B., jer.) ladrón.
team [tim] *s.* 1. equipo, grupo (de jugadores, colaboradores, científicos, etc.). 2. yunta, yugada, tronco, tiro, atelaje. 3. camada de puercos; cría de patos. 4. (ant.) progenie, linaje. —*v.t.* 1. uncir, enyugar, enganchar. 2. transportar por medio de una yunta (de animales). 3. (G.B.) dar (trabajo) a contratista (que emplea un grupo de trabajadores). —*v.i.* 1. trabajar como tronquista. 2. **t. up (with)** asociarse (con), unir fuerzas (con); **t. up together,** unir fuerzas, formar un equipo.
teammate ['timˌmeɪt] *s.* compañero de equipo.
team spirit, espíritu de equipo, espíritu de cooperación.
teamster [-stər, B -stə] *s.* 1. tronquista, carretero, carrero, carretonero. 2. conductor de camión profesional.
teamwork [-ˌwɜrk, B -ˌwɜk] *s.* 1. trabajo en equipo o colectivo. 2. solidaridad, cooperación, coordinación, espíritu de grupo.
tea party, 1. té, reunión por la tarde para tomar el té. 2. (jer.) bochinche, altercado, escaramuza.
teapot ['tiˌpɑt, B -ˌpɔt] *s.* tetera.
teapoy [-ˌpɔɪ] *s.* (anglo-ind.) mesita ornamental de tres patas; mesita de té.
tear [tɪr, B tɪə] *s.* 1. lágrima. 2. gota (ej., de resina). 3. (*pl.*) lágrimas, lloro, llanto. 4. **to be in tears,** estar llorando; **to burst into tears,** saltarle or saltársele a uno las lágrimas; **to hold back one's tears,** beberse las lágrimas; **to move to tears,** conmover, hacer llorar; **to shed tears,** llorar, verter lágrimas; **to wipe away one's tears,** enjugarse las lágrimas. —*v.i.* verter lágrimas.
tear [tɛr, B tɛə] *v.t.* (*pret.* TORE [tɔr, B tɔ]; *p.p.* TORN [tɔrn, B tɔn]; *p.pr.* TEARING) 1. desgarrar, romper, rasgar, despedazar. 2. (gen. con *away, out, off* o *from,* etc.) arrancar, separar con violencia. 3. (fig.) dividir, separar; perturbar, atormentar, torturar. 4. **t. down,** arrancar (un afiche de la pared), derribar, demoler (un edificio), desarmar (una máquina); (fig.) denigrar, manchar (reputación); **t. oneself away,** desgarrarse, separarse (contra su voluntad); **t. open,** abrir precipitada o violentamente; **t. out,** arrancar, separar con violencia; **t. up,** romper; hacer pedazos; desarraigar, sacar de raíz. —*v.i.* 1. separarse, romperse, rasgarse, hacerse pedazos. 2. **t. along,** pasar a toda velocidad; **t. around,** andar apresurada o excitadamente; llevar una vida desordenada; **t. at,** romper precipitadamente (ej., envoltura); **t. away** (u **off**), irse corriendo; **t. into,** acometer, agredir, caer encima; **t. out,** salir con ímpetu. —*s.* 1. desgarradura, rasgadura, rotura, desgarro. 2. prisa, ímpetu, precipitación. 3. (jer. E.U.) jarana.
teardown ['tɛrˌdaʊn, B 'tɛəˌ-] *s.* demolición; desarmadura.
teardrop ['tɪrˌdrɑp, B 'tɪəˌdrɔp] *s.* lágrima; joya del arete.
tearful [-fəl] *a.* 1. lagrimoso, lacrimoso, plañidero, llorón. 2. lagrimoso, lloroso, conmovedor.
tearfully [-fəlɪ] *adv.* llorosamente, lleno de lágrimas.
tearfulness [-fəlnəs] *s.* estado lagrimoso; tristeza, desconsuelo.
tear gas, gas lacrimoso, gas lacrimógeno.
tearjerker [-ˌdʒɜrkər, B -ˌdʒɜkə] *s.* (jer.) relato o drama ramplón o excesivamente sentimental.
tearless [-ləs] *a.* sin lágrimas.
tearoom ['tiˌrum, -ˌrʊm] *s.* salón de té.
tea rose, (bot.) rosa (de) té.
tear sheet ['tɛr-, B 'tɛə-] (impr.) página suelta (de un periódico), comprobante del anuncio (que se envía al anunciador).
tearstain ['tɪrˌsteɪn, B 'tɪəˌ-] *s.* mancha o huella de lágrima.
teary ['tɪrɪ, B 'tɪərɪ] *a.* (TEARIER; TEARIEST) 1. lagrimoso, lacrimoso. 2. lloroso, conmovedor.
tease [tiz] *v.t.* 1. importunar, fastidiar, embromar (Amer.), tomar el pelo a. 2. despedazar, desmenuzar (para examen microscópico). 3. cardar, carduzar, peinar (paños). —*s.* 1. fastidio, molestia, importunación. 2. embromador, cócora.
teasel ['tizəl] *s.* 1. (bot.) cardencha. 2. cardencha, carda (instrumento que sirve para cardar). —*v.t.* (*pret., p.p.* TEASELED O TEASELLED; *p.pr.* TEASELING O TEASELLING) carmenar, cardar (paño), sacar (el pelo) con la carda.
teaseler, teaseller [-zələr, B -lə] *s.* pelaire, cardador, carmenador.
teaser ['tizər, B -zə] *s.* 1. cócora, embromador (Amer.). 2. problema difícil, rompecabezas intrigante. 3. cosa tentadora e incitadora. 4. (jer.) mujer que provoca intencionadamente el deseo sexual sin llegar a satisfacerlo.
tea service, t. set, juego de té, servicio de té.
tea shop, (pr. G.B.) salón de té.
teasingly ['tizɪŋlɪ] *adv.* 1. en broma, en chanza. 2. con aire provocativo o incitante, provocativamente.
teaspoon ['tiˌspun] *s.* cucharilla o cucharita de té.
teaspoonful [-ˌfʊl] *s.* (*pl.* TEASPOONFULS O TEASPOONSFUL) cucharilla o cucharita llena, cucharadita.
teat [tɪt, B tit] *s.* teta, tetilla, pezón.
tea table, mesita de té.
teatime ['tiˌtaɪm] *s.* hora del té.
tea towel, albero, secador (de platos), paño de cocina.
tea tray, bandeja del té.
tea wagon, mesa rodante, carrito de té.
teazel, teazle, *vars. de* **teasel.**
tech. *abrev. de* 1. **technical,** técnico. 2. **technically,** técnicamente. 3. **technology,** tecnología.
tech [tɛk] *s.* (jer.) escuela tecnológica.
teched [tɛtʃt] *a.* (jer.) tocado, medio loco, chiflado.
technetium [tɛk'niʃɪəm] *s.* (quím.) tecnecio.
technic ['tɛknɪk] *s.* 1. técnica. 2. (*pl.*) (sing. o pl. en const.) métodos técnicos. —*a.* técnico.
technical ['tɛknɪkəl] *a.* 1. técnico. 2. de aspecto legal, calificado por la ley como, según la ley.
technical adviser, asesor técnico.
technical college, escuela politécnica.
technicality [ˌtɛknə'kælətɪ] *s.* (*pl.* TECHNICALITIES) 1. tecnicidad. 2. tecnicismo, voz técnica. 3. punto o detalle técnico.
technically ['tɛknɪkəlɪ] *adv.* 1. técnicamente. 2. conforme a la ley (estricta); a la letra.
technical overdraft, (com.) sobregiro aparente, sobregiro técnico.
technician [tɛk'nɪʃən] *s.* técnico, especialista, experto técnico.
Technicolor (TM) ['tɛknɪˌkʌlər, B -ə] *s.* 1. (foto.) tecnicolor. 2. t., (fig.) colorido brillante, colores deslumbrantes, colores chillones.
technique [tɛk'nik] *s.* técnica.
technochemistry ['tɛknoʊ'kɛmətrɪ] *s.* química industrial.
technocracy [tɛk'nɑkrəsɪ, B -'nɔk-] *s.* tecnocracia.
technocrat ['tɛknəˌkræt] *s.* tecnócrata.
technological [ˌtɛknə'lɑdʒɪkəl, B -'lɔdʒ-] **technologic** [-'lɑdʒɪk, B -'lɔdʒ-] *a.* tecnológico.
technologist [tɛk'nɑlədʒəst, B -'nɔl-] *s.* técnico, especialista; tecnólogo.
techonology [-dʒɪ] *s.* (*pl.* TECHNOLOGIES) tecnología.
techy, *var. de* **tetchy.**
tectonic [tɛk'tɑnɪk, B -'tɔn-] *a.* 1. estructural, arquitectónico, arquitectural. 2. (geol.) tectónico.
tectonic earthquake, (geof.) terremoto tectónico, sismo de dislocación.
tectonics [-ɪks] *s. pl.* (*sing. o pl. en const.*) 1. arte de la construcción. 2. (geol.) tectónica, estructura terrestre.
tectrix ['tɛktrɪks] *s.* (*pl.* TECTRICES [-trəˌsiz, B tɛk'traɪ-]) (zool.) tectriz.
ted [tɛd] *v.t.* (*pret., p.p.* TEDDED; *p.pr.* TEDDING) (agr.) henificar, henear (pasto, césped, etc.).
tedder ['tɛdər, B -ə] *s.* (agr.) henificadora (máquina).
teddy bear ['tɛdɪ-] osito de felpa o de trapo, osito de juguete.
Te Deum [teɪ'deɪəm, B 'ti'di-] (relig.) tedéum.
tedious ['tidɪəs] *a.* tedioso, aburrido, fastidioso.
tediously [-lɪ] *adv.* aburridamente, tediosamente.
tediousness [-nəs] *s.* tedio.
tedium ['tidɪəm] *s.* tedio, aburrimiento, fastidio, hastío.

tee [ti] *s.* (*pl.* TEES) 1. (la letra) te. 2. **to a t.,** a la perfección, exactamente. —*a.* en forma de (la letra) te.
tee, *s.* 1. marca, meta, hito (en un juego). 2. (golf) tee, punto de partida. —*v.t., v.i.* (golf) colocar la pelota en un tee; **t. off,** dar el primer golpe a la pelota; (fig.) empezar, comenzar.
teel [til] *var. de* **til.**
teem [tim] *v.i.* 1. (con *with*) rebosar o estar lleno (de); hervir (de). 2. (ant.) parir, llevar en las entrañas. —*v.t.* (ant.) producir, generar, abundar (algo en alguna parte).
teeming ['timɪŋ] *a.* 1. prolífico, fecundo; abundante. 2. apiñado, atestado.
teen [tin] *s.* (ant.) lesión; dolor; ira, vejación.
teen, *var. de* **teen-age.**
teen-age ['tin,eɪdʒ] *a.* de la adolescencia.
teen-ager [-ər, B -ə] *s.* joven de 13 a 19 años de edad, adolescente.
teener ['tinər, B -nə] *var. de* **teen-ager.**
teenie-weenie, *var. de* **teeny-weeny.**
teens [tinz] *s.* (*pl.*) números o años de edad entre 13 y 19 años; adolescencia; **to be in one's t.,** tener entre 13 y 19 años, ser (un) adolescente.
teeny ['tinɪ] *a.* (TEENIER; TEENIEST) (fam.) pequeñito, menudo, chiquitín.
teeny-weeny [-'winɪ] *a.* (fam.) chiquirritillo, chiquitito.
teepee, *var. de* **tepee.**
tee shirt, *var. de* **T-shirt.**
teeter ['titər, B -ə] *v.i.* 1. balancearse, columpiarse, oscilar. 2. tambalear(se), bambolear(se); ir tambaleando, andar trastabillando. 3. vacilar, titubear. —*s.* balanceo, vaivén; columpio.
teeterboard [-,bɔrd, B -,bɔd] *s.* 1. tabla de un sube y baja. 2. trampolín en forma de balancín de tabla (para disparar al que está de pie en un extremo cuando alguien salta sobre el otro).
teeth [tiθ] *pl. de* **tooth.**
teethe [tið] *v.i.* echar dientes, dentar.
teething ['tiðɪŋ] *s.* dentición.
teething ring, chupadero, chupador, aro para ayudar a la dentición.
teethridge ['tiθ,rɪdʒ] *s.* (anat.) alvéolo, alveolo.
teetotal ['ti,toʊtəl, B ti'toʊt-] *a.* 1. abstemio, partidario de la templanza. 2. (fam.) entero, completo, total, absoluto.
teetotaler [-'toʊtələr, B -'toʊtlə] *s.* abstemio.
teetotalism [-əl,ɪzəm] *s.* abstinencia, templanza.
teetotalist [-əst] *s.* (G.B.) abstemio.
teetotum [ti'toʊtəm, B 'titoʊ'tʌm] *s.* perinola, perindola.
Teflon (TM) ['tɛflɑn] *s.* Teflon, Teflón, Tefal; **a T. bullet,** una bala Teflon.
teg [tɛg] *s.* (G.B.) oveja de dos años.
tegmen ['tɛgmən] *s.* (*pl.* TEGMINA [-mənə]) (anat., zool., bot.) tegmen.
tegmental [tɛg'mɛntəl] *a.* (anat., zool., bot.) tegmental.
tegmentum [-əm] *s.* (*pl.* TEGMENTA [-ə]) *var. de* **tegument.**
tegula ['tɛgjələ] *s.* (*pl.* TEGULAE [-,li]) (zool.) tégula.
tegular [-lər, B -lə] *a.* tegular.
tegument [-mənt] *s.* (anat., zool., bot.) tegumento.
tegumentary [,tɛgjə'mɛntərɪ] *a.* (anat., zool., bot.) tegumentario.
te-hee ['ti'hi] *s.* risa entre dientes, risa burlona. —*v.i.* reír entre dientes.
teil tree [til-] (bot.) tilo, alfóncigo, tarebinto.
tektite ['tɛktaɪt] *s.* (min.) tectita.
telamon ['tɛlə,mɑn, B -mən] *s.* (*pl.* TELAMONES [,tɛlə'moʊniz]) (arq.) telamón, atlante.
telangiectasis [tɛl,ændʒɪ'ɛktəsəs] *s.* (*pl.* TELANGIECTASES [-,siz]) (med.) telangiectasia.
telangiectatic [-ɛk'tætɪk] *a.* (med.) telangiectásico.
telautograph [tɛl'ɔtə,græf, B -grɑf] *s.* telautógrafo, aparato que transmite texto y fotos por cable.
telecast ['tɛlɪ,kæst, B -,kɑst] *v.t., v.i.* (*pret., p.p.* TELECAST O TELECASTED; *p.pr.* TELECASTING) teledifundir, transmitir por televisión. —*s.* teledifusión, transmisión televisada.
telecommunication [,tɛlɪkə,mjunə'keɪʃən] *s.* telecomunicación.
teleconference *s.* teleconferencia.
telecourse ['tɛlɪ,kɔrs, B -,kɔs] *s.* curso de estudios televisado.
telectroscope [tə'lɛktrə,skoʊp] *s.* telectroscopio.
teledu ['tɛlə,du] *s.* (zool.) teledu.
telefilm ['tɛlə,fɪlm] *s.* película para televisión.
telega [tɪ'lɛgə, B -'leɪgə] *s.* telega (carro de transporte usado en Rusia).
telegauge ['tɛlə,geɪdʒ] *s.* teleindicador, indicador a distancia.
telegenic [,tɛlə'dʒɛnɪk] *a.* (t.v.) telegénico.
telegony [tə'lɛgənɪ] *s.* (biol.) telegonía.
telegram ['tɛlə,græm] *s.* telegrama. —*v.t.* (*pret., p.p.* TELEGRAMMED; *p.pr.* TELEGRAMMING) telegrafiar.
telegraph [-,græf, B -,grɑf] *s.* (teleg.) 1. telégrafo. 2. telegrama. —*v.t.* telegrafiar. —*v.i.* mandar un telegrama.
telegraph code, clave telegráfica.
telegrapher [tə'lɛgrəfər, B -fə] *s.* telegrafista.
telegraphic [,tɛlə'græfɪk] *a.* telegráfico.
telegraphically [-ɪkəlɪ] *adv.* telegráficamente.
telegraphist [tə'lɛgrəfəst] *s.* telegrafista.
telegraph key, manipulador, llave telegráfica.
telegraphone [tə'lɛgrə,foʊn] *s.* telegráfono.
telegraph operator, telegrafista.
telegraph pole, poste telegráfico, poste de telégrafo.
telegraph shovel, pala para hoyos.
telegraphy [tə'lɛgrəfɪ] *s.* telegrafía.
telekinesis [,tɛləkə'nisəs, B -kaɪ-] *s.* (parasicología) telequinesis.
telelectric [-'lɛktrɪk] *s.* teleléctrico, mando electrónico a distancia.
telelens ['tɛlɪ,lɛnz] *s.* (foto.) teleobjetivo.
Telemachus [tə'lɛməkəs] *s.* (mitol.) Telémaco, hijo de Odiseo y Penélope.
telemanometer [,tɛləmə'nɑmətər, B -'nɔmɪtə] *s.* telemanómetro.
telemechanics [-mə'kænɪks] *s.* telemecánica.
telemechanism [-'mɛkə,nɪzəm] *s.* telemecanismo, mando mecánico a distancia.
telemeter ['tɛlə,mitər, B -ə] *s.* telémetro, distanciómetro.
telemetric [,tɛlə'mɛtrɪk] *a.* telemétrico, distanciométrico.
telemetry [tə'lɛmətrɪ] *s.* telemetría.
telencephalon [,tɛlɛn'sɛfə,lɑn, B -lɔn] *s.* (med.) telencéfalo.
teleobjective [,tɛlɪəb'dʒɛktɪv] *s.* (foto.) teleobjetivo.
teleological [,tilɪə'lɑdʒɪkəl, B -'lɔdʒ-] *a.* (filos.) teleológico.
teleology [-'ɑlədʒɪ, B -'ɔl-] *s.* (filos.) teleología.
teleost ['tɛlɪ,ɑst, B -ɔst] **teleostean** [,tɛlɪ'ɑstɪən, B -'ɔs-] *s., a.* (ict.) teleósteo.
telepathic [,tɛlə'pæθɪk] *a.* telepático.
telepathically [-ɪkəlɪ] *adv.* telepáticamente.
telepathist [tə'lɛpəθəst] *s.* telepatista.
telepathy [-θɪ] *s.* telepatía.
telephone ['tɛlə,foʊn] *s.* teléfono; **to be on the t.,** estar hablando por teléfono. —*v.t.* telefonear. —*v.i.* llamar por teléfono.
telephone book, guía telefónica, guía de teléfonos.
telephone booth or **box,** (G.B.) cabina o casilla de teléfono.
telephone directory, guía telefónica, guía de teléfonos.
telephone exchange, central telefónica, central de teléfonos.
telephone message, telefonema, despacho telefónico.
telephone number, número de teléfono.
telephone operator, telefonista.
telephone receiver, receptor telefónico.
telephone switchboard, tablero o pizarra de distribución telefónica.
telephonic [,tɛlə'fɑnɪk, B -'fɔn-] *a.* telefónico.
telephonically [-ɪkəlɪ] *adv.* telefónicamente.
telephonist ['tɛlə,foʊnəst, B tə'lɛfə-] *s.* telefonista.
telephonograph [,tɛlə'foʊnə,græf, B -grɑf] *s.* telefonógrafo.
telephony [tə'lɛfənɪ] *s.* telefonía.
telephoto [-'foʊtoʊ] *a.* (foto.) telefotográfico.
telephotograph [,tɛlə'foʊtə,græf, B -grɑf] *s.* telefotografía.
telephotographic [-,foʊtə'græfɪk] *a.* telefotográfico.
telephotography [-fə'tɑgrəfɪ, B -'tɔg-] *s.* telefotografía.
telephoto lens, (foto.) teleobjetivo, lente de largo alcance.
telephotometer [,tɛləfoʊ'tɑmətər, B -'tɔmɪtə] *s.* telefotómetro.
teleplay ['tɛlə,pleɪ] *s.* drama para televisión.
teleprinter [-,prɪntər, B -ə] *s.* teletipo, teleimpresor.
TelePrompter (TM) (E.U.) [-,prɑmptər, B -,prɔmptə] *s.* (t.v.) teleprompter, autocue.
teleran [-,ræn] *s.* (aer.) telerán, telerradar.
telergy ['tɛlərdʒɪ, B -ədʒɪ] *s.* telepatía.
telescope [-ə,skoʊp] *s.* telescopio. —*v.i.* telescoparse. —*v.t.* 1. telescopar. 2. (fig.) comprimir, condensar.
telescopic [,tɛlə'skɑpɪk, B -'skɔp-] *a.* 1. telescópico (observación, lente, etc.). 2. telescópico, de secciones compresibles.
telescoping gage, calibre telescópico.
Telescopium [-'skoʊpɪəm] *s.* (astr.) Telescopio.
telespectroscope [-'spɛktrə,skoʊp] *s.* telespectroscopio.
telestereoscope [,tɛlə'stɛrɪə,skoʊp, B -'stɪər-] *s.* telestereoscopio.
telesthesia [,tɛləs'θiʒə, B -'θisɪə] *s.* telestesia (percepción psíquica para ver hechos u objetos muy distantes).
telestich, telestic [tə'lɛstɪk] *s.* acróstico.
telethermograph [,tɛlə'θɜrmə,græf, B -'θɜmə,grɑf] *s.* teletermómetro registrador.
telethermometer [-θər'mɑmətər, B -θə'mɔmɪtə] *s.* teletermómetro.
telethermoscope [-'θɜrmə,skoʊp, B -'θɜmə-] *s.* teletermoscopio.
Teletype (TM) (E.U.) ['tɛlə,taɪp] *s.* 1. teletipo. 2. comunicación por medio de teletipo. —*v.t., v.i.* enviar (mensajes) por teletipo.
teletypewriter [-'taɪp,raɪtər, B -ə] *s.* teletipo, teleimpresor, telescriptor.
teletypist [-əst] *s.* operador de teletipo.
teleutospore [tə'lutə,spɔr, B -'ljutə,spɔ] *s.* (bot.) teleutóspora.
teleutosporic [-,lutə'spɔrɪk, B -,ljut-] *a.* (bot.) teleutospórico.
teleview ['tɛlə,vju] *v.t., v.i.* ver por televisión.
televiewer [-ər, B -ə] *s.* televidente, espectador de televisión.

televise [ˈtɛləˌvaɪz] *v.t., v.i.* televisar, transmitir por televisión.
television [-ˌvɪʒən] *a.* televisivo. —*s.* televisión; tele (fam.).
television addict, teleadicto.
televisionally [ˌtɛləˈvɪʒənəlɪ] *adv.* por televisión.
television broadcasting, teledifusión.
television camera, cámara de televisión, cámara televisora.
television screen, pantalla del televisor.
television set, televisor, aparato de televisión.
television transmitter, transmisor de televisión, teletransmisor.
television tube, tubo de televisión, tubo catódico.
telex [ˈtɛlɛks] *s.* 1. télex, sistema de comunicación internacional directo. 2. mensaje enviado o recibido por este medio. —*v.i.* enviar mensajes por télex.
telfer, telferage, *vars. de* **telpher, telpherage.**
telic [ˈtɛlɪk] *a.* intencional, dirigido a un fin.
teliospore [ˈtilɪəˌspɔr, B -ˌspɔ] *s.* (bot.) telióspora, teliospora.
teliosporic [ˌtilɪəˈspɔrɪk] *a.* (bot.) teliospórico.
telium [ˈtilɪəm] *s.* (bot.) telio.
tell [tɛl] *v.t.* (*pret., p.p.* TOLD [tould] *p.pr.* TELLING) 1. decir, contar, narrar, referir, relatar. 2. revelar ej., *it told a tale,* eso reveló mucho. 3. (con *of* o *about*) informar (sobre), dar parte (de). 4. contar (dinero, votos, etc.); enumerar, numerar. 5. **all told,** contando todo; **t. off,** (mil.) separar (contando), destacar o designar (para un servicio); (jer.) regañar, reprender; **t. one to (do),** mandar u ordenar a uno (hacer), decirle a uno que (haga); **t. that to the marines!** (fam.) a otro perro con ese hueso, ¡cuéntaselo a tu abuela!; **t. (someone) where to get off,** (jer.) poner (a alguien) en su sitio; **to tell you the truth,** a decir verdad. —*v.i.* 1. relatar. 2. producir efecto, tener importancia. 3. **I t. you,** (yo) le aseguro, (yo) le digo; **t. against,** perjudicar, ser perjudicial para; **t. of,** dar un informe (sobre), hablar (de); **t. on,** afectar a, hacer mella en; informar sobre, delatar, ej., *don't t. on me,* no me delates; **you're telling me!** (jer.) ¡me lo vas a decir! ¡mire a quién se lo cuenta!; **you never can tell,** las apariencias engañan.
teller [ˈtɛlər, B -ə] *s.* 1. relator, narrador. 2. computador, contador; escrutador de votos. 3. recibidor, pagador (en un banco).
telling [-ɪŋ] *a.* 1. efectivo, eficaz. 2. revelador, expresivo, significante.
tellingly [-lɪ] *adv.* expresivamente.
telltale [-ˌteɪl] *s.* 1. chismoso, cuentista, correveidile; soplón. 2. indicación, indicio, señal. 3. reloj marcador o registrador (de la entrada y salida de empleados, etc.). 4. (mar.) registrador de rumbo (junto al timón). 5. (f.c.) dispositivo de aviso, señal de peligro. —*a.* revelador, delator.
tellurate [ˈtɛljəˌreɪt, B -rət] *s.* (quím.) telurato.
tellurian [təˈlʊrɪən, B -ˈljʊər-] *a.* telúrico. —*s.* morador de la tierra.
telluric [-ɪk] *a.* 1. telúrico, terrestre. 2. (quím.) telúrico (relativo al telurio).
telluride [ˈtɛljəˌraɪd] *s.* (quím.) telururo.
tellurite [-ˌraɪt] *s.* 1. (quím.) telurito. 2. (min.) telurita.
tellurium [təˈlʊrɪəm, B -ˈljʊər-] *s.* (quím.) telurio.
tellurous [ˈtɛljərəs] *a.* (quím.) teluroso.
telly [ˈtɛlɪ] *s.* (fam., G.B.) televisión; aparato de televisión, televisor.
telodynamic [ˌtɛloudaɪˈnæmɪk] *a.* teledinámico.
telolecithal [ˌtɛləˈlɛsəθəl] *s.* (biol.) telolécito.
telome [ˈtiloum] *s.* (bot.) teloma.
telophase [ˈtɛləˌfeɪz] *s.* (biol.) telofase.
telpher [ˈtɛlfər, B -fə] *s.* teleférico, alambrecarril (esp. eléctrico). —*v.t.* transportar por teleférico.
telpherage [ˈtɛlfərɪdʒ] *s.* teleferaje, sistema de transporte teleférico.
telson [ˈtɛlsən] *s.* (zool.) telson.
temblor [ˈtɛmblər, B -blə] *s.* (E.U.) temblor de tierra.
temerarious [ˌtɛməˈrɛrɪəs, B -ˈrɛər-] *a.* temerario, imprudente, precipitado.
temerariously [-lɪ] *adv.* temerariamente.
temerity [təˈmɛrətɪ] *s.* temeridad, audacia, imprudencia, precipitación.
temper [ˈtɛmpər, B -pə] *v.t.* 1. templar (metal, cristal); amasar (arcilla); (pint.) templar (colores). 2. temperar, templar, moderar, mitigar. 3. (mús.) templar (un instrumento). 4. (fig.) templar, aguerrir (soldados, tropa, etc.). 5. (raro) ajustar, concordar. 6. (ant.) combinar, mezclar. —*v.i.* templarse (metal). —*s.* 1. temple (de un metal o cristal, una mezcla, etc.). 2. temple, genio, carácter, humor, disposición (del ánimo). 3. ecuanimidad, compostura, serenidad. 4. irritación, cólera, mal genio. 5. substancia templadora; liga, metal añadido (en una aleación). 6. (pint.) templa. 7. (ant.) constitución (corporal). 8. **a fit of t.,** una rabieta, un acceso de cólera; **out of t.,** fuera de (sus) casillas, de mal temple; **to fly into a t.,** montar en cólera; **to keep one's t.,** dominarse, contenerse; **to lose one's t.,** perder la paciencia, enojarse; **to show t.,** estar de mal genio, estar malhumorado.
tempera [-pərə] *s.* (pint.) pintura al temple.
temperable [-pərəbəl] *a.* templable.
temperament [ˈtɛmprəmənt] *s.* 1. temperamento, constitución, complexión, naturaleza. 2. temperamento, disposición, humor. 3. temperación, templadura. 4. (mús.) temperamento. 5. (ant.) temperatura; temperie, clima.
temperamental [ˌtɛmprəˈmɛntəl] *a.* temperamental; excitable, sensible, emocional.
temperamentally [-əlɪ] *adv.* 1. por naturaleza o índole. 2. de manera temperamental, temperamentalmente.
temperance [ˈtɛmpərəns] *s.* temperancia, templanza, moderación, continencia, abstinencia (esp. de bebidas alcohólicas).
temperate [-ət] *a.* 1. templado, temperado. 2. (mús.) templado.
temperately [-lɪ] *adv.* templadamente, temperadamente.
temperateness [-nəs] *s.* templanza, temperancia.
Temperate Zone, *s.* (geog.) zona templada.
temperature [ˈtɛmprətʃər, B -tʃə] *s.* 1. temperatura. 2. fiebre, calentura. 3. (ant.) temperamento; templanza.
temperature correction, (meteor.) corrección por temperatura.
temperature gradient, (meteor.) pendiente de temperatura.
temperature indicator, termómetro, indicador de temperatura.
temperature recorder, registrador de temperatura.
temperature stress, esfuerzo por temperatura o de temperatura.
tempered [ˈtɛmpərd, B -pəd] *a.* 1. dispuesto, inclinado (bien, mal, etc.). 2. templado, moderado. 3. (mús.) modificado a temperamento.
temperer [-pərər, B -pərə] *s.* 1. templador. 2. aliviador, mitigador. 3. máquina mezcladora (de cemento, cal, etc.).
tempering [-pərɪŋ] *a.* templador. —*s.* templadura, temple.
temper mill, (metal.) laminador de temple.
temper pin, (esco.) 1. perno regulador de un torno de hilar. 2. (mús.) clavija de violín.
temper screw, (mec.) tornillo graduador.
tempest [ˈtɛmpəst] *s.* 1. tempestad, borrasca, tormenta. 2. (fig.) tumulto, agitación borrascosa. 3. **t. in a teapot,** tempestad en un vaso de agua. —*v.t.* agitar, conmover violentamente.
tempestuous [tɛmˈpɛstʃuəs, B -tju-] *a.* tempestuoso, turbulento, borrascoso.
tempestuously [-lɪ] *adv.* tempestuosamente.
tempestuousness [-nəs] *s.* carácter tempestuoso.
templar [ˈtɛmplər, B -plə] *s.* 1. **T.,** (hist.) templario. 2. (G.B.) abogado o estudiante de derecho (que pertenece a la orden de abogados del Temple en Londres). 3. (E.U.) templario (miembro de cierta orden masónica).
template [-plət] *s.* 1. (arq.) solera. 2. patrón, calibre, plantilla, modelo. 3. (mar.) gálibo.
temple [ˈtɛmpəl] *s.* 1. templo, santuario, iglesia. 2. (fig.) templo. 3. (anat.) sien. 4. (tej.) templén. 5. **T.,** una de las sociedades de abogados que hay en Londres.
templet, *var. de* **template.**
tempo [ˈtɛmpou] *s.* (*pl.* TEMPI [-pi] o TEMPOS) 1. (mús.) compás, tempo. 2. (fig.) ritmo, paso.
temporal [ˈtɛmpərəl] *a.* (anat.) temporal.
temporal, *a.* 1. temporal, del tiempo. 2. temporal, transitorio, pasajero. 3. temporal, secular, profano.
temporal bone, (anat.) (hueso) temporal.
temporality [ˌtɛmpəˈrælətɪ] *s.* 1. temporalidad, carácter temporal. 2. (relig.) (*gen. pl.*) temporalidades.
temporally [ˈtɛmpərəlɪ] *adv.* temporalmente, transitoriamente.
temporarily [ˌtɛmpəˈrɛrəlɪ, B ˈtɛmpərər-] *adv.* temporalmente, momentáneamente.
temporary [ˈtɛmpəˌrɛrɪ, B -rərɪ] *a.* temporaneo, temporario; temporero (obrero); interino (persona designada).
temporary cartilage, (biol.) cartílago temporal, cartílago de osificación.
temporary duty, (mil.) servicio interino.
temporization [ˌtɛmpərəˈzeɪʃən, B -raɪ-] *s.* contemporización.
temporize [ˈtɛmpəˌraɪz] *v.i.* contemporizar, temporizar.
temporizer [-ər, B -ə] *s.* contemporizador, contemporizadora.
tempt [tɛmpt] *v.t.* 1. tentar, seducir. 2. tentar, inducir, instigar, incitar. 3. tentar, provocar. 4. probar, arriesgar. 5. **t. (one) into,** tentar (a uno); **t. (one) into (doing),** tentar o provocar (a uno) a que (haga); **t. (one) to (do),** tentar (a uno) a (hacer), tentar (a uno) a que (haga).
temptable [ˈtɛmptəbəl] *a.* susceptible a tentación.
temptation [tɛmpˈteɪʃən] *s.* tentación; **to fall into t.,** caer en la tentación.
tempter [ˈtɛmptər, B -tə] *s.* tentador; **the T.,** el tentador (el diablo).
tempting [-tɪŋ] *a.* tentador, atractivo, seductor.
temptingly [-lɪ] *adv.* de manera tentadora o seductora, tentadoramente.
temptress [-trəs] *s.* tentadora, mujer seductora.
ten [tɛn] *s.* 1. diez. 2. (fam.) billete de diez dólares. —*a.* diez.
tenability [ˌtɛnəˈbɪlətɪ] *s.* validez (de una teoría, hipótesis, argumento, etc.).
tenable [ˈtɛnəbəl] *a.* sostenible, defendible, defensible.
tenace [ˈtɛneɪs, B -əs] *s.* (naipes) tenaza.
tenacious [təˈneɪʃəs] *a.* 1. tenaz, resistente, cohesivo. 2. tenaz, adhesivo, pegajoso. 3. retentiva (memoria). 4. tenaz, pertinaz, persistente.

tenaciously [-lɪ] *adv.* tenazmente, con firmeza.
tenaciousness [-nəs] *s.* tenacidad, pertinacia, firmeza.
tenacity [tə'næsətɪ] *s.* tenacidad; (fís.) tenacidad.
tenaculum [tə'nækjələm] *s.* (*pl.* TENACULA [-lə]) (med., ento.) tenáculo.
tenaille, tenail [tə'neɪl] *s.* (fort.) tenaza.
tenaillon [tə'nɑ'joʊn, B -'nælɪən] *s.* (fort.) tenallón.
tenancy ['tɛnənsɪ] *s.* (der.) tenencia, posesión; inquilinato, arrendamiento.
tenant ['tɛnənt] *s.* 1. (der.) arrendatario, inquilino. 2. habitante, morador, ocupante. —*v.t.* tener en arriendo.
tenantable [-əbəl] *a.* 1. (der.) arrendable. 2. habitable, ocupable.
tenant farmer, agricultor arrendatario.
tenantless [-ləs] *a.* desarrendado, deshabitado.
tenantry ['tɛnəntrɪ] *s.* 1. tenencia, posesión. 2. inquilinato, arriendo. 3. conjunto de inquilinos.
tench [tɛntʃ] *s.* (ict.) tenca.
Ten Commandments, (bíbl.) diez mandamientos.
tend [tɛnd] *v.i.* **t. on,** asistir, atender, servir (como criado o asistente); **t. to,** atender a. —*v.t.* 1. atender, cuidar (a enfermo, planta, máquina, etc.); **I will t. bar today,** estaré de barman hoy; **I will t. the fire tonight,** vigilará el fuego esta noche. 2. (ant.) acompañar (como criado o asistente).
tend [tɛnd] *v.i.* 1. dirigirse, moverse. 2. **t. (to do),** tener el efecto de, contribuir a, tender a, propender a, inclinarse a; servir para. —*v.t.* (mar.) vigilar (una soga, cadena, etc. para impedir que se enrede).
tendance ['tɛndəns] (ant.) *s.* 1. ministración; atención, cuidado, servicio. 2. comitiva, séquito.
tendency [-dənsɪ] *s.* (*pl.* TENDENCIES) tendencia, inclinación.
tendentious [tɛn'dɛntʃəs, B -'dɛnʃəs] *a.* tendencioso.
tendentiously [-lɪ] *adv.* de manera tendenciosa, tendenciosamente.
tendentiousness [-nəs] *s.* carácter tendencioso.
tender ['tɛndər, B -də] *s.* 1. servidor; guarda, vigilante, guardián; peón de albañil. 2. (mar.) buque nodriza. 3. (mar.) transbordador, alijadora, gabarra, patache. 4. (f.c.) ténder, alijo.
tender ['tɛndər, B -də] *v.t.* 1. (der.) ofrecer (suma, dinero, etc.) en pago (de una obligación). 2. ofrecer, proponer, presentar (presupuesto, servicios, renuncia, etc.). —*s.* 1. (der.) oferta formal de pago (de una obligación). 2. oferta, ofrecimiento, propuesta (esp. en una licitación).
tender, *a.* (TENDERER; TENDEREST) 1. tierno, blando, suave, muelle. 2. tierno, débil, delicado, frágil. 3. tierno, afectuoso, amoroso, cariñoso. 4. (con *of, over* o *upon*) considerado, cuidadoso, solícito (con). 5. tierno, inmaduro, joven. 6. delicado, fino, suave. 7. sensible, emotivo, impresionable, susceptible. 8. de tono suave y delicado (color). 9. delicado, difícil, arriesgado (tema, asunto, etc.). 10. (mar.) celoso. —*v.t., v.i.* 1. enternecer(se). 2. (ant.) tratar con ternura. —*s.* (ant.) consideración, miramiento, cuidado.
tender age, edad tierna, primeros años.
tenderfoot [-ˌfʊt] *s.* (*pl.* TENDERFEET [-ˌfit] o TENDERFOOTS) 1. bisoño, novato, inexperto. 2. (E.U.) colono recién llegado.
tenderhearted [-'hɑrtəd, B -'hɑt-] *a.* bondadoso, compasivo; impresionable, susceptible.
tenderize ['tɛndəˌraɪz] *v.t.* suavizar, ablandar (carne).
tenderling [-dərlɪŋ, B -dəlɪŋ] *s.* 1. persona consentida, mimada o delicada; criatura. 2. pitón de asta de venado.
tenderloin [-dərˌlɔɪn, B -dəˌ-] *s.* 1. filete de solomillo, lomo. 2. bajos fondos (de una ciudad).
tenderly ['tɛndərlɪ, B -dəlɪ] *adv.* tiernamente.
tender-minded [-'maɪndəd] *a.* idealista, iluso, soñador.
tenderness [-nəs] *s.* terneza, ternura; afecto, cariño; sensibilidad, delicadeza.
tending ['tɛndɪŋ] *a.* tendente, tendiente.
tendinous ['tɛndənəs] *a.* (anat.) tendinoso.
tendon ['tɛndən] *s.* (anat.) tendón.
tendril ['tɛndrəl] *s.* zarcillo, tijereta, vitícula.
tendrillous [-drələs] *a.* (bot.) zarcilloso.
Tenebrae ['tɛnəˌbreɪ, B -bri] *s. pl.* (*sing. o pl. en const.*) (relig.) tinieblas.
tenebrific [ˌtɛnə'brɪfɪk] *a.* que produce tenebrosidad.
tenebrious [tə'nɛbrɪəs] *var. de* **tenebrous.**
tenebrous ['tɛnəbrəs] *a.* tenebroso, obscuro, lóbrego, sombrío.
tenement ['tɛnəmənt] *s.* 1. casa, habitación de alquiler; apartamento, departamento, vivienda. 2. casa de vecindad, conventillo. 3. habitación, morada. 4. (der.) tierras o inmuebles en tenencia.
tenementary [ˌtɛnə'mɛntərɪ] *a.* formado por casas de vecindad.
tenement house, casa de vecindad (gen. dilapidada), conventillo (Amer.).
tenesmus [tə'nɛzməs] *s.* (med.) tenesmo, pujo.
tenet ['tɛnət, B 'tin-] *s.* principio, dogma, doctrina.
tenfold ['tɛnˌfoʊld] *a.* décuplo. —*adv.* diez veces.
Tenn. *abrev. de* **Tennessee,** Tennessee (E.U.).
tenner ['tɛnər, B -ə] *s.* (fam., E.U.) billete de diez dólares; (G.B.) billete de diez libras esterlinas.
Tennessee [ˌtɛnə'si] Tennessee, estado de los E.U.
tennis ['tɛnəs] *s.* (dep.) tenis.
tennis shoes, zapatos de gimnasia, zapatos o zapatillas de tenis.
tenon ['tɛnən] *s.* (carp.) espiga, almilla, barbilla. —*v.t.* 1. espigar, desquijerar, despatillar. 2. ensamblar a espiga.
tenonitis [ˌtɛnə'naɪtəs] *s.* (med.) tenonitis, tenontitis, inflamación de un tendón.
tenor ['tɛnər, B -ə] *s.* 1. contenido, significado, tenor. 2. carácter, índole. 3. tendencia, curso, rumbo. 4. (der.) copia exacta. 5. (mús.) tenor; viola. 6. (com.) plazo (de una letra de cambio). —*a.* (mús.) de tenor.
tenosynovitis [ˌtɛnoʊˌsɪnə'vaɪtəs] *a.* (med.) tendosinovitis.
tenotomy [tə'nɑtəmɪ, B -'nɔt-] *s.* (*pl.* TENOTOMIES) (med.) tenotomía.
tenpenny ['tɛnˌpɛnɪ, B -pənɪ] *a.* 1. (G.B.) que vale diez peniques, de diez peniques. 2. (puntilla o clavo) de tres pulgadas de largo.
tenpenny nail, clavo de tres pulgadas.
tenpin [-ˌpɪn] *s.* 1. bolo (de madera). 2. (*pl.*) juego de bolos (que se practica con diez bolos de madera).
tenrec ['tɛnrɛk] *s.* (zool.) tenrec.
tense [tɛns] *s.* (gram.) tiempo (del verbo). —*a.* tenso, tirante, tieso, estirado. —*v.t.* poner en tensión, tensionar. —*v.i.* volverse tenso.
tensely ['tɛnslɪ] *adv.* con tensión, tensamente.
tenseness [-nəs] *s.* tensión, tirantez.
tensible ['tɛnsəbəl] *a.* extensible, capaz de tensión.
tensile ['tɛnsəl, B -saɪl] *a.* 1. tensor, extensible, dúctil, flexible. 2. de tensión.
tensile strength, (fís.) resistencia a la tensión, resistencia a la tracción.
tensility [tɛn'sɪlətɪ] *s.* facilidad para ponerse tenso.
tensimeter [tɛn'sɪmətər, B -tə] *s.* (fís.) manómetro.
tensiometer [ˌtɛnsɪ'ɑmətər, B -'ɔmɪtə] *s.* tensiómetro, instrumento que mide la intensidad de la tensión.
tension ['tɛntʃən, B 'tɛnʃən] *s.* 1. tensión, tirantez. 2. tensión, ansiedad mental; nerviosidad. 3. tirantez (de relaciones, etc.). 4. (mec.) mecanismo tensor; regulador de tensión; freno (de lanzadera de telares). 5. (elec.) tensión, potencial. 6. (mec.) tensión, tracción. —*v.t.* tensar.
tensional [-əl] *a.* de tensión.
tensional stress, esfuerzo o fatiga de tensión.
tensionless [-ləs] *a.* libre de tensión.
tension spring, resorte tensor, muelle tensor.
tension test, (ing.) ensayo de tensión.
tension wrench, llave indicadora o de tensión.
tensity ['tɛnsətɪ] *s.* tensión, tirantez.
tensive [-sɪv] *a.* tirante, tensor.
tenson ['tɛnsən] *s.* (lit.) tensón.
tensor ['tɛnsər, -sɔr, B -sə] *s.* (anat., geom.) tensor.
ten-strike ['tɛnˌstraɪk] *s.* 1. tiro que derriba todos los bolos. 2. (fam.) golpe decisivo, éxito completo.
tent [tɛnt] *s.* 1. tienda, tienda de campaña, toldo, carpa (Amer.). 2. (med.) cámara (esp. de oxígeno). 3. (med.) lechino, tapón. —*v.i.* acampar bajo tiendas, alojarse en tienda. —*v.t.* 1. alojar en tiendas. 2. cubrir con un toldo. 3. (med.) mantener abierta (una herida, etc.) con lechino o tapón.
tentacle ['tɛntəkəl] *s.* (bot., zool.) tentáculo.
tentacled [-kəld] *a.* (zool., bot.) tentaculado.
tentacular [tɛn'tækjələr, B -lə] *a.* (zool., bot.) tentacular.
tentative ['tɛntətɪv] *a.* 1. tentativo, de ensayo, experimental, provisorio. 2. incierto, vacilante.
tentatively [-lɪ] *adv.* 1. experimentalmente, a título de ensayo. 2. inciertamente, vacilantemente.
tentativeness [-nəs] *s.* carácter experimental, calidad de experimental.
tent caterpillar, (ento.) lagarta.
tented ['tɛntəd] *a.* entoldado, cubierto con toldos.
tenter ['tɛntər, B-tə] *s.* (tej.) rambla, tendedor, rama tensora, marco de tender. —*v.t.* enramblar (paños).
tenterhook [-ˌhʊk] *s.* escarpia, alcayata; **to be on tenterhooks,** estar en ascuas, estar preso de ansiedad.
tenth [tɛnθ] *s.* 1. décimo. 2. diez (en fechas). 3. (mús.) décima. —*a.* décimo.
tenthly ['tɛnθlɪ] *adv.* en décimo lugar.
tenth-rate [-'reɪt] *a.* de ínfima categoría, de pésima calidad.
tentmaker ['tɛntˌmeɪkər, B -ə] *s.* tendero (el que hace tiendas de campaña).
tent pole, mástil de una tienda de campaña.
tent show, espectáculo circense (bajo una tienda).
tent stitch, (cost.) punto tallo.
tenuity [tɛ'nuətɪ, B -'nju-] *s.* 1. tenuidad, debilidad, delgadez, esbeltez. 2. enrarecimiento (de fluidos o gases). 3. sencillez (de estilo).
tenuous ['tɛnjuəs] *a.* 1. tenue; débil, delgado. 2. raro, enrarecido (fluido, gas, etc.). 3. (fig.) tenue, insubstancial.
tenuously [-lɪ] *adv.* tenuemente, débilmente.
tenuousness [-nəs] *s.* 1. tenuidad, debilidad. 2. rareza (de un fluido, gas, etc.).
tenure ['tɛnjər, B -jʊə] *s.* 1. posesión, tenencia, pertenencia. 2. ejercicio (de un oficio o cargo).
teosinte [ˌtiə'sɪntɪ] *s.* (bot.) teocinte.

tepee ['tipi] *s.* tepee, xipi (tienda típica de los indios pieles rojas).
tepefaction [ˌtɛpə'fækʃən] *s.* templadura.
tepefy ['tɛpəˌfaɪ] *v.t., v.i.* entibiarse, irse poniendo templado o tibio.
tephigram ['tɛfəˌgræm] *s.* (meteor.) tefígrama.
tephrite ['tɛfraɪt] *s.* (min.) tefrita.
tephroite [-roʊˌaɪt] *s.* (min.) tefroíta.
tepid ['tɛpəd] *a.* 1. tibio, templado. 2. (fig.) tibio (interés, etc.).
tepidarium [ˌtɛpɪ'dɛrɪəm, B -'dɛər-] *s.* (*pl.* TEPIDARIA [-ə]) tepidario.
tepidity [tə'pɪdətɪ] *s.* tibieza.
tepidly ['tɛpədlɪ] *adv.* tibiamente.
tepidness [-nəs] *s.* tibieza.
tequila [tə'kilə] *s.* 1. agave, maguey. 2. tequila.
teratogeny [ˌtɛrə'tɑdʒənɪ, B -'tɔdʒ-] *s.* (med.) teratología, estudio de las condiciones que originan los monstruos fisiológicos.
teratoid ['tɛrəˌtɔɪd] *a.* (med.) teratoide.
teratological [ˌtɛrətə'lɑdʒɪkəl, B -'lɔdʒ-] *a.* (med.) teratológico.
teratology [-'tɑlədʒɪ, B -'tɔl-] *s.* (med.) teratología.
teratoma [-'toʊmə] *s.* (med.) teratoma.
terbium ['tɜrbɪəm, B 'tɜbɪ-] *s.* (quím.) terbio.
terce [tɜrs, B tɜs] *s.* (relig.) tercia (hora canónica).
tercel ['tɜrsəl, B 'tɜsəl] *var. de* **tiercel.**
tercentenary [ˌtɜrsɛn'tɛnərɪ, B ˌtɜsɛn'-tinərɪ] *a.* de tres siglos. —*s.* tricentenario.
tercentennial [ˌtɜrsɛn'tɛnɪəl, B ˌtɜsɛn-] *a.* de tres siglos. —*s.* tricentenario.
terceroon ['tɜrsəˌrun, B tɜsə'run] *s.* tercerón, tercerona; hijo de una persona blanca y otra mulata.
tercet ['tɜrsət, B 'tɜsɪt] *s.* 1. (poét.) terceto, tercerilla. 2. (mús.) tresillo.
terebene ['tɛrəˌbin] *s.* (quím.) terebeno.
terebic [tə'rɛbɪk] *a.* (quím.) terébico.
terebinth ['tɛrəˌbɪnθ] *s.* (bot.) terebinto, cornicabra.
terebinthic [ˌtɛrə'bɪnθɪk] *a.* relativo a la trementina.
terebinthine [-θən, B -θaɪn] *a.* de trementina.
terebratula [ˌtɛrə'brætʃələ, B -'brætjʊ-] *s.* (*pl.* TEREBRATULAE [-ˌli]) (zool.) terebrátula.
teredo [tə'ridoʊ] *s.* (*pl.* TEREDOS O TEREDINES [-dɪˌniz]) (zool.) tiñuela, broma.
Teresian [tə'riʒən, B -'risɪən] *a., s.* teresa (monja carmelita).
terete [tə'rit] *a.* (bot.) terete.
tergal ['tɜrgəl, B 'tɜgəl] *a.* (zool.) tergal.
tergiversate ['tɜrdʒɪvərˌseɪt, B 'tɜdʒɪvɜs-eɪt] *v.i.* 1. tergiversar. 2. apostatar; renegar.
tergiversation [ˌtɜrdʒɪvər'seɪʃən, B ˌtɜdʒɪvɜ'-] *s.* 1. tergiversación, deformación de un hecho. 2. deserción; apostasía.
tergiversator ['tɜrdʒɪvərˌseɪtər, B 'tɜdʒɪv-ɜˌseɪtə] *s.* tergiversador, tergiversadora.
tergum ['tɜrgəm, B 'tɜgəm] *s.* (*pl.* TERGA [-gə]) (zool.) térgum, tergo.
teriyaki [ˌtɛrɪ'jɑkɪ] *s.* (cocina) plato japonés de carne o pescado sazonado con salsa de soja.
term [tɜrm, B tɜm] *s.* 1. término, duración, período. 2. (*pl.*) términos, condiciones. 3. término, expresión, vocablo. 4. (*pl.*) relaciones (en el trato). 5. (arq.) término. 6. período académico. 7. (der., com.) término, plazo, vencimiento. 8. (der.) posesión, pertenencia, tenencia (de tierras); (período de) sesiones (de un tribunal). 9. (der.) condena. 10. (lóg.) término (de un silogismo). 11. (mat.) término. 12. (ant.) límite, confín, fin; condiciones, circunstancias. 13. **in terms of,** desde el punto de vista de; **not on any terms,** bajo ningún concepto; en ninguna circunstancia; **to be on bad terms (with),** estar en malas relaciones (con); **to be on good terms (with),** estar en buenas relaciones (con); **to bring (someone) to terms,** hacer aceptar (a alguien) condiciones; **to come to terms,** llegar a un acuerdo. —*v.t.* llamar, calificar de.
termagancy ['tɜrməgənsɪ, B 'tɜmə-] *s.* turbulencia, carácter pendenciero.
termagant [-gənt] *s.* virago, marimacho. —*a.* turbulenta, pendenciera, regañona (mujer).
termer ['tɜrmər, B 'tɜmə] *s.* condenado (a prisión), convicto, penado.
terminability [ˌtɜrmənə'bɪlətɪ, B ˌtɜm-] *s.* terminabilidad.
terminable ['tɜrmənəbəl, B 'tɜm-] *a.* terminable, limitable.
terminable annuity, (com.) renta reembolsable.
terminal ['tɜrmənəl, B 'tɜm-] *a.* 1. terminal, último, final. 2. periódico. 3. (bot.) terminal. —*s.* 1. extremidad, extremo, final, remate. 2. estación terminal; estación de carga. 3. (gram.) terminación. 4. (arq.) acabado. 5. (elec.) borne, terminal. 6. (med.) terminal.
terminal block, (elec.) bloque terminal; tablero de bornes.
terminal board, (elec.) tablero terminal.
terminal leave, (mil.) licencia final de separación, permiso final.
terminally [-əlɪ] *adv.* 1. periódicamente. 2. por el extremo.
terminal velocity, (aer.) velocidad terminal.
terminate ['tɜrməˌneɪt, B 'tɜmɪ-] *v.t.* 1. terminar, finalizar, finiquitar, concluir. 2. limitar, confinar. —*v.i.* 1. terminar(se), acabar(se). 2. estar limitado. 3. **t. in,** tener la terminación de, terminar en (letra, sufijo, etc.). —[-nət] *a.* 1. (gram.) perfectivo. 2. (mat.) finito.
termination [ˌtɜrmə'neɪʃən, B ˌtɜmɪ-] *s.* 1. terminación, final, conclusión. 2. limitación, confinamiento. 3. resultado. 4. (gram.) terminación, desinencia. 5. **to bring to a t.,** poner término a, concluir.
terminational [-əl] *a.* 1. final (acento, sílaba). 2. (gram.) flexional, desinencial.
terminative ['tɜrməˌneɪtɪv, B 'tɜmɪnətɪv] *a.* terminativo; determinativo.
terminator [-ˌneɪtər, B -ə] *s.* terminador; (astr.) terminador.
terminological [ˌtɜrmənə'lɑdʒɪkəl, B ˌtɜmɪnə'lɔdʒ-] *a.* terminológico.
terminologically [-kəlɪ] *adv.* en terminología.
terminology [ˌtɜrmə'nɑlədʒɪ, B ˌtɜmɪ'nɔl-] *s.* (*pl.* TERMINOLOGIES) terminología.
term insurance, seguro de plazo fijo.
terminus ['tɜrmənəs, B 'tɜmɪ-] *s.* (*pl.* TERMINI [-naɪ] O TERMINUSES) 1. límite, confín. 2. poste limítrofe, mojón. 3. terminación, fin, meta. 4. estación terminal (de ferrocarril, ómnibus interurbano, etc.).
termite ['tɜrˌmaɪt, B 'tɜmaɪt] *s.* (ento.) comején, termita, termes.
termless ['tɜrmləs, B 'tɜm-] *a.* 1. ilimitado. 2. incondicional.
termor ['tɜrmər, B 'tɜmə] *s.* (der.) poseedor de bienes por un plazo fijo o de por vida.
term paper, (E.U.) composición de examen trimestral (en colegio o universidad).
termtime [-ˌtaɪm] *s.* (E.U.) período escolar; período de sesiones.
tern [tɜrn, B tɜn] *s.* 1. (orn.) golondrina de mar, gaviotín. 2. terno (en la lotería).
ternary ['tɜrnərɪ, B 'tɜnərɪ] *a.* 1. (mat., quím., bot.) ternario, trino. 2. tercero (de una serie, orden o rango).
ternate [-ˌneɪt, B -nət] *a.* (bot.) trifoliado.
terne [tɜrn, B tɜn] *s.* aleación de estaño y plomo.
terneplate ['tɜrnˌpleɪt, B 'tɜn-] *s.* chapa aplomada, lámina de estaño emplomado, chapa plomo-estaño.
terpene ['tɜrpin, B 'tɜpin] *s.* (quím.) terpeno.
terpenic [tɜ'pɪnɪk, B tɜ'-] *a.* (quím.) terpénico.
terpin ['tɜrpən, B 'tɜpɪn] *s.* (quím.) terpino.
terpineol [tɜr'pɪnɪˌoʊl, B tɜ'-ˌɔl] *s.* (quím.) terpineol.
terpin hydrate, (quím.) terpina.
terpinol ['tɜrpənəl, B 'tɜpɪ-] *s.* (quím.) terpino, terpinol, terpineol.
Terpsichore [tɜrp'sɪkərɪ, B tɜp-] *s.* (mitol.) Terpsícore, la musa de la danza.
terpsichorean [ˌtɜrpsɪkə'riən, B tɜp-] *a.* 1. **T.,** de Terpsícore. 2. de la danza, del baile.
terra ['tɛrə] *s.* (lat.) tierra (el planeta).
terra alba ['tɛrə'ælbə] (com.) yeso; caolín; magnesia.
terrace ['tɛrəs] *s.* 1. terraplén. 2. terraza, terrado, terrero, azotea. 3. galería abierta. 4. bancal, balate, parata (Amer.). 5. crujía de casas (construidas en terreno elevado). 6. (E.U.) jardín central (que divide una avenida). —*v.t.* 1. terraplenar. 2. abancalar.
terracer [-ər, B -ə] *s.* máquina terrazadora.
terra-cotta [ˌtɛrə'kɑtə, B -'kɔtə] *s.* 1. terracota. 2. color terracota.
terra firma [-'fɜrmə, B -'fɜmə] (lat.) tierra firme.
terrain [tə'reɪn, B 'tɛreɪn] *s.* terreno; (geol.) terreno.
terra incognita ['tɛrəɪn'kɑgnətə, B -'kɔg-] (*pl.* TERRAE INCOGNITAE ['tɛri-ˌti]) (lat.) tierra virgen, campo virgen (en cuanto a conocimientos).
Terramycin [ˌtɛrə'maɪsən] *s.* (farm.) terramicina (marca de fábrica).
terrane [tə'reɪn] *s.* (geol.) terreno.
terrapin ['tɛrəpən] *s.* (zool.) terrapene.
terraqueous [tɛr'eɪkwɪəs] *a.* terráqueo.
terrarium [tə'rɛrɪəm, B -'rɛər-] *s.* (*pl.* TERRARIA [-ə] O TERRARIUMS) terrario.
terrazzo [tə'ræzoʊ, -'rɑtsoʊ] *s.* terrazo, piso veneciano, piso de mármol brecha.
terrene [tə'rin] *a.* 1. terrenal, mundano, mundanal. 2. terrenal, terrestre. —*s.* tierra; terreno.
terreplein ['tɛrəˌpleɪn, B 'tɛəˌ-] *s.* (fort.) plataforma, terraplén.
terrestrial [tə'rɛstrɪəl] *a.* 1. terrestre, terreno, térreo, terrino. 2. terrenal, mundano. —*s.* terrícola.
terrestrial horizon, (fotgmt.) horizonte terrestre.
terrestrial latitude, (nav.) latitud terrestre.
terret ['tɛrət] *s.* portarriendas, anilla.
terre-verte ['tɛrˌvɛrt, B 'tɛəˌvɛət] *s.* (min.) tierra verde, tierra de Verona, glauconita.
terrible ['tɛrəbəl] *a.* 1. terrible, aterrador, pavoroso, espantoso, terrorífico. 2. (fam.) terrible, atroz, tremendo.
terribleness [-nəs] *s.* lo terrible.
terribly [-blɪ] *adv.* terriblemente.
terricolous [tə'rɪkələs] *a.* 1. (zool.) terrícola. 2. (bot.) terrestre.
terrier ['tɛrɪər, B -ə] *s.* 1. (zool.) terrier. 2. (der.) catastro, registro de la propiedad.
terrific [tə'rɪfɪk] *a.* 1. terrífico, terrorífico, espantoso, pavoroso. 2. (fam.) brutal, grande, extraordinario, magnífico, excelente.
terrifically [-ɪkəlɪ] *adv.* pavorosamente, espantosamente.
terrify ['tɛrəˌfaɪ] *v.t.* aterrorizar, aterrar, espantar, amedrentar.
terrigenous [tɛ'rɪdʒənəs] *a.* terrígeno.

territorial [ˌtɛrə'tɔrɪəl] *a.* 1. territorial, distrital, regional. 2. (der.) territorial, jurisdiccional. 3. (mil.) territorial (ejército, reserva, etc.). —*s.* soldado de la fuerza territorial.
territorialism [-ˌɪzəm] *s.* supremacía de la clase terrateniente (en un estado).
territoriality [ˌtɛrəˌtɔrɪ'ælətɪ] *s.* territorialidad.
territorialization [-ələ'zeɪʃən, B -laɪ-] *s.* (E.U.) conversión en territorio federal.
territorialize [-'tɔrɪəˌlaɪz] *v.t.* (E.U.) convertir en territorio federal, organizar en forma territorial.
territorial jurisdiction, (der.) jurisdicción territorial.
territorially [-ɪəlɪ] *adv.* en forma territorial o regional.
territorial sea, (der.) mar territorial.
territorial waters, (der.) aguas jurisdiccionales, aguas territoriales.
territory ['tɛrəˌtɔrɪ, B -tərɪ] *s.* (*pl.* TERRITORIES) 1. territorio (de un estado, ciudad, etc.). 2. (E.U., Can., Aust.) territorio federal. 3. (com.) territorio, área, zona (asignada a un vendedor, etc).
terror ['tɛrər, B -ə] *s.* 1. terror, pavor, espanto, pánico. 2. persona o cosa terrorífica. 3. (fam.) chiquillo travieso, malcriado. 4. **the T.,** (hist.) el Terror (época durante la Revolución Francesa).
terrorism [-ərˌɪzəm] *s.* terrorismo.
terrorist [-ərəst] *s.* terrorista.
terroristic [ˌtɛrər'ɪstɪk] *a.* terrorista.
terrorization [-ə'zeɪʃən, B -aɪ-] *s.* terror, terrorismo.
terrorize ['tɛrərˌaɪz] *v.t.* aterrorizar, aterrar.
terry ['tɛrɪ] *s.* (*pl.* TERRIES) tejido esponja, tejido de rizo, tela esponja.
terry cloth, tela (de tejido) esponja, tela de toalla.
terse [tɜrs, B tɜs] *a.* sucinto, conciso, breve.
tersely ['tɜrslɪ, B 'tɜslɪ] *adv.* sucintamente, concisamente, brevemente.
terseness [-nəs] *s.* concisión, brevedad.
tertial ['tɜrʃəl, B 'tɜʃəl] *a.* (orn.) terciario (díc. de las plumas que nacen en el húmero de las aves). —*s.* pluma terciaria.
tertian [-ʃən] (med.) *a.* terciana (fiebre). —*s.* terciana, fiebre terciana.
tertiary ['tɜrʃɪˌɛrɪ, B 'tɜʃərɪ] *a.* 1. terciario (en orden o grado), tercero. 2. (relig., quím., geol.) terciario. —*s.* (*pl.* TERTIARIES) 1. (relig., geol.) terciario. 2. (orn.) pluma terciaria.
tervalent [tər'veɪlənt, B tə'-] *a.* (quím.) trivalente.
terylene ['tɛrəlin] *s.* (tej.) terileno.
terza rima ['tɛrtsə'rimə, B 'tɛət-] (poét.) terceto, tercia rima.
terzetto [tɛrt'sɛtoʊ, B tɜt-] *s.* (*pl.* TERZETTOS o TERZETTI) (mús.) terceto, trío.
tessellate ['tɛsəˌleɪt] *v.t.* taracear, poner teselas en. — [-lət] *a.* teselado.
tessellated [-əd] 1. teselado. 2. abigarrado, moteado.
tessellation [ˌtɛsə'leɪʃən] *s.* teselado, taracea, mosaico.
tessera ['tɛsərə] *s.* (*pl.* TESSERAE [-ˌri]) 1. tesela, abáculo. 2. (hist.) tésera.
tessitura [ˌtɛsə'tʊrə, B -'tʊərə] *s.* (mús.) tesitura.
test [tɛst] *s.* 1. examen. 2. prueba, ensayo, experimento. 3. piedra de toque, criterio normal. 4. (psic.) test. 5. (pr. G.B.) copela. 6. (zool.) testa, concha. 7. **to put to the t.,** poner a prueba. —*v.t.* 1. examinar, poner a prueba, probar. 2. (quím.) analizar, probar. 3. (pr. G.B.) copelar (metales).
testa ['tɛstə] *s.* (*pl.* TESTAE [-ˌti]) (bot.) testa.
testable ['tɛstəbəl] *a.* probable, verificable.
testacean [tɛs'teɪʃən] *s.* (zool.) testáceo.
testaceous [-ʃəs] *a.* (zool.) testáceo.
testacy ['tɛstəsɪ] *s.* (der.) condición de (morir) testado.
testament ['tɛstəmənt] *s.* 1. **T.,** (bíbl.) Testamento. 2. (der.) testamento.
testamentary [ˌtɛstə'mɛntərɪ] *a.* (der.) testamentario.
testate ['tɛsˌteɪt, B -tɪt] *a.* (der.) testado.
testator ['tɛsteɪtər, B tɛs'teɪtə] *s.* (der.) testador.
testatrix [tɛs'teɪtrɪks] *s.* (fam.) (*pl.* TESTATRICES [-trɪˌsiz]) testadora.
test ban, acuerdo entre naciones para abstenerse de llevar a cabo pruebas de explosiones atómicas.
test boring, (geol., petróleo) perforacíon de prueba, cala, sondeo, sondaje de exploración.
test case, (der.) causa instrumental, acción constitutiva, caso de prueba.
test chamber, (ing.) cámara de experimentación.
test-drive ['tɛstdraɪv] *v.t.* probar (en carretera), someter a prueba de carretera.
test drive, prueba de carretera.
tested ['tɛstəd] *a.* ensayado; probado.
tester ['tɛstər, B -tə] *s.* 1. (quím.) probador, ensayador; reactivo. 2. pabellón (de cama); baldaquín, dosel (del altar).
test flight, (aer.) vuelo de prueba.
testicle ['tɛstɪkəl] *s.* (anat.) testículo, testes.
testicular [tɛs'tɪkjələr, B -lə] *a.* (anat.) testicular.
testiculate [-lət] *a.* (bot.) testiculado.
testification [ˌtɛstəfə'keɪʃən] *s.* testificación, atestiguación, atestación.
testifier ['tɛstəˌfaɪər, B -faɪə] *s.* testigo.
testify ['tɛstəˌfaɪ] *v.i.* (*pret., p.p.* TESTIFIED; *p.pr.* TESTIFYING) 1. ser testigo, dar testimonio. 2. declarar, manifestar, aseverar. 3. (der.) rendir testimonio. 4. **t. to,** testificar, atestiguar; probar, evidenciar. —*v.t.* 1. atestiguar, atestar, testificar, testimoniar. 2. (der.) atestiguar bajo juramento.
testily ['tɛstəlɪ] *adv.* enojosamente, con irritación, irritadamente.
testimonial [ˌtɛstə'moʊnɪəl] *s.* 1. testimonial, certificado. 2. testimonio, atestado. 3. tributo, homenaje. —*a.* testimonial.
testimony ['tɛstəˌmoʊnɪ, B -mənɪ] *s.* (*pl.* TESTIMONIES) 1. testimonio, atestación, evidencia. 2. afirmación, aseveración, declaración. 3. (relig.) Tablas de la Ley; las Sagradas Escrituras.
testiness ['tɛstɪnəs] *s.* irritación, irascibilidad.
testing ground, terreno de pruebas, banco de pruebas.
testis ['tɛstəs] *s.* (*pl.* TESTES [-ˌtiz]) (anat.) teste.
test match, (criquet) partidos entre equipos nacionales.
teston ['tɛstən] **testoon** [tɛ'stun] *s.* (hist.) testón.
testosterone [təs'tɑstəˌroʊn, B -'tɔs-] *s.* (bioquím.) testosterona.
test paper, (quím.) papel indicador, papel reactivo.
test pattern, (E.U.) carta de ajuste.
test pilot, (aer.) piloto de pruebas.
test tube, (quím.) tubo de ensayo, probeta.
test-tube ['tɛsˌtub, B -tjub] *a.* producido en el tubo de ensayo, de probeta.
testudinal [tɛs'tudənəl, B -'tjud-] *a.* (zool.) testudíneo.
Testudinata [ˌtɛsˌtudə'nɑtə, B -tjudɪ'neɪtə] *s. pl.* (zool.) testudiniados.
testudinate [tɛs'tudənət, B -'tju-] *a., s.* (zool.) testudiniado.
testudo [-'tudoʊ, B -'tju-] *s.* (*pl.* TESTUDINES [-dɪˌniz]) (hist.) testudo.
testy ['tɛstɪ] *a.* (TESTIER; TESTIEST) 1. enojadizo, irritable, quisquilloso (persona). 2. malhumorado, disgustado (tono, respuesta, etc.).
Tet [tɛt] *s.* (vietnamita) Año Nuevo Lunar en los países del Asia, el cual se celebra durante tres días.
tetanic [tɛ'tænɪk] *a.* (fisiol., med.) tetánico.
tetanize ['tɛtənˌaɪz] *v.t.* (fisiol.) tetanizar.
tetanus ['tɛtənəs] *s.* (med., fisiol.) tétanos.
tetany [-ɪ] *s.* (*pl.* TETANIES) (med.) tetania.
tetartohedral [təˌtɑrtoʊ'hidrəl, B -ˌtɑtoʊ'-hɛd-] *a.* tetartoédrico (cristal).
tetchily ['tɛtʃəlɪ] *adv.* (hum., dial.) quisquillosamente, irritablemente, irasciblemente.
tetchiness [-ɪnəs] *s.* (hum., dial.) naturaleza quisquillosa, irritabilidad, irascibilidad.
tetchy ['tɛtʃɪ] *a.* (hum., dial.) quisquilloso, irritable, irascible.
tête-a-tête ['teɪtə'teɪt] (fr.) *a.* de cara a cara, confidencial. —*adv.* cara a cara, en privado. —*s.* 1. conversación confidencial o privada (entre dos personas). 2. confidente (mueble).
tether ['tɛðər, B -ə] *s.* 1. traílla, maniota, traba, correa, atadura (para apersogar animales). 2. resistencia, fuerzas, recursos (de una persona). 3. **at the end of one's t.,** al límite de sus fuerzas, en las últimas. —*v.t.* apersogar, trabar, atar.
tetrabasic [ˌtɛtrə'beɪsɪk] *a.* (quím.) tetrabásico.
tetraborate [-'bɔrˌeɪt] *s.* (quím.) tetraborato.
tetrabranch ['tɛtrəˌbræŋk] *s.* (zool.) tetrabranquiado.
tetrabranchiate [ˌtɛtrə'bræŋkɪət] *a.* (zool.) tetrabranquiado. —*s.* nautilo.
tetrabromide [-'broʊˌmaɪd] *s.* (quím.) tetrabromuro.
tetrachloride [-'klɔraɪd] *s.* (quím.) tetracloruro.
tetrachord ['tɛtrəˌkɔrd, B -kɔd] *s.* (mús.) tetracordio.
tetrachordal [ˌtɛtrə'kɔrdəl, B -'kɔd-] *a.* (mus.) de tetracordio.
tetracid [tɛ'træsəd] *s.* (quím.) tetrácido.
tetracycline [ˌtɛtrə'saɪklin] *s.* (farm.) tetraciclina.
tetrad ['tɛtræd] *s.* 1. (biol.) tetrada, tétrade. 2. (bot.) tétrade. 3. (quím.) átomo o elemento tetravalente.
tetradrachm ['tɛtrəˌdræm] *s.* (numis.) tetradracma.
tetradymite [tɛ'trædəˌmaɪt] *s.* (min.) tetradimita.
tetradynamous [ˌtɛtrə'daɪnəməs] *a.* (bot.) tetradínamo.
tetraethyl lead [-'ɛθəl-] (quím.) tetraetilplomo.
tetrafluoride [-'flʊrˌaɪd, B -'flʊər-] *s.* (quím.) tetrafluoruro.
tetragon ['tɛtrəˌgɑn, B -gən] *s.* (geom.) tetrágono.
tetragonal [tɛ'trægənəl] *a.* (geom.) tetragonal.
tetragram ['tɛtrəˌgræm] *s.* (gram.) tetragrámaton.
Tetragrammaton [ˌtɛtrə'græməˌtɑn, B -tɔn] *s.* (relig.) tetragrámaton.
tetragynous [ˌtɛtrə'dʒaɪnəs, B tɛ'trædʒɪnəs] *a.* (bot.) tetrágino.
tetrahedral [ˌtɛtrə'hidrəl, B -'hɛdrəl] *a.* (geom.) tetraédrico.
tetrahedrite [-ˌdraɪt] *s.* (min.) tetraedrita.
tetrahedron [-drən] *s.* (*pl.* TETRAHEDRONS o TETRAHEDRA [-drə]) (geom.) tetraedro.
tetralogy [tɛ'trælədʒɪ] *s.* tetralogía.
tetramerous [-'træmərəs] *a.* (bot., zool.) tetrámero.
tetrameter [-'træmətər, B -tə] *s.* (poét.) tetrámero.

tetrandrous [-'trændrəs] *s.* (bot.) tetrandro.
tetrapetalous [ˌtɛtrə'pɛtələs] *a.* (bot.) tetrapétalo.
tetraploid ['tɛtrəˌplɔɪd] *a.* (fisiol.) tetraploide.
tetraploidy [-ˌplɔɪdɪ] *s.* (fisiol.) tetraploidía.
tetrapterous [tɛ'træptərəs] *a.* (ento.) tetráptero.
tetrarch ['tɛtrɑrk, B 'titrɑk] *s.* 1. (hist.) tetrarca. 2. príncipe subordinado, reyezuelo.
tetrarchy [-trɑrkɪ, B -trɑkɪ] *s.* tetrarquía, gobierno bajo el mando de cuatro jefes; estado dividido en cuatro gobiernos.
tetraspore ['tɛtrəˌspɔr, B -ˌspɔ] *s.* (bot.) tetráspora, tetraspora.
tetrasporic [ˌtɛ-'spɔrɪk] *a.* (bot.) tetraspórico.
tetrastich ['tɛtrəˌstɪk] *a.* (poét.) tetrástrofo.
tetrastichal [tɛ'træstɪkəl] **tetrastichic** [ˌtɛtrə'stɪkɪk] *a.* (poét.) tetrástico.
tetrastichous [tɛ'træstɪkəs] *a.* (bot.) tetrástico.
tetrastyle ['tɛtrəˌstaɪl] *s.* (arq.) tetrástilo. —*a.* que consta de cuatro pilares o columnas.
tetrasyllabic [ˌtɛtrəsə'læbɪk] *a.* (gram.) tetrasílabo.
tetrasyllable ['tɛtrəˌsɪləbəl] *s.* (gram.) tetrasílabo, cuatrisílabo.
tetratomic [ˌtɛtrə'tɑmɪk, B -'tɔm-] *a.* (quím.) tetratómico, tetraatómico.
tetravalence [-'veɪləns] *s.* (quím.) tetravalencia.
tetravalent [-lənt] *a.* (quím.) tetravalente.
tetrode ['tɛtroʊd] *s.* (electrón.) tétrodo.
tetroxide [tɛ'trɑkˌsaɪd, B -'trɔk-] *s.* (quím.) tetróxido.
tetryl ['tɛtrəl] *s.* (quím.) tetrilo, butilo; tetril (explosivo).
tetter ['tɛtər, B -ə] *s.* 1. (med.) herpes, albarazo; sarpullido; empeine. 2. (vet.) albarazo, blanca morfea.
Teucrian ['tukrɪən, B 'tju-] *a., s.* (hist.) teucro, troyano.
Teuton ['tutən, B 'tju-] *a., s.* teutón, alemán, germano.
Teutonic [tu'tɑnɪk, B tju'tɔn-] *a.* teutónico. —*s.* (idioma) teutónico.
Teutonism ['tutənˌɪzəm, B 'tju-] *s.* 1. creencia en la superioridad de la raza teutónica o germana. 2. civilización o cultura teutónica.
teutonization [ˌtutənə'zeɪʃən, B ˌtjutənaɪ-] *s.* germanización.
teutonize ['tutənˌaɪz, B 'tju-] *v.t.* germanizar, hacer teutónico. —*v.i.* hacerse teutónico.
Tex. *abrev. de* **Texas,** Tejas (E.U.).
Texan ['tɛksən] *a., s.* tejano, del estado de Tejas (E.U.).
Texas ['tɛksəs] *s.* Tejas, estado de los E.U. —*a.* de Tejas, tejano.
Texas fever, (vet.) fiebre de Tejas.
Texas leaguer, (béisbol) tiro de béisbol en que la pelota cae fuera del cuadrado que forman las bases pero dentro del campo del juego.
Texas Ranger, policía montado del Estado de Tejas (E.U.).
text [tɛkst] *s.* 1. texto. 2. tópico, tema, ej., *to stick to one's t.,* ceñirse uno al tema. 3. texto, libro de texto.
textbook ['tɛkstˌbʊk] *s.* libro de texto.
text edition, edición para uso escolar o universitario.
text hand, carácter de letra gruesa.
textile ['tɛksˌtaɪl, -təl, B -taɪl] *a.* textil. —*s.* textil, tejido, material textil.
textual ['tɛkstʃʊəl, B -tjʊəl] *a.* textual.
textualism [-ˌɪzəm] *s.* adhesión rígida a la letra del texto; adhesión rígida a las Escrituras.
textualist [-əst] *s.* textualista.
textually [-ɪ] *adv.* textualmente.
textuary ['tɛkstʃʊˌɛrɪ, B -tjʊərɪ] *a.* textual, literal.
textural ['tɛkstʃʊrəl, B -tjʊərəl] *a.* textural.
texture ['tɛkstʃər, B -tʃə] *s.* 1. textura, contextura. 2. tela, tejido, obra tejida. 3. (fig.) textura, estructura, organización (de una obra de arte).
Th *símb. de* **thorium,** torio (Th).
T.H. *abrev. de* **Territory of Hawaii.**
Thai [taɪ] *a., s.* tai, tais, thai, de Tailandia.
Thailand ['taɪlænd] *s.* Tailandia.
thalamencephalon [ˌθæləmɛn'sɛfəˌlɑn, B -ˌlɔn] *s.* (anat.) talamencéfalo.
thalamic [θə'læmɪk] *a.* (anat.) talámico.
thalamifloral [-ɪ'flɔrəl] **thalamiflorous** [-əs] *a.* (bot.) talamifloro.
thalamite ['θæləˌmaɪt] *s.* talamite (remero en galera).
thalamus ['θæləməs] *s.* (*pl.* THALAMI [-ˌmaɪ]) (anat., bot.) tálamo.
thalassic [θə'læsɪk] *a.* talásico.
thalassocracy [ˌθælə'sɑkrəsɪ, B -'sɔk-] *s.* (pol.) talasocracia.
thalassography [ˌθælə'sɑgrəfɪ, B -'sɔg-] *s.* oceanografía, ciencia de lo relativo al mar.
thaler, *var. de* taler.
Thalia [θə'laɪə] *s.* (mitol.) Talía, la musa del teatro; una de las tres gracias.
thallic ['θælɪk] *a.* (quím.) tálico.
thallium ['θælɪəm] *s.* (quím.) talio.
thalloid ['θælɔɪd] *a.* (bot.) taloide.
thallophyte [-əˌfaɪt] *s.* (bot.) talofita.
thallous ['θæləs] *a.* (quím.) talioso.
thallus ['θæləs] *s.* (*pl.* THALLI [-ˌlaɪ] o THALLUSES) (bot.) talo.
Thames [tɛmz] *s.* Támesis, río de Inglaterra.
than [ðæn, ðən] *conj.* 1. que (comparativo), ej., *you are older t. he,* Ud. es más viejo que él, *he's not taller t. I,* él no es más alto que yo. 2. (delante de números) de, ej., *less t. five,* menos de cinco, *more t. once,* más de una vez. 3. que, ej., *not more t. five,* no más que cinco. 4. del que, de la que; de lo que, ej., *less money t. needed,* menos dinero del que necesitaba, *it is farther t. I thought,* está más lejos de lo que pensaba. 5. que, de lo que, ej., *he speaks Spanish better than he writes it,* habla el castellano mejor (de lo) que lo escribe.
Thanatos ['θænətɑs, B -tɔs] *s.* (mitol.) Tánatos, personificación de la muerte.
thane [θeɪn] *s.* 1. (Ingl., hist.) caballero, gentilhombre (título antiguo de honor equivalente a barón). 2. (esco., hist.) barón, señor; jefe de un clan.
thank [θæŋk] *s.* (*ú. sólo en pl.*) agradecimiento, gracias, gratitud; **thanks,** (*interj.*) gracias; **thanks to,** gracias a, merced a. —*v.t.* agradecer, dar gracias a; **I'll t. you to,** te agradeceré que, ej., *I'll t. you to be quiet,* hága (n) me el favor de guardar silencio, *I'll t. you not to mention his name again,* hazme el favor de no volver a mencionar su nombre; **t. God** ¡a Dios gracias! ¡gracias a Dios!; **t. you,** gracias, gracias a Ud.; **to have (only) oneself to t.,** tener (uno mismo) la culpa, ser (uno mismo) responsable.
thankful ['θæŋkfəl] *a.* agradecido, reconocido.
thankfully [-fəlɪ] *adv.* agradecidamente.
thankfulness [-fəlnəs] *s.* agradecimiento, gratitud, reconocimiento.
thankless [-ləs] *a.* 1. ingrato, desagradecido. 2. ingrato, no apreciado (trabajo, tarea, etc.).
thanklessly [-lɪ] *adv.* desagradecidamente.
thanklessness [-nəs] *s.* desagradecimiento, ingratitud.
thank offering, (bíbl.) acción de gracias.
thanksgiving [ˌθæŋks'gɪvɪŋ] *s.* 1. acción de gracias; reconocimiento por las mercedes recibidas (esp. de Dios). 2. oración de agradecimiento.
Thanksgiving Day, (E.U.) día de acción de gracias (cuarto jueves de noviembre).
thankworthy ['θæŋkˌwɜrðɪ, B -ˌwɜðɪ] *a.* digno de gratitud o reconocimiento, meritorio.
thapsia ['θæpsɪə] *s.* (bot.) tapsia, caña hedionda.
that [ðæt] (*pron. demostrativo; pl.* THOSE [ðoʊz] 1. ése, ésa, eso; aquél, aquélla, aquello. 2. otro, ej., *he went to this doctor and t.,* fue de un médico a otro. 3. [ðæt, ðət] (*pron. rel., pl.* THAT) que, ej., *all t.,* cuanto(s) que, todo(s) que, *the best t. we can do,* lo mejor que podemos hacer. 4. quien, el que, la que, lo que, ej., *the box t. you put the jewels in,* el estuche en (el) que Ud. puso las alhajas, *the person t. you got it from,* la persona de quien lo ha recibido Ud. 5. **and all t.,** y cosas por el estilo, y todo lo demás; **and t.,** y cosas por el estilo; y así por el estilo; **at t.,** así, sin más; todavía, más aún, para colmo, además; considerándolo todo, pensándolo bien; **for all t.,** a pesar de eso, sin embargo; de todos modos, ej., *he's very sick for all t.,* él está muy enfermo de todos modos; **like t.,** así, de ese modo; **so t.'s t.!** ¡así es pues! ¡no hay nada que hacer!; **this, t., and the other,** una cosa y otra, varios asuntos; **to put this and t. together,** atar cabos, sacar conclusiones; **upon t.,** luego, entonces, sobre esto; **t. is, t. is to say,** es decir, esto es; **t.'s right!** ¡correcto! ¡así es!; **what's t. you say?** ¿qué cosa dice Ud.? —*a.* (*pl.* THOSE) 1. ese, esa; aquel, aquella, ej., *look at t. dog,* mire ese perro. 2. él, aquél (que) (seguido de un p.p.), ej., *the best method is t. employed by the Americans,* el mejor método es el empleado (o aquél que es empleado) por los americanos. 3. **t. way,** de ese modo, de esa manera; **to be t. way about,** estar enamorado de; estar aficionado a. —*conj.* 1. que, ej., *she said t. he came early,* dijo que él vino temprano. 2. a fin de (que), para (que), ej., *he lives t. he may eat,* vive para comer. 3. **in t.,** por cuanto; **so t.,** de modo que, de suerte que; con tal que; para que. —*adv.* 1. tanto, tan; así. 2. hasta, ej., *I will go t. far,* hasta ahí llego. 3. (dial.) muy. 4. **t. many,** tantos; **t. much,** tanto.
thatch [θætʃ] *s.* 1. bálago, barda, paja. 2. techumbre de paja, techo de bálago. 3. (fam.) pelo tupido, greñas. —*v.t.* bardar, empajar, techar con paja o bálago.
thatched roof, techumbre de paja, techo de bálago.
thatching ['θætʃɪŋ] *s.* bálago, paja, material para empajar.
thaumatrope ['θɔməˌtroʊp] *s.* (fís.) taumátropo.
thaumaturge ['θɔməˌtɜrdʒ, B -tɜdʒ] **thaumaturgist** [-əst] *s.* taumaturgo, autor de prodigios.
thaumaturgic [ˌθɔmə'tɜrdʒɪk, B -'tɜdʒ-] **thaumaturgical** [-ɪkəl] *a.* taumatúrgico, pertinente a la magia o los milagros.
thaumaturgy ['θɔməˌtɜrdʒɪ, B -tɜdʒɪ] *s.* taumaturgia, magia, milagros.
thaw [θɔ] *v.i.* 1. derretirse, disolverse, liquidarse, licuarse. 2. (fig.) volverse cordial, ponerse afable, ablandarse. 3. (*v. impers.*) deshelarse, calentarse, entibiarse (el clima). —*v.t.* derretir, disolver, liquidar, licuar, deshelar. —*s.* 1. deshielo, derretimiento. 2. (fig.) ablandamiento (en relaciones, etc.).
Th. D. *abrev. de* **Doctor of Theology,** Doctor en Teología.
the, (cuando no lleva acento, ante consonante: [ðə] ante vocal: [ðɪ] con acento: [ði]) *art.* el, la, lo, los, las, ej., *the brave,* los valientes, *the beautiful,* lo hermoso, *the best,* lo mejor, *ten cents*

the copy, diez centavos el ejemplar. —*adv.* cuanto, por cuanto; tanto, tanto más; mientras más; **the (more, less,** etc.) . . ., **the (more, better,** etc.), cuanto (más, menos, etc.) . . ., tanto (más, mejor, etc.); **the sooner the better,** mientras más pronto, tanto mejor.

Theaceae [θɪˌeɪsɪi] *s. pl.* (bot.) teáceas.

theaceous [θɪ'eɪʃəs] *a.* (bot.) teáceo.

theanthropism [θɪ'ænθrəˌpɪzəm] *s.* (teo.) teantropía.

thearchy ['θiɑrkɪm, B -ɑkɪ] *s.* (*pl.* THEARCHIES) teocracia, gobierno de los dioses; orden o jerarquía de los dioses.

theater ['θiətər, B 'θɪətə] *s.* 1. teatro. 2. anfiteatro, ej., *operating t.,* anfiteatro quirúrgico. 3. teatro, escena, lugar (de los acontecimientos), ej., *t. of war,* escena de la guerra. 4. teatro, arte dramático; drama.

theatergoer [-ˌgoʊər, B -ˌgoʊə] *s.* amigo de frecuentar los teatros; teatrero (Amer.).

theatergoing [-ˌgoʊɪŋ] *s.* afición al teatro; (el) ir al teatro, ej., *t. is his favorite pastime,* ir al teatro es su pasatiempo predilecto.

theater-in-the-round [-tərɪnðə'raʊnd] *s.* anfiteatro, teatro circular o arena.

theatine ['θiətaɪn] *a., s.* (relig.) teatino.

theatre, *var. de* **theater.**

theatrical [θɪ'ætrɪkəl] *a.* 1. teatral, teátrico, escénico, dramático. 2. teatral, artificial, artificioso, afectado.

theatricalism [-kəˌlɪzəm] *s.* teatralidad.

theatricalize [-kəˌlaɪz] *v.t.* 1. dramatizar, adaptar para el teatro. 2. exhibir o presentar de modo teatral o en forma ostentosa.

theatrically [-kəlɪ] *adv.* teatralmente.

theatricals [-kəlz] *s. pl.* 1. funciones teatrales (esp. de aficionados). 2. modales teatrales.

theatrics [θɪ'ætrɪks] *s. pl.* 1. representación teatral. 2. efectos teatrales.

thebain [θɪ'beɪən] **thebaine** ['θibəˌin, B -ˌaɪn] *s.* (quím.) tebaína.

Theban ['θibən] *a., s.* tebano, tebeo, de Tebas.

Thebes [θibz] *s.* (hist.) Tebas, antigua ciudad de Egipto.

theca ['θikə] *s.* (*pl.* THECAE [-si]) (anat., bot.) teca.

thecal ['θikəl] **thecate** [-kət] *a.* (anat., bot.) tecal.

thé dansant [ˌteɪˌdɑn'sɑn] (*pl.* THÉS DANSANTS) té bailable, té danzant.

thee [ði] *pron.* 1. (ant.) te, a tí (caso objectivo de la segunda pers. del sing. del pron. pers.). 2. tú (en el lenguaje de los cuáqueros).

theelin ['θilən] *s.* (bioquím.) telina.

theft [θɛft] *s.* 1. hurto, robo, ratería, substracción. 2. (ant.) cosa hurtada.

thegn, *var. de* **thane.**

theine ['θiən] *s.* (quím.) teína.

their [ðɛr, B ðɛə] *a.* su, suyo, suya, de ellos, de ellas.

theirs [ðɛrz, B ðɛəz] *pron. pos.* (los) suyos, (las) suyas, de ellos, de ellas; (el) suyo, (la) suya.

theism ['θiɪzəm] *s.* teísmo, creencia en un dios o dioses.

theist [-əst] *s., a.* teísta.

theistic [θi'ɪstɪk] **theistical** [-tɪkəl] *a.* teísta.

thelitis [θɪ'laɪtəs] *s.* (med.) telitis.

them [ðɛm, ðəm] *pron.* los, las, les; (a) ellos, (a) ellas; **to t.,** les, a ellos.

thematic [θɪ'mætɪk] *a.* temático.

theme [θim] *s.* 1. tema, asunto, materia. 2. composición, ensayo. 3. (gram.) tema, radical, parte esencial (de un vocablo). 4. (mús.) tema, motivo (de una composición).

theme song, (mús.) cortina musical, canción característica o principal (de una opereta, película, etc.).

Themis ['θiməs] *s.* (mitol.) Temis, diosa de la ley y la justicia.

themselves [ðəm'sɛlvz, ðɛm-] *pron.* 1. ellos mismos, ellas mismas; (a) sí, (a) sí mismos, (a) sí mismas. 2. (a) sí mismo. 3. *a veces se lo traduce con el v. refl. en castellano,* ej., *they hurt t.,* se lastimaron. 4. **by t.,** solos, solas; **with t.,** consigo (mismos, mismas).

then [ðɛn] *adv.* 1. entonces, en aquel tiempo, a la sazón. 2. luego, después, en seguida. 3. entonces, en tal caso. 4. pues, por consiguiente, en consecuencia, por lo tanto. 5. **and t.,** con esto, y entonces; **and what t.?** ¿y qué pasó? ¿y qué más? ¿y qué siguió?; **but t.,** por otra parte, pero en tal caso, pero por otro lado, pero al mismo tiempo; **now and t.,** de cuando en cuando, de vez en cuando; **now . . . t. . . .,** ya . . . ya . . .; ora . . . ora . . .; **now t., well t.,** ahora bien, (tenemos) pues; **t. and there,** ahí mismo, al momento, al punto. —*a.* de entonces, de aquellos días, de aquel tiempo, de aquel entonces, de aquella época, ej., *the t. king,* el entonces rey, el rey de aquella época, el rey de aquel entonces. —*s.* aquel tiempo; **before t.,** antes de eso; **by t.,** para entonces; **from t. on,** desde entonces, de allí en adelante; **since t.,** desde aquel tiempo, desde aquella ocasión; **until t.,** hasta entonces; hasta luego.

thenar ['θiˌnɑr, B -nə] *s.* (anat.) ténar.

thence [ðɛns] *adv.* 1. de allí, desde allí. 2. de ahí, por eso. 3. (ant.) desde entonces, desde aquel momento.

thenceforth [ðɛns'fɔrθ, B -'fɔθ] *adv.* desde entonces.

thenceforward [-'fɔrwərd, B -'fɔwəd] **thenceforwards** [-wərdz, B -wədz] *adv.* desde entonces; desde allí en adelante, de allí en adelante.

theobromine [ˌθiə'broʊmin, B θɪ-maɪn] *s.* (quím.) teobromina.

theocentric [ˌθiə'sɛntrɪk] *a.* (teo.) teocéntrico.

theocracy [θɪ'ɑkrəsɪ, B -'ɔk-] *s.* (*pl.* THEOCRACIES) teocracia, país gobernado por un dios o por sacerdotes que suponen actuar bajo mandato divino.

theocrat ['θiəˌkræt] *s.* teócrata.

theocratic [ˌθiə'krætɪk] **theocratical** [-ɪkəl] *a.* teocrático.

theodicy [θɪ'ɑdəsɪ, B -'ɔd-] *s.* (filos.) teodicea.

theodolite [-əˌlaɪt] *s.* teodolito, instrumento de precisión para medir ángulos verticales y horizontales.

theogonic [ˌθiə'gɑnɪk, B -'gɔn-] *a.* teogónico, de la genealogía de los dioses.

theogony [θɪ'ɑgənɪ, B -'ɔg-] *s.* teogonía, genealogía de los dioses mitológicos.

theologian [ˌθiə'loʊdʒən] *s.* teólogo.

theological [-'lɑdʒɪkəl, B θɪə'lɔdʒ-] **theologic** [-ɪk] *a.* teológico, teologal, teólogo.

theologically [-kəlɪ] *adv.* teológicamente.

theologize [θɪ'ɑləˌdʒaɪz, B -'ɔl-] *v.i.* teologizar. —*v.t.* dar carácter religioso o teológico a.

theologue ['θiəˌlɔg, -ˌlɑg, B 'θɪəlɔg] *s.* (fam.) teólogo; estudiante de teología.

theology [θɪ'ɑlədʒɪ, B -'ɔl-] *s.* (*pl.* THEOLOGIES) teología, estudio de Dios y de doctrinas religiosas.

theomachy [θɪ'ɑməkɪ, B -'ɔm-] *s.* teomaquia, lucha contra los dioses; lucha entre los dioses.

theomania [ˌθioʊ'meɪnɪə] *s.* teomanía, manía de creerse Dios.

theonomous [θɪ'ɑnəməs, B -'ɔn-] *a.* gobernado por Dios.

theopathy [-'ɑpəθɪ, B -'ɔp-] *s.* (*pl.* THEOPATHIES) experiencia mística; éxtasis religioso.

theophany [θɪ'ɑfənɪ, B -'ɔf-] *s.* (*pl.* THEOPHANIES) teofanía, aparición o manifestación patente de una divinidad.

theophylline [ˌθiə'fɪlin] *s.* (quím.) teofilina.

theorbo [θɪ'ɔrboʊ, B -'ɔboʊ] *s.* (mús.) tiorba.

theorem ['θiərəm, 'θɪrəm, B 'θɪər-] *s.* teorema; (mat.) teorema.

theoretical [ˌθiə'rɛtɪkəl, B θɪ-] **theoretic** [-ɪk] *a.* 1. teórico. 2. teorizante.

theoretically [-kəlɪ] *adv.* teóricamente.

theoretician [ˌθiərə'tɪʃən, B ˌθɪə-] **theorist** ['θiərəst, B 'θɪə-] *s.* teórico.

theorize ['θiəˌraɪz, B 'θɪə-] *v.i.* teorizar, especular.

theorizer [-ər, B -ə] *s.* teorizante.

theory ['θiərɪ, 'θɪrɪ, B 'θɪə-] *s.* (*pl.* THEORIES) teoría.

theory of evolution, teoría de la evolución.

theosophical [ˌθiə'sɑfɪkəl, B θɪə'sɔf-] *a.* (rel., filos.) teosófico.

theosophist [θɪ'ɑsəfəst, B -'ɔs-] *s.* teósofo, teósofa, iluminista.

theosophy [-fɪ] *s.* (rel., filos.) teosofía.

therapeusis [ˌθɛrə'pjusəs] *s.* (*pl.* THERAPEUSES [-ˌsiz]) (med.) terapéutica.

therapeutic [-'pjutɪk] *a.* terapéutico.

therapeutically [-ɪkəlɪ] *adv.* con método terapéutico, terapéuticamente.

therapeutics [-ɪks] *s. pl.* (*sing.* o *pl. en const.*) terapéutica.

therapeutist [-əst] *s.* (med.) terapeuta.

therapy ['θɛrəpɪ] *s.* terapia.

there [ðɛr, B ðɛə] *adv.* 1. allí, ahí, allá. 2. en eso, en cuanto a eso, con eso, ej., *t. I agree with you,* en eso concuerdo con Ud., *you had him t.,* tú le agarraste con eso. 3. **you t.,** ¡usted! ¡oiga!; **here and t.,** acá y allá; irregularmente; **I have been t. before,** (jer.) eso no es nada nuevo para mí; **not to be all t.,** (jer.) estar medio trastornado, tener un tornillo flojo; **t. it is, you see,** ve, allí está el busilis; **t. you are,** eso es; ahí tiene; **t. or thereabouts,** más o menos, aproximadamente; **to get t.,** llegar, arribar; (jer.) tener éxito, triunfar. —*s.* ese lugar, aquel punto. —*interj.* 1. ¡mira! ¡vaya! ¡toma! 2. ya (ú. en forma repetida como expresión de consuelo), ej., *t., t., don't cry now!* ¡ya, ya, no llores más!

thereabouts ['ðɛrəbaʊts, B 'ðɛər-] **thereabout** [-əbaʊt] *adv.* 1. por ahí, por allí, por allá, cerca, alrededor. 2. aproximadamente, más o menos.

thereafter [ðɛr'æftər, B ðɛər'ɑftə] *adv.* 1. después de, de allí en adelante, subsecuentemente. 2. (ant.) según esto.

thereat [-'æt] *adv.* 1. ahí, allí, allá, en aquel punto y lugar. 2. luego, sobre eso, por eso.

thereby [ðɛr'baɪ, B 'ðɛə'-] *adv.* 1. con eso, con lo cual, por medio de eso. 2. por eso, debido a eso, así, de tal modo. 3. por ahí, por allí, alrededor.

therefor [-'fɔr, B ðɛə'fɔ] *adv.* por esto, para esto, por eso, para eso.

therefore ['ðɛrˌfɔr, B 'ðɛəfɔ] *adv.* por lo tanto, por consiguiente, por ende, en consecuencia, debido a eso.

therefrom [ðɛr'frʌm, -'frɑm, B ðɛə'frɔm] *adv.* de allí, de ahí; de eso, de aquello.

therein [-'ɪn, B ðɛər-] *adv.* 1. adentro. 2. en eso, en ese respecto.

thereinafter [ˌðɛrɪn'æftər, B ˌðɛərɪn'ɑftə] *adv.* en adelante, en lo sucesivo, posteriormente, después.

thereinbefore [-bɪ'fɔr, B -'fɔ] *adv.* (der.) anteriormente, (dicho o mencionado) más arriba, antes (en documentos, etc.).

thereinto [ðɛr'ɪntu, B ðɛər-] *adv.* (ant.) dentro de eso, dentro de esto.
thereof [-'ʌv, B -'ɔv] *adv.* de eso, de esto, de allí, de ahí.
thereon [-'ɑn, B -'ɔn] *adv.* 1. encima, encima de eso. 2. (ant.) luego, sobre eso.
thereto [ðɛr'tu, B ðɛə'-] *adv.* 1. a eso, a ello. 2. (ant.) además.
theretofore [ˌðɛrtə'fɔr, B ˌðɛətə'fɔ] *adv.* hasta entonces, antes de eso.
thereunder [ðɛr'ʌndər, B ðɛər'ʌndə] *adv.* debajo, bajo eso, por debajo.
thereupon ['ðɛrəˌpɑn, B 'ðɛərə'pɔn] *adv.* 1. encima de eso, por encima. 2. por lo tanto, por consiguiente. 3. luego, sobre eso.
therewith [ðɛr'wɪð, -'wɪθ, B ðɛə'-] *adv.* 1. con eso, con esto. 2. (ant.) en seguida, inmediatamente.
therewithal [ˌðɛrwɪð'ɔl, B ˌðɛəwɪð-] *adv.* 1. con eso, con esto. 2. (ant.) a más, además.
theriaca [θɪ'raɪəkə] **theriac** ['θɪrɪˌæk, B 'θɪər-] *s.* (farm.) teríaca, triaca.
theriacal [-kəl] *a.* (farm.) teriacal, triacal.
theriomorphic [ˌθɪrɪə'mɔrfɪk, B ˌθɪərɪə'-mɔfɪk] *a.* que tiene forma animal (díc. de las antiguas divinidades o sus representaciones).
therm [θɜrm, B θɜm] *s.* (fís.) termia, caloría pequeña, mil unidades térmicas inglesas.
thermae ['θɜrˌmi, B 'θɜˌ-] *s. pl.* (hist.) termas.
thermaesthesia, *var. de* **thermesthesia.**
thermal ['θɜrməl, B 'θɜməl] *a.* termal.
thermal alarm, termoavisador, alarma térmica.
thermal barrier, (aer.) muro térmico, muro del calor.
thermal coefficient, coeficiente térmico o de expansión por calor.
thermal cutout, (elec.) cortacircuito técnico, disyuntor termal.
thermal efficiency, (fís.) rendimiento térmico.
thermal insulation, aislamiento térmico.
thermal spring, manantial de aguas termales.
thermal unit, unidad térmica.
thermesthesia [ˌθɜrməs'θiʒə, B ˌθɜməs'θizjə] *s.* (fisiol.) termestesia.
thermic ['θɜrmɪk, B 'θɜmɪk] *a.* térmico.
Thermidor [-məˌdɔr, B -ˌdɔ] *s.* (hist.) termidor.
thermion ['θɜrmˌaɪən, B θɜ'maɪ-] *s.* (fís.) termión.
thermionic [ˌθɜrmɪ'ɑnɪk, B ˌθɜmɪ'ɔnɪk] *a.* (fís.) termiónico.
thermionic current, (fís.) corriente termiónica.
thermionics [-ɪks] *s. pl.* (fís.) (*sing. en const.*) termiónica.
thermionic tube, t. valve, (elec.) válvula termiónica.
thermistor ['θɜrˌmɪstər, B 'θɜmɪstə] *s.* (elec.) resistencia térmica.
Thermit ['θɜrˌmɪt, B 'θɜˌ-] *s.* (quím.) termita.
thermoammeter [ˌθɜrmoʊ'æmətər, B ˌθɜmoʊ-tə] *s.* (elec.) amperímetro térmico, termoamperímetro.
thermoanesthesia, thermoanaesthesia [ˌθɜrmoʊˌænɛs'θiʒə, B ˌθɜmoʊ-'θizjə] *s.* (med.) termoanestesia.
thermobarograph [-mə'bærəˌgræf, B -ˌgrɑf] *s.* (fís.) termobarógrafo.
thermobarometer [-bə'rɑmətər, B -'rɔmɪtə] *s.* termobarómetro.
thermocautery [-'kɔtərɪ] *s.* (cir.) termocauterio.
thermochemical [-'kɛmɪkəl] *a.* termoquímico.
thermochemistry [-əstrɪ] *s.* termoquímica.
thermocoagulation [ˌθɜrmoʊkoʊˌægjə'leɪʃən, B θɜmə-] *s.* (med.) termocoagulación.
thermoconductor [-kən'dʌktər, B -tə] *s., a.* (fís.) termoconductor.
thermocouple ['θɜrməˌkʌpəl, B 'θɜmə-] *s.* (elec.) pila termoeléctrica, par térmico, termocupla, termo par.
thermoduric [ˌθɜrmoʊ'durɪk, B ˌθɜmoʊ'-djʊər-] *a.* (med.) termodúrico.
thermodynamic [-daɪ'næmɪk] *a.* termodinámico.
thermodynamic efficiency, (fís.) rendimiento termodinámico.
thermodynamics [-ɪks] *s. pl.* (*sing.* o *pl. en const.*) termodinámica.
thermoelectric [-ɪ'lɛktrɪk] *a.* termoeléctrico.
thermoelectric couple, t. pair, (elec.) par termoeléctrico, par térmico.
thermoelectricity [-ɪˌlɛk'trɪsətɪ] *s.* (elec.) termoelectricidad.
thermoelectric thermometer, termómetro termoeléctrico.
thermoelectromotive [-trə'moʊtɪv] *a.* termoelectromotriz (fuerza, energía).
thermoelectron [-ɪ'lɛkˌtrɑn, B -ˌtrɔn] *s.* (fís.) termoelectrón.
thermoelement [ˌθɜrmoʊ'ɛləmənt, B ˌθɜmoʊ-] *s.* (elec.) termoelemento.
thermogenesis [-'dʒɛnəsəs] *s.* termogénesis, producción de calor por un cuerpo animal mediante procesos fisiológicos.
thermogenetic [-dʒə'nɛtɪk] *a.* (fisiol.) termogenético.
thermogenic [-'dʒɛnɪk] *a.* (fisiol.) termógeno.
thermogram ['θɜrməˌgræm, B 'θɜmə-] *s.* termograma, lectura registrada por un termómetro automático.
thermograph [-ˌgræf, B -ˌgrɑf] *s.* termógrafo, termómetro automático.
thermographic [ˌθɜrmə'græfɪk, B ˌθɜmə-] *a.* (tip.) termográfico.
thermography [θər'mɑgrəfɪ, B θɜ'mɔg-] *s.* (tip.) termografía.
thermojunction [ˌθɜrmoʊ'dʒʌŋkʃən, B ˌθɜmə-] *s.* (elec.) termounión.
thermokinematics [-ˌkɪnə'mætɪks] *s. pl.* (elec., fís.) termocinemática.
thermolabile [-'leɪbəl] *a.* (bioquím.) termolábil.
thermology [θər'mɑlədʒɪ, B θə'mɔl-] *s.* termología.
thermolysis [-əsəs] *s.* (quím., fisiol.) termólisis.
thermolytic [ˌθɜrmə'lɪtɪk, B ˌθɜmə-] *a.* (quím., fisiol.) termolítico.
thermomagnetic [-moʊmæg'nɛtɪk] *s.* (elec., fís.) termomagnético, piromagnético.
thermometer [θər'mɑmətər, B θə'mɔmɪtə] *s.* termómetro.
thermometric [ˌθɜrmə'mɛtrɪk, B ˌθɜmə-] *a.* termométrico.
thermometric pressure column, (fís.) columna termométrica.
thermometry [θər'mɑmətrɪ, B θə'mɔm-] *s.* (fís.) termometría.
thermonuclear [ˌθɜrmoʊ'nuklɪər, B ˌθɜmoʊ'njuklɪə] *a.* termonuclear.
thermoperiodism [-'pɪrɪəˌdɪzəm, B -'pɪər-] **thermoperiodicity** [-ˌpɪrɪə'dɪsətɪ, B -ˌpɪər-] *s.* (biol.) termoperiodicidad.
thermophile ['θɜrməˌfaɪl, B 'θɜmə-] *s.* (biol.) termófilo.
thermophysics [ˌθɜrmoʊ'fɪzɪks, B θɜmoʊ-] *s. pl.* (*sing. en const.*) termofísica.
thermopile ['θɜrməˌpaɪl, B 'θɜmə-] *s.* (fís.) termopila.
thermoplastic [ˌθɜrmə'plæstɪk, B ˌθɜmə-] *a.* (fís.) termoplástico. —*s.* substancia termoplástica.
thermoplasticity [-plæs'tɪsətɪ] *s.* calidad de termoplástico.
thermopump ['θɜrmoʊˌpʌmp, B 'θɜmoʊ-] *s.* termobomba.
Thermopylae [θər'mɑpəli, B θɜ'mɔp-] *s. pl.* (hist.) Termópilas, desfiladero donde los espartanos intentaron detener a los persas.
thermoregulation [ˌθɜrmoʊˌrɛgjə'leɪʃən, B ˌθɜmoʊ-] *s.* (fís.) termorregulación.
thermoregulator [-'rɛgjəˌleɪtər, B -ə] *s.* (fís.) termorregulador.
thermoregulatory [-ləˌtɔrɪ, B -ˌrɛgjʊ'leɪtərɪ] *a.* (fís.) termorregulador.
thermos ['θɜrməs, B 'θɜmɔs] *s.* termo, termos.
thermoscope ['θɜrməˌskoʊp, B 'θɜmə-] *s.* (fís.) termoscopio.
thermoscopic [ˌθɜrmə'skɑpɪk, B ˌθɜmə'skɔp-] *a.* (fís.) termoscópico.
thermosetting ['θɜrmoʊˌsɛtɪŋ, B 'θɜmoʊ-] *a.* termofraguante, termoestable, duroplástico (díc. de los plásticos que no pueden remodelarse después de calentados).
thermosiphon [ˌθɜrmə'saɪfən, B ˌθɜmə-] *s.* termosifón.
thermostability [-moʊstə'bɪlətɪ] *s.* estabilidad térmica.
thermostable [-'steɪbəl] *a.* termoestable.
thermostat ['θɜrməˌstæt, B 'θɜmə-] *s.* termóstato, termostato.
thermostatic [ˌθɜrmə'stætɪk, B ˌθɜmə-] *a.* termostático.
thermostatic valve, válvula de gobierno termostático.
thermotank ['θɜrməˌtæŋk, B 'θɜmə-] *s.* caja térmica (para calefacción o enfriamiento).
thermotaxis [ˌθɜrmə'tæksəs, B ˌθɜmə-] *s.* (biol., fisiol.) termotaxismo.
thermotherapy [-moʊ'θɛrəpɪ] *s.* (med.) termoterapia.
thermotropism [θər'mɑtrəˌpɪzəm, B θɔ'mɔ-] *s.* (biol.) termotropismo.
Thersander [θər'sændər, B θə'-də] *s.* (mitol.) Tersandro, aliado griego en la guerra de Troya.
Thersites [θər'saɪtiz, B θɜ'-] *s.* (mitol.) Tersites, guerrero griego en la guerra de Troya.
thesaurus [θɪ'sɔrəs] *s.* (*pl.* THESAURI [-ˌaɪ] o THESAURUSES) 1. diccionario de ideas afines, ideológico, de sinónimos; enciclopedia; libro de referencia; (fig.) tesoro (de conocimientos, citas famosas, etc.) 2. tesorería; almacén.
these [ðiz] *pl. de* **this.**
Theseus ['θiˌsus, -sɪəs, B -ˌsjus] *s.* (mitol.) Teseo, héroe que mató al Minotauro.
thesis ['θisəs] *s.* (*pl.* THESES [-ˌsiz]) tesis; [B 'θɛsɪs] (mús., filos., poét.) tesis.
Thespiae ['θɛspɪˌi] *s.* (mitol.) Tespias, ciudad griega situada al pie del monte Helicón.
thespian ['θɛspɪən] *a.* 1. **T.,** de Tespis. 2. dramático (arte). —*s.* actor, actriz.
Thespian Maids, (mitol.) las Tespíadas, las Musas.
Thespis ['θɛspəs] *s.* (hist.) Tespis, poeta griego supuesto creador de la tragedia.
Thespius ['θɛspɪəs] *s.* (mitol.) Tespios, fundador de la ciudad de Tespias.
Thess. *abrev. de* **Thessalonians,** Epístola de San Pablo a los Tesalonicenses (Tes.).
Thessalian [θɛ'seɪlɪən] *a., s.* tesálico, tesaliense, tesalio, tésalo.
Thessalonian [ˌθɛsə'loʊnɪən] *a.* tesalonicense, tesalónico. —*s.* tesalonicense, tesalónico, tesalónica; **Thessalonians,** (*sing. en const.*) (bíbl.) Epístola (de San Pablo) a los Tesalonicenses.
Thessalonica [-'lɑnɪkə, B -lə'naɪ-] **Thesalonike** [-lə'nikɪ] *s.* Tesalónica, antiguo nombre de Salónica.

Thessaly ['θɛsəlɪ] *s.* Tesalia, región al E. de Grecia.
theta ['θeɪtə, B 'θitə] *s.* theta, octava letra del alfabeto griego.
Thetis ['θitəs, B 'θɛt-] *s.* (mitol.) Tetis, nereida madre de Aquiles.
theurgical [θɪ'ɜrdʒəkəl, B -'ɜdʒə-] *a.* teúrgico, propio de la teúrgia, mágico.
theurgist ['θiərdʒəst, B -ɜdʒɪst] *s.* teúrgo, mago.
theurgy [-dʒɪ] *s.* (hist., relig.) teúrgia, practicas mágicas encaminadas a establecer relación con deidades benéficas.
thew [θju] *s.* 1. (*ú. gen. en pl.*) tendón, músculo. 2. (*pl.*) fuerza muscular; (fig.) vigor (físico o mental).
thewy ['θjuɪ] *a.* (THEWIER; THEWIEST) musculoso; vigoroso.
they [ðeɪ] *pron.* 1. ellos, ellas. 2. (*en forma indefinida*) la gente, los hombres, ej., *t. say,* la gente dice, se dice.
they'd [ðeɪd] *contr. de* **they had, they would.**
they'll [ðeɪl] *contr. de* **they will, they shall.**
they're [ðɛr, 'ðeɪər, B 'ðɛə] *contr. de* **they are.**
they've [ðeɪv] *contr. de* **they have.**
Thia ['θaɪə, B 'θiə] *s.* (mitol.) Tea, Teia, hija de Urano.
Thiamine ['θaɪəˌmin] *s.* (quím.) tiamina.
thiazine [-ˌzin] *s.* (quím.) tiazina.
thiazole [-ˌzoʊl] *s.* (quím.) tiazol.
thick [θɪk] *a.* 1. grueso, espeso. 2. de espesor, de grosor, ej., *five inches t.,* cinco pulgadas de espesor (o de grosor). 3. denso, compacto, tupido, atestado, lleno, relleno. 4. espeso, condensado. 5. turbio, confuso, borroso; brumoso (tiempo); impenetrable, profundo (oscuridad, silencio); sofocante, bochornoso (aire, calor). 6. apagado (voz); indistinto (habla). 7. fuerte, marcado (acento). 8. pesado, obtuso, torpe, estúpido. 9. (fam.) íntimo. 10. (fam.) insolente, insoportable. 11. **a bit t., a little too t., rather t.,** (jer., G.B.) demasiado, más de lo razonable; **to be t. with,** estar lleno de; (fam.) tener mucha intimidad con. *—s.* 1. grueso, espesor, grosor. 2. lo más denso, lo más tupido o recio. 3. estúpido, zonzo. 4. **in the t. of it,** en lo más reñido (de la pelea, disputa, etc.); **through t. and thin,** contra viento y marea, a toda costa; en las buenas o en las malas. *—adv.* 1. densamente, tupidamente. 2. abundantemente. 3. turbiamente, confusamente. 4. **to lay it on t.,** ser efusivo en demasía, ser exagerado en cumplidos.
thicken ['θɪkən] *v.t.* 1. espesar, condensar. 2. hacer más grueso. 3. hacer indistinto (habla). *—v.i.* 1. espesarse, condensarse. 2. volverse más numeroso o denso. 3. volverse más grueso. 4. complicarse, intrincarse, embrollarse.
thickener [-ər, B -ə] *s.* espesador; condensador.
thickening [-ɪŋ] *s.* 1. espesamiento, engrosamiento. 2. espesador.
thicket ['θɪkət] *s.* espesura, maleza, soto, matorral, broza.
thicketed [-əd] *a.* poblado de maleza.
thickhead ['θɪkˌhɛd] *s.* (fam.) estúpido, torpe, cabeza dura, cabezón.
thickheaded [-əd] *a.* estúpido, torpe.
thickish [-ɪʃ] *a.* algo espeso o denso.
thick-knee [-ˌni] *s.* (orn.) alcaraván, charadrio.
thickly ['θɪklɪ] *adv.* 1. densamente, tupidamente. 2. abundantemente. 3. turbiamente, confusamente. 4. en voz apagada; indistintamente.
thickness [-nəs] *s.* 1. grueso, grosor. 2. espesor, densidad. 3. espesura. 4. cuerpo, consistencia. 5. capa, estrato. 6. estupidez, torpeza.
thickness gage, (mec.) lengüeta calibradora, galgas calibradas.
thickset [-'sɛt] *a.* 1. denso, muy poblado, abundante. 2. grueso, fornido, corpulento. *—s.* espesura, maleza, soto, matorral, broza.
thick-skinned [-'skɪnd] *a.* 1. de pellejo grueso. 2. (fig.) insensible, duro; sinvergüenza. 3. **to be t.-s.,** tener buen o mucho estómago.
thick-skulled [-'skʌld] *a.* torpe; estúpido.
thick-witted [-'wɪtəd] *a.* torpe, estúpido, imbécil.
thief [θif] *s.* (*pl.* THIEVES) ladrón, ratero, caco, hurtador.
thieve [θiv] *v.t., v.i.* robar, hurtar.
thieveless ['θivləs] *a.* (esco.) indiferente, sin rumbo; inútil, sin provecho; yermo, frío; aborrecible.
thievery [-ərɪ] *s.* robo, hurto. latrocinio, ratería.
thieves' latin, jerga propia de los ladrones.
thieving ['θivɪŋ] *a.* propio de robo o de ladrones; ladrón.
thievish [-ɪʃ] *a.* 1. ladrón, ratero, sisador. 2. ladronesco.
thievishly [-lɪ] *adv.* como un ladrón, ladronamente.
thievishness [-nəs] *s.* latrocinio; rapacidad.
thigh [θaɪ] *s.* (anat.) muslo.
thighbone ['θaɪˌboʊn] *s.* (anat.) fémur.
thigmotaxis [ˌθɪgmə'tæksəs] *s.* (biol.) tigmotaxismo.
thigmotropism [θɪg'mɑtrəˌpɪzəm, B -'mɔ-] *s.* (biol.) tigmotropismo.
thill [θɪl] *s.* limonera, lanza de carruaje.
thimble ['θɪmbəl] *s.* 1. dedal. 2. (mar.) guardacabo. 3. (mec.) manguito.
thimbleberry [-ˌbɛrɪ] *s.* (bot.) (variedad de) frambueso americano.
thimbleful [-ˌfʊl] *s.* (cantidad que cabe en un) dedal; poquito (díc. esp. de líquidos).
thimblerig [-ˌrɪg] *s.* fullería hecha con tres tacitas y un guisante o bola pequeña. *—v.t.* (*pret., p.p.* THIMBLERIGGED; *p.pr.* THIMBLERIGGING) estafar con el juego de las tres tacitas y el guisante; petardear, timar.
thimblerigger [-ər, B -ə] *s.* fullero que estafa con las tres tacitas y el guisante.
thimbleweed [-ˌwid] *s.* 1. (variedad de) aster americano. 2. (variedad de) anémone americano.
thin [θɪn] *a.* (THINNER; THINNEST) 1. delgado, fino, tenue. 2. delgado, cenceño, flaco, enjuto, descarnado; magro. 3. claro, ralo, no denso, fluido (líquido). 4. escaso, poco (ganancia, público, etc.), ej., *t. hair,* cabello ralo. 5. raro, enrarecido (aire). 6. de poca consistencia; aguado (sopa, cerveza, etc.). 7. (fig.) débil, de poco volumen (voz). 8. insubstancial, inadecuado, débil, poco convincente (argumento, excusa, etc.). 9. transparente (pretexto, etc.) 10. (foto.) de poca densidad, con poco contraste. 11. **that's too t.,** (fam.) eso es inverosímil; **t. on top,** (fam.) calvo; **to be as t. as a reed,** estar en los huesos; **to disappear into t. air,** hacerse humo. *—adv.* delgadamente, finamente, tenuemente. *—v.t.* (*pret., p.p.* THINNED; *p.pr.* THINNING) 1. adelgazar. 2. atenuar, ralear. 3. aclarar; entresacar (pelo, árboles). 4. diluir, enrarecer. 5. **t. out,** hacer menos denso. *—v.i.* 1. adelgazar, enflaquecer. 2. diluirse; enrarecerse.
thine [ðaɪn] (ant., poét.) *pron.* tuyo, tuya, el tuyo, la tuya. *—a.* tu, tus.
thing [θɪŋ] *s.* 1. cosa, objeto. 2. cosa, asunto, cuestión, materia. 3. (fam.) persona, tipo; criatura, chico, chica, ej., *poor* (*little*) *t.* ¡pobre criatura! ¡pobrecito! *a spiteful t.,* un tipo malicioso, *a pretty t.,* una chica guapa. 4. (*pl.*) efectos (personales); ropa, ej., *I got my things together,* recogí mis cosas o mi ropa. 5. (der.) cosa, bien, propiedad. 6. **a dumb t.,** un zonzo; una bobota; **above all things,** ante todo; muy especialmente; **as things stand,** tal como están las cosas; **for one t.,** por un lado, en primer término; **how's things?** (fam.) ¿qué tal? ¿cómo te va?; **it's just the t.,** eso viene de perilla, es justamente lo que me (nos, etc.) falta; **it is the real t.,** esto es genuino, esto va en serio; **no such t.,** nada de eso; **not the t.,** no lo apropiado; **not to know the first t. about it,** no saber nada de; **of all things!** ¡qué sorpresa! ¡vaya desastre!; **old t.,** ¡viejo! ¡vieja! ¡compadre! ¡hermano!; **one of those things,** una de esas cosas que pasan, una de esas cosas raras; **soft t.,** trabajo fácil y bien pagado; **the t. is,** es que, la verdad es que, ej., *the t. is he did not know what to do,* es que (o la verdad es que) él no sabía qué (debía) hacer; lo más importante es, ej., *the t. was to get home,* lo más importante era llegar a casa; **there's no such t.,** no hay tal cosa; **to have a t. about,** (fam.) estar obsesionado con; **to have not a thing,** no tener nada; **to know a t. or two,** (fam.) saber cuántas son cinco; tener experiencia, ser astuto; **to make a good t. of,** (fam.) sacar provecho de, obtener ganancia de; **to see things,** ver visiones, padecer alucinaciones; **to take things easy,** dar tiempo al tiempo; **to tell someone a t. or two,** decirle a uno cuatro verdades.
thingamabob, thingamajig, *vars. de* **thingumbob, thingumajig.**
thing-in-itself [ˌθɪŋɪnɪt'sɛlf] *s.* (*pl.* THINGS-IN-THEMSELVES [ˌθɪŋzɪnðəm'sɛlvz]) (filos.) cosa-en-sí, realidad final o metafísica; noúmeno.
things personal, (der.) bienes personales.
things real, (der.) bienes inmuebles.
thingumbob ['θɪŋəməˌbɑb, B -ˌbɔb] **thingumajig** [-ˌdʒɪg] *s.* (fam.) el comose-llama, el que-te-dije, la cosa esa, quídam.
think [θɪŋk] *v.t.* (*pret., p.p.* THOUGHT [θɔt]; *p.pr.* THINKING) 1. pensar; concebir, idear. 2. creer, considerar, juzgar, ej., *t. (something) right,* creer conveniente o apropiado (algo). 3. pensar, meditar, reflexionar, ej., *he will t. himself silly,* con tanto meditar se volverá tonto. 4. pensar, intentar, proponerse. 5. tener la mente llena de, pensar siempre en. 6. **t. little of,** tener en poco; **t. matters over,** pensar bien las cosas; **t. much of,** tener en buen concepto, estimar mucho; **t. nothing of,** restar importancia a; menospreciar, tener en poco; **t. out,** considerar cuidadosamente, desarrollar (plan, solución, etc.); **t. over,** pensar bien, meditar; **t. up,** inventar, imaginar. *—v.i.* 1. pensar; raciocinar, razonar. 2. opinar, suponer, creer. 3. recordar, acordarse, pensar en, ej., *I always t. of you,* me acuerdo siempre de ti. 4. **I don't t. so, I t. not,** no me parece, creo que no; **I t. so,** creo que sí, me parece que sí; **I thought so!** ¡me lo figuraba!; **I wouldn't t. of (doing) it,** ni pensarlo; **let me t.,** déjeme pensar; **t. about,** considerar, reflexionar sobre; **t. again,** volver a pensarlo, reconsiderar; **t. aloud,** pensar en voz alta; **t. better of,** cambiar de opinión acerca de; tener mejor opinión de (alguien); **t. highly of,** tener en alto concepto; **t. ill of,** tener mala opinión de; **t. of,** pensar en, considerar; no olvidar, acordarse de; idear, inventar; imaginar; **t. twice,** pensarlo dos veces, reflexionar bien. *—s.* 1. ejercicio mental, raciocinio. 2. idea, pensamiento.
thinkable ['θɪŋkəbəl] *a.* 1. concebible. 2. realizable, posible.
thinker [-ər, B -ə] *s.* pensador.
thinking [-ɪŋ] *a.* pensante, pensador; racional; **to put on one's t. cap,** avivar uno el seso. *—s.* parecer, opinión, juicio, pensamiento; reflexión;

to my way of t., a mi parecer, en mi concepto, en mi opinión.
thinkingly [-lɪ] *adv.* cuerdamente, racionalmente.
thinly ['θɪnlɪ] *adv.* 1. delgadamente, finamente, tenuemente. 2. escasamente (vestido, etc.). 3. insuficientemente (disimulado, etc.).
thinner ['θɪnər, B -ə] *s.* diluyente, diluente, adelgazador (esp. de pintura).
thinness [-nəs] *s.* 1. delgadez, tenuidad. 2. delgadez, flaqueza. 3. poca consistencia; raleza. 4. (fig.) debilidad (de voz; del argumento, etc.). 5. (fig.) transparencia (de un pretexto, etc.). 6. (foto.) poca densidad, poco contraste (de un negativo).
thin-skinned [-'skɪnd] *a.* 1. de piel delgada, fina. 2. (fig.) sensible, sensitivo, susceptible.
thioacetic acid [ˌθaɪoʊə'sitɪk-] (quím.) ácido tioacético.
thio acid ['θaɪoʊ-] (quím.) tioácido.
thioarsenate [ˌθaɪoʊ'ɑrsəˌneɪt, B -'ɑsənɪt] **thioarseniate** [-ɑr'siniˌeɪt, B -ɑ'-] *s.* (quím.) tioarseniato.
thioarsenite [-ˌnaɪt] *s.* (quím.) tioarsenito.
thiocarbamide [-'kɑrbəˌmaɪd, B -'kɑbə-] *s.* (quím.) tiocarbamida.
thiocyanate [-'saɪəˌneɪt] *s.* (quím.) tiocianato.
thiocyanic [-saɪ'ænɪk] *a.* (quím.) tiociánico.
Thiokol ['θaɪəˌkɔl] *s.* (quím.) tiocol.
thionate [-ˌneɪt] *s.* (quím.) tionato.
thionic [θaɪ'ɑnɪk, B -'ɔn-] *a.* (quím.) tiónico.
thionic acid, (quím.) ácido tiónico.
thionine ['θaɪəˌnin] *s.* (quím) tionina.
thionyl [-ˌnɪl] *s.* (quím.) tionilo.
thiophene [-ˌfin] *s.* (quím.) tiofeno.
thiophosphoric acid [ˌθaɪoʊˌfɑs'fɔrɪk-, B -ˌfɔs-] (quím.) ácido tiofosfórico.
thiosinamine [-sɪn'æmɪn, B -'sɪnəˌmaɪn] *s.* (quím.) tiosinamina.
thiosulfate [-'sʌlfeɪt] *s.* (quím.) tiosulfato.
thiosulfuric [-ˌsʌl'fjʊrɪk, B -'fjʊər-] *a.* (quím.) tiosulfúrico.
thiouracil [-'jʊrəˌsɪl, B -'jʊər-] *s.* (quím.) tiouracilo.
thiourea [-jʊ'riə, B -'jʊərɪə] *s.* (quím.) tiourea.
third [θɜrd, B θɜd] *a.* tercero, tercio, terciario. —*s.* 1. tercero, tercio, terzuelo, tercera parte. 2. tres (en fechas). 3. (astr., geom.) tercero (sexagésima parte de un segundo de tiempo o de arco). 4. (*pl.*) (der.) tercera parte de los bienes personales (de esposo muerto intestado que hereda la viuda); herencia de viuda. 5. (mús.) tercera; tercer tono (de la escala).
third base, (béisbol) tercera base.
third boiler, meladora de azúcar (Caribe).
third class, 1. tercera clase, clase turista (en un barco). 2. **t. c. mail,** (E.U.) impresos (enviados por correo).
third-class ['θɜrd'klæs, B 'θɜd'klɑs] *a.* 1. de tercera clase. 2. (fig.) de baja categoría, inferior. —*adv.* en tercera clase.
third degree, (E.U.) interrogatorio con coacción o tortura.
third-degree burn [-dɪ'gri-] (med.) quemadura de tercer grado.
third dimension, tercera dimensión.
third estate, (pol.) estado general, estado llano, estado común.
third eyelid, membrana nictitante, tercer párpado (de ciertos animales).
third force, (pol.) tercera fuerza, fuerza intermedia.
third house, (fam., pol.) grupo que defiende intereses especiales, cabilderos.
thirdly ['θɜrdlɪ, B 'θɜd-] *adv.* en tercer lugar.
third party, 1. (esp. der.) tercero, tercera persona. 2. (E.U., pol.) tercer partido, cualquier partido político independiente de los dos partidos mayoritarios.
third party risks, (seguros) riesgos contra tercera persona.
third person, (gram.) tercera persona.
third rail, (elec.) tercer riel, carril conductor, riel conductor o de toma.
third-rate ['θɜrd'reɪt, B 'θɜd-] *a.* de tercer orden; de mala calidad, inferior.
third ventricle, (anat.) ventrículo tercero, ventrículo medio.
third wire, (elec.) conductor neutro.
Third World, (pol.) el Tercer Mundo.
thirl [θɜrl, B θɜl] *v.t.* (dial., G.B.) 1. perforar, taladrar. 2. hacer estremecer.
thirlage ['θɜrlɪdʒ, B 'θɜlɪdʒ] *s.* (Esco., hist.). 1. derecho feudal que obligaba a los vasallos a efectuar la molienda en un molino determinado. 2. impuesto sobre la molienda.
thirst [θɜrst, B θɜst] *s.* 1. sed. 2. (fig.) sed, apetito, ansia, anhelo, deseo. —*v.i.* 1. tener sed. 2. **t. for** (o **after**), (fig.) tener sed de, estar sediento de, ansiar, anhelar, apetecer.
thirster ['θɜrstər, B 'θɜstə] *s.* sediento, sedienta.
thirstiness [-stɪnəs] *s.* sed.
thirsty ['θɜrstɪ, B 'θɜstɪ] *a.* 1. sediento. 2. (fig.) sediento, ansioso, anhelante. 3. sediento, seco, agostado, árido (tierra, terreno, etc.). 4. (fam.) que provoca sed. 5. **to be t. for,** tener sed de.
thirsty work, trabajo que produce sed al que lo realiza.
thirteen [ˌθɜr'tin, B 'θɜ'-] *s.* trece. —*a.* de trece.
thirteenth [-'tinθ] *s.* 1. decimotercio, trezavo. 2. trece (en fechas). —*a.* decimotercio, decimotercero, trezavo.
thirtieth ['θɜrtɪəθ, B 'θɜt-] *s.* 1. trigésimo, treintavo. 2. treinta (en fechas). —*a.* trigésimo, treintavo.
thirty ['θɜrtɪ, B 'θɜtɪ] *s.* treinta; **thirties,** números o años de treinta a treintinueve; **t. all,** (tenis) treinta iguales. —*a.* de treinta.
thirty-eight ['θɜrtɪ'eɪt, B 'θɜtɪ-] *s.* 1. treinta y ocho, treintaiocho. 2. pistola de calibre treinta y ocho.
thirty-second note [-'sɛkənd-] (mús.) fusa.
thirty-second rest, (mús.) silencio de fusa.
thirty-two [-'tu] *s.* 1. treinta y dos, treintaidós. 2. pistola de calibre treinta y dos.
thirty-twomo [-moʊ] (impr.) *a.* en treintaidosavo. —*s.* libro en treintaidosavo.
this [ðɪs] *pron.* (*pl.* THESE [ðiz]) éste, ésta, esto; **t. and that,** esto y aquello; **t., that and the other,** esto, eso y aquello; una cosa y la otra, varias cosas. —*a.* este, esta; **t. day,** hoy (día); **t. way,** por acá, por este camino; así, de este modo. —*adv.* tanto, tan; **t. much,** esta cantidad, así tanto; esto.
Thisbe ['θɪzbɪ] *s.* (mitol.) Tisbe, amada de Píramo.
thistle ['θɪsəl] *s.* (bot.) cardo.
thistledown [-ˌdaʊn] *s.* (bot.) vilano del cardo, papo.
thistly ['θɪslɪ] *a.* cubierto de cardos; (fig.) espinoso, difícil.
thither ['θɪðər, B 'ðɪðə] *adv.* allá, hacia allá, más allá. —*a.* ulterior, lejano, remoto, del otro lado.
thitherto [-'tu, ˌθɪð-, B ˌðɪð-] *adv.* hasta ese tiempo, hasta esa oportunidad, hasta entonces.
thitherward ['θɪðərwərd, B 'ðɪðəwəd] **thitherwards** [-wərdz, B -wədz] *adv.* hacia allá, para allá, en esa dirección.
tho [ðoʊ] *contr. de* **though,** (fam.) aunque, a pesar.
thole [θoʊl] **tholepin** ['θoʊlˌpɪn] *s.* 1. (mar.) escálamo, tolete. 2. (agr.) asidero del mango de la guadaña.
Thomas Aquinas ['tɑməsə'kwaɪnəs, B 'tɔm-næs] (filos., teo.) Santo Tomás de Aquino.
Thomism ['toʊˌmɪzəm] *s.* (filos., teo.) tomismo, doctrinas de Santo Tomás de Aquino.
Thomist [-məst] *s., a.* tomista, perteneciente a la doctrina de Santo Tomás de Aquino.
Thomistic [toʊ'mɪstɪk] *a.* (filos., relig.) tomístico.
thong [θɔŋ] *s.* correa, tirilla de cuero, correhuela.
Thor [θɔr, B θɔ] *s.* (mitol.) Tor, Thor, dios escandinavo de la lluvia y el trueno.
thoracic [θə'ræsɪk, B θɔ-] *a.* (anat.) torácico.
thoracic duct, (anat.) conducto torácico.
thoracothomy [ˌθɔrə'kɑtəmɪ, B -'kɔt-] *s.* (*pl.* THORACOTOMIES) (med.) toracotomía.
thorax ['θɔrˌæks] *s.* (*pl.* THORAXES O THORACES [θə'reɪˌsiz]) (anat.) tórax.
thoria ['θɔrɪə] *s.* (quím.) torina.
thorianite [-ˌnaɪt] *s.* (min.) torianita.
thoric ['θɔrɪk] *a.* (min.) tórico.
thoride [-ˌaɪd] *s.* (quím.) torido.
thorite [-aɪt] *s.* (min.) torita.
thorium ['θɔrɪəm] *s.* (min.) torio.
thorn [θɔrn, B θɔn] *s.* 1. espina, púa. 2. (bot.) endrino; espino, oxiacanta. 3. letra rúnica para el sonido de la th inglesa. 4. **to have a t. in one's flesh (o in one's side),** tener una espina clavada.
thorn apple, 1. (bot.) baya del espino. 2. (bot.) higuera loca, chamico (Am.); borrachero.
thornback ['θɔrnˌbæk, B 'θɔn-] *s.* 1. (ict.) raya con púa. 2. (zool.) (variedad de) cangrejo europeo.
thornbush [-ˌbʊʃ] *s.* arbusto espinoso; maleza espinosa.
thorned [θɔrnd, B θɔnd] *a.* espinoso, lleno de espinas.
thornless ['θɔrnləs, B 'θɔn-] *a.* sin espinas.
thorny ['θɔrnr, B 'θɔnɪ] *a.* (THORNIER; THORNIEST) 1. espinoso. 2. (fig.) espinoso, arduo, intrincado, enmarañado, embrollado.
thoron ['θɔrˌɑn, B -ˌɔn] *s.* (quím.) torón.
thorough ['θɜroʊ, ↓ə, 'ʧ--rə] *a.* 1. completo, cabal, acabado. 2. consumado, perfecto. 3. cuidadoso, concienzudo; minucioso, detallado. 4. (raro) atravesador. —*s.* **T.,** (G.B., hist.) política tiránica durante Carlos I. —*prep., adv.* (ant.) por.
thorough bass, (mús.) bajo cifrado.
thoroughbrace ['θɜrəˌbreɪs, B 'θʌrə-] *s.* tira de cuero de suspensión (en un carruaje).
thoroughbred [-ˌbrɛd] *a.* 1. de pura sangre, de pura raza o casta (esp. caballo). 2. perfecto, consumado, diestro. 3. primoroso, excelente. —*s.* 1. caballo de carrera de pura sangre. 2. persona bien parecida.
thoroughfare [-ˌfɛr, B -ˌfɛə] *s.* 1. carretera, vía pública; calle transitada. 2. pasaje, tránsito. 3. **no t.,** no hay paso, la calle (está) cerrada.
thoroughgoing [-'goʊɪŋ] *a.* cabal, completo, esmerado, minucioso, extremadamente cuidadoso.
thoroughly ['θɜroʊlɪ, -əlɪ, B 'θʌrəlɪ] *adv.* 1. completamente, cabalmente. 2. concienzudamente, minuciosamente; detalladamente.
thoroughness [-nəs] *s.* cumplimiento, entereza; perfección; minuciosidad, escrupulosidad.
thoroughpaced ['θɜrəˌpeɪst, B 'θʌrə-] *a.* 1. entrenado en todos los pasos. 2. (fig.) cabal, completo, consumado.
thoroughpin [-ˌpɪn] *s.* (vet.) dilatación o tumefacción sinovial (encima del jarrete del caballo).
thoroughwax [-ˌwæks] *s.* (bot.) perfoliada.
thoroughwort [-ˌwɜrt, B -ˌwɜt] *s.* (bot.) eupatorio.

thorp [θɔrp, B θɔp] *s.* (ant.) villorrio, caserío, aldea.
those [ðoʊz] *pl. de* **that.**
thou [ðaʊ] *pron.* (ant., poét.) tú. —*v.t., v.i.* (ant.) tutear.
thou [θaʊ] *s.* (jer.) (*pl.* THOU O THOUS) mil dólares; mil libras esterlinas.
though [ðoʊ] *conj.* aunque, a pesar de que, aun cuando, si bien, bien que; **as t.,** como si. —*adv.* sin embargo, no obstante, con todo.
thought [θɔt] *s.* 1. pensamiento, reflexión. cogitación. 2. percepción, apreciación. 3. pensamiento, idea, concepción, noción, ej., *a happy t.,* una idea feliz. 4. (*pl.*) punto de vista, opinión (de uno). 5. atención, cuidado, esmero, solicitud. 6. preocupación, ej., *his one t.,* su única preocupación. 7. **on second t.,** pensándolo mejor; **to give t. to,** pensar en, acordarse de, meditar sobre; **to have thoughts of (doing),** acariciar la idea de (hacer); **to take t.,** considerar.
thought [θɔt] *pret., p.p. de* **think.**
thoughtful [θɔtfəl] *a.* 1. pensativo, meditativo, meditabundo. 2. atento, considerado. 3. cuidadoso, precavido.
thoughtfully [-fəlɪ] *adv.* 1. pensativamente, con aire pensativo. 2. cuidadosamente, con reflexión, con consideración.
thoughtfulness [-fəlnəs] *s.* 1. cuidado, previsión. 2. atención, esmero, solicitud.
thoughtless [-ləs] *a.* 1. incauto, imprudente; irreflexivo, precipitado, atolondrado. 2. descuidado, negligente. 3. desconsiderado, desatento.
thoughtlessly [-lɪ] *adv.* 1. incautamente, imprudentemente; irreflexivamente, precipitadamente, atolondradamente. 2. descuidadamente, negligentemente. 3. desconsideradamente, desatentamente.
thoughtlessness [-nəs] *s.* 1. imprudencia; irreflexión, precipitación, atolondramiento. 2. descuido, negligencia. 3. desconsideración, desatención.
thought-out ['θɔtˌaʊt] *a.* bien considerado, bien deliberado, muy pensado.
thought-read [-ˌrid] *v.t.* 1. leer el pensamiento a (alguien). 2. adivinar (los planes, etc.) que (uno) tiene en mente.
thought transference, transmisión del pensamiento, telepatía.
thought wave, onda telepática.
thoughtway [-ˌweɪ] *s.* modo de pensar (característico de un grupo, tiempo o cultura particulares).
thousand ['θaʊzənd] *a.* mil. —*s.* mil, millar; **one in a t.,** muy raro; excelente.
thousandfold [-ˌfoʊld] *a.* de mil. —*adv.* mil veces, mil veces más.
Thousand Island dressing, (cocina) mayonesa sazonada, salsa hecha de mayonesa, pasta de tomate y pepinillos.
thousand-legger [ˌθaʊzənd'lɛgər, B -ə] *s.* (ento.) milpiés, cochinilla.
thousandth ['θaʊzəntθ] *a., s.* milésimo.
Thrace [θreɪs] *s.* (hist.) Tracia, antigua provincia romana.
Thracian ['θreɪʃən] *a., s.* tracio, trace, traciano.
thraldom, thralldom ['θrɔldəm] *s.* esclavitud, servidumbre.
thrall [θrɔl] *v.t.* (ant.) esclavizar, sojuzgar, avasallar. —*s.* 1. esclavo, siervo. 2. esclavitud, servidumbre.
thrash [θræʃ] *v.t.* 1. trillar, desgranar (trigo, etc.). 2. (fig.) (gen. con *over*) trillar, machacar, repasar, estudiar o examinar una y otra vez. 3. batir, abatanar. 4. sacudir (brazo, pierna). 5. azotar, tundar, zurrar. 6. aplastar, derrotar, infligir una severa derrota a. 7. **t. out (a problem, a plan,** etc.), discutir a fondo, resolver discutiendo (un problema, un plan, etc.). —*v.i.* 1. trillar el grano. 2. agitarse, revolverse, moverse violentamente. —*s.* (dep.) pataleo usado al nadar en estilo libre.
thrasher ['θræʃər, B -ə] *s.* 1. (agr.) trillador, desgranador; máquina desgranadora o trilladora. 2. (ict.) zorra de mar.
thrasher, *s.* (orn.) especie de sinsonte.
thrashing [-ɪŋ] *s.* 1. azotaina, paliza, zurra. 2. (agr.) trilla, desgranamiento.
thrashing floor, (agr.) era.
thrashing machine, (agr.) trillo, trilladora.
thrasonical [θreɪ'sɑnɪkəl, B θrə'sɔn-] *a.* jactancioso, fanfarrón, fachendoso.
thrasonically [-kəlɪ] *adv.* con jactancia.
thrave [θreɪv] *s.* (dial.) medida de veinticuatro gavillas; atado, haz, manojo; multitud, muchedumbre, caterva.
thread [θrɛd] *s.* 1. hilo. 2. filamento (metálico o vegetal); fibra, hilito; hilo (de araña, gusano de seda, etc.). 3. hilo (de agua); rayo fino (de luz); filón, vena o veta delgada (de mineral). 4. (fig.) hilo, ilación, conexión. 5. (mec.) filete, rosca (de tornillo). 6. **the t. of life,** el hilo de la vida; **to gather up the threads,** relacionar puntos tratados separadamente, atar cabos; **to hang by a t.,** pender de un hilo; **to lose its t.,** rodarse (perno, tornillo); **to lose the t. of,** perder el hilo de; **to resume** (o **to take up**) **the t. (of),** reasumir el hilo (de la narración, discurso, etc.). —*v.t.* 1. enhebrar, enhilar, ensartar. 2. pasar por, atravesar; colarse o abrirse paso por (esp. dificultosamente). 3. entretejer. 4. (mec.) roscar, enroscar, aterrajar, filetear. 5. **t. one's way,** abrirse paso, colar (con cautela o dificultad). —*v.i.* 1. (cocina) ponerse (el almíbar) a punto de hilo. 2. **t. through,** colarse por.
threadbare ['θrɛdˌbɛr, B -ˌbɛə] *a.* 1. raído, gastado. 2. (fig.) trillado, repetido, común.
thread cutter, (mec.) máquina o herramienta de roscar.
threaded ['θrɛdəd] *a.* (mec.) roscado, fileteado.
threaded joint, junta atornillada, unión roscada.
threader [-ər, B -ə] *s.* 1. enhebrador. 2. (mec.) terraja.
threadfin [-ˌfɪn] *s.* (ict.) pez parecido al mújol.
threadfish [-ˌfɪʃ] *s.* (ict.) zapatero.
thread gage, calibre o pantilla para roscas.
threading ['θrɛdɪŋ] *s.* enrosque.
threading die, cojinete de roscar, dado.
threading machine, (maq.) máquina de roscar, tarrajadora, fileteadora.
threadless [-ləs] *a.* sin rosca (unión, conexión).
threadlike [-ˌlaɪk] *a.* filiforme.
thread mark, hilo de seguridad (que se pone al papel moneda para evitar su falsificación).
thread roller, (mec.) laminador de roscas.
threadworm [-ˌwɜrm, B -ˌwɜm] *s.* (zool.) ascáride, nematodo, oxiuro, lombricilla.
thready ['θrɛdɪ] *a.* 1. filiforme, delgado, filamentoso. 2. débil (voz, pulso, etc.).
threap [θrip] *v.t.* (pr. esco.) 1. regañar, reprender. 2. insistir en.
threat [θrɛt] *s.* amenaza. —*v.t., v.i.* (ant., dial.) amenazar.
threaten ['θrɛtən] *v.t.* amenazar, amagar, conminar; **t. to (do),** amenazar (hacer), amenazar con (hacer); **t. with,** amenazar con (un cuchillo, revólver, etc.); amenazar de (muerte, castigo, etc.). —*v.i.* 1. proferir amenazas. 2. tener aspecto amenazante; presagiar algún mal o calamidad.
threatening [-ɪŋ] *a.* amenazador.
threateningly [-lɪ] *adv.* con amenazas, de modo amenazador, amenazantemente.
three [θri] *s., a.* tres.
three-base hit ['θri'beɪs-] (béisbol) lanzamiento que permite al bateador alcanzar la tercera base.
three-centered arch [-ˌsɛntərd-, B -təd-] (arq.) arco zarpanel.
three cleft, (bot.) trífido.
three-color [-ˌkʌlər, B -ə] *a.* (foto., impr.) tricrómico.
three-color photography, tricromía.
three-cornered [-'kɔrnərd, B -'kɔnəd] *a.* 1. triangular; de tres picos (sombrero). 2. triple (empate); entre tres contendientes.
three-cornered hat, tricornio, sombrero de tres picos.
three-D ['θri'di] *a.* tridimensional. —*s.* representación tridimensional; (cine) película tridimensional.
three-decker [-'dɛkər, B -ə] *s.* 1. (mar.) barco de tres cubiertas (esp. buque de guerra). 2. edificio o estructura de tres pisos. 3. emparedado de tres capas de pan y dos de carne, embutido, etc.
three-deep, en tres filas o hileras.
three-dimensional [-də'mɛntʃənəl, B -'mɛnʃən-] *a.* tridimensional.
threefold [-ˌfoʊld] *a.* compuesto de tres; de tres veces, triple, triplo, tresdoble. —*adv.* tres veces, por triplicado, triplemente.
three-handed [-'hændəd] *a.* (naipes) (jugado o que se puede jugar) a tres manos.
three hundred, trescientos.
three hundredth, tricentésimo.
three-leaved ['θri'livd] *a.* (bot.) trifilo.
three-legged [-'lɛgd, -'lɛgəd] *a.* de tres pies.
three-mile limit [-'maɪl-] (der.) límite de tres millas (de jurisdicción marítima).
three of a kind, (póker) pierna.
threepence ['θrɪpəns, B 'θrɛp-] *s.* tres peniques; moneda de tres peniques.
threepenny [-ənɪ, 'θriˌpɛnɪ, B 'θrɛpənɪ] *a.* 1. de tres peniques. 2. (fig.) de poco valor, pobre, barato, mezquino. 3. **a t. bit,** una moneda de tres peniques.
three-phase ['θri'feɪz] *a.* (elec.) trifasico.
three-ply [-'plaɪ] *a.* de tres capas, láminas o hilos.
three-point landing [-'pɔɪnt-] (aer.) aterrizaje en tres puntos.
three-quarter [-'kwɔrtər, B -'kwɔtə] *s.* (rugby) zaguero medio.
three-quarter binding, encuadernación a tres cuartos.
three R's, (fam., hum.) lectura, escritura y aritmética (como bases de la educación).
threescore ['θri'skɔr, B -'skɔ] *a.* tres veintenas, sesenta.
threesome [-səm] *a.* hecho o ejecutado por tres personas. —*s.* juego o danza para tres personas; partido de golf en el que un jugador juega su pelota contra las de otros dos.
three-square [-'skwɛr, B -'skwɛə] *a.* triangular (díc. de cierta clase de lima).
three-stringed [-ˌstrɪŋd] *a.* de tres cuerdas.
three-way switch [-'weɪ-] conmutador de tres direcciones, llave de tres puntos.
three-way valve, válvula de tres pasos, llave de tres conductos.
thremmatology [ˌθrɛmə'tɑlədʒɪ, B -'tɔl-] *s.* (biol.) trematología.
threnode ['θriˌnoʊd, B 'θrɛnˌoʊd] *var. de* **threnody.**
threnodic [θrɪ'nɑdɪk, B -'nɔd-] *a.* fúnebre.
threnodist ['θrɛnədəst] *s.* compositor de trenos.
threnody ['θrɛnədɪ] *s.* (*pl.* THRENODIES) treno, canto fúnebre, lamentación.
thresh [θrɛʃ] *v.t.* 1. trillar, desgranar (trigo, etc.). 2. (fig.) (gen. con *over*) trillar, machacar, batir, repasar, estudiar o examinar una y otra vez. 3.

(raro) azotar, tundar, zurrar. —*v.i.* 1. trillar el grano. 2. agitarse, revolverse, moverse violentamente.
thresher ['θrɛʃər, B -ə] *s.* 1. trillador; (máquina) trilladora. 2. (ict.) zorra de mar.
thresher shark, (ict.) zorra de mar (especie de tiburón).
threshing machine [-ɪŋ] (máquina) trilladora.
threshold ['θrɛʃˌould, -ˌhould] *s.* 1. umbral, tranco. 2. (fig.) entrada, principio, comienzo, punto inicial. 3. (fisiol., psic.) umbral, limen. 4. **to be on the t. of,** estar en los umbrales de; **to cross the t.,** pisar el umbral, atravesar el umbral.
threshold frequency, (fís.) frecuencia crítica.
threshold of hearing, t. of audibility, umbral de audibilidad.
threshold visibility, visibilidad mínima.
threw [θru] *pret. de* **throw.**
thrice [θraɪs] *adv.* 1. tres veces. 2. repetidamente, muy, en sumo grado.
thrift [θrɪft] *s.* 1. economía, frugalidad, ahorro. 2. medra, crecimiento vigoroso (como el de una planta). 3. (pr. esco.) trabajo lucrativo; ocupación provechosa. 4. (bot.) césped de Olimpo. 5. (ant.) prosperidad.
thriftily ['θrɪftəlɪ] *adv.* económicamente, frugalmente, con ahorro.
thriftiness [-tɪnəs] *s.* frugalidad, economía.
thriftless ['θrɪftləs] *a.* manirroto, derrochador, malgastador.
thrifty ['θrɪftɪ] *a.* (THRIFTIER; THRIFTIEST) 1. económico, frugal, ahorrativo. 2. floreciente, próspero.
thrill [θrɪl] *v.t.* 1. emocionar, hacer estremecer, turbar (de emoción). 2. hacer vibrar o temblar. —*v.i.* 1. emocionarse, conmoverse; estremecerse de emoción. 2. vibrar, temblar. —*s.* 1. emoción, agitación, excitación, estremecimiento. 2. (med.) tremor, vibración.
thriller ['θrɪlər, B -ə] *s.* 1. novela sensacional, p. ext. novela de misterio, o policiaca. 2. espectáculo emocionante; cosa excitante.
thrilling [-ɪŋ] *a.* emocionante; conmovedor.
thrillingly [-lɪ] *adv.* de manera o modo emocionante.
thrips [θrɪps] *s.* (*pl.* THRIPS) (ento.) trips, tisanóptaro.
thrive [θraɪv] *v.i.* (*pret.* THROVE [θrouv] o THRIVED; *p.p.* THRIVED o THRIVEN ['θrɪvən]; *p.pr.* THRIVING) 1. medrar (planta, animal). 2. (fig.) medrar, prosperar, enriquecerse; tener éxito.
thriving ['θraɪvɪŋ] *a.* próspero, floreciente.
thrivingly [-lɪ] *adv.* prósperamente, florecientemente.
thro [θru] (ant.) *var. de* **through.**
throat [θrout] *s.* 1. garganta, gola. 2. (fig.) garganta (de una montaña); pasaje, paso; angostura, estrechez; gollete (de una botella). 3. tragante (de horno). 4. (mar.) cruz (del ancla). 5. **to clear one's t.,** aclarar la voz; **to cut one's own t.,** (fig.) arruinarse a sí mismo; **to cut one's t.,** cortarse la garganta; **to jump down one's t.,** regañarle a uno, chillarle a uno; **to lie in one's t.,** mentir descaradamente; **to stick in one's t.,** atascársele a uno en la garganta (ej., una espina); **to take by the t.,** coger por la garganta (para estrangular); **to thrust** (o **ram**) **down one's t.,** meterle a uno por las narices, insistir en que uno tome nota de (algo). —*v.t.* hablar o cantar con voz gutural.
throatband ['θroutˌbænd] **throatlatch** [-ˌlætʃ] *s.* ahogadero (de la cabezada de una caballería).
throatily [-əlɪ] *adv.* guturalmente, roncamente.
throating ['θroutɪŋ] *s.* (arq.) goterón.
throat microphone, micrófono de garganta, laringófono.
throaty [-ɪ] *a.* (THROATIER; THROATIEST) gutural, ronco.
throb [θrɑb, B θrɔb] *v.i.* (*pret., p.p.* THROBBED; *p.pr.* THROBBING) 1. latir, palpitar, pulsar (el corazón, el pulso, etc.). 2. (fig.) vibrar, temblar (con emoción, pasión, etc.). —*s.* latido, palpitación, pulsación, pulsada.
throe [θrou] *s.* 1. dolor extremo, agonía, angustia, congoja; (*pl.*) dolores del parto. 2. (*gen. pl.*) esfuerzo penoso. 3. **in the throes of,** ajetreándose en; a punto de.
thrombase ['θrɑmˌbeɪs, B 'θrɔm-] *s.* (bioquím.) trombasa.
thrombin [-bən] *s.* (bioquím.) trombina, trombasa.
thrombocyte [-bəˌsaɪt] *s.* (fisiol.) trombocito.
thromboembolism [ˌθrɑmbou'ɛmbəˌlɪzəm, B ˌθrɔm-] *s.* (med.) tromboembolia.
thrombogen ['θrɑmbədʒən, B 'θrɔm-] *s.* (bioquím.) trombógeno.
thrombokinase [ˌθrɑmbou'kaɪnˌeɪs, B ˌθrɔm-] *s.* (bioquím.) trombocinasa, tromboquinasa.
thrombophlebitis [-flɪ'baɪtəs] *s.* (med.) tromboflebitis.
thromboplastic [-'plæstɪk] *a.* (bioquím.) tromboplástico.
thromboplastin [-'plæstən] *s.* (bioquím.) tromboplastina.
thrombosis [θrɑm'bousəs, B θrɔm-] *s.* (med.) trombosis.
thrombus ['θrɑmbəs, B 'θrɔm-] *s.* (*pl.* THROMBI [-ˌbaɪ]) (med.) trombo.
throne [θroun] *s.* 1. trono. 2. (fig.) trono, dignidad de rey. 3. (*pl.*) (relig.) tronos (espíritus bienaventurados que forman el tercer coro). —*v.t.* entronizar, elevar al trono. —*v.i.* ocupar el trono.
throne room, sala del trono.
throng [θrɔŋ] *s.* gentío, multitud, muchedumbre, caterva, tropel de gente. —*v.i.* apinarse, amontonarse; moverse o pasar en tropel. —*v.t.* 1. abrumar, aplastar, apretar (a uno la multitud). 2. atestar, llenar (calle, plaza, etc. con gentío).
throstle ['θrɑsəl, B 'θrɔs-] *s.* 1. (orn.) tordo. 2. telar continuo.
throttle ['θrɑtəl, B 'θrɔt-] *s.* 1. garganta, gaznate, garguero, tráquea. 2. (mot.) válvula de estrangulación. —*v.t.* 1. estrangular, ahogar, sofocar. 2. (mot.) (ú. gen. con *down*) obturar, estrangular (los gases o vapores de una máquina); reducir la velocidad de (un motor). —*v.i.* asfixiarse, sofocarse.
throttlehold [-ˌhould] *s.* control absoluto, dominio opresivo.
throttle lever, (mot.) palanquita de estrangulación, manija de admisión, mariposa, obturador de la gasolina.
throttle valve, 1. válvula de admisión; válvula de estrangulación. 2. regulador (en locomotora). 3. regulador de mariposa (de una chimenea). 4. (aut.) acelerador.
through [θru] *prep.* 1. por, a través de. 2. por, de un extremo a otro de. 3. durante, del principio al fin de. 4. por medio de, por conducto de, mediante; a causa de, gracias a, debido a, a consecuencia de. 5. (E.U.) desde . . . hasta, ej., *open Monday t. Saturday,* abierto desde el lunes hasta el sábado. —*adv.* 1. al través, de lado a lado, de parte a parte, de un extremo a otro. 2. de principio a fin, hasta el final. 3. completamente, enteramente. 4. **t. and t.,** por completo, de cabo a rabo; repetidas veces; hasta los tuétanos; **to be t.,** (fam.) haber terminado, no poder más; **to be t. with,** (fam.) haber terminado con, no querer ver más; **to carry t.,** llevar a cabo. —*a.* 1. de paso libre, de vía libre, preferencial (calle o carretera). 2. que atraviesa por completo. 3. directo (tren o vapor).
through bolt, perno pasante, tornillo pasante.
through bridge, puente de paso a través, puente de tablero inferior.
through-ither ['θruəðər, B -ɪðə] **through-other** [-əðər, B -ʌðə] *adv.* (pr. esco.) en confusión; con promiscuidad.
throughout [θru'aut] *prep.* por todo, en todo, a lo largo de; durante todo. —*adv.* en cada parte, a cada parte; en todas partes; en todo respecto.
throughput ['θruˌput] *s.* rendimiento, producto; gasto.
through traffic, (f.c) tráfico de larga distancia.
throughway [-ˌweɪ] *s.* autopista, carretera de acceso limitado.
throve [θrouv] *pret. de* **thrive.**
throw [θrou] *v.t.* (*pret.* THREW [θru]; *p.p.* THROWN [θroun]; *p.pr.* THROWING) 1. arrojar, lanzar, tirar, echar; despedir, desprender. 2. derribar, echar por tierra, tumbar (a opositor, un caballo a jinete, etc.) 3. dirigir, echar (una mirada); mover rápidamente (brazo, cabeza, etc.); echar (el cuerpo); lanzar, asestar (un golpe). 4. mudar la piel (una culebra); perder (una herradura el caballo); echar, descartar (una carta en juegos de naipes). 5. producir (cosecha). 6. parir (una camada). 7. modelar en un torno (vasijas). 8. torcer (hilo). 9. echar (dados). 10. organizar, dar, ej., *t. a party,* dar una fiesta. 11. armar, hacer, ej., *t. a scene,* hacer una escena, armar escándalo. 12. echar (una llave de lucha), mover (una palanca). 13. perder intencionalmente, regalar (una carrera, contienda, etc.). 14. **t. a bridge,** tender un puente; **t. a fit,** arrebatarse, enfurecerse; **t. about,** esparcir, derrochar (dinero); **t. aside,** desechar, poner de lado; **t. away,** arrojar, tirar, botar (Am.) (fig.) desperdiciar, desechar; **t. back,** echar atrás, contrarrestar; reflejar; **t. down,** echar por tierra, derribar; **t. good money after bad,** malgastar dinero al tratar de recuperar pérdidas; **t. in,** dar de adehala, dar de más, dar de yapa (Am.); añadir; intercalar, interponer (una palabra, observación, etc.); conectar (una llave, etc.); **t. in one's hand,** pasar, no entrar (en un juego de naipes, esp. póker); (fig.) renunciar, abandonar; **t. in one's lot with,** compartir la suerte de; **t. in one's face,** echar en cara, reprochar; **t. in the clutch,** embragar; **t. off,** desechar, deshacerse de, librarse de; quitarse (máscara); desviar, descarriar; despistar; improvisar (poema, discurso), soltar (agudezas); quitarse apresuradamente (ropa); **t. on** (u **over**), echarse encima (ropa, saco, etc.); **t. one a kiss;** tirarle un beso a uno; **t. one's weight about,** hacer gala uno de la propia autoridad o importancia; **t. oneself at,** arremeter a o contra (enemigo, oponente, etc.); asediar, tratar de captar el afecto de; **t. oneself down,** echarse (en un lecho, al suelo, etc.); **t. oneself into,** entregarse por completo a (trabajo, diversiones, etc.); **t. oneself on** (o **upon**), poner toda su confianza en; **t. open,** abrir de par en par; **t. out,** echar fuera, expeler; botar (Am.); proferir (indirecta, sugestión), insinuar; descartar, rechazar (proyecto, plan, etc.); distraer, desconcertar, confundir; **t. out on one's ear,** poner de patitas en la calle; **throw out one's chest,** sacar el pecho; **t. out the clutch,** desembragar; **t. over,** abandonar, desamparar, desertar; **t. the book at (someone),** aplicar todo el rigor de la ley o de un castigo a (alguien); **t. up,** levantar rápidamente, alzar; abandonar,

dejar; renunciar; arrojar, devolver, vomitar (la comida); **to be thrown together,** juntarse casualmente. —*v.i.* arrojar, tirar, lanzar; **t. about,** revolverse, agitarse; **t. back,** volver al tipo originario; **t. up,** vomitar. —*s.* 1. tiro, tirada, echada, lanzamiento. 2. bufanda ligera; manta de viaje, cobertor ligero. 3. (geol.) falla, dislocación. 4. (mec.) carrera, juego. 5. (dep.) lanzamiento. 6. **at a stone's t.,** a tiro de piedra, muy cerca.

throwaway ['θroʊəˌweɪ] *s.* volante, hoja suelta, folleto, circular.

throwback [-ˌbæk] *s.* 1. reversión, atavismo, tipo o caso atávico. 2. retroceso, vuelta atrás.

thrower [-ər, B -ə] *s.* 1. arrojador, tirador. 2. (tej.) torcedor de sedas. 3. alfarero (que modela en un torno). 4. (dep.) lanzador.

thrown [θroʊn] *p.p. de* **throw.**

throwout ['θroʊˌaʊt] *s.* desembrague, desacople.

throw rug, alfombra pequeña.

throwster ['θroʊstər, B -stə] *s.* torcedor de seda.

thru [θru] *contr. de* **through,** (fam.) a través.

thrum [θrʌm] *s.* 1. (tej.) cabo o extremidad de la urdimbre; cadillos; fleco, cairel, borla; hilo basto. 2. (*gen. pl.*) desperdicios de hilaza basta. 3. (*pl.*) (mar.) cabos cortos para hacer palletes. 4. (esco.) partícula, pedazo; enredo, maraña. 5. **thread and t.,** justos y pecadores. —*v.t.* (*pret., p.p.* THRUMMED; *p.pr.* THRUMMING) 1. cairelar, orlar, guarnecer con borlas o flecos. 2. (mar.) hacer palletes.

thrum, *v.i.* 1. rasguear o tocar mal un instrumento de cuerda. 2. sonar monótonamente. —*v.t.* 1. tocar (un instrumento) distraída o monótonamente. 2. relatar o repetir tediosamente. —*s.* sonido monótono.

thrush [θrʌʃ] *s.* 1. (med.) afta. 2. (vet.) higo.

thrush, *s.* (orn.) tordo, malvía, zorzal, petirrojo.

thrust [θrʌst] *v.t.* (*pret., p.p.* THRUST; *p.pr.* THRUSTING) 1. empujar, impeler o extender con fuerza. 2. **t. aside,** descartar, rechazar (propuesta, etc.); **t. down,** echar abajo (palanca, manubrio, etc.); **t. in,** meter en, zampar en; interponer (una palabra); **t. into,** meter en, apretujar en (bolsillo, etc.); **t. on** (o **upon**), imponer, forzar a aceptar (tarea, responsabilidad, etc.); **t. oneself forward,** llamar la atención hacia sí mismo; **t. out,** echar fuera; sacar; **t. through,** atravesar, traspasar, clavar, punzar, apuñalar. —*v.i.* 1. (gen. con *on, to, forward,* etc.) avanzar a empellones, abrirse paso por la fuerza. 2. extenderse. 3. **t. at,** acometer o embestir con puñal (u otra arma punzante). —*s.* 1. empuje, empujón. 2. estocada, lanzada. 3. arremetida, embestida. 4. fuerza propulsora, velocidad de salida (de un cohete o motor a reacción). 5. (mil.) ataque de penetración. 6. (geol.) corrimiento, paraclasa. 7. (mec.) empuje axial; presión (entre partes). 8. (arq.) empuje (de un arco).

thrust bearing, (mec.) cojinete de empuje, quicionera.

thruster ['θrʌstər, B -tə] *s.* arribista.

thruway ['θruˌweɪ] *s.* autopista.

Thucydides [θu'sɪdəˌdiz, B θju-] *s.* (hist.) Tucídides, historiador griego.

thud [θʌd] *s.* 1. golpe. 2. baque, batacazo (ruido sordo). —*v.t., v.i.* (*pret., p.p.* THUDDED; *p.pr.* THUDDING), dar un baque; caer o chocar con un ruido sordo.

thug [θʌg] *s.* 1. (hist.) thug (miembro de una antigua secta asesina de la India). 2. ladrón, malhechor, bandolero; matón.

thuggery ['θʌgərɪ] *s.* bandolerismo, bandidaje.

thuggish [-ɪʃ] *a.* rufianesco.

thuja ['θudʒə, B 'θju-] *s.* (bot.) tuya.

thuja oil, aceite de tuya.

Thule ['θulɪ, B 'θjuli] *s.* (hist.) Tule, región que los antiguos consideraban que era la más septentrional del mundo.

thulia ['θulɪə, B 'θju-] *s.* (quím.) óxido de tulio.

thulium [-lɪəm] *s.* (quím.) tulio.

thumb [θʌm] *s.* 1. pulgar, pólice. 2. (arq.) óvolo, cuarto bocel. 3. **all thumbs,** torpe; **rule of t.,** método práctico; **thumbs up!** (jer.) ¡buena suerte!; **to be thumbs down on,** desaprobar, estar en contra de, oponerse a; **to have (someone) under one's t.,** tener (a alguien) de la oreja; **to twiddle one's thumbs,** estar ocioso, no hacer nada. —*v.t.* 1. ensuciar o ajar con los dedos o manoseando mucho; manosear (las teclas del piano, etc.); tocar (música) torpemente. 2. hojear (un libro, etc.). 3. **t. one's nose,** hacer morisquetas de burla (tocando la nariz con el pulgar de la mano extendida).

thumb clamp, (mec.) grampa de mariposa.

thumb index, uñero, índice alfabético (al borde de las páginas de un diccionario, etc.).

thumbkin ['θʌmkɪn] *s.* (hist.) empulgueras (antiguo instrumento de tortura).

thumbnail ['θʌmˌneɪl] *s.* uña del pulgar. —*a.* del tamaño de la uña del pulgar; pequeño, condensado, reducido (artículo, relato, etc.).

thumbnail nut, tuerca de mariposa o manual.

thumbnail sketch, retrato en miniatura, descripción breve pero acertada (de un sujeto o una situación).

thumbprint [-ˌprɪnt] *s.* impresión del pulgar, huella digital.

thumbscrew [-ˌskru] *s.* 1. (mec.) tornillo de mariposa o de orejas. 2. (hist.) empulgueras (antiguo instrumento de tortura).

thumb switch, (elec., rad.) pulsador.

thumbtack [-ˌtæk] *s.* chinche, chincheta, tachuela.

thump [θʌmp] *s.* puñada, porrazo, puñetazo; baque, ruido sordo. —*v.t.* apuñear, majar, apalear, aporrear. —*v.i.* 1. dar golpes, golpear pesadamente. 2. latir fuertemente (el corazón).

thumping ['θʌmpɪŋ] *a.* (fam.) enorme, colosal; excelente.

thunder ['θʌndər, B -də] *s.* 1. trueno. 2. (fig.) trueno, tronido; estruendo, estrépito, fragor. 3. amenaza o censura severa. 4. **to steal someone's t.,** adelantarse a, robarle la idea a (alguien). —*v.i.* 1. tronar, haber o sonar truenos. 2. (con *down, along, past,* etc.) pasar con estruendo (por). 3. **t. against** (o **at**), tronar contra, fulminar censuras contra; t. into, caer o entrar con estruendo; **t. on,** golpear estrepitosamente. —*v.t.* 1. fulminar (censuras, excomuniones, etc.). 2. **t. on** (o **upon**), asestar (golpes pesados) a.

thunderbird [-ˌbɜrd, B -ˌbɜd] *s.* pájaro mítico que produce el trueno y el rayo (según las creencias del indio norte-americano).

thunderbolt [-ˌboʊlt] *s.* 1. rayo, descarga de un rayo. 2. piedra de rayo. 3. (fig.) rayo.

thunderclap [-ˌklæp] *s.* tronido.

thundercloud [-ˌklaʊd] *s.* nubarrón, nube tormentosa (cargada de electricidad).

thunderer ['θʌndərər, B -ə] *s.* tronador, fulminador; **the T.,** Júpiter.

thunderhead ['θʌndərˌhɛd, B -dəˌ-] *s.* (meteor.) masa de cúmulos (que precede generalmente a una tronada).

thundering ['θʌndərɪŋ] *a.* 1. tronante, tonante. 2. descomunal, extraordinario, excepcional.

thunderingly [-lɪ] *adv.* 1. con truenos o tronidos. 2. estruendosamente, estrepitosamente.

thunderous [-əs] *a.* atronador, tronador, tronitoso.

thunderously [-lɪ] *adv.* con truenos, con un ruido ensordecedor, atronadoramente.

thunderpeal ['θʌndərˌpil, B -dəˌ-] *s.* tronido, fragor del trueno.

thundershower [-ˌʃaʊər, B -ə] **thundersquall** [-ˌskwɔl] *s.* chubasco con truenos, borrasca con truenos.

thunderstick [-ˌstɪk] *s.* bramadera (instrumento que usan los pastores para llamar al rebaño).

thunderstone [-ˌstoʊn] *s.* piedra de rayo.

thunderstorm [-ˌstɔrm, B -ˌstɔm] *s.* tronada.

thunderstricken [-ˌstrɪkən] *var. de* **thunderstruck.**

thunderstroke [-ˌstroʊk] *s.* rayo (con trueno).

thunderstruck [-ˌstrʌk] *a.* atónico, estupefacto, turulato, pasmado, asombrado.

thurible ['θʊrəbəl, B 'θjʊər-] *s.* (relig.) turíbulo, incensario.

thurifer [-əfər, B -fə] *s.* (relig.) turiferario.

thurify [-ˌfaɪ] *v.t.* (*pret., p.p.* THURIFIED; *p.pr.* THURIFYING) turificar, incensar.

Thuringian [θʊ'rɪndʒɪən, B θjʊə-] *a., s.* turingiano, de un antiguo estado de Alemania Central.

Thurs. *abrev. de* **Thursday,** jueves (juev.).

Thursday ['θɜrzdɪ, B 'θɜz-] *s.* jueves.

thus [ðʌs] *adv.* 1. así, de este o ese modo, de esta manera, en estos términos. 2. tanto, hasta. 3. así, por esto, por eso, así que. 4. por ejemplo. 5. **t. far,** hasta aquí, hasta ahora.

thwack [θwæk] *v.t.* golpear con algo pesado; aporrear, pegar. —*s.* porrazo; golpe seco y sonoro.

thwart [θwɔrt, B θwɔt] *a.* 1. transversal, transverso, travieso, travesero. 2. (ant.) perverso; intratable. —*adv.* al o a través de, través. —*s.* (mar.) banco de remeros, banco de bogar. —*v.t.* 1. contrariar, desbaratar, frustrar, impedir, bloquear, obstruir. 2. (ant.) pasar a través de.

thwartwise ['θwɔrtˌwaɪz, B 'θwɔt-] *a.* transversal, transverso. —*adv.* al través, a través, en cruz.

thy [ðaɪ] *a. pos.* (ant., poét.) tu, tus.

Thyestean [θaɪ'ɛstɪən] *a.* 1. de Tiestes, personaje mitológico que devoró a sus hijos. 2. (fig.) caníbal.

thylacine ['θaɪləˌsaɪn] *s.* (zool.) yabí, lobo de Tasmania.

thyme [taɪm] *s.* (bot.) tomillo.

Thymelaeaceae [ˌθɪməlɪ'eɪsɪˌi] *s. pl.* (bot.) timeleáceas.

thymelaeaceous [-'eɪʃəs] *a.* (bot.) timeleáceo.

thymic ['θaɪmɪk] *a.* (anat., fisiol.) tímico.

thymol ['θaɪˌmɔl] *s.* (quím.) timol.

thymonucleic [ˌθaɪmoʊnu'kliɪk, B nju-] *a.* (quím.) timonucleico.

thymus ['θaɪməs] *s.* (anat.) timo.

thymy ['taɪmɪ] *a.* lleno de tomillos; que huele a tomillo.

thyratron ['θaɪrəˌtrɑn, B 'θaɪərəˌtrɔn] *s.* (electrón.) tiratrón.

thyroid ['θaɪˌrɔɪd] *a.* (anat.) tiroideo. —*s.* 1. (anat.) tiroides (cuerpo o glándula). 2. (farm.) tiroidina.

thyroidectomy [ˌθaɪˌrɔɪ'dɛktəmɪ] *s.* (med.) tiroidectomía.

thyroid gland, (anat.) glándula tiroides.

thyroiditis [-'daɪtəs] *s.* (med.) tiroiditis.

thyrotoxic [-roʊ'tɑksɪk, B -'tɔk-] *a.* (med.) tirotóxico.

thyrotoxicosis [-ˌtɑksə'koʊsəs, B -ˌtɔk-] *s.* (med.) tirotoxicosis.

thyrotrophin [θaɪ'rɑtrəfən, B ˌθaɪərə'troʊ-] **thyrotropin** [-pən] *s.* (fisiol.) tirotropina.

thyroxine [θaɪ'rɑkˌsin, B θaɪə'rɔk-] *s.* (bioquím.) tiroxina.
thyrse [θɜrs, B θɜs] *s.* (bot.) tirso.
thyrsoid ['θɜrˌsɔɪd, B 'θɜˌ-] **thyrsoidal** [θɜr'sɔɪdəl, B θɜ'-] *a.* (bot.) tirsoide.
thyrsus ['θɜrsəs, B 'θɜsəs] *s.* (*pl.* THYRSI [-saɪ]) 1. (relig. romana) tirso (vara adornada con hojas de parra que servía de cetro a Baco). 2. (bot.) tirso.
thysanopteran [ˌθaɪsə'nɑptərən, B ˌθɪsə'-nɔp-] *a.*, *s.* (ento.) tisanóptero.
Thysanura [-'nʊrə, B -'njʊərə] *s. pl.* (ento.) tisanuros.
thysanuran [-'nʊrən, B -'njʊər-] *a.*, *s.* (ento.) tisonuro.
thyself [ðaɪ'sɛlf] *pron.* (ant.) tú mismo, ti mismo.
ti [ti] *s.* (mús.) si.
Ti *símb. de* **titanium,** titanio (Ti).
tiara [tɪ'ærə, -'ɛr-, B -'ɑr-] *s.* 1. tiara (del papa). 2. corona, diadema (como adorno de cabeza).
Tiber ['taɪbər, B -bə] *s.* Tíber, río de Italia.
Tiberius [taɪ'bɪrɪəs, B -'bɪər-] *s.* (hist.) Tiberio, emperador romano.
Tibet [tə'bɛt] el Tíbet, región autónoma de China al N. de los montes Himalaya.
Tibetan [-'bɛtən] *a.*, *s.* tibetano, del Tíbet.
tibia ['tɪbɪə] *s.* (*pl.* TIBIAE [-ɪˌi] o TIBIAS) 1. (anat.) tibia. 2. (ento.) cuarta articulación de la pata. 3. (mús.) tibia.
tibial [-ɪəl] *a.* (anat.) tibial, de la tibia.
tibiotarsal [ˌtɪbɪə'tɑrsəl, B -'tɑsəl] *a.* (anat.) tibiotarsiano.
tibourbou [tə'bʊrbu, B tɪ'bʊəbu] *s.* (bot.) erizo.
tic [tɪk] *s.* (med.) tic.
tical [tɪ'kɑl] *s.* (*pl.* TICALS o TICAL) tical (unidad monetaria de Tailandia).
tic douloureux ['tɪkˌdulə'ru, B -'rɜ] (med.) tic doloroso de la cara.
tick [tɪk] *s.* (ento.) ácaro, garrapata, rezno, pito, mosca borriquera.
tick, *s.* 1. funda (de colchón, almohada o almohadón). 2. cutí, cotí.
tick [tɪk] *v.t.* 1. hacer tictac (un reloj). 2. latir, palpitar. 3. funcionar. 4. **t. away,** pasar (díc. del tiempo); **t. over,** (G.B.) marchar en vacío (un motor); (fig.) marcar el paso. —*v.t.* (gen. con *off*) 1. marcar con una contraseña, contramarcar. 2. marcar, contar, medir, registrar (díc. de un instrumento que hace tictac). 3. **t. away,** marcar el paso (de los minutos, del tiempo, como el reloj); **t. (someone) off,** (fam.) reprender (a uno), sermonear (a uno); **t. out,** comunicar o imprimir (noticias, cotizaciones, etc.; díc. del telégrafo, teletipo, etc.). —*s.* 1. tictac. 2. instante, momento, segundo. 3. contramarca, contraseña. 4. (fam.) crédito, fiado; cuenta de crédito.
ticked [tɪkt] *a.* 1. punteado, abigarrado, veteado, moteado. 2. listado (piel de un animal).
ticker ['tɪkər, B -ə] *s.* 1. receptor telegráfico, teleimpresor. 2. (fam.) reloj. 3. (jer.) el corazón.
ticker tape, cinta de teleimpresor.
ticket ['tɪkət] *s.* 1. billete, boleta, boleto (Am.); entrada. 2. certificado, licencia, permiso, pase. 3. marbete, etiqueta, rótulo. 4. (aut.) multa, boleta (Arg.), papeleta (Perú). 5. (pol., E.U.) lista de candidatos, candidatura; programa (de un partido). 6. (mil.) (jer. G.B.) licencia absoluta. 7. **that's the t.** ¡eso es lo que se necesita! ¡eso es lo que queríamos! —*v.t.* 1. rotular, marcar, poner etiqueta a. 2. (E.U.) proveer de billetes, vender pasaje a.
ticket agency, agencia de viajes, agencia de turismo; agencia de billetes (de teatro, conciertos, cine, etc.).
ticket agent, 1. agente de viajes. 2. vendedor de billetes (para el teatro, conciertos, etc.), taquillero.
ticket collector, revisor, recaudador de boletos de pasaje (en trenes, tranvías, autobuses, etc.).
ticket holder, poseedor de un billete, boleto o entrada.
ticket office, taquilla, despacho de billetes, boletería (Amer.).
ticket of leave, (G.B.) libertad condicional (de condenado).
ticket window, taquilla, ventanilla, boletería.
tick fever, 1. (med.) fiebre de las Montañas Rocosas. 2. (vet.) fiebre de Tejas.
ticking ['tɪkɪŋ] *s.* (tej.) cutí, cotí, terliz.
tickle ['tɪkəl] *v.i.* hormiguear, sentir cosquillas, hormigueo o picazón. —*v.t.* 1. hacerle cosquillas a, cosquillear. 2. divertir, entretener; halagar, deleitar. —*s.* cosquilleo, hormigueo; cosquillas.
tickler ['tɪklər, B 'tɪklə] *s.* 1. algo que cosquillea o estimula. 2. (ten.) libro uxiliar de obligaciones por pagar, libro diario. 3. (fam.) problema difícil, rompecabezas.
tickler coil, (elec.) bobina de regeneración, bobina de reacción.
tickling [-lɪŋ] *s.* cosquillas.
ticklish [-lɪʃ] *a.* 1. cosquilloso. 2. (fig.) cosquilloso, quisquilloso, puntilloso, susceptible (carácter). 3. delicado, espinoso, crítico (situación, problema, etc.).
ticklishness [-nəs] *s.* naturaleza cosquillosa o quisquillosa, sensibilidad, susceptibilidad.
ticktack ['tɪkˌtæk] *s.* tictac, tic tac.
ticktacktoe [ˌtɪkˌtæk'toʊ] *s.* tres en raya (juego).
ticktock ['tɪkˌtɑk, B -ˌtɔk] *s.* tictac (de un reloj grande).
tic-tac-toe, *var. de* **ticktacktoe.**
tidal ['taɪdəl] *a.* de marea, relativo al flujo de la marea.
tidal current, corriente de la marea.
tidal epoch, retraso de la marea máxima después del plenilunio.
tidal flood, maremoto.
tidal harbor, puerto navegable sólo durante la pleamar.
tidal wave, 1. aguaje, marejada, oleada (causada por terremoto o ventarrón). 2. (fig.) marejada (movimiento o conmoción públicos).
tidbit ['tɪdˌbɪt] *s.* 1. (E.U.) bocado, bocadito, golosina. 2. chismecito inofensivo; noticia agradable.
tiddledywinks ['tɪdəldɪˌwɪŋks] **tiddlywinks** ['tɪdlɪ-] *s. pl.* juego cuyo objeto es embocar pequeños discos dentro de una vasija.
tide [taɪd] *s.* 1. marea. 2. (fig.) ola, corriente (de opinión, popularidad, etc.). 3. (poét.) arroyo, corriente, inundación. 4. (ant.) época, estación, período de tiempo, oportunidad. 5. **priming of the tides,** adelanto diario de la marea; **to swim (o go) with the t.,** bailar al son que tocan, dejarse llevar por la corriente, seguir la corriente; **to turn the t.,** cambiar la suerte, cambiar el curso (de los acontecimientos). —*a.* de marea. —*v.i.* 1. crecer (la marea); levantarse (las olas). 2. navegar o deslizarse con la marea (un barco). —*v.t.* 1. hacer llevar o flotar con la marea. 2. **t. (someone) over,** ayudar (a alguien) a salir del apuro; alcanzar, ej., *we have water enough to t. us over until help comes,* tenemos agua suficiente para alcanzarnos hasta que recibamos ayuda.
tide gage, mareómetro, mareógrafo, escala de marea.
tide gate, compuerta de marea.
tidehead ['taɪdˌhɛd] *s.* límite de subida de la marea.
tideland [-ˌlænd, -lənd] *s.* marisma; zona costera.
tideless [-ləs] *a.* sin marea.
tide lock, esclusa contra la marea.
tidemark [-ˌmɑrk, B -ˌmɑk] *s.* 1. marca de marea (alta o baja). 2. (fig.) límite extremo (alto o bajo).
tide rip, onda de marea.
tidesman ['taɪdzmən] **tidewaiter** ['taɪdˌweɪtər, B -ə] *s.* vista, inspector de aduanas (que vigila el desembarco de mercaderías).
tide table, tabla de mareas (que indica la altura de la marea en un lugar a diferentes horas del día durante un año).
tidewater ['taɪdˌwɔtər, -'wɑt-, B -ˌwɔtə] *s.* 1. agua de marea. 2. playa, orilla del mar.
tideway [-ˌweɪ] *s.* canal de mareas.
tidily ['taɪdəlɪ] *adv.* 1. aseadamente, pulcramente. 2. ordenadamente.
tidiness [-ɪnəs] *s.* 1. aseo, pulcritud, limpieza; orden. 2. sentido del orden.
tidings ['taɪdɪŋz] *s. pl.* noticias, nuevas; informes.
tidy ['taɪdɪ] *a.* (TIDIER; TIDIEST) 1. limpio, aseado, pulcro; ordenado, metódico. 2. (fam.) regular, adecuado. 3. (fam.) considerable, substancial, bastante grande. —*v.t.* (*pret., p.p.* TIDIED; *p.pr.* TIDYING) ordenar, poner en orden, arreglar; limpiar, asear. —*v.i.* (gen. con *up*) sentar orden. —*s.* (*pl.* TIDIES) tapete, antimacasar (que se pone en el respaldo y los brazos de un sillón).
tie [taɪ] *v.t.* (*pret., p.p.* TIED; *p.pr.* TYING o TIEING) 1. atar, amarrar, liar. 2. (fig.) unir, enlazar. 3. entrelazar, trenzar (una guirnalda, corona de flores, etc.); hacer el nudo de (la corbata). 4. empatar (partido); igualar (puntaje). 5. (mús.) ligar (notas). 6. **t. a can to,** (jer.) deshacerse de, librarse de; **t. down,** sujetar; (fig.) tener amarrado; **t. in,** conectar; **t. in with,** relacionar con, adaptar a; **t. the knot,** (fig.) casar, casarse; **t. to,** ligar a, sujetar a; limitar a, confinar a; **t. together,** anudar; **t. up,** restringir, limitar; reservar o destinar (para determinado propósito); inmovilizar; obstruir, paralizar. —*v.i.* 1. unirse, cerrarse, conectarse. 2. (con *with*) empatar (con equipo opositor, etc.), quedar o salir pata o patas (con). 3. **t. in with,** relacionarse con, adaptarse a; **t. into,** arremeter, embestir; regañar, reprender. —*s.* 1. lazo, cordón, cinta. 2. atadura, ligadura, ligazón. 3. (fig.) vinculación, enlace. 4. (fig.) lazo, vínculo, unión. 5. traba, obligación. 6. corbata. 7. (*pl.*) zapatos de lazo (de hombre). 8. empate. 9. (mús.) ligadura; ligado. 10. (arq., ing.) riostra, traviesa, travesaño, durmiente. 11. (f.c.) traviesa, durmiente (Amer.). 12. **to play off a t.,** jugar un partido de desempate.
tie bar, (f.c.) barra separadora (entre las dos agujas de cambio).
tie beam, (const.) tirante, viga tirante.
tied column, (const.) columna zunchada.
tie-dye ['taɪˌdaɪ] *s.* método para estampar o adornar telas y piezas de ropa con dibujos al azar, amarrándolas en secciones y sumergiéndolas ligeramente en la mezcla del tinte.
tie-in [-ˌɪn] *s.* enlace, conexión.
tie-joint [-ˌdʒɔɪnt] *s.* (carp.) encepadura.
tiemannite ['timəˌnaɪt] *s.* (min.) tiemannita.
tiepin ['taɪˌpɪn] *s.* alfiler de corbata.
tie plate, (f.c.) placa de asiento, placa de defensa.
tier [tɪr, B tɪə] *s.* 1. fila, hilera, ringlera. 2. fila de palcos (de teatro). —*v.t., v.i.* arreglar o estar arreglado en hileras o filas; amontonar(se) en hileras.

tierce [tɪrs, B tɪəs] *s.* 1. tercerola (barril de mediana cabida). 2. tercera, [B tɜs] tercia (de naipes). 3. (relig.) tercia (hora inmediata después de prima). 4. (esgr.) tercera (parada y posición de la mano). 5. (ant.) tercio, tercera parte.
tiercel ['tɪrsəl, B 'tɪəsəl] *s.* (caza) terzuelo, torzuelo.
tierce major, (naipes) tercera mayor.
tierceron ['tɪrsərən, B 'tɪər-] *s.* (arq.) tercelete.
tie rod, (mec.) barra tirante, varilla de tensión; (aut.) barra de dirección.
tier table, mesita de varios tableros o de niveles escalonados.
tie-up ['taɪˌʌp] *s.* 1. enlace, conexión, asociación. 2. establo de vacas. 3. paralización, atoramiento, embotellamiento (del tráfico, etc.). 4. (E.U.) interrupción, paro (de máquinas, de una industria). 5. (mar.) amarradero.
tiff [tɪf] *s.* 1. riña, altercado, pendencia. 2. (raro) trago o sorbo de licor o ponche. —*v.i.* (anglo-ind.) almorzar, merendar.
tiffany ['tɪfənɪ] *s.* gasa de muselina.
tiffin ['tɪfən] (anglo-ind.) *s.* almuerzo, merienda. —*v.i., v.t.* almorzar, merendar.
tiger ['taɪgər, B -gə] *s.* 1. tigre. 2. (fig.) tigre, fiera (persona cruel). 3. (E.U.) vítor, grito final, última aclamación. 4. (fam.) oponente formidable (en un juego, competencia, etc.). 5. (G.B.) paje, lacayo. 6. **to have a t. by the tail,** estar metido en un lío, verse en una situación difícil e inesperada.
tiger beetle, (ento.) cicindela.
tiger cat, 1. (zool.) gato montés; gato cerval, ocelote, tigrillo. 2. gato (doméstico) atigrado.
tigereye ['taɪgərˌaɪ] *var. de* **tiger's-eye.**
tigerflower [-gərˌflauər, B -gəˌflauə] *s.* (bot.) cacomite.
tigerish ['taɪgərɪʃ] *a.* 1. de tigre, como un tigre. 2. violento, feroz, terrible, cruel.
tiger lily, (bot.) azucena atigrada, trigidia.
tiger moth, (ento.) artia.
tiger's-eye ['taɪgərzˌaɪ, B -gəz-] *s.* (min.) ojo de gato.
tiger shark, (ict.) tiburón tigre; alecrín.
tiger weasel, (zool.) vormela.
tight [taɪt] *a.* 1. apretado, ajustado. 2. estrecho, angosto; ajustado, ceñido. 3. cerrado (ej., vuelta de un camino). 4. tirante, tieso, teso, atesado. 5. bien cerrado, hermético; impermeable; estanco (barco, etc.). 6. (fig.) difícil, apurado (situación). 7. severo, riguroso, estricto. 8. compacto, denso. 9. (fig.) sucinto, breve (estilo, lenguaje, etc.). 10. (fam.) cicatero, tacaño. 11. reñido (contienda, carrera, etc.). 12. bien formado, ordenado, bonito, decente. 13. (fam.) ahumado, achispado, bebido. 14. (com.) escaso, difícil de obtener (díc. de dinero o de mercaderías). —*adv.* estrechamente, apretadamente, ajustadamente; **hold t.,** ¡agárrense bien!
tighten ['taɪtən] *v.t., v.i.* estrechar(se), ajustar(se), apretar(se); **to t. one's belt,** apretarse el cinturón, prepararse para los embates de la vida.
tightener [-ər, B -ə] *s.* tensor.
tightening line [-ɪŋ-] (const.) cable atesador, cable de compensación o de tensión.
tightfisted ['taɪt'fɪstəd] *a.* (fam.) tacaño, cicatero.
tight fit, (mec.) ajuste forzado o apretado.
tight-fitting [-'fɪtɪŋ] *a.* muy ajustado.
tight laced, (fam.) estricto, severo.
tight-lipped [-'lɪpt] *a.* 1. con los labios firmes o tensos. 2. taciturno, callado, poco comunicativo, reservado.
tightly [-lɪ] *adv.* estrechamente, apretadamente, ajustadamente.
tight-mouthed ['taɪt'mauðd, -'mauθt, B -'mauðd] *a.* callado, reservado.
tightness [-nəs] *s.* 1. tensión, tirantez. 2. estrechez. 3. apretura. 4. (fam.) tacañería.
tightrope [-ˌroup] *s.* cuerda floja. —*a.* de cuerda floja.
tights [taɪts] *s. pl.* (traje de) malla (de los bailarines, acróbatas, gimnastas, etc.); medias enterizas de malla.
tightwad ['taɪtˌwɑd, B -ˌwɔd] *s.* (jer., E.U.) tacaño, cicatero, avaro.
tightwire [-ˌwaɪr, B -ˌwaɪə] *s.* cuerda floja.
tiglic ['tɪglɪk] *a.* (quím.) tíglico.
tiglon ['taɪˌglɑn, B -glən] *s.* cría híbrida de tigresa y león.
tigon [-ˌgɑn, B -gən] *var. de* **tiglon.**
tigress ['taɪgrəs] *s.* tigresa.
tigrine [-grən, B -ˌgraɪn] *a.* atigrado.
tigrish [-grɪʃ] *var. de* **tigerish.**
tike, *var. de* **tyke.**
til [tɪl] *s.* (bot.) sésamo.
tilbury ['tɪlˌbɛrɪ, B -bərɪ] *s.* tílburi, coche ligero de dos pasajeros.
tilde ['tɪldə, B tɪld] *s.* 1. tilde, virgulilla que se pone sobre ciertas letras, ej., la ñ. 2. reparo, crítica leve.
tile [taɪl] *s.* 1. teja, tejado. 2. azulejo, losa, baldosa; loseta, baldosín, enlosado. 3. atanor (de cañería). 4. (fam.) sombrero de copa; chistera. 5. **on the tiles,** (jer.) de juerga; **to have a t. loose,** (jer.) tener un tornillo flojo, estar medio loco. —*v.t.* tejar, trastejar, enlosar, embaldosar, azulejar.
tilefish ['taɪlˌfɪʃ] *s.* (ict.) lofolátilo.
tile floor, embaldosado.
tile kiln, tejar (taller o fábrica).
tiler [-ər, B -ə] *s.* 1. tejero, azulejero; enlosador, tejador, trastejador, solador. 2. portero de logia (de masones).
tile roof, tejado, techo de tejas.
tile tea, té comprimido en panes.
Tiliaceae [ˌtɪlɪ'eɪsɪˌi] *s. pl.* (bot.) tiliáceas.
tiliaceous [-'eɪʃəs] *a.* (bot.) tiliáceo.
tiling ['taɪlɪŋ] *s.* tejado, trastejadura, trastejo; enlosado, embaldosado, azulejería.
till [tɪl] *prep.* 1. hasta (cierto tiempo). 2. [tʌl] (esco.) a. —*conj.* hasta que. —*v.t., v.i.* cultivar, laborar, labrar.
till, *s.* 1. caja, cajón o gaveta para guardar dinero (en un banco o una tienda). 2. (geol.) morena.
tillable ['tɪləbəl] *a.* cultivable, laborable, arable.
tillage [-ɪdʒ] *s.* cultivo, labranza, labor.
tiller ['tɪlər, B -ə] *s.* 1. agricultor, labrador. 2. cultivadora (máquina agrícola). 3. (mar.) caña del timón. 4. renuevo, retoño, vástago. —*v.i.* renovarse, retoñar (las plantas).
tillite ['tɪlˌaɪt] *s.* (geol.) tilita.
tilt [tɪlt] *s.* toldo, cubierta, tendal. —*v.t.* entoldar.
tilt, *v.t.* 1. inclinar, ladear, voltear, volcar. 2. apuntar (la lanza), dar (una lanzada); arremeter (adversario, enemigo, etc.). —*v.i.* 1. inclinarse, reclinarse, ladearse. 2. justar, tomar parte en un torneo. 3. **t. at,** acometer, arremeter contra; criticar; **t. at windmills,** arremeter contra molinos de viento. —*s.* 1. justa, torneo, certamen. 2. lanzada, golpe; (fig.) altercado, disputa. 3. rapidez, velocidad. 4. inclinación. 5. declive. 6. (E.U.) balancín de tabla. 7. **(at) full t.,** a toda velocidad.
tilter ['tɪltər, B -ə] *s.* 1. justador, torneador. 2. mecanismo u obrero que vierte (hierro fundido, vidrio, etc.).
tilth [tɪlθ] *s.* 1. agricultura, cultivo, labranza, labor. 2. tierra cultivada, capa labrada (de tierra).
tilt hammer, martinete de báscula.
tilting ['tɪltɪŋ] *s.* inclinación; vuelco. —*a.* inclinado, ladeado.
tilting level, nivel basculante.
tiltmeter ['tɪltˌmitər, B -ə] *s.* medidor de inclinación, inclinómetro.
tiltyard [-ˌjɑrd, B -ˌjɑd] *s.* palestra, arena.
timbal ['tɪmbəl] *s.* (mús.) timbal, atabal, tamboril.
timbale ['tɪmbəl, B tæm'bɑl] *s.* (cocina) timbal, molde o cubilete de arroz o pasta, relleno de marisco, pollo o carne.
timber ['tɪmbər, B -bə] *s.* 1. maderamen, maderaje, madera de construcción. 2. viga, madero. 3. (fig.) madera, materia. 4. monte, bosque. 5. (const. naval) cuaderna, mango de madera. —*v.t.* enmaderar; entibar (excavaciones en minas); enramar (las cuadernas de buques).
timber cruiser, estimador de madera en pie (en bosques).
timbered [-bərd, B -bəd] *a.* 1. enmaderado. 2. arbolado, boscoso.
timber forest, bosque maderable.
timberhead ['tɪmbərˌhɛd, B -bəˌ-] *s.* (mar.) gambota.
timber hitch, (mar.) vuelta de braza.
timber-hitch [-ˌhɪtʃ] *v.t.* (mar.) amarrar con vueltas de braza o cabo.
timbering ['tɪmbərɪŋ] *s.* maderamen, maderaje; entibación, asnado (en minas).
timberland [-bərˌlænd, B -bəˌ-] *s.* bosque (de árboles maderables); tierra o zona boscosa.
timberline [-ˌlaɪn] *s.* límite de la vegetación arbórea.
timberman [-mən, B -ˌmæn] *s.* entibador, ademador (en minas).
timber merchant, negociante en madera o en árboles maderables.
timber right, derechos de monte o de bosque (sobre la madera en pie).
timber wolf, (zool.) lobo gris norteamericano.
timberwork ['tɪmbərˌwɜrk, B -bəˌwɜk] *s.* maderaje, maderamen.
timber yard, maderería, taller o almacén de maderas.
timbre ['tæmbər, 'tɪm-, B 'tæmbrə] *s.* (mús., fon., her.) timbre.
timbrel ['tɪmbrəl] *s.* (mús.) antiguo tipo de pandereta, adufe.
timbreled, timbrelled [-brəld] *a.* tocado al son de pandereta(s).
Timbuktu [ˌtɪmˌbʌk'tu] *s.* 1. Tombuctú, Tombouctou, ciudad de Mali, África occidental. 2. (fig., E.U.) el quinto infierno, cualquier lugar remoto.
time [taɪm] *s.* 1. tiempo. 2. tiempo, período, duración, lapso. 3. tiempo, época, era, edad. 4. rato, instante, momento. 5. tiempo, ocasión, oportunidad, ej., *now is your t.,* ahora es su oportunidad, *t. is (was) ripe,* la ocasión es (era) propicia, el tiempo es (era) oportuno. 6. tiempo, hora; ej., *it is t. to leave,* es hora de irse, *my t. is drawing near,* se acerca mi hora (de la muerte). 7. vez, veces, ej., *four times six is twenty four,* cuatro veces seis son veinticuatro. 8. (com.) horario (de trabajo); sueldo, paga (por hora). 9. (mús.) tiempo, compás, ritmo, cadencia. 10. (poét.) mora (unidad de duración). 11. (gram.) tiempo. 12. **against t.,** contra el reloj; con toda premura; **all in good t.,** todo a su tiempo, vamos por partes; **all the t.,** todo el tiempo; (E.U.) siempre, en todo; **a long t.,** mucho tiempo; **a long t. ago,** hace mucho tiempo, mucho tiempo ha; **any t.,** a cualquier hora, cuando quiera; **at a t.,** a la vez; **at no t.,** en ningún momento, nunca; **at one t.,** en un tiempo, anteriormente; **at some t. or other,** en una u otra ocasión, un día u otro; **at the present t.,** al presente, en la actualidad; **at the**

same t., al mismo tiempo; a la vez; no obstante; **at the wrong t.**, en un mal momento, fuera de tiempo; **at this t. of day,** (fig.) a estas alturas (de las negociaciones, acontecimientos, etc.); **at times,** a ratos, a veces; **behind the times,** (fig.) atrasado, anticuado, fuera de moda; **behind t.**, atrasado; **between times,** en los intervalos; **by that t.**, para entonces; **each t.**, cada vez; **every t.**, cada vez; siempre; **for all t.**, para siempre; **for some t.**, durante algún tiempo; **for the last t.**, por última vez (te advierto, digo, etc.); **for the t. being,** por ahora, por lo pronto, en el entretanto; **from this t.**, desde hoy; **from t. to t.**, de tiempo en tiempo, de vez en cuando, ocasionalmente; **good t.**, buen rato, momento agradable; **hard** (o **bad**) **t.**, mal rato; **hard** (o **bad**) **times,** tiempos difíciles (para vivir); **in a short t.**, en breve, dentro de poco; **in good t.**, temprano; a tiempo; **in my t.**, en mis días, en mis tiempos; **in no t.**, en un dos por tres, en seguida; **in the nick of t.**, justo a tiempo, al momento preciso; **in the course of t.**, andando el tiempo; **in t.**, a tiempo; con tiempo; andando el tiempo, más adelante; (mús.) con ritmo, a compás; acompasado; **in two** (**three,** etc.) **hours' t.**, en (el transcurso de) dos (tres, etc.) horas; **it will last our t.**, durará hasta el fin de nuestra era; **many a t., many times,** muchas veces, a menudo; **on t.**, puntual; puntualmente; **out of t.**, fuera de sazón; demasiado tarde; (mús.) fuera de tiempo, desacompasado; **the good old times,** los buenos tiempos de antaño; **the t. is ripe,** este es el momento, la ocasión es oportuna; **the t. of day,** la hora del día; **the t. of one's life,** un rato magnífico; **t. and again, t. after t.**, repetidas veces; **t. enough,** (fam.) con tiempo, a tiempo (para); **t. is money,** el tiempo es oro; **t. off,** horas libres; **t. will show** (o **tell**), el tiempo lo dirá; **to be far on in her t.**, estar bastante avanzada (en el embarazo); **to be serving one's t.**, estar de aprendiz, trabajar como principiante; **to beat t.**, (mús.) marcar el compás (con la mano, un palo, etc.); **to bide one's t.**, tomarse tiempo; **to do t.**, cumplir una condena; **to gain t.**, ganar tiempo; **to have a good t.**, divertirse, pasar un rato agradable; **to have no t. for,** no tener tiempo para; **to keep good** (o **bad**) **t.**, andar bien (o mal) (el reloj); **to keep t.**, (mús.) seguir el compás; moverse en armonía; **to kill t.**, matar el tiempo; **to lose t.**, perder el tiempo; atrasarse (reloj); **to make good t.**, correr a buena velocidad (auto, etc.); **to make t.**, ganar tiempo; **to mark t.**, marcar el paso; **to pass the t.**, pasar el tiempo; **to pass the t. away,** matar el tiempo; **to serve t.**, cumplir una condena; **to take one's t.**, tomarse tiempo; **to waste t.**, desperdiciar o gastar el tiempo; **two** (**three,** etc.) **at a t.**, de dos (tres, etc.) en dos; **what is the t.?** ¿qué hora es? —*v.i* (raro), seguir el compás; moverse en armonía. —*v.t.* 1. fijar la hora o el tiempo de. 2. regular (reloj, espoleta de bomba, etc.). 3. hacer a compás (pasos de baile, movimientos); hacer a tiempo oportuno; escoger el momento para (acción, observación). 4. (dep.) registrar o cronometrar el tiempo de (ganador, etc.). —*a.* 1. de tiempo; del tiempo. 2. a plazos.

time and a half, tiempo y medio, sobretiempo, salario y medio.

time and tide, tiempo y sazón.

time bill, (com.) letra a día fijo, letra a plazo o a término.

time bomb, bomba de tiempo, bomba de acción retardada.

time capsule, cápsula del tiempo.

time card, tarjeta registradora o marcador de hora.

timecard ['taɪm,kɑrd, B 'taɪm,kɑd] *s.* horario; itinerario.

time chart, mapa de husos horarios.

time clock, reloj registrador, de tiempo (que marca la hora de entrada y salida de los empleados u obreros).

time-consuming [-kən'sumɪŋ, B -'sju-] *a.* 1. que exige o demanda mucho tiempo. 2. malgastador de tiempo.

timed [taɪmd] *a.* 1. de duración determinada (ejercicio, examen, etc.). 2. retardada (explosión). 3. hecho en un (buen, mal, etc.) momento, ej., *an ill-t. remark,* una observación hecha en un mal momento, una observación inoportuna.

time deposit, (com.) depósito a plazo, depósito a término fijo.

time draft, (com.) giro a plazo, letra de cambio a plazo, orden de pago a plazo.

time exposure, (foto.) exposición de tiempo; pose de tiempo.

time fuse, espoleta de tiempo.

time-honored ['taɪm,ɑnərd, B -,ɔnəd] *a.* tradicional, consagrado por el tiempo, venerable.

time immemorial, tiempos perdidos en la historia.

timekeeper [-,kipər, B -pə] *s.* 1. reloj, cronómetro. 2. (mús.) marcador de tiempo. 3. (dep.) cronometrador, cronometrista.

time killer, 1. desocupado, ocioso. 2. pasatiempo.

time lag, intervalo, retardo (entre la causa y el efecto), período de retraso.

timeless ['taɪmləs] *a.* 1. eterno, infinito. 2. sin fecha, sin limitación de tiempo. 3. (ant.) prematuro, inoportuno.

timeliness [-lɪnəs] *s.* 1. puntualidad. 2. oportunidad.

time loan, (com.) préstamo a plazo fijo.

time lock, cerradura de tiempo.

timely ['taɪmlɪ] *adv.* (ant.) oportunamente, a tiempo. —*a.* (TIMELIER; TIMELIEST) puntual; oportuno.

time money, (com.) dinero (prestado) a plazo fijo.

time note, (com.) letra de cambio a plazo fijo, pagaré.

time of climb, (aer.) tiempo de subida.

time of departure, hora de salida.

timeous ['taɪməs] *a.* (esco.) oportuno.

time-out ['taɪm'aʊt] *s.* (*pl.* TIME-OUTS) 1. intermedio, intervalo. 2. (dep.) interrupción, suspensión temporal (de un partido, acto ceremonial, etc.). 3. tiempo de descanso (que se toma dentro de un horario de trabajo).

timepiece [-,pis] *s.* reloj, cronómetro.

timepleaser [-,plizər, B -zə] *s.* (ant.) persona servil; contemporizador.

timer ['taɪmər, B -mə] *s.* 1. contador, cronometrador, cronometrista. 2. cronógrafo, cronómetro. 3. distribuidor del encendido (en motores).

timesaving ['taɪm,seɪvɪŋ] *a.* que ahorra o economiza tiempo.

timeserver [-,sɜrvər, B -,sɜvə] *s.* contemporizador, oportunista.

timeserving [-vɪŋ] *a.* contemporizador, adulador, servil. —*s.* contemporización, oportunismo.

timesharing ['taɪm,ʃerɪŋ] *s.* (comput.) trabajo en tiempo compartido, utilizacion compartido; de tiempo compartido (sistema).

time sheet, hoja o planilla de jornales devengados.

time signal, señal horaria (esp. en la radio).

time signature, (mús.) llave de tiempo.

time slice, (comput.) fracción de tiempo.

time study, estudio de la productividad y eficiencia del trabajo en función del tiempo.

time switch, interruptor horario, interruptor de reloj.

timetable ['taɪm,teɪbəl] *s.* 1. horario; itinerario. 2. guía de salidas y llegadas (de trenes, aviones, etc.).

timework [-,wɜrk, B -,wɜk] *s.* trabajo a jornal, trabajo por hora o por día.

timeworker ['taɪm,wɜrkər, B -,wɜkə] *s.* jornalero, jornalera; trabajador a destajo.

timeworn [-,wɔrn, B -,wɔn] *a.* 1. usado, trillado, gastado. 2. anticuado, viejo.

time yield, (const.) deformación inelástica resultante de la aplicación continua de carga; escurrimiento plástico.

time zone, huso horario.

timid ['tɪməd] *a.* tímido, timorato, apocado.

timidity [tə'mɪdətɪ] *s.* timidez.

timidly ['tɪmədlɪ] *adv.* tímidamente.

timidness [-nəs] *s.* timidez.

timing ['taɪmɪŋ] *s.* 1. habilidad de escoger el momento oportuno; oportunidad. 2. (mús.) sentido del ritmo o compás. 3. (mot.) puesta a punto; regulación del encendido, distribución del encendido. 4. (dep.) acierto, ritmo correcto (en los movimientos).

timing gear, (mot.) engranaje de distribución.

timing quadrant, (mec.) sector de reglaje.

timing relay, (elec.) relai de acción retardada.

timocracy [taɪ'mɑkrəsɪ, B -'mɔk-] *s.* (pol.) timocracia.

timocratic [,taɪmə'krætɪk] **timocratical** [-ɪkəl] *a.* timocrático.

Timon ['taɪmən] *s.* Timón, filósofo griego.

timorous ['tɪmərəs] *a.* timorato, tímido, miedoso.

timorously [-lɪ] *adv.* tímidamente, miedosamente.

timorousness [-nəs] *s.* timidez, pusilanimidad.

timothy ['tɪməθɪ] *s.* (bot.) fleo.

timpani ['tɪmpənɪ] *s. pl.* (*sing. o pl. en const.*) (mús.) tímpanos, timbales.

timpanist [-nəst] *s.* timbalero.

tin [tɪn] *s.* 1. (quím.) estaño. 2. hojalata, lata. 3. lata (de conservas, tabaco, etc.). 4. (jer.) mosca, parné, plata (Amer.), dinero. —*v.t.* (*pret. p.p.* TINNED; *p.pr.* TINNING) 1. estañar. 2. cubrir con hojalata. 3. (pr. G.B.) enlatar, envasar (conservas). —*a.* de hojalata.

tinamou ['tɪnə,mu] *s.* (orn.) tinamú.

tin-bearing ['tɪn,berɪŋ, B -,beər-] *a.* (geol.) estañífero.

tincal ['tɪŋkəl] *s.* (min.) atíncar, tincal.

tin can, (jer., mar.) destructor.

tinct [tɪŋkt] *a.* (poét.) teñido, matizado, sazonado delicadamente. —*v.t.* (ant.) impregnar; teñir, tinturar. —*s.* (poét.) tintura, colorido.

tinctorial [tɪŋk'tɔrɪəl] *a.* tintóreo, colorativo.

tincture ['tɪŋktʃər, B -tʃə] *s.* 1. tintura, disolución medicinal. 2. (fig.) matiz, aspecto. 3. (fig.) traza, vestigio, huella. 4. (poét.) colorante, tinte. 5. (her.) esmalte. —*v.t.* 1. tinturar, teñir, colorar. 2. (fig.) impregnar, sazonar, matizar.

tindalo ['tɪndə,loʊ] *s.* (bot.) tindalo.

tinder ['tɪndər, B -də] *s.* yesca, mecha.

tinderbox [-,bɑks, B -,bɔks] *s.* 1. yesquero, esquero (bolsa para yescas). 2. (fig.) polvorín.

tinder fungus, (bot.) hongo yesquero.

tindery [-dərɪ] *a.* como yesca, seco e inflamable.

tine [taɪn] *s.* diente (de tenedor); punta, púa (de horca, astas, etc.).

tinea ['tɪnɪə] *s.* (med.) tiña.

tineid [-ɪəd] *s.* (ento.) tineido.

tin fish, (jer.) (mar.) torpedo.

tinfoil ['tɪn,fɔɪl] *s.* hojuela o papel de estaño, platina (Am.).

ting [tɪŋ] *s.* tintín. —*v.t.* (pret., p.p. TINGED; *p.pr.* TINGING) hacer tintinear. —*v.i.* tintinear, tintinar.

tinge [tɪndʒ] *v.t.* (pret., p.p. TINGED; *p.pr.* TINGING) 1. teñir, tinturar, colorar. 2. (fig.) teñir, matizar, alterar (de envidia, ira, etc.). —*s.* 1. matiz, tinte. 2. gustillo, dejo. 3. traza, vestigio.

tingle ['tɪŋgəl] *v.i.* 1. sentir picazón o comezón, hormiguear; estremecerse (de entusiasmo). 2. tintinear, tintinar. 3. zumbar (los oídos). —*v.t.* 1. picar, causar hormigueo. 2. (p. ext.) estimular. —*s.* 1. picazón, hormigueo; estremecimiento. 2. zumbido (en los oídos).

tin god, ídolo de barro, dios falso.

tinguaite ['tɪŋgwəˌeɪt] (geol.) tinguaita.

tin hat, (jer., mil.) casco de acero.

tinhorn ['tɪnˌhɔrn, B -ˌhɔn] *a.* (jer.) 1. de poca monta. 2. charro, de oropel, de relumbrón. —*s.* tahúr de poca monta.

tinily ['taɪnəlɪ] *adv.* diminutivamente.

tininess [-nɪnəs] *s.* tamaño diminuto.

tinker ['tɪŋkər, B -kə] *s.* 1. hojalatero, calderero, remendón, latonero, chapistero. 2. chapucero, chambón, chafallón. 3. chambonada, chapucería. 4. (ict.) caballa, escombro. —*v.i.* 1. trabajar mal, reparar chambonamente. 2. **t. at,** ocuparse ineficazmente con o en. —*v.t.* frangollar, chafallar, chapucear; **t. up,** remendar chapuceramente, apañar.

tinkerer [-kərər, B -ə] *s.* chapucero, chafallón.

tinker's damn, fruslería, bagatela, nadería; **I don't care a t.'s d.,** me importa un bledo.

tinkle ['tɪŋkəl] *v.i.* retiñir, tintinear, campanillear. —*v.t.* hacer retiñir, tintinear o campanillear. —*s.* retintín, tintineo, campanilleo.

tinkling [-klɪŋ] *s.* tintín, retintín, tintineo, campanilleo.

tinman ['tɪnmən] *s.* hojalatero, estañero.

tinned [tɪnd] *a.* 1. estañado. 2. (comida) en lata.

tinner ['tɪnər, B -ə] *s.* 1. estañero, hojalatero, estañador. 2. minero de estaño. 3. (G.B.) envasador de latas de conserva.

tinnily [-əlɪ] *adv.* agudamente, con sonido de hojalata.

tinniness [-ɪnəs] *s.* agudez (de voz).

tinnitus [tə'naɪtəs] *s.* (med.) tinnitus.

tinny ['tɪnɪ] *a.* (TINNIER; TINNIEST) 1. estañoso, que contiene (mucho) estaño. 2. parecido al estaño. 3. agudo, metálico (voz, sonido).

tin opener, (G.B.) abrelatas.

tin ore, (geol.) casiterita, mineral de estaño.

Tin Pan Alley, 1. (E.U.) distrito de Nueva York frecuentado por compositores y editores de música popular. 2. los compositores y editores de música popular en conjunto.

tinplate ['tɪn'pleɪt] *s.* hojalata, hoja de lata, chapa o lámina estañada.

tin-plate, *v.t.* estañar.

tin pyrites, (min.) pirita de estaño, estannita.

tin roof, *s.* tejado de cinc, techo de hojalata.

tinsel ['tɪnsəl] *s.* 1. oropel, bricho; lentejuela; hilo de oro o plata. 2. (fig.) oropel, relumbrón. —*a.* 1. de bricho, cubierto de lentejuelas. 2. (fig.) de oropel, de relumbrón, chillón. —*v.t.* (*pret., p.p.* TINSELED o TINSELLED; *p.pr.* TINSELING o TINSELLING) adornar con brichos, lentejuelas; oropelar.

tin sheet, *s.* hojalata.

tin shop, hojalatería.

tinsmith ['tɪnˌsmɪθ] *s.* hojalatero, estañero.

tin spar, (geol.) casiterita.

tin spirit, solución de estaño (usada como mordiente).

tinstone [-ˌstoʊn] *s.* (min.) casiterita, estaño vidrioso.

tint [tɪnt] *s.* 1. matiz, tinte, tono, color. 2. color templado. 3. (pint.) media tinta. 4. (impr.) grisado, sombreado; fondo (de color claro). —*v.t.* matizar, colorar, teñir.

tinter ['tɪntər, B -ə] *s.* tintorero.

tintinnabulary [ˌtɪntə'næbjəˌlerɪ, B -lərɪ] *a.* con tintineo, de campanilla, acompañado de retintines.

tintinnabulation [-ˌnæbjə'leɪʃən, B 'tɪn-] *s.* tintineo, campanilleo, retintín.

tintless ['tɪntləs] *a.* incoloro.

tintometer [tɪn'tɑmətər, B -tɔmɪtə] *s.* tintómetro.

tintype ['tɪnˌtaɪp] *s.* (foto.) ferrotipo.

tinware [-ˌwer, B -ˌweə] *s.* artículos de hojalata.

tinwork [-ˌwɜrk, B -ˌwɜk] *s.* 1. obra de estaño; artículos de estaño. 2. (*pl.*) (*sing. o pl. en const.*) hojalatería.

tiny ['taɪnɪ] *a.* (TINIER; TINIEST) diminuto, menudo, minúsculo, chiquitín, chiquirritín.

tiny tot, 1. chiquitín, niño pequeño. 2. (*pl.*) gente menuda.

tip [tɪp] *v.t.* (*pret., p.p.* TIPPED; *p.pr.* TIPPING) 1. inclinar, ladear. 2. saludar (quitándose el sombrero). 3. **t. into,** verter (líquido) en; **t. out,** derramar; **t. over,** volcar. —*s.* 1. inclinación, ladeo. 2. descargadero (de carbón, basura, etc.). —*v.i.* 1. inclinarse, ladearse. 2. **t. over,** volcarse.

tip, *s.* 1. punta, extremidad, extremo; cabo, ápice, cúspide. 2. herrete, casquillo, regatón (de bastón, etc.). 3. puntera, bigotera (del zapato). 4. boquilla (del soplete). 5. **from t. to toe,** de pies a cabeza; **on the t. of one's toes,** en la punta de los pies; **to have it on the t. of one's tongue,** tenerlo en la punta de la lengua. —*v.t.* (*pret., p.p.* TIPPED; *p.pr.* TIPPING) 1. guarnecer, poner herrete o casquillo a, poner regatón a. 2. quitar la punta a. 3. **t. in,** (impr.) encañonar (pliego, hoja, etc.).

tip, *v.t.* 1. dar un golpecito a, golpear o tocar ligeramente. 2. (dep.) dar un golpe rasante a (la pelota) con el borde del palo. 3. (fam.) avisar o informar por debajo de cuerda. 4. dar propina a. 5. **t. off,** prevenir, advertir secretamente; poner (a uno) sobre aviso; pasarle a uno la voz o el dato. —*v.i.* dar propina. —*s.* 1. golpecito, palmadita. 2. informe, soplo (dado en secreto); indicio. 3. propina, gratificación. 4. **a straight t.,** un buen consejo, una información correcta.

tipcart ['tɪpˌkɑrt, B -ˌkɑt] *s.* volquete, camión volquete.

tipcat ['tɪpˌkæt] *s.* billalda, ballarda, tala (juego).

tipi, *var. de* **tepee.**

tip-off [-ˌɔf] *s.* advertencia secreta, informe dado por debajo de cuerda.

tippet ['tɪpət] *s.* 1. palatina, esclavina. 2. (G.B.) (relig.) bufanda grande de color negro usada por el clero en el coro.

tipple ['tɪpəl] *v.t.* beber repetida y prolongadamente; empinar el codo, ser bebedor. —*v.i.* beborrotear, traguear (Am.). —*s.* bebida alcohólica, licor, trago.

tipple, *s.* (E.U.) 1. mecanismo de vuelco. 2. volcadero; planta para la criba del carbón.

tippler ['tɪplər, B -lə] *s.* borrachín, bebedor.

tipsily [-səlɪ] *adv.* como borracho.

tipsiness [-sɪnəs] *s.* chispa, borrachera, embriaguez.

tip speed, (ing.) velocidad periférica.

tipstaff ['tɪpˌstæf, B -ˌstɑf] *s.* alguacil de vara, ministril; vara de justicia.

tipster ['tɪpstər, B -stə] *s.* (fam.) uno que vende informes secretos, datero (Am.).

tipsy ['tɪpsɪ] *a.* (TIPSIER; TIPSIEST) 1. achispado, chispo, calamocano, algo borracho. 2. (fig.) vacilante; sesgado, oblicuo, ej., *a t. angle,* un ángulo oblicuo.

tiptoe ['tɪpˌtoʊ] *s.* punta del pie; **on t.,** de (o en) puntillas; (fig.) alerta, sobre aviso. —*v.i.* andar de puntillas. —*a.* 1. de puntillas, alerta; ansioso. 2. cauto, cauteloso; furtivo, escondido, clandestino. —*adv.* de puntillas.

tip-top [-'tɑp, B -'tɔp] *s.* cumbre, cima (de un cerro; de la perfección, felicidad, etc.). —*a.* de primera, excelente. —*adv.* en primer lugar, perfectamente.

tirade [taɪ'reɪd] *s.* diatriba, perorata, andanada.

Tirana [tɪ'rɑnə] *s.* Tirana, capital de Albania.

tire [taɪr, B 'taɪə] *v.t.* 1. cansar, fatigar, agotar, rendir. 2. (fig.) cansar, aburrir, fastidiar. —*v.i.* cansarse. —*s.* (dial.) cansancio, fatiga, lasitud.

tire, (ant.) *v.t.* ataviar; peinar. —*s.* (ant.) atavío; vestido; tocado (de mujer).

tire, *s.* 1. llanta, cubierta, neumático. 2. calce, bandaje, llanta (de hierro). —*v.t.* poner llantas o neumáticos a.

tire chains, cadenas antideslizantes, cadenas de rueda, cadenas para nieve.

tired [taɪrd, B 'taɪəd] *a.* cansado, fatigado, rendido; **t. out,** exhausto.

tiredly [-lɪ] *adv.* cansadamente.

tiredness [-nəs] *s.* cansancio, fatiga, lasitud.

tire gage, manómetro para neumáticos, medidor de presión para neumáticos.

tire iron, (aut.) desmontador de neumáticos.

tireless ['taɪrləs, B 'taɪəlɪs] *a.* incansable, infatigable.

tirelessly [-lɪ] *adv.* incansablemente.

tirelessness [-nəs] *s.* perseverancia incansable, energía inagotable.

tire pump, (aut.) inflador, bomba de neumáticos, bomba de inflar.

tire rack, (aut.) portaneumáticos.

tire remover, desmontador de neumáticos, llantera.

Tiresias [taɪ'risɪəs, B -æs] *s.* (mitol.) Tiresias, profeta ciego de las leyendas griegas.

tiresome ['taɪrsəm, B 'taɪəsəm] *a.* tedioso, aburrido, cansado, pesado, molesto; **how t.!** ¡qué pesado!

tiresomely [-lɪ] *adv.* tediosamente, cansadamente, pesadamente.

tire spreader, (aut.) desplegador, ensanchador de neumáticos.

tire tread, rodadura, banda de rodamiento.

tire tube, (aut.) cámara, tubo de neumático.

tirewoman ['taɪrˌwʊmən, B 'taɪəˌ-] *s.* (ant.) doncella, criada, mucama (Am.).

tiringroom ['taɪrɪŋˌrum, -ˌrʊm, B 'taɪər-] *s.* (ant.) cuarto de vestir, esp. camarín (de un teatro).

tiro, *var. de* **tyro.**

Tirol, *var. de* **Tyrol.**

tirrivee ['tɜrəˌvi, B tɪrə'vi] *s.* (esco.) berrinche, pataleta, rabieta; conmoción, perturbación, revuelo.

'tis [tɪz] *contr. de* **it is.**

tisane [tɪ'zæn] *s.* (farm.) tisana.

tissue ['tɪʃu] *s.* 1. (tej.) gasa, tisú, gloria, tejido de seda. 2. (fig.) red (ej., de mentiras), trama. 3. (biol.) tejido. 4. papel de seda. —*v.t.* (raro) tejer, entretejer.

tissue paper, papel de seda.

tit [tɪt] *s.* (ant.) jaca, caballito, jaco, jamelgo.

tit, *s.* (jer.) teta, pezón.

tit, *s.* (orn.) paro; paro carbonero, herrerillo.

Tit. *abrev. de* **Titus,** Epístola de San Pablo a Tito (Tit.).

Titan ['taɪtən] *s.* 1. (mitol.) Titán, cualquiera de los hijos de Urano y Gea. 2. (fig.) titán, gigante, coloso. —*a.* titánico, gigantesco, colosal.

titanate ['taɪtənˌeɪt] *s.* (quím.) titanato.

titanesque [ˌtaɪtən'ɛsk] *a.* titánico.

titanic [taɪ'tænɪk] *a.* 1. titánico, gigantesco, colosal; inmenso. 2. **T.,** (mitol.) titánico. 3. (quím.) titánico.

titanic acid, (quím.) ácido titánico.

titanically [-ɪkəlɪ] *adv.* titánicamente.

titaniferous [ˌtaɪtən'ɪfərəs] *a.* (quím.) titanífero.

titanite ['taɪtənˌaɪt] *s.* (min.) titanita.

titanium [taɪ'teɪnɪəm] *s.* (quím.) titanio.
titanium dioxide, (quím.) dióxido de titanio.
titanium steel, acero al titanio.
titanium white, blanco de titanio.
titanosaur [taɪ'tænəˌsɔr, B -ˌsɔ] *s.* (pal.) titanosaurus.
titanous [taɪ'tænəs, B 'taɪtənəs] *a.* (quím.) titanoso, de titanio.
titbit ['tɪtˌbɪt] *s.* golosina, gollería, bocado predilecto, bocadito.
titer ['taɪtər, B -ə] *s.* (quím., med., fisiol.) título.
tit for tat, uno por otro, golpe por golpe.
tithable ['taɪðəbəl] *a.* diezmable.
tithe [taɪð] *v.t.* diezmar. —*v.i.* pagar el diezmo. —*s.* 1. diezmo. 2. décima parte. 3. minucia, fracción.
tither ['taɪðər, B -ðə] *s.* diezmero, dezmero.
tithing [-ðɪŋ] *s.* 1. cobro o pago del diezmo. 2. diezmo. 3. (G.B.) (der.) pequeña división administrativa (formada por diez vecinos y sus familias).
titi [tɪ'ti] *s.* (zool.) tití.
Titian ['tɪʃən, B 'tɪʃɪ-] *s.* 1. Ticiano, pintor veneciano. 2. **t.,** (color) castaño rojizo, rojo amarillento, rojo veneciano (díc. del cabello).
titillate ['tɪtəlˌeɪt] *v.t.* 1. cosquillear. 2. hacerle cosquillas a uno, excitar agradablemente, aguijonear.
titillation [ˌtɪtəl'eɪʃən] *s.* 1. cosquilleo. 2. excitación agradable.
titillative ['tɪtəlˌeɪtɪv] *a.* excitante, inquietante (para los sentidos).
titivate ['tɪtəˌveɪt] *v.t., v.i.* (fam.) acicacalar(se), emperifollar(se), emperejilar(se).
titivation [ˌtɪtə'veɪʃən] *s.* acicalamiento, acicaladura.
titlark ['tɪtˌlɑrk, B -ˌlɑk] *s.* (orn.) motacila, azuzanieves, nevatilla.
title ['taɪtəl] *s.* 1. título. 2. (der., com.) título, derecho; libro, publicación. 3. (*pl.*) (cine, t.v.) letreros, rótulos. 4. (dep.) campeonato. 5. (ant.) cartel. —*v.t.* 1. titular, intitular. 2. conferir título a, nombrar. —*a.* titular, ej., *t. page,* primera página (diarios, periódicos), portada, cabezal (libros).
titled [-əld] *a.* titulado, con título.
title deed, (der.) escritura de propiedad, título traslativo de dominio.
titled person, persona con título nobiliario.
titleholder ['taɪtəlˌhoʊldər, B -də] *s.* 1. titulado. 2. (dep.) poseedor del título, campeón.
title page, portada (de un libro); primera página (de un periódico).
title role, t. part, (teat.) papel principal.
titlist [-əst] *s.* (dep.) campeón.
titmouse ['tɪtˌmaʊs] *s.* (orn.) paro; paro carbonero; herrerillo.
Titoism ['titoʊˌɪzm] *s.* (pol.) titoísmo, doctrina política del mariscal Tito de Yugoslavia.
titrate ['taɪˌtreɪt] (quím.) *v.t.* titular. —*v.i.* efectuar una titulación.
titration [taɪ'treɪʃən] *s.* (quím.) titulación.
titre, (G.B.) *var. de* **titer.**
tit-tat-toe [ˌtɪˌtæ'toʊ] *var. de* **ticktacktoe.**
titter ['tɪtər, B -ə] *v.i.* reír entre dientes, reír con disimulo. —*s.* risita entre dientes, risita ahogada o disimulada.
tittivate, tittivation, *vars. de* titivate, titivation.
tittle ['tɪtəl] *s.* 1. tilde, vírgula. 2. ápice, pizca, jota, adarme.
tittle-tattle ['tɪtəlˌtætəl] *s.* cháchara, chismorreo, chismería. —*v.i.* chacharear, chismear, comadrear.
tittle-tattler [-ər, B -ə] *s.* chismoso.
tittup ['tɪtəp] *s.* salto, brinco, corcovo, cabriola de contento. —*v.i.* (*pret., p.p.* TITTUPED o TITTUPPED; *p.pr.* TITTUPING o TITTUPPING) corvetear, cabriolar, retozar, brincar.
titubation [ˌtɪtʃʊ'beɪʃən, B ˌtɪtjʊ-] *s.* (med.) titubeo, titubación.
titular ['tɪtʃələr, B 'tɪtjʊlə] *a.* 1. titular. 2. nominal (que existe sólo en nombre). —*s.* titular.
titular bishop, obispo de título, obispo de anillo.
titularly [-lɪ] *adv.* con sólo el título.
titulary [-ˌlɛrɪ, B -lərɪ] *a.* titular. —*s.* que tiene título, el que tiene título o derecho (a algo).
Titus ['taɪtəs] *s.* 1. (relig.) Tito, discípulo y compañero del apóstol San Pablo. 2. (hist.) Tito, emperador romano.
tizzy ['tɪzɪ] *s.* (*pl.* TIZZIES) 1. alboroto, sobresalto, excitación; confusión, aturdimiento. 2. (jer. G.B.) (moneda de) seis peniques.
TKO *abrev. de* **technical knockout,** knockout técnico (boxeo).
Tl *símb. de* **thallium,** talio (Tl).
T.L. *abrev. de* **total loss,** pérdida total.
Tlepolemus [tlə'pɑləməs, B -'pɔl-] *s.* (mitol.) Tlepólemo, hijo de Hércules, muerto durante la guerra de Troya.
tlo *abrev. de* **total loss only,** pérdida total solamente (seguros).
Tm *símb. de* **thulium,** tulio (Tm).
T-man ['tiˌmæn] *s.* (E.U., fam.) agente del Departamento del Tesoro.
tmesis [tə'misəs, B 'tmisɪs] *s.* (gram.) tmesis.
TNT ['tiˌɛn'ti] *abrev. de* **trinitrotoluene,** trinitrotolueno (T.N.T.).
to [tu, tʊ, tə] *prep.* 1. a, hacia, en dirección a o de ej., *give it to him,* déselo a él, *to the north,* hacia el norte. 2. en, ej., *I told him to his face,* se lo dije en su propia cara, *from door to door,* de puerta en puerta. 3. para, a (con la intención de, con el fin de), ej., *he came to see you,* él vino para (o a) verte. 4. hasta (indicando efecto o resultado), ej., *I am soaked to the bone,* estoy calado hasta los huesos. 5. con, ej., *she has been very good to them,* ha sido muy buena con ellos. 6. según, de acuerdo a, ej., *to my way of thinking,* de acuerdo con mi modo de pensar. 7. por (en honor de), ej., *a toast to you,* un brindis por ti. 8. a (indicando correspondencia, proporción), ej., *A is to B as C is to D,* A es a B, como C es a D. 9. a, hasta (indicando fin de un período de tiempo), ej., *from Monday to Saturday,* de lunes a sábado; *she will be here from six to seven,* ella estará aquí desde las seis hasta las siete. 10. hasta (indicando grado o extensión), ej., *true to the end,* fiel hasta el fin. 11. por (indicando proporción o cantidad relativa), ej., *four quarts to the gallon,* cuatro litros por galón. 12. a (indicando algo que encuentra respuesta o reacción), ej., *I will answer to that later,* responderé a eso más adelante. 13. a (indicando el fin o meta de una actividad), ej., *he took to singing,* comenzó a aprender canto. 14. para (indicando relación o interés), ej., *he was like a father to me,* fue un padre para mí. 15. a (indicando el destinatario de una acción o beneficio), ej., *title to the property,* título a la propiedad. 16. menos, para (indicando el tiempo que falta para completar la hora), ej., *five (minutes) to seven,* siete menos cinco (minutos), cinco (minutos) para las siete. 17. para, a, ante (indicando resultado), ej., *to my great surprise, I heard him sing,* para mi gran sorpresa, le oí cantar, *to the surprise of the audience, she started to sing,* ante la sorpresa del público, ella empezó a cantar. 18. por (indicando acción futura), ej., *there's still much to do,* queda todavía mucho por hacer. 19. no se traduce en castellano cuando sirve para introducir el infinitivo, ej., *to be or not to be,* ser o no ser. 20. no se traduce en castellano cuando sustituye al infinitivo al fin de la frase, ej., *I meant to call but I had no time to,* quise llamarte pero no tuve tiempo (de hacerlo). — [tu] adv. 1. para acá. 2. cerca, a mano. 3. (mar) de bolina.
t.o. *abrev. de* **turn over,** sigue (en la página) siguiente; al dorso (de la página).
toad [toʊd] *s.* 1. (zool.) sapo, escuerzo. 2. (fig.) persona desagradable o repelente.
toadeater ['toʊdˌitər, B -ə] *s.* quitamotas, adulador servil, pelotillero, lameculos.
toadfish [-ˌfɪʃ] *s.* (ict.) pejesapo.
toadflax [-ˌflæks] *s.* (bot.) linaria, lino bastardo.
toad spit, t. spittle, (ento.) baba de cuclillo.
toadstone [-ˌstoʊn] *s.* (min.) estelión, estelón.
toadstool [-ˌstul] *s.* seta, hongo; esp. hongo venenoso.
toady ['toʊdɪ] *s.* (*pl.* TOADIES) adulador servil, quitamotas. —*v.i.* (*pret., p.p.* TOADIED; *p.pr.* TOADYING) adular servilmente, ser adulador.
toadyism [-ˌɪzəm] *s.* adulación servil.
to and fro, de acá para allá, de un lado a otro.
to-and-fro ['tuən'froʊ] *a.* alternativo; de vaivén. —*adv.* de acá para allá, de un lado a otro.
toast [toʊst] *v.t., v.i.* tostar(se). —*s.* tostada; **a piece of t.,** una tostada; **to have (one) on t.,** (jer.) tener (a uno) a su merced.
toast, *s.* brindis. —*v.t.* brindar a o por; beber a la salud o en honor de.
toaster ['toʊstər, B -tə] *s.* 1. brindador, el que brinda. 2. tostadora (de pan, eléctrica); tostador (de café, etc.).
toasting [-tɪŋ] *a.* de o para tostar. —*s.* tostadura, tueste.
toasting fork, horquilla o tenedor de tostar.
toastmaster ['toʊstˌmæstər, B -ˌmɑstə] *s.* maestro de ceremonias (que presenta a los oradores de sobremesa en un banquete).
toast rack, portatostadas.
tobacco [tə'bækoʊ] *s.* (*pl.* TOBACCOS) tabaco.
tobacco box, tabaquera.
tobacco field, tabacal.
tobacco jar, pote de tabaco.
tobacco mildew, moho azul (enfermedad de la planta del tabaco).
tobacco mosaic, mosaico del tabaco (virus que ataca las plantas del tabaco).
tobacconist [tə'bækənəst] *s.* (G.B.) tabaquero, estanquero.
tobacco pouch, bolsa de tabaco, tabaquera.
tobacco worm, (ento.) oruga del tabaco.
to-be [tə'bi] *a.* (*ú. gen. en combinaciones de palabras*) futuro, ej., *the bride-to-be,* la futura novia.
toboggan [tə'bɑgən, B -'bɔg-] *s.* (dep.) tobogán. —*v.i.* 1. deslizarse en tobogán. 2. caer, precipitarse, bajar rápidamente (los valores en la bolsa, precios, etc.).
toby ['toʊbɪ] *s.* (*pl.* TOBIES) 1. pichel, vaso grande (gen. en forma de hombre gordo). 2. cigarro delgado de calidad inferior.
toccata [tə'kɑtə] *s.* (mús.) tocata.
Tocharian [toʊ'kærɪən, B tə'kɛər-] *s.* (hist.) tocario, tocariano, pueblo del Asia central.
tocher ['tɑkər, B 'tɔkə] *s.* (esco.) dote.
tocologist [toʊ'kɑlədʒəst, B tə'kɔl-] *s.* (med.) tocólogo.
tocology [-dʒɪ] *s.* (med.) tocología.
tocopherol [-'kɑfəˌrɔl, B -'kɔf-] *s.* (bioquím.) tocoferol.
tocororo [ˌtoʊkə'roʊroʊ] *s.* (orn.) tocororo.
tocsin ['tɑksən, B 'tɔk-] *s.* 1. campana de alarma. 2. toque a rebato; rebato, alarma.
tod [tɑd, B tɔd] *s.* (ant.) 1. medida de peso para lana (apr. 28 lbs.). 2. (G.B.) matorral, espesura.
today [tə'deɪ] *adv.* 1. hoy, en este día. 2. al presente, hoy (en) día. —*s.* (el día de) hoy; el presente, actualidad.

toddle ['tɑdəl, B 'tɔd-] *v.i.* andar a tatas, hacer pinitos; andar tambaleándose (como un niño que da los primeros pasos). —*s.* pinito, pino; tambaleo.
toddler ['tɑdlər, B 'tɔdlə] *s.* niño que empieza a andar.
toddy ['tɑdɪ, B 'tɔdɪ] *s.* (*pl.* TODDIES) 1. savia de palmera. 2. ponche.
to-do [tə'du] *s.* (fam.) alharaca, alboroto, baraunda; **much t.-d. about nothing,** mucho ruido y pocas nueces.
toe [toʊ] *s.* 1. dedo del pie. 2. punta del pie. 3. punta (de media, calzado, patín, etc.). 4. uña o pezuña (de los animales). 5. (mec.) talón, reborde, pestaña, saliente, brazo; gorrón, base de talud, fondo del barreno. 6. **from top to t.,** de pies a cabeza; **to be on one's toes,** estar alerta, estar despierto; **to tread on one's toes,** herir los sentimientos de uno; **toes up,** muerto. —*v.t.* 1. proveer de punteras, remendar la punta de (calcetín, zapato). 2. tocar con la punta del pie (línea de partida). 3. (carp.) clavar oblicuamente; asegurar con clavos (un puntal). 4. **t. the line (o mark),** (fig.) observar las reglas, conformarse, respetar la línea (de un grupo o partido). —*v.i.* 1. (con *in* o *out*) pararse o andar con las puntas de los pies torcidas (hacia adentro o afuera). 2. andar de puntillas.
toe box, refuerzo de la puntera (del zapato).
toe cap, puntera (del zapato).
toed [toʊd] *a.* 1. que tiene (cierto número de) dedos (en el pie), ej., *a five-t. bird,* un pájaro que tiene cinco dedos (en el pie). 2. (carp.) metido oblicuamente (un clavo); asegurado con clavos oblicuos (díc. de un puntal).
toe dance, danza o baile sobre la punta de los pies.
toe-dance ['toʊˌdæns, B -ˌdɑns] *v.i.* bailar sobre la punta de los pies.
toe-dancer [-ər, B -ə] *s.* bailarín o bailarina de ballet.
toehold [-ˌhoʊld] *s.* 1. asimiento o lugar de soporte para las puntas de los pies (ej., en una subida o escalamiento). 2. (fig.) agarradero, arraigo precario; punto de apoyo. 3. (lucha) llave en la que el agresor dobla el pie de su oponente.
toe-in [-ˌɪn] *s.* (aut.) convergencia (de las ruedas delanteras).
toeless [-ləs] *a.* sin puntera (zapato).
toenail [-ˌneɪl] *s.* 1. uña del dedo del pie. 2. clavo oblicuo. —*v.t.* (carp.) clavar oblicuamente.
toe-out [-ˌaʊt] *s.* (aut. divergencia.
toepiece [-ˌpis] *s.* puntera (del calzado).
toff [tɑf, B tɔf] *s.* (jer. G.B.) gomoso, currutaco, pisaverde.
toffee ['tɑfi, B 'tɔfɪ] *s.* melcocha, arropía; **he can't sing for t.,** (jer. G.B.) no sabe cantar en absoluto.
toffee-nosed [-ˌnoʊzd] *a.* (jer. G.B.) presumido, tieso, estirado; pretencioso, presuntuoso.
toffy, *var. de* **toffee.**
toft [tɔft, tɑft, B tɔft] *s.* (G.B. dial.) 1. casa para habitación y sus terrenos. 2. colina, collado.
tog [tɑg, B tɔg] *s.* 1. (*pl.*) (fam.) ropa, vestidos (esp. para ocasión, deportes, etc. especificados). 2. (jer.) chaqueta, americana. 3. (*pl.*) (Aust.) traje de baño. —*v.t.* (*pret., p.p.* TOGGED; *p.pr.* TOGGING) (gen. con *out* o *up*) (fam.) acicalar, engalanar, vestir.
toga ['toʊgə] *s.* (*pl.* TOGAS O TOGAE [-dʒi]) 1. (hist.) toga. 2. toga, vestidura talar (de un juez, catedrático, etc.).
togaed [-gəd] *a.* togado.
together [tə'gɛðər, B -ə] *adv.* 1. juntamente. 2. juntos, en conjunto. 3. uno con otro. 4. a un tiempo, al mismo tiempo, simultáneamente. 5. continuamente, continuadamente, sin interrupción. 6. conjuntamente; de (común) acuerdo. 7. mutuamente, entre sí, (*ú. de modo pleonástico después de verbos como:* **add, multiply, join, cooperate,** etc.). 8. **to get t.,** juntar, reunir, acopiar; reunirse; **to go t.,** ir juntos; ser novios; **to live t.,** vivir juntos; **t. with,** junto con.
togetherness [-nəs] *s.* 1. unidad, uniformidad. 2. solidaridad, compañerismo. 3. simultaneidad.
toggery ['tɑgərɪ, B 'tɔg-] *s.* (*pl.* TOGGERIES) (fam.) ropa, vestidos; (G.B.) ropería.
toggle ['tɑgəl, B 'tɔg-] *s.* 1. (mec.) fiador atravesado. 2. (mec.) palanca acodada; tensor de rana (para alambres). 3. junta de codillo; articulación de rodillera. 4. (mar.) cazonete (de aparejo). —*v.t.* 1. proveer de junta de codillo. 2. (mar.) asegurar con cazonete.
toggle bolt, tornillo articulado, tornillo de fiador.
toggle joint, (mec.) junta de codillo, articulación de rodillera.
toggle press, prensa de palanca acodillada, prensa de rótula.
toggle switch, (elec.) interruptor de palanca, interruptor de volquete.
toil [tɔɪl] *v.i.* 1. trabajar asiduamente, afanarse, atrafagar. 2. (con *along, up,* etc.) moverse con gran dificultad o con mucho esfuerzo. —*s.* 1. tráfago, fatiga, afán, faena, trabajo pesado. 2. (ant.) lucha, contienda.
toil, *s.* 1. red (para la caza). 2. (*pl.*) (fig.) red, maraña, trampa.
toile [twɑl] *s.* tela ligera y transparente de hilo o algodón, lienzo.
toiler ['tɔɪlər, B -ə] *s.* trabajador, trabajadora.
toilet ['tɔɪlət] *s.* 1. tocado, arreglo, acicalamiento. 2. retrete, excusado, inodoro. 3. (raro) vestido, atavío, traje. 4. (med.) limpiadura (de una herida, parte del cuerpo, etc.). 5. (ant.) tocador.
toilet articles, artículos de tocador.
toilet case, neceser.
toilet paper, t. tissue, papel higiénico.
toilet powder, talco.
toilet room, retrete, excusado; tocador.
toiletry ['tɔɪlətrɪ] *s.* (*pl.* TOILETRIES) artículo de tocador.
toilet set, juego de tocador.
toilet soap, jabón de tocador, jabón de olor, jaboncillo.
toilette [twɑ'lɛt] *s.* 1. tocado, arreglo. 2. vestido, traje (esp. de tarde o de noche).
toilet water, agua de tocador, agua de Colonia.
toilful ['tɔɪlfəl] *a.* trabajoso, afanoso, laborioso.
toilfully [-fəlɪ] *adv.* trabajosamente, laboriosamente.
toilsome [-səm] *a.* laborioso, trabajoso, afanoso; penoso.
toilsomely [-lɪ] *adv.* laboriosamente, trabajosamente.
toilsomeness [-nəs] *s.* laboriosidad, fatiga.
toilworn ['tɔɪlˌwɔrn, B -ˌwɔn] *a.* rendido por la fatiga.
Tokay [toʊ'keɪ] *s.* 1. uva de Tokay. 2. (vino) tokai.
token ['toʊkən] *s.* 1. señal, signo, indicación, muestra. 2. símbolo. 3. distintivo, rasgo característico; insignia, divisa (de autoridad, derecho, identidad, etc.). 4. prenda, recuerdo. 5. ficha, tanto (usados como moneda, billete, pase, etc.). 6. **by the same t.,** por la misma razón, por el mismo motivo; **in t. of,** en señal de. —*a.* simbólico, nominal.
tokenism [-ˌɪzəm] *s.* (E.U.) la admisión nominal y en número muy limitado de una minoría religiosa o racial, esp. negros, en puestos de trabajo, escuelas, asociaciones, etc., para cumplir aparentemente con la ley o aplacar a la opinión pública.
token money, 1. moneda despreciada. 2. moneda nominal.
token payment, pago parcial o nominal (en señal de buena fe).
tokology, *var. de* **tocology.**
Tokyo ['toʊkɪˌoʊ] *s.* Tokio, capital de Japón.
tola ['toʊlə] *s.* unidad de peso en la India (apr. 12 gramos).
tolbooth ['toʊlˌbuθ, B 'tɔl-] *s.* (esco.) municipio; cárcel municipal.
told [toʊld] *pret., p.p. de* **tell.**
tole, *var. de* **toll.**
tole [toʊl] *s.* lata esmaltada o laqueada (para confeccionar bandejas, lámparas, cajas ornamentales, etc.).
Toledan [tə'lidən, B tɔ'leɪd-] *a., s.* toledano, de Toledo.
Toledo [-'lidoʊ, B -'leɪd-] *s.* (*pl.* TOLEDOS) espada u hoja toledana.
tolerability [ˌtɑlərə'bɪlətɪ, B ˌtɔl-] *s.* aceptabilidad.
tolerable ['tɑlərəbəl, B 'tɔl-] *a.* 1. tolerable, sufrible, llevadero. 2. mediano, pasadero, regular, aceptable.
tolerably [-blɪ] *adv.* 1. tolerablemente. 2. medianamente, aceptablemente.
tolerance ['tɑlərəns, B 'tɔl-] *s.* tolerancia; (tec.) tolerancia.
tolerant [-ənt] *a.* tolerante; (med.) tolerante.
tolerantly [-lɪ] *adv.* con tolerancia, indulgentemente, tolerantemente.
tolerate ['tɑləˌreɪt, B 'tɔl-] *v.t.* tolerar; soportar, sufrir, aguantar.
toleration [ˌtɑlə'reɪʃən, B ˌtɔl-] *s.* 1. tolerancia, permiso tácito. 2. tolerantismo.
tolerator ['tɑləˌreɪtər, B 'tɔl-ə] *s.* uno que tolera (injusticia, etc.).
tolidine ['tɑləˌdin, B 'tɔl-] *s.* (quím.) tolidina.
toll [toʊl] *s.* 1. peaje, portazgo, pontaje. 2. impuesto, derecho. 3. derecho de transporte. 4. (tele.) tarifa por llamada de larga distancia, tasa. 5. (fig.) tributo (de vidas, etc.); bajas, número de víctimas (en una batalla, siniestro, etc.), ej., *road t.,* (fig.) número de víctimas en accidentes de carretera. 6. (dial.) maquila, derecho de molienda. 7. **to take t. (of),** infligir una pérdida (a). —*v.t.* cobrar peaje o portazgo a, imponer peaje a. —*v.i.* cobrar peaje o portazgo.
toll, *v.t.* tentar, atraer (la caza, los peces, animales domésticos).
toll, *v.t.* tañer, tocar (la campana), sonar (la hora, etc.). —*v.i.* sonar; doblar, tocar a muerto (campanas) ej., *for whom the bell tolls,* por quien dobla la campana. —*s.* tañido; doble de las campanas.
tollage ['toʊlɪdʒ] *s.* peaje, portazgo; derecho.
toll bar, barrera de peaje.
tollbooth ['toʊlˌbuθ, B 'tɔl-] *s.* caseta o garita de peaje, cabina de peaje.
toll bridge, puente de peaje.
toll call, (tele.) llamada a larga distancia; llamada interurbana.
toller ['toʊlər, B -ə] *s.* el que cobra peaje.
toller, *s.* perro entrenado (de caza).
tollgate ['toʊlˌgeɪt] *s.* barrera de peaje.
tollhouse [-ˌhaʊs] *s.* cabina del peajero (en la barrera de peaje).
tollkeeper [-ˌkipər, B -ə] *s.* peajero, portazguero.
toll line, (tele.) línea de larga distancia, línea.
Toltec ['toʊltɛk, 'tɑl-, B 'tɔl-] **Toltecan** [-ən] *a., s.* (hist.) tolteca.
tolu [toʊ'lu] *s.* (med.) bálsamo de tolú.
toluate ['tɑljʊˌeɪt, B 'toʊl-] *s.* (quím.) toluato.

toluene [-ˌin] *s.* (quím.) tolueno.
toluic [tə'luɪk, B toʊ'lju-] *a.* (quím.) toluico.
toluidine [tə'luəˌdin, B -'lju-] *s.* (quím.) toluidina.
toluidine blue, (quím.) azul de toluidina.
toluol ['tɑljʊˌɔl, B 'toʊl-] *s.* (quím.) toluol.
tolyl ['tɑləl, B 'tɔl-] *s.* (quím.) tolil, tolilo.
Tom [tɑm, B tɔm] *s.* 1. diminutivo de Tomás. 2. **t.,** macho (del gato y algunos otros animales), ej., *t. turkey,* pavo.
tomahawk ['tɑməˌhɔk, B 'tɔm-] *s.* tomahawk, hacha de guerra de los indios norteamericanos; **to bury the t.,** envainar la espada; hacer la paz. —*v.t.* herir o matar con un tomahawk.
tomalley ['tɑmˌælɪ, B tə'mælɪ] *s.* (cocina) hígado de langosta.
Tom and Jerry, bebida caliente de ron, azúcar, canela y huevos.
tomato [tə'meɪtoʊ, B -'mɑt-] *s.* (*pl.* TOMATOES) 1. (bot.) tomatera, tomate. 2. tomate (fruto).
tomato catsup, salsa de tomate.
tomb [tum] *s.* tumba, sepulcro, sepultura; **the t.,** (fig.) la tumba, el fin, la muerte. —*v.t.* sepultar, enterrar.
tombac ['tɑmˌbæk, B 'tɔm-] *s.* (joy.) tumbaga, tumbago (Am.) (aleación empleada en joyería).
tombless ['tumləs] *a.* sin tumba; insepulto.
tomblike [-ˌlaɪk] *a.* parecido a la tumba, sepulcral.
tombolo ['tɑmbəˌloʊ, B 'tɔm-] *s.* (geol.) tómbolo.
tomboy ['tɑmˌbɔɪ, B 'tɔm-] *s.* niña o jovencita aficionada a los juegos o deportes masculinos, marimacho.
tomboyish [-ɪʃ] *a.* propio de la niña intrépida o atrevida en sus juegos; como un marimacho.
tombstone ['tumˌstoʊn] *s.* piedra o lápida sepulcral.
tomcat ['tɑmˌkæt, B 'tɔm-] *s.* gato (macho).
tomcod [-ˌkɑd, B -ˌkɔd] *s.* (ict.) (especie de) bacalao pequeño.
Tom, Dick and Harry, fulano, zutano y mengano; **every T. D. and H.,** (gen. despec.) todos, todo el mundo (sin distinción).
tome [toʊm] *s.* 1. tomo, volumen. 2. libraco.
tomentose [toʊ'mɛnˌtoʊs] *a.* (bot.) tomentoso.
tomentum [toʊ'mɛntəm, B tə-] *s.* (*pl.* TOMENTA [-tə]) (bot.) tomento.
tomfool ['tɑm'ful, B 'tɔm-] *a., s.* mentecato, zopenco.
tomfoolery [-ərɪ] *s.* 1. mentecatada, necedad, payasada. 2. disparate, tontería.
Tommy ['tɑmɪ, B 'tɔmɪ] *s.* (*pl.* TOMMIES) soldado (raso) inglés.
Tommy Atkins [-'ætkɪnz] soldado raso inglés (nombre ficticio usado como modelo en los impresos oficiales).
tommy gun, (mil.) metralleta, pistola automática.
tommy-gun [-ˌgʌn] *v.t.* ametrallar (con metralleta o pistola automática).
tommyrot [-ˌrɑt, B -ˌrɔt] *s.* (jer.) tontería, idiotez.
tomography [toʊ'mɑgrəfɪ, B tə'mɔg-] *s.* (med.) tomografía.
tomorrow [tə'mɑroʊ, B -'mɔr-] *adv.* mañana. —*s.* mañana; **the day after t.,** pasado mañana.
tompion ['tɑmpɪən, B 'tɔm-] *var. de* tampion.
Tom Thumb, Pulgarcito (p. ext. enano).
tomtit ['tɑm'tɪt, B 'tɔm-] *s.* (orn.) paro carbonero, herrerillo, reyezuelo.
tom-tom ['tɑmˌtɑm, B 'tɔmˌtɔm] *s.* tamtam, tantán.
ton [tʌn] *s.* (*pl.* TONS o TON) 1. tonelada. 2. (mar.) tonelada (100 pies cúbicos). 3. (*pl.*) montones, ej., *tons of money,* montones de dinero.
tonal ['toʊnəl] *a.* tonal.
tonality [toʊ'nælətɪ] *s.* (mús., pint.) tonalidad.
tone [toʊn] *s.* 1. tono. 2. temperamento, humor, genio. 3. (med., fisiol.) tono, tonicidad. 4. (mús., pint., fon.), tono. 5. metal, timbre (de la voz); entonación, inflexión. 6. **to change one's t.,** mudar el tono; **to lower one's t.,** bajar el tono. —*v.t.* 1. entonar. 2. dar tono a, modificar el tono de, matizar. 3. afinar, templar (instrumentos musicales). 4. (foto.) colorar. 5. **t. down,** bajar o suavizar el tono de, moderar(se), paliar; **t. up,** (med.) entonar, tonificar. —*v.i.* 1. tomar un tono. 2. armonizar, entonar (colores). 3. **t. in with,** combinarse o unirse armoniosamente con.
tone arm, brazo (de tocadiscos).
tone color, (mús.) timbre.
tone control, (rad.) control de tono.
tone-deaf ['toʊnˌdɛf] *a.* que tiene mal oído, falto de oído musical.
toneless [-ləs] *a.* mate, sin tono.
tonelessly [-lɪ] *adv.* sin tono, sin expresión, en voz apagada.
tone poem, (mús.) poema sinfónico.
tonetic [toʊ'nɛtɪk] *a.* (filol.) tonético, relativo al tono de una lengua.
tonetics [-ɪks] *s. pl.* (*sing. en const.*) tonética.
tong [tɔŋ, tɑŋ, B tɔŋ] *v.t.* asir o sujetar con tenazas; **t. oysters,** arrancar ostras con tenazas. —*v.i.* usar tenazas para sacar o recoger.
tong, *s.* (chino) sociedad, hermandad; (E.U.) sociedad secreta de los residentes chinos esp. en la costa del Océano Pacífico.
tonga ['tɑŋgə, B 'tɔŋ-] *s.* (anglo-ind.) vehículo liviano de dos ruedas (gen. para cuatro personas).
tongs [tɔŋz, tɑŋz, B tɔŋz] *s. pl.* (*sing. o pl. en const.*) alicates, tenazas, mordazas, pinzas, tenacillas.
tongue [tʌŋ] *s.* 1. lengua. 2. lengua (de res, ternera, reno, etc. usada como alimento). 3. (fig.) habla, lengua. 4. idioma, lengua, lenguaje. 5. lengua, lengüeta (de zapato); badajo, espiga (de campana); clavillo (de hebilla); vara, lanza (de carro). 6. (geog.) lengua, punta (de tierra). 7. (carp.) lengüeta, espiga. 8. (mús.) lengüeta. 9. (f.c.) punta (movible) de cambiavía. 10. **to find one's t.,** recobrar uno el habla; **to give** (o **throw**) **t.,** exclamar, echar a ladrar, dar aullidos (perro al dar con la pista); **to have a long t.,** tener mucha lengua, ser blando de boca; **to have it on the tip of one's t.,** tenerlo en la punta de la lengua; **to hold one's t.,** callarse; **to put** (o **stick**) **out one's t.,** sacar la lengua; **to wag one's t.,** írsele a uno la lengua; chismear; **watch your t.,** ten cuidado con lo que dices; **(with one's) t. in one's cheek,** escarnecidamente; con ironía disimulada. —*v.i.* 1. extenderse (la tierra en una lengua). 2. (mús.) producir tonos con la lengua. 3. (raro) hablar; charlar, parlotear. —*v.t.* 1. lamer, tocar con la lengua. 2. cortar lengüeta(s) en, machihembrar. 3. (mús.) producir (tonos) con la lengua. 4. (ant.) regañar.
tongue and groove, (carp.) lengüeta y ranura.
tongue and groove joint, (carp.) ensambladura de lengüeta y ranura, unión machihembrada.
tongued [tʌŋd] *a.* que tiene (cierta) lengua; provisto de lengüeta.
tongue grafting, (agr.) injerto de acoplamiento, injerto de lengüeta.
tongue-lash ['tʌŋˌlæʃ] *v.t.* reprender.
tongue-lashing [-ɪŋ] *s.* reprensión severa, regaño fuerte.
tongueless [-ləs] *a.* 1. sin lengua. 2. mudo, sin habla.
tongue-tie [-ˌtaɪ] *s.* (med.) anquiloglosia. —*v.t.* hacer callar.
tongue-tied [-ˌtaɪd] *a.* (fig.) con la lengua atada, tímido para hablar, cohibido al hablar; mudo; **to get t.-t.,** trabársele a uno la lengua.
tongue twister, trabalenguas.
tongue worm, (ento.) landrilla.
tonguing and grooving plane ['tʌŋɪŋ-] (carp.) cepillo para hacer lengüetas y ranuras.
tonic ['tɑnɪk, B 'tɔn-] *a.* tónico; (mús., pint., filol., fon.) tónico. —*s.* 1. (med.) tónico. 2. (mús., fon.) tónica.
tonic accent, (fon.) acento tónico, acento de altura.
tonicity [toʊ'nɪsətɪ] *s.* (fisiol.) tonicidad.
tonic spasm, (med.) espasmo tetánico o tónico.
tonic water, agua tónica.
tonight [tə'naɪt] *adv.* esta noche. —*s.* esta noche, la noche de hoy.
toning ['toʊnɪŋ] *s.* entonación.
tonite ['toʊnaɪt] *s.* (quím.) tonita.
tonka bean ['tɑŋkə-, B 'tɔŋ-] 1. (bot.) sarapia, cumarú. 2. haba tonca.
Tonkin ['tɑn'kɪn, B 'tɔŋ-] *s.* Tonkín, Tonquín, antiguo estado en la Indochina francesa, hoy parte de Vietnam del Norte.
Tonkinese [ˌtɑnkə'niz, B ˌtɔŋ-] *a., s.* tonquinés, de Tonquín o Tonkín.
tonnage ['tʌnɪdʒ] *s.* 1. tonelaje. 2. (com.) derechos de tonelaje.
tonnage deck, (mar.) cubierta de arqueo.
tonnage dues, (mar.) derechos de tonelaje.
tonneau [tə'noʊ, B 'tɔnoʊ] *s.* (*pl.* TONNEAUS o TONNEAUX [-'noʊz, B -noʊz]) (aut.) compartimiento posterior.
tonometer [toʊ'nɑmətər, B -'nɔmɪtə] *s.* 1. tonómetro, medidor de tonos. 2. tonómetro, instrumento para medir la tensión (en el globo ocular) y la presión.
tonometry [-trɪ] *s.* tonometría.
tons burden [tʌnʒ-] (mar.) arqueo, capacidad.
tonsil ['tɑnsəl, B 'tɔn-] *s.* (anat.) tonsila, amígdala.
tonsillar [-sələr, B -lə] *a.* (anat.) tonsilar.
tonsillectomy [ˌtɑnsə'lɛktəmɪ, B ˌtɔn-] *s.* (med.) tonsilectomía, amigdalectomía.
tonsillitis [-'laɪtəs] *s.* (med.) tonsilitis, amigdalitis.
tonsillotomy [-'lɑtəmɪ, B -'lɔt-] *s.* (med.) tonsilotomía, amigdalotomía.
tonsorial [tɑn'sɔrɪəl, B tɔn-] *a.* barberil, relativo a o propio de barbero.
tonsure ['tɑntʃər, B 'tɔnʃə] *s.* (relig.) tonsura. —*v.t.* tonsurar.
tontine ['tɑnˌtin, B tɔn'tin] *s.* (com.) tontina.
tonus ['toʊnəs] *s.* (fisiol.) tono; esp. tono muscular, tonicidad.
too [tu] *adv.* 1. también, asimismo, igualmente; del mismo modo; además. 2. demasiado; excesivamente. 3. de veras, ej., *I meant to do it t.,* de veras quise hacerlo. 4. **t. bad!** ¡qué lástima!; **t. many,** demasiados; **t. much,** demasiado; el colmo, insoportable, ej., *this is really t. much,* esto ya es el colmo, esto es insoportable.
took [tʊk] *pret. de* **take.**
tool [tul] *s.* 1. herramienta, útil. 2. (fig.) instrumento, medio. 3. máquina herramienta. —*v.t.* 1. labrar, trabajar. 2. dotar o equipar de herramientas; mecanizar. 3. (enc.) filetear, decorar con hierro. 4. (jer.) conducir (un coche); transportar, llevar (en un vehículo). —*v.i.* 1. usar herramientas. 2. instalar máquinas o dar herramientas. 3. (jer.) (con *along, through,* etc.) dirigirse o pasear en coche (por, a través de, etc.).
toolbox ['tulˌbɑks, B -ˌbɔks] *s.* caja de herramientas.
tool cabinet, armario para herramientas.

tool chest, caja de herramientas.
toolhead [-ˌhɛd] *s.* (mec.) cabezal giratorio.
toolholder [-ˌhoʊldər, B -də] *s.* portaherramientas.
toolhouse [-ˌhaʊs] *s.* cobertizo, almacén para herramientas, depósito de herramientas.
tooling ['tulɪŋ] *s.* trabajo de herramientas, montaje.
tool kit, juego de herramientas.
toolmaker ['tulˌmeɪkər, B -kə] *s.* fabricante de herramientas; herrero de harramientas; tallador de herramientas.
toolmaking [-kɪŋ] *s.* fabricación de herramientas, manufactura de herramientas.
toolroom [-ˌrum, -ˌrʊm] *s.* depósito de herramientas.
tool steel, acero de herramientas.
toom [tum] *a.* (pr. esco.) vacío.
toon [tun] *s.* (bot.) cedro de Singapur.
toot [tut] *v.t.* tocar, sonar (cuerno de caza, bocina, pito, etc.). *—v.i.* emitir bocinazos o pitazos; sonar (la bocina, el pito, etc.). *—s.* trompetazo, pitazo, bocinazo.
tooth [tuθ] *s.* (*pl.* TEETH [tiθ]). 1. diente. 2. diente, púa, mella. 3. (bot.) diente. 4. (mec.) diente, leva, álabe. 5. **armed to the teeth,** armado hasta los dientes; **by the skin of one's teeth,** por poco, por un pelo; **decayed t.,** diente cariado; **long in the teeth,** viejo (díc. pr. de caballos); **to cast (something) in one's teeth,** echarle (algo) en cara a uno; **to cut one's teeth,** endentecer, echar los dientes; **to fight t. and nail,** luchar con dientes y uñas, darse íntegro a la lucha; **to have a sweet t.,** ser muy goloso; **to put teeth into,** reforzar, fortalecer; aumentar la eficacia de; **to set** (o **put**) **one's teeth on edge,** dar dentera a uno; **to show one's teeth,** (fig.) enseñar o mostrar los dientes. *—v.t.* 1. dentar, endentar. 2. mellar; cortar en dientes. *—v.i.* endentar, engranar.
toothache ['tuθˌeɪk] *s.* dolor de muelas, dolor de dientes.
tooth and nail, a brazo partido, encarnizadamente; con todos los medios.
toothbrush [-ˌbrʌʃ] *s.* cepillo de dientes.
toothed [tuθt, B tuðd] *a.* 1. dentado, dentellado. 2. de (ciertos) dientes (ú. gen. en palabras compuestas), ej., *a sharp-t. tiger,* un tigre de dientes afilados. 3. (bot.) dentado. 4. (arq.) en adaraja. 5. (mec.) dentado; endentado.
tooth harrow, (mec.) grada de dientes.
toothily ['tuθəlɪ] *adv.* mostrando los dientes, ej, *he smiled t.,* sonrió mostrando los dientes.
toothing [-ɪŋ] *s.* 1. dentición. 2. (arq.) adaraja. 3. (mec.) dentado.
toothing plane, (carp.) cepillo dentado.
toothless [-ləs] *a.* 1. desdentado, sin dientes, desmolado, edentado. 2. (fig.) ineficaz.
toothpaste [-ˌpeɪst] *s.* pasta dentífrica, pasta de dientes, dentífrico.
toothpick [-ˌpɪk] *s.* mondadientes, limpiadientes, palillo.
toothpick holder, caja de mondadientes, palillero.
tooth powder, polvo dentífrico.
toothsome ['tuθsəm] *a.* gustoso, sabroso, apetitoso, p. ext. atractivo.
toothsomely [-lɪ] *adv.* gustosamente, apetitosamente.
toothsomeness [-nəs] *s.* sabor agradable.
toothwort [-ˌwɜrt, B -ˌwɜt] *s.* (bot.) dentaria.
toothy ['tuθɪ] *a.* (TOOTHIER; TOOTHIEST) 1. dentudo. 2. mostrando los dientes (sonrisa, etc.).
tootle ['tutəl] *v.i., v.t.* tocar suavemente; tocar repetida o continuamente (esp. la flauta).
tootsy-wootsy ['tʊtsɪ'wʊt-, B 'tʊtsɪ'wut-] *s.* (*pl.* TOOTSY-WOOTSIES) (habla infantil o afectiva) queridita.
top [tɑp, B tɔp] *s.* 1. cima, cumbre, pico, cúspide. 2. (fig.) cumbre, cima. 3. parte superior, parte de arriba; superficie (de tierra); coronilla (de la cabeza); cabeza (de una página); tablero (de la mesa); copa (de un árbol); copete (del calzado); corte superior (de un libro); chaqueta (de un pijama). 4. tapa (de un barril, de una olla, etc.); fuelle (de un carruaje); capota, toldo (de un automóvil). 5. primer puesto, primera fila; primero (entre todos), ej., *he came out t. of the class,* terminó (como) primero en la clase. 6. máximo, máximum, sumo grado, lo mejor, culminación. 7. (bot.) tallo, hojas de encima (de cebolla, zanahoria, remolacha, etc.). 8. (mar.) cofa. 9. (aut.) toma directa, la más alta velocidad. 10. (*pl.*) (naipes) las cartas de más valor. 11. (dep.) efecto vertical (que se imparte a la pelota por un golpe rasante en su parte superior). 12. **at the t. of,** a la cabeza de; **at the t. of one's voice,** a voz en cuello; **from t. to bottom,** de arriba abajo; **from t. to toe,** de pies a cabeza; **on t.,** encima; (fig.) a la cabeza, en la cumbre; victoriosamente; **on t. of,** además de, por colmo de; **over the t.,** (mil.) saliendo de la trinchera (al atacar), al asalto; **the t. of the morning to you,** (Irl.) muy buenos días; **the tops,** (jer.) la flor de la canela; **to blow one's t.,** (jer.) volverse loco (de entusiasmo o emoción); salir uno de sus casillas, perder la paciencia, montar en cólera; **to come to the t.,** (fig.) llegar a la cumbre, ganar fama (en una profesión, carrera, etc.). *—v.t.* (*pret., p.p.* TOPPED [tɑpt, B tɔpt]; *p.pr.* TOPPING) 1. podar, desmochar. 2. coronar, rematar. 3. cubrir (con otro tinte, capa, etc.). 4. llegar a la cima de, levantarse sobre. 5. aventajar, sobrepujar, dominar. 6. superar, mejorar (marca, calidad, etc.). 7. salvar, pasar encima de (obstáculo, etc.). 8. (quím.) hacer una destilación primaria de (petróleo crudo). 9. (golf) golpear (la pelota) en la parte superior. 10. **t. off,** rematar, concluir, completar; **t. up,** llenar al tope. *—v.i.* **t. off (with),** completar (con), rematar (con). *—a.* 1. cimero, último. 2. principal; de alta categoría, eminente. 3. excelente, brillante. 4. máximo, ej., *at t. speed,* a máxima velocidad.
top, *s.* trompo, peón, peonza (juguete); **to sleep like a t.,** dormir como un tronco.
topaz ['toʊˌpæz] *s.* 1. topacio. 2. colibrí, picaflor (Am.).
top billing, 1. (teat.) primer lugar en cartelera (de un actor o actriz). 2. sitio preferencial o prominente (de una noticia, artículo, anuncio, etc. en periódico, publicidad, etc.).
top boot, bota alta.
topcoat ['tɑpˌkoʊt, B 'tɔp-] *s.* abrigo ligero, sobretodo, gabán.
top dead center, (ing.) punto muerto superior.
top die, (mec.) contramatriz.
top dog, 1. (fam.) persona o grupo que está a la cabeza; posición de máximo poder o prestigio. 2. el que manda, mandamás. 3. vencedor (esp. en una contienda muy disputada).
top-drawer [-ˌdrɔr, B -ˌdrɔ] *a.* 1. de la más alta categoría; excelente, eminente, supremo. 2. de la más alta clase, aristocrático.
top-dress [-ˌdrɛs] *v.t.* 1. abonar la superficie de (suelo). 2. revestir la superficie de (tierra, camino, etc.), recebar (carreteras).
top-dressing [-ɪŋ] *s.* 1. abono aplicado a la superficie. 2. recebo.
tope [toʊp] *v.i.* (ant.) beber con exceso habitualmente.
tope, *s.* 1. (ict.) tiburón europeo. 2. estupa (santuario budista).
topee [toʊ'pi, B 'toʊpi] *s.* (anglo-ind.) casco tropical (esp. el hecho de corcho).
toper ['toʊpər, B -pə] *s.* borrachín, bebedor.
topflight ['tɑp'flaɪt, B 'tɔp-] *a.* sobresaliente, excelente, eminentísimo.
topful, topfull [-'fʊl] *a.* lleno hasta el borde, repleto.
topgallant [-'gælənt, B tə'gæl-] (mar.) *s.* juanete. *—a.* de juanete.
topgallant mast, (mar.) mastelerillo de juanete.
top-hamper ['tɑp'hæmpər, B 'tɔp-pə] *s.* (mar.) pesos altos; superestructuras; palos y jarcias.
top hat, sombrero de copa, chistera.
top-heavy [-ˌhɛvɪ] *a.* 1. (que es) más pesado arriba que abajo; inestable. 2. más grueso o abultado en la parte superior. 3. (com.) demasiado capitalizado.
Tophet ['toʊfət] *s.* (bíbl.) infierno; caos completo.
top-hole ['tɑp'hoʊl, B 'tɔp-] *a.* (jer., G.B.) excelente.
tophus ['toʊfəs] *s.* (*pl.* TOPHI [-ˌfaɪ]) (med.) tofo.
topi, *var. de* **topee.**
topiary ['toʊpɪˌɛrɪ, B -pjərɪ] *a.* de jardinería (artística u ornamental). *—s.* (*pl.* TOPIARIES) arte de la jardinería; jardín ornamental.
topic ['tɑpɪk, B 'tɔp-] *s.* 1. asunto, tema, materia, tópico. 2. (ret., lóg.) (*gen. pl.*) tópicos.
topical [-ɪkəl] *a.* 1. tópico, local. 2. corriente, del día. 3. temático.
topicality [ˌtɑpə'kælətɪ, B ˌtɔp-] *s.* (*pl.* TOPICALITIES) 1. carácter local. 2. asunto de interés local, asunto local.
topically ['tɑpɪkəlɪ, B 'tɔp-] *adv.* localmente.
topkick ['tɑp'kɪk, B 'tɔp-] *s.* (jer., E.U.) sargento primero.
topknot [-ˌnɑt, B -ˌnɔt] *s.* moño alto; copete (de cintas, plumas, etc.).
topless [-ləs] *a.* sin parte superior. *—s.* ropa de baño o vestido que deja descubierto el torso.
toploftiness [-ˌlɔftɪnəs] *s.* vanidad; desdén.
toplofty [-tɪ] *a.* (fam.) copetudo, vanidoso, hinchado, pomposo; desdeñoso.
topman [-mən] *s.* 1. minero de superficie. 2. (mar.) vigía; juanetero.
topmast [-ˌmæst, -məst, B -ˌmɑst] *s.* (mar.) mastelero.
top milk, capa de crema (que sube a la superficie de la leche fresca).
topmost ['tɑpˌmoʊst, B 'tɔp-] *a.* (que es el) más alto o más elevado; máximo, predominante.
top-notch [-'nɑtʃ, B -'nɔtʃ] *a.* (fam.) superior, sobresaliente, excelente; encumbrado, eminente; de calidad inmejorable.
top-notcher [-ər, B -ə] *s.* as, persona sobresaliente; uno de los mejores, ej., *he is a t.-n. among tennis players,* él es uno de los mejores jugadores de tenis.
topographer [tə'pɑgrəfər, B -'pɔgrəfə] *s.* topógrafo.
topographic [ˌtɑpə'græfɪk, B ˌtɔp-] **topographical** [-ɪkəl] *a.* topográfico.
topographical latitude, latitud geodésica.
topographically [-ɪkəlɪ] *adv.* topográficamente.
topographical plane, plano topográfico o acotado, planialtimetría.
topographical survey, levantamiento topográfico, altimetría.
topography [tə'pɑgrəfɪ, B -'pɔg-] *s.* topografía.
topologic [ˌtɑpə'lɑdʒɪk, B ˌtɔpə'lɔdʒ-] **topological** [-ɪkəl] *a.* topológico; regional.

topology [tə'pɑlədʒɪ, B -'pɔl-] *s.* 1. (mat.) topología. 2. (med.) topografía, anatomía regional.
toponym ['tɑpə,nɪm, B 'tɔp-] *s.* topónimo, nombre de un lugar.
toponymic [,tɑpə'nɪmɪk, B ,tɔp-] **toponymical** [-ɪkəl] *a.* toponímico.
toponymy [tə'pɑnəmɪ, B -'pɔn-] *s.* toponimia.
topper ['tɑpər, B 'tɔpə] *s.* 1. (fam.) chistera, sombrero de copa. 2. (fam. G.B.) persona excelente; cosa extraordinaria. 3. abrigo corto, sobretodo, abrigo de entretiempo.
topping [-ɪŋ] *s.* 1. punta, extremidad, coronamiento, esp. copete, moño. 2. acabado; capa final (en mampostería). 3. destilación primaria (del petróleo). 4. (cocina) remate, coronamiento (en helados, tortas, etc.). *—a.* 1. distinguido, eminente, destacado. 2. (pr. G.B.) excelente.
topping lift, (mar.) perigallo, amantillo.
topple ['tɑpəl, B 'tɔp-] *v.i.* 1. caerse, venirse abajo, volcarse. 2. tambalear(se). *—v.t.* derribar, volcar, hacer caer.
tops [tɑps, B tɔps] *a.* (*ú. sólo predicativamente*) (lo) mejor, (el) más destacado o eminente.
topsail ['tɑp,seɪl, -səl, B 'tɔp-] *s.* (mar.) gavia.
top-secret [-'sikrət] *a.* (E.U., mil., dip.) estrictamente confidencial, archisecreto.
top sergeant, (fam. mil.) sargento primero.
topside [-'saɪd] *s.* (mar.) borda. *—adv.* 1. (mar.) en la cubierta. 2. arriba, encima.
topsoil [-,sɔɪl] *s.* mantillo, capa vegetal superior, tierra mantillosa o negra, humus.
top spin, efecto vertical (impartido a una bola o pelota).
topstitch [-,stɪtʃ] *v.t.* aplicar puntadas paralelas a la costura de (una prenda de vestir, como adorno).
topstone [-,stoʊn] *s.* (arq.) albardilla, coronamiento.
topsy-turvily ['tɑpsɪ'tɜrvəlɪ, B 'tɔpsɪ'tɜvɪ-] *adv.* patas arriba, en desorden.
topsy-turvy [-'tɜrvɪ, B -'tɜvɪ] *adv.* patas arriba, en desorden. *—a.* trastornado, desbarajustado; revuelto. *—s.* desbarajuste; desorden; confusión.
topsy-turvydom [-dəm] *s.* (hum.) desorden completo.
top timber, (mar.) barraganete.
top view, (dib.) vista de planta, vista desde arriba.
toque [toʊk] *s.* toca; cualquier sombrero de mujer ajustado y sin ala.
tor [tɔr, B tɔ] *s.* tolmo, tormo, peñasco.
Torah ['toʊrə, 'tɔrə, B 'tɔrə] *s.* (*pl.* TOROTH [-'roʊt] o TORAHS) (relig.) 1. el Antiguo Testamento. 2. el Pentateuco. 3. tora, la ley judaica comprendida en el Talmud.
torch [tɔrtʃ, B tɔtʃ] *s.* 1. antorcha. 2. antorcha de acetileno, antorcha a soplete. 3. (pr. G.B.) linterna eléctrica. 4. (jer.) **to carry a t. for,** estar enamorado de; **to hand on the t.,** (fig.) entregar o pasar la antorcha (a la generación siguiente).
torchbearer ['tɔrtʃ,bɛrər, B 'tɔtʃ,bɛərə] *s.* 1. hachero. 2. (fig.) el que porta la antorcha (de una idea, movimiento político, etc.).
torchlight [-,laɪt] *s.* luz de antorcha.
torchon lace ['tɔr,ʃɑn-, B 'tɔʃən-] encaje de hilo basto.
torch singer, cantante de canciones (melancólicas) de amor.
torch song, canción en la que se suele lamentar el amor no correspondido.
torch welding, soldadura a soplete.
torchwood ['tɔrtʃ,wʊd, B 'tɔtʃ-] *s.* 1. (bot.) ñámbar. 2. madera resinosa (inflamable).
tore [tɔr, B tɔ] *s.* 1. (arq.) torés; toro, bocel, moldura cilíndrica. 2. (geom.) toro.
tore [tɔr, B tɔ] *pret. de* **tear.**
toreador ['tɔrɪə,dɔr, B -,dɔ] *s.* torero.
tori, *pl. de* **torus.**
toric ['tɔrɪk] *a.* (ópt.) tórico.
torii ['tɔrɪ,i] *s.* (arq.) torii (pórtico construido cerca de un templo sintoísta).
torment [tɔr'mɛnt, B tɔ'-] *v.t.* 1. atormentar, angustiar, afligir. 2. agitar, revolver (mar, agua, atmósfera, etc.). 3. vejar, acosar, hostigar. 4. (raro) torturar. — ['tɔr,mɛnt, B 'tɔ,-] *s.* 1. tormento, tortura. 2. (fig.) tormento, angustia, congoja.
tormentil ['tɔrmən,tɪl, B 'tɔmən-] *s.* (bot.) tormentila, consuelda roja.
tormentingly [tɔr'mentɪŋlɪ, B tɔ'-] *adv.* de modo atormentador.
tormentor [-ər, B -ə] *s.* 1. atormentador. 2. (cinem.) pantalla insonorizada. 3. (teat.) bastidor.
torn [tɔrn, B tɔn] *p.p. de* **tear.**
tornadic [tɔr'neɪdɪk, B tɔ'-] *a.* de tornado, propio de un tornado.
tornado [-'neɪdoʊ] *s.* (*pl.* TORNADOES o TORNADOS) tornado; (fig.) explosión, estallido, andanada.
tornillo [tɔr'nijoʊ, B tɔ'-] *s.* (*pl.* TORNILLOS) (bot.) tornillo.
toroid ['tɔrɔɪd] *s.* (geom.) toroide.
torose [-,oʊs, B tə'roʊs] *a.* (bot.) toruliforme.
torpedo [tɔr'pidoʊ, B tɔ'-] *s.* (*pl.* TORPEDOES) 1. (ict.) torpedo, tremielga, tembladera. 2. (mar.) torpedo. 3. cohetecillo (que estalla al ser arrojado contra una superficie dura). 4. (jer., E.U.) pistolero, asesino pagado. *—v.t.* (mar. y fig.) torpedear.
torpedo boat, torpedero, lancha torpedera.
torpedo-boat destroyer [-,boʊt-] cazatorpedero, contratorpedero.
torpedo body, carrocería en forma de torpedo, carrocería aerodinámica de automóvil.
torpedoman [-,mæn, -mən] *s.* (mar.) torpedista.
torpedo net, red de defensa contra torpedos.
torpedo tube, tubo lanzatorpedos.
torpid ['tɔrpəd, B 'tɔpɪd] *a.* 1. tórpido, adormecido, aletargado, entumecido, entorpecido, inerte. 2. pesado, inactivo, apático; torpe, estúpido.
torpid, *s.* (G.B.) bote de carrera de ocho remos (construido en forma de tingladillo, usado en las carreras de cuaresma en Oxford); carrera de cuaresma entre botes de ocho remos.
torpidity [tɔr'pɪdətɪ, B tɔ'-] *s.* entorpecimiento, apatía, pesadez, indiferencia.
torpidly ['tɔrpədlɪ, B 'tɔpɪd-] *adv.* torpemente, apáticamente.
torpidness [-nəs] *s.* torpeza, entorpecimiento; apatía, pesadez.
torpor ['tɔrpər, B 'tɔpə] *s.* 1. entumecimiento, adormecimiento, entorpecimiento. 2. apatía, indiferencia.
torporific [,tɔrpə'rɪfɪk, B ,tɔpə-] *a.* soporífico, soporífero.
torque [tɔrk, B tɔk] *s.* 1. (hist.) torques (collar). 2. (mec.) par torsor, par de torsión, par motor, momento torsor, momento torsional o de torsión.
torque converter, convertidor de torsión.
torque gage, indicador de torsión.
torque meter, torsiómetro, medidor de torsión.
torrefaction [,tɔrə'fækʃən] *s.* torrefacción.
torrefy ['tɔrə,faɪ] *v.t.* (*pret., p.p.* TORREFIED; *p.pr.* TORREFYING) someter a torrefacción, oxidar en caliente.
torrent ['tɔrənt, 'tɑr-, B 'tɔr-] *s.* 1. torrente, corriente violenta (de agua, lava, etc.). 2. (fig.) raudal, torrente (de preguntas, injurias, etc.). *—a.* torrentoso, torrencial, correntoso.
torrential [tɔ'rɛntʃəl, tə-, B tɔ'rɛnʃəl] *a.* torrencial, torrentoso, correntoso.
torrentially [-'rɛntʃəlɪ, B -'rɛnʃ-] *adv.* a modo de torrente, como un torrente.
torrid ['tɔrəd, 'tɑr-, B 'tɔr-] *a.* 1. tórrido, ardiente, abrasador. 2. (fig.) ardiente, ardoroso, fervoroso.
torridity [tɔ'rɪdətɪ] *s.* calor abrasador, sumo ardor.
torridly ['tɔrədlɪ, 'tɑr-, B 'tɔr-] *adv.* ardorosamente, ardientemente.
torridness [-nəs] *s.* calor abrasador, sumo ardor.
torrid zone, zona tórrida.
torsade [tɔr'sɑd, -'seɪd, B tɔ'-] *s.* (cost.) torzal.
torsion ['tɔrʃən, B 'tɔʃən] *s.* 1. torsión, torcimiento, torcedura. 2. (mec.) torsión.
torsional [-əl] *a.* de torsión.
torsional moment, (fís.) momento de torsión.
torsional strength, resistencia a la torsión.
torsion balance, (fís.) balanza de torsión.
torsion bar, (aut.) barra de torsión.
torsion meter, torsiómetro.
torsion pendulum, péndulo de torsión.
torsk [tɔrsk, B tɔsk] *s.* (ict.) especie de bacalao.
torso ['tɔrsoʊ, B 'tɔsoʊ] *s.* (*pl.* TORSOS o TORSI [-,si]) torso.
tort [tɔrt, B tɔt] *s.* (der.) entuerto, agravio, daño (indemnizable en juicio civil y que no se origina en un incumplimiento de contrato).
torticollis [,tɔrtə'kɑləs, B ,tɔtɪ'kɔl-] *s.* (med.) tortícolis.
tortile ['tɔrtəl, B 'tɔtaɪl] *a.* 1. torcido, doblado. 2. (bot.) enroscado, enrollado.
tortilla [tɔr'tijə, B tɔ'til-] *s.* (Méx., cocina) tortilla (de maíz).
tortoise ['tɔrtəs, B 'tɔt-] *s.* 1. tortuga, galápago. 2. (hist.) testudo, bóveda baja.
tortoiseshell ['tɔrtə,ʃɛl, B 'tɔtə-] *s.* 1. concha de carey, carey. 2. (ento.) carey (variedad de mariposa). *—a.* de carey, semejante al carey.
tortricid ['tɔrtrəsəd, B 'tɔtrɪ-] *a.* (ento.) tortrícido.
tortuosity [,tɔrtʃʊ'ɑsətɪ, B ,tɔtjʊ'ɔs-] *s.* (*pl.* TORTUOSITIES) 1. tortuosidad, sinuosidad. 2. (fig.) tortuosidad, carácter solapado. 3. recoveco, recodo, revuelta, meandro.
tortuous ['tɔrtʃʊəs, B 'tɔtjʊ-] *a.* 1. tortuoso, sinuoso, laberíntico. 2. (fig.) tortuoso, solapado, artificioso, torcido.
tortuously [-lɪ] *adv.* 1. tortuosamente, sinuosamente, torcidamente. 2. (fig.) tortuosamente, solapadamente.
tortuousness [-nəs] *s.* 1. tortuosidad, sinuosidad. 2. (fig.) tortuosidad, carácter solapado.
torture ['tɔrtʃər, B 'tɔtʃə] *s.* tortura, tormento. *—v.t.* 1. torturar, atormentar, dar tormento a. 2. (fig.) tergiversar, torcer (el significado, palabras, etc.).
torturer [-tʃərər, B -ə] *s.* torturador, atormentador.
torturous [-tʃərəs] *a.* torturador, atormentador, cruelmente doloroso.
torus ['tɔrəs] *s.* (*pl.* TORI [-aɪ]) 1. (anat.) toro, torus. 2. (arq.) torés, bocel. 3. (bot., geom.) toro.
Tory ['tɔrɪ] *s.* (*pl.* TORIES) 1. (G.B., pol.) conservador. 2. (E.U., hist.) realista, fidelista (persona que durante la guerra de la independencia favorecía a Inglaterra). 3. **t.,** conservador empedernido, reaccionario. *—a.* conservador.
Toryism [-,ɪzəm] *s.* (pol.) conservadurismo, doctrina del partido conservador.
tosh [tɑʃ, B tɔʃ] *s.* (G.B., jer.) disparate, idiotez, tontería.
toss [tɔs, tɑs, B tɔs] *v.t.* 1. mover o echar de un lado a otro, pelotear con. 2. agitar, sacudir, menear, blandir. 3. tirar, arrojar (pelota, peso,

etc.); arrojar o tirar con desenvoltura o descuido; lanzar al aire (una moneda); coger (a alguien el toro). 4. echar atrás; erguir con desdén u orgullo (la cabeza). 5. **t. aside,** echar a un lado, apartar; **t. (someone) in a blanket,** mantear (a alguien); **t. oars,** arbolar los remos, levantar los remos en saludo; **t. off,** tomar de golpe (un trago); hacer (algo) rápidamente o sin esfuerzo; **t. out,** echar afuera; **t. up,** preparar rápidamente (comida, plato, etc.). —*v.i.* 1. revolverse (por insomnio, intranquilidad, etc.). 2. lanzar al aire una moneda, apostar con una moneda, apostar a cara o cruz. 3. **t. and turn,** revolverse, dar vueltas en la cama; **t. (someone) for,** jugar (con alguien) a cara o cruz por (derecho, posesión de una cosa, etc.); **t. up,** lanzar una moneda al aire, jugar a cara o cruz. —*s.* 1. lanzamiento, echada. 2. sacudida. 3. apuesta a cara o cruz. 4. **to take a t.,** ser lanzado del caballo; **to win the t.,** ganar la apuesta, ganar a cara o cruz.

tosspot ['tɔsˌpɑt, 'tɑs-, B 'tɔsˌpɔt] *s.* borrachín, bebedor.

toss-up [-ˌʌp] *s.* 1. cara o cruz, lanzamiento de una moneda. 2. probabilidad o azar parejos.

toston [toʊ'stoʊn] *s.* (numis.) tostón.

tot [tɑt, B tɔt] *v.t.* (*pret., p.p.* TOTTED; *p.pr.* TOTTING) (ú. gen. con *up*) sumar, totalizar. —*v.i.* **t. up,** aumentarse, acumularse; **t. up to,** (fig.) equivaler a, significar. —*s.* niño de corta edad, nene.

total ['toʊtəl] *a.* 1. total, todo, entero. 2. total, completo, cabal. *s.* 1. todo, total, totalidad. 2. suma, total. —*v.t.* (*pret., p.p.* TOTALED O TOTALLED; *p.pr.* TOTALING O TOTALLING) 1. sumar, verificar el total de. 2. sumar, totalizar, ascender a un total de. —*v.i.* sumar.

total abstinence, abstinencia de bebidas alcohólicas.

total disability, incapacidad absoluta, invalidez absoluta.

total eclipse, (astr.) eclipse total.

totalisator, *var. de* **totalizator.**

totalism [-ˌɪzəm] *s.* totalitarismo.

totalistic [ˌtoʊtəl'ɪstɪk] *a.* totalitario, absoluto.

totalitarian [-ˌtælə'tɛrɪən, B -'tɛər-] *a., s.* totalitario.

totalitarianism [-ˌɪzəm] *s.* totalitarismo.

totality [toʊ'tælətɪ] *s.* totalidad.

totalization [ˌtoʊtələ'zeɪʃən, B -aɪ'zeɪ-] *s.* totalización.

totalizator ['toʊtələˌzeɪtər, B -aɪˌzeɪtə] *s.* totalizador.

totalize ['toʊtəlˌaɪz] *v.t.* 1. totalizar, sumar. 2. resumir.

totalizer [-ˌaɪzər, B -zə] *s.* totalizador.

totally ['toʊtəlɪ] *adv.* totalmente, en conjunto, completamente, enteramente.

total utility, (e.p.) utilidad total.

total war, guerra total.

totaquine ['toʊtəˌkwin, B -ˌkwaɪn] **totaquina** [ˌtoʊtə'kinə, B -'kwaɪnə] *s.* (farm.) totaquina.

tote [toʊt] *v.t.* 1. (fam., E.U.) cargar, llevar. 2. totalizar, sumar. —*s.* 1. carga, peso. 2. totalizador.

tote bag, bolsa, bolso (gen. de tela o paja).

totem ['toʊtəm] *s.* (antrop.) tótem.

totemic [toʊ'tɛmɪk] *a.* totémico.

totemism ['toʊtəˌmɪzəm] *s.* totemismo.

totemistic [toʊtə'mɪstɪk] *a.* totémico.

totem pole, mástil o poste totémico.

tother, t'other ['tʌðər, B -ə] *a., pron.* (dial.) (el) otro, (la) otra.

totipalmate [ˌtoʊtə'pælˌmeɪt] *a.* (zool.) totipalmado.

totipotent [toʊ'tɪpətənt] *a.* (biol.) totipotencial.

totter ['tɑtər, B 'tɔtə] *v.i.* tambalear(se), bambolear(se); estar por desplomarse, amenazar ruina.

tottering [-ərɪŋ] *a.* tambaleante, bamboleante; a punto de derrumbarse.

totteringly [-lɪ] *adv.* tambaleando, con bamboleo.

tottery [-ərɪ] *a.* tambaleante, bamboleante; ruinoso.

toucan ['tuˌkæn, -ˌkɑn, B 'tukən] *s.* (orn.) tucán.

touch [tʌtʃ] *v.t.* 1. tocar. 2. tocar, alcanzar, llegar a. 3. (fig.) equiparar, igualar. 4. (gen. con *in*) delinear, trazar, esbozar (rasgos, contornos, etc. en una pintura). 5. afectar, conmover, enternecer. 6. tocar, aludir a, referirse a (tema, asunto, etc.). 7. concernir, atañer, tocar a (alguien). 8. matizar, teñir. 9. dañar ligeramente, afectar; corromper. 10. (en frases negativas) afectar, tener efecto en; abordar, resolver (problema, etc.). 11. (fam.) dar un sablazo a, ej., *I touched him for five bucks,* le di un sablazo de cinco dólares. 12. (ant.) tocar, pulsar (teclas o cuerdas de un instrumento). 13. **t. down,** (fútbol, E.U.) tocar tierra (con la pelota) detrás de la raya de la meta (para marcar tantos); **t. off,** esbozar (un dibujo), trazar o hacer (un esbozo) rápidamente; disparar (un cañón); desencadenar, provocar; **t. one's hat,** saludar con un toque de la mano en el sombrero; **t. (one) to the quick,** tocar en lo vivo (a uno); **t. up,** corregir, retocar; dar los últimos toques a; avivar (caballo, etc. con el látigo); estimular (la memoria); **t. wood,** (fig.) tocar madera. —*v.i.* 1. tocar(se), estar en contacto. 2. **t. at,** tocar en, hacer escala en (puerto); **t. down,** aterrizar (avión); **t. on** (o **upon**), aludir a, mencionar casualmente; tratar levemente (tema); (fig.) rayar en, acercarse a. —*s.* 1. toque, tocamiento, tacto, palpamiento. 2. (sentido del) tacto. 3. tacto, sensibilidad; sensación táctil, sensación, percepción. 4. contacto, comunicación. 5. toque, retoque, ej., *finishing touches,* retoques finales. 6. toque, mano, estilo; rasgo característico. 7. punzada (de dolor, conciencia, etc.); ataque ligero (de una enfermedad), ej., *a t. of grippe,* un ligero ataque de gripe. 8. pizca, rastro, vestigio. 9. mancha, defecto. 10. imanación (por contacto). 11. (fútbol Am.) terreno fuera de las líneas laterales del campo de juego. 12. (jer.) sablazo. 13. (ant.) toque, piedra de toque. 14. **by t.,** al tacto; **in t. with,** en contacto con, en comunicación o relaciones con; al corriente de; **near t.,** zafada venturosa, escapada por un pelo; **out of t. with** no estar al corriente de; sin relaciones con; **to get in t. with,** ponerse en comunicación o contacto con; **to keep in t.,** mantenerse en contacto; seguir la correspondencia; **to lose one's t.,** perder el tiento, perder la mano; **to put to the t.,** poner a prueba; **to win by a t.,** ganar por puesta de mano.

touchable ['tʌtʃəbəl] *a.* tocable, tangible.

touch and go, 1. vaivén, alternación rápida. 2. carácter precario o incierto. 3. **to be t. a. g.,** pender de un hilo, ser cuestión de suerte.

touch-and-go [-ən'goʊ] *a.* precario, incierto, arriesgado.

touchback [-ˌbæk] *s.* (fútbol E.U.) posición del jugador o jugada en que éste se encuentra detrás de la línea de su propia meta y en posesión del balón.

touchdown [-ˌdaʊn] *s.* 1. (aer.) aterrizaje. 2. (fútbol E.U.) tanto (marcado al tocar el suelo con el balón detrás de la meta del adversario).

touched [tʌtʃt] *a.* 1. tocado, chiflado; **t. in the head,** tocado de la cabeza. 2. enternecido, conmovido.

touch football, variedad de fútbol norteamericano en que sólo se toca al jugador que lleva el balón en vez de atajarlo.

touchhole ['tʌtʃˌhoʊl] *s.* (mil.) fogón, oído del cañón.

touchily [-əlɪ] *adv.* 1. quisquillosamente, de modo quisquilloso. 2. con irritación, irritadamente.

touchiness [-ɪnəs] *s.* 1. susceptibilidad, sensibilidad. 2. irritabilidad, irascibilidad.

touching [-ɪŋ] *a.* conmovedor, enternecedor, patético, emocionante. —*prep.* (ant., lit.) tocante a, con respecto a, en cuanto a.

touchingly [-lɪ] *adv.* de modo conmovedor, conmovedoramente, patéticamente, en forma enternecedora, enternecedoramente.

touch-in-goal ['tʌtʃɪn'goʊl] *s.* (fútbol E.U.) ángulo exterior del campo (formado por las líneas de base y laterales).

touchline [-ˌlaɪn] *s.* (fútbol) línea lateral.

touchmark [-ˌmɑrk, B -ˌmɑk] *s.* marca de fábrica grabada en peltre.

touch-me-not [-mɪˌnɑt, B -ˌnɔt] *s.* (bot.) 1. balsamina, hierba de Santa Catalina. 2. cohombrillo amargo, pepino.

touchneedle [-ˌnidəl] *s.* aguja de prueba (de aleación fija de oro para examinar otras aleaciones).

touchstone [-ˌstoʊn] *s.* 1. (min.) piedra de toque, basanita, jaspe negro. 2. (fig.) examen, criterio de prueba.

touch system, sistema (de mecanografía) al tacto.

touch-type ['tʌtʃˌtaɪp] *v.t.* mecanografiar al tacto.

touch-typing [-ɪŋ] *s.* mecanografía al tacto.

touchwood [-ˌwʊd] *s.* hupe, yesca.

touchy ['tʌtʃɪ] *a.* (TOUCHIER; TOUCHIEST) 1. quisquilloso, susceptible, delicado, ej., *a t. business,* un asunto delicado. 2. quisquilloso, enojadizo (persona).

tough [tʌf] *a.* 1. firme, fuerte, duro. 2. estropajoso, correoso. 3. glutinoso, viscoso. 4. resistente, robusto, vigoroso, de pelo en pecho. 5. (fig.) tieso, recio, firme. 6. testarudo, tenaz. 7. (E.U.) alborotador, pendenciero, rufián; rudo, vulgar. 8. (fam.) difícil, penoso, arduo; desagradable, adverso, desfavorable, malo, ej., *don't make it any tougher,* no hagas las cosas más difíciles, *t. luck,* mala suerte. —*s.* (E.U.) villano, malvado, rufián.

tough customer, 1. persona difícil (de trato). 2. tipo duro, tipo peligroso.

toughen ['tʌfən] *v.t.* 1. endurecer, atiesar; templar. 2. volver correoso. 3. (fig.) endurecer, hacer tenaz, dar firmeza o dureza a. —*v.i.* 1. endurecerse, atiesarse; templarse. 2. volverse correoso. 3. (fig.) endurecerse, volverse tenaz.

toughie ['tʌfɪ] *s.* 1. matón, rufián, persona ruda. 2. problema difícil.

tough-minded [-'maɪndəd] *a.* poco sentimental, realista, (de carácter) duro.

toughness ['tʌfnəs] *s.* firmeza, dureza; resistencia, fortaleza.

toughy, *s.* (*pl.* TOUGHIES) *var. de* **toughie.**

toupee [tu'peɪ, B 'tupeɪ] *s.* 1. tupé. 2. postizo pequeño, copete de cabello postizo.

tour [tʊr, B tʊə] *s.* 1. viaje de turismo, excursión; recorrido, peregrinación, paseo, vuelta; circuito. 2. turno, tanda, jornada, período. 3. (G.B., mil.) turno de servicio, turno de guardia. 4. **on t.,** de viaje, en gira; **to make a t.,** hacer un viaje; **to make a t. of,** recorrer. —*v.i.* hacer un viaje, hacer un recorrido. —*v.t.* 1. viajar por, hacer un viaje en, recorrer. 2. (teat.) presentar (obra) en un recorrido.

touraco ['tʊrəˌkoʊ, B 'tʊər-] *s.* (orn.) variedad de cuco africano.

tourbillion [tʊr'bɪljən, B tʊə'-] *s.* 1. torbellino. 2. cohete (de fuegos artificiales) que asciende en forma de espiral.
tour de force [ˌtʊrdə'fɔrs, B 'tʊədə'fɔs] (fr.) proeza, exhibición de fuerza o destreza, realización ingeniosa.
touring ['tʊrɪŋ, B 'tʊər-] *a.* turístico, de turismo.
touring car, automóvil de turismo.
tourism [-ˌɪzəm] *s.* turismo.
tourist ['tʊrəst, B 'tʊər-] *s.* turista. —*a.* turístico, de turista(s).
tourist card, tarjeta de turista (que sirve en lugar de pasaporte).
tourist class, clase turista, segunda clase, clase económica (en buques y aviones de pasajeros).
tourist court, motel.
tourist resort, complejo turístico.
tourist trade, turismo.
tourist traffic, turismo, movimiento turístico.
tourmaline ['tʊrmələn, -ˌlin, B 'tʊəməlɪn] *s.* (min.) turmalina.
tournament ['tʊrnəmənt, 'tɜr-, B 'tʊənə-] *s.* 1. (hist.) justa, torneo. 2. torneo, certamen, competencia, concurso, contienda.
tourney ['tʊrnɪ, 'tɜr-, B 'tʊənɪ] *s.* torneo, justa, lid. —*v.i.* tornear, justar, lidiar.
tourniquet ['tʊrnɪkət, 'tɜr-, B ' tʊənɪˌkeɪ] *s.* (med.) torniquete.
tournois [tʊr'nwɑ, B tɜn'wɑ] *a.* (numis.) tornés.
tour of inspection, gira de inspección.
touse [taʊz] *v.t.* (dial.) enmarañar, desmelenar (los cabellos).
tousle ['taʊzəl] *v.t.* enmarañar, desmelenar, desgreñar, despeinar. —*s.* desgreño, greña, cabello revuelto.
tout [taʊt] *v.i.* 1. (con *for*) (ocuparse en) solicitar o pescar (apuestas, clientes, etc.), cabildear. 2. (pr. G.B.) espiar los entrenamientos de los caballos de carrera. 3. (E.U.) dar información sobre caballos de carrera. —*v.t.* 1. (fam.) solicitar, importunar, molestar. 2. (G.B.) espiar (caballos de carrera). 3. (E.U.) dar información sobre (los caballos). —*s.* 1. solicitador (de clientela, apuestas, etc.). 2. (G.B.) espía de los entrenamientos de los caballos. 3. (E.U.) persona que vende información sobre caballos de carrera. 4. **on the t.,** al acecho, a la mira.
touter ['taʊtər, B -ə] *s. var. de* **tout.**
touzle, *var. de* **tousle.**
tow [toʊ] *v.t.* remolcar, atoar, toar, sirgar, halar. —*s.* 1. remolque, atoaje. 2. sirga, (maroma de) remolque; remolcador. 3. remolque, acoplado (auto o barco que se remolca). 4. **in the t. of,** remolcado por; **to take in t.,** dar remolque a, llevar a remolque; (fig.) tomar a su cuidado; guiar; **with (someone) in t.,** seguido por (alguien), ej., *he entered with his secretary in t.,* entró seguido por su secretaria.
tow, *s.* estopa.
towage ['toʊɪdʒ] *s.* 1. remolque. 2. derechos de remolque.
toward [tɔrd, B 'toʊəd] *a.* 1. próximo, en preparación, inminente. 2. (ant.) dócil, tratable; favorable, propicio.
toward [tɔrd, tə'wɔrd, B -'wɔd] **towards** [tɔrdz, tə'wɔrdz, B -'wɔdz] *prep.* 1. hacia, en la dirección de. 2. hacia, para con; en relación a, con respecto a. 3. próximo a, cercano a. 4. para, ej., *the government's efforts t. improving the situation,* los esfuerzos del gobierno para mejorar la situación. 5. hacia, cerca de, alrededor de (lugar u hora).
towardliness ['toʊərdlɪnəs, 'tɔrd-, B 'toʊəd-] *s.* (ant.) docilidad, obediencia.
towardly [-lɪ] *a.* 1. acogedor, afable. 2. (ant.) favorable, propicio; dócil, tratable.
towboat ['toʊˌboʊt] *s.* remolcador.
tow car, grúa-remolque.
towed flight, (avia.) vuelo remolcado.
towel ['taʊəl] *s.* toalla; **to throw in the t.,** (boxeo, fig.) tirar la esponja, dejar la capa al toro, darse por vencido. —*v.t.* (*pret., p.p.* TOWELED O TOWELLED; *p.pr.* TOWELING O TOWELLING) secar o frotar con toalla.
toweling, towelling [-ɪŋ] *s.* género o tela para toalla.
towel rack, toallero.
tower ['taʊər, B -ə] *s.* 1. torre. 2. torreón, fortaleza, ciudadela. 3. (fig.) baluarte, defensa. —*v.i.* 1. encumbrarse, elevarse. 2. (fig.) **t. above,** descollar entre, destacarse entre, ej., *he towers above his contemporaries,* él descuella (o se destaca) entre sus contemporáneos.
tower clock, reloj de torre.
towered [-ərd, B -əd] **towery** [-ərɪ] *a.* torreado, guarnecido de torres.
towering [-ərɪŋ] *a.* 1. altísimo, enorme, imponente. 2. extremado, intenso, violento (pasión, ira, etc.). 3. desmesurado, desmedido (ej., ambición).
tower wagon, camión andamio, camión de torre.
towhead ['toʊˌhɛd] *s.* persona pelirrubia (cuyos cabellos son casi blancos).
towheaded [-əd] *a.* pelirrubio (de un rubio blanquecino).
towhee [ˌtoʊ'hi, B taʊ-] *s.* (orn.) carcachil, totochil.
towing ['toʊɪŋ] *s.* remolque, servicio de grúa.
towing charges, derechos de remolque.
to wit, a saber, es decir.
towline ['toʊˌlaɪn] *s.* sirga, cable de remolque.
town [taʊn] *s.* 1. pueblo, poblado, población; ciudad. 2. (dial. G.B.) villa, aldea, lugar; municipio. 3. **in t.,** en la ciudad; **(out) on the t.,** de parranda, de francachela; **out of t.,** fuera de la ciudad, ausente; **the t.,** (fig.) la ciudad, la vida urbana; **to go to t.,** (fam., G.B.) andar de jarana; echar la casa por la ventana, no escatimar gastos; **to paint the t. red,** ir de parranda, ir de juerga.
town and gown, (G.B.) gente del pueblo y miembros de la Universidad (de Oxford o Cambridge); (fig.) todo el mundo.
town car, coche sedán de cuatro puertas (con un vidrio que separa el compartimento de pasajeros).
town clerk, secretario de ayuntamiento.
town council, concejo, concejo municipal.
town councillor, (G.B.) concejal.
town crier, (hist.) pregonero, voceador.
town hall, ayuntamiento, municipio, municipalidad, concejo.
town house, casa particular en la ciudad.
town meeting, cabildo, ayuntamiento; concejo municipal.
town planning, urbanismo.
township ['taʊnˌʃɪp] *s.* 1. municipio, ayuntamiento, municipalidad. 2. área de treinta y seis millas cuadradas (de terrenos públicos). 3. (G.B., hist.) unidad territorial de administración (constituída por uno o varios feudos o parroquias). 4. (Can.) subdivisión de algunas provincias.
townsman ['taʊnzmən] *s.* 1. habitante de la ciudad, ciudadano. 2. conciudadano.
townspeople [-ˌpipəl] *s.* 1. vecinos del pueblo, lugareños. 2. ciudadanos, gente de la ciudad.
town talk, *s.* comidilla, hablilla de un pueblo.
townswoman [-ˌwʊmən] *s.* 1. mujer habitante de la ciudad, ciudadana. 2. conciudadana.
townwear ['taʊnˌwɛr, B -wɛə] *s.* vestido serio (de color o corte); traje de vestir, traje de tarde.
towpath ['toʊˌpæθ, B -pɑθ] *s.* camino de sirga (que se usa para remolcar una embarcación por un canal).
towrope [-ˌroʊp] *s.* sirga, maroma de remolque.
tow truck, grúa-remolque, camión grúa.
toxaemia, toxaemic, *vars de* **toxemia, toxemic.**
toxalbumin [ˌtɑksæl'bjumən, B ˌtɔk-] *s.* (bioquím.) toxalbúmina.
toxemia [tɑk'simɪə, B tɔk-] *s.* (med.) toxemia.
toxemic [-mɪk] *a.* (med.) toxémico.
toxic ['tɑksɪk, B 'tɔk-] *a.* tóxico.
toxic anaemia, (med.) anemia tóxica.
toxicant [-sɪkənt] *a.* tóxico. —*s.* veneno.
toxication [ˌtɑksə'keɪʃən, B ˌtɔk-] *s.* intoxicación.
toxicity [tɑk'sɪsətɪ, B tɔk-] *s.* toxicidad.
toxicogenic [ˌtɑksəkoʊ'dʒɛnɪk, B ˌtɔk-] *a.* (fisiol., med.) toxicogénico, toxicógeno.
toxicological [ˌtɑksəkə'lɑdʒɪkəl, B ˌtɔk-'lɔdʒ-] *a.* toxicológico.
toxicologist [-'kɑlədʒəst, B -'kɔl-] *s.* toxicólogo.
toxicology [-'kɑlədʒɪ, B -'kɔl-] *s.* toxicología.
toxicosis [-'koʊsəs] *s.* (med.) toxicosis.
toxic waste, residuos tóxicos.
toxin ['tɑksən, B 'tɔk-] *s.* (bioquím.) toxina.
toxin-antitoxin [-'æntɪˌtɑksən, B -ˌtɔk-] *s.* toxinantitoxina.
toxiphobia [ˌtɑksə'foʊbɪə, B ˌtɔk-] *s.* (med.) toxifobia; toxicofobia.
toxoid ['tɑkˌsɔɪd, B 'tɔk-] *s.* (med.) toxoide.
toxophilite [tɑk'sɑfəˌlaɪt, B tɔk'sɔf-] *s.* aficionado al tiro de arco; arquero.
toxoplasmosis [ˌtɑksəˌplæz'moʊsəs, B ˌtɔk-] *s.* (med.) toxoplasmosis.
toy [tɔɪ] *s.* 1. juguete. 2. chuchería, fruslería, baratija; nadería, futilidad. 3. (ant.) flirteo, coqueteo; pasatiempo; deporte; travesura, extravagancia. —*v.i.* jugar, juguetear, divertirse; **t. with,** jugar con; acariciar, dar vueltas a (una idea). —*a.* 1. de juego. 2. diminuto.
toy bank, alcancía, hucha.
toy dealer, el que comercia en juguetes.
toy dog, perro faldero, perrito.
toy fish, pez ornamental, pez de acuario.
toyish ['tɔɪɪʃ] *a.* 1. menudo, de juguete. 2. juguetón, frívolo.
toyishness [-nəs] *s.* puerilidad, niñería.
toyon ['tɔɪˌɑn, B -ən] *s.* (bot.) tollón.
toy shop, t. store, juguetería, tienda de juguetes.
toy soldier, soldadito de plomo, soldado de juguete.
trabeated ['treɪbɪˌeɪtəd] *a.* construido de vigas horizontales, arquitrabado.
trabecula [trə'bɛkjələ] *s.* (anat., zool., bot.) trabécula.
trabecular [-lər, B -lə] **trabeculate** [-lət] *a.* (anat., zool., bot.) trabecular, trabeculado.
trace [treɪs] *s.* 1. rastro, huella, pista, pisada. 2. (geof.) línea de registro. 3. pizca, vestigio, ápice, sombra, señal, indicio. 4. trazado, trazo. 5. (geom.) traza. 6. **without leaving a t.,** sin dejar el menor indicio. —*v.t.* 1. trazar, delinear, dibujar. 2. (t. con *over*) calcar. 3. (fig.) señalar, indicar. 4. (*gen. en p.p.*) adornar con tracería (ventanas, etc.). 5. rastrear, seguir la pista de. 6. seguir, averiguar, investigar, buscar; descubrir, hallar, encontrar. 7. (t. con *back*) reconstruir, deducir o averiguar el origen de (por medio de vestigios); comprobar la filiación de (antepasados). 8. (ant.) escudriñar.
trace, *s.* 1. tirante, tiradera; ronzal. 2. (*pl.*) arreos, guarniciones. 3. (mec.) brazo transmisor (de movimiento). 4. **to kick over the traces,** rebelarse; salirse de la rutina.

traceable ['treɪsəbəl] *a.* susceptible de ser hallado o descubierto.
trace element, (biol.) microelemento, elemento menor.
tracelessly [-ləslɪ] *adv.* sin (dejar) rastro, sin dejar huella.
tracer [-ər, B -ə] *s.* 1. investigador, inquisidor. 2. cédula de investigación o reclamo (de envíos postales extraviados, etc.). 3. delineante, diseñador, trazador. 4. calcador, tiralíneas; patrón de calcomanía (para costura). 5. (quím.) indicador radioactivo; cuerpo indicador. 6. (mil.) compuesto trazador.
tracer atom, (fís.) átomo marcado.
tracer bullet, bala trazadora.
tracery [-ərɪ] *s.* (arq.) tracería.
trachea ['treɪkɪə, B trə'kiə] *s.* (*pl.* TRACHEAE) (anat., bot., ento.) tráquea.
tracheal [-kɪəl, B -'ki-] *a.* traqueal.
tracheal tissue, (bot.) tejido traqueal.
tracheary ['treɪkɪˌɛrɪ, B -ərɪ] *a.* (zool.) traqueal.
tracheid ['treɪkɪəd] *s.* (bot.) traqueida.
tracheitis [ˌtreɪkɪ'aɪtəs] *s.* (med.) traqueítis.
tracheotomy [-'ɑtəmɪ, B ˌtrækɪ'ɔt-] *s.* (med.) traqueotomía.
trachoma [trə'koʊmə] *s.* (med.) tracoma.
trachomatous [trə'kɑmətəs, B -'kɔm-] *a.* (med.) tracomatoso.
trachyandesite [ˌtrækɪ'ændəˌzaɪt, B ˌtreɪ-] *s.* (geol.) traqueandesita.
trachyte ['trækˌaɪt, 'treɪˌkaɪt] *s.* (min.) traquita.
trachytic [trə'kɪtɪk] *a.* (geol.) traquítico.
tracing ['treɪsɪŋ] *s.* 1. calco; calcado. 2. rastreo. 3. trazado.
tracing paper, papel de calcar.
track [træk] *s.* 1. huella, pisada, estampa (de hombre o animal); rodada, carril, carrilera (de vehículo), estela (de barco, etc.). 2. curso, camino, senda, sendero. 3. ruta, trayectoria, recorrido. 4. vía férrea, línea, rieles, carriles; trocha (ancha o angosta). 5. (fig.) sucesión (de ideas, acontecimientos, etc.). 6. oruga, banda de rodamiento (de tanques, tractores, etc.). 7. (dep.) pista (de carreras), carreras atléticas (que se practican en pistas). 8. **in one's tracks,** allí mismo, donde se encuentra uno; **off the t.,** descarrilado; (fig.) por los cerros de Úbeda, desviado, distraído (de un tema de que se trata); **on the right t.,** por buen camino; **to be on (someone's) t.,** estar sobre la pista de (alguien); **to jump the tracks,** descarrilar; **to keep t. of,** seguir con atención, estar al día con, mantenerse informado sobre (los sucesos del momento); acordarse u ocuparse de; **to lose t. of,** perder de vista; **to make tracks,** (jer.) irse, marcharse; **to make tracks for,** (jer.) ir a, dirigirse **a; the wrong side of the tracks,** la parte pobre de una comunidad residencial. —*v.t.* 1. seguir la pista o huella de, rastrear; investigar, descubrir, deducir. 2. (E.U.) dejar pisadas en, dejar huellas de (lodo, etc.). 3. rastrear (satélites artificiales, cohetes, etc.). 4. recorrer, atravesar. 5. **t. down,** perseguir y atrapar; cazar; averiguar el origen de. —*v.i.* 1. estar en alineación (ruedas). 2. dejar huellas. 3. (rad.) leer, seguir el surco (de disco de gramófono).
trackage ['trækɪdʒ] *s.* 1. (f.c.) red de vías. 2. remolque.
track-and-field [-ən'fild] *a.* (dep.) de campo y pista (díc. de ciertas pruebas atléticas).
track circuit, circuito de vía.
track cycling, (dep.) ciclismo en pista.
tracker ['trækər, B -ə] *s.* 1. rastreador. 2. (mil.) perseguidor, aparato seguidor del blanco.
track gage, t. gauge, (f.c.) patrón de ancho, vara de trocha, gálibo, calibre de entrevía.
tracking [-ɪŋ] *s.* 1. rastreo. 2. (rad.) lectura (del sonido grabado en discos, cinta magnética etc.). 3. (astronáut.) localización. 4. (mil.) persecución.
tracking radar, (rad.) radar de persecución.
tracking station, (aeroesp.) estación seguimiento, centro de rastreo.
track jack, (f.c.) gato de vía, levantarrieles.
tracklayer [-ˌleɪər, B -ə] *s.* 1. instalador de carriles, tendedor de vía. 2. vehículo oruga, vehículo de cadena.
tracklaying [-ˌleɪɪŋ] *s.* (f.c.) tendido, instalación de rieles o carriles.
trackless ['trækləs] *a.* 1. sin caminos, no pisado (selva, etc.). 2. sin huellas, que no deja huellas (pisadas, etc.). 3. sin rieles, sin vía.
trackless trolley, trolebús.
trackman [-mən] **trackwalker** [-ˌwɔkər, B -ə] *s.* (f.c.) guardavía, corredor de vía, inspector o vigilante de vías.
track meet, (dep.) concurso de juegos atléticos de pista y campo.
track pan, (f.c.) canaleta de toma en marcha, artesa de vía.
track record, historial, antecedentes.
tracksuit ['træksut] *a.* equipo de deportes, chándal.
trackwork [-ˌwɜrk, B -wɜk] *s.* cálculo y construcción del sistema de carriles de las vías férreas.
tract [trækt] *s.* 1. tracto, trecho; extensión, espacio, zona, región. 2. (anat., zool.) sistema (de órganos). 3. (relig.) tracto (versículo que se canta antes del evangelio). 4. (ant., poét.) duración, período, espacio (de tiempo). 5. folleto, opúsculo.
tractability [ˌtræktə'bɪlətɪ] *s.* 1. docilidad. 2. ductilidad, maleabilidad.
tractable ['træktəbəl] *a.* 1. tratable, manejable, dócil. 2. dúctil, maleable.
tractableness [-bəlnəs] *s.* 1. docilidad. 2. ductilidad, maleabilidad.
tractably [-blɪ] *adv.* dócilmente.
tractate ['trækˌteɪt] *s.* tratado (escrito, libro); ensayo.
tractile ['træktəl, B -taɪl] *a.* dúctil.
tractility [træk'tɪlətɪ] *s.* ductilidad.
traction ['trækʃən] *s.* 1. tracción, arrastre. 2. fricción adhesiva (de las ruedas sobre la vía).
tractional [-əl] *a.* de tracción.
traction engine, tractor, locomotora o máquina de arrastre.
traction wheel, (mec.) rueda de tracción, polea impulsora.
tractive [-tɪv] *a.* de tracción, de arrastre, tractivo.
tractive force, (ing.) fuerza de arrastre, potencia o fuerza tractora.
tractor ['træktər, B -tə] *s.* 1. tractor; máquina de arrastre. 2. (aer.) aeroplano de hélice delantera.
tractor crane, grúa de tractor, grúa móvil.
tractor engine, motor tractor o delantero.
tractor plow, (agr.) arado mecánico.
tractor propeller, (aer.) hélice tractora, hélice delantera.
trade [treɪd] *s.* 1. oficio, ocupación, profesión. 2. negocio, comercio; (G.B.) comercio al por menor. 3. arte, artesanía, industria. 4. comerciantes (colectivamente); gremio. 5. clientela. 6. (E.U.) trueque, canje, cambio. 7. viento alisio. 8. **by t.,** de profesión; **in t.,** en canje; **the t.,** (fam., G.B.) los abastecedores (de alimentos) con licencia; **to be in t.,** comerciar al por menor; tener una tienda, ser tendero. —*v.t.* 1. trocar, canjear, cambiar. 2. cambiar de (sombreros, sitios, etc.). 3. vender (influencia, favor político, etc.). 4. **t. in,** dar un objeto usado como pago inicial por otro nuevo; **t. off,** deshacerse de (algo) por trueque. —*v.i.* 1. (gen. con *in*) comerciar, traficar (en algo). 2. (gen. con *at*) comprar, hacer sus compras (en una tienda, etc.). 3. **t. on,** aprovecharse de, abusar de (buena voluntad, ignorancia, etc.). —*a.* de comercio, comercial, mercantil; industrial.
trade acceptance, letra comercial (aceptada).
trade agreement, 1. tratado comercial, acuerdo de intercambio (entre naciones). 2. pacto colectivo (entre patrones y gremios obreros).
trade discount, (com.) descuento comercial, descuento usual del ramo.
trade dollar, (E.U., hist.) dólar (usado en el comercio con el Oriente).
trade fair, exposición industrial.
trade-in ['treɪdˌɪn] *s.* trueque de venta; artículo o aparato que se entrega como primer pago por otro nuevo o mejor.
trademark [-ˌmɑrk, B -mɑk] *s.* marca de fábrica, marca registrada, marca comercial. —*v.t.* registrar la marca de (un artículo); poner marca de fábrica a (un artículo).
trade name, 1. nombre comercial registrado. 2. razón social.
trader [-ər, B -ə] *s.* 1. comerciante, mercader, mercante, tratante, traficante, negociante. 2. buque mercante, buque carguero.
trade route, 1. ruta de comercio (ej., de una caravana). 2. vía marítima.
trade school, escuela de artes y oficios, escuela industrial.
trade secret, secreto comercial o industrial, secreto de fábrica.
tradesman ['treɪdzmən] *s.* tendero, comerciante al por menor; empleado de tienda.
tradesmen's entrance, puerta de servicio.
tradespeople [-ˌpipəl] *s. pl.* tenderos, comerciantes al por menor.
tradeswoman [-ˌwʊmən] tendera.
trade union, sindicato; gremio de obreros.
trade unionism, sindicalismo.
trade unionist, sindicalista.
trade war, guerra comercial.
trade winds, (mar.) vientos alisios.
trading ['treɪdɪŋ] *s.* trato, comercio. —*a.* 1. mercantil. 2. venal, que se vende.
trading account, (ten.) cuenta de compra y venta.
trading post, tienda general o de intercambio; (ant.) factoría.
trading stamp, sello de premio, estampilla de propaganda (que se puede canjear por mercadería).
tradition [trə'dɪʃən] *s.* tradición.
traditional [-əl] *a.* tradicional.
traditionalism [-ˌɪzəm] *s.* tradicionalismo.
traditionalist [-əst] *s., a.* tradicionalista.
traditionalistic [trəˌdɪʃənə'lɪstɪk] *a.* tradicionalista.
traditionally [trə'dɪʃənəlɪ] *adv.* tradicionalmente.
traditionary [-ˌɛrɪ, B -ərɪ] *a.* tradicional.
traditionless [-ləs] *a.* carente de tradiciones.
traditor ['trædətər, B -tə] *s.* (*pl.* TRADITORES [ˌtrædə'tɔriz]) (hist.) traidor (entre los antiguos cristianos durante las persecuciones).
traduce [trə'dus, B -'djus] *v.t.* calumniar, difamar, vilipendiar; denigrar, detractar.
traducement [-mənt] *s.* calumnia, difamación.
traducer [-ər, B -ə] *s.* calumniador; denigrador, detractor.

traducianism [trə'duʃən,ɪzəm, B -'dju-] *s.* (teo.) traducianismo.
traffic ['træfɪk] *s.* 1. tráfico, tránsito, circulación (de vehículos, peatones, etc.). 2. transporte, transportación. 3. movimiento, pasajeros o mercancías (transportados). 4. tráfico, negocio. 5. (fig.) intercambio (ej., de ideas). 6. tratos, relaciones. 7. **all that the t. will bear,** todo lo posible en las circunstancias actuales. —*v.i.* (*pret., p.p.* TRAFFICKED; *p.pr.* TRAFFICKING) traficar, negociar.
traffic beam, (aut.) luz de pase, luz de cruce.
traffic circle, círculo de tráfico, glorieta de tráfico.
traffic control, regulación del tráfico.
traffic cop, t. policeman, policía de tráfico.
traffic court, juzgado de circulación, juzgado de tráfico, audiencia territorial; sala de tránsito (arq.).
traffic engineering, ingeniería de tránsito (que trata del diseño de calles y del control del tráfico o tránsito).
traffic island, isla o zona de seguridad (para peatones).
traffic jam, atascamiento o embotellamiento del tráfico, aglomeraciones, tapón.
trafficker ['træfɪkər, B -ə] *s.* traficante, negociante.
traffic lane, vía o pista (de tránsito).
traffic light, luz de tráfico, semáforo.
traffic manager, 1. (f.c.) director de tráfico. 2. (com.) jefe de despachos.
traffic policeman, agente de tráfico.
traffic sign, señal de tráfico, luz de tráfico.
traffic violation, infracción de las reglas de tráfico.
tragacanth ['trægə,kænθ] *s.* (bot.) (arbusto y goma del) tragacanto, adraganto, alquitira.
tragedian [trə'dʒidɪən] *s.* trágico, dramaturgo (autor o actor trágico).
tragedienne [-,dʒidɪ'ɛn] *s.* (actriz) trágica.
tragedy ['trædʒədɪ] *s.* (*pl.* TRAGEDIES) 1. tragedia, drama. 2. (fig.) tragedia, suceso funesto.
tragic [-ɪk] *a.* 1. trágico, dramático. 2. (fig.) trágico, infausto, funesto.
tragical [-ɪkəl] *a.* trágico.
tragically [-kəlɪ] *adv.* trágicamente.
tragicalness [-kəlnəs] *s.* carácter trágico o funesto.
tragicomedy [,trædʒɪ'kɑmədɪ, B -'kɔm-] *s.* tragicomedia.
tragicomic [-ɪk] **tragicomical** [-ɪkəl] *a.* tragicómico, jocoserio.
tragopan ['trægə,pæn] *s.* (orn.) tragopán.
tragus ['treɪgəs] *s.* (*pl.* TRAGI) (anat.) trago.
T rail ['ti,reɪl] (f.c.) riel de hongo, riel de patín, riel de Vignoles, carril americano.
trail [treɪl] *v.t.* 1. arrastrar. 2. traer o llevar consigo (en los zapatos, pies, etc.). 3. rastrear, perseguir. 4. venir detrás de, seguir el paso de; quedarse detrás de. 5. **t. arms,** (mil.) bajar o suspender el arma (con una mano y paralela al suelo). —*v.i.* 1. descolgarse, colgar; arrastrarse. 2. rezagarse, quedarse atrás. 3. trepar (plantas). 4. emanar, flotar, esparcirse (humo, niebla, etc.). 5. **t. behind,** rezagarse, retrasarse; **t. off,** apagarse, desvanecerse (voz, sonido). —*s.* 1. cola (de cometa, vestido, etc.). 2. rastro, huella, pisada; pista. 3. sendero, trocha, vereda. 4. (mil.) suspensión (de armas). 5. (mil.) gualdera, contera.
trail bike, moto de motocross, moto de trial.
trailblazer ['treɪl,bleɪzər, B -zə] *s.* 1. precursor, explorador, pionero, colonizador. 2. promotor, innovador, pionero.
trailblazing [-zɪŋ] *a.* precursor, explorador, innovador.
trailer [-ər, B -ə] *s.* 1. (cinem.) sinopsis, avance publicitario (de una película). 2. (carro de) remolque, remolque habitable, casa-remolque.
trailer camp, campamento para casas-remolques.
trailer truck, camión con remolque.
trailing [-ɪŋ] *a.* 1. rastrero, remolcado. 2. rezagado. 3. colgante.
trailing aerial, (rad.) antena colgante.
trailing arbutus, (bot.) espigea rastrera.
trailing edge, (aer.) borde de salida, borde de escape.
trailing wheel, (f.c.) rueda trasera o zaguera.
trail net, red barredera.
trail rope, cuerda guía, cuerda freno.
train [treɪn] *s.* 1. cola (de traje). 2. séquito, comitiva, escolta. 3. procesión, fila o columna (de personas o cosas); serie, sucesión (de ideas, pensamientos, etc.). 4. secuela. 5. tren (de ferrocarril). 6. reguero de pólvora. 7. (mec.) tren, movimiento. 8. (mil.) tren de campaña, convoy. —*v.t.* 1. disciplinar, educar, instruir, preparar. 2. ejercitar, entrenar; adiestrar, amaestrar. 3. apuntar, dirigir, enfocar (arma, mira del fusil, etc.). 4. guiar, poner en espaldera (plantas). 5. (raro) remolcar, arrastrar. —*v.i.* 1. ejercitarse, adiestrarse, entrenarse. 2. disciplinarse, educarse, instruirse. 3. (fam.) ir en tren, viajar en tren.
trainable ['treɪnəbəl] *a.* disciplinable, educable.
trainband [-,bænd] *s.* (G.B., hist.) banda armada.
trainbearer [-,bɛrər, B -ə] *s.* 1. paje (que sostiene la cola de un traje). 2. (relig.) caudatario.
train crash, accidente ferroviario.
train dispatcher, despachador de trenes.
trained [treɪnd] *a.* 1. adiestrado. 2. entrenado, experimentado. 3. experto, ej., *nothing escaped his t. eye,* nada escapó a su mirada experta.
trained nurse, enfermera diplomada.
trainee [,treɪ'ni] *s.* 1. aprendiz, practicante. 2. (mil.) recluta.
trainer ['treɪnər, B -ə] *s.* 1. (dep.) entrenador. 2. preparador (de caballos). 3. amaestrador (de animales).
train ferry, transbordador de trenes.
training [-ɪŋ] *s.* enseñanza, instrucción, preparación, entrenamiento, aprendizaje, adiestramiento, ejercitación, ej., *in t.,* entrenándose (atleta, bailarín, etc.). —*s.* de enseñanza, de entrenamiento, instructor.
training camp, (mil.) campo de entrenamiento.
training college, (G.B.) escuela para maestros, escuela normal.
training flight, (aer.) vuelo de entrenamiento.
training schedule, programa de instrucción.
training school, 1. escuela práctica, escuela vocacional. 2. reformatorio, escuela correccional.
training ship, buque escuela.
trainload ['treɪn,loʊd] *s.* carga de un tren completo.
trainman [-mən, -,mæn] *s.* ferroviario, vagonero, empleado ferroviario.
train-mile [-'maɪl] *s.* (f.c.) milla recorrida por un tren (tomada como unidad).
train mileage, kilometraje por tren (total de tren millas).
train oil, aceite de ballena, aceite de pescado.
traipse [treɪps] *v.i.* (fam.) patullar, cazcalear, patear, andar de un lado para otro. —*v.t.* cazcalear por, pisar. —*s.* caminata penosa.
trait [treɪt, B treɪ] *s.* rasgo, cualidad característica, peculiaridad.
traitor ['treɪtər, B -ə] *s.* traidor.
traitorous [-ərəs] *a.* traidor, traicionero, infiel, pérfido.
traitorously [-lɪ] *adv.* traidoramente, traicioneramente.
traitorousness [-nəs] *s.* traición, deslealtad, perfidia.
traitress ['treɪtrəs] *s.* traidora.
Trajan ['treɪdʒən] *s.* (hist.) Trajano, emperador romano nacido en España.
traject [trə'dʒɛkt] *v.t.* (ant.) atravesar, traspasar.
trajection [-'dʒɛkʃən] *s.* (ant.) travesía, pasaje.
trajectory [-tərɪ, B 'trædʒɪk-] *s.* (*pl.* TRAJECTORIES) 1. trayectoria. 2. curva del proyectil hacia el blanco.
tram [træm] *s.* hilo de trama, seda trama, trama de seda.
tram, *s.* 1. vagoneta (de mina). 2. barquilla (de un transportador aéreo). 3. (fam., G.B.) tranvía. 4. *forma abrev. de* **tramway, tramroad.** —*v.t.* (*pret., p.p.* TRAMMED; *p.pr.* TRAMMING) acarrear o transportar en una vagoneta.
tram, *s.* (mec.) 1. compás de varas. 2. calibre de alineación o ajuste. —*v.t.* alinear, reajustar (con un compás de varas).
tramcar ['træm,kɑr, B -kɑ] *s.* 1. vagoneta. 2. (pr. G.B.) tranvía, coche de tranvía.
tramline [-,laɪn] *s.* (G.B.) línea de tranvía.
trammel ['træməl] *s.* 1. traba, manea o maniota (que se pone a los caballos). 2. (fig.) (*gen. pl.*) traba, impedimento, obstáculo, estorbo. 3. trasmallo (de pescar). 4. llares, trébedes. 5. (mec.) elipsógrafo; compás de varas. —*v.t.* (*pret., p.p.* TRAMMELED O TRAMMELLED; *p.pr.* TRAMMELING O TRAMMELLING) 1. trabar, echar trabas a (caballo, etc.). 2. (fig.) trabar, impedir, estorbar, obstaculizar. 3. interceptar (como en una red), pescar con trasmallo.
tramontane [trə'mɑnteɪn, B -'mɔn-] *a.* tramontano, trasmontano; transalpino. —*s.* forastero, extranjero.
tramp [træmp] *v.i.* 1. caminar pesadamente, patullar. 2. vagar, andar sin rumbo, cazcalear, callejear. —*v.t.* 1. hollar, conculcar, pisotear, patear. 2. recorrer a pie, caminar por. —*s.* 1. vago, vagabundo. 2. (fam.) ramera. 3. paseo, caminata. 4. trapa (ruido de pisadas). 5. estoperol, placa de metal para proteger la suela de los zapatos. 6. (mar.) carguero de servicio irregular.
trample ['træmpəl] *v.i.* patullar; **t. on** (o **upon** u **over**), pisotear, ajar (lit. y fig.). —*v.t.* pisotear, hollar. —*s.* 1. pisoteo. 2. ruido de pisadas.
trampler [-plər, B -plə] *s.* pisador, conculcador.
trampoline ['træmpə,lin, B -lɪn] *s.* (dep.) trampolín, cama elástica.
tramp ship, t. steamer, (mar.) carguero de servicio irregular.
tramroad ['træm,roʊd] *s.* (min.) rieles, carriles, vía para vagonetas.
tramway [-,weɪ] *s.* 1. rieles, carriles. 2. (G.B.) tranvía.
trance [træns, B trɑns] *s.* 1. estupor. 2. trance, estado hipnótico. 3. éxtasis, arrobamiento, rapto. —*v.t.* (pr. poét.) extasiar, arrobar.
tranquil ['træŋkwəl] *a.* (TRANQUILER O TRANQUILLER; TRANQUILEST O TRANQUILLEST) tranquilo, quieto, calmo, sosegado, sereno.
tranquility [træŋ'kwɪlətɪ] *s.* tranquilidad, sosiego, calma.
tranquilization [,træŋkwələ'zeɪʃən, B -laɪ-] *s.* aquietamiento.
tranquilize ['træŋkwə,laɪz] *v.t., v.i.* tranquilizar(se), calmar(se), sosegar(se), serenar(se).
tranquilizer [-,laɪzər, B -zə] *s.* tranquilizador, tranquilizante, calmante.
tranquillity, *var. de* **tranquility.**
tranquillize, tranquillizer, *var. de* **tranquilize, tranquilizer.**

tranquilly ['træŋkwəlɪ] *adv.* tranquilamente, sosegadamente, serenamente.
tranquilness [-nəs] *s.* tranquilidad, sosiego, serenidad, calma.
transact [træn'sækt, -'zækt] *v.i.* negociar, traficar, comerciar. —*v.t.* llevar a cabo, ejecutar; gestionar, tramitar.
transaction [-'sækʃən, -'zæk-] *s.* 1. negociación, gestión. 2. transacción, trato, convenio, negocio. 3. (*pl.*) actas, memorias (esp. de sociedades científicas). 4. (der.) transacción.
transactional [-ʃənəl] *a.* de transacción.
transactor [-tər, B -tə] *s.* negociante, comerciante, tramitador, gestor.
transalpine [træns'ælˌpaɪn, trænz-] *a.* transalpino.
transamination [ˌtrænsˌæmə'neɪʃən, ˌtrænz-] *s.* (bioquím., quím.) transaminación.
trans-Andean [ˌtræns'ændɪən, ˌtrænz-] *a.* transandino.
transatlantic [-ət'læntɪk] *a.* transatlántico.
transcalent [træns'keɪlənt] *a.* diatérmano, que permite el paso del calor.
transceiver [træn'sivər, B -və] *s.* radio transmisor-receptor, transceptor.
transcend [-'sɛnd] *v.t.* 1. traspasar, exceder. 2. sobrepasar, superar, sobresalir. 3. (filos., teo.) ser trascendente para (la razón, creencia, etc.). —*v.i.* (filos., teo.) trascender, transcender.
transcendence [-'sɛndəns] **transcendency** [-dənsɪ] *s.* trascendencia, transcendencia.
transcendent [-dənt] *a.* 1. trascendental, extraordinario, sobresaliente. 2. (filos., teo.) trascendente.
transcendental [ˌtrænsˌɛn'dɛntəl] *a.* 1. trascendental, transcendental, extraordinario, sobresaliente. 2. sobrenatural. 3. (filos.) transcendental. 4. (mat.) transcendente.
transcendentalism [-ˌɪzəm] *s.* (filos.) trascendentalismo.
transcendentalist [-əst] *s., a.* trascendentalista.
transcendentally [-əlɪ] *adv.* trascendentalmente.
transcendently [træn'sɛndəntlɪ] *adv.* de manera trascendental, trascendentalmente.
transcontinental [ˌtrænsˌkɑntə'nɛntəl, B -ˌkɔn-] *a.* transcontinental.
transcribe [træn'skraɪb] *v.t.* 1. transcribir (texto, dictado, etc.). 2. (mús.) transcribir, adaptar. 3. (fon.) transcribir, representar (los sonidos) con signos. 4. (rad.) grabar (música, discursos, etc. para la radiodifusión).
transcript ['trænskrɪpt] *s.* trasunto, copia, apógrafo (esp. de documentos).
transcription [træn'skrɪpʃən] *s.* transcripción; (mús.) transcripción; adaptación; (rad.) transcripción, grabación.
transcrystalline [ˌtræns'krɪstələn, trænz-, B -laɪn] *a.* (metal.) transcristalino.
transcutaneous [-kju'teɪnɪəs] *a.* (med.) transcutáneo.
transducer [-'dusər, B -'djusə] *s.* (fís.) transductor.
transect [træn'sɛkt] *v.t.* cortar transversalmente.
transection [-'sɛkʃən] *s.* corte transversal.
transept ['trænˌsɛpt] *s.* (arq.) crucero, transepto; brazo del crucero.
transeptal [træn'sɛptəl] *a.* (arq.) crucero.
transfer [træns'fɜr, B -'fɜ] *v.t.* (*pret., p.p.* TRANSFERRED; *p.pr.* TRANSFERRING) 1. transferir, pasar, trasladar, transbordar. 2. (impr.) reportar. 3. calcar, trasladar (dibujo, etc.). 4. (der.) transferir, traspasar. —*v.i.* cambiar, transbordar (de tren, línea, etc.). — ['trænsˌfɜr, B -fə] *s.* 1. transferencia, traslado, trasposición, transbordo. 2. calcomanía. 3. (der.) transferencia, cesión. 4. (E.U.) billete de transbordo. 5. (f.c.) vía o estación de transbordo.
transferability [ˌtrænsˌfɜrə'bɪlətɪ] *s.* (der.) transferibilidad.
transferable [træns'ɪɜrəbəl] *a.* (der.) transferible, cesible.
transfer crane, (f.c.) grúa de transbordo.
transferee [ˌtrænsfər'i] *s.* cesionario.
transference [træns'fɜrəns, B 'trænsfərəns] *s.* 1. transferencia; entrega, cesión, traspaso, traslación de dominio; traslado. 2. (psic.) trasferencia (de los sentimientos y los deseos).
transferential [ˌtrænsfə'rɛntʃəl, B -'rɛnʃəl] *a.* de traspaso o transferencia.
transferer [træns'fɜrər, B -ə] *s.* (der.) transferidor, cesionista, cedente.
transfer factor, (rad.) factor de propagación.
transfer impedance, (elec.) impedancia de traspaso o de transferencia.
transfer paper, papel de calcar.
transfer switch, (elec.) conmutador.
transfiguration [trænsˌfɪgjə'reɪʃən] *s.* transfiguración, transformación; **T.,** (relig.) Transfiguración (de Jesucristo).
transfigure [-'fɪgjər, B -'fɪgə] *v.t.* 1. transfigurar, transformar. 2. exaltar, idealizar.
transfinite [-'faɪˌnaɪt] *a.* (mat.) transfinito.
transfinite cardinal, (mat.) (número) cardinal transfinito.
transfinite ordinal, (mat.) (número) ordinal transfinito.
transfix [-'fɪks] *v.t.* 1. traspasar, atravesar, espetar. 2. (fig.) paralizar, inmovilizar.
transfixion [-'fɪkʃən] *s.* transfixión.
transform [træns'fɔrm, B -'fɔm] *v.t.* 1. transformar, transfigurar, convertir. 2. (elec., mat.) transformar, trasformar. — ['trænsˌfɔrm, B -ˌfɔm] *s.* 1. (lingüística) una de las reglas para lograr transformaciones gramaticales en oraciones simples. 2. (mat.) proceso o resultado de una transformación matemática.
transformable [-əbəl] *a.* transformable.
transformation [ˌtrænsfər'meɪʃən, B -fə'-] *s.* 1. transformación, conversión. 2. postizo, peluca.
transformative [træns'fɔrmətɪv, B -'fɔmət-] *a.* transformativo.
transformer [-'fɔrmər, B -'fɔmə] *s.* (elec.) transformador.
transformer coil, bobina transformadora.
transformer core, núcleo del transformador.
transformism [-ˌmɪzəm] *s.* (biol.) transformismo.
transformist [-məst] *a., s.* (biol.) transformista.
transformistic [ˌtrænsfər'mɪstɪk, B -fə'-] *a.* transformista.
transfusable [træns'fjuzəbəl] *a.* transfusible.
transfuse [træns'fjuz] *v.t.* 1. transfundir, transvasar, decantar, trasegar. 2. impregnar. 3. (med.) hacer una transfusión de (ej. sangre); (med.) hacer una transfusión a (una persona).
transfuser [-'fjuzər, B -zə] *s.* transfusor.
transfusible [-zəbəl] *a.* transfusible.
transfusion [-ʒən] *s.* transfusión, trasiego; (med.) transfusión (de sangre).
transgress [træns'grɛs, trænz-] *v.t.* 1. transgredir, violar, quebrantar, infringir. 2. traspasar (límites, fronteras, etc.). —*v.i.* 1. infringir o transgredir la ley; pesar. 2. propasarse, excederse, extralimitarse.
transgression [-'grɛʃən] *s.* 1. transgresión, infracción. 2. pecado.
transgressive [-'grɛsɪv] *a.* transgresivo.
transgressor [-'grɛsər, B -ə] *s.* 1. transgresor, infractor. 2. pecador.
transhumance [-'hjuməns, B træns-] *s.* trashumación.
transhumant [-mənt] *a.* trashumante.
transience ['træntʃəns, B -zɪəns] **transiency** [-tʃənsɪ, B zɪən-] *s.* (*pl.* TRANSIENCIES) transitoriedad.
transient [-tʃənt, B -zɪənt] *a.* 1. pasajero, transitorio, momentáneo, efímero. 2. transeúnte. 3. (fís.) transiente. 4. (mús.) de enlace (díc. de una modulación no esencial). —*s.* 1. transeúnte, huésped pasajero. 2. (fís.) fenómeno transiente; sonido transiente. 3. (elec.) oscilación momentánea.
transient current, (elec.) corriente momentánea.
transiently [-lɪ] *adv.* temporalmente, transitoriamente, de paso.
transientness [-nəs] *s.* transitoriedad.
transient voltage, (elec.) tensión momentánea o transitoria.
transilluminate [ˌtrænsə'luməˌneɪt, ˌtrænz-, B -'lju-] *v.t.* iluminar por transparencia, pasar luz a través de (un órgano para examen médico).
transillumination [-əˌlumə'neɪʃən, B -ˌlju-] *s.* transiluminación.
transistor [-'ɪstər, B -tə] *s.* (electrón.) transistor.
transistorize [-təˌraɪz] *v.t.* (electrón.) transistorizar.
transistor radio, radio a transistores.
transit ['trænsət, -zət] *s.* 1. tránsito; paso, pasaje. 2. conducción, transporte. 3. transición. 4. (astr.) tránsito; culminación. 5. (top.) tránsito. 6. **in t.,** de tránsito, en tránsito, de paso. —*v.t.* 1. atravesar, pasar por, transitar por. 2. (fig.) invertir (el anteojo del teodolito de tránsito). —*v.i.* transitar.
transit instrument, 1. (astr.) anteojo meridiano. 2. (top.) teodolito de tránsito.
transition [træns'ɪʃən, trænz-, B træn'sɪʒən] *s.* 1. transición. 2. (mús.) transición (esp. modulación transitoria); cambio (repentino) de llave.
transitional [-əl] *a.* de transición.
transitive ['trænsətɪv, -zə-] *a.* 1. transitivo, transitorio. 2. (gram.) transitivo, activo (verbo). —*s.* (gram.) verbo transitivo.
transitively [-lɪ] *adv.* transitivamente.
transitiveness [-nəs] *s.* carácter transitivo.
transitman ['trænsətmən, -zət-] (f.c.) encargado del tránsito.
transitorily [ˌtrænsə'tɔrəlɪ, -zə-, B 'trænsɪtər-] *adv.* transitoriamente.
transitoriness ['trænsəˌtɔrɪnəs, -zə-, B -tər-] *s.* transitoriedad.
transitory [-ˌtɔrɪ, B -tərɪ] *a.* transitorio.
transit theodolite, (top.) teodolito de tránsito.
Trans-Jordan [træns'dʒɔrdən, trænz-, B -'dʒɔdən] *s.* antiguo nombre de Jordania, Transjordania.
translatable [-'leɪtəbəl] *a.* traducible.
translate [-'leɪt] *v.t.* 1. traducir, descifrar. 2. cambiar, transformar. 3. transferir, trasladar. 4. transportar, arrobar, embelesar. 5. (relig.) trasladar (obispo de una sede a otra). 6. (teleg.) retransmitir (por relevador). 7. (mec.) impartir movimiento de traslación a. —*v.i.* 1. prestarse a traducción, ser traducible (bien, mal, etc.). 2. actuar como traductor.
translation [-'leɪʃən] *s.* 1. traducción; versión. 2. traslación, remoción (de restos, etc.). 3. (mec.) traslación. 4. (teleg.) retransmisión (automática por relevador).

translational [-əl] *a.* (mec.) de traslación.
translative [-'leɪtɪv] *a.* 1. traslativo, trasladante. 2. de traducciones, traductor.
translator [-'leɪtər, B -ə] *s.* traductor, intérprete.
transliterate [-'lɪtəˌreɪt] *v.t.* trasliterar, representar los sonidos de una lengua con las letras de otra.
transliteration [ˌtrænsˌlɪtə'reɪʃən, ˌtrænz-] *s.* trasliteración.
translucence [træns'lusəns, trænz-] **translucency** [-ənsɪ] *s.* translucidez.
translucent [-ənt] *a.* translúcido.
translucently [-lɪ] *adv.* con translucidez, translucidamente.
translucid [træns'lusəd, trænz-] *a.* translúcido.
translunar [-'lunər, B -nə] *a.* translunar.
transmarine [-mə'rin] *a.* transmarino, ultramarino (región, ruta, pueblo, etc.).
transmigrate [-'maɪˌgreɪt, B -maɪ'greɪt] *v.i.* transmigrar.
transmigration [-maɪ'greɪʃən] *s.* transmigración.
transmigrator [-'maɪˌgreɪtər, B -maɪ'greɪtə] *s.* transmigrador.
transmigratory [-'maɪgrəˌtɔrɪ, B -tərɪ] *a.* transmigrador.
transmissibility [-ˌmɪsə'bɪlətɪ] *s.* transmisibilidad.
transmissible [-'mɪsəbəl] *a.* transmisible.
transmission [træns'mɪʃən, trænz-] *s.* 1. transmisión. 2. (aut.) transmisión, cambio de velocidades; caja de cambio o de engranajes. 3. (rad.) transmisión.
transmission assembly, (aut.) conjunto de la transmisión.
transmission belt, correa transmisora, banda de transmisión.
transmission case, caja de transmisión, caja de velocidades.
transmission factor, coeficiente de transmisión.
transmission gear engranaje de transmisión.
transmissive [-'mɪsɪv] *a.* transmisor, transmisible.
transmit [-'mɪt] *v.t.* (*pret., p.p.* TRANSMITTED; *p.pr.* TRANSMITTING) 1. transmitir, remitir. 2. transmitir (enfermedad, cualidades). 3. conducir (calor, luz, corriente, etc.). 4. (rad., t.v.) transmitir (señal).
transmittable [-əbəl] *a.* transmisible.
transmittance [-əns] *s.* 1. transmisión. 2. (fís., rad.) transmitencia.
transmitter [-ər, B -ə] *s.* (rad., teleg., t.v.) transmisor.
transmitting antenna, (rad.) antena de transmisión, antena transmisora.
transmitting set, (rad.) aparato transmisor.
transmitting station, (rad.) estación transmisora o emisora.
transmogrification [ˌtrænsˌmɑgrəfə'keɪʃən, ˌtrænz-, B -mɔg-] *s.* (hum.) transformación mágica.
transmogrify [-'mɑgrəˌfaɪ, B -'mɔg-] *v.t.* (*pret., p.p.* TRANSMOGRIFIED; *p.pr.* TRANSMOGRIFYING) (hum.) transformar (como por encanto o magia).
transmontane [-'mɑnˌteɪn, B -'mɔn-] *a.* transmontano.
transmutability [-ˌmjutə'bɪlətɪ] *s.* transmutabilidad.
transmutable [-'mjutəbəl] *a.* transmutable, trasmutable.
transmutableness [-nəs] *s.* transmutabilidad.
transmutably [-'mjutəblɪ] *adv.* transmutablemente.
transmutation [-mju'teɪʃən] *s.* (fís., quím., alquimia) trasmutación, transmutación; (biol.) transformismo.
transmutative [-'mjutətɪv] *a.* transmutativo, transmutativo.
transmute [-'mjut] *v.t., v.i.* (quím., fís.) transmutar.
transmuter [-ər, B -ə] *s.* transmutador.
transoceanic [ˌtrænsˌoʊʃɪ'ænɪk, B 'trænz-] *a.* transoceánico.
transom ['trænsəm] *s.* 1. travesaño, durmiente, dintel. 2. barra horizontal (de una cruz, horca, etc.). 3. (arq.) montante, lumbre. 4. (mar.) yugo (de popa).
transonic [træn'sɑnɪk, B -'sɔn-] *a.* (fís.) transónico.
transpacific [ˌtrænspə'sɪfɪk] *a.* transpacífico.
transpadane ['trænspəˌdeɪn] *a.* (geog.) transpadano.
transparence [træns'pærəns, B -'pɛər-] **transparency** [-ənsɪ] *s.* (*pl.* TRANSPARENCIES) 1. transparencia, diafanidad. 2. transparente (para letreros). 3. (foto.) diapositiva.
transparent [-ənt] *a.* 1. transparente, translúcido. 2. (poét.) luminoso, brillante. 3. (fig.) transparente, obvio; franco, cándido.
transparently [-lɪ] *adv.* de modo transparente, transparentemente.
transpicuous [-'pɪkjʊəs] *a.* transparente.
transpierce [-'pɪrs, B -'pɪəs] *v.t.* atravesar, traspasar; penetrar.
transpiration [ˌtrænspə'reɪʃən] *s.* transpiración; (bot.) transpiración.
transpiratory [-'spaɪrəˌtɔrɪ, B -'spaɪərətərɪ] *a.* (bot.) transpiratorio.
transpire [træns'paɪr, B -'paɪə] *v.t.* transpirar. —*v.i.* 1. transpirar, rezumarse. 2. trascender, traslucirse. 3. (fam.) acontecer, suceder. 4. revelarse, dejar ver, dejar conocer, llegar a saberse (por indicios).
transplacental [ˌtrænsplə'sɛntəl] *a.* (med.) transplacentario.
transplant [træns'plænt, B -'plɑnt] *v.t.* 1. trasplantar. 2. (fig.) trasladar, trasplantar (a otro país). 3. (med.) trasplantar. — ['trænsˌplænt, B -plɑnt] *s.* trasplante.
transplantable [-əbəl] *a.* trasplantable.
transplantation [ˌtrænsˌplæn'teɪʃən, B -plɑn-] *s.* trasplante.
transplanter [træns'plæntər, B -'plɑntə] *s.* trasplantador (persona o instrumento).
transponder [-'pɑndər, B -'pɔndə] *s.* radiofaro de respuesta.
transpontine [-'pɑnˌtaɪn, B -'pɔn-] *a.* del otro lado del puente; (G.B.) de la parte sur del Támesis (en Londres).
transport [træns'pɔrt, B -'pɔt] *v.t.* 1. transportar, acarrear. 2. (fig.) arrebatar. 3. (hist.) deportar, desterrar (criminal a colonia penal). ['trænsˌpɔrt, B -pɔt] *s.* 1. transporte, transportación, conducción, acarreo. 2. arrobamiento, rapto; arranque, acceso, ej., *in a t. of rage,* en un arranque de cólera. 3. buque o avión de transporte. 4. transporte, movilidad.
transportability [ˌtrænsˌpɔrtə'bɪlətɪ, B -ˌpɔt-] *s.* capacidad de ser transportado, transportabilidad.
transportable [-'pɔrtəbəl, B -'pɔt-] *a.* transportable.
transportation [ˌtrænspər'teɪʃən, B -pɔ'-] 1. transportación, transporte, conducción, acarreo. 2. (hist.) deportación (a colonia penal).
transporter [træns'pɔrtər, B -'pɔtə] *s.* transportador, porteador.
transporter bridge, puente transbordador.
transporting [-ɪŋ] *a.* 1. transportador, de transporte. 2. arrebatador.
transposal [-'poʊzəl] *s.* transposición.
transpose [-'poʊz] *v.t.* 1. transponer. 2. (mat.) transponer (ej., un término de una ecuación). 3. (mús.) transportar a otra llave u otro tono. 4. (raro) transferir, transportar.
transposer [-'poʊzər, B -'poʊzə] *s.* transponedor.
transposition [ˌtrænspə'zɪʃən] *s.* 1. transposición, traspuesta. 2. (mat.) transposición. 3. (mús.) transportación, transporte.
transputer [træns'pjutər] *s.* (comput.) transputor.
trans-Pyrenean [trænsˌpɪrɪ'niən] *a.* transpirenaico.
transsexual [træns˛sɛkʃuəl] *a., s.* transexual.
transship [-'ʃɪp] *v.t.* transbordar.
transshipment [-mənt] *s.* transbordo.
trans-Siberian ['trænssaɪ'bɪrɪən, B -'bɪər-] *a* transiberiano.
transubstantiate [ˌtrænsəb'stæntʃɪˌeɪt, B -'stænʃɪ-] *v.t.* transubstanciar(se).
transubstantiation [-ˌstæntʃɪ'eɪʃən, B -ˌstænʃɪ-] *s.* (teo.) transubstanciación.
transudate [træn'sudət, B -'sjud-] *s.* (med.) trasudado.
transudation [ˌtrænˌsu'deɪʃən, B -ˌsju-] *s.* trasudación.
transude [træn'sud, B -'sjud] *v.i.* trasudarse, trazumarse, rezumarse.
transuranium [ˌtrænsjə'reɪnɪəm] **transuranic** [-'rænɪk] *a.* (quím.) transuranio, transuránico.
transvaluate [træns'væljʊˌeɪt, trænz-] *v.t.* volver a valuar (sobre una base diferente).
transvaluation [-ˌvæljʊ'eɪʃən] *s.* nueva valuación o valoración (hecha sobre una base distinta).
transvase [-'veɪs] *v.t.* transvasar.
transversal [-'vɜrsəl, B -'vɜsəl] *a.* transversal. —*s.* (geom.) línea transversal.
transversally [-səlɪ] *adv.* transversalmente.
transverse ['trænsˌvɜrs, 'trænz-, B -vɜs] *s.* 1. travesaño, pieza transversa. 2. (anat.) músculo transverso. 3. (geom.) eje transverso. — [træns'vɜrs, trænz-, B -'vɜs] *a.* transverso.
transverse colon, (anat.) colon transverso.
transversely [træns'vɜrslɪ, trænz-, B -'vɜslɪ] *adv.* en forma transversa, atravesando, transversalmente.
transverse section, (dib.) sección o corte transversal.
transvestism [-'vɛsˌtɪzəm] *s.* (med.) transvestismo, transvestitismo.
transvestite [-ˌtaɪt] *s.* transvestita.
Transylvanian [ˌtrænsəl'veɪnɪən] *a.* transilvano, de Transilvania (región de Rumania).
trap [træp] *s.* 1. trampa, armadijo, garlito, cepo, red, lazo. 2. (fig.) trampa, artimaña, ardid. 3. escotillón. 4. coche ligero de dos ruedas. 5. (mús.) (*gen. pl.*) instrumento(s) de percusión (de la orquesta). 6. (dep.) lanzaplatos, lanzadiscos (para disparar pichones de barro). 7. (golf) obstáculo (de arena). 8. (mec.) sifón, tubo en U (para obturación hidráulica); bombillo inodoro, sifón de tubería sanitaria. 9. (jer.) pico, boca; **to shut one's t.,** cerrar el pico. 10. **to fall into a t.,** caer en la trampa; **to spring a t.,** hacer saltar una trampa. —*v.t.* (*pret., p.p.* TRAPPED; *p.pr.* TRAPPING) 1. coger en la trampa, entrampar; atrapar. 2. proveer de una trampa o trampas. 3. proveer de sifones. —*v.i.* armar trampas (para la caza); cazar con trampas.
trap, *s.* 1. (*pl.*) (fam.) equipaje, bártulos; pertenencias personales. 2. (ant.) jaez, adorno de las caballerías. —*v.t.* adornar, enjaezar (caballos, etc.).

trap, *s.* (geol.) roca trapeana.
trapdoor ['træp'dɔr, B -'dɔ] *s.* trampa; (teat.) escotillón, pescante; (min.) puerta de ventilación.
trapeze [træ'piz, B trə-] *s.* trapecio (de gimnasia o circo).
trapeze artist, gimnasta de trapecio; trapecista, volatinero.
trapezial [-'pizɪəl] *a.* (geom.) trapecial.
trapeziform [-zəˌfɔrm, B -ˌfɔm] *a.* trapezoidal.
trapezist [-zəst] *s.* gimnasta de trapecio; trapecista, volatinero.
trapezium [-zɪəm] *s.* (*pl.* TRAPEZIUMS O TRAPEZIA [-ə]) 1. (geom., E.U.) trapezoide; (G.B.) trapecio. 2. (anat.) (hueso) trapecio.
trapezius [-zɪəs] *s.* (anat.) trapecio.
trapezohedron [trəˌpizoʊ'hidrən, B ˌtræpə-] *s.* trapezoedro.
trapezoid ['træpəˌzɔɪd] *s.* 1. (geom., E.U.) trapecio, (G.B.) trapezoide. 2. (anat.) (hueso) trapezoide.
trapezoid, trapezoidal [ˌtræpə'zɔɪdəl] *a.* (geom., E.U.) trapecial; (G.B.) trapezoidal.
trapper ['træpər, B -ə] *s.* trampero, cazador de pieles.
trappings [-ɪŋz] *s.* (*gen. pl.*) 1. jaeces, arreos, aderezos (de las caballerías). 2. adornos, atavíos.
Trappist ['træpəst] *s.* (relig.) trapense.
trapse, *var. de* **traipse.**
trapshooter ['træpˌʃutər, B -ə] *s.* (dep.) tirador de tiro al platillo o al plato.
trapshooting [-ɪŋ] *s.* (dep.) tiro al platillo, tiro de pichón.
trap shot, (tenis) (golpe de) medio voleo.
trash [træʃ] *s.* 1. basura, desecho, desperdicio. 2. hojarasca, paja, broza. 3. cachivache, trasto. 4. (fig.) hojarasca, disparate, tontería, patarata. 5. quídam; gentuza, canalla. 6. bagazo (de caña). —*v.t.* podar, escamondar; desbrozar (esp. caña de azúcar).
trash, *v.t.* (ant.) poner trabanco a (un perro). —*s.* (dial., G.B.) trabanco, trangallo, tramojo.
trash can, basurero, cubo de la basura, tacho de basura (Amer.).
trashiness ['træʃɪnəs] *s.* mala calidad.
trashrack [-ˌræk] *s.* rejilla coladera, rejilla para impedir la entrada de cuerpos extraños en una tubería.
trashy [-ɪ] *a.* (TRASHIER; TRASHIEST) 1. baladí, fútil; malo, de mala calidad. 2. despreciable, vil.
trauma ['traʊmə, B 'trɔmə] *s.* (*pl.* TRAUMATA [-mətə] O TRAUMAS) (med.) trauma, lesión.
traumatic [trə'mætɪk, B trɔ-] *a.* (med.) traumático.
traumatism ['traʊməˌtɪzəm, B 'trɔ-] *s.* (med.) traumatismo, traumatosis.
traumatize [-ˌtaɪz] *v.t.* 1. (med.) lesionar, herir (esp. durante una operación quirúrgica). 2. (psic.) traumatizar.
travail [trə'veɪl, B 'trævˌeɪl] *s.* 1. dolores de parto. 2. afán, fatiga. 3. congoja, dolor, tormento. —*v.i.* 1. sufrir los dolores del parto. 2. fatigarse, afanarse.
trave [treɪv] *s.* (arq.) viga transversal, travesaño.
travel ['trævəl] *v.i.* (*pret., p.p.* TRAVELED O TRAVELLED; *p.pr.* TRAVELING O TRAVELLING) 1. viajar. 2. pasar, moverse, correr. 3. hacer viajes (vendedor comercial); (t. con *for*) ser viajante (de una firma). 4. (mec.) (con *along, in,* etc.) correr (por, en, etc.). 5. (jer.) ir o moverse rápidamente. 6. (dial.) andar, caminar. 7. **t. light,** viajar con poco equipaje; **t. in style,** viajar de lujo. —*v.t.* viajar por (país, región, etc.); recorrer, cubrir (distancia); conducir, arrear (rebaño, ganado, etc.). —*s.* 1. viaje. 2. tráfico, movimiento. 3. (*pl.*) descripciones de viajes, ej., *she likes to read about my travels,* a ella le gusta leer descripciones de mis viajes. 4. (mec.) recorrido, carrera, corrida, movimiento (ej., de un pistón); desplazamiento.
travel agency, t. bureau, agencia de viajes.
travel agent, agente de viajes.
traveled, travelled [-əld] *a.* 1. que ha viajado mucho. 2. trillado, muy frecuentado (camino). 3. (geol.) errático.
traveler, traveller [-ələr, B -lə] *s.* 1. viajero; viajante; turista. 2. (mec.) corredera; carretilla, artefacto movible. 3. (mar.) racamento, raca.
traveler's check, cheque de viajero, cheque de turista.
traveler's joy, (bot.) hierba de los lazarosos, hierba de los pordioseros.
traveler's tale, patraña, cuento, invención.
traveling ['trævəlɪŋ] *a.* 1. de viaje, para viajes; para viajar. 2. viajero; viajante. 3. (mec.) corredizo, móvil, ambulante, desplazable. —*s.* (cine) travelín.
traveling bag, t. case, maleta de viaje, maletín.
traveling crane, grúa corrediza, puentegrúa, grúa de puente.
traveling expenses, gastos de viaje, viáticos.
traveling salesman, agente viajero, viajante (de comercio).
traveling speed, (mec.) velocidad de traslación, velocidad de marcha.
travel mechanism, mecanismo de avance.
travelogue, travelog ['trævəˌlɔg, -ˌlɑg, B -lɔg] *s.* narración de un viaje; película documental sobre un viaje.
traversable [trə'vɜrsəbəl, B -'vɜs-] *a.* 1. atravesable. 2. (der.) negable, contestable.
traverse [trə'vɜrs, B 'trævəs] *v.t.* 1. cruzar, recorrer, caminar o pasar por, atravesar. 2. estorbar, impedir; contrariar, frustrar. 3. examinar o escudriñar con cuidado; discutir a fondo (un tema). 4. (der.) negar, oponerse a, impugnar. 5. trasladar, mover o girar lateral o transversalmente. 6. (carp.) cepillar de través. —*v.i.* 1. atravesarse; cruzarse; hacer vaivén, moverse de un lado a otro; caminar; ir de un sitio a otro. 2. girar, dar vueltas. 3. (top.) trazar una poligonal, trazar un itinerario. — ['trævərs, B -əs] *s.* 1. travesaño, travesero, crucero, traviesa. 2. paso, pasaje, travesía (de una distancia). 3. camino oblicuo, curso en zigzag. 4. (der.) negación, impugnación, objeción legal. 5. (mec.) giro o movimiento lateral; carrera, juego. 6. (fort.) traversa, través. 7. (top.) línea quebrada; línea transversal. —*a.* transversal; atravesado, cruzado. —*adv.* (ant.) de través, en sentido transversal.
traverse board, (mar.) rosa naútica o de los vientos.
traverse circle, (fort.) círculo en que se mueve la cureña.
traverse drill, taladro de ajuste lateral, taladro ranurador.
traverse feed, (mec.) avance lateral.
traverse fire, (mil.) fuego cruzado.
traverse jury, (der.) jurado (de juicio).
traverse line, (top.) poligonal.
traverser [trə'vɜrsər, B 'trævəsə] *s.* 1. (der.) negante, negador. 2. (f.c.) transbordador, transportador (mecanismo o dispositivo). 3. correa transportadora.
traverse shaper, limadora de cabeza móvil.
traverse survey, (top.) trazado de una poligonal, poligonación, itinerario.
traverse table, (top., mar.) tabla de coordenadas de longitud y latitud.
travertine ['trævərˌtin, B -vətɪn] **travertin** [-tən] *s.* (min.) travertino (mármol italiano).
travesty ['trævəstɪ] *s.* (*pl.* TRAVESTIES) parodia, farsa, imitación burlesca, caricatura. —*v.t.* (*pret., p.p.* TRAVESTIED; *p.pr.* TRAVESTYING) parodiar, imitar grotescamente.
travois [trə'vɔɪ] **travoise** [-'vɔɪz] *s.* (*pl.* TRAVOIS O TRAVOISES) rastra primitiva, narria (de los indios de N. América).
trawl [trɔl] *s.* 1. red barredera, jábega, boliche. 2. (t. **t.-line**) palangre. —*v.t., v.i.* pescar a la rastra o rastreando.
trawler ['trɔlər, B -ə] *s.* 1. jabeguero; palangrero. 2. jábega (barco de pesca rastreador).
tray [treɪ] *s.* 1. bandeja, salvilla; platillo (de balanza); cajón, gaveta (de ropero, baúl, etc.). 2. (dial.) artesa, cubeta, cuba.
treacherous ['trɛtʃərəs] *a.* traicionero, traidor, alevoso, pérfido; engañoso, falaz.
treacherously [-lɪ] *adv.* traidoramente, alevosamente, a traición.
treacherousness [-nəs] *s.* alevosía, carácter traicionero; perfidia, falsedad.
treachery ['trɛtʃərɪ] *s.* traición; perfidia, felonía, falsedad.
treacle ['trikəl] *s.* 1. (pr. G.B.) melaza, melado, meladura. 2. (hist.) triaca.
treacly [-kəlɪ] *a.* 1. melado. 2. (fig.) dulzarrón, empalagoso.
tread [trɛd] *v.t.* (*pret.* TROD, [trɑd, B trɔd]; *p.p.* TRODDEN ['trɑdən, B 'trɔdən] O TROD; *p.pr.* TREADING) 1. pisar, hollar. 2. (gen. con *down*) pisotear, patullar; (fig.) pisotear, abrumar, aplastar, oprimir. 3. cubrir (distancia) pisando; andar por (camino, etc.). 4. pisar, cubrir (el gallo a la gallina). 5. (aut.) reencauchar (neumático). 6. **t. back,** desandar; **t. the stage** (o **boards**), ser actor; **t. water,** pedalear en el agua (para mantenerse a flote). —*v.i.* 1. andar, caminar; moverse (a pie), poner el pie; dar un paso, dar pasos. 2. juntarse, copularse (las aves). 3. **t. in someone's (foot) steps,** (fig.) seguir los pasos (o el ejemplo) de otro; **t. lightly,** (fig.) ir con tiento, mirar donde se pisa; **t. on** (o **upon**), hollar, pisar; **t. on air,** (fig.) estar muy contento, transportarse de gozo; **t. on eggs,** (fig.) andar pisando huevos, proceder con suma cautela; **t. on the heels of,** pisarle los talones a; **t. on (someone's) toes,** (fig.) ofender a (alguien); **where angels fear to t.,** donde los ángeles no se aventuran a pisar (situación o lugar difícil de vencer). —*s.* 1. pisada, huella (en el suelo, tierra, etc.). 2. piso, paso, pisada. 3. suela (del zapato o estribo); cara, llanta, estrías (de rueda, neumático, etc.). 4. escalón o peldaño (de escalera). 5. galladura, chalaza (del huevo). 6. anchura de vía, trocha (de vehículos).
treadle ['trɛdəl] *s.* (mec.) cárcola, pedal. —*v.i.* pedalear, operar un pedal.
treadmill [-ˌmɪl] *s.* 1. molino de rueda de andar. 2. (fig.) noria, tráfago, rutina.
treas. *abrev de* **treasurer,** tesorero.
treason ['trizən] *s.* 1. alta traición. 2. traición, deslealtad (a una causa, amigo, etc.); perfidia.
treasonable [-əbəl] *a.* traicionero, traidor.
treasonably [-əblɪ] *adv.* traidoramente, cometiendo alta traición.
treasonous [-əs] *a.* traicionero, traidor.
treasurable ['trɛʒərəbəl] *a.* apreciable, precioso.
treasure ['trɛʒər, B -ə] *s.* 1. tesoro, caudal. 2. (fig.) tesoro, preciosidad. —*v.t.* 1. tesorar; acumular (riquezas). 2. apreciar mucho, guardar como un tesoro (esp. en la memoria).

treasure house, (fig.) mina (de noticias, información, etc.).
treasure hunt, caza del tesoro.
treasurer [-ərər, B -ərə] *s.* tesorero, tesorera.
treasurership [-ərˌʃɪp, B -əʃɪp] *s.* tesorería.
treasure-trove ['trɛʒərˌtroʊv, B -əˌ-] *s.* 1. (der.) tesoro hallado, tapado (Amer.). 2. (fig.) descubrimiento valioso.
treasury [-ərɪ] *s.* 1. tesorería. 2. tesoro (público), erario, fisco; ministerio de hacienda. 3. (fig.) tesoro; (libro de datos, información, etc.).
Treasury Department, (E.U.) Ministerio de Hacienda.
treasury note, (E.U.) bono fiscal (para el pago de impuestos, derechos, etc.).
treasury stock, (com.) acciones en caja, acciones amortizadas, acciones de tesorería.
treat [trit] *v.i.* 1. (con *with*) negociar, tratar (con). 2. (con *of*) tratar (de, sobre), versar (sobre). 3. dar o pagar un convite. —*v.t.* 1. tratar (alguna materia, tema, etc.); (gen. con *as*) considerar, tomar (en broma, etc.). 2. tratar (a persona, cosa), dar (buen o mal) trato a. 3. convidar, invitar. 4. tratar, atender (a los enfermos); curar, dar tratamiento a (una enfermedad, mal, etc.). 5. (quím.) tratar (una substancia). 6. **t. oneself to,** permitirse el placer de, darse el lujo de; **t. (someone) to,** convidar (a alguien) a (cenar, etc.); convidar (a alguien) con (algo), ej., *I'll t. you to an ice cream,* te convido a un helado. —*s.* 1. obsequio, agasajo, convite, convidada. 2. solaz, placer, deleite.
treatable ['tritəbəl] *a.* tratable, curable (enfermedad, dolencia, etc.).
treater [-ər, B -ə] *s.* tratador, negociador.
treatise ['tritəs, B -ɪz] *s.* 1. tratado (libro, escrito). 2. (ant.) relación, narración.
treatment ['tritmənt] *s.* 1. trato, tratamiento. 2. régimen; terapéutica.
treaty ['tritɪ] *s.* (*pl.* TREATIES) tratado, pacto, convenio, trato; **to sign a t.,** firmar un convenio o tratado.
treaty port, puerto abierto (por tratado) al comercio extranjero.
treble ['trɛbəl] *a.* 1. triple, triplo, tríplice, tresdoble. 2. (mús.) de tiple, atiplado, sobreagudo. —*s.* 1. (mús.) tiple, soprano. 2. tono atiplado, voz aguda. 3. (rad.) (tonos) agudos. —*v.t.* triplicar. —*v.i.* 1. triplicarse. 2. cantar tiple o soprano.
treble clef, (mús.) clave de sol.
treble staff, (mús.) pentagrama que lleva la clave de sol.
trebly ['trɛblɪ] *adv.* tres veces, triplicadamente, triplemente.
trebuchet [ˌtrɛbə'ʃɛt, B -jə-] **trebucket** ['triˌbʌkət, B 'trɛ-] *s.* (hist.) especie de catapulta.
tredecillion [ˌtridɪ'sɪljən] *s.* (E.U.) unidad seguida de 42 ceros; (G.B.) unidad seguida de 78 ceros.
tree [tri] *s.* 1. árbol. 2. palo, madero, garrote, estaca, poste. 3. (ant.) La Cruz. 4. horca. 5. **at the top of the t.,** (fig.) en la cumbre de su profesión; **to bark up the wrong t.,** (fig.) estar despistado, seguir una pista errada; **up a t.,** (fam.) entre la espada y la pared, en un aprieto. —*v.t.* 1. hacer refugiarse en un árbol (a una persona o animal). 2. (fig.) poner en aprieto, arrinconar. 3. poner (zapato) en horma.
tree cactus, (bot.) pitahaya.
tree climber, (orn.) trepatroncos.
tree crab, (zool.) cangrejo de los cocoteros.
tree fern, (bot.) helecho arbóreo, helecho arborescente.
tree frog, (zool.) rana arbórea, rana de San Antonio, calamite.
tree heath, (bot.) (especie de) brezo con flores blancas.
treeless ['triləs] *a.* sin árboles.
tree line, límite de la vegetación arbórea.
treenail ['triˌneɪl] *s.* clavija, espiga, tarugo.
tree of heaven, (bot.) árbol del cielo, ailanto, barniz del Japón, maque.
tree of knowledge, (bíbl.) árbol de la ciencia del bien y del mal.
tree of life, (bíbl.) árbol de la vida.
tree pruner, podador de árboles.
tree shrew, (zool.) tupaya.
tree stump, tocón.
tree surgeon, curador de árboles, persona especializada en el cuidado de los árboles.
tree surgery, curación de los árboles (por medio de cortes).
tree toad, (zool.) rana arbórea, rana de San Antonio.
treetop ['triˌtɑp, B -tɔp] *s.* copa (de árbol); (*pl.*) cima de árboles.
tree trunk, tronco de un árbol.
treflé, treflée [trɛf'leɪ] **trefly** ['trɛflɪ] *a.* (her.) trebolado.
trefoil ['triˌfɔɪl, B 'trɛfɔɪl] *s.* 1. (bot.) trifolio, trébol. 2. (arq.) trifolio.
trefoil arch, (arq.) arco trebolado.
trehalose [trɪ'hɑlˌoʊs] *s.* (quím.) trehalosa.
treillage ['treɪlɪdʒ] *s.* emparrado, varaseto (para enredaderas); enrejado, espaldera.
trek [trɛk] *v.t.* (*pret., p.p.* TREKKED; *p.pr.* TREKKING) (pr. África del S.) tirar, arrastrar. —*v.i.* 1. (pr. África del S.) viajar en carromato. 2. mudarse, trasladarse. 3. hacer una caminata o recorrido fatigoso; avanzar lenta y laboriosamente. —*s.* 1. (pr. África del S.) viaje en carromato. 2. migración; jornada, viaje (esp. largo o arduo); caminata, recorrido fatigoso.
trellis ['trɛləs] *s.* enrejado, varaseto, espaldera. —*v.t.* 1. hacer trepar (plantas) en una espaldera. 2. proveer de espaldera. 3. entrelazar, entretejer.
trellised [-əst] *a.* provisto de espaldera.
trelliswork [-əsˌwɜrk, B -wɜk] *s.* enrejado, varaseto.
trematode ['trɛməˌtoʊd] *s.* (ento.) trematode, trematodo.
tremble ['trɛmbəl] *v.i.* 1. temblar, estremecerse, vibrar; tiritar (de frío). 2. (fig.) temblar, trepidar (de miedo, ansiedad, etc.), ej., *I t. at the idea,* la (sola) idea me hace temblar. —*s.* 1. temblor, estremecimiento. 2. (*pl.*) (vet.) tembladera (del ganado).
trembler [-blər, B -blə] *s.* (elec.) temblador; interruptor intermitente.
tremblingly [-blɪŋlɪ] *adv.* trémulamente.
trembly [-blɪ] *a.* (fam.) tembleque, temblón, trémulo.
tremendous [trɪ'mɛndəs] *a.* 1. tremendo, formidable, asombroso. 2. (fam.) tremendo, enorme, extraordinario.
tremendously [-lɪ] *adv.* enormemente, extremadamente.
tremolant ['trɛmələnt] *s.* registro de trémolo (en el órgano).
tremolite ['trɛməˌlaɪt] *s.* (min.) tremolita.
tremolo ['trɛməˌloʊ] *s.* (*pl.* TREMOLOS) (mús.) trémolo.
tremor ['trɛmər, B -ə] *s.* 1. tremor, temblor. 2. estremecimiento, vibración, trepidación. 3. (fig.) emoción nerviosa, conmoción.
tremulant [-jələnt] *a.* tremulante, tremulento, trémulo.
tremulous [-ləs] *a.* 1. trémulo, tembloroso. 2. tímido, temeroso.
tremulously [-lɪ] *adv.* trémulamente.
tremulousness [-nəs] *s.* timidez, ansiedad.
trench [trɛntʃ] *v.t.* 1. tallar, grabar. 2. surcar, zanjar. 3. atrincherar. —*v.i.* 1. abrirse camino (un torrente de lava, etc.). 2. hacer trincheras; atrincherarse. 3. **t. on** (o **upon**), (fig.) invadir, abusar de; lindar con, rayar en. —*s.* 1. foso, fosa, canal, cuneta, zanja; acequia, cauce. 2. (mil.) trinchera. 3. fosa submarina.
trenchancy ['trɛntʃənsɪ] *s.* 1. agudeza. 2. mordacidad.
trenchant [-tʃənt] *a.* 1. incisivo, agudo, penetrante. 2. mordaz, cáustico (lenguaje, estilo, crítica, etc.). 3. nítido, bien definido.
trenchantly [-lɪ] *adv.* 1. agudamente, con penetración. 2. mordazmente, cáusticamente. 3. nítidamente.
trench coat, trinchera, impermeable.
trench digger, (maq.) excavadora de zanjas.
trenched [trɛntʃt] *a.* 1. con surcos o canales. 2. (mil.) provisto de trincheras.
trencher ['trɛntʃər, B -tʃə] *s.* 1. plato trinchero; tabla para rebanar la carne asada. 2. (ant.) cuchillo; trinchante. 3. zanjadora (máquina). 4. el que abre zanjas o fosos.
trencherman [-mən] *s.* 1. persona que tiene buen diente, que come con fruición. 2. (ant.) parásito, gorrón.
trench fever, (med.) fiebre de las trincheras.
trench foot, t. feet, (med.) pie de trinchera.
trenching machine, zanjadora, cavadora de zanjas.
trench knife, (mil.) cuchillo de monte.
trench mortar, (mil.) mortero de trinchera.
trench mouth, (med.) angina de Vincent, enfermedad de Vincent.
trench warfare, guerra de trinchera a trinchera.
trend [trɛnd] *v.i.* 1. dirigirse, tender. 2. inclinarse. —*s.* 1. dirección, curso, rumbo. 2. tendencia, inclinación, giro (de acontecimientos, opinión, etc.).
trepan [trɪ'pæn] *s.* (med., min.) trépano. —*v.t.* (*pret., p.p.* TREPANNED; *p.pr.* TREPANNING) (med., min.) trepanar.
trepan, (ant.) *s.* engañador, impostor; trampa. —*v.t.* enredar, entrampar; estafar, timar.
trepanation [ˌtrɛpə'neɪʃən] *s.* (med.) trepanación.
trepang [trɪ'pæŋ] *s.* (zool.) holoturia, cohombro de mar.
trephination [ˌtrɛfə'neɪʃən] *s.* (med.) trepanación.
trephine [trɪ'faɪn, B -'fin] *s.* (med.) trefina. —*v.t.* operar con trefina, trepanar.
trepidation [ˌtrɛpə'deɪʃən] *s.* 1. perturbación, ansiedad nerviosa, azoramiento. 2. trepidación, vibración.
treponema [ˌtrɛpə'nimə] *s.* (*pl.* TREPONEMATA [-mətə] o TREPONEMAS) (bact.) treponema.
trespass ['trɛspəs, -ˌpæs, B 'trɛspəs] *v.i.* 1. estar ilegalmente, entrar sin derecho (en algún lugar). 2. errar, pecar. 3. (der.) traspasar o transgredir un límite; violar o infringir la ley. 4. **no trespassing,** prohibido el paso; **t. against,** pecar contra, ofender; **t. on** (o **upon**), entrar sin derecho a o en; abusar de (paciencia, hospitalidad, etc.); infringir, conculcar (los derechos de otro). —*s.* 1. entrada sin derecho. 2. infracción, violación. 3. ofensa, pecado. 4. (der.) transgresión, violación. 5. **forgive us our trespasses,** perdónanos nuestras deudas (oración del Padrenuestro).
trespasser [-ər, B -ə] *s.* 1. intruso. 2. pecador. 3. (der.) violador, transgresor.
tress [trɛs] *s.* 1. trenza, bucle, rizo (esp. de cabello). 2. (*pl.*) cabellera (esp. de mujer).

tressed [trɛst] *a.* trenzado.
tressure ['trɛʃər, B -ə] *s.* (her.) trechor.
trestle ['trɛsəl] *s.* 1. caballete. 2. bastidor. 3. (ing.) caballete, puente o viaducto de caballete.
trestle bridge, puente de caballetes.
trestle horse, (carp.) caballete, burro de aserrar.
trestletree [-ˌtri] *s.* (mar.) bao de los palos.
trestlework [-ˌwɜrk, B -wɜk] *s.* estructura o armazón de caballetes; castillejo; obra sobre pilares.
tret [trɛt] *s.* (com.) deducción por merma, rebaja.
trews [truz] *s.* (*pl.*) calzón de tartán (esp. el que se lleva debajo de la falda escocesa).
trey [treɪ] *s.* tres (en naipes, dados o dominó).
triable ['traɪəbəl] *a.* (der.) procesable, enjuiciable.
triacid [traɪ'æsəd] *s., a.* (quím.) triácido.
triad ['traɪˌæd, B -əd] *s.* 1. tríada (de dioses, síntomas, etc.); terno, trinca. 2. (mús.) acorde perfecto (mayor o menor). —*a.* (quím.) trivalente.
triadelphous [ˌtraɪə'dɛlfəs] *a.* (bot.) triadelfo.
triadic [traɪ'ædɪk] *a.* 1. trino. 2. (quím.) trivalente.
trial ['traɪəl] *s.* 1. ensayo, prueba, experimento, tanteo. 2. tentativa, esfuerzo. 3. tribulación, mortificación; vejación, molestia. 4. (der.) juicio, pleito, vista, proceso. 5. **on t.,** a prueba, a título de prueba; **to be on** (o **to stand**) **t.,** estar sujeto a juicio; **to bring** (o **to put**) **to t.,** encausar, enjuiciar; **to give (someone) a t.,** emplear (a alguien) a prueba, darle una oportunidad a (alguien); **to give (something) a t.,** probar (algo); **to take on t.,** tomar a prueba. —*a.* de ensayo, de prueba.
trial and error, tanteo, método de tanteos; ensayo, prueba (a base de la eliminación de errores).
trial balance, (com.) balance de comprobación, balance de saldos.
trial balloon, (lit. y fig.) globo de prueba, globo experimental, globo de ensayo.
trial by jury, (der.) juicio por jurado.
trial by ordeal, (hist.) juicios de Dios, ordalías.
trial flight, (avia.) vuelo de prueba.
trial jury, (der.) jurado procesal, jurado de juicio.
trial lawyer, abogado litigante.
trial pit, (min.) calicata.
trial run, 1. recorrido o marcha de prueba. 2. (fig.) ensayo, prueba, experimento.
triandrous [traɪ'ændrəs] *a.* (bot.) triandro.
triangle ['traɪˌæŋgəl] *s.* 1. (geom.) triángulo. 2. escuadra, cartabón. 3. (mús.) triángulo (instrumento). 4. (fig.) triángulo, (enredo o complicación amorosa de tres personas), ej., *the eternal t.,* el eterno triángulo.
triangular [traɪ'æŋgjələr, B -lə] *a.* 1. triangular, triangulado, triángulo. 2. tripartito, ej., *a t. agreement,* acuerdo tripartito. 3. (mil.) triangular.
triangular compass, compás de tres piernas.
triangularity [-ˌæŋgjə'lærətɪ] *s.* carácter o aspecto triangular.
triangularly [-'æŋgjələrlɪ, B -ləlɪ] *adv.* triangularmente.
triangulate [traɪ'æŋgjələt] *a.* triangulado. —[-ˌleɪt] *v.t.* triangular.
triangulation [-ˌæŋgjə'leɪʃən] *s.* triangulación.
triarchy ['traɪˌɑrkɪ, B -ɑkɪ] *s.* (*pl.* TRIARCHIES) gobierno de tres personas; triunvirato.
Triassic [traɪ'æsɪk] *a., s.* (geol.) triásico.
triatic stay [traɪ'ætɪk-] (mar.) estay de seguridad.
triatomic [ˌtraɪə'tɑmɪk, B -'tɔm-] *a.* (quím.) triatómico.
triaxial [traɪ'æksɪəl] *a.* (geom., mec.) triaxial, triaxil.
triazine ['traɪəˌzin, B traɪ'æzaɪn] *s.* (quím.) triazina.
triazole ['traɪəˌzoʊl, B traɪ'æzoʊl] *s.* (quím.) triazol.
tribadism ['trɪbəˌdɪzəm] *s.* tribadismo, homosexualidad femenina, lesbianismo.
tribal ['traɪbəl] *a.* tribal, de tribu.
tribally [-bəlɪ] *adv.* en forma tribal, en tribus.
tribasic [traɪ'beɪsɪk] *a.* (quím.) tribásico.
tribe [traɪb] *s.* 1. tribu (comunidad indígena). 2. (fam.) la familia propia.
tribesman ['traɪbzmən] *s.* miembro de una tribu.
triboelectric [ˌtraɪboʊɪ'lɛktrɪk] *a.* triboeléctrico.
triboelectricity [-ɪˌlɛk'trɪsətɪ] *s.* triboelectricidad, electricidad producida por frotación.
triboluminescence [-lumə'nɛsəns] *s.* (fís.) triboluminiscencia, triboluminescencia.
triboluminescent [-ənt] *a.* (fís.) triboluminiscente, triboluminescente.
tribometer [traɪ'bɑmətər, B -'bɔmɪtə] *s.* tribómetro.
tribrach ['traɪbræk, B 'trɪbræk] *s.* (poét.) tribraquio.
tribromide [traɪ'broʊˌmaɪd] *a.* (quím.) tribromuro.
tribromoethanol [ˌtraɪˌbroʊmoʊ'ɛθəˌnɔl] *s.* (quím.) tribromoetanol.
tribulation [ˌtrɪbjə'leɪʃən] *s.* tribulación, congoja, aflicción.
tribunal [traɪ'bjunəl, trɪb'ju-] *s.* 1. tribunal; juzgado, sala de justicia. 2. (fig.) tribunal, foro.
tribunate ['trɪbjəˌneɪt, B -nət] *s.* (hist.) tribunado.
tribune ['trɪbjun, trɪb'jun, B 'trɪbjun] *s.* 1. (hist.) tribuno. 2. (fig.) tribuno, defensor de los derechos del pueblo.
tribune, *s.* tribuna.
tribuneship [-ˌʃɪp] *s.* tribunado.
tributary ['trɪbjəˌtɛrɪ, B -tərɪ] *a.* 1. tributario, subordinado, súbdito; contributivo. 2. tributario (río o corriente). —*s.* (*pl.* TRIBUTARIES) tributario.
tribute ['trɪbjut] *s.* 1. (hist.) tributo (pagado por un vasallo o estado). 2. (fig.) tributo, contribución, ofrenda, ej., *floral tributes,* ofrendas florales. 3. (fig.) alabanza, homenaje, ej., *the tributes of his admirers,* las alabanzas de sus admiradores, *to pay t. to,* rendir homenaje a.
trice [traɪs] *v.t.* (mar.) levantar; izar y amarrar; ligar (velas, etc.). —*s.* momento, instante, tris; **in a t.,** en un abrir y cerrar de ojos, en un periquete.
tricentennial [ˌtraɪsɛn'tɛnɪəl] *a.* de trescientos años. —*s.* tricentenario.
triceps ['traɪˌsɛps] *s.* (*pl.* TRICEPSES O TRICEPS) (anat.) tríceps.
trichiasis [trɪ'kaɪəsəs] *s.* (med.) triquiasis.
trichina [trɪ'kaɪnə] *s.* (*pl.* TRICHINAE [-ˌni]) (zool.) triquina.
trichinization [ˌtrɪkənə'zeɪʃən, B -naɪ-] *s.* triquinización.
trichinize ['trɪkəˌnaɪz] *v.t.* volver triquinoso, infectar con triquina.
trichinosis [ˌtrɪkə'noʊsəs] *s.* (med.) triquinosis.
trichinous [trɪ'kaɪnəs, B 'trɪkə-] *a.* triquinoso.
trichite ['trɪkˌaɪt] *s.* (min.) triquita.
trichloride [traɪ'klɔrˌaɪd] *s.* (quím.) tricloruro.
trichloroacetic acid [ˌtraɪˌklɔroʊə'sitɪk-] (quím.) ácido tricloroacético.
trichocephalus [ˌtrɪkə'sɛfələs] *s.* (zool.) tricocéfalo.
trichogyne ['trɪkəˌdʒaɪn] *s.* (bot.) tricógina.
trichoid ['trɪkˌɔɪd] *a.* tricoide, parecido al pelo.
trichologist [trə'kɑlədʒəst, B -'kɔl-] *s.* tricólogo.
trichology [-dʒɪ] *s.* tricología.
trichome ['trɪkˌoʊm] *s.* (bot.) tricoma.
trichomonad [ˌtrɪkə'mɑnˌæd, B -'mɔn-] *s.* (zool.) tricomonádido.
trichomoniasis [ˌtrɪkəmə'naɪəsəs] *s.* (vet.) tricomoniasis.
trichophytosis [ˌtrɪkəfaɪ'toʊsəs] *s.* (med.) tricofitosis.
trichopteran [trɪ'kɑptərən, B -'kɔp-] *s.* (ento.) tricóptero.
trichosis [trə'koʊsəs] *s.* (med.) tricosis.
trichotomic [ˌtrɪkə'tɑmɪk, B -'tɔm-] *a.* tricotómico, dividido en tres partes, clases, etc.
trichotomous [trɪ'kɑtəməs, B -'kɔt-] *a.* tricótomo.
trichotomy [-mɪ] *s.* tricotomía.
trichroism ['traɪˌkroʊˌɪzəm] *s.* (fís.) tricroísmo.
trichromatic [ˌtraɪkroʊ'mætɪk] *a.* tricromático.
trichromatism [traɪ'kroʊməˌtɪzəm] *s.* tricromatismo.
trichuriasis [ˌtrɪkjə'raɪəsəs] *s.* (*pl.* TRICHURIASES [-ˌsiz]) (med.) tricuriasis.
trichuris [trə'kjurəs] *s.* (zool.) tricocéfalo.
tricipital [traɪ'sɪpətəl] *a.* 1. tricipital. 2. (anat.) tríceps.
trick [trɪk] *s.* 1. truco, ardid. 2. travesura, jugarreta, treta. 3. maña, costumbre, hábito peculiar. 4. turno, tanda. 5. (naipes) baza. 6. (E.U.) muñeca (niño gracioso, muchacha guapa). 7. **to be up to one's tricks,** estar haciendo de las suyas; **to do the t.,** resolver el problema, servir su propósito, surtir efecto; **to go back to one's old tricks,** volver uno a las andadas, volver a sus andanzas; **to play a dirty t. on (someone),** hacer una mala jugada a (alguien); **you can't teach an old dog new tricks,** viejo es Pedro para cabrero. —*v.t.* 1. trampear, burlar, engañar; estafar, embaucar. 2. **to t. into,** obligar con engaño; conseguir fraudulentamente (que alguien haga algo); **t. out of,** quitar o despojar con engaño. —*a.* 1. de truco. 2. mañoso.
tricker ['trɪkər, B -ə] *s.* tramposo, embustero.
trickery [-ərɪ] *s.* maña, trampería, embrollo, embuste.
trickily ['trɪkəlɪ] *adv.* 1. engañosamente. 2. intrincadamente.
trickiness [-ɪnəs] *s.* carácter engañoso o dificultoso.
trickish [-ɪʃ] *a.* tramposo, engañoso; mañoso, difícil, intrincado.
trickishly [-lɪ] *adv.* engañosamente, con trampa, tramposamente.
trickle ['trɪkəl] *v.i.* 1. gotear, destilar, chorrear, escurrir. 2. entrar, salir, pasar gradual e irregularmente. 3. **t. out,** (fig.) salir paulatinamente (noticia, información, etc.). —*s.* hilo, chorro delgado, goteo.
tricklet ['trɪklət] *s.* hilo de agua, arroyuelo.
trick or treat, (fam., E.U.) o una jugarreta o un regalo (amenaza en la noche de Halloween); **to go trick or treating,** salir a recorrer casas amenazando con una jugarreta si no se recibe un regalo.
trickster ['trɪkstər, B -stə] *s.* tramposo, embustero.
tricksy [-sɪ] *a.* 1. juguetón, retozón, travieso. 2. (ant.) garboso; tramposo.

tricktrack [ˈtrɪkˌtræk] *s.* (juego de) chaquete.

tricky [ˈtrɪkɪ] *a.* (TRICKIER; TRICKIEST) 1. tramposo, engañoso, falso. 2. (fam.) mañoso, difícil, dificultoso; intrincado; delicado.

triclinic [traɪˈklɪnɪk] *a.* (min.) triclínico (esp. cristales).

triclinium [-ˈklɪnɪəm] *s.* (hist.) triclinio.

tricolor [ˈtraɪˌkʌlər, B ˈtrɪkələ] *s.* bandera tricolor (esp. la de Francia). —*a.* tricolor.

tricorn [-ˌkɔrn, B ˈtraɪˌkɔn] *s.* tricornio, tricorne. —*s.* (sombrero) tricornio.

tricorne [-ˌkɔrn, B -ˌkɔn] *s.* tricornio, sombrero de tres picos.

tricot [ˈtrikou] *s.* (fr.) 1. tricot, malla. 2. traje de malla (para bailarines).

tricrotic [traɪˈkrɑtɪk, B -ˈkrɔt-] *a.* (fisiol.) tricroto, tricrótico.

tricrotism [ˈtraɪkrəˌtɪzəm] *s.* (fisiol.) condición tricrótica (díc. del pulso en el que hay triple latido).

trictrac, *var. de* **tricktrack.**

tricuspid [traɪˈkʌspəd] **tricuspidate** [-pəˌdeɪt] *a.* tricúspide.

tricuspid valve, (anat.) válvula tricúspide.

tricycle [ˈtraɪˌsɪkəl] *s.* triciclo.

tricycle landing gear, (avia.) tren de aterrizaje triciclo.

tricyclic [traɪˈsaɪklɪk, B -ˈsɪk-] *a.* (quím) tricíclico.

tridacna [trəˈdæknə] *s.* (zool.) tridacna.

tridactyl [traɪˈdæktəl] *a.* tridáctilo.

trident [ˈtraɪdənt] *s.* 1. (mitol.) tridente. 2. fisga, arrejaque. —*a.* tridente.

tridentate [traɪˈdɛnˌteɪt] *a.* tridente.

Tridentine [traɪˈdɛntən, B -ˌtaɪn] *a.* tridentino.

tridimensional [ˌtraɪdəˈmɛntʃənəl, B -ˈmɛnʃən-] *a.* tridimensional.

tridimensionality [-ˌmɛntʃəˈnælətɪ, B -ˌmɛnʃə-] *s.* aspecto o condición tridimensional.

triduum [ˈtrɪdʒʊəm, B ˈtrɪdjʊ-] *s.* (relig.) triduo.

triecious, *var. de* **trioecious.**

tried [traɪd] *a.* 1. probado, seguro (remedio, receta, etc.). 2. comprobado, fiel, confiable (amigo, etc.). 3. probado, atribulado, afligido.

triennial [traɪˈɛnɪəl] *a.* trienal, trieñal. —*s.* 1. trienio. 2. tercer aniversario.

triennially [-əlɪ] *adv.* cada tres años.

triennium [-əm] *s.* (*pl.* TRIENNIA [-ə] o TRIENNIUMS) trienio.

triens [ˈtraɪɛnz] *s.* (*pl.* TRIENTES [traɪˈɛnˌtiz]) (numis.) triente.

trier [ˈtraɪər, B -ə] *s.* ensayador, experimentador; examinador; cateador; comprobador, verificador.

trierarch [ˈtraɪəˌrɑrk, B -ˌrɑk] *s.* (hist.) trierarca.

trierarchy [-rɑrkɪ, B -ˌrɑkɪ] *s.* (hist.) trierarquía.

trifacial [traɪfeɪʃəl] (anat.) *a.* trifacial. —*s.* nervio trifacial.

trifid [ˈtraɪˌfɪd] *a.* trífido.

trifle [ˈtraɪfəl] *s.* 1. bagatela, friolera, nadería, menudencia, fruslería. 2. tiritaña, bagatela, miseria, suma insignificante. 3. (*ú. adverbialmente*) algo, un poquito, ej., *he is a t. angry,* él está algo molesto. 4. bizcocho borracho con mostachón, conserva de frutas y crema batida. 5. variedad de peltre (usado para pequeños utensilios). 6. **to stop at trifles,** pararse en pelillos, ser cuidadoso en demasía. —*v.i.* 1. chancear, bromear, retozar, travesear. 2. hablar con frivolidad. 3. **t. with,** juguetear con (cosas); tratar con ligereza, jugar con (sentimientos, tema, personas, etc.). —*v.t.* **t. away,** malgastar, despilfarrar.

trifler [-flər, B -flə] *s.* persona frívola; chancero, burlón.

trifling [-flɪŋ] *a.* 1. frívolo, ligero. 2. insignificante, baladí, trivial.

triflingly [-lɪ] *adv.* frívolamente, trivialmente.

trifocal [traɪˈfoukəl] *a.* trifocal. —*s. pl.* lentes o anteojos trifocales.

trifoliate [-ˈfoulɪət] **trifoliated** [-ˌeɪtəd] *a.* (bot.) trifoliado.

trifoliolate [-lɪəˌleɪt] *a.* (bot.) trifoliolado.

trifolium [-lɪəm] *s.* (bot.) trifolio.

triforium [traɪˈfɔrɪəm] *s.* (*pl.* TRIFORIA [-ə]) (arq.) triforio.

triform [ˈtraɪˌfɔrm, B -ˌfɔm] *a.* triforme.

trifurcate [traɪˈfɜrkət, B -ˈfɜkɪt] *a.* trifurcado. — [ˈtraɪfɜrˌkeɪt, B traɪˈfɜ,-] *v.i.* trifurcarse.

trifurcation [ˌtraɪfɜrˈkeɪʃən, B -fɜˈ-] *s.* trifurcación.

trig [trɪg] *a.* 1. acicalado, elegante; apuesto. 2. estirado, relamido. 3. (dial.) firme, vigoroso, sano. —*v.t., v.i.* (*pret., p.p.* TRIGGED; *p.pr.* TRIGGING) **t. out (o up),** (dial., pr. G.B.) acicalar, ataviar.

trig, (pr. dial.) *v.t.* calzar, trabar, atar (las ruedas). —*s.* 1. calzo, galga. 2. (fam.) trigonometría.

trigeminal [traɪˈdʒɛmənəl] *a.* (anat.) trigémino. —*s.* nervio trigémino.

trigeminal neuralgia, (med.) neuralgia del nervio trigémino.

trigger [ˈtrɪgər, B -ə] *s.* gatillo, disparador. —*v.t.* 1. apretar el gatillo de, disparar (fusil, etc.). 2. (fig.) (t. con *off*) provocar, desatar.

trigger circuit, (rad.) circuito activador de disparo.

triggerfish [-ˌfɪʃ] *s.* (ict.) pez ballesta.

trigger guard, guardamonte.

trigger-happy [-ˌhæpɪ] *a.* propenso a disparar impulsivamente; irresponsable, arrebatado (en el uso de armas de fuego o en asuntos que pueden precipitar una guerra); agresivo, beligerante.

triggerman [-mən, -ˌmæn] *s.* pistolero, asesino profesional; guardaespaldas de un tahúr.

trigger mechanism, (arm.) mecanismo de disparo, mecanismo del disparador.

trigger pull, (arm.) resistencia del disparador.

triglyph [ˈtraɪˌglɪf] *s.* (arq.) tríglifo.

trigon [ˈtraɪgɑn, B -gən] *s.* 1. (raro) (geom.) trígono, triángulo. 2. (astrol.) trígono. 3. (mús.) trigón (instrumento antiguo de cuerdas).

trigonal [ˈtrɪgənəl] *a.* (geom.) trigonal.

trigonometer [ˌtrɪgəˈnɑmətər, B -ˈnɔmɪtə] *s.* trigonómetro.

trigonometric [-nəˈmɛtrɪk] **trigonometrical** [-trɪkəl] *a.* trigonométrico.

trigonometric function, función o razón trigonométrica.

trigonometric line, (geom.) línea trigonométrica.

trigonometry [ˌtrɪgəˈnɑmətrɪ, B -ˈnɔm-] *s.* trigonometría.

trigraph [ˈtraɪˌgræf, B -ˌgrɑf] *s.* conjunto de tres letras que representan un solo sonido.

trihedral [traɪˈhidrəl, B -ˈhɛdrəl] *a.* (geom.) triédrico.

trihedron [-drən] *s.* (*pl.* TRIHEDRONS O TRIHEDRA [-drə]) (geom.) triedro.

trihydrate [-ˈhaɪˌdreɪt] *s.* (quím.) trihidrato.

trilateral [-ˈlætərəl] *a.* (geom.) trilátero.

trilaterally [-rəlɪ] *adv.* en forma trilátera.

trilby [ˈtrɪlbɪ] *s.* (pr. G.B.) (*pl.* TRILBIES) sombrero de paño.

trilinear [traɪˈlɪnɪər, B -ə] *a.* (mat.) trilineal.

trilingual [-ˈlɪŋgwəl] *a.* trilingüe.

triliteral [-ˈlɪtərəl] *a.* trilítero. —*s.* palabra trilítera.

triliteralism [-ˌɪzəm] *s.* carácter triliteral (de idiomas, esp. los semíticos).

trilith [ˈtraɪˌlɪθ] **trilithon** [traɪˈlɪˌθɑn, B ˈtraɪlɪˌθɔn] *s.* trilito.

trill [trɪl] *v.t.* 1. pronunciar con gorjeos. 2. (fon.) pronunciar con vibración. —*v.i.* 1. gorjear, hablar o cantar gorjeando. 2. (mús.) trinar. —*s.* 1. gorjeo. 2. (fon.) vibración; vibrante. 3. (mús.) trino.

trillion [ˈtrɪljən] *s., a.* 1. (E.U.) billón. 2. (G.B.) trillón.

trilobate [traɪˈlouˌbeɪt] **trilobated** [-əd] **trilobed** [ˈtraɪˈloubd] *a.* (bot.) trilobulado.

Trilobita [ˌtraɪləˈbaɪtə] *s. pl.* (pal.) trilobites.

trilobite [ˈtraɪləˌbaɪt] *s.* (pal.) trilobita.

trilocular [traɪˈlɑkjələr, B -ˈlɔkjʊlə] **triloculate** [-lət] *a.* trilocular.

trilogy [ˈtrɪlədʒɪ] *s.* (*pl.* TRILOGIES) trilogía.

trim [trɪm] *v.t.* (*pret., p.p.* TRIMMED; *p.pr.* TRIMMING) 1. arreglar, ordenar; adornar, decorar; guarnecer, ataviar. 2. cercenar, recortar; podar, mondar (árbol, etc.); despabilar (vela, etc.). 3. (fig.) cercenar, reducir, ajustar (gastos, presupuesto, etc.). 4. (fam.) pelar, timar. 5. (fam.) reprochar, reprender; castigar, corregir; zurrar. 6. (fam.) derrotar, vencer (en juego). 7. (carp.) desbastar, cepillar, acepillar, alisar, azolar (la madera). 8. (mar.) adrizar (un buque); orientar (las velas); estibar (la carga). 9. (aer.) equilibrar, balancear (dirigible, avión, etc.). 10. **t. down,** reducir; **t. off** (o **away**), recortar, podar; despabilar (vela); **t. one's sails,** (fig.) adaptarse, amoldarse; **t. up,** acicalar, ataviar, hermosear. —*v.i.* 1. ser neutral, nadar entre dos aguas; actuar según las conveniencias. 2. (mar.) balancear (bien o mal). —*s.* 1. orden, condición, arreglo, disposición, estado. 2. vestido, atavío. 3. adorno, aderezo; decoración de escaparate. 4. guarnición; acabado interior (de un automóvil). 5. (arq.) chambrana, adornos de madera. 6. (mar.) asiento (de un buque); arrumaje (de la carga); orientación (de las velas). 7. (aer.) compensación. 8. recorte, desecho. 9. **in good t.,** en buen estado, en forma. —*a.* (TRIMMER; TRIMMEST) 1. pulcro, bonito; compacto. 2. bien parecido, apuesto. 3. (ant.) en orden, bien acondicionado; excelente —*adv.* en regla, en orden.

trimembral [trɪˈmɛmbrəl] *a.* trimembre.

trimer [ˈtraɪmər, B -mə] *s.* (quím.) trímero.

trimerous [ˈtrɪmərəs, B ˈtraɪm-] *a.* (bot., ento.) trimero.

trimester [traɪˈmɛstər, ˈtraɪˌmɛs-, B traɪˈmɛstə] *s.* trimestre.

trimestral [traɪˈmɛstrəl] **trimestrial** [-trɪəl] *a.* trimestral.

trimeter [ˈtrɪmətər, B -ə] *a., s.* (poét.) trímetro.

trimeter verse, (poét.) verso trímetro.

trimethadione [ˌtraɪˌmɛθəˈdaɪoun] *s.* (farm.) trimetadiona.

trimethylamine [ˌtraɪˈmɛθələˌmin, B -ˌmɛˈθɪl-] *s.* (quím.) trimetilamina.

trimetric [traɪˈmɛtrɪk] *a.* 1. (poét.) trímetro. 2. trimétrico (cristal).

trimetrical [-trɪkəl] *s.* (poét.) trímetro.

trimetric projection, (geom.) proyección trimétrica.

trimly [ˈtrɪmlɪ] *adv.* en regla, en orden.

trimmer [ˈtrɪmər, B -ə] *s.* 1. recortadora, desbastadora, cepilladora. 2. contemporizador, oportunista. 3. (mar.) estibador. 4. (arq.) cabio. 5. (elec.) condensador de ajuste, condensador de corrección.

trimming [-ɪŋ] *s.* 1. ajuste, compostura, arreglo; compensación. 2. guarnición, adorno; (*pl.*) accesorios, arrequives, aderezos, piezas de adorno. 3. (carp.) cepillado. 4. (jer.) derrota, zurra.
trimming tab, (aer.) aleta compensadora, aleta de compensación.
trimming tank, (ing.) tanque de equilibrio.
trimness [-nəs] *s.* aspecto ordenado, pulcritud.
trimolecular [ˌtraɪmə'lɛkjələr, B -lə] *a.* (quím.) de tres moléculas, trimolecular.
trimonthly [traɪ'mʌnθlɪ] *a.* trimensual.
trimorph ['traɪˌmɔrf, B -ˌmɔf] *s.* trimorfo.
trimorphic [traɪ'mɔrfɪk, B -'mɔfɪk] **trimorphous** [-fəs] *a.* trimorfo.
trimorphism [-ˌfɪzəm] *s.* trimorfismo.
trimotor ['traɪˌmoʊtər, B -ə] *s.* (aeroplano) trimotor.
Trinacrian [trɪ'neɪkrɪən, B traɪ-] *a.* trinacrio, de Trinacria (antiguo nombre de Sicilia).
trinal ['traɪnəl] *a.* 1. triple, trino, tresdoble. 2. (gram.) trial. —*s.* (gram.) trial.
trinary ['traɪnərɪ] *a.* ternario.
trindle ['trɪndəl] (dial., G.B.) *s.* rueda, ruedecilla, esp. rueda de carretilla. —*v.t., v.i.* rodar, hacer rodar.
trine [traɪn] *a.* 1. triple, trino, de tres partes. 2. (astrol.) en trígono. 3. (fig.) propicio. —*s.* 1. (astrol.) trígono. 2. tríada, trinidad; (relig.) **the T.,** la Trinidad.
Trinidad and Tobago ['trɪnəˌdædəndtoʊ'beɪgoʊ] Trinidad y Tobago, islas de las Antillas que forman un estado conjunto.
Trinidad asphalt, chapapote.
Trinitarian [ˌtrɪnə'tɛrɪən, B -'tɛər-] *a.* 1. (relig.) de la Trinidad, creyente en la Trinidad. 2. triple, trino. —*s.* 1. creyente en la Trinidad. 2. trinitario, ciudadano de Trinidad y Tobago.
Trinitarianism [-əˌnɪzəm] *s.* (relig.) 1. doctrina de la Trinidad. 2. creencia en la doctrina de la Trinidad.
trinitrocresol [traɪˌnaɪtroʊ'kriˌsɔl, B -trə'krɛ-] *s.* (quím.) trinitrocresol.
trinitroglycerin [-'glɪsərən] *s.* (quím.) trinitroglicerina.
trinitrotoluene [-'tɑljʊˌin, B -'tɔl-] *s.* (quím.) trinitrotolueno (T.N.T).
Trinity ['trɪnətɪ] *s.* 1. (teo.) Trinidad. 2. (relig.) Domingo de la Santísima Trinidad. 3. **t.,** trinidad, tríada, trinca.
Trinity Sunday, (relig.) domingo de la Santísima Trinidad.
trinket ['trɪŋkət] *s.* 1. dije, bujería, chuchería, alhaja pequeña. 2. baratija, bagatela. —*v.i.* intrigar; conspirar.
trinketry [-kətrɪ] *s.* dijes, chucherías, alhajas pequeñas.
trinkums [-kəmz] *s. pl.* (Esco.) baratijas, bagatelas, naderías.
trinomial [traɪ'noʊmɪəl] *a.* 1. (mat.) de trinomio. 2. (biol.) trinomial. —*s.* 1. (mat.) trinomio. 2. (biol.) nombre trinomial.
trio ['trioʊ] *s.* (*pl.* TRIOS) 1. trío, tres, trinca, ternario, terno. 2. (mús.) trío, terceto.
triode ['traɪˌoʊd] *s.* (electrón.) tríodo.
trioecious [traɪ'iʃəs] *a.* (bot.) trioico.
triolein [traɪ'oʊlɪən] *s.* (quim.) trioleína.
triolet ['traɪələt, B 'trioʊˌlɛt] *s.* (poét.) octava (en la que el primer verso se repite en el cuarto y en el séptimo, y el segundo en el octavo).
triose ['traɪˌoʊs] *s.* (quím.) triosa.
trioxide [traɪ'ɑkˌsaɪd, B -'ɔk-] *s.* (quím.) trióxido.
trip [trɪp] *v.i.* (*pret., p.p.* TRIPPED; *p.pr.* TRIPPING) 1. ir brincando; moverse con pasos rápidos; bailar con ligereza. 2. (t. con *over*) dar un traspié, tropezar (con o contra). 3. (fig.) tropezar, errar, pecar, cometer un desliz. 4. trabarse la lengua. 5. (raro) viajar, hacer un viaje. —*v.t.* 1. (t. con *up*) hacer tropezar, echar una zancadilla a; (fig.) hacer fallar; detener. 2. (gen. con *up*) coger en falta, coger en una mentira. 3. (mar.) desgarrar (ancla); izar (verga, mastelero). 4. (mec.) soltar, disparar. 5. (ant.) ejecutar (una danza) con ritmo y gracia. 6. **t. the light fantastic,** bailar con agilidad. —*s.* 1. viaje, excursión, recorrido. 2. paso ligero y ágil. 3. traspié, tropiezo; paso en falso, desliz, error, equivocación. 4. zancadilla. 5. (mec.) trinquete; escape, disparo. 6. (jer., E.U.) alucinaciones causadas por drogas como L.S.D.
tripartite [traɪ'pɑrˌtaɪt, B -'pɑˌ-] *a.* tripartito.
tripartition [ˌtraɪpɑr'tɪʃən, B -pɑ'-] *s.* tripartición.
tripe [traɪp] *s.* 1. tripa, mondongo, callos, ventrón. 2. (jer.) tonterías, disparates, necedades.
tripedal ['traɪpɪdəl, B traɪ'pidəl] *a.* de tres pies.
tripersonal [traɪ'pɜrsənəl, B -'pɜsən-] *a.* de tres personas.
tripetalous [-'pɛtələs] *a.* (bot.) tripétalo.
trip gear, (mec.) mecanismo de desenganche o de disparo.
trip-hammer ['trɪpˌhæmər, B -ə] *s.* (mec.) martinete de fragua, martillo pilón, martillo de caída.
triphenylmethane [ˌtraɪˌfɛnəl'mɛθˌeɪn] *s.* (quim.) trifenilmetano.
triphibious [traɪ'fɪbɪəs] *a.* que utiliza fuerzas aéreas, navales y terrestres en ataque coordinado.
triphthong ['trɪfˌθɔŋ, 'trɪp-, B 'trɪfˌθɔŋ] *s.* triptongo.
triphyline ['trɪfəˌlin] **triphylite** [-ˌlaɪt] *s.* (min.) trifilina.
tripinnate [traɪ'pɪnˌeɪt] *a.* (bot.) tripinnaticompuesta (hoja).
triplane ['traɪˌpleɪn] *s.* (aer.) triplano.
triple ['trɪpəl] *a.* triple, triplo, tríplice, tresdoble. —*s.* 1. triple, triplo. 2. (béisbol) bateo que permite al bateador llegar a la tercera base. —*v.t.* triplicar. —*v.i.* 1. triplicar. 2. (béisbol) ganar la tercera base gracias a un golpe.
triple-acting [-'æktɪŋ] *a.* de triple efecto.
Triple Alliance, (hist.) Triple Alianza.
triple-expansion engine [-ɪk'spæntʃən-, B -'spænʃən-] (mot.) máquina de vapor de triple expansión.
triple measure, (mús.) compás ternario.
triple-nerved [-'nɜrvd, B -'nɜvd] *a.* (bot.) triplinerve, triplinervio.
triple play, (béisbol) jugada que pone fuera de juego a tres corredores de base.
triple-space [-'speɪs] *v.t.* espaciar (texto) dejando dos líneas en blanco. —*v.i.* escribir (a máquina) dejando dos líneas en blanco.
triplet ['trɪplət] *s.* 1. terno (conjunto de tres cosas). 2. tripleto; (*pl.*) trillizos. 3. (mús.) tresillo. 4. (poét.) terceto, tercerilla (estrofa de tres versos).
triple-throw switch ['trɪpəlˌθroʊ-] (elec.) interruptor de tres cuchillas.
triple time, (mús.) compás ternario.
trip lever, palanca de disparo, palanquita de desenganche.
triplex ['trɪpˌlɛks] *a.* triple, triplo, tríplice, tresdoble.
triplex glass, vidrio tríplex.
triplicate ['trɪplɪkət] *a.* 1. triple, triplo. 2. tercera (copia), triplicado. —*s.* ejemplar triple, triplicado; **in t.,** en triplicado, con dos copias. —[-ləˌkeɪt] *v.t.* triplicar.
triplication [ˌtrɪplə'keɪʃən] *s.* triplicación.
triplicity [tri'plɪsətɪ] *s.* 1. triplicidad. 2. (astrol.) trígono.
triplite ['trɪpˌlaɪt] *s.* (min.) triplita.
triploblastic [ˌtrɪploʊ'blæstɪk] *a.* (zool.) triploblástico.
triploid ['tripˌlɔɪd] *a.* (biol.) triploide. —*s.* individuo triploide.
triploidy [-ɪ] *s.* (biol.) triploidía.
triply ['trɪplɪ] *adv.* en grado triple, tres veces, triplemente.
tripod ['traɪˌpɑd, B -ˌpɔd] *s.* trípode.
tripodal ['trɪpədəl] *a.* de tres pies.
tripody [-dɪ] *s.* (*pl.* TRIPODIES) (poét.) verso trímetro.
tripoli [-lɪ] *s.* (min.) trípol, trípoli.
Tripoli ['trɪpəlɪ] *s.* Trípoli, capital de Libia.
Tripolitan [trɪ'pɑpətən, B -'pɔl-] *a., s.* tripolitano, de Trípoli.
tripos ['traɪˌpɑs, B -ˌpɔs] *s.* (*pl.* TRIPOSES) 1. (G.B.) examen para obtener el grado (en la Universidad de Cambridge). 2. (ant.) trípode.
tripper ['trɪpər, B -ə] *s.* 1. (pr. G.B.) excursionista, turista. 2. (mec.) desenganchador, disparador, volteador, tumbador.
trippet [-ət] *s.* (mec.) leva o palanca que golpea otra pieza a intervalos regulares.
trippingly [-ɪŋlɪ] *adv.* ágilmente, rápidamente, velozmente.
tripping transformer, (elec.) transformador de desenganche.
trip relay, (elec.) relai disparador.
tripterous ['trɪptərəs] *a.* (bot.) tripteroide.
triptych ['trɪptɪk] *s.* tríptico, retablo de tres hojas.
triquetrous [traɪ'kwitrəs] *a.* triangular.
triradiate [traɪ'reɪdɪət] *a.* trirradiado.
trirectangular [ˌtraɪrɛk'tæŋgjələr, B -lə] *a.* (geom.) trirrectángulo.
trireme ['traɪˌrim] *s.* (hist.) trirreme.
trisaccharide [traɪ'sækəˌraɪd] *s.* (quím.) trisacárido.
Trisagion [trɪ'sɑjɔn, B -'sægɪən] *s.* (*pl.* TRISAGIA [-jə, B -ə]) trisagio.
trisect [traɪ'sɛkt] *v.t.* (geom.) trisecar.
trisection [-'sɛkʃən] *s.* (geom.) trisección.
trisector [-'sɛktər, B -tə] *s.* (geom.) trisector, trisectriz.
trismic ['trɪzmɪk] *a.* (med.) trísmico.
trismus [-məs] *s.* (med.) trismo.
trisoctahedron [ˌtrɪsˌɑktə'hidrən, B -ˌɔktə'hɛ-] *s.* trisoctaedro.
trisodium [traɪ'soʊdɪəm] *a.* (quím.) trisódico.
trisomic [-'soʊmɪk] *a.* (biol.) trisómico.
Tristan ['trɪstən] *s.* (lit.) Tristán, amante de Isolda, personajes de leyenda inmortalizados en la ópera de Richard Wagner.
tristeza [trə'steɪzə] *s.* 1. (vet.) tristeza bovina, fiebre de Tejas. 2. (bot.) podredumbre de las raicillas de los cítricos.
tristful [trɪstfəl] *a.* (ant.) triste, apesadumbrado.
tristfully [-fəlɪ] *adv.* (ant.) tristemente.
tristich ['trɪstɪk] *s.* (poét.) terceto, tercerilla.
tristichous [-tɪkəs] *a.* (bot.) trístico.
Tristram ['trɪstrəm] *s. var. de* **Tristan.**
tristylous [traɪ'staɪləs] *a.* (bot.) de tres estilos.
trisulfide [-'sʌlfaɪd] *s.* (quím.) trisulfuro.
trisyllabic [ˌtraɪsə'læbɪk] *a.* trisílabo, trisilábico.
trisyllabically [-ɪkəlɪ] *adv.* en forma trisílaba.
trisyllable [traɪ'sɪləbəl] *s.* (gram.) trisílabo.
trite [traɪt] *a.* gastado, trillado, trivial.
tritely ['traɪtlɪ] *adv.* trivialmente.
triteness [-nəs] *s.* trivialidad.
tritheism ['traɪθiˌɪzəm] *s.* (teo.) triteísmo.

tritheist [-əst] *s., a.* (teo.) triteísta.
tritheistic [ˌtraɪθiˈɪstɪk] **tritheistical** [-tɪkəl] *a.* (teo.) triteísta.
tritium [ˈtrɪtɪəm] *s.* (quím.) tritio.
tritoma [ˈtrɪtəmə] *s.* (bot.) tritoma.
Triton [ˈtraɪtən] *s.* 1. (mitol.) Tritón, dios marino con cuerpo de hombre y cola de pez. 2. (zool.) tritón (molusco o salamandra).
triton [ˈtraɪˌtɑn, B -tɔn] *s.* (fís.) tritón.
tritone [-ˌtoʊn] *s.* (mús.) trítono.
triturable [ˈtrɪtʃərəbəl] *a.* triturable.
triturate [ˈtrɪtʃəˌreɪt] *v.t.* triturar. — [-rət, B -ˌreɪt] *s.* substancia triturada.
trituration [ˌtrɪtʃəˈreɪʃən] *s.* 1. trituración. 2. (farm.) polvo triturado.
triturator [ˈtrɪtʃəˌreɪtər, B -ə] *s.* trituradora (máquina).
triumph [ˈtraɪəmf] *s.* 1. triunfo, victoria. 2. júbilo, exultación. 3. **in t.,** en triunfo. —*v.i.* 1. (t. con *over*) triunfar (sobre, de), obtener la victoria (sobre). 2. exultar.
triumphal [traɪˈʌmfəl] *a.* triunfal.
triumphal arch, arco de triunfo, arco triunfal.
triumphant [-fənt] *a.* 1. triunfante, victorioso, exitoso. 2. exultante, regocijado. 3. (ant.) triunfal, magnífico.
triumphantly [-lɪ] *adv.* triunfantemente, triunfalmente.
triumvir [traɪˈʌmvər, B trɪˈʊmvə] *s.* (*pl* TRIUMVIRS O TRIUMVIRI [-vəˌraɪ, B -ˌri]) (hist.) triunviro.
triumviral [-vərəl] *a.* (hist.) triunviral.
triumvirate [-rət] *s.* triunvirato.
triune [ˈtraɪjun] *a.* (teo.) trino y uno. —*s.* tríada; **T.,** Trinidad.
trivalence [traɪˈveɪləns, B ˈtraɪvə-] *s.* (quím.) trivalencia.
trivalency [-lənsɪ, B traɪˈveɪ-] *s.* (*pl.* TRIVALENCIES) *var. de* **trivalence.**
trivalent [-lənt] *a.* (quím.) trivalente.
trivalve [ˈtraɪˌvælv] *a.* trivalvo.
trivet [ˈtrɪvət] *s.* 1. trípode, soporte de tres pies. 2. trébedes (para poner al fuego sartenes, peroles, etc.). 3. salvamanteles (de metal). 4. (G.B.) **right as a t.,** perfectamente bien.
trivia [ˈtrɪvɪə] *s. pl.* trivialidades, bagatelas, banalidades.
trivial [-ɪəl] *a.* trivial, banal, insignificante, común, trillado.
triviality [ˌtrɪvɪˈælətɪ] *s.* (*pl.* TRIVIALITIES) trivialidad, banalidad.
trivialize [ˈtrɪvɪəˌlaɪz] *v.t.* trivializar, hacer trivial; convertir en una trivialidad.
trivially [-lɪ] *adv.* trivialmente, banalmente.
trivial name, (quím.) nombre trivial.
trivium [ˈtrɪvɪəm] *s.* (*pl.* TRIVIA [-ə]) (hist., zool.) trivio.
triweekly [traɪˈwiklɪ] *a.* trisemanal. —*adv.* cada tres semanas, tres veces a la semana. —*s.* publicacíon trisemanal.
trocar [ˈtroʊˌkɑr, B -ˌkɑ] *s.* (med.) trocar.
trochaic [troʊˈkeɪɪk] *a., s.* (poét.) trocaico.
trochaic verse, (poét.) verso trocaico.
trochal [ˈtroʊkəl, B ˈtrɔk-] *a.* (zool.) trocal.
trochanter [troʊˈkæntər, B -ə] *s.* (anat.) trocánter.
trochanteral [-ərəl] *a.* (anat.) trocantéreo.
trochar, *var. de* **trocar.**
troche [ˈtroʊkɪ, B troʊʃ] *s.* (farm.) trocisco, pastilla.
trochee [ˈtroʊki] *s.* (poét.) troqueo.
trochelminth [ˈtrɑkəlˌmɪnθ, B ˈtrɔk-] *s.* (zool.) troquelminto.
trochilus [ˈtrɑkələs, B ˈtrɔk-] *s.* (*pl.* TROCHILI [-ˌlaɪ]) (orn.) colibrí, pájaro mosca, picaflor.
trochlea [-lɪə] *s.* (anat.) tróclea.
trochlear [-lɪər, B -ə] *a.* 1. (anat.) troclear. 2. (bot.) trocleariforme.
trochoid [ˈtroʊˌkɔɪd] *s.* (geom.) trocoide. —*a.* (anat.) trocoide.
trochoidal [troʊˈkɔɪdəl] *a.* (anat.) trocoide.
trochophore [ˈtrɑkəˌfɔr, B ˈtrɔkəˌfɔ] *s.* (zool.) trocófora.
trod [trɑd, B trɔd] *pret. de* **tread.**
trodden [ˈtrɑdən, B ˈtrɔd-] *p.p. de* **tread.**
troglodyte [ˈtrɑgləˌdaɪt, B ˈtrɔg-] *s.* 1. troglodita. 2. (fig.) ermitaño. 3. (orn.) troglodita.
troglodytic [ˌtrɑgləˈdɪtɪk, B ˌtrɔg-] *a.* troglodítico.
trogon [ˈtroʊˌgɑn, B -ˌgɔn] *s.* (orn.) trogón; quetzal, surucuá, tocororo.
troika [ˈtrɔɪkə] *s.* 1. troica, troika, trineo ruso tirado por tres caballos. 2. grupo de tres, triunvirato.
Troilus [ˈtrɔɪləs, B ˈtroʊɪ-] *s.* (mitol.) Troilo, amante de Cresida en los romances medievales inspirados en las leyendas de Aquiles.
Trojan [ˈtroʊdʒən] *a.* troyano. —*s.* 1. troyano, natural de Troya. 2. valiente.
Trojan horse, (mitol.) caballo de Troya.
troll [troʊl] *s.* gnomo, enano, ser sobrenatural (en la mitología teutónica).
troll, *v.t.* 1. revolver, hacer rodar. 2. cantar en sucesión, cantar en voz alta; cantar alegremente, celebrar cantando. 3. pescar arrastrando el anzuelo; pescar en (un lago, etc.); (fig.) tentar, atraer. 4. (ant.) pasar en ronda o círculo, hacer circular. —*v.i.* 1. hablar rápidamente. 2. cantar o jugar en forma jovial y alegre. 3. pescar arrastrando el anzuelo. 4. (ant.) rodar, vagar. —*s.* 1. repetición, rutina. 2. rondel, cantar que se entona en partes sucesivas; canto de personas en círculo. 3. sedal con anzuelo y cebo; cebo (de pescar).
trolley [ˈtrɑlɪ, B ˈtrɔlɪ] *s.* (*pl.* TROLLEYS) 1. (G.B.) carreta, carretón. 2. trole, cargador, carretilla, carrillo. 3. (f.c., elec.) trole, polea o colector de corriente (de tranvías). 4. tranvía. 5. **to be off (one's) t.,** haber perdido la chaveta, habérsele caído un tornillo. —*v.t., v.i.* (*pret., p.p.* TROLLEYED O TROLLIED; *p.pr.* TROLLEYING O TROLLYING) llevar o viajar en un tranvía.
trolleybus [-ˌbʌs] *s.* trolebús.
trolley car, tranvía eléctrico.
trolley harp, horqueta de trole.
trolley hoist, montacargas colgante; guinche colgante.
trolley line, línea de tranvía.
trolleyman [-mən, -ˌmæn] *s.* conductor del trole o tranvía, motorista.
trolley pole, pértiga de trole.
trolley rail, carril conductor.
trolley shoe, (f.c., elec.) patín de contacto.
trolley wire, alambre conductor del trole.
trolling [ˈtroʊlɪŋ] *s.* pesca a flor de agua desde un bote en movimiento.
trollop [ˈtrɑləp, B ˈtrɔl-] *s.* 1. maritornes, mujer sucia y desaliñada. 2. gorrona, ramera, suripanta.
trolly, *s.* (*pl.* TROLLIES) *var. de* **trolley.**
trombidiasis [ˌtrɑmbəˈdaɪəsəs, B ˌtrɔm-] *s.* (vet.) trombidiosis, trombiculosis.
trombone [trɑmˈboʊn, ˈtrɑmˌboʊn, B trɔmˈboʊn] *s.* (mús.) trombón, sacabuche.
trombonist [-əst] *s.* trombón (músico).
trommel [ˈtrɑməl, B ˈtrɔm-] *s.* (min.) zaranda, trómel.
trompe [trɑmp, B trɔmp] *s.* trompa (ventilador hidráulico para las forjas).
trompe l'oeil [trɔmpˈlɔjə] *s.* (fr.) ilusión óptica.
trona [ˈtroʊnə] *s.* (min.) trona.
trone [troʊn] *s.* (pr. esco.) báscula para pesos grandes.
troop [trup] *s.* 1. tropa, turba, caterva; bandada (de aves); rebaño. 2. tropel, enjambre. 3. (*pl.*) ejército, tropas, soldados. 4. (mil.) escuadrón (de caballería). 5. (raro) compañía (de actores). —*v.i.* 1. andar o deambular en grupos o cuadrillas. 2. apiñarse, agruparse, juntarse, atroparse. 3. **t. in,** entrar en tropel; **t. off (o out),** marcharse (o salir) en tropel. —*v.t.* **t. the colour,** (G.B.) rendir honores a la bandera (ante las tropas reunidas, esp. en público).
troop carrier, (mil.) avión de transporte de tropas.
trooper [ˈtrupər, B -pə] *s.* 1. soldado de caballería. 2. caballo de guerra. 3. (Aust.) policía montado. 4. (G.B.) buque de transporte de tropas. 5. (E.U.) policía de la guardia civil (de un estado). 6. (mil.) (soldado) paracaidista. 7. **to swear like a t.,** blasfemar como un arriero.
troop horse, caballo de guerra, caballo de armas.
troop school, curso de instrucción militar.
troopship [ˈtrupˌʃɪp] *s.* buque transporte.
troop train, tren militar.
troostite [ˈtruˌstaɪt] *s.* (min.) troostita.
trop. *abrev. de* **tropic,** trópico, **tropical,** tropical.
tropaeolaceous [troʊˌpioʊˈleɪʃəs] *a.* (bot.) tropeoláceo, tropeoleo.
tropaeolin [trəˈpiəlɪn, B troʊ-] *s.* (quím.) tropeolina.
tropaeolum [-ləm] *s.* (bot.) tropeolácea, tropeolea.
trope [troʊp] *s.* (ret.) tropo.
tropeine [ˈtroʊpɪˌin] *s.* (quím.) tropeína.
tropeolin, *var. de* **tropaeolin.**
trophic [ˈtrɑfɪk, B ˈtrɔf-] *a.* (fisiol.) trófico.
trophied [ˈtroʊfɪd] *a.* adornado de trofeos.
trophoblast [ˈtrɑfəˌblæst, B ˈtrɔf-] *s.* (embr.) trofoblasto.
trophoneurosis [ˌtrɑfənʊˈroʊsəs, B ˌtrɔfənjʊə-] *s.* (med.) trofoneurosis.
trophoplasm [ˈtrɑfəˌplæzəm, B ˈtrɔf-] *s.* (biol.) trofoplasma.
trophozoite [ˌtrɑfəˈzoʊaɪt, B ˌtrɔf-] *s.* (zool.) trofozoito.
trophy [ˈtroʊfɪ] *s.* (*pl.* TROPHIES) trofeo.
tropic [ˈtrɑpɪk, B ˈtrɔp-] *s.* (astr., geog., biol.) trópico; **Tropics,** zona tórrida o tropical. —*a.* tropical.
tropical [-ɪkəl] *a.* 1. tropical. 2. (fig.) fervoroso, pasional. 3. (ret.) trópico.
tropical storm, vendaval, tormenta de los trópicos.
tropical year, (astr.) año trópico.
tropic bird, (orn.) rabijunco.
tropic of Cancer, (astr.) trópico de Cáncer.
tropic of Capricorn, (astr.) trópico de Capricornio.
tropine [ˈtroʊpin, B -ˌpaɪn] *s.* (quím.) tropina.
tropism [ˈtroʊˌpɪzəm, B ˈtrɔpˌɪz-] *s.* (biol.) tropismo.
tropistic [troʊˈpɪstɪk, B trə-] *a.* (biol.) del tropismo, trópico.
tropologic [ˌtroʊpəˈlɑdʒɪk, ˌtrɑpə-, B ˌtrɔpəˈlɔdʒ-] **tropological** [-ɪkəl] *a.* tropológico.
tropologically [-ɪkəlɪ] *adv.* en forma tropológica.
tropology [troʊˈpɑlədʒɪ, B trəˈpɔl-] *s.* (*pl.* TROPOLOGIES) tropología.
tropopause [ˈtroʊpəˌpɔz, ˈtrɑpə-, B ˈtrɔp-] *s.* (meteor.) tropopausa.
tropophyte [-ˌfaɪt] *s.* (bot.) tropófita.
troposphere [-ˌsfɪr, B -ˌsfɪə] *s.* (meteor.) troposfera.
trot [trɑt, B trɔt] *v.i.* (*pret., p.p.* TROTTED; *p.pr.* TROTTING) trotar; pasar o ir al trote; **t. along,** (fam.) moverse, menearse. —*v.t.* 1. hacer trotar.

2. recorrer al trote. 3. **t. out,** hacer trotar (al caballo); (fig.) sacar a relucir. —*s.* 1. trote (del caballo y de ciertos cuadrúpedos). 2. paseo a caballo; carrera entre trotadores. 3. paso vivo; actividad intensa. 4. (raro) niñito (que hace pinitos). 5. (jer., E.U.) chuleta (traducción ilícita usada en las lecciones o exámenes). 6. (ant., despec.) mujer anciana. 7. **the trots,** (jer.) diarrea.

trot, *s.* (pesca) palangre; ramal del palangre.

troth [trɔθ, trɑθ, B troʊθ] *s.* 1. fidelidad, lealtad. 2. voto o promesa de fe, palabra, empeño. 3. (ant.) esponsales. 4. **to plight one's t.,** empeñar la palabra, dar palabra (esp. de casamiento). —*v.t.* prometer, empeñar, dar (la palabra); contraer esponsales con (alguien).

trothplight ['trɔθˌplaɪt, 'trɑθ-, B 'troʊθ-] (ant.) *s.* desposorios, esponsales. —*v.t.* desposar, contraer esponsales con (alguien).

trotline ['trɑtˌlaɪn, B 'trɔt-] *s.* (dep.) palangre, espinel.

Trotskyism ['trɑtskɪˌɪzəm, B 'trɔt-] *s.* (pol.) trotskismo, doctrinas políticas de León Trotsky.

Trotskyite [-ˌaɪt] *a., s.* trotskista, partidario de Trotsky o sus doctrinas políticas.

trotter ['trɑtər, B 'trɔtə] *s.* 1. trotón, trotador. 2. pie de cerdo, patita de chancho (Amer.) (como alimento).

trotyl ['troʊtəl] *s.* (quím.) trotil.

troubadour ['trubəˌdɔr, B -ˌdʊə] *s.* (fr.) trovador.

trouble [trʌbəl] *v.t.* 1. inquietar, alterar, preocupar, angustiar. 2. afligir, hostigar. 3. incomodar, molestar, importunar, estorbar. 4. agitar, perturbar, disturbar, revolver. 5. **may I t. you?** ¿me hace Ud. el favor?; **to be troubled with,** padecer de; **to fish in troubled waters,** pescar en río revuelto; **t. oneself,** molestarse. —*v.i.* 1. incomodarse, darse la molestia, molestarse. 2. inquietarse, preocuparse, apurarse. 3. **why should I t. to explain?** ¿por qué tengo que molestarme en dar una explicación? —*s.* 1. disturbio, perturbación, agitación. 2. contratiempo, infortunio, dificultad; incomodidad, inconveniencia. 3. inquietud, preocupación; vejación, pena, aflicción. 4. esfuerzo, molestia. 5. mal, enfermedad, ej., *lung t.,* enfermedad del pulmón. 6. (mec.) avería, ej., *engine t.,* avería del motor. 7. **no t. at all,** no es molestia, con mucho gusto; **not to be worth the t.,** no valer la pena; **that's the t.,** ahí está el busilis, ésa es la dificultad; **the t. is (that),** lo malo es que; **to ask for t.,** (fam.) buscarse líos; **to be in t.,** hallarse en un apuro; estar en un aprieto; **to be looking for t.,** buscarle cinco pies al gato; **to get into t.,** meterse en líos; **to give t.,** dar molestia; **to have t. with (someone or something),** tener dificultades con (alguien o algo); **to make t.,** causar dificultades; **to put oneself to the t. to (do),** tomarse la molestia de (hacer); **to stir up t.,** encender la mecha, armar un lío; **to take the t. to (do),** tomarse la molestia de, tomarse el trabajo de (hacer); **to take (much, little) t. to (do),** emplear (mucho, poco) cuidado en (hacer); **what's the t.?** ¿qué pasa?

troubled [-əld] *a.* 1. preocupado (ojos, cara, expresión, etc.). 2. agitado, disturbado (zona, área, atmósfera, etc.).

trouble-free ['trʌbəl'fri] *a.* 1. sin defectos, sin desperfectos, ininterrumpido (funcionamiento, etc.). 2. libre de disturbios (zona, área, etc.).

trouble light, luz o farol de emergencia.

troublemaker ['trʌbəlˌmeɪkər, B -kə] *s.* perturbador, alborotador, camorrista.

troubler ['trʌblər, B -lə] *s.* perturbador, alborotador.

troubleshooter [-əlˌʃutər, B -ə] *s.* 1. reparador (de desperfectos en un motor, red eléctrica, instalaciones, etc.). 2. (fig.) mediador (en dificultades, desavenencias, discordias).

troublesome [-səm] *a.* 1. penoso, pesado, gravoso, fastidioso, incómodo, dificultoso. 2. molesto, enfadoso, importuno.

troublesomely [-lɪ] *adv.* molestamente, enfadosamente, con importunidad, importunamente.

troublesomeness [-nəs] *s.* importunidad, pesadez, porfía.

troublous ['trʌbləs] *a.* 1. inquieto, agitado, turbulento. 2. inquietante, perturbador.

trough [trɔf] *s.* 1. camellón, abrevadero; comedero, gamella, pesebre. 2. artesa, pileta, batea (Amer.); dornajo, amasadera; gamellón (para pisar uvas, etc.). 3. canal, conducto (de agua); canalón (del tejado). 4. depresión, vaguada, hondonada. 5. seno (de dos olas). 6. (meteor.) línea de máxima depresión (barométrica).

trounce [traʊns] *v.t.* zurrar, azotar, vapulear; derrotar abrumadoramente (en deportes, juego, etc.).

troupe [trup] *s.* compañía, esp. viajera (de actores o de circo).

trouper ['trupər, B -pə] *s.* actor en una compañía teatral (esp. viajera); **old t.,** actor veterano.

troupial [-pɪəl] *s.* (orn.) trupial, turpial.

trousers ['traʊzərz, B -zəz] *s. pl.* pantalones, calzones; **to wear the t.,** (G.B.) calzarse o llevar los pantalones, ponerse los calzones.

trousseau [trusoʊ] *s.* (fr.) (*pl.* TROUSSEAUX [-soʊz] o TROUSSEAUS) 1. ajuar (de novia). 2. (ant.) atado, lío, paquete.

trout [traʊt] *s.* (ict.) trucha.

trout lily, (bot.) diente de perro.

trouty ['traʊtɪ] *a.* rico en truchas (río).

trouvère [tru'vɛər, B -'vɛə] *s.* (fr.) trovero, trovador.

trove [troʊv] *s.* 1. hallazgo, descubrimiento. 2. colección, tesoro.

trover ['troʊvər, B -və] *s.* (der.) acción reivindicatoria (de una cosa mueble o de su valor).

trow [troʊ] *v.i., v.t.* (ant.) creer; pensar; suponer.

trowel ['traʊəl] *s.* badilejo, llana, paleta; fratás, palustre, trulla (de albañil); desplantador (de jardinero). —*v.t.* (*pret., p.p.* TROWELED o TROWELLED; *p.pr.* TROWELING o TROWELLING) palustrear, fratasar, allanar, emparejar con la llana.

troy [trɔɪ] *a.* troy, del peso troy.

Troy, *s.* Troya, antigua ciudad de Asia Menor.

troy weight, peso troy, sistema de pesos cuya unidad es la libra de 12 onzas.

truancy ['truənsɪ] *s.* 1. briba, tuna; haraganería. 2. ausencia injustificada de la escuela o del trabajo.

truant [-ənt] *s.* 1. haragán, tunante. 2. novillero. 3. **to play t.,** hacer novillos, hacer la rabona. —*v.i.* hacer novillos; tunar, correr la tuna, andar a la briba. —*a.* 1. holgazán, haragán, tunante. 2. que hace novillos.

truce [trus] *s.* (mil.) tregua; cese, pausa, respiro. —*v.i.* concertar o firmar una tregua.

truck [trʌk] *v.t., v.i.* trocar, cambiar, permutar; feriar, cambalachear, trujamanear. —*s.* 1. trueque, cambio, permuta; barata, cambalache. 2. comercio, tráfico, trato; **to have no t. with,** no asociarse, no tener tratos con. 3. efectos menudos (para vender o trocar), buhonería; (esp. E.U.) hortalizas para el mercado. 4. pago de salarios en especie. 5. (fam.) fruslería, baratijas; disparate, tontería; basura.

truck, *s.* 1. carro, carretón; vagoneta; camión, camioneta; autocamión; carretilla de mano; (G.B.) furgón de plataforma. 2. (f.c.) bogie o boggie, carretilla. 3. ruedecilla (esp. ruedecilla fuerte para la cureña de un cañón). 4. (mar.) galleta (de asta o mástil). —*v.t.* acarrear, transportar en camión; llevar en vagoneta o carro. —*v.i.* ser carretero o camionero.

truckage ['trʌkɪdʒ] *s.* camionaje; acarreo.

truck driver, camionero.

trucker [-ər, B -ə] *s.* 1. hortelano, verdulero (esp. el que cultiva hortalizas para el mercado). 2. (Esco.) buhonero.

trucker, *s.* camionero, carretero, carretonero, conductor de camión.

truck farm, huerto de hortalizas (para el mercado).

truck horse, caballo de tiro.

trucking ['trʌkɪŋ] *s.* acarreo, camionaje.

truckle ['trʌkəl] *s.* ruedecilla; rodaja (de muebles). —*v.t., v.i.* mover(se) o rodar sobre ruedecillas o rodajas; hacer rodar.

truckle, *v.i.* **t. to,** someterse servilmente a; servir para ganar favores de, halagar, adular.

truckle bed, carriola.

truckler ['trʌklər, B -lə] *s.* servilón, servilona, adulador, aduladora.

truckline ['trʌkˌlaɪn] *s.* empresa camionera, empresa de transporte vial.

truckload [-ˌloʊd] *s.* camionada, carrada; carretada.

truckman [-mən] *s.* camionero, carretero; carrero.

truck system, (com.) sistema de pago de salarios en especie.

truck tractor, tractor de camión, camión tractor.

truck trailer, camión acoplado, camión de remolque.

truculence ['trʌkjələns] **truculency** [-lənsɪ] *s.* 1. truculencia, fiereza, crueldad. 2. belicosidad, pugnacidad. 3. agresividad, insolencia.

truculent [-lənt] *a.* 1. truculento, feroz, cruel. 2. belicoso, pugnaz. 3. agresivo, insultante, insolente. 4. vituperioso. 5. (raro) destructivo.

truculently [-lɪ] *adv.* 1. con truculencia, truculentamente, ferozmente, cruelmente. 2. belicosamente. 3. agresivamente, insolentemente.

trudge [trʌdʒ] *v.i.* caminar con trabajo, caminar pesada o cansadamente. —*s.* marcha penosa, caminata larga y difícil.

trudgen stroke ['trʌdʒən-] (dep.) brazada a la marinera.

true [tru] *a.* (TRUER; TRUEST) 1. verdadero, cierto, real. 2. verídico, veraz. 3. (con *to*) fiel, leal, constante (a); fidedigno, digno (de). 4. verdadero, genuino, legítimo, puro, natural. 5. (con *to*) conforme (a regla, patrón, norma, modelo, etc.). 6. correcto, exacto, preciso, estricto; fiel (copia, traducción, etc.). 7. (biol.) puro, típico (de su clase). 8. (geol., top., mec.) justo, a plomo, a nivel, alineado. 9. (ant.) honesto, honrado, recto. 10. **t. to life,** conforme con la realidad, exactamente, propiamente, naturalmente; **to come t.,** realizarse, resultar cierto; **to run t. to form** (o **type**), obrar o suceder como era de esperarse. —*adv.* 1. conforme a la verdad, verídicamente, honradamente. 2. en línea recta, sin desviación; con exactitud. —*s.* 1. (gen. con *the*) lo verdadero, lo real. 2. posición correcta, calidad de ser exacto. 3. **in t.,** alineado; **out of t.,** desarreglado, desalineado, mal dispuesto, inexacto. —*v.t.* (*pret., p.p.* TRUED; *p.pr.* TRUING o TRUEING) alinear, rectificar, ajustar (rueda, herramienta, etc.).

true bearing, (top., mar.) rumbo verdadero.

true bill, (der.) acusación aprobada por el gran jurado.

true blue, 1. persona leal, partidario fiel. 2. (ant.) color o tinte azul indeleble.
true-blue ['tru'blu] *a.* leal, fiel, constante.
trueborn [-'bɔrn, B -'bɔn] *a.* legítimo, verdadero (por nacimiento), ej., *a t. Englishman,* inglés de nacimiento.
true-bred [-'brɛd] *a.* de casta o raza legítima (esp. animales).
true copy, copia fiel.
true course, (mar., aer.) rumbo verdadero.
true-false test [-'fɔls-] prueba de cierto o falso (para determinar la veracidad o falsedad de una serie de proposiciones).
truehearted [-'hɑrtəd, B -'hɑt-] *a.* leal, fiel.
trueheartedness [-nəs] *s.* lealtad, fidelidad.
true horizon, 1. (astr.) horizonte racional. 2. (mar.) horizonte real.
true-life ['tru'laɪf] *a.* de la vida real, ej., *a t.-l. story,* una historia de la vida real.
truelove [-'lʌv] *s.* enamorado, enamorada.
truelove knot, true-lover's knot [-'lʌvərz-, B -əz-] nudo o lazo que no se desata fácilmente; emblema de amor ideal.
true meridian, meridiano astronómico.
trueness [-nəs] *s.* 1. fidelidad. 2. sinceridad. 3. verdad. 4. exactitud.
truepenny [-ˌpɛnɪ] *s.* (ant.) tipo honesto (persona digna de confianza).
true ribs, (anat.) costillas verdaderas.
true time, hora solar.
true-to-life, realista, verosímil.
true watt, (elec., electrón.) vatio efectivo.
truffle ['trʌfəl] *s.* (bot.) trufa, criadilla de tierra.
truism ['truˌɪzəm] *s.* 1. truismo, perogrullada; trivialidad. 2. axioma.
trull [trʌl] *s.* (ant.) ramera, perendeca, prostituta.
truly ['trulɪ] *adv.* 1. verdaderamente, en verdad. 2. honestamente, propiamente, genuinamente, lealmente, sinceramente. 3. con exactitud, correctamente. 4. fielmente, lealmente. 5. de hecho; en realidad, efectivamente, de veras. 6. **I'm t. sorry,** lo siento de verdad; **yours t.,** su seguro servidor.
trump [trʌmp] *s.* 1. triunfo, palo de triunfo (en juegos de naipes). 2. (fam.) buen sujeto, buena persona. 3. **no t.,** (bridge) sin triunfo; **to turn up trumps,** (fam.) superar las expectativas; tener un golpe de fortuna. *—v.t.* 1. matar con un triunfo. 2. vencer, ganar a, sobrepujar, aplastar, dejar sin palabra. 3. **t. up,** forjar, inventar, fabricar. *—v.i.* triunfar, jugar (del palo del) triunfo.
trump, *s.* 1. (poét., ant.) trompa, trompeta. 2. (Esco., Irl.) birimbao. *—v.i., v.t.* (ant.) tocar (la trompa); anunciar a son de trompa.
trump card, (lit., fig.) carta de triunfo; **higher t.,** carta mayor de triunfo; **to play one's t. c.,** (fig.) jugar su mejor carta.
trumped-up ['trʌmpt'ʌp] *a.* fraudulento, fraguado, falso.
trumpery ['trʌmpərɪ] *s.* (*pl.* TRUMPERIES) 1. baratija, cachivache, bujería, hojarasca. 2. (fig.) disparate, tontería. *—a.* de oropel, cursi, charro; inventado, engañoso.
trumpet ['trʌmpət] *s.* 1. (mús.) trompeta. 2. trompetero, trompeta. 3. trompetilla. 4. corneta acústica. 5. (S. de E.U.) (*pl.*) (bot.) sarracenia. 6. **to blow one's own t.,** darse charol, cantar sus propias alabanzas. *—v.t.* anunciar o proclamar a son de trompeta. *—v.i.* 1. tocar la trompeta, trompetear. 2. barritar, berrear (el elefante).
trumpet creeper, (bot.) jazmín trompeta.
trumpeter [-ər, B -ə] *s.* 1. (mús., mil.) trompetero, trompeta; corneta (en la orquesta). 2. (fig.) portavoz, pregonero. 3. (orn.) agamí trompeta.
trumpet fish, (ict.) centrisco, chocha de mar, trompetero.
trumpet flower, (bot.) 1. jazmín trompeta. 2. madreselva.
trumpet honeysuckle, (bot.) madreselva.
trumpetlike ['trʌmpətˌlaɪk] *a.* 1. atrompetado. 2. como de una trompeta (sonido).
trumpet vine, (bot.) jazmín trompeta.
trumpetweed [-ˌwid] *s.* (bot.) eupatorio maculado; eupatorio purpúreo.
truncate ['trʌŋkeɪt] *v.t.* truncar, troncar; desmochar, podar. *—a.* truncado, trunco.
truncated cone [-əd-] (geom.) cono truncado.
truncation [ˌtrʌŋ'keɪʃən] *s.* truncamiento, tronca.
truncheon ['trʌntʃən] *s.* 1. bastón, vara (esp. del policía). 2. cachiporra, tranca. *—v.t.* (ant.) zurrar con cachiporra.
trundle ['trʌndəl] *s.* 1. rodaja, rodillo, ruedecilla. 2. carretilla de mano. 3. (mec.) piñón, linterna; barrote de linterna. *—v.t.* 1. rodar (aro de niños, cilindro, etc.). 2. (gen. con *along, down,* etc.) ir rodando. *—v.t.* 1. hacer rodar. 2. llevar en carretilla, transportar en carrito.
trundle bed, carriola.
trundle-tail [-ˌteɪl] *s.* (ant.) perro de cola crespa o rizada; perro cruzado.
trunk [trʌŋk] *s.* 1. tronco (de árbol, del cuerpo, de una familia, arterial, etc.); tórax (de un insecto). 2. baúl, cofre. 3. maletera (Amer.), valija (del automóvil). 4. proboscis, esp. trompa (de elefante). 5. (*pl.*) trusa. 6. pozo, cañón, conducto (de ventilación, descarga, etc.); tubería maestra o principal (de abastecimientos, de alcantarillas, etc.). 7. línea principal telefónica (entre dos centrales, línea interurbana). 8. (arq.) fuste (de columna). 9. (mar.) mamparo encerrador de escotilla. *—a.* troncal, principal, del tronco.
trunk call, (pr. G.B.) llamada de larga distancia.
trunk crane, grúa automóvil, camión grúa, carro grúa.
trunk dealer, baulero, cofrero.
trunk engine, (mec.) máquina de vástago tubular; máquina de émbolo de tronco.
trunkfish ['trʌŋkˌfɪʃ] *s.* (ict.) chapín, cofre.
trunk line, 1. (f.c.) línea principal. 2. (tele.) línea interurbana o principal. 3. (mil.) línea de enlace; línea de abastecimiento principal.
trunk piston, (mec.) émbolo de tronco, émbolo abierto.
trunnel ['trʌnəl] *var. de* **treenail.**
trunnion ['trʌnjən] *s.* (arm., mec.) muñón, gorrón.
truss [trʌs] *v.t.* 1. (t. con *up*) liar, atar. 2. embroquetar (las piernas y alas de las aves), espetar las piernas de (las aves). 3. (ing.) atirantar, apuntalar, armar. 4. (mar.) atrozar. 5. (gen. con *up*) apretar, ajustar (vestido); (ant.) ahorcar (reo). *—s.* 1. haz, atado, lío (esp. de paja o heno); (G.B.) atado de heno de 56 o 60 libras; atado de paja de 36 libras. 2. (arq.) ménsula, cartela, can, canecillo, modillón; (ing.) armazón, armadura (de techo o tejado). 3. (med.) braguero (para hernia). 4. (bot.)mazorca, racimo (de una flor). 5. (mar.) troza.
truss beam, (const.) viga armada o reforzada.
truss bridge, puente de armadura, puente de celosía.
trussing['trʌsɪŋ] *s.* 1. amarradura, amarre, ligadura. 2. (ing.) armadura, refuerzo.
trust [trʌst] *s.* 1. confianza, fe, creencia (en una persona). 2. expectación; esperanza. 3. tarea, deber, encargo, obligación. 4. responsabilidad, cuidado, custodia, cargo. 5. (der.) fideicomiso. 6. (com.) trust, consorcio. 7. (raro) confiabilidad, integridad, honradez. 8. **in t.,** en administración; en fideicomiso; **on t.,** a crédito, al fiado; **to take on t.,** creer o aceptar a ojos cerrados. *—v.i.* 1. (con *in* o *to*) confiar en, fiarse de. 2. abrigar esperanza; esperar, ej., *I t. you will write,* espero que escribirás. *—v.t.* 1. confiar en, contar con, fiarse de. 2. dar fe a, creer. 3. (con *to, with* o *in*) encomendar (a), depositar (en). 4. dar crédito a, fiar a. 5. **to be trusted,** gozar de confianza; **t. (someone) with (something),** confiar (algo) a (alguien), ej., *you can't t. him with money,* no se le puede confiar dinero.
trust account, (fin.) cuenta de registro.
trust certificate, (com.) certificado de participación en una sociedad inversionista.
trust company, compañía de depósito, sociedad de fideicomiso, banco fiduciario.
trust deed, (der.) escritura fiduciaria, contrato de fideicomiso; título constitutivo de hipoteca.
trustee [ˌtrʌs'ti] *s.* (der.) fiduciario, síndico, fideicomisario, patrono, depositario, consignatario; miembro del directorio de una institución. *—v.t.* encomendar a un fiduciario o síndico. *—v.i.* actuar como fiduciario o síndico.
trusteeship [-ˌʃɪp] *s.* 1. cargo del fiduciario o fideicomisario. 2. administración fiduciaria (de un territorio).
trust estate, (der.) bienes de fideicomiso.
trustful ['trʌstfəl] *a.* confiado.
trustfully [-fəlɪ] *adv.* confiadamente.
trustfulness [-fəlnəs] *s.* confianza plena.
trust fund, fondo fiduciario (de dinero, valores, títulos, obligaciones, etc.).
trustily ['trʌstəlɪ] *adv.* fielmente, lealmente.
trustiness [-tɪnəs] *s.* fidelidad, probidad.
trusting [-tɪŋ] *a.* que confía; confiado.
trustingly [-lɪ] *adv.* confiadamente.
trustless ['trʌtləs] *a.* 1. indigno de confianza, desleal. 2. desconfiado, receloso.
trust territory, territorio bajo administración fiduciaria.
trustworthiness [-ˌwɜrðɪnəs, B -ˌwɜðɪ-] *s.* confiabilidad, integridad, honradez.
trustworthy [-ðɪ] *a.* confiable, fiable, fidedigno, seguro.
trusty ['trʌstɪ] *a.* (TRUSTIER; TRUSTIEST) confiable, fiel, leal. *—s.* persona confiable, persona digna de confianza; (E.U.) presidiario considerado digno de confianza y que se ha merecido ciertos privilegios.
truth [truθ] *s.* (*pl.* TRUTHS [truðz, truθs]) 1. verdad, realidad. 2. exactitud, corrección, validez. 3. veracidad, sinceridad, honestidad. 4. (pr. G.B.) posición correcta; **out of t.,** desalineado. 5. **T.** (Ciencia Cristiana) Verdad, Dios. 6. **in t.,** (lit.) a la verdad, en verdad, en realidad, seriamente; **of a t.,** (ant.) de veras, por supuesto, en verdad; **to speak the t.,** a decir verdad.
truthful ['truθfəl] *a.* verídico. veraz.
truthfully [-fəlɪ] *adv.* verídicamente, con verdad, verazmente.
truthfulness [-fəlnəs] *s.* veracidad.
truth serum, (crim., psic.) suero de la verdad.
truth value, *s.* (lóg.) veracidad o falsedad de una proposición.
try [traɪ] *v.t.* (*pret., p.p.* TRIED; *p.pr.* TRYING) 1. probar, poner a prueba (cualidad, persona, paciencia, etc.). 2. probar, ensayar, intentar, procurar. 3. (der.) someter a juicio (persona); ver (causa, litigio); (con *for*) procesar, juzgar (por asesinato, robo, etc.). 4. irritar, exasperar. 5. forzar, cansar (la vista, nervios, etc.). 6. (t. con *up*) acepillar (madera). 7. refinar, purificar. 8. (ant.) demostrar, comprobar, verificar. 9. querer + *inf.,* ej. *it is trying to rain,* quiere llover. — **to be tried for one's life,** ser juzgado por un crimen que puede costarle (a uno) la cabeza; **t. on,** probarse (ropa, zapatos, etc.); **t. (it, tricks, etc.) on**

with (someone), probar el efecto de (algo, un truco, etc.) en (alguien); **t. one's hand at,** probar su habilidad en (algo); probar su suerte en (juego, etc.); **t. out,** someter a prueba, probar; fundir (grasa de ballena); **t. to (do),** tratar de (hacer), probar a (hacer). —*v.i.* procurar, esforzarse; tratar de (hacer); **t. and (do),** (fam.) tratar de (hacer), ej., *t. and be patient,* trate de tener paciencia; **t. for,** tratar de lograr (entendimiento, mejores relaciones, etc.); competir para, solicitar (empleo, oficio, etc.); **t. hard,** esforzarse mucho. —*s.* (*pl.* TRIES) 1. prueba, ensayo, intento. 2. (rugby) tanto, marca (señalado poniendo la pelota en la línea de la meta contraria o detrás de ella). 3. **to have a t. at it,** hacer el intento; **to make a t. at,** intentar.

trying ['traɪɪŋ] *a.* molesto, exasperante, irritante; penoso, angustioso, difícil, ej., *a t. time,* un rato difícil.

trying plane, (carp.) garlopín, garlopa.

tryma ['traɪmə] *s.* (bot.) trima.

tryout ['traɪ,aʊt] *s.* 1. prueba de aptitud (de un participante, concursante, actor, etc.). 2. experimento. 3. (E.U.) ensayo (de una obra teatral).

trypanosome [trɪp'ænə,soʊm, B 'trɪpənə-] *s.* (zool.) tripanosoma.

trypanosomiasis [-,ænəsə'maɪəsəs, B ,trɪpənoʊsə-] *s.* (med.) tripanosomiasis.

tryparsamide [trɪp'ɑrsə,maɪd, B -'ɑsə-] *s.* (farm.) triparsamida.

trypsin ['trɪpsən] *s.* (bioquím.) tripsina.

trypsinogen [trɪp'sɪnədʒən] *s.* (fisiol.) tripsinógeno.

tryptic ['trɪptɪk] *a.* (fisiol.) tríptico.

tryptophan [-tə,fæn] **tryptophane** [-,feɪn] *s.* (bioquím.) triptofano.

trysail ['traɪ,seɪl, -səl] *s.* (mar.) vela cangreja.

trysail mast, (mar.) esnón.

try square, (carp.) escuadra de comprobación.

tryst [trɪst, B traɪst] *s.* 1. cita (esp. de amantes); lugar de cita. 2. (Esco., dial.) mercado, feria. —*v.t., v.i.* (ant.) acordar o concertar(se) una cita con; acudir a una cita.

tsade ['tsɑdə, -dɪ] *s.* sadhé (letra hebrea).

tsar [tsɑr, B zɑ] *var. de* **czar.**

tsetse ['tsɛtsɪ, 'tɛtsɪ] *s.* mosca tsetsé.

T-shirt ['ti,ʃɜrt, B -,ʃɜt] *s.* camiseta interior con manga corta; polera (Amer.).

T-square [-,skwɛr, B -,skwɛə] escuadra en T, regla T. doble escuadra.

T-tube [-,tub, B -,tjub] *s.* tubo en T.

T.U. *abrev. de* **trade union,** sindicato.

Tuareg ['twɑ,rɛg] *s.* tuareg, lenguaje y miembro de las tribus bereberes de África.

tuatara [,tuə'tɑrə] *s.* (zool.) tuatara, tuatera.

tub [tʌb] *s.* 1. tina, barril, cuba, tonel, artesón. 2. tina, bañera, bañadera (Amer.); (fam.) baño de tina. 3. (fam.) buque viejo y lento; persona gorda o corpulenta. 4. tonelete o barrilillo (como medida de capacidad variable). 5. (min.) cubeta, balde (para transportar mineral o carbón). —*v.t.* (*pret., p.p.* TUBBED; *p.pr.* TUBBING) 1. encubar, entubar. 2. bañar en tina. —*v.i.* bañarse, lavarse.

tuba ['tubə, B 'tju-] *s.* (mús.) tuba.

tubal ['tubəl, B 'tju-] *a.* (med.) tubárico, tubario.

tubate [-,beɪt] *a.* (bot.) tubular, tubuloso.

tubber ['tʌbər, B -ə] *s.* barrilero, tonelero.

tubby ['tʌbɪ] *a.* (TUBBIER; TUBBIEST) gordiflón, rechoncho.

tube [tub, B tjub] *s.* 1. tubo; caño. 2. cámara de aire (de neumáticos). 3. túnel subterráneo (para ferrocarriles); ferrocarril subterráneo (en Londres). 4. (anat.) trompa, tubo. 5. (bot.) tubo, caño, cañón, cañuto, conducto. 6. (elec.) tubo, válvula. —*v.t.* entubar; proveer de tubo(s).

tube foot, (zool.) pie ambulacral.

tubeless ['tubləs, B 'tjub-] *a.* sin cámara (llanta neumática).

tube of force, (fís.) tubo de fuerzas.

tuber ['tubər, B 'tjubə] *s.* 1. (bot.) tubérculo. 2. (anat.) tuberosidad, tubérculo.

tubercle [-kəl] *s.* (bot., anat., med.) tubérculo.

tubercle bacillus, (bact.) bacilo de Koch, bacilo de la tuberculosis.

tubercled [-kəld] *a.* tuberculado.

tubercular [tʊ'bɜrkjələr, B tju'bɜkjʊlə] *a.* 1. (med.) tuberculoso. 2. tuberculado, tubercular. —*s.* (med.) tuberculoso, tuberculosa.

tuberculate [-lət] *a.* tuberculado; tubercular, tuberculoso.

tuberculated [-,leɪtəd] *a.* tuberculado.

tuberculation [-,bɜrkjə'leɪʃən, B -,bɜkjʊ-] *s.* tuberculización, tuberculación.

tuberculin [-'bɜrkjələn, B -'bɜkjʊ-] *s.* (bact.) tuberculina.

tuberculoid [-,lɔɪd] *a.* (med.) tuberculoide.

tuberculosis [tʊ,bɜrkjə'loʊsɪs, B tju,bɜkjʊ-] *s.* (med.) tuberculosis.

tuberculotoxin [-'bɜrkjəloʊ,tɑksən, B -'bɜkjʊlə,tɔk-] *s.* (med.) tuberculotoxina.

tuberculous [-ləs] *a.* tuberculoso.

tuberose ['tub,roʊz, B 'tjubə-] *s.* (bot.) tuberosa, nardo.

tuberosity [,tubə'rɑsətɪ, B ,tjubə'rɔs-] *s.* (*pl.* TUBEROSITIES) (anat.) tuberosidad.

tuberous ['tubərəs, B 'tju-] *a.* tuberoso.

tuberous comfrey, (bot.) consuelda menor.

tuberous root, (bot.) raíz tuberosa.

tube saw, sierra tubular.

tube shaped, tubular.

tubicolous [tʊ'bɪkələs, B tjʊ-] *a.* (zool.) tubícola.

tubiform ['tubə,fɔrm, B 'tjubɪ,fɔm] *a.* tubiforme.

tubing ['tubɪŋ, B 'tju-] *s.* 1. entubado, tubería, tubuladura, cañería. 2. material para tubos, trozo de tubo.

tubular [-bjələr, B -lə] *a.* tubular.

tubular boiler, caldera multitubular.

tubulate [-lət] *a.* tubulado.

tubulature [-lətʃər, B -tʃə] *s.* 1. tubuladura. 2. tubería.

tubule ['tubjul, B 'tju-] *s.* (anat.) túbulo.

tubuliferous [,tubjə'lɪfərəs, B ,tju-] *a.* (ento.) tubulífero.

tubulous ['tubjələs, B 'tju-] *a.* tubuloso, tubulado.

tubulure [-,lʊr, B -,lʊə] *s.* tubuladura (de una retorta, etc.).

tuck [tʌk] *v.t.* 1. (cost.) alforzar, plegar, doblar (tela, etc.). 2. apretar. 3. poner en lugar abrigado o cómodo. 4. **t. away,** ocultar; comer vorazmente, tragar; **t. in,** apretujar en, meter en (el bolsillo el dinero, en el pantalón, la camisa, etc.); arropar (a alguien en cama, etc.); acostar (a criatura, etc.); **t. oneself in,** arrebujarse; **t. up,** arropar (a alguien en cama, etc.); acostar (a criatura, etc.); arremangar, sobarcar. —*v.i.* 1. doblarse, plegarse. 2. caber ajustadamente, encajar(se) bien. 3. (pr. G.B.) **t. in** (o **into**), comer (algo) con buen apetito. —*s.* 1. alforza, pliegue, dobladillo. 2. (natación) salto mortal. 3. (jer., G.B.) comestibles, esp. pasteles y dulces. 4. (E.U.) vitalidad, energía. 5. (mar.) arca de popa.

tuck, *s.* (hist.) espadín, estoque.

tucker ['tʌkər, B -ə] *s.* 1. (cost.) escote (adorno en el cuello de la camisa). 2. alforzador (de la máquina de coser). 3. (pr. Aust.) comida.

tucker out, (fam., E.U.) dejar agotado, dejar hecho polvo; **all tuckered out,** hecho polvo, molido, cansado.

tucker-bag [-,bæg] *s.* (pr. Aust.) alforja, mochila (para llevar comida).

tucket ['tʌkət] *s.* trompetazo, clarinada.

tuck-in ['tʌk,ɪn] *s.* (jer., G.B.) comilona.

tuck-shop [-,ʃɑp, B -,ʃɔp] *s.* (jer., G.B.) dulcería, confitería, pastelería.

tucu-tucu ['tuku'tuku] **tuco-tuco** ['tukoʊ'tukoʊ] *s.* (zool.) tucutuco.

Tues. *abrev. de* **Tuesday,** martes (mart.).

Tuesday ['tuzdɪ, B 'tjuz-] *s.* martes.

tufa ['tufə, B 'tju-] *s.* (geol.) tufo, toba (caliza o calcárea).

tufaceous [tu'feɪʃəs, B tju-] *a.* tufáceo, tobáceo.

tuff [tʌf] *s.* tufo, toba (piedra volcánica).

tuffaceous [tʌ'feɪʃəs] *a.* tufáceo, tobáceo.

tuft [tʌft] *s.* 1. copete, penacho, cresta; tupé, moño; mechón (de pelo). 2. manojo, hacecillo. 3. borla. 4. montecillo, elevación. 5. basta, puntadas; botón sujetador (en colchones, etc.). —*v.t.* 1. adornar con borlas o penachos. 2. fijar el relleno de (los colchones) con hilos o botones.

tufted ['tʌftəd] *a.* copetudo, empenachado.

tufter [-tər, B -tə] *s.* colchonero.

tufthunter ['tʌft,hʌntər, B -ə] *s.* adulón, quitamotas.

tufting needle ['tʌftɪŋ-] aguja colchonera.

tufty [-tɪ] *a.* (TUFTIER; TUFTIEST) empenachado.

tug [tʌg] *v.t.* (*pret., p.p.* TUGGED; *p.pr.* TUGGING) 1. tirar de. 2. arrastrar, halar, jalar (Amer.), remolcar. —*v.i.* 1. tirar con fuerza. 2. esforzarse, luchar. —*s.* 1. tirón, estirón, jalón (Amer.). 2. esfuerzo, lucha. 3. cuerda, cadena de remolque. 4. contratirante (en los arreos). 5. remolcador (barco).

tugboat ['tʌg,boʊt] *s.* remolcador (barco).

tug of war, 1. (dep.) competencia en que dos bandos tiran de extremos opuestos de una cuerda. 2. (fig.) lucha crítica, esfuerzo supremo (entre dos bandos).

tui ['tuɪ] *s.* (orn.) tui, tuy.

tuille [twil] *s.* faldar (parte de la armadura antigua).

tuition [tʊ'ɪʃən, B tju-] *s.* 1. enseñanza, instrucción. 2. derechos de matrícula, cuota que se paga por la instrucción.

tuitional [-əl] *a.* de enseñanza.

tularemia [,tulə'rimɪə, B ,tju-] *s.* (med., vet.) tularemia.

tule ['tulɪ, B -leɪ] *s.* (bot.) tule.

tulip ['tuləp, B 'tju-] *s.* (bot.) tulipán.

tulip tree, (bot.) tulipero, tulipanero.

tulipwood [-,wʊd] *s.* madera del tulipanero.

tulle [tul, B tjul] *s.* tul.

tumble ['tʌmbəl] *v.i.* 1. dar volteretas, brincar, saltar (esp. en acrobacia). 2. tumbar, caer pesadamente, caerse, dar en tierra, desplomarse. 3. dar tumbos, dar vueltas (por ej., un proyectil en el aire); voltearse. 4. rodar, revolcarse. 5. tambalearse, ir bamboleándose. 6. caer, bajar (los precios). 7. (fam.) darse cuenta, comprender. 8. **t. down,** derrumbarse, desplomarse, venirse abajo; **t. in,** encajar (una pieza de madera dentro de otra); **t. into** (o **upon**), tropezar con; **t. into bed,** tumbarse (en la cama); **t. out,** salir a montones, salir tumultuosamente; levantarse (de la cama); **t. to (something),** (fam.) caer en la cuenta de (algo); (G.B.) adaptarse a; **t. to someone's game,** verle el juego a alguien. —*v.t.* 1. tumbar, derribar. 2. demoler, desplomar, derrumbar. 3. desordenar, revolver, desarreglar (ropa, objetos); despeinar (cabello). 4. revolver en tambor (metales para pulirlos, cueros para ablandarlos, etc.). 5. **t. into,** echar desordenadamente en. —*s.* 1. caída. 2. vuelco, voltereta (esp.

en acrobacia). 3. tumbo (de las olas, etc.). 4. desorden, confusión. 5. montón, montones. 6. **to give a t. to,** mostrar interés por; **to take** (o **have**) **a** (**slight, nasty,** etc.) **t.,** dar un tumbo, rodar, caerse (ligeramente, aparatosamente, etc.).

tumble bay, (hidr.) amortiguador de energía, lecho amortiguador.

tumblebug [-ˌbʌg] *s.* (ento.) escarabajo pelotero.

tumbledown [-ˌdaʊn] *a.* destartalado, arruinado.

tumble-dry ['tʌmbəl'draɪ] *v.t.* secar en secadora.

tumble-dryer [tʌmbəl'draɪər] *s.* secadora.

tumbler ['tʌmblər, B -blə] *s.* 1. vaso. 2. acróbata, volatinero, saltimbanqui. 3. guarda, tumbador, volcador (de una cerradura). 4. seguro de escopeta. 5. tambor (giratorio, de limpieza, desarenador, etc.). 6. tentempié, tentetieso, dominguillo (juguete). 7. (mec.) muñequilla (en cigüeñal, eje, etc.); volcador, pestillo. 8. perro conejero. 9. (orn.) pichón volteador.

tumbler switch, (elec.) interruptor de volquete.

tumbleweed ['tʌmbəlˌwid] *s.* (bot.) planta rodadora.

tumbling ['tʌmblɪŋ] *s.* acrobacia.

tumbling barrel, tambor de limpieza o de frotación, molino a tambor.

tumbrel, tumbril ['tʌmbrəl] *s.* 1. carreta, carretón, chirrión. 2. (ant.) carro de artillería. 3. (hist.) silla de chapuzar (en que se ataba a la persona para sumergirla en el agua).

tumefacient [ˌtumə'feɪʃənt, B ˌtju-] *a.* (med.) tumefaciente.

tumefaction [-'fækʃən] *s.* tumefacción.

tumefy ['tuməˌfaɪ, B 'tju-] *v.t., v.i.* (*pret., p.p.* TUMEFIED; *p.pr.* TUMEFYING) tumefacer(se).

tumescence [tu'mɛsəns, B tju-] *s.* tumescencia.

tumescent [-ənt] *a.* tumescente.

tumid ['tuməd, B 'tju-] *a.* 1. hinchado. 2. protuberante, prominente. 3. (fig.) túmido, hinchado, pomposo (estilo, etc.).

tumidity [tu'mɪdətɪ, B tju-] *s.* (fig.) hinchazón, pomposidad.

tumidly ['tumədlɪ, B 'tju-] *adv.* (fig.) pomposamente.

tumidness [-nəs] *s.* (fig.) hinchazón, pomposidad.

tummy ['tʌmɪ] *s.* (*pl.* TUMMIES) (fam.) barriguita, barriga.

tummyache ['tʌmɪeɪk] *s.* (fam.) dolor de barriga, dolor de tripa.

tumor, (pr. G.B.) **tumour** ['tumər, B 'tjumə] *s.* tumor, hinchazón, bulto.

tumorous ['tumərəs, B 'tjum-] *a.* tumoroso.

tump [tʌmp] *s.* (dial., G.B.) loma, montecillo; grupo de árboles en una elevación; montón.

tumpline ['tʌmpˌlaɪn] *s.* correa que se lleva alrededor de la cabeza o de los hombros para llevar peso sobre la espalda.

tumular ['tumjələr, B 'tju-lə] *a.* tumulario.

tumult ['tuˌmʌlt, B 'tju-] *s.* tumulto, alboroto; conmoción.

tumultuary [tʊ'mʌltʃʊˌɛrɪ, B tju'mʌltjʊərɪ] *a.* tumultuario.

tumultuous [-əs] *a.* tumultuoso, agitado, alborotado.

tumultuously [-lɪ] *adv.* tumultuosamente.

tumultuousness [-nəs] *s.* estado tumultuoso, turbulencia.

tumulus ['tumjələs, B 'tju-] *s.* (*pl.* TUMULI [-ˌlaɪ]) túmulo.

tun [tʌn] *s.* tonel para vino (esp. el de una capacidad de 252 galones).

tuna ['tunə, B 'tju-] *s.* 1. (bot.) tuna, higuero de tuna. 2. tuna, higo chumbo, nopal.

tuna, *s.* (ict.) atún.

tunable, tuneable ['tunəbəl, B 'tju-] *a.* 1. afinable, templable (instrumentos de música). 2. (rad.) sintonizable. 3. (ant.) armonioso, melodioso; concordante.

tundra ['tʌndrə] *s.* tundra, desiertos en la región ártica esp. Rusia y Laponia.

tune [tun, B tjun] *s.* 1. aire, tonada, son. 2. tono (correcto), consonancia. 3. (fig.) armonía, concordancia (de mente o temperamento). 4. **in t.,** en tono; afinado; **in t. with,** en armonía con; **out of t.,** desentonado, desafinado; **to be out of t. with,** (fig.) no armonizar con, no estar en armonía con; **to change one's t.,** (fig.) ensayar por otra vía; cambiar de tono (al hablar); **to put out of t.,** destemplar; **to the t. of,** por la cantidad de. —*v.t.* 1. afinar, templar (instrumento). 2. (fig.) (con *to*) ajustar, adaptar (algo a finalidad, circunstancias, etc.). 3. (con *with*) armonizar (con). 4. (poét.) entonar, cantar, modular. 5. **t. in,** (rad., t.v.) sintonizar; **t. out,** (rad., t.v.) desintonizar; **t. up,** (mús.) afinar; (mec.) afinar, poner a punto (un motor, etc.). —*v.i.* asonar, armonizar; **t. in on,** (rad., t.v.) sintonizar; **t. in,** (jer., E.U.) estar o estarse al tanto de; **t. out,** (jer., E.U.) retirarle el apoyo, la simpatía a una causa; **t. up,** afinar (orquesta); entonar (cantante, músico); ajustar, afinar (motor, etc.).

tuneful ['tunfəl, B 'tjun-] *a.* 1. armonioso, melodioso, musical. 2. sonoro.

tunefully [-fəlɪ] *adv.* armoniosamente, melodiosamente, musicalmente.

tuneless [-ləs] *a.* 1. desentonado, disonante, discordante. 2. silencioso, enmudecido, mudo.

tuner ['tunər, B 'tjunə] *s.* 1. afinador. 2. (rad.) sintonizador.

tune-up ['tunˌʌp, B 'tjun-] *s.* 1. puesta a punto, afinamiento (de un motor, etc.). 2. prueba preliminar; ejercicio previo.

tung oil ['tʌŋ-] aceite de palo, aceite de tung.

tungstate ['tʌŋˌsteɪt] *s.* (quím.) tungstato.

tungsten ['tʌŋstən] *s.* (quím.) tungsteno.

tungsten carbide, acero al carburo tungsteno.

tungsten lamp, lámpara (incandescente con filamento) de tungsteno.

tungsten ochre, (metal.) trióxido de tungsteno nativo, tungstenita.

tungsten steel, acero al tungsteno.

tungstic [-stɪk] *a.* túngstico.

tungstic acid, (quím.) ácido túngstico.

tungstite [-ˌstaɪt] *s.* (min.) tungstita.

Tungus [tʊŋ'guz] *s.* (*pl.* TUNGUS O TUNGUSES) tungus.

Tungusic [-'guzɪk] *a., s.* tungúsico.

tunic ['tunɪk, B 'tju-] *s.* 1. (hist.) túnica. 2. túnica, blusa. 3. (anat., bot., zool.) túnica. 4. (relig.) tunicela, túnica. 5. cubierta natural de plantas, animales, etc.

tunica ['tunɪkə, B 'tju-] *s.* (*pl.* TUNICAE [-nəˌki]) (anat.) túnica.

tunicate [-kət, -ˌkeɪt] **tunicated** [-ˌkeɪtəd] *a.* (bot., zool.) tunicado.

tunicin ['tunəsən, B 'tju-] *s.* (bioquím.) tunicina.

tunicle ['tunɪkəl, B 'tju-] *s.* (relig.) tunicela.

tuning coil ['tunɪŋ-, B 'tju-] (rad.) bobina sintonizadora.

tuning condenser, (rad.) condensador de sintonía.

tuning dial, (rad.) cuadrante de sintonización.

tuning eye, (rad.) indicador de sintonía, ojo mágico.

tuning fork, (mús.) diapasón.

tuning hammer, (mús.) afinador (llave de).

tuning knob, (rad.) botón de sintonía, botón de sintonización.

Tunis ['tunɪs, B 'tju-] *s.* Túnez, capital de Tunicia.

Tunisia [tu'niʒə, B tju'nɪzɪə] *s.* Tunicia (antes Túnez).

Tunisian[-ʒən, B -zɪən] *a., s.* tunecino, de Tunicia.

tunnage *var. de* **tonnage.**

tunnel ['tʌnəl] *s.* 1. túnel. 2. (min.) socavón, galería. 3. (raro) tubo de chimenea. —*v.t.* (*pret., p.p.* TUNNELED O TUNNELLED; *p.pr.* TUNNELING O TUNNELLING) construir (un túnel debajo de); perforar un túnel en. —*v.i.* (gen. con *through, into,* etc.) pasar o atravesar horadando.

tunneler, tunneller [-ər, B -ə] *s.* descombradora de cuchara.

tunnel vision, 1. (ópt.) visión de túnel. 2. (fig.) estrechez de miras.

tunny ['tʌnɪ] *s.* (*pl.* TUNNIES O TUNNY) (ict.) atún.

tup [tʌp] *s.* 1. (pr. G.B.) (zool.) morueco, carnero padre. 2. maza, mazo, calzo, martillo, martinete. —*v.t.* (*pret., p.p.* TUPPED; *p.pr.* TUPPING) (pr. G.B.) cubrir (a la hembra el morueco).

Tupamaros [ˌtupə'mɑroʊz] *s.* tupamaros, nombre de las guerrillas urbanas en Uruguay, derivado de Túpac Amaru, cacique indio que se rebeló contra los españoles.

tupelo ['tupəˌloʊ, B 'tju-] *s.* (*pl.* TUPELOS) (bot.) nisa.

Tupi [tu'pi, B 'tupɪ] *s.* (*pl.* TUPI O TUPIS) tupi, tupí, pueblo indio que habita partes de Brasil y Paraguay.

Tupian [-ən] *a.* tupi, tupí, de la tribu de los Tupis del bajo Amazonas.

Tupi-Guarani [tuˌpiˌgwɑrə'ni, B 'tupɪ-] *s.* tupí-guaraní, idioma y dialectos aborígenes de una vasta región de Sudamérica.

tuppence ['tʌpəns] **tuppenny** [-pənɪ] *s.* (fam.) dos peniques.

tuque [tuk, B tjuk] *s.* gorra tejida canadiense.

Turanian [tʊ'reɪnɪən, B tjʊə-] *a., s.* turanio, turaní, de una región de Turquestán.

turban ['tɜrbən, B 'tɜbən] *s.* turbante.

turban buttercup, (bot.) francesilla, marimoña.

turbaned [-bənd] *a.* tocado con turbante.

turbellarian [ˌtɜrbə'lɛrɪən, B 'tɜbə'lɛər-] *s., a.* (zool.) turbelario.

turbeth ['tɜrbəθ, B 'tɜbɪθ] *var de* **turpeth.**

turbid ['tɜrbəd, B 'tɜbɪd] *a.* 1. turbio, túrbido, espeso. 2. confuso, perplejo. 3. turbulento.

turbidimeter [ˌtɜrbə'dɪmətər, B ˌtɜbɪ-ə] *s.* turbidímetro.

turbidimetric [-də'mɜtrɪk] *a.* turbidimétrico.

turbidity [-'bɪdətɪ] *s.* turbiedad.

turbidly ['tɜrbədlɪ, B 'tɜbɪd-] *adv.* turbiamente.

turbidness [-nəs] *s.* turbiedad, turbulencia, confusión, perplejidad.

turbinal ['tɜrbənəl, B 'tɜbən-] *a.* (anat.) turbinado, turbinal. —*s.* (hueso) turbinado.

turbinate [-bənət] *a.* (bot.) turbinado.

turbine ['tɜrbən, -ˌbaɪn, B 'tɜbɪn] *s.* turbina.

turbit ['tɜrbət, B 'tɜbɪt] *s.* (orn.) paloma de corbata.

turbith ['tɜrbəθ, B 'tɜbɪθ] *var. de* **turpeth.**

turbo ['tɜrboʊ, B 'tɜboʊ] *s.* 1. turbina. 2. *forma abrev. de* **turbosupercharger.**

turboalternator [ˌtɜrboʊ'ɔltərˌneɪtər, B ˌtɜboʊ'ɔltə,-ə] *s.* turboalternador.

turboblower ['tɜrboʊˌbloʊər, B 'tɜboʊ-ə] *s.* turbosoplador.

turbocharger [-ˌtʃɑrdʒər, B -ˌtʃɑdʒə] *s.* turbina alimentadora, turbocompresor, sobrealimentador de turbina.

turbocompressor [ˌtɜrboʊkəm'prɛsər, B ˌtɜboʊ-ə] *s.* turbocompresor.

turbodynamo [-'daɪnəmoʊ] *s.* turbodínamo.
turbofan ['tɜrboʊˌfæn, B 'tɜboʊ-] *s.* turboventilador.
turbogenerator [ˌtɜrboʊ'dʒɛnəˌreɪtər, B 'tɜboʊ-ə] *s.* turbogenerador.
turbojet ['tɜrboʊˌdʒɛt, B 'tɜboʊ-] *s.* (avión) turborreactor.
turbojet engine, (aer.) turborreactor.
turbomachine [-məˌʃin] *s.* turbomáquina.
turbomotor [-ˌmoʊtər, B -ə] *s.* turbomotor.
turboprop[-ˌprɑp, B -'prɔp] *s.* 1. turbopropulsor, turbohélice. 2. avión turbopropulsor.
turbo-propeller engine [ˌtɜrboʊprə'pɛlər-, B ˌtɜboʊ-ə] **turboprop-jet engine** [-'prɑpˌdʒɛt, B -'prɔp] (aer.) turbopropulsor, turbohélice.
turbopump ['tɜrboʊˌpʌmp, B 'tɜboʊ-] *s.* turbobomba.
turboramjet engine [ˌtɜrboʊ'ræmˌdʒɛt-, B ˌtɜboʊ-] (aer.) turborreactor de doble flujo.
turbosupercharger [-'supərˌtʃɑrdʒər, B -'sjupəˌtʃɑdʒə] *s.* turbosobrealimentador, turbosupercargador.
turbot ['tɜrbət, B 'tɜbət] *s.* (*pl.* TURBOT O TURBOTS) (ict.) turbo, rodaballo.
turbulence ['tɜrbjələns, B 'tɜbju-] *s.* turbulencia.
turbulency [-lənsɪ] *s.* (*pl.* TURBULENCIES) *var. de* **turbulence.**
turbulent [-lənt] *a.* turbulento.
turbulent airflow, (aer.) régimen turbulento.
turbulent flow, 1. (hidr.) flujo turbulento. 2. (aer.) régimen turbulento.
turbulently [-lɪ] *adv.* turbulentamente.
Turcoman, *s.* (*pl.* TURCOMANS) *var. de* **Turkoman.**
turd [tɜrd, B tɜd] *s.* 1. (vulg.) excremento (trozo de). 2. (jer., vulg.) persona de poco valor.
tureen [tə'rin] *s.* sopera.
turf [tɜrf, B tɜf] *s.* (*pl.* TURFS O TURVES [tɜrvz, B tɜvz]) 1. césped, tepe. 2. turba. 3. **the t.,** pista de carrera de caballos; carreras de caballos (como deporte). —*v.t.* encespedar, cubrir con césped o tepes; **t. out,** (jer., pr. G.B.) echar, arrojar.
turfman ['tɜrfmən, B 'tɜf-] *s.* turfista, turfman.
turfy ['tɜrfɪ, B 'tɜfɪ] *a.* (TURFIER; TURFIEST) 1. cubierto de turba o césped. 2. semejante a la turba o al césped.
turgescent [tɜr'dʒɛsənt, B ˌtɜ'-] *a.* (poét.) turgente, túrgido, abultado; (fig.) ampuloso, pomposo (estilo, lenguaje).
turgid ['tɜrdʒəd, B 'tɜdʒəd] *a.* 1. turgente, hinchado, abultado. 2. ampuloso, pomposo.
turgidity [ˌtɜr'dʒɪdətɪ, B ˌtɜ'-] *s.* ampulosidad, pomposidad.
turgidly ['tɜrdʒədlɪ, B 'tɜdʒəd-] *adv.* ampulosamente, pomposamente.
turgidness [-nəs] *s.* ampulosidad, pomposidad.
turgite ['tɜrˌdʒaɪt, B 'tɜˌ-] *s.* (min.) turgita.
turgor ['tɜrgər, B 'tɜgə] *s.* (fisiol., bot.) turgor.
turion ['tʊrɪˌɑn, B 'tjʊərɪən] *s.* (bot.) turión.
Turk [tɜrk, B tɜk] *s.* 1. turco. 2. (raza de) caballo turco. 3. musulmán. 4. (ant.) tirano, persona bárbara. 5. **the Grand T.,** el gran Turco (sultán de Turquía).
Turkestan [ˌtɜrkəs'tæn, B ˌtɜkɪs'tɑn] *s.* Turquestán.
turkey ['tɜrkɪ, B 'tɜkɪ] *s.* 1. **T.,** Turquía. 2. (orn.) pavo. 3. (jer.) fracasdo, fiasco; fracasado. 4. **to talk t.,** (fam.) hablar claramente.
turkey buzzard, (orn.) zopilote, gallinazo, aura (Amer.).
turkey-cock [-ˌkɑk, B -ˌkɔk] **turkey-gobbler** [ˌtɜrkɪ'gɑblər, B ˌtɜkɪ'gɔblə] *s.* 1. pavo macho. 2. (fam.) presumido.
turkey oak, (bot.) rebollo, mesto.
Turkey red, rojo turco, grancé.
Turkic ['tɜrkɪk, B 'tɜkɪk] *a.* turco (díc. de una subfamilia de las lenguas uralaltaicas).
Turkish [-kɪʃ] *a.* turco, turquesco. —*s.* turco, lengua turca.
Turkish bath, baño turco.
Turkish delight, T. paste, confite gelatinoso rociado con azúcar.
Turkish empire, imperio otomano.
Turkish saddle, (anat.) silla turca.
Turkish towel, toalla rusa, toalla de felpa gruesa.
Turkism ['tɜrˌkɪzəm, B 'tɜˌ-] *s.* costumbres, creencias, principios e instituciones turcas; (raro) expresión idiomática turca, modismo turco.
Turkoman ['tɜrkəmən, B 'tɜkə-] *s.* turcomano, miembro de las tribus de origen turco que viven en algunas regiones del Cercano Oriente y de la Unión Soviética.
Turkomanic [ˌtɜrkə'mænɪk, B tɜkə-] *a.* turcomano.
Turk's-cap lily, (bot.) martagón.
Turk's head, 1. (mar.) barrilete. 2. (G.B.) escobillón.
turmaline *var. de* **tourmaline.**
turmeric ['tɜrmərɪk, B 'tɜm-] *s.* (bot.) cúrcuma, batatilla.
turmeric paper, (quím.) papel de cúrcuma.
turmoil ['tɜrˌmɔɪl, B 'tɜˌ-] *s.* confusión, agitación, disturbio, alboroto, tumulto, baraúnda.
turn [tɜrn, B tɜn] *v.t.* 1. volver, voltear (Amer.) (cabeza, ojos, etc.). 2. hacer girar, dar vuelta a (rueda, grifo, llaves, etc.); volver (la página). 3. invertir, revolver; volver, virar (Amer.) (un vestido, chaqueta, etc.). 4. torcer (el tobillo). 5. convertir, transformar, cambiar. 6. alterar, afectar; trastornar, perturbar. 7. agriar, volver agrio, ej., *this heat will t. the milk,* este calor agriará la leche. 8. traducir (texto). 9. dar la vuelta a, doblar (esquina). 10. desviar, ej., *will turn a bullet,* puede desviar una bala. 11. cumplir (cierto número de años), ej., *he just turned fifteen,* acaba de cumplir quince años. 12. dar (la hora), ej., *it just turned ten,* acaban de dar las diez. 13. formular, moldear, componer una frase, verso, etc.). 14. mover, comerciar con (capital, mercadería); ganar. 15. tornear. 16. **t. about,** dar vuelta a; **t. a deaf ear to,** hacer oídos sordos a; **t. against,** hacer reñir, enemistar con; **t. an honest penny,** ganarse la vida honradamente; **t. around,** dar vuelta a; voltear; hacer girar; tergiversar, torcer (palabras de uno); **t. aside,** desviar; **t. away,** volver (la cabeza); desviar; negar la entrada a, no admitir, no atender; rechazar; **t. back,** volver atrás, hacer regresar o retroceder; retrasar (el reloj); **t. down,** plegar, doblar hacia abajo; poner boca abajo; bajar (el gas, la luz de la lámpara, etc.); rechazar, rehusar; **t. from,** desviar de, apartar de, rechazar; **t. in,** entregar; entregar a la policía; **t. into,** convertir en, volver en; **t. loose,** dejar libre; desatar, desencadenar (a una persona); **t. off,** cerrar (la llave del agua, gas, etc.); apagar (la luz, radio); cortar (el agua, la luz, etc.); **t. on,** abrir la llave (del agua, gas, luz, etc.); encender (la luz, radio, etc.); fijar (los ojos, mirada) en; (jer.) atraer (sexualmente, etc.), por ej., *she turns me on,* ella me atrae; iniciar en el uso de drogas; **t. one's back on,** (fig.) volver la espalda; **t. one's coat,** volver la casaca, cambiar de opinión; **t. out,** echar, arrojar, expulsar; doblar o torcer hacia afuera (el pie, etc.); producir, fabricar; **t. over,** trastornar, volcar; pasar, entregar, ceder (al cumplise un turno); (com.) hacer negocios por (la suma de); **t. over a new leaf,** (fig.) volver la hoja, comenzar de nuevo, enmendarse; **t. (something) over in one's mind,** pensar (algo) bien; considerar (algo) a fondo; **t. over to,** dejar al cuidado o a cargo de; traspasar a; **t. round,** dar vuelta a; voltear; **t. tail,** mostrar los talones; **t. (the brain, the head) of,** (lit., fig.) volver loco; **t. the cold shoulder to,** desairar; **t. the scale(s),** cambiar el orden de las cosas; determinar, decidir; **t. the stomach,** causar asco; **t. the tables,** cambiar la suerte, volver la tortilla; **t. the trick,** lograr, llevar a cabo; **t. thumbs down on,** condenar a, rechazar; **t. to,** volver hacia, dirigir hacia, inclinar hacia; **t. to (account, advantage, profit),** sacar provecho de, aprovechar; **t. up,** doblar o plegar hacia arriba, arremangar; alzar, levantar (cuello del abrigo, etc.); poner boca arriba; descubrir (un naipe, etc.); desenterrar, sacar a luz; (fam.) encontrar, descubrir; cavar, revolver (la tierra); poner más fuerte (la radio, gas, etc.); **t. up one's nose at,** desdeñar, despreciar; **t. upside down,** poner patas arriba. —*v.i.* 1. dar la vuelta, volverse. 2. girar, rodar. 3. virar; cambiar (de religión, partido, etc.). 4. revolver (se), dar vueltas, ej., *my stomach turns,* se me revuelve el estómago, *my head turns,* me da vueltas la cabeza. 5. curvarse, doblarse. 6. cambiar, ej., *the tide turns,* cambia la marea; (fig.) cambia la suerte. 7. volverse, ponerse (pálido, serio, agrio, etc.); hacerse, volverse, tornarse (traidor, héroe, etc.). 8. volverse, agriarse, acedarse, ranciarse; cuajarse. 9. cambiar de color (esp. hojas). 10. tornearse (bien, mal, etc.). 11. **t. about,** dar vuelta, volverse; **t. against,** volverse contra, rebelarse contra; **t. around,** dar vuelta, dar una vuelta completa; **t. aside,** volver las espaldas; desviarse; **t. back,** volverse; retroceder; **t. down,** doblarse hacia abajo; doblar por, ej., *t. down a street,* doblar por una calle; **t. in,** entrar o regresar a casa; (fam.) acostarse; **t. into,** entrar en; convertirse en; **t. off,** desviarse, torcer, cambiar de rumbo; desalentar, apagar; disgustar; **t. on** (o **upon**) volverse contra, acometer a; **t. on,** tomar drogas, esp. con el propósito de agudizar los sentidos; **t. out,** resultar, salir; acudir, presentarse, asistir; **t. out to be,** venir a ser, resultar ser; **t. over,** volcar (bote, carruaje, etc.); voltearse, dar vueltas; (avia.) capotar; **t. over,** (imper.) a la vuelta (de la página); **t. round,** voltearse; cambiar de frente, cambiar de opinión; **t. round and round,** dar vueltas; **t. to,** torcer hacia, volver hacia (ej., una calle a la izquierda o derecha); recurrir a, acudir a, dirigirse a, ej., *I did not know which way to t.,* no sabía adónde dirigirme; convertirse en; ponerse a trabajar; **t. up,** doblarse hacia arriba; llegar, apersonarse; aparecer; sobrevenir, ocurrir; reaparecer, ser encontrado. —*s.* 1. vuelta, revolución, ej., *a t. of the wheel,* una vuelta de la rueda. 2. movimiento, ej., *with a neat t. of the wrist,* con un movimiento hábil de la muñeca. 3. vuelta, viraje; curva, recodo. 4. espiral, rosca; vuelta (de un rollo); torcimiento, torcedura. 5. vuelta, paseo, caminata. 6. favor, servicio; pasada, ej., *ill* (o *bad*) *t.,* mala pasada. 7. momento, rato, trecho. 8. turno, vez; ocasión, oportunidad. 9. cambio, alteración. 10. rumbo, dirección; giro (de la conversación, frase, etc.). 11. cariz, aspecto, faz. 12. disposición, inclinación; habilidad. 13. requerimiento, ej., *it served your t.,* satisfizo tu requerimiento. 14. sobresalto, ej., *it gave me quite a t.,* me dio un fuerte sobresalto, me dio un vuelco el corazón. 15. (mús.) melisma (de cuatro notas). 16. (teat.) acto corto, número (de variedades, etc.). 17. (impr.) letra vuelta,

letra volcada, cabeza de muerto. 18. (mec.) torno. 19. **at every t.,** a cada paso, a cada rato; **at the t. of (the century,** etc.), al terminar (el siglo, etc.); **by turns,** por turnos; **in t.,** a su vez; **one good t. deserves another,** amor con amor se paga; **out of t.,** fuera de lugar; fuera de orden; **to be one's t.,** tocarle a uno, ej., *now it's our t.,* ahora (nos) toca a nosotros; **to have a t. for,** tener habilidad para; **to take a t.,** dar una vuelta, ej., *I took a t. in the garden,* di una vuelta en el jardín, *he took a t. to the right,* dio una vuelta a la derecha; torcer, ej., *the road took a t. to the left,* el camino torció a la izquierda; **to take a t. for the better,** estar mejorando, empezar a mejorar; **to take a t. for the worse,** estar empeorando, empezar a empeorarse; **to take turns** (at), turnar(se), alternar (en); **turn of mind,** inclinación, disposición, carácter.

turnabout ['tɜrnəˌbaʊt, B 'tɜn-] *s.* 1. cambio de partido o bando; cambio de posición. 2. renegado, tránsfuga. 3. (E.U.) tiovivo.

turnaround [-əˌraʊnd] *s.* 1. espacio para dar la vuelta (un vehículo). 2. cambio completo, giro total. 3. operación de desembarque y embarque, de carga y descarga. 4. (com.) procesamiento. 5. **t. time,** (comput.) tiempo de devolución, tiempo de repuesta.

turnbuckle [-ˌbʌkəl] *s.* (mec.) tornillo, tensor, templador, torniquete.

turncap [-ˌkæp] *s.* caperuza giratoria de chimenea.

turncoat [-ˌkoʊt] *s.* renegado, tránsfuga.

turndown [-ˌdaʊn] *a.* que puede ser doblado hacia abajo; caído (díc. del cuello de camisa). —*s.* rechazo, rechazamiento.

turned comma, (impr.) coma invertida.

turned-up nose, nariz respingona.

turner ['tɜrnər, B 'tɜnə] *s.* 1. tornero, fustero. 2. gimnasta, volatinero.

turner's lathe, torno.

turnery [-nərɪ] *s.* (mec.) tornería.

turn indicator, (aut.) indicador de viraje.

turning [-nɪŋ] *s.* 1. vuelta, rotación, viraje, giro. 2. recodo, meandro, ángulo (del camino), esquina (de la calle). 3. trabajo de tornería, moldeamiento (en el torno); composición (de una frase pulida, etc.).

turning chisel, (mec.) escoplo de torno, formón de tornero, asentador.

turning point, 1. momento crucial, punto decisivo. 2. (top.) punto de cambio.

turnip ['tɜrnəp, B 'tɜnɪp] *s.* 1. (bot.) nabo. 2. (fam.) reloj grueso de bolsillo.

turnix ['tɜrnɪks, B 'tɜnɪks] *s.* (orn.) variedad de codorniz.

turnkey ['tɜrnˌki, B 'tɜn-] *s.* carcelero, alcaide, llavero de una cárcel.

turnoff [-ˌɔf] *s.* 1. desvío (de un camino o carretera). 2. desviación, cambio (de rumbo, ruta, etc.).

turnout [-ˌaʊt] *s.* 1. salida. 2. concurrencia, reunión (para un propósito especial). 3. equipaje, vestido, atavío. 4. carruaje (con sus caballos, servidumbre y equipo). 5. (pr. G.B.) huelga; huelguista. 6. producción, rendimiento. 7. (f.c.) apartadero, desviadero.

turnover [-ˌoʊvər, B -və] *a.* doblado o vuelto hacia abajo. —*s.* 1. vuelco, trastorno. 2. cambio, trasiego. 3. empanada, tarta. 4. movimiento total (de transacciones comerciales, ventas, etc.); producción (de un día, mes, etc.); productividad. 5. cambio de personal; rotación.

turnpike [-ˌpaɪk] *s.* 1. barrera de portazgo o peaje. 2. camino de portazgo; carretera, autopista (esp. con pago de peaje).

turnscrew [-ˌskru] *s.* destornillador.

turn signal, (aut., E.U.) intermitente, direccional (Col., Mex.), señalizador (Chile).

turnsole [-ˌsoʊl] *s.* (bot.) 1. girasol, mirasol, heliotropo. 2. pensel.

turnspit [-ˌspɪt] *s.* asador giratorio.

turnstile ['tɜrnˌstaɪl, B 'tɜn-] *s.* torniquete, molinete.

turnstile antenna, (rad.) antena de torno, antena de molinete.

turnstone [-ˌstoʊn] *s.* (orn.) revuelvepiedras.

turn-switch [-ˌswɪtʃ] *s.* (elec.) interruptor giratorio.

turntable [-ˌteɪbəl] *s.* 1. plataforma giratoria (de ferrocarril). 2. platina portadiscos (de fonógrafo), plato giradiscos. 3. mesa giratoria, soporte giratorio.

turnup [-ˌʌp] *a.* vuelto o doblado hacia arriba; respingona (nariz). —*s.* 1. dobladillo (del pantalón). 2. (pr. G.B.) zacapela, riña, bronca, gresca. 3. **t. for the books,** (fam., G.B.) sorpresa, suceso inesperado.

turpentine ['tɜrpənˌtaɪn, B 'tɜpən-] *s.* 1. trementina. 2. (bot.) terebinto. 3. esencia de trementina, aguarrás. —*v.t.* 1. saturar o frotar con trementina; aplicar trementina a. 2. extraer trementina de (coníferas).

turpeth ['tɜrpəθ, B 'tɜpɪθ] *s.* 1. (bot.) turbit (planta y raíz). 2. (min.) turbit mineral.

turpitude ['tɜrpəˌtud, B 'tɜpɪtjud] *s.* vileza, bajeza, ruindad, depravación.

turquoise ['tɜrˌkwɔɪz, B 'tɜkwɑz] *s.* 1. (min.) turquesa. 2. (**t. turquoise blue**) azul turquesa.

turquoise blue, azul turquesa.

turret ['tɜrət, B 'tʌr-] *s.* 1. torrecilla. 2. (mec.) portaherramientas giratorio. 3. (foto.) portaobjetivos giratorio. 4. (mil.) torreta, torre blindada; (aer.) cúpula o torre blindada (del ametrallador de un avión). 5. (hist.) (mil.) torre móvil.

turret drill, (mec.) taladradora radial.

turreted [-əd] *a.* 1. guarnecido de torre(s), torreado. 2. (zool.) turriculado (apl. a las conchas de ciertos moluscos).

turret gun, (mil.) cañón de torre, pieza de torreta.

turret lathe, (mec.) torno (de) revólver, torno de torrecilla.

turret toolpost, poste portaherramienta (de) revólver.

turriculate [tə'rɪkjələt] *a.* turriculado.

Turridae ['tɜrəˌdi, B 'tʌr-] *s. pl.* (zool.) túrridos.

turtle ['tɜrtəl, B 'tɜt-] *s.* 1. (zool.) tortuga, galápago, tortuga de mar, carey. 2. (ant.) tórtola. 3. **to turn t.,** voltearse patas arriba; (mar.) zozobrar. —*v.i.* cazar tortugas (esp. como una ocupación).

turtleback [-ˌbæk] *s.* 1. caparazón de tortuga. 2. (mar.) cubierta de caparazón.

turtledove [-ˌdʌv] *s.* (orn.) tórtola.

turtleneck [-ˌnɛk] *a.* con cuello arrollado *or* vuelto. —*s.* 1. cuello arrollado, cuello vuelto. 2. suéter con cuello arrollado o vuelto, pulóver con cuello arrollado o vuelto.

turtle shell, carey.

Tuscan ['tʌskən] *a.* 1. toscano, natural de Toscana, región de Italia. 2. (arq.) toscano. —*s.* toscano, toscana (habitante e idioma).

Tuscan Order, (arq.) orden Toscano.

Tuscany [-kənɪ] *s.* la Toscana (región de Italia).

Tuscarora [ˌtʌskə'rɔrə] *s.* tuscarora, tribu de indios de E.U.

tusche ['tʊʃə] *s.* líquido empleado en litografía y dibujo.

tush [tʌʃ] *s.* colmillo; esp. canino de un caballo. —*interj.* ¡bah!

tushed [tʌʃt] *a.* colmilludo (caballo).

tusk [tʌsk] *s.* 1. colmillo (de animales). 2. diente grande y saliente. 3. (carp.) espiga o almilla pequeñas. —*v.t.* excavar o rasgar con el colmillo; herir con el colmillo.

tusked [tʌskt] *a.* colmilludo, provisto de colmillos.

tusker ['tʌskər, B -kə] *s.* elefante o jabalí colmilludo; animal provisto de colmillos.

tusk tenon, (carp.) almilla reforzada (por una o más espigas).

tussah ['tʌsə] *s.* 1. (zool.) gusano de seda de la India. 2. tusor, tussor (seda).

tussive ['tʌsɪv] *a.* (med.) tusivo.

tussle ['tʌsəl] *v.i.* forcejear, pugnar, agarrarse. —*s.* forcejeo, agarrada, riña, pugna.

tussock ['tʌsək] *s.* montecillo de hierbas.

tussock moth, (ento.) lagarta.

tussore ['tʌsɔr, B -ə] *var. de* **tussah.**

tut [tʌt] *interj.* ¡tate! ¡basta! ¡bah! ¡vaya!

Tutankhamen, Tutankhamon [ˌtuˌtæŋ-k'ɑmən] *s.* (hist.) Tutankamón, Tutankamen, faraón de la decimoctava dinastía.

tutelar [-ələr, B -ə] *a.* tutelar.

tutelar angel, ángel de la guarda.

tutelar saint, santo patrón.

tutelary [-əlˌɛrɪ, B -ərɪ] *a.* tutelar. —*s.* entidad tutelar.

tutiorism ['tuʃɪəˌrɪzəm, B 'tju-] *s.* (teo.) tuciorismo.

tutiorist [-rəst] *s.* (teo.) tuciorista.

tutor ['tutər, B 'tjutə] *s.* 1. preceptor, maestro particular; (G.B.) preceptor asignado (profesor que vigila los estudios y la disciplina de un grupo de estudiantes, pr. en las Universidades de Oxford y Cambridge). 2. (der.) tutor, curador. —*v.t.* 1. ser tutor o guardián de. 2. enseñar, instruir. 3. (ant., fig.) dominar, frenar (pasiones, a sí mismo, etc.). 4. instruir secretamente, aleccionar bajo mano (esp. a un testigo). —*v.i.* 1. ser maestro o instructor particular, vivir de la enseñanza particular. 2. (E.U.) tomar lecciones particulares.

tutorage [-ərɪdʒ] *s.* 1. (der.) tutoría, tutela, tutoría, guarda. 2. patronato. 3. enseñanza, instrucción, guía.

tutoress [-rəs] *s.* (der.) tutora.

tutorial [tu'tɔrɪəl, B tju-] *a.* 1. (der.) tutelar. 2. preceptoril. —*s.* clase dada por un preceptor asignado (en las Universidades de Oxford y Cambridge).

tutorship ['tutərˌʃɪp, B 'tjutə,-] *s.* tutela, tutoría.

tutoyer [ˌtutwɑ'jeɪ] *v.t.* (fr.) tutear, tratar con familiaridad.

tutsan ['tʌtsən] *s.* (bot.) todasana, todabuena.

tutti ['tutɪ, B 'tʊtɪ] *s., a., adv.* (mús.) tutti, todos (los instrumentos).

tutti-frutti [ˌtutɪ'frutɪ, B 'tʊtɪˌfrʊtɪ] *s.* (italiano) tutti frutti (helado o golosina de muchas clases de fruta).

tut-tut ['tʌt'tʌt] *interj.* ¡tate! ¡basta! ¡bah! ¡vaya!

tutty ['tʌtɪ] *s.* (min.) atutía, tucía.

tutu ['tuˌtu] *s.* tutú (faldita corta que usan las bailarinas de ballet).

tux [tʌks] *forma abrev. de* **tuxedo,** esmoquin, smoking.

tuxedo [ˌtʌk'sidoʊ] *s.* esmoquin, traje de etiqueta masculino.

tuyère [twi'ɛr, B -'jɛə] *s.* (metal.) tobera (en hornos).

TV *abrev. de* **television,** televisión (TV).

TV dinner, comida completa preparada, congelada y lista para servir.

T.V.A. *abrev. de* **Tennessee Valley Authority,** Agencia del Valle del Tennessee (encargada del desarrollo hidráulico e hidroeléctrico de la cuenca del río Tennessee).

twaddle ['twɑdəl, B 'twɔd-] *v.i., v.t.* decir tonterías, disparatar, cotorrear. —*s.* 1. patrañas, tonterías, disparates. 2. cotorreo, habladuría.
twaddler ['twɑdlər, B 'twɔdlə] *s.* 1. disparatador. 2. charlatán.
twain [tweɪn] *a.* (poét.) dos. —*s.* (poét.) 1. dos. 2. (un) par.
twang [twæŋ] *v.i.* 1. producir un sonido vibrante. 2. hablar por la nariz, hablar con voz nasal, ganguear. —*v.t.* 1. puntear (guitarra, etc.). 2. decir (una palabra) con sonido nasal. 3. dar un tirón a la cuerda de (un arco, etc.); disparar (una flecha). —*s.* 1. tañido o punteado vibrante (de un instrumento de cuerda). 2. tonillo nasal, gangueo.
twang, *var. de* **tang.**
twankay ['twæŋˌkeɪ] *s.* variedad de té verde.
tweak [twik] *v.t.* pellizcar retorciendo; dar un pellizco retorcido a. —*s.* pellizco retorcido; pellizcón.
tweed [twid] *s.* paño asargado de lana; tweed; (*pl.*) vestidos de paño asargado de lana.
tweedle ['twidəl] *v.t., v.i.* 1. cantar o silbar. 2. atraer por medio de la música. 3. tocar un instrumento.
Tweedledum and Tweedledee [ˌtwidəl'dʌmənˌtwidəl'di] dos individuos o cosas que difieren sólo en nombre.
tweedy ['twidɪ] *a.* 1. (TWEEDIER; TWEEDIEST) de paño asargado, como paño asargado. 2. (fig.) díc. de la persona que viste ropa de tweed.
'tween [twin] *contr. de* **between.**
tweese, *var. de* **tweeze.**
tweet [twit] *s.* gorjeo, piada. —*v.i.* gorjear, piar.
tweeter ['twitər, B -ə] *s.* (rad.) altavoz agudos, bafle de agudos, tweeter.
tweeze [twiz] *s.* (anat.) estuche de cirugía. —*v.t.* sacar o arrancar con pinzas.
tweezers ['twizərz, B -zəz] *s. pl.* (*sing. o pl. en const.*) pinzas, tenacillas, tenazuelas, bruselas.
twelfth [twɛlfθ] *s.* 1. dozavo, duodécimo. 2. doce (en fechas). —*a.* duodécimo, doceno, dozavo.
Twelfth Day, día de Reyes, Epifanía.
Twelfth Night, 1. Noche de Reyes. 2. la fiesta de la Epifanía.
Twelfth Night Cake, roscón de Reyes, rosca de Reyes.
twelve [twɛlv] *a., s.* doce; **the T.,** (bíbl.) los doce apóstoles.
twelvefold ['twɛlvˌfoʊld] *a.* doce veces mayor. —*adv.* doce veces.
twelvemo [-ˌmoʊ] (impr.) *a.* en dozavo. —*s.* libro en dozavo.
twelvemonth [-ˌmʌnθ] *s.* (G.B.) (un) año.
twelve-tone [-'toʊn] *a.* (mús.) de los doce sonidos, dodecafónico.
twentieth ['twɛntɪəθ] *s.* 1. veintavo, vigésimo. 2. veinte (en las fechas). —*a.* vigésimo, veintavo; veinte (ordinal).
twenty ['twɛntɪ] *a.* veinte. —*s.* 1. veinte. 2. (billete de) veinte dólares. 3. **the twenties,** los años veinte, la tercera década (de la vida o de un siglo).
twentyfold [-ˌfoʊld] *a.* veinte veces mayor. —*adv.* veinte veces.
twenty odd, veintitantos.
twenty-one [ˌtwɛntɪ'wʌn] *s.* 1. veintiuno. 2. veintiuno (juego de naipes).
twenty-twenty (o 20/20) vision, acuidad normal de la vista o sea la facultad de poder ver claramente a veinte pies de distancia lo que el ojo normal ve a esa distancia.
twenty-two [-'tu] *s.* 1. veintidós. 2. rifle o pistola de calibre veintidós.
twerp [twɜrp, B twɜp] *s.* (jer.) tipejo, desgraciado.
twibil, twibill ['twaɪˌbɪl] *s.* (hist.) hacha de dos filos.
twice [twaɪs] *adv.* dos veces; doblemente, al doble; **t. as many** (o **as much**), el doble, otro(s) tanto(s); **t. that quantity,** el doble de esa cantidad; **(he is) t. the man he was,** (es) dos veces más hombre que antes.
twice-laid ['twaɪs'leɪd] *a.* hecho de cuerda usada (díc. de otra cuerda).
twice-told [-'toʊld] *a.* dicho dos veces, repetido; trillado, gastado.
twiddle ['twɪdəl] *v.t.* hacer girar (esp. los pulgares). —*v.i.* 1. entretenerse ociosa o distraídamente; ocuparse en fruslerías. 2. revolverse, rodar. 3. **t. one's thumbs,** no hacer nada, matar el tiempo; **t. with,** jugar con. —*s.* vuelta ligera.
twig [twɪg] *v.t.* (G.B.) (*pret., p.p.* TWIGGED; *p.pr.* TWIGGING) 1. observar, percibir. 2. (fam.) comprender, entender. —*s.* 1. ramita, varilla. 2. (anat.) vaso capilar. 3. vara divinatoria, varilla mágica.
twilight ['twaɪˌlaɪt] *s.* 1. crepúsculo. 2. (fig.) decadencia, ocaso. —*a.* crepuscular; obscuro, sombrío.
twilight sleep, (med.) sueño crepuscular.
twilit ['twaɪlɪt] *a.* iluminado a media luz, crepuscular.
twill [twɪl] *s.* tela cruzada, sarga, cruzadillo. —*v.t.* (tej.) cruzar (la tela), tejer con líneas diagonales.
twilled silk, tela cruzada de seda.
twill weave, tejido o ligamento en líneas diagonales, tejido en cadenilla.
twin [twɪn] *a.* gemelo, doble. —*s.* 1. gemelo, mellizo. 2. **Twins,** (astr.) Géminis, Gemelos. 3. agregado de cristales, macla. —*v.i.* (*pret., p.p.* TWINNED; *p.pr.* TWINNING) 1. parir gemelos. 2. formarse en agregado (cristales). —*v.t.* 1. parear, emparejar. 2. vincular.
twin beds, camas gemelas.
twin bill, programa de dos partidos, programa doble (de béisbol, cine, etc.).
twinborn ['twɪnˌbɔrn, B -bɔn] *a.* mellizo, gemelo.
twin brother, hermano gemelo; **the T. Brothers** (o **Brethren**), (astr., mitol.) Cástor y Pólux.
twin-cylinder ['twɪn'sɪləndər, B -də] *a.* de dos cilindros, de cilindros gemelos.
twine [twaɪn] *s.* 1. (hilo) bramante, cordel, guita, torzal. 2. enroscadura, retorcedura; repliegue. 3. entretejedura, entrelazamiento; enredo. —*v.t.* 1. retorcer, torcer. 2. entretejer, entrelazar; tejer (guirnalda, corona de flores, etc.). 3. ceñir, envolver, cercar. —*v.i.* 1. serpentear. 2. **t. about** (o **round**), dar vueltas alrededor, abrazar.
twin-engine ['twɪn'ɛndʒən] **twin-engined** [-dʒənd] *a.* bimotor.
twiner ['twaɪnər, B -ə] *s.* planta trepadora.
twinflower ['twɪnˌflaʊər, B -ə] *a.* (bot.) (especie de) madreselva.
twinge [twɪndʒ] *v.t.* causar un dolor agudo a, punzar. —*v.i.* sentir un dolor agudo. —*s.* 1. dolor agudo, punzada. 2. remordimiento (de conciencia). 3. asomo (de envidia, temor, etc.). 4. **to have a t. of conscience,** remorderle a uno la conciencia.
twi-night ['twaɪˌnaɪt] *a.* (E.U.) de programa doble (de béisbol), en el que el primer partido empieza en las últimas horas de la tarde.
twink [twɪŋk] *v.i.* (ant.) retiñir, tintinear.
twinkle ['twɪŋkəl] *v.i.* 1. pestañear, parpadear. 2. centellear, escintilar, destellar, titilar. 3. menearse, moverse rápidamente. —*v.t.* hacer centellear o titilar (luz, ojos, etc.). *s.* 1. pestañeo, guiñada, guiño. 2. destello, centelleo, titilación. 3. meneo rápido (del pie, etc. al bailar). 4. instante, momento.
twinkling [-klɪŋ] *s.* 1. pestañeo, parpadeo, guiñada, guiño. 2. destello, centelleo, titilación. 3. momento, instante; **in a t., in the t. of an eye,** en un abrir y cerrar de ojos.
twinning ['twɪnɪŋ] *s.* 1. gestación de mellizos. 2. acoplamiento; pareo; junta o unión (de dos personas u objetos relacionados). 3. (rad.) duplicidad (en el cuarzo).
twin-screw [-'skru] *a.* (mar.) de doble hélice, de hélices gemelas.
twin sister, hermana gemela.
twirl [twɜrl, B twɜl] *v.t.* 1. hacer girar. 2. (béisbol) arrojar (la pelota). —*v.i.* dar vueltas. —*s.* 1. rotación, vuelta, giro. 2. enroscadura.
twist [twɪst] *v.t.* 1. torcer, retorcer; doblar, doblegar. 2. enrollar, arrollar, enroscar. 3. trenzar. 4. torcer, dislocar (tobillo, muñeca, etc.). 5. deformar, descomponer, desfigurar (cara, facciones, etc.). 6. (fig.) torcer, viciar (palabras, significado, etc.). 7. **t. in** (o **into**), entrelazar, entretejer; **t. off,** romper retorciendo; **t. one's way,** serpentear. —*v.i.* 1. retorcerse, enroscarse. 2. contorcerse, contorsionarse. 3. serpentear, serpear, culebrear. 4. girar con efecto (una bola). 5. **t. and turn,** dar vueltas (en la cama); **t. around,** dar una vuelta repentina. —*s.* 1. cordoncillo, torzal. 2. rosca (de pan); rollo (de tabaco). 3. torsión, torcedura. 4. vuelta, giro. 5. efecto (dado a la pelota o bola). 6. curva, vuelta (de un río, camino, etc.). 7. paso (de una hélice). 8. sesgo, peculiaridad (de la mente, del carácter, etc.). 9. tergiversación (del significado). 10. peripecia. 11. esguince, torcimiento (del tobillo, muñeca, etc.). 12. (mec.) esfuerzo de rotación; tensión torsional. 13. ardid, truco. 14. (jer.) mujer, muchacha; (Mex., P. Rico) chamaca. 15. **to give a t. to,** retorcer; dar efecto a (la pelota o bola); tergiversar, alterar el significado de (palabras, hechos, etc.); **t. of the wrist,** (fig.) juego de manos, destreza, tino.
twist drill, barrena o broca espiral, barrena salomónica o de caracol, broca helicoidal, mecha espiral.
twisted ['twɪstəd] *a.* torcido, retorcido.
twisted surface, superficie alabeada.
twister [-tər, B -tə] *s.* 1. torcedor (persona o aparato); cordelero, soguero, cabestrero, guitero; torcedero (aparato). 2. (béisbol) pelota (arrojada) con efecto, pelota curvada. 3. (E.U.) torbellino, tornado, tromba. 4. impostor, trapacero. 5. rompecabezas, problema difícil.
twist moment, (ing.) momento torcional.
twist stitch, (cost.) punto de cordoncillo, punto torcido.
twit [twɪt] *v.t.* (*pret., p.p.* TWITTED; *p.pr.* TWITTING) 1. mofarse de, burlar(se), ridiculizar. 2. reprender por, escarnecer por, sacar en cara (flojera, mendacidad, etc.). —*s.* 1. mofa, burla, chacota. 2. reprensión, escarnio. 3. (jer., G.B.) bobo, tonto.
twitch [twɪtʃ] *v.t.* halar a sacudidas; tirar o sacudir bruscamente. —*v.i.* crisparse, contorcerse, convelerse; **t. at,** tirar bruscamente de, dar un tirón a. —*s.* 1. tirón, sacudida, estirón repentino. 2. crispatura, crispadura, crispamiento espasmódico (de músculos, facciones, etc.). 3. punzada, dolor agudo. 4. (vet.) bocado.
twitch grass, (bot.) grama.
twitter ['twɪtər, B -ə] *v.i.* 1. gorjear, chirriar (los pájaros). 2. reír a medias, reír con disimulo. 3. temblar de agitación; excitarse, agitarse. —*v.t.* decir con voz chirriadora. —*s.* 1. gorjeo, chirrido (de los pájaros). 2. risita sofocada, risa a medias. 3. agitación, estremecimiento.
twixt [twɪkst] (poét., dial.) *contr. de* **betwixt.**

two [tu] *a.* dos. —*s.* dos; **by twos,** de dos en dos; **in two,** en dos; **in t. twos,** (G.B.) en un santiamén; **one or t.,** unos cuantos, un par de; **to put t. and t. together,** atar cabos, caer en cuenta; **t. of a kind,** tal para cual.

two-base hit, (beisbol) golpe con que el bateador gana la segunda base.

two-bit ['tu'bɪt] *a.* 1. (E.U.) de un cuarto de dólar. 2. (fig.) insignificante, de poca monta.

two-by-four [-bə'fɔr, B -'fɔ] *a.* 1. de dos por cuatro (pulgadas, pies, etc.). 2. (fig., fam.) pequeño, insignificante; mezquino; miserable. —*s.* madera de dos por cuatro (pies, pulgadas, etc.).

two-car garage, garaje de dos plazas.

two-cycle [-ˌsaɪkəl] *a.* de dos tiempos.

two-decker [-'dɛkər, B -ə] *a.* de dos puentes (barco); de dos pisos (autobús); de dos niveles, de dos capas (emparedado, etc.).

two-dimensional [-də'mɛntʃənəl, B -'mɛnʃən-] *a.* 1. bidimensional. 2. (fig.) superficial, frívolo (estilo, novela, etc.).

two-edged [-'ɛdʒd] *a.* (lit., fig.) de dos filos.

two-faced [-'feɪst] *a.* 1. de dos caras. 2. (fig.) falso, doble.

two-facedly [-'feɪsədlɪ, -'feɪstlɪ] *adv.* doblemente, con duplicidad.

twofer ['tufər, B -fə] *s.* dos entradas por el precio de una, entrada rebajada de precio.

two-fisted [-'fɪstəd] *a.* (fam.) viril, vigoroso, fuerte.

twofold [-ˌfoʊld] *a.* doble; de dos clases o aspectos. —*adv.* al doble, dos veces.

two-handed [-'hændəd] *a.* 1. de dos manos; para dos manos. 2. (fig.) grande, fornido, fuerte. 3. ambidextro.

two-headed [-'hɛdəd] *a.* bicéfalo, de dos cabezas.

two hundred, doscientos.

two hundredth, ducentésimo.

two-image photogrammetry, fotogrametría por imágenes dobles, estereofotogrametría.

two-legged [-ˌlɛgəd, -ˌlɛgd] *a.* de dos patas o pies.

two-master ['tu'mæstər, B -'mɑstə] *s.* (mar.) barco de dos palos.

two pairs, (póker) par doble.

twopence ['tuˌpɛns, B 'tʌpəns] *s.* 1. (G.B.) dos peniques; moneda de dos peniques. 2. (fig.) pequeñez, insignificancia.

twopenny ['tuˌpɛnɪ, B 'tʌpənɪ] *a.* 1. (del valor) de dos peniques. 2. (fig.) despreciable, sin valor, barato.

twopenny-halfpenny ['tʌpənɪ'heɪpənɪ] *a.* (G.B.) 1. de dos y medio peniques. 2. (fig.) mezquino, miserable, raquítico.

two-phase ['tu'feɪz] *a.* (elec.) bifásico, difásico.

two-ply [-ˌplaɪ] *a.* de dos capas; de dos tramas; de dos hilos o hebras.

two-point perspective, perspectiva angular o de dos conjuntos.

two-point seismograph, (geof.) sismógrafo de dos componentes.

two-pole [-ˌpoʊl] *a.* (elec.) bipolar.

two-seater [-'sitər, B -ə] *s.* biplaza, vehículo de dos plazas.

two-sided [-'saɪdəd] *a.* 1. de dos lados; bilateral. 2. doble, falso, hipócrita. 3.con dos aspectos, con dos apariencias (tesis, argumento, etc.).

twosome ['tusəm] *s.* 1. pareja (de personas o cosas). 2. (golf) partido de simples (entre dos jugadores).

two-step [-ˌstɛp] *s.* (mús.) danza de salón. —*v.i.* bailar esta danza.

two-stroke engine, motor de dos tiempos.

two-throw [-'θroʊ] *a.* de dos direcciones, bidireccional.

two-time [-'taɪm] *v.t.* engañar (a cónyuge, amante), traicionar (a socio, cómplice, etc.).

two-tongued [-'tʌŋd] *a.* falso, doble.

two-track [-ˌtræk] *a.* de doble vía.

two-way [-'weɪ] *a.* 1. de dos sentidos, de doble sentido (tráfico, movimiento, calle, etc.). 2. de doble uso (cuello de camisa, ropa, etc.). 3. mutuo, recíproco. 4. (rad.) bilateral (comunicación, enlace, etc.).

two-way radio, (rad.) aparato emisor y receptor, transceptor.

two-way switch, (elec.) conmutador de dos direcciones.

two-way valve, válvula de doble paso.

two-wire [-waɪr, B -'waɪə] *a.* (elec.) bifilar.

Tychonian [taɪ'koʊnɪən] **Tychonic** [-'kɑnɪk, B -'kɔn-] *a.* (astr.) ticónico.

tycoon [taɪ'kun] *s.* 1. **T.,** taicún (título dado al shogún del Japón). 2. magnate (industrial o comercial); hombre de negocios de gran poder e influencia.

tye [taɪ] *s.* (mar.) ostaga.

tying, *p.pr. de* **tie.**

tyke [taɪk] *s.* 1. perro; perro de raza indefinida. 2. (fam.) niñito, chiquillo. 3. (dial., esco.) persona torpe.

tymbal, *var. de* **timbal.**

tymp [tɪmp] *s.* (metal.) timpa.

tympan ['tɪmpən] *s.* 1. (arq.) tímpano, panel. 2. (impr.) tímpano (pliegos de cubrir). 3. (mús.) tímpano, atabal, timbal.

tympani, *var. de* **timpani.**

tympanic [tɪm'pænɪk] *a.* (anat.) timpánico.

tympanic antrum, (anat.) antro timpánico.

tympanic bone, (anat.) hueso del tímpano.

tympanic membrane, (anat.) membrana timpánica.

tympanist ['tɪmpənəst] *s.* timbalero, atabalero.

tympanites [ˌtɪmpə'naɪtiz] *s.* (med.) timpanitis, timpanismo (distensión por gases, esp. del estómago).

timpanitic [-'nɪtɪk] *a.* (med.) timpanítico.

tympanitis [-'naɪtəs] *s.* (med.) timpanitis, otitis media.

tympanum ['tɪmpənəm] *s.* (*pl.* TYMPANUMS o TYMPANA [-nə]) 1. (anat.) tímpano (oído medio; membrana timpánica). 2. (arq.) tímpano. 3. (elec.) diafragma (de un teléfono). 4. (mús.) tímpano, atabal.

tympany [-nɪ] *s.* 1. (med.) timpanismo, timpanitis. 2. (ant.) ampulosidad.

Tyndareus [tɪn'dɛrɪəs, B -'dɛər-] *s.* (mitol.) Tíndaro, esposo de Leda, padre de Clitemnestra y Cástor.

tyne, *var. de* **tine.**

typ. *abrev de* 1. **typographic,** tipográfico. 2. **typography,** tipografía.

typal ['taɪpəl] *a.* de un tipo o tipos; típico.

type [taɪp] *s.* 1. tipo, clase, especie, género. 2. tipo, signo, emblema, distintivo. 3. tipo, norma, ejemplar, modelo, ej., *t. of chivalry,* modelo de caballería. 4. (biol., fisiol.) tipo, grupo. 5. (impr.) tipo, carácter, letra. —*v.t.* 1. prefigurar; representar; simbolizar. 2. escribir a máquina, mecanografiar. 3. (med.) determinar el grupo de (sangre). —*v.i.* escribir a máquina.

type bar, línea de linotipia.

type body, (impr.) árbol del tipo.

typecase ['taɪpˌkeɪs] *s.* (impr.) caja tipográfica, caja de tipo, caja de imprenta.

typecast [-ˌkæst, B -ˌkɑst] *v.t.* 1. asignar (a un actor) los papeles que concuerdan mejor con sus habilidades o características físicas. 2. identificar (a un actor) con un personaje o un papel.

typeface [-ˌfeɪs] *s.* (impr.) carácter de letra, tipo de letra.

type founder, (impr.) fundidor de tipos, diseñador de tipos.

typefoundry [-ˌfaʊndrɪ] *s.* (impr.) fundición de tipos.

type gauge, (impr.) tipómetro.

type genus, (biol.) género tipo.

type-high ['taɪp'haɪ] *a.* (impr.) de la altura de tipos.

type metal, (impr.) metal tipográfico, metal de imprenta.

type page, (impr.) plana, molde, caja.

typescript [-ˌskrɪpt] *s.* texto escrito a máquina.

typeset [-ˌsɛt] *v.t.* (impr.) componer (tipo).

typesetter [-ər, B -ə] *s.* (impr.) 1. compositor, tipógrafo, cajista, tipógrafo cajista, paquetero. 2. máquina de componer.

typesetting [-ɪŋ] (impr.) *s.* composición, composición tipográfica. —*a.* de componer, de composición.

type species, t. specimen, (biol.) especie tipo.

typewrite ['taɪpˌraɪt] *v.t., v.i.* mecanografiar, escribir a máquina.

typewriter [-ər, B -ə] *s.* 1. máquina de escribir. 2. mecanógrafo, dactilógrafo.

typewriter ribbon, cinta para máquina de escribir, cinta de máquina.

typewriting [-ɪŋ] *s.* 1. mecanografía, dactilografía. 2. texto escrito a máquina.

typewritten ['taɪpˌrɪtən] *p.p. de* **typewrite.** —*a.* escrito a máquina.

Typhaceae [taɪ'feɪsɪˌi] *s. pl.* (bot.) tifáceas.

typhaceous [-ʃəs] *a.* (bot.) tifáceo.

typhlitis [tɪf'laɪtəs] *s.* (med.) tiflitis.

typhlology [tɪf'lɑlədʒɪ, B -'lɔl-] *s.* (med.) tiflología.

typhlosis [-'loʊsəs] *s.* (med.) tiflosis.

typhogenic [ˌtaɪfə'dʒɛnɪk] *a.* (med.) tifogénico, tifógeno.

typhoid ['taɪfɔɪd] *a.* (med.) tifóidico, tifódico; tifoideo. —*s.* (med.) fiebre tifoidea.

typhoid fever, (med.) fiebre tifoidea, fiebre estérica, fiebre abdominal.

typhoon [taɪ'fun] *s.* tifón.

typhous ['taɪfəs] *a.* tífico.

typhus ['taɪfəs] *s.* (med.) tifus.

typic ['tɪpɪk] *a.* típico.

typical [-ɪkəl] *a.* típico, característico, representativo, emblemático, simbólico.

typicality [ˌtɪpə'kælətɪ] *s.* carácter típico.

typically ['tɪpɪkəlɪ] *adv.* típicamente.

typicalness [-kəlnəs] *s.* carácter típico.

typification [ˌtɪpəfə'keɪʃən] *s.* simbolización.

typify ['tɪpəˌfaɪ] *v.t.* (*pret., p.p.* TYPIFIED; *p.pr.* TYPIFYING) 1. simbolizar, representar. 2. ser ejemplo o modelo de.

typing ['taɪpɪŋ] *s.* mecanografía, dactilografía.

typist [-pəst] *s.* mecanógrafo, mecanógrafa, dactilógrafo, dactilógrafa, tipiadora.

typo [-ˌpoʊ] *s.* (fam.) error tipográfico.

typo., typog. 1. *abrev de* **typography,** tipografía. 2. **typographer,** tipógrafo.

typograph [-pəˌgræf, B -ˌgrɑf] *v.t.* producir (sellos postales) por impresión tipográfica.

typographer [taɪ'pɑgrəfə, B -'pɔg-fə] *s.* tipógrafo.

typographic [ˌtaɪpə'græfɪk] **typographical** [-ɪkəl] *a.* tipográfico.

typographical error, errata, yerro o error de imprenta.

typographically [-ɪkəlɪ] *adv.* tipográficamente.

typographic art, arte tipográfico o gráfico.

typography [taɪ'pɑgrəfɪ, B -'pɔg-] *s.* tipografía.

typolithography [ˌtaɪpoʊlɪ'θɑgrəfɪ, B -'θɔg-] *s.* tipolitografía.
typological [ˌtaɪpə'lɑdʒɪkəl, B -'lɔdʒ-] *a.* tipológico.
typology [taɪ'pɑlədʒɪ, B -'pɔl-] *s.* tipología, estudio de tipos o clasificaciones.
typometry [-'pɑmətrɪ, B -'pɔm-] *s.* (impr.) tipometría.
tyramine ['taɪrəˌmin] *s.* (quím.) tiramina.
tyrannic [tɪ'rænɪk] **tyrannical** [-ɪkəl] *a.* tiránico, despótico.
tyrannically [-kəlɪ] *adv.* tiránicamente, tiranamente.
tyrannicalness [-kəlnəs] *s.* naturaleza tiránica.
tyrannicide [-əˌsaɪd] *s.* 1. tiranicidio. 2. tiranicida.
tyrannize ['tɪrəˌnaɪz] *v.i.* (gen. con *over*) ejercer dominio (sobre). —*v.t.* tiranizar, oprimir.
tyrannizer [-ər, B -ə] *s.* tirano.
tyrannosaur [tə'rænəˌsɔr, B -ˌsɔ] *s.* (pal.) tiranosauro.
tyrannous ['tɪrənəs] *a.* tirano, despótico.
tyrannously [-lɪ] *adv.* tiránicamente.
tyranny ['tɪrənɪ] *s.* tiranía, despotismo.
tyrant ['taɪrənt, B 'taɪə-] *s.* tirano, déspota.
tyrant flycatcher, (ento.) papamoscas, doral americano.
tyre, (pr. G.B.) *var. de* **tire,** llanta.
Tyre [taɪr, B 'taɪə] *s.* (hist.) Tiro, antigua ciudad fenicia.
Tyrian ['tɪrɪən] *a., s.* tirio, de Tiro, antigua ciudad fenicia.
Tyrian purple, púrpura de Tiro.
tyro ['taɪˌroʊ, B 'taɪə-] *s.* aprendiz, bisoño.
tyrocidine, tyrocidin [ˌtaɪrə'saɪdən, B ˌtaɪə-] *s.* (bioquím.) tirocidina.
Tyrol [tə'roʊl, B 'tɪrəl] *s.* Tirol, región de Europa Central.
Tyrolean [tə'roʊlɪən] **Tyrolese** [ˌtɪrə'liz] *a., s.* tirolés, natural de Tirol.
tyrosinase ['taɪrəsənˌeɪs, B 'taɪə-] *s.* (biol.) tirosinasa.
tyrosine [-rəˌsin] *s.*(bioquím.) tirosina.
tyrothricin [ˌtaɪrə'θraɪsən, B ˌtaɪə-] *s.* (bioquím.) tirotricina.
Tyrrhenian [tə'rinɪən] *s.* el (mar) Tirreno. —*a.* tirreno, del mar Tirreno.
Tyrtaeus [tɜr'tiəs, B tɜ'-] *s.* (lit.) Tirteo, poeta elegíaco griego.
tzar, tzarina, *vars. de* **tsar, tsarina.**
tzetze, *var. de* **tsetse.**
tzigane [tsɪ'gɑn] *a., s.* gitano, zíngaro, cíngaro.

U

U [ju] *s.* u, vigésima primera letra del alfabeto inglés.
U *símb. de* **uranium,** uranio. —*s.* cualquier objeto en forma de U. —*a.* en forma de U.
U.A.R. *abrev. de* **United Arab Republic,** República Árabe Unida (RAU).
UAW (E.U.) *abrev. de* **United Automobile Workers,** unión de los trabajadores de la industria automotriz.
U-bar ['juˌbɑr, B -ˌbɑ] *s.* barra en U.
Ubiquitarian [juˌbɪkwə'tɛrɪən] *a., s.* (relig.) ubiquitario.
ubiquitous [jʊ'bɪkwətəs] *a.* ubicuo.
ubiquitously [-lɪ] *adv.* en forma ubicua, ubicuamente.
ubiquitousness [-nəs] *s.* ubicuidad, ubiquidad.
ubiquity [-wətɪ] *s.* ubicuidad, ubiquidad.
U-boat ['juˌboʊt] *s.* submarino alemán.
U bolt, perno en (forma de) U.
udder ['ʌdər, B 'ʌdə] *s.* ubre, teta, mama.
udometer [ju'dɑmətər, B ju'dɔmɪtə] *s.* (meteor.) udómetro, pluviómetro.
udometric [ˌjudə'mɛtrɪk] *a.* (meteor.) udométrico, pluviométrico.
udomograph [ju'dɑməˌgræf, B -'dɔməˌgrɑf] *s.* (meteor.) pluviómetro registrador.
UFO *abrev. de* **unidentified flying object,** objeto volador no identificado (OVNI).
Ugaritic [ˌjugə'rɪtɪk, ugə-] *s.* (filol.) ugarítico.
ugh [ʌg] *interj.* ¡uf!
uglification [ˌʌglɪfɪ'keɪʃən] *s.* afeamiento.
uglify ['ʌglɪˌfaɪ] *v.t.* afear.
uglily ['ʌgləlɪ] *adv.* feamente.
ugliness [-lɪnəs] *s.* fealdad.
ugly [-ʌglɪ] *a.* (UGLIER; UGLIEST)1. feo 2. repugnante, repulsivo, asqueroso. 3. feo, desfavorable, amenazador (aspecto, rumor, noticia, etc.). 4. desagradable, ofensivo. 5. reprensible, terrible. 6. peligroso, temible, ej., *an u. customer,* un tipo peligroso. 7. **as u. as sin, más** feo que Picio, más feo que el pecado.
ugly duckling, 1. patito feo (con referencia a un cuento de Andersen). 2. (fam.) alguien o algo que de pronto mejora o se embellece notablemente.
Ugrian ['ugrɪən, 'ju-] *s., a.* ugro, ugrio, de ciertos pueblos de Siberia y Hungría.
UHF *abrev. de* **ultrahigh frequency,** frecuencia ultraelevada.
uhlan ['uˌlɑn, B -lən] *s.* (mil.) ulano, lancero de caballería en los antiguos ejércitos austriaco, ruso y alemán.
uintaite, uintahite [jʊ'ɪntəˌaɪt] *s.* (min.) uintahíta, uintaíta.
U.K. *abrev. de* **United Kingdom,** Reino Unido.
ukase [ju'keɪs, B -'keɪz] *s.* 1. ucase, decreto del zar. 2. (fig.) ucase, orden gubernativa injusta y tiránica.
Ukraine, the [ju'kreɪn] *s.* Ucrania.
Ukrainian [ju'kreɪnɪən] *a.* ucraniano, ucranio. —*s.* 1. ucranio, natural de Ucrania. 2. ucraniano (lengua).
ukulele [ˌjukə'leɪlɪ] *s.* (mús.) ukelele, pequeña guitarra de Hawai.
ulcer ['ʌlsər, B -sə] *s.* 1. (med.) úlcera. 2. (fig.) llaga. —*v.i.* ulcerarse.
ulcerate [-səˌreɪt] *v.t.* ulcerar. —*v.i.* ulcerarse.
ulceration [ˌʌlsə'reɪʃən] *s.* (med.) ulceración.
ulcerative ['ʌlsəˌreɪtɪv, -rətɪv] *a.* (med.) ulcerativo.
ulcerous [-sərəs] *a.* ulceroso.
ulema [ˌulə'mɑ, B 'ulɪmə] *s.* (relig.) ulema, académico musulmán versado en Teología y Derecho.
uliginose [jʊ'lɪdʒənəs] *a.* (bot.) uliginoso.
ulitis [jʊ'laɪtɪs] *s.* (med.) ulitis.
ullage ['ʌlɪdʒ] *s.* (com.) merma de un tonel.
ulmaceous [ʌl'meɪʃəs] *a.* (bot.) ulmáceo.
ulmin ['ʌlmən] *s.* (quím.) ulmina.
ulna ['ʌlnə] *s.* (*pl.* ULNAE [-ni] o ULNAS) (anat.) ulna, cúbito.
ulnar ['ʌlnər, B 'ʌlnə] *a.* (anat.) ulnar, cubital.
ulster ['ʌlstər, B 'ʌlstə] *s.* 1. úlster (especie de) gabán largo de origen irlandés. 2. **U.,** Úlster, provincia de Irlanda del Norte.
ulterior [ʌl'tɪrɪər, B -'tɪərɪə] *a.* 1. ulterior. 2. remoto. 3. oculto, latente. 4. siguiente, subsecuente, futuro.
ulteriorly [-lɪ] *adv.* ulteriormente.
ultima ['ʌltəmə] *s.* (gram., poética) última sílaba.
ultimacy [-sɪ] *s.* ultimidad.
ultimate ['ʌltəmət] *a.* 1. último, final. 2. fundamental; primario, elemental. 3. extremo, sumo; máximo. 4. último, remoto. —*s.* 1. esencia. 2. conclusión, punto final. 3. colmo.
ultimately [-lɪ] *adv.* últimamente, por último, finalmente.
ultimateness [-nəs] *s.* ultimidad.
ultimate strength, (ing.) resistencia a rotura o fallo, fatiga de ruptura, resistencia final.
ultima Thule, 1. última Tule (isla más septentrional según los antiguos). 2. (fig.) región remota. 3. lo último, el summum, el colmo.
ultimatum [ˌʌltə'meɪtəm] *s.* (*pl.* ULTIMATUMS o ULTIMATA [-tə]) ultimátum.
ultimo ['ʌltəmoʊ] *a.* último, próximo pasado (mes).
ultra ['ʌltrə] *a.* extremo, excesivo; exagerado. —*s.* 1. (lit.) ultraísta. 2. ultra, extremista, radical.
ultracentrifugation [ˌʌltrəsɛnˌtrɪfjə'geɪʃən] *s.* ultracentrifugación.
ultracentrifuge [-'sɛntrəˌfjudʒ] *s.* ultracentrífuga, ultracentrifugadora.
ultraconservative [-kən'sɜrvətɪv, B -'sɛvə-] *s., a.* archiconservador.
ultracritical [-'krɪtɪkəl] *a.* hipercrítico.
ultradyno [-'daɪnoʊ] *s.* (rad.) ultradino.
ultrafashionable [-'fæʃənəbəl] *a.* ultraelegante.
ultrahigh frequency ['ʌltrəˌhaɪ-] (elec.) frecuencia ultraalta.
ultraism ['ʌltrəˌɪzəm] *s.* ultraísmo, extremismo.
ultraist [-trəəst] *a., s.* extremista.
ultraistic [ˌʌltrə'ɪstɪk] *a.* extremista.
ultramarine [-mə'rin] *a.* ultramarino, del otro lado del mar. —*s.* 1. ultramar, azul de ultramar, azul ultramarino. 2. azul ultramarino, color de ultramar.
ultramicrochemistry [-ˌmaɪkroʊ'kɛməstrɪ] *s.* ultramicroquímica.
ultramicrometer [-maɪ'krɑmətər, B -'krɔmɪtə] *s.* ultramicrómetro.
ultramicroscope [-'maɪkrəˌskoʊp] *s.* ultramicroscopio.
ultramicroscopic [-ˌmaɪkrə'skɑpɪk, B -'skɔp-] *a.* ultramicroscópico.
ultramicroscopy [-maɪ'krɑskəpɪ, B -'krɔs-] *s.* ultramicroscopía.
ultramodern [-'mɑdərn, B -'mɔdən] *a.* ultramoderno.
ultramodernist [-əst] *s.* modernista extremado.
ultramontane [-'mɑnˌteɪn, B -'mɔn-] *a., s.* 1. ultramontano, del otro lado de los montes. 2. (relig.) papista, ultracatólico.
ultramontanism [-'mɑntənˌɪzəm, B -'mɔn-] *s.* ultramontanismo.
ultramundane [-'mʌnˌdeɪn] *a.* ultramundano, ultraterreno.
ultranationalism [-'næʃənəˌlɪzəm] *s.* nacionalismo extremo.
ultranationalist [-nələst] *a., s.* nacionalista extremado.
ultrared [-'rɛd] *a., s.* ultrarrojo, infrarrojo.
ultrared rays, rayos ultrarrojos o infrarrojos.
ultrashort [-'ʃɔrt, B -'ʃɔt] *a.* (rad.) ultracorta (onda).
ultrashort wave, (rad.) onda ultracorta, onda extracorta.
ultrasonic [-'sɑnɪk, B -'sɔnɪk] *a.* 1. supersónico (velocidad, etc.) 2. ultrasónico, ultrasonoro (frecuencia, onda, etc.). —*s.* ultrasonido, onda ultrasónica, frecuencia ultrasonora.
ultrasonics [-'sɑnɪks, B -'sɔnɪks] *s. pl.* (*sing. en const.*) supersónica, ultraacústica (ciencia).
ultrasound [-'saʊnd] *s.* ultrasonido.
ultraviolet [-'vaɪələt] *a., s.* (fís.) ultravioleta, ultraviolado.
ultraviolet lamp, lámpara (de radiación) ultravioleta.
ultraviolet light, radiación ultravioleta.
ultraviolet ray, rayo ultravioleta.
ultravirus [-'vaɪrəs] *s.* (bact.) ultravirus.
ululant ['ʌljələnt, B 'jul-] *a.* ululante, aullador.
ululate [-ˌleɪt] *v.i.* ulular, aullar.
ululation [ˌʌljə'leɪʃən, ˌul-, B ˌjul-] *s.* ululato, aullido.
Ulysses [jʊ'lɪsiz] *s.* (mitol.) Ulises, héroe de *La Odisea* de Homero.
umbel ['ʌmbəl] *s.* (bot.) umbela.
umbellar [-bələr, B -lə] *a.* (bot.) umbelar.
umbellate ['ʌmbəˌleɪt, ˌʌm'bɛlət] **umbellated** ['ʌmbəˌleɪtəd] *a.* (bot.) umbelado.
umbelliferous [ˌʌmbə'lɪfərəs] *a.* (bot.) umbelífero.
umbellulate [-'bɛljələt] *a.* (bot.) umbelular.
umbellule ['ʌmbəlˌjul, B ʌm'bɛl-] *s.* (bot.) umbélula.
umber ['ʌmbər, B -bə] *s.* 1. (pint.) tierra de sombra. 2. ocre obscuro. 3. (ict.) tímalo. —*a.* de color ocre obscuro. —*v.t.* teñir de color ocre obscuro; obscurecer.
umber, *s.* (ict.) tímalo.

umbilical [ˌʌm'bɪlɪkəl] *a.* (anat.) umbilical.
umbilical cord, 1. (anat.) cordón umbilical. 2. (astronáut.) conexión eléctrica o alimentadora de un proyectil antes del lanzamiento; conexión de un astronauta con la nave madre, mientras éste se encuentra flotando en el espacio.
umbilicate [-kət] **umbilicated** [-ˌkeɪtəd] *a.* umbilicado.
umbilication [-ˌbɪlə'keɪʃən] *s.* (anat.) umbilicación.
umbilicus [ʌm'bɪlɪkəs, ˌʌmbə'laɪkəs] *s.* (*pl.* UMBILICI [-kaɪ] o UMBILICUSES) (anat., bot., fig.) ombligo.
umbiliform [ʌm'bɪləˌfɔrm, B -ˌfɔm] *a.* umbilicado.
umble pie ['ʌmbəl-] (cocina) pastel relleno de menudos de venado.
umbles ['ʌmbəlz] *s.* (ant., cocina) menudos, (esp. de venado).
umbo ['ʌmboʊ] *s.* (*pl.* UMBONES [ˌʌm'booniz] UMBOS) 1. (anat., zool.) umbo. 2. (bot.) umbón. 3. cazoleta (centro saliente de un escudo o broquel).
umbonate [-bəˌneɪt] *a.* (bot.) umbonado.
umbra ['ʌmbrə] *s.* (*pl.* UMBRAE [-bri] o UMBRAS) 1. (astr.) cono de sombra (del eclipse solar o lunar); sombra (fondo negro de las manchas solares). 2. (fig.) sombra (persona que sigue a otro). 3. (ict.) pichihuén.
umbrage ['ʌmbrɪdʒ] *s.* 1. (ant.) sombra, umbría. 2. umbráculo; follaje. 3. (ant.) sospecha. 4. ofensa, pique, resentimiento. 5. (ant.) umbra, sombra. 6. **to take u. (at),** ofenderse, resentirse (por).
umbrageous [ˌʌm'breɪdʒəs] *a.* 1. umbroso, umbrío, sombrío, sombroso. 2. resentido, suspicaz.
umbrageously [-lɪ] *adv.* 1. con sombra. 2. suspicazmente.
umbral ['ʌmbrəl] *a.* tenebroso, oscuro.
umbral cone, (astr.) cono de sombra, cono de penumbra.
umbra tree, (bot.) ombú, bellasombra.
umbrella [ʌm'brɛlə] *s.* 1. paraguas; parasol, sombrilla. 2. (mil.) cobertura aérea. 3. (zool.) umbrela (parte del cuerpo de las medusas con forma de sombrilla).
umbrella leaf, (bot.) (variedad norteamericana de) cérbero.
umbrella plant, (bot.) juncia africana.
umbrella stand, paragüero, bastonera, sombrillera.
umbrella tree, (bot.) (variedad americana de) magnolia.
Umbria ['ʌmbrɪə] *s.* Umbría, región de Italia.
Umbrian [-brɪən] *a.* de Umbría. —*s.* 1. natural de Umbría, Italia. 2. umbrío, umbro (lengua).
umbriferous [ʌm'brɪfərəs] *a.* umbroso, umbrátil.
umiak ['umɪˌæk] *s.* umiak, umiac (bote esquimal).
umlaut ['ʊmˌlaʊt] *a.* 1. (fon.) metafonía. 2. diéresis, crema (signo ortográfico). —*v.t.* poner diéresis sobre (palabra, letra); modificar por metafonía.
umpirage ['ʌmˌpaɪrɪdʒ] *s.* arbitraje, arbitración, arbitramento, arbitramiento; tercería; (der.) arbitraje.
umpire ['ʌmpaɪr, B -paɪə] *s.* 1. (der.) tercero, árbitro, compromisario. 2. (dep.) árbitro. —*v.t.* arbitrar, juzgar como árbitro. —*v.i.* actuar como árbitro.
umpteen ['ʌmp'tin] *a.* (fam.) muchísimo, incontable, innumerable.
umpteenth [-'tinθ] *a.* (fam.) enésimo.

'un [ən] *pron.* (fam., dial.) uno, tipo, sujeto, ej., *he is a queer 'un,* es un tipo raro.
UN *abrev. de* **United Nations,** (Organización de las) Naciones Unidas, ONU, *f.*
unabashed [ˌʌnə'bæʃt] *a.* desenvuelto, desenfadado; descarado, descocado.
unabated [-'beɪtəd] *a.* no disminuido; cabal.
unabbreviated [ˌʌnə'briviˌeɪtəd] *a.* íntegro, completo, no abreviado.
unable [ˌʌn'eɪbəl] *a.* inhábil, incapaz, impotente; imposibilitado; **to be u. to (do),** no poder (hacer), serle a uno imposible (hacer).
unabridged [-ə'brɪdʒd] *a.* no resumido, no abreviado, íntegro, completo.
unabsolved [-əb'zɑlvd, -'sɑlvd, B -'zɔlvd] *a.* no absuelto.
unaccented [ʌn'æksɛntəd, B ˌʌnæk'sɛntəd] *a.* sin acento, átono, inacentuado.
unacceptable [ˌʌnək'sɛptəbəl] *a.* inaceptable.
unaccessible [ˌʌnək'sɛsəbəl] *a.* inaccesible, no accesible.
unaccommodated [-ə'kɑməˌdeɪtəd, B -ə'kɔm-] *a.* 1. no equipado. 2. sin acomodo, desacomodado, sin alojamiento.
unaccompanied [-ə'kʌmpənɪd] *a.* solo, no acompañado.
unaccomplished [-ə'kɑmplɪʃt, B -'kɔm-] *a.* 1. incompleto, no acabado. 2. falto de experiencia o cualidades.
unaccountable [-'kaʊntəbəl] *a.* 1. inexplicable, extraño, misterioso. 2. irresponsable, falto de responsabilidad.
unaccountably [-blɪ] *adv.* inexplicablemente, misteriosamente.
unaccounted [-'kaʊntəd] *a.* **u. for,** inexplicado; no hallado, no encontrado.
unaccustomed [-'kʌstəmd] *a.* 1. insólito, no usual, no común, extraño. 2. desacostumbrado, inhabituado.
unacknowledged [ˌʌnək'nɑlɪdʒd, B -'nɔl-] *a.* 1. ignorado, no reconocido. 2. no declarado. 3. por contestar (una carta).
unacquainted [-'kweɪntəd] *a.* (ú. gen. con *with*) no versado (en), ignorante (de); **to be u. with,** no conocer (a alguien); ignorar.
unadaptability [-ˌdæptə'bɪlətɪ] *s.* inadaptabilidad.
unadaptable [-'dæptəbəl] *a.* inadaptable.
unadapted [-'dæptəd] *a.* inadaptado.
unadaptedness [-nəs] *s.* inadaptación.
unaddable [ˌʌn'ædəbəl] *a.* insumable.
unadjusted [ˌʌnə'dʒʌstəd] *a.* no ajustado, no regulado o arreglado; inadaptado.
unadoptable [-'dɑptəbəl, B -'dɔp-] *a.* inadoptable.
unadopted [-'dɑptəd, B -'dɔp-] *a.* 1. no adoptado, no empleado. 2. (G.B.) no mantenido por las autoridades locales (díc. de caminos).
unadorned [-'dɔrnd, B -'dɔnd] *a.* sin adorno, llano, liso, simple.
unadulterated [-'dʌltəˌreɪtəd] *a.* no adulterado, puro, sin mezcla, genuino, natural.
unadvised [ˌʌnəd'vaɪzd] *a.* 1. indiscreto, imprudente. 2. inconsiderado, precipitado.
unadvisedly [-'vaɪzədlɪ] *adv.* 1. indiscretamente, imprudentemente. 2. inconsiderablemente, precipitadamente.
unaesthetic [-ɛs'θɛtɪk, B -is-] *a.* antiestético.
unaffected [-ə'fɛktəd] *a.* 1. inafectado, natural, sincero, genuino, sencillo. 2. no influido, inalterado.
unaffectedness [-nəs] *s.* naturalidad, sinceridad, ingenuidad.
unaided [ˌʌn'eɪdəd] *a.* sin ayuda, solo.
unaligned [ˌʌnə'laɪnd] *a.* no alineado, no aliado, no comprometido (entre los grupos competidores de naciones).

unallowable [-'laʊəbəl] *a.* inadmisible, no permisible.
unalloyed [-'lɔɪd] *a.* 1. sin mezcla, sin impurezas. 2. (fig.) puro.
unalterable [ˌʌn'ɔltərəbəl] *a.* inalterable, invariable, inmutable.
unalterableness [-nəs] *s.* inalterabilidad.
unalterably [-'ɔltərəblɪ] *adv.* inalterablemente.
unaltered [-'ɔltərd, B -'ɔltəd] *a.* inalterado.
unambiguous [-æm'bɪgjʊəs] *a.* inequívoco, claro de expresión, sin ambigüedad.
unambitious [-æm'bɪʃəs] *a.* falto de ambiciones.
un-American [-ə'mɛrəkən] *a.* poco americano; antiamericano, antinorteamericano.
unamusing [ˌʌnə'mjuzɪŋ] *a.* aburrido.
unanalyzable [ʌn'ænəˌlaɪzəbəl] *a.* inanalizable, no analizable.
unaneled [ˌʌnə'nild] *a.* (ant.) sin haber recibido la extremaunción.
unanimated [ʌn'ænəˌmeɪtəd] *a.* inanimado.
unanimity [ˌjunə'nɪmətɪ] *s.* unanimidad.
unanimous [jʊ'nænəməs] *a.* unánime.
unanimously [-lɪ] *adv.* unánimemente.
unanimousness [-nəs] *s.* unanimidad.
unanswerable [ˌʌn'ænsərəbəl, B -'ɑn-] *a.* incontestable, irrefutable, irrebatible.
unanswerableness [-nəs] *s.* incontestabilidad.
unanswerably [-blɪ] *adv.* incontestablemente, de manera irrefutable, irrefutablemente.
unanswered [ˌʌn'ænsərd, B -'ɑnsəd] *a.* por contestar, no contestado, dejado sin contestación.
unapostolic [ʌnˌæpəs'tɑlɪk, B -'tɔl-] *a.* contrario al uso apostólico; sin autoridad apostólica.
unappealable [ˌʌnə'piləbəl] *a.* (der.) inapelable.
unappealing [-ɪŋ] *a.* poco atractivo.
unappeasable [-'pizəbəl] *a.* que no puede ser apaciguado; implacable.
unappeasably [-blɪ] *adv.* sin dejarse apaciguar; implacablemente.
unappetizing [ˌʌn'æpəˌtaɪzɪŋ] *a.* poco apetitoso.
unappreciative [-ə'priʃɪətɪv] *a.* ingrato, desagradecido.
unapprehensive [ʌnˌæprɪ'hɛnsɪv] *a.* inaprensivo, desaprensivo.
unapproachability [ˌʌnəˌproʊtʃə'bɪlətɪ] *s.* inaccesibilidad.
unapproachable [-'proʊtʃəbəl] *a.* 1. inaccesible; inalcanzable, inasequible. 2. inabordable. 3. sin igual. 4. esquivo, de pocos amigos.
unapproachableness [-nəs] *s.* inaccesibilidad.
unappropriated [ˌʌnə'proʊprɪˌeɪtəd] *a.* sin dueño, libre; baldío, realengo (terreno).
unapproved [ˌʌnə'pruvd] *a.* desaprobado, no aprobado.
unapt [ˌʌn'æpt] *a.* 1. inadecuado, no apropiado. 2. inepto, inhábil, lerdo. 3. desacostumbrado, inacostumbrado.
unaptly [-lɪ] *adv.* 1. de manera inadecuada, inadecuadamente. 2. ineptamente, lerdamente.
unaptness [-nəs] *s.* 1. ineptitud. 2. improbabilidad.
unargued [ˌʌn'ɑrgjud, B -'ɑgjud] *a.* no discutido, no debatido; no disputado.
unarm [ˌʌn'ɑrm, B -'ɑm] *v.t.* (ant.) desarmar.
unarmed [-'ɑrmd, B -'ɑmd] *a.* 1. desarmado. 2. (bot., zool.) inerme.
unarranged [ˌʌnə'reɪndʒd] *a.* 1. sin arreglo; no arreglado, no convenido. 2. (mús.) no adaptado.
unartificial [ʌnˌɑrtə'fɪʃəl, B -ˌɑtɪ-] *a.* natural, no artificioso.
unartistic [ˌʌnɑr'tɪstɪk, B -ɑ'tɪs-] *a.* no artístico.

unascertainable [ʌnˌæsər'teɪnəbəl, B -ˌæsə'-] *a.* inaveriguable.
unascertained [-'teɪnd] *a.* inaveriguado, no comprobado.
unashamed [ˌʌnə'ʃeɪmd] *a.* desvergonzado, sinvergüenza.
unasked [-'æskt, B -'ɑskt] *a.* 1. no solicitado, espontáneo. 2. no llamado, no convidado, no invitado.
unaspirated [ʌn'æspəˌreɪtəd] *a.* (fon.) no aspirado.
unassailable [ˌʌnə'seɪləbəl] *a.* inexpugnable, irreductible.
unassembled [-'sɛmbəld] *a.* (mot., mec.) desarmado, desmontado.
unassertive [-'sɜrtɪv, B -'sɜtɪv] *a.* retraído, modesto, tímido.
unassignable [-'saɪnəbəl] *a.* intransferible.
unassimilable [-'sɪmələbəl] *a.* no asimilable, no absorbible.
unassisted [-ə'sɪstəd] *a.* por sí solo, sin ayuda.
unassuming [-'sumɪŋ, B -'sju-] *a.* modesto, recatado; retraído, discreto.
unassumingly [-lɪ] *adv.* modestamente, sin pretensiones; discretamente, retraídamente.
unattached [ˌʌnə'tætʃt] *a.* 1. suelto, separado, libre; soltero, no comprometido. 2. no asignado, no incorporado. 3. (der.) no embargado. 4. (mil.) de reemplazo.
unattainable [-'teɪnəbəl] *a.* inasequible, inalcanzable, irrealizable.
unattempted [-'tɛmptəd] *a.* no ensayado, no intentado, no experimentado.
unattended [-'tɛndəd] *a.* desatendido; solo.
unattested [-'tɛstəd] *a.* injustificado, sin confirmación o corroboración.
unattire [ˌʌnə'taɪr, B -'taɪə] *v.t., v.i.* desvestir(se).
unattractive [ˌʌnə'træktɪv] *a.* sin atractivo.
unau [jʊ'nɔ, B 'junɔ] *s.* (zool.) unau, perezoso de dos dedos.
unauspicious [ˌʌnɔ'spɪʃəs] *a.* desfavorable, no propicio.
unauthorized [ʌn'ɔθəˌraɪzd] *a.* desautorizado.
unavailable [ˌʌnə'veɪləbəl] *a.* 1. inasequible, inaccesible. 2. no obtenible, agotado (libro u otro artículo).
unavailing [-'veɪlɪŋ] *a.* inútil, ineficaz, vano, infructuoso.
unavailingly [-lɪ] *adv.* inútilmente, ineficazmente, vanamente, infructuosamente.
unavoidable [ˌʌnə'vɔɪdəbəl] *a.* inevitable, ineludible, ineluctable.
unavoidably [-blɪ] *adv.* inevitablemente.
unaware [-'wɛr, B -'wɛə] *a.* ignorante(de), ajeno(a); inconsciente; **to be u. of,** no percatarse de, no tener conocimiento de. *—adv.* (poét.) de improviso, sin saberlo.
unawareness [-nəs] *s.* inconsciencia, inadvertencia, desconocimiento.
unawares [-'wɛrz, B -'wɛəz] *adv.* 1. inadvertidamente, inopinadamente, sin saberlo. 2. de improviso, sorpresivamente, repentinamente, inesperadamente. 3. **at u.,** (ant.) de improviso; **to take** (o **catch**) **u.,** coger desprevenido.
unbacked [ˌʌn'bækt] *a.* 1. sin ayuda, sin apoyo, sin respaldo. 2. sin apuesta. 3. cerril, sin domar (caballo).
unbaked [ˌʌn'beɪkt] *a.* no cocido, crudo (ladrillo, teja).
unbalance [-'bæləns] *v.t.* desequilibrar, trastornar. *—s.* desequilibrio.
unbalanced [-ənst] *a.* 1. no equilibrado, no contrapesado. 2. (fig.) desequilibrado, trastornado (mente, carácter, etc.). 3. (com.) que no cuadra (cuenta, etc.).
unbalanced phases, (elec.) fases desequilibradas.
unballast [ˌʌn'bæləst] *v.t.* (mar.) deslastrar.
unballasted [-əstəd] *a* 1. desprovisto de lastre; no equilibrado. 2. (fig.) inestable, instable, inseguro.
unbandage [-'bændɪdʒ] *v.t.* desvendar.
unbank [-'bæŋk] *v.t.* avivar (el fuego) removiendo las cenizas.
unbar [ˌʌn'bɑr, B -'bɑ] *v.t.* (*pret., p.p.* UNBARRED; *p.pr.* UNBARRING) desatrancar.
unbarred [-'bɑrd, B -'bɑd] *a.* 1. desatrancado (puerta, etc.); abierto. 2. que no está marcado con barras o franjas.
unbated [-'beɪtəd] *a.* (ant.) no disminuido.
unbearable [-'bɛrəbəl, B -'bɛər-] *a.* intolerable, insoportable, insufrible, inaguantable.
unbearably [-blɪ] *adv.* intolerablemente.
unbeatable [-'bitəbəl] *a.* invencible.
unbeaten [-'bitən] *a.* 1. invicto, insuperado. 2. no pisado, no frecuentado.
unbecoming [ˌʌnbɪ'kʌmɪŋ] *a.* 1. impropio, indecoroso, indigno. 2. que sienta mal (vestido, etc.).
unbecomingly [-lɪ] *adv.* 1. impropiamente, indecorosamente. 2. con mal gusto.
unbecomingness [-nəs] *s.* impropiedad, indecoro.
unbegotten [-bɪ'gɑtən, B -'gɔt-] *a.* ingénito, no engendrado.
unbeknown [ˌʌnbɪ'noʊn] **unbeknownst** [ˌʌnbɪ'noʊnst] *a.* desconocido, ignorado, no conocido, no sabido. *—adv.* (gen. con *to*) sin conocimiento (de), por sorpresa (de).
unbelief [ˌʌnbə'lif] *s.* descreimiento; incredulidad, escepticismo.
unbelievable [-'livəbəl] *a.* increíble.
unbelievably [-blɪ] *adv.* increíblemente.
unbeliever [-'livər, B -'livə] *s.* 1. incrédulo, escéptico. 2. infiel, irreligioso, ateo.
unbelieving [-'livɪŋ] *a.* 1. descreído, incrédulo, escéptico. 2. ateo, infiel, no creyente.
unbelievingly [-lɪ] *adv.* desconfiadamente, escépticamente; incrédulamente.
unbelt [ˌʌn'bɛlt] *v.t.* desceñir, desatar el cinturón de (espada, etc.).
unbend [ˌʌn'bɛnd] *v.t.* 1. enderezar, desencorvar. 2. relajar (la mente). 3. (mar.) desenvergar. *—v.i.* 1. enderezarse, desencorvarse. 2. ponerse cómodo, sentirse en confianza. 3. ponerse afable, ablandarse.
unbending [-ɪŋ] *a.* 1. inconmovible, inflexible, resoluto, riguroso. 2. frío, reservado, poco afable.
unbendingly [-ɪŋlɪ] *adv.* 1. inflexiblemente, rigurosamente. 2. fríamente, sin afabilidad.
unbendingness [-ɪŋnəs] *s.* 1. inflexibilidad, rigor. 2. frialdad, falta de afabilidad.
unbeseeming [ˌʌnbɪ'simɪŋ] *a.* indecente, indecoroso, impropio.
unbeseemingly [-lɪ] *adv.* indecentemente, indecorosamente, impropiamente.
unbeseemingness [-nəs] *s.* indecencia, impropiedad.
unbiased [ˌʌn'baɪəst] *a.* imparcial, neutral.
unbiblical [ˌʌn'bɪblɪkəl] *a.* que no está en la Biblia, no autorizado por la Biblia.
unbidden [ʌn'bɪdən] **unbid** [-'bɪd] *a.* 1. espontáneo, no pedido o solicitado. 2. no invitado.
unbind [-'baɪnd] *v.t.* desatar, desamarrar, desligar.
unbitted [ˌʌn'bɪtəd] *a.* sin freno, sin bridas.
unbleached [-'blitʃt] *a.* sin blanquear.
unblemished [-'blɛmɪʃt] *a.* inmaculado, impoluto.
unblenched [-'blɛntʃt] *a.* impávido, imperté-rrito.
unblessed, unblest [-'blɛst] *a.* 1. no bendito, no consagrado; profano. 2. impío, maldito; desgraciado, infortunado. 3. (relig.) excomulgado.
unblock [-'blɑk, B -'blɔk] *v.t., v.i.* (naipes) establecer (palo en la mano de otro jugador saliendo con carta de alto valor).
unblooded [-'blʌdəd] *a.* sin casta, que no es de pura sangre (caballo).
unblushing [-'blʌʃɪŋ] *a.* desvergonzado, sinvergüenza.
unblushingly [-lɪ] *adv.* desvergonzadamente, sin vergüenza.
unbodied [-'bɑdɪd, B -'bɔd-] *a.* 1. incorpóreo, no corpóreo; sin cuerpo; separado del cuerpo. 2. sin forma, amorfo.
unbolt [ˌʌn'boʊlt] *v.t., v.i.* desatrancar, desbarretar el cerrojo de (la puerta, ventana, etc.).
unbolted [-'boʊltəd] *a.* 1. desatrancado. 2. no cernido (harina).
unbonnet [-'bɑnət, B -'bɔn-] *v.t.* quitar el sombrero o bonete a. *—v.i.* descubrirse.
unbonneted [-ətəd] *a.* descubierto, sin sombrero.
unborn [-'bɔrn, B -'bɔn] *a.* nonato, no nacido aún; venidero, futuro (generación, etc.).
unbosom [-'bʊzəm] *v.t.* revelar (secretos, confidencias, etc.), confesar; **u. oneself (to),** abrir o descubrir uno su pecho (a), desahogarse (con).
unbottomed [-'bɑtəmd, B -'bɔt-] *a.* insondable, sin fondo.
unbound [-'baʊnd] *a.* 1. no encuadernado, sin encuadernar, en rústica. 2. desatado, suelto, libre.
unbounded [-əd] *a.* 1. ilimitado, infinito. 2. desenfrenado.
unbowed [-'baʊd] *a.* 1. no inclinado, derecho. 2. no subyugado, no domado.
unbrace [-'breɪs] *v.t.* 1. aflojar, soltar, desabrochar, desasegurar. 2. debilitar; relajar. 3. destemplar (un tambor).
unbraid [-'breɪd] *v.t.* destrenzar, destejer; desenredar, desenmarañar.
unbranched [-bræntʃt, B -'brɑntʃt] *a.* 1. sin ramas. 2. no ramificado.
unbreakable [ˌʌn'breɪkəbəl] *a.* irrompible, infrangible; inquebrantable, indestructible.
unbreathable [-'briðəbəl] *a.* irrespirable.
unbred [-'brɛd] *a.* 1. sin instrucción, no entrenado. 2. sin casta (animal). 3. malcriado, mal educado.
unbridle [ˌʌn'braɪdəl] *v.t.* 1. desembridar (a los caballos). 2. (fig.) desenfrenar.
unbridled [-'braɪdəld] *a.* 1. desembridado. 2. (fig.) desenfrenado, descomedido, licencioso.
unbroken [-'broʊkən] *a.* 1. intacto, entero. 2. ininterrumpido, continuo. 3. inviolada (ley). 4. no superado, vigente (marca deportiva). 5. indómito, bravío, cerrero (caballo).
unbuckle [-'bʌkəl] *v.t.* deshebillar; desprender.
unbuild [-'bɪld] *v.t.* demoler, arrasar, derribar, derruir.
unbuildable [-əbəl] *a.* inconstruible.
unbuilt [-'bɪlt] *a.* 1. no construido. 2. sin construir, sin construcciones (terreno).
unburden [-'bɜrdən, B -'bɜd-] *v.t.* descargar, quitar la carga; (fig.) aliviar, desahogar (conciencia, alma, etc.); **u. oneself (of),** desahogarse (de).
unburied [-'bɛrɪd] *a.* insepulto.
unburned [-'bɜrnd, B -'bɜnd] **unburnt** [-'bɜrnt, B -'bɜnt] *a.* no quemado; no cocido (ladrillo, etc.).
unbury [ˌʌn'bɛrɪ] *v.t.* desenterrar, exhumar.

unbusinesslike [-'bɪznəsˌlaɪk] *a.* poco práctico; inexperto, ineficaz; contra la ética (en los negocios).
unbutton [-'bʌtən] *v.t., v.i.* 1. desabotonar, desabrochar. 2. (fig.) desahogarse.
unbuttoned [-'bʌtənd] *a.* 1. no abotonado. 2. sin botones. 3. (fig.) no restringido, desenvuelto, desenfrenado. 4. (fig.) debilitado, descompuesto.
uncage [-'keɪdʒ] *v.t.* soltar de la jaula; (fig.) libertar.
uncalled [-'kɔld] *a.* no llamado, no pedido; **u. for,** inapropiado, impertinente; no reclamado; innecesario.
uncanceled [-'kænsəld] *a.* 1. sin cancelar (sello postal). 2. no anulado, no rescindido.
uncannily [-'kænəlɪ] *adv.* 1. sobrenaturalmente, extrañamente, misteriosamente. 2. (esco.) peligrosamente, arriesgadamente.
uncanniness [-'kænɪnəs] *s.* 1. carácter sobrenatural o extraño; naturaleza misteriosa. 2. (esco.) peligrosidad.
uncanny [-'kænɪ] *a.* 1. sobrenatural, misterioso, extraño. 2. (esco.) peligroso, arriesgado.
uncap [-'kæp] *v.t.* destapar. —*v.i.* quitarse el sombrero, descubrirse.
uncared-for [ˌʌn'kɛrdˌfɔr, B -'kɛədˌfɔ] *a.* desamparado, descuidado, abandonado.
uncase [-'keɪs] *v.t.* 1. desenvainar. 2. revelar. 3. (mil.) desplegar (la bandera).
uncaused [-'kɔzd] *a.* 1. no creado, increado. 2. no causado, no originado.
unceasing [-'sisɪŋ] *a.* incesante, continuo.
unceasingly [-lɪ] *adv.* incesantemente, sin cesar.
unceremonious [-ˌsɛrə'moʊnɪəs] *a.* 1. familiar, informal, que no guarda ceremonias. 2. abrupto, descortés.
unceremoniously [-lɪ] *adv.* 1. informalmente, familiarmente, sin ceremonia. 2. descortésmente.
uncertain [ˌʌn'sɜrtən, B ʌn'sɜtən] *a.* 1. incierto, indefinido, dudoso, dubitativo, problemático. 2. indeterminado. 3. inseguro, indeciso, perplejo, irresoluto, vacilante. 4. inconstante, variable, cambiable.
uncertainly [-lɪ] *adv.* inciertamente, inseguramente, vacilantemente; indeterminadamente, indefinidamente.
uncertainness [-nəs] *s.* incertidumbre, indeterminación, indecisión, vacilación.
uncertainty [-tɪ] *s.* (*pl.* UNCERTAINTIES) 1. incertidumbre; indeterminación, indecisión, inseguridad. 2. lo incierto, cosa incierta, duda.
uncertainty principle, (fís.) principio de incertidumbre.
unchain [ˌʌn'tʃeɪn] *v.t.* desencadenar, libertar.
unchallenged [-'tʃæləndʒd] *a.* 1. no retado. 2. indisputable. 3. **to go u.,** no tener rival.
unchancy [-'tʃænsɪ, B -'tʃɑn-] *a.* (esco.) malaventurado, malhadado; peligroso.
unchangeability [ʌnˌtʃeɪndʒə'bɪlətɪ] *s.* inalterabilidad, invariabilidad, inmutabilidad, inconmutabilidad.
unchangeable [ˌʌn'tʃeɪndʒəbəl] *a.* inalterable, invariable, incambiable, inmutable, inconmutable.
unchangeableness [-nəs] *s.* inalterabilidad, invariabilidad, inmutabilidad, inconmutabilidad.
unchangeably [-blɪ] *adv.* inalterablemente, invariablemente, sin cambio.
unchanged [ˌʌn'tʃeɪndʒd] *a.* invariado, inalterado.
uncharged [ˌʌn'tʃɑrdʒd, B -'tʃɑdʒd] *a.* sin carga, no cargado (batería, etc.).
uncharitable [ˌʌn'tʃærətəbəl] *a.* poco caritativo, duro, falto de benevolencia, severo, rígido.
uncharitableness [-nəs] *s.* falta de benevolencia, severidad, rigidez, dureza.
uncharitably [-blɪ] *adv.* sin benevolencia o caridad, severamente, rígidamente, duramente.
uncharted [-'tʃɑrtəd, B 'ʌn'tʃɑtɪd] *a.* inexplorado, desconocido.
unchaste [ˌʌn'tʃeɪst] *a.* incontinente, inmoral, lascivo.
unchastely [-lɪ] *adv.* sin castidad, sin continencia; lascivamente.
unchastity [-'tʃæstətɪ] *s.* falta de castidad, incontinencia.
unchristian [ˌʌn'krɪstʃən] *a.* 1. poco cristiano, pagano, gentil. 2. anticristiano. 3. incivilizado, bárbaro.
unchurch [ˌʌn'tʃɜrtʃ, B -'tʃɜtʃ] *v.t.* 1. expulsar o excluir de la iglesia, excomulgar. 2. despojar de una iglesia.
unchurched [-'tʃɜrtʃt, B -'tʃɜtʃt] *a.* que no pertenece a ninguna iglesia.
unci, *pl. de* **uncus.**
uncial ['ʌntʃəl, B -sɪəl] *a., s.* uncial, tipo de letra usado antiguamente.
unciform ['ʌnsəˌfɔrm, B -fɔm] *a., s.* (anat.) unciforme.
uncinaria [ˌʌnsə'nærɪə] *s.* (med.) uncinaria, anquilostoma.
uncinariasis [ˌʌnˌsɪnə'raɪəsəs] *s.* (med.) uncinariasis, anquilostomiasis.
uncinate ['ʌnsəˌneɪt, B -nɪt] *a.* uncinado, en forma de garfio.
uncinus [ˌʌn'saɪnəs] *s.* (*pl.* UNCINI [-naɪ]) (zool.) uncina.
uncircumcised [ˌʌn'sɜrkəmˌsaɪzd, B -'sɜkəm-] *a.* 1. incircunciso, no circuncidado, incircuncidado. 2. (fig.) gentil, no judío; pagano.
uncircumcision [ˌʌnˌsɜrkəm'sɪʒən, B -ˌsɜkəm-] *s.* 1. falta de circuncisión. 2. (bíbl.) la gente no circuncisa; la gentilidad.
uncircumscribed [ˌʌn'sɜrkəmˌskraɪbd, B -'sɜkəm-] *a.* incircunscripto.
uncircumstantial [-ˌsɜrkəm'stænʃəl, B -ˌsɜkəm-] *a.* sin detalles, no minucioso.
uncivil [ˌʌn'sɪvəl] *a.* 1. no civilizado, bárbaro. 2. incivil, descortés.
uncivilizable [ˌʌn'sɪvəˌlaɪzəbəl] *a.* incivilizable.
uncivilized [-ˌlaɪzd] *a.* incivilizado, bárbaro, salvaje.
uncivilly [-'sɪvəlɪ] *adv.* incivilmente, descortésmente.
unclad [ˌʌn'klæd] *a.* desvestido, desnudo.
unclaimed [ˌʌn'kleɪmd] *a.* no reclamado (carta, correo, etc.).
unclasp [ˌʌn'klæsp, B -'klɑsp] *v.t.* 1. desabrochar. 2. separar (las manos que se han estrechado).
unclassifiable [ˌʌn'klæsəˌfaɪəbəl] *a.* inclasificable.
unclassified [-ˌfaɪd] *a.* no clasificado; no clasificado como secreto.
uncle ['ʌŋkəl] *s.* 1. tío. 2. (jer.) prestamista. 3. **to cry (holler,** etc.) **u.,** rendirse.
unclean [ˌʌn'klin] *a.* sucio, inmundo, desaseado; impuro.
uncleanliness [-'klɛnlɪnəs] *s.* desaseo; impureza.
uncleanly [ˌʌn'klɛnlɪ] *a.* desaseado; impuro. —[-klinlɪ] *adv.* desaseadamente; impuramente.
uncleanness [-'klinnəs] *s.* suciedad, inmundicia, desaseo; impureza.
unclench [-'klɛntʃ] *v.t.* 1. relajar (el puño). 2. desasir, soltar. —*v.i.* abrirse (el puño).
Uncle Sam ['ʌŋkəl'sæm] (fam.) el Tío Sam, figura que representa a los E.U.
Uncle Tom [-'tɑm, B -'tɔm] (fam., E.U.) Tío Tom, negro que adopta una actitud servil frente al blanco (del personaje de la obra *La Cabaña del Tío Tom*).
unclinch [ˌʌn'klɪntʃ] *var. de* **unclench.**
uncloak [ˌʌn'kloʊk] *v.t.* 1. desencapotar. 2. (fig.) desencapotar, desenmascarar. —*v.i.* desencapotarse.
unclog [-'klɑg, B -'klɔg] *v.t.* desatancar, desatascar.
uncloister [-'klɔɪstər, B -'klɔɪstə] *v.t.* exclaustrar, permitir que abandone el claustro (a un religioso).
unclose [-'kloʊz] *v.t.* abrir, revelar.
unclothe [-'kloʊð] *v.t.* 1. desvestir, desarropar. 2. desnudar, despojar. 3. (fig.) descubrir, revelar.
unclouded [-'klaʊdəd] *a.* claro, despejado, sin nubes.
unco ['ʌŋkoʊ] *a.* (pr. esco.) 1. extraño, desconocido; misterioso, raro. 2. extraordinario. —*adv.* extremadamente, notablemente, muy. —*s.* (esco.) 1. (*pl.*) nuevas, noticias. 2. extraño, forastero.
uncoagulable [ˌʌnˌkoʊ'ægjələbəl] *a.* incoagulable.
uncock [-'kɑk, B -'kɔk] *v.t.* desmontar, poner el seguro de, bajar el percutor de (arma).
uncognizant [-'kɑgnəzənt, B -'kɔg-] *a.* inconsciente, sin conocimiento de (un hecho, una situación, etc.).
uncoil [-'kɔɪl] *v.t., v.i* desenrollar(se), desarrollar(se).
uncoined [-'kɔɪnd] *a.* no acuñado.
uncollectible [-kə'lɛktəbəl] *a.* incobrable.
uncolored [-'kʌlərd, B -'kʌləd] *a.* 1. (pint.) no coloreado. 2. (fig.) incoloro, sin exageración, sin aumento; imparcial.
uncombed [ˌʌn'koʊmd] *a.* despeinado.
uncombinable [ˌʌnkəm'baɪnəbəl] *a.* incombinable.
uncomeliness [ˌʌn'kʌmlɪnəs] *s.* fealdad; desaire.
uncomely [-'kʌmlɪ] *a.* feo; desairado.
uncomfortable [-'kʌmftəbəl, -'kʌmfərtə-, B -'kʌmftəbəl] *a.* 1. incómodo. 2. desagradable, molesto, penoso, embarazoso. 3. intranquilo. 4. inquietante.
uncommercial [ˌʌnkə'mɜrʃəl, B -'mɜʃəl] *a.* 1. no comercial. 2. contrario a las usanzas comerciales.
uncommitted [ˌʌnkə'mɪtəd] *a.* no comprometido, imparcial, sin tomar una posición.
uncommon [ˌʌn'kɑmən, B -'kɔmən] *a.* poco común, no usual, infrecuente, raro, extraño, excepcional, extraordinario.
uncommonly [-lɪ] *adv.* extraordinariamente, notablemente.
uncommonness [-nəs] *s.* infrecuencia, rareza.
uncommunicative [-kə'mjunəˌkeɪtɪv, -nɪkətɪv] *a.* poco comunicativo, poco informativo; reservado, taciturno.
uncompensable [ˌʌnkəm'pɛnsəbəl] *a.* incompensable, irresarcible.
uncomplaining [ˌʌnkəm'pleɪnɪŋ] *a.* no quejoso, impasible.
uncompleted [ˌʌnkəm'plitəd] *a.* inacabado, incompleto, sin terminar.
uncomplimentary [-ˌkɑmplə'mɛntərɪ, B -ˌkɔm-] *a.* poco halagüeño, desfavorable; despectivo, ofensivo.
uncompromising [-'kɑmprəˌmaɪzɪŋ, B -'kɔm-] *a.* inflexible, intransigente, irreconciliable, inexorable.

uncompromisingly [-lɪ] *adv.* inflexiblemente, inexorablemente, de manera intransigente, intransigentemente.
unconcern [-kən'sɜrn, B -'sɜn] *s.* desinterés, indiferencia, desapego, desprendimiento; despreocupación.
unconcerned [-'sɜrnd, B -'sɜnd] *a.* desinteresado, indiferente, desprendido, desapegado; despreocupado.
unconcernedly [-'sɜrnədlɪ, B -'sɜnɪd-] *adv.* indiferentemente; despreocupadamente.
unconcernedness [-nəs] *s.* desinterés, indiferencia, desprendimiento, desapego; despreocupación.
unconditional [ˌʌnkən'dɪʃənəl] *a.* incondicional.
unconditionally [-ɪ] *adv.* incondicionalmente.
unconditional surrender, capitulación o rendición incondicional.
unconditioned [-'dɪʃənd] *a.* 1. incondicional. 2. no acondicionado, natural, innato. 3. (psic.) instintivo, espontáneo, no aprendido.
unconfessable [ˌʌnkən'fɛsəbəl] *a.* inconfesable.
unconfined [ˌʌnkən'faɪnd] *a.* ilimitado; libre, sin trabas, sin obstáculos.
unconfirmed [ˌʌnkən'fɜrmd, B -fɜmd] *a.* no confirmado.
unconformable [-'fɔrməbəl, B -'fɔm-] *a.* 1. disconforme, desconforme. 2. (geol.) discordante.
unconformity [-ətɪ] *s.* (*pl.* UNCONFORMITIES) 1. inconformidad, desconformidad, disidencia. 2. (geol.) discordancia (falta de continuidad en los estratos).
uncongenial [-'dʒinjəl, -'dʒiniəl] *a.* 1. incompatible, que no congenia. 2. antipático, desagradable.
unconnected [ˌʌnkə'nɛktəd] *a.* inconexo, discontinuo, interrumpido.
unconquerable [ˌʌn'kɑŋkərəbəl, B -'kɔŋ-] *a.* 1. inconquistable, invencible, indomable. 2. insuperable.
unconquered [-kərd, B -kəd] *a.* invicto, no conquistado.
unconscientious [-kɑntʃɪ'ɛntʃəs, B -kɔnʃɪ-] *a.* inconsciente, irresponsable.
unconscientiousness [-nəs] *s.* inconsciencia, irresponsabilidad.
unconscionable [-'kɑntʃənəbəl, B -'kɔnʃən-] *a.* 1. desrazonable, desmedido, excesivo, exorbitante. 2. inmoral, falto de escrúpulo. 3. injusto, chocante.
unconscionably [-blɪ] *adv.* 1. desmedidamente, exorbitantemente. 2. sin escrúpulo.
unconscious [-'kɑntʃəs, B -'kɔnʃəs] *a.* 1. inconsciente. 2. desmayado, sin conocimiento. 3. (con *of*) inconsciente (de), ignorante (de). 4. no intencional; instintivo. 5. **the u.,** (psic.) el inconsciente; lo inconsciente; **to become u.,** perder el sentido, desmayarse.
unconsciously [-lɪ] *adv.* inconscientemente.
unconsciousness [-nəs] *s.* inconsciencia.
unconsidered [ˌʌnkən'sɪdərd, B -'sɪdəd] *a.* 1. inconsiderado, irreflexivo. 2. insignificante.
unconstitutional [-ˌkɑnstə'tuʃənəl, B -ˌkɔnstɪ'tjuʃ-] *a.* inconstitucional.
unconstitutionality [-ˌtuʃə'nælətɪ, B -ˌtju-] *s.* inconstitucionalidad.
uncontainable [ˌʌnkən'teɪnəbəl] *a.* incontenible.
uncontaminated [ˌʌnkən'tæmɪˌneɪtəd] *a.* incontaminado, puro, limpio.
uncontemplated [-'kɑntəmˌpleɪtəd, B -'kɔntɛmˌpleɪtɪd] *a.* inesperado, impensado.
uncontrollable [ˌʌnkən'troʊləbəl] *a.* incontrolable, ingobernable; indomable, irrefrenable.
uncontrolled [-'troʊld] *a.* 1. no controlado, no dominado, no gobernado. 2. no vigilado.
unconventional [-kən'vɛntʃənəl, B -'vɛnʃ-] *a.* 1. informal, despreocupado. 2. original, inacostumbrado, desacostumbrado.
unconventionality [-ˌvɛntʃə'nælətɪ, B -ˌvɛnʃə-] *s.* 1. informalidad, despreocupación. 2. originalidad.
uncork [-'kɔrk, B -'kɔk] *v.t.* 1. descorchar. 2. (fig.) destapar; soltar.
uncorrectable [ˌʌnkə'rɛktəbəl] *a.* incorregible (error, manuscrito, etc.).
uncorrected [-'rɛktəd] *a.* no corregido.
uncorrupted [ˌʌnkə'rʌptəd] *a.* incorrupto.
uncountable [ˌʌn'kaʊntəbəl] *a.* incontable, innumerable.
uncounted [-'kaʊntəd] *a.* no contado, innumerable.
uncouple [-'kʌpəl] *v.t.* 1. desparejar, deshacer (una pareja); esp. soltar de la tirilla (una pareja de perros). 2. desenganchar, desacoplar.
uncourteous [-'kɜrtɪəs, B -'kɜtɪəs] *a.* descortés, desatento.
uncourtly [-'kɔrtlɪ, B -'kɔt-] *a.* grosero, rústico, mal educado.
uncouth [-'kuθ] *a.* 1. tosco, rústico, inculto; descortés, grosero, brusco, rudo. 2. desgarbado, torpe. 3. (ant.) misterioso; raro, extraño.
uncouthly [-lɪ] *adv.* groseramente, bruscamente, rudamente.
uncouthness [-nəs] *s.* tosquedad, rusticidad; grosería, brusquedad, rudeza.
uncover [ʌn'kʌvər, B -ə] *v.t.* 1. descubrir, destapar. 2. (fig.) revelar, descubrir, destapar, dejar al descubierto. 3. desabrigar, desarropar; quitarse el sombrero de (la cabeza). —*v.i.* descubrirse, quitarse el sombrero.
uncovered [-'kʌvərd, B -'kʌvəd] *a.* 1. descubierto, desabrigado, destapado, desarropado. 2. (com.) descubierto.
uncowl [ˌʌn'kaʊl] *v.t.* quitar la capucha de (o a).
uncreated [ˌʌnkrɪ'eɪtəd] *a.* increado.
uncritical [ˌʌn'krɪtɪkəl] *a.* 1. que no discrimina. 2. sin reservas, incondicional.
uncriticizable [-'krɪtəˌsaɪzəbəl] *a.* incriticable.
uncross [-'krɔs] *v.t.* descruzar.
uncrown [-'kraʊn] *v.t.* descoronar, destronar, deponer.
uncrowned [-'kraʊnd] *a.* que no lleva corona; no coronado.
uncrystallizable [ˌʌn'krɪstəˌlaɪzəbəl] *a.* incristalizable.
unction ['ʌŋkʃən] *s.* 1. unción, ungimiento. 2. ungüento, untura. 3. unción, devoción. 4. beatería.
unctuosity [ˌʌŋktʃu'ɑsətɪ, B -'ɔsɪtɪ] *s.* untuosidad.
unctuous ['ʌŋktʃuəs, B -tjuəs] *a.* 1. untuoso, untoso, grasiento, aceitoso. 2. plástico, moldeable (arcilla). 3. devoto, fervoroso. 4. mojigato, hipócrita, farisaico.
unctuously [-lɪ] *adv.* hipócritamente, farisaicamente.
unctuousness [-nəs] *s.* 1. untuosidad. 2. beatería, mojigatería.
uncultivated [ˌʌn'kʌltəˌveɪtəd] *a.* 1. yermo, baldío, no cultivado. 2. inculto, rústico, grosero.
uncultured [ˌʌn'kʌltʃərd, B -'kʌltʃəd] *a.* inculto, rústico.
uncurl [ˌʌn'kɜrl, B -'kɜl] *v.t., v.i.* desrizar(se), desencrespar(se); desenrollar(se).
uncus ['ʌŋkəs] *s.* (*pl.* UNCI ['ʌnsai]) (anat.) uncus.
uncustomed [ˌʌn'kʌstəmd] *a.* libre de derechos de aduana.
uncut [ˌʌn'kʌt] *a.* 1. no cortado, no tallado, en bruto (esp. piedras preciosas). 2. (impr.) que tiene los bordes sin cortar (libro). 3. completo, sin cortes (libro, película).
undamaged [ˌʌn'dæmɪdʒd] *a.* indemne, ileso, intacto.
undamped [ˌʌn'dæmpt] *a.* 1. (fís., electrón.) no amortiguado. 2. no refrenado, no disminuido; no descorazonado.
undated [ˌʌn'deɪtəd] *a.* sin fecha.
undaunted [ˌʌn'dɔntəd] *a.* intrépido, denodado; impávido, impertérrito.
undauntedly [-lɪ] *adv.* intrépidamente, denodadamente.
undauntedness [-nəs] *s.* intrepidez, arrojo, valentía.
undé, undée [ʌn'deɪ] *a.* (her.) ondeado, ondeante.
undecagon [ʌn'dɛkəˌgɑn, B -gən] *s.* (geom.) undecágono, endecágono.
undeceive [ˌʌndɪ'siv] *v.t.* desengañar, desilusionar.
undecided [ˌʌndɪ'saɪdəd] *a.* no resuelto; indeciso, irresoluto; dudoso.
undecillion [ˌʌndɪ'sɪljən] *s.* (E.U.) unidad seguida de 36 ceros; (G.B.) unidad seguida de 66 ceros.
undecipherable [ˌʌndɪ'saɪfərəbəl] *a.* indescifrable, ininteligible.
undecisive [ˌʌndɪ'saɪsɪv] *a.* no decisivo.
undeclinable [ˌʌndɪ'klaɪnəbəl] *a.* indeclinable (oferta, invitación, etc.); (gram.) indeclinable.
undecylenic acid [ˌʌnˌdɛsə'lɛnɪk-] (quím.) ácido undecilénico.
undefeated [ˌʌndɪ'fitəd] *a.* invicto.
undefended [ˌʌndɪ'fɛndəd] *a.* indefenso (díc. esp. de la acción judicial).
undeferrable [ˌʌndɪ'fɜrəbəl] *a.* inaplazable, impostergable.
undefiled [ˌʌndɪ'faɪld] *a.* impoluto, inmaculado, sin mancha.
undefinable [ˌʌndɪ'faɪnəbəl] *a.* indefinible, indeterminable.
undefined [ˌʌndɪ'faɪnd] *a.* indefinido.
undelayable [ˌʌndɪ'leɪəbəl] *a.* impostergable.
undeliberate [ˌʌndɪ'lɪbərət] *a.* indeliberado.
undeliberately [-lɪ] *adv.* indeliberadamente.
undeliberateness [-nəs] *s.* indeliberación.
undelivered [ˌʌndɪ'lɪvərd, B -'lɪvəd] *a.* sin entregar, no entregado (carta, paquete postal, etc.).
undemanding [ˌʌndɪ'mændɪŋ, B -'mɑnd-] *a.* poco exigente, modesto.
undemonstrable [ˌʌndɪ'mɑnstrəbəl, B -'mɔn-] *a.* indemostrable.
undemonstrative [ˌʌndɪ'mɑnstrətɪv, B -'mɔn-] *a.* reservado, poco expresivo, no efusivo.
undeniable [-'naɪəbəl] *a.* 1. innegable, indisputable, incontestable. 2. legítimo, muy bueno, excelente.
undeniably [-blɪ] *adv.* indisputablemente.
under ['ʌndər, B 'ʌndə] *prep.* 1. debajo de, bajo de, bajo. 2. bajo (ej., la mesa, la autoridad, órdenes, etc.); so (pretexto, pena, etc.). 3. en, ej., *u. the circumstances,* en (o bajo) las circunstancias, *u. repair,* en reparación, en compostura. 4. inferior a, (por) menos de, menos que, ej., *it can not be bought u. $50,* no se puede comprarlo por menos de $50. 5. en la época de, en tiempo de. 6. según, conforme a. 7. **to be known u. the name of,** ser conocido por o bajo el nombre de; **u. a cloud,** (fig.) desacreditado; en desgracia;

u. arms, bajo las armas; **u. consideration,** en consideración, bajo consideración; **u. contract,** bajo contrato; conforme al contrato; **u. cover,** (fig.) subrepticiamente; al abrigo, a cubierto; **u. cultivation,** en cultivo; **u. fire,** en combate, bajo el fuego enemigo; criticado; **u. full sail,** (mar.) a toda vela; **u. hatches,** (mar.) debajo de la cubierta; (fig.) escondido; muerto; **u. lock and key,** bajo llave, encerrado; **u. oath,** bajo juramento; **u. one's breath,** susurrando; **u. one's nose,** (fig.) en las barbas de uno, en sus (propias) narices; **u. one's wing,** (fig.) bajo su ala o protección; **u. pain of,** bajo pena de, so pena de; **u. penalty of (death,** etc.), so pena de (muerte, etc.); **u. sentence of,** condenado a, bajo sentencia de; **u. separate cover,** por separado, en sobre aparte, bajo cubierta separada; **u. steam,** bajo presión; **u. the care of,** al cuidado de; **u. the command of,** al mando de; **u. the hand and seal of,** firmado y sellado por; **u. the lee of,** al abrigo de; **u. the rose,** en secreto; **u. the sun,** bajo el sol, en todas partes; **u. the weather,** indispuesto; **u. this act,** (der.) con arreglo a esta ley; **u. way,** en camino, en marcha; principiando; andando. —*adv.* 1. debajo, bajo, abajo. 2. menos. — **to be under an obligation to,** deber favores a (alguien); **to bring u.,** subyugar, someter, vencer; **to go u.,** sucumbir; fracasar; hundirse; **to keep u.,** oprimir, mantener sojuzgado o sometido; **to knuckle u.,** doblegarse ante, ceder a. —*a.* 1. inferior. 2. subalterno, subordinado, dependiente. 3. menor.

underachieve [ˌʌndərə'tʃiv] *v.i.* rendir menos (en estudios escolares) de lo posible o esperado.

underachiever [-ər, B -ə] *s.* alumno cuyo nivel de rendimiento está por debajo del corriente.

underact [ˌʌndə'rækt] *v.t.* interpretar (un papel) mal o reprimidamente; representar sin brillo (un drama). —*v.i.* actuar sin énfasis (en un drama).

underage [ˌʌndə'reɪdʒ] *a.* menor de edad, falto de edad (necesaria).

underarm ['ʌndəˌrɑrm, B 'ʌndəˌrɑm] *a.* 1. que está bajo el brazo. 2. clandestino, secreto. —*adv.* sin levantar las manos (más arriba de la altura del hombro). —*s.* (anat.) axila.

underbelly ['ʌndərˌbɛlɪ, B 'ʌndəˌ-] *s.* parte inferior (de un cuerpo o masa); (fig.) parte más débil o vulnerable.

underbid [ˌʌndər'bɪd, B ˌʌndə'-] *v.t.* 1. ofrecer o vender a menor precio que; hacer propuesta más baja que. 2. ofrecer menos del valor de; rebajar. 3. (naipes) declarar (una mano) debajo de su fuerza.

underbodice ['ʌndərˌbɑdɪs, B 'ʌndəˌbɔdɪs] *s.* cubrecorsé.

underbody [-ˌbɑdɪ, B -ˌbɔdɪ] *s.* 1. parte inferior del cuerpo de un animal. 2. la parte inferior de un vehículo.

underbred [ˌʌndər'brɛd, B -də'-] *a.* 1. de raza impura, de raza mixta. 2. vulgar, sin urbanidad, malcriado.

underbrush ['ʌndərˌbrʌʃ, B -dəˌ-] *s.* maleza, broza, monte bajo.

underbuy [ˌʌndər'baɪ, B -də'-] *v.t.* comprar una cantidad insuficiente de (un artículo).

undercarriage ['ʌndərˌkærɪdʒ, B -dəˌ-] *s.* 1. (mec.) chasis, bastidor (que sostiene la carrocería). 2. (aer.) tren de aterrizaje.

undercharge [ˌʌndər'tʃɑrdʒ, B -də'tʃɑdʒ] *v.t.* 1. cobrar de menos. 2. (mil.) cargar (un arma) con poco explosivo. — ['ʌndərˌtʃɑrdʒ, B 'ʌndəˌtʃɑdʒ] *s.* 1. precio insuficiente, cobro de menos. 2. (mil.) carga insuficiente.

underclass ['ʌndərˌklæs, B -dəˌklɑs] *s.* 1. (educ.) (*gen. pl.*) (estudiantes de) los dos primeros años de la universidad. 2. (sociol.) clase marginada.

underclassman [ˌʌndər'klæsmən, B -də'klɑs-] *s.* estudiante (universitario) del primero o segundo año.

underclothes ['ʌndərˌklouz, B -dəˌklouðz] *s. pl.* ropa interior.

underclothing [-ˌklouðɪŋ] *s.* ropa interior.

undercoat [-ˌkout] *s.* 1. chaqueta interior. 2. pelaje corto cubierto por otro más largo. 3. capa de base, primera mano, mano interior (de pintura, etc.).

underconsumption [ˌʌndərkən'sʌmʃən, B -dəkən-] *s.* infraconsumo.

undercool [-'kul] *v.t.* (fís., quím.) sobreenfriar, subenfriar.

undercover [-'kʌvər, B 'ʌndəˌkʌvə] *a.* secreto, clandestino, confidencial.

undercover agent, agente secreto; espía.

undercroft ['ʌndərˌkrɔft, B -dəˌ-] *s.* (ant.) cuarto subterráneo, cripta.

undercurrent [-ˌkɜrənt, B -ˌkʌrənt] *s.* 1. corriente submarina o subfluvial. 2. (fig.) corriente oculta (de opiniones contrarias a las expresadas públicamente).

undercut [ˌʌndər'kʌt, B -də'-] *v.t.* 1. (lit., fig.) socavar. 2. cincelar (obra de relieve). 3. vender o trabajar a menor precio que. 4. (golf) dar un golpe oblicuo a (la pelota). 5. (tenis) cortar (la pelota). —*v.i.* 1. socavar una superficie o la posición, etc. de una persona. 2. (tenis) cortar la pelota. — ['ʌndərˌkʌt B 'ʌndəˌ-] —*s.* 1. socava, socavación. 2. (cocina, E.U.) solomillo; (G.B.) lomo. 3. (golf) golpe sesgado. 4. (tenis) corte sesgado.

undercutter ['ʌn-ˌkʌtər, B -ə] *s.* (maq.) muescador; portasierra para corte inferior; socavadora.

underdeveloped [ˌʌn-dɪ'vɛləpt] *a.* 1. subdesarrollado (país, región). 2. insuficientemente desarrollado (músculo, cuerpo, etc.). 3. (foto.) insuficientemente revelado.

underdeveloped countries, países subdesarrollados.

underdevelopment [-'vɛləpmənt] *s.* 1. subdesarrollo (de un país, región, etc.). 2. desarrollo insuficiente (de un músculo, cuerpo, etc.). 3. (foto.) revelado insuficiente.

underdo [-'du] *v.t.* 1. hacer de menos, hacer menos de lo necesario. 2. soasar, medio asar.

underdog ['ʌndərˌdɔg, B -dəˌ-] *s.* 1. aquél que no es el favorito (en competencia, deportes, etc.); el que se espera que pierda (en una elección, etc.). 2. (fig.) víctima (de la injusticia social, persecución, etc.); desvalido, (el) más débil; **the underdogs,** los de abajo, la gente pobre, los desvalidos.

underdone [ˌʌndər'dʌn, B -də'-] *a.* soasado, a medio asar (esp. carnes).

underdrainage ['ʌndərˌdreɪnɪdʒ, B -dəˌ-] *s.* desagüe subterráneo.

underdrawers [-ˌdrɔrz, B -ˌdrɔz] *s. pl.* calzoncillos.

underemployment [ˌʌndərɪm'plɔɪmənt] *s.* 1. empleo deficiente; empleo parcial (de la mano de obra). 2. incapacitación laboral (en tipo de trabajo y salario).

underestimate [-'ɛstəˌmeɪt] *v.t.* 1. tasar en menos, avaluar debajo de su precio. 2. menospreciar, desestimar, tener en menos. — [-mət] *s.* 1. valuación por debajo del precio, subvaluación; presupuesto demasiado bajo. 2. menosprecio, desestima.

underestimated [-'ɛstəˌmeɪtəd] *a.* poco estimado, inestimado; tasado por debajo del precio real.

underestimation [-ˌɛstə'meɪʃən] *s.* 1. valuación por debajo del precio. 2. menosprecio, desestimación.

underexpose [-ɪks'pouz] *v.t.* (foto.) exponer insuficientemente.

underexposure [-'pouʒər, B -'pouʒə] *s.* exposición, insuficiente.

underfed [-'fɛd, B -də'-] *a.* desnutrido, mal alimentado.

underfeed [-'fid] *v.t.* 1. desnutrir, alimentar insuficientemente. 2. alimentar (una caldera, etc.) por la parte inferior.

underfoot [-'fʊt] *adv.* 1. bajo los pies (esp. en el piso, en el suelo); a los pies. 2. en el camino, estorbando.

undergarment ['ʌndərˌgɑrmənt, B -dəˌgɑmənt] *s.* prenda interior (de vestir).

undergird [ˌʌndər'gɜrd, B -də'gɜd] *v.t.* 1. ceñir por debajo, cinchar. 2. (fig.) apuntalar.

underglaze [-'gleɪz, B 'ʌndəˌgleɪz] *a.* aplicado antes de vidriar (díc. de los colores para decorar objetos de porcelana o cerámica).

undergo [-'gou, B ˌʌn-] *v.t.* 1. ser sometido a. sufrir. 2. sostener, experimentar, pasar por.

undergraduate [-'grædʒuət] *s.* estudiante universitario (no graduado o no licenciado).

underground ['ʌndərˌgraund, B -dəˌ-] *a.* 1. subterráneo. 2. (fig.) clandestino, secreto, subrepticio. 3. (fig.) no comercial o convencional (filmes, publicaciones, etc.). —*s.* 1. subterráneo, sótano, espacio o conducto debajo de tierra. 2. ferrocarril subterráneo. 3. movimiento clandestino de resistencia; organización clandestina revolucionaria o subversiva. [ˌʌn-'graund] —*adv.* 1. bajo tierra. 2. a escondidas, ocultamente, secretamente.

underground movement, movimiento clandestino.

Underground Railroad, (hist., E.U.) organización clandestina que ayudaba a escapar a los esclavos.

undergrown [ˌʌndər'groun, B 'ʌndə'-] *a.* 1. de pequeña estatura. 2. de desarrollo incompleto.

undergrowth ['ʌndərˌgrouθ, B -dəˌ-] *s.* broza, maleza, monte bajo.

underhand [-ˌhænd] *a.* 1. clandestino, secreto, solapado, disimulado; falso, socarrón, fraudulento. 2. ejecutado sin levantar las manos (más arriba de la altura del hombro). —*adv.* 1. bajo mano, por debajo de cuerda, clandestinamente, secretamente, disimuladamente. 2. sin levantar las manos (más arriba de la altura del hombro).

underhanded [ˌʌndər'hændəd, B -də'-] *a.* 1. clandestino, secreto, disimulado, solapado. 2. escaso de mano de obra.

underhandedly [-lɪ] *adv.* bajo mano, por debajo de cuerda, clandestinamente, disimuladamente.

underhandedness [-nəs] *s.* disimulo, engaño, socarronería.

underhung [-'hʌŋ] *a.* 1. sobresaliente (díc. de la quijada inferior); que tiene la quijada inferior sobresaliente. 2. suspendido debajo de los ejes (díc. del bastidor del chasis de un vehículo).

underlaid [-'leɪd] *p.p. de* **underlay.** —*a.* 1. subyacente. 2. (que tiene algo) colocado o puesto por debajo.

underlay [-'leɪ] *v.t.* 1. cubrir o tender por el fondo de. 2. poner por debajo de, poner como soporte a. 3. (impr.) levantar o reforzar con calzo o realce. —*s.* (impr.) calzo, realce.

underlet [-'lɛt] *v.t.* 1. arrendar a un precio menor (que el verdadero). 2. subarrendar.

underlie [-'laɪ] *v.t.* 1. estar debajo de, extenderse debajo de. 2. (fig.) sostener, sustentar, servir de fundamento, ser la razón o base de (idea, revolución, etc.). 3. (fin.) preceder como título o garantía a (otro). 4. (ant.) estar sujeto a, asumir responsabilidad por.

underline ['ʌndərˌlaɪn, B ˌʌndə'laɪn] *v.t.* 1. subrayar. 2. (fig.) subrayar, acentuar, recalcar. — ['ʌndərˌlaɪn, B -dəˌ-] *s.* 1. raya (debajo de una palabra, etc.). 2. contorno inferior (de esa parte del cuerpo de un animal).

underling ['ʌndərlɪŋ, B -dəlɪŋ] *s.* dependiente, subalterno, subordinado.

underlip [-ˌlɪp] *s.* (anat.) labio inferior, labio mandibular.

underlying [ˌʌndər'laɪɪŋ, B -də'-] *a.* 1. implícito, fundamental. 2. (fin.) precedente (título, derecho, etc.).

underman [-'mæn] *v.t.* no dotar de tripulación o guarnición suficiente (barco, fortaleza, etc.).

undermine [-'maɪn] *v.t.* 1. socavar, minar, trasminar. 2. (fig.) socavar, destruir insidiosamente, arruinar subrepticiamente, debilitar paulatinamente (posición, salud, etc.).

undermodulation [-ˌmɑdʒə'leɪʃən, B -ˌmɔdjʊ-] *s.* (rad.) modulación insuficiente.

undermost ['ʌndərˌmoʊst, B -dəˌ-] *a.* ínfimo, último (en lugar, orden, rango, etc.).

underneath [ˌʌndər'niθ, B -də'-] *adv.* debajo, abajo, bajo, por debajo. —*prep.* debajo de, bajo.

undernourish [-'nɜrɪʃ, B -'nʌrɪʃ] *v.t.* desnutrir, alimentar de modo deficiente.

undernourished [-'nɜrɪʃt, B -'nʌrɪʃt] *a.* desnutrido, mal alimentado.

undernourishment [-'nɜrɪʃmənt, B -'nʌrɪʃ-] *s.* desnutrición, alimentación deficiente.

underpaid [-'peɪd] *a.* mal pagado; insuficientemente retribuido.

underpants ['ʌndərˌpænts, B -dəˌ-] *s. pl.* calzoncillos.

underpart [-ˌpɑrt, B -ˌpɑt] *s.* 1. parte inferior (del cuerpo de un animal). 2. (teat., cinem.) papel secundario.

underpass [-ˌpæs, B -ˌpɑs] *s.* paso por debajo, paso inferior (esp. de una carretera por debajo de una línea de ferrocarril).

underpay [ˌʌndər'peɪ, B -də'-] *v.t.* pagar mal (a empleado, trabajo, etc.); pagar menos de lo justo por (trabajo, servicio, etc.).

underpin [-'pɪn] *v.t.* 1. socalzar, apuntalar; sotomurar, recalzar (cimientos). 2. (fig.) sostener, defender.

underpinning ['ʌndərˌpɪnɪŋ, B -dəˌ-] *s.* 1. (arq.) apuntalamiento, socalzado; sotomuración, recalce, recalzo. 2. (fam.) (*gen. pl.*) piernas (de una persona).

underplay [ˌʌndər'pleɪ, B -də'-] *v.t.* 1. jugar naipe más bajo que (otro naipe en la mano). 2. interpretar (un papel) mal o reprimidamente; representar sin brillo (un drama). —*v.i.* actuar sin énfasis (en un drama).

underplot ['ʌndərˌplɑt, B 'ʌndəˌplɔt] *s.* acción secundaria (en un drama).

underprice [ˌʌndər'praɪs, B -də'-] *v.t., v.i.* cobrar por debajo del precio; ganar a un competidor rebajando los precios.

underprivileged [-'prɪvəlɪdʒd] *a.* desamparado, desvalido; menesteroso, necesitado, pobre; que no goza de las ventajas de la mayoría.

underproduction [-prə'dʌkʃən] *s.* producción insuficiente, baja producción.

underproof [-'pruf] *a.* de menos de 50% de contenido alcohólico.

underquote [-'kwoʊt] *v.t.* cotizar a menor precio (que otro); cotizar un precio menor que.

underrate [-'reɪt] *v.t.* menospreciar, despreciar, desestimar.

underripe [-'raɪp] *a.* medio maduro.

underrun [-'rʌn] *v.t.* correr o pasar por debajo de.

underscore [-'skɔr, B -'skɔ] *v.t.* 1. subrayar. 2. (fig.) subrayar, acentuar, recalcar. — ['ʌndərˌskɔr, B 'ʌndəˌskɔ] *s.* raya (debajo de una palabra, etc.).

undersea [-'si] *a.* submarino. —*adv.* bajo la superficie del mar.

underseas [-'siz] *adv.* bajo la superficie del mar.

undersecretariat [-ˌsɛkrə'tɛriət] *s.* subsecretaría.

undersecretary [-'sɛkrəˌtɛrɪ, B -'sɛkrətərɪ] *s.* subsecretario.

undersecretaryship [-ʃɪp] *s.* subsecretaría.

undersell [-'sɛl] *v.t.* 1. vender más barato que. 2. malbaratar, malvender.

undersexed [-'sɛkst] *a.* de baja líbido, hiposexuado.

undershirt ['ʌndərˌʃɜrt, B -dəˌʃɜt] *s.* camiseta (interior).

undershoot [ˌʌndər'ʃut, B -də'-] *v.t.* 1. quedar corto (del blanco, al disparar, etc.). 2. (aer.) quedarse corto de pista (al aterrizar).

undershot ['ʌndərˌʃɑt, B -dəˌʃɔt] *a.* 1. sobresaliente (díc. de los dientes incisivos inferiores); que tiene la quijada inferior sobresaliente. 2. de impulsión por abajo (díc. de una rueda hidráulica).

undershot gate, (hidr.) compuerta de descarga inferior.

undershrub [-ˌʃrʌb] *s.* planta aparrada.

underside [-ˌsaɪd] *s.* lado de abajo, superficie que está debajo; la parte oculta.

undersign [ˌʌndər'saɪn, B -də'-] *v.t.* subscribir, firmar al pie de un escrito. — **the undersigned,** el (o los) infrascrito(s), el (o los) suscrito(s), el (o los) abajo firmante(s).

undersize [-'saɪz] **undersized** [-'saɪzd] *a.* 1. de tamaño menor que lo común o normal, muy pequeño. 2. bajito, achaparrado.

underskirt ['ʌndərˌskɜrt, B -dəˌskɜt] *s.* enagua, enaguas, fustán (Amer.).

underslung [ˌʌndər'slʌŋ, B -də'-] *a.* colgante, suspendido de las ballestas, suspendido de los ejes (díc. del armazón de un vehículo).

undersong ['ʌndərˌsɔŋ, B -dəˌ-] *s.* el estribillo de una canción; canción acompañante.

undersparred [-ˌspɑrd, B -ˌspɑd] *a.* (mar.) con vergas demasiado pequeñas para extender debidamente las velas.

understaffed [ˌʌn-'stæft, B -'stɑft] *a.* con pocos empleados, corto de personal.

understand [ˌʌndər'stænd, B -də'-] *v.t.* 1. comprender. 2. entender, tener entendido; presumir, suponer. 3. dar por sentado, sobrentender. 4. (gram.) suplir. 5. **be it understood,** entiéndase; **it being understood that,** bien entendido que; **that is understood,** está entendido, por supuesto; **to be understood,** sobreentenderse; **to give one to u.,** dar a entender a uno; **to make (one) u.,** hacer (a uno) comprender; **to make oneself understood,** hacerse comprender; **u. each other,** comprenderse; entenderse (mutuamente). —*v.i.* 1. comprender, tener comprensión, ser comprensivo. 2. creer, tener entendido.

understandability [-ˌstændə'bɪlətɪ] *s.* comprensibilidad.

understandable [-'stændəbəl] *a.* comprensible; **it's u.,** se comprende.

understandably [-blɪ] *adv.* comprensiblemente, de manera comprensible, explicablemente, naturalmente; **u. so,** con razón.

understanding [-'stændɪŋ] *s.* 1. comprensión, entendimiento, interpretación. 2. inteligencia, discernimiento, raciocinio. 3. armonía, correspondencia. 4. opinión, interpretación. 5. arreglo, acuerdo. 6. **beyond one's u.,** más allá de la capacidad de comprensión (de uno); **on the u. that,** a condición de que; **to come to (o reach) an u.,** llegar a un acuerdo. —*a.* comprensivo, tolerante, compasivo.

understandingly [-lɪ] *adv.* con tolerancia, tolerantemente, compasivamente, comprensivamente.

understate [-'steɪt] *v.t.* 1. exponer inadecuadamente, argüir en forma deficiente. 2. quitar importancia a, subestimar (dificultad, peligro, etc.). 3. decir o exponer con modestia o reticencia.

understatement [-mənt] *s.* declaración exageradamente modesta; **it was an u.,** subestimó la realidad.

understock [-'stɑk, B -'stɔk] *v.t.* (com.) tener o proveer de menos inventario del necesario o aprobado.

understood [ˌʌndər'stʊd, B -də'-] *p.p. de* **understand.** —*a.* sobrentendido, subentendido, implícito.

understrapper ['ʌndərˌstræpər, B -dəˌstræpə] *s.* subordinado, dependiente, subalterno.

understudy [-ˌstʌdɪ] *v.t.* (teat.) aprender (un papel) para reemplazar a otro actor (en caso necesario). —*s.* (teat.) sobresaliente; actor suplente o substituto.

undersurface [-ˌsɜrfəs, B -ˌsɜfəs] *s.* lado de abajo, superficie inferior, superficie de fondo.

undertake [ˌʌndər'teɪk, B -də-] *v.t.* 1. emprender, acometer, intentar. 2. garantizar, prometer. 3. encargarse de, tomar a su cargo. 4. (ant.) trabar, comenzar (una batalla, contienda, discusión, etc.). 5. **u. to (do),** obligarse a, comprometerse a (hacer). —*v.i.* (ant.) (con *for*) ser fiador o garante (de).

undertaker [-'teɪkər, B -ə] *s.* 1. empresario, contratista. 2. ['ʌndərˌteɪk-, B -dəˌ-] funerario, empresario de funeraria, agente de entierros.

undertaking [-'teɪkɪŋ] *s.* 1. empresa, empeño. 2. promesa, compromiso, garantía. 3. ['ʌndərˌteɪk-, B -dəˌ-] oficio del empresario de funeraria.

undertenant ['ʌndərˌtɛnənt, B -dəˌ-] *s.* subarrendatario, subinquilino.

under-the-counter [-ðə'kaʊntər, B -'kaʊntə] *a.* disimulado, hecho por lo bajo, ilegal, ilícito.

undertone [-ˌtoʊn] *s.* 1. voz baja. 2. color apagado, color amortiguado o mortecino. 3. matiz de fondo. 4. (fig.) tendencia latente.

undertow [-ˌtoʊ] *s.* (mar.) resaca, contracorriente, corriente de fondo.

undertravel [-'trævəl] *s.* (mec.) carrera incompleta.

undertrick [-ˌtrɪk] *s.* (naipes) caída (cada una de las bazas que el jugador deja de cumplir).

undertrump [ˌʌndər'trʌmp, B -də'-] *v.t., v.i.* (naipes) cubrir con un triunfo más bajo (que el puesto por otro jugador).

undervaluation [ˌʌndərˌvæljʊ'eɪʃən, B -dəˌ-] *s.* avalúo inferior (al valor real).

undervalue [-'vælju] *v.t.* 1. tasar en menos (del valor real). 2. menospreciar, desapreciar, desestimar.

underwaist ['ʌndərˌweɪst, B -dəˌ-] *s.* camisa o camiseta interior (de niño).

underwater [-ˌwɔtər, B -ˌwɔtə] *a.* 1. subacuático, submarino. 2. de debajo de la línea de flotación (de un barco).

underwater fishing, caza submarina.

underway [-ˌweɪ] *a.* (hecho) en camino; (hecho) en movimiento, ej., *u. fueling,* toma de gasolina mientras un vehículo se mueve.

underwear ['ʌndərˌwɛr, B -dəˌwɛə] *s.* ropa interior.

underweight ['ʌndərˌweɪt, B -dəˌ-] *s.* falta de peso, peso menor que el normal o requerido. —*a.* falto de peso, que no tiene el peso normal o requerido.

underwing [-ˌwɪŋ] *s.* (ento.) ala posterior (esp. de ciertas mariposas).

underwood [-ˌwʊd] *s.* maleza, monte bajo, broza.

underwork [ˌʌndər'wɜrk, B -də'wɜk] *v.i.* trabajar menos de lo debido. —*v.t.* trabajar por menos sueldo que otro. —*s.* trabajo de rutina.

underworld ['ʌndərˌwɜrld, B -dəˌwɜld] *a.* (de la hampa) hampesco. —*s.* 1. el otro mundo; infiernos. 2. antípoda (lugar de la tierra diametralmente opuesto a otro). 3. hampa, gente de mal vivir, bajos fondos. 4. (ant.) la tierra, mundo terrenal.

underwrite ['ʌndəˌraɪt] *v.t.* 1. subscribir. 2. asegurar (esp. contra riesgos marítimos). 3. (fin.) subscribir (una emisión de valores). —*v.i.* trabajar en seguros.

underwriter ['ʌndəˌraɪtər, B -ˌraɪtə] *s.* 1. (com.) asegurador, empresa aseguradora. 2. (fin.) suscriptor (de una emisión de valores).

undescribable [ˌʌndɪs'kraɪbəbəl] *a.* indescriptible.

undeserved [ˌʌndɪ'zɜrvd, B -'zɜvd] *a.* inmerecido.

undeservedly [-'zɜrvədlɪ, B -'zɜvəd-] *adv.* inmerecidamente.

undeserving [-'zɜrvɪŋ, B -'zɜvɪŋ] *a.* desmerecedor, indigno.

undesigned [ˌʌndɪ'zaɪnd] *a.* involuntario, no intencional.

undesigning [-'zaɪnɪŋ] *a.* sincero, sencillo, cándido.

undesirable [-'zaɪrəbəl] *a.* indeseable. —*s.* persona indeseable.

undestroyable [-dɪ'strɔɪəbəl] *a.* indestructible.

undetachable [ˌʌndɪ'tætʃəbəl] *a.* inseparable, inamovible.

undetectable [-dɪ'tɛktəbəl] *a.* inaveriguable, que no se puede descubrir.

undeterminable [-dɪ'tɜrmənəbəl, B -'tɜm-] *a.* indeterminable.

undetermined [-'tɜrmənd, B -'tɜmənd] *a.* indeterminado.

undeveloped [ˌʌndɪ'vɛləpt] *a.* 1. sin desarrollar, rudimentario. 2. (foto.) sin revelar, no revelado.

undeviating [ʌn'diviˌeɪtɪŋ] *a.* recto, constante, fiel.

undies ['ʌndɪz] *s. pl.* (fam.) prendas íntimas (esp. de mujer).

undigested [ˌʌndɪ'dʒɛstəd] *a.* 1. indigesto, no digerido; no asimilado. 2. no clasificado, no ordenado (datos, etc.).

undignified [ʌn'dɪgnəˌfaɪd] *a.* indecoroso, falto de dignidad.

undiluted [ˌʌndɪ'lutəd, B -'ljut-] *a.* no diluido, concentrado.

undiminished [ˌʌndə'mɪnɪʃt] *a.* sin merma; constante.

undine [ʌn'din, 'ʌndin] *s.* (mitol.) ondina, ninfa de las aguas.

undiplomatic [ˌʌndɪplə'mætɪk] *a.* poco diplomático, descortés.

undirected [ˌʌndə'rɛktəd, ˌʌndaɪ-] *a.* 1. no dirigido, que no tiene gobierno. 2. no dirigido, que no tiene señas o sobrescrito (ej., una carta).

undiscernible [-dɪ'sɜrnəbəl, B -'sɜnə-] *a.* imperceptible, invisible.

undischarged [-dɪs'tʃɑrdʒd, B -'tʃɑdʒd] *a.* 1. no ejecutado, incumplido (deber, etc.). 2. no pagado, no liquidado (deuda, obligación). 3. no desembarcado, por desembarcar (carga).

undisciplined [ʌn'dɪsəplənd] *a.* indisciplinado, indómito.

undiscriminating [ˌʌndɪs'krɪməˌneɪtɪŋ] *a.* sin sentido crítico, fácil de complacer.

undisguised [ˌʌndɪs'gaɪzd] *a.* sin disfraz; franco, abierto, no disimulado.

undismayed [ˌʌndɪs'meɪd] *a.* impávido, intrépido; perseverante.

undisposed [ˌʌndɪs'poʊzd] *a.* 1. poco dispuesto, contrario. 2. no distribuido, no colocado, no vendido.

undisputed [ˌʌndɪs'pjutəd] *a.* indisputable, incontestable.

undissociated [-dɪ'soʊʃɪˌeɪtəd] *a.* (quím., fís.) sin disociar (electrónicamente).

undissolvable [ˌʌndɪ'zɑlvəbəl, B -'zɔlv-] *a.* indisoluble.

undistinct [ˌʌndɪs'tɪŋkt] *a.* indistinto.

undistinguishable [ˌʌndɪs'tɪŋgwɪʃəbəl] *a.* indistinguible.

undistorted [-'tɔrtəd, B -'tɔtɪd] *a.* 1. no adulterado, sin falsificación. 2. (rad., electrón.) sin distorsión.

undisturbed [-dɪs'tɜrbd, B -'tɜbd] *a.* 1. inalterado, sereno. 2. sin ser molestado o perturbado.

undivided [ˌʌndɪ'vaɪdəd] *a.* 1. indiviso, íntegro, entero. 2. completo, todo, ej., *you have my u. attention,* le escucho con toda atención.

undividedly [-lɪ] *adv.* indivisamente, íntegramente, enteramente.

undivided profits, (com.) utilidades a distribuir.

undo [ʌn'du] *v.t.* 1. desatar, desabrochar, desligar, deshacer (un nudo). 2. anular, desvirtuar; redimir. 3. arruinar, perder. 4. descomponer, perturbar, trastornar. 5. seducir.

undoer [-'duər, B -'duə] *s.* 1. destructor. 2. seductor.

undoing [ʌn'duɪŋ] *s.* 1. anulación, revocación (de lo hecho). 2. ruina, pérdida.

undomesticated [ˌʌndə'mɛstɪˌkeɪtəd] *a.* no domesticado.

undone [ʌn'dʌn] *a.* 1. sin hacer, por hacer. 2. arruinado, destruido, perdido. 3. desatado, desligado. 4. **to come u.,** deshacerse, desatarse; **to leave u.,** dejar sin hacer, dejar sin terminar.

undouble [ʌn'dʌbəl] *v.t.* desdoblar, desplegar, desenvolver.

undoubted [ʌn'daʊtəd] *a.* no dudado; indudable, indubitable.

undoubtedly [-lɪ] *adv.* indudablemente, sin duda.

undramatic [ˌʌndrə'mætɪk] *a.* poco dramático, carente de dramatismo.

undrape [ʌn'dreɪp] *v.t.* quitar cortinas o colgaduras a; quitar el velo a.

undraw [ʌn'drɔ] *v.t.* descorrer, abrir (cortinas, etc.).

undreamed-of [-'drimdˌʌv, -ˌɑv, B -ɔv] **undreamt-of** [-'drɛmt-] *a.* no soñado, inopinado, inesperado.

undress [ʌn'drɛs] *v.t.* 1. desnudar, desvestir. 2. desguarnecer, despojar. 3. quitar el vendaje de (una herida). —*v.i.* desvestirse, desnudarse. —*s.* ropa de casa, traje sencillo.

undried [ʌn'draɪd] *a.* húmedo, sin secar.

undrinkable [ʌn'drɪŋkəbəl] *a.* impotable, no bebible.

undryable [ʌn'draɪəbəl] *a.* insecable.

undue [-'du, B -'dju] *a.* 1. no vencido (documento). 2. indebido, inmoderado, excesivo, desmedido. 3. impropio, inapropiado (comportamiento, conducta, etc.).

undulant ['ʌndʒələnt, B -djʊ-] *a.* ondulante, undulante.

undulant fever, (med.) fiebre ondulante, fiebre (de) Malta.

undulate [-ˌleɪt] *v.i.* 1. ondular, undular, ondear. 2. fluctuar (sonido). —*v.t.* 1. hacer ondular o serpentear. 2. ondular (papel, superficie de lago, etc.). — [-lət] *a.* ondeado, ondulado.

undulated [-ˌleɪtəd] *a.* ondeado, ondulado.

undulation [ˌʌndʒə'leɪʃən, B -djʊ-] *s.* 1. ondulación, undulación, ondeo. 2. pulsación (del sonido).

undulatory ['ʌndʒələˌtɔrɪ, B -djʊlətərɪ] *a.* ondulatorio, undulatorio, ondulante, ondoso, undoso.

undulatory theory, (fís.) teoría ondulatoria (de la luz).

unduly [ʌn'dulɪ, B -'dju-] *adv.* 1. indebidamente, excesivamente. 2. impropiamente.

undutiful [-'dutɪfəl, B -'dju-] *a.* desobediente; ingrato; irrespetuoso.

undying [ʌn'daɪɪŋ] *a.* imperecedero, perpetuo, eterno.

unearned [-'ɜrnd, B -'ɜnd] *a.* 1. no ganado, inmerecido. 2. (com.) no devengado.

unearned increment, (com.) plusvalía, mayor valía, plusvalor.

unearth [-'ɜrθ, B -'ɜθ] *v.t.* 1. desenterrar, excavar (tesoro, etc.); exhumar. 2. (fig.) desenterrar, sacar a la luz, descubrir (secreto, etc.).

unearthliness [-lɪnəs] *s.* carácter sobrenatural, apariencia o aire ultramundanos.

unearthly [-lɪ] *a.* 1. no terrenal, sobrenatural. 2. espantoso, aterrador. 3. absurdo, extraño, fantástico.

uneasily [ʌn'izəlɪ] *adv.* 1. inquietamente, desasosegadamente. 2. preocupadamente, ansiosamente.

uneasiness [ʌn'izɪnəs] *s.* 1. inquietud, desasosiego. 2. preocupación, ansiedad.

uneasy [ʌn'izɪ] *a.* (UNEASIER, UNEASIEST) 1. inquieto, intranquilo, desasosegado. 2. preocupado, ansioso. 3. embarazoso, incómodo. 4. inquietante, perturbador (sospecha, etc.). 5. inestable, precario.

uneatable [ʌn'itəbəl] *a.* incomible, no comestible.

uneconomic [-ˌɛkə'nɑmɪk, B -ˌikə'nɔmɪk] *a.* no económico, poco lucrativo.

uneducated [-'ɛdʒəˌkeɪtəd] *a.* no educado, inculto, ignorante.

unemployable [ˌʌnɪm'plɔɪəbəl] *a.* que no puede ser empleado. —*s.* persona incapacitada (por vejez, etc.) para tener un empleo.

unemployed [ˌʌnɪm'plɔɪd] *a.* 1. desocupado, desempleado; cesante. 2. sin utilizar, inutilizado, no usado. 3. no invertido, improductivo. 4. **the u.,** los desocupados, los desempleados.

unemployment [ˌʌnɪm'plɔɪmənt] *s.* desocupación, desempleo; cesantía.

unemployment benefits, beneficios del seguro contra desempleo.

unemployment insurance, seguro de desempleo, seguro contra la desocupación.

unencumbered [ˌʌnɪn'kʌmbərd, B -'kʌmbəd] *a.* 1. desembarazado, libre de trabas. 2. libre de gravámenes u obligaciones, saneado.

unending [ʌn'ɛndɪŋ] *a.* inacabable, interminable, sin fin.

unendowed [-ɪn'daʊd] *a.* sin dote, sin fondos.

unendurable [-ɪn'dʊrəbəl, B -'djʊər-] *a.* insoportable, inaguantable, insufrible.

unengaged [ˌʌnɪn'geɪdʒd] *a.* 1. no comprometido, libre de compromisos. 2. desocupado, libre.

un-English [ʌn'ɪŋglɪʃ] *a.* ajeno al carácter inglés.

unenjoyable [ˌʌnɪn'dʒɔɪəbəl] *a.* penoso, desagradable.

unenlightened [ˌʌnɪn'laɪtənd] *a.* no instruido, ignorante.

unenterprising [-'ɛntərˌpraɪzɪŋ, B -'ɛntəˌ-] *a.* sin iniciativa, tímido.

unentertaining [-ɛntər'teɪnɪŋ, B -tə'-] *a.* poco divertido, aburrido.
unenthusiastic [-ɪnˌθuzɪ'æstɪk, B -ˌθjuzɪ-] *a.* apático, indolente.
unenviable [ʌn'ɛnvɪəbəl] *a.* poco envidiable.
unequal [ʌn'ikwəl] *a.* 1. desigual; diferente. 2. desigual, accidentado, irregular (superficie, terreno, etc.). 3. **u. to,** inadecuado para; incapaz de, no capacitado para.
unequaled [ʌn'ikwəld] *a.* sin igual, sin par, único, sin rival; sobresaliente, excelente.
unequally [ʌn'ikwəlɪ] *adv.* desigualmente.
unequivocal [ˌʌnɪ'kwɪvəkəl] *a.* inequívoco, indudable; claro.
unequivocally [-kəlɪ] *adv.* sin ambages, claramente.
unerring [ʌn'ɜrɪŋ] *a.* infalible, certero.
unerringly [-lɪ] *adv.* infaliblemente, certeramente.
unescapable [ˌʌnɪs'keɪpəbəl] *a.* inevitable, ineludible.
UNESCO [jʊ'nɛskoʊ] *abrev. de* **United Nations Educational, Scientific and Cultural Organization,** Organización de las Naciones Unidas para la Educación, la Ciencia y la Cultura (UNESCO).
unessential [ˌʌnə'sɛnʃəl] *a.* no esencial, innecesario, insignificante, de poca importancia.
unestimated [ʌn'ɛstəmeɪtəd] *a.* inestimado.
unethical [ʌn'ɛθɪkəl] *a.* poco ético.
uneven [-'ivən] *a.* 1. desigual, accidentado. 2. desigual, diferente. 3. cambiante, sin uniformidad. 4. impar (número).
unevenly [-lɪ] *adv.* desigualmente, irregularmente.
unevenness [-nəs] *s.* desigualdad, irregularidad, aspereza.
uneventful [ˌʌnɪ'vɛntfəl] *a.* sin acontecimientos notables, sin novedad; plácido.
unexampled [ˌʌnɪg'zæmpəld, B -'zɑm-] *a.* sin ejemplo, sin igual, sin precedente, nunca visto, único.
unexceptionable [ˌʌnɪk'sɛpʃənəbəl] *a.* 1. irreprochable, intachable, irreprensible. 2. (der.) irrecusable.
unexceptionably [-blɪ] *adv.* irreprochablemente, de manera intachable, intachablemente.
unexceptional [-'sɛpʃənəl] *a.* nada excepcional, común, corriente, ordinario.
unexciting [ˌʌnɪk'saɪtɪŋ] *a.* trivial, aburrido.
unexpected [ˌʌnɪks'pɛktəd] *a.* inesperado, imprevisto, impensado.
unexpectedly [-lɪ] *adv.* inesperadamente, de improviso, de repente.
unexpired [-ɪk'spaɪrd, B -'spaɪəd] *a.* no caducado, vigente.
unexplainable [ˌʌnɪks'pleɪnəbəl] *a.* inexplicable, incomprensible.
unexplained [ˌʌnɪks'pleɪnd] *a.* inexplicado.
unexploitable [ˌʌnɛks'plɔɪtəbəl] *a.* inexplotable.
unexploited [ˌʌnɛks'plɔɪtəd] *a.* inexplotado.
unexplored [-ɪk'splɔrd, B -'splɔd] *a.* inexplorado.
unexposed [ˌʌnɪks'poʊzd] *a.* 1. no revelado, no descubierto. 2. (foto.) no expuesto.
unexpressed [ˌʌnɪks'prɛst] *a.* inexpresado; sobrentendido, tácito.
unexpressive [-'prɛsɪv] *a.* 1. inexpresivo, sin expresión, poco expresivo. 2. (ant.) inefable.
unexpurgated [ʌn'ɛkspərˌgeɪtəd, B -'ɛkspəˌ-] *a.* no expurgado, íntegro (texto).
unextendible [ˌʌnɪks'tɛndəbəl] *a.* improrrogable.
unextinguishable [ˌʌnɪk'stɪŋgwɪʃəbəl] *a.* inextinguible.
unfadable [ʌn'feɪdəbəl] *a.* 1. no desteñible, indeleble (color, etc.). 2. imborrable, imperecedero, inolvidable.
unfading [ʌn'feɪdɪŋ] *a.* inmarcesible, inmarchitable.
unfailing [ʌn'feɪlɪŋ] *a.* 1. incansable, persistente. 2. inagotable, indefectible, cierto, seguro. 3. leal, fiel. 4. infalible.
unfailingly [-lɪ] *adv.* 1. incansablemente. 2. indefectiblemente. 3. lealmente, fielmente. 4. infatigablemente.
unfair [-'fɛr, B -'fɛə] *a.* 1. injusto, inicuo. 2. desleal (competencia). 3. desfavorable (viento, corriente, etc.). 4. (dep.) incorrecto, sucio.
unfairly [-lɪ] *adv.* 1. injustamente, de mala fe. 2. (dep.) suciamente, con trampa.
unfairness [-nəs] *s.* 1. injusticia, falta de equidad. 2. incorrección.
unfaith [ʌn'feɪθ] *s.* falta de fe, incredulidad.
unfaithful [ʌn'feɪθfəl] *a.* 1. infiel, infidente, desleal, no cumplidor, que rompe una promesa o un contrato. 2. infiel, inexacto, erróneo. 3. infiel (al cónyuge), adúltero.
unfaithfully [-fəlɪ] *adv.* infielmente, deslealmente.
unfaithfulness [-fəlnəs] *s.* infidelidad, deslealtad, perfidia.
unfalsifiable [ˌʌn'fɔlsəˌfaɪəbəl] *a.* infalsificable.
unfaltering [ʌn'fɔltərɪŋ] *a.* resuelto, firme, constante.
unfamiliar [-fə'mɪljər, B -'mɪljə] *a.* no muy conocido, no muy familiar, ajeno, extraño; **u. with,** ignorante de, desconocedor de, no familiarizado con, poco versado en.
unfamiliarity [ˌʌnfəˌmɪlɪ'ærɪtɪ] *s.* desconocimiento.
unfamiliarly [-fə'mɪljərlɪ, B -'mɪljəlɪ] *adv.* con poco conocimiento.
unfashionable [ʌn'fæʃənəbəl] *a.* fuera de moda, inelegante.
unfasten [-'fæsən, B -'fɑs-] *v.t.* desatar, soltar, aflojar; desabrochar, desenganchar.
unfathered [-'fɑðərd, B -'fɑðəd] *a.* 1. ilegítimo, bastardo. 2. no identificado, de origen desconocido.
unfathomable [ʌn'fæðəməbəl] *a.* insondable.
unfavorable [ʌn'feɪvərəbəl] *a.* desfavorable, desventajoso, no procipio, adverso, contrario.
unfavorably [-blɪ] *adv.* desfavorablemente, desventajosamente.
unfeasible [ˌʌn'fizəbəl] *a.* impracticable, irrealizable.
unfeeling [ʌn'filɪŋ] *a.* insensible, indiferente, impasible; cruel, sin sentimientos.
unfeelingly [-lɪ] *adv.* insensiblemente, cruelmente.
unfeelingness [-nəs] *s.* insensibilidad, dureza de corazón.
unfeigned [ˌʌn'feɪnd] *a.* genuino, real, verdadero; sincero, franco.
unfeignedly [ʌn'feɪnədlɪ] *adv.* sinceramente, sin fingimiento.
unfeignedness [-nəs] *s.* sinceridad, candor.
unfetter [-'fɛtər, B -'fɛtə] *v.t.* 1. destrabar, desencadenar. 2. libertar, redimir.
unfilled [ˌʌn'fɪld] *a.* 1. no llenado, vacío (botella, etc.). 2. (com.) no ejecutado, no despachado (pedido, etc.).
unfinished [ʌn'fɪnɪʃt] *a.* 1. inconcluso, no acabado; incompleto; imperfecto. 2. (tej.) crudo (díc. de ciertas telas de lana). 3. no barnizado, sin pulir.
Unfinished Symphony, (mús.) Sinfonía Inconclusa (Schubert, Mahler).
unfit [ʌn'fɪt] *a.* 1. inadecuado, no apropiado, impropio; inservible. 2. incapaz, inepto, incompetente. 3. **to be u. for,** no servir para. —*v.t.* inhabilitar, incapacitar, descalificar.
unfitly [-lɪ] *adv.* ineptamente; de manera inadecuada o inconveniente.
unfitness [-nəs] *s.* 1. ineptitud, incompetencia, falta de aptitud. 2. impropiedad. 3. estado de salud deficiente (esp. obesidad).
unfitted [-'fɪtəd] *a.* 1. sin aptitudes. 2. no armado; sin guarniciones.
unfitting [-'fɪtɪŋ] *a.* impropio, indigno.
unfix [ˌʌn'fɪks] *v.t.* aflojar, desligar, soltar, desprender.
unflagging [ʌn'flægɪŋ] *a.* incansable, incesante.
unflattering [ˌʌn'flætərɪŋ] *a.* poco halagüeño, poco halagador.
unfledged [ʌn'flɛdʒd] *a.* 1. implume. 2. (fig.) inmaduro, inexperimentado, novel, novato.
unfleshly [ʌn'flɛʃlɪ] *a.* espiritual, no carnal.
unflinching [ʌn'flɪntʃɪŋ] *a.* intrépido, impávido; resuelto, decidido.
unflinchingly [-lɪ] *adv.* intrépidamente, impávidamente; resueltamente, decididamente.
unfold [ʌn'foʊld] *v.t.* 1. desdoblar, desenrollar; desenvolver, desplegar, abrir, extender. 2. (fig.) desplegar, exponer, revelar, dar a conocer, descubrir, poner en claro. —*v.i.* 1. desdoblarse, desplegarse, abrirse. 2. desarrollarse (una historia, cuento, etc.).
unforced [ˌʌn'fɔrst, B -'fɔst] *a.* espontáneo, voluntario, natural, no forzado.
unforeseeable [ʌnfɔr'siəbəl, B -fɔ'-] *a.* imprevisible.
unforeseen [-'sin] *a.* imprevisto, inesperado, improviso, impensado.
unforgettable [-fər'gɛtəbəl, B -fə'gɛt-] *a.* inolvidable.
unforgettably [-blɪ] *adv.* de manera inolvidable, inolvidablemente.
unforgivable [-fər'gɪvəbəl, B -fə'-] *a.* imperdonable, indisculpable, inexcusable.
unforgiving [-'gɪvɪŋ] *a.* implacable, inexorable.
unformed [ˌʌn'fɔrmd, B -'fɔmd] *a.* 1. no formado. 2. sin madurez. 3. informe, disforme, amorfo; desorganizado.
unfortunate [ʌn'fɔrtʃənət, B -'fɔtʃ-] *a.* desafortunado, infortunado, infeliz, desgraciado, desdichado, malaventurado. —*s.* infortunado, desgraciado.
unfortunately [-lɪ] *adv.* desgraciadamente, infelizmente, infortunadamente.
unfounded [ʌn'faʊndəd] *a.* infundado.
unfreeze [ˌʌn'friz] *v.t.* 1. deshelar, descongelar. 2. liberar (precios, materias primas, etc.) de control o de regulaciones. 3. descongelar (fondos, sueldos, salarios).
unfrequented [ˌʌnfrɪ'kwɛntəd] *a.* solitario, poco frecuentado.
unfriended [ʌn'frɛndəd] *a.* solitario, desamparado, sin amigos.
unfriendliness [ʌn'frɛndlɪnəs] *s.* 1. falta de amistad o benevolencia, hostilidad, enemistad. 2. inhospitalidad.
unfriendly [ʌn'frɛndlɪ] *a.* 1. no amigable, hostil, enemigo. 2. desfavorable, no propicio. 3. inhóspito, inhospitalario (paisaje, playa, etc.).
unfrock [-'frɑk, B -'frɔk] *v.t.* expulsar, deponer, privar (a un sacerdote o ministro del culto) del derecho a ejercer sus funciones.
unfruitful [ˌʌn'frutfəl] *a.* infructuoso, infructífero, estéril; no remunerativo.
unfruitfully [-fəlɪ] *adv.* infructuosamente.
unfruitfulness [-fəlnəs] *s.* infructuosidad, esterilidad.

unfulfilled [ˌʌnfʊlˈfɪld] *a.* 1. insatisfecho (deseo, necesidad, etc.); incumplido (promesa, etc.). 2. frustrado, insatisfecho.
unfulfillment [-ˈfɪlmənt] *s.* 1. incumplimiento (de una promesa, etc.). 2. frustración; insatisfacción.
unfunded [ʌnˈfʌndəd] *a.* (com.) no consolidado; flotante; sin depósito de fondos.
unfurl [-ˈfɜrl, B -ˈfɜl] *v.t.* 1. desdoblar, desarrollar, extender; desplegar (bandera). 2. (mar.) largar (la vela). —*v.i.* desarrollarse, extenderse.
unfurnished [-ˈfɜrnɪʃt, B -ˈfɜnɪʃt] *a.* desamueblado, desamoblado (casa, piso, departamento, etc.).
ungainliness [ʌnˈgeɪnlɪnəs] *s.* torpeza, inhabilidad, desgarbo, falta de gracia.
ungainly [ʌnˈgeɪnlɪ] *a.* torpe, inhábil, desmañado, desgarbado. —*adv.* torpemente, desgarbadamente.
ungallant [ʌnˈgælənt] *a.* falto de caballerosidad, desatento, descortés.
ungenerous [ʌnˈdʒɛnərəs] *a.* 1. falto de generosidad, desconsiderado. 2. tacaño, mezquino.
ungenerously [-lɪ] *adv.* sin generosidad; con mezquindad, mezquinamente; severamente.
ungentlemanly [ʌnˈdʒɛntəlmənlɪ] *a.* indigno o impropio de un caballero, mal educado, rudo.
ungifted [ʌnˈgɪftəd] *a.* sin talento.
ungird [ˌʌnˈgɜrd, B -ˈgɜd] *v.t.* desceñir, desfajar; desatar, desamarrar, desligar; descinchar (bestias).
ungirt [ˌʌnˈgɜrt, B -ˈgɜt] *a.* 1. desceñido. 2. flojo, suelto.
unglazed [ʌnˈgleɪzd] *a.* 1. sin vidriar, no vidriado (objetos de alfarería). 2. sin cristales, sin vidrio(s) (ventana). 3. no satinado.
unglossable [ʌnˈglɔsəbəl] *a.* inglosable.
unglue [ʌnˈglu] *v.t., v.i.* despegar(se), desencolar(se).
ungodliness [-ˈgɑdlɪnəs, -ˈgɔd-, B -ˈgɔd-] *s.* 1. impiedad, irreligión. 2. maldad, vileza, perversidad.
ungodly [-lɪ] *a.* (UNGODLIER; UNGODLIEST) 1. impío, irreligioso, profano. 2. malvado, vil, perverso. 3. (fam.) atroz, execrable, nefando.
ungotten [-ˈgɑtən, B -ˈgɔtən] **ungot** [-ˈgɑt, B -ˈgɔt] *a.* (jer.) 1. no conseguido, no obtenido. 2. (ant.) no engendrado.
ungovernable [-ˈgʌvərnəbəl, B -ˈgʌvən-] *a.* ingobernable, inmanejable, indisciplinable.
ungraceful [ʌnˈgreɪsfəl] *a.* desgarbado, falto de gracia, inelegante, deslucido; torpe, chabacano.
ungracefully [-fəlɪ] *adv.* sin gracia, deslucidamente, desgarbadamente.
ungracefulness [-fəlnəs] *s.* torpeza, falta de elegancia o gracia.
ungracious [ʌnˈgreɪʃəs] *a.* 1. descortés, poco afable. 2. desagradable, mal educado.
ungraciously [-lɪ] *adv.* con displicencia; sin gracia.
ungrammatical [ˌʌngrəˈmætɪkəl] *a.* antigramatical, incorrecto.
ungraspable [ʌnˈgræspəbəl, B -ˈgrɑs-] *a.* 1. inasible, inaprensible. 2. incomprensible, inconcebible.
ungrateful [ʌnˈgreɪtfəl] *a.* ingrato, desagradecido, malagradecido, desagradable.
ungratefully [-fəlɪ] *adv.* ingratamente, desagradecidamente.
ungratefulness [-fəlnəs] *s.* ingratitud, desagradecimiento.
unground circuit [-ˈgraʊnd-] (elec.) circuito sin conexión a tierra.
ungrudgingly [ʌnˈgrʌdʒɪŋlɪ] *adv.* de buena gana, sin quejarse.
ungual [ˈʌŋgwəl] *a.* (zool.) ungular, ungueal, unguinal, relativo a las uñas.
unguard [ʌnˈgɑrd, B -ˈgɑd] *v.t.* desguarnecer, quitar el resguardo o protección a.
unguarded [-ˈgɑrdəd, B -ˈgɑdɪd] *a.* 1. desguarnecido, indefenso. 2. incauto, imprudente, indiscreto. 3. desprevenido. 4. **in an u. moment,** en un momento de descuido.
unguardedly [-lɪ] *adv.* incautamente; imprudentemente.
unguent [ˈʌŋgwənt] *s.* ungüento.
unguiculate [ʌŋˈgwɪkjʊlət, -ˌleɪt] *a., s.* (zool.) unguiculado.
unguis [ˈʌŋgwəs] *s.* (*pl.* UNGUES [-gwiz]) 1. (zool.) úngula. 2. (bot.) unguículo.
ungula [ˈʌŋgjʊlə] *s.* (*pl.* UNGULAE [-jʊˌli]) 1. (zool.) úngula. 2. (bot.) unguículo.
ungular [-lər, B -lə] *a.* (zool., bot.) ungular, ungueal, unguinal.
Ungulata [ˌʌŋgjʊˈleɪtə] *s.pl.* (zool.) ungulados.
ungulate [ˈʌŋgjʊlət, B -ˌleɪt] *a., s.* (zool.) ungulado.
unhackneyed [ʌnˈhæknɪd] *a.* no trillado, original.
unhallow [ʌnˈhæloʊ] *v.t.* (ant.) profanar, violar.
unhallowed [ʌnˈhæloʊd] *a.* 1. no consagrado. 2. profano, impío. 3. inmoral, licencioso.
unhampered [-ˈhæmpərd, B -ˈhæmpəd] *a.* libre de trabas, desembarazado.
unhand [ʌnˈhænd] *v.t.* soltar de las manos, desasir.
unhandsome [ʌnˈhænsəm] *a.* 1. feo, falto de belleza. 2. impropio, indigno. 3. descortés, grosero.
unhandy [ʌnˈhændɪ] *a.* 1. torpe, desmañado. 2. incómodo, inconveniente (esp. para manejar con las manos).
unhappily [ʌnˈhæpəlɪ] *adv.* 1. infelizmente, desdichadamente, desconsoladamente. 2. desgraciadamente, lamentablemente.
unhappiness [-ɪnəs] *s.* desgracia, infelicidad, infortunio, desdicha.
unhappy [ʌnˈhæpɪ] *a.* (UNHAPPIER; UNHAPPIEST) 1. infeliz, desdichado, desgraciado, triste, desconsolado. 2. desafortunado, malhadado. 3. desacertado, poco feliz, impropio. 4. (ant.) dañino, nocivo.
unharmed [-ˈhɑrmd, B -ˈhɑmd] *a.* indemne, incólume, intacto, ileso.
unharmonious [-hɑrˈmoʊnɪəs, B -hɑˈ-] *a.* inarmónico, poco armonioso, discordante.
unharness [-ˈhɑrnəs, B -ˈhɑnɪs] *v.t.* desenjaezar, desaparejar, desguarnecer (animales de tiro).
unhealthily [ʌnˈhɛlθəlɪ] *adv.* de manera enfermiza o insalubre, enfermizamente, insalubremente.
unhealthiness [-ˈhɛlθɪnəs] *a.* insalubridad; carácter enfermizo.
unhealthy [-ˈhɛlθɪ] *a.* (UNHEALTHIER; UNHEALTHIEST) 1. insalubre, malsano, nocivo. 2. enfermo, indispuesto; achacoso, enfermizo. 3. riesgoso, peligroso. 4. corruptor, degradante (costumbres, ambiente, etc.).
unheard [ˌʌnˈhɜrd, B -ˈhɜd] *a.* 1. no oído, no escuchado. 2. desatendido, desoído.
unheard-of [-ˌʌv, -ˌɑv, B -ɔv] *a.* 1. inaudito, sin precedente, extraño. 2. desconocido, sin fama.
unheeded [ʌnˈhidəd] *a.* desatendido, desoído, despreciado.
unheedful [ʌnˈhidfəl] *a.* desatento, descuidado, negligente.
unheedingly [ʌnˈhidɪŋlɪ] *adv.* sin prestar atención, con aire distraído.
unhesitating [ʌnˈhɛzəˌteɪtɪŋ] *a.* pronto, listo, resuelto, decidido; perseverante.
unhesitatingly [-lɪ] *adv.* sin titubear, prontamente, resueltamente, decididamente; continuamente, ininterrumpidamente.
unhewn [ʌnˈhjun] *a.* no labrado, en bruto.
unhinge [ʌnˈhɪndʒ] *v.t.* 1. desgoznar, desgonzar. 2. alterar, desequilibrar, desquiciar, trastornar (la mente).
unhitch [ʌnˈhɪtʃ] *v.t.* desenganchar, desatar, desprender, soltar.
unholiness [ʌnˈhoʊlɪnəs] *s.* impiedad, maldad.
unholy [ʌnˈhoʊlɪ] *s.* (UNHOLIER; UNHOLIEST) 1. profano, impío. 2. vil, malvado. 3. (fam.) atroz, tremendo, terrible.
unhonored [ˌʌnˈɑnərd, B -ˈɔnəd] *a.* 1. no respetado, irreverenciado. 2. rechazado (cheque).
unhood [ʌnˈhʊd] *v.t.* descaperuzar, descapirotar; desenmascarar, quitar el disfraz a.
unhook [ʌnˈhʊk] *v.t.* desenganchar, desabrochar.
unhoped-for [-ˈhoʊptˌfɔr, B -ˌfɔ] *a.* inesperado, imprevisto; nunca soñado.
unhorse [-ˈhɔrs, B -ˈhɔs] *v.t.* desarzonar; desmontar.
unhouseled [ʌnˈhaʊzəld] *a.* (ant.) que no ha recibido la eucaristía.
unhuman [ʌnˈhjumən] *a.* ajeno al hombre, que no es humano.
unhurried [-ˈhɜrɪd, B -ˈhʌrɪd] *a.* lento, pausado, no apresurado.
unhurt [-ˈhɜrt, B -ˈhɜt] *a.* ileso, incólume, indemne.
unhygienic [ˌʌnhaɪdʒɪˈɛnɪk, B -ˈdʒinɪk] *a.* antihigiénico.
Uniate, Uniat [ˈjunɪət] *s.* (relig.) uniato.
uniaxial [ˌjunɪˈæksɪəl] *a.* uniáxico, uniaxil (cristal).
unicameral [ˌjunɪˈkæmərəl] *a.* unicameral (legislatura).
UNICEF [ˈjunəˌsɛf] *abrev. de* **United Nations Children's Fund,** Fondo de las Naciones Unidas para la Infancia (UNICEF).
unicellular [ˌjunɪˈsɛljələr, B -lə] *a.* (biol.) unicelular.
unicellularity [-ˌsɛljəˈlærətɪ] *s.* (biol.) unicelularidad.
unicolor [ˈjunəˌkʌlər, B -ˌkʌlə] *a.* monócromo, de un solo color.
unicorn [ˈjunəˌkɔrn, B -ˌkɔn] *s.* 1. (mitol.) unicornio, caballo fantástico con un cuerno largo en medio de la frente. 2. **U.,** (astro.) Unicornio.
unicorn fish, (ict.) unicornio de mar, unicornio marino.
unicycle [ˈjunɪˌsaɪkəl] *a.* monociclo (velocípedo de una sola rueda).
unidentified [ˌʌnaɪˈdɛntəˌfaɪd] *a.* no identificado.
unidentified flying object, (*abrev.* **UFO**) objeto volador no identificado (OVNI).
unidirectional [ˌjunɪdəˈrɛkʃənəlˌ] *a.* unidireccional, de un solo sentido.
unidirectional current, (elec.) corriente directa.
unifiable [ˈjunəˌfaɪəbəl] *a.* que puede ser unificado, unificable.
unification [ˌjunəfəˈkeɪʃən] *s.* unificación.
unified field theory, (fís.) teoría del campo unificado.
unifier [ˈjunɪˌfaɪər, B -ˌfaɪə] *s.* unificador, unificadora.
unifilar [ˌjunɪˈfaɪlər, B -ˈfaɪlə] *a.* unifilar, de un solo hilo o cable.
uniflorous [-ˈflɔrəs] *a.* (bot.) unifloral.
unifoliate [ˌjunɪˈfoʊlɪət] *a.* (bot.) unifoliado.
unifoliolate [ˌjunɪˈfoʊlɪəˌleɪt] *a.* (bot.) unifoliolado.

uniform [ˈjunəˌfɔrm, B -ˌfɔm] *a.* uniforme. —*s.* 1. uniforme. 2. **in full u.,** con uniforme de gala. —*v.t.* uniformar, hacer uniforme.
uniformed [-ˌfɔrmd, B -ˌfɔmd] *a.* uniformado.
uniformity [ˌjunəˈfɔrmətɪ, B -ˈfɔmɪtɪ] *s.* uniformidad.
uniformity coefficient, coeficiente de uniformidad, coeficiente uniforme.
uniform load, (ing.) carga uniforme.
uniformly [ˈjunəˌfɔrmlɪ, B -fɔm-] *adv.* uniformemente.
uniform motion, (ing.) velocidad uniforme.
uniformness [-nəs] *s.* uniformidad.
unify [ˈjunəˌfaɪ] *v.t.* (*pret., p.p.* UNIFIED; *p.pr.* UNIFYING) unificar, unir.
unijugate [jʊˈnɪdʒəˌgeɪt, ˌjunɪˈdʒugət] *a.* (bot.) uniyugado.
unilateral [ˌjunɪˈlætərəl] *a.* unilateral.
unilocular [ˌjunɪˈlɑkjələr, B -ˈlɔkjʊlə] *a.* (bot.) unilocular.
unimaginable [ˌʌnɪˈmædʒənəbəl] *a.* inimaginable.
unimpaired [-ɪmˈpɛrd, B -ˈpɛəd] *a.* incólume, no mermado, intacto.
unimpeachable [ˌʌnɪmˈpitʃəbəl] *a.* intachable, irrecusable; irreprochable, inculpable.
unimpeachably [ˌʌnɪmˈpitʃəblɪ] *adv.* irreprochablemente.
unimportance [-ˈpɔrtəns, B -ˈpɔtəns] *s.* insignificancia, poca importancia.
unimportant [-ˈpɔrtənt, B -ˈpɔtənt] *a.* insignificante, poco importante.
unimprovable [ˌʌnɪmˈpruvəbəl] *a.* inmejorable.
unimproved [ˌʌnɪmˈpruvd] *a.* no mejorado; no usado o empleado; baldío, inculto, yermo; no urbanizado.
uninflammable [ˌʌnɪnˈflæməbəl] *a.* ininflamable, incombustible.
uninflected [ˌʌnɪnˈflɛktəd] *a.* (gram.) sin inflexiones (idioma).
uninfluenced [ʌnˈɪnflʊənst] *a.* no influenciado, no influido, no afectado.
uninformed [-ɪnˈfɔrmd, B -ˈfɔmd] *a.* inculto, ignorante, mal informado.
uninhabitable [ˌʌnɪnˈhæbətəbəl] *a.* inhabitable.
uninhabited [ˌʌnɪnˈhæbətəd] *a.* inhabitado, deshabitado, despoblado.
uninheritable [ˌʌnɪnˈhɛrɪtəbəl] *a.* que no se puede heredar, inheredable.
uninhibited [ˌʌnɪnˈhɪbətəd] *a.* 1. libre de inhibiciones. 2. franco, desembarazado (risa, sonrisa, etc.). 3. desenfrenado.
uninitiated [ˌʌnɪˈnɪʃɪˌeɪtəd] *a.* profano, ignorante, que carece de conocimientos, no iniciado (en una materia).
uninjured [-ˈɪndʒərd, B -ˈɪndʒəd] *a.* ileso, indemne.
uninspired [-ɪnˈspaɪrd, B -ˈspaɪəd] *a.* falto de inspiración, trivial, aburrido.
uninstructed [-ɪnˈstrʌktəd] *a.* sin aviso, que no ha recibido aviso o instrucciones.
uninsured [-ɪnˈʃʊrd, B -ʃʊəd] *a.* no asegurado, sin seguro.
unintelligence [ˌʌnɪnˈtɛlədʒəns] *s.* falta de inteligencia.
unintelligent [ˌʌnɪnˈtɛlədʒənt] *a.* falto de inteligencia, sin inteligencia.
unintelligible [-ˈtɛlədʒəbəl] *a.* ininteligible, no inteligible.
unintentional [-ˈtɛnʃənəl] *a.* no intencional, involuntario, casual.
unintentionally [-ɪ] *adv.* sin intención.
uninterested [ʌnˈɪntrəstəd] *a.* 1. no interesado, indiferente, apático. 2. desinteresado, desprendido.
uninteresting [ʌnˈɪntrəstɪŋ] *a.* falto de interés, aburrido, insípido.
uninterred [ˌʌnɪnˈtɜrd, B -ˈtɜd] *a.* insepulto.
uninterrupted [ˌʌnɪntəˈrʌptəd] *a.* ininterrumpido, continuo.
uninterruptedly [-lɪ] *adv.* sin interrupción.
unintimidated [ˌʌnɪnˈtɪməˌdeɪtəd] *a.* no intimidado.
uninuclear [ˌjunɪˈnuklɪər, B -ˈnjuklɪə] *a.* uninuclear, de un núcleo.
uninvested [ˌʌnɪnˈvɛstəd] *a.* 1. no invertido (capital, etc.). 2. no investido (de una dignidad, etc.).
uninvited [ˌʌnɪnˈvaɪtəd] *a.* no invitado, sin invitación.
uninviting [ˌʌnɪnˈvaɪtɪŋ] *a.* 1. no atractivo. 2. repelente, repugnante.
union [ˈjunjən] *s.* 1. unión, coalición, asociación; fusión. 2. unión, concordia, armonía. 3. unión, cofederación, alianza. 4. unión (sexual); matrimonio. 5. emblema o símbolo de unión (en banderas, etc.). 6. sindicato; gremio de obreros. 7. (mec.) unión; tuerca de unión. 8. (mat.) unión. 9. **The U.,** los Estados Unidos; (G.B.) El Reino Unido. 10. asociación estudiantil en una Universidad de los E.U.; sede de esta organización.
union card, tarjeta de miembro del sindicato.
union catalog, catálogo colectivo de varias bibliotecas.
unionism [ˈjunjəˌnɪzəm] *s.* sindicalismo, gremialismo.
unionist [-nəst] *s.* sindicalista, gremialista.
unionization [ˌjunjənəˈzeɪʃən, B -naɪ-] *s.* sindicación, agremiación, sindicalización (Amer.).
unionize [ˈjunjəˌnaɪz] *v.t.* sindicar, agremiar, sindicalizar (Amer.).
Union Jack, (E.U., mar.) bandera con el emblema que representa la unión de los Estados; (G.B.) pabellón nacional.
Union of South Africa, Unión Sudafricana.
Union of Soviet Socialist Republics, (hist.) Unión de Repúblicas Socialistas Soviéticas (URSS).
union shop, fábrica o taller que emplea sólo obreros agremiados.
union suit, ropa interior de cuerpo entero.
uniparental [ˌjunɪpəˈrɛntəl] *a.* (med.) partenogénico, unigénito.
uniparous [juˈnɪpərəs] *a.* (zool., bot.) unípara.
uniped [ˈjunəˌpɛd] *a.* unípede, de un solo pie.
unipersonal [ˌjunəˈpɜrsənəl, B -ˈpɜs-] *a.* unipersonal.
uniplanar [ˌjunɪˈpleɪnər, B -ˈpleɪnə] *s.* (mec.) uniplanar.
unipod [ˈjunəˌpɑd, B -ˌpɔd] *s.* soporte unípede.
unipolar [ˌjunɪˈpoʊlər, B -ˈpoʊlə] *a.* (fís., anat.) unipolar.
unipotent [ˌjuˈnɪpətənt] *a.* (biol.) unipotencial.
unique [juˈnik] *a.* único, singular.
uniquely [juˈniklɪ] *adv.* singularmente, originalmente, extraordinariamente.
uniqueness [juˈniknəs] *s.* unicidad, singularidad.
unisexual [ˌjunɪˈsɛkʃʊəl, B -ˈsɛksjʊəl] *a.* 1. (bot., zool.) unisexual. 2. (jer., E.U.) dic. de la moda o vestimenta diseñada tanto para el hombre como para la mujer.
unison [ˈjunəsən, -nəzən] *s.* 1. (mús.) unisonancia. 2. armonía, acuerdo, concordancia. 3. **in u.,** al unísono. —*a.* unísono, unisón.
unisonous [juˈnɪsənəs] **unisonal** [-əl] *a.* unisón, unísono.
unit [ˈjunət] *s.* 1. unidad, elemento. 2. (biol., mat.) unidad. 3. (mec., elec.) unidad, grupo (de máquinas, etc.) que funciona como un todo.
unitage [ˈjunətɪdʒ] *s.* especificación de la unidad (en un sistema de medida, etc.); conjunto de unidades.
Unitarian [ˌjunəˈtɛrɪən] *a., s.* (relig.) unitario.
Unitarianism [-ˌɪzəm] *s.* (relig.) unitarismo.
unitary [ˈjunəˌtɛrɪ, B ˈjunɪtərɪ] *a.* 1. unitario. 2. compuesto de unidades. 3. integrado. 4. (mat., fís.) unitario.
unitary theory, (fís.) teoría unitaria, teoría del campo unificado.
unit character, (biol.) carácter dominante.
unite [jʊˈnaɪt] *v.t.* 1. unir. 2. reunir, aunar. —*v.i.* unirse.
united [jʊˈnaɪtəd] *a.* unido.
United Arab Emirates, Emiratos Árabes Unidos.
United Arab Republic, (hist.) República Árabe Unida.
united front, (pol.) frente único.
United Kingdom, Reino Unido.
unitedly [jʊˈnaɪtədlɪ] *adv.* unidamente.
United Nations, Naciones Unidas.
United States, Estados Unidos; (*ú. t. adjetivamente*) estadounidense, de los Estados Unidos.
United States of America (the), *m. sing.* los Estados Unidos de America.
United States of Mexico, *m. pl.* Estados Unidos Mexicanos.
unit factor, (biol.) gen o factor principal.
unit heater, unidad de calefacción, calentador unitario.
unitive [ˈjunətɪv] *a.* unitivo.
unit load, carga por unidad, carga unitaria o específica.
unit magnetic pole, (fís.) polo magnético unitario.
unit price, (econ.) precio unitario, precio por unidad.
unity [ˈjunətɪ] *s.* (*pl.* UNITIES) 1. unidad. 2. acuerdo, concordia, unión. 3. continuidad, coherencia. 4. (mat.) unidad. 5. **the unities,** (teat.) las unidades aristotélicas (tiempo, acción, lugar).
univ. *abrev. de* 1. **universal,** universal. 2. **university,** universidad.
univalence [ˌjunɪˈveɪləns] **univalency** [-lənsɪ] *s.* (quím.) univalencia.
univalent [ˌjunɪˈveɪlənt] *a.* (quím.) univalente.
univalve [ˈjunɪˌvælv] *a., s.* (zool.) univalvo.
univalvular [ˌjunɪˈvælvjələr, B -lə] *a.* (zool.) univalvular.
universal [ˌjunəˈvɜrsəl, B -ˈvɜsəl] *a.* universal, cósmico; global, comprensivo. —*s.* 1. (lóg.) proposición universal. 2. (filos.) universal. 3. (mec.) universal.
universal agent, (der.) apoderado general.
universal chuck, (maq.) mandril o plato universal.
Universalism [-ˌɪzəm] *s.* (teo.) universalismo.
Universalist [-əst] *a., s.* (teo.) universalista.
universality [ˌjunəvɜrˈsælətɪ, B -vɜˈ-] *s.* universalidad.
universalization [ˌjunəˌvɜrsələˈzeɪʃən, B -ˌvɜsəlaɪ-] *s.* universalización.
universalize [-ˈvɜrsəˌlaɪz, B -ˈvɜsə-] *v.t.* universalizar.
universal joint, (mec.) junta o unión universal, acoplamiento o articulación universal, cardán, junta cardánica.
universal language, lengua universal.
universal lathe, (maq.) torno universal.
universal legacy, legado a título universal.
universally [ˌjunəˈvɜrsəlɪ, B -ˈvɜsə-] *adv.* universalmente.
universalness [-səlnəs] *s.* universalidad.

universal succession, (der.) sucesión universal.

universe ['junəˌvɜrs, B -ˌvɜs] *s.* 1. universo, cosmos, mundo. 2. sistema (filosófico, matemático, etc.) completo e independiente. 3. **u. of discourse,** (lóg.) extensión de una idea o concepto.

university [ˌjunə'vɜrsətɪ, B -'vɜsɪtɪ] *s.* (*pl.* UNIVERSITIES) universidad.

university degree, título universitario.

univocal [ju'nɪvəkəl] *a., s.* unívoco, (palabra) de un solo significado.

unjoin [ʌn'dʒɔɪn] *v.t.* separar, desunir, dividir.

unjoint [ʌn'dʒɔɪnt] *v.t.* desarticular; (mec.) desensamblar.

unjointed [ʌn'dʒɔɪntəd] *a.* desarticulado.

unjudged [ʌn'dʒʌdʒd] *a.* no juzgado, sin juzgar, pendiente de juicio.

unjust [ʌn'dʒʌst] *a.* 1. injusto, inicuo. 2. (ant.) deshonesto, pérfido.

unjustifiable [ˌʌn'dʒʌstəˌfaɪəbəl] *a.* injustificable, inexcusable.

unjustifiably [-ˌfaɪəblɪ] *adv.* injustificadamente, inexcusablemente.

unjustified [-ˌfaɪd] *a.* injustificado.

unjustifiedly [-lɪ] *adv.* injustificadamente.

unjustly [-'dʒʌstlɪ] *adv.* injustamente, inicuamente.

unjustness [-nəs] *s.* injusticia, iniquidad.

unkempt [ʌn'kɛmpt] *a.* 1. despeinado, desgreñado, desmelenado. 2. desarreglado, desaseado.

unkenned [ʌn'kɛnd] *a.* (dial.) extraño, raro, desconocido.

unkennel [ʌn'kɛnəl] *v.t.* 1. hacer salir de su guarida (a un animal). 2. descubrir, revelar.

unkind [ʌn'kaɪnd] *a.* 1. poco amable, severo, rudo, cruel. 2. riguroso, duro (clima, tiempo).

unkindliness [-lɪnəs] *s.* falta de amabilidad, aspereza, dureza.

unkindly [-lɪ] *adv.* poco amablemente, de manera poco amable; rudamente, severamente. —*a.* poco afable; duro, rudo.

unkindness [-nəs] *s.* falta de bondad, dureza, crueldad.

unkingly [ʌn'kɪŋlɪ] *a.* impropio o indigno de un rey.

unknit [ʌn'nɪt] *v.t., v.i.* destejer(se); deshilar(se).

unknot [ʌn'nɑt, B -'nɔt] *v.t.* desamarrar, desatar, desanudar.

unknowable [ʌn'noʊəbəl] *a.* inconocible, incognoscible, inescrutable.

unknowingly [-ɪŋlɪ] *adv.* sin saber, inadvertidamente.

unknown [ʌn'noʊn] *a.* desconocido; ignorado, ignoto, incógnito; **u. to,** ignorado por. —*s.* 1. (mat.) incógnita. 2. **the u.,** lo desconocido, lo ignoto.

unknown quantity, (mat. y fig.) incógnita.

Unknown Soldier, Soldado Desconocido.

unlabeled [ʌn'leɪbəld] *a.* sin rótulo, sin etiqueta.

unlabored [ʌn'leɪbərd, B -'leɪbəd] *a.* 1. espontáneo, no elaborado, sencillo. 2. sin cultivar (terreno, campo).

unlace [ʌn'leɪs] *v.t.* 1. desenlazar, desatar. 2. desabrochar (un vestido).

unlade [ʌn'leɪd] *v.t.* descargar.

unladylike [ʌn'leɪdɪˌlaɪk] *a.* impropio de una dama.

unlaid [ˌʌn'leɪd] *a.* 1. no colocado o puesto. 2. no apaciguado. 3. destorcido (cuerda, etc.).

unlamented [ˌʌnlə'mɛntəd] *a.* no llorado, no lamentado.

unlash [ʌn'læʃ] *v.t.* desatar; deshacer.

unlatch [ʌn'lætʃ] *v.t.* abrir (la puerta) levantando el picaporte. —*v.i.* abrirse, soltarse.

unlawful [ˌʌn'lɔfəl] *a.* ilegal, ilícito; ilegítimo.

unlawfully [ʌn'lɔfəlɪ] *adv.* ilegalmente, ilícitamente; ilegítimamente.

unlawfulness [-fəlnəs] *s.* ilegalidad, ilicitud; ilegitimidad.

unlay [ˌʌn'leɪ] *v.t., v.i.* (mar.) destorcer, descolchar (una cuerda).

unlead [ˌʌn'lɛd] *v.t.* 1. sacar plomo de (una bala, etc.). 2. (impr.) llenar (espacio entre líneas).

unleaded [ˌʌn'lɛdəd] *a.* 1. despojado de plomo; no cubierto con plomo. 2. (impr.) desinterlineado, lleno (sin espacio entre líneas).

unlearn [ˌʌn'lɜrn, B -'lɜn] *v.t.* desaprender, olvidar (lo aprendido); deshacerse de (hábito).

unlearned [ˌʌn'lɜrnəd, B -'lɜnɪd] *a.* 1. indocto, iliterato; ignorante. 2. [-'lɜrnd, B -'lɜnd] no aprendido.

unleash [ˌʌn'liʃ] *v.t.* 1. quitar la traílla a. 2. (fig.) desatar, desencadenar; soltar, liberar.

unleavened [ˌʌn'lɛvənd] *a.* ázimo, ácimo, sin levadura (pan).

unless [ʌn'lɛs] *conj.* a menos que, a no ser que. —*prep.* excepto, salvo, con excepción de.

unlettered [ˌʌn'lɛtərd, B -'lɛtəd] *a.* 1. iletrado, ignorante, iliterato, analfabeto. 2. desprovisto de letras.

unlevelled [ˌʌn'lɛvəld] *a.* desnivelado.

unlicensed [ˌʌn'laɪsənst] *a.* 1. no autorizado, sin autorizar; sin licencia, sin permiso. 2. sin restricciones, desenfrenado.

unlicked [ˌʌn'lɪkt] *a.* desmañado, torpe; crudo.

unlike [ˌʌn'laɪk] *a.* disímil, desemejante, distinto, diferente, diverso, desigual. —*prep.* 1. impropio de, indigno de; no característico de. 2. (de una manera) diferente de, no como.

unlikelihood [-lɪhʊd] **unlikeliness** [-lɪnəs] *s.* improbabilidad.

unlikely [-lɪ] *a.* improbable, remoto; inverosímil.

unlikeness [-nəs] *s.* desemejanza, disimilitud, diferencia, diversidad, desigualdad.

unlimber [ˌʌn'lɪmbər, B -'lɪmbə] *v.t.* 1. (mil.) desenganchar el avantrén de (un cañón). 2. alistar para la acción. —*v.i.* hacer preparativos para la acción.

unlimited [ˌʌn'lɪmətəd] *a.* 1. ilimitado, inmenso, infinito, incalculable. 2. sin restricciones.

unlined [ˌʌn'laɪnd] *a.* 1. sin forro; no forrado. 2. sin rayar (papel); sin arrugas (rostro).

unlink [ˌʌn'lɪŋk] *v.t.* separar, desconectar.

unliquidated [ʌn'lɪkwəˌdeɪtəd] *a.* 1. sin liquidar. 2. (com.) pendiente de pago.

unlisted [ˌʌn'lɪstəd] *a.* 1. (bolsa) no cotizado (acciones, valores, etc.). 2. no registrado, fuera de la lista.

unlive [ˌʌn'lɪv] *v.t.* vivir hasta que se borre u olvide (un error, crimen, etc.).

unload [ˌʌn'loʊd] *v.t.* 1. descargar, desembarcar. 2. descargar, aligerar, exonerar, liberar. 3. desahogar, desahogarse de (remordimiento, pena, etc.). 4. descargar, quitar la carga de (un arma). 5. (bolsa) vender en grandes cantidades, deshacerse de (acciones). —*v.i.* quitarse un peso de encima.

unloader [-'loʊdər, B -'loʊdə] *s.* descargador.

unlock [-'lɑk, B -'lɔk] *v.t.* 1. abrir la cerradura de (puerta, etc.). 2. (fig.) desencerrar; descubrir, revelar (secretos, etc.). 3. liberar, desencadenar.

unlooked-for [ˌʌn'lʊktˌfɔr, B -fɔ] *a.* inesperado, imprevisto, inopinado.

unloose [ʌn'lus] **unloosen** [ʌn'lusən] *v.t.* soltar, desatar, aflojar, desencadenar; liberar.

unlosable [ʌn'luzəbəl] *a.* imperdible (objeto, apuesta, etc.).

unlovely [ʌn'lʌvlɪ] *a.* poco amable, poco seductor, sin gracia, desgarbado, desagradable.

unluckily [ˌʌn'lʌkəlɪ] *adv.* desafortunadamente, desgraciadamente.

unluckiness [-ɪnəs] *s.* infortunio, desgracia, desdicha; mala suerte.

unlucky [ʌn'lʌkɪ] *a.* (UNLUCKIER; UNLUCKIEST) 1. desgraciado, desdichado. 2. desafortunado, infortunado, lamentable, deplorable. 3. infausto, aciago, de mal agüero. 4. **to be u.,** tener mala suerte.

unmade [ˌʌn'meɪd] *a.* increado; deshecho; arruinado; desarreglado.

unmaidenly [ʌn'meɪdənlɪ] *a.* impropio de una doncella.

unmake [ˌʌn'meɪk] *v.t.* 1. deshacer, arruinar, aniquilar, destruir. 2. degradar, destituir, deponer.

unman [ˌʌn'mæn] *v.t.* 1. emascular, castrar; afeminar. 2. acobardar; debilitar. 3. privar de personal (barco, fortaleza, etc.).

unmanageable [ʌn'mænədʒəbəl] *a.* difícil de manejar, inmanejable, intratable, indisciplinable.

unmanliness [ˌʌn'mænlɪnəs] *s.* 1. falta de caballerosidad; cobardía. 2. afeminamiento.

unmanly [-lɪ] *a.* 1. impropio de un hombre, poco caballeroso, cobarde. 2. afeminado.

unmanned [ˌʌn'mænd] *a.* 1. sin hombres; despoblado. 2. no tripulado. 3. (ant.) indómito (halcón).

unmannered [ˌʌn'mænərd, B -'mænəd] *a.* malcriado, mal educado, incivil, descortés, rudo.

unmannerliness [-'mænərlɪnəs, B -əlɪ-] *s.* rudeza, descortesía, incivilidad, mala crianza, malacriadez (Amer.).

unmannerly [-'mænərlɪ, B -'mænəlɪ] *a.* rudo, descortés, incivil, malcriado, mal educado (persona); descomedido, descortés (comportamiento, acto). —*adv.* rudamente, descortésmente.

unmarked [-'mɑrkt, B -'mɑkt] *a.* 1. sin marca, no marcado. 2. sin letrero (calle, etc.). 3. inadvertido.

unmarketable [ˌʌn'mɑrkətəbəl, B -'mɑkət-] *a.* invendible, incomerciable.

unmarriageable [ˌʌn'mærɪdʒəbəl] **unmarriable** [ˌʌn'mærɪəbəl] *a.* incasable.

unmarried [ʌn'mærɪd] *a.* soltero, célibe.

unmask [ʌn'mæsk, B -'mɑsk] *v.t.* desenmascarar. —*v.i.* desenmascararse, quitarse la máscara.

unmast [-'mæst, B -'mɑst] *v.t.* (mar.) desarbolar.

unmatched [ˌʌn'mætʃt] *a.* único, sin par, inigualado; dispar, desigual.

unmeaning [ˌʌn'minɪŋ] *a.* 1. vacuo, sin expresión (cara, etc.). 2. sin sentido, falto de significación.

unmeant [ˌʌn'mɛnt] *a.* involuntario, sin intención.

unmeasurable [ˌʌn'mɛʒərəbəl] *a.* inmensurable; inmenso, inconmensurable.

unmeasured [-'mɛʒərd, B -'mɛʒəd] *a.* 1. no medido. 2. infinito, ilimitado. 3. desmedido, inmoderado.

unmeet [ˌʌn'mit] *a.* impropio, inconveniente.

unmeetness [-nəs] *s.* inconveniencia.

unmellowed [ʌn'mɛloʊd] *a.* inmaduro.

unmentionable [-'mɛnʃənəbəl] *a.* impropio, que no debe mencionarse, infando. —*s. pl.* (hum.) prendas íntimas; pantalones interiores de mujer.

unmerchantable [-'mɜrtʃəntəbəl, B -'mɜtʃənt-] *a* invendible, no comerciable.

unmerciful [-'mɜrsɪfəl, B -'mɜsɪ-] *a.* despiadado, inclemente, cruel.

unmercifully [-fəlɪ] *adv.* despiadadamente, cruelmente.

unmerited [ˌʌn'mɛrətəd] *a.* inmerecido, inmérito.
unmeritedly [-lɪ] *adv.* inmerecidamente.
unmesh [ʌn'mɛʃ] *v.t.* desengranar.
unmilitary [-'mɪləˌtɛrɪ, B -tərɪ] *a.* no militar; falto de porte marcial.
unmindful [ˌʌn'maɪndfəl] *a.* descuidado, desatento, negligente, olvidadizo; **not u. of,** teniendo presente; **u. of,** sin pensar en, descuidando.
unmistakable [ˌʌnmɪs'teɪkəbəl] *a.* inequívoco, inconfundible, obvio, evidente.
unmistakably [-'teɪkəblɪ] *adv.* obviamente, evidentemente, sin lugar a equivocarse.
unmitigated [ˌʌn'mɪtɪˌgeɪtəd] *a.* 1. no mitigado, no suavizado, duro, severo. 2. completo, absoluto (bribón, verdad, etc.).
unmitigatedly [-lɪ] *adv.* duramente, severamente.
unmixed [ˌʌn'mɪkst] *a.* no mezclado, sin mezcla, puro, simple.
unmoor [ˌʌn'mʊr, B -'mʊə] *v.t.* (mar.) desamarrar, desaferrar (un barco). —*v.i.* (mar.) soltar amarras, levantar las áncoras (barco).
unmoral [-'mɔrəl] *a.* amoral.
unmorally [-əlɪ] *adv.* amoralmente.
unmortified [-'mɔrtəˌfaɪd, B -'mɔtə-] *a.* inmortificado.
unmotivated [ˌʌn'moʊtəˌveɪtəd] *a.* inmotivado.
unmounted [ˌʌn'maʊntəd] *a.* 1. no montado, a pie (policía, etc.). 2. sin montar, no engastado (piedra preciosa, joya, etc.). 3. sin marco (pintura, etc.).
unmovable [ˌʌn'muvəbəl] *a.* inmovible.
unmoved [-'muvd] *a.* inalterado, impasible, indiferente.
unmoving [-'muvɪŋ] *a.* inmóvil, inmoble, inmoto.
unmuffle [ˌʌn'mʌfəl] *v.t.* descubrir, destapar.
unmusical [ˌʌn'mjuzɪkəl] *a.* 1. no musical, discordante. 2. falto de musicalidad.
unmuzzle [ˌʌn'mʌzəl] *v.t.* quitar el bozal a; (fig.) dejar hablar.
unnail [ʌn'neɪl] *v.t.* desclavar.
unnamable, unnameable [ˌʌn'neɪməbəl] *a.* 1. innombrable, indesignable, innominable. 2. inefable, que no se puede mencionar (esp. vicio).
unnatural [ˌʌn'nætʃərəl] *a.* artificial; afectado, forzado; desnaturalizado; inhumano; anormal, monstruoso.
unnaturally [-əlɪ] *adv.* artificialmente; afectadamente, forzadamente; anormalmente.
unnaturalness [-əlnəs] *s.* artificialidad, afectación; anormalidad.
unnavigable [ʌn'nævɪgəbəl] *a.* innavegable.
unnecessarily ['ʌnˌnɛsə'sɛrəlɪ, B ʌn'nɛsɪsərɪlɪ] *adv.* innecesariamente, superfluamente, inútilmente.
unnecessary [ʌn'nɛsəˌsɛrɪ, B -sərɪ] *a.* innecesario, superfluo, inútil.
unnegotiable [ˌʌnnɪ'goʊʃɪəbəl] *a.* 1. innegociable; no comerciable; invendible. 2. (fam.) intransitable.
unneighbourly [-'neɪbərlɪ, B -'neɪbəlɪ] *a.* adusto, poco amable, descortés (con sus vecinos).
unnerve [-'nɜrv, B -'nɜv] *v.t.* acobardar, amilanar, desalentar, desconcertar.
unnoticeable [ʌn'noʊtəsəbəl] *a.* imperceptible.
unnoticed [-əst] *a.* inadvertido, desapercibido.
unnumbered [-'nʌmbərd, B -'nʌmbəd] *a.* 1. innumerable. 2. no numerado, sin numeración, sin número.
UNO ['junoʊ] *abrev. de* **United Nations Organization,** Organización de las Naciones Unidas (ONU).

unobjectionable [ˌʌnəb'dʒɛkʃənəbəl] *a.* inobjetable, irreprochable.
unobliging [ˌʌnə'blaɪdʒɪŋ] *a.* poco servicial, nada servicial, desacomedido (Amer.).
unobservable [ˌʌnəb'zɜrvəbəl, B -'zɜvə-] *a.* inobservable.
unobservance [-vəns] *s.* inobservancia.
unobservant [-vənt] *a.* 1. distraído, descuidado, desatento. 2. (con *of*) inobservante (de reglas, leyes, etc.).
unobserved [-'zɜrvd, B -'zɜvd] *a.* inadvertido, desapercibido; inobservado.
unobserving, *a.* distraído, descuidado, desatento.
unobstructed [ˌʌnəb'strʌktəd] *a.* no obstruido, libre.
unobtainable [ˌʌnəb'teɪnəbəl] *a.* inasequible, no obtenible.
unobtrusive [ˌʌnəb'trusɪv] *a.* discreto, modesto, moderado, recatado.
unoccupied [ʌn'ɑkjəˌpaɪd, B -'ɔk-] *a.* 1. desocupado, vacante, vacío. 2. desocupado, ocioso. 3. (mil.) no ocupado (territorio, país, etc.).
unoffending [ˌʌnə'fɛndɪŋ] *a.* inofensivo, inocuo.
unofficial [ˌʌnə'fɪʃəl] *a.* no oficial, extraoficial.
unofficially [ˌʌnə'fɪʃəlɪ] *adv.* extraoficialmente.
unopened [ʌn'oʊpənd] *a.* sin abrir, cerrado.
unopposed [ˌʌnə'poʊzd] *a.* sin (encontrar) oposición.
unorganized [ʌn'ɔrgəˌnaɪzd, B -'ɔgə-] *a.* 1. no organizado. 2. (biol.) sin estructura orgánica. 3. (sociol.) no agremiado. 4. (lóg.) carente de método.
unoriginal [ˌʌnə'rɪdʒənəl] *a.* poco original, sin originalidad.
unorthodox [ʌn'ɔrθəˌdɑks, B -'ɔθəˌdɔks] *a.* no ortodoxo, heterodoxo.
unostentatious [ˌʌnˌɑstən'teɪʃəs, B -ˌɔs-] *a.* sin ostentación, modesto, sencillo, llano.
unostentatiously [-lɪ] *adv.* sin ostentación, sencillamente.
unowned [ʌn'oʊnd] *a.* sin dueño; (der.) mostrenco.
unpacified [ʌn'pæsəˌfaɪd] *a.* turbulento, amotinado.
unpack [ʌn'pæk] *v.t.* desempaquetar, desempacar, desembalar, desenfardar.
unpacking [-ɪŋ] *s.* desempaque, desembalaje.
unpaged [ʌn'peɪdʒd] *a.* de páginas no numeradas.
unpaid [ʌn'peɪd] *a.* 1. no pagado, pendiente de pago, impago (Amer.). 2. sin paga, irremunerado.
unpaired [ˌʌn'pɛrd, B -'pɛəd] *a.* no apareado, no pareado.
unpalatable [ˌʌn'pælətəbəl] *a.* 1. desabrido, insípido. 2. (fig.) desagradable.
unparalleled [ʌn'pærəˌlɛld] *a.* sin par, inigualado, sin ejemplo, sin paralelo.
unpardonable [ʌn'pɑrdənəbəl, B -'pɑd-] *a.* imperdonable, inexcusable, irremisible.
unpardonably [-əblɪ] *adv.* imperdonablemente.
unparliamentary [-ˌpɑrlə'mɛntərɪ, B -ˌpɑlə-] *a.* contrario a las reglas o usos parlamentarios.
unpartisan [-'pɑrtəzən, B -'pɑtɪ-] *a.* 1. no afiliado a ningún partido. 2. imparcial.
unpassionate [ʌn'pæʃənət] *a.* desapasionado, tranquilo.
unpatriotic [-ˌpeɪtrɪ'ɑtɪk, B 'ʌnˌpætrɪ'ɔt-] *a.* poco patriótico, antipatriótico.
unpatronized [ˌʌn'peɪtrəˌnaɪzd, B -'pæ-] *a.* 1. sin patrocinio o patrocinador. 2. sin clientela.

unpaved [ʌn'peɪvd] *a.* sin pavimento, sin pavimentar; desempedrado.
unpayable [ʌn'peɪəbəl] *a.* impagable.
unpeg [ʌn'pɛg] *v.t.* desclavijar.
unpen [ʌn'pɛn] *v.t.* soltar (ganado) del redil; dejar libre (a un preso).
unpeople [ʌn'pipəl] *v.t.* despoblar.
unperceivable [-pər'sivəbəl, B -pə'-] *a.* imperceptible.
unperceived [-'sivd] *a.* desapercibido, inadvertido.
unperfect [-'pɜrfɪkt, B -'pɜfɪkt] *a.* imperfecto.
unperforated [-'pɜrfəˌreɪtəd, B -'pɜfə-] *a.* (filat.) sin perforar.
unpersuadable [-pər'sweɪdəbəl, B -pə'-] *a.* impersuasible.
unperturbed [-pər'tɜrbd, B -pə'tɜbd] *a.* inalterado, sereno.
unperused [ˌʌnpə'ruzd] *a.* no leído, no revisado, no hojeado.
unphilanthropic [-fɪlən'θrɑpɪk, B -'θrp-] *a.* poco humanitario.
unpicked [ʌn'pɪkt] *a.* 1. no escogido. 2. no recogido (díc. de flores y frutos).
unpile [ʌn'paɪl] *v.t.* desamontonar.
unpin [ʌn'pɪn] *v.t.* 1. desenclavar, desprender. 2. (ajedrez) desclavar.
unpinioned [ʌn'pɪnjənd] *a.* desatado.
unplaced [ʌn'pleɪst] *a.* (llegado) fuera del marcador (caballo en carrera).
unplagued [ʌn'pleɪgd] *a.* no atormentado por; **u. by,** libre de (dolor, fastidio, etc.).
unplait [ʌn'pleɪt, B -'plæt] *v.t.* destrenzar.
unplanned [ʌn'plænd] *a.* no planeado, no premeditado, no intencional; casual, accidental.
unplanted [ʌn'plæntəd] *a.* no cultivado (terreno, etc.).
unpleaded [ʌn'plidəd] *a.* (der.) no defendido; no alegado.
unpleasant [ʌn'plɛzənt] *a.* desagradable, molesto, ingrato, antipático.
unpleasantly [-lɪ] *adv.* desagradablemente.
unpleasantness [-nəs] *s.* 1. carácter desagradable. 2. disgusto, enfado. 3. desazón; desagrado.
unpledged [ʌn'plɛdʒd] *a.* no empeñado (palabra, etc.).
unplowed [ʌn'plaʊd] *a.* (agr.) inculto, no arado.
unplug [-'plʌg] *v.i.* desenchufar, desconectar; destupir.
unplumbed [ʌn'plʌmd] *a.* 1. no sondeado, no medido. 2. (fig.) no entendido, no investigado.
unpolished [ˌʌn'pɑlɪʃt, B -'pɔlɪʃt] *a.* áspero, tosco; sin pulir, deslustrado; rudo, basto, grosero, zafio.
unpolished diamond, diamante en bruto.
unpolitic [-'pɑlətɪk, B -'pɔl-] *a.* impolítico, imprudente, indiscreto.
unpolitical [ˌʌnpə'lɪtəkəl] *a.* apolítico, poco interesado en la política.
unpolled [ʌn'poʊld] *a.* no entrevistado; no inscrito como votante.
unpolluted [ˌʌnpə'lutəd] *a.* impoluto, incontaminado, inmaculado, puro.
unpopular [ʌn'pɑpjələr, B -'pɔpjʊlə] *a.* impopular.
unpopularity [-ˌpɑpjə'lærətɪ, B -ˌpɔp-] *s.* impopularidad.
unposted [ʌn'poʊstəd] *a.* 1. no despachado (carta, etc.). 2. no informado, ignorante.
unpostponable [ˌʌnpoʊst'poʊnəbəl] *a.* inaplazable, impostergable.
unpractical [ʌn'præktɪkəl] *a.* poco práctico, inservible, inútil.
unpracticed [ʌn'præktəst] *a.* inexperto, sin práctica.

unprecedented [ʌn'prɛsəˌdɛntəd] *a.* sin precedente, nunca visto; inaudito.
unprecise [ˌʌnprɪ'saɪs] *a.* impreciso, indefinido, indeterminado.
unpredictable [ˌʌnprɪ'dɪktəbəl] *a.* 1. imposible de predecir, incalculable (evento). 2. inconstante, incierto, caprichoso (persona).
unprejudiced [ʌn'prɛdʒədəst] *a.* sin prejuicios, sin predisposición, imparcial.
unpremeditated [ˌʌnprɪ'mɛdəˌteɪtəd] *a.* impremeditado, indeliberado.
unpremeditatedly [-lɪ] *adv.* impremeditadamente, indeliberadamente.
unpremeditation [ˌʌnprɪˌmɛdə'teɪʃən] *s.* impremeditación, indeliberación.
unprepared [ˌʌnprɪ'pɛrd, B -'pɛəd] *a.* desprevenido; no preparado.
unpreparedness [-nəs] *s.* falta de preparación; descuido.
unprepossessing [ˌʌnpripə'zɛsɪŋ] *a.* poco atractivo, poco impresionante.
unpresentable [ˌʌnprɪ'zɛntəbəl] *a.* impresentable; desaliñado.
unpressed [ʌn'prɛst] *a.* 1. no planchado; no apretado (botón, etc.). 2. no forzado, voluntario.
unpretending [ˌʌnprɪ'tɛndɪŋ] *a.* modesto, sin pretensiones.
unpretentious [-'tɛnʃəs] *a.* 1. modesto, sin pretensiones, sencillo. 2. franco, sincero.
unprevailing [ˌʌnprɪ'veɪlɪŋ] *a.* ineficaz, nulo.
unpreventable [ˌʌnprɪ'vɛntəbəl] *a.* inevitable, ineludible, ineluctable.
unpriced [ʌn'praɪst] *a.* sin precio fijo; sin precio marcado.
unprincipled [ʌn'prɪnsəpəld] *a.* sin principios, sin conciencia; amoral.
unprintable [ʌn'prɪntəbəl] *a.* impublicable; indecente, obsceno.
unprinted [ʌn'prɪntəd] *a.* no impreso, sin imprimir.
unproductive [-prə'dʌktɪv] *a.* improductivo, infructuoso.
unprofessed [ˌʌnprə'fɛst] *a.* no declarado, no revelado (intención, propósito, etc.).
unprofessional [ˌʌnprə'fɛʃənəl] *a.* 1. no profesional, no técnico. 2. reñido con la ética profesional, impropio, no ético.
unprofitable [-'prɑfɪtəbəl, B -'prɔfɪt-] *a.* improductivo; inútil, infructuoso, desventajoso.
unprofitableness [-nəs] *s.* improductividad; inutilidad.
unprofitably [-əblɪ] *adv.* inútilmente, sin provecho.
unprolific [ˌʌnprə'lɪfɪk] *a.* poco prolífico, estéril, infecundo.
unprolongable [-prə'lɔŋəbəl] *a.* improrrogable.
unpromising [-'prɑməsɪŋ, B -'prɔm-] *a.* poco prometedor, poco atractivo.
unprompted [-'prɑmptəd, B -'prɔmptɪd] *a.* no sugerido, espontáneo.
unpronounceable [ˌʌnprə'naʊnsəbəl] *a.* impronunciable.
unpropitious [ˌʌnprə'pɪʃəs] *a.* desfavorable, no propicio.
unproportioned [-prə'pɔrʃənd, B -'pɔʃənd] *a.* desproporcionado.
unpropped [-'prɑpt, B -'prɔpt] *a.* desapuntalado, sin apoyo.
unprosperous [ʌn'prɑspərəs, B -'prɔs-] *a.* no lucrativo, impróspero; desafortunado.
unprotected [ˌʌnprə'tɛktəd] *a.* desvalido, desamparado, indefenso.
unproved [ʌn'pruvd] **unproven** [ʌn'pruvən] *a.* no comprobado; (der.) no probado.
unprovided [ˌʌnprə'vaɪdəd] *a.* (gen. con *with*) desprovisto, desabastecido (de); **u. for,** desamparado, abandonado; (der.) sin recurso para.
unprovoked [ˌʌnprə'voʊkt] *a.* no provocado, inmotivado, infundado.
unpruned [ʌn'prund] *a.* no podado, sin podar.
unpublished [ʌn'pʌblɪʃt] *a.* no publicado, inédito.
unpunished [ʌn'pʌnɪʃt] *a.* impune, sin castigo.
unquailing [ʌn'kweɪlɪŋ] *a.* resuelto; animoso.
unqualified [-'kwɑləˌfaɪd, B -'kwɔl-] *a.* 1. inhábil, incompetente, incapaz. 2. sin título, sin licencia o autorización, desautorizado. 3. inhabilitado. 4. incondicional, ilimitado, absoluto, completo, entero.
unqualifiedly [-lɪ] *adv.* incondicionalmente, ilimitadamente, completamente, enteramente.
unquenchable [ʌn'kwɛntʃəbəl] *a.* inextinguible; insaciable.
unquestionable [ʌn'kwɛstʃənəbəl] *a.* incuestionable, indiscutible, indisputable.
unquestionably [-əblɪ] *adv.* incuestionablemente, indiscutiblemente, indudablemente.
unquestioned [-'kwɛstʃənd] *a.* no sujeto a interrogación (testigo, etc.); incuestionable.
unquestioning [ʌn'kwɛstʃənɪŋ] *a.* incondicional, sin restricción.
unquiet [ʌn'kwaɪət] *a.* 1. agitado, inquieto, desasosegado; perturbado emocionalmente. 2. turbulento (época, etc.). 3. ruidoso.
unquote [ʌn'kwoʊt] *v.i.* cerrar comillas (después de una cita).
unracked [-'rækt] *a.* no trasegado (el vino).
unraked [-'reɪkt] *a.* no rastrillado.
unravel [ʌn'rævəl] *v.t.* 1. desenmarañar, desenredar, deshilar. 2. (fig.) desenmarañar, desembrollar, aclarar, descifrar. —*v.i.* desenredarse, deshilarse.
unravelment [-mənt] *a.* desenlace (de una obra).
unreachable [ʌn'ritʃəbəl] *a.* inalcanzable.
unread [ʌn'rɛd] *a.* 1. no leído, sin leer. 2. poco leído, no versado (en literatura), inculto.
unreadable [ʌn'ridəbəl] *a.* 1. ilegible. 2. que no vale la pena leer. 3. incomprensible, oscuro.
unreadiness [-'rɛdɪnəs] *s.* falta de preparación; lentitud.
unready [-'rɛdɪ] *a.* desprevenido; no preparado; lento, lerdo.
unreal [ʌn'ril, B -'rɪəl] *a* irreal, ilusorio, quimérico, imaginario, ficticio.
unrealistic [-ˌrɪə'lɪstɪk] *a.* poco práctico, no realista; irreal.
unreality [ˌʌnrɪ'ælətɪ] *s.* irrealidad.
unrealizable [ʌn'riəˌlaɪzəbəl] *a.* irrealizable.
unreaped [ʌn'ript] *a.* no segado, no cosechado.
unreason [ʌn'rizən] *s.* sinrazón; irracionalidad; locura.
unreasonable [-əbəl] *a.* irrazonable, irracional, inmoderado.
unreasonableness [-əbəlnəs] *s.* 1. irracionalidad; sinrazón. 2. exorbitancia, inmoderación.
unreasonably [-əblɪ] *adv.* irracionalmente; inmoderadamente.
unreasoning [-ɪŋ] *a.* irracional, ilógico; irreflexivo.
unreclaimed [ˌʌnrɪ'kleɪmd] *a.* 1. no reclamado. 2. sin mejorar, inculta (tierra).
unrecognizable [ʌnˌrɛkəg'naɪzəbəl] *a.* que no puede reconocerse.
unreconcilable [-ˌrɛkən'saɪləbəl] *a.* incompatible, irreconciliable, intransigente, implacable.
unreconciled [-'rɛkənˌsaɪld] *a.* no resignado, no reconciliado.
unreconstructed [ˌʌnrikən'strʌktəd] *a.* intransigente, retrógrado.
unrecoverable [ˌʌnrɪ'kʌvərəbəl] *a.* irrecuperable; irreparable.
unrecovered [-'kʌvərd, B -'kʌvəd] *a.* no recobrado, irrecobrable.
unredeemable [-'dimәbəl] *a.* irredimible.
unredeemed [ˌʌnrɪ'dimd] *a.* 1. no redimido. 2 irredento (territorio).
unreel [ʌn'ril] *v.t., v.i.* desenrollar (se).
unreeve [ʌn'riv] *v.t.* (mar.) despasar, desguarnir (el cabrestante).
unrefined [ˌʌnrɪ'faɪnd] *a.* no refinado, impuro, tosco, torpe, rudo.
unrefined sugar, azúcar quebrada, azúcar prieta.
unreflecting [ˌʌnrɪ'flɛktɪŋ] *a.* irreflexivo.
unregarded [ˌʌnrɪ'gɑrdəd, B -'gɑdɪd] *a.* desatendido, descuidado, desdeñado, despreciado.
unregardful [-fəl] *a.* negligente, descuidado.
unregenerate [ˌʌnrɪ'dʒɛnərət] *a.* no regenerado; incorregible; impenitente, incontrito, impío.
unrelenting [ˌʌnrɪ'lɛntɪŋ] *a.* inexorable, inflexible, implacable; riguroso, tenaz.
unrelentingly [-lɪ] *adv.* inexorablemente, inflexiblemente, sin tregua.
unreliable [ˌʌnrɪ'laɪəbəl] *a.* 1. poco serio, no confiable, indigno de confianza; incierto, inestable. 2. que funciona mal (maquinaria).
unrelieved [ˌʌnrɪ'livd] *a.* 1. uniforme, monótono, sin variación. 2. no aliviado, no sosegado (dolor, pena, etc.).
unreligious [ˌʌnrɪ'lɪdʒəs] *a.* irreligioso.
unremitting [ˌʌnrɪ'mɪtɪŋ] *a.* perseverante, incansable, incesante.
unremittingly [-lɪ] *adv.* con perseverancia, perseverantemente, incansablemente.
unremunerated [ˌʌnrɪ'mjunəˌreɪtəd] *a.* irremunerado, no remunerado, sin paga.
unremunerative [-ˌreɪtɪv, B -rət-] *a.* no lucrativo, poco remunerador.
unrenewable [ˌʌnrɪ'nuəbəl, B -'nju-] *a.* irrenovable; (com.) improrrogable.
unrenounceable [ˌʌnrɪ'naunsəbəl] *a.* irrenunciable.
unrented [ʌn'rɛntəd] *a.* desalquilado.
unrepairable [ˌʌnrɪ'pɛrəbəl, B -'pɛər-] *a.* incomponible, irreparable.
unrepealable [ˌʌnrɪ'piləbəl] *a.* inabrogable.
unrepealed [ˌʌnrɪ'pild] *a.* no revocado, no abrogado, no derogado, en vigencia, vigente.
unrepentant [ˌʌnrɪ'pɛntənt] **unrepenting** [-ɪŋ] *a.* impenitente, incontrito.
unrepining [ˌʌnrɪ'paɪnɪŋ] *a.* resignado.
unreplaceable [ˌʌnrɪ'pleɪsəbəl] *a.* irreemplazable.
unreported [ˌʌnrɪ'pɔrtəd, B -'pɔtɪd] *a.* no comunicado, no denunciado (crimen, etc.).
unreprievable [ˌʌnrɪ'privəbəl] *a.* inconmutable (sentencia de muerte).
unrequested [ˌʌnrɪ'kwɛstəd] *a.* espontáneo, no solicitado.
unrequited [ˌʌnrɪ'kwaɪtəd] *a.* no correspondido (amor, etc.).
unrescindable [ˌʌnrɪ'sɪndəbəl] *a.* irrescindible.
unreserve [-'zɜrv, B -'zɜv] *s.* falta de reserva; franqueza, sinceridad.
unreserved [-'zɜrvd, B -'zɜvd] *a.* 1. no reservado, libre (asiento, cuarto, etc.). 2. sin reservas, sin restricción, incondicional (admiración, aprobación, etc.). 3. franco, abierto.
unreservedly [-'zɜrvədlɪ, B -'zɜvɪd-] *adv.* sin reserva, francamente, abiertamente.
unreservedness [-nəs] *s.* franqueza, abertura de corazón.

unresistant [ˌʌnrɪ'zɪstənt] *a.* sin resistencia, dócil.
unresisted [-təd] *a.* no obstruido, no impedido.
unresisting [-tɪŋ] *a.* que no ofrece resistencia.
unresolvable [ˌʌnrɪ'zɑlvəbəl, B -'zɔl-] *a.* indisoluble; insoluble.
unresolved [-'zɑlvd, B -'zɔlvd] *a.* 1. irresoluto, indeterminado, indeciso. 2. no resuelto, no aclarado.
unresponsive [ˌʌnrɪ'spɑnsɪv, B -'spɔn-] *a.* insensible, no impresionable; indiferente.
unrest [ʌn'rɛst] *s.* 1. inquietud, desasosiego, intranquilidad, zozobra. 2. disturbio, desorden.
unrestrainable [ˌʌnrɪ'streɪnəbəl] *a.* irrefrenable, incontenible; irreprimible.
unrestrained [-'streɪnd] *a.* 1. desenfrenado, licencioso. 2. libre, espontáneo.
unrestrainedly [-'streɪnədlɪ] *adv.* 1. desenfrenadamente, licenciosamente. 2. libremente, espontáneamente, con soltura.
unrestricted [ˌʌnrɪs'trɪktəd] *a.* ilimitado, sin restricción, sin trabas.
unrevealable [ˌʌnrɪ'viləbəl] *a.* irrevelable.
unrevealed [ˌʌnrɪ'vild] *a.* no divulgado, irrevelado, no revelado.
unrhymed [ʌn'raɪmd] *a.* sin rima.
unriddle [ʌn'rɪdəl] *v.t.* descifrar, resolver; adivinar; desentrañar.
unrifled [ʌn'raɪfəld] *a.* de ánima lisa, no rayado (díc. del cañón de armas de fuego).
unrig [ʌn'rɪg] *v.t.* (mar.) desarbolar, desenjarciar, desaparejar (el barco); desencapillar (las vergas).
unrighteous [ʌn'raɪtʃəs] *a.* 1. malo, perverso, pecador. 2. injusto, inicuo.
unrighteously [-lɪ] *adv.* 1. con perversidad o maldad, pecaminosamente. 2. injustamente, inicuamente.
unrighteousness [-nəs] *s.* 1. maldad, perversidad. 2. injusticia, iniquidad.
unrip [ʌn'rɪp] *v.t.* 1. cortar, desgarrar, desprender (costura). 2. (fig.) revelar, descubrir.
unripe [ʌn'raɪp] *a.* inmaturo, inmaduro; verde, no maduro.
unripeness [-nəs] *s.* 1. condición de verde o inmaduro de un fruto. 2. condición de inmadurez, falta de madurez.
unrivaled, unrivalled [ʌn'raɪvəld] *a.* sin rival; sin igual, sin par, incomparable.
unrivet [ʌn'rɪvət] *v.t.* quitar los remaches a, desclavar.
unrobe [ʌn'roʊb] *v.t., v.i.* desvestir(se); desnudar(se).
unroll [ʌn'roʊl] *v.t.* 1. desenrrollar, desarrollar. 2. desplegar; exhibir, descubrir. *—v.i.* desenrollarse.
unromantic [ˌʌnroʊ'mæntɪk] *a.* poco romántico, prosaico.
unroof [ˌʌn'ruf, -'rʊf, B -'ruf] *v.t.* destechar, destapar, descubrir.
unroot [ˌʌn'rut, -'rʊt, B -'rut] *v.t.* erradicar, desarraigar; extirpar.
unrove [ʌn'roʊv] *a.* (mar.) desguarnido (de un motón).
UNRRA ['ʌnrɑ] *abrev. de* **United Nations Relief and Rehabilitation Administration,** Administración de Ayuda y Rehabilitación de las Naciones Unidas.
unruffled [ʌn'rʌfəld] *a.* 1. tranquilo, inalterado, sereno. 2. calmo, calmoso (mar, agua).
unruled [ʌn'ruld] *a.* 1. sin rayar (papel). 2. independiente, no gobernado.
unruliness [ʌn'rulɪnəs] *s.* 1. indocilidad, indisciplina; rebeldía. 2. turbulencia, inquietud.
unruly [ʌn'rulɪ] *a.* (UNRULIER; UNRULIEST) 1. indócil, indisciplinable, ingobernable; refractario; revoltoso, levantisco. 2. turbulento, inquieto.
unsaddle [ʌn'sædəl] *v.t.* 1. desensillar (bestias). 2. derribar (a un jinete).
unsafe [ʌn'seɪf] *a.* inseguro; peligroso; inhospitalario (ej., playa, área, lugar).
unsafety [-tɪ] *s.* inseguridad; peligro.
unsaid [ʌn'sɛd] *a.* no dicho, no pronunciado; **to leave u.,** dejar de decir, dejar de mencionar.
unsalable, unsaleable [ʌn'seɪləbəl] *a.* invendible.
unsalaried [ʌn'sælərɪd] *a.* no asalariado.
unsalted [ʌn'sɔltəd] *a.* sin sal, no salado.
unsanctioned [ʌn'sæŋkʃənd] *a.* desautorizado, no aprobado.
unsanitary [ˌʌn'sænəˌtɛrɪ, B -tərɪ] *a.* insalubre, malsano; antihigiénico.
unsatisfactory [ˌʌnsætəs'fæktərɪ] *a.* no satisfactorio; inaceptable, inadecuado.
unsatisfied [ʌn'sætəsˌfaɪd] *a.* insatisfecho.
unsatisfying [-ˌfaɪɪŋ] *a.* poco satisfactorio, nada satisfactorio, deficiente, insuficiente.
unsaturate [ʌn'sætʃərət] *s.* (quím.) compuesto no saturado.
unsaturated [ʌn'sætʃəˌreɪtəd] *a.* no saturado.
unsavory [ʌn'seɪvərɪ] *a.* 1. insípido, soso, desabrido. 2. (fig.) desagradable, ofensivo; deshonroso.
unsay [ʌn'seɪ] *v.t.* retractar, desdecirse de, retractarse de.
unscalable [ʌn'skeɪləbəl] *a.* no escalable (cerro, etc.).
unscathed [ʌn'skeɪðd] *a.* ileso, indemne, incólume, intacto, sano y salvo.
unscholarly [-'skɑlərlɪ, B -'skɔləlɪ] *a.* 1. indigno de una persona docta (comportamiento, etc.). 2. poco erudito, inexacto.
unschooled [ʌn'skuld] *a.* 1. no aprendido, natural, innato (talento, etc.). 2. no entrenado, no preparado, no acostumbrado. 3. **u. in,** ignorante de, sin instrucción en (oficio, tema, etc.).
unscientific [ˌʌnsaɪən'tɪfɪk] *a.* acientífico, anticientífico.
unscramble [ʌn'skræmbəl] *v.t.* 1. desenrollar, desembrollar. 2. descifrar (mensaje en clave).
unscreened [ʌn'skrind] *a.* 1. no cribado. 2. no filmado, no adaptado para el cine. 3. no examinado, no investigado.
unscrew [ʌn'skru] *v.t.* desatornillar, destornillar, desenroscar; desenganchar, separar. *—v.i.* destornillarse, separarse.
unscrupulous [ʌn'skrupjʊləs] *a.* inescrupuloso.
unscrupulously [-lɪ] *adv.* de modo inescrupuloso, inescrupulosamente.
unscrupulousness [-nəs] *s.* inescrupulosidad.
unseal [ʌn'sil] *v.t.* romper el sello de, abrir.
unseam [ʌn'sim] *v.t.* abrir las costuras de, descoser.
unsearchable [-'sɜrtʃəbəl, B -'sɜtʃ-] *a.* inescrutable, impenetrable; inexplorable.
unseasonable [ʌn'sizənəbəl] *a.* fuera de tiempo, intempestivo, inoportuno, extemporáneo; fuera de sazón.
unseasonableness [-nəs] *s.* 1. condición de lo inoportuno. 2. condición de lo que está fuera de estación (frutos, etc.).
unseasonably [-əblɪ] *adv.* inoportunamente.
unseasoned [ʌn'sizənd] *a.* 1. sin sazonar; insípido, soso. 2. (fig.) inmaturo, inexperto.
unseat [ʌn'sit] *v.t.* 1. quitar del asiento; desarzonar. 2. destituir; desaforar (de un cuerpo legislativo).
unseated [-'sitəd] *a.* 1. destituido. 2. sin asiento(s).
unseaworthy [-'siˌwɜrðɪ, B -ˌwɜðɪ] *a.* innavegable.
unseconded [ʌn'sɛkəndəd] *a.* no apoyado, no secundado.
unseeing [ʌn'siɪŋ] *a.* 1. ciego. 2. vago (ojos, mirada).
unseemliness [ʌn'simlɪnəs] *s.* impropiedad, indecencia.
unseemly [ʌn'simlɪ] *a.* impropio, indecoroso, indecente. *—adv.* impropiamente, indecorosamente, indecentemente.
unseen [ʌn'sin] *a.* 1. no visto; invisible. 2. a primera vista (traducción). 3. inadvertido, desapercibido.
unsegregated [ʌn'sɛgrəˌgeɪtəd] *a.* no segregado; libre de segregación (racial).
unselfish [ʌn'sɛlfɪʃ] *a.* generoso, desprendido, altruista.
unselfishness [-nəs] *s.* generosidad, altruismo.
unserviceable [ʌn'sɜrvəsəbəl, B -'sɜvɪ-] *a.* inútil, inservible; incapaz de ser reparado (televisor, radio, etc.).
unserviceableness [-nəs] *s.* inutilidad.
unset [ʌn'sɛt] *a.* 1. no montado (piedra preciosa, joya). 2. no fraguado (cemento, yeso, etc.).
unsettle [ʌn'sɛtəl] *v.t.* 1. desarreglar, descomponer, desordenar. 2. alterar, inquietar, perturbar. *—v.i.* desarreglarse, descomponerse.
unsettled [ˌʌn'sɛtəld] *a.* 1. inestable, instable, perturbado; inconstante, variable; errante. 2. indeciso, incierto, dudoso. 3. inestable, irregular (vida, hábitos, etc.). 4. despoblado, inhabitado. 5. desequilibrado (mente). 6. (com.) por pagar, no liquidado, pendiente. 7. (der.) no dispuesto, sin liquidar; yacente (herencia).
unsettling [-'sɛtlɪŋ] *a.* inquietante, perturbador.
unsevered [-'sɛvərd, B -əd] *a.* no separado, indiviso, entero.
unsew [-'soʊ] *v.t.* descoser, deshilvanar, deshacer.
unsex [-'sɛks] *v.t.* privar de la sexualidad, esp. quitar los atractivos femeninos a (una mujer).
unshackle [-'ʃækəl] *v.t.* desherrar; desaherrojar, desengrilletar, libertar, desencadenar.
unshakable, unshakeable [-'ʃeɪkəbəl] *a.* inconmovible, firme.
unshaken [-kən] *a.* firme, sin temblar.
unshaped [-'ʃeɪpt] *a.* no formado, sin forma, informe.
unshapely [-'ʃeɪplɪ] *a.* desproporcionado.
unshapen [-pən] *a.* 1. no formado, sin forma, informe. 2. informe, deforme, disforme; malhecho, contrahecho.
unsharable, unshareable [ˌʌn'ʃɛrəbəl, B -'ʃɛər-] *a.* incompartible.
unshaven [-'ʃeɪvən] *a.* no afeitado, sin afeitar, sin rasurar.
unsheathe [-'ʃið] *v.t.* desenvainar (la espada).
unshed [-'ʃɛd] *a.* no derramada (lágrima).
unshell [-'ʃɛl] *v.t.* descascarar.
unsheltered [-'ʃɛltərd, B -təd] *a.* descubierto, no protegido, desamparado; inhospitalario, inhóspito (hogar).
unship [-'ʃɪp] *v.t.* 1. desembarcar; descargar. 2. (mar.) desarmar (un remo).
unshod [-'ʃɑd, B -'ʃɔd] *a.* descalzo; desherrado (caballo).
unshorn [-'ʃɔrn, B -'ʃɔn] *a.* no tonsurado.
unshorn sheep, ovejas no esquiladas.
unshrinkable [-'ʃrɪŋkəbəl] *a.* que no se encoge (tela, etc.).
unshrinking [-kɪŋ] *a.* intrépido, inquebrantable.
unsicker [-'sɪkər, B -ə] *a.* (ant., esco.) indigno de confianza.
unsight [ˌʌn'saɪt] *a.* no visto, no examinado.
unsighted [-əd] *a.* 1. no avistado (buque, etc.). 2. sin mira (arma de fuego).
unsightliness [-lɪnəs] *s.* fealdad.

unsightly [-lɪ] *a.* feo, de aspecto desagradable.

unsized [-'saɪzd] *a.* desencolado, sin apresto (papel).

unskilled [-'skɪld] *a.* inexperto, imperito; desmañado.

unskilled labor, mano de obra no calificada, labor manual sencilla.

unskilled laborer, peón de pico y pala; obrero no especializado.

unskilled workman, u. worker, obrero no especializado.

unskillful [ˌʌn'skɪlfəl] *a.* desmañado, torpe.

unskillfully [-fəlɪ] *adv.* desmañadamente, torpemente.

unskillfulness [-fəlnəs] *s.* desmaña, torpeza.

unsling [-'slɪŋ] *v.t.* 1. quitar del cabestrillo; descolgar. 2. (mar.) deslingar, quitar la eslinga a.

unsmokable [-'smoʊkəbəl] *a.* infumable.

unsnap [-'snæp] *v.t.* desabrochar.

unsnarl [-'snɑrl, B -'snɑl] *v.t.* (lit., fig.) desenmarañar, desenredar.

unsociability [-ˌsoʊʃə'bɪlətɪ] *s.* insociabilidad.

unsociable [ˌʌn'soʊʃəbəl] *a.* insociable, intratable, huraño; solitario; reservado.

unsociableness [-bəlnəs] *s.* insociablidad.

unsociably [-blɪ] *adv.* de manera insociable, insociablemente.

unsocial [-'soʊʃəl] *a.* insociable, huraño; antisocial.

unsold [-'soʊld] *a.* no vendido, rezagado (mercadería).

unsolder [ˌʌn'sɑdər, -'sɔd-, B -'sɔldə] *v.t.* desoldar; (fig.) dividir, partir.

unsolderable [-ərəbəl] *a.* insoldable.

unsoldierly [-'soʊldʒərlɪ, B -dʒəlɪ] *a.* indigno de un soldado; poco propio de un soldado.

unsolicited [ˌʌnsə'lɪsətəd] *a.* no solicitado, no pedido.

unsolvable [-'sɑlvəbəl, B -'sɔl-] *a.* insoluble, irresoluble.

unsolved [-'sɑlvd, B -'sɔlvd] *a.* no solucionado; sin resolver.

unsophisticated [-sə'fɪstəˌkeɪtəd] *a.* no sofisticado, natural, sencillo, puro, cándido, inexperto.

unsophistication [-səˌfɪstə'keɪʃən] *s.* naturalidad, sencillez; falta de refinamiento; inexperiencia.

unsought [-'sɔt] *a.* no solicitado, no buscado, no pedido (ayuda, consejo, etc.).

unsound [ˌʌn'saʊnd] *a.* 1. defectuoso; falso, erróneo. 2. falto de vigor, enfermizo; poco firme; ligero (sueño). 3. **of u. mind,** fuera de juicio, insano, demente.

unsounded [-əd] *a.* no sondeado, insondable.

unsoundly [-lɪ] *adv.* 1. defectuosamente. 2. erróneamente.

unsoundness [-nəs] *s.* 1. inexactitud, incorrección, falsedad. 2. falta de solidez.

unsparing [-'spɛrɪŋ, B -'spɛər-] *a.* 1. profuso, abundante; generoso, pródigo. 2. cruel, despiadado.

unsparingly [-lɪ] *adv.* 1. pródigamente. 2. despiadadamente.

unspeak [ˌʌn'spik] *v.t.* (ant.) desdecirse de, retractarse de.

unspeakable [-əbəl] *a.* 1. indescriptible, inefable. 2. incalificable, abominable, atroz.

unspeakably [-əblɪ] *adv.* 1. inexpresablemente, indeciblemente. 2. abominablemente, atrozmente, insoportablemente.

unspecialized [-'spɛʃəˌlaɪzd] *a.* no especializado; (biol.) no específico.

unspecified [-'spɛsəˌfaɪd] *a.* no especificado.

unspent [-'spɛnt] *a.* inexhausto; no gastado.

unspoiled [-'spɔɪld] **unspoilt** [-'spɔɪlt] *a.* 1. no corrompido, fresco, natural, no averiado, intacto. 2. no consentido, no mimado (niño).

unspontaneous [-spɑn'teɪnɪəs, B -spɔn-] *a.* no espontáneo, forzado, artificial.

unsportsmanlike [-'spɔrtsmənˌlaɪk, B -'spɔts-] *a.* antideportivo.

unspotted [-'spɑtəd, B -'spɔt-] *a.* sin mancha, inmaculado, impoluto.

unsprung [-'sprʌŋ] *a.* sin muelles, sin resortes.

unstable [-'steɪbəl] *a.* 1. inestable, instable. 2. fluctuante, irregular; vacilante. 3. (quím.) inestable (compuesto). 4. (fís.) radioactivo.

unstableness [-bəlnəs] *s.* inestabilidad.

unstably [-blɪ] *adv.* de manera inestable, inestablemente.

unstamped [ˌʌn'stæmpt] *a.* sin sellar, sin estampilla (carta, paquete, etc.).

unstate [-'steɪt] *v.t.* privar de estado o dignidad, degradar.

unsteadily [-'stɛdəlɪ] *adv.* inconstantemente.

unsteadiness [-dɪnəs] *s.* inestabilidad, inconstancia.

unsteady [-'stɛdɪ] *a.* 1. inseguro, inestable; tambaleante. 2. inconstante. 3. desigual, irregular. 4. fluctuante, intermitente.

unsteel [-'stil] *v.t.* ablandar, enternecer.

unstep [-'stɛp] *v.t.* (mar.) desmontar (ej., un mástil).

unstick [-'stɪk] *v.t.* soltar, desprender (algo clavado, pegado o agarrado).

unstinted [ˌʌn'stɪntəd] *a.* no escatimado, ilimitado, abundante.

unstinting [-'stɪntɪŋ] *a.* generoso.

unstitch [-'stɪtʃ] *v.t.* descoser.

unstop [-'stɑp, B -'stɔp] *v.t.* destaponar, destapar, abrir; dar paso a.

unstrained [-'streɪnd] *a.* 1. no forzado, relajado. 2. no filtrado.

unstrap [-'stræp] *v.t.* quitar las correas a.

unstratified [-'strætəˌfaɪd] *a.* no estratificado.

unstressed [-'strɛst] *a.* (fon.) átono, sin acento, inacentuado; sin énfasis.

unstring [ˌʌn'strɪŋ] *v.t.* 1. desensartar. 2. desencordar, desencordelar. 3. desatar, aflojar. 4. debilitar, trastornar, ej., *nerves unstrung by fear,* nervios debilitados por el miedo.

unstrung [-'strʌŋ] *a.* 1. debilitado, trastornado, nervioso, enervado. 2. desencordado, desensartado (collar).

unstuck [-'stʌk] *a.* 1. suelto, flojo, aflojado. 2. **to come u.,** desmoronarse, caer en desorden, desarreglarse.

unstudied [-'stʌdɪd] *a.* 1. natural, no afectado. 2. **u. in,** no versado en, sin conocimientos de.

unsubmissive [-səb'mɪsɪv] *a.* insumiso, rebelde.

unsubmissiveness [-nəs] *s.* insumisión.

unsubstantial [-səb'stæntʃəl, B -'stænʃəl] *a.* 1. insubstancial, poco sólido. 2. irreal, sin fundamento sólido. 3. ligero (díc. de comidas).

unsubstantiality [-səbˌstæntʃɪ'ælətɪ, B -ˌstænʃɪ-] *s.* insubstancialidad.

unsubstantially [-səb'stæntʃəlɪ, B -'stænʃə-] *adv.* insubstancialmente.

unsubstantiated [-səb'stæntʃɪˌeɪtəd, B -'stænʃɪ-] *a.* no confirmado, no respaldado.

unsuccess [ˌʌnsək'sɛs] *s.* fracaso, fiasco, malogro.

unsuccessful [-fəl] *a.* fracasado, desafortunado; poco próspero.

unsuccessfully [-fəlɪ] *adv.* sin éxito, infructuosamente.

unsuitability [-ˌsutə'bɪlətɪ, B -ˌsjut-] *s.* impropiedad.

unsuitable [-'sutəbəl, B -'sjut-] *a.* impropio, inservible, inadecuado.

unsuited [-'sutəd, B -'sjut-] *a.* impropio, no apropiado; inadaptado.

unsullied [-'sʌlɪd] *a.* inmaculado, impoluto.

unsung [-'sʌŋ] *a.* 1. no cantado. 2. (fig.) no alabado. 3. (poét.) no celebrado en canción o verso; olvidado.

unsupported [-sə'pɔrtəd, B -'pɔt-] *a.* sin apoyo, sin sostén.

unsure [-'ʃʊr, B -'ʃʊə] *a.* inseguro.

unsurmountable [-sər'maʊntəbəl, B -sə'-] *a.* insuperable, invencible (dificultad, obstáculo).

unsurpassed [-sər'pæst, B -sə'pɑst] *a.* no superado.

unsuspected [ˌʌnsə'spɛktəd] *a.* insospechado.

unsuspecting [-ɪŋ] *a.* confiado, ingenuo, sin recelo.

unswathe [-'swɑð, B -'sweɪð] *v.t.* desenvolver, desvendar, desfajar.

unswayed [-'sweɪd] *a.* no influido, no influenciado, no guiado (por pasiones, promesas, etc.).

unswear [-'swɛr, B -'swɛə] *v.t.* retractarse de; abjurar.

unsweetened [-'switənd] *a.* no endulzado.

unswerving [-'swɜrvɪŋ, B -'swɜv-] *a.* inmutable, constante.

unsworn [-'swɔrn, B -'swɔn] *a.* no juramentado.

unsymmetrical [-sə'mɛtrɪkəl] *a.* asimétrico, disimétrico.

unsympathetic [ˌʌnsɪmpə'θɛtɪk] *a.* 1. sin compasión, indiferente, antagónico, hostil. 2. **u. to,** opuesto a, contrario a.

unsystematic [-sɪstə'mætɪk] *a.* sin sistema, poco sistemático.

untactful [-'tæktfəl] *a.* importuno, desatinado.

untainted [-'teɪntəd] *a.* 1. incorrupto, no contaminado. 2. sin mancha o tacha.

untalented [-'tæləntəd] *a.* sin talento, incapaz.

untamable [-'teɪməbəl] *a.* indomable.

untamed [-'teɪmd] *a.* indomado, bravío.

untangle [-'tæŋgəl] *v.t.* desenredar, desenmarañar; resolver.

untaught [-'tɔt] *a.* 1. no enseñado; instintivo, natural. 2. sin instrucción, ignorante.

untaxed [-'tækst] *a.* libre de impuesto (s).

unteach [-'titʃ] *v.t.* hacer olvidar (creencia, etc.); enseñar lo contrario de.

untempered [ˌʌn'tɛmpərd, B -pəd] *a.* 1. no templado, dulce, suave (acero, etc.). 2. (fig.) destemplado, inmoderado.

untenable [-'tɛnəbəl] *a.* 1. insostenible, indefendible, indefensible (idea, opinión, etc.). 2. inhabitable.

untenanted [-'tɛnəntəd] *a.* vacío, desocupado, desalquilado.

unthankful [ˌʌn'θæŋkfəl] *a.* 1. ingrato, desagradecido, malagradecido (Amer.). 2. no agradecido, no reconocido (trabajo, tarea, etc.).

unthankfully [-fəlɪ] *adv.* desagradecidamente.

unthinkable [-'θɪŋkəbəl] *a.* inconcebible, inimaginable, impensable.

unthinking [-kɪŋ] *a.* irreflexivo, inconsiderado, precipitado.

unthinkingly [-lɪ] *adv.* 1. irreflexivamente, inconsideradamente. 2. instintivamente.

unthought-of [-'θɔtəv, B -ɔv] *a.* inconcebible, inesperado.

unthread [-'θrɛd] *v.t.* 1. desensartar, desenhebrar; deshebrar. 2. encontrar el camino por (un laberinto, etc.). 3. desembrollar (una situación).

unthrifty [-'θrɪftɪ] *a.* derrochador, gastador.

unthrone [-'θroʊn] *v.t.* destronar, derrocar.

untidily [-'taɪdəlɪ] *adv.* 1. desaliñadamente. 2. desordenadamente.
untidiness [-dɪnəs] *s.* 1. desaliño, desaseo. 2. falta del sentido de orden.
untidy [ˌʌn'taɪdɪ] *a.* (UNTIDIER; UNTIDIEST) 1. desaliñado, desaseado. 2. descuidado, desordenado.
untie [-'taɪ] *v.t.* 1. desatar; desamarrar, deshacer (un nudo); desprender; soltar, aflojar. 2. resolver. —*v.i.* desatarse, desamarrarse.
until [ən'tɪl] *prep.* hasta, ej., *his name was unknown u. tonight,* su nombre era desconocido hasta esta noche. —*conj.* hasta que, ej., *he kept on working u. he died,* siguió trabajando hasta que murió.
untile [ˌʌn'taɪl] *v.t.* desembaldosar, quitar las tejas.
untillable [-'tɪləbəl] *a.* (agr.) incultivable.
untilled [-'tɪld] *a.* inculto, agreste (terreno, campo).
untimeliness [-'taɪmlɪnəs] *s.* inoportunidad, carácter inoportuno o prematuro, inconveniencia.
untimely [-'taɪmlɪ] *a.* intempestivo, inoportuno, extemporáneo; prematuro; **to have an u. end,** malograrse. —*adv.* intempestivamente, a destiempo, inoportunamente; prematuramente.
untiring [-'taɪrɪŋ, B -'taɪər-] *a.* infatigable, incansable; constante.
untitled [-'taɪtəld] *a.* 1. sin título. 2. sin derecho.
unto ['ʌntu, -tʊ] *prep.* (ant., poét.) hasta; hacia.
untold [ˌʌn'toʊld] *a.* 1. nunca dicho, no narrado. 2. indecible, incalculable.
untouchable [-'tʌtʃəbəl] *a.* intocable, intangible. —*s.* intocable (individuo de una casta inferior en la India).
untouched [-'tʌtʃt] *a.* 1. no tocado, intacto, ileso. 2. insensible, no conmovido.
untoward [ˌʌn'toʊərd, B -əd] *a.* 1. adverso, desfavorable, contrario. 2. inconveniente, desagradable, vejatorio; desafortunado.
untowardness [-nəs] *s.* 1. adversidad, inconveniencia. 2. testarudez.
untraceable [-'treɪsəbəl] *a.* 1. que no se puede ubicar, imposible de encontrar. 2. inescrutable, que no deja marca o huellas.
untractable [-'træktəbəl] *a.* intratable.
untrained [-'treɪnd] *a.* no entrenado, falto de preparación; no acostumbrado; inexperto.
untrammelled [-'træməld] *a.* libre de trabas; no confinado o limitado.
untransferable [-træns'fɜrəbəl] *a.* intransferible.
untranslatability [-trænsˌleɪtə'bɪlətɪ, -trænz-] *s.* intraducibilidad.
untranslatable [-'leɪtəbəl] *a.* intraducible.
untraveled [ˌʌn'trævəld] *a.* 1. que no ha viajado. 2. no visitado, no frecuentado (por viajeros); inexplorado.
untread [-'trɛd] *v.t.* repasar, volver sobre los pasos de, desandar.
untreated [-'tritəd] *a.* sin tratar, no tratado (enfermedad, afección, etc.).
untried [-'traɪd] *a.* 1. no probado, experimental. 2. (der.) no procesado.
untrimmed [-'trɪmd] *a.* sin adornos, sin guarniciones; sin recortar.
untrod [-'trɑd, B -'trɔd] **untrodden** [-ən] *a.* no pisado, no hollado, virgen (tierra, nieve, etc.).
untroubled [-'trʌbəld] *a.* no molestado o perturbado; quieto, tranquilo; claro, transparente.
untrue [-'tru] *a.* 1. falso, inexacto. 2. engañoso, infiel, desleal.
untruly [-lɪ] *adv.* 1. falsamente. 2. engañosamente, deslealmente.
untruss [-'trʌs] *v.t.* (ant.) desatar, desempaquetar; desvendar.
untrustful [ˌʌn'trʌstfəl] *a.* desconfiado, receloso, suspicaz.
untrustworthy [-ˌwɜrðɪ, B -ˌwɜðɪ] *a.* indigno de confianza; inseguro, precario.
untrusty [-'trʌstɪ] *a.* pérfido, traidor.
untruth [-'truθ] *s.* 1. falsedad, mentira. 2. (ant.) infidelidad, traición.
untruthful [-fəl] *a.* falso, mentiroso, mendaz.
untruthfully [-fəlɪ] *adv.* falsamente.
untruthfulness [-fəlnəs] *s.* falsedad, falsía.
untuck [-'tʌk] *v.t.* desenfaldar, desdoblar.
untune [-'tun, B -'tjun] *v.t.* poner fuera de tono; desarreglar, descomponer.
untutored [-'tutərd, B -'tjutəd] *a.* 1. sin instrucción, inculto. 2. sencillo, ingenuo.
untwine [ˌʌn'twaɪn] *v.t.* 1. destorcer, desenrollar; desenmarañar. 2. (fig.) disolver, deshacer. —*v.i.* destorcerse, desenrollarse.
untwist [-'twɪst] *v.t., v.i.* destorcer(se), desenrollar.
unused [-'juzd] *a.* 1. no usado o empleado, nuevo, inutilizado, sin uso. 2. [-'just] (con *to*) no acostumbrado (a), no habituado (a).
unusual [-'juʒʊəl] *a.* inusual, raro, extraordinario, inusitado, insólito.
unusually [-əlɪ] *adv.* extraordinariamente.
unusualness [-əlnəs] *s.* carácter insólito, rareza; notabilidad.
unutterable [-'ʌtərəbəl] *a.* 1. inexpresable, indecible, inefable. 2. (fam., G.B.) completo, consumado (tonto, etc.).
unutterably [-əblɪ] *adv.* inexpresablemente, indeciblemente.
unvaccinated [-'væksəˌneɪtəd] *a.* no vacunado.
unvalued [-'væljud] *a.* 1. desapreciado, inestimado; desestimado, menospreciado. 2. sin valuación.
unvanquished [ˌʌn'væŋkwɪʃt] *a.* invicto, no derrotado.
unvarnished [-'vɑrnɪʃt, B -'vɑnɪʃt] *a.* 1. sin barnizar. 2. (fig.) sencillo, puro, ej., *the u. truth,* la pura verdad.
unvarying [-'vɛrɪɪŋ, B -'vɛər-] *a.* invariado, invariable, inmutable.
unveil [-'veɪl] *v.t.* quitar el velo a; descubrir, revelar. —*v.i.* quitarse el velo.
unventilated [-'vɛntəlˌeɪtəd] *a.* no ventilado.
unverifiable [-'vɛrəˌfaɪəbəl] *a.* inaveriguable, que no se puede verificar.
unverified [-'vɛrəˌfaɪd] *a.* no verificado, no comprobado.
unversed [-'vɜrst, B -'vɜst] *a.* no versado, no instruido (en).
unvocal [-'voʊkəl] *a.* taciturno, reservado; poco hablador; sin facilidad de palabra.
unvoice [-'vɔɪs] *v.t.* (fon.) ensordecer.
unvoiced [ˌʌn'vɔɪst] *a.* 1. no expresado. 2. (fon.) sordo.
unvoicing [-'vɔɪsɪŋ] *s.* (fon.) ensordecimiento.
unvouched for [ˌʌn'vaʊtʃtˌfɔr, B -ˌfɔ] no garantizado, no verificado.
unwalled [-'wɔld] *a.* sin murallas, sin cerca, abierto.
unwanted [-'wɑntəd, -'wɔnt-, B -'wɔnt-] *a.* 1. no deseado, superfluo. 2. indeseable.
unwanted guest, invitado de piedra.
unwarily [-'wɛrəlɪ, B -'wɛər-] *adv.* incautamente.
unwariness [-ɪnəs] *s.* imprudencia, falta de cautela.
unwarlike [-'wɔrˌlaɪk, B -'wɔˌ-] *a.* pacífico, no bélico.
unwarned [-'wɔrnd, B -'wɔnd] *a.* desprevenido, sin aviso previo.
unwarrantable [-'wɔrəntəbəl] *a.* injustificable; indefendible, insostenible.
unwarrantably [-əblɪ] *adv.* injustificablemente.
unwarranted [-əd] *a.* 1. injustificado. 2. desautorizado. 3. no garantizado.
unwarrantedly [-ədlɪ] *adv.* 1. injustificadamente. 2. sin autorización.
unwary [-'wɛrɪ, B -'wɛərɪ] *a.* incauto, imprudente; desprevenido.
unwashed [-'wɔʃt, -'wɑʃt, B -'wɔʃt] *a.* no lavado, sin lavar, desaseado.
unwatered [-'wɔtərd, -'wɑt-, B -'wɔtəd] *a.* 1. sin agua (ciudad, etc.). 2. sin abrevar (ganado, caballo, etc.). 3. no diluido, no aguado (vino, leche, etc.). 4. seco, sin riego.
unwavering [-'weɪvərɪŋ] *a.* firme, constante.
unwaveringly [-ɪŋlɪ] *adv.* sin vacilar, firmemente.
unweaned [-'wind] *a.* sin destetar.
unwearied [-'wɪrɪd, B -'wɪər-] *a.* no cansado, fresco.
unwearying [-'wɪrɪɪŋ, B -'wɪərɪ-] *a.* incansable, persistente, perseverante.
unweave [ˌʌn'wiv] *v.t.* 1. destejer. 2. (fig.) desenredar, desembrollar.
unwed [-'wɛd] *a.* célibe, soltero, soltera.
unwelcome [-'wɛlkəm] *a.* 1. mal recibido, mal acogido. 2. inoportuno.
unwell [-'wɛl] *a.* 1. enfermo, indispuesto. 2. menstruante. 3. **to feel u.,** sentirse mal.
unwept [-'wɛpt] *a.* no llorado; no lamentado.
unwholesome [-'hoʊlsəm] *a.* 1. insalubre, malsano. 2. inmoral, dañino.
unwieldily [-'wildəlɪ] *adv.* pesadamente.
unwieldiness [-dɪnəs] *s.* pesadez, incomodidad.
unwieldy [-'wildɪ] *a.* pesado, abultado, difícil de manejar.
unwilled [-'wɪld] *a.* involuntario, sin intención.
unwilling [ˌʌn'wɪlɪŋ] *a.* renuente, reacio; contrario; maldispuesto, ej., *u. to* (*do something*), maldispuesto a (hacer algo).
unwillingly [-lɪ] *adv.* de mala gana.
unwillingness [-nəs] *s.* mala gana, renuencia.
unwind [-'waɪnd] *v.t.* desenvolver, desenrollar, desenredar. —*v.i.* 1. desenvolverse. 2. relajarse, serenarse.
unwired [-'waɪrd, B -'waɪəd] *a.* no alambrado; sin alambres.
unwisdom [-'wɪzdəm] *s.* falta de cordura o discreción; insensatez; tontería, desatino.
unwise [-'waɪz] *a.* indiscreto, imprudente; tonto, necio.
unwisely [-lɪ] *adv.* imprudentemente; neciamente.
unwish [-'wɪʃ] *v.t.* dejar de desear (algo).
unwithering [-'wɪðərɪŋ] *a.* inmarchitable, inmarcesible.
unwitting [ˌʌn'wɪtɪŋ] *a.* 1. inconsciente, inadvertido. 2. sin intención.
unwittingly [-lɪ] *adv.* inconscientemente, inadvertidamente.
unwomanly [-'wʊmənlɪ] *a.* impropio de una mujer; poco femenino.
unwonted [-'wɔntəd, B -'woʊnt-] *a.* 1. desacostumbrado, inusual, desusado, inusitado, raro. 2. (ant.) no acostumbrado, no familiar o familiarizado.
unwontedly [-lɪ] *adv.* desacostumbradamente, inusitadamente.
unwontedness [-nəs] *s.* rareza.
unwooded [-'wʊdəd] *a.* sin árboles, pelado, raso.
unworkable [-'wɜrkəbəl, B -'wɜk-] *a.* 1. impracticable. 2. inexplotable.
unworkmanlike [-mənˌlaɪk] *a.* chapucero, sin maña, hecho sin cuidado (trabajo).

unworldliness [-'wɜrldlɪnəs, B -'wɜld-] *s.* 1. carácter ultramundano; espiritualidad. 2. ingenuidad, sencillez.
unworldly [-lɪ] *a.* 1. no terrenal, ultramundano; espiritual. 2. ingenuo, sencillo.
unworn [ˌʌn'wɔrn, B -'wɔn] *a.* 1. no gastado, no usado. 2. no trillado, fresco, original (idea, chiste, etc.).
unworthily [-'wɜrðəlɪ, B -'wɜðɪ-] *adv.* indignamente, sin mérito.
unworthiness [-ðɪnəs] *s.* indignidad, falta de mérito.
unworthy [-ðɪ] *a.* indigno, desmerecedor, sin mérito; frívolo.
unwounded [-'wundəd] *a.* ileso, indemne, sin daño o herida.
unwoven [-'woʊvən] *p.p. de* **unweave.**
unwrap [-'ræp] *v.t.* desenvolver, desempaquetar.
unwreathe [-'rið] *v.t.* destorcer; desenrollar.
unwrinkle [-'rɪŋkəl] *v.t.* desarrugar.
unwritten [-'rɪtən] *a.* 1. oral, tradicional. 2. no escrito, en blanco.
unwritten law, (der.) derecho no escrito; derecho consuetudinario.
unwrought [ˌʌn'rɔt] *a.* en bruto, en estado bruto, no elaborado.
unwrought wax, cera virgen.
unyielding [-'jildɪŋ] *a.* 1. inflexible, inconmovible, obstinado (persona). 2. firme, rígido, duro (objeto).
unyoke [-'joʊk] *v.t.* 1. libertar de un yugo, desenyugar (Amer.); desuncir. 2. separar, desunir.
unzip [-'zɪp] *v.t.* abrir la cremallera o cierre relámpago (Am.) en (prenda de vestir). *—v.i.* abrirse por cremallera.
up [ʌp] *adv.* 1. arriba, más arriba, para arriba, hacia arriba, ej., *from ten dollars up,* de diez dólares para arriba. 2. allá, acá, ej., *a man came up and looked at me,* un hombre se me acercó y me miró, *go up and ask him,* vaya y pregúntele. 3. en pie, derecho; de pie. 4. más fuerte; enteramente, completamente; bien (dando énfasis), ej., *clean up your room,* limpia bien tu cuarto, *eat up your food,* come toda tu comida, *speak up,* hable más fuerte. 5. con ventaja o ganancia; en igualdad, ej., *our side is two up,* nuestro bando está con una ventaja de dos (puntos. tantos, etc.), *after an hour's play I was ten dollars up,* después de una hora de juego había ganado diez dólares, *the score is five up,* el tanteador está parejo con cinco (puntos, tantos, etc.) por bando. 6. (dep.) en la silla, ej., *with an unknown jockey up,* con un jinete desconocido en la silla (de un caballo de carrera). 7. (G.B.) en la universidad, ej., *he stayed up the whole summer,* se quedó en la universidad todo el verano. 8. **to be all up with,** no haber remedio para, acabarse para, ej., *it's all up with him,* no hay remedio para él, todo se acabó para él; **to be up,** estar levantado; estar en el aire, estar volando; haber crecido o subido, ej., *the river is up,* ha subido el (nivel del) río, *corn is up,* el (precio del) maíz ha subido; quedar construído, ej., *the house was up in two weeks,* la casa quedó construída en dos semanas; haberse levantado, haber salido, ej., *the sun is up,* el sol ha salido, *the whole country is up already,* se ha levantado ya todo el país, *the wind is up,* se ha levantado el viento; haber(se) expirado o terminado, haberse cumplido, ej., *time is up,* ha expirado el plazo, se ha cumplido el tiempo, ha llegado la hora; **to be up against,** tener que hacer frente a, tener que luchar con; **to be up against it,** estar en apuros; **to be up and about,** estar levantado (gen. temprano); estar restablecido (de enfermedad); **to be up and doing,** estar levantado y haciendo cosas, estar levantado y trabajando; **to be up early,** levantarse temprano (de la cama); **to be up for,** haber sido presentado para, ej., *the matter is up for approval,* el asunto ha sido presentado para su aprobación; ser procesado, ej., *he is up for stealing,* va a ser procesado por robo; **to be up in,** ser versado o perito en; **to be up late,** acostarse tarde, velar; **to be up on,** estar informado de, tener conocimiento de (noticias, etc.); estar al día en, no atrasarse en o con (trabajo, estudios, etc.); **to be up to,** estar a la altura de; ser capaz de cumplir con, ser competente para (tarea, trabajo, etc.); estar metido en, estar tramando (algo); estar enterado de, estar prevenido contra (trucos, etc.); estar conforme a, ej., *it is up to standard,* está conforme a la norma; incumbir a, corresponder a, depender de, ser asunto de, ej., *it is up to you,* esto incumbe a ti, esto te corresponde, esto depende de ti, es asunto tuyo; **tu get up,** levantarse (de la cama, la silla, etc.); **to go up,** subir; **to live up to one's income,** gastar todo lo que se gana; **up!** (o **up with you!**) ¡levántate!; ¡arriba!; **up above,** allá arriba; **up and down,** de arriba abajo, de un lado a otro, por todas partes; **up in arms,** en armas, alzado, rebelado; **up to,** hasta; **up do date,** al día; hasta la fecha; **what is up?** ¿qué pasa?; **what is up with you?** ¿qué te pasa? *—prep.* hacia arriba de, a lo largo de, a lo alto de; hacia dentro de; contra, en contra de; **he went up the stairs,** subió la escalera; **up country,** al interior (del país); **up the river,** río arriba; **up the street,** calle arriba; **up the wind,** contra el viento. *—a.* inclinado; ascendente, de subida, ej., *up escalator,* escalera (móvil) de subida, *up train,* tren que viaja al norte. *—s.* 1. altura, tierra elevada, subida. 2. (fig.) prosperidad. 3. **on the up-and-up,** (fam.) honesto; mejorándose (negocios, perspectivas, etc.). *—v.i.* (*pret., p.p.* UPPED; *p.pr.* UPPING) 1. levantarse; subir; animarse. 2. **up and,** ponerse de repente a, ej., *(then) he up (s) and says,* (entonces) él se pone de repente a decir. *—v.t.* 1. levantar. 2. aumentar, elevar, ej., *u. prices,* elevar precios, *u. production,* aumentar la producción.
up-and-coming ['ʌpən'kʌmɪŋ] *a.* 1. prometedor. 2. con aire de éxito.
up-and-down [ˌʌpən'daʊn] *a.* 1. oscilante, fluctuante (precios, fortuna); con altibajos (años); cambiante (voz, sonido). 2. muy escarpado, perpendicular. 3. desigual, accidentado (terreno); montañoso.
upas ['jupəs] *s.* 1. (bot.) upas, antiaris. 2. upas, antiar (resina tóxica). 3. (fig.) ponzoña, veneno.
upbeat ['ʌpˌbit] *s.* (mús.) compás o nota inacentuadas. *—a.* optimista, animado, alegre.
upbraid [ˌʌp'breɪd] *v.t.* reconvenir, reprochar, recriminar, echar en cara; **u. for** (o **with**), reconvenir por (o con).
upbraiding [-ɪŋ] *s.* reconvención, reproche, recriminación.
upbringing ['ʌpˌbrɪŋɪŋ] *s.* crianza, educación.
upbuild [ˌʌp'bɪld] *v.t.* construir, edificar, erigir; componer, armar.
upbuilder [-ər, B -ə] *s.* constructor.
upcast ['ʌpˌkæst, B -kɑst] *s.* pozo de ventilación. *—a.* dirigido hacia arriba.
upchuck [-ˌtʃʌk] *v.t., v.i.* (fam.) vomitar, devolver.
upcoming [-ˌkʌmɪŋ] *a.* próximo, venidero, cercano.
upcountry ['ʌp'kʌntrɪ] *a.* del interior, de tierra adentro. *—s.* interior (de un país, etc.). — [ˌʌp'kʌntrɪ] *adv.* (fam.) en el interior, hacia el interior, tierra adentro.
upcurrent [-ˌkɜrənt, B -ˌkʌ-] *s.* (meteor.) corriente ascendente.
update [ˌʌp'deɪt] *v.t.* poner al día.
updo ['ʌpˌdu] *s.* (fam.) moño, rodete alto, peinado hacia arriba.
updraft [-ˌdræft, B -ˌdrɑft] *s.* corriente ascendente, tiro, (ej., de aire).
upend [ˌʌp'ɛnd] *v.t., v.i.* poner(se) de punta, poner(se) derecho, ponerse vertical.
upgrade ['ʌpˌgreɪd] *s.* rampa, cuesta o pendiente en subida; **on the u.,** ascendente, progresivo. *—a.* ascendente.
upgrade [ˌʌp'greɪd] *v.t.* 1. mejorar. 2. subir, ascender. 3. sustituir (un producto de calidad inferior) por otro mejor y más caro.
upgrowth ['ʌpˌgroʊθ] *s.* crecimiento; aumento, desarrollo.
upheaval [ˌʌp'hivəl] *s.* 1. solevantamiento (esp. de la corteza terrestre). 2. trastorno, cataclismo; revuelta.
upheave [-'hiv] *v.t., v.i.* solevantar(se), alzarse.
upheld [-'hɛld] *pret., p.p. de* **uphold.**
uphill ['ʌpˌhɪl] *s.* cuesta ascendente. — ['ʌp'hɪl] *adv.* cuesta arriba. — ['ʌpˌhɪl] *a.* 1. ascendente. 2. de situación elevada. 3. (fig.) dificultoso, penoso; laborioso.
uphold [ˌʌp'hoʊld] *v.t.* 1. sostener, mantener, tener erguido. 2. levantar, elevar. 3. sostener, sustentar, defender (principio, tésis, etc.).
upholder [-ər, B -ə] *s.* defensor; sostenedor.
upholster [əp'hoʊlstər, B -stə] *v.t.* 1. poner colgaduras a, guarnecer. 2. tapizar, entapizar (muebles).
upholsterer [-stərər, B -stərə] *s.* tapicero.
upholstery [-stərɪ] *s.* 1. tapizado (de un mueble). 2. tapicería (arte del tapicero).
UPI *abrev. de* **United Press International,** Prensa Unida Internacional.
upkeep ['ʌpˌkip] *s.* mantenimiento, conservación; gastos de conservación o manutención.
upland [-lənd] *s.* terreno elevado, tierra alta; meseta, altiplanicie. *—a.* 1. alto; de tierras elevadas. 2. rústico.
upland cotton, algodón de altura.
uplander [-ləndər, B -də] *s.* montañés; persona de las tierras altas.
uplift ['ʌpˌlɪft] *s.* 1. elevación, levantamiento. 2. (fig.) influencia edificante; exaltación moral; mejoramiento (cultural, social, etc.). 3. (geol.) levantamiento. 4. sostén (para el pecho). — [ʌp'lɪft] *v.t.* 1. elevar, edificar (esp. social, intelectual o moralmente). 2. alzar, levantar, elevar.
upmost ['ʌpˌmoʊst] *a.* más alto, más elevado; supremo, último, lo más (que se pueda).
upon [ə'pɔn, -'pɑn, B -'pɔn] *prep.* en, a; sobre, encima de; por; con; **to go u.,** guiarse por, ser guiado por, ej., *u. my advice,* por consejo mío; **u. my honor!** ¡a fe mía!; **u. my word!** por mi palabra!; **u.** (o **on**) the whole, mirándolo todo.
upper ['ʌpər, B -ə] *a.* 1. superior, más elevado, de arriba, de encima. 2. exterior.(ropa). 3. (geol.) superior. 4. (geog.) alto. 5. **the u. regions,** las regiones etéreas. *—s.* 1. pala del calzado; (*pl.*) cabezada (del calzado). 2. litera superior (en coche-cama o camarote de buques). 3. dentadura (postiza) superior. 4. (*pl.*) (G.B.) botines o polainas cortas de paño. 5. **on one's uppers,** sin dinero, en aprietos.
upper atmosphere, (meteor.) atmósfera superior, atmósfera de altura.
upper berth, litera superior (en coche cama o camarote de buques).
upper case, (impr.) caja alta.
uppercase [ˌʌpər'keɪs, B -ə'-] *a.* (impr.) mayúscula, versal, de caja alta (letra).

upper circle, (teat.) segundo piso, anfiteatro.
upper-class [ˌʌpər'klæs, B -ə'klɑs] *a.* 1. de las clases altas, aristocrático. 2. de los últimos años o grados (en las escuelas).
upper classes, clases altas.
upperclassman [-'klæmən, B -'klɑs-] *s.* estudiante de los últimos años o grados.
upper crust, (fam.) clases altas, alta sociedad.
uppercut ['ʌpərˌkʌt, B-əˌ-] *s.* (box) gancho de abajo arriba, uppercut. —*v.t., v.i.* asestar un gancho de abajo arriba (a).
upper echelongs, altas esferas.
upper hand, dominio, ventaja; maestría; **to get the u. h. (of),** obtener dominio (sobre), llegar a controlar; **to hold the u. h.,** llevar la voz cantante.
Upper House, cámara alta (del parlamento).
upper millstone, *s.* muela, corredera.
uppermost [-ˌmoʊst] *a.* 1. más alto, más elevado. 2. supremo, último. 3. predominante. —*adv.* en primer lugar; en posición predominante.
Upper Nile, Nilo Alto.
Upper Palatinate, (hist.) (el) Alto Palatinado, electorado del Sacro Imperio Romano.
upper regions, cielo, paraíso, el más allá.
upper story, 1. piso alto. 2. (hum., G.B.) cabeza, cerebro; **off one's u. s.,** chiflado, (que está) mal de la azotea.
upperworks ['ʌpərˌwɜrks, B -əˌwɜks] *s. pl.* (mar.) obra muerta.
uppish ['ʌpɪʃ] *a.* arrogante; orgulloso; encopetado, altivo, altanero, presumido.
uppishly [-lɪ] *adv.* altivamente, altaneramente.
uppishness [-nəs] *s.* altivez, altanería.
uppity ['ʌpətɪ] *a.* 1. (fam.) encopetado, altivo, altanero, presumido. 2. (E.U., despec.) que quiere salirse de su sitio, quo no se conforma con su posición social.
uppityness [-nəs] *a.* altivez, presuntuosidad.
upraise [ˌʌp'reɪz] *v.t.* levantar; elevar.
uprear [-'rɪr, B -'rɪə] *v.t.* levantar, exaltar; erigir. —*v.i.* levantarse.
upright ['ʌpˌraɪt] *a.* 1. derecho, vertical, enhiesto, recto. 2. (fig.) recto, probo, honesto, equitativo, justo. —*adv.* 1. verticalmente. 2. (fig.) rectamente, con justicia. —*s.* 1. montante, pie derecho, pierna, paral, soporte, apoyo. 2. piano vertical, piano recto. 3. (*pl.*) (fútbol) postes (del arco).
uprightly [-lɪ] *adv.* 1. verticalmente. 2. (fig.) rectamente, con justicia.
uprightness [-nəs] *s.* 1. verticalidad. 2. (fig.) rectitud.
upright piano, piano vertical.
upright projection, alzado, proyección vertical.
uprise [ˌʌp'raɪz] *v.t.* 1. levantarse. 2. subir, ascender. 3. crecer gradualmente (el sonido). 4. sublevarse. — ['ʌpˌraɪz] *s.* 1. levantamiento. 2. subida, pendiente.
uprising ['ʌpˌraɪzɪŋ, B ʌp'raɪ-] *s.* levantamiento, sublevación, sedición, insurrección.
uproar ['ʌpˌrɔr, B -ˌrɔ] *s.* tumulto, alboroto, conmoción.
uproarious [ʌp'rɔrɪəs] *a.* 1. tumultuoso, ruidoso, estruendoso. 2. hilarante.
uproariously [-lɪ] *adv.* 1. tumultuosamente, ruidosamente. 2. extremadamente (chistoso).
uproot [ˌʌp'rut] *v.t.* desarraigar, descuajar, descepar; (fig.) desarraigar.
uprooter [-ər, B -ə] *s.* desarraigador; extirpador.
ups and downs, altibajos, vaivenes, vicisitudes.
upset ['ʌpˌsɛt] *a.* trastornado, perturbado; enfadado. — [ʌp'sɛt] *v.t.* 1. volcar, tumbar. 2. desbaratar, desarreglar, dar al traste. 3. trastornar, perturbar; enfadar. 4. (mec.) recalcar. 5. (dep.) vencer inesperadamente. 6. **to u. the applecart,** arruinar todo. —*v.i.* volcarse. — ['ʌpˌsɛt] *s.* 1. vuelco. 2. contratiempo, trastorno. 3. malestar. 4. (mec.) recalco; recalcador. 5. (dep.) derrota o victoria inesperada; resultado sorprendente.
upset price, precio mínimo fijado, precio de base (en subasta o remate público).
upsetter [ʌp'sɛtər, B -ə] *s.* (mec.) prensa para cortar llantas.
upshot ['ʌpˌʃɑt, -ˌʃɔt] *s.* resultado, conclusión; **the u. of it is that,** total que.
upside [-ˌsaɪd] *s.* parte superior; lo de arriba.
upside down, al revés, con lo de arriba abajo, patas arriba; en confusión; **to turn everything u. d.,** poner todo en desorden.
upside-down [ˌʌpˌsaɪd'daʊn] *a.* al revés, invertido, revuelto.
upside-down cake, torta volteada, pastel aderezado con frutas en el fondo del molde.
upsilon ['jupsəˌlɑn, 'ʌp-, B jupˌsaɪlən] *s.* upsilón, vigésima letra del alfabeto griego.
upspring [ˌʌp'sprɪŋ] *v.i.* levantarse de un salto; brotar, nacer. — ['ʌpˌsprɪŋ] *s.* (ant.) salto, brinco en el aire.
upstage ['ʌp'steɪdʒ] *adv* al fondo de la escena, hacia el fondo de la escena. —*a.* 1. situado al fondo de la escena. 2. (fam.) altanero, arrogante. — [ʌp-] *v.t.* 1. desairar, tratar con altanería. 2. (teat.) robar la escena a.
upstairs ['ʌp'stɛrz, B -'stɛəz] *adv.* 1. arriba, en el piso de arriba. 2. en posición elevada. 3. (aer.) a mucha altura. —*a.* 1. de arriba; del piso alto. 2. arriba de las escaleras. —*s. pl.* (*sing. o pl. en const.*) piso de arriba; piso superior.
upstanding [ˌʌp'stændɪŋ] *a.* 1. derecho, erguido. 2. (fig.) recto, probo, honrado.
upstart [ʌp'stɑrt, B -'stɑt] *v.t., v.i.* sobre-saltar(se). — ['ʌpˌstɑrt, B -ˌstɑt] *a., s.* advenedizo, nuevo rico.
upstate ['ʌpˌsteɪt] (E.U.) *a* del área rural, de la región al norte (de un estado). —*s.* área rural, región norteña (de un estado esp. con relación a una ciudad).
upstater [-'steɪtər, B -ə] *a.* persona oriunda de la región norteña (de un estado), norteño, norteña.
upstream [-strim] *adv.* 1. aguas arriba, río arriba. 2. a contracorriente, contra la corriente.
upstroke [-ˌstroʊk] *s.* 1. trazo (de pluma, etc.) por arriba. 2. (mec.) carrera ascendente, carrera de ascenso.
upsurge [-ˌsɜrdʒ, B -ˌsɜdʒ] *s.* repunte, acrecencia súbita, ascenso rápido.
upsweep [ʌp'swip] *v.t., v.i.* empinar(se); encumbrar(se). — ['ʌpˌswip] *s.* 1. superficie inclinada hacia arriba; subida. 2. estilo de peinado (con el cabello en alto y recogido en la coronilla).
upswept ['ʌpˌswɛpt] *a.* 1. dirigido o curvado hacia arriba. 2. peinado hacia arriba (cabello).
upswing [ʌp'swɪŋ] *v.i.* mejorar, perfeccionarse. — ['ʌpˌswɪŋ] *s.* 1. vuelta hacia arriba, movimiento hacia arriba. 2. (com.) mejora, alza.
upsy-daisy ['ʌpsə'deɪzɪ] *interj.* **¡upa!**
uptake ['ʌpˌteɪk] *s.* 1. comprensión, entendimiento, captación. 2. canal de salida de la chimenea; tubo o conducto de ventilación. 3. **quick on the u.,** rápido para entender, inteligente; **slow on the u.,** duro de mollera, lento para el entender.
upthrow [-ˌθroʊ] *s.* (geol.) solevantamiento.
upthrust [-ˌθrʌst] *s.* 1. levantamiento. 2. (geol.) solevantamiento.
up-to-date [ˌʌptə'deɪt] *a.* 1. (que va) hasta la fecha; reciente. 2. de última moda; moderno. 3. **to bring up-to-d.,** poner al corriente (a alguien); poner al día (algo).
up-to-dateness [-nəs] *s.* modernidad.
uptown ['ʌp'taʊn] *adv.* 1. hacia el norte de la ciudad. 2. hacia el distrito residencial (de una ciudad). —*a.* 1. de los barrios al norte (en una ciudad). 2. del distrito residencial.
uptrend [-ˌtrɛnd] *s.* tendencia ascendente.
upturn [ʌp'tɛrn, B -'tɜn] *v.t., v.i.* 1. volver(se) hacia arriba. 2. trastornar(se), volcar(se). — ['ʌpˌtɜrn, B -ˌtɜn] *s.* 1. vuelta hacia arriba. 2. (com.) mejora, alza.
upturned nose, nariz respingona.
UPU *abrev. de* **Universal Postal Union,** Unión Postal Universal.
upward ['ʌpwərd, B -wəd] *adv.* 1. hacia arriba. 2. hacia el interior. 3. más arriba, encima. 4. desde, ej., *from his youth u.,* desde su juventud. 5. **and u.,** y más (todavía); **u. of,** más de. —*a.* hacia arriba; ascendente, ej., *prices show an u. tendency,* los precios muestran una tendencia ascendente.
upwardly [-lɪ] *adv.* ascendentemente.
upwards [-wərdz, B -wədz] *adv. var. de* upward.
upwind ['ʌp'wɪnd] *adv.* contra el viento. —*a.* contrario al viento.
uracil ['jʊrəsɪl] *s.* (quím.) uracilo.
uraemia, uraemic, *var. de* **uremia, uremic.**
uraeus [jʊ'riəs] *s.* (*pl.* URAEI [-ˌaɪ]) (relig. egipcia) símbolo de áspide sagrado.
Ural-Altaic [ˌjʊrəlˌæl'teɪɪk, B ˌjʊər-] *a.* uralo-altaico, uraloaltaico, uralaltaico (grupo de idiomas).
Uralian [jʊ'reɪlɪən] *a.* de los Urales.
uralite ['jʊrəˌlaɪt, B 'jʊər-] *s.* (min.) uralita.
uranalysis, *var. de* **urinalysis.**
uranate ['jʊrəˌneɪt, B 'jʊər-] *s.* (quím.) uranato.
Urania [jʊ'reɪnɪə] *s.* (mitol.) Urania, musa de la astronomía.
Uranian [-nɪən] *a.* uranio, celestial.
uranic [jʊ'rænɪk] *a.* (quím.) uránico.
uranide ['jʊrəˌnaɪd, B 'jʊər-] *s.* (quím.) uranio.
uraninite [jʊ'rænəˌnaɪt] *s.* (min.) uraninita.
uranite ['jʊrəˌnaɪt, B 'jʊər-] *s.* (min.) uranita.
uranium [jʊ'reɪnɪəm] *s.* (quím.) uranio.
uranocircite [ˌjʊrənoʊ'sɜrˌsaɪt, B ˌjʊər-'sɜˌ-] *s.* (min.) uranocircita.
uranographer [ˌjʊrə'nɑgrəfər, B -'nɔg-fə] *s.* uranógrafo.
uranographist [-fəst] *s.* uranógrafo.
uranography [-fɪ] *s.* uranografía.
uranolite [jʊ'rænəˌlaɪt] *s.* (geol.) uranolito, uranófana.
uranological [ˌjʊrənoʊ'lɑdʒɪkəl, B ˌjʊər-'lɔdʒ-] *a.* uranológico.
uranology [-'nɑlədʒɪ, B -'nɔl-] *s.* uranología.
uranometry [-'nɑmətrɪ, B -'nɔm-] *s.* uranometría.
uranophane [jə'rænəˌfeɪn] *s.* (min.) uranofano, uranofana.
uranospinite [ˌjʊrə'nɑspəˌnaɪt, B ˌjʊərə'nɔs-] *s.* (min.) uranospinita.
uranothallite [-noʊ'θæˌlaɪt] *s.* (min.) uranotalita.
uranothorite [-noʊ'θɔrˌaɪt] *s.* (min.) uranotorita.
uranotil [jə'rænəˌtɪl] *s.* (min.) uranotilo.
uranous [jʊ'reɪnəs, B 'jʊərə-] *a.* (quím.) uranoso.
Uranus ['jʊrənəs, B 'jʊər-] *s.* (mitol.) Urano, personificación del cielo, padre de los titanes.
uranyl ['jʊrəˌnɪl, B 'jʊər-] *s.* (quím.) uranilo.
urate ['jʊrˌeɪt, B 'jʊər-] *s.* (quím.) urato.
urban ['ɜrbən, B 'ɜbən] *a.* urbano, característico de la ciudad.

urban district, distrito urbano.
urbane [ˌɜr'beɪn, B ɜ'-] *a.* cortés, urbano.
urbanely [-lɪ] *adv.* cortésmente, urbanamente.
urbaneness [-nəs] *s.* urbanidad, cortesía.
urbanism ['ɜrbəˌnɪzəm, B 'ɜbə-] *s.* 1. modo de vivir urbano, costumbres urbanas. 2. urbanismo. 3. urbanización.
urbanist [-nəst] *s.* urbanista.
urbanite [-ˌnaɪt] *s.* habitante de la ciudad, ciudadano.
urbanity [ɜr'bænətɪ, B ɜ'-] *s.* (*pl.* URBANITIES) urbanidad, cortesía.
urbanization [ˌɜrbənə'zeɪʃən, B ˌɜbənaɪ-] *s.* urbanización.
urbanize ['ɜrbəˌnaɪz, B 'ɜbə-] *v.t.* urbanizar.
urbiculture [-ˌkʌltʃər, B -tʃə] *s.* cultura urbana, asuntos urbanos.
urceolate ['ɜrsɪələt, B 'ɜsɪ-] *a.* (bot.) urceolado.
urceolus [ˌɜr'siələs, B ɜ'-] *s.* (*pl.* URCEOLI [-laɪ]) (bot.) urceólo.
urchin ['ɜrtʃən, B 'ɜtʃɪn] *s.* 1. (zool.) erizo. 2. (zool.) erizo de mar. 3. rapacejo, chiquillo, pilluelo, golfillo.
Urdu ['ʊrˌdu, 'ɜr-, B 'ʊədu] *s.* urdu, lenguaje derivado del hindi, idioma oficial de Paquistán.
urea [jʊ'riə, B 'jʊərɪə] *s.* (bioquím.) urea.
ureal [-'riəl, B -rɪəl] *a.* (bioquím.) ureal.
urease ['jʊrɪˌeɪs, B 'jʊər-] *s.* (bioquím.) ureasa.
Uredinales [jʊˌrɛdə'neɪliz, B -ˌridɪ-] *s. pl.* (bot.) uredinales, uredíneas.
uredinium [ˌjʊrə'dɪnɪəm, B ˌjʊər-] *s.* (*pl.* UREDINIA [-ə]) uredinio.
uredinous [jʊ'rɛdənəs, B -'ridɪ-] *a.* (bot.) uredíneo, uredinal.
urediospore [jʊ'ridɪəˌspɔr, B -ˌspɔ] *s.* (bot.) uredospora.
uredium [-dɪəm] *s.* (*pl.* UREDIA [-ə]) (bot.) uredio.
uredo [jʊ'riˌdoʊ] *s.* (med.) uredo.
ureide ['jʊrɪˌaɪd, B 'jʊər-] *s.* (quím.) ureído.
uremia [jʊ'rimɪə, B jʊə-] *s.* (med.) uremia.
uremic [-mɪk] *a.* (med.) urémico.
ureter [ˌjʊ'ritər, B -tə] *s.* (anat.) uréter.
ureteral [-tərəl] **ureteric** [ˌjʊrə'tɛrɪk, B jʊər-] *a.* (anat.) ureteral, uretérico.
urethan ['jʊrəˌθæn, B 'jʊər-] **urethane** [-θeɪn] *s.* (quím.) uretano.
urethra [ju'riθrə, B jʊə-] *s.* (*pl.* URETHRAE [-θri] o URETHRAS) (anat.) uretra.
urethral [-θrəl] *a.* (anat.) uretral.
urethritis [ˌjʊrɪ'θraɪtəs, B ˌjʊər-] *s.* (med.) uretritis.
urethroscope [jʊ'riθrəˌskoʊp, B jʊə-] *s.* (med.) uretroscopio.
urethroscopy [ˌjʊrɪ'θrɑskəpɪ, B ˌjʊərɪ'θrɔs-] *s.* (med.) uretroscopía.
uretic [jə'rɛtɪk, B jʊə-] *a.* (anat.) urético.
urge [ɜrdʒ, B ɜdʒ] *v.t.* 1. instar, exhortar. 2. impeler, incitar, estimular. 3. impulsar, impeler, empujar; apresurar, apremiar. 4. recomendar, propugnar o pedir con insistencia (medidas, acción, etc.). 5. insistir en, destacar. —*v.i.* 1. (con *for, against,* etc.) abogar (por), argüir (contra). 2. apresurarse, ir rápidamente. —*s.* impulso, instinto.
urgency ['ɜrdʒənsɪ, B 'ɜdʒən-] *s.* urgencia, premura.
urgent [-dʒənt] *a.* urgente, apremiante, perentorio.
urgently [-lɪ] *adv.* urgentemente.
urger ['ɜrdʒər, B 'ɜdʒə] *s.* el que apremia o acucia.
urging [-ɪŋ] *s.* apremio, instancia.
uric ['jʊrɪk, B 'jʊər-] *a.* (fisiol., quím.) úrico.

urinal [-ənəl] *s.* 1. orinal. 2. urinario, urinal.
urinalysis [ˌjʊrə'næləsəs, B jʊər-] *s.* (med.) urinálisis, uranálisis.
urinary ['jʊrəˌnɛrɪ, B 'jʊərɪnərɪ] *a.* urinario, relativo a la orina y a los órganos que la producen o expelen.
urinary bladder, (anat.) vejiga urinaria, vejiga de la orina.
urinary calculus, (med.) cálculo urinario.
urinary tract, (anat.) vías urinarias.
urinate ['jʊrəˌneɪt, B 'jʊər-] *v.i.* orinar.
urination [ˌjʊrə'neɪʃən, B jʊər-] *s.* urinación.
urine ['jʊrən, B 'jʊər-] *s.* orina, orines.
uriniferous [ˌjʊrə'nɪfərəs, B jʊər-] *a.* (anat.) urinífero.
urinogenital [-noʊ'dʒɛnətəl] *a.* (anat.) urinogenital, urogenital.
urinometer [-'nɑmətər, B -'nɔmɪtə] *s.* urinómetro.
urinous ['jʊrənəs, B 'jʊər-] **urinose** [-ˌnoʊs] *a. urinoso, urinario.*
urn [ɜrn, B ɜn] *s.* 1. urna. 2. jarra, cafetera, tetera.
urobilin [ˌjʊrə'baɪlən, B jʊər-] *s.* (bioquím.) urobilina.
urochrome ['jʊrəˌkroʊm, B 'jʊər-] *s.* (bioquím.) urocromo.
urocyst [-ˌsɪst] *s.* (anat.) urocisto.
Urodela [ˌjʊrə'dilə, B jʊər-] *s. pl.* (zool.) urodelos.
urodelan [-lən] *s.* (zool.) urodelo.
urodele ['jʊrəˌdil, B 'jʊər-] *s.* (zool.) urodelo.
urodynia [ˌjʊrə'dɪnɪə, B jʊər-] *s.* (med.) urodinia.
urogenital [ˌjʊroʊ'dʒɛnətəl, B jʊər-] *a.* (anat.) urogenital.
urogenous [jə'rɑdʒənəs, B -'rɔdʒ-] *a.* (fisiol.) urógeno.
urography [-'rɑgrəfɪ, B -'rɔg-] *s.* urografía.
urolith ['jʊrəˌlɪθ, B 'jʊər-] *s.* (med.) urolito.
urolithiasis [ˌjʊrələ'θaɪəsəs, B ˌjʊər-] *s.* (med.) urolitiasis.
urolithic [-'lɪθɪk] *a.* (med.) urolítico.
urologic [-'lɑdʒɪk, B -'lɔdʒ-] **urological** [-ɪkəl] *a.* urológico.
urologist [jʊ'rɑlədʒəst, B jʊə'rɔl-] *s.* (med.) urólogo.
urology [-dʒɪ] *s.* (med.) urología.
uropatagium [ˌjʊroʊpə'teɪdʒɪəm, B ˌjʊər-] *s.* (zool.) uropatagio.
urophein [ˌjʊrə'fiən, B jʊər-] *s.* (bioquím.) urofeína.
uropod ['jʊrəˌpɑd, B 'jʊərəpɔd] *s.* (zool.) urópodo.
uropoiesis [ˌjʊrəˌpɔɪ'isəs, B ˌjʊər-] *s.* (med.) uropoyesis.
uropygial [-'pɪdʒɪel] *a., s.* (orn.) uropigio.
uropygial gland, (orn.) glándula uropigia.
uropygium [-əm] *s.* (orn.) uropigio.
uroscopic [-'skɑpɪk, B -'skɔp-] *a.* (med.) uroscópico.
uroscopist [jʊ'rɑskəpəst, B jʊə'rɔs-] *s.* (med.) uroscopista.
uroscopy [-kəpɪ] *s.* (med.) uroscopia.
urosis [jʊ'roʊsəs, B jʊə-] *s.* (med.) urosis.
urotoxy ['jʊrəˌtɑksɪ, B 'jʊərəˌtɔk-] *s.* (fisiol.) urotoxia.
uroxanthin [ˌjʊrə'zænθɪn, B jʊər-] *s.* (bioquím.) uroxantina.
ursa ['ɜrsə, B 'ɜsə] *s.* (zool.) osa.
Ursa Major, (astr.) Osa Mayor.
Ursa Minor, (astr.) Osa Menor.
ursine ['ɜrˌsaɪn, B 'ɜˌ-] *a.* ursino, osuno, propio del oso.
ursine baboon, (zool.) chacma.
ursine dasyure [-'dæsɪjʊr, B -jʊə] (zool.) dasiuro.

ursine howler, (zool.) araguato, aluato, carayá, mono aullador.
Ursuline ['ɜrsələn, B 'ɜsjʊlaɪn] *s., a.* (relig.) ursulina.
urticaceous [ˌɜrtə'keɪʃəs, B ˌɜtɪ-] *a.* (bot.) urticáceo.
urticant ['ɜrtəkənt, B 'ɜtɪ-] *a.* (med.) urticante.
urticaria [ˌɜrtə'kɛrɪə, B ˌɜtɪ'kɛər-] *s.* (med.) urticaria.
urticate ['ɜrtəˌkeɪt, B 'ɜtɪ-] *v.t.* 1. producir comezón (como las ortigas). 2. causar urticaria.
urtication [ˌɜrtə'keɪʃən, B ˌɜtɪ-] *s.* (med.) urticación.
urubu [ˌʊrə'bu] *s.* (orn.) urubú.
urucu [ˌʊrə'ku] *s.* (bot.) urucú.
Uruguay ['jʊrəˌgwaɪ, B 'ʊrʊ-] *s.* el Uruguay.
Uruguayan [ˌjʊrə'gwaɪən, B ˌʊrʊ-] *a., s.* uruguayo.
urus ['jʊrəs, B 'jʊər-] *s.* (zool.) uro.
us [ʌs] *pron.* (*caso complementario de* **we**) nos; nosotros, nosotras.
US *abrev. de* **United States,** Estados Unidos.
USA *abrev. de* 1. **United States of America,** Estados Unidos de Norteamérica (E.U.). 2. **United States Army,** Ejército de los Estados Unidos.
usability [ˌjuzə'bɪlətɪ] *s.* valor práctico, utilidad.
usable ['juzəbəl] *a.* servible, utilizable, usable, aprovechable, practicable.
usableness [-nəs] *s.* valor práctico, utilidad.
usable range, (rad.) gama utilizable de frecuencia.
USAF *abrev de* **United States Air Force,** Fuerza Aérea de los Estados Unidos.
usage ['jusɪdʒ, B -zɪdʒ] *s.* 1. uso, usanza, costumbre. 2. trato, tratamiento. 3. uso común, empleo (de una palabra o frase en un sentido particular).
usance ['juzəns] *s.* 1. (com.) plazo (a que se debe pagar una letra de cambio en el exterior). 2. (ant.) uso; empleo; costumbre; interés (pagado por dinero).
Usbek,Usbeg, *vars. de* **Uzbek, Uzbeg.**
USCG *abrev. de* **United States Coast Guard,** Guardacostas de los Estados Unidos.
use [juz] *v.t.* 1. usar, emplear, utilizar, hacer uso de, valerse de. 2. consumir, gastar, desgastar. 3. tratar, portarse con, proceder con. 4. **ill-use,** maltratar, abusar; **u. bad language,** renegar, blasfemar; **u. one's own judgment,** usar su propio criterio; **u. up,** consumir, agotar; **you may u. my name,** puede referirse a mí, puede dar mi nombre como referencia. —*v.i.* (*ú solamente en pret., esp. seguido de* **to**) soler, acostumbrar, ej., *I used to take the bus,* yo solía tomar el ómnibus, *didn't u. to answer,* no acostumbraba contestar. — [jus] *s.* 1. uso, empleo, aplicación. 2. uso, usanza, costumbre; práctica, hábito. 3 (der.) uso, usufructo; goce. 4. utilidad, provecho; objeto, finalidad. 5. rito, liturgia. 6. **in u.,** en uso; usándose; **no u.,** inútil, de nada sirve; que no viene al caso; **out of u.,** fuera de uso; fuera de moda; **to be of no u.,** ser inservible, ser inútil; **to have no u. for,** no tener ocasión de emplear (algo); no necesitar; no gustarle a uno, no aguantar, detestar; **to make u. of,** hacer uso de, usar de, valerse de; utilizar (algo); aprovecharse de (alguien); **to put to u.,** poner en servicio, poner en uso; **what's the use?** ¿para qué? ¿qué importa?
useable, useableness, *vars. de* **usable, usableness.**
used [just] *a.* 1. habituado, acostumbrado. 2. [juzd] usado, gastado, viejo, de segunda mano. 3. **to be u. to,** estar acostumbrado a; **to get u.**

to, habituarse a, acostumbrarse a; **u. up,** agotado; avejentado.
useful ['jusfəl] *a.* 1. útil, provechoso, beneficioso, ventajoso. 2. (jer., G.B.) excelente, eficaz.
usefully [-fəlɪ] *adv.* útilmente, provechosamente, ventajosamente.
usefulness [-fəlnəs] *s.* utilidad, provecho.
useless [-ləs] *a.* inútil, inservible; ineficaz, inepto.
uselessly [-lɪ] *adv.* inútilmente.
uselessness [-nəs] *s.* inutilidad.
user ['juzər, B -zə] *s.* 1. consumidor, comprador. 2. (der.) usuario.
user friendly, fácil de usar.
usher ['ʌʃər, B -ə] *s.* 1. ujier, conserje, portero. 2. aposentador, acomodador (en cine, teatro, etc.) 3. (ant.) profesor o instructor auxiliar, profesor asistente (de colegio). 4. (G.B.) sotamaestro. —*v.t.* 1. acomodar, aposentar. 2. **u. in,** introducir, anunciar; escoltar.
USIA *abrev. de* **United States Information Agency,** Agencia de Información de los Estados Unidos.
USM *abrev. de* **United States Mail,** Correos de los Estados Unidos.
USMC *abrev. de* **United States Marine Corps,** Infantería de Marina de los Estados Unidos.
USN *abrev. de* **United States Navy,** Marina de los Estados Unidos.
USNR *abrev. de* **United States Naval Reserve,** Reserva Naval de los Estados Unidos.
usquebaugh ['ʌskwɪˌbɔ] *s.* whiski (de Irl. y Esco.).
U.S.S. *abrev. de* **United States Ship,** Buque de los Estados Unidos.
USSR *abrev. de* **Union of Soviet Socialist Republics,** (hist.) Unión de Repúblicas Socialistas Soviéticas (URSS).
ustulation [ˌʌstʃə'leɪʃən, B -tjʊ-] *s.* (farm.) ustulación.
usual ['juʒʊəl, 'juʒəl] *a.* usual, acostumbrado, corriente, habitual; **as u.,** como de costumbre; **the u.,** lo de siempre (refiriéndose a comidas, bebidas, etc.).
usually [-əlɪ] *adv.* usualmente, por lo general, por regla general, acostumbradamente, habitualmente.
usucapion [ˌjuzə'keɪpɪən, B juzjʊ-] *s.* (der. romano) usucapión.
usucapt ['juzəˌkæpt, B 'juzjʊ-] *v.t.* (der. romano) usucapir.
usufruct [-ˌfrʌkt] (der.) *s.* usufructo. —*v.t.* usufructuar.
usufructuary [ˌjuzə'frʌktʃʊˌɛrɪ, B ˌjuzjʊ-tjʊərɪ] (der.) *s.* usufructuario, usufructuador. —*a.* usufructuario, usuario.
usurer ['juʒərər, B -ə] *s.* usurero, logrero.
usurious [jʊ'ʒʊrɪəs, B -'zjʊər-] *a.* usurero, logrero, con usura.
usuriously [-lɪ] *adv.* usurariamente.
usurp [jʊ'sɜrp, B -'zɜp] *v t.* usurpar, arrebatar, arrogarse. —*v.i.* **u. on** (o **upon**), desposeer; cometer usurpación.
usurpation [ˌjusər'peɪʃən, B -zə'-] *s.* usurpación (esp. del poder soberano).
usurper [jʊ'sɜrpər, B -'zɜpə] *s.* usurpador, usurpadora.
usury ['juʒərɪ] *s.* usura, logro, interés excesivo (por un préstamo); **to practice u.,** usurear, usurar.
ut [ʌt, B ʊt] *s.* (mús.) ut, do.
Ut. *abrev. de* **Utah,** Utah (E.U.).
Utah ['juˌtɔ, -tɑ] *s.* Utah, estado de los E.U.
Ute [jut] *s.* (*pl.* UTE o UTES) ute, yute, tribu de indios de E.U.
utensil [jʊ'tɛnsəl] *s.* utensilio; (*pl.*) útiles.
uterine ['jutərən, B -raɪn] *a.* (anat.) uterino.
uterus ['jutərəs] *s.* (*pl.* UTERI [-ˌaɪ]) (anat.) útero.
utile ['jutəl, B -taɪl] *a.* (ant.) útil, práctico, provechoso.
utilitarian [jʊˌtɪlə'tɛrɪən, B ˌjutɪlə'tɛər-] *a.* 1. utilitario. 2. (filos.) utilitarista. —*s.* (filos.) utilitario, utilitarista.
utilitarianism [-ɪzəm] *s.* (filos.) utilitarismo.
utility [jʊ'tɪlətɪ] *s.* 1. utilidad, conveniencia, provecho. 2. (t. **public u.**) (empresa de) servicio público. 3. (*pl.*) (com.) servicios públicos (acciones de una empresa de servicio público). —*a.* 1. de uso práctico; de calidad corriente. 2. suplente.
utilizable ['jutəˌlaɪzəbəl] *a.* utilizable, aprovechable.
utilization [ˌjutələ'zeɪʃən, B -laɪ-] *s.* utilización, aprovechamiento.
utilize ['jutəˌlaɪz] *v.t.* utilizar, aprovechar, valerse de, servirse de.
utilizer [-ər, B -ə] *s.* utilizador.
utmost ['ʌtˌmoʊst] *a.* 1. extremo, más distante. 2. sumo, máximo, ej., *he did it with the u. care,* lo hizo con sumo (o máximo) cuidado. —*s.* lo sumo, lo mayor, lo más, lo máximo, lo más posible; **one's u.,** lo más que uno puede hacer; **to do one's u.,** hacer todo lo posible; **to the u.,** a más no poder.
Uto-Aztecan [ˌjuˌtoʊ'æzˌtɛkən] *a.* uto-azteca, uteazteca, grupo de diferentes tribus indias de E.U. que descienden de un tronco común.
utopia [jʊ'toʊpɪə] *s.* 1. utopía. 2. **U.,** Utopía, isla imaginaria descrita por Santo Tomás Moro.
utopian [-pɪən] *a.* utópico. —*s.* utopista, visionario.
utopianism [-əˌnɪzəm] *s.* idea utópica.
utopian socialism, (hist., pol.) socialismo utópico.
utopism ['jutəˌpɪzəm] *s.* ideas utopistas, filosofía utopista.
utricle ['jutrɪkəl] *s.* (anat., bot.) utrículo.
utricular [jʊ'trɪkjələr, B -lə] *a.* (anat., bot.) utricular.
utriculate [-lət] *a.* utriculado.
utriculitis [jʊˌtrɪkjə'laɪtəs] *s.* (med.) utriculitis.
utriculus [jʊ'trɪkjələs] *s.* (anat.) utrículo.
utter ['ʌtər, B -ə] *a.* completo, total, entero, absoluto, cabal; **u. nonsense,** tontería consumada.
utter, *v.t.* 1. pronunciar, articular, expresar, decir. 2. revelar, divulgar. 3. poner en circulación, emitir (esp. moneda falsa, documentos falsos, etc.).
utterable [-ərəbəl] *a.* articulable, decible, pronunciable.
utterance [-ərəns] *s.* 1. pronunciación, expresión. 2. declaración, aserción, dicho. 3. lenguaje, estilo. 4. emisión (esp. de moneda o documentos falsos).
utterance, *s.* (ant.) último suspiro, muerte.
utterer [-ərər, B -ərə] *s.* 1. pronunciador, divulgador. 2. el que hace circular (moneda falsa, etc.).
utterly ['ʌtərlɪ, B -əlɪ] *adv.* totalmente, completamente, absolutamente, enteramente.
uttermost [-ˌmoʊst] *a.* 1. extremo, más distante. 2. sumo, máximo. —*s.* lo sumo, lo mayor, lo máximo, lo más.
U-tube ['juˌtub, B -ˌtjub] *s.* tubo en U.
uvanite ['juvəˌnaɪt] *s.* (min.) uvanita.
uvarovite [jʊ'vɑrəˌvaɪt, B -'vær-] *s.* (min.) uvarovita.
uvea ['juvɪə] *s.* (anat.) úvea.
uveal [-vɪəl] *a.* (anat.) uveal.
uveal tunica, (anat.) túnica uveal.
uveitic [ˌjuvɪ'ɪtɪk] *a.* (med.) uveítico.
uveitis [ˌjuvɪ'aɪtəs] *s.* (med.) uveítis.
uviol glass ['juˌvaɪəl-] (ópt.) lente uviol, vidrio transparente a los rayos ultravioletas.
uvula ['juvjələ] *s.* (*pl.* UVULAS o UVULAE [-ˌli]) (anat.) úvula.
uvular [-lər, B -lə] *a.* (anat., fon.) uvular. —*s.* (fon.) sonido uvular.
uvulitis [ˌjuvjə'laɪtəs] *s.* (med.) uvulitis.
uxorial [ʌk'sɔrɪəl] *a.* uxorio, de la esposa.
uxoricide [-əˌsaɪd] *s.* 1. uxoricida (marido que mata a su esposa). 2. uxoricidio.
uxorious [-ɪəs] *a.* excesivamente amoroso con su (propia) esposa, (demasiado) sumiso a su esposa.
uxoriously [-əslɪ] *adv.* con complacencia excesiva (para la esposa).
uxoriousness [-əsnəs] *s.* complacencia (con la esposa).
Uzbek ['ʊzˌbɛk, B 'ʌz-] **Uzbegs** [-ˌbɛgz] *s.* 1. uzbeco, miembro de un grupo de pueblos sedentarios del Turquestán. 2. lenguaje de estos pueblos.
Uzbekistan [ʊzˌbɛkɪ'stæn, B ʌz-] *s.* Uzbekistán, república de la Unión Soviética, en Asia central.

V

V [vi] v, vigésima segunda letra del alfabeto inglés.
v *s.* (fam.) billete de cinco dólares. —*a.* en forma de v; **v. motor,** (aut.) motor de cilindros convergentes o en v; **v. tool,** cincel para ranuras triangulares.
V *símb. de* **vanadium,** vanadio (V).
Va. *abrev. de* **Virginia,** Virginia (E.U.).
V.A. *abrev. de* **Vice-Admiral,** Vicealmirante.
v.a. *abrev. de* **volt-ampere,** voltamperio.
vacancy ['veɪkənsɪ] *s.* (*pl.* VACANCIES) 1. vacancia, vacante (cargo o empleo vacantes). 2. vacío, vacuidad. 3. (raro) ocio, desocupación. 4. **V.,** se alquila (casa, cuarto, local, etc.).
vacant [-kənt] *a.* 1. vacante (oficio, empleo); desocupado (casa, trono, etc.); baldío (terreno). 2. desocupado, ocioso, ej., *a few v. hours,* unas pocas horas ociosas. 3. vago, inexpresivo (ej., mirada); vacuo, vacío (mente, interés, pensamiento).
vacantly [-lɪ] *adv.* vagamente, sin expresión.
vacate ['veɪˌkeɪt, veɪ'keɪt, B və-] *v.t.* 1. dejar vacante, desocupar, evacuar. 2. (der.) anular, invalidar, revocar, rescindir. —*v.i.* vacar, irse, salir, marcharse.
vacation [veɪ'keɪʃən, B və-] *s.* 1. vacación, vacaciones, asueto. 2. suspensión, cesación, receso (de actividades). 3. **to be on v.,** estar de vacaciones.
vacationer [-ər, B -ə] **vacationist** [-əst] *s.* persona que está de vacaciones; veraneante.
vaccinal ['væksənəl, B væk'saɪn-] *a.* (med.) vacunal.
vaccinate ['væksəˌneɪt] *v.t.* (med.) vacunar, inocular; inmunizar.
vaccination [ˌvæksə'neɪʃən] *s.* (med.) vacunación, inoculación, inmunización.
vaccinator ['væksəˌneɪtər, B -ə] *s.* (med.) vacunador (persona o instrumento).
vaccine [væk'sin, B 'vækˌsin] *a.* 1. vacuna. 2. vacunal. —*s.* vacuna.
vaccine lymph, (med.) linfa vacuna.
vaccine therapy, vacunoterapia.
vaccinia [væk'sɪnɪə] *s.* (med.) vaccinia.
vacciniaceous [vækˌsɪnɪ'eɪʃəs] *a.* (bot.) vaccinieo.
vacillant ['væsələnt] *a.* vacilante.
vacillate ['væsəˌleɪt] *v.i.* 1. vacilar, oscilar; fluctuar, ondear. 2. vacilar, titubear, hesitar.
vacillating [-ɪŋ] *a.* 1. vacilante; irresoluto, inconstante. 2. fluctuante, oscilante.
vacillatingly [-lɪ] *adv.* con vacilación, vacilantemente.
vacillation [ˌvæsə'leɪʃən] *s.* 1. vacilación, oscilación. 2. vacilación, irresolución, titubeo. 3. fluctuación, vaivén.
vacillatory ['væsələˌtɔrɪ, B -tərɪ] *a.* vacilatorio.
vacua, *pl. de* **vacuum.**
vacuity [væ'kjuətɪ, və-] *s.* (*pl.* VACUITIES) 1. vacuidad. 2. vacío, hueco. 3. vaciedad, inanidad, fatuidad; inexpresividad.
vacuo ['vækjuˌoʊ, B -jʊ-] *s.* el vacío; **in v.,** en el vacío.
vacuolar [ˌvækjʊ'oʊlər, B -lə] *a.* (biol.) vacuolar.
vacuolate ['vækjʊəˌleɪt] **vacuolated** [-əd] *a.* (biol.) vacuolado.
vacuolation [ˌvækjʊə'leɪʃən] *s.* (biol.) vacuolización.
vacuole ['vækjʊˌoʊl] *s.* (biol.) vacuola.
vacuous ['vækjʊəs] *a.* 1. vacuo, vacío. 2. necio, fatuo. 3. vacío, ocioso.
vacuousness [-nəs] *s.* 1. vacuidad. 2. necedad, fatuidad.
vacuum ['vækjʊəm, -jʊm] *s.* (*pl.* VACUUMS o VACUA [-jʊə]) vacío. —*a.* 1. vacuo, vacío. 2. al vacío, de vacío. 3. aspirante. —*v.t.* (fam.) limpiar con aspiradora de polvo.
vacuum booster, multiplicador de fuerza al vacío.
vacuum bottle, v. flask, termo (recipiente, botella).
vacuum brake, freno de vacío, freno neumático, vacuofreno.
vacuum cleaner, aspiradora (de polvo), barredora eléctrica.
vacuum drier, desecador a vacío.
vacuum filter, filtro al vacío.
vacuum gauge, vacuómetro, manómetro al vacío.
vacuumize ['vækjəˌmaɪz, B -jʊə-] *v.t.* 1. producir vacío en, vaciar de aire. 2. limpiar al vacío; secar o envasar al vacío.
vacuum-packed [ˌvækjʊəm'pækt] *a.* envasado al vacío.
vacuum pan, tacho al vacío.
vacuum pump, bomba aspirante, bomba de vacío.
vacuum seal, sellado al vacío.
vacuum tube, (electrón.) tubo al vacío, tubo de vacío.
vacuum valve, ventosa al vacío, válvula de vacío.
vade mecum ['veɪdɪ'mikəm] (*pl.* VADE MECUMS) vademécum, cartera, portafolio; libreta de apuntes.
V. Adm. *abrev. de* **Vice-Admiral,** Vicealmirante.
vagabond ['vægəˌbɑnd, B -ˌbɔnd] *a., s.* 1. vagabundo, errante. 2. gitano. —*v.i.* vagabundear, vagar.
vagabondage [-ɪdʒ] *s.* 1. vagabundaje, vagabundeo, vagancia. 2. vagabundos (en conjunto).
vagabondish [-ɪʃ] *a.* de vagabundo.
vagabondism [-ˌɪzəm] *s.* vagabundeo (colectivo).
vagabondize [-ˌaɪz] *v.i.* vagabundear.
vagal ['veɪgəl] *a.* (anat.) vagal (nervio).
vagarious [və'gɛrɪəs, -'gær-, B -'gɛər-] *a.* caprichoso, antojadizo.
vagary ['veɪgərɪ] *s.* (*pl.* VAGARIES) capricho, antojo, humorada, extravagancia, excentricidad.
vagile ['vædʒel, B -ˌaɪl] *a.* ágil, ligero.
vagina [və'dʒaɪnə] *s.* (*pl.* VAGINAE [-ni] o VAGINAS) 1. (anat.) vagina. 2. (bot.) vaina.
vaginal ['vædʒənəl, B və'dʒaɪnəl] *a.* (anat.) vaginal.
vaginalectomy [ˌvædʒənə'lɛktəmɪ] *s.* (med., cir.) vaginalectomía.
vaginate ['vædʒəˌneɪt] **vaginated** [-əd] *a.* 1. vaginado. 2. envainado, enfundado.
vaginicolous [ˌvædʒə'nɪkələs] *a.* (med.) vaginícola.
vaginitis [-'naɪtəs] *s.* (med.) vaginitis.
vaginotomy [-'nɑtəmɪ, B -'nɔt-] *s.* (cir.) vaginotomía.
vaginula [və'dʒɪnjələ, B -'dʒaɪn-] *s.* vagínula.
vagitus [-'dʒaɪtəs] *s.* (med.) vagido (primer grito del recién nacido).
vagotomy [veɪ'gɑtəmɪ, B -'gɔt-] *s.* (med.) vagotomía.
vagotonia [ˌveɪgə'toʊnɪə] *s.* (med.) vagotonía.
vagotropic [-'trɑpɪk, B -'trɔp-] *a., s.* (med.) vagotrópico, vagotropo.
vagrancy ['veɪgrənsɪ] *s.* vagancia, vagabundeo.
vagrant [-grənt] *s.* vagabundo, vagamundo, vago, pelafustán, pelagatos. —*a.* vagabundo, vagamundo, vago.
vagrantly [-lɪ] *adv.* (poét.) vagarosamente.
vague [veɪg] *a.* vago, indefinido, incierto, impreciso, dudoso.
vaguely ['veɪglɪ] *adv.* vagamente, indefinidamente, inciertamente, imprecisamente.
vagueness [-nəs] *s.* vaguedad, imprecisión.
vagus ['veɪgəs] *s.* (*pl.* VAGI [-dʒaɪ]) (anat.) vago, nervio vago.
vail [veɪl] (ant.) *v.i.* aprovecharse, beneficiarse, obtener ganancia. —*s.* gratificación, propina.
vail, (ant.) *v.t.* 1. bajar, dejar caer, sumergir, dejar sumergir. 2. quitar (sombrero, etc.).
vain [veɪn] *a.* 1. vano, insubstancial. 2. vano, fútil, inútil, estéril, infructuoso. 3. vanidoso, envanecido; vacío; presumido, ostentoso, fantasioso; frívolo. 4. (raro) insignificante, mezquino, miserable. 5. (ant.) tonto, bobo. 6. **in v.,** en vano.
vainglorious [veɪn'glɔrɪəs] *a.* vanaglorioso, jactancioso.
vaingloriously [-lɪ] *adv.* vanagloriosamente, jactanciosamente.
vaingloriousness [-nəs] *s.* vanagloria, jactancia.
vainglory ['veɪnˌglɔrɪ, B ˌveɪn'glɔrɪ] *s.* vanagloria, jactancia.
vainly ['veɪnlɪ] *adv.* vanamente; inútilmente.
vainness [-nəs] *s.* vanidad; inutilidad, futilidad, envanecimiento.
vair [vɛr, B vɛə] *s.* vero, marta cebellina (piel); (her.) vero.
valance ['væləns] *s.* 1. cenefa; doselera. 2. guardamalleta.
valanced [-ənst] *a.* con cenefa.
vale [veɪl] *s.* (poét.) val, valle. —*interj.* (lat.) ¡adiós!
valediction [ˌvælə'dɪkʃən] *s.* vale, adiós, despedida.
valedictorian [-dɪk'tɔrɪən] *s.* (E.U.) alumno que pronuncia el discurso de despedida.
valedictory [-'dɪktərɪ] *a.* de despedida. —*s.* (*pl.* VALEDICTORIES) discurso de despedida.
valence ['veɪləns] *s.* (quím.) valencia.
Valencian [və'lɛntʃɪən, B -'lɛnʃɪ-] *a., s.* valenciano, de Valencia.
Valenciennes [vəˌlɛnsɪ'ɛnz, B ˌvælənsɪ'ɛn] *s.* (fr.) encaje de Valenciennes.
valentine ['vælənˌtaɪn] *s.* 1. enamorado o enamorada (esp. a quien se envía saludos el día de San Valentín). 2. misiva que se envía el día de San Valentín.

Valentine Day, Valentine's Day, día de San Valentín (14 de febrero); (E.U.) día de los enamorados.
vale of tears, valle de lágrimas.
valerate ['vælə,reɪt] *s.* (quím.) valerato, valerianato.
valerian [və'lɪrɪən, B -'lɪər-] *s.* (bot.) valeriana.
valerianaceous [-,lɪrɪə'neɪʃəs, B -,lɪər-] *a.* (bot.) valerianáceo.
valerianate [və'lɪrɪə,neɪt, B -'lɪər-] *s.* (quím.) valerianato.
valeric acid [-'lɪrɪk-, B -'lɪər-] (quím.) ácido valérico.
valet ['vælət, væ'leɪ, B 'vælɪt] *s.* (fr.) asistente (personal o criado, camarero; paje de hotel). —*v.t.* servir como criado o camarero.
valet de chambre, (fr.) ayuda de cámara.
valetudinarian [,vælə,tudən'ɛrɪən, B -,tjudɪ'nɛər-] *a., s.* valetudinario, enfermizo, impedido, delicado.
valetudinarianism [-,ɪzəm] *s.* estado valetudinario.
valetudinary [-'tudən,ɛrɪ, B -'tjudɪnərɪ] *a.* valetudinario, enfermizo. —*s.* (raro) valetudinario, valetudinaria.
valgus ['vælgəs] *s.* (med.) valgus (esp. de los pies). —*a.* torcido hacia afuera.
Valhalla [væl'hælə] *s.* (mitol.) Valhala, refugio paradisíaco donde los dioses germánicos reciben a los héroes caídos en batalla.
vali ['vɑlɪ] *s.* valí (gobernador musulmán).
valiance [væljəns] *s.* (ant.) bravura, valentía, valor.
valiant [-jənt] *a., s.* valiente, valeroso, bravo.
valiantly [-lɪ] *adv.* valientemente.
valiantness [-nəs] *s.* valentía, bravura.
valid ['væləd] *a.* 1. valedero. 2. (der.) válido, vigente (contrato, etc.).
validate ['vælə,deɪt] *v.t.* validar; ratificar, confirmar.
validation [,vælə'deɪʃən] *s.* validación; ratificación, confirmación.
validity [və'lɪdətɪ] *s.* validez, valor.
validly ['vælədlɪ] *adv.* válidamente, valederamente.
validness [-nəs] *s.* validez.
valine ['væl,in] *s.* (quím.) valina.
valise [və'lis, B -'liz] *s.* (fr.) maleta, valija, saco de viaje.
Valkyrie [væl'kɪrɪ, B -'kɪərɪ] *s.* (mitol.) valquiria, doncella del dios Odín en la saga germánica.
vallate ['væl,eɪt] *a.* vallado, cercado.
vallation [væ'leɪʃən] *s.* (ant.) muralla, vallado, valladar.
vallecula [væ'lɛkjələ] *s.* (*pl.* VALLECULAE [-,li]) (anat., bot.) valécula.
vallecular [-lər, B -lə] *a.* (anat., bot.) valecular.
valleculate [-lət] *a.* (anat., bot.) valeculado.
valley ['vælɪ] *s.* 1. valle, cuenca. 2. (arq.) lima hoya.
valor, (G.B.) **valour** ['vælər, B -ə] *s.* valor, valentía, coraje, ánimo, brío.
valorization [,vælərə'zaɪʃən, B -raɪ-] *s.* valorización.
valorize ['vælə,raɪz] *v.t.* valorar, valorizar.
valorous ['vælərəs] *a.* valeroso, valiente.
valorously [-lɪ] *adv.* valerosamente, valientemente.
valorousness [-nəs] *s.* valentía, valor.
valse [vɑls] *s.* (fr.) (mús.) vals, valse.
valuable ['væljʊəbəl, 'væljə-] *a.* valioso, costoso; estimable, apreciable. —*s. pl.* objetos de valor, objetos preciados.
valuable consideration, (der.) causa valiosa, causa onerosa.
valuableness [-nəs] *s.* alto valor.
valuably [-blɪ] *adv.* útilmente, valiosamente.
valuate ['væljʊ,eɪt] *v.t.* avaluar, avalorar, valorar, tasar.
valuation [,væljʊ'eɪʃən] *s.* 1. valuación, evaluación, valoración, valorización; tasación, avalúo. 2. valor estimado, precio fijado. 3. apreciación, estimación.
valuational [-əl] *a.* de valoración, de avalúo.
valuator ['væljʊ,eɪtər, B -ə] *s.* tasador, avaluador.
value ['vælju] *s.* 1. valor, valía, mérito, aprecio. 2. lo que vale (alguien o algo) ej., *he learnt the v. of a true friend,* se dio cuenta de lo que vale un amigo leal. 3. valor, precio, coste, monta, importe. 4. (arte) valor (proporción luminosa de una parte de una pintura). 5. (mús.) valor, duración (de una nota). —*v.t.* 1. valorar, valorizar, avaluar, tasar. 2. apreciar, considerar, estimar, tener en mucho.
value-added tax['vælju'ædəd] impuesto al valor agregado, impuesto sobre el valor añadido (Esp.).
valued [-jud] *a.* apreciado, estimado, ej., *v. friend,* amigo apreciado, *a painting v. at ten thousand dollars,* un cuadro estimado en diez mil dólares.
value in account, (ten.) valor en cuenta.
value increase, plusvalía.
valueless ['væljuləs] *a.* 1. sin valor, inútil, inservible. 2. insignificante, baladí; fútil, despreciable.
valuer [-ər, B -ə] *s.* valuador, tasador.
value received, (com.) valor recibido.
valuta [və'lutə] *s.* (econ.) valuta.
valval ['vælvəl] *a.* valvular, valvar, relativo a las valvas o válvulas.
valvate ['væl,veɪt, B -vɪt] *a.* (bot., zool.) valvado, valvulado, valvular.
valve [vælv] *s.* 1. (anat.) válvula. 2. (bot.) ventalla, valva. 3. (zool.) valva. 4. (mús.) válvula de llave. 5. (pr. G.B.) (electrón.) válvula, tubo electrónico. 6. (mec.) válvula, llave.
valve amplifier, (electrón.) amplificador de válvulas.
valve box, (mot.) caja de válvulas, caja de distribución.
valve cap, (aut.) tapón de válvula, capuchón de válvula (de neumáticos).
valve chest, (mot.) caja de distribución.
valve gear, (mot.) mecanismo de distribución (por válvulas); aparejo de válvula.
valve grinder, (maq.) amoldadora de asientos de máquina, refrenador o rectificador de válvulas.
valve-in-head engine ['vælvən'hɛd-] motor con válvulas en la culata.
valveless ['vælvləs] *a.* sin válvulas.
valve lift, (mec.) alza o carrera de válvula.
valve lifter, (mec.) levantaválvulas, desmontaválvulas.
valve refacer, refrentador de válvulas.
valve rod, (mec.) vástago de válvula; (mot.) vástago del distribuidor.
valve seat, (mec.) asiento de la válvula.
valve spring, (mec.) muelle de válvula.
valve stem, (mot.) vástago de válvula; barra del distribuidor, varilla de distribución.
valve travel, (mec.) carrera de la válvula; carrera del distribuidor.
valve trimmings, (mot.) guarniciones o reglajes de la válvula.
valve trombone, trombón de pistones.
valviform ['vælvə,fɔrm, B -,fɔm] *a.* valviforme.
valvula ['vælvjələ] *s.* (*pl.* VALVULAE [-,li]) (anat.) válvula.
valvular [-lər, B -lə] *a.* valvular.
valvulate [-,leɪt] *a.* valvulado.
valvule [-vjul, B -vjʊl] *s.* valvulilla.
valvulitis [,vælvjə'laɪtəs] *s.* (med.) valvulitis.
vambrace ['væm,breɪs] *s.* (arm.) avambrazo.
vamoose [væ'mus, B və-] *v.i.* (jer.) marcharse, largarse, irse precipitadamente.
vamp [væmp] *s.* 1. empella, pala, cabezada (del zapato). 2. remiendo, parche. 3. (mús.) acompañamiento a ritmo pero improvisado. —*v.t.* 1. poner empella en. 2. (mús.) acompañar con improvisación, improvisar. 3. **v. up,** remendar, parchar, fraguar, inventar (excusa, etc.).
vamp, (jer.) *s.* vampiresa, aventurera. —*v.t.* seducir, tentar; engatusar.
vamper ['væmpər, B -ə] *s.* remendón.
vampire ['væm,paɪr, B -,paɪə] *s.* 1. vampiro. 2. (fig.) vampiro, explotador, parásito, chupador (Amer.). 3. vampiresa, aventurera. 4. (teat.) escotillón pequeño. 5. (zool.) vampiro (murciélago americano).
vampirism [-,ɪzəm, B -,paɪər-] *s.* 1. vampirismo (creencia en los vampiros). 2. (fig.) vampirismo.
vamplate ['væm,pleɪt] *s.* (arm.) arandela (en lanza).
van [væn] *s.* 1. camión de mudanzas, camión de carga cubierto, carromato. 2. (f.c.) furgón de carga, galera.
van, *s.* 1. (dial.) bioldo. 2. (poét.) ala. 3. (mil.) vanguardia.
vanadate ['vænə,dəɪt] *s.* (quím.) vanadato, vanadiato.
vanadic [və'neɪdɪk, B -'næd-] *a.* (quím.) vanádico.
vanadic acid, (quím.) ácido vanádico.
vanadinite [-ən,aɪt] *s.* (min.) vanadinita.
vanadium [-'neɪdɪəm] *s.* (quím.) vanadio.
vanadium steel, acero de vanadio, acero al vanadio.
vanadous [və'neɪdəs, B 'vænə-] *a.* (quím.) vanadioso.
Van Allen radiation belt [væn'ælən-] (fís.) cinturón de Van Allen, capa de Van Allen.
Vandal ['vændəl] *a.* vándalo, vandálico. —*s.* vándalo, vándala; (fig.) vándalo, destructor.
vandalism [-,ɪzəm] *s.* vandalismo.
vandalistic [,vændəl'ɪstɪk] *a.* vandálico.
Vandyke [væn'daɪk] *s.* 1. barba puntiaguda. 2. valona (cuello o capa a lo Van Dyck).
vane [veɪn] *s.* 1. veleta (para indicar la dirección del viento), giraldilla. 2. aspa (de molino); paleta (de hélice). 3. barbas (de pluma). 4. pluma estabilizadora (en el extremo de la flecha). 5. (const.) tablilla de mira (del cuadrante), pínula. 6. (mar.) grímpola, cataviento; pínula.
vaned [veɪnd] *a.* provisto de veleta, aspa de molino, paleta o hélice.
vaned disc, (mec.) rueda de paletas.
vang [væŋ] *s.* (mar.) osta.
vanguard ['væn,gɑrd, B -,gɑd] *s.* vanguardia, avanzada.
vanguardism [-,ɪzəm] *s.* (lit.) vanguardismo.
vanguardist [-əst] *s., a.* vanguardista.
vanilla [və'nɪlə] *s.* (*pl.* VANILLAS) (bot.) vainilla.
vanilla bean, (vaina de la) vainilla.
vanillic [və'nɪlɪk] *a.* vainíllico.
vanillin [-ən] *s.* (quím.) vainillina.
vanish ['vænɪʃ] *v.i.* desaparecer, desvanecerse, esfumarse, disiparse; **v. into thin air,** (fig.) hacerse humo, desaparecer.
vanishing cream [-ɪŋ-] crema de base (cosmético que no deja huella cuando se frota en el cutis).
vanishing point, (dib.) punto de (la) vista, punto de fuga.

vanity ['vænətɪ] *s.* (*pl.* VANITIES) 1. cosa vana, cosa fútil o inútil. 2. vanidad, futilidad. 3. vanidad, vanagloria, presunción, engreimiento, envanecimiento; ostentación. 4. neceser; estuche de polvos, estuche de afeites, polvera de bolsillo. 5. (**t. vanity table**) tocador.
vanity box, v. case, neceser.
vanity fair, 1. (lit.) feria de vanidades. 2. el mundo social.
vanning test ['vænɪŋ-] (quím.) ensayo por agitación.
vanquish ['væŋkwɪʃ] *v.t.* 1. vencer, conquistar, derrotar; subyugar. 2. (fig.) dominar, subyugar (pasiones, etc.).
vanquishable [-əbəl] *a.* vencible, conquistable, subyugable.
vanquisher [-ər, B -ə] *s.* vencedor, conquistador.
vantage ['væntɪdʒ, B 'vɑnt-] *s.* 1. ventaja. 2. posición ventajosa, superioridad. 3. (tenis) ventaja.
vantage ground, posición o situación ventajosa.
vantage point, 1. lugar ventajoso; posición ventajosa. 2. (dep.) punto.
vanward ['vænwərd, B -wəd] *a.* de vanguardia, delantero.
vapid ['væpəd] *a.* insípido, soso, insulso.
vapidity [væ'pɪdətɪ] *s.* insipidez, sosera, insulsez.
vapidly ['væpədlɪ] *adv.* insípidamente, insulsamente, sosamente.
vapidness [-nəs] *s.* insipidez, sosera, insulsez.
vapor, (G.B.) **vapour** ['veɪpər, B -pə] *s.* 1. vapor, vaho. 2. niebla, bruma; humo; exhalación, hálito, tufo. 3. quimera, sueño, fantasmagoría. 4. (ant.) (*pl.*) vapores (acceso de hipocondría). —*v.i.* 1. vaporear, vaporar, avahar. 2. vaporizarse, evaporarse. 3. jactarse, alardear, baladronear; disparatar.
vapor bath, baño de vapor.
vapor heating, calefacción a vapor.
vaporific [,veɪpə'rɪfɪk] *a.* vaporífero, vaporoso.
vaporing, (G.B.) **vapouring** ['veɪpərɪŋ] *a.* 1. que vaporea, que evapora. 2. jactancioso. —*s.* (*gen. pl.*) jactancia, baladronada(s), alarde(s); disparate(s).
vaporish [-ɪʃ] *a.* 1. vaporoso. 2. (fig.) melancólico, hipocondríaco.
vaporizable ['veɪpə,raɪzəbəl] *a.* vaporable, evaporable.
vaporization [,veɪpərə'zeɪʃən, B -raɪ-] *s.* vaporización.
vaporize ['veɪpə,raɪz] *v.t.* vaporizar, vaporar, vaporear, evaporar, volatizar. —*v.i.* 1. vaporizarse, vaporarse, vaporearse, evaporarse. 2. jactarse, alardear, baladronear; disparatar.
vaporizer [-,raɪzər, B -zə] *s.* vaporizador, pulverizador.
vapor lock, (mot.) bolsa de vapor.
vaporous ['veɪpərəs] *a.* 1. vaporoso, gaseoso, etéreo; nebuloso, brumoso. 2. (fig.) fugaz, insubstancial; caprichoso, quimérico.
vaporousness [-nəs] *s.* vaporosidad.
vapor pressure, v. tension, (fís.) presión de vapor.
vapor trail, (aer.) estela de vapor.
vapory, (G.B.) **vapoury** ['veɪpərɪ] *a.* 1. vaporoso. 2. vago, indefinido, borroso (contornos, etc.).
vaquero [vɑ'kɛroʊ, B -'kɛər-] *s.* (*pl.* VAQUEROS) (neol.) vaquero, pastor de ganado vacuno.
var [vɑr, B vɑ] *s.* (elec.) voltamperio reactivo.
var. *abrev. de* **variant,** variante.
vara ['vɑrə] *s.* vara (medida de longitud).
var-hour-meter ['vɑr,aʊr-, B -aʊə,-] *s.* varhorímetro.
variability [,vɛrɪə'bɪlətɪ, B ,vɛər-] *s.* variabilidad.
variable ['vɛrɪəbəl, B 'vɛər-] *a.* 1. variable, cambiable. 2. variable, alterable, veleidoso, inestable, inconstante, mudable, tornadizo. —*s.* 1. (mat.) variable, cantidad variable. 2. (mar.) viento variable; (*pl.*) región de vientos variables; calmas.
variable capacitor, v. condenser, (elec.) condensador variable.
variable gear, (ing.) engranaje de multiplicación variable.
variable inductor, (elec.) inductor variable.
variable motion, (mec.) movimiento variado.
variableness [-nəs] *s.* variabilidad, inconstancia, ligereza.
variable pitch, (aer.) paso regulable.
variable quantity, (mat.) cantidad variable.
variable-speed gear ['vɛrɪəbəl,spid-, B 'vɛər-] (mot.) engranaje de velocidad regulable.
variable star, (astr.) estrella (de magnitud) variable.
variable time fuse, espoleta de tiempos, espoleta de proximidad.
variably ['vɛrɪəblɪ, B 'vɛər-] *adv.* 1. variablemente. 2. alternativamente.
variance ['vɛrɪəns, B 'vɛər-] *s.* 1. variación, diferencia, desviación. 2. disensión, discrepancia, desavenencia. 3. **to be at v. (with),** estar en desacuerdo (con), discrepar (con), reñir (con).
variant [-ənt] *a.* 1. variante, diferente, vario. 2. discrepante. 3. (raro) variable, cambiable. —*s.* variante.
variate [-,eɪt] *s.* (estadística) variable.
variation [,vɛrɪ'eɪʃən, B ,vɛər-] *s.* 1. variación, cambio, mutación, variedad, mudanza. 2. (mat., astr., biol., mús., aer.) variación. 3. (gram.) inflexión.
variational [-əl] *a.* de variación, con variación.
variative ['vɛrɪ,eɪtɪv, B 'vɛər-] *a.* de variación, variable.
varicella [,værə'sɛlə] *s.* (med.) varicela.
variceloid [-,ɔɪd] *a.* (med.) variceloide.
varices, *pl. de* **varix.**
varicocele ['værəkə,sil] *s.* (med.) varicocele.
varicolored, (G.B.) **varicoloured** ['vɛrɪ,kʌlərd, B 'vɛər-əd] *a.* multicolor, polícromo, de varios colores; abigarrado.
varicose ['værə,koʊs] *a.* (med.) varicoso.
varicosis [,værə'koʊsəs] *s.* (med.) varicosis.
varicosity [-'kɑsətɪ, B -'kɔs-] *s.* varicosidad.
varicotomy [-'kɑtəmɪ, B -'kɔt-] *s.* (med.) varicotomía, varicectomía.
varied ['vɛrɪd, B 'vɛər-] *a.* variado, vario; diverso.
variegate ['vɛrɪə,geɪt, B 'vɛər-] *v.t.* 1. jaspear, abigarrar, vetear. 2. (fig.) variar, dar variedad a, diferenciar; diversificar.
variegated [-əd] *a.* abigarrado, jaspeado, veteado, entrelistado; matizado; rayado.
variegation [,vɛrɪə'geɪʃən, B ,vɛərɪ'geɪ-] *s.* variedad de colores; jaspeadura, abigarramiento, veteado.
varietal [və'raɪətəl] *a.* 1. relativo a la variedad. 2. de distinta variedad, ej., vino que lleva el nombre de la variedad de uva.
variety [və'raɪətɪ] *s.* (*pl.* VARIETIES) 1. variedad, diversidad. 2. variedad, surtido. 3. (teat.) variedades. 4. (biol.) variedad. 5. **v. is the spice of life,** en la variedad está el gusto.
variety meat, vísceras, entrañas comestibles.
variety show, (teat.) función de variedades.
variety store, bazar (esp. de artículos baratos).
variform ['vɛrə,fɔrm, B 'vɛərɪ,fɔm] *a.* diversiforme.
variocoupler ['vɛrɪoʊ,kʌplər, B 'vɛərɪə-lə] *s.* (elec.) varioacoplador.
variola [,vɛrɪ'oʊlə, B və'raɪə-] *s.* (med.) viruela.
variolar [-lər, B -lə] *a.* (med.) varioloso, variólico.
variolate ['vɛrɪə,leɪt, B 'vɛər-] *a.* (med.) parecido a la viruela (como lesión).
variolation [,vɛrɪə'leɪʃən, B ,vɛər-] *s.* (med.) variolación, variolización.
variole ['vɛrɪ,oʊl, B 'vɛər-] *s.* 1. (bot.) fóvea. 2. (min.) esférula (de variolita).
variolic [vɛrɪ'ɑlɪk, B ,vɛərɪ'ɔl-] *a.* variólico.
variolite ['vɛrɪə,laɪt, B 'vɛər-] *s.* (min.) variolita.
varioloid [,vɛrɪ'oʊ,lɔɪd, B 'vɛərɪə-] *s.* (med.) varioloide.
variolous [-ləs, B və'raɪə-] *a.* (med.) 1. varioloso, variólico. 2. varioloso, afectado de viruela. 3. con cicatrices como las que deja la viruela.
variometer [,vɛrɪ'ɑmətər, B -'ɔmɪtə] *s.* (elec.) variómetro.
variorum [-'ɔrəm] *s.* edición o texto anotados. —*a.* 1. anotado, con notas (texto o libro). 2. de varias fuentes.
various ['vɛrɪəs, B 'vɛər-] *a.* 1. vario, diverso, variado, diferente, mudable. 2. varios, numerosos, múltiples. 3. (ant.) inconstante, cambiable.
variously [-lɪ] *adv.* variamente; diversamente.
variousness [-nəs] *s.* variedad, diversidad.
varisized ['vɛrɪ,saɪzd, B 'vɛər-] *a.* de varios tamaños.
varistor [væ'rɪstər, B və'rɪstə] *s.* (rad.) varistor.
varix ['værɪks, B 'vɛər-] *s.* (*pl.* VARICES ['værə,siz]) (med.) varice, variz, várice.
varlet ['vɑrlət, B 'vɑlɪt] *s.* 1. bribón, pícaro, truhán, golfo. 2. (ant.) lacayo, sirviente; paje.
varletry [-lətrɪ] *s.* (ant.) canalla, populacho, chusma.
varmeter ['vɑr,mitər, B 'vɑ,-] *s.* (elec.) contador de voltamperios reactivos.
varmint ['vɑrmənt, B 'vɑmɪnt] *s.* 1. canalla, bribón. 2. sabandija, zorro (Amer.).
varnish ['vɑrnɪʃ, B 'vɑnɪʃ] *v.t.* 1. barnizar, embarnizar. 2. (fig.) embellecer (la verdad, etc.); paliar, mitigar (culpa, etc.); disimular. —*s.* 1. barniz, charol; capa de barniz. 2. mogate, vidriado. 3. (fig.) brillo exterior, apariencia; paliación, embellecimiento.
varnisher [-ər, B -ə] *s.* barnizador, charolista.
varnish tree, (bot.) variedad de árboles que producen laca y resinas de las que se hace el barniz.
varsity ['vɑrsətɪ, B 'vɑsɪ-] *s.* 1. universidad. 2. (dep.) equipo titular (de la universidad). —*a.* 1. universitario. 2. que representa la universidad.
varsoviana [,vɑrsoʊ'vjɑnə, B ,vɑsoʊ-] **varsovienne** [-'vjɛn, B -vɪ'ɛn] *s.* (mús.) varsoviana, danza y música polacas parecidas a la mazurca.
varus ['vɛrəs, B 'vɛər-] *s.* (med.) pie zambo o contrahecho, esp. pie talus o calcáneo. —*a.* varus (díc. esp. de las extremidades inferiores); estevado, patiestevado, patituerto.
varve [vɑrv, B vɑv] *s.* (geol.) varve.
vary ['vɛrɪ, B 'vɛərɪ] *v.t.* (*pret., p.p.* VARIED; *p.pr.* VARYING) 1. variar, cambiar, mudar; diversificar; discrepar. 2. (mús.) variar (de ritmo, armonía, intervalo, etc.). —*v.i.* 1. variar, cambiar, alterarse; alternar. 2. (con *from*) diferenciarse, diferir, desviarse (de).
varying [-ɪŋ] *a.* variante, variable.
varying hare, (zool.) liebre mímica.
varyingly [-lɪ] *adv.* variablemente.
varying motion, (mec.) movimiento variado.

vas [væs] *s.* (anat.) vaso, conducto.
vascular ['væskjələr, B -lə] *a.* (anat., bot., zool.) vascular, vasculoso.
vascular bundle, (bot.) fascículo vascular.
vascularity [ˌvæskjə'lærətɪ] *s.* (anat., bot., zool.) vascularidad.
vascular plants, (bot.) plantas vasculares.
vascular tissue, (bot.) tejido vascular.
vasculose ['væskjəˌlous] *a.* (bot.) vasculoso.
vasculum ['væskjələm] *s.* (*pl.* VASCULA [-lə]) caja de lata usada por botánicos para recoger plantas.
vas deferens ['væs'dɛfərənz] (anat., zool.) conducto deferente.
vase [veɪs, veɪz, B vɑz] *s.* jarrón, vaso; florero.
vasectomy [væs'ɛktəmɪ] *s.* (med.) vasectomía.
Vaseline (TM) ['væsəˌlin, ˌvæsə'lin] *s.* vaselina.
vasiform ['veɪsəˌfɔrm, B 'veɪzəˌfɔm] *a.* vasiforme, en forma de vaso.
vasoconstriction [ˌveɪzoukən'strɪkʃən, ˌveɪs-, ˌvæs-, B ˌvæs-] *s.* (fisiol.) vasoconstricción.
vasoconstrictive [-'strɪktɪv] *a.* (fisiol.) vasoconstrictor.
vasoconstrictor [-tər, B -tə] *a.* (fisiol.) vasoconstrictor.
vasodilatation [-ˌdɪlə'teɪʃən, B -ˌdaɪleɪ-] *s.* (fisiol.) vasodilatación.
vasodilator [-daɪ'leɪtər, B -ə] *a.* (fisiol.) vasodilatador.
vasoinhibitor [-ɪn'hɪbətər, B -ə] *s.* (fisiol.) (agente o droga) vasoinhibidor.
vasoinhibitory [-əˌtɔrɪ, B -ɪtərɪ] *a.* (fisiol.) vasoinhibidor.
vasomotor [-'moutər, B 'veɪz-ə] *a.* (fisiol.) vasomotor.
vasopressin [-'prɛsən] *s.* (fisiol.) vasopresina.
vasospasm ['veɪzouˌspæzəm, 'væs-, B 'veɪs-] *s.* (fisiol.) vasospasmo, espasmo vascular.
vasospastic [ˌveɪzou'spæstɪk, ˌvæs-, B 'veɪs-] *a.* (fisiol.) vasospástico.
vasovagal [-'veɪgəl] *a.* (fisiol.) vasovagal.
vassal ['væsəl] *s.* 1. (hist.) vasallo. 2. (fig.) vasallo, siervo, esclavo. —*a.* 1. vasallo. 2. servil, tributario.
vassalage [-ɪdʒ] *s.* 1. vasallaje. 2. (fig.) servidumbre, dependencia (esp. política).
vast [væst, B vɑst] *a.* 1. vasto, amplio, espacioso, dilatado, extenso. 2. vasto, inmenso, enorme. 3. (ant.) yermo, baldío, desierto. —*s.* 1. (poét.) inmensidad, infinito. 2. (dial., G.B.) gran cantidad.
vastitude ['væstəˌtud, B 'vɑstɪˌtjud] *s.* vastedad, inmensidad.
vastity [-tətɪ] *s.* (*pl.* VASTITIES) (raro) vastedad, inmensidad.
vastly ['væstlɪ, B 'vɑst-] *adv.* en sumo grado, sumamente, muy, muchísimo, vastamente.
vastness [-nəs] *s.* vastedad, inmensidad.
vasty ['væstɪ, B 'vɑs-] *a.* (ant.) inmenso, enorme.
VAT *abrev. de* **value-added tax,** impuesto al valor agregado (IVA).
vat [væt] *s.* tina, tanque, cuba. —*v.t.* (*pret., p.p.* VATTED; *p.pr.* VATTING) poner o tratar en una tina o cuba.
vat dye, colorante de cuba o de tina.
vat-dyed ['væt'daɪd] *a.* teñido con colorantes de tina.
vatic ['vætɪk] *a.* profético, vaticinador, agorero.
Vatican ['vætɪkən] *s.* Vaticano. —*a.* vaticano, del Vaticano.
Vatican City, Ciudad del Vaticano.
vaticide ['vætəˌsaɪd] *s.* asesino o asesinato de un profeta.
vaticinal [və'tɪsənəl, B væ-] *a.* profético, profetal.
vaticinate [-ˌeɪt] *v.i., v.t.* vaticinar, profetizar, predecir; adivinar, pronosticar, augurar.
vaticination [-ˌtɪsə'neɪʃən] *s.* vaticinio, pronóstico, presagio, augurio.
vaticinator [-'tɪsənˌeɪtər, B -ə] *s.* vaticinador.
vat paper, papel de tina, papel de mano.
vaudeville ['vɔdvəl, B 'voudəvɪl] *s.* (teat.) variedades, teatro de variedades; función de variedades.
vaudevillian [ˌvɔd'vɪljən, B ˌvoud-] (teat.) *s.* escritor o artista de teatro de variedades. —*a.* de variedades.
Vaudois [vou'dwɑ, B 'voudwɑ] *s. pl.* (fr.) (relig.) valdenses.
vault [vɔlt] *s.* 1. bóveda, cúpula, cimborrio. 2. cueva, bodega, subterráneo, sibil. 3. cripta, tumba. 4. (anat.) bóveda. 5. (fig.) firmamento, cielo. —*v.t.* (arq.) voltear, abovedar.
vault, *s.* 1. salto con garrocha, salto con pértiga. 2. salto, corcovo (de un caballo). —*v.t.* saltar con garrocha o pértiga; saltar (un obstáculo, cerco, etc.) apoyándose en la(s) mano(s).
vaulted ['vɔltəd] *a.* abovedado, arqueado.
vaulter [-tər, B -tə] *s.* saltador con garrocha, volteador.
vaulting [-tɪŋ] *s.* construcción abovedada, bóveda.
vaulting, *a.* 1. saltador. 2. de salto, usado para saltar (en ejercicios gimnásticos).
vaulting-horse [-ˌhɔrs, B -ˌhɔs] *s.* caballo de salto, potro de madera (para gimnasia).
vaulty ['vɔltɪ] *a.* como una bóveda, abovedado.
vaunt [vɔnt, vɑnt, B vɔnt] *v.i.* vanagloriarse, jactarse, alardear, ufanarse. —*v.t.* jactarse de, ostentar. —*s.* 1. jactancia, alarde, ostentación. 2. fanfarronada, palanganada (Amer.).
vaunt-courier ['vɔnt'kurɪər, 'vɑnt-, B 'vɔnt-ə] *s.* (fr.) 1. precursor, explorador. 2. (ant.) soldado de una avanzada.
vaunter [-ər, B -ə] *s.* jactancioso, fanfarrón, blasonador; farolón (Amer.).
vauntful [-fəl] *a.* jactancioso, vanaglorioso, fanfarrón.
vauntingly [-ɪŋlɪ] *adv.* jactanciosamente, fanfarronamente.
vaunty ['vɔntɪ] *a.* (VAUNTIER; VAUNTIEST) (Esco.) orgulloso; vano, vanidoso; jactancioso.
vaward ['vɑˌwɔrd, B -wəd] *s.* (ant.) vanguardia (de tropas); frente, puesto delantero.
V belt, (mec.) correa trapezoidal o en V, banda V.
V branch, bifurcación.
VC *abrev. de* **Viet Cong,** Vietcong.
VCR *abrev. de* **videocassette recorder,** magnetoscopia, video.
VD *abrev. de* **venereal disease,** enfermedad venérea.
V-Day ['viˌdeɪ] *s.* día de la victoria, día del triunfo.
VDU *abrev. de* **visual display unit,** (comput.) pantalla (de visualización), monitor, terminal.
've [v, əv] *contr. de* **have.**
VE *abrev. de* **victory in Europe,** victoria en Europa.
veal [vil] *s.* (carne de) ternera.
veal chop, v. cutlet, chuleta de ternera.
veal pie, pastel de ternera.
vealer ['vilər, B -lə] *s.* ternero cuya carne es apropiada para comer.
vectograph ['vɛktəˌgræf, B -ˌgrɑf] *s.* (ing.) vectógrafo.
vector ['vɛktər, B -tə] *s.* 1. (biol.) vector, portador. 2. (mat.) vector. 3. (astr.) radio vector.
vector addition, adición geométrica o de vectores.
vector algebra, algebra vectorial.
vector analysis, (mat.) análisis vectorial.
vector field, (mat.) campo vectorial.
vectorial [vɛk'tɔrɪəl] *a.* (mat.) vectorial.
vector potential, (mat.) potencial vector.
vector product, (mat.) producto vectorial.
vector sum, (mat.) suma vectorial.
Veda ['veɪdə] *s.* Veda, texto sagrado del hinduismo; (*pl.*) los cuatro libros sagrados del hinduismo.
Vedaic [və'deɪɪk] *a.* védico, relativo al Veda.
Vedantic [veɪ'dɑntɪk, B vɛ'dæn-] *a.* 1. (filos.) vedantista. 2. védico.
Vedantism [-ˌtɪzəm] *s.* (filos.) vedantismo.
Vedantist [-təst] *s.* vedantista.
vedette [vɪ'dɛt] *s.* 1. (mil.) centinela de avanzada. 2. vedette, estrella de teatro, artista de fama.
Vedic ['veɪdɪk] *a.* védico, de los vedas (forma pristina del Sánscrito).
veep [vip] *s.* (fam.) vicepresidente.
veer [vɪr, B vɪə] *v.i.* 1. desviarse; cambiar de dirección, cambiar de condición o posición (a otra). 2. (meteor.) variar (el viento en el mismo sentido de las agujas del reloj). 3. (mar.) virar, rolar. —*v.t.* virar, dirigir (el buque) a otro rumbo. —*s.* cambio (de curso, dirección, etc.); desviación.
veer, *v.t.* (mar.) arriar, aflojar, largar (cabo, cadena del ancla, etc.); **v. and haul,** halar a estrepadas; (fig.) vacilar, titubear.
veery ['vɪrɪ, B 'vɪərɪ] *s.* (*pl.* VEERIES) (orn.) (variedad de) tordo norteamericano.
vegetable ['vɛdʒtəbəl, 'vɛdʒətəbəl] *a.* vegetal. —*s.* vegetal, verdura, hortaliza, legumbre.
vegetable butter, manteca o mantequilla vegetal.
vegetable garden, huerto de legumbres, huerto de verduras.
vegetable hair, v. horsehair, crin vegetal.
vegetable ivory, 1. marfil vegetal. 2. (nuez de) tagua.
vegetable kingdom, reino vegetal.
vegetable market, verdulería.
vegetable marrow, (bot.) calabacín.
vegetable mold, tierra vegetal, mantillo.
vegetable oil, aceite vegetal.
vegetable plate, plato de legumbres (sin carne).
vegetable soup, sopa de verduras.
vegetable stew, menestra, potaje de verduras.
vegetable tallow, grasa vegetal (usada en la elaboración de velas o jabón).
vegetable wax, cera vegetal.
vegetal ['vɛdʒətəl] *a.* 1. vegetal. 2. (biol.) vegetativo, vegetante.
vegetarian [ˌvɛdʒə'tɛrɪən, B -'tɛər-] *a., s.* vegetariano, vegetalista.
vegetarianism [-ˌɪzəm] *s.* vegetarianismo (régimen alimenticio).
vegetate ['vɛdʒəˌteɪt] *v.i.* vegetar (las plantas); (fig.) vegetar.
vegetation [ˌvɛdʒə'teɪʃən] *s.* vegetación.
vegetative ['vɛdʒəˌteɪtɪv, B -tətɪv] *a.* vegetativo, vegetante.
vegetatively [-lɪ] *adv.* de manera vegetativa.
vegetativeness [-nəs] *s.* capacidad vegetativa.
vehemence ['viəməns] *s.* vehemencia, intensidad; impetuosidad.
vehement [-mənt] *a.* vehemente, fogoso, impetuoso.
vehemently [-lɪ] *adv.* vehementemente, impetuosamente.
vehicle ['viɪkəl] *s.* 1. vehículo, carruaje. 2. medio, excipiente.
vehicle road, camino carretero.

vehicular [vɪ'hɪkjələr, B -lə] *a.* de o para vehículos, transportado por vehículo.
V-eight ['vi'eɪt] *s.* (automóvil con) motor de ocho cilindros en V.
veil [veɪl] *s.* 1. velo. 2. (fig.) velo, cubierta, máscara, antifaz, disfraz. 3. (anat., zool.) velo. 4. **to draw a v. over,** correr o echar velo sobre; **to lift the v.,** descorrer el velo; **to take the v.,** (fig.) tomar los hábitos. —*v.i.* velar, encubrir(se); disfrazar(se); ocultar(se); tapar(se).
veiled [veɪld] *a.* 1. con velo. 2. (fig.) velado, disfrazado; indirecto.
veiling ['veɪlɪŋ] *s.* 1. acción de cubrir con un velo. 2. velo, cortina. 3. material para velos.
vein [veɪn] *s.* 1. (anat.) vena. 2. (fig.) vena, humor, genio. 3. (bot.) vena, nervio. 4. vena, veta (en mármol, madera, etc.). 5. vena, vena de agua (subterránea). 6. grieta, rendija, quebradura (en cualquier substancia). 7. (geol., min.) vena, venero, veta, filón. 8. (ento.) nervio (del ala de un insecto). —*v.t.* jaspear, vetear; marcar con venas.
veined [veɪnd] *a.* 1. venoso, veteado, avetado. 2. (bot.) nervado. 3. (geol.) en forma de filón.
veining ['veɪnɪŋ] *s.* red de venas; (anat.) venoso.
veinless ['veɪnləs] *a.* desprovisto de venas.
veinlet [-lət] *s.* (bot.) venilla.
veinstone [-ˌstoʊn] *s.* (min.) ganga.
veinule [-jul] **veinulet** [-jələt] *s.* (bot.) venilla, venula.
veiny ['veɪnɪ] *a.* venoso, lleno de venas; veteado (hojas, mármol, etc.).
vela, *pl. de* **velum.**
velamen [və'leɪmən] *s.* (*pl.* VELAMINA [-'læmənə]) (anat., bot.) velamen.
velar ['vilər, B -lə] *a.* (anat., fon.) velar. —*s.* (fon.) (sonido) velar.
velarium [vɪ'lɛrɪəm, B -'lɛər-] *s.* (hist.) velario, toldo que cubría los circos y anfiteatros en la antigua Roma.
velarization [ˌvilərə'zeɪʃən, B -raɪ-] *s.* (fon.) velarización.
velarize ['viləˌraɪz] *v.t.* (fon.) velarizar.
velate ['vilət, -ˌleɪt] *a.* (bot., zool.) velado.
veld, veldt [fɛlt, B vɛlt] *s.* veld, estepa (en el África meridional).
velitation [ˌvɛlə'teɪʃən] *s.* (ant.) escaramuza, refriega; disputa.
velleity [vɛ'liətɪ] *s.* veleidad.
vellicate ['vɛləˌkeɪt] (raro) *v.t.* pellizcar; titilar, velicar.
vellication [ˌvɛlə'keɪʃən] *s.* (med.) sacudimiento muscular espasmódico.
vellum ['vɛləm] *s.* 1. vitela, pergamino. 2. pergamino; manuscrito en (papel) pergamino. 3. papel pergamino. —*a.* de vitela, avitelado.
vellum paper, papel pergamino, papel apergaminado, papel avitelado.
velocimeter [ˌvɛlə'sɪmətər, B -ə] *s.* velocímetro.
velocipede [və'lɑsəˌpid, B -'lɔs-] *s.* velocípedo.
velocity [-'lɑsətɪ, B -'lɔs-] *s.* velocidad, rapidez, celeridad.
velocity head, (hidr.) carga de velocidad o altura dinámica.
velocity of escape, (astr.) velocidad de escape, velocidad de liberación.
velocity ratio, (ing.) relación de velocidad.
velodrome ['viləˌdroʊm] *s.* velódromo.
velour [və'lʊr, B -'lʊə] *s.* (tej.) veludillo (tipo de tejido parecido al terciopelo).
velum ['viləm] *s.* (*pl.* VELA [-lə]) (anat., zool.) velo; (anat.) velo del paladar.
velure [vɛ'lʊr, B 'vɛljə] *s.* (fr.) (ant.) terciopelo, terciopelado, velludo.

velutinous [və'lutənəs] *a.* (bot., ento.) velloso, aterciopelado.
velvet ['vɛlvət] *s.* 1. (tej.) terciopelo, velludo. 2. (zool.) piel velluda (en las astas de los ciervos durante su crecimiento). 3. (jer.) ganancia limpia. 4. **on v.,** en posición de ventaja; con buenas ganancias (en el juego). —*a.* 1. de terciopelo, terciopelado, aterciopelado. 2. (fig.) suave, ligero.
velveteen [ˌvɛlvə'tin] *s.* 1. (tej.) pana, velludillo, terciopelo de algodón. 2. (*pl.*) ropas (esp. pantalones) de pana.
velvet grass, (bot.) heno blanco.
velvetleaf ['vɛlvətˌlif] *s.* (bot.) alcotán.
velvet tamarind, (bot.) tamarindo montero.
velvety ['vɛlvətɪ] *a.* 1. terciopelado, aterciopelado. 2. blando, suave, sedoso.
Ven. *abrev. de* **Venerable,** Venerable.
vena ['veɪnə, B 'vi-] *s.* (anat.) vena.
vena cava ['veɪnə'kɑvə, B 'vinə'keɪvə] (anat.) vena cava.
vena contracta [-kən'træktə] (hidr.) chorro contraído o contracto, vena contraída.
venal ['vinəl] *a.* venal, comprable, sobornable.
venality [vɪ'nælətɪ, B vi-] *s.* venalidad, corruptibilidad.
vena portae ['veɪnə'pɔrtˌi, B 'vinə'pɔti] (anat.) vena porta.
venatic [vɪ'nætɪk] *a.* venatorio, relativo a la caza.
venation [veɪ'neɪʃən, B vɪ-] *s.* (ento., bot.) nervadura, disposición de las venas.
vend [vɛnd] *v.t.* 1. vender (esp. como buhonero). 2. expender. 3. divulgar, decir públicamente. —*v.t.* 1. venderse. 2. efectuar ventas.
vendace ['vɛndəs] *s.* (*pl.* VENDACE O VENDACES) (ict.) corégono.
vendee [vɛn'di] *s.* comprador, compradora, adquiridor, adquiridora.
vendémiaire [ˌvɑndeɪmaɪ'ɛr, B -'ɛə] *s.* (hist.) vendimiario.
vender, *var. de* **vendor.**
vendetta [vɛn'dɛtə] *s.* (neol.) (*pl.* VENDETTAS) vendetta, venganza.
vendibility [ˌvɛndə'bɪlətɪ] *s.* posibilidad de venta (de un artículo).
vendible ['vɛndəbəl] *a.* vendible. —*s.* (*gen. pl.*) artículos vendibles.
vending machine, distribuidor automático (de cigarrillos, sellos, etc.), máquina expendedora.
vendition [vɛn'dɪʃən] *s.* (der.) vendición, venta.
vendor ['vɛndər, B -ˌdɔ] *s.* 1. vendedor; buhonero. 2. distribuidor automático.
vendue [vɛn'du, B -'dju] *s.* almoneda, subasta.
veneer [və'nɪr, B -'nɪə] *s.* 1. chapa, hoja de madera, revestimiento, baño (oro, plata). 2. (fig.) barniz, apariencia superficial o falaz. —*v.t.* 1. chapear, enchapar; revestir, cubrir. 2. (fig.) disfrazar, disimular; ocultar.
veneering [-ɪŋ, B -'nɪər-] *s.* chapeado, enchapado, revestimiento.
venenate ['vɛnəˌneɪt] *v.t.* envenenar, inyectar veneno en (díc. de una serpiente, etc.).
venepuncture ['vɛnəˌpʌŋktʃər, B -tʃə] *s.* (med.) venepuntura, venepunción.
venerability [ˌvɛnərə'bɪlətɪ] *s.* venerabilidad, respetabilidad.
venerable ['vɛnərəbəl] *a.* venerable, venerado, reverenciable.
venerableness [-nəs] *s.* venerabilidad, respetabilidad.
venerably [-blɪ] *adv.* venerablemente.
venerate ['vɛnəˌreɪt] *v.t.* venerar, reverenciar; honrar, respetar.
veneration [ˌvɛnə'reɪʃən] *s.* veneración, reverencia; respeto; homenaje; culto.

venerator ['vɛnəˌreɪtər, B -ə] *s.* venerador, veneradora.
venereal [və'nɪrɪəl, B -'nɪər-] *a.* venéreo.
venereal disease, (med.) enfermedad venérea.
venereologist [vəˌnɪrɪ'ɑlədʒəst, B -ˌnɪərɪ'ɔl-] *s.* especialista en enfermedades venéreas.
venereology [-dʒɪ] **venerology** [ˌvɛnə'rɑlədʒɪ, B -'rɔl-] *s.* venereología.
venery ['vɛnərɪ] *s.* (ant.) venus, deleite sexual; acto carnal, acto venéreo.
venery, *s.* (ant.) montería; caza.
venesect ['vɛnəˌsɛkt] *v.t.* practicar la venesección.
venesection [ˌvɛnə'sɛkʃən] *s.* flebotomía; sangría.
Venetian [və'niʃən] *a., s.* veneciano, de Venecia.
Venetian blind, persiana.
venetian chalk, talco gráfico.
Venetian glass, cristal de Murano.
Venetic [və'nɛtɪk] *a., s.* (filol.) véneto.
Venezuela [ˌvɛnə'zweɪlə] *s.* Venezuela.
Venezuelan [-lən] *a, s.* venezolano, de Venezuela.
venge [vɛndʒ] *v.t., v.i.* vengar(se).
vengeance ['vɛndʒəns] *s.* venganza; **with a v.,** con creces, con extremo; en sumo grado, de veras, con toda el alma.
vengeful ['vɛndʒfəl] *a.* vengativo, vindicativo.
vengefully [-fəlɪ] *adv.* vindicativamente.
vengefulness [-fəlnəs] *s.* espíritu vengativo, ánimo vengativo.
V-engine ['viˌɛndʒən] *s.* motor en V.
venial ['vinɪəl] *a.* venial, perdonable, excusable, leve.
veniality [ˌvinɪ'ælətɪ] *s.* venialidad.
venially ['vinɪəlɪ] *adv.* venialmente.
venialness [-əlnəs] *s.* venialidad.
venial sin, (relig.) pecado venial.
Venice ['vɛnəs] *s.* Venecia, ciudad de Italia.
venipuncture, *var. de* **venepuncture.**
venire [və'naɪrɪ, B -'naɪərɪ] *s.* (der.) mesa de jurados.
venire facias [-'feɪʃɪəs, B -æs] (der.) auto de convocación del jurado.
venireman [və'naɪrɪmən, B -'naɪər-] *s.* (der.) persona designada como jurado.
venison ['vɛnəsən, B 'vɛnzən] *s.* carne de venado.
venom ['vɛnəm] *s.* 1. veneno (de serpientes, escorpiones, etc.), ponzoña. 2. (fig.) veneno, malicia, malignidad, rencor, maldad.
venomous [-əs] *a.* 1. venenoso, ponzoñoso, tóxico. 2. (fig.) venenoso, malicioso, maligno.
venomously [-lɪ] *adv.* venenosamente, ponzoñosamente; maliciosamente, malignamente.
venomousness [-nəs] *s.* 1. calidad de venenoso. 2. maldad, rencor.
venosity [vɪ'nɑsətɪ, B -'nɔs-] *s.* venosidad.
venostasis [ˌvinə'steɪsəs] *s.* (med.) venostasis.
venous ['vinəs] *a.* (anat., bot., zool.) venoso; veteado.
venous blood, sangre negra, sangre venosa.
vent [vɛnt] *s.* 1. ventosa, respiradero, abertura, pasaje, paso. 2. tronera, lumbrera (en muralla, costado de buque, etc.). 3. oído, fogón (en armas de fuego). 4. orificio, agujero (de instrumentos de viento). 5. (fig.) salida, desahogo, desfogue. 6. (pr. esco.) humero, cañón de chimenea. 7. (zool.) ano, abertura anal o cloacal. 8. **to give v. to (one's indignation, wrath,** etc.), dar rienda suelta a (indignación, ira, etc.). —*v.t.* 1. abrir respiradero(s) en, proveer de abertura(s) u orificio(s). 2. dar salida a. 3. (fig.) dar rienda suelta a, desfogar, desahogar, expresar públicamente.
ventage ['vɛntɪdʒ] *s.* pequeña abertura u orificio; respiradero.

ventail ['vɛn͵teɪl] *s.* (hist.) ventalle, visera del casco.
venter ['vɛntər, B -ə] *s.* 1. (anat., zool.) vientre; protuberancia; concavidad, cavidad. 2. (der.) matriz, seno.
vent flue, conducto de ventilación.
venthole ['vɛnt͵hoʊl] *s.* respiradero (ventana).
ventiduct ['vɛntə͵dʌkt] *s.* conducto de ventilación; ventosa; resolladero.
ventilate ['vɛntəl͵eɪt] *v.t.* 1. ventilar, airear, orear (Amer.). 2. oxigenar (ej., la sangre). 3. divulgar, expresar o examinar públicamente; exponer, discutir. 4. (ant.) ahechar.
ventilation [͵vɛntəl'eɪʃən] *s.* ventilación; aeración, respiración, oreo.
ventilative ['vɛntəl͵eɪtɪv] *a.* que ventila.
ventilator [-ər, B -ə] *s.* ventilador.
ventilator belt, correa de ventilación.
ventilatory [-ə͵tɔrɪ, B -ətərɪ] *a.* que ventila, de ventilación.
ventral ['vɛntrəl] *a.* (anat., zool., bot.) ventral, abdominal.
ventral decubitus [-də'kjubətəs] decúbito prono o ventral.
ventral hernia, (med.) hernia abdominal.
ventrally [-trəlɪ] *adv.* en posición ventral, sobre el vientre.
ventricle ['vɛntrɪkəl] *s.* (anat.) ventrículo.
ventricular [vɛn'trɪkjələr, B -lə] *a.* ventricular.
ventriculus [-ləs] *s.* (*pl.* VENTRICULI [-͵laɪ]) (zool.) ventrículo.
ventriloquial [͵vɛntrə'loʊkwɪəl] *a.* de ventriloquia.
ventriloquism [vɛn'trɪlə͵kwɪzəm] *s.* ventriloquia.
ventriloquist [-kwəst] *s.* ventrílocuo.
ventriloquize [-͵kwaɪz] *v.i., v.t.* hablar como ventrílocuo.
ventriloquy [-kwɪ] *s.* ventriloquia.
ventrolateral [͵vɛntrə'lætərəl] *a.* (anat.) ventrolateral.
ventromedial [-'midɪəl] *a.* ventromedial.
venture ['vɛntʃər, B -tʃə] *s.* 1. empresa, negocio; acto aventurado, negocio arriesgado, especulación. 2. (ant.) riesgo, ventura, albur, cosa arriesgada. 3. **at a v.,** al azar, a la buena ventura. —*v.t.* 1. exponer a un peligro, arriesgar, aventurar. 2. aventurar (opinión, conjetura, etc.). 3. (raro) confiar en. 4. **nothing ventured nothing gained,** quien no arriesga no gana; quien no se aventura no pasa la mar. —*v.i.* atreverse, osar; arrojarse; aventurarse, arriesgarse, correr el albur; **v. on** (o **upon**), arriesgarse con o en; **v. out,** salir (con riesgo).
venture capital, (com.) capital empresario, capital arriesgado.
venturer ['vɛntʃərər, B -ərə] *s.* aventurero.
venturesome ['vɛntʃərsəm, B -tʃəsəm] *a.* 1. aventurado, arriesgado, riesgoso, azaroso. 2. emprendedor; osado, atrevido.
venturesomely [-lɪ] *adv.* arriesgadamente, riesgosamente, azarosamente, osadamente.
venturesomeness [-nəs] *s.* carácter aventurero, arrojo, temeridad, atrevimiento.
venturi [vɛn'tʊrɪ, B -'tʊərɪ] *s.* tubo de Venturi, venturi.
venturous ['vɛntʃərəs] *a.* 1. aventurado, arriesgado, riesgoso, azaroso. 2. aventurero, emprendedor. 3. audaz, osado, atrevido, arrojado.
venturously [-lɪ] *adv.* arriesgadamente, riesgosamente, azarosamente.
venturousness [-nəs] *s.* arrojo, temeridad, osadía.
venue ['vɛnju] *s.* 1. (der.) jurisdicción (en que se ha cometido un crimen o en que tiene lugar un litigio); escrito que designa el lugar en que debe realizarse el litigio; cláusula de una declaración jurada que indica el lugar donde fue firmada; **change of v.,** cambio de tribunal en un pleito. 2. (esgr.) pase.
venule ['vɛnjul] *s.* (anat., biol.) vénula.
Venus ['vinəs] *s.* 1. (mitol.) Venus, diosa romana del amor y la belleza. 2. (astr.) Venus. 3. (fig.) venus, amor sexual. 4. (alquimia) venus, cobre (metal).
Venushair [-͵hɛr, B -͵hɛə] *s.* (bot.) (variedad de) adianto o culantrillo.
Venusian [vɪ'nuʒən, B -'njuzɪən] *a.* (astr.) del planeta Venus.
Venus's-flytrap ['vinəsəz'flaɪ͵træp] *s.* (bot.) atrapamoscas, dionea.
Venus's navelwort, (bot.) ombligo de Venus, hierba de bálsamo, vasillo.
Venus's slipper, (bot.) chapín de Venus, zueco.
veracious [və'reɪʃəs] *a.* veraz, verídico.
veraciously [-lɪ] *adv.* verídicamente.
veraciousness [-nəs] *s.* veracidad.
veracity [və'ræsətɪ] *s.* 1. veracidad. 2. exactitud, precisión. 3. (la) verdad.
veranda, verandah [və'rændə] *s.* barandal, balcón, mirador, galería, terraza, pórtico.
veratric [və'rætrɪk] *a.* (quím.) verátrico.
veratridine [-'rætrə͵din] *s.* (quím.) veratridina.
veratrine ['vɛrə͵trin, B -traɪn] *s.* (farm.) veratrina.
veratrum [və'reɪtrəm] *s.* (bot., med.) veratro.
verb [vɜrb, B vɜb] *s.* (gram.) verbo.
verbal ['vɜrbəl, B 'vɜbəl] *a.* 1. verbal, de palabra, oral. 2. (gram.) verbal. 3. literal. —*s.* (gram.) substantivo derivado de un verbo, deverbal, postverbal.
verbal auxiliary, verbo auxiliar.
verbal contract, contrato verbal o de palabra.
verbalism [-͵ɪzəm] *s.* 1. expresión verbal. 2. verbalismo. 3. verbosidad, verborrea.
verbalist [-əst] *s.* 1. literalista. 2. verbalista.
verbalization [͵vɜrbələ'zeɪʃən, B ͵vɜbəlaɪ-] *s.* transformación en verbo, verbalización.
verbalize ['vɜrbə͵laɪz, B 'vɜbə-] *v.t.* 1. dar expresión a, poner en palabras. 2. transformar en verbo, verbalizar. —*v.i.* expresarse con verbosidad.
verbalizer [-ər, B -ə] *s.* persona verbosa.
verbally [-lɪ] *adv.* verbalmente.
verbal noun, (gram.) substantivo derivado de un verbo (ej., el gerundio inglés); deverbal, postverbal.
verbatim [vɜr'beɪtəm, B vɜ'-] *a., adv.* al pie de la letra, palabra por palabra.
verbena [vər'binə, B və'-] *s.* (bot.) verbena, hierba sagrada.
verbenaceous [͵vɜrbə'neɪʃəs, B ͵vɜbɪ-] *a.* (bot.) verbenáceo.
verbiage ['vɜrbɪɪdʒ, B 'vɜbɪ-] *s.* verbosidad, verborrea, palabrería.
verbify ['vɜrbə͵faɪ, B 'vɜbə-] *v.t.* (*pret., p.p.* VERBIFIED; *p.pr.* VERBIFYING) transformar en verbo.
verbose [vər'boʊs, B vɜ'-] *a.* verboso, difuso; palabrero.
verbosely [-lɪ] *adv.* con verbosidad, verbosamente.
verboseness [-nəs] *s.* verbosidad, ampulosidad; labia, palabrería.
verbosity [-'bɑsətɪ, B -'bɔsɪ-] *s.* verbosidad, verborrea; palabrería.
verdancy ['vɜrdənsɪ, B 'vɜd-] *s.* 1. verdor, verdín, verdura, verdina. 2. inocencia.
verdant [-ənt] *a.* 1. verde, verdoso; fresco. 2. (fig.) verde, inocente, cándido, inexperto.
verd antique [vɜrd-, B vɜd-] (min.) verde antiguo; mármol serpentino; pátina verde.
verderer, verderor ['vɜrdərər, B 'vɜdərə] *s.* (G.B.) (hist.) guarda mayor del bosque real.
verdict ['vɜrdɪkt, B 'vɜdɪkt] *s.* veredicto, fallo, sentencia; **to bring in a v.,** dictar un veredicto.
verdict of guilty, fallo condenatorio.
verdigris ['vɜrdə͵gris, B 'vɜdɪgrɪs] *s.* cardenillo, verdete, verdín, moho.
verdin ['vɜrdən, B 'vɜd-] *s.* (orn.) variedad de paro.
verditer ['vɜrdətər, B 'vɜdɪtə] *s.* cardenillo, verde de montaña, verde de tierra (pigmento).
verdure ['vɜrdʒər, B 'vɜdʒə] *s.* 1. verdor (esp. de la vegetación); lozanía, verdura, verdín; fronda. 2. (fig.) verdor, frescura, vigor.
verdured [-dʒərd, B -dʒəd] *a.* cubierto de verdor.
verdurous [-dʒərəs] *a.* lozano; fresco, vigoroso, verdoso.
Verein [və'raɪn, B fə-] *s.* (alemán) asociación, sociedad.
verge [vɜrdʒ, B vɜdʒ] *s.* 1. borde, filo, límite, margen, canto, vera. 2. cetro, vara (como emblema de poder). 3. (arq.) fuste (de una columna). 4. árbol del volante (de un reloj). 5. (ant.) jurisdicción. 6. **on** (o **upon**) **the v. of,** al borde de, a punto de, a un tris de. —*v.i.* 1. declinar, inclinarse (hacia); acercarse a, aproximarse a, tender a. 2. **v. on** (**o upon**), estar al borde de, llegar casi hasta; rayar en.
verger ['vɜrdʒər, B 'vɜdʒə] *s.* 1. sacristán, cuidador (de una iglesia). 2. (G.B.) macero (de un obispo o juez).
Vergil ['vɜrdʒəl, B 'vɜdʒɪl] *s.* Virgilio, poeta latino, autor de la *Eneida*.
Vergilian [vɜr'dʒɪlɪən, B vɜ'-] *a.* virgiliano, del poeta Virgilio.
verglas [vɛr'glɑ, B vɛə'-] *s.* capa fina de hielo (sobre la roca).
veridical [və'rɪdɪkəl, B vɛ-] *a.* 1. verídico. 2. genuino, real.
veridically [-kəlɪ] *adv.* verídicamente.
verifiable ['vɛrə͵faɪəbəl] *a.* comprobable, verificable.
verification [͵vɛrəfə'keɪʃən] *s.* verificación, comprobación, demostración.
verificative ['vɛrəfə͵keɪtɪv] *a.* verificativo.
verifier ['vɛrə͵faɪər, B -ə] *s.* verificador.
verify [-͵faɪ] *v.t.* (*pret., p.p.* VERIFIED; *p.pr.* VERIFYING) 1. verificar, comprobar, demonstrar, constatar, confirmar, ratificar. 2. (der.) autenticar, refrendar, afirmar bajo juramento.
verily ['vɛrəlɪ] *adv.* en verdad, ciertamente, verdaderamente, realmente.
verisimilar [͵vɛrə'sɪmələr, B -lə] *a.* verosímil, verisímil.
verisimilarly [-lɪ] *adv.* verosímilmente.
verisimilitude [-sə'mɪlə͵tud, B -͵tjud] *s.* verosimilitud, verisimilitud.
verism ['vɪr͵ɪzəm, B 'vɪər-] *s.* realismo, verismo, crudeza (en arte, literatura).
verist [-əst] *s., a.* realista, verista.
veristic [͵vɪr'ɪstɪk, B ͵vɪər-] *a.* realista.
veritable ['vɛrətəbəl] *a.* verdadero, real.
veritably [-blɪ] *adv.* verdaderamente, realmente.
verity ['vɛrətɪ] *s.* verdad, hecho, realidad.
verjuice ['vɜr͵dʒus, B 'vɜ͵-] *s.* 1. agraz, zumo ácido (de la uva u otras frutas). 2. (fig.) aspereza, amargura, sinsabor, disgusto, mordacidad.
vermeil ['vɜrməl, B 'vɜmeɪl] *s.* (fr.) 1. (poét.) color bermejo. 2. vermeil, plata sobredorada. —*a.* 1. (poét.) bermellón, bermejo. 2. dorado.

vermian ['vɜrmɪən, B 'vɜmɪ-] *a.* vermicular, vermiforme.
vermicelli [ˌvɜrmə'tʃɛlɪ, B ˌvɜmɪ'sɛlɪ] *s.* fideos delgados, fideos cabellos de ángel.
vermicide ['vɜrməˌsaɪd, B 'vɜmɪ-] *s.* (med.) vermicida, vermífugo.
vermicular [vɜr'mɪkjələr, B vɜ'-lə] *a.* 1. vermicular, vermiforme. 2. (arq.) vermiculado.
vermiculate [-ˌleɪt] *v.t.* hacer labrado rugoso en (madera, como adorno). —[-lət] *a.* 1. de labrado rugoso. 2. vermicular, vermiforme. 3. vermiculoso.
vermiculated [-ˌleɪtəd] *a.* (arq.) vermiculado.
vermiculation [-ˌmɪkjə'leɪʃən] *s.* (med.) vermiculación.
vermiculite [-'mɪkjəˌlaɪt] *s.* (min.) vermiculita.
vermiculose [-ˌloʊs, B -ˌmɪkjə'loʊs] **vermiculous** [-ləs, B -'mɪkjə-] *a.* vermicular.
vermiform ['vɜrməˌfɔrm, B 'vɜmɪˌfɔm] *a.* vermiforme, de forma de gusano.
vermiform appendix, (anat.) apéndice vermiforme.
vermiform process, (anat.) 1. vermis (del cerebelo). 2. proceso vermiforme.
vermifuge [-ˌfjudʒ] *a., s.* (farm.) vermífugo.
vermilion, vermillion [vər'mɪljən, B və'-] *s.* 1. bermellón, cinabrio. 2. color bermejo. —*v.t.* colorear con cinabrio; enrojar.
vermin ['vɜrmən, B 'vɜmɪn] *s.* (*pl.* VERMIN) (*ú. pr. con sentido de pl.*) 1. sabandija. 2. (fig.) sabandija; canalla, bribón.
vermination [ˌvɜrmə'neɪʃən, B ˌvɜmɪ-] *s.* (med.) verminación.
verminosis [-'noʊsəs] *s.* (med.) verminosis.
verminous ['vɜrmənəs, B 'vɜmɪ-] *a.* verminoso.
vermivorous [vɜr'mɪvərəs, B vɜ'-] *a.* (zool.) vermívoro.
Vermont [vər'mɑnt, B vɜ'mɔnt] *s.* Vermont, estado de los E.U.
vermouth [vɜr'muθ, B 'vɜməθ] *s.* vermut, vermú.
vernacular [vər'nækjələr, B və'-lə] *a.* vernáculo; vulgar. —*s.* idioma vernacular, dialecto, habla local.
vernacularism [-ləˌrɪzəm] *s.* modismo, localismo.
vernacularly [-lərlɪ, B -ləlɪ] *adv.* en lenguaje vernacular, en habla local.
vernal ['vɜrnəl, B 'vɜn-] *a.* 1. vernal, primaveral. 2. (fig.) fresco, juvenil.
vernal equinox, equinoccio vernal o de primavera.
vernal grass, (bot.) grama de olor, grama de prados.
vernalize [-ˌaɪz] *v.t.* (agr.) vernalizar.
vernalization [ˌvɜrnələ'zeɪʃən, B ˌvɜnəlaɪ-] *s.* (agr.) vernalización.
vernally ['vɜrnəlɪ, B 'vɜn-] *adv.* 1. primaveralmente. 2. (fig.) juvenilmente.
vernation [vər'neɪʃən, B və'-] *s.* (bot.) vernación.
vernier ['vɜrnɪər, B 'vɜnjə] *s.* nonio, vernier.
vernier caliper, (mec.) calibre de nonio, calibre a vernier.
vernier compass, (mar.) brújula de nonio.
vernier gauge, (mec.) pie de rey, calibrador.
vernier micrometer, micrómetro de precisión, calibre micrométrico.
Veronal ['vɛrəˌnɔl, B -ənəl] *s.* (farm.) veronal.
Veronese [ˌvɛrə'niz] *a.* veronés, veronense. —*s.* (*pl.* VERONESE) veronés, veronesa, veronense.
veronica [və'rɑnɪkə, B -'rɔn-] *s.* 1. (bot.) verónica. 2. (relig.) lienzo de la Verónica. 3. (taur.) verónica, lance con la capa extendida entre las dos manos.
verruca [və'rukə] *s.* (*pl.* VERRUCAE [-ki]) verruga.
verrucose [-ˌkoʊs] **verrucous** [-kəs] *a.* verrugoso, verrucoso.
verrucosity [ˌvɛru'kɑsətɪ, B -'kɔs-] *s.* verrucosis.
Versailles [vər'saɪ, B vɛə'-] *s.* Versalles, ciudad cercana a París, antigua residencia de los Luises.
versant ['vɜrsənt, B 'vɜs-] *a.* 1. interesado. 2. experimentado. 3. **v. with,** versado en, conocedor de.
versant, *s.* cuesta, pendiente, declive, vertiente; inclinación.
versatile ['vɜrsətəl, B 'vɜsəˌtaɪl] *a.* 1. versátil, flexible, polifacético. 2. (bot., zool.) versátil.
versatilely [-ɪ] *adv.* en forma versátil, con versatilidad.
versatileness [-nəs] **versatility** [ˌvɜrsə'tɪlətɪ, B ˌvɜsə-] *s.* versatilidad.
verse [vɜrs, B vɜs] *s.* 1. verso. 2. estancia, estrofa. 3. (bíbl.) versículo. —*v.i., v.t.* versificar.
verse, *v.t.* **v. oneself in,** familiarizarse con, adquirir experiencia en.
versed [vɜrst, B vɜst] *a.* versado, instruido, perito.
versed, *a.* (mat.) verso.
versed cosine, (mat.) coseno verso.
versed sine, (mat.) seno verso.
verse maker, versificador.
verse making, versificación.
verseman ['vɜrsmən, B 'vɜs-] *s.* versificador, metrista, metrificador.
verse-monger [-ˌmʌŋgər, -ˌmɑŋ-, B -ˌmʌŋgə] *s.* poetastro.
verser ['vɜrsər, B 'vɜsə] *s.* versificador.
versicle [-sɪkəl] *s.* versículo.
versicolor ['vɜrsɪˌkʌlər, B 'vɜsɪˌkʌlə] **versicolored** [-ərd, B -əd] *a.* 1.versicolor, multicolor; policolor; cambiante; jaspeado, abigarrado. 2. tornasolado, iridiscente.
versicular [ˌvɜr'sɪkjələr, B ˌvɜ'-lə] *a.* de versículos, (dividido) en versículos.
versification [ˌvɜrsəfə'keɪʃən, B ˌvɜsɪ-] *s.* 1. versificación, metrificación. 2. métrica; poética.
versifier ['vɜrsəˌfaɪər, B 'vɜsɪ-ə] *s.* versificador, metrista, metrificador, rimador.
versify [-ˌfaɪ] *v.i.* (*pret., p.p.* VERSIFIED; *p.pr.* VERSIFYING) versificar. —*v.t.* 1. versificar, metrificar. 2. relatar o escribir en verso, rimar, versear, trovar.
versine ['vɜrˌsaɪn, B 'vɜˌ-] **versin** [-ˌsaɪn, B -sɪn] *s.* (mat.) seno verso.
version ['vɜrʒən, -ʃən, B 'vɜʃən] *s.* 1. versión. 2. (med.) versión. 3. (mús.) interpretación, ejecución. 4. exposición.
versional [-əl] *a.* de una versión (de la Biblia), relativo a la versión o interpretación.
vers libre [vɛr'librə, B vɛə'-] (fr.) verso libre.
verso ['vɜrsoʊ, B 'vɜsoʊ] *s.* (*pl.* VERSOS) reverso (de página o moneda), dorso; (impr.) página par.
verst [vɜrst, B vɜst] *s.* versta, medida rusa de longitud.
versus ['vɜrsəs, B 'vɜsəs] *prep.* (der.) contra, con; (dep.) contra, versus (Amer.).
vert [vɜrt, B vɜt] *s.* 1. toda planta con hojas verdes en un bosque; (G.B.) derecho o privilegio de cortar árboles en el bosque. 2. (her.) color verde, sinople.
vertebra ['vɜrtəbrə, B 'vɜt-] *s.* (*pl.* VERTEBRAE [-bri] o VERTEBRAS) (anat., zool.) vértebra.
vertebral [-brəl] *a.* (anat., zool.) vertebral.
vertebral column, (anat.) columna vertebral.
vertebrate [-brət, -ˌbreɪt] *a.* 1. vertebrado. 2. (fig.) de estructura sólida, bien organizado. —*s.* (zool.) vertebrado.
vertebration [ˌvɜrtə'breɪʃən, B ˌvɜt-] *s.* 1. segmentación en vértebras. 2. (fig.) estructuración.
vertex ['vɜrˌtɛks, B 'vɜˌ-] *s.* (*pl.* VERTEXES o VERTICES [-təˌsiz]) 1. (geom.) vértice. 2. (astr.) cenit, zenit. 3. (anat.) vértice (del cráneo). 4. cúspide, cima, cumbre, ápice.
vertical ['vɜrtɪkəl, B 'vɜt-] *a.* 1. vertical, perpendicular. 2. del vértice, (situado) en el vértice. —*s.* vertical, perpendicular, cenital.
vertical angles, (geom.) ángulos verticales.
vertical circle, (astr.) vertical.
vertical clearance, (const.) franqueo superior, altura libre.
vertical envelopment, (mil.) envolvimiento vertical.
vertical fin, 1. (zool.) aleta dorsal, anal y caudal. 2. (aer., avia.) plano vertical, plano de deriva.
verticality [ˌvɜrtə'kælətɪ, B ˌvɜt-] *s.* verticalidad.
vertically ['vɜrtɪkəlɪ, B 'vɜt-] *adv.* verticalmente.
verticalness [-kəlnəs] *s.* verticalidad.
vertical plane, plano vertical.
vertical point, (top.) punto V, punto nadiral.
vertical rudder, (aer.) timón de dirección, plano de deriva.
vertical stabilizer, (aer.) estabilizador vertical.
vertical turn, (aer.) viraje a la vertical.
vertical union, sindicato o gremio industrial.
vertices, *pl. de* **vertex.**
verticil ['vɜrtəˌsɪl, B 'vɜt-] *s.* (bot.) verticilo.
verticillate [ˌvɜrtə'sɪlət, B ˌvɜt-] *a.* verticilado.
verticity [vɜr'tɪsətɪ, B vɜ'-] *s.* verticidad, giro.
vertiginous [vɜr'tɪdʒənəs, B vɜ'-] *a.* vertiginoso.
vertiginously [-lɪ] *adv.* vertiginosamente.
vertigo ['vɜrtɪˌgoʊ, B 'vɜtɪ-] *s.* (*pl.* VERTIGOES o VERTIGINES [ˌvɜr'tɪdʒəˌniz, B ˌvɜ'-]) 1. (med.) vértigo, vahído, desvanecimiento. 2. (vet.) vértigo, modorra (del ganado caballar y bovino).
vertu, *var. de* **virtu.**
Vertumnus [vər'tʌmnəs, B və'-] *s.* (mitol.) Vertumno, dios romano de las estaciones del año.
vervain ['vɜrˌveɪn, B 'vɜˌ-] *s.* (bot.) verbena.
vervain sage, (bot.) gallocresta, rinanto.
verve [vɜrv, B vɜv] *s.* 1. estro, numen, inspiración. 2. vigor, vitalidad, entusiasmo. 3. (ant.) talento, aptitud. 4. (teat.) vis cómica.
vervet ['vɜrvət, B 'vɜvət] *s.* especie de mico del África del Sur.
very ['vɛrɪ] *a.* 1. puro, completo, verdadero, absoluto, ej., *the v. truth,* la pura verdad, *the veriest fool must know it,* hasta el más tonto lo sabe. 2. exacto, preciso; idéntico, real, mismo, ej., *in that v. moment,* en ese preciso instante, *in the v. heart of the city,* en el mismo centro de la ciudad. 3. (esp. con *the, this* o *that*) mismo, propio, mismísimo, idéntico, ej., *this v. night,* esta misma noche, *his v. children turned against him,* sus propios hijos se volvieron contra él, *for that v. reason,* por esa misma razón, por eso mismo. 4. mero, simple, solo, ej., *the v. idea of doing it,* la sola idea de hacerlo. 5. **at the v. end,** al final de todo. —*adv.* 1. muy, mucho, sumamente. 2. de veras, en efecto, ej., *it's the v. best cheese you can buy,* éste es de veras el mejor queso que puede Ud. comprar. 3. **v. many,** muchísimos; **v. much,** mucho, muchísimo; **v. much so,** muchísimo, en sumo grado; **v. well,** muy bien, está bien.
very high frequency, (rad.) frecuencia muy alta.

Very light, bengala Very.
very low frequency, (rad.) frecuencia muy baja.
vesania [və'seɪnɪə] *s.* (med.) vesania, locura.
vesica [və'sikə, B 'vɛsɪ-] *s.* (*pl.* VESICAE [-si]) (anat.) vejiga (esp. la urinaria).
vesical ['vɛsɪkəl] *a.* (anat.) vesical.
vesicant [-kənt] *a., s.* (med.) vesicante.
vesicate ['vɛsə,keɪt] *v.t., v.i* (med.) ampollar(se), avejigar(se).
vesication [,vɛsə'keɪʃən] *s.* (med.) vesicación.
vesicatory ['vɛsɪkə,tɔrɪ, B -,keɪtərɪ] *a.* vesicante, vesicatorio, vejigatorio. —*s.* (*pl.* VESICATORIES) vesicatorio, vejigatorio.
vesicle ['vɛsɪkəl] *s.* (anat., med., bot., zool.) vesícula, vejiguilla.
vesicula [və'sɪkjələ] *s.* (anat., med.) vesícula.
vesicular [-lər, B -lə] *a.* (anat., med.) vesicular.
vesicula seminalis [-,sɛmə'næləs] (anat.) vesícula seminal.
vesiculate [-lət] *a.* vesiculado. — [-,leɪt] *v.t.* formar vesículas en. —*v.i.* tornarse vesicular.
vesiculation [və,sɪkjə'leɪʃən] *s.* vesiculación.
vespal ['vɛspəl] *a.* de avispas.
vesper ['vɛspər, B -pə] *s.* 1. **V.,** (astr.) Véspero, lucero de la tarde. 2. campana que llama a vísperas. 3. (*pl.*) (relig.) vísperas. 4. (ant.) tarde, atardecer. —*a.* vespertino, de la tarde.
vesperal [-pərəl] *s.* 1. (relig.) vesperal. 2. funda protectora (para cubrir los lienzos del altar entre las ceremonias). —*a.* vespertino.
vespertilionid [,vɛspər'tɪlɪənɪd, B -pə'-] *s.* (zool.) vespertiliónido.
Vespertilionidae [-,tɪlɪ'ɑnədi, B -'ɔnɪ-] *s. pl.* (zool.) vespertiliónidos.
vespertine ['vɛspər,taɪn, B -pə,-] **vespertinal** [,vɛspər'taɪnəl, B -pə'-] *a.* vespertino.
vespiary [-pɪ,ɛrɪ, B -ərɪ] *s.* (*pl.* VESPIARIES) avispero.
vespid ['vɛspəd] *a., s.* (ento.) véspido.
Vespidae [-pədi] *s. pl.* (ento.) véspidos.
Vespucci [vɛs'putʃɪ] *s.* (Américo) Vespucio (geógrafo y navegante, uno de los primeros en viajar al Nuevo Mundo).
vessel ['vɛsəl] *s.* 1. vasija, recipiente, receptáculo, vaso. 2. embarcación, buque, barco, bajel. 3. avión, aeroplano. 4. (bíbl.) vaso, recipiente (de gracia, virtudes). 5. (anat., zool.) vaso, ej., *blood v.,* vaso sanguíneo. 6. (bot.) vaso, canal.
vest [vɛst] *s.* 1. chaleco. 2. (pr. G.B.) camiseta. 3. chaqueta, chaquetilla (de mujer). 4. (hist.) túnica, chaqueta antigua. 5. (ant.) manto; atavío; vestidura, vestido. —*v.t.* 1. vestir (esp. con las vestiduras eclesiásticas). 2. invertir (dinero). 3. **v. in,** conferir (dignidad, derechos, etc.), adjudicar, ceder, consignar (propiedad); **v. with,** investir con o de, dotar de. —*v.i.* 1. vestirse, ponerse vestiduras. 2. **v. in,** tener validez (para), pertenecer (**a**).
vesta ['vɛstə] *s.* 1. **V.,** (mitol.) Vesta. 2. (G.B.) cerilla; fosforito de madera.
vestal ['vɛstəl] *a.* vestal. —*s.* 1. (hist.) vestal. 2. virgen, doncella.
vested ['vɛstəd] *a.* 1. vestido, revestido. 2. (der.) establecido, consumado; protegido por la ley.
vested estate, (der.) propiedad en dominio pleno.
vested interest, (der.) interés establecido, interés creado.
vested rights, (der.) derechos adquiridos.
vestee [vɛs'ti] *s.* pechera, chaquetilla (esp. de traje de mujer).
vestiary ['vɛstɪ,ɛrɪ, B -ərɪ] *s.* (*pl.* VESTIARIES) 1. vestidura; vestimentas. 2. vestuario (en conventos, etc.).
vestibular [vɛs'tɪbjələr, B -lə] *a.* vestibular.
vestibule ['vɛstə,bjul] *s.* 1. vestíbulo, salón de entrada (hotel, etc.); portal, zaguán, atrio. 2. (f.c.) pasillo cubierto, fuelle de conexión (entre dos coches de pasajeros). 3. (anat., zool.) vestíbulo.
vestibuled [-,bjuld] *a.* con vestíbulo.
vestibule school, escuela de capacitación (para el personal de una fábrica).
vestige ['vɛstɪdʒ] *s.* 1. vestigio, huella, rastro, traza, reliquia. 2. (biol.) vestigio, rudimento.
vestigial [vɛs'tɪdʒɪəl] *a.* (med.) vestigial, rudimentario; atrofiado.
vesting ['vɛstɪŋ] *s.* tela o corte para chalecos.
vestment ['vɛstmənt] *s.* 1. vestidura, prenda, vestido de ceremonia. 2. vestidura, vestimenta (de sacerdote).
vest-pocket ['vɛst,pɑkət, B -'pɔk-] *a.* diminuto, de bolsillo.
vestry ['vɛstrɪ] *s.* (*pl.* VESTRIES) 1. sacristía, vestuario (de la iglesia). 2. capilla anexa (a la iglesia); salón parroquial. 3. junta parroquial protestante (administradora). 4. (ant.) ropero, armario, guardarropa.
vestryman [-mən] *s.* miembro de la junta parroquial protestante.
vesture ['vɛstʃər, B -tʃə] (poét.) *s.* vestidura, indumento; cobertura, cubierta. —*v.t.* vestir; cubrir.
vesuvian [və'suvɪən] *s.* 1. (min.) vesubianita. 2. fósforo grande (usado antiguamente para prender cigarros).
vesuvianite [-ə,naɪt] *s.* (min.) vesubianita.
Vesuvius [və'suvɪəs] *s.* Vesubio, volcán al S.E. de Nápoles.
vet [vɛt] *s.* (fam.) *forma abrev. de* **veteran,** veterano, ex combatiente.
vet. *abrev de* 1. **veterinary,** veterinaria. 2. **veterinarian,** veterinario.
vet, *v.t.* (*pret., p.p.* VETTED; *p.pr.* VETTING) 1. (vet.) examinar o tratar un animal enfermo. 2. (fig.) examinar, revisar, corregir.
vetch [vɛtʃ] *s.* (bot.) vicia, veza, algarroba, arveja, arvejera.
vetchling ['vɛtʃlɪŋ] *s.* (bot.) áfaca, áfaga.
veteran ['vɛtərən] *s.* 1. veterano; experto, práctico. 2. (E.U.) veterano, ex combatiente. 3. árbol viejo de grueso tronco. —*a.* veterano; experimentado, experto, práctico.
Veterans Day, (E.U.) Día de los Veteranos (el 11 de noviembre).
veterinarian [,vɛtərən'ɛrɪən, B -'ɛər-] *s.* veterinario, albéitar.
veterinary ['vɛtərən,ɛrɪ, B -ərɪ] *s.* (*pl.* VETERINARIES) veterinario, albéitar. —*a.* veterinario.
veterinary science, veterinaria.
veterinary surgeon, (G.B.) veterinario, albéitar.
vetiver ['vɛtəvər, B -və] *s.* (bot.) vetiver.
veto ['vitoʊ] *s.* (*pl.* VETOES) veto. —*v.t.* (*pret., p.p.* VETOED; *p.pr.* VETOING) poner veto a, vetar (Amer.).
vetoer [-ər, B -ə] *s.* él que ejerce el veto.
vex [vɛks] *v.t.* 1. fastidiar, molestar, irritar. 2. hostigar, acosar. 3. agitar, inquietar, angustiar. 4. discutir, debatir. —*v.i.* **v. over,** preocuparse por, inquietarse por.
vexation [vɛk'seɪʃən] *s.* 1. fastidio, molestia. 2. disgusto, desazón, enojo. 3. chinchorrería.
vexatious [-ʃəs] *a.* 1. enfadoso, fastidioso, molesto. 2. agitado, angustiado.
vexatiously [-lɪ] *adv.* molestamente, importunamente, fastidiosamente.
vexatiousness [-nəs] *s.* 1. importunidad, carácter enfadoso, irritante. 2. molestia.
vexed [vɛkst] *a.* enfadado, irritado.
vexedly ['vɛksədlɪ, 'vɛkstlɪ] *adv.* con irritación, molestamente, irritadamente.
vexillary ['vɛksə,lɛrɪ, B -lərɪ] *s.* (*pl.* VEXILLARIES) (hist.) vexilario. —*a.* (bot.) vexilar.
vexillum [vɛk'sɪləm] *s.* (*pl.* VEXILLA [-ə]) 1. (hist.) vexilo. 2. (orn.) vexilo (barba de la pluma). 3. (bot.) vexilo, estandarte (pétalo superior o posterior de la corola).
VHF *abrev. de* **very high frequency,** frecuencia muy alta.
V.I. *abrev. de* **Virgin Islands,** Islas Vírgenes.
via ['vaɪə, 'viə, B 'vaɪə] *prep.* por (la vía de); vía, por vía, ej., *via air mail,* por vía aérea.
viability [,vaɪə'bɪlətɪ] *s.* viabilidad.
viable ['vaɪəbəl] *a.* viable.
viaduct ['vaɪə,dʌkt] *s.* viaducto.
vial ['vaɪəl] *s.* redoma, frasco; pomo, botellita.
viameter [vaɪ'æmɪtər, B -ə] *s.* (meteor.) odómetro.
viand ['vaɪənd] *s.* vianda; (*pl.*) provisiones, vitualla(s).
viatic [vaɪ'ætɪk] *a.* de viático; del viaje.
viaticum [-'ætɪkəm] *s.* (*pl.* VIATICA [-kə] o VIATICUMS) 1. viático, provisiones de viaje. 2. (relig.) viático.
viator [-'eɪtər, B -ə] *s.* (*pl.* VIATORES [,vaɪə'tɔriz]) viajero, viajante.
vibrancy ['vaɪbrənsɪ] *s.* vibración, resonancia.
vibrant [-brənt] *a.* 1. vibrante. 2. lleno de vitalidad (ej., personalidad).
vibrantly [-lɪ] *adv.* vibrantemente.
vibrate ['vaɪ,breɪt, B vaɪ'breɪt] *v.t.* vibrar. —*v.i.* 1. vibrar, oscilar, cimbrarse; estremecer. 2. (fig.) vacilar, titubear. 3. (fig.) emocionarse.
vibratile ['vaɪbrətəl, B -,taɪl] *a.* vibrátil, vibratorio.
vibratility [,vaɪbrə'tɪlətɪ] *s.* vibratilidad, capacidad vibrátil.
vibrating ['vaɪbreɪtɪŋ, B vaɪ'breɪt-] *a.* 1. vibrante. 2. oscilante. 3. trepidante.
vibration [vaɪ'breɪʃən] *s.* 1. vibración, oscilación. 2. (fig.) vacilación, titubeo. 3. (fís.) vibración.
vibrationless [-ləs] *a.* sin vibración.
vibrative ['vaɪ,breɪtɪv, B vaɪ'breɪt-] *a.* vibratorio.
vibrato [vɪ'brɑtoʊ] *s.* (mús.) vibrato.
vibrator ['vaɪ,breɪtər, B vaɪ'breɪtə] *s.* 1. (elec.) vibrador, interruptor intermitente. 2. (rad.) oscilador.
vibratory ['vaɪbrə,tɔrɪ, B -tərɪ] *a.* vibratorio.
vibrio ['vɪbrɪ,oʊ] *s.* (bact.) vibrión.
vibriosis [,vɪbrɪ'oʊsəs] *s.* (med.) edema maligno, edema gaseoso.
vibrissa [vaɪ'brɪsə] *s.* (*pl.* VIBRISSAE [-i]) (anat., zool., orn.) vibrisa, vibriza.
vibrograph ['vaɪbrə,græf, B -,grɑf] *s.* vibrógrafo.
vibrometer [vaɪ'brɑmətər, B -'brɔmɪtə] *s.* vibrómetro.
vibroscope ['vaɪbrə,skoʊp] *s.* vibroscopio.
viburnum [vaɪ'bɜrnəm, B -'bɜnəm] *s.* (bot.) viburno, mundillo, geldre.
vicar ['vɪkər, B -ə] *s.* 1. vicario, delegado. 2. (relig. anglicana) sacerdote de una parroquia (cuyos diezmos pertenecen a una casa religiosa o seglar); párroco. 3. (relig. episcopal) pastor a cargo de una capilla dependiente.
vicarage ['vɪkərɪdʒ] *s.* 1. beneficios del párroco. 2. residencia del párroco. 3. curato. 4. (raro) vicaría, vicariato.
vicar apostolic, (*pl.* VICARS APOSTOLIC) (relig.) vicario apostólico.
vicarate ['vɪkərət] *s.* vicariato, vicaría.
vicaress [-əs] *s.* vicaria.
vicar forane ['vɪkərfə'reɪn, B -ə'fɔreɪn] (*pl.* VICARS FORANE) (relig.) vicario foráneo.
vicar-general [-'dʒɛnərəl] *s.* (*pl.* VICARSGENERAL) 1. (relig. anglicana) representante de los Arzobispos de Canterbury o York. 2. (G.B.)

(hist.) representante eclesiástico del rey. 3. (relig. católica) vicario general.
vicarial [vaɪˈkɛrɪəl, B -ˈkɛər-] *a.* 1. vicario. 2. vicarial, de la vicaría.
vicariate [-ət] *s.* vicariato, vicaría.
vicarious [vaɪˈkɛrɪəs, B -ˈkɛər-] *a.* 1. vicario, delegado. 2. indirecto (placer, pena, sacrificio, etc.). 3. (med.) vicario (díc. esp. de una hemorragia substitutiva de un período menstrual).
vicariously [-lɪ] *adv.* 1. de vicario, por substitución. 2. indirectamente.
Vicar of Christ, Vicario de Jesucristo (el Papa).
vicarship [ˈvɪkər͵ʃɪp, B -ə͵-] *s.* 1. vicariato, vicaría. 2. (relig. anglicana) oficio del sacerdote parroquial, curato.
vice [vaɪs] *s.* 1. vicio, inmoralidad; corrupción, depravación. 2. vicio, defecto, imperfección, falta. 3. **V.,** (hist.) bufón que personificaba el vicio (en moralidades inglesas).
vice [ˈvaɪsɪ] *prep.* en lugar de, en vez de. — [vaɪs] *prefijo,* vice, suplente, adjunto, segundo, alterno.
vice admiral [vaɪs-] vicealmirante.
vice admiralty, vicealmirantazgo.
vice-chancellor [ˈvaɪsˈtʃænsələr, B -ˈtʃɑnsələ] *s.* 1. vicecanciller. 2. (der.) canciller ayudante.
vice-consul [-ˈkɑnsəl, B -ˈkɔn-] *s.* vice-cónsul.
vice-consulate [-ət] *s.* viceconsulado.
vice-consulship [-͵ʃɪp] *s.* viceconsulado.
vicegerency [-ˈdʒɪrənsɪ, B -ˈdʒɛr-] *s.* vicegerencia, representación, suplencia, lugartenencia.
vicegerent [-ənt] *s.* vicegerente, representante, delegado, vicario, suplente.
vice-governor [-ˈgʌvənər, B -nə] *s.* vicegobernador.
vice-king [-ˈkɪŋ] *s.* virrey.
vicennial [vaɪˈsɛnɪəl] *a.* vicenal.
vice-presidency [ˈvaɪsˈprɛzədənsɪ] *s.* vicepresidencia.
vice-president [-dənt] *s.* vicepresidente; vicepresidenta.
vice-presidential [-͵prɛzəˈdɛntʃəl, B -ˈdɛnʃəl] *a.* vicepresidencial.
vice-queen [-ˈkwin] *s.* virreina.
viceregal [-ˈrigəl] *a.* virreinal.
vice-regent [-ˈridʒənt] *s.* vicegobernador; vicerregente.
vicereine [ˈvaɪs͵reɪn] *s.* virreina.
viceroy [-͵rɔɪ] *s.* 1. virrey. 2. (ento.) variedad de mariposa americana.
viceroyal [͵vaɪsˈrɔɪəl] *a.* virreinal.
viceroyalty [-tɪ] *s.* virreinato.
viceroyship [ˈvaɪs͵rɔɪ͵ʃɪp] *s.* virreinato.
vice squad, (E.U.) patrulla policial para combatir el vicio.
vice-treasurer [-ˈtrɛʒərər, B -ə] *s.* vicetesorero.
vice versa [ˈvaɪsɪˈvɜrsə, B -ˈvɜsə] vice-versa.
Vichy water [ˈvɪʃɪ-, B ˈviʃɪ-] agua (mineral) de Vichy; agua mineral.
vicinage [ˈvɪsənɪdʒ] *s.* 1. vecindad, vecindario. 2. cercanía(s), inmediaciones.
vicinal [-əl] *a.* 1. vecinal. 2. vecino, adyacente.
vicinity [vəˈsɪnətɪ] *s.* (*pl.* VICINITIES) 1. vecindad, vecindario. 2. cercanía(s), inmediaciones, alrededores.
vicious [ˈvɪʃəs] *a.* 1. vicioso, inmoral, depravado; malvado, perverso. 2. vicioso, defectuoso, imperfecto. 3. viciado, impuro, inmundo. 4. nocivo, malsano. 5. arisco, indomado, bravo (animal). 6. malicioso, maligno, rencoroso.
vicious circle, círculo vicioso.
viciously [-lɪ] *adv.* 1. viciosamente, inmoralmente. 2. malignamente. 3. fieramente.
viciousness [-nəs] *s.* 1. malignidad, maldad, perversidad. 2. braveza, fiereza (de animales).
vicissitude [vəˈsɪsə͵tud, B -͵tjud] *s.* 1. vicisitud. 2. cambio, mudanza.
vicissitudinary [-͵sɪsəˈtudən͵ɛrɪ, B -ˈtjudənərɪ] **vicissitudinous** [-əs] *a.* vicisitudinario, lleno de vicisitudes.
victim [ˈvɪktəm] *s.* 1. víctima. 2. (der.) interfecto.
victimize [-tə͵maɪz] *v.t.* 1. hacer víctima, victimar. 2. engañar, estafar, embaucar.
victimizer [-ər, B -ə] *s.* victimario.
victor [ˈvɪktər, B -tə] *s.* vencedor, triunfador. —*a.* victorioso, vencedor, triunfante.
victoria [vɪkˈtɔrɪə] *s.* 1. victoria (coche descubierto de cuatro ruedas). 2. (bot.) victoria regia, irupé.
Victorian [-ɪən] *a.* 1. victoriano, de la época en que reinaba la reina Victoria de Inglaterra (1837-1901). 2. estirado, pomposo; mojigato, conservador.
Victorian age, era victoriana.
Victorianize [-ə͵naɪz] *v.t.* transformar al estilo de la era victoriana.
victoriate [-ət] *s.* (numis.) victoriato.
victorious [vɪkˈtɔrɪəs] *a.* victorioso, vencedor, triunfante.
victoriously [-lɪ] *adv.* victoriosamente.
victory [ˈvɪktərɪ] *s.* (*pl.* VICTORIES) victoria; triunfo.
victress [-trəs] *s.* vencedora, ganadora, triunfadora.
Victrola [vɪkˈtroʊlə] *s.* (ant.) (marca comercial) victrola, fonógrafo.
victual [ˈvɪtəl] *s.* comida; *pl.* vitualla(s), víveres, viandas, manjares. —*v.t.* (*pret., p.p.* VICTUALED o VICTUALLED; *p.pr.* VICTUALING o VICTUALLING) avituallar, vituallar. —*v.i.* 1. alimentarse. 2. proveerse de víveres, avituallarse.
victualer, victualler [-ər, B -ə] *s.* 1. abastecedor, proveedor, vivandero. 2. cantinero. 3. buque abastecedor.
vicuña [vɪˈkunjə, B -ˈkjunə] *s.* 1. (zool.) vicuña. 2. (lana o tejido de) vicuña.
vide [ˈvaɪdɪ] *v.* véase, véanse.
vide ante [-ˈæntɪ] véase lo anterior.
vide infra [-ˈɪnfrə] véase más abajo o adelante.
videlicet [vəˈdɛlə͵sɛt, B -ˈdilɪ-] *adv.* a saber, es decir, esto es.
video [ˈvɪdɪ͵oʊ] *a.* de video, de vídeo (Esp.). —*s.* video, vídeo (Esp.) —*v.t.* grabar.
video arcade, sala recreativa (con videojuegos).
video camara, videocamara.
videocassette [ˈvɪdɪoʊkəˈsɛt] *s.* videocasete, videocassete, videocassette.
videocassette recorder, magnetoscopia, video, vídeo (Esp.).
video clip, videoclip.
video club, videoclub.
videoconference [ˈvɪdɪoʊˈkɑnfərəns] *s.* videoconferencia.
videodisc, videodisk [ˈvɪdɪoʊdɪsk] *s.* videodisco.
video film, película de video, videofilm.
video frequency, (t.v.) videofrecuencia, frecuencia de imagen o de visión.
video game, videojuego.
videogenic [ˈvɪdɪoʊˈdʒɛnɪk] *a.* que se presta a ser transmitido por televisión.
video library, videoteca.
video piracy, videopiratería.
videophone [ˈvɪdɪoʊfoʊn] *s.* videófono, videoteléfono.
videoprojector [ˈvɪdɪoʊprəˈdʒɛktər] *s.* videoproyector.
video recorder, aparto de video, video, vídeo (Esp.).
video recording, 1. (*tape*) video, vídeo (Esp.) (*cinta*). 2. (*process*) grabación en video, grabación en vídeo (Esp.), videograbación (*acto*).
videotape [ˈvɪdɪoʊteɪp] *s.* cinta de video, videocinta, video (Esp.). —*v.t.* grabar en video, grabar en video (Esp.), videograbar.
videotape recorder, video, videograbadora.
videotape recording, video, vídeo (Esp.), videograma; videograbación (*acto*).
videotaping [ˈvɪdɪoʊteɪpɪn] *s.* videograbación.
videotex [ˈvɪdɪoʊtɛks] **videotext** [ˈvɪdɪoʊtɛkst] *s.* videotex, videotexto.
vide supra [ˈvaɪdɪˈsuprə] véase arriba.
vidette, *var. de* **vedette.**
vidicon [ˈvɪdɪ͵kɑn, B -͵kɔn] *s.* (t.v.) vidicón.
viduity [vɪˈduətɪ, B -ˈdju-] *s.* viudez.
vie [vaɪ] *v.i.* (*pret., p.p.* VIED; *p.pr.* VYING) competir, rivalizar; contender. —*v.t.* (ant.) cotejar, contraponer; apostar, arriesgar.
Vienna [vɪˈɛnə] *s.* Viena, capital de Austria.
Vienna sausage, salchicha de Viena.
Viennese [͵viəˈniz] *a.* vienés. —*s.* (*pl.* VIENNESE) vienés.
Vientiane [vjɛnˈtjɑn] *s.* Vientiane, capital de Laos.
Vietcong [vɪˈɛtˈkɑŋ, B ˈvjɛtˈkɔŋ] *s.* 1. Vietcong, guerrilleros y grupos de combate que forman el Ejército de Liberación Nacional de Vietnam del Sur. 2. vietcong, miembro de este grupo.
Vietminh [ˈviətˈmɪn, B ˈvjɛt-] *s.* (*pl.* VIETMINH) vietmin, miembro de la liga revolucionaria que luchó contra los franceses por la independencia de Vietnam.
Vietnam [-ˈnɑm, B -ˈnæm] *s.* Vietnam. **North Vietnam,** Vietnam del Norte; **South Vietnam,** Vietnam del Sur.
Vietnamese [͵viətnəˈmiz, B ͵vjɛt-] *a., s.* vietnamés, vietnamita.
vietnik [ˈvjɛtnɪk] *s.* (jer., E.U.) opositor a la intervención militar en Vietnam.
view [vju] *s.* 1. vista, mirada; inspección. 2. panorama, paisaje; perspectiva. 3. (pint., foto.) vista, cuadro. 4. opinión, parecer, ej., *he took a favorable v.,* él se formó una opinión favorable. 5. propósito, intención, mira. 6. (ant., dial.) apariencia, aspecto. 7. **at first v.,** a primera vista; **in v. of,** en vista de; **on v.,** en exhibición; **to be** (o **come**) **in v. (of),** estar (presentarse) a la vista (de); alcanzar a ver, avistar; **to have in v.,** tener por objeto; tener en mente, tener en consideración; **to take a closer v. (of),** examinar más de cerca; **with a v. to,** con el propósito de, con miras a. —*v.t.* 1. mirar, escrutar, inspeccionar, examinar. 2. (fig.) contemplar, considerar, ej., *the subject may be viewed in different ways,* el asunto puede considerarse de diferentes maneras.
viewer [ˈvjuər, B -ə] *s.* 1. veedor, inspector. 2. espectador; televidente. 3. (foto.) visor.
viewfinder [-͵faɪndər, B -də] *s.* (foto., fotmgt.) visor.
view halloo, grito proferido por el cazador al avistar un zorro.
viewless [-ləs] *a.* 1. sin opinión, indiferente. 2. (poét., ret.) invisible.
viewpoint [-͵pɔɪnt] *s.* punto de vista.
viewy [ˈvjuɪ] *a.* (VIEWIER; VIEWIEST) (fam.) 1. visionario, teorizante, impráctico. 2. espectacular, llamativo, ostentoso.
vigesimal [vaɪˈdʒɛsəməl] *a.* vigesimal, vigésimo.
vigil [ˈvɪdʒəl] *s.* 1. vigilia, vela, velación, desvelo. 2. (relig.) (*gen. en pl.*) vigilia. 3. **to keep v.,** velar, trasnochar.

vigilance ['vɪdʒələns] *s.* 1. vigilancia, cuidado. 2. desvelo.
vigilance committee, (E.U.) junta de vigilancia.
vigilant [-lənt] *a.* vigilante, atento.
vigilante [ˌvɪdʒə'læntɪ] *s.* (E.U.) vigilante (miembro de una banda de ciudadanos que se auto-eligen como policías).
vigilantly ['vɪdʒələntlɪ] *adv.* vigilantemente.
vigintillion [ˌvaɪˌdʒɪn'tɪljən] *s.* (E.U.) unidad seguida de 63 ceros; (G.B.) unidad seguida de 120 ceros.
vignette [vɪn'jɛt] *s.* 1. (impr.) marmosete. 2. ilustración esfumada. 3. (fig.) descripción en miniatura, esquicio, croquis. 4. (arq.) ornamento (esp. de palmitas, volutas, etc.). —*v.t.* 1. hacer una viñeta de (fotografía, retrato, etc.). 2. (fig.) describir en miniatura.
vigor, (pr. G.B.) **vigour** ['vɪgər, B -ə] *s.* 1. vigor, vitalidad, fuerza, tesón. 2. vigor, verdor, lozanía. 3. vigor, vigencia, validez.
vigorous ['vɪgərəs] *a.* 1. vigoroso, fuerte, enérgico. 2. lozano.
vigorously [-lɪ] *adv.* vigorosamente, enérgicamente, con tesón.
vigorousness [-nəs] *s.* 1. vigorosidad, energía. 2. lozanía.
Viking ['vaɪkɪŋ] *s.* vikingo, explorador o pirata escandinavo que asediaba las costas de Europa en los siglos VIII y IX.
vilayet [vɪlaɪ'ɛt, B vɪ'lɑjɛt] *s.* vilayato (división administrativa de Turquía).
vile [vaɪl] *a.* 1. vil, bajo, soez. 2. repugnante, detestable, odioso. 3. (fam.) pésimo, abominable.
vilely ['vaɪllɪ] *adv.* vilmente, bajamente, abyectamente.
vileness [-nəs] *s.* vileza, abyección, bajeza.
vilification [ˌvɪləfə'keɪʃən] *s.* 1. difamación, denuesto, calumnia. 2. (raro) envilecimiento.
vilifier ['vɪləˌfaɪər, B -ə] *s.* difamador, denostador, calumniador.
vilify [-ˌfaɪ] *v.t.* (*pret., p.p.* VILIFIED; *p.pr.* VILIFYING) 1. difamar, denostar, calumniar. 2. (raro) envilecer, corromper.
vilipend ['vɪləˌpɛnd] *v.t.* (lit.) vilipendiar, desacreditar, despreciar.
vill [vɪl] *s.* (hist.) división administrativa y política; aldea.
villa ['vɪlə] *s.* villa, quinta, casa de campo.
villadom [-dəm] *s.* (G.B.) la sociedad suburbana.
village ['vɪlɪdʒ] *s.* aldea, pueblo, caserío. —*a.* aldeano.
villager [-ər, B -ə] *s.* aldeano, lugareño.
villagery [-ɪdʒrɪ, B -ɪdʒərɪ] *s.* (conjunto de) aldeas o pueblos.
villain ['vɪlən] *s.* 1. maleante, infame, malvado, villano. 2. (teat.) villano, bribón, malo; pillo. 3. (apl. a niños) pilluelo. 4. (hist.) siervo de la gleba (en el sistema feudal). 5. (ant.) patán, rústico.
villainous [-əs] *a* 1. malvado, bellaco, villano, ruin. 2. abominable, pésimo, miserable.
villainously [-lɪ] *adv.* 1. malvadamente, bellacamente, villanamente. 2. abominablemente, pésimamente, miserablemente.
villainy ['vɪlənɪ] *s.* (*pl.* VILLAINIES) 1. villanía, vileza, infamia. 2. villanía, maldad, depravación.
villanage, *var. de* **villenage.**
villanella [ˌvɪlə'nɛlə] *s.* (*pl.* VILLANELLE [-ɪ]) (mús.) villanesca, antigua cancioncilla de origen napolitano.
villanelle [-'nɛl] *s.* (fr.) villanela, poema corto de origen francés.
villatic [vɪ'lætɪk] *a.* rural, rústico.
villein ['vɪlən] *s.* (hist., Ingl.) siervo de la gleba (en el sistema feudal).
villenage [-ɪdʒ] *s.* (fr.) (hist.) villanaje, villanería.
villosity [vɪl'ɑsətɪ, B -'ɔs-] *s.* (bot., zool. anat.) vellosidad.
villous ['vɪləs] *a.* (bot., zool.) velloso.
villus ['vɪləs] *s.* (*pl.* VILLI [-ˌaɪ]) (anat., embr., bot.) vello; microvellosidad.
vim [vɪm] *s.* fuerza, vigor, energía, brío; espíritu.
vimineous [vaɪ'mɪnɪəs, B vɪ-] *a.* (bot.) vimíneo.
vina ['vinə] *s.* (mús.) vina, antiguo instrumento de cuerdas originario de la India.
vinaceous [vaɪ'neɪʃəs] *a.* de color vinoso.
vinaigrette [ˌvɪnɪ'grɛt, B ˌvɪneɪ-] *s.* 1. vinagrera. 2. (cocina) vinagreta (salsa).
vinaigrette sauce, salsa vinagreta.
vinal ['vaɪnəl] *a.* vínico, vinoso; de vino.
vinca ['vɪŋkə] *s.* (bot.) vincapervinca, hierba doncella.
Vincent's angina ['vɪnsənts-] (med.) angina de Vincent.
vincetoxicum [ˌvɪnsə'tɑksəkəm, B -'tɔk-] *s.* (bot.) vencetósigo, berza de perro, berza perruna.
vincible ['vɪnsəbəl] *a.* vencible, conquistable.
vinculum ['vɪŋkjələm] *s.* (*pl.* VINCULA [-lə] o VINCULUMS) (mat.) vínculo.
vindicable ['vɪndɪkəbəl] *a.* justificable, defendible (proposición, conducta, etc.).
vindicate ['vɪndəˌkeɪt] *v.t.* 1. vindicar, justificar (principio, acto, etc.). 2. (der.) vindicar, reivindicar. 3. (ant.) librar, libertar.
vindication [ˌvɪndə'keɪʃən] *s.* 1. vindicación. 2. (der.) reivindicación.
vindicative [vɪn'dɪkətɪv, B 'vɪndɪ-] *a.* (ant.) vindicativo.
vindicator ['vɪndəˌkeɪtər, B -ə] *s.* vindicador, defensor.
vindicatory [-dɪkəˌtɔrɪ, B -ˌkeɪtərɪ] *a.* 1. vindicatorio, justificativo. 2. vengativo.
vindictive [vɪn'dɪktɪv] *a.* vengativo, vindicativo.
vindictive damages, (der.) daños punitivos.
vindictively [-lɪ] *adv.* vindicativamente, por venganza.
vindictiveness [-nəs] *s.* carácter vengativo.
vine [vaɪn] *s.* (bot.) 1. vid, parra. 2. enredadera.
vineal ['vɪnɪəl] *a.* vínico.
vine arbor, emperrado, pérgola; quiosco enramado.
vine beetle, (ento.) escarabajuelo.
vine borer, (ento.) pulgón de las viñas.
vine branch, sarmiento, pámpano.
vine bud, botón.
vine-clad ['vaɪnˌklæd] *a.* cubierto de viñas o enredaderas.
vinedresser ['vaɪnˌdrɛsər, B -ə] *s.* viñador, viñatero (Amer.).
vine fretter, (zool.) gusano revoltón.
vinegar ['vɪnɪgər, B -gə] *s.* 1. vinagre. 2. (fig.) mordacidad.
vinegar eel, anguílula del vinagre.
vinegarish [-gərɪʃ] *a.* (fig.) avinagrado, vinagroso.
vinegarroon [ˌvɪnɪgə'run] *s.* (ento.) vinagrón (alacrán gigante de Méx. y del sudoeste de los E.U.).
vinegar worm, (ento.) anguílula del vinagre.
vinegary ['vɪnɪgərɪ] *a.* vinagroso; avinagrado, agrio.
vine grower, vitícola, viticultor.
vine growing, viticultura.
vine grub, v. louse, (zool.) gusano revoltón.
vine leaf, pámpana, hoja de parra.
vine-like ['vaɪnˌlaɪk] *a.* aparrado.
vine pest, (ento.) filoxera.
vinery ['vaɪnərɪ] *s.* (*pl.* VINERIES) 1. invernadero para el cultivo de vides. 2. emparrado.
vine shoot, sarmiento.
vinestock ['vaɪnˌstɑk, B -ˌstɔk] *s.* cepa (de la vid).
vineyard ['vɪnjərd, B -jəd] *s.* 1. viña, viñedo. 2. (fig.) viña, campo de labores (esp. espirituales).
vineyardist [-əst] *s.* viñador.
vineyard keeper, viñador, viñalero (Amer.).
vinic ['vaɪnɪk] *a.* vínico.
vinic ether, éter vínico.
vinicultural [ˌvɪnə'kʌltʃərəl] *a.* vinícola.
viniculture ['vɪnəˌkʌltʃər, B -tʃə] *s.* viticultura.
viniculturist [ˌvɪnə'kʌltʃərəst] *s.* vinicultor.
viniferous [vaɪ'nɪfərəs] *a.* vinífero.
vinification [ˌvɪnəfə'keɪʃən] *s.* vinificación.
vinose ['vaɪnoʊs] *a.* 1. vinoso. 2. de color de vino.
vinosity [vaɪ'nɑsətɪ, B -'nɔs-] *s.* vinosidad.
vinous ['vaɪnəs] *a.* 1. vinoso. 2. de color vinoso.
vintage ['vɪntɪdʒ] *s.* 1. vendimia. 2. cosecha (de la uva) ej., *wine of the 1917 v.,* vino de la cosecha de 1917. 3. (fig.) origen, cepa. —*a.* 1. de vendimia. 2. puro, de una sola cosecha (vino). 3. añejo (licor, vino); antiguo, clásico; de años, anticuado. 4. típico, característico; de lo mejor.
vintager [-ər, B -ə] *s.* vendimiador.
vintage wine, vino añejo.
vintage year, 1. año de cosecha excelente (que produce vino de primera calidad). 2. (fig.) año de éxitos.
vintner ['vɪntnər, B -nə] *s.* vinatero.
viny ['vaɪnɪ] *a.* (VINIER; VINIEST) cubierto de vides y enredaderas.
vinyl ['vaɪnəl] *s.* (quím.) vinilo.
vinyl alcohol, (quím.) alcohol vinílico.
vinyl chloride, (quím.) cloruro de vinilo.
vinylic [vaɪ'nɪlɪk] *a.* vinílico.
Vinylite ['vaɪnəlˌaɪt] *s.* vinilita.
vinyl plastic, plástico de vinilo.
vinyl resin, resina de vinilo.
viol ['vaɪəl] *s.* (mús.) viola antigua.
viola [vɪ'oʊlə] *s.* (mús.) viola, instrumento de cuerda algo más grande (y de registro más grave) que el violín.
viola [vaɪ'oʊlə, B 'vaɪə-] *s.* (bot.) viola.
violable ['vaɪələbəl] *a.* que se puede violar, violable.
violaceae [ˌvaɪə'leɪsɪˌi] *s. pl.* (bot.) violáceas.
violaceous [-'leɪʃəs] *a.* 1. violáceo, violado (color). 2. violácea (planta).
viola da braccio [vɪ'oʊlədə'brɑtʃoʊ] (mús.) viola tenor.
viola da gamba [-'gɑmbə, B -'gæm-] (mús.) viola de gamba.
viola d'amore [-dɑ'mɔreɪ] (mús.) viola de amor.
violate ['vaɪəˌleɪt] *v.t.* 1. violar, infringir (ley, tratado, etc.). 2. violar, estuprar (a mujer). 3. violar, profanar, invadir, perturbar (santuario, retiro, etc.).
violation [ˌvaɪə'leɪʃən] *s.* violación.
violator ['vaɪəˌleɪtər, B -ə] *s.* violador, transgresor.
violence ['vaɪələns] *s.* 1. violencia. 2. **to do v. to,** hacer daño a; reñir con, ej., *it does v. to my principles,* eso riñe con mis principios.
violent [-lənt] *a.* violento.
violently [-lɪ] *adv.* violentamente.
violet ['vaɪələt] *s.* 1. (bot.) violeta. 2. (color) violeta, violáceo, violado. 3. especie de mariposa (de color violeta). —*a.* violado, violáceo.
violet ray, (fís.) rayo violeta.

violin [ˌvaɪəˈlɪn] *s.* 1. violín. 2. violinista.
violinist [-əst] *s.* violinista.
violinmaker [-ˌmeɪkər, B -ə] *s.* fabricante de violines.
violist [vɪˈoʊləst] *s.* (mús.) el que toca la viola.
violle [vjɔl] *s.* (fís.) violle (unidad óptica antigua).
violoncellist [ˌvaɪələnˈtʃɛləst] *s.* violoncelista, violonchelista.
violoncello [-ˈtʃɛloʊ] *s.* (mús.) violoncelo, violonchelo.
violone [vjoʊˈloʊneɪ, B ˈvaɪəloʊn] *s.* (mús.) violón, contrabajo.
viosterol [vaɪˈɑstəˌrɔl, B -ˈɔs-] *s.* (farm.) viosterol.
VIP [ˈviaɪˈpi] *abrev. de* **very important person,** *s.* (fam.) persona muy importante, VIP; **he was given V. treatment,** lo trataron como a un VIP.
VIP lounge, sala VIP, sala para persones muy importantes.
viper [ˈvaɪpər, B -pə] *s.* (zool.) **víbora;** (fig.) víbora.
viperine [-pəˌraɪn] *a.* viperino, vipéreo.
viperish [-rɪʃ] *a.* (fig.) viperino, vipéreo.
viperous [-rəs] *a.* viperino, vipéreo.
viper's bugloss, (bot.) viperina.
viper's grass, (bot.) escorzonera, salsifí de España, salsifí negro.
virago [vəˈrɑgoʊ] *s.* (*pl.* VIRAGOES o VIRAGOS) 1. mujer regañona, mujer de mal genio, sierpe, arpía. 2. (ant.) virago, marimacho.
vireo [ˈvɪrɪˌoʊ] *s.* (orn.) vireo.
vireonine [-ɪoʊˌnaɪn, B -ɪə-] *a., s.* (orn.) vireónido.
virescence [vəˈrɛsəns] *s.* (bot.) virescencia.
virescent [-ənt] *a.* (bot.) virescente.
virgate [ˈvɜrˌgeɪt, B ˈvɜgɪt] *s.* (hist.) antigua medida británica de tierra.
virgate, *a.* (bot.) de forma de vara, enhiesto; ramoso.
Virgil [ˈvɜrdʒəl, B ˈvɜdʒəl] *s.* Virgilio, poeta romano, autor de la Eneida.
Virgilian, *var. de* **Vergilian.**
virgin [ˈvɜrdʒən, B ˈvɜdʒɪn] *s.* 1. virgen, doncella. 2. (astr.) Virgo (constelación). 3. **the V.,** la Virgen María. —*a.* 1. virgen. 2. inicial, primero.
virginal [-əl] *a.* virginal. —*s.* (mús.) virginal (espineta antigua).
virgin beeswax, cera virgen.
virgin birth, 1. (teo.) parto virginal (de María). 2. partenogénesis.
virgin honey, miel virgen.
Virginia [vərˈdʒɪnjə, B vəˈ-] Virginia, estado de los E.U.
Virginia creeper [vərˈdʒɪnjə-, B vəˈ-] (bot.) enredadera de Virginia, guan.
Virginia fence, cerca en zigzag.
Virginian [-jən] *a., s.* virginiano, de Virginia, estado del S. de E.U.
Virginia reel, un baile folklórico estado-unidense.
Virginia snakewort, (bot.) serpentaria virginiana.
Virginia stock, (bot.) mahonesa.
Virginia trumpet flower, (bot.) jazmín trompeta.
Virgin Islands, Islas Vírgenes (grupo de islas del Caribe).
virginity [vərˈdʒɪnətɪ, B vɜˈ-] *s.* virginidad, doncellez.
virginium [-ˈdʒɪnɪəm] *s.* (quím.) virginio.
Virgin Mary, Virgen María.
virgin's bower, (bot.) clemátide, aján, clematis de los Alpes, hierba de los lazarosos, hierba de los pordioseros.
virgin wool, lana virgen, lana en rama.
virgulate [ˈvɜrgjələt, B ˈvɜgjʊ-] *a.* virgular.
virgule [-gjul] *s.* (tip.) vírgula, virgulilla.
viricidal [ˌvaɪrəˈsaɪdəl, B ˌvaɪərə-] *a.* (med.) viricida, virucida.
viricide [ˈvaɪrəˌsaɪd, B ˈvaɪərə-] *s.* substancia viricida.
virid [ˈvɪrəd] *a.* verde brillante.
viridescence [ˌvɪrəˈdɛsəns] *s.* verdor.
viridescent [-ənt] *a.* verdoso.
viridian [vəˈrɪdɪən] *s.* verde cromo.
viridity [-ətɪ] *s.* verdor; frescura.
virile [ˈvɪrəl, B -ˌaɪl] *a.* 1. viril, varonil; macho. 2. dominante, imperioso (carácter, etc.); vigoroso (estilo literario, etc.).
virilism [-ˌɪzəm] *s.* (med.) virilismo.
virility [vəˈrɪlətɪ] *s.* virilidad.
virole [vɪˈroʊl] *s.* (her.) virol.
virologist [vaɪˈrɑlədʒəst, B ˌvaɪəˈrɔl-] *s.* (med.) experto en virología.
virology [-dʒɪ] *s.* (med.) virología.
virosis [vaɪˈroʊsəs] *s.* (med.) virosis.
virtu [ˌvɜrˈtu, B vɜˈ-] *s.* 1. afición a objetos de arte o antigüedades. 2. objetos de arte, antigüedades, curiosidades (colectivamente).
virtual [ˈvɜrtʃʊəl, B ˈvɜtʃ-] *a.* virtual; implícito.
virtual axis, (ing.) eje instantáneo de rotación.
virtual energy, (ing.) energía potencial.
virtual focus, (ópt.) foco virtual.
virtual image, (fís., ópt.) imagen virtual.
virtuality [ˌvɜrtʃʊˈælətɪ, B ˌvɜtʃʊ-] *s.* virtualidad.
virtually [ˈvɜrtʃʊəlɪ, B ˈvɜtʃ-] *adv.* virtualmente.
virtual velocity, (mec.) velocidad virtual.
virtual voltage, (elec.) voltaje efectivo.
virtue [ˈvɜrtʃʊ, B ˈvɜtju] *s.* 1. virtud, rectitud, moralidad. 2. (*pl.*) (relig.) virtudes (quinto coro de ángeles). 3. virtud, castidad (esp. de mujer). 4. **by (o in) v. of,** en virtud de; **of easy v.,** fácil (mujer); **to make a v. of,** convertir en virtud (algo que no lo es).
virtueless [-ləs] *a.* sin virtud(es), amoral.
virtuosa [ˌvɜrtʃʊˈoʊsə, B ˌvɜtjʊ-] *s.* virtuosa (en las bellas artes, esp. en música).
virtuosic [-ˈɑsɪk, B -ˈɔs-] *a.* virtuoso.
virtuosity [-ətɪ] *s.* virtuosismo, virtuosidad.
virtuoso [-ˈoʊsoʊ, B -zoʊ] *s.* (*pl.* VIRTUOSOS o VIRTUOSI [-si]) 1. virtuoso, artista de gran técnica. 2. conocedor; coleccionista.
virtuous [ˈvɜrtʃʊəs, B ˈvɜtʃ-] *a.* 1. virtuoso. 2. poderoso, eficaz.
virtuously [-lɪ] *adv.* virtuosamente.
virtuousness [-nəs] *s.* virtud, condición de virtuoso.
virucide [ˈvaɪrəˌsaɪd, B ˈvaɪərə-] *s.* substancia virucida.
virulence [ˈvɪrələns] *s.* 1. virulencia; acrimonia. 2. malignidad, encono.
virulency [-lənsɪ] *s.* (*pl.* VIRULENCIES) *var. de* **virulence.**
virulent [-lənt] *a.* virulento.
virulently [-lɪ] *adv.* con virulencia, virulentamente.
virus [ˈvaɪrəs, B ˈvaɪərəs] *s.* 1. virus. 2. (ant.) veneno.
visa [ˈvizə] *s.* 1. visado, visa (del pasaporte). 2. visto bueno, refrendación, refrendo. —*v.t.* (*pret., p.p.* VISAED [-zəd]; *p.pr.* VISAING [-zəŋ]) visar (un pasaporte); poner el visto bueno, refrendar (un documento).
visage [ˈvɪzɪdʒ] *s.* 1. semblante, rostro. 2. apariencia, aspecto.
visaged [-ɪdʒd] *a.* de rostro, cara o semblante.
visard, *var. de* **vizard.**
vis-à-vis [ˌvɪzəˈvi, B ˈvizɑvi] *s.* (fr.) (*pl.* VIS-À-VIS) 1. persona que está enfrente o está cara a cara con otra (esp. en ciertas danzas). 2. conversación íntima (entre dos personas). 3. confidente (mueble). —*adv.* frente a frente, cara a cara. —*prep.* frente a, comparado con, respecto a.
Visayan [vəˈsaɪən] *a., s.* visayo, de las islas Visayas o Bisayas (Filipinas).
viscacha [vɪsˈkɑtʃə, B -ˈkæ-] *s.* (zool.) vizcacha.
viscera [ˈvɪsərə] *s. pl.* (*sing.* VISCUS [ˈvɪskəs]) (anat.) vísceras, entrañas.
visceral [-rəl] *a.* 1. visceral, abdominal. 2. (fig.) hondo, íntimo, instintivo (sentimiento, etc.); crudo, realista (drama, etc.).
visceromotor [ˌvɪsərəˈmoʊtər, B -ə] *a.* (fisiol.) visceromotor.
viscid [ˈvɪsəd] *a.* viscoso, glutinoso, pegajoso.
viscidity [vɪˈsɪdətɪ] *s.* (*pl.* VISCIDITIES) viscosidad, glutinosidad.
viscometer [vɪsˈkɑmətər, B -ˈkɔmɪtə] *s.* viscosímetro.
viscose [ˈvɪsˌkoʊs] *a.* 1. viscoso, glutinoso, pegajoso. 2. de viscosa. —*s.* (quím.) viscosa.
viscosity [vɪsˈkɑsətɪ, B -ˈkɔs-] *s.* (*pl.* VISCOSITIES) viscosidad.
viscount [ˈvaɪˌkaʊnt] *s.* vizconde.
viscountcy [-sɪ] *s.* (*pl.* VISCOUNTCIES) vizcondado (título).
viscountess [-əs] *s.* vizcondesa.
viscounty [-ɪ] *s.* (*pl.* VISCOUNTIES) vizcondado (título o territorio).
viscous [ˈvɪskəs] *a.* viscoso, glutinoso, pegajoso.
viscous flow, (hidr.) flujo laminar o viscoso.
viscousness [-nəs] *s.* viscosidad.
viscous vortex, (aer., hidr.) torbellino viscoso, vortice viscoso.
viscus, (raro) *sing. de* **viscera.**
vise (pr. G.B.) **vice** [vaɪs] *s.* prensa de tornillo, tornillo de banco, cárcel. —*v.t.* coger o apretar con prensa de tornillo.
visé [ˈviˌzeɪ] *s., v.t.* (fr.) *var. de* **visa.**
Vishnu [ˈvɪʃnu] *s.* Visnú, Vishnú, segundo miembro de la Trinidad en la Teología hindú.
Vishnuism [-ˌɪzəm] *s.* (relig.) visnuismo, vishnuismo.
visibility [ˌvɪzəˈbɪlətɪ] *s.* (*pl.* VISIBILITIES) visibilidad.
visible [ˈvɪzəbəl] *a.* visible; notorio, manifiesto.
visible horizon, (geog.) horizonte sensible o natural.
visibleness [-nəs] *s.* visibilidad.
visibly [-blɪ] *adv.* visiblemente.
Visigoth [ˈvɪzəˌgɑθ, B -gɔθ] *s.* visigodo.
Visigothic [ˌvɪzəˈgɑθɪk, B -ˈgɔθ-] *a.* visigótico, visigodo.
vision [ˈvɪʒən] *s.* 1. visión, aparición, fantasía, fantasma. 2. visión, vista. 3. imaginación, previsión, clarividencia. —*v.t.* ver en una visión, evocar en una visión, imaginar.
visional [-əl] *a.* 1. claro, gráfico (relato, interpretación, etc.). 2. irreal, imaginario.
visionariness [ˈvɪʒəˌnɛrɪnəs, B -nərɪ-] *s.* naturaleza visionaria, naturaleza quimérica.
visionary [ˈvɪʒəˌnɛrɪ, B -nərɪ] *a.* 1. visionario, quimérico, imaginario. 2. impracticable, utópico. —*s.* (*pl.* VISIONARIES) visionario, soñador.
visionless [-ənləs] *a.* 1. privado de la vista, ciego. 2. falto de visión, sin inspiración.
visit [ˈvɪzət] *v.t.* 1. visitar. 2. vivir como huésped con. 3. (bíbl.) visitar, enviar, imponer, infligir (castigos, etc.); otorgar, bendecir con (premios, salvación, etc.). —*v.i.* 1. hacer visitas, ir de visita. 2. (fam.) charlar, platicar. 3. (bíbl.) imponer castigos. —*s.* 1. visita, visitación. 2. (der.) reconocimiento a un barco neutral en virtud del derecho de búsqueda.
visitable [-əbəl] *a.* visitable, que se puede visitar; sujeto a inspección o reconocimiento.

visitant [-ənt] *s.* 1. aparición, visión. 2. (orn.) ave de paso. 3. (poét., ret.) visitante.
visitation [ˌvɪzəˈteɪʃən] *s.* 1. visitación, visita (esp. oficial). 2. disposición divina, gracia o castigo del cielo. 3. **V.,** (relig.) Visitación. 4. (zool.) migración ocasional (de un gran número de animales).
visitator [ˈvɪzəˌteɪtər, B -ə] *s.* (relig.) visitador oficial.
visitatorial [ˌvɪzətəˈtɔrɪəl] *a.* del visitador (autoridad, jurisdicción, oficio, etc.).
visiting card [ˈvɪzətɪŋ-] tarjeta de visita.
visiting fireman, (fam., hum.) huésped ilustre.
visiting nurse, enfermera visitante, enfermera ambulante.
visiting professor, profesor visitante.
visitor [ˈvɪzətər, B -ə] *s.* visitante, visita.
visor [ˈvaɪzər, B -zə] *s.* 1. visera (de una gorra, un yelmo, etc.). 2. (fig.) máscara, disfraz.
visored [-zərd, B -zəd] *a.* 1. con visera, provisto de visera. 2. (fig.) enmascarado, disfrazado.
vista [ˈvɪstə] *s.* vista, perspectiva, panorama.
visual [ˈvɪʒʊəl, B ˈvɪzjʊ-] *a.* 1. visual. 2. visible.
visual acuity, agudeza o acuidad visual.
visual aid, ayuda visual, medio visual.
visual angle, (ópt.) ángulo visual.
visual-aural radio range [-ˈɔrəl-] (aer.) radiofaro direccional visual-auditivo.
visualization [ˌvɪʒʊələˈzeɪʃən, B ˌvɪzjʊəlaɪ-] *s.* 1. formación de una imagen mental. 2. acción de hacer visible.
visualize [ˈvɪʒʊəˌlaɪz, B ˈvɪzjʊə-] *v.t.* 1. imaginarse, representar(se) en la mente. 2. concebir, planear. —*v.i.* formarse una imagen mental.
visualizer [-ˌlaɪzər, B -zə] *s.* persona de memoria visual o gráfica.
visual line, (ópt.) rayo visual, línea visual.
visual purple, (bioquím.) púrpura visual.
visual ranging, (fotgmt.) colimación, cálculo de distancia por aparato óptico.
visual ray, (ópt.) rayo visual.
visual tuning, (t.v.) sintonización óptica, sintonización visual.
vita [ˈvaɪtə] *s.* pequeño resumen autobiográfico.
vitaceous [vaɪˈteɪʃəs] *a.* (bot.) vitáceo.
vital [ˈvaɪtəl] *a.* 1. vital. 2. (fig.) vital, esencial. 3. fatal, mortal, ej., *a v. wound,* una herida mortal. 4. (raro) vivo, viviente; vivaz, animado. —*s. pl.* 1. órganos vitales. 2. partes esenciales.
vital force, (filos.) impulso vital.
vitalism [-ˌɪzəm] *s.* (filos., biol.) vitalismo.
vitalist [-əst] *a., s.* vitalista.
vitalistic [ˌvaɪtəlˈɪstɪk] *a.* vitalista.
vitality [vaɪˈtælətɪ] *s.* vitalidad.
vitalization [ˌvaɪtələˈzeɪʃən, B -əlaɪ-] *s.* vitalización.
vitalize [ˈvaɪtəlˌaɪz] *v.t.* 1. vitalizar, vivificar. 2. vigorizar, animar.
Vitallium [vaɪˈtælɪəm] *s.* (med.) vitalio.
vitally [ˈvaɪtəlɪ] *adv.* vitalmente, de manera vital; **it is v. important,** es de importancia vital.
vital statistics, 1. estadística demográfica. 2. (hum.) medidas (del cuerpo de una mujer).
vitamer [ˈvaɪtəmər, B -mə] *s.* (quím.) vitámero.
vitamin [ˈvaɪtəmən, B ˈvɪt-] *s.* vitamina.
vitamin deficiency, deficiencia o carencia de vitaminas, avitaminosis.
vitaminic [ˌvaɪtəˈmɪnɪk, B ˌvɪt-] *a.* vitamínico.
vitaminize [ˈvaɪtəməˌnaɪz, B ˈvɪt-] *v.t.* 1. proveer de o suplir con vitaminas. 2. (fig.) vigorizar.
vita rays, (biol.) rayos ultravioletas, biológicos.
vitascope [ˈvaɪtəˌskoʊp] *s.* proyector cinematográfico primitivo.
vitellin [vaɪˈtɛlən, və-] *s.* (bioquím.) vitelina, ovovitelina.
vitelline [-ən, B -ˌaɪn] *a.* 1. vitelina, relativo a la membrana que envuelve la yema del huevo. 2. vitelina, dícese de la bilis de color amarillo subido.
vitellus [-əs] *s.* (biol.) vitelo.
vitiate [ˈvɪʃɪˌeɪt] *v.t.* 1. viciar, contaminar, corromper. 2. viciar, invalidar (un contrato, pacto, etc.).
vitiated [-əd] *a.* viciado.
vitiation [ˌvɪʃɪˈeɪʃən] *s.* 1. corrupción, contaminación. 2. invalidación.
vitiator [ˈvɪʃɪˌeɪtər, B -ə] *s.* corruptor.
viticultural [ˌvɪtəˈkʌltʃərəl] *a.* vitícola.
viticulture [ˈvɪtəˌkʌltʃər, B -tʃə] *s.* viticultura.
viticulturer [ˌvɪtəˈkʌltʃərər, B -ə] **viticulturist** [-əst] *s.* viticultor, vitícola.
vitiligo [ˌvɪtəlˈaɪgoʊ] *s.* (med.) vitiligo.
vitreosity [ˌvɪtrɪˈɑsətɪ, B -ˈɔs-] *s.* vidriosidad.
vitreous [ˈvɪtrɪəs] *a.* vítreo.
vitreous body, (anat.) cuerpo (o humor) vítreo (del ojo).
vitreous electricity, electricidad vítrea.
vitreous enamel, esmalte vítreo.
vitreous humor, (anat.) humor vítreo (del ojo).
vitreousness [-nəs] *s.* vidriosidad.
vitreous silver, (geol.) plata vítrea, argentina.
vitrescent [vɪˈtrɛsənt] *a.* vitrescible.
vitrescible [vɪˈtrɛsəbəl] *a.* vitrescible, vitrificable.
vitric [ˈvɪtrɪk] *a.* vítreo, vidrioso.
vitrifaction [ˌvɪtrəˈfækʃən] *s.* vitrificación.
vitrifiable [ˈvɪtrəˌfaɪəbəl] *s.* vitrificable.
vitrification [ˌvɪtrəfəˈkeɪʃən] *s.* vitrificación.
vitriform [ˈvɪtrəˌfɔrm, B -ˌfɔm] *a.* vítreo, vidrioso.
vitrify [ˈvɪtrəˌfaɪ] *v.t., v.i.* (*pret., p.p.* VITRIFIED; *p.pr.* VITRIFYING) vitrificar(se).
vitriol [ˈvɪtrɪəl] *s.* 1. (quím.) vitriolo. 2. (fig.) virulencia (de palabras); sarcasmo. —*v.t.* (*pret., p.p.* VITRIOLED O VITRIOLLED; *p.pr.* VITRIOLING O VITRIOLLING) (metal.) bañar en vitriolo.
vitriolated [ˈvɪtrɪəˌleɪtəd] *a.* (quím.) vitriolado.
vitriolic [ˌvɪtrɪˈɑlɪk, B -ˈɔl-] *a.* 1. vitriólico. 2. (fig.) violento, mordaz, sangriento (crítica, injuria, etc.).
vittle, *var. de* **victual.**
vituline [ˈvɪtʃʊˌlaɪn, B ˈvɪtjʊ-] *a.* becerril.
vituperable [vaɪˈtupərəbəl, B vɪˈtju-] *a.* vituperable.
vituperate [-ˌreɪt] *v.t., v.i.* vituperar.
vituperation [vaɪˌtupəˈreɪʃən, B vɪˌtju-] *s.* vituperación, vituperio; denuesto.
vituperative [-ˈtupərətɪv, B -ˈtju-] *a.* vituperioso, vituperador.
vituperatively [-lɪ] *adv.* vituperiosamente.
vituperator [-ˌreɪtər, B -ə] *s.* vituperador, vituperante.
vituperatory [-rəˌtɔrɪ, B -tərɪ] *a.* vituperante, vituperioso.
viva [ˈvivə] *interj., s.* ¡viva!
vivacious [vəˈveɪʃəs, vaɪ-] *a.* 1. vivaracho, vivaz. 2. (bot.) vivaz.
vivaciously [-lɪ] *adv.* con vivacidad, vivamente.
vivaciousness [-nəs] *s.* vivacidad, viveza.
vivacity [-ˈvæsətɪ] *s.* vivacidad, viveza.
vivandière [ˌviˌvɑnˈdjɛr, B -ˈdjɛə] *s.* (fr.) (hist.) vivandera, cantinera.
vivarium [vaɪˈvɛrɪəm, B -ˈvɛər-] *s.* (*pl.* VIVARIA [-ə] O VIVARIUMS) vivero.
viva voce [ˈvaɪvəˈvoʊsɪ] *a.* verbal, oral. —*adv.* de palabra, de viva voz.
viverrine [vaɪˈvɛrən, B ˈvaɪvəˌraɪn] *a.* (zool.) vivérrido.
vives [vaɪvz] *s.* (vet.) adivas.
vivid [ˈvɪvəd] *a.* 1. vivo, vívido, gráfico (relato, descripción, etc.). 2. vivo, claro, intenso (recuerdo, impresión, etc.). 3. vivo, brillante, reluciente (color).
vividly [-lɪ] *adv.* claramente, gráficamente; intensamente; al vivo.
vividness [-nəs] *s.* 1. claridad, intensidad. 2. brillo (de colores).
vivific [vaɪˈvɪfɪk] *a.* vivificante, vivificador.
vivification [ˌvɪvəfəˈkeɪʃən] *s.* vivificación.
vivify [ˈvɪvəˌfaɪ] *v.t.* (*pret., p.p.* VIVIFIED; *p.pr.* VIVIFYING) vivificar; avivar, animar.
vivifying [-ɪŋ] *a.* vivificador, vivificante.
viviparity [ˌvaɪvəˈpærətɪ, B ˌvɪ-] **viviparousness** [vaɪˈvɪpərəsnəs, B vɪ-] *s.* (zool., bot.) viviparida.
viviparous [vaɪˈvɪpərəs, B vɪ-] *a.* (zool., bot.) vivíparo.
vivisect [ˈvɪvəˌsɛkt, B ˌvɪvɪˈsɛkt] *v.t.* disecar (un animal vivo). —*v.i.* practicar la vivisección.
vivisection [ˌvɪvəˈsɛkʃən] *s.* vivisección.
vivisectional [-əl] *a.* de vivisección.
vivisectionist [-əst] *s.* 1. vivisector. 2. partidario de la vivisección.
vivisector [ˈvɪvəˌsɛktər, B ˌvɪvɪˈsɛktə] *s.* vivisector.
vivisectorium [ˌvɪvəsɛkˈtɔrɪəm] *s.* vivisectorio.
vixen [ˈvɪksən] *s.* 1. zorra, raposa. 2. (fig.) mujer regañona y colérica, arpía.
vixenish [-ɪʃ] *a.* 1. zorruno. 2. (fig.) regañona y colérica.
viz. *abrev de* **videlicet.**
vizard [ˈvɪzərd, B -əd] *s.* máscara, disfraz.
vizier, vizir [vəˈzɪr, B -ˈzɪə] *s.* visir, ministro musulmán.
vizierate [-ət, B -ˈzɪər-] *s.* visirato.
vizierial [-ɪəl] *a.* del visir.
viziership [-ˌʃɪp, B -ˈzɪəˌ-] *s.* visirato, visirazgo.
vizor, vizored, *vars. de* **visor, visored.**
V-J Day [ˈviˈdʒeɪ-] *abrev. de* **victory in Japan,** día de la victoria sobre el Japón (agosto 15 de 1945).
VLF *abrev. de* **very low frequency,** frecuencia muy baja.
vocable [ˈvoʊkəbəl] *s.* vocablo, voz, término.
vocabular [voʊˈkæbjələr, B -lə] *a.* verbal, de palabras.
vocabulary [voʊˈkæbjəˌlɛrɪ, və-, B -lərɪ] *s.* vocabulario, léxico.
vocabulary entry, artículo del vocabulario (en un diccionario o léxico).
vocal [ˈvoʊkəl] *a.* 1. vocal; verbal, oral. 2. (con *with*) resonante (de voces, gorjeo de pájaros, etc.). 3. clamoroso, vocinglero, voceador. 4. (fon.) vocal; vocálico. —*s.* (fon.) vocal.
vocal cords, (anat.) cuerdas vocales.
vocalic [voʊˈkælɪk, və-] *a.* vocálico.
vocalism [ˈvoʊkəlˌɪzəm] *s.* 1. vocalización, articulación. 2. canto, técnica o arte de cantar. 3. (fon.) vocalismo; conversión en vocal, vocalización.
vocalist [-əst] *s.* cantante, vocalista.
vocality [voʊˈkælətɪ] *s.* 1. carácter vocal. 2. dicción, elocuencia (de un orador, etc.).
vocalization [ˌvoʊkələˈzeɪʃən, B -kəlaɪ-] *s.* (mús., fon.) vocalización.
vocalize [ˈvoʊkəlˌaɪz] *v.t.* 1. articular, pronunciar. 2. (fon.) convertir en vocal, vocalizar. 3. (filol.) proveer de vocales (texto árabe o hebreo). —*v.i.* 1. emitir sonidos articulados. 2. (mús.) vocalizar.

vocally [-ɪ] *adv.* vocalmente; verbalmente.
vocal organ, órgano de la voz.
vocation [voʊ'keɪʃən] *s.* vocación; oficio, profesión, carrera; **to mistake one's v.,** errar uno la vocación.
vocational [-əl] *a.* 1. vocacional (escuela, consejo, guía, etc.). 2. profesional (experiencia, formación, etc.).
vocational education, instrucción vocacional.
vocational training, formación vocacional.
vocational experience, experiencia profesional.
vocational guidance, orientación vocacional o profesional.
vocational school, escuela vocacional, escuela de artes y oficios.
vocational training, formación profesional.
vocative ['vɑkətɪv, B 'vɔk-] *a., s.* (gram.) (caso) vocativo.
vocatively [-lɪ] *adv.* en vocativo.
vociferance [voʊ'sɪfərəns] *s.* vociferación.
vociferant [-ənt] *a.* vociferante, vociferador, vocinglero, clamoroso.
vociferate [-əˌreɪt] *v.i., v.t.* vociferar, vocear, gritar.
vociferation [voʊˌsɪfə'reɪʃən] *s.* vociferación, clamor.
vociferator [-'sɪfəˌreɪtər, B -ə] *s.* vociferador.
vociferous [-ərəs] *a.* vociferador, clamoroso, ruidoso.
vociferously [-lɪ] *adv.* con clamor, a voces, a gritos.
vociferousness [-nəs] *s.* vocinglería.
vocoder ['voʊˌkoʊdər, B -ə] *s.* (electrón.) vocoder.
voder ['voʊdər, B -ə] *s.* (electrón.) voder.
vodka ['vɑdkə, B 'vɔd-] *s.* vodka (licor).
vodun [voʊ'dun] *var. de* **voodocism.**
vogue [voʊg] *s.* boga, moda; **the v.,** la moda; **to be in v.,** estar de moda o en boga.
voguish ['voʊgɪʃ] *a.* 1. a la moda, elegante, de buen tono. 2. de popularidad pasajera.
voice [vɔɪs] *s.* 1. voz. 2. (gram.) voz (activa o pasiva). 3. (mús.) voz, cantante. 4. (fon.) sonoridad (de consonantes). 5. (ant.) rumor; fama, reputación. 6. **at the top of one's v.,** a voz en cuello; **in a loud v.,** en voz alta; **in a low v.,** en voz baja; **to be in v.,** estar en buena voz (cantante); **to give v. to,** expresar; **to have a v. in (a matter),** tener voz en (un asunto); **to raise one's v.,** alzar la voz; **veiled v.,** voz empañada; **with one v.,** a una voz, por unanimidad. —*v.t.* 1. expresar, manifestar; dar expresión a; divulgar. 2. (mús.) afinar (cañones del órgano). 3. (fon.) sonorizar.
voice coil, (rad.) bobina móvil de altavoz, bobina de la voz.
voiced [vɔɪst] *a.* 1. (*ú. en compuestos*) de (cierta) voz, ej., *harsh-v.,* de voz chillona. 2. expresado, dicho. 3. (fon.) sonoro, sonorizado.
voiceful ['vɔɪsfəl] *a.* (poét.) sonoro, sonante, resonante.
voiceless [-ləs] *a.* 1. mudo. 2. (fon.) sordo, no sonoro.
Voice of America, (rad.) la Voz de América.
voice pipe, tubo portavoz.
void [vɔɪd] *a.* 1. vacío, vacuo, hueco. 2. vacante, vaco, desocupado. 3. (con *of*) falto, carente, desprovisto (de). 4. (der.) nulo, inválido, írrito; anulable. 5. (poét., ret.) inútil; vano, ineficaz; inservible. —*s.* 1. vacuo, vacío; claro, laguna. 2. (fig.) (sensación de) vacuidad o futilidad. 3. (naipes) fallo (falta de un palo en la mano), ej., *I have a v. in spades,* tengo fallo a espadas. —*v.t.* 1. evacuar, descargar. 2. vaciar, desocupar. 3. (der.) anular, invalidar, irritar; inutilizar.
voidable ['vɔɪdəbəl] *a.* (esp. der.) anulable.
voidance ['vɔɪdəns] *s.* 1. vaciamiento. 2. (relig.) vacante. 3. (der.) anulación, invalidación.
void coefficient, (ing.) coeficiente cavitario.
voided ['vɔɪdəd] *a.* 1. vaciado. 2. vacante. 3. (der.) inválido, anulado.
voider [-ər, B -ə] *s.* 1. vaciador. 2. anulador.
voidness [-nəs] *s.* 1. vacío, vacuidad. 2. invalidez, nulidad.
voile [vɔɪl] *s.* (fr.) (tej.) espumilla; gasa de algodón.
voix celeste [ˌvwɑseɪ'lɛst, B -sɪ-] (fr.) (mús.) voz celestial (registro de tono suave y trémulo del órgano).
volant ['voʊlənt] *a.* (fr.) 1. (zool.) volante, volador, voladero. 2. (her.) volante. 3. (poét.) ágil, veloz, ligero.
Volapük ['voʊləˌpʊk, B 'vɔlə-] *s.* volapuk (idioma universal inventado en 1879).
volar ['voʊlər, B -lə] *a.* (anat.) palmar o plantar.
volary ['voʊlərɪ] *s.* (*pl.* VOLARIES) pajarera, averío.
volatile ['vɑlətəl, B 'vɔləˌtaɪl] *a.* 1. volátil, evaporable, vaporable. 2. (fig.) volátil, veleidoso, fugaz, transitorio. 3. explosivo. 4. (raro) volante, volador.
volatileness [-nəs] *s.* 1. volatilidad. 2. fugacidad. 3. volubilidad.
volatility [ˌvɑlə'tɪlətɪ, B ˌvɔl-] *a.* volatilidad.
volatilization [ˌvɑlətələ'zeɪʃən, B vɔˌlæ-] *s.* vulcanizacion.
volatilize ['vɑlətəlˌaɪz, B vɔ'lætɪl-] *v.t., v.i.* volatilizar(se).
volcanic [vɑl'kænɪk, B vɔl-] *a.* volcánico.
volcanically [-ɪkəlɪ] *adv.* volcánicamente.
volcanic ash, ceniza volcánica; lava pulverizada, escorial.
volcanic glass, (min.) vidrio volcánico, obsidiana.
volcanicity [ˌvɑlkə'nɪsətɪ, B ˌvɔl-] *s.* volcanicidad, vulcanismo.
volcanic rock, roca volcánica.
volcanism ['vɑlkəˌnɪzəm, B 'vɔl-] *s.* (geol.) volcanismo, vulcanismo.
volcanist [-nəst] *s.* (geol.) experto en vulcanología.
volcanization [ˌvɑlkənə'zeɪʃən, B -naɪ-] *s.* volcanización.
volcanize ['vɑlkəˌnaɪz, B 'vɔl-] *v.t.* someter a calor volcánico, afectar por calor volcánico (rocas, minerales, etc.).
volcano [vɑl'keɪnoʊ, B vɔl-] *s.* (*pl.* VOLCANOES o VOLCANOS) volcán; **to be on the edge of a v.,** (fig.) estar sobre un volcán, vivir en peligro constante.
volcanologist [ˌvɑlkə'nɑlədʒəst, B ˌvɔlkə'-nɔl-] *s.* vulcanólogo, experto en vulcanología.
volcanology [-dʒɪ] *s.* vulcanología.
vole [voʊl] *s.* (naipes) bola, capote; **to go the v.,** (fig.) jugar el todo por el todo.
vole, *s.* (zool.) ratón campestre, ratón de agua.
volery, *var. de* **volary.**
volitant ['vɑlətənt, B 'vɔl-] *a.* (zool.) volante, volador.
volition [voʊ'lɪʃən, və-] *s.* volición, voluntad; **of one's own v.,** de su propia voluntad (de uno).
volitional [-əl] *a.* volitivo, relativo a la voluntad.
volitive ['vɑlətɪv, B 'vɔl-] *a.* volitivo, voluntario.
volley ['vɑlɪ, B 'vɔlɪ] *s.* (*pl.* VOLLEYS) 1. descarga cerrada, andanada, salva (de cañonazos, etc.); rociada, lluvia (de flechas, piedras, etc.). 2. (fig.) estallido, andanada, torrente (de juramentos, palabras, etc.). 3. (dep.) voleo, volea (de la pelota). —*v.t.* (*pret., p.p.* VOLLEYED o VOLLIED; *p.pr.* VOLLEYING) 1. lanzar (una descarga). 2. (fig.) lanzar (juramentos, preguntas, etc.). 3. (dep.) volear, golpear o lanzar de voleo (la pelota). —*v.i.*(dep.) hacer un voleo.
volleyball [-ˌbɔl] *s.* (dep.) vóleibol; volley ball.
volplane ['vɑlˌpleɪn, B 'vɔl-] (aer.) *v.i.* planear, deslizarse en aeroplano. —*s.* planeo, vuelo planeado, vuelo cernido.
Volsci ['vɑlˌsaɪ, B 'vɔlski] *s. pl.* (hist.) volscos, antiguo pueblo conquistado por los romanos.
Volsung ['vɑlsʊŋ, B 'vɔl-] *s.* (mitol.) Volsungo, personaje de la saga escandinava.
volt [voʊlt, B vɔlt] *s.* 1. (equit.) vuelta (que da un caballo trotando de lado). 2. (esgr.) salto para evitar una estocada.
volt [voʊlt] *s.* (elec.) voltio.
Volta effect ['voʊltə-, B 'vɔl-] (fís.) efecto Volta.
voltage ['voʊltɪdʒ] *s.* (elec.) voltaje, tensión.
voltage amplification, (elec.) amplificación de tensión.
voltage coil, (elec.) bobina de tensión.
voltage divider, (elec.) reductor de voltaje o de tensión.
voltage doubler, (rad.) duplicador de voltaje.
voltage drop, (elec.) caída de tensión.
voltage rating, (elec.) voltaje nominal.
voltage regulator, (elec.) regulador de voltaje, regulador de tensión.
voltage transformer, (elec.) transformador de tensión, transformador de voltaje.
voltaic [vɑl'teɪɪk, B vɔl-] *a.* (elec.) voltaico.
voltaic battery, (elec.) pila voltaica.
voltaic cell, (elec.) elemento voltaico.
voltaic couple, (elec.) par voltaico.
voltaic electricity, electricidad voltaica o dinámica.
voltaic pile, (elec.) pila de Volta, pila voltaica.
Voltairean, Voltairian [voʊl'tɛrɪən, B vɔl'-tɛər-] *a., s.* volteriano, del filósofo francés, Voltaire.
Voltairianism [-ˌɪzəm] *s.* volterianismo.
voltaism ['voʊltəˌɪzəm, 'vɑl-, B 'vɔl-] *s.* voltaísmo, galvanismo.
voltameter [voʊl'tæmətər, B vɔl-ə] *s.* (fís.) voltámetro, voltiamperímetro.
voltametric [ˌvoʊltə'mɛtrɪk, B ˌvɔl-] *a.* (fís.) voltamétrico.
voltammeter ['voʊlt'æmˌitər, B -'æmɪtə] *s.* (fís.) voltamperímetro, voltiamperímetro.
volt-ampere [-'æmˌpɪr, B -pɛə] *s.* (elec.) voltamperio.
Volta's pile, pila de Volta, pila voltaica.
volte face [ˌvɔlt'fɑs] cambio de opinión, cambio de actitud.
voltmeter ['voʊltˌmitər, B -ə] *s.* (elec.) voltímetro.
volubility [ˌvɑljə'bɪlətɪ, B ˌvɔl-] *s.* 1. facundia, verbosidad, afluencia. 2. volubilidad.
voluble ['vɑljəbəl, B 'vɔl-] *a.* 1. facundo, verboso, suelto de lengua, charlatán, afluente. 2. voluble, rotativo, rotante. 3. (bot.) voluble.
volubleness [-nəs] *s.* 1. facundia, verbosidad. 2. volubilidad.
volubly [-blɪ] *adv.* con facundia.
volume ['vɑljəm, -jʊm, B 'vɔl-] *s.* 1. volumen, tomo. 2. volumen, bulto, masa, cantidad; capacidad, caudal. 3. volumen, fuerza (de sonido). 4. (geom.) volumen. 5. (raro) volumen (rollo de papel o pergamino). —*v.i.* abultarse, expandirse.
volume control, (rad.) regulador de volumen.
volumed [-jəmd, -jʊmd] *a.* 1. masivo, voluminoso. 2. (raro) (*ú. en compuestos*) en (tantos) volúmenes o tomos, ej., *a two-volumed dictionary,* un diccionario en dos volúmenes.
volume damper, (a.a.) regulador o compuerta de tiro.

volume level, nivel sonoro.
volume production, producción en masa.
volumeter ['valjʊˌmitər, B vɔ'ljumɪtə] *s.* (fís.) volúmetro.
volumetric [ˌvaljʊ'mɛtrɪk, B ˌvɔl-] *a.* volumétrico.
volumetrically [-trɪkəlɪ] *adv.* volumétricamente.
volumetric analysis, (quím.) análisis volumétrico.
volumetry [və'lumətrɪ, B -'lju-] *s.* volumetría.
volume unit, decibelio.
voluminosity [vəˌlumə'nasətɪ, B -ˌljumɪ'nɔs-] *s.* 1. abultamiento. 2. multiplicidad, numerosidad, abundancia. 3. verbosidad.
voluminous [-'lumənəs, B -'lju-] *a.* 1. voluminoso. 2. copioso (notas, datos, etc.); prolijo (autor, escritor, carta, etc.). 3. enrollado, serpenteado, lleno de circunvoluciones.
voluminously [-lɪ] *adv.* copiosamente, voluminosamente.
voluminousness [-nəs] *s.* 1. abultamiento. 2. multiplicidad, numerosidad, abundancia. 3. prolijidad.
voluntarily [ˌvalən'tɛrəlɪ, B 'vɔləntər-] *adv.* voluntariamente.
voluntariness ['valənˌtɛrɪnəs, B 'vɔləntər-] *s.* voluntariedad.
voluntarism [-təˌrɪzəm] *s.* (filos.) voluntarismo.
voluntary ['valənˌtɛrɪ, B 'vɔləntərɪ] *a.* voluntario. —*s.* (*pl.* VOLUNTARIES) 1. voluntario. 2. (mús.) improvisación (esp. en el órgano).
voluntary consideration, (der.) causa lucrativa.
voluntary conveyance, (der.) cesión gratuita.
voluntaryism [-ˌɪzəm] *s.* (filos.) voluntarismo.
voluntary muscle, (anat.) músculo voluntario.
volunteer [ˌvalən'tɪr, B ˌvɔlən'tɪə] *s.* 1. voluntario. 2. (der.) actor, ejecutante o representante voluntarios. 3. (der.) adquiriente a título gratuito. —*a.* 1. voluntario. 2. de voluntarios. —*v.t.* ofrecer o contribuir voluntariamente. —*v.i.* 1. ofrecerse como voluntario. 2. alistarse o servir como voluntario.
voluptuary [və'lʌptʃʊˌɛrɪ, B -'lʌptjʊərɪ] *s.* (*pl.* VOLUPTUARIES) voluptuoso, sibarita. —*a.* voluptuoso, sensual.
voluptuate [-ˌeɪt] *v.i.* regodearse; sumirse en el lujo.
voluptuous [və'lʌptʃʊəs] *a.* voluptuoso, sensual.
voluptuously [-lɪ] *adv.* voluptuosamente.
voluptuousness [-nəs] *s.* voluptuosidad.
volute [və'lut, B -'ljut] *s.* 1. (arq.) voluta. 2. (zool.) espira o hélice (de una concha). 3. (zool.) voluta (molusco). —*a.* 1. espiral, en espiral, de caracol. 2. (mec.) helicoidal.
volute chamber, (mec.) caja de voluta, caja espiral.
volute compass, (dib.) compás de espirales.
volute pump, (mec.) bomba centrifugadora en cuerpo de caracol.
volute spring, (mec.) resorte de espiral, resorte de espira cónica.
volution [və'luʃən, B -'lju-] *s.* 1. (zool.) espira o hélice (deuna concha). 2. (anat.) circunvolución.
volva ['valvə, B 'vɔl-] *s.* (bot.) volva.
Volvocaceae [ˌvalvə'keɪsɪˌi, B ˌvɔl-] *s. pl.* (bot.) volvocáceas.
volvulus ['valvjələs, B 'vɔl-] *s.* (med.) vólvulo, volvo.
vomer ['voʊmər, B -mə] *s.* (anat., zool.) vómer.
vomerine [-məˌraɪn] *a.* (anat., zool.) vomeriano.
vomica ['vamәkə, B 'vɔm-] *s.* (med.) vómica.
vomicine ['vaməˌsin, B 'vɔm-] *s.* (quím.) vomicina.
vomit ['vamət, B 'vɔm-] *s.* 1. vómito. 2. emético, vomitivo. —*v.i.* 1. vomitar, arrojar. 2. ser vomitado, salir con violencia. —*v.t.* vomitar, arrojar.
vomiting gas [-ətɪŋ-] (mil.) agresívo emético.
vomitive [-ətɪv] *s., a.* vomitivo, emético.
vomitory [-əˌtɔrɪ, B -tərɪ] *a.* vomitorio, vomitivo, emético. —*s.* (*pl.* VOMITORIES) 1. (hist.) vomitorio (en circos y teatros). 2. (ant.) emético, vomitivo.
vomiturition [ˌvamətʃə'rɪʃən, B ˌvɔm-] *s.* (med.) vomiturición.
vomitus ['vamətəs, B 'vɔm-] *s.* (med.) vómito.
V-one (V-1) *abrev de* **flying bomb,** bomba volante.
voodoo ['vudu] *s.* 1. vodú, vudú, voduismo. 2. hechicero o brujo, que practica el vodú. —*v.t.* hechizar, embrujar.
voodooism [-ˌɪzəm] *s.* voduismo, creencias religiosas basadas en la magia.
voodooist [-əst] *s.* practicante del voduismo; hechicero o brujo.
voracious [vɔ'reɪʃəs, və-] *a.* 1. voraz. 2. insaciable. 3. glotón.
voraciously [-lɪ] *adv.* vorazmente.
voracity [-'ræsətɪ] *s.* voracidad.
vortex ['vɔrˌtɛks, B 'vɔˌ-] *s.* (*pl.* VORTEXES o VORTICES [-təˌsiz]) 1. vórtice. 2. vorágine, torbellino.
vortex tunnel, (aer.) túnel aerodinámico vertical.
vortical [-tɪkəl] *a.* vortiginoso, voraginoso.
vorticella [ˌvɔrtə'sɛlə, B ˌvɔtɪ-] *s.* (*pl.* VORTICELLAE [-i] o VORTICELLAS) (biol.) vorticela.
vorticose ['vɔrtəˌkoʊs, B 'vɔtɪ-] *a.* vortiginoso, voraginoso.
vortiginous [vɔr'tɪdʒənəs, B vɔ'-] *a.* (ant.) vortiginoso, voraginoso.
Vosges [voʊʒ] *s.* Vosgos (montes del N.E. de Francia).
votaress ['voʊtərəs] *s.* adicta, entusiasta; devota; partidaria ferviente.
votary ['voʊˌtərɪ] *s.* (*pl.* VOTARIES) adicto, entusiasta; devoto; partidario ferviente.
vote [voʊt] *s.* 1. voto. 2. votación, sufragio. 3. sufragio, derecho de voto. 4. (fig.) voz, voto, parecer dictamen. 5. voto, votante. 6. **the v.,** la votación (conjunto de votos emitidos); **to put to the v.,** someter a votación. —*v.i.* votar, dar voto; **v. against,** votar en contra; votar en contra de (algo o alguien); **v. for,** votar por, votar a favor de (algo o alguien); **v. that,** proponer que. —*v.t.* 1. votar por, elegir o determinar por votos. 2. (fam.) declarar, señalar. 3. **v. down** votar en contra; derrotar, desaprobar; **v. in,** elegir (a oficio, etc.) por votación.
voteless ['voʊtləs] *a.* sin voto.
vote of censure, voto de censura.
vote of confidence, voto de confianza.
voter ['voʊtər, B -ə] *s.* votante, votador, elector.
voting [-ɪŋ] *s.* votación. —*a.* de votación, electoral.
voting machine, máquina registradora de votos electorales.
voting paper, (G.B.) balota.
voting precinct, distrito electoral.
voting trust, fideicomiso electoral.
votive ['voʊtɪv] *a.* votivo.
votive mass, misa votiva.
votive offering, exvoto.
vouch [vaʊtʃ] *v.t.* 1. comprobar, verificar; compulsar. 2. (der.) citar, emplazar (al defensor de un título). 3. (ant.) atestiguar, testimoniar; defender, sostener; garantizar, avalar. —*v.i.* **v. for,** responder de, garantizar (algo); responder por, salir fiador por (alguien); atestiguar, confirmar (algo).
vouchee [vaʊ'tʃi] *s.* 1. fiado, garantizado. 2. (der.) defensor del título.
voucher ['vaʊtʃər, B -tʃə] *s.* 1. comprobante. 2. certificado; documento probatorio. 3. fiador, garante. 4. comprobación; prueba. —*v.t.* autenticar con comprobante.
vouchsafe [vaʊtʃ'seɪf] *v.t.* 1. conceder, otorgar, dispensar; dignarse a dar. 2. (ant.) garantizar.
vouchsafement [-mənt] *s.* concesión, condescendencia.
voussoir [vu'swar, B -'swa] *s.* (fr.) (arq.) dovela.
vow [vaʊ] *s.* 1. voto, promesa solemne (a Dios o a alguna deidad); promesa de fidelidad o lealtad. 2. afirmación solemne, aseveración. 3. **to be under v.,** haber tomado un voto. —*v.t.* 1. comprometerse a; prometer solemnemente, jurar. 2. afirmar solemnemente, aseverar. —*v.i.* afirmar, aseverar.
vowel ['vaʊəl, vaʊl] *s.* (gram.) vocal. —*a.* vocal, vocálico.
vowel harmony, (filol.) armonía vocálica.
vowelization [ˌvaʊələ'zeɪʃən, B -laɪ-] *s.* inserción de puntos vocálicos (en texto árabe o hebreo).
vowelize ['vaʊəˌlaɪz] *v.t.* proveer de puntos vocálicos (texto árabe o hebreo).
vowel point, punto vocálico (en el hebreo y en el árabe).
vow of chastity, (relig.) voto de castidad.
vow of poverty, (relig.) voto de pobreza.
vox [vaks, B vɔks] *s.* voz.
vox angelica ['vaksæn'dʒɛlɪkə, B 'vɔks-] (mús.) voz angélica (registro del órgano).
vox humana [-hju'manə] (mús.) voz humana (registro del órgano).
vox populi [-'papjəˌlaɪ, B -ˌpɔp-] opinión pública.
voyage ['vɔɪɪdʒ] *s.* viaje (esp. por mar o aire), travesía. —*v.i.* viajar por mar, navegar; viajar por aire; hacer viajes. —*v.t.* viajar por, atravesar.
voyager [-ər, B -ə] *s.* viajero, pasajero (de un buque).
V. P. *abrev de* **Vice-President,** vicepresidente.
V-particle ['vɪˌpartɪkəl, B -ˌpat-] *s.* (fís.) partícula V.
V-shaped, en forma de V.
V-sign, signo de la victoria; **to give the V.,** hacer la V de la victoria.
Vt. *abrev de* **Vermont,** Vermont.
VT *abrev. de* **variable time,** tiempo variable.
VT fuze ['vi'ti-] (mil.) espoleta de radioproximidad, espoleta de tiempo variable.
VTOL *abrev. de* **vertical takeoff and landing,** despegue y aterrizaje vertical.
V-two (V-2) proyectil de largo alcance empleado por Alemania en la Segunda Guerra mundial.
vug, vugg, vugh [vʌg] *s.* (geol.) vug, geoda pequeña, drusa.
Vulcan ['vʌlkən] *s.* (astr., mitol.) Vulcano.
vulcanian [ˌvʌl'keɪnɪən] *a.* 1. **V.,** (mitol.) Vulcanio. 2. volcánico.
vulcanicity [-kə'nɪsətɪ] *s.* volcanicidad.
vulcanism ['vʌlkəˌnɪzəm] *s.* (geol.) vulcanismo, plutonismo.
vulcanite [-ˌnaɪt] *s.* vulcanita. —*a.* de vulcanita.
vulcanizable [-ˌnaɪzəbəl] *a.* vulcanizable.
vulcanizate [-nəˌzeɪt] *s.* artículo vulcanizado.
vulcanization [ˌvʌlkənə'zeɪʃən, B -naɪ-] *s.* vulcanización.
vulcanize ['vʌlkəˌnaɪz] *v.t.* vulcanizar. —*v.i.* ser vulcanizado.
vulcanized fiber [-ˌnaɪzd-] fibra vulcanizada.

vulcanized rubber, caucho vulcanizado.
vulcanologist [ˌvʌlkə'nɑlədʒəst, B -'nɔl-] *s.* vulcanólogo, experto en vulcanología.
vulcanology [-dʒɪ] *s.* (geol.) vulcanología.
vulgar ['vʌlgər, B -gə] *a.* 1. vulgar. 2. **the v.,** el vulgo.
vulgar era, era vulgar, era común, era cristiana.
vulgar fraction, (mat.) quebrado o fración común.
vulgarian [ˌvʌl'gɛrɪən, -'gær-, B -'gɛər-] *s.* persona vulgar, esp. ricacho, ricachón.
vulgarism ['vʌlgəˌrɪzəm] *s.* 1. vulgarismo. 2. vulgaridad, grosería, ordinariez, patanería.
vulgarity [ˌvʌl'gærətɪ] *s.* (*pl.* VULGARITIES) vulgaridad, grosería, ordinariez, trivialidad.
vulgarization [-gərə'zeɪʃən, B -raɪ-] *s.* vulgarización.
vulgarize ['vʌlgəˌraɪz] *v.t.* 1. vulgarizar. 2. adocenar.
vulgarizer [-ər, B -ə] *s.* vulgarizador.
vulgarly ['vʌlgərlɪ, B -gəlɪ] *adv.* vulgarmente.
vulgarness [-nəs] *s.* vulgaridad.
vulgate ['vʌlˌgeɪt, -gət] *s.* 1. **V.,** Vulgata. 2. p. ext. texto comúnmente aceptado.
vulgus ['vʌlgəs] *s.* (*pl.* VULGUSES) 1. vulgo, plebe. 2. (G.B.) composición breve en latín o griego (que se hacía como ejercicio en algunas escuelas).
vulnerability [ˌvʌlnərə'bɪlətɪ] *s.* vulnerabilidad.
vulnerable ['vʌlnərəbəl] *a.* 1. vulnerable. 2. (bridge) vulnerable. 3. **v. to,** (fig.) susceptible a, indefenso contra (ataque, censura, etc.).
vulnerableness [-nəs] *s.* vulnerabilidad.
vulnerary ['vʌlnəˌrɛrɪ, B -rərɪ] *a.* vulnerario. —*s.* (*pl.* VULNERARIES) vulnerario.
vulpine ['vʌlˌpaɪn] *a.* 1. vulpino, zorruno. 2. ladino, astuto.
vulpinite ['vʌlpəˌnaɪt] *s.* (min.) vulpinita.
vulture ['vʌltʃər, B -tʃə] *s.* (orn.) buitre, catartes.
vulturine [-tʃərˌaɪn] **vulturous** [-əs] *a.* buitrero.
vulva ['vʌlvə] *s.* (anat.) vulva.
vulval [-vəl] **vulvar** [-vər, B -və] *a.* (anat.) vulvar.
vulvitis [ˌvʌl'vaɪtəs] *s.* (med.) vulvitis.
vulvovaginitis [ˌvʌlvoʊˌvædʒə'naɪtəs] *s.* (med.) vulvovaginitis.
vying ['vaɪɪŋ] *p.pr. de* **vie.** —*a.* emulador, rival.
vyingly [-lɪ] *adv.* con emulación, rivalizando.

W

W ['dʌbəlju] *s.* w, vigésima tercera letra del alfabeto inglés.

W. *abrev. de* 1. **west,** oeste (O). 2. **western,** occidental. 3. **Washington,** Washington. 4. **Wednesday,** miércoles.

w. *abrev. de* 1. **week,** semana. 2. **wife,** esposa. 3. **with,** con.

W *simb. de* **wolfram,** tungsteno (W).

wa' [wɔ, wɑ] (esco.) *var. de* **wall.**

Waaf [wæf] *s.* (*pl.* WAAFS) (G.B.) miembro del cuerpo auxiliar femenino de la Real Fuerza Aérea (en la segunda guerra mundial).

wab [wæb, B wɑb] (esco.) *var. de* **web.**

wabble ['wɑbəl, B 'wɔb-] *s.* (ento.) larva de moscardón (que infesta a las ardillas).

wabble, *var. de* **wobble.**

WAC [wæk] *abrev. de* **Women's Army Corps,** Cuerpo Militar Femenino de los E.U.

wacke ['wækə] *s.* (geol.) roca parda arenisca y basáltica.

wackily ['wækəlɪ] *adv.* absurdamente, excéntricamente, alocadamente.

wackiness [-ɪnəs] *s.* excentricidad, extravagancia.

wacky ['wækɪ] *a.* (WACKIER; WACKIEST) (jer.) absurdo, excéntrico, loco, ilógico.

wad [wɑd, B wɔd] *s.* 1. lío, fajo (de paja, papel, billetes, estopa, etc.). 2. taco (que se coloca en ciertas armas de fuego y en cartuchos). 3. rollo o fajo de billetes (de dinero). 4. (jer.) montón (de dinero), dineral, fortuna. —*v.t.* (*pret., p.p.* WADDED; *p.pr.* WADDING) 1. apiñar, apretar (papel, fieltro, estopa, etc.). 2. atacar (un arma de fuego, cartucho, bala en cartucho). 3. acolchar, enguatar, emborrar; (fig.) proteger.

wad, *s.* (esco., der.) prenda, empeño; **in w.,** empeñado, en prenda.

wadding ['wɑdɪŋ, B 'wɔd-] *s.* guata (para acolchar); relleno (para vestidos); tacos (en armas de fuego).

waddle ['wɑdəl, B 'wɔd-] *v.i.* (*pret., p.p.* WADDLED; *p.pr.* WADDLING) anadear, nanear, andar como un pato. —*s.* andar del patojo, contoneo, andar de pato.

waddy ['wɑdɪ, B 'wɔdɪ] (Aust.) *s.* cachiporra, maza (usada por los aborígenes). —*v.t.* atacar con cachiporra, dar un cachiporrazo a.

wade [weɪd] *v.i.* 1. ir vadeando (en agua, arena, lodo, nieve, etc.). 2. (fig.) pasar o avanzar con dificultad o esfuerzo. 3. chapotear. 4. **w. in** (o **into**), atacar denodadamente, arremeter; empezar a trabajar resueltamente; **w. through,** cruzar vadeando; (fig.) leer con dificultad (un libro largo o tedioso, etc.). —*v.t.* vadear.

wader ['weɪdər, B -ə] *s.* 1. vadeador. 2. (orn.) ave zancuda. 3. (*pl.*) botas altas impermeables (usadas para vadear).

wadi ['wɑdɪ, B 'wɔdɪ] *s.* (*pl.* WADIES) uadi, arroyada (en el África y Asia).

wading bird ['weɪdɪŋ-] ave zancuda.

wading pool, piscina de poca profundidad.

wady, *s.* (*pl.* WADIES) *var. de* **wadi.**

wae [weɪ] (dial.) *var. de* **woe.**

waesucks ['weɪˌsʌks] *interj.* (esco.) ¡ay! (como exclamación de dolor o pena).

Waf [wæf] *s.* (*pl.* WAFS) miembro del cuerpo femenino de la Fuerza Aérea de E.U.

wafer ['weɪfər, B -fə] *s.* 1. hostia, barquillo. 2. oblea (para pegar sobres, etc.). 3. (relig.) hostia. 4. (mec.) chapa, disco (usado como válvula, diafragma, etc.). —*v.t.* pegar o cerrar con oblea.

wafer socket, (rad.) zócalo de discos, portaválvula de chapas.

waff [wæf] *s.* (pr. esco.) 1. señal, seña (hecha con la mano). 2. bocanada, fumarada; vaharada. 3. ojeada, vistazo. 4. fantasma, espectro, aparecido. —*v.t., v.i.* (esco.) señalar con la mano; aletear, menearse.

waffie ['wæfɪ, B 'wɑ-] *s.* (esco.) vago, vagabundo.

waffle ['wɑfəl, 'wɔf-, B 'wɔf-] *s.* wafle, especie de panqueque (Amer.), barquillo o torta con estrías, hecha con una plancha de molde cuadriculado.

waffle iron, waflera (molde de cuadritos para hacer wafles).

waft [wɑft, wæft, B wɑft] *v.t.* llevar por el aire, llevar por el aire, llevar sobre el agua. —*v.i.* flotar, boyar, sobrenadar. —*s.* 1. seña (hecha con las manos); ondeo; aletada. 2. mecedura, fluctuación. 3. onda; corriente, soplo, oreo (de viento, etc.); ligera emanación (de olor). 4. (mar.) gallardete o banderín de señales.

waftage ['wɑftɪdʒ, 'wæf-, B 'wɑf-] *s.* paso o conducción por el aire o sobre el agua.

wafter [-tər, B -tə] *s.* (mec.) disco giratorio o paleta de ventilador.

wafture [-tʃər, B -tʃə] *s.* fluctuación; lo que es llevado por la brisa o por las olas del mar.

wag [wæg] *v.t.* (*pret., p.p.* WAGGED; *p.pr.* WAGGING) menear, mover o sacudir ligeramente; **it is the tail that wags the dog,** (fig.) el (los) que debería(n) obedecer, dirige(n) (a un partido, organización, etc.); **w. its tail,** colear, mover la cola; **w. one's finger at,** amonestar, reprender. —*v.i.* 1. oscilar, tambalear, balancearse. 2. moverse, agitarse, menearse. 3. anadear, nanear. 4. (ant.) irse, largarse. —*s.* 1. meneo (de la cabeza, del dedo, de la cola, etc.); coleada, coleo. 2. burlón, bromista.

wage [weɪdʒ] *v.t.* 1. librar, trabar (combate, guerra, etc.). emprender (campaña, etc.). 2. (dial., G.B.) ajornalar, contratar. 3. (ant.) empeñar, pignorar; apostar, arriesgar; intentar. —*v.i.* estar en curso, prevalecer (por cierto tiempo). —*s.* 1. salario, paga, sueldo, haber, jornal. 2. (fig.) (*gen. pl.*) fruto, producto. 3. (ant.) empeño, fianza; compromiso.

wage dividend, participación en los beneficios (que reciben los empleados y obreros de una empresa).

wage earner, asalariado, obrero, trabajador.

wage freeze, congelación de salarios.

wageless ['weɪdʒləs] *a.* no pagado (empleo, trabajador, etc.).

wage level, nivel de salarios.

wager ['weɪdʒər, B -dʒə] *s.* 1. apuesta; parada, postura. 2. (ant.) caución, prenda; promesa. 3. (hist.) prueba (juicio de Dios). 4. **to lay a w.,** hacer una apuesta. —*v.t.* 1. apostar, poner (apuesta). 2. arriesgar, aventurar. —*v.i.* apostar.

wagerer [-dʒərər, B -ə] *s.* apostador.

wager of battle, (hist.) prueba del duelo, juicio de Dios mediante desafío.

wager of law, (hist.) prueba de la compurgación.

wage scale, escala de sueldos, escala de haberes.

wageworker ['weɪdʒˌwɜrkər, B -ˌwɜkə] *s.* asalariado, obrero, trabajador.

waggery ['wægərɪ] *s.* (*pl.* WAGGERIES) chocarrería, bufonada, travesura, chanza, chunga, broma.

wagging tongues ['wægɪŋ-] malas lenguas.

waggish [-ɪʃ] *a.* chocarrero, bufón, travieso, bromista; (hecho) en broma.

waggishly [-lɪ] *adv.* en broma, con chacota.

waggishness [-nəs] *s.* carácter chocarrero.

waggle ['wægəl] *v.i.* oscilar, balancearse, menearse; tambalearse, ondearse. —*v.t.* menear. —*s.* meneo, contoneo (de las caderas, etc.), tambaleo.

wagglingly ['wæglɪŋlɪ] *adv.* con anadeo o meneo, contoneándose.

waggly [-lɪ] *a.* vacilante.

waggon, waggoner, (G.B.) *vars. de* **wagon, wagoner.**

Wagnerian [vɑg'nɪrɪən, B -'nɪər-] *s.* (mús.) wagneriano, seguidor o admirador de la música de Richard Wagner. —*a.* wagneriano, propio o relativo a Wagner o sus óperas.

wagon, (pr. G.B.) **waggon** ['wægən] *s.* 1. carro, carretón, vagoneta, vagón. 2. (G.B., f.c.) vagón de carga, furgón. 3. furgoneta, rubia, camioneta, automóvil rural. 4. cochecito (de juguete). 5. **W.,** (astr.) Carro. 6. **to be** (o **to go**) **on the w.,** abstenerse de bebidas alcohólicas; **to hitch one's w. to a star,** mirar muy alto, poner el tiro muy lejos. —*v.t.* transportar en vagón. —*v.i.* viajar en carro.

wagonage [-ɪdʒ] *s.* 1. (ant.) transporte por vagón; porte, carretaje, precio de acarreo. 2. conjunto de vagones.

wagoner [-ər, B -ə] *s.* 1. carretero. 2. (astr.) Cochero, Auriga.

wagonette [ˌwægə'nɛt] *s.* carriocoche, birlocho, tartana (coche ligero con pescante elevado y dos filas de asientos).

wagonful ['wægənˌfʊl] *s.* carretada.

wagon-lit [vægoʊn'li, B 'vægɔn-] *s.* (*pl.* WAGON-LITS o *wagons-lits*) (f.c.) cochecama, vagón-dormitorio, litera.

wagonload ['wægənˌloʊd] *s.* carretada.

wagon master, (mil.) vaguemaestre.

wagon train, tren de carga.

wagonwright [-ˌraɪt] *s.* carretero.

wagtail ['wægˌteɪl] *s.* (orn.) aguzanieves, pezpita, motacila, apuranieves, avecilla de las nieves.

Wahhabi [wə'hɑbɪ] **Wahhabite** [-ˌaɪt] *s.* (relig.) wahabí, wehabí, seguidor de la doctrina mahometana más conservadora.

Wahhabism [-ˌɪzəm] *s.* (relig.) doctrina wahabita, secta conservadora dentro de la religión mahometana que se opone a toda práctica no sancionada por el Corán.

wahoo ['wɑˌhu, 'wɔ- B wə'hu] *s.* (bot.) evónimo, bonetero (arbusto).
wahoo, *s.* 1. (bot.) olmo racimoso. 2. (bot.) (variedad de) tilo. 3. (ict.) peto, wahoo.
waif [weɪf] *s.* 1. expósito; niño extraviado o abandonado. 2. bien mostrenco; animal extraviado. 3. (ant.) (*pl.*) cosas robadas y abandonadas por el ladrón en su huida. 4. (mar.) gallardete, banderín de señales.
waif property, (der.) bienes mostrencos.
waifs and strays, (G.B.) 1. pertenencias, baratijas. 2. niños sin hogar, expósitos.
wail [weɪl] *v.t., v.i.* gemir; sollozar; lamentar(se), deplorar; aullar, gemir (el viento). —*s.* gemido; sollozo; lamento.
wailer ['weɪlər, B -ə] *s.* gimoteador, gimoteadora.
wailful [-fəl] *a.* 1. doloroso, triste, quejoso; sollozante. 2. (fig.) que aúlla, gemidor (díc. del viento).
wailfully [-fəlɪ] *adv.* dolorosamente, tristemente.
wailing [-ɪŋ] *s.* lamento, gemido.
Wailing Wall, (hist., relig.) Muro de los Lamentos, Muro de las Lamentaciones (en Israel).
wain [weɪn] *s.* 1. **the W.** (astr.) Carro de David, Osa Mayor. 2. (poét.) carromato.
wainscot ['weɪnˌskoʊt, -ˌskɑt, B -skət] *s.* revestimiento, friso (esp. de madera), arrimadillo; enmaderado, enmaderamiento; alfarje. —*v.t.* (*pret., p.p.* WAINSCOTED o WAINSCOTTED; *p.pr.* WAINSCOTING o WAINSCOTTING) revestir (las paredes) con madera; poner frisos de madera a (las paredes).
wainscoting, wainscotting [-ɪŋ] *s.* encuadernado, revestimiento, paneles (de madera).
wainwright ['weɪnˌraɪt] *s.* carretero.
waist [weɪst] *s.* 1. cintura, talle. 2. talle, corpiño, jubón, blusa. 3. (mar.) combés. 4. (zool.) cintura, clitelo.
waistband ['weɪstˌbænd] *s.* cinturón, pretina, cinto.
waistcloth [-ˌklɔθ] *s.* pampanilla, taparrabo.
waistcoat ['wɛskət, 'weɪstˌkoʊt, B 'weɪst-] *s.* 1. chaleco. 2. justillo.
waister ['weɪstər, B -stə] *s.* (mar.) (raro) marinero inepto o de pobre condición física (al que destinan a un puesto de poca importancia en el combés del buque).
waistline ['weɪstˌlaɪn] *s.* talle, cintura, pretina.
wait [weɪt] *v.i.* 1. esperar, aguardar, estar esperando, estar a la expectativa. 2. **to keep (someone) waiting,** hacer esperar (a alguien); **w. for,** esperar (algo o a alguien); **w. on** (o **upon**), servir a, atender a (alguien); presentar sus respetos a, hacer una visita de cortesía a (jefe, persona de rango superior, etc.); ser consecuencia de, ocurrir a raíz de; (dep.) seguir de cerca (a competidor en carrera); **w. on** (o **at**) **table,** servir a la mesa; trabajar de camarero; **w. up,** velar (esperando); **w. up for (someone),** esperar (a alguien) sin acostarse, esperar (a alguien) levantado. —*v.t.* 1. esperar, aguardar. 2. servir, atender (a una mesa el camarero). 3. demorar (la comida). 4. **w. out,** aguardar (hasta) que termine. —*s.* 1. espera, demora; pausa. 2. (hist.) (*gen. pl.*) músico; juglar; murga de nochebuena. 3. (ant.) sereno, vigilante. 4. **to lay w.,** hacer emboscada; **to lie in w.,** estar al acecho; **to lie in w. for,** acechar, tender una emboscada a.
wait-a-bit ['weɪtəˌbɪt] *s.* (bot.) 1. zarzaparrilla. 2. espino, oxiacanto.
waiter ['weɪtər, B -ə] *s.* 1. mozo, camarero. 2. bandeja, salvilla. 3. (ant.) vigilante, velador.
waiting ['weɪtɪŋ] *s.* espera, período de espera. —*a.* que espera, de espera.
waiting list, lista de espera (ej., para un nombramiento).
waiting maid, criada de servicio, camarera, doncella.
waiting man, criado de servicio.
waiting room, sala de espera, antesala.
waitress ['weɪtrəs] *s.* camarera.
waive [weɪv] *v.t.* 1. renunciar a, desistir de (un derecho, alegato, etc.). 2. diferir, postergar. 3. dejar, descartar. 4. (ant.) abandonar (cosas robadas).
waiver ['weɪvər, B -və] *s.* (der.) renuncia, abandono.
wake [weɪk] *v.i.* (*pret.* WAKED o WOKE [woʊk]; *p.p.* WAKED o WOKEN [ˌwoʊkən]; *p.pr.* WAKING) 1. despertar(se). 2. revivir, resucitar. 3. (ant.) estar despierto. 4. (ant.) trasnochar. 5. **w. (up) to,** (fig.) llegar a apreciar, darse cuenta de; **w. up,** despertar(se); (fig.) despabilarse. —*v.t.* 1. despertar. 2. resucitar. 3. (dial.) velar (a un muerto). 4. **w. up,** despertar; (fig.) despertar (recuerdos, etc.); despabilar (a alguien). —*s.* 1. vela, velación, vigilia. 2. velatorio, velorio. 3. (relig. anglicana) verbena, kermesse, fiesta anual del santo patrón de una iglesia.
wake, *s.* estela (de buque, avión, etc.), aguaje (de buque); **in the w. of,** inmediatamente después de, como secuela o resultado de, a raíz de.
wakeful ['weɪkfəl] *a.* 1. insomne. 2. (fig.) despierto, vigilante, alerta.
wakefully [-fəlɪ] *adv.* en vela, insomne; alertamente.
wakefulness [-fəlnəs] *s.* 1. estado insomne, insomnio. 2. vigilancia, desvelo, vigilia.
wakeless [-ləs] *a.* profundo (díc. del sueño).
waken ['weɪkən] *v.i.* despertar(se); **w. to the point (fact,** etc.), (fig.) caer en la cuenta. —*v.t.* despertar.
wakerife ['weɪkˌraɪf] *a.* (esco.) vigilante, alerta.
wake-robin [-ˌrɑbən, B -ˌrɔb-] *s.* (bot.) 1. (G.B.) aro, yaro. 2. (E.U.) arísaro, rabiacana, candil, candilillos, frailillos.
wake-up [-ˌʌp] *s.* (E.U., fam.) pájaro carpintero.
waking [-ɪŋ] *s.* 1. despertar. 2. vela, vigilia. 3. velorio. —*a.* 1. despierto. 2. vigilante, alerta.
waking hours, horas de vela.
Walachia, Walachian, *vars. de* **Wallachia, Wallachian.**
waldgrave ['wɑldˌgreɪv, B 'wɔld-] *s.* (hist.) guardián principal del bosque en el imperio alemán antiguo.
Waldorf salad ['wɔlˌdɔrf-, B -dɔf-] (cocina) ensalada de manzana, apio y nueces, con mayonesa.
wale [weɪl] *s.* 1. roncha, cardenal, verdugón. 2. reborde. 3. lomo (de tierra); bollo (en tela). 4. (*pl.*) cintas (de un barco). —*v.t.* sacar ronchas en (la piel el golpe de látigo, etc.), marcar con cardenales.
wale, (dial., G.B.) *s.* selección; cosa elegida; lo más escogido. —*v.t.* escoger, seleccionar.
Waler ['weɪlər, B -lə] *s.* caballo de guerra (importado de Australia para el ejército inglés en la India).
Walhalla [vɑl'hɑlə, B væl'hælə] *var. de* **Valhalla.**
walk [wɔk] *v.i.* 1. caminar, andar, ir a pie. 2. ir al paso (caballo, etc.). 3. andar, pasar, moverse, ir, marchar. 4. pasear (se), deambular. 5. (béisbol) caminar, pasar a primera base (por haber servido mal la pelota el lanzador). 6. **w. about,** deambular; **w. after,** ir tras de; **w. away,** irse, marcharse; **w. away from,** distanciarse de, sacar ventaja fácilmente a (competidor, caballo, etc. en carrera); salir ileso de (accidente); **w. back,** regresar (a pie); **w. down the hill,** bajar (a pie) la colina; **w. down a street,** pasar o ir por una calle; **w. in,** entrar, pasar adelante; **w. in on (someone),** caerle por sorpresa a, sorprender a (alguien); **w. into,** (jer.) arremeter, atacar, maltratar; **w. into a trap,** caer en una trampa; **w. off,** marcharse; abandonar (trabajo, empleo, etc.); **w. off** (o **away**) **with,** llevarse, salirse con, alzarse con; **w. on air,** (fig.) rebosar de felicidad; **w. out,** salir, irse; declararse en huelga; **w. out of (meeting,** etc.), abandonar (reunión, etc.); **w. out on (someone),** abandonar, dejar a su suerte, dejar en apuros (a alguien); **w. through,** repasar a la ligera (libro, papel de teatro, etc.); hacer superficialmente (trabajo, etc.); **w. together,** pasearse o marchar juntos; **w. up,** subir (a pie); acercarse; **w. up and down,** pasearse de arriba abajo. —*v.t.* 1. caminar, recorrer (a pie); pasar sobre. 2. hacer caminar, llevar a caminar o pasear, llevar de paseo. 3. acompañar, caminar con. 4. (béisbol) dar oportunidad (a un jugador) para que llegue a la primera base. 5. **w. (someone) off his feet,** cansar (a alguien) haciéndole caminar; **w. the boards,** (fig.) ser actor; **w. the chalk,** probar (a la policía) que no está uno ebrio (caminando entre dos líneas blancas pintadas en el suelo); **w. the horses,** poner los caballos al paso; **w. the streets,** andorrear; ser prostituta. —*s.* 1. paseo, caminata. 2. modo de andar, paso, porte; andadura (de caballo). 3. clase social, estado, condición, ej., ***people in all walks of life,*** personas de toda condición. 4. avenida, alameda, paseo; acera; senda, sendero; pasillo. 5. ruta (de un vendedor o mendigo, ambulante), ronda (de policía). 6. pasto, corral, cercado (para animales). 7. (dep.) concurso de caminata. 8. (béisbol) base ganada a raíz de cuatro lanzamientos defectuosos. 9. **to go for a w.,** ir de paseo, salir a pasear; **to take a w.,** dar un paseo.
walkaway ['wɔkəˌweɪ] *s.* triunfo fácil.
walker ['wɔkər, B -ə] *s.* caminante, paseante, peatón.
walkie-talkie [-'tɔkɪ] *s.* transmisor-receptor portátil; transceptor portátil, walkie-talkie.
walk-in ['wɔkˌɪn] *a.* 1. con entrada para personas (cuarto frigorífico, alacena etc.). 2. con puerta a la calle. —*s.* 1. cuarto frigorífico grande. 2. (E.U.) victoria electoral fácil.
walking ['wɔkɪŋ] *a.* 1. andante, caminante, paseante; andador, ambulante. 2. de andar, para andar. 3. de balancín, oscilante, móvil. 4. guiado por un hombre a pie (díc. de ciertas maquinarias agrícolas de tracción animal). —*s.* 1. caminata, paseo. 2. paso, modo de andar.
walking beam, balancín.
walking cane, bastón.
walking chair, andador para niños.
walking delegate, delegado sindical, visitador sindical.
walking dragline, (const.) draga ambulante o andadora.
walking encyclopedia, (fig.) enciclopedia ambulante (díc. de una persona bien instruida).
walking fern, (bot.) helecho rastrero.
walking gentleman, (teat.) segundo galán, actor secundario.
walking lady, (teat.) segunda dama, actriz secundaria.
walking leaf, (bot.) helecho rastrero.
walking library, (fig.) enciclopedia ambulante, erudito.
walking pace, paso de andadura.
walking papers, (fam.) orden o carta de despido; despido (de un empleo).
walking stick, 1. bastón. 2. (ento.) caballo de palo.

walking ticket, *var. de* **walking papers.**
walking tour, excursión a pie.
Walkman (TM) ['wɔk,mæn] *s.* walkman.
walk-on ['wɔk,ɔn, -,ɑn-, B -,ɔn] *s.* (teat.) papel breve (gen. sin hablar).
walkout [-,aʊt] *s.* (fam. E.U.) huelga, paro.
walkover [-,oʊvər, B -və] *s.* 1. (fam.) triunfo fácil. 2. faena o trabajo fácil.
walk-up [-,ʌp] *s.* apartamento en un edificio sin ascensor.
walkway [-,weɪ] *s.* 1. pasillo, pasaje, andén, pasarela (esp. en barcos, fábricas, etc.). 2. (E.U.) camino ancho (ej., en un jardín).
Walkyrie [vɑl'kɪrɪ, B væl'kɪərɪ] *s.* Valquiria, doncella de Odín en la mitología nórdica.
wall [wɔl] *s.* 1. pared, muro, tabique, tapia. 2. (*gen. pl.*) muralla, fortificaciones. 3. (fig.) barrera. 4. (bot.) membrana, vaina. 5. (anat.) pared. 6. (min.) salbanda, respaldo (de filones). 7. **to drive** (o **push**) **to the w.,** poner (a otro) entre la espada y la pared; obligar a ceder; vencer, aplastar; **to go to the w.,** verse acosado, estar en calzas prietas; caer en bancarrota; fracasar, salir perdiendo; **to run one's head against the w.,** darse uno contra la pared; **to see through a brick w.,** ser clarividente; **walls have ears,** las paredes oyen; **with one's back to the w.,** acorralado, luchando solo. —*v.t.* 1. emparedar, tapiar, cercar, murar. 2. amurallar, fortificar. 3. **w. in,** amurallar; (fig.) emparedar; **w. off,** separar (por una pared); **w. up,** encerrar con muro, tapiar.
wallaby ['wɑləbɪ, B 'wɔl-] *s.* (*pl.* WALLABIES o WALLABY) (zool.) wallabi.
Wallachia [wɑ'leɪkɪə, B wɔ-] *s.* (hist.) Valaquia, antiguo principado hoy parte de Rumania.
Wallachian [-kɪən] *a., s.* valaco, natural o propio de Valaquia.
wallah ['wɑlə, B 'wɔlə] *s.* (anglo-ind.) (*ú. gen. en compuesto*) agente, hacedor, sirviente, encargado.
wallaroo [,wɑlə'ru, B ,wɔl-] *s.* (zool.) especie de canguro.
wallboard ['wɔl,bɔrd, B -,bɔd] *s.* tabla u hoja de fibra prensada; madera laminada para pared.
wallbracket [-,brækət] *s.* palomilla, ménsula; soporte asegurado a la pared.
wall clock, reloj de pared.
wall creeper, (orn.) pico murario.
walled [wɔld] *a.* amurallado, fortificado.
wallet ['wɑlət, B 'wɔl-] *s.* 1. cartera, billetera. 2. (ant.) morral, saco, bolsa.
wallet-size photo, foto tamaño carnet.
walleye ['wɔl,aɪ] *s.* 1. ojo albino; ojo overo. 2. (med.) leucoma; estrabismo divergente. 3. (ict.) pez de ojos saltones.
walleyed [-,aɪd] *a.* 1. de ojos albinos, que sufre de leucoma o de estrabismo divergente. 2. de mirada fija o en blanco (como persona afectada de leucoma). 3. de mirada penetrante o fiera.
wall fern, (bot.) polipodio común.
wallflower [-,flaʊər, B -ə] *s.* 1. (bot.) alelí amarillo. 2. (fam.) chica que se queda sin pareja en los bailes.
wall germander, (bot.) camedrio, camedris.
wall hanging, colgadura de pared, tapiz o lienzo artístico que se cuelga en la pared.
wallie, *var. de* **wally.**
wall knot, (mar.) piña (especie de nudo).
wall louse, (ento.) chinche.
wall of partition, (fig.) línea divisoria.
Walloon [wɑ'lun, B wɔ-] *s.* 1. valón, habitante de una región de Bélgica. 2. valón, lengua de los valones. —*a.* valón.
wallop ['wɑləp, B 'wɔl-] *v.i.* 1. apresurarse, abalanzarse. 2. bambolearse; avanzar o correr tambaleando. —*v.t.* (fam.) 1. azotar, zurrar; golpear con fuerza. 2. (fig.) aplastar, derrotar decisivamente. —*s.* 1. (fam.) golpe fuerte, golpazo. 2. impacto; alboroto, sobresalto. 3. **to pack a w.,** ser capaz de asestar un golpe fortísimo, tener un puño duro. —*adv.* con ruido sordo.
wallop, *v.i.* (esco., dial.) hervir, bullir.
walloper [-ər, B -ə] *s.* (fam.) persona que golpea con fuerza (esp. un boxeador).
walloping [-ɪŋ] *a.* grande, enorme; impresionante. —*s.* (fam.) zurra, tunda, paliza.
wallow ['wɑloʊ, B 'wɔl-] *v.i.* 1. revolcarse (en el fango, agua, etc. o en placeres, vicios, etc.). 2. nadar (en dinero, la opulencia). 3. undular, surtir o brotar con remolinos (humo, llamas, etc.). —*s.* 1. revuelco. 2. revolcadero, bañadero (de animales); depresión, hondón (en el terreno). 3. (fig.) estado o condición (de depravación, miseria, etc.).
wall painting, pintura al fresco, pintura mural.
wallpaper ['wɔl,peɪpər, B -pə] *s.* papel de empapelar, papel pintado, papel tapiz para paredes. —*v.t., v.i.* empapelar.
wall pellitory, (bot.) parietaria, cañarroya; albahaquilla de río.
wall pepper, (bot.) siempreviva.
wall plate, 1. (arq.) carrera, solera, viga de apoyo (sobre un muro). 2. (mec.) placa de apoyo o de asiento (para asegurar maquinaria).
wall plug, (elec.) toma de enchufe de pared, caja de contacto en la pared.
wall radiator, radiador de pared.
wall rock, (min.) roca estéril; roca de los respaldos.
wall rocket, (bot.) raqueta, jaramago, balsamita.
wall rue, (bot.) (variedad de) ruda.
wall salt-petre, espuma de nitro, afronitro.
wall tile, azulejo.
wall tree, (bot.) árbol de espaldera.
wally ['weɪlɪ] *a.* (WALLIER; WALLIEST) (esco.) excelente, fino; robusto.
walnut ['wɔl,nʌt] *s.* 1. nuez (de nogal). 2. nogal (árbol y madera). 3. color de nogal.
walnut color, nogalina.
walnut colored, noguerado, de color (de) nogal.
walnut stain, nogalina.
walnut tree, nogal (árbol).
walnut wood, nogal (madera).
walrus ['wɔlrəs, 'wɑl-, B 'wɔl-] *s.* (zool.) morsa.
walrus mustache, (fam.) bigotes de morsa, bigote espeso y caído.
waltz [wɔlts, B wɔls] *s.* vals (música y baile). —*v.i.* valsar; **w. off with,** ganar fácilmente (premio, etc.). —*v.t.* valsar con; **w. through,** pasar (examen, prueba, etc.) con suma facilidad.
waltzer ['wɔltsər, B 'wɔlsə] *s.* valsador, el que baila valses.
waly ['weɪlɪ] *interj.* (esco., N. de Ingl.) ¡ay! ¡oh! (como exclamación de pena).
wamble ['wɑmbəl, B 'wɔm-] *v.i.* 1. tambalear(se), bambolear(se); retorcerse, hacer eses. 2. sentir náusea. 3. dar rugidos (el estómago). —*s.* 1. tambaleo, andar vacilante. 2. rugido (del estómago).
wame [weɪm] *s.* (pr. esco.) vientre, barriga.
wampish ['wæmpɪʃ] *v.i.* (esco.) fluctuar, oscilar; balancearse, columpiarse.
wampum ['wɑmpəm, B 'wɔm-] *s.* 1. cuentas cilíndricas hechas de conchas (usadas por los indios norteamericanos como moneda). 2. (jer.) guita, plata (dinero).
wampumpeag [-,pig] *s.* cuentas hechas de conchas de color púrpura (usadas por los indios norteamericanos como moneda de menor valor).
wan [wɑn, B wɔn] *a.* 1. pálido, descolorido; macilento; lánguido, enfermizo. 2. tenue, empañado (luz, etc.). 3. (ant.) triste, pesaroso. —*v.i.* (*pret., p.p.* WANNED; *p.pr.* WANNING) empalidecer; languidecer; demacrarse.
wand [wɑnd, B wɔnd] *s.* 1. vara; varilla mágica, varita de virtudes. 2. cetro. 3. tablilla usada como marca (en arquería). 4. (dial.) ramita, varilla; renuevo, retoño (esp. de sauce).
wander ['wɑndər, B 'wɔndə] *v.i.* 1. vagar, errar. 2. pasear. 3. delirar, desvariar, disparatar. 4. **w. from,** desviarse de, descarriarse de; **w. off the point,** andarse por las ramas. —*v.t.* vagar a través de. —*s.* vagabundeo; paseo.
wanderer [-dərər, B -ə] *s.* 1. vagabundo, peregrino, nómada. 2. persona vaga, indecisa o extraviada.
wandering [-ɪŋ] *a.* 1. vagabundo, errante; nómada. 2. ondulante, sinuoso. 3. delirante, disparatado. —*s.* 1. (*ú. gen. en pl.*) peregrinación; viaje. 2. extravío, aberración. 3. delirio. 4. divagación.
wandering albatross, (orn.) albatros errante.
wandering cell, (anat.) leucocito.
wandering jenny, (bot.) hierba de la moneda.
Wandering Jew, 1. judío errante. 2. **w. j.,** (bot.) sangría, cordobán.
wandering kidney, (med.) riñón flotante.
wanderingly ['wɑndərɪŋlɪ, B 'wɔn-] *adv.* 1. divagando; como un vagabundo. 2. en delirio.
wanderlust ['wɑndər,lʌst, B 'wɔndə,-] *s.* impulso de viajar; pasión por los viajes; instinto de nómada.
wanderoo [,wɑndə'ru, B ,wɔn-] *s.* (zool.) wanderu.
wane [weɪn] *v.i.* 1. menguar, disminuir, decrecer. 2. decaer, declinar; debilitarse. —*s.* 1. mengua, disminución; decadencia, declinación. 2. cuarto menguante (de la luna). 3. defecto, merma (en un tablón). 4. **on the wane,** menguando; decayendo, disminuyendo.
waney ['weɪnɪ] *a.* 1. menguante; disminuido. 2. defectuoso, mermado (un tablón).
wangle ['wæŋgəl] *v.i.* 1. culebrear, serpentear, zigzaguear (en un gentío). 2. (fig.) desenredarse. 3. prevaricar, recurrir a engañifas. —*v.t.* 1. menear, blandir. 2. cazar, obtener por medio de engañifas, conseguir con artimañas; trampear. 3. manipular, falsificar (cuentas, etc.).
wangler [-glər, B -glə] *s.* trampeador, gorrón.
wanigan ['wɑnɪgən, B 'wɔn-] *s.* casa flotante.
waning ['weɪnɪŋ] *adj.* menguante. —*s.* mengua, disminución.
wanion ['wɑnjən, B 'wɔn-] *s.* (ant.) venganza, maldición.
wanly ['wɑnlɪ, B 'wɔn-] *adv.* lánguidamente, débilmente.
wanna ['wɑnə] (fam.) *abrev. de.* **want to.**
wannabe ['wɑnəbi] *s.* (jer.) aspirante.
wanness [-nəs] *s.* palidez; languidez.
want [wɑnt, wɔnt, B wɔnt] *v.t.* 1. necesitar, requerir, ej., *the matter wants careful study,* el asunto necesita un estudio cuidadoso, *bricklayers wanted,* se necesitan albañiles. 2. desear, anhelar, querer, ej., *I w. you to go,* quiero que (te) vayas, *I w. to thank you,* deseo agradecerle, *tell John I w. him,* dígale a Juan que (quiero que) venga (a verme). 3. carecer de, tener falta de, faltar (algo) a, ej., *the statue wants the head,* a la estatua le falta la cabeza. 4. **not to be wanted,** no ser bien recibido, ser ingrata la presencia (de uno), ej., *you are not wanted here,* Ud. no es bien recibido aquí, su presencia es ingrata aquí; **to be wanted,** hacer falta; ser requerida su presencia (de uno); ser llamado (al teléfono, etc.). —*v.i.* 1. (gen. con *for*) estar necesitado (de); estar privado (de), estar (sin), ej., *he never wants for friends,* nunca está sin amigos. 2. (pr. con

in, of o *to*) carecer (de), faltar (a alguien, etc.); ser deficiente (en), estar falto (de), ej., *the roof of the building is wanting,* falta el techo al edificio, *he is wanting in judgment,* está falto de juicio. 3. querer (ir en alguna dirección), ej., *the dog wants out,* el perro quiere salir. —*s.* 1. necesidad, indigencia, privación. 2. necesidad, cosa necesitada. 3. falta, carencia. 4. deseo, anhelo. 5. **for w. of,** por falta de; **to be in w.,** estar necesitado; **to be in w. of,** necesitar, hacer falta a uno.

want ad, (fam.) aviso, anuncio, oferta o demanda (en un periódico).

wantage ['wɑntɪdʒ, 'wɔnt-, B 'wɔnt-] *s.* deficiencia; merma, déficit.

wanted ['wɑntəd, 'wɔnt-, B 'wɔnt-] *a.* 1. se necesita, se busca, ej., *w. expert mechanic* (*cook,* etc.), se necesita mecánico experto (cocinera, etc.). 2. buscado, ej., *w. dead or alive,* se busca vivo o muerto. 3. (en avisos clasificados) se solicita.

wanting [-ɪŋ] *a.* 1. falto; ausente. 2. deficiente, defectuoso. 3. (dial.) carente de inteligencia. 4. (ant.) necesitado, indigente. 5. **w. in,** falto de, carente de. —*prep.* sin, menos.

wanton ['wɑntən, 'wɔnt-, B 'wɔnt-] *a.* 1. perverso, insensible, cruel; inexcusable, injustificable. 2. desenfrenado, extravagante, caprichoso (humor, genio, imaginación, etc.). 3. sensual, lascivo, licencioso. 4. exuberante, frondoso (vegetación). 5. jovial, juguetón, retozón. 6. (ant.) indisciplinado, desobediente, indomable, indócil. —*s.* 1. libertino. 2. niño juguetón o travieso. 3. (ant.) niño consentido o mimado. 4. mujer de costumbres libres, impúdica. —*v.i.* 1. actuar con crueldad. 2. ser atrevido o impúdico; vivir licenciosamente. 3. coquetear. —*v.t.* (raro) desperdiciar (el tiempo) frívolamente.

wantonly [-lɪ] *adv.* 1. insensiblemente, cruelmente. 2. desenfrenadamente, caprichosamente, sin motivo. 3. licenciosamente, sin pudor.

wantonness [-nəs] *s.* 1. perversidad, insensibilidad, crueldad. 2. desenfreno, extravagancia, capricho. 3. sensualidad, lascivia. 4. exuberancia, frondosidad (de la vegetación).

wany, *var. de* **waney.**

wap [wæp, B wɔp] (dial.) *var. de* **whop.**

wap, (dial.) *v.t.* envolver, doblar; atar. —*s.* envoltura.

wapiti ['wɑpətɪ, B 'wɔp-] *s.* (zool.) wapití.

wappenschawing ['wæpən͵ʃɔɪŋ] *s.* (esco.) exhibición de armamento; revista de armas.

wapper-jawed ['wɑpər͵dʒɔd, B 'wɔpə͵-] *a.* 1. (E.U.) de quijada torcida o desviada; de mandíbula sobresaliente. 2. (G.B.) de boca torcida.

war [wɔr, B wɔ] *s.* 1. guerra. 2. (ant.) armamento; fuerzas armadas. 3. **sinews of w.,** los medios (financieros, materiales, etc.) de guerra; **to be at w. (with),** estar en guerra (con); **to be on a w. footing,** estar en pie de guerra; **to carry the w. into the enemy's country,** (fig.) contraatacar, responder agresivamente, reaccionar tomando la ofensiva; **to declare w. (upon),** declarar la guerra (contra); **to be off to the wars,** ir a la guerra; **to go to w.,** declarar la guerra; **to make** (o **wage**) **w. (on),** hacer guerra (a); **to roll back the tide of w.,** rechazar una invasión; **w. to the death,** guerra a muerte, lucha a muerte. —*v.i.* (*pret., p.p.* WARRED; *p.pr.* WARRING) 1. hacer guerra, estar en guerra, guerrear. 2. (fig.) luchar, disentir.

war aim, fines de la guerra.

war baby, 1. niño nacido durante la guerra. 2. (fam.) ganga o beneficio debido a la guerra.

warble ['wɔrbəl, B 'wɔbəl] *v.i.* 1. gorjear, trinar. 2. (E.U.) gorgoritear; cantar. —*v.t.* 1. cantar trinando. 2. (fig.) expresar a voz en cuello. —*s.* gorjeo, trino; gorgorito.

warble fly, moscardón (cuyas larvas viven bajo la piel de varios mamíferos).

warbler [-blər, B -blə] *s.* 1. cantor, gorjeador. 2. (orn.) sílvido; curruca.

warbling [-blɪŋ] *s.* canto, gorjeo. —*adj.* canoro; susurrante.

war bride, desposada de un movilizado en plena guerra.

war chest, recaudación pública para fines benéficos o campaña política.

war crime, crimen de guerra, que comete una nación o ejército beligerante en contra de los convenios internacionales y principios humanos.

war criminal, criminal de guerra, persona de posición responsable y ventajosa que se ensaña contra el enemigo en una guerra.

war cry, grito de guerra, grito de combate.

ward [wɔrd, B wɔd] *v.t.* 1. resguardar, vigilar. 2. **w. off,** parar, detener (golpe, puñalada. etc.); apartar, desviar, rechazar. —*s.* (ant.) guardián, custodio.

ward, *s.* 1. pupilo, menor o huérfano bajo tutela. 2. barrio, cuartel, distrito (de una ciudad). 3. sala, crujía, pabellón (de un hospital); celda, pabellón (de una cárcel o prisión). 4. (*pl.*) guardas (de llave o cerradura). 5. defensa, protección. 6. (G.B., hist.) cierta división de condados. 7. (ant.) guarnición; plaza fuerte, posición defensiva.

war dance, danza de guerra.

ward chief, (pol.) jefe político de un barrio.

warded ['wɔrdəd, B 'wɔdəd] *a.* (provisto) de guardas (cerradura o llave).

warden ['wɔrdən, B 'wɔd-] *s.* 1. guarda, guardián: vigilante; celador, custodio. 2. alcaide, carcelero. 3. capillero (de una iglesia). 4. (hist.) alcalde. 5. (G.B.) director (de colegio, de la casa de moneda, etc.).

wardens and vestry, mayordomos y junta parroquial.

wardenship ['wɔrdən͵ʃɪp, B 'wɔd-] *s.* 1. guardianía. 2. alcaidía, celaduría.

war department, (E.U.) ministerio de guerra.

warder [-ər, B -ə] *s.* 1. guardián, vigilante, sereno. 2. (G.B.) carcelero. 3. (hist.) bastón de mando. 4. (fig.) fuerte, baluarte.

ward heeler, (fam.) ayudante o secuaz de jefe político.

wardress ['wɔrdrəs, B 'wɔdrəs] *s.* guardiana.

wardrobe ['wɔrd͵roʊb, B 'wɔd-] *s.* 1. guardarropa (local o armario); ropero (armario). 2. vestuario, ropa; guardarropía (en el teatro).

wardrobe trunk, baúl ropero, baúl de camarote.

wardroom ['wɔrd͵rum, -͵rʊm, B 'wɔd-] *s.* (mar., mil.) cámara de oficiales; comedor de oficiales.

wardship ['wɔrd͵ʃɪp, B 'wɔd-] *s.* 1. tutela, patronato. 2. pupilaje.

ware [wɛr, B wɛə] *s.* 1. (*ú. esp. en palabras compuestas*) objetos, artículos, ej., *glassw.,* artículos de vidrio. 2. (*pl.*) mercaderías, mercancías. 3. alfarería, loza, porcelana.

ware, (ant.) *a.* 1. enterado; sabedor. 2. cauteloso; prudente. —*v.t.* hacer caso a, guardarse de.

ware, *v.t.* (esco.) gastar; otorgar, conferir; malgastar.

war effort, esfuerzo bélico, esfuerzo en conjunto de una población para producir lo necesario para abastecer su ejército en guerra.

warehouse ['wɛr͵haʊs, B 'wɛə͵-] *s.* almacén, depósito. — [-͵haʊz] *v.t.* almacenar.

warehouse keeper, guardalmacén.

warehouseman [-mən] *s.* almacenero, guardalmacén, almacenista.

warehouse rent, almacenaje.

warehousing system [-͵haʊzɪŋ-] sistema de almacenaje.

wareroom [-͵rum, -͵rʊm] *s.* tienda, almacén.

warfare ['wɔr͵fɛr, B 'wɔ͵fɛə] *s.* 1. contienda armada; guerra; operaciones militares. 2. contienda, lucha, conflicto.

war fever, ardor bélico, celo de un beligerante en un estado de guerra.

war flail, (ant., mil.) mangual.

war footing, estado de preparación para la guerra; **on a w. f.,** en pie de guerra.

war game, (mil.) maniobras de guerra (en campo abierto o sobre un mapa, etc.), simulacro de guerra.

warhead ['wɔr͵hɛd, B 'wɔ͵-] *s.* cono u ojiva de combate (de torpedos, proyectiles nucleares, etc.); sección explosiva de un proyectil.

war-horse [-͵hɔrs, B -͵hɔs] *s.* 1. caballo de guerra. 2. (fam.) (esp. **old w. h.**) veterano. 3. obra trillada (musical o teatral).

warily ['wɛrəlɪ, B 'wɛər-] *adv.* cautelosamente.

war industry, industria especializada en material de guerra.

wariness [-ɪnəs] *s.* cautela, precaución.

warison ['wærɪsən] *s.* grito de batalla, señal de asalto.

warlike ['wɔr͵laɪk, B 'wɔ͵-] *a.* 1. guerrero, belicoso. 2. militar, marcial.

warlikeness [-nəs] *s.* belicosidad; marcialidad.

war loan, empréstito de guerra; préstamo que solicita una nación o una empresa para fines o preparativos bélicos.

warlock [-͵lɑk, B -͵lɔk] *s.* brujo, hechicero; mago.

warlord [-͵lɔrd, B -͵lɔd] *s.* 1. jefe militar. 2. tirano agresivo que domina por medio del terror.

warm [wɔrm, B wɔm] *a.* 1. caliente, caluroso. 2. cálido (clima, país, etc.). 3. abrigador (vestido, vestimenta, etc.). 4. abrigado, cómodo, confortable, reconfortado, ej., *w. with wine,* reconfortado por el vino. 5. caluroso, cordial, cariñoso (sentimiento, saludo, ofrecimiento, etc.); afectuoso, amoroso (disposición, temperamento, etc.). 6. ardiente, acalorado, animado (disputa, debate, etc.). 7. ardiente, entusiasmado (admirador, partidario, etc.). 8. calentito, fresco, reciente. 9. cálido (color). 10. entrado en calor; (fig.) acostumbrado (al trabajo en oficina, etc.). 11. caliente (ú. en juego de niños al acercarse al objeto escondido). 12. **to be w.** (impers.) hacer calor (díc. del tiempo); tener calor (una persona); **to grow w.,** volverse cálido o afectuoso; **to keep w.,** conservar caliente (cosas); abrigar del frío, calentar (personas); **w. as toast,** calentito. —*v.t.* 1. calentar, caldear. 2. (fig.) hacer aceptar o apreciar (plan, idea, etc.); inspirar simpatías en, entusiasmar. 3. **w. over,** recalentar (comida); **w. up,** recalentar (comida), hacer entrar en calor (el cuerpo, ej., un trago de licor). —*v.i.* 1. calentarse. 2. **w. to** (o **toward**), volverse amistoso con, empezar a simpatizar con; **w. up,** entrar en calor; (fig.) tomar bríos, entusiasmarse. —*s.* (dial.) calor; calentamiento, calefacción.

warm-blooded ['wɔrm'blʌdəd, B 'wɔm-] *a.* 1. de sangre caliente. 2. (fig.) apasionado, ardiente.

warmed-over ['wɔrmd͵oʊvər, B 'wɔmd͵oʊvə] *a.* recalentado (comida).

warmer ['wɔrmər, B 'wɔmə] *s.* calentador, ej., *foot w.,* calentador de pies, calentapiés.

warm front, (meteor.) frente caliente; frente cálido.

warmhearted ['wɔrm'hɑrtəd, B 'wɔm'hɑt-] *a.* afectuoso, bondadoso, simpático.

warmheartedly [-lɪ] *adv.* afectuosamente, cariñosamente.
warmheartedness [-nəs] *s.* afecto, bondad.
warming pad ['wɔrmɪŋ-, B 'wɔmɪŋ-] almohadilla eléctrica.
warming pan, calentador de cama.
warmly ['wɔrmlɪ, B 'wɔm-] *adv.* calurosamente, cariñosamente, afectuosamente; con entusiasmo.
warmness [-nəs] *s.* 1. calor. 2. cariño, afectuosidad.
warmonger ['wɔrˌmʌŋgər, -ˌmɑŋ-, B 'wɔˌmʌŋgə] *s.* atizador de la guerra, fomentador de la guerra.
warmongering [-gərɪŋ] *s.* incitación a la guerra.
warmth [wɔrmθ, B wɔmθ] *s.* 1. calor (moderado). 2. simpatía, cordialidad; entusiasmo, ardor. 3. (pint.) efecto radiante (de colores cálidos).
warn [wɔrn, B wɔn] *v.t.* 1. avisar, prevenir; alertar, poner sobre aviso. 2. advertir, amonestar, apercibir.
warner ['wɔrnər, B 'wɔnə] *s.* amonestador.
warning [-nɪŋ] *s.* aviso, advertencia; **let this be a w. to you,** que esto te sirva de escarmiento; **to give w.,** dar aviso (del cese de un arriendo o empleo); **to take w.,** hacer caso a la advertencia, andar sobre aviso. —*a.* amonestador; de advertencia.
warning horn, bocina de alarma.
warning indicator, dispositivo de aviso o de alarma.
warningly [-lɪ] *adv.* a modo de aviso; en tono amonestador.
warning sign, señal de advertencia.
War Office, (G.B.) Ministerio de Guerra.
War of Independence, Guerra de la Independencia.
war of nerves, guerra de nervios.
War of Secession, (E.U.) guerra de Secesión, la Guerra Civil de 1861.
warp [wɔrp, B wɔp] *s.* 1. (tej.) urdimbre, urdiembre. 2. alma, armazón (de la llanta). 3. torcedura, combadura, alabeo. 4. (fig.) sesgo (de la mente); perversión. 5. (mar.) espía. 6. limo dejado por una crecida de río. —*v.t.* 1. torcer, retorcer, encorvar; combar, empandar, alabear. 2. pervertir, descarriar (la mente). 3. interpretar mal, torcer, falsear (sentido, relato, texto, etc.). 4. (aer.) alabear (el ala para mantener el equilibrio). 5. (mar.) mover (una embarcación) con espía, remolcar, halar. —*v.i.* 1. torcerse; alabearse, pandear, curvarse. 2. (mar.) espiar, ir a remolque. 3. (fig.) desviarse, apartarse.
war paint, 1. pintura que se ponían ciertas tribus primitivas para ir a la guerra. 2. (fam.) vestido ceremonial, gala, traje de lujo; adornos, atavíos. 3. (jer.) cosméticos, maquillaje.
warp and woof, 1. trama y urdimbre. 2. (fig.) fundamento, base.
warpath ['wɔrˌpæθ, B 'wɔˌpɑθ] *s.* senda que seguían los indios norteamericanos para atacar al enemigo; **on the w.,** (fig.) buscando pendencia; de mal humor; propenso a pelear.
warp beam, (tej.) enjulio, enjullo, ensullo.
warped [wɔrpt, B wɔpt] *a.* combado, adunco.
warped surface, (geom.) superficie alabeada.
warper ['wɔrpər, B 'wɔpə] *s.* urdidor (máquina o persona).
warping [-ɪŋ] *s.* 1. combadura, alabeo. 2. urdidura. 3. (mar.) remolque.
warping buoy, (mar.) boya de espía.
warplane ['wɔrˌpleɪn, B 'wɔˌ-] *s.* avión de guerra, avión militar.
war profiteer, logrero de guerra, comerciante que se beneficia de una guerra.

warrant ['wɔrənt, 'wɑr-, B 'wɔr-] *s.* 1. auto, decreto, orden, mandamiento. 2. garantía, comprobante, certificado. 3. autorización, poder. 4. justificación, fundamento. 5. libramiento, orden de pago. 6. (der.) orden de detención, orden de prisión; citación (ante un juez). 7. (com.) certificado de opción (para comprar acciones). 8. (mil.) patente, nombramiento de asimilado. 9. (G.B.) certificado de depósito. —*v.t.* 1. asegurar, certificar, aseverar, atestiguar. 2. garantizar (contra daños, pérdidas, etc.); responder de, garantizar. 3. autorizar, sancionar, aprobar. 4. justificar. 5. **I'll w.,** no hay duda, sin duda.
warrantable [-əbəl] *a.* justificable, garantizable.
warrantably [-blɪ] *adv.* con razón, con justificación, justificadamente.
warrantee [ˌwɔrən'ti, ˌwɑr-, B ˌwɔr-] *s.* (der.) garantizado, persona garantizada.
warranter ['wɔrəntər, 'wɑr-, B 'wɔrənte] *s.* (der.) garante, fiador.
warrant of arrest, (der.) orden de detención, orden de arresto, orden de captura.
warrant officer, (mil.) suboficial, oficial asimilado; (mar.) oficial de mar; contramaestre.
warrantor [ˌwɔrən'tɔr, ˌwɑr-, B 'wɔrənˌtɔ] *s.* (der.) garante, fiador.
warranty ['wɔrəntɪ, 'wɑr-, B 'wɔr-] *s.* (*pl.* WARRANTIES) 1. garantía, seguridad. 2. justificación, autorización. 3. (der.) garantía. 4. (hist.) garantía formal (de un título a un feudo franco).
warranty clause, (der.) cláusula de evicción y saneamiento.
warranty deed, (der.) escritura de propiedad con garantía de título.
warranty of title, (der.) garantía de título.
warren ['wɔrən, 'wɑr-, B 'wɔr-] *s.* 1. conejera, conejar, madriguera de conejos; vivar. 2. (fig.) conejera (lugar habitado por muchas personas); barrio populoso. 3. lugar vedado (reservado para la cría de ciertos animales).
warrener [-ər, B -ə] *s.* 1. (hist.) guardabosques. 2. el que está al cuidado de las conejeras.
warrior ['wɔrɪər, 'wɑr-, B 'wɔrɪə] *s.* guerrero.
war risk insurance, seguro contra el riesgo de guerra.
warsaw ['wɔrsɔ, B 'wɔsɔ] *s.* (ict.) guasa.
Warsaw, *s.* Varsovia, capital de Polonia.
Warsaw Pact, the, (hist.) el Pacto de Varsovia.
war service chevron, (mil.) divisa conmemorativa de campaña.
warship ['wɔrˌʃɪp, B 'wɔˌ-] *s.* navío, buque de guerra.
warsle, warstle ['wɑrsəl, B 'wɑs-] *v.i., v.t.* (esco.) luchar; forcejear. —*s.* lucha.
wart [wɔrt, B wɔt] *s.* 1. verruga, pequeño tumor. 2. (bot.) verruga.
warthog ['wɔrtˌhɔg, -ˌhɑg, B 'wɔtˌhɔg] *s.* (zool.) jabalí verrugoso, facócero, suido africano.
wartime ['wɔrˌtaɪm, B 'wɔˌ-] *s.* tiempo, período, época de guerra.
warty ['wɔrtɪ, B 'wɔtɪ] *a.* verrugoso, averrugado.
war whoop, grito de guerra (esp. de los indios norteamericanos).
war widow, viuda de guerra, viuda de un combatiente.
warworn ['wɔrˌwɔrn, B 'wɔˌwɔn] *a.* gastado por la guerra.
wary ['wærɪ, 'werɪ, B 'weərɪ] *a.* (WARIER; WARIEST) cauteloso, cuidadoso, circunspecto, precavido.
war zone, zona de guerra.
was [wʌz, wɑz, wəz, B wɔz] *primera y tercera personas sing. del pret. de* **be.**

wash [wɔʃ, wɑʃ, B wɔʃ] *v.t.* 1. lavar. 2. bañar (orillas, ojo, herida, etc.); regar (una comarca, región, etc. el río o canal); mojar, humedecer. 3. excavar (canal, hueco, etc. el agua). 4. arrastrar, llevarse (algo el agua), ej., *a wave washed him overboard,* una ola lo arrastró por la borda. 5. lavar (mineral). 6. lavar (dibujo con aguadas); dar un baño (de color) a, bañar, dorar, platear, azogar. 7. (fig.) purificar, limpiar. 8. **w. away,** quitar lavando; arrastrar (algo el agua); **w. down,** baldear, limpiar; **w. down with,** acompañar (comida, etc.) con, ej., *sausages washed down with beer,* salchichas acompañadas con cerveza; **w. off,** sacar o quitar lavando; **w. one's face,** lavarse la cara; **w. one's hands,** (fig.) lavarse las manos, eludir una responsabilidad; **w. oneself,** lavarse; **w. out,** quitar lavando; limpiar lavando; lavar por dentro; deslavar, arrastrar, derrumbar (un puente el río crecido, etc.); suspender (evento deportivo, mitin, etc.) debido a la lluvia; **w. up,** lavar (los platos, la vajilla, etc.); varar, arrojar (a la playa las olas, el mar, etc.), ej., *it was washed up by the sea,* fue varado por el mar. —*v.i.* 1. (t. con *up*) lavarse. 2. lavar la ropa; ser lavandera. 3. no desteñir (se); sufrir el lavado (bien o mal). 4. (con *along, out*) ser llevado (por el agua), flotar (sobre el agua); (con *in, into*) entrar en, inundar (el mar, etc.); (con *over*) fluir o pasar sobre, anegar. 5. (fam.) ser creído o aceptado, soportar examen. 6. **w. away,** derrumbarse; **w. off,** salir en el lavado; **w. out,** desteñir(se); desvanecerse; fracasar, ser incapaz; **w. up,** lavar los platos (después de la comida). —*s.* 1. lavado, lavadura, lavamiento, lavatorio. 2. jabonado, ropa para el lavado; ropa lavada. 3. jabonaduras, lavazas, desperdicios. 4. loción (cosmética). 5. baño, capa delgada (que se aplica a una superficie). 6. flujo de agua, golpe de agua. 7. derrubio, erosión (por acción del mar o río). 8. aluvión, depósito. 9. aguazal, charca, marisma. 10. estela, aguas turbulentas (detrás de la hélice). 11. (aer.) estela turbulenta (del aire detrás del avión). 12. (O. de E.U.) lecho desecado (de una corriente). 13. bebida aguada. 14. (pint.) acuarela. 15. (meteor.) estela, turbulencia. 16. cono aluvial. 17. **it will all come out in the w.,** (fig.) todo sale en la lavada (o en el lavado), al final todo se solucionará o aclarará.
Wash. *abrev. de* **Washington,** Washington (E.U.).
washable ['wɔʃəbəl, 'wɑʃ-, B 'wɔʃ-] *a.* lavable.
wash and wear, que no se plancha después de lavado (camisa, prenda, etc.), de lavar y poner (Esp.).
wash ball, bola de jabón perfumado.
washbasin [-ˌbeɪsən] *s.* jofaina, palangana, lavabo.
washboard [-ˌbɔrd, B -ˌbɔd] *s.* 1. tabla de lavar. 2. (carp.) rodapié. 3. (mar.) falca, batidero.
washboiler [-ˌbɔɪlər, B -lə] *s.* caldera para hervir la ropa.
wash boring, (petróleo) perforación con lavado, sondeo con inyección de agua, sondeo hidráulico.
wash bottle, (frasco) depurador de gases.
washbowl ['wɔʃˌboul, 'wɑʃ-, B 'wɔʃ-] *s.* jofaina, palangana, lavabo, lavatorio (Amer.).
washcloth [-ˌklɔθ] *s.* paño para lavarse (la cara o el cuerpo).
washday [-ˌdeɪ] *s.* día de lavado (de la ropa), día de la colada (Esp.).
washed-out ['wɔʃtˌaut, 'wɑʃt-, B 'wɔʃt-] *a.* 1. desteñido, descolorido, desvaído. 2. (fam.) agotado, extenuado, rendido; desmoralizado.
washed-up [-'ʌp] *a.* (fam.) arruinado, acabado, fracasado.

washer ['wɔʃər, 'wɑʃ-, B 'wɔʃə] *s.* 1. lavador, limpiador, depurador; (foto.) lavador. 2. arandela. 3. máquina de lavar.
washerman [-mən] *s.* lavandero.
washerwoman [-ˌwʊmən] *s.* lavandera.
washery [-ərɪ] *s.* (*pl.* WASHERIES) (min.) lavadero.
washhouse ['wɔʃˌhaʊs, 'wɑʃ-, B 'wɔʃ-] *s.* lavadero.
washing [-ɪŋ] *s.* 1. lavado; ablución. 2. baño, capa delgada. 3. jabonado, ropa para el lavado, ropa lavada. 4. (*pl.*) lavazas. 5. (min.) lava. 6. (*pl.*) (min.) lavadero; mineral (esp. oro) acumulado (después del lavado).
washing machine, máquina de lavar, lavadora.
washing powder, polvo para lavar.
washing soda, sosa para lavar; sosa para blanquear, sal de soda (Am.).
Washington ['wɔʃɪŋtən, 'wɑʃ-, B 'wɔʃ-] *s.* 1. Washington, capital de los Estados Unidos de Norte América. 2. estado al N.O. de los E.U.
Washington palm, (bot.) washingtonia, palma de Castilla.
Washington pie, (E.U.) bizcocho con relleno de crema o conserva de frutas.
washleather ['wɔʃˌlɛðər, 'wɑʃ-, B 'wɔʃˌ-lɛðə] *s.* gamuza, pedazo de piel (que se usa para limpiar).
wash-off ['wɔʃˌɔf, 'wɑʃ-, B 'wɔʃ-] *a.* que se destiñe.
washout [-ˌaʊt] *s.* 1. derrubio, derrumbamiento, derrumbe, corrimiento (de tierras). 2. persona inútil o incapaz; fiasco, fracaso (en un examen, competencia, etc.); chancleta (persona inepta).
washpot [-ˌpɑt, B -ˌpɔt] *s.* bacía.
washrag [-ˌræg] *s.* paño para lavar (platos, suelo, etc.).
washroom [-ˌrum, -ˌrʊm] *s.* lavabo, gabinete de aseo.
wash sale, venta ficticia de acciones (con fines especulativos).
washstand [-ˌstænd] *s.* 1. palanganero. 2. lavabo, lavamanos.
washtub [-ˌtʌb] *s.* tina de lavar, cuba de colada, artesa.
washwoman [-ˌwʊmən] *s.* lavandera.
washy ['wɔʃɪ, 'wɑʃɪ, B 'wɔʃɪ] *a.* (WASHIER; WASHIEST) 1. débil, flojo; acuoso, aguado. 2. diluido, débil (color, perfil). 3. (fig.) insípido, insulso; enervado, vago (sentimiento, estilo, etc.). 4. (raro) húmedo, mojado.
wasn't ['wʌzənt, 'wɑz-, B 'wɔz-] *contr. de* **was not.**
wasp [wɑsp, wɔsp, B wɔsp] *s.* (ento.) avispa.
WASP (fam., E.U.) *abrev. de* **white Anglo-Saxon Protestant,** blanco anglosajón y protestante.
waspish ['wɑspɪʃ, 'wɔs-, B 'wɔs-] *a.* 1. colérico, irascible, enojadizo, irritable. 2. delgado, esbelto.
waspishly [-lɪ] *adv.* coléricamente, de manera irritable.
waspishness [-nəs] *s.* mal genio, irritabilidad.
wasp waist, talle de avispa, cintura de avispa.
wasp-waisted ['wɑspˌweɪstəd, 'wɔsp-, B 'wɔsp-] *a.* de talle de avispa; muy ceñido o entallado.
wassail ['wɑsəl, wɑ'seɪl, B 'wɔseɪl] (hist.) *s.* 1. brindis antiguo. 2. bebida ceremonial (hecha de cerveza o vino aromatizado con especias, azúcar, manzanas asadas, etc.). 3. juerga de borrachera. —*v.i.* festejar, jaranear. —*v.t.* brindar por.
wassail bowl, ponchera.
wassailer [-ər, B -ə] *s.* (hist.) festejador, juerguista.
Wassermann reaction ['wɑsərmən-, 'vɑs-, B 'wɔsəmən-] (med.) reacción de Wassermann.
wastage ['weɪstɪdʒ] *s.* 1. despilfarro, derroche, desperdicio. 2. pérdida, desgaste, merma.
waste [weɪst] *a.* 1. desierto, desolado, baldío, yermo. 2. asolado, devastado. 3. rechazado, desechado, superfluo, sobrante, residual. 4. de desagüe, de escape. 5. excreto, excremental, excrementicio. 6. **to lay w.,** asolar, devastar, arrasar; **to lie w.,** estar eriazo o inculto (tierra). —*v.t.* 1. malgastar, desperdiciar, dilapidar, disipar. 2. consumir, gastar, mermar. 3. devastar, desolar, destruir. 4. enflaquecer, debilitar, marchitar, amenguar. 5. **w. one's breath,** gastar saliva en balde; **w. (one's) time,** perder el tiempo. —*v.i.* desgastarse, gastarse, debilitarse, enflaquecerse; **w. away,** menguar; marchitarse, demacrarse, consumirse. —*s.* 1. desierto, erial, yermo. 2. desperdicio, pérdida (de tiempo, dinero, etc.). 3. consunción, emaciación, demacración. 4. despojos, desperdicios, desechos, basura. 5. aguas de albañal. 6. borra, hilacha de algodón; estopa. 7. (geol.) erosión. 8. **to go** (o **to run) to w.,** ser desperdiciado, no usarse.
wastebasket ['weɪstˌbæskət, B -ˌbɑs-] *s.* canasto, cesto de papeles, papelera.
wasted ['weɪstəd] *a.* 1. devastado, asolado, arrasado. 2. demacrado, enflaquecido. 3. malgastado, inútil.
wasteful ['weɪstfəl] *a.* 1. pródigo, derrochador, manirroto. 2. ruinoso, antieconómico.
wastefully [-fəlɪ] *adv.* pródigamente.
wastefulness [-fəlnəs] *s.* 1. prodigalidad. 2. gasto inútil.
waste gate, válvula de expulsión.
waste iron, chatarra.
wasteland ['weɪstˌlænd] *s.* tierra eriaza, erial, páramo.
waste matter, desperdicios, residuos.
waste mold, (esc.) molde desechable.
wasteness [-nəs] *s.* (raro) desolación; aridez.
wastepaper [-'peɪpər, B -pə] *s.* papel viejo o usado, papel de desecho.
wastepaper basket, canasto, cesto para papeles, papelera.
waste pile, (min.) escombrera.
waste pipe, tubo de desagüe, tubo de evacuación.
waste product, 1. desecho de fabricación. 2. producto residual (de las actividades vitales del cuerpo).
waster ['weɪstər, B -tə] *s.* 1. malgastador, derrochador, pródigo. 2. pieza defectuosa, material rechazado.
waste silk, borra de seda.
waste steam, vapor de escape.
wasting [-tɪŋ] *a.* 1. devastador, arrollador; asolador. 2. debilitador, enervante. —*s.* desgaste, agotamiento; extenuación, consunción.
wastrel ['weɪstrəl] *s.* 1. derrochador, malgastador, manirroto, pródigo. 2. vagabundo, vago.
wastry [-trɪ] *s.* (esco.) derroche, prodigalidad.
watch [wɑtʃ, B wɔtʃ] *v.i.* 1. velar, hacer vigilia. 2. mirar, estar a la expectativa. 3. vigilar. 4. esperar, aguardar. 5. **w. for,** esperar, estar atento a; **w. out!** ¡cuidado!; **w. out for,** estar a la mira de, estar atento a; tener cuidado con; **w. over,** vigilar sobre, velar. —*v.t.* 1. mirar, ver (ej., televisión, un partido de fútbol, etc.). 2. vigilar, observar, prestar atención a, fijarse en. 3. cuidar, custodiar. 4. tener cuidado con. 5. esperar, aguardar. 6. **w. one's step,** tener cuidado (con lo que uno hace). —*s.* 1. vigilancia, cuidado. 2. sereno, vigilante, guardia, guarda; patrulla. 3. turno de guardia. 4. reloj de bolsillo. 5. cronómetro de barco. 6. (mar.) guardia; servicio. 7. (hist.) cuarto (de la noche); velación, vigilia. 8. (esco.) (colina usada como) atalaya, vigía. 9. **on the w.,** alerta, en guardia; **to keep (a) w.,** estar de guardia; **to keep w. over,** vigilar, velar.
watchband ['wɑtʃˌbænd, B 'wɔtʃ-] *s.* correa de reloj (de) pulsera.
watchcase [-ˌkeɪs] *s.* caja de reloj.
watch chain, cadena de reloj.
watch charm, dije, ornamento que pende de la cadena del reloj.
watchdog [-ˌdɔg] *s.* 1. perro guardián. 2. (fig.) guardián, guardia, vigilante.
watcher ['wɑtʃər, B 'wɔtʃə] *s.* 1. vigilante. 2. observador. 3. velador. 4. (pol.) vigilante o delegado de un partido en el lugar en que se celebran elecciones.
watch fire, hoguera de campamento (como señal o para el uso de un guardia, vigilante, etc.).
watchful [-fəl] *a.* 1. vigilante, atento, alerta. 2. (ant.) desvelado, despierto.
watchfulness [-fəlnəs] *s.* vigilancia, cuidado.
watch glass, cristal de reloj.
watchmaker ['wɑtʃˌmeɪkər, B 'wɔtʃˌm-eɪkə] *s.* relojero.
watchmaking [-kɪŋ] *s.* relojería. —*a.* relojero.
watchman [-mən] *s.* vigilante, guardián, sereno, velador.
watch night, noche de vigilia, esp. noche vieja (víspera de año nuevo).
watch pocket, faltriquera de reloj, bolsillo del reloj.
watch spring, muelle de reloj.
watchtower [-ˌtaʊər, B -ə] *s.* garita, atalaya, vigía.
watchword [-ˌwɜrd, B -ˌwɜd] *s.* 1. santo y seña, consigna, contraseña. 2. lema.
watchwork [-ˌwɜrk, B -ˌwɜk] *s.* mecanismo de reloj.
water ['wɔtər, 'wɑt-, B 'wɔtə] *s.* 1. agua. 2. (*pl.*) aguas (territoriales, etc.). 3. (joy.) agua (de piedras preciosas). 4. aguas (en tela, seda, etc.). 5. acuarela. 6. (fisiol.) agua (orina, lágrimas, etc.). 7. (farm.) agua (de Colonia, de azahar, de rosas, etc.). 8. (com.) acciones diluidas, capital inflado. 9. **above (below) w.,** sobre (bajo) la superficie del agua; **by w.,** por barco; **in deep water(s),** (fig.) en honduras, en dificultades; **in hot w.,** en apuros; **in low w.,** (fig.) deprimido, alicaído; apurado, sin dinero; **in smooth w.,** (fig.) libre de dificultades; **it doesn't hold w.,** (fig.) esto no se puede sostener, esto no convencerá a nadie (díc. de argumento, tesis, relato, etc.); **like w.,** como agua, en abundancia; **much w. has flowed under the bridge,** ha pasado mucho tiempo; **of the first w.,** (fig.) (calidad) de la mejor clase, de primera; **on the w.,** navegando; **still waters run deep,** (fig.), del agua mansa líbreme Dios que de la brava me libro yo; **written in w.,** efímero, pasajero; **to fish in troubled waters,** pescar en río revuelto; **to go through fire and w.,** (fig.) pasarlas negras, pasar las de Caín; **to hold (one's) w.,** contener la orina; **to keep one's head above w.,** (fig.) salir a flote; mantenerse a flote; **to make w.,** hacer aguas, orinar; hacer agua (buque, etc.); **to throw cold w. on (plan, project,** etc.), (fig.) desanimar de la ejecución de, restar mérito a (un plan, proyecto, etc.). —*v.t.* 1. mojar, rociar, salpicar. 2. dar de beber a; abrevar. 3. mañar, regar. 4. dar aguas a (una tela). 5. aguar, echar agua en, diluir (leche, vino, etc.). 6. (com.) diluir (acciones); inflar (capital). 7. **w. down,** suavizar, moderar. —*v.i.* 1. llenarse de agua, hacerse agua, ej., *his mouth watered,* la boca se le hizo agua. 2. llorar (los ojos). 3. tomar agua, aprovisionarse (de agua), ej., *the ship put into port to w.,* el barco atracó en el puerto para tomar agua. 4. beber agua

(animales). —*a.* 1. acuático. 2. acuoso, de agua. 3. para agua. 4 hidráulico.

waterage ['wɔtərɪdʒ, 'wɑt-, B 'wɔt-] *s.* (G.B.) barcaje.

water back, calentador de agua, depósito donde se calienta el agua (en el fogón de una cocina).

water bag, 1. bolsa para agua. 2. (zool.) redecilla, segundo estómago (del camello). 3. (embr.) bolsa de las aguas.

water ballast, (mar.) lastre de agua.

water ballet, ballet acuático.

water bar, (arq.) plancha obturadora.

water bath, 1. baño de agua. 2. baño María.

water-bearer ['wɔtərˌbɛrər, 'wɑt-, B 'wɔtəˌbɛərə] *s.* aguador, azacán, aguatero (Am.).

water-bearing [-ɪŋ] *a.* acuífero (suelo, etc.).

water bed, cama de agua.

water beetle, (ento.) ditisco.

water bird, ave acuática.

water biscuit, galleta quebradiza, elaborada con harina y agua.

water blister, (med.) ampolla, vejiguilla o vesícula llena de agua.

water bloom, flor de agua.

waterboard ['wɔtərˌbɔrd, 'wɑt-, B 'wɔtəˌbɔd] *s.* (mar.) cubichete.

waterborne [-ˌbɔrn, B -ˌbɔn] *a.* 1. a flote, flotante. 2. fluvial, marítimo (tráfico, etc.). 3. propagado por el agua (ej., enfermedad).

water bottle, 1. garrafa (para agua). 2. cantimplora (del soldado).

water boy, aguador, aguatero (Amer.).

waterbrain [-ˌbreɪn] *s.* (vet.) modorra, tornada.

water brash, (med.) pirosis, sensación de ardor en el estómago.

waterbuck [-ˌbʌk] *s.* (zool.) kobo, kob.

water bucket, cubo de agua, balde de agua.

water buffalo, (zool.) búfalo, búfalo de la India, carabao.

water bug, (ento.) chinche de agua; garapito.

water carriage, transporte marítimo, transporte fluvial.

water carrier, 1. aguador, azacán. 2. nube de lluvia. 3. depósito de agua. 4. **W. C.,** (astr.) Acuario.

water cask, barrica de agua.

water chestnut, castana de agua.

water chinquapin, (bot.) nelumbio, nelumbio brillante.

water clock, reloj de agua, clepsidra.

water closet, excusado, retrete, inodoro, wáter (Amer.).

water color, (pint.) acuarela.

watercolor ['wɔtərˌkʌlər, 'wɑt-, B 'wɔtəˌkʌlə] *s.* acuarela. —*a.* de acuarela; a la acuarela.

watercolorist [-ərəst] *s.* acuarelista.

water column, 1. (f.c.) columna de agua. 2. indicador del nivel de agua.

water-cool [-ˌkul] *v.t.* enfriar por agua, hidroenfriar.

water-cooled [-ˌkuld] *a.* enfriado por agua, refrigerado por agua.

water cooler, fuente (de agua potable refrigerada), bebedero.

water-cooling [-ˌkulɪŋ] *s.* refrigeración o enfriamiento por agua.

watercourse [-ˌkɔrs, B -ˌkɔs] *s.* 1. corriente de agua. 2. madre o lecho (de un arroyo, río, etc.); canal, conducto. 3. (der.) derecho de aguas.

watercraft ['wɔtərkræft, 'wɑt-, B 'wɔtəˌkrɑft] *s.* 1. habilidad en la navegación y deportes acuáticos. 2. barco, buque, embarcación; embarcaciones (en conjunto).

water crake, (orn.) tordo de agua; mirlo de agua.

watercress [-ˌkrɛs] *s.* (bot.) berro, mastuerzo, balsamita mayor.

water culture, (agr.) hidroponía, hidroponia.

water cure, 1. cura de aguas, hidroterapia. 2. (hist.) tormento de toca.

water curing, (constr.) curado al agua.

water dog, 1. (zool.) perro de aguas. 2. (hum.) lobo de mar; nadador excelente.

water drive, (hidr.) impulsión por agua, empuje hidrostático.

watered ['wɔtərd, 'wɑt-, B 'wɔtəd] *a.* 1. abundante en agua. 2. aguado, diluido.

watered silk, (tej.) muaré, moaré.

waterer [-ərər, B -ə] *s.* 1. aguador, azacán. 2. regador. 3. abrevador (de ganado).

waterfall [-ərˌfɔl, B -əˌ-] *s.* cascada, catarata, salto de agua.

water-fast [-ˌfæst, B -ˌfɑst] *a.* 1. a prueba de agua; insoluble. 2. (esco.) estanco, hermético.

water faucet, grifo.

water fennel, (bot.) enante.

waterfinder [-ˌfaɪndər, B -də] *s.* rabdomante.

water flea, (ento.) pulga de agua, pulga acuática.

waterfowl [-ˌfaʊl] *s.* ave acuática.

waterfront [-ˌfrʌnt] *s.* 1. terreno ribereño o costero. 2. zona portuaria, zona de los muelles.

water gap, abra, boca, garganta, hondonada (entre montañas por donde fluye una corriente).

water gas, (quím.) gas de agua.

water gate, puerta de esclusa, compuerta.

water gauge, 1. indicador del nivel de agua. 2. hidrómetro.

water germander, (bot.) escordio, ajote.

water glass, 1. reloj de agua, clepsidra. 2. vaso (para beber agua). 3. caja con fondo de vidrio (que sirve para examinar objetos que se encuentran debajo del agua). 4. indicador de nivel, tubo de nivel (en calderas, etc.). 5. (quím.) vidrio soluble o líquido.

water gum, (bot.) árbol del caucho.

water hammer, (hidr.) 1. martillo de agua, ariete hidráulico. 2. golpe de ariete (en tuberías de agua, etc.).

water-hardened ['wɔtərˌhɑrdənd, 'wɑt-, B 'wɔtəˌhɑd-] *a.* (metal.) templado en agua.

water head, (ing.) carga hidrostática.

water heater, calentador de agua.

water hemlock, (bot.) cicuta.

water hen, (orn.) gallina de agua, gallareta, fúlica.

water hole, 1. charco, charca. 2. hoyo en (una superficie de) hielo.

water hyacinth, (bot.) jacinto de agua.

water ice, sorbete, granizada, granizado.

water-inch ['wɔtərɪntʃ, 'wɑt-, B 'wɔt-] *s.* paja de agua (medida antigua).

wateriness [-ɪnəs] *s.* acuosidad.

watering [-ɪŋ] *s.* 1. riego, regadura. 2. lagrimeo. —*a.* 1. regador, que riega. 2. abrevador. 3. lacrimoso, que lagrimea. 4. con aguas termales, de baños (díc. de lugares).

watering boat, barco aguador, transporte de agua potable o de riego.

watering can, regadera de plantas y flores.

watering cart, carro regador.

wateringhole [-ˌhoʊl] *s.* 1. charco, charca. 2. aguadero.

watering place, 1. balneario, lugar de baños; baños termales. 2. abrevadero; aguadero, aguaje.

watering trough, 1. abrevadero. 2. (f.c.) canaleta de toma en marcha, artesa de vía.

waterish [-ɪʃ] *a.* aguado, acuoso; aguanoso, aguachento (Amer.).

water jacket, (mot.) camisa o chaqueta de agua; camisa de enfriamiento.

water jug, jarra, aguamanil; porrón.

water jump, zanja con agua (como obstáculo en carreras de caballos).

waterless ['wɔtərləs, 'wɑt-, B 'wɔtələs] *a.* sin agua, seco, árido.

water level, 1. nivel hidrostático. 2. nivel del agua. 3. línea de flotación. 4. nivel de agua (instrumento).

water lily, (bot.) ninfea, nenúfar.

waterline [-ˌlaɪn] *s.* 1. (mar.) línea de flotación. 2. orilla del agua.

waterlog [-ˌlɔg, -ˌlɑg, B -ˌlɔg] *v.t.* (*pret., p.p.* WATERLOGGED ; *p.pr.* WATERLOGGING) anegar, inundar; llenar o saturar de agua.

waterlogged [-ˌlɔgd, -ˌlɑgd, B -ˌlɔgd] *a.* anegado, inundado; saturado de agua.

Waterloo [-ˌlu, B ˌwɔtə'lu] *s.* (fig.) derrota decisiva; **to meet one's w.,** sufrir una derrota decisiva; **the candidate met his W. because of the campaign expenses,** el candidato se le llegó su San Martín a causa de los gastos de la campaña electoral.

water main, cañería matriz, cañería de acueducto; tubería maestra.

waterman ['wɔtərmən, 'wɑt-, B 'wɔtəmən] *s.* (mar.) barquero, botero, **remero.**

watermanship [-ˌʃɪp] *s.* (mar.) oficio o habilidad de un barquero; destreza para remar o nadar.

watermark [-ˌmɑrk, B -ˌmɑk] *s.* 1. marca de nivel del agua. 2. (impr.) filigrana, marca de agua. —*v.t.* marcar con agua imprimir con filigrana.

watermelon [-ˌmɛlən] *s.* (bot.) sandia, melón de agua, badea.

water meter, contador de agua, medidor de agua.

water mill, molino de agua.

water moccasin, (zool.) mocasín de agua, serpiente de agua.

water motor, hidromotor, motor de agua.

water nymph, (mitol.) náyade, ninfa de las aguas.

water oak, (bot.) roble de agua.

water of crystallization, (quím.) agua de cristalización.

water of hydration, (quím.) agua de hidratación.

water ouzel, (orn.) tordo de agua, mirlo de agua.

water ox, (zool.) búfalo, búfalo de la India.

water parsnip, (bot.) berrera, berraza, berra, arsáfraga.

water parting, divisoria (de aguas).

water pipe, 1. narguile. 2. caño de agua, tubería de agua.

water pistol, pistola de agua (juguete).

water plane, hidroavión, hidroplano.

water plantain, (bot.) alisma, llantén de aguas, lirón.

water polo, (dep.) polo acuático, waterpolo.

waterpot ['wɔtərˌpɑt, wɑt-, B 'wɔtəˌpɔt] *s.* (ant.) regadera.

waterpower [-ˌpaʊər, B -ə] *s.* 1. fuerza hidráulica, energía hidráulica, energía hidroeléctrica; fuerza de agua. 2. salto de agua.

water pox, (med.) varicela.

waterproof [-ˌpruf] *a.* impermeable. —*s.* 1. material impermeable; hidrófugo. 2. (pr. G.B.) impermeable. —*v.t.* impermeabilizar.

waterproofer [-ər, B -ə] *s.* impermeabilizador, producto que impermeabiliza.

waterproofing [-ɪŋ] *s.* 1. impermeabilización. 2. material impermeable.

water rail, (orn.) polla de agua; rey de codornices, bitor.

water ram, (hidr.) ariete hidráulico.

water rat, 1. (zool.) rata de agua, satirio; rata almizclada. 2. (jer.) hampón de puerto.

water reed, (bot.) caña acuática.

water-repellent ['wɔtərɪ'pɛlənt, 'wɑt-, B 'wɔtərɪ-] *a.* impermeable; impermeabilizado, hidrófugo (*tela*).

water-resistant [-rɪ'zɪstənt] *a.* impermeable; impermeabilizado, hidrófugo (*tela*).
water rights, derechos ribereños; derechos de agua, derechos acuáticos, (riegos) aprovechamiento de aguas; servidumbre de aguas.
water sail, (mar.) arrastraculo.
water sapphire, (min.) zafiro de agua.
waterscape ['wɔtər,skeɪp, 'wɑt-, B 'wɔtə,-] *s.* (pint.) paisaje marino, marina.
water scorpion, (ento.) escorpión de agua, chinche de agua.
water seal, cierre hidráulico, cierre de agua.
watershed [-,ʃɛd] *s.* 1. divisoria (de aguas). 2. cuenca, vertiente, hoya.
waterside ['wɔtər,saɪd, 'wɑt-, B 'wɔtə,-] *s.* ribera, orilla, borde del agua, litoral.
water skater, *var. de* **water strider.**
water ski, (dep.) esquí náutico, esquí acuático.
water-ski [-,ski] *v.i.* (dep.) hacer esquí acuático.
water skin, odre, bota (para beber).
water skipper, *var. de* **water strider.**
water snake, (zool.) serpiente de agua, mocasín.
water-soak [-,soʊk] *v.t.* remojar, empapar (de agua), embeber.
water softener, (producto) ablandador, neutralizador del agua.
water-soluble [-,sɑljəbəl, B -,sɔl-] *a.* 1. soluble en agua. 2. (bioquím.) hidrosoluble (díc. de vitaminas).
water spaniel, espaniel de aguas.
water spider, (zool.) araña de agua.
water sport, deporte acuático.
waterspout ['wɔtər,spaʊt, 'wɑt-, B 'wɔtə,-] *s.* 1. pico o boquilla de manguera, surtidor. 2. canalón (que recoge el agua en los tejados). 3. tromba marina, manga, torbellino. 4. orificio de distribución (de turbinas).
water sprite, personaje imaginario que vive en las aguas; ninfa, náyade, nereida, ondina.
water strider, (ento.) tejedor, zapatero, andarríos.
water supply, abastecimiento de agua, suministro o provisión de agua.
water system, 1. sistema fluvial; red de aguas corrientes. 2. abastecimiento de agua.
water table, 1. nivel hidrostático, nivel superior de agua subterránea, nivel freático. 2. (arq.) retallo de derrame.
water tank, aljibe, depósito, tanque de agua.
water thrush, (orn.) 1. tordo de agua, mirlo de agua. 2. curruca americana.
watertight [-,taɪt] *a.* 1. a prueba de agua, estanco; impermeable, hermético. 2. sin escapatorias (documento, contrato, etc.), sin un punto flaco (argumento, etc.).
watertight bulkhead, (mar.) mamparo estanco.
watertight compartment, (mar.) compartimiento estanco.
water tower, 1. tanque de agua, depósito de agua, torre de agua. 2. aparato contra incendios con tubería vertical extensible.
water trough, abrevadero.
watertube boiler ['wɔtər,tub-, 'wɑt-, B 'wɔtə,tjub-] caldera acuotubular.
water turbine, turbina hidráulica.
water vapor, vapor acuoso, vapor producido por la evaporación de agua.
water-vascular [-'væskjələr, B -lə] *a.* (zool.) acuovascular (sistema).
water wagon, furgón de agua.
water wall, pantalla de agua.
water wave, 1. onda de agua. 2. ondulación al agua (del cabello).
water-wave [-,weɪv] *v.t.* ondular al agua (el cabello).
waterway ['wɔtər,weɪ, 'wɑt-, B 'wɔtə,-] *s.* 1. vía de agua, vía fluvial, canal navegable. 2. (mar.) trancanil.
waterweed [-,wid] *s.* hierba acuática, planta silvestre acuática.
waterwheel [-,hwil, -,wil] *s.* 1. rueda hidráulica; turbina hidráulica. 2. rueda de paletas (de un barco). 3. noria.
water wings, nadaderas, salvavidas en forma de alas.
water witch, rabdomante, persona que adivina la presencia de agua subterránea.
water witching, rabdomancia.
waterworks [-,wɜrks, B -,wɜks] *s.pl.* 1. planta de agua potable, instalación de agua corriente; sistema de abastecimiento de agua. 2. (jer.) fuente de lágrimas; **to turn on the w.,** echarse a llorar.
waterworn [-,wɔrn, B -,wɔn] *a.* pulido o gastado por el agua.
watery ['wɔtərɪ, 'wɑt-, B 'wɔt-] *a.* 1. acuoso, aguoso, aguanoso, aguachento (Am.) (fruta, vegetales, etc.). 2. lloroso, lagrimoso, lacrimoso (ojos); baboso, salivoso (labios). 3. aguado, diluido (vino, sopa, solución, etc.); (fig.) insípido, endeble (estilo, discurso, etc.). 4. pálido, desteñido (color).
watt [wɑt, B wɔt] *s.* (fís.) vatio, wat.
wattage ['wɑtɪdʒ, B 'wɔt-] *s.* (elec.) vatiaje.
Watteau back [wɑ'toʊ-, B 'wɔtoʊ-] espalda de un vestido con grandes pliegues que no están sujetos en la cintura (como en los cuadros de Watteau).
watter ['wɑtər, B 'wɔtə] *s.* (elec.) (*ú. en compuestos*) de (tantos) vatios, cj., *twenty-five w.*, aparato (bombilla, motor, etc.) de veinticinco vatios.
watt-hour ['wɑt,aʊr, B 'wɔt,aʊə] *s.* (elec.) vatio-hora, vatihora.
watt-hour meter, contador de vatio-hora.
wattle ['wɑtəl, B 'wɔt-] *s.* 1. zarzo, estera, armazón de juncos. 2. (*pl.*) mimbres, juncos (para cercos, vallas, tejados de paja, etc.). 3. valla de mimbres. 4. barba, carnosidad (que cuelga del cuello de algunas aves y de algunos reptiles); barbilla (de peces). 5. (Aust.) acacia. —*v.t.* 1. construir con zarzos o esteras. 2. enzarzar. 3. entretejer o entrelazar en zarzo (mimbres, juncos, etc.).
wattled [-əld] *a.* 1. enzarzado. 2. con barba (ave); con barbilla (pez).
wattless ['wɑtləs, B 'wɔt-] *a.* (elec.) devatiado, desvatado, sin vatios.
wattmeter [-,mitər, B -ə] *s.* (elec.) vatímetro.
waul [wɔl] *v.i.* gritar, chillar, maullar.
wave [weɪv] *v.i.* 1. ondear, undular (trigo); flamear, flotar (bandera, etc.); ondular, rizarse (cabello). 2. señalar con un ademán, hacer señales. —*v.t.* 1. mover de un lado a otro, agitar (el brazo, una lámpara, etc.); blandir (espada, pistola, etc.). 2. hacer señales o señas con. 3. hacer ademán de. 4. ondular, rizar (el pelo). 5. (tej.) formar aguas en, dar aguas o visos a. 6. **w. aside** (o **away**), echar a un lado, desechar, apartar (con un ademán); **w. farewell,** decir adiós (con el brazo, pañuelo, etc.). —*s.* 1. ola, onda. 2. (fig.) ola (de calor, atracos, prosperidad, etc.). 3. (fig.) oleada, ej., *to attack in waves,* atacar en oleadas. 4. ondulación (del cabello). 5. movimiento de la mano, ademán. 6. (fís.) onda. 7. **the wave(s),** (poét.) agua, piélago, mar.
Wave, *s.* (E.U.) miembro del cuerpo auxiliar femenino de la marina de guerra.
wave band, (rad.) banda de ondas, faja de ondas, rango o gama de ondas.
waved [weɪvd] *a.* 1. ondulado, ondeado. 2. con aguas (tela, seda, etc.).
wave detector, (rad.) detector de ondas.
wave front, (fís.) frente o avanzada de la onda.
wave guide, (rad.) guía de ondas.
wavelength ['weɪv,lɛŋθ, -,lɛŋkθ] *s.* (fís.) longitud de onda.
waveless [-ləs] *a* sin olas, calmado, sosegado (mar, aguas).
wavelet [-lət] *s.* pequeña ola marina.
wave mechanics, (fís.) mecánica de ondas.
wavemeter ['weɪv,mitər, B -ə] *s.* ondímetro, ondómetro, odámetro.
waver ['weɪvər, B -və] *v.i.* 1. vacilar, titubear, hesitar. 2. tambalear, bambolear. 3. oscilar, fluctuar (la luz, llama, etc.). —*a.* 1. oscilación. 2. vacilación.
waverer [-vərər, B -ə] *s.* (fig.) veleta (persona mudable o irresoluta).
waveringly [-vərɪŋlɪ] *adv.* 1. de modo vacilante, con indecisión. 2. de manera oscilante; trémulamente.
wavery [-vərɪ] *a.* vacilante, irresoluto, inconstante.
wave theory, (fís.) teoría ondulatoria de la luz.
wave train, (fís.) tren de ondas.
wave trap, (rad.) selector de ondas.
wave winding, (elec.) devanado ondulado, devanado en espiral, devanado en serie.
wavily ['weɪvəlɪ] *adv.* en forma ondulante, ondulantemente.
waviness [-vɪnəs] *s.* calidad de ondeado, aspecto ondulante.
wavy ['weɪvɪ] *a.* (WAVIER; WAVIEST) 1. ondeado, ondulado, undoso, ondulante. 2. sinuoso, ondulado, ondulatorio.
wawl [wɔl] *v.i.* (esco.) llorar, lamentarse, dar alaridos.
wax [wæks] *v.i.* 1. crecer (la luna). 2. hacerse, ponerse (gordo, alegre, enojado, etc.). 3. **w. and wane,** (fig.) sufrir altibajos.
wax, *s.* 1. cera (de abejas, vegetal, mineral, etc.). 2. (med.) cerumen, cera, cerilla (de los oídos). 3. matriz de cera (para la fabricación de discos fonográficos). 4. **to mould (one) like w.,** moldear (a uno) como la cera. —*v.t.* encerar, untar con cera.
wax, *s.* (fam.) rabieta, rabia, enfado.
wax bean, judía, alubia, habichuela (con vaina de color crema).
waxberry ['wæks,bɛrɪ] *s.* (*pl.* WAXBERRIES) (bot.) 1. árbol de cera; pimientilla. 2. bolita de nieve.
wax cake, pan de cera.
wax candle, cirio.
wax chandler, cerero.
wax cloth, linóleo, tela encerada.
waxed paper [wækst-] papel parafinado, papel encerado.
waxen ['wæksən] *a.* 1. céreo. 2. cubierto de cera. 3. ceroso, blando. 4. de brillo ceroso. 5. (fig.) pálido.
wax end, hilo encerado (de los zapateros).
waxer [-sər, B -sə] *s.* encerador.
wax etching, (impr.) electrotipia en cera.
waxiness [-sɪnəs] *s.* consistencia cerosa; aspecto ceroso.
waxing [-sɪŋ] *s.* 1. enceramiento. 2. grabación (fonográfica) en disco de cera.
wax light, cirio.
wax match, cerilla, fósforo de cera.
wax model, w. modeling, modelado en cera.
wax myrtle, (bot.) árbol de cera, arrayán brabántico.
wax painting, pintura al encausto, encausto a la cera.
wax palm, (bot.) 1. (variedad de) palmera de los Andes. 2. carandaí, carnauba, palmera del Brasil.

wax paper, papel parafinado, papel encerado.
wax plant, (bot.) cerifior.
wax pocket, cavidad secretora de cera.
wax taper, velita, cirio delgado y de color vistoso (gen. para candelabro de mesa de comedor).
wax tree, (bot.) árbol de la cera.
waxwing [ˈwæksˌwɪŋ] *s.* (orn.) picotera.
waxwork [-ˌwɜrk, B -ˌwɜk] *s.* 1. figura de cera. 2. *pl.* (*sing. o pl. en const.*) museo de cera.
waxy [ˈwæksɪ] *a.* 1. (WAXIER; WAXIEST) ceroso, cereo, encerado. 2. (fam., G.B.) enfadado.
way [weɪ] *s.* 1. vía, camino; ruta. 2. dirección, rumbo. 3. paso, camino; espacio, sitio. 4. avance, progreso, pasaje. 5. distancia, trecho. 6. (fig.) modo, manera; medio, camino; método, procedimiento. 7. moda; estilo. 8. aspecto, respecto. 9. modo de obrar, comportamiento, curso. 10. hábito, costumbre, peculiaridad. 11. condición, estado. 12. esfera, campo de acción, ocupación. 13. (*pl.*) anguilas de grada, rampa (en un astillero). 14. (tej.) dirección del tejido (en la tela). 15. (der.) servidumbre de paso, derecho de paso, derecho de vía. 16. (mec.) guia, resbaladera. 17. **across the w.,** al otro lado, en frente; **a good w.,** un buen trecho; **a great w. off,** muy lejos, muy distante; **all the w.,** por todo el camino; en todo, del todo; hasta el fin; **all the w. down,** a lo largo de; **any w.,** de cualquier modo, de todas maneras, de cualquier manera; en todo caso, en cualquier caso; **both ways,** ambos lados, las dos caras; (apuesta) a ganador y placé (de caballos); **by the w.,** por el camino; de paso, a propósito, dicho sea de paso; **by w. of,** por la vía de, por vía de; por modo de, a título de, a guisa de, a manera de; **covered w.,** camino cubierto, paso cubierto; camino desenfilado; (mil.) galería cubierta; **each w.,** de cada lado, en cualquier forma; **every w.,** por todas partes, por cualquier lado; de cualquier modo, por cualquier medio; **in a bad w.,** en mal estado, en malas condiciones; **in a big w.,** en gran escala; **in a small w.,** en pequeña escala; **in a w.,** de cierta manera, hasta cierto punto, en cierto modo; **in every w.,** desde todo punto de vista, en todo respecto; **in my own w.,** a mi modo, a mi manera; **in no w.,** de ningún modo, de ninguna manera; **it is only his w.,** él es así, es su manera de ser, es su modo; **nothing out of the w.,** (fig.) nada fuera de lo común, nada extraordinario; **on the w.,** de camino, de paso; **on the w. out,** a la salida, saliendo; **on the w. to,** camino de, con rumbo a; **out of the w.,** escondido; lejano, remoto, perdido; hecho, despachado; (fig.) fuera de lo común, extraordinario; (imper.) ¡a un lado!; **parting of the ways,** (fig.) momento de decisión, disyuntiva; **permanent w.,** (f.c.) vía permanente; **right of w.,** derecho de paso; **that is the w. to do it,** así se hace, muy bien hecho; **that w.,** por ahí, por allí; de ese modo, así; **the other w. around,** al contrario, al revés; **the W. of the Cross,** (relig.) Vía Crucis, Estaciones de la Cruz; **the w. of the world,** costumbres de moda; **this w.,** por acá, por aquí; **to be a long w. off,** estar lejos de, no llegar a; estar en gran forma; **to be in the family w.,** (fam.) estar embarazada; **to be in the w.,** estar en el camino, estorbar, ser obstáculo, incomodar; **to be on the w.,** viajar, estar de viaje; acercarse, venir; **to be set in one's ways,** estar apegado a sus hábitos, estar acostumbrado a una forma de vida; **to be under w.,** estar navegando (barco); estar en marcha, estar en camino; estar progresando; **to clear the w.,** quitar obstáculos (del camino); facilitar el camino; **to come one's w.,** (fig.) presentarse (oportunidad, etc.) a uno, caerle a uno en suerte; **to feel one's w.,** tentar o tantear el camino; proceder con tiento; **to feel the same w.,** sentir lo mismo, ser de la misma opinión; **to find a w.,** encontrar la manera o la forma; **to find the w.,** encontrar el camino, llegar a destino; **to force one's w.,** abrirse paso o camino por la fuerza; forzar su entrada; **to get in the w.,** situarse en medio, obstaculizar, entrometerse; **to get out of the w.,** quitar(se) de en medio, quitarse de encima, hacer lugar; **to give w.,** ceder, retroceder; dejar pasar; partirse, romperse (cuerda, tabla, etc.); (mar.) remar fuertemente; **to give w. to,** (fig.) entregarse a; **to go a long w. towards;** (fig.) contribuir mucho a, hacer un esfuerzo considerable para; **to go** (o **take**) **one's own w.,** (fig.) seguir su propio camino, actuar independientemente; **to go one's w.,** partir; irse por su propio camino, seguir su camino; (fig.) apartarse; **to go out of one's w.,** (fig.) tomarse la molestia, hacer un esfuerzo extraordinario; **to go the same w.,** llevar el mismo camino, llevar el mismo rumbo; **to go the w. of all flesh, to go the w. of all earth, to go the w. of nature,** morir, volver el polvo al polvo; **to have a w. (with),** manejar bien, saber guiar, tener poder de persuasión (con); tener don de gentes, saber congraciarse; **to have it both ways,** usar ambas alternativas; **to have** (o **get**) **one's (own) w.,** salirse con la suya, hacer lo que se quiere; **to keep out of the w.,** estarse a un lado, no obstruir el paso; **not to know which w. to turn,** no saber dónde meterse o esconderse; (fig.) no saber a qué atenerse, no saber en quién cobijarse, no saber a quién pedir ayuda; **to know one's w. around,** (fig.) ser conocedor; ser experimentado o experto; **to lead the w.,** enseñar el camino; entrar el primero, ir primero; (fig.) guiar, dar el ejemplo; **to look the other w.,** mirar a otro lado, desviar la vista; hacerse el que no ve; **to lose one's** (o **the**) **w.,** perderse, andar perdido, extraviarse, desviarse; **to make one's w.,** abrirse paso, avanzar; (fig.) hacer carrera, acreditarse, prosperar; **to make w.,** hacer lado, hacer lugar; (fig.) prosperar; **to make w. for,** dar paso a, abrir paso para, ceder paso a; hacer lugar para; **to mend one's ways,** mejorar de conducta, mudar de vida, llevar vida distinta; **to pave the w.,** (fig.) preparar el terreno, allanar el terreno, allanar el camino; **to pay one's w.,** pagar su parte (de los gastos de viaje, etc.); **to pick one's w.,** avanzar, progresar; **to put someone in the w. of something,** dar oportunidad a alguien para; **to put out of the w.,** sacar de encima, apartar; quitar de en medio; matar en secreto, asesinar; **to rub (someone) the wrong w.,** (fig.) molestar, enojar (a alguien); **to see one's w. to,** encontrar la manera de, ver el modo de; **to stand in the w.,** obstaculizar, ser obstáculo; **to work one's w. (through),** abrirse camino, abrirse paso (por); **to work one's w. through,** (fig.) pagar con su trabajo los gastos (de los estudios, la universidad, etc.); **w. in,** entrada; **w. out,** salida; **where there's a will there's a w.,** querer es poder; **which w.?** ¿por dónde? ¿en qué dirección? —*a.* intermedio.
waybill [ˈweɪˌbɪl] *s.* hoja de ruta, carta de porte.
way car, 1. (f.c.) vagón de cola, furgón de cola. 2. vagón de carga ligera.
wayfarer [-ˌfɛrər, B -ˌfɛərə] *s.* caminante, viajero.
wayfaring [-ɪŋ] *a.* caminante, viajero.
wayfaring tree, (bot.) viburno, lantana.
waygoing [-ˌgoʊɪŋ] *s.* (pr. esco.) partida, marcha; adiós.
waylay [ˈweɪˌleɪ, B weɪˈleɪ] *v.t.* 1. acechar, saltear. 2. abordar.
waylayer [-ər, B -ə] *s.* acechador, salteador.
waylaying [-ɪŋ] *s.* acechanza, acecho.
waymark [-ˌmɑrk, B -ˌmɑk] **waypost** [-ˌpoʊst] *s.* mojón, hito.
Way of the Cross, (relig.) Vía Crucis.
ways and means, medios y arbitrios.
wayside [ˈweɪˌsaɪd] *s.* borde del camino, orilla o costado del camino. —*a.* (situado) al borde del camino.
way station, (E.U.) estación intermedia, estación de paso, estación de tránsito, apeadero (del ferrocarril).
way train, (f.c.) tren de escala, tren local.
wayward [ˈweɪwərd, B -wəd] *a.* 1. díscolo, voluntarioso, desobediente; avieso, descarriado. 2. irregular, caprichoso. 3. adverso, contrario (suerte).
waywardly [-lɪ] *adv.* 1. de modo díscolo, caprichosamente, voluntariosamente. 2. irregularmente, caprichosamente. 3. adversamente.
waywardness [-nəs] *s.* 1. indocilidad, desobediencia. 2. adversidad, perversidad (de la suerte, etc.).
wayworn [-ˌwɔrn, B -ˌwɔn] *a.* fatigado del viaje.
W by N *abrev. de* **west by north,** oeste cuarta al noroeste.
W by S *abrev. de* **west by south,** oeste cuarta al suroeste.
w.c. [ˈdʌblju'si] *abrev de* **water closet,** inodoro, wáter (Am.).
W.D. *abrev. de* **War Department,** Departamento de Guerra.
we [wi] *pron.* nosotros, nosotras.
weak [wik] *a.* 1. débil, endeble, frágil. 2. débil, enfermizo, enclenque. 3. (fig.) débil, irresoluto. 4. débil, deficiente, ineficaz (argumento, pruebas, etc.). 5. ralo, aguado (té, café, etc.), suave (licor, cerveza, etc.). 6. poco, incompleto, ej., *w. crew,* tripulación incompleta. 7. blando (trigo), pobre (harina). 8. flojo (estilo). 9. (gram.) regular, débil (díc. de verbos o su conjugacion). 10. (fon.) no acentuada, átona (sílaba). 11. (foto.) sin contraste. 12. **the weaker sex,** el sexo débil (las mujeres); **to grow w.,** debilitarse; **to have a w. stomach,** (fig.) ser cobarde.
weak demand, (com.) poca demanda.
weaken [ˈwikən] *v.t., v.i.* debilitar(se), atenuar(se); aflojar(se).
weakening [-ɪŋ] *s.* debilitamiento, enervamiento. —*a.* debilitante, enervante.
weakfish [ˈwikˌfɪʃ] *s.* (ict.) pez marino comestible de las costas de E.U.
weakhanded [-ˈhændəd] *a.* 1. escaso de braceros; escaso de mano de obra. 2. de manos débiles.
weakheaded [-ˈhɛdəd] *a.* 1. de cabeza débil. 2. poco inteligente.
weakhearted [-ˈhɑrtəd, B -ˈhɑt-] *a.* (fig.) apocado, pusilánime, timorato.
weak-kneed [-ˈnid] *a.* 1. débil de rodillas. 2. (fig.) falto de energías, falto de resolución, irresoluto; servil.
weakling [ˈwiklɪŋ] *s., a.* 1. canijo, enclenque, enteco. 2. tímido, apocado.
weakly [-lɪ] *a.* (WEAKLIER; WEAKLIEST) enfermizo, achacoso, enclenque.
weak market, (com.) mercado flojo.
weak-minded [ˈwikˈmaɪndəd] *a.* pobre de espíritu, simple, mentecato.
weak-mindedness [-nəs] *s.* mentecatería, simpleza.
weak point, (fig.) (el) punto débil.
weak side, (fig.) (el) lado flaco.
weal [wil] *s.* 1. bienestar, prosperidad, felicidad; **the public** (o **general**) **w.,** el bienestar público. 2. (ant.) riqueza; cuerpo político, el estado.

weal, *s.* verdugo, verdugón, roncha, cardenal.
weald [wild] *s.* región boscosa; llanura, campo abierto.
wealth [wɛlθ] *s.* 1. riqueza, caudal, opulencia; (fig.) abundancia, profusión. 2. (ant.) bienestar, prosperidad.
wealthily ['wɛlθəlɪ] *adv.* ricamente, opulentamente.
wealthiness [-θɪnəs] *s.* riqueza, opulencia.
wealthy ['wɛlθɪ] *a.* (WEALTHIER; WEALTHIEST) 1. rico, adinerado, acaudalado, opulento. 2. (con *in*) abundante.
wealthy, *s.* (bot.) variedad de manzana americana de color rojo brillante.
wean [win] *v.t.* 1. destetar, desmamar. 2. (con *from*) (fig.) separar; desacostumbrar; independizar.
wean, *s.* (esco.) infante, niñito, criatura.
weaner ['winər, B -ə] *s.* 1. destetadera. 2. becerro destetado, cordero (u otro animal) destetado.
weanling [-lɪŋ] *s.* niño o animal destetado.
weapon ['wɛpən] *s.* arma; proyectil. —*v.t.* armar.
weaponless [-ləs] *a.* desarmado, sin armas; indefenso.
weaponry [-rɪ] *s.* armería, arte de fabricar armas; armamento.
wear [wɛr, B wɛə] *v.t.* (*pret.* wore [wɔr, B wɔ]; *p.p.* WORN [wɔrn, B wɔn]; *p.pr.* WEARING) 1. llevar o traer puesto (vestido, traje, etc.); calzar (zapato, guante); usar; vestir de, ej., *w. green,* vestir de verde, *w. uniform,* vestir de uniforme. 2. gastar (ropa, etc.). 3. desgastar, consumir, deteriorar (esp. por uso). 4. cansar, fatigar, agotar. 5. soportar, llevar (encima), ej., *he wears his years well,* él lleva bien sus años, está bien conservado. 6. exhibir, mostrar (sonrisa, cara adusta, etc.). 7. llevar (bandera, colores; díc. del barco). 8. (mar.) virar (al barco) a sotavento. 9. **w. away,** pasar, gastar (tiempo) lenta o tediosamente; desgastar, corroer; **w. down,** gastar, desgastar; (fig.) cansar, acabar con (resistencia, paciencia, etc.); **w. off,** gastar; **w. one's hair (short, long,** etc.), llevar o usar el pelo (corto, largo, etc.); **w. out,** gastar; (fig.) aguantar, soportar, resistir (tormenta, etc.); cansar, fatigar, agotar; **w. out one's welcome,** abusar uno de la hospitalidad; **w. the pants,** (fam.) llevar los pantalones (díc. de una persona autoritaria); **w. the crown,** reinar, ser rey o reina; **w. the gown,** ser abogado o juez; **w. the sword,** ser soldado, seguir la carrera militar; **w. the willow,** llevar luto; lamentar (la muerte o desaparición de alguien). —*v.i.* 1. durar, perdurar; resistir (uso); conservarse, ej., *this cloth won't w.,* esta tela no resistirá, esta tela no va a durar (mucho), *she wears well,* (fig.) ella se conserva bien, ella no aparenta sus años. 2. gastarse, desgastarse. 3. (raro) amoldarse, ajustarse (con el uso al cuerpo; díc. de ropas). 4. (mar.) virar a sotavento. 5. **w. away,** gastarse, consumirse, mermarse, corroerse; alargarse, prolongarse (el tiempo, el día, etc.); **w. off,** desgastarse, borrarse; disiparse, desaparecer; **w. on,** irritar (los nervios, etc.); pasar (lentamente), alargarse, prolongarse (el tiempo, el día, etc.); **w. out,** gastarse; acabarse, terminarse. —*s.* 1. uso (de artículo de vestir). 2. moda, boga, ej., *to be in general w.,* estar de moda. 3. ropa, artículo de vestir. 4. desgaste, gasto. 5. durabilidad. 6. **for everyday w.,** para todo trote; **to be the worse for w.,** estar bien gastado; **to have in w.,** usar, llevar (ropa); usar, hacer uso de.
wearable ['wɛrəbəl, B 'wɛər-] *a.* que se puede usar, llevar o vestir.
wear and tear, deterioro causado por el uso; desgaste natural.
wearer [-ər, B -ə] *s.* el que lleva, usa, o viste.
wearied ['wɪrɪd, B 'wɪər-] *a.* 1. cansado, agotado. 2. aburrido, fastidiado.
weariful [-ɪfəl] *a.* 1. tedioso, fastidioso, pesado. 2. fatigado, cansado.
wearifulness [-nəs] *s.* tedio.
weariless ['wɪrɪləs, B 'wɪər-] *a.* infatigable, incansable.
wearily [-lɪ] *adv.* cansadamente, fatigadamente.
weariness [-nəs] *s.* cansancio, fatiga, lasitud.
wearing ['wɛrɪŋ, B 'wɛər-] *a.* 1. de vestir, para vestir. 2. desgastador; fatigoso, agotador.
wearing apparel, prendas de vestir, indumentaria.
wearingly [-lɪ] *adv.* fatigosamente.
wearing surface, (mec.) capa de desgaste o de rodamiento, carpeta de desgaste.
wearish ['wɪrɪʃ, B 'wɪərɪʃ] *a.* (esco.) insípido; enfermizo, delicado.
wearisome ['wɪrɪsəm, B 'wɪər-] *a.* 1. fatigoso, penoso. 2. tedioso, fastidioso, pesado.
wearisomely [-lɪ] *adv.* 1. fatigosamente, penosamente. 2. pesadamente.
wearisomeness [-nəs] *s.* tedio, fastidio.
weary ['wɪrɪ, B 'wɪərɪ] *a.* (WEARIER; WEARIEST) 1. cansado, fatigado. 2. tedioso, fastidioso. 3. (con *of*) aburrido (de), hastiado (de). —*v.t., v.i.* (*pret., p.p.* WEARIED; *p.pr.* WEARYING) 1. cansar(se), fatigar(se). 2. hastiar(se), aburrir(se). 3. enfadar, molestar.
weasand ['wizənd] *s.* 1. (ant.) garguero, gaznate. 2. tráquea.
weasel ['wizəl] *s.* 1. (zool.) comadreja. 2. (jer.) chivato, soplón. 3. vehículo para nieve. —*v.i.* 1. emplear subterfugios, ser equívoco. 2. (jer.) chivarse, dar el soplo.
weasel word, palabra equívoca, declaración ambiguo.
weather ['wɛðər, B -ə] *s.* 1. tiempo, clima. 2. mal tiempo, ej., *under stress of w.,* obligado por el mal tiempo (a hacer algo). 3. **in the w.,** a la intemperie; **to make good w. of it,** (mar.) aguantar el tiempo, aguantar bien la tormenta (barco); **under the w.,** (fam.) indispuesto, con malestar; en dificultades financieras; bebido, emborrachado. —*v.t.* 1. orear, airear; curtir o madurar a la intemperie (por la acción del aire). 2. aguantar (el temporal); (fig.) resistir a, sobrevivir a (la adversidad). 3. (mar.) ganar el barlovento de, doblar (un cabo, etc.) por el barlovento. —*v.i.* 1. curtirse a la intemperie. 2. resistir a la intemperie. —*a.* 1. del tiempo, de tiempo; meteorológico; atmosférico. 2. (mar.) de barlovento, del lado del viento.
weatherability [ˌwɛðərə'bɪlətɪ] *s.* resistencia a la intemperie.
weather-beaten ['wɛðərˌbitən, B -əˌ-] *a.* curtido por la intemperie (rostro, rasgos, etc.); gastado o deteriorado por la intemperie.
weatherboard [-ˌbɔrd, B -bɔd] *s.* 1. (carp.) tabla solapada, tabla de chilla. 2. (mar.) lado del viento (en un barco). —*v.t.* cubrir con tablas solapadas, revestir de tablas de chilla.
weatherboarding [-ɪŋ] *s.* solapadura de tablas, tablas solapadas, tablas de chilla, chillado.
weather-bound [-ˌbaʊnd] *a.* anclado (barco en puerto); detenido por el mal tiempo (personas).
weather bureau, oficina meteorológica.
weather changes, cambios atmosféricos.
weather chart, mapa meteorológico, carta del tiempo.
weathercock [-ˌkɑk, B -kɔk] *s.* 1. giralda, giraldilla, veleta. 2. (fig.) veleta, persona inconstante.
weather conditions, condiciones atmosféricas.
weather deck, (mar.) cubierta superior.
weathered [-ərd, B -əd] *a.* 1. curtido por la intemperie. 2. (arq.) inclinado (vertiente de tejado o de cornisa).
weathered oak, roble ahumado.
weather eye, capacidad para pronosticar cambios del tiempo; **to keep one's w. e. open,** (fig.) estar alerta.
weather forecast, pronóstico del tiempo.
weather gauge, (mar.) posición a barlovento (de un barco respecto a otro); (fig.) posición de ventaja o superioridad.
weatherglass ['wɛðərˌglæs, B -əglɑs] *s.* barómetro.
weathering [-ərɪŋ] *s.* 1. acción corrosiva de los elementos naturales; alteración o desgaste debidos a los agentes atmosféricos. 2. (arq.) vertiente (de tejado o de cornisa).
weathering test, prueba de intemperismo.
weatherly [-ərlɪ, B -əlɪ] *a.* (mar.) capaz de navegar de bolina (barco).
weatherman [-ˌmæn] *s.* (fam.) meteorologista, meteorólogo.
weather map, mapa meteorológico.
weather molding, (arq.) vertiente (de cornisa).
weatherproof [-ˌpruf] *a.* a prueba de intemperie; protegido del mal tiempo. —*v.t.* hacer a prueba de intemperie, hacer resistente al mal tiempo.
weather satellite, satélite metereológico.
weather sheets, (mar.) escotas de barlovento.
weather ship, buque meteorológico.
weather side, costado de barlovento.
weather signal, señal para indicar las variaciones del tiempo.
weather station, estación meteorológica.
weather strip, burlete.
weather-strip ['wɛðərˌstrɪp, B -əˌ-] *v.t.* proveer de burletes.
weathertight [-ˌtaɪt] *a.* a prueba de intemperie.
weather vane, veleta, giraldilla.
weather-wise [-ˌwaɪz] *a.* que presiente los cambios del tiempo o de la opinión pública.
weatherworn [-ˌwɔrn, B -ˌwɔn] *a.* gastado o deteriorado por la intemperie.
weave [wiv] *v.t.* (*pret.* WOVE [woʊv]; *p.p.* WOVEN ['woʊvən]; *p.pr.* WEAVING) 1. tejer, tramar; trenzar; entrelazar, entretejer. 2. (fig.) tejer, fabricar, maquinar, urdir, forjar. 3. **w. one's way,** avanzar con virajes repetidos. —*v.i.* 1. tejer en telar. 2. entretejerse; entrelazarse. 3. seguir en un curso tortuoso o serpenteado. 4. **get weaving,** (jer., G.B.) ¡manos a la obra! ¡vamos!; **w. through (a crowd),** abrirse paso por (una muchedumbre) zigzagueando. —*s.* tejido, textura.
weaver ['wivər, B -və] *s.* 1. tejedor, tejedora, tejedera. 2. (orn.) tejedor.
weaverbird [-ˌbɜrd, B -ˌbɜd] *s.* (orn.) tejedor, ondarríos.
weaver's knot, nudo llano.
web [wɛb] *s.* 1. tela, tejido (de hilos, de araña, etc.); telaraña. 2. red, malla, cadena (de f.c., carreteras, etc.). 3. (fig.) enredo, maraña (de mentiras, etc.). 4. (zool.) membrana (de los palmípedos). 5. barba, pelo (de pluma). 6. (arq.) nervio (de estructura); tejido, trabazón (de armazón). 7. alma de viga o de riel. 8. paletón (de la llave). 9. (impr.) (bobina o rollo de) papel continuo. 10. (fig.) artificio engañoso, trampa. —*v.t.* (*pret., p.p.* WEBBED; *p.pr.* WEBBING) enmarañar, enredar, embrollar.
webbed [wɛbd] *a.* 1. tejido. 2. unido por una telilla o membrana. 3. (orn.) palmeado.
webbing ['wɛbɪŋ] *s.* tira de tela gruesa, cincha, correa de tejido (usados en tapicería, para cinturones, cananas, etc.).

webby [-ɪ] *a.* enmarañado (cabello, etc.).
weber [ˈwɛbər, B ˈveɪbə] *s.* (elec.) weber, weberio (unidad de flujo magnético).
webfoot [ˈwɛbˌfʊt] *s.* 1. pata palmeada. 2. palmípedo.
web-footed [-əd] *a.* palmeado, palmípedo.
web frame, (mar.) bulárcama, sobreplán.
web member, (arq.) pieza de enrejado, pieza de armadura.
web press, prensa rotativa con papel continuo, prensa rotativa de alimentación continua.
webster [ˈwɛbstər, B -stə] *s.* (ant.) tejedor, tejedora, tejedera.
wecht [wɛkt] (esco.) *var. de* **weight.**
wed [wɛd] *v.t.* (*pret.* WEDDED; *p.p.* WEDDED O WED; *p.pr.* WEDDING) 1. casarse con, tomar por esposa o marido. 2. casar. 3. (fig.) unir, aunar. 4. **(to be) wedded to,** (estar) dedicado o pegado a (ocupación, pasatiempo, teoría, etc.). —*v.i.* casarse, contraer matrimonio.
Wed. *abrev. de* **Wednesday,** miércoles (miér.).
wedding [ˈwɛdɪŋ] *s.* boda, bodas, nupcias, casamiento, matrimonio. —*a.* 1. nupcial (velo, traje, etc.). 2. de bodas (día, noche, torta, etc.). 3. de novios (viaje).
wedding anniversary, aniversario de boda.
wedding march, marcha nupcial.
wedding ring, anillo de boda, sortija de matrimonio, alianza.
wedge [wɛdʒ] *s.* 1. cuña, calce, calza, alzaprima. 2. tajada, trozo, ej., *a w. of cake,* una tajada de torta. 3. (mil.) cúneo. —*v.t.* 1. calzar, acuñar. 2. (raro) hender, partir o abrir con cuña. 3. (gen. con *in*) apretar, encajar; entremeter. —*v.i.* encajarse, agarrotarse.
wedge shell, (zool.) coquina.
wedgie [ˈwɛdʒɪ] *s.* zapato de cuña (de mujer).
wedgy [ˈwɛdʒɪ] *a.* cuneiforme, en forma de cuña.
wedlock [ˈwɛdˌlɑk, B -lɔk] *s.* matrimonio, estado matrimonial, connubio.
Wednesday [ˈwɛnzdɪ] *s.* miércoles.
wee [wi] *a.* (WEER; WEEST) pequeñito, chiquito, chirriquitín, chiquitín, diminuto. —*s.* (esco.) pizca, triza; **to bide a w.,** (esco.) esperarse un poco.
weed [wid] *s.* 1. mala hierba; maleza, cizaña. 2. alga marina. 3. (fam.) tabaco; cigarro, habano. 4. (jer.) marihuana. 5. caballo o ganado demacrado (esp. el inepto para la cría). —*v.t.* 1. desherbar, desyerbar, escardar, sachar, desmalezar. 2. **w. out,** (fig.) arrancar, extirpar, suprimir, eliminar, erradicar (lo dañino o inútil). —*v.i.* escardar las malas hierbas.
weed, *s.* 1. (*gen. pl.*) prenda de vestir, esp. ropas de luto. 2. cinta de crespón de luto (que se usa en los sombreros de hombre), franja de luto (en chaqueta o saco de hombre).
weeded [ˈwidəd] *a.* 1. desherbado, desyerbado. 2. cubierto de malas hierbas, enmalezado.
weeder [-ər, B -ə] *s.* desyerba, escarda, azadilla, almocafre, sacho; escardador, desmalezador.
weedhook [-ˌhʊk] *s.* escarda, azadillo.
weediness [-ɪnəs] *s.* estado enmalezado o herboso.
weeding [-ɪŋ] *s.* escarda, deshierba.
weed-killer [-ˌkɪlər, B -ə] *s.* herbicida.
weedless [-ləs] *a.* libre de mala hierba.
weedy [-ɪ] *a.* (WEEDIER; WEEDIEST) 1. que abunda en malas hierbas, cubierto de malas hierbas, enmalezado. 2. (fam.) larguirucho, flacucho.
week [wik] *s.* semana; **a w.,** por semana, ej., *twice a w.,* dos veces por semana, *fifty dollars a w.,* cincuenta dólares por semana; **a w. of Sundays,** siete semanas, mucho tiempo; **a w. from today,** dentro de una semana.
weekday [ˈwikˌdeɪ] *s.* día de trabajo, día laborable, día de entresemana, día de semana (Amer.).
weekdays [-ˌdeɪz] *adv.* en cada día de trabajo, en días de trabajo, durante la semana.
weekend [-ˌɛnd] *s.* fin de semana. —*v.i.* pasar el fin de semana (esp. de visita o de paseo).
weekend bag, maletín (para viajes de fin de semana).
week-ender [-ˌɛndər, B -də] *s.* 1. excursionista de fin de semana. 2. maletín (para viajes de fin de semana).
weekends [-ˌɛndz] *adv.* a fines de (cada) semana.
weekly [-lɪ] *adv.* semanalmente, hebdomadariamente, por semana. —*a.* semanal, semanario, hebdomadario. —*s.* (*pl.* WEEKLIES) semanario, revista semanal.
ween [win] *v.i., v.t.* (ant.) suponer(se); imaginar(se), creer(se).
weeny [ˈwinɪ] *a.* (WEENIER; WEENIEST) chiquito, chiquitito.
weep [wip] *v.i.* (*pret., p.p.* WEPT [wɛpt]; *p.pr.* WEEPING) 1. llorar. 2. (fig.) gotear, chorrear, escurrirse, sudar. 3. (bot.) llorar. —*v.t.* 1. llorar, llorar por, lamentar, deplorar. 2. llorar, derramar, verter (lágrimas). 3. (bot.) llorar, exudar. 4. **w. one's eyes out,** llorar a mares, llorar a lágrima viva; **w. oneself out,** llorar a más no poder; **w. out,** decir llorando. —*s.* (fam.) lloro, lágrimas, llanto.
weeper [ˈwipər, B -pə] *s.* 1. llorador, lloraduelos. 2. plañidera. 3. gasa o señal de luto; (*pl.*) velo de viuda. 4. (jer.) cuento, novela o película muy sentimental o melodramática.
weep hole, (const.) agujero de drenaje.
weeping [-pɪŋ] *a.* 1. llorón, lloroso, plañidero. 2. (fig.) lluvioso. 3. (bot.) llorón.
weeping ash, (bot.) fresno llorón.
weepingly [-lɪ] *adv.* llorosamente, con llanto.
weeping willow, (bot.) sauce llorón, sauce de Babilonia, desmayo.
weep pipe, (mec.) tubo de drenaje o de goteo.
weepy [-pɪ] *a.* llorón. —*s.* (jer.) cuento, novela o película muy sentimental.
weevil [ˈwivəl] *s.* (ento.) gorgojo, calapatillo, mordihuí, gusano del trigo.
weeviled, weevilled [-vəld] *a.* gorgojoso.
wee-wee [ˈwiˌwi] *v.i.* (lenguaje infantil) hacer pipí, orinar. —*s.* (fam.) pipí.
weft [wɛft] *s.* 1. (tej.) trama. 2. textura, tejido.
weigh [weɪ] *v.t.* 1. pesar; sopesar. 2. (fig.) medir, pesar, considerar (palabras, razones, etc.). 3. (mar.) levar (anclas); (raro) poner a flote (barco hundido). 4. **w. down,** hacer inclinar, sobrecargar; (fig.) abrumar, oprimir, afligir, acongojar; **w. in,** pesar (a pugilista o jinete) antes de la competencia; **w. out,** pesar (mercadería para la venta); dar o dividir por peso; pesar (a pugilista o jinete) después de la competencia. —*v.i.* 1. pesar, ser pesado. 2. (fig.) pesar, importar, entrar en cuenta. 3. (mar.) levar anclas. 4. **w. in,** pesarse, ser pesado (pugilista o jinete) antes de la competencia; aparecer, llegar de improviso; **w. in with,** presentar, producir (argumento, opinión, etc.) con aire triunfante; **w. into (someone),** acometer, atacar (a alguien); **w. on** (o **upon**), (fig.) pesar sobre, gravar, ser enredoso o gravoso para; **w. out,** pesarse, ser pesado (pugilista o jinete) después de la competencia; **w. with,** importar a, ser de importancia para.
weigh, *var. de* **way** (ú. en **under w.,** en camino, en marcha).
weighable [ˈweɪəbəl] *a.* que puede ser pesado o vendido a peso.
weighed [weɪd] *a.* 1. pesado. 2. experimentado, probado.
weigher [ˈweɪər, B -ə] *s.* pesador.
weighing [-ɪŋ] *s.* peso, pesada. —*a.* de pesar, para pesar.
weighing machine, weighing scale, balanza, báscula.
weight [weɪt] *s.* 1. peso. 2. pesa, unidad de peso. 3. pesa (para presionar, contrabalancear, etc.). 4. (fig.) peso, importancia, influencia, autoridad. 5. (dep.) peso; pesos, barra de pesos. 6. valor relativo (en estadística). 7. **by w.,** por peso; **to lose w.,** adelgazar, bajar de peso; **to pull one's w.,** hacer su parte; **to put on w.,** subir de peso; **to put the w.,** (dep.) lanzar el peso; **to throw one's w. about,** darse (demasiada) importancia. —*v.t.* 1. poner un peso o pesa a. 2. hacer más pesado (fraudulentamente). 3. cargar, sobrecargar. 4. sopesar. 5. asignar valor a (factor o elemento estadístico). 6. (esquí) trasladar el peso (del cuerpo) a. 7. **w. down,** (fig.) abrumar, agobiar.
weighted [ˈweɪtəd] *a.* 1. cargado con peso. 2. cargada (seda). 3. lastrado (proyectiles).
weightily [-əlɪ] *adv.* 1. pesadamente. 2. con mucho peso, con gran fuerza.
weightiness [-ɪnəs] *s.* 1. ponderosidad, pesadez. 2. (fig.) solidez, fuerza, importancia.
weightless [-ləs] *a.* sin peso, ingrávido.
weightlessness [-nəs] *s.* ingravidez, antigravedad.
weight lifter, (dep.) levantador de pesas, halterófilo, halterofilista.
weight lifting, (dep.) levantamiento de pesas, halterofilia.
weight watcher, persona que cuida la línea.
weighty [-ɪ] *a.* (WEIGHTIER; WEIGHTIEST) 1. pesado, ponderoso. 2. de peso, ponderable, importante, grave.
weir [wɪr, B wɪə] *s.* 1. presa, vertedero, vertedor, azud, esclusa. 2. cañal, encañizada.
weird [wɪrd, B wɪəd] *a.* 1. sobrenatural, espectral, misterioso, fantasmagórico. 2. extraño, raro, fantástico. 3. (ant.) fatal, del destino; hechiceresco; **the w. sisters,** las Parcas; las brujas (en el drama "Macbeth" de Shakespeare). —*s.* (esco.) sino, destino, suerte, esp. mala fortuna; **to dree one's w.,** (esco.) conformarse con su suerte.
weirdly [ˈwɪrdlɪ, B ˈwɪəd-] *adv.* sobrenaturalmente, misteriosamente; extrañamente.
weirdness [-nəs] *s.* misterio, carácter misterioso; extrañeza, rareza.
Weismannism [ˈvaɪˌsmɑnˌɪzəm] *s.* (biol.) weismanismo.
wejack [ˈwidʒæk] *s.* (zool.) (variedad americana de) marta.
welch [wɛltʃ, B wɛlʃ] **welcher** [ˈwɛltʃər, B ˈwɛlʃə] *vars. de* **welsh, welsher.**
welcome [ˈwɛlkəm] *a.* 1. bienvenido, bien llegado, recibido con agrado o beneplácito. 2. grato, agradable, placentero (noticias, etc.). 3. **to make one w.,** dar una calurosa bienvenida a uno; **you are w.,** (E.U.) ¡no hay de qué! ¡de nada!; **you are w. to it,** está a su disposición; quédese con él si quiere; (irón.) buen provecho le haga. —*s.* bienvenida, buena acogida; **to outstay one's w.,** abusar de la hospitalidad (prolongando una visita más tiempo del conveniente). —*v.t.* 1. dar la bienvenida a. 2. acoger o recibir con beneplácito o satisfacción. —*interj.* ¡sea(s) bienvenido! ¡bienvenidos!; w. to Chicago!, ¡bienvenido a Chicago!
welcomely [-lɪ] *adv.* agradablemente, placenteramente.
welcomeness [-nəs] *s.* buena acogida.
welcomer [-ər, B -ə] *s.* recibidor, saludador.

weld [wɛld] *s.* (bot.) gualda (planta y tinte).
weld, *v.t.* 1. soldar. 2. (fig.) unir, juntar, reunir. 3. **w. into,** (fig.) integrar en. —*v.i.* soldarse, ser soldable. —*s.* (punto de) soldadura.
weldable ['wɛldəbəl] *a.* soldable.
welder [-dər, B -də] *s.* soldador (persona); soldadora (máquina).
welding [-dıŋ] *s.* soldadura. —*a.* de soldar, para soldar.
welding goggles, gafas de soldar.
welding helmet, casquete o casco de soldar.
welding mask, careta de soldar.
weldment ['wɛldmənt] *s.* conjunto de partes soldadas, ensambladura soldada.
weldor ['wɛldər, B -də] *s.* soldador (hombre).
weld rod, varilla de soldar o de soldadura.
weld torch, 1. lámpara de soldar. 2. soplete.
welfare ['wɛlˌfɛr, B -fɛə] *s.* 1. bienestar, bien, prosperidad, bienandanza, felicidad. 2. asistencia social. 3. (E.U.) prestaciones sociales; **to be on w.,** recibir prestaciones del tesoro público.
welfare society, sociedad benéfica.
welfare state, (pol.) estado benefactor, estado de asistencia y seguridad social.
welfare work, obra de asistencia social, obra de bienestar social.
welfare worker, asistente social.
welkin ['wɛlkən] *s.* (ant.) firmamento, cielo, bóveda celeste.
well [wɛl] *s.* 1. pozo (de agua, petróleo, gas, sal, etc.). 2. (lit., fig.) fuente, manantial, venero, origen. 3. cavidad, espacio encerrado, receptáculo. 4. vaso o copa de tintero. 5. (G.B., der.) recinto para los abogados (en salas de tribunal). 6. (arq.) caja o pozo de escalera o ascensor. 7. (mar.) pozo. 8. vivar de pesca, pozo de barco pescador. —*v.i.* manar, brotar, fluir. —*v.t.* verter, derramar, vaciar.
well, *adv.* (BETTER; BEST) 1. bien. 2. con propiedad, razonablemente, honestamente, con razón, ej., *I could not (very)* w. refuse him, no pude honestamente rehusarle, *he laughs, as w. he may,* él ríe, y con razón. 3. muy, mucho, ej., *it speaks w. for his honesty,* eso dice mucho de su honradez. 4. **as w.,** también, a la vez; con igual razón, ej., *you may as w. know it now,* no hay razón para que no lo sepas ahora; **as w. as,** así como también; además de; **jolly w.,** muy bien, mucho, muchísimo (*ú. como expresión enfática*), ej., *he is jolly w. right,* él tiene muchísima razón; **that is just as w.,** está muy bien así, es mejor así; **to do w.,** (fig.) progresar, prosperar; **w. ahead,** muy adelante; **w. done!** ¡bravo! ¡bien hecho!; **w. up in,** bien preparado en, experto en. —*a.* 1. bueno, bien; satisfactorio, adecuado, apropiado, conveniente. 2. en buena salud, sano; curado. 3. **to get w.,** sanar, restablecerse, mejorar (de salud); **to look w.,** tener buena apariencia, lucir bien; verse bien; **to mean w.,** tener buenas intenciones; **w. and good,** santo y bueno; tanto mejor.
well, *interj.* ¡bueno!; ¡vaya! ¡vamos! ¡toma!
we'll [wil] *contr. de* **we shall** o **we will.**
well-advised [ˌwɛləd'vaızd] *a.* 1. prudente, cuerdo. 2. oportuno, acertado, afortunado (acto, medida, etc.).
well-aimed ['wɛl'eımd] *a.* acertado, certero.
well-appointed [-ə'pɔıntəd] *a.* bien amueblado; bien equipado.
well-attended ['wɛlə'tɛndəd] *a.* muy concurrido, con mucho público.
wellaway [ˌwɛlə'weı] *interj.* (ant.) ¡ay de mí!.
well-balanced ['wɛl'bælənst] *a.* 1. bien equilibrado; bien proporcionado. 2. (fig.) equilibrado, sensato.
well-behaved [-bı'heıvd] *a.* 1. de buena conducta; de buenos modales. 2. bien adiestrado (animal).
well-being [-'biıŋ] *s.* bienestar; comodidad.
well-beloved [ˌwɛlbı'lʌvd] *a.* bien amado.
well borer, pocero, el o lo que cava pozos.
wellborn ['wɛl'bɔrn, B -'bɔn] *a.* bien nacido, de buena prosapia, de buena familia.
well-bred [-'brɛd] *a.* 1. bien criado, bien educado; de maneras refinadas. 2. de buena casta o raza (díc. de animales).
well-built [-'bılt] *a.* de buena complexión, bien hecho (persona).
well casing, entubado de pozos, tubería de revestimiento.
well-chosen [-'tʃouzən] *a.* bien escogido, acertado (frase, palabras, etc.).
well-conditioned [ˌwɛlkən'dıʃənd] *a.* 1. bien condicionado, bien dispuesto. 2. en buena condición (física).
well-connected [-kə'nɛktəd] *a.* bien vinculado, de buena familia, con influencias o buenas relaciones.
well-content [-kən'tɛnt] *a.* contento, satisfecho.
well curbing, brocal (de pozo).
well digger, pocero.
well-disposed [-dıs'pouzd] *a.* bien intencionado; dispuesto; receptivo, de buen talante.
well-doer ['wɛl'duər, B -ə] *s.* bienhechor, benefactor.
welldoing [-ıŋ] *s.* buenas obras, beneficencia. —*a.* benéfico.
well-done [-'dʌn] *a.* 1. bien hecho. 2. (cocina) bien asado, bien cocido (filete).
well-dressed [-'drɛst] *a.* bien vestido, sobriamente elegante.
well-educated ['wɛl'ɛdʒəkeıtəd] *a.* culto, instruido.
well-favored [-'feıvərd, B -vəd] *a.* bien parecido, agraciado.
well-fed [-'fɛd] *a.* bien nutrido, bien alimentado; regordete.
well-fixed [-'fıkst] *a.* (fam.) acomodado, próspero, rico.
well-founded [-'faundəd] *a.* fundado, fundamentado.
well-groomed [-'grumd] *a.* 1. acicalado, arreglado, aseado. 2. bien almohazado, cuidadosamente atendido (caballo). 3. limpio, cuidado (animal doméstico).
well-grounded [-'graundəd] *a.* 1. bien asentado, de base firme. 2. (fig.) bien fundado.
well-handled [-'hændəld] *a.* bien dirigido, hábilmente conducido, administrado eficientemente.
wellhead ['wɛlˌhɛd] *s.* 1. fuente, manantial, venero. 2. (fig.) fuente.
well-heeled [-'hild] *a.* (jer.) adinerado, acomodado, fondeado (Amer.).
well-hung ['wɛl'hʌŋ] *a.* 1. (cul., G.B.) bien manido. 2. (jer.) bien dotado (*hombre*).
well-informed [-ın'fɔrmd, B -'fɔmd] *a.* 1. bien informado. 2. de amplios conocimientos, enterado.
Wellington ['wɛlıŋtən] *s.* Wellington, capital de Nueva Zelandia.
Wellington ['wɛlıŋtən] *s.* bota alta cuya parte delantera llega arriba de la rodilla.
well-intentioned ['wɛlın'tɛntʃənd, B -'tɛnʃənd] *a.* bien intencionado.
well-kept [-'kɛpt] *a.* bien cuidado, bien conservado, bien tenido.
well-knit [-'nıt] *a.* 1. bien construido; de contextura sólida (cuerpo). 2. bien estructurado (argumento, historia, etc.).
well-known [-'noun] *a.* muy conocido, consabido; familiar.
well-looking [-'lʊkıŋ] *a.* atractivo, de buena apariencia.
well-mannered [-'mænərd, B -əd] *a.* de buenas maneras, de buenos modales, cortés.
well-meaning [-'minıŋ] **well-meant** [-'mɛnt] *a.* bien intencionado; honrado, sincero.
well-meant ['wɛl'mɛnt] *a.* dado con la mejor intención.
well-nigh [-'naı] *adv.* casi; poco menos que.
well-off [-'ɔf] *a.* acomodado, adinerado, próspero.
well-oiled [-'ɔıld] *a.* 1. bien aceitado. 2. (jer., G.B.) achispado, ahumado, ajumado. 3. eficiente.
well-ordered ['wɛl'ɔrdərd, B -'ɔdəd] *a.* bien ordenado, bien dispuesto.
well-read [-'rɛd] *a.* leído, instruido, ilustrado, culto.
well-remembered [-rı'mɛmbərd, B -bəd] *a.* de buena reputación; de grata memoria.
well-reputed [-rı'pjutəd] *a.* prestigioso.
well-rounded ['wɛl'raundəd] *a.* 1. completo, equilibrado (vida); polifacético (persona). 2. (fig.) curvilíneo (mujer).
well-set [-'sɛt] *a.* 1. bien establecido. 2. robusto, fornido.
wellsite ['wɛlzaıt] *s.* (min.) welsita.
well-spent [-'spɛnt] *a.* bien empleado (tiempo, dinero, etc.).
well-spoken ['wɛl'spoukən] *a.* 1. bienhablado, cortés. 2. bien dicho, acertado (palabras, etc.).
wellspring [-ˌsprıŋ] *s.* (lit., fig.) fuente, manantial, venero.
well-stocked [-'stɑkt, B -'stɔkt] *a.* bien provisto; con un surtido amplio.
well-suited [-'sutəd, B -'sjut-] *a.* apropiado, adecuado.
well-sweep [-ˌswip] *s.* cigüeñal, cigoñal (del pozo).
welltempered [-'tɛmpərd, B -pəd] *a.* 1. bien templado (acero, espada, etc.). 2. de buen temperamento. 3. (mús.) bien templado.
well-thought-of [wɛl'θɔtˌʌv, B -ɔv] *a.* bien mirado, de buena reputación.
well-timbered ['wɛl'tımbərd, B -bəd] *a.* 1. bien enmaderado, con maderamen fuerte (casa, edificio). 2. bien proporcionado (caballo). 3. que abunda en árboles madereros (terreno).
well-timed [-'taımd] *a.* 1. oportuno. 2. preciso, exacto.
well-to-do [-tə'du] *a.* próspero, acomodado.
well-turned [-'tɜrnd, B -'tɜnd] *a.* 1. bien formado (figura, cuerpo). 2. pulido (frase, palabras). 3. redondeado, bien formado (pie de mesa, columna, etc.).
well water, agua de pozo.
well-wisher [-ˌwıʃər, B -ə] *s.* bienqueriente; persona que da el parabién.
well-wishing [-ıŋ] *a.* bienqueriente.
well-worn [-'wɔrn, B -'wɔn] *a.* 1. gastado, desgastado; raído; anticuado, trillado. 2. usado con propiedad.
Welsbach ['wɛlzˌbæk] *s.* quemador de gas.
welsh ['wɛlʃ] *v.i.* (jer.) 1. alzarse con el santo y la limosna. 2. **w. on,** dejar de pagar fraudulentamente (apuesta, deuda, etc.); no cumplir con (promesa, palabra, etc.).
Welsh, *a.* galés, de Gales. —*s.* 1. idioma galés. 2. (*pl.*) habitante de Gales (península de G.B.).
welsher ['wɛlʃər, B -ə] *s.* estafador, pícaro.
Welsh corgi, (zool.) perro galés (de piernas cortas y cabeza parecida a la del zorro).
Welshman [-mən] *s.* galés, de Gales, G.B.
Welsh onion, *s.* (bot.) cebolleta.
Welsh rabbit, W. rarebit, (cocina) plato de queso derretido, cerveza y leche, servido sobre tostadas.

Welsh terrier, (zool.) terrier galés, terrier de pelo recio.

welt [wɛlt] *s.* 1. ribete, vivo (en prendas de vestir); vira (del zapato). 2. costurón, roncha, verdugo, cardenal. 3. latigazo. 4. (carp.) refuerzo. —*v.t.* 1. ribetear; poner vira a (zapato). 2. levantar ronchas en (cuerpo, etc.). 3. dar una paliza a.

Weltanschauung [ˈvel͵tɑn͵ʃaʊəŋ] *s.* (alemán, filos.) cosmovisión, visión universal de la vida y el hombre.

welter [ˈwɛltər, B -tə] *v.i.* 1. revolcarse (en agua, lodo, cieno, etc.). 2. (fig.) encenagarse, sumergirse (en vicios, etc.). 3. elevarse y caer tumultuosamente, agitarse. —*s.* 1. tumulto, confusión. 2. (fig.) revolcadero, cenegal.

welter, *s.* (fam.) pugilista de peso medio mediano.

welterweight [-͵weɪt] *s.* 1. peso extra (de 12,7 kilos que se le pone a un caballo de carreras). 2. (boxeo) peso medio (o semi) mediano; pugilista de peso medio.

wen, *s.* runa (adoptada en el antiguo alfabeto inglés) con el valor fonético de la w.

wench [wɛntʃ] *s.* 1. moza, muchacha, mozuela. 2. campesina, criada, sirvienta. 3. (ant.) ramera, prostituta. —*v.i.* mocear.

wencher [ˈwɛntʃər, B -tʃə] *s.* mujeriego, aficionado a las mujeres.

wend [wɛnd] *v.t.* seguir (camino); **w. one's way,** encaminarse. —*v.i.* seguir su camino, ir, pasar.

Wendish [ˈwɛndɪʃ] *a.* vendo, wendo. —*s.* (idioma) vendo o wendo.

wennish [ˈwɛnɪʃ] **wenny** [-ɪ] *a.* (med.) como un lobanillo, que tiene un lobanillo.

went [wɛnt] *pret. de* **go.**

wentletrap [ˈwɛntəl͵træp] *s.* (zool.) molusco marino de concha en espiral.

wept [wɛpt] *pret., p.p. de* **weep.**

were [wɜr, wər, B wɜ, wə] *segunda pers. sing., primera, segunda y tercera pers. pl. del pret. indic. y todo el pret. del subj. del verbo* **to be.**

we're [wɪr, B wɪə] *contr. de* **we are.**

weren't [wɜrnt, B wɜnt] *contr. de* **were not.**

werewolf [ˈwɪr͵wʊlf, ˈwɛr-, B ˈwɪə͵-] *s.* 1. (mitol.) hombre lobo. 2. (med.) licántropo (hombre que se cree lobo).

wergild [ˈwɜr͵gɪld, B ˈwɜ͵-] *s.* (hist.) indemnización que debían pagar los parientes de un asesino a los parientes de la víctima.

wernerite [ˈwɜrnə͵raɪt, B ˈwɜnə-] *s.* (min.) wernerita.

wert [wɜrt, wərt, B wɜt] (hist., poét.) *pret. segunda pers. de* **be.**

Wesleyan [ˈwɛzlɪən] *a.* (relig.) wesleyano, de Wesley. —*s.* wesleyano, metodismo.

west [wɛst] *s.* oeste, occidente; **the W.,** el Oeste (de Estados Unidos); el Occidente, el Mundo Occidental. —*a.* occidental, del oeste, que viene del oeste (díc. del viento). —*adv.* hacia el oeste, en el oeste; **w. of,** al oeste de; **to go w.,** (jer.) morir; declinar; arruinarse.

westbound [ˈwɛst͵baʊnd] *a.* con rumbo al oeste.

west by north, (mar.) oeste cuarta al noroeste.

west by south, (mar.) oeste cuarta al suroeste.

West End, (G.B.) barrio elegante de Londres.

wester [ˈwɛstər, B -tə] *v.i.* virar o dirigirse hacia el oeste. —*s.* poniente, céfiro (esp. tempestuoso).

westerliness [-lɪnəs] *s.* dirección oeste.

westerly [-lɪ] *s.* (*pl.* WESTERLIES) poniente, céfiro, viento del oeste. —*a.* occidental, que viene del oeste; que va hacia el oeste.

western [-tərn, B -tən] *a.* 1. occidental. 2. **W.,** del Oeste (de Estados Unidos). —*s.* 1. occidental. 2. oriundo o residente del Oeste (de los Estados Unidos). 3. película o novela del oeste o de vaqueros.

Westerner [-ər, B -ə] *s.* oriundo o habitante del Oeste, (esp. de los Estados Unidos).

West Germany, (hist.) Alemania Occidental.

Western Hemisphere, Hemisferio Occidental.

westernize [ˈwɛstər͵naɪz, B -tə͵-] *v.t., v.i.* hacer(se) occidental.

westernmost [-tərn͵moʊst, B -tən-] *a.* el más occidental, del extremo occidental.

western paper birch, (bot.) abedul blanco de Norte América.

Western Roman Empire, (hist.) Imperio de Occidente.

West German, de Alemania Occidental.

West Indian, *a.* de las Indias Occidentales, antillano. —*s.* natural de las Antillas, antillano.

West Indian corkwood, madera de balsa, palo de balsa.

West Indies, Indias Occidentales, las Antillas.

westing [ˈwɛstɪŋ] *s.* (mar.) pasaje o deriva hacia el oeste (del barco).

west-northwest [ˈwɛst͵nɔrθˈwɛst, B -͵nɔθ-] *s.* oesnoroeste, oesnorueste.

Westphalian [wɛstˈfeɪljən] *a., s.* Westfaliano, de la provincia alemana de Westfalia.

West Pointer, (E.U.) cadete graduado de la academia militar de West Point.

west-southwest [ˈwɛst͵saʊθˈwɛst] *s.* oessudoeste, oessudueste.

West Virginia [-vərˈdʒɪnjə, B vəˈ-] *s.* Virginia Occidental, estado de los E.U.

westward [-wərd, B -wəd] *a.* que va hacia el oeste, que mira o da al oeste. —*adv.* hacia el oeste.

westwards [-wərdz, B -wədz] *adv.* hacia el oeste.

west wind, (viento) poniente, céfiro.

wet [wɛt] *a.* (WETTER; WETTEST) 1. mojado, empapado, húmedo. 2. lluvioso (clima, día, etc.). 3. fresco, no seco todavía, ej., *w. paint,* pintura fresca. 4. (E.U., hist.) de licor, ej., *w. cargo,* cargamento de licor; bebidas alcohólicas (durante la época de la ley seca). 5. (tec.) al agua, húmedo; hecho por vía húmeda, ej., *w. extraction of copper,* extracción del cobre por vía húmeda. 6. conservado en líquido. 7. (jer.) erróneo, equivocado, descarriado. 8. (jer., G.B.) aguado, apagado, tonto; empalagoso, sentimental. 9. **to be mad as a w. hen,** tener un arrebato de cólera; **to be w. behind the ears,** (fig.) estar con la leche en los labios, ser un imberbe; **w. to the skin,** calado hasta los huesos, hecho una sopa. —*s.* 1. mojadura, mojada; humedad; agua. 2. lluvia, tiempo lluvioso. 3. (E.U.) antiprohibicionista. —*v.t.* (*pret., p.p.* WET O WETTED; *p.pr.* WETTING) 1. mojar, remojar, empapar; humedecer, humectar. 2. orinar en, mojar (la cama, etc.). 3. **w. down,** humedecer rociando con agua; **w. one's whistle,** (fam.) mojar el gaznate, beber un trago. —*v.i.* 1. mojarse, empaparse. 2. orinar.

wetback [ˈwɛt͵bæk] *s.* (derog., E.U.) mojado, espalda mojada.

wet bargain, negocio concertado y celebrado con bebida.

wet blanket, (fig.) aguafiestas.

wet-blanket [-ˈblæŋkət] *v.t.* desalentar, desanimar, deprimir.

wet-bulb thermometer, termómetro de depósito húmedo, termómetro húmedo o de ampolleta húmeda.

wet cell, (elec.) pila húmeda.

wet cooper, fabricante de barriles para líquidos.

wet cupping, (med.) ventosa escarificada o abierta.

wet dock, (mar.) dique flotante, dársena, dársena de flote, dique de marea.

wet dream, orgasmo involuntario durante el sueño.

wet floor, (señal) piso mojado.

wet goods, (com.) líquidos envasados (esp. licores, vinos).

wether [ˈwɛðər, B -ə] *s.* (zool.) carnero llano, carnero castrado.

wetland [ˈwɛt͵lænd] *s.* tierra húmeda, tierra pantanosa.

wetly [-lɪ] *adv.* en estado húmedo, con humedad, húmedamente.

wetness [-nəs] *s.* humedad.

wet nurse, ama de leche o de crianza, nodriza.

wet-nurse [-͵nɜrs, B -͵nɜs] *v.t.* 1. criar (la nodriza al niño). 2. (fig.) mimar, dedicar sumo cuidado a.

wet pack, (med.) tratamiento con lienzos húmedos.

wet plate, (foto.) placa de colodión.

wet process, (quím.) vía húmeda, procedimiento húmedo.

wet rot, putrefacción húmeda.

wet steam, (tec.) vapor saturado, vapor húmedo.

wettable [ˈwɛtəbəl] *a.* mezclable con agua (polvos indisolubles, etc.).

wet through, empapado, hecho una sopa.

wetting [-ɪŋ] *s.* mojada, mojadura; remojo, calada.

wet wash, ropa lavada aún húmeda; ropa preparada para la plancha.

we've [wiv] *contr. de* **we have.**

WFTU *abrev. de* **World Federation of Trade Unions,** Federación Mundial de Sindicatos.

whack [hwæk, wæk] *v.t.* 1. (fam.) pegar, golpear rápida y ruidosamente; vapulear. 2. (pr. G.B.) batir, derrotar (en un juego). 3. (jer.) **w. up,** hacer el reparto de, repartir (el botín); hacer rápidamente, fabricar apresuradamente. —*v.i.* dar golpes, repartir golpazos. —*s.* 1. golpe fuerte, bofetón, bofetada; palmada. 2. intento, tentativa; prueba. 3. parte, porción, lote.

whacker [ˈhwækər, ˈwækər, B -ə] *s.* (jer.) cosa grande, gigante; mentirón.

whacking [-ɪŋ] (fam.) *s.* tunda, zurra, vapuleo. —*a.* colosal, enorme, ingente. —*adv.* enormemente.

whacky [-ɪ] *var. de* **wacky.**

whale [hweɪl, weɪl] *s.* 1. (zool.) ballena. 2. (fam.) persona o cosa enorme o excelente. 3. **a w. at,** (fam.) un as en, excelente en, ducho en, ej., *a w. at football,* un as en fútbol; **a w. for,** loco por, muy aficionado a, ej., *a w. for chess,* loco por el ajedrez, muy aficionado al ajedrez; **a w. of a,** enorme, extraordinario, ej. *a w. of a difference,* una diferencia enorme, *a w. of a story,* un cuento extraordinario. —*v.i.* cazar ballenas.

whale, *v.t.* (fam.) zurrar, vapulear, dar una tunda a; derrotar, aplastar (en contienda).

whaleback [ˈhweɪl͵bæk, ˈweɪl-] *s.* vapor de carga con cubierta convexa.

whaleboat [-͵boʊt] *s.* 1. bote ballenero. 2. bote o gasolinera con ambos extremos en forma de proa inclinada.

whalebone [-͵boʊn] *s.* (barba de) ballena.

whalecalf [-͵kæf, B -͵kɑf] *s.* ballena joven, ballenato.

whale louse, (zool.) piojo de mar.

whale oil, aceite de ballena.

whaler [-ər, B -ə] *s.* 1. ballenero, cazador de ballenas. 2. buque ballenero.

whaling [-ɪŋ] *s.* 1. caza de ballenas. 2. (E.U., poét.) la vida azarosa del marino que trabajaba en un barco ballenero.

wham [hwæm, wæm] *s.* 1. golpe fuerte. 2. pum (sonido de un golpe fuerte). —*v.t.* golpear o batir ruidosamente. —*v.i.* chocar o estallar ruidosamente.

whammy ['hwæmɪ, 'wæm-] *s.* (*pl.* WHAMMIES) (jer.) mal de ojo, aojo, mala sombra.

whang [hwæŋ, wæŋ] *s.* (G.B.) pedazo grande, pedazo grueso.

whang, *v.t.* 1. golpear con fuerza. 2. (esco.) zurrar, vapulear. —*v.i.* sonar como un bombo. —*s.* golpe resonante.

whangee [hwæŋ'gi, wæŋ'gi] *s.* bastón de bambú.

whap, *var. de* **whop.**

wharf [hwɔrf, wɔrf, B wɔf] *s.* (*pl.* WHARVES [hwɔrvz, wɔrvz, B wɔvz] o WHARFS) 1. muelle, desembarcadero, descargadero; fondeadero. 2. (ant.) malecón, ribera. —*v.t.* atracar a un muelle, llevar a un muelle (barco); almacenar (mercadería) en un muelle, guardar en dársena.

wharfage ['hwɔrfɪdʒ, 'wɔr-, B 'wɔfɪdʒ] *s.* 1. muellaje, amarraje, derechos de muelle. 2. conjunto de muelles (de un puerto).

wharfinger [-fɪndʒər, B -dʒə] *s.* administrador de un muelle, fiel de muelle; (G.B.) representante del armador en el muelle.

wharfmaster ['hwɔrf,mæstər, 'wɔrf-, B 'wɔf,mastə] *s.* administrador o encargado de un muelle.

wharve [hwɔrv, wɔrv, B wɔv] *s.* (tej.) nuez (del huso).

what [hwɑt, wɑt, B wɔt] *pron. interrogativo.* 1. qué, qué cosa; cuál, ej., *w. is that?* ¿qué es eso? *w. is it made of?* ¿de qué (cosa) está hecho? *w. is your telephone number?* ¿cuál es su número de teléfono? *w. will people say?* ¿qué dirá la gente? 2. cómo, ej., *what! do you really mean it?* ¡cómo! ¿lo dice Ud. en serio? 3. **I know w.,** tengo una idea, ya sé (qué hacer); **I'll tell you w.,** te voy a decir una cosa; **no matter w.,** no importa qué; **so w.?** (fam.) ¿y qué?; **w.?** ¿qué (dices)?; **w. about, w. of,** qué te parece, qué hay en cuanto a, qué se sabe de, qué noticias hay de; qué haremos para resolver, qué remedio habrá contra, ej., *w. about John?* ¿qué se sabe de Juan? *w. of the war?* ¿qué noticias hay de la guerra? *w. about absenteeism?* ¿qué haremos para resolver el ausentismo?; **w. does it matter?** ¿qué importa?; **w. else?** ¿qué más? ¿qué otra cosa?; **w. for,** ¡para qué! ¿con qué fin? ¿por qué razón?; **(and) w. have you,** (jer.) (y) cosas por el estilo; **w. if,** qué le parece, qué ocurriría si, ej., *w. if I were to do it?* ¿qué le parece si lo hago yo? ¿qué ocurre si yo lo hago?; **w. is he?** ¿cuál es su profesión?; **w. is he like?** ¿cómo es él?; **w. is that all about?** ¿a qué viene todo eso?; **w. is the idea?** (jer.) ¿qué pretende hacer? ¿qué pasa?; **w. next?** después de esto ¿qué? ¿y ahora qué?; **w. not,** (y) qué sé yo; **well, w. of it?** bueno, ¿y qué? —*pron. rel.* 1. el que, lo que, los que, ej., *w. is called public opinion,* lo que se llama opinión pública, *tell me w. you know,* cuéntame lo que sabes. 2. **come w. will** (o **may**), suceda lo que suceda, venga lo que quiera; **to know w.'s w.,** estar enterado, conocer bien el asunto; **w. is more,** más aún; lo que es peor; **w. it takes,** lo que es necesario (para), las capacidades (para). —*a.* 1. qué, qué tal, qué mas, ej., *w. a nuisance!* ¡qué fastidio! *w. a. pity!* ¡qué lástima! *w. good* (o *use*) *is it?* ¿para qué sirve? ¿qué utilidad tiene? *w. plan will he try?* ¿qué plan intentará? *w. lovely flowers!* ¡qué flores más preciosas! 2. el que, lo que, todo lo que, ej., *lend me w. money you have,* préstame (todo) el dinero que tengas, *we will give you w. help is possible,* le daremos (toda) la ayuda que sea posible. —*adv.* cuánto, cuál, cómo, ej., *w. he has suffered!* ¡cuánto ha sufrido!

whate'er [hwɑt'ɛr, wɑt-, B wɔt'ɛə] (poét.) *var. de* **whatever.**

whatever [-'ɛvər, B -ə] *pron.* cualquier cosa que, lo que, todo lo que, ej., *do w. you like,* haz lo que quieras, *w. happens,* suceda lo que suceda, *w. it may be,* lo que sea. —*a.* 1. cualquier, de cualquier clase; cualquier . . . . . que, cualquiera que sea. 2. (*en negación e interrogación*) ninguno, de ninguna clase, ej., *there is no doubt w.,* no queda ninguna duda, *is there no chance w.?* ¿no hay ninguna probabilidad?

whatnot ['hwɑt,nɑt, 'wɑt-, B -nɔt] *s.* 1. rinconera, estante liviano (para chucherías). 2. baratija, chisme.

what's [hwɑts, wɑts, B wɔts] *contr. de* **what is, what has** o **what does.**

whatsoe'er [,hwɑtsoʊ'ɛr, wɑt-, B ,wɔt-'ɛə] (poét.) *var. de* **whatsoever.**

whatsoever [-'ɛvər, B -ə] *var. enfática de* **whatever.**

whaup [hwɔp, wɔp] *s.* (esco., orn.) zarapito.

wheal [hwil, wil] *s.* (med.) roncha; grano, postilla.

wheat [hwit, wit] *s.* (bot.) trigo (planta y grano).

wheat cake, tortilla de masa hecha con harina de trigo.

wheatear ['hwit,ɪr, 'wit-, B 'wit,ɪə] *s.* (orn.) culiblanco, triguero.

wheaten [-ən] *a.* 1. triguero. 2. (hecho) de trigo.

wheatfield [-,fild] *s.* trigal.

wheat germ, germen de trigo.

wheatgrowing [-,groʊɪŋ] *a.* triguero; productor de trigo.

wheat rust, (bot.) anublo de trigo.

Wheatstone bridge [-,stoʊn-, B -stən-] (elec.) puente de Wheatstone.

wheatworm [-,wɜrm, B -wɜm] *s.* (zool.) gusano de trigo.

wheedle ['hwidəl, 'widəl] *v.i.* lisonjear, halagar; **w. into,** persuadir o inducir con halagos (a hacer algo), ganar o conseguir con halagos; **w. (something) out of (someone),** sonsacar (algo) con maña a (alguien), obtener (algo) con halagos de (alguien).

wheedler ['hwidlər, 'wid-, B -lə] *s.* lagotero, engatusador.

wheel [hwil, wil] *s.* 1. rueda. 2. (aut.) volante, timón (Car.). 3. (mar.) (rueda del) timón. 4. (*pl.*) rodaje, engranaje; maquinaria. 5. girándula (de fuegos artificiales). 6. (fam.) bicicleta. 7. voltereta, volantín (Amer.). 8. refrán, estribillo (de una canción). 9. (mil.) conversión, giro (que hace una fila de soldados), ej., *left w.!* ¡girar a la izquierda! 10. (jer.) persona importante, alto cargo (en una empresa, etc.). **11. fifth wheel,** rodete; rueda de repuesto (de automóvil); (fig.) objeto superfluo; **Fortune's w.,** la rueda de la fortuna; **to go on wheels,** (fig.) marchar sobre ruedas (asunto, causa, etc.); **to grease the wheels,** (fam.) aceitar los engranajes; **to take the w.,** llevar el volante, conducir, manejar (Amer.); **to turn wheels,** dar volteretas; **wheels of government,** mecanismos gubernativos; **wheels within wheels,** maquinaria intrincada; (fig.) fuerzas esotéricas. —*v.t.* 1. hacer rodar; mover o llevar sobre ruedas. 2. acarrear o transportar en carretilla. 3. empujar o pasear en sillón de ruedas. 4. hacer girar, revolver. 5. proveer de ruedas. —*v.i.* 1. girar, rodar, moverse sobre ruedas. 2. montar bicicleta. 3. (mil.) conversar, girar sobre un flanco. 4. **w. about** (o **around**), dar vuelta, girar sobre los talones, ir en círculos o curvas; (fig.) cambiar de opinión.

wheel aligner, (auto.) alineador de ruedas.

wheel and axle, (mec.) cabría.

wheel animal, w. animalcule, (zool.) rotífero.

wheel barometer, barómetro de cuadrante.

wheelbarrow ['hwil,bæroʊ, 'wil-] *s.* carretilla. —*v.t.* transportar en carretilla.

wheelbase [-,beɪs] *s.* (aut.) distancia entre ejes, batalla.

wheel boss, (mec.) cubo de rueda.

wheelchair [-,tʃɛr, B -'tʃɛə] *s.* silla de ruedas.

wheel dresser, rectificador de ruedas abrasivas.

wheeled [hwild, wild] *adv.* 1. de ruedas. 2. rodante.

wheeler ['hwilər, 'wi-, B -lə] *s.* 1. carretillero (en fábricas, sitios de construcción, etc.). 2. carretero, aperador; fabricante de ruedas. 3. caballo de varas. 4. vapor de ruedas. 5. (*ú. esp. en compuestos*) vehículo de (cierto número o clase de) ruedas, ej., *four-w.,* coche de cuatro ruedas.

wheelhorse ['hwil,hɔrs, 'wil-, B -'hɔs] *s.* 1. caballo de varas. 2. (fig.) colaborador eficiente (esp. en una organización política).

wheelhouse [-,haʊs] *s.* (mar.) timonera.

wheeling [-ɪŋ] *s.* 1. transporte sobre ruedas. 2. estado transitable (de un camino carretero).

wheel lathe, torno para rueda.

wheel load, carga sobre una rueda.

wheel lock, (hist.) llave giratoria de fusil con pedernal.

wheelman [-mən] *s.* 1. (mar.) timonel, timonero. 2. ciclista.

wheel puller, sacarrueda, extractor de ruedas.

wheel rope, (mar.) guardín del timón.

wheelsman ['hwilzmən, 'wilz-] *s.* (mar.) timonel, timonero.

wheel track, carril.

wheelwork ['hwil,wɜrk, 'wil-, B -wɜk] *s.* ruedas engranadas, rodaje.

wheelwright [-,raɪt] *s.* ruedero, carretero, aperador.

wheen [hwin, win] *a.* (dial., G.B.) unos cuantos, algunos. —*s.* gran cantidad, montón.

wheeze [hwiz, wiz] *v.i.* respirar asmáticamente, resollar con dificultad o silbido, gañir, jadear. —*v.t.* **w. out,** decir resollando. —*s.* 1. jadeo, resuello asmático o silboso. 2. (jer.) chiste, dicho, agudeza (esp. trillado).

wheezily ['hwizəlɪ, 'wi-] *adv.* con resuello jadeante o asmático.

wheeziness [-zɪnəs] *s.* timbre asmático (de la voz).

wheezy [-zɪ] *a.* que resuella con dificultad, jadeante.

whelk [hwɛlk, wɛlk, B wɛlk] *s.* (zool.) buccino.

whelk, *s.* (med.) póstula, pápula; roncha.

whelm [hwɛlm, wɛlm] *v.t., v.i.* (poét., ret.) sumergir, anegar; abrumar, aplastar, sobrepujar.

whelp [hwɛlp, wɛlp] *s.* 1. cachorro. 2. (despec.) mozalbete. 3. (mar.) (*gen. pl.*) guardainfantes. 4. (mec.) diente de rueda de cadena. —*v.t., v.i.* parir (perra o hembra de otros animales carnívoros).

when [hwɛn, wɛn] *adv.* 1. ¿cuándo? ¿en qué tiempo? ej., *I don't know w. it was,* no sé cuándo fue, *w. did he leave?* ¿cuándo salió? *w. did I suggest such a thing?* ¿cuándo fue que propuse yo tal cosa? 2. **say w.,** diga cuándo (debo cesar o comenzar), diga hasta dónde (díc. al servir una bebida a alguien). —*conj.* 1. cuando, aun cuando, ej., *he lied when he need not have done so,* él mintió (aun) cuando no hubiera sido menester hacerlo, *w. it rains he stays at home,* cuando llueve, él se queda en casa. 2. si, ej., *you shall have it w. you ask politely,* lo recibirás si lo pides cortésmente. 3. al (hacer), ej., *he hailed me w. he saw me,* me saludó al verme. 4. **w. Greek meets Greek,** cuando compiten fuerzas parejas. —*pron.* cuándo, ej., *since w.?* ¿desde

cuándo? *till w. can you stay?* ¿hasta cuándo puedes quedarte? —*s.* tiempo, fecha, ocasión (de un suceso).
whenas [hwɛn'æz, wɛn-] *conj.* (ant.) cuando, aun cuando.
whence [hwɛns, wɛns] (poét., lit.) *adv.* de dónde. —*conj.* de dónde, ej., *no one knows w. she comes,* nadie sabe de dónde viene ella, *return w. you came,* vuelve al sitio de dónde viniste.
whencesoever ['hwɛnssoʊˌɛvər, 'wɛns-, B -ə] *conj.* de dondequiera, de cualquier parte que sea.
whene'er [hwɛn'ɛr, wɛn-, B -'ɛə] (poét.) *var. de* **whenever.**
whenever [-'ɛvər, B -ə] *adv., conj* cuando quiera que, en cualquier momento que; cada vez que, tan pronto como.
whensoever ['hwɛnsoʊˌɛvər, 'wɛn-, B -ə] *var. enfática de* **whenever.**
where [hwɛr, wɛr, B wɛə] *adv.* dónde, adónde, en dónde, por dónde; **w. are you going?** ¿a dónde va usted? **w. are you looking?** ¿dónde está usted mirando? —*conj.* donde, adonde, en donde, por donde; dónde, ej., *send him w. he will be taken care of,* envíelo donde lo cuiden, *the place w. he was born,* el lugar donde él nació, *they showed me w. they were,* me enseñaron dónde paraban. —*s.* lugar.
whereabout, *var. de* **whereabouts.**
whereabouts ['hwɛrəˌbaʊts, 'wɛr-, B 'wɛər-] *adv.* dónde, por dónde, cerca de dónde, ej., *w is the post office?* ¿por dónde queda la oficina de correos? —*conj.* donde, por donde. —*s. pl.* (*sing o pl en const.*) paradero, ubicación (aproximada), ej., *his present w. is* (o *are*) *unknown,* se desconoce su paradero actual.
whereas [hwɛr'æz, wɛr-, B wɛər-] *conj.* 1. por cuanto, visto que, en vista de que, puesto que, considerando que. 2. en tanto que, mientras que. —*s.* (*pl.* WHEREASES) (der.) considerando; preámbulo.
whereat [-'æt] *conj.* a lo cual, con lo cual.
whereby [-'baɪ, B wɛə'-] *adv.* (ant.) por qué medio, cómo, ej., *w. shall we know him?* ¿por qué cosa lo conoceremos? —*conj.* por medio del cual, según el cual, ej., *the signs w. he shall be known,* los signos por los cuales lo conoceremos.
where'er [-'ɛr, B wɛər'ɛə] (poét.) *contr. de* **wherever.**
wherefore ['hwɛrˌfɔr, 'wɛr-, B 'wɛəfɔ] *adv.* por qué, por qué motivo; por lo que, por lo cual. —*s.* porqué, causa, razón, motivo.
wherefrom [-ˌfrʌm, -ˌfrɑm, B -frɔm] *conj.* desde donde, de lo cual.
wherein [hwɛr'ɪn, wɛr-, B wɛr-] *adv.* en qué, en dónde, en qué respecto, en qué punto, ej., *w. am I mistaken?* ¿en qué respecto estoy equivocado? —*conj.* en que, donde.
whereinsoever [-soʊ'ɛvər, B -ə] *var. enfática de* **wherein.**
whereinto [-'ɪntu] *conj.* en donde, en que, en lo cual.
whereof [-'ʌv, B -'ɔv] *conj.* de que, de lo que, ej., *he knows w. he speaks,* él sabe de qué habla. —*adv.* (ant.) de qué.
whereon [-'ɔn, -'ɑn, B -'ɔn] *conj.* en que, sobre (el, la, lo) que, ej., *a foundation w. to build,* cimientos en que construir. —*adv.* (ant.) en qué.
wheresoever [-'ɛvər, B -ə] *var. enfática de* **wherever.**
wherethrough ['hwɛrˌθru, 'wɛr-, B 'wɛəˌ-] *conj.* a través de lo cual, por medio de lo cual.
whereto [-ˌtu] *adv.* adónde, para qué. —*conj.* adonde, a lo que, a lo cual.
whereunto [hwɛr'ʌntu, wɛr-, B wɛər-] (ant.) *var. de* **whereto.**
whereupon ['hwɛrəˌpɔn, 'wɛr-, -ˌpɑn, B ˌwɛərə'pɔn] *conj.* 1. en que, sobre que. 2. después de lo cual, sobre lo cual, entonces.
wherever [hwɛr'ɛvər, wɛr-, B wɛər'ɛvə] *adv.* dónde. —*conj.* dondequiera que, en cualquier parte que sea.
wherewith ['hwɛrˌwɪð, 'wɛr-, B wɛə'wɪθ] *adv.* (ant.) con qué. —*conj.* con que, con lo cual. —*pron.* lo necesario para, medios para, con qué, ej., *the w. to buy food,* los medios para comprar comida.
wherewithal [-ˌɔl, B ˌwɛəwɪ'ðɔl] *adv.* con que, con lo cual. —*s.* requisitos, medios, cumquibus, dinero, ej., *he doesn't have the w. for a new suit,* no tiene dinero para un vestido nuevo.
wherry ['hwɛrɪ, 'wɛrɪ] *s.* (*pl.* WHERRIES) (mar.) lancha, chalana; esquife.
whet [hwɛt, wɛt] *v.t.* (*pret., p.p.* WHETTED; *p.pr.* WHETTING) 1. afilar, sacar filo a. 2. (fig.) despertar, estimular (deseo, interés, curiosidad, etc.). 3. abrir (el apetito). —*s.* 1. (fig.) estímulo. 2. estimulante; aperitivo. 3. (dial.) tanda o turno de trabajo.
whether ['hwɛðər, 'wɛð-, B -ə] *conj.* si, ej., *I don't know w. he will be here,* no sé si (él) estará aquí, *w. we stay or we go,* (ya) sea que nos quedemos o nos vayamos, *we have to win w. by hook or by crook,* tenemos que ganar de cualquier manera; **w. or not,** en todo caso, de todos modos. —*pron.* (ant.) cuál (de dos).
whetstone ['hwɛtˌstoʊn, 'wɛt-] *s.* piedra de afilar, afiladera, amoladera.
whetter [-ər, B -ə] *s.* 1. afilador. 2. (fig.) estimulante.
whew [hwu] *interj.* (hum.) ¡vaya! ¡zambomba! —*s.* silbido.
whey [hweɪ, weɪ] *s.* suero (de la leche).
whey-face ['hweɪˌfeɪs, 'weɪ-] *s.* cara pálida, rostro lívido, ceniciento.
whey-faced [-ˌfeɪst] *a.* pálido (esp. de miedo), lívido.
which [hwɪtʃ, wɪtʃ] *pron.* 1. (*interrogativo*) cuál, quién, ej., *I asked him w. was right,* le pregunté cuál era correcto, *w. is w.?* ¿cuál es cuál? ¿cuál es el uno y cuál es el otro? *w. of you will come with me?* ¿quién de ustedes quiere acompañarme? 2. que; el cual, la cual, lo cual, los cuales, las cuales; el que, la que, lo que, los que, las que; cosa que; ej., *the meeting, w. was held in the theater, was a failure,* la reunión, que se llevó a cabo en el teatro, fue un fracaso, *the house in w. he lives,* la casa en que vive; *the book of w. I was speaking,* el libro del cual hablaba, *for w. reason,* razón por la cual, *he said he saw me there, w. was a lie,* dijo que me había visto allí, lo cual era mentira, *I told him to go, w. he did,* le dije que se fuera, cosa que él hizo. 3. (ant., dial.) quien, que, el cual (ref. a personas), ej., *our Father, w. art in Heaven,* Padre nuestro, que estás en los Cielos. 4. **all (of) w.,** todo lo cual, todos los cuales; **both of w.,** que (han hecho o no hecho, etc.) . . . ambos. —*a.* cuál, cuáles (de ellos); qué; que; el cual, la cual, lo cual, los cuales, las cuales, ej., *w. men are guilty?* ¿cuáles hombres son culpables? *w. sister did he marry?* ¿con cuál de las hermanas se casó? *w. way shall we go?* ¿qué camino tomamos?
whichever [hwɪtʃ'ɛvər, wɪtʃ-, B -ə] *pron.* cualquiera, cualesquiera (que sea), ej., *take w. comes first,* tome cualquiera que venga primero. —*a.* cualquier, ej., *w. way you take it will lead you there,* cualquier camino que tomes te llevará allí.
whichsoever [ˌhwɪtʃsoʊ'ɛvər, ˌwɪtʃ-, B -ə] *var. enfática de* **whichever.**
whicker ['hwɪkər, 'wɪk-, B -ə] *v.i.* (fam.) relinchar. —*s.* relincho.
whidah, *var. de* **whydah.**
whiff [hwɪf, wɪf] *s.* 1. soplo, vaharada; fumada, fumarada. 2. olor o sabor fugaz, ej., *to get a w. of,* percibir un olor de. 3. (fam., G.B.) cigarro corto. —*v.i.* 1. soplar. 2. echar bocanadas de humo (fumando pipa, etc.). 3. olfatear. —*v.t.* 1. soplar. 2. exhalar; echar (humo, etc.).
whiffet ['hwɪfət, 'wɪf-] *s.* (fam., E.U.) persona insignificante, pelagatos, nulidad.
whiffle [-əl] *v.i.* 1. soplar en ráfagas ligeras (el viento). 2. vacilar (la llama); revolotear (hojas, etc. en el aire). 3. (fig.) vacilar, titubear. —*v.t.* despedir, expulsar, disipar (con un soplo).
whiffler ['hwɪflər, 'wɪf-, B -lə] *s.* (fig.) veleta; persona evasiva.
whiffler *s.* (G.B., hist.) soldado u oficial que despejaba el camino para una procesión.
whiffletree [-əlˌtri] *s.* volea, balancín (de coche).
Whig [hwɪg, wɪg] *s.* 1. (hist., E.U.) miembro de un partido político del siglo pasado, predecesor del actual Partido Republicano. 2. (G.B.) Whig, miembro del Partido Liberal.
whigmaleerie [ˌhwɪgmə'lɪrɪ, ˌwɪgmə-, B -'lɪərɪ] *s.* (esco.) capricho; cosa extraña o caprichosa.
while [hwaɪl, waɪl] *s.* rato, tiempo; **a little w.,** un ratito; **a little w. ago,** hace apenas un rato, no hace mucho; **all the w.,** todo ese tiempo; **a long w.,** largo rato; **a long w. ago,** hace mucho tiempo; **a w. after,** poco después; **a w. ago,** hace rato; **for a w.,** por algún tiempo; **once in a w.,** de vez en cuando; **the w.,** entre tanto, mientras tanto; **to make it worth one's w.,** recompensar a uno, pagar por su tiempo y esfuerzo a uno. —*conj.* mientras (que), en tanto, ej., *w. there is life there is hope,* mientras hay vida hay esperanza, *I have remained poor w. my brother has made a fortune,* yo sigo siendo pobre en tanto que mi hermano ha hecho una fortuna. —*v.t.* (gen. con *away*) pasar (el rato); entretener, engañar (el tiempo, la hora, etc.); pasar (el tiempo, la tarde, etc.) divirtiéndose.
whiles [hwaɪlz, waɪlz] *adv.* (esco.) a veces. —*conj.* (ant.) mientras.
whilom ['hwaɪləm, 'waɪl-] (poét., ant.) *adv.* antes, antiguamente, antaño, en otro tiempo. —*a.* antiguo, de antes, de antaño, que fue, ej., *his w. friend,* su amigo de antaño.
whilst [hwaɪlst, waɪlst] (pr. G.B.) *var. de* **while.**
whim [hwɪm, wɪm] *s.* 1. capricho, antojo. 2. (min.) malacate.
whimbrel ['hwɪmbrəl, 'wɪm-] *s.* (orn.) zarapito real.
whimper ['hwɪmpər, 'wɪm-, B -pə] *v.i.* lloriquear, plañir, gimotear. —*s.* lloriqueo, plañido, gimoteo.
whimperingly [-pərɪŋlɪ] *adv.* lloriqueando, entre plañidos.
whimsey, *var. de* **whimsy.**
whimsical ['hwɪmzɪkəl, 'wɪm-] *a.* 1. caprichoso, caprichudo, extravagante, antojadizo. 2. raro, extraño.
whimsicality [ˌhwɪmzə'kælətɪ, ˌwɪm-] *s.* rareza, singularidad, capricho, fantasía.
whimsically ['hwɪmzɪkəlɪ, 'wɪm-] *adv.* caprichosamente, extravagantemente.
whimsicalness [-kəlnəs] *s.* rareza, singularidad, extravagancia, carácter caprichoso.
whimsied ['hwɪmzɪd, 'wɪm-] *a.* antojadizo, caprichoso, caprichudo.
whimsy [-zɪ] *s.* (*pl.* WHIMSIES) capricho, antojo, extravagancia.

whim-wham ['hwɪm,hwæm, 'wɪm,wæm] *s.* (jer.) 1. chuchería, fruslería, adorno charro. 2. antojo, capricho. 3. (*pl.*) ataque de nervios, nerviosismo.

whin [hwɪn, wɪn] *s.* (bot.) tojo, aliaga, aulaga, hiniesta, retama de escoba.

whin, *s.* (min.) roca basáltica dura.

whinchat ['hwɪn,tʃæt, 'wɪn-] *s.* (orn.) pratíncola, cagaestacas.

whine [hwaɪn, waɪn] *v.i.* gimotear, plañir, gemir. —*v.t.* (gen. con *out*) expresar gimoteando, decir en voz lastimosa. —*s.* gimoteo, plañido, quejido, gemido.

whiningly ['hwaɪnɪŋlɪ, 'waɪn-] *adv.* plañideramente; con gemidos.

whinny ['hwɪnɪ, 'wɪnɪ] *v.i.* (*pret., p.p.* WHINNIED; *p.pr.* WHINNYING) relinchar. —*s.* relincho, relinchido.

whinstone ['hwɪn,stoʊn, 'wɪn-] *s.* roca (basáltica) dura.

whiny ['hwaɪnɪ, 'waɪnɪ] *a.* (WHINIER; WHINIEST) plañidero, gimoteador, gemidor.

whip [hwɪp, wɪp] *v.t.* (*pret., p.p.* WHIPPED o WHIPT; *p.pr.* WHIPPING) 1. azotar, fustigar, flagelar, dar latigazos a; zurrar, vapulear. 2. (con *in, off, on, together*) arrear con latigazos; dirigir imperiosamente. 3. (fig.) fustigar, zaherir, censurar severamente. 4. (fam.) vencer, batir, ganar a; superar. 5. mover o lanzar súbitamente. 6. batir (huevos, crema, etc.). 7. (gen. con *about, around* u *over*) enrollar o envolver con cuerdecilla. 8. (mar.) izar con candaliza. 9. (cost.) sobrecoser. 10. pescar en (río, etc.) con caña. 11. (jer., G.B.) alzarse con, escamotear. 12. **w. away,** arrebatar, llevarse de golpe; **w. off,** arrebatar, quitar súbitamente; **w. out,** sacar de repente; **w. up,** agarrar, coger en un instante; (fig.) estimular, intensar, intensificar, excitar (pasiones, etc.). —*v.i.* 1. (con *about, behind, in,* etc.) moverse rápidamente; obrar con ligereza. 2. (con *away, off,* etc.) echar a correr; marcharse de prisa. 3. **w. round,** volverse de repente. —*s.* 1. látigo, azote, zurriago, fusta. 2. latigazo, azote. 3. aspa de molino de viento. 4. (mec.) izador, cuerda y poleas. 5. cochero, mayoral. 6. (caza) perrero. 7. (pol.) caudillo de un partido (en un cuerpo legislativo). 8. (cocina) batidor; postre de batidos. 9. (rad.) antena flexible.

whipcord ['hwɪp,kɔrd, 'wɪp-, B -kɔd] *s.* 1. tralla; trenza de látigo. 2. género o tela basta y fuerte con estrías diagonales.

whip grafting, (agr.) injerto de acoplamiento.

whip hand, mano que maneja el látigo; p. ext. dominio, mando, control; **to have the w. h. of,** dominar completamente, tener en su poder (a alguien).

whiplash [-,læʃ] *s.* latigazo.

whipped cream, crema chantilly, crema (de nata) batida.

whipper [-ər, B -ə] *s.* 1. azotador. 2. (cocina) batidor.

whipper-in [,hwɪpər'ɪn, ,wɪp-] *s.* (*pl.* WHIPPERS-IN) (caza) perrero.

whippersnapper ['hwɪpər,snæpər, 'wɪp-, B -ə,-ə] *s.* títere, mequetrefe, arrapiezo.

whippet ['hwɪpət, 'wɪp-] *s.* 1. perro lebrel. 2. (t. **whippet tank**) (mil.) tanque ligero.

whipping ['hwɪpɪŋ, 'wɪp-] *s.* 1. azotamiento, zurriagazo, vapuleo, paliza, tunda. 2. (cocina) batimiento. 3. (cost.) sobrecostura.

whipping boy, víctima propiciatoria, cabeza de turco, chivo expiatorio.

whipping post, (hist.) poste de flagelación.

whippletree [-əl,tri] *var. de* **whiffletree.**

whippoorwill [,hwɪpər'wɪl, ,wɪp-, B 'wɪpʊə,wɪl] *s.* (orn.) chotacabras norte-americano, dormilón, atajacaminos.

whippy ['hwɪpɪ, 'wɪpɪ] *a.* muy elástico; como un látigo.

whip ray, (ict.) raya con púa, raya vaca.

whip-round [-,raʊnd] *s.* (pr. G.B.) colecta (de dinero).

whipsaw [-,sɔ] *s.* sierra cabrilla. —*v.t.* 1. aserrar (con sierra cabrilla). 2. (fig.) pelar (en juego de azar); hacer perder (en negocios, etc.).

whipstaff [-,stæf, B -,stɑf] *s.* (mar.) pinzote, puno del látigo.

whip stall, (aer.) entrada en pérdida durante una ascensión vertical (en que la nariz del avión se cimbra violentamente).

whipster [-stər, B -stə] *s.* 1. mequetrefe. 2. azotador.

whipstitch [-,stɪtʃ] *v.t.* (cost.) sobrecoser.

whipstock [-,stɑk, B -stɔk] *s.* puño o man, go del látigo.

whip top, peonza, trompo.

whipworm [-,wɜrm, B -wɜm] *s.* (ento.) (especie de) triquina.

whir [hwɜr, wɜr, B wɜ] *v.i.* (*pret., p.p.* WHIRRED; *p.pr.* WHIRRING) 1. zumbar, girar o vibrar zumbando. 2. volar zumbando. —*v.t.* llevar zumbando. —*s.* 1. zumbido. 2. aleteo.

whirl [hwɜrl, wɜrl, B wɜl] *v.i.* 1. girar, remolinear; dar vueltas violentes. 2. pasar o volar rápidamente. —*v.t.* 1. hacer girar rápidamente, remolinear. 2. llevar en remolinos (hojas el viento, etc.). —*s.* 1. giro, vuelta, revolución, rotación, remolino. 2. alboroto, ajetreo, conmoción; confusión (mental). 3. ensayo, prueba.

whirlbone ['hwɜrl,boʊn, 'wɜrl-, B 'wɜl-] *s.* (anat.) rótula.

whirligig [-ɪ,gɪg] *s.* 1. perinola. 2. tiovivo, caballitos. 3. (ento.) girino, escribano del agua, tejedera; esquila. 4. (fig.) giros, cambios, ej., *w. of time,* giros de la suerte, cambios de la fortuna.

whirlpool ['hwɜrl,pul, 'wɜrl-, B 'wɜl-] *s.* remolino, vorágine.

whirlpool bath, piscina de hidromasaje.

whirlwind [-,wɪnd] *s.* torbellino, remolino de viento, manga de viento; **to sow the wind and reap the w.,** sembrar viento y cosechar tempestades.

whirly ['hwɜrlɪ, 'wɜr-, B 'wɜlɪ] *a.* (WHIRLIER; WHIRLIEST) remolineante. —*s.* pequeño torbellino.

whirlybird [-,bɜrd, B -,bɜd] *s.* (jer.) helicóptero.

whirr, *var. de* **whir.**

whirry ['hwɜrɪ, B 'wɜrɪ] *v.t., v.i.* (*pret., p.p.* WHIRRIED; *p.pr. whirrying*) (esco.) girar, remolinear; zumbar.

whish [hwɪʃ, wɪʃ] *v.i.* zumbar o silbar; moverse con zumbido suave. —*s.* zumbido suave (ej., de una varita que corta el aire).

whisht [hwɪʃt, wɪʃt] *interj.* (pr. esco.) ¡chitón! ¡punto en boca!

whisk [hwɪsk, wɪsk] *s.* 1. movimiento rápido; movimiento de una escobilla o cepillo. 2. (cocina) batidor. 3. atado de paja, atado de plumas o pelos; escobilla, cepillo; plumero; matamoscas. —*v.i.* escurrirse rápidamente; pasar de prisa. —*v.t.* 1. (gen. con *away* u *off*) quitar rápidamente, arrebatar, arrancar; cepillar, barrer (mota, polvo, mosca, etc.). 2. batir (huevos, crema, etc.).

whisk broom, escobilla de ropa.

whisker ['hwɪskər, 'wɪs- B -kə] *s.* 1. pelo de la barba; (*pl.*) patillas. 2. bigotes (del gato, etc.). 3. (mar.) (*gen. pl.*) arbotantes del bauprés.

whiskered [-kərd, B -kəd] *a.* patilludo; barbudo; bigotudo.

whiskery [-kərɪ] *a.* bigotudo; hirsuto.

whiskey ['hwɪskɪ, 'wɪs-] *s.* whiski.

whiskey sour, whiski con gotas amargas, azúcar, jugo de limón y hielo picado.

whisky, *var. de* **whiskey.**

whisper ['hwɪspər, 'wɪs-, B -pə] *v.i.* 1. cuchichear, murmurar, susurrar. 2. (fig.) susurrar, sugerir. 3. secretear. —*v.t.* 1. decir al oído de. 2. pronunciar cuchicheando; (fig.) murmurar secretamente. —*s.* 1. cuchicheo, susurro, murmullo. 2. secreteo.

whisperer [-pərər, B -pərə] *s.* cuchicheador, susurrador.

whispering [-pərɪŋ] *s.* 1. cuchicheo, susurro. 2. murmuración, chismorreo. —*a.* 1. susurrante, susurrador. 2. murmurador, susurrón.

whisperingly [-lɪ] *adv.* susurrando.

whist [hwɪst, wɪst] *interj.* (dial.) ¡chitón! —*s.* whist (juego de naipes).

whistle ['hwɪsəl, 'wɪs-] *v.i.* 1. silbar, chiflar; piar (aves). 2. pitar, tocar un pito, pitear (Amer.). 3. pasar o volar con un sonido silbante. 4. **w. for,** llamar con un silbido; (fig.) anhelar o buscar en vano. —*v.t.* 1. silbar (una canción, etc.). 2. llamar con un silbido. —*s.* 1. silbato, pito, chiflo. 2. (fam.) gaznate, garganta, boca. 3. silbo, silbido, rechifla, chifla. 4. **to wet one's w.,** mojar el gaznate, remojar la palabra.

whistle-blower ['hwɪsəl,bloʊər] *s.* denunciante, soplón, acusete.

whistler ['hwɪslər, 'wɪs-, B -lə] *s.* 1. silbador. 2. roncador (caballo de carrera). 3. (orn.) clángula. 4. (zool.) marmota norteamericana.

whistle-stop [-əl,stɑp, B -,stɔp] *s.* 1. pequeña estación, apeadero (en que los trenes sólo se detienen a una señal); villorrio, aldea. 2. (E.U.) visita corta (de un candidato político a pequeños pueblos, sin bajarse del tren). —*v.t.* (E.U.) hacer una gira política por las pequeñas comunidades.

whistling [-lɪŋ] *s.* silbo, silbido, chiflido.

whistling buoy, (mar.) boya de silbato, boya de pito o sirena.

whistling kettle, pava con silbato.

whit [hwɪt, wɪt] *s.* ápice, jota, punto, pizca; **not to care a w.,** no importar un ápice (a uno).

white [hwaɪt, waɪt] *a.* 1. blanco. 2. cano (pelo, barba). 3. transparente, incoloro (aire, agua, luz). 4. pálido. 5. (fig.) puro, inocente; inocuo, inofensivo, suave, limpio (chiste, cuento, mentira). 6. (E.U.) decente, honesto, honrado. 7. (pol.) reaccionario; realista; contrarrevolucionario. 8. **to go w.,** ponerse pálido. —*s.* 1. (color) blanco. 2. clara (del huevo). 3. blanco del ojo, esclerótica. 4. vestido blanco. 5. blanco, persona de la raza blanca. 6. (ajedrez, damas) (las piezas) blancas. 7. (ant.) blanco o centro del blanco (en ballestería). —*v.t.* (ant.) blanquear, emblanquecer.

white alder, (bot.) aliso blanco.

white alloy, metal blanco.

white ant, (ent.) comején, hormiga blanca, termita.

white antimony, (metal.) antimonio blanco.

whitebait ['hwaɪt,beɪt, 'waɪt-] *s.* (ict.) arenque joven; sardineta; boquerón.

white basil, (bot.) alcino.

whitebeam [-,bim] *s.* (bot.) mostellar, mostajo, mojera.

white bear, (zool.) oso blanco, oso polar.

whitebeard [-,bɪrd, B -,bɪəd] *s.* (hombre) anciano, hombre barbicano.

white beet, (bot.) acelga.

white birch, (bot.) abedul blanco.

white blood cell, (fisiol.) glóbulo blanco, corpúsculo blanco (en la sangre).

white book, (pol.) libro blanco (informe oficial sobre asuntos gubernamentales empastado en blanco).

white-breasted [-ˈbrɛstəd] *a.* pechiblanco.
white bronze, bronce rico en estaño.
white bryony, (bot.) brionia blanca, nueza blanca.
whitecap [ˈhwaɪtˌkæp, ˈwaɪt-] *s.* 1. (*gen. en pl.*) cabrillas, palomas, palomillas (que se forman en el mar). 2. **W.,** (E.U., hist.) miembro de una sociedad secreta que trataba de imponer sus principios por la fuerza.
white chip, 1. ficha blanca para póker (gen. de valor mínimo). 2. (fig.) bagatela, friolera, nadería.
white-collar [-ˈkɑlər, B -ˈkɔlə] *a.* empleado (de oficina), oficinista profesional (en contraste con el obrero).
white cooper, cubero (fabricante de cubos, cubas, etc.).
white corpuscle, (fisiol.) corpúsculo blanco, glóbulo blanco.
white crop, cereal, esp. el ya maduro que blanquea en la planta.
whited [-əd] *a.* 1. blanqueado. 2. enjalbegado.
white damp, gas venenoso de las minas de carbón.
whited sepulcher, (bíbl.) sepulcro blanqueado.
white Dutch clover, (bot.) trébol blanco, trébol rastrero.
white earth, (min.) tierra blanca, tierra de Segovia.
white elephant, 1. (fig.) elefante blanco (cosa costosa y sin ninguna utilidad), posesión que trae más problemas que ventajas. 2. (zool.) elefante albino.
white-faced [ˈhwaɪtˌfeɪst, ˈwaɪt-] *a.* 1. pálido. 2. cariblanco (caballo).
white feather, pluma blanca (símbolo de cobardía); **to show the w.f.,** mostrarse cobarde.
white fir, (bot.) abeto blanco.
whitefish [-ˌfɪʃ] *s.* (ict.) corégono; esturión blanco.
white flag, bandera blanca (de parlamento o rendición).
white flux, (metal.) castina blanca de carbonato potásico.
white-footed [-ˌfʊtəd] *a.* patialbo, patiblanco.
white fox, (zool.) zorro ártico, zorro blanco.
white fraxinella, (bot.) díctamo blanco, fresnillo.
white friar, carmelita (fraile).
white-fronted [-ˌfrʌntəd] *a.* cariblanco.
white gold, oro blanco, aleación blanquizca de oro.
white goods, 1. ropa blanca (mantelería, toallas, sábanas, etc.). 2. aparatos domésticos (con acabado en porcelana blanca como cocinas, refrigeradoras, etc.).
white goosefoot, (bot.) señiglo, cenizo, armuelle borde, berza de pastor.
white gum, (bot.) gomero.
white-handed [-ˈhændəd] *a.* 1. maniblanco. 2. (fig.) inocente, puro.
whitehead [-ˌhɛd] *s.* 1. (orn.) ave de cabeza blanca. 2. (med.) acné miliar.
white-headed [-əd] *a.* 1. de cabeza blanca; de plumaje blanco. 2. rubio (de pelo). 3. afortunado.
white-headed eagle, (orn.) águila blanca.
white heat, 1. calor blanco. 2. (fig.) fiebre, sumo acaloramiento, frenesí.
white hellebore, (bot.) eléboro blanco, verdegambre.
white horses, cabrillas, palomas, palomillas (que se forman en el mar).
white-hot [ˈhwaɪtˌhɑt, ˈwaɪt-, B -ˈhɔt] *a.* 1. de calor blanco, calentado al blanco. 2. (fig.) ardoroso, frenético.
White House, Casa Blanca (residencia del Presidente de E.U.).
white iron, fundición blanca; hierro estañado, hojalata.
white lead, blanco de plomo, albayalde, cerusa.
white leather, cuero curtido en alumbre y sal.
white-leaved rockrose, (bot.) estepa blanca, estepilla, jara blanca.
white lie, mentirilla, mentira inocente, mentira oficiosa.
white lily, azucena.
white-lipped peccary, (zool.) báquira labiada, pécari labiado.
white list, 1. lista de gente favorecida, digna de confianza. 2. (com., E.U.) lista de las transacciones de la bolsa.
white-livered [ˈhwaɪtˈlɪvərd, ˈwaɪt-, B -ˈlɪvəd] *a.* cobarde, pusilánime.
white lupine, (bot.) lupino, altramuz.
whitely [-lɪ] *adv.* blancamente, con blancura.
white magic, magia blanca.
white man's burden, (la supuesta) obligación de la raza blanca (de llevar su civilización a las regiones pobladas por otras razas).
white matter, (anat.) substancia blanca (del cerebro y médula espinal).
white meat, (cocina) carne de pechuga (del ave); carne de ternera, cerdo o conejo.
white metal, metal blanco.
white mica, mica blanca, moscovita.
white mulberry, (bot.) morera, morera blanca.
white mustard, (bot.) mostaza blanca.
whiten [ˈhwaɪtən, waɪt-] *v.t., v.i.* blanquear(se), emblanquecer(se); descolorar(se).
whitener [-ər, B -ə] *s.* blanqueador.
whiteness [-nəs] *s.* 1. blancura, albura, albor. 2. palidez.
White Nile, Nilo Blanco, el tramo del Nilo antes de llegar a Khartum.
whitening [-ənɪŋ] *s.* 1. blanqueo, emblanquecimiento. 2. lechada, yeso blanco, blanco de España.
white noise, (rad., electrón.) ruido blanco.
white oak, (bot.) roble blanco de América.
white paper, informe oficial (sobre asuntos gubernamentales), libro blanco.
white pepper, (bot.) pimienta blanca.
white perch, (ict.) perca blanca.
white pine, (bot.) pino blanco.
white plague, (med.) peste blanca (tisis o tuberculosis pulmonar).
white poplar, (bot.) álamo blanco.
white potato, (bot.) patata o papa blanca, papa de Irlanda.
white primary, (hist., E.U.) elección primaria (sólo) para votantes de la raza blanca.
white print, fotocopia blanca, fotocalco blanco, copia heliográfica.
white pyrite, (geol.) marcasita.
white race, raza blanca.
white rat, (zool.) rata albina.
white rot, carne de gallina (en maderas).
White Russia, Bielorrusia, Rusia Blanca.
White Russian, ruso blanco; bielorruso.
whites [hwaɪts, waɪts] *s. pl.* 1. (med.) flores blancas, flujo blanco, leucorrea. 2. flor de harina, harina (de) flor.
white sage, (bot.) ontina; tomillo blanco, santónico.
white sale, venta de ropa blanca; venta de artículos domésticos (con acabado en porcelana blanca; cocinas, refrigeradoras, etc.).
white salt, sal blanca.
white sandalwood, (bot.) sándalo blanco.
white satin, 1. (bot.) hierba de la plata. 2. (ento.) especie de mariposa nocturna.
white sauce, (cocina) salsa blanca, bechamel.
white slave, esclava blanca (mujer forzada a vivir en la prostitución, víctima de la trata de blancas).
white slaver, traficante de blancas, traficante en mujeres para la prostitución.
white slavery, w. slave traffic, trata de blancas.
whitesmith [ˈhwaɪtˌsmɪθ, ˈwaɪt-] *s.* 1. estañero, hojalatero. 2. trabajador que pule y galvaniza el hierro.
white stocking, pata blanca (del caballo).
white stonecrop, (bot.) siempreviva menor, uva de gato.
white sugar, azúcar blanca, refinada.
white supremacist, partidario de la supremacía (de la raza) blanca.
white supremacy, supremacía (de la raza) blanca.
white sweet clover, (bot.) trébol de olor blanco.
whitetail [-ˌteɪl] *forma abrev. de* **white-tailed deer.**
white-tailed deer, (zool.) ciervo de Virginia.
white-tailed eagle, (orn.) águila calva; (G.B.) melión.
white-tailed gnu, (zool.) ñu negro.
white-tailed sea eagle, (orn.) melión.
whitethroat [ˈhwaɪtˌθroʊt, ˈwaɪt-] *s.* (orn.) andahuertos, curruca.
white tie, 1. corbatín blanco. 2. frac, atuendo masculino de gala.
white trash, (S. de E.U., despec.) blancos pobres.
white vitriol, (quím.) caparrosa blanca.
white wagtail, (orn.) caudatrémula, motacila, aguzanieves, aguanieves, nevatilla, nevereta, andarríos.
whitewall [-ˌwɔl] *s.* (aut.) neumático de costado blanco, neumático de banda blanca.
white walnut, (bot.) nogal blanco americano.
whitewash [ˈhwaɪtˌwɔʃ, ˈwaɪt-, -ˌwɑʃ, B ˈwaɪtˌwɔʃ] *v.t.* 1. enjalbegar, encalar, blanquear (pared, cerca, etc.). 2. (fig.) excusar, absolver, exonerar (a alguien); encubrir, disimular (faltas, defectos, etc. de alguien). 3. derrotar por completo, dejar zapatero (al contrario en el juego). —*s.* 1. jalbegue, lechada, blanqueo; blanquete (afeite). 2. (fig.) exoneración, absolución; disimulo, encubrimiento (de faltas, vicios, etc.). 3. derrota absoluta (sin un tanto a favor de uno).
whitewasher [-ər, B -ə] *s.* 1. enjalbegador, blanqueador, encalador. 2. (fig.) encubridor.
whitewashing, *s.* blanqueo, encalado, enlucido.
white water, agua espumosa (ej., la de rápidos, cataratas, etc.).
white water lily, (bot.) ninfea, nenúfar.
white way, (fig.) avenida brillantemente iluminada.
white whale, (zool.) beluga.
white wheat, (bot.) trigo albar, trigo albarejo, trigo candeal, mijo ceburro.
white willow, (bot.) sauce blanco.
whitewing [ˈhwaɪtˌwɪŋ, ˈwaɪt-] *s.* barrendero uniformado de blanco, en gen. persona uniformada de blanco.
whitewood [-ˌwʊd] *s.* (bot.) 1. tulipero, tilo. 2. álamo americano.
whither [ˈhwɪðər, ˈwɪð-, B -ə] *adv.* adónde. —*conj.* adonde.
whithersoever [ˌhwɪðərsoʊˈɛvər, ˌwɪð-, B ˌwɪðəsoʊˈɛvə] *conj.* adondequiera.
whitherward [ˈhwɪðərwərd, ˈwɪð-, B -əwəd] **whitherwards** [-wərdz, B -wədz] *adv.* en qué dirección; hacia dónde.
whiting [ˈhwaɪtɪŋ, ˈwaɪt-] *s.* (ict.) 1. merluza. 2. romero.
whiting, *s.* blanco de España, yeso blanco.
whitish [-ɪʃ] *a.* blanquizco, blanquecino, blancuzco.
whitishness [-nəs] *s.* color blanquecino.
whitlow [ˈhwɪtloʊ, ˈwɪt-] *s.* (med.) panadizo.

whitlow grass, (bot.) 1. draba. 2. saxífraga.
whitlowwort [-ˌwɜrt, B -wɜt] *s.* (bot.) nevadilla, sanguinaria menor.
Whitmonday [-ˌmʌndɪ] *s.* lunes de Pentecostés.
Whitsun [-sən] *a.* de Pentecostés.
Whitsunday [-ˈsʌndɪ] *s.* domingo de Pentecostés.
Whitsuntide [-sənˌtaɪd] *s.* semana de Pentecostés (esp. la que sigue al domingo de Pentecostés); esp. domingo, lunes y martes de Pentecostés.
whittle [ˈhwɪtəl, ˈwɪ-] *s.* (G.B.) cuchillo grande. —*v.t.* 1. sacar pedazos a (un trozo de madera) con un cuchillo, tallar, mondar. 2. **w. away,** gastar poco a poco (ej., una herencia); **w. down** (u **off**), cernenar, reducir o acortar gradualmente. —*v.i.* cortar pedazos de una madera.
whittling [-təlɪŋ] *s.* astilla de madera (cortada con un cuchillo).
whity [ˈhwaɪtɪ, ˈwaɪtɪ] *a.* (WHITIER; WHITIEST) blanquecino, blancuzco, blanquizco.
whiz [hwɪz, wɪz] *v.i.* (*pret., p.p.* WHIZZED; *p.pr.* WHIZZING) 1. pasar muy aprisa, pasar con un silbido o zumbido, volar con la velocidad de un rayo. 2. zumbar, silbar (proyectiles). 3. **w. by,** rehilar (flecha, lanza, etc.). —*v.t.* hacer girar hasta oír un silbido o zumbido. —*s.* (*pl.* WHIZZES) zumbido, silbido.
whiz, *s.* (*pl.* WHIZZES) mago, as, fenómeno.
whiz-bang [ˈhwɪzˌbæŋ, ˈwɪz-] *s.* (jer.) 1. granada o proyectil de alta velocidad (cuyo zumbido es casi simultáneo con su explosión). 2. buscapiés, petardo. 3. bomba voladora. 4. (fig.) fenómeno, maravilla. —*a.* fenomenal, maravilloso.
whiz kid, (fam.) lince, prodigio.
whizz, *var. de* **whiz** (zumbar, zumbido, etc.).
whizzer [-ər, B -ə] *s.* 1. bramadera, zumba. 2. centrífuga para secar (granos, azúcar, algodón nitratado, etc.).
who [hu] *pron.* 1. quién(es). 2. que, quien(es). 3. (ant.) el que, la que, los que, las que; **as w. should say,** como si alguien dijera.
WHO *abrev. de* **World Health Organization,** Organización Mundial de la Salud (OMS).
who's who, quien es quien (libro de biografías de personas notables).
whoa [woʊ] *interj.* ¡so! ¡cho! ¡jo!
whodunit [huˈdʌnət] *s.* (jer.) novela policial; drama o película policiaca.
whoever [huˈɛvər, B -ə] *pron.* quienquiera que, cualquiera que; quien, el que, la que.
whole [hoʊl] *a.* 1. entero, todo. 2. entero, intacto, indemne, ileso. 3. carnal (de la misma madre y padre), ej., *w. brother,* hermano carnal. 4. entero, completo, cabal. —*s.* 1. total, totalidad. 2. conjunto, todo, suma. 3. **as a w.,** en conjunto; **on** (o **upon**) **the w.,** en general, mirándolo todo.
whole gale, (mar.) temporal.
wholehearted [ˈhoʊlˈhɑrtəd, B -ˈhɑtɪd] *a.* 1. sincero, franco. 2. cordial. 3. entusiasta.
wholeheartedly [-lɪ] *adv.* sinceramente, de todo corazón; con tesón, tesoneramente.
wholeheartedness [-nəs] *s.* 1. sinceridad. 2. cordialidad. 3. entusiasmo.
whole hog, sin restricción, enteramente; **to go the w. h.,** no quedarse a medias, no refrenarse, no contenerse.
whole meal bread, pan integral.
whole milk, leche completa, leche sin desnatar.
wholeness [-nəs] *s.* 1. todo, totalidad. 2. integridad, entereza.
whole note, (mús.) semibreve, redonda.
whole number, (mat.) entero, número entero.
wholesale [ˈhoʊlˌseɪl] *s.* venta o comercio (al) por mayor; **by w.,** (al) por mayor. —*a.* 1. al por mayor, mayorista. 2. en grande, en masa. —*adv.* 1. (al) por mayor. 2. en masa. —*v.t., v.i.* vender(se) (al) por mayor.
wholesaler [-ər, B -ə] *s.* mayorista.
wholesome [ˈhoʊlsəm] *a.* 1. sano, saludable, salubre, salutífero. 2. (fig.) saludable, sano, seguro; prudencial, prudente. 3. (raro) favorable, propicio.
wholesomely [-lɪ] *adv.* saludablemente.
wholesomeness [-nəs] *s.* cualidad de lo sano, salubridad.
whole-souled [-ˈsoʊld] *a.* sincero.
whole step, w. tone, (mús.) tono completo.
wholewheat flour [-ˈhwit-, -wit-] harina de trigo entero.
who'll [hul] *contr. de* **who will** o **who shall.**
wholly [ˈhoʊlɪ] *adv.* totalmente, enteramente, completamente, por completo.
whom [hum] *pron.* a quién(es); a quien(es), que, al que, al cual.
whomever [ˌhumˈɛvər, B -ə] *pron.* a quienquiera, a cualquiera.
whomp [hwɑmp, wɑmp, B wɔmp] *s.* estallido, estampido; trueno (de armas de fuego). —*v.t.* 1. batir o golpear con ruido, cascar; derrotar abrumadoramente, aplastar (en deportes). 2. **w. up,** excitar, mover, alborotar; armar apresuradamente, chapucear, frangollar. —*v.i.* caer con estrépito, hacer un impacto ruidoso.
whomsoever [ˌhumsoʊˈɛvər, B -ə] *pron.* a quienquiera, a cualquiera.
whoop [hwup, B hup] *interj.* ¡hurra! ¡anda! ¡vamos! ¡dale! —*v.i.* 1. gritar, vocear. 2. huchear. 3. ulular. 4. toser jadeando. —*v.t.* 1. alentar o vitorear a gritos, incitar o insultar a gritos. 2. (gen. con *up*) aumentar, subir. 3. **w. it up,** (jer.) alborotar, armar una gritería; jaranear. —*s.* 1. grito, alarido. 2. clamoreo. 3. chillido (del búho). 4. estertor de la tos ferina. 5. pizca, ápice, nonada. 6. **not to care a w.,** no importar(le) un pito.
whoop-de-do, whoop-de-doo [ˌhupdɪˈdu] *s.* bullicio, alboroto, actividad bulliciosa; disputa (política) acalorada.
whoopee [ˈwʊpi] *interj.* ¡hurra! ¡viva! ¡vamos! —*s.* (jer.) gran parranda; holgorio, jolgorio, parranda o diversión bulliciosa; **to make w.,** (jer.) tener una diversión alegre y bulliciosa.
whooping cough, (med.) tos ferina, tos convulsiva, coqueluche.
whooping crane, *s.* (orn.) tipo de grulla blanca conocida por su grito característico.
whoopla [ˈhuˌplɑ] *s.* (jer.) 1. conmoción, alharaca, alboroto. 2. holgorio ruidoso, jarana.
whoosh [hwuʃ, wuʃ] *v.i.* pasar como una exhalación, pasar como un silbido. —*s.* silbido (ej., de un proyectil).
whop [hwɑp, wɑp, B wɔp] *v.i., v.t.* golpear rápidamente; batir, azotar; derrotar por completo. —*s.* golpazo.
whopper [ˈhwɑpər, ˈwɑp-, B ˈwɔpə] *s.* (fam.) cosa enorme o extraordinaria; mentira o bola colosal.
whopping [-ɪŋ] *a.* (fam.) colosal, enorme, grandísimo.
whore [hɔr, B hɔ] *s.* puta, prostituta, ramera. —*v.i.* 1. putañear. 2. (bíbl.) adorar dioses falsos. —*v.t.* (ant.) prostituir.
whoredom [ˈhɔrdəm, B ˈhɔdəm] *s.* 1. prostitución, putaísmo, putanismo. 2. (bíbli.) idolatría.
whorehouse [-ˌhaʊs] *s.* casa de prostitución, prostíbulo.
whoremaster [-ˌmæstər, B -ˌmɑstə] *s.* chulo; alcahuete.
whoremastery [-tərɪ] *s.* alcahuetería.
whoremonger [-ˌmʌŋgər, -ˌmɑŋ-, B -ˌmʌŋgə] *s.* (ant.) hombre putañero; chulo, alcahuete.
whoreson [-sən] *s.* 1. bastardo. 2. (fam.) rufián, chulo.
whorish [ˈhɔrɪʃ] *a.* putesco, lascivo.
whorl [hwɔrl, wɔrl, B wɜl] *s.* 1. espiral. 2. (bot.) verticilo. 3. (zool.) espira (del caracol marino). 4. (dactiloscopia) verticilo. 5. (tej.) tortera o tortero, volante de la rueca, nuez (del huso).
whorled [hwɔrld, wɔrld, B wɜld] *a.* (bot.) verticilado.
whort [hwɜrt, wɜrt, B wɜt] **whortle** [ˈhwɜrtəl, ˈwɜr-, B ˈwɜtəl] *s.* (bot.) (variedad de) arándano.
whortleberry [-ˌbɛrɪ] *s.* (bot.) arándano, anavia.
whose [huz] *a.* cuyo, cuya, cuyos, cuyas, de quien(es). —*pron.* de quien(es), de quién(es).
whosesoever [ˌhuzsoʊˈɛvər, B -ə] *a.* de quienquiera.
whosoever [ˌhusoʊˈɛvər, B -ə] *pron.* quienquiera que, cualquiera que; quien, el que, la que, los que, las que.
why [hwaɪ, waɪ] *adv.* ¿por qué? ¿para qué? ¿a qué —*conj.* porque; por lo (el. la) cual; **that is w.,** por eso es que. —*interj.* ¡toma!; pues; **w., certainly,** por supuesto, ciertamente, desde luego; **w., yes,** pues, sí; sí, pues. —*s.* 1. (el) porqué, (la) causa. 2. problema desconcertante, enigma. 3. **the whys and wherefores,** todos los detalles, todos los aspectos, las minucias.
whydah [ˈhwɪdə, ˈwɪd-] *s.* (orn.) tejedor.
WI *abrev. de* **West Indies,** Indias Occidentales, Antillas.
wick [wɪk] *s.* mecha, pabilo, torcida.
wicked [ˈwɪkəd] *a.* 1. malo, malvado, inicuo, perverso. 2. feroz, bravo (díc. de animales). 3. vil, bajo; desagradable. 4. travieso, revoltoso.
wickedly [-lɪ] *adv.* inicuamente, perversamente; desagradablemente.
wickedness [-nəs] *s.* maldad, iniquidad, perversidad.
wicker [ˈwɪkər, B -ə] *s.* 1. mimbre. 2. cestería; artículos de mimbre. —*a.* mimbroso, de mimbre.
wickerwork [-ˌwɜrk, B -wɜk] *s.* cestería; artículos de mimbre.
wicket [ˈwɪkət] *s.* 1. portillo, postigo; portezuela, entrada de torniquete. 2. ventanilla (de banco, de correos, etc.). 3. puertecilla de desagüe (ej., de un canal). 4. meta (en criquet). 5. aro (en croquet).
wicketkeeper [-ˌkipər, B -pə] *s.* guardameta (en criquet).
wicking [ˈwɪkɪŋ] *s.* torcida, pabilo, material para mechas.
wickiup [ˈwɪkɪˌʌp] *s.* choza o cabaña (de ciertas tribus indias nómadas del S. de E.U.).
wicopy [-əpɪ] *s.* (*pl.* WICOPIES) (bot.) 1. tilo, tilo americano. 2. (variedad de) arce. 3. sauce.
widdershins [ˈwɪdərʃənz, B -əʃɪnz] *adv.* en sentido contrario al de las agujas del reloj; a contramano.
widdy [ˈwɪdɪ] *s.* (*pl.* WIDDIES) (esco.) cuerda de mimbre; mimbre; dogal.
wide [waɪd] *a.* 1. ancho. 2. del ancho de, de ancho, ej., *three meters w.,* de tres metros de ancho. 3. ancho, holgado, suelto. 4. dilatado, muy abierto (ej., ojos). 5. comprensivo, vasto; extenso; ilimitado, excesivo, ej., *a w. generalization,* una generalización excesiva. 6. (gen. con *of*) remoto, lejano, apartado, distante (de); fuera, lejos (del blanco, caso, verdad, etc.). 7. (agr.) rica en grasas y carbohidratos (díc. de una ración alimenticia para animales). 8. (fon.) relajada (díc. de las vocales). 9. (jer., G.B.) despierto, vivo. 10. (raro) (con *of*) diferente. —*adv.* 1. lejos, a gran distancia. 2. anchamente, de par en par. 3. **far and w.,**

por todas partes, por todos lados; **to go w.,** errar el blanco (tiro, proyectil); **w. apart,** muy separados o alejados; **w. open,** de par en par. *—s.* 1. (criquet) pelota lanzada fuera del alcance del bateador. 2. (poét.) anchura; espacio o extensión anchos.

wide-angle ['waɪd'æŋgəl] *a.* (foto., ópt.) granangular, de ángulo ancho.

wide-angle lens, gran angular.

wide-awake [-ə'weɪk] *a.* despabilado; (fig.) despabilado, despierto.

wide-eyed [-'aɪd] *a.* 1. con los ojos muy abiertos. 2. (fig.) atónito, pasmado, asombrado. 3. (fig.) puro, cándido (inocencia, ingenuidad).

widely [-lɪ] *adv.* 1. lejos, a gran distancia. 2. excesivamente. 3. muy, mucho; anchamente, holgadamente.

widemouthed [-'maʊðd] *a.* 1. bocudo, bocón. 2. (fig.) boquiabierto. 3. (fig.) descarado, desvergonzado (denuesto, blasfemia, etc.). 4. (arm.) desbocado (pieza de artillería).

widen ['waɪdən] *v.t., v.i.* ensanchar(se), dilatar(se), extender(se), ampliar(se).

widener [-ənər, B -ə] *s.* instrumento o aparato para ensanchar.

wideness [-nəs] *s.* anchura, ancho.

wide-open [-'oʊpən] *a.* abierto de par en par; abierto a la vida licenciosa (ciudad, lugar).

wide-open spaces, llanuras, praderas, campo libre, abierto.

widespread [-'sprɛd] *a.* 1. extendido. 2. difundido, esparcido, diseminado, propalado, propagado.

wide-spreading ['waɪd'sprɛdɪŋ] *a.* extenso; de mucho alcance.

widgeon ['wɪdʒən] *s.* 1. (orn.) mareca, pato marrueco; cerceta, zarceta. 2. (ant.) simplón, gaznápiro.

widget ['wɪdʒət] *s.* 1. dispositivo mecánico, artefacto. 2. adminículo, chisme, pieza o accesorio cuyo nombre real no se conoce.

widish ['waɪdɪʃ] *a.* bastante ancho, tirando a ancho.

widow ['wɪdoʊ] *s.* 1. viuda. 2. (naipes) baceta. 3. (impr.) viuda (línea corta sobrante de la columna o página anterior). *—v.t.* 1. dejar viuda. 2. (gen. con *of*) privar (de) (una cosa necesaria o estimada). 3. (ant.) sobrevivir como viuda de. *—a.* (dial.) enviudado; privado, despojado.

widow bird, (orn.) viuda dominicana.

widowed [-oʊd] *a.* viudo.

widower [-oʊər, B -ə] *s.* viudo.

widowhood ['wɪdoʊˌhʊd] *s.* viudez.

widow's cruse, (bíbl.) vasija de la viuda.

widow's mite, (bíbl.) el óbolo de la viuda.

widow's walk, plataforma de observación (de una casa en la costa del mar).

width [wɪdθ, wɪtθ] *s.* 1. anchura, ancho. 2. amplitud, liberalidad (de mente, opiniones, etc.). 3. (tej.) corte (de calicó, tela, etc.).

widthwise ['wɪdθˌwaɪz] *adv.* a lo ancho.

wield [wild] *v.t.* 1. esgrimir (el sable, la espada, etc.), manejar (brocha, herramienta, etc.). 2. (fig.) empuñar (el cetro); ejercer (autoridad, el poder). 3. **w. the pen,** escribir; **w. the willow,** (jer., G.B.) jugar criquet.

wieldable ['wildəbəl] *a.* manejable.

wielder [-dər, B -də] *s.* esgrimidor.

wieldy [-dɪ] *a.* (WIELDIER; WIELDIEST) manejable.

wiener ['winər, B -nə] *s.* salchicha de Viena.

Wiener schnitzel ['vinərˌʃnɪtsəl, B -nəˌ-] escalope de ternera a la vienesa.

wienerwurst ['winərˌwərst, B -nəˌwɜst] *s.* salchicha de Viena.

wife [waɪf] *s.* (*pl.* WIVES [waɪvz]) esposa, señora, mujer; **to take a w.,** tomar mujer, casarse.

wifehood ['waɪfˌhʊd] *s.* estado de la mujer casada.

wifeless [-ləs] *a.* soltero; viudo; sin esposa.

wifelike [-ˌlaɪk] *a.* como una mujer casada; de esposa. *—adv.* al modo, a la manera de una esposa.

wifeliness [-lɪnəs] *s.* 1. aire de mujer casada. 2. comportamiento característico de una esposa.

wifely [-lɪ] *a.* de esposa, de casada; propio de una esposa.

wig [wɪg] *s.* peluca. *—v.t.* (*pret., p.p.* WIGGED; *p.pr.* WIGGING) 1. poner peluca a. 2. (G.B.) echar una reprimenda a, censurar, reprender severamente.

wigan ['wɪgən] *s.* (tej.) entretela tiesa de algodón.

wigeon *var. de* **widgeon.**

wigged [wɪgd] *a.* con peluca, de peluca.

wigging ['wɪgɪŋ] *s.* (fam., G.B.) reprimenda, regaño, reprensión.

wiggle ['wɪgəl] *v.i.* menearse rápidamente; culebrear. *—v.t.* menear rápidamente. *—s.* 1. meneo, culebreo. 2. potaje de mariscos o pescado con guisantes.

wiggler ['wɪglər, B -lə] *s.* 1. (ento.) larva o ninfa de mosquito. 2. lo que se menea o culebrea.

wiggly [-lɪ] *a.* ondulante, sinuoso, movedizo como un gusano.

wight [waɪt] *s.* (hum., ant.) criatura, ser viviente. *—a.* (ant., dial.) 1. bravo, valiente; fuerte; poderoso. 2. ruidoso; activo.

wigmaker ['wɪgˌmeɪkər, B -kə] *s.* fabricante o vendedor de pelucas.

wigwag ['wɪgˌwæg] *v.t., v.i.* (*pret., p.p.* WIGWAGGED; *p.pr.* WIGWAGGING) (mil., mar.) comunicar(se) por señales, señalar con banderolas o luces. *—s.* (mil., mar.) comunicación por señales o banderolas; mensaje de señales.

wigwam ['wɪgˌwɑm, B -wæm] *s.* 1. wigwam (tienda o vivienda de los indios de N.Amér.). 2. (E.U., jer.) local empleado por un partido político, para asambleas, etc.

wikiup, *var. de* **wickiup.**

wilco ['wɪlkoʊ] *interj.* (rad.) se actuará conforme (a instrucciones recibidas).

wild [waɪld] *a.* 1. salvaje, bravío, indomesticado, chúcaro (Amer.) (animal); silvestre, rusticano, bravío, no cultivado, cimarrón (planta) (Amer.). 2. inculto, desierto, desolado, despoblado (región, terreno, etc.). 3. salvaje, bárbaro, incivilizado. 4. bravo, indomado, cerril. 5. fiero, feroz. 6. desenfrenado, turbulento, alborotado; desordenado, desarreglado; bullicioso, desbordante; disoluto, licencioso. 7. infundado, errático (teoría, suposición, etc.); extravagante, estrafalario; visionario, alocado. 8. impetuoso, brioso, fogoso, vehemente. 9. violento. 10. alocado, loco, frenético. 11. errado, desviado (tiro, golpe, etc.). 12. (naipes) (que sirve) de comodín (carta). 13. **the w. men,** los extremistas (de un partido político, etc.); **to be w. about (someone),** (fam.) estar loco por (alguien); **to be w. about (something),** (fam.) entusiasmarse locamente por (algo); **to drive w.,** volver loco. *—adv.* 1. violentamente. 2. desatinadamente, alocadamente; sin pies ni cabeza. 3. sin cultivo. 4. **to run w.,** crecer en estado salvaje; (fig.) propagarse desmesuradamente. *—s.* 1. desierto, selva; tierra virgen, yermo; despoblado. 2. estado silvestre o natural. 3. **in the w.,** en estado natural; como planta silvestre; **the w.,** la naturaleza; **the wilds,** región primitiva, selva.

wild allspice, (bot.) benjuí.

wild and woolly, bullicioso y poco refinado.

wild artichoke, (bot.) alcachofa silvestre, alcaucil, alcaucí.

wild ass, (zool.) onagro.

wild basil, (bot.) clinopodio, alcino.

wild beast, fiera; animal salvaje.

wild boar, (zool.) jabalí, jabalina.

wild brier, (bot.) rosal silvestre, escaramujo, agavanzo.

wild capulin, (bot.) capulí cimarrón.

wild card, 1. comodín (en un juego de cartas). 2. (fig.) imponderable. 3. (comput.) comodín.

wild carrot, (bot.) zanahoria silvestre, dauco, biznaga.

wildcat ['waɪldˌkæt] *s.* 1. (zool.) gato montés; lince. 2. (fig.) fiera, persona de carácter indómito o bravío. *—a.* 1. ilícito, no autorizado, ilegal. 2. atolondrado; descabellado. 3. quimérico, sin fundamento. 4. de ensayo, perforado al azar (pozo de petróleo). *—v.i.* catear en busca de petróleo.

wildcat bank, (E.U., hist.) banco que emitía billetes sin respaldo.

wildcat strike, huelga no autorizada (por el sindicato obrero).

wildcatter [-ər, B -ə] *s.* (fam.) 1. buscador de petróleo (que perfora pozos al azar). 2. gestor de empresas o negocios descabellados.

wild celery, (bot.) esmirnio, perejil macedonio, apio caballar, apio equino.

wild chestnut, 1. (bot.) castaño silvestre, castaño regoldo, castaño regoldano, castaño borde. 2. castaña regoldana (fruto).

wildebeest ['wɪldəˌbist] *s.* (*pl.* WILDEBEESTS o WILDEBEEST) (zool.) ñu azul, ñu negro.

wilder ['wɪldər, B -də] (ant., poét.) *v.t.* despistar, confundir, aturdir. *—v.i.* extraviarse, vagar.

wilderment [-mənt] *s.* (ant., poét.) aturdimiento, perplejidad.

wilderness ['wɪldərnəs, B -dənɪs] *s.* 1. desierto, selva; yermo. 2. soledad, ej., *w. of sea,* soledad del mar. 3. (con *of*) multitud confusa, mezcolanza, mar (de cosas). 4. (ant.) rusticidad, tosquedad, selvatiquez.

wilderness area, (E.U.) territorio conservado en su estado virgen (en un parque nacional, etc.).

wild-eyed ['waɪld'aɪd] *a.* 1. de mirada furiosa; frenético, agitado. 2. extremista; irracional.

wild fig, (bot.) higuera silvestre, cabrahígo, cornicabra.

wildfire [-ˌfaɪr, B -ˌfaɪə] *s.* 1. fuego griego. 2. fuego fatuo. 3. incendio destructivo. 4. fucilazo, relámpago. 5. (ant.) erisipela; sarpullido. 6. **to spread like w.,** correr como un reguero de pólvora, extenderse como una mancha de aceite (noticia, chisme, etc.).

wild flax, (bot.) camelina; linaria, lino bastardo.

wild flower, flor del campo, flor silvestre.

wildfowl ['waɪldˌfaʊl] *s.* aves silvestres, aves de caza.

wildfowler [-lərm, B -lə] *s.* cazador de aves silvestres.

wildfowling [-lɪŋ] *s.* caza o cacería de aves silvestres.

wild goat, (zool.) cabra montés.

wild goose, (orn.) ganso silvestre.

wild-goose chase ['waɪld'gus-] (fig.) persecución inútil; empresa quimérica.

wild hazel, (bot.) avellana silvestre, nochizo.

wild honey, miel silvestre.

wild honeysuckle, (bot.) azalea.

wild hyacinth, (bot.) jacinto silvestre.

wild indigo, (bot.) índigo o añil silvestre.

wilding [-ɪŋ] *s.* 1. planta silvestre; esp. manzana silvestre. 2. animal salvaje o silvestre. *—a.* (ant.) inculto; indomesticado.

wild land, yermo, páramo.

wild leek, (bot.) ajipuerro, puerro silvestre.

wild lettuce, (bot.) lechuga silvestre.
wildlife ['waɪld,laɪf] *s.* fauna silvestre; animales salvajes; caza.
wildling [-lɪŋ] *s.* planta silvestre; animal silvestre.
wildly [-lɪ] *adv.* 1. violentamente. 2. desatinadamente, alocadamente, sin pies ni cabeza.
wild madder, (bot.) 1. rubia, granza (planta y raíz). 2. variedad de galio.
wild mandrake, (bot.) manzana de mayo.
wild marjoram, (bot.) orégano.
wild mint, (bot.) poleo.
wild mustard, (bot.) variedad de mostaza silvestre (que crece como mala hierba en los cultivos de cereales).
wildness ['waɪldnəs] *s.* 1. salvajismo, salvajez, selvatiquez, ferocidad, fiereza, brutalidad. 2. locura, desvarío. 3. (ant.) desierto, yermo, selva o tierra virgen.
wild oat, 1. (bot.) avena loca o silvestre. 2. **to sow one's w. oats,** cometer excesos juveniles; correr sus mocedades.
wild olive, 1. (bot.) acebuche, olivo silvestre. 2. acebuchina (fruto).
wild onion, (bot.) ceborrincha, cebolla silvestre.
wild orach, (bot.) ceñiglo, cenizo, armuelle borde.
wild pansy, (bot.) pensamiento silvestre, trinitaria.
wild parsnip, (bot.) chirivía silvestre.
wild pear, 1. (bot.) peral silvestre, guadapero, peruétano, piruétano. 2. (bot.) cermeño. 3. peruétano; cermeña (frutas).
wild pink, (bot.) 1. clavel silvestre. 2. pegamoscas americana.
wild rice, (bot.) tuscarora, arroz de la India, arroz salvaje.
wild rose, (bot.) escaramujo oloroso, agavanzo.
wild rye, (bot.) ballico, vallico.
wild sage, (bot.) gallocresta, orvalle, rinanto.
wild teasel, (bot.) escobilla.
wild thyme, (bot.) serpol.
Wild West, (el) indómito Oeste (el Oeste de los E.U. durante la época de la colonización).
wildwood ['waɪld,wʊd] *s.* bosque virgen, selva.
wild yam, (bot.) ñame silvestre.
wile [waɪl] *s.* 1. ardid, estratagema, superchería, treta. 2. astucia, artería. —*v.t.* 1. (con *away, into*) atraer, inducir con ardides, seducir. 2. (gen. con *away*) pasar (el rato o tiempo).
wilful, *var. de* **willful.**
wilily ['waɪləlɪ] *adv.* astutamente, arteramente.
wiliness [-lɪnəs] *s.* artería, astucia.
will [wɪl] *s.* 1. voluntad, deseo, albedrío, intención. 2. última voluntad, testamento. 3. **at w.,** a gusto, a voluntad, a discreción; **thy w. be done,** hágase tu voluntad; **to do (something) with a w.,** hacer (algo) con mucha voluntad, empeñarse en hacer (algo); **to have one's w.,** conseguir uno su propósito; salirse uno con la suya; **to make one's w.,** hacer testamento; **where there's a w. there's a way,** querer es poder. —*v.t.* (*pret., condicional* WOULD [wʊd]) 1. determinar, disponer, mandar, ordenar, decretar. 2. sugestionar, inducir (por fuerza de voluntad, hipnotismo, etc.). 3. (der.) legar, dejar en testamento. 4. (ant.) querer, desear. —*v.i.* 1. tener (la) voluntad. 2. querer, desear. 3. gustarle a uno; ocurrírsele a uno. 4. **if you w.,** si Ud. quiere.
will, *v. aux.* (*pret. y condicional* WOULD) 1. en segunda y tercera pers. ú. para formar un declaración o una pregunta en futuro simple o modo condicional, ej., *you w. hear about it tomorrow,* mañana tendrá Ud. noticias (acerca) de eso, *he would have been killed if he had let go,* él se habría matado si se hubiera soltado, *w. you hear from him soon?* ¿recibirás noticias de él pronto? 2. en primera pers. ú. para formar una declaración futura o condicional expresando intención o deseo, ej., *I w. not be caught again,* no me cogerán otra vez, *I would not have gone if you had warned me in time,* yo no habría ido si usted me hubiera advertido a tiempo. 3. en primera pers. en oraciones subordinadas para formar un futuro simple, una declaración condicional o una pregunta, ej., *you said I would never manage,* dijiste que yo nunca podría hacerlo. 4. en segunda y tercera personas en oraciones subordinadas para formar una declaración futura o condicional expresando intención o deseo, ej., *you promised you would not be caught again,* prometiste que no te volverían a coger. 5. hacer o suceder siempre, soler, ej., *accidents w. happen,* siempre habrá accidentes, *he w. get excited over trifles,* siempre alborota por pequeñeces, *he would sit there every night,* solía sentarse allí todas las noches.
willable ['wɪləbəl] *a.* que puede ser determinado o deseado.
willed [wɪld] *a.* (*ú. en compuestos*) de voluntad (fuerte, débil, etc.), ej., *strong-w.,* de voluntad recia.
willemite ['wɪlə,maɪt] *s.* (min.) villemita.
willet ['wɪlət] *s.* (orn.) (variedad americana de) agachadiza.
willful, wilful ['wɪlfəl] *a.* 1. voluntario, intencional, premeditado. 2. voluntarioso, obstinado, testarudo.
willfully, wilfully [-fəlɪ] *adv.* 1. voluntariamente, intencionalmente. 2. voluntariosamente, obstinadamente, testarudamente.
willfulness, wilfulness [-fəlnəs] *s.* 1. intención, premeditación. 2. voluntariedad, obstinación, testarudez.
willies ['wɪlɪz] *s. pl.* 1. (jer., E.U.) nerviosidad, repeluzno, escalofríos (de temor o adversión). 2. los espíritus de las doncellas que fueron desdichadas en amores (según una antigua leyenda germana).
willie-waught ['wɪlɪ,wɑkt] *s.* (esco.) trago grande.
willing ['wɪlɪŋ] *a.* 1. dispuesto, listo, llano. 2. voluntario, pronto. 3. deseoso. 4. (filos.) volitivo. 5. **God w.,** Dios mediante, si Dios quiere.
willingly [-lɪ] *adv.* voluntariamente; gustosamente, de buena gana.
willingness [-nəs] *s.* buena voluntad, buena gana, gusto.
williwaw ['wɪlɪ,wɔ] *s.* 1. ráfaga fría, tramontana (en costas montañosas). 2. turbulencia, remolino.
will-less ['wɪlləs] *a.* 1. sin voluntad; falto de voluntad, abúlico. 2. sin intención, involuntario. 3. sin testamento, intestado.
will-o'-the-wisp [,wɪləðə'wɪsp] *s.* 1. fuego fatuo. 2. ilusión, quimera.
will-o'-the-wispish [-'wɪspɪʃ] *a.* (G.B.) ilusorio, quimérico.
willow ['wɪloʊ] *s.* 1. (bot.) sauce, salce. 2. (mec.) diablo (máquina para limpiar algodón o lana). 3. (fam.) paleta de criquet, bate; **to handle the w.,** batear. —*v.t.* limpiar (fibras) con diablo.
willower ['wɪloʊər, B -ə] *s.* (mec.) diablo (máquina para limpiar algodón o lana).
willow herb, (bot.) camenerio, lisimaquia, arroyuela.
willow oak, (bot.) roble de los E.U. (con hojas parecidas a las del sauce).
willow pattern, diseño de azul o rojo representando un paisaje de inspiración china, que aparece en algunas vajillas.
willowware ['wɪloʊ,wɛr, B -,wɛə] *s.* vajilla con un dibujo específico de inspiración china.
willowish [-ɪʃ] *a.* parecido al sauce.
willowy [-oʊɪ] *a.* 1. poblado de sauces. 2. mimbreño, sarguero. 3. (fig.) cimbreño, esbelto y alto (persona).
willpower ['wɪl,paʊr, B -,paʊə] *s.* fuerza de voluntad.
will to power, 1. (filos.) voluntad de potencia. 2. ansias de poder (ej., de un dictador).
willy ['wɪlɪ] *v.t.* (*pret., p.p.* WILLIED; *p.pr.* WILLYING) limpiar (fibras) con diablo. —*s.* (mec.) diablo (máquina para limpiar algodón o lana).
willy-nilly ['wɪlɪ'nɪlɪ] *adv.* quieras o no quieras, de buen o mal grado.
Wilson's thrush ['wɪlsənz-] (orn.) tordo canoro.
wilt [wɪlt] *v.i.* 1. agostarse, marchitarse, secarse. 2. (fig.) marchitarse, descaecer, languidecer; amilanarse. —*v.t.* marchitar, ajar. —*s.* marchitamiento; marchitez.
wilt, (ant.) *segunda pers. sing. pres. ind. de* **will.**
Wilton ['wɪltən] *s.* especie de alfombra de Bruselas.
wily ['waɪlɪ] *a.* (WILIER; WILIEST) artero, taimado, ladino.
wimble ['wɪmbəl] *s.* barrena, taladro; (carp.) berbiquí. —*v.t.* taladrar, barrenar, horadar.
wimple ['wɪmpəl] *s.* 1. toca, griñón. 2. (esco.) vuelta, recodo (de un camino); ardid, treta. —*v.t.* 1. vestir con toca o griñón; velar, cubrir con velo. 2. doblar, plegar, colocar en pliegues o plegados. 3. rizar, hacer ondear (la superficie del agua). —*v.i.* 1. caer en pliegues. 2. ondear, rizarse (el agua). 3. (esco.) serpentear (ej., una corriente o riachuelo).
win [wɪn] *v.i.* (*pret., p.p.* WON [wʌn]; *p.pr.* WINNING) 1. ganar, triunfar; prevalecer. 2. lograr un fin; avanzar, lograr pasar. 3. **w. at (chess,** etc.), ganar en (ajedrez, etc.); **w. free,** librarse, desembarazarse; **w. out,** salir victorioso, triunfar (entre muchos); **w. through,** lograr pasar por, lograr éxito, terminar exitosamente; **w. upon,** adquirir importancia para (alguien); ganar la voluntad de (uno). —*v.t.* 1. ganar; conseguir, lograr, obtener, adquirir. 2. ganar, ganarse, merecer (elogios, distinción, etc.). 3. ganar, conquistar, granjear, captarse (voluntad, afecto, estima, etc.); persuadir, inducir (a hacer algo). 4. ganar, alcanzar, llegar a, ej., *w. access,* ganar acceso, *w. the shore,* ganar la orilla. 5. extraer (metal, carbón, etc.) 6. **w. one's bread,** ganarse el pan; **w. one's spurs,** ser armado caballero; (fig.) consagrarse; **w. one's way,** avanzar luchando, abrirse camino; **w. over (someone),** ganarse o conquistar la amistad (apoyo, voluntad, etc.) de (alguien); **w. the favor of,** caer en gracia a; **w. the field,** quedar señor del campo; **w. victory,** conquistar la victoria, triunfar. —*s.* triunfo, victoria.
win, *v.t.* (esco.) secar (ej., heno) a la intemperie; aventar (grano). —(esco., dial.) *var. de* **wind.**
wince [wɪns] *v.i.* recular, encogerse, respingar, sobresaltarse (de dolor, miedo, etc.). —*s.* 1. respingo, sobresalto. 2. devanadora de tintorero.
winch [wɪntʃ] *s.* 1. manubrio, cigüeña. 2. (mec.) montacargas, malacate. —*v.t.* izar por medio de un montacargas o malacate.
Winchester ['wɪn,tʃɛstər, B -tʃɪstə] *s.* winchester, (marca de fábrica) fusil o rifle de repetición.
wind [wɪnd] *s.* 1. viento. 2. (*pl.*) puntos cardinales. 3. resuello, aliento, respiración. 4. (fig.) palabrería, palabras vanas; aire, nada; viento, vanidad. 5. viento, olor, rastro. 6. (mús.) instrumento(s) de viento; (*pl.*) músicos que tocan los instrumentos de viento (en una orquesta). 7. (jer.) plexo solar. 8. viento, ventosidad, flatulencia. 9. **against the w.,** contra el viento; **before**

the w., con el viento; **between w. and water,** (fig.) en posición precaria o riesgosa; **contrary w.**, viento en contra, viento desfavorable; **down the w.**, con el viento; **fair w.**, viento favorable o propicio; **from the four winds,** de todas partes; **in the w.'s eye** (o **in the teeth of the w.**), contra el viento, de cara al viento; **into the w.**, (mar.) contra el viento; **off the w.**, (mar.) con viento en popa; **on a w.**, (mar.) con viento de bolina; **second w.**, fuerzas renovadas; **south w.**, viento del sur, austro; **the w. rises,** el viento se levanta o cobra fuerza; **there's something in the w.**, (fig.) algo flota en el aire, algo se avecina; **to break w.**, soltar ventosidades, ventosear; **to catch** (o **to get**) **one's w.**, recobrar el aliento; **to find out how the w. blows** (o **lies**), (fig.) ver de qué lado sopla el viento; **to fling** (o **cast**) **caution,** etc. **to the w.**, olvidar toda cautela, etc.; **to get** (o **to take**) **w.**, tomar el viento; **to get w. of,** dar con el viento de (la caza); (fig.) enterarse de, intuir, barruntar, percibir en el aire; **to go like the w.**, ir como el viento; **to have one's w. taken,** recibir un golpe en la boca del estómago; quedar sin aliento; **to hit one in the w.**, golpear a uno en la boca del estómago; **to recover one's w.**, recobrar el aliento; **to run like the w.**, correr como una liebre; **to sail** (o **to be**) **close** (o **near**) **to the w.**, ceñir el viento, navegar de bolina; (fig.) estar al borde de lo indecente o ilegal (al hablar u obrar); **to take** (o **to get**) **the w. of,** tomar el viento de; **to take the w. out of one's sails,** (fig.) apagarle a uno los fuegos; **to the four winds,** a los cuatro vientos; **up the w.**, (mar.) contra el viento; **w. ahead,** (mar.) con viento de proa. —*v.t.* 1. airear, orear; ventilar. 2. husmear, olfatear. 3. quitar el resuello a, dejar sin aliento. 4. dejar recobrar el aliento a (ej., un caballo). 5. regular el paso de aire en (un tubo del órgano).

wind [waɪnd] *v.t.* (*pret., p.p.* WOUND [waʊnd] o WINDED; *p.pr.* WINDING) 1. arrollar; enrollar, enroscar; devanar, ovillar, encanillar (hilo, etc.). 2. envolver, cubrir con envoltura. 3. curvar, torcer, mover sinuosamente. 4. dar cuerda a (reloj, etc.). 5. (mar.) levantar o izar (con torno, molinete, cabrestante, etc.); virar (al barco). 6. **w. off,** desenrollar, desenvolver; **w. one's way,** serpentear, dar muchos rodeos para llegar; **w. one's way into (affections,** etc.), congraciarse con, ganarse el afecto de; **w. (a person) round one's little finger,** tener uno (a otra persona) bajo su influencia; **w. up,** enrollar por completo; levantar con torno; templar (cuerdas del violín, etc.); dar cuerda a (reloj); (fig.) avivar, animar, excitar, poner tenso; concluir, finalizar, terminar; liquidar (sociedad, negocio, asuntos, etc.). —*v.i.* 1. torcerse, encorvarse. 2 torcer, serpentear, culebrear (camino, río, etc.). 3. (mar.) virar. 4. dar pasos recruzados (caballo). 5. **w. around,** rodear, enroscarse (a); **w. up,** (fig.) terminar, acabar; liquidarse (compañía, sociedad, etc.). —*s.* 1. combadura. 2. rollo, bobina.

wind [waɪnd, wɪnd] *v.t.* (pret., p.p. WOUND, (raro) WINDED; *p.pr.* WINDING) soplar; tocar o hacer sonar (trompeta, clarín, etc.).

windage ['wɪndɪdʒ] *s.* 1. (arm.) viento, huelgo (de un proyectil). 2. (arm.) fricción del viento, desvío (de un proyectil) por efecto del viento; correcciónviento. 3. (mar.) superficie (de un barco) expuesta al viento. 4. resistencia al viento (estructuras).

windbag [-ˌbæg] *s.* 1. fuelle (de la gaita). 2. (jer.) persona pretensiosa y charlatana.

windblown [-ˌbloʊn] *a.* 1. movido, batido o desarreglado por el viento. 2. (peinado) de cabellos cortos que cubren las sienes como arremolinados por el viento.

wind-borne [-ˌbɔrn, B -bɔn] *a.* llevado por el viento (polen, etc.).

windbound [-ˌbaund] *a.* (mar.) detenido por vientos contrarios.

wind brace, contraviento, pieza de refuerzo contra el viento.

windbreak [-ˌbreɪk] *s.* 1. línea o grupo de árboles o estructuras para cortar el viento. 2. abrigo contra el viento, guardabrisa.

windbreaker [-ˌbreɪkər, B -kə] *s.* chaqueta o cazadora generalmente con capucha usada para las actividades al aire libre.

wind-broken [-ˌbroʊkən] *a.* (vet.) enfisematoso (díc. de los caballos).

windburn [-ˌbɜrn, B -ˌbɜn] *s.* irritación (de la piel) causada por el viento.

wind-chill factor ['wɪndtʃɪl] *s.* sensación térmica.

wind cone, (meteor.) manga de aire; (avia.) indicador cónico de la direccion del viento.

winded [-əd] *a.* falto de aliento, sin resuello.

winder ['waɪndər, B -də] *s.* 1. (mec.) devanador, devanadera, carretel, argadijo, argadillo, canilla. 2. llave para dar cuerda. 3. planta trepadora, enredadera. 4. (arq.) escalón de vuelta, escalón de abanico.

windfall ['wɪndˌfɔl] *s.* 1. fruta caída del árbol. 2. suerte inesperada o súbita; ganga, breva, cucaña, cosa llovida o caída del cielo.

windflaw [-ˌflɔ] *s.* ráfaga de viento, racha.

windflower [-ˌflaʊər, B -ə] *s.* (bot.) anemone, anémona.

windgall [-ˌgɔl] *s.* 1. (vet.) aventadura; agalla. 2. parhelio, parhelia.

wind gap, abra, garganta, paso (en la montaña).

wind harp, (mús.) arpa eolia.

windhover [-ˌhʌvər, -ˌhɑv-, B -hɔvə] *s.* (orn.) cernícalo.

windily ['wɪndəlɪ] *adv.* con un efecto borrascoso; ampulosamente, con mucha palabrería.

windiness [-dɪnəs] *s.* 1. ventosidad, flatulencia. 2. hinchazón, verbosidad, pomposidad. 3. ventolera (de aire).

winding ['waɪndɪŋ] *s.* 1. devanado; bobina, bobinado. 2. arrollamiento, torcedura, torsión, retorcimiento; enroscadura. 3. recodo, recoveco; serpenteo. 4. paso recruzado (de un caballo). 5. vuelta, giro, rodeo. —*a.* sinuoso, tortuoso; serpentino; en espiral; de caracol (escalera, etc.).

winding engine, (min.) máquina de extracción.

winding frame, (tej.) devanadera, devanador, argadillo.

windingly [-lɪ] *adv.* tortuosamente, serpenteando.

winding sheet, mortaja, sudario.

winding up, liquidación, conclusión, desenlace.

wind instrument, (mús.) instrumento de viento.

windjammer ['wɪndˌdʒæmər, B -ə] *s.* (fam., mar.) buque de vela; marinero de un buque de vela.

windlass ['wɪndləs] *s.* 1. (mec.) torno, cabria, árgana. 2. (mar.) molinete. 3. (min.) malacate. —*v.t., v.i.* izar con el torno o molinete.

windle ['wɪndəl] *v.i.* (esco.) devanar o encanillar hilaza; dar vueltas, serpentear; ventiscar (nieve).

windless ['wɪndləs] *a.* sin viento, encalmado; sin resuello.

windlestraw ['wɪndəlˌstrɔ] *s.* (G.B.) hierba seca, bálago (que se usa para hacer cuerdas o para trenzar).

windmill ['wɪndˌmɪl] *s.* 1. molino de viento. 2. molinete, molinillo (juguete). 3. (*pl.*) (fig.) molinos de viento, enemigos imaginarios. 4. (jer.) helicóptero. 5. **to tilt at windmills,** (fig.) arremeter contra molinos de viento.

window ['wɪndoʊ] *s.* 1. ventana; vidriera; ventanal. 2. ventanilla (de coches, tren, etc.). 3. cristal, vidrio (de ventana); hoja de vidrio; ventanilla transparente (en los sobres). 4. escaparate, vitrina, vidriera (Amer.) (de tienda). 5. (mil.) cinta perturbadora (del radar). 6. **to look out of the w.**, mirar por la ventana. —*v.t.* proveer de ventanas.

window blind, persiana, celosía (en el interior), contraventana, postigo (en el exterior).

window box, 1. caja de contrapesos (de ventanas de guillotina). 2. macetero.

window-dress [-ˌdrɛs] *v.t.* poner vistoso, hermosear, aderezar.

window dresser, escaparatista, decorador de escaparates.

window dressing, 1. decorado de escaparates. 2. (fig.) relumbrón, oropel.

window envelope, sobre con ventanilla transparente.

window fastener, pasador o cerrojo de ventana.

window glass, *s.* cristal o vidrio de ventana.

windowpane ['wɪndoʊˌpeɪn] *s.* cristal o vidrio de ventana, hoja de vidrio.

window post, jamba de ventana.

window sash, bastidor o marco de vidriera.

window screen, alambrera, mosquitero de ventana.

window seat, asiento o banco interior al pie de una ventana.

window shade, cortinilla.

window-shop [-'ʃɑp, B -ʃɔp] *v.i.* mirar los escaparates sin comprar; vitrinear (Amer.).

window shutter, contraventana.

window sill, apoyo de la ventana; antepecho de la ventana.

window trimmer, escaparatista, decorador de escaparates o vitrinas.

windpipe ['wɪndˌpaɪp] *s.* tráquea, gaznate.

wind-pollinated [-'pɑləˌneɪtəd, B -'pɔl-] *a.* (bot.) fertilizado por acción del viento (plantas).

windproof [-ˌpruf] *a.* a prueba de viento.

wind rose, diagrama de los vientos reinantes (en un lugar determinado).

windrow ['wɪndˌroʊ] *s.* 1. hilera de heno, hilera de gavillas (puestas a secar). 2. hilera de hojas secas o polvareda formada por el viento. 3. camellón, caballete, lomo (entre dos surcos o al margen del camino). —*v.t.* arreglar en hileras.

wind sail, (mar.) manguera de viento.

wind scale, escala de vientos (para registrar su fuerza y velocidad).

windscreen [-ˌskrin] *a.* (G.B.) parabrisas, guardabrisa.

windscreen wiper, (G.B.) limpiaparabrisas.

wind shake, resquebradura en la madera de árboles (causada por vientos fuertes).

windshield [-ʃild] *s.* parabrisas, guardabrisa, cortaviento, guardaviento.

windshield wiper, (aut.) limpiaparabrisas, desempañador.

wind sleeve, w. sock, manga de viento.

Windsor tie ['wɪnzər-, B -zə-] corbata ancha de seda atada con doble lazo.

wind sprint, (dep.) carrera corta de entrenamiento (para ejercitar los pulmones).

windstorm ['wɪndˌstɔrm, B -ˌstɔm] *s.* ventarrón, vendaval, huracán.

windsucker [-ˌsʌkər, B -ə] *s.* (vet.) caballo que sufre de aerofagia.

wind sucking, (vet.) aerofagia.

windsurf ['wɪndsɜrf] *v.i.* hacer surf a vela, practicar el windsurf hacer windsurfing.

windsurfer ['wɪndˌsɜrfər] *s.* 1. tablista, surfista. 2. tabla de windsurf.

windsurfing ['wɪndˌsɜrfɪŋ] *s.* windsurf, windsurfing, surf a vela.

windswept [-ˌswɛpt] *a.* barrido o arrastrado por el viento.

wind tee, (aer.) T de aterrizaje, "T" indicadora del viento.

wind tunnel, (aer.) túnel aerodinámico.

windup ['waɪnd,ʌp] *s.* 1. conclusión, clausura, cierre, final, desenlace. 2. (béisbol) movimiento circular del brazo para tomar impulso (antes de lanzar la pelota). 3. (dep.) final de partida. —*a.* (con mecanismo) de cuerda (juguete, etc.).

windward ['wɪndwərd, B -wəd] *s.* barlovento. —*adv.* a barlovento. —*a.* 1. hacia el viento. 2. del lado expuesto al viento.

Windward Islands, Islas de Barlovento.

wind-wing [-,wɪŋ] *s.* (aut.) ventana cortaviento.

windy ['wɪndɪ] *a.* (WINDIER; WINDIEST) 1. ventoso, expuesto al viento, barrido por el viento; borrascoso, tempestuoso. 2. (fig.) verboso, pomposo, ampuloso; fútil, frívolo. 3. flatulento. 4. (pr. G.B.) asustado, miedoso, nervioso.

wine [waɪn] *s.* 1. vino. 2. color de vino tinto, rojo obscuro. 3. **in w.,** bebido; **over the walnuts and the w.,** de sobremesa; **when the w. is in the wit is out,** el vino embota el entendimiento; **to take w. with,** beber en compañía de. —*v.i.* beber vino. —*v.t.* convidar con vino; **to w. and dine,** agasajar, tratar con suma hospitalidad.

winebag ['waɪn,bæg] *s. var. de* **wineskin,** bota de vino, odre; (fig.) odre (persona que bebe vino en exceso).

winebibber [-,bɪbər, B -ə] *s.* borrachín, bebedor.

winebibbing [-ɪŋ] *s.* beber desmesurado de vino. —*a.* bebedor.

wine card, lista de vinos (en un restaurante).

wine cellar, bodega de vino.

wine-colored [-,kʌlərd, B -əd] *a.* de color de vino, rojo obscuro.

wine cooler, garapiñera, recipiente para enfriar vino.

wine dealer, vinatero, detallista de vinos y licores.

wine gallon, galón de 231 pulgadas cúbicas.

wineglass [-,glæs, B -,glɑs] *s.* copa (para vino).

winegrower [-,groʊər, B -ə] *s.* viñador, viñatero (Amer.).

winegrowing [-ɪŋ] *s.* industria vinícola, vinicultura. —*a.* vinícola.

wine merchant, vinatero mayorista.

wine palm, (bot.) palma de vino.

winepress ['waɪn,prɛs] *s.* lagar, trujal.

winepresser [-ər, B -ə] *s.* lagarero.

winery [-ərɪ] *s.* (*pl.* WINERIES) lagar; vinatería, vinería (Amer.).

Winesap ['waɪn,sæp] *s.* (E.U.) manzana roja de invierno.

wineshop ['waɪn,ʃɑp, B -ʃɔp] *s.* vinatería; taberna.

wineskin [-,skɪn] *s.* odre, bota de vino, cuero, pellejo de vino.

wine taster, 1. catavinos, catador de vinos. 2. catavino (tubo).

wing [wɪŋ] *s.* 1. ala. 2. aleta (de coche, auto, etc.); aleta (de sillón); hoja (de una puerta); aspa (de molino); oreja, orejeta (de tuerca). 3. ala, sector (de una casa, edificio, etc.). 4. ala, facción, bando (de un partido, movimiento, etc.). 5. (mil.) ala, flanco (de tropa); brigada o escuadra aéreas; (*pl.*) (G.B.) insignia de piloto. 6. (teat.) bastidor, bambalina; (*pl.*) (los) dos lados del escenario. 7. (fam.) brazo (esp. aquél con que se lanza). 8. (dep.) alero, jugador de ala. 9. (arq.) ala. 10. **on the w.,** al vuelo, volando; **to clip one's wings,** (fig.) cortarle las alas a uno; **to take under one's w.,** (fig.) tomar bajo la protección de uno; **to take w.,** alzar o levantar el vuelo, echar a volar. —*v.t.* 1. (lit., fig.) dar alas a. 2. emplumar (una flecha). 3. añadir alas a (un edificio). 4. atravesar volando. 5. herir en el ala o en el brazo; herir ligeramente. —*v.i.* volar, aletear.

wing and wing, (mar.) con las velas tendidas en botalones a ambos lados.

wing area, (aer.) superficie o alcance de las alas.

wing bow, tectriz o cobija de color en el ala (de un ave).

wing case, (ento.) ala protectora, élitro.

wing chair, sillón de orejas.

wing collar, cuello doblado, cuello de pajarita.

wing cover, (ento.) ala protectora, élitro.

wing covert, tectriz, cobija (del ala de un ave).

wingding ['wɪŋ,dɪŋ] *s.* fiesta animada, jolgorio ruidoso.

winged [wɪŋd] *a.* 1. alado, alífero. 2. (fig.) sublime, elevado; rápido. 3. (poét.) alífero, alígero.

winged god, (mitol.) Mercurio.

winged horse, (mitol.) Pegaso, caballo alado.

wing flap, (aer.) alerón.

wing-footed ['wɪŋ'fʊtəd] *a.* (poét.) alípede, alípedo, veloz.

wingless [-ləs] *a.* sin alas, áptero.

winglet [-lət] *s.* ala pequeña, alita.

wing lift, (aer.) sustentación.

winglike [-,laɪk] *a.* en forma de ala, aliforme.

wing loading, (aer.) carga alar, intensidad de la carga, carga por unidad de superficie de sustentación.

wingman [-mən] *s.* (aer.) piloto de flanco.

wing nut, tuerca de orejas, tuerca de alas.

wingover ['wɪŋ,oʊvər, B -və] *s.* (aer.) medio rizo.

wing rail, (f.c.) contrarriel, contracarril.

wing resistance, (aer.) resistencia activa.

wing screw, tuerca de orejas, tuerca de alas.

wing-shaped [-,ʃeɪpt] *a.* aliforme, en forma de ala.

wing shooting, tiro al vuelo.

wingspan ['wɪŋ,spæn] *s.* (aer.) envergadura (de las alas).

wingspread [-,sprɛd] *s.* envergadura de las alas (de un avión, insecto o ave).

wing transom, (mar.) yugo principal.

wing wall, (ing.) muro de aleta.

wingy [-ɪ] *a.* (WINGIER; WINGIEST) 1. alado, alífero. 2. en forma de ala.

wink [wɪŋk] *v.i.* 1. parpadear, pestañear. 2. (gen. con *at*) guiñar el ojo (a); (fig.) tolerar, disimular, hacer la vista gorda, fingir ignorancia (de). 3. centellear, titilar (estrellas, luces, etc.). 4. **like winking,** (jer.) en un abrir y cerrar de ojos. —*v.t.* 1. guiñar (el ojo). 2. hacer (algo) parpadeando; **she winked back her tears,** ella parpadeó para contener sus lágrimas. —*s.* 1. guiño, pestañeo, parpadeo. 2. guiño, seña, insinuación. 3. sueño, siesta. 4. instante, momento. 5. **in a w.,** en un dos por tres, en un abrir y cerrar de ojos; **not to sleep a w. (all night,** etc.), no pegar los ojos (en toda la noche, etc.); pasar la noche en blanco (o en claro); **to take forty winks,** descabezar un sueño; **to tip the w. to (someone),** (jer.) avisar, advertir (a alguien), pasar(le) el dato a (alguien).

winker ['wɪŋkər, B -kə] *s.* 1. anteojera (para caballos). 2. (fam.) (*pl.*) los ojos, las pestañas.

winkle ['wɪŋkəl] *s.* (zool.) caracol marino. —*v.t.* (ú. gen. con *out*) 1. desalojar, extraer, sacar de. 2. eliminar.

winkle, *var. de* **twinkle.**

winnable ['wɪnəbəl] *a.* ganable, que puede ganarse.

winner ['wɪnər, B -ə] *s.* ganador, vencedor, triunfador.

winner's circle, cercado para el (caballo) ganador (junto a la pista de carreras).

winning [-ɪŋ] *s.* 1. triunfo, victoria. 2. (*gen. pl.*) ganancias, lucro. 3. (min.) campo de explotación; pozo (de minas). —*a.* 1. ganador, victorioso, triunfante, vencedor. 2. atractivo, cautivador, simpático.

winningly [-lɪ] *adv.* atractivamente, persuasivamente.

winning manners, don de gentes.

winning post, poste de llegada, (poste de la) meta.

winning side, partido triunfante, ganador.

winnock ['wɪnək] *s.* (esco.) ventana.

winnow ['wɪnoʊ] *v.t.* 1. beldar, bieldar, despajar, aventar. 2. (gen. con *out*) (fig.) seleccionar, entresacar; analizar. 3. (poét.) batir (el aire, las alas). —*v.i.* 1. aventar grano. 2. aletear. —*s.* 1. bieldo. 2. aventamiento. 3. batimiento, aleteo.

winnower [-ər, B -ə] *s.* (máquina) aventadora.

winnowing [-ɪŋ] *s.* aventamiento; zarandeo.

winnowing fork, bieldo.

winnowings [-ɪŋz] *s. pl.* tamo, polvillo de paja.

wino ['waɪ,noʊ] *s.* (*pl.* WINOS) (jer.) borrachín, borracho (dado a beber vino).

winrace ['wɪn,reɪs] *s.* velocidad máxima alcanzada por un caballo victorioso.

winsome ['wɪnsəm] *a.* 1. atractivo, atrayente, agradable; simpático, gracioso. 2. alegre.

winsomely [-lɪ] *adv.* 1. graciosamente. 2. alegremente.

winsomeness [-nəs] *s.* gracia, atractivo.

winter ['wɪntər, B -tə] *s.* invierno. —*v.i.* invernar, pasar el invierno; **w. on,** pasar el invierno comiendo (semillas, musgo, etc.). —*v.t.* hacer invernar. —*a.* invernal, hibernal.

winterberry [-,bɛrɪ] *s.* (*pl.* WINTERBERRIES) (bot.) acebo, agrifolio.

winterbourne [-,bɔrn, -,bʊrn, B -,bɔn] *s.* arroyuelo que fluye sólo en época de lluvias.

winter cherry, (bot.) alquequenje, vejiguilla, vejiga de perro.

winter clothes, ropa de invierno, ropa de abrigo.

winter crookneck, (bot.) calabaza de invierno.

winterer ['wɪntərər, B -tərə] *s.* morador o huésped de la temporada invernal.

winterfeed ['wɪntər,fid, B -tə,-] *v.t., v.i.* alimentar(se), proveer de alimento al ganado durante el invierno cuando no hay pastos disponibles. —*s.* forraje para el invierno.

wintergreen [-,grin] *s.* 1. (bot.) pirola; gaulteria. 2. aceite de gaulteria.

winter-hardy [-,hɑrdɪ, B -hɑdɪ] *a.* resistente al frío (díc. de plantas).

winterish ['wɪntərɪʃ] *a.* invernizo; casi invernal.

winterization [,wɪntərə'zeɪʃən, B -raɪ-] *s.* acondicionamiento para el invierno.

winterize ['wɪntə,raɪz] *v.t.* acondicionar para el invierno.

winter-kill ['wɪntər,kɪl, B -tə,-] *v.t., v.i.* (E.U.) destruir o perecer (plantas) por el frío (del invierno).

winterly [-lɪ] *a.* invernal, invernizo, hibernal.

winter pasture, invernadero.

winter quarters, 1. (mil.) cuarteles de invierno. 2. residencia de invierno.

winter resort, balneario de invierno, lugar de vacaciones de invierno.

winter rose, (bot.) eléboro negro.

winter savory, (bot.) hisopillo, guisopillo, morquera.

winter season, la temporada de invierno, la invernada.

winter solstice, (astr.) solsticio de invierno, solsticio hiemal.

winter squash, (bot.) cidrayote.

wintertide [-,taɪd] *s.* estación invernal, invernada.

winter wheat, (bot.) trigo otoñal, trigo de invierno.
wintle ['wɪntəl] *v.i.* (esco.) tambalear, bambolear. —*s.* tambaleo, bamboleo.
wintry ['wɪntrɪ] *a.* (WINTRIER; WINTRIEST) 1. invernizo. 2. frío, helado; tormentoso.
winy ['waɪnɪ] *a.* (WINIER; WINIEST) 1. vinoso. 2. afectado por el vino.
winze [wɪnz] *s.* 1. (min.) pozo ciego, pozo de comunicación. 2. (esco.) maldición, imprecación.
wipe [waɪp] *v.t.* enjugar o limpiar frotando; **w. away** (u off), quitar (polvo, suciedad, etc.) frotando; enjugar (lágrimas); **w. off the slate,** (fig.) cancelar la cuenta; hacer borrón y cuenta nueva; **w. one's boots on,** (fig.) abusar, humillar; **w. one's eyes,** enjugarse las lágrimas; **w. out,** estregar por dentro; (fig.) destruir, extirpar, aniquilar, borrar con; enjugar, cancelar (deuda); **w. the floor with,** (fig.) aporrear, sopetear; derrotar por completo; humillar; **w. up,** limpiar, secar (el suelo con un trapo, etc.); limpiar, quitar (suciedad, agua, etc. del suelo). —*s.* 1. manotada, revés, bofetada, cachetada (Amer.). 2. remoque, pulla, befa, mofa. 3. limpión, limpiadura. 4. (jer.) pañuelo. 5. (mec.) leva.
wiper ['waɪpər, B -pə] *s.* 1. limpiador, desempañador; trapo, paño (para limpiar). 2. (elec.) contacto deslizante (ej., de un reóstato). 3. (mec.) excéntrica; álabe, leva; manecilla del controlador. 4. (aut.) limpiaparabrisas.
wire [waɪr, B waɪə] *s.* 1. alambre. 2. alambrado, alambrera. 3. telégrafo; telegrama, cable. 4. línea (imaginaria) de llegada (en carreras de caballos). 5. cuerda (de piano o arpa). 6. **to pull wires,** (fig.) tocar resortes, usar de influencias (para lograr algo); intrigar; **under the w.,** en la meta, en la línea de llegada (de carreras de caballos); al último momento; **under w.,** cercado con alambrado. —*v.t.* 1. proveer de alambre; ensartar en alambre; conectar con alambre, alambrar; armar con alambraje. 2. cablegrafiar, telegrafiar. —*v.i.* telegrafiar, cablegrafiar.
wire brush, cepillo metálico, cepillo de alambre.
wire cloth, tejido de alambre, tela metálica.
wire coat, capa de pelo duro (díc. de perros).
wirecutter ['waɪrˌkʌtər, B 'waɪəˌ-ə] *s.* cortaalambres.
wired [waɪrd, B waɪəd] *a.* 1. reforzado por alambre, con armazón de alambre. 2. armado (con conexiones de alambre). 3. revestido de alambre (botellas, etc.). 4. alambrado, cercado con alambre.
wiredancer ['waɪrˌdænsər, B 'waɪəˌdɑnsə] *s.* volatinero, volatinera, equilibrista.
wiredancing [-ɪŋ] *s.* volatines, baile de la cuerda floja.
wired radio, radio de circuito cerrado.
wiredraw [-ˌdrɔ] *v.t.* 1. trefilar (metal). 2. (fig.) sutilizar, limar demasiado.
wiredrawer [-ˌdrɔər, B -ə] *s.* obrero trefilador.
wiredrawn [-ˌdrɔn] *a.* (fig.) excesivamente sutil y detallado (distinciones, diferencias, etc.).
wire entanglement, (fort.) alambrada.
wire fabric, tejido o malla de alambre.
wire fence, alambrado, cerca alambrada.
wire fuse, (elec.) alambre fusible.
wire gauze, gasa de alambre.
wire glass, vidrio armado, vidrio alambrado o reforzado, cristal armado.
wirehair ['waɪrˌher, B 'waɪəˌhɛə] *s.* terrier de pelo fuerte o duro.
wirehaired [-ˌherd, B -ˌhɛəd] *a.* de pelo fuerte (perro).
wirehaired terrier, (zool.) terrier escocés (de pelo fuerte o duro).
wireless [-ləs] *a.* 1. inalámbrico. 2. (pr. G.B.) de radio, radiofónico. —*s.* (pr. G.B.) radio, aparato radiorreceptor. —*v.t., v.i.* (pr. G.B.) transmitir o comunicar por radio.
wireless telegraphy, telegrafía inalámbrica o sin hilos; radiotelegrafía.
wireless telephone, radioteléfono.
wireless telephony, telefonía inalámbrica o sin hilos; radiotelefonía.
wireman [-mən] *s.* electricista de obras, guardalíneas.
wire-mesh spring mattress ['waɪrˌmɛʃ-, B 'waɪə-] colchón de tela metálica.
wire nail, alfiler de París.
wire netting, alambrera, alambre tejido, tela metálica.
Wirephoto (TM) [-ˌfoʊtoʊ] *s.* 1. belinógrafo (*maquina*). 3. belinograma (*foto*).
wirepuller [-ˌpʊlər, B -ə] *s.* intrigante, maquinador, manipulador.
wirepulling [-ɪŋ] *s.* (fig.) intriga, maquinación, uso de influencias (para conseguir algún propósito en una organización, partido político, etc.).
wirer ['waɪrər, B 'waɪərə] *s.* 1. electricista de obras, guardalíneas. 2. cazador que usa trampas de alambre.
wire-record [ˌwaɪrrɪ'kɔrd, B ˌwaɪərɪ'kɔd] *v.t.* grabar en alambre magnético.
wire recorder, magnetófono, grabadora de alambre.
wire recording, grabación en alambre magnético.
wire rope, cable metálico, cable de alambre o de acero.
wire service, servicio cablegráfico de noticias.
wire solder, alambre de soldadura.
wiretap ['waɪrˌtæp, B 'waɪə-] *v.i.* interceptar las líneas telefónicas (o telegráficas). —*s.* 1. conectador para la interceptación de líneas telefónicas. 2. escucha telefónica, interceptación de líneas telefónicas.
wiretapper [-ər, B -ə] *s.* persona que intercepta líneas telefónicas.
wiretapping [-ɪŋ] *s.* interceptación de líneas telefónicas (o telegráficas).
wireway [-ˌweɪ] *s.* (elec.) canal de alambres, conducto superficial de alambres, red eléctrica.
wire wheel, rueda de rayos de alambre.
wirework [-ˌwɜrk, B -wɜk] *s.* alambrera, tela metálica.
wireworks [-ˌwɜrks, B -wɜks] *s. pl.* fábrica de alambres; trefilería.
wireworm [-ˌwɜrm, B -wɜm] *s.* (ento.) 1. larva del escarabajo de resorte. 2. ciempiés.
wiriness ['waɪrɪnəs, B 'waɪərɪ-] *s.* calidad de recio y nervudo.
wiring ['waɪrɪŋ, B 'waɪərɪŋ] *s.* 1. instalación alámbrica, tendido eléctrico, canalización eléctrica. 2. colocación de alambres.
wiring diagram, diagrama de instalación alámbrica, esquema alámbrico, esquema de conexiones.
wirra ['wɪrə] *interj.* (Irl.) ¡ay! ¡ay de mí!
wiry ['waɪrɪ, B 'waɪərɪ] *a.* (WIRIER; WIRIEST) 1. de alambre. 2. fuerte, resistente, nervudo, delgado pero fuerte. 3. metálico, agudo (díc. del sonido).
wis [wɪs] *v.t.* (ant.) saber bien.
Wis., Wisc. *abrev. de* **Wisconsin,** Wisconsin (E.U.).
Wisconsin [wɪs'kɑnsən, B -'kɔn-] *s.* Wisconsin, estado de los E.U.
wisdom ['wɪzdəm] *s.* 1. sabiduría, sapiencia, sagacidad, cordura. 2. (hist.) conocimientos, erudición, instrucción.
wisdom tooth, muela del juicio, cordal; **to cut one's w. teeth,** madurar con los años.
wise [waɪz] *s.* manera, modo, forma; **in any w.,** de cualquier modo; **in no w.,** de ninguna manera.
wise, *a.* 1. sabio, sagaz, cuerdo. 2. juicioso, prudente, sensato. 3. (jer.) conocedor, bien informado. 4. (ant.) docto. 5. **a word to the w. is enough,** al buen entendedor pocas palabras; **the W. Men,** los reyes magos; **to be none the wiser,** no saber más que antes, no comprender mejor que antes; **to get w.,** (jer.) caer en el chiste, darse cuenta del chiste; **to get w. to,** (jer.) darse cuenta de; **to put one w. to,** (jer.) abrirle los ojos a uno respecto a, poner a uno al tanto de. —*v.t.* **w. up,** (jer.) abrirle los ojos a (uno), poner al tanto a (uno). —*v.i.* **w. up,** (jer.) caer en el chiste.
wise, *v.t.* (esco.) guiar, dirigir; instruir, persuadir.
wiseacre ['waɪzˌeɪkər, B -kə] *s.* (fam., hum.) sabihondo, sabelotodo, sabidillo; sabidilla, marisabidilla.
wisecrack [-ˌkræk] *s.* agudeza, salida aguda, comentario chistoso. —*v.i.* lanzar agudezas, hacer comentarios chistosos o agudos.
wisecracker [-ər, B -ə] *s.* persona que tiene salidas frescas o chistosas.
wise guy, (jer.) el que presume de viveza, experiencia, etc., con cierta insolencia.
wise move, un acierto.
wisenheimer ['waɪzənˌhaɪmər, B -mə] *s.* (jer.) sabelotodo, sabidillo.
wisent ['viˌzɛnt, B 'wi-] *s.* (zool.) bisonte europeo.
wisewoman ['waɪzˌwʊmən] *s.* 1. adivina, hechicera, sortílega. 2. partera, comadrona.
wish [wɪʃ] *v.t.* 1. desear, anhelar. 2. querer, desear, pedir, ej., *I w. he were here,* quisiera que él estuviese aquí, *we w. you to do it,* queremos que Ud. lo haga, *I w. to see it,* desearía verlo. 3. **I w. I knew,** ¡ojalá lo supiera!; **it is to be wished (that),** es deseable (que); **w. a Merry Christmas,** dar las Pascuas; desear Feliz Navidad; **w. (something) on (someone),** forzar, imponer (algo) a (alguien); **w. one well (ill),** desear buena (mala) suerte a uno; **w. one were dead,** desear morir, preferir la muerte; **w. someone happiness,** desear la felicidad de alguien. —*v.i.* **w. for,** desear, anhelar. —*s.* deseo, anhelo; (*pl.*) deseos, votos; **best wishes,** muchos recuerdos, un abrazo, saludos; **to make a w.,** expresar un deseo.
wishbone ['wɪʃˌboʊn] *s.* espoleta (de la pechuga de las aves).
wisher [-ər, B -ə] *s.* el que desea.
wishful [-fəl] *a.* deseoso, ansioso, anhelante, ávido.
wishfully [-fəlɪ] *adv.* anhelosamente, con anhelo.
wishfulness [-fəlnəs] *s.* anhelo, carácter anhelante.
wishful thinking, ilusiones, sueños; **to indulge in w. t.,** ponerse a soñar, anticipar lo que se anhela.
wishing well, pozo de los deseos.
wish-wash ['wɪʃˌwɔʃ, -ˌwɑʃ, B -ˌwɔʃ] *s.* aguachirle, aguapié, bebida o infusión aguada.
wishy-washy ['wɪʃɪˌwɔʃɪ, -ˌwɑʃɪ, B -ˌwɔʃɪ] *a.* 1. flojo, débil, aguado (licor, té, etc.). 2. insípido, insulso, desabrido (conversación, lectura, etc.). 3. sin energía, sin convicciones, falto de entereza, sin carácter.
wisp [wɪsp] *s.* 1. hacecillo, manojito (de hierba, paja, etc.), mechón (de pelo). 2. (fig.) rastro, vestigio; jirón (de humo, niebla, etc.). 3. fuego fatuo. 4. **a wisp of a girl,** una chiquilla menuda. —*v.t.* hacer atados de, reunir en haz, hacer manojos de.
wispy ['wɪspɪ] *a.* (WISPIER; WISPIEST) espigado, delgado; pequeño.
wist [wɪst] (ant.) *pret., p.p. de* **wit.**

wistaria [wɪs'tɛrɪə, B -'tɛər-] **wisteria** [-'tɪr-, B -'tɪər-] *s.* (bot.) glicina.
wistful ['wɪstfəl] *a.* añorante, nostálgico, pensativo y melancólico.
wistfully [-fəlɪ] *adv.* con añoranza, con anhelo, con más deseos que esperanzas.
wistfulness [-fəlnəs] *s.* anhelo, aire esperanzado; añoranza, nostalgia; disposición pensativa.
wit [wɪt] *s.* 1. ingenio, inteligencia, entendimiento. 2. juicio, cordura, sensatez. 3. agudeza, sutileza, sal, gracia, ingenio. 4. persona viva e ingeniosa. 5. **to be at one's wits' end,** no saber qué hacer, estar desesperado o perplejo; **to be out of one's wits,** estar fuera de sí, perder los estribos; **to have (o to keep) one's wits about one,** estar en sus cinco sentidos; ser inteligente o despierto; **to live by one's wits,** vivir de su ingenio; **to lose one's wits,** perder el juicio; **to use one's wits,** valerse de su propio ingenio.
wit, (*pret.* WIST [wɪst] *p.pr.* WITTING) 1. (ant.) *v.t., v.i.* saber. 2. **to wit,** es decir, a saber.
witan ['wɪˌtɑn] *s. pl.* (hist., G.B.) miembro(s) del consejo, consejo.
witch [wɪtʃ] *s.* 1. bruja, hechicera. 2. tarasca, vejarrona. 3. (fam.) hechicera, mujer encantadora. 4. (dial.) brujo, mago. —*v.t.* embrujar, hechizar, encantar, fascinar.
witchcraft ['wɪtʃˌkræft, B -ˌkrɑft] *s.* 1. hechicería, brujería. 2. fascinación, embrujo.
witch doctor, exorcista, hechicero, curandero (de una tribu).
witch-elm, *var. de* **wych-elm.**
witchery [-ərɪ] *s.* (*pl.* WITCHERIES) 1. hechicería, brujería. 2. fascinación, embrujo.
witches' sabbath ['wɪtʃəz-] aquelarre, reunión de brujas.
witchgrass ['wɪtʃˌgræs, B -ˌgrɑs] *s.* (bot.) grama, bermuda, bermuda-grass, gramilla colorada, pata de perdiz, agropiro.
witch hazel, 1. (bot.) hamamelis. 2. agua de hamamelis, hamametina.
witch-hunt [-ˌhʌnt] *s.* caza de brujas, persecución de brujas; (fig., E.U.) persecución de disidentes, persecución política basada en calumnias.
witching [-ɪŋ] *s.* brujería, hechicería. —*a.* hechicero, encantador.
witch moth, (ento.) noctuido.
witchy [-ɪ] *a.* (WITCHIER; WITCHIEST) 1. hechicero. 2. brujesco.
wite [waɪt] *v.t.* (pr. esco.) culpar, echar la culpa a, censurar. —*s.* culpa, censura.
witenagemot, witenagemote ['wɪtənəgəˌmoʊt] *s.* (hist.) antiguo consejo anglosajón formado por los nobles prelados y oficiales administrativos.
with [wɪð, wɪθ] *prep.* 1. con. 2. para, ej., *w. God all things are possible,* todo es posible para Dios, *it's holiday time w. us,* es el período de vacaciones para nosotros. 3. por, ej., *they will vote w. the Democrats,* ellos votarán por los demócratas. 4. de, ej., *I am stiff w. cold,* estoy pasmado de frío, *he is silent w. shame,* él está mudo de vergüenza, *the glass is overflowing w. wine,* el vaso rebosa de vino. 5. a, ej., *it rests w. you to decide,* a ti te corresponde tomar una decisión, *the next move is w. you,* le toca a Ud. la próxima jugada, *w. all speed,* a toda velocidad, a toda prisa. 6. **he is one w. us,** está de nuestra parte; **to be w. it,** (jer.) seguir el ritmo o la corriente, estar en ambiente; **to begin w.,** en primer término, por lo pronto; **w. child,** embarazada; **w. God,** (fig.) con Dios, en el cielo; **w. me,** conmigo; **w. no,** sin; **w. that,** con eso, dicho esto; **w. time,** andando el tiempo; con el tiempo; **w. you,** contigo; con Ud(s).
withal [wɪð'ɔl, wɪθ-] *adv.* 1. además. 2. con todo, sin embargo. —*prep.* (ant.) con.
withdraw [-'drɔ] *v.t.* 1. retirar, quitar, sacar; apartar. 2. retractar, revocar, desdecir. —*v.i.* 1. retirarse, apartarse, separarse. 2. (pol.) retirar la moción (en el parlamento). 3. (mil.) replegarse.
withdrawal [-'drɔəl] *s.* 1. retiro. 2. separación, remoción. 3. (mil.) retirada, repliegue.
withdrawal symptom, síntoma de abstinencia.
withdrawing room [-'drɔɪŋ-] (ant.) gabinete, salita privada, ante-alcoba.
withdrawn [-'drɔn] *a.* 1. aislado, apartado. 2. reservado, tímido.
withe [wɪθ, wɪð, waɪð] *s.* 1. mimbre, junco. 2. (mec.) mango flexible. —*v.t.* (dial.) atar con mimbres o juncos.
wither ['wɪðər, B -ə] *v.t.* 1. marchitar, agostar, ajar. 2. (fig.) dañar; helar, fulminar (con la mirada, etc.), dejar atónito. —*v.i.* 1. marchitarse, agostarse, ajarse. 2. (fig.) marchitarse, languidecer, deteriorarse.
witherband [-ˌbænd] *s.* pieza sujetafustes (de la silla de montar).
withered ['wɪðərd, B -əd] *a.* 1. marchito, mustio. 2. desecado, arrugado (rostro, etc.).
witheredness [-nəs] *s.* marchitez, marchitamiento, sequedad.
withering ['wɪðərɪŋ] *a.* en proceso de marchitarse, ajarse o agotarse.
witherite ['wɪðəˌraɪt] *s.* (min.) witerita.
withe rod, (bot.) (variedad de) viburno.
withers ['wɪðərz, B -əz] *s. pl.* cruz (del caballo o de otros animales).
withershins ['wɪðərˌʃɪnz, B -əˌ-] *var. de* **widdershins.**
withhold [wɪθ'hoʊld, wɪð-] *v.t.* 1. detener, retener, contener, impedir. 2. negar, rehusar (permiso, autorización, etc.). —*v.i.* **w. from,** abstenerse de.
withholding tax, (der.) impuesto de retención, impuesto retenido.
within [-'ɪn] *adv.* dentro, adentro, por (a) dentro, en el interior, interiormente; **clean w. and without,** limpio por dentro y (por) fuera; sin mácula; **to make pure w.,** purificar el espíritu; **to stay w.,** quedarse adentro, no salir. —*prep.* 1. dentro de, adentro de. 2. dentro de, en el espacio de, ej., *w. an hour,* dentro de una hora. 3. al alcance de, ej., *w. sight,* al alcance de la vista. 4. a poco de, cerca de, ej., *w. some three miles of the shore,* a unas tres millas de la costa. 5. **to keep w. bounds;** mantener a raya; **to live w. one's income,** vivir de acuerdo a sus ingresos; **to run w. oneself,** correr sin esfuerzo; **w. an ace (of),** as un paso (de), a un pelo (de), a punto (de); **w. an inch (of),** (fig.) a dos dedos (de); **w. a short distance,** a poca distancia; **w. call,** al alcance de la voz, a poca distancia; **w. doors,** puertas adentro, en la casa, dentro de la casa; **w. reach,** a tiro, cerca; al alcance de la mano; **w. the law,** dentro de la ley. —*s.* interior; **from w.,** de adentro.
withindoors [-ˌdɔrz, B -ˌdɔz] *adv.* puertas adentro, dentro de la casa, en la casa.
without [-'aʊt] *adv.* fuera, afuera, por fuera, en el exterior, exteriormente. —*prep.* 1. fuera de, afuera; de. 2. más allá de. 3. sin, ej., *w. my permission,* sin mi permiso. 4. sin (hacer), sin que (haga), ej., *he looked at John w. saying a word,* miraba a Juan sin decir palabra, *they sold the house w. my knowing it,* ellos vendieron la casa sin que yo lo supiera. 5. **it goes w. saying,** se sobreentiende, huelga decir; **to do (o to go) w.,** pasar(se) sin; **w. doubt,** ciertamente; sin ninguna duda; **w. end.** sin fin; infinito, eterno. —*s.* exterior; **from w.,** desde afuera. —*conj.* (dial.) a menos que, salvo que.
withoutdoors [-ˌdɔrz, B -ˌdɔz] *adv.* fuera de la casa, en el exterior.
withstand [-'stænd] *v.t.* 1. resistir a, oponerse a. 2. aguantar, soportar, sufrir. 3. (ant.) obstruir.
withy ['wɪðɪ] *s.* (*pl.* WITHIES) mimbre, junco. —*a.* mimbreño; flexible, ágil.
witless ['wɪtləs] *a.* necio, tonto, estúpido.
witlessly [-lɪ] *adv.* neciamente, tontamente, estúpidamente.
witlessness [-nəs] *s.* necedad, tontera, estupidez.
witling ['wɪtlɪŋ] *s.* persona que se las da de ingeniosa o aguda sin serlo.
witloof ['wɪtˌloʊf] *s.* (bot.) 1. achicoria, chicoria. 2. escarola, endibia.
witness ['wɪtnəs] *s.* 1. testimonio, atestación; confirmación, prueba. 2. testigo. 3. **in w. whereof,** en fe de lo cual; **to bear (someone) w.,** corroborar lo sostenido, confirmar lo manifestado (por alguien); **to bear w. to,** atestiguar; **to call to w.,** tomar por testigo, llamar para atestiguar; **w. for the defense,** testigo de descargo; **w. for the prosecution,** testigo de cargo. —*v.t.* 1. testificar, atestiguar, dar testimonio de, dar pruebas de. 2. presenciar, ser testigo de; p. ext. ser la escena de. 3. firmar como testigo. —*v.i* (con *for, against*) dar testimonio (por, contra); **w. to (something)** atestiguar (algo).
witness stand, (pr. G.B.) **w. box,** banquillo o estrado de los testigos.
witted ['wɪtəd] *a.* ingenioso.
witticism [-əˌsɪzəm] *s.* agudeza, ocurrencia, chiste, gracia.
wittily [-əlɪ] *adv.* ingeniosamente, graciosamente, ocurrentemente.
wittiness [-ɪnəs] *s.* ingenio, agudeza; gracia, donosura.
witting ['wɪtɪŋ] *s.* (dial.) información, noticias. —*a.* 1. instruido, sabedor. 2. hecho adrede, intencional.
wittingly [-lɪ] *adv.* a sabiendas, adrede, de propósito, ex profeso.
wittol ['wɪtəl] *s.* (ant.) cornudo a sabiendas, marido que consiente el adulterio de su mujer.
witty ['wɪtɪ] *a.* (WITTIER; WITTIEST) ingenioso, agudo, chistoso, gracioso, ocurrente.
wive [waɪv] (raro) *v.i.* desposarse (con una mujer). —*v.t.* desposar; casar (a); tomar por esposa.
wivern ['waɪvərn, B -vɜn] *a.* (her.) dragón alado.
wives, *pl. de* **wife.**
wiz [wɪz] *s.* (jer.) mago, as, fenómeno, prodigio.
wizard ['wɪzərd, B -əd] *s.* 1. hechicero, mago, brujo. 2. (fam.) mago, as, fenómeno. 3. (ant.) sabio. —*a.* (jer., pr. G.B.) excelente, tremendo, fenomenal.
wizardly [-lɪ] *a.* hechicero, mágico, maravilloso, asombroso, propio de magos.
wizardry [-rɪ] *s.* (*pl.* WIZARDRIES) hechicería, magia, brujería.
wizen ['wɪzən] *v.t., v.i.* marchitar(se), agostar(se). —*a.* marchito, agostado.
wizened [-ənd] *a.* acartonado, enjuto, magro; marchito, seco.
WMO *abrev. de* **World Meteorological Organization,** Organización Meteorológica Mundial (OMM).
WNW *abrev. de* **west-northwest,** oesnoroeste (ONO).
WO *abrev. de* 1. **War Office,** Ministerio de Guerra. 2. **warrant officer,** suboficial.
woad [woʊd] *s.* 1. (bot.) glasto, hierba pastel. 2. glasto, tinte azul (extraído del glasto).
woadwaxen ['woʊdˌwæksən] *s.* (bot.) retama de tintes.

woald [woʊld] *var. de* **weld.**
wobble ['wɑbəl, B 'wɔb-] *v.i.* 1. bambolear, tambalear. 2. fluctuar, temblar (voz, sonido). 3. (fig.) vacilar, titubear, ser inconstante. *—v.t.* hacer tambalear (se). *—s.* 1. bamboleo, tambaleo. 2. fluctuación.
wobble pump, (aer.) bomba de mano para combustible.
wobble saw, (maq.) sierra elíptica, o excéntrica, sierra circular oscilante.
wobbling ['wɑblɪŋ, B 'wɔb-] *a.* bamboleante, inestable.
wobbly [-lɪ] *a.* (WOBBLIER; WOBBLIEST) 1. tambaleante, bamboleante. 2. fluctuante, temblorosa, temblante (voz). 3. vacilante, indeciso, inconstante.
woe [woʊ] *interj.* (poét.) ¡ay!; **w. is me!** ¡ay de mí! ¡pobre de mí!; **w. be to,** maldito sea, desdichado el que. *—s.* pesar, aflicción, miseria; (*gen. pl.*) calamidad, infortunio; **weal and w.,** las buenas y las malas, prosperidad y adversidad.
woebegone ['woʊbɪˌgɔn, -ˌgɑn, B -ˌgɔn] *a.* 1. desconsolado, melancólico, abatido. 2. desolado (lugar).
woebegoneness [-nəs] *s.* abatimiento, desaliento.
woeful ['woʊfəl] *a.* 1. afligido, apenado, adolorido. 2. lastimero, lamentable, deplorable. 3. miserable, desgraciado.
woefully [-fəlɪ] *adv.* apesaradamente, tristemente, con pena; lamentablemente; miserablemente.
woefulness [-fəlnəs] *s.* pesadumbre, pena, tristeza.
woke, *pret. de* **wake.**
woken ['woʊkən] (ant., dial.) *p.p. de* **wake.**
wold [woʊld] *s.* campiña ondulada y sin bosques; rasa, llanura.
wolf [wʊlf] *s.* (*pl.* WOLVES [wʊlvz]) 1. (zool.) lobo. 2. piel de lobo. 3. (ento.) larva de polillas o escarabajos (que infestan los graneros). 4. persona rapaz; zorro. 5. seductor, libertino. 6. (mús.) disonancia de acordes. 7. **to cry w.,** dar la alarma sin causa; **to hold the w. by the ears,** ver (uno) las orejas al lobo; **to keep the w. from the door,** ganar lo suficiente para no sufrir hambre; **w. in sheep's clothing,** lobo con piel de oveja, hipócrita. *—v.t.* (t. con *down*) devorar, engullir, comer grosera o vorazmente.
wolf cub, lobato, lobezno, cachorro de lobo.
wolf dog, perro lobo.
Wolffian body ['wʊlfɪən-] (embr.) cuerpo de Wolff.
wolffish ['wʊlfˌfɪʃ] *s.* (ict.) lobo de mar.
wolfhound [-ˌhaʊnd] *s.* (zool.) barsoí, bórzoi, galgo ruso.
wolfish ['wʊlfɪʃ] *a.* 1. lobuno. 2. (fig.) feroz, rapaz.
wolfishly [-lɪ] *adv.* ferozmente, con rapacidad.
wolfishness [-nəs] *s.* rapacidad, ferocidad.
wolfling ['wʊlflɪŋ] *s.* lobato, lobezno.
wolf pack, (mil., mar.) flotilla de submarinos para ataque simultáneo.
wolfram ['wʊlfrəm] *s.* 1. (quím.) volframio. 2. (min.) volframita.
wolframic [wʊl'fræmɪk] *a.* volfrámico.
wolframite ['wʊlfrəˌmaɪt] *s.* (min.) volframita, wolframita.
wolfsbane ['wʊlfsˌbeɪn] *s.* (bot.) matalobos, luparia, acónito, uva lupina, uva verga.
wollastonite ['wʊləstəˌnaɪt] *s.* (min.) wolastonita.
wolver ['wʊlvər, B -və] *s.* cazador de lobos, lobero.
wolverine [ˌwʊlvə'rin, B 'wʊlvərin] *s.* 1. (zool.) glotón de América. 2. **W.** (E.U.) natural o habitante (del estado) de Michigan.
Wolverine State, (E.U.) Estado de Michigan.
wolves, *pl. de* **wolf.**
woman ['wʊmən] *s.* (*pl.* WOMEN ['wɪmən]) 1. mujer, hembra. 2. la mujer, las mujeres, el sexo femenino. 3. **she's a young w. already,** ya es toda una mujer, ya está hecha una mujer; **there's a w. in it,** hay una mujer metida en esto, hay faldas de por medio; **tied to a woman's apron-strings,** atado a las faldas de una mujer; **to make an honest w. of,** (hum) tomar por esposa; **to play the w.,** comportarse como una mujer.
woman friend, amiga.
woman hater, misógino, enemigo de las mujeres.
womanhood ['wʊmənˌhʊd] *s.* 1. estado o condición de mujer. 2. feminidad, femineidad, carácter femenino, cualidades femeninas. 3. las mujeres colectivamente, el sexo femenino.
womanish [-ɪʃ] *a.* 1. mujeril, femenil, femenino. 2. afeminado.
womanishly [-lɪ] *adv.* 1. en forma mujeril, como una mujer. 2. afeminadamente.
womanishness [-nəs] *s.* 1. feminidad, femineidad. 2. afeminación, afeminamiento.
womanize [-ˌaɪz] *v.t.* afeminar, tornar afeminado.
womanizer [-zər, B -zə] *s.* tenorio, don Juan, aficionado a las faldas.
womankind [-ˌkaɪnd] *s.* (las) mujeres (en general); (el) sexo femenino; **one's w.,** mujeres de la familia de uno; rama femenina de la familia.
womanlike [-ˌlaɪk] *a.* mujeril, femenil, de mujer, femenino.
womanliness [-lɪnəs] *s.* feminidad, femineidad, naturaleza femenina, carácter mujeril.
womanly ['wʊmənlɪ] *a.* mujeril, femenino, propio de una mujer. *—adv.* mujerilmente, femeninamente.
woman of the street, prostituta, mujer de la vida.
woman of the world, mujer de mundo, mujer experimentada.
woman servant, sirvienta, criada, mucama (Amer.).
woman's rights, derechos de la mujer.
woman suffrage, sufragio femenino, voto femenino.
woman suffragist, sufragista.
woman voter, electora.
woman writer, escritora.
womb [wum] *s.* 1. (anat.) útero, matriz. 2. (fig.) entrañas, seno. 3. **falling of the w.,** prolapso del útero.
wombat ['wɑmˌbæt, B 'wɔmbət] *s.* (zool.) uombat, oso australiano.
women, *pl. de* **woman.**
womenfolk ['wɪmənˌfoʊk] *s. pl.* las mujeres (de una familia, tribu o sociedad).
Women's Lib, Women's Liberation, Movimiento de Liberación Femenina.
womp [wɑmpˌwɔmp, B wɔmp] *s.* (t.v.) mancha hiperluminosa.
won [wʌn, woʊn] *v.i.* (*pret., p.p.* WONNED; *p.pr.* WONNING) (ant.) habitar, morar, residir.
won [wʌn] *pret., p.p. de* **win.**
wonder ['wʌndər, B -də] *s.* 1. maravilla. 2. milagro, ej., *it's a w. he survived,* es un milagro que él haya sobrevivido. 3. (fig.) maravilla, joya; prodigio, ej., *the boy is a w.,* el niño es un prodigio. 4. admiración; curiosidad. 5. **for a w.,** por excepción, por milagro; **nine days' w.,** suceso de interés pasajero; **(it is) no w. that,** no es de extrañarse que, es natural (que); **small w.,** no es de extrañarse; **the seven wonders of the world,** las siete maravillas del mundo; **the w. is (that),** lo que sorprende es (que); **to do wonders,** hacer maravillas; (con *for, to* o *with*) tener un efecto extraordinario (para); **to work wonders,** hacer milagros; tener un efecto extraordinario. *—v.i.* 1. (ú. gen. con *at*) maravillarse (de), extrañarse (de); sorprenderse (de). 2. tener curiosidad, preguntarse, desear saber. 3. **I w.,** (fam.) lo dudo; **I shouldn't w.,** no me sorprendería. *—v.t.* (ant.) admirar, maravillarse de.
wonderberry [-ˌbɛrɪ] *s.* (bot.) solano, hierba mora.
wonder child, niño prodigio.
wonder drug, droga milagrosa, medicamento maravilloso.
wonderful [-fəl] *a.* maravilloso, admirable, prodigioso, estupendo.
wonderfully [-fəlɪ] *adv.* maravillosamente, admirablemente, prodigiosamente, a las mil maravillas, estupendamente.
wonderfulness [-fəlnəs] *s.* aspecto maravilloso; prodigiosidad.
wonderingly ['wʌndərɪŋlɪ] *adv.* 1. con admiración. 2. con curiosidad. 3. con duda, dudosamente.
wonderland ['wʌndərˌlænd, B -dəˌ-] *s.* tierra o país de las maravillas; reino de las hadas, mundo fantástico.
wonderment [-mənt] *s.* 1. admiración, maravilla. 2. curiosidad. 3. sorpresa, extrañeza.
wonder-stricken [-ˌstrɪkən] **wonderstruck** [-ˌstrʌk] *a.* admirado, maravillado, atónito.
wonderwork [-ˌwɜrk, B -ˌwɜk] *s.* acto milagroso, prodigio; trabajo maravilloso.
wonder-worker [-kər, B -kə] *s.* mago.
wonder-working [-kɪŋ] *a.* de efecto milagroso.
wondrous ['wʌndrəs] *a.* maravilloso, admirable; prodigioso. *—adv.* (poét.) maravillosamente.
wondrously [-lɪ] *adv.* maravillosamente; prodigiosamente.
wondrousness [-nəs] *s.* carácter maravilloso, prodigiosidad.
wonky ['wɑŋkɪ, B 'wɔŋ-] *a.* (WONKIER; WONKIEST) (jer., G.B.) inseguro, tambaleante, precario, débil.
wont [wɔnt, woʊnt, wʌnt, B woʊnt] *a.* habituado, acostumbrado; **to be w. (to),** tener la costumbre (de), soler. *—s.* costumbre, hábito. *—v.t., v.i.* (*pret.* WONT; *p.p.* WONT o WONTED; *p.pr.* WONTING) (poét.) acostumbrar(se), habituar(se).
won't [woʊnt] *contr. de* **will not.**
wonted ['wɔntəd, 'woʊn-, 'wʌn-, B 'woʊn-] *a.* acostumbrado; habitual, usual.
wontedly [-lɪ] *adv.* acostumbradamente; habitualmente, usualmente.
wontedness [-nəs] *s.* costumbre, hábito, habituación.
woo [wu] *v.t., v.i.* 1. cortejar, galantear, requebrar (a una mujer). 2. perseguir, buscar, tratar de alcanzar (fama, fortuna, etc.).
wood [wʊd] *s.* 1. madera. 2. leña. 3. madero, palo, madera aserrada. 4. (*gen. pl.*) bosque, selva, monte. 5. (mús.) instrumento. (de viento) de madera; (*pl.*) maderas. 6. (golf.) palo con cabeza de madera. 7. (bolos) bola. 8. **the w.,** tonel, candiota, pipa (de vino, cerveza, etc.); **from the w.,** del tonel; **he cannot see the w. for the trees,** los árboles no le dejan ver el bosque; **out of the woods,** (fam.) a salvo, libre de preocupaciones, ansiedad o dificultad; **to take to the woods,** escapar al monte. *—a.* 1. de madera; para madera; en madera. 2. de bosque. 3. (t. **woods**) silvestre, de los bosques (díc. de plantas, etc.). *—v.t.* 1. poblar de árboles. 2. abastecer de leña. *—v.i.* recoger leña (en el bosque, etc.).
wood alcohol, (quím.) alcohol de madera, alcohol metílico.

wood anemone, (bot.) anemone silvestre.
wood betony, (bot.) 1. betónica. 2. (variedad de) gallarito.
woodbin [ˈwʊdˌbɪn] *s.* leñera.
woodbine [-ˌbaɪn] *s.* (bot.) 1. madreselva. 2. (E.U.) enredadera de Virginia.
wood block, 1. adoquín de madera. 2. (impr.) boj, grabado al boj.
wood-block [-ˌblɑk, B -ˌblɔk] *a.* (impr.) grabado al boj.
wood borer, carcoma.
wood-carver [-ˌkɑrvər, B -ˌkɑvə] *s.* tallista, tallador en madera.
wood carving, talla en madera, entalladura de madera; tallado en madera.
woodchat [-ˌtʃæt] *s.* (orn.) 1. tordo asiático. 2. alcaudón, verdugo.
woodchopper [-ˌtʃɑpər, B -ˌtʃɔpə] *s.* leñador, talador, leñatero.
woodchuck [-ˌtʃʌk] *s.* (zool.) marmota de Norte América.
wood coal, 1. carbón vegetal. 2. lignito.
woodcock [ˈwʊdˌkɑk, B -ˌkɔk] *s.* 1. (orn.) coalla, becada, gallina sorda, gallineta, becacina. 2. (ant.) simplón, papanatas.
woodcraft [-ˌkræft, B -ˌkrɑft] *s.* 1. habilidad de orientarse en los bosques, conocimiento práctico de la vida del bosque. 2. (habilidad en) trabajos de madera.
woodcut [-ˌkʌt] *s.* (impr.) boj, grabado en madera, xilografía.
woodcutter [-ər, B -ə] *s.* leñador, hachero, aserrador.
wood dealer, maderero (el que comercia en maderas).
wooded [-əd] *a.* arbolado, boscoso, enselvado, ej., *densely w.,* cubierto de arbolado, cubierto de espeso arbolado.
wooden [ˈwʊdən] *a.* 1. de madera, de palo, ej., *w. bowl,* escudilla o cuenco de madera, *w. leg,* pata de palo, *w. spoon,* cuchara de palo. 2. (fig.) tieso, rígido, ej., *w. motions,* movimientos rígidos. 3. inexpresivo, estoico (mirada, cara); torpe (maneras, etc.). 4. **don't take any w. nickels** (fam., E.U.) no dejes que te engañen.
wooden face, cara de palo, expresión impasible.
wood engraver, grabador en madera.
wood engraving, (impr.) grabado en madera.
woodenhead [ˈwʊdənˌhɛd] *s.* (fam.) zopenco, zoquete, estúpido.
wooden-headed [-əd] *a.* zopenco, zoquete, estúpido.
wooden horse, (ant.) potro de madera (antiguo castigo en el ejército).
wooden Indian, 1. (E.U.) indio de madera, (figura que antes se colocaba delante de las tiendas de cigarros). 2. (fam.) persona impasible.
wooden leg, pata de palo, pierna artificial, pierna postiza.
woodenly [-lɪ] *adv.* 1. rígidamente. 2. (fig.) inexpresivamente, estoicamente.
woodenness [-nəs] *s.* (fig.) rigidez; insensibilidad, estoicismo.
wooden shoe, zueco (de madera).
woodenware [-ˌwɛr, B -ˌwɛə] *s.* utensilios de madera para mesa y cocina.
wood file, lima para madera.
wood grouse, (orn.) urogallo.
wood hyacinth, (bot.) campánula europea.
wood ibis, (orn.) tántalo.
woodiness [ˈwʊdɪnəs] *s.* consistencia leñosa.
woodland [-ˌlænd] *s.* monte, bosque, región arbolada. — [-lənd] *a.* boscoso, de bosque, selvático, silvestre.
woodlot [-ˌlɑt, B -ˌlɔt] *s.* área reservada para la conservación del bosque.
wood louse, (ento.) cochinilla, porqueta.
woodman [-mən] *s.* 1. hombre del bosque. 2. (G.B.) guardabosque; silvicultor.
woodnote [-ˌnoʊt] *s.* 1. canto de pájaro silvestre; canto natural o salvaje. 2. (G.B.) poesía espontánea, verso improvisado.
wood nymph, 1. (mitol.) ninfa de los bosques, napea, dríada, dríade, oréade. 2. (ento.) variedad de mariposa de colorido vistoso. 3. (orn.) colibrí, picaflor.
wood paper, papel de celulosa.
woodpecker [-ˌpɛkər, B -ə] *s.* (orn.) carpintero, pájaro carpintero, picamaderos, picaposte, picarrelincho, picarro, pico, pito.
wood pigeon, (orn.) 1. paloma torcaz. 2. (E.U.) (variedad de) paloma silvestre.
woodpile [-ˌpaɪl] *s.* pila de leña, montón de leña, tinada.
woodprint [-ˌprɪnt] *s.* (impr.) grabado en boj.
wood pulp, pulpa o pasta de madera (usada para hacer papel).
wood pussy, (E.U., zool.) mofeta, zorrillo.
wood rasp, escofina para madera.
woodruff [-wʊdrʌf] *s.* (bot.) asperilla, rubilla, hepática estrellada, reina de los bosques, hierba de las siete sangrías.
wood screw, tornillo para madera.
wood shavings, virutas de madera, acepilladuras.
woodshed [ˈwʊdˌʃɛd] *s.* leñera, leñero, alero para proteger la leña.
woodsia [ˈwʊdzɪə] *s.* (bot.) variedad de helecho.
woodsman [ˈwʊdzmən] *s.* hombre de bosque, leñador.
wood sorrel, (bot.) acedera menor, acederilla, acetosilla.
wood spirit, 1. (mitol.) silvano, espíritu del bosque. 2. (quím.) metanol, alcohol metílico, alcohol de madera.
woodsy [ˈwʊdzɪ] *a.* (WOODSIER; WOODSIEST) boscoso; selvático.
wood tar, alquitrán vegetal.
wood thrush, (orn.) (variedad de) tordo norteamericano.
woodturner [-ˌtɜrnər, B -ˌtɜnə] *s.* torneador en madera, tornero en madera.
woodwaxen [-ˌwæksən] *s.* (bot.) retama de tintes, retama de tintoreros.
woodwinds [-ˌwɪndz] *s. pl.* (mús.) maderas, instrumentos (de viento) de madera (clarinete, oboe, etc.).
wood-wool [-ˌwʊl] *s.* viruta fina de madera (usada para empaquetar o en vendajes quirúrgicos).
woodwork [-ˌwɜrk, B -ˌwɜk] *s.* enmaderado, maderaje, maderamen; labrado de carpintería.
woodworker [-kər, B -kə] *s.* carpintero; tallador (de madera).
woodworking [-kɪŋ] *a.* de labrar madera, de carpintería. —*s.* carpintería; talla en madera.
woodworm [-ˌwɜrm, B -wɜm] *s.* (ento.) carcoma.
woody [ˈwʊdɪ] *a.* (WOODIER; WOODIEST) 1. arbolado, boscoso, enselvado. 2. de madera; lignoso, leñoso. 3. a madera, ej., *it has a w. smell,* tiene sabor a madera, huele a madera.
woodyard [ˈwʊdˌjɑrd, B -ˌjɑd] *s.* maderería, almacén de maderas, deposito de maderas.
wooer [ˈwʊər, B ˈwʊə] *s.* pretendiente, galán, cortejador.
woof [wʊf, B wuf] *s.* (tej.) 1. trama. 2. tejido, tela, género.
woofer [ˈwʊfər, B -ə] *s.* (rad.) altavoz graves.
wool [wʊl] *s.* 1. lana. 2. ropa o vestido de lana. 3. lanosidad, vello (esp. de plantas); cabello rizado, (esp. de los negros). 4. **dyed in the w.,** teñido en rama; (fig.) intransigente, acérrimo; **(to) go for w. and come home shorn,** ir por lana y salir trasquilado; **much cry and little w.,** mucho ruido y pocas nueces; **to pull the w. over someone's eyes,** engañar a uno como a uno niño. —*a.* de lana, lanar.
wool-bearing [ˈwʊlˌbɛrɪŋ, B -ˌbɛərɪŋ] *a.* lanar, que produce lana.
wool card, carda.
wool clip, producto de la esquila, producción (anual) de lana.
wool combing, cardadura.
woold [wuld] *v.t.* (mar.) trincar.
woolding [ˈwuldɪŋ] *s.* (mar.) reata.
woolen [ˈwʊlən] *a.* (hecho) de lana. —*s.* tela o tejido de lana; (*gen. pl.*) ropa de lana.
wooler [-ər, B -ə] *s.* animal lanar, animal que produce lana.
wool fat, grasa de la lana, lanolina.
woolfell [ˈwʊlˌfɛl] *s.* (G.B.) zalea.
wool-gather [-ˌgæðər, B -ə] *v.i.* soñar despierto. —*v.t.* recoger lana.
woolgathering [-ərɪŋ] *s.* (fig.) absorción, distracción. —*a.* absorto, distraído, ensimismado.
wool grease, grasa de la lana, lanolina.
woolgrowing [-ˌgroʊɪŋ] *s.* cría de ganado lanar.
wool-hall [-ˌhɔl] *s.* (G.B.) mercado de lanas, mercado de productos de lana.
wooliness, *var. de* **woolliness.**
woollen, (pr., G.B.) *var. de* **woolen.**
woolliness [ˈwulɪnəs] *s.* lanosidad, vellosidad.
woolly [ˈwʊlɪ] *a.* (WOOLLIER; WOOLLIEST) 1. lanudo, lanoso; lanuginoso, lanado. 2. rizado, ensortijado, pasudo (Car.) (cabello). 3. (fig.) impreciso, vago, indefinido, confuso (ideas, mente, estilo, etc.); empañado (sonido, voz). 4. (fam.) varonil, pujante; rudo (como los hombres del antiguo O este de E.U.). 5. (bot.) pubescente, velloso. —*s.* (*pl.* WOOLLIES) 1. (jer.) prenda de lana, esp. ropa interior de lana. 2. (O. de E.U., Aust.) carnero, oveja.
woolly bear, (ento.) larva peluda de los gusanos de seda.
woolly-headed [-ˌhɛdəd] *a.* 1. de pelo crespo o rizado, (de cabello) pasudo (Car.). 2. de ideas confusas, de pensamientos desordenados.
woolpack [ˈwʊlˌpæk] *s.* 1. fardo o bala de lana. 2. (meteor.) cúmulo grande.
woolsack [-ˌsæk] *s.* 1. saco de lana, fardo de lana. 2. (G.B.) cojín que sirve de asiento al Lord Canciller (en la Cámara de los Lores).
woolshed [-ˌʃɛd] *s.* puesto o lugar de esquileo.
woolskin [-ˌskɪn] *s.* zalea, vellón.
woolsorters' disease [-ˌsɔrtərz-, B -ˌsɔtəz-] (med.) ántrax pulmonar.
wool stapler, lanero (que clasifica y vende la lana).
wooly, *var. de* **woolly.**
woozily [ˈwuzəlɪ, ˈwʊz-, B ˈwʊz-] *adv.* aturdidamente, confusamente, ofuscadamente.
wooziness [-zɪnəs] *s.* aturdimiento, ofuscación.
woozy [ˈwuzɪ, ˈwʊ-, B ˈwu-] *a.* (WOOZIER; WOOZIEST) aturdido, ofuscado.
wop [wɑp, B wɔp] *s.* (jer., despec.) italiano, bachicha, bachiche (despec., Amer.).
Worcester sauce [ˈwʊstər-, B -tə-] **Worcestershire sauce** [-ʃɪr-, ʃər-, B -ʃɪə-] salsa inglesa.
word [wɜrd, B wɜd] *s.* 1. palabra. 2. palabra (de honor), promesa. 3. noticia, información; aviso, recado, mensaje. 4. santo y seña, contraseña. 5. voz, orden, mandato. 6. (*pl.*) letra (de una composición musical). 7. (*pl.*) disputa, contienda verbal. 8. (ant.) dicho, adagio, sentencia breve, apotegma. 9. **a man of his w.,** hombre de palabra, hombre que cumple lo prometido; **a**

w. in time, una palabra a tiempo, un consejo a tiempo; **a w. out of season,** una palabra a destiempo; interferencia; **by w. of mouth,** verbalmente, de palabra; **in a** (o **one**) **w.,** en una palabra, en resumidas cuentas, en resumen; **in other words,** en otros términos, en otras palabras; **in so many words,** en esas mismas palabras, exactamente así; claramente, sin ambages; **in the words of,** según las palabras de, como dice; **in w.,** de palabra; **in w. and deed,** de palabra y obra; **mark my words,** tome nota de lo que digo, advierta mis palabras; **my w.!** ¡válgame Dios!; **on my w.,** bajo mi palabra; a fe mía; **on one's w. of honor,** bajo su palabra (de uno); **The W.,** (relig.) la Palabra, el Verbo (de Dios); **to break one's w.,** romper su promesa, faltar uno a su palabra; **to bring w.,** traer noticias; **to eat one's words,** comerse sus palabras, retractarse; **to give** (o **to pledge**) **one's w.,** dar o empeñar uno su palabra; **to give the w. to,** dar la palabra de (hacer algo); **to have a w. to say,** tener algo (importante) que decir; **to have a w. with,** tener unas palabras con, hablar cuatro palabras con, hablar con; **to have no words,** no tener palabras, quedarse estupefacto; **to have the last w.,** decir la última palabra; **to have w. from,** recibir noticias de (una persona); **to have w. of,** saber acerca de, recibir noticias de (una persona mediante otra); **to have words with,** trabarse en palabras con, cruzar palabras con; **to keep one's w.,** cumplir o mantener uno su palabra; **to leave w.,** dejar dicho; **to put in** (o **to say**) **a good w. for,** decir unas palabras en favor de, recomendar; **to send w. (of),** mandar mensaje, enviar nuevas (de); **to suit the action to the w.,** cumplir (uno) con lo dicho, obrar según lo indicado; **to take one at his w.,** tomarle la palabra a uno; **to take one's w. for it,** fiarse de la palabra de uno; **to take the words out of one's mouth,** quitarle a uno la(s) palabra(s) de la boca; **to twist one's words,** torcer las palabras de uno; **to waste one's words,** hablar en vano; **upon my w.,** bajo mi palabra. —*interj.* ¡válgame Dios!; **w. for w.,** palabra por palabra, literalmente, textualmente. —*v.t.* formular, redactar; expresar con palabras; enunciar. —*v.i.* (ant.) hablar, disertar, discursar.

wordage ['wɜrdɪdʒ, B 'wɜd-] *s.* palabrería.

word blindness, (med.) alexia, ceguera verbal.

wordbook [-ˌbʊk] *s.* 1. vocabulario, diccionario, lexicón. 2. libreto (de una ópera u opereta).

word-deaf [-ˌdɛf] *a.* (med.) afásico.

word-for-word [ˌwɜrdfər'wɜrd, B 'wɜdfə'wɜd] *a., adv.* literal, textual, palabra por palabra.

wordily ['wɜrdəlɪ, B 'wɜd-] *adv.* con verbosidad, verbosamente, redundantemente.

wordiness [-ɪnəs] *s.* verbosidad, palabrería, redundancia.

wording [-ɪŋ] *s.* estilo, redacción, fraseología; términos, texto (de un mensaje, cable, etc.).

wordless [-ləs] *a.* falto de palabras, (fig.) mudo.

wordmonger [-ˌmʌŋgər, -ˌmɑŋ-, B -ˌmʌŋgə] *s.* palabrero; fanfarrón.

word of command, (mil.) voz de mando.

word-of-mouth [ˌwɜrdəv'maʊθ, B ˌwɜd-] *a.* comunicado verbalmente.

word-painter ['wɜrdˌpeɪntər, B 'wɜd-ə] *s.* escritor hábil, vívido en las descripciones.

word-perfect [-'pɜrfɪkt, B -'pɜfɪkt] *a.* que sabe (su papel, un verso, etc.) al pie de la letra.

word picture, descripción vívida.

wordplay [-ˌpleɪ] *s.* juego de palabras; agudeza (s), dicho(s) agudo(s); intercambio de sutilezas.

word processing, tratamiento de textos, procesamiento de textos, proceso de palabras.

word processor, procesador de textos, procesador de palabras.

word square, cuadrado de palabras idénticas en sentido vertical y horizontal.

word stress, acentuación, acento (de las sílabas de una palabra).

wordy [-ɪ] *a.* (WORDIER; WORDIEST) verboso, redundante.

wore [wɔr, B wɔ] *pret. de* **wear.**

work [wɜrk, B wɜk] *s.* 1. trabajo, labor, faena; empleo, ocupacíon. 2. obra, acto. 3. obra, producto. 4. obra (musical, literaria, etc.). 5. (*pl.*) obras (de construcción, ingeniería, etc.). 6. (*pl.*) fábrica, taller. 7. (*pl.*) maquinaria, mecanismo, movimiento. 8. (mil.) (*gen. pl.*) fortificación, fuerte. 9. **a good day's w.,** una buena labor, un buen trabajo del día; **a learned w.,** una obra erudita; **all in a day's w.,** rutina diaria; gajes del oficio; **all w. and no play,** demasiado trabajo, trabajo sin descanso; **at w.,** trabajando; obrando; en juego, ej., *powerful influences are at w.,* están en juego poderosas influencias; **good w.,** buena obra; **let's get to w.,** ¡manos a la obra!; **the works,** (jer.) (el) todo; una zurra, una paliza severa; la muerte (por asesinato); **to be out of w.,** no tener trabajo, estar sin empleo; **to give (someone) the works,** (jer.) dar una paliza severa a (alguien); asesinar; **to look for w.,** buscar trabajo o empleo; **to make short w. of,** terminar con prontitud; deschacerse rápidamente de; acabar pronto con; vencer rápidamente; **to shoot the works,** (jer.) revelar todo, hablar sin reservas; apostar todo (el dinero); jugarse el todo por el todo. —*a.* de trabajo; para el trajabo. —*v.i.* (*pret., p.p.* WORKED o WROUGHT [rɔt]; *p.pr.* WORKING) 1. trabajar, laborar, estar empleado (en una empresa, oficina, etc.). 2. funcionar, operar. 3. resultar, salir bien; surtir efecto. 4. obrar, tener efecto. 5. pasar lentamente, progresar laboriosamente. 6. poder labrarse (madera, etc.) 7. fermentar. 8. **w. against,** obrar en contra de, oponerse a; tener efecto adverso sobre; **w. at,** trabajar en, ocuparse de; **w. away,** trabajar continuamente, seguir trabajando; **w. down,** descender poco a poco, bajar con cuidado o dificultad; **w. free,** soltarse (con el uso, movimiento, etc.); desatarse (debido a movimiento); **w. in,** trabajar en; entrar, insertarse (ilustración, etc.) en (texto, libro, etc.); adaptarse a; **w. into,** entrar en, penetrar en; **w. loose,** aflojarse; **w. on** (o **upon**), trabajar en, esta ocupado en; influir en, persuadir, incitar; obrar sobre, afectar; **w. out,** salir bien surtir efecto; **w. out at,** resultar en (una suma); **w. round,** cambiar de dirección, virar (viento, etc.) ej., *the ship is working round,* el barco está virando; **w. through,** penetrar, atravesar a fuerza de trabajo, abrirse paso por (muchedumbre, etc.); **w. up (to),** avanzar gradualmente (hacia), tender (a) (cierto fin, crisis, etc.). —*v.t.* 1. labrar, trabajar; formar, moldear.2. efectuar, realizar, llevar a cabo, lograr; producir. 3. poner en funcionamiento, hacer funcionar, accionar (máquina, etc.); hacer trabajar (a persona, animal, etc.); trabajar (a un caballo). 4. (con *in, through,* etc.) hacer pasar, meter (en, por, etc.). 5. manejar (negocio, plantación, etc.)∝plotar (mina); tener a su cargo (un distrito, departamento, sección de ventas, etc.). 6. disponer, arreglar. 7. calcular, resolver (una suma, un problema). 8. coser, bordar. 9. impeler, excitar, inducir. 10. **w. down,** hacer bajar; **w. in,** hacer entrar, meter; insertar (ilustración, tema, etc.); insinuar gradualmente; **w. into,** meter en, intercalar en; inducir, mover; **w. off,** deshacerse de; hacer pasar (cólera, indignación, etc.); lograr vender; pagar con el trabajo (deuda, etc.); **w. one's head off,** trabajar duro, trabajar hasta más no poder; **w. one's way through,** abrirse camino por; pagar uno los gastos con su trabajo; **w. one's will upon,** imponer su voluntad a; **w. out,** calcular, encontrar (suma, etc.), resolver (problema, etc.); agotar (mina, una persona con el trabajo); lograr, alcanzar con dificultad; desarrollar, elaborar (plan, proyecto, etc.); **w. over,** alterar, rehacer; **w. up,** preparar, elaborar; estimular, excitar.

workability [ˌwɜrkə'bɪlətɪ, B ˌwɜkə-] *s.* practicabilidad, viabilidad.

workable ['wɜrkəbəl, B 'wɜkə-] *a.* 1. laborable, labradero. 2. factible, practicable, viable. 3. explotable (mina).

workableness [-bəlnəs] *s.* practicabilidad, viabilidad.

workaday [-kəˌdeɪ] *a.* 1. laborable (día), cuotidiano, de uso diario. 2. (fig.) prosaico, ordinario, vulgar.

workbag ['wɜrkbæg, B 'wɜk-] *s.* bolsa de herramientas o implementos; esp. bolsa de costura.

workbasket [-ˌbæskət, B -ˌbɑs-] *s.* costurero, neceser de costura.

workbench [-ˌbɛntʃ] *s.* banco de taller, banco o mesa de trabajo; banco de carpintero.

workbook [-ˌbʊk] *s.* 1. manual de estudios, (libro de) texto. 2. manual de trabajo. 3. cuaderno de ejercicios (de colegial o estudiante).

workbox [-ˌbɑks, B -bɔks] *s.* caja de herramientas.

work camp, campo de trabajo (para voluntarios); campo de trabajo forzado (para prisioneros).

workday [-ˌdeɪ] *s.* día laborable, día de trabajo, día útil; jornada (laboral). —*a.* 1. cuotidiano, diario, de cada día. 2. prosaico, ordinario, vulgar.

worked-up ['wɜrkt'ʌp, B 'wɜkt-] *a.* excitado, agitado.

worker ['wɜrkər, B 'wɜkə] *s.* 1. trabajador, obrero, operario. 2. (ento.) abeja u hormiga obrera.

worker bee, (ento.) abeja obrera, abeja neutra.

work farm, granja-correccional (para delincuentes menores de edad).

workflow ['wɜrkfloʊ, B 'wɜk-] *s.* circuito de producción.

workfolk [-ˌfoʊk]**workfolks** *s. pl.* trabajadores, obreros, operarios.

work force, 1. destacamento de trabajadores. 2. potencial de mano de obra (de una nación, comunidad, etc.).

workhorse [-ˌhɔrs, B -hɔs] *s.* 1. caballo de trabajo, caballo de tiro. 2. (fig.) persona conocida por ser muy trabajadora.

workhouse [-ˌhaʊs] *s.* 1. (E.U.) correccional, casa de corrección. 2. (G.B.) asilo, hospicio, casa de caridad. 3. (ant.) taller, obrador.

working ['wɜrkɪŋ, B 'wɜkɪŋ] *a.* 1. trabajador. 2. laboral, de trabajo. 3. adecuado, suficiente (mayoría parlamentaria, conocimientos, etc.); utilizable, practicable, que sirve o funciona (hipótesis, etc.). —*s.* 1. funcionamiento, operación. 2. contorsión; estremecimiento. 3. (*gen. pl.*) excavación, mina, cantera. 4. explotación (mina); laboreo; (mar.) maniobra.

working asset, (com.) activo realizable.

working capacity, capacidad de servicio o de funcionamiento.

working capital, (ten.) capital circulante, capital en giro; capital activo, capital de explotación.

working class, clase obrera.

working-class ['wɜrkɪŋˌklæs, B 'wɜk-ˌklɑs] *a.* de clase obrera.

working day, día de trabajo, día laborable o útil; jornada.

working drawing, (arq., mec.) dibujo de trabajo, plano de taller, plano de ejecución, plano de construcción, montea.

working face, frente de ataque, faz de labores (en minas); fondo de labores (en túneles).

working fluid, (mec.) fluido motor, fluido operante.

working hypothesis, hipótesis de trabajo.

working load, carga de servicio, carga de trabajo.

workingman [-ˌmæn] *s.* jornalero, obrero, operario, trabajador.

working model, modelo de guía, esquema, maqueta.

working papers, 1. permiso oficial de trabajo (de un menor). 2. (ten.) papeles de trabajo.

working pressure, (mec.) presión de trabajo.

working speed, velocidad de trabajo, velocidad de funcionamiento.

working stroke, (mot.) carrera de trabajo, carrera de encendido.

working voltage, (elec.) tensión del servicio.

workless [ˈwɜrkləs, B ˈwɜk-] *a.* desempleado, desocupado, cesante, sin empleo, parado (obrero).

work load, 1. cantidad o cuota de trabajo (esperada de un empleado, grupo de trabajadores, etc. durante cierto período de tiempo). 2. cantidad de trabajo que ejecuta una máquina en un tiempo establecido.

workman [-mən] *s.* trabajador, obrero, operario.

workmanlike [-ˌlaɪk] **workmanly** [-lɪ] *a.* 1. esmerado, bien ejecutado, primoroso. 2. (despec.) sin genio, sin brillantez, sin nada más que habilidad técnica, (esp. de obras de arte).

workmanship [ˈwɜrkmənˌʃɪp, B ˈwɜk-] *s.* 1. artificio, destreza, pericia. 2. confección, hechura; mano de obra.

workmate [-ˌmeɪt] *s.* (pr. G.B.) compañero de trabajo.

workmen's compensation insurance, seguro social obrero.

work of art, obra de arte.

work of charity, obra de caridad.

work of the devil, obra del diablo.

workout [-ˌaʊt] *s.* 1. prueba, ensayo (para determinar capacidad o habilidad). 2. (dep.) ejercicio de entrenamiento.

workpeople [-ˌpipəl] *s. pl.* (pr. G.B.) obreros, operarios, gente de trabajo.

workroom [-ˌrum, -ˌrʊm] *s.* obrador, taller, sala o gabinete de trabajo.

works council, (G.B.) comité de trabajadores (para la discusión de problemas de relaciones industriales).

workshop [ˈwɜrkˌʃɑp, B ˈwɜkˌʃɔp] *s.* obrador, taller.

work-shy [-ˌʃaɪ] *a.* flojo, perezoso, vago.

work stoppage, paro, suspensión del trabajo.

worktable [-ˌteɪbəl] *s.* mesa de trabajo, esp. mesa (con gavetas) para labor; mesita-costurero.

work-to-rule [ˈwɜrktəˈrul] *s.* (G.B.) huelga pasiva, huelga de celo (Esp.), trabajo a reglamento (S. Amer.).

work-up [-ˌʌp] *s.* (impr.) levantamiento, espacio levantado (en el pliego); alzamiento (de caracteres).

workweek [-ˌwik] *s.* horas trabajadas en una semana.

workwoman [-ˌwʊmən] *s.* trabajadora, obrera, operaria.

world [wɜrld, B wɜld] *s.* 1. mundo. 2. (fig.) mar, inmensidad, ej., *a. w. of trouble,* un mar de dificultades. 3. (fig.) (*pl.*) montones, sinnúmero. 4. **for all the w.,** exactamente, bajo todos los conceptos; **for the world.** (*ú. gen en negación*) por nada del mundo; **half the w.,** medio mundo, un montón de gente; **in the w.,** en el mundo entero; **it's the same the w. over,** en todas partes se cuecen habas; **not for all the w.,** por nada del mundo; **nothing in the w.,** nada en absoluto; **the other w.,** el otro mundo; **the w. to come,** el otro mundo; **to be out of this w.,** ser algo nunca visto; **to bring into the w.,** traer (o echar) al mundo; **to carry the w. before one,** alcanzar un éxito nunca visto; **to come to the w.,** venir al mundo; **to know the w.,** (fig.) tener experiencia; **to make the best of both worlds,** reconciliar intereses mundanos y espirituales; **to see the w.,** ver mundo; **to the w.,** (jer.) completamente, de remate, ej. *drunk to the w.,* completamente borracho, borracho de remate; **to think the w. of,** tener muy alto concepto de, estimar sobremanera; **where in the w.,** dónde diablos, ej., *where in the w. is that book?* ¡dónde diablos está ese libro?

World Bank, Banco Mundial.

world-beater [ˈwɜrldˌbitər, B ˈwɜld-ə] *s.* campeón del mundo, el (la, lo) mejor en el mundo.

World Court, Tribunal Internacional de Justicia.

world-famous [-ˈfeɪməs] *a.* de fama mundial, mundialmente famoso.

world history, historia universal.

worldliness [-lɪnəs] *s.* mundanalidad, espíritu mundano.

worldling [-lɪŋ] *s.* persona mundana.

worldly [-lɪ] *a.* (WORLDLIER; WORLDLIEST) 1. mundano, mundanal, terreno, terrenal, terrestre. 2. seglar, secular, profano. 3. corrido, avezado en las cosas del mundo.

worldly-minded [ˌwɜrldlɪˈmaɪndəd, B ˈwɜld-] *a.* mundano, de intereses materiales.

worldly-mindedness [-nəs] *s.* mundanería, mundanalidad.

worldly-wise [ˈwɜrldlɪˌwaɪz, B ˈwɜld-] *a.* avezado en las cosas del mundo.

world map, mapamundi, planisferio.

world power, potencial mundial.

world record, récord mundial, marca mundial.

world-record holder, plusmarquista mundial.

world series, (E.U.) serie mundial (serie de encuentros de béisbol entre los campeones de las dos ligas mayores de E.U. para decidir el campeonato profesional).

World's Fair, exposición universal.

world-shaking [-ˌʃeɪkɪŋ] *a.* sensacional; importante, de enormes consecuencias, que afecta o importa a todo el mundo.

World War, guerra mundial.

world-weariness [-ˌwɪrɪnəs, B -ˌwɪər-] *s.* aburrimiento de la vida, cansancio de las cosas del mundo.

world-weary [-ˌwɪrɪ, B -ˌwɪərɪ] *a.* cansado de este mundo, cansado de la vida; aburrido de los placeres materiales.

world-wide [-ˈwaɪd] *a.* global, mundial.

World-Wide Web, telaraña mundial.

worm [wɜrm, B wɜm] *s.* 1. gusano, lombriz; helminto. 2. (fig.) gusano (persona insignificante o vil). 3. rosca, filete (de tornillo); serpentín de alambique; (mec.) tornillo sin fin. 4. (*pl.*) lombrices, helmintiasis. 5. (anat.) vermis, apéndice vermiforme. 6. (zool.) lita, landrilla. 7. **w. of conscience,** (fig.) remordimiento de (la) conciencia. —*v.i.* 1. arrastrarse o deslizarse como un gusano. 2. **w. into.** insinuarse en; **w. out of,** salir laboriosamente de. —*v.t.* 1. librar de gusanos o lombrices. 2. quitar (la lita) al perro. 3. (mar.) entrañar (un cabo). 4. **w. oneself into,** introducirse en (como un gusano); (fig.) insinuarse en (confidencia, etc.); **w. one's way (in, through,** etc.), pasar arrastrándose (adentro, por, etc.); **w. out (of),** sonsacar (a), arrancar con artimañas (a).

worm drive, (mec.) trasmisión por tornillo sin fin, mando a sinfín.

worm-eaten [ˈwɜrmˌitən, B ˈwɜm-] *a.* 1. agusanado, apolillado, carcomido. 2. (fig.) anticuado, inservible.

worm fence, cerca de zigzag.

worm gear, (mec.) engranaje de tornillo sin fin, engranaje helicoidal; rueda de tornillo sin fin.

wormhole [-ˌhoʊl] *s.* agujero o picadura de gusano.

wormlike [-ˌlaɪk] *a.* vermiforme, vermicular.

wormroot [-ˌrut] *s.* (bot.) espigelia.

wormseed [-ˌsid] *s.* 1. (bot.) santónico. 2. (bot.) pazote, pasote, apasote, hierba hormiguera, hierba de Santa María del Brasil. 3. (farm.) semencontra, santónico (cabezuela de la planta).

worm wheel, (mec.) rueda dentada de tornillo sin fin.

wormwood [-ˌwʊd] *s.* 1. (bot.) ajenjo, absintio, alosna. 2. (fig.) amargor, amargura, mortificación.

wormy [ˈwɜrmɪ, B ˈwɜmɪ] *a.* (WORMIER; WORMIEST) 1. gusaniento, gusanoso, agusanado. 2. carcomido, apolillado. 3. vermiforme. 4. (fig.) rastrero, servil; tortuoso, solapado.

worn [wɔrn, B wɔn] *p.p. de* **wear.**

worn joke, chiste trillado, broma gastada.

worn-out [ˈwɔrnˈaʊt, B ˈwɔn-] *a.* gastado, raído; agotado, cansado, rendido.

worriment [ˈwɜrɪmənt, B ˈwʌrɪ-] *s.* inquietud, preocupación; molestia.

worrisome [-səm] *a.* 1. aprensivo, inquieto, preocupado. 2. molesto, fastidioso, inquietante.

worry [ˈwɜrɪ, B ˈwʌrɪ] *v.t.* (*pret., p.p.* WORRIED; *p.pr.* WORRYING) 1. sacudir y lacerar con los dientes. 2. atormentar, acosar; fastidiar, importunar, molestar. 3. preocupar, inquietar. 4.**w. oneself,** inquietarse, preocuparse (indebidamente); **w. out,** (fig.) resolver (problema, etc.) abordándolo una y otra vez. —*v.i.* 1. preocuparse, inquietarse, incomodarse. 2. mover esforzándose; (con *through* o *along*) pasar a duras penas; componérselas con dificultad. 3. **I should w.,** (fam.) ¡qué me importa! —*s.* (*pl.* WORRIES) 1. tormento, molestia. 2. preocupación, inquietud, ansiedad, zozobra.

worrywart [-ˌwɔrt, B -ˌwɔt] *s.* persona aprensiva, dada a preocuparse.

worse [wɜrs, B wɜs] *a.* peor; **to be none the w. for (it),** no haberlo dañado en absoluto (la experiencia, el percance, etc.); no ser menos aceptable o deseable; **to get (o to grow) w., empeorar(se)** (esp. un enfermo); **to make (it) w.,** (para) empeorar; **w. and w.,** de mal en peor, peor que peor; **w. luck,** por mala suerte, desgraciadamente; **w. than ever,** peor que nunca. —*s.* 1. algo peor, cosa peor. 2. **a change (o turn) for the w.,** empeoramiento; **to go from bad to w.,** ir de mal en peor; **to have the w., (of),** salir perdiendo (de), ser derrotado (en). —*adv.* peor, menos bien, de modo peor; **to be w. off,** quedar peor, estar en situación peor (que antes).

worsen [ˈwɜrsən, B ˈwɜs-] *v.t., v.i.* empeorar(se), agravar(se).

worsening [-ənɪŋ] *s.* empeoramiento.

worship [ˈwɜrʃəp, B ˈwɜʃɪp] *s.* 1. adoración, culto; reverencia. 2. merced, señoría, ej., *your w.,* vuestra merced, usía. 3. (ant.) dignidad, mérito; reputación. —*v.t.* (*pret., p.p.* WORSHIPED

O WORSHIPPED; *p.pr.* WORSHIPING O WORSHIPPING) 1. adorar, rendir culto (a); reverenciar. 2. (fig.) idolatrar, adorar.

worshiper [-ər, B -ə] *s.* adorador, cultor, devoto.

worshipful [-fəl] *a.* 1. adorador. 2. (como tratamiento gen. con. **the,** G.B.) honorable, estimable, venerable.

worshipfully [-fəlɪ] *adv.* con adoración, respetablemente, venerablemente.

worshipless [-ləs] *a.* no adorado, no venerado.

worshipper, (pr. G.B.) *var. de* **worshiper.**

worst [wɜrst, B wɜst] *a.* peor; pésimo, malísimo. —*s.* lo peor, lo más malo, lo pésimo; **at (the) w.,** en la peor situación posible, en su peor aspecto; en el peor de los casos, a peor andar; **if w. comes to w.,** si pasa lo peor; **to get the w. of it,** llevar la peor parte, ser derrotado; **to have the w. (of),** ser derrotado (en); **to make the w. of,** considerar o revelar el peor aspecto de (algo). —*adv.* pésimamente, del peor modo posible. —*v.t.* aventajar, vencer, derrotar, superar.

worsted ['wʊstəd] *s.* (tej.) 1. estambre. 2. tela de lana peinada.

wort [wɜrt, B wɜt] *s.* (*ú. gen. en vocablos compuestos*) (bot.) planta, hierba, ej., *madwort* (raspilla; camelina).

wort, *s.* mosto de cerveza, cerveza sin fermentar.

worth [wɜrθ, B wɜθ] *prep.* 1. valorado en tal precio; digno de, merecedor de. 2. **for all one is w.,** con todas las fuerzas, a más no poder; **no to be w. damn,** (jer.) no valer nada, no servir para nada; **to be w.,** valer; merecer; valer la pena; tener, poseer, ej., *it is w. a fortune,* vale una fortuna, *what is it w.?* ¿cuánto vale esto? *it is not w. doing,* no vale la pena hacerlo, *he spent all he was w. on this scheme,* gastó todo lo que tenía en este proyecto; **to be w. one's salt,** servir muy bien, valer mucho; ser digno del nombre; **to be w. one's weight in gold,** valer su peso en oro. —*s.* 1. valor, valía, ej., *of little w.,* de poco valor. 2. mérito, excelencia, ej., *men of great w.,* hombres de gran mérito. 3. riqueza, fortuna, ej., *their joint w. is well over a million,* sus fortunas en conjunto llegan a mucho más de un millón. 4.**w. of,** por (un) valor de, ej., *$100 w. of spare parts,* repuestos por (un) valor de $100.

worth, *v.i.* (ant.) tornarse, volverse.

worthful ['wɜrθfəl, B 'wɜθ-] *a.* 1. meritorio, estimable, apreciado. 2. valioso, estimado.

worthily ['wɜrðəlɪ, B 'wɜðɪ-] *adv.* 1. dignamente. 2. merecidamente, como corresponde.

worthiness [-ɪnəs] *s.* dignidad; mérito, merecidamente.

worthless ['wɜrθləs, B 'wɜθ-] *a.* 1. sin valor, inservible, inútil. 2. despreciable.

worthlessly [-lɪ] *adv.* inútilmente, sin provecho; **to live w.,** llevar una vida inútil o sin provecho.

worthlessness [-nəs] *s.* inutilidad; falta de valor o mérito.

worth while, *a.* **to be w.,** valer la pena, ser de mérito.

worthwhile ['wɜrθ'hwaɪl, -'waɪl, B 'wɜθ-] *a.* de mérito, digno de atención, ej. *a. worthwhile book,* un libro de mérito, un libro digno de atención.

worthwhileness [-nəs] *s.* mérito, utilidad.

worthy ['wɜrðɪ, B 'wɜðɪ] *a.* (WORTHIER; WORTHIEST) 1. apreciable, meritorio, digno; estimable, respetable. 2. (ant.) merecido. 3. **w. of,** acreedor a, digno de, merecedor de, ej., *w. of notice,* digno de notarse, *w. of the name,* digno de tal nombre. —*s.* (*pl.* WORTHIES) persona ilustre, notabilidad, prócer.

wot [wɑt, B wɔt] (ant.) *primera y tercera pers. sing. pres. indic. de* **wit** (saber).

Wotan ['vɔtɑn, 'voʊ-] *s.* (mitol.) Wodan, Wotan, dios germánico identificado con el dios escandinavo Odín.

would [wʊd, wəd] *pret. de* **will.**

would [woʊld] (bot.) *var. de* **weld.**

would-be ['wʊd,bi] *a.* supuesto, pretendido; aspirante, que pretende ser.

wouldn't ['wʊdənt] *contr. de* **would not.**

wouldst [wʊdst] (ant.) *segunda pers. del pret. de* **will.**

wound [wund] *s.* 1. herida, lesión, llaga. 2. (fig.) herida, agravio, ofensa. —*v.t., v.i.* herir; **w. to the quick,** herir en lo vivo.

wound [waʊnd] *pret., p.p. de* **wind.**

wounded ['wundəd] *a.* herido; **the w.,** los heridos.

woundless [-ləs] *a.* ileso, sin heridas.

woundwort [-,wɜrt, B -,wɜt] *s.* (bot.) vulneraria.

wove [woʊv] *pret., p.p. de* **weave.**

woven ['woʊvən] *p.p. de* **weave.**

wove paper, papel avitelado.

wow [waʊ] *s.* (rad., electrón.) aullido, ululación (del sonido reproducido).

wow, (jer.) *s.* éxito notable. —*v.t.* (jer.) embelesar, cautivar, conquistar.

wowser ['waʊzər, B -zə] *s.* (pr. Aust.) puritano, formalista.

WRAC [ræk] *abrev. de* **Women's Royal Army Corps,** Sección Femenina del Ejército de G.B.

wrack [ræk] *s.* 1. nave naufragada; ruinas, despojos, restos. 2. naufragio. 3. algas secas (arrojadas por el mar a la playa). 4. (esco.) yerba, maleza. —*v.t.* hacer naufragar; arruinar, demoler.

wrack, *var. de* **rack.**

wrackful ['rækfəl] *a.* destructivo, injurioso.

WRAF *abrev. de* **Women's Royal Air Force,** Sección Femenina de la Real Fuerza Aérea de G.B.

wraith [reɪθ] *s.* aparecido, fantasma, espectro.

wrangle ['ræŋgəl] *v.i.* reñir, pendenciar, disputar, altercar, pelotear, argüir. —*v.t.* 1. obtener arguyendo, conseguir a la fuerza. 2. (O. de E.U.) rodear (ganado). —*s.* riña, pendencia, disputa, altercado, pelotera.

wrangler [-glər, B -glə] *s.* 1. pendenciero, pleitista, disputador. 2. (O. de E.U.) vaquero, resero, manadero.

wrap [ræp] *v.t.* (*pret. y p.p.* WRAPPED; *p.pr.* WRAPPING) enrollar, envolver, cubrir; **to be wrapped up in,** (fig.) estar absorto en (algo); estar prendado de, estar entregado o dedicado a (alguien); **w. around,** doblar alrededor de; **w. up,** envolver, enrollar; cubrir, apañar, arropar; concluir, finalizar. —*v.i.* **w. round (o around),** doblarse alrededor; **w. up (in),** envolverse, arroparse (en); quedar envuelto (en). —*s.* 1. manta, frazada, mantón, pañolón, bufanda, cobija (Amer.), bata; **to put one's wraps on,** abrigarse. 2. vuelta, doblamiento. 3. (*esp. en pl.*) cubierta, cobertura, cubertura. 4. **to keep under wraps,** mantener en secreto, ej., *the plan was kept under wraps,* (fig.) el plan se mantuvo en secreto.

wraparound ['ræpə,raʊnd] *s.* 1. capa, manto. 2. pliego inserto de cuatro páginas (en un libro).

wrapper [-ər, B -ə] *s.* 1. envoltura; funda, cubierta, cobertura. 2. tabaco de hoja (para cigarros). 3. sobrecubierta (de libro). 4. bata, peinador.

wrapping [-ɪŋ] *s.* envoltura, cubierta.

wrapping paper, papel de envolver o embalar.

wrap-up [-,ʌp] *s.* resumen de noticias, relato o sumario condensado de noticias.

wrasse [ræs] *s.* (ict.) labro.

wrath [ræθ, B rɔθ] *s.* ira, cólera, furia. —*a.* (ant.) muy irascible, violento, turbulento.

wrathful ['ræθfəl, B 'rɔθ-] *a.* airado, iracundo, furioso, colérico.

wrathfully [-fəlɪ] *adv.* airadamente, furiosamente, coléricamente.

wrathy [-ɪ] *a.* (WRATHIER; WRATHIEST) airado, iracundo, furioso, colérico.

wreak [rik] *v.t.* descargar, dar rienda suelta a (la cólera); **w. vengeance (o punishment) on,** infligir venganza (o castigo) a.

wreakful ['rikfəl] *a.* vengativo, vindicativo.

wreath [riθ] *s.* (*pl.* WREATHS [riðz]) 1. corona (de flores, hojas, etc.), guirnalda, festón. 2. espiral (de humo). 3. (poét.) circulo (de bailarines, espectadores, etc.).

wreathe [rið] *v.t.* 1. retorcer. 2. entrelazar, tejer (guirnaldas o coronas). 3. enguirnaldar, ceñir. 4. envolver, ej., *his face was wreathed in smiles,* su rostro estaba envuelto en sonrisas. 5. **w. round,** rodear, enroscar. —*v.i.* 1. retorcerse, contorsionarse. 2. salir o subir en espirales, serpentear (humo, etc.).

wreathy ['riðɪ] *a.* retorcido, espiral; serpenteado, serpenteante.

wreck [rɛk] *s.* 1. naufragio, zozobra; ruina, fracaso. 2. buque naufragado, restos de un naufragio; restos, pecios, destrozos. 3. (der.) bienes varados de un naufragio. 4. **to be a (o an old) w.,** estar hecho un cascajo; estar muy estropeado. —*v.t.* 1. hacer naufragar, (hacer) zozobrar, (hacer) hundir, echar a pique. 2. destrozar, destruir (tren, avión, etc.); demoler (edificio). 3. arruinar; desbaratar (planes, empresa, esperanzas, etc.); deshacer (nervios, etc.). —*v.i.* 1. naufragar, zozobrar, hundirse, irse a pique. 2. destrozarse, destruirse. 3. fracasar, arruinarse.

wreckage ['rɛkɪdʒ] *s.* restos de un naufragio, pecios; despojos, ruinas, restos.

wrecked [rɛkt] *a.* náufrago (marinero, etc.).

wrecker ['rɛkər, B -ə] *s.* 1. demoledor, derribador; persona que trata de causar naufragios para hacer pillaje. 2. (mar.) salvador de buques, buque de salvamento. 3. (aut.) camión de auxilio, carro grúa, coche taller.

wrecking [-ɪŋ] *s.* salvamento, salvataje; demolición (de edificios, etc.).

wrecking amendment, (pol.) modificación de un proyecto de ley con intención de frustrar su principal finalidad.

wrecking ball, bola rompedora o demoledora (para derribos).

wrecking bar, barra sacaclavos, barra cuello de ganso.

wrecking car, (aut.) camión de auxilio, carro grúa.

wrecking crane, 1. grúa demoledora. 2. (fc.) grúa de auxilio o de salvamento.

wren [rɛn] *s.* (orn.) reyezuelo, ratona, abadejo, régulo.

Wren, *s.* (G.B.) miembro del servicio femenino de la marina.

wrench [rɛntʃ] *s.* 1. torcedura violenta, arranque o tirón torcido. 2. pena o dolor agudo. 3. (med.) distensión, esguince, desguince, dislocadura, luxación; detorsión, distorsión. 4. (mec.) llave, llave de tuerca. —*v.t.* 1. torcer o retorcer violentamente; arrebatar torciendo; forzar, forcejar torciendo. 2. dislocar, desencajar, sacar de quicio. 3. (fig.) tergiversar, torcer, deformar, alterar (el sentido de una frase, los hechos, etc.).

wrest [rɛst] *v.t.* 1. (gen. con *from*) arrancar torciendo, arrebatar con violencia. 2. (fig.) torcer, deformar, falsear. —*s.* 1. torsión violenta, torcimiento. 2. llave o palanca para afinar (piano, arpa, etc.).

wrester ['rɛstər, B -ə] *s.* tergiversador, tergiversadora.

wrestle ['rɛsəl] *v.i.* 1. luchar. 2. pelear, lidiar. 3. forcejear (con), pugnar (con o contra). —*v.t.* luchar con, pelear con. —*s.* 1. lucha, partido de lucha. 2. contienda, pugna.
wrestler ['rɛslər, B -lə] *s.* luchador.
wrestling [-lɪŋ] *s.* (dep.) lucha.
wrest pin, clavija (de pianos, arpas, etc.).
wrest plank, (mús.) clavijero (del piano).
wretch [rɛtʃ] *s.* 1. desdichado, desgraciado, infeliz. 2. hombre degradado, canalla, sinvergüenza.
wretched ['rɛtʃəd] *a.* 1. miserable, infeliz, desdichado. 2. lastimoso, doloroso, funesto. 3. despreciable, vil, detestable, sinvergüenza. 4. pésimo, malísimo.
wretchedly [-lɪ] *adv.* 1. miserablemente. 2. vilmente. 3. pésimamente.
wretchedness [-nəs] *s.* 1. miseria, desdicha, desgracia. 2. bajeza, ruindad, vileza.
wriggle ['rɪgəl] *v.i.* 1. menearse, agitarse, serpentear, culebrear; retorcerse, contorcerse. 2. **w. away** (u **off**), escapar(se) culebreando, escabullirse; **w. into,** insinuarse en; **w. out of (a difficulty,** etc.), librarse de (una dificultad, etc.). —*v.t.* menear (cola, mano, etc.); hacer serpentear; **w. one's way,** deslizarse serpenteando. —*s.* meneo, contorsión; serpenteo, culebreo.
wriggler ['rɪglər, B -lə] *s.* larva de mosquito.
wriggling [-lɪŋ] *s.* meneo, ondulación, coleadura, serpenteo.
wriggly [-lɪ] *a.* sinuoso, tortuoso, serpenteante.
wright [raɪt] *s.* (*ú. gen. en vocablos compuestos*) artífice, autor, ej., *shipwright,* constructor naval, *playwright,* dramaturgo.
wring [rɪŋ] *v.t.* (*pret., p.p.* WRUNG [rʌŋ] *p.pr.* WRINGING) 1. torcer violentamente, retorcer, forzar con torcedura. 2. (fig.) atormentar, torturar (el ánimo, espíritu, etc.). 3. **w. from,** obtener por extorsión, arrancar (dinero); sacar por fuerza (la verdad); sonsacar (mediante amenazas, etc.), ej., *w. a. confession from a prisoner,* arrancar una confesión a un preso; **w. (someone's) hand,** dar un apretón de mano a (alguien); **w. off,** arrancar retorciendo; **w. one's hands,** retorcerse las manos; **w. out,** retorcer, estrujar (ropa húmeda); exprimir (agua); **w. the neck of,** torcer el pescuezo de; **wringing wet,** empapado. —*s.* 1. torsión. 2. estrujamiento. 3. apretón (de manos).
wringer ['rɪŋər, B -ə] *s.* máquina o rodillo para exprimir (ropa húmeda, etc.); máquina de escurrir ropa.
wrinkle ['rɪŋkəl] *s.* 1. arruga. 2. (fam.) método, técnica, truco. —*v.i.* arrugarse, encarrujarse. —*v.t.* arrugar, encarrujar, fruncir; **w. one's brow,** fruncir o arrugar el ceño o entrecejo.
wrinkled [-kəld] *a.* arrugado, rugoso, encarrujado.
wrinkly [-klɪ] *a.* arrugado, rugoso.
wrist [rɪst] *s.* 1. (anat.) muñeca; codillo (en los cuadrúpedos). 2. puño (de la camisa). 3. (mec.) pasador de pistón.
wristband ['rɪst,bænd] *s.* puño de camisa, bocamanga.
wristlet [-lət] *s.* 1. manguito para la muñeca; muñequera. 2. (jer.) esposas.
wristlock [-,lɑk, B -,lɔk] *s.* (lucha) llave con que se retuerce la muñeca al adversario.
wrist pin, (mec.) pasador de pistón, pasador de articulación, bolón.
wristwatch [-,wɑtʃ, B -,wɔtʃ] *s.* reloj (de) pulsera.
writ [rɪt] *s.* 1. escrito, escritura. 2. (der.) auto, mandato, mandamiento, oficio, orden judicial, decreto judicial, ejecutoria. 3. **the Holy Writ,** la Sagrada Escritura.
writ of summons, (der.) emplazamiento.
write [raɪt] *v.t.* (*pret.* WROTE [rout] *p.p.* WRITTEN ['rɪtən] o (ant.) WRIT [rɪt]; *p.pr.* WRITING) 1. escribir. 2. escribir (en), escribir con, ej., *w. German well,* escribir bien en o el alemán, *w. in ink,* escribir con tinta. 3. **w. a good hand,** tener buena letra; **w. down,** apuntar, anotar; describir o representar como; denigrar o desdorar por escrito; (ten.) rebajar el valor de, castigar (un activo); reducir el valor nominal de (acciones); **w. in,** insertar en, intercalar en; **w. off,** (ten.) castigar; (fig.) dar por perdido; **w. oneself,** calificarse, titularse; **w. oneself out,** acabársele a uno las ideas (de escritor); **w. out,** formular por escrito; escribir en forma completa, escribir sin abreviar (una palabra); extender (cheque, orden, etc.); **w. up,** poner al día, actualizar (diario, libros contables, etc.); dar forma a, elaborar, redactar (relato o artículo a base de datos, información, etc.); dar bombo a, bombear (esp. en la prensa); (ten.) valorar en demasía (una partida del activo); aumentar el precio de. —*v.i.* 1. escribir. 2. **w. away,** dejar correr la pluma, escribir mucho y rápido; **w. back,** contestar por escrito; **w. down,** escribir para las masas; **w. for a living,** ganarse la vida como escritor; **w. in for,** solicitar por escrito; **w. on,** seguir escribiendo; escribir sobre (un tema) o acerca de (un asunto).
write-down ['raɪt,daun] *s.* (ten.) castigo, rebaja del valor (de un activo).
write-off [-,ɔf] *s.* (ten.) castigo.
writer [-ər, B -ə] *s.* 1. escritor, autor. 2. (esco., der.) abogado; procurador. 3. **the w.,** el que escribe, el suscrito (en cartas, documentos, etc.).
writer's cramp, mogigrafía, grafospasmo, calambre de los escribientes.
write-up ['raɪt,ʌp] *s.* 1. (ten.) valoracion indebida del activo. 2. crítica, evaluación crítica (de un film, pieza teatral); descripción propagandística (de un producto), relato (de un suceso).
writhe [raɪð] *v.t.* 1. retorcerse (de dolor); contorsionarse, contorcerse. 2. serpentear, culebrear. 3. (fig.) angustiarse, amargarse. —*v.t.* retorcer en espiras o pliegues. —*s.* retorcimiento, contorsión.
writhen ['rɪðən] *a.* (poét.) retorcido, contorsionado.
writhing ['raɪðɪŋ] *s.* retorcimiento, contorsión.
writing ['raɪtɪŋ] *s.* 1. escritura. 2. letra, caligrafía. 3. inscripción. 4. escrito, composición escrita. 5. el escribir (como arte o profesión). 6. **at this w., at the present w.,** al momento de escribir la presente; **in one's own w.,** de su puño y letra; **in w.,** por escrito; **to put (something) in w.,** formular (algo) por escrito.
writing case, estuche de artículos de escribir.
writing desk, escritorio.
writing pad, taco para escribir, bloc de papel.
writing paper, papel de escribir, papel de cartas.
writ of attachment, (der.) mandamiento de embargo, providencia de secuestro.
writ of certiorari, (der.) auto de avocación.
writ of error, (der.) auto de casación.
writ of execution, (der.) auto ejecutivo, mandamiento de ejecución; ejecutoria.
writ of habeas corpus, (der.) auto de habeas corpus.
writ of right, 1. (G.B., hist.) mandato que tendía a proteger a los arrendatarios feudales en el disfrute de su dominio sometiendo sus juicios a la corte señorial. 2. (E.U., der.) mandato reivindicatorio (para reintegrar a sus dueños propiedades injustamente retenidas).
writ of summons, (der.) emplazamiento.
written ['rɪtən] *p.p. de* **write.** —*a.* escrito; impreso.
written accent, acento ortográfico.
WRNS [rɛnz] *abrev. de* **Women's Royal Air Force,** Sección Femenina de la Armada Real de G.B.
wrong [rɔŋ] *a.* 1. malo, impropio, censurable. 2. indebido, incorrecto. 3. equivocado, erróneo, errado, desacertado, falso (respuesta, medida, solución, etc.). 4. malo, descompuesto, estropeado, malogrado (Amer.). 5. **born on the w. side of the tracks,** ser de humilde condición; **in the w. place,** mal colocado, mal situado; **it's w. to tell a lie,** está mal decir mentiras; **to be the w. (house, book,** etc.), no ser (la casa, el libro, etc.) que se busca; **to be w.,** no tener razón, equivocarse (persona); estar mal hecho (cosa); andar mal (reloj); ser erróneo (razonamiento, ideas, etc.);**to be (o go) w. with,** pasarle (algo) a, ej., *something is w. with him,* algo le pasa, *something went w. with my car,* algo le ha pasado a mi coche; **to do the w. thing,** hacer lo indebido; **to go the w. way,** equivocarse de camino; **to get out on the w. side of the bed,** levantarse con el pie izquierdo; **to say the w. thing,** decir una cosa desatinada; **to take the w. way,** ir por mal camino; tomar a mal; **what's w. with . . .?** (fam.) ¿qué tiene de malo . . .?; **w. move,** jugada o medida equivocada, mal paso; **w. side out,** al revés; al envés. —*s.* mal, daño, agravio, entuerto, injuria, injusticia; **can two wrongs make a right?** ¿pueden dos entuertos hacer un derecho?; **to be in the w.,** no tener razón, ser culpable; **to do w.,** obrar mal; **to do (one) w.,** ser injusto con (uno), juzgar mal (a uno); hacer daño a (uno); **to do w. to,** agraviar a, hacer daño a; **to know right from w.,** distinguir entre el bien y el mal; **to put (someone) in the w.,** hacer parecer culpable (a alguien); poner en una posición censurable. —*adv.* 1. mal, sin razón, sin causa, injustamente. 2. al revés; equivocadamente, erróneamente. 3. **don't get me w.,** entiéndame bien, no me interprete mal; **to get (someone) in w.,** (fam.) malquistar; dejar mal parado (a alguien); **to go w.,** salir mal; darse a la mala vida; equivocarse; descomponerse, estropearse; dejar de funcionar. —*v.t.* hacer mal a, causar perjuicio a, ser injusto con, agraviar, injuriar, ofender.
wrongdoer ['rɔŋ,duər, B -ə] *s.* malhechor, malvado, pecador.
wrongdoing [-ɪŋ] *s.* fechoría, maldad.
wrong font, (impr.) letra de otra fuente, matriz de otro tipo.
wrongful [-fəl] *a.* 1. injusto, inicuo, malo, injurioso. 2. ilícito, ilegal, ilegítimo.
wrongfully [-fəlɪ] *adv.* 1. injustamente, sin razón. 2. ilícitamente, ilegalmente, ilegítimamente.
wrongfulness [-fəlnəs] *s.* 1. maldad, injusticia. 2. ilicitud, ilegalidad, ilegitimidad.
wrongheaded ['rɔŋ'hɛdəd] *a.* terco, obstinado.
wrongheadedly [-lɪ] *adv.* tercamente, obstinadamente.
wrongheadedness [-nəs] *s.* terquedad, obstinación (en error).
wrongly ['rɔŋlɪ] *adv.* 1. mal, sin razón, sin causa, injustamente. 2. al revés; equivocadamente, erróneamente.
wrongness [-nəs] *s.* 1. injusticia; maldad. 2. error.
wrong note, (mús.) nota falsa.
wrong number, (tele.) número equivocado.
wrote [rout] *pret. de* **write.**
wroth [rɔθ, B rouθ] *a.* (G.B.) iracundo, airado, enojado.
wrought [rɔt] *pret., p.p. de* **work.** —*a.* 1. forjado, fraguado; hecho al martillo. 2. trabajado, labrado, elaborado.

wrought iron, (metal.) hierro forjado o fraguado; hierro dulce.

wrought-iron casting, fundición de hierro maleable.

wrought-up ['rɔt'ʌp] *a.* sobreexcitado, perturbado, muy conmovido.

wrung [rʌŋ] *pret. p.p. de* **wring.**

wry [raɪ] *v.i., v.t.* (*pret., p.p.* WRIED; *p.pr.* WRYING) enroscar(se), torcer(se). —*a.* (WRIER; WRIEST) 1. torcido, doblado, deformado, sesgado. 2. tergiversado, contrario; pervertido. 3. irónico, burlón. 4. **to make a w. face,** hacer una mueca (de disgusto, etc.), torcer el gesto en desagrado.

wryly ['raɪlɪ] *adv.* irónicamente.

wryneck ['raɪˌnɛk] *s.* 1. (med.) tortícolis, torticoli, torticolis. 2. (fam.) persona con el cuello torcido. 3. (orn.) torcecuello, hormiguero.

WSW *abrev. de* **west-southwest,** oessudoeste (OSO).

wulfenite ['wʊlfəˌnaɪt] *s.* (min.) wulfenita.

wurst [wɜrst, B wɜst] *s.* (alemán) salchicha, embutido, embuchado.

wurzel ['wɜrzəl, B 'wɜzəl] *s.* (bot.) remolacha forrajera.

W. Va. *abrev. de* **West Virginia,** Virginia Occidental (E.U.).

WVS *abrev. de* **Women's Voluntary Service,** Servicio Femenino Voluntario (G.B.).

wych-elm ['wɪtʃˌɛlm] *s.* (bot.) olmo escocés.

Wycliffe ['wɪklɪf] *s.* Wiclef, Wycliffe, teólogo y reformador religioso inglés.

wye [waɪ] *s.* (letra) ye, (letra) i griega.

wyliecoat ['waɪlɪˌkoʊt] *s.* (esco.) camiseta; enaguas.

Wyo. *abrev. de* **Wyoming,** Wyoming (E.U.).

Wyoming [waɪ'oʊmɪŋ] *s.* Wyoming, estado de los E.U.

wyvern, *var. de* **wivern.**

X

X [ɛks] *s.* x, vigésima cuarta letra del alfabeto inglés.

xanthate ['zænθeɪt] *s.* (quím.) jantato, xantato.

xanthein ['zænθiɪn] *s.* (quím.) xanteína.

xanthene ['zænˌθin] *s.* (quím.) xanteno.

xanthene dye, (quím.) tinte de xanteno.

xanthic ['zænθɪk] *a.* 1. (quím.) jántico, xántico. 2. amarillento, amarillejo (díc. esp. de flores).

xanthin ['zænθən] *s.* (quím.) xantina.

xanthine ['zænˌθin] *s.* (bioquím.) xantina, jantina.

Xanthippe, Xantippe [zæn'tɪpɪ] *s.* Jantipa, Xantipa, esposa de Sócrates, p. ext. mujer colérica, de carácter áspero.

xanthochroid ['zænθəˌkrɔɪd] (etnol.) *a.* rubio. —*s.* persona rubia.

xanthoderm ['zænθəˌdɜrm, B -ˌdɜm] *a.* (antrop.) xantodermo, de piel amarilla. —*s.* xantodermo, persona perteneciente a una de las razas de piel amarilla.

xanthoderma [ˌzænθə'dɜrmə, B -'dɜmə] *s.* (med.) xantoderma, xantodermía.

xanthogen ['zænθədʒən] *s.* (quím.) xantógeno.

xanthoma [zæn'θoumə] *s.* (*pl.* XANTHOMAS o XANTHOMATA [-mətə]) (med.) xantoma.

xanthophyll ['zænθəˌfɪl] *s.* (bioquím.) xantófila, jantofila, pigmento amarillo de las flores y frutos.

xanthopsia [zæn'θɑpsɪə, B -'θɔp-] *s.* (med.) xantopsia.

xanthopsin [zæn'θɑpsɪn, B -'θɔp-] *s.* (bioquím.) xantopsina.

xanthosis [zæn'θousɪs] *s.* (med.) xantosis.

xanthous ['zænθəs] *a.* 1. xantodermo, amarillo, de coloración amarillenta. 2. rubio, de cabello claro.

xanthoxylin [zæn'θɑksələn, B -'θɔk-] *s.* (quím., farm.) xantoxilina.

x-axis ['ɛksˌæksəs] *s.* 1. (elec.) eje eléctrico-cristal de cuarzo. 2. (avia.) eje longitudinal. 3. (mat.) eje horizontal, sistema de coordenadas rectangulares.

x bracing, diagonales cruzadas, aspas, crucetas.

X chromosome, (biol.) cromosoma X.

Xe *simb. de* **xenon,** xenón (Xe).

xebec ['zibɛk] *s.* (mar.) jabeque.

xenia ['zinɪə] *s.* (bot.) xenia.

xenium ['zinɪəm] *s.* (*pl.* XENIA [-nɪə]) xenia.

Xenoclea [ˌzɪnə'kliə] *s.* (mitol.) Xenoclea, sibila que se negó a profetizar cuando llegó Hércules a Delfos.

Xenocrates [zɪ'nɑkrəˌtiz, B -'nɔk-] *s.* Xenócrates, Jenócrates, filósofo griego.

xenodiagnosis [ˌzɛnouˌdaɪɪg'nousəs] *s.* (med.) xenodiagnosis.

xenogamy [zə'nɑgəmɪ, B -'nɔg-] *s.* (bot.) xenogamia.

xenogenesis [ˌzɛnou'dʒɛnəsəs] *s.* (biol.) xenogénesis.

xenolith ['zɛnəlɪθ] *s.* (min.) xenolita.

xenomania [ˌzɛnə'meɪnɪə] *s.* afición, atracción hacia lo extranjero.

xenomorphic [ˌzɛnə'mɔrfɪk, B -'mɔfɪk] xenomorphous [-'mɔrfəs, B -'mɔfəs] *a.* 1. (min.) xenomorfo, xenomórfico. 2. de forma extraña.

xenon ['ziˌnɑn, B 'zɛnɔn] *s.* (quím.) xenon, xenón.

Xenophanes [zɪ'nɑfəˌniz, B -'nɔf-] *s.* Jenófanes, Xenófanes, poeta y filósofo griego.

xenophile ['zɛnəˌfaɪl] *s.* xenófilo, xenófila, persona aficionada a lo extranjero.

xenophilous [zə'nɑfələs, B -'nɔf-] *a.* xenófilo, inclinado, aficionado a lo extranjero.

xenophobe [-ˌfoub] *s.* xenófobo, xenófoba, persona que tiene aversión a lo extranjero.

xenophobia [ˌzɛnə'foubɪə] *s.* xenofobia, odio o aversión a lo extranjero.

xenophobic [ˌzɛnə'foubɪk] *a.* xenófobo, que odia a lo extranjero.

Xenophon ['zɛnəfən] *s.* Jenofonte, historiador griego.

xerasia [zɪ'reɪsɪə] *s.* (med.) xerasia.

xeric ['zɪrɪk] *a.* (bot.) 1. seco, deficiente de humedad. 2. xerofítico.

xerographic [ˌzɪrə'græfɪk] *a.* xerográfico.

xerography [zə'rɑgrəfɪ, B -'rɔg-] *s.* (foto.) xerografía.

xerophagia [zɪrə'feɪdʒɪə] **xerophagy** [zə'rɑfədʒɪ, B -'rɔf-] *s.* (relig.) xerofagia, ayuno riguroso durante la Semana Santa, practicado por los fieles de la Iglesia Ortodoxa.

xerophilous [zə'rɑfələs, B -'rɔf-] *a.* (bot.) xerófilo.

xerophthalmia [ˌzɪrˌɑf'θælmɪə, B -ˌɔf-] *s.* (med.) xeroftalmia.

xerophyte ['zɪrəˌfaɪt] *s.* (bot.) xerófita, planta adaptada a climas secos.

xerophytic [ˌzɪrə'fɪtɪk] *a.* (bot.) xerofítico.

xerosis [zɪ'rousəs] *s.* (med.) xerodermia.

Xerox (TM) ['zɪrɑks-, B -ɔks-] Xerox; **to make a X. of, to make a X. copy of,** xerocopiar, xerografiar, photografiar.

Xerox copy, Xerox, fotocopia.

Xerox machine, fotocopiadora.

Xerxes ['zɜrksiz, B 'zɜk-] *s.* Jerjes, rey de Persia.

xi [zaɪ, B saɪ] *s.* xi, decimocuarta letra del alfabeto griego.

xiphias ['zɪfɪəs] *s.* (ict.) jifia.

xiphisternum [ˌzɪfɪ'stɛrnəm, B -'stɜnəm] *s.* (*pl.* XIPHISTERNA [-nə]) (anat.) xifisternón.

xiphoid ['zɪfˌɔid] (anat.) *a.* xifoideo. —*s.* xifoides.

Xiphosura [ˌzɪfə'sʊrə] *s. pl.* (zool.) xifosuros.

xiphosuran [-'surən] *a., s.* (zool.) xifosuro, jifosuro.

Xmas ['krɪsməs] *s. var. de* **Christmas,** Navidad.

X-radiation ['ɛksˌreɪdɪ'eɪʃən] *s.* 1. irradiación con rayos X. 2. emanación de rayos X.

X ray, 1. (fís.) rayo X, rayo Roentgen. 2. radiografía.

X-ray ['ɛksˌreɪ] *v.t.* radiografiar, fotografiar con los rayos X; tratar o examinar por medio de los rayos X. —*a.* radiográfico, de rayos X.

X-ray photograph, radigrafía, radiografía, fotografía con los rayos X, roentgenograma.

x-ray print, radiografía.

x-ray spectrum, espectro de los rayos X.

X-ray therapy, (med.) radioterapia.

x-ray tube, (fís.) tubo de rayos X.

xylan ['zaɪlæn] *s.* (quím.) xilana, xilano.

xylary ray ['zaɪlərɪ] (bot.) rayo medular.

xylem ['zaɪləm] *s.* (bot.) xilema, parte leñosa de los árboles y plantas.

xylene ['zaɪˌlin] *s.* (quím.) xileno.

xylic ['zaɪlɪk] *a.* (quím.) xílico.

xylic acid, (quím.) ácido xílico.

xylidine ['zaɪləˌdin, B -daɪn] *s.* (quím.) xilidina.

xylobalsamum [ˌzaɪlə'bɔlsəməm] *s.* (farm.) xilobálsamo.

xylocarpous [ˌzaɪlə'kɑrpəs, B -'kɑpəs] *a.* (bot.) de fruto duro.

xylograph ['zaɪləˌgræf, B -ˌgrɑf] *s.* xilografía (impresión), grabado en madera.

xylographer [zaɪ'lɑgrəfər, B -'lɔgrəfə] *s.* xilógrafo.

xylographic [ˌzaɪlə'græfɪk] **xylographical** [-ɪkəl] *a.* xilográfico.

xylography [zaɪ'lɑgrəfɪ, B -'lɔg-] *s.* xilografía (arte).

xyloid ['zaɪlɔɪd] *a.* xiloide, parecido a la madera, relativo a la madera.

xyloidin [zaɪ'lɔɪdɪn] *s.* (quím.) xiloidina.

xylol ['zaɪˌlɔl] *s.* (quím.) xilol, xileno.

xylophage ['zaɪləˌfeɪdʒ] *s.* (ento.) xilófago.

xylophagous [zaɪ'lɑfəgəs, B -'lɔf-] *a.* xilófago, que se alimenta de madera.

xylophone ['zaɪləˌfoun, 'zɪlə-] *s.* (mús.) xilófono, instrumento parecido a la marimba.

xylose ['zaɪˌlous] *s.* (quím.) xilosa.

xylotile ['zaɪləˌtaɪl] *s.* (quím.) xilotila.

xylotomous [zaɪ'lɑtəməs, B -'lɔt-] *a.* (ento.) xilótomo.

xylotomy [zaɪ'lɑtəmɪ, B -'lɔt-] *s.* corte microscópico de la madera (con micrótomo).

x-y recorder, (ing.) registrador de dos coordenadas, registrador bidimensional.

xyst [zɪst] **xystus** ['zɪstəs] *s.* (arq.) pórtico, galería.

xyster ['zɪstər, B -tə] *s.* (med.) xister, raspador (para huesos).

Y

Y [waɪ] *s.* y, vigésima quinta letra del alfabeto inglés.
Y *símb. de* **yttrium,** itrio (Y).
yabber ['jæbər, B -ə] *v.i.* (Aust.) cotorrear, charlar, platicar (Méx.). —*s.* cotorreo, plática.
yacca ['jækə] *s.* (bot.) yaca.
yacht [jɑt, B jɔt] *s.* yate. —*v.i.* competir en regata de yates; dar un paseo en yate; navegar o viajar en yate.
yachting ['jɑtɪŋ, B 'jɔt-] *s.* la navegación o manejo de un yate (considerado como deporte); paseo en yate.
yacht race, regata de yates.
yachtsman ['jɑtsmən, B 'jɔts-] *s.* dueño o timonel de yate; aficionado al deporte de los yates.
yachtsmanship [-ˌʃɪp] **yachtmanship** ['jɑtmən-, B 'jɔt-] *s.* el arte de conducir un yate.
yack, *var. de* **yak,** cotorrear.
yaff [jæf] *v.i.* (esco.) ladrar, regañir. —*s.* ladrido, gañido (del perro).
yager ['jeɪgər, B -gə] *s.* 1. *var. de* **jaeger.** 2. (hist., E.U.) rifle de cañón corto.
yagi ['jɑgɪ] *s.* (*pl.* YAGIS) (rad., t.v.) antena Yagi.
yahoo ['jeɪhu, B jə'hu] *s.* 1. bestia, patán, bruto. 2. (lit.) **Y.,** brutos con forma humana que aparecen en "Los viajes de Gulliver" de Swift.
Yahweh ['jɑweɪ, B jɑ'weɪ] **Yahveh, Yahvè** ['jɑveɪ] *s.* (bíbl.) Yahvé, Jehová, Jehovah.
Yahwism ['jɑˌwɪzəm] **Yahvism** [-ˌvɪz-] *s.* adoración de Yahvé.
yak [jæk] *s.* (zool.) yak, buey montaraz del Tíbet.
yak, *v.i.* (*pret., p.p.* YAKKED; *p.pr.* YAKKING) (jer.) cotorrear, parlotear, charlar.
Yakima ['jækəˌmɔ] *a.* yaquina, yakina. —*s.* (*pl.* YAKIMA O YAKIMAS) yaquina, yakina.
yam [jæm] *s.* (bot.) 1. ñame (planta y raíz). 2. (S. de E.U.) camote, batata.
yammer ['jæmər, B -ə] *s.* 1. (fam.) plañido; grito, lloriqueo. 2. parloteo, plática. —*v.i.* 1. plañir, lloriquear. 2. parlotear, platicar. 3. gruñir, protestar. 4. producir un ruido fuerte y persistente.
yank [jæŋk] (fam.) *s.* tirón, estirón. —*v.t.* (ú. gen. con *out* u *off*) sacar de un tirón, arrancar violentamente. —*v.i.* dar un tirón.
Yank, *s.* (fam.) yanqui.
Yankee ['jæŋkɪ] *s.* yanqui. —*a.* propio o característico de los yanquis.
Yankeedom [-dəm] *s.* tierra de los yanquis, yanquilandia; los yanquis.
Yankeeism [-ˌɪzəm] *s.* yanquismo.
Y antenna, (rad.) antena adaptada en delta.
yap [jæp] *s.* 1. ladrido, gañido. 2. (jer.) cháchara. 3. (jer.) patán, rústico. 4. (jer.) boca. —*v.i.* (*pret., p.p.* YAPPED; *p.pr.* YAPPING) 1. ladrar, gañir (el perro). 2. (jer.) charlar tontamente; chacharear ruidosamente; insistir machaconamente; parlotear.
yapok, yapock [jə'pɑk, B -'pɔk] *s.* (zool.) yapok.
Yarborough ['jɑrˌbɜrə, B 'jɑbərə] *s.* (whist, bridge) mano sin cartas más altas que nueve.
yard [jɑrd, B jɑd] *s.* 1. yarda. 2. (mar.) verga. 3. **to man the yards,** disponer(se) los marineros sobre las vergas (en salutación).
yard, *s.* 1. corral, cercado, patio. 2. (f.c.) patio. 3. **the Y.,** (G.B.) Scotland Yard (cuartel general de policía en Londres). 4. astillero. —*v.t.* (gen. con *up*) acorralar, apriscar, encerrar o guardar en un corral.
yardage ['jɑrdɪdʒ, B 'jɑd-] *s.* 1. longitud en yardas; superficie en yardas cuadradas; volumen en yardas cúbicas. 2. acorralamiento (de ganado en una estación de f.c., etc.); derecho de acorralamiento.
yardarm ['jɑrdˌɑrm, B 'jɑdɑm] *s.* (mar.) penol.
yardbird [-ˌbɜrd, B -ˌbɜd] *s.* 1. ordenanza (soldado). 2. recluta bisoño.
yard goods, géneros de pieza.
yardman [-mən] *s.* 1. (mar.) marinero que maneja las vergas. 2. empleado en un depósito de madera. 3. (f.c.) encargado del patio.
yardmaster [-ˌmæstər, B -ˌmɑstə] *s.* (f.c.) superintendente o jefe de patio.
yardstick [-ˌstɪk] *s.* 1. yarda, vara de una yarda de largo. 2. (fig.) criterio, norma, patrón.
yare [jɛr, B jɛə] *a.* (ant.) listo, pronto; activo.
yarely ['jɛrlɪ, B 'jɛəlɪ] *adv.* (ant.) pronto, presto.
yareta [jɑ'reɪtə, B -ɑ] *s.* (bot.) llareta.
yarn [jɑrn, B jɑn] *s.* 1. hilaza, hilo, hilado. 2. (fam.) cuento, historieta; cuento increíble, andaluzada. 3. **to spin a y.,** contar un cuento (largo e increíble). —*v.i.* (fam.) contar historias (increíbles).
yarn-dye ['jɑrnˌdaɪ, B 'jɑn-] *v.t.* teñir en hilo (antes de fabricarse el tejido).
yarning chisel ['jɑrnɪŋ-, B 'jɑn-] escoplo calafateador de estopa.
yarrow ['jæroʊ] *s.* (bot.) milenrama, milhojas, altarreina, artemisa bastarda.
yashmak [jɑʃ'mɑk, B 'jæʃmæk] *s.* velo doble con que las musulmanas se cubren el rostro.
yataghan ['jætəˌgæn, B -gən] *s.* yatagán, sable turco.
yaud [jɔd, jɑd, B jɔd] *s.* (esco.) caballo de trabajo, rocín.
yauld [jɔld] *a.* (esco.) alerto; activo.
yaup, *var. de* **yawp.**
yaupon ['juˌpɑn, B 'joʊˌpɔn] *s.* (bot.) apalachina.
yaw [jɔ] *v.i.* 1. (mar.) guiñar, dar guiñadas. 2. (aer.) dar guiñadas, desviarse (de la línea recta de vuelo). —*s.* 1. (mar.) guiñada. 2. (aer.) guiñada, desvío, desviación, derrape.
yaw axis, (avia.) eje vertical.
yawing moment ['jɔɪŋ-] (aer.) momento de guiñada.
yawl [jɔl] 1. yola. 2. balandra, queche. 3. (dial.) aullido, ululato, grito.
yawn [jɔn] *v.i.* 1. bostezar. 2. abrirse (desmesuradamente), estar abierta en todo su ancho. —*v.t.* decir bostezando. —*s.* 1. bostezo. 2. abertura, cavidad.
yawning ['jɔnɪŋ] 1. abierto; profundo (precipicio, etc.). 2. bostezante, bostezador, que bosteza.
yawp [jɔp] *s.* (fam.) alarido; gañido; gritería, grito (ej., de un ave). —*v.i.* (fam.) dar alaridos.
yaws [jɔz] *s. pl.* (med.) frambesia, pián, botón de amboina, mal de pinto.
y axis, 1. (avia.) eje transversal. 2. (mat.) eje vertical, en el sistema de coordenadas rectangulares.
Yb *símb. de* **ytterbium,** iterbio (Yb).
Y branch, bifurcación (de tubería).
Y chromosome, cromosoma Y.
Y connection, (elec.) conexión de estrella, montaje en estrella.
ye [ji] *pron.* (ant., lit.) vosotros, vosotras, vos, os.
ye [ji, ði, ðə] *art.* (ant.) el, la, los, las.
yea [jeɪ] *adv.* 1. sí (como voto). 2. y aun, y hasta, además. —*s.* sí, voto afirmativo, voto a favor.
yean [jin] *v.t., v.i.* parir (la oveja o cabra).
yeanling ['jinlɪŋ] *s.* cordero a cabrito mamantón. —*a.* recién nacido.
year [jɪr, B jɜ] *s.* 1. año. 2. (*pl.*) años, edad. 3. **a. y.,** por año, anual(mente); **by the y.,** por año; **from y. to y.,** año tras año, cada año; **in the y. one,** (fig.) el año de la nana; **in years,** entrado en años, de edad; **in years to come,** en años venideros; **of late years,** en los últimos años, en años recientes; **once a y.,** una vez al año; cada año; **y. by y.,** año tras año, cada año; **y. in y. out,** durante años (sucesivos), sin interrupción.
year-end ['jɪr'ɛnd] *a.* de fin de año. —*s.* fin de año.
yearbook ['jɪrˌbuk, B 'jɜˌ-] *s.* anuario.
yearling [-lɪŋ] *s.* primal, añojo, añal, borro. —*a.* primal, añal.
yearlong [-'lɔŋ] *a.* que dura un año, para todo el año.
yearly [-lɪ] *a.* anual. —*adv.* anualmente, cada año; una vez al año, al año.
yearn [jɜrn, B jɜn] *v.t.* (gen. con *for* o *after*) anhelar, ansiar, desear vivamente, suspirar por, añorar.
yearning ['jɜrnɪŋ, B 'jɜnɪŋ] *s.* anhelo, deseo vivo.
yearningly [-lɪ] *adv.* anhelosamente.
year of grace, año de gracia.
year-round ['jɪr'raʊnd, B 'jɜ'-] *a.* abierto (por) todo el año (hotel, teatro, etc.); practicable durante todo el año (deporte, etc.).
yeast [jist] *s.* 1. levadura. 2. giste (de cerveza). 3. espuma. 4. (fig.) fermento. —*v.i.* fermentar; espumar, hacer espuma.
yeast cake, pastilla de levadura.
yeasty ['jistɪ] *a.* 1. semejante a la levadura. 2. (fig.) exuberante, inquieto; frívolo, trivial.
yegg [jɛg] **yeggman** ['jɛgmən] *s.* (jer.) ladrón (esp. de cajas fuertes).
yelk [jɛlk] *var. de* **yolk.**
yell [jɛl] *v.i.* dar alaridos, gritar, adllar. —*v.t.* decir a gritos. —*s.* 1. alarido, grito, aullido. 2. (E.U., Can.) grito distintivo y típico de un colegio o universidad (con que los estudiantes alientan a sus compañeros en competencias atléticas).
yellow ['jɛloʊ] *a.* 1. amarillo. 2. rubio (pelo). 3. amarillento, amarillejo, amarilloso (debido a enfermedad, edad, etc.). 4. (fig.) blanco, cobarde, medroso. 5. (fig.) sensacional, escandaloso (periódico, prensa, etc.). 6. (ant.) receloso,

suspicaz, celoso. —*s.* 1. amarillo (color o tinte). 2. yema (del huevo). 3. (*pl.*) ictericia (esp. de animales domésticos). 4. (ant.) ánimo receloso, celos. —*v.i.* amarillecer, amarillear, enmarillecerse. —*v.t.* volver amarillo, teñir de amarillo.
yellow agate, (min.) ceracate.
yellow-billed cuckoo [-ˌbɪld-] (orn.) cuclillo de pico amarillo.
yellow birch, (bot.) abedul amarillo.
yellowbird [-ˌbɜrd, B -ˌbɜd] *s.* (orn.) jilguero de América; dominguito.
yellow bugle, (bot.) pinillo.
yellow camomile, (bot.) manzanilla loca.
yellow daisy, (bot.) rudbequia; aurora común, flor de una hora.
yellow-dog [-ˌdɔg] *a.* 1. vil, despreciable, cobarde. 2. antisindicalista.
yellow-dog contract, contrato de (empleo) con obrero que no es miembro del sindicato, o que se compromete a no afiliarse a él durante el tiempo que dure su empleo.
yellow earth, (min.) tierra amarilla, almagre.
yellow elder, (bot.) retama, trompetilla, borla de San Pedro, retamo (Amer.).
yellow fever, (med.) fiebre amarilla.
yellow flag, 1. (mar.) bandera amarilla, (insignia de la cuarentena). 2. (bot.) ácoro bastardo, ácoro palustre, falso ácoro.
yellow goatsbeard, (bot.) barba cabruna.
yellowhammer [ˈjɛloʊˌhæmər, B -ə] *s.* (orn.) emberizo, verderol, verderón, pájaro tonto, ave tonta; (E.U.) picamaderos.
yellow iris, (bot.) ácoro bastardo, ácoro palustre, ácoro falso.
yellowish [-ɪʃ] *a.* amarillento, amarillejo, amarilloso.
yellow jack, 1. (med.) fiebre amarilla. 2. bandera amarilla (como insignia de cuarentena). 3. (ict.) jurel.
yellow jacket, (ento.) (especie de) avispa con pintas amarillas.
yellow lead ore, (min.) plomo amarillo, wulfenita.
yellowlegs [ˈjɛloʊˌlɛgz] *s. pl.* (*sing o pl. en const.*) (orn.) zarapito, sarapico.
yellow metal, 1. oro. 2. latón (con 40% de cinc).
yellow mombin [-moʊmˈbin] (bot.) jobo.
yellowness [-nəs] *s.* amarillez.
yellow oak, roble amarillo.
yellow ocher, (min.) ocre amarillo.
Yellow Pages (TM), (tele.) páginas amarillas.
yellow peril, peligro amarillo (que supuestamente representa la raza amarilla para la civilización occidental o los intereses de la raza blanca).
yellow phosphorus, fósforo blanco.
yellow pine, (bot.) pino amarillo, pino del incienso.
yellow plum, ciruela de yema.
yellow poplar, (bot.) tulipanero, liriodendro.
yellow poppy, (bot.) chicalote, argemone, amapola espinosa.
yellow pyrites, (geol.) calcopirita.
Yellow Sea, mar Amarillo, entre la China y Corea.
yellow spot, (anat.) mancha amarilla (de la retina).
yellow spruce, (bot.) abeto amarillo o rojo; picea del Pacífico.
yellowthroat [ˈjɛloʊˌθroʊt] *s.* (orn.) curruca americana.
yellow vetch, (bot.) arveja silvestre.
yellow warbler, (orn.) silvia amarilla.
yellow water lily, (bot.) nenúfar amarillo.
yellowweed [-ˌwid] *s.* (bot.) 1. vara de San José. 2. gualda. 3. hierba jacobea, hierba de Santiago.
yellowwood [-ˌwʊd] *s.* (bot.) fustete; pino amarillo; sándalo amarillo.
yelp [jɛlp] *v.i., v.t.* gañir, aullar (el perro). —*s.* gañido, aullido.
Yemen [ˈjɛmən] *s.* Yemen, país al S. de la península arábica.
Yemeni [-ənɪ] **Yemenite** [-ˌnaɪt] *a., s.* yemenita.
yen [jɛn] *s.* (*pl.* YEN) yen (unidad monetaria del Japón).
yen, (jer.) *s.* ansia, anhelo, ganas; propensión. —*v.i.* anhelar, ansiar, desear intensamente, tener el capricho, tener ganas.
yeoman [ˈjoʊmən] *s.* 1. (hist., G.B.) pequeño terrateniente o agricultor. 2. (G.B.) alabardero o guardia del rey; voluntario de un cuerpo de caballería. 3. (mar.) oficinista de a bordo, encargado de las señales; pañolero. 4. (hist.) asistente; criado, sirviente del rey.
yeoman of the guard, (G.B.) alabardero o guardia del rey; continuo.
yeomanry [-rɪ] *s.* (*pl.* YEOMANRIES) 1. pequeños terratenientes (de cierto lugar en conjunto). 2. (G.B.) cuerpo de voluntarios de caballería.
yeoman's service, yeoman service, ayuda leal, buen servicio.
yerk [jɜrk, B jɜk] *v.t.* (G.B.) 1. azotar, zurrar. 2. excitar, alborotar. 3. levantarse de pronto.
yes [jɛs] *adv.* 1. sí; **y. indeed,** sí por cierto, ya lo creo; **y.?** ¿sí? ¿ah, sí? ¿de veras? —*s.* (*pl.* YESES) (el) sí; **to say y.,** dar el sí, asentir.
ye'se [jis] (esco., dial.) *abrev. de* **ye shall.**
yes-man [ˈjɛsˌmæn] *s.* sacristán de amén; empleado o subordinado servil.
yester [ˈjɛstər, B -tə] *a.* (poét) pasado, de ayer, de antaño.
yesterday [ˈjɛstərˌdɪ, -ˌdeɪ, B -tədɪ] *s.* ayer; **I (he, she) was not born y.,** yo (él, ella) no he (ha) nacido ayer, no soy (es) tan ingenuo (ingenua); **it is but of y.,** es de origen reciente. —*adv.* ayer. —*a.* del ayer, de tiempos pasados o recientes.
yestereve [-tərˈiv] **yesterevening** [-nɪŋ] (ant.) *s.* (la) tarde de ayer; (la) noche de ayer. —*adv.* ayer en la tarde; ayer noche, anoche.
yestermorn [-tərˈmɔrn, B -təˈmɔn] **yestermorning** [-ˈmɔrnɪŋ, B -ˈmɔnɪŋ] (ant.) *s.* (la) mañana de ayer. —*adv.* ayer por la mañana, en la mañana de ayer.
yesternight [-ˈnaɪt] (ant.) *s.* (la) noche de ayer. —*adv.* ayer (en la) noche, anoche.
yesternoon [-ˈnun] (ant.) *s.* (el) mediodía de ayer. —*adv.* ayer al mediodía, al mediodía de ayer.
yesterweek [-ˈwik] *s., adv.* (ant.) la semana pasada.
yesteryear [-ˈjɪr, B -ˈjɜ] (poét.) *s.* el año pasado; (fig.) años pasados. —*adv.* antaño.
yestreen [jɛsˈtrin] *s.* (esco.) tarde o noche de ayer. —*adv.* ayer en la tarde; anoche.
yet [jɛt] *adv.* 1. todavía, aún. 2. (*en preguntas*) ya, ej., *is he gone yet?* ¿ya se fue él? 3. más, aún. 4. sin embargo, con todo; aun así. 5. **as y.,** hasta ahora. —*conj.* empero, mas, pero, sin embargo.
yew [ju] *s.* (bot.) tejo.
Yggdrasil [ˈɪgdrəˌsɪl, B -ˌdræsəl] *s.* Ygdrasil (fresno que simboliza el universo en la mitol. noruega).
Y grouping, (elec.) montaje en Y, montaje en estrella.
Y-gun [ˈwaɪˌgʌn] *s.* cañón doble antisubmarino (para lanzar bombas de profundidad).
YHA *abrev. de* **Youth Hostels Association,** Asociación de Albergues de Juventud.
Yiddish [ˈjɪdɪʃ] *a., s.* yídish.
yield [jild] *v.t.* 1. producir; (com.) rendir, redituar, devengar. 2. ceder, dejar, renunciar. 3. rendir, entregar. 4. conceder, admitir. 5. (ant.) devolver, destituir. 6. **y. the palm,** (fig.) ceder la victoria, renunciar al triunfo; **y. up,** rendir, entregar; descubrir, revelar (ej., secreto). —*v.i.* 1. flaquear, ceder, doblegarse. 2. rendirse, sucumbir. 3. ser productivo; dar (mucha, poca) utilidad. 4. **y. to,** ceder a, consentir a, dar preferencia a. —*s.* 1. producto, beneficio, rendimiento. 2. (com.) cosecha.
yielding [ˈjildɪŋ] *a.* 1. productivo. 2. blando, maleable, flexible. 3. complaciente, condescendiente, acomodadizo.
yieldingly [-lɪ] *adv.* sin resistencia, con complacencia o condescendencia.
yield point, (ing.) punto cedente o de deformación, límite elástico aparente.
yield ratio, (ing.) límite de elasticidad.
yield strenght, (ing.) límite elástico.
yield temperature, (metal.) temperatura de fusión.
yill [jɪl] (esco.) *var. de* **ale.**
yin [jɪn] (esco.) *var. de* **one.**
yip [jɪp] *v.i.* (*pret., p.p.* YIPPED; *p.pr.* YIPPING) (fam.) gañir, aullar. —*s.* gañido, aullido (del perro).
yippee [ˈjɪpɪ] *interj.* ¡hurra!
yird [jɪrd, B jɜd] (esco., N. de Ingl.) tierra.
ylang-ylang, *var. de* **ilang-ilang.**
Y level, nivel en Y, nivel de horquetas.
YMCA *abrev. de* **Young Men's Christian Association,** Asociación de Jóvenes Cristianos.
YMHA *abrev. de* **Young Men's Hebrew Association,** Asociación de Jóvenes Hebreos.
yodel [ˈjoʊdəl] *v.t., v.i.* (*pret., p.p.* YODELED o YODELLED; *p.pr.* YODELING o YODELLING) cantar a la manera de los montañeses del Tirol. —*s.* canto con cambios repentinos del tono natural al falsete.
yoga [ˈjoʊgə] *s.* yoga, yoguismo.
yoghurt, *var. de* **yogurt.**
yogi [ˈjoʊgɪ] **yogin** [-gən] yoghi, yogui, el que practica el yoga.
yogurt [ˈjoʊgərt, B ˈjɔgət] *s.* yogur, yogurt.
yohimbine [joʊˈhɪmˌbin] *s.* (quím.) yohimbina.
yoicks [jɔɪks] *interj.* (G.B.) grito con que se azuza a los perros.
yoke [joʊk] *s.* 1. yugo. 2. balancín (para llevar pesos). 3. canesú, hombrillo (de camisa). 4. (*pl. gen.* YOKE) yunta (de animales). 5. (fig.) yugo, unión, enlace (esp. del matrimonio). 6. (fig.) yugo, férula, servidumbre. 7. tirante (de campana). 8. (mec.) horquilla; grapa, abrazadera; varilla de unión o conexión, varilla de maniobra. 9. (mar.) yugo (del timón). 10. (aer.) palanca de mando. 11. **to throw off the y.,** sacudir el yugo, liberarse. —*v.t.* 1. uncir, enyugar; acoplar. 2. (fig.) aparear, emparejar, unir (esp. en matrimonio). 3. (raro) oprimir, esclavizar, forzar, sojuzgar. —*v.i.* (gen. con *together* o *with*) aparearse; trabajar juntos.
yoke elm, (bot.) carpe.
yokefellow [ˈjoʊkˌfɛloʊ] *s.* compañero de fatigas; amigo íntimo; cónyuge.
yokel [ˈjoʊkəl] *s.* patán, paleto.
yoldring [ˈjɔldrɪŋ] *s.* (esco.) (orn.) ave tonta.
yolk [joʊk] *s.* 1. yema (de huevo). 2. churre, juarda, suarda, pringue (de la lana). 3. (embr.) vitelo (nutritivo).
yolk sac, (embr.) saco vitelino.
yolky [ˈjoʊkɪ] *a.* pringoso, grasoso (lana).
Yom Kippur [ˌjɔmˈkɪpər, B -ə] (relig.) yom kipur, solemne fiesta judía celebrada con ayuno y ceremonias.
yon [jɑn, B jɔn] **yond** [jɑnd, B jɔnd] *a., adv.* (ant., dial.) *vars. de* **yonder.** —*pron.* (ant.) aquello.
yonder [ˈjɑndər, B ˈjɔndə] *adv.* allí, allá, acullá. —*a.* aquel, de allá.

yoo-hoo [ˈjuˌhu] *interj.* ¡hola! ¡eh!
yore [jɔr, B jɔ] *s.* tiempos antiguos; **of y.,** antiguamente, antaño, en otro tiempo.
Yorkist [ˈjɔrkəst, B ˈjɔkɪst] *s.* (G.B., hist.) partidario de la casa real de York, esp. en las Guerras de las Rosas.
York rite [ˈjɔrk-, B ˈjɔk-] un rito masónico; secta masónica que cuenta con 13 grados.
Yorkshire pudding [ˈjɔrkˌʃɪr-, B ˈjɔkʃə-] masa que se hornea en la salsa natural del asado.
Yoruba [ˈjɔrəbə] *s.* 1. yoruba, miembro de una tribu africana. 2. yoruba, lenguaje de esta tribu.
you [ju, jʊ] *pron.* 1. tú, usted; vosotros, ustedes; te, a ti, le, la, a usted; os, a vosotros, les, a ustedes. 2. (ant.) sí mismo; **get y. gone,** !váyase!; **sit y. down,** ¡siéntese Ud.! *—pron. impers.* uno, se, ej., *it makes y. jump,* eso le hace saltar a uno, *what are y. to do with a man like this?* ¿qué se hace con un hombre como éste?
you-all [ˈjuˈɔl, jɔl, B juˈɔl] *pron.* (dial., S. de E.U.) ustedes, vosotros, vosotras.
you'd [jud, jʊd] *contr. de* **you had** o **you would.**
you'll [jul, jʊl] *contr. de* **you will** o **you shall.**
young [jʌŋ] *a.* (YOUNGER [ˈjʌŋgər, B -gə] YOUNGEST [ˈjʌŋgəst]) 1. joven. 2. mozo, juvenil. 3. (fig.) inexperto, novato. 4. hijo, joven, ej., *y. Smith,* el joven Smith, *Pliny the younger,* Plinio el joven. 5. **in my y. days,** en mis tiempos mozos, en mi juventud; **my y. man (woman),** mi enamorado(a); **the night is still y.,** la noche es joven todavía; **the y.,** la gente joven, la juventud; **to grow y. again,** rejuvenecer(se). *—s.* 1. (*pl.*) jóvenes, juventud. 2. hijuelos, cría (de animales); **with y.,** preñada.
young and old, todo el mundo.
youngberry [ˈjʌŋˌbɛrɪ] *s.* (bot.) (especie de) zarzamora híbrida.
young blood, (la) juventud, gente joven; vigor o frescura juveniles.
younger [ˈjʌŋgər, B -gə] *a. comp de* **young,** más joven; menor, ej., *he's y. than you,* él es más joven (o menor) que Ud.; menor, ej., *his y. daughter,* su hija menor.
youngest [ˈjʌŋgəst] *a. superl. de* **young,** el (la) más joven (de), ej., *he is the y. of my children,* él es el más joven de mis hijos, *she is my y. daughter,* ella es la más joven de mis hijas.
young fellow, joven, mozo.
young girl, muchacha, joven, chica, mozuela.
youngish [ˈjʌŋɪʃ] *a.* bastante joven; de aire juvenil (díc. de gente madura); más bien joven.
young lady, señorita.
youngling [-lɪŋ] *s.* 1. jovencito, mocito, mozuelo. 2. cría (animal pequeño).
young love, amor juvenil.
young people, los jóvenes, la gente joven.
young person, joven, persona joven.
youngster [jʌŋstər, B -stə] *s.* 1. jovenzuelo, jovencito, mozalbete. 2. potro, potrillo.
young things, gente joven, jóvenes (especialmente las muchachas).
Young Turk, rebelde (en un partido político esp. el de tendencias progresistas o liberales).
young 'un [ˈjʌŋən] (*ú. gen. como vocativo*) jovencito.
younker [ˈjʌŋkər, B -kə] *s.* 1. (ant.) caballero joven, señorito. 2. joven, chico.
your [jʊr, jər, B jɔ] *a.* tu, tus, vuestro, vuestros, su, sus, de usted, de ustedes; de uno.
yours [jʊrz, jɔrz, B jɔz] *pron. pos.* (el) tuyo, (los) tuyos, (el) suyo, (los) suyos, (los) vuestros, (el) de Ud., (los) de Uds., ej., *I like y. better,* me gusta más el tuyo, *is he a friend of y.?* ¿él es amigo tuyo? ¿es amigo de Ud.?; **what's y.?** (fam.) ¿qué va a tomar? ¿qué (bebida) puedo servirle?
yourself [jʊrˈsɛlf, jər-, B jɔˈ-] *pron. de la segunda pers. del sing forma enfática o reflexiva* (*pl.* YOURSELVES [-ˈsɛlvz]) tú mismo, vosotros mismos; usted(es) mismo (s); ti, te, se, ej., *have you hurt y.?* ¿te has lastimado? *you said so y.,* tú mismo lo has dicho; **be y.!** ¡no pierdas los estribos! ¡domínate!; **by y.,** solo; **you are not quite y. today,** ¡tú no estás hoy en tus cabales!
yours truly, 1. (*ú. como formula convencional de despedida en cartas*) atentamente, su atto. y s.s. 2. (hum. *con referencia a sí mismo*) su servidor, el suscrito, un servidor.
youth [juθ] *s.* (*pl.* YOUTHS [juðz, juθs, B juðz]) 1. juventud. 2. la juventud, la gente joven, los jóvenes. 3. joven, muchacho. 4. **his extreme y. saved him from the draft,** se salvó del servicio militar por ser tan joven.
youth club, club juvenil.
youthful [ˈjuθfəl] *a.* 1. juvenil; vigoroso. 2. joven, nuevo, fresco.
youthfully [-fəlɪ] *adv.* con vigor juvenil; como un joven.
youthfulness [-fəlnəs] *s.* juventud, frescura o vigor juvenil.
youth hostel, albergue para jóvenes viajeros.
you've [juv, jʊv] *contr. de* **you have.**
yow [joʊ] (dial.) *var. de* **ewe.**
yowl [jaʊl] *v.i.* dar alaridos, aullar. *—v.t.* proferir entre alaridos. *—s.* alarido, aullido.
yo-yo [ˈjoʊjoʊ] *s.* yo-yo, yoyo, yoyó (juguete).
yperite [ˈipəˌraɪt] *s.* (quím.) yperita, iperita, gas mostaza.
Y plates, (rad.) placas de desviación vertical (en tubos de cátodo).
yr. *abrev. de* 1. **year,** año. 2. **your,** suyo, suya.
y switch, (f.c.) cambiavía en Y, cambio de desvío doble.
Yt *símb. de* **yttrium,** itrio (Y).
ytterbia [ɪˈtɜrbɪə, B ɪˈtɜbɪə] *s.* (quím.) iterbina.
ytterbium [-bɪəm] *s.* (quím.) iterbio.
yttria [ˈɪtrɪə] *s.* (quím.) itria.
yttric [-rɪk] *a.* (quím.) ítrico.
yttriferous [ɪˈtrɪfərəs] *a.* intrífero.
yttrium [ˈɪtrɪəm] *s.* (quím.) itrio.
yttrium metal, metal de itrio.
Yucatan [ˌjukəˈtæn, B -ˈtɑn] *s.* (el) Yucatán, península de México.
Yucatec [ˈjukəˌtɛk] *s.* yucateco, yucateca.
Yucatecan [ˌjukəˈtɛkən] *a.* yucateco.
yucca [ˈjʌkə] *s.* (bot.) yuca, mandioca.
Yugoslav [ˈjugoʊˌslɑv, -ˌslæv] *a., s.* yugoeslavo, yugoslavo.
Yugoslavia [ˌjugoʊˈslɑvɪə] *s.* (hist.) Yugoslavia, Yugoeslavia.
Yugoslavian [-ɪən] *a., s.* (hist.) yugoeslavo, yugoslavo.
Yukon [ˈjukɑn, B -kɔn] *s.* 1. el (río) Yukón. 2. Yukón, territorio en el Canadá.
Yule [jul] *s.* Navidad, Natividad, pascua de Navidad.
Yule log, nochebueno, tronco navideño, tronco grande con que se inicia la fogata hogareña la noche de Navidad.
Yuletide [ˈjulˌtaɪd] *s.* Navidad, Natividad, pascua de Navidad.
Yuman [ˈjumən] *a.* yuma, propio de un grupo de tribus indias de E.U.
yummy [ˈjʌmɪ] *a.* (YUMMIER; YUMMIEST) (fam.) delicioso, riquísimo.
yurt [jʊrt, B juət] *s.* yurta, habitáculo o tienda redonda usada por los mongoles y turcos del Asia Central.
YWCA *abrev. de* **Young Women's Christian Association,** Asociación de Jóvenes Cristianas.
YWHA *abrev. de* **Young Women's Hebrew Association,** Asociación de Jóvenes Hebreas.
ywis, *var. de* **iwis.**

Z

Z [zi, B zɛd] *s.* z, vigésima sexta letra del alfabeto inglés.
zaffer, zaffre ['zæfər, B -ə] *s.* (min.) zafre.
Zambia ['zæmbɪə] *s.* Zambia.
zamia ['zeɪmɪə] *s.* (bot.) zamia.
zamindar [zəˌmin'dɑr, B -'mɪndɑ] *s.* (angloind., hist.) 1. terrateniente. 2. recaudador de impuestos sobre tierras.
zander ['zændər, B -də] *s.* (ict.) variedad de lucio o sello.
zaniness ['zeɪnɪnəs] *s.* tontería, ridiculez; extravagancia.
zany ['zeɪnɪ] *s.* (*pl.* ZANIES) 1. simplón, papanatas. 2. burlador, bromista, tonto. 3. (despec.) adulón. 4. bufón, payaso. —*a.* (ZANIER; ZANIEST) tonto, alocado; ridículo, absurdo; estrafalario.
Zanzibar ['zænzəˌbɑr, B ˌzænzɪ'bɑ] *s.* Zanzíbar, isla al E. de la costa de África, hoy parte de Tanzania.
zap [zæp] *tr.v.* (coll.) liquidar; (comput.) eliminar, borrar. —*interj.* (coll.) ¡zas!
Zarathustra [ˌzærə'θustrə] *s.* (relig.) Zaratustra, Zoroastro, profeta persa, fundador de la religión que lleva su nombre.
zaratite ['zɑrəˌtaɪt, B 'zæ-] *s.* (min.) zaratita.
zareba, zariba [zə'ribə] *s.* estacada o empalizada provisional (de ramas de arbustos, etc. hecha originalmente en África para proteger pueblos, campamentos, etc.).
zax [zæks] *s.* herramienta para recortar y horadar pizarras de techar.
zayin ['zɑjən] *s.* zain, séptima letra del alfabeto hebreo.
zeal [zil] *s.* celo, fervor, ardor, ahínco.
Zealand ['zilənd] *s.* Seeland, Seelandia, Selandia (isla de Dinamarca).
zealot ['zɛlət] *s.* 1. fanático, partidario acérrimo; entusiasta. 2. **Z.,** (his.) zelote.
zealotry [-ətrɪ] *s.* fanatismo.
zealous ['zɛləs] *a.* celoso, fervoroso, entusiasta.
zealously [-lɪ] *adv.* celosamente, fervorosamente; con ardor.
zealousness [-nəs] *s.* carácter fervoroso; entusiasmo.
zebec, zebeck, *vars. de* **xebec.**
Zebedee ['zɛbədɪ, B -əˌdi] *s.* (bíbl.) Zebedeo, padre de los apóstoles San Juan y Santiago.
zebra ['zibrə] *s.* (zool.) cebra.
zebra crossing, (G.B.) cebra, cruce para peatones señalado con rayas en el pavimento.
zebrine [-ˌbraɪn] *a.* cebrado, con aspecto de cebra, con marcas o rayas de cebra.
zebroid [-ˌbrɔɪd] *s.* (zool.) cebroide.
zebu ['zibu] *s.* (zool.) cebú.
Zechariah [ˌzɛkə'raɪə] *s.* 1. (bíbl.) Zacarías. 2. (bíbl.) (el) libro de Zacarías.
zed [zɛd] *s.* (G.B.) (letra) zeta, zeda, ceda.
zedoary ['zɛdoʊˌɛrɪ, B -ərɪ] *s.* (bot.) cedoaria.
zee [zi] *s.* (E.U.) (letra) zeta, zeda, ceda.
Zeeland ['zilənd, B 'zeɪ-] *s.* Zelanda, Zelandia.
Zeelander [-ləndər, B -də] *s.* zelandés, zelandesa, celandés, celandesa.
zein ['ziən] *s.* (bioquím.) zeína, ceína.
zemindar, *var. de* **zamindar.**
zenana [zə'nɑnə, B zɛ-] *s.* zenana, harén en la India y Persia.
Zend-Avesta [ˌzɛndə'vɛstə] *s.* (relig.) Zendavesta, libros sagrados del zoroastrismo.
zenith ['zinəθ, B 'zɛnɪθ] *s.* 1. (astr.) cenit, zenit. 2. (fig.) cenit, apogeo.
zenithal [-əl] *a.* cenital.
zenith tube, (astr.) telescopio cenital.
Zeno ['zinoʊ] *s.* Zenón, filósofo griego.
zeolite ['ziəˌlaɪt] *s.* (geol.) ceolita, zeolita.
zephyr ['zɛfər, B -ə] *s.* 1. céfiro, poniente, favonio. 2. (tej.) céfiro. 3. **Z.,** (mitol.) Céfiro, el viento Oeste personificado.
zeppelin ['zɛpələn, 'zɛplən] *a.* zepelín, dirigible.
zero ['zɪroʊ, B 'zɪər-] *s.* (*pl.* ZEROS O ZEROES) 1. cero. 2. (fig.) nada; cero a la izquierda, nadie, nulidad. 3. **Z.,** Cero (avión de guerra japonés). 4. **to fly at z.,** (aer.) volar a una altura menor de mil pies. —*a.* (meteor.) cero. —*v.t.* (*pret., p.p.* ZEROED; *p.pr.* ZEROING) (ú. gen. con *in*) 1. centrar la puntería sobre (blanco, posiciones enemigas, etc.). 2. centrar la puntería de (un arma de fuego). —*v.i.* **z. in (on),** centrar la puntería (sobre).
zero alignment, (ópt.) línea de fe.
zero cutout, (mec.) interruptor de vacío.
zero-g, (astronáut.) gravedad nula.
zero hour, hora cero (hora de ataque; momento crítico).
zest [zɛst] *s.* gusto, sabor; deleite, placer.
zestful ['zɛstfəl] *a.* sabroso; lleno de viveza, alegre, vivo.
zestfully [-fəlɪ] *adv.* con gusto o sabor, sabrosamente; con viveza.
zestfulness [-fəlnəs] *s.* gusto, sumo placer.
zesty ['zɛstɪ] *a.* (ZESTIER; ZESTIEST) gustoso, sabroso; deleitoso.
zeta ['zeɪtə, B 'zitə] *s.* zeta, sexta letra del alfabeto griego.
Zetes ['zitiz] *s.* (mitol.) Zeteo, argonauta, hijo de Boreas.
Zethus ['ziθəs] *s.* (mitol.) Zetos, hijo de Zeus que construyó las murallas de Tebas.
zeugma ['zugmə, B 'zjug-] *s.* (gram., ret.) zeugma, zeuma, ceugma.
Zeus [zus, B zjus] *s.* (mitol.) Zeus, deidad máxima del panteón griego, rey del Olimpo.
zibeline, zibelline ['zɪbəˌlin, B -ˌlaɪn] *s.* (tej.) cebellina.
zibet, zibeth ['zɪbət] *s.* (zool.) gato de algalia, civeta de la India.
ziggurat ['zɪgəˌræt] *s.* (arte., hist.) zigurat (pirámide babilónica con un templo en su vértice).
zigzag ['zɪgˌzæg] *s.* zigzag. —*a.* en zigzag, zigzagueante, ej., *z. course,* recorrido en zigzag, *z. trench,* trinchera en zigzag o zigzagueante. —*adv.* en zigzag. —*v.i.* (*pret., p.p.* ZIGZAGGED; *p.pr.* ZIGZAGGING) mover(se) en zigzag, zigzaguear. —*v.t.* hacer zigzaguear, dar forma de zigzag a.
zigzag winding, (elec.) devanadora de zigzag.
zillion ['zɪljən] *s.* (fam.) número astronómico. —*a.* enorme, astronómico (número, cantidad).
zinc [zɪŋk] *s.* (quím.) cinc, zinc. —*v.t.* (*pret., p.p.* ZINCED O ZINCKED; *p.pr.* ZINCING O ZINCKING) bañar en cinc, revestir de cinc, galvanizar.
zincate ['zɪŋˌkeɪt] *s.* (quím.) cincato.
zinc blende, (min.) blenda de cinc, esfalerita.
zinc bloom, (min.) flor de cinc.
zinc carbonate, (min.) carbonato de cinc, calamina.
zinc chloride, (quím.) cloruro de cinc.
zinciferous [zɪŋ'kɪfərəs] *a.* cincífero, que contiene cinc.
zincify ['zɪŋkəˌfaɪ] *v.t.* (*pret., pp.* ZINCIFIED; *p.pr.* ZINCIFYING) revestir o impregnar de cinc, galvanizar.
zincite [-ˌkaɪt] *s.* (min.) cincita.
zincky [-kɪ] *a.* (ZINCKIER; ZINCKIEST) (min.) cíncico.
zincograph ['zɪŋkəˌgræf, B -ˌgrɑf] *s.* cincograbado. —*v.t.* grabar en cinc; reproducir mediante cincograbado.
zincographer [zɪŋ'kɑgrəfər, B -'kɔgrəfə] *s.* cincograbador.
zincographic [ˌzɪŋkə'græfɪk] **zincographical** [-ɪkəl] *a.* cincográfico.
zincography [zɪŋ'kɑgrəfɪ, B -'kɔg-] *s.* cincografía.
zinc ointment, (farm.) ungüento de cinc.
zincous ['zɪŋkəs] *a.* (quím.) cíncico, de cinc, del cinc.
zinc oxide, (quím.) óxido de cinc, cincita.
zinc sulfate, (quím.) sulfato de cinc.
zinc sulfide, (quím.) sulfuro de cinc.
zinc white, (quím.) blanco de cinc.
zincy, *a.* (ZINCIER; ZINCIEST) *var. de* **zincky.**
zing [zɪŋ] *s.* 1. zumbido estridente. 2. (fig.) brío, ánimo, entusiasmo. —*v.i.* zumbar como una bala.
Zingiberaceae [ˌzɪndʒəbə'reɪsɪˌi] *s. pl.* (bot.) cingiberáceas, zingiberáceas.
zingiberaceous [-'reɪʃəs] *a.* (bot.) cingiberáceo, zingiberáceo.
zinkenite ['zɪŋkəˌnaɪt] *s.* (min.) zinkenita.
zinky, *a.* (ZINKIER; ZINKIEST) *var. de* **zincky.**
zinnia ['zɪnɪə, 'zɪnjə] *s.* (bot.) cinnia, zinia.
Zion ['zaɪən] *s.* (bíbl.) 1. Sión, colina en Jerusalén en la que se erigía el templo. 2. p. ext., el pueblo hebreo. 3. (fig.) el cielo, el paraíso.
Zionism [-ˌɪzəm] *s.* sionismo, movimiento en favor del retorno de los judíos a Israel.
Zionist [-əst] *s., a.* sionista.
Zionistic [ˌzaɪə'nɪstɪk] *a.* sionista.
zip [zɪp] *s.* 1. silbido, zumbido (ej., de una bala). 2. (fig.) brío, vigor, energía, vitalidad. —*v.i.* (*pret., p.p.* ZIPPED; *p.pr.* ZIPPING) 1. silbar, zumbar (como una bala). 2. **z. about** (o **around** o **by**), actuar con energía, mover o pasar como un rayo; **z. out,** salir rápido, salir como disparado. —*v.t.* **z. open,** abrir con cremallera, abrir la cremallera de; **z. up,** cerrar con cremallera; cerrar la cremallera de.
zip code, código postal.
zip gun, fusil improvisado (hecho con un tubo de cañería, con percutor actuado por una cinta elástica para disparar balas de calibre 22).

zipper ['zɪpər, B -ə] *s.* cremallera, cierre relámpago (Amer.).
zippered [-ərd, B -əd] *a.* (provisto) de cremallera; cerrado con cremallera.
Zipporah [zɪ'pɔrə] *s.* (bíbl.) Séfora, esposa de Moisés.
zippy ['zɪpɪ] *a.* (ZIPPIER; ZIPPIEST) (fam.) brioso, vivaz.
zircon ['zɜrˌkɑn, B 'zɜˌkɔn] *s.* (min.) circón, zircón.
zirconate ['zɜrkəˌneɪt, B 'zɜkə-] *s.* (quím.) circonato.
zirconia [ˌzɜr'koʊnɪə, B zə'-] *s.* (quím.) circona.
zirconic [-'kɑnɪk, B -'kɔn-] *a.* (quím.) circónico.
zirconium [-'koʊnɪəm, B ˌzɜ'-] *s.* (quím.) circonio, zirconio.
zirconium oxide, (quím.) circona.
zither ['zɪðər, 'zɪθ-, B 'zɪðə] *s.* (mús.) cítara.
zitherist [-ərəst] *s.* citarista, el que toca la cítara.
zoa, *pl. de* **zoon.**
zoantharian [ˌzoʊˌæn'θɛrɪən, B -'θɛər-] *a., s.* (zool.) zoantario.
zoanthropy [zoʊ'ænθrəpɪ] *s.* (med.) zoantropía.
zodiac ['zoʊdɪˌæk] *s.* (astron.) zodiaco, zodíaco.
zodiacal [zoʊ'daɪəkəl] *a.* (astron.) zodiacal.
zoea [zoʊ'iə] *s.* (*pl.* ZOEAE [-'iˌi] o ZOEAS) (zool.) zoe, zoea.
Zoïlus ['zoʊɪləs, B 'zɔɪləs] *s.* 1. Zoilo, retórico y filósofo griego, conocido principalmente por sus críticas a Homero. 2. p. ext. crítico implacable.
zoisite ['zɔɪˌsaɪt] *s.* (min.) zoisita.
zoism ['zoʊˌɪzəm] *s.* (filos.) zoísmo, teoría del principio vital.
Zomba ['zɑmbə, B 'zɔmbə] *s.* Zomba, capital de Malawi.
zombi, zombie ['zɑmbɪ, B 'zɔm-] *s.* 1. cadáver resucitado por medio de magia negra. 2. (jer.) tipo raro, persona excéntrica; persona que parece actuar mecánicamente y bajo una influencia extraña. 3. bebida fuerte (de licores mezclados con ron y jugo de fruta).
zonal ['zoʊnəl] **zonary** [-ərɪ] *a.* zonal; de zonas, en zonas.
zonate [-eɪt] **zonated** [-əd] *a.* con (las) zonas marcadas.
zonation [zoʊ'neɪʃən] *s.* 1. división en zonas, zonificación (Amer.). 2. (biol., geog.) distribución en zonas.
zone [zoʊn] *s.* 1. zona. 2. (ant., poét.) faja, cintura. —*v.t.* dividir en zonas, distribuir o disponer por zonas; marcar con zonas, zonificar (Amer.).
zone of influence, zona de influencia.
zonular ['zoʊnjələr, B -lə] *a.* (anat.) zonular.
zonule ['zoʊnjul] *s.* (anat.) zónula.
zoo [zu] *s.* (jardín) zoológico, zoo.
zoocecidium [ˌzoʊəsə'sɪdɪəm] *s.* (*pl.* ZOOCECIDIA [-ə]) (bot.) zoocecidio.
zooflagellate [ˌzoʊə'flædʒələt] *s.* (zool.) zooflagelado.
zoogamete [-gə'mit, B -'gæmˌit] *s.* (bot.) zoogámeta.
zoogenic [-'dʒɛnɪk] **zoogenous** [zoʊ'ɑdʒənəs, B -'ɔdʒ-] *a.* zoogénico, propio de los animales.
zoogeographic [ˌzoʊəˌdʒiə'græfɪk] **zoogeographical** [-ɪkəl] *a.* zoogeográfico.
zoogeography [-dʒɪ'ɑgrəfɪ, B -'ɔg-] *s.* zoogeografía.
zooglea [zoʊ'ɑglɪə, B ˌzoʊə'gliə] *s.* (med.) zooglea.
zoographic [ˌzoʊə'græfɪk] **zoographical** [-ɪkəl] *a.* zoográfico.
zoography [zoʊ'ɑgrəfɪ, B -'ɔg-] *s.* zoografía.
zooid ['zoʊˌɔɪd] *s.* (zool.) zooide.
zooidal [zoʊ'ɔɪdəl] *a.* (zool.) zooide.
zoolater [zoʊ'ɑlətər, B -'ɔlətə] *s.* zoólatra, persona que rinde culto a los animales.
zoolatry [-ətrɪ] *s.* zoolatría.
zoolith [zoʊəlɪθ] *s.* (geol.) zoolito.
zoolithic [zoʊə'lɪθɪk] *a.* zoolítico.
zoological [-'lɑdʒɪkəl, B -'lɔdʒ-] *a.* zoológico.
zoological garden [B zʊ'lɔdʒ-] jardín zoológico.
zoologist [zoʊ'ɑlədʒəst, B -'ɔl-] *s.* zoólogo, zoóloga.
zoology [-dʒɪ] *s.* (*pl.* ZOOLOGIES) zoología.
zoom [zum] *v.i.* 1. volar zumbando. 2. (aer.) subir en ángulo abrupto. 3. (cinem., foto.) acercarse o alejarse la cámara muy rápidamente (al fotografiar una escena). —*s.* 1. zumbido. 2. (aer.) tirón.
zoometry [zoʊ'ɑmətrɪ, B -'ɔm-] *s.* zoometría.
zoom lens, (foto.) objetivo zoom, objetivo de distancia focal variable.
zoomorphic [ˌzoʊə'mɔrfɪk, B -'mɔfɪk] *a.* zoomórfico, de forma animal, con forma de animal.
zoomorphism [-ˌfɪzəm] *s.* (antrop.) zoomorfismo.
zoon ['zoʊˌɑn, B -ˌɔn] *s.* (*pl.* ZOA [-ə]) (zool.) zoon.
zoonosis [zoʊ'ɑnəsəs, B ˌzoʊə'noʊ-] *s.* (med.) zoonosis.
zooparasite [ˌzoʊə'pærəˌsaɪt] *s.* zooparásito, animal parásito.
Zoophaga [zoʊ'ɑfəgə, B -'ɔf-] *s. pl.* (zool.) zoófagos, mamíferos carnívoros.
zoophagous [-gəs] *s.* zoófago, carnívoro.
zoophilous [zoʊ'ɑfələs, B -'ɔf-] *a.* (bot.) zoófilo.
zoophobia [ˌzoʊə'foʊbɪə] *s.* zoofobia, miedo anormal a los animales.
zoophoric [-'fɔrɪk] *a.* (arq.) zooforico.
zoophorus [zoʊ'ɑfərəs, B -'ɔf-] *s.* (arq.) zoóforo.
zoophyte ['zoʊəˌfaɪt] *s.* (zool.) zoófito.
zoophytology [ˌzoʊəfaɪ'tɑlədʒɪ, B -'tɔl-] *s.* zoofitología.
zooplankton [ˌzoʊə'plæŋktən] *s.* (zool.) zooplanctnon.
zooplasty ['zoʊəˌplæstɪ] *s.* (med.) zooplastia.
zoosperm [-ˌspɜrm, B -ˌspɜm] *s.* (med.) 1. zoospermo, zoospermio. 2. (bot.) zoospora.
zoosporangium [ˌzoʊəspə'rændʒɪəm] *s.* (*pl.* ZOOSPORANGIA [-ə]) (bot.) zoosporangio.
zoospore ['zoʊəˌspɔr, B -ˌspɔ] *s.* (bot., zool.) zoospora.
zootaxy [-tæksɪ] *s.* (zool.) zootaxia.
zootechnical [ˌzoʊə'tɛknɪkəl] *a.* zootécnico.
zootechnics [-nɪks] *s. pl.* (*sing. en const.*) zootecnia.
zootechny ['zoʊəˌtɛknɪ] *s.* (*pl.* ZOOTECHNIES) zootecnia.
zootherapy [ˌzoʊə'θɛrəpɪ] *s.* (vet.) zooterapia.
zootomic [-'tɑmɪk, B -'tɔm-] **zootomical** [-ɪkəl] *a.* zootómico.
zootomy [zoʊ'ɑtəmɪ, B -'ɔt-] *s.* zootomía.
zoot suit ['zut-] (jer., E.U.) antiguo traje de petimetre (que se caracterizaba por la chaqueta ancha hasta las rodillas y pantalones muy anchos en las caderas y muy ajustados en los tobillos).
Zoroaster [ˌzoʊroʊ'æstər, B ˌzɔroʊ-tə] *s.* (relig.) Zoroastro, Zaratustra, profeta persa fundador del mazdeísmo.
Zoroastrian [-'æstrɪən] *a.* (relig.) zoroástrico.
Zoroastrianism [-ˌɪzəm] *s.* zoroastrismo o mazdeísmo, religión fundada por Zoroastro.
zortzico [zɔr'sikoʊ, B zɔ'-] *s.* zorcico, canción y danza popular vasca.
zoster ['zoʊstər, 'zɑs-, B 'zɔstə] *s.* 1. (med.) soster, herpe zoster, zona. 2. (hist.) cinturón (de los antiguos griegos).
Zouave [zu'ɑv, zwɑv] *s.* (mil.) zuavo, soldado argelino de vistoso uniforme, que antiguamente Francia incorporaba a su ejército de infantería.
zounds [zaʊndz] *interj.* (ant.) ¡voto al chápiro! ¡cáspita!
Zr *símb. de* **zirconium,** circonio (Zr).
zucchetto [zu'kɛtoʊ] *s.* (italiano) solideo.
zucchini [-'kinɪ] *s.* (*pl.* ZUCCHINI o ZUCCHINIS) (bot.) calabacín, variedad de calabaza, zapallito italiano (Amer.).
Zulu ['zulu] *s. a.* zulú (tribu africana).
Zululand [-ˌlænd] *s.* Zululandia, territorio al N. de Natal en África del Sur.
Zuñi ['zunɪ, B -njɪ] *s.* (*pl.* ZUÑI o ZUÑIS) zuñi (indio mejicano).
Zuñian [-ən] *a.* zuñi.
zwieback ['swiˌbæk, 'zwaɪ-, B 'zwi-] *s.* bizcocho muy tostado de marcado sabor a canela.
Zwinglian ['zwɪŋglɪən] *a.* (relig.) zwingliano, de Zwinglio. —*s.* seguidor de (la doctrina teocrática de) Zwinglio.
Zwinglianism [-əˌnɪzəm] *s.* (relig.) zwinglianismo.
zygapophysis [ˌzaɪgə'pɑfəsəs, B -'pɔf-] *s.* (*pl.* ZYGAPOPHYSES [-ˌsiz]) (anat., zool.) cigapófisis, zigapófisis.
zygodactyl [ˌzaɪgə'dæktəl] *a., s.* (zool.) cigodáctilo, zigodáctilo.
zygodactylous [-tələs] *a.* (zool.) cigodáctilo, zigodáctilo.
zygogenesis [-'dʒɛnəsəs] *s.* (biol.) cigogénesis, zigogénesis.
zygoma [zaɪ'goʊmə] *s.* (*pl.* ZYGOMATA [-mətə]) (anat.) cigoma, zigoma.
zygomatic [ˌzaɪgə'mætɪk] *a.* (anat., zool.) cigomático, zigomático.
zygomatic arch, (anat.) arco cigomático o zigomático.
zygomorphic [-'mɔrfɪk, B -'mɔfɪk] (biol.) zigomorfo, cigomorfo, cigomórfico, zigomórfico.
zygomorphism [-ˌfɪzəm] *s.* (biol.) cigomorfismo, zigomorfismo.
zygophyllaceous [ˌzaɪgoʊfə'leɪʃəs] *a.* (bot.) cigofiláceo, zigofiláceo.
zygophyte ['zaɪgəˌfaɪt] *s.* (bot.) cigófita, zigófita.
zygosis [zaɪ'goʊsəs] *s.* (*pl.* ZYGOSES [-ˌsiz]) (bot., zool.) cigosis, zigosis.
zygospore ['zaɪgəˌspɔr, B -ˌspɔ] *s.* (bot.) cigospora, zigospora, cigosporo, zigosporo.
zygote [zaɪgoʊt] *s.* (biol.) cigota, zigota, cigoto, zigoto.
zygotene ['zaɪgəˌtin] *s.* (biol.) cigoteno, zigoteno.
zymase ['zaɪˌmeɪs] *s.* (bioquím.) cimasa, zimasa.
zyme [zaɪm] *s.* (med.) cimo, zimo.
zymogen ['zaɪmədʒən] *s.* (bioquím.) cimógeno, zimógeno.
zymogenesis [ˌzaɪmə'dʒɛnəsəs] *s.* (bioquím.) cimogénesis, zimogénesis.
zymogenic [-'dʒɛnɪk] *a.* (bioquím.) cimógeno, zimógeno.
zymology [zaɪ'mɑlədʒɪ, B -'mɔl-] *s.* (med.) cimología, zimología.
zymolysis [-əsəs] *s.* (bioquím.) cimólisis, zimólisis.
zymometer [zaɪ'mɑmətər, B -'mɔmɪtə] *s.* (rad.) cimómetro, zimómetro.
zymoplastic [ˌzaɪmə'plæstɪk] *a.* (bioquím.) cimoplástico, zimoplástico.
zymoscope ['zaɪməˌskoʊp] *s.* (rad.) cimoscopio, zimoscopio.
zymosis [zaɪ'moʊsəs] *s.* (med.) cimosis, zimosis.
zymotic [-'mɑtɪk, B -'mɔt-] *a.* (med.) cimótico, zimótico.
zymurgy ['zaɪmərdʒɪ, B -ˌmɜdʒɪ] *s.* (quím.) cimurgia, zimurgia.

PART II

Spanish-English

PARTE II

Español-Inglés

Brief Outline of Spanish Pronunciation

letter	*approximate sound*
a	Like **a** in American English **father:** *casa, padre, alma.*
b	At the beginning of a word and when preceded by **m,** like English **b** in **bass, amber:** *beso, ambos;* much softer when it is between vowels or followed by **l** or **r:** *abanico, doble, abrir.*
c	Before **e** or **i** like English **th** in **thin, thaw** — in most of Spain; like English **c** in **center, cipher** — in America and Southern Spain (Andalusia): *cinco, dice, centro, cepo;* before **a, o, u,** the same as in English **cow, cop, croup,** but without aspiration or explosion: *cama, comer, cutis, croquis.*
ch	Like English **ch** in **child:** *chico, ochenta.*
d	At the beginning of a word and after **n,** like English **d** in **day, dance,** but without aspiration or explosion: *día, donde;* in all other positions it resembles the English **th** in **this, that, those:** *cada, piedra, sordo, Madrid.*
e	Like English **e** in **pet, mess, set:** *perro, mesa, seto.*
f	Like in English **fat, free:** *foca, afuera, frito.*
g	When followed by **a, o, u,** or a consonant, like **g** in English **go, great,** but without aspiration or explosion: *gato, gorra, guapo, grande, glotón;* before **e** and **i** like a strongly aspirated English **h** in **house, ha!** (or **ch** in German **Bach**): *gente, ágil;* the **u** in **ue** and **ui** is silent after **g,** unless marked with a dieresis: *guerra, guía* are pronounced like English **guest** and **guild;** *güiro, agüero* like English **Guinevere** and **Guelph.**
h	Always silent (except after **c,** see letter **ch** above): *hijo, almohada.*
i	Like English **see, meat:** *pino, grito, camino.*
j	Like a strongly aspirated English **h** in **house** (or German **ch** in **Bach**): *jarro, fijo, jota.*
k	Like English **k,** but without aspiration or explosion: *kilo, kimono.*
l	Like English **l** in **list, lamb:** *luz, cola, sal.*
ll	Like English **ly** in **halyard, million:** *calle, pollo, llanta;* regional American variations are like English **y** in **youth,** and like English **s** in **measure** (this last one in Uruguay and Argentina).
m	Like English **m** in **man, among:** *más, jamón, amado.*
n	Like English **n** in **now, note:** *lana, pan, número;* before hard **c** and hard **g,** like English **ng** in **singer:** *banco, tengo.*
ñ	Like English **ny** in **canyon, onion:** *mañana, añil.*
o	Like English **o** in **cord:** *dos, rojo, orden.*
p	Like English **p** in **pot, probe,** but without aspiration or explosion: *pelo, pronto, aparte.*
q	Like English **k,** but without aspiration or explosion: *quitar, aquel* (it is always followed by **ui** or **ue,** but the **u** is silent).
r	At the beginning of a word or after **n, l, s,** it is pronounced like **rr** (see below): *roto, enredo, alrededor, israelí;* in all other positions it is pronounced somewhat like the American English **dd** in **caddie, Eddy:** *cara, pero.*
rr	It is strongly trilled and pronounced like the rolled **r** in Scottish **burn:** *perro, carro, arroz.*
s	Like English **s** in **seam, salt, essay:** *casa, crisis, sitio.*
t	Like English **t** in **star, top,** but without aspiration or explosion: *tenso, lata, atar.*
u	Like English **u** in **brute, rule:** *rudo, abrupto, unir.* (It is silent in the combinations **gue** and **gui** — unless marked with a dieresis — and always silent when preceded by a **q;** see letters **g** and **q** above).
v	Unless emphasis is desired at the beginning of a word (*Valencia, ¡viva!, Valparaíso*), this letter is pronounced, in all positions, like the Spanish **b.**
w	Originally pronounced like **v** or **b;** nowadays, in imitation of the English **w,** it is pronounced like **gu** in **Guam, guacamole;** thus **Washington** and **watt,** pronounced by many Spanish speakers, can sound like *Guashington* and *gwatt.*
x	Exactly like English **x** in **examine, exact:** *máximo, éxito;* in some parts of Spain, certain words such as *auxilio, exacto,* are pronounced as if the **x** were an English **s;** in the words *México, mexicano,* the **x** is pronounced as if it were a **j** (for the former spelling, *Méjico, mejicano*).
y	Like English **y** in **young:** *ya, cuyo.* A regional variant (in Argentina and Uruguay) produces a sound like English **s** in **measure** — see letter **ll** above.
z	In most of Spain it is pronounced like English **th** in **think, thwart:** *zambullida, zancos;* in America and Southern Spain (Andalusia) like English **s** in **seam, soft, essay.**

The treatment of Spanish diphthongs and triphthongs is beyond the scope of this brief review. However, here are some equivalent sounds to initiate the reader into the approximate pronunciation of the most common ones:

ai—ay	Like English **i** in **fight:** *laico, baile, ¡ay!*
au	Like English **ou** in **round:** *pausa, raudo.*
ei—ey	Like English **ey** in **they:** *reina, mamey.*
eu	Like **e** and **o** in **get to:** *pleura, deuda.*
oi—oy	Like English **oi** in **voice:** *oigo, voy.*
ia—ya	Like English **ya** in **yard:** *piano, yarey.*
ua	Like **w** and **a** in **what:** *cuarto, aguante.*
ie—ye	Like English **ye** in **yesterday:** *pie, yerno.*
ue	Like **w** and **e** in **when:** *puede, renuente.*
oi—yo	Like English **yo** in **yoke:** *miope, yodo.*
uo	Like English **uo** in **quote:** *vacuo, cuota.*
iu—yu	Like English **yu** in **Yuma:** *triunfo, ayuda.*
ui—uy	Like English **we** in **weed:** *ruido, muy.*
iai	Like English **yi** in **yipe:** *confiáis, fastidiáis.*
iei	Like the English word **yea:** *enviéis, confiéis.*
uai—uay	Like English **wi** in **wife:** *aguáis, Uruguay.*
uei—uey	Like English **wei** in **weight:** *atenuéis, buey.*

Pronunciation of the Spanish Alphabet

The IPA symbols show you how the letters of the alphabet should be read.

a [ɑ], **b** [be] or [be ˈlarga], **c** [se] or [θe], **d** [de], **e** [e], **f** [ˈefe], **g** [xe], **h** [ˈatʃe], **i** [i], **j** [ˈxota], **k** [ka], **l** [ˈele], **m** [ˈeme], **n** [ˈene], **ñ** [ˈeɲe], **o** [o], **p** [pe], **q** [ku], **r** [ˈere], **s** [ˈese], **t** [te], **u** [u], **v** [be] or [be ˈkorta], **w** [ˈdoʙle ʙe], **x** [ˈekis], **y** [i grjega], **z** [ˈseta] or [ˈθeta].

Elements of Spanish Grammar

Note

The following is only a brief review meant to help the reader understand the examples and expressions used in the body of this dictionary. In no way does this section constitute a complete treatise of Spanish grammar.

THE NOUN

The Gender

1. MASCULINE are most Spanish nouns ending in *o, e, i, u, j, l, n, r, s, t, x.*

Some exceptions: *mano* (hand), *sangre* (blood), *leche* (milk), *hurí* (houri), *tribu* (tribe), *miel* (honey), *imagen* (image), *flor* (flower), *tos* (cough), and most words of Greek origin ending in *is,* such as *tesis* (thesis), *hipótesis* (hypothesis), *síntesis* (synthesis), etc.

Also masculine are: names of rivers, oceans, mountains, days of the week, months of the year; names of countries, provinces, cities and towns — except those ending in *a;* names of male persons and animals and the notes of the scale (do, re, mi, fa, sol, etc.).

2. FEMININE are most Spanish nouns ending in *a, d, -ión, z, -umbre* and *-ie,* e.g. *casa* (house), *actitud* (attitude), *lección* (lesson), *paz* (peace), *muchedumbre* (multitude, crowd), *efigie* (effigy).

Some exceptions: *día* (day), *tranvía* (trolley car, tramway) and many nouns of Greek origin, e.g. *clima* (climate), *dilema* (dilemma), *planeta* (planet), *poema* (poem), *problema* (problem), *telegrama* (telegram), etc. Other exceptions: *ataúd* (coffin), *césped* (lawn, grass), *laúd* (lute), *centurión* (centurion), *gorrión* (sparrow), *arroz* (rice), *pez* (fish — live), *barniz* (varnish).

Also feminine are the names of the letters of the alphabet; of countries, provinces, cities and towns ending in *a;* names of female persons and animals.

Some nouns can be either masculine or feminine, according to the sex of the person in question, e.g. *idiota* (idiot), *telefonista* (telephone operator), *mártir* (martyr), *suicida* (suicide). Others take on the gender according to the meaning required, e.g. *el cura* (priest), *la cura* (cure); *el orden* (order —sequence), *la orden* (order — command).

Other nouns can be either masculine or feminine, although their meaning is the same, e.g. *azúcar* (sugar), *mar* (sea), *arte* (art). N.B. *arte* is always feminine in the plural: *las artes* (the arts).

In certain nouns of common gender, the sex is indicated by placing *macho* (male) or *hembra* (female) after the noun, e.g. *la perdiz macho* or *hembra* (the male or female partridge), *el águila macho* or *hembra* (the male or female eagle).

The Plural

The plural of Spanish nouns is formed by adding *s* to words ending in an unaccented vowel, e.g. *pluma-plumas* (pens, feathers), *carta-cartas* (letters, cards); by adding *-es* to words which end in an accented vowel or consonant, e.g. *rubí-rubíes* (rubies), *autoridad-autoridades* (authorities).

Some exceptions: *papá-papás, mamá-mamás, sofá-sofás, café-cafés.*

THE ARTICLE

The Definite Article

MASCULINE: *el, los* FEMININE: *la, las*
NEUTER: *lo*

1. The definite article agrees in number and gender with the noun it accompanies, e.g. *el caballo* (the horse), *las mujeres* (the women).

2. The masculine singular article, however, is used before feminine nouns which begin with accented *a* or *ha,* e.g. *el agua* (water), *el hambre* (hunger), *el águila,* (eagle).

3. The masculine singular article becomes attached to a preceding *a* or *de* to form *al* and *del,* e.g. *fueron al cine* (they went to the movies), *volvió del colegio* (he returned from school).

4. The definite article is used more frequently in Spanish than in English. The additional uses are:

a) With nouns used in a general sense, e.g. *me gustan las manzanas* (I like apples), *el hombre y su ambiente* (man and his environment).

b) Usually with the names of professions, arts, sports and sciences, e.g. *el periodismo* (journalism), *la cacería* (hunting), *la escultura* (sculpture — the art), *la medicina* (medicine — the science).

c) With abstract nouns, e.g. *la libertad* (freedom, liberty).

d) With the names of some countries, e.g. *la Argentina, el Japón* (Japan).

e) Usually with the names of languages — except after *estudiar* (to study), *hablar* (to speak) and the prepositions *de* (of) and *en* (in) —, e.g. *el inglés es difícil* (English is difficult), *estudia ruso* (he studies Russian), *profesor de alemán* (German teacher).

f) With the names of seasons, e.g. *el invierno* (winter), *la primavera* (spring).

g) Before titles, e.g. *el señor Sánchez, el presidente Roosevelt* — except in direct address: *¿cómo está, señor Sánchez?* (how are you, Mr. Sanchez?).

h) Often before parts of the body and articles of clothing where English uses possessive adjectives, e.g. *me rompí el dedo* (I broke my finger), *ponte la chaqueta* (put on your jacket).

i) Before proper names qualified by an adjective, *el pobre Juan* (poor John).

j) In expressions of time, e.g. *son las diez* (it's ten o'clock), *a la una* (at one o'clock).

k) With weights and measurements of time, e.g. *cuesta siete pesetas la onza* (it costs seven pesetas an ounce), *gana cien dólares a la semana* (he earns one hundred dollars a week).

l) With such words as *colegio* (school), *cárcel* (jail), e.g. *fue al colegio* (he went to school), *está en la cárcel* (he is in jail).

5. The definite article is omitted before the number of the title of a king, pope, etc., e.g. *Jorge V* (George the Fifth), *Pío XII* (Pius the Twelfth).

6. The neuter article *lo* is used with the masculine singular of the adjective or past participle, e.g. *lo bello* (the beautiful), *lo increíble* (the incredible, the incredible thing), *lamentamos lo ocurrido* (we regret what has happened).

The Indefinite Article

MASCULINE: *uno, unos* FEMININE: *una, unas*

1. The indefinite article agrees with the noun in both gender and number, e.g. *un amigo* (a friend), *unas casas* (some houses, a few houses).

2. The masculine singular article, however, must be used before feminine nouns which begin with accented *a* or *ha,* e.g. *un alma* (a soul), *un hada* (a fairy).

3. Unlike the definite article, the indefinite article is used less in Spanish than in English. It is omitted in the following cases:

a) Before unmodified nouns denoting nationality, rank or occupation in a general sense after the verbs *ser* (to be) and *parecer* (to seem), e.g. *es española* (she is a Spaniard), *mi hermano es médico* (my brother is a doctor), BUT: *mi hermano es un médico famoso* (my brother is a famous doctor), *parece que es bailarina* (it seems she is a ballerina), BUT: *parece una bailarina* (she looks like a ballerina).

b) Before *otro, cierto, cien, mil, medio, tal, ¡qué . . !,* e.g. *mañana será otro día* (tomorrow will be another day), *cierto amigo tuyo* (a certain friend of yours), *cien veces* (a hundred times), *medio kilo* (a half kilo), *de tal palo tal astilla* (a chip off the old block), *¡qué sorpresa!* (what a surprise!).

c) After *con* (with) or *sin* (without) when the singleness or individuality of the following noun is not important, e.g. *una casa con piscina* (a house with a swimming pool), *salió sin sombrero* (she went out without a hat).

THE ADJECTIVE

Descriptive Adjectives

1. There are two kinds of descriptive adjectives in Spanish:

a) Those with one form for each gender, e.g. *pequeño-pequeña* (small), *encantador-encantadora* (charming).

b) Those with one form for both genders, e.g. *grande* (large, great), *común* (common), *azul* (blue), *capaz* (capable), *fiel* (faithful).

2. Spanish adjectives form the plural in the same way as Spanish nouns.

3. Spanish adjectives agree in number and gender with the nouns they qualify.

4. If an adjective qualifies a group of two or more nouns of different genders, the adjective will be in the masculine, e.g. *la casa y el jardín son muy hermosos* (the house and the garden are very beautiful).

5. Spanish adjectives usually follow the noun when they describe a quality, but they may also precede it when stressing a quality inherent in the noun, or when they are purely ornamental, e.g. *la silla tapizada* (the upholstered chair), *el fiero león* (the fierce lion).

6. Spanish adjectives usually precede the noun when they are demonstrative or possessive, or when they describe quantity, e.g. *mis libros* (my books), *veinte hombres* (twenty men), *aquel niño* (that child).

7. Nearly all Spanish adjectives may be used with the corresponding article to form a noun, e.g. *es un estudioso* (he is a studious person), *el tímido* (the timid one), *lo mejor es esperar* (the best [thing] is to wait).

Demonstrative Adjectives

MASCULINE: *este, estos* (this, these); *ese, esos; aquel, aquellos* (that, those).

FEMININE: *esta, estas* (this, these); *esa, esas; aquella, aquellas* (that, those).

Possessive Adjectives

1st PERSON: *mi, mis* (my); *nuestro, nuestros; nuestra, nuestras* (our).

2nd PERSON: *tu, tus; vuestro, vuestros; vuestra, vuestras* (your).

FORMAL: *su, sus* (your); same form used for masculine and feminine, whether addressing one or more persons.

3rd PERSON: *su, sus* (his, her, its, their); same form used for masculine and feminine, whether referring to one or more persons.

Interrogative Adjectives

¿qué? (what?); *¿cuál?* (which?); *¿cuánto? ¿cuánta?* (how much?; *¿cuántos? ¿cuántas?* (how many?).

THE ADVERB

1. *Adverbs of Manner*

a) Most adverbs of manner are formed by attaching the suffix *-mente* to the feminine singular of some adjectives, e.g. *ridículamente* (ridiculously — from the adjective *ridículo*), or to the common form of others, e.g. *felizmente* (happily — from the adjective *feliz*).

When two or more adverbs occur together, only the last one bears the suffix *-mente,* e.g. *se expresó clara y concisamente* (he expressed himself clearly and concisely).

b) Other adverbs have the same form as the masculine singular of the adjective, e.g. *no habla muy claro* (he doesn't speak very clearly), *camina rápido* (walk quickly).

c) Still others have various forms, e.g. *aprisa* (fast), *así* (like this, this way, thus), *bien* (well), *despacio* (slowly), etc.

2. Adverbs of time, place, quantity; interrogative, indefinite, demonstrative and relative adverbs have various forms, e.g. *ayer* (yesterday), *hoy* (today), *lejos* (far, far away), *allí* (there, over there), *algo* (some), *nada* (nothing), *adelante* (forward), *demasiado* (too much), etc.

COMPARISON OF ADJECTIVES AND ADVERBS

In most cases, the comparison of Spanish adjectives and adverbs is formed by placing *más* (more) before the positive, e.g. *hermoso* (beautiful), *más hermoso, claramente, más claramente* (clearly, more clearly). Some have irregular comparatives, e.g.

Adjective	Adverb	Comparison
bueno (good)	*bien* (well)	*mejor* (better)
malo (bad)	*mal* (badly)	*peor* (worse)
mucho (much)	*mucho* (much)	*más* (more)
poco (little)	*poco* (little)	*menos* (less)

In comparative constructions, the English word "than is translated by *que,* except when followed by an indication of quantity or number, in which case *de* is used, e.g. *soy más alto que él* (I am taller than he-him), *es mejor esperar aquí que salir tan tarde* (it is better to wait here than to go out so late), *cuesta más de cien dólares* (it costs more than one hundred dollars), *menos de siete años* (less than seven years).

The superlative is formed by adding the corresponding definite article before the comparative, e.g. *es el más grande de todos* (it is the largest of all), *el torero más famoso de España* (the most famous bullfighter in Spain).

PRONOUNS

Personal Pronouns

Subject	Object	Prepositional	
yo	*me*	*mí*	I
tú	*te*	*ti*	you
él	*lo-le*	*él*	he, it
ella	*la-le*	*ella*	she, it
nosotros(-tras)	*nos*	*nosotros(-tras)*	we
vosotros(-tras)	*os*	*vosotros(-tras)*	you (plural)
ellos-ellas	*los-las-les*	*ellos-ellas*	they

a) *tú* and *vos* (*vos* more commonly used in parts of America, especially in Argentina) are used to address children, relatives and friends. Although *vosotros* is the plural of *tú* and is used in Spain, *ustedes* is always used as the plural of both *tú* and *vos* in America.

b) *usted* is used in formal address — with strangers, persons of rank — and often, too, to reprimand a child.

c) The forms *le-les* become *se* when they occur with another object pronoun of the third person, e.g. *se lo di* (I gave it to him), NOT *le lo di.*

d) The object forms are always attached to the infinitive, gerund and imperative affirmative, e.g. *debes verla* (you should-must see her), *terminó dándoselo* (he ended up giving it to him), *cómpramelo* (buy it for me).

In all other cases the object form precedes the verb, e.g. *la vi ayer* (I saw her yesterday), *no lo hagas* (do not do it), *no me lo digas* (do not tell me).

e) The preposition *con,* together with *mí, ti, sí,* forms the composite words *conmigo, contigo, consigo* (with me-myself, with you-yourself, with him-himself — her-herself, it-itself, they-themselves).

f) The pronoun *lo* sometimes can be translated by "so" or left untranslated, e.g. *¿es Picasso un buen pintor? sí lo es.* (is Picasso a good painter? yes, he is.) *te lo dije* (I told you so).

Reflexive Pronouns

	Prepositional	
me	*mí, mí mismo-ma*	myself
te	*ti, ti mismo-ma*	yourself
se	*sí, sí mismo-ma*	himself, herself, itself
nos	*nosotros-tras, nosotros-tras mismos-mas*	ourselves
os	*vosotros-tras, vosotros-tras mismos-mas*	yourselves
se	*sí, sí mismos-mas*	yourselves
se	*sí, sí mismos-mas*	themselves

The reflexive pronoun is used with much greater frequency in Spanish than in English. Some uses are:

a) When the action of the verb is reflected back on the subject, e.g. *se quemó* (he burned himself), *se lava las manos* (he washes his hands).

b) To indicate reciprocity, e.g. *no se saludaron* (they did not greet each other).

c) To form the passive, e.g. *aquí se habla español* (Spanish [is] spoken here), *se canceló el concierto* (the concert was canceled).

d) To form the impersonal construction "one" or "you" plus verb, e.g. *se aprende trabajando* (one learns by working), *no se oye nada* (one can't hear a thing).

e) To indicate a change from one condition to another (very often translated into English by "get and "become"), e.g. *se enriqueció* (he became rich), *se emborrachó* (he got drunk), *no te enojes* (don't get angry).

Reflexive pronouns are appended to the infinitive, gerund and affirmative imperative, but in all other cases they precede the verb, e.g. *mirarse* (to look at oneself), *cómpratelo* (buy it — for yourself), *no te marches* (don't go).

The prepositional form is used after a preposition, where English uses the reflexive form, e.g. *lo compré para mí* (I bought it for myself), *se ríe de sí mismo* (he laughs at himself).

Relative Pronouns

The most frequently used relative pronouns are:

que (who, whom, which, that).
quien-quienes (who, whom, that).
cuyo-cuya, cuyos-cuyas (whose).
lo que (what, e.g. *lo que dijiste resultó ser verdad,* what you said turned out to be true).
lo que (which, e.g. *llegó tarde, lo que en él es raro,* he arrived late, which in him is unusual).

Demonstrative Pronouns

éste-ésta (this); *éstos-éstas* (these); *esto* (this).
ése-ésa (that); *ésos-ésas* (those); *eso* (that).
aquél-aquélla (that); *aquéllos-aquéllas* (those); *aquello* (that).

Possessive Pronouns

el mío, la mía; los míos, las mías (mine)
el nuestro, la nuestra; los nuestros, las nuestras (ours)
el tuyo, la tuya; los tuyos, las tuyas (yours — singular)
el suyo, la suya; los suyos, las suyas (yours — formal)
el vuestro, la vuestra; los vuestros, las vuestras (yours — plural)
el suyo, la suya; los suyos, las suyas (his, hers)
el suyo, la suya; los suyos, las suyas (theirs)

Interrogative Pronouns

quién-quiénes (who); *qué* (what); *cuál* (which, which one, what); *cuáles* (which, which ones); *cuánto-cuánta* (how much); *cuántos-cuántas* (how many).

THE PREPOSITION

For a thorough treatment of all Spanish prepositions and their meanings, uses and examples, we refer the reader to each one, listed alphabetically, in the body of this dictionary.

THE VERB

There are three conjugations, distinguished by the ending of the infinitive: *-ar, -er, -ir.* The endings and conjugations given below are applicable to all regular verbs.

INFINITIVE	*lavar*	*correr*	*subir*
GERUND	*lavando*	*corriendo*	*subiendo*
PAST PARTICIPLE	*lavado*	*corrido*	*subido*

Indicative

Present

(*lav*) *-o, -as, -a, -amos, -áis, -an.*
(*corr*) *-o, -es, -e, -emos, -éis, -en.*
(*sub*) *-o, -es, -e, -imos, -ís, -en.*

Imperfect

(*lav*) *-aba, -abas, -aba, -ábamos, -abais, -aban.*
(*corr*) (*sub*) } *-ía, -ías, -ía, -íamos, -íais, -ían.*

Preterite

(*lav*) *-é, -aste, -ó, -amos, -asteis, -aron.*
(*corr*) (*sub*) } *-í, -iste, -ió, -imos, -isteis, -ieron.*

Future

(*lavar*) (*correr*) (*subir*) } *-é, -ás, -á, -emos, -éis, -án.*

Conditional

(*lavar*) (*correr*) (*subir*) } *-ía, -ías, -ía, -íamos, -íais, -ían.*

Subjunctive

Present

(*lav*) *-e, -es, -e, -emos, -éis, -en.*
(*corr*) (*sub*) } *-a, -as, -a, -amos, -áis, -an.*

Imperfect

(*lav*) *-ara, -aras, -ara, -áramos, -arais, -aran.*
-ase, -ases, -ase, -ásemos, -aseis, -asen.
(*corr*) (*sub*) } *-iera, -ieras, -iera, -iéramos, -ierais, -ieran.*
-iese, -ieses, -iese, -iésemos, -ieseis, -iesen.

Future (infrequent)

(*lav*) *-are, -ares, -are, -áremos, -areis, -aren.*
(*corr*) (*sub*) } *-iere, -ieres, -iere, -iéremos, -iereis, -ieren.*

The perfect (compound) forms of all the tenses (Indicative and Subjunctive) are conjugated with *haber:*

Present	Preterite	Imperfect	Future	Conditional
he	*hube*	*había*	*habré*	*habría*
has	*hubiste*	*habías*	*habrás*	*habrías*
ha	*hubo*	*había*	*habrá*	*habría*
hemos	*hubimos*	*habíamos*	*habremos*	*habríamos*
habéis	*hubisteis*	*habíais*	*habréis*	*habríais*
han	*hubieron*	*habían*	*habrán*	*habrían*

Imperative

The imperative have two forms, the singular and the plural of the second person in the present:

lava, lavad; corre, corred; sube, subid

To express command or exhortation in the first person plural and both forms of the third person, the corresponding forms of the present subjunctive are used.

Irregular Verbs

Irregular verbs are those which do not follow the regular patterns of conjugation. Some changes are radical, others orthographical.

a) Radical changes:

pensar-pienso
mover-muevo
sentir-sintamos

b) Orthographical changes:

sacar-saqué *cazar-cacé* *llegar-llegué*	in order to preserve original sound of consonants.
tañir-taño *leer-leyó*	suppression of vowel as redundant.
confiar-confío *situar-sitúo*	written accent to split up diphthong of infinitive.

Some verbs may combine radical and orthographical changes.

WE REFER YOU TO THE TABLE OF IRREGULAR VERBS.

Uses of the Subjunctive

The subjunctive is widely used in Spanish, mainly:

a) In conditional sentences, when the condition is contrary to fact, e.g. *si Juan viniera(se), te avisaríamos* (if John should [were to] come, we would let you know).

b) To replace the conditional perfect, e.g. *te lo hubiera(se)-prestado . . . te lo habría prestado . . .* (I would have lent it to you . . .).

c) In subordinate clauses dependent on:

Verbs, adjectives, interjections, etc. expressing wanting, ordering, advising, requesting, permitting, forbidding, causing, necessity, e.g. *él quería que lo hicieras* (he wanted you to do it), *ojalá que no llueva* (let's hope it doesn't rain), *te aconsejo que no vengas* (I advise you not to come), *es preciso que obremos rápido* (we must work quickly).

Verbs or adjectives expressing not knowing or believing, negation or doubt, e.g. *dudo que lleguemos a tiempo* (I doubt we will arrive on time), *no creía que lo hubiéramos hecho* (he would not believe that we had done it), *es inútil que trates de negarlo* (it's useless for you to try to deny it).

Expressions of possibility or probability and conjunctions introducing future, hypothetical or contrary ideas or actions; in general, all statements involving conjecture or guesswork, e.g. *es posible (probable) que venga* (it is possible that he will come), *serviré la comida en cuanto esté lista* (I will serve the meal as soon as it is ready), *apenas termine me iré a casa* (as soon as I finish I will go home), *por inteligente que sea no podrá resolver este problema* (however intelligent he may be he won't be able to solve this problem), *no puedes entrar a menos que — a no ser que — tengas un boleto* (you can't go in unless you have a ticket), *te lo presto con tal que — a condición de que — no lo rompas* (I'll lend it to you on condition that you don't break it).

Relative pronouns referring to an unspecified antecedent in general statements, e.g. *no hay quien me ayude* (there is no one to help me), *¿existe un coche que no se descomponga?* (is there a car which does not break down?), *buscamos una máquina que no haga ruido* (we are looking for a machine that will not make noise).

Verbs of sorrow, fear and emotion; verbs and expressions of surprise, e.g. *me extraña que digas eso* (I'm surprised to hear you say that), *es raro que haya llegado tarde* (it's strange that he should have been late).

The Passive Voice

The passive voice is formed by the verb *ser* plus the past participle of the main verb, e.g. *fue seguido por dos hombres* (he was followed by two men). However, Spanish tends to avoid this form of the passive by using the reflexive, a verb in the third person plural or the active voice, e.g. *estos libros se publicaron hace años* (these books were published years ago), *aún no han establecido la causa del incendio* (the cause of the fire has not been determined yet), *lo siguieron dos hombres* (he was followed by two men).

Accentuation

1. In the majority of Spanish words the stress falls on the last or the next to the last syllable, according to the following simple rules:

a) The next to the last syllable is stressed in words ending in a vowel, *n* or *s*, e.g. *mesa, taberna, solemne, margen, martes, crisis.*

b) The last syllable is stressed in words ending in a consonant (except *n* or *s*), e.g. *avestruz, andar, merced, correr, reloj, laurel.*

c) Written accent is employed when stress does not fall in accordance with the above rules, e.g. *lápiz, dátil, bambú, ámbito, pasión, amén, revés, jesuítico.*

2. Words with identical spelling are usually distinguished by a written accent, e.g. *este* (adjective), *éste* (pronoun); *solo* (adjective), *sólo* (adverb); *se* (reflexive pronoun), *sé* (of the verbs *saber* and *ser*); *mi* (possessive adjective), *mí* (reflexive pronoun).

3. Pronouns, adjectives and adverbs, when used interrogatively or exclamatorily, are also distinguished by a written accent, e.g. *no sé cómo lo hizo* (I don't know how he did it), *¿cómo estás?* (how are you?), *¡qué extraordinario!* (how extraordinary!), *¿a quién seleccionaste?* (who did you choose?) *dime cuáles prefieres* (tell me which ones you prefer).

4. In cases where adjacent strong and weak vowels do not form a diphthong (i.e. when the two vowels are pronounced separately), the weak vowel always carries a written accent — even when the two vowels are separated by an *h,* which is always silent — e.g. *país, raíz, baúl, acentúa, búho, vahído.*

5. Monosyllabic words have no written accent, except when, in accordance with rule No. 2 above, there are two with identical spelling but different meaning, e.g. *te* (second person pronoun), *té* (tea); *mi* (possessive adjective), *mí* (pronoun); *de* (preposition), *dé* (of the verb *dar*), *si* (conjunction), *sí* (yes or reflexive pronoun); *mas* (conjunction), *más* (adjective-adverb); *se* (reflexive pronoun); *sé* (of the verbs *ser* and *saber*).

6. The word *o* has a written accent when it stands between numerals, e.g. 6 *ó* 7 (6 or 7).

7. The first element in a compound word drops the written accent, e.g. *decimoséptimo* (*décimo* and *séptimo:* seventeenth), *asimismo* (*así* and *mismo:* likewise). Exceptions are adverbs ending in *-mente,* e.g. *fácilmente* (easily) and compound words separated by a hyphen, e.g. *teórico-práctico* (theoretical and practical).

Abbreviations Used in This Dictionary

Part II: Spanish-English

a.	adjective
abbrev.	abbreviation
(a.c.)	air conditioning
(acc.)	accounting
(acous.)	acoustics
adv.	adverb
(aer.)	aeronautics
(aeroesp.)	aerospace
(agr.)	agriculture
(Amer.)	America
(anat.)	anatomy
(And.)	Andes
(Angl.)	Anglicism
(anth.)	anthropology
appl.	applied
(arch.)	archaic
(archeol.)	archeology
(archit.)	architecture
(Arg.)	Argentina
(arm.)	arms; armaments
art.	article
(art.)	fine arts
(artil.)	artillery
(astrol.)	astrology
(astron.)	astronomy
(astronaut.)	astronautics
aug.	augmentative
(Aust.)	Australia
(auto.)	automobile
aux.	auxiliary
(avia.)	aviation
(bac.)	bacteriology
(Bib.)	Bible
(biochem.)	biochemistry
(biol.)	biology
(bkb.)	bookbinding
(bldg.)	building (trade)
(Bol.)	Bolivia
(bot.)	botanical
C.	century
(C. Amer.)	Central America
(Can.)	Canada
(Canar. I.)	Canary Islands
(Car.)	Caribbean region
(carp.)	carpentry
(cart.)	cartography
(cer.)	ceramics
(chem.)	chemistry
(Chile)	Chile
(cine.)	cinema
(civ. engin.)	civil engineering
(Col.)	Colombia
(coll.)	colloquial
(com.)	commerce
comp.	comparative
(comput.)	computer
conj.	conjunction
contr.	contraction
(C. Rica)	Costa Rica
(crim.)	criminology
(cryst.)	crystallography
(Cuba)	Cuba
(cul.)	culinary
def.	defective; definite
dem.	demonstrative
(dent.)	dentistry
(derog.)	derogatory
(dial.)	dialect
dim.	diminutive
(dipl.)	diplomacy
(Dom. Rep.)	Dominican Republic
(dressm.)	dressmaking
E.	East
(ecc.)	ecclesiastical
(ecol.)	ecology
(econ.)	economics
(Ecuad.)	Ecuador
(educ.)	education
e.g.	for example
(elec.)	electricity
(electron.)	electronics
(Eng.)	England
(engin.)	engineering
(ento.)	entomology
(equit.)	equitation
esp.	especially
(ethnol.)	ethnology
f.	feminine
(fen.)	fencing
(fig.)	figurative
(fort.)	fortification
(Fr.)	French
(gal.)	gallicism
(G.B.)	Great Britain
gen.	generally
(geol.)	geology
(geom.)	geometry
(geoph.)	geophysics
ger.	gerund
(gram.)	grammar; grammatical
(Guar.)	Guarani (origin)
(Guat.)	Guatemala
(her.)	heraldry
(hist.)	history
(Hond.)	Honduras
(hum.)	humorous
(hunt.)	hunting
(hydr.)	hydraulic; hydraulics
(ichth.)	ichthyology
i.e.	that is to say
imper.	imperative
imp. u.	improper use
(ind.)	industry
indef.	indefinite
indic.	indicative
inf.	infinitive
interj.	interjection
interrog.	interrogative
invar	invariable
(iron.)	ironical
irr.	irregular
i.v.	intransitive verb
(jewel.)	jewelry
(journ.)	journalism
(Lat.)	Latin
(law)	law
(ling.)	linguistics
(lit.)	literature
(log.)	logic
m.	masculine
(mach.)	machinery
(mar.)	maritime; nautical
(mas.)	masonry
(math.)	mathematics
(mech.)	mechanics
(med.)	medicine
(metal.)	metallurgy
(metaph.)	metaphysics
(meteorol.)	meteorology
(Mex.)	Mexico
(mil.)	military
(min.)	mining; mineralogy
(mus.)	music
(myth.)	mythology
n.	noun
N.	North
(neol.)	neologism
neut.	neuter
(Nic.)	Nicaragua
(numis.)	numismatics
(obs.)	obsolete
(ophthal.)	ophthalmology
(opt.)	optics
(ornith.)	ornithology
(p.)	painting
(paleon.)	paleontology
(Pan.)	Panama
(Par.)	Paraguay
past part.	past participle
pers.	person; personal
(Peru)	Peru
(pet.)	petrology; petrole
(pharm.)	pharmaceutics
(philat.)	philately
(Phil. I.)	Philippine Islands
(philol.)	philology
(philos.)	philosophy
(phonet.)	phonetics
(photgmt.)	photogrammetry
(photog.)	photography
(phys.)	physics
(physiol.)	physiology
pl.	plural
(poet.)	poetry; poetic
(pol.)	politics
pos.	possessive
pre.	prefix
prep.	preposition
pret.	preterite
pres.	present
(P. Rico)	Puerto Rico
(print.)	printing
pron.	pronoun
(psyc.)	psychology
(Quech.)	Quechua (origin)
(rad.)	radio
(rare)	rare
rec.	reciprocal
ref.	refer to; reference
reflex.	reflexive
(reg.)	regional
(rel.)	religion
(rhet.)	rhetoric
r.v.	reflexive verb
(ry.)	railway
S.	South
(Salv.)	El Salvador
(S. Amer.)	South America
(sb.)	shipbuilding
(sculp.)	sculpture
(señal)	public sign
(sew.)	sewing
sing.	singular
(sl.)	slang
(sociol.)	sociology
(Sp.)	Spain
(sport.)	sports
subj.	subjunctive
super.	superlative
(surg.)	surgery
(surv.)	surveying
sym.	symbol
(taur.)	tauromachy
(tech.)	technology
(tel.)	television; telecommunications
(tex.)	textiles
(theat.)	theater
(theol.)	theology
(TM)	trademark
(top.)	topography
(trig.)	trigonometry
tr. v.	transitive verb
(Urug.)	Uruguay
(U.S.)	United States
var.	variant
(Ven.)	Venezuela
(vet.)	veterinary
(vulg.)	vulgar; vulgarism
W.	West
(zool.)	zoology

A

A, *f.* a, first letter of the Spanish alphabet; **a por a y b por b,** point by point.

a, *prep.* to, in, at, according to, on, by, for. 1. Direction and movement, *a)* to, *voy a Roma,* I am going to Rome; *b)* at, *se fue a ellos como un león,* he went at them like a lion; *c)* used eliptically, *a la cárcel,* to prison with him. 2. Interval of time, *a)* to, *de diez a doce,* from ten to twelve; *b)* in, *a unos pocos días,* in a few short days; *c)* after, *a los tres días,* after three days. 3. Place in time, *a)* at, *al mediodía,* at noon, *a las diez,* at ten o'clock; *b)* on, *a la mañana siguiente,* on the following morning, *a su llegada,* on his arrival. 4. Contraposition, to, *cara a cara,* face to face. 5. Accord, *a)* to, *a mi pesar,* to my regret; *b)* according to, *a la ley de Castilla,* (arch.) according to the law of Castille; *c)* at, *a su disposición,* at your disposal. 6. Location, *a)* at, *lo cogieron a la puerta,* they caught him at the door; *b)* on, *a bordo,* on board; *c)* by, *al lado de la casa,* by the house. 7. Price and rate, *a)* at, *a veinte soles el kilo,* at twenty soles a kilo; *b)* at, *a toda velocidad,* at full speed. 8. Manner, *a)* on, *a caballo,* on horseback; *b)* by, *poco a poco,* little by little; *c)* in, *a la inglesa,* in the English manner, *a lo caballero,* in a gentlemanly fashion; *d)* with, *lo asediaron a preguntas,* they besieged him with questions. 9. Instrument, *a)* by, *tejido a mano,* woven by hand, *a fuerza bruta,* by brute force; *b)* used adjectivally in phrases, *canto a dos voces,* a two-part song. 10. Used jussively, *a ver,* let's see; *a comer,* let's eat. 11. Used to indicate the indirect object, *dí un hueso al perro,* I gave the dog a bone. 12. Used before the names of people, personified names, sometimes the names of towns and occasionally other nouns in the objective case, *encontré a María,* I met Mary; *se debe respetar a los ancianos,* one should respect old people.

A *abbrev. of* **unidad angstrom,** angstrom unit (A).

A *sym. of* **argón,** argon (A).

aarónico, ca, *a.* (Bib.) Aaronic, pertaining to Aaron.

aaronita, (Bib.) *a.* Aaronic. —*m., f.* descendant of Aaron.

aba, *interj.* (arch.) watch out! —*m.* 1. aba (woolen garment). 2. patriarch, elder (in the Middle East).

abab, *m.* (arch.) free Turkish seaman employed on the galleys in the absence of slaves.

ababa, *f.* (bot.) poppy.

ababán, *m.* (Arg., Par.) small wild tree from S. Amer. used in the manufacture of supports for other trees.

ababillarse, *r.v.* (Chile, Mex.) to have an infirmity of the stifle (horses and other quadrupeds).

ababol, *m.* 1. (bot.) poppy. 2. (fig.) a simple-minded or foolish person.

abacá, *m.* 1. (bot.) abacá, a name for manila hemp. 2. cloth made from this fiber.

abacería, *f.* grocery store, grocer's.

abacero, ra, *m., f.* grocer.

abachí, *m.* (Guar., Arg., Par.) a variety of pineapple.

abacial, *a.* abbatial, of an abbey, abbot or abbess.

ábaco, *m.* 1. abacus, calculating frame. 2. (archit.) abacus, the uppermost slab of a capital or column. 3. (min.) washing trough, esp. for gold.

abacora, *var. of* **albacora.**

abacorado, da, *a.* (Peru, Ven.) frightened, chickened-out (sl.).

abacorar, *tr.v.* 1. (Amer.) to attack; to pursue relentlessly, harass; to corner. 2. (Amer.) to subject, overcome. 3. (Amer.) to catch, surprise. 4. (Cuba) to stockpile; to hoard, to corner the market. 5. to smooch (sl.) while dancing.

abactor, ra, *m., f.* (Arg.) horse or cattle thief, rustler.

abad, *m.* 1. abbot. 2. *var. of* **abadejo,** blister beetle.

abada, *f.* rhinoceros.

abadejo, *m.* 1. (ornith.) kinglet. 2. (ichth.) cod, codfish. 3. (ento.) blister beetle, Spanish fly, cantharis.

abadengo, ga, *a.* abbatial. —*m.* abbey.

abadernar, *tr.v.* (mar.) to fasten with short ropes.

abadesa, *f.* 1. abbess. 2. (Chile, sl.) madam (of a brothel).

abadí, *a.* pertaining to descendants of Mohammed ben Ismail ben Abad, founder of the Kingdom of Seville in the 11th C. —*m.* descendant of Mohammed ben Ismail ben Abad.

abadía, *f.* abbey; rank of an abbot or abbess, abbacy.

abadiado, *m.* abbacy, abbotship (the rank, jurisdiction and territory).

abadiato, *m.* abbotship, abbacy.

ab aeterno, *adv.* (Lat.) since time immemorial.

abafo, fa, *a.* undyed.

abajadero, *m.* slope, incline, gradient.

abajador, *m.* stable man, helper (who lowers tools and equipment to those working underground, e.g. in a mine).

abajamiento, *m.* the action of lowering; descent.

abajar, *tr.v., r.v. var. of* **bajar.**

abajeño, ña, *m., f.* (Amer.) a person native to or coming from the coastland or any lowland. —*a.* pertaining or relative to the coastland or lowland.

abajo, *adv.* down; below, downstairs, underneath. — **¡a.!** down with, e.g. *a. el tirano,* down with the tyrant; **boca a.,** face down; **cuesta a.,** downhill; **de arriba a.,** from top to bottom; **echar a.,** to overthrow; destroy, demolish; **traer a.,** to bring down, overthrow; to bring (the house, i.e. theater) down (with applause).

abalance, abalancé, *ref.* **abalanzar.**

abalanzar, (*ref. 53*) *tr.v.* 1. to balance, make balance, to counterweight. 2. to throw violently, fling. —*r.v.* to throw or hurl oneself; to pounce, attack; to venture upon recklessly, launch into. — **abalanzarse a,** to launch into; **abalanzarse sobre,** to pounce upon, attack, throw oneself upon.

abalar, *tr.v., r.v.* (Sp.) to move, shake.

abalaustrado, da, *a.* balustered.

abalaustrar, *tr.v.* (Cuba) to install balusters in.

abaldonadamente, *adv.* courageously, fearlessly; audaciously.

abaldonar, *tr.v.* to debase, vilify; to insult, affront, offend.

abaleador, ra, *m., f.* 1. one who separates grain from chaff. 2. (Amer.) gunman, gunmoll.

abaleadura, *f.* 1. action of separating grain from chaff. 2. chaff.

abalear, *tr.v.* 1. (agr.) to separate grain from chaff. 2. (Amer.) to fire on, shoot at; to wound or kill with a gunshot.

abaleo, *m.* 1. (agr.) separation of grain from chaff. 2. broom for separating chaff from grain. 3. plant used in the manufacture of this broom.

abalice, abalicé, *ref.* **abalizar.**

abalizamiento, *m.* buoying; marking with buoys or caution signals.

abalizar, (*ref. 53*) *tr.v.* to mark with buoys; to mark an airstrip, airport runway or roadway detour with some kind of caution or directional markers. —*r.v.* (mar.) to take bearings.

abalonado, da, *a.* balloonlike.

abalone, *m.* (zool.) abalone, a large edible mollusk.

abalorio, *m.* 1. bead. 2. bead necklace. 3. (*pl.*) adornments.

abaluartado, da, *a.* fortified, bastioned.

abaluartar, *tr.v.* to fortify with bastions.

aballar, *r.v., tr.v.* to move. —*tr.v.* (p.) to tone down, soften (lines or colors).

aballestar, *tr.v.* (mar.) to haul or make taut (a rope or cable).

abama, *f.* (bot.) bog asphodel.

abanar, *tr.v.* to cool or ventilate with a fan.

abandalice, abandalicé, *ref.* **abandalizar.**

abandalizar, (*ref. 53*) *tr.v., var. of* **abanderizar.**

abanderado, *m.* 1. standard-bearer. 2. (fig.) follower of a cause, joiner of a movement.

abanderamiento, *m.* 1. (mar.) registration (of a ship). 2. joining a cause or a movement.

abanderar, *tr.v.* (mar.) to register a ship (usually a merchant ship) under the flag of a particular nation; to provide a ship with registration documents. —*i.v.* to join, to take up someone's cause, e.g. *me voy a abanderar,* I'm going to join.

abanderice, abandericé, *ref.* **abanderizar.**

abanderizador, ra, *m., f.* ringleader; agitator; person who organizes a movement. —*a.* pertaining to a person who agitates for a cause.

abanderizar, (*ref. 53*) *tr.v.* to agitate for a cause, to proselytize and recruit followers. —*r.v.* band together; (Amer.) to join (a political party, etc.).

abandonado, da, *past part. of* **abandonar.** —*a.* 1. abandoned, forsaken. 2. careless, negligent, lax; slovenly, lazy, shiftless.

abandonamiento, *m.* abandoning, abandonment. 2. slovenliness, sloth, carelessness.

abandonar, *tr.v.* 1. to leave, go out of. 2. to abandon, desert. 3. to give up, renounce (right, etc.). —*i.v.* to resign. —*r.v.* 1. to surrender to, yield to (vices); (theol.) to surrender (to God). 2. (fig.) to become slovenly or careless. 3. to despair.

abandonismo, *m.* defeatism.

abandonista, *a., m., f.* defeatist.

abandono, *m.* 1. abandonment, desertion. 2. abandon, unrestraint, dissoluteness, debauchery, carelessness. 3. (law) renunciation (of rights). 4. (theol.) complete surrender (to God).

abanicar, *(ref. 50) tr.v.* 1. to fan. 2. (taur.) to wave the cape before the bull (and thus test his reactions). —*r.v.* to fan oneself.
abanicazo, *m.* a swat delivered with a fan.
abanico, *m.* 1. fan; fan-shaped object. 2. (coll.) sword, sabre. 3. (mar.) shears, improvised crane. 4. (Cuba) signal at a railway fork. 5. (archit.) fan window. 6. (bldg.) hoisting gin. — **a. aluvial,** alluvial fan; **a. de deyección,** (geol.) debris cone; **a. eductor,** exhaust fan; **a. eléctrico,** (Mex.) electric fan.
abanillo, *m.* 1. ruff; ruffle. 2. mechanical fan.
abanino, *m.* gauze frill or trimming (to adorn a low neckline or décolletage).
abanique, abaniqué, *ref.* **abanicar.**
abaniquear, *tr.v.* (coll.) to fan.
abaniqueo, *m.* 1. fanning. 2. (coll.) excessive gesticulation while speaking. 3. (auto.) shimmy.
abaniquería, *f.* fan shop or factory.
abaniquero, ra, *m., f.* fan maker or vendor.
abano, *m.* ceiling fan; flychaser.
abanto, *a.* dull, stupid; (taur.) slow, dimwitted (bull). —*m.* (ornith.) Egyptian vulture.
abañador, ra, *m., f.* sifter or sorter (of grain).
abañadura, *f.* sifting or sorting (of grain).
abañar, *tr.v.* to sift or sort grain with a special sifter or screen.
abarajar, *tr.v., var. of* **barajar.**
abaratamiento, *m.* cheapening; the action and effect of lowering the price or the quality.
abaratar, *tr.v.* 1. to make cheaper, cheapen. 2. to lower, reduce (prices). —*i.v., r.v.* to get or become cheaper, to fall in price or quality.
abarbechar, *tr.v.* to plow in preparation for sowing or leaving land fallow.
abarbetar, *tr.v.* (mar.) to lash; to serve, seize (a cable).
abarca, *f.* 1. wooden shoe, clog. 2. (Sp.) sandal.
abarcable, *a.* 1. that can be embraced or clasped. 2. (fig.) that can be grasped, understood, encompassed (e.g. an idea).
abarcado, da, *a.* sandaled, wearing sandals, wearing clogs or wooden shoes.
abarcador, ra, *a.* all-embracing, comprehensive. —*m., f.* gatherer, embracer; hoarder, monopolizer.
abarcadura, *f.* embrasure, inclusion; encompassment.
abarcamiento, *m., var. of* **abarcadura.**
abarcar, *(ref. 50) tr.v.* 1. to embrace, take in, encompass; to comprise, contain, include. 2. to embrace, clasp. 3. to take in (with the eye). 4. (fig.) to undertake, embark upon (many things at the same time). 5. (Amer.) to monopolize, corner (the market). 6. (Ecuad., coll.) to hatch. 7. (hunt.) to surround a stretch of woodland where the game is thought to be). — **quien mucho a. poco aprieta,** one should not bite off more than one can chew.
abarcón, *m.* iron ring clamped on the central pole of a carriage.
abaritonado, da, *a.* baritone-like (said of voices or musical instruments).
abarloar, *tr.v.* (mar.) to bring (a ship) alongside. —*r.v.* to come alongside.
abarque, abarqué, *ref.* **abarcar.**
abarquero, ra, *m., f.* sandal maker or vendor.
abarquillado, da, *a.* curled up; cone-shaped.
abarquillamiento, *m.* the act of curling, bending, or wrapping into a roll.
abarquillar, *tr.v.* to curl, bend or curve a sheet of paper, metal or some other material into a roll (similar to the shape of a boat).
abarracar, *(ref. 50) i.v., r.v.* (mil.) to set up camp, to build barracks.
abarrado, da, *a.* said of defective cloth flecked with an extraneous strand in the weave.
abarraganamiento, *m.* concubinage, illicit cohabitation.
abarraganarse, *iv.* to live in concubinage, to cohabit illicitly.
abarrajado, da, *a.* (Chile, Peru, coll.) bold, shameless, libidinous, libertine.
abarrajar, *tr.v.* 1. to attack and rout, overwhelm (an enemy). 2. to hurl, hurtle. —*r.v.* 1. (S. Amer.) to become corrupt or depraved, become a scoundrel. 2. (Amer.) to slip, fall.
abarrajo, *m.* (Peru) a fall, a stumble; **tonto de a.,** a dumbell, a fool.
abarramiento, *m.* 1. hurtling. 2. shaking.
abarrancadero, *m.* 1. precipice. 2. (fig.) difficult business or situation.
abarrancamiento, *m.* 1. falling, or putting (something) into ditches, gullies, etc. 2. a difficulty (in business or some situation).
abarrancar, *(ref. 50) tr.v.* 1. to form cracks, gulleys or ditches in. 2. to throw or put into a gorge, ravine or ditch. —*i.v.* (mar.) to run aground. —*r.v.* 1. to fall or go into a gorge, ravine or ditch. 2. (mar.) to run aground. 3. (fig.) to become involved in great difficulties, get into a jam or a fix.
abarranque, abarranqué, *ref.* **abarrancar.**
abarraque, abarraqué, *ref.* **abarracar.**
abarrar, *tr.v.* 1. to hurl, hurtle. 2. to shake vigorously.
abarredera, *f.* 1. broom. 2. net. 3. (fig.) anything that sweeps or cleans.
abarrisco, *adv.* all jumbled together.
abarrotado, da, *a.* crowded, completely full; well-stoked (store).
abarrotador, ra, *m., f.* 1. (Amer.) general store keeper. 2. one who crowds, monopolizes or hoards.
abarrotamiento, *m.* crowding, massing; stocking-up of goods.
abarrotar, *tr.v.* 1. to strengthen with bars, bar up. 2. (bldg.) to place a waler or strongback in. 3. (mar.) to stow, secure or fix securely with short iron bars (cargo); to fill completely (a ship) with cargo; fill (shop) with goods; stock full, crowd up a place. 4. (Chile, Guat.) to corner (the market). 5. (Cuba, coll.) to win with lower cards in a game of manilla.
abarrote, *m.* 1. (*pl.*) (Mex.) grocery store. 2. (Amer.) provisions, food-stuffs. 3. (mar.) small package to secure the stowing of cargo.
abarrotería, *f.* (C. Amer.) general store, grocery store.
abarrotero, ra, *m., f.* (Amer.) general store keeper or grocer.
abarse, *r.v.* to get out of the way (*def. v., used only in the inf. and imper.*).
abasí, *a.* pertaining to the Abbas, dynasty of first caliph of the Abbassides.
Abasidas, *m.* (*pl.*)Abbassides, the dynasty of caliphs claiming descendancy from Abbas, Mohammed's uncle.
abastamiento, *m.* provisioning, supplying or furnishing with necessary provisions.
abastanza, *f.* copiousness, abundance, plenty.
abastar, *tr.v.* to provision, supply or furnish with necessary provisions. —*r.v.* to satisfy or content oneself.
abastardar, *i.v., var. of* **bastardear.**
abastecedor, ra, *a.* supplying. —*m., f.* supplier, purveyor.
abastecer, *(ref. 45) tr.v.* to supply, provide; **a. de,** to supply or furnish with.
abastecimiento, *m.* supply; supplying, provisioning; providing; (*pl.*) supplies, stores; **a. de combustible,** fueling.
abastero, *m.* 1. (Chile) wholesale livestock or cattle dealer. 2. (Cuba) supplier, purveyor.
abastezca, abastezco, *ref.* **abastecer.**
abastionar, *tr.v.* to fortify with bastions.
abasto, *m.* provisioning, supplying; (*pl.*) supplies, provisions, esp. foodstuffs. — **dar** or **darse a. para,** to cope with, be able to manage or handle; **mercado de a.,** (Arg., Sp.) wholesale marketplace.
abatanar, *tr.v.* 1. to full, to shrink and thicken cloth. 2. (fig.) to beat, hit, maltreat.
abatatado, da, *a.* 1. (S. Amer.) scared, intimidated. 2. (P. Rico) stocky, lumpy (person).
abatatar, *tr.v.* (Arg., Urug.) to frighten, scare, intimidate. —*r.v.* to become frightened or intimidated; to become embarrassed.
abate, *m.* 1. abbot, an ecclesiastic of the minor orders. 2. a foreign priest (in Spain) esp. one who is French or Italian.
abatí, *m.* (Arg., Par.) 1. corn, maize. 2. an alcoholic drink distilled from corn.
abatible, *a.* 1. collapsible. 2. (mar.) descending, that which can be lowered.
abatida, *f.* (fort.) abatis, a fortification of barbed wire; a barricade of branches facing the opponent.
abatidamente, *adv.* dejectedly, despondently, dispiritedly.
abatidero, *m.* drainage ditch, sluiceway.
abatido, da, *past part. of* **abatir.** —*a.* 1. dejected, disheartened, crestfallen. 2. contemptible, despicable, abject. 3. depreciated, fallen in price or quality (said of perishable goods and fruit). —*m.* (Cuba, coll.) slatting, boarding (for making crates, etc.).
abatimiento, *m.* 1. dejection, dejectedness, depression, low spirits, discouragement. 2. (mar., aer.) leeway, drift. 3. knocking down; demolition; cutting down; shooting down (of plane). 4. lowering, hauling down. 5. (mil., mar.) dismantling, disassembling.
abatir, *tr.v.* 1. to knock down; to demolish; to cut down (e.g. tree); to shoot down (e.g. plane). 2. to lower, take down, haul down (e.g. flag); to lay flat. 3. to crush, dishearten, discourage, lower one's spirits. 4. to humiliate. 5. (mar., mil.) to dismantle, take apart, disassemble. —*i.v.* (mar., aer.) to fall off, tend to leeward. —*r.v.* 1. to lose heart, become dispirited or disheartened. 2. to humble oneself. 3. to dive, swoop (bird of prey).
abatismo, *m.* power of the abbots; body of abbés.
abayado, da, *a.* (bot.) berrylike.
abayuncarse, *r.v.* (Guat.) to acquire the manners and behavior of a boor.
abazón, *m.* (zool.) cheek pouch (of certain mammals, used for depositing food prior to mastication).
abderitano, na, *a.* Abderian, pertaining to one of two ancient cities, in Spain and Thrace called Abdera.
abdicación, *f.* abdication; renouncing, giving up.
abdicar, *(ref. 50) tr.v.* to abdicate; to give up, relinquish, renounce; **a. la corona,** to give up or relinquish the crown; **a. los derechos,** to give up one's rights. —*i.v.* to abdicate; **a. en favor de,** to abdicate in favor of.
abdicativamente, *adv.* by proxy.
abdicativo, va, *a.* abdicative, pertaining to abdication.
abdique, abdiqué, *ref.* **abdicar.**
abdomen, *m.* (anat., zool.) abdomen.
abdominal, *a.* abdominal.
abducción, *f.* (log., physiol., anat.) abduction.
abducir, *(ref. 47) tr.v.* (physiol., anat.) to abduce, abduct.

abductor, *a.* (anat.) abducent. —*m.* (anat.) abductor, abducent muscle.
abecé, *m.* 1. a-b-c, the alphabet. 2. (fig.) basics, basis, fundamentals. — **no saber el abecé,** (fig.) not to know the ABCs.
abecedario, *m.* 1. alphabet. 2. primer for teaching the alphabet. 3. alphabetical index or list. 4. rudiments. — **a. manual,** manual alphabet, sign language.
abedul, *m.* (bot.) birch; birchwood; (Mex.) toothed alder.
abeja, *f.* 1. (ento.) bee. 2. busy bee, hard worker. 3. (astron.) **A.,** Musca. — **a. albañila,** mason bee; **a. carpintera,** carpenter bee; **a. reina** or **maestra,** queen bee; **a. neutra** or **obrera,** worker bee.
abejar, *m.* apiary.
abejarrón, *m.* 1. (ento.) bumblebee. 2. (Amer.) any droning insect.
abejaruco, *m.* 1. (ornith.) bee eater. 2. (fig.) gossip, gossipmonger.
abejera, *f.* 1. apiary. 2. (bot.) lemon balm, sweet balm, garden balm; beewort.
abejero, ra, *m., f.* bee keeper. —*m.* (ornith.) bee eater.
abejón, *m.* 1. (ento.) drone; bumblebee.
abejorreo, *m.* hum, droning (of insects); (coll.) hum (of conversation).
abejorro, *m.* 1. (ento.) bumblebee; cockchafer. 2. (fig.) a person who is a bore.
abejucado, da, *a.* (Car.) rattan-like, reed-like.
abejucarse, *r.v.* (Car., Mex.) to become reedy (a climbing vine).
abejuela, *f. dim. of* abeja, small bee.
abejuno, na, *a.* pertaining to a bee, bee-like.
abellacado, da, *past part. of* **abellacar.** —*a.* mischievous, devilish (said of children); artful, cunning, villainous, mean (said of adults).
abellacar, (*ref. 50*) *tr.v., r.v.* to make or become vile, villainous, knavish, deceitful.
abellaque, abellaqué, *ref.* **abellacar.**
abellotado, da, *a.* acorn-shaped.
abelmosco, *m.* (bot.) abelmosk; (Mex.) okra, gumbo.
abemoladamente, *adv.* sweetly, caressingly, gently, softly.
abemolar, *tr.v.* 1. (mus.) to put into a minor key. 2. (fig.) to soften, sweeten (the voice).
abencerraje, *m.* member of a Moorish family, famous in Spain for its rivalry with the Cegri family; **Cegríes y Abencerrajes,** (fig.) Capulets and Montagues.
abenuz, *m.* (bot.) ebony, the tree and its wood.
aberenjenado, da, *a.* shaped or colored like an eggplant.
abería, *f.* (coll.) bush used for quickset hedges.
aberración, *f.* 1. aberration, slip, error, deviation. 2. (astron., biol., med., opt., physiol., psyc.) aberration. 3. (Amer.) stubbornness, wrongheadedness, bullheadedness. — **a. cromática,** (opt.) chromatic aberration; **a. de esfericidad,** (opt.) spherical aberration; **¡qué a.!** what an absurdity!
aberrante, *a.* aberrant; unusual, not normal.
aberrar, *i.v.* to err, to be mistaken; to deviate from the norm; to walk, move, or act erratically.
abertal, *a.* 1. cracked, split (said of land cracked or fissured by drought). 2. open (said of unfenced lands). —*m.* split, crack, opening.
abertura, *f.* 1. opening (to a cave, hole, or enclosure). 2. opening, crack, fissure, crevice. 3. valley. 4. cove, inlet. 5. frankness, openness. 6. (phonet.) openness (of vowels). 7. (opt., phys., photog.) aperture. — **a. de ahorro,** slot (for night deposits at a bank); **a. numérica,** (phys.) numerical aperture.
abesana, *f., var. of* **besana.**
abesón, *m.* (bot.) common dill.
abestiado, da, *a.* beast-like, brutish.
abestializado, da, *a., var. of* **abestiado.**
abestiarse, *r.v.* (coll.) to become brutalized or brutish.
abéstola, *f.* (agr.) plowstaff.
abetal, abetar, *m.* fir forest or grove.
abete, *m.* hook for holding cloth while it is being sheared.
abetinote, *m.* fir tree resin.
abeto, *m.* (bot.) fir; **a. blanco,** white fir, silver fir; **a. del norte, a. falso** or **rojo,** spruce.
abetuna, *f.* fir tree shoot or sprout.
abetunado, da, *past part. of* **abetunar.** —*a.* 1. blacked, blackened. 2. pitch-like, tar-like. 3. tarred, covered with pitch or tar. 4. black and lustrous like shoe polish.
abetunar, *tr.v.* 1. to black, blacken, cover with shoe polish. 2. to cover with pitch or tar.
abey, *m.* (bot.) jacaranda; **a. hembra,** mimosa; **a. macho,** rosewood, mahogany.
abiar, *m.* (bot.) oxeye, field camomile.
Abidján, *m.* Abidjan, capital of Ivory Coast.
abieldar, *tr.v., var. of* **beldar.**
abiertamente, *adv.* openly, candidly, frankly.
abierto, ta, *irr. past part. of* **abrir.** —*a.* 1. open; dilated; flat, clear, unobstructed (commonly said of level country). 2. (fig.) open, unaffected, sincere, candid, frank; tolerant, liberal; generous. — **a cielo** abierto, in the open air; **cuenta abierta,** (com.) open account; **caballo abierto,** horse with distended chest muscles; **campo abierto,** open country; **embarcación abierta,** open boat.
abietáceo, a, *a.* (bot.) abietineous. —*f.* (*pl.*) Abietineae.
abietino, *m., var. of* **abetinote.**
abigarradamente, *adv.* in a badly matched manner (said of colors or a collection of things).
abigarrado, *past part. of* **abigarrar.** —*a.* 1. pertaining to badly combined or clashing colors. 2. pertaining to an orderless collection of ill-assorted things.
abigarramiento, *m.* a collection of badly matched or ill-assorted colors or things; the action or effect of putting together such colors or things.
abigarrar, *tr.v.* to crowd together a collection of things without any order; to put together a variety of clashing colors.
abigeato, *m.* (law) cattle stealing, rustling.
abigeo, *m.* (law) cattle thief, rustler.
abigotado, da, *a.* having a large thick mustache.
abinar, *tr.v.* to plow the land a second time.
ab initio, *adv.* (Lat.) from the beginning; from time immemorial.
ab intestato, *adv.* (Lat.) 1. (to die) intestate. 2. (fig.) carelessly; with abandon.
abintestato, *m.* judicial procedure for settling or probating an intestate estate.
abiogenesia, *f.* (biol.) abiogenesis, spontaneous generation.
abiogénesis, *f.* (biol.) abiogenesis, spontaneous generation.
abiogenético, ca, *a.* (biol.) abiogenetic.
abiótico, ca, *a.* (biol.) abiotic.
abipón, *a., m., f.* Abipon, pertaining to a race of Indians that inhabited the Argentinian Chaco.
ab irato, *adv.* (Lat.) in anger, thoughtlessly.
abisagrar, *tr.v.* to install hinges (on doors, etc.).
abisal, *a.* 1. *var. of* **abismal.** 2. (geol.) abyssal, deep-seated.
abiselar, *tr.v., var. of* **biselar.**
abisinio, nia, *a., m., f.* Abyssinian, pertaining to Ethiopia, its language, and its people. —*f.* A., Abyssinia, former name of Ethiopia.
abismado, da, *past part. of* **abismar.** —*a.* 1. depressed, dejected. 2. amazed. 3. absorbed in deep meditation. 4. (her.) centrally figured on an escutcheon.
abismal, *a.* abysmal, deep, profound, unfathomable; incomprehensible.
abismar, *tr.v.* 1. to overwhelm, perplex, confuse, baffle; to humble. 2. to horrify, appall; to depress. 3. to spoil, ruin. 4. to throw into an abyss. —*r.v.* 1. to give oneself up (to), plunge (into), surrender (to) (grief, contemplation, etc.). 2. (Amer.) to be amazed. 3. (Dom. Rep.) to become ruined, spoiled. — **abismarse en,** to give oneself up to, plunge into, become absorbed in.
abismático, *a.* deep, profound.
abismo, *m.* 1. abyss, chasm. 2. hell. 3. (her.) central field on an escutcheon. — **estar al borde del a.,** to be on the verge of doom.
abitadura, *f.* (mar.) bitting, fastening cables around bitts.
abitaque, *m.* rafter, beam, joist.
abitar, *tr.v.* (mar.) to fasten the anchor cable to bitts, bitt.
abitón, *m.* bitt, a deck post to which cables or ropes are secured (when anchoring a ship).
abizcochado, da, *a.* resembling a biscuit or cake in shape, richness and flavor.
abjurable, *a.* (coll.) retractable.
abjuración, *f.* abjuration, disavowal, recantation under oath, renunciation.
abjurar, *tr.v.* to abjure, disavow, recant, renounce.
ablación, *f.* 1. (med.) ablation, surgical removal of any part of the body. 2. (geol.) wearing away, erosion.
ablactación, *f.* (med.) ablactation, weaning.
ablandabrevas, *m., f.* (fig., coll.) good-for-nothing, a useless person.
ablandador, ra, *a.* softening; mollifying. —*m., f.* softener; mollifier.
ablandamiento, *m.* softening; soothing, mollification.
ablandante, *a.* softening, mollifying.
ablandar, *tr.v.* 1. to soften. 2. (fig.) to pacify; to mitigate or assuage (anger, ire, etc.). 3. to loosen; to soften. —*r.v.* 1. to soften. 2. to be pacified; to be mitigated or assuaged (anger, etc.). 3. to calm down or lessen in force (the wind). —*i.v.* 1. to improve (winter weather); to begin to thaw. 2. to calm down or lessen in force (the wind).
ablandativo, va, *a.* softening, mollifying.
ablandecer, (*ref. 45*) *tr.v.* 1. to soften. 2. to pacify, mollify. 3. to loosen. 4. to smooth.
ablandezca, ablandezco, *ref.* **ablandecer.**
ablano, *m., var. of* **avellano.**
ablativo, *m.* (gram.) ablative; **a. absoluto,** (gram.) ablative absolute.
ablefaria, *f.* (med.) ablepharia, congenital absence of eyelids.
ablegado, *m.* ablegate, papal envoy who takes the insignia of office to a newly named cardinal.
ablepsia, *f.* (med.) ablepsia, loss of eyesight, blindness.
ablución, *f.* 1. ablution, a washing of the body, esp. as a religious ceremony of purification. 2. the liquid used for such ceremony.
abluente, *a., m.* (med.) abluent.
ablusado, da, *a.* bloused, loose (worn loosely).
abnegación, *f.* abnegation, self-denial, selflessness.
abnegadamente, *adv.* with abnegation, unselfishly, altruistically.
abnegado, da, *past part. of* **abnegar.** —*a.* self-sacrificing, altruistic.
abnegar, (*ref. 67*) *tr.v.* to forego, renounce, abnegate. —*r.v.* to deny oneself, give up one's self-interests, desires, or passions.

abnegué, *ref.* **abnegar.**
abniego, abniegue, *ref.* **abnegar.**
abobado, da, *a.* stupid, dim-witted.
abobamiento, *m.* stupidity, stultification.
abobar, *tr.v.* to make stupid, stupefy, stultify. —*r.v.* to become stupid.
abobra, *f.* (bot.) decorative creeper.
abocadear, *tr.v.* 1. to wound or hurt by biting. 2. to take bites or mouthfuls of.
abocado, da, *past part. of* **abocar.** —*a.* mild, said of a blend of sherry containing dry and sweet wine. —*m.* any pleasant smooth wine.
abocamiento, *m.* 1. biting. 2. approaching. 3. meeting, interview, conference. 4. bringing into position (troops, artillery). 5. (mar.) entering (port, strait, etc.).
abocar, (*ref. 50*) *tr.v.* 1. to seize with the mouth, to bite. 2. to decant, to pour. 3. to bring into position (troops, guns). —*r.v.* to meet, have an interview or conference. —*i.v.* (mar.) to enter a channel or strait.
abocardado, da, *past part. of* **abocardar.** —*a.* trumpet-shaped, flared (said most commonly of firearms, such as the blunderbuss).
abocardar, *tr.v.* to ream or widen the mouth of a tube or hole.
abocardo, *m.* (mar., min.) a kind of drill or auger.
abocelado, da, *a.* (archit.) having the form of a semicircular convex molding or beading.
abocetado, da, *a.* (p.) sketched.
abocetar, *tr.v.* (p.) to sketch.
abochornado, da, *past part. of* **abochornar.** —*a.* 1. stifling, suffocating, very hot. 2. (fig.) embarrassed, mortified; blushing, flushed.
abochornar, *tr.v.* 1. to embarrass, to make one blush. 2. (agr.) to wilt or wither (from excessive heat). —*r.v.* to blush with embarrassment, to be mortified.
abocinado, da, *a.* 1. trumpet-shaped, flared. 2. (equit.) with drooping head (horses).
abocinamiento, *m.* flaring, widening.
abocinar, *tr.v.* to widen or flare the end of a tube or pipe like a trumpet or funnel. —*i.v.* (coll.) to fall flat on one's face.
abofarse, *r.v.* 1. to become spongy; to swell up, become puffy, bloated. 2. (fig.) to act sleepy.
abofeteador, ra, *a.* slapping. —*m., f.* slapper.
abofetear, *tr.v.* to slap (the face).
abogacía, *f.* law (as a subject or profession).
abogada, *f.* woman lawyer; (coll.) lawyer's wife; (fig.) mediator.
abogadear, *i.v.* (coll.) to practice law in a dishonorable manner.
abogaderas, *f.* (*pl.*) (S. Amer.) specious arguments, quibbling.
abogadesco, ca, *a.* pertaining to a lawyer (usually derog.).
abogadil, *a.* (derog.) pertaining to a lawyer.
abogadillo, *m.* (coll., derog.) mediocre lawyer, small town lawyer.
abogadismo, *m.* excessive interference of lawyers and application of their methods in public affairs, or in issues outside of their competence.
abogado, *m.* 1. lawyer, barrister, attorney, solicitor. 2. (fig.) mediator. — **a. acusador** or **fiscal,** prosecuting attorney; **a. defensor,** lawyer for the defense; **a. del diablo,** (fig.) devil's advocate; **a. de oficio,** public defender, court-appointed attorney; **recibirse de a.,** to pass the bar exams.
abogador, *m.* beadle or sexton of a brotherhood, who informs members of the feast days, etc. on which they should meet.
abogaducho, *m.* (coll., derog.) inexperienced or incompetent lawyer.
abogamiento, *m.* (arch.) defense, pleading; (fig.) intercession, mediation.
abogar, (*ref. 51*) *i.v.* 1. to plead, to defend. 2. (fig.) to intercede; to advocate. — **a. por,** to advocate; to plead for.
abogue, abogué, *ref.* **abogar.**
abohetado, da, *a.* swollen, puffy, bloated.
abolaga, *f.* (bot.) furze, whin, gorse.
abolengo, *m.* ancestry, lineage; (law) inheritance, patrimony.
abolición, *f.* abolition; repeal, revocation, abrogation.
abolicionismo, *m.* abolitionism, **esp. the** cause opposing slavery.
abolicionista, *a., m., f.* abolitionist, esp. one who opposed slavery.
abolir, (*ref. 78*) *tr.v.* to abolish; to revoke, repeal.
abollado, da, *past part. of* **abollar.** —*a.* 1. dented, bruised. 2. (coll.) broke, penniless.
abolladura, *f.* dent, bruise.
abollar, *tr.v.* 1. to dent, bruise. 2. to emboss. 3. to stun or confound. —*r.v.* to get dented, e.g. *se me abolló un guardafango,* one of the fenders on my car got dented.
abollón, *m., var. of* **abolladura.**
abollonar, *tr.v.* 1. to emboss. 2. (Arg.) to shed buds (plants).
abolorio, *m., var. of* **abolengo.**
abolsado, da, *a.* 1. baggy, puckered; full of air pockets (as in a badly painted wall). 2. bag-like, loose-fitting.
abolsarse, *r.v.* 1. to form pockets or bags; to pucker. 2. (mas.) to blister, become blistered or full of bubbles.
abomaso, *m.* (vet.) abomasum, fourth stomach of a ruminant.
abombado, da, *past part. of* **abombar.** —*a.* 1. (coll.) faint, light in the head; dizzy; confused. 2. (S. Amer.) stagnant. 3. (Arg., Chile, Nic., coll.) stoned, bombed, plastered (sl.), drunk.
abombar, *tr.v.* 1. to make convex. 2. to stun, bewilder, confuse. —*i.v.* to pump. —*r.v.* 1. (Amer.) to start to rot, go bad; to become stagnant. 2. (Arg., Chile, Nic.) to get drunk. 3. (Cuba) to become overripe (fruit). 4. to become convex.
abominable, *a.* abominable, hateful; ugly.
abominablemente, *adv.* abominably; hatefully.
abominación, *f.* abomination, execration.
abominar, *tr.v.* to abominate; **to hate,** abhor, loathe. —*i.v.* **a. de,** to abominate.
abonable, *a.* 1. payable, e.g. *a. en cuotas mensuales,* payable in monthly installments. 2. of land that can be fertilized.
abonado, da, *past part. of* **abonar.** —*a.* reliable, trustworthy. —*m., f.* 1. subscriber, customer, user. 2. season-ticket holder. 3. fertilized land. 4. (Arg., Par., Urug.) teacher's pet.
abonador, *m.* 1. worker who spreads the fertilizer. 2. guarantor, bondsman; person who vouches for another. 3. cooper's auger.
abonamiento, *m.* 1. vouching, guaranteeing, backing. 2. (com.) bail, security. 3. (agr.) spreading of fertilizer, fertilizing. 4. subscription; steady patronage.
abonanzar, (*ref. 53*) *i.v.* 1. to grow calm, clear up (the weather, a storm). 2. (fig.) to clear up, get better (difficult situation).
abonar, *tr.v.* 1. to stand as security for, bail, back, vouch for, guarantee. 2. to improve. 3. to affirm. 4. to fertilize, spread fertilizer on. 5. to buy a subscription. 6. (com.) to credit (in a bank account); to pay. — **a. en cuenta a,** to credit to the account of. —*i.v.* to become calm (weather). —*r.v.* to subscribe, to buy a season ticket for, e.g. *me aboné a esta pensión,* I've become a steady guest at this boarding house.
abonaré, *m.* (com.) I.O.U.; promissory note; due-bill.
abonero, ra, *m., f.* (Mex.) street merchant or vendor who sells on installments.
abono, *m.* 1. manure, fertilizer. 2. subscription; season ticket. 3. payment, installment.
aboque, aboqué, *ref.* **abocar.**
aboquillado, da, *past part. of* **aboquillar.** —*a.* shaped like a mouthpiece.
aboquillar, *tr.v.* 1. to put a mouthpiece on (something). 2. (archit.) to splay, flare, widen the mouth of. 3. to bevel.
aboral, *a.* (med., zool.) aboral, opposite to or away from the mouth.
abordable, *a.* 1. approachable, accessible. 2. (mar.) able to be boarded.
abordador, ra, *a.* (mar.) boarding (said of a party of armed men attacking a ship). —*m.* (mar.) boarder.
abordaje, *m.* (mar.) boarding (act of boarding a ship); **¡al a.!,** board the ship! (with hostile intentions).
abordar, *tr.v.* 1. (mar.) to board. 2. to crash or bump one ship against another through carelessness, accident, or with hostile intentions. 3. (mar.) to bring into dock, dock. 4. (fig.) to approach (someone with a suggestion, etc.). 5. (fig.) to undertake, tackle (a difficult assignment). —*i.v.* (mar.) to put into port.
abordo, *m., var. of* **abordaje.**
aborigen, *a.* aboriginal; indigenous. —*m., f.* aborigine, aboriginal.
aborlonado, da, *a.* (Col., Chile) ribbed, striped (caused by a defect in weaving).
aborrachado, da, *a.* bright red, flaming red.
aborrajarse, *r.v.* to dry up, shrivel (wheat, before kernels are completely formed).
aborrascado, *a.* stormy, cloudy (weather, sky, etc.).
aborrascarse, (*ref. 50*) *r.v.* to become stormy, cloudy, inclement (weather).
aborrasque, *ref.* **aborrascarse.**
aborrecedor, ra, *a.* hating. —*m., f.* hater, loather, detester.
aborrecer, (*ref. 45*) *tr.v.* 1. to hate, abhor, detest. 2. (of birds) to abandon (brood or nest). 3. to bother, annoy; to bore someone.
aborrecible, *a.* hateful, loathsome, detestable.
aborreciblemente, *adv.* abhorrently, hatefully.
aborrecidamente, *adv.* with hate or loathing, very reluctantly.
aborrecimiento, *m.* loathing, detestation, hate, aversion.
aborregado, da, *a.* lacking initiative, sheep-like, clinging to the herd.
aborregarse, (*ref. 51*) *r.v.* 1. to become covered with fleecy clouds (the sky). 2. (Peru) to become stupid, act stupidly, listlessly.
aborregue, *ref.* **aborregarse.**
aborrezca, aborrezco, *ref.* **aborrecer.**
aborricarse, (*ref. 50*) r.v. (Cuba, Chile, Peru, coll.) to become dull, slow, or stupid.
aborrique, aborriqué, *ref.* **aborricarse.**
abortador, *m.* abortionist.
abortamiento, *m.* 1. miscarriage, abortion. 2. abortion (miscarriage caused artificially).
abortar, *tr.v.* to abort (a landing; a plan). —*i.v.* 1. to have a miscarriage, abort. 2. to have an abortion, abort. 3. (fig.) to miscarry, fail. 4. (biol.) to abort, become stunted in development (organ of plant or animal). 5. (med.) to disappear (a disease) before its time.
abortista, *a.* pro-choice. —*mf.* 1. pro-choicer. 2. (med.) abortionist. —*f.* woman who has had an abortion.
abortivo, va, *a.* abortion-inducing. —*m.* abortifacient (agent which causes an abortion).

aborto, *m.* 1. miscarriage. 2. abortion (miscarriage caused artificially). 3. miscarriage (of a plan). 4. (coll.) a very ugly person. — **a. contagioso,** (vet.) contagious abortion; **a. espontáneo,** miscarriage; **a. terapéutico,** therapeutic abortion.
abortón, *m.* aborted quadruped, prematurely born quadruped; skin of aborted lamb.
aborujar, *tr.v., i.v.* 1. to make or become lumpy. 2. to wrap or bundle up in bedclothes or warm clothing.
abotagamiento, *m.* swelling, puffiness.
abotargarse, (*ref. 51*) *r.v.* to become swollen, puffy, bloated (generally because of illness).
abotargue, abotargué, *ref.* **abotargarse.**
abotijarse, *r.v.* to get bloated; to become potbellied.
abotinado, da, *a.* gaiter-shaped; shaped like a high shoe, legging, or spat.
abotonador, *m.* buttonhook.
abotonadura, *f., var. of* **botonadura.**
abotonar, *tr.v., r.v.* to button, button up. —*i.v.* 1. to bud (plants). 2. to form buttons on egg white (of an egg cooked in water). 3. (Nic.) to adulate, flatter fawningly.
abovedado, da, *past part. of* **abovedar.** —*a.* arched, vaulted.
abovedar, *tr.v.* to vault, arch, crown.
ab ovo, *adv.* (Lat.) (said of narratives) from the beginning or from a very remote time.
aboyado, da, *a.* 1. rented with oxen to till it (a farm). 2. (Amer.) buoy-like, buoy-shaped.
aboyar, *tr.v.* 1. to provide with oxen (a farm). 2. (mar.) to mark with buoys. —*i.v.* to float, to buoy up.
abozalar, *tr.v.* to muzzle (a dog, etc.).
abra, *f.* 1. small bay, cove. 2. dale, valley. 3. fissure, crack. 4. (mar.) distance between masts. 5. (Amer.) leaf (of a door), pane (of a window). 6. clearing (in a wood); path (through the underbrush); (Nic.) trail.
abracadabra, *m.* abracadabra, a word supposed to have magical and curing powers, used in incantations, etc.
abracar, *tr.v.* (Cuba, Mex.) to embrace, to encompass.
abrace, abracé, *ref.* **abrazar.**
abracijarse, *r.v.* to embrace, embrace one another.
abracijo, *m.* (coll.) embrace, hug.
Abrahán, *m.* Abraham; **Seno de A.,** Abraham's bosom.
abrahonar, *tr.v.* (coll.) to grasp by the arms, to grasp by the upper part of the sleeves.
abrasadamente, *adv.* ardently.
abrasador, ra, *a.* burning, searing.
abrasamiento, *m.* 1. burning. 2. passion, ardor.
abrasante, *a.* scorching, burning.
abrasar, *tr.v.* 1. to burn. 2. to overheat. 3. to dry up, parch, nip, squelch (plants). 4. (fig.) to consume, squander. 5. (fig.) to embarrass, squash. 6. (fig.) to inflame with passion. —*i.v.* to burn, be very hot. —*r.v.* 1. to dry up, become parched (by the heat), be nipped (by the cold). 2. to burn. 3. (fig.) to be roasting or boiling, be very hot. 4. (fig.) to be consumed, burn (with passion, anger, etc.). — **abrasarse de,** to be consumed with (love); **abrasarse en deseos de +** *inf.,* to be dying to + *inf.;* **abrasarse vivo,** to be roasting or boiling, be very hot; **¡ que te abrasas!** watch out! you're getting hot (or near the mark).
abrasilado, da, *a.* Brazil red, of the color of brazilwood.
abrasión, *f.* 1. abrasion; abrading. 2. (geol.) erosion. 3. (med.) abrasion, superficial excoriation. 4. (med.) intestinal irritation produced by strong laxatives.
abrasivo, va, *a., m.* abrasive.
abravecer, (*ref. 45*) *tr.v.* to infuriate.
abravezca, abravezco, *ref.* **abravecer.**
abraxas, *m.* abraxas, abrasax, a mystical word used as a charm and engraved on talismans.
abrazada, *f.* embrace.
abrazadera, *f.* 1. clamp, band, clasp, brace, clip. 2. (print.) brace, bracket. — **sierra a.,** lumberman's saw; **a. tapafuga,** leak clamp.
abrazado, da, *past part. of* **abrazar.** —*a.* (sl.) in jail, arrested, in the clink.
abrazador, ra, *a.* 1. embracing. 2. (bot.) without a petiole, not petiolate.
abrazamiento, *m.* embracing.
abrazante, *a.* 1. embracing. 2. (bot.) not petiolate, without a petiole.
abrazar, (*ref. 53*) *tr.v.* 1. to embrace, hug, clasp. 2. (fig.) to contain, include, embrace, take in. 3. to join, adopt, embrace (a religion, etc.). 4. (fig.) to take on, to take charge of (business). —*r.v.* to embrace, embrace one another.
abrazo, *m.* 1. embrace, hug. 2. (fig.) carnal embrace, sexual act. — **un b., Carlos,** best wishes, Charles; regards, Charles; love, Charles.
abreacción, *f.* (psyc.) abreaction.
abreboca, *m., f.* 1. (Arg.) featherbrain, absent-minded person. 2. appetizer, tidbit.
abrebotellas, *m.* bottle opener.
abrecartas, (*pl.* **abrecartas**) *m.* letter-opener.
ábrego, *m.* south wind, Auster (poet.).
abrelatas, (*pl.* **abrelatas**) *m.* can-opener.
abrenuncio, *interj.* (Lat.) (coll.) fie! by no means!
abrepuño, *m.* 1. (bot.) centaury. 2. (*pl.*) crowfoot (Ranunculus muricatus).
abretonar, *tr.v.* (mar.) to fix the guns at the side of the ship, facing from stern to prow.
abrevadero, *m.* watering place, drinking trough.
abrevador, ra, *a.* watering. —*m., f.* one who waters cattle. —*m.* drinking trough
abrevar, *tr.v.* 1. to water (cattle, soil, streets); to soak (skin, in tanning). 2. to give a drink to; to administer (a potion) to. 3. to slake (thirst).
abreviación, *f.* abbreviation; shortening; abridgement.
abreviadamente, *adv.* in short, in brief, briefly; succinctly.
abreviado, da, *past part. of* **abreviar.** —*a.* condensed, succinct, concise; sparse.
abreviador, ra, *a.* abbreviating; abridging, condensing, shortening. —*m., f.* 1. abbreviator, abridger. 2. (ecc.) abbreviator, Vatican official who abbreviates manuscripts and writs.
abreviaduría, *f.* (ecc.) post of abbreviator.
abreviamiento, *m., var. of* **abreviación.**
abreviar, *tr.v.* 1. to reduce, shorten; to abbreviate, abridge; to cut short. 2. to accelerate; to hurry. —*r.v.* (C. Amer.) to hurry, to make haste. — **¡abrevia!** hurry up.
abreviatura, *f.* 1. abbreviation, contraction. 2. (ecc.) post of abbreviator in Vatican. 3. compendium or resume. — **en a.,** (coll.) with brevity; speedily, hastily.
abriboca, *a.* (Arg.) distracted; absent-minded; open-mouthed (with wonder), befuddled, etc.
abribonado, da, *past part. of* **abribonarse.** —*a.* rascally, roguish, scampish.
abribonarse, *r.v.* to become a rogue or rascal.
abridero, ra, *a.* freestone, a variety of peach.
abridor, ra, *a.* opening. —*m.* 1. can opener; bottle opener. 2. freestone (peach). 3. (agr.) grafting knife. 4. earring worn immediately after piercing the ears. 5. (arch.) iron rod used for opening fluted collars. — **a. de láminas,** (print.) engraver, cutter.
abrigada, *f., var. of* **abrigadero.**
abrigadero, *m.* 1. sheltered place; (mar.) shelter, haven, cove. 2. (Amer.) lair, hideout.
abrigado, *past part. of* **abrigar.** —*m.* sheltered place, shelter.
abrigador, ra, *a.* 1. protective, warm (clothing). 2. (Mex.) concealing. —*m.* (Mex.) concealer, harborer (of a criminal).
abrigaño, *m., var. of* **abrigadero.**
abrigar, (*ref. 51*) *tr.v.* 1. to shelter, protect; to protect from the cold, wrap up (in warm clothing). 2. (fig.) to harbor (suspicions); cherish, have (hopes, plans, etc.). 3. (mar.) to harbor. 4. (fig.) to help, assist, aid; protect. 5. (equit.) to grip (a horse) with the knees. —*r.v.* 1. to wrap oneself up (in warm clothing). 2. to take shelter.
abrigo, *m.* 1. overcoat; wrap. 2. shelter, sheltered place. 3. (mil.) shelter; cover. 4. (fig.) help, protection. 5. (mar.) harbor, inlet, cove. 6. (archeol.) small, shallow cave. 7. (Arg.) blanket; quilt. — **al a. de,** sheltered by, protected by, under cover of; **estar al a. de,** to be protected by; **a. antiaéreo,** bomb shelter.
ábrigo, *m., var. of* **ábrego.**
abrigue, abrigué, *ref.* **abrigar.**
abril, *m.* 1. April. 2. (fig.) springtime; early youth. 3. (*pl.*) the years of early youth. — **estar hecho un a.,** to look very handsome (a man) or beautiful (a woman); **tener trece abriles,** to be thirteen years old.
abrileño, ña, *a.* pertaining to April; typical of April.
abrillantado, da, *a.* 1. highly polished, glossy. 2. (Amer.) glazed (fruit).
abrillantador, *m.* gem-cutter and polisher, lapidary; instrument for cutting and polishing jewels.
abrillantar, *tr.v.* 1. to cut and polish (precious stones). 2. to make glitter and sparkle, polish. 3. (fig.) to enhance, give luster to. 4. (Amer.) to glaze, crystallize (fruit).
abrimiento, *m.* opening.
abrinquinado, da, *a.* (coll.) delicate, fragile; (Sp.) prettified.
abrir, *irr. past part.:* **abierto.** *tr.v.* to open; to undo; to unlock; to unfasten; to spread out, open out. 2. to open, begin, inaugurate (studies, campaigns, sessions, etc.). 3. to open, set up (a shop, business). 4. to dig. 5. to open, cut, construct (roads, canals). 6. to split, crack. 7. to open (a hand of cards, a list, gunfire). 8. (Amer.) to clear (woodlands). — **a. calle,** to make way; **¡a. cancha!** gangway; **a. el apetito,** to whet the appetite; **a. los cimientos,** to dig the foundations; **a. crédito,** to give (someone) credit, advance money; **a. una lámina,** to engrave a plate; **a. un libro,** to cut the pages of a book; **a. la licitación,** to open the bidding; **a. la mano,** to be generous; to accept bribes; **a. los ojos,** to open one's eyes, realize the truth; **abrirle los ojos a,** to open (someone's) eyes; **a. paso,** to make way; **a. una cuenta,** to open an account; **a. una procesión** or **marcha,** to lead or head a procession or march. —*i.v.* 1. to open. 2. to spread, spread out (fire from gun). 3. to clear up (weather). 4. (mar.) to float free (ship which was aground). 5. (Amer.) to run away. 6. (Amer.) to back out, withdraw (from a commitment). — **a. el día,** to dawn (the day). —*r.v.* to open. 2. to split, crack, open. 3. to spread, spread out (fire from gun). 4. (Amer.) to leave stealthily and suddenly. 5. to open ranks. 6. (Amer.) to swerve out (a motor car). — **abrirse con alguien,** to confide in or unbosom oneself to someone; **abrirse paso,** to make way for oneself; **abrirse de piernas,** (vulg.) to seek a sexual embrace, to surrender oneself.

abrir, *m.* opening; **en un a. y cerrar de ojos,** in the twinkling of an eye.
abro, *m.* (bot.) Indian licorice.
abrocatelado, da, *var. of* **abroquelado.**
abrochador, ra, *m.* buttonhook. —*f.* (Arg., Urug.) stapler.
abrochadura, *f. ref.* **abrochamiento.**
abrochamiento, *m.* buttoning; fastening, lacing.
abrochar, *tr.v.* 1. to button up, lace up, do up; to fasten with hooks and eyes. 2. (Mex.) to catch, to apprehend.
abrogación, *f.* abrogation, repeal, revocation, annulment.
abrogar, (*ref. 51*) *tr.v.* (law) to abrogate, repeal; revoke, abolish, annul.
abrogarse, *r.v.* (Amer.) to assume, to take upon oneself.
abrogatorio, ria, *a.* abrogative.
abrogue, abrogué, *ref.* **abrogar.**
abrojal *m.* thistly, thorny patch.
abrojín, *m.* (zool.) murex, a variety of mollusk.
abrojo, *m.* 1. (bot.) caltrop, star thistle; thorn, thistle. 2. thistle-shaped device (used in the whip of a flagellant). 3. (mil.) caltrop. 4. (coll.) (*pl.*) sorrows, grief. 5. (mar.) (*pl.*) sharp rocks (at surface level).
abroma, *m.* (bot.) devil's cotton.
abromado, da, *a.* (mar.) misted over, obscured by heavy fog or mist.
abromarse, *r.v.* (mar.) to become covered with barnacles.
abroncar, (*ref. 50*) *tr.v.* 1. (coll.) to annoy, irritate; to disgust; to bore. 2. to embarrass, show up, make blush. 3. to tell off, reprimand severely. 4. to boo, to hiss. —*r.v.* to get annoyed, irritated, disgusted, bored.
abronque, abronqué, *ref.* **abroncar.**
abroquelado, da, *past part. of* **abroquelar.** —*a.* (bot.) shield-shaped, peltate.
abroquelar, *tr.v.* 1. (mar.) to boxhaul, to veer sharply instead of tacking normally. 2. to shield, protect, defend. —*r.v.* to shield oneself, defend oneself.
abrótano, *m.* (bot.) southernwood; **a. hembra,** lavender cotton.
abrotoñar, *i.v.* (bot.) to bud, sprout.
abrumador, ra, *a.* overwhelming, crushing, oppressive. —*m., f.* oppressor.
abrumadoramente, *adv.* overwhelmingly, oppressively.
abrumar, *tr.v.* 1. to overwhelm, oppress; to crush. 2. (fig.) to weary, annoy. 3. (fig.) to embarrass a person by showering him with praise, attentions, reproaches, accusations, mockery, etc. —*r.v.* to become cloudy, foggy or misty.
abruñeiro, *m.* (N. of Sp., bot) sloe (fruit).
abruptamente, *adv.* abruptly.
abrupto, ta, *a.* 1. steep, abrupt; craggy, rugged, rough. 2. abrupt, sudden.
abrutado, da, *a.* brutish, bestial, uncouth.
abruzarse, *r.v.* to lie face down, to lie prone.
abruzo, za, *a., m., f.* Abruzzian. —*m.* (*pl.*) Abruzzi, mountains and region in Italy.
absceso, *m.* (med.) abscess.
abscisa, *f.* (geom.) abscissa.
abscisión, *f.* 1. abscission, separation. 2. (fig.) interruption or renunciation.
absenta, *f.* absinthe (liquor).
absentina, *f.* (chem.) absinthin.
absentismo, *m.* absenteeism (applied to landlords and landowners).
absentista, *a.* pertaining to absenteeism (of landlords). *m., f.* absentee landlord.
ábsida, *f., var. of* **ábside.**
absidal, *a.* apsidal, of an apse or apsis.
ábside, *m., f.* (archit.) apse. —*m.* (astron.) apsis.
absidiola, *f.* apse chapel.
absíntico, ca, *a.* absinthic.
absintio, *m.* (bot.) absinthium, absinthe, wormwood.
absintismo, *m.* (med.) absinthism.
absit, *interj.* (Lat.) God forbid!
absolución, *f.* absolution, acquittal; **a. de la demanda,** finding for the defendant, dismissal of the complaint; **a. de la instancia,** acquittal (due to lack of evidence); **a. general,** granting, by certain religious orders, of indulgences on certain days of the year; **a. libre,** verdict of not guilty, acquittal.
absoluta, *f.* 1. dogmatic assertion. 2. (mil., coll.) discharge or separation from the armed forces.
absolutamente, *adv.* 1. absolutely, entirely, completely; definitely. 2. absolutely not.
absolutismo, *m.* absolutism; despotism.
absolutista, *a., m., f.* absolutist.
absoluto, ta, *a.* 1. absolute. 2. independent, unrestricted, unlimited. 3. imperious, domineering. — **lo absoluto,** the absolute, ultimate; **en absoluto,** not at all (used in negative sentences); absolutely not; **dominio absoluto,** (law) freehold.
absolutorio, ria, *a.* (law) absolvent, absolving, acquitting.
absolvederas, *f.* (*pl.*) (coll.) facility in giving absolution.
absolvedor, ra, *a.* absolving, absolvent. —*m., f.* absolver, absolvent.
absolvente, *a.* absolvent, absolving.
absolver, (*ref. 34*) *tr.v.* to absolve; to acquit.
absorbefaciente, *a., m.* (med.) absorbefacient.
absorbencia, *f.* absorption; absorbency; **a. específica, specific absorptive index.**
absorbente, *m.* absorbent. —*a.* absorbing.
absorber, *tr.v.* (lit., fig.) to absorb.
absorbible, *a.* absorbable.
absorbimiento, *m., var. of* **absorción.**
absorción, *f.* absorption.
absortar, *tr.v.* to engross, engage wholly, entrance. —*r.v.* to be engrossed, entranced.
absorto, ta *irr. past part. of* **absorber.** —*a.* entranced, absorbed, engrossed; **estar a. en,** to be absorbed in.
abstemio, mia, *a.* abstemious; non-drinking (of alcoholic beverages). —*m., f.* abstainer, non-drinker, teetotaler.
abstención, *f.* abstention.
abstencionismo, *m.* (polit.) nonparticipation.
abstencionista, *a.* abstaining. —*m., f.* abstainer.
abstenerse, (*ref. 23*) *r.v.* to abstain, to deprive oneself of something; to refrain; **a. de** + *inf.*, to abstain or refrain from + *ger.*
abstenga, abstengo, *ref.* **abstenerse.**
abstergente, *a.* abstergent, purifying. —*m.* abstergent, a cleansing application or medicine.
absterger, (*ref. 57*) *tr.v.* (med.) to cleanse, purify.
absterja, absterjo, *ref.* **absterger.**
abstersión, *f.* (med.) abstersion, cleansing, purifying.
abstersivo, va, *a.* (med.) abstergent, abstersive, cleansing, purifying.
abstinencia, *f.* abstinence; fasting.
abstinente, *a.* abstinent, abstemious.
abstinentemente, *adv.* abstinently, abstemiously.
abstracción, *f.* abstraction; introspection, concentration.
abstraccionismo, *m.* abstractionism.
abstraccionista, *m., f.* abstractionist; (art.) creator of abstract art.
abstractamente, *adv.* abstractly.
abstractivo, va, *a.* abstractive.
abstracto, ta, abstract; **en abstracto,** in abstract; **arte abstracto,** abstract art.
abstraer, (*ref. 24*) *tr.v.* to abstract. —*i.v.* **a. de,** to do without. —*r.v.* to withdraw, become withdrawn or lost in thought; **abstraerse de,** to do without.
abstraído, da, *a.* 1. engrossed, abstracted, absorbed (in ideas); absent-minded. 2. withdrawn.
abstraiga, abstraigo, *ref.* **abstraer.**
abstraje, abstrajera, abstrajese, *ref. abstraer.*
abstrayendo, *ref.* **abstraer.**
abstruso, sa, *a.* abstruse, recondite; obscure.
abstuve, abstuviera, abstuviese, *ref.* **abstenerse.**
absuelto, ta, *irr. past part. of* **absolver.**
absuelva, absuelvo, *ref.* **absolver.**
absurdamente, *adv.* absurdly.
absurdidad, *f.* absurdity.
absurdo, da, *a.* absurd. —*m.* absurdity.
abubilla, *f.* (ornith.) hoopoe.
abuchear, *tr.v.* to hiss, boo, catcall, jeer at.
abucheo, *m.* hissing, booing, catcalling, jeering.
abuela, *f.* grandmother; (fig.) elderly lady; **cuéntaselo a tu a.,** (fig., coll.) tell it to the marines!
abuelastro, tra, *m.* stepgrandfather. —*f.* stepgrandmother.
abuelita, *f.* 1. grandmother (dim. or term of endearment). 2. (Chile) baby's bonnet.
abuelo, *m.* 1. grandfather; (*pl.*) grandparents; (fig.) grandad, elderly man. 2. (lottery) number 90. 3. (fig.) (*pl.*) the fine locks of hair on the nape of a woman's neck.
abuenar, *tr.v.* 1. (Arg.) to calm, pacify. 2. to improve the behavior of a child or a pet.
abuhado, da, *a.* swollen, bloated.
abuhardillado, da, *a.* like a small garret; dormer-windowed; like a dormer window.
abuje, *m.* (Cuba, ento.) chigger, jigger, red bug; mite.
abulaga, *f., var. of* **aulaga.**
abulense, *a.* of or from Avila. —*m., f.* native or inhabitant of Avila. — **la magnífica catedral a.,** the magnificent cathedral of Avila.
abulia, *f.* (psyc.) abulia, lack of willpower, loss of energy.
abúlico, ca, *a.* (psyc.) abulic, lacking willpower or energy.
abullonado, da, *a.* balloonlike, (sleeve, skirt, etc.).
abullonar, *tr.v.* to emboss, to embroider thickly; (sew.) to puff up.
abultado, da, *a.* bulky; swollen; protruding.
abultamiento, *m.* 1. enlarging, augmenting. 2. heap, pile. 3. swelling; prominence.
abultar, *tr.v.* 1. to augment, enlarge; to swell. 2. (fig.) to exaggerate. 3. (sculp.) to prepare the initial shape (of a sculpture). —*i.v.* to be bulky, to take up room.
abundamiento, *m.* abundance; **a mayor a.,** moreover, furthermore.
abundancia, *f.* abundance, plenty, great quantity; **de la a. del corazón habla la boca,** one speaks about that which is most in one's thoughts; **nadar en la a.,** to be on easy street (to be in the midst of plenty).
abundancial, *a.* (gram.) said of adjectives which express the idea of abundance.
abundante, *a.* abundant, plentiful, copious.
abundantemente, *adv.* abundantly.
abundar, *i.v.* to abound, teem; **a. en,** to abound in or with, teem with; **a. en,** to agree with, to persist in, stick to (an opinion, idea, etc.); **lo que abunda no daña,** you can't have too much of a good thing.

Abundio, (Sp., coll.) **más tonto que A.,** dunce, dumbell.
abundo, *adv.* (arch.) abundantly.
abundosamente, *adv.* abundantly.
abundoso, sa, *a.* abundant.
abuñolado, da, *a.* bun-shaped; (like a fritter), puff-shaped.
abuñolar, (*ref. 33*) *tr.v.* (cul.) to fry eggs, etc., on both sides, to turn over (in frying).
abuñuela, abuñuele, *ref.* **abuñolar.**
abuñuelado, da, *a., var. of* **abuñolado.**
abuñuelar, *tr.v., var. of* **abuñolar.**
¡abur! *interj.* (coll.) good-bye! so long! ciao!
aburar, *tr.v.* to burn; to scorch.
aburelado, da, *a.* dark red.
aburguesarse, *r.v.* to become bourgeois; (coll.) to follow the easy path in life.
aburrado, da, *a.* similar to a donkey or burro (e.g. said of coarse and gross persons). *—f.* (Mex.) destined for mule-breeding (a mare).
aburrarse, *r.v.* to become brutish, stupid.
aburrición, *f.* 1. (coll.) *var. of* **aburrimiento.** 2. (Amer.) aversion, antipathy.
aburridamente, *adv.* tediously, boringly.
aburrido da, *a.* boring, tedious, tiresome; bothersome.
aburridor, ra, *a.* boring, tedious, tiresome; bothersome.
aburrimiento, *m.* boredom, tedium. — **¿que a.!** what a drag ! what a bore!
aburrir, *tr.v.* 1. to annoy, to bore, tire, weary. 2. (coll.) to spend (money, time). 3. to leave, abandon. *—r.v.* to grow tired, become bored; **aburrirse como una ostra,** to get bored stiff; **aburrirse con, de** or **por,** to get bored with; **aburrirse de +** *inf.*, to get tired of + *ger.*
aburujar, *tr.v., r.v., var. of* **aborujar.**
abusador, ra, *a.* (coll.) abusive. *—m., f.* a person who is abusive, a bully.
abusante, *a.* abusive.
abusar, *i.v.* **a de,** to abuse, misuse, make bad use of; to take advantage of, impose on; to maltreat, mistreat; (Car.) to rape, violate.
abusión, *f.* 1. abuse. 2. piece of nonsense, absurdity, contradiction. 3. superstition; augury, omen. 4. (rhet.) abuse, misuse of terms, catachresis.
abusionero, ra, *a.* superstitious; pertaining to divination or fortune-telling.
abusivamente, *adv.* abusively, incorrectly; illegally.
abusivo, va, *a.* 1. abusive, misapplied, incorrectly used. 2. outrageous (prices, interest). 3. (Amer.) cruel, bullying, brutal, bad, e.g. *no seas abusivo,* don't be such a bully. *—m., f.* (Amer.) person who misuses his position or authority; someone who takes advantage; brute, bully.
abuso, *m.* 1. abuse, misuse. 2. abuse, injustice; imposition. — **a. de autoridad,** abuse or misuse of authority; **a. de cargo,** misuse of position or post; **a. de confianza,** breach of confidence or trust; **a. deshonestos,** indecent assault; **a. sexual infantil** child abuse.
abusón, na, *a.* said of a person who misuses his power or authority. *—m., f.* one who misuses his power or authority; a bully.
abyección, *f.* 1. abjectness, degradation, abjection, abasement. 2. dejection, depression.
abyecto, ta, *a.* 1. abject, wretched, miserable. 2. despicable, base, low, vile.
a/c *abbrev. of* 1. **a cargo de,** charged to. 2. **a cuenta de,** on account of.
A.C. *abbrev. of* 1. **Año de Cristo,** Anno Domini, in the year of our Lord (AD). 2. **América Central,** Central America.
acá, *adv.* here, over here, hither; **a. y allá, a. y acullá,** here and there, everywhere; **de anoche a.,** overnight, from one day to another; **de ayer a.,** since yesterday; **¿ de cuándo a.?** since when?; **desde entonces a.,** since then; **más a.,** closer over here, closer, nearer; **muy a.,** right over here; **por a.,** around here; **tan a.,** so close; **tan a., como puedas,** as far over here as you can; **de a. para allá,** to and fro, from pillar to post.
acabable, *a.* finishable, exhaustible.
acabadamente, *adv.* completely, perfectly.
acabado, da, *past part. of* **acabar.** *—a.* 1. perfect, complete. 2. finished, worn-out, exhausted. *—m.* finish (manner or style of finishing a piece of work, final effect given).
acabador, ra, *a.* finisher, surfacer, dresser.
acabalar, *tr.v.* to complete, finish.
acaballadero, *m.* 1. stud farm for horses and donkeys. 2. mating season for horses and donkeys.
acaballado, da, *a.* horse-like; horsy, like a horse's head (a face).
acaballar, *tr.v.* to service (a mare).
acaballerado, da, *a.* gentlemanly, gentlemanlike.
acaballerar, *tr.v., r.v.* to treat or behave as a gentleman.
acaballonar, *tr.v.* (agr.) to raise ridges in, furrow.
acabamiento, *m* .1. completion, finishing; end, termination. 2. death. 3. (Arg., Urug., vulg.) orgasm.
acabañar, *i.v.* to build cabins or huts (said of shepherds).
acabar, *tr.v.* 1. to finish, complete, terminate. 2. to give a fine finish to (a piece of carpentry, etc.). 3. to finish up, use up completely. 4. (S. Amer., coll.) to disparage, slander, speak ill of. *—i.v.* 1. to end, finish. 2. (Arg., Urug., vulg.) to have an orgasm, to come (vulg.). 3. to die; to die out, become extinct. — **a. con,** to put an end to, kill; to finish with (a friend, etc.); to use up completely, e.g. *ellos han acabado con sus recursos,* they have used up their resources; **a. de,** to have just, e.g. *acabo de comer,* I have just eaten; **a. por,** to finish by, end up by, e.g. *acabaron por casarse,* they ended up by getting married, *él acabó por entenderlo,* he finally understood it. *—r.v.* 1. to finish, end. 2. to die out, become extinct. 3. to run out of, e.g. *se me acabó la plata,* I ran out of money. — **y se acabó,** and that's the end of it; **se acabó lo que se daba, sanseacabó,** (coll.) that's the end of the question.
acabe, *m.* (P. Rico) celebration at the end of the coffee harvest.
acabellado, da, *a.* light brown, light chestnut.
acabestrillar, *i.v.* to go hunting with a stalking ox.
acabijo, *m.* (coll.) end, finish.
acabildar, *tr.v.* to call together, organize into a group (to pursue some intention or plan).
acabiray, *m.* (Guar., Arg., Par.) bald-headed buzzard.
acabo, *m., var. of* **acabamiento.**
acabóse, *m.* (coll.) the end, the limit, the last straw. — **¡ esto es el a.!** this is the last straw!
acabronado, da, *a.* 1. like a billygoat. 2. (Sp.) cowardly.
acacia, *f.* 1. (bot.) acacia. 2. (pharm.) gum arabic. — **a. bastarda,** (bot.) sloe, black-thorn; **a blanca o falsa,** (bot.) locust tree; **a. rosa,** (bot.) rose acacia.
acacianos, *m.* (*pl.*) heretics, followers of Acacius.
acacoyol, *m.* (Mex., bot.) Job's tears.
acacharse, *r.v.* 1. (coll.) to bend down. 2. (Chile, Peru) to become unsalable because of being shop-soiled or out of fashion.
acachetar, *tr.v.* (taur.) to finish off the bull with the **puntilla** (a short dagger used by bullfighters).
acachetear, *tr.v.* to slap in the face.
academia, *f.* 1. academy. 2. A., Academe, the academic community. 3. (art.) a full-figure study of a nude. 4. (Arg., Urug.) a top-notch football or soccer team. — **a. de baile,** dance school; **a. de conductores, a. de choferes** driving school; **a. de corte y confección** dressmaking school; **a. de idiomas,** language school; **a de peluquería** beautician's school; **a. militar** military academy.
académicamente, *adv.* academically.
academicismo, *m.* academicism, classicism.
académico, ca, *a.* academic. *—m., f.* academician; **a. de número,** regular member.
academista, *m., f.* teacher, pupil, or member of an academy.
academizar, (*ref. 53*) *tr.v.* to academize.
Acadia, *f.* Acadia, original name of Nova Scotia and New Brunswick (Canadian provinces).
acaecedero, ra, *a.* contingent, possible, eventual
acaecer, (*ref. 45*) *i.v.* to happen (used only in infinitive and in third person *sing.* and *pl.*), e.g. *acaeció una desgracia,* a misfortune has occurred.
acaecimiento, *m.* event, incident, occurrence.
acaezca, *ref.* **acaecer.**
acafresna, *f.* (bot.) service tree.
acahe, *m.* Paraguayan mockingbird.
acahual, *m.* 1. (Mex.) sunflower. 2. (Mex.) tall grass (used for covering fallow fields). 3. (Mex.) hillock, hill.
acairelar, *tr.v.* to border, put a fringe on, to embroider elaborately.
acajú, (*pl.* **acajúes**) *m.* (bot.) acajou, cashew nut and tree.
acal, *m.* (Mex.) canoe; boat.
acalabrotar, *tr.v.* (mar.) to weave into a cable (three ropes of three strands each).
acalacas, *f.* (ento., Peru) ant (about the size of a grasshopper).
acalambrarse, *r.v.* to get a cramp or cramps, have an attack of cramps.
acalefo, *a.* (zool.) acalephan. *—m.* (zool.) acaleph, acalephan; (*pl.*) Acalepha, Acalephae.
acalenturarse, *r.v.* to become feverish.
acalia, *f.* (bot.) marshmallow.
acallador, ra, *a.* silencing, quieting.
acallantar, *tr.v., var. of* **acallar.**
acallar, *tr.v.* 1. to silence, quiet, hush. 2. (fig.) to pacify, calm down.
acaloradamente, *adv.* vehemently, heatedly; angrily.
acalorado, da, *past part. of* **acalorar.** *—a.* vehement, heated; angry.
acaloramiento, *m.* ardor, excitement, vehemence, passion.
acalorar, *tr.v.* 1. to heat or warm up. 2. to tire. 3. to encourage; to inspire. 4. to arouse, stir up, incite, inflame. *—r.v.* 1. to get hot or warm. 2. to get heated, excited or worked up; to get heated (a discussion).
acaloro, *var. of* **acaloramiento.**
acalote, *m.* (Mex.) part of a river which is cleared of floating weeds in order to permit the passage of canoes.
acamar, *tr.v.* to flatten, beat or knock (plants or crops) flat (storms or winds). *—r.v.* to be knocked flat, be flattened (plants or crops). *—i.v.* 1. to sway and bend with the wind and the rain (plants, crops). 2. to lie in rest for the night (farm animals).
acamastronarse, *r.v.* (coll.) to become artful or cunning.
acambrayado, da, *a.* (tex.) cambric-like.

acamellado, da, *a.* camel-like, resembling a camel (said of buff or tan shades).
acamellonar, *tr.v.* (Mex.) *var. of* **acaballonar.**
acampada, *f.* camping; campground.
acampamento, *m., var. of* **campamento.**
acampanado, da, *past part. of* **acampanar.** —*a.* bell-bottomed (trousers); flared; **falda a.,** flared skirt.
acampanar, *tr.v* to give the shape of bell, make bell-shaped.
acampar, *i.v., tr.v., r.v.* to camp, to encamp; (fig.) to halt and rest.
acampo, *m.* pasture.
ácana, *f.* (bot.) acana; (bot.) bully tree; a sapotaceous tree of the Antilles.
acanalado, da, *past part. of* **acanalar.** —*a.* channeled; channel-shaped; fluted, grooved, ribbed, striated.
acanalador, *m.* (carp.) grooving tool; rabbet plane.
acanaladora, *f.* channeling, quarrying or grooving machine.
acanaladura, *f.* (archit.) groove, fluting, stria, striation; channel molding.
acanalar, *tr.v.* to groove, flute, striate; to cut a channel in, channel, give the form of a channel.
acanallado, da, *a.* despicable, currish, worthless.
acanallar, *tr.v.,* to corrupt; to deprave. —*r.v.* to become base or depraved, to keep bad company.
acancerarse, *r.v., var. of* **cancerarse.**
acandilado, da, *a.* erect, straight as a candle.
acanelado, da, *a.* cinnamon-colored, cinnamon-flavored.
acanelonar, *tr.v.* to beat with a knotted whip.
acanillado, da, *a.* ribbed, striped (caused by a defect in weaving).
acanilladura, *f.* a defect caused by thread of different thickness or color in the weave.
acansinarse, *r.v., var. of.* **cansarse.**
acantáceo, a, *a.* (bot.) acanthaceous. —*f.* acanthaceous plant; (*pl.*) Acanthaceae.
acantalear, *i.v.* (Sp.) to hail or rain very hard.
acantarar, *tr.v.* to measure in pitcherfuls.
acantear, *tr.v.* to throw stones at; to stone.
acantilado, da, *a.* 1. steep. 2. having underwater shelves, steep rocks or banks. —*m.* cliff; escarpment.
acantilar, *tr.v.* 1. to run (a ship) aground or on the rocks. 2. to dredge. —*r.v.* to run aground, run on the rocks.
acantio, *m.* (bot.) cotton thistle.
acanto, *m.* 1. (bot.) acanthus, bear's breech. 2. (archit.) acanthus.
acantocéfalo, la, *a.* (zool.) acanthocephalan. —*m.* (*pl.*) Acantohcephala.
acantoide, *a.* acanthoid, acanthous; spiny, spiny-shaped.
acántolis, *m.* (Cuba) thorny-backed reptile.
acantonamiento, *m.* 1. (mil.) cantonment, quartering (of troops); quarters. 2. a place where troops are billeted.
acantonar, *tr.v.* to quarter, billet (troops). —*r.v.* to be quartered or billeted. — **acantonarse en,** to limit oneself or one's activities to (a particular sphere of studies, interest, etc.).
acantopterigio, gia, *a.* (ichth.) acanthopterygian. —*m.* acanthopterygian; (*pl.*) Acanthopterygii.
acañaverear, *tr.v.* to wound with sharp pointed canes, an ancient form of torture.
acañonear, *tr.v.* (mil.) to shell or bombard with heavy artillery.
acañutado, da, *a.* bamboo-like, reed-like; cylindrical.
acaobado, da, *a.* mahogany-colored.
acapacle, *m.* (Mex.) cane believed to have medicinal qualities.
acaparador, ra, *a.* hoarding. —*m., f.* 1. hoarder. 2. a person involved in black market operations (especially in war-time).
acaparamiento, *m.* 1. hoarding, buying up (to create a scarcity of goods to be resold at greater profit). 2. cornering (of the market). 3. monopolization (of the conversation). 4. taking possession, getting hold (of).
acaparar, *tr.v.* 1. to buy up, hoard. 2. to corner the market. 3. to take possession of, get hold of. 4. to monopolize (the conversation).
acaparrarse, *r.v.* to come to terms or to an agreement (as in a bargain).
acaparrosado, da, *a.* copperas-colored; blotchy.
acapillar, *tr.v.* to catch, capture; to trap, ensnare.
acápite, *m.* (Amer.) separate paragraph.
acapizarse, *r.v.* (coll.) to fight by grabbing the opponent's head.
acaponado, da, *a.* 1. effeminate, unmanly. 2. sexless, capon-like.
acapuchar, *tr.v.* to shape into a hood.
acapullarse, *r.v.* 1. to envelop or wrap itself into a cocoon. 2. to take the shape of a blossom or a bud.
acaracolado, da, *a.* wavy, spiral-shaped, winding; shaped like a seashell.
acaraira, *f.* (Cuba) *var. of* **caraira.**
acarambanado, da, *a., var. of* **carambanado.**
acaramelado, da, *a.* 1. caramel-coated. 2. caramel-hued. 3. (fig.) sugary, syrupy, mellifluous. 4. (coll.) blissfully enamored.
acaramelar, *tr.v.* to cover with caramel. —*r.v.* 1. (coll.) to be excessively gallant, to exude charm. 2. to become crystalized (fudge, toffee.) 3. to get carried away by sentimental love. — **acaramelarse con,** (coll.) to fall in love with.
acarar, *tr.v.* to confront; to face; to brave.
acardenalar, *tr.v.* to bruise, beat black and blue. —*r.v.* to become covered with welts, become black and blue.
acardia, *f.* (med.) lack of a heart (in the fetus).
acareamiento, *m.* a face-to-face confrontation.
acarear, *tr.v., var. of* **acarar.**
acariasis, *f.* (med.) acariasis.
acariciador, ra, *a.* caressing; tender, loving. —*m., f.* one who fondles or caresses.
acariciante, *a.* caressing.
acariciar, *tr.v.* 1. to caress, fondle. 2. (fig.) to treat tenderly and lovingly. 3. to cherish, harbor (hopes, a dream). 4. (fig.) to touch or brush against (something) very lightly.
acariciarse, *tr.v.* to fondle or caress oneself or one another. — **a. las barbas,** to stroke one's beard.
acárido, *m.* (zool.) acarid, mite.
acariñar, *tr.v.* (Amer.) to fondle or caress; to treat lovingly.
acarminar, *tr.v.* to dye or tint red; to redden (something).
acarnerado, da, *a.* with a sheep-like head (said of horses).
ácaro, *m.* (ento.) acarus, mite; **a. de la sarna,** itch mite; **a. del queso, a. doméstico,** cheese mite.
acarodermatitis, *f.* skin inflammation produced by the acarus.
acaroide, *a.* (bot., med.) acaroid.
acárpico, ca, *a.* (bot.) acarpous.
acarpo, pa, *a.* (bot.) acarpous.
acarraladura, *f.* (Chile, Peru) run, ladder (in a stocking).
acarralar, *tr.v.* to skip a thread in weaving. —*r.v.* to wither (grapevines) due to frost.
acarrarse, *r.v.* to seek shade (said of sheep).
acarrascado, da, *a.* like an evergreen oak.
acarreadizo, za, *a.* portable, movable.
acarreamiento, *m.* 1. transportation; cartage. 2. (*pl.*) supplies.
acarrear, *tr.v.* 1. to transport, convey, carry, cart. 2. to entail, occasion, cause (damage, misfortune). —*r.v.* to bring upon oneself, incur.
acarreo, *m.* transportation; cartage, freight. — **tierras de acarreo,** alluvium; sand or clay deposits left by moving waters.
acarretear, *tr.v.* (coll.) *var. of* **carretear.**
acarreto, *m.* transportation; freight, cartage; hilo de a., pack thread, twine.
acarroñar, *tr.v.* (Col., coll.) to intimidate. —*r.v.* to become intimidated.
acartonado, da, *a.* (Amer.) 1. resembling pasteboard; stiff. 2. dried-up by age; withered (a person).
acartonar, *tr.v.* to give the appearance of cardboard. —*r.v.* 1. to become like cardboard. 2. (coll.) to become withered (with age).
acasamatado, da *a.* (fort.) 1. casemated, protected with a casemate. 2. like a casemate.
acaseramiento, *m.* (Peru, Chile, coll.) faithful patronage; habit of buying at the same store.
acaserarse, *r.v.* (Chile, Peru) to become a regular customer (of a store); (Chile, Peru) to become attached (to) or fond (of).
acaso, *m.* chance, accident. —*adv.* perhaps, maybe; by chance, by accident. — **por si a.,** just in case.
acastañado, da, *a.* brownish, chestnut-colored.
acastellanado, da, *a.* Castilian-like, having adopted Castilian ways.
acastillado, da, *a.* castle-like.
acastorado, da, *a.* like beaver fur.
acatable, *a.* worthy of respect; venerable.
acatadamente, *adv.* respectfully, with respect.
acataléctico, *a.* acatalectic; **verso a.,** acatalectic verse. —*m.* acatalectic (verse).
acatalecto, *a., m., var. of* **acataléctico.**
acatalepsia, *f.* (med.) acatalepsia.
acatamiento, *m.* 1. observance, compliance, e.g. *el a. de una ley,* the observance of a law. 2. respect, reverence, acceptance.
acatar, *tr.v.* 1. to obey, observe, respect (law, rules, etc.). 2. to revere, respect, venerate. 3. (Amer.) to notice, realize.
acatarrar, *tr.v.* (Mex., Chile, coll.) to annoy. —*r.v.* to catch a cold.
acatechitli, *m.* (ornith.) Mexican finch (Fringilla mexicanus).
acates, *m.* 1. faithful friend. 2. (myth.) **A.,** Achates, Aeneas' faithful friend (in Virgil's *Aeneid*).
acato, *m.* reverence, respect; **darse a.,** to realize, notice; **hacer a.,** to be respectful.
acatólico, ca, *a.* non-Catholic (Christian); said of one who rejects papal authority.
acaudado, da, *a.* (bot.) acaudal.
acaudalado, da, *a.* wealthy, opulent, rich.
acaudalar, *tr.v.* to amass, accumulate (a fortune, knowledge, etc.).
acáudeo, a, *a.* (med., zool.) acaudal.
acaudillador, ra, *a.* leading, commanding. —*m.* leader, commander.
acaudillamiento, *m.* leadership, command.
acaudillar, *tr.v.* to lead, command. —*r.v.* to elect a leader or commander.
acaule, *a.* (bot.) acaulescent, having no visible stem.
acautelarse, *r.v., var. of* **cautelarse.**
Acaya, *f.* Achaea, ancient province in the N. Peloponnesus.
accedente, *a.* acceding (said of treaties between princes).
acceder, *i.v.* to accede, agree; **a. a,** to accede to, agree to.
accesibilidad, *f.* accessibility.
accesible, *a.* accessible, attainable; (fig.) approachable, easy to talk with, affable, accessible.

accesión, *f.* 1. accession, acquiescence, agreement. 2. accessory. 3. access, entry. 4. (law) accession. 5. (med.) attack or accession of intermittent fever.
accésit, *m.* second prize (in scientific, literary, or artistic competitions).
acceso, *m.* 1. access; approach; entrance; admittance. 2. approachableness, accessibility, e.g. *una persona de fácil a.,* an easily approached person. 3. (archit.) passage, corridor. 4. outburst, fit, access (e.g. of anger, etc.). 5. (med.) attack, access (of fever, coughing, etc.). — **ganar a. a,** to gain access to; **tener a. a,** to have access to.
accesoria, *f.* annex, additional but separate wing or building; (*pl.*) street-level rooms of a building or large house, usually rented to individual tenants.
accesorio, ria, *a.* accessory. —*m.* 1. accessory; fixture, attachment. 2. (theat.) props.
accidentado, da, *past part. of* **accidentar.** —*a.* uneven, irregular, rough (terrain, surface, etc.). 2. troubled, difficult, agitated (life, journey, etc.). —*m., f.* victim of an accident.
accidental, *a.* 1. accidental, chance, happening by chance, e.g. *un encuentro a.,* an accidental or chance meeting. 2. accidental, caused by accident, e.g. *muerte a.,* accidental death. 3. accidental, incidental, contingent. 4. acting, temporary, e.g. *director a.,* acting director. —*m.* (mus.) accidental.
accidentalmente, *adv.* accidentally.
accidentar, *r.v.* to have an accident; to be hurt or injured. —*tr.v.* to cause an accident; to injure, hurt in an accident.
accidentario, ria, *a., var. of* **accidental.**
accidente, *m.* 1. accident, mishap, occurrence causing injury, e.g. *a. aéreo, a. de avión,* plane crash, *a. de auto, a. de coche,* automobile accident, *a. ferroviario,* train crash. 2. accident, unexpected event, e.g. *se encontraron por a.,* they met by chance. 3. accident, accidental, nonessential property; (philos., log.) accident. 4. fainting fit or spell. 5. (fig.) fit, outburst, sudden passion. 6. accident, unevenness, irregularity (of surface, terrain, etc.). 7. (gram.) accident. 8. (mus.) accidental. 9. (med.) complication (in an illness). 10. (theol.) (*pl.*) material manifestation of bread and wine after consecration. — **seguro contra accidentes,** accident insurance; **a. de trabajo,** occupational accident.
Accio, *m.* (hist.) Actium, where Octavian defeated the forces of Mark Antony and Cleopatra.
acción, *f.* 1. action, activity; effect; act, deed; gesture, gesticulation. 2. (law) lawsuit, action. 3. (mil.) action, battle. 4. (com.) share, stock. 5. (p.) action, pose. 6. (lit.) action, story or incidents in a drama, novel, etc. 7. (phys.) action (of one body on another). 8. (Peru) raffle ticket. — **a. al portador,** (com.) bearer share, nonregistered share; **a. constitutiva,** (law) test case; **a. de gracias,** expression of thanks, thanksgiving; **a. directa,** direct action; **a. eslabonada,** (phys.) chain reaction; **a. nominativa,** (com.) registered stock; **a. ordinaria,** (com.) common stock; **a. preferente,** preferred stock; **a. refleja,** (physiol.) reflex action; **dejar sin a., quitar la a. (a alguien),** to deprive (someone) of freedom of action; **ganar (a alguien)la a.,** to beat (someone) to it (coll.); **mala a.,** evil deed, double-crossing.
accionado, da, *a.* 1. driven, propelled, powered. 2. acted, expressed by gestures.
accionamiento, *m.* driving, propelling; drive. — **a. eléctrico,** (mec.) electric drive; **a. por cadena,** (mec.) chain drive; **a. por fricción,** (auto.) friction drive; **a. manual,** manual operation.
accionar, *tr.v.* 1. to put in motion, propel, drive. 2. (Amer.) to bring a legal action against. —*i.v.* to gesticulate.
accionario, a, *a.* stock.
accionista, *m., f.* shareholder, stockholder.
accípitre, *m.* (ornith.) accipiter, bird of prey.
accisa, *f.* indirect tax on food.
Accra, Accra, capital of Ghana.
acebadamiento, *m., var. of* **encebadamiento.**
acebadar, *tr.v., r.v., var. of* **encebadar.**
acebal, *m., var. of* **acebeda.**
acebeda, *f.* holly grove, holly wood.
acebedo, *m., var. of* **acebeda.**
acebo, *m.* (bot.) holly.
acebollado, da, *a.* 1. having cup shake or ring shake (timber). 2. damaged (timber). 3. like an onion, onion-shaped, onion-flavored.
acebolladura, *f.* ring shake, cup shake (in timber); damage (present in timber).
acebrado, da, *a., var. of* **cebrado.**
acebuchal, *a.* of or related to the wild olive. —*m.* grove of wild olive **trees.**
acebuche, *m.* wild olive (tree).
acebucheno, na, *a.* of or related to the wild olive.
acebuchina, *f.* wild olive (fruit).
acece, acecé, *ref.* **acezar.**
acechadera, *f.* lookout post, observation post: ambush.
acechadero, *m., var. of* **acechadera.**
acechador, ra, *a.* ambushing, lurking, watching, observing. —*m., f.* ambusher, waylayer; observer, watcher, spy.
acechamiento, *m.* the action of ambushing, waylaying, lurking; watching, observing, spying on.
acechanza, *f., var. of* **acecho.**
acechar, *tr.v.* to lie in ambush for, lie in wait for; to watch, observe, spy on, be on the lurk.
aceche, *m.* copperas, vitriol.
acecho, *m.* 1. watching, observation; lying in wait or ambush. 2. observation post. — estar **al a.** or **en an.,** to lie in wait or ambush; to watch, observe, be on the lookout.
acechón, *a.* (coll.) ambushing, lurking; watching, observing. — **hacer** la **acechona,** coll.) to lie in wait or ambush; to watch, observe.
acecido, *m.* (coll.) *var. of* **acezo.**
acecinar, *tr.v.* to cure (meat) by salting and smoking. —*r.v.* to become thin or lean with age.
acedamente, *adv.* bitterly, sourly.
acedar, *tr.v.* 1. to sour, make bitter. 2. to upset the stomach with acidity, heartburn. 3. (fig.) to displease, annoy, vex. —*r.v.* 1. to go sour, become bitter. 2. to get annoyed. 3. to fade, wilt (plants).
acedera, *f.* (bot.) sorrel; **a. menor,** wood sorrel.
acederaque, *m.* chinaberry, bead tree, azedarach.
acederilla, *f.* (bot.) alleluia, wood sorrel, woodwaxen, oxalis.
acederón, *m.* variety of sorrel.
acedía, *f.* 1. acidity, sourness. 2. heartburn or acid indigestion. 3. unpleasantness, roughness, uncouthness (of manner). 4. (ichth.) plaice, flounder.
acedo, da, *a.* 1. acid, sour. 2. disagreeable, unpleasant, rough, harsh (in manner). —*m.* sour sap (of trees).
acefalía, *f.* 1. acephalia, acephalism, headlessness. 2. (fig.) lack of a leader.
acefalismo, *m.* 1. acephalia, acephalism, headlessness. 2. (fig.) lack of a leader. 3. sect and doctrine of the Acephali.
acéfalo, la, *a.* 1. acephalous, headless. 2. of the Acephali (5th C. heretics). 3. acephalous, leaderless, headless. 4. (zool.) acephalous. —*m.* 1. (*pl.*) Acephali (5th C. heretics). 2. (zool.) acephal, (*pl.*) Acephala.
aceguero, *m.* woodsman who collects timber and brush.
aceifa, *f.* military expedition conducted by the Saracens in summer.
aceitada, *f.* 1. spilled oil. 2. oiling. 3. pastry made with oil.
aceitar, *tr.v.* to oil, smear with oil.
aceitazo, *m.* thick, dirty oil; lubricating oil.
aceite, *m.* oil. — **a. de abeto,** fir tree resin; **a. de almendras,** almond oil; **a. de anís,** aniseed brandy; **a. de ballena,** whale oil; **a. de cada,** juniper oil; **a. de coco,** coconut oil; **a. de hígado de bacalao,** cod-liver oil; **a. de María,** calaba oil; **a. de hojuela,** oil pressed from olive skins; **a. de linaza,** linseed oil; **a. de mesa,** salad oil; **a. de oliva,** olive oil; **a. de palma,** palm oil; **a. de palo,** oil of copaiba; **a. de pepa de algodón,** cotton-seed oil; **a. de ricino,** castor oil; **a. de rosas,** attar of roses; **a. de vitriolo,** sulphuric acid; **a. esencial, essential oil; a. fijo,** heavy oil; **a. mineral,** mineral oil; petroleum; **a. onfacino,** omphacine oil, oil extracted from unripe olives; **a. serpentino,** medicinal oil used against worms; **a. vegetal,** vegetable oil; **a. virgen,** first oil extracted from the olive; **a. volátil,** volatile oil.
aceitera, *f.* 1. oil cruet, oil container; (mec.) oiler, oil cup (for oiling machinery). 2. (ento.) oil beetle. 3. (*pl.*) cruets.
aceitero, ra, *a.* 1. oiler; oil vendor. 2. (bot.) mountain damson, marupa.
aceitillo, *m.* 1. (Cuba, P. Rico) satinwood, paradise tree. 2. cosmetic oil.
aceitón, *m.* 1. heavy lubricating oil. 2. olive oil dregs. 3. sticky liquid secreted by certain insects on plants causing fungus.
aceitoso, sa, *a.* oily, greasy.
aceituna, *f.* olive (fruit); **a. corval,** large olive; **a. de la reina,** queen olive; **a. manzanilla,** manzanilla olive; **a. picudilla,** small beaked olive; **a. rellena,** stuffed olive; **a. zapatera,** dried or stale olive; **a. zorzaleña,** very small round olive; **llegar a las aceitunas,** to arrive late.
aceitunado, da, *a.* olive green. —*f.* olive crop.
aceitunero, ra, *m., f.* olive picker; olive vendor. —*m.* storeroom or storehouse where the olives are cured.
aceituní, *m.* rich oriental cloth used in the Middle Ages; arabesque work.
aceitunillo, *m.* 1. wild olive. 2. (bot.) (Cuba) laurel (Beilschmiedia pendula).
aceituno, *m.* olive tree; (Hond.) tree bearing olive-like fruit. — **a. silvestre,** West Indian variety of storax, West Indian hardwood tree.
acelajado, da, *a.* crossed with colored clouds (said of the sky).
aceleracion, *f.* acceleration. — **a. de gravedad,** acceleration of gravity.
acelerada, *f.* acceleration.
aceleradamente, *adv.* speedily, swiftly, quickly; hastily.
acelerador, ra, *a.* accelerating; (anat.) accelerator (nerve, muscle). —*m.* (anat., chem., mec., photog.) accelerator. — **a. lineal,** (phys.) linear accelerator.
aceleramiento, *m., var. of* **aceleración.**
acelerar, *tr.v.* to speed up, hurry; to accelerate. — **a. el paso,** to hasten one's step. —*i.v.* to hurry, hasten.
aceleratriz, (*pl.* **aceleratrices**) *a.* accelerative, acceleratory; **fuerza a.,** accelerating force.
acelerómetro, *m.* (phys.) accelerometer.
acelga, *f.* (bot.), chard, Swiss chard; **cara de a.,** (coll.) sourpuss (sl.), sullen face.

acémila, *f.* 1. mule, beast of burden. 2. (coll.) brute, boor; rough, ill-mannered person. 3. (arch.) tax, tribute.
acemilado, da, *a.* mule-like, resembling a beast of burden.
acemilar, *a.* of or pertaining to mules or muleteers.
acemilería, *f.* 1. mule stable. 2. the job or business of mule-keeping.
acemilero, ra, *a.* of or pertaining to mules and mule stables. *—m.* muleteer.
acemita, *f.* bran bread, wholemeal bread.
acemite, *m.* 1. wholemeal flour, graham flour; middlings, comminuted, finely ground bran. 2. porridge.
acendrado, da, *past part. of* **acendrar.** *—a.* pure, stainless, spotless; without blemish.
acendramiento, *m.* purification, refinement.
acendrar, *tr.v.* to purify, refine (metals); (fig.) to make pure or stainless.
acensar, *tr.v., var. of* **acensuar.**
acensuador, *m., var. of* **censualista.**
acensuar, (*ref. 55*) *tr.v.* 1. to take the census. 2. to assess or tax (property).
acento, *m.* 1. accent, stress. 2. accent, manner of speaking, lilt (local or national). 3. (*pl.*) accents, language. — **a. agudo,** acute accent; **a. circunflejo,** circumflex accent; **a. de intensidad,** stress accent; **a. grave,** grave accent; **a. tónico, a. prosódico,** tonic accent; **a. métrico,** metrical accent; **a. ortográfico,** written accent; **a. secundario,** (phonet.) secondary stress.
acentrico, *a.* acentric, centerless; off-center.
acentuación, *f.* accentuation.
acentuadamente, *adv.* 1. with a marked accent. 2. (fig.) markedly; conspicuously, noticeably.
acentuado, da, *past part. of* **acentuar.** *—a.* 1. accented, stressed. 2. accentuated, prominent.
acentuador, ra, *m., f.* person who speaks slowly with emphasis.
acentual, *a.* (gram.) accentual.
acentuar, (*ref. 55*) *tr.v.* 1. to accent, stress orally (certain syllable). 2. to accent, mark with an accent. 3. to accentuate, emphasize. *—r.v.* 1. to be accented or stressed. 2. to be accentuated or emphasized; to stand out.
aceña, *f.* water-driven flour mill; water wheel.
aceñero, *m.* water mill keeper.
acepar, *i.v.* to take root.
acepción, *f.* meaning, acceptation; **a. de personas,** favoritism; **segunda a.,** the second meaning (in order of the common uses of a word).
acepilladora, *f.* plane, planing machine, surfacer.
acepilladura, *f.* 1. (carp.) planing. 2. (*pl.*) wood shavings.
acepillar, *tr.v.* 1. to plane. 2. to brush; to dress. 3. (coll.) to polish.
aceptabilidad, *f.* acceptability.
aceptable, *a.* acceptable.
aceptablemente, *adv.* acceptably.
aceptación, *f.* 1. acceptance; (com.) acceptance. 2. approval, approbation. — **a. de personas,** favoritism; **a. bancaria,** (com.) bank acceptance.
aceptadamente, *adv.* acceptedly.
aceptador, ra, *a.* accepting. *—m., f.* accepter; (com.) acceptor (of bills). — **a. de personas,** discriminator, one who discriminates unfairly between people.
aceptante, *a.* accepting. *—m., f.* accepter.
aceptar, *tr.v.* 1. to accept, to honor; (com.) to accept (checks, drafts, bills of exchange). 2. to approve, sanction; **a.** + *inf.,* to agree to + *inf.*
acepto, ta, *a.* acceptable, agreeable, pleasing.
aceptor, *m.* (chem., phys.) acceptor.
acequia, *f.* irrigation ditch or trench; drain, trench; (Amer.) gutter (at the side of a road).
acequiador, *m.* trench-maker, ditch digger.
acequiar, *tr.v.* to dig irrigation ditches or trenches in. *—i.v.* to dig irrigation ditches or trenches.
acequiero, *m.* irrigation ditch keeper, man who maintains irrigation ditches and regulates their use.
acera, *f.* 1. pavement, sidewalk. 2. row of houses on either side of the street. 3. (archit.) facing, face, surface of a wall; stone forming wall surface.
aceración, *f.* (metal.) tempering, hardening.
acerado, da, *past part. of* **acerar.** *—a.* 1. steely, steel-like; made of steel, steel (as *a.*); strong. 2. (fig.) mordant, biting, barbed (e.g. style). 3. (mas.) faced with mortar. 4. (bot.) spiky.
acerar, *tr.v.* 1. to steel, turn into steel. 2. to mix with tincture of steel, impart to a solution the medicinal qualities of steel. 3. to plate with steel (copper plates). 4. to strengthen, steel, temper. 5. to make mordant or biting (e.g. style). *—r.v.* to strengthen or steel oneself, become tempered, steeled or strengthened.
acerar, *tr.v.* 1. to provide with pavement or sidewalks. 2. (archit.) to lay the facing stones (of a wall).
acerbamente, *adv.* cruelly, harshly, severely, bitterly.
acerbidad, *f.* 1. bitterness, sourness, acerbity, asperity. 2. severity, harshness, bitterness.
acerbísimamente, *adv.* very cruelly, harshly, or bitterly.
acerbo, ba, *a.* 1. sour, bitter, rough. 2. harsh, cruel, severe, bitter.
acerca de, *prep.* about, concerning, with regard to.
acercamiento, *m.* approximation, bringing near; nearness; the action of drawing near, getting closer; (pol.) rapprochement.
acercar, (*ref. 50*) *tr.v.* to bring or place near or nearer. *—r.v.* to approach, draw near; **acercarse a,** to approach; (fig.) to begin to grasp a thought.
ácere, *m., var. of* **arce.**
acería, *f.* steel mill.
acerico, *m.* (Sp.) pincushion; small cushion or pillow.
acerillo, *m., var. of* **acerico.**
aceríneo, a, *a.* (bot.) aceraceous. *—m.* (*pl.*) Aceraceae.
acerino, na, *a.* (poet.) steel-like. *—f.* semi-precious stone resembling a steel chip.
acerista, *m.* steel technician or manufacturer.
acernadar, *tr.v.* (vet.) to apply ash poultices to (horses).
acero, *m.* 1. steel. 2. (fig.) steel, sword, weapon; (*pl.*)arms. 3. tincture of steel.— **a. al aluminio,** aluminium steel; **a. al manganeso,** manganese steel; **a. al níquel,** nickel steel; **a. al titanio,** titanium steel; **a. al tungsteno,** tungsten steel; **a. cromado,** chromium steel; **a. damasquinado,** damascened steel; **a. de liga** or **aleación,** alloy steel; **a. dulce,** soft steel; **a. duro,** hard steel; **a. estructural** or **de construcción,** structural steel; **a. fundido,** cast steel; **a. inoxidable,** stainless steel; **a. relamido,** rerolled steel; **tener buenos aceros,** to have a lot of courage or pluck.
acerola, *f.* (bot.) azarole; haw, fruit of the hawthorn.
acerolo, *m.* hawthorn (shrub).
acerque, acerqué, *ref.* **acercar.**
acérrimamente, *adv.* strongly, staunchly; vigorously.
acérrimo, ma, *a.* 1. all-out, staunch, utter, absolute. 2. tenacious, fanatic, zealous (friend or enemy), rabid. 3. extremely acrid.
acerrojar, *tr.v.* to lock, bolt.
acertadamente, *adv.* correctly, accurately, rightly.
acertado, da, *past part. of* **acertar.** *—a.* correct, right, proper; accurate.
acertador, ra, *m.* good guesser.
acertamiento, *m., var. of* **acierto.**
acertar, (*ref. 29*) *tr.v.* 1. to hit upon; to guess right; to find, at last. 2. (tail.) to match (pattern of fabric). *—i.v.* 1. to be correct, be right; to do just the right thing; to succeed, be successful. 2. to guess right or correctly. 3. (agr.) to survive, thrive (plants). — **a. a,** to hit (a target); **a. a** + *inf.;* to happen to + *inf.;* **a. con,** to find, get to, come upon.
acertijo, *m.* riddle, conundrum.
aceruelo, *m.* 1. small pack-saddle. 2. pin-cushion.
acervo, *m.* 1. cultural equipment, values. 2. heap, pile. 3. common property (of restricted group). 4. (law) undivided estate. 5. heap of loose grain.
acérvulo, *f.* (anat.) acervulus cerebri, brain sand.
acescencia, *f.* acescence, acetic fermentation.
acescente, *a.* acescent, turning sour, slightly sour.
acetábulo, *m.* 1. (anat., zool.) acetabulum. 2. acetabulum, ancient liquid measure.
acetaldehído, *m.* (chem.) acetaldehyde.
acetamida, *f.* (chem.) acetamide.
acetanilida, *f.* (chem.) acetanilide, acetanilid.
acetato, *m.* (chem.) acetate; **a. cúprico** or **de cobre,** copper acetate; **a. de etilo,** ethyl acetate; **a. de vinilo,** vinyl acetate.
acético, ca, *a.* acetic.
acetificación, *f.* acetification.
acetificar, (*ref. 50*) *tr.v., r.v.* to acetify, turn into vinegar or acetic acid.
acetifique, acetifiqué, *ref.* **acetificar.**
acetilcolina, *f.* (pharm.) acetylcholine.
acetileno, *m.* (chem.) acetylene.
acetilo, *m.* (chem.) acetyl.
acetímetro, *m.* acetimeter, acetometer, instrument for measuring acetic acid content.
acetín, *m.* barberry.
acetite, *m.* former name for acetic oxide; copper acetate.
acetocelulosa, *f.* (chem.) cellulose acetate, acetocellulose.
acetofenetidina, *f.* (chem.) acetophenetidin.
acetol, *m.* (chem.) acetol.
acetomiel, *m.* (pharm.) a syrup compound containing honey and vinegar.
acetona, *f.* (chem.) acetone.
acetonemia, *f.* (med.) acetonemia.
acetosa, *f.* (bot.) sorrel.
acetosidad, *f.* acetosity, acidity.
acetosilla, *f.* (bot.) wood sorrel.
acetoso, sa, *a.* acetous, acetose, acid.
acetre, *m.* 1. small bucket for lifting water from the well. 2. the holy water basin (at the entrance of a church).
acetrinar, *tr.v.* to turn greenish yellow (an object). *—r.v.* to become greenish yellow (with illness or rage).
acezar, (*ref. 53*) *i.v.* to pant, gasp.
acezo, *m.* panting.
acezoso, sa, *a.* panting, gasping.
achabacanar, *tr.v.* to make cheap, crude or shoddy.
achacable, *a.* imputable, attributable.
achacana, *f.* (bot., Amer.) a variety of artichoke.
achacar, (*ref. 50*) *tr.v.* to impute, attribute.
achacosamente, *adv.* ailingly.
achacosidad, *f.* sickliness, weakness.
achacoso, sa, *a.* sickly, ailing; indisposed, slightly ill.
achachay, *interj.* 1. (Quech., Ecuad.) expressing cold. 2. (Col.) expressing approval. *—m.* children's game.
achaflanado, da, *a.* beveled, feather-edged; slanted.

achaflanador, *m.* beveling tool.
achaflanadura, *f.* slant, beveling.
achaflanar, *tr.v.* to bevel, chamfer, splay.
achagrinado, da, *a.* imitating fine morocco leather.
achagual, *m.* (ichth.) elephant fish.
achahuistlarse, *r.v.* (Mex.) to become rusty; to spoil (grain).
achajuanarse, *r.v.* (Col.) to get winded or tired (said of animals).
achampañado, da, *a.* champagne-type, champagne-like, sparkling (wines).
achanchar, *tr.v.* 1. (Chile, Peru) to check (in checkers). 2. (Chile) to cause (a player) to remain with a double, unable to play it (in dominoes). —*r.v.* 1. (Peru) to become embarrassed, become worried. 2. (Arg., Urug.) to get fat.
achantarse, *r.v.* 1. (coll.) to hide, lie low. 2. (coll.) to conform, submit, comply.
achaparrado, da, *past part. of* **achaparrarse.** —*a.* 1. shrub-sized, shrubby, stunted (plants). 2. chubby, plump and short.
achaparrarse, *r.v.* 1. to grow or become stunted, become shrubby. 2. (coll.) to become chubby.
achapinarse, *r.v.* (Guat.) to adopt Guatemalan customs.
achaplinarse, *r.v.* (Amer.) to adopt mannerisms characteristic of the movie actor Charles Chaplin.
achaque, *m.* 1. slight illness, indisposition, ailment. 2. (coll.) period (menstruation). 3. pregnancy. 4. matter, subject. 5. excuse, pretext, motive, cause. 6. (C. Rica) fainting spell of pregnant women. 7. weakness, failing, fault.
achaque, achaqué, *ref.* **achacar.**
achaquero, *m.* judge of a council of cattlemen who imposed fines on cattle thieves.
achaquiento, *a., var. of* **achacoso.**
acharado, da, *a.* (coll., Sp.) jealous.
achares, *m., pl.* (coll., Sp.) jealousy.
acharolado, da, *a.* 1. varnished, varnish-like, lacquer-like. 2. like patent leather.
acharolar, *tr.v., var. of* **charolar.**
achatado, da, *a.* flat, flat-nosed.
achatamiento, *m.* flattening.
achatar, *tr.v.* to flatten. —*r.v.* to become flat.
achechar, *tr.v.* (Mex.) to pamper.
achicado, da, *past part. of* **achicar.** —*a.* 1. shortened. 2. childish.
achicador, ra, *a.* diminishing, reducing. —*m.* (mar.) bailing scoop, bailer.
achicadura, *f.* 1. reduction, diminution. 2. (mar.) bailing.
achicamiento, *m., var. of* **achicadura.**
achicar, (*ref. 50*) *tr.v.* 1. to lessen, reduce; to make smaller; to shorten (a dress). 3. to intimidate, cow, humble, humiliate. 4. (Col.) to kill. —*r.v.* 1. to get smaller, reduce. 2. to be intimidated, cowed or squashed; to feel small; to get cold feet, get scared.
achichado, da, *a.* intoxicated.
achicharradero, *m.* (coll., fig.) sweltering overheated room or place.
achicharrante, *a.* sizzling; sweltering, broiling.
achicharrar, *tr.v.* 1. to sizzle, burn, fry or broil too much; to scorch, heat excessively. 2. to bother, annoy. 3. (Amer.) to squash, crush. —*r.v.* to get burned, to swelter, e.g. *me estoy achicharrando,* I'm sweltering (in the sun, with the heat).
achicharronarse, *r.v.* (Mex.) to shrivel, wrinkle up.
achichinque, *m.* 1. (min.) scooper, bailer (ridding mine of water). 2. (Mex.) faithful servant, constant servant; flatterer.
achicopalarse, *r.v.* (Mex.) to lose heart, to become discouraged.
achicoria, *f.* (bot.) chicory.
achicorial, *m.* chicory field.
achiguarse, (*ref. 52*) *r.v.* (Arg., Chile) to sag, bend; to develop a paunch.
achilarse, *r.v.* (Col.) to become cowardly.
achimero, *m.* (Guat.) peddler.
achimes, *m., pl.* (Guat.) the peddler's stock, cart and merchandise.
achinado, da, *a.* (Amer.) Chinese-like; having almond-shaped eyes.
achinar, *tr.v.* (coll.) 1. to intimidate, scare. 2. to murder. 3. to corner (a checker).
achinelado, da, *a.* slipper-shaped.
achinelar, *tr.v.* to give the form of a slipper.
achinería, *f.* (Amer.) peddlery, canvassing.
achiotal, *m.* plantation of annatto trees.
achiote, *m.* (bot.) annatto tree.
achique, *m.* scooping, bailing, draining.
achique, achiqué, *ref.* **achicar.**
achiquillado, da, *a., var. of* **aniñado.**
achiquitar, *tr.v.* (Amer.) to lessen, reduce; to make smaller.
achirlar, *tr.v.* (Arg.) to thin down.
achispado, da, *past part. of* **achispar.** —*a.* tipsy, merry, lit-up.
achispar, *tr.v.* to make (someone) merry or tipsy (with liquor). —*r.v.* to become merry, tipsy, to get high or lit-up (sl.).
achocadura, *f.* 1. throwing or hurling against a wall; hitting, striking, injuring, hurting. 2. knock, blow; bruise, wound, injury.
achocar, (*ref. 50*) *tr.v.* 1. to throw or hurl against a wall. 2. to hurt, injure; to hit, strike. 3. (coll.) to hoard (money). —*i.v.* (P. Rico, Dom. Rep.) to faint, lose consciousness.
achocolatado, da, *a.* chocolate-colored.
achocharse, *r.v.* (coll.) to begin to dote, become senile.
acholado, da, *a.* (Amer.) 1. like a mestizo or half-breed; 2. abashed, cowed.
acholador, ra, *a.* (Amer.) abashing.
acholar, *tr.v.* (Chile, Peru) to make (someone) feel small, to embarrass. —*r.v.* to become embarrassed, feel small.
acholo, *m.* (Amer.) embarrassment.
achololе, *m.* (Mex.) excess irrigation waters which run off the fields.
achololear, *i.v.* (Mex.) to drain off excess irrigation waters.
acholencado, da, *a.* (Mex.) sickly, feeble.
achololera, *f.* (Mex.) ditch for draining excess irrigation waters.
acholloncarse, (*ref. 50*) *r.v.* (Chile) to squat.
achoque, achoqué, *ref.* **achocar.**
achote, *m.* (bot.) *var. of* **achiote.**
achubascarse, (*ref. 50*) *r.v.* to cloud over and threaten rain.
achubasque, *ref.* **achubascarse.**
achucutado, da, *a.* (Quech., Amer.) disheartened, dismayed.
achucutarse, achucuyarse, *r.v.* (Quech.) to be intimidated, scared or cowed.
achuchado, da, *a.* (coll.) difficult.
achuchador, ra, *m., f.* bully.
achuchamiento, *m.* blow, jostling.
achuchar, *tr.v.* 1. (coll.) to crush, crumple, squeeze. 2. (coll.) to push, jostle. —*r.v.* (Amer.) to be afflicted with fever.
achucharrar, *tr.v.* (Amer.) to crush, crumple. —*r.v.* (Mex.) to shrink back; to become cowed.
achuchón, *m.* 1. (coll.) push, shove. 2. (coll.) crushing, squeezing; squeeze.
achuete, *m.* (bot.) annatto tree.
achulado, da, *a.* (coll.) uncouth, rude, caddish.
achulapado, da, *a.* (coll.) 1. sassy; self-assured. 2. brazen.
achulaparse, *r.v., var. of* **achularse.**
achularse, *r.v.* to become uncouth, rude, caddish.
achunchamiento, *m.* (Chile, Peru) brow-beating, squashing, humiliation; shyness, timidity.
achunchar, *tr.v.* (Chile, Peru) to cow, browbeat, humiliate, squash. —*r.v.* 1. to become cowed, withdrawn or browbeaten. 2. to become afraid or scared.
achune, *f.* (bot.) nettle.
achuntar, *tr.v.* (Chile) to hit the target, hit the bull's-eye.
achuñuscar, (*ref. 50*) *tr.v.* (Chile) to crush, squeeze, press.
achura, *f.* (Quech., Arg.) offal; innards, entrails.
achurador, *m.* (Arg.) gutter, person who eviscerates or dresses butchered meat.
achurar, *tr.v.* 1. (Arg.) to gut, eviscerate, remove offal from (butchered meat). 2. (Arg.) to knife, butcher (someone).
achurrar, *tr.v.* (Pan.) to flatten.
achurruscar, *tr.v.* (Chile) to squeeze.
aciago, ca, *a.* unfortunate; ominous, fateful.
acial, *m.* 1. barnacle (instrument that, clamped to lip or ear of animals, stops them from moving). 2. (Ecuad., Guat.) whip, switch.
aciano, *m.* (bot.) cornflower, bluebottle.
acianos, *m.* (bot.) heath, heather (Erica scoparia).
acíbar, *m.* 1. aloes. 2. (fig.) bitterness, sorrow, annoyance.
acibarar, *tr.v.* 1. to make bitter with aloes. 2. (fig.) to embitter.
acibarrar, *tr.v., var. of* **abarrar.**
aciberar, *tr.v.* to pulverize; to grind finely.
acicalado, da, *past part. of* **acicalar.** —*a.* 1. spruced up, smart, well-groomed. 2. polished, burnished.
acicalador, ra, *a.* polishing, burnishing. —*m.* polisher, polishing or burnishing tool.
acicaladura, *f.* smartness, elegance, nattiness; pulchritude.
acicalamiento, *m., var. of* **acicaladura.**
acicalar, *tr.v.* 1. to spruce up; to dress, shave, clean, ornament smartly. 2. to polish, burnish (weapons). 3. (archit.) to finish, put a finish on (a wall, etc.). —*r.v.* to dress up, make oneself smart, spruce up, dress in style.
acicate, *m.* pointed Moorish spur; (fig.) spur, goad.
acicatear, *tr.v.* to incite, to spur on.
acíclico, ca, *a.* (elec.) acyclic.
acícula, *f.* (bot.) acicula, aciculum.
aciculado, da, *a.* (bot., zool.) aciculate.
acicular, *a.* acicular; bristly, spiny, needlelike.
acículo, *m.* (zool.) aciculum.
aciche, *m.* paving hammer, brick hammer.
acidalio, lia, *a.* pertaining to Venus, Venus-like.
acidaque, *m.* obligatory dowry given by Mohammedan to his wife.
acidez, *f.* acidity; sourness.
acidia, *f.* laziness, indolence.
acídico, *a.* acidic, acid-forming.
acidífero, ra, *a.* (chem.) acidiferous, acid-containing.
acidificación, *f.* (chem.) acidification.
acidificar, (*ref. 50*) *tr.v.* to acidify.
acidimetría, *f.* acidimetry, measurement of acidity of liquids.
acidímetro, *m.* acidimeter.
acidioso, sa, *a.* lazy, indolent.
acidismo, *m.* (med.) acidosis.
ácido, da, *a.* 1. acid; sour, tart. 2. (fig.) sour, rough, uncouth. —*m.* (chem.) acid; **á. acético,** acetic acid; **á. arsénico,** arsenic acid; **á. arsenioso,** arsenious acid; **á. ascórbico,** ascorbic acid; **á. aspártico** or **asparagínico,** aspartic acid; **á. benzoico,** benzoic acid; **á. bórico,** boracic or

boric acid; **á. carbónico,** carbonic acid; **á. carmínico,** carminic acid; **á. cianhídrico,** hydrocyanic acid; **á. cinámico,** cinnamic acid; **á. cítrico,** citric acid; **á. clorhídrico,** hydrochloric acid; **á. clórico,** chloric acid; **á. esteárico,** stearic acid; **á. fénico,** phenic acid or carbolic acid; **á. fluorhídrico,** hydrofluoric acid; **á. fórmico,** formic acid; **á. fulmínico,** fulminic acid; **á. gentísico,** gentisic acid; **á. glutámico** or **glutamínico,** glutamic or glutaminic acid; **á. glicérico,** glyceric acid; **á. graso,** fatty acid; **á. hidriódico,** hydriodic acid; **á. láctico,** lactic acid; **á. muriático,** muriatic acid; **á. nítrico,** nitric acid; **á. pantoténico,** pantothenic acid; **á. para-aminobenzoico,** para-aminobenzoic acid; **á. oxalico,** oxalic acid; **á. pícrico,** picric acid; **á. prúsico,** prussic acid; **á. salicílico,** salicylic acid; **á. silícico,** silicic acid; **á. sulfhídrico,** sulphydric acid; **á. sulfúrico,** sulfuric acid; **á. sulfuroso,** sulfurous acid; **á. tartárico** or **tártrico,** tartaric acid; **á. úrico,** uric acid; **a prueba de ácidos,** acid-fast.

acidófilo, la, *a., m.* acidophile, acidophil.

acidorresistente, *a.* acid-resistant, acid-proof, acid-fast.

acidosis, *f.* (med.) acidosis.

acidular, *tr.v.* to acidulate. —*r.v.* to become acidulous or slightly sour.

acídulo, la, *a.* acidulous, sour.

acientífico, ca, *a.* unscientific.

acierte, acierto, *ref.* **acertar.**

acierto, *m.* 1. good shot; success; good idea, successful plan. 2. ability, skill. 3. wisdom, good judgment or sense. 4. coincidence. — **con a.,** successfully, skillfully, right on target; **un a.,** a wise move.

aciforme, *a.* (bot.) aciform; needleshaped, sharp.

ácigos, *a.* azygous. —*f.* (anat.) azygous, azygous vein.

aciguatado, da, *a.* 1. pale, yellow. 2. suffering from fish poisoning.

aciguatar, *tr.v.* (reg.) to watch, observe.

aciguatarse, *r.v.* to get fish poisoning.

acijado, da, *a.* copperas-colored, vitriol-colored.

acije, *m.* copperas, vitriol.

acijoso, sa, *a.* containing copperas.

acilo, *m.* (chem.) acyl.

ácimo, *a., var. of* **ázimo.**

acimut, *m.* (astron.) azimuth.

acimutal, *a.* (astron.) azimuthal.

acinaciforme, *a.* (bot.) acinaciform.

acincelar, *tr.v., var. of* **cincelar.**

acinesia, *f.* (med.) akinesia, paralysis of the motor nerves.

acínico, ca, *a.* (med.) acinic, acinous, acinar.

aciniforme, *a. aciniform.*

ácino, *m.* (anat., bot.) acinus.

acinoso, sa, *a.* (med.) acinous, acinic.

ación, *f.* stirrup strap.

acionera, *f.* (S. Amer.) stirrup bar.

acionero, *m.* maker of stirrup straps.

acipado, da, *a.* (tex.) closely woven.

acirate, *m.* boundary, limit; ridge separating two plots of garden; path or walk separating two rows of trees.

acitara, *f.* 1. wall; thick wall forming the side of a house. 2. railing of a bridge. 3. saddle or chair cover.

acitrón, *m.* candied citron.

aclamación, *f.* acclamation. — **por a.,** by acclamation, unanimously.

aclamador, ra, *a.* acclaiming. —*m., f.* acclaimer.

aclamar, *tr.v.* 1. to acclaim, applaud. 2. to hail, approve.

aclámide, *a.* (bot.) achlamydeous.

aclaración, *f.* clarification, explanation. — **a. de sentencia,** (law) amendment of the judge's decision.

aclarador, ra, *a.* clarifying, explanatory. —*m.* (tech.) clarifier.

aclarar, *tr.v.* 1. to clarify, make clear or clearer. 2. to clarify, explain, clear up. 3. to thin (e.g. thick sauce). 4. to thin out, space out. 5. to clear (the voice). 6. to rinse (clothes), wash (minerals). 7. to sharpen (one's senses). 8. to relax (the face). 9. (mar.) to disentangle, unravel. —*i.v.* 1. to become clear (the sky), clear up (the weather). 2. to dawn, break (day). —*r.v.* 1. to become clear, be clarified (liquid; problem). 2. to clear up, brighten (the weather), become clear (the sky). 3. to thin out, become thinner or more spaced out. 4. reveal one's inner feelings, to open one's heart.

aclaratorio, ria, *a.* explanatory, clarifying.

aclarecer, (*ref. 45*) *tr.v., var. of* **aclarar.**

aclareo, *m.* spacing out; making sparse.

aclarezca, aclarezco, *ref.* **aclarecer.**

aclástico, ca, *a.* (opt.) aclastic.

aclavelado, da, *a.* carnation-like (**in shape** or fragance).

acle, *m.* (bot.) acle, tree.

acleido, da, *a.* (zool.) acleidian, aclidian.

aclimatable, *a.* able to acclimatize.

aclimatación, *f.* acclimatization.

aclimatar, *tr.v.* to acclimatize. —*r.v.* to become acclimatized, acclimated.

aclínico, ca, *a.* (phys.) aclinic.

aclocar, (*ref. 69*) *i.v.* to brood (hens). —*r.v.* to stretch out, lie down; to become broody (hens).

acloqué, *ref.* **aclocar.**

aclorhidria, *f.* (med.) achlorhydria.

aclorhídrico, ca, *a.* achlorhydric.

aclueco, *ref.* **aclocar.**

aclueque, *ref.* **aclocar.**

accla, *f.* virgin of the Sun (in the lore of the Incas).

acme, *f.* (med.) acme, crisis (of a disease).

acné, *f.* (med.) acne.

acobardamiento, *m.* intimidation; cowardliness, cowardice.

acobardar, *tr.v.* to intimidate, daunt, frighten. —*r.v., i.v.* to become frightened; to turn cowardly.

acobijar, *tr.v.* (agr.) to mulch.

acobijo, *m.* (agr.) mulch.

acobrado, da, *a.* copper-colored.

acocarse, (*ref. 50*) *r.v.* to become worm-ridden (fruit).

acoceador, ra, *a.* kicking.

acoceamiento, *m.* kick, kicking.

acocear, *tr.v.* 1. to kick. 2. (coll.) to ill-treat, maltreat, kick about.

acocil, *m.* (Mex.) fresh-water shrimp.

acocotar, *tr.v., var. of* **acogotar.**

acocote, *m.* (Mex.) long calabash perforated at both ends used to extract the sweet juice of the maguey plant by suction.

acocullado, da, *a.* (Peru, Bol., coll.) high with drink, lit up, drunk; merry.

acocharse, *r.v.* to crouch, cower, duck.

acochinar, *tr.v.* 1. (coll.) to make dirty or mess up. 2. to assassinate. 3. to silence, scare, intimidate. 4. to corner a piece (in checkers).

acodado, da, *a.* bent in the form of an elbow. — **tubo acodado,** (mec.) joint.

acodadura, *f.* 1. (agr.) layering, layerage. 2. (archit.) propping, shoring. 3. (carp.) squaring (timber).

acodalamiento, *m.* (archit.) shoring, propping; stay, shore, support.

acodalar, *tr.v.* (archit.) to prop, shore.

acodar, *tr.v.* 1. to lean the arm or elbow on. 2. (agr.) to layer (vines or plants). 3. (archit.) to prop, shore, stay. 4. (carp.) to square (timber). 5. (vet.) to drive (nails) into the sensitive part of the hoof (shoeing a horse improperly). —*r.v.* to lean or rest on one's elbow.

acoderamiento, *m.* (mar.) bringing the broadside to bear.

acoderar, *tr.v.* (mar.) to bring the broadside to bear, to anchor broadside on.

acodiciar, *tr.v.* to covet, long for, desire.

acodillar, *tr.v.* 1. to bend into an elbow or angle. 2. to beat, defeat (in certain card games). —*i.v.* to sink to the knees (quadrupeds). —*r.v.* (Chile) to suffer from girth sores.

acodo, *m.* 1. (agr.) shoot. 2. (archit.) projection or raised border around a voussoir or an opening in a wall.

acogedizo, za, *a.* easily or indiscriminately adapted or adaptable.

acogedor, ra, *a.* cozy, friendly, welcoming, inviting, e.g. *un ambiente acogedor,* a friendly or inviting atmosphere, *un cuarto acogedor,* a cozy room. —*m., f.* harborer, protector.

acoger, (*ref. 62*) *tr.v.* 1. to welcome, receive hospitably. 2. to shelter, protect, harbor. 3. to pasture, give pasture to. 4. to accept (news, doctrines). —*r.v.* to take refuge, shelter; to make use of, resort to. — **acogerse a,** to take refuge in; **acogerse en casa de un amigo,** to take refuge in a friend's house; **acogerse a la ley,** stay within the law.

acogeta, *f.* asylum, refuge, place of shelter.

acogida, *f.* 1. welcome, reception. 2. asylum, refuge, haven. 3. meeting place. 4. withdrawal. 5. protection, shelter. 6. approval, acceptance. 7. (com.) acceptance. — **dar buena a. a un giro,** (com.) to honor a draft; **tener buena a.,** to be well received, be welcomed, be given a warm welcome.

acogido, da, *past part. of* **acoger.** —*m., f.* inmate of poorhouse. —*m.* pasturing fee.

acogimiento, *m., var. of* **acogida.**

acogollar, *tr.v.* (agr.) to cover up tender plants (to protect them from wind and frost). —*i.v., r.v.* to sprout, bud (cabbage, lettuce, etc.).

acogombradura, *f.* (agr.) banking, hilling, earthing (of plants).

acogombrar, *tr.v.* to bank, earth, hill (plants).

acogotar, *tr.v.* 1. to kill, kill by a blow on the back of the neck. 2. (coll.) to knock down (grabbing someone by the back of the neck). 3. to intimidate, subdue.

acogullado, da, *a.* shaped like a monk's cowled habit.

acohombrar, *tr.v.* to bank, earth, hill (plants).

acoja, acojo, *ref.* **acoger.**

acojinamiento, *m.* (mec.) cushioning.

acojinar, *tr.v.* to pad, stuff, quilt. 2. (mec.) to cushion.

acolada, *f.* 1. accolade. 2. the embrace following the knighting ceremony.

acolar, *tr.v.* (her.) to unite (two coats of arms) under one crown; to decorate (a coat of arms) with special marks of distinction.

acolchado, da, *a.* padded, quilted. —*m.* 1. padding, quilting. 2. facing, covering (of matted straw or reeds used in dike fortifications).

acolchar, *tr.v.* 1. to pad, stuff, quilt; to cushion. 2. (mar.) to lay, to intertwine (strands of rope).

acolchonar, *tr.v.* (Amer.) *var. of* **acolchar.**

acólita, *f.* nun acting as an acolyte in a religious ceremony.

acolitado, *m.* (ecc.) order of acolytes.

acólito, *m.* 1. acolyte; altar boy. 2. disciple or follower.

acollador, *m.* (mar.) lanyard.
acollar, (*ref. 33*) *tr.v.* (agr.) to bank up with earth, cover with earth (base of tree). 2. (mar.) to caulk (a ship). 3. (mar.) to tighten, tauten (lanyards).
acollarado, da, *past part. of* **acollarar.** —*a.* having a neck of a different color from the rest of the body (birds, etc.).
acollarar, *tr.v.* 1. to put a collar on (an animal). 2. to leash together (dogs); (Arg., Chile) to tie together. —*r.v.* 1. (Chile) to hold each other by the neck. 2. (Arg., Urug.) to live in concubinage; (coll.) to get hitched, get married.
acollonar, *tr.v.* to scare, frighten, intimidate. —*r.v.* to become scared or frightened; to cower. to turn cowardly.
acolmillado, *a.* sharp-toothed, well-set (saw).
acombar, *tr.v., var. of* **combar.**
acomedido, da, *past part. of* **acomedirse.** —*a.* (Amer.) accommodating, obliging.
acomedimiento, *m.* (Peru) willingness to help, helpfulness.
acomedirse, (*ref. 39*) *r.v.* (Amer.) to volunteer, to oblige.
acometedor, ra, *a.* aggressive, attacking. —*m., f.* aggressor, attacker.
acometer, *tr.v.* 1. to attack, rush upon. 2. to undertake, attempt. 3. to overtake, overcome (illness, sleep, etc.). 4. (mas., min.) to converge, join (galleries in a mine; pipes). — **a. a** + *inf.*, to begin or start + *ger.*, decide to + *inf.*
acometida, *f.* 1. attack, assault. 2. connection, link-up (a pipe with the main pipe).
acometiente, *a.* 1. attacking. 2. enterprising.
acometimiento, *m.* 1. attack, assault. 2. sewer connection (between subsidiary and main channel).
acometividad, *f.* aggressiveness.
acomodable, *a.* adjustable, adaptable, accommodating.
acomodación, *f.* 1. accommodation, arrangement. 2. (physiol.) accommodation (of the eye).
acomodadamente, *adv.* 1. comfortably. 2. neatly, tidily.
acomodadizo, za, *a.* accommodating; adaptable, pliable, yielding.
acomodado, da, *a.* 1. comfortably off, rich, well-to-do (coll.). 2. comfort-loving, sybaritic. 3. moderate, reasonable (price). 4. (Arg.) having an easy job, or a privileged position obtained through personal influence rather than merit.
acomodador, ra, *m.* usher. —*f.* usherette.
acomodamiento, *m.* 1. agreement, arrangement; (law) transaction. 2. accommodation; lodging, quartering.
acomodar, *tr.v.* 1. to accommodate, find a place for. 2. to arrange, put in order, put straight. 3. to put in, place, e.g. *a. la aguja en la jeringa,* to put the needle in the syringe. 4. to find employment for, place; to employ, take on. 5. to adapt, adjust, accommodate. 6. to reconcile, conciliate. 7. to accommodate, furnish, provide. —*i.v.* to suit, fit; to be suitable. —*r.v.* 1. to accommodate oneself, find oneself a seat; to find or settle into a comfortable position. 2. to adapt or adjust oneself; to conform. 3. to be reconciled. 4. to conform to. — **acomodarse con alguien,** to be reconciled with someone; **acomodarse de camarero,** to get employed as a waiter; **acomódense ustedes,** find yourselves a seat or place, make yourselves comfortable.
acomodaticio, cia, *a.* 1. accommodating, obliging. 2. opportunistic (who changes side, doctrine, etc., when it is to his advantage). 3. (iron.) flexible (interpretation, meaning).
acomodo, *m.* 1. employment, job. 2. arrangement, adjustment. 3. lodging, accommodation. 4. (Amer.) sinecure, convenient job or position obtained through personal influence rather than merit.
acompañado, da, *past part. of* **acompañar.** —*a.* 1. accompanied, attended. 2. busy, frequented.
acompañador, ra, *a.* accompanying. —*m., f.* companion; attendant; (mus.) accompanist.
acompañamiento, *m.* 1. accompanying, accompaniment. 2. company, retinue, escort. 3. (theat.) extra. 4. (mus.) accompaniment.
acompañanta, *f.* female companion; chaperone.
acompañante, *a.* accompanying. —*m., f.* 1. companion; attendant; escort; (mus.) accompanist. 2. (mar.) timepiece used in astronomical observations.
acompañar, *tr.v.* 1. to accompany; to go with; to escort. 2. to enclose, send with (e.g. in a letter). 3. (mus.) to accompany. 4. to sympathize with, e.g. *te acompaño en tu desgracia,* I sympathize with you in your misfortune. 5. (her., p.) to adorn (principal motif or subject) with other motifs. —*r.v.* 1. to be accompanied; to accompany oneself, e.g. *me acompaño muy bien yo misma,* I accompany myself quite nicely. 2. to consult one another; to hold a consultation.
acompasadamente, *adv.* rhythmically.
acompasado, da, *a.* 1. rhythmic. 2. slow, monotonous (speech). 3. leisurely (walk).
acompasar, *tr.v.* 1. to measure (with a compass or a metronome). 2. to apportion exactly (time, expenses). 3. (mus.) to divide into bars. 4. to give a rhythm to (one's speech).
acomplejado, da, *a.* suffering from complexes or inhibitions.
acomplejar, *tr.v.* to cause someone's complexes or inhibitions. —*r.v.* to suffer from a complex, psychic disturbance or inhibition.
acomplexionado, da, *a., var. of* **complexionado.**
acomunarse, *r.v.* to unite, ally, confederate, associate.
acona, *f.* (bot.) eugenia.
Aconcagua, *m.* highest peak in the Western Hemisphere (in the Argentinian Andes).
aconcagüino, na, *a.* of or from Aconcagua. —*m., f.* native or inhabitant of the Chilean province of Aconcagua.
aconchabamiento, *m.* (Peru) *var. of* **conchabanza.**
aconchabarse, *r.v., var. of* **conchabarse.**
aconchadillo, *m.* (cul.) the preparation and marinading of a certain stew.
aconchar, *tr.v.* 1. to push to a safe place. 2. (mar.) to embay, force toward the shore. —*r.v.* 1. to back against, back away. 2. (mar.) to run firmly aground. 3. (mar.) to come alongside easily (two ships or vessels). 4. (Chile) to get clarified (a liquid, by settling of sediment). 5. (taur.) to back up against the barrier (the bull).
acondicionado, da, *a.* conditioned. — **aire acondicionado,** air conditioning; **bien a.,** of a good disposition; well-appointed (quarters); of good quality; **con aire acondicionado,** air-conditioned; **mal a.,** of a bad disposition; in poor condition; of poor quality.
acondicionador, ra, *a.* conditioning. —*m.* conditioner. — **a. de aire,** air conditioner.
acondicionamiento, *m.* the act of conditioning or preparing a situation, climate, etc.
acondicionar, *tr.v.* 1. to condition, outfit, prepare, e.g. *están acondicionando a los soldados para luchar en la selva,* they are conditioning or preparing the soldiers to fight in the jungle. 2. to appoint, recondition, repair, renovate, e.g. *a. un barco,* to recondition or outfit a ship. 3. to condition (the air). 4. to hollow out (precious stone to increase its sparkle). —*r.v.* to be conditioned; to condition oneself.
acondrito, *m.* (geol.) achondrite.
acondroplasia, *f.* (med.) achondroplasia.
acondroplástico, ca, *a.* achondroplastic.
acongojadamente, *adv.* in or with anguish, afflictedly, distressfully.
acongojador, ra, *a.* distressing, anguishing.
acongojante, *a.* distressing, anguishing.
acongojar, *tr.v.* to anguish, afflict, distress. —*r.v.* to be afflicted, distressed or anguished.
aconitina, *f.* (chem.) aconitine.
acónito, *m.* (bot.) aconite, monkshood, wolfsbane.
aconsejable, *a.* advisable.
aconsejado, da, *a.* prudent, sensible. — **mal a.,** imprudent, ill-advised.
aconsejador, ra, *a.* advising, counseling. —*m., f.* adviser, counselor.
aconsejar, *tr.v.* to advise, counsel; **a.** + *inf.*, to advise to + *inf.* — *r.v.* to seek or take advice. — **aconsejarse con** or **de,** to consult, seek the advice of; **aconsejarse con la almohada,** to sleep on it (e.g. a problem).
aconsonantar, *tr.v., i.v.* to make (a word) rhyme with another; to rhyme.
acontecedero, ra, *a.* possible (a chance or event).
acontecer, (*ref. 45*) *i.v.,* to happen, come about, come to pass.
acontecido, da, *past part. of* **acontecer.** —*a.* sad, depressed, dejected (face).
acontecimiento, *m.* event, happening, incident.
acontezca, *ref.* **acontecer.**
acopado, da, *a.* 1. like the crown or top of a tree. 2. cupped, cup-like, cup-shaped (like a calyx). 3. (vet.) cupped, cup-shaped, round and hollow (hoof).
acopar, *tr.v.* 1. to trim (crown of tree), to shape. 2. (mar.) to shape (plank of lumber to convenient shape). —*i.v.* 1. to become cup-shaped, cup. 2. to form a crown (trees, plants).
acopetado, da, *a.* tufted, crowned.
acopiador, ra, *m., f.* gatherer, collector, verifier, classifier; storer, supplier.
acopiamiento, *m., var. of* **acopio.**
acopiar, *tr.v.* to gather, collect, classify; to store (information).
acopio, *m.* gathering, collecting, storing (information or ideas); inventory or quantity (of supplies).
acoplado, da, *a.* connected; joined, coupled; (fig.) shacked up (sl.), living together (couple). — **a. directamente,** (mec.) direct-connected. —*m.* (S. Amer.) trailer (vehicle).
acopladura, *f., var. of* **acoplamiento.**
acoplamiento, *m.* 1. coupling, connecting, joining, splicing. 2. adjustment; concubinate. 3. connection, joint, splice; (carp.) splice; (elec.) connection, coupling. 4. (biol.) coupling, linkage. — **a. capacitativo,** (elec.) capacitive coupling; **a. cónico,** (mec.) cone coupling; **a. de bridas,** (mec.) flange coupling; **a. de fricción,** (mec.) friction coupling; **a. de garras,** (mec.) claw or jaw coupling; **a. de pestaña,** (mec.) flange coupling; **a. de cascada,** (elec.) cascade rectifier circuit; **a. estrecho** or **cerrado,** (elec.) close coupling; **a. inductive,** (elec.) inductive coupling; **a. universal,** (mec.) universal coupling; **coeficiente de a.,** (elec.) coupling coefficient; **a. gradual,** step connection; **a. telescópico,** sliding coupling.
acoplar, *tr.v.* 1. to couple; to connect; to join; to scarf; to hitch up, yoke together. 2. to mate, pair, bring together. 3. to reconcile, bring together. —*r.v.* 1. to mate. 2. to shack-up (sl.), "to live in sin" with someone; to join together. 3. to be reconciled. — **acoplarse a,** (coll.) to join, to adjust oneself.

acople, *m.* (Chile, mec.) coupling (also acoplo).
acoque, *ref.* **acocarse.**
acoquinamiento, *m.* intimidation, cowering.
acoquinar, *tr.v.* to intimidate, scare, frighten. —*r.v.* to become frightened, intimidated or scared, e.g. *me acoquiné al final,* I chickened out (sl.) at the end.
acorace, acoracé, *ref.* **acorazar.**
acorar, *tr.v.* (rare) to anguish, grieve, afflict, sadden. —*r.v.* 1. to wither, wilt, die (plants) due to climatic changes. 2. to anguish, grieve.
acorazado, *m.* battleship. —*a.* armored; armorclad. — **división acorazada,** armored division.
acorazamiento, *m.* armoring, armor-plating, armor.
acorazar, (*ref. 53*) *tr.v.* to armor, armorplate (ships, etc.). —*r.v.* (coll.) to steel oneself (e.g. against pain, onslaught, situation, etc.).
acorazonado, da, *a.* heart-shaped.
acorchado, da, *a.* cork-like, spongy.
acorchamiento, *m.* shrivelling, withering; turning soft or spongy.
acorchar, *tr.v.* to cover or line with cork. —*r.v.* 1. to go spongy or soft. 2. to shrivel, become stale (fruit). 3. to become torpid, go to sleep (limbs of the body).
acordada, *f.* 1. (law) court resolution, order or ruling; authorization; court warning. 2. fraternity established in Mexico in 1710 to combat highwaymen; jail where such highwaymen were imprisoned.
acordadamente, *adv.* 1. unanimously, by common consent. 2. after due consideration.
acordado, da, *past part. of* **acordar.** —*a.* 1. agreed, agreed upon. 2. sensible, prudent. — **lo acordado,** that which has been agreed upon.
acordanza, *f.* 1. agreement, harmony. 2. recollection, memory.
acordar, (*ref. 33*) *tr.v.* 1. to decide, resolve; to agree, agree upon. 2. to reconcile, conciliate. 3. to remind, bring to mind. 4. (arch.) to remember. 5. (mus.) to harmonize, tune. 6. (p.) to compose or arrange (colors) harmoniously. 7. to grant, give. — **a.** + *inf.,* to agree to + *inf.* — *i.v.* 1. to harmonize, agree. 2. (arch.) to realize, understand; to find out. —*r.v.* 1. to remember, recollect. 2. to agree, come to an agreement; to be agreed. — **acordarse** + *inf.,* to agree to + *inf.;* to be agreed to + *inf.;* **acordarse con,** to come to an agreement with; **acordarse de,** to remember; **acordarse de** + *inf.,* to remember to + *inf.;* **si mal no me acuerdo,** if I remember correctly, if I'm not mistaken.
acorde, *a.* 1. in agreement, in accord, agreed, e.g. *estamos acordes,* we are in agreement. 2. harmonious (sounds, colors). 3. tuned, in tune (instruments). —*m.* (mus.) chord; triad. — **a. perfecto,** perfect triad; **a. perfecto mayor,** major triad; **a. perfecto menor,** minor triad.
acordelar, *tr.v.* 1. to measure with a cord or measuring chain. 2. to mark off with a cord (lines or perimeters).
acordemente, *adv.* by common consent.
acordeón, *m.* accordion.
acordeonista, *m., f.* accordionist.
acordonado, da, *past part. of* **acordonar.** —*a.* 1. surrounded, cordoned off. 2. laced (shoes, boots). 3. cord-like. 4. (Mex.) lean, thin.
acordonamiento, *m.* 1. cordoning off, surrounding. 2. milling (of coins).
acordonar, *tr.v.* 1. to fasten or tie with a cord. 2. to mill (coins). 3. to surround, cordon off. 4. (C. Amer., Cuba) to prepare (land for sowing).
acores, *m.* (*pl.*) (med.) achores, scald head.
acornado, da, *a.* (her.) with horns of a different hue or material (from the rest of the animal represented in the coat-of-arms).
acornar, (*ref. 33*) *tr.v., var. of* **acornear.**
acorneador, ra, *a.* butting (bull, ram, etc.).
acornear, *tr.v.* to butt (with horns); to gore.
ácoro, *m.* (bot.) calamus, sweet flag. — **á. bastardo, á. palustre, á. falso,** yellow flag or iris, flagon.
acorralamiento, *m.* the act of corralling, rounding up; cornering, trapping.
acorralar, *tr.v.* 1. to corral, drive into a corral or pen (cattle); to corner, trap (a person). 2. to frighten, scare, intimidate.
acorrer, *tr.v.* (arch.) to help, assist, aid. —*i.v.* to run to the aid (of someone). —*r.v.* to take refuge or shelter.
acorro, *m.* (obs.). *var. of* **socorro.**
acorrucarse, *r.v., var. of* **acurrucarse.**
acorruque, acorruqué, *ref.* **acorrucarse.**
acortamiento, *m.* 1. shortening; reduction, cutting down, lessening. 2. (astron.) curtation.
acortar, *tr.v.* to shorten; to reduce, lessen, cut down. —*r.v.* 1. to become or get shorter; to be reduced or shortened. 2. to be timid, shy or bashful. 3. to draw back, shy (a horse).
acorullar, *tr.v.* (mar.) to ship the oars.
acorvar, *tr.v., var. of* **encorvar.**
acosadamente, *adv.* (rare) harassingly.
acosador, ra, *a.* harassing. —*m., f.* harasser; pursuer; hounder.
acosamiento, *m.* harassing, harassment; pursuit; hounding.
acosar, *tr.v.* 1. to harass; to pursue. 2. to spur on, race (a horse). 3. to harass, pester, hound, hem in, e.g. *le acosaron a preguntas,* they harassed him with questions.
acosijar, *tr.v.* (Mex.) (coll.) to overwhelm, to oppress.
acosmismo, *m.* (philos.) acosmism.
acoso, *m., var. of* **acosamiento.**
acostada, *f.* the act of lying down, sleeping, reclining.
acostado, da, *past part. of* **acostar.** —*a.* 1. lying down; stretched out; in bed. 2. (her.) couchant.
acostamiento, *m.* 1. laying down; lying down. 2. support, favor, protection. 3. (arch.) stipend.
acostar, (*ref. 33*) *tr.v.* 1. to lay down; to put to bed. 2. to bring close (to). 3. (mar.) to bring alongside. —*i.v.* 1. to list, lean to one side. 2. to reach the shore. —*r.v.* 1. to go to bed, lie down. 2. to approach. 3. (mar.) to go alongside. 4. to list, lean to one side. 5. to adhere, incline. — **acostarse con,** to go to bed with, sleep with.
acostumbradamente, *adv.* customarily.
acostumbrar, *tr.v.* to accustom. —*i.v.* to be accustomed, be in the habit of. — **a.** + *inf.,* to be accustomed to, be in the habit of + *ger.* — *r.v.* to get accustomed to; *acostumbrarse a,* to get or become accustomed to + *inf.* or *ger.*
acotación, *f.* 1. annotation; marginal note. 2. (theat.) stage direction. 3. (top.) elevation mark (on a map). 4. *var. of* **acotamiento.**
acotada, *f.* tree nursery (in land that has been set aside by law for the purpose of reforestation).
acotamiento, *m.* delimitation; limit, boundary, boundary mark.
acotar, *tr.v.* 1. to mark the boundaries or limits of, delimit, stake out. 2. to reserve (land) for certain use. 3. to fix, specify. 4. to prune or trim the branches of. —*r.v.* to take refuge in another district.
acotar, *tr.v.* 1. to annotate, make marginal notes in; to remark, observe, say, note. 2. to accept. 3. (coll.) to choose, select. 4. to be in agreement with somebody. 5. (top.) to mark elevations or dimensions on.
acotejar, *tr.v.* (Amer.) to arrange. —*r.v.* to make oneself comfortable.
acotejo, *m.* (Cuba) arrangement.
acotiledón, *a.* (bot.) acotyledonous. —*m.* (bot.) acotyledon; (*pl.*) (bot.) Acotyledona.
acotiledóneo, a, *a.* acotyledonous. —*f.* acotyledon; (*pl.*) (bot.) Acotyledons.
acotillo, *m.* sledge hammer.
acoyundar, *tr.v.* to yoke (oxen).
acoyuntar, *tr.v.* (agr.) to hitch together (two beasts of burden of different owners in order to make a pair).
acoyuntero, *m.* (agr.) each of the farmers who provide a horse to make a pair.
acracia, *f.* 1. acracy, anarchy. 2. (med.) asthenia, acratia.
ácrata, *a.* anarchical, anarchistic. —*m., f.* anarchist.
acre, *a.* 1. acrid, harsh, pungent. 2. mordant, bitter, caustic, biting. —*m.* 1. (med.) fever accompanied by an itching sensation. 2. acre (land measure).
acrecencia, *f.* increase, growth; accretion; (law) accretion; property obtained by accretion.
acrecentamiento, *m.* increase, augmentation, growth.
acrecentante, *a.* increasing; incremental.
acrecentar, (*ref. 29*) *tr.v.* 1. to increase, augment. 2. to promote, advance (someone in a job). —*r.v.* to grow, increase.
acrecer, (*ref. 45*) *tr.v.* to augment, increase. —*i.v.* **a. a,** to be transferred to, devolve upon. —*r.v.* to increase, grow, grow larger.
acreciente, acreciento, *ref.* **acrecentar.**
acrecimiento, *m., var. of* **acrecencia.**
acreción, *f.* (min., med.) accretion.
acreditado, da, *past part. of* **acreditar.** —*a.* accredited; reputable.
acreditar, *tr.v.* 1. to accredit; to guarantee, vouch for. 2. give a reputation or name, make famous. 3. (com.) to credit (in an account). —*r.v.* to become famous, get a reputation or name. — **acreditarse como,** to get a name or reputation as; **acreditarse por,** to become famous for.
acreditativo, va, *a.* accrediting.
acreedor, ra, *a.* 1. credit, e.g. *un saldo acreedor,* a credit balance. 2. deserving. — **a. a,** deserving; **ser a. a,** to deserve. —*m., f.* creditor.
acreencia, *f.* (Amer.) credit, favorable balance in an account.
acremente, *adv.* acridly, bitterly, mordantly, caustically.
acrezca, acrezco, *ref.* **acrecer.**
acriance, acriancé, *ref.* **acrianzar.**
acrianzar, (*ref. 53*) *tr.v.* to raise, rear, bring up.
acribador, ra, *a.* sifting. —*m., f.* sifter.
acribadura, *f.* sifting; (*pl.*) siftings.
acribar, *tr.v.* 1. to sift. 2. to riddle with holes, riddle.
acribillar, *tr.v.* 1. to riddle with holes; to riddle, e.g. *acribillar a balazos,* to riddle with bullets. 2. to harass, hound.
acrídido, *a.* (ento.) acridian. —*m.* (ento.) acridid; (*pl.*) Acrididae.
acridina, *f.* (chem.) acridine.
acriflavina, *f.* (pharm.) acriflavine.
acrílico, ca, *a.* (chem.) acrylic.
acriminación, *f.* incrimination, accrimination, accusation (of a crime).
acriminador, ra, *a.* incriminating, accusatory. —*m., f.* accuser.
acriminar, *tr.v.* 1. to incriminate, accuse (of a crime); to impute (blame on someone). 2. to exaggerate the gravity of (a crime).
acrimonia, *f.* sourness, tartness, bitterness (of taste); acrimony, sharpness, severity, harshness (said of words, character, etc.).
acrimonioso, sa, *a.* acrimonious.

acriollado, da, *a.* person who has adopted Spanish-American customs or speech.
acriollarse, *r.v.* (S. Amer.) to adopt Spanish American ways.
acrisoladamente, *adv.* honestly, virtuously.
acrisolado, da, *past part. of* **acrisolar.** *—a.* honest, virtuous, upright. *—m.* glasswork.
acrisolar, *tr.v.* 1. to refine (metals); to purify, cleanse. 2. to clarify, reveal, (truth, etc.).
acristalado, *a.* 1. glass-like; glazed. 2. glassed in.
acristianar, *tr.v.* (coll.) to christen, baptize. 2. (coll.) to Christianize, make Christian.
acritud, *f., var. of* **acrimonia.**
acroamático, ca, *a.* acroamatic, oral.
acrobacia, *f.* acrobatics; stunt.
acróbata, *m., f.* acrobat.
acrobático, ca, *a.* acrobatic.
acrobatismo, *m.* acrobatics, acrobatism.
acrocárpeo, a, *a.* (bot.) acrocarpous.
acrocarpio, a, *a.* (bot.) acrocarpous. *—f.* (bot.) (*pl.*) Acrocarpi.
acrocarpo, pa, *a.* (bot.) acrocarpous.
acrocéfalo, la, *a.* (med.) acrocephalous.
acrodonte, *a., m.* (zool.) acrodont.
acródromo, ma, *a.* (bot.) acrodrome.
acroe, *m., var. of* **acroy.**
acrofobia, *f.* acrophobia, fear of height.
acrógeno, na, *a.* (bot.) acrogenous, acrogenic.
acroleína, *f.* (chem.) acrolein.
acromado, da, *a.* chrome-like.
acromatice, acromaticé, *ref.* **acromatizar.**
acromatico, ca, *a.* achromatous, achromatic, colorless; (bot., opt.) achromatic.
acromatina, *f.* (biol.) achromatin.
acromatismo, *m.* (opt.) achromatism.
acromatizar, (*ref. 53*) *tr.v.* (opt.) to achromatize, to correct a chromatic aberration.
acromatopsia, *f.* (med.) achromatopsia, color blindness.
acromegalia, *f.* (med.) acromegalia, acromegaly.
acromial, *a.* (anat.) acromial.
acromiano, na, *a.* (anat.) acromial.
acrómico, ca, *a.* (anat.) achromic, achromatous.
acromión, *m.* (anat.) acromion.
acrónico, ca, *a.* (astron.) acronical.
acropétalo, la, *a.* (bot.) acropetal.
acrópolis, *f.* acropolis, citadel.
acrospiro, *m.* (bot.) acrospire.
acrósporo, ra, *a.* (biol.) acrosporous. *—f.* (biol.) acrospore.
acróstico, ca, *a.* acrostic, acrostical. *—m.* acrostic.
acrostolio, *m.* (mar.) acrostolium, acroterium, beak, beakhead.
acrotera, *f.* (archit.) acroterium (ornament or statue placed on the angles of a pediment in classical buildings).
acroteria, *f., var. of* **acrotera.**
acroterio, *m.* (archit.) pediment.
acrotismo, *m.* (med.) acrotism, absence or weakness of the pulse.
acroy, *m.* gentleman-in-waiting of the House of Burgundy.
acsu, *f.* (Bol.) skirt of coarse material worn by Indian women.
acta, *f.* 1. minutes, record (of proceedings); (*pl.*) records. 2. certificate, document; result sheet, certificate of results (of examinations, elections, etc.). 3. (*pl.*) life, acts and deeds (of martyrs). — **a. notarial,** notarial certificate; **levantar un a.,** to draw up a document or certificate.
actea, *f.* (bot.) dwarf elder, danewort.
Acteón, *m.* (myth.) Actaeon.
actina, *f.* 1. (physiol.) actin (muscular protein). 2. (zool.) actine.
actinia, *f.* (zool.) actinia, sea anemone.
actínico, ca, *a.* (chem.) actinic.
actínido, *m.* (chem.) actinide; (*pl.*) actinide series.
actiniforme, *a.* (med.) actiniform.
actinio, *m.* (chem.) actinium.
actinismo, *m.* actinism; radiation properties which produce chemical changes.
actinógrafo, *m.* (photog.) actinograph.
actinoide, *a.* actinoid; ray-like.
actinolita, *f.* (min.) actinolite, amphibole.
actinometría, *f.* (phys.) actinometry.
actinométrico, ca, *a.* (opt.) actinometric.
actinómetro, *m.* (opt.) actinometer.
actinomices, *m.* (*pl.*) (med.) actinomyces.
actinomicético, ca, *a.* (bac.) actinomycetous.
actinomiceto, *m.* (bac.) actinomycete.
actinomicina, *f.* (med.) actinomycin.
actinomicosis, *f.* (vet.) actinomycosis.
actinomorfo, fa, *a.* (biol.) actinomorphic, actinomorphous.
actinón, *m.* (chem.) actinon.
actinota, *f., var. of* **actinolita.**
actinoterapia, *f.* (med.) actinotherapy.
actinozoos, *m.* (*pl.*) (zool.) actinozoans.
actitud, *f.* 1. attitude, frame of mind, outlook. 2. position, posture.
activación, *f.* activation, triggering; (elec.) firing.
activador, *m.* (chem., physiol.) activator, promoter; energizer.
activamente, *adv.* actively.
activar, *tr.v.* to activate; to hasten, expedite.
actividad, *f.* activity, action. — **en a.,** in operation, in action; **en plena a.,** in full operation; **esfera de a.,** field of action.
activismo, *m.* activism.
activista, *a., m., f.* activist.
activo, va, *a.* active. *—m.* (com.) assets; **a. corriente** or **realizable,** current assets; **a. fijo** or **permanente,** capital assets.
acto, *m.* 1. act; action. 2. ceremony, act, function. 3. (theat.) act. 4. (hist.) actus (Roman lineal measurement). 5. (philos.) act, actus. 6. (educ.) thesis. — **a. bélico, a. de guerra,** act of war; **a. continuo** or **seguido,** immediately afterwards; **a. de conciliación,** proceedings for conciliation; **a. de contrición,** act of contrition; **a. de posesión,** possessory action; **a. de presencia,** token attendance or appearance; **a. fallido,** Freudian slip; **a. humano,** (theol.) act of free will; **a. jurídico,** legal proceeding, juristic act, act of law; **acto particular,** (law) private act; **a reflejo,** reflex action; **a. sexual,** sexual act; **en a.,** in the act; (philos.) in act, in actu; **en el a.,** immediately. — **hacer a. de presencia,** to put in an appearance.
actomiosina, *f.* (physiol.) actomyosin.
actor, *m.* theatrical performer, actor. — **a. substituto** or **suplente,** understudy; **primer a.,** leading man. *—m., f.* (law) actor, claimant, plaintiff; **a. civil,** plaintiff.
actriz, (*pl.* **actrices**) *f.* actress.
actuación, *f.* 1. performance (of actor, football player, etc.); action, behavior, conduct, e.g. *no me ha gustado la a. del ministro en este asunto,* I did not like the minister's handling of this affair. 2. (law) action, proceeding; (*pl.*) proceedings.
actuado, da, *past part. of* **actuar.** *—a.* trained, skilled, experienced; **lo a.,** (law) the steps that have already been taken in a legal action.
actual, *a.* 1. present, current, factual. 2. (philos.) actual, real.
actualice, actualicé, *ref.* **actualizar.**
actualidad, *f.* present time; present situation or condition; (*pl.*) news, current events.— **en la a.,** at present, at the present time; **ser de gran a.,** to be very topical at the present moment, be constantly in the news at the present time; **perder a.,** to become obsolete, to lose interest, to go out of fashion.
actualizar, (*ref. 53*) *tr.v.* 1. to bring up to date. 2. to actualize, put into effect.
actualmente, *adv.* at present, at the present time.
actuante, *m., f.* student who defends a thesis in a university or college.
actuar, (*ref. 55*) *i.v.* 1. to act, work, e.g. *hay que a. pronto,* we must act fast. 2. (theat., cine.) to act, perform. 3. to act, produce effects, e.g. *el calor actúa sobre los cuerpos,* heat acts on or produces effects in bodies. 4. to act, behave. 5. to be in action. 6. to defend a thesis (in a university). 7. (law) to prosecute, bring an action.
actuarial, *a.* actuarial; pertaining to the insurance actuary.
actuario, *m.* (law) actuary, clerk of a court of justice; **a. de seguros,** insurance actuary.
actuosidad, *f.* diligence.
actuoso, sa, *a.* diligent.
acuache, *m.* (Mex.) pal, buddy, chum, friend.
acuadrillar, *tr.v.* 1. to band together (men). 2. to command, lead (a band of men). 3. (Chile) to gang up on and attack (someone). *—r.v.* to band together, form a band.
acuafortista, *m., var. of* **aguafuertista.**
acuanauta, *m., f.* aquanaut.
acuantiar, *tr.v.* to assess the value or worth of a thing; to determine quantity or amount.
acuarela, *f.* water color, water-color painting, aquarelle.
acuarelista, m. water-color painter, water-colorist, aquarellist.
acuarelístico, ca, *a.* pertaining to water-color.
acuario, *m.* aquarium.
Acuario, *m.* (astron.) Aquarius.
acuartelado, da, *past part. of* **acuartelar.** *—a.* 1. (mil.) billeted. 2. (her.) quartered, divided into quarters.
acuartelamiento, *m.* 1. the act of billeting. 2. (mil.) troops; quarters.
acuartelar, *tr.v.* 1. (mil.) to quarter, billet; to keep troops in barracks or on the alert. 2. to divide land into plots. 3. (mar.) to flat or haul in the jib. *—r.v.* to take up quarters.
acuarteronado, da, *a.* said of a quadroon, a person who has one Negro grandparent.
acuartillado, da, *a.* bent in the quarters under a heavy load (said of pack animals).
acuartillar, *i.v.* to bend in the quarters under a heavy load or weight (said of pack animals).
acuate, *m.* (Mex.) water snake with black and yellow head.
acuático, ca, *a.* 1. aquatic; living or growing in water. 2. pertaining to water.
acuátil, *a., var. of* **acuático.**
acuatinta, *f.* aquatint.
acuatizaje, *m.* (aer.) landing on water.
acuatizar, (*ref. 53*) *i.v.* (aer.) to land on water.
acubado, da, *a.* 1. bucket-shaped. 2. cube-shaped.
acubilar, *tr.v.* to round up (cattle).
acúbito, *m.* (hist.) Roman sofa.
acuchamarse, *r.v.* (Ven.) to become sad or languid.
acuchamiento, *m.* (Chile) agglomeration.
acucharado, da, *a.* spoon-shaped.
acuchillado, da, *past part. of* **acuchillar.** *—a.* 1. slashed, stabbed. 2. (dressm.) gored, slashed. 3. prudent, cautious through experience.
acuchillador, ra, *a.* 1. quarrelsome, brawling. 2. stabbing. *—m., f.* 1. quarrelsome person, brawler, troublemaker. 2. stabber. *—m.* planer, man who planes wooden floors.

acuchillar, *tr.v.* 1. to knife, stab. 2. to plane (wooden floors). 3. (dressm.) to gore, slash. 4. to thin out (plants in seedbed). —*r.v.* to fight with knives or swords.
acuchucar, *tr.v.* (Chile) to squeeze, squash.
acuchuchar, *var. of* **acuchucar.**
acucia, *f.* 1. meticulousness, zeal, diligence. 2. yearning, longing.
acuciadamente, *adv., var. of* **acuciosamente.**
acuciador, ra, *a.* meticulous, zealous; diligent.
acuciamiento, *m.* hastening, goading, driving, urging, prodding.
acuciante, *pres. part. of* acuciar.
acuciar, *tr.v.* 1. to hasten, urge, drive; to goad, prod. 2. to yearn for. 3. to stimulate. 4. (arch.) to take great care.
acuciosamente, *adv.* 1. meticulously, conscientiously, diligently. 2. yearningly, longingly.
acuciosidad, *f.* meticulousness, conscientiousness, zeal, diligence, great care.
acucioso, sa, *a.* 1. meticulous, conscientious, zealous, diligent. 2. eager, keen.
acuclillado, da, *a.* squatting.
acuclillarse, *r.v.* to squat.
acudiente, *m.* (Col.) students' counselor or tutor.
acudimiento, *m.* aid, assistance, help.
acudir, *i.v.* 1. to go; to present oneself; to attend, be present, e.g. *a. a la cita puntualmente,* to arrive punctually (for an appointment). 2. to help, aid, succor. 3. to reply, respond. 4. to be productive or fruitful (land). 5. to respond. — **a. a,** to resort to (person, medicine); **a. en socorro de,** to go to help.
acueducto, *m.* aqueduct.
ácueo, a, *a.* aqueous, watery.
acuerdado, da, *a.* aligned (as with a rope).
acuerde, acuerdo, *ref.* **acordar.**
acuerdo, *m.* 1. agreement, understanding, consent, resolution. 2. agreement, pact. 3. agreement, accord, accordance, harmony. — **de a.,** in agreement; **de a. con,** in accordance with; **estar de a.,** to be in agreement; **llegar a un a.,** to come to or reach an agreement or understanding; **ponerse** or **quedar de a.,** to agree, come to an agreement; **por a. común, de común a.,** by common consent or agreement; **vivir en perfecto a.,** to live in perfect harmony.
acuerne, acuerno, *ref.* **acornar.**
acuerpado, da, *a.* (Col.) hefty, husky.
acuerpar, *tr.v.* (C. Amer.) to defend, support (someone).
acueste, acuesto, *ref.* **acostar.**
acuicultura, *f.* aquiculture.
acuidad, *f.* acuity, sharpness (of the senses); **a. estereoscópica,** stereoscopic acuity.
acuidarse, *r.v.* to be preoccupied with.
acuífero, ra, *a.* aquiferous, water-bearing.
acuilmarse, *r.v.* (Amer.) to grieve; to lose heart or courage.
acuitadamente, *adv.* with grief or affliction, sorrowfully.
acuitar, *tr.v.* to afflict, grieve. —*r.v.* to grieve.
ácula, *f.* (bot.) a Eurasian herb (Scandix australis).
aculado, da, *a.* 1. (zool.) aculeate. 2. (her.) rampant (said of a horse). —*m.* (*pl.*) (zool.) Aculeata.
acular, *tr.v.* 1. to make (a horse, cart etc.) back up. 2. (coll.) to corner (someone). —*r.v.* (mar.) to run astern into shallows or onto a shoal.
aculebrinado, da, *a.* (mil.) long-muzzled (cannon); in the shape of a culverin.
aculeiforme, *a.* aculeiform; sharp or pointed as a needle.
acúleo, a, *a.* (zool.) aculeate. —*m.* sting.
aculeolado, da, *a.* (bot.) aculeolate, aculeate.
aculéolo, *m.* (bot.) aculeus.
acullá, *adv.* there, opposite, on the other side, yonder.
acullicar, *tr.v.* (S. Amer.) to chew (coca leaves).
aculturación, *f.* (sociol.) adoption of a higher culture, adoption of another culture.
aculturarse, *r.v.* (sociol.) to adopt the culture traits of another group.
acumetría, *f.* (med.) acoumetry.
acúmetro, *m.* acumeter, acoumeter, acoutemeter.
acuminado, da, *a.* acuminate, tapering, pointed.
acumuchar, *tr.v.* (Chile) to accumulate, to heap.
acumulable, *a.* accumulative.
acumulación, *f.* accumulation; gathering. — **a. a base de intereses,** (com.) interest method of accumulation.
acumuladero, *m.* (Mex.) cave, lair; animal's hideaway.
acumulador, ra, *a.* accumulating. —*m., f.* accumulator. —*m.* (elec.) accumulator, storage battery; **a. compensador** or **flotante,** (elec.) floating battery; **a. cargado,** active cell.
acumulamiento, *m.* accumulation.
acumular, *tr.v.* 1. to accumulate, amass. 2. to charge with, accuse of. 3. (law) to try jointly. 4. (Arg., Col.) to attribute, impute.
acumulativamente, *adv.* jointly, accumulatively.
acumulativo, va, *a.* accumulative, cumulative.
acunar, *tr.v.* to cradle, to rock (the cradle).
acuñación, *f.* 1. coining, minting. 2. wedging.
acuñado, *a.* 1. coined, minted. 2. sealed, affixed. 3. wedged. —*m.* wedging; locking; jamming; (print.) lockup, quoining (of a form); quoins (collectively of a form).
acuñador, ra, *a.* minting, coining. —*m.* 1. minter, coiner. 2. (print.) shooting stick.
acuñamiento, *m.* wedging, jamming.
acuñar, *tr.v.* 1. to wedge, put a wedge or wedges in; to lock, jam (a machine); (print.) to quoin, lock up (a form in a chase). 2. to coin or mint; to stamp in die. 3. to affix a seal.
acuorrefrigerado, da, *a.* water-cooled.
acuosidad, *f.* wateriness, aqueousness.
acuoso, sa, *a.* aqueous, watery; juicy (said of fruit).
acupe, *m.* (Ven.) a drink made of fermented corn.
acupuntura, *f.* (surg.) acupuncture.
acure, *m.* (Ven.) guinea pig.
acurí, *m.* (Col., Ven.) agouti, a rodent.
acurrado, da, *a.* (Cuba) affected (imitating Andalusian speech and manners).
acurrarse, *r.v.* (Cuba) to imitate Andalusian speech and manners.
acurrucado, da, *a.* curled-up like a cat; cozy.
acurrucarse, (*ref. 50*) *r.v.* 1. to curl up; to get cozy and comfortable. 2. (fig.) to cower, back up or hide.
acurrullar, *tr.v.* (mar.) to furl (sails).
acurruque, acurruqué, *ref.* **acurrucarse.**
acus. *abbrev. of* **acusativo,** accusative (acc.).
acusable, *a.* impeachable.
acusación, *f.* accusation, charge, impeachment.
acusado, da, *past part. of* **acusar.** —*m., f.* accused.
acusador, ra, *a.* accusing. —*m., f.* accuser.
acusante, *a.* accusing, prosecuting.
acusar, *tr.v.* 1. to accuse, charge; impeach. 2. to denounce, give away, inform on. 3. to acknowledge (receipt of letter, etc.). 4. to announce, call (winning cards). 5. to show, reveal, e.g. *los papeles industriales acusaron la baja más pronunciada,* the market index showed the most pronounced drop. — **a. de,** to accuse of. —*r.v.* to confess; **acusarse de** + *inf.,* to confess + *ger.* — **a. asombro,** to register surprise; **a. desorden,** to reveal disorder.
acusativo, *m.* (gram.) accusative case.
acusatorio, ria, *a.* accusatory, accusing.
acuse, *m.* 1. acknowledgment (of receipt). 2. announcement of winning cards; winning card.
acusetas, *m.* (C. Amer., Col., coll.) *var. of* **acusón.**
acusete, *m.* (Amer.) *var. of* **acusón.**
acusón, na, *a.* talebearing. —*m., f.* (coll.) telltale, tattletale, sneak, talebearer.
acústica, *f.* (phys.) acoustics.
acústico, ca, *a.* acoustic; **trompetilla a.,** eartrumpet; **tubo a.,** speaking tube.
acutángulo, *a.* acute-angled.
acutí, *m.* (Arg., Par., zool.) agouti.
acutómetro, *m.* (phys.) audiometer.
adacilla, *f.* (bot.) variety of sorghum.
adafina, *f.* stew which the Spanish Jews used to place on glowing embers on Friday evening to eat on the Sabbath.
adagial, *a.* proverbial.
adagio, *m.* 1. proverb, adage. 2. (mus., ballet) slow, measured, graceful passage.
adaguar, (*ref. 52*) *i.v....* to drink (cattle).
adala, *f.* (mar.) pump dale.
adalid, *m.* commander, military leader; leader, head (of a party, corporation or school).
adamadamente, *adv.* gently, softly.
adamado, da, *a.* 1. womanish, effeminate. 2. elegant, delicate. 3. pretending to be genteel or elegant (said of a coarse person).
adamadura, *f.* 1. token of affection. 2. love-sickness. 3. infatuation.
adamantino, na, *a.* adamantine.
adamar, *tr.v.* to woo, court. —*r.v.* to become effeminate, become slim and delicate like a woman.
adamascado, da, *a.* like damask, damask.
adamascador, *m.* damask manufacturer.
adámico, ca, *a.* (geol.) deposited by ebb tides (land).
Adamismo, *m.* Adamitism, doctrine and sect of the Adamites.
adamita, *a.* Adamitic, of the Adamites. —*m., f.* Adamite, member of one of the religious sects which held their meetings in the nude.
adán, *m.* 1. **A.,** Adam. 2. (coll.) ragamuffin, scruffy urchin. 3. (coll.) slovenly apathetic fellow. — **en traje de A.,** in one's birthday suit, naked; **manzana de A.,** Adam's apple.
adaptabilidad, *f.* adaptability.
adaptable, *a.* adaptable; flexible.
adaptación, *f.* adaptation; acclimatization.
adaptado, da, *a.* adapted; adjusted.
adaptador, ra, *a.* adapting, adjusting. —*m.* (mec.) adapter; transition piece, fitting; **a. de antena,** antenna adapter; **a. de onda,** wave adapter; **a. de válvula,** valve adapter; **a. para tubería,** casing adapter.
adaptante, *a.* adapting.
adaptar, *tr.v.* to adapt, adjust. —*r.v.* to adapt, adjust or accustom oneself, conform.
adaraja, *f.* (bldg.) toothing.
adarce, *m.* salt residue left on objects touched by sea water.
adardear, *tr.v.* to wound with darts.
adarga, *f.* oval or heart-shaped leather shield, target.
adargar, (*ref. 51*) *tr.v.* to protect with a shield; to defend, protect.
adargue, adargué, *ref.* **adargar.**
adarguero, *m.* shield maker; one who uses a shield or target.
adarme, *m.* 1. ancient Arabic measure. 2. (coll.) drib, driblet, drop, bit. — **por adarmes,** very sparingly, stingily, (coll.) in dribs and drabs.
adarvar, *tr.v.* to **stun, daze.** —*r.v.* to be stunned, bewildered or dazed.
adarve, *m.* (mil.) narrow path behind the parapet or bastion of a fortress; (coll.) protection, defense.

adatar, *tr.v.* to credit (in an account).
adax, *m.* (zool.) addax.
adaza, *f.* (bot.) sorghum.
Addis-Abeba, Addis Ababa, capital of Ethiopia.
A. de C. *abbrev. of* **Año de Cristo,** Anno Domini, in the year of our Lord (AD).
adecenamiento, *m.* division into or formation in tens.
adecenar, *tr.v.* to divide into or form in tens.
adecentar, *tr.v.* to make presentable. —*r.v.* to make oneself presentable, smarten oneself up, dress up.
adecuación, *f.* fitting, adapting.
adecuadamente, *adv.* 1. correctly, properly, fittingly, suitably. 2. adequately, sufficiently.
adecuado, da, *past part. of* **adecuar.** —*a.* 1. correct, right, proper, fit, fitting, appropriate. 2. adequate, sufficient.
adecuar, *tr.v.* to adapt, fit.
adefagia, *f.* (med.) adephagia, insatiable hunger.
adéfago, ga, *a.* (med., ento.) **adephagous.** —*m.* (ento.) adephagan; (*pl.*) **Adephaga.**
adefera, *f.* (archit.) small tile used in friezes and pavements.
adefesio, *m.* 1. rubbish, nonsense. 2. ridiculous costume or dress. 3. mess, scarecrow, ridiculous figure.
adefina, *f., var. of* **adafina.**
adehala, *f.* extra, something given for good measure; tip, gratuity.
adehesado, *m.* pasture land.
adehesamiento, *m.* pasture land; converting into pasture land.
adehesar, *tr.v.* to convert into pasture, prepare land for pasture.
A. de J.C. *abbrev. of* **antes de Jesucristo,** ante Cristum, before Christ (B.C.).
adelantadamente, *adv.* in advance, beforehand.
adelantado, da, *past part. of* **adelantar.** —*a.* 1. advanced, precocious (said of a child). 2. rash, bold. 3. early (fruit, plants). 4. fast (a clock, etc.). — **por a.,** in advance. —*m.* governor of a frontier province; **a. de mar,** commander of sea expedition, empowered to govern the lands he may discover and conquer.
adelantador, ra, *a.* advancing. —*m., f.* advancer, one who advances, extends. — **adelantador de fases,** (elec.) phase advancer.
adelantamiento, *m.* 1. advance, progress, improvement. 2. post of a governor of a frontier province; territory under jurisdiction of a governor of a frontier province.
adelantar, *tr.v.* 1. to move or bring forward or ahead, advance; to set ahead (e.g. a watch). 2. to advance, pay in advance, make (a payment) in advance. 3. to get ahead of, go past; to outdo, surpass, outstrip, beat, excel. 4. to advance, speed up, make faster (e.g. job, work); to quicken, hasten (one's step). 5. to advance, make progress or advance, make advances in. 6. to improve, increase. —*i.v.* 1. to go fast, gain (a watch). 2. to advance, progress, improve (student in studies; sick person in illness). 3. to run, go faster than rider wishes (horse). —*r.v.* 1. to go forward, go ahead, get ahead. 2. to gain, go fast (a watch). — **adelantarse a,** to get ahead of; to beat, surpass, outstrip, outdo, excel; **a. dinero,** to advance money.
adelante, *adv.* ahead, **farther** on; **forward,** onward. —¡a.! forward!; come in!; **de aquí en a.,** de **hoy en a.,** henceforth, from now on; **en lo a.,** in the future; **llevar a.,** to go ahead with, carry on with, carry out, perform; **más a.,** farther on; **por el camino a.,** up ahead, **farther** on; **salir a.,** to come through, come out well or ahead.
adelanto, *m.* 1. advance, progress. 2. (com.) advance payment, advance. — **a. en cuenta corriente,** overdraft.
adelfa, *f.* (bot.) oleander; rosebay.
adelfal, *m.* oleander field, field of oleanders; rosebay bush or field.
adelfilla, *f.* (bot.) spurge laurel (Daphne laureola).
adelgace, adelgacé, *ref.* **adelgazar.**
adelgazador, ra, *a.* slimming; thinning.
adelgazamiento, *m.* slimming, getting thinner; slimness, slenderness, thinness.
adelgazar, (*ref. 53*) *tr.v.* 1. to make thin, slim or slender. 2. to refine, purify. 3. to discuss with extreme subtlety, split hairs about. 4. to stretch (wire). 5. to taper, plane thin (wood). — **a. la voz,** to raise the pitch of one's voice. —*i.v.* 1. to slim; to get thin or slim; to taper. 2. to split hairs, discuss with extreme subtlety. —*r.v.* to slim; to get thin or slim; to taper.
A. del S. *abbrev. of* **América del Sur, South** America (S.A.).
adema, *f.* (min.) *var. of* **ademe.**
ademador, *m.* (min.) timberman, shorer, workman who makes or installs stays, shores or props.
ademadora, *f.* ax used in mine timbering.
ademán, *m.* gesture, look, attitude; (*pl.*) manners. — **en a. de,** as if about to, getting ready to; **hacer a. de,** to make a move to.
ademar, *tr.v.* (min.) to shore, prop.
además, *adv.* moreover, furthermore; exceedingly; **a. de,** besides, in addition to.
ademe, *m.* (min.) pit prop, shore, strut; shoring.
adempribio, *m.* (Arg.) common pasture ground.
adenalgia, *f.* adenalgia, glandular pains.
adenectomía, *f.* (med.) adenectomy.
adenia, *f.* (med.) adenia.
adenina, *f.* (med.) adenine.
adenitis, *f.* (med.) adenitis.
adenocarcinoma, *m.* (med.) adenocarcinoma.
adenófora, *f.* (bot.) bellflower, Canterbury bell (Campanula odorifera).
adenoideo, a, *a.* (anat.) adenoidal, adenoid.
adenoides, *m.* (*pl.*) (med.) adenoids.
adenología, *f.* (anat.) adenology.
adenológico, ca, *a.* (med.) adenological.
adenoma, *m.* (med.) adenoma.
adenopatía, *f.* (med.) adenopathy.
adenosina, *f.* (biochem.) adenosine.
adensar, *tr.v.* to thicken, muddle; to condense.
adentelladura, *f.* (mec.) gears, toothing.
adentellar, *tr.v.* to bite (gears); (bldg.) to leave toothing in a wall.
adentrar, *tr.v., r.v.* to search deeper into a subject, e.g. *adentremos en el tema,* let's get into the subject.
adentro, *adv.* within, inside; **mar a.,** out to sea; **puertas a.,** in private; **ser muy de a.,** to be like one of the family; **tierra a.,** inland. —*m.* (*pl.*) innermost self; **para sus adentros,** to oneself, to himself. —*interj.* come in, enter.
adepto, ta, *a.* adept, initiated.
aderece, aderecé, *ref.* **aderezar.**
aderezamiento, *m.* 1. seasoning, flavoring, dressing. 2. embellishing, adorning.
aderezar, (*ref. 53*) *tr.v.* 1. to adorn, embellish, dress. 2. to season, flavor, dress (food, drinks). 3. to prepare, make ready. 4. to dress, treat (fabrics). 5. to mend, repair. —*r.v.* to adorn oneself, dress up; to get ready.
aderezo, *m.* 1. seasoning, flavoring, condiment, dressing. 2. adorning, ornamentation, adornment; finery. 3. preparation. 4. gum starch (used in stiffening textiles). 5. set (jewelry). 6. harness, trappings (of a horse). 7. ornamentation (on swords, daggers, jewelry, etc.).
adermina, *f.* (med.) adermin.
aderra, *f.* thin esparto rope; rush rope.
adestrado, da, *past part. of* **adestrar.** —*a.* (her.) having a bearing or division on the right hand side of the escutcheon.
adestrador, ra, *a., m., f., var. of* **adiestrador.**
adestramiento, *m., var. of* **adiestramiento.**
adestrar, (*ref. 29*) *tr.v., var. of* **adiestrar.**
adeudado, da, *a.* indebted.
adeudamiento, *m.* indebtedness.
adeudar, *tr.v.* 1. to owe. 2. to pay, be liable to pay (taxes). 3. to debit (in an account). —*r.v.* to go into debt.
adeudo, *m.* 1. debt. 2. customs duty. 3. (com.) debit.
adeveras, *adv.* (Amer., coll.) really, truly.
adherencia, *f.* 1. adherence, adhesion, sticking. 2. attachment, appendage, addition. 3. (med.) adhesion. 4. relationship, bond.
adherente, *a.* adherent. —*m., f.* adherent, follower; subscriber. —*m.* (*pl.*) implements, equipment.
adherido, da, *a.* 1. glued, stuck. 2. joined (to a cause, party, etc.).
adherir, (*ref. 42*) *tr.v.* to affix, stick on. —*i.v.* to stick, adhere. —*r.v.* 1. to stick, adhere. 2. to adhere, agree, support, join. — **adherirse a,** to stick or adhere to; to adhere to, agree with, support, join, e.g. *me adhiero a lo que dices,* I agree with what you say, *todos los obreros se han adherido a la huelga,* all the workers joined the strike.
adhesión, *f.* 1. adhesion, sticking. 2. adherence, loyalty, support, adhesion. 3. (phys.) adhesion, molecular attraction. 4. (law) assent, acceptance, agreement.
adhesividad, *f.* adhesiveness.
adhesivo, va, *a.* adhesive.
adhiera, adhiero, *ref.* **adherir.**
adhiriendo, adhiriera, adhiriese, adhirió, *ref.* **adherir.**
ad hoc, expressly. — **comité a. h.,** ad hoc committee.
adiabático, ca, *a.* adiabatic.
adiado, da, *a.* appointed (day).
adiafa, *f.* (hist.) present or refreshment given to seamen at the end of a voyage.
adiaforesis, *m.* (med.) adiaphoresis.
adiamantado, da, *a.* adamantine, diamond-like.
adiamantar, *tr.v.* to set diamonds into (something).
adiano, na, *a.* (obs.) strong, vigorous.
adiar, *tr.v.* to set, fix, appoint (day, date).
adiatermancia, *f.* (phys.) adiathermancy.
adiatérmico, ca, *a.* adiathermic.
adiaván, *m.* (bot.) wild coconut palm (Cocos mamilaris).
adicción a díe, (law) addictio in diem, agreement releasing vendor from contract to sell in case of a better offer.
adicción in díem, *var. of* **adicción a díe.**
adición, *f.* 1. addition; adding; (math.) addition. 2. footnote, marginal note. 3. (Amer.) check (hotel, restaurant). — **a. de herencia,** acceptance of a legacy.
adicionador, ra, *a.* adding. —*m., f.* adder.
adicional, *a.* additional.
adicionar, *tr.v.* 1. to add, add to. 2. to extend, prolong.
adicto, ta, *a.* 1. devoted, fond, attached. 2. addicted, e.g., *a. a las drogas,* addicted to drugs. —*m., f.* follower, supporter. — **a. a la buena música,** fond of good music.
adiestrable, *a.* trainable.
adiestrado, da, *past part. of* **adiestrar.** —*a.* 1. trained (person, horse, etc.). 2. (her.) flanked on the right of the escutcheon by another bearing.

adiestrador, ra, *a.* training, teaching. —*m., f.* teacher, trainer, guide.
adiestramiento, *m.* teaching, training, instruction. — **a. industrial,** industrial training.
adiestrar, *tr.v.* to teach, train, instruct; to make proficient or skillful; to guide, lead. —*r.v.* to train oneself, teach oneself; to become proficient or skilled; to receive training or instruction. — **adiestrarse a** + *inf.*, to teach or train oneself to + *inf.*
adiestro, adiestre, *ref.* **adestrar.**
adietar, *tr.v.* to put on a diet. —*r.v.* to go on a diet.
adifés, *a.* (Guat.) difficult, costly. —*adv.* (Ven.) on purpose.
adinamia, *f.* (med.) adynamia, prostration.
adinámico, ca, *a.* (med.) adynamic, lacking strength.
adinerado, da, *a.* rich, wealthy, well-to-do.
adinerar, *tr.v.* (coll.) to convert into money; *r.v.* to become rich.
adintelado, *a.* (archit.) straight, flat (arch).
ad interim, (Lat.) ad interim, provisionally.
adiós, *interj.* good-bye! what do you know! —*m.* farewell. good-bye, adieu.
adipal, *a.* fatty (tissue, etc.).
adipocira, *f.* (chem.) adipocere.
adiposidad, *f.* adiposity.
adiposis, *f.* (med.) obesity, adiposis.
adiposo, sa, *a.* adipose.
adipsia, *f.* (med.) adipsia, lack of thirst.
adir, *tr.v.* (law) to accept, receive (inheritance).
aditamento, *m.* 1. addition. 2. attachment, fixture. — **por a.,** in addition.
aditicio, cia, *a.* added, additional.
aditivo, va, *a.* additive. —*m.* 1. admixture, additive. 2. (elec.) addition agent.
ádito, *m.* adytum (inner sanctum of ancient temples).
adivas, *f.* (*pl.*) (vet.) vives, strangullion, strangles (inflammatory swelling in the throat of animals).
adive, *m.* (zool.) jackal.
adivinable, *a.* guessable; predictable, foretellable, prognosticable.
adivinación, *f.* prophecy; divination, prediction; guessing. — **a. del pensamiento,** mind reading.
adivinador, ra, *a.* divinatory, prophetic. —*m., f.* prophesier, diviner, soothsayer, augur; guesser. — **a. del pensamiento,** mind reader.
adivinaja, *f.* (coll.) riddle, puzzle, conundrum.
adivinamiento, *m.* divination.
adivinanza, *f.* riddle, conundrum, puzzle.
adivinar, *tr.v.* 1. to guess. 2. to prophesy, foretell, divine. 3. to solve (a riddle). 4. to read (someone's mind or thought); to tell (someone's fortune).
adivinatorio, ria, *a.* divinatory, prophetic.
adivino, na, *m., f.* prophet, soothsayer, seer, fortuneteller.
adj. *abbrev. of* **adjetivo,** adjective (adj.).
adjetivación, *f.* 1. conversion into an adjective, use as an adjective. 2. qualification (of noun by adjective).
adjetivadamente, *adv.* adjectivally.
adjetival, *a.* adjectival.
adjetivar, *tr.v.* 1. (gram.) to use adjectivally, use as an adjective. 2. (gram.) to qualify (noun with adjectives). 3. to call, name, apply a name to. —*r.v.* (gram.) to become an adjective, assume the function of an adjective.
adjetivo, va, *a.* (gram.) adjective, adjectival. —*m.* adjective; **a. gentilicio,** proper adjective.
adjudicación, *f.* adjudging, awarding (of a prize, etc.).
adjudicador, ra, *m., f.* awarder, adjudger.
adjudicar, (*ref. 50*) *tr.v.* to award, adjudge. —*r.v.* to appropriate.
adjudicativo, va, *a.* adjudicative.
adjudicatorio, ria, *m., f.* grantee, awardee, person who receives a prize or an award.
adjudique, adjudiqué, *ref.* **adjudicar.**
adjunción, *f.* 1. adjoining, adjunction, addition. 2. (law) adjunction. 3. (rhet.) zeugma.
adjuntar, *tr.v.* to enclose, attach (e.g. in a letter).
adjunto, ta, *a.* attached, accompanying, adjunct; enclosed (in a letter). —*m., f.* adjunct, colleague, associate. —*m.* 1. addition. 2. (gram.) adjunct.
adjutor, ra, *a.* helping, assisting. —*m., f.* helper, assistant.
adleriano, na, *a.* Adlerian, related to Alfred Adler's interpretation of Freud's theories.
ad libitum, (mus.) ad libitum, at will, freely.
adminicular, *tr.v.* (law) to corroborate; to help, strengthen, fortify.
adminículo, *m.* 1. adminicle, help, support. 2. (law) adminicle, corroborative evidence or proof. 3. utensil, instrument, (*pl.*) emergency equipment or utensils.
administración, *f.* 1. administration. 2. manager's office. — **consejo de a.,** board of directors; **en a.,** in trust, managed by an administrator and not the owner; **por a.,** officially, by the government (by an official body).
administrador, ra, *a.* administrating. —*m., f.* administrator, manager, trustee; **a. concursal,** (law) receiver or trustee in bankruptcy; **a. de correos,** postmaster; **a. de negocios,** business manager; **a. judicial,** administrator of an estate; **a. suplente,** acting manager.
administrar, *tr.v.* 1. to administer, manage, direct. 2. to administer (medicine, the sacraments). 3. to deal, give (blows, kicks).
administrativamente, *adv.* administratively.
administrativo, va, *a.* administrative.
administratorio, ria, *a., var. of* **administrativo.**
admirable, *a.* admirable.
admirablemente, *adv.* admirably.
admiración, *f.* 1. admiration. 2. wonder, surprise, amazement. 3. exclamation point (¡ !).
admirado, da, *past part. of* **admirar.** —*a.* admired; astonished.
admirador, ra, *m., f.* admirer. —*a.* admiring.
admirar, *tr.v.* 1. to admire. 2. to amaze, surprise. —*r.v.* to marvel, wonder, be surprised or amazed. — **admirarse de,** to wonder or marvel at, be surprised or amazed at.
admirativamente, *adv.* admiringly.
admirativo, va, *a.* admiring; admirable.
admisibilidad, *f.* admissibility.
admisible, *a.* admissible.
admisión, *f.* 1. admission, acceptance; reception. 2. (engin.) intake, entry.
admitido, da, *past part. of* **admitir.** —*a.* admitted, recognized; received, accepted.
admitir, *tr.v.* 1. admit, let in, receive, accept. 2. to admit, agree to, recognize, concede, grant. 3. to permit, allow, admit. — **a. una reclamación,** to accept a claim.
admonición, *f.* admonition, warning.
admonitor, ra, *m., f.* monitor, admonisher; nun or monk who supervises the observance of the rules.
adnata, *f.* (anat.) conjunctiva.
adnato, ta, *a.* (bot., zool.) adnate, congenitally joined.
adnominal, *a.* (gram.) adnominal.
adobado, da, *past part. of* **adobar.** —*m.* well-seasoned, marinaded meat.
adobador, ra, *a.* pickling, preserving; curing, tanning. —*m., f.* 1. pickler, preserver. 2. tanner, dresser (of skins). 3. repairer, mender.
adobadura, *f.* dressing.
adobamiento, *m.* 1. pickling, preserving. 2. seasoning, flavoring. 3. tanning, dressing (of hides); dressing (of fabrics). 4. repairing, mending.
adobar, *tr.v.* 1. to season, flavor, prepare, marinate. 2. to repair, mend. 3. to pickle, preserve. 4. to tan, dress (hides); to dress (fabrics). 5. to fit, shape (shoe to horse's hoof). 6. to strengthen, give body to (wines).
adobasillas, *m.* chair mender.
adobe, *m.* 1. sun-dried clay brick. 2. fetters, shackles.
adobeño, ña, *a.* resembling or pertaining to adobe.
adobera, *f.* 1. adobe mold, adobe brick mold; adobe factory, adobe brick factory. 2. (Mex.) adobe-shaped cheese.
adobería, *f.* 1. adobe brick factory. 2. tannery.
adobío, *m.* front part of a blast furnace.
adobo, *m.* 1. pickling, preserving. 2. seasoning, flavoring, preparing. 3. tanning, dressing (of hides); dressing (of fabrics). 4. pickle, marinade, pickling sauce; seasoning sauce, dressing. 5. dressing (for tanning hides and for preparing fabrics). 6. cosmetic. 7. pickled meat, pickled pork.
adocenadamente, *adv.* in a vulgar manner.
adocenado, da, *past part. of* **adocenar.** —*a.* common, ordinary.
adocenamiento, *m.* 1. sale by the dozen. 2. grouping or dividing into dozens.
adocenar, *tr.v.* 1. to divide, put into dozens. 2. to consider low-class. —*r.v.* to become common, vulgar or low-class.
adoctrinamiento, *m.* indoctrination, instruction, teaching.
adoctrinar, *tr.v.* to indoctrinate, instruct.
adolecente, *a.* suffering, sick. —*m., f.* patient.
adolecer, (*ref. 45*) *i.v.*, to fall sick, become ill; **a. de,** to suffer from. —*r.v.* to sympathize, be sorry.
adoleciente, *a., var. of* **adolecente.**
adolescencia, *f.* adolescence.
adolescente, *a., m., f.* adolescent.
adolezca, adolezco, *ref.* **adolecer.**
adolorado, da, *a., var. of* **dolorido.**
adolorar, *tr.v.* to ache.
adolorido, da, *a., var. of* **dolorido,** suffering, afflicted; in pain.
adomiciliar, *tr.v., r.v., var. of* **domiciliar,** to domicile, to take up one's abode.
Adonai, *m.* Adonai (Hebrew name for God).
adonde, *adv., conj.* where, whither.
adondequiera, *adv.* wherever, anywhere.
adonice, adonicé, *ref.* **adonizarse.**
adónico, *a., m.* (poet.) Adonic.
adonio, *a., m., var. of* **adónico.**
adonis, *m.* 1. **A.,** (myth.) Adonis. 2. Adonis, beautiful youth.
adonizarse, (*ref. 53*) *r.v.* to adorn or beautify oneself, spruce oneself, make oneself smart or elegant.
adopción, *f.* adoption.
adopcionismo, *m.* (theol.) adoptionism, adoptionist heresy.
adopcionista, *a., m.* adoptionist.
adoptable, *a.* adoptable.
adoptado, da, *past part. of* **adoptar.** —*a.* adopted.
adoptador, ra, *a.* adopting. —*m., f.* adopter.
adoptante, *a.* adopting. —*m., f.* adopter.
adoptar, *tr.v.* to adopt.
adoptivo, va, *a.* foster, adopted, adoptive, e.g. *un hijo adoptivo,* a foster or adopted child, *un padre adoptivo,* a foster father, *una patria adoptiva,* an adopted country.
adoquín, *m.* paving stone, paving block.
adoquinado, *m.* pavement, paving.
adoquinar, *tr.v.* to pave.

ador, *m.* time to irrigate, to water the land.
adorable, *a.* adorable.
adoración, *f.* 1. worship. 2. adoration, idolatry.
adorado, da, *a.* adored; **mi adorado tormento,** (fig.) my beloved.
adorador, ra, *a.* 1. worshipping. 2. adoring, idolizing. —*m., f.* 1. worshipper. 2. adorer, idolizer.
adorante, *a.* 1. worshipping. 2. adoring, idolizing.
adorar, *tr.v.* 1. to worship. 2. to adore, idolize, love. 3. to prostrate oneself before the Pope (newly elected cardinals). 4. to hold in great esteem; to respect. —*i.v.* to pray, worship.
adoratorio, *m.* 1. temple in which American Indians worshippped their idols. 2. portable altar.
adoratriz, *f.* nun belonging to a religious order which reforms fallen women.
adormecedor, ra, *a.* soporific.
adormecer, (*ref. 45*) *tr.v.* to put to sleep, make drowsy; to lull to sleep; to calm, soothe, quiet. —*r.v.* to fall asleep; to become drowsy; to become numb. — **a. en,** to surrender to, give oneself up to (vices, etc.).
adormecido, da, *past part. of* **adormecer.** —*a.* 1. drowsy, sleepy. 2. numb, gone to sleep (limbs).
adormeciente, *a.* soporiferous.
adormecimiento, *m.* 1. falling asleep, going to sleep. 2. sleepiness, drowsiness, torpor. 3. numbness (of limb).
adormezca, adormezco, *ref.* **adormecer.**
adormidera, *f.* (bot.) opium poppy.
adormilarse, *r.v., var. of* **adormitarse.**
adormir, (*ref. 38*) *tr.v., r.v., var. of* **adormecer.**
adormitarse, *r.v.* to doze, drowse.
adornado, da, *a.* adorned; decorated, ornamented.
adornador, ra, *a.* adorning, beautifying. —*m., f.* adorner, decorator.
adornamiento, *m.* adornment, decoration.
adornante, *a.* adorning, beautifying.
adornar, *tr.v.* 1. to adorn. 2. to grace (with virtues, qualities, etc.). — **a. con,** to adorn with.
adornista, *m.* decorator.
adorno, *m.* 1. ornament, adornment, decoration. 2. grace, accomplishment. 3. (bot.) (*pl.*) balsam, balsamine.
adorote, *m.* (Amer.) wheelbarrow.
adosado, da, *a.* affixed, placed (as on a wall).
adosar, *tr.v.* to stand or place near; **a. a,** to stand against, place against or near to; (her.) to place with the back to.
adoselado, *a.* canopied.
adquiera, adquiero, *ref.* **adquirir.**
adquirente, *a.* acquiring. —*m.* acquirer; buyer, purchaser.
adquirible, *a.* acquirable, obtainable.
adquirido, da, *a.* acquired. — **bienes adquiridos,** acquired wealth.
adquiridor, ra, *a.* acquiring. —*m., f.* acquirer; buyer, purchaser.
adquiriente, *a., var. of* **adquirente.**
adquirir, (*ref. 43*) *tr.v.* to acquire.
adquisición, *f.* acquisition.
adquisidor, ra, *a., m., f., var. of* **adquiridor.**
adquisitivo, va, *a.* 1. (law) acquisitive. 2. buying, e.g. *poder adquisitivo,* buying power (e.g. of a currency).
adra, *f.* 1. turn, go (coll.) 2. section of the population of a town; neighborhood.
adragante, *a.* (pharm.) tragacanth (gum).
adraganto, *m.* (bot.) tragacanth.
adral, *m.* sideboard, side boards or planks (of a cart or wagon).
adrede, *adv.* on purpose, deliberately.
adredemente, *adv., var. of* **adrede.**
adrenalina, *f.* (biochem., pharm.) adrenalin, adrenaline.
adrenérgico, ca, *a.* (med.) adrenergic.
adrenocorticotrópico, ca, *a.* (med.) adrenocorticotropic.
adresógrafo, *m.* Addressograph.
adrián, *m.* 1. bunion. 2. magpie nest.
Adriano, *m.* Adrian; Hadrian, Roman emperor born in Southern Spain.
adriático, ca, *a., m.* Adriatic (sea, coast).
adrice, adricé, *ref.* **adrizar.**
adrizamiento, *m.* (mar.) righting.
adrizar, (*ref. 53*) *tr.v.* (mar.) to right. —*r.v.* (mar.) to right itself, recover an upright position.
adrolla, *f., var. of* **trapaza,** fraud, trick.
adrollero, *m.* cheat, swindler, fraud.
adrubado, da, *a.* deformed.
adscribir, *tr.v.* 1. attach, appoint, assign. 2. to ascribe, attribute.
adscripción, *f.* 1. attachment, assignment. 2. attribution; ascription, inscription.
adscripto, ta, *irr, past part, of* **adscribir.** —*a.* attached, assigned.
adsorbente, *a.* adsorbent.
adsorber, *tr.v.* to adsorb.
adsorción, *f.* (chem.) adsorption.
adstringente, *a., var. of* **astringente.**
adstringir, (*ref. 62*) *tr.v., var. of* **astringir.**
aduana, *f.* customs, custom house; **a. seca,** island custom house; **en la a.,** in bond; **pasar por la a.,** to go through customs; **pasar por todas las aduanas,** to undergo a close examination.
aduanal, *a.* pertaining to the custom house.
aduanar, *tr.v.* to register and pay duty for (goods) at the custom house.
aduanero, ra, *a.* customs. —*m.* customs official; exciseman.
aduar, *m.* Bedouin settlement or encampment; gypsy camp; Indian encampment.
adúcar, *m.* coarse silk made from outer part of cocoon; coarse silk, coarse silk cloth.
aducción, *f.* (zool.) adduction.
aducir, (*ref. 47*) *tr.v.* to adduce, cite (as proof).
aductor, *a.* (physiol.) adducent. —*m.* (anat.) adductor (muscle).
aduendado, da, *a.* ghost-like, elfin-like.
adueñarse, *r.v.* to take possession; **a. de,** to take possession of.
aduerma, aduermo, *ref.* **adormir.**
adufe, *m.* 1. Moorish tambourine. 2. (coll.) foolish person, fool.
adufero, ra, *m., f.* tambourine player.
aduja, *f.* (mar.) coil, fake (of a rope, cable etc.).
adujar, *tr.v.* (mar.) to coil, fake (rope). —*r.v.* (mar.) to curl up (into any space).
aduje, adujera, adujese, *ref.* **aducir.**
adul, *m.* 1. legal advisor to a cadi in Morocco. 2. reliable person, man worthy of one's confidence. 3. notary, clerk.
adula, *f.* 1. common pasture. 2. each of the plots of land watered by the same irrigation ditch. 3. herd of cattle grazing on common pasture. 4. time to irrigate.
adulación, *f.* adulation, flattery.
adulador, ra, *a.* adulating, flattering, adulatory. —*m., f.* flatterer.
adulante, *a.* adulating, flattering, adulatory.
adular, *tr.v.* to adulate, flatter.
adularia, *f.* (min.) adularia.
adulatorio, ria, *a.* adulatory, flattering.
adulce, adulcé, *ref.* **adulzar.**
adulero, *m.* shepherd guarding common herd or flock.
adulete, *a., m., f.* (Amer.) *var. of* **adulón.**
adulo, *m.* (Chile, Guat.) *var. of* **adulación.**
adulón, na, *a.* (coll.) flattering, fawning. —*m., f.* flatterer, fawner, bootlicker, apple polisher, soft-soaper.
adulteración, *f.* adulteration.
adulterado, da, *past part. of* **adulterar.** —*a.* adulterated.
adulterador, ra, *a.* adulterating. —*m., f.* adulterator.
adulterante, *a.* adulterating.
adulterar, *tr.v.* to adulterate. —*i.v.* to commit adultery. —*r.v.* to become adulterated.
adulterinamente, *adv.* adulterously.
adulterino, na, *a.* adulterine; false.
adulterio, *m.* adultery.
adúltero, ra, *a.* adulterous. —*m.* adulterer. —*f.* adulteress.
adulto, ta, *a.* 1. adult, mature. 2. fully grown, adult (plant). 3. highly or fully developed (language). —*m., f.* adult.
adulzamiento, *m.* softening of metal.
adulzar, (*ref. 53*) *tr.v.* 1. to sweeten (foods). 2. to make more ductile, soften (metal).
adulzorar, *tr.v.* to sweeten, to soften. —*r.v.* to become sweet tempered, become sweeter.
adumbración, *f.* (p.) shade, shadow.
adumbrar, *tr.v.* (p.) to shade.
adunar, *tr.v.* to unite, join together; to unify.
adunco, ca, *a.* aduncous, curved, bent, warped.
adundarse, *r.v.* (C. Amer.) *var. of* **atontarse.**
adunia, *adv.* in abundance, abundantly.
adurir, *tr.v.* (arch.) to burn.
adurmiendo, adurmiera, adurmiese, adurmió, *ref.* **adormir.**
adustez, *f.* austerity, severity, grimness, sternness.
adustión, *f.* burning.
adusto, ta, *irr. past part. of* **aducir.** —*a.* 1. austere, grim, severe, stern. 2. (Ven.) inflexible, stubborn.
aduzca, aduzco, *ref.* **aducir.**
adv. *abbrev. of* adverbio, adverb (adv.).
advección, *f.* (meteorol.) advection.
advenedizo, za, *a.* 1. newly arrived; foreign. 2. parvenu, upstart. —*m., f.* 1. immigrant, foreigner, newcomer, outsider. 2. (derog.) parvenu, upstart.
advenga, advengo, *ref.* **advenir.**
advenidero, ra, *a.* future, forthcoming.
advenimiento, *m.* 1. arrival, coming; advent. 2. accession to the throne. — **segundo** a., Second Coming of Christ.
advenir, (*ref. 26*) *i.v.* to come, arrive.
adventicio, cia, *a.* adventitious. —*f.* (anat.) adventitia.
adventismo, *m.* (rel.) Adventism.
adventista, *a., m., f.* Adventist.
adveración, *f.* attestation, confirmation, certification.
adverado, da, *a.* (law) attested, witnessed.
adverar, *tr.v.* to attest, authenticate (a document).
adverbial, *a.* (gram.) adverbial.
adverbialice, adverbialicé, *ref.* **adverbializar.**
adverbializar, (*ref. 53*) *tr.v.* (gram.) to adverbialize, convert into an adverb. —*r.v.* to become an adverb.
adverbialmente, *adv.* (gram.) adverbially.
adverbio, *m.* (gram.) adverb; **a. de lugar,** adverb of place; **a. de tiempo,** adverb of time; **a. de cantidad,** adverb of quantity; **a. de modo,** adverb of manner.
adversamente, *adv.* adversely.
adversario, ria, *m., f.* adversary, opponent.
adversativo, va, *a.* (gram.) adversative.
adversidad, *f.* adversity, misfortune.
adverso, sa, *a.* adverse.
advertencia, *f.* 1. warning, advice. 2. notice. 3. foreword, preface (in a book).
advertidamente, *adv.* knowingly, with forewarning.

advertido, da, *past part. of* **advertir.** *—a.* capable, skillful, clever.
advertimiento, *m.* warning, notice.
advertir, (*ref. 42*) *tr.v.* 1. to observe, notice, note. 2. to draw to (someone's) notice, tell, inform, notify; to warn, advise. *—i.v.* to realize. *—r.v.* to become aware (of), notice.
adviento, *m.* (ecc.) Advent, the four weeks preceding Christmas.
advierta, advierto, *ref.* **advertir.**
advine, *ref.* **advenir.**
adviniendo, adviniera, adviniese, *ref.* advenir.
advocación, *f.* name given to a church, chapel, or altar dedicated to the Virgin or a saint.
adyacencia, *f.* adjacency, contiguity.
adyacente, *a.* adjacent, adjoining, contiguous.
aechadero, *m., var. of* **ahechadero.**
aechador, ra, *a., var. of* **ahechador.**
aechar, *tr.v., var. of* **ahechar.**
aecho, *m., var. of* **ahecho.**
aeda, *m., var. of* **aedo.**
aedo, *m.* bard, singer of epic poetry (in ancient Greece).
aeración, *f.* 1. (med.) aeration, ventilation. 2. (med.) aeration. 3. the action of charging liquid with gas or air.
aerar, *tr.v.* to aerate.
aereador, *m.* aerator. — **a. de rocío,** spray aerator; **a. de boquilla,** nozzle aerator; **a. de escobilla,** brush aerator.
aéreo, a, *a.* 1. air, aerial. 2. (coll.) subtle, volatile. — **agregado aéreo,** air attaché; **correo aéreo,** airmail; **fuerza aérea,** air force; **raíz aérea,** aerial root; **vía aérea,** air route.
aerífero, ra, *a.* aeriferous, conveying air.
aerificación, *f.* aerification, aeration.
aerificar, (*ref. 50*) *tr.v.* to aerify, gasify.
aeriforme, *a.* aeriform.
aeroamortiguador, *m.* air-damper.
aerobacia, *f.* aerobatics.
aerobalística, *f.* aeroballistics.
aeróbico, ca, *a.* aerobic.
aerobio, bia, *a.* aerobic. *—m.* (biol.) aerobe.
aerobiosis, *f.* aerobiosis.
aeroclub *m.* flying club.
aerodinamica, *f.* aerodynamics.
aerodinámico, ca, *a.* aerodynamical, aerodynamic; streamlined.
aerodromo, *m.* airport, aerodrome.
aeroembolismo, *m.* (med.) aeroembolism, air bends, decompression sickness.
aeroenfriador, *m.* air cooler, air cooling unit.
aeroespacial *a.* aerospace.
aerofagia, *f.* (med.) aerophagia, spasmodic air swallowing.
aerofaro, *m.* airway beacon, aerial beacon.
aerofobia, *f.* (med.) aerophobia, morbid fear of air.
aerófobo, ba, *a.* aerophobic, suffering from aerophobia.
aeróforo, ra, *a.* aeriferous, conveying air.
aerofotografía, *f.* aerial photography, aerophotography.
aerofotográfico, ca, *a.* aerophotographical, aerophotographic.
aerofotogrametría, *f.* aerial photogrammetry.
aerofumigación *f.* crop dusting.
aerografía, *f.* aerography.
aerógrafo, *m.* 1. (rad.) aerograph. 2. airbrush.
aerograma, *m.* aerogram; radiogram.
aerolínea, *f.* airline.
aerolítico, ca, *a.* aerolitic.
aerolito, *m.* aerolite, meteoric stone.
aerología, *f.* aerology.
aerológico, ca, *a.* aerological.
aeromancia, *f.* aeromancy; predictions of future events based on the weather.
aeromántico, ca, *a.* aeromantic. *—m., f.* aeromancer, one who predicts the future by interpreting the weather.
aeromarítimo, ma, *a.* aeromarine, air sea.
aeromecánica, *f.* aeromechanics.
aeromedicina, *f.* (med.) aeromedicine.
aerometría. *f.* aerometry.
aerómetro, *m.* aerometer.
aeromodelismo, *m.* construction of model airplanes.
aeromodelista, *m., f.* maker or designer of model airplanes.
aeromodelo, *m.* model airplane.
aeromoza, *f.* air hostess.
aeronato, ta, *a.* born in an airplane in flight.
aeronauta, *m., f.* aeronaut.
aeronáutica, *f.* aeronautics.
aeronáutico, ca, *a.* aeronautical, aeronautic.
aeronaval, *a.* air-sea.
aeronave, *f.* airship.
aeronavegable, *a.* air-worthy.
aeroneurosis, *f.* (med.) aeroneurosis.
aeropiratería, *f.* (Mex.) air piracy; skyjacking.
aeroplano, *m.* aeroplane; **a. propulsor,** pusher airplane.
aeropostal, *a.* air-mail.
aeropuerto, *m.* airport. — **a. aduanero,** customs airport; **a. franco,** customs-free airport.
aerorrefrigerar, *tr.v.* to air-cool; to aircondition.
aeroscopio, aeróscopo, *m.* aeroscope.
aerosfera, *f.* aerosphere.
aerosol, *m.* aerosol, spray can.
aerostación, *f.* ballooning.
aeróstata *m., f.* balloonist.
aerostática, *m.* aerostatics.
aerostático, ca, *a.* aerostatical, aerostatic.
aeróstato, *m.* (aer.) aerostat, dirigible, balloon.
aerotecnia, *f.* science dealing with the use of air in industry.
aerotécnico, ca, *a.* aerotechnical. *—m., f.* aerotechnician.
aeroterapia, *f.* (med.) aerotherapy, aerotherapeutics.
aerotermo, *m.* aerothermal, hot-air furnace.
aerotermodinámica, *f.* (phys.) aerothermodynamics.
aeroterrestre, *a.* (mil.) air-land, air-ground.
aerotransportado, d ı, *a.* airborne.
aerovía, *f.* airway.
aeta, 1. *m., f.* (Phil. I.) member of a mountain tribe. *—a.* pertaining to that tribe.
afabilidad, *f.* affability.
afable, *a.* affable.
afablemente, *adv.* affably.
afabulación, *f.* moral (of a fable); sequence of events constituting a narrative.
áfaca, *f.* (bot.) lathyrus (Lathyrus aphaca).
afacetado, da, *a.* faceted.
afagia, *f.* (med.) aphagia.
afamado, da, *a.* famous, renowned.
afamar, *tr.v.* to make famous. *—r.v.* to become famous.
afamiliado, da, *a.* (Dom. Rep.) related by marriage.
afán, *m.* 1. eagerness, zeal, anxiety, keenness, keen desire. 2. manual work, physical work; exhausting work. 3. (Col.) haste, e.g. *no puedo hablarte, tengo a.,* I can't talk to you, I'm in a hurry.
afanadamente, *adv., var. of* **afanosamente.**
afanado, da, *a.* 1. eager, zealous; hardworking. 2. (Col.) rushed, hurried.
afanador, ra, *a.* hard-working, painstaking; eager, zealous, diligent. *—m., f.* 1. hard worker, drudge. 2. laborer; manual work. 3. (coll.) thief.
afanar, 1. to press, hurry, harry, harass. 2. (coll.) to rob, steal. 3. (C. Amer.) to earn (money). *—i.v.* 1. to work hard or eagerly. 2. to do physical work. *—r.v.* to work hard or eagerly, strive, toil; to take a lot of trouble. — **afanarse por** + *inf.,* to work hard or eagerly to + *inf.,* strive to + *inf.;* **afanarse por nada,** to get upset for no reason.
afaneso, *m.* (min.) arsenite of copper.
afaníptero, ra, *a.* (ento.) aphanipterous. *—m.* (*pl.*) (ento.) Aphaniptera.
afanita, *var. of* **anfibolita.**
afanítico, ca, *a.* (min.) aphanitic.
afanosamente, *adv.* eagerly, zealously, painstakingly.
afanoso, sa, *a.* 1. hardworking; eager, keen. 2. laborious, hard (work).
afarallonado, da, *a.* cliff-like, craggy, rugged.
afarolado, da, *a.* (taur.) pertaining to a pass in the game, where the matador swings the cape above his head. — **un lance a., a swinging pass.**
afarolarse, *r.v.* (Amer.) to get excited, get alarmed, to make a fuss (coll.).
afasia, *f.* (med.) aphasia, loss of speech.
afásico, ca, *a.* aphasic, aphasiac.
afeador, ra, *a.* uglifying, defacing. *—m., f.* defacer (lit., fig.).
afeamiento, *m.* 1. uglifying, defacing, deformation. 2. blemishing (of reputation).
afear, *tr.v.* 1. to make ugly, deform, deface. 2. to speak ill of, to discredit, blemish (someone's reputation).
afeblecerse, (*ref. 45*) *r.v.* to become thin, weak or feeble.
afeblezca, afeblezco, *ref.* **afeblecerse.**
afección, *f.* 1. affection, fondness (for). 2. (med.) affection, disease. 3. affect, impression. 4. (ecc.) right of bestowing a benefice.
afectable, *a.* (coll.) impressionable.
afectación, *f.* affectation.
afectadamente, *adv.* affectedly.
afectado, da, *past part. of* **afectar.** *—a.* 1. affected; artificial. 2. afflicted. 3. affected, concerned.
afectar, *tr.v.* 1. to affect; to have an effect on; to damage, injure. 2. to affect, concern, have to do with. 3. to sadden, afflict, grieve. 4. to affect, feign, assume, put on. 5. to yearn for, desire. 6. (law) to affect, encumber, pledge, mortgage.
afectísimo, ma, *a. super. of* **afecto,** e.g. *su afectísimo servidor,* your obedient servant.
afectividad, *f.* affectivity, emotionality.
afectivo, va, *a.* affective, emotional, e.g. *vida afectiva,* emotional life; sentimental, e.g. *es de gran valor afectivo,* it has great sentimental value.
afecto, ta, *a.* affectionate. — **a. a,** fond of; attached to; assigned to; allocated to; subject to; **a. de,** affected by, suffering from (a disease). *—m.* 1. emotion, feeling. 2. affection, fondness, attachment, love, e.g. *a. a,* affection or fondness for. 3. (med.) affection, disease. 4. (p.) vividness, liveliness (in interpretation of subject).
afectuosamente, *adv.* affectionately.
afectuosidad, *f.* affection.
afectuoso, sa, *a.* 1. affectionate, loving. 2. (p.) expressive, vivid.
afeitada, *f.* shave; shaving.
afeitadamente, *adv.* ornately, handsomely, beautifully.
afeitado, da, *past part. of* **afeitar.** *—a.* 1. shaved. 2. painted, made up. *—m.* (taur.) shaving off (the tips of the bull's horns).
afeitadora, *f.* electric razor, shaver.
afeitar, *tr.v.* 1. to shave; to trim, clip (hedge, tree, horse's tail); (taur.) to shave off (tips of bull's horns). 2. to beautify, embellish, make beautiful.

—*r.v.* 1. to shave, have a shave. 2. to beautify oneself, make up (one's face).
afeite, *m.* 1. embellishment, adornment. 2. cosmetic, make-up.
afelio, *m.* (astron.) aphelion.
afelpado, da, *a.* plushy, nappy; velvet-textured.
afelpar, *tr.v.* 1. to make like or give the appearance of velvet or plush (to material). 2. (mar.) to patch a sail with tar and snips of canvas.
afeminación, *f.* effeminacy; affectation.
afeminadamente, *adv.* effeminately.
afeminado, da, *past part. of* **afeminar.** —*a.* effeminate.
afeminamiento, *m., var. of* **afeminación.**
afeminar, *tr.v.* to make effeminate. —*r.v.* to become effeminate.
aferente, *a.* (biol.) afferent.
aféresis, *f.* (gram.) aphaeresis, omission of one or more letters at the beginning of a word.
aferradamente, *adv.* tenaciously.
aferrado, da, *a.* **a. a,** attached to, fixed to, e.g. *es un hombre a. a su modo de vivir,* he is very attached to his way of life.
aferramiento, *m.* 1. grasping, seizing. 2. clinging (to), insistence (on). 3. (mar.) furling; hooking; mooring.
aferrar, (*ref.* 29) *tr.v.* 1. to grasp, seize. 2. (mar.) to furl; to hook; to anchor, moor. —*i.v.* 1. (mar.) to anchor, moor. 2. to insist. —*r.v.* 1. to grasp one another. 2. to be or become fastened together with grappling irons (ships). 3. to cling, hold. 4. to insist; **aferrarse a,** to cling to, hold on to (life, an opinion, etc.); **aferrarse a que** + *indic.,* to insist or maintain that + *indic.,* e.g. *yo me aferro a que fueron los Vikingos que descubrieron América,* I insist that it was the Vikings who discovered America.
aferruzado, da, *a.* angry, irate.
afervorar, *tr.v., r.v., var. of* **enfervorizar.**
afervorice, afervoricé, *ref.* **afervorizar.**
afervorizar, (*ref.* 53) *tr.v., r.v., var. of* **enfervorizar.**
afestonado, da, *a.* festooned.
affaire, *m.* (Fr.) affaire, affair.
Afganistán, *m.* Afghanistan.
afgano, na, *a., m., f.* Afghan; native of Afghanistan.
afiance, afiancé, *ref.* **afianzar.**
afianzamiento, *m.* 1. fastening, securing. 2. security, guarantee, bail. 3. support, prop; (fig.) backing, support.
afianzar, (*ref.* 53) *tr.v.* 1. to fasten, secure. 2. to fix with supports, prop, support; (fig.) to back up, support, strengthen (regime, etc.). 3. to guarantee, vouch for, stand bail, security or guarantee for. 4. to hold, grasp. —*r.v.* to make oneself secure or fast; to hold on fast; **afianzarse a,** to hold on fast to; **afianzarse en** or **sobre,** to make oneself secure or fast in.
afición, *f.* 1. liking, taste, fondness, enthusiasm, e.g. *tener a. a,* to have a liking or taste for, like, be fond of, be an enthusiast or fan of; *tomar a. a,* to take a liking to; *cobrar a. a,* to become fond of; to get to like. 2. fans, enthusiasts; the expert public. 3. zeal, keenness, eagerness.
aficionado, da, *m., f.* (mus., sport.) 1. fan, enthusiast. 2. amateur; beginner. —*a.* fond of, having a liking for.
aficionador, ra, *a.* inspiring fondness or affection.
aficionar, *tr.v.* to induce a liking for. —*r.v.* **aficionarse a,** to become fond of; to develop a liking for, become enthusiastic about.
afiche, *m.* poster, placard; advertising sign.
afidávit, *m.* (law) affidavit.
áfido, *m.* (ento.) aphid, aphis; (*pl.*) aphides, Aphididae.
afiebrado, da, *past part. of* **afiebrarse.** —*a.* feverish.
afiebrarse, *r.v.* (Amer.) to become feverish.
afielar, *tr.v., var. of* **enfielar.**
afierre, afierro, *ref.* **aferrar.**
afijar, *tr.v.* to affix, fasten, secure.
afijo, *m.* (gram.) affix. —*a.* affixal (said of pronouns suffixed to the verb).
afilacuchillos, *m.* knife sharpener.
afiladera, *f.* whetstone, hone.
afilado, da, *a.* sharp, slender; fine-drawn (face, fingers, nose).
afilador, ra, *a.* sharpening. —*m.* 1. sharpener, man who sharpens (knives, scissors, etc.). 2. razor strop; (Amer.) whetstone, hone. 3. sharpening or grinding machine.
afiladura, *f.* sharpening, whetting, honing, stropping.
afilalápiz, (*pl.* **afilalápices**) *m.* pencil sharpener.
afilamiento, *m.* slenderness, finely-drawn quality (of face, nose or fingers).
afilar, *tr.v.* 1. to sharpen, to whet, grind, strop. 2. (Arg., Urug.) to court, to woo. —*r.v.* to grow thin or pointed (face, beard, nose).
afiliación, *f.* affiliation.
afiliado, da, *a.* affiliated (to group or organization). —*m., f.* a member of a group or an organization.
afiliar, *tr.v.* to affiliate, join. —*r.v.* to join, become affiliated; **afiliarse a,** to join, become affiliated with.
afiligranado, da, *a.* filigreed; fine, delicate.
afiligranar, *tr.v.* 1. to filigree; to adorn or embellish finely.
afillar, *tr.v.* (Sp., reg.) to adopt.
áfilo, la, *a.* (bot.) aphyllous, leafless.
afilón, *m.* razor strop; knife sharpener.
afilorar, *tr.v.* (Cuba, P. Rico) to adorn, embellish.
afilosofado, da, *a.* said of one who pretends to be a deep thinker.
afín, *a.* akin, kindred, allied, connected, related. —*m., f.* related by affinity.
afinación, *f.* 1. tuning (of musical instrument). 2. finishing, refining.
afinadamente, *adv.* 1. in tune. 2. in a refined manner.
afinado, da, *past part. of* **afinar.** —*a.* tuned (said of voice, musical instruments).
afinador, ra, *m.* tuner (of piano, harp, etc.); tuning key. —*a.* tuning; finishing; refining.
afinadura, *f., var. of* **afinación.**
afinamiento, *m.* 1. tuning (of musical instrument). 2. finishing, completion. 3. refining. 4. refinement, polish (of manners).
afinar, *tr.v.* 1. to tune (musical instrument). 2. to perfect, complete, finish, put finishing touches to. 3. to refine (metals). 4. to make (a person) refined or polished. 5. (bkb.) to affix (cover) in correct place; to trim edges of cover. 6. (print.) to finish (stereotype plate). —*i.v.* to sing or play in tune. —*r.v.* to become refined or polished (in manners).
afincado, da, *a.* rooted, settled in; (Arg., Col.) domiciled.
afincadamente, *adv.* obstinately, tenaciously.
afincar, (*ref.* 50) *i.v.* to buy real estate. —*r.v.* 1. to settle down, take up residence. 2. to buy real estate.
afine, *a., var. of* **afín.**
afinidad, *f.* 1. affinity, relationship; similarity. 2. affinity, empathy, kinship by election. 3. (biol., chem., math.) affinity. — **a. de intereses,** similarity of interests; **a. electiva,** elective affinity; **por a.,** by marriage.
afino, *m.* refining (of metals).
afirmación, *f.* affirmation.
afirmadamente, *adv.* firmly, definitely, certainly.
afirmado, da, *past part. of* **afirmar.** —*a.* firm, secure; assured. —*m.* roadbed (upon which asphalt is poured).
afirmador, ra, *a.* affirming. —*m., f.* affirmer.
afirmante, *a.* affirmative. —*m., f.* person who affirms or attests.
afirmar, *tr.v.* 1. to affirm, assert. 2. to strengthen, secure, fasten, make firm or fast. 3. (Chile, Mex.) to give, deal (blows). —*r.v.* 1. to make oneself secure or steady, sit fast, stand fast, hold fast. 2. to stand firmly (by one's opinions). 3. (fenc.) to thrust firmly, attack boldly.
afirmativa, *f.* 1. word or phrase denoting assent. 2. an affirmative statement or proposition.
afirmativamente, *adv.* in the affirmative.
afirmativo, va, *a.* affirmative.
afirolar, *tr.v.* (Cuba) to adorn, embellish.
afistular, *tr.v.* (med.) to make fistulous. —*r.v.* to become fistulous.
aflacar, *tr.v.* (sl.) *var. of* **enflaquecer.**
aflamencado, da, *a.* (Sp., coll.) said of a person who adopts an Andalusian accent or Spanish gypsy manners and idioms.
aflatarse, *r.v.* (Hond., Nic.) to be sad, grieve, lose heart.
aflato, *m.* 1. breeze, wind. 2. afflatus, inspiration, creative impulse.
aflautado, da, *a.* high-pitched; pitched high and sharp like a flute.
aflechado, da, *a.* shaped like an arrow.
aflicción, *f.* affliction; misery, distress.
aflictivo, va, *a.* saddening, distressing, afflictive.
aflicto, ta, *irr. past part. of* **afligir.**
afligente, *a.* afflicting.
afligidamente, *adv.* in deep affliction, sorrowfully, sadly.
afligido, da, *past part. of* **afligir.** —*a.* sorrowful, grieved, distressed; upset.
afligimiento, *m., var. of* **aflicción.**
afligir, (*ref.* 62) *tr.v.* to afflict, distress, sadden. —*r.v.* to grieve, be grieved, be upset, be distressed; **afligirse con** or **por,** to be grieved or distressed by.
aflija, aflijo, *ref.* **afligir.**
aflijón, na, *a.* (Chile, coll.) always distressed or grieving, gloomy.
aflogístico, ca, *a.* aphlogistic, burning without producing flames.
aflojamiento, *m.* slackening, relaxing; lessening, diminution.
aflojar, *tr.v.* 1. to loosen, slacken. 2. (coll., Amer.) to let go, to pay, cough up, pay up (sl.). —*i.v.* to slacken, become slack (in one's studies, etc.); (coll.) to diminish (heat). —*r.v.* to become loose or slack; to weaken.
aflorado, da, *a.* 1. of the finest flour. 2. excellent, fine, first class. 3. (geol.) outcropping.
afloramiento, *m.* (geol.) outcropping, outcrop; rock exposure.
aflorar, *i.v.* (geol.) to outcrop. —*tr.v.* to sift, cribble.
afluencia, *f.* 1. abundance, affluence; crowd, throng. 2. eloquence, volubility, loquacity. 3. flowing. — **hora de mayor** or **máxima a.,** rush hour.
afluente, *a.* 1. flowing, affluent, copious, abundant. 2. voluble, loquacious. —*m.* tributary, affluent.
afluentemente, *adv.* abundantly, affluently, copiously.
afluir, (*ref.* 48) *i.v.* 1. to flow. 2. to congregate, to appear in great numbers. 3. to flow into (a river, etc.).

aflujo, *m.* (med.) afflux, affluxion.
aflús, *a.* (Arg., Bol., Mex., coll.) penniless, broke (sl.).
afluxionarse, *r.v.* 1. (Col., Cuba) to catch cold. 2. (C. Amer.) to get swollen, swell up.
afluya, *ref.* **afluir.**
afluyendo, afluyera, afluyese, *ref.* **afluir.**
afluyo, *ref.* **afluir.**
afmo. *abbrev. of* **afectísimo,** sincerely or very truly (yours).
afofarse, *r.v.* to become soft, spongy or flabby.
afogarar, *tr.v.* to burn, overcook. —*r.v.* to burn, become burned (food).
afollado, *m.* 1. puckered, pleated (clothes). 2. ballooned, baggy (trousers). 3. collapsible (carriage hood, etc.).
afollador, *m.* (Mex.) bellows operator, worker who operates the bellows.
afollar, (*ref. 33*) *tr.v.* 1. to blow (with bellows). 2. to pleat, fold, pucker. 3. (mas.) to botch. —*r.v.* (mas.) to become blistered or full of bubbles (walls).
afondar, *tr.v., i.v., r.v.* to sink, submerge; to hit bottom (lit., fig.).
afonía, *f.* (med.) aphonia, loss of voice.
afónico, ca, *a.* aphonic, voiceless. — **estar a.,** to have lost one's voice; **volverse a.,** to lose one's voice.
áfono, na, *a.* aphonic, voiceless.
aforado, *past part. of* **aforar.** —*a.* privilege, possessing a privilege. —*m., f.* possessor of a privilege or exemption.
aforador, *m.* estimator, assessor, appraiser; gauger.
aforamiento, *m.* valuing, appraising; gauging, measuring; granting of privileges.
aforar, (*ref. 33*) *tr.v.* 1. to value, appraise, estimate the value of; to measure, gauge. 2. to accord or grant privileges. 3. (coll.) to issue invoices. 4. (theat.) to conceal the sides of the stage from the audience.
aforisma, *f.* (vet.) **aneurysm.**
aforismo, *m.* aphorism, adage.
aforístico, ca, *a.* aphoristic.
aforo, *m.* 1. appraisal, estimation (of value). 2. gauging, measurement. 3. seating capacity (of a theater or auditorium).
aforrador, ra, *a.* lining. —*m., f.* liner, person who lines (clothing, pipes, casing, upholstery, etc.).
aforrar, *tr.v.* 1. to line (an inner surface); to cover (books, furniture, etc.). 2. (mar.) to serve (a cable). —*r.v.* 1. to put on heavy underclothing. 2. to eat and drink well.
aforro, *m.* lining; (mar.) serving, sheathing.
afortunadamente, *adv.* fortunately, luckily.
afortunado, da, *a.* 1. fortunate, lucky; happy. 2. (mar.) stormy. — **un barco a.,** at the mercy of the winds (a ship).
afortunar, *tr.v.* to make (someone) happy.
afosarse, *r.v.* (mil.) to entrench oneself, dig in.
afoscarse, (*ref. 50*) *r.v.* (mar.) to become hazy or misty.
afótico, ca, *a.* aphotic, without light.
afrailado, da, *past part. of* **afrailar.** —*a.* (print.) with blank patches.
afrailamiento, *m.* trimming, pruning (of a tree).
afrailar, *tr.v.* (agr.) to trim, prune (trees, shrubs).
afrancesado, da, *a.* 1. fond of French styles and customs. 2. affecting French manners or customs. —*m., f.* one who affects or adopts French manners, style or customs; a person who supports French policies.
afrancesamiento, *m.* the process of becoming French-like in customs or manners.
afrancesar, *tr.v.* to make French-like, Gallicize. —*r.v.* to become French-like or Gallicized.
afranelado, da, *a.* flannel-like, textured like flannel.
afranjado, da, *a.* striped; bordered (clothing, cloth, flag, coat-of-arms).
afrecharse, *r.v.* (Chile) to get sick from overeating of bran (animals).
afrecho, *m.* bran.
afrenillar, *tr.v.* (mar.) to lash; to bridle (the oars).
afrenta, *f.* 1. affront, insult. 2. disgrace, dishonor; shame.
afrentador, ra, *a.* insulting, offending. —*m., f.* offender.
afrentar, *tr.v.* to affront, insult; to humiliate. —*r.v.* to be ashamed; to blush; **afrentarse de,** to be ashamed of.
afrentosamente, *adv.* insultingly.
afrentoso, sa, *a.* insulting, offending.
afretado, da, *past part. of* **afretar.** —*a.* 1. like a border or fringe, fringed. 2. (mar.) scrubbed, cleaned.
afretar, *tr.v.* (mar.) to scrub, clean.
africado, da, *a.* (phonet.) affricative. —*f.* affricate.
africanice, *ref.* **africanizar.**
africanismo, *m.* 1. Africanism, African word or expression. 2. African influence.
africanista, *m., f.* Africanist, student of African culture.
africanizar, (*ref. 53*) *tr.v.* to Africanize. —*r.v.* to become Africanized.
africano, na, *a., f., m.* African. —*m.* (Hond.) a kind of dessert.
áfrico, *m.* South wind.
afrikaans *m.* Afrikaans
afrikaner *a., m., f.* Afrikaner.
afrisonado, da, *a.* hairy and large (said of horses).
afro, *a., m.* African. —*m.* the natural hair style of the Black people.
afroamericano, na, *a.* (U.S.) Afro-American.
afrocubano, na, *a.* Afro-Cuban.
afrodisíaco, ca, *a., m.* aphrodisiac.
Afrodita, *f.* (myth.) Aphrodite, Greek goddess of love and beauty.
afronitro, *m.* saltpeter.
afrontado, da, *past part. of* **afrontar.** —*a.* (her.) face to face, facing (animals in an escutcheon, etc.).
afrontamiento, *m.* facing, confronting, confrontation.
afrontar, *tr.v.* to face, confront, defy (danger, risk, etc.); to bring or put face to face, confront (people). —*i.v.* to face.
afrontilar, *tr.v.* (Mex.) to tie (cattle) by the horns to a post (in order to subdue or slaughter the animal).
afta, *f.* (med.) aphtha; fever blister, cold sore.
aftoso, sa, *a.* (med.) aphthous.
afuelle, afuello, *ref.* **afollar.**
afuera, *adv.* outside; out. — **¡a.!** get out. — (fort.) glacis, embankment surrounding a fortress.
afueras, *f., pl.* outskirts, suburbs.
afuera, afuero, *ref.* **aforar.**
afueteadura, *f.* (Car., Peru) whipping.
afuetear, *tr.v.* (Car., Peru) to whip.
afufa, *f.* (coll.) flight; **estar sobre las afufas,** to be about to flee; **tomar las afufas,** to run away, flee.
afufar, *i.v., r.v.* (coll.) to escape, flee.
afufón, *m.* (coll.) *var. of* **afufa.**
afumarse, *r.v.* (Col., coll.) to get drunk; to get stoned (sl.).
afusilar, *tr.v.* (vulg.) *var. of* **fusilar.**
afusión, *f.* (med.) **affusion.**
afuste, *m.* (mil.) gun carriage, gun mounting.
afutrarse, *r.v.* (Chile) to dress up, dress elegantly.
Ag *sym. of* **argento,** argentum (Ag) silver.
agá, *m.* aga, agha, officer in the Turkish Army.
agabachar, *tr.v.* (Sp.) to cause to adopt French customs. —*r.v.* to adopt French customs.
agacé, *a.* of or belonging to an Indian tribe at the mouth of the Paraguay river.
agachada, *f.* 1. (coll.) trick, stratagem. 2. stooping, crouching; ducking.
agachadera, *f.* (Chile, ornith.) a kind of lark.
agachadiza, *f.* (ornith.) snipe. — **hacer la a.,** (coll.) to duck, duck out of view.
agachaparse, *r.v., var. of* **agazaparse.**
agachar, *tr.v.* to lower, bend (the head or body). —*r.v.* 1. to crouch, squat; to stoop, duck; to cower. 2. (coll.) to bear abuse for the sake of future advantage. 3. to withdraw from society or go into seclusion for a short time.
agachón, *m.* (Mex., sl.) coward.
agalbanado, da, *a.* lazy, idle; indolent.
agalerar, *tr.v.* (mar.) to tip (a canvas or awning) so that rain can run off.
agalla, *f.* 1. (bot.) gall, nutgall, gallnut. 2. (ichth.) gill; (ornith.) side of head, temple. 3. (*pl.*) tonsils. 4. (*pl.*) angina. 5. (coll.) (*pl.*) guts, courage, bravery. 6. (vet.) windgall, incipient blister. 7. (*pl.*) boring rod thread. 8. (Amer.) greed, desire. 9. (Ecuad.) hooked stick for reaching. — **tener muchas agallas,** to have guts or courage; (Amer.) to be shameless, to have the nerve or gall to + *inf.*
agallado, da, *a.* galled, steeped in an infusion of gallnuts. —*m.* decoction of gallnuts (used in dying processes).
agalladura, *f., var. of* **galladura.**
agallegado, da, *a.* (Amer.) said of a person who although born in Latin America speaks Spanish like a Spaniard.
agallón, *m.* 1. large gallnut. 2. large silver bead; large (wooden) rosary bead. 3. (archit.) echinus, molding.
agallonado, da, *a.* (archit.) decorated with moldings.
agalludo, da, *a.* 1. (Amer.) greedy, grasping. 2. astute, dishonest, unscrupulous. 3. (Arg., Chile) bold, daring.
agáloco, *m.* (bot.) agalloch, agalwood, aloe (wood).
agalmatolita, *f.* agalmatolite, Chinese soapstone.
agama, *f.* (Cuba) kind of crab.
Agamenón, *m.* (myth.) Agamemnon, leader of the Greek heroes in the Trojan Wars.
agamí, (*pl.* **agamíes**) *m.* (ornith.) trumpeter, South American aquatic bird.
agamitar, *i.v.* (hunt.) to imitate the call of the fawn.
ágamo, ma, *a.* (bot.) agamic, agamous.
agamogénesis, *f.* (biol.) agamogenesis, asexual reproduction.
agamogenético, ca, *a.* (biol.) agamogenetic, agamic, agamous.
agamuzado, da, *a., var. of* **gamuzado.**
agangrenarse, *r.v., var. of* **gangrenarse.**
Aganipe, *f.* (myth.) Agannipe, sacred fountain of the Greek muses.
agañotar, *tr.v.* to choke, strangle.
agapanto, *m.* (bot.) agapanthus, African lily.
ágape, *m.* agape, a love feast (fig.) banquet, party.
agarabatado, da, *a.* 1. hooked, hook-shaped. 2. scribbled, scrawled.
agarbado, da, *a., var. of* **garboso.**
agarbanzado, *a.* buff-colored, chick-pea colored.
agarbar, *r.v.* to stoop, crouch.
agarbillar, *tr.v.* (agr.) to sheave, bind into sheaves.
agareno, na, *a.* descended from Agar, Moslem, Mohammedan. —*f.* (Sp.) a compliment to a good-looking woman (among the gypsies).
agárico, *m.* (bot.) agaric.

agarrada, *f.* (coll.) dispute, quarrel; fight, scrap.

agarradera, *f.* 1. (Amer.) handle, holder. 2. handgrip, strap. 3. pot holder. 4. oven glove. 5. (coll.) influence, pull. 6. (mar.) anchorage. — **a. de cable, cable clip.**

agarrado, da, *past part. of* **agarrar.** —*a.* 1. (coll.) tight-fisted, close-fisted, tight, miserly, stingy. 2. cheek-to-cheek, said of a dance in which the partners are tightly embraced.

agarrador, ra, *a.* 1. grasping, seizing. 2. (Chile, Ecuad., Peru) heady, intoxicating, strong (liquor). —*m.* 1. potholder, flatiron holder. 2. (coll.) policeman, constable, cop, catch-pole, bailiff.

agarrafador, ra, *a.* gripping, seizing. —*m.* 1. worker who handles baskets containing crushed olives ready for pressing. 2. bottler, person who bottles wine or oil in large glass containers.

agarrafar, *tr.v.* to grab or seize hard. —*r.v.* to seize one another (violently).

agarrama, *f., var. of* **garrama.**

agarrante, *a.* 1. gripping, grasping. 2. (coll.) miserly, stingy.

agarrar, *tr.v.* 1. to grasp, seize, grab, catch hold of; to take. 2. to capture, catch. 3. (coll.) to get, catch (a cold). 4. to catch unawares, surprise (doing something). 5. to seize, catch (someone or an illness). 6. (coll.) to get, obtain. — **a. de,** to seize by, take by, e.g. *le agarré de la mano,* I seized or took him by the hand. —*i.v* to stick (paint); to take, take root (plant). —*r.v.* 1. to hold on, get hold. 2. to come to blows with, come to grips with, grapple with one another, e.g. *agarrarse a golpes,* to come to blows. — **agarrarse de,** hold onto, get or grab hold of; (coll.) **agarrársela con uno,** (coll.) to pick on someone.

agarre, *m.* (Amer., coll.) influence, pull.

agarro, *m.* (coll.) grasp, grasping.

agarrochador, *m.* (taur.) goader; the picador who pricks the bull.

agarrochar, *tr.v.* 1. (taur.) to goad, prick (the bull with a lance). 2. (mar.) to tighten (the sailyard line).

agarrón, *m.* 1. (Amer.) grab, grasp; jerk. 2. quarrel, dispute; scrap, fight.

agarrotado, da, *past part. of* **agarrotar.** —*a.* 1. stiff. 2. (mec.) seized up, stuck due to lack of grease (said of machine parts).

agarrotamiento, *m.* 1. garrotting, execution by garrote. 2. (mec.) seizing up, sticking of machine parts (due to lack of grease).

agarrotar, *tr.v.* 1. to execute by garrote. 2. to tie or bind. 3. to press; to choke. —*r.v.* 1. to stiffen, get stiff or become rigid; e.g. *las manos se me han agarrotado del frío,* my hands have become stiff from the cold. 2. (mec.) to stick due to lack of grease (machine parts); to seize-up.

agasajador, ra, *a.* entertaining, e.g. *el comité a.,* the entertainment committee. —*m., f.* host, entertainer.

agasajar, *tr.v.* to give a banquet or dinner for, lionize, entertain splendidly; to treat attentively, regale or shower with gifts or attentions.

agasajo, *m.* 1. reception, dinner, banquet; invitation; token or mark of esteem; kindness.

ágata, *f.* (min.) agate; **á. musgosa,** (min.) moss agate.

agauchado, da, *a.* gaucho-like, person who has adopted gaucho customs.

agaucharse, *r.v.* to adopt the customs of the gauchos.

agavanzo, *m.* (bot.) dog rose.

agave, *f.* (bot.) agave, century plant.

agavillador, *m., f.* sheaver, binder, one who sheaves. —*f.* combine, harvester.

agavillar, *tr.v.* 1. to sheave, tie or bind into sheaves. 2. to band together, form into a band or gang. —*r.v.* to band together.

agazapar, *tr.v.* (coll.) to catch, seize. —*r.v.* (coll.) to stoop, crouch; to stalk, ambush.

agencia, *f.* 1. agency. 2. diligence, activity. 3. (Chile) pawnshop. — **a. de cobro,** collection agency (for delinquent payments); **a. de colocaciones** or **empleos,** employment agency; **a. de contactos,** dating service; **a. de prensa** or **noticias,** news service; **a. de publicidad,** advertising agency; **a. de viajes,** travel agency; **a. de funeraria,** funeral parlor; **a. inmobiliaria,** real estate agency; **a. publicitaria,** advertising agency.

agenciar, *tr.v.* to get, obtain; to negotiate. —*i.v.* to procure through industry or astuteness. —*r.v.* to obtain for oneself; e.g. *me las agencié para corseguir estos boletos,* I connived to get these tickets.

agenciero, *m.* (Chile) pawnbroker; (Cuba) mover, trucker; (Arg., Urug.) bookie, lottery vendor.

agencioso, sa, *a.* diligent.

agenda, *f.* agenda; notebook, memorandum, memo book, pocket diary (for appointments, etc.). — **a. cultural,** entertainment guide; **a. de bolsillo,** pocket diary; **a. de despacio,** memo pad (for a desk); **a. de trabajo,** engagement book.

agenesia, *f.* (med.) agenesis; (anat.) developmental defect.

agente, *m.* agent; factor; (chem.) agent. — **a. de aduana,** customhouse broker; **a. de bolsa, a. de cambio, a. de cambio y bolsa,** stockbroker; **a. de policía,** policeman; **a. de propiedad inmobiliaria,** real estate agent, realtor; **a. de seguros,** insurance agent; **a. de trafico,** traffic policeman; **a. de viajes,** travel agent; **a. inmobiliario,** real estate agent, realtor; **a. literario,** literary agent; **a. provocador,** agent provocateur; **a. secreto,** secret agent; **a. viajero,** traveling salesman.

agerasia, *f.* (med.) agerasia, old age free from ailments.

agérato, *m.* (bot.) ageratum.

agermanarse, *r.v.* 1. (arch.) to join a guild. 2. to cohabitate with a person of the opposite sex.

agestado, da, *a.* **bien a.,** with a pleasant look; **mal a.,** with an unpleasant look or mien.

agestarse, *r.v.* to make a face, grimace; to gesture.

agestión, *f.* accumulation; sediment, deposit.

agibílibus, *m.* (coll.) resourcefulness, enterprise, cleverness; (coll.) resourceful or ingenious person.

agible, *a.* feasible, practicable.

agigantado, da, *a.* gigantic; extraordinary.

agigantar, *tr.v.* to make enormous; to exaggerate, to blow out of proportion. —*r.v.* to become enormous.

agigotar, *tr.v.* to chop; to mince.

ágil, *a.* agile, nimble; quick.

agilidad, *f.* agility, nimbleness; quickness; speed.

agilitar, *tr.v.* 1. to make agile, nimble or quick. 2. to empower, enable; to facilitate. 3. to speed up. —*r.v.* to become agile, nimble or quick.

agilizar, (*ref. 53*) *tr.v., var. of* **agilitar.**

ágilmente, *adv.* agilely, nimbly; quickly.

agio, *m.* agio, premium paid on converting from one currency to another; speculation; stockjobbing; usury.

agiotador, *m., var. of* **agiotista.**

agiotaje, *m., var. of* **agio.**

agiotista, *m.* speculator, stockjobber; moneychanger.

agitable, *a.* agitable, shakable; excitable.

agitación, *f.* 1. agitation, disturbance. 2. waving; shaking. 3. roughness (of sea).

agitado, da, *past part. of* **agitar.** —*a.* agitated, shaken.

agitador, ra, *a.* agitating; stirring. —*m., f.* agitator. —*m.* (chem.) stirring rod, stirrer.

agitanado, da, *a.* 1. gypsy-like; having adopted gypsy manners of speech and behavior. 2. (Sp.) of a rich olive-hued complexion (complimentary); swarthy.

agitante, *a.* agitating.

agitar, *tr.v.* 1. to shake, to wave; to stir. 2. to agitate, excite, rouse (a crowd); to disturb, disquiet (the mind). —*r.v.* 1. to wave; to shake. 2. to become agitated or excited. 3. to get rough (sea).

aglomeración, *f.* agglomeration; crowd, multitude. — **aglomeraciones,** traffic tie-ups; **aglomeraciones urbanas,** built-up urban areas.

aglomerado, da, *past part. of* **aglomerar.** —*a.* crowded, full. —*m.* 1. coal brick, briquette. 2. (geol.) agglomerate.

aglomerante, *m.* binder, agglutinant, binding material.

aglomerar, *tr.v., r.v.* to agglomerate, gather; to mix.

aglutinación, *f.* agglutination; adhesion.

aglutinado, da, *a.* agglutinate; joined or pasted together.

aglutinante, *a.* agglutinant, agglutinative; adhesive.

aglutinar, *tr.v.;* to bring together, unite. —*r.v.* to agglutinate, to cake.

aglutinina, *f.* (biochem.) agglutinin.

agnación, *f.* (law) agnation; kinship through the male or father's side.

agnado, da, *a., m., f.* agnate, related through the male or father's side; akin.

agnaticio, cia, *a.* agnatic, related through the male or father's side.

agnición, *f.* (poet.) recognition of someone in a dramatic work.

agnocasto, *m.* (bot.) chaste tree, hemp tree, monk's pepper tree.

agnomento, *m., var. of* **cognomento.**

agnominación, *f.* (rhet.) paronomasia.

agnosia, *f.* (med.) agnosia.

agnosticismo, *m.* (philos.) agnosticism.

agnóstico, ca, *a., m., f.* agnostic.

agnus, *m., var. of* **agnusdéi.**

agnusdéi, *m.* (rel.) 1. Agnus Dei (Lamb of God), a representation of the Lamb. 2. an invocation said thrice in the Roman Catholic mass.

agobiado, da, *past part. of* **agobiar.** —*a.* 1. stooping. 2. (coll.) tired, worn out. 3. (coll.) overwhelmed, confused, at a loss. 4. humiliated, vanquished.

agobiador, ra, *a.* overwhelming, oppressive; (coll.) tiring, exhausting.

agobiante, *a.* overwhelming; oppressive; (coll.) stifling (heat).

agobiar, *tr.v.* 1. to overwhelm, oppress (with work, cares, etc.); to depress, dispirit; to exhaust, fatigue completely. 2. to weigh down; to bend, double; to humiliate. —*r.v.* to stoop, bend, be weighed down; be exhausted.

agobio, *m.* oppression, exhaustion, depression; burden.

agogia, *f.* (min.) drain.

agolar, *tr.v.* (mar.) to furl (the sails).

agolpamiento, *m.* crowding together; pile-up, heap; piling up.

agolpar, *tr.v., r.v.* to crowd together; to heap up, pile up, to rush.

agolletar, *t.v.* to place or wrap something around the neck of a bottle.

agonal, *a.* agonistic; competitive, combative. —*m.* (*pl.*) agonia (Roman festivals).

agonía, *f.* 1. agony, torment, extreme pain. 2. agony, death throes; end.

agonice, agonicé, *ref.* **agonizar.**

agónico, ca, *a.* 1. death, e.g. *estertor agónico,* death rattle. 2. agonizing, in agony. —*f.* (phys.) agonic line.
agonioso, sa, *a.* (coll.) insistent, pestering, pressing, anxious.
agonista, *m., f.* wrestler.
agonística, *f.* agonistics.
agonístico, ca, *a.* agonistic; competitive, combative.
agonizante, *a.* 1. agonizing. 2. dying, moribund. —*m.* 1. monk who ministers to those about to die. 2. counselor who helps students in their work (in some universities), tutor.
agonizar, (*ref. 53*) *tr.v.* 1. (coll.) to plague, annoy, pester, harass. 2. to attend, minister to (the dying). —*i.v.* 1. to be in agony. 2. to be dying, be in the throes of death. 3. to yearn, long, die. 4. to be about to go out or be extinguished (light); to be on its last legs; to be about to finish or end; **a. por** + *inf.*, to be dying for or longing to + *inf.*
ágono, na, *a.* (geom.) agonic, having no angles.
ágora, *f.* agora, market or public square in ancient Greece; meeting place, assembly point.
agora, *adv.* (sl.) *var. of* **ahora.**
agorafobia, *f.* agoraphobia, fear of open spaces.
agorar, (*ref. 35*) *tr.v.* to predict, prophesy, foretell, prognosticate.
agorero, ra, *a.* 1. presaging, oracular. 2. ill-omened, ominous. 3. superstitious. —*m., f.* 1. augur, presager, oracle, prognosticator; fortune teller. 2. presager or foreteller of doom.
agorgojarse, *r.v.* (agr.) to become infested with weevils (grain), wormed.
agorronar, *tr.v.* to rub (a newborn motherless lamb or foal) with the blood or placenta from another sheep or mare so that she will adopt it as her own.
agostadero, *m.* (agr.) summer pasture; summer-pasture time; pasturing.
agostado, da, *a.* dried up, parched, withered.
agostador, *m.* (agr.) laborer who plants vines.
agostamiento, *m.* 1. parching, drying-up. 2. summer plowing. 3. summer grazing.
agostar, *tr.v.* 1. to plow in August. 2. to parch, wither, dry up. —*r.v.* to become parched or dried up, to dry up. —*i.v.* to graze or pasture on stubble in August.
agosteño, ña, *a.* pertaining to the month of August.
agostero, *a.* pasturing in stubble fields. —*m.* 1. (agr.) harvest helper. 2. religious mendicant who gathers grain donations in August.
agostía, *f.* summer employment.
agostino, na, *a.* (pertaining to) August.
agostizo, za, *a.* 1. pertaining to the month of August. 2. weak, sickly. 3. born or foaled in August.
agosto, *m.* August; harvest; harvest time. — **hacer uno su a.,** to make hay while the sun shines, make a profit.
agotable, *a.* exhaustible.
agotado, da, *past part. of* **agotar.** —*a.* 1. sold-out (tickets, merchandise, etc.). 2. (Amer.) dead (battery, motor, etc.); exhausted, drained.
agotador, ra, *a.* exhausting, tiring, draining.
agotamiento, *m.* extreme fatigue, exhaustion.
agotante, *a.* exhausting, tiring, fatiguing, draining.
agotar, *tr.v.* 1. to exhaust, wear out, tire completely. 2. to use up, consume completely. —*r.v.* 1. to become exhausted or worn out. 2. to be used up, be consumed completely, give out, run out (supplies, etc.); to be selling out, be sold out (theater tickets, merchandise, edition of book, etc.).
agovía, *f., var. of* **alborga.**

agozcado, da, *a.* snapping, yapping (dog).
agracejina, *f.* (bot.) barberry (fruit).
agracejo, *m.* 1. (bot.) barberry. 2. (Cuba) terebinth tree.
agraceño, ña, *a.* sour, tart, sharp; verjuice-like.
agracera, *f.* verjuice container, container for the juice of unripe grapes.
agracero, ra, *a.* grapevine bearing unripening fruit.
agraciadamente, *adv.* graciously, charmingly; gracefully.
agraciado, da, *a.* 1. graceful, gracious, charming. 2. pretty, good-looking, attractive. 3. lucky, e.g. *el número agraciado,* the lucky number (in a lottery). —*m., f.* winner (in a lottery, raffle, etc.).
agraciar, *tr.v.* 1. to grace, adorn, embellish, add charm to. 2. to favor (with). 3. to reward, honor; to award. 4. to pardon (a criminal).
agracillo, *m.* (bot.) barberry (bush).
agradabilísimo, ma, *a. super.* of **agradable,** most agreeable or pleasant; most charming.
agradable, *a.* agreeable, pleasant, pleasing; charming.
agradablemente, *adv.* agreeably, pleasantly; charmingly.
agradador, ra, *a.* eager to please, pleasing.
agradamiento, *m., var. of* **agrado.**
agradar, *i.v.* to be pleasing, please.
agradecer, (*ref. 45*) *tr.v.* to thank, thank for, e.g. *le agradecí su ayuda,* I thanked him for his help; to be thankful for, e.g. *agradezco cualquier ayuda,* I am thankful for any help.
agradecidamente, *adv.* gratefully, thankfully.
agradecido, da, *a.* grateful, thankful.
agradecimiento, *m.* gratitude, gratefulness, thanks, thankfulness.
agradezco, agradezca, *ref.* **agradecer.**
agrado, *m.* 1. charm, affability. 2. liking, pleasure. — **de su a.,** to one's liking.
agrafia, *f.* (med.) agraphia.
agramadera, *f.* (agr.) hemp or flax scutcher; scutch, brake.
agramado, *m.* (agr.) scutching, braking.
agramador, ra, (agr.) *a.* scutching. —*m.* scutcher (person); scutcher, scutch (machine).
agramar, *tr.v.* (agr.) 1. to brake, scutch (flax or hemp). 2. to beat, flog.
agramilar, *tr.v.* (mas.) 1. to trim or shape (bricks), to make (bricks) equal (in size). 2. to paint (a wall) imitating bricks.
agramiladora, *f.* trimming machine.
agramiza, *f.* stalk of hemp (left after scutching).
agrandamiento, *m.* 1. enlarging, enlargement, increase. 2. (Amer.) aggrandizement.
agrandar, *tr.v.* to enlarge, make larger. —*r.v.* 1. to increase, to grow larger. 2. (Amer.) to face up to a challenge or to a dangerous situation, usually with success.
agranujado, da, *a.* 1. roguish, scoundrelly. 2. granular, grain-shaped; filled with grain.
agranulocito, *m.* (biol.) agranulocyte.
agranulocitosis, *f.* (med.) agranulocytosis.
agrario, ria, *a.* agrarian. —*m., f.* agrarian. **reforma a.,** agrarian reform.
agrarismo, *m.* agrarianism.
agravación, *f.* aggravation, worsening.
agravador, ra, *a.* aggravating, worsening.
agravamiento, *m.* aggravation, worsening.
agravante, *a.* aggravating. — **circunstancias agravantes,** aggravating circumstances.
agravantemente, *adv.* aggravatingly.
agravar, *tr.v.* 1. to aggravate, make worse. 2. to increase, make heavier (taxes, etc.). 3. to oppress. 4. to exaggerate. 5. to weigh down, make heavier. —*r.v.* to get worse, aggravate (illness, etc.).

agravatorio, ria, *a.* aggravating; (law) mandatory, compulsory, demanding compliance with an issued order.
agraviadamente, *adv.* offensively.
agraviado, da, *past part. of* **agraviar.** —*a.* injured, wronged, humiliated, offended.
agraviador, ra, *a.* wronging, injuring, damaging; offensive. —*m., f.* offender, injurer.
agraviamiento, *m.* offense; injury, wrong.
agraviante, *a., var. of* **agraviador.**
agraviar, *tr.v.* 1. to wrong; to injure, damage; to offend, insult, affront. 2. to overtax, oppress. —*r.v.* 1. to get worse (an illness). 2. to take offense, become offended.
agravio, *m.* wrong; insult, affront, offense; harm, injury; (law) damage, injury. — **en a. de,** harmful to, injurious to.
agravioso, sa, *a.* offensive, insulting; injurious.
agraz, *m.* 1. verjuice, sour grape juice; sour or unripe grape; verjuice drink. 2. alpine currant. 3. (fig.) annoyance, displeasure. — **echar (a uno) el agraz en el ojo,** to say something unpleasant (to someone); **en agraz,** prematurely, unseasonably.
agrazada, *f.* verjuice drink.
agrazar, (*ref. 53*) *i.v.* to taste sour. —*tr.v.* to vex, annoy.
agrazón, *m.* 1. wild grape; grape or bunch of grapes that never ripen. 2. wild gooseberry bush. 3. (fig.) annoyance, displeasure, disgust.
agrecillo, *m., var. of* **agracillo.**
agredido, da, *past part. of* **agredir.** —*a.* assaulted; injured, wounded.
agredir, (*ref. 78*) *tr.v.* to assault, attack.
agregable, *a.* addable; attachable.
agregación, *f.* 1. addition. 2. attachment.
agregado, da, *past part. of* **agregar.** —*a.* (bot.) aggregate. —*m.* 1. aggregate (collection; total); (math.) aggregate, total. 2. (bldg.) aggregate (hard material used in concrete); (geol.) aggregate, aggregate rock. 3. (Arg., Par., Urug., coll.) freeloader. 4. attaché. — **a. aéreo, comercial, diplomático, militar** or **naval,** air, commercial, diplomatic, military or naval attaché; **a. escalonado** or **graduado,** (bldg.) graded aggregate; **a. grueso,** coarse aggregate; **a. bituminoso,** bituminous aggregate.
agregaduría, *f.* adjunct office of a diplomatic attaché or a public official.
agregar, (*ref. 51*) *tr.v.* 1. to add. 2. to appoint, assign, attach. —*r.v.* 1. to join. — **agregarse a,** to join.
agregativo, va, *a.* (pharm.) composite, compound; aggregative.
agregue, agregué, *ref.* **agregar.**
agremán, *m.* passementerie; elaborate embroidery work made with ribbon, beads and gimp.
agremiación, *f.* 1. unionization, syndication. 2. union, syndicate.
agremiado, da, *a.* unionized, organized (labor). —*m., f.* union member.
agremiar, *tr.v.* to unionize, syndicate. —*r.v.* to become unionized or syndicated.
agresión, *f.* aggression. — **pacto de no a.,** (polit.) non-aggression pact.
agresivamente, *adv.* aggressively.
agresividad, *f.* aggressiveness.
agresivo, va, *a.* aggressive, hostile, offensive.
agresor, ra, *m., f.* aggressor; assailant.
agreste, *a.* wild, uncultivated; rustic; rough.
agrete, *a.* sourish, tart.
agriado, da, *a.* sour, surly, sullen, ill-humored.
agriamente, *adv.* sourly; harshly, bitterly.
agriar, *tr.v.* 1. to make sour. 2. to annoy, exasperate. —*r.v.* 1. to become sour. 2. to become irritated or exasperated.

agriaz, *m.* (bot.) chinaberry, bead tree.
agrícola, *a.* agricultural, agrarian. —*m., f.* agriculturist, farmer.
agricultor, ra, *m., f.* agriculturist, farmer.
agricultura, *f.* agriculture, farming.
agridulce, *a.* bittersweet, sweet-and-sour.
agrietamiento, *m.* cracking; (geol.) fissuring, jointing.
agrietar, *tr.v., r.v.* to split, crack.
agrifada, *a.* (print.) aldine (type).
agrifolio, *m.* (bot.) holly tree.
agrilla, *f., var. of* **acedera.**
agrillarse, *r.v.* to sprout.
agrimensor, *m.* surveyor.
agrimensura, *f.* surveying.
agrimonia, *f.* (bot.) agrimony, liverwort.
agringado, a, *a.* (Amer., derog.) having adopted gringo (N. American) customs.
agringarse, *r.v.* (Amer., derog.) to adopt gringo (N. American) customs.
agrio, ria, *a.* 1. sour, acid. 2. sour, disagreeable (character, speech). 3. discordant, unharmonious (colors). —*m.* sourness, sour juice; (*pl.*) sour-fruit trees, citrus trees.
agrión, *m.* 1. callosity on a horse's knee. 2. (bot.) chinaberry, bead tree.
agripalma, *f.* (bot.) motherwort.
agrisado, da, *a.* grayish, greyish.
agro, *m.* farmland; farming.
agro, gra, *a.* sour. —*m.* 1. sourness. 2. citron jelly.
agrobiología, *f.* agrobiology.
agrología, *f.* agrology, the science of agricultural production.
agrológico, ca, *a.* agrological.
agromicrobiología, *f.* agromicrobiology.
agronomía, *f.* agronomy.
agronómico, ca, *a.* agronomical.
agrónomo, *m.* agronomist. —*a.* agronomical.
agropecuario, ria, *a.* pertaining to farming and animal husbandry.
agroquímica, *f.* agrochemistry, agricultural chemistry.
agror, *m.* sourness, bitterness.
agróstide, *f.* (bot.) bent grass.
agrostología, *f.* (bot.) agrostology, the science of grasses.
agrumar, *tr.v.* to curdle, clot, lump. —*r.v.* to become curdle or clotted.
agrupación, *f.* group; collection, assembly; crowd, gathering; social unit, club. — **a. coral,** (mus.) choral society, choir.
agrupado, da, *past part. of* **agrupar.** —*a.* 1. grouped, assembled. 2. pertaining to the conformation of a horse. — **bien a.,** with a good croup.
agrupador, ra, *a.* grouping. —*m., f.* person who gathers others into a group.
agrupamiento, *m.* 1. crowd, group; gathering, assembling. 2. pile, heap.
agrupar, *tr.v., r.v.* 1. to group, assemble. 2. to heap or pile on.
agrura, *f.* sourness; acidity; citrus orchard; (*pl.*) citrus fruits, sour fruits.
agua, *f.* 1. water. 2. distilled liquid, e.g. *a. de rosas,* rose water. 3. rain. 4. (archit.) slope (of roof). 5. (mar.) leak (in a ship). 6. (mar.) tide. 7. (*pl.*) water, sparkle, glint (in precious stone). 8. (*pl.*) wavy lustrous pattern (on silk, etc.). 9. (*pl.*) urine, water. 10. (*pl.*) waters, mineral springs. 11. (*pl.*) waters, seas. 12. (*pl.*) course, route. 13. (*pl.*) current. — **a pan y a.,** on bread and water; **a. amoniacal,** ammonia water; **a. bendita,** holy water; **a. blanca,** (chem.) lead acetate water; **a. cibera,** water used to irrigate soil; **a. corriente,** running water; **a. cruda,** hard water; **a. cuaderna,** (mar.) bilge water; **a. de azahar,** orange-flower water; **a. de borrajas,** unimportant thing, trifle; **a. de cal,** lime water; **a. de cepas,** (coll.) wine; **a. de colonia,** eau de cologne; **a. del amnios,** (physiol.) amniotic fluid; **a. delgada,** soft water; **a. de lluvia,** rain water; **a. de rosas,** rose water; **a. de Seltz,** seltzer water, soda water; **a. de socorro,** emergency baptism, administered without solemnities in cases of emergency; **a. dulce,** fresh water; **a. dura,** hard water; **a. fuerte,** (chem.) aqua fortis, strong water, nitric acid; **a. gaseosa,** carbonated water; **a. gorda,** hard water; **a. llovediza, a. lluvia,** rain water; **a. manantial,** spring water; **a. mineral,** mineral water; **a. muerta,** stagnant water; **a. oxigenada,** (chem.) hydrogen peroxide; **a. nieve,** sleet; **a. pesada,** (chem.) heavy water; **a. potable,** drinking water; **a. regia,** (chem.) aqua regia, solution of hydrochloric and nitric acids; **a. roja,** hot water; **a. sal,** fresh water to which salt is added; **a. salada,** salt water; **a. salobre,** salt water; **a. termal,** hot-spring water; **a. tónica,** tonic water; **a. viento,** driving rain; **a. viva,** running water, fresh water; **aguas abajo,** downstream; **aguas arriba,** upstream; **aguas de creciente,** (mar.) rising tide; **aguas del timón.** (mar.) wake (of a ship); **aguas de menguante,** (mar.) ebb tide; **aguas falsas,** seeping waters; **aguas firmes,** well or spring water; **aguas jurisdiccionales,** territorial waters; **aguas llenas,** high tide; **aguas muertas,** (mar.) neap tides; **aguas negras,** sewage, sewage water; **aguas pluviales,** rainwater; **aguas residuales,** sewage; **aguas servidas,** sewage; **aguas vertientes,** spring or mountain water; rain water; **aguas vivas.** (mar.) spring tides; **bailarle el a. delante a.** to be ingratiating to, try to please; **como a.,** in great abundance; **echar a. en el mar,** to carry coals to Newcastle; **echar toda el a. al molino,** to go all out, make every effort (to get something); **estar con el agua al cuello,** to be in deep (or hot) water; **estar entre dos aguas,** to be in doubt, be undecided; **hacerse a. en la boca,** to melt in one's mouth; **hacérsele (a uno) a. la boca,** (coll.) to make one's mouth water; **¡hombre al a.!** man overboard; **irse (algo) al agua,** to crumble, go to pieces (a project, idea, etc.); **irsele (a uno) las aguas,** (coll.) to urinate (due to sudden shock, fear, emotion, etc.); **llevar el a. a su molino,** (coll.) to monopolize everything for one's own benefit; **no hallar uno a. en el mar,** to be unable to do the simplest thing; **sacar a. de las piedras,** to derive some benefit from seemingly hopeless circumstances; **sin decir a. va,** suddenly, without a word of warning; **tan claro como el a.,** very clear; obvious.
aguacal, *m.* whitewash.
aguacatal, *m.* 1. avocado (alligator pear) orchard, plantation of avocado trees. 2. (coll., Hond.) testicle. 3. (Guat.) loafer, lazybones.
aguacate, *m.* 1. avocado tree; avocado, alligator pear. 2. pear-shaped emerald.
aguacero, *m.* 1. shower, downpour, 2. host, shower (of misfortunes, etc.). 3. (Cuba) a kind of glow-worm.
aguacha, *f.* stagnant water.
aguachacha, *f.* (C. Amer.) poorly prepared or blended food or drink.
aguachar, *tr.v.* 1. to flood, fill with water. 2. to tame, break (horse). —*r.v.* 1. to become flooded or waterlogged. 2. (Arg.) to become fat (horse). —*m.* puddle, pool.
aguacharnar, *tr.v.* to flood, waterlog.
aguachento, ta, *a.* (Amer.) watery.
aguachinarse, *r.v.* (Mex.) to become waterlogged (land, crops, etc.).
aguachirle, *f.* 1. inferior wine; slipslop, watery wine or liquor. 2. trifle.
aguacibera, *f.* water used to irrigate soil sowed when dry.
aguacil, *m.* 1. *var. of* **alguacil.** 2. (Amer.) dragonfly.
aguada, *f.* 1. watering place; source of water. 2. (mar.) water supply. 3. (min.) flood (in mine). 4. colored wash (for toning down whitewash); (p.) gouache, wash; water color, gouache sketch. 5. (*pl.*) water. 6. (Amer.) water trough, watering place.— **hacer a.,** (mar.) to take on water; **pintura a la a.,** gouache painting.
aguadero, ra, *a.* waterproof (clothing). —*m.* 1. watering place, watering station, drinking trough; water hole. 2. place where logs are rolled into the river. —*f.* wing feather; (*pl.*) frame placed on horses for carrying water.
aguadija, *f.* (med.) water (in blisters, wounds, etc.).
aguado, da, *past part. of* **aguar.** —*a.* 1. watery; watered, diluted. 2. dull, boring, lifeless (party, person). 3. abstemious. 4. (Guat., Ecuad.) weak, washed-out. 5. (Ven.) tasteless (fruit). —*m., f.* (coll.) wet blanket, dull, lifeless person.
aguador, ra, *m., f.* water vendor. —*m.* rung (of water wheel).
aguaducho, *m.* 1. flood of water. 2. conduit, water course. 3. water vending stall, refreshments stand.
aguadulce, *m.* (Col., Costa Rica) *var. of* aguamiel.
aguadura, *f.* 1. (vet.) (a kind of) founder. 2. abscess (on a horse's hoof).
aguafiestas, *m., f.* (coll.) spoilsport, wet blanket, party pooper, kill-joy.
aguafuerte, *f.* etched plate; etching.
aguafuertista, *m., f.* (art.) etcher.
aguagoma, *f.* (p.) gum water.
aguaí, *m.* (Arg., Par.) *var. of* **aguay.**
aguaitacaimán, *m.* (Cuba, ornith.) martineta.
aguaitacamino, *m.* (ornith.) goatsucker.
aguaitada, *f.* (Amer., coll.) watching, observing; look.
aguaitador, ra, *a.* (Amer.) watching, observing. —*m., f.* observer, watcher.
aguaitamiento, *m.* (Amer.) watching, observing; look.
aguaitar, *tr.v.* to watch, keep watch on, observe; to spy on; to look at, have a look at. —*i.v.* to have a look.
aguaite, *m.* (Chile, coll.) *var. of* **aguaitamiento;** (Mex., coll.) *var. of* **espera.**
aguajaque, *m.* fennel gum or resin.
aguaje, *m.* 1. watering place; water hole; drinking trough. 2. (Guat., Hond.) reprimand. 3. (P. Rico) exaggeration. 4. (Ecuad., Guat.) heavy shower, downpour. 5. (mar.) tidal wave; strong current; tidal water. 6. water supply (on board ship). 7. wake (of a ship). 8. whirlpool, eddy, (around the rudder). 9. spirit, fortitude, gumption.
aguají, (*pl.* **aguajíes**) *m.* 1. (ichth.) gag, grouper, bonaci. 2. (Cuba) sauce made of chili, onions, garlic, lemon juice and water.
aguajirarse, *r.v.* (Cuba, P. Rico) to become countrified; to adopt rural customs.
aguamala, *f.* (zool.) jellyfish.
aguamanil, *m.* water jug, wash jug; washbowl, wash basin; washstand.
aguamanos, *m.* water for washing hands; water jug; wash basin.
aguamar, *m.* (zool.) jellyfish.
aguamarina, *f.* (min.) aquamarine.
aguamelado, da, *a.* soaked in syrup, syrupy.
aguamiel, *f.* hydromel, honey and water; (Amer.) cane sugar and water; (Mex.) maguey juice (from which pulque is made).
aguandero, *m.* (Col.) *var. of* **aguador.**

aguanés, sa, *a.* (Chile) *var. of* **yaguané.**
aguanieve, *f.* sleet.
aguanieves, *f.* (ornith.) white wagtail.
aguanosidad, *f.* (physiol.) body fluids.
aguanoso, sa, *a.* watery, aqueous, very moist.
aguantable, *a.* bearable, tolerable.
aguantaderas, *f.* *(pl.)* (Amer.) **tener a.,** to be very tolerant.
aguantador, ra *a.* (coll.) resistent; enduring, strong.
aguantar, *tr.v.* 1. to bear, endure; to stand, tolerate, put up with. 2. to hold up, bear, sustain. 3. to hold (one's breath). 4. (mar.) to tauten. — **a. carros y carretas,** (coll.) to put up with everything. —*i.v.* 1. to hold on, hold out. 2. (taur.) to stand firm, to move the left foot forward for the kill; —*r.v.* 1. to control oneself, contain oneself. 2. (coll.) (Amer.) to stop, halt.
aguante, *m.* fortitude, patience; endurance, resistance (to toil or fatigue).
aguañón, *a.* **maestro a.,** engineer in hydraulic construction.
aguapé, *m.* (Arg., Par., bot.) water hyacinth.
aguapié, *m.* watery wine.
aguar, (*ref. 52*) *tr.v.* 1. to dilute, water down. 2. to spoil (party, pleasure, etc.). 3. (fig.) to attenuate; to make less unpleasant or burdensome. 4. to throw into water. 5. (Hond.) to water (cattle). —*r.v.* 1. to become diluted or watery. 2. to become flooded or inundated. 3. to become boring or dull (party). 4. (vet.) to become ill from drinking water while perspiring (horse).
aguará, *m.* (Amer.) a variety of red fox.
aguarachay, *m.* (Amer.) a kind of grey fox.
aguaraibá, *m.* (Arg., Par., Urug., bot.) terebinth tree.
aguarapado, *a.* (Mex., Col., P. Rico) said of a beverage resembling sugarcane juice.
aguardada, *f.* wait, waiting.
aguardadero, *m.* hunter's blind or hideout.
aguardador, ra, *a.* waiting. —*m., f.* waiter, person who waits.
aguardar, *tr.v.* 1. to wait for, await; to expect. 2. to await, be in store, e.g. *no sé lo que me aguarda,* I don't know what awaits me or what is in store for me. 3. to wait for, grant, e.g. *te aguardaremos tres días,* we will give you three days more, we will wait three days more for you. —*i.v.* to wait.
aguardentería, *f.* liquor shop; saloon.
aguardentero, ra, 1. *m., f.* liquor seller. 2. *f.* liquor flask.
aguardentoso, sa, *a.* 1. brandy, brandy-like. 2. smelling of brandy. 3. mixed or fortified with brandy. 4. raucous, harsh (voice).
aguardiente, *m.* brandy, spirituous liquor; **a. de cabeza,** first distillate; first sample of brandy taken from still; a. **de caña,** rum.
aguardillado, da, *a.* (archit.) garret-like.
aguardo, *m.* hiding place; (hunt.) hunter's blind.
aguaribay, *m.* (bot.) *var. of* **aguaraibá.**
aguarse, *r.v.* (coll.) to lose heart, become discouraged.
aguarrás, *m.* oil of turpentine.
aguasal, *f., var. of* **salmuera.**
aguasarse, *r.v.* (Chile, Arg., Urug.) to become countryfied, take on rural customs.
aguate, *m.* (Mex., Hond.) prickle.
aguatero, *m.* (Amer.) water carrier, water seller.
aguatocha, *f.* water pump.
aguaturma, *f.* (bot.) Jerusalem artichoke.
aguaverde, *m.* (zool.) jellyfish.
aguaviento, *m.* driving rain, rainy gusts.
aguavientos, *m.* (bot.) Jerusalem sage.
aguavilla, *f.* (bot.) bearberry.
aguay, *m.* (bot.) star apple.
aguaza, *f.* aqueous humor; sap, juice (exuded by some plants and fruits).
aguazal, *m.* large pool or puddle; **marsh,** fen.
aguazar, (*ref. 53*) *tr.v.* to flood, waterlog. —*r.v.* to become flooded, waterlogged, or marshy.
aguazo, *m.* (p.) gouache.
aguazoso, sa, *a., var. of* aguanoso.
aguazul, *m., var. of* **algazul.**
aguazur, *m., var. of* **aguazul.**
aguce, agucé, *ref.* **aguzar.**
agudamente, *adv.* sharply; keenly, acutely; wittily.
agudez, *f., var. of* **agudeza.**
agudeza, *f.* 1. sharpness; acuteness; keenness. 2. witty remark, witticism.
agudice, agudicé, *ref.* **agudizar.**
agudizar, (*ref. 53*) *tr.v.* to sharpen, make more keen or acute. —*r.v.* to become more serious, get worse (illness).
agudo, da, *a.* 1. sharp (blade, point; pain, etc.). 2. acute, keen, sharp (mind, intelligence). 3. witty, clever. 4. acute, coming rapidly to a crisis (illness). 5. keen, sharp (eyesight, etc.). 6. acute, serious, e.g. *un problema agudo,* a serious problem. 7. pungent (smell). 8. high-pitched, sharp (voice, sound). 9. (gram.) acute (accent); oxytone, accented on the last syllable. 10. (geom.) acute. 11. fast, brisk, speedy.
aguedita, *f.* (bot.) bitterbush.
agüeitar, *tr.v.* (Amer.), *var. of* **aguaitar.**
agüela, *f.* (coll.) grandmother.
agüelo, *m.* (coll.) grandfather.
agüera, *f.* ditch for catching rainwater.
agüere, agüero, *ref.* **agorar.**
agüerista, *a.* (Col.) superstitious.
agüero, *m.* augury, omen, presage, sign. — **ser de buen** or **mal a.,** to be good or bad luck, to be of good or ill omen.
aguerrido, da, *past part. of* **aguerrir.** —*a.* hardened, doughty, bold, brave.
aguerrir, (*ref. 78*) *tr.v.* to accustom or inure to war, harden. —*r.v.* to become accustomed or inured to war.
aguijada, *f.* 1. goad, spur. 2. plowstaff, paddle used for cleaning plowshares.
aguijador, ra, *a.* goading, spurring, inciting. —*m., f.* goader, inciter.
aguijadura, *f.* goading, spurring.
aguijar, *tr.v.* to goad, spur on; (fig.) to incite, spur on, urge on. —*i.v.* to hurry, hurry along.
aguijatorio, ria, *a.* (law, arch.) mandatory (said of judicial order from higher court to lower court).
aguijón, *m.* barb, sharp point on the end of a goad; sting (of insects); spur; prickle, thorn; (fig.) stimulus, goad.
aguijonada, *f., var. of* **aguijonazo.**
aguijonamiento, *m.* goading, spurring, pricking.
aguijonazo, *m.* prick, sting.
aguijoneador, ra, *a.* pricking, goading.
aguijonear, *tr.v.* to goad, prick, incite, spur on, urge on.
águila, *f.* 1. (ornith.) eagle. 2. eagle (emblem; medal, decoration). 3. silver piece worth ten reales, minted in Spain during the reign of Emperor Charles V; Mexican twenty dollar gold piece; eagle, American ten dollar gold piece. 4. (Chile) child's kite. 5. (fig.) astute person. 6. (astron.) **A.,** Aquila. — **á. barbuda,** (ornith.) bearded eagle; **á. blanca,** (ornith.) white-headed eagle; **á. calva,** (ornith.) bald eagle; **á. caudal, á. caudalosa,** (ornith.) golden eagle; **á. culebrera,** (ornith.) snake buzzard, harrier eagle; **á. doble,** double eagle, American twenty dollar gold piece; **á. explayada,** (her.) two-headed eagle with wings extended; **á. grande,** spread eagle (in skating); **á. imperial,** (ornith.) imperial eagle; **á. marina,** (ornith.) sea eagle; **¿á. o sol?** (Mex.) heads or tails?; **á. pasmada,** (her.) eagle with wings closed; **á. pescadora,** (ornith.) osprey; **á. real,** (ornith.) golden eagle; **ser un á.,** to be very efficient; **tener mirada de águila,** to be lynx-eyed.
aguileña, *f.* (bot.) columbine.
aguileño, ña, *a.* aquiline.
aguilera, *f.* eagle's nest, aeyrie.
aguililla, *a.* very fast (horse). —*m., f.* (Ecuad., Chile) cheat, swindler.
aguilón, *m.* 1. large eagle. 2. arm, jib, boom (of crane). 3. diagonal tied beam (of gabled roof). 4. gable (of roof). 5. beveled tile (of gabled roof). 6. square clay drainpipe. 7. (her.) eagle without beak or talons.
aguilote, *m.* (bot.) Mexican tomato with poisonous root.
aguilucho, *m.* eaglet.
aguín, *m.* (bot.) dwarf pine.
aguinaldo, *m.* 1. Christmas bonus, New Year's gift 2. Christmas carol. 3. (bot.) aguinaldo, wild convulvulus creeper that blooms at Christmas.
agüista, *m., f.* one who goes to a spa for a cure.
agüita, *f.* 1. *dim. of* **agua,** water. 2. water that has been flavored with aromatic herbs (e.g. anise, jasmine, etc.). 3. (Peru, coll.) money.
aguizgar, (*ref. 51*) *tr.v.* to goad, spur on, urge on.
aguizgue, aguizgué, *ref.* **aguizgar.**
aguja, *f.* 1. needle (knitting, gramophone, engraver's, etc.); hatpin; firing-pin (of a gun, rifle, etc.); spike; dowel. 2. needle, obelisk; spire, steeple. 3. thin wire used for cleaning the priming hole of a rifle. 4. hand (of a clock); style (of a sundial). 5. (mar.) compass. 6. (ry.) switch rail; (*pl.*) switch, point. 7. wooden support (for a bridge). 8. (carp.) brad, finishing nail. 9. (cul.) meat pie. 10. (ichth.) needlefish, hornfish. 11. (agr.) graft. 12. (print.) wrinkle formed accidentally (on page during printing). 13. needle, blasting needle pricker. 14. (Amer.) upright, stake, post (forming a fence or barricade). 15. (bot.) lady's comb, shepherd's needle. 16. (*pl.*) front ribs (of an animal). 17. (*pl.*) disease of horses. — **a. capotera,** darning needle; **a. colchonera,** bodkin, quilting or tufting needle; **a. de bitacora,** see **a. de marear; a. de enjalmar,** saddler's needle, harness maker's needle; **a. de crochet,** crochet hook; **a. de fogón,** (artil.) gun pin; **a. de gancho,** crochet needle; **a. de inclinación,** (phys.) dipping needle; **a. de mar,** (ichth.) pipefish, needlefish; **a. de marcar,** theodolite; **a. de marear,** mariner's needle, compass; **a. de mechar,** larding needle; **a. de media,** knitting needle; **a. de pastor,** (bot.) lady's comb, shepherd's needle; **a. de punto,** knitting needle; **a. de radio,** (med.) radium needle; **a. de toque,** (jewel.) testing needle used by jewelers to ascertain the content of gold or silver in any object; **a. de verdugado,** largest needle used by tailors; **a. de espartera,** needle used for making reed mats; **a. hipodérmica,** (med.) hypodermic needle; **a. loca,** compass needle (which does not point North); **a. magnética,** magnetic needle; compass needle; **alabar sus agujas,** (coll.) to blow one's own trumpet; **buscar una a. en un pajar,** to look for a needle in a haystack; **conocer** or **entender la a. de marear,** to know the ins and outs of business, know business from A to Z; **cuartear la a.,** (mar.) to box the compass.
agujadera, *f.* needlewoman.
agujal, *m.* (mec.) hole (left in **mud walls** by dowel used to hold boards of **wall** mold in place).
agujazo, *m.* needle prick, pin prick.

agujerar, *tr.v., r.v., var. of* **agujerear.**
agujerear, *tr.v.* to pierce, perforate, **prick,** puncture; to make holes in, bore, **drill.** *—r.v.* to become riddled with holes.
agujerito, *m.* little hole; finger hole.
agujero, *m.* 1. hole; **a. de cuerda,** keyhole (of clock). 2. (fig.) lair, hideaway. 3. pincushion, needlecase.
agujeruelo, *m. dim. of* **agujero,** small hole.
agujeta, *f.* 1. lace, cord, thong, **latchet** (tipped with tags to tie up or **secure** trousers or other clothing). 2. (*pl.*) aches and pains felt after prolonged exertion. 3. (Sp.,Ven.) ornamental hatpin. 4. (print.) unsightly wrinkle in the paper. 5. (Amer.) large needle, knitting needle.
agujetero, ra, *m., f.* (Amer.) pincushion, needlecase.
agujón, *m. aug. of* **aguja,** large needle.
agujuela *f.* 1. *dim. of* **aguja,** small needle. 2. brad, finishing nail.
aguosidad, *f.* watery humor, lymph.
aguoso, sa, *a., var. of* **acuoso.**
agur! *interj.* (coll.) farewell, goodbye, so long.
agusanado, da, *a.* 1. wormy, worm-ridden. 2. (Cuba, sl.) person who becomes counter-revolutionary.
agusanamiento, *m.* 1. worminess, **the act** of becoming worm-ridden. 2. (Cuba, sl.) the act of becoming counter-revolutionary.
agusanarse, *r.v.* 1. to become worm-eaten or worm-ridden. 2. (Cuba, sl.) to become counter-revolutionary.
agustina, *f.* (bot.) variety of anemone.
agustinianismo, *m.* (philos., rel.) **Augustinianism.**
agustiniano, na, *a., m., f.* Augustinian.
agustino, na, *a., m., f.* Augustinian (monk or nun).
agutí, *m.* (zool.) agouti.
aguzadero, ra, *a.* sharpening, whetting. *—m.* (hunt.) place where boars habitually root and sharpen their tusks. *—f.* sharpener, whetstone.
aguzado, da, *past part. of* **aguzar.** *—a.* 1. sharp, pointed. 2. keen, smart.
aguzador, ra, *a.* sharpening; stimulating. *—m., f.* sharpener (person). *—f.* whetstone, sharpener.
aguzadura, *f.* 1. sharpening, whetting; sharpness. 2. steel used to forge new cutting edge on plow.
aguzamiento, *m.* sharpening, whetting.
aguzanieves, *f.* (ornith.) white wagtail.
aguzar, (*ref. 53*) *tr.v.* 1. to sharpen, whet. 2. to stimulate, arouse, excite. — **a. el ingenio,** to sharpen one's wits; **a. el oído,** to prick up one's ear; **a. la vista,** to strain one's eyes.
aguzonazo, *m.* thrust, lunge.
¡ah! *interj.* ah!
Ah *abbrev. of* **amperio-hora, amperhora,** ampere-hour (amp-hr).
ahacado, *a.* stocky, pony-like, small (horse).
ahajar, *tr.v., var. of* **ajar.**
ahebrado, da, *a.* fibrous, thready, stringy.
ahechadero, *m.* sifting yard, place for sifting (grain).
ahechador, ra, *a.* sifting. *—m., f.* sifter (of grain).
ahechaduras, *f.* (*pl.*) siftings, chaff.
ahechar, *tr.v.* to sift, cribble (grain).
ahecho, *m.* sifting, cribbling.
ahelear, *tr.v.* 1. to make bitter. 2. (fig.) to embitter, sadden. *—i.v.* to taste bitter, have a bitter taste.
ahelgado, da, *a., var. of* **helgado.**
ahembrado, da, *a.* effeminate.
aherrojamiento, *m.* shackling, putting in chains; (fig.) oppression, subjugation.
aherrojar, *tr.v.* to put in irons, shackle; (fig.) to oppress, subjugate.
aherrumbrar, *tr.v.* to give the color or taste of iron. *—r.v.* to take on the taste or color of iron; to rust.
ahervorarse, *r.v.* to become heated by fermentation (stored grain).
ahí, *adv.* there; **a. no más,** just over there; **a.** or **de a.,** in this or that way, hence; **de a. a poco,** after a short time; **de a. en adelante,** from then on; **de ahí que,** with the result that; and that is why, that explains why; **por a.,** over there, that way; around there, thereabouts, more or less; **por a. lejos,** far away.
ahidalgadamente, *adv., var. of* **hidalgamente.**
ahidalgado, da, *a.* gentlemanly, noble, chivalrous.
ahigadado, da, *a.* 1. brave, courageous, 2. liver-colored.
ahijadera, *f.* sucklings in a flock or herd (collectively).
ahijadero, *m.* breeding place for sheep.
ahijado, da, *m., f.* godchild; protegé. *—m.* godson. *—f.* goddaughter.
ahijador, *m.* shepherd in charge of breeding pens.
ahijamiento, *m., var. of* **prohijamiento.**
ahijar, *tr.v.* 1. to adopt. 2. to place (young animals) with their mothers or foster-mothers. 3. (fig.) to impute, attribute. *—i.v.* 1. to procreate, bear (children). 2. to bud, sprout.
¡ahijuna! *interj.* (Arg., Chile, Urug.) expressing admiration or surprise.
ahilado, da, *a.* 1. gentle (breeze). 2. faint (voice). *—m.* (Ven., coll.) row (of trees or plants).
ahilamiento, *m.* weakness, faintness.
ahilar, *tr.v.* to line up, put in line. *—i.v.* to go in line or single file. *—r.v.* 1. to faint (from hunger); to become thin (through illness). 2. to become sour (wine), mouldy (yeast, cheese, etc.). 3. to grow tall and branchless due to density of planting or to grow weak and stunted due to lack of light (trees).
ahilo, *m.* faintness, weakness.
ahincadamente, *adv.* zealously; earnestly, eagerly.
ahincado, da, *a.* zealous, eager.
ahincar, (*ref. 50*) *tr.v.* to urge, press (eagerly). *—r.v.* to hasten, hurry.
ahínco, *m.* zeal, eagerness.
ahínque, ahinqué, *ref.* **ahincar.**
ahitamiento, *m.* 1. delimitation, marking of boundaries with landmarks. 2. indigestion (from overeating).
ahitar, *tr.v.* 1. to delimit, mark out the boundaries of (with landmarks). 2. to cause indigestion, to bloat. *—r.v.* to get bloated or flatulent, get indigestion.
ahitera, *f.* (coll.) acute indigestion.
ahito, ta, *a.* 1. gorged, bloated, stuffed. 2. (coll.) annoyed, fed up. *—m.* indigestion, overeating.
ahobachonado, da, *a.* (coll.) lazy, idle.
ahobachonarse, *r.v.* (coll.) to become lazy.
ahocicar, (*ref. 50*) *tr.v.* 1. to defeat (an opponent) in an argument. 2. to rub (dog's) nose in its dirt (as a form of training). *—i.v.* 1. to acknowledge defeat in an argument. 2. (mar.) to pitch and plunge (boat). 3. to fall flat on one's face.
ahocinarse, *r.v.* to stream through narrow gorges (rivers).
ahocique, ahociqué, *ref.* **ahocicar.**
ahogadero, ra, *a.* suffocating, choking. *—m.* 1. hangman's rope. 2. (coll.) crush, overcrowded place. 3. throat latch or band, halter; necklace, choker. 4. cauldron of hot water for drowning the silkworm chrysalis.
ahogadizo, za, *a.* 1. easily drowned or stifled. 2. non-floating (said of wood which sinks in water). 3. harsh, rough (fruit hard to swallow).
ahogado, da, *past part. of* **ahogar.** *—a.* 1. unventilated, stuffy. 2. muffled (cry, shout). 3. (chess) stalemated. *—m., f.* drowned or suffocated person.
ahogador, ra, *a.* choking, stifling, suffocating. *—m., f.* choker. *—m.* 1. choker, necklace. 2. throat latch or band. 3. (Nicar.) *var. of* **ahorcadora.**
ahogagato, *m.* a small tidbit or delicacy, made with yucca starch.
ahogar, (*ref. 51*) *tr.v.* 1. to drown; to suffocate, stifle, choke, smother. 2. to smother, put out, extinguish (fire). 3. to drown, kill (plants) with too much water; to choke (plants) through lack of space. 4. to flood, submerge. 5. to harass, oppress, overwhelm. 6. to smother, suppress (passions, rebellions, etc.). 7. (Col., Peru) to stew. 8. (chess) to stalemate. *—r.v.* 1. to drown; to choke, suffocate; to be drowned; to be choked or suffocated; to drown or choke oneself. 2. to feel suffocated or choked, be stifled. 3. to be choked (plants through lack of space); to be drowned, be killed by too much water (plants). 4. to feel overwhelmed, overcome or oppressed. 5. to submerge, sink. 6. (mar.) to ship water (at the prow). — **ahogarse en un vaso de agua,** to make a mountain out of a mole hill.
ahogaviejas, *f.* (bot.) a Eurasian herb (Scandix australis).
ahogo, *m.* 1. shortness of breath; choking. 2. (mec.) flooding (of motor by gasoline). 3. distress, anguish, affliction. 4. poverty, necessity, period of poverty. 5. haste, hurry. 6. (Col., Peru) stewing sauce.
ahogue, ahogue, *ref.* **ahogar.**
ahoguijo, *m.* 1. congestion of the chest, shortness of breath. 2. (vet.) quinsy (swollen throat).
ahoguío, *m.* (coll.) congestion of the chest, shortness of breath.
ahombrado, da, *a.* (coll.) mannish, masculine (said of a boy or a woman).
ahombrar, *r.v.* (coll.) to become mannish.
ahondamiento, *m.* deepening.
ahondar, *tr.v.* 1. to deepen, make deeper; to put in deeper. 2. to dig deeply into, examine or study profoundly. *—i.v.* 1. to go down deep, delve. 2. to delve deeply (into), study profoundly. — **a. en,** to go down deep into, to delve deeply into, study profoundly. *—r.v.* to go down deeper; to worsen (e.g. an illness).
ahonde, *m.* 1. deepening. 2. (min.) depth of excavation required to obtain title to a mine.
ahora, *adv.* 1. now, at present. 2. just, e.g. *ahora me lo han dicho,* they have just told me. 3. soon, in a moment, e.g. *ahora escribiré,* I shall write soon. — **a. mismo,** at once; **hasta a.,** until now, so far; (coll.) so long, see you soon; **por a.,** for the present; **a. bien,** well, now then; nevertheless.
ahorca, *f.* (coll., Ven.) present, gift.
ahorcado, da, *past part. of* **ahorcar.** *—m., f.* hanged person; (rare) person condemned to be hanged.
ahorcadora, *f.* (Guat., Hond.) kind of wasp.
ahorcadura, *f.* hanging.
ahorcajarse, *r.v.* to sit astride.
ahorcamiento, *m.* hanging; execution by hanging.
ahorcaperros, *m.* (mar.) hitch, running bowline.
ahorcar, (*ref. 50*) *tr.v.* 1. to hang (to execute). 2. to abandon, leave (studies, religious life). 3. (Arg., Mex., Urug.) to lend money at usury rates. *—r.v.* to hang oneself.
ahorita, *adv.* (Amer., coll.) recently; right now; very soon.
ahormar, *tr.v.* 1. to fit, mold. 2. to bring to reason. 3. to break in (shoes, etc.). 4. (taur.) to put (a bull) in position ready for the kill. 5. (equit.) to maneuver horse's head into position. *—r.v.* to fit, become adjusted to.

ahornagamiento, *m.* withering by heat (plants); parching (of land by excessive heat).
ahornagar, (*ref. 51*) *tr.v.* to parch, wither. —*r.v.* to become parched or withered.
ahornague, *ref.* **ahornagar.**
ahornar, *tr.v.* to put in an oven. —*r.v.* to burn on the outside while still unbaked inside (bread).
ahorque, ahorqué, *ref.* **ahorcar.**
ahorquillado, da, *a.* 1. forked. 2. in the shape of a hairpin.
ahorquillar, *tr.v.* to prop up with forks (branches of a tree); to give the shape of a hairpin. —*r.v.* to become forked.
ahorradamente, *adv.* freely, easily.
ahorrado, da, *past part. of* **ahorrar.** —*a* 1. free. 2. economical, thrifty. 3. saved (money, efforts, etc.).
ahorrador, ra, *a.* thrifty. —*m., f.* a person who saves money.
ahorramiento, *m.* saving (money, time, etc.).
ahorrar, *tr.v.* 1. to save, e.g. *a. dinero,* to save money, *esta máquina me ha ahorrado mucho tiempo,* this machine has saved me a lot of time. 2. to save, spare. 3. to free, emancipate. —*r.v.* 1. to save or spare oneself, e.g. *ahorrarse tiempo,* to save oneself time, *ahorrarse trabajo,* to save oneself work. 2. to restrain oneself. — **no ahorrárselas con nadie,** to speak or act freely, be straightforward, be blunt.
ahorrativa, *f., var. of* **ahorro.**
ahorrativo, va, *a.* 1. thrifty, economical. 2. tight, miserly. 3. economy, economizing, e.g. *medidas ahorrativas,* economy measures.
ahorría, *f.* 1. (agr.) barrenness. 2. freedom.
ahorrista, *m., f.* (Amer.) saver (of money).
ahorro, *m.* saving, economy; (*pl.*) savings.
ahoyadura, *f.* hole, hole-making, hole-digging.
ahoyar, *tr.v.* to dig holes in. —*i.v.* to dig holes.
ahuata, (bot.) dogbane.
ahuate, *m.* (Mex., C. Amer.) small prickly hairs (of sugar cane, corn).
ahuatoso, sa, *a.* (Mex., C. Amer.) prickly, fuzzy (referring to the corn and sugar cane plant).
ahuciar, *tr.v.* (C. Amer.) to encourage, give encouragement, hope, or confidence.
ahuchador, ra, *n.* hoarder. —*a.* hoarding, miserly.
ahuchar, *tr.v.* 1. to hoard; to keep in a safe place. 2. to call a hawk by repeatedly yelling out the word hucho. 3. (Col., Mex., Ven.) to sic (a dog on someone). 4. (coll.) to tease, stir up, incite.
ahuchear, *tr.v.* (coll.) to hiss, whistle at, boo.
ahucheo, m. (coll.) hissing, booing, whistling.
ahuecadera, *f.* hollowing tool.
ahuecado, da, *past part. of* **ahuecar.** —*a.* hollow.
ahuecador, *m.* 1. hollower. 2. hollowing tool. 3. hoop, bustle or crinoline (of a dress).
ahuecamiento, *m.* 1. hollowing; loosening. 2. (coll.) conceit, vanity, boast.
ahuecar, (*ref. 50*) *tr.v.* 1. to make hollow, hollow out; to fluff up, loosen (wool); to loosen, turn over, dig (earth). 2. to make (the voice) deep and solemn. —*i.v.* (coll.) to scram (sl.), leave. —*r.v.* (coll.) to become vain, put on airs; to boast, swagger.
ahuehué, *m., var. of* **ahuehuete.**
ahuehuete, *m.* (bot., Mex.) ahuehuete, Montezuma, coniferous tree similar to the cypress.
ahueque, ahuequé, *ref.* **ahuecar.**
ahuesado, da, *past part. of* **ahuesarse.** —*a.* 1. bone-like, bone-colored, bone-hard. 2. (Chile, Peru) out of fashion, passé, old-fashioned.
ahuesarse, *r.v.* 1. (Chile, Peru) to become unsalable (due to damage or being out of fashion); to go out of style, become passé. 2. (Amer.) to lose weight, to become bony.
ahuevado, da, *a.* (Pan., derog.) person who lacks back bone; softy.
ahuevar, *tr.v.* 1. to clarify (wine) with egg white. 2. to make egg-shaped.
ahuizote, *m.* 1. (Mex.) otter. 2. (Mex.) nuisance (person). 3. (C. Rica) augury, witchcraft.
ahulado, *m.* (C. Amer.) oilcloth, waterproofed cloth. —*a.* waterproof; (Amer.) rubberized.
ahumada, *f.* smoke signal.
ahumadero, *m.* smokehouse.
ahumado, da, *past part. of* **ahumar.** —*a.* 1. smoked (glass, salmon, etc.). 2. dark, sun (eyeglasses). —*m.* smoking, curing.
ahumar, *tr.v.* 1. to smoke, cure (in smoke). 2. to fill with smoke, smoke up. —*i.v.* 1. to smoke, fume, emit smoke. 2. (coll.) to get drunk or tipsy. —(with aspirate h) *r.v.* 1. to get filled with smoke, get smoked up. 2. (coll.) to get drunk or tipsy. 3. to become black or blackened by smoke. 4. to get a smoky taste, taste of smoke. — **ahumársele a uno el pescado,** (coll.) to get annoyed.
ahunche, *m.* (Col.) refuse, residue.
ahusado, da, *past part. of* **ahusar.** —*a.* tapered; spindle-shaped; cone-shaped.
ahusamiento, *m.* tapering.
ahusar, *tr.v.* to give the shape of a spindle; to taper. —*r.v.* to taper.
ahuyentador, ra, *a.* scaring. —*m., f.* scarer. —*m.* scarecrow.
ahuyentar, *tr.v.* to drive or chase away; to shoo away; to banish (thoughts, doubts, cares, passion).
AIEA *abbrev. of* **Agencia Internacional de Energía Atómica,** International Atomic Energy Agency (IAEA).
AID *abbrev. of* **Agencia para el Desarrollo Internacional,** Agency for International Development (AID).
AIF *abbrev. of* **Asociación Internacional de Fomento,** International Development Association (IDA).
aiguaste, *m.* (Guat., Hond., cul.) sauce made from flour, chili and other spices, used to flavor meat.
aijada, *f., var. of* **aguijada.**
ailanto, *m.* (bot.) ailanthus, tree of heaven.
aillo, *m.* 1. lariat with copper balls on one end used by the Peruvian Indians for hunting. 2. (Bol., Peru) class, cast or family; faction within a tribe.
aimará, *a., m., f.* Aymara (S. Amer. Indian); member and language of this tribe.
aimarista, *m., f.* specialist in Aymara culture.
aína, *adv.* soon; easily; almost.
aínas, *adv.* not as easy as it may seem.
aindamáis, *adv.* (coll.) moreover, furthermore.
aindiado, da, *a.* (Amer.) Indianlike.
airadamente, *adv.* angrily.
airado, da, *a.* angry, vexed, irate. — **vida a.,** prostitution.
airamiento, *m.* angering; anger, wrath, fury.
airampo, *m.* (bot.) a species of cactus used as a coloring agent.
airar, *tr.v.* to anger; to irritate; to annoy. —*r.v.* to get angry.
aire, *m.* 1. air; draft; wind; atmosphere. 2. air, look, appearance, mien. 3. (*pl.*) airs, vanity, conceit, 4. pace, gait (of a horse). 5. triviality, trivial thing. 6. style, elegance, ease, naturalness, stylishness. 7. (coll.) crick, wryneck, torticollis. 8. (mus.) air, tune. — **a. acondicionado,** air-conditioning; **a. adicional** or **suplementario,** (physiol.) supplemental air; **a. arrachado,** bumpy air; **a. aspirado,** inhaled air, admission air; **a. comprimido,** (phys.) compressed air; **a. contaminado,** polluted air; **a. de familia,** family resemblance; **a. líquido,** (phys.) liquid air; **al a.,** without foundation, without basis; mounted with clips at the edges and having no base setting (precious stones); into the air, e.g. *disparar al a.,* to fire into the air; **al a. libre,** outdoors, in the open air; **azotar el a.,** (coll.) to toil in vain; **darle a uno el a. de,** (coll.) to get wind of, hear of; **darle a uno un a.,** (coll.) to get an ache or pain (in the neck, back, etc.); **darse aires,** to put on airs; **darse un a. a,** to look like; **de buen** or **mal a.,** in a good or bad temper or mood; **dejar en el a.,** to leave undecided, pending or in the air; **estar en el a.,** to be undecided, be in the air; **hablar al a.,** to talk idly, make empty talk; **salir al a.,** to go on the air, go on the radio; **tener un a. a,** to be like, resemble; **tomar el a.,** to get some fresh air, go for a walk.
aireación, *f.* airing, ventilation, aeration.
aireador, *m.* aerator.
airear, *tr.v.* to air, ventilate; to aerate; to publicize or bring to light; **a. los granos,** to winnow. —*r.v.* 1. to take the air, refresh oneself in the air. 2. to catch cold.
aireo, *m.* airing, ventilation; aeration.
airón, *m.* 1. (ornith.) grey heron. 2. crest (of certain birds); plume, aigrette, panache (adornment.).
airosamente, *adv.* 1. stylishly, with style, elegantly. 2. successfully, with flying colors.
airosidad, *f.* style, elegance, stylishness.
airoso, sa, *a.* 1. stylish, elegant, graceful, self-assured. 2. successful, e.g. *salir a.,* to come out (of something) successfully, come through with flying colors. 3. airy, windy.
aislable, *a.* 1. capable of being isolated. 2. able to be insulated.
aislación, *f.* insulation.
aislacionismo, *m.* isolationism.
aislacionista, *a., m., f.* isolationist.
aisladamente, *adv.* isolatedly.
aislado, da, *past part. of* **aislar.** —*a.* isolated; in isolation or seclusion, e.g. *vivir a.,* to live in isolation or seclusion.
aislador, ra, *a.* insulating; isolating. —*m.* insulator; **a. de cadena,** (elec.) string insulator.
aislamiento, *m.* 1. isolation. 2. insulation.
aislante, *m.* insulant, insulating, insulator; **a. hidrófugo,** water-repellent insulant.
aislar, *tr.v.* 1. to isolate. 2. (phys., elec.) to insulate. —*r.v.* to isolate oneself; to retire, withdraw.
aj, *m.* illness, indisposition, complaint; (*pl.*) illnesses, aches and pains.
aja, *f.* adze, chip-ax.
ajá, *interj.* (coll.) that's right! aha! (expression of approval).
ajabeba, *f.* Moorish flute.
ajacho, *m.* (Bol.) strong drink made of chicha and chili.
ajada, *f.* sauce made of bread soaked in garlic, water and salt.
ajadamente, *adv.* languidly.
ajado, da, *past part. of* **ajar.** —*a.* 1. sad, withered. 2. garlicky.
ajajá, *interj., var. of* **¡ajá!**
ajambado, da, *a.* (C. Amer.) hearty, voracious.
ajamiento, *m.* 1. rumpling; mussing; crumpling; spoiling. 2. insult.
ajamonarse, *r.v.* 1. (coll.) to acquire a middle age spread (a woman). 2. (Chile) to grow old and withered.
ajar, *tr.v.* 1. to spoil, mar, tarnish; to rumple, muss, crumple. 2. to insult. —*r.v.* to become tarnished; to become rumpled, crumpled, mussed. —*m.* garlic field.
ajaraca, *f.* bow, garland or knot ornamentation (in Arabic architecture).

ajaracado, *m.* ornamentation in the form of bows, garlands or knots (found in Arabic architecture).
ajarafe, *m.* 1. tableland, plateau. 2. flat roof.
ajaspajas, *f.* (*pl.*) bagatelle, trifle.
aje, *m.* 1. illness, indisposition; (*pl.*) aches and pains. 2. (bot.) a kind of yam. 3. (ento.) cochineal insect from which a yellow dye is obtained.
ajea, *f.* 1. (bot.) mugwort. 2. brushwood.
ajear, *i.v.* to cry like a partridge.
ajebe, *m.* rock alum.
ajedrea, *f.* (bot.) savory.
ajedrecista, *m.* chess player.
ajedrez, *m.* 1. chess; chess set. 2. (mar.) latticed wood barrier used to impede boarding by raiding party.
ajedrezado, da, *a.* checkered.
ajedrezar, *tr.v.* to combine colors.
ajenabe, *m., var. of* **jenabe.**
ajenabo, *m., var. of* **jenabe.**
ajenación, *f. var. of* **enajenación.**
ajenar, *tr.v., var. of* **enajenar.**
ajengibre, *m., var. of* **jengibre.**
ajenjo, *m.* absinthe (plant and drink), wormwood.
ajeno, na, *a.* 1. belonging to another, of another. 2. foreign, alien. 3. strange, different. 4. (fig.) distant, far away, remote, detached. — **a. a,** foreign or alien to; **a. de,** free of, devoid of, lacking; ignorant of, unaware of; **no codiciéis el bien ajeno,** do not covet thy neighbor's goods; **estar a. de sí,** to be detached.
ajenuz, *m.* (bot.) love-in-a-mist; field fennel.
ajeo, *m.* cry of a pursued partridge. — **perro de a.,** setter (dog).
ajerezado, da, *a.* like sherry, sherry-type (wine). — **coñac a.,** sherry-flavored brandy.
ajero, ra, *m., f.* garlic vendor. —*m.* owner of a garlic field.
ajesuitado, da, *a.* 1. Jesuitical, Jesuit-like. 2. (fig., Amer.) crafty.
ajete, *m.* 1. *dim. of* **ajo,** young garlic plant. 2. (bot.) wild leek. 3. garlic sauce.
ajetrear, *tr.v.* to tire, fatigue, bustle and bustle about. —*r.v.* to bustle about, wear oneself out.
ajetreo, *m.* bustling about, bustle.
ají, *m.* (*pl.* **ajíes**) (bot.) bell pepper; capsicum; chili pepper.
ajiaceite, *m.* garlic and oil sauce.
ajiaco, *m.* 1. (Amer.) stew made of vegetables and meat. 2. (Cuba) muddle, jumble, mixture.
ajicero, ra, *m.* chili sauce container. —*m., f.* (Chile) person who sells chili.
ajicola, *f.* glue made of kidskin boiled with garlic (used in paints).
ajicomino, *m.* garlic and cumin seed sauce.
ajiche, *a.* (Guat.), thin, run down.
ajigolear, *tr.v.* (Mex.) to urge, hurry.
ajilar, *i.v.* 1. (Amer.) to go to a specific place. 2. (Cuba) to walk hurriedly.
ajilimoje, *m., var. of* **ajilimójili.**
ajilimójili, *m.* 1. bell pepper, garlic and vinegar sauce. 2. (*pl.*) (coll.) extras. — **con todos sus ajilimójilis,** (coll.) including everything, the works (sl.).
ajillo, *m.* mixture of crushed garlic, green pepper, bread crumbs, oil, vinegar, and salt. — **calamares al a.,** squid in garlic sauce.
ajimez, *m.* (archit.) mullioned window.
ajipuerro, *m.* (bot.) wild leek (Allium porrum).
ajironar, *tr.v.* 1. to tear to shreds 2. to make an uneven edge (on a skirt or other garment).
ajiseco, *m.* 1. dried chili. 2. slightly piquant green pepper. 3. (Peru) purple-colored gamecock.
ajizal, *m.* green pepper field.
ajo, *m.* 1. garlic; garlic clove; garlic sauce. 2. (coll.) ladies' cosmetic. 3. (coll.) secret or shady affair or business. 4. (coll.) coarse expression. — **a. blanco,** sauce made of raw garlic, bread crumbs, salt, oil and vinegar; **a. cañete, castañete, castañuelo,** reddish variety of garlic; **a. cebollino,** small garlic; **a. chalote,** shallot; **a. de Valdestillas,** (coll.) costly, extra; **a.̇ porro** or **puerro,** leek; **andar en el a.,** to be in the know; **revolver el a.,** to stir up trouble; **soltar ajos y cebollas,** to swear, curse; **tieso como un a.,** straight as a rod.
ajó, *interj.* (Amer.) 1. word used to encourage children to begin to speak. 2. my goodness! wow!
ajobar, *tr.v.* to carry on the back.
ajobero, ra, *a.* carrying, bearing. —*m., f.* carrier, bearer.
ajobilla, *f.* (zool.) variety of mollusk found on the coast of Spain.
ajobo, *m.* 1. bearing, carrying. 2. load, burden, 3. hardship, fatigue, burden.
ajofaina, *f., var. of* **aljofaina.**
ajolín, *m.* (ento.) black bedbug.
ajolote, *m.* (zool.) axolotl, edible lake salamander.
ajomate, *m.* (bot.) conferva, bright green alga (Rhizoclonium rivulare).
ajonje, *m.* 1. birdlime. 2. (bot.) carline thistle.
ajonjear, *tr.v.* (Col.) to spoil, indulge, pamper, pet.
ajonjeo *m.* (Col.) indulging, spoiling, pampering, petting.
ajonjera, *f.* (bot.) carline thistle. — **a. juncal,** gum succory.
ajonjero, *m., var. of* **ajonjera.**
ajonjo, *m., var. of* **ajonje.**
ajonjolí, *m.* 1. (bot.) sesame seed. 2. (Ven.) tapeworm larvae (of pigs).
ajonuez, *m.* (cul.) garlic and nutmeg sauce.
ajoqueso, *m.* (cul.) garlic and cheese sauce.
ajorar, *tr.v.* to move, drive (by force).
ajorca, *f.* bangle, bracelet; anklet.
ajordar, *i.v.* (Arg.) to raise one's voice.
ajornalar, *tr.v.* to hire by the day. —*r.v.* to work by the day.
ajorrar, *tr.v.* to drag (timber) to a freight station.
ajotar, *tr.v.* 1. (Amer.) to tease, incite (a dog). 2. to prejudice a person against another.
ajote, *m.* (bot.) water germander.
ajuagas, *f.* (*pl.*) (vet.) malanders, sores on the hoof.
ajuanetado, da, *a., var. of* **juanetudo.**
ajuaneteado, da, *a., var. of* **juanetudo.**
ajuar, *m.* 1. dowry. 2. trousseau. 3. household furniture and effects.
ajuarar, *tr.v.* to furnish.
ajudiado, da, *a.* having Jewish traits.
ajuglarado, da, *a.* minstrel-like, juggler-like, buffoon-like.
ajuglarar, *tr.v.* to juggle. —*i.v.* to perform like a minstrel or a buffoon.
ajuiciado, da, *past part. of* **ajuiciar.** —*a.* sensible, prudent, judicious, wise.
ajuiciar, *i.v.* to become sensible or prudent. —*tr.v.* 1. to make sensible or prudent. 2. *var. of* **enjuiciar,** to judge.
ajumarse, *r.v.* (coll.) (vulg.) to get drunk.
ajuncia, *f.* (Col.) anguish.
ajuno, na, *a.* like garlic, tasting of garlic.
ajupar, *tr.v.* (Pan.) to tease, incite.
ajustabilidad, *f.* adjustability.
ajustable, *a.* adjustable.
ajustadamente, *adv.* 1. tightly. 2. justly, rightly. 3. by a small margin or amount, e.g. *ganar a.,* to win by a small margin.
ajustado, da, *past part. of* **ajustar.** —*a.* 1. tight, tight-fitting. 2. just, correct, right.
ajustador, ra, *a.* adjusting. —*m.* 1. adjuster; fitter, machinist; (print.) justifier. 2. (Car.) brassiere. 3. (jewel.) ring-guard (to stop large ring from slipping off the finger). — **a. de reclamaciones,** claims adjuster; **a. mecánico,** metal fitter; tool maker, model maker.
ajustamiento, *m., var. of* **ajuste.**
ajustar, *tr.v.* 1. to adjust; to fit; to adapt. 2. to tighten, make tight or tighter; to take in (e.g. a dress). 3. to arrange (a marriage), make, negotiate (peace), settle, come to an agreement on (a court action). 4. to control, moderate. 5. to reconcile, bring together. 6. to pay, settle (an account); to adjust (insurance claims). 7. to fix (a price). 8. to contract, hire, engage. 9. to deal, give (blows). 10. (print.) to make up; to justify. 11. (mec.) to adjust, regulate. 12. (Col.) to skimp, use economically, economize on. — **a. las cuentas,** to settle accounts. —*i.v.* 1. to fit. 2. to be tight (dress), pinch (shoe). — **ahí es donde le ajusta a uno el zapato,** that's where the shoe pinches. —*r.v.* 1. to conform, adjust or adapt oneself. 2. to fit. 3. to tighten, e.g. *ajustarse el cinturón,* to tighten one's belt. 4. to get hired or contracted. 5. to come to an agreement. 6. to be made or negotiated (peace), be arranged (a marriage), be settled (court case). 7. to accord, be in accordance, e.g. *no ajustarse a la realidad,* to be unrealistic. 8. (taur.) to fight close.
ajuste, *m.* 1. adjustment; fitting. 2. hiring engaging. 3. setting (of price). 4. agreement; settlement; arrangement. 5. reconciliation. 6. (acous.) scaling. 7. (print.) make-up. 8. (C. Amer.) gratuity, extra. — **tubo de a.,** adapting pipe; **a. conificado,** taper fit; **a. exacto,** close fit.
ajustero, ra, *a.* (Col.) contracting. —*m., f.* contractor.
ajusticiado, da, *past part. of* **ajusticiar.** —*m., f.* executed criminal.
ajusticiamiento, *m.* execution (of a criminal).
ajusticiar, *tr.v.* to execute (a criminal).
ajustón, *m.* 1. (Amer.) punishment, illtreatment. 2. (Ecuad.) *var. of* **apretón.**
al, *contraction of* **a** *and* **el.** 1. on, about, **al** + *inf.,* on + *ger.,* e.g. *al despertarme,* on waking up, *al llegar,* about to arrive. 2. to the, at, at the *(followed by a masculine noun),* e.g. *al parque,* to the park, *al desayuno,* at breakfast.
Al *sym. of* **aluminio,** aluminum, aluminium (Al).
ala, *f.* 1. wing (of bird, plane, building, etc.). 2. wing, protection, e.g. *bajo su a.,* under one's wing. 3. brim (of hat). 4. (archit.) eaves (of roof). 5. row, line. 6. wing, side, faction, e.g. *a. derecha* or *izquierda,* right or left wing. 7. (mil., mar.) wing, flank. 8. (anat.) ala, wing. 9. (bot.) wing (foliaceous, membranous or woody expansion). 10. (bot.) elecampane. 11. (fort.) wing, curtain. 12. (mar.) upper-studding sail. 13. (mec.) propeller blade. 14. (*pl.*) courage, valor, spirit. 15. wing (in soccer). — **a. del corazón,** (med.) auricle; **a. ranurada,** slotted wing; **a. sinclinal,** (geol.) trough limb; **a. de molino,** windmill vane; **a. de mosca,** (sl.) cheating trick (at cards); brad, tack; **ahuecar el a.,** to get going, beat it (sl.), run away; **arrastrar el a.,** to court, woo; **caérsele a uno las alas,** to lose heart; **cortarle a uno las alas,** to discourage, throw a wet blanket on someone's plans; to clip someone's wings, limit someone's scope; **dar alas,** to encourage; **de alas delta,** (aer.) delta-wing; **tomar** alas, to take liberties; **volar uno con sus propias alas,** to stand on one's own feet.
¡alá! *interj., var. of* **¡Hala!**
Alá, *m.* Allah.
alabado, *past part. of* **alabar.** —*m.* 1. hymn sung in honor of the Eucharist. 2. (Amer.) song of watchmen and field workers at dawn. — **al a.,** (Chile, coll.) at daybreak.
alabador, ra, *a.* praising. —*m., f.* praiser.

alabamiento, *m., var. of* **alabanza.**
alabancero, ra, *a.* flattering. —*m., f.* flatterer.
alabancia, *f.* boast, brag.
alabancioso, sa, *a.* (coll.) boastful, bragging.
alabandina, *f.* (min.) alabandite, manganblende.
alabanza, *f.* praise, commendation; glory.
alabar, *tr.v.* to praise, extol. —*i.v.* (Mex.) to sing the alabado. —*r.v.* to boast; **alabarse a sí mismo,** to blow one's horn.
alabarda, *f.* (mil.) halberd.
alabardado, da, *a.* halberd-shaped.
alabardazo, *m.* blow with a halberd.
alabardero, *m.* 1. halberdier. 2. (coll.) hired fan (theat.), one of a claque.
alabastrado, da, *a.* alabaster, alabaster-like, alabastrine.
alabastrina, *f.* sheet of selenite or gypseous alabaster (used instead of window glass).
alabastrino, na, *a.* alabaster, alabastrine.
alabastrita, alabastrites, *f.* gypseous alabaster, selenite.
alabastro, *m.* alabaster; **a. oriental,** oriental alabaster; **a. yesoso,** gypseous alabaster, selenite.
álabe, *m.* 1. (hydr.) bucket, vane, blade (of water wheel); (mec.) cog, tooth (on wheel). 2. drooping branch of a tree. 3. lining mat in carts. 4. (archit.) eaves. — **á. difusor,** diffusion vane; **á. delfector,** deflector or redirecting vane.
alabeado, da, *past part. of* **alabear.** —*a.* 1. warped, buckled. 2. cambered.
alabear, *tr.v.* 1. to camber. 2. to warp, make warped (wood). —*r.v.* to warp.
alábega, *f., var. of* **albahaca.**
alabeo, *m.* warping.
alabesa, *f.* short spear.
alabiado, da, *a.* ragged-edged (of badly milled coins).
alacate, *m.* (Mex.) gourd, pumpkin.
alacayuela, *f.* (bot.) a cistaceous plant with yellow flowers found in the mountains of Southern Spain.
alacena, *f.* 1. cupboard, closet. 2. (mar.) locker.
alaciarse, *r.v., var. of* **enlaciarse.**
alaco, *m.* 1. (Hond.) wastrel, good-for-nothing. 2. (Hond., El Salv.) rag, tatter.
alacrán, *m.* 1. (ento.) scorpion. 2. fastener, link (for metal button). 3. bridle-bit ring. 4. (Arg., Col.) backbiter, slanderer. — **a. cebollero,** (ento.) male cricket; **a. marino,** (ichth.) angler.
alacranado, da, *a.* 1. bitten by a scorpion. 2. disease-ridden, vice-ridden.
alacrancillo, *m.* (bot.) heliotrope.
alacranear, *i.v.* (Arg.) to backbite, be a backbiter.
alacranera, *f.* (bot.) scorpion grass.
alacridad, *f.* alacrity, diligence.
alacha, alache, *f.* (ichth.) small sardine, anchovy.
alada, *f.* fluttering of wings.
aladar, *m.* lock of hair falling over the temple (gen. used in *pl.*).
aladear, *tr.v.* (Ecuad.) to withdraw one's esteem.
aladica, *f.* (ento.) winged ant.
aladierna, *f., m.* (bot.) buckthorn.
aladierno, *m., var. of* **aladierna.**
Aladino, *m.* Aladdin. — **A. y la lámpara maravillosa,** Aladdin and the magic lamp.
alado, da, *a.* 1. winged, having wings. 2. swift. 3. (bot.) alate, wing-shaped.
aladrada, *f.* furrow.
aladrar, *tr.v.* to plow.
aladrería, *f.* (Sp.) farming tools; furrows left by the plow.
aladrero, *m.* 1. (min.) timberman. 2. maker or repairer of farming tools.
aladro, *m.* plow.
aladroque, *m.* (ichth.) small sardine, anchovy (Sardinella allecia).
alafia, *f.* (coll.) mercy, pardon, pity (used mainly with **pedir**).
alafre, *a.* (Ven.) base, vile.
álaga, *f.* wheat with long yellow grain; grain of this wheat.
alagadizo, za, *a.* easily waterlogged.
alagar, (*ref. 51*) *tr.v.* to make waterlogged. —*r.v.* to become waterlogged.
alagartado, da, *a.* 1. lizard-like (in coloring), variegated. 2. (C. Amer.) stingy, miserly.
alagartarse, *r.v.* 1. (Mex.) to stand with legs splayed (horses). 2. (C. Amer.) to become stingy.
alague, *ref.* **alagar.**
alajor, *m.* tribute formerly paid by tenants to landowners.
alajú, (*pl.* **alajúes**) *m.* paste of almonds, nuts and honey.
alalá, *m.* popular song of Northern Spain.
alalia, *f.* (med.) aphonia, loss of speech.
alalimón, *m.* children's game in which the participants sing a song beginning with **alalimón.**
alalino, na, *a.* dumb, mute.
alama, *f.* yellow-flowered leguminous plant.
alamanda, *f.* (bot.) allamanda.
alamar, *m.* 1. frog (ornamental loop sewed on as a fastener). 2. trimming, fringe, tassel.
alambicadamente, *adv.* elaborately, ornately, with an elaborate style.
alambicado, da, *past part. of* **alambicar.** —*a.* 1. elaborate, ornate, intricate, complicated (style). 2. given sparingly or bit by bit.
alambicamiento, *m.* 1. distillation. 2. elaborateness, ornateness (of style).
alambicar, (*ref. 50*) *tr.v.* 1. to distill. 2. to pore over. 3. to make excessively subtle (language, style, concepts). 4. (coll.) to reduce (price) as much as possible.
alambique, alambiqué, *ref.* **alambicar.**
alambique, *m.* 1. still, alembic. 2. (Amer., S. Spain) distillery. — **por a.,** in dribs and drabs, sparingly.
alambiquería, *f.* (Cuba, P. Rico) distillery.
alambiquero, *m.* (Cuba) owner or manager of a still or distillery.
alambor, *m.* 1. (archit.) bevel cut (of stone or wood). 2. (fort.) scarp, rough slope.
alamborado, da, *a.* beveled.
alambrado, da, *past part. of* **alambrar.** —*a.* fenced off with wire netting. —*m.* wire fence, barbed wire fence; wire netting, wire mesh. —*f.* (mil.) wire entanglement; barbed wire fence.
alambrar, *tr.v.* to surround with a wire fence.
alambre, *m.* 1. wire. 2. copper. 3. cowbells, sheepbells. — **a. alimentador,** feed wire; **a. de guardia,** (elec.) guard wire; **a. de púas,** barbed wire; **a. de soldadura,** wire solder; **a. forrado,** covered wire, **a. cargado,** live wire; **a. aislado,** insulated wire.
alambrear, *i.v.* to peck at the cage wire (partridge).
alambrecarril, *m.* cable or funicular railway, cableway.
alambrera, *f.* 1. wire screen (for doors, windows); wire cover (used to cover foods). 2. fender (for a fire), fireguard.
alambrería, *f.* wire shop.
alameda, *f.* public walk lined with trees; promenade lined with poplars; poplar cove.
alamedero, *m.* (Mex.) keeper of a poplar grove or public walk.
alamín, *m.* (arch.) 1. clerk appointed to check weights and measures and set prices for foodstuffs. 2. building inspector. 3. judge dealing with distribution of water and irrigation offenses.
alaminazgo, *m.* office of the **alamín.**
álamo, *m.* (bot.) poplar. — **a. alpino, a. líbico,** trembling poplar; **a. blanco,** white poplar; **a. negro,** black poplar; **a. temblón,** aspen tree.
alampar, *i.v., r.v.* (Sp., reg.) to yearn, long, crave, e.g. *estoy alampado por beber,* I'm longing for a drink.
alamud, *m.* (arch.) square bolt, iron bar (used as bolt for doors or windows).
alanceador, ra, *a.* lancing, spearing, wounding. —*m.* lancer.
alancear, *tr.v.* 1. to lance, spear, wound with a lance. 2. (fig.) to criticize, censure.
alandrearse, *r.v.* to become dry, stiff and blanched (silkworms).
alanés, *m.* (zool., Mex.) a species of large deer.
alanina, *f.* (chem.) alanine.
alano, na, *m., f.* wolf hound. —*a.* pertaining to the Alani, early invaders of Spain.
alantoico, ca, *a.* (med.) allantoic.
alantoides, *a.* allantoid. —*f.* (anat.) allantois.
alanzar, (*ref. 53*) *tr.v.* to lance, spear, wound with a lance or spear.
alapí, *m.* (ornith., C. Amer.) ant-eating bird.
alaqueca, *f.* (min.) carnelian.
alaqueque, *m., var. of* **alaqueca.**
alar, *m.* 1. eaves. 2. (hunt.) horsehair snare (for catching partridges). 3. (Amer.) sidewalk.
alárabe, *a., m., f.* Arab, Arabian.
alarde, *m.* 1. display, ostentation, show, braggadocio. 2. inspection, review (of troops). 3. muster roll. 4. visit of judge to prisoners. 5. fortnightly review of pending work (made by state tribunals). 6. examination of hive made by bees when they leave and enter. — **hacer a. de,** to make a show of, show off about, boast of, brag of; **a. de fuerza,** show of strength.
alardear, *i.v.* to boast; **a. de,** to boast about. —**a. de rico,** he boasts about how rich he is.
alardeo, *m.* ostentation, showing off (coll.), bragging.
alardoso, sa, *a.* ostentatious.
alarga, *f.* **dar la a.** 1. to let out more string (for kite). 2. (Sp., reg.) to foster excessive familiarity.
alargada, *f.* 1. extension, lengthening. 2. (mar.) subsiding of the wind.
alargadera, *f.* 1. lengthening bar (for compass or drill). 2. (chem.) adapter, nozzle.
alargado, da, *a.* extended, elongated, lengthened, stretched.
alargador, ra, *a.* extending, lengthening, stretching.
alárgama, *f.* (bot.) African rue.
alargamiento, *m.* lengthening, extension, stretching.
alargar, (*ref. 51*) *tr.v.* 1. to lengthen, extend, make longer. 2. to stretch, stretch out (leg, arm). 3. to open wide, e.g. *a. la vista,* to keep one's eyes open; to open, prick up (one's ears). 4. to hand (something to someone). 5. to let out, play out (cable, rope). 6. to stretch (salary, rations, etc.). 7. to push away, drive away, separate. —*r.v.* 1. to lengthen, grow or get longer. 2. (mar.) to veer aft (wind). 3. to expatiate, enlarge.
alargue, alargué, *ref.* **alargar.**
alarguez, *m.* (bot.) barberry, aspalathus.
alaria, *f.* (potter's) fettling iron.
alarida, *f.* hue and cry, loud shouting.
alarido, *m.* howl, scream, shout; Moorish war cry.
alarifazgo, *m.* office of an architect or master builder.
alarife, *m.* 1. architect, master builder; mason. 2. (Arg.) astute, clever fellow.
alarije, *a.* large red (grape).

alario, ria, *a.* alary, alar; shaped like a wing.
alarma, *f.* 1. alarm; warning. 2. **alarm,** fright, anxiety. — **a. aérea, air-raid** warning; **a. contra robos** or **ladrones,** burglar alarm; **a. de incendios,** fire alarm; **dar la a.,** to give or sound the alarm; **falsa a.,** false alarm; **poner la a.,** to set the alarm.
alarmador, ra, *a.* alarming.
alarmante, *a.* alarming.
alarmar, *tr.v.* 1. to alarm; disquiet. 2. to call to arms. —*r.v.* to become alarmed or frightened.
alármega, *f.* (bot.) African rue.
alarmismo, *m.* alarmism.
alarmista, *a., m., f.* alarmist.
alaroz, *m.* screen-door frame.
alaste, *a.* (C. Rica, Nic.) slippery, viscous.
alastrar, *tr.v.* to throw (the ears) back (animals). —*r.v.* to lie flat, lie close to the ground to avoid discovery (animals).
a látere, *m.* (coll.) constant companion, bosom friend.
alaterno, *m., var. of* **aladierna.**
alatinado, da, *a.* affected, Latinlike (language).
alatrón, *m.* foam of niter, saltpeter.
alavanco, *m.* wild duck.
alavense, *a., m., f.* Alavese, of or from the province of Alava, Spain.
alavés, sa, *a., m., f.* Alavese.
alavesa, *f.* short lance.
alazán, na, *a.* sorrel-colored, chestnut-colored, reddish-brown. —*m., f.* sorrel-colored horse or mare.
alazana, *f.* olive oil press.
alazano, na, *a., m., f., var. of* **alazán.**
alazo, *m.* blow with a wing.
alazor, *m.* (bot.) safflower, bastard saffron.
alba, *f.* 1. dawn, daybreak; first rays of light before sunrise. 2. (ecc.) alb, religious vestment. 3. (mil.) last watch of the night. — **rayar** or **romper el a.,** the dawn breaks.
albacara, *f.* 1. (fort.) outer tower of fortress where the cattle were kept. 2. round, projecting tower.
albacea, *m.* (law) executor. —*f.* executrix.
albaceazgo, *m.* (law) executorship, office of administrator of an estate.
albacetense, *a., m., f., var. of* **albaceteño.**
albaceteño, ña, *a., m., f.* of or from the Spanish province of Albacete.
albacora, *f.* 1. early fig. 2. (ichth.) albacore, bonito, tuna.
albada, *f.* 1. aubade, morning serenade. 2. (bot.) soapwort.
albahaca, *f.* (bot.) sweet basil.
albahaquero, *m.* flowerpot, jardiniere.
albahaquilla, *f.* **a. de río,** (bot.) pellitory, wall pellitory.
albaicín, *m.* 1. hilly part of town. 2. **A.,** Gypsy quarter of Granada.
albaida, *f.* (bot.) anthyllis (Anthyllis cistoides).
albalá, *m., f.* (arch.) public or private document of attestation; royal grant or charter.
albanado, da, *a.* sleepy.
albanecar, *m.* (carp.) triangle formed by the two sides of sloping roof.
albanega, *f.* 1. hair net; net for catching rabbits. 2. (archit.) spandrel; pendentive.
albaneguero, *m.* (sl.) dice-player, crapshooter.
albanés, sa, *a., m., f.* Albanian. —*m.* Albanian (language).
Albania, *f.* Albania.
albano, na, *a., m., f.* Albanian.
albañal, *m.* 1. sewer. 2. cesspool; slop basin or can. 3. (fig.) filth, foulness. — **salir por el a.,** (fig., coll.) to come out badly from some experience.
albañalero, *m.* sewer builder; sewer cleaner.
albañar, *m., var. of* **albañal.**
albañil, *m.* mason, bricklayer.
albañila, *a.* **abeja a.,** mason bee.
albañilería, *f.* masonry; bricklaying. — **a. de piedra bruta,** rubblework, rubble masonry; **a. de piedra labrada, a. de hilera,** ashlar masonry.
albaquía, *f.* balance due of a debt.
albar, *a.* white. —*m.* whitish unwatered soil or land.
albarán, *m.* 1. "for rent" sign. 2. public or private document of attestation. 3. (com.) duplicate note of purchase.
albarazado, da, *a.* 1. whitish. 2. black or grey streaked with red. 3. (Mex.) half-breed, of Chinese and mestizo parents. 4. (med.) leprous.
albarazo, *m.* 1. (med., vet.) ringworm, tetter. 2. (med.) alphos, white leprosy.
albarca, *f., var. of* **abarca.**
albarcoque, *m., var. of* **albaricoque.**
albarcoquero, *m., var. of* **albaricoquero.**
albarda, *f.* 1. packsaddle. 2. (cul.) lardon, strip of fat bacon. 3. (Guat., Hond.) peasant's rawhide saddle. — **a. gallinera,** flat packsaddle; **a. sobre a.,** (coll.) time after time.
albardado, da, *a.* saddlebacked, with different colored skin on the back.
albardán, *m.* buffoon, jester, fool.
albardanería, *f.* buffoonery, jesting.
albardar, *tr.v., var. of* **enalbardar.**
albardear, *tr.v.* 1. (C. Amer.) to saddle a wild horse (in the process of breaking it). 2. (Hond.) to annoy.
albardela, *f.* breaking saddle, training saddle (for breaking horses).
albardería, *f.* 1. packsaddle-maker's shop. 2. packsaddle making.
albardero, *m.* packsaddle maker.
albardilla, *f.* 1. breaking or training saddle (used in breaking horses). 2. thick wool (on sheep's back). 3. lining (on the handles of clipper's shears). 4. water carrier's shoulder pad. 5. iron holder. 6. (bldg.) coping. 7. ridge (dividing garden beds or plots); ridge of mud (forming in paths after rain and use by traffic). 8. mud (sticking to plough-shares). 9. (cul.) lardon (strips of bacon used in roasting meat). 10. (cul.) batter. 11. trick used by cardsharps.
albardín, *m.* (bot.) matweed (Lygeum spartum).
albardinar, *m.* matweed patch or field.
albardón, *m.* 1. large packsaddle; riding saddle (used in Andalusia). 2. (S. Amer.) ridge of fertile land (between lakes, river or canals). 3. (Hond., mas.) coping.
albardonería, *f., var. of* **albardería.**
albardonero, *m., var. of* **albardero.**
albarejo, *a.* **trigo a.,** white wheat. —*m.* white wheat; white bread.
albareque, *m.* fine-mesh fishing net.
albarico, *a., m., var. of* **albarejo.**
albaricoque, *m.* 1. (bot.) apricot (fruit). 2. apricot tree.
albaricoquero, *m.* (bot.) apricot tree.
albarigo, *a., m., var. of* **albarejo.**
albarillo, *m.* 1. fast tune played on the guitar to accompany dancing or ballads. 2. white apricot. 3. white-apricot tree.
albarino, *m.* (obs.) white cosmetic, ceruse.
albariza, *f.* salt lake.
albarizo, za, *a.* whitish (soil). —*m.* white soil.
albarra, *f.* (bot.) a kind of plum tree.
albarrada, *f.* 1. unmortared stone wall, terrace of earth (contained by such a wall); earthen wall; earthen or stone barricade, defensive earthwork. 2. earthenware bottle.
albarrana, *f., var. of* **albarranilla,**
albarranilla, *f.* (bot.) squill.
albarraz, *m.* 1. (med.) alphos, white leprosy. 2. (bot.) lousewort.
albarrazado, da, *a.* mottled, multicolored.
albarsa, *f.* fisherman's basket.
albatoza, *f.* small covered boat.
albatros, *m.* (ornith.) albatross.
albayaldado, da, *a.* coated with white lead.
albayaldar, *tr.v.* to coat with white lead.
albayalde, *m.* white lead, ceruse.
albazano, na, *a.* of dark-chestnut color.
albazo, *m.* 1. (Ecuad., Mex.) action fought at dawn. 2. (Chile, Peru) morning serenade.
albear, *i.v.* 1. to turn white; to be whitish. 2. (Arg.) to get up early.
albedo, *m.* (astron.) albedo, reflecting power of an illuminated body.
albedrío, *m.* 1. free will (gen. with **libre**). 2. whim, caprice, fancy. 3. unwritten law, precedent. — **al a. de alguien,** as one sees fit; **rendir el a.,** to submit.
albéitar, *m.* veterinarian.
albeitería, *f.* veterinary science.
albeldar, *tr.v., var. of* **bieldar.**
albellanino, *m.* (bot.) cornel tree.
albellón, *m., var. of* **albollón.**
albenda, *f.* embroidered white linen hangings.
albendera, *f.* 1. woman who makes and embroiders hangings. 2. (coll.) gadabout, loafer (female).
albengala, *f.* gauze worn as adornment on Moorish turban.
albentcla, *f.* fine-meshed fishing net.
alberca, *f.* 1. pool, reservoir, tank. 2. pond or vat for steeping hemp or flax.
albérchiga, *f., var. of* **albérchigo.**
alberchigal, *m.* peach orchard.
albérchigo, *m.* 1. peach (fruit). 2. peach tree.
alberchiguero, *m.* 1. peach tree. 2 (reg.) apricot tree.
albercón, *m. aug. of* **alberca,** large reservoir or tank.
albercoque, *m., var. of* **albaricoque.**
albercoquero, *m., var. of* **albaricoquero.**
albergada, *f.* 1. (mil., arch.) camping site. 2. (arch.) lodging, shelter.
albergador, ra, *a.* sheltering. —*m., f.* shelterer.
albergar, (*ref. 51*) *tr.v.* to give lodging to, lodge; to shelter, harbor. —*i.v., r.v.* to take lodgings, lodge; to shelter, take shelter.
albergue, albergué, *ref.* **albergar.**
albergue, *m.* lodging; shelter, refuge; den, lair (of animals); hostel; **a. de jóvenes,** youth hostel.
alberguería, *f.* 1. inn. 2. poorhouse.
alberguero, ra, *m., f.* inn-keeper.
albero, ra, *a.* whitish. —*m.* 1. whitish **earth.** 2. dishcloth.
alberque, *m., var. of* **alberca.**
alberquero, ra, *m., f.* caretaker of reservoirs, pools or tanks.
albertita, *f.* (min.) black asphalt.
albescencia, *f.* albescence.
albicante, *a.* whitening, bleaching.
albido, da, *a.* whitish.
albigense, *a., m., f.* Albigensian, **native of** Albi; (*pl.*) Albigenses, 12th C. French heretics who condemned the use of sacraments and the hierarchy of the Church.
albihar, *m.* (bot.) oxeye.
albillo, lla, *a.* **uva a.,** variety of soft white grape; **vino a.,** wine made with that grape.
albín, *m.* 1. (min.) bloodstone, hematite. 2. (p.) dark carmine color.
albina, *f.* 1. salt marsh. 2. salt (left in salt marsh).

albinismo, *m.* albinism.
albino, na, *a.* albino, albinic. *—m., f.* 1. albino. 2. (Mex.) octoroon, offspring of a quadroon and a Caucasian.
Albión, *m.* (poet.) Albion (England).
albita, *f.* (min.) albite, white feldspar.
albitana, *f.* 1. plant fence. 2. (mar.) apron.
albo, ba, *a.* (poet.) white.
alboaire, *m.* tile-work (in archways).
albogón, *m.* 1. ancient wooden bass flute. 2. instrument resembling a bagpipe.
albogue, *m.* 1. flageolet; pastoral flute. 2. cymbal.
alboguear, *i.v.* 1. to play the flute. 2. to clash cymbals.
alboguero, ra, *m., f.* flute or flageolet maker or player.
albohol, *m.* (bot.) bindweed; red poppy.
albollón, *m.* drain, gutter; sewer.
albóndiga, *f.* meatball, fish ball.
albondiguilla, *f., var. of* **albóndiga.**
albor, *m.* 1. whiteness. 2. light of dawn. 3. dawn, beginning. — **a.** or **albores de la vida,** infancy, youth.
alborada, *f.* 1. dawn. 2. dawn attack, **action** fought at dawn. 3. (mil.) reveille. 4. aubade, dawn serenade or music.
albórbola, *f.* cheering, joyful shouts.
alborear, *i.v.* to dawn.
alborga, *f.* rope-soled sandal used by Spanish peasants.
albornía, *f.* glazed cup-shaped vessel.
alborno, *m.* (bot.) alburnum.
albornoz, (*pl.* **albornoces**) *m.* 1. coarse woolen cloth. 2. burnoose (hooded cloak worn by the Arabs and Moors).
alboroce, alborocé, *ref.* **alborozar.**
alboronía, *f.* stew of tomatoes, eggplant, pumpkin and green pepper.
alboroque, *m.* treat or refreshment taken or given on sealing a business deal.
alborotadamente, *adv.* excitedly, noisily, confusedly.
alborotadizo, za, *a.* excitable; restive.
alborotado, da, *past part. of* **alborotar.** *—a.* impetuous, headstrong, rash.
alborotador, ra, *a.* trouble-making, agitating. *—m., f.* agitator, troublemaker.
alborotapueblos, *m., f.* 1. agitator, rabblerouser. 2. (coll.) lively person, the life of the party.
alborotar, *tr.v.* to stir up, arouse, agitate, incite; to cause to mutiny or riot. *—i.v.* to make noise or a racket. *—r.v.* to riot, mutiny; to get excited or agitated; to get rough (the sea).
alboroto, *m.* 1. tumult, uproar, clamor; riot, disturbance; confusion, disorder; hubbub, fuss; alarm, unrest; (Mex.) joy, jubilation. 2. (Amer.) honey-coated popcorn.
alborotoso, sa, *a.* (Cuba) *var. of* **alborotador.**
alborozadamente, *adv.* joyfully, rejoicingly; exultingly; delightedly.
alborozador, ra, *a.* bringing great joy or jubilation. *—m., f.* bringer of joy.
alborozar, (*ref. 53*) *tr.v.* to delight, enrapture, overjoy, elate. *—r.v.* to feel elated or overjoyed.
alborozo, *m.* joy, jubilation, delight; gaiety.
alborto, *m.* (bot.) strawberry tree.
albotín, *m.* (bot.) terebinth.
albriciar, *tr.v.* 1. (Sp.) to give good news or glad tidings to. 2. to congratulate.
albricias, *f.* (*pl.*) 1. gift or reward given to one bringing good news; gift given in celebration of a happy event. 2. vents in casting molds. *—interj.* good news! congratulations. — **ganar las a.,** to be the first to congratulate.
albuca, *m.* (bot.) asphodel.
albudeca, *f.* poor quality melon.
albufera, *f.* lagoon, lake.
albugíneo, a, *a.* 1. albugineous. 2. (zool.) entirely white.
albugo, *m.* (med.) albugo, leucoma; white spot (on nails).
albuhera, *f.* pond, tank, reservoir.
álbum, (*pl.* **álbumes**) *m.* album. — **á. de autografos,** autograph album; **á. de estampillas** or **sellos de correo,** stamp album; **á. de recortes,** scrapbook.
albumen, *m.* (bot.) albumen.
albúmina, *f.* (biochem.) albumin. — **a. de leche,** lactalbumin.
albuminado, da, *past part. of* **albuminar.** *—a.* (photog.) emulsified.
albuminar, *tr.v.* (photog.) to emulsify.
albuminímetro, *m.* albuminimeter.
albuminoide, *m.* albuminoid.
albuminoideo, a, *a.* albuminoid, albuminoidal.
albuminómetro, *m., var. of* **albuminímetro.**
albuminosa, *f.* (biochem.) albumose.
albuminoso, sa, *a.* albuminous.
albuminuria, *f.* (med.) albuminuria.
albuminúrico, ca, *a.* albuminuric.
albumosa *f.* (biochem., bot.) albumose.
albur, *m.* 1. (fig.) risk, hazard, chance. 2. first two cards drawn by the dealer in the game of monte. 3. (*pl.*) lansquenet, card game. 4. (ichth.) bleak, river fish. — **correr un a.,** to take a risk, venture.
albura, *f.* 1. perfect whiteness. 2. white of egg. 3. (bot.) alburnum, sapwood. — **doble a.,** (bot.) defect in wood texture.
alburente, *a.* soft and spongy (wood).
alburero, *m.* (cards) lansquenet player.
alburiar, *tr.v.* (C. Rica) to deceive, delude.
alburno, *m.* (bot.) alburnum, sapwood.
alca, *f.* (ornith.) auk.
alcabala, *f.* sales tax. — **a. del viento,** sales tax paid by foreign merchant.
alcabalatorio, ria, *m.* sales-tax register.
alcabalero, *m.* sales-tax collector; tax-collector.
alcabuco, *m., var. of* **arcabuco.**
alcacel, *m., var. of* **alcacer.**
alcacer, *m.* green barley; barley field. — **estar ya duro el a. para zampoñas,** (coll.) to be past the age for learning or doing things, be over the hill; **retozarle a uno el a.,** (coll.) to be very merry or jolly, romp about.
alcachofa, *f.* 1. artichoke (plant and fruit). 2. (mec.) filter.
alcachofado, da, *a.* artichoke-like. *—m.* artichoke stew.
alcachofal, *m.* artichoke field.
alcachofar, *m., var. of* **alcachofal.**
alcachofero, ra, *a.* artichoke. *—m., f.* artichoke seller. *—f.* 1. artichoke (plant).
alcací, *m., var. of* **alcacil.**
alcacil, *m.* wild artichoke.
alcadafe, *m.* receptacle to catch liquid spilled when drawing from a tap.
alcahaz, (*pl.* **alcahaces**) *m.* large bird cage.
alcahazada, *f.* cageful of birds.
alcahazar, (*ref. 53*) *tr.v.* to put in a cage, keep in a cage.
alcahuete, ta, *m., f.* 1. procurer, pimp, pander; procuress, madame. 2. (coll.) one who aids and abets. 3. (coll.) gossiper. *—m.* (theat.) entr'acte curtain, intermission curtain.
alcahuetear, *tr.v.* to procure (for prostitution). *—i.v.* to pimp, procure, be a pander, procurer or procuress.
alcahutería, *f.* 1. procuring, pandering, pimping. 2. (coll.) aiding, abetting. 3. (coll.) trickery.
alcaicería, *f.* raw-silk exchange, Moorish customs house where dealers brought raw silk for tax assessment; raw silk market or bazaar.
alcaico, *a.* (poet.) Alcaic verse.
alcaide, *m.* 1. governor or warden of a castle, fortress or prison. 2. superintendent of a wheat exchange.
alcaidesa, *f.* governor's or warden's wife.
alcaidía, *f.* 1. post of governor or warden of a castle, fortress or prison. 2. territory under the control of the governor of a castle or fortress. 3. cattle toll paid for crossing the territory of certain governors.
alcalá, *m.* (arch.) castle, fortress, citadel.
alcalaíno, na, *a.* of or from Alcalá de Henares, Spain (birthplace of Cervantes). *—m., f.* native or inhabitant of Alcalá de Henares.
alcaldada, *f.* 1. abuse of authority. 2. stupid or foolish remark.
alcalde, *m.* 1. mayor. 2. magistrate. 3. caller (one who calls the figures of a dance), master of ceremonies. 4. card game for six; card game similar to brisque played by three; dummy (cards). — **a. de barrio,** official to whom mayor delegates his powers in a certain section of a city; **a. del mes de enero,** enthusiastic or zealous new employee; **a. de monterrilla,** small town mayor; **a. mayor,** magistrate who exercises ordinary jurisdiction in a town; **a. ordinario,** village magistrate exercising ordinary jurisdiction; magistrate in a city district; **a. pedáneo,** puisne or junior judge; **tener el padre a.,** (fig.) to have a friend at court.
alcadesa, *f.* mayoress; wife of a mayor.
alcaldesco, ca, *a.* (derog.) mayoral, pertaining to mayors or their office.
alcaldía, *f.* mayoralty; mayor's office.
alcaleño, ña, *a.* of or from Alcalá del Júcar, Spain. *—m., f.* native or inhabitant of Alcalá del Júcar.
alcalescencia, *f.* (chem.) alkalescence.
alcalescente, *a.* alcalescent.
álcali, *m.* (chem.) alkali.
alcalice, alcalicé, *ref.* **alcalizar.**
alcalífero, ra, *a.* alkaline.
alcalificante, *a.* alkalifying.
alcalificar, (*ref. 50*) *tr.v.* to alkalify.
alcalimetría, *f.* (chem.) alkalimetry.
alcalímetro, *m.* (chem.) alkalimeter.
alcalinidad, *f.* (chem.) alkalinity.
alcalino, na, *a.* alkaline.
alcalización, *f.* (chem.) alkalization.
alcalizar, (*ref. 53*) *tr.v.* (chem.) to alkalize.
alcaloide, *m.* (chem.) alkaloid.
alcaloideo, a, *a.* (chem.) alkaloid, alkaloidal.
alcalosis, *f.* (med.) alkalosis.
alcaller, *m.* potter.
alcallería, *f.* earthenware, pottery, earthenware pots.
alcamar, *m.* Peruvian bird of prey.
alcamonero, ra, *a.* (Ven.) meddlesome.
alcamonías, *f.* 1. (*pl.*) spices, herbs. 2. (coll.) trickery, tricks. *—m.* (*sing.*) (coll.) pimp, go-between.
alcana, *f.* (bot.) henna.
alcaná *f.* street market.
alcance, alcancé, *ref.* **alcanzar.**
alcance, *m.* 1. reach, arm's length; **range** (of a gun, the eye, etc.); (fenc.) reach; (*pl.*) scope, e.g. *todavía no se saben los alcances del proyecto,* the scope of the project is not yet known. 2. (*pl.*) intelligence, ability, talent, capacity. 3. pursuit, chase. 4. late or special post, special delivery. 5. import, significance. 6. (com.) balance due, deficit; (mil.) credits, money due to a soldier. 7. last minute news, late news. 8. (print.) take (of a copy to be set), portion of copy which a compositor receives for typesetting. — **al a. de,** within reach of; within range of; **al a. de la**

mano, within hands reach; **al a. de la vista,** within eyeshot; **al a. del oído,** within earshot; **a. eficaz,** (mil.) effective range; **andarle** or **irle a uno a** or **en los alcances,** (coll.) to watch, spy on, follow; **a su a.,** within one's reach; within one's power; **dar a. a,** to catch up with, overtake, reach; **de gran a.,** long-range; **de mucho a.,** far-reaching (e.g. measures); **fuera del a.,** out of reach; out of range; **salir en el alcance de,** to get within the reach of; **tener alcances,** to have ability, be able or talented; **a. dañino,** lethal range, damaging range; **a. óptico,** optical range, or path.

alcancía, *f.* 1. money box, coin bank, piggy bank. 2. earthen ball, missile stuffed with flowers or cinders. 3. (mil.) fire grenade, blazing pot full of pitch and other inflammable material thrown at the enemy. 4. (Amer.) alms box, collection box, poor box.

alcándara, *f.* 1. falcon's perch. 2. clothes rack. 3. (N. Africa) sloped road leading to the casbah.

alcandía, *f.* (bot.) sorghum.

alcandial, *m.* millet or sorghum field.

alcandor, *m.* (arch.) a kind of cosmetic.

alcandora, *f.* beacon, signal fire.

alcándora, *f., var. of* **alcándara.**

alcanfor, *m.* camphor.

alcanforada, *f.* (bot.) camphor scented shrub.

alcanforar, *tr.v.* to camphorate. *—r.v.* (Amer.) to disappear, vanish.

alcanforero, *m.* (bot.) camphor tree.

alcántara, *f.* 1. wooden cover over loom treadle to protect velvet. 2. (Cuba) water jug.

alcantarilla, *f.* 1. sewer; culvert, drain. 2. small bridge. 3. (Mex.) cubical water tank.

alcantarillado, *f.* sewage system, sewerage.

alcantarillar, *tr.v.* to lay or install sewers in.

alcantarillero, *m.* sewer keeper.

alcantarino, na, *a.* of or from Alcántara. *—m., f.* native or inhabitant of Alcántara, Portugal.

alcanzable, *a.* attainable, reachable.

alcanzadizo, za, *a.* easily reached or obtained.

alcanzado, da, *past part. of* **alcanzar.** *—a.* in debt, needy, short of money, hard up (coll.)

alcanzador, ra, *a.* pursuing. *—m., f.* pursuer.

alcanzadura, *f.* (vet.) overreach, attaint, contusion or bruise on the pastern of a horse.

alcanzar, (*ref. 53*) *tr.v.* 1. to reach, catch up with, get up to. 2. to reach, reach up to, e.g. *no puedo alcanzarlo,* I can't reach it. 3. to take hold of, reach out and take; (Amer.) to hand, pass, reach, e.g. *alcánzame la sal, por favor,* pass the salt, please. 4. to obtain, get, attain. 5. to live at the same time as. 6. to understand, grasp. 7. to be able to see, smell or hear. 8. to get to, reach. *—i.v.* 1. to reach, e.g. *él prometió pintar el cuarto hasta donde alcanzara su mano,* he promised to paint the room up to where his hand reached. 2. to have a long (or short) range, e.g. *los cañones modernos alcanzan lejos,* modern guns have a long range. 3. to be sufficient, last, e.g. *el dinero que me dio no me alcanzó,* the money he gave me was not sufficient. **— a. a** + *inf.,* to manage to + *inf.,* be able to + *inf. —r.v.* 1. to touch. 2. (vet.) to overreach (horses).

alcaparra, *f.* (bot.) caper (plant and fruit); (Ecuad.) (*pl.*) agave buds (eaten pickled). **— a. de Indias,** Indian cress, garden nasturtium.

alcaparrado, da, *a.* dressed or flavored with capers.

alcaparral, *m.* caper field.

alcaparrera, *f.* (bot.) caper (bush).

alcaparro, *m.* (bot.) caper (bush).

alcaparrón, *m.* large caper (berry).

alcaparrosa, *f., var. of* **caparrosa.**

alcaraván, *m.* (ornith.) stone curlew, thick-knee (Burhinus ccdicnemus).

alcaravea, *f.* (bot.) caraway (plant and seed)

alcaravenero, *a.* said of hawk trained to pursue the stone curlew.

alcarceña, *f.* (bot.) tare, true bitter vetch.

alcarceñal, *m.* bitter vetch field.

alcarchofa, *f., var. of* **alcachofa.**

alcarcil, *m., var. of* **alcaucil.**

alcareño, ña, *a.* of or from Alcalá de Guadaira, Spain. *—m., f.* native or inhabitant of Alcalá de Guadaira.

alcarracero, ra, *m., f.* maker or seller of earthenware water-cooling jugs. *—m.* shelf for water-cooling jugs.

alcarraza, *f.* earthenware water-cooling jug.

alcarreño, ña, *a.* of or from la Alcarria, Spain. *—m., f.* native or inhabitant of la Alcarria.

alcarría, *f.* arid plateau.

alcartaz, (*pl.* **alcartaces**) *m.* paper cone (for holding sweets, etc.).

alcatara, *f., var. of* alquítara.

alcatenes, *m.* (arch.) medicine made of linseed and copperas used for treating sores and ulcers of hunting dogs and falcons.

alcatifa, *f.* 1. fine rug or tapestry. 2. (bldg.) bed of cinders (for leveling a surface before tiling).

alcatraz, (*pl.* **alcatraces**) *m.* (ornith.) pelican; solan; gannet (Sula bassana).

alcaucí, (*pl.* **alcaucíes**) *m., var. of* **alcaucil.**

alcauciar, *tr.v.* (Amer., sl.) to execute by firing squad.

alcaucil, *m.* wild artichoke.

alcaudón, *m.* (ornith.) butcher bird, shrike (Lanius excubitor).

alcayata, *f.* 1. hooked nail, tenterhook, spike; (ry.) track spike. 2. (Col.) oil lamp.

alcazaba, *f.* 1. citadel; fort; castle. 2. a community or settlement perched high on sloping land (Spain and N. Africa).

alcázar, *m.* 1. castle, fortress. 2. (Sp., hist.) king's palace. 3. (mar.) poop deck, quarter deck.

alcazuz, (*pl.* **alcazuces**) *m.* (bot.) licorice (Glycyrrhiza glabra).

alce, alcé, *ref.* **alzar.**

alce, *m.* 1. (zool.) elk, moose. 2. cut (in cards); portion of cards cut. 3. (print.) working up of sheets for printing, putting sheets in order. 4. (Cuba) gathering of cut sugar cane.

alcedo, *m.* maple grove.

Alcestes, *f.* (myth.) Alcestis.

alcino, *m.* (bot.) wild basil.

alción, *m.* 1. (ornith.) halcyon; kingfisher; Chinese swallow. 2. (astron.) **A.,** Alcyone.

Alcione, *f.* 1. (myth.) Halcyon, Alcyone. 2. (astron.) Alcyone.

alcioneo, *a.* halcyon. *—m.* 1. (myth.) **A.,** Alcyoneus. 2. (*pl.*) halcyon days.

alcionio, *m.* (zool.) colony of alcionarians, polypary.

alcionito, *m.* (zool.) fossilized colony of alcionarians.

alcista, *a.* rising, bull, bullish, tending to rise (stock market, etc.), e.g. *tendencia a.,* tendency to rise. *—m., f.* stock speculator, bull.

alcoba, *f.* 1. bedroom, alcove. 2. pointer case (of a balance or scales). 3. place for public weighing. 4. fishing net.

alcobilla, *f.* 1. *dim. of* **alcoba,** small bedroom or alcove, 2. pointer case (of a balance or scales).

alcocarra, *f.* face, grimace, gesture.

alcofa, *f.* two-handled fruit basket, hamper.

alcohol, *m.* 1. alcohol. 2. (min.) **galeno.** 3. kohl (cosmetic used in the East to stain eyelids). **— a, absoluto,** absolute alcohol; **a. amílico,** amyl alcohol; **a. de grano,** grain alcohol; **a. de madera,** wood alcohol; **a. de 90 grados,** 90% denatured alcohol; **a. desnaturalizado,** denatured alcohol; **a. etílico,** ethyl or grain alcohol; **a. laurilo,** lauryl alcohol; **a. metílico,** methyl or wood alcohol; **a. propílico,** propyl alcohol; **a. vinílico,** vinyl alcohol.

alcoholado, da, *past part. of* **alcoholar.** *—a.* with black rimmed eyes (animals). *—m.* (pharm.) alcoholate, spirits.

alcoholar, *tr.v.* 1. to blacken (eyelid borders, eyelashes, eyebrows or hair) with kohl. 2. to bathe (eyes) with collyrium. 3. to distill alcohol from. 4. (mar.) to tar after caulking. 5. (pharm.) to pulverize.

alcoholato, *m.* (pharm., chem.) alcoholate.

alcoholaturo, *m.* (pharm.) solution made from medicinal herbs and alcohol.

alcoholero, ra, *a.* maker or seller of alcohol. *—f.* 1. alcohol factory. 2. kohl pot or jar. 3. vessel for antimony or alcohol.

alcoholice, alcoholicé, *ref.* **alcoholizar.**

alcohólico, ca, *a., m., f.* alcoholic.

Alcohólicos Anónimos, Alcoholics Anonymous.

alcoholificación, *f.* alcoholic fermentation.

alcoholímetro, *m.* alcoholometer.

alcoholismo, *m.* alcoholism.

alcoholización, *f.* 1. fortification (of wines). 2. (chem.) alcoholization, conversion into alcohol.

alcoholizado, da, *past part. of* **alcoholizar.** *—a.* suffering from alcoholism. *—m., f.* patient suffering from alcoholism.

alcoholizar, (*ref. 53*) *tr.v.* 1. to add alcohol to; to fortify (wine). 2. (chem.) to alcoholize, convert into alcohol. *—r.v.* to become an alcoholic.

alcohometría, *f.* (chem.) alcoholometry.

alcohómetro, *m., var. of* **alcoholímetro.**

alcolla, *f.* large round flask or ampulla with narrow neck.

alconcilla, *f.* (arch.) rouge (cosmetic).

alcor, *m.* hill.

Alcorán, *m.* Alkoran, the Koran, the sacred book of the Moslems.

alcoránico, ca, *a.* Koranic.

alcoranista, *m.* scholar, expounder or teacher of the Koran.

alcorano, na, *a.* Koranic.

alcorce, alcorcé, *ref.* **alcorzar.**

alcorce, *m.* shortening, short cut.

alcorcí, (*pl.* **alcorcíes**) *m.* trinket, small jewel.

alcornocal, *m.* cork oak grove or wood.

alcornoque, *m.* 1. (bot.) cork oak. 2. blockhead. **— cabeza de a.,** blockhead, dimwit.

alcornoqueño, ña, *a.* pertaining to the cork tree.

alcorque, *m.* 1. cork-soled clog. 2. small irrigation ditch around plants.

alcorza, *f.* sugar icing.

alcorzado, da, *past part. of* **alcorzar.** *—a.* 1. (fig., coll.) mellifluous. 2. extremely courteous or refined.

alcorzar, (*ref. 53*) *tr.v.* 1. to coat with sugar icing. 2. (coll.) to adorn.

alcotán, *m.* 1. (ornith.) lanner, bird of prey similar to the falcon. 2. (bot.) velvet-leaf (Cessampilas pareira).

alcotana, *f.* stonecutter's hammer or mattock; pickaxe.

alcrebite, *m.* sulfur.

alcribís, *m.* (metal.) tuyère.

alcribite, *m.* sulfur.

alcubilla, *f.* water tank, reservoir; basin.

alcubiyi, *f.* (ornith.) crested lark.

alcucero, ra, *a.* 1. (coll.) sweet-toothed. *—m., f.* maker or seller of oil containers or jars.

alcuño, *m.* (obs.) sobriquet, nickname.

alcuza, *f.* oil container or jar; (C. Amer., Col.) earthenware bottle; (Chile, Ecuad., Peru) cruet.
alcuzada, *f.* jarful of oil.
alcuzcucero, *m.* bowl in which couscous is prepared.
alcuzcuz, (*pl.* **alcuzcuces**) *m.* couscous, Moorish dish.
aldaba, *f.* 1. door knocker. 2. latch; bolt, crossbar. 3. hitching ring (for tying horses to). — **agarrarse uno a** or **de buenas aldabas, tener buenas aldabas,** (coll.) to have pull, have influence.
aldabada, *f.* 1. knock with a door knocker. 2. (coll., fig.) advice, warning. 3. (coll.) pangs (of conscience).
aldabazo, *m.* 1. loud knock with a door knocker. 2. (fig.) pang of conscience.
aldabear, *i.v.* to knock, knock with a door knocker.
aldabeo, *m.* knocking, rapping (with door knocker).
aldabía, *f.* horizontal crossbeam.
aldabilla, *f.* 1. small latch, catch. 2. small door knocker.
aldabón, *m.* large knocker; large handle (of a trunk or chest).
aldabonazo, *m.* loud knocking.
aldana, *f.* (Col.) bone added to a dish to enhance the flavor.
aldea, *f.* village, hamlet.
aldeaniego, ga, *a.* rustic, rural; pertaining to a village.
aldeanismo, *m.* rural or rustic turn of speech; parochialism.
aldeano, na, *a.,* village; rustic, rural, country. —*m., f.* villager.
aldehído, *m.* (chem.) aldehyde; **a. glicérico,** glyceraldehyde; **a. fórmico,** formaldehyde.
aldehuela, *f.* small hamlet or village.
aldeneja, *f.* (bot.) honeywort.
aldeorrio, *m.* out of the way small village.
aldeorro, *m., var. of* **aldeorrio.**
alderredor, *adv.* around, about.
aldino, na, *a.* (print.) Aldine.
aldiza, *f.* (bot.) bluebottle.
aldol, *m.* (chem.) aldol.
aldorta, *f.* (ornith.) small white crested egret.
aldosa, *f.* (chem.) aldose.
aldrán, *m.* 1. seller of wine to shepherds. 2. foreman, head shepherd.
aldúcar, *m.* coarse silk.
ale, *f.* ale.
alea, *f.* verse of the Koran.
aleación, *f.* alloy. — **a. delta,** delta metal; **a. encontrada,** gold alloy.
alear, *i.v.* 1. to flutter or flap its wings; to move one's arms like wings. 2. to get better, recover, e.g. *ir aleando,* to be recovering, getting better (from sickness, fatigue). —*tr.v.* (metal.) to alloy.
aleatorio, ria, *a.* aleatory, contingent; depending on chance.
alebrado, da, *a.* timid, fearful.
alebrarse, (*ref.* 29) *r.v.* 1. to throw one-self flat on the ground. 2. to become frightened or scared, cower in fear.
alebrastarse, *r.v., var. of* **alebrestarse.**
alebrestarse, *r.v.* 1. to throw oneself flat on the ground. 2. to become alarmed or flustered. 3. to rear up (horse).
alebronar, *tr.v.* to frighten, intimidate. —*r.v.* to become frightened or scared.
alecantina, *f.* (Ecuad.) constant scolding.
aleccionador, ra, *a.* instructive, instructing. — **serle a uno aleccionadora (una cosa),** to teach one a lesson, e.g. *esta experiencia le ha sido muy aleccionadora,* this experience has taught him a lesson.
aleccionamiento, *m.* instruction, teaching, training.
aleccionar, *tr.v.* to instruct, teach, train.
alece, *m.* 1. (ichth.) small variety of sardine (Sardinella allecia). 2. fish dish prepared with red mullet.
alecrín, *m.* 1. (ichth.) tiger shark. 2. (bot.) verbenaceous tree with mahogany-like wood (Holocalix balansae).
alectoria, *f.* stone found in the maw of cocks, formerly thought to have medicinal value.
aleche, *m., var. of* **haleche.**
alechugar, (*ref.* 51) *tr.v.* 1. to curl like a lettuce leaf. 2. (dressm.) to pleat, shirr (like a ruff).
alechugue, alechugué, *ref.* **alechugar.**
alechuguinado, da, *a.* dandy-like.
alechuguinar, *tr.v., r.v.* to adopt the manners and dress of a dandy or dude.
aleda, *f.* **cera a.,** first wax spread by bees on the beehive.
aledaño, ña, *a.* bordering, adjoining. —*m.* common boundary, border, limit.
alef, *m.* aleph, alef; **a. cero,** (math.) alephnull.
alefangina, *f.* (pharm.) purgative pills made of spices.
alefriz, (*pl.* **alefrices**) *m.* (mar.) mortise, rabbet (on keel, stem or stem post).
alegación, *f.* allegation, argument.
alegamar, *tr.v.* to fertilize with mud or silt. —*r.v.* to fill up or become filled up with silt or mud.
aleganarse, *r.v., var. of* **alegamarse.**
alegar, (*ref.* 51) *tr.v.* 1. to allege, contend. 2. to state, declare.
alegato, *m.* (law) allegation.
alegatorio, ria, *a.* pertaining to allegation.
alegoría, *f.* allegory.
alegóricamente, *adv.* allegorically.
alegorice, alegoricé, *ref.* **alegorizar.**
alegórico, ca, *a.* allegorical, allegoric.
alegorizar, (*ref.* 53) *tr.v.* to allegorize.
alegra, *f.* (mar.) reamer, pump auger.
alegrador, ra, *a.* gladdening, cheering. —*m.* 1. paper spill (a small roll of paper for lighting cigars, fires, etc.). 2. (*pl.*) (taur.) banderillas. 3. (mec.) reamer.
alegradura, *f.* (med.) periosteotomy, seraping of the bone.
alegrante, *a.* gladdening, cheering.
alegrar, *tr.v.* 1. to make happy, cheer, gladden. 2. enliven, make lively; (fig.) to revive, poke (a fire); to make brighter (a light). 3. (mar.) to slacken (cables); to lighten (a ship) of ballast. 4. (taur.) to incite (the bull) to charge. —*r.v.* 1. to be happy; to feel glad or happy. 2. (coll.) to become merry or tipsy. — **alegrarse de, con** or **por,** to be or feel happy with or glad about.
alegrar, *tr.v.* 1. (rare) to scrape. 2. (med.) to scrape (the bone), perform a periosteotomy on. 3. (mar.) to ream, make larger (a hole).
alegre, *a.* 1. merry, lighthearted, cheerful, happy; lively. 2. bright, lively (colors). 3. (coll., fig.) tipsy, high (from alcoholic drink). 4. (coll., fig.) lucky, fortunate. 5. (coll., fig.) risqué, off-color. 6. (coll., fig.) reckless, daring; careless.
alegremente, *adv.* gaily, merrily, lightheartedly, happily.
alegrete, ta, *a.* frolicsome, waggish, gay.
alegreto, *adv., m.* (mus.) allegretto, moderately fast.
alegría, *f.* 1. happiness; gaiety, merriment, lightheartedness, joy. 2. (bot.) sesame. 3. nougat of honey, nuts and sesame seeds. 4. (mar.) opening of a loophole or gunport. 5. (*pl.*) public festivities or celebrations. 6. (*pl.*) one of the purest of flamenco chants and dances.
alegro, *adv., m.* (mus.) allegro, fast tempo.
alegrón, na, *a.* 1. (Amer.) very gay, merry or cheerful. 2. (Mex.) flirtatious. —*m.* 1. (coll.) unexpected and sudden joy. 2. (coll.) sudden brief blaze. 3. (Mex.) flirt.
alegue, alegué, *ref.* **alegar.**
alejado, da, *past part. of* **alejar.** —*a.* distant, remote.
alejamiento, *m.* moving apart; moving away; alienation, estrangement; withdrawal.
Alejandría, *f.* Alexandria, city in Egypt.
alejandrino, na, *a.* 1. Alexandrian, from Alexandria. 2. Alexandrine. —*m.* (poet.) alexandrine (verse). —*m., f.* Alexandrian, native of Alexandria.
Alejandro, *m.* Alexander; **A. Magno,** Alexander the Great.
alejar, *tr.v.* 1. to remove to a distance, put farther away. 2. to estrange, alienate. 3. to keep at a distance. —*r.v.* 1. to withdraw, move away, leave; to go far away. 2. to become estranged or alienated.
alejija, *f.* barley porridge spiced with sesame.
alejur, *m., var. of* **alajú.**
alelamiento, *m.* stupidity, foolishness.
alelar, *tr.v.* to stupefy, bewilder. —*r.v.* to become stupefied.
alelí, (*pl.* **alelíes**) *m.* (bot.), *var. of* **alhelí.**
alelismo, *m.* (biol.) allelism.
alelomórfico, ca, *a.* (biol.) allelomorphic.
alelomorfismo, *m.* (biol.) allelomorphism.
alelomorfo, *m.* (biol.) allelomorph, allele.
aleluya, *interj.* alleluia, hallelujah (expression of joy). —*m., f.* hallelujah (anthem praising God). —*m.* Easter time. —*f.* 1. small religious print given away at Easter time; a religious text (generally in verse). 2. small milk cake given away by nuns at Easter time. 3. (bot.) wood sorrel (Oxalis acetosella). 4. (coll.) poor painting. 5. (coll.) poor verses, doggerel. 6. (coll.) bag of bones, very thin person or animal. 7. (coll.) joy. 8. (Amer.) (coll.) flimsy excuse.
alema, *f.* 1. allotted quantity of irrigation water. 2. (*pl.*) (Bol.) public baths (in a river).
alemán, na, *a., m., f.* German. —*m.* German (language); **alto a.,** High German; **alto a. antiguo,** Old High German; **bajo a.,** Low German.
alemana, *f., var. of* **alemanda.**
alemanda, *f.* allemande, Spanish court dance of the Renaissance.
alemanesco, *a., var. of* **alemanisco.**
Alemania, *f.* Germany. — **A. Occidental,** West Germany; **A. Oriental,** East Germany.
alemánico, ca, *a.* Germanic, German.
alemanisco, ca, *a.* Germanic. —*m.* damask table linen.
alenguar, (*ref.* 52) *tr.v.* to discuss, negotiate (the leasing of pasture lands).
alentada, *f.* long breath.
alentadamente, *adv.* spiritedly; gallantly; bravely.
alentado, da, *past part. of* **alentar.** —*a.* 1. tireless. 2. brave, spirited; gallant. 3. haughty. 4. (Amer.) healthy. 5. (Arg.) comforting; invigorating.
alentador, ra, *a.* encouraging, inspiring.
alentar, (*ref.* 29) *i.v.* to breathe. —*tr.v.* to encourage, cheer, inspire. —*r.v.* 1. to be encouraged. 2. (C. Amer., Col.) to give birth. 3. (Col., Ecuad.) to clap, applaud.
alentoso, sa, *a.* brave, spirited.
Alenzón, *m.* Alençon, city of France, famous for its lace.
aleonado, da, *a.* tawny; brindled, in the colors of the lion.
aleonar, *tr.v.* (Amer.) to stir up, agitate (generally for fun or through enthusiasm).

alepín, *m.* bombazine, a fine wool fabric.
alerce, *m.* (bot.) larch; **a. africano,** sandarac tree; **a. europeo,** European larch (Larix decidua).
alergeno, *m.* (med.) allergen.
alergia, *f.* (med.) allergy.
alérgico, ca, *a.* allergic. — **ser a. a,** to be allergic to (also used fig.).
alergina, *f.* (med.) allergen.
alergista, allergist.
alero, *m.* 1. (archit.) eaves. 2. splashboard, mudguard (of a carriage). 3. side of a partridge snare. — **a. corrido,** (archit.) eave along a wall that has no cornice; **a. de chaperón,** (archit.) eave without corbels; **a. de mesilla,** (archit.) eave that projects horizontally forming a cornice.
alero, *a.* said of a young stag (deer) that has not yet sired.
alerón, *m.* (aer.) aileron; **a. compensado,** balanced aileron; **a. ranurado,** slotted aileron.
alerta, *adv.* on the alert, vigilantly, alertly. — **estar a.,** to be on the alert or on the look out. —*interj.* look out! watch out! —*m.* alert, alarm; **dar el a.,** to give the alert, sound the alarm.
alertamente, *adv.* alertly.
alertar, *tr.v.* to alert, sound the alarm, put (someone) on the alert.
alerto, ta, *a.* alert, vigilant, watchful.
alerzal, *m.* larch wood or grove.
alesnado, da, *a.* pointed, sharp.
aleta, *f.* 1. fin (of a fish, car, etc.); flipper, fin (used for swimming and skin diving). 2. blade (of propeller, turbine). 3. small wing 4. leaf (of a hinge). 5. (archit.) alette, a wing of a building or a buttress. 6. (anat.) ala, wing (of nose). 7. (mar.) (*pl.*) fashion pieces. — **a. compensadora** or **de compensación,** (aer.) trimming tab; **a. de bauprés,** (mar.) bee; **a. de semáforo,** semaphore blade.
aletada, *f.* flapping or fluttering of wings.
aletargado, da, *a.* sluggish, sleepy, drowsy.
aletargamiento, *m.* lethargy, sluggishness, drowsiness; apathy.
aletargar, (*ref.* 51) *tr.v.* to make lethargic. —*r.v.* to become lethargic.
aletargue, aletargué, *ref.* **aletargar.**
aletazo, *m.* 1. blow with a wing or fin. 2. (Cuba, Chile) fisticuff, punch; slap. 3. (Hond.) swindle or theft.
aletear, *i.v.* 1. to flap (wings or fins), flutter. 2. to wave one's arms like wings.
aleteo, *m.* 1. flapping or fluttering of wings. 2. palpitation, accelerated beating (of the heart).
aleto, *m.* (ornith.) osprey, fish hawk.
aletoscopio, *m.* alethoscope.
aletría, *f.* (Sp., reg., cul.) noodles.
aleudar, *tr.v.* to leaven, add yeast to (bread). —*r.v.* to rise, become fermented.
aleurita, *f.* (bot.) Aleurites (genus of the spurge family); tung tree, tung oil tree.
aleurómetro, *m.* aleurometer, instrument used to test the quality of gluten in flour.
aleurona, *f.* (bot., biochem.) aleurone, a seed protein.
alevantar, *tr.v.* (coll.) to raise, lift. —*r.v.* (coll.) to get up.
aleve, *a.* treacherous, perfidious. —*m.* treachery; traitor.
alevemente, *adv.* treacherously.
alevilla, *f.* (ento.) a kind of moth.
alevín, *m.* 1. fingerlings used to stock rivers, lakes, etc. 2. (fig.) a young beginner or initiate in some discipline or profession.
alevosa, *f.* (vet.) ranula (a cyst formed under the tongue).
alevosamente, *adv.* treacherously.
alevosía, *f.* perfidy, treachery; **con a.,** treacherously.
alevoso, sa, treacherous, perfidious.
alexia, *f.* alexia, a loss of the ability to read (caused by a brain lesion).
alexifármaco, ca, a. (med.) alexipharmic, acting as an antidote. —*m.* antidote.
aleya, *f.* verse of the Koran.
aleznado, da, *a.* (bot.) pointed.
alezo, *m.* 1. (med.) abdominal support or girdle (worn by mothers after child birth).
alfa, *f.* alpha, first letter of the Greek alphabet. — **a. y omega,** alpha and omega, the beginning and the end.
alfábega, *f.* (bot.) sweet basil.
alfabéticamente, *adv.* alphabetically.
alfabetice, alfabeticé, *ref.* **alfabetizar.**
alfabético, ca, *a.* alphabetical. — **en orden alfabético,** in alphabetical order.
alfabetización, *f.* 1. alphabetization, arrangement in alphabetical order. 2. teaching to read and write; literacy; **campaña de a.,** literacy campaign.
alfabetizar, (*ref.* 53) *tr.v.* 1. to alphabetize, put in alphabetical order. 2. to teach to read and write, make literate.
alfabeto, *m.* alphabet; **a. Braille,** Braille alphabet; **a. Fonético Internacional,** International Phonetic Alphabet; **a. Morse,** Morse code.
alfaguara, *m.* gushing stream.
alfahar, *m.* pottery; potter's workshop.
alfahararería, *f.* pottery, ceramics.
alfaharero, *m.* potter.
alfajía, *f.* (carp.) wood for door or window frames.
alfajor, *m.* paste made of almonds, walnuts and honey; cake made with this paste; (Amer.) pastry filled with a sweet filling; (Ven.) confection made of cassava flour, molasses, pineapple and ginger.
alfalfa, *f.* alfalfa.
alfalfal, *m.* alfalfa field.
alfalfar, *m.* alfalfa field.
alfalfe, *m.* alfalfa.
alfana, *f.* strong, large horse.
alfandoque, *m.* 1. (Col., Peru) paste made of molasses, cheese, anise and ginger. 2. (C. Amer., Col.) musical instrument made of bamboo.
alfaneque, *m.* (ornith.) lanner, African falcon.
alfanjado, da, *a.* scimitar-shaped, crescent-shaped.
alfanjazo, *m.* scimitar wound or blow.
alfanje, *m.* 1. scimitar. 2. (ichth.) swordfish.
alfanjete, *m. dim. of* **alfanje,** small scimitar.
alfaque, *m.* sandbar, sand bank at the mouth of a river.
alfaqueque, *m.* (hist.) 1. officer in charge of ransoming slaves or prisoners of war. 2. courier.
alfaquí, (*pl.* **alfaquíes**) *m.* alfaqui, a teacher or expounder of the Koran and Mohammedan law.
alfar, *a.* said of a horse that raises the head too much while galloping. —*m.* 1. pottery; potter's workshop. 2. clay. —*i.v.* to raise the head too much while galloping (a horse).
alfaraz, (*pl.* **alfaraces**) *m.* Arab light cavalry horse.
alfarda, *f.* 1. (hist.) tax paid by Moors and Jews in Christian kingdoms; irrigation tax; special tax (Morocco). 2. (archit.) beam, strut (of a frame).
alfardilla, *f.* 1. gold or silver braid. 2. straw plait or mat.
alfardón, *m.* 1. washer, metal ring. 2. irrigation tax. 3. girder, heavy beam. 4. hexagonal glazed tile.
alfareme, *m.* Moorish face veil.
alfarería, *f.* pottery, pottery making factory, or ceramics shop. — **a. vidriada,** glazed pottery.
alfarero, *m.* potter.
alfargo, *m.* central beam of an oilpress.
alfarje, *m.* grinder, instrument for grinding olives; place where the grinder is housed.
alfarje, *m.* carved and ornate wood ceiling; parquet, ornate wood flooring.
alfarjía, *f.* (carp.) wood frame for doors and windows.
alfazaque, *m.* (ento.) a kind of scarab.
alfeiza, *f., var. of* **alféizar.**
alfeizado, da, *a.* having a splay or embrasure.
alféizar, *m.* (archit.) embrasure, recess of a door or window; (archit.) splay of door or window, slope or bevel at the sides of a door or window; (Amer.) window sill.
alfeñicarse, (*ref.* 50) *r.v.* 1. (coll.) to affect refinement and daintiness. 2. (coll.) to become or grow very thin.
alfeñique, alfeñiqué, *ref.* **alfeñicarse.**
alfeñique, *m.* 1. sugar paste. 2. (coll.) thin, delicate person. 3. (coll.) affectation, finickiness.
alferazgo, *m.* 1. ensigncy, ensignship, second lieutenantship. 2. (S. Amer.) religious festival which is paid for by one or more persons.
alferecía, *f.* 1. epilepsy. 2. ensigncy, second lieutenantship.
alférez, (*pl.* **alféreces**) *m.* 1. (mil.) ensign, standard bearer; second lieutenant; **a. alumno,** officer cadet; **a. de fragata,** (mar.) ensign, rank equivalent to second lieutenant in the army; **a. de navío,** (mar.) lieutenant. 2. (S. Amer.) person chosen to pay the expenses of a party, ball, etc.
alferraz, *m.* small bird of prey used in falconry.
alficoz, (*pl.* **alficoces**) *m.* (bot.) squash.
alfil, *m.* bishop (chess). — **a. dama,** queen's bishop.
alfiler, *m.* 1. pin; pin, brooch 2. (bot.) Cuban wood-bearing tree. 3. (*pl.*) pin money (money given to wives for private expenses); (*pl.*) tip given to servants. 4. (*pl.*) children's game. 5. (*pl.*) (bot.) stork's bill. — **a. de corbata,** tiepin, scarfpin; **a. de nodriza** or **imperdible,** safety pin; **a. de París,** wire nail; **con todos sus alfileres** or **de veinticinco alfileres,** (coll.) dressed to the nines, dressed in style, dressed to kill (referring to women); **no caber un a.,** to be full to the top, be full to bursting; **pegar** or **prender con a.,** (coll.) to fix or put together shakily; (coll.) to learn superficially (for an exam).
alfilerazo, *m.* 1. pinprick. 2. large pin.
alfilerillo, *m.* 1. (Arg., Col., Chile, bot.) alfilaria, pin clover, pin grass. 2. (Mex., ento.) tobacco borer.
alfilete, *m.* semolina, coarsely ground durum (wheat) meal.
alfiletero, *m.* pincushion.
alfiz, (*pl.* **alfices**) *m.* (archit.) panel of a Moorish arch that starts from the impost or from the floor.
alfolí, (*pl.* **alfolíes**) *m.* 1. granary. 2. salt warehouse.
alfoliero, *m.* granary or salt warehouse keeper.
alfolinero, *m., var. of* **alfoliero.**
alfombra, *f.* carpet, rug; (fig.) covering, blanket, carpet, e.g. *a. de flores,* flower carpet. — **a. trenzada,** braided rug; **a. persa,** Persian rug.
alfombrado, *m.* carpeting, floor covering.
alfombrar, *tr.v.* to carpet, cover the floor with carpets.
alfombrero, ra, *m., f.* carpet maker; carpet salesman.
alfombrilla, *f.* 1. (med.) German measles. 2. small rug; mat.
alfombrista, *m.* carpet dealer or salesman; carpet maker and installer.
alfóncigo, *m.* (bot.) pistachio (tree and fruit).
alfonsearse, *r.v.* (arch.) to make fun of, mock.
alfonsí, *a., var. of* **alfonsino.**
alfónsigo, *m., var. of* **alfóncigo.**

Alfonsinas, *f.* (*pl.*) (astron.) Alphonsine Tables.
alfonsino, na, *a.* Alphonsine, pertaining to the Alphonsos (Spanish kings). —*m.* coin minted during the reign of Alphonso the Wise (Spanish king).
alfonsismo, *m.* policy supporting the Alphonsos (Spanish kings).
alforce, alforcé, *ref.* **alforzar.**
alforfón, *m.* (bot.) buckwheat; buckwheat grain.
alforja, *f.* 1. (*gen. pl.*) saddlebag; double knapsack. 2. provisions for the road.
alforjero, ra, *a.* pertaining to a saddlebag. —*m., f.* saddlebag maker or seller. —*m.* mendicant friar.
alforjón, *m.* (bot.) buckwheat.
alforjuela, *f. dim. of* **alforja,** small knapsack or saddlebag.
alforza, *f.* 1. tuck, pleat. 2. (coll.) large scar.
alforzar, (*ref. 53*) *tr.v.* to pleat, tuck.
alfoz, (*pl.* **alfoces**) *m., f.* suburb; borough, district.
alga, *f.* (bot.) alga, seaweed.
algaba, *f.* wood, forest.
algaida, *f.* 1. thicket, thick brushland. 2. sand dune.
algalia, *f.* 1. civet, musk-like oil used in perfumery. 2. (bot.) abelmosk, musk hibiscus. 3. (med.) catheter. —*m.* (zool.) civet cat.
algaliar, *tr.v.* to perfume with civet.
algara, *f.* 1. party of mounted marauders, marauding party. 2. attack by mounted marauders. 3. thin skin (of onion, etc.).
algarabía, *f.* 1. Arabic (language). 2. (coll.) din, clamor, jabbering; (coll.) babble, babbling; gibberish. 3. scribbling, scrawling. 4. (bot.) centaury, knapweed or other wiry bush employed in making brooms.
algarabiado, da, *a.* Arabic-speaking. —*m., f.* Arabic-speaking person.
algarada, *f.* 1. din, shouting, uproar. 2. mounted party of marauders.
algarero, ra, *a.* prattling, chattering, jabbering. —*m.* mounted marauder, member of a raiding party.
algarrada, *f.* 1. catapult (Roman weapon). 2. bull baiting. 3. bullfight with young bulls. 4. the herding of bulls.
algarroba, *f.* 1. (bot.) vetch; carob; mesquite. 2. carob bean. 3. (*pl.*) (Cuba) mangrove roots attached to fishing lines.
algarrobal, *m.* vetch field or patch; carob tree grove.
algarrobar, *i.v.* (Cuba) to prepare a line for fishing.
algarrobero, ra, *n.* (bot.) carob tree.
algarrobillo, *m.* (Arg.) carob bean.
algarrobina, *f.* (Peru) syrup made from carob beans, used in the preparation of cocktails.
algarrobo, *m.* (bot.) carob tree. — **a. loco,** Judas tree.
algavaro, *m.* (ento.) a kind of beetle.
algazara, *f.* 1. tumult, din, clamor. 2. Moorish war cry.
algazul, *m.* (bot.) saltwort.
álgebra, *f.* algebra. — **á. vectorial,** vector algebra.
algebraico, ca, *a.* algebraic.
algébrico, ca, *a.* algebraic.
algebrista, *m., f.* 1. algebraist. 2. (arch., med.) bonesetter, surgeon specializing in fractures.
algecireño, na, *a.* of or from Algeciras, S. Spain. —*m., f.* native or inhabitant of Algeciras.
algente, *a.* (poet.) algid, cold; chilly; icy.
algidez, *f.* algidity, coldness.
álgido, da, *a.* 1. algid, icy; (med.) algid. 2. (coll.) intense, active; heated (discussion).
algina, *f.* (chem.) algin.
algo, *indef. pron.* something; a little, a smattering. — **a. es a.** or **más vale a. que nada,** something is better than nothing; **por a.,** for some reason. —*adv.* somewhat, rather.
algodón, *m.* 1. cotton (plant and cloth). 2. (Cuba, bot.) swamp milkweed. 3. (*pl.*) cotton and silk scraps put in bottom of inkwells to prevent the pen from absorbing too much ink. 4. (*pl.*) ear plugs (of cotton). — **a. absorbente,** absorbent cotton; **a. de azúcar,** cotton candy; **a. en rama,** raw cotton; **a. hidrófilo,** absorbent cotton; **a. pima,** pima cotton; **a. pólvora, pólvora de a.,** guncotton, cotton powder; **estar criado entre algodones,** (coll.) to have been pampered or brought up very delicately; **a. artificial,** cellulose cotton; **a. blanqueado,** bleached cotton.
algodonal, *m.* cotton field or plantation; cotton plant.
algodonar, *tr.v.* to cover, fill, or stuff with cotton.
algodoncillo, *m.* (bot.) swamp milkweed.
algodonero, ra, *a.* cottony, pertaining to cotton. —*m., f.* cotton dealer; cotton grower. —*m.* cotton plant.
algodonita, *f.* (chem.) algodonite, copper arsenide.
algodonosa, *f.* (bot.) plant similar to cotton which grows in the Mediterranean coast (Diotis candidissima).
algodonoso, sa, *a.* cottony, cotton-like.
algofobia, *f.* algophobia, abnormal fear of pain.
algoide, *a.* (bot.) algoid, **alga-like.**
Algol, *m.* (astron.) Algol, a star in the constellation of Perseus.
algolagnia, *f.* (med.) algolagnia, sexual pleasure derived from experiencing or inflicting pain; masochism or sadism.
algología, *f.* algology, the study of algae.
algonquino, na, *a.* Algonkian, Algonquian, Algonquin. —*m.* Algonquian (language and linguistic family). —*m., f.* Algonquian Indian (N. America).
algor, *m.* (med.) algor, chill.
algorfa, *f.* grain loft.
algorín, *m.* olive bin in an oil mill; olive bin yard.
algoritmia, *f.* algorism, the Arabic system of numbers.
algorítmico, ca, *a.* algorithmic.
algoritmo, *m.* algorism, algorithm.
algorza, *f.* thatch put over a mud wall.
algoso, sa, *a.* algous, full of algae.
alguacil, *m.* 1. police, constable, warrant officer; bailiff. 2. (arch.) minister of justice, magistrate, judge. 3. (arch.) governor (of city or region). 4. (taur.) official dressed in black who leads the parade into the ring, receives the keys of the bull pen (**toril**) and presents triumphant bullfighters with an ear, tail, etc., as trophies. 5. skeleton key (used by burglars). 6. (ento.) jumping spider. 7. (Arg.) (ento.) dragonfly.
alguacila, *f.* (coll.), *var. of* **alguacilesa.**
alguacilazgo, *m.* office or post of a constable, warrant officer or bailiff.
alguacilejo, *m.* (derog.) petty constable.
alguacilesa, *f.* police constable's wife; bailiff's wife.
alguacilía, *f.* office or post of constable or bailiff.
alguacililllo, *m.* (taur.) assistant to the alguacil.
alguaquida, *f.* torch made of straw dipped in sulphur.
alguien, *indef. pron.* somebody, someone.
algún, *a.* apocope of **alguno** used only before masculine singular nouns. — **a. tanto,** a little somewhat, rather.
alguno, na, *a.* 1. some, any. 2. some, moderate, e.g. *de a. importancia,* of moderate importance. 3. not any, e.g. *no hay duda alguna,* there is not any doubt, *en manera alguna,* in no way whatever; *no tengo dinero alguno,* I haven't any money. — **alguna vez,** sometime, sometimes; **a. que otro,** some, a few. —*indef. pron.* someone; (*pl.*) some, e.g., *¿ha venido a.?* has anyone arrived?
alhacena, *f., var. of* **alacena.**
alhaja, *f.* 1. jewel, gem. 2. valuable ornament; fine piece of furniture. 3. (fig.) gem, jewel, (highly prized thing or person). — **¡buena a.!** (iron.) rogue, good-for-nothing.
alhajado, da, *a., m., f.* (Col.) rich, wealthy, well-to-do.
alhajar, *tr.v.* 1. to adorn with jewels, bejewel. 2. to provide with furniture, furnish.
alhajú, (*pl.* **alhajúes**) *m., var. of* **alajú.**
alhajuela, *f. dim. of* **alhaja,** trinket, small jewel.
alhámega, *f.* (bot.) African rue.
alhamí, (*pl.* **alhamíes**) *m.* tile-covered stone bench built against a wall.
alhandal, *m.* (pharm.) colocynth.
alharaca, *f.* ado, fuss, outcry. — **hacer alharacas,** to make a fuss.
alharaquiento, ta, *a.* pertaining to a person or event, etc., that causes a hubbub, fuss, flurry of activity, racket, outcry, etc.
alhargama, *f., var. of* **alharma.**
alharma, *f.* (bot.) African rue.
alhelí, (*pl.* **alhelíes**) *m.* (bot.) stock, gilly-flower.
alhelicillo, *m.* (bot.) sweet alyssum, alyssum.
alheña, *f.* 1. (bot.) henna. 2. henna, powder made from henña leaves. 3. (bot.) privet. 4. (bot.) water plantain. 5. rust, mildew, blight (of wheat). — **hecho una a., molido como una a.,** (coll.) worn-out, fagged out, exhausted; shattered; broken to pieces.
alheñar, *tr.v.* to dye with henna. — r.v. to be affected by rust, mildew or blight, become blighted (wheat).
alhócigo, *m., var. of* **alfóncigo.**
alhoja, *f.* (ornith.) lark.
alholí, *m., var. of* **alfolí.**
alholva, *f.* (bot.) fenugreek.
alholvar, *m.* fenugreek field.
alhóndiga, *f.* public granary; corn exchange; grain exchange.
alhondigaje, *m.* (Mex.) warehouse fees, storage fees.
alhondiguero, *m.* keeper of a public granary or wheat exchange.
alhorma, *f.* Moorish camp.
alhorre, *m.* (med.) meconium, first feces of a baby; newborn infant's rash.
alhoz, (*pl.* **alhoces**) *m.* suburb, borough, district.
alhucema, *f.* (bot.) lavender.
alhucemilla, *f.* (bot.) a kind of lavender.
alhuceña, *f.* (bot.) cruciferous plant with flowers on spikes, bearing an edible fruit.
alhumajo, *m.* (bot.) pine needles.
alhurreca, *f.* salt residue left on objects by sea water.
ali, *m.* (cards) a hand with two or three cards of a kind.
aliabierto, ta, *a.* open-winged.
aliacán, *m.* (med.) jaundice.
aliacanado, da, *a.* (med.) jaundiced, suffering from jaundice.
aliáceo, a, *a.* alliaceous, garlicky, smelling or tasting of garlic.
aliadas, *f.* (arch.) Christmas bonus given to foundry workers in the Basque country.
aliado, da, *past part. of* **aliar.** —*a.* allied. —*m., f.* ally.
aliadófilo, la, *a., m., f.* pro-Ally, said of those in favor of the Allies in World War I.
aliaga, *f.* (bot.) furze, gorse.
aliagar, *m.* gorse thicket.
alianza, *f.* 1. alliance, union. 2. **alliance,** pact (treaty of alliance). 3. (Amer.) wedding ring. 4. alliance, connection or union through marriage. 5. (bot., zool.) alliance, group of families. — **A.**

Cuádruple, (hist.) Quadruple Alliance; **Santa A.,** (hist.) Holy Alliance; **A. Triple,** (hist.) Triple Alliance.
aliar, (*ref. 54*) *tr.v.* (rare) to ally, join together. —*r.v.* to ally, become allied, make an alliance, form an alliance.
aliara, *f.* drinking horn.
aliaria, *f.* (bot.) garlic mustard.
alias, *adv.* alias, otherwise known as. —*m.* name, nickname.
aliblanca, *f.* 1. (Col.) laziness, indolence; lethargy, sluggishness, drowsiness. 2. (Cuba) wild dove.
alible, *a.* nourishing, nutritive.
álica, *f.* pottage made with spelt and vegetables.
alicaído, da, *a.* 1. with drooping wings. 2. (coll.) drooping, weak, languishing. 3. (coll.) crestfallen, downcast, down-in-the-mouth, discouraged.
alicántara, *f.* (zool.) viper.
alicante, *m.* (zool.) viper.
alicantina, *f.* (coll.) trick, ruse, stratagem.
alicantino, na, *a.* pertaining to the city or province of Alicante, Spain. —*m., f.* native or inhabitant of Alicante.
alicatado, *m.* arabesque or Moorish tiling.
alicatar, *tr.v.* 1. to tile. 2. to trim or cut (tiles) into the required shape.
alicate, *m.* 1. (*pl.*) pliers, pincers; tongs. 2. (P. Rico) accomplice, helper.
alicer, *m.* (archit.) dado or wainscoting of tiles.
aliciente, *m.* incentive, inducement.
alicortar, *tr.v.* to clip or injure the wings of a bird.
alicorto, ta, *a.* 1. having short wings. 2. (fig.) unimaginative; (fig.) unaspiring.
alicrejo, *m.* 1. (Amer.) hack, nag, old horse. 2. (C. Rica) ugly person; frightening insect.
alicuanta, *a., f.* (math.) aliquant.
alícuota, *a., f.* (math.) aliquot.
alicurco, ca, *a.* (Chile) cunning, astute, sagacious.
alicuz, (*pl.* **alicuces**) (Hond.) *m.* exploiter; smart alec; a shrewd and unscrupulous person.
alidada, *f.* alidade, instrument for surveying and mapping. — **a. azimutal,** azimuth finder; **a. niveladora,** leveling alidade.
aliebre, aliebro, *ref.* **alebrarse.**
alineable, *a.* alienable.
alienación, *f.* 1. alienation; transfer, sale. 2. (med.) alienation, mental derangement; insanity.
alienado, da, *past part. of* **alienar.** —*a.* insane, mad. —*m., f.* alienated person.
alienar, *tr.v.* to alienate, transfer, sell, give away. —*r.v.* to become alienated.
alienígena, *a.* alien, foreign. —*m., f.* alien, foreigner.
alienígeno, na, *a.* strange, unnatural.
alienismo, *m.* (med.) alienism, study or treatment of diseases of the mind; psychiatry.
alienista, *m., f.* (med.) alienist, psychiatrist.
aliente, aliento, *ref.* **alentar.**
aliento, *m.* 1. breath; breathing. 2. encouragement. 3. spirit, vigor, enterprise, courage. — **dar a.,** to encourage, give encouragement (coll.); **de un a.;** all in one breath; without stopping; **cobrar a.,** to take courage; **recobrar el a.,** to get one's breath back; **sin a.,** breathless.
alifafe, *m.* 1. (coll.) indisposition, complaint, illness. 2. (vet.) callous tumor on the hock (of a horse).
alifar, *tr.v.* (Sp. reg.) to polish, burnish.
alifático, ca, *a.* (chem.) aliphatic.
alífero, ra, *a.* pertaining to wings.
aliforme, *a.* aliform, shaped like a wing.
aligación, *f.* 1. alloy, mixture. 2. tie, bond, union.
aligamiento, *m., var. of* **aligación.**
aligar, (*ref. 51*) *tr.v.* 1. to tie, bind; to unite. 2. to mix, alloy (metals).
aligator, *m.* (zool.) alligator.
aliger, *m.* (arch.) cross guard (of a sword).
aligeramiento, *m.* 1. easing, alleviation. 2. lightening. 3. hastening, hurrying; shortening.
aligerar, *tr.v.* 1. to lighten, make lighter. 2. to alleviate, relieve, ease. 3. to shorten; to hasten, accelerate. —*i.v.* to hasten, hurry.
alígero, ra, *a.* 1. (poet.) winged. 2. (poet.) fleet, fast.
aligonero, *m.* (bot.) hackberry tree (Celis australis).
aligue, aligué, *ref.* **aligar.**
aligustre, *m.* (bot.) privet (Ligustrum vulgare).
alijador, *m.* 1. (mar.) lighter, a kind of barge used for unloading other vessels. 2. (mar.) seaman on a lighter. 3. (tex.) operator of a cotton gin.
alijar, *m.* 1. wasteland. 2. common pasture-land. 3. Bedouin camp or settlement. —*tr.v.* 1. to unload, lighten (a ship) of cargo; to land (contraband). 2. to gin cotton.
alijarar, *tr.v.* to divide (wasteland) for cultivation.
alijarero, *m.* person who farms a plot of wasteland.
alijariego, ga, *a.* pertaining to wasteland.
alijo, *m.* 1. unloading, lightening (of ship). 2. ginning (of cotton). 3. contraband, smuggling.
alilaya, *f.* (Amer.) frivolous excuse. —*m., f.* (Mex.) cunning, clever person.
alileno, *m.* (chem.) allylene.
alilo, *m.* (chem.) allyl.
alim, *m.* (bot.) spurge tree.
alimanisco, ca, *a.* (Col.) damask (cloth).
alimaña, *f.* 1. animal, predatory animal. 2. (fig.) despicable person.
alimañero, *m.* game keeper or warden employed in killing off predatory animals.
alimentación, *f.* feeding; food; nutrition, nourishment; (mec.) feeding, feed. — **a. forzada** or **a presión.** (mec.) force feed; **a. por gotas,** (auto.) drip feed; **a. por gravedad,** (mec.) gravity feed; **a. intermitente,** ratchet feed; **conductor de a.,** feed wire; **de a. por flotador,** (auto.) float-feed (carburetor); **a. anódica,** plate power supply.
alimentado, da, *past part. of* **alimentar.** —*a.* fed; fired; e.g. *a. a petróleo,* oil-fired.
alimentador, ra, *a.* feeding, nourishing. —*m., f.* one who pays an allowance (for food). —*m.* feeder; stoker; a. **automático,** automatic feeder; self-feeder; **a. principal,** (elec.) trunk feeder.
alimental, *a.* alimental, alimentary, nourishing.
alimentante, *a.* feeding, nourishing. —*m., f.* (law) maintainer, one who pays alimony or an allowance.
alimentar, *tr.v.* 1. to feed; to nourish; (mec.) to feed (a machine with fuel); to encourage, nurture. 2. (law) to maintain, pay alimony or an allowance to. — **a. un deseo,** (fig.) to nurture a wish. —*i.v.* to be nourishing, be nutritious. —*r.v.* to feed; **alimentarse con** or **de,** to feed on; to live on.
alimentario, *a.* alimentary, nourishing. —*m.* (law) recipient of alimony or maintenance.
alimenticio, cia, *a.* nutritional, nutritive, food, e.g. *valor alimenticio,* food value.
alimentista, *m., f.* recipient of alimony or maintenance.
alimento, *m.* 1. food; fuel; (*pl.*) food, foodstuffs. 2. encouragement, sustenance. 3. (*pl.*) allowance, alimony. — **a. combustible,** carbohydrate food; **a. reparador,** nitrogenous protein food; **a. congelado,** frozen food; **a. deshidratado,** dehydrated food; **a. precocinado,** precooked food.
alimentoso, sa, *a.* nutritious, nourishing.
álimo, *m.* (bot.) orach.
alimoche, *m.* (ornith.) Egyptian vulture.
alimón, al a. (taur.) a pass made with the cape held by two bullfighters.
alimonarse, *r.v.* to turn yellowish from disease (leaves).
alindado, da, *past part. of* **alindar.** —*a.* pretending elegance; dandified, foppish.
alindamiento, *m.* marking of limits or boundaries.
alindar, *tr.v.* to mark the limits or boundaries of. —*i.v.* to border, adjoin, be next (to); **a. con,** to border, adjoin, be next to.
alindar, *tr.v.* to adorn, embellish, make beautiful. —*r.v.* to primp oneself, make oneself beautiful; to spruce up; to become dandified.
alineación, *f.* 1. alignment, aligning; tracking. 2. (sport.) line-up, lineup, formation or composition of a team. 3. parallel arrangement.
alineador, *m.* aligning tool.
alinear, *tr.v.* 1. to align, put in line, line up. 2. to make up, compose, form (a team). —*r.v.* to line up, get into a line, form a line.
aliñado, da, *past part. of* **aliñar.** —*a.* 1. neat, clean. 2. spiced. —*m.* (Ven.) spiced brandy or liquor.
aliñador, ra, *a.* spicing, seasoning. —*m.* (Chile) bonesetter.
aliñar, *tr.v.* 1. to spice, flavor, season, dress. 2. to put in order, groom, make tidy and attractive. 3. to prepare. 4. (Chile) to set (bones). —*r.v.* to spruce up, groom oneself.
aliño, *m.* 1. dressing, seasoning. 2. cleanliness, neatness, attractiveness; tidying up; sprucing up. 3. preparation. 4. (*pl.*) (arch.) apparatus, instrument, equipment.
aliñoso, sa, *a.* 1. neat, attractive. 2. careful, conscientious, hardworking.
alioli, *m.* garlic and olive-oil sauce.
alionín, *m.* (ornith.) titmouse.
alipata, *m.* (bot.) blind-your-eyes, milky mangrove, Philippine poison tree.
alípede, *a.* (poet.) wing-footed (as the bat), aliped; (zool.) aliped. —*m.* (zool.) aliped.
alípedo, da, *a.* (poet.) wing-footed, aliped; (zool.) aliped. —*m.* (zool.) aliped.
alipego, *m.* (C. Amer.) bonus, little gift given to the buyer (in a store).
aliquebrado, da, *past part. of* **aliquebrar.** —*a.* (coll.) crestfallen, disheartened.
aliquebrar, (*ref. 29*) *tr.v.* to break the wings of. —*r.v.* to break its wings (a bird).
aliquiebre, aliquiebro, *ref.* **aliquebrar.**
alirrojo, ja, *a.* red-winged.
alisado, *past part. of* **alisar.** —*m.* polishing, smoothing; reaming.
alisador, ra, *a.* smoothing; planing; surfacing. —*m., f.* smoother, planer, surfacer, polisher. —*m.* finishing tool, surfacing or polishing instrument; reamer, instrument for smoothing inside of a cylinder; smoother, wooden instrument for smoothing candles.
alisadura, *f.* 1. smoothing, polishing. 2. (*pl.*) shavings, chips.
alisar, *tr.v.* to smooth, polish, plane, make smooth, surface; to ream; to smooth, sleek (hair). —*r.v.* to smooth, sleek (one's hair). —*m.* alder grove.
aliseda, *f.* alder grove.
alisios, *a.* **vientos a.,** trade winds.
alisma, *f.* (bot.) water plantain.
aliso, *m.* (bot.) alder. — **a. blanco,** birch, white alder; **a. negro,** black alder (Alnus ferruginea).
alistado, da, *past part. of* **alistar.** —*a.* 1. striped. 2. recruited, enlisted.
alistador, *m.* recruiter, enlister, enroller.
alistamiento, *m.* 1. enlistment, recruitment, recruiting. 2. levy, draft recruits.
alistar, *tr.v.* 1. (mil.) to recruit, enlist, enroll; to draft. 2. to warn, forewarn. 3. to make ready, prepare for. —*r.v.* 1. to enlist. 2. to get ready. —*i.v., tr.v.* to rouse, enliven; to sharpen the wits.

alistonar, *tr.v.* to lath.
aliteración, *f.* 1. alliteration, repetition of the same initial sound in two or more words of a phrase. 2. (rhet.) paronomasia, punning.
aliterado, da, *a.* alliterated.
alitienzo, *m., var. of* **labiérnago.**
alitierno, *m.* (bot.) alatern, alaternus, buckthorn.
aliviadero, *m.* spillway, outlet (letting excess water escape).
aliviador, ra, *a.* alleviating; comforting, consoling. —*m.* lever which controls the millstone in grading flour.
alivianar, *tr.v., var. of* **aliviar.**
aliviar, *tr.v.* 1. to lighten, lessen, make lighter (e.g. weight, work, etc.); to ease, alleviate, lessen (pain, burden, etc.). 2. to relieve (someone of weight, trouble, etc.); to take, remove. 3. to comfort, soothe, console. 4. to quicken (one's step). —*r.v.* to be relieved, get relief, e.g. *aliviarse del dolor,* to get relief from the pain.
alivio, *m.* relief, alleviation.
alizar, *m.* 1. (archit.) frieze of glazed tiles. 2. glazed tile.
alizari, *m.* (bot.) madder.
alizarina, *f.* (chem.) alizarin, alizarine; madder (red dye).
aljaba, *f.* quiver (for arrows).
aljafana, *f.* washbasin.
aljama, *f.* 1. assembly of Moors or Jews. 2. mosque; synagogue. 3. ghetto, Jewish quarter; Moorish quarters, casbah.
aljamía, *f.* (arch.) Spanish (Moorish name for the language); Spanish written in Arabic characters.
aljamiado, da, *a.* speaking Moorish Spanish or aljamía; (Spanish) written in Arabic characters.
aljarafe, *m.* tableland, plateau; flat roof.
aljarfa, *f.* (arch.) center of a fishing net.
aljarfe, *m., var. of* **aljarfa.**
aljebana, *f.* washbasin.
aljecería, *f.* 1. gypsum or plaster factory or shop. 2. plaster work, plastering.
aljecero, *m.* gypsum or plaster manufacturer or seller.
aljerife, *m.* (arch.) large fishing net.
aljerifero, *m.* (arch.) fisherman using an aljerife or large fishing net.
aljez, (*pl.* **aljeces**) *m.* gypsum.
aljezar, *m.* gypsum quarry.
aljezón, *m.* plaster debris or rubble (used for rebuilding).
aljibe, *m.* 1. cistern, tank, reservoir. 2. (Col.) well. 3. (mar.) tank boat; waterboat; tanker.
aljibero, *m.* tanks or reservoir keeper.
aljofaina, *f.* washbasin.
aljófar, *m.* 1. seed pearl; imperfect or irregularly shaped pearls. 2. (poet.) pearl, drop (e.g. of dew).
aljofifa, *f.* floor cloth, mop.
aljofifar, *tr.v.* to clean with a floor cloth or mop.
aljonje, *m.* 1. bird lime. 2. (bot.) carline thistle.
aljonjera, *f.* (bot.) carline thistle (also **aljonjero**).
aljonjolí, (*pl.* **aljonjolíes**) *m.* (bot.) sesame.
aljor, *m.* (min.) gypsum.
aljoroce, aljorocé, *ref.* **aljorozar.**
aljorozar, (*ref. 53*) *tr.v.* (mas.) to plaster, cover with mortar.
aljura, *f.* jubbah, Moorish overcoat with narrow, short sleeves.
alka-seltzer *m.* Alka-Seltzer (TM).
alkermes, *m.* alkermes, brandy flavored with bay leaves, mace, nutmeg, cloves and cinnamon, colored with the kermes insect or cochineal.
allá, *adv.* there, yonder, over there; in the other world; far away, way back, e.g. *a. en la China,* far away in China, *a. en mis mocedades,* way back in my youth. — **a. tú, él, ella** or **ellos,** that's your, his, her or their affair; **el más a.,** the other world, life after death; **más a.,** farther, further; **más a. de,** beyond, farther than.
allanador, ra, *a.* smoothing, levelling. —*m., f.* 1. leveler. 2. burglar; official searcher (of house, building, etc.).
allanamiento, *m.* 1. smoothing, levelling; flattening. 2. agreement, acquiescence. 3. burglary, housebreaking; searching (premises by police). 4. (law) acceptance (of claim by defendant). — **a. de morada,** official entry and search; breaking into a house.
allanar, *tr.v.* 1. to smooth, level, flatten. 2. to get around, overcome (difficulties). 3. to pacify, subdue. 4. to enter, break into; to search, raid (house, building, etc.). —*r.v.* 1. to agree, conform, yield, submit. 2. to tumble down, fall flat. 3. to become a commoner (a nobleman).
allegadero, ra, *a., var. of* **allegador.**
allegadizo, za, *a.* collected without selection, bundled together at random.
allegado, da, *past part. of* **allegar.** —*a.* near, close; related. —*m., f.* 1. relation, relative. 2. follower, adherent, partisan, supporter.
allegador, ra, *a.* gathering, collecting. —*m., f.* gatherer, collector. —*m.* rake or board for gathering thrashed wheat; (fire) poker.
allegamiento, *m.* 1. gathering, collection. 2. relationship, kinship.
allegar, (*ref. 51*) *tr.v.* 1. to gather, collect. 2. to put or place near. 3. to gather (thrashed wheat) into piles. 4. to add. —*i.v.* to arrive. —*r.v.* 1. to adhere, agree, join. 2. to arrive. 3. to approach, draw near. — **allegarse a,** to agree with, join, adhere to.
allegue, allegué, *ref.* **allegar.**
allende, *adv.* beyond, on the other side; moreover, furthermore. —*prep.* beyond; besides, in addition to. — **de a los mares,** from overseas, from far away.
allí, *adv.* there; then, on that occasion; por allí, that way.
alloza, *f.* green almond.
allozar, *m.* almond tree grove.
allozo, *m.* almond tree; wild almond tree.
alludel, *m., var. of* **aludel.**
allulla, *f.* (Amer.) shortbread.
alma, *f.* 1. soul, spirit; heart. 2. spirit, liveliness, vigor, energy. 3. backbone, core, essence. 4. human being, soul, e.g. *no había un alma en la plaza,* there wasn't a soul in the square. 5. core, center, stem (the firm center of any instrument or construction); core, heart, center (central strand of a rope or cable); core (of a dam); (bldg.) web, stem. 6. (artil.) bore (of a gun). 7. lower part of the sword hilt, comprising the knuckle bows, head of the blade and guard. 8. (mus.) soundpost (small post under the bridge in stringed instrument). 9. (bldg.) scaffold pole. — **agradecer con** or **en el a.,** to thank from the bottom of one's heart; **a. atravesada, a. de Caín, a. de Judas,** malevolent and warped person; **a. de caballo,** (coll.) unscrupulous and heartless person, Iago; **a. de cántaro,** (coll.) tactless and unfeeling person; **a. de Dios,** saint, saintly person or soul; **a. en pena,** ghost; (fig.) melancholy person; **arrancársele el a.,** to break someone's heart; **caérsele a uno el a. a los pies,** to be bitterly disappointed, have one's heart sink; **no tener a.,** to be heartless or callous; to be unscrupulous; **partir el a. a,** to break one's heart; **paseársele el a. por el cuerpo,** to be very lazy or indolent; **sacarse el a.,** (Amer.) to work one's fingers to the bone, work like mad; **tener el a. en un hilo,** to have one's heart in one's mouth.
almacén, *m.* 1. warehouse, storehouse; storeroom. 2. wholesale store. 3. (Amer.) grocery store. 4. (mil.) magazine. — **a. afianzado,** bonded warehouse; **a. de agua,** (mar.) water cask; **a. de pólvora,** (powder) magazine; **a. de víveres,** grocery store.
almacenado, *m.* amount of wine laid in vats for aging. —*a.* stored away; stacked up; accumulated.
almacenaje, *m.* storage or warehouse fees. — **a. al aire libre** or **al descubierto,** open storage.
almacenamiento, *m.* 1. storing; storage. 2. stored goods.
almacenar, *tr.v.* to store, stack, put in a warehouse; to accumulate, hoard.
almacenero, *m.* warehouse-keeper or watchman.
almacenista, *m., f.* warehouse owner; wholesale store keeper; warehouse or wholesale store assistant; (Amer.) wholesale food supplier.
almaceno, na, *a., var. of* **amaceno.**
almáciga, *f.* 1. mastic (resin). 2. nursery, seedbed.
almacigado, da, *a.* (Amer.) bay colored (cattle); brunet, brunette (person).
almacigar, (*ref. 51*) *tr.v.* to perfume with mastic.
almácigo, *m.* 1. (bot.) mastic tree. 2. species of terebinth (Terebinthus americana). 3. seedbed.
almacigue, almacigué, *ref.* **almacigar.**
almaciguero, ra, *a.* pertaining to a nursery or seedbed.
almádana, *f.* sledge hammer.
almadaneta, *f.* small sledge hammer.
almadearse, *r.v.* (rare) *var. of* **almadiarse.**
almádena, *f.* stone hammer, spalling hammer, sledge hammer.
almadeneta, *f.* small stone or sledge hammer, spalling hammer.
almadía, *f.* a kind of canoe used in India; raft.
almadiar, *i.v., r.v.* to get sea sick.
almadiero, *m.* raftsman; canoeist.
almádina, *f., var. of* **almádana.**
almadraba, *f.* 1. tuna or tunny fishing. 2. tuna fishing waters, net, season. — **a. de buche,** tuna fishing in a circle of nets to trap the fish; **a. de tiro,** tuna fishing with hand nets.
almadrabero, ra, *a.* pertaining to tuna fishing. —*m.* tuna fisherman.
almadreña, *f.* clog, wooden shoe.
almadreñero, *m.* clogmaker.
almágana, *f.* 1. (Hond.) sledge hammer. 2. (Hond.) layabout, sloth, sluggard.
almaganeta, *f., var. of* **almádana.**
almagesto, *m.* almagest, a medieval book of astrology.
almagra, *f., var. of* **almagre.**
almagradura, *f.* coloring with red ochre.
almagral, *m.* red ochre bed or deposit.
almagrar, *tr.v.* 1. to color with red ochre. 2. to defame. 3. (vulg.) to wound, draw blood.
almagre, *m.* red ochre.
almagrera, *f.* container (for red ochre).
almagrero, ra, *a.* rich in red ochre; bearing red ochre.
almaizal, *m., var. of* **almaizar.**
almaizar, *m.* 1. Moorish headgear or veil. 2. (ecc.) humeral, humeral veil.
almaizo, *m.* (bot.) hackberry.
almajal, *m.* (bot.) saltwort or glasswort patch or field.
almajaneque, *m.* (mil.) battering-ram.
almajar, *m.* (bot.) saltwort or glasswort patch or field.
almajara, *f.* hotbed, patch well fertilized to induce seed germination.
almajo, *m.* (bot.) saltwort, glasswort.
almalafa, *f.* full-length Moorish robe.

alma-máter, *f.* (Amer.) alma mater, the school or college that one attended; (fig.) guiding spirit, driving force.
almanaque, *m.* almanac, calendar; — **hacer almanaques,** (fig.) to muse, to be pensive.
almanaquero, ra, *m.* 1. almanac dealer or maker. 2. (derog.) painter of banal scenes or hackneyed subjects.
almandina, *f.* (jewel.) almandine, almandite; deep red garnet.
almandino, *a.* (jewel.) almandine, e.g. *granate almandino,* almandine garnet.
almanguena, *f.* red ochre.
almanta, *f.* space between two furrows; space between rows of olive trees or grape vines.
almarada, *f.* 1. three-edged poniard. 2. sandalmaker's needle. 3. iron poker (used in sulfur foundry).
almarbatar, *tr.v.* (carp.) to join (two pieces of wood) together.
almarbate, *m.* strut joining two pieces of wood.
almarcha, *f.* village situated on low land.
almarga, *f.* marlpit.
almariete, *m.* small cupboard, closet.
almario, *m.* cupboard, closet.
almarjal, *m.* 1. marshland, swampland. 2. (bot.) saltwort or glasswort patch.
almarjo, *m.* 1. (bot.) glasswort. 2. barilla, crude soda ash.
almaro, *m.* (bot.) cat thyme.
almarrá, *m.* cotton gin.
almarraja, *f.* perforated glass bottle used for sprinkling or watering plants.
almarraza, *f., var. of* **almarraja.**
almártaga, *f.* 1. (chem.) litharge, yellow lead oxide. 2. head-piece formerly added to the horse's harness (also **almártega**).
almártiga, *f.* 1. *var. of* **almártaga.** 2. (Col.) a good-for-nothing, lazy person.
almartigón, *m.* halter (for tying animals to the stall).
almaste, *m., var. of* **almástiga.**
almástiga, *f.* mastic (resin).
almastigado, da, *a.* containing mastic.
almatrero, *m.* shad-net fisherman.
almatriche, *m.* irrigation canal.
almatroque, *m.* shad net.
almazara, *f.* oil-mill.
almazarero, *m.* oil-mill operator.
almazarrón, *m., var. of* **almagre.**
almea, *f.* 1. storax, storax balsam; dried storax bark. 2. alma, almah, almeh, Arab woman who improvises verses and dances for a living.
almecina, *f.* hackberry (fruit).
almeja, *f.* mussel, clam.
almejar, *m.* clam bed.
almejí, (*pl.* **almejíes**) *f.* small robe used by Spanish Moors (also **almejía**).
almena, *f.* merlon, a parapet or battlement between two openings or crenels.
almenado, da, *past part. of* **almenar.** —*a.* having merlons; merlon shaped. —*m.* battlements.
almenaje, *m.* battlements.
almenar, *m.* cresset, torchholder. —*tr.v.* (fort.) to top with merlons (a fortification).
almenara, *f.* 1. beacon, signal fire. 2. large candelabrum. 3. (reg.) return ditch, overflow ditch.
almendra, *f.* 1. (bot.) almond (fruit and nut); kernel (of any drupaceous fruit). 2. almond-shaped diamond. 3. cut glass drop (of chandelier). 4. (Cuba, fig.) excellent, first-rate. 5. (archit.) almond, almond-shaped decoration on molding. — **a. amarga,** bitter almond; **a. dulce,** sweet almond; **a. garapiñada,** candied almond; **a. mollar,** soft-shelled almond; **de la media a.,** finicky, fastidious.
almendrada, *f.* almond milk, drink made of milk, almonds and sugar.
almendrado, da, *a.* almond-shaped. —*m.* marzipan, marchpane, almond paste.
almendral, *m.* 1. almond grove. 2. almond tree.
almendrar, *tr.v.* (archit.) to decorate with almond-moldings.
almendrate, *m.* almond stew.
almendrera, *f.* almond tree. — **florecer la a.,** to become prematurely grey.
almendrero, *m.* 1. almond tree. 2. almond dish or bowl (for serving almonds).
almendrilla, *f.* 1. almond-shaped locksmith's file. 2. fine coal; fine gravel. 3. (geol.) conglomerate of fine stones.
almendro, *m.* (bot.) almond tree. — **a. amargo,** bitter almond tree.
almendrón, *m.* (bot.) Malabar almond (tree and fruit).
almendruco, *m.* green almond.
almenilla, *f.* merlon-shaped decoration.
almeriense, *a.* of or pertaining to Almería. —*m., f.* native or inhabitant of Almería, Spain.
almete, *m.* 1. (arch.) helmet. 2. (arch.) soldier wearing a helmet.
almez, (*pl.* **almeces**) *m.* hackberry (tree).
almeza, *m.* hackberry (fruit).
almezo, *m., var. of* **almez.**
almiar, *m.* haystack.
almiarar, *tr.v.* to stack (hay).
almíbar, *m.* syrup.
almibarado, da, *a.* very sweet, syrupy; flattering, honeyed (words).
almibarar, *tr.v.* to cover or coat with syrup; (fig.) to sweeten, honey (one's language) in order to convince someone of something.
almicantarada, *f., var. of* **almicantarat.**
almicantarat, *f.* (astron.) almucantar, a small circle of the celestial sphere parallel to the horizon, used for determining the height of stars.
almidón, *m.* starch. — **a. de maíz,** cornstarch, corn flour.
almidonado, da, *past part. of* **almidonar.** —*a.* 1. starched. 2. extremely smart and spruce. —*m.* starching.
almidonar, *tr.v.* to starch (laundry).
almidoneria, *f.* starch factory.
almifor, *m.* (sl.) horse.
almifora, *f.* (sl.) mule.
almiforero, *m.* (sl.) horse or mule thief.
almijara, *f.* (Sp.) oil tank.
almijarero, *m.* oil-depot keeper or watchman.
almilla, *f.* 1. (arch.) short, tight-fitting jacket or blouse (worn under the armor). 2. (carp.) tenon. 3. breast of pork.
almimbar, *m.* pulpit (in a mosque).
alminar, *m.* minaret, turret of a mosque.
almiquí, *m.* (Cuba) almique, solenodon, an insectivorous mammal of Cuba and Haiti.
almiranta, *f.* 1. (mar.) vice admiral's ship. 2. (coll.) admiral's wife.
almirantazgo, *m.* 1. admiralty. 2. harbor dues. 3. admiralship, rank of admiral.
almirante, *m.* 1. admiral. 2. (arch.) woman's headgear.
almirez, (*pl.* **almireces**) *m.* metal mortar.
almizate, *m.* central panel of a carved wooden ceiling.
almizcate, *m.* yard or patio between two houses.
almizclar, *tr.v.* to perfume with musk.
almizcle, *m.* musk.
almizcleña, *f.* grape hyacinth.
almizcleño, ña, *a.* musky.
almizclera, *f.* (zool.) desman; muskrat.
almizclero, ra, *a.* musky. —*m.* (zool.) musk deer.
almo, ma, *a.* 1. (poet.) nourishing, nurturing. 2. holy, venerable.
almocadén, *m.* 1. infantry captain (in Spanish Morocco). 2. (Morocco) mayor of a district.
almocafre, *m.* rake, small hoe; weeding and transplanting trowel.
almocárabe, *m.* (archit., carp.) bowshaped decoration.
almocarbe, *m., var. of* **almocárabe.**
almocatracia, *f.* (arch.) tax on woolen goods.
almocela, *f.* 1. hood. 2. straw mattress.
almocrí, *m.* reader of the Koran (in a mosque).
almodí, (*pl.* **almodíes**) *m., var. of* **almudí.**
almodón, *m.* flour made from dampened wheat.
almodrote, *m.* 1. sauce for eggplant made with oil, garlic, cheese, etc. 2. (coll.) potpourri, hodgepodge.
almófar, *m.* chain mail coif (worn under the helmet).
almofía, *f., var. of* **jofaina.**
almoflate, *m.* harness maker's knife.
almofrej, *m.* camp bed or sleeping bag.
almofrez, (*pl.* **almofreces**) *m., var. of* **almofrej.**
almogama, *f.* (mar.) loof frame.
almogavár, *m.* (arch.) raider, marauder.
almogavarear, *i.v.* (arch.) to raid, maraud.
almogavaría, *f.* raiders, marauders, raiding party. (also **almogavería**).
almohace, almohacé, *ref.* **almohazar.**
almohacear, *tr.v., var. of* **almohazar.**
almohada, *f.* 1. pillow; cushion. 2. (archit.) bolster (in Ionic architecture). 3. (artil.) bolster, block of wood that supports the gun mounting. 4. (mar.) bolster (cushion or piece of soft wood to stop chafing). — **consultar con la a.,** (coll.) to sleep on the matter, think over carefully; **dar a.,** to bestow a grandeeship (a ceremony in which the queen raises a lady to nobility by having her sit in front of her on a cushion); **tomar la a.,** to receive a grandeeship.
almohadado, da, *a.* cushioned.
almohadazo, *m.* blow with a pillow.
almohade, *a.* Almohad, Almohade. —*m.* (*pl.*) Almohades (Islamic dynasty ruling in North Africa and Spain in the 12th century).
almohadilla, *f.* 1. small cushion; small pad; sewing cushion; (Amer.) pincushion. 2. (Chile, Peru) flatiron holder. 3. (archit.) bolster (in Ionic architecture). 4. (archit.) boss (on ashlar masonry). 5. (vet.) callus (on the back of a horse where the saddle rests). — **a. eléctrica,** electric pad; **a. higiénica,** sanitary napkin.
almohadillado, da, *past part. of* **almohadillar.** —*a.* 1. padded, cushioned. 2. (archit.) raised, bossed (masonry). —*m.* 1. (archit.) bossage, bosses. 2. (mar.) wooden paneling between iron hull and armor plating of a ship.
almohadillar, *tr.v.* (archit.) to boss (stone) by beveling the edges so that the stones are in relief.
almohadón, *m.* 1. cushion, pillow. 2. (archit.) springer, first stone of an arch.
almohatre, *m.* (chem.) sal ammoniac.
almohaza, *f.* curry comb.
almohazador, *m.* currier, groom (of horses).
almohazar, (*ref. 53*) *tr.v.* to curry, curry-comb.
almojábana, *f.* 1. cheese cake. 2. cruller, fritter.
almojarifazgo, *m.* 1. ancient import or export duty. 2. post of customs officer.
almojarife, *m.* 1. royal tax collector. 2. customs officer.
almojaya, *f.* (archit.) putlog, put-log, a short piece of lumber that supports a scaffolding floor.
almojerifazgo, *m., var. of* almojarifazgo.
almojerife, *m., var. of* almojarife.
almona, *f.* shad-fishing waters.

almóndiga, *f., var. of* albóndiga.
almondiguilla, *f., var. of* **almóndiga.**
almoneda, *f.* public auction; clearance sale.
almonedar, *tr.v.* to auction, sell by auction.
almonedear, *tr.v., var. of* **almonedar.**
almoraduj, *m., var. of* almoradux.
almoradux, *m.* (bot.) marjoram.
almorávide, *a.* Almoravid, Almoravide. *—m.* (*pl.*) Almoravides (Islamic dynasty ruling in Spain from 1093 to 1148).
almorcé, *ref.* **almorzar.**
almorejo, *m.* (bot.) foxtail (Setoria glauca).
almorí, *m.* honey pastry.
almoronía, *f., var. of* **alboronía.**
almorrana, *f.* (med.) hemorrhoid; (*pl.*) hemorrhoids, piles.
almorraniento, ta, *a.* hemorrhoidal, suffering from hemorrhoids or piles. *—m., f.* person suffering from piles.
almorrón, *m.* (reg., Sp.) ridge of earth separating plots of land.
almorta, *f.* (bot.) purple vetch.
almorzada, *f.* double handful; the amount contained by the two hands cupped together. 2. (Mex.) generous dinner.
almorzar, (*ref. 70*) *i.v.* to breakfast or (more often) to lunch. *—tr.v.* to eat (something) for lunch or breakfast.
almotacén, *m.* 1. inspector of weights and measures; weights and measures office. 2. administrator of royal estates. 3. Moroccan market overseer.
almotacenazgo, *m.* office of the inspector of weights and measures.
almotacenía, *f.* 1. fee paid to the inspector of weights and measures. 2. office of the inspector of weights and measures.
almotazaf, *m., var. of* **almotacén.**
almotazanía, *f., var. of* **almotacenía.**
almozárabe, *a., m., f., var. of* **mozárabe.**
almud, *m.* ancient land and grain measure.
almudada, *f.* (arch.) ground in which an **almud** of seed was sown.
almudejo, *m.* weight (for weighing dry goods).
almudero, *m.* official keeper of public weights and measures (to weigh grain and vegetables).
almudí, (*pl.* **almudíes**) *m.* public granary; wheat market, corn exchange.
almudín, *m., var. of* **almudí.**
almuecín, *m.* muezzin, Mohammedan who calls to prayer.
almuédano, *m.* muezzin, Mohammedan who calls to prayer.
almuercera, *f.* (Mex.) food stall keeper.
almuercería, *f.* (Mex.) food stall, snack stall.
almuérdago, *m.* mistletoe.
almuertas, *f.* (arch.) tax on grain.
almuerza, *f., var. of* almorzada.
almuerza, almuerzo, *ref.* almorzar.
almuerzo, *m.* 1. lunch (sometimes, breakfast). 2. luncheon service or set.
almunia, *f.* orchard, farm.
alna, *f.* ell, linear measurement of approximately one meter.
alnado, da, *m.* stepson. *—f.* stepdaughter.
álnico, *m.* (metal.) alnico, any of various iron alloys used in making permanent magnets.
alobadado, da, *a.* 1. (vet.) suffering from carbuncular tumors. 2. bitten by a wolf.
alobado, da, *a.* infested with wolves (game reserve).
alobunado, da, *a.* wolf-like (especially hair color).
alocadamente, *adv.* crazily; rashly, recklessly.
alocado, da, *a.* crazy, mad, insane; rash, ill-considered.
alocar, (*ref. 50*) *tr.v. r.v., var. of* **enloquecer.**
alocucíon, *f.* allocution, address, talk.
alodial, *a.* (law) allodial.
alodio, *m.* (law) allodium, land held in absolute ownership without feudal over-lord.
áloe, *m.* 1 (bot.) aloe. 2. (pharm.) aloes. 3. (bot.) agalloch.
aloético, ca, *a.* aloetic.
alófana, *f.* (min.) allophane, hydrous aluminum silicate.
aloína, *f.* (chem.) aloin, bitter yellow purgative obtained from aloes.
aloja, *f.* 1. mead, drink made from water, honey and spices. 2. (Chile, Arg.) kind of beer (made from maize or carob bean pods).
alojado, da, *past part. of* **alojar.** *—m., f.* guest, lodger. *—m.* soldier billeted in a civilian house.
alojamiento, *m.* 1. (action) lodging, boarding (of civilians); billeting, quartering (of soldiers). 2. (place) lodgings (of civilians); billet, quarters (of soldiers); (mil.) camp.
alojar, *tr.v.* to lodge, put up, give accomodation to; to quarter, billet (troops). *—r.v.* 1. to lodge, take lodgins; to be billeted or quartered. 2. to lodge, get lodged.
alojería, *f.* store where mead (**aloja**) is made and sold.
alojero, ra, *m., f.* person who makes or sells mead (**aloja**). *—m.* 1. mead stall. 2. theatre box near the orchestra pit.
alomado, da, *past part. of* **alomar.** *—a.* 1. arched. 2. with an arched back (horses).
alomar, *tr.v.* 1. (agr.) to furrow, plow into furrows. 2. (equit.) to distribute equally (the load on a horse). *—r.v.* 1. to grow strong and fit for breeding (horses). 2. to become arch-backed (a horse).
alomerismo, *m.* (chem.) allomerism.
alometria, *f.* (bot.) allometry.
alométrico, ca, *a.* (bot.) allometric.
alomorfismo, *m.* (min., chem.) allomorphism.
alomorfo, fa, *a.* (min., chem.) allomorphic. *—m.* (min., chem.) allomorph.
alón, *a.* (Amer.) wide-brimmed (hat). *—m.* plucked wing (of any fowl).
alondra, *f.* (ornith.) lark.
alongado, da, *past part. of* **alongar.** *—a.* elongated, prolonged, long.
alongamiento, *m.* 1. lengthening; extension; prolongation. 2. separation, distance.
alongar, (*ref. 72*) *tr.v.* 1. to prolong, extend; to lengthen, stretch. 2. to remove, put at a distance. *—r.v.* to move away, go away.
alongué, *ref.* **alongar.**
alonsito, *m.* (ornith., Arg., Urug.) baker bird.
alonso, *a.* (agr.) bearded (wheat).
alópata, *a.* (med.) allopathic. *—m.* allopath, allopathist.
alopatía, *f.* allopathy.
alopáticamente, *adv.* allopathically.
alopático, ca, *a.* allopathic.
alopátrico, ca, *a.* (bot.) allopatric.
alopecia, *f.* (med.) alopecia, baldness.
alopecuro, *m.* (bot.) meadow foxtail (Alopecurus pratensis).
alopiado, *a., var. of* **opiado.**
aloque, aloqué, *ref.* alocarse.
aloque, *a.* light red (color); rosé (wine). *—m.* rosé wine; mixture of red and white wine.
aloquecerse, (*ref. 45*) *r.v., var. of* **enloquecerse.**
aloquezca, aloquezco, *ref.* **aloquecerse.**
aloquín, *m.* stone wall in a wax bleachery.
alora, *adv.* (arch.) readily.
alorarse, *r.v.* (Sp., reg.) to become tanned from sun and wind.
alorritmia, *f.* (med.) allorhythmia.
alosa, *f.* (ichth.) shad.
alosna, *f.* (bot.) wormwood, absinthe.
alotar, *tr.v.* (mar.) 1. *var. of* **arrizar.** 2. to stow (a net).
alotérmico, ca, *a.* having a different temperature.
alotermo, ma, *a.* having a different temperature.
alotropía, *f.* allotropy.
alotrópico, ca, *a.* allotropic.
alotropismo, *m.* allotropism.
alpaca, *f.* 1. (zool.) alpaca. 2. alpaca (wool and cloth). 3. nickel silver, German silver.
alpacón, *m.* (Chile) thick and coarse wool.
alpamato, *m.* (bot., Arg.) variety of myrtle (Myrtus thea).
alpañata, *f.* 1. chamois leather (used by potter to smooth earthenware vessels before baking them in kiln). 2. reddish clay.
alparcear, *tr.v.* to match animals from different owners.
alparcería, *f.* (coll.) 1. *var. of* **aparcería.** 2. (Sp.) gossiping.
alparcero, ra, *a.* (Sp.) gossipy.
alpargata,, *f.* espadrille, hemp sandal.
alpargatado, da, *past part. of* **alpargatar.** *—a.* sandal-like.
alpargatar, *i.v.* to make hemp or rope sandals.
alpargate, *m., var. of* **alpargata.**
alpargatería, *f.* shop where hemp sandals are made and sold.
alpargatero, ra, *m., f.* hemp sandal maker.
alpargatilla, *m., f.* 1. *dim. of* **alpargata,** small hemp sandal. 2. (coll.) cunning, crafty person.
alpartaz, (*pl.* **alpartaces**) *m.* piece of chain mail used to protect union of helmet and breastplate.
alpatana, *f.* (Sp.) tool, agricultural implement.
alpax, *m.* (metal.) alpax.
alpechín, *m.* dark, smelly juice oozing from a pile of olives; (Amer.) tart juice (squeezed from some fruits).
alpechinera, *f.* earthenware vessel for receiving juice oozing from olives.
alpende, *m.* tool shed, tool house; lean-to.
alpérsico, *m.* (bot.) peach (fruit and tree).
Alpes, *m. pl.* Alps; **A. Dináricos,** Dinaric Alps; **A. Lepontinos,** Lepontine Alps; **A. Marítimos,** Maritime Alps.
alpestre, *a.* 1. alpine; 2. (fig.) mountainous, wild.
alpinismo, *m.* (sport.) alpinism, mountain climbing.
alpinista, *m., f.* (sport.) alpinist, mountain climber.
alpino, na, *a.* Alpine (capitals used when referring specifically to the Alps); alpine (when referring to any high mountain region).
alpiste, *m.* (bot.) canary grass; birdseed. — **dejar a uno a.,** to leave (someone) out; **quedarse (uno) a.,** to be left out (of a project into which one has put much effort).
alpistela, *f., var. of* **alpistera.**
alpistera, *f.* sesame seed cake.
alpistero, *m.* sieve for birdseed.
alpujarreño, ña, *a.* from or of Alpujarras, Spain. *—m., f.* native or inhabitant of Alpujarras.
alquequenje, *m.* (bot.) alkekengi, winter cherry, Chinese lantern (plant and fruit, used as a diuretic).
alquería, *f.* 1. grange, farmhouse. 2. hamlet.
alquermes, *m.* alkermes, liquor or aromatic brandy colored with the kermes insect or cochineal.
alquerque, *m.* in olive oil mills, the place where olive pulp from first pressing is shredded.
alquez, (*pl.* **alqueces**) *m.* wine measure (of 384 pints).
alquezar, *m.* river dam.
alquibla, *f.* point towards which Moslems face while praying.

alquicel, *m.* 1. Moorish cape of white wool. 2. seat cover.
alquicer, *m., var. of* **alquicel.**
alquifol, *m.* (chem.) galena, native lead sulfide used to glaze pottery.
alquilable, *a.* rentable, leasable, hirable.
alquiladizo, za, *a.* (derog.) mercenary, for hire (appl. to people). —*m., f.* (derog.) mercenary.
alquilador, ra, *m., f.* lessor, hirer; tenant.
alquilamiento, *m.* renting, letting, leasing; hiring.
alquilar, *tr.v.* to let, lease; to rent; to hire. —*r.v.* to hire oneself out; to be for rent. — **se alquila,** for rent, for hire.
alquiler, *m.* rent, rental (money paid for leasing or renting). — **de a.,** for hire; **auto de a.,** taxicab, car for hire.
alquilón, na, *a.* (derog.) mercenary, **for** hire (appl. to people). —*m., f.* mercenary, hireling.
alquimia, *f.* alchemy.
alquímicamente, *adv.* alchemically.
alquímico, ca, *a.* alchemic, alchemical.
alquimila, *f.* (bot.) lion's foot, ladies' mantle.
alquimista, *m.* alchemist.
alquinal, *m.* woman's veil or headdress.
alquitara, *f.* still, alembic. — **por a.,** little by little, sparingly, stingily (coll.).
alquitarar, *tr.v.* to distill.
alquitira, *f.* (bot.) tragacanth.
alquitrán, *m.* tar, pitch; mixture of pitch, grease, resin, and oil. — **a. de carbón, a. de hulla, a.** mineral, mineral or coal tar; **a. de turba,** peat tar; **a. vegetal,** wood tar.
alquitranado, da, *a.* tarred; tarry. —*m.* (mar.) tarpaulin.
alquitranar, *tr.v.* to tar, coat with tar or pitch.
alrededor, *adv.* around. — **a.** de, around, about. —*m. (pl.)* **alrededores,** outskirts, environs.
alrota, *f.* tow, flax residue.
Alsacia, *f.* Alsace; **A. Lorena,** Alsace-Lorraine, France.
alsaciano, na, *c., m., f.* Alsatian. —*m.* Alsatian (language).
álsine, *f.* (bot.) chickweed; scorpion grass.
alta, *f.* 1. certificate of discharge (from a hospital). 2. entry into or admittance to a body, profession, etc.; (mil.) certificate of return to or entry into active service; return to or entry into active service. 3. tax declaration; tax declaration form. 4. ancient court dance; dancing exercise. 5. (fenc.) public fencing bout. 6. (coll.) tower; (coll.) window. — **dar de a.,** (mil.) to mark down, take note of a soldier's return to unit or a recruit's reporting to unit; **dar de a., dar el a.,** to discharge (patient) from hospital, to declare (a patient) cured; **darse de a.,** to join, become a member.
altabaca, *f.* (bot.) field inula, elecampane (Inula viscosa).
altabaque, *m.* wicker basket.
altabaquillo, *m.* (bot.) bindweed (Convolvulus arvensis).
altacimut, *m.* (astron.) altazimuth.
altaico, ca, *a.* Altaic, Altaian, of or from the Altai Mountains (Central Asia).
altamandría, *f.* (bot.) knotgrass (Polygonum aviculare).
altamente, *adv.* highly, extremely, e.g. *a. apreciado,* highly appreciated.
altamisa, *f.* (bot.) mugwort (Artemisa vulgaris).
altamisilla, *f.* (Cuba), *var. of* **artemisilla.**
altana, *f.* (coll.) temple.
altanar, *i.v.* (coll.) to marry.
altaneramente, *adv.* haughtily, arrogantly; high-handedly.
altanería, *f.* 1. haughtiness, arrogance. 2. falconry, hunting with high-flying birds of prey. 3. heights. 4. high flying, soaring (of birds of prey).
altanero, ra, *a.* 1. haughty, arrogant. 2. high flying, soaring.
altanos, *a.* **vientos altanos,** (mar.) winds that blow alternately from land to shore and vice versa.
altar, *m.* 1. altar. 2. (astron.) **A.,** Ara. 3. (min.) altar, flue bridge, bridge wall. 4. (fig.) religion. — **a. mayor,** high altar; **llevar al a.,** to marry, to lead to the altar; **poner (a alguien) en un altar,** (fig.) to put (someone) on a pedestal, to idolize.
altarero, *m.* altar maker; altar dresser.
altaricón, na, *a.* hefty, husky.
altarreina, *f.* (bot.) yarrow, milfoil (Achillae millefolium).
altavoz, (*pl.* **altavoces**) *m.* (rad.) loud-speaker; **a. electrodinámico,** (rad.) dynamic speaker.
altea, *f.* (bot.) althea.
altear, *tr.v.* 1. to raise, make something higher. 2. (Arg., Par.) to stop (someone). —*r.v.* to rise (land).
alterabilidad, *f.* alterability.
alterable, *a.* alterable.
alteración, *f.* 1. alteration, change. 2. anger, irritation. 3. disturbance, commotion. 4. dispute, argument, disagreement.
alteradizo, za, *a.* changeable, variable; fickle.
alterado, da, *past part. of* **alterar.** —*a.* 1. altered, changed. 2. agitated, disturbed, upset. 3 angry, annoyed, irritated.
alterador, ra, *a.* altering; disturbing, disquieting.
alterante, *a., m.* (med.) alterative.
alterar, *tr.v.* 1. to alter, change. 2. to disquiet, disturb, agitate. 3. to annoy, irritate. —*r.v.* 1. to undergo change, change, alter. 2. to become agitated. 3. to become irritated or annoyed.
alterativo, va, *a.* alterative, causing change.
altercación, *f.* altercation, dispute, disagreement.
altercado, *m., var. of* **altercación.**
altercador, ra, *a.* argumentative, wrangling. —*m., f.* wrangler, argumentative person.
altercante, *a.* argumentative, wrangling.
altercar, (*ref. 50*) *i.v., r.v.* to disagree, argue, quarrel.
alter ego, *m.* (Lat.) alter ego, other self.
alternabilidad, *f.* ability to be alternated.
alternable, *a.* able to be alternated.
alternación, *f.* alternation.
alternadamente, *adv.* alternately.
alternado, da, *a.* alternate.
alternador, *m.* (elec.) alternator, alternating current generator; **a. bifásico,** two-phaser, diphaser.
alternancia, *f.* alternation; **a. dc generaciones,** (biol.) alternation of generations.
alternante, *a.* alternating.
alternar, *tr.v.* to alternate, interchange. —*i.v.* 1. to alternate, take turns. 2. to alternate, succeed or happen by turns. — **a con,** to mix with, have social intercourse with, be friendly with.
alternativa, *f.* 1. alternative; choice, option. 2. (taur.) ceremony (during a bullfight) in which a bullfighter is acknowledged as a full-fledged matador and is invited to take part in the game with a recognized bullfighter.
alternativamente, *adv.* alternately.
alternativo, va, *a.* alternating, alternate; **cultivo a.,** crop rotation.
alterno, na, *a.* alternating; (elec.) alternating; (geom., bot.) alternate. — **corriente alterna,** (elec.) alternating current.
altero, *m.* (Mex.) pile, heap.
alteroso, sa, *a.* (mar.) unstable, top-heavy, too high in the freeboard (said of a ship).
alterque, alterqué, *ref.* **altercar.**
alteza, *f.* 1. A., Highness (title). 2. height, elevation; sublimity.
altibajo, *m.* 1. brocaded velvet. 2. (fenc.) downward thrust. 3. (*pl.*) (coll.) undulating land, rise and fall of land. 4. (*pl.*) (coll.) ups and downs (of fortune).
altígrafo, *m.* altigraph, altitude recorder.
altilocuencia, *f.* grandiloquence.
altilocuente, *a.* grandiloquent.
altilocuo, cua, *a.* grandiloquent.
altillo, *m.* 1. hillock, rise (in the ground). 2. (S. Amer.) attic, garret.
altimetría, *f.* altimetry.
altímetro, tra, *a.* altimetrical. —*m.* altimeter; **a. aneroide,** aneroid altimeter; **a. barométrico,** barometric altimeter.
altipampa, *f.* (Arg., Bol.) high plateau.
altiplanicie, *f.* altiplano, high plateau, high tableland.
altiplano, *m., var. of* **altiplanicie.**
altiscopio, *m.* (mar.) altiscope, periscope.
altísimo, ma, *a.* very high, highest; **El A.,** God.
altisonancia, *f.* high-flown style or language, bombast.
altisonante, *a.* high-flown, bombastic, high-sounding, pompous (language).
altisonantemente, *adv.* pompously, bombastically.
altísono, na, *a.* high-flown, pompous, bombastic, high-sounding.
altitonante, *a.* (poet.) thundering.
altitud, *f.* height, altitude, elevation. — **a. barométrica,** (meteorol.) pressure altitude.
altivamente, *adv.* haughtily, arrogantly; proudly.
altivar, *tr.v.* (rare) to make proud or arrogant. —*r.v.* to become proud or arrogant.
altivecer, (*ref. 45*) *tr.v.* to make haughty, arrogant or proud. —*r.v.* to become haughty, arrogant or proud.
altivez, *f.* haughtiness, pride, arrogance.
altiveza, *f., var. of* **altivez.**
altivo, va, *a.* 1. haughty, proud, arrogant. 2. lofty, high.
alto, ta, *a.* 1. high, tall; elevated, e.g. *un edificio* or *un hombre alto,* a tall building or man, *terreno alto,* high ground. 2. upper, e.g. *el piso alto,* the upper floor; **Cámara Alta,** Upper Chamber; **Alto Volta,** Upper Volta. 3. high, swollen (river, sea), e.g. *marea alta,* high tide. 4. high, upper, superior, e.g. *un alto funcionario,* a high official; **la alta sociedad,** high society; **la clase alta,** the upper classes. 5. high, refined, excellent; **alta cocina,** haute cuisine, the art of fine cooking. 6. (acous.) high, loud, e.g. *léelo en voz alta,* read it aloud. 7. high, serious, grave, e.g. *fiebre alta,* high fever, *alta traición,* high treason. 8. high, raised, e.g. *precios altos,* high prices, *talle alto,* high waistline. 9. high, late, advanced, e.g. *a altas horas de la noche,* late at night; **la Alta Edad Media,** the Late Middle Ages. 10. high, open, e.g. *en alta mar,* on the high seas. 11. high, intense, e.g. *alta tensión,* high tension; **alto horno,** blast furnace. 12. (art.) high-raised; **alto relieve,** high relief, alto-relievo. 13. high, lofty, elevated, e.g. *altos principios,* high principles. —*m.* 1. height, elevation; hillock. 2. (Amer.) heap, pile. 3. (mus.) alto. 4. (*pl.*) upstairs, the upper stories, the upper floor. — **alta atmósfera,** upper atmosphere; **alta fidelidad,** high fidelity; **alta frecuencia,** high frequency; **alta peluquería,** hairstyling; **altas esferas,** upper echelons; **altas presiones,** high pressure; **alta traición,** high treason; **alto cargo,** high-ranking position; **alto mando,** high-ranking officer; **altos y bajos,** ups and downs **alto voltaje,** high voltage; **de lo alto,** from above; **de lo alto de,** from the heights of; **en alto,** on high; **irse por**

todo lo alto, to go all out; **pasar por alto,** to ignore, omit; overlook, excuse.
alto, *adv.* 1. high up, up high, high. 2. loud, loudly, aloud.
alto, *m.* stop, halt; — **dar el alto a,** to order to stop; **hacer a.,** to stop, halt, make a halt; **poner a. a,** to put a stop or halt to. —*interj.* halt; **¡a. ahí!** halt! stop there!; **¡a. al fuego!** cease fire!
altoparlante, *m.* (rad.) loudspeaker, speaker.
altor, *m., var. of* **altura.**
altozanero, *m.* (Col.) porter.
altozano, *m.* 1. hillock, knoll. 2. higher or upper part (of a town). 3. (Col., Ven., C. Amer.) porch (of a church); (Col., Ven.) raised terrace (of a house).
altramuz, (*pl.* **altramuces**) *m.* (bot.) lupine (plant and fruit).
altruismo, *m.* altruism.
altruista, *a.* altruistic. —*m., f.* altruist.
altura, *f.* 1. height, altitude, elevation; tallness. 2. summit, top, height. 3. pitch (of sound). 4. (mar.) altitude. 5. (*pl.*) Heaven, the Heavens, the Highest. 6. (astron.) altitude. — **a. de polo,** the elevation of the pole or of any of the heavenly bodies; **a. barométrica,** barometric height; **a. calculada,** (avia.) rated altitude; **a. dinámica,** (hydr.) velocity head; **a. manométrica,** (meteorol., hydr.) manometric head, static lift; **a. real,** (avia.) actual height; **a estas alturas,** at this point, now, at this advanced stage; **a la a. de,** level with; at, as far up as; ((mar.) off; **a. de franqueo** or **paso,** clearance height; **ascendió a las alturas,** (Bib.) He ascended to Heaven; **estar a la a. de,** to be up to, be equal to; to be level with; **estar a la a. de las circunstancias,** to be equal to the occasion; **Gloria a Dios en las alturas,** Glory to God in Heaven; **ponerse a la a. de las circunstancias,** to rise to the occasion.
alúa, *f.* (Arg., ento.) firefly, glowworm.
alubia, *f.* (bot.) kidney bean, French bean.
alubiar, *m.* bean field.
aluciar, *tr.v.* to polish, burnish. —*r.v.* to spruce oneself up, get dressed up.
alucinación, *f.* hallucination.
alucinadamente, *adv.* deludedly, erroneously.
alucinador, ra, *a.* hallucinatory, delusive. —*m.* hallucinogen.
alucinamiento, *m., var. of* **alucinación.**
alucinante, *a.* hallucinating, dazzling, tricky.
alucinar, *tr.v.* to hallucinate; to delude, dazzle, trick, deceive. —*r.v.* to be deceived or deluded.
alucinatorio, ria, *a.* hallucinatory, hallucinating.
alucita, *f.* (ento.) corn moth, moth causing damage to wheat.
alucón, *m.* (ornith.) barn owl.
alud, *m.* avalanche.
aluda, *f.* (ento.) winged ant.
aludel, *m.* (chem.) aludel.
aludido, da, *past part. of* **aludir.** —*a.* above-mentioned, referred to.
aludir, *i.v.* to allude, refer to.
aludo, da, *a.* large-winged; wide-brimmed.
alujar, *tr.v.* (C. Amer.) to polish.
alumbra, *f.* (rare), *var. of* **excava.**
alumbrado da *past part. of* **alumbrar.** —*a.* 1. lighted, lit. 2. (Arg., Chile, coll.) lit-up, tight, tipsy, merry. —*m.* 1. lighting, street lighting. 2. (*pl.*) Alumbrados, Illuminati, 16th C. mystic Spanish sect seeking illumination by and union with God. — **a. de gas,** gas lighting; **a. fluorescente,** fluorescent lighting; **a. indirecto,** indirect lighting; **a. antideslumbrante,** non-glare lighting; **a. rasante,** grazing lighting; **a. vertical,** overhead lighting.
alumbrado, da, *past part. of* **alumbrar.** —*a.* treated with alum.
alumbrador, ra, *a.* illuminating, lighting. —*m., f.* (ant.) lighter, linkboy.
alumbramiento, *m.* 1. illumination, lighting. 2. (fig.) childbirth.
alumbrante, *a.* illuminating. —*m.* 1. (theat.) lighting engineer; light technician. 2. linkboy.
alumbrar, *tr.v.* 1. to illuminate, light, light up, give light to. 2. to enlighten, illuminate. 3. (fig.) to give birth to. 4. (agr.) to remove bank of soil from (vines). 5. to discover (subterranean waters). 6. to give sight to (the blind). 7. (Amer.) to examine (an egg) against the light. —*i.v.* 1. to give light, e.g. *a. bien* or *mal,* to give a good or poor light, give a lot of or little light. —*r.v.* (Arg., Chile, coll.) to get tipsy or tight, get lit-up.
alumbrar, *tr.v.* to treat with alum.
alumbre, *m.* (chem.) alum; **a. crómico,** chrome alum; **a. de amonio,** ammonia alum; **a. de pluma,** crystallized alum; **a. sacarino, a. zucarino,** (med.) astringent solution of sugar and alum; **a. sódico,** soda alum.
alumbrera, *f.* alum mine.
alumbroso, sa, *a.* aluminous, containing alum.
alúmina, *f.* (chem.) alumina, aluminum oxide.
aluminato, *m.* (chem.) aluminate.
aluminiar, *tr.v.* to aluminize, to aluminum-plate.
alumínico, ca, *a.* aluminous.
aluminio, *m.* aluminum, aluminium; **a. en polvo,** aluminum powder; **papel de a.,** aluminum foil; **a. anodizado,** anodized aluminum; **a. fundido,** (metal.) cast aluminum; **a. cromado,** chromeplated or chromatized aluminum.
aluminita, *f.* (min.) aluminite, websterite, aluminum sulfate.
aluminoso, sa, *a.* aluminous, consisting of alum.
aluminotermia, *f.* (mec.) aluminothermy, aluminothermica.
alumnado, *m.* student body.
alumno, na, *m., f.* pupil, disciple, student.
alunado, da, *a.* 1. mad, lunatic. 2. (vet.) having spasms. 3. spoiled (bacon).
alunamiento, *m.* (mar.) curve of boltrope.
alunarado, da, *a.* spotted with moles; polka-dotted.
alunarse, *r.v.* 1. to spoil (bacon). 2. to become sore or inflamed (sores, wound). 3. (Col., Ven.) to become galled or chafed.
alunice, alunicé, *ref.* **alunizar.**
alunita, *f.* (min.) alunite.
alunizaje, *m.* lunar landing, moon landing.
alunizar, (*ref. 53*) *i.v.* to land on the moon.
alusión, *f.* allusion, reference; **a. personal,** personal allusion, innuendo.
alusivo, va, *a.* allusive.
alustrar, *tr.v.* to polish, put a shine on.
alutación, *f.* (min.) gold nugget.
alutrado, da, *a.* otter-colored.
aluvial, *a.* alluvial.
aluvión, *m.* 1. flood, alluvion. 2. (fig.) flood, torrent (of people, things, etc.). 3. alluvium, alluvial deposit; (law) alluvion. — **de a.,** formed by alluvial deposit.
alveario, *m.* (anat.) alveary.
álveo, *m.* river bed, bed of a stream.
alveolado, *a.* (bldg.) alveolated, honeycombed.
alveolar, *a.* (anat., phonet.) alveolar.
alvéolo, *m.* (anat., phonet.) alveolus, alveole; (bot.) alveola; cell, alveolus (of honeycomb).
alverja, *f., var. of* **arveja.**
alverjana, *f., var. of* **arvejana.**
alverjilla, *f.* (bot., Ecuad.) sweet **pea.**
alverjón, *m., var. of* **arvejón.**
alvino, na, *a.* (med.) alvine.
alza, *f.* 1. rise, increase (e.g. in prices). 2. (mil.) backsight (on a rifle). 3. leather added to the last to increase the size of a shoe. 4. (print.) overlay. 5. each of the wooden parts of movable press. — **jugar al a.,** to speculate on the rise of prices, bull the market; **a. y baja,** rise and fall in stocks; **en a.,** (Amer.) rising, prosperous; **a. abatida,** (mil.) battle sight, low range; **a. automática,** (mil.) automatic sight; (hydr.) automatic flashboard; **a. fija,** (mil.) block sight; **a. móvil,** (hydr.) flashboard, wicket.
alzacuello, *m.* 1. high, stiff collar on a dress. 2. clerical collar with fancy tie.
alzada, *f.* 1. height (of a horse). **2. (law)** appeal (in governmental litigation).
alzadamente, *adv.* for a lump sum.
alzadera, *f.* counter-weight used in jumping.
alzadizo, za, *a.* easily lifted.
alzado, da, *past part. of* **alzar.** —*a.* 1. fraudulently bankrupt. 2. fixed, settled (sum of money). 3. (Amer.) wild; in heat. 4. (Amer., fig.) spoilt, insolent. 5. (Amer.) rebellious, insurrectionary. —*m.* 1. raising, lifting. 2. (archit.) elevation (geometrical projection of a building). 3. (mar.) height (of a ship). 4. rebel, guerrilla.
alzadura, *f.* lifting, raising; rising, elevation.
alzafuelles, *m., f.* flatterer, toady, sycophant.
alzamiento, *m.* 1. lifting, raising; rising; rise (e.g. of prices). 2. higher bid (at an auction). 3. rising, rebellion, uprising. — **a. de bienes,** fraudulent bankruptcy.
alzapaño, *m.* curtain hook or holder (holding curtain to side of window or door).
alzapelo, la, *a.* (Guat., fig.) cowardly, irresolute.
alzapié, *m.* snare (for birds, animals, etc.).
alzaprima, *f.* 1. crowbar, lever; wedge. 2. bridge (on string instruments).
alzaprimar, *tr.v.* 1. to lever, raise with a lever. 2. to incite, arouse, stir up.
alzapuertas, *m.* (theat.) extra, supernumerary.
alzar, (*ref. 53*) *tr.v.* 1. to raise, lift; to heave, hoist; (ecc.) to elevate (the host). 2. to pick up; to lift, steal, make off with. 3. to hide. 4. to gather (the harvest). 5. to raise (game). 6. (mas.) to give, hand (plaster). 7. (print.) to work up, put (printed sheets) in order. — **a. bandera,** to revolt; **a. el codo,** to drink to excess; **a. la mano,** to threaten; **a. velas,** to set sail; **a. la voz,** to raise one's voice. —*r.v.* 1. to rise; to tower (mountains, buildings); to soar (birds). 2. to rise, rebel, mutiny. 3. to go fraudulently bankrupt. 4. to leave a card game when winning. 5. (law) to appeal. 6. (Amer.) to escape and run wild, go berserk (animals). — **alzarse con,** to make off with, steal; **alzarse en armas,** to rise in arms.
alzo, *m.* (C. Amer.) theft, robbery.
Am *symb. of* **americio,** americium (Am).
a.m. *abbrev. of* **ante meridiem,** (Lat.) ante meridiem (a.m.), before noon.
ama, *f.* 1. lady or mistress of the house; woman owner, proprietress; landlady. 2. housekeeper; head maid. 3. nursemaid, nanny; wet nurse. — **a. de brazos,** (Col., Chile) nursemaid; **a. de casa,** housewife; **a. de cria,** wet nurse; **a. de gobierno,** housekeeper; **a. de leche,** wet nurse; **a. de llaves,** housekeeper; **a. seca,** dry nurse, nursemaid.
amabilidad, *f.* amiability, affability, kindness.
amabilísimo, ma, *a. super. of* **amable,** very amiable, kind or friendly.
amable, *a.* kind, courteous, amiable, affable, friendly.
amablemente, *adv.* amiably, affably, kindly.
amacayo, *m.* (bot., Amer.) fleur-de-lis.
amaceno, na, *a.* damson. —*m.* (bot.) damson tree. —*f.* damson plum.
amachambrar, *tr.v.* (mas.) to feather. —*r.v.* (Chile) to cohabit.

amachetear, *tr.v.* to hack with a machete.
amachinarse, *r.v.* (Amer.) to cohabit, live in concubinage.
amacho, cha, *a.* (Arg.) strong, outstanding.
amacigado, da, *a.* yellow-colored, mastic-colored.
amación, *f.* platonic love.
amacollar, *i.v., r.v.* (bot.) to sprout a cluster or clusters of shoots.
amado, da, *past part. of* **amar.** —*a., m., f.* beloved.
amador, ra, *a.* loving, fond. —*m., f.* lover.
amadrigar, *(ref. 51) tr.v.* to shelter, receive well (especially someone who is not worthy of it). —*r.v.* to hide, burrow (animals); to withdraw oneself from society, go into seclusion.
amadrigue, amadrigué, *ref.* **amadrigar.**
amadrinado, da, *past part. of* **amadrinar.** —*a.* (Arg.) said of animals not used to being separated from the herd.
amadrinamiento, *m.* coupling, yoking (of horses).
amadrinar, *tr.v.* 1. to couple, yoke together (horses). 2. to sponsor, support, help, favor; to be godmother to; to act as sponsor for (bride or bridegroom at wedding). 3. (S. Amer.) to train (horses) to follow a leader. 4. (mar.) to splice, join, couple (two things for reinforcement).
amadroñado, da, *a.* resembling a **madroño,** a species of large cherry.
amaestradamente, *adv.* masterfully, dexterously, skillfully.
amaestrado, da, *past part. of* **amaestrar.** —*a.* 1. skilled, trained, experienced. 2. tame, trained, e.g. *un oso amaestrado,* a trained bear.
amaestrador, ra, *a.* training, coaching. —*m., f.* trainer, coach.
amaestradura, *f.* artifice, trick, ruse.
amaestramiento, *m.* training, coaching, teaching.
amaestrar, *tr.v.* 1. to train, coach, teach. 2. (coll.) to tame.
amagadura, *f.* (vet.) chafing on a horse's hoof.
amagamiento, *m.* (Amer.) 1. threat; menacing gesture. 2. deep gorge.
amagar, *(ref. 51) tr.v.* 1. to make threatening gestures. 2. to feign, simulate, feint. —*i.v.* 1. to be impending, be imminent. 2. to appear. — **a. a** + *inf.,* to show signs of + *ger.,* threaten to + *inf.,* seem about to + *inf.* —*r.v.* 1. (coll.) to hide. 2. (S. Amer.) to threaten each other mockingly.
amago, *m.* 1. sign, indication, beginning, outbreak. 2. threat, menace. 3. mock attack.
amague, amagué, *ref.* **amagar.**
amainador, *m.* (min.) cager, onsetter, man who handles the bucket at the top of the mine shaft.
amainar, *tr.v.* 1. (mar.) to lower, shorten (sails). 2. (min.) to bring (buckets of minerals) to the surface. 3. to calm, lessen, reduce. —*i.v.* 1. to subside, lessen, die down (winds). 2. to yield, give up, desist from (some enterprise, plan, wish, etc.).
amaine, *m.* 1. lowering, shortening (of sails). 2. subsiding, lessening (wind). 3. yielding, desisting. 4. relaxation, calming.
amaitinar, *tr.v.* to stalk, spy on, watch, observe.
amajadar, *tr.v.* 1. to keep (sheep) in a field to fertilize it. 2. to fence in, put in a fold (sheep). —*i.v.* to go into the fold, seek shelter in the fold.
amajanar, *tr.v.* to mark out the boundaries of (a field) with piles of stones.
¡amalaya! *interj.* (Amer.) God grant! I wish!
amalayar, *tr.v.* (Arg., Mex.) to wish deeply (for something to happen).
amalecita, *a., m.* (Bib.) Amalekite.
amalequita, *a., var. of* **amalecita.**
amalgama, *f.* amalgam; mixture.
amalgamación, *f.* amalgamation; mixture.
amalgamador, ra, *a.* amalgamating. —*m.* amalgamator.
amalgamar, *tr.v.* to amalgamate; to mix.
amalgamiento, *m., var. of* **amalgamación.**
amallarse, *r.v.* (Chile, coll.) to leave (a gambling party) when one is winning.
amamantador, ra, *a.* suckling. —*f.* suckler, one who suckles.
amamantamiento, *m.* suckling, nursing.
amamantar, *tr.v.* to suckle, nurse.
amán, *m.* peace, amnesty (Moorish expression).
amanal, *m.* (Mex.) reservoir, tank.
amancay, (*pl.* **amancaes**) *m.* (bot., Chile. Peru) Peruvian daffodil (Hymenocallys amancaes); (Arg.) hippeastrum (Hipeastrum ambiguum).
amancebamiento, *m.* concubinage, illicit cohabitation.
amancebarse, *r.v.* to live in concubinage, cohabit illicitly.
amancillar, *tr.v.* 1. (fig.) to stain, tarnish. 2. to disgrace, defame. 3. to soil, deface.
amanear, *tr.v.* to fetter, chain, hobble (a horse).
amanecer, *(ref. 45) i.v.* 1. to dawn, break (the day). 2. to wake up, be at daybreak (in a certain place or condition). 3. (fig.) to begin to appear or manifest itself, dawn. —*r.v.* to stay awake all night (studying, partying, etc.) e.g. *me amanecí estudiando, I stayed up all night studying.* — **no por mucho madrugar amanece más temprano,** do not rely only upon an early start. —*m.* dawn, daybreak; **al a.,** at daybreak.
amanecida, *f., var. of* **amanecer.**
amaneciente, *a.* dawning, beginning to appear.
amaneradamente, *adv.* affectedly, mannered, in a mannered fashion.
amanerado, da, *past part. of* **amanerarse.** —*a.* 1. mannered, affected. 2. (Amer.) excessively courteous, polite; effeminate.
amaneramiento, *m.* 1. affectation, affectedness. 2. mannerism, affected or mannered style.
amanerarse, *r.v.* to become mannered or affected, act affectedly.
amanezca, amanezco, *ref.* amanecer.
amaniatar, *tr.v.* to manacle, tie the hands of.
amanita, *f.* (bot.) amanita, very poisonous agaric mushroom.
amanitina, *f.* amanita toxin.
amanojado, da, *a.* bunched, in bunches or in the shape of a bunch.
amanojar, *tr.v.* to bundle, bunch, gather in bunches.
amansado, da, *past part. of* **amansar.** —*a.* tamed.
amansador, ra, *a.* taming; appeasing, soothing. —*m., f.* tamer; soother, appeaser. —*m.* (Amer.) horse breaker. —*f.* (Arg., fig.) long wait (in a public office waiting room); waiting room.
amansamiento, *m.* taming, breaking; pacification, soothing.
amansar, *tr.v., r.v.* to tame (wild animal, one's character); to break (a horse); to pacify, soothe.
amanse, *m., var. of* **amansamiento.**
amantar, *tr.v.* (coll.) to cloak, cover (someone) with a cloak or garment.
amante, *a.* loving, fond. —*m.* lover, concubine; (*pl.*) lovers. —*f.* mistress, concubine.
amante, *m.* (mar.) rope, pendant.
amantillar, *tr.v.* (mar.) to top the lifts.
amantillo, *m.* (mar.) lift, topping lift.
amanuense, *m.* amanuensis, clerk; secretary.
amanzanamiento, *m.* (Arg.) division of land into blocks, parcels or squares.
amanzanar, *tr.v.* (Arg.) to divide land into blocks, parcels or squares.
amañado, da, *past part. of* **amañar.** —*a.* 1. skillful, clever. 2. faked, fixed.
amañar, *tr.v.* to fix up cleverly, fake; to do cleverly. —*r.v.* to find a way or manage (to do something), become clever (at doing something), get the knack (of doing something).
amaño, *m.* 1. skill, ability, cleverness, aptitude, dexterity. 2. (fig.) trick, intrigue. 3. (*pl.*) tools, instruments.
amapola, *f.* (bot.) poppy; (Cuba, bot.) althea.
amapuches, *m., pl.* (Cuba) tools, gear.
amar, *tr.v.* to love; to be fond of.
amaracino, na, *a.* of marjoram.
amáraco, *m.* (bot.) *var. of* **mejorana,** sweet marjoram.
amaraje, *m.* (aer.) landing on water.
amarantáceo, a, *a.* (bot.) amaranthaceous. —*f.* amaranth; (*pl.*) Amaranthaceae.
amarantina, *f.* (bot.) globe amaranth (Gomphrena globosa).
amaranto, *f.* (bot.) amaranth. —*a.* crimson-colored.
amarar, *i.v.* (aer.) to land on water.
amarchantarse, *r.v.* (Cuba, Mex., Ven.) to become a regular customer, an habitué.
amarecer, *(ref. 45) tr.v.* to mate (**ram** with ewe).
amargado, da, *a.* embittered.
amargaleja, *f.* (bot.) sloe (fruit).
amargamente, *adv.* bitterly.
amargar, *(ref. 51) tr.v.* to make bitter; (fig.) to embitter, make bitter; to annoy, irritate, exasperate. —*i.v.* to be bitter. —*r.v.* to become bitter; to become embittered; to get annoyed or exasperated.
amargo, ga, *a.* 1. bitter. 2. (fig.) painful, distressing, grievous. 3. annoyed, irritated. —*m.* 1. bitterness, bitter taste. 2. (cul.) sweetmeat made from bitter almonds. 3. (*pl.*) bitters (liquor). 4. (Arg., Urug.) maté without sugar.
amargón, *m.* (bot.) dandelion.
amargor, *m.* 1. bitterness, acridity. 2. (fig.) bitterness, grief, sorrow.
amargosamente, *adv., var. of* **amargamente.**
amargoso, sa, *a.* bitter. —*m.* (bot.) service tree.
amargue, amargué, *ref.* **amargar.**
amarguera, *f.* (bot.) buplever (Bupleurum fruticosum).
amarguillo, *m.* sweetmeat made from bitter almonds.
amargura, *f.* bitterness; (fig.) bitterness, grief, affliction.
amaricado, da, *a.* (coll.) effeminate.
amariconado, da, *a.* (coll.) effeminate, unmanly.
amarilidáceo, a, *a.* (bot.) amaryllidaceous. —*f.* amaryllidaceous plant; (*pl.*) Amaryllidaceae.
amarilídeo, a, *a., var. of* **amarilidáceo.**
amarilis, *f.* (bot.) amarylis.
amarilla, *f.* 1. (coll.) gold coin, Spanish doubloon. 2. (vet.) sheep jaundice.
amarillear, *i.v.* 1. to be yellowish; to show a yellow tinge; to turn yellow. 2. to go pale.
amarillecer, *(ref. 45) i.v.* to turn yellow.
amarillejo, ja, *a.* yellowish.
amarillento, ta, *a.* yellowish.
amarilleo, *m.* yellow tinge; yellowishness.
amarillez, *f.* yellowness.
amarillo, lla, *a.* yellow. —*m.* 1. yellow (color). 2. lethargy of silkworms (during foggy weather). 3. (Arg.) wild tamarind (Pithecolobium tortum). — **a. de cromo,** chrome yellow; **fiebre amarilla,** (med.) yellow fever.
amarinar, *tr.v., var. of* **marinar.**
amariposado, da, *a.* butterfly-like.
amaritud, *f., var. of* **amargor.**
amarizarse, *(ref. 53) r.v.* to copulate (sheep). —*i.v.* (Amer.), (aer.) to land on the water.
amaro, *m.* (bot.) common clary.

amaromar, *tr.v., var. of* **amarrar.**
amarra, *f.* 1. mooring line, cable or rope. 2. martingale, strap fastened to girth and bit to stop a rearing horse. 3. (*pl.*) (fig.) protection, support, backing. 4. (*pl.*) (fig.) ties, obligations (moral, social, etc.).
amarraco, *m.* (cards) score of five points in the card game of **mus.**
amarradero, *m.* hitching ring; hitching post; (mar.) mooring post, bollard, moorings.
amarradijo, *m.* (C. Amer.) badly tied knot.
amarrado, da, *past part. of* **amarrar. —***a.* 1. (Chile) stiff, slow. 2. (Amer.) tight, stingy, mean.
amarradura, *f.* tying, fastening; (mar.) mooring, moorage; knot.
amarraje, *m.* moorage, dues paid for mooring.
amarrar, *tr.v.* 1. to tie; to tie up, bind; to lash, make fast; (mar.) to moor, tie up. 2. to stack, shuffle in such a way that certain cards remain together. *—r.v.* **amarrársela,** (C. Amer., Col., coll.) to get drunk.
amarrazones, *m., pl.* (mar.) ground tackle.
amarre, *m.* 1. tying, fastening; (mar.) mooring, moorage; tie, splice, knot. 2. stacking of cards, shuffling cards in such a way that certain cards remain together, e.g. *hacer un a.,* to stack cards.
amarrete, *a.* (Amer., coll.) mean, stingy, tightfisted. *—m., f.* mean or stingy person, tightwad (sl.).
amarrido, da, *a.* dejected, gloomy, sad.
amarro, *m.* tying, fastening, tie.
amarteladamente, *adv.* infatuatedly.
amartelado, da, *past part. of* **amartelar. —***a.* infatuated, madly in love, lovestruck, lovesick.
amartelamiento, *m.* infatuation, lovesickness.
amartelar, *tr.v.* 1. to drive mad, torment with love, passion or jealousy. 2. to enamor, inspire love or passion in. *—r.v.* to fall deeply in love; to become absorbed in one another (lovers).
amartillar, *tr.v.* 1. to hammer. 2. to cock (a gun). 3. (fig.) to secure, fix (deal, business).
amarulencia, *f.* resentment, bitterness.
amasadera, *f.* (cul.) kneading bowl.
amasadero, *m.* kneading room.
amasado, da, *a.* (Cuba) pulpy (avocado, etc.), soft, crumby (bread).
amasador, ra, *a.* kneading. *—m., f.* kneader.
amasadura, *f.* 1. kneading. 2. dough.
amasamiento, *m.* 1. kneading (of dough). 2. (med.) massage, massaging.
amasandería, *f.* (Col., Chile) bakery.
amasandero, ra, *m., f.* (Col., Chile) baker.
amasar, *tr.v.* 1. to knead; to mix. 2. (fig.) to amass, heap together, e.g. *a. fortuna,* to amass a fortune. 3. to massage. 4. (coll.) to arrange, settle.
amasia, *f.* (Amer.) common-law wife, concubine.
amasiato, *m.* (Amer.) concubinage.
amasijo, *m.* 1. kneading. 2. piece of dough. 3. (bldg.) quantity of plaster or mortar. 4. (coll.) mess, hodgepodge, potpourri. 5. (coll.) pact, agreement, plot.
amatar, *tr.v.* (Ecuad.) to cause sores on a horse by friction of the harness.
amate, *m.* (bot.) amate, Mexican fig tree.
amateur, *a., m., f., gal. for* **aficionado.**
amatista, *f.* amethyst.
amatividad, *f.* amativeness, disposition to sexual love.
amativo, va, *a.* amative.
amatorio, ria, *a.* amatory.
amaurosis, *f.* (med.) amaurosis; **a. fugax,** (avia., med.) flight blindness (of aviators).
amauta, *m.* (Bol., Peru) Amauta, sage of the Incas; elder with moral authority in an Indian village.
amayorazgar, (*ref. 51*) *tr.v.* (law) to entail, convert into an entailment.
amayuela, *f.* (zool.) mussel.
amazacotado, da, *a.* 1. stodgy, lumpy (food). 2. (fig.) dull, incoherent, formless (works of art).
amazona, *f.* 1. (myth.) Amazon; (fig.) masculine woman, amazon. 2. (fig.) horsewoman. 3. long riding skirt. 3. (ornith.) Amazon (parrot).
Amazonas (el), *m.* Amazon (river and jungle).
amazónico, ca, *a.* Amazonian. — **la selva a.,** the Amazonian jungle.
amazonita, *f.* (min.) amazonite.
ambages, *m.* (*pl.*) ambages, circumlocution, beating about the bush; **hablar sin a.,** to talk turkey.
ambagioso, sa, *a.* ambiguous, roundabout, circumlocutory.
ámbar, *m.* 1. (min.) amber. 2. delicate perfume. — **á. gris,** ambergris; **á. negro,** black amber, jet; **á pardillo,** ambergris; **ser un á.,** (fig., coll.) to be clear, transparent (liquors, esp. wine).
ambarina, *f.* (bot.) abelmosk, algalia; (Cuba) scabiosa.
ambarino, na, *a.* amber-like, amber.
Amberes, *m.* Antwerp, city of Belgium.
amberino, na, *a.* of or from Antwerp. *—m., f.* inhabitant or native of Antwerp, Belgium.
ambiciar, *tr.v., var. of* **ambicionar.**
ambición, *f.* ambition; drive.
ambicionar, *tr.v.* to desire, yearn or long for.
ambiciosamente, *adv.* ambitiously.
ambicioso, sa, *a.* 1. ambitious. 2. climbing (plants). *—m., f.* ambitious person.
ambidextro, tra, *a.* ambidextrous.
ambidiestro, tra, *a., var. of* **ambidextro.**
ambientación, *f.* 1. giving atmosphere. 2. adjustment to environment, surroundings or situation.
ambiental, *a.* environmental, pertaining to surroundings.
ambientar, *tr.v.* to give atmosphere. *—r.v.* to get used to one's environment or surroundings.
ambiente, *a.* surrounding, ambient. *—m.* 1. atmosphere, e.g. *este restaurante no tiene a.,* this restaurant has no atmosphere. 2. social group, layer, e.g. *a. aristocrático,* aristocratic milieu. 3. ambiance, atmosphere, environment, e.g. *él tiene buen a. en su trabajo,* he works in a pleasant atmosphere. 4. (Arg., Chile, Urug.) room, chamber, e.g. *departamento de dos ambientes,* two-room apartment.
ambigú, *m.* 1. buffet supper. 2. refreshment counter; buffet bar.
ambiguamente, *adv.* ambiguously.
ambigüedad, *f.* ambiguity, ambiguousness.
ambiguo, gua, *a.* 1. ambiguous, uncertain, doubtful, dubious. 2. (gram.) common (either masculine or feminine).
ambir, *m.* (Col., Ven.) tobacco juice.
ámbito, *m.* 1. ambit, boundary, circumference, perimeter, boundary line, limit. 2. ambit, scope, extent.
ambivalencia, *f.* ambivalence.
ambivalente, *a.* ambivalent.
ambiversión, *f.* (psyc.) ambiversion.
amblador, ra, *a.* ambling.
ambladura, *f.* amble, gait;
amblar, *i.v.* to amble.
amblehuelo, *m.* wax candle (weighing two pounds).
ambleo, *m.* 1. thick wax candle. 2. large candlestick.
ambligonio, *a.* (geom.) obtuse-angled (triangle).
ambliopía, *f.* (med.) amblyopia (weakness of sight).
amblioscopio, *m.* (opt.) amblyoscope.
ambo, *m.* 1. prize given to the bearer of two tickets which, added together, equaled the number of the winning ticket in the lottery; turning up of two contiguous numbers in the same row (in lotto or bingo). 2. (Arg., Chile, tail.) two-piece suit, suit (without a waistcoat).
ambón, *m.* ambo, pulpit.
ambos, bas, *a., indef. pron.* both; **a. a dos,** both.
ambrosía, *f.* 1. (myth., fig.) ambrosia. 2. (bot.) ambrosia, ragweed.
ambrosíaco, ca, *a.* ambrosial.
ambrosiano, na, *a.* Ambrosian, pertaining to St. Ambrose.
ambucia, *f.* (Chile) hunger, voracity, greediness.
ambuciento, ta, *a.* (Chile) hungry, greedy.
ambuesta, *f.* double handful.
ambulación, *f.* ambling, strolling.
ambulacral, *a.* (zool.) ambulacral.
ambulacro, *m.* 1. (zool.) ambulacrum. 2. passage, corridor (in catacombs). 3. tree-lined walk, avenue or promenade.
ambulancia, *f.* ambulance.
ambulanciero, ra, *m., f.* ambulance driver.
ambulante, *a.* 1. ambulant, traveling, moving, e.g. *vendedor a.,* peddler, huckster. 2. itinerant; walking. *—m.* railway, post-office, or mail clerk.
ambular, *i.v.* to ambulate, stroll.
ambulativo, va, *a.* ambulatory, wandering, roving.
ambulatorio, ria, *a.* ambulatory. *—m.* welfare center; public clinic.
ambustión, *f.* burning; (med.) cauterization.
ameba, *f.* (zool.) amoeba.
amebeo, *a.* amoebaean (verse).
amebiasis, *f.* (med.) amoebiasis.
ameboideo, a, *a.* amoeboid.
amechar, *tr.v.* 1. to insert a wick in (a lamp, candle, etc.). 2. (cul.) *var. of* **mechar,** to lard a cut of meat.
amedrantar, *tr.v., var. of* **amedrentar,** to frighten, scare, intimidate.
amedrentador, ra, *a.* frightening, scaring. *—m., f.* frightener, scarer.
amedrentar, *tr.v.* to frighten, scare, intimidate. *—r.v.* to become frightened, scared, or intimidated.
ámel, *m.* district chief (among the Arabs).
amelar, *i.v.* to make honey (bees).
amelcochado, da, *a.* 1. (Cuba) sentimental. 2. (Mex., Par.) with the consistency of molasses candy or taffy.
amelcochar, *tr.v.* (Cuba, Mex., P. Rico) to make into taffy or molasses candy. *—r.v.* 1. to become like taffy. 2. (Cuba) to pretend to like, feign liking or pleasure. 3. (Cuba) to fall in love; to become sentimental (when falling in love).
amelga, *f.* each of several plots of land dividing a field to facilitate even plowing and sowing.
amelgado, da, *a.* uneven, unevenly sown (wheat). *—m.* (Sp.) marking of boundaries or limit (of fields); boundary mark or mound.
amelgador, *m.* ridger, plowman.
amelgar, (*ref. 51*) *tr.v.* 1. to furrow at regular intervals (to facilitate even sowing). 2. (Sp.) to mark the boundaries of (fields).
amelgue, amelgué, *ref.* **amelgar.**
amelía, *f.* district governed by an **ámel.**
amelo, *m.* (bot.) aster.
amelonado, da, *a.* 1. melon-shaped, melon-like. 2. (coll.) madly in love, love-struck.
amelonarse, *r.v.* (coll.) to fall madly in love.
amembrillado, da, *a.* quince-shaped, quince-like.
amén, *interj., m.* amen. — **en un decir a.,** immediately, in a jiffy; **decir a. a todo,** to agree with everything. *—adv.* 1. except, with the exception of. 2. apart from. — **a. de,** in addition to, besides; **a. de que,** unless.

amenace, amenacé, *ref.* **amenazar.**
amenamente, *adv.* pleasantly, agreeably.
amenaza, *f.* threat, menace.
amenazador, ra, *a.* threatening, menacing. —*m., f.* threatener.
amenazante, *a.* threatening, menacing.
amenazar, (*ref. 53*) *tr.v.* to threaten. — **a.** + *inf.*, to threaten to + *inf.*, e.g. *amenazó denunciarlo,* he threatened to report him, *amenaza llover,* it's threatening to rain; **a. con,** to threaten with, e.g. *a. con un látigo,* to threaten with a whip; **a. con** + *inf.*, to threaten to + *inf.*, e.g. *lo amenazó con denunciarlo,* he threatened to report him.
amencia, *f.* (med.) amentia, mental derangement, madness.
amenguador, ra, *a.* 1. lessening, diminishing. 2. defamatory, belittling.
amenguamiento, *m.* 1. lessening, reduction. 2. belittlement, defamation.
amenguar, (*ref. 52*) *tr.v.* 1. to reduce, diminish, lessen. 2. to defame; to belittle, insult. —*i.v.* to reduce, grow less, lessen.
amenice, amenicé, *ref.* **amenizar.**
amenidad, *f.* amenity, pleasantness, agreeableness.
amenizar, (*ref. 53*) *tr.v.* 1. to make pleasant, make agreeable, make charming. 2. to enliven, make interesting.
ameno, na, *a.* pleasant, agreeable, charming.
amenorrea, *f.* (med.) amenorrhea, suppression of menstrual period.
amentáceo, a, *a.* (bot.) amentaceous. —*f.* (bot.) (*pl.*) Amentiferae.
amentar, *tr.v.* to lace up, tie (shoes); to tie, fasten with a strap.
amento, *m.* (bot.) ament, catkin, cattail.
ameos, *m.* (bot.) bishop's weed (Ammi majus).
amerar, *tr.v.* to mix (with water). —*r.v.* to soak through, filter through, percolate, seep (moisture, water).
amerengado, da, *a.* 1. meringue-like. 2. (coll.) affected, prim and finicky; obsequious.
América Central, *f.* Central America.
América del Norte, *f.* North America.
América del Sur, *f.* South America.
americana, *f.* (sport.) jacket, coat.
americanice, americanicé, *ref.* **americanizar.**
americanismo, *m.* 1. Americanism, Spanish word particular to Spanish America. 2. admiration for American things.
americanista, *m., f.* Americanist.
americanizacíon, *f.* Americanization.
americanizar, (*ref. 53*) *tr.v.* to Americanize, make North American, make Spanish American. —*r.v.* to become Americanized, acquire North American habits and customs, acquire Spanish American customs.
americano, na, *a., m., f.* 1. American. 2. (Amer.) North American.
americio, *m.* (chem.) americium.
amerindio, dia, *m., f.* Amerindian.
ameritar, *tr.v., r.v.* (Amer.) to merit.
amesquite, *m.* (bot., Mex.) a kind of fig.
amestizado, da, *a.* mestizo-like, mixed.
ametalado, da, *a.* metallic; (fig.) metallic (sounds).
ametista, *f., var. of* **amatista.**
ametrallador, *m.* (artil.) machine gunner.
ametralladora, *f.* machine gun.
ametrallamiento, *m.* machine-gunning; (fig.) slaughter.
ametrallar, *tr.v.* to machine-gun.
amétrope, *a.* (med.) ametropic.
ametropía, *f.* (med.) ametropia.
ameyal, *m.* (Mex.) filtering pool (for reservoir).
amezquindarse, *r.v.* (rare) to become sad.
amfetamina, *f.* (pharm.) amphetamine.
ami, *m.* (bot.) bishop's weed (Ammi majus).
amia, *f.* (ichth.) cub shark, lamia.
amianto, *m.* (min.) amianthus, asbestos; **a. ligniforme,** (min.) rock wood.
amiba, *f., var. of* **ameba,** (zool.) amoeba.
amibiano, na, *a.* amoebic, amoeban.
amibiasis, *f.* (med.) amebiasis.
amibocito, *m.* (biol.) amoebocyte.
amiboideo, *a.* (zool.) amoeboid, ameboid.
amical, *a.* (gal.) friendly.
amicísimo, ma, *a. super. of* **amigo,** most friendly, very friendly.
amida, *f.* (chem.) amide.
amidógeno, *m.* (chem.) amidogen.
amidol, *m.* (chem.) amidol.
amiento, *m.* (arch.) leather strap.
amigabilidad, *f.* friendliness, affability.
amigable, *a.* 1. amicable, affable, friendly. 2. harmonious, concordant.
amigablemente, *adv.* amicably, affably.
amigacho, *m. aug., derog. of* **amigo.**
amigar, (*ref. 51*) *tr.v.* to bring together, make (others) friends. —*r.v.* 1. to become friends (after a fight or estrangement), to become reconciled. 2. to live in concubinage, cohabit.
amigazo, *m.* (Amer.) great friend, pal; (Arg.) *derog. of* **amigo.**
amígdala, *f.* (anat.) tonsil, amygdala.
amigdaláceo, a, *a.* almond shape; (bot.) amygdalaceous. —*f.* amygdalaceous plant; (*pl.*) Amygdalaceae.
amigdalino, na, *a.* amygdaline. —*f.* (chem.) amygdalin.
amigdalitis, *f.* (med.) tonsilitis.
amigdaloide, *a.* (geol.) amygdaloid.
amigo, ga, *a.* 1. friendly; fond (of). 2. (poet.) kind, benign. — **es muy amigo mío,** he is a great friend of mine; **ser a. de,** to be fond of, have a taste or liking for. —*m.* 1. friend; comrade, buddy; boyfriend. 2. lover, paramour. 3. beam upon which miners stand to go up and down a mine shaft. — **a. íntimo** or **del alma,** bosom friend, close friend; **a. de pelillo** or **de taza de vino,** (coll.) fair-weather friend; **a. hasta las aras,** good and faithful friend; **pie de a.,** bracket, brace. —*interj.* well, well!, that's it!. —*f.* 1. friend; girlfriend; sweetheart. 2. mistress, concubine.
amigote, *m.* (coll.) *aug. of* **amigo, great** friend, buddy, pal.
amigue, amigué, *ref.* **amigar.**
amiguísimo, ma, *a.* very friendly.
amiláceo, a, *a.* amylaceous, starchy, containing starch.
amilanado, da, *a.* cowardly; pusillanimous; timid.
amilanamiento, *m.* fright, cowardliness, cowardice; intimidation.
amilanar, *tr.v.* to cow, frighten, intimidate, terrify, scare; to dispirit, dishearten. —*r.v.* to become cowed, intimidated; frightened or scared, get cold feet; to flag.
amilasa, *f.* (biochem.) amylase.
amileno, *m.* (chem.) amylene.
amílico, *a.* (chem.) amylic. —*m.* (coll.) bad wine or brandy, rotgut.
amillaramiento, *m.* tax assessment.
amillarar, *tr.v.* to assess (property) for taxes.
amillonado, da, *a.* 1. opulent, wealthy, extremely rich. 2. (arch.) subject to tax.
amilo, *m.* (chem.) amyl.
amilobacteria, *f.* (bac.) amylobacterium.
amiloideo, a, *a.* amyloid.
amilosis. *f.* (med.) amyloidosis.
amín, *m.* tax collector (in Morocco).
amina, *f.* (chem.) amine.
amínico, ca, *a.* (chem.) aminic.
aminoácido, *m.* (chem.) amino acid.
aminoración, *f.* reduction, diminution, lessening.
aminorar, *tr.v.* to diminish, reduce, lessen.
amir, *m.* ameer, amir, emir.
amistad, *f.* 1. friendship, amity. 2. friend. — **hacer buenas amistades,** to make good friends; **hacer a.,** (coll.) to make up, make friends again, become reconciled; **romper la a.,** to quarrel, fall out; **trabar a.,** to strike up a friendship, make friends.
amistar, *tr.v.* to bring together, make friends; to reconcile (enemies). —*r.v.* to become or make friends; to become reconciled.
amistosamente, *adv.* amicably, cordially, in a friendly manner.
amistoso, sa, *a.* friendly, amicable.
amitigar, (*ref. 51*) *tr.v., var. of* **mitigar.**
amito, *m.* (ecc.) amice.
amitosis, *f.* (biol.) amitosis.
Ammán, Amman, capital of Jordan.
amnesia, *f.* (med.) amnesia, loss of memory.
amnésico, ca, *a.* (med. amnesic.
amnícola, *a.* (zool.) riparial, riparian, growing on river banks.
amnios, *m.* (anat.) amnion, foetal sac.
amniota, *a.* (zool.) amniote, amniotic.
amniótico, ca, *a.* (anat.) amniotic.
amnistía, *f.* amnesty, pardon.
amnistiar, *tr.v.* to grant amnesty.
amo, *m.* master (of the house); head (of the family); owner, proprietor; boss, foreman, overseer. — **ser el amo de la casa,** to be the master of the house.
amoblar, (*ref. 33*) *tr.v., var. of* **amueblar,** to furnish.
amochar, *i.v.* to cut off (with a short machete).
amodita, *f.* viper (Vipera berus).
amodorrado, da, *a.* drowsy, sleepy, heavy.
amodorramiento, *m.* drowsiness, heaviness, sleepiness.
amodorrarse, *r.v.* to become drowsy, grow sleepy.
amodorrecer, (*ref. 45*) *tr.v.* to make drowsy.
amodorrido, da, *a.* drowsy, sleepy.
amófilo, la, *a.* (zool.) ammophilius, living or growing in sand.
amogollarse, *r.v.* (P. Rico) to become moldy or musty.
amogotado, da, *a.* (mar.) mound-like, knoll-shaped.
amohecer, (*ref. 45*) *tr.v., r.v., var. of* **enmohecer.**
amohinar, *tr.v.* to irritate, annoy. —*r.v.* to become irritable or annoyed.
amojamado, da, *past part. of* **amojamar.** —*a.* thin, lean.
amojamamiento, *m.* leanness, gauntness; emaciation.
amojamar, *tr.v.* to dry and salt (tuna fish). —*r.v.* to become lean, emaciated or drawn.
amojelar, *tr.v.* (mar.) to nip (a cable).
amojonador, *m.* one who fixes boundaries.
amojonamiento, *m.* 1. delimitation, marking with boundaries, marking of boundaries. 2. boundaries, boundary, limit.
amojonar, *tr.v.* to delimit, mark with boundaries, mark the boundaries of.
amojosao, *m.* (Arg., coll.) gaucho's knife.
amol, *m., var. of* **amole.**
amoladera, *a.* **piedra a.,** grindstone, whetstone. —*f.* whetstone, grindstone.
amolado, da, *past part. of* **amolar.** —*a.* (Amer.) bothered, annoyed; hurt (feelings).

amolador, *m.* grinder, sharpener.
amoladura, *f.* grinding, sharpening; (*pl.*) grindstone dust, grindings.
amolanchín, *m.* sharpener.
amolar, (*ref. 33*) *tr.v.* 1. to sharpen, grind, whet. 2. (fig.) to annoy, pester, irritate. 3. (fig.) to become thinner, to lose weight.
amoldable, *a.* moldable, malleable.
amoldador, ra, *a.* forming, molding. —*m., f.* molder.
amoldamiento, *m.* molding.
amoldar, *tr.v.* 1. to mold, model, fashion; fit, adapt. —*r.v.* to adapt oneself, conform.
amole, *m.* (bot., Amer.) soap plant (used in Mexico as soap).
amollador, ra, *a.* slackening, easing off. —*m., f.* (in the game of reversi) one who plays a low card while holding a high one.
amollante, *a.* slackening, easing off.
amollar, *i.v.* 1. to yield, cede, give in. 2. (in the game of reversi) to play low (while holding in reserve a higher card than that played by opponent). —*tr.v., i.v.* (mar.) to ease off, loosen, slacken, play out (cable).
amollentar, *tr.v.* to soften.
amolletado, da, *a.* roll-shaped, rolled.
amomo, *m.* (bot.) amomum.
amonama, *f.* (Ecuad.) honeycomb (of underground hive).
amonarse, *r.v.* (coll.) to get drunk.
amondongado, da, *a.* (coll.) fat, fat, coarse, slovenly; flabby.
amonedación, *f.* minting, coining.
amonedado, da, *past part. of* **amonedar.** —*a.* (Amer.) rich, well-off (person).
amonedar, *tr.v.* to mint, coin.
amonestación, *f.* 1. admonition. 2. warning, advice. 3. (*pl.*) (marriage) banns. — **correr las amonestaciones,** to publish the banns.
amonestador, ra, *a.* admonishing; warning. —*m., f.* admonisher.
amonestamiento, *m.* admonition, admonishment.
amonestante, *a.* admonishing.
amonestar, *tr.v.* 1. to reprove, admonish; to advise, warn. 2. to publish the banns of. —*r.v.* to have one's banns published.
amoniacal, *a.* ammoniacal.
amoníaco, ca, *a.* ammoniac, ammoniacal, e.g. *sal amoníaca,* sal ammoniac. —*m.* 1. ammonia. 2. ammoniac, gum resin.
amónico, ca, *a.* (chem.) ammonic, ammonical.
amonio, *m.* (chem.) ammonium.
amonita, *a.* (Bib.) Ammonitish. —*m., f.* (Bib.) Ammonite. —*f.* (paleon.) ammonite.
amontar, *tr.v.* to put to flight, chase away. —*r.v.* 1. to flee, run away, take flight. 2. to take cover or shelter.
amontazgar, (*ref. 51*) *tr.v., var. of* **montazgar.**
amontillado, *m.* amontillado, pale dry sherry.
amontonadamente, *adv.* in a heap, piled together.
amontonador, ra, *a.* accumulating, gathering. —*m., f.* gatherer, accumulator.
amontonamiento, *m.* pile, heap; accumulation, piling up.
amontonar, *tr.v.* to pile together, heap together; to cram together. —*r.v.* 1. to pile up, collect, accumulate; to crowd together. 2. to get angry, fly into a fury. 3. (fig., coll.) to cohabit, live in concubinage.
amor, *m.* 1. love; gentleness, kindness, affection. 2. darling, love, beloved, sweetheart. 3. devotion, zeal, eagerness. 4. (*pl.*) love affairs. 5. (*pl.*) words of endearment; compliments; flattery. 6. (*pl.*) (bot.) hedgehog parsley. — **a. al uso,** (bot.) confederate rose, cotton rose (Hibiscus mutabilis); **a. con a. se paga,** love is rewarded with love; **a. cortés,** courtly love; **a. de hortelano,** (bot.) bedstraw, cleavers; foxtail, burdock; **a. libre,** free love; **a. propio,** pride, self-esteem; self-respect; **al a. de la lumbre** or **del fuego,** near the fireside or firelight; **con mil amores, de mil amores,** with the greatest of pleasure; **en el a. y la guerra todo vale,** all's fair in love and war; **hacer el a.,** to make love; **¡por a. de Dios!** for God's sake!; **a. patrio,** patriotism.
amoragar, (*ref. 51*) *tr.v.* to cook over a fire, barbecue.
amoral, *a.* amoral. —*m., f.* amoralist.
amoralidad, *f.* amorality.
amoralismo, *m.* amoralism.
amoratado, da, *past part. of* **amoratar.** —*a.* livid, blue, purple; (Amer.) black and blue. — **a. de frío,** blue with cold; **un ojo amoratado,** black eye, shiner.
amoratar, *tr.v., r.v.* to turn or go blue or purple.
amorcar, (*ref. 50*) *tr.v., var. of* **amurcar.**
amorcillo, *m.* 1. amourette, passing or trifling love affair. 2. amorino, amourette, figurine of Cupid.
amordace, amordacé, *ref.* **amordazar.**
amordazador, ra, *a.* gagging; muzzling; silencing. —*m., f.* gagger; muzzler; silencer.
amordazamiento, *m.* gagging (of a person); muzzling (of a dog); (fig.) silencing; muzzling, gagging.
amordazar, (*ref. 53*) *tr.v.* to gag (a person); to muzzle (a dog); (fig.) to silence, muzzle, gag.
amorecer, (*ref. 45*) *tr.v.* to cover or serve (a female sheep). —*r.v.* to be in heat or in rut (sheep).
amorezca, *ref.* **amorecer.**
amorfía, *f.* 1. amorphism, amorphousness. 2. (med.) amorphia, organic deformity.
amorfo, fa, *a.* amorphous, shapeless.
amorgar, (*ref. 51*) *tr.v.* to stupefy (fish) with fetid olive pulp.
amorgue, amorgué, *ref.* amorgar.
amoricones, *m.* (*pl.*) (coll.) flirting looks; candid behavior of young couples in love.
amorío, *m.* (coll.) minor love affair; fling, crush.
amoriscado, da, *a.* Moorish-looking; Moorish.
amormado, da, *a.* (vet.) glandered, affected with glanders.
amormío, *m.* (bot.) sea daffodil.
amorosamente, *adv.* lovingly, affectionately.
amoroso, sa, *a.* 1. loving, affectionate, kind, e.g. *carta amorosa,* love letter. 2. soft, malleable (land). 3. mild, balmy, pleasant (weather).
amorque, amorqué, *ref.* **amorcar.**
amorrar, *i.v.* 1. (coll.) to hang or lower one's head. 2. (coll.) to sulk, become sullen. 3. (mar.) to pitch at the bow. —*r.v.* (coll.) 1. to hang or lower one's head. 2. to sulk, become sullen. —*tr.v.* 1. (mar.) to make (a ship) pitch at the bow. 2. (mar.) to beach head-on.
amorreo, a, *a., m., f.* (Bib.) Amorite.
amorriñarse, *r.v.* (Amer.) to become sullen and sad.
amorrionado, da, *a.* (rare) helmet-like, helmet-shaped.
amorronar, *tr.v.* (mar.) to roll and tie a flag at certain intervals (in order to hoist it as a distress signal).
amorrongarse, (*ref. 51*) *r.v.* 1. (reg.) to fall asleep in someone's arms (a child). 2. (Cuba) to become frightened, scared.
amortajador, ra, *m., f.* undertaker, mortician.
amortajamiento, *m.* shrouding, laying out (of the dead).
amortajar, *tr.v.* 1. to shroud, lay out, prepare (the dead) for burial. 2. to conceal, cover, disguise.
amortecer, (*ref. 45*) *tr.v.* to dull, dim (light); to tone down, soften (color); to cushion, soften (blow); to deaden, muffle (noise). —*r.v.* 1. to faint, swoon. 2. to be muffled or deadened (noise); to grow dim or dull (light, color); to be cushioned or softened (blow).
amortecimiento, *m.* 1. dulling, dimming; cushioning, softening; deadening, muffling; cooling. 2. fainting.
amortezca, amortezco, *ref.* **amortecer.**
amortice, amorticé, *ref.* **amortizar.**
amortiguación, *f.* muffling, deadening, damping (of sound, noise, etc.); softening, cushioning (of blow, bang, shock); dimming, dulling (of light); toning down, softening (of color); damping, dampening (of fire).
amortiguado, a, *past part. of* **amortiguar.** —*a.* muffled; softened. — **a. por aire,** air-dampened; **a. por topes de goma,** rubber-cushioned.
amortiguador, ra, *a.* muffling, dulling, deadening; damping; dimming, dulling; softening, absorbing, cushioning. —*m.* shock absorber; door check; bumper, snubber. — **a. de chispas,** (elec.) spark arrester; **a. de faroles, a. de luces,** (auto.) headlight dimmer; **a. de ruido,** silencer, muffler; **a. de sonido,** sound absorber.
amortiguamiento, *m., var. of* **amortiguación.**
amortiguar, (*ref. 52*) *tr.v.* to muffle, deaden, damp (sound, noise); to soften, cushion (blow, bang, shock); to dim, dull (light); to tone down, soften (color); to damp, dampen (fire).
amortizable, *a.* amortizable; payable.
amortización, *f.* amortization.
amortizar, (*ref. 53*) *tr.v.* 1. to amortize, to write off, pay off, refund. 2. to abolish (jobs in an office, etc.). 3. to depreciate (machinery).
¡amos, anda! *interj.* (Sp.) you don't say! go on! you're telling me!
amoscamiento, *m.* (coll.) irritation, anger, peevishness.
amoscarse, (*ref. 50*) *r.v.* 1. to get angry or irritated, to get vexed. 2. (Cuba) to blush, get confused.
amosque, amosqué, *ref.* **amoscarse.**
amosquilarse, *r.v.,* to take shelter (cattle) against flies in a cool or shaded place.
amostace, amostacé, *ref.* **amostazar.**
amostachado, da, *a.* whiskered, mustachioed.
amostazar, (*ref. 53*) *tr.v.* (coll.) to irritate, annoy. —*r.v.* 1. to get irritated, or annoyed. 2. (Amer.) to become embarrassed or confused.
amotinado, da, *past part. of* **amotinar.** —*a.* seditious, mutinous. —*m., f.* mutineer, rebel, rioter.
amotinador, ra, *a.* seditious, mutinous; rabble-rousing, agitating. —*m., f.* agitator, rabble-rouser; mutineer, rebel, rioter.
amotinamiento, *m.* mutiny, uprising, rebellion, riot.
amotinar, *tr.v.* to agitate, incite to riot or mutiny; (fig.) to stir up, agitate, disquiet. —*r.v.* to mutiny, riot, rebel.
amoto, *m.* (Sp., sl.) motorcycle.
amover, (*ref. 34*) *tr.v.* to remove, dismiss (from a job).
amovible, *a.* removable; detachable.
amovilidad, *f.* removability.
ampalagua, *f.* (Arg.) a kind of boa constrictor.
amparador, ra, *a.* sheltering, protecting. —*m., f.* shelterer, protector.
amparar, *tr.v.* 1. to protect, shelter, give sanctuary; to deal with, to cover. 2. (Amer.) to acquire the right to work (a mine). 3. (Ven.) to borrow. —*r.v.* to shelter or protect oneself, seek shelter or sanctuary; to avail oneself of the protection or favor (of someone or something).
amparo, *m.* shelter, sanctuary; protection, aid, favor.

ampáyar, ampáyer *m., f.* (Col.) umpire.
ampelídeo, a, *a.* (bot.) ampelideous, ampelidaceous. —*f.* (*pl.*) Ampelidaceae, vine family.
ampélido, *m.* (ornith.) a species of passerine bird.
ampelita, *f.* (min.) ampelite.
ampelografía, *f.* the science of vine growing.
ampelógrafo, *m.* expert in viticulture.
ampelopsis, *f.* (bot.) ampelopsis.
amper, *m.* (elec.) ampere.
amperaje, *m.* (elec.) amperage.
amperímetro, *m.* ammeter, amperemeter. — **a. calórico,** hot-wire ammeter; **a. de abrazadera,** (elec.) clamp ammeter; **a. térmico,** thermal ammeter, thermoammeter.
amperio, *m.* (elec.) ampere; **a. hora,** ampere-hour; **a.-pie,** ampere-foot; **a.-vuelta,** ampere-turn.
amperómetro, *m., var. of* **amperímetro.**
amplexicaulo, la, *a.* (bot.) amplexicaul, clasping the stem.
ampliable, *a.* enlargeable, expandable.
ampliación, *f.* enlargement, expansion; magnification.
ampliador, ra, *a.* amplifying, enlarging. —*m., f.* amplifier, enlarger. —*f.* (photog.) enlarger, (apparatus).
ampliamente, *adv.* amply, copiously, fully.
ampliar, (*ref. 54*) *tr.v.* to extend, enlarge, amplify; (photog.) to enlarge; **a. el plazo,** to extend the time, to prolong the deadline.
ampliativo, va, *a.* enlarging, amplifying, amplificatory.
amplificación, *f.* amplification, magnification, enlargement. — **a. reflejada,** (rad.) reflex amplification; **coeficiente** or **factor de a.,** (elec.) amplification factor; **a. de tensión,** (elec.) voltage amplification; **a. en cascada** or **multigradual,** (elec.) cascade amplification; **a. de potencia,** power amplification; **a. dinámica,** dynamic magnification.
amplificador, ra, *a.* amplifying. —*m.* (elec.) magnifier, amplifier; enlarger; (rad.) amplifier; loudspeaker. — **a. de reacción positiva,** (elec., rad.) feedback or regenerative amplifier; **a. realimentado,** (elec., rad.) feedback coil; **a. simetrico, equilibrado** or **en contrafase,** push-pull amplifier; **a. de audiofrecuencia,** (rad.) audiofrequency or audio amplifier.
amplificar, (*ref. 50*) *tr.v.* to amplify; to enlarge.
amplificativo, va, a. amplificatory, enlarging, amplificative.
amplifique, amplifiqué, *ref.* **amplificar.**
amplio, a, *a.* ample, extensive, comprehensive; large, roomy.
amplísimo, a, *a. super. of* **amplio.**
amplitud, *f.* amplitude, size, extent, magnitude, range, coverage, scope.
ampo, *m.* 1. shining whiteness. 2. snowflake.
ampolla, *f.* 1. blister; bladder. 2. bubble (in boiling water). 3. ampulla, globular-bodied flask or glass; (ecc.) cruet, ampulla (container for wine and water in the Mass); (med.) ampoule (small bottle containing medicine).
ampollar, *tr.v.* 1. to blister, cause blisters on. 2. to make hollow. —*r.v.* 1. to blister, become blistered. 2. to become hollow.
ampolleta, *f.* 1. small vial, small bottle. 2. sandglass, hourglass, sand clock. 3. time necessary for the sand in one bubble of a sand-clock to pass to the other. 4. (Chile) lightbulb.
ampulosamente, *adv.* verbosely, pompously, redundantly, bombastically.
ampulosidad, *f.* verbosity, pomposity, redundancy, bombast.
ampuloso, sa, *a.* verbose, pompous, full of redundancies, bombastic.
amputación, *f.* amputation.
amputado, da, *past part. of* **amputar.** —*m., f.* amputee.
amputar, *tr.v.* to amputate, truncate.
Amsterdam, Amsterdam, capital of the Netherlands.
amuchachado, da, *a.* boyish, girlish.
amuchar, *tr.v.* (Amer.) to multiply, grow.
amueblar, *tr.v.* to furnish (a house, etc.).
amueble, amueblo, *ref.* **amueblar.**
amuelar, *tr.v.* to stack (wheat).
amuele, amuelo, *ref.* **amuelar.**
amueva, amuevo, *ref.* **amover.**
amugamiento, *m.* delimitation, marking boundaries, marking of boundaries.
amugronador, ra, *a.* (agr.) layering. —*m., f.* (agr.) one who layers.
amugronar, *tr.v.* (agr.) to layer (vines); (Chile) to layer (any plant).
amujerado, da, *a.* effeminate, womanish.
amujeramiento, *m.* effeminacy, womanishness.
amular, *i.v.* to be sterile. —*r.v.* 1. to become temporarily or permanently barren (a mare). 2. (Mex.) to become useless. 3. (coll.) to become stubborn (like a mule).
amulatado, da, *a.* mulatto-like, mulatto-colored, swarthy.
amuleto, *m.* amulet, charm.
amunicionar, *tr.v., var. of* **municionar.**
amuñecado, da, *a.* doll-like.
amura, *f.* 1. (mar.) bow timbers, planking at the side of a ship where it begins to narrow towards the prow. 2. tack of a sail.
amurada, *f.* ceiling, inside timbers of a ship.
amurallar, *tr.v.* to wall, fortify with walls.
amurar, *tr.v.* 1. (mar.) to haul in (the lower corner of a sail) with a tack. 2. (Arg., coll.) to jail, imprison.
amurcar, (*ref. 50*) *tr.v.* (taur.) to gore.
amurco, *m.* (taur.) goring, blow with the horns.
amurque, *ref.* **amurcar.**
amurrarse, *r.v.* (Amer.) to become sad, downcast.
amurriñarse, *r.v.* to contract dropsy (an animal).
amusco, ca, *a.* dark brown colored, dark brown.
amusgar, (*ref. 51*) *tr.v.* 1. to throw back the ears (an animal about to kick, bite, etc.). 2. to squint (to see better). —*i.v.* to throw back the ears (animals). —*r.v.* 1. (Hond.) to become embarrassed, draw back. 2. (Arg.) to concede, to give up.
amusgue, amusgué, *ref.* **amusgar.**
amuso, *m.* marble slab decorated with a compass rose.
amustiar, *tr.v.* to wither.
an-, *pre,* lack of, e.g. *analfabetismo,* lack of literacy.
ana, *f.* 1. ell (measurement). 2. ana, sign used to indicate equal quantities in medical prescriptions.
ana-, *pre.* 1. opposition: **anacrónico,** anachronistic. 2. superposition: **anatema,** anathema. 3. repetition: **anabaptista,** Anabaptist.
anabaptismo, *m.* (rel.) Anabaptism.
anabaptista, *a., m., f.* (rel.) Anabaptist.
anabí, (*pl.* **anabíes**) *m., var. of* **nabí,** Arab prophet.
anabiosis, *f.* (biol.) anabiosis.
anabólico, ca, *a.* (biol.) anabolic.
anabolismo, *m.* (biol.) anabolism.
anacarado, da, *a.* mother-of-pearl, inlaid with mother-of-pearl.
anacardiáceo, a, *a.* (bot.) anacardiaceous. —*f.* (*pl.*) (bot. Anacardiaceae.
anacárdico, ca, *a.* (chem.) anacardic.
anacardina, *f.* (pharm.) mixture made of cashew nuts (formerly used for restoring the memory).
anacardo, *m.* (bot.) cashew tree; cashew nut.
anaclástico, ca, *a.* (phys.) anaclastic.
anaclinal, (geol.) anaclinal.
anaco, *m.* loose skirt worn by the Indian women of Bolivia, Peru and Ecuador.
anacoluto, *m.* (gram.) anacoluthon.
anaconda, *f.* (zool.) anaconda.
anacoreta, *m.* anchoret, anchorite, hermit. —*f.* anchoress.
anacorético, ca, *a.* anchoretic, anchoritic.
anacreóntico, ca, *a., m.* Anacreontic, pertaining to the style of the Greek poet, Anacreon.
anacrónicamente, *adv.* anachronistically.
anacrónico, ca, *a.* anachronistic; dated.
anacronismo, *m.* anachronism.
ánade, *m., f.,* duck; goose; **á. silvestre** or **real,** mallard.
anadear, *i.v.* to waddle.
anadeja, *f.* duckling.
anadino, na, *m., f.* duckling.
anadiplosis, *f.* (rhet.) anadiplosis.
anadón, *m.* 1. duckling. 2. non-floating wood.
anadromo, ma, *a.* (zool.) anadromous.
anaerobio, *a.* (biol.) anaerobic, anaerobical. —*m.* anaerobe.
anaerobiosis, *f.* (biol.) anaerobiosis.
anafalla, *f., var. of* **anafaya.**
anafase, *f.* (biol.) anaphase.
anafaya, *f.* faille, ribbed silk fabric of plain weave.
anafe, *m.* portable stove.
anafilaxia, *f., var. of* **anafilaxis.**
anafilaxis, *f.* (med.) anaphylaxis.
anáfora, *f.* 1. (rhet.) anaphora, repetition. 2. anaphora, eucharistic prayer of consecration in the divine liturgy (Greek Orthodox Church).
anafórico, ca, *a.* anaphoric, anaphorical.
anafre, *m., var. of* **anafe,** portable oven.
anafrodisia, *f.* (med.) anaphrodisia, absence of sexual desire.
anafrodisíaco, ca, *a. m.* (med.) anaphrodisiac.
anafrodita, *a.* anaphroditous, abstaining from sexual pleasure.
anaglífico ca, *a.* (archit.) anaglyphical.
anáglifo, *m.* 1. (archit.) anaglyph, vase or figure decorated in low unpolished relief. 2. anaglyph, a composite picture printed in two colors that produces a three-dimensional image when viewed through spectacles having lenses of corresponding colors.
anaglifoscopio, *m.* anaglyphoscope.
anagnórisis, *f.* (poet.) anagnorisis, recognition.
anagoge, *m., var. of* **anagogía.**
anagogía, *f.* 1. anagoge, mystic or spiritual meaning of words. 2. anagoge, mystic detachment or rapture.
anagógico, ca, *a.* anagogic, anagogical.
anagrama, *m.* anagram.
anagramático, ca, *a.* anagrammatic.
anagramatismo, *m.* anagrammatism.
anagramatista, *m., f.* anagrammatist.
anagramatizador, ra, *m., f.* anagrammatist.
anagramatizar, (*ref. 53*) *tr.v.* to anagrammatize, make into anagrams.
anagramista, *m., f., var. of* **anagramatista.**
anahao, *m.* (bot.) anahau, anahao, a tall Philippine palm.
anaiboa, *m.* (Cuba) toxic juice obtained from yucca root.
anal, *a.* (anat.) anal.
analcima, *f.* (min.) analcime, analcite.
analcitita, *f.* (geol.) analcitite, analcimite.
analectas, *f.* (*pl.*) analects, anthology.
analema, *f.* (astron.) analemma.
analepsia, *f.* (med.) analepsis, convalescence, recovery.
analéptico, ca, *a.* (med.) analeptic, restoring strength.

anales, *m.* (*pl.*) annals.
analfabético, ca, *a.* illiterate.
analfabetismo, *m.* illiteracy.
analfabeto, ta, *a., m., f.* illiterate.
analgeno, *m.* (pharm., chem.) analgen.
analgesia, *f.* (med.) analgesia, insensibility to pain.
analgésico, ca, *a.* analgesic, producing analgesia. —*m.* analgesic, agent producing analgesia, painkiller, pain-reliever.
analice, analicé, *ref.* **analizar.**
análisis, *m., f.* analysis. — **a. cualitativo,** (chem.) qualitative analysis, analysis of the elements in a compound; **a. cuantitativo,** (chem.) quantitative analysis, analysis to find the quantity of each element; **a. de sangre,** blood test or analysis; **a. espectral,** (phys.) spectrum analysis; **a. vectorial,** vector analysis; **a. electrolítico,** (chem.) electroanalysis; **a. ponderal,** gravimetric analysis.
analista, *m., f.* 1. analyst, psychoanalyst. 2. annalist, historian, chronicler.
analístico, ca, *a.* annalistic, pertaining to the annals or history.
analíticamente, *adv.* analytically.
analítico, ca, *a.* analytic, analytical. —*f.* (philos.) analytics.
analizable, *a.* analyzable.
analizador, ra, *a.* analyzing. —*m., f.* analyst; analyzer. —*m.* (opt.) analyzer; **a. de harmónicos,** (rad.) harmonic analyzer; **a. de ondas,** (rad.) wave analyzer.
analizar, (*ref.* 53) *tr.v.* to analyze.
análogamente, *adv.* analogously, similarly.
analogía, *f.* analogy.
analógicamente, *adv.* analogically.
analógico, ca, *a.* analogical.
analogismo, *m.* (log.) analogism.
analogizar, (*ref.* 53) *tr.v. to analogize.*
análogo, ga, *a.* analogous, similar.
anamita, *a., m., f.* Annamese (language and people of a region of Vietnam).
anamnesis, *f.* (med.) anamnesis.
anamnéstico, ca, *a.* (med.) anamnestic.
anamórfico, ca, *a.* (biol.) anamorphic.
anamorfosis, *f.* (biol.) anamorphosis.
anamú, (*pl.* **anamúes**) *m.* (bot). (Cuba, P. Rico, Ven.) garlic-scented herb (Petiveria alliacea).
ananá, *m., var. of* **ananás.**
ananás, *m.* (bot.) pineapple (plant and fruit).
ananké, *m.* (Greek) destiny, fate.
anapelo, *m.* (bot.) aconite, monkshood, wolfsbane.
anapéstico, ca, *a.* (poet.) anapaestic.
anapesto, *m.* (poet.) anapaest.
anaplastia, *f.* (surg.) anaplasty, plastic surgery.
anaptixis, *f.* (phonet.) anaptyxis.
anaquel, *m.* shelf, cupboard.
anaquelería, *f.* case of shelves, shelving, bookshelves.
anaranjado, da, *a.* orange-colored. —*m.* orange (the color).
anarquía, *f.* anarchy.
anárquicamente, *adv.* anarchically.
anarquice, anarquicé, *ref.* **anarquizar.**
anárquico, ca, *a.* anarchic, anarchical.
anarquismo, *m.* anarchism.
anarquista, *a.* anarchistic. —*m., f.* anarchist.
anarquizar, (*ref.* 53) *tr.v.* to make anarchic, spread anarchy in a country or a body of people.
anasarca, *f.* (med.) anasarca.
anascote, *m.* (tex.) fine serge.
anastasia, *f.* (bot.) mugwort.
anastigmático, ca, *a.* (opt.) anastigmatic.
anastomice, *ref.* **anastomizarse.**
anastomizarse, (*ref.* 53) *r.v.* to anastomose.
anastomosarse, *r.v.* (bot., zool.) to anastomose.
anastomosis, *f.* (anat., biol.) anastomosis.
anastomótico, ca, *a.* (bot., anat.) anastomotic.
anástrofe, *m.* (rhet.) anastrophe.
anata, *f.* yearly income; benefits accrued from yearly work, pension, etc.
anatasa, *f.* (min.) anatase.
anatema, *m., f.* anathema.
anatematice, anatematicé, *ref.* **anatematizar.**
anatematismo, *m.* anathematism, anathemization, excommunication.
anatematizador, ra, *a.* anathematizing. —*m., f.* anathematizer.
anatematizar, (*ref.* 53) *tr.v.* 1. to anathematize, excommunicate. 2. to condemn, curse.
anatomía, *f.* anatomy.
anatómicamente, *adv.* anatomically.
anatómico, ca, *a.* anatomic, anatomical. —*m., f.* anatomist.
anatomista, *m., f.* anatomist.
anatomizar, (*ref.* 53) *tr.v.* 1. to anatomize, dissect. 2. to delineate, emphasize (bones and muscles).
anátropo, pa, *a.* (bot.) anatropous.
anay, *m.* 1. (ento.) anay, white ant, termite. 2. (bot.) anay.
anca, *f.* haunch (animals); croup (horses); hind quarters; (coll.) buttocks, thighs (esp. a woman's); (coll.) rump, buttock; **a ancas** or **a las ancas,** behind, on the rump; (coll.) accompanying, together with; **ancas de rana,** frogs' legs; **dar ancas vueltas,** (Mex.) to give odds; **llevar** or **traer a las ancas a otro,** (coll.) to support, maintain somebody else.
ancado, da, *a.* (vet.) stringhalted. —*m.* pillion rider (person seated behind rider on the same horse).
ancaramita, *f.* (geol). ankaramite.
ancestral, *a.* ancestral.
anchamente, *adv.* widely, largely, broadly.
anchar, *tr.v., i.v.* to broaden, widen, enlarge.
ancheta, *f.* 1. (Amer.) small amount of goods (to be sold). 2. profit, gain (from any deal). 3. small or unprofitable business deal. 4. (Arg., Bol., Col.) silliness, foolishness. 5. (Ecuad., Mex., Peru) bargain, good deal.
anchi, *m.* 1. (Arg.) soup made with corn, water, sugar and lemon. 2. (Chile) barley or wheat meal.
anchicorto, ta, *a.* wide and short.
ancho, cha, *a.* wide, broad; full, ample; loose, loose-fitting (clothes). — **a mis, a tus, a sus anchas** or **anchos,** freely, unrestrictedly, as one pleases; **estar** or **sentirse a sus anchas,** to be or feel at home or at ease; **estar** or **ponerse muy** or **tan ancho,** to be or become conceited or vain; **quedarse tan ancho,** not to worry, keep calm (about what has been done or said); **tener la manga muy ancha,** to be too tolerant. —*m.* width, breadth; **a. de banda,** (rad.) bandwidth; **tener tantos metros de a.,** to be so many meters wide; **a. de la vía,** (ry.) track gauge.
anchoa, *f.* anchovy.
anchor, *m., var. of* **anchura,** width, breadth, size.
anchova, *f.* anchovy.
anchoveta, *f. dim. of* **anchoa,** anchovy.
anchura, *f.* 1. width, breadth. 2. (fig.) latitude, license, freedom, laxness, laxity. — **a. de banda,** (rad.) bandwidth; **a. de paso,** (mec.) clearance width.
anchuroso, sa, *a.* extensive, wide, spacious, large.
ancianía, *f.* seniority (in military hierarchy).
ancianidad, *f.* old age.
anciano, na, *a.* old, aged. —*m.* old man; elder; eldest friar in a military order. —*f.* old woman.
ancla, *f.* anchor; (sl.) hand. — **a. de la esperanza,** sheet anchor; **a. de leva,** bower, bower anchor; **a. flotante,** drift anchor, drogue; **argolla del a.,** anchor ring; **arrastrar el a.,** to drag the anchor; **brazo del a.,** anchor arm; **caña del a.,** anchor shank; **cepo del a.,** anchor stock; **cruz del a.,** anchor throat; **diamante del a.,** anchor crown; **echar anclas,** to cast or drop anchor, (coll.) to stay firmly in a place; **encepar el a.,** to stock the anchor; **estar al a.,** to be at anchor; **galga del a., anchor back; levar anclas,** to weigh anchor; **oreja del a.,** anchor fluke, anchor palm; **pico del a.,** anchor bill; **a. de seta,** mushroom anchor; **a. sin cepo,** stockless anchor.
ancladero, *m.* anchorage, anchoring place.
anclaje, *m.* (mar.) anchoring (action); (mar.) anchorage, anchoring place; (mar.) anchorage, anchoring dues.
anclar, *i.v.* (mar.) to anchor, cast anchor; (mar.) to be anchored.
anclote, *m.* 1. (mar.) kedge anchor. 2. (Mex.) small barrel, keg.
anco, *m.* (Arg., Bol., Peru) a variety of pumpkin (cucurbita maxima).
ancón, *m.* 1. cove, bay. 2. (Mex.) corner, nook. 3. (archit.) ancon, bracket, corbel. 4. (P. Rico) raft. 5. (Col.) space between two hills.
anconada, *f.* cove, bay.
áncora, *f.* 1. (mar., fig.) anchor. 2. (fig.) shelter. 3. anchor-like mechanism of a clock.
ancorar, *i.v.* (mar.) to anchor, drop anchor.
ancorca, *f.* yellow ocher.
ancorel, *m.* (mar.) anchor-stone (stone used to anchor the float of a fish net).
ancorería, *f.* anchor workshop or forge.
ancorero, *m.* anchor maker.
ancorque, *m.* (rare) *var. de* **ancorca.**
ancua, *f.* (Arg., Chile) toasted maize.
ancuco, *m.* (Bol.) nougat (made from peanuts or almonds and honey).
ancudo, da, *a.* big rumped (animal); with big buttocks (person).
ancusa, *f.* (bot.) oxtongue, bugloss, alkanet; **a. de tintes,** alkanet.
ancuviña, *f.* tomb, grave (of Chilean Indians).
anda, *f.* (Amer.) *var. of* **andas.**
andábata, *m.* gladiator.
andada, *f.* 1. thin, hard-baked bread. 2. walking, long walk, hike. 3. (*pl.*) tracks (of wild animals). — **volver uno a las andadas,** (coll.) to go back to one's old tricks.
andadera, *f.* (bldg.) traveler, traveling derrick or scaffold.
andaderas, *f.* (*pl.*) go-cart, stroller (for teaching children to walk).
andadero, ra, *a.* 1. easily passable (on foot). 2. wandering, roving.
andado, da, *past part. of* **andar.** —*a.* 1. beaten, trodden (path); frequented (street). 2. common, ordinary. 3. shabby, rather worn (clothes). —*m.* 1. (Hond.) gait. 2. stepson. —*f.* stepdaughter.
andador, ra, *a.* 1. wandering, roving. 2. fast-walking, swift. —*m., f.* walker; wanderer, rover. —*m.* 1. (law) court messenger. 2. courier, messenger. 3. path (in vegetable garden). 4. go-cart, stroller (for teaching children to walk). 5. (*pl.*) reins (to support child beginning to walk). — **poder andar sin a.,** (coll.) to be able to take care of oneself, be able to shift for oneself, be able to stand on one's own feet.
andadura, *f.* gait, pace; going, walking. — **paso de andadura,** (equit.) amble, gait.
andahuertas, *m.* (ornith.) beccafico, fig-pecker.
andalón, na, *a.* (C. Amer., Mex.) wandering, roving.
Andalucía, *f.* Andalusia, region of Spain.
andalucismo, *m.* Andalusianism, word or expression particular to Andalusia; love of Andalusian things.

andalucita, *f.* (min.) andalusite.
andaluz, za, (*pl.* **andaluces**) *a., m., f.* Andalusian; **ser muy a.,** to be witty, gay.
andaluzada, *f.* (coll.) exaggeration; boasting, bragging; **decir andaluzadas,** to boast, brag; to exaggerate.
andamiada, *f.* scaffolding, scaffold.
andamiaje, *m., var. of* **andamiada.**
andamiar, *tr.v.* to scaffold.
andamio, *m.* 1. scaffold, scaffolding; platform; granstand. 2. (coll.) footwear, shoes. — **a. colgado,** hanging scaffold; **a. óseo,** skeleton; **a. tubular,** pipe scaffold.
andana, *f.* 1. row, tier. 2. shelves. — **llamarse a.,** to go back on one's word.
andanada, *f.* 1. (mar.) broadside. 2. covered grandstand (in bull ring). 3. (coll.) sharp reproof, reprimand. — **soltar una a.,** to give a dressing down; **tener por andanadas,** (Arg.) to have plenty, too much of.
andancia, *f.* 1. event, occurrence. 2. (Amer.) light epidemic illness.
andando, andandito, *interj.* right away, immediately; let's go!
andaniño, *m.* go-cart, stroller.
andante, *a.* walking; errant, e.g. *caballero a.,* knight errant. —*adv.* (mus.) andante, moderately slow.
andantesco, ca, *a.* of or about knighthood or knight errantry.
andantino, *adv.* (mus.) andantino.
andanza, *f.* occurrence, event. **buena a.,** good fortune or luck; **mala a.,** ill fortune, bad luck; **volver a las andanzas,** to go back to one's old tricks, be up to one's old tricks again.
andar, (*ref. 1*) *i.v.* 1. to walk; to go, move; to amble; to travel. 2. to go, work, function. 3. to pass, go by, elapse. 4. to be, feel, e.g. *¿cómo andas?* how are you, how do you feel? 5. to be, go, e.g. *¿cómo andan los negocios?* how's business, how's business going? **a. alegre,** to be happy, gay. 6. (mar.) to fall off to leeward. — **a más** or **todo a.,** at full speed; **¡anda!** away with you, go on, beat it, scram!; **¡ándale!** (coll.) right!; **a.** + *ger.,* to have been + *ger.,* e.g. *me anda fastidiando todo el día,* he's been annoying me all day; **a. a caballo,** to ride horseback; **a. a derechas** or **derecho,** to behave or act in an honest or upright manner; **anda a freír espárragos,** (coll.) go jump in the lake; **a. a gatas,** to go on all fours, crawl; **a. a la que salta,** (coll.) to be on the lookout for every opportunity; **a. a tientas,** to grope in the dark; **dime con quien andas y te diré quien eres,** one shall be known by the company one keeps; **a. con,** to handle, e.g. *es peligroso a. con pólvora,* it is dangerous to handle gun-powder; **a. con cuidado,** to take care, be careful; **a. de acá para allá,** to go from here to there, wander or rove about; **a. de broma,** to be joking; **a. de juerga,** to go or be on a spree; **a. en,** to be mixed up in, e.g. *a. en pleitos,* to be mixed up in trouble; to go through, search, e.g. *lo encontré andando en los cajones,* I found him going through the drawers; **a. en boca de todos, a. de boca en boca,** to be on everybody's lips, be common knowledge; **a. por** + *inf.,* to try to + *inf.;* **a. por las nubes,** to be absent minded; **a. sin cuidado,** to be careless, not to take care; not to worry; **a. tras,** to be after, look for, pursue; **¿cómo andas, anda, andamos de?** how are you, he, she, we, etc. fixed for? e.g. *cómo andas de dinero?* how are you fixed for money? —*r.v. to go;* **andarse a** + *inf.,* to be engaged in + *ger.,* set about + *ger.;* **andarse con** or **en,** to be full of, have, employ, use, e.g. *siempre se anda con bromas,* he is always full of jokes; **andarse por las ramas,** to beat about the bush. —*tr.v.* to go, to cover, walk (a certain distance); to walk or go up or down (road or street). —*m.* 1. walk, pace, gait. 2. behavior, manner.
andaraje, *m.* 1. wheel of chain pump. 2. frame of a garden roller.
andaraz, *a.* (poet.) wayfaring (person). — (*pl.* **andaraces**) *m.* (zool.) hutia (Capromus melanurus).
andariego, ga, *adj.* wandering, roving. —*m., f.* gadabout, rover, wanderer.
andarin, na, *adj.* walking. —*m., f.* tireless walker.
andarina, *f., var. of* **andorina.**
andarivel, *m.* 1. cable ferry; ferry cable. 2. (mar.) safety ropes (on a ship). 3. (mar.) single whip. 4. (Cuba) small ferry-boat. 5. (Cuba, imp. u.) (*pl.*) a plethora of objects.
andarraya, *f.* a table game similar to checkers.
andarríos, *m.* 1. (ornith.) white wagtail (Motacilla alba). 2. (ento.) water skipper (Hydrametra stagnorum).
andas, *f.* (*pl.*) portable platform; stretcher, litter; bier. — **en a. y volandas,** speedily, quickly, rapidly.
andel, *m.* track, path.
andén, *m.* 1. railway platform; path, footpath; footway, pavement, sidewalk (esp. of a bridge). 2. pier, boat landing. 3. railing parapet. 4. shelf. 5. (Arg., Bol., Peru) (*pl.*) cultivation terraces (in the Andes). — **a. de cabeza,** (ry.) end platform; **a. de entrevía,** (ry.) island platform.
andenería, *f.* (Peru) terracing, terraces (for cultivation in the Andes).
andero, *m.* platform bearer, litter bearer, pallbearer.
Andes, *m.* (pl.) Andes.
andesina, *f.* (min.) andesine.
andesita, *f.* (geol.) andesite.
andinismo, *m.* mountain-climbing in the Andes.
andinista, *m., f.* mountain climber in the Andes.
andino, na, *a.* Andean.
andirá, (Arg., Par.) vampire.
ándito, *m.* sidewalk; pavement.
andoba, *m.* (sl.) guy, Mac, Buster (gen. in third person).
andola, *f.* popular song of the 17th century.
andolina, *f.* (ornith.) swallow.
andón, na, *a.* (Amer.) fast, fast-walking (said of horses).
andorga, *f.* (coll.) belly, abdomen; **llenar la a.,** (coll.) to eat your fill.
andorina, *f.* (ornith.) swallow.
Andorra, *f.* Andorra.
andorra, *f.* (coll.) bustler, gadabout.
andorrano, na, *a., m., f.* Andorran.
andorrear, *i.v.* (coll.) to bustle about, gadabout.
andorrero, ra, *a.* roaming, roving; gadding. —*m., f.* gadabout; roamer, rover.
andosco, ca, *a.* two-year-old (cattle).
andradita, *f.* (min.) andradite.
andrajero, ra, *m., f.* ragpicker, ragdealer.
andrajo, *m.* 1. rag, tatter. 2. wretch, good-for-nothing, scoundrel. 3. piece of rubbish, useless thing.
andrajosamente, *adv.* raggedly, wretchedly.
andrajoso, sa, *a.* ragged, tattered.
andriana, *f.* peignoir; negligée, housecoat.
andrino, na, *f.* (bot.) sloe, sloe plum (fruit). —*m.* sloe tree.
androcéfalo, la, *a.* (anat.) androcephalous.
androceo, *m.* (bot.) androecium, male organs of a flower.
androcracia, *f.* (sociol.) male supremacy.
androfobia, *f.* (med.) androphobia, abnormal dread of men.
andrógeno, na, *a.* (biochem.) androgenic. —*m.* androgen.
androginia, *f.* (bot., zool.) androgyny.
andrógino, na, *a.* 1. (bot.) androgynous. 2. (zool.) androgynous, hermaphroditic. 3. (arch., astrol.) androgynous (planets). —*m., f.* androgyne.
androide, *m.* android, an automaton resembling a human being (science fiction).
androlatría, *f.* androlatry, worship of a man as a divine being.
andrómeda, *f.* (astron., myth.) Andromeda.
andrómina, *f.* (coll.) trick, lie, fraud, story.
androsemo, *m.* (bot.) androseme.
androsterona, *f.* (biochem.) androsterone.
andujareño, ña, *a.* of or from Andújar, Spain. —*m., f.* native or inhabitant of Andújar.
andullo, *m.* 1. (mar.) canvas-layer (to protect the swivel blocks and harpings of a ship). 2. long rolled tobacco leaf; bundle of tobacco leaves (used to form a pack); (Cuba) plug tobacco, chewing tobacco. — **mascar a.,** to chew tobacco.
andurriales, *m.* (*pl.*) byways, out-of-the-way places, (coll.) boondocks.
anduve, anduvieron, anduviera, anduviese, *ref.* **andar.**
anea, *f.* (bot.) cattail, bulrush.
anear, *tr.v.* to measure by ells. —*m.* bulrush patch.
aneblar, (*ref. 29*) *tr.v.* to cloud, make dark; to make misty or foggy. —*r.v.* to become misty or foggy; to cloud over, become cloudy.
anécdota, *f.* anecdote.
anecdotario, *m.* collection of anecdotes.
anecdótico, ca, *a.* 1. anecdotal. 2. nonessential, irrelevant.
anecdotista, *m., f.* anecdotist.
aneciarse, *r.v.* to become stupid.
anegable, *a.* floodable, subject to inundation.
anegación, *f.* 1. drowning. 2. inundation, flooding.
anegadizo, za, *a.* liable to flooding, subject to flooding.
anegamiento, *m.* 1. drowning. 2. inundation, flooding.
anegar, (*ref. 67*) *tr.v.* 1. to drown; to sink. 2. to flood, inundate. —*r.v.* 1. to drown; to sink. 2. to become flooded or inundated. 3. (fig.) to overwhelm; to annoy. — **a. en llanto,** to be overcome by tears.
anegociado, da, *a.* busy; having many businesses.
anejar, *tr.v., var. of* **anexar,** to annex; to join, attach.
anejín, *m., var. of* **anejir.**
anejir, *m.* rhymed proverb set to music; musical ditty.
anejo, ja, *a.* annexed, attached; dependent; **llevar anejo,** to carry with it. —*m.* 1. annex. 2. church dependent on another one. 3. rural district joined to a borough.
aneldo, *m.* (bot.) dill.
aneléctrico, ca, *a.* (phys.) anelectric.
anélido, *a., m.* (zool.) annelid; (*pl.*) Annelida.
anemia, *f.* (med.) anemia, anaemia; **a. perniciosa,** pernicious anemia; **a. hipocrómica,** hypochromic anemia.
anémico, ca, *a.* anemic, anaemic. —*m., f.* 1. person suffering from anemia. 2. (coll.) weakling.
anemocordio, *m.* Aeolian harp.
anemofilia, *f.* (bot.) anemophily.
anemófilo, la, *a.* (bot.) anemophilous.
anemografía, *f.* (phys.) anemography.
anemográfico, ca, *a.* anemographic.
anemógrafo, *m.* 1. anemoscope, instrument for recording the direction of the wind. 2. expert in anemography.

anemograma, *m.* (meteorol.) anemogram.
anemología, *f.* (phys.) anemology.
anemometría, *f.* (phys.) anemometry.
anemómetro, *m.* anemometer, wind gauge (measuring the force and velocity of the wind). — **a. de molinete,** vane anemometer; **a. registrador,** recording anemometer.
anémona, anemona, anemone, *f.* 1. (bot.) anemone. 2. (zool.) sea anemone, actinia (a polyp). — **a. de mar,** sea anemone.
anemoscopio, *m.* (phys.) anemoscope.
anepigráfico, ca, *a.* uninscribed.
anequín, *adv.* **de a.,** per head (system of paying for each animal sheared).
anaeróbico, *a.* (biol.) anaerobic.
anerobio, *m.* (imp. u.) *var. of* **anaerobio.**
aneroide, *a., m.* aneroid; **a. de topógrafo,** surveying aneroid.
aneroidógrafo, *m.* aneroidograph.
anestesia, *f.* anesthesia, anaesthesia. — **a. de bloque,** block anesthesia; **a. de conducción,** conduction anesthesia; **a. espinal,** spinal anesthesia; **a. general,** general anesthesia; **a. local,** local anesthesia; **a. medular,** spinal anesthesia.
anestesiador, *m.* anesthetist, anaesthetist.
anestesiar, *tr.v.* to anesthetize, anaesthetize; (fig.) to bore stiff (coll.).
anestésico, ca, *a., m.* anesthetic, anaesthetic; **a. general,** general anesthetic; **a. local,** local anesthetic.
anestesiología, *f.* (med.) anesthesiology.
anestesiólogo, ga, *m., f.* anesthesiologist.
anestesista, *m., f.* anesthetist, anaesthetist.
aneurisma, *m., f.* (med.) aneurism, aneurysm.
aneurismático, ca, *a.* (med.) aneurysmatic.
anexar, *tr.v.* to annex; to join, attach, incorporate.
anexidades, *f.* (*pl.*) adjuncts, appurtenances, accessories.
anexión, *f.* annexation.
anexionamiento, *m.* (Arg., Chile) *var. of* **anexión.**
anexionar, *tr.v., var. of* **anexar.**
anexionismo, *m.* annexationism.
anexionista, *a., m., f.* annexationist.
anexo, xa, *a.* annexed, attached; incorporated; dependent. —*m.* annex.
anfesibena, *f., var. of* **anfisbena.**
anfetamina, *f.* (pharm.) amphetamine.
anfiartrosis, *f.* (anat.) amphiarthrosis.
anfibio, bia, *a.* amphibious, amphibian. —*m.* 1. (zool.) amphibian; (*pl.*) Amphibia. 2. amphibian (vehicle able to travel on land and in water).
anfibología, *f.* amphibology, ambiguity in syntax, equivocation.
anfibológico, ca, *a,* amphibological, ambiguous.
anfibiótico, ca, *a.* (ento.) amphibiotic.
anfíbol, *m.* (min.) amphibole.
anfibolita, *f.* (min.) amphibolite.
anfibología, *f.* (rhet.) amphibology.
anfibológico, ca, *a.* amphibological.
anfíbraco, *m.* (poet.) amphibrach.
anfictión, *m.* (hist.) amphictyon, deputy to the council or congress held by an amphictyony.
anfictionado, *m.* (hist.) office of amphictyon.
anfictionía, *f.* (hist.) amphictyony.
anfidiploide, *a.* (biol.) amphidiploid.
anfímacro, *m.* (poet.) amphimacer.
anfión, *m.* opium.
anfioxo, *m.* (zool.) amphioxus.
anfípodo, *m.* (zool.) amphipod; (*pl.*) Amphipoda.
anfipróstilo, *m.* (archit.) amphiprostyle.
anfisbena, *f.* 1. (myth., hist.) amphisbaena. 2. (zool.) amphisbaenian (a worm-like lizard).
anfiscio, *m.* (geog.) inhabitant of the torrid zone, amphiscian.
anfisibena, *f., var. of* **anfisbena.**
anfiteatro, *m.* 1. amphitheatre. 2. (theat.) balcony. — **a. anatómico,** dissecting room (of hospital or medical school); **a. quirúrgico,** operating theater or room.
anfitrión, *m.* 1. (coll.) host (one who entertains). 2. (myth.) **A.,** Amphitryon.
Anfitrite, *f.* (myth.) Amphitrite, goddess of the sea.
anfítropo, pa, *a.* (bot.) amphitropous.
ánfora, *f.* 1. amphora. 2. (Mex.) ballot box. 3. (*pl.*) (ecc.) cruet, ampullas (vessels for holding holy oils).
anfótero, ra, *a.* (chem.) amphoteric.
anfractuosidad, *f.* 1. anfractuosity, tortuousness. 2. (anat.) sulcus, anfractuosity (depressions separating the convolutions of the brain).
anfractuoso, sa, *a.* anfractuous, tortuous, circuitous, winding.
angaité, *m.,* (Arg., Bol., Par.) Indian language.
angaria, *f.* (mar.) angary (compulsory service exacted by government; forcible seizure of shipping for public use).
angarillada, *f.* wheelbarrow-load; pannier-load.
angarillar, *tr.v.* to put panniers on (a horse, etc.).
angarillas, *f. pl.* 1. wheelbarrow. 2. panniers. 3. cruet stand.
angarillear, *tr.v.* (Chile) to transport in panniers.
angaripola, *f.* 1. calico, printed cotton. 2. (*pl.*) furbelows, gaudy ornaments.
ángaro, *m.* beacon (warning fire).
angarria, *f.* (Col.) rough, worn-out leather.
angarrio, *m.* (Amer.) lean and hungry looking person.
angas, *f. pl.* (Amer.) **por a. o por mangas,** by hook or by crook.
angazo, *m.* 1. scoop net for catching shellfish. 2. (agr.) harrow, large rake.
ángel, *m.* 1. angel. 2. (artil.) crossbar shot. 3. opportunity to play on top of the table itself (in pool). — **á. custodio** or **de la guarda,** guardian angel; **á. malo** or **de las tinieblas,** devil; **tener á.,** to have grace or charm; **tener mal á.,** to lack grace or charm; **tener mucho á.,** to have a lot of charm; **estar pasando un á.,** said of a moment of silence in a conversation.
angélica, *f.* 1. (bot.) angelica. 2. (pharm.) purgative mixture. 3. (ecc.) lesson sung on Saturday of Holy Week to bless the candles. — **a. carlina,** carline thistle.
angelical, *a.* angelical, angelic.
angelicalmente, *adv.* angelically.
angelice, angelicé, *ref.* **angelizarse.**
angelico, *m.* (reg., Sp.) *dim. of* **ángel,** little angel, dear little child.
angélico, ca, *a.* 1. angelic, angelical. 2. (chem.) angelic (acid).
angelín, *m.* (bot.) angelin, cabbage tree (Andira inermis).
angelito, *m. dim of* **ángel,** little angel, dear little child. — **estar uno con los angelitos,** (coll.) to be in the clouds, be unaware of what is happening; to be asleep.
angelizarse, (*ref. 53*) *r.v.* to become good or saintly. —*tr.v.* to make angelical.
angelón, *m. aug. of* **ángel,** large figure of an angel. — **a. de retablo,** (coll.) plump and fat-cheeked person.
angelote, *m.* 1. *aug. of* **ángel,** large figure of an angel. 2. (coll.) chubby, good-natured child; (coll.) simple, quiet-natured person. 3. (ichth.) angelfish.
ángelus, *m.* Angelus.
angevino, na, *a.* (hist.) Angevin.
angina, *f.* (med.) angina, quinsy. — **a. de pecho,** angina pectoris; **a. de Vincent,** Vincent's angina.
angioclasto, *m.* (med.) angioclast, pincer-like instrument to stop the flow in an artery.
angiocolitis, *f.* (med.) angiocholitis.
angiografía, *f.* (anat.) angiography.
angioleucitis, *f.* (med.) angioleucitis, lymphangitis, inflammation of the lymph vessels.
angiología, *f.* (anat.) angiology.
angioma, *m.* (med.) angioma, small tumor.
angiospermo, ma, *a.* (bot.) angiospermous. —*f.* (bot.) angiosperm, (*pl.*) Angiospermae.
angla, *f.* cape of land, promontory.
anglesita, *f.* (min.) anglesite.
anglicanismo, *m.* (rel.) Anglicanism.
anglicanizado, da, *a.* anglicized.
anglicano, na, *a., m., f.* (rel.) Anglican.
anglicismo, *m.* Anglicism.
anglo, gla, *a.* Anglian; English. —*m., f.* 1. Anglo; Englishman; English-speaking person. 2. (U.S.) name given to English-speaking Americans by the Chicanos or Mexican-Americans in the S.W.
angloamericano, na, *a., m., f.* Anglo-American.
anglocatólico, ca, *a., m., f.* Anglo-Catholic.
angloespañol, ñola, *a.* English-Spanish.
anglófilo, la, *a., m., f.* Anglophile.
anglófobo, ba, *a., m., f.* Anglophobe.
angloindio, dia, *a.* Anglo-Indian.
anglomanía, *f.* Anglomania.
anglómano, na, *a., m., f.* Anglomaniac, Anglomane.
anglonormando, da, *a., m., f.* Anglo-Norman.
angloparlante, *a.* English-speaking.
anglosajón, na, *a., m., f.* Anglo-Saxon.
angola, *f.* (Hond.) sour milk.
angolán, *m.* (bot.) alangium.
angora, *m.* angora (cat or goat).
angorra, *f.* canvas or leather apron.
angostar, *tr.v., i.v., r.v.* to narrow; to contract.
angosto, ta, *a.* narrow, tight, close.
angostura, *f.* 1. narrowness; narrow place, path or passage. 2. angostura (aromatic bitter bark).
angra, *f.* bay, cove, inlet.
angrelado, da, *a.* engrailed, indented at the edge.
angstrom, *m.* (phys.) angstrom.
angú, *m.* (C. Rica, Pan.) a plantain-and-meat dish.
anguarina, *f.* sleeveless farmer's smock.
anguila, *f.* 1. eel. 2. (mar.) (*pl.*) ways (inclined structure on which a vessel is supported in launching). — **a. eléctrica,** electric eel; **anguilas de cabo,** whip (in the galleys).
anguilazo, *m.* whiplash, blow with a whip.
anguilero, ra, *a.* eel, for eels (basket).
anguiliforme, *a.* (zool.) anguiliform.
anguílula, *f.* (zool.) vinegar worm.
anguina, *f.* (vet.) inguinal vein.
angula, *f.* elver, grig, young eel.
angulado, da, *a.* angular, sharp-cornered.
angular, *a.* angular. — **piedra a.,** keystone.
angularmente, *adv.* angularly.
angulema, *f.* 1. hemp cloth. 2. (*pl.*) flattery, cajolery. — **hacer angulemas, venir con angulemas,** (coll.) to fawn upon, flatter.
ángulo, *m.* (geom.) angle; corner, angle (formed by two walls). — **á. agudo,** (geom.) acute angle; **á. complementario,** (geom.) complementary angle; **á. complementario de situación,** (mil.) complementary angle of site; **á. crítico,** (aer., opt.) critical angle; **á. de ataque,** (aer.) angle of attack; **á. de deriva,** (aer., mar.) drift angle; **á. de despeje,** clearance angle; **á. de desviación** or **desvío,** angle of deflection; **á. de escora,** (mar.) keeling angle; **á. de incidencia,** (phys.) angle of incidence; **á. del objetivo,** (mil.) target angle; **á. del ojo,** corner of the eye; **á. de pérdida,** (aer.) angle of stall; **á. de planeo,** (aer.) gliding angle; **á. de reflexión,** (phys.) angle of

reflection; **á. de refracción,** (phys.) angle of refraction; **á. de retraso** or **atraso,** (elec.) angle of lag; **á. de tiro,** (artil.) angle of elevation; **á. entrante,** re-entrant angle; **á. esférico,** (geom.) spherical angle; **á. facial,** (zool.) facial angle, degree of prognathism; **á. horario,** (astron.) hour angle; **á. llano,** (geom.) straight angle; **á. muerto,** blind spot; **á. obtuso,** (geom.) obtuse angle; **á. recto,** right angle; **á. reflejo,** (geom.) reflex angle; **ángulos adyacentes,** adjacent angles; **ángulos alternos,** (geom.) alternate angles; **ángulos correspondientes,** (geom.) corresponding angles; **ángulos opuestos por el vértice,** (geom.) vertically opposite angles; **á. suplementario,** (geom.) supplementary angle; **á. visual,** (opt.) visual angle; **á. de retraso,** (elec.) angle of lag, phase angle; **á. de rumbo,** (geoph.) angle of strike; **á. descendente,** (top.) angle of depression; **á. incluso,** included angle.

angulosidad, *f.* angularity.

anguloso, sa, *a.* angular, sharp-cornered, angled.

angurria, *f.* 1. (coll.) strangury (painful discharge of urine). 2. (Amer.) inordinate appetite; greed, avarice.

angurriento, ta, *a.* (Amer.) greedy, avaricious.

angustia, *f.* anguish, anxiety, distress, affliction.

angustiadamente, *adv.* anguishingly, anxiously.

angustiado, da, *past part. of* **angustiar.** —*a.* 1. anguished, afflicted, anxious. 2. greedy, grasping, miserly. 3. (Mex.) short, narrow.

angustiador, ra, *a.* distressing, anguishing, grieving.

angustiar, *tr.v.* to distress, afflict, disturb. —*r.v.* to become distressed or disturbed.

angustiosamente, *adv.* anxiously, distressfully.

angustioso, sa, *a.* 1. distressed, afflicted. 2. distressing, afflicting, anguishing.

anhelación, *f.* 1. yearning, longing. 2. gasping (for breath).

anhelante, *a.* yearning, longing.

anhelar, *tr.v.* to yearn for, long for. —*i.v.* 1. to gasp, breathe hard. 2. to yearn, long. — **a.** + *inf.;* to yearn or long to + *inf.;* **a. hacer,** to long to do; **a. por,** to yearn or long for.

anhélito, *m.* gasping, heavy breathing, shortness of breath.

anhelo, *m.* yearning, longing, ardent desire.

anhelosamente, *adv.* yearningly, longingly.

anheloso, sa, *a.* 1. eager, yearning, desirous, e.g. *a. de,* eager for, desirous of, yearning for. 2. breathless, panting; difficult, heavy (breathing).

anhídrido, *m.* (chem.) anhydride. — **a. arsenioso,** arsenic trioxide; **a. bórico,** boron trioxide; **a. carbónico,** carbon dioxide; **a. nítrico,** nitric oxide (nitrogen pentoxide); **a. sulfúrico,** sulfur trioxide; **a. sulfuroso,** sulfur dioxide.

anhidrita, *f.* (min.) anhydrite.

anhidro, dra, *a.* (chem.) anhydrous.

anhidrosis, *f.* (med.) anhydrosis.

aní, *m.* (*pl.* **aníes**) (ornith.) ani, common ani.

anidar, *i.v.* to nest (birds); to dwell, live. —*tr.v.* to shelter, give refuge, harbor. —*r.v.* to nest; to dwell, live.

aniebla, anieble, *ref.* **aneblar.**

anieblar, *tr.v., var. of* **aneblar.**

aniego, *m., var. of* **anegación.**

aniego, aniegue, *ref.* **anegar.**

anilina, *f.* (chem.) aniline.

anilla, *f.* ring, hoop, loop, curtain ring; (*pl.*) gymnasium rings. — **a. de servilleta,** (Amer.) napkin ring.

anillado, da, *past part. of* **anillar.** —*a.* 1. curled, kinky. 2. (zool.) annelidan, annulated (animal). —*m.* (zool.) annelid.

anillar, *tr.v.* 1. to form into rings, shape like a ring. 2. to fasten with rings. 3. to make rings. 4. to mark birds with rings on their feet.

anillejo, te, *m. dim. of* **anillo,** small ring.

anillo, *m.* 1. ring, small hoop; (finger) ring. 2. (archit.) annulet, annulus; (zool., anat.) annulus. 3. cigar band (band around cigar indicating its make and name). 4. (*pl.*) (sl.) shackles. 5. ring, arena of the bullring. — **a. de boda,** wedding ring; **a. de bolas,** (mec.) ball race; **a. de compromiso,** engagement ring; **a. del émbolo** or **pistón,** piston ring; **a. de los Nibelungos,** (myth., mus.) Ring of the Nibelung; **a. del Pescador,** St. Peter's ring, papal seal; **a. de lubricación,** oil ring; **a. colector,** (elec.) slip or collector ring; **a. de levas,** (mech.) cam ring; **a. de pedida,** engagement ring; **a. de retículo,** cross-hair ring; **a. sincronizador,** (auto.) synchronizing ring; **a. de seguridad,** guard ring; **a. de torsión,** torque ring; **a. sombrerete,** cowl ring; **a. de remate,** (bldg.) cap ring; **a. de Saturno,** (astron.) Saturn's ring; **a. pastoral,** bishop's ring; **de a.,** honorary; **caer** or **venir como a. al dedo,** (coll.) to fit like a glove, to be just the thing needed.

ánima, *f.* 1. soul, spirit; soul in pain or purgatory. 2. (artil.) bore (of a gun). 3. (mec.) cable center, core. 4. (*pl.*) tolling of bells to summon people to pray for the dead. — **á. en pena,** ghost, wraith; soul in purgatory.

animación, *f.* 1. animation, liveliness; bustle, movement. 2. lively crowd.

animadamente, *adv.* animatedly, in a lively manner.

animado, da, *past part. of* **animar.** —*a.* lively, animated. — **ser muy a.,** to be a lot of fun, the soul of the party.

animador, ra, *a.* 1. enlivening, animating. 2. encouraging. —*m., f.* 1. (rad., theat., tel.) emcee, master of ceremonies; entertainer; (Sp.) crooner, singer. 2. animator, enlivener.

animadversión, *f.* 1. enmity, ill-will. 2. animadversion, adverse criticism, censure.

animal, *a.* 1. animal. 2. animal, physical, carnal. 3. stupid; ignorant, uncouth. — **instinto a.,** animal instinct. —*m.* 1. animal. 2. (coll.) fool, idiot; uncouth person. — **a. de tiro,** draft animal.

animalada, *f.* stupidity, stupid remark or action.

animálculo, *m.* animalcule.

animalejo, *m.* (derog.) *dim. of* **animal,** small animal.

animalice, animalicé, *ref.* **animalizar.**

animalidad, *f.* animality.

animalismo, *m.* animalism.

animalista, *m., f.* animalist.

animalización, *f.* animalization.

animalizar, (*ref.* 53) *tr.v.* to animalize. —*r.v.* to become animalized; to become stupid or brutish.

animalucho, *m.* (derog.) repulsive animal.

animar, *tr.v.* to animate, enliven; to give life to, vitalize; to encourage. — **a. a** + *inf.,* to encourage to + *inf.,* e.g. *a. a cantar,* to encourage to sing. —*r.v.* 1. to become lively or animated; to take heart, be encouraged; to cheer up. 2. to feel like, get interested, decide, e.g. *quizás se anime a venir también,* perhaps he'll feel like coming too.

anime, *m.* (bot.) courbaril, West Indian locust tree; courbaril (resin).

animero, *m.* beggar who receives alms in return for prayers for the dead.

anímico, ca, *a.* psychic, mental.

animismo, *m.* (rel.) animism.

animista, *m., f.* animist.

animita, *f.* (Cuba) glowworm.

ánimo, *m.* 1. spirit, courage, valor, fortitude. 2. spirit, energy, vitality, drive, go (coll.). 3. intention, mind, desire. 4. encouragement. — **¡ánimo!** courage! come on! cheer up!; **caer** or **caerse de á.,** to become disheartened or discouraged, lose heart; **dar á.,** to encourage; **dilatar el á.,** to cheer up, give heart to; to take heart, cheer up; **estado de á.,** mood, frame of mind; **estar de á. para,** to be in the mood for, feel like; **hacerse á. de** + *inf.,* to make up one's mind to + *inf.;* **tener á. de** + *inf.,* to intend to + *inf.,* **tener á. para** + *inf.,* to be in the mood for + *ger.*

animosamente, *adv.* 1. courageously, valiantly. 2. spiritedly, cheerfully.

animosidad, *f.* animosity, enmity.

animoso, sa, *a.* 1. courageous, brave, bold, resolute. 2. spirited, cheerful.

aniñadamente, *adv.* childishly.

aniñado, da, *a.* childish.

aniñarse, *r.v.* to become childish.

anion, *m.* (elec.) anion.

aniquilable, *a.* destructible, able to be annihilated.

aniquilador, ra, *a.* annihilating, destructive. —*m., f.* annihilator, destroyer.

aniquilamiento, *m.* annihilation.

aniquilar, *tr.v.* to annihilate, wipe out, exterminate. —*r.v.* 1. to be annihilated or wiped out. 2. to decline or deteriorate greatly (health, property); to waste away (health). 3. to humble oneself.

anís, *m.* 1. (bot.) anise (plant). 2. anise, aniseed (seed); sugar-coated aniseed. 3. anisette (anise-flavored liqueur).

anisado, da, *past part. of* **anisar.** —*m.* anisette (anise-flavored liqueur).

anisar, *m.* anise field. —*tr.v.* to flavor with anise.

aniseiconia, *f.* (med.) aniseikonia.

anisete, *m.* anisette (liqueur).

anisilo, *m.* (chem.) anisyl.

anisodonte, *a.* (anat., zool.) anisodont, uneven-toothed.

anisófilo, *a.* (bot.) anisophyllous, with uneven leaves.

anisogamia, *f.* (biol.) anisogamy.

anisómero, ra, *a.* (zool.) anisomerous, with uneven floral organs in every whorl.

anisométrico, ca, *a.* (bot., geom., geol., min.) anisometric, unsymmetrical.

anisometropía, *f.* (opt.) anisometropia.

anisopétalo, la, *a.* (bot.) anisopetalous, with uneven petals.

anisotropía, *f.* (min., phys.) anisotropy, anisotropism.

anisotrópico, ca, *a.* (phys.) anisotropic.

anisotropismo, *m.* (bot.) anisotropy, anisotropism.

anisótropo, pa, *a.* (phys.) anisotropic.

anito, *m.* (Phil. I.) family idol, fetish, ancestral spirit.

anivelar, *tr.v.* to even; to level.

aniversario, ria, *a.* anniversary. —*m.* anniversary; memorial service.

¡anjá! *interj.* (Amer.) well! hmm!

anjeo, *m.* coarse canvas, burlap.

anjova, *f.* (Can. I.) salt mackerel.

Ankara, *f.* Ankara, capital of Turkey.

annamita, *a., m., f.* Annamese, native of Annam (Vietnam).

ano, *m.* (anat.) anus.

anoa, *f.* (zool.) anoa, small wild buffalo of the Celebes Islands.

anóbidos, *m.* (ento.) (*pl.*) Anobiidae, family of small hard-bodied beetles.

anoche, *adv.* last night.

anochecedor, ra, *a.* staying up late. —*m., f.* (coll.) night owl, person who goes to bed late.

anochecer, (*ref.* 45) *i.v.* 1. to grow or get dark, fall (the night), e.g. *está anocheciendo,* night is falling, it's getting dark. 2. to be or arrive at nightfall. —*r.v.* to grow or get dark.

anochecer, *m.* nightfall, dusk; **al anochecer,** at nightfall or dusk.
anochecida, *f., var. of* **anochecer.**
anochecido, *adv.* at dusk.
anochezca, anochezco, *ref.* **anochecer.**
anódico, ca, *a.* anodic, anodal, anode, e.g. *rayos anódicos,* anode rays.
anodinia, *f.* anodynia, absence of pain.
anodino, na, *a.* 1. anodyne, assuaging pain. 2. insipid, colorless. 3. insignificant. 4. innocuous, inoffensive, harmless. —*m.* anodyne.
ánodo, *m.* (phys.) anode.
anofeles (*pl.* **anofeles**) *m.* (ento.) anopheles (mosquito).
anolis, *m.* (zool.) anoli, anole.
anomalía, *f.* anomaly; **a. gravimétrica,** gravity anomaly.
anomalístico, ca, *a.* (astron.) anomalistic.
anómalo, la, *a.* anomalous.
anomuro, ra, *a.* (zool.) anomuran. —*m.* (zool.) anomuran, (*pl.*) Anomura.
anón, na, *m., f.* (bot., Amer.) sweetsop, soursop, custard apple.
anona, *f.* (hist.) annona, supply of provisions.
anonáceo, a, *a.* (bot.) annonaceous. —*f.* (*pl.*) Annonaceae.
anonadación, *f.* 1. annihilation, destruction. 2. crushing, depression (of spirits, etc.).
anonadamiento, *m., var. of* **anonadación.**
anonadar, *tr.v.* 1. to annihilate, destroy, crush. 2. to crush, depress or dishearten completely, crush one's spirit. —*r.v.* 1. to be annihilated or destroyed. 2. to be crushed, become completely depressed. — **me dejó anonadado,** he left me baffled.
anoncillo, *m.* (Cuba, bot.) genip.
anónimamente, *adv.* anonymously.
anonimato, *m.* anonymity.
anonimia, *f.* anonymity.
anónimo, ma, *a.* anonymous. —*m.* 1. anonym, pseudonym. 2. anonymous article or letter.
anoploterio, *m.* (paleon.) anoplotherium.
anopluro, ra, *a.* (zool.) anopluriform. —*m.* sucking louse, (*pl.*) Anoplura.
anorak, *m.* anorak, hooded, waterproof jacket (originally worn by Eskimos).
anorexia, *f.* (med.) anorexia, lack of appetite.
anoria, *f., var. of* **noria.**
anormal, *a.* abnormal.
anormalidad, *f.* abnormality.
anormalmente, *adv.* abnormally.
anortita, *f.* (min.) anorthite.
anorza, *f.* (bot.) bryony (Bryonia alba).
anosmia, *f.* (med.) anosmia, loss or impairment of the sense of smell.
anotación, *f.* 1. annotation, note, comment. 2. writing down, taking down. 3. score (of points in game. — **a. preventiva,** (law) provisional notation (of pending suit).
anotador, ra, *a.* annotating. —*m., f.* annotator. —*m.* 1. scorekeeper; scorer (of goals). 2. scorecard; scoreboard. —*f.* (cine.) script girl.
anotar, *tr.v.* 1. to annotate, write notes on, make notes on. 2. to make a note of, write down, take down, jot. 3. to remark, point out, comment. 4. to score (e.g. a goal). 5. to keep score.
anovelado, da, *a.* like a novel, in the form of a novel.
anoxemia, *f.* (med.) anoxemia, anoxaemia, deficient oxygenation of the blood.
anqueador, ra, *a.* ambling (horse).
anquear, *i.v.* to amble (horse).
anquera, *f.* (Mex.) leather cover for a horse's rump.
anquialmendrado, da, *a.* narrow-rumped (horse).
anquiboyuno, na, *a.* bony-rumped, having a rump like an ox (horse).
anquiderribado, da, *a.* low-rumped (horse).
anquílope, *m.* (med.) small tumor near the inner corner of the eye.
anquilosamiento, *m.* ankylosing, anchylosing; (fig.) rusting; aging.
anquilosarse, *r.v.* 1. to ankylose, become ankylosed. 2. to stop, halt (the progress of something). 3. (fig.) to rust; to become passé (ideas, etc.).
anquilosis, *f.* (med.) ankylosis, anchylosis.
anquilóstoma, *m.* (zool.) hookworm.
anquilostomiasis, *f.* (med.) ankylostomiasis, hookworm disease.
anquirredondo, da, *a.* with a fleshy round rump (horse).
anquiseco, ca, *a.* lean-rumped (horse).
ansa, *f.* (hist.) Hanse, Hanseatic League (medieval merchant league of various free German towns).
ánsar, *m.* (ornith.) graylag goose; goose.
ansarería, *f.* goose farm.
ansarero, ra, *m., f.* gooseherd, goose keeper.
ansarino, na, *a.* pertaining to geese. —*m.* gosling.
ansarón, *m., var. of* **ánsar.**
anseático, ca, *a.* Hanseatic, pertaining to the medieval league of free German towns.
ansí, *adv.* (arch.) *var. of* **así.**
ansia, *f.* 1. anxiety, anguish. 2. yearning, longing. 3. (fig.) torture. 4. (*pl.*) nausea, sickness.
ansiadamente, *adv., var. of* **ansiosamente.**
ansiar, (*ref. 54 and regular*) *tr.v.* to yearn for, long for. — **a.** + *inf.,* to long or yearn to + *inf.,* e.g. *a. volar,* to yearn to fly or flee.
ansiático, ca, *a., var. of* **anseático.**
ansiedad, *f.* anxiety; worry.
ansina, *adv.* (arch.) *var. of* **así.**
ansiosamente, *adv.* anxiously.
ansioso, sa, *a.* anxious; worried; eager. — a. de, anxious for, yearning for, eager for.
anta, *f.* 1. (zool.) elk. 2. (Amer.) tapir. 3. (archeol.) menhir, megalith. 4. (archit.) anta.
antagalla, *f.* (mar.) spritsail reef bands.
antagallar, *tr.v.* (mar.) to reef (the spritsail).
antagónico, ca, *a.* antagonistic, opposed, opposing, contrary.
antagonismo, *m.* antagonism, opposition; rivalry.
antagonista, *m., f.* antagonist, rival, opponent, adversary. —*m.* 1. (anat.) antagonist, counteracting muscle or nerve. 2. (mec.) reactive spring.
antana, (coll.) **llamarse a.,** to go back on one's word.
antanaclasis, *f.* (rhet.) antanaclasis, repetition of a word but giving it a different or contrary sense.
antañada, *f.* (rare) dated news.
antañazo, *adv.* (coll.) a long time ago.
antaño, *adv.* 1. long ago, of yore. 2. last year.
antañón, na, *a.* very old, ancient.
antarca, *adv.* (Arg., Bol.) on one's back, supine.
Antares, *m.* (astron.) Antares.
antártico, ca, *a.* antarctic. — **círculo polar a.,** Antarctic Circle.
Antártida, *f.* Antarctica, the land area around the S. Pole.
ante, *prep.* before, in front of, in the presence of; in view of, with regard to. — **a. todo,** above all, first of all. —*m.* 1. elk; African antelope, bubal. 2. buckskin, buff. 3. (Mex.) tapir. 4. first course (of dinner). 5. (Peru) cold fruit and wine punch.
anteado, da, *a.* buff-colored.
antealtar, *m.* (ecc.) chancel.
anteanoche, *adv.* night before last, two nights ago.
anteanteanoche, *adv.* three nights ago.
anteanteayer, *adv.* three days ago.
anteantenoche, *adv., var. of* **anteanteanoche.**
anteantier, *adv., var. of* **anteanteayer.**
anteayer, *adv.* the day before yesterday. — **anteayer tarde** or **noche,** the day before yesterday in the afternoon or the night before last.
antebrazo, *m.* forearm; (vet.) shoulder (quadrupeds).
anteburro, *m.* (zool.) Mexican tapir.
antecama, *f.* bedside rug.
antecámara, *f.* antechamber, outer chamber, anteroom. — **a. de compresión,** air lock.
antecapilla, *f.* antechapel, anteroom or vestibule of a chapel.
antecedente, *a.* antecedent, preceding. —*m.* 1. (gram., log., math.) antecedent. 2. (*pl.*) background, case history, record, e.g. *tiene malos antecedentes,* he has a bad record. — **antecedentes criminales,** criminal record.
antecedentemente, *adv.* previously, before.
anteceder, *tr.v., i.v.* to antecede, precede, go before.
antecesor, ra, *a.* previous, former, preceding. —*m., f.* predecessor. —*m.* forefather, ancestor.
anteclásico, ca, *a.* pre-classical, proto-classical (art, literature, etc.).
anteco, ca, *a.* (geog.) antoecian, antiscian; on the same meridian, but on opposite sides of the equator.
antecocina, *f.* pantry, small storeroom for table and kitchenware.
antecoger, (*ref. 57*) *tr.v.* to pick up (a person, thing) and carry (him or it) in front.
antecoja, antecojo, *ref.* **antecoger.**
antecolumna, *f.* (archit.) column of a porch.
antecoro, *m.* antechoir, the entrance leading to the choir.
antecristo, *m., var. of* **anticristo.**
antedata, *f.* antedate.
antedatar, *tr.v.* to antedate.
antedecir, (*ref. 7*) *tr.v.* to foretell, predict.
antedespacho, *m.* antechamber, vestibule; waiting room of an office.
antedía, *adv.* a few days before; beforehand.
antedicho, cha, *past part. of* **antedecir.** —*a.* aforesaid, foregoing, above-mentioned.
antediciendo, *ref.* **antedecir.**
antediga, antedigo, *ref.* **antedecir.**
antedije, antedijera, antedijese, *ref.* **antedecir.**
antediluviano, na, *a.* antediluvian.
antefija, *f.* (archit.) antefix; eaves, gable end.
antefirma, *f.* 1. closing (of a letter). 2. title affixed before a signature.
antefoso, *m.* (fort.) outer moat.
anteguerra, *f.* pre-war period.
antehistórico, ca, *a.* prehistoric.
anteiglesia, *f.* 1. atrium, porch, portico (of a church). 2. parish church, parish (district).
anteislámico, ca, *a.* pre-Islamic.
antejo, *m.* (bot.) Cuban wood-bearing tree.
antelación, *f.* previousness, precedence, anteriority, anticipation, advance. — **con a.,** in advance, with anticipation; in good time.
antelar, *tr.v.* (Chile, Mex.) to anticipate.
antelia, *f.* (meteorol.) anthelion.
antellevar, *tr.v.* (Mex.) to run down (a pedestrian).
antemano, *adv.* **de a.,** beforehand, in advance.
antemeridiano, na, *a.* antemeridian, before noon, (a. m.).
antemio, *m.* (archit.) anthemion.
antemural, *m.* (fort.) defense, rampart, protection.
antena, *f.* 1. (rad.) antenna, aerial; **en a.,** on the air; 2. (zool.) antenna (sensory organ). 3. (mar.) lateen yard. — **a. adaptada en delta,** (rad.) Y antenna; **a. antiparasitaria,** (rad.) noise-reducing antenna; **a. compensadora** (rad.), balancing

antenna; **a. binomia,** binomial array; **a. de conejo,** rabbit ears, indoor antenna; **a. de cuadro,** radio loop, loop antenna; **a. de haz,** beam antenna; **a. de radar,** radar dish; **a. parabólica** satellite dish, parabolic antenna.
antenacido, da, *a.* prematurely born.
antenado, da, *m.* stepson. *—f.* stepdaughter.
antenatal, *a.* antenatal, prenatal.
antenoche, *adv.* 1. the night before last. 2. (coll.) before nightfall, before dusk.
antenombre, *m.* title (prefixed to a name, such as **don,** etc.).
anténulas, *f.* (*pl.*) (zool.) antennule.
antenupcial, *a.* prenuptial.
anteojera, *f.* 1. spectacle-case. 2. blinder, blinker (for a horse). 3. eyepatch.
anteojero, *m.* maker or vendor of eyeglasses.
anteojos, *m.* (*pl.*) 1. eyeglasses, spectacles. 2. binoculars, spyglasses, opera glasses. 3. blinkers (horse). — **a. de larga vista, a. prismáticos,** binoculars; **a. de campaña,** field glasses; **anteojo de puntería,** sighting telescope.
antepagar, (*ref. 51*) *tr.v.* to pay in advance, pay beforehand.
antepague, antepagué, *ref.* **antepagar.**
antepalco, *m.* (theat.) anteroom to a box.
antepasado, da, *past part. of* **antepasar.** *—a.* of a period preceding another already elapsed, e.g. *el año antepasado,* the year before last. *—m.* ancestor, predecessor.
antepasar, *i.v.* (rare) to precede, go before.
antepechado, da, *a.* parapeted, with a railing; with a sill (window).
antepecho, *m.* 1. railing, rail (of balcony, bridge, etc.); sill (of window); (fort.) parapet, breastwork. 2. breast collar (of a harness). 3. (tex.) breast beam (loom). 4. (min.) bench.
antepenúltimo, ma, *a.* antepenultimate.
antepondré, *ref.* **anteponer.**
anteponer, (*ref. 15*) *tr.v.* 1. to place in front, place before. 2. to prefer, give preference to. *—r.v.* to place oneself in front.
anteponga, antepongo, *ref.* **anteponer.**
anteporta, *f., var. of* **anteportada.**
anteportada, *f.* fly leaf, half title, bastard title.
anteposición, *f.* anteposition (placing before).
anteproyecto, *m.* draft, preliminary plan, preliminary design. — **a. de ley,** draft bill.
antepuerta, *f.* 1. portiere (curtain hanging in front of a door). 2. (fort.) inner gate.
antepuerto, *m.* 1. high ground before a mountain pass. 2. (mar.) outer port.
antepuesto, ta, *irr. past part. of* **anteponer.**
antepuse, *ref.* **anteponer.**
antepusiera, antepusiese, *ref.* **anteponer.**
antequino, *m.* (archit.) cavetto, a concave molding.
antera, *f.* (bot.) anther.
anteridio, *m.* (bot.) antheridium.
anterior, *a.* previous, former, preceding; front; (anat., zool.) anterior. — **a. a,** previous to, prior to.
anterioridad, *f.* anteriority, precedence, previousness. — **con a.,** beforehand.
anteriormente, *adv.* previously, formerly.
antero, *m.* tanner, leather worker.
anterozoide, *m.* (bot.) antherozoid.
antes, *adv.* 1. before, formerly, previously. 2. rather, sooner than. — **a. de,** before, e.g. *a de noche* or *ayer,* before last night or yesterday; **a. de +** *inf.,* before + *ger.* or *indic.,* e.g. *a. de llegar al cruce,* before getting or before one gets to the crossroads; rather than + *inf.,* e.g. *me mataría a. de hacer eso,* I would rather kill myself than do that; **a. (de) que** + *subj.,* before + *indic.,* e.g. *a.* (*de*) *que venga,* before he comes; rather than let or allow + *inf.,* e.g. *eliminarían a sus agentes a.* (*de*) *que cayesen en manos del enemigo,* they would eliminate their agents rather than let them fall into the hands of the enemy; **a.** + *inf.* **que** + *inf.,* rather than, e.g. *a. morir que entregarse,* rather die than surrender; **a. mencionado,** above-mentioned; **de a.,** (coll.) formerly, previously; **cuanto a.,** as soon as possible. *—a.* previous. e.g. *el día a.,* the previous day, the day before. *—conj.* rather, on the contrary, e.g. *el buen pensador no teme a la soledad, antes la desea,* the deep thinker doesn't fear loneliness, rather he seeks it.
antesacristía, *f.* anteroom to a sacristy.
antesala, *f. ante-chamber, anteroom, vestibule.* — **hacer a.,** to be kept waiting, to cool one's heels waiting for someone.
antesalazo, *m.* (Mex.) long wait to see an important person.
antesis, *f.* (bot.) anthesis.
antestatura, *f.* (fort.) improvised entrenchment or rampart.
antetemplo, *m.* porch of a temple.
antevea, anteveo, *ref.* **antever.**
antevenga, antevengo, *ref.* **antevenir.**
antevenir, (*ref. 26*) *i.v.* to precede, go before.
antever, (*ref. 27*) *tr.v.* to foresee.
anteví, anteviendo, anteviera, anteviese, *ref.* **antever.**
antevine, *ref.* **antevenir.**
anteviniendo, anteviniera, anteviniese, *ref.* **antevenir.**
antevíspera, *f.* day before yesterday, two days ago.
antevisto, ta, *irr. past part. of* **antever.**
antiácido, da, *a.* antacid, antiacid, acid-resisting.
antiadherente, *a.* nonstick.
antiéreo, a, *a.* antiaircraft. *—m.* antiaircraft gun.
antiafrodisíaco, ca, *a., m.* (pharm.) anaphrodisiac.
antialcohólico, ca, *a.* antialcoholic.
antialcoholismo, *m.* antialcoholism.
antialérgico, -ca, *a.* antiallergenic.
antiamericano, -na, *a.* un-American.
antiar, *m.* antiar, upas tree (containing poisonous sap).
antiarina, *f.* (chem.) antiarin.
antiartístico, ca, *a.* unaesthetic, contrary to art forms.
antiartrítico, ca, *a.* (med.) antiarthritis.
antiasmático, ca, *a.* (med.) antiasthmatic.
antibactérico, ca, *a.,* antibacterial.
antibalístico, -ca, *a.* antiballistic.
antibaquio, *m.* (poet.) antibacchius.
antibelicista, *a.* antiwar; pacifist. *—m.f.* pacifist.
antibiosis, *f.* (biol.) antibiosis.
antibiótico, ca, *a., m.* (med.) antibiotic.
anticanónico, ca, *a.* anticanonical.
anticapacitivo, va, *a.* (elec., chem.) anticapacitive.
anticatalizador, *m.* (chem.) anticatalyst.
anticatarral, *a.* (med.) anticatarrhal.
anticátodo, *m.* (phys.) anticathode.
anticatólico, ca, *a.* anti-Catholic.
anticiclón, *m.* (meteorol.) anticyclone, high pressure area.
anticiclónico, ca, *a.* anticyclonic.
anticientífico, ca, *a.* unscientific, opposed to science.
anticipación, *f.* 1. anticipation. 2. (rhet.) prolepsis, procatalepsis. — **con a.,** in advance.
anticipadamente, *adv.* in advance.
anticipado, da, *past part. of* **anticipar.** *—a.* in advance (e.g. payment). *—f.* sudden blow, unexpected thrust.
anticipador, ra, *a.* anticipatory. *—m., f.* anticipator.
anticipamiento, *m., var. of* **anticipación.**
anticipar, *tr.v.* 1. to bring forward, advance; anticipate, hasten. 2. to anticipate, pay beforehand; to advance, lend (money). 3. to point out in advance, tell in advance. — **a. agradecimientos,** to thank in advance. *—r.v.* to be early, come early (e.g. train, rains, etc.); **anticiparse a.,** to anticipate, foresee, e.g. *anticiparse a sus deseos,* to anticipate one's wishes; to forestall, e.g. *me anticipé a mi adversario,* I beat my opponent to it.
anticipo, *m.* 1. anticipation. 2. advance, advance payment.
anticlástico, *m.* (math.) anticlastic.
anticlerical, *a., m.* anticlerical.
anticlericalismo, *m.* anticlericalism.
anticlímax, *m.* anticlimax.
anticlinal, *a.* anticlinal. *—m.* (geol.) anticline.
anticlinorio, *m.* (geol.) anticlinorium.
anticloro, *m.* (chem.) antichlor.
anticoagulante, *a., m.* anticoagulant.
anticohesor, *m.* (rad.) anticoherer.
anticolinérgico, ca, *a., m.* (physiol.) anticholinergic.
anticolinesterasa, *f.* (physiol.) anticholinesterase.
anticomunismo, *m.* anticommunism.
anticomunista, *a., m., f.* anticommunist.
anticoncepcional, *a.* contraceptive (measures, device, practices etc.).
anticoncepcionismo, *m.* contraception (ideas, policy, etc.).
anticonformista, *a., m., f.* anticonformist, nonconformist.
anticongelador, *m.* de-icer, anti-icer.
anticongelante, *m.* antifreeze. *—a.* antifreezing.
anticonstitucional, *a.* anticonstitutional, unconstitutional.
anticorrosivo, va, *a., m., f.* anticorrosive, rust-resisting, non-corrosive.
anticresis, *f.* (law) antichresis.
anticresista, *m., f.* (law) creditor in an antichretic contract.
anticrético, ca, *a.* (law) antichretic.
anticristiano, na, *a.* antichristian.
anticristo, *m.* Antichrist.
anticrítico, *m.* anticritic.
anticuado, da, *a.* antiquated, old fashioned, out-of-date, obsolete.
anticuar, *tr.v.* to make antiquated, make old or out-of-date. *—r.v.* to become antiquated or out-of-date.
anticuario, *m.* antiquarian, antiquary; antique dealer.
anticuchero, ra, *m., f.* (Peru) roast meat vendor.
anticucho, *m.* (Peru) marinated meat or fowl skewered on a strip of cane and roasted over a brazier with a sauce of chili pepper.
anticuerpo, *m.* (bac.) antibody.
antidáctilo, *m.* (poet.) anapest.
antidemocrático, ca, *a.* antidemocratic, undemocratic.
antideportivo, va, *a.* unsporting.
antideslizante, *a.* nonslipping; nonskid, antiskid (car tires).
antideslumbrante, *a.* antiglare.
antidetonante, *a.* antiknock. *—m.* antiknock, antidetonant, fuel dope.
antidiftérico, ca, *a.* (med.) antidiphtheritic.
antidinástico, ca, *a.* antidynastic, contrary to a reigning dynasty.
antidotario, *m.* 1. antidotary, pharmacopoeia. 2. place in a drugstore for antidotes.

antídoto, *m.* antidote.
antieconómico, ca, *a.* uneconomic, unprofitable.
antiemético, ca, *a., m.* (pharm.) antiemetic.
antiepiléptico, ca, *a., m.* antiepileptic.
antier, *adv., var. of* **anteayer.**
antiesclavismo, *m.* antislavery.
antiesclavista, *a., m., f.* abolitionist.
antiescorbútico, ca, *a., m.* antiscorbutic.
antiescrofuloso, sa, *a.* antiscrofulous.
antiespasmódico, ca, *a., m.* antispasmodic.
antiestético, ca, *a.* unaesthetic.
antievangélico, ca, *a.* antievangelical.
antifaz, (*pl.* **antifaces**) *m.* mask.
antifebril, *a.* antifebrile, antipyretic.
antifebrina, *f.* (chem.) acetanilide.
antifederalista, *m.* antifederalist.
antifeminismo, *m.* antifeminism.
antifeminista, *a., m., f.* antifeminist.
antifernales, *a.* **bienes a.,** (law) property transferred to wife in marriage contract.
antifidelista, *a.* opposed to Fidel Castro and/or his policies.
antiflogístico, ca, *a., m.* (med.) antiphlogistic.
antífona, *f.* 1. antiphon, verse or verses sung or recited before and after the psalms. 2. (coll.) posterior, backside, behind.
antifonal, *a.* antiphonal. —*m.* antiphonal, antiphonary (book containing antiphons).
antifonario, *a.* antiphonal. —*m.* 1. antiphonary. 2. (coll.) backside, behind.
antifonero, ra, *m., f.* precentor, choir director.
antífrasis, *f.* (rhet.) antiphrasis.
antifricción, *a.* antifriction, e.g. *un metal a.,* an antifriction metal. — **dispositivo de a.,** antifriction device.
antigás, *a.* used against gas, e.g. *máscara a.,* gas mask.
antigénico, ca, *a.* (med.) antigenic.
antígeno, na, *a.* (med.) antigenic. —*m.* antigen.
Antígona, *f.* (myth.) Antigone, daughter of Oedipus.
antigramatical, *a.* ungrammatical.
antigravedad, *f.* weightlessness.
antigripal, *a.* used against influenza.
antigualla, *f.* antique; old-fashioned dress or piece of furniture; jalopy, (old car); old story, (*pl.*) ancient history; old custom.
antiguamente, *adv.* in other times; formerly.
antiguamiento, *m.* antiquation.
antiguar, *tr.v.* to make antiquated. —*i.v.* to acquire seniority of service (in a post or employment). —*r.v.* to become antiquated, become old-fashioned, become out-of-date.
antigubernamental, *a.* antigovernment, antigovernmental.
antigüedad, *f.* 1. antiquity, ancient times. 2. service, years of service (in an employment), seniority. 3. (*pl.*) antiques.
antiguo, gua, *a.* old; ancient, antique; **a. régimen,** ancien régime. — **a la antigua** or **a lo antiguo,** in the old-fashioned way; **de antiguo,** since early times; **en lo antiguo,** in olden times. —*m.* (*pl.*) the ancients.
Antiguo Testamento, (Bib.) Old Testament.
antihelmíntico, ca, *a., m.* (med.) vermifuge.
antiherrumboso, sa, *a.* rust-resisting.
antihigiénico, ca, *a.* unhygienic, unsanitary.
antihigroscópico, ca, *a.* (phys.) nonhygroscopic.
antihistamina, *f.* (pharm.) antihistamine.
antihistamínico, ca, *a., m.* (pharm.) antihistaminic.
antiimperialismo, *m.* anti-imperialism.
antiimperialista, *a., m.* anti-imperialist.
antiinflacionista, *a.* anti-inflationary.
antijurídico, ca, *a.* illegal, unlawful.
antilegal, *a.* illegal, unlawful.
antiliberal, *a.* antiliberal.
antillano, na, *a., m., f.* West Indian, Antillean, Caribbean.
Antillas, *f.* (*pl.*) West Indies, the Antilles. — **A. Francesas,** French Antilles; **A. Mayores,** Greater Antilles; **A. Menores,** Lesser Antilles.
antilogaritmo, *m.* antilogarithm.
antilogía, *f.* antilogy, contradiction.
antilógico, ca, *a.* antilogical.
antílope, *m.* (zool.) antelope.
antimacasar, *m.* antimacassar, furniture guard or slipcover.
antimagnético, ca, *a.* antimagnetic, nonmagnetic.
antimalárico, ca, *a., m.* antimalarial.
antimasónico, ca, *a.* antimasonic.
antimateria, *f.* (phys.) antimatter.
antimilitarismo, *m.* antimilitarism.
antimilitarista, *a., m., f.* antimilitarist.
antimisil *a.* antiballistic. —*m.* antiballistic missile.
antimonárquico, ca, *a.* antimonarchic, antimonarchical.
antimonial, *a.* (chem.) antimonial, containing antimony.
antimoniato, *m.* (chem.) antimonate, salt of antimonic acid.
antimónico, ca, *a.* (chem.) antimonic.
antimonio, *m.* (metal.) antimony, regulus.
antimonita, to, *f.* (geol.) antimonite, stibnite. —*m.* (chem.) antimonite.
antimonopolio, *a.* antitrust.
antimoral, *a.* unmoral, immoral.
antinatural, *a.* unnatural.
antinefrítico, ca, *a.* (med.) antinephritic.
antineurálgico, ca, *a.* (med.) antineuralgic.
antineutrino, *m.* (phys.) antineutrino.
antineutrón, *m.* (phys.) antineutron.
antinodo, *m.* (rad., phys.) antinode.
antinomia, *f.* (law) antinomy.
antinomiano, na, *a.* (rel.) antinomian.
antinómico, ca, *a.* antinomic, contradictory.
antioqueno, na, *a.* Antiochian, of or pertaining to Antioch, ancient capital of Syria. —*m., f.* Antiochian.
antioqueño, ña, *a.* of or from Antioquia (Colombia). —*m., f.* native or inhabitant of Antioquia.
antioxidante, *a., m.* antioxidant; antirust, rustproof.
antipalúdico, ca, *a.* antimalarial.
antipapa, *m.* antipope, illegitimate pretender to the papacy.
antipapado, *m.* antipapacy, illegitimate papacy.
antipapista, *a.* antipapistical, antipapist. —*m., f.* antipapist.
antipara, *f.* 1. screen. 2. gaiter, legging.
antiparásito, ta, *a.* (elec., rad.) antiparasitic, suppressing atmospherics or static. —*m.* (elec., rad.) noise suppressor, device for suppressing atmospherics or static.
antiparero, *m.* soldier wearing gaiters.
antiparras, *f.* (*pl.*) (coll.) spectacles, goggles, specs (coll.), glasses.
antipartícula, *f.* (phys.) antiparticle.
antipatía, *f.* dislike, antipathy, aversion.
antipatice, antipaticé, *ref.* **antipatizar.**
antipático, ca, *a.* 1. disagreeable, unpleasant. 2. antipathetic.
antipatinador, ra, *a.* antiskid (also **antipatinante).**
antipatizar, (*ref. 53*) *i.v.* (Amer.) to dislike, feel antipathy, feel an aversion towards someone or something.
antipatriótico, ca, *a.* unpatriotic.
antipedagógico, ca, *a.* contrary to the principles of teaching; antipedagogic, antipedagogical.
antipendio, *m.* antependium, altarfront.
antiperistáltico, ca, *a.* (zool.) antiperistaltic.
antiperístasis, *f.* antiperistasis.
antipirético, ca, *a., m.* (med.) antipyretic, antifebrile.
antipirina, *f.* (med.) antipyrine.
antípoda, *a.* antipodal. —*m.* 1. antipode, antithesis. 2. (*pl.*) antipodes (places or people on diametrically opposite parts of the globe).— **Antípodas,** (geog.) Antipodes (islands).
antipoético, ca, *a.* antipoetic, unpoetic.
antipolilla, *a.* mothproof. —*m.* moth killer.
antipontificado, *m., var. of* **antipapado.**
antiprogresista, *a., m., f.* reactionary, conservative.
antiprotón, *m.* (phys.) antiproton.
antipútrido, da, *a., m.* (med.) antiputrescent, rot-resistant.
antiquísimo, ma, *a. super. of* **antiguo,** ancient, very old.
antiquismo, *m.* archaism.
antirrábico, ca, *a.* (med.) antirabies.
antirreglamentario, ria, *a.* against regulations, against rules.
antirreligioso, sa, *a.* antireligious.
antirresonante, *a.* soundproof.
antirreumático, ca, *a., m.* antirheumatic.
antiscio, *a., var. of* **anteco,** antiscian.
antisemita, *a.* anti-Semitic. —*m., f.* anti-Semite.
antisemítico, ca, *a.* anti-Semitic.
antisemitismo, *m.* anti-Semitism.
antisepsia, *f.* (med.) antisepsis.
antiséptico, ca, *a.* (med.) antiseptic. —*m.* antiseptic.
antisifilítico, ca, *a.* (med.) antisyphilitic.
antisísmico, ca, *a.* earthquake-proof.
antisocial, *a.* antisocial, unsociable.
antisonoro, ra, *a.* soundproof.
antispasto, *m.* (poet.) an iamb and a trochee.
antistrofa, *f.* (poet.) antistrophe.
antisubmarino, na, *a.* (mil.) antisubmarine.
antisuero, *m.* (med.) antiserum.
antitanque, *a.* (mil.) antitank. — **batería a.,** antitank battery.
antitérmico, ca, *a.* 1. (med.) antipyretic. 2. heatproof.
antítesis, (*pl.* **antitesis**) *f.* antithesis.
antitetánico, ca, *a.* anti-tetanus.
antitético, ca, *a.* antithetic, antithetical.
antitipo, *m.* antitype.
antitóxico, ca, *a.* antitoxic.
antitoxina, *f.* (med.) antitoxin, antibody.
antitrago, *m.* (anat.) antitragus, thicker part of external ear.
antituberculoso, sa, *a.* (med.) antitubercular.
antivaho, *a. invar.* mistproof (*windshield*).
antiveneno, *m.* (med.) antivenin.
antivenéreo, a, *a.* (med.) antivenereal.
antiviral, antivirulento, ta, *a.* antiviral.
antlerita, *f.* (geol.) antlerite, native copper sulphate.
antociana, *f.* (biochem.) anthocyanin.
antocianina, *f.* (biochem.) anthocyanin.
antodio, *m.* (bot.) anthodium.
antófago, ga, *a.* (zool.) anthophagous.
antofita, *f.* (bot.) anthophyte.
antojadizamente, *adv.* capriciously; in a fickle manner.
antojadizo, za, *a.* capricious; whimsical, fickle.
antojado, da, *past part. of* **antojarse.** —*a.* ficle, full of whims and fancies, having a whim or a fancy.
antojarse, *r.v.* to fancy, feel like, have a notion to, e.g. *no hace más que lo que se le antoja,* he does only what he feels like doing; to want,

fancy, take a fancy to, e.g. *se me antojó la flor,* I took a fancy to the flower; to have a notion, think, feel, e.g. *se me antoja que va a llover,* I have a notion that it's going to rain.
antojera, *f., var. of* **anteojera.**
antojito, *m.* appetizer, delicacy; (*pl.*) (Arg., Mex.) tidbits, hors d'oeuvres.
antojo, *m.* 1. whim, fancy, caprice (esp. of a pregnant woman); notion, fancy, idea. 2. (*pl.*) moles, birthmarks. 3. (sl.) irons, chains. — **a su antojo,** as one pleases; **tener antojos,** (Amer., coll.) to be pregnant (woman).
antología, *f.* anthology.
antoniano, na, *a.* of or from the order of St. Anthony. —*m.* member of the order of St. Anthony.
antonimia, *f.* (rhet.) antonymy.
antónimo, ma, *a.* antonymous. —*m.* antonym.
antonomasia, *f.* (rhet.) antonomasia (synecdote in which the name of a well-known person is used instead of an appellative or vice versa); **por antonomasia,** metaphorically.
antonomástico, ca, *a.* (rhet.) antonomastical, antonomastic.
antor, *m.* (law, Sp.) vendor of stolen goods acquired in good faith.
antorcha, *f.* torch, flambeau; welding torch; (fig.) beacon-light, guide; inspiration. — **a. a soplete,** blowtorch; **a. soldadora,** welding torch.
antorchar, *tr.v., var. of* **entorchar.**
antorchero, *m.* cresset, torch holder or socket; sconce.
antoría, *f.* (law, Sp.) right to reclaim stolen goods.
antosta, *f.* (Sp.) fragment or piece of ceiling.
antozoario, *a.* (zool.) anthozoan, anthozoic.
antozoo, *a.* (zool.) anthozoan, anthozoic. —*m.* (*pl.*) Anthozoa.
antraceno, *m.* (chem.) anthracene.
antracífero, ra, *a.* (geol.) anthraciferous.
antracina, *f.* (chem.) anthracine.
antracita, *f.* anthracite, hard coal.
antracítico, ca, *a.* anthracitic.
antracnosis, *f.* (bot.) anthracnose.
antracosis, *f.* (med.) anthracosis, lung disease caused by coal dust.
ántrax, *m.* (med.) anthrax, carbuncle, malignant boil.
antro, *m.* cavern, cave, grotto; (fig.) den (of iniquity); (anat.) antrum. — **a. timpánico,** (anat.) tympanic antrum.
antropocéntrico, ca, *a.* (philos.) anthropocentric.
antropocentrismo, *m.* (philos.) anthropocentrism.
antropofagia, *f.* anthropophagy, cannibalism.
antropófago, ga, *a.* anthropophagous, cannibalistic. —*m., f.* anthropophagus, cannibal; (*pl.*) anthropophagi, cannibals.
antropogenia, *f.* anthropogeny.
antropógeno, na, *a.* anthropogenic.
antropografía, *f.* anthropography.
antropográfico, ca, *a.* anthropographic.
antropoide, *a., m.* (zool.) anthropoid.
antropoideo, a, *a.* (zool.) anthropoidal, anthropoid. —*m.* anthropoid, anthropoid ape.
antropolatría, *f.* anthropolatry, man-worship.
antropología, *f.* anthropology, the study of man.
antropológico, ca, *a.* anthropological.
antropólogo, *m.* anthropologist.
antropómetra, *m.* expert in anthropometry.
antropometría, *f.* anthropometry.
antropométrico, ca, *a.* anthropometric, anthropometrical.
antropomórfico, ca, *a.* anthropomorphic.
antropomorfismo, *m.* anthropomorphism.
antropomorfo, fa, *a.* (zool.) anthropomorphous, anthropoid. —*m.* (zool.) anthropomorph, (*pl.*) Anthropomorpha, anthropoid apes.
antroponimia, *f.* (sociol.) onomastics, onomatology, study of the formation of names and surnames.
antroponímico, ca, *a.* onomastic, concerning the study of names and surnames.
antropónimo, *m.* surname.
antropopiteco, *m.* (paleon.) anthropopithecus.
antruejada, *f.* carnival trick or joke, practical joke.
antruejo, *m.* carnival, three days of carnival before Lent.
antuerpiense, *a.* Antwerp, of or from Antwerp, Belgium. —*m., f.* inhabitant or native of Antwerp.
antuviado, da, *a.* (Mex.) precocious, early. —*f.* (coll.) unexpected blow.
antuviar, *tr.v.* 1. (coll.) to hit unexpectedly. 2. to forestall, anticipate.
antuvión, *m.* (coll.) sudden blow or attack; (fig.) person who delivers a blow first. — **de a.,** suddenly, unexpectedly; **jugar de a.,** (coll.) to beat (someone) to it.
anual, *a.* annual, yearly.
anualidad, *f.* 1. annual occurrence. 2. yearly payment, yearly rent; annuity, year's pay. — **a. incondicional,** annuity certain; **a. pasiva,** annuity payable.
anualmente, *adv.* annually, yearly.
anuario, *m.* 1. yearbook; yearly report. 2. trade or professional directory.
anúbada, *f., var. of* **anúteba.**
anubado, da, *a.* cloudy, clouded, overcast.
anubarrado, da, *a.* cloudy, clouded, overcast.
anublado, da, *past part. of* **anublar.** —*a.* cloudy, clouded, overcast.
anublar, *tr.v.* 1. to cloud; to dim, obscure, darken. 2. to tarnish (reputation), cloud (happiness). 3. to wither (plants). —*r.v.* 1. to cloud over, become cloudy or overcast. 2. to be dampened (joy), to tarnish (reputation). 3. to wither (plants). 4. to fade, disappear (hope).
anublo, *m., var. of* **añublo.**
anucar, *tr.v.* (Quech., Arg.) to wean a child.
anudador, ra, *a.* knotting, tying, joining. —*m.* (tex.) piecer, worker who ties threads together. —*f.* (mec.) knotter.
anudadura, *f., var. of* **anudamiento.**
anudamiento, *m.* knotting, tying; joining.
anudar, *tr.v.* 1. to tie knots in, tie a bow in. 2. to tie together; to join, connect. 3. to continue, pick up (a story, an interrupted conversation). —*r.v.* 1. to get knotted, become tied together. 2. to unite, join together, become joined or united. 3. to become stuntet, withered (plants, animals, etc.).
anuencia, *f.* consent, agreement.
anuente, *a.* consenting, agreeing.
anulable, *a.* annullable, revocable, voidable.
anulación, *f.* annulment, abrogation, nullification. — **a. del juicio,** mistrial.
anulado, da, *past part. of* **anular.** —*a.* annulled, cancelled. — **a. por completo,** cancelled in toto.
anulador, ra, *a.* annulling, abrogating, revoking. —*m., f.* annuller, abrogator, revoker.
anular, *tr.v.* 1. to annul, make null and void, revoke, nullify. 2. to withdraw power or authority from. —*r.v.* 1. to be humiliated. 2. to be passed over (not promoted). 3. to be deprived of power or authority. 4. (math.) to cancel out. —*a.* annular, ring-shaped. —*m.* ring finger.
anulativo, va, *a.* able to annul, voiding, nullifying.
anulete, *m.* (her.) annulet.
ánulo, *m.* (archit.) annulet.
anuloso, sa, *a.* composed of rings; annular, ring-shaped.
anunciación, *f.* 1. announcement. 2. **A.,** (ecc.) Annunciation.
anunciador, ra, *a.* announcing; advertising. —*m., f.* announcer; advertiser; **cartel anunciador,** billboard. —*m.* (elec.) annunciator.
anunciante, *a.* advertising. —*m., f.* advertiser.
anunciar, *tr.v.* 1. to announce; to advertise. 2. to forebode, presage.
anuncio, *m.* 1. announcement. 2. omen, prognostication. 3. advertisement; (tel.) commercial; **a. destacado,** display advertisement; **anuncios breves** or **clasificados** or **por palabras,** classified ads.
anuo, nua, *a.* annual, yearly.
anuresis, *f.* (med.) anuresis, anuria.
anurético, ca, *a.* (med.) anuretic.
anuria, *f.* (med.) anuria, anuresis.
anúrico, ca, *a.* (med.) anuric.
anuro, ra, *a.* (zool.) anurous, tailless. —*m.* (zool.) anuran; (*pl.*) Anura.
anúteba, *f.* 1. call to war, call to arms. 2. (arch.) contribution (in work or money) toward repairs on a fortress. 3. group of people engaged in those repairs.
anverso, *m.* obverse (of coins, medals, etc.).
anzolero, *m.* fishhook maker or seller.
anzuelo, *m.* 1. fishhook. 2. (coll.) lure, bait, attraction, allurement. — **picar** or **tragarse el a., caer en el a.,** (coll.) to fall into the trap, go for the bait, swallow the hook.
aña, *m.* (Peru) *var. of* **añas.**
añacal, *m.* 1. corn porter (who carries wheat to mill). 2. baker's board (for carrying bread).
añada, *f.* 1. season, year, period. 2. strip of land. 3. yearly crop; alternate harvest.
añadido, *past part. of* **añadir.** —*m.* 1. addition, supplement. 2. toupee, hairpiece.
añadidura, *f.* addition; extra weight or measure (given by tradesman over correct weight of item purchased). — **de a.,** extra, for good weight or measure; **por a.,** moreover, besides, in addition (often implying "to make matters worse").
añadir, *tr.v.* to add; to pad.
añafea, *f.* wrapping paper, brown paper.
añafil, *m.* 1. long Moorish trumpet. 2. Moorish trumpeter.
añafilero, *m.* Moorish trumpeter.
añagaza, *f.* 1. bird decoy or lure. 2. trick, snare, bait.
añal, *a.* 1. annual, yearly. 2. year old (cattle). —*m., f.* yearling (calf, kid or lamb). —*m.* offering in memory of a dead person a year after his death.
añalejo, *m.* ecclesiastical calendar.
añapa, *f.* (Arg., Chile) drink made with carob beans; (Bol.) carob bean meal. — **hacer a. una cosa,** to break something to smithereens.
añapanco, *m.* (bot., Bol.) lady-of-the-night cactus.
añas, *f.* 1. (Peru, zool.) conepate, small white striped skunk (Conepatus chinga). 2. (S. Amer.) a species of fox.
añascar, (*ref. 50*) *tr.v.* 1. (coll.) to collect or gather together bit by bit. 2. to tangle, muddle. —*r.v.* to get tangled or muddled up.
añasco, *m.* tangle, muddle.
añasque, añasqué, *ref.* **añascar.**
añejamiento, *m.* aging.
añejar, *tr.v.* to age; to cure. —*r.v.* to age; to mature; to go stale.
añejo, ja, *a.* old, aged (said of wine); old; stale.
añero, ra, *suffix,* e.g. **quinceañera** fifteen-year-old girl.
añicos, *m.* (*pl.*) fragments, smithereens. — **hacerse a.,** (coll.) to exert oneself to the utmost, do one's utmost; to be broken or smashed to smithereens.

añil, *m.* 1. indigo (plant, dye, color). 2. blue, bluing (used in laundering).
añilal, *m.* (Col.) indigo field.
añilar, *tr.v.* to dye indigo, blue.
añilería, *f.* indigo plantation and processing plant.
añinero, *m.* worker or dealer in lambskins.
añino, na, *a.* year-old, yearling (lambs). *—m.* 1. yearling (lamb). 2. (*pl.*) fleecy lambskin; lamb's wool.
año, *m.* year. — **a. académico,** academic year; **a. anomalístico,** (astron.) anomalistic year; **a. árabe,** lunar year; **a. astral,** (astron.) astral year; **a. bisiesto,** leap year; **a. civil,** civil year, calendar year; **a. climatérico,** climacteric year; calamitous year; **a. común,** common lunar year; **a. defectivo,** defective year; **a. de gracia,** year of grace, year of Our Lord; **a. luz,** (astron.) light-year; **a. económico,** fiscal year; **a. emergente,** year starting on any set date and ending on the same date the following year; **a. en curso,** current year; **a. escolar,** school year; **a. fiscal,** fiscal year; **a. intercalar,** leap year; **a. lectivo,** school year; **a. lunar,** (astron.) lunar year; **a. luz,** (astron.) light year; **a. político,** civil year; **a. sabático,** sabbatical; **a. sideral** or **sidéreo,** sidereal year; **a. trópico,** tropical year; **a. y vez,** (said of land) planted every other year, (said of fruit trees) bearing fruit every other year; **de buen a.,** fat and healthy; **el a. verde,** (Arg., Par., Ven.) never; **en el a. de la nana,** years ago, many years ago, in the year one; **entrado en años,** advanced or getting on in years; **entre a.,** during the year; **¡ Feliz Año Nuevo!** Happy New Year; **ganar a.,** (coll.) to pass final examinations; **los años veinte, treinta,** etc., the Twenties, Thirties, etc.); **perder a.,** (coll.) to fail final examinations; **por el a. . . . ,** around the year . . . ; **quitarle años a uno,** to take years off one, make one look younger; **tener tantos años,** to be so many years old; **¿cuántos años tiene usted?** how old are you?
añojal, *m.* fallow land, land left fallow for a period of time.
añojo, ja, *m., f.* yearling (calf or lamb).
añoranza, *f.* 1. nostalgia; sadness, grief. 2. loneliness (due to absence or loss).
añorar, *tr.v.* to pine for, miss; to grieve for. *—i.v.* to pine, feel nostalgic; to grieve.
añoso, sa, *a.* old, aged, advanced in years.
añublar, *tr.v., var. of* **anublar.**
añublo, *m.* mildew, blight (on wheat, etc.).
añudador, ra, *a., var. of* **anudador.**
añudadura, *f., var. of* **añudamiento.**
añudamiento, *m.* knotting, tying, joining.
añudar, *tr.v., var. of* **anudar.**
añusgar, (*ref. 51*) *i.v.* 1. to choke. 2. to get angry or annoyed.
añusgue, añusgué, *ref.* **añusgar.**
aojada, *f.* (Col.) skylight, bull's-eye, transom.
aojador, ra, *a.* bewitching. *—m., f.* hoodooer, jinxer.
aojamiento, *m.* bewitching, hoodooing, jinxing; spell, curse.
aojar, *tr.v.* 1. to bewitch, jinx, give (a person) the evil eye. 2. (fig.) to spoil, break, render useless.
aojo, *m.* evil eye, spell, charm, curse.
Aónides, *f.* (*pl.*) the Muses.
aoristo, *m.* aorist, aorist tense (in Greek).
aorta, *f.* (anat.) aorta.
aórtico, ca, *a.* (anat.) aortic, aortal.
aortitis, *f.* (med.) aortitis.
aovado, da, *a.* oval, egg-shaped; (bot.) ovate.
aovar, *i.v.* to lay eggs.
aovillarse, *r.v.* to curl up, roll up into a ball; to shrink.
apa, al a. (Chile) carried on one's back. *—interj.* exclamation to encourage oneself or another to get up or lift a weight; (Mex.) exclamation denoting puzzlement or surprise.
apabilar, *tr.v.* to trim (a candlewick).
apabullamiento, *m.* 1. (coll.) squashing, crushing, flattening. 2. (coll.) silencing, crushing, squashing.
apabullar, *tr.v.* 1. (coll.) to crush, squash, flatten. 2. (coll.) to silence, crush, squash (e.g. with arguments). — **no me apabulles,** don't overwhelm me.
apabullo, *m.* 1. (coll.) squashing, crushing, flattening. 2. (coll.) silencing, squashing, crushing.
apacentadero, *m.* pasture, grazing ground.
apacentador, ra, *a.* 1. pasturing, grazing. 2. nourishing, fostering. *—m., f.* nourisher, fosterer. *—m.* shepherd, herdsman.
apacentamiento, *m.* 1. pasturing, grazing; fodder, feed. 2. nourishing, fostering, feeding.
apacentar, (*ref. 33*) *tr.v.* 1. to graze, pasture (cattle). 2. to teach, instruct. 3. to feed, nourish, foster (desires, passions). 4. (Peru) to pacify. *—r.v.* 1. to graze, pasture. 2. to feed.
apache, *a., m., f.* Apache (Indians). *—m.* 1. apache, criminal, thug. 2. (Mex.) raincoat.
apacheta, *f.* mound of stones erected by Andean Indians as a sign of devotion to a divinity. — **hacer la a.,** (Arg.) to enrich oneself.
apachico, *m.* (Peru) bundle, package.
apachurrar, *tr.v.* to crush, squash, mangle.
apacibilidad, *f.* mildness, placidness; gentleness.
apacible, *a.* mild, placid; gentle; balmy (weather).
apaciblemente, *adv.* mildly, placidly; gently.
apaciente, apaciento, *ref.* **apacentar.**
apaciguador, ra, *a.* soothing, calming, pacifying, appeasing. *—m., f.* pacifier, calmer, appeaser.
apaciguamiento, *m.* pacification, calming, appeasement. — **política de a.,** policy of appeasement.
apaciguar, (*ref. 52*) *tr.v.* to pacify, soothe, calm, appease. *—r.v.* to calm down, become or grow calm.
apacle, *m.* (Nahuatl, Mex.) a medicinal herb.
apadrinador, ra, *a.* sponsoring, backing, supporting; protecting. *—m., f.* sponsor, backer, supporter. *—m.* patron; protector; second. *—f.* patroness; protectress.
apadrinamiento, *m.* sponsoring, backing; seconding (in duel); protection.
apadrinar, *tr.v.* to sponsor; to act as a godfather to; to act as a sponsor for bride or bridegroom at a wedding; to patronize, back; to protect; to second (in a contest or duel); (Arg.) to accompany, ride alongside (someone who is training an unbroken horse). *—r.v.* to avail oneself of someone's help or protection.
apagable, *a.* extinguishable, quenchable.
apagabroncas, (*pl.* **apagabroncas**) *m.* (coll.) bouncer, person who throws undesirable customers out of a night club, bar, or restaurant.
apagadizo, za, *a.* slow to burn, of difficult combustion.
apagado, da, *past part. of* **apagar.** *—a.* 1. out (fire). 2. slaked (lime). 3. hushed, muffled (sounds). 4. listless, lifeless, spiritless (people). 5. dull, faded (colors).
apagador, ra, *a.* extinguishing, dimming; dulling. *—m., f.* extinguisher (person). *—m.* 1. extinguisher, quencher; snuffer (for candles). 2. (mus.) damper; soft-pedal (of a piano).
apagafuego, *m.* fire extinguisher.
apagaincendios, (*pl.* **apagaincendios**) *m.* fire extinguisher; fire engine.
apagallamas, (*pl.* **apagallamas**) *m.* fire extinguisher.
apagamiento, *m.* 1. extinguishing; switching off; going out; going off. 2. slaking. 3. toning down; dimming. 4. fading, subsiding.
apagapenol, *m.* (mar.) leech line.
apagar, (*ref. 51*) *tr.v.* 1. to put out (fire, light); to switch off (light, radio, electricity); to extinguish (fire). 2. to slake (lime). 3. to silence (enemy fire), to deaden (sound). 4. to tone down (colors). 5. to dim, turn down (lights). 6. to dispel, drive away, placate, appease (ill-feeling). — **apagarle a uno los fuegos,** to take the wind out of one's sails; **apaga y vámonos,** let's go; how absurd; how disgusting. *—r.v.* 1. to go out (fire, light); to go off (light, radio); to fail (electricity). 2. to fade, subside, be driven away or dispelled (anger, etc.).
apagavelas, *m.* 1. candle snuffer or extinguisher. 2. (fig.) killjoy.
apagón, *m.* 1. blackout (when electricity fails). 2. (Cuba, Mex.) cigar or coal that dies out often. 3. (Mex.) fast-starting horse that slows down gradually.
apague, apagué, *ref.* **apagar.**
apainelado, *a.* (archit.) **arco a.,** basket handle arch, elliptic arch.
apaisado, da, *a.* oblong, rectangular, of greater width than height.
apaisanarse, *r.v.* (Arg.) to acquire rural or country customs, to become countrified.
apajarado, da, *a.* (Chile, Arg.) scatterbrained. *—m.* (Cuba) effeminate man.
apalabrar, *tr.v.* to arrange beforehand; to discuss beforehand. *—r.v.* to come to an agreement.
Apalaches, *m.* (*pl.*) Appalachian Mountains (U.S.).
apalachina, *f.* (bot.) type of buckthorn.
apalancamiento, *m.* levering, leverage.
apalancar, (*ref. 50*) *tr.v.* to lever, raise or move with a lever.
apalanque, apalanqué, *ref.* **apalancar.**
apalastrarse, *r.v.* 1. (Col., P. Rico, Dom. Rep.) to become faint or weak. 2. (Dom. Rep.) to get worse (illness).
ápale, *interj.* (Mex.) exclamation to indicate surprise or to caution someone.
apaleada, *f.* (Arg., Mex.) *var. of* **apaleo.**
apaleador, ra, *a.* cudgeling, beating. *—m.* beater, cudgeler, assaulter.
apaleamiento, *m.* beating, clubbing, cudgeling.
apalear, *tr.v.* 1. to beat, cudgel, club; to beat (a rug) with a stick; to knock off (fruit) with a pole. 2. to winnow (grain). 3. to shovel. — **a. oro** or **plata,** to be very rich.
apaleo, *m.* 1. winnowing; winnowing season. 2. beating, thrashing.
apalmada, *a.* **mano apalmada,** (her.) hand appaumé.
apalpar, *tr.v.* to touch, feel.
apamparse, *r.v.* (Arg.) to become dazed, bewildered.
apanado, da, *past part. of* **apanar.** *—a.* (Chile, Ecuad., Peru) covered with breadcrumbs, breadcrumbed. *—m.* 1. (Chile, Ecuad., Peru) steak dipped in egg and breadcrumbs. 2. (Peru, sl.) beating, thrashing (of a person).
apanalado, da, *a.* honeycombed.
apanar, *tr.v.* 1. (Peru, Ecuad., Chile) to dip in egg and breadcrumbs. 2. (Peru, sl.) to beat up, give a thrashing to (a person).
apancora, *f.* (Chile) spiny crab, sea hedgehog.
apandar, *tr.v.* (coll.) to pinch, swipe, lift, steal.
apandillar, *tr.v.* to form into a gang. *—r.v.* to form a gang, band together.
apandorgarse, *r.v.* (Peru) *var. of* **apoltronarse.**
apangarse, (*ref. 51*) *r.v.* (C. Amer.) to duck, stoop, bend down.

apaniaguado, da, apaniguado, da, *m., f., var. of* **paniaguado.**
apaniaguarse, *r.v.* (Col., P. Rico, Ven.) to plot, conspire.
apanojado, da, *a.* (bot.) panicled, paniculate, paniculated.
apantallado, da, *a.* 1. (elec.) shielded, screened. 2. (Mex.) stupid, foolish.
apantallar, *tr.v.* (rad.) to screen, to shield.
apantanar, *tr.v.* to make swampy or boggy; to flood, waterlog. —*r.v.* to become waterlogged; to become swampy or boggy.
apantuflado, da, *a.* 1. shaped like a slipper. 2. (fig.) unkempt, disheveled.
apañado, da, *past part. of* **apañar.** —*a.* 1. skillful, clever, handy, ingenious. 2. (coll.) suitable, fit. 3. thick or wooly (cloth).
apañador, ra, *m., f.* 1. seizer; pilferer, thief. 2. (Amer.) one who covers up for someone else.
apañadura, *f.* 1. seizing; taking, stealing. 2. preparing, dressing. 3. mending, repairing; repair. 4. (Amer.) protecting. 5. (*pl.*) trimming, edging, border.
apañalarse, *r.v.* (Mex.) to take shelter in a comfortable and safe place.
apañamiento, *m.* 1. seizing; taking, stealing. 2. preparing, dressing. 3. mending, repairing; repair. 4. (Amer.) protection.
apañar, *tr.v.* 1. to pick up; to seize; to steal, take. 2. (Peru) to gather (cotton). 3. to dress, prepare, make smart. 4. (coll.) to wrap up (in warm clothing). 5. (coll.) to mend, repair. 6. (Amer.) to protect, cover up for, make excuses for. —*r.v.* to manage, find a way (to do something). — **apañarselas,** (Amer.) to manage, find a way.
apaño, *m.* 1. seizing; taking, stealing. 2. (coll.) repair, patch, mend. 3. (coll.) knack, ability. 4. (coll.) lover.
apañuscador, ra, *a.* 1. (coll.) crumpling, crushing. 2. (coll.) stealing, pilfering. —*m., f.* 1. (coll.) crumpler. 2. (coll.) pilferer, thief.
apañuscar, (*ref. 50*) *tr.v.* 1. (coll.) to crumple, crush. 2. to take, steal, cop (coll.), swipe (coll.). 3. (Ven.) to crush together.
apañusque, apañusqué, *ref.* **apañuscar.**
apapagayado, da, *a.* parrot-like, aquiline (nose).
aparador, ra, *m., f.* shoe or boot closet. —*m.* 1. sideboard, dresser; (ecc.) credence (table near the altar). 2. workshop. 3. (Mex.) show window, display window. 4. (Hond.) cold drink; afternoon refreshment. — **estar de aparador,** (coll.) to be dressed up and ready to receive (visitors).
aparadura, *f.* (mar.) garboard, garboard strake.
aparar, *tr.v.* 1. to prepare, arrange; to dress, trim, adorn. 2. (carp.) to plane, dub (planks, boards); to dress with an adz. 3. (agr.) to weed, dress. 4. to close (uppers of shoe). 5. to catch or gather with one's hands, skirt or cloak; stretch out one's hand, skirt or cloak for. 6. to peel (fruit). 7. to hand, reach, give.
aparasolado, da, *a.* parasol-shaped; (bot.) umbellate.
aparatarse, *r.v.* 1. to get ready; dress up, spruce up. 2. (Col.) to become overcast and threatening (the sky).
aparatero, ra, *a.* (Chile) showy, spectacular; ostentatious.
aparato, *m.* 1. apparatus, device, appliance, fixture, gadget, machine; (coll.) airplane; (coll.) television set, radio set. 2. pomp, show, ostentation. 3. (anat.) system; **a. circulatorio,** circulatory system; **a. digestivo,** digestive system; **a. respiratorio,** respiratory system. 4. (med.) syndrome. 5. (med.) appliance, bandage, dressing. — **a. auditivo,** hearing aid; **a. crítico,** critical apparatus; **a. de seguridad,** safety device; **a. de mando,** control mechanism; **a. eléctrico,** thunder and lightning; **a. ortopédico,** surgical appliance; **a. volador,** (obs.) flying machine.
aparatoso, sa, *a.* spectacular, showy; ostentatious.
aparcamiento, *m.* parking (of vehicles).
aparcar, (*ref. 50*) *tr.v.* to park or deposit (war material) in a munitions camp or park; to park (a car).
aparcería, *f.* 1. (agricultural) partnership; sharecropping (sharing benefits between tenant farmer and landowner). 2. (Arg.) friendship, comradeship.
aparcero, ra, *m., f.* 1. partner; sharecropper. 2. (Amer.) companion, friend.
apareamiento, *m.* 1. matching; pairing off. 2. mating.
aparear, *tr.v.* 1. to match; to pair off, form into pairs. 2. to mate (animals). —*r.v.* 1. to pair off. 2. to mate.
aparecer, (*ref. 45*) *i.v., r.v.* to appear; to show up, turn up.
aparecido, *past part. of* **aparecer.** —*m.* ghost, specter.
aparecimiento, *m.* apparition, appearing.
aparedar, *tr.v.* to wall up.
aparejadamente, *adv.* aptly, suitably. — **a. acompañado,** suitably accompanied.
aparejado, da, *past part. of* **aparejar.** —*a.* apt, fit, suitable.
aparejador, *m.* foreman builder, overseer; rigger; one who lays out the work.
aparejar, *tr.v.* 1. to prepare, get ready. 2. to dress with care. 3. to harness, saddle. 4. (mar.) to rig, fit out. 5. to prime (canvas), size (with gum or plaster prior to gilding). —*r.v.* to get ready.
aparejería, *f.* (Amer.) saddlery, harness shop.
aparejo, *m.* 1. tackle, block and fall. 2. harness, riding gear. 3. (mar.) rigging. 4. equipment, gear, kit, (*pl.*) tools, instruments, utensils, materials. 5. priming, sizing (action), (*pl.*) priming, sizing, filler (substance). 6. (archit.) layout. 7. (mas.) bond. 8. preparation, arrangement. 9. providing, provision (of materials). — **a. cruzado,** (bldg.) cross or Dutch bond; **a. de cadena,** chain block; **a. de gata,** (mar.) cat tackle; **a. diferencial,** differential hoist, chain block.
aparencial, *a.* (philos.) having only apparent existence.
aparentar, *tr.v.* to feign, simulate, pretend; to look, appear. — **aparenta ser más joven,** he (she) seems younger.
aparente, *a.* 1. apparent, seeming. 2. suitable, fitting, apt. 3. visible. 4. apparent, clear, evident.
aparentemente, *adv.* apparently, seemingly.
aparezca, aparezco, *ref.* **aparecer.**
aparición, *f.* 1. appearance, apparition. 2. apparition, specter, ghost. — **a. gradual,** (cine., tel.) fade-in.
apariencia, *f.* 1. appearance, aspect, look. 2. likelihood, probability. 3. (*pl.*) (theat.) scenic drop. — **salvar las apariencias,** to keep up appearances; **en a.,** apparently.
aparque, aparqué, *ref.* **aparcar.**
aparrado, da, *a.* 1. spreading, growing horizontally, vinelike. 2. squat, stubby, short and fat.
aparragarse, (*ref. 51*) *r.v.* (Amer.) to become squat or stubby; to crouch.
aparrague, aparragué, *ref.* **aparragarse.**
aparrandado, da, *a.* (C. Rica) fatigued from nocturnal revelry.
aparrar, *tr.v.* to espalier, train (branches of tree) horizontally.
aparroquiado, da, *past part. of* **aparroquiar.** —*a.* established in a parish.
aparroquiar, *tr.v.* to get new customers or clients for; (Chile) to get new parishioners for. —*r.v.* to become a parishioner.
apartadamente, *adv.* privately, separately.
apartadero, *m.* 1. siding (for trains), side road, sidetrack (for trolleys); side route (for boats). 2. grazing field (at side of road for passing cattle). 3. sorting room (for wool). 4. (taur.) individual pen. 5. (Mex.) penning, corralling (of cattle). — **a. muerto,** (ry.) dead-end siding.
apartadijo, *m.* 1. recess, alcove, niche. 2. small part, portion. — **hacer apartadijos,** to divide into portions.
apartadizo, za, *a.* retiring, unsociable. —*m.* alcove, recess, niche.
apartado, da, *past part. of* **apartar.** —*a.* 1. remote, distant. 2. different, distinct. 3. withdrawn, remote. —*m.* 1. back room, side room. 2. post office box; post or mail separated for special delivery or disposal. 3. penning, corralling (bulls). 4. committee member of a cattle ranchers' cooperative. 5. (law) section, article (of a decree or law). 6. (min.) smelting house.
apartador, ra, *m., f.* sorter, separater, divider. —*m.* 1. copper refining dish. 2. retort for refining silver. 3. (Ecuad.) goad, stick for driving cattle.
apartamento, *m.* room; apartment, (G.B.) flat.
apartamiento, *m.* 1. separation; moving away, withdrawal, retirement; remoteness, seclusion. 2. retreat, haven, remote place. 3. apartment, (G.B.) flat. 4. withdrawal, waiver (of a court action).
apartar, *tr.v.* 1. to separate; to take aside, take to one side; to put or brush to one side; to drive away, drive off, push away, remove. 2. to dissuade. 3. to sort, classify (wool). 4. to divide into flocks. 5. to pen, put into corrals. 6. (ry.) to shunt. 7. (Mex., min.) to extract (gold from silver ingots). — **a. el grano de la paja,** to separate the wheat from the chaff. —*i.v.* (hunt.) to follow the scent. —*r.v.* 1. to go away, leave, move away, go off, withdraw, retire. 2. to get divorced, divorce. 3. (law) to withdraw from a law suit, desist.
aparte, *adv.* apart; aside, on one side; apart from, besides. — **a. de,** apart from, besides. —*m.* 1. (theat.) aside (remark on stage). 2. new paragraph. 3. (Arg.) penning, corralling (in rodeo).
apartheid [a'partej] *m.* apartheid.
apartidar, *tr.v., r.v.* to take sides with, back, support.
apartijo, *m.* 1. alcove, recess. 2. small portion.
apartotel, *m.* apartment hotel.
aparvar, *tr.v.* to heap together (grain for threshing); (fig.) to heap together, gather, collect.
apasionadamente, *adv.* passionately, vehemently; unfairly, in a biased way.
apasionado, da, *a.* 1. passionate. 2. mad (about), devoted (to), ardently fond (of), e.g. *a. por ella,* madly in love with her.
apasionamiento, *m.* passion, vehemence, emotion, excitement, enthusiasm.
apasionante, *a.* exhilarating, exciting.
apasionar, *tr.v.* 1. to impassion; to excite, fill with enthusiasm. 2. to torment, afflict. —*r.v.* to become impassioned or excited. — **apasionarse por,** to be or become passionately fond of, develop great enthusiasm for, be or become mad about, be or become very enthusiastic about.
apasote, *m.* (bot.) wormseed.
apastar, *tr.v.* to graze, pasture.
apaste, *m.* (Guat., Hond., Mex.) earthenware tub with handles.
apatanado, da, *a.* rough, coarse, rude, ill-mannered.
apatía, *f.* apathy, indifference.
apático, ca, *a.* apathetic.

apatita, *f.* (min.) apatite.
apátrida, *a.* stateless. —*m., f.* 1. stateless person. 2. (Arg.) a person who does not love his country.
apatusco, *m.* 1. (coll.) ornament, decoration, piece of finery. 2. (coll.) utensil, tool. 3. (Ven.) intrigue, fraud.
apayasar, *tr.v.* to make farcical or ridiculous. —*r.v.* to act the clown.
apazote, *m.* (Amer., bot.) wormseed.
apea, *f.* 1. hobble (for horses). 2. (min.) mine prop, pit prop.
apeadero, *m.* 1. horse block, mounting block. 2. resting place, wayside inn; small wayside station or bus depot. 3. (coll.) temporary lodging place, pied-à-terre.
apeador, ra, *a.* surveying. —*m.* surveyor.
apealar, *tr.v.* (Amer.) to hobble (horse).
apeamiento, *m.* 1. dismounting; alighting. 2. propping, shoring (of a building). 3. surveying.
apear, *tr.v.* 1. to help dismount; to help get down, help get out (of a carriage, etc.). 2. to fetter, hobble, shackle (a horse); to scotch, chock (a wheel). 3. to survey, mark boundaries of (land). 4. to fell (a tree). 5. to overcome, surmount (difficulties). 6. (coll.) to dissuade. 7. (archit.) to shore, stay, prop (a building, etc.). 8. (archit.) to lower (from its place); (Mex.) to bring down, lower. 9. (C. Amer.) to tell off, rebuke. — **a. el tratamiento,** to dispense with honorary titles. —*r.v.* 1. to dismount (from a horse); to alight, get out (from a carriage). 2. to be dissuaded, decide otherwise. 3. to lodge, put up, stay.
apechar, *i.v.* **a. con,** to accept stoically, put up with.
apechugar, (*ref.* *51*) *tr.v.* 1. (Amer.) to take, steal, make off with. 2. (Peru, Ecuad.) to grab, seize, take hold of. —*i.v.* to buffet with the chest. — **a. con,** to put up with, accept stoically.
apechugue, apechugué, *ref.* **apechugar.**
apedace, apedacé, *ref.* **apedazar.**
apedazar, (*ref.* *53*) *tr.v.* 1. to tear to pieces, to bits. 2. to mend, patch, repair.
apedernalado, da, *a.* hard, flinty.
apedreado, da, *past part. of* **apedrear.** —*a.* variegated, spotted, speckled.
apedreador, ra, *m., f.* stoner, stone thrower.
apedreamiento, *m.* 1. stoning; stoning to death. 2. hail, hail storm; damage caused by hail.
apedrear, *tr.v.* to stone; to attack by stoning. —*impers. v.* to hail. —*r.v.* to be damaged through hail (crops).
apedreo, *m., var. of* **apedreamiento.**
apegadamente, *adv.* fondly, affectionately.
apegarse, (*ref.* *51*) *r.v.* 1. to become fond (of), become attached (to). 2. (Ecuad.) to approach.
apego, *m.* fondness, affection, attachment.
apegualar, *i.v.* (Arg., Chile) to tie the bridle to a ring on the saddle.
apegue, apegué, *ref.* **apegarse.**
apelable, *a.* (law) appealable.
apelación, *f.* 1. appeal. 2. (coll.) medical consultations. — **interponer a.,** (law) to appeal, file an appeal; **no hay or no tiene a.,** (coll.) there is no way out (no remedy).
apelado, da, *past part. of* **apelar.** —*a.* (law) of an appellee, pertaining to an appellee. —*m., f.* (law) appellee.
apelado, da, *a.* evenly colored (horses).
apelambrar, *tr.v.* to lime (hides), to remove hair.
apelante, *a.* appellant, appealing. —*m., f.* appellant.
apelar, *i.v.* 1. to appeal, make an appeal. 2. to appeal, have recourse. 3. to refer. — **a. a,** to appeal to; to have recourse to; **a. a, ante or para,** to appeal to, make an appeal to (e.g. a higher court). 4. to be of the same color (horses).
apelativo, *a., m.* (gram.) appellative. —*m.* (Amer.) surname.
apeldar, *i.v.* (coll.) to take to flight, flee, run away. — **apeldarlas,** to run away, flee, to take it on the lam (sl.).
apelde, *m.* 1. dawn chime, ringing of a bell before daybreak (in Franciscan monasteries). 2. (coll.) flight, running away.
apellar, *tr.v.* to dress (leather).
apellidador, ra, *a.* naming. —*m., f.* name giver. —*m.* clansman, warrior (belonging to a group having the same surname).
apellidamiento, *m.* 1. naming. 2. calling, summoning.
apellidar, *tr.v.* 1. to call, name. 2. to call by the surname. 3. to call, to summon. —*r.v.* to be called, be named.
apellidero, *m.* clansman, warrior (belonging to a group having the same surname).
apellido, *m.* 1. surname, family name, last name; name; nickname. 2. clan, host brought together by the same surname.
apelmace, apelmacé, *ref.* **apelmazar.**
apelmazadamente, *adv.* compactly, heavily.
apelmazar, (*ref.* *53*) *tr.v.* to compress, make compact. —*r.v.* to become compact or compressed.
apelotonar, *tr.v.* to form into balls. —*r.v.* to form balls, curl up.
apena, *adv., var. of* **apenas.**
apenado, da, *a.* 1. sorry, sad; embarrassed. 2. shy, bashful.
apenar, *tr.v.* to sadden, cause pain to. —*r.v.* to feel sad or sorrowful; to grieve; (C. Amer.) to feel shy or embarrassed in company.
apenas, *adv.* scarcely, barely, hardly. —*conj.* no sooner than, as soon as. — **a. si,** scarcely, hardly.
apencar, (*ref.* *50*) *i.v.* (coll.) **a. con,** to accept stoically, put up with.
apendectomía, *f.* (med.) appendectomy.
apéndice, *m.* 1. appendage, appurtenance, adjunct. 2. appendix (of a book). 3. (coll.) appendage, crony, hanger-on. 4. (aer.) appendix (tube at bottom of balloon). 5. (biol., zool.) appendage, appendix; (anat.) appedix. — **a. cecal,** vermicular or **vermiforme,** (anat.) appendix, vermiform appendix.
apendicectomía, *f.* (med.) appendectomy.
apendicitis, *f.* (med.) appendicitis.
apendicular, *a.* appendicular.
Apeninos, *m.* (*pl.*) Apennines (mountains in Italy).
apenque, apenqué, *ref.* **apencar.**
apensionar, *tr.v.* to pension, grant a pension to. —*r.v.* (Chile) to become sad or distressed.
apeñuscar, (*ref.* *50*) *tr.v.* (Amer.) to press together, crush. —*r.v.* to crowd or cram together.
apeñusque, apeñusqué, *ref.* **apeñuscar.**
apeo, *m.* 1. surveying (an estate); (law) document attesting the boundaries and limits of an estate. 2. shoring up (a building); (bldg.) shores, props, stays.
apeonar, *i.v.* to run (a bird).
apepsia, *f.* (med.) apepsia.
apepu, *m.* (Amer.) orange-like tree and its fruit.
aperador, *m.* 1. foreman of a farm or mine. 2. wheelwright.
aperar, *tr.v.* 1. to make or repair (wagons, farm equipment). 2. (Ven., Arg.) to saddle, harness. —*r.v.* (Amer.) to provide oneself with clothes, food or tools.
apercepción, *f.* (psyc.) apperception.
aperceptivo, va, *a.* (psyc.) apperceptive.
apercibimiento, *m.* 1. provision, furnishing; preparation. 2. (law) warning, caution. 3. awareness.
apercibir, *tr.v.* 1. to provide, furnish; to prepare, arrange. 2. to warn, caution. 3. to observe, notice, perceive. 4. (law) to warn, caution. — **apercibirse de,** to become aware of; to provide oneself with.
apercollar, (*ref.* *33*) *tr.v.* 1. to seize by the neck. 2. (coll.) to kill by a blow on the neck. 3. (coll.) to snatch, grasp, seize.
aperdigar, (*ref.* *51*) *tr.v.* to broil lightly.
aperdigue, aperdigué, *ref.* **aperdigar.**
apereá, *m.* (Amer.) cavy, guinea pig (Cavia aparea or Cavia pamperum).
apergaminado, da, *past part. of* **apergaminarse.** —*a.* parchment-like; wrinkled.
apergaminarse, *r.v.* (coll.) to become lean and wrinkled.
aperiódico, ca, *a.* (phys.) aperiodic.
aperitivo, va, *a.* appetizing; (med.) aperient, aperitive. —*m.* 1. appetizer; aperitif, (pre-meal drink). 2. (med.) aperitive, aperient.
aperlado, da, *a., var. of* **perlado.**
apernador, ra, *a.* (hunt.) seizing game by the leg.
apernar, (*ref.* *29*) *tr.v.* (hunt.) to seize (game) by the leg.
apero, *m.* 1. tools, equipment, gear, outfit; (Amer.) riding gear, saddle. 2. farm draft animals.
aperreado, da, *past part. of* **aperrear.** —*a.* difficult, wearisome, (coll.) dog-like. — (Mex.) **¡qué vida más a.!** it's a dog's life.
aperreador, ra, *a.* (coll.) wearisome, annoying. —*m., f.* pest, nuisance, plague.
aperrear, *tr.v.* 1. to set dogs on. 2. (coll.) to plague, pester, weary, annoy, fatigue. —*r.v.* 1. to get annoyed, grow weary or fatigued. 2. (coll.) to be obstinate, stand one's ground obstinately.
aperreo, *m.* annoyance, trouble; work, toil.
apersogar, (*ref.* *51*) *tr.v.* to tether, tie; to string together.
apersogue, apersogué, *ref.* **apersogar.**
apersonado, da, *past part. of* **apersonarse.** —*a.* **bien a.,** personable, presentable, of good presence; **mal a.,** not presentable.
apersonamiento, *m.* (law) appearance.
apersonarse, *r.v.* to appear, appear in person, present oneself; (law) to appear.
apertura, *f.* 1. opening, beginning, commencement (of work, studies, etc.); opening (in chess). 2. opening or reading of a will. 3. move, step, e.g. *el partido centrista hizo una a. a la izquierda,* the center party moved to the left.
apesadumbrado, da, *a.* burdened; afflicted, saddened, grieved.
apesadumbrar, *tr.v.* to distress, grieve. —*r.v.* to be grieved, be distressed. — **apesadumbrarse de or con,** to be grieved or distressed by or at.
apesaradamente, *adv.* sorrowfully, sadly.
apesarado, da, *a.* (Arg., Chile), *var. of* **apesadumbrado.**
apesarar, *tr.v., r.v., var. of* **apesadumbrar.**
apesgamiento, *m.* 1. load, burden. 2. burdening, fatiguing, tiring.
apesgar, (*ref.* *51*) *tr.v.* to burden, fatigue, tire.
apesgue, apesgué, *ref.* **apesgar.**
apestante, *a.* smelly, stinking.
apestar, *tr.v.* 1. to infect with the plague. 2. to corrupt, vitiate. 3. to annoy, tire, irritate, bore. — **estar apestado de,** to be lousy with. —*i.v.* to stink, smell. —*r.v.* 1. to be infected with the plague, catch the plague. 2. (Col., Peru) to catch cold.
apestillar, *tr.v.* 1. to fasten, secure, tackle. 2. (coll.) to catch and tie (a person).
apestoso, sa, *a.* 1. foul-smelling, stinking. 2. annoying, irritating. — **ser un a.,** to be a bore or a pest.
apétala, *a.* (bot.) apetalous, having no petals.
apetecedor, ra, *a.* desiring, craving, longing.
apetecer, (*ref.* *45*) *tr.v.* to long for, yearn for, crave for.

apetecible, *a.* appetizing; desirable, tempting.
apetencia, *f.* appetite, hunger; desire, craving.
apetezca, apetezco, *ref.* **apetecer.**
apetite, *m.* 1. appetizing sauce. 2. stimulant, spur, incentive.
apetitivo, va, *a.* 1. appetitive. 2. appetizing, delicious, tasty.
apetito, *m.* appetite. — **a. concupiscible,** sexual appetite or desire; **abrir** or **despertar el a.,** to whet the appetite.
apetitoso, sa, *a.* appetizing; tasty, delicious.
ápex, *m.* 1. (astron.) solar apex, apex of the sun's motion or way. 2. (anat.) apex.
apezonado, da, *a.* nipple-shaped.
apezuñar, *i.v.* to dig hooves into the ground (horses or cattle).
apiadador, ra, *a.* pitying, filled with pity, tender-hearted.
apiadar, *tr.v.* 1. to fill with pity. 2. to pity, treat with pity. —*r.v.* to have pity, be filled with pity. — **apiadarse de,** to have pity on.
apianar, *tr.v.* to soften, lower (sound or voice).
apiaradero, *m.* tally, account of number of livestock.
apical, *a.* apical. —*f.* apical consonant.
apicararse, *r.v.* to become cunning, become a rogue.
ápice, *m.* 1. apex, top, tip, point, vertex, summit. 2. apex, tittle, jot, orthographical sign. 3. iota, jot, whit, fraction. 4. (coll.) crisis, crux. — **estar en los ápices de,** (coll.) to understand completely, know from A to Z; **(no) importar un á.,** (not) to care a whit.
apícola, *a.* apicultural, pertaining to the bee.
apículo, *m.* (bot.) apiculus.
apicultor, ra, *m., f.* apiculturist, beekeeper.
apicultura, *f.* apiculture, beekeeping industry.
apichonado, a, *m., f.* (Chile) in love.
apichu, *m.* (Bol., Peru, Quech.) sweet potato.
apierna, apierne, *ref.* apernar.
apilada, *f.* smoked and dried chestnut.
apilamiento, *m.* piling up, heaping up; pile.
apilar, *tr.v.* 1. to pile up, heap up. 2. (coll.) to amass, hoard (money).
apilonar, *tr.v.* (Amer.) to heap up, pile up.
apimplarse, *r.v.* (coll.) to get drunk, get high.
apimpollarse, *r.v.* 1. to bud, sprout (plants). 2. to spruce, smarten up.
apiñado, da, *past part. of* **apiñar.** —*a.* 1. cone-shaped. 2. crammed or packed together.
apiñadura, *f., var. of* **apiñamiento.**
apiñamiento, *m.* crowding or cramming together; crush, crowd.
apiñar, *tr.v., r.v.* to crowd, cram or pack together.
apiñonado, da, *a.* (Mex.) dark-skinned (person).
apio, *m.* (bot.) celery. — **a. caballar, cimarrón** or **equino,** smallage, wild celery; **a. de ranas,** crowfoot; buttercup.
apiolar, *tr.v.* 1. to gyve (a hawk); to tie (a dead animal) by the legs. 2. (coll.) to capture, arrest. 3. (coll.) to kill.
apiparse, *r.v.* (coll.) to gorge (food), overeat; to drink oneself silly.
apir, *m.* (S. Amer.) mine worker.
apiramidado, da, *a.* pyramid-shaped.
apirear, *tr.v.* (Chile) to transport, carry (minerals).
apirético, ca, *a.* (med.) apyretic.
apirexia, *f.* (med.) apyrexia, absence or intermission of fever.
apirgüinarse, *r.v.* (Chile, vet.) to suffer from distomatosis, distomiasis or fascioliasis.
apiri, *m.* (S. Amer., Quech.) mine worker.
apirularse, *r.v.* (Chile) to dress or spruce up.
apis, *m.* (bot.) goosefoot.
apisonador, ra, *a.* tamping; rolling. —*m.* tamper (tool for tamping). —*f.* steam roller, roller.
apisonamiento, *m.* tamping, ramming; rolling; packing down.
apisonar, *tr.v.* to ram down, tamp, pound or pack down; to roll flat.
apitiguarse, (*ref. 52*) *r.v.* (Chile) to become depressed, disheartened or dismayed.
apitonado, da, *a.* punctilious, fussy, fastidious.
apitonamiento, *m.* growing (horn); sprouting, budding.
apitonar, *i.v.* to grow horns; to sprout, bud. —*tr.v.* to break (an egg shell) with its beak (bird). —*r.v.* (coll.) to quarrel, insult one another.
apívoro, ra, *a.* apivorous.
apizarrado, da, *a.* slate-colored.
aplacable, *a.* appeasable, placable.
aplacador, ra, *a.* calming, soothing, placating. —*m., f.* calmer, soother, placator.
aplacamiento, *m.* appeasement, soothing, calming, placating.
aplacar, (*ref. 50*) *tr.v.* to placate, appease, calm, soothe.
aplace, aplacé, *ref.* **aplazar.**
aplacer, (*ref. 13*) *tr.v., i.v.* to please. —*r.v.* to be pleased, take pleasure.
aplacerado, da, *a.* (mar.) level, smooth and shallow.
aplacible, *a.* agreeable, pleasant.
aplaciente, *a.* pleasing, satisfying.
aplanacalles, *m., f. pl.* (Amer.) idler, loafer; stroller.
aplanadera, *f.* leveler; tamper; road roller.
aplanador, ra, *a.* leveling, rolling, flattening. —*m., f.* leveler, roller, flattener. —*m.* tamper (tool for tamping). —*f.* steam roller.
aplanamiento, *m.* 1. leveling, flattening. 2. (coll.) dismay, discouragement.
aplanante, *ref.* **aplanar.**
aplanar, *tr.v.* 1. to level, flatten, smooth (surfaces). 2. (coll.) to stun, bowl over (with news). —*r.v.* 1. to collapse, fall down (a building). 2. (coll.) to become subdued, lose one's vigor, lose heart, become discouraged. — **a. las calles,** (Amer.) to loaf around.
aplanchado, *a.* ironed, well pressed.
aplanchador, ra, *m., f.* ironer, presser.
aplanchar, *tr.v.* to iron, press.
aplanético, ca, *a.* (opt.) aplanatic.
aplantillar, *tr.v.* to cut or carve according to a pattern; to work to a template.
aplaque, aplaqué, *ref.* **aplacar.**
aplastamiento, *m.* crushing, flattening.
aplastante, *a.* 1. crushing, overwhelming, e.g. *victoria a.,* overwhelming victory. 2. exhausting, e.g. *calor a.,* exhausting heat.
aplastar, *tr.v.* 1. to crush, squash, flatten. 2. to crush, overwhelm, put down (rebellion, uprising, etc.). 3. (coll.) to leave speechless, stun, astound, crush, squash. 4. (Arg.) to tire, weary. —*r.v.* to become crushed (by overwork, heat, fatigue).
aplatanado, da, *a.* indolent, passive, apathetic. —*m., f.* (Cuba, P. Rico) a foreigner who has adapted himself to local conditions or who adopts local speech and customs; one who "goes native".
aplatanamiento, *m.* 1. indolence, apathy; growing indolent or apathetic. 2. action and effect of going native or adopting local habits.
aplatanarse, *r.v.* 1. to grow or become lazy, indolent or apathetic. 2. (Cuba, P. Rico) to settle down, get used to the country in which one lives and adopt its customs, e.g. *se aplatanó,* he's gone native.
aplaudidor, ra, *a.* applauding. —*m., f.* applauder.
aplaudir, *tr.v.* 1. to applaud, clap. 2. (fig.) to applaud, commend, praise (decision, etc.).
aplauso, *m.* 1. applause. 2. approbation. — **a. cerrado,** deafening applause.
aplayar, *i.v.* to overflow, inundate, flood the banks (river).
aplazable, *a.* deferable, postponable.
aplazamiento, *m.* 1. summoning. 2. postponement.
aplazar, (*ref. 53*) *tr.v.* 1. to summon. 2. to postpone. 3. (Arg., Urug.) to fail an exam, to flunk.
aplebeyar, *tr.v.* to make common or vulgar; to degrade, debase. —*r.v.* to become common or vulgar.
aplicable, *a.* applicable.
aplicación, *f.* 1. application (such as lotion, poultice, etc.). 2. application, zeal, industry, assiduousness, keenness. 3. appliqué (ornament).
aplicado, da, *past part. of* **aplicar.** —*a.* 1. studious, industrious, zealous. 2. applied (e.g. art, sciences).
aplicar, (*ref. 50*) *tr.v.* 1. to apply, put, place, e.g. *a. una capa de pintura sobre otra,* to apply one coat of paint on another. 2. to apply, use, employ, make use of. 3. to assign; to devote. 4. to apply, bring to bear on. 5. to impute, attribute. 6. (law) to adjudge. —*r.v.* 1. to be applied, used or employed. 2. to apply, devote or dedicate oneself. 3. to apply, be pertinent, have a bearing on.
aplique, apliqué, *ref.* **aplicar.**
aplique, *m.* 1. (theat.) complementary piece of stage scenery. 2. wall light or lamp.
aplita, *f.* (geol.) aplite.
aplomado, da, *past part. of* **aplomar.** —*a.* 1. poised, self-assured, serious, solemn. 2. lead-colored.
aplomar, *tr.v.* 1. make heavier. 2. (bldg.) to plump (a wall). 3. (bldg.) to make or build vertically. —*i.v.* to be plumb, perpendicular. —*r.v.* 1. to become heavier. 2. to collapse, fall to the ground. 3. to become serious or settled (in character).
aplomo, *m.* 1. aplomb, poise, self-assurance. 2. conformation (alignment) of a horse's (or other animal's) feet and legs. 3. verticality, perpendicularity. 4. plumb (bob and line).
apnea, *f.* (med.) apnea, suspension of respiration.
apoastro, *m.* (astron.) apogee.
apocadamente, *adv.* 1. timidly, irresolutely, pusillanimously. 2. humbly.
apocado, da, *past part. of* **apocar.** —*a.* 1. bashful, timid, vacillating, pusillanimous. 2. humble, shy.
apocador, ra, *a.* reducing, lessening.
Apocalipsis, *m.* (Bib.) Apocalypse.
apocalíptico, ca, *a.* apocalyptic; (coll.) chaotic.
apocamiento, *m.* 1. timidity, vacillation, irresolution, pusillanimity. 2. depression, low spirits.
apocar, (*ref. 50*) *tr.v.* 1. to lessen, reduce; to limit, restrict, cramp. 2. to cow, humble, intimidate. —*r.v.* to become cowed, humble oneself; to get intimidated or scared, get cold feet.
apocárpico, ca, *a.* (bot.) apocarpous.
apocatástasis, *f.* (philos.) apocatastasis.
apócema, *f.* (pharm.) potion, apozem.
apochongamiento, *m.* (Arg., Urug.) fear, cowardice.
apochongarse, *r.v.* (Arg., Urug.) to fear, to cow, to draw back.
apócima, *f.* (pharm.) potion, apozem.
apocináceo, a, *a.* (bot.) apocynaceous. —*f.* (*pl.*) Apocynaceae.
apócopa, *f.* (gram.) *var. of* **apócope.**
apocopar, *tr.v.* (gram.) to apocopate, shorten a word by dropping the last sound or sounds.
apócope, *f.* (gram.) apocope.
apócrifamente, *adv.* apocryphally.
apócrifo, fa, *a.* Apocryphal, pertaining to the Apocrypha; apocryphal, unauthentic.

apocromático, ca, *a.* (opt.) apochromatic.
apodador, ra, *a.* nicknaming. *—m., f.* a person who nicknames.
apodar, *tr.v.* to nickname.
apodencado, da, *a.* hound-like (dog).
apoderado, da, *past part. of* **apoderar.** *—a.* empowered, authorized. *—m.* attorney; manager; agent. — **constituir apoderado,** (law) to grant power of attorney.
apoderamiento, *m.* 1. power of attorney; empowering, authorization. 2. appropriation, seizing, taking possession.
apoderar, *tr.v.* to empower, grant the power of attorney to. *—r.v.* **apoderarse de,** to appropriate, seize, take possession of, take hold of, seize power.
apodia, *f.* apodia, congenital absence of feet.
apodíctico, ca, *a.* (log.) apodictic, apodictical.
apodo, *m.* nickname, agnomen, sobriquet.
ápodo, da, *a.* (zool.) apodal, having no feet.
apódosis, *f.* (gram.) apodosis.
apófice, *f.* (archit.) apophyge.
apófisis, *f.* 1. (anat., zool., geol., bot.) apophysis. 2. (anat.) process (of a bone), e.g. *a. acromial,* acromial process. — **a. alveolar,** alveolar process; **a. basilar,** basilar process; **a. cigomática,** (anat.) zygomatic process; **a. clinoides,** clinoid process; **a. coracoides,** coracoid process; **a. pterigoides,** (med.) pterygoid process.
apofonía, *f.* (phonet.) apophony, ablaut.
apogeo, *m.* (astron.) apogee; (fig.) apogee, height (of fame, power, etc.).
apógrafo, *m.* apograph, transcript.
apolilladura, *f.* moth hole.
apolillamiento, *m.* damage caused by moths.
apolillar, *tr.v.* to damage (clothes, by moths). *—r.v.* to become moth-eaten (clothes).
apolinar, *a.* (poet.) *var. of* **apolíneo.**
apolíneo, *a.* (poet.) Apollonian.
apolismado, da, *a.* (Amer.) damaged; worn; soiled.
apolismar, *tr.v.* (Amer.) to damage, to wear; to soil.
apolítico, ca, *a.* apolitical, nonpolitical.
Apolo, *m.* (myth.) Apollo, Greek and Roman god of the Arts, Poetry and Medicine.
apologética, *f.* (rel.) apologetics.
apologético, ca, *a.* apologetic, defensive, praising, justificatory.
apología, *f.* 1. defense, justification, praise, apologia, apology. 2. (coll.) eulogy, panegyric.
apologice, apologicé, *ref.* **apologizar.**
apológico, ca, *a.* pertaining to apologues or fables.
apologista, *m., f.* apologist, defender, praiser.
apologizar, (*ref. 53*) *tr.v.* to defend, praise, apologize.
apólogo, *m.* apologue, fable.
apoltronado, da, *a.* lazy, idle; sedentary.
apoltronamiento, *m.* laziness, idleness.
apoltronarse, *r.v.* to become sedentary; to become lazy or idle.
apolvillarse, *r.v.* (Chile, agr.) to become infested with bunt (wheat parasite).
apomazar, (*ref. 53*) *tr.v.* to polish or smooth with a pumice stone.
apomorfina, *f.* (chem.) apomorphine.
aponeurosis, *f.* (anat.) aponeurosis.
aponeurótico, ca, *a.* (anat.) aponeurotic.
apontocar, (*ref. 50*) *tr.v.* to prop up, hold up.
apontoque, apontoqué, *ref.* **apontocar.**
apoplegía, *f.* (med.) apoplexy. — **que te da una a.,** (coll.) don't get so excited.
apoplético, ca, *a., m., f.* (med.) apoplectic.
apoque, apoqué, *ref.* **apocar.**
apoquinar, *tr.v.* (sl.) to pay up, cough up, fork over, come across with (information, payment, etc.).
aporca, *f.* (Chile) *var. of* **aporcadura.**
aporcador, ra, *a.* hilling, earthing over; banking up. *—m., f.* a person who earths over vegetables or banks soil around trees.
aporcadura, *f.* (agr.) hilling, earthing over (vegetables); banking up soil around trees.
aporcar, (*ref. 50*) *tr.v.* (agr.) to hill, bank up with soil, earth over.
aporisma, *m.* (med.) ecchymema.
aporismarse, *r.v.* to develop an ecchymema.
aporque, aporqué, *ref.* **aporcar.**
aporque, *m., var. of* **aporcadura.**
aporrar, *i.v.* (coll.) to be left speechless.
aporrarse, *r.v.* (coll.) to be a bore or a nuisance; to become annoying or boring.
aporreado, da, *past part. of* **aporrear.** *—a.* wretched, miserable, hard. *—m.* (Cuba) highly seasoned stew of beef or cod.
aporreador, ra, *m., f.* a person who beats, ill-treats or abuses.
aporreadura, *f., var. of* **aporreo.**
aporreamiento, *m., var. of* **aporreo.**
aporreante, *a.* cudgeling, beating.
aporrear, *tr.v.* 1. to cudgel, club, beat. 2. to swat (flies). 3. to bother, annoy. 4. to abuse, ill-treat. *—r.v.* to slave, work one's fingers to the bone. — **porque te quiero te aporreo,** (coll.) I mistreat you because I love you.
aporreo, *m.* cudgeling, clubbing, beating.
aporretado, da, *a.* short and stubby (fingers).
aporrillarse, *r.v.* (med.) to swell and become stiff (the joints).
aportación, *f.* 1. contribution. 2. dowry.
aportadera, *f.* pannier, grape tub.
aportadero, *m.* 1. port, harbor. 2. stopping-off point.
aportar, *i.v.* 1. to put into port. 2. to arrive or get (somewhere) by chance or accident. 3. to arrive. *—tr.v.* 1. to contribute, bring, e.g. a share. 2. to bring (a dowry).
aporte, *m.* contribution.
aportillar, *tr.v.* 1. (mil.) to pierce, make a breach in (a wall). 2. to break. *—r.v.* to fall down, collapse.
aposentador, ra, *a.* accommodating. *—m.* 1. host, accommodator. 2. a kind of chamberlain or master of the royal house. 3. (mil.) billeting officer.
aposentaduría, *f.* office of the chamberlain.
aposentamiento, *m.* 1. lodging, accommodation. 2. room, lodgings.
aposentar, *tr.v.* to lodge, put up, accommodate, house. *—r.v.* to take rooms, lodge.
aposento, *m.* 1. room, chamber. 2. lodging. 3. (arch., theat.) box. 4. (Cuba, P. Rico) master bedroom.
aposesionar, *tr.v.* to give possession. *—r.v.* to take possession.
aposición, *f.* (gram.) apposition.
apositivo, va, *a.* (gram.) appositional, appositive.
apósito, *m.* (med.) dressing; poultice.
aposta, *adv., var. of* **adrede,** on purpose.
apostadamente, *adv.* (coll.) *var. of* **adrede,** on purpose.
apostadero, *m.* 1. post station. 2. (mar.) naval station. 3. (mar.) naval command (district).
apostante, *a.* betting, wagering.
apostar, (*ref. 33*) *tr.v.* 1. to bet, wager. 2. to post, station. — **a. a** or **por,** to bet on; **a. que,** to bet that. *—i.v.* 1. to compete, vie. 2. to bet. *—r.v.* 1. to station or post oneself. 2. to compete, vie.
apostasía, *f.* apostasy.
apóstata, *m., f.* apostate; renegade.
apostatar, *i.v.* to apostatize, become an apostate.
apostema, *f.* (med.) *var. of* **postema,** aposteme, abscess.
apostemar, *tr.v.* (med.) to form or cause an abscess on. *—r.v.* to abscess, become full of abscesses.
apostemero, *m.* (med.) *var. of* **postemero,** large lancet.
apostemoso, sa, *a.* abscessed.
a posteriori, *adv.* (Lat.) a posteriori; based on experience; subsequent.
apostilla, *f.* footnote, annotation, brief explanation.
apostillar, *tr.v.* to annotate.
apostillarse, *r.v.* (med.) to become marked with scabs.
apóstol, *m.* apostle.
apostolado, *m.* 1. apostolate. 2. propagation of new ideas.
apostólicamente, *adv.* 1. apostolically. 2. (coll.) poorly, modestly.
apostólico, ca, *a.* apostolic.
apostrofar, *tr.v.* 1. to apostrophize, direct an apostrophe at. 2. (coll.) to insult, abuse.
apóstrofe, *m., f.* 1. (rhet.) apostrophe (address). 2. (coll.) insult.
apóstrofo, *m.* apostrophe (orthographic sign).
apostura, *f.* bearing, grace.
apotegma, *m.* apothegm, apophthegm, maxim.
apotema, *f.* (geom.) apothem.
apoteósico, ca, *a.* glorious, grandiose, magnificent.
apoteosis, (*pl.* **apoteosis**) *f.* apotheosis.
apoteótico, ca, *a., var. of* **apoteósico.**
apotrerar, *tr.v.* 1. (Chile, Ecuad.) to divide a ranch into pasture plots. 2. (Cuba to put (cattle) to pasture.
apoyabrazos, *m.* armrest.
apoyacabezas, *m.* headrest.
apoyadura, *f.* flow of milk (to the udders).
apoyar, *tr.v.* 1. to rest, lean. 2. to support, hold up, prop up. 3. to support, aid, help. 4. to confirm, uphold, support. 5. to let down (flow of milk). 6. to droop, drop the head (horses). *—i.v.* to rest, lean; to be supported. *—r.v.* 1. to lean, rest; to be supported. 2. to lean, rely (on someone for help). 3. to be based, be founded. — **apoyarse en,** to base one's opinions on.
apoyatura, *f.* (mus.) appoggiatura, grace note.
apoyo, *m.* 1. support, backing; protection, help, aid. 2. prop, support, stay. — **a. de fuego,** (mil.) fire support; **a. de rodillos,** (mec.) roller bearing.
apozarse, (*ref. 53*) *r.v.* (Amer.) to become stagnant (waters); to form a pool.
APRA *abrrev. of* **Alianza Popular Revolucionaria Americana,** (Peru) American People's Revolutionary Alliance.
apraxia, *f.* (med.) apraxia.
apreciable, *a.* 1. appreciable, considerable. 2. estimable, fine, worthy of esteem.
apreciación, *f.* appreciation, estimation, value.
apreciadamente, *adv.* appreciatively.
apreciador, ra, *a.* appreciative. *—m., f.* appraiser.
apreciar, *tr.v.* 1. to esteem, hold in esteem, value, appreciate, e.g. *lo aprecio mucho,* I hold him in great esteem, *aprecio lo que tú haces,* I appreciate what you are doing. 2. to judge, appreciate, e.g. *hay que a. estas cosas en el terreno,* one has to judge these things on the spot. 3. to appreciate (judge critically), e.g. *él no sabe a. el vino,* he doesn't know how to judge good wine. 4. to appreciate, value, appraise, calculate the value of.
apreciativo, va, *a.* appreciative.
aprecio, *m.* 1. appreciation, estimation, esteem, value. 2. (Mex.) attention. — **no hacer a. a,** not to pay attention to.
aprehender, *tr.v.* 1. to apprehend, catch, capture; (law) to embargo, seize. 2. to apprehend, conceive, understand.
aprehensión, *f.* 1. apprehension, fear. 2. apprehension, perception, conception, understanding. 3. apprehension, capture; (law) seizure, embargo.

aprehensivo, va, *a.* 1. apprehensive, perceptive. 2. afraid.
apremiadamente, *adv.* urgently, pressingly; with constraint (as in a judicial or administrative order).
apremiador, ra, *a.* pressing, compelling, urgent; oppressive. —*m., f.* compeller, urger.
apremiante, *a.* urgent, pressing, compelling; oppressing.
apremiantemente, *adv.* urgently, pressingly, compellingly; oppressively.
apremiar, *tr.v.* 1. to press, urge. 2. to compel, oblige. 3. to hurry, harass, hound.
apremio, *m.* 1. pressure, constraint, harassment. 2. (law) judicial order (to compel compliance); administrative order (to enforce payment of taxes). — **apremios físicos,** physical coercion; **apremios ilegales,** maltreatment.
aprendedor, ra, *a.* learning. —*m., f.* learner.
aprender, *tr.v.* to learn. — **a. a** + *inf.,* to learn to + *inf.,* eg. *a. a tocar el piano,* to learn to play the piano; **aprender haciendo,** to learn by doing.
aprendiz, za, *m., f.* apprentice; beginner.
aprendizaje, *m.* apprenticeship; learning. — **hacer el a.,** to serve one's apprenticeship; **pagar el a.,** (coll.) to pay for one's inexperience.
aprensador, ra, *a.* pressing. —*m., f.* presser.
aprensadura, *f.* (rare) *var. of* **prensadura.**
aprensar, *tr.v.* 1. to press, squeeze. 2. to oppress, afflict, distress.
aprensión, *f.* fear, misgiving, apprehension, qualm.
aprensivo, va, *a.* apprehensive, uneasy, fearful.
apresador, ra, *a.* capturing; seizing. — **barco apresador,** privateer. —*m., f.* captor. —*m.* privateer.
apresamiento, *m.* capture, seizure; arrest.
apresar, *tr.v.* to capture, seize, arrest, take prisoner; to grasp, seize (with claws, teeth).
apreso, sa, *a.* rooted (tree or plant which has taken roots).
aprestar, *tr.v.* 1. to prepare, make ready, equip. 2. to dress (textiles). —*r.v.* to prepare oneself, get ready.
apresto, *m.* 1. preparation; equipment, gear. 2. dressing (of textiles); sizing (of canvas prior to painting), size (substance used). 3. material used for dressing textiles.
apresuración, *f., var. of* **apresuramiento.**
apresuradamente, *adv.* hurriedly, hastily, precipitatedly.
apresurado, da, *past part. of* **apresurar.** —*a.* hurried, hasty, precipitated.
apresuramiento, *m.* haste, hastiness; acceleration; precipitation, eagerness.
apresurar, *tr.v.* to hurry, hasten. —*r.v.* to make hasten, hurry. — **apresurarse a** or **por** + *inf.,* to hasten or hurry to + *inf.,* e.g. *apresurarse por tomar el tren,* to hurry to take the train.
apretadamente, *adv.* 1. tightly, closely. 2. insistently.
apretadera, *f.* 1. strap (for tightening, compressing or fastening (*gen. pl.*). 2. (*pl.*) (coll.) pressure, insistence (used to make someone do something).
apretadero, *m.* girdle, truss (for hernias, etc.).
apretadizo, za, *a.* compressible, easily tightened.
apretado, da, *past part. of* **apretar.** —*a.* 1. difficult, dangerous. 2. (coll.) mean, close-fisted, stingy (cool.). 3. squashed, tightly-packed. 4. short, brief; close, e.g. *un resultado a.,* a close score. —*m.* formerly, a name given to a closely-knit type of handscript.
apretador, ra, *a.* tightening; pressing; squashing, squeezing. —*m.* 1. tightener. 2. short sleeveless, tight-fitting jacket or bodice. 3. baby's harness (bodice with reins attached, to guide an infant's first steps). 4. (obs.) bellyband (to protect infant's navel). 5. hairband; barrette; hair clasp.
apretadura, *f.* tightening, pressing, constricting; pressure, compression, constriction.
apretamiento, *m., var. of* **aprieto.**
apretante, *a.* tightening, compressing, constricting; squeezing, squashing.
apretar, (*ref. 29*) *tr.v.* 1. to press; to hug, hold tight; to squash, squeeze; to press, cram or squash together; to tighten (screw, rope. etc.); to tense (muscles); to pinch (shoes); to be too tight (a dress); to grip, shake (hands); to grit (teeth), clench (fist). 2. to harass, harry, pursue relentlessly, plague, dun. 3. to distress, worry, afflict. 4. to tighten up, make more severe (discipline, laws; siege); to treat more severely. 5. to beseech, press, urge; to coerce, constrain, oblige. 6. (p.) to heighten light and shade (in a picture) with dashes of dark colors. — **a. la mano,** to shake hands, shake (someone's) hand; to become more strict, tighten the reins; to be mean, miserly or stingy; **a. los talones,** to take to one's heels; **quien mucho abarca poco aprieta,** grasp all, lose most. —*i.v.* 1. to pinch (shoes), be tight (dress). 2. to get worse (pain), increase, get heavier (rain). — **a. a correr,** (coll.) to start running, break into a run; **a. con,** to close in on, attack, come to grips with. —*r.v.* 1. to cram or crowd together. 2. to grieve, afflict oneself, worry, be distressed.
apretazón, *f.* (coll.) congestion, crush, crowd; squeeze.
apretón, *m.* 1. grip, squeeze, hug, pressure. 2. (coll.) dash, sprint, spurt. 3. sudden effort or exertion. 4. (coll.) conflict, struggle, difficulty. 5. (coll.) violent griping pains. 6. crush (of people). 7. (p.) dark coloring (applied to a picture to heighten contrast of light and shade). — **a. de manos,** a warm handshake.
apretujar, *tr.v.* (coll.) to squeeze or press hard; to jam, crowd, crush or cram together. —*r.v.* to crowd, jam or cram together.
apretujón, *m.* (coll.) tight squeeze, crush; push, jam.
apretura, *f.* 1. (coll.) jam, crush (of people); confined space. 2. difficulty, fix. 3. scarcity, shortage, lack (esp. of food).
aprevenir, (*ref. 26*) *tr.v.* (Col., Guat.) *var. of* **prevenir.**
aprevine, *ref.* **aprevenir.**
apreviniendo, apreviniera, apreviniese, *ref.* **aprevenir.**
apriesa, *adv.* (arch.) *var. of* **aprisa.**
aprietatuercas, *m.* nut-driver, nut runner or setter.
apriete, aprieto, *ref.* **apretar.**
aprieto, *m.* 1. trouble, difficulty, fix, distress, straits. 2. jam, crush (of people). — **poner en aprietos,** to put someone on the spot; **sacar de un a.,** help someone out of a jam.
aprimar, *tr.v.* to refine, perfect.
apriorismo, *m.* (philos.) apriorism.
apriorista, *m., f.* apriorist.
apriorístico, ca, *a.* aprioristic.
aprisa, *adv.* promptly, quickly.
apriscar, (*ref. 50*) *tr.v.* to gather sheep into the fold, gather cattle into the pen.
aprisco, *m.* corral, fold, pen; place of refuge.
aprisionar, *tr.v.* to imprison; to capture; to tie, bind.
aprisque, aprisqué, *ref.* **apriscar.**
aproar, *i.v.* (mar.) to turn the prow.
aprobación, *f.* approval, approbation; passing (examination).
aprobado, *past part. of* **aprobar.** —*m.* pass (lowest mark for passing an examination).
aprobador, ra, *a.* approving. —*m., f.* approver.
aprobante, *a.* approving. —*m., f.* approver.
aprobanza, *f.* approval.
aprobar, (*ref. 33*) *tr.v.* 1. to approve, ratify, confirm; to pass (a bill in parliament). 2. to approve of, agree with. 3. to pass (examination). —*i.v.* to pass, pass an examination.
aprobativo, va, *a., var. of* **aprobatorio.**
aprobatoriamente, *adv.* approvingly.
aprobatorio, ria, *a.* approbatory, approving.
aproches, *m.* (*pl.*) 1. (mil.) approaches. 2. neighborhood.
aprontamiento, *m.* quick preparation; prompt delivery or payment.
aprontar, *tr.v.* 1. to dispose of (something) promptly or quickly; to prepare, foresee. 2. to pay immediately, hand over at once.
apronte, *m.* (Chile, Arg.) trial run (of horse).
apropiable, *a.* appropriable.
apropiación, *f.* 1. appropriation, taking possession. 2. fitting, adapting.
apropiadamente, *adv.* appropriately, fittingly, suitably.
apropiado, da, *past part. of* **apropiar.** —*a.* appropriate, proper, fitting, suitable.
apropiador, ra, *a.* appropriating. —*m., f.* appropriator.
apropiar, *tr.v.* 1. to give possession of. 2. to fit, adapt, suit. 3. (Amer.) to appropriate (funds). —*r.v.* to take possession. — **apropiarse de,** to appropriate, take possession of, seize.
apropincuación, *f.* approach, approaching.
apropincuarse, *r.v.* (rare) to approach.
a propósito, *adv.* 1. by the way. 2. intentionally.
apropósito, *m.* short play or sketch.
aprovechable, *a.* usable; available.
aprovechadamente, *adv.* 1. profitably, beneficially. 2. shrewdly, slyly.
aprovechado, da, *past part. of* **aprovechar.** —*a.* 1. hard-working, diligent. 2. economical; thrifty. 3. shrewd, sly, opportunistic.
aprovechador, ra, *a.* 1. diligent. 2. shrewd, sly, opportunistic. —*m., f.* person who takes advantage or makes use of people and circumstances, opportunist.
aprovechamiento, *m.* 1. use, utilization; exploitation, development. 2. application industriousness, diligence. — **a. de aguas,** (law) water rights; **a. forestal,** forest produce.
aprovechar, *tr.v.* 1. to use or employ profitably, make use of, take advantage of. 2. (mar.) to luff whenever the wind permits. —*i.v.* 1. to be useful, be of use, be profitable. 2. to progress, improve. —*r.v.* to take advantage. — **aprovecharse de,** to take advantage of, avail oneself of.
aprovisionador, *m.* supplier, purveyor.
aprovisionamiento, *m.* supplying, provisioning; supplies, provisions.
aprovisionar, *tr.v.* to provision, supply.
aproximación, *f.* 1. closeness, nearness; (math.) approximation. 2. consolation prize (in lotteries). — **a. controlada desde tierra,** (aer.) ground-controlled approach.
aproximadamente, *adv.* approximately, about, around, more or less.
aproximado, da, *past part. of* **aproximar.** —*a.* approximate, close.
aproximar, *tr.v.* to approximate; to bring close or move near. —*r.v.* to approach, come near or nearer, get close to.
aproximativo, va, *a.* approximate.
apruebe, aprueba, *ref.* **aprobar.**
ápside, *m.* (astron.) apsis.
apsiquia, *f.* (med.) apsychia, loss of consciousness.
aptamente, *adv.* aptly, fitly, suitably.

aptar, *tr.v.* to adapt, accommodate, adjust.
aptérix, *m.* (ornith.) apteryx, kiwi.
áptero, ra, *a.* (ento.) apteral, apterous, wingless.
aptitud, *f.* aptitude, fitness, ability, capability.
apto, ta, *a.* apt, fit, capable.
apuchinarse, *r.v.* (Cuba, coll.) to satiate or gorge oneself.
apuesta, *f.* wager, bet; stake. — **de apuesta** or **sobre a.,** (coll.) spiritedly, stubbornly, with determination.
apuestamente, *adv.* handsomely, elegantly, gracefully.
apueste, apuesto, *ref.* **apostar.**
apuesto, ta, *past part. of* **aponer.** —*a.* handsome, good-looking, fine-looking, elegant.
apulgarar, *i.v.* to press with the thumb.
apulgararse, *r.v.* to become soiled with small spots (white clothing).
apulso, *m.* (astron.) appulse.
apunado, da, *a.* (Arg., Bol., Chile, Peru) sick with soroche or altitude sickness.
apunarse, *r.v.* (S. Amer.) to get altitude sickness or soroche.
apunchar, *tr.v.* to cut the teeth in (combs).
apuntación, *f.* 1. noting, noting down, notation, note. 2. pointing, aiming. 3. (mus.) notation.
apuntado, da, *past part. of* **apuntar.** —*a.* 1. pointed; (her.) counterpointed. 2. (Chile) drunk.
apuntador, ra, *m., f.* 1. (theat.) prompter. 2. (mil.) gunner, gun layer. 3. time keeper; recorder. —*f.* pointing tool.
apuntalamiento, *m.* propping, shoring; support; trench bracing.
apuntalar, *tr.v.* to prop, shore, support, brace.
apuntamiento, *m.* 1. note, noting, noting down, notation. 2. sharpening, pointing. 3. pointing, aiming. 4. (law) case summary.
apuntar, *tr.v.* 1. to point, aim; to train, aim (gun); to lay (gun). 2. to point to, point at, point out, indicate. 3. to underline, mark (something in a text in order to find it later). 4. to note, note down, write down, make a note of. 5. to outline, sketch. 6. to baste; to tack; to fasten temporarily. 7. to sharpen; to point. 8. (coll.) to patch, darn, stitch, sew, mend. 9. to prompt, whisper the answer to; (theat.) to prompt. 10. to mention, remark upon in passing. 11. to put up, bet, stake (money). 12. to hint, suggest. 13. (print.) to fasten (the sheets) in the register points. —*i.v.* 1. to aim, e.g. *a. muy alto,* to aim high. 2. to appear; to begin to break, e.g. *el día apuntó,* the day began to break; **a. y no dar,** to promise and not comply. —*r.v.* 1. to begin to go sour (wine). 2. (coll.) to begin to get tipsy. 3. to write or sign one's name on a list or subscription. 4. (Mex.) to sprout.
apunte, *m.* 1. note; noting; memorandum, notation. 2. sketch, outline. 3. (theat.) promptbook, prompter's copy; prompter's voice, prompting; prompter. 4. stake, wager; person who stakes against the banker. 5. eccentric person. 6. (coll.) rogue, rascal. — **libro de apuntes,** notebook.
apuntillar, *tr.v.* (taur.) to deal the coup de grace to the bull with a dagger.
apuñalado, da, *past part. of* **apuñalar.** —*a.* dagger-shaped.
apuñalar, *tr.v.* to stab, knife.
apuñalear, *tr.v., var. of* **apuñalar.**
apuñar, *tr.v.* 1. to seize, grasp, grip. 2. to punch, pummel. —*i.v.* to clench one's fist.
apuñear, *tr.v.* (coll.) to punch, pummel.
apuñetear, *tr.v, var. of* **apuñear.**
apuracabos, *m. pl.* save-all (device in candlestick permitting total consumption of the candle).
apuración, *f.* 1. purification, finishing; clarification. 2. (fig.) verification, investigation. 3. push, forcing. 4. trouble, annoyance, bother.
apuradamente, *adv.* 1. hurriedly, hastily. 2. at the exact or right time, punctually. 3. precisely, carefully, with great care.
apurado, da, *past part. of* **apurar.** —*a.* 1. hard-up, needy, e.g. *a. de,* hard-up for, short of (money). 2. dangerous, difficult, hard. 3. careful, carefully done; exact, precise. 4. rushed, in a hurry, e.g. *estamos apurados,* we're in a hurry.
apurador, ra, *a.* purifying, refining. —*m., f.* purifier, refiner. —*m.* 1. save-all (device in candlestick permitting total consumption of candle). 2. (min.) ore washer.
apuramiento, *m., var. of* **apuración.**
apuranieves, *f.* (ornith.) wagtail.
apurar, *tr.v.* 1. to purify, refine. 2. to use up, drink up, drain, finish up. 3. to terminate, finish. 4. to verify, check; scrutinize. 5. to hurry up. 6. to annoy, vex, irritate. —*r.v.* 1. to worry, get anxious. 2. to hurry, make haste. 3. to finish up, drink up, drain, e.g. *apuró la botella,* he finished up the bottle.
apure, *m.* 1. (min.) purification, refining. 2. (min.) residue of sifted lead after washing.
apuro, *m.* 1. difficult or awkward situation, difficulty, jam, fix (usually in *pl.*), e.g. *estar* or *poner en apuros,* to be or put in a jam or fix. 2. hurry, haste. 3. hardship, need, want.
apurón, na, *a.* (Amer., coll.) hurrying, person who hurries himself or others.
aquejador, ra, *a.* troubling, worrisome, afflicting.
aquejar, *tr.v.* to afflict, trouble, worry; to grieve.
aquejoso, sa, *a.* afflicted, troubled, worried; grieved.
aquejumbrarse, *r.v.* (Amer.) to grumble, moan.
aquel, *m.,* **aquella,** *f.* (*pl.* **aquellos** *m.,* **aquellas** *f.*) *dem. a.* that (*pl.* those).
aquél, *m.,* **aquélla,** *f.* (*pl.* **aquéllos** *m.,* **aquéllas** *f.*) *dem. pron.* that, that one (*pl.* those, those ones); he (*m.*), she (*f.*), they (*pl.*); the former (in contrast with the latter).
aquel, *m.* (coll.) grace, charm, attraction, appeal.
aquelarre, *m.* sabbat, witches' sabbath.
aquello, *neut. pron.* that, that thing.
aquende, *adv.* (arch.) on this side.
aquenio, *m.* (bot.) achene, akene.
aqueo, a, *a., m., f.* (hist.) Achaean, Achaian, of the ancient Greek province of Achaea.
aquerenciado, da, *past part. of* **aquerenciar.** —*a.* (Mex.) enamored, in love.
aquerenciarse, *r.v.* to become fond. — **a. a,** to become fond of, become attached to.
aquese, sa, so, *dem. pron.* (poet.) that.
aqueste, ta, to, *dem. pron.* (poet.) this.
aqueta, *f.* (ento.) cicada.
aquí, *adv.* 1. here. 2. now. 3. then, at that point. — **a. dentro,** in here, e.g. *les espero a. dentro,* I shall wait for you in here; **de a. en adelante,** from now on; **por a.,** here, this way, e.g. *venga Ud. por a.,* come this way.
aquiescencia, *f.* acquiescence, consent, assent.
aquiescente, *a.* acquiescent, consenting.
aquietador, ra, *a.* quieting, soothing, calming, pacifying.
aquietadoramente, *adv.* soothingly, pacifyingly.
aquietamiento, *m.* soothing, quieting, pacifying, calming; stillness.
aquietante, *a.* soothing, calming, pacifying.
aquietar, *tr.v.* to soothe, pacify, calm. —*r.v.* to calm down, become quiet.
aquifoliáceo, cea, *a.* (bot.) aquifoliaceous, with hollylike leaves. —*f.* (*pl.*) (bot.) Aquifoliaceae.
aquifolio, *m.* (bot.) holly, holly tree.
aquilatamiento, *m.* 1. assay, evaluation (of number of carats in gold, jewels, etc.). 2. appraisal (of character).
aquilatar, *tr.v.* 1. to assay, appraise, calculate quality or value (of gold, precious stones). 2. to appraise, evaluate, calculate worth or merit of (person, thing). 3. to purify, refine.
aquilea, *f., var. of* **milenrama.**
aquileño, *m.* (sl.) person with a bent for thievery.
Aquiles, *m.* Achilles. — **talón de Aquiles,** Achilles' heel.
aquilífero, *m.* Roman standard bearer.
aquilino, na, *a.* (poet.) aquiline. — **nariz a.,** Roman or aquiline nose.
aquillado, da, *a.* keel-like; (mar.) long-keeled (ship).
aquilón, *m.* Boreas, north wind.
aquilonal, *a.* north, northerly; wintry.
aquilonar, *a., var. of* **aquilonal.**
aquintralarse, *r.v.* (Chile) to become covered with mistletoe (tree, shrubs); to be attacked by a disease caused by mistletoe.
Aquisgrán, *m.* Aix-la-Chapelle, Aachen.
aquistador, ra, *a.* acquisitive, acquiring.
aquistar, *tr.v.* to acquire, obtain, get.
aquitano, na, *a., m., f.* (hist.) Aquitanian, of the Roman province of Aquitania.
aquivo, va, *a.* (hist.) Achaean, Achaian, of the ancient Greek province of Achaea. —*m., f.* Achaean.
ara, *f.* 1. altar. 2. (astron.) **A.,** Ara, Altar. — **acogerse a las aras,** to seek asylum, take refuge; **en aras de,** for the sake of, in honor of. —*m.* (ornith.) macaw.
árabe, *a., m., f.* Arab, Arabian. —*m.* Arabic (language).
arabesco, ca, *a.* 1. Arabian, Arabic. 2. arabesque. —*m.* (art., ballet) arabesque.
Arabia, *f.* Arabia. — **A. Saudita,** Saudi Arabia.
arabice, arabicé, *ref.* **arabizar.**
arábico, ca, *a., var. of* **arábigo.**
arábigo, ga, *a.* Arabian, Arabic. —*m.* Arabic (language). — **estar en a.,** (coll.) to be Greek (*hard to understand*).
arabio, bia, *a., m., f.* Arab, Arabian.
arabismo, *m.* Arabism (Arabic expression).
arabista, *m., f.* Arabist, student of Arabic language and culture.
arabización, *f.* Arabization.
arabizar, (*ref. 53*) *tr.v.* to Arabize, make Arabic. —*i.v.* to adopt Arabian customs.
arable, *a.* arable.
aracanto, *m.* (Peru) giant sea-weed.
aracarí, *m.* (ornith.) aracari, kind of toucan.
aráceo, cea, *a.* (bot.) araceous. —*f.* (*pl.*) Araceae, the Arum family.
arácnido, da, *a.* (zool.) arachnidan. —*m.* arachnid; (*pl.*) Arachnida, arachnidan family.
aracnoideo, a, *a.* arachnoid.
aracnoides, *a.* (anat.) arachnoid. —*f.* (anat.) arachnoid (membrane).
aracnología, *f.* (zool.) arachnology.
arada, *f.* plowing; plowed land; day's plowing.
arado, *m.* plow; plowing. — **a. de reja múltiple,** gang plow; **a. rotatorio,** rotary plow; **a. desarraigador,** rooting plow; grub hook.
arador, ra, *a.* plowing (implement). —*m.* 1. plowman, tiller. 2. (ento.) itch mite.
aradro, *m.* (reg., Sp.) plow.
aradura, *f.* plowing, tillage.
aragonés, sa, *a.* Aragonese, of the Spanish region of Aragon. —*m., f.* Aragonese. — **el gran a.,** the great Aragonese (Goya, the painter).
aragonito, *m.* (min.) aragonite.
araguaney, *m.* (Ven., bot.) tecoma (Tecoma spectabilis).
araguato, *m.* (zool.) araguato, ursine howler, howling monkey.

araguirá, *m.* (ornith.) red-breasted bird of the Fringillidae family (Coryphospingus cucullatus rubescens).
aralia, *f.* (bot.) aralia.
araliáceo, a, *a.* (bot.) araliaceous. —*f.* araliad; (*pl.*) Araliaceae.
arambel, *m.* 1. arras, wall tapestry, hanging screen. 2. (coll.) rag, tatter, shred.
arambeloso, sa, *a.* ragged, tattered.
arameo, a, *a., m., f.* Aramean. —*m.* Aramaic (language).
aramio, *m.* (agr.) fallow field.
arana, *f.* trick, swindle.
araná, *m.* (Ven.) rustic straw hat.
arancel, *m.* tariff. — **a. proteccionista,** protective tariff.
arancelario, ria, *a.* tariff, pertaining to tariffs.
arancelarse, *r.v.* (Guat.) to become a habitual customer of a shop, a store, a café, etc.; to become an habitué.
arandanedo, *m.* (bot.) bilberry orchard.
arándano, *m.* (bot.) bilberry bush; bilberry (fruit).
arandela, *f.* 1. bobèche, rim (of a candlestick). 2. (mec.) washer. 3. (mil.) vamplate, hand guard on handle of a lance (to protect hand). 4. ruff; ruffled collar and cuffs. 5. (agr.) funnel-shaped insect trap (placed around the trunk of a tree). 6. candlestick, candelabrum. 7. (S. Amer.) dress or shirt ruffles, frill. 8. (mar.) hatch, half-port. — **a. acopada,** cup washer; **a. fijadora,** check washer.
arandillo, *m.* (ornith.) marsh warbler.
arandón, *m.* (bot.) daphne (Daphne aquilaria).
aranero, ra, *a.* tricking, swindling. —*m., f.* trickster; swindler.
aranés, sa, *a.* from the valley of Arán (in the Pyrenees).
araniego, *a.* (said of the hawk) caught with a net.
aranoso, sa, *a., var. of* **aranero.**
aranzada, *f.* (arch.) land measure of about five hectares, or almost an acre.
araña, *f.* 1. (ento.) spider. 2. chandelier. 3. bird net. 4. (coll.) hard worker, hustler, go-getter. 5. prostitute, whore. 6. (bot.) love-in-the-mist. 7. (ichth.) greater weaver, stingbull. 8. (mar.) crowfoot, running rigging (for suspending an awning). 9. (Amer.) light carriage. — **a. de agua,** (zool.) water spider; **a. de mar,** (zool.) sea spider, spider crab; **a. picacaballos,** (ento.) chigoe (small arachnid which bores into horse's hooves).
arañada, *f.* scratch.
arañador, ra, *a.* scratching. —*m., f.* scratcher.
arañamiento, *m.* scratching; scratch.
arañando, *adv.* barely, hardly. — **aprobar exámenes a.,** to pass exams by the skin of one's teeth.
arañar, *tr.v.* 1. to scratch. 2. (coll.) to scrape together (money). —*r.v.* to scratch oneself.
arañazo, *m.* scratch, scrape.
arañero, ra, *a.* wild, untamed (hawk).
arañil, *a.* spidery.
araño, *m.* scratching; scratch; scrape; scraping.
arañuela, *f.* 1. (bot.) love-in-the-mist. 2. (ento.) crop-eating grub.
arañuelo, *m.* 1. (ento.) red spider. 2. (ento.) crop-eating grub. 3. bird net.
arapaima, *f.* (ichth.) arapaima.
aráquida, *f.* peanut.
arar, *m.* (bot.) sandarac tree.
arar, *tr.v.* to plow; to furrow, wrinkle; (fig.) to plow through (water, snow).
arara, *m.* (Bol.) species of parrot.
araroba, *f.* (bot.) araroba (Andina araroba).
arate, *m.* dullness, heaviness.
arate cavate, humdrum, plodding routine; dullness, unimaginativeness, uncouthness.
araucanista, *m., f.* expert in Araucan and the Araucanians.
araucano, na, *a., m., f.* Araucanian, Araucan. —*m.* Araucan (language). — **La Araucana,** Chile's great national epic written by Alonso de Ercilla, circa 1570.
araucaria, *f.* (bot.) araucaria (Araucaria araucana). — **a. excelsa,** (bot.) Norfolk Island pine (Araucaria excelsa).
arauja, *f.* (bot.) species of milkweed (Arauja albens).
aravico, *m.* a poet of the ancient tribes of Peru.
arbalestrilla, *f.* arbalest, early form of sextant.
arbellón, *m., var. of* **albollón.**
arbicuajer, *m.* (bot.) wild resiniferous tree from Cuba.
arbitrable, *a.* arbitrable, subject to arbitration.
arbitración, *f.* (law) arbitration.
arbitrador, ra, *a.* arbitrating, judging. —*m., f.* arbiter, arbitrator, judge.
arbitraje, *m.* 1. arbitration, arbitrage. 2. (com.) arbitrage. 3. (sport.) referee or umpire.
arbitral, *a.* (law) arbitral, pertaining to arbitration or refereeing.
arbitramento, *m.* arbitration, arbitrament.
arbitramiento, *m., var. of* **arbitramento.**
arbitrante, *a.* arbitrating, refereeing.
arbitrar, *tr.v.* 1. (sport.) to referee, umpire, to judge, decide, arbitrate. 2. to gather together, get together. —*i.v.* to arbitrate; (sport.) to referee, umpire.
arbitrariamente, *adv.* 1. arbitrarily, highhandedly. 2. by arbitration.
arbitrariedad, *f.* arbitrariness, highhandedness.
arbitrario, ria, *a.* 1. arbitrary, high-handed. 2. arbitral, arbitrary.
arbitrativo, va, *a.* arbitral, arbitrary.
arbitratorio, ria, *a.* (law) arbitral.
arbitrero, ra, *a.* arbitral, arbitrary. —*m.* crank politician or reformer.
arbitrio, *m.* 1. discretion, free will. 2. scheme, means, way, expedient, device. 3. adjudication, decision, judgment. 4. (*pl.*) rates, tariff charges. — **libre a.,** free will.
arbitrista, *m., f.* crank politician or reformer.
árbitro, ra, *a.* independent, free, autonomous. —*m.* arbiter, judge, (sport.) referee, umpire; official.
árbol, *m.* 1. (bot.) tree. 2. (mec.) axle, arbor, spindle, shaft. 3. (print.) body, type body, shank, stem. 4. (mar.) mast. 5. (mus.) axle (governing registers of an organ). 6. (jewel.) watchmaker's graver or burin. 7. body of a shirt. 8. (archit.) crown post of winding stairs. 9. (Chile) clothes rack. — **á. botella** (bot.) bottle tree; **á. cardán,** (auto.) cardan shaft; **á. cigüeñal,** (mech.) crankshaft; **á. de costados,** family or genealogical tree; **á. de Diana,** (chem.) arbor Dianae; **á. de dirección,** (auto.) steering shaft; **á. de distribución** or **de levas,** (mech.) camshaft; **á. de fuego,** frame for fireworks; **á. de Judas,** (bot.) Judas tree; **á. de la cera,** (bot.) Chinese tallow tree; wax myrtle; **á. de la ciencia** or **del bien y del mal,** tree of knowledge; **á. de levas,** (mec.) camshaft; **á. de la vida,** (Bib.) tree of life; (bot.) arborvitae, tree of life; (anat.) arbor vitae; **á. del cielo,** (bot.) ailanthus; **á. del clavo,** (bot.) clove tree; **á. del diablo,** (bot.) sandbox tree; **á. del incienso,** (bot.) incense tree; **á. del lizo,** (tex.) comb or implement for separating warp-threads; **á. del pan,** (bot.) breadfruit tree; **á. del Paraíso,** (bot.) Russian olive, oleaster; **á. del tipo,** (print.) type body; **á. de María,** (bot.) calaba tree; **á. de Navidad,** Christmas tree; **á. de Pascua** (And.) Christmas tree; **á. de pie,** tree springing from seed, not from scion; **á. genealógico,** family tree; **á. gomífero,** (bot.) gum tree; **á. motor,** (mec.) drive shaft; **á. padre,** tree left after others have been cut down to re-forest area; **á. propulsor,** driving shaft, (auto.) propeller shaft.
arbolado, da, *a.* wooded. —*m.* 1. trees (covering tract of land). 2. (sl.) tall, hefty man.
arboladura, *f.* (mar.) masts and yards; rigging.
arbolar, *tr.v.* 1. to hoist, raise aloft. 2. to put against. 3. (mar.) to mast. 4. to swell (high seas). —*r.v.* to rear (horse).
arbolario, ria, *a.* (coll.) harebrained, scatterbrained. —*m., f.* madcap, scatterbrain; person who colors or exaggerates a tale.
arboleda, *f.* grove, wood; a pleasant, shady corner in the country or in a garden.
arboledo, *m.* woodland.
arbolejo, *m. dim. of* **árbol,** small tree.
arbolete, *m.* 1. *dim. of* **árbol,** small tree. 2. branch stuck into the ground, to which lime twigs are attached for catching birds. 3. core of grapeshot, iron rod to which nine iron balls were attached to form a duster of grapeshot.
arbolillo, *m.* 1. *dim. of* **árbol.** 2. (min.) side of blast furnace.
arbolista, *m., f.* arborist.
arbollón, *m., var. of* **albollón.**
arborecer, (*ref. 45*) *i.v.* to grow into a tree (a sapling).
arbóreo, a, *a.* arboreal, wooded.
arborescencia, *f.* arborescence.
arborescente, *a.* arborescent.
arboricultor, *m.* (agr.) arboriculturist.
arboricultura, *f.* (agr.) arboriculture, tree cultivation.
arboriforme, *a.* arboriform, tree-shaped.
arborización, *f.* (geol.) arborization, natural branch-like design found on some stones.
arborizar, *tr.v.* to forest; to landscape with trees.
arbotante, *m.* 1. (archit.) flying buttress. 2. (mar.) hoisting beam, outlooker, cleat on hull for securing lines.
arbustivo, va, *a.* shrub-like.
arbusto, *m.* shrub, bush.
arca, *f.* 1. chest, coffer; ark; (*pl.*) coffers. 2. tempering oven (for glass). 3. (*pl.*) (anat.) hollows underneath the ribs. — **a. cerrada,** (coll.) clam, reticent person; **a. de agua,** water tank, reservoir, water tower; **a. de la alianza,** (Bib.) Ark of the Covenant; **a. del cuerpo,** trunk (of the body); **a. del pan,** (coll.) breadbasket (sl.), stomach; **a. del testamento,** (Bib.) Ark of the Covenant; **a. de Noé,** Noah's Ark; (ichth.) arkshell (a species of mollusk); (coll.) lumber room of trunk; **hacer arcas,** (fig.) to loosen the purse strings.
arcabucear, *tr.v.* to shoot with a harquebus.
arcabucería, *f.* 1. troop or body of harquebusiers; harquebusade, volley from harquebuses; harquebuses. 2. harquebus factory or shop.
arcabucero, *m.* 1. harquebusier. 2. harquebus maker.
arcabucete, *m. dim. of* **arcabuz,** small harquebus.
arcabuco, *m.* dense woodland or brush, thicket.
arcabucoso, sa, *a.* densely wooded.
arcabuz, (*pl.* **arcabuces**) *m.* 1. (arch., mil.) harquebus. 2. harquebusier.
arcabuzazo, *m.* 1. (arch., mil.) harquebus shot. 2. harquebus shot wound.
arcacil, *m., var. of* **alcacil.**
arcada, *f.* 1. (archit.) arcade; archway, arch. 2. retching (used more often in the *pl.*). 3. (mus.) bowing (in playing stringed instruments).

árcade, *a., m., f.* Arcadian, of or pertaining to Arcadia.
Arcadia, *f.* 1. Arcadia, ancient region of the Peloponnesus. 2. (fig.) any place of bucolic serenity and simplicity.
arcádico, ca, *a., var. of* **arcadio.**
arcadio, dia, *a.* Arcadian.
arcador, *m.* wool loosener (person who loosens up wool fibers).
arcaduz, (*pl.* **arcaduces**) *m.* 1. pipe, conduit; aqueduct. 2. bucket of a water wheel. 3. (coll.) way, means.
arcaico, ca, *a.* archaic; obsolete.
arcaísmo, *m.* archaism.
arcaísta, *m., f.* archaist, one who uses archaisms.
arcaizante, *a.* archaizing.
arcaizar, (*ref. 53*) *tr.v.* to archize, make archaic. —*i.v.* to use archaisms.
arcanamente, *adv.* mysteriously.
arcángel, *m.* archangel.
arcangélico, ca, *a.* archangelic.
arcano, na, *a.* arcane, esoteric, recondite; secret, hidden. —*m.* arcanum, secret.
arcar, (*ref. 50*) *tr.v., var. of* **arquear.** 1. to arch, bend. 2. to loosen up, fluff (fibers of wool).
arcatura, *f.* (archit.) arcature.
arce, *m.* (bot.) maple tree.
arcedianato, *m.* archdeaconry, land under archdeacon's jurisdiction.
arcediano, *m.* archdeacon.
arcedo, *m.* maple grove.
arcén, *m.* edge, border, bank; curbstone (of a well).
archa, *f.* type of halberd.
archi, *pre.* arch, prefix indicating preeminence or superiority, e.g. *archienemigo,* archenemy.
archibribón, na, *a.* very lazy. —*m., f.* 1. layabout, loafer, (coll.) bum. 2. rogue or scoundrel.
archicofrade, *m., f.* member of a confraternity.
archicofradía, *f.* confraternity.
archidiácono, *m., var. of* arcediano, archdeacon.
archidiócesis, *f.* archdiocese.
archiducado, *m.* archduchy, the rank of archduke.
archiducal, *a.* archducal.
archiduque, *m.* archduke.
archiduquesa, *f.* archduchess.
archimandrita, *m.* (ecc.) archimandrite.
archimillonario, ria, *a., m., f.* multimillionaire.
archipámpano, *m.* (hum.) imaginary tycoon or self-styled magnate; (coll.) big noise.
archipiélago, *m.* archipelago.
archisabido, da, *a.* well-known.
architriclino, *m.* head steward in charge of banquets (in Greek and Roman times).
archivado, da, *past part. of* **archivar.** —*a.* (coll.) out of style, old-fashioned, unfashionable.
archivador, ra, *a.* archiving, filing. —*m., f.* file clerk, archivist. —*m.* filing cabinet.
archivar, *tr.v.* to file (documents in filing cabinet), put into a file, stow; to archive, put into archives; (coll.) to file away, pigeonhole.
archivero, *m.* archivist (person in charge of archives); file clerk.
archivista, *m., var. of* **archivero.**
archivístico, ca, *a.* archival.
archivo, *m.* 1. archives, records, annals; archive, archives, place where archives or records are kept; (office) files, file. 2. trustworthy person. 3. mine, abundant source, e.g. *a. de sabiduría,* fountain of knowledge.
archivolta, *f.* (archit.) archivolt.
arcifinio, nia, *a.* having natural boundaries (territory).
arcilla, *f.* clay, argil. — **a. figulina,** potter's clay; **a. refractaria,** fire clay.
arcillar, *tr.v.* to loam, improve soil with clay.
arcilloarenoso, sa, *a.* (geol.) argillarenaceous.
arcilloso, sa, *a.* clayey, clayish, argillaceous.
arción, *m.* fretwork design used in medieval architecture.
arciprestazgo, *m.* archpriesthood; land under jurisdiction of an archpriest.
arcipreste, *m.* archpriest.
arco, *m.* 1. (geom., astron., elec.) arc. 2. bow (weapon). 3. (mus.) bow (of violin, etc.). 4. (archit., anat.) arch. 5. (sport.) goal. 6. hoop (of barrel). — **a. abocinado,** (archit.) splayed arch; **a. adintelado,** (archit.) flat arch; **a. alveolar,** (anat.) alveolar arch; **a. angrelado,** (archit.) foiled arch; **a. a nivel,** (archit.) flat arch, straight arch; **a. apainelado,** (archit.) basket-handle arch; **a. apuntado,** (archit.) pointed or ogival arch; lancet arch; **a. árabe,** (archit.) Moorish arch; **a. botarate,** (archit.) flying buttress; **a. cantante,** (elec.) singing arc; **a. carpanel,** (archit.) basket-handle arch; **a. cegado** or **ciego,** (archit.) blind arch; **a. cigomático,** (anat.) zygomatic arch; **a. cojo,** (archit.) rampant arch; **a. conopial,** (archit.) ogee arch; **a. crucero** or **ojivo,** (archit.) transverse or cross rib (of groined arch or cross vault); **a. de agalla,** (zool.) gill arch; **a. de descarga,** (archit.) discharging or relieving arch; **a. de herradura,** (archit.) horseshoe arch; **a. de iglesia,** (coll.) difficult task; **a. de medio punto** or **de centro pleno,** (archit.) round arch, semicircular arch; **a. del proscenio,** (theat.) proscenium arch; **a. de sierra,** hacksaw frame; **a. de todo punto** or **de punto entero,** (archit.) equilateral arch; **a. de triunfo,** triumphal arch; **a. de violín,** violin bow; **a. diurno,** (astron.) diurnal arc; **a. enviajado** or **aviajado,** (archit.) skew arch; **a. escarzano,** (archit.) segmental arch; **a. iris,** rainbow; **a. lanceolado,** (archit.) lanceolate arch; **a. ojival,** (archit.) gothic arch, lancet arch, ogival arch; **a. perpiaño,** (archit.) arch supporting barrel vault; **a. ojival equilátero,** (archit.) equilateral arch; **a. ojival rebajado,** (archit.) blunt arch; segmental arch; **a. pelviano,** (anat.) pelvic arch; **a. peraltado,** (archit.) stilted arch; **a. político,** political spectrum; **a. por tranquil.** (archit.) rampant arch; **a. quinquefoliado,** (archit.) quinquefoliate arch; **a. realzado,** (archit.) stilted arch; **a. rebajado,** (archit.) segmental arch; **a. apuntado,** (archit.) stilted arch; **arcos caídos,** fallen arches (of feet); **a. taquimétrico,** stadia arc; **a. tercelete,** (archit.) intermediate rib (of groined arch or cross vault); **a. toral,** (archit.) each of the four arches supporting the cupola of a building; **a. trebolado,** (archit.) trefoil arch; **a. triunfal,** arch of triumph; memoriad arch; (archit.) triumphal arch (in early church); **a. voltaico,** (elec.) voltaic arc.
arcón, *m. aug. of* **arca,** large chest.
arconte, *m.* (hist.) archon, Athenian magistrate.
arcosa, *f.* (geol.) arkose.
arctado, *a.* having to be ordained within a specified limit of time (app. to ordinands).
arcuación, *f.* curvature (of an arch).
arda, *f., var. of* **ardilla.**
ardalear, *i.v.* 1. to space out; to thin out. 2. to grow sparse, to fail to mature (said of the vine and its fruit).
ardea, *f., var. of* **alcaraván.**
ardentía, *f.* 1. *var. of* **ardor.** 2. burning; burning, sting, smarting. 3. pyrosis, heartburn. 4. phosphorescence (of the sea).
ardentísimamente, *adv.* very ardently or fervidly.
arder, *i.v.* 1. to burn, blaze. 2. to burn, sting, smart. 3. (poet.) to blaze, shine, glitter. 4. (fig.) to be in a feverish state (of excitement). 5. to rot (manure). — **a. de** or **en,** to burn with (love, hate, passion, etc.); **a. en,** to be ablaze or rage with (war, etc.); **la cosa está que arde,** (fig.) things are pretty hot. —*tr.v.* to burn. —*r.v.* 1. to burn. 2. to spoil (through excess heat or dampness); to rot, go bad (corn, olives, tobacco, etc.).
ardero, ra, *a.* squirrel hunting (dog). —*m.* squirrel dog.
ardeviejas, *f. pl.* (bot.) furze, gorse, spiny shrub.
ardid, *a.* astute, cunning. —*m.* trick, ruse, device, stratagem, artifice.
ardido, da, *past part. of* **arder.** —*a.* 1. brave, courageous, daring, bold. 2. (Amer.) irritated, annoyed, burned up.
ardiente, *a.* 1. burning. 2. (fig.) burning (fever), parching (thirst). 3. (fig.) ardent, passionate, fervent, burning, fiery. 4. (fig., poet.) red.
ardientemente, *adv.* ardently.
ardilla, *f.* 1. (zool.) squirrel. — **a. de la tierra,** (zool.) ground squirrel; gopher; **a. gris,** (zool.) gray squirrel; **a. listada,** (zool.) chipmunk; **a. voladora,** or **volante,** (zool.) flying squirrel. 2. (coll.) go-getter (in business).
ardimiento, *m.* 1. burning. 2. (fig.) bravery, courage.
ardínculo, *m.* (vet.) abscess in gangrenous wounds of horses.
ardiondo, da, *a.* courageous, brave.
ardite, *m.* ancient Spanish coin of little value; trifle. — **no vale un a.,** it's not worth a dime.
ardor, *m.* 1. ardor, passion, fervor, vehemence. 2. keenness, zeal, eagerness. 3. courage, valor, intrepidity. 4. heat. 5. (fig.) brilliance, radiance.
ardora, *f.* phosphorescence (of the sea) indicating the presence of a school of sardines.
ardorada, *f.* blush.
ardorosamente, *adv.* ardently, fervently, fierily; enthusiastic.
ardoroso, sa, *a.* ardent, fervent, fiery.
arduamente, *adv.* arduously, strenuously, with difficulty.
arduidad, *f.* arduousness.
arduo, dua, *a.* arduous, hard, strenuous, difficult.
ardurán, *m.* (bot.) African sorghum.
área, *f.* 1. area. 2. are (square measure). — **á. de castigo,** (sport.) penalty area; **á. de recreo,** playground; **á. de reposo,** rest area; **á. de servicio,** service area; **á. metropolitana,** metropolitan area; **á. pequeña** or **chica,** goal area.
areca, *f.* (bot.) areca palm; areca palm nut; betel palm.
arecuna, *m.* (Ven.) a Carib people.
arefacción, *f.* drying.
areito, *m.* ceremonial song and dance of Central American and Caribbean Indians.
arel, *m.* large sieve (for wheat).
arelar, *tr.v.* to sieve, sift (wheat).
arena, *f.* 1. sand. 2. filings, grindings (of metal), small particles (of minerals). 3. arena (of a bullring, boxing ring, etc.). 4. (fig.) battlefield. 5. (med.) (*pl.*) gallstones. — **a. movediza,** quicksand; **a. muerta,** pure sand, unmixed with earth and therefore useless for cultivation; **edificar sobre a.,** to build upon sand (on weak foundations); **sembrar en la a.,** to labor in vain, sow on barren ground.
arenáceo, a, *a.* arenaceous, sandy.
arenadora, *f.* sand spreader, sander.
arenal, *m.* sandy ground; sand pit; quicksand.
arenalejo, *m. dim. of* **arenal,** small sandy place or sand pit.
arenar, *tr.v.* to sand, cover with sand; to rub with sand. —*r.v.* to become covered or filled with sand.
arencar, (*ref. 50*) *tr.v.* to dry and salt (sardines).

arencón, *m.* large herring.
arenero, ra, *m., f.* sand dealer or vendor. —*m.* (ry.) sandbox; sand trap, settling basin; grit chamber. —*f.* (Mex.) sandblasting machine.
arenga, *f.* harangue; speech; (fig.) any impassioned and long-winded argument; (coll.) dispute, quarrel.
arengador, ra, *a.* haranguing. —*m., f.* haranguer.
arengar, (*ref. 51*) *tr.v., i.v.* to harangue.
arengue, arengué, *ref.* **arengar.**
arenguista, *m.* (Mex.) *var. of* **arengador.**
arenícolo, la, *a.* (zool.) arenicolous. —*f.* lugworm; (*pl.*) Arenicola.
arenilla, *f.* 1. fine sand used for drying ink; pounce. 2. (med.) calculus, gallstone. 3. (*pl.*) granulated saltpeter used in gunpowder.
arenisca, *f.* (min.) sandstone.
arenisco, a, *a.* sandy, mixed with sand.
arenoso, sa, *a.* sandy, gritty, arenaceous.
arenque, arenqué, *ref.* **arencar.**
arenque, *m.* (ichth.) herring.
arenquera, *f.* herring net.
aréola, *f.* (anat., med., bot.) areola.
areolación, *f.* (biol.) areolation.
areolado, da, *a.* (biol.) areolate.
areolar, *a.* (biol.) areolar.
areometría, *f.* (chem.) hydrometry, areometry.
areómetro, *m.* areometer, hydrometer.
areopagita, *m.* Areopagite, member of the Areopagus (Athenian high court).
areópago, *m.* 1. Areopagus, highest court in ancient Athens. 2. (iron.) panel of experts, e.g. *la Real Academia es el a. de la lengua española,* the Royal Academy is the A. of the Spanish language.
areosístilo, *a., m.* (archit.) araeosystyle.
areóstilo, *a., m.* (archit.) araeostyle.
arepa, *f.* (Amer.) cornmeal griddlecake. — **hacer a.,** (vulg.) to make love (lesbians).
arepera, *f.* (Amer.) 1. pan for making arepa. 2. (Col.) lesbian.
arequipa, *f.* (Mex.) type of milk pudding.
arequipeño, ña, *a.* of or from Arequipa, Peru. —*m., f.* native or inhabitant of Arequipa.
ares, expression used to denote marvelous or wonderful things. — **poseer ares y mares,** (coll.) to own the world; **contar ares y mares,** to tell tall stories; **hacer ares y mares,** to do wonders.
arestil, *m.* (vet.) rash, skin eruption.
arestín, *m.* 1. (bot.) dark blue umbelliferous plant. 2. (med., vet.) rash, skin eruption. 3. displeasure, annoyance.
arestinado, da, *a.* (vet.) suffering from a rash or skin eruption.
arete, *m.* earring.
aretúsea, *f.* (bot.) arethusa (bog orchid).
arfada, *f.* (mar.) pitching.
arfar, *i.v.* (mar.) to pitch.
arfil, *m., var. of* **alfil.**
argadijo, *m.* 1. reel, bobbin. 2. frame for lower part of statue or effigy. 3. (coll.) noisy, blustering, meddlesome person. 4. set of small tools or instruments.
argadillo, *m.* 1. reel, bobbin. 2. frame for lower part of a statue or effigy. 3. (coll.) noisy, blustering, meddlesome person. 4. large wicker basket.
argado, *m.* trick, prank.
argalí, *m.* (zool.) argali, Asian wild sheep.
argalia, *f.* (surg.) catheter.
argallera, *f.* (carp.) plane, cooper's tool for cutting grooves, reed plane.
argamandel, *m.* rag, tatter.
argamandijo, *m.* (coll.) set of small tools or instruments.
argamasa, *f.* (mas.) mortar.
argamasar, *tr.v.* 1. to mix (mortar). 2. to cement, mortar. —*i.v.* to mix mortar.
argamasón, *m.* large piece of mortar.
argán, *m.* (bot.) argan tree.
árgana, *f.* (mec.) crane.
árganas, *f.* (*pl.*) wicker baskets used as packsaddles.
arganel, *m.* (astron.) small metal ring (in an astrolabe).
arganeo, *m.* (mar.) anchor ring.
árgano, *m.* (mec.) crane.
argavieso, *m.* squall, heavy rain shower.
argayo, *m.* 1. (Sp.) landslide, e.g. *a. de nieve,* avalanche. 2. woolen cloak worn by monks of the Dominican Order.
Argel, *m.* Algiers, capital of Algeria.
argel, *a.* with a white right foot (horse).
Argelia, *f.* Algeria.
argelino, na, *a., m., f.* Algerian.
argema, *f.* (med.) argema, corneal ulcer.
argemone, *f.* (bot.) argemone, prickly poppy.
argén, *m.* (her.) argent.
argentada, *f.* cosmetic formerly used by ladies.
argentado, da, *a.* 1. silvered, silvery. 2. silver-plated.
argentador, ra, *a.* silvering. —*m.* silversmith.
argentán, *m.* nickel silver, German silver.
argentar, *tr.v.* 1. to silver, plate with silver. 2. to decorate with silver. 3. to silver, make silvery.
argentario, *m.* 1. silversmith. 2. master of the mint, mintmaster.
argénteo, a, *a.* silvery, shiny like silver; silver-plated.
argentería, *f.* 1. silver or gold embroidery. 2. embellishment, adornment. 3. high flown expression with little content.
argentero, *m.* silversmith.
argentífero, ra, *a.* argentiferous, containing silver.
Argentina, *f.* Argentina, the Argentine.
argentina, *f.* 1. (bot.) silverweed. 2. (min.) argentine.
argentinismo, *m.* Argentinism, word or expression peculiar to Argentina.
argentino, na, *a.* 1. silvery. 2. Argentine. —*m., f.* Argentine, Argentinian (native of Argentina). —*m.* argentino, Argentine gold coin worth five pesos.
argentita, *f.* (min.) argentite (silver ore).
argento, *m.* (poet.) argent, silver. — **a. vivo,** quicksilver; **a. vivo sublimado,** (chem.) mercuric chloride, corrosive sublimate.
argentoso, sa, *a.* argentous, mixed with silver.
argila, *f.* clay.
argiloso, sa, *a.* clayey, clayish.
argilla, *f.* clay.
arginina, *f.* (chem.) arginine.
argirodita, *f.* (min.) argyrodite.
argirol, *m.* (pharm.) argyrol.
argivo, va, *a., m., f.* (hist.) Argive.
argo, *m.* (chem.) argon.
argol, *m.* (chem.) argol.
argólico, ca, *a.* Argive, pertaining to Argolis.
Argólida, *f.* (hist.) Argolis, ancient Greek region.
argolla, *f.* 1. ring, hoop, band. 2. type of croquet. 3. pillory. 4. collar, necklace. 5. tie, bond, shackle, fetter. 6. (Amer.) alliance; ring or group of vested interests, trust. — **a. de compromiso,** engagement ring; **a. de matrimonio,** wedding ring; **formar a.,** (C. Amer.) to form a monopoly or trust; **tener a.,** (coll.) to have pull.
argolleta, *f. dim. of* **argolla,** little ring, band or hoop.
argollón, *m. aug. of* **argolla,** large ring, band or hoop.
árgoma, *f.* (bot.) furze, gorse.
argomal, *m.* gorse thicket.
argón, *m.* (chem.) argon.
argonauta, *m.* 1. (myth.) Argonaut, follower of Jason. 2. (zool.) argonaut, paper nautilus.
argos, *m.* (hist., myth., astron.) Argus, Argo.
argot, *m.* (gal., coll.) argot, jargon.
argucia, *f.* sophistry, subtlety; specious argument or reasoning.
argüe, *m.* (mar.) capstan, windlass.
árguenas, *f.* (*pl.*) 1. wheelbarrow. 2. panniers, saddlebags.
arguenero, *m.* 1. (Chile) maker or vendor of saddlebags or panniers. 2. (Chile) fruit or vegetable vendor who brings his produce in saddlebags or panniers.
árgueñas, *f.* (*pl.*) *var. of* **árguenas.**
argüir, (*ref. 49*) *tr.v.* 1. to argue, reason, e.g. *él arguyó que no tenía obligación alguna con su familia,* he argued that he had no obligation to his family. 2. to imply, indicate, argue. 3. to deduce, prove, argue. 4. to accuse, allege; **a. de,** to accuse of being. —*i.v.* to argue.
argüitivo, va, *a.* argumentative.
argumentación, *f.* argumentation, reasoning, argument.
argumentador, ra, *a.* arguing. —*m., f.* arguer.
argumentante, *a.* arguing. —*m., f.* arguer.
argumentar, *tr.v., i.v.* to argue; to dispute.
argumentativo, va, *a.* argumentative, characterized by or consisting of argument or reasoning.
argumentista, *m., f.* 1. arguer. 2. script or scenario writer.
argumento, *m.* 1. argument, reasoning, (log., philos.) argument. 2. plot (of a play or film); theme, subject, argument (of a book, film). 3. (astron., math.) argument. 4. summary, synopsis. 5. (Car.) argument, dispute. — **a. Aquiles,** decisive piece of reasoning proving a thesis; **a. cornuto,** (log.) dilemma; **a. ontológico,** (philos.) ontological argument.
arguya, *ref.* **argüir.**
arguyendo, arguyera, arguyese, *ref.* **argüir.**
arguyente, *a.* arguing. —*m., f.* **arguer.**
arguyo, *ref.* **argüir.**
aria, *f.* (mus.) aria.
Ariadna, *f.* (myth.) Ariadne, Cretan princess who helped Theseus escape from the Labyrinth.
arica, *f.* (Ven., coll.) wild bee.
aricado, *m.* (agr.) superficial plowing.
aricar, (*ref. 50*) *tr.v.* (agr.) to plow superficially, plow the surface of, harrow.
aridarse, *r.v.* (Mex.) *var. of* **aridecerse.**
aridecer, (*ref. 45*) *tr.v.* (agr.) to make arid, parch. —*i.v., r.v.* to become arid or barren, become parched.
aridez, *f.* aridity, barrenness, aridness.
aridezca, *ref.* **aridecer.**
árido, da, *a.* 1. arid, barren, dry. 2. arid, uninteresting, tedious. —*m.* (*pl.*) dry commodities (grain, vegetables, etc.).
Aries, *m.* (astron.) Aries.
arieta, *f.* (mus.) arietta, short aria.
arietario, ria, *a.* of or pertaining to a battering ram.
ariete, *m.* 1. battering ram. 2. ram, armored steamship with an iron beak. — **a. hidráulico,** (mec.) ram, hydraulic ram.
arietino, na, *a.* resembling a ram's head.
arigue, *m.* (Phil. I.) squared timber.
arije, *a., var. of* **alarijo.**
arijo, ja, *a.* (agr.) light, easily tilled (land).
arilado, da, *a.* (bot.) arillate.
arilo, *m.* (bot.) aril.
arillo, *m.* 1. neck stock frame (of clerics). 2. earring.

arimaspe, *m., var. of* **arimaspo.**
arimaspo, *m.* (myth.) Arimasp, one-eyed man of Scythia.
arimez, (*pl.* **arimeces**) *m.* (archit.) ressaut, projection (in buildings as reinforcement or ornament).
ario, ria, *a., m., f.* 1. Aryan, formerly applied to the Indo-European language family. 2. improperly used by the Nazis to designate a non-Semitic European.
arique, *m.* (Cuba) 1. strip of royal palm bark (used for tying). 2. (fig.) hay. — **no ha soltado el a.,** he still has hay in his hair.
arísaro, *m.* (bot.) wake-robin.
arisblanco, ca, *a.* white-awned (wheat, barley, etc.).
ariscarse, (*ref. 50*) *r.v.* to become surly; to become angry.
arisco, ca, *a.* surly, rude, churlish; shy, skittish.
arisnegro, gra, *a.* black-awned (wheat, barley, etc.).
arisprieto, ta, *a., var. of* **arisnegro.**
arista, *f.* 1. (geom.) edge (formed by intersection of two planes); (archit.) arris (edge formed by meeting of two surfaces); edge (of a sword); (fort.) edge, salient angle (intersection of two planes of a glacis). 2. (bot.) awn, arista; (ento.) arista (tip of antenna of Diptera). 3. chaff (left after scutching flax). — **a. cortante,** cutting edge; **a. viva,** sharp edge; draft edge.
aristado, da, *a.* 1. awned, bearded. 2. edged.
Aristarco, *m.* 1. Aristarchus, Greek critic and grammarian. 2. **a.,** (derog.) severe critic.
aristino, *m.* (vet.) *var. of* **arestín.**
aristocracia, *f.* aristocracy.
aristócrata, *m., f.* aristocrat.
aristocráticamente, *adv.* aristocratically.
aristocratice, *ref.* **aristocratizar.**
aristocrático, ca, *a.* aristocratic.
aristocratizar, (*ref. 53*) *tr.v.* to make aristocratic.
Aristófanes, *m.* (hist., lit.) Aristophanes, Athenian dramatist.
aristofánico, ca, *a.* Aristophanic.
aristoloquia, *f.* (bot.) aristolochia, birthwort.
aristoloquiáceo, a, *a.* (bot.) aristolochiaceous. —*f.* (*pl.*) Aristolochiaceae.
aristón, *m.* 1. (archit.) edge, corner (of a building). 2. (mus.) barrel organ, hurdygurdy.
aristoso, sa, *a.* awned, bearded.
Aristóteles, *m.* (hist.) Aristotle, Greek philosopher.
aristotélico, ca, *a., m., f.* Aristotelian.
aristotelismo, *m.* Aristotelianism.
aritenoide, *m.* (anat.) arytenoid.
aritenoideo, a, *a.* (anat.) arytenoid.
aritmética, *f.* arithmetic.
aritméticamente, *adv.* arithmetically.
aritmético, ca, *a.* arithmetical. —*m., f.* arithmetician.
aritmógrafo, *m., var. of* **aritmómetro.**
aritmomanía, *f.* mania for numbers.
aritmómetro, *m.* adding machine.
arjorán, *m.* (bot.) Judas tree.
arlar, *tr.v.* to bunch (fruits).
arlequín, *m.* 1. **A.,** Harlequin (in commedia dell'arte). 2. harlequin, buffoon; (coll.) ridiculous person. 3. harlequin or Neapolitan ice cream. — **a. de frutas,** (Cuba) mixed fruit dessert.
arlequinada, *f.* harlequinade.
arlequinesco, ca, *a.* harlequinesque.
arlo, *m.* 1. (bot.) barberry. 2. bunch of fruit.
arlota, *f., var. of* **alrota.**
arma, *f.* 1. weapon; (*pl.*) arms, weapons. 2. (mil.) branch of an army. 3. (taur.) horn; (*pl.*) natural defenses (of any animal). 4. (*pl.*) troops, army (of a nation); army, military profession. 5. (*pl.*) parts (of certain instruments). 6. (*pl.*) arms, bearings, heraldic devices; coat of arms, escutcheon. 7. (*pl.*) fighting, feats of arms. — **¡a las armas!** to arms!; **alzarse en armas,** to rebel, rise; **a. arrojadiza,** missile, thrown or projected weapon (spear, arrow, etc.); **a. atómica,** atomic weapon; **a. automática,** automatic, automatic weapon; **a. blanca,** weapon with a blade (e.g. sword, bayonet, etc.); **a. de chispa,** flintlock, flintlock weapon; **a. de fuego,** firearm; **a. de percusión,** percussion lock weapon; **a. de repetición,** repeating firearm; **a. negra,** foil, blunted sword (used in learning fencing); **armas blancas,** (her.) heraldic devices of a new knight which were not put on his shield until he had earned them in battle; **armas falsas,** (her.) heraldic bearings in disagreement with the rules; **de armas tomar,** of action, resolute, bold, energetic, e.g. *es un hombre de armas tomar,* he's a man of action; **descansar las armas,** (mil.) to stand at ease; **estar en a.** or **en armas,** to be engaged in a civil war, be up in arms; **hacer armas,** to make war; to fight; to threaten with a weapon; **pasar por las armas,** (mil.) to execute; **presentar las armas,** to present arms; **rendir las armas,** (mil.) to surrender, lay down arms (to the enemy); **sobre las armas,** (mil.) ready for action; **tocar el a., tocar a.,** to sound the call to arms; **tomar armas** or **las armas,** to take up arms.
armada, *f.* 1. navy; fleet, armada. — **A. Invencible,** (hist.) Spanish Armada. 2. (hunt.) line of hunters; line of beaters. 3. (S. Amer.) circular shape (of lassos coiled for throwing).
armadera, *f.* (mar.) main rib or timber (of a ship's frame).
armadía, *f.* raft, float.
armadijo, *m.* trap, snare (for game).
armadilla, *f.* (sl.) gambling money (given to somebody to gamble on one's behalf).
armadillo, *m.* (zool.) armadillo.
armado, da, *past part. of* **armar.** —*a.* 1. armed; (her.) armed. 2. reinforced (concrete). 3. (Mex., P. Rico) stubborn. —*m.* 1. man in armor in a procession. 2. (Mex.) armadillo. 3. (Arg.) handrolled cigarette.
armador, ra, *m., f.* assembler, fitter. —*m.* 1. shipowner. 2. corsair, privateer. 3. recruiter (of sailors for cod and whale fishing). 4. doublet, jacket.
armadura, *f.* 1. armor, armature. 2. frame, framework, shell, truss; (fig.) framework. 3. (anat.) frame, skeleton. 4. (elec.) armature. 5. (mus.) key signature, accidents. 6. (mar.) iron ring. — **a. volada,** cantilever truss.
armaga, *f.* (bot.) rue (Ruta graveolens).
Armagedón, *m.* (Bib.) Armageddon.
armajal, *m.* swamp, marsh, fen.
armajo, *m.* (bot.) glasswort.
armamentista, *a.* armaments, e.g. *carrera a.,* armaments race.
armamento, *m.* armament; armaments, weapons.
armar, *tr.v.* 1. to arm, provide or furnish with arms. 2. to prime, cock, load (gun for firing); to fix (bayonets); to tighten, tense, tauten (string of bow, spring of any mechanism in general). 3. to assemble, put together, put up, mount, pitch (a tent), stack (rifles), set (a trap). 4. to base, found, build, construct, establish. 5. to cause, create (a scandal, trouble, etc.). 6. (mar.) to provision, fit out, equip (a ship). 7. to equip. 8. to arrange, organize, prepare. 9. to reinforce, strengthen. 10. to lay, put (silver or gold on other metals). 11. to leave (a tree) with a shoot for guiding growth. 12. (Arg.) to roll, make (a cigarette). — **a. caballero,** to confer knighthood, to knight; **armarla,** to cause a row; **a. un escándalo,** to create a scandal; **a. un jaleo,** to kick up a fuss. —*i.v.* to fit, suit; to go (with). —*r.v.* 1. to arm, arm oneself; (fig.) to arm oneself (e.g. with patience). 2. to start, break out (a quarrel, trouble, row, scandal, etc.), e.g. *se armó la gorda, la de San Quintín* or *la de Dios es Cristo,* a tremendous quarrel, fight or row broke out. 3. (C. Amer., Mex.) to balk, stop, halt, be unwilling to go on (an animal); to balk, be stubborn or obstinate (a person). 4. (Amer.) to get what one wants; to get rich, make a pile, make a killing.
armario, *m.* closet, wardrobe; cupboard.
armatoste, *m.* 1. hulk, cumbersome ugly thing; (coll.) hulk, slob, fat useless person. 2. trap, snare. 3. leading device on a crossbow.
armazón, *f.* framework, frame; assembling, assemblage (of a piece of furniture). —*m.* skeleton, frame.
armelina, *f.* ermine skin.
armella, *f.* eyebolt, staple, screw eye.
armelluela, *f. dim. of* **armella,** eyebolt, staple.
armenio, nia, *a., m., f.* Armenian. —*m.* Armenian (language).
armería, *f.* 1. armory, arsenal. 2. armory (armorer's workshop; gunsmith trade).
armero, *m.* 1. armorer, gunsmith. 2. gun rack; arms rack.
armífero, ra, *a., var. of* **armígero.**
armígero, ra, *a.* 1. (poet.) bearing arms, armored. 2. warlike. —*m.* armor-bearer, squire.
armilar, *a.* armillary, armillary sphere.
armilla, *f.* (archit.) surbase, torus, principal part of the base of a column.
armiñado, da, *past part. of* **armiñar.** —*a.* 1. ermined. 2. ermine-white, spotless.
armiñar, *tr.v.* to make ermine-white.
armiño, *m.* 1. (zool.) ermine, ermine (fur). 2. (fig.) purity, spotlessness. 3. white spot or mark near the hoof of a horse.
armipotente, *a.* (poet.) mighty in war.
armisonante, *a.* (poet.) clanging and ringing with arms.
armisticio, *m.* armistice.
armón, *m.* (artil.) limber.
armonía, *f.* 1. harmony, agreement, cordiality. 2. (mus.) harmony.
armónica, *f.* 1. (mus.) harmonica, mouth organ. 2. (mus.) harmonica (form of glockenspiel with glass bars instead of metal ones).
armónicamente, *adv.* harmonically.
armonice, armonicé, *ref.* **armonizar.**
armónico, ca, *a.* harmonic. —*m.* (mus.) harmonic, overtone.
armonio, *m.* (mus.) harmonium, a small reed organ.
armoniosamente, *adv.* harmoniously.
armonioso, sa, *a.* harmonious.
armonizable, *a.* harmonizable, able to be harmonized.
armonización, *f.* harmonization.
armonizar, (*ref. 53*) *tr.v.* to harmonize.
armuelle, *m.* (bot.) orach (Atriplex hortense). — **a. borde,** wild orach, white goosefoot.
arna, *f.* beehive.
arnacho, *m.* (bot.) restharrow.
arnadi, (*pl.* **arnadíes**) *m.* candy containing almonds, nuts, etc.
arnaucho, *m.* (Peru) small very hot chile pepper.
arnés, *m.* 1. (*pl.*) harness. 2. armor. 3. any set of trappings, tools; equipment, outfit.
árnica, *f.* (bot., pharm.) arnica.
arnicina, *f.* crystalline alkaloid extracted from arnica flowers.
arnillo, *m.* (ichth.) Acanthopterygian fish from the Antilles (Apsilus dentatus).

aro, *m.* 1. hoop, ring; (auto.) tire rim. 2. (Amer.) wedding band or ring. 3. (Arg., Chile) drop earring. 4. (bot.) cuckoopint, arum; **a. de Etiopía,** (bot.) calla lily, arum lily. — **a. del émbolo** or **pistón,** piston ring; **entrar por el a.,** (coll.) to yield to something unwillingly, do something unwillingly.
¡aro! *interj.* (Chile) expression used to interrupt someone who is singing, dancing, etc. with the offer of a drink. —*m.* interruption.
aroideo, a, *a.* (bot.) aroid. —*f.* aroid, plant of arum family; (*pl.*) Araceae.
aroma, *m.* aroma, perfume, scent, fragrance. —*f.* (bot.) aroma, huisache flower.
aromal, *m.* (Cuba) aroma or huisache patch.
aromar, *tr.v., var. of* **aromatizar.**
aromatice, aromaticé, *ref.* **aromatizar.**
aromaticidad, *f.* fragrance, scent; aromatic quality.
aromático, ca, *a.* aromatic, fragrant, scented.
aromatización, *f.* aromatization.
aromatizante, *a.* aromatizing, perfuming.
aromatizar, (*ref. 53*) *tr.v.* to aromatize, perfume, scent.
aromo, *m.* (bot.) aromo, huisache.
aromoso, sa, *a., var. of* **aromático.**
aron, *m.* (bot.) cuckoopint, arum.
arpa, *f.* (mus.) harp. — **a. eolia,** aeolian harp; **tronar como a. vieja,** (coll.) to come to an unfortunate and sudden end, come to a bad end.
arpado, da, *past part. of* **arpar.** —*a.* 1. serrated, toothed. 2. (poet.) sweet-voiced, dulcet-toned (bird song).
arpadura, *f.* scratch.
arpar, *tr.v.* to scratch, claw, tear with nails or claws; to tear to tatters.
arpegio, *m.* (mus.) arpeggio.
arpella, *f.* (ornith.) marsh harrier.
arpende, *m.* old Spanish land measurement.
arpeo, *m.* (mar.) grappling iron, grapnel; cant hook. — **arpeos de pie,** climbing irons.
arpía, *f.* 1. (myth.) Harpy (evil creature part woman, part bird). 2. (coll.) harpy, shrew. 3. harpy, rapacious person. 4. (ornith.) harpy eagle.
arpillador, *m.* (Mex.) packer, wrapper, person who covers (bales, etc.) with burlap.
arpilladura, *f.* (Mex.) covering with burlap or sackcloth.
arpillar, *tr.v.* (Mex.) to cover with burlap or with sackcloth.
arpillera, *f.* 1. *var. of* **harpillera.** 2. burlap, bagging.
arpir, *m.* (Amer.) 1. (Aymara) porter, carrier. 2. mine hand.
arpista, *m., f.* (mus.) harpist, harper.
arpón, *m.* 1. harpoon, spear. 2. (archit. clamp.
arponado, da, *past part. of* **arponar.** —*a.* harpoon-like; pronged, ragged (bolt).
arponar, arponear, *tr.v.* to harpoon.
arponero, *m.* 1. harpooner. 2. harpoon maker.
arqueada, *m.* 1. (mus.) bow, stroke of bow. 2. retching, nausea.
arqueador, *m.* (mar.) 1. ship surveyor, ship gauger. 2. wool beater.
arqueaje, *m.* 1. (mar.) gauging, surveying (of ships). 2. (mar.) tonnage.
arqueamiento, *m., var. of* **arqueaje.**
arquear, *tr.v.* 1. to arch. 2. to beat (wool). 3. to gauge, survey (a ship). —*i.v.* to retch, be sick with nausea.
arquegonio, *m.* (bot.) archegonium.
arquéntero, *m.* (zool.) archenteron.
arqueo, *m.* 1. arching, bending. 2. beating (of wool). 3. (mar.) gauging, surveying (of ships). 4. (mar.) tonnage, capacity (of a ship). 5. (acc.) audit; appraisal of assets. — **a. bruto,** (mar.) gross tonnage; **a. neto,** net tonnage.
arqueolítico, ca, *a.* of the Stone Age.
arqueología, *f.* archaeology.
arqueológico, ca, *a.* archaeological.
arqueólogo, *m.* archaeologist.
arquería, *f.* 1. arcade. 2. (Mex.) aqueduct.
arquero, *m.* 1. cashier, teller (bank, treasury, etc.). 2. archer (soldier). 3. hooper, cooper, hoopmaker (for casks, barrels). 4. (sport.) goalkeeper.
arquetípico, ca, *a.* archetypal.
arquetipo, *m.* archetype.
arquetón, *m. aug. of* **arqueta,** big chest or coffer.
arquibanco, *m.* bench or seat with drawers.
arquidiócesis, *f.* archidiocese.
arquiepiscopal, *a.* archiepiscopal.
Arquímedes, *m.* (hist.) Archimedes, Greek physicist and mathematician.
arquimesa, *f.* writing desk, bureau.
arquisinagogo, *m.* principal of a synogogue.
arquitecto, *m.* architect.
arquitectónico, ca, *a.* architectonic, architectural.
arquitectura, *f.* architecture.
arquitectural, *a.* architectural.
arquitrabe, *m.* (archit.) architrave.
arquivolta, *f.* (archit.) archivolt.
arrabá, *m.* (archit.) rectangular ornament that frames the arches of doors and windows in Arabic architecture.
arrabal, *m.* suburb; (*pl.*) outskirts (of a town); (Amer.) city slums.
arrabalero, ra, *a.* 1. suburban. 2. (coll.) ill-bred, uncouth, coarse. —*m., f.* 1. suburbanite. 2. ill-bred person.
arrabiatar, *tr.v.* (C. Amer.) to tie head to tail in single file. —*r.v.* (C. Amer.) to submit slavishly.
arrabillado, da, *a.* blighted (wheat).
arrabio, *m.* (metal.) cast iron.
arracacha, *f.* 1. (bot.) arracacha. 2. (fig., Col.) nonsense, stupidity.
arracada, *f.* drop earring.
arracimado, da, *past part. of* **arracimar.** —*a.* clustered, in clusters.
arracimarse, *r.v.* to gather in clusters.
arraclán, *m.* (bot.) alder buckthorn, alder dogwood.
arráez, (*pl.* **arráeces**) *m.* 1. Arabian or Moorish leader; captain of a Moorish ship; (Phil. I.) ship's captain or master; leader, foreman (on a tuna fishing expedition).
arraigadamente, *adv.* fixedly, securely.
arraigadas, *f.* (*pl.*) (mar.) futtock shrouds.
arraigado, da, *past part. of* **arraigar.** —*a.* 1. deeply-rooted. 2. possessing real estate. —*m.* (mar.) lashing, mooring (line or chain).
arraigán, *m.* (Cuba) Chinese tallow tree.
arraigante, *a.* deep-rooting, securing, secure.
arraigar, (*ref. 51*) *tr.v.* 1. to fix, root, establish firmly. 2. (Amer.) to confine (someone) to the town limits. —*i.v.* 1. to take root. 2. to become deeply rooted (habits, vices, etc.). 3. (law) to give bail, bond or surety. —*r.v.* to settle, establish oneself in a place.
arraigo, *m.* 1. settling (in a place), taking root. 2. real estate, landed property.
arraigue, arraigué, *ref.* **arraigar.**
arralar, *i.v., var. of* **ralear.**
arramblar, *tr.v.* 1. to cover (land) with sand and gravel (a rushing river, flood, etc.). 2. to sweep away, carry away. —*r.v.* to become (land) covered with sand and gravel (due to a flood, etc.).
arramplar, *tr.v.* (fig.) to ransack, strip of everything.
arrancaclavos, *m.* nail puller, claw bar.
arrancada, *f.* 1. starting jerk, sudden start (of ship, car, train, etc.); sudden increase of speed. 2. sudden charge or attack.
arrancadera, *f.* cowbell worn by tame cattle used in leading the herd.
arrancadero, *m.* starting point.
arrancado, da, *past part. of* **arrancar.** —*a.* (coll.) broke, penniless, poor.
arrancador, ra, *m.* 1. starter. 2. anything that pulls out or wrenches. — **a. automático,** self-starter.
arrancadura, *f.* pulling out, extraction.
arrancamiento, *m., var. of* **arrancadura.**
arrancapinos, *m.* (coll.) small person; (fig.) dwarf.
arrancar, (*ref. 50*) *tr.v.* 1. to pull up, uproot; to pull out, extract; to tear off, tear away, pull off; to wrench, snatch, snatch away, seize, take; to get, obtain. 2. to heave (a sigh); to spit, expectorate. 3. (mar.) to make (a ship) go faster. 4. (Amer.) to start (a motor). —*i.v.* 1. to start; to set off, set out, leave; to set sail. 2. (mar.) to pick up speed. 3. to originate, come (from). 4. (archit.) to spring (vault or arch from impost).
arrancasiega, *f.* 1. (agr.) reaping (wheat) while at the same time pulling out plants too small to be cut by the scythe. 2. poor quality grain. 3. dispute, quarrel.
arranchar, *tr.v.* 1. (mar.) to skirt, sail close to. 2. to haul close aft, brace (sails). 3. (Amer.) to seize, snatch, take. —*r.v.* 1. to eat together. 2. (Mex., Ven.) to settle down.
arranciarse, *r.v., var. of* **enranciarse.**
arrancón, *m.* sudden start, abrupt takeoff.
arranque, arranqué, *ref.* **arrancar.**
arranque, *m.* 1. fit, outburst (of anger, passion, etc.). 2. beginning, start. 3. (archit.) springing (point at which arch begins). — **línea de a.,** spring line. 4. (biol.) base, beginning (of a limb or of any part of animal or plant). 5. (mec.) starter, starting gear (of car); starting (of car). 6. witty remark, sally. 7. pulling out, pulling up. 8. wrench, wrenching, snatching, seizing. — **a. en frío,** cold starting.
arranquera, *f.* (Cuba, Mex., P. Rico) lack of money, poverty.
arrapar, *tr.v.* to snatch away, seize, take away by force.
arrapiezo, *m.* 1. rag, tatter. 2. urchin, ragamuffin.
arrapo, *m.* 1. *var. of* **harapo,** rag, tatter. 2. insignificant quantity, whit.
arras, *f.* (*pl.*) 1. pledge, token (of a contract). 2. thirteen coins given by bridegroom to bride at wedding. 3. (law) gift made by husband to the wife; dowry.
arrasado, da, *past part. of* **arrasar.** —*a.* satiny, satin-like.
arrasadura, *f.* leveling with a strickle.
arrasamiento, *m.* razing, demolition; destruction.
arrasar, *tr.v.* 1. to smooth, level. 2. to raze, destroy, demolish. 3. to fill to the brim. 4. to level with a strickle. —*r.v.* 1. to fill with tears (eyes). 2. to clear, become clear (the sky).
arrastraculo, *m.* (mar.) driver, water sail.
arrastradamente, *adv.* 1. (coll.) imperfectly, defectively. 2. arduously, laboriously. 3. unhappily, with a heavy heart.
arrastradera, *f.* (mar.) lower studding-sail.
arrastradero, *m.* 1. log path (over which logs are dragged). 2. place through which dead bulls are dragged from the bullring.
arrastradizo, za, *a.* 1. trailing, dragging. 2. beaten, frequented (path).
arrastrado, da, *past part. of* **arrastrar.** —*a.* 1. wretched, miserable. 2. roguish, rascally. —*m., f.* rogue, rascal, scamp.

arrastramiento, *m.* dragging, towing, trailing.
arrastrante, *a.* dragging, towing, trailing. —*m.* applicant for a scholarship.
arrastrapiés, *m.* shuffling or dragging feet.
arrastrar, *tr.v.* 1. to pull, drag, pull along, haul, tow; to carry away, sweep away; to drag, shuffle (one's feet); to drag down (e.g. into disgrace, misfortune, etc.). 2. to draw (cards). 3. to attract, pull, draw; to convince, win over. 4. to drag out (one's life). —*i.v.* 1. to drag, trail. 2. to crawl, creep; to slide, slither. 3. to draw cards. —*r.v.* 1. to drag, trail; (fig.) to drag, be tedious. 2. to creep, crawl; to slide, slither. 3. to crawl, cringe, lower oneself.
arrastre, *m.* 1. dragging, towing; haulage, drayage; (taur.) dragging out of bull (at end of bullfight); drawing of trumps or certain suit (in cards). 2. (min.) slope of an adit. 3. (min., Mex.) silver mill. 4. (Arg., Cuba, Urug.) pull, influence; (Dom. Rep.) political pull or influence. — **estar para el a.,** to be a wreck; **pesca de a.,** trawler fishing; **a. capilar,** (chem.) capillary entrainment.
arrastrojarse, *r.v.* (Col.) become overgrown with weeds, underbrush.
arrate, *m.* pound (weight), avoirdupois.
arratonado, da, *a.* gnawed or eaten by mice or rats.
arrayán, *m.* (bot.) myrtle. — **a. brabántico,** wax myrtle.
arrayanal, *m.* myrtle field.
arráyaz, (*pl.* **arráyaces**) *m., var. of* **arráez.**
arraz, (*pl.* **arraces**) *m., var. of* **arráez.**
¡arre! *interj.* get up! giddap! —*m.* (coll.) nag, old nag; toy horse.
arreada, *f.* 1. (Mex., Arg.) rustling, cattle stealing. 2. (Arg., Urug.) recruiting; shanghaiing.
arreado, da, *past part. of* **arrear.** —*a.* 1. (coll.) impoverished, poor. 2. (Amer., coll.) slow, lazy, sluggish.
arreador, *m.* 1. (Amer.) small whip (for driving or herding cattle). 2. olive harvester. 3. muleteer.
arrear, *tr.v.* 1. to drive, herd, prod (cattle). 2. (Arg., Mex.) to steal, rustle (cattle). 3. to hurry, urge on. 4. to hit, strike. 5. (Arg., Urug.) to recruit, shanghai. —*i.v.* to hurry, hasten. — **¡arrea!** (coll.) hurry up! get moving!; (coll.) nonsense! (interjection used to indicate disagreement).
arrear, *tr.v.* 1. to harness. 2. to decorate, embellish.
arrebañaderas, *f. pl.* hook, grappling hooks.
arrebañador, ra, *a.* scraping, gathering, collecting. —*m., f.* gatherer, collector, scraper.
arrebañadura, *f.* 1. (coll.) gathering up completely; eating up completely; finishing off. 2. (*pl.*) leavings, left-overs.
arrebañar, *tr.v.* 1. to gather up completely. 2. to eat up completely, finish the last bits of (food), to scrape the plate clean.
arrebatadamente, *adv.* headlong, precipitately, rashly; violently.
arrebatadizo, za, *a.* violent, prone to violence; rash, impetuous.
arrebatado, da, *past part. of* **arrebatar.** —*a.* 1. impetuous, rash. 2. violent. 3. (coll.) crazy.
arrebatador, ra, *a.* 1. captivating, arresting, charming. 2. violent. 3. exciting, stirring.
arrebatamiento, *m.* 1. snatching, seizing, carrying away. 2. fury, rage, passion. 3. ecstasy, rapture.
arrebatapuñadas, *m.* bully, brawler.
arrebatar, *tr.v.* 1. to snatch, snatch away, seize, e.g. *le arrebataron la carta,* they snatched the letter away from him; to carry off, carry away. 2. to carry away, move, stir, arouse or excite powerfully; to charm, attract, captivate. 3. to parch, dry up (crops). —*r.v.* 1. to get or be carried away, be seized, be stirred (by anger, passion, mystic ecstasy, etc.), e.g. *se arrebató de ira,* he was seized with anger, he flew into a rage. 2. to become parched (crops); to be burned (food).
arrebatiña, *f.* scramble, grabbing, scuffle; free-for-all.
arrebato, *m.* 1. fury, fit, rage. 2. ecstasy, rapture.
arrebatoso, sa, *a.* quick, sudden.
arrebol, *m.* red (of clouds, sunset); rouge, cosmetic; rosiness (of cheeks); (*pl.*) red tinted clouds.
arrebolada, *f.* red tinted clouds.
arrebolar, *tr.v.* to redden, make red; to rouge. —*r.v.* 1. to redden, turn red. 2. to make up, rouge. 3. (Ven.) to dress up, adorn oneself. 4. (Col.) to make a fuss.
arrebolera, *f.* 1. rouge box. 2. (bot.) four-o'clock, marvel of Peru.
arrebozar, (*ref. 53*) *tr.v.* 1. to muffle up (face); (fig.) to hide, conceal, cover up. 2. (Peru, cul.) to coat with or cook in batter. —*r.v.* 1. to muffle up one's face. 2. to swarm, cluster (insects).
arrebozo, *m., var. of* **rebozo.**
arrebujadamente, *adv.* confusedly, jumbled.
arrebujar, *tr.v.* to jumble or bundle together. —*r.v.* to wrap oneself (in bedclothes, cloak, etc.).
arrechera, *m.* (Amer.) lust, lechery.
arrecharse, *r.v.* (Amer.) to get sexually aroused.
arrecho, cha, *a.* 1. (Amer.) sexually excited, in heat, lustful. 2. (Amer.) brave, spirited.
arrechucho, *m.* 1. (coll.) fit, sudden impulse or outburst. 2. sudden and passing indisposition.
arreciar, *tr.v.* to make stronger. —*i.v.* 1. to get stronger, put on weight. 2. to grow worse, grow more severe or violent. —*r.v.* to grow worse, grow more severe or violent. — **arrecia la lluvia,** it's raining harder.
arrecife, *m.* 1. (mar.) reef. 2. stone paved road; roadbed, gravel bed of road.
arrecirse, (*ref. 78*) *r.v.* to become numb (a limb) due to cold.
arredilar, *tr.v.* to put (sheep, cattle) in a pen or corral.
arredomado, da, *a.* artful, cunning, sly.
arredondear, *tr.v., r.v., var. of* **redondear.**
arredramiento, *m.* 1. moving back, backing away. 2. fright, fear.
arredrar, *tr.v.* to move away, remove; to drive back, move back; to frighten or scare away. —*r.v.* to draw back, shrink back; to move away, back away; to become frightened, be scared.
arredro, *adv.* back, backwards.
arregazado, da, *past part. of* **arregazar.** —*a.* turned up (point, tip), upturned.
arregazar, (*ref. 53*) *tr.v.* to tuck up or gather on one's lap.
arregladamente, *adv.* following the rules; in an orderly manner.
arreglado, da, *past part. of* **arreglar.** —*a.* 1. orderly; tidy, neat. 2. moderate, reasonable. — **arreglado a,** according to, in accordance with.
arreglador, *m.* (com.) surveyor, valuer (of averages).
arreglar, *tr.v.* 1. to arrange, put in order, tidy up, put straight, make attractive. 2. to arrange, settle, fix up; to solve, put straight or right. 3. to mend, repair. 4. (mus.) to arrange. 5. to punish, correct. 6. (Amer.) to doctor, castrate (a cat). 7. (mar.) to check, adjust (chronometers). —*r.v.* 1. to be arranged, settled or fixed. 2. to conform, agree. 3. to dress up, smarten or tidy oneself up. — **arreglarse con,** to conform to, to agree with; to come to an agreement with; **arreglárselas,** to manage.
arreglo, *m.* 1. tidying up, putting straight; arrangement (of furniture, of flowers); **a. floral,** flower arrangement. 2. repair, mending. 3. arrangement, agreement, settlement, compromise. 4. (mus.) arrangement. 5. (coll.) cohabitation, concubinage. — **a. personal,** personal appearance; **con a. a,** according to, in accordance with.
arregostarse, *r.v.* (coll.) to grow fond of, acquire a taste for.
arregosto, *m.* (coll.) liking, taste (for).
arrejacar, (*ref. 50*) *tr.v.* (agr.) to harrow.
arrejaco, *m.* (ornith.) swift.
arrejada, *f.* (agr.) plowstaff, paddle for cleaning soil from plowshare.
arrejaque, *m.* 1. three-pronged fishing spear. 2. (ornith.) swift.
arrejerar, *tr.v.* (mar.) to make (a ship) fast by casting two anchors fore and one aft.
arrejonado, da, *a.* (bot.) lanceolate, spear-like (leaves).
arrelde, *m.* (arch.) four pound weight.
arrellanarse, 1. *r.v.* to stretch out, make oneself comfortable. 2. (fig.) to enjoy one's work.
arremangado, da, *past part. of* **arremangar.** —*a.* turned up; tucked up.
arremangar, (*ref. 51*) *tr.v.* to turn up, roll up (sleeves, cuffs), tuck up (skirt). —*r.v.* 1. to turn up, roll up (sleeves, cuffs), tuck up (skirt). 2. (coll.) to make a firm decision, take a firm stand.
arremango, *m.* tucking up; tuck (in tucked up clothes).
arremangue, arremangué, *ref.* **arremangar.**
arrematar, *tr.v.* (coll.) to end, complete, finish, put an end to.
arremedar, *tr.v., var. of* **remedar.**
arremetedero, *m.* (mil.) weak point of a fortress, point to be attacked in a fortress.
arremetedor, ra, *a.* attacking, assaulting. —*m., f.* assailant, attacker, aggressor.
arremeter, *tr.v.* to assail, attack, assault. —*i.v.* 1. to rush forth, launch forth, attack. 2. (coll.) to shock, be offensive (to look at). — **a. contra,** to rush at, attack; **a. contra molinos de viento,** to tilt at windmills.
arremetida, *f.* assault, attack.
arremetimiento, *m., var. of* **arremetida.**
arremolinadamente, *adv.* in a turmoil; in a whirl.
arremolinado, da, *a.* whirling, eddying; milling around, crowding around.
arremolinarse, *r.v.* 1. to mill around, crowd around. 2. to form whirls (water, wind).
arrempujar, *tr.v., var. of* **rempujar** (improper use).
arrempujón, *m., var. of* **empujón** (improper use).
arremueco, *m., var. of* **arremuesco.**
arremuesco, *m.* (Col.) caress.
arrendable, *a.* leasable, rentable.
arendación, *f., var. of* **arrendamiento.**
arrendadero, *m.* hitching ring, iron ring used for tying a horse to its stall in the stable.
arrendado, da, *past part. of* **arrendar.** —*a.* 1. rented, leased. 2. obedient to the rein (a horse).
arrendador, ra, *m., f.* lessor, landlord; tenant, lessee, hirer. —*m.* 1. (sl.) fence, receiver of stolen goods. 2. hitching ring (to which a horse is tied).
arrendajo, *m.* 1. (ornith.) jay, mocking bird. 2. (coll.) mimic.
arrendamiento, *m.* renting, letting; lease; rent.
arrendante, *m., f.* lessor, landlord, renter. 2. lessee, renter, tenant.
arrendar, (*ref. 29*) *tr.v.* 1. to rent, let, lease. 2. to rent, hold or occupy under a lease. 3. to hitch, tie up (a horse). 4. to train (a horse). 5. (fig.) to secure, tie. 6. to mimic.

arrendatario, ria, *a.* leasing, renting. —*m., f.* lessee, tenant.
arrendaticio, cia, *a.* (law) pertaining to rent.
arrenquín, *m.* 1. (Amer.) leader (of a team of pack animals). 2. helper (hired by cartmen, muleteers, travelers). 3. inseparable friend, buddy.
arreo, *m.* 1. ornament, decoration. 2. (*pl.*) harness, trappings (of a horse). 3. accessories, appurtenances.
arreo, *adv.* successively, uninterruptedly.
arrepanchigarse, (*ref. 51*) *r.v.* (coll.) *var. of* **repantigarse,** to stretch or sprawl (oneself) in a chair.
arrepápalo, *m.* doughnut, fritter.
arrepentido, da, *a.* repentant. —*m., f.* penitent.
arrepentimiento, *m.* 1. repentance. 2. (p.) correction (to a painting).
arrepentirse, (*ref. 42*) *r.v.* to repent, regret. — **a. de,** to repent, repent for (e.g. one's sins, etc.); **a. de** + *perfect inf.* to repent or regret + *ger.*, e.g. *a. de reñir,* to regret quarreling.
arrepienta, arrepiento, *ref.* **arrepentirse.**
arrepistar, *tr.v.* to pulp, grind (rags) into a pulp (in paper making).
arrepisto, *m.* grinding, pulping (of rags).
arrepticio, cia, *a.* possessed (by the devil).
arrequesonarse, *r.v.* to become curdled, sour, go bad (milk).
arrequife, *m.* iron bearing (supporting the pressing cylinder of a cotton gin).
arrequintar, *tr.v.* (Amer., coll.) to tighten with a cord or bandage.
arrequive, *m.* 1. decorative fringe or border (of a dress); (*pl.*) finery, adornments, ornaments, trappings. 2. (*pl.*) circumstances.
arrestado, da, *past part. of* **arrestar.** —*a.* audacious, bold, daring.
arrestallamas, *m.* (mec.) flame arrester.
arrestar, *tr.v.* to arrest; detain. —*r.v.* **arrestarse a,** to tackle boldly, take on resolutely.
arresto, *m.* 1. arrest; imprisonment, detention. 2. (*pl.*) boldness, daring, enterprise, spirit. — **a. domicillario,** house arrest; **bajo a.,** under arrest; **a. mayor,** imprisonment (up to 6 months); **a. menor,** imprisonment (up to a month); **a. preventivo,** preventive detention.
arretín, *m.* moreen, woolen cloth.
arretranca, *f., var. of* **retranca.**
arrevesado, da, *a.* intricate, difficult.
arrezafe, *m.* (bot.) 1. cotton thistle. 2. bramble, bramble patch.
arrezagar, (*ref. 51*) *tr.v.* to tuck up, hitch up, roll up. 2. to raise.
arria, *f.* team (of pack animals), drove of beasts.
arriada, *f.* 1. (mar.) hauling down, taking in (a sail), slacking off (of cable). 2. (reg.) flood, freshet, washout.
arrial, *m., var. of* **arriaz.**
arrianismo, *m.* Arianism.
arriano, na, *a., m., f.* (rel.) Arian.
arriar, *tr.v.* 1. (mar.) to haul down (sails, flags); to slacken, cast off (a rope, line, chain). 2. *tr.v.* to flood, inundate. —*r.v.* to become flooded or inundated.
arriata, *f., var. of* **arriate.**
arriate, *m.* 1. narrow flower border (along-side wall). 2. highway, road. 3. **cane** trellis.
arriaz, (*pl.* **arriaces**) *m.* quillon (of a sword hilt); grip (of a sword).
arriba, *adv.* 1. (position) above, upstairs (in a house), overhead (in the sky), aloft (in a ship). 2. (movement) up, upwards, upstairs. — **aguas a.,** upstream; **¡a.!** up with! (exclamation of support); **a. citado,** above-mentioned; **a. las manos,** hands up!; **cuesta a.,** uphill; **de a.,** from above; **de a. abajo,** from beginning to end; from top to bottom; **más a.,** higher up; **para a.,** up, upwards; **río a.,** upstream, upriver.
arribada, *f.* 1. arrival. 2. (mar.) leeward tack. 3. (Arg.) violent and insolent answer or response. — **a. forzosa,** (law) emergency or forced arrival (of ship at a port due to bad weather); **estar de a.,** (mar.) to be making an emergency arrival.
arribaje, *m.* arrival of a ship to port.
arribar, *i.v.* 1. to arrive. 2. (coll.) to recover, recuperate. 3. (mar.) to drift with the wind. 4. (mar.) to fall off to leeward. — **a. a,** to reach, get to, arrive at. —*r.v.* to recover, recuperate.
arribazón, *m.* abundance of fish in a port or along the coast.
arribeño, ña, *m., f.* 1. (Amer.) highlander. 2. (Arg., Par.) stranger, outlander, foreigner.
arribismo, *m.* social-climbing; opportunism.
arribista, *m.* social climber; arriviste, upstart.
arribita, *adv.* (coll.) slightly above, further up.
arribo, *m.* arrival.
arricés, *m.* 1. buckle of a stirrup strap. 2. (Ven.) runt, bum, insignificant and despicable person.
arricesa, *f., var. of* **arricés.**
arricete, *m.* sandbank, shoal.
arridar, *tr.v.* (mar.) to tauten (the standing rigging of a ship).
arriende, arriendo, *ref.* **arrendar.**
arriendo, *m., var. of* **arrendamiento.**
arriera, *f.* (Col., Mex.) large red ant very destructive to crops.
arriería, *f.* muleteering, driving of pack animals.
arriero, *m.* 1. muleteer. 2. (ornith.) large Cuban cuckoo.
arriesgadamente, *adv.* riskily, hazardously, daringly.
arriesgado, da, *past part of* **arriesgar.** —*a.* 1. risky, hazardous, dangerous. 2. bold, daring.
arriesgar, (*ref. 51*) *tr.v.* to risk, venture. —*r.v.* to take a risk. — **arriesgarse a** + *inf.*, to risk + *ger.*, e.g. *a. a perder,* to risk losing.
arriesgón, *m.* risk, hazarding, risking.
arriesgue, arriesgué, *ref.* **arriesgar.**
arrimadero, *m.* support, prop, stay.
arrimadillo, *m.* 1. mat, wainscotting. 2. game of marbles.
arrimadizo, za, *m., f.* hanger-on, sycophant, person who hangs around influential people in order to obtain favors.
arrimador, *m.* backlog (log placed in a fireplace to support other logs).
arrimadura, *f.* moving near; moving together.
arrimar, *tr.v.* 1. to put, place or bring near. 2. (mar.) to stow (cargo). 3. to give, deal (blows). 4. to put, place or push to one side; to put aside, lay aside, lay down, give up. 5. to get rid of, ignore, shelve, take no further notice of. — **a. el hombro,** to lend a hand; to put one's shoulder to the wheel. —*r.v.* 1. to approach, get near, place oneself near. 2. to rest, lean. 3. to join together. 4. to move over, move up, move or squash together (e.g. to make room on a seat). 5. (coll.) to cohabit, live in concubinage. — **arrimarse a,** to approach, get near to, come close to; to seek the protection or favor of; to move up to; to lean or rest against.
arrime, *m.* place near the goal (in bowling).
arrimo, *m.* 1. moving near, placing near or beside. 2. support, protection, help. 3. attachment, fondness. 4. party wall; curtain wall.
arrimón, *m.* 1. loiterer, loafer, idler. 2. hanger-on, sycophant, parasite. — **estar de a.,** (coll.) to hang around, loiter, be waiting or watching; **hacer el a.,** (coll.) to stagger along leaning against walls (because of drunkenness).
arrinconado, da, *past part. of* **arrinconar.** —*a.* 1. distant, remote, out of the way. 2. (fig.) neglected, forgotten.
arrinconamiento, *m.* retreat, retirement, withdrawal.
arrinconar, *tr.v.* 1. to put away, lay aside; to ignore, forsake (a person), e.g. *a. a un amigo,* to ignore or pay no attention to a friend; to give up, abandon, e.g. *a. los libros,* to give up studying, *a. el bastón,* to relinquish command. 2. to corner, drive (someone) into a corner. —*r.v.* (coll.) to retire, retreat, withdraw (from the world).
arrinquín, *m.* (Amer.) devoted servant.
arriñonado, da, *a.* kidney-shaped.
arriostrar, *tr.v.* to brace, stay.
arriquín, *m., var. of* **arrinquín.**
arriscadamente, *adv.* boldly, audaciously, daringly.
arriscado, da, *past part. of* **arriscar.** —*a.* 1. craggy; jagged. 2. bold, daring, resolute. 3. agile, gallant, graceful. 4. (Amer.) turned-up (nose).
arriscador, ra, *m., f.* olive picker, gleaner of olives.
arriscamiento, *m.* daring, boldness, resoluteness.
arriscar, (*ref. 50*) *tr.v.* to risk, hazard, dare. —*r.v.* 1. to take a risk. 2. to plunge over a cliff (cattle). 3. to become ruffled, get angry. 4. to become vain or conceited. 5. (rare) to take refuge among the rocks. 6. (Peru) to dress elegantly, dress up.
arrisco, *m., var. of* **riesgo,** risk.
arritmia, *f.* 1. lack of rhythm. 2. (med.) arrhythmia (alteration in the rhythm of the heartbeat, either in timing or force).
arrítmico, ca, *a.* arrhythmic, arrhythmical.
arrivismo, *m.* social-climbing, opportunism.
arrivista, *m., f.* social climber, opportunist.
arrizar, (*ref. 53*) *tr.v.* (mar.) to reef, lash or tie securely.
arroaz, (*pl.* **arroaces**) *m.* (zool.) dolphin.
arroba, *f.* arroba (weight of 25 lbs. and Spanish liquid measure varying from 2.6 to 3.6 gallons).
arrobadera, *f.* (Chile) leveling harrow.
arrobadizo, za, *a.* prone to or feigning ecstasy or rapture.
arrobado, da, *past part. of* **arrobar.** —*a.* ecstatic, rapturous.
arrobador, ra, *a.* entrancing, causing rapture or ecstasy.
arrobamiento, *m.* ecstasy, entrancement, rapture.
arrobar, *tr.v.* to enrapture, entrance, enchant. —*r.v.* to be enraptured, entranced or enchanted.
arrobero, ra, *a.* weighing one arroba. —*m., f.* baker.
arrobo, *m.* ecstasy, transport.
arrocabe, *m.* (arch.) 1. top crossbeam. 2. wooden frieze.
arrocado, da, *a.* distaff-shaped.
arrocero, ra, *a.* rice. —*m., f.* rice grower; rice dealer.
arrochelarse, *r.v.* (Col., Ven.) to balk, rear (a horse).
arrocinado, da, *past part. of* **arrocinar.** —*a.* 1. nag-like. 2. bestial. 3. (coll.) infatuated.
arrocinar, *tr.v.* (coll.) to brutalize, bestialize. —*r.v.* 1. (coll.) to become brutalized. 2. (coll.) to fall madly in love.
arrodajarse, *r.v.* (C. Rica) to sit cross-legged.
arrodelar, *tr.v.* to protect with a buckler. —*r.v.* to be protected or protect oneself with a buckler.
arrodillado, da, *a.* kneeling, on one's knees.
arrodilladura, *f., var. of* **arrodillamiento.**
arrodillamiento, *m.* kneeling.
arrodillar, *tr.v.* to make (someone) kneel. —*i.v., r.v.* to kneel down.

arrodrigar, (*ref. 51*) *tr.v. var. of* **arrodrigonar.**
arrodrigonar, *tr.v.* (agr.) to stake, prop up (vines).
arrodrigue, arrodrigué, *ref.* **arrodrigar.**
arrogación, *f.* 1. adoption. 2. arrogation, claiming (of rights, faculties, etc.).
arrogancia, *f.* arrogance, haughtiness, gallantry; bravery.
arrogante, *a.* haughty, arrogant; brave; gallant, poised.
arrogantemente, *adv.* arrogantly; gallantly; bravely.
arrogar, (*ref. 51*) *tr.v.* (law) to adopt, arrogate (someone). *—r.v.* to arrogate, arrogate to oneself, claim, assume (rights, faculties, etc.).
arrogue, arrogué, *ref.* **arrogar.**
arrojadamente, *adv.* intrepidly, audaciously, daringly.
arrojadizo, za, *a.* easily thrown; for throwing, to be thrown (missile).
arrojado, da, *past part. of* **arrojar.** *—a.* intrepid, daring, bold, rash.
arrojar, *tr.v.* 1. to fling, hurl; to throw. 2. (fig.) to show, leave, yield (figures, accounts, information). 3. (coll.) to vomit, throw up, puke (vulg.). *—r.v.* 1. to throw oneself, plunge. 2. to rush, dash (at someone), fall (upon someone). 3. to launch, venture (into an enterprise). — **a. dividendos,** to pay dividends; **a. un promedio,** (com.) to strike an average; **a. un saldo,** (com.) to show a balance.
arroje, *m.* 1. man who drops as a counterweight to raise the curtain in a theatre. 2. (*pl.*) place from where these men jump.
arrojo, *m.* daring, boldness.
arrollable, *a.* able to be rolled, rollable.
arrollado, *past part. of* **arrollar.** *—m.* 1. (Arg., Chile) pork sausage. 2. (Arg., Chile, Peru) rolled beef, rolled roast. 3. (Río de la Plata) jelly roll.
arrollador, ra, *a.* overwhelming; crushing; sweeping; irresistible; devastating.
arrollamiento, *m.* rolling; winding; (elec.) winding. — **a. del inducido,** (elec.) armature winding; **a. en tambor,** (elec.) drum winding; **a. inductor,** (elec.) field winding; **a. anular,** (elec.) ring winding.
arrollar, *tr.v.* 1. to roll up; to roll, wind. 2. to sweep or carry away. 3. to run (someone) down or over (a car, bus, etc.). 4. to defeat, crush. 5. to override, ride roughshod over, ignore, pay no attention to (laws, etc.). 6. to overwhelm, leave speechless or dumbfounded, confuse, mix (someone) up (coll.). 7. (Amer.) to rock (a child).
arromadizar, (*ref. 53*) *tr.v.* to cause a cold. *—r.v.* to catch a cold.
arromance arromancé, *ref.* **arromanzar.**
arromanzar, (*ref. 53*) *tr.v.* 1. (arch.) to translate into the vernacular (i.e. any romance language.). 2. to translate into Spanish.
arromar, *tr.v.* to blunt, dull. *—r.v.* to become blunt or dull.
arromper, *tr.v.* (coll., Sp.) to break, plow (untilled land).
arrompido, *past part. of* **arromper.** *—m.* ground broken for tilling.
arronzar, (*ref. 53*) *tr.v.* (mar.) to move with levers, lever (a heavy object). *—i.v.* (mar.) to drift to leeward.
arropamiento, *m.* wrapping up, muffling up (against the cold).
arropar, *tr.v.* 1. to clothe, wrap with clothes. 2. to add syrup (to wine). *—r.v.* to clothe oneself, wrap up.
arrope, *m.* 1. syrup, grape syrup; (pharm.) syrup. 2. (Amer.) sweet made of fruits.
arropea, *f.* fetter, shackle, hobble (for horses).
arropera, *f.* syrup jar or container; grape syrup jar or container.
arropía, *f.* taffy.
arropiero, ra, *m., f.* maker or vendor of taffy.
arrostrado, da, *past part. of* **arrostrar.** *—a.* **bien a.,** endowed with pleasant features or countenance.
arrostrar, *tr.v.* to face, confront; to defy. *—i.v.* to face. — **a. con or por,** to face. *—r.v.* to go out to face or meet (enemy, a problem, etc.).
arroyada, *f.* 1. valley (through which a rivulet runs); channel, gulley (made by rivulet or stream). 2. flood, freshet.
arroyadero, *m.* gully, channel.
arroyar, *tr.v.* to form gullies or channels. *—r.v.* to become gullied or full of gullies.
arroyarse, *r.v.* to become infected with smut or blight (cereal plants).
arroyo, *m.* 1. stream, brook; bed (of a brook or stream); gutter, water course; (S. Amer.) small navigable river. 2. small town street. — **plantar en el a.,** (coll.) to put out of the house; to dismiss, fire (coll.).
arroyuela, *f.* (bot.) purple loosestrife.
arroyuelo, *m.* brooklet.
arroz, *m.* rice. — **a. con leche,** rice pudding; **a. con mango,** (coll., Cuba) a messy affair; **a. en blanco,** boiled rice; **a. integral,** brown rice; **a. salvaje,** wild rice.
arrozal, *m.* rice field, rice paddy.
arruar, (*ref. 55*) *i.v.* (hunt.) to grunt (a boar while fleeing from hunters).
arruchar, *tr.v.* (coll.) to clean out (in gambling).
arrufado, da, *a.* (mar.) sheered, curved.
arrufadura, *f.* (mar.) sheer (of a ship).
arrufaldado, da, *a.* with the brim turned up (hat).
arrufar, *tr.v.* (mar.) to form the sheer of. *—i.v.* to have a sheer, curve upwards. *—r.v.* (arch.) to become enraged or irritated; to snarl (dogs).
arrufianado, da, *a.* depraved, vicious, roguish.
arrufo, *m.* (mar.) *var. of* **arrufadura.**
arruga, *f.* wrinkle (in skin), crease (in clothes), fold (in paper); (geol.) ruga, fold (in the ground).
arrugación, *f., var. of* **arrugamiento.**
arrugamiento, *m.* wrinkling; creasing, rumpling; wrinkle.
arrugar, (*ref. 51*) *tr.v.* to wrinkle (skin); to crease, crumple (clothes); to knit (the brow). *—r.v.* 1. to wrinkle, knit (the brow); to become wrinkled, creased or crumpled. 2. to shrink, shrivel.
arrugia, *f.* (min.) 1. induced caving method employed by Spanish miners to mine gold. 2. gold mine.
arrugue, arrugué, *ref.* **arrugar.**
arruinador, ra, *a.* ruining, destructive. *—m., f.* ruiner; destroyer.
arruinamiento, *m.* ruin; ruining; destroying, destruction.
arruinar, *tr.v.* to ruin; to destroy. *—r.v.* to be ruined or destroyed.
arrullador, ra, *a.* lulling; soothing. *—m., f.* flatterer.
arrullar, *tr.v.* 1. to lull or sing to sleep. 2. to coo (dove) 3. to court, woo, bill and coo to.
arrullo, *m.* 1. cooing (of doves). 2. billing and cooing, love words (of sweethearts). 3. lullaby. 4. rustle, pleasant whisper.
arruma, *f.* 1. (mar.) division or partition in hold (for stowing cargo). 2. (Chile) pile (of objects).
arrumaco, *m.* 1. (coll.) caress, sign of affection. 2. (coll.) adornment, extravagant decoration. — **hacer arrumacos,** to show affection.
arrumaje, *m.* (mar.) stowage (of cargo on a ship).
arrumar, *tr.v.* 1. to stow (cargo). 2. (Amer.) to pile together, pile up. *—r.v.* to become overcast (the sky).
arrumazón, *f.* 1. (mar.) stowage (cargo). 2. (mar.) bank of clouds (on the horizon).
arrumbación, *f.* 1. menial chores (performed in a wine cellar). 2. navigating, plotting the course; setting the bearing (of a ship).
arrumbada, *f.* (mar.) wales in a rowing galley.
arrumbador, ra, *a.* navigating, steering. *—m.* 1. navigator, steersman. 2. worker in a wine cellar.
arrumbamiento, *m.* (mar.) course.
arrumbar, *tr.v.* 1. to cast aside, stow away, store. 2. to overwhelm someone (as to force him to be silent in a conversation), to floor, to confound. 3. to ignore, cast aside, neglect someone. 4. (mar.) to determine the direction; to place in line. *—i.v.* to set the bearings, plot the course (of a ship). *—r.v.* to be seasick.
arrunflar, *tr.v.* to collect (cards of the same suit). *—r.v.* to have a flush hand (in cards).
arrurruz, *m.* arrowroot (starch).
arrutar, *tr.v.* to scare away (birds).
arsáfraga, *f.* (bot.) water parsnip.
arsenal, *m.* 1. shipyard, dockyard, navy yard. 2. arsenal, munitions depot; (fig.) arsenal, storehouse.
arseniato, *m.* (chem.) arsenate.
arsenical, *a.* arsenical.
arsenicismo, *m.* (med.) chronic arsenic poisoning.
arsénico, ca, *a.* (chem.) arsenic. *—m.* arsenic. — **a. blanco,** arsenious anhydride.
arsénido, *m.* (chem.) arsenide.
arsenioso, sa, *a.* (chem.) arsenious, arsenous.
arsenito, *m.* (chem.) arsenite.
arseniuro, *m.* (chem.) arsenide.
arsina, *f.* (chem.) arsine.
arsolla, *f.* (bot.) milk thistle.
art. *abbrev. of* **artículo,** article.
arta, *f.* (bot.) plantain. — **a. de agua,** (bot.) fleawort.
artado, *a., var. of* **arctado.**
artal, *m.* (arch.) pie, pastry.
artalejo, *m., var. of* **artalete.**
artalete, *m. dim. of* **artal,** small pastry or pie.
artanica, *f.* (bot.) cyclamen.
artanta, *f.* (bot.) matico.
arte, *m., f.* 1. art, fine arts. 2. art, skill, craft, knack, astuteness, cleverness, cunning. 3. fishing tackle or gear. — **bellas artes,** fine arts; **artes de pesca,** nets; **artes menores,** crafts; **artes y oficios,** arts and crafts; **el a. por el a.,** art for art's sake; **malas artes,** evil means; **no ser or no tener a. ni parte en,** to have nothing to do with; **por amor** al a., free, gratis; **por a. del diablo,** by unnatural means, as if helped by the devil; **por a. de magia,** by magic.
artefacto, *m.* appliance, device, contrivance; artifact; fixture; fixture. — **artefactos de baño, artefactos sanitarios,** bathroom fixtures; **artefactos eléctricos,** electrical appliances.
artejo, *m.* 1. knuckle (of the fingers). 2. (zool.) arthromere, segment.
Artemis, Artemisa, *f.* (myth.) Artemis, Greek goddess of hunting.
artemisa, *f.* (bot.) mugwort, sagebrush. — a. bastarda, (bot.) yarrow.
artemisia, *f.* (bot.) *var. of* **artemisa.**
artemisilla, *f.* (Cuba, bot.) bastard feverfew.
artera, *f.* iron stamp (for marking bread).
arteramente, *adv.* craftily, cunningly, astutely.
arteria, *f.* 1. (anat.) artery. 2. (fig.) **artery,** main road, main street. — **a. celíaca,** (anat.) coeliac artery, coeliac axis; **a. coronaria,** coronary artery; **a. emulgente,** renal artery; **a. ranina,** lingual artery.
artería, *f.* cunning, astuteness, craftiness.
arterial, *a.* arterial. — **circulación a.,** arterial circulation.

arterialización, *f.* arterialization, changing of venous to arterial blood (in lungs).
arteriografía, *f.* arteriography.
arteriola, *f.* arteriole, small artery.
arteriología, *f.* arteriology.
arteriosclerosis, *f.* (med.) arteriosclerosis, hardening of the arteries.
arterioso, sa, *a.* arterial, arterious.
arteriotomía, *f.* (surg.) arteriotomy.
arteriovenoso, sa, *a.* arteriovenous.
arteritis, *f.* (med.) arteritis (inflammation of the arteries).
artero, ra, *a.* wily, cunning, crafty, artful.
artesa, *f.* trough, kneading trough. — **a. de vía,** (ry.) track pan.
artesanado, *m.* craftsmen, guild.
artesanía, *f.* 1. handicrafts, craftsmanship, artisanry. 2. craftsmen (the occupation).
artesano, na, *m., f.* craftsman, artisan.
artesiano, na, *a.* artesian (well).
artesilla, *f.* trough (of a well).
artesón, *m.* 1. kitchen trough, wash tub. 2. (archit.) coffer, caisson. 3. (archit.) caissoned or coffered ceiling.
artesonado, da, *past part. of* **artesonar.** —*a.* (archit.) **coffered, caissoned.** —*m.* (archit.) caissoned or coffered ceiling.
artesonar, *tr.v.* (archit.) to coffer, caisson.
artesuela, *f. dim. of* **artesa,** small trough.
artético, ca, *a.* arthritic.
ártico, ca, *a.* arctic.
articulación, *f.* 1. articulation. 2. (Chile, law) question. 3. (bot.) geniculation. 4. (anat.) joint. 5. clear enunciation. — **a. giratoria,** swivel joint; **a. universal,** (mech.) universal joint.
articuladamente, *adv.* clearly, distinctly.
articulado, da, *past part. of* **articular.** —*a.* 1. articulated. 2. articulated, articulate, jointed. —*m.* 1. (zool.) articulate; (*pl.*) (zool.) Articulata. 2. series of articles (of a law, treaty, etc.); (law) series of proofs (presented by the litigant).
articulador, ra, *a.* (law) argumentative. —*m.* (Peru, law) wily lawyer, one who easily finds articles (of law) with which to oppose the adversary (in a lawsuit).
articular, *a.* articular, pertaining to joints.
articular, *tr.v.* 1. to articulate, enunciate, pronounce; (phonet.) to articulate, form (speech sounds). 2. to articulate, join, joint. 3. (law) to formulate (questions). 4. to divide into articles.
articulario, ria, *a.* articular.
articulatorio, ria, *a.* articulatory.
articulista, *m., f.* writer of articles; feature writer.
artículo, *m.* 1. article (clause, section or distinct portion of a law, parliamentary bill or any writing). 2. article, essay (in magazine, newspaper, etc.). 3. article, commodity, item of merchandise. 4. (gram.) article. 5. (law) incidental question (in a case). 6. (zool.) articulation, joint. 7. entry (in a dictionary). — **a. adicional,** adjunct, addendum (to a law); **a. de comercio,** article, ware, item of merchandise; **a. de fe,** article of faith; **a. de fondo,** (jour.) editorial, leading article; **a. de muerte,** the last moment before death, article of death, the point of death; **a. de previo pronunciamiento,** (law) dilatory exception; **a. de primera necesidad,** basic commodity; **a. definido or determinado,** (gram.) definite article; **artículos de belleza,** cosmetics; **artículos de consumo,** consumer goods **artículos de escritorio,** stationery; **artículos de tocador,** toiletries; **a. genérico, indefinido or indeterminado,** (gram.) indefinite article; **artículos de novedad,** novelties.
artífice, *m., f.* 1. artificer, craftsman, skilled workman, artisan. 2. (fig.) author, architect, person.
artificial, *a.* artificial.
artificialmente, *adv.* artificially.
artificiero, *m.* (mil.) artificer, one who prepares ammunition.
artificio, *m.* 1. artifice, trick, ruse. 2. artifice, skill, ingenuity. 3. device, contrivance, appliance.
artificiosamente, *adv.* 1. ingeniously, skillfully; craftily, artfully. 2. artificially.
artificioso, sa, *a.* 1. skillful, ingenious; artful, cunning, crafty. 2. elaborate, artificial, unnatural (e.g. literary style).
artiga, *f.* 1. clearing and plowing (of land). 2. cleared and plowed land.
artigar, (*ref. 51*) *tr.v.* to clear and break up (land).
artillado, *m.* ship's artillery; stronghold's artillery.
artillar, *tr.v.* 1. to mount cannon on, furnish with artillery. 2. to make ready (the artillery on a ship, fort, etc.).
artillería, *f.* artillery; **a. de avancarga,** muzzle-loading artillery; **a. de batalla or de campana,** field artillery; **a. de costa,** coast artillery; **a. de montaña,** light mountain artillery; **a. de plaza, a. de sitio,** siege artillery; **a. de retrocarga,** breech loading artillery; **a. gruesa,** heavy artillery; **a. ligera, montada,** rodada or volante, light field artillery; **clavar la a.,** to spike the guns; **desmontar** la a., to dismount the artillery.
artillero, *m.* 1. gunner, artilleryman. 2. (min.) blaster, powderman.
artilugio, *m.* (derog.) 1. worthless contraption, gadget. 2. contrivance. 3. tool.
artimaña, *f.* 1. trick, ruse, strategem. 2. (hunt.) snare, trap, gin.
artimón, *m.* 1. (mar.) mizzenmast. 2. mizzen, mizzenmast sail.
artina, *f.* (bot.) boxthorn berry.
artiodáctilo, la, *a.* (zool.) artiodactyl, artiodactylous. —*m.* artiodactyl; (*pl.*) Artiodactyla.
artista, *m., f.* artist. — **a. invitado, guest** artist.
artísticamente, *adv.* artistically.
artístico, ca, *a.* artistic.
artizar, (*ref. 53*) *tr.v.* to perform ingeniously.
arto, *m.* (bot.) boxthorn.
artocarpáceo, a, *a.* (bot.) *var. of* **artocárpeo.**
artocárpeo, a, *a.* (bot.) artocarpous. —*f.* artocarpad, artocarpus; (*pl.*) Artocarpus, artocarpous family.
artolas, *f.* (*pl.*) mule chair; saddle for two riders, back-to-back.
artos, *m., var. of* **arto.**
artralgia, *f.* (med.) arthralgia.
artrítico, ca, *a., m., f.* (med.) arthritic.
artritis, *f.* (med.) arthritis.
artritismo, *m.* (med.) arthritism.
artrografía, *f.* (anat.) arthrography.
artrología, *f.* (anat.) arthrology.
artrómeto, *m.* (zool.) arthromere.
artropatía, *f.* (med.) arthropathy.
artrópodo, da, *a.* (zool.) arthropodal, arthropod. —*m.* arthropod; (*pl.*) Arthropods.
artrosis, *f.* (anat.) arthrosis.
artuña, *f.* ewe which has lost its newborn lamb.
Arturo, *m.* (astron.) Arcturus.
aruco, *m.* (Col., Ven., ornith.) crested screamer.
aruera, *f.* (Arg.) terebinth tree.
arugas, *f.* (*pl.*) (bot.) common feverfew.
árula, *f.* (archeol.) small altar.
arundíneo, a, *a.* arundinaceous, arundineous, reedy, cane-like.
aruñar, *tr.v.* (coll.) to scratch, claw.
aruñazo, *m.* (coll.) scratch.
aruño, *m.* (coll.) scratch.
arúspice, *m.* haruspex, soothsayer.
aruspicina, *f.* haruspicy.
arveja, *f.* (bot.) vetch (Vicia monantha); vetch seed; (S. Amer.) green pea. — **a. silvestre,** yellow vetch, meadow pea.
arvejal, *m.* vetch field; (S. Amer.) green pea garden.
arvejana, *f., var. of* **arveja.**
arvejar, *m., var. of* **arvejal.**
arvejera, *f.* (bot.) vetch (Vicia monantha).
arvejo, *m.* (bot.) green pea.
arvense, *a.* (bot.) growing in sown fields (plants).
arzobispado, *m.* 1. archbishopric. 2. archbishop's see.
arzobispal, *a.* archiepiscopal.
arzobispo, *m.* archbishop.
arzolla, *f.* 1. (bot.) centaury. 2. (bot.) milk thistle. 3. unripe almond.
arzón, *m.* fore or hind bow of a saddle; saddletree.
as, *m.* 1. ace (in cards, dice). 2. ace, wizard, person who excels at something. 3. ancient Roman coin. — **ser un as,** to excel at something, be a wizard; **as de guía,** (mar.) bowline; **as del volante,** (auto.) speed king; **as del fútbol,** (sport.) soccer star.
As *sym. of* **arsénico,** arsenic (As).
asa, *f.* 1. handle. 2. (fig.) opportunity, pretext. 3. sap of certain plants. 4. (sl.) ear. — **en asas,** akimbo; **ser del a.,** to be on intimate terms, be an intimate or bosom friend.
asá, *adv.* (coll.) **así, asá,** so-so, middling, fair.
asacar, (*ref. 50*) *tr.v.* 1. to invent. 2. to pretend, feign. 3. to impute.
asación, *f.* 1. roasting. 2. (pharm.) decoction.
asacristanado, da, *a.* like a sacristan or sexton.
asadero, ra, *a.* fit for roasting. —*m.* (fig.) a very hot place.
asado, da, *past part. of* **asar.** —*m.* 1. roast meat. 2. (Arg.) barbecue (outdoor party). — **a. al horno,** baked; **a. a la parrilla,** grilled.
asador, *m.* spit, roasting jack; barbecue.
asadora, *f.* rotisserie, grill.
asadura, *f.* 1. offal, innards, entrails; liver and lungs. 2. (coll.) sluggishness. — **echar las asaduras,** to work very hard, toil like a slave.
asaeteador, *m.* archer, bowman.
asaetear, *tr.v.* 1. to shoot or kill (someone) with an arrow. 2. (fig.) to vex, annoy.
asafétida, *f.* (bot.) asafetida.
asainetado, da, *a.* (theat.) farcical, burlesque.
asainetear, *tr.v.* to flavor with salt and pepper.
asalariado, da, *past part. of* **asalariar.** —*a.* salaried. —*m., f.* 1. salaried worker. 2. (derog.) hireling, mercenary.
asalariar, *tr.v.* to fix a salary or wage for; to pay a salary or wage. —*r.v.* to work for a salary.
asalmerar, *tr.v.* (mas.) to give the upper part of an abutment a sloping plane (where an arch or vault will rest).
asalmonado, da, *a.* 1. salmon-like. 2. salmon pink.
asaltador, ra, *a.* assaulting, attacking. —*m., f.* attacker, assailant.
asaltar, *tr.v.* to assault, storm (fortress); to assault, attack (person); (fig.) to strike suddenly (a thought, illness, death).
asalto, *m.* 1. assault; attack; storm, storming; (fenc.) thrust. 2. type of ticktacktoe, noughts and crosses. 3. round (in boxing); (fenc.) fencing bout. 4. (coll.) surprise party. — **a. y agresión,** (law) assault and battery; **tomar por a.,** to take by storm.
asamblea, *f.* assembly, meeting, congress; (mil.) assembly. — **a. constitutiva,** organization meeting; **a. de accionistas,** stockholders meeting; **A. General,** General Assembly (U.N.); **a. plenaria,** plenary session.
asambleísta, *m., f.* member of an assembly.
asar, *tr.v.* to roast. —*r.v.* (fig.) to roast, feel very hot.
asarabácara, asáraca, *f.* (bot.) asarabacca, hazelwort.

asardinado, da, *a.* (mas.) rowlocked (laid in rowlocks).
asarero, *m.* (bot.) blackthorn, sloe tree.
asargado, da, *a.* twilled, serge-like (textile).
asarina, *f.* (bot.) figwort (Antirrhinum asarina).
ásaro, *m.* (bot.) asarum, hazelwort.
asativo, va, *a.* (pharm.) decocted, boiled in its own juice.
asayé, *m.* (Bol.) palm fiber frail or basket.
asaz, *adv.* (poet.) abundantly, very much. —*a.* much, a lot of, many.
asbestino, na, *a.* asbestine.
asbesto, *m.* (min.) asbestos.
ascalonia, *f.* (bot.) shallot.
áscar, *m.* the army (in Morocco).
áscari, *m.* Moroccan infantryman.
ascariasis, *f.* (med.) ascariasis.
ascáride, *f.* (zool.) ascarid, intestinal worm.
ascaridiasis, ascaridiosis, *f.* (med.) ascariasis.
ascendencia, *f.* 1. ancestry. 2. authority, power, influence, ascendancy.
ascendente, *a.* ascending, rising, ascendant, upward (e.g. trend in prices). —*m.* (astrol.) ascendant.
ascender, (*ref. 30*) *i.v.* to ascend, mount, climb; (fig.) to advance (in business), rise (in status). — **a. a,** to amount to, add up to. —*tr.v.* to raise, promote (in rank).
ascendiente, *a.* ascending, ascendant. —*m., f.* ascendant, ancestor, forefather. —*m.* (moral) ascendancy, power, influence, authority.
ascensión, *f.* 1. ascension, rising. 2. (ecc.) **A.,** Ascension (of Jesus and festival celebrating it). 3. exaltation (of a pope or king). — **a. recta,** (astron.) **right** ascension.
ascensional, *a.* (astrol.) ascensional.
ascensionista, *m., f.* 1. balloonist. 2. mountain climber, alpinist.
ascenso, *m.* (fig.) promotion (in rank or position); step (in a career); (rare) ascent, rise. — **a. muerto,** (mar.) dead rise.
ascensor, *m.* elevator, lift; hoist. — **a. automático,** automatic elevator; **a. de carga,** freight elevator.
ascensorista, *m., f.* elevator operator.
asceta, *m., f.* ascetic, hermit; anchorite.
asceterio, *m.* colony of hermits or anchorites.
ascética, *f.* asceticism, ascetic doctrine.
ascético, ca, *a.* ascetic.
ascetismo, *m.* asceticism, profession and doctrine of asceticism.
ascidia, *f.* 1. (zool.) ascidian; Ascidia (genus). 2. (bot.) ascidium.
asciende, asciendo, *ref.* **ascender.**
ascio, cia, *a., m., f.* (geog.) ascian.
ásciro, *m.* (bot.) St.-Peter's-wort.
ascítico, ca, *a.* (med.) ascitic. —*m., f.* person suffering from ascites or abdominal dropsy.
ascitis, *f.* (med.) ascites, abdominal dropsy.
asclepiadáceo, a, *a.* (bot.) asclepiadaceous. —*f.* (bot.) asclepiad; (*pl.*) Asclepiadaceae.
Asclepio, *m.* (myth.) Asclepius, Greek god of medicine and healing.
asco, *m.* 1. nausea; disgust; disgusting thing. 2. (coll.) fear. — **dar a. a alguien,** to disgust someone; **estar hecho un a.,** (coll.) to look extremely dirty; **hacer ascos a,** (coll.) to turn up one's nose at.
ascomiceto, ta, *a.* (bot.) ascomycetous. —*m.* (bot.) ascomycete; (*pl.*) Ascomycetes.
ascórbico, ca, *a.* ascorbic. — **ácido a., ascorbic** acid, vitamin C.
ascosidad, *f.* loathsomeness, foulness, repulsiveness.
ascoso, sa, *a.* nauseating, repulsive, disgusting, loathsome.
ascospora, *f.* (bot.) ascospore.
ascua, *f.* glowing ember. — **a. de oro, glittering** object; **arrimar el a. a su sardina,** (coll.) to look after one's own interests; **estar en ascuas,** (coll.) to be on edge.
aseadamente, *adv.* cleanly, neatly.
aseado, da, *past part. of* **asear.** —*a.* clean, neat.
asear, *tr.v.* to clean, tidy. —*r.v.* to clean or tidy oneself up.
asechador, ra, *a.* trapping, ensnaring, deceiving. —*m., f.* ensnarer, deceiver, trapper.
asechamiento, *m., var. of* **asechanza.**
asechanza, *f.* trap, snare. — **armar una a.,** to set a trap.
asechar, *tr.v.* to trick, snare, deceive, lay traps for.
asecho, *m., var. of* **asechanza.**
asedado, da, *a.* silky, smooth (as silk).
asedar, *tr.v.* to make silky or smooth.
asediador, ra, *a.* besieging. —*m., f.* besieger.
asediar, *tr.v.* to besiege, lay siege to, blockade; to harass, pester, hound.
asedio, *m.* siege, blockade.
aseglararse, *r.v.* to become worldly (clergy).
asegundar, *tr.v.* to repeat (an action) immediately.
asegurable, *a.* insurable.
aseguración, *f.* insurance, insurance policy.
asegurado, da, *past part. of* **asegurar.** —*a.* insured, safeguarded; assured. —*m., f.* insured person. — **a. por fianza,** bonded.
asegurador, ra, *a.* insuring; safeguarding; fastening, assuring. —*m., f.* insurance man, insurer, underwriter.
aseguramiento, *m.* 1. securing; fastening. 2. assuring, assurance. 3. protection, making safe. 4. insurance, insuring.
asegurar, *tr.v.* 1. to secure, make secure, safe or stable; to fasten, fix securely. 2. to insure, guarantee; (com.) to insure. 3. to assure, tell with assurance, e.g. *te aseguro que va a venir,* I assure you that he is going to come. 4. to make safe, protect. 5. to reassure, free from fear or anxiety. 6. to imprison, seize, lock up. —*r.v.* 1. to make sure, find out for sure. 2. (com.) to insure oneself. 3. to reassure oneself.
aseidad, *f.* (metaph.) aseity.
asemejar, *tr.v.* 1. to make resemble, make alike. 2. to liken, compare. —*i.v., r.v.* to be alike, be similar. — **a. a,** to resemble, be like.
asendereado, da, *past part. of* **asenderear.** —*a.* 1. exhausted or worn out by work and troubles. 2. expert, skillful.
asenderear, *tr.v.* 1. to make a path through. 2. to pursue or follow through paths.
asenso, *m.* 1. assent, agreement, consent. 2. credence, belief. — **dar a.,** to give credit to, believe; to agree with.
asentada, *f.* sitting, session.
asentaderas, *f.* (*pl.*) (coll.) seat, buttocks.
asentadillas, *adv.* (equit.) side saddle.
asentado, da, *past part. of* **asentar.** —*a.* judicious, sensible; stable, settled.
asentador, *m.* 1. wholesale dealer in foodstuffs. 2. blacksmith's turning chisel. 3. razor strop. 4. (Mex., print.) planer.
asentamiento, *m.* 1. settling (of foundations). 2. settlement, encampment. 3. (law) recording, writing down (of facts in ledger).
asentar, (*ref. 29*) *tr.v.* 1. to write down, note down, record, register (in a ledger). 2. to seat. 3. to press, smooth, iron (clothes); to make lie flat (lapel, pleat); to level, make smooth, tamp down (newly-laid floor or road). 4. to sharpen, hone, put an edge on. 5. to fix, put or set firmly; to build, erect, lay the foundations of (a building), found (a city), set up (a camp); to consolidate, put on a firm footing. 6. to set, put (e.g. on the throne, in authority, etc.). 7. to make, agree upon (a treaty, agreement). 8. to deal, give (blows). 9. to affirm, confirm; to take as a fact or as definite. 10. to impress (on the mind). 11. (Arg., Peru) to agree with (food). 12. (law) to put (plaintiff) in possession of defendant's estate. —*i.v.* 1. to fit, suit (clothes). 2. to rest, be. —*r.v.* 1. to settle down, settle oneself; to perch, settle, alight (bird on branch). 2. to settle (foundations of building). 3. to settle, go to the bottom (liquids, sediments of liquids). 4. to gall, chaff (harness). 5. to establish oneself (e.g. in a position). 6. to lie flat (lapel of coat, etc.). — **a. al debe,** to debit; **a. al haber,** to credit; **a. una partida,** to make an entry.
asentimiento, *m.* consent, assent.
asentir, (*ref. 42*) *i.v.* to assent, concur, agree.
asentista, *m.* contractor, supplier (of goods to army, navy, etc.).
aseñorado, da, *a.* 1. lordly, high and mighty. 2. gentlemanly, refined, ladylike.
aseo, *m.* cleanliness, neatness, tidiness.
asépalo, la, *a.* (bot.) asepalous.
asepsia, *f.* (med.) asepsis.
aséptico, ca, *a.* (med.) aseptic.
asequible, *a.* 1. attainable, obtainable, available (object). 2. approachable, accessible (person).
aserción, *f.* assertion, declaration, affirmation.
aserenar, *tr.v.* to make calm or tranquil, to quiet. —*r.v.* to become calm, calm down.
asermonado, da, *a.* sermonlike, moralistic, preachy.
aserradero, *m.* sawmill.
aserradizo, za, *a.* fit to be sawed, for sawing.
aserrado, da, *past part. of* **aserrar.** —*a.* (bot.) serrated, serrate.
aserrador, ra, *a.* sawing. —*m.* sawyer. —*f.* power saw. — **a. de banda,** band saw.
aserradura, *f.* sawing; cut (of saw); (*pl.*) sawdust.
aserrar, (*ref. 29*) *tr.v.* to saw.
aserrear, *tr.v.* (Chile, coll.) to saw.
aserrín, *m.* sawdust.
aserruchar, *tr.v.* (Amer.) to saw, cut (with handsaw).
asertivamente, *adv.* assertively.
asertivo, va, *a.* assertive.
aserto, *m.* assertion, affirmation.
asertor, ra, *m., f.* assertor, affirmant.
asertorio, *a.* (law) **juramento a.,** assertory oath.
asesar, *tr.v.* to make sensible, put some sense into. —*i.v.* to become sensible.
asesinar, *tr.v.* 1. to assassinate; to murder. 2. (fig.) to upset or annoy greatly.
asesinato, *m.* assassination; murder.
asesino, na, *a.* murdering, murderous. —*m., f.* murderer, homicide; assassin.
asesor, ra, *a.* counselling, advising. —*m., f.* counsellor, advisor.
asesoramiento, *m.* counsel, advice.
asesorar, *tr.v.* to advise, counsel. —*r.v.* to take advice; to get or seek advice. — **asesorarse con alguien,** to take someone's advice; to get or seek advice from someone.
asesoría, *f.* 1. adviser's or consultant's office and fee. 2. advising, counseling.
asestadura, *f.* 1. aiming, pointing. 2. giving, dealing (of blows); firing (of shots).
asestar, *tr.v.* 1. to aim, point, level (weapon); to direct (one's eyes). 2. to deal, give, deliver (blows), fire (shot).
aseveración, *f.* affirmation, asseveration.
aseveradamente, *a.* affirmatively.
aseverar, *tr.v.* to asseverate, affirm, assert.
aseverativo, va, *a.* affirmative, assertive.

asexual, *a.* asexual.
asfaltado, da, *past part. of* **asfaltar.** *—m.* asphalting; asphalt paving.
asfaltar, *tr.v.* to asphalt.
asfáltico, ca, *a.* asphaltic; bituminous.
asfalto, *m.* asphalt.
asfíctico, ca, *a.* asphyctic, asphyxial.
asfixia, *f.* (med.) asphyxia.
asfixiador, ra, *a.* asphyxiating.
asfixiante, *a.* 1. asphyxiating, asphyxiant. 2. sweltering, sultry (weather, atmosphere). — **hace un calor a.,** it's very hot (weather).
asfixiar, *tr.v.* to asphyxiate, smother. *—r.v.* to be asphyxiated, suffocate.
asfíxico, ca, *a., var. of* **asfíctico.**
asfódelo, *m.* (bot.) asphodel.
asga, asgo, *ref.* **asir.**
así, *a.* such, e.g. *un niño así,* such a child; *así es la vida,* such is life. *—adv.* 1. so, thus, in this manner, this (that) way, like this (that), e.g. *¡así se habla!* that's the way to talk! 2. so much, in such a way, e.g. *¿así he cambiado?* have I changed so much? 3. as well, as, both, e.g. *así los maestros como los alumnos,* teachers as well as pupils. 4. may, e.g. *así te pese,* may you live to regret it. 5. around, thereabouts, e.g. *diez dólares o así,* ten dollars or so. 6. likewise, like, e.g. *así el padre como el hijo,* like father, like son. — **así así,** middling, fair; **así nada más,** (S. Amer.) **así no más,** just like that, e.g. *así no más rompió a diluviar,* it began pouring, just like that; **así o asá,** anyway you put it, one way or the other; **así que, así como,** as soon as; **así sea,** so be it; **así y todo,** with it all, even so; **aun así,** even so, even then; **por decirlo así,** so to speak; **tan or tanto es así, que ... tanto es así, que ...** so much so, that ... ; **y así sucesivamente,** and so forth and so on. *—conj.* 1. even though, even if, although, e.g. *iremos así llueva,* we'll go even if it rains. **2. así que, así pues,** so, then, e.g. **así que** or **así pues, te quedas,** so you're staying, then. 3. **y así, así que,** and so, thus therefore, e.g. *le ayudamos, así que (y así) pudo casarse,* we helped him and so he was able to get married.
Asia, *f.* Asia. — **A. Menor,** Asia Minor.
asiático, ca, *a., m., f.* Asian, Asiatic.
asibilación, *f.* (phonet.) assibilation.
asibilar, *tr.v.* (phonet.) to assibilate.
asicar, *tr.v.* (Dom. Rep.) to harass, molest.
asidera, *f.* (Arg.) rigging or saddle strap (used to tie a lasso).
asidero, *m.* 1. handle; handhold. 2. (fig.) pretext. 3. (*pl.*) (mar.) tow ropes.
asiduamente, *adv.* assiduously.
asiduidad, *f.* 1. assiduity. 2. frequency.
asiduo, dua, *a.* 1. assiduous. 2. frequent.
asienta, asiente, asiento, *ref.* **asentar;** asentir.
asiento, *m.* 1. seat, chair; seat (in congress, court). 2. site, spot (of town or building); (Amer.) mining town, site or territory; (Cuba) agricultural center. 3. bottom (of bottle, etc.). 4. sediment. 5. sinking, settling (of a building). 6. peace treaty. 7. contract (for providing food, etc., to the army or other organization). 8. jotting, entry (in ledger). 9. bit (of a bridle). 10. bar, seat of the bit (in horse's mouth). 11. indigestion. 12. bed of mortar. 13. stability, permanence. 14. prudence, judgment, maturity. 15. order, arrangement. 16. (mec.) bearing, seat, support. 17. (sl.) seat, behind, buttocks. 18. (*pl.*) semi-spherical pearls. 19. (*pl.*) linen reinforcements (on shirt collars and cuffs). — **a. corredizo,** sliding seat; **a. de colmenas,** open apiary; **a. de débito or cargo,** (acc.) debit entry; **a. de molino,** millstone; **a. de pastor,** (bot.) furze, gorse; **a. de presentación,** (law) entry or recording in property registry; **a. eyectable, lanzable** or **proyectable,** (aer.) ejection seat; **de a.,** permanently; **hacer a.,** to settle (a building), establish oneself, settle (person); **tomar a.,** to take a seat.
asierre, asierro, *ref.* **aserrar.**
asignable, *a.* assignable.
asignación, *f.* 1. allowance; salary. 2. assignation.
asignado, *past part. of* **asignar.** *—m.* 1. (Ecuad.) part of wages paid in kind. 2. assignat (paper money issued during the French Revolution).
asignar, *tr.v.* to give, apportion, allot, assign, e.g. *le han asignado un sueldo de veinte mil soles,* they have given him a salary of twenty thousand soles, *le han asignado la embajada en Berlín,* they have given him the ambassadorship in Berlin. — **a. fondos,** to make an appropriation.
asignatario, ria, *m., f.* (Amer., law) beneficiary, legatee.
asignatura, *f.* course, subject (in school). — **aprobar una a.,** to pass a subject; **suspender una a.,** to fail a subject.
asilado, da, *past part. of* **asilar.** *—m., f.* 1. political refugee, person who has been given asylum. 2. inmate (of an institution).
asilamiento, *m.* granting or giving asylum, sheltering.
asilar, *tr.v.* to give or grant asylum (to political refugees); to place in an institution, home, etc. *—r.v.* to take asylum, take refuge.
asilla, *f. dim. of* **asa,** small handle.
asilo, *m.* 1. home (for the aged, orphans, etc.). 2. asylum, sanctuary, refuge. — **a. de huérfanos,** orphanage; **a. de pobres,** poorhouse; **buscar a.,** to seek asylum; **dar a.,** to shelter.
asilvestrado, da, *a.* grown wild (from a cultivated plant).
asimao, *m.* (bot.) rhamnaceous wild shrub from the Phil. I.
asimetría, *f.* asymmetry.
asimétrico, ca, *a.* asymmetric, asymmetrical.
asimiento, *m.* 1. grasping, holding. 2. (fig.) fondness, attachment.
asimilable, *a.* assimilable.
asimilación, *f.* assimilation.
asimilar, *tr.v.* 1. to assimilate, absorb (food; knowledge, facts). 2. to assimilate, incorporate, take in. 3. (phonet.) to assimilate.
asimilativo, va, *a.* assimilative, assimilating.
asimilista, *a.* in favor of assimilation of ethnical or linguistic minorities.
asimina, *f.* (bot.) papaw.
asimismo, *adv., var. of* **así mismo,** likewise, also.
asimplado, da, *a.* simple, ingenuous.
asina, *adv.* (coll.), *var. of* **así.**
asincrónico, ca, *a.* asynchronous.
asincronismo, *m.* asynchronism.
asindético, ca, *a.* (gram.) asyndetic.
asindeton, *m.* (rhet.) asyndeton.
asinergia, *f.* (anat.) asynergia.
asinino, na, *a.* asinine.
asintiendo, asintiera, asintiese, asintió, *ref.* asentir.
asintomático, ca, *a.* (med.) asymptomatic.
asíntota, *f.* (geom.) asymptote.
asintótico, ca, *a.* (geom.) asymptotic, asymptotical.
asir, (*ref. 2*) *tr.v.* to grasp, seize. — **asidos del brazo,** arm in arm; **a. de,** to grasp or seize by. *—i.v.* to take root. *—r.v.* to grab hold of one another; (fig.) fight, come to blows; **asirse a, de** or **en,** to seize, grab, grab hold of; **asirse con,** to grapple with, come to blows with.
asirio, ria, *a., m., f.* Assyrian. *—m.* Assyrian (language). *—f.* **A.,** Assyria.
asiriología, *f.* Assyriology, study of Assyria.
asiriólogo, *m.* Assyriologist.
asistencia, *f.* 1. attendance, presence. 2. help, aid, assistance. 3. (Mex.) parlor, living room. 4. (Peru) first-aid post, health-service clinic. 5. (*pl.*) (monetary) allowance. — **a. social,** welfare work, public assistance.
asistenta, *f.* (female) assistant, attendant; servant, maid.
asistente, *a.* attending; assisting. *—m.* 1. attendant, assistant. 2. (arch.) syndic, city official (among Roman Catholics). 3. monk assisting Superior. 4. (mil.) orderly.
asistir, *tr.v.* to help, aid, assist; to attend, take care of, nurse; to accompany; to serve, attend upon. *—i.v.* to be present; to follow suit (in cards). — **a. a,** to attend, be present at.
asistolia, *f.* (med.) asystole.
asistólico, ca, *a.* (med.) asystolic.
asma, *f.* (med.) asthma.
asmático, ca, *a., m., f.* (med.) asthmatic.
asna, *f.* 1. ass, she-ass. 2. (*pl.*) (carp.) rafters.
asnacho, *m.* (bot.) restharrow, cammock.
asnada, *f.* (coll.) stupidity, foolishness, asininity.
asnado, *m.* (min.) pit prop, side-wall timber.
asnal, *a.* 1. asinine, pertaining to an ass or a donkey. 2. (coll.) brutish, bestial. 3. asinine, stupid.
asnallo, *m.* (bot.) cammock, restharrow.
asnalmente, *adv.* 1. riding a donkey or ass. 2. (coll.) brutishly, bestially. 3. asininely, stupidly.
asnejón, *m. aug. of* **asno,** ass, dolt, idiot.
asnería, *f.* 1. (coll.) pack of donkeys. 2. (coll.) stupidity, foolishness, asininity.
asnilla, *f.* 1. prop, shoring, stanchion, strut. 2. trestle.
asnillo, *m.* (ento.) insectivorous coleopteron.
asnino, na, *a.* (coll.) pertaining to an ass, donkey; asinine.
asno, *m.* (zool.) ass, donkey, jackass; (fig.) ass, dolt.
asobarcar, (*ref. 50*) *i.v., var. of* **sobarcar,** to take under the arm.
asobinarse, *r.v.* to lay prostrate on the ground, unable to move (an animal); to fall in a heap.
asocarronado, da, *a.* roguish, knavish; cunning, designing (person).
asociación, *f.* 1. association, union, partnership. 2. (sport.) association football, soccer. — **a. de ideas,** association of ideas; **a. gremial,** trade union; **a. sindical,** labor union.
asociacionismo, *m.* (psyc.) associationism, (theory holding all psychic phenomena can be explained by the law of association of ideas).
asociado, da, *past part. of* **asociar.** *—a.* associated. *—m., f.* associate, partner.
asociamiento, *m.* association.
asociar, *tr.v.* 1. to associate, link, connect. 2. to join, unite, combine. *—r.v.* to become partners. — **asociarse a or con,** to become a partner of; to join.
asociativo, va, *a.* associative.
asocio, *m.* (S Amer., coll.) association, company.
asolación, *f.* devastation, destruction, razing.
asolador, ra, *a.* destroying, demolishing, devastating. *—m., f.* destroyer.
asolamiento, *m.* devastation, destruction, havoc, laying waste.
asolanar, *tr.v.* to spoil, damage crops (east wind).
asolapar, *tr.v.* to set (tiles, shingles) so they overlap.
asolar, (*ref. 33*) *tr.v.* 1. to devastate, lay waste, destroy. 2. to parch, dry up, scorch (crops, land, etc.). *—r.v.* 1. to settle (sediment). 2. to become parched, dried up or scorched (crops, land, etc.).
asoldar, (*ref. 33*) *tr.v.* to hire, employ. *—r.v.* to engage oneself for a salary, hire oneself out.

asoleada, *f.* (Amer.) sunstroke, insolation.
asoleado, da, *past part. of* **asolear.** *—a.* (Amer.) dumb, stupid, foolish.
asolear, *tr.v.* to sun, put in the sun, bleach in the sun; to expose (animals) to sun-stroke. *—r.v.* to bask in the sun, sun oneself; to tan oneself, get tanned.
asoleo, *m.* 1. sunning, basking in the sun. 2. (mil.) drying of powder in the sun when already granulated. 3. (vet.) illness in certain animals causing palpitations and shortness of breath.
asolvamiento, *m.* clogging, obstruction (of any duct).
asolvar, *tr.v.* (arch.) *var. of* **azolvar,** to clog, obstruct.
asomada, *f.* 1. brief appearance. 2. place from where something can be seen, lookout.
asomagado, da, *a.* (Ecuad.) sleepy.
asomar, *i.v.* to begin to appear or be seen. *—tr.v.* to show, stick out, put out (the head through an opening); to let show or be seen. *—r.v.* 1. to look or lean out, e.g. *asomarse a* or *por la ventana,* to look or lean out of the window. 2. (coll.) to begin to get tipsy or lit up. 3. to delve superficially into a subject.
asombradizo, za, *a.* timid, easily frightened, scary, jumpy.
asombrador, ra, *a.* astonishing, astounding, surprising.
asombrar, *tr.v.* 1. to amaze, astonish, astound. 2. to shade, shadow; to darken; to make (a hue) darker. 3. to frighten, astound. *—r.v.* 1. to be amazed, astonished or astounded. 2. to be frightened. — **asombrarse de,** to be amazed or astonished at.
asombro, *m.* 1. amazement, astonishment. 2. fright, surprise. 3. marvel, amazing person or thing.
asombrosamente, *adv.* amazingly, astonishingly, astoundingly.
asombroso, sa, *a.* astonishing, amazing.
asomo, *m.* 1. peep, peek, glimpse. 2. hint, clue, sign. 3. conjecture, suspicion. — **ni por a.,** not by the longest stretch of the imagination, not by a long shot; by no means.
asonada, *f.* riot, mutiny, protest demonstration.
asonancia, *f.* (poet., rhet.) assonance, harmony.
asonantar, *i.v.* (rhet.) to be assonant, assonate. *—tr.v.* (rhet.) to make assonant.
asonante, *a., f.* assonant.
asonar, (*ref. 33*) *i.v.* to be assonant, to accord, correspond (sounds).
asordante, *a.* deafening.
asordar, *tr.v.* to deafen.
asorocharse, *r.v.* 1. (Amer.) to suffer from altitude sickness; to get altitude sickness. 2. (Amer., coll.) to blush.
asosegar, (*ref. 67*) *tr.v., i.v., r.v., var. of* **sosegar.**
asosegué, asosiego, asosiegue, *ref.* **asosegar.**
asotanar, *tr.v.* to dig or excavate for a cellar or basement.
aspa, *f.* 1. cross, St. Andrew's cross, crossed wooden beams, x-shaped figure. 2. spool, reel (for yarn). 3. wheel, vanes, sails (of a windmill); sail, vane (of a windmill). 4. (her.) saltier, saltire. 5. (min.) intersection (of two veins). 6. (S. Amer.) (*pl.*) horns. 7. (Chile) size, extension (of a mine). — **en a.,** cross-wise.
aspadera, *f.* (mec.) spool, reel (to wind thread).
aspado, da, *past part. of* **aspar.** *—a.* 1. with arms extended like a cross. 2. cross-shaped, in the form of a cross. 3. (her.) with a saltier. *—m., f.* penitent who had his arms tied to a bar in the form of a cross.
aspador, ra, *a.* (tex.) reeling. *—m., f.* reeler, spooler. *—m.* reel, spool.
aspálato, *m.* (bot.) aspalathus.
aspalto, *m.* (p.) dark transparent color.
aspar, *tr.v.* 1. to wind, reel (thread). 2. to crucify. 3. (coll.) to annoy, vex. *—r.v.* to writhe, contort oneself (with pain, etc.).
asparagina, *f.* (chem.) asparagine.
aspaventar, *tr.v.* to frighten, scare.
aspaventero, ra, *a., m., f.* fussy, fussing, effusive, expressing exaggerated fear, admiration or excitement.
aspaviento, *m.* fuss, fussiness, exaggerated demonstration of fear, surprise, emotion or excitement. — **hacer aspavientos,** to make, kick up or cause a fuss.
aspecto, *m.* 1. aspect, appearance, countenance, look. 2. aspect, side, e.g. *es el a. moral del asunto el que no me gusta,* it is the moral aspect of the affair which I don't like. 3. (astron., astrol., gram.) aspect.
ásperamente, *adv.* roughly, harshly; rudely, gruffly.
asperarteria, *f.* (arch.) trachea, windpipe.
asperear, *i.v.* to have a sour or acrid taste.
asperete, *m.* tartness, sourness (in certain fruits).
aspereza, *f.* 1. roughness, asperity. 2. roughness, ruggedness (of terrain). 3. harshness (of voice). 4. sourness, tartness (of fruit). 5. harshness, severity, gruffness (of character).
asperges, *m.* 1. (coll.) Asperges, chant beginning with the words "Asperges me, Domine." 2. (coll.) sprinkling, aspersion. 3. (coll.) holy water (sprinkled in the Asperges).
asperidad, *f., var. of* **aspereza.**
asperiego, ga, *a.* pertaining to a variety of sour apple (fruit or tree).
asperilla, *f.* (bot.) woodruff.
asperillo, *m.* tartness, sourness (of green fruit).
asperjar, *tr.v.* to sprinkle; to sprinkle with holy water.
áspero, ra, *a.* 1. rough, rugged. 2. harsh (voice). 3. sour (fruit). 4. harsh, gruff, severe (character).
asperón, *m.* grindstone, gritstone.
aspérrimo, ma, *a. super. of* **áspero,** very rough.
aspersión, *f.* aspersion, sprinkling.
aspersorio, *m.* sprinkler.
aspérula, *f.* (bot.) woodruff.
áspid, *m.* 1. (zool.) asp. 2. culverin.
áspide, *m., var. of* **áspid.**
aspidistra, *f.* (bot.) aspidistra.
aspilla, *f.* dipstick (to measure wine in a container).
aspillar, *tr.v.* to measure (wine) with a dipstick.
aspillera, *f.* (fort.) loophole, embrasure, crenel, machicolation.
aspiración, *f.* 1. aspiration; inhalation; suction, draft. 2. aspiration, hope, ambition. 3. (phonet.) aspiration. 4. (mus.) short pause. — **a. de renta,** income expected; **a. mecánica,** forced draft; **a. normal,** natural draft.
aspirado, da, *past part. of* **aspirar.** *—a., f.* (phonet.) aspirate.
aspirador, ra, *a.* suction, sucking; inhaling. *—m.* aspirator; suction pipe. *—f.* vacuum cleaner. **a. de polvo,** vacuum cleaner, dust exhauster.
aspirante, *a.* suction, sucking; inhaling. — **bomba a.,** suction pump. *—m.* aspirant, candidate; applicant; (mar.) midshipman. — **a. a oficial,** officer candidate.
aspirar, *tr.v.* 1. to inhale, breathe in; to suck in, draw in. 2. (phonet.) to aspirate. *—i.v.* to aspire. — **a. a,** to aspire to.
aspirina, *f.* (med.) aspirin.
asquear, *i.v.* to be or feel nauseated or disgusted. *—tr.v.* to nauseate, disgust, revolt.
asquerosamente, *adv.* revoltingly, loathsomely, nauseatingly.
asquerosidad, *f.* filth, foulness; loathsomeness, vileness.
asqueroso, sa, *a.* disgusting, loathsome, revolting, nauseating; filthy.
asquístico, *a.* (geol.) aschistic.
asta, *f.* 1. pike, lance, spear; staff (of lance, spear, pike); flagpole, flagstaff. 2. horn (of an animal); beam (main trunk of antler). 3. (mar.) rib, frame-member (of a ship). 4. (mar.) truck (of a mast); (mar.) pennant staff. 5. handle (of a tool). — **a media a.,** at half mast; **dejar en las astas del toro,** to desert someone in difficulty.
ástaco, *m.* (zool.) crawfish, crayfish.
astado, da, *a.* horned, having horns. *—m.* 1. (taur.) bull. 2. Roman pikeman; pike bearer.
Astarté, *f.* (myth.) Astarte, goddess of love and fertility.
astaticidad, *f.* (phys.) astaticism.
astático, ca, *a.* (phys.) astatic.
astatinio, *m.* (chem.) astatine.
asteísmo, *m.* (rhet.) asteism, gentle irony or banter.
astenia, *f.* (med.) asthenia.
asténico, ca, *a., m., f.* (med.) asthenic.
aster, *m.* (bot.) aster.
asteria, *f.* 1. (min.) asteriated opal. 2. (zool.) starfish.
asterisco, *m.* asterisk.
asterismo, *m.* (astron., cryst., phys.) asterism.
astero, *m.* 1. Roman pikeman; pike bearer. 2. pike maker.
asteroide, *a.* (zool.) asteroid, starlike. *—m.* (astron.) asteroid, planetoid.
asteroideo, *m.* (zool.) asteroid; (*pl.*) Asteroidea.
astifino, *a.* (taur.) (said of a bull) with tapered, sharp horns.
astigmático, ca, *a.* (med., opt.) astigmatic.
astigmatismo, *m.* (med., opt.) astigmatism.
astigmómetro, *m.* (med., opt.) astigmometer.
astil, *m.* helve, handle, haft; shaft (arrow); beam (of a scale); quill, shaft (of a feather); stem (of key).
astilejos, *m.* (*pl.*) (astron.) *var. of* **astillejos.**
astilla, *f.* splinter, sliver, chip, fragment. — **de tal palo, tal a.,** like father, like son, a chip off the old block; **sacar a.,** (coll.) to obtain a share or part of the profit, get a cut (coll.).
astillar, *tr.v.* to splinter, chip; to break to pieces, destroy.
astillazo, *m.* blow or prick from a flying chip or splinter.
Astillejos, *m.* (*pl.*) (astron.) Castor and Pollux.
astillero, *m.* 1. spear or lance rack. 2. shipyard, dockyard. 3. lumber yard; lumber warehouse. 4. (Mex.) wood chopping site.
astillón, *m. aug. of* **astilla,** big chip or splinter.
astilloso, sa, *a.* 1. brittle, fragile, easily splintered. 2. splintery, having splinters.
ástomo, ma, *a.* (biol.) astomatous.
astracán, *m.* astrakhan (fur).
astracanada, *f.* (coll., theat.) farce, burlesque.
astrágalo, *m.* 1. (bot.) tragacanth (Astragalus gummifer); tragacanth gum. 2. (archit., artil.) astragal, molding around a column or cannon muzzle. 3. (anat.) astragalus, ankle bone.
astral, *a.* astral.
astreñir, (*ref. 41*) *tr.v., var. of* **astringir.**
astricción, *f.* astriction, binding.
astrictivo, va, *a.* astrictive, astringent, styptic.
astricto, ta, *irr. past part. of* **astringir.** *—a.* 1. constrited, compressed. 2. (fig.) compelled, bound, obligated.
astrífero, ra, *a.* (poet.) starry, star-studded.
astringencia, *f.* astringency; astriction, constriction.
astringente, *a.* astringent.
astringir, (*ref. 62*) *tr.v.* 1. to astringe, constrict, compress. 2. to hold, constrain, repress. 3. (fig.) to oblige, compel.

astrinja, astrinjo, *ref.* **astringir.**
astriñendo, astriñera, astriñese, *ref.* **astreñir.**
astriñir, (*ref. 66*) *tr.v., var. of* **astringir.**
astro, *m.* star.
astrobotánica, *f.* astrobotany.
astrocito, *m.* (anat.) astrocyte.
astrofísica, *f.* astrophysics.
astrofísico, ca, *a.* astrophysical.
astrofotografía, *f.* astrophotography.
astrofotográfico, ca, *a.* astrophotographic.
astrofotometría, *f.* astrophotometry.
astrofotométrico, ca, *a.* astrophotometric.
astrografía, *f.* astrography.
astrográfico, ca, *a.* astrographic.
astrógrafo, *m.* astrograph, photographic telescope.
astrolabio, *m.* (astron.) astrolabe.
astrolito, *m.* aerolite, meteoric stone.
astrologar, (*ref. 51*) *tr.v.* to prognosticate, forecast or foretell by the stars.
astrología, *f.* astrology.
astrológico, ca, *a.* astrological.
astrólogo, ga, *a.* astrologic, astrological. *—m., f.* astrologer.
astrometeorología, *f.* astrometeorology.
astronauta, *m.* astronaut, cosmonaut.
astronáutica, *f.* astronautics.
astronave, *f.* spaceship.
astronavegación, *f.* astronavigation, celestial navigation.
astronavío, *m.* spaceship.
astronomía, *f.* astronomy.
astronómicamente, *adv.* astronomically.
astronómico, ca, *a.* 1. astronomic, astronomical. 2. (coll.) astronomical, enormous, gigantic.
astrónomo, *m.* astronomer.
astroquímica, *f.* astrochemistry.
astrosamente, *adv.* filthily, in a slovenly fashion.
astrosfera, *f.* (biol.) astrosphere.
astroso, sa, *a.* 1. wretched, miserable. 2. (fig.) shabby, ragged. 3. vile, despicable.
astucia, *f.* 1. astuteness, cleverness, shrewdness, cunning. 2. trick, ruse, stratagem.
astucioso, sa, *a.* astute, clever, shrewd, cunning.
asturiano, na, *a., m., f.* Asturian, from the province of Asturias (Spain).
asturión, *m.* 1. (ichth.) sturgeon. 2. pony, small horse.
astutamente, *adv.* astutely, cunningly, shrewdly.
astuto, ta, *a.* astute, cunning, shrewd.
asuardado, da, *a.* stained, soiled (cloth).
asubiadero, *m.* (Sp., reg.) shelter from the rain.
asubiar, *i.v.* to guard against the rain.
asueto, *m.* short holiday, half holiday. — **día de a.,** day off, day's holiday; **tarde de a.,** afternoon off, half holiday.
asumir, *tr.v.* 1. to assume (responsibilities, command; great proportions). 2. to raise, elevate.
Asunción, Asuncion, capital of Paraguay.
asunción, *f.* 1. assumption, taking on (e.g. of authority, command, etc.). 2. (ecc.) **A.,** Assumption. 3. elevation (to a post, dignity, etc.).
asuncionista, *m.* a member of the religious order of the Augustinians of the Assumption.
asunto, *irr. past part. of* **asumir.** *—m.* subject, topic; matter, affair. — **tener muchos asuntos entre manos,** to have many irons in the fire; **a. pendiente,** pending business; **asuntos exteriores,** foreign affairs; **vamos al a.,** let's get down to business.
asuramiento, *m.* burning; parching, scorching.
asurar, *tr.v.* 1. to burn (stews, meats, etc.); to parch, scorch (crops). 2. to worry. *—r.v.* 1. to get burned; to become parched or scorched. 2. to be worried. 3. to be very hot.
asurcado, da, *past part. of* **asurcar.** *—a.* furrowed.
asurcano, na, *a.* neighboring (lands or farmers).
asurcar, (*ref. 50*) *tr.v.* to furrow.
asuso, *adv., var. of* **arriba.**
asustadizo, za, *a.* (coll.) scary, fearful, timid.
asustado, da, *a.* frightened, scared.
asustador, *a.* scaring, frightening, alarming.
asustar, *tr.v.* to scare, frighten. *—r.v.* to be scared or frightened. — **asustarse de, por or con, to be frightened at or by; asustarse de +** *inf.* to be afraid to + *inf.,* be frightened to + *inf.,* e.g. *me asusto de pensarlo,* it scares me to think about it.
asutilar, *tr.v., var. of* **sutilizar.**
At *sym. of* **astatinio,** astatine (At).
atabacado, da, *a.* tobacco-colored.
atabal, *m.* (mus.) tabor, tambour, timbrel, drum.
atabalear, *i.v.* 1. to pound (running horses). 2. to drum (with the fingers).
atabalejo, *m.* small drum.
atabalero, *m.* tambour player.
atabalete, *m.* small drum.
atabanado, da, *a.* white spotted (horse).
atabardillado, da, *a.* like typhus or spotted fever.
atabe, *m.* vent (in water pipes).
atabernado, *a.* sold by the bottle or glass, retailed (wine).
atabladera, *f.* (agr.) leveling board (used) on freshly sown land).
atablar, *tr.v.* to level (with a leveling board).
atacable, *a.* vulnerable.
atacadera, *f.* tamping stick, rammer (for ramming down explosives).
atacado, da, *past part. of* **atacar.** *—a.* (coll.) 1. irresolute, vacillating, timid. 2. (coll.) stingy, niggardly.
atacador, ra, *a.* aggressive, attacking. *—m., f.* aggressor, attacker. *—m.* (mil.) rammer, ramrod.
atacadura, *f.* 1. fastening, buttoning. 2. ramming, thrusting.
atacamiento, *m., var. of* **atacadura.**
atacamita, *f.* (min.) atacamite.
atacante, *a.* attacking, assailing. *—m., f.* attacker, assailant.
atacar, (*ref. 50*) *tr.v.* 1. to attack, assault. 2. to refute, attack, contradict (e.g. argument). 3. (chem.) to corrode, eat away. 4. to tamp or ram down (powder in charge); to pack, jam, stuff. 5. to fasten, button up, do up. 6. to attack (an illness), overcome (sleep). 7. to begin, make a start on, attack. — **a. en oleadas,** to attack in waves. *—r.v.* to fasten or button up.
ataché, *m.* (gal.) attaché.
atacir, *m.* (astrol.) division of the celestial arch into twelve parts; zodiac (figure showing these divisions).
atacola, *f.* strap for tying up horse's tail.
ataderas, *f. pl.* (coll.) garters.
atadero, *m.* 1. cord, rope. 2. halter ring or hook; place where a thing is tied. 3. (coll.) garter. — **no tener a.,** (coll.) to be topsy turvy, be in disorder; to make no sense.
atadijo, *m.* 1. poorly packed or ill-shaped bundle. 2. rope, cord.
atado, da, *past part. of* **atar.** *—a.* bashful, easily embarrassed. *—m.* bundle, parcel.
atador, ra, *a.* tying, binding, fastening. *—m., f.* tier binder. *—m.* (sheaf) binder.
atadura, *f.* 1. tying, binding, fastening. 2. strap, cord, string. 3. union, bond, link. 4. hindrance, restriction.
atafagar, (*ref. 51*) *tr.v.* 1. to suffocate stifle, smother (especially by strong odors). 2. (coll.) to annoy, pester, plague. *—r.v.* to suffocate, be stifled.
atafea, *f.* surfeit, satiation.
atafetanado, da, *a.* taffeta-like.
atagallar, *i.v.* (mar.) to crowd sail, sail with sails full.
ataguía, *f.* (construction) cofferdam.
ataharre, *m.* broad crupper (to prevent horse's harness from slipping forward).
atahona, *f., var. of* **tahona.**
atahonero, *m., var. of* **tahonero.**
atahorma, *f.* (ornith.) harrier eagle.
ataifor, *m.* 1. small round Moorish table. 2. deep dish.
atairar, *tr.v.* to put or make moldings in (door and window frames).
ataire, *m.* molding (in door and window frames).
ataja, *f.* (Arg.) *var. of* **ataharre.**
atajada, *f.* (Chile) interception, hindrance, obstruction.
atajadero, *m.* barrage, dike (to direct water into new channel for irrigation).
atajadizo, *m.* 1. partition. 2. small plot or segment of land.
atajador, ra, *a.* intercepting, obstructing, hindering. *—m.* 1. interceptor, obstructor. 2. (Amer.) drover, cattle driver.
atajamiento, *m.* interception; stopping; halting.
atajante, *a.* intercepting.
atajaprimo, *m.* (Cuba) colonial dance similar to the creole tap or clog dance (also called **zapateo cubano**).
atajar, *tr.v.* 1. to intercept, head off, stop, halt; to interrupt, cut short, butt in on (speaker, conversation, etc.). 2. to divide, partition (land, etc.); to divide (cattle) into flocks or herds. 3. to cut (manuscript), cross out (parts to be omitted in manuscript). *—i.v.* to take a short cut. *—r.v.* 1. (fig.) to feel embarrassed or perplexed; to feel afraid. 2. (Sp.) to get drunk.
atajasolaces, *m.* (sl.) wet-blanket, party pooper.
atajea, *f., var. of* **atarjea.**
atajía, *f., var. of* **atarjea.**
atajo, *m.* 1. shortcut; (fig.) shortcut, quick method. 2. division, segment, portion. 3. (fenc.) direct thrust. 4. cut (in a text). 5. group, band; string, pack. — **echar por un a.,** to take a short cut; to dodge, duck, avoid.
atalajar, *tr.v.* (mil.) to harness (horses).
atalaje, *m.* 1. (artil.) team of horses; harness. 2. (coll.) outfit, equipment.
Atalanta, *f.* (myth.) Atalanta.
atalantar, *tr.v.* 1. to stun, daze, shock. 2. to please, suit. *—r.v.* 1. to be stunned or bewildered. 2. to rush, hurry.
atalaya, *f.* watchtower; lookout, vantage point. *—m.* lookout; observer; watcher; spy.
atalayador, ra, *a.* watching, observing; spying, prying. *—m., f.* lookout, guard; observer; pryer.
atalayar, *tr.v.* to watch, observe; to spy on, snoop on.
atalayero, *m.* (mil.) scout, lookout.
atalayuela, *f.* small watchtower or lookout.
ataludar, *tr.v.* to slope.
ataluzar, (*ref. 53*) *tr.v., var. of* **ataludar.**
atalvina, *f.* porridge made with milk and almonds.
atamiento, *m.* (coll.) timidity, meekness, pusillanimity, shyness.
atanasia, *f.* 1. (bot.) costmary. 2. (print.) English type, 14-point type. 3. (poet., philos.) immortality (from the Greek).
atanasiano, na, *a.* (rel.) Athanasian.
Atanasio, *m.* (rel.) Athanasius. — **credo de A.,** Athanasian Creed.
atanco, *m.* (rare) obstacle, barrier, obstruction.
atanor, *m.* water pipe; ceramic or concrete water duct.

atanquía, *f.* 1. depilatory cream. 2. coarse silk (outer part of the cocoon which cannot be spun).
atañedero, ra, *a.* pertinent, concerning.
atañer, (*ref. 59*) *i.v.* to concer (*def. v. used only in 3rd pers.*).
atapialar, *tr.v.* (Ecuad., coll.) to enclose with earth walls, build walls around.
atapuzar, (*ref. 53*) *tr.v.* (Ven.) to cram, stuff, fill.
ataque, ataqué, *ref.* **atacar.**
ataque, *m.* 1. attack, assault. 2. (mil.) earthworks, siege trenches. 3. (med.) attack, fit (of apoplexy, etc.). — **a. de detención,** (mil.) holding attack; **a. de fijación,** (mil.) secondary attack.
ataquiza, *f.* (agr.) layering (of vine shoots, etc.).
ataquizar, (*ref. 53*) *tr.v.* to layer (a vine shoot).
atar, *tr.v.* 1. to tie, bind; to lace up. 2. to tie, bind, restrict, restrain. 3. (fig.) to reconcile, relate. — **a. cabos,** to put two and two together; **no a. ni desatar,** to talk nonsense, talk incoherently; to get or lead nowhere, solve nothing. —*r.v.* 1. to get tied up (in difficulties). 2. to stick (to an opinion).
atarace, ataracé, *ref.* **atarazar.**
ataracea, *f., var. of* **taracea,** inlay, marquetry.
ataracear, *tr.v., var. of* **taracear.**
atarantado, da, *past part. of* **atarantar.** —*a.* 1. bitten by a tarantula. 2. (coll.) restless and noisy. 3. stunned, frightened, scared.
atarantamiento, *m.* consternation, shock.
atarantar, *tr.v.* to stun, daze, shock. —*r.v.* 1. to be stunned or bewildered. 2. to rush, hurry.
ataraxia, *f.* ataraxy, ataraxia, state of extreme placidity or serenity.
atarazana, *f.* 1. dockyard. 2. rope-workers' shed.
atarazar, (*ref. 53*) *tr.v.* to bite or tear off.
atardecer, (*ref. 45*) *i.v.* to draw towards evening, grow late.
atardecer, *m.* late afternoon.
atardezca, *ref.* **atardecer,**
atareado, da, *past part. of* **atarear.** —*a.* busy, occupied.
atarear, *tr.v.* to give work to someone. —*r.v.* to occupy or busy oneself; **me atareo en contar,** I busy myself counting.
atarjea, *f.* 1. brick casing around pipes (for protection). 2. pipe, piping, drainpipe, conduit.
atarquinar, *tr.v.* to cover with mud. —*r.v.* to be covered with mud.
atarraga, *f.* (bot.) elecampane, inula.
atarragar, (*ref. 51*) *tr.v.* 1. to fit, shape (shoe to horse's foot). 2. (Ven.) to nail. —*r.v.* (Amer.) to eat excessively.
atarrajar, *tr.v., var. of* **aterrajar.**
atarraya, *f.* casting net.
atarugamiento, *m.* 1. embarrassment, confusion. 2. pegging, fastening with pegs or pins. 3. plugging, stopping up. 4. stuffing, packing.
atarugar, (*ref. 51*) *tr.v.* 1. to dowel, fasten or fix together with pegs or pins. 2. to plug, stop up. 3. (coll.) to silence, squelch, leave with nothing to say. 4. (coll.) to stuff, pack. 5. to fill, bloat. —*r.v.* 1. to be silenced, feel confused or embarrassed. 2. to stuff oneself (with food).
atarugue, atarugué, *ref.* **atarugar.**
atasajado, da, *past part. of* **atasajar.** —*a.* (coll.) stretched out (on horseback).
atasajar, *tr.v.* 1. to cut into slices (meat). 2. to salt or corn meat.
atascadero, *m.* 1. mudhole, slough, muddy place (where vehicles, etc. get bogged down). 2. stumbling block, obstacle.
atascado, da, *a.* 1. obstinate, stubborn, dogged. 2. stuck, blocked.
atascamiento, *m.* obstruction.
atascar, (*ref. 50*) *tr.v.* 1. to stop up, clog (pipes, drains). 2. to calk (a ship). 3. to hamper, impede, hinder. —*r.v.* 1. to clog, become clogged. 2. (coll.) to get stuck, become bogged down.
atasco, *m.* obstruction.
atasque, atasqué, *ref.* **atascar.**
¡atatay! *interj.* (Quech., Ecuad.) expression of revulsion or loathing.
ataúd, *m.* coffin, casket.
ataudado, da, *a.* coffin-shaped.
ataujía, *f.* 1. damascene work, damascening (inlaying of metal-work with gold or silver designs). 2. high quality craftsmanship, work of art.
ataujiado, da, *a.* damascened, decorated with damascene work.
ataurique, *m.* (archit.) ornamental plaster-work.
ataviar, *tr.v.* to deck, adorn. —*r.v.* to attire oneself, deck oneself out.
atávico, ca, *a.* atavistic.
atavío, *m.* dress, adornment; (*pl.*) finery.
atavismo, *m.* atavism.
ataxia, *f.* (med.) ataxia, ataxy. — **a. locomotriz progresiva,** (med.) locomotor ataxia.
atáxico, ca, *a., m., f.* (med.) ataxic.
atece, atecé, *ref.* **atezar.**
atecomate, *m.* (Mex.) drinking cup.
atecorralar, *tr.v.* (Mex.) to fence or wall in with an unmortared wall.
atediante, *a.* tiresome, wearisome, tedious.
atediar, *tr.v.* to bore, tire, weary, cause tedium. —*r.v.* to become bored, tired or weary.
ateísmo, *m.* atheism.
ateísta, *a.* atheistic. —*m., f.* atheist.
atejo, *m.* (Col.) parcel, package, bundle.
atelaje, *m.* 1. (artil.) team of draft horses. 2. harness.
atelana, *f.* Roman one-act play or farce.
ateles, *m.* (zool.) ateles, spider monkey.
atemorice, atemoricé, *ref.* **atemorizar.**
atemorizar, (*ref. 53*) *tr.v.* to terrify, frighten. —*r.v.* to be terrified or frightened.
atemperación, *f.* moderation, tempering.
atemperador, ra, *a.* moderating, tempering. —*m.* (phys.) moderator (to slow neutrons in a reactor).
atemperante, *a.* moderating, tempering.
atemperar, *tr.v.* 1. to soothe, calm, pacify. 2. to moderate, temper. 3. to adjust, accommodate. 4. to bring to a bearable or convenient temperature. 5. (metal.) to temper (steel). 6. to warm up (a furnace, crucible, etc.). —*r.v.* 1. to calm down, become calm. 2. to become moderate, temperate. 3. to become tempered.
atenacear, *tr.v.* 1. to tear the flesh from (someone) with pincers; to torture. 2. to tie down securely.
Atenas, *f.* Athens, capital of Greece.
atenazar, (*ref. 53*) *tr.v.* 1. to gnash, clench (the teeth). 2. to tear the flesh from (someone) with pincers; to torture. 3. to tie down securely.
atención, *f.* 1. attention, heed. 2. attention, civility, kindness, courtesy. 3. (wool-trade) contract of sale at current but unspecified price. 4. (*pl.*) work, obligations, duties, responsibilities. — **¡a.!** (mil.) attention!; pay attention; **en a. a,** bearing in mind, considering, in view of; **estar en a.,** to stand at attention; **llamar la a.,** to attract or draw one's attention; to surprise, be surprising; **llamarle la a. a uno,** to call or draw (someone's) attention, bring to (someone's) notice (i.e. to make him notice his mistake, etc.); **ponerse en a.,** to come to attention; **prestar a.,** to pay attention.
atendedor, ra, *m., f.* (print.) proofreader's assistant, copyholder, reading boy.
atendencia, *f.* attention.
atender, (*ref. 30*) *tr.v.* 1. to pay attention. 2. to attend to, take care of, look after; to serve, wait on (e.g. tables in restaurant); to attend, nurse (a patient). 3. to keep in mind, be aware of. 4. to await, wait for. —*i.v.* 1. to attend, pay attention. 2. to attend, be present. 3. (print.) to follow copy while proofreader reads aloud. — **a. a,** to attend to, look after; to wait on, serve; to attend, be present at.
atendible, *a.* worthy of attention or consideration.
atendré, atendría, *ref.* **atenerse.**
Atenea, *f.* (myth.) Pallas Athena.
atenebrarse, *r.v.* to cloud over, darken.
ateneísta, *m., f.* member of an athenaeum.
ateneo, *m.* athenaeum, cultural or scientific association.
ateneo, a, *a., m., f.* (poet.) Athenian.
atenerse, (*ref. 23*) *r.v.* **atenerse a,** to depend on, rely on; to follow, observe, abide by, be guided by.
atenga, atengo, *ref.* **atenerse.**
ateniense, *a., m., f.* Athenian.
atenor, *m.* (Col., Ecuad., coll.), *var. of* **atanor.**
atenorado, da, *a.* (mus.) tenor-like (voice and instrument).
atentación, *f.* (law) illegal procedure, illegality.
atentadamente, *adv.* 1. prudently, cautiously. 2. illegally, unlawfully.
atentado, da, *past part. of* **atentar.** —*a.* judicious, moderate, prudent, discreet. —*m.* 1. illegal procedure, illegality. 2. aggression against the government or a person representing authority; crime, offense, criminal assault or attack. — **a. contra la vida de,** attempt on (someone's) life.
atentamente, *adv.* 1. attentively, respectfully. 2. yours truly or sincerely (used to close a letter).
atentar, (*ref. 33*) *tr.v.* to attempt to commit (a crime). —*i.v.* to attempt a crime, offense, etc. — **a. contra,** to make an attempt against; to attempt a crime, offense, etc. against. —*r.v.* to control or restrain oneself.
atentatorio, ria, *a.* illegal, unlawful.
atento, ta, *irr. past part. of* **atender.** —*a.* 1. attentive, heedful. 2. polite, courteous, civil.
atenuación, *f.* 1. attenuation. 2. extenuation. 3. (rhet.) litotes.
atenuador, *m.* (elec.) attenuator. — **a. de escalera,** (rad.) ladder attenuator.
atenuante, *a.* 1. attenuating. 2. extenuating (circumstances).
atenuar, (*ref. 55*) *tr.v.* 1. to attenuate, make thin. 2. to extenuate, serve as excuse for (crime). 3. to soften (a request or demand).
ateo, a, *a.* atheistic. —*m., f.* atheist.
ateperetarse, *r.v.* (C. Amer.) to become bewildered or confused.
atepocate, *m.* (Mex.) tadpole.
atercianado, da, *a.* suffering from tertian or intermittent fever. —*m., f.* person suffering from intermittent fever.
aterciopelado, da, *a.* velvety, velour-like.
aterecerse, (*ref. 45*) *r.v.* to become numb with cold.
aterido, da, *past part. of* **aterir.** —*a.* numb with the cold.
aterimiento, *m.* numbness from cold, growing numb.
aterir, *tr.v.* to numb. —*r.v.* to become numb with cold (*def. v. used only in inf. and past part.*).
atermancia, *f.* (phys.) athermancy.
atérmano, na, *a.* (phys.) athermanous.
ateroma, *m.* (med.) atheroma.
ateromasia, *f.* (med.) atheromasia.
ateromatosis, *f.* (med.) atheromatosis.
ateromatoso, sa, *a.* (med.) atheromatous.
aterosis, *f.* (med.) atherosis.
aterrada, *f.* (mar.) landfall (approaching land).
aterrado, da, *past part. of* **aterrar.** —*a.* terrified; appalled, e.g. *estoy a. con esa noticia,* I'm appalled at the news.

aterrador, ra, *a.* terrifying, fearful.
aterrajar, *tr.v.* 1. (mec.) to thread, cut the thread on (a screw). 2. to shape moldings on with a modeling board.
aterraje, *m.* (mar.) approaching land; (aer.) landing.
aterramiento, *m.* 1. terror, fear. 2. dejection; humiliation.
aterrar, (*ref. 32*) *tr.v.* 1. to knock down; to demolish, destroy. 2. to cover with earth. 3. to dump (slag, rubble). 4. to terrify. —*i.v.* to reach land, to land. —*r.v.* 1. (mar.) to approach land. 2. to be terrified.
aterrerar, *tr.v.* (min.) to dump (slag or rubbish).
aterrice, aterricé, *ref.* **aterrizar.**
aterrilladura, *f.* (Cuba) sunburn; sunstroke.
aterrillarse, *r.v.* (Cuba) to get sunburned.
aterrizaje, *m.* (aer.) landing; (mar.) landfall, approaching land; **a. a ciegas,** (aer.) blind or instrument landing; **a. con motor parado** or **con hélice calada,** (aer.) dead-stick landing; **a. de precisión,** (aer.) spot landing; **a. forzoso,** (aer.) forced landing; **pista de a.,** landing strip.
aterrizar, (*ref. 53*) *i.v.* (aer.) to land. — **a. corto,** (aer.) to undershoot.
aterronar, *tr.v.* to clot, make lumpy. —*r.v.* to become lumpy, clot.
aterrorice, aterroricé, *ref.* **aterrorizar.**
aterrorizar, (*ref. 53*) *tr.v.* to terrify, frighten. —*r.v.* to become terrified.
ates, *m.* (bot.) a sweetsop widely cultivated in the Philippine Islands.
atesorar, *tr.v.* 1. to treasure, store up, hoard. 2. to possess (virtues, etc.).
atestación, *f.* attestation, testimony, affidavit.
atestado, *past part. of* **atestar.** —*m.* affidavit, sworn statement; (*pl.*) testimonials.
atestado, da, *a.* stubborn, obstinate.
atestadura, *f.* 1. stuffing, cramming. 2. must used to top up wine casks.
atestamiento, *m.* stuffing, cramming.
atestar, (*reg. and ref. 33*) *tr.v.* 1. to stuff, pack, fill, cram. 2. to top up (wine casks) with must.
atestar, *tr.v.* (law) to attest, testify, witness.
atestiguación, *f.* (law) attestation, testimony, deposition.
atestiguamiento, *m., var. of* **atestiguación.**
atestiguar, (*ref. 52*) *tr.v.* to attest, testify, depose.
atetado, da, *past part. of* **atetar.** —*a.* breast-shaped.
atetar, *tr.v.* to suckle (commonly applied to animals).
atetillar, *tr.v.* (agr.) to dig a trench around (the base of trees) leaving a mound of soil against the trunk base.
atezado, da, *past part. of* **atezar.** —*a.* sunburned, tanned; dark-skinned, swarthy.
atezamiento, *m.* 1. smoothness, glossiness. 2. darkening, swarthiness.
atezar, (*ref. 53*) *tr.v.* 1. to make smooth and glossy. 2. to darken, make dark. —*r.v.* to become tanned or sunburned, get dark or swarthy.
atibar, *tr.v.* (min.) to pack, fill up (galleries and shafts).
atiborrar, *tr.v.* to pack, stuff, fill; to cram, gorge, stuff (with food). —*r.v.* 1. to stuff oneself (with food). 2. (fig.) to fill the head with ideas, etc.
atice, aticé, *ref.* **atizar.**
aticismo, *m.* Atticism, classicism.
aticista, *m., f.* Atticist, classicist.
ático, ca, *a., m., f.* (hist., geog.) Attic. —*m.* 1. Attic (dialect). 2. (archit.) attic (garret; pediment).
atienda, atiendo, *ref.* **atender.**
atiente, atiento, *ref.* **atentar.**
atierre, atierro, *ref.* **aterrar.**
atierre, *m.* 1. (min.) cave-in. 2. (Mex.) filling up with earth.
atiesar, *tr.v.* to stiffen, harden; to tighten, tauten. —*r.v.* to become hard or stiff; to become tight or taut.
atieste, atiesto, *ref.* **atestar.**
atifle, *m.* potter's trivet, clay utensil used by potters to keep pieces separate while they bake.
atigrado, da, *a.* striped (like a tiger's skin).
atijara, *f.* 1. merchandise, commerce. 2. freight charge. 3. reward, recompense.
atijarero, *m.* carrier.
Atila, *m.* (hist.) Attila, king of the Huns.
atildado, da, *past part. of* **atildar.** —*a.* tidy, neat, elegant.
atildadura, *f., var. of* **atildamiento.**
atildamiento, *m.* 1. marking with a tilde. 2. criticism, censure. 3. tidying, cleaning, smartening up; neatness, tidiness.
atildar, *tr.v.* 1. to write a tilde. 2. to censure, criticize. 3. to arrange, clean, tidy, adorn. —*r.v.* to smarten oneself up.
atinadamente, *adv.* cleverly, prudently, sensibly.
atinar, *tr.v.* 1. to find. 2. to guess, hit upon. —*i.v.* **a. a,** to find, come upon, stumble on; to hit (target); to guess, hit upon; a. a + *i. f.,* to manage to + *inf.,* succeed in + *ger.,* e.g. *atino a encontrar,* I manage to find; **a. con,** to find, come upon, stumble on, to guess, hit upon; **a. en,** to guess.
atinca, *m.* (Chile, coll.) *var. of* **atíncar.**
atíncar, *m.* (chem.) borax.
atinconar, *tr.v.* (min.) to prop up (walls of a mine).
atinente, *a.* relevant, pertinent.
atingencia, *f.* 1. (Amer.) connection, relation. 2. (Mex.) judgment, prudence; skill.
atingente, *a., var. of* **atinente.**
atingir, (*ref. 62*) *tr.v.* (Peru, Chile) to oppress, tyrannize.
atinja, atinjo, *ref.* **atingir.**
atiparse, *r.v.* (C. Rica) to gorge or stuff oneself (with food).
atiplado, da, *past part. of* **atiplar.** —*a.* piercing, high-pitched (voice or tone).
atiplar, *tr.v.* to raise the pitch of (musical instrument), to treble. —*r.v.* to become sharp (tone or voice).
atipujarse, *r.v.* (Guat., Hond.) *var. of* **atiparse.**
atiquizar, (*ref. 53*) *tr.v.* (Hond.) to whip up, rouse, stir up, incite.
atirantar, *tr.v.* 1. to secure, tie, brace with ties. 2. to tauten, tighten, make tight.
atiriciarse, *r.v.* to get jaundice.
atisbadero, *m.* (Amer.) peephole.
atisbador, ra, *a.* watching, observing. —*m., f.* watcher, observer.
atisbadura, *f.* watching, observing.
atisbar, *tr.v.* to watch, observe, examine.
atisbo, *m.* 1. watching, observation. 2. (fig.) glimpse, sign, suspicion.
atisuado, da, *a.* tissue-like.
¡atiza! *interj.* really! gee! (expression of surprise).
atizacandiles, *m.* (coll.) meddlesome servant.
atizadero, *m.* (fire) poker.
atizador, ra, *a.* 1. stirring, inflaming, inciting. 2. poking. —*m.* 1. (fire) poker. 2. feeder (of an oil press).
atizar, (*ref. 53*) *tr.v.* 1. to poke (fire). 2. to trim (wick). 3. to inflame, stir up (feelings). 4. (coll.) to give, deal, strike (blow with stick, foot).
atizonar, *tr.v.* (mas.) to bond (wall) with headers; (mas.) to embed (a beam) in wall. —*r.v.* to become blighted (plants).
atlante, (*pl.* **atlantes**) *m.* 1. (archit.) atlas, telamon, male figure as support of an entablature. 2. (fig.) mainstay, prop (person who remains firm in the execution of a project).
atlántico, ca, *a.* Atlantic. —*m.* **A.,** Atlantic (ocean).
Atlántida, *f.* (myth.) Atlantis, the lost continent, supposed to have existed W. of Gibraltar on the Atlantic ocean.
Atlántidas, *f.* (*pl.*) (astron., myth.) Atlantides.
atlas, *m.* 1. atlas (collection of maps; group of illustrations attached to a volume). 2. (anat.) atlas, first vertebra of the neck. 3. **A.,** (myth.) Atlas.
atleta, *m.* 1. athlete; gymnast. 2. (fig.) staunch defender.
atlético, ca, *a.* athletic.
atletismo, *m.* athletics.
atmiatría, *f.* (med.) atmiatry, atmiatrics, treatment of disease by vapors or gases.
atmómetro, *m.* (meteorol., chem.) atmometer.
atmósfera, *f.* atmosphere.
atmosférico, ca, *a.* atmospheric. —*f.* (rad.) static, atmospherics.
atoar, *tr.v.* 1. (mar.) to tow. 2. (mar.) to warp.
atocha, *f.* (bot.) esparto grass.
atochada, *f.* barrage, small dam (made of esparto and earth).
atochal, *m.* esparto field.
atochar, *m., var. of* **atochal.**
atochar, *tr.v.* 1. to stuff or fill with esparto; by extension, to pack tightly with any substance. 2. (mar.) to blow, press or jam (sail) against the rigging (wind). —*r.v.* to become jammed or wedged (cable).
atochero, ra, *m., f.* esparto carrier.
atochón, *m.* esparto reeds or rushes; (bot.) esparto.
atocinado, da, *past part. of* **atocinar.** —*a.* (coll.) fat, fleshy (person).
atocinar, *tr.v.* 1. to cut up (pig); to make into bacon. 2. (coll.) to murder. —*r.v.* 1. (coll.) to become irritated or annoyed. 2. (coll.) to fall madly in love.
atocle, *m.* (Mex.) damp fertile soil.
atojar, *tr.v.* (C. Rica, Cuba) to sic, incite (a dog).
atol, *m.* (Amer.) *var. of* **atole.**
atole, *m.* (Amer.) drink prepared with cornmeal gruel. — **dar a. con el dedo,** (coll., Mex.) to pull the wool over someone's eyes, deceive, trick.
atoleadas, *f.* (*pl.*) (Hond.) festivities at which **atole** is served.
atolero, ra, *m., f.* **atole** maker or vendor.
atolillo, *m.* thin **atole** made for the sick or for young children.
atolladero, *m.* 1. mire, bog. 2. obstruction, handicap. 3 (Amer., coll.) predicament. — **estar metido en un a.,** to be in a fix or a jam.
atollar, *i.v., r.v.* 1. to get bogged down or stuck in the mud. 2. (coll.) to get stuck in a place or situation.
atolón, *m.* atoll.
atolondradamente, *adv.* 1. recklessly, without reflection, rashly, precipitately. 2. confusedly, in a confused or bewildered manner.
atolondrado, da, *past part. of* **atolondrar.** —*a.* 1. hare-brained, reckless, rash, precipitate. 2. confused, bewildered, stunned.
atolondramiento, *m.* 1. confusion, bewilderment. 2. recklessness, rashness.
atolondrar, *tr.v.* to confuse, bewilder, stupefy. —*r.v.* to be confused, bewildered or stupefied.
atomice, atomicé, *ref.* **atomizar.**
atomicidad, *f.* (chem.) atomicity.
atómico, ca, *a.* atomic. — **bomba a.,** atom bomb; **desintegracíon a.,** (phys.) atomic fission; **energía a.,** (phys.) atomic energy; **número a.,** (chem.) atomic number; **peso a.,** (chem.) atomic weight; **pila a.,** (phys.) atomic pile, nuclear reactor; **proyectil a.,** atomic missile; **submarino a.,**

nuclear submarine; **teoría a.,** (phys.) atomic or nuclear theory.
atomismo, *m.* (philos.) atomism.
atomista, *m., f.* (philos.) atomist.
atomístico, ca, *a.* atomistic.
atomización, *f.* atomization, atomizing.
atomizador, *m.* atomizer, spray; aerosol bomb. — **a. de pintura,** paint sprayer.
atomizar, (*ref. 53*) tr.v. to atomize, pulverize.
átomo, *m.* atom. — **a. activo,** (phys.) hot atom; **á. fisionado,** split atom; **átomogramo,** (chem., phys.) gram-atom, gram-atomic weight.
atona, *f.* ewe that raises another's lamb.
atonal, *a.* (mus.) atonal.
atonalidad, *f.* (mus.) atonality.
atondar, *tr.v.* (equit.) to spur, urge on (horse).
atonía, *f.* (med.) atony, lack of muscle tone.
atónico, ca, *a.* 1. (med., gram.) atonic. 2. (gram.) unaccented.
atónito, ta, *a.* astonished, amazed, astounded.
átono, na, *a.* 1. (gram., med.) atonic. 2. (gram.) unaccented.
atontadamente, *adv.* stupidly, foolishly.
atontamiento, *m.* stupefaction, stunning.
atontar, *tr.v.* to stun, stupefy, bewilder. —*r.v.* to become stunned, stupefied or bewildered.
atopile, *m.* (Mex.) foreman in charge of irrigation waters.
Ator, *f.* (myth.) Hathor, Egyptian goddess of love and joy.
atoramiento, *m.* obstruction, blockage, clogging, choking.
atorar, *tr.v.* 1. to obstruct, stop up, clog. 2. to cut or chop into firewood. —*r.v.* to become clogged, obstructed or stopped up; to choke.
atormentadamente, *adv.* tormentedly, anxiously, distressedly.
atormentador, ra, *a.* tormenting; torturing. —*m., f.* tormentor; torturer.
atormentar, *tr.v.* 1. to torment, cause pain; to torture. 2. (artil.) to shell, bombard.
atornasolado, da, *a.* shot, irridescent, changeable (cloth, etc.).
atornillador, *m.* screwdriver.
atornillar, *tr.v.* 1. to screw, screw on; to fix with a screw. 2. (Amer.) to disturb, importune, molest.
atoro, *m.* (Amer.) *var. of* **atoramiento.**
atorozonarse, *r.v.* (vet.) to suffer from enteritis or colic.
atorrante, *a.* (Arg.) loafing, lazy. —*m., f.* loafer, bum.
atorrantismo, *m.* (Arg.) loafing, bumming about.
atorrar, *i.v.* (Arg.) to loaf about, laze, bum, be a bum or loafer.
atortillar, *tr.v.* (Chile) *var. of* **atortujar,** to flatten.
atortojar, *tr.v.* 1. (Ven.) to squeeze, flatten, squash. 2. (Cuba, Ven.) to worry, frighten, intimidate.
atortolar, *tr.v.* (coll.) to worry, frighten, intimidate. —*r.v.* to get frightened.
atortorar, *tr.v.* (mar.) to frap, tighten, strengthen.
atortujar, *tr.v.* to squeeze, flatten, squash.
atorunado, da, *a.* (Chile) strong, hefty.
atosigador, ra, *a.* 1. toxic, poisonous. 2. harrying, harassing. —*m., f.* 1. poisoner. 2. harrier, harasser.
atosigamiento, *m.* 1. poisoning. 2. harassing, harrying, pressuring.
atosigar, (*ref. 51*) *tr.v.* 1. to poison. 2. to harass, harry, press, pressure. —*r.v.* to become harassed or worried.
atosigue, atosigué, *ref.* **atosigar.**
atóxico, ca, *a.* atoxic, non-poisonous.
atrabajado, da, *a.* 1. overworked, hardworked. 2. laboriously contrived, artificial, unnatural.
atrabajar, *tr.v.* (rare) to make someone work, burden with overwork.
atrabancado, da, *past part. of* **atrabancar.** —*a.* 1. (Mex.) reckless, thoughtless, rash. 2. (Cuba, reg. Sp.) obstructing, obstructed (with furniture, etc.).
atrabancar, (*ref. 50*) *tr.v.* 1. to clear objects quickly or hastily. 2. to obstruct or crowd (with objects, etc.).
atrabanco, *m.* 1. hastiness, hurry. 2. obstruction.
atrabanque, atrabanqué, *ref.* **atrabancar.**
atrabiliario, ria, *a.* 1. (med., anat.) atrabiliary, atrabilious. 2. (coll.) ill-tempered, dyspeptic. — **cápsula atrabiliaria** (anat.) atrabiliary capsule.
atrabilioso, sa, *a.* (med.) atrabiliary, atrabilious.
atrabilis, *f.* 1. (med.) black bile, atrabile. 2. bad temper.
atracada, *f.* 1. (Cuba, Mex.) blowout (sl.), big feed. 2. (Cuba) quarrel. 3. (mar.) docking, berthing.
atracadero, *m.* (mar.) berth, dock, pier, mooring (for small craft).
atracado, da, *past part. of* **atracar.** —*a.* 1. (Chile) harsh, severe, unbending (person). 2. (Chile) niggardly, miserly, stingy, mean. 3. surfeited, full (with food).
atracador, *m.* (sl.) holdup man.
atracar, (*ref. 50*) *tr.v.* 1. to holdup, waylay, assault. 2. (coll.) to stuff, fill (with food). 3. to bring up or close, place near; (mar.) to bring alongside. 4. (Chile) to deal with harshly, beat. —*i.v.* (mar.) to go or come alongside, moor, dock, berth. —*r.v.* 1. to stuff or gorge oneself. 2. (Cuba, Hond.) to quarrel (with one another).
atracción, *f.* 1. attraction. 2. (*pl.*) amusements, diversions. — **parque de atracciones,** amusement park; **a. capilar,** (phys.) capillary attraction.
atraco, *m.* robbery, holdup, stickup.
atracón, *m.* (coll.) 1. blowout, big feed. 2. surfeit, excess.
atractivo, va, *a.* attractive. —*m.* attractiveness, attraction.
atractriz, *a.* (phys.) attractive. — **fuerza a.,** power of attraction.
atraer, (*ref. 24*) *tr.v.* to attract, draw.
atrafagar, (*ref. 51*) *i.v.* to toil, strive, exert oneself. —*r.v.* to fuss or fidget.
atrafague, atrafagué, *ref.* **atrafagar.**
atragantamiento, *m.* choking.
atragantarse, *r.v.* 1. to choke. 2. (coll.) to get confused, embarrassed or mixed up (while speaking). 3. (fig., coll.) to dislike, find (something) difficult to swallow.
atraíble, *a.* attractable.
atraicionar, *tr.v.* to betray.
atraidorado, da, *a.* treacherous, traitorous.
atraiga, atraigo, *ref.* **atraer.**
atraillar, *tr.v.* 1. to leash (dogs). 2. (hunt.) to trail or stalk game (guided by dog on leash). 3. to bind securely, hold fast.
atraimiento, *m.* attraction.
atraje, atrajera, atrajese, *ref.* **atraer.**
atramojar, *tr.v.* (Col., Ven.) to leash.
atrampar, *tr.v.* to trap, ensnare, catch. —*r.v.* 1. to fall into a trap, be trapped, ensnared or caught. 2. to catch, stick (bolt which will not open). 3. (coll.) to become involved, entangled or mixed up (in difficulties).
atramuz, (*pl.* **atramuces**) *m.* (bot.) lupine.
atrancar, (*ref. 50*) *tr.v.* 1. to bar, bolt (door). 2. to obstruct, clog. —*i.v.* 1. (coll.) to stride, take long steps or strides. 2. (coll.) to skim, read hastily. —*r.v.* 1. to shut (oneself) in (putting a bar across the door). 2. (Mex.) to become stubborn, be insistent.
atranco, *m.* difficulty, hindrance, obstacle.
atranque, atranqué, *ref.* **atrancar.**
atranque, *m., var. of* **atranco.**
atrapamoscas, *f.* (bot.) Venus' flytrap.
atrapar, *tr.v.* 1. (coll.) to catch, trap. 2. (coll.) to get, obtain. 3. (coll.) to deceive, take in, ensnare.
atraque, atraqué, *ref.* **atracar.**
atraque, *m.* (Peru) traffic jam.
atrás, *adv.* back, backward; behind; back, ago, e.g. *algunos años a.,* some years back or ago; **¡a.!** back! get back!; **a. de,** behind; **dar marcha a.,** to go into reverse, back up; **dar un paso a.,** to take a step backwards; **dejar a.,** to leave behind; **días a.,** days back or ago; **echarse a.,** to back out; withdraw; **hacerse a.,** to move back; **hacia a.,** back, backwards; **quedarse a.,** to stay or lag behind; **volver los ojos a.,** to turn one's eyes back.
atrasado, da, *past part. of* **atrasar.** —*a.* 1. slow (clock, watch). 2. backward (child in school; country in development). 3. back (payment, issue of magazine, etc.). 4. late, e.g. *el tren viene atrasado,* the train will arrive late, is delayed. 5. behind, in arrears, e.g. *él está muy a. en sus pagos,* he is behind or very much in arrears with his payments; **a. de noticias,** not abreast of the news.
atrasar, *tr.v.* to retard, delay; to postdate (event, document); to retard, slow down (a clock); to set back (a clock). —*i.v.* to go slow, be slow (a clock). —*r.v.* to get or stay behind, lag behind; to be late; to lose, be or go slow (a clock); to fall into arrears.
atraso, *m.* delay; slowness; backwardness; (*pl.*) arrears.
atravesado, da, *past part. of* **atravesar.** —*a.* 1. cross-eyed, squint-eyed, cock-eyed. 2. mongrel, crossbred (animal). 3. (fig.) wicked, evil.
atravesador, ra, *a.* traversing, crossing.
atravesaño, *m., var. of* **travesaño.**
atravesar, (*ref. 29*) *tr.v.* 1. to put or lay across. 2. to pierce, run through. 3. to block, obstruct, impede. 4. to cross, cross over, go over, go through. 5. (in card games) to stake, wager, bet; to play (a trump). 6. (Amer.) to buy up, monopolize, corner. 7. to put the evil eye on, bewitch. 8. (mar.) to lay to (a ship). — **a. en,** to lay or put (something) across (road, stream, etc.). —*r.v.* 1. (mar.) to lie to. 2. to be in the way, obstruct, impede. 3. to interrupt, butt in; to join in; to meddle. 4. to wrangle, quarrel, have a quarrel. 5. to stake, bet, wager. — **atravesársele a uno una persona,** to find someone unpleasant or unbearable; **atravesársele a uno alguien,** to have a quarrel with someone, come up against someone.
atraviese, atravieso, *ref.* **atravesar.**
atrayendo, *ref.* **atraer.**
atrayente, *a.* attractive, appealing.
atreguado, da, *a.* 1. mad, deranged. 2. under truce.
atreguar, (*ref. 52*) *tr.v.* to give or grant a truce. —*r.v. to agree to a truce.*
atrepsia, *f.* (med.) athrepsia.
atresia, *f.* (med.) atresia.
atresnalar, *tr.v.* (agr.) to shock, arrange (sheaves) in shocks.
atreverse, (*ref. 27*) *r.v.* to dare; venture; **a. a +** *inf.,* to dare to + *inf.* e.g. *a. a decir,* to dare (to) say; **a. con** or **contra,** to be insolent to, insulting or offensive toward.
atreví, atreviendo, atreviera, atreviese, *ref.* **atreverse.**
atrevidamente, *adv.* 1. daringly, boldly. 2. impudently, impertinently, insolently.
atrevido, da, *irr. past part. of* **atreverse.** —*a.* 1. daring, bold. 2. impudent, insolent, impertinent.

atrevimiento, *m.* 1. daring, boldness. 2. impudence, insolence, impertinence.
atribución, *f.* 1. attribution. 2. function, duty, obligation; (*pl.*) powers, authority, jurisdiction.
atribuir, (*ref. 48*) *tr.v.* 1. to attribute, ascribe to. 2. to confer, grant. —*r.v.* to confer on oneself.
atribulación, *f.* tribulation.
atribuladamente, *adv.* distressedly, distressfully, afflictedly.
atribular, *tr.v.* to distress, afflict. —*r.v.* to become distressed or afflicted.
atributivo, va, *a.* attributive.
atributo, *m.* 1. attribute. 2. (log., gram.) predicate. 3. (Hond.) wooden platform or stand for carrying religious images in processions.
atribuya, atribuyendo, atribuyó, *ref.* atribuir.
atrición, *f.* attrition, contrition, repentance.
atril, *m.* lectern; music stand.
atrilera, *f.* ornamental cover for lectern or music stand.
atrincar, (*ref. 50*) *tr.v.* 1. (Amer.) to tie fast, bind. 2. (Cuba) to tighten.
atrincheramiento, *m.* entrenchment, line of trenches.
atrincherar, *tr.v.* to entrench, surround with trenches. —*r.v.* to entrench oneself, dig in.
atrinchilar, *tr.v., r.v.* (Mex.) to corner (someone).
atrinque, atrinqué, *ref.* **atrincar.**
atrio, *m.* 1. (archit.) atrium; porch, hall. 2. (min.) upper end of washing trough.
atrípedo, da, *a.* (zool.) black-footed.
atrirrostro, tra, *a.* (ornith.) black-beaked.
atrito, ta, *a.* contrite, repented.
atrocidad, *f.* 1. atrocity. 2. (coll.) enormity, excess. 3. (coll.) stupidity, stupid action or remark.
atrochar, *i.v.* to go by a cross path, take a short cut.
atrofia, *f.* atrophy.
atrofiar, *tr.v.* to atrophy, cause atrophy. —*r.v.* to atrophy, suffer from atrophy, become atrophied.
atrófico, ca, *a.* atrophic.
atrojar, *tr.v.* to garner, store in bins (grain). —*r.v.* 1. (Mex., coll.) to be stumped or beaten (unable to solve a problem). 2. (Mex., coll.) to calm down (horse).
atrompetado, da, *a.* trumpet-mouthed, wide-mouthed (gun); fleshy and crooked (nose).
atronadamente, *adv.* rashly, impetuously, hastily.
atronado, da, *a.* precipitate, hasty, impetuous.
atronador, ra, *a.* thundering, thunderous, deafening.
atronadura, *f.* 1. fissure, crack (in tree). 2. (vet.) crepance (of a horse).
atronamiento, *m.* 1. deafening. 2. stupefying, stunning.
atronar, (*ref. 33*) *tr.v.* 1. to deafen. 2. to stun, stupefy. 3. to stop up the ears of (a horse) to avoid its shying. 4. to stun (cattle); to kill (a bull) by a blow on the nape of the neck. —*r.v.* to be frightened or killed by thunder (animals).
atronerar, *tr.v.* to make loopholes, portholes, or embrasures in.
atropado, da, *past part. of* **atropar.** —*a.* (agr.) gathered into sheaves or bundles (branches).
atropar, *tr.v.* to assemble, or group into troops or gangs; to gather (branches, hay). —*r.v.* to assemble in gangs or troops.
atropelladamente, *adv.* hastily, tumultuously.
atropellado, da, *past part. of* **atropellar.** —*a.* hasty, precipitate. —*f.* assault, onset, violent attack.
atropellador, ra, *a.* trampling; transgressing, violating. —*m., f.* trampler; abuser; transgressor, violator.
atropellamiento, *m., var. of* **atropello.**
atropellaplatos, *f.* (hum.) clumsy house servant.
atropellar, *tr.v.* 1. to trample down, trample under foot; to run over, knock down. 2. to ride roughshod over, treat abusively. 3. to abuse, revile. 4. to disregard, violate, ride roughshod over (laws, obligations, feelings, etc.). 5. to do hurriedly or hastily. —*i.v.* to disregard, violate, ride roughshod over (laws, feelings, obligations, etc.); to override, pay no attention to. —*r.v.* to act hastily or hurriedly; to speak quickly.
atropello, *m.* outrage, abuse, maltreatment; attack, assault.
atropina, *f.* (chem., pharm.) atropine.
atroz, (*pl.* **atroces**) *a.* 1. atrocious, brutal, savage. 2. (coll.) enormous, huge, tremendous.
atrozar, *tr.v.* (mar.) to truss a yard.
atrozmente, *adv.* 1. atrociously, horribly. 2. enormously.
atruchado, da, *a.* trout-colored.
atruhanado, da, *a.* villainous, rascally, roguish.
atte. *abbrev. of* **atentamente,** yours sincerely, faithfully or truly (in closing a letter).
atucuñar, *tr.v.* (Hond.) to stuff, pack, cram. —*r.v.* (Hond.) to stuff oneself (with food).
atuendo, *m.* 1. pomp, ostentation. 2. apparel, attire.
atufadamente, *adv.* peevishly, crossly, angrily.
atufado, da, *past part. of* **atufar.** —*a.* 1. wearing side locks. 2. (Arg.) angry, annoyed. 3. (Cuba, Guat.) vain, arrogant.
atufamiento, *m., var. of* **atufo.**
atufar, *tr.v.* 1. to overcome with fumes. 2. to anger, annoy. —*r.v.* 1. to be overcome by fumes. 2. to get angry. 3. to go sour (wines). 4. (Ecuad.) to become giddy, confused, dazed. 5. (Guat.) to grow haughty, put on airs. — **atufarse con, de** or **por,** to get angry with or at.
atufo, *m.* annoyance, anger.
Au *sym. of* **aurum (oro),** aurum (gold) (Au).
atún, *m.* 1. (ichth.) tuna fish. 2. (coll.) rough, ignorant person. — **la pesca del a.,** tuna-fishing.
atunara, *f.* tuna-fishing ground.
atunera, *f.* tuna fish hook.
atunero, ra, *m., f.* tuna fish dealer. — *m.* tuna fisherman.
aturar, *tr.v.* (coll.) to close tightly.
aturdidamente, *adv.* dazedly, dizzily; confusedly.
aturdido, da, *past part. of* **aturdir.** —*a.* 1. dazed, stunned, giddy. 2. bewildered, amazed.
aturdidor, ra, *a.* stunning; bewildering, amazing.
aturdimiento, *m.* daze, stun; shock, upset, confusion; (med.) vertigo, dizziness.
aturdir, *tr.v.* 1. to daze, stun. 2. to bewilder, confuse, agitate, perturb. 3. (med.) to produce vertigo or giddiness. —*r.v.* 1. to be dazed or stunned. 2. to become bewildered, confused, agitated or perturbed. 3. (med.) to become giddy.
aturquesado, da, *a.* turquoise blue, turquoise-like.
aturrullamiento, *m.* bewilderment, perplexity, confusion.
aturrullar, *tr.v.* (coll.) to confuse, bewilder, puzzle, baffle. —*r.v.* (coll.) to get confused, bewildered, puzzled or baffled.
aturullar, *tr.v., var. of* **aturrullar.**
atusador, ra, *a.* trimming, shearing; grooming. —*m., f.* trimmer, shearer (gen. of locks or hair).
atusar, *tr.v.* 1. to trim (hair or plants). 2. to comb and smooth, groom (hair). —*r.v.* to dress very fancily.
atutía, *f.* 1. tutty, impure zinc oxide. 2. medicinal ointment made of tutty.
atuve, atuviera, atuviese, *ref.* **atenerse.**
auca, *f.* 1. (ornith.) gray wild goose. 2. goose (game). 3. (Bol.) bowler hat, derby hat.
audacia, *f.* audacity, daring boldness.
audaz, (*pl.* **audaces**) *a.* audacious, daring, bold.
audazmente, *adv.* audaciously, daringly, boldly.
audibilidad, *f.* (rad.) audibility.
audible, *a.* audible.
audición, *f.* 1. hearing, audition. 2. audition, sense of hearing. 3. broadcast, program. 4. audition, tryout (for part in play, etc.).
audiencia, *f.* 1. audience, hearing. 2. audience chamber. 3. royal tribunal, high court of justice. 4. district under courts' jurisdiction. 5. tribunal building. 6. (público) audience; **de mucha a.,** (tel.) with a large audience, with many viewers. — **a. nacional,** supreme court; **a. pública,** public hearing; **a. territorial,** police court, traffic court; **dar a.,** to grant an audience; **hacer a.,** to meet and decide law cases.
audífono, *m.* audiphone, hearing aid; (rad.) headphone, earphone.
audio, *a.* (rad.) audio.
audioamplificador, *m.* (rad.) audio or audiofrequency amplifier.
audiofrecuencia, *f.* (rad.) audio-frequency.
audiograma, *m.* audiogram.
audiómetro, *m.* (phys.) audiometer.
audiovisual, *a.* audio-visual. — **material auxiliar a.,** audio-visual aids.
auditivo, va, *a.* auditive, auditory, aural. — **aparato auditivo,** earphone, receiver.
auditor, *m.* 1. legal adviser, judge, judge advocate. 2. (com.) auditor, one who audits accounts. — **a. de guerra,** judge advocate, legal adviser for the Army; **a. de la nunciatura,** Papal Nuncio's adviser on ecclesiastical law; **a. de marina,** judge advocate for the Navy.
auditoría, *f.* 1. auditorship; auditing. 2. office of judge advocate.
auditorio, ria, *a.* auditory, aural. —*m.* 1. audience. 2. auditorium.
auge, *m.* 1. summit, apex, apogee, e.g. *en esta época España se encontraba en el a. de su esplendor,* at this time Spain was at the height of her splendor; (astron.) apogee. 2. popularity, vogue, e.g. *esta moda tenía gran a. en el siglo dieciocho,* this fashion was very popular in the eighteenth century. 3. rise, boom, e.g. *el cobre está en a.,* copper is booming, copper is rising.
augita, *m.* (min.) augite.
augur, *m.* augur; auspex (in ancient Rome, a priest who interpreted the omens).
auguración, *f.* augury, divination by omens.
augurar, *tr.v.* to augur, divine, foretell, prognosticate.
augurio, *m.* augury, omen, presage.
augustal, *a.* Augustan, pertaining to the Augustan Age in Roman history.
augustamente, *adv.* augustly, majestically.
augusto, ta, *a.* august, majestic.
aula, *f.* 1. classroom, lecture hall. 2. (poet.) palace.
aulaga, *f.* (bot.) furze, whin, gorse (Ulex australis or europea). —**a. vaquera,** whin (Ulex boeticus).
áulico, ca, *a.* aulic, courtly. —*m., f.* courtier.
aulladero, *m.* (hunt.) grounds where wolves howl.
aullador, ra, *a.* howling. —*m.* (zool.) howler monkey.
aullante, *a.* howling.
aullar, *i.v.* to howl, wail, yell, cry.
aullido, aúllo, *m.* howl, wail.
aumentable, *a.* increasable, augmentable, enlargeable.
aumentación, *f.* (rhet.) climax.
aumentado, da, *a.* (mus.) augmented.
aumentador, ra, *a., m., f.* augmenting, enlarging, enlarger.
aumentar, *tr.v.* to augment, increase, enlarge. — **aumentarle el sueldo a alguien,** to raise someone's salary. —*i.v.* to increase, augment. —*r.v.* to increase, augment.

aumentativo, va, *a.* (gram.) augmentative.
aumento, *m.* increase, enlargement, augmentation; raise (in salary). — **ir en a.,** to be on the increase.
aun, *adv.* even, yet, although, still; **a. cuando,** even though, even if.
aún, *adv.* yet, still; **a. no,** not yet; **a. más, más a.,** furthermore, moreover.
aunamiento, *m.* combining, joining.
aunar, *tr.v.* to unite, join; to mix, combine. —*r.v.* to unite, join together; to combine.
aunche, *m.* (Col.) residue, leftovers.
aunque, *conj.* although, even though. — **a. no quieras,** even if you don't want to; **A. Ud. No Lo Crea de Ripley,** Ripley's Believe It or Not.
¡aúpa! *interj.* up! come up! get up!
aupar, *tr.v.* 1. (coll.) to help up, lift. 2. to exalt, praise.
auque, *m.* (Chile) fine potter's clay.
aura, *f.* 1. aura, air, atmosphere, e.g. *le rodeaba un a. de misterio,* an aura of mystery surrounded her. 2. gentle breeze; breath, exhalation, aura. 3. popularity, public approval. 4. (med.) aura. —*m.* (ornith.) turkey buzzard, vulture.
auranciáceo, a, *a.* (bot.) aurantiaceous. —*f.* aurantiaceous plant; (*pl.*) Aurantiaceae.
áureo, a, *a.* gold, golden, aureate. —*m.* (numis.) aureus (coin).
aureola, *f.* 1. (theol., meteorol.) aureole. 2. aureole, halo. 3. (med., bot., anat.) aureola. 4. aureole, line left around a stain.
aureolar, *tr.v.* to adorn with a halo; (fig.) to exalt or glorify.
aureomicina, *f.* (med.) aureomycin.
aurero, *m.* (Cuba) flock of turkey buzzards.
áurico, ca, *a.* (chem.) auric, of gold, golden.
aurícula, *f.* (anat., bot.) auricle.
auriculado, da, *a.* auriculate.
auricular, *a.* auricular. —*m.* 1. little finger. 2. (tel.) earpiece, receiver; earphone.
aurífero, ra, *a.* auriferous, gold-bearing.
auriga, *m.* 1. (poet.) auriga, charioteer. 2. (astron.) **A., Auriga.**
aurígero, ra, *a., var. of* **aurífero.**
aurista, *m.* aurist, ear specialist.
aurívoro, ra, *a.* (poet.) craving for gold.
aurochs, *m.* (zool.) aurochs, European bison.
aurora, *f.* 1. aurora, dawn (of the day, of time). 2. (ecc.) morning service. 3. pink or rosy (color). 4. drink made with milk, almonds and cinnamon; (Bol.) type of **chicha** (fermented drink). 5. (Amer., ornith.) small owl. — **a. austral,** aurora australis; **a. boreal,** aurora borealis; **despunta** or **rompe la a.,** the dawn is breaking.
auroral, *a.* auroral, pertaining to the aurora.
aurragado, da, *a.* badly tilled and cultivated (soil).
auscultación, *f.* (med.) auscultation.
auscultar, *tr.v.* (med.) to auscultate, examine by auscultation.
ausencia, *f.* absence. — **tener buenas** or **malas ausencias,** to have good or bad news (of persons absent); **brillar uno por su a.,** to be conspicuous by (one's) absence.
ausentado, da, *past part. of* **ausentar.** —*a.* absent.
ausentar, *tr.v.* to send or keep away (people, etc.). —*r.v.* to absent oneself, to disappear.
ausente, *a.* absent. — **a. sin licencia,** (mil.) awol, absent without leave. —*m., f.* absentee. —*m.* (law) missing person.
ausentismo, *m.* absenteeism.
ausoles, *m.* (*pl.*) 1. (C. Amer.) volcanic cracks. 2. (Salv.) geysers.
auspiciar, *tr.v.* (Amer.) to back, support, sponsor.
auspicio, *m.* 1. omen, augury, auspice. 2. (*pl.*) auspices, patronage, sponsorship. — **bajo los auspicios de,** under the auspices of.
auspicioso, sa, *a.* auspicious, favorable.
austenita, *f.* (metal.) austenite.
austeramente, *adv.* austerely.
austeridad, *f.* austerity.
austero, ra, *a.* austere.
austral, *a.* southern, austral. — **continente a.,** Antarctica; **polo a.,** south pole.
Australia, *f.* Australia. — **A. Meridional,** South Australia.
australiano, na, *a., m., f.* Australian.
Austria, *f.* Austria.
austríaco, ca, *a., m., f.* Austrian.
austro, *m.* 1. auster, south wind. 2. south.
austroasiático, ca, *a.* austroasiatic.
ausubo, *m.* (bot.) a West Indian fruit tree of the sapodilla family.
autarcía, *f., var. of* **autarquía.**
autarquía, *f.* 1. autarchy, absolute sovereignty. 2. autarky, autarchy, economic self-sufficiency.
autárquico, ca, *a.* autarchic, autarchical; autarkic, autarkical.
auténtica, *f.* 1. certification (of authenticity). 2. authorized copy.
autenticación, *f.* authentication.
auténticamente, *adv.* authentically.
autenticar, (*ref.* 50) *tr.v.* to authenticate.
autenticidad, *f.* authenticity.
auténtico, ca, *a.* authentic, genuine.
autentificar, (*ref.* 50) *tr.v.* (neol.) to authenticate.
autentifique, autentifiqué, *ref.* **autentificar.**
autentique, autentiqué, *ref.* **autenticar.**
autillo, *m.* 1. private decree of the Inquisition. 2. (ornith.) tawny owl.
autismo, *m.* (psyc.) autism.
auto, *m.* automobile, motorcar. — **a. patrullero,** prowl car, squad car.
auto, *m.* 1. judicial decree, decision or ruling. 2. (*pl.*) file, record or proceedings of a case. — **a. acordado,** (law) supreme court ruling arrived at with participation of all its branches; **a. de fe,** (rel.) auto da fe; **a. sacramental,** (theat.) allegorical or religious play.
autoabsorción, *f.* self-absorption.
autoalimentador, ra, *a., m., f.* self-feeding, self-feeder.
autoalineamiento, *m.* self-alignment.
autoamortizable, *a.* self-liquidating.
autoamortizar, (*ref.* 53) *r.v.* to be self-liquidating.
autoanálisis, *m.* (psyc.) self-analysis.
autobiografía, *f.* autobiography.
autobiográfico, ca, *a.* autobiographical.
autoblasto, *m.* (bot.) autoblast.
autobombo, *m.* self-praise, blowing of one's own trumpet.
autobote, *m.* power boat.
autobús, *m.* bus, omnibus, autobus.
autocamión, *m.* motor truck.
autocapacidad, *f.* (elec.) self-capacitance.
autocar, *m.* coach, autocar, bus.
autocarril, *m.* (Amer.) electric or diesel railway car.
autocatálisis, *f.* (biol.) autocatalysis.
autocebador, ra, *a.* (mec.) self-priming.
autocentrado, da, *a.* (mec.) self-centering.
autocine, *m.* (Chile) drive-in motion-picture theater.
autoclástico, *a.* (geol.) autoclastic.
autoclave, *m.* autoclave, sterilizer; retort.
autocracia, *f.* (polit.) autocracy.
autócrata, *m., f.* autocrat, chief of state with limitless powers; (fig.) a tyrant.
autocrático, ca, *a.* autocratic, autocratical.
auto-crítico, ca, *a.* self-critical. —*f.* self-criticism.
autoctonía, *f.* autochthony.
autóctono, na, *a.* autochthonic, autochthonous; aboriginal, domestic, native. —*m., f.* autochthon; native.
autodestrucción, *f.* self-destruction.
autodeterminación, *f.* self-determination.
autodeterminismo, *m.* (philos.) self-determination.
autodidacto, ta, *a.* autodidact, self-taught. —*m., f.* self-taught person.
autodino, *m.* (rad.) autodyne.
autodisciplinado, da, *a.* self-disciplined.
autodisparador, *m.* self-timer.
autódromo, *m.* motorcar race track, motordrome.
autoedición, *f.* desktop publishing.
autoempleo, *m.* self-employment.
autoencendido, *m.* self-ignition.
autoendurecible, *a.* (metal.) self-hardening.
autoengaño, *m.* self deception.
autoenvenenamiento, *m.* (med.) autointoxication.
autoerotismo, *m.* (psyc.) autoerotism.
autoescuela, *f.* driving school.
autoestima, *f.* self esteem.
autoestopista, *m., f.* hitchhiker.
autoexcitación, *f.* (elec.) self-excitation.
autofecundación, *f.* (bot.) close fertilization, self-fertilization, self-pollination.
autofecundado, da, *a.* (bot.) self-pollinated.
autofecundante, *a.* (bot.) autogamous.
autofertilización, *f.* self-fertilization.
autófito, *m.* (bot.) autophyte.
autogamia, *f.* (bot.) autogamy.
autogamo, ma, *a.* (bot.) autogamous.
autogenerador, *a.* (chem.) self-generative.
autogénesis, *f.* autogenesis.
autógeno, na, *a.* autogenous (soldering). —*f.* welding.
autogiro, *m.* autogiro, autogyro.
autogobierno, *m.* self-government.
autografía, *f.* autography, lithographic reproduction of writing or drawing.
autografiar, (*ref.* 54) *tr.v.* to autograph, sign, write one's autograph in (book, photo, program, etc.).
autográfico, ca, *a.* autographical, autographic.
autógrafo, fa, *a.* autographic, by the author's hand. —*m.* autograph. — **cazador de autógrafos,** autograph hunter.
autohipnosis, *f.* (med.) autohypnosis.
autoignición, *f.* self-ignition.
autoinducción, *f.* (elec.) self-induction.
autoinducido, da, *a.* (elec.) self-induced.
autoinductancia, *f.* (elec.) self-inductance, coefficient of self-induction.
autoinfección, *f.* (med.) autoinfection.
autoinflamación, *f.* self-ignition; spontaneous combustion.
autointoxicación, *f.* (med.) autointoxication, autotoxemia.
autolimitación, *f.* self-limitation.
autolisado, *m.* (biol.) autolysate.
autolisina, *f.* (med.) autolysin.
autólisis, *f.* (biochem.) autolysis.
automación, *f.* automation.
autómata, *m.* automaton, robot.
automáticamente, *adv.* automatically.
automático, ca, *a.* automatic. —*m.* clasp.
automatismo, *m.* automatism.
automatización, *f.* automatization.
automatizar, (*ref.* 53) *tr.v.* to automatize.
automedonte, *m.* (fig.) coachman, charioteer.
autómnibus, *m., var. of* **autobús.**
automotor, ra, *a.* automotive, automobile, self-propelling. —*m.* diesel or electric railway coach, railcar.
automotriz, *f. a.* automotive, self-propelling.

automóvil, *a.* self-propelling, automotive. —*m.* automobile, motorcar. — **a. de mando,** (mil.) command car.
automovilismo, *m.* motoring.
automovilista, *m., f.* motorist; motoring enthusiast, automobilist.
automovilístico, ca, *a.* pertaining to motoring.
autonomía, *f.* 1. autonomy, self-determination. 2. cruising range (of a ship, airplane, etc.).
autonómicamente, *adv.* autonomously.
autonómico, ca, *a.* autonomous, autonomic.
autonomista, *m., f.* autonomist.
autónomo, ma, *a.* 1. autonomous. 2. (physiol., anat.) autonomic.
autopista, *f.* throughway, expressway; turnpike.
autoplastia, *f.* (surg.) autoplasty, autografting.
autoplástico, ca, *a.* autoplastic.
autopolinización, *f.* (bot.) self-pollination.
autopotencial, *m.* (geoph.) self-potential.
autopropagado, da, *a.* self-propagating.
autopropulsión, *f.* self-propulsion.
autopropulsor, ra, *a.* self-moving.
autoprotección, *f.* 1. self-protection. 2. fail-safe (automatic system of protection against failure in the discharge of a nuclear device).
autopsia, *f.* autopsy.
autópsido, da, *a.* metallic-looking (mineral).
autor, ra, *m., f.* 1. author, authoress. 2. perpetrator (of a crime). —*m.* (arch.) theatrical manager.
autoría, *f.* (arch.) managership, post of manager (of theater or theatrical company).
autorice, autoricé, *ref.* **autorizar.**
autoridad, *f.* 1. authority. 2. pomp, show, display. — **con a.,** authoritatively, with authority, e.g. ***él** habla con a. sobre este asunto,* he speaks authoritatively on this subject.
autoritariamente, *adv.* authoritatively; imperiously, despotically.
autoritario, ria, *a.* authoritarian; imperious, bossy (coll.). —*m., f.* authoritarian, martinet, despot.
autoritarismo, *m.* authoritarianism.
autoritativo, va, *a.* authoritative.
autorizable, *a.* authorizable.
autorización, *f.* authorization.
autorizadamente, *adv.* authoritatively; with authorization.
autorizado, da, *past part. of* **autorizar.** —*a.* authoritative.
autorizador, ra, *a.* authorizing. —*m., f.* authorizer.
autorizamiento, *m., var. of* **autorización.**
autorizante, *a.* authorizing.
autorizar, (*ref. 53*) *tr.v.* 1. to authorize, empower. 2. to authorize, permit. 3. (law) to authenticate or legalize with a signature (a document). — **a. a** + *inf.,* to authorize to + *inf.,* e.g. *te autorizo a firmar por mí,* I authorize you to sign for me.
autorradiación, *f.* (phys.) self-radiation.
autorregistrador, ra, *a.* (tel.) self-recording.
autorregulador, ra, *a.* self-regulating.
autorretrato, *m.* self-portrait.
autorrotativo, va, *a.* self-rotating.
autoservicio, *m.* self-service.
autosoma, *m.* (biol.) autosome.
auto-stop, *m.* hitchhiking; **hacer a.,** to hitchhike; **mi amigo me cogió en a.,** my friend gave me a ride.
autosuficiencia, *f.* self-sufficiency.
autosugestión, *f.* autosuggestion, self-suggestion.
autotemplable, *a.* (metal.) self-hardening.
autotemplado, da, *a.* (metal.) self-hardened.
autoterapia, *f.* (med.) autotherapy.
autotipia, *f.* (photog.) autotypy.
autotitulado, da, *a.* (Amer.) self-styled.
autotomía, *f.* (biol.) autotomy.
autotoxemia, *f.* (med.) autotoxemia.
autotoxina, *f.* (med.) autotoxin.
autotransformador, *m.* (elec.) balancing coil, autotransformer.
autotrofia, *f.* (bot., bac.) autotrophy.
autótrofo, fa, *a.* (bot.) autotrophic.
autovía, *f.* 1. diesel or electric railway coach. 2. automobile highway.
autumnal, *a.* autumnal.
autunita, *f.* (min.) autunite.
Auvernia, *f.* Auvergne, region of France.
auvernia, *f.* (Cuba) lemon verbena.
auxiliador, ra, *a.* helping, aiding. —*m., f.* helper, assistant.
auxiliante, *a.* helping, aiding.
auxiliar, *a.* auxiliary, helping; (gram.) auxiliary. —*m., f.* auxiliary; helper, assistant; substitute, aide.
auxiliar, *tr.v.* 1. to help, aid, assist. 2. to attend, comfort.
auxiliaría, *f.* assistantship; assistant professorship.
auxiliatorio, ria, *a.* (law) mandatory, pertaining to an order of a superior court to compel compliance with a decree of a lower court. —*f.* mandatory order, mandamus.
auxilio, *m.* help, aid, assistance, relief. — **primeros auxilios,** first aid.
auximón, *m.* (bot.) auximone.
auyama, *f.,* (Amer., bot.) gourd; pumpkin.
Av. *abbrev. of* **avenida,** avenue (Av.).
avacado, da, *a.* pot-bellied and spiritless (horse).
avadar, *i.v., r.v.* to become shallow and fordable (river).
avahar, *tr.v.* 1. to breathe on, blow vapor on. 2. to warm with breath or vapor. —*i.v.* to steam, emit vapor.
aval, *m.* (com.) endorsement (guaranteeing payment of a draft, a promissory note); written guarantee (of someone's good conduct).
avalancha, *f.* avalanche.
avalar, *tr.v.* (com.) to guarantee (payment of a promissory note) with an endorsement; to answer for (a person) with an endorsement.
avalentado, da, *a.* swaggering; bragging.
avalentamiento, *m.* braggadocio, boastfulness, swagger.
avalentar, *tr.v.* to give encouragement to.
avalentonado, da, *a.* swaggering, bragging, boastful.
avalista, *m., f.* endorser; guarantor, backer.
avallar, *tr.v.* to fence in (a property).
avalorar, *tr.v.* 1. to value, appraise, rate, set value on. 2. to encourage.
avaluación, *f., var. of* **valuación,** valuation, appraisal.
avaluar, (*ref. 55*) *tr.v.* to value, appraise, calculate the value of.
avalúo, *m.* valuation, appraisal.
avambrazo, *m.* vambrace (part of medieval armor).
avance, avancé, *ref.* **avanzar.**
avance, *m.* 1. advance; (mil.) advance, attack. 2. (com.) advance, payment in advance; balance sheet; budget, estimate. 3. trailer, preview (of film). 4. removable front (of carriage body). 5. (mec.) feed, advance. 6. (min.) heading (end of a gallery). 7. (ry.) lead, frog distance. 8. (elec.) lead, pitch. — **a. angular,** (elec., mec.) angular pitch; **a. de fase,** (elec.) phase lead or displacement; **a. noticioso,** (tel.) preview of the news.
avanecerse, (*ref. 45*) *r.v.* to shrivel, go bad (fruit).
avantal, *m., var. of* **devantal,** apron.
avante, *adv.* ahead; **a. a toda máquina,** full steam ahead.
avantrén, *m.* (mil.) limber (of a gun carriage).
avanzada, *f.* (mil.) outpost; advance guard, scouting detachment.
avanzado, da, *a.* 1. advanced. — **de edad a.,** advanced in years. 2. advanced, avantgarde (ideas, etc.).
avanzar, (*ref. 53*) *tr.v.* 1. to advance, move or push forward. 2. to propose, breach, put forward (a subject, plan, etc.). —*i.v.* 1. (mil.) to advance (troops). 2. to progress, make progress; to move on, get on (to better things). 3. to near (an end); to move forward (in time). —*r.v.* to advance.
avanzo, *m.* 1. balance sheet. 2. budget, cost estimate.
avaramente, *adv.* avariciously.
avaricia, *f.* avarice; greediness, cupidity.
avariciosamente, *adv.* avariciously; greedily.
avaricioso, sa, *a.* avaricious; greedy.
avarientamente, *adv.* avariciously; greedily.
avariento, ta, *a.* avaricious, greedy. —*m., f.* miser.
avariosis, *f.* (Amer.) syphilis.
avaro, ra, *a.* avaricious; greedy, miserly. —*m., f.* miser.
avasallador, ra, *a.* subduing, subjecting, subjugating. —*m., f.* subjugator, subduer.
avasallamiento, *m.* subjection, subjugation.
avasallar, *tr.v.* to subdue, subjugate; to subject. —*r.v.* to become a subject or vassal; to submit.
avatar, *m.* (myth.) each one of Vishnu's reincarnations.
Avda. *abbrev. of* **avenida,** avenue (Av.).
ave, *f.* 1. bird, fowl. 2. (astron.) **A.,** Apus (constellation). — **a. canora,** songbird; **a. corredora,** flightless bird; **a. de caza,** game bird; **a. del Paraíso,** (ornith.) bird of paradise; **a. de paso,** migratory bird; (coll.) rolling stone, person who does not stay for long in one place; **a. de rapiña,** bird of prey; (coll.) trickster, confidence man; **A. Fénix,** (astron.) Phoenix (constellation); **a. fría,** (ornith.) lapwing; **a. lira,** (ornith.) lyrebird; **a. nocturna,** nocturnal bird; (coll.) night owl; **a. pasajera,** migratory bird; **a. rapaz** or **rapiega,** bird of prey; **a. zonza,** (ornith.) yellow-hammer.
Ave. *abbrev. of* **avenida,** avenue (Ave.).
avece, avecé, *ref.* **avezar.**
avechucho, *m.* ugly bird; (coll., fig.) unpleasant person.
avecilla, *f. dim. of* **ave,** birdie, little bird. — **a. de las nieves,** (ornith.) wagtail.
avecinar, *tr.v.* 1. to domicile. 2. to bring or place near. —*r.v.* 1. to approach, draw near. 2. to take up residence.
avecindamiento, *m.* 1. settling, taking up residence. 2. domicile.
avecindar, *tr.v.* to domicile. —*r.v.* to take up residence, establish oneself (in a district, town).
avefría, *f.* (ornith.) lapwing.
avejentar, *tr.v., r.v.* to age prematurely.
avejigar, (*ref. 51*) *tr.v., i.v., r.v.* to blister, vesicate.
avellana, *f.* hazelnut. — **a. de la India, a.** índica, myrobalan, cherry plum.
avellanado, da, *a.* hazel colored. — **a. y cincelado,** countersunk and chipped (rivet).
avellanador, *m.* (mec.) countersinking bit.
avellanal, avellanar, *m.* grove of hazel trees.
avellanar, *tr.v.* to countersink. —*r.v.* to shrivel, wither.
avellaneda, do, *f., m. var. of* **avellanar.**
avellanero, ra, *m., f.* hazelnut seller. —*f.* hazel tree.
avellano, *m.* (bot.) hazel tree.
avemaría, *f.* 1. Ave María, Hail Mary (prayer). 2. Angelus. — **al a.,** at dusk or nightfall; **en un a.,** in a flash; **¡Ave Maria¡** *interj.* Good Heavens!

avena, *f.* 1. oats. 2. (poet.) oat, **pastoral.** pipe. — **a. loca,** wild oats.
avenado, da, *a.* lunatic, crazy.
avenal, *m.* oat field.
avenamiento, *m.* draining, drainage.
avenar, *tr.v.* to drain.
avenate, *m.* oatmeal gruel.
avenenar, *tr.v., var. of* **envenenar.**
avenencia, *f.* agreement, compromise, accord.
avenga, avengo, *ref.* **avenir.**
aveníceo, a, *a.* oat-like, avenaceous.
avenida, *f.* 1. avenue, concourse, urban road. 2. flood, freshet. 3. gathering. 4. (mil.) approach, way of access.
avenido, da, *past part. of* **avenir.** —*a.* **bien a.,** in agreement; **mal a.,** in disagreement.
avenidor, ra, *a.* conciliatory, mediatory. —*m., f.* reconciler, mediator.
aveniente, *a.* agreeing, compromising; reconciling.
avenimiento, *m.* agreeing, compromising; agreement, compromise.
avenir, (*ref. 26*) *tr.v.* to reconcile, bring to terms, conciliate. —*i.v.* to happen, occur (*used only in inf. and 3rd pers. sing. and pl.*). —*r.v.* 1. to agree, come to an agreement. 2. to become reconciled. 3. to become adjusted or adapted; to conform. 4. to harmonize, combine. — **avenirse a + *inf.*,** to agree to + *inf.*, e.g. *me avengo a pagar,* I agree to pay.
aventador, ra, *a.* winnowing. —*m., f.* winnower. —*m.* 1. winnowing fork; scutcher. 2. fan; small esparto fan. —*f.* 1. winnowing machine. 2. (min.) suction valve.
aventadura, *f.* (vet.) windgall, soft tumor generally on a horse's fetlock.
aventajado, da, *past part. of* **aventajar.** —*a.* 1. outstanding, superior. 2. advantageous, profitable. —*m.* (mil., arch.) private soldier receiving additional pay.
aventajar, *tr.v.* 1. to surpass, excel. 2. to advance, give an advantage to, put ahead. —*r.v.* 1. to excel, surpass. 2. to advance, get ahead.
aventamiento, *m.* 1. fanning. 2. winnowing. 3. blowing.
aventar, (*ref. 33*) *tr.v.* 1. to fan. 2. to winnow. 3. to blow along. 4. (coll.) to expel, drive out (a person). 5. (Cuba) to air (sugar) in the sun. 6. (Amer.) to throw. —*r.v.* 1. to swell up, become inflated. 2. (coll.) to flee, escape, blow (sl.). 3. (Amer.) to throw oneself; to jump, dive.
aventón, *m.* (Amer.) push, shove.
aventura, *f.* 1. adventure. 2. risk, danger, hazard; vicissitude.
aventurado, da, *a.* 1. daring, bold. 2. risky, hazardous.
aventurar, *tr.v.* 1. to risk, e.g. *no voy a a. mi capital,* I'm not going to risk my capital. 2. to venture, hazard (e.g. an opinion). —*r.v.* to venture, risk oneself, take a risk. — **aventurarse a + *inf.*,** to risk + *ger.;* to venture to + *inf.*, e.g. *me aventuraré a invertir,* I'll risk investing.
aventureramente, *adv.* adventurously, daringly.
aventurero, ra, *a.* 1. adventurous, venturesome. 2. (Amer.) grown out of season (maize, rice, etc.). 3. sown on unirrigated land. —*m.* 1. adventurer (person who seeks adventure or partakes in a hazardous enterprise). 2. adventurer, volunteer, soldier of fortune, free lance. 3. (mar.) volunteer midshipman. 4. peddler, hawker. 5. (Mex.) casually hired drover. —*f.* adventuress.
averdugar, (*ref. 51*) *tr.v.* (vet.) to adjust or tighten (horseshoe) excessively causing lesions.
averdugue, *ref.* **averdugar.**
avergoncé, *ref.* **avergonzar.**
avergonzar, (*ref. 71*) *tr.v.* 1. to shame, put to shame. 2. to embarrass. —*r.v.* 1. to be ashamed, feel ashamed. 2. to feel or get embarrassed. — **avergonzarse de + *inf.*,** to be ashamed to + *inf.*, e.g. *me avergüenzo de pedir,* I am ashamed to ask; **avergonzarse por,** to be ashamed of.
avergüence, *ref.* **avergonzar.**
avergüenzo, *ref.* **avergonzar.**
avería, *f.* 1. damage; failure, breakdown. 2. (com., mar.) average; **a. gruesa,** general or gross average; **a. simple,** particular average. 3. aviary. 4. flock of birds.
averiar, (*ref. 54*) *tr.v.* to damage. —*r.v.* to be or become damaged or spoiled; to break down.
averiguable, *a.* ascertainable, investigable.
averiguación, *f.* ascertainment, inquiry.
averiguadamente, *adv.* assuredly, certainly.
averiguador, ra, *a.* investigating, inquiring. —*m., f.* investigator, inquirer.
averiguamiento, *m., var. of* **averiguación.**
averiguar, (*ref. 52*) *tr.v.* to ascertain, find out, inquire into. —*i.v.* (Hond., Mex.) to argue, dispute.
averío, *m.* flock of domestic fowl.
averno, *m.* (poet.) hell, Avernus.
averroísmo, *m.* (philos.) Averroism.
averroísta, *a.* (philos.) Averroistic. —*m., f.* Averroist.
averrugado, da, *a.* warty, full of warts.
averrugarse, (*ref. 51*) *r.v.* to develop warts, become warty, become full of or covered with warts.
aversión, *f.* aversion, dislike; hate.
Avesta, *m.* (rel.) Avesta, Zoroastrian scriptures.
avestruz, (*pl.* **avestruces**) *m.* (ornith.) ostrich. — **a. de América,** (ornith.) American ostrich, rhea, ñandu.
avetado, da, *a.* veined, streaked, striped.
avetarda, *f., var. of* **avutarda.**
avetoro, *m.* (ornith.) bittern.
avezar, (*ref. 53*) *tr.v.* to accustom. —*r.v.* to become accustomed.
aviación, *f.* aviation; air force.
aviador, ra, *a.* preparing, equipping. —*m., f.* preparer, equipper. —*m.* 1. pilot, aviator, flyer; (mil.) airman. 2. calking auger. 3. (Amer.) supplier or financier of miners or farmers. 4. (Cuba) sodomite, bugger, homosexual. —*f.* airwoman, aviatrix, flyer.
aviamiento, *m.* preparation; equipping.
aviar, (*ref. 54*) *tr.v.* 1. to prepare; to equip; to supply, provide. 2. to make ready, prepare. 3. (Amer.) to equip or supply (farmer, miner, etc.) with equipment or money; (Chile) to finance (mining works). — **a. de** or **con,** to provide with; **estar aviado,** (coll.) to be in a fix or jam, be beset by difficulties. —*i.v.* (coll.) to hurry, make haste. —*r.v.* to get ready, prepare.
Avicena, *m.* Avicenna, Arab physician. — **más mató la cena, que sanó A.,** the cure is worse than the ill.
aviciar, *tr.v.* (agr.) to make plants grow rank.
avícola, *a.* pertaining to bird-raising, poultry-breeding.
avicultor, ra, *m., f.* poultry breeder, aviculturist.
avicultura, *f.* poultry breeding, aviculture.
ávidamente, *adv.* avidly; greedily.
avidez, *f.* avidity, avidness; greed, cupidity.
ávido, da, *a.* avid, greedy.
aviejar, *tr.v., r.v., var. of* **avejentar.**
avienta, *f.* winnowing.
aviente, aviento, *ref.* **aventar.**
aviento, *m.* pitchfork; winnowing fork.
aviesamente, *adv.* perversely, malevolently.
avieso, sa, *a.* 1. twisted, distorted. 2. perverse, malicious.
avigorar, *tr.v.* to invigorate, revive.
avilantarse, *r.v.* to become impudent, be insolent.
avilantez, *f.* insolence, forwardness, boldness, audacity.
avilanteza, *f., var. of* **avilantez.**
avilés, sa, *a.* of or from Avila, Spain. —*m., f.* native or inhabitant of Avila.
avillanado, da, *a.* rustic, rude, low, boorish; debased.
avillanamiento, *m.* boorishness; debasement.
avillanar, *tr.v.* to debase. —*r.v.* to become boorish or debased.
avinagradamente, *adv.* (coll.) sourly, acridly; roughly, harshly.
avinagrado, da, *a.* (coll.) vinegary, crabbed.
avinagrar, *tr.v.* to sour, make sour. —*r.v.* 1. to turn sour; to turn into vinegar. 2. (fig.) to become embittered.
avinca, *f.* (bot.) a variety of Peruvian pumpkin.
avine, *ref.* **avenir.**
aviniendo, aviniera, aviniese, *ref.* **avenir.**
aviñonense, *a.* of or from Avignon, France. —*m., f.* native or inhabitant of Avignon.
avío, *m.* 1. prevention, foresight. 2. preparation, provisioning; provisions, food; (*pl.*) (coll.) equipment, kit. 3. (Amer.) loan (to farmer or miner). 4. (Chile, Peru) complete harness for riding. — **¡al a.!** (coll.) hurry up! get on with it.
avión, *m.* 1. airplane, plane, aircraft. 2. (ornith.) martin, European swift. — **a. a chorro,** or **reacción,** jet plane, jet; **a. cisterna,** tanker; **a. de bombardeo,** bomber; **a. de carga,** cargo plane; **a. de caza,** pursuit plane, fighter; **a. de combate,** combat aircraft; **a. de hélice,** propeller-driven aircraft; **a. nodriza,** tanker; **a. supersónico,** supersonic plane; **a. turborreactor,** turbojet; **por a.,** by air.
avioneta, *f.* small airplane, sports plane.
avisadamente, *adv.* prudently, wisely, cautiously.
avisado, da, *past part. of* **avisar.** —*a.* prudent, sagacious, cautious. — **mal a.,** rash, reckless.
avisador, ra, *a.* 1. informing. 2. warning. —*m.* messenger.
avisar, *tr.v.* 1. to inform. 2. to advise; to warn.
aviso, *m.* 1. notice; advertisement. 2. information, news. 3. warning, admonishment; (taur.) warning (to a bullfighter) that time for the next phase of the game is running out. 4. (mar.) dispatch boat. — **andar** or **estar sobre a.,** to be on one's guard; **a. clasificado,** classified ad; **a. fúnebre,** death notice; **dar a. de,** to inform of; **sobre a.,** on the alert.
avispa, *f.* 1. (ento.) wasp. 2. (coll.) shrewd person.
avispado, da, *past part. of* **avispar.** —*a.* (coll.) clever, sharp, quick-witted, aware, alert, shrewd.
avispar, *tr.v.* 1. to whip, spur. 2. (coll.) to make quick-witted, bright or alert. —*r.v.* 1. (fig.) to worry, fret, get worried. 2. (coll.) to become bright and alert.
avispero, *m.* 1. wasp's nest. 2. swarm of wasps. 3. (coll.) imbroglio, mess, muddled affair. 4. (med.) hives, carbuncle.
avispón, *m.* (ento.) hornet.
avistar, *tr.v.* to descry, sight. —*r.v.* to meet (to discuss business).
avitaminosis, *f.* (med.) avitaminosis.
avitelado, da, *a.* vellum-like, parchment-like.
avituallamiento, *m.* victualing, provisioning.
avituallar, *tr.v.* to provision, victual, provide goods.
avivadamente, *adv.* briskly, lively, vividly.
avivador, ra, *a.* enlivening, reviving. —*m.* 1. (carp.) quirk. 2. (carp.) quirking plane.
avivamiento, *m.* enlivening; heightening; reviving.

avivar, *tr.v.* 1. to enliven, liven up, brighten up, animate; to excite, inflame (passion, etc.). 2. to poke (fire), turn up (light), brighten, heighten (color). *—i.v., r.v.* 1. to hatch (silkworm eggs). 2. to revive, liven up, brighten.
avizor, *m.* watcher, observer. — **estar a ojo a.,** to be on the lookout, attentive to.
avizorador, ra, *a.* watching, observing. *—m., f.* watcher, observer.
avizorante, *a.* watching, watchful, observant.
avizorar, *tr.v.* to watch, observe; to spy.
-avo, -ava, *suffix* added to numerals to express a fraction of the whole.
avocación, *f.* (law) transfer of a case from a lower to a higher court.
avocamiento, *m., var. of* **avocación.**
avocar, (*ref. 50*) *tr.v.* 1. to remove (a case) to a higher court. 2. to take over (a business deal from an inferior).
avocastro, *m.* (Chile, Peru) ungainly person.
avoceta, *f.* (ornith.) avocet.
avogadro, *m.* (phys.) **número de a.,** the number of molecules in a mass of a substance.
avolcanado, da, *a.* volcanic (area).
avoque, avoqué, *ref.* **avocar.**
avucasta, *f., var. of* (ornith.) **avutarda.**
avugo, *m.* (bot.) a variety of small green pear.
avuguero, *m.* (bot.) a kind of pear tree bearing small fruits.
avulsión, *f.* (surg.) avulsion, extirpation.
avutarda, *f.* (ornith.) great bustard.
avutardado, da, *a.* bustard-like.
axial, *a.* axial, axal, pertaining to an axis.
axila, *f.* 1. armpit. 2. (bot.) axil, axilla.
axilar, *a.* axillary, axillar, pertaining to the axilla or axil.
axinita, *f.* (min.) axinite.
axiología, *f.* (philos.) axiology.
axiológico, ca, *a.* axiological.
axioma, *f.* axiom; maxim.
axiomático, ca, *a.* axiomatic, self-evident.
axiómetro, *m.* (mar.) telltale, instrument for indicating the direction of the helm.
axis, *m.* (anat.) axis (second vertebra of the neck).
axo, *m.* woolen garment worn by Peruvian Indians.
axoideo, a, *a.* (anat.) axial, pertaining to the axis (vertebra).
axón, *m.* (anat., physiol.) axon, axone, neurite.
¡ay! *interj.* ouch! alas! woe! — **¡ay de mí!** alas! woe is me! *—m.* sigh, moan, lament; **tiernos ayes,** tender sighs; **estar en un a.,** to be in pain.
aya, *f.* governess, nanny, nursemaid.
ayacuá, *m.* (Arg.) malignant sprite (of Indian folklore).
ayahuasca, *f.* (bot., S. Amer.) narcotic plant from which a drink inducing delirium and hallucinations is obtained (Banisteria mettalicolor).
ayapana, *f.* (bot., S. Amer.) ayapana, medicinal plant from the Amazon.
ayate, *m.* (Mex.) cloth made from the fiber of the maguey.
ayear, *i.v.* to sigh, lament, moan.
ayeaye, *m.* (zool.) aye-aye, lemur.
ayecahue, *m.* 1. (Chile) slovenly person; urchin, bum. 2. (Chile) (*pl.*) ridiculous or extravagant attire.
ayer, *adv.* yesterday; only yesterday, a short time ago. — **de a. acá, de a. a hoy,** quickly, rapidly, overnight, from one day to another. *—m.* yesterday, past.
ayermar, *tr.v.* to lay waste; to turn into desert or wasteland. *—r.v.* to become wasteland or desert.
ayo, *m.* tutor, guardian.
ayocote, *m.* (Mex.) large kidney bean.
ayoguascle, *m.* (Mex.) pumpkin seed.
ayote, *m.* (Mex.) pumpkin; gourd. — **dar ayotes,** (S. Amer., coll.) to turn down (a suitor).
ayotera, *f.* (C. Amer., bot.) pumpkin (plant).
ayotete, *m.* (Mex., bot.) ornamental climbing plant.
ayúa, *f.* (C. Amer., bot.) prickly ash.
ayuda, *f.* 1. help, aid, assistance. 2. financial help, supplementary allowance. 3. (med.) enema, clyster. 4. syringe. 5. prod, prick, lash (given to a horse). — **a. de cámara,** valet; **a. memoria,** aide-mémoire; **a. de parroquia,** chapel of ease; **a. de vecino,** outside help. *—m.* (mar.) preventer-rope.
ayudado, da, *past part. of* **ayudar.** *—a.* (taur.) with both hands (when handling the sword).
ayudador, ra, *a.* helping, aiding. *—m., f.* helper.
ayudanta, *f.* female assistant.
ayudante, *a.* helping. *—m.* assistant; aide; (mil.) adjutant. — **a. de campo,** aide-de-camp; **a. de cátedra,** assistant professor; **a. de dirección,** assistant director; **a. de montes,** overseer; **a. de obras públicas,** civil engineer's assistant; **a. general,** (mil.) adjutant general; **Ayudante Técnico Sanitario,** Registered Nurse.
ayudantía, *f.* assistantship; office of assistant; (mil.) adjutancy; adjutant's office.
ayudar, *tr.v.* to help, aid, assist. — **a. a** + *inf.,* to help to + *inf.,* help + *inf.,* e.g. *a. a escapar,* to help to escape; **a. y encubrir,** (law) to aid and abet.
ayuga, *f.* (bot.) mock cypress.
ayuiñandi, *m.* (bot., Arg.) wild laureaceous shrub used in making incense (Nectandra porphyria).
ayún, *m.* (bot.) fruit tree of the Moluccas used for dyeing.
ayunador, ra, *a.* fasting. *—m., f.* faster, person who fasts.
ayunante, *a.* fasting.
ayunar, *i.v.* to fast; to do without.
ayuno, na, *a.* 1. fasting, unfed. 2. ignorant, uninformed. — **en ayunas, en ayuno,** fasting, unfed, before breakfast; **estar en ayunas** or **en ayuno,** not to have eaten, be unfed; (fig.) to be all at sea, not to understand. *—m.* fasting, fast. — **a. natural,** (rel.) fasting from midnight on.
ayunque, *m., var. of* **yunque,** anvil.
ayuntamiento, *m.* 1. town hall, city hall. 2. town, city or borough council. 3. reunion, meeting. 4. copulation, sexual intercourse.
ayuntar, *tr.v.* (rare), *var. of* **juntar.**
ayuso, *adv.* (arch.) downward, below.
ayustar, *tr.v.* (mar.) to splice (ropes); to scarf (timber).
ayuste, *m.* (mar.) splicing, scarfing; splice.
azabachado, da, *a.* jet, jet-black.
azabache, *m.* 1. (min.) jet. 2. (ornith.) coal tit or titmouse. 3. (*pl.*) jet trinkets or ornaments.
azabachero, *m.* 1. worker in jet. 2. vendor of jet ornaments.
azabara, *f.* (bot.) aloe.
azacán, na, *a.* menial, drudging, toiling. *—m., f.* drudge, slave. — **estar** or **andar hecho un a.,** to work very hard, keep one's nose to the grindstone. *—m.* water carrier.
azacanarse, *r.v.* to work very hard, toil.
azacanear, *i.v.* to work very hard, toil.
azache, *f.* inferior silk made from the outside of the cocoon. *—a.* inferior (silk).
azacuán, *m.* (ornith., Guat.) kite.
azada, *f.* (agr.) hoe.
azadada, *f.,* **azadazo,** *m.* blow given with a hoe.
azadilla, *f.* garden or weeding hoe.
azadón, *m. aug. of* **azada,** grub hoe. — **a. de peto** or **pico,** pick, pickax, mattock; **a. mecánico,** (bldg.) trench hoe, backdigger.
azadonada, *f.* blow dealt with a hoe.
azadonar, *tr.v.* to hoe, spade, dig with a hoe or pick.
azadonazo, *m.* blow dealt with a hoe.
azadonero, *m.* hoer, person who works with a hoe.
azafata, *f.* (aer.) stewardess, hostess.
azafate, *m.* flat wicker basket, low-edged wicker tray; (Amer.) tray.
azafrán, *m.* 1. (bot.) saffron (Crocus sativa). 2. saffron (food coloring and flavoring). 3. (mar.) rudderstock. — **a. bastardo, romí** or **romín,** bastard saffron; **a. de Marte,** (chem.) iron oxide.
azafranado, da, *a.* 1. saffron, saffron-colored. 2. (Mex.) red-haired.
azafranal, *m.* saffron patch, saffron field.
azafranar, *tr.v.* to dye with saffron; to add saffron to (a liquid, dish, etc.).
azafranero, ra, *m., f.* saffron grower; saffron dealer.
azagadero, azagador, *m.* cattle path, cattle trail.
azagaya, *f.* assagai, javelin, light spear.
azahar, *m.* orange, lemon or citron blossom.
azainadamente, *adv.* perfidiously, slyly.
azal, *f.* (bot.) a variety of Portuguese black grape.
azalá, *m.* Mohammedan prayer.
azalea, *f.* (bot.) azalea.
azamboero, azambogo, azamboo, *m.* (bot.) citron tree.
azanahoriate, *m.* 1. (cul.) candied carrot. 2. (coll.) honeyed compliment.
azanca, *f.* (min.) underground spring.
azanoria, *f., var. of* **zanahoria,** carrot.
azaque, *m.* religious tribute offered by Mohammedans.
azar, *m.* 1. chance, hazard. 2. misfortune, accident, mischance. 3. losing card, losing throw. 4. cushion side (of billiard pocket). 5. hazard, hazard corner, obstacle (in game of pelota). — **al a.,** at random.
azarandar, *tr.v., var. of* **zarandar.**
azarante, *a.* bewildering, frightening.
azarar, *tr.v.* to fluster, rattle, embarrass, confuse. *—r.v.* 1. to miscarry, go awry. 2. to get flustered, rattled; to become embarrassed or confused.
azarbe, *m.* main drainage ditch.
azarbeta, *f.* small drainage ditch.
azarcón, *m.* 1. minimum, red lead, lead oxide. 2. (p.) bright orange.
azarearse, *r.v.* 1. (Chile, Guat., Hond.) to get flustered, rattled, embarrassed or confused. 2. (Chile, Peru) to get annoyed or irritated.
azarja, *f.* spindle for winding raw silk.
azarolla, *f.* (bot.) haw, fruit of the hawthorn.
azarollo, *m.* (bot.) hawthorn.
azarosamente, *adv.* hazardously; unfortunately.
azaroso, sa, *a.* 1. risky, hazardous. 2. troubled, unsettled. 3. difficult, unpleasant.
azcona, *f.* (arch.) javelin used by the Basques.
azemar, *tr.v.* to smooth down.
ázimo, *a.* unleavened (bread).
azimut, *m.* (astron., top.) azimuth. — **a. azumido,** assumed azimuth; **a. terrestre,** ground azimuth; **a. verdadero,** true azimuth.
azimutal, *a.* (astron.) azimuthal.
aznacho, *m.* (bot.) cluster pine, pinaster.
aznallo, *m.* 1. (bot.) cluster pine, pinaster. 2. (bot.) restharrow.
azoado, da, *past part. of* **azoar.** *—a.* (chem.) nitrogenous.
azoar, *tr.v.* (chem.) to nitrogenize, impregnate with nitrogen. *—r.v.* to become nitrogenized or impregnated with nitrogen, absorb nitrogen.
azoato, *m.* (chem.) nitrate.
azocar, (*ref. 50*) *tr.v.* (mar.) to tighten up (a knot); (Cuba) to press too tightly, pack too close. — **tabaco azocado,** pressed tobacco leaves.
ázoe, *m.* (chem.) nitrogen.

azofaifa, *f.* (bot.) jujube (fruit).
azofaifo, fa, *m., f.* (bot.) jujube (tree).
azófar, *m.* brass, latten.
azofra, *f.* unpaid labor exacted for public works.
azogadamente, *adv.* (coll.) in a flurry, flurriedly, quickly.
azogamiento, *m.* 1. quicksilvering, coating with quicksilver. 2. (coll.) agitation, worry.
azogar, (*ref. 51*) *tr.v.* 1. to quicksilver, coat with quicksilver. 2. to slake (lime). —*r.v.* 1. (med.) to get mercury poisoning. 2. (coll.) to get disturbed, agitated, troubled or upset.
azogue, azogué, *ref.* **azogar.**
azogue, *m.* 1. quicksilver, mercury. 2. market place. — **ser un a.,** (coll.) to be restless, be a jack-in-the-box.
azoguería, *f.* (min.) amalgamating works.
azoguero, *m.* (min.) amalgamator.
azoico, *a.* 1. (chem.) azoic, nitric, nitrogenous. 2. (geol.) azoic, before life.
azolar, (*ref. 53*) *tr.v.* (carp.) to dub, trim (wood) with an adze.
azolvar, *tr.v.* to block, clog (a drain). —*r.v.* to become blocked or clogged.
azolve, *m.* (Mex.) mud, silt (blocking conduit).
azoque, azoqué, *ref.* **azocar.**
azor, *m.* (ornith.) goshawk.
azorada, *f.* (Col.) confusion, bewilderment.
azoramiento, *m.* confusion, bewilderment.
azorante, *a.* confusing, bewildering; startling.
azorar, *tr.v.* to startle, alarm; to confuse, bewilder; to incite, rouse. —*r.v.* to be startled, alarmed, excited, confused or bewildered.
azorencarse, (*ref. 50*) *r.v.* (C. Amer.) *var. of* atontarse.
azorenque, azorenqué, *ref.* **azorencarse.**
Azores, *f.* (*pl.*) Azores Islands.
azoro, *m.* 1. (Peru, Mex., P. Rico) confusion, bewilderment. 2. (C. Amer.) ghost, apparition, sprite.
azorocarse, (*ref. 50*) *r.v.* (Hond.) to be startled, alarmed or frightened.
azoroque, azoroqué, *ref.* **azorocarse.**
azorrado, da, *past part. of* **azorrarse.** —*a.* 1. fox-like, foxy. 2. sleepy, drowsy.
azorramiento, *m.* drowsiness, dullness, sleepiness.
azorrarse, *r.v.* to get drowsy, drowse.
azotable, *a.* deserving a whipping.
azotacalles, *m., f.* (coll.) gadabout, lounger, loafer, bum.
azotado, da, *past part. of* **azotar.** —*a.* motley, variegated; (Chile) brindled, striped. —*m.* (ecc.) flagellant.
azotador, ra, *a.* whipping, lashing. —*m., f.* flogger, whipper.
azotaina, *f.* (coll.) beating, flogging, lashing.
azotamiento, *m.* flogging; scourging, thrashing.
azotar, *tr.v.* to flog, whip, scourge, thrash; to flail; to pound or beat upon (as the surf). —*r.v.* 1. to flog oneself. 2. (Arg., Urug., Bol.) to plunge, dive.
azotazo, *m.* 1. lash, lashing. 2. smack, spanking.
azote, *m.* 1. whip, cat o'nine tails, tawse, strap, scourge. 2. lash (with a whip). 3. pounding, beating (of sea), lashing (of wind). 4. (fig.) scourge (person, personification of evil). 5. (*pl.*) whipping, flogging.
azotea, *f.* 1. flat roof, terraced roof. 2. (Arg.) adobe house with flat roof.
azotera, *f.* (equit., S. Amer.) ends of the reins used as a whip.
azotina, *f., var. of* **azotaina.**
azteca, *a.* Aztec. —*m., f.* Aztec. —*m.* Aztec (language).
aztor, *m.* (ornith.) falcon.
azua, *f.* (Peru) **chicha,** beer-like drink.
azúcar, *m.,* or *f.* sugar. — **a. blanca,** refined white sugar; **a. blanquilla,** semi-refined sugar; **a. cande** or **candi,** rock candy; **a. de caña,** cane sugar; **a. de cortadillo,** cube sugar, lump sugar; **a. de leche,** lactose; **a. de lustre,** caster sugar; **a. de pilón,** loafsugar; **a. en cubos,** cube sugar; **a. en pancitos,** sugar lumps; **a. en polvo,** icing or powdered sugar; **a. en terrón,** lump sugar; **a. morena, a. prieta,** brown sugar; **a. quebrada,** demerara sugar, unrefined sugar; **a. refinado,** refined sugar; **a. rubia,** (Amer.) brown sugar.
azucarado, da, *past part. of* **azucarar.** —*a.* sugary, sweet; (fig.) sugared, honeyed.
azucarar, *tr.v.* 1. to sugar, coat or ice with sugar; to sweeten. 2. (coll.) to sweeten, soften (person, thing). —*r.v.* to crystallize, go sugary (syrup in preserves).
azucarera, *f.* 1. sugar bowl. 2. sugar mill or factory.
azucarero, ra, *a.* pertaining to sugar. —*m.* 1. foreman in sugar mill, sugar expert. 2. sugar producer, manufacturer or magnate. 3. sugar bowl. 4. (ornith.) honey creeper.
azucarillo, *m.* fondant made of syrup, egg white and lemon dissolved in water, a refreshing drink.
azuce, azucé, *ref.* **azuzar.**
azucena, *f.* 1. (bot.) Madonna or white lily. 2. (fig.) pure, delicate person or thing. — **a. anteada,** (bot.) day lily, fire lily (Hemerocallis fulva).
azuche, *m.* (engin.) pile shoe, pile ferrule.
azud, *m.* 1. irrigation water wheel. 2. diversion dam (for irrigation).
azuda, *f., var. of* **azud.**
azuela, *f.* adz. — **a. curva,** spout adz; **a. ferrocarrilera,** railroad adz.
azuele, azuelo, *ref.* **azolar.**
azufaifa, *f.* (bot.) jujube (berry).
azufaifo, *m.* (bot.) jujube (tree). — **a. loto,** lotus tree.
azufrado, da, *past part. of* **azufrar.** —*a.* sulfureous; sulfur-colored. —*m.* sulfuring, sulfurization, sulfuration.
azufrador, ra, *a.* sulfuring, sulfurizing. —*m.* 1. sulfurator, machine for bleaching and drying clothes. 2. (agr.) sulfur sprayer, sulfuring machine (for spraying grapevines).
azuframiento, *m.* sulfuring, sulfurization, sulfuration.
azufrar, *tr.v.* 1. to sulfur, sulfurize, sulfurate. 2. to fumigate with sulphur.
azufre, *m.* sulphur, sulfur; brimstone. — **a. vegetal,** lycopodium powder; **a. vivo,** brimstone, native sulfur.
azufrera, *m.* sulfur mine.
azufrón, *m.* (min.) powdered pyrites.
azufroso, sa, *a.* sulfurous, sulfureous.
azul, *a.* blue, azure. —*m.* blue; **a. acerado,** electric blue; **a. celeste,** sky blue; **a. de cobalto,** cobalt blue; **a. de metileno,** (chem.) methylene blue; **a. de montaña,** natural copper carbonate; **a. de prusia,** Prussian blue; **a. de toluidina,** (chem., med.) toluidine blue; **a. de ultramar,** ultramarine; **a. marino,** navy blue; **a. turquesa,** turquoise blue; **a. turquí,** indigo.
azulado, da, *a.* bluish, blue. — **a. por recocción,** blue-annealed.
azulaque, *m.* mortar, mastic (for filling pipe joints).
azular, *tr.v.* to dye or color blue.
azulear, *i.v.* to be bluish, look bluish; to turn blue.
azulejar, *tr.v.* to tile, lay tiles.
azulejería, *f.* 1. tiling, tile work. 2. tile making.
azulejero, *m.* tiler, tile maker.
azulejo, *a.* bluish. —*m.* 1. glazed tile. 2. (ornith.) indigo bunting; blue tanager; bluebird. 3. (bot.) bluebell. 4. (Chile, ichth.) blue shark.
azulenco, ca, *a.* bluish, blue.
azulete, *m.* blue rinse or tint, bluing.
azulillo, *m.* (Ven.) indigo dye.
azulino, na, *a.* bluish.
azulona, *f.* (ornith., Car.) blue dove.
azumagarse, (*ref. 51*) *r.v.* (Chile) to rust, get rusty.
azumague, *ref.* **azumagarse.**
azumar, *tr.v.* to dye or bleach (hair).
azúmbar, *m.* 1. (bot.) water plantain. 2. (bot.) spikenard. 3. storax (resin).
azumbrado, da, *a.* 1. measured in **azumbres** (equivalent to 4 pints liquid measure). 2. (coll.) drunk, tipsy (coll.).
azumbre, *f.* liquid measure equivalent to 4 pints.
azur, *a., m.* (her.) azure.
azurina, *f.* (chem.) azurine.
azurita, *f.* (min.) azurite.
azurronarse, *r.v.* to remain attached to husk (wheat grain).
azurumbarse, *r.v.* (Guat., Hond.) to become confused or bewildered.
azuzador, ra, *a.* instigating, inciting. —*m., f.* instigator, inciter.
azuzar, (*ref. 53*) *tr.v.* to sic (dogs); to incite, stir up, rouse.

B

B, *f.* b, second letter of the Spanish alphabet.
Ba *sym. of* **bario,** barium (Ba).
BA *abbrev. of* **Buenos Aires,** Buenos Aires.
Baal, *m.* (hist., Bib.) **Baal. — culto de B.,** cult of Baal.
baalita *a., m., f.* (hist., Bib.) Baalite.
baba *f.* 1. drivel, slaver; slime, slimy secretion (of slugs, worms and plants). — **caérsele a uno la b. por,** to dote on, drool over (someone or something); **babas frías,** (Col.) a fool.
babada, *f., var. of* **babilla.**
babadero, *m., var. of* **babador.**
babador, *m.* bib; protective cloth or small apron worn under the chin.
babanuco, *m.* (Chile) cloth pad (worn on the head underneath heavy loads).
babaza, *f.* 1. slime, mucous secretion. 2. (zool.) slug.
babazorro, rra, *a.* 1. rustic, rough. 2. (hum.) pertaining to the inhabitants of Alava, Spain.
babear, *i.v.* 1. to dribble, slaver, salivate. 2. to secrete slime (plants, snails). 3. (coll.) to dote (on), drool (over).
babel, *m., f.* 1. babel, bedlam, confusion. 2. **B.,** Babel. — **la Babel de Hierro,** (poet.) New York City.
babélico, ca, *a.* 1. Babelic. 2. noisy; disorderly, unintelligible.
babeo, *m.* dribbling, slavering; salivating, secretion of slime.
babera, *f.* 1. beaver (of helmet). 2. bib.
babero, *m., var. of* **babador.**
baberol, *m.* beaver (of helmet).
Babia, *f.* (geog.) region in the mountains of León, Spain. — **estar** or **quedarse en B.,** to fail to understand something; to be wrapped up in one's own thoughts.
babieca, *a.* doltish, lazy and stupid. —*m., f.* (coll.) dolt, lazy and stupid person. —*m.* (hist.) **B.,** El Cid's horse.
babilar, *m.* axle (on which a mill hopper revolves).
babilonia, *f.* 1. (coll.) babel, bedlam; confusion. 2. **B.,** Babylon.
babilónico, ca, *a.* 1. (hist.) Babylonian (pertaining to Babylon). 2. ostentatious, magnificent, Babylonian.
babilonio, nia, *a., m., f.* Babylonian, of or pertaining to the ancient city of Babylon.
babilla, *f.* 1. (vet.) stifle, knee; muscles and tendons around the stifle or knee. 2. (Mex.) swelling of a fractured bone; humor secreted by fractured bones.
babiney, *m.* (Cuba, reg.) puddle, pool of muddy rainwater.
babirusa, *m.* (zool.) babirusa, East Indian wild pig.
babismo, *m.* (rel.) Babism.
bable, *m.* dialect spoken in the province of Asturias, Spain.
babón, na, *a., var. of* **baboso.**
babor, *m.* (mar.) port(side).
babosa, *f.* 1. (zool.) slug. 2. (Cuba, vet.) babesiasis, Texas or blackwater fever (of cattle). 3. cattle tick (parasite which causes Texas fever). 4. (Ven.) kind of snake.
babosear, *tr.v.* to dribble over; to cover with slime, secrete slime over. —*i.v.* (coll.) to drool (over), dote (on).
baboseo, *m.* (coll.) dribbling, slavering.
babosilla, *f.* (zool.) small variety of slug.
baboso, sa, *a.* 1. dribbling, (of one who dribbles a lot). 2. (coll.) immature, callow. 3. (Amer.) foolish, stupid. 4. (coll.) mushy. —*m., f.* 1. dribbler, driveler. 2. immature or callow person. 3. (Amer.) fool, stupid person. 4. (ichth.) blenny.
baboyana, *f.* (Cuba, zool.) small blue-tailed lizard (Ameiva auberi).
babucha, *f.* 1. mule, babouche. 2. (Mex.) shoe with high uppers tied with a cord.
babuino, *m.* (zool.) baboon.
babujal, *m.* 1. (Cuba) evil spirit (popularly believed to haunt the countryside and enter human bodies). 2. (Cuba) person who has made a pact with the devil.
babunuco, *m.* (Amer.) cloth pad worn on the head for carrying heavy loads.
baca, *f.* baggage rack atop a stagecoach.
bacalada, *f.* salted codfish.
bacaladero, ra, *a.* pertaining to codfish. —*m.* codfisher (ship).
bacalao, *m.* 1. (ichth.) codfish. 2. (cul.) salted codfish cooked in a tomato sauce (traditional fare of the Basque provinces). — **b. de Escocia,** hake; **cortar el b.,** (coll.) to have the upper hand (in something, with somebody); to wear the pants, be the master.
bacallao, *m., var. of* **bacalao.**
bacallar, *m.* rustic, peasant.
bacan, *m.* 1. (Arg., Urug.) idler, loafer. 2. dandy. 3. (Cuba) cornmeal tamale cooked in a banana leaf. —*a.* rich, but of dubious taste.
bacanal, *a.* bacchanalian. —*f.* bacchanal, bacchanalia, orgy; (*pl.*) Bacchanalia, Bacchanals (festival of Bacchus).
bacante, *f.* 1. bacchante; (*pl.*) Bacchae. 2. (fig.) drunken woman, lush (coll.).
bacao, *m.* (Phil. I., bot.) mangrove.
bácara, *f.* (bot.) clary, an aromatic herb.
bacará, *m.* baccarat, twenty-one, black-jack (a card game).
bácaris, *f., var. of* **bácara.**
bacelar, *m.* vine arbor, grape arbor.
bacera, *f.* (vet.) anthrax.
baceta, *f.* stock, widow (cards left after dealing a hand).
bachaco, *m.* (Ven., Col.) large red ant.
bachata, *f.* (Cuba, P. Rico) spree; gay drinking party.
bachatear, *i.v.* (Cuba, P. Rico) to make merry and have fun at a party. — **vamos a b.,** let's go on a binge.
bachatero, ra, *a., m., f.* happy-go-lucky (person).
bache, *m.* 1. pothole, hole. 2. (fig.) accidental interruption in a continuous activity. 3. (theat.) a dead moment affecting the rhythm and action of the performance.
bachear, *tr.v.* to repair holes in (the roadway). —*i.v.* to become full of potholes (roads, streets).
bacheo, *m.* road mending, patching.
bachicha, *m., f.* 1. (S. Amer., derog.) Italian, dago (derog.). 2. (S. Amer., derog.) Italian language. —*f.* (*pl.*) (Mex.) dregs (of drinks). — **me bebi hasta las bachichas,** I drank to the dregs.
bachiche, *m., f., var. of* **bachicha.**
bachiller, *m., f.* 1. graduate of the equivalent of junior college in the U.S.A. 2. holder of a bachelor's degree; baccalaureate.
bachiller, ra, *a.* loquacious, garrulous; pedantic. —*m., f.* (coll.) prater, babbler.
bachillerada, *f.* prattle, babble.
bachilleramiento, *m.* 1. conferring or obtaining a bachelor's degree. 2. graduation, commencement ceremony (after obtaining a bachelor's degree).
bachillerar, *tr.v.* to confer a bachelor's degree. —*r.v.* to obtain such degree, to graduate.
bachillerato, *m.* 1. bachelor's degree. 2. courses leading to a bachelor's degree.
bachillerear, *i.v.* (coll.) to babble, prate, chatter.
bachillería, *f.* 1. babble, prattle. 2. (coll.) unfounded statement, nonsense.
bacia, *f.* basin, receptacle; barber's shaving basin.
baciforme, *a.* (bot.) bacciform, berry-shaped.
báciga, *f.* 1. card game played by two or more persons, each with three cards. 2. winning point made in this game.
bacilar, *a.* 1. (biol.) bacillary, bacillar. 2. (min.) coarse-fibered.
baciliforme, *a.* (bot.) bacilliform.
bacilo, *m.* (biol.) bacillus.
bacillar, *m.* 1. newly planted vineyard. 2. vine arbor.
bacín, *m.* 1. large chamber pot (of glazed earthenware). 2. beggar's bowl. 3. (coll.) contemptible man.
bacinada, *f.* 1. slops thrown from a chamber pot. 2. (coll.) dirty trick.
bacinejo, *m. dim. of* **bacín,** small chamber pot.
bacinero, ra, *m., f.* person who passes the collection plate (in church).
bacineta, *f.* small bowl or pot; poor box.
bacinete, *m.* 1. basinet (helmet). 2. cuirassier. 3. (anat.) pelvis.
bacinica *f.* small chamber pot.
bacinilla, *f., var. of* **bacinica.**
bacisco, *m.* (min.) ore-flux used in quick-silver mines.
bacitracina, *f.* (med.) bacitracin.
Baco, *m.* (myth.) Bacchus, Roman god of wine and revelry, identified with Dionysus, his Greek counterpart.
baconiano, na, *a.* (philos.) Baconian, pertaining to the thought and writings of the English philosopher, Francis Bacon. —*m., f.* person who follows the doctrines of Francis Bacon.
bacteremia, bacteriemia *f.* (med.) bacteremia.
bacteria, *f.* (bot., biol.) bacterium; (*pl.*) bacteria.
bacteriano, na, *a.* bacterial.
bactericida, *a.* bactericidal. —*m.* bactericide.
bactérico, ca, *a.* bacteric, bacterial.
bacterina, *f.* (med.) bacterin.
bacteriofagia, *f.* (bac.) bacteriophagy.
bacteriófago, ga, *a.* bacteriophagic. —*m.* bacteriophage.

bacteriólisis, *f.* bacteriolysis.
bacteriología, *f.* bacteriology, the science that studies bacteria.
bacteriológico, ca, *a.* bacteriological. — **guerra b.,** germ warfare.
bacteriólogo, ga, *m., f.* bacteriologist.
bacterioscopía *f.* (biol., med.) bacterioscopy.
bacteriostasis, *f.* (bot.) bacteriostasis.
bacteriostático, ca, *a.* (bac.) bacteriostatic.
bacterioterapia *f.* (med.) bacteriotherapy.
bacterización, *f.* (med.) bacterization.
bacteroide, *a.* bacteroid, bacteroidal.
bactriano, na, *a., m., f.* (hist., geog.) Bactrian. —*f.* Bactria, Bactriana.
bacuey, *m.* (Cuba) wild plant whose leaves, in alcoholic infusion, are said to stimulate fecundity in women.
baculiforme, *a.* baculiform, in the shape of a rod.
báculo, *m.* 1. walking stick, staff. 2. (fig.) aid, comfort, support. — **b. pastoral,** bishop's crosier.
bada, *f., var. of* **abada.**
badajada, *f.* 1. stroke of the clapper against the bell. 2. (coll.) nonsense.
badajazo, *m., var. of* **badajada.**
badajear, *i.v.* (coll.) to talk nonsense incessantly.
badajo, *m.* 1. clapper, tongue of a bell. 2. (coll.) prattler, chatterbox.
badajocense, *a.* of or from Badajoz. —*m., f.* inhabitant or native of Badajoz, Spain.
badajoceño, ña, *a.* of or from Badajoz, Spain. —*m., f.* native or inhabitant of Badajoz.
badal, *m., var. of* **aciar.**
badán, *m.* trunk, barrel (of animal body).
badana, *f.* 1. dressed sheepskin. — **zurrar (a uno) la badana,** (coll.) to give (someone) a hiding; to insult. 2. hatband. —*m.* (*pl.*) lazy person, e.g. *tu marido es un badanas,* your husband is a good-for-nothing.
badano, *m.* chisel (used in boat building).
badea, *f.* 1. insipid cucumber or watermelon. 2. (Col.) a highly appreciated kind of melon. 3. (coll.) something tasteless. 4. (coll.) lazybones.
badén, *m.* 1. gutter, gully (made by rainfall). 2. a paved trench or water conduit built across a road.
baderna, *f.* (mar.) thrummed cable, plaited cord or rope (used to lash down the tiller, secure cable to capstan, etc.).
badián, *m.* (bot.) Chinese anise; star anise.
badiana, *f.* (bot.) Chinese anise; badian, fruit of the Oriental anise tree, used as a medicine and as a flavoring.
badil, *m.* fire shovel or poker (a fireplace tool).
badila, *f.* fire shovel or poker. — **dar a uno con la b. en los nudillos,** to give one a rap over the knuckles, to reprehend.
badilazo, *m.* blow with a fire shovel.
badilejo, *m.* mason's trowel.
badina, *f.* shallow pool; small pond.
badminton, *m.* badminton (racket game).
badomía, *f.* nonsense, absurdity.
badulacada, *f., var. of* **bellaquería.**
badulaque, *a.* good-for-nothing, unreliable, deceitful. —*m.* 1. (arch.) kind of cosmetic. 2. good-for-nothing (person). 3. fool, nincompoop.
badulaquear, *i.v.* (Amer.), *var. of* **bellaquear.**
badulaquería, *f.* (Amer.), *var. of* **bellaqueria.**
baezano, na, *a.* of or from Baeza, Spain. —*m., f.* inhabitant or native of Baeza.
baga, *f.* 1. pod of the flax plant. 2. rope used to tie packs onto animals.
bagá, *m.* custard apple, soursop.
bagacera, *f.* drying shed (for bagasse in sugar cane mill).
bagaje, *m.* 1. (mil.) baggage, equipment. 2. beast of burden, pack horse or mule. 3. equipment, machinery, resources, e.g. *b. intelectual,* intellectual equipment. 4. knowledge, experience.
bagajero, *m.* (mil.) baggage driver.
bagar, (*ref. 51*) *i.v.* to pod, form pods and seeds (flax).
bagarino, *m.* free and paid oarsman (as opposed to a galley slave).
bagasa, *f.* prostitute.
bagatela, *f.* 1. bagatelle, trifle. 2. (Chile) bagatelle (the game).
bagazal, *m.* 1. (Cuba) place to store the bagasse. 2. custard apple grove or patch.
bagazo, *m.* flax husk or straw; bagasse (residue of sugar cane or beet after the extraction of the juice); pulp (residue of various fruits after extraction of juice).
Bagdad, *m.* Baghdad, Bagdad.
bagre, *m.* 1. (ichth.) catfish. 2. (S. Amer.) unpleasant person; ugly, slovenly woman. —*a.* 1. (C. Amer.) smart, clever. 2. (Bol., Col.) vulgar, illbred, coarse. 3. (Mex.) foolish, stupid.
bagual, *a.* 1. (S. Amer.) wild, untamed (horses, etc.). 2. (S. Amer.) ill-mannered, unsociable. —*m.* 1. wild horse, mustang. 2. (S. Amer.) oaf, lout, uncouth person.
bagualada, *f.* 1. (Arg.) herd of wild horses. 2. (fig.) stupidity, foolishness.
baguarí, *m.* (ornith.) a South American stork.
bague, *ref.* **bagar.**
baguío, *m.* (Phil. I.) baguio, tropical cyclone.
¡bah! *interj.* used to express disbelief or contempt.
Bahama, *f.* Bahama Islands. — **Gran B.,** Grand Bahama; **las Bahamas,** the Bahamas.
bahareque, *m.* (Col., Ven.), *var. of* **bajareque.**
baharí, *m.* (ornith.) red-legged sparrow hawk.
bahía, *f.* bay; harbor.
bahorrina, *f.* 1. slops, refuse; filth. 2. (fig., coll.) riffraff, rabble, mob.
bahuno, *m., var. of* **bajuno.**
baila, *f.* (ichth.) scorpion fish (Scorpaena similis).
bailable, *a.* danceable. — **música b.,** dance music. —*m.* dance number (in an opera, play, etc.).
bailadero, *m.* public dancing hall.
bailador, ra, *a.* dancing. —*m., f.* dancer.
bailante, *a.* dancing. —*m.* (Arg.) orgy.
bailaor, ra, *m., f.* professional Flamenco dancer. —*a.* dancing (referring only to flamenco or Gypsy style).
bailar, *tr.v.* 1. to dance. 2. to spin, make (a top) spin. —*i.v.* 1. to dance. 2. to spin (a top). 3. to be excited or agitated, be in a whirl or flutter. 4. to prance (a horse). — **b. al son que tocan,** to swim with the tide; **sacar a b.,** to invite to dance.
bailarín, na, *m., f.* dancer, professional dancer. —*f.* ballerina.
baile, *m.* 1. dance. 2. ball, dance. 3. ballet. — **b. de figuras,** square dance, figure dance; **b. de etiqueta,** dress ball; **b. de San Vito,** (med.) St. Vitus' dance, chorea; **b. de máscaras or de disfraces,** masquerade or costume ball.
baile, *m.* (arch.) alderman, bailiff, sheriff.
bailete, *m.* short ballet (performed in the course of a play).
bailía, *f.* bailiwick.
bailiaje, *m.* commandery in the Order of the Knights of St. John of Jerusalem.
bailiazgo, *m., var. of* **bailía.**
bailío, *m.* knight-commander of the Order of St. John.
bailotear, *i.v.* (coll.) to dance a lot or clumsily.
bailoteo, *m.* 1. clumsy dancing. 2. (Cuba) improvised dance party.
baivel, *m.* miter square, bevel square (used by masons).
baja, *f.* 1. drop, fall (in prices, taxes, etc.). 2. (mil.) casualty, loss. 3. (mil.) document registering the absence or loss of a soldier. 4. withdrawal, retirement (from a club, profession, etc.); **form for** declaring withdrawal from activities subject to taxation. 5. sick leave; **b. por maternidad,** maternity leave. — **dar b. una cosa,** to drop in value; **dar de b.,** to drop (a person) from a membership list; (mil.) to mark absent; to discharge (a soldier); **darse de b.,** to retire; to withdraw from membership of a club or society; **jugar a la b.,** (com.) to speculate on a fall in prices on the stock exchange.
bajá, *m.* pasha.
bajaca, *f.* (Ecuad.) woman's hair ribbon.
bajada, *f.* descent, way or path down; downward slope, declivity. — **en b.,** sloping downwards; **b. de aguas,** gutter; **b. de bandera,** minimum fare; b. **pluvial,** (bldg.) leader, downspout.
bajador, *m.* (Chile) check rein.
bajalato, *m.* dignity, office and jurisdiction of a pasha.
bajamar, *f.* low tide. — **b. más baja,** lowest low tide; **b. media,** mean low tide.
bajamente, *adv.* (fig.) basely, abjectly, meanly.
bajar, *tr.v.* 1. to lower, let down; to bring down, take down. 2. to go down (stairs, hill, etc.). 3. to turn down (radio, gas, electricity), lower, dim (lights). 4. to reduce, lower (prices). 5. to lower, bow (one's head). — **bajarle a uno los humos,** to take someone down a peg. —*i.v.* 1. to go or come down, descend; to alight, get down, get off. 2. to fall, drop (prices, temperature). —*r.v.* to go or come down, descend; to alight, get down, get off; **bajarse de las nubes,** to come down to earth.
bajareque, *m.* 1. (Cuba) dilapidated house or hut. 2. (Amer.) wall made of plaited cane and mud.
bajel, *m.* ship, vessel.
bajelero, *m.* owner or master of a ship.
bajera, *f.* 1. (Arg., Urug.) saddle blanket. 2. (Amer.) bad tobacco.
bajero, ra, *a.* 1. lower, under. 2. said of a garment, e.g. *falda b.,* underskirt.
bajete, *m.* 1. (mus.) baritone. 2. (mus.) exercise in harmony in the bass clef. 3. (derog.) short person.
bajeza, *f.* 1. base action, baseness, vileness. 2. lowliness, lowness. — **b. de ánimo,** timidity, pusillanimity.
bajial, *m.* marsh.
bajío, *m.* 1. shallows, shoal, sandbank. 2. (Amer.) low-lying ground. — **dar en un b.,** to come across a serious difficulty, get stuck.
bajista, *m., f.* (com.) bear, stock exchange operator speculating on a fall in prices.
bajo, *m.* 1. low-lying land, depression, hollow. 2. shoal, sandbank. 3. (mus.) bass (voice or instrument, singer or player); bass, bass part (of a vocal or instrumental score); lowest note of a chord. 4. (mar.) deep. 5. (*pl.*) horse's hoofs; four feet of a horse. 6. (*pl.*) ground floor. 7. (*pl.*) hem, border (of dress or trousers). — **b. profundo,** basso profundo; **b. continuo,** drone bass, continuo.
bajo, ja, *a.* 1. low (thing, place), short (person). 2. downstairs (floor, room, etc.). 3. lowered, downcast (head, eyes, etc.). 4. quiet (color). 5. base (metal). 6. early (Easter and other movable feasts). 7. late, e.g. *baja Edad Media,* Late Middle Ages. 8. low, despicable, base (person, character, action, etc.). 9. common, coarse, vulgar (expressions, language, habits, etc.). 10. low, cheap (price). 11. deep (sound, voice). 12. low, soft, faint. — **bajas pasiones,** animal passions; **bajas presiones,** low pressure; **b. de agujas,** (equit.) low-withered (horse); **b. Latin,** Low latin; **b. relieve,** (art.) bas relief; **b. ley,** (min.) low grade (ore); **b. octanaje, low-octane; bajos fondos,** underworld.

bajo, *prep.* under, below, beneath. — **b. juramento,** under oath; **b. las circunstancias,** under the circumstances; **b. llave,** under lock and key; **b. pena de,** under penalty of; **b. tierra,** buried.
bajo, *adv.* 1. down, below, underneath. 2. low, softly, in a low voice. — **por lo b.,** cautiously; in an undertone.
bajoca, *f.* (Sp., reg.) string bean.
bajomando, *m.* (auto.) underdrive.
bajón, *m.* 1. sharp decline, drop (in wealth, health, etc., gen. used with the verb **dar**). 2. (mus.) instrument resembling a bassoon.
bajonao, *m.* (ichth., Cuba) jolthead porgy.
bajonazo, *m. aug. of* **bajo,** (taur.) low thrust of the matador's sword (a foul).
bajoncillo, *m.* (mus.) an instrument resembling a tenor or alto bassoon.
bajonista, *m.* bassoonist, bassoon player.
bajorrelieve, *m.* (sculp.) bas-relief.
bajuelo, la, *a. dim. of* **bajo,** rather low, lowish, shortish.
bajuno, na, *a.* low, vile, base.
bajura, *f.* lowness (of place); shortness (of stature).
bakelita, *f.* bakelite.
bala, *f.* 1. bullet, cannon ball, shot. 2. (sport) shot, weight. 3. bale (of cotton, etc.). 4. (print.) printer's inking ball. — **a prueba de b.,** bullet-proof; **b. de fogueo,** blank, blank round; **b. de goma,** rubber bullet; **b. de plástico,** plastic bullet; **b. de salva,** blank, blank round; **b. expansiva,** dumdum bullet; **b. perdida,** stray bullet; (fig.) idler, good-for-nothing; **b. trazante,** tracer bullet; **lanzamiento de b.,** (sport.) shot put, putting the shot or weight; **lanzar la b.,** (sport.) to put the weight; **tirar con b.,** to get straight to the point.
balaca, *f.* (Amer.) boast, boasting. — **echar balacas,** to boast.
balacada, *f.* (Ecuad.) *var. of* **balaca.**
balada, *f.* (poet., mus.) ballad; ballade.
baladí, *a.* trifling, trivial, banal.
balador, ra, *a.* bleating, baaing (animal).
baladrar, *i.v.* to shout, scream, shriek; to whoop.
baladre, *m.* (bot.) oleander, rosebay.
baladrero, ra, *a.* shouting, screaming, shrieking; loud-mouthed. —*m., f.* shouter.
baladro, *m.* shout, scream, shriek, cry; screech, whoop.
baladrón, na, *a.* boastful, blustering; (Ecuad.) roguish, knavish. —*m., f.* swaggerer, braggart.
baladronada, *f.* boast, brag, boastful remark; bravado.
baladroncar, *i.v.* to boast, brag; to swagger; to bully.
balagar, *m.* hayrick, haystack.
bálago, *m.* 1. straw, chaff, grain stalk. 2. thick lather, soapsuds, soap ball. 3. straw rick, mow.
balagre, *m.* (Hond.) liana used for making fish traps.
balaguero, *m.* haystack, hayrick, mow; heap of chaff.
balaj, *m., var. of* **balaje.**
balaje, *m.* (min.) balas, balas ruby; spinel ruby (a semiprecious stone).
balalaika, *f.* (mus.) balalaika.
bálamo, *m.* (mar., N. Spain) school of fish.
balance, *m.* 1. rocking; swinging, swaying; (fenc.) balancing, poising; (mar.) rolling, rocking. 2. (fig.) vacillation, hesitation, wavering. 3. (com.) balance; balance sheet. 4. (Cuba, coll.) rocking chair. — **b. de comercio** or **comercial,** balance of trade; **b. de poder,** (polit.) balance of power; **b. general consolidado,** (acc.) consolidated balance, sheet; **b. pendiente,** outstanding balance, balance due; **b. calórico,** heat balance.
balanceador, ra, *a.* rocking, swaying.
balancear, *i.v.* 1. to rock, sway; (mar.) to roll. 2. (fig.) to vacillate, waver, hesitate, be in doubt or perplexed. —*tr.v.* to balance, to achieve a degree of equilibrium between. —*r.v.* to rock, sway, or swing.
balanceo, *m.* swinging, swaying, rocking; (mar.) rolling.
balancero, *m., var. of* **balanzario.**
balancín, *m.* 1. whippletree, splinter bar (of coach). 2. balancing pole (of tightrope walker). 3. (mec.) beam, lever, rod; rocker arm. 4. minting mill. 5. (*pl.*) (mar.) sheets, yard lifts. 6. (mar.) outrigger (of canoe). 7. (ento.) halter, balancer, poiser. 8. seesaw. 9. rocking chair, rocker. 10. bascule; beam of a scale. 11. pump-jack. — **b. compensador,** (mec.) equalizing beam.
balandra, *f.* (mar.) sloop, single-masted sail boat.
balandrán, *m.* cassock with tippet or stole, gen. worn by monks.
balandrista, *m.* captain or owner of a sloop.
balandro, *m.* small sloop; (Cuba) fishing smack.
balanitis, *f.* (med.) balanitis.
bálano, *m.* 1. (anat.) glans, balanus, penis. 2. (zool.) acorn barnacle.
balano, *m., var. of* **bálano.**
balanófago, ga, *a.* (zool.) barnacle-eating (animal).
balante, *a.* bleating. —*m.* (sl.) sheep.
balanza, *f.* 1. balance, scale. 2. judgment, comparative estimate. 3. (astron.) **B.,** Libra, Scales, Balance. — **b. cambista,** (econ.) foreign exchange balance; **b. de baño,** bathroom scale; **b. de cocina,** kitchen scales; **b. de comercio,** (econ.) balance of trade; **b. de cruz,** beam and scales; **b. de pagos,** (econ.) balance of payments; **en b.,** in the balance, undecided; **b. de precisión,** analytical balance; **b. tolva,** weigh hopper.
balanzario, *m.* weighmaster (in the mint).
balanzón, *m.* 1. cleaning pan (for gold or silver). 2. (Sp., Mex.) grain-sorting sieve.
balao, *m.* (bot.) gurjun tree (Dipterocarpus vernicifluus).
balaquear, *i.v.* (Arg., Col.) to boast, brag; to swagger.
balar, *i.v.* to bleat. — **b. por,** (fig.) to pine for someone; to crave something.
balarrasa, *m.* 1. (coll.) rotgut, hooch, moonshine. 2. (coll., fig.) rogue, hothead.
balastaje, *m.* ballasting.
balastar, *tr.v.* (ry.) to ballast.
balastera, *f.* ballast pit; stone or gravel quarry.
balasto, *m.* 1. (ry.) ballast. 2. gravel bed (spread on roads prior to final paving).
balastro, *m., var of* **balasto.**
balata, *f.* 1. (poet., mus.) ballade; dancing song. 2. (bot.) balata, bully tree. 3. balata gum.
balate, *m.* 1. terrace boundary; sloping terrace. 2. border (of a ditch). 3. (zool.) sea cucumber, trepang; slug.
balausta, *f.* (bot.) balausta (a fruit similar to the pomegranate).
balaustra, *f.* variety of the pomegranate tree.
balaustrada, *f. f.* balustrade; banister.
balaustrado, da, *past part. of* **balaustrar.** —*a.* banister or baluster-shaped; balustered; enclosed or ornamented with a balustrade.
balaustral, *a., var. of* **balaustrado.**
balaustre, *m.* 1. baluster, banister. 2. (Col., Ecuad.) bricklayer's trowel.
balaústre, *m., var. of* **balaustre.**
balay, *m.* 1. (Amer.) wicker basket. 2. (Cuba) wooden bowl used to wash rice before cooking it.
balazo, *m.* shot; bullet wound. — **ser un b. para,** (Peru, Chile) to be a whiz at (coll.); **no me entra ni a balazos,** (Amer.) I can't stand it (him, her).
balboa, *m.* balboa (Panamanian monetary unit).
balbucear, *i.v.* 1. to stammer, stutter; to babble. 2. (fig.) to say sweet nothings.
balbucencia, *f.* stammering, stuttering; babbling.
balbuceo, *m., var. of* **balbucencia.**
balbuciente, *a.* stammering, stuttering; babbling (like a child).
balbucir, *i.v.* to stammer, stutter; to babble.
balbusardo, *m.* (ornith.) osprey, fish hawk.
Balcanes, *m.* (*pl.*) Balkans, European peninsula.
balcánico, ca, *a.* Balkan.
balcarrotas, *f.* (*pl.*) (Amer.) side whiskers, sideburns; (Mex.) locks of hair falling over sides of face (worn by Mexican Indians).
balcón, *m.* 1. balcony; balcony railing. 2. vantage point, observation site.
balconaje, *m.* balconies, row of balconies.
balconcillo, *m.* 1. little balcony. 2. (theat.) parquet circle. 3. (taur.) gallery above the bull pen (where the bullfighters' family and friends are seated).
balconear, *i.v.* (coll.) to flirt from the balcony.
balda, *f.* 1. shelf (of cupboard or wardrobe). 2. a worthless bargain, trifle. 3. crossbar (to secure a door).
baldado, da, *a.* crippled. —*m., f.* cripple, invalid.
baldadura, *f.* physical disability or incapacity.
baldamiento, *m., var. of* **baldadura.**
baldaquín, *m.* 1. baldachin, canopy; dais. 2. (arch.) ciborium.
baldaquino, *m., var. of* **baldaquín.**
baldar, *tr.v.* 1. to cripple, maim, disable, incapacitate. 2. to trump (at cards). 3. to inconvenience, obstruct; to annoy greatly. —*r.v.* to become crippled, disabled or incapacitated, be maimed.
baldazo, *m.* 1. a blow administered with a bucket. 2. the action of washing or flushing with the contents of a pail.
balde, *m.* pail, bucket. — **b. basculante,** dump or contractor's bucket; **b. excavador,** digging bucket; **b. grampa,** clamshell or grab bucket.
balde, *adv.* **de b.,** free, gratis, without cause, without motive; **en b.,** in vain, of no use; **estar de b.,** to be superfluous; to be idle.
baldeadora, *f.* flusher.
baldear, *tr.v.* 1. to wash or flush down (the deck, floor, etc.) with buckets of water. 2. to bail out (a pond, well, etc.).
baldeo, *m.* washing or flushing down with buckets of water.
baldés, *m.* soft sheepskin (for gloves, etc.).
baldíamente, *adv.* in vain, uselessly; idly.
baldío, a, *a.* 1. uncultivated, untilled; waste. 2. vacant (land, lot). 3. baseless, unfounded (argument, etc.). 4. idle, shiftless (person). —*m.* uncultivated land, wasteland.
baldo, a, *a.* 1. void of, lacking, out of (a suit in cards). 2. (Col., P. Rico, vulg.) crippled, maimed. —*m.* void, lack (a suit in cards). —*f.* closet shelf.
baldón, *m.* blot, blemish (on honor); affront, insult.
baldonador, ra, *a.* insulting, offensive. —*m., f.* affronter, insulter.
baldonar, *tr.v.* to affront, insult.
baldonear, *tr.v.* to affront, insult. —*r.v.* to be affronted or insulted.
baldosa, *f.* 1. floor tile. 2. ancient string instrument.
baldosado, *m.* tiled floor.
baldosador, *m.* tile layer.
baldosar, *tr.v.* to tile a floor, to lay tiles.
baldosín, *m.* small floor tile.
baldosón, *m. aug. of* **baldosa,** large paving tile, flagstone.
baldragas, *m.* sluggard, slacker, listless fellow.
balduque, *m.* narrow red tape used in offices to tie up bundles of business papers.

balea, *f.* large broom (for sweeping threshing floors).
baleador, ra, *a.* shooting. —*m., f.* shooter.
balear, *a.* Balearic. —*m., f.* native or inhabitant of the Balearic Islands. —*f., pl.* **Baleares,** Balearics; **las Islas Baleares,** the Balearic Islands. **B.,** Balearic Isles. —*m.* dialect of the Catalonian language, spoken in the Balearic Islands.
balear, *tr.v.* 1. (Amer.) to shoot, shoot down; to fire upon, shoot at, shoot to death. 2. (Sp.) to separate grain from chaff.
baleárico, ca, *a.* Balearic.
baleario, ria, *a.* Balearic.
balénido, *m.* (zool.) balaenid; (*pl.*) balaenidae.
baleo, *m.* 1. floor mat. 2. wicker fan (for fanning fire). 3. (Amer.) shooting spree, shoot-out (U.S.).
balería, *f.* ammunition; bullet supply.
balerío, *m., var. of* **balería.**
balero, *m.* 1. bullet mold. 2. (Col., Mex.) cup and ball (children's game).
baleta, *f. dim. of* **bala,** small bale, small bundle.
balhurria, *f.* (sl.) riffraff, trash, scum (people).
Bali, *f.* 1. Bali, island province of Indonesia. 2. Balinese, the Malayan language spoken in Bali. 3. Asian snake.
balido, *m.* bleat, bleating (of sheep, goat, deer).
balimbín, *m.* (Phil. I., bot.) carambola, a fruit-bearing tree.
balín, *m. dim. of* **bala,** small bullet, small caliber bullet, pellet (of air pistol); (*pl.*) shot, buckshot.
balinero, *m.* (mec.) ball race; ball bearing.
balinés, sa, *a., m., f.* Balinese.
balista, *f.* ballista, ancient military machine.
balístico, ca, *a.* ballistic. —*f.* ballistics.
balistocardiografía, *f.* (med.) ballistocardiography.
balistocardiograma, *m.* (med.) ballistocardiogram.
balita, *f.* (Phil. I.) land measure of about two thirds of an acre.
balitadera, *f.* (hunt.) reed pipe used for calling deer.
balitar, *i.v.* to bleat insistently or repeatedly.
balitear, *i.v., var. of* **balitar.**
baliza, *f.* (mar.) buoy; survey pole; marker, beacon. — **b. delimitadora,** (avia.) boundary marker; **b. fija,** beacon, range marker.
balizamiento, *m., var. of* **abalizamiento,** (mar.) marking with buoys.
balizar, (*ref. 53*) *t.r.v.* (mar.) to mark with buoys or beacons.
ballena, *f.* 1. (zool.) whale. 2. whalebone, baleen; corset steel or stay. 3. (astron.) **B.,** Cetus, Whale.
ballenato, *m.* whale calf.
ballener, *m.* whale-shaped medieval vessel.
ballenero, ra, *a.* whaling (boat, expedition); whale (oil, fat). —*m.* 1. whaler. 2. whaleboat.
ballesta, *f.* 1. ballista, crossbow, arbalest. 2. bird snare. 3. carriage or car spring.
ballestada, *f.* crossbow shot.
ballestazo, *m.* wound caused by crossbow shot.
ballestear, *tr.v.* (hunt.) to shoot, shoot at with a crossbow.
ballestera, *f.* embrasure or loophole for crossbow.
ballestería *f.* 1. corps of crossbowmen; crossbowmen's quarters. 2. crossbow armory, store of crossbows. 3. hunt with a crossbow.
ballestero, *m.* 1. crossbowman. 2. crossbow maker. 3. king's gun bearer or armorer.
ballestilla, *f.* 1. small whippletree (of carriages). 2. cheating trick (in cards). 3. (astron.) cross-staff. 4. (mar.) bowshaped fishing gear. 5. (vet.) fleam (lancet for letting blood).
ballestón, *m.* large crossbow or arbalest.
ballestrinque, *m.* (mar.) clove hitch.
ballet, *m.* ballet.
ballico, *m.* (bot.) Italian rye grass.
ballueca, *f.* (bot.) wild oat.
balneario, ria, *m.* bathing or beach resort, watering place, spa. —*a.* pertaining to bathing in a public place.
balneoterapia, *f.* (med.) balneotherapy.
balompié, *m.* soccer (U.S., Can.) football (game).
balón, *m.* 1. large bale or bundle. 2. ball, football, basketball. 3. cylinder tank (for gas). 4. balloon, glass flask. 5. gas bag, oxygen bag. — **b. de oxígeno,** oxygen tank; **b. de papel,** bundle of 24 reams.
baloncesto, *m.* basketball (game).
balonvolea, *m.* volleyball.
balota, *f.* ballot (voting ball); (Peru) numbered slip of paper for drawing random questions (in school examinations).
balotada, *f.* (equit.) ballotade.
balotaje, *m.* (Amer.) balloting, voting.
balotar, *i.v.* to vote with a ballot.
balsa, *f.* 1. raft, float. 2. pool, pond. 3. sludge collector (in oilmills). 4. (Mex.) swamp. 5. (Amer.) balsa wood. — **b. de aceite,** (coll.) quiet, tranquil place or person; **b. salvavidas,** life raft.
balsadera, ro, *m., f.* ferry, ferrying point or station.
balsamera, *f.* flacon for balsam.
balsamerita, *f., var. of* **balsamera.**
balsámico, ca. *a.* balsamic, healing, balmy.
balsamina, *f.* (bot.) balsam apple; (bot.) garden balsam.
balsamita, *f.* (bot.) wall rocket (Diplotaxis virgata). — **b. mayor,** (bot.) watercress.
bálsamo, *m.* 1. balsam, balm. 2. (fig.) balm (something that soothes or comforts). — **b. de copaiba,** copaiba balsam; **b. de Judea** or **de la Meca,** opobalsam, balm of Gilead; **b. del Canadá,** Canada balsam; **b. del Perú,** balsam of Peru; **b. de María,** calaba balsam; **b. de Tolú,** balsam of Tolu.
balsear, *tr.v.* to ferry across a river on a raft.
balsero, ra, *m., f.* raftsman, ferryman or woman.
balso, *m.* (mar.) sling, loop for lifting men or goods aboard.
balsopeto, *m.,* 1. (arch.) large pouch carried next to the breast. 2. (coll.) bosom, breast.
Baltasar, *m.* (Bib.) Belshazzar. — **cena** or festín de B., Belshazzar's feast; opulence, sumptuosity.
bálteo, *m.* 1. (arch.) military belt or sash (part of insignia). 2. (astron.) B., Orion's belt.
báltico, ca, *a.* Baltic. —*m.* Baltic (sea). —*m., f.* Balt, native of the Baltic States.
baluarte, *m.* (fort.) bulwark, bastion; (fig.) bulwark, support, defense.
baluma, *f.* 1. (Cuba) bundle; heap, pile. 2. (mar.) after-leech rope.
balumba, *f.* 1. bulky bundle or parcel; big jumble of things. 2. (Amer.) noise, uproar, racket, shindy.
balumbo, *m.* cumbersome or bulky thing.
balumoso, sa, *a.* (Amer.) voluminous, bulky, cumbersome.
bamba, *f.* 1. (Hond.) silver coin (five pesetas). 2. (Ven.) silver coin (half peso). 3. Mexican dance. — **caballito de B.,** good-for-nothing person; useless thing.
bambalear, *i.v., r.v., var. of* **bambolear.**
bambalina, *f.* (theat.) fly, (*pl.*) flies. — **entre bambalinas,** (fig.) behind the scenes.
bambalinón, *m.* (theat.) large fly (used to reduce the scenery).
bambanear, *i.v., r.v., var. of* **bambolear.**
bambarria, *a.* stupid, foolish. —*m., f.* (coll.) fool, idiot. —*f.* fluke, scratch (in billiards).
bambarrión, *m.* (cool.) *aug. of* **bambarria,** big fool, big idiot.
bambita, *f.* (Guat.) half a real, small silver coin.
bambochada, *f.* painting representing a drunken feast, with grotesque figures.
bamboche, *m.* (coll.) chubby, ruddy-faced person.
bambolear, *i.v., r.v.* to sway; to swing; to reel, totter.
bamboleo, *m.* reeling, tottering; swaying; swinging.
bambolla, *f.* 1. (coll.) show, sham, ostentation. 2. blister; bubble. 3. (fig.) boast, lie.
bambollero, ra, *a.* (coll.) ostentatious, pretentious, showy.
bambonear, *i.v., r.v., var. of* **bambolear.**
bamboneo, *m., var. of* **bamboleo.**
bambú, (*pl.* **bambúes**) *m.* (bot.) bamboo. — **cortina de b.,** (pol.) Bamboo Curtain (China).
bambuc, *m., var. of* **bambú.**
bambuco, *m.* (Col.) popular dance.
bambudal, *m.* (Ecuad.) bamboo grove.
bampuche, *m.* (Ecuad.) decorative clay figures (on a balustrade).
banaba, *f.* (bot.) banaba, a Philippine tree.
banago, *m.* (bot.) banago.
banal, *a.* banal, trivial.
banalidad, *f.* banality, triviality.
banana, *f.* (bot.) banana (tree and fruit).
bananal, *m., var. of* **bananar.**
bananar, *m.* (Amer.) banana grove.
bananero, ra, *a.* pertaining to the banana —*f.* banana plantation. —*m.* banana tree.
banano, *m.* (bot.) banana tree; (Amer.) banana (fruit).
banas, *f.* (*pl.*) (arch., Mex.) banns (of marriage).
banasta, *f.* large wickerwork basket, hamper.
banastero, ra, *m., f.* basket maker; basket seller.
banasto, *m.* round basket.
banca, *f.* 1. bench, form. 2. stall, stand (market). 3. (com.) banking. 4. banker; baccarat (card game). 5. bank, money put up by a banker. 6. banca, Philippine canoe. — **hacer saltar la b.,** to break the bank; **tener b.,** (Arg., Urug., coll.) to be influential, to have pull.
bancada, *f.* 1. large stone bench; large bench or table; shearing bench (for cloth). 2. cloth (to be sheared). 3. (archit.) piece of masonry. 4. (mar.) rower's bench, bank, thwart. 5. (min.) stope.
bancal *m.* 1. rectangular garden plot. 2. berm, bench, terrace. 3. sand bar, sand bank. 4. bench cover. 5. (bot.) bancal, Philippine wood-bearing tree.
bancalero, *m.* maker of bench covers.
bancario, ria, *a.* banking, financial. — **empleado b.,** bank worker or employee.
bancarrota, *f.* bankruptcy; (fig.) bankruptcy, disgrace, discredit. — **ir a la b.,** to go bankrupt; **estar en b.,** to be bankrupt; (fig.) to be broke, penniless.
bancaza, *f.* (mec.) bedplate; heavy bench.
bancazo, *m.* (Cuba) steel bedframe supporting the rollers of a sugar mill.
bance, *m.* bar, rail (for closing road or entrance to a rural property).
banco, *m.* 1. bench, seat, form; pew; **b. de carpintero,** workbench. **2.** work table, carpenter's bench. 3. money changer's table, counter. 4. (com.) bank. 5. (Cuba) banker (in games); baccarat. 6. checkpiece (of bridle). 7. sand bank, sand bar; **b. de arena,** sandbank; **b. de coral,** coral reef; **b. de niebla,** fog bank; **b. de nieve,** snowdrift, snowbank. 8. (Col.) plain, plateau; (Ecuad.) fertile alluvial land. 9. shoal, school

(of fish). 10. (geol.) stratum. 11. (mar.) rower's bench, bank, thwart. 12. (mas.) course, row of bricks. 13. (min.) outcrop. 14. (mec.) bed; **b. de pruebas,** test bed; (fig.) testing ground. — **b. agrícola,** farm loan bank; **b. de ahorros,** savings bank; **b. de datos,** data base, data bank; **b. de descuento,** discount bank; **b. de emisión,** bank of issue; **b. de esperma** or **semen,** sperm bank; **b. de hielo,** ice floe; **b. de inversiones,** investment bank; **b. de la paciencia,** (mar.) bench on the quarter deck; **estar en el b. de la paciencia,** (fig.) to bear (grievance, annoyance) in silence; **b. de liquidación,** clearing house; **b. de memoria,** memory bank; **b. de órganos,** organ bank; **b. de piedra,** vein, lode (in a quarry); **b. de reserva, reserve bank; b. de sangre,** blood bank; **b. emisor,** bank of issue; **b. hipotecario,** mortgage bank; **B. Mundial,** World Bank.

banda, *f.* 1. band, stripe, strip; (rad., phys., bot., zool.) band. 2. sash (for decorations). 3. band, gang. 4. (mus.) band (military, circus, etc.). 5. party, faction (political). 6. flock, covey. 7. side. 8. cushion (on billiard table). 9. (rel.) humeral veil. 10. (cine.) track, e.g. *b. sonora,* sound track. 11. (dressm.) ornamental border; band; ribbon. 12. (Amer.) cord, string (for pants.). 13. (her.) bend. 14. (mar.) side (of ship). 15. (*pl.*) (print.) rails (on which platen of press runs). — **b. de desgarre,** (aer.) rip panel; **b. de embrague,** clutch band; **b. de frecuencia,** (rad.) frecuency band; **b. de ondas,** (rad.) wave band; **b. de sonido,** sound track; **b. de transmisión,** transmission belt; **b. germinativa,** (bot.) germinal band; **b. sonora,** sound track; **cerrarse uno a la b.,** to stand firm, stick to one's guns; **b. eslabonada,** endless belt; **b. portadora,** (elec.) carrier band; **b. transportadora,** conveyor belt.

bandada, *f.* flock, covey (of birds); (fig.) a group of noisy children.

bandaje, *m.* (gal.) tire. — **b. del inducido,** (mec. armature band.

bandarria, *f., var. of* **mandarria,** (mar.) iron maul (used by calkers).

bandazo, *m.* (mar.) lurch, violent heave or roll to one side (of a ship).

bandeado, da, *past part. of* **bandear.** —*a.* striped.

bandear, *i.v.* to rock, sway, move from side to side. —*r.v.* to shift for oneself, e.g. *me las bandeo bien,* I manage allright. —*tr.v.* 1. (C. Amer.) to chase someone; to wound. 2. (S. Amer.) to change political affiliation. 3. (S. Amer.) to cross (a lake, river or brook).

bandeja, *f.* tray. — **servir en bandeja de plata,** (fig.) to pamper someone.

bandera, *f.* flag, pennon, pennant; banner; standard; colors (of infantry). — **a banderas desplegadas,** openly, freely; **alzar b.,** (mar.) to strike the colors; **arriar b.,** to surrender; **b blanca or de paz,** white flag, flag of truce; **b. de señales,** signal flag; **b. morrón,** (mar.) distress flag; **b. negra,** Jolly Roger; **batir banderas,** (mil.) to dip or strike the flag (as a salute); **levantar banderas,** to call to arms, rally troops; **jurar la b.,** to swear allegiance to the flag.

bandereta, *f. dim. of* **bandera,** small flag, pennant.

bandería, *f.* band, faction, party.

banderilla, *f,* 1. (taur.) banderilla, barbed dart. 2. (coll.) trick, joke. 3. (coll.) dig, barbed or satirical remark. 4. (print.) correction note pasted on proof. 5. tidbit, hors d'oeuvre on a cocktail stick. — **b. de fuego,** (taur.) barb or banderilla with fireworks attached; **clavar, plantar** or **poner una b.,** (coll.) to taunt, goad, tease.

banderillazo, *m.* (Amer., coll.) touch, hit (for a loan) (sl.).

banderillear, *tr.v.* (taur.) to place banderillas on the bull.

banderillero, *m.* banderillero (bullfighter who is particularly deft at placing banderillas).

banderín, *m.* 1. small flag, pennant. 2. infantry guide (on maneuvers). 3. recruiting post.

banderizar, (*ref. 53*) *tr.v., var. of* **abanderizar.**

banderizo, za, *a.* 1. partisan. 2. (fig.) fiery, excitable, seditious.

banderola, *f.* 1. banderole, bannerol, pennon, streamer (attached to a lance). 2. (ry.) switch target. 3. surveying flag.

bandidaje, *m.* banditry; (fig.) abuse.

bandido, da, *m., f.* bandit, outlaw, brigand, highwayman.

bandín *m.* (mar.) rowing bench in the galleys (near the stern).

bando, *m.* 1. faction, party. 2. flock, covey. 3. school of fish. 4. edict, law; proclamation; (*pl.*) banns. — **echar b.,** to issue a law or edict.

bandola, *f.* 1. bandore, mandolin. 2. (mar.) jury mast or rigging.

bandolera, *f.* 1. female bandit. 2. bandoleer (for carrying gun and bullets across the chest. — **salieron en b.,** they left in a fury.

bandolerismo, *m.* banditry; (fig.) abuse.

bandolero, *m.* bandit, brigand, outlaw; (fig.) bully; shady character.

bandolín, *m.* mandolin, bandore.

bandolina, *f.* 1. bandoline, hair pomade. 2. mandolin, bandore.

bandolinista, *m., f.* mandolin player.

bandolón, *m.* large mandolin; large banduria or bandore.

bandolonista, *m.* mandolin player.

bandoneón, *m.* (mus.) large concertina, used esp. in Argentina.

bandujo, *m.* (Sp.) large sausage.

bandullo, *m.* (coll.) guts, entrails.

bandurria, *f.* 1. (mus.) bandurria, bandore, guitar-like instrument. 2. (S. Amer., ornith.) stork, ibis.

bandurrista, *m.* bandurria player.

BANESTO, m. abbrev. **Banco Español de Credito.**

bangaño, ña, *m., f.* (Amer.) gourd, vessel made from a gourd.

Bangkok, Bangkok, capital of Thailand.

Bangladesh, Bangladesh.

baniano, *m.* 1. banian, merchant (in India). 2. (bot.) banyan, banian.

banjo, *m.* (mus.) banjo.

banquear, *tr.v.* 1. (Col.) to level, flatten, make level or flat. 2. to excavate. 3. (aer.) to bank (a plane).

banqueo, *m.* (Col.) clearing and leveling of ground.

banquero, *m.* banker (commerce and gambling).

banqueta, *f.* 1. stool; footstool. 2. footway, gangway (along a large sewer). 3. (fort.) banquette. 4. (Mex., Guat.) sidewalk.

banquete, *m.* banquet; feast.

banqueteado, da, *past part. of* **banquetear.** —*a.* (Ecuad.) shameless, **barefaced.**

banqueteador, ra, *a.* banqueting. —*m., f.* banquet-giver, host.

banquetear, *tr.v.* to banquet, feast. —*i.v., r.v.* to attend a banquet; to feast.

banquillo, *m.* 1. *dim. of* **banco,** small stool. 2. (law) dock, defendant's seat. 3. (Amer.) gallows. 4. (Cuba) axle supports of the rollers of a sugar mill.

banquisa, *f.* ice floe, ice pack.

bantú, (*pl.* **bantúes**) —*m., f.* member of any of the Negroid tribes of southern and equatorial Africa. —*a.* pertaining to the Bantus or their languages.

banzo, *m.* 1. cheek of a frame (e.g. of a ladder, chair back, embroidery frame, etc.). 2. sloping side of an irrigation ditch.

baña, *f., var. of* **bañadero.**

bañadera, *f.* (Amer.) bathtub, bath.

bañadero, *m.* water hole, wallow (where wild animals bathe).

bañado, *past part. of* **bañar.** —*m.* 1. chamber pot. 2. (Arg., Urug.) swampland, marshland. — **b. de cinc,** zinc-coated; **b. en estaño,** tin-dipped.

bañador, ra, *a.* bathing. —*m., f.* bather. —*m.* 1. dipping vat or tub. 2. bathing costume or suit.

bañar, *tr.v.* 1. to bathe. 2. to bathe, give a bath, to bathe. 3. to bathe, wash, lave. 4. to coat, dip, cover, e.g. *bañado en almíbar,* coated with syrup. 5. to bathe, wet, moisten, e.g. *bañado en sudor,* bathed in sweat. 6. to bathe, fill, cover, e.g. *un cuarto bañado de luz,* a room bathed in light, *bañado de gloria,* covered with glory. 7. to leave a border on (the sole of a shoe). —*r.v.* 1. to bathe, swim, take a bath. 2. to have a bath, bathe.

bañera, *f.* bath, bathtub.

bañero, *m.* bathhouse owner or keeper.

bañil, *m.* water hole, wallow (where wild animals bathe).

bañista, *m., f.* bather, swimmer.

baño, *m.* 1. bath (action of bathing). 2. bath, bathtub. 3. bathroom; toilet, lavatory. 4. (*pl.*) baths, spa, watering resort. 5. coat, coating (of icing, etc.). 6. bagnio, ancient Moorish prison. 7. (metal.) melt, mass of molten metal. 8. (chem.) bath (medium in which something is placed to regulate its temperature). 9. (chem.) bath, solution. — **b. de aire comprimido,** (med.) compressed air bath; **b. de arena,** (chem.) sand bath; **b. de asiento,** sitz bath; **b. de barro,** mud bath; **b. de María,** (cul.) double boiler, bain-marie; **b. de sol,** sun bath; **b. de vapor,** steam bath; **b. fijador,** (photog.) fixative, fixing solution; b. **revelador,** developing solution; **b. turco,** Turkish bath.

bao, *m.* (mar.) beam; crosstree.

baobab, *m.* (bot.) baobab tree.

baptisia, *f.* (bot.) baptisia.

baptismo, *m.* (*rel.*) *var. of* **bautismo.**

baptista, *m., f.* (*rel.*) *var. of* **bautista.**

baptisterio, *m.* baptistry, baptistery.

baque, *m.* thud, thump, violent bump (of falling object).

baqueano, na, *a., var. of* **baquiano.**

baquear, *i.v.* (mar.) to sail with the current.

baquelita, *f.* (chem.) bakelite.

baquero, *m.* loose garment, smock.

baqueta, *f.* 1. ramrod. 2. switch (used by horse-breakers). 3. (archit.) reed, bead (molding). 4. (*pl.*) (mus.) drumsticks. — **tratar a la b.,** to treat (someone) despotically, contemptuously, harshly; **carrera de baquetas,** running the gauntlet.

baquetazo, *m.* blow with a ramrod.

baqueteado, da, *past part. of* **baquetear.** —*a.* (fig.) used to or inured to hard work.

baquetear, *tr.v.* 1. to force someone to run the gauntlet. 2. to harass, vex, bother. 3. (coll.) to mistreat.

baqueteo, *m.* 1. harassment, vexation. 2. exhaustion, fatigue.

baquetón, *m.* (archit.) large bead molding.

baquetudo, da, *a.* (Cuba) sluggish, indolent.

baquía, *f.* 1. familiarity with a region. 2. (Amer.) manual skill or dexterity.

baquiano, na, *a.* skillful, expert —*m., f.* expert on a region. —*m.* guide, scout.

baquiar, *tr.v.* (Mex.) to teach, train.

báquico, ca, *a.* bacchic, bacchanalian.
baquio, *m.* (poet.) bacchius, metrical foot of one short syllable followed by two long ones.
báquira, *m.* (zool.) peccary, wild pig.
bar, *m.* 1. bar, barroom. 2. (phys.) bar, a unit of pressure equal to one million dynes per square centimeter.
baraca, *f.* (rel.) baraka, divine power attributed to Mohammedan hermits.
baracuta, *f.* (Hond., ichth.) barracuda.
baracutey, *a.* (Cuba) mateless (bird or fowl); celibate, single, living alone (person).
barahunda, *f.* tumult, uproar, confusion.
baraja, *f.* 1. pack, deck (of cards). 2. quarrel, fight. 3. (Hond.) medicinal root. — **entrarse en b.,** to throw one's hand in (in cards and figuratively); **entrarse** or **meterse en b., echarse en la b.,** (fig.) to throw one's hand in, give up; **jugar con dos barajas,** (coll.) to play a double game; **peinar la b.,** to riffle the cards; **echar la suerte de la b.,** to read one's fortune in the cards.
barajadura, *f.* 1. shuffling (cards). 2. jumble, confusion, mix-up. 3. quarrel, dispute.
barajar, *tr.v.* 1. to shuffle (cards); to mix together, jumble together. 2. to stop (a throw in dice); (Chile, Mex., Arg.) to stop, halt, impede; (Arg., Urug.) to catch, intercept (things thrown). 3. to check, rein in (horse). —*i.v.* to quarrel. —*r.v.* to be mixed, jumbled or muddled together.
baraje, *m., var. of* **barajadura.**
baranda, *f.* 1. railing, banister. 2. cushion (of billiard table).
barandado, barandaje, *m., var. of* **barandilla.**
barandal, *m.* 1. upper and lower beam to which balusters are attached. 2. rail, railing.
barandilla, *f.* railing, banister.
barangay, *m.* 1. (Phil. I.) balangay, barangay (a small boat). 2. (Phil. I.) barangay, village.
barangayán, *m.* (Phil. I.) large clinker built canoe.
barata, *f.* 1. cheapness. 2. barter, exchange. 3. bargain sale.
baratador, ra, *a.* bartering, trading. —*m., f.* barterer, trader.
baratamente, *adv.* cheaply, inexpensively.
baratear, *tr.v.* to sell cheaply or at a discount.
baratería, *f.* (law) barratry, fraudulent sale.
baratero, ra, *a.* (Amer.) cheap, cheapskate. —*m.* man who exacts money from gamblers.
baratía, *f.* (Col.) cheapness.
baratija, *f.* (*gen. pl.*) trinket, bauble, notions.
baratillero, ra, *m., f.* peddler, hawker.
baratillo, *m.* 1. second-hand goods, knick-knack, bric-a-brac. 2. second-hand shop or stall, bric-a-brac shop or stall. 3. bargain sale. —*a.* cheap, inexpensive.
barato, ta, *a.* inexpensive, cheap. —*m.* bargain. — **de b.,** free, gratis; **echar a b.,** to shout down, heckle; **lo b. sale caro,** cheap things turn out to be expensive. —*adv.* cheaply, inexpensively.
báratro, *m.* (poet.) hell.
baratura, *f.* cheapness, low price.
baraúnda, *f.* tumult, uproar, confusion.
baraustar, *tr.v.* 1. to aim, deal, give (a blow). 2. to ward off.
barba, *f.* 1. chin. 2. beard, whiskers. 3. wattle, gill (of a bird). 4. first swarm (leaving the beehive); top part of beehive. 5. shaving, shave. 6. (vet.) ranula (tumor). 7. (*pl.*) rootlets, root hairs (of plants, etc.). 8. (*pl.*) deckle edges (of paper). 9. (*pl.*) barbs, the lateral filaments from the shaft of a feather. — **a b. regalada,** abundantly, liberally; **b. a b.,** face to face; **b. cabruna,** (bot.) yellow goatsbeard; **b. cerrada,** thick beard; **b. de ballena,** whalebone, whalebone, baleen; **barbas de chivo,** goatee beard; **echar a las barbas,** to throw in one's face; **en las barbas de,** in the presence of; in one's face, under one's nose; **hacer la b.,** to shave, trim one's beard or moustache; **hacer la b. a,** to flatter, fawn upon; to bother, annoy; **papel de barbas,** deckle-edged paper; **poner las barbas en remojo,** to prepare oneself, take precautions; **Dios da barbas al que no tiene quijada,** opportunities come to those who don't need them; **por b.,** apiece, per head; **subirse a las barbas de,** to be insolent to. —*m.* character actor who plays old men's parts. — **B. Azul,** Bluebeard.
barbacana, *f.* 1. low wall surrounding a churchyard. 2. (fort.) barbican. 3. (fort.) loophole, embrasure.
barbacoa, *f.* 1. (Amer.) platform bed, board bed supported on props, makeshift cot. 2. (Amer.) small lookout platform; small hut on piles. 3. (Amer.) wooden or reed lattice frame (for preserving grain, fruit, etc.); (C. Rica) trellis for vines. 4. (Amer.) barbecue (frame for roasting meat); barbecued meat.
barbada, *f.* 1. lower jaw (of a horse). 2. curb chain, curb strap (of a bit). 3. (ichth.) dab, flounder.
barbado, da, *a.* bearded. —*m.* seedling; shoot, offshoot. — **plantar de b.,** to plant as a seedling, transplant.
barbaja, *f.* 1. (bot.) out-leaved viper's grass. 2. (*pl.*) first roots.
barbaján, *a.* (Cuba, Mex.) uncouth, ill-mannered. —*m.* lout, oaf.
barbajuelas, *f.* (*pl.*) (agr.) first roots.
barbar, *i.v.* 1. to grow a beard. 2. to breed (bees). 3. (agr.) to take root.
bárbaramente, *adv.* 1. barbarously, brutally, savagely. 2. (coll.) enormously, tremendously.
barbáricamente, *adv.* barbarically, barbarously.
barbarice, barbaricé, *ref.* **barbarizar.**
barbárico, ca, *a.* barbaric, barbarian.
barbaridad, *f.* 1. (coll.) crass stupidity, very foolish act, great mistake; piece of nonsense, (*pl.*) nonsense, rubbish. 2. (coll.) enormous amount, pile, e.g. *una b. de dinero,* an enormous amount of money. 3. barbarity, outrage, atrocity, excess. — **decir barbaridades,** to talk nonsense.
barbarie, *f.* barbarism; savagery, cruelty; rusticity, lack of culture. — **revertir a la b.,** to revert to barbarianism.
barbarija, *f.* (bot.) laurustine.
barbarismo, *m.* 1. barbarism, use of words not accepted as standard. 2. piece of nonsense, crass stupidity, great mistake. 3. barbarism, savagery. 4. (poet.) barbarians; barbarian hordes.
barbarizar, (*ref. 53*) *tr.v.* 1. to make barbarous, barbarize. 2. to fill with barbarisms (a language). —*i.v.* to talk nonsense, make outrageous statements.
bárbaro, ra, *a.* 1. barbarian (pertaining to the barbarians). 2. barbarous, barbaric (cruel, savage; uncivilized). 3. rash, reckless. 4. (coll.) enormous, tremendous, terrific, huge. —*m., f.* 1. barbarian. 2. rash or reckless person.
barbarote, ta, *m., f. aug. of* **bárbaro.**
Barbarroja, *m.* (hist.) Barbarossa.
barbasco, *m.* (bot.) great mullein.
barbato, *a.* (astron.) bearded (comet).
barbaza, *f. aug. of* **barba,** large beard.
barbear, *tr.v.* 1. to reach with the chin. 2. (Mex.) to flatter. 3. (Mex., Col.) to bulldog, throw (a steer) to the ground. —*i.v.* to barber. — **b. con,** to reach almost up to.
barbechada, *f.* plowing; fallowing.
barbechar, *tr.v.* to plow for sowing; to fallow.
barbechera, *f.* 1. fallow fields. 2. fallowing season; plowing season. 3. plowing; fallowing.
barbecho, *m.* fallow. — **firmar como en un b.,** to sign without examining what one is signing.
barbera, *a.* (Amer.) red (wine). —*f.* barber's wife.
barbería, *f.* 1. barbershop. 2. barbering, barber's trade.
barberil, *a.* (coll.) barber-like, pertaining to a barber.
barbero, *m.* 1. barber. 2. (Mex.) flatterer, apple polisher.
barberol, *m.* (ento.) part of the lower lip of a masticating insect.
barbeta, *f.* 1. (mil.) barbette. 2. (mar.) racking. — **a b.,** in barbette.
barbián, na, *a.* (coll.) self-assured, easy-mannered, elegant; bold. —*m.* blade, gallant.
barbiblanco, *a.* grey-bearded.
barbicacho, *m.* ribbon or scarf tied under the chin.
barbicano, *a.* gray-bearded.
barbicela, *f.* (zool.) barbicel.
barbiespeso, *a.* thick-bearded.
barbihecho, *a.* newly-shaven.
barbijo, *m.* (Arg.) chin strap.
barbilampiño, *a.* beardless, smooth-faced; sparsely bearded.
barbilindo, *a.* dandified, effeminate.
barbilla, *f.* 1. point or tip of the chin. 2. barbel, fleshy appendage on the lips of a fish. 3. (carp.) tenon, rabbet. 4. (vet.) ranula, frog-tongue (tumor under the tongue). —*m.* (*pl.*) (Col.) sparsely-bearded man.
barbillera, *f.* 1. roll of tow wrapped around boiling tubs of wine to drain off the must. 2. chin bandage (to close the mouth of the dead).
barbilucio, *a., var. of* **barbilindo.**
barbiluengo, *a.* long-bearded.
barbinegro, *a.* black-bearded, dark-bearded.
barbiponiente, *a.* 1. (coll.) downy-cheeked, growing a beard. 2. (coll.) beginning, new, incipient.
barbiquejo, *m.* 1. chin strap, bonnet ribbon. 2. (mar.) bobstay. 3. (Amer.) halter. 4. (Cuba) wild pigeon.
barbirrojo, *a.* red-bearded.
barbirrubio, *a.* blond-bearded.
barbirrucio, *a.* salt-and-pepper-bearded.
barbitaheño, *a.* red-bearded.
barbital, *m.* (med., chem.) barbital, a barbiturate used as an hypnotic.
barbiteñido, *a.* having a dyed beard.
barbitonto, ta, *a.* stupid-looking, foolish-looking.
barbiturato, *m.* (chem.) barbiturate.
barbitúrico, ca, *a.* barbituric. —*m.* (chem.) barbituric acid; a barbiturate.
barbo, *m.* (ichth.) barbel. — **b. de mar,** mullet.
barbón, *m.* 1. bearded man. 2. billy goat. 3. (rel.) Carthusian lay brother.
barboquejo, *m.* chin strap, bonnet ribbon; (Cuba) (imp. u.) shoelace, corset lace.
barbotaje, *m.* (mec.) splash.
barbotar, *i.v., tr.v.* to mumble, mutter.
barbote, *m.* 1. visor, beaver (of a helmet). 2. small silver plug embedded in the lower lip as a sign of rank among some Argentinian Indians.
barbotear, *i.v.* to mutter; to gabble, jabber.
barbucha, *f. derog. of* **barba,** unkempt beard, straggly beard.
barbudo, da, *a.* thickly-bearded. —*m.* 1. bearded man. 2. (bot.) rootlet.
bárbula, *f.* (ornith.) barbule.
barbulla, *f.* (coll.) babble, gabbling, jabbering.
barbullar, *i.v.* (coll.) to gabble, jabber.
barbullón, na, *a.* chattering, babbling. —*m., f.* gabbler, jabberer.
barbusano, *m.* laurel of the Canary Islands (Apollonias canariense).

barca, *f.* small boat. — **b. de pasaje,** ferryboat.
barcada, *f.* 1. boatload. 2. boat trip.
barcaje, *m.* 1. transportation by boat, ferrying. 2. freight charge; boat fare.
barcal, *m.* trough or bowl for collecting wine.
barcarola, *f.* (mus.) barcarole, gondolier's song.
barcaza, *f.* lighter, barge.
barcelonense, *a., m., f., var. of* **barcelonés.**
barcelonés, sa, *a.* of or from Barcelona. —*m., f.* native of Barcelona.
barceno, na, *a., var. of* **barcino.**
barceo, *m.* (bot.) matweed (Lygeum spartum).
barchilón, na, *m.* (Amer.) orderly, male nurse's aide (in hospital). —*f.* (Amer.) nurse's aide.
barcia, *f.* chaff (of grain); siftings.
barcina, *f.* 1. (Amer.) esparto net sack. 2. bundle of straw.
barcino, na, *a.* 1. roan, brindled (animal). 2. (Arg.) turncoat, opportunist (politician).
barco, *m.* 1. boat, ship, vessel. 2. shallow ravine or gorge. — **b. a motor,** motorboat; **b. de carga** or **mercante,** freighter, cargo ship; **b. de guerra,** warship; **b. de pesca,** fishing boat; **b. de vapor,** steamboat; **b. de vela,** sailboat; **b. fantasma,** ghost ship; **b. madre,** mother ship.
barcolongo, *m.* (arch.) long narrow boat.
barcoluengo, *m., var. of* **barcolongo.**
barda, *f.* 1. bard (armor for a horse). 2. thatch (on fence or wall). 3. (mar.) thundercloud.
bardado, da, *a.* 1. barded, equipped with bards (horse's gear). 2. thatched.
bardaguera, *f.* (bot.) willow (Salix oleaefolia).
bardal, *m.* 1. thatched fence or wall. 2. (bot.) bramble.
bardana, *f.* (bot.) burdock. — **b. menor,** (bot.) hedgehog parsley.
bardar, *tr.v.* to thatch (fences or walls).
bardiota, *m.* (hist.) member of the Imperial body-guard (in Byzantine Empire).
bardo, *m.* bard, poet.
bardoma, *f.* (Amer.) dirt, filth, mud.
baremo, *m.* ready reckoner, book of tables.
bargueño, *m.* carved and inlaid credenza or desk.
barí, *a.* (sl.) excellent, wonderful (a Spanish Gypsy expression).
baría, *f.* (phys.) barye, microbar.
baribal, *m.* (zool.) black bear.
baricentro, *m.* (engin.) barycenter.
bárico, ca, *a.* (chem.) baric.
bario, *m.* (chem.) barium.
barisfera, *f.* (geol.) barysphere.
barita, *f.* (min.) baryta, barium oxide.
baritel, *m.* (min.) winch (employed in mines to hoist water or ore).
barítico, ca, *a.* (chem.) barytic.
baritina, *f.* (min.) barite, barium sulphate, heavy spar.
barítono, *m.* (mus.) baritone.
barjuleta, *f.* haversack, knapsack.
barloa, *f.* (mar.) mooring cable, cable used to moor ships side by side.
barloar, *tr.v.* (mar.) to bring a ship alongside (another ship or a wharf). —*r.v., i.v.* to come alongside.
barloventear, *i.v.* 1. (mar.) to ply to windward. 2. (coll.) to rove about, wander, ramble.
barlovento, *m.* (mar.) windward.
barnabita, *m.* (rel.) Barnabite, a member of the Order of Saint Paul.
barnacla, *m.* (ornith.) barnacle goose.
barnice, barnicé, *ref.* **barnizar.**
barniz, (*pl.* **barnices**) *m.* 1. varnish; glaze (porcelain, pottery). 2. cosmetic. 3. smattering, superficial or partial knowledge (of a subject). 4. (print.) compound used to prepare printer's ink. — **b. del Japón,** (bot.) ailanthus, tree of heaven.
barnizado, *past part. of* **barnizar.** —*m.* 1. varnish (coat of varnish). 2. varnishing.
barnizador, ra, *a.* **varnishing.** —*m.* varnisher.
barnizadura, *f.* 1. varnish (coat of varnish). 2. varnishing.
barnizar, (*ref. 53*) *tr.v.* to varnish.
barodinámica, *f.* (meteorol.) barodynamics.
barógrafo, *m.* (meteorol.) barograph.
barograma, *m.* (phys.) barogram.
barometría, *f.* (meteorol.) barometry, the process of measuring atmospheric pressure.
barométrico, ca, *a.* barometric, barometrical.
barómetro, *m.* barometer. — **b. aneroide,** aneroid barometer; **b. de cubeta,** cup barometer; **b. de mercurio,** mercurial barometer; **b. holostérico,** holosteric barometer; **b. altimétrico,** altitude barometer.
barometrógrafo, *m.* (meteorol.) barometrograph.
barón, *m.* baron (title of nobility).
baronesa, *f.* baroness (title of nobility).
baronía, *f.* barony, baronage.
baróscopo, baroscopio, *m.* (meteorol.) baroscope, an instrument for registering the variations of atmospheric pressure.
barotermógrafo, *m.* (meteorol.) barothermograph, an instrument for recording pressure and temperature.
baroto, *m.* baroto, dug-out canoe used in the Phil., I.
barquear, *tr.v., i.v.* to cross (river, lake) in a boat.
barqueo, *m.* going by boat; crossing in a boat.
barquero, *m.* boatman; ferryman.
barqueta, *f.* small boat.
barquete, *m.* small boat or ship.
barquía, *f.* (Sp.) fishing boat.
barquichuelo, *m.* small boat or ship.
barquilla, *f.* 1. cone-shaped mold. 2. (aer.) balloon basket; nacelle (car of airship). 3. (mar.) log (apparatus for measuring speed of ship). 4. *var. of* **barquillo.**
barquillero, ra, *m., f.* maker or vendor of ice-cream cones. —*m.* ice-cream cone mold.
barquillo, *m.* cone (for ice cream, etc.).
barquín, *m.* blacksmith's bellows.
barquinazo, *m.* 1. (coll.) hard jolt or jar (of a coach or carriage); fall from a coach or carriage. 2. (Mex.) the thud of a falling body.
barquinera, *f., var. of* **barquín.**
barquino, *m.* wineskin.
barra, *f.* 1. bar; ingot; lever, crowbar; bar of iron used in a pitching game; (mec.) rod. 2. bar, railing (separating judges from public); counter, bar; barroom, tavern. 3. sand bar, sandbank. 4. stripe, colored thread (defect in cloth). 5. (her., mus.) bar. 6. (mar.) irons, fetters. 7. metal hoop (on pool table). 8. bar (where) the bit fits into the horse's mouth. 9. (Chile) a game of tag played by teams. 10. (Amer.) kind of stocks. 11. (Amer.) public (in courtroom); fans, supporters, public. 12. (Amer., min.) share (in a mine). 13. (*pl.*) arched trees (of a packsaddle). 14 (*pl.*) perforated side pieces (of an embroidery frame). 15. (Arg., Urug., coll.) gang, group of friends. 16. (Amer.) mouth (of river). 17. long loaf of bread. 18. candy bar. — **b. alimentadora,** feed rod; **b. angular,** (ry.) angle bar; **b. colectora,** (elec.) busbar; **b. colisa,** (mec.) swivel bar; **b. cuello de ganso,** wrecking bar; **b. de distribución,** (elec.) busbar; **b. de labios,** lipstick; **b. de torsión,** (auto.) torsion bar; **b. de vaivén,** (tex.) traverse bar; **b. espaciado** or **espaciadora,** space bar (of typewriter); **b. fija,** horizontal bar; **b. imanada,** bar magnet; **b. sacaclavos,** wrecking bar; **barras paralelas,** parallel bars; **b. T,** (bldg.) T bar; b. **tirante,** tie rod; **b. transversal,** crossbar.
barrabás, *m.* 1. (coll.) scoundrel, rogue, rascal. 2. **B.,** (Bib.) Barrabas.
barrabasada, *f.* rude or uncouth action, rash act; base or dirty trick.
barraca, *f.* cabin, hut, shack; (Amer.) warehouse, storehouse; barracks.
barrachel, *m.* chief bailiff.
barracón, *m.* 1. *aug. of* **barraca.** 2. (Amer.) market stall. 3. (Cuba) living quarters for rural workers.
barracuda, *f.* (ichth.) barracuda.
barrado, da, *past part, of* **barrar.** —*a.* 1. (tex.) flecked with different colored threads, streaked. 2. (her.) barred.
barragán, *m.* barracan, waterproof cloth of coarse wool or goat's hair; barracan, barracan coat.
barragana, *f.* concubine.
barraganería, *f.* concubinage.
barraganete, *m.* (mar.) top-timber, futtock.
barrajar, *tr.v.* (Arg.) to knock down.
barraje, *m.* dike, barrage.
barral, *m.* demijohn of about 25 pints.
barramunda, *f.* (ichth.) barramunda.
barranca, *f., var. of* **barranco.**
barrancal, *m.* rugged area full of gorges or ravines.
barranco, *m.* 1. ravine, deep hollow, gorge, gully. 2. precipice, cliff. 3. (coll.) difficulty, obstacle.
barrancoso, sa, *a.* 1. full of ravines or gorges. 2. craggy; steep.
barranquear, *tr.v.* to drag (timber) through gorges and gullies.
barranquera, *f., var. of* **barranco.**
barraquero, ra, *m., f.* (Amer.) owner or manager of a warehouse or storehouse. —*m.* (reg., Sp.) builder of cottages.
barraquillo, *m.* (mil.) short, light field gun.
barrar, *tr.v.* to smear with mud.
barrar, *tr.v., var. of* **barrear.**
barreal, *m.* mudhole; clay pit.
barrear, *tr.v.* to barricade, block up, to bar; to fasten with a bar; to fasten or bind with iron hoops. —*i.v.* to graze (a knight's armor, with a lance). —*r.v.* to entrench.
barreda, *f., var. of* **barrera,** barrier, wooden fence or breastwork.
barredera, *f.* street-sweeping machine.
barredero, ra, *a.* sweeping; dragging. —*m.* baker's long-handled broom.
barredor, ra, *a.* sweeping. —*m., f.* **sweeper.** — **b. eléctrica,** vacuum cleaner.
barredura, *f.* sweeping; (*pl.*) sweepings, refuse; chaff.
barrejobo, *m.* (Amer.) clearing, clean sweep.
barrelleta, *f.* (bot.) saltwort (Salsola vermiculata).
barreminas, (*pl.* **barreminas**) *m.* (mar., mil.) mine sweeper.
barrena, *f.* 1. (mec.) drill, auger; bit (of drill). 2. (aer.) spin. — **b. de cruz** or **de filo de cruz,** star drill; **b. de extensión** or **expansión,** extension bit; **b. de mano,** hand drill; **b. de ojo,** ring auger; **b. picada,** (aer.) tail spin; **b. picadora,** (mec.) chopping bit; **b. plana,** (aer.) flat spin; **entrar en b.,** to go into a spin (airplane); **b. adamantina,** adamantine drill; **b. cortanúcleo,** core bit; **b. espiral,** twist drill, auger bit; **b. salomónica,** twist drill; screw auger.
barrenado, da, *past part. of* **barrenar.** —*a.* (coll.) crazy, screwy, mad.
barrenador, ra, *m.* drill runner; auger, drill. —*f.* drill.
barrenar, *tr.v.* 1. to bore, drill. 2. (mar.) to scuttle. 3. to foil, frustrate, scotch (someone's plans). 4. to violate, infringe (law).
barrendero, ra, *m., f.* sweeper, street cleaner (person).

barrenero, *m.* 1. drill maker or dealer. 2. (min.) driller, blaster.
barrenillo, *m.* 1. (ento.) boring insect, borer. 2. (bot.) disease produced by borer insect. 3. stubbornness. 4. (coll.) constant worry, idée fixe.
barreno, *m.* 1. (mec.) large drill or auger. 2. bore hole; blast hole, blasting hole. 3. haughtiness, pride, vanity. 4. (Chile, Mex.) mania, pet idea. — **dar b.,** (mar.) to scuttle (a ship); **llevarle el b. a uno,** (Mex., coll.) to humor someone; **b. cebado,** (min.) missed hole; **barrenos limitadores,** (min.) line holes.
barreña, *f., var. of* **barreño.**
barreño, *m.* earthenware tub (for washing dishes, etc.).
barrer, *tr.v.* 1. to sweep; (mar.) to rake; (fig.) to sweep away, carry away. 2. to graze, touch. —*i.v.* to sweep. — **al b.,** (com.) on an average; **b. con,** (fig.) to sweep away, get rid of; **b. hacia adentro,** (fig.) to look out for oneself, have an eye on one's interests. —*r.v.* (Mex.) to shy (horse).
barrera, *f.* 1. barrier; fence; road block; tollgate; (ry.) level crossing gate. 2. (mil.) barrage. 3. (taur.) barrier around the bull ring; first row of seats. — **b. antitanque,** (mil.) antitank barrier; **b. de cruce,** (ry.) crossing gate; **b. de golpe,** (ry.) automatic crossing gate; **b. del sonido,** sound barrier; **b. de minas,** (mar.) mine barrier; **b. de peaje,** toll gate; **b. de potencial,** (phys.) potential barrier; **b. generacional,** generation gap; **b. rasante,** (mil.) creeping barrage.
barrera, *f.* 1. clay pit. 2. crockery cupboard. 3. heap of soil left after saltpeter has been extracted.
barrero, *m.* 1. potter. 2. clay pit. 3. mud hole, bog. 4. (Amer.) salt marsh. —*a.* (Arg., Urug.) said of race horse that runs well on a muddy track (good mud-runner).
barreta, *f.* 1. (min., mas.) small bar, crowbar. 2. shoe lining. 3. (Mex.) bricklayer's hammer.
barretear, *tr.v.* to bind or fasten with hoops (barrels, kegs, etc.).
barretero, *m.* (min.) cutter, digger (one who works with a pick).
barretina, *f.* Catalan men's cap.
barretón, *m.* (Col.) miner's pick.
barriada, *f.* neighborhood, quarter, district.
barrial, *m.* mudhole, bog, mire, clay pit.
barrica, *f.* medium-sized barrel, cask.
barricada, *f.* barricade.
barrido, *past part. of* **barrer.** —*m.* 1. sweeping. 2. sweepings, refuse.
barriga, *f.* 1. belly, stomach. 2. pregnancy. 3. belly (of a flask or jar). — **b. llena, corazón contento,** a full stomach, a happy heart.
barrigón, na, *a.* (coll.) big-bellied, pot-bellied. —*m.* (coll., Cuba) child.
barrigudo, da, *a.* big-bellied, pot-bellied.
barriguera, *f.* cinch, bellyband (of a draft horse).
barril, *m.* 1. barrel, cask. 2. (Amer.) hexagonal kite. — **comer del b.,** (Col.) to eat food of poor quality; **irse al b.,** (Cuba) to go into bankruptcy.
barrilada, *f.* capacity of a barrel.
barrilaje, *m.* (Mex.) stock of barrels.
barrilame, barrilamen, *m.* 1. stock of barrels. 2. barrel factory.
barrilejo, *m.* small barrel.
barrilería, *f.* 1. stock of barrels. 2. barrel factory; barrel store.
barrilero, *m.* cooper, barrel maker or vendor.
barrilete, *m.* 1. (carp.) clamp, dog. 2. hexagonal kite. 3. cylinder (of a revolver). 4. (mar.) mouse (knot). 5. (mus.) cylindrical piece of the clarinet next to the mouthpiece. 6. small barrel, keg. 7. (zool.) fiddler crab. 8. (Amer.) (ichth.) bonito. 9. (Mex.) assistant lawyer or solicitor.
barrilico, illo, ito, *m. dim. of* **barril,** keg, rundlet, small barrel, firkin.
barrilla, *f.* 1. (bot.) barilla, saltwort (Salsola soda). 2. barrilla, soda ash. 3. (Bol., Peru) native copper. — **b. de borde,** (bot.) saltwort (Salsola kali); **b. de Alicante,** bot.) saltwort (Salsola Webbi).
barrillar, *m.* 1. barilla plantation. 2. barilla pits, where barilla is burned to extract soda ash.
barrillero, ra, *a.* producing or containing barilla.
barrillo, *m.* pimple.
barrio, *m.* district, quarter, ward. — **el otro b.,** (coll.) the other world; **b. chino,** Chinatown; (Sp.) red-light district; **b. comercial,** business district; **b. de invasión** or **espontáneo,** shanty town; **B. Latino,** Latin Quarter; **b. obrero,** blue-collar neighborhood; **b. periférico,** suburb; **barrios bajos,** slums.
barrisco, *adv.* all jumbled together.
barrista, *m., f.* gymnast who performs on the horizontal bar.
barrizal, *m.* mud hole, bog, mire; clay pit.
barro, *m.* 1. mud; clay. 2. earthenware vessel made of fragrant clay. 3. piece of rubbish or junk. 4. (Arg., Urug.) blunder, mistake. — **b. blanco,** potter's clay; **b. cocido,** terra cotta; **tener b. a mano,** to have plenty of money at hand.
barro, *m.* pimple; (vet.) whelk, tumor.
barroco, ca, *a.* 1. baroque. 2. (fig.) elaborate, ornate.
barrocho, *m.* barouche (topless carriage with two double seats facing each other).
barrón, *m.* 1. big bar. 2. (bot.) beach grass.
barroquismo, *m.* 1. baroque style. 2. eleborate, ornate taste.
barroso, sa, *a.* 1. muddy. 2. reddish, terracotta colored. 3. pimply, pimpled (face).
barrote, *m.* 1. thick bar, rail. 2. round rung (of a ladder). 3. (carp.) cross brace, wooden brace. 4. (*pl.*) (mar.) scantlings, battens.
barrotín, *m.* (mar.) intermediate beam.
barrueco, *m.* 1. baroque pearl, irregularly-shaped pearl. 2. (geol.) nodule.
barrumbada, *f.* 1. (coll.) boast, brag. 2. (coll.) extravagance, ostentatious expenditure.
barruntador, ra, *a.* guessing, surmising. —*m., f.* guesser.
barruntamiento, *m.* surmising, guessing.
barruntar, *tr.v.* to guess, surmise, conjecture, e.g. *barrunto mal tiempo,* I think we'll have foul weather.
barrunte, *m.* conjecture, guess; sign, clue.
barrunto, *m.* 1. guess, conjecture. 2. (Mex., P. Rico) strong north wind.
bartola, a la b., without a care in the world; **echarse, tenderse** or **tumbarse a la b.,** to lie back without a care in the world; (Arg., Mex., Urug.) to idle, loaf.
bartolear, *i.v.* (Chile) to idle, loaf, e.g. *tú siempre bartoleando,* and you, loafing, as usual.
bartolillo, *m.* small meat or cream-filled pastry.
bartolina, *f.* small, dark cell or dungeon.
bartular, bartulear, *i.v.* (Chile) to ponder, muse.
bartuleo, *m.* (Chile) pondering, musing.
bártulos, *m.* (*pl.*) household goods, goods and chattels; implements. — **liar los bártulos,** (coll.) to pack up, gather one's belongings (preparatory to moving or a journey); **preparar los b.,** (coll.) to get one's tools ready for work.
barú, (*pl.* **barúes**) *m.* (bot.) sugar palm.
baruca, *f.* (coll.) stratagem, trick, ruse (to prevent something).
barullento, ta, *a.* (Arg., Par., Urug.), *var. of* **barullero.**
barullero, ra, *a.* rowdy, noisy, boisterous, e.g. *¡qué fiesta tan barullera!* what a noisy party!
barullo, *m.* (coll.) confusion, disorder, tumult, uproar.
barya, *f.* (phys.) barye.
barzal, *m.* blackberry field; bramble-covered ground.
barzón, *m.* 1. stroll, ramble. 2. (agr.) yoke ring to which the plow is attached.
barzonear, *i.v.* to ramble, stroll about.
basa, *f.* basis, foundation; (archit.) base.
basada, *f.* (mar.) cradle, stocks (frame on which a ship is built).
basal, *a.* (med.) basal, fundamental, basic.
basáltico, ca, *a.* (geol.) basaltic.
basalto, *m.* (geol.) basalt.
basamento, *m.* (archit.) base and pedestal (of column), base, foundation.
basanita, *f., var. of* **basalto.**
basar, *tr.v.* 1. to base, support, found (an opinion, etc.). 2. to build; to put on a base. —*r.v.* to be based. — **basarse en,** to base one's ideas, judgment or opinions on; to rely on.
basáride, *f.* (zool.) bassarisk, cacomistle.
basca, *f.* 1. nausea, queasiness (*gen. used in pl.*). 2. rabidness (in a dog). 3. (coll.) fit, impulse. 4. (vet.) fatal sheep disease characterized by convulsions. — **dar bascas,** to make someone feel sick.
bascosidad, *f.* filth, dirt; (Ecuad.) dirty or vulgar word.
bascoso, sa, *a.* 1. queasy, nauseated, feeling sick. 2. (Ecuad.) dirty, coarse.
báscula, *f.* 1. platform scale. 2. (fort.) bascule (seesaw machine for raising the drawbridge). — **b.-puente,** weighbridge; **b.-tolva,** weighing batcher; **b.-vagones,** car dumper.
basculador, *m.* 1. tip-up truck, tipcart. 2. dumper, rocker. 3. (min.) tippleman; any tipping device.
basculante, *a.* tiltable, swivel-mounted. — **ventana b.,** hopper window; **camión b.,** dump truck.
bascular, *i.v.* to tip, tilt, rock; to fall.
bascunana, *f.* (bot.) variety of durum wheat.
base, *f.* 1. base, foundation (on which something is built or rests). 2. base, bottom, lower part. 3. basis, foundation (of a principle, argument, idea, doctrine, etc.). 4. (sport.) base (in baseball, etc.). 5. base, station (military, naval, of an expedition, etc.), e.g. *b. aérea,* air base, *b. naval,* naval base or station, *b. de operaciones,* operational base. 6. militant core or nucleus, cadre (of political party in each district). — **a b. de,** as the basic ingredients, e.g. *este coctel se hace a b. de gin y jugo de naranja,* this cocktail is made with gin and orange juice as the basic ingredients; **b. ática,** (archit.) Attic base; **b. imponible,** tax base; **b. meta,** home plate (in baseball); **en b. a** (coll.) on the basis of.
básico, ca, *a.* basic.
báside, basidio, *m.* (bot.) basidium.
basidial, *a.* (bot.) basidial.
basidiomiceto, *a.* (bot.) basidiomycetous. —*m.* (bot.) basidiomycete, (*pl.*) Basidiomycetes.
basidióspora, *f.* (bot.) basidiospore.
basificar, (*ref. 50*) *tr.v.* to basify.
basifijo, ja, *a.* (bot.) basifixed.
basilar, *a.* (anat.) basilar.
Basilea, *f.* Basle, Basel, city in Switzerland.
basilea, *f.* (sl.) gallows.
basilense, *a., var. of* **basiliense.**
basílica, *a.* (anat.) basilic (vein). —*f.* 1. basilica. 2. (anat.) basilic vein.
basilical, *a.* basilican.
basilicón, *a., m.* basilicon (ointment).
basiliense, *a.* of or from Basle. —*m., f.* inhabitant or native of Basle, Switzerland.

basilio, lia, *a., m.* (rel.) Basilian (of the Order of St. Basil).
basilisco, *m.* 1. (myth., zool.) basilisk. 2. (artil.) basilisk (large cannon shooting stone shot). — **estar hecho un b.,** (coll.) to be furious, be enraged.
basipeto, ta, *a.* (bot.) basipetal.
basketball, basket, *m.* basketball.
basketbol, *m.* basketball.
basketbolista, *m.* basketball player.
basofilia, *f.* (biol.) basophilia.
basófilo, la, *a.* (biol.) basophile, basophilic, basophilous. —*m.* (biol.) basophile.
basquear, *i.v.* to feel sick or queasy. —*tr.v.* to nauseate, make queasy or sick.
básquet, basquet, *m.* basketball.
básquetbol, basquetbol, *m.* basketball.
basquetbolero, ra, *m., f.* basketball player.
basquetbolista, *a.* basketball. —*m., f.* basketball player.
basquetero, ra, *m., f.* basketball player.
basquilla, *f.* (vet.) fatal disease in sheep characterized by convulsions.
basquiña, *f.* basquine, top petticoat, formerly worn by Spanish and Basque women.
basta, *f.* 1. basting, tacking; basting stitch. 2. (Amer.) hem; (Amer.) trouser cuff (U.S.), turnup (G.B.). 3. tufting stitch, stitch pulled through a mattress. —*interj.* enough! that's enough!
bastaje, *m.* porter, carrier.
bastamente, *adv.* roughly, coarsely, crudely.
bastante, *a.* enough, sufficient. —*adv.* 1. enough, sufficiently. 2. fairly, rather, quite.
bastantear, *tr.v.* (law) to acknowledge or recognize (power of attorney) as valid.
bastantemente, *adv.* sufficiently.
bastanteo, *m.* (law) acknowledgement or recognition of power of attorney; certificate of validity.
bastantero, *m.* (law) official who checks validity of power of attorney.
bastar, *i.v.* to suffice, be enough or sufficient.
bastarda, *f.* 1. bastard file. 2. (artil.) bastard, small culverin.
bastardeamiento, *m.* degeneration, decline, deterioration.
bastardear, *i.v.* to degenerate, deteriorate, decline. —*tr.v.* to debase; to adulterate.
bastardelo, *m.* notary's notebook or ledger.
bastardeo, *m.* degeneration, decline, deterioration.
bastardía, *f.* 1. bastardy, illegitimacy. 2. wickedness, baseness, dastardliness.
bastardilla, *f.* (mus.) a flute.
bastardillo, lla, *a.* (print.) italic. —*m., f.* italics.
bastardo, da, *a.* bastard; (print.) bastard. —*m., f.* bastard. —*m.* 1. (zool.) boa. 2. (mar.) parrel, parral. 3. (print.) bastard type.
baste, *m.* (sew.) basting, tacking.
baste, *m.* saddle pad.
bastear, *tr.v.* (sew.) to baste, tack.
bastedad, *f.* roughness, coarseness.
basterna, *m.* (*pl.*) people formerly inhabiting the Podolian and Ukranian regions of U.S.S.R. —*f.* chariot used by the **basternas;** covered Roman litter.
bastero, *m.* person who makes or sells packsaddles.
basteza, *f.* coarseness, roughness.
bastida, *f.* (mil.) siege tower.
bastidor, *m.* 1. frame; framework, easel; window sash; screen. 2. (theat.) wing, side flat. 3. (mar.) frame supporting propeller axle. 4. (Cuba, Dom. Rep.) bed spring. — **b. de las placas,** (photog.) plate holder; **entre bastidores,** in the wings; (coll.) behind the scenes, secretly; **b. auxiliar,** (auto.) subframe; **b. inferior,** underframe.
bastilla, *f.* 1. (sew.) hem; basting stitch. 2. **B.,** (hist.) the Bastille. — **día de la B.,** Bastille Day (July 14th).
bastillado, da, *a.* (her.) with inverted merlons.
bastillar, *tr.v.* (sew.) to hem.
bastillear, *tr.v.* (Chile), *var. of* **bastillar.**
bastimentar, *tr.v.* to provision, victual, supply with provisions.
bastimento, *m.* 1. supplies, provisions, victuals (for a city, army, etc.). 2. (rare) vessel, ship. 3. mattress tufting.
bastión, *m.* (fort.) bastion.
bastionado, da, *a.* (fort.) bastioned.
basto, *m.* 1. packsaddle; (Amer.) saddle pad. 2. ace of clubs, club (card); (*pl.*) clubs, suit of the Spanish pack.
basto, ta, *a.* 1. rough, coarse; **gross. 2.** (tex.) homespun.
bastón, *m.* 1. cane, walking stick; truncheon; baton (of authority). 2. (fig.) authority, command. 3. roller (of silk frame). 4. (her.) pale, vertical bar (on escutcheon). — **b. de esquiar,** ski pole; **dar b.,** to stir (ropy wine); **empuñar el b.,** to take command, seize the reins.
bastonada, *f., var. of* **bastonazo.**
bastonazo, *m.* blow given with a cane, bastinado.
bastoncillo, *m.* 1. narrow ribbon (for trimming). 2. (anat.) rod (in the retina); bastoncillos **de Neper,** Napier's bones or rods.
bastonear, *tr.v.* 1. to cane, beat with a stick, cudgel. 2. to stir (ropy wine) with a stick.
bastoneo, *m.* caning, basting, cudgeling.
bastonera, *f.* umbrella stand, cane stand.
bastonero, *m.* 1. master of ceremonies, caller (of the figures at a dance). 2. one who makes or sells walking sticks. 3. assistant warden (in a prison). 4. (Ven.) ruffian.
basura, *f.* 1. garbage, rubbish, refuse; sweepings, dirt; horse manure. 2. (Cuba) usable tobacco cuttings. — **estar para la b.,** to be a wreck, to be useless or worn out; **prohibido tirar b.** or **se prohibe tirar b.** (señal) no littering; don't throw out garbage.
basural, *f.* (Amer.) dump, garbage dump.
basurero, *m.* 1. rubbish or garbage collector, garbage man (U.S.), dustman (G.B.). 2. garbage can, dustbin; refuse dump, dump.
basuriento, ta, *a.* (Amer.) full of garbage.
basurita, *f.* (coll., Cuba) tip, gratuity.
Basutolandia, *f.* Basutoland, former name of Lesotho, country in Africa.
bata, *f.* 1. dressing gown, robe, housecoat; gown or dress; **b. de baño,** bathrobe. 2. long, ruffled dress with a train, formerly worn by Southern Spanish and Caribbean women.
bata, *m.* (Phil. I.) young native servant.
batacazo, *m.* 1. thud, bump (of a falling person). 2. (Amer.) unexpected win by a racehorse.
bataclana, *f.* (Amer.) show girl, chorus girl, striptease dancer.
batahola, *f.* noise, hubbub, uproar; bustle, hurly-burly.
batalla, *f.* 1. battle, combat, engagement; battle order, battle positions; joust, tournament; (fig.) battle, struggle, agitation (of mind). 2. groove or notch in crossbow (to nock arrow in). 3. saddle seat. 4. (mec.) wheel base. 5. (fenc.) fencing bout. — **b. campal,** pitched battle; free-for-all; **campo de b.,** battlefield; **de b.,** (coll.) hard-wearing, everyday (things made for daily use); **en b.,** (mil.) with an extended front; (mil.) in battle order or positions; **librar b.,** to do battle, join in battle; **orden de b.,** battle array; **presentar b.,** to offer battle.
batallador, ra, *a.* 1. warring, battling. 2. enterprising, hard-working. —*m.* 1. warrior, battler, fighter. 2. fencer.
batallar, *i.v.* 1. to fight, battle, struggle. 2. to argue, contend, dispute. 3. to waver, hesitate, vacillate. 4. (fenc.) to fence.
batallero, ra, *m., f.* (Mex., coll.) bustler, meddler, busybody.
batallola, *f., var. of* **batayola.**
batallón, *m.* battalion.
batallona, *a.* (coll.) **cuestión b.,** bone of contention; moot point.
batán, *m.* 1. (tex.) fulling mill. 2. a boys' game.
batanadura, *f.* (tex.) fulling (cloth.)
batanar, *tr.v.* 1. (tex.) to full (cloth). 2. to beat, hit, maltreat.
batanear, *tr.v.* (coll.) to shake, pummel, beat.
batanero, *m.* (tex.) fuller.
batanga, *f.* bamboo outrigger (on Phil. I. canoes).
bataola, *f., var. of* **batahola.**
batata, *f.* 1. (bot.) sweet potato (Ipomoea batatas). 2. (Arg., coll.) shyness, bashfulness, timidity. — **dulce de b.,** sweet potato pudding.
batatal, batatar, *m.* sweet potato field.
batatazo, *m.* (Amer.) win by an outsider (racing). — **dar un b.,** to win unexpectedly, win against all odds.
bátavo, va, *a., m., f.* Batavian, native of Batavia, former name of Djakarta, capital of Indonesia.
batayola, *f.* 1. (mar.) rail. 2. (mar.) oilcloth-covered box for storing crew's hammocks.
bate, *m.* 1. bat, baseball bat, cricket bat. 2. (ry.) tamping pick.
batea, *f.* 1. washtub; foot basin; pan. 2. flat-bottomed boat, punt. 3. (ry.) flatcar.
bateador, ra, *m.* hitter, batter (in baseball or cricket). 2. (ry.) tamping bar, tamper. —*f.* power tamper.*tr.v.* 1. to hit, bat (ball in cricket or baseball). 2. (ry.) to tamp (ties).
batel, *m.* 1. small boat or vessel. 2. (*p.l.*) (sl.) gang, band (of thieves and ruffians).
batelero, ra, *m., f.* boatman (of small boat or vessel).
bateo, *m.* 1. (sport.) batting. 2. (ry.) tamping. 3. (coll.) baptism.
batería, *f.* 1. (artil.) battery. 2. (elec.) battery. 3. battery (of instruments, devices, lights, etc.). 4. (mus.) battery (percussion section of orchestra or band). 5. (theat.) footlights. 6. battering, bombardment; breach (caused by bombardment). — **b. C,** (rad.) C battery; **b. costera,** (mil.) shore battery; **b. seca,** dry battery; **b. anódica,** (rad.) anode or plate battery; **b. elevadora,** (elec.) booster battery; **b. compensadora,** (elec.) floating battery; buffer battery; **b. de acumuladores,** storage battery; **b. de cocina,** kitchen utensils, pots and pans.
batey, *m.* (Cuba) 1. the grounds occupied by a sugar mill and ancillary installations. 2. collective of sugar-making machinery. 3. (hist.) Arawak or Siboney Indian settlement.
batibio, *m.* (zool.) bathybius.
batiboleo, *m.* (Mex.) noise, bustle, hubbub, hurly-burly.
batiborrillo, batiburrillo, *m.* hodgepodge, medley.
baticabeza, *m.* (ento.) skipjack, snapping beetle.
baticola, *f.* 1. crupper. 2. (Bol.) loin cloth. 3. (Par.) diaper.
baticolearse, *r.v.* (Hond.) to become chafed by the crupper (horse's tail).
baticulo, *m.* 1. (mar.) auxiliary cable. 2. (mar.) small gaff or boom. — **mástil de b.,** ringtail boom; **vela de b.,** ringtail sail, ringsail.
batida, *f.* 1. (hunt.) battue, beating (to flush out the game). 2. raid, search, e.g. *b. de la policía,* police raid. 3. minting. 4. (Car.) attack (of fighting cock).

batidera, *f.* 1. mortar or concrete shovel (for mixing concrete). 2. instrument for cutting honeycombs. 3. stirrer (in glass-making). 4. nap of a churn. 5. (tex.) scutcher.

batidero, *m.* 1. uninterrupted beating or striking. 2. uneven or rutted ground. 3. (*pl.*) (mar.) washboard. 4. (mar.) reinforcement on sail (to protect it from rubbing).

batido, da, *past part. of* **batir.** —*a.* 1. variegated or shot, chatoyant (silk). 2. trodden, beaten (path). —*m.* 1. (cul.) batter. 2. beating (of metal, wool, batter, etc.). 3. whipped cocktail. 4. (Amer.) milkshake.

batidor, ra, *a.* beating. —*m.* 1. beater, e.g. *b. de oro* or *plata,* gold or silver beater. 2. scout, reconnoiterer; outrider. 3. (hunt.) beater. 4. (cul.) beater, whisk. 5. comb. 6. (Amer.) chocolate pot. —*f.* (Amer., cul.) beater, whisk, churn.

batiente, *a.* beating. — **reírse a mandíbula b.,** to laugh one's head off. —*m.* 1. jamb (of a door or window). 2. surf-beaten spot on coast or dike. 3. damper (of piano). 4. (fort.) timber placed on the sill of an embrasure to protect it from wear by gun-carriage wheels. 5. (mar.) vertical frame of a gun port.

batígrafo, *m.* bathygraphic camera (for deep-water photography).

batihoja, *m.* gold or silver beater; sheet-metal worker.

batilongo, *m.* (Cuba) long, loose smock or dressing gown.

batimán, *m.* (dance) battement, quick whipping movement of raised leg.

batimento, *m.* (p.) shadow, shade.

batimetría, *f.* bathymetry, the science of measuring the depth of large bodies of water.

batimétrico, ca, *a.* bathymetric, bathymetrical.

batimiento, *m.* 1. beating. 2. (phys.) beat.

batín, *m.* wrapper, short dressing gown or housecoat.

batino, *m.* Philippine tree of the dogbane family (Alstonia macrophylla).

batintín, *m.* gong.

bationdeo, *m.* fluttering of a banner, flag or curtain.

batiportar, *tr.v.* (mar.) to emplace (artillery) by resting it against the top of the port sill.

batiporte, *m.* (mar.) sill (of gun port).

batiportes, *m.* (*pl.*) port-sills.

batir, *tr.v.* 1. to beat, hammer, strike. 2. to beat, defeat. 3. to beat, outdo (record). 4. to beat, whip, mix (batter, mixtures, etc.). 5. (tex.) to beat (wool, fibers). 6. (mil.) to batter, bombard. 7. to demolish, knock down (wall, building, etc.). 8. to take down (tent). 9. to beat upon (rain, sun, wind, waves). 10. to flap, beat (wings, oars). 11. to brush or comb upwards. 12. to arrange (reams of paper). 13. to mint (coin.). 14. to beat, range over, scour, search. 15. (bkb.) to flatten newly-bound books by hammering. 16. (Chile, Peru, Guat.) to rinse (clothes). — **a hierro caliente b. de repente,** strike while the iron is hot; **b. el vuelo,** to fly; **b. los talones,** to take to one's heels; **b. palmas,** to clap hands, to applaud. —*i.v.* 1. to beat violently (the heart). 2. (Arg., sl.) to confess. —*r.v.* to fight; **batirse a duelo,** to fight a duel; batirse **en retirada,** to beat a retreat.

batíscafo, *m.* bathyscaphe, deep-sea research vessel.

batisfera, *f.* bathysphere, a reinforced deep-diving chamber.

batista, *f.* (tex.) batiste, cambric.

bato, *m.* 1. simpleton. 2. (Arg., Bol.) (ornith.) jabiru. 3. (Chile, Hond., Mex.) shepherd in Nativity scenes.

bató, *m.* (Hond.) large canoe.

batojar, *tr.v.* to knock down (fruit from a tree) with a stick.

batolítico, ca, *a.* (geol.) batholithic.

batolito, *m.* (geol.) batholith.

batología, *f.* (rhet.) battology (needless repetition).

batómetro, *m.* (phys.) bathometer.

batracio, cia, *a.* (zool.) batrachian. —*m.* (zool.) batrachian, (*pl.*) Batrachia.

batraco, *m.* (vet.) tongue tumor.

batro, *m.* (bot., Chile) cattail.

batuda, *f.* acrobatic jumps (on a springboard).

batuecas, estar **uno en las** b., (coll.) to daydream, to be in the clouds, to woolgather.

batuque, *m.* (Arg., Urug.) uproar, rumpus, hubbub, shindy.

batuquear, *tr.v.* 1. (Col., Cuba, Guat.) to shake, shake up. 2. (Guat.) to reprimand severely. —*i.v.* (Arg.) to cause an uproar, rumpus or row.

baturrillo, *m.* hodgepodge, hash, mishmash, potpourri; (fig., mus.) medley.

baturro, rra, *a.* uncouth, rustic. —*m., f.* (Sp.) Aragonese peasant.

batuta, *f.* (mus.) baton. — **llevar la b.,** (coll.) to be in command, to preside, be the boss.

baúl, *m.* 1. trunk, chest. 2. (coll.) belly, paunch. — **b. mundo,** Saratoga trunk; **henchir** or **llenar el b.,** to fill one's belly, gorge oneself.

baulería, *f.* (Cuba) trunk factory.

baulero, *m.* trunk maker or seller.

bauprés, *m.* (mar.) bowsprit. — **b. móvil,** reefing bowsprit.

bausa, *f.* (Peru) laziness, idleness, loafing.

bausán, na, *a.* (Amer.) lazy, idling, loafing. —*m., f.* 1. manikin, effigy. 2. simpleton, fool, idiot.

bautice, bauticé, *ref.* **bautizar.**

bautismal, *a.* baptismal.

bautismo, *m.* baptism; christening. — **b. del aire,** first flight in an airplane; **b. de fuego,** baptism of fire, first combat; **romperle el b. a uno,** (coll.) to beat the hell out of, knock someone's block off.

bautista, *a.* (rel.) Baptist. —*m.* 1. baptist, baptizer, **el B.,** St. John the Baptist. 2. (rel.) Baptist (member of the Baptist Church).

bautisterio, *m.* (rel.) baptistry, baptistery.

bautizante, *a.* baptizing. —*m., f.* baptizer.

bautizar, (*ref.* 53) *tr.v.* 1. to baptize; to christen. 2. (hum). to dilute (wine) with water.

bautizo, *m.* baptism; christening, christening party.

bauxita, *f.* (min.) bauxite (aluminum ore).

bávaro, ra, *a., m., f.* Bavarian.

Baviera, *f.* Bavaria, a state in West Germany.

baya, *f.* 1. berry. 2. (bot.) star of Bethlehem. 3. (Cuba, bot.) kind of calabash tree. 4. (Cuba, zool.) mussel. 5. (Chile) grape juice.

bayadera, *f.* bayadere, female dancer and singer of India.

bayahonda, *f.* (Dom. Rep., bot.) acacia.

bayal, *a.* (tex.) cambric-like.

bayal, *m.* lever used to move stones in a quarry.

bayarte, *m.* wheelbarrow, handbarrow; stretcher, litter.

bayeta, *f.* 1. baize; thick flannel. 2. dust cloth; floor mop. —*m.* (Col.) lazy, unkempt man. — **arrastrar bayetas,** to be smart enough to go to college; to put on such airs.

bayetón, *m.* 1. heavy thick woolen cloth. 2. (Col.) long woolen poncho.

bayo, ya, *a.* bay. —*m.* 1. bay horse. 2. silkworm butterfly (used as bait in fly-fishing). 3. (Chile) bier.

bayoco, *m.* 1. ancient Italian copper coin. 2. (Sp.) unripe or withered fig.

bayón, *m.* sack made from talipot palm leaves.

Bayona, *f.* Bayonne (French city). — **arda B.,** never mind the cost, a fig for the expense.

bayonense, bayonés, sa, *a.* from or of Bayonne, France. —*m., f.* inhabitant or native of Bayonne.

bayoneta, *f.* bayonet. — **a la b.,** (mil.) with fixed bayonets; **armar la b., calar la b.,** (mil.) to fix bayonets.

bayonetazo, *m.* bayonet thrust; bayonet wound or blow.

bayoque, *m., var. of* **bayoco.**

bayosa, *f.* (sl.) sword.

bayú, (*pl.* **bayúes**) *m.* (Cuba) brothel.

bayuca, bayunca, *f.* (coll.) tavern, inn.

bayunco, ca, *a.* (Guat.) coarse, rough, uncouth.

baza, *f.* trick (at caras); b. **de caída,** (bridge) down-trick; **b. ganada,** (bridge) acquired trick; **b. usurpadora,** (bridge) appropriated trick; **hacer** b., to win a trick; to prosper, succeed; **meter b.,** (coll.) to interfere, to butt in; **no dejar meter b.,** (coll.) to monopolize the conversation; **no poder meter b.,** (coll.) not to be able to get a word in edgeways; **soltar la b.,** to let a trick go (at cards).

bazar, *m.* bazaar; market place, fair.

bazo, za, *a.* yellowish brown. —*m.* (anat.) spleen.

bazofia, *f.* 1. refuse, garbage. 2. slop, swill, inedible food. 3. pigswill, hogwash, pig food.

bazuca, bazuco, *f.* (mil.) bazooka.

bazuar, (*ref.* 50) *tr.v.* to shake, shake up (things).

bazuque, bazuqué, *ref.* **bazucar.**

bazuquear, *tr.v., var. of* **bazucar.**

bazuqueo, *m.* shaking.

bco. *abbrev. of* **banco,** bank.

be, *m.* baa, bleat (sheep).

Be *sym. of* berilio, beryllium (Be).

beata, *f.* 1. devout or pious woman; lay sister. 2. (coll.) very zealous church woman. 3. (Sp., coll.) peseta (coin).

beatería, *f.* sanctimony, affected piety; bigotry.

beaterio, *m.* community house for lay sisters.

beatificación, *f.* beatification.

beatíficamente, *adv.* beatifically.

beatificante, *a.* beatifying.

beatificar, (*ref.* 50) *tr.v.* 1. to beatify. 2. (Guat., Hond.) to give extreme unction to (sick or dying person). 3. (rel.) to confer sainthood on.

beatífico, ca, *a.* beatific.

beatifique, beatifiqué, *ref.* **beatificar.**

beatilla, *f.* (tex.) betille, fine linen.

beatitud, *f.* 1. beatitude. 2. Beatitude (title given to the Pope). 3. happiness, bliss.

beatnik [' b i t n i k] *m.,f.* beatnik.

beato, ta, *a.* 1. blessed, happy. 2. beatified. 3. devout, pious. 4. exaggeratedly pious. —*m., f.* 1. beatified person. 2. devout or pious person. 3. overpious person. —*m.* 1. man who wears clerical dress without belonging to any definite order. 2. (coll.) zealous churchgoer.

beatón, na, *m., f.* hypocrite, bigot.

bebé, *m.* baby; babe.

bebeco, ca, *a.* (Col.) albino.

bebedero, ra, *a.* drinkable. —*m.* 1. water trough, drinking dish; watering place. 2. spout (of drinking vessel). 3. (*pl.*) hemming strips, hem reinforcement. 4. (Peru) refreshment stand. —*f.* (Col., Mex.) drinking bout.

bebedizo, za, *a.* drinkable, potable. —*m.* (medicinal, poisonous, love) potion or philter.

bebedor, ra, *a.* drinking. —*m., f.* heavy drinker, boozer; lush (sl.).

bebelera, *f.* (coll.) unquenchable thirst.

beber, *tr.v.* 1. to drink. 2. to drink in, imbibe (ideas, doctrines). — **b. los vientos por,** to sigh or long for. —*i.v.* to drink. — **b. a la salud de,** to drink to (someone's) health; **b. como una cuba,** (coll.) to drink like a fish; **b. de,** to drink from or out of.

beberaje, *m.* (Arg., Urug.) beverage, esp. alcoholic.
beberrón, na, *a.* (coll.) boozy, hard-drinking. —*m., f.* hard drinker, drunkard.
bebestible, *a.* (coll.) drinkable. —*m.* (Amer.) drink. — **los bebestibles y los comestibles,** (hum.) food and drink.
bebezón, *f.* 1. (Col.) drinking bout. 2. (Cuba) intoxicating drink.
bebible, *a.* (coll.) drinkable, pleasant to drink.
bebida, *f.* drink. — **darse a la b.,** to take to drink.
bebido, da, *past part. of* **beber.** —*a.* tipsy, drunk. —*m.* drink.
bebienda, *f.* drink, beverage.
bebirina, *f.* (chem.) bebeerine.
bebistrajo, *m.* (coll.) brew, concoction (liquor); (coll.) unpleasant concoction.
beborrotear, *i.v.* (coll.) to tripple, sip.
beca, *f.* 1. scholarship, fellowship. 2. grant (of a scholar). 3. scholar. 4. sash (worn over academic gown). 5. hood (of gown).
becabunga, *f.* (bot.) speedwell.
becacina, *f.* (ornith.) snipe; (ornith.) woodcock.
becada, *f.* (ornith.) woodcock.
becado, da, *m., f.* recipient of a scholarship or fellowship.
becafigo, *m.* (ornith.) figpecker, beccafico.
becar, *tr.v.* to award or grant a scholarship or fellowship.
becario, ria, *m., f.* scholarship student, fellow, scholar, recipient of a scholarship.
becasina, *f.* (ornith.) woodcock.
becerra, *f.* 1. yearling calf. 2. (bot.) snapdragon.
becerrada, *f.* (taur.) bullfight with yearling bulls.
becerrero, *m.* herdsman who tends yearling calves.
becerril, *a.* pertaining to a calf.
becerrillo, *m. dim. of* **becerro,** calfskin.
becerro, *m.* 1. bull calf; yearling bull; calfskin. 2. church, monastery or community register (for property, privileges). — **b. de oro,** (Bib.) the golden calf, riches, Mammon; **b. marino,** (zool.) seal, sea calf.
becoquín, *m.* cap with earflaps.
becoquino, *m.* (bot.) honeywort.
becqueriana, *f.* short lyric poem (in the style of Gustavo Adolfo Bécquer).
becuadrado, *m.* (mus.) first of Gregorian modes.
becuadro, *m.* (mus.) natural sign.
Bechuanalandia, *f.* Bechuanaland, former name of present Botswana, country in Africa.
bedano, *m.* (carp.) large chisel.
bedel, *m.* beadle, warden, proctor or custodian in schools and colleges.
bedelía, *f.* post of usher or caretaker (in a school or college).
bedelio, *m.* (pharm.) bdellium.
bederre, *m.* (sl.) executioner.
beduino, na, *a., m., f.* Bedouin, nomadic Arab. —*m.* (fig.) barbarian, villain, ruffian.
beduro, *m.* (mus.) *var. of* **becuadrado.**
befa, *f.* 1. jeer, taunt, gibe. 2. gross or obscene remark.
befabemí, *m.* (mus.) hypophrygian mode.
befar, *i.v.* to blow, snort (horse). —*tr.v.* to jeer at, gibe at, scoff at, mock, ridicule.
befo, fa, *a.* 1. having a thick underlip; blubber-lipped. 2. knock-kneed. —*m.* 1. lip (of an animal). 2. (zool.) monkey.
begardo, da, *var. of* **beguino.**
begohmio, *m.* (elec.) begohm.
begonia, *f.* (bot.) begonia.
begoniáceo, a, *a.* (bot.) begoniaceous. —*f.* (*pl.*) Begoniaceae.
beguina, *f.* (rel.) Beguine, member of lay sisterhood.
beguino, na, *m.* (rel.) Beguin, Beghard. —*f.* (rel.) Beguine.
begum, begún, *f.* begum, princess (in India); lady of rank (in Moslem societies).
behaviorismo, *m.* behaviorism.
behetría, *f.* 1. (hist.) free town under its own chosen prince or seigneur. 2. (fig.) confusion, disorder.
Beirut, Beirut, capital of Lebanon.
béisbol, *m.* baseball.
beisbolero, ra, beisbolista, *m., f.* baseball player.
beisbolístico, ca, *a.* baseball.
bejín, *m.* 1. (bot.) puffball. 2. (coll.) cross-patch, irritable or touchy person. 3. whining child.
bejuca, *f.* (Col.) poisonous snake.
bejucal, *m.* place overgrown with reeds.
bejuco, *m.* (bot.) liana, reed.
bejuquear, *tr.v.* (Amer.) to beat, thrash with a reed.
bejuqueda, *f.* 1. place overgrown with reeds or lianas. 2. (Amer.) beating, thrashing.
bejuquera, *f.* (P. Rico) *var. of* **bejucal.**
bejuquero, *m.* 1. (Ven.) *var. of* **bejucal.** 2. (Col.) confusing situation.
bejuquillo, *m.* 1. Chinese gold necklace. 2. (bot.) ipecac, ipecacuanha.
Belcebú, *m.* 1. (Bib.) Beelzebub. 2. **b.,** demon, devil.
belcho, *m.* (bot.) joint fir, ephedra.
beldad, *f.* 1. beauty. 2. beauty, belle, beautiful woman.
beldar, (*ref. 29*) *tr.v.* to winnow with a fork.
belduque, *m.* (Amer.) large pointed knife.
belemnita, *f.* (paleon.) belemnite.
belén, *m.* 1. B., Bethlehem. 2. crib, Christmas creche. 3. (coll.) bedlam, confusion, disorder. 4. (coll.) risky or hazardous business; **meterse en belenes,** to get into trouble, get into difficulties.
beleño, *m.* (bot.) henbane.
belérico, *m.* (bot.) myrobalan.
belesa, *f.* (bot.) leadwort.
belez, (*pl.* **beleces**) *m.* 1. vessel, bowl. 2. piece of furniture.
belezo, *m., var. of* **belez.**
belfo, fa, *a.* with a thick underlip. —*m.* lip (of a quadruped).
belga, *a., m., f.* Belgian.
Bélgica, *f.* Belgium.
bélgico, ca, *a.* Belgian, pertaining to Belgium.
Belgrado, *m.* Belgrade, capital of Yugoslavia.
bélicamente, *adv.* bellicosely, belligerently.
Belice, *m.* Belize, port city and capital of British Honduras.
belicismo, *m.* militarism, agressiveness, bellicosity.
belicista, *a.* militaristic, aggressive, bellicose.
bélico, ca, *a.* warlike, martial, bellicose.
belicosamente, *adv.* bellicosely, belligerently.
belicosidad, *f.* bellicosity.
belicoso, sa, *a.* bellicose, belligerent, warlike; aggressive quarrelsome.
beligerancia, *f.* belligerence; **conceder** or **dar b. a uno,** to consider somebody important enough to contend with.
beligerante, *a.* belligerent. —*m.* belligerent (nation at war).
belígero, ra, *a.* (poet.) bellicose, warlike.
belinún, *m.* (Arg., Urug., coll.) simpleton.
belio, *m.* (phys.) bel.
belísono, na, *a.* martial-sounding.
belitre, *a.* (coll.) low, mean, base. —*m.* rogue, ruffian, scoundrel.
belitrero, *m.* (sl.) swindler of thieves.
beliz, *m.* (Mex.) valise, small suitcase.
bellacada, *f.* 1. *var. of* **bellaquería.** 2. den of rogues.
bellacamente, *adv.* 1. cunningly, artfully. 2. basely, meanly, wickedly.
bellaco, ca, *a.* 1. astute, artful, cunning. 2. wicked, rascally, low. 3. (Arg., Urug.) balky (horse). 4. (Ecuad., Pan.) brave. 5. (P. Rico) lecherous; sexually aroused. —*m., f.* scoundrel, rascal, rogue.
bellacuelo, *m. aim. of* **bellaco.**
belladona, *f.* (bot.) belladonna.
bellamente, *adv.* beautifully, perfectly, gracefully.
bellaquear, *i.v.* 1. to cheat, trick, swindle. 2. (Arg., Urug.) to rear, buck (horses). 3. (Arg., Urug.) to be stubborn.
bellaquería, *f.* cunning, artfulness, trickery, swindling, cheating; roguery, wickedness.
bellasombra, *f.* (bot.) umbra tree.
belleza, *f.* beauty. — **belleza exótica,** glamour girl; **decir bellezas,** to speak with charm and delicacy.
bellido, da, *a.* beautiful, lovely.
bello, lla, *a.* beautiful, fair, lovely. — **bellas artes,** fine arts.
bellota, *f.* 1. acorn. 2. carnation bud. 2. small perfume jar. 4. decorative pompon. 5. (anat.) glans. — **b. de mar,** (zool.) acorn barnacle.
bellote, *m.* nail with acorn-shaped head, large round-headed nail.
bellotear, *i.v.* to feed on acorns (livestock).
bellotera, *f.* acorn picker or vendor; acorn harvest time; acorn harvest; acorn fodder.
bellotero, *m.* 1. person who picks or sells acorns. 2. acorn fodder. 3. acorn-bearing tree.
belorta, *f.* (agr.) iron band or clasp (securing sheath to beam of plow).
beluario, *m.* lion tamer.
beluga, *f.* (zool.) beluga, white whale.
belvedere, *m.* belvedere, gazebo.
bembo, ba, *a.* 1. (Cuba, Mex., P. Rico) thick-lipped. 2. (Mex.) stupid, foolish. —*m., f.* (Mex.) dolt, simpleton. —*m.* (Ecuad., Peru, P. Rico) mouth, snout; (Cuba) thick lip. —*f.* (Car., Ven.) thick lip, thick mouth; (Peru) snout, mouth. — **radio bemba,** (Cuba, coll.) the grapevine, gossip which circulates by word of mouth.
bembón, na, *a.* (Amer.) blubber-lipped, thick-lipped. — **negro bembón,** (Cuba) affectionate term for a young black man.
bembudo, da, *a.* (Amer.), *var. of* **bembón.**
bemol, *a.* (mus.) flat. —*m.* (mus.) flat, flat sign. — **b. doble,** double flat; **tener bemoles,** (coll.) to be very difficult, be a tough assignment.
bemolado, da, *past part. of* **bemolar.** —*a.* (mus.) lowered a semitone.
bemolar, *tr.v.* (mus.) to lower a semitone.
ben, *m.* (bot.) horseradish tree.
benarriza, *f.* (ornith.) ortolan.
bencedrina, *f.* (pharm.) benzedrine.
bencénico, ca, *a.* pertaining to benzene.
benceína, *f.* (chem.) benzein.
benceno, *m.* (chem.) benzene.
bencílico, ca, *a.* (chem.) benzilic.
bencilo, *m.* (chem.) benzyl.
bencina, *f.* (chem.) benzine.
bendecidor, ra, *a.* blessing. —*m., f.* one who blesses.
bendecir, (*ref. 3*) *tr.v.* to bless; to consecrate.
bendición, *f.* 1. blessing, benediction. 2. grace (said before meal). — **bendiciones nupciales,** wedding ceremony; **echar la b. a,** (coll.) to be finished with, have done with.
bendiga, bendigo, *ref.* **bendicir.**
bendije, bendijera, bendijese, *ref.* **bendecir.**
bendito, ta, *irr. past part. of* **bendecir.** —*a.* 1. holy, blessed. 2. happy, blissful. 3. simple, simple-minded. — **agua b.,** holy water; **como pan bendito,** (to sell) like hot cakes; **ser un bendito,** to

be simple or simple-minded. —*interj.* (P. Rico), **¡ay, bendito!** Dear Lord! (expressing pain, surprise or pity).

benedícite, *m.* (ecc.) Benedicite (canticle); benedicite, grace, prayer before meals; exeat, travel permit granted to ecclesiastics.

benedicta, *f.* (pharm.) medicinal powder mixed with honey or syrup.

benedictino, na, *a., m., f.* (rel.) Benedictine. —*m.* Benedictine (liqueur).

benefactor, ra *a., m., f., var. of* **bienhechor.**

beneficencia, *f.* 1. beneficence, charity. 2. welfare organization or institution, charity organization; public welfare office.

beneficentísimo, ma, *a. super. of* **benéfico,** very beneficent, charitable or kind.

beneficiación, *f.* benefitting.

beneficiado, da, *m., f.* one who receives the proceeds of a benefit performance. —*m. (ecc.)* beneficiary (one who holds a benefice).

beneficiador, ra, *a.* benefitting, improving. —*m., f.* 1. benefactor. 2. developer (of land). 3. processer (of ores). 4. exploiter (of a mine).

beneficial, *a.* pertaining to ecclesiastical benefices.

beneficiar, *tr.v.* 1. to benefit, profit, help. 2. to develop, cultivate (land). 3. to work, exploit (mines, etc.). 4. to process (ores). 5. to purchase (a post, job). 6. to administer (excise revenue). 7. to sell below par (shares, etc.). 8. (Amer.) to slaughter and sell (cattle, etc.). —*i.v.* to benefit. —*r.v.* to profit. — **beneficiarse de** or **con,** to benefit by, profit by.

beneficiario, ria, *m., f.* beneficiary, person designated to receive income of a trust estate; the one named to receive proceeds or benefits (e.g. in an insurance policy).

beneficio, *m.* 1. benefit; profit, gain. 2. development, cultivation (of land). 3. working, exploitation (of mines). 4. smelting, processing (of ores). 5. (Amer.) slaughtering and selling (of cattle, etc.). 6. (ecc.) benefice. 7. buying of a post. 8. sale of shares, etc., below par. 9. benefit, benefit performance. 10. (law) right (by law or privilege). 11. (Chile) fertilizer. — **a b. de,** for the benefit of; **b. amovible** or **amovible ad nútum.** (ecc.) benefice withdrawable by a grantor; **b. bruto,** gross profit; **b. de bandera,** tax reduction on merchandise transported by ships of a nation's own merchant marine; **b. de deliberar,** (law) opportunity of deliberation (in which the heir can postpone acceptance of inheritance until inventory has been made); **b. de inventario,** (law) benefit of inventory, right granted to heir to accept inheritance without being obliged to pay debts amounting to more than the inheritance; **b. de justicia gratuita,** entitlement to legal aid; **b. extrasalarial,** fringe benefit; **b. líquido,** net profit; **b. neto,** net profit; **b. por acción,** earnings per share; **b. simple,** (ecc.) sinecure; **b. social,** fringe benefit; **a. b. de inventario,** (fig.) with reservations, cautiously; **hombre sin oficio ni b.,** man without a cent or a job.

beneficioso, sa, *a.* beneficial, profitable, useful.

benéfico, ca, *a.* charitable, beneficent, kind.

benemérito, ta, *a.* worthy, meritorious (gen. a title given to patriots). — **El Benemérito,** (Mex.) Benito Juárez; **La Benemérita (Guardia Civil),** (Sp., hum.) The Civil Guard (rural police).

beneplácito, *m.* approval, consent.

benevolencia, *f.* benevolence, kindness.

benevolente, *a.* benevolent, kind.

benévolo, la, *a.* benevolent, kind.

bengala, *f.* 1. **B.,** Bengal (country). 2. a variety of muslin. 3. (bot.) Indian cane. 4. (mil.) baton. 5. Bengal light (fireworks). — **b. de señales,** signal flare.

bengalí, (*pl.* **bengalíes**) *a.* Bengal, Bengalese, Bengali. —*m., f.* Bengali, Bengalese. —*m.* 1. Bengali (language). 2. (ornith.) bengali (Uraeginthus bengalus).

bengalina, *f.* (tex.) bengaline.

benignamente, *adv.* benignly, kindly, benevolently.

benignidad, *f.* benignity, benignancy, kindness.

benigno, na, *a.* 1. benign, kind, affable, benevolent. 2. mild, temperate (climate). 3. (med.) benign.

benito, ta, *a., m., f.* (rel.) Benedictine.

benjamín, *m.* Benjamin, baby, youngest son in a family.

benjamita, *a.* (Bib.) descending from or pertaining to Benjamin. —*m., f.* Benjamite.

benjuí, *m.* benzoin, benjamin (aromatic balsam).

bentónico, ca, *a.* (biol.) benthonic, benthal.

bentonita, *f.* (metal.) bentonite.

bentos, *m.* (biol.) benthos.

benzaldehido, *m.* (chem.) benzaldehyde.

benzamida, *m.* (chem.) benzamide.

benzoato, *m.* (chem.) benzoato; **b. de sodio,** (chem.) sodium benzoate.

benzocaína, *f.* (med.) benzocaine.

benzofenona, *f.* (chem.) benzophenone.

benzoico, ca, *a.* (chem.) benzoic.

benzoílo, *m.* (chem.) benzoil.

benzoína, *f.* (chem.) benzoin.

benzol, *m.* (chem.) benzol.

beocio, cia, *a.* 1. Boeotian. 2. stupid, dull. —*m., f.* Boeotian. —*f.* **B.,** Boeotia, region of ancient Greece.

beodez, *f.* drunkenness.

beodo, da, *a., m., f.* drunk.

beorí, (*pl.* **beoríes**) *m.* (zool.) Brazilian tapir.

beotismo, *m.* stupidity, dullness, coarseness, grossness.

beque, *m.* 1. (mar.) head (of ship). 2. chamber pot. 3. (*pl.*) (mar) beakhead, crew's latrines.

bequeriana, *f.* love poem (in the style of Gustavo Adolfo Bécquer).

bequista, *m.* (Amer.) scholarship holder, scholarship student.

berbén, *m.* (Mex., med.) type of scurvy.

berberecho, *m.* (zool.) cockle (Cardium edule), an edible shell fish.

berberí, (*pl.* **berberíes**) *a., m., f.* Berber, pertaining to a Moslem tribe of N. Africa, its culture or language.

berbería, *f.* 1. B., Barbary, a region in Northern Africa, chiefly inhabited by Berbers. 2. (bot., Hond.) oleander.

berberidáceo, a, berberídeo, a, *a.* (bot.) berberidaceous. —*f.* berberid; (*pl.*) Berberidaceae.

berberis. *m., var. of* **bérbero.**

bérbero, *m.* 1. (bot.) barberry. 2. mixture made from barberries.

berbí, *a.* woven from uncombed threads (said of cloth made in Verviers).

berbiquí, (*pl.* **berbiquíes**) *m.* (carp.) bit brace, bitstock; **b. de pecho,** breast drill, belly brace; **b. acodado,** angular bitstock; **b. de matraca,** ratchet brace.

berceo, *m.* kind of esparto grass.

bercial, *m.* ground overgrown with esparto grass.

beréber, berebere, *m., f.* Berber, a member of one of several Moslem tribes in N. Africa.

berengario, ria, *a., m., f.* (rel., hist.) Berengarian.

berenjena, *f.* (bot.) eggplant. — **b. catalana,** morada or **moruna,** common variety of eggplant; **b. de huevo,** egg-shaped eggplant Solanum ovigerum); b. **zocata,** over-ripe yellow eggplant.

berenjenal, *m.* 1. eggplant patch. 2. predicament, jam, fix, difficulties; **meterse uno en buen b.** or **mal b.** or un b., (coll.) to get into a fix, jam, predicament or difficulties.

berenjenín, *m.* cylindrical eggplant.

bergamota, *f.* (bot.) bergamot (lime, pear), its fruit and essence.

bergamote, bergamoto, *m.* (bot.) bergamot tree.

bergante, *m.* shameless scoundrel, blackguard, ruffian, scoundrel.

bergantín, *m.* (mar.) brig. — **b. goleta,** brigantine.

beriberi, *m.* (med.) beriberi.

berilio, *m.* (chem.) beryllium.

berilo, *m.* (min.) beryl.

berkelio, *m.* (chem.) berkelium.

berlanga, *f.* card game like rummy in which the object is to collect three cards of a kind.

Berlín, *m.* Berlin; **B. Occidental** and **Oriental,** West and East Berlin.

berlina, *f.* 1. berlin, a four-wheeled, two seater carriage. 2. closed front compartment (of stagecoach or railway carriage). — **en b.**, in a ridiculous position.

berlinés, sa, *a,* from or of Berlin. —*m., f.* Berliner.

berlinga, *f.* clothesline pole; rod or pole used to stir molten metal; (mar.) spar, round timber; pole holding up clothes line.

berlingar, (*ref. 51*) *tr.v.* to stir (molten metal).

berlingue, berlingué, *ref.* **berlingar.**

berma, *f.* (fort.) berm, ground at the foot of a rampart.

bermejal, *m.* (Cuba) large expanse of reddish soil.

bermejear, *i.v.* to become reddish.

bermejizo, za, *a.* reddish. —*m.* (zool.) fruit bat, flying fox.

bermejo, ja, *a.* bright red (color); **La Torre Bermeja,** the Red Tower (one of the historic buildings of the Alhambra).

bermejón, na, *a.* red, reddish.

bermejuela, *f.* (ichth.) bitterling (Rhodeus amarus).

bermejuelo, la, *a. dim. of* **bermejo,** reddish.

bermejura, *f.* bright redness.

bermellón, *m.* vermilion.

bermuda, *f.* (bot.) Bermuda grass.

bermudiana, *f.* (bot.) grassflower.

Berna, *f.* Bern, Berne, capital of Switzerland.

bernardina, *f.* (coll.) boastful lie, whopper, (sl.) tall tale.

bernardo, da, *a., m., f.* (ecc.) Bernardine.

bernegal, *m.* cup with scalloped edges; (Canar. I., Ven.) earthen jar (to collect filtered water).

bernés, sa, *m., f.* Bernese, native of Bern, Switzerland.

bernia, *f.* 1. rug, rough woolen cloth. 2. rug cloak or cape. —*m., f.* (Hond.) loafer,

berquelio, *m.* (chem.) berkelium.

berra, *f.* (bot.) tall watercress.

berraña, *f.* (bot.) variety of inedible watercress.

berraza, *f.* (bot.) water parsnip, tall watercress.

berrear, *i.v.* to bleat, low, bellow (animals); to shriek, scream; (fig.) to bellow, shout, sing off key, to cry (a child) with shrieks.

berrenchín, *m.* 1. steaming breath (of an angry boar). 2. (coll.) tantrum, fit of anger.

berrendo, da, *a.* two-colored, spotted. —*m.* deer-like wild mammal found in the Mexican highlands.

berrengue, berrenque, *m.* (S. Amer.) short, thick whip.

berreo, *m., var. of* **berrinche.**

berrera, *f.* (bot.) water parsnip.

berretín, *m.* (Arg., Urug.) 1. stubbornness. 2. obsession, fixation.

berriadora, *f.* (Col.) drunken spree or bout.

berrido, *m.* bellow, low (of an animal); (fig.) shriek; off-key note (in singing).

berrín, *m.* crosspatch, touchy, irascible person.

berrinche, *m.* 1. (coll.) rage, tantrum. 2. (Mex.) smell of the male animal caused by genital discharge.

berrinchudo, da, *a.* 1. (Amer.) touchy, irascible, bad-tempered. 2. (Mex.) in heat (animal). 3. (sl., Mex.) sexually aroused (person).
berrizal, *m.* watercress bed.
berro, *m.* (bot.) watercress.
berrocal, *m.* craggy or rocky area.
berroqueña, *a.* granite, granitic. —*f.* granite.
berrueco, *m.* 1. (med.) small tumor in the pupil of the eye. 2. granitic crag or tor. 3. baroque pearl.
bersagliero, (*pl.* **bersaglieri**) *m.* Bersagliere, Italian infantry soldier.
berta, *f.* bertha, deep lace collar (on women's dresses).
bertillonaje, *m.* Bertillon system, bertillonage (a system of personal identification antedating fingerprinting).
berza, *f.* (bot.) cabbage. — **b. de pastor,** (bot.) white goosefoot; b. **de perro,** (bot.) vincetoxicum, milkweed (Vincetoxicum album); **estar en b.,** to be in the blade (crops); **mezclar berzas con capachos,** (coll.) to bring in irrelevant details; **picar la b.,** to be a neophyte.
berzal, *m.* cabbage field.
berzas, berzotas, *m. pl.* ignorant or stupid person.
besador, ra, *a.* kissing. —*m., f.* one who kisses.
besalamano, *m.* unsigned note in the third person and bearing the abbreviation B.L.M. (kisses your hand).
besamanos, *m.* 1. court ceremony to show allegiance to royalty, formerly including hand-kissing. 2. manner of greeting by kissing a person's hand, hand kiss.
besamel, besamela, *f.* white sauce (prepared with flour, cream and butter).
besana, *f.* 1. first furrow (in plowing). 2. furrowing, series of parallel furrows.
besante, *m.* 1. bezant, ancient Byzantine coin. 2. (her.) bezant.
besar, *tr.v.* to kiss; (coll.) to touch lightly, graze. — **b. la mano or b. los pies,** to pay respects to; **bésame mucho, Antonio,** give me a lot of kisses, Anthony. —*r.v.* 1. to kiss, kiss one another. 2. (coll.) to bump heads, collide head-on (with someone).
besico, *m. dim. of* **beso,** little kiss. — **b. de monja,** (bot.) balloon vine.
beso, *m.* 1. kiss. 2. bump, collision. — **b. de Judas,** (fig.) kiss of Judas, treacherous kiss; **b. de paz,** kiss of peace.
besotear, (Mex.) *var. of* **besuquear.**
bestezuela, *f. dim. of* **bestia,** small beast.
bestia, *f.* animal, beast; **b. de albarda,** ass, donkey; **b. de carga,** beast of burden; **gran b.,** tapir. —*m., f.* (coll.) blockhead, fool, dunce, idiot, ass. —*a.* stupid, doltish.
bestiaje, *m.* beasts of burden, team of pack animals.
bestial, *a.* 1. bestial, brutal, savage. 2. (coll.) terrific, fabulous, tremendous. —*m.* (rare) beast (cow, horse, mule, donkey).
bestialice, bestialicé, *ref.* **bestializarse.**
bestialidad, *f.* 1. bestiality, brutality, savagery. 2. bestiality, carnal intercourse with an animal. 3. (coll.) stupidity, foolishness; stupid or foolish remark. 4. (coll.) tremendous amount.
bestializarse, (*ref.* 53) *r.v.* to become beast-like or brutalized.
bestialmente, *adv.* bestially.
bestiame, *m. var. of* **bestiaje.**
bestiario, *m.* 1. bestiary, medieval fables about animals. 2. Roman gladiator who fought against beasts.
bestión, *m. aug. of* **bestia,** big beast; (archit.) triton, fantastic ornamental figure, half-man half-beast.
béstola, *f.* plowstaff (for scraping plowshare).
besucador, ra, *a.* (coll.) kissing. —*m., f.* kisser (person).
besucar, (*ref.* 50) *tr.v.* (coll.) *var. of* **besuquear.**
besucón, na, *a., m., f.* (coll.) *var. of* **besucador.**
besugada, *f.* a large dish of sea bream.
besugo, *m.* (ichth.) sea bream (Pagellus controdontus); (ichth.) red porgy.
besuguera, *f.* 1. porgy or sea bream vendor. 2. fish pan or casserole (for cooking fish).
besuguero, *m.* porgy or sea bream vendor; fish hook used to catch sea bream.
besuguete, *m. dim. of* **besugo,** red sea bream.
besuque, besuqué, *ref.* **besucar.**
besuquear, *tr.v.* (coll.) to lavish kisses on, to kiss repeatedly.
besuqueo, *m.* (coll.) repeated kissing; smooching (sl.).
beta, *f.* 1. beta, second letter of the Greek alphabet. 2. (mar.) rope, cable. 3. piece of tape, bit of thread.
betabel, *m.* (Mex.) beet, beetroot.
betaína, *f.* (chem.) betaine.
betanaftol, *m.* (chem.) beta-naphtol.
betarraga, betarrata, *f.* beet, beetroot.
betatrón, *m.* (phys.) betatron.
betel, *m.* (bot.) betel.
beteraga, beterraga, *f.* (Chile, Peru) *var. of* **betarraga.**
bético, ca, *a., m., f.* of the Spanish region formerly called Bética, today Andalusia.
betijo, *m.* piece of laurel branch inserted in the mouth of a young goat to prevent suckling but permitting it to graze.
betlemita, *a., m., f.* Bethlemite, of Bethlehem.
betlemítico, ca, *a.* Bethlemitc.
betónica, *f.* (bot.) betony. — **b. coronaria,** (bot.) gillyflower, wild carnation.
Betsabé, *f.* (Bib.) Bathsheba, mother of Solomon, wife of David.
betuláceo, a, *a.* (bot.) betulaceous (of the birch family). —*f.* (*pl.*) (bot.) Betulaceae.
betumen, *m.* (min.) bitumen.
betuminoso, sa, *a.* bituminous.
betún, *m.* 1. bitumen, pitch, tar; pine tar. 2. shoe polish. 3. mastic used to seal joints between pipes. 4. (Cuba) water in which the veins of tobacco leaves have been saturated, used to moisten tobacco leaf. 5. (Chile) cake icing.
betunar, *tr.v.* to polish (shoes).
betunear, *tr.v.* (Cuba) to moisten (tobacco leaves) with water in which the veins of tobacco leaves have been saturated.
betunería, *f.* 1. tar, pitch or bitumen factory or shop. 2. shoe polish factory or shop.
betunero, *m.* 1. tar or pitch manufacturer or dealer. 2. shoe polish manufacturer or dealer. 3. bootblack, shoe-shine boy.
bevatrón, *m.* (phys.) bevatron.
bey, *m.* bey, Turkish governor
bezaar, *m., var. of* **bezoar.**
bezante, *m.* (her.) bezant.
bezar, *m., var. of* **bezoar.**
bezo, *m.* 1. thick lip. 2. proud flesh (in a wound).
bezoar, *m.* (med.) bezoar.
bezoárdico, ca, *a., var. of* **bezoárico.**
bezoárico, ca, *a.* bezoardic, antidotal. —*m.* bezoardio, antidote. — **b. mineral,** bezoar mineral, antimony oxide.
bezote, *m.* ring worn in the lower lip by South American Indians.
bezudo, da, *a.* thick-lipped, blubber-lipped.
bi- prefix meaning two or twice, e.g. *bicorne,* two-horned, *bicéfalo,* two-headed.
Bi *sym. of* **bismuto,** bismuth (Bi).
biaba, *f.* (Arg., Urug.) beating, thrashing, whipping.
biajaca, *f.* freshwater Cuban fish about a foot long (Mandopsis tetracanthus).
biajaiba, *f.* edible Caribbean fish with reddish forked tail (Neomaenis synagrys).
biangular, *a.* biangular, two-angled.
biarca, *m.* quartermaster and paymaster (of the Roman militia).
biarticulado, da, *a.* biarticulate.
bias, *m.* (rad.) bias.
biasar, *tr.v.* (rad.) to bias.
biatómico, ca, *a.* (chem.) biatomic.
biauricular, *a.* biauricular.
biáxico, ca *a.* biaxial.
biaxil, *a.* biaxial.
biaza, *f.* leather knapsack or saddlebag.
bibásico, ca, *a.* (chem.) bibasic.
bibelot, *m.* 1. doll, toy, knick-knack, figurine. 2. (Ven.) jewel, valuable object.
biberón, *m.* nursing bottle, baby's bottle.
bibí, (*pl.* **bibíes**) *m.* 1. (Arg.) type of lily. 2. (P. Rico) baby's pacifier.
bibicho, *m.* (Hond.) cat.
bibijagua, *f.* 1. type of destructive ant (Atta insularis). 2. (Cuba) busybee (person).
Biblia, *f.* Bible.
bíblico, ca, *a.* biblical.
bibliobús, *m.* mobile library.
bibliofilia, *f.* bibliophilism, love of books.
bibliófilo, *m.* bibliophile, bibliophilist.
bibliografía, *f.* bibliography.
bibliográfico, ca, *a.* bibliographic, bibliographical.
bibliógrafo, fa, *m., f.* bibliographer.
bibliología, *f.* bibliology.
bibliomancia, *f.*, bibliomancy, divination by the interpretation of a passage chosen at random, esp. from the Bible.
bibliomanía, *f.* bibliomania, a craze for collecting books, esp. rare ones.
bibliómano, *m.* bibliomaniac.
bibliopola, *m.* bibliopole, bookseller (of rare books).
bibliopólico, ca, *a.* bibliopolic.
biblioteca, *f.* 1. library. 2. (Amer.) bookcase, bookstand. — **b. circulante,** lending library; **b. de consulta,** reference library.
bibliotecario, ria, *m., f.* librarian, bibliothecary.
bibliotecnia, *f.* knowledge of the art of book printing and bookbinding.
biblioteconomía, *f.* library science, library management.
bibona, *f.* (bot.) aralia (Aralia capitata).
bicable, *a.* double-cable.
bical, *m.* male salmon.
bicameral, *a.* bicameral.
bicameralismo, *m.* doctrine supporting the bicameral system.
bicamerismo, *m.* legislature consisting of two chambers.
bicapsular, *a.* (bot.) bicapsular, bicarpellary.
bicarbonatado, da, *a.* containing bicarbonate.
bicarbonato, *m.* (chem.) bicarbonate; **b. de sosa** or **de sodio,** sodium bicarbonate.
bicarburo, *m.* (chem.) dicarbide; **b. de hidrogeno,** ethylene.
bicéfalo, la, *a.* bicephalic, bicephalous, two-headed; **águila b.,** two-headed eagle.
bicentenario, *m.* bicentenary.
bíceps, (*pl.* **bíceps**) *m.* (anat.) biceps; **b. braquial,** biceps brachii; **b. femoral,** biceps femoris.
bicerra, *f.* (zool.) mountain goat.
bicha, *f.* 1. (coll.) snake. 2. (archit.) triton, ornamental figure half-man half-beast. 3. (Col.) bug, small animal. 4. (P. Rico, sl.) penis.
bichar, *tr.v.* (Arg., Urug.) to spy on, watch, observe.
bicharraco, *m.* 1. ugly-looking animal. 2. (fig.) ugly-looking or contemptible person.

biche, *a.* 1. (Col.) unripe (fruit). 2. (Col.) feeble, sickly (person). 3. (Mex.) soft, spongy. —*m.* (Peru) large pot.
bicheadero, *m.* (Arg.) watchtower.
bichear, *tr.v.* to spy on, watch, observe.
bichero, *m.* (mar.) boathook.
bichín, *m.* (Hond.) harelip.
bicho, *m.* 1. bug, insect, (*pl.*) vermin. 2. animal, beast; (taur.) bull. 3. (coll.) person, fellow, freak, queer character or customer. 4. (Peru) spite, envy. 5. (sl., Amer.) penis. — **b. viviente,** living soul, e.g. *no hay b. viviente,* there's not a living soul; **mal b.,** malevolent fellow, ugly character; **todo b. viviente,** everyone.
bichoco, ca, *a.* 1. (Amer.) disabled by weakness or old age (a horse). 2. (coll.) disabled (person.).
bici, *m.* (coll.) bike, cycle, bicycle.
bicicleta, *f.* bicycle; **b. de carreras,** racing bicycle; **b. de montaña,** mountain bike; **b. fija** or **de ejercicio,** exercise bike.
bicíclico, ca, *a.* bicyclic.
biciclo, *m.* velocipede (with the pedal fixed on the front wheel).
bicilíndrico, *a.* (engin.) twin-cyclinder.
bicípite, *a.* bicipital, two-headed.
bicloruro, *m.* (chem.) bichloride, dichloride.
bicoca, *f.* 1. (coll.) trifle, bagatelle. 2. (Arg., Chile, coll.) calotte, skullcap. 3. (Chile, coll.) flick (with the fingers).
bicolor, *a.* bicolored, two-colored.
bicóncavo, va, *a.* (geom.) biconcave, double-concave.
bicónico, *a.* biconical.
biconvexo, xa, *a.* (geom.) biconvex, double-convex.
bicoque, *m.* (Bol.) knock on the head with the knuckles of the hand.
bicoqueta, *f.* (Peru) cap with ear flaps; tall kind of biretta.
bicoquete, bicoquín, *m.* cap with droopy ear-flaps; double-pointed cap.
bicorne, *a.* (poet.) two-horned, bicorn; two-cornered.
bicornio, *m.* two-cornered hat.
bicos, *m.* (*pl.*) small gold trimmings and studs (formerly used to adorn velvet caps).
bicromatado, da, *a.* (chem.) bichromated.
bicromato, *m.* (chem.) bichromate, dichromate; **b. de potasio,** (chem.) potassium dichromate; **b. de sodio,** (chem.) sodium dichromate.
bicromía, *f.* (print.) two-color print.
bicrón, *m.* (phys.) bicron.
bicuento, *m.* (math.) billion (G.B.), million millions (U.S.).
bicúspide, *a., m.* (dent.) bicuspid.
BID *abbrev. of* **Banco Interamericano de** Desarrollo, Interamerican Development Bank.
bidé, *m.* (Fr.) bidet, oval toilet fixture used for personal hygiene.
bidel, *m.* (Amer.) *var. of* **bidé.**
bidentado, da, *a.* bidentate, two-pronged.
bidente, *a.* bidentate. —*m.* two-pronged hoe or spade.
bidón, *m.* (Fr.) large can, tin can; steel drum.
biela, *f.* (mec.) connecting rod, pitman; **b. motriz,** connecting or main driving rod; **b. paralela** or **de acoplamiento,** coupling or side rod.
bielda, *f.* 1. (agr.) wooden rake (with six or seven-bar grating, used to gather and carry chaff or straw). 2. winnowing.
bieldada, *f.* pitchforkful (load carried on winnowing fork).
bieldar, *tr.v.* (agr.) to winnow with a pitchfork.
bieldo, *m.* (agr.) winnowing fork.
bielga, *f.* (reg., Sp.) large winnowing fork, used to make haystacks.
bielgo, *m., var. of* **bieldo.**
Bielorrusia, *f.* Byelorussia, White Russia, a republic of the USSR.
bien, *m.* 1. good, goodness, e.g. *distinguir entre el b. y el mal,* to distinguish between good and evil. 2. good, welfare, benefit. 3. (*pl.*) wealth; possessions; assets, goods, property, estate. — **b. común,** commonweal, public welfare; **bienes adventicios,** (law) adventitious property, acquired by a son under paternal control through his own efforts or inherited from relatives or strangers, providing it is not derived from the father; **bienes alodiales,** (law) allodial property (free from liens or charges); **bienes comunales** or **concejiles,** communal or civic property; **bienes de capital,** capital assets; **bienes de consumo,** consumer goods; **bienes de equipo,** capital assests; **bienes de fortuna,** worldly goods or possessions, wealth; **bienes dotales,** dowry; **bienes forales,** (law) leasehold estate; **bienes fungibles,** (law) fungible goods; **bienes gananciales,** (law) property acquired during married life, property of conjugal partnership; **bienes inmuebles,** see **bienes raíces; bienes mostrencos,** (law) waif property, escheated goods; **bienes muebles,** goods and chattels, personal or movable property; **bienes profecticios,** (law) profectitious property, acquired by a son under paternal control, through or deriving from his father; **bienes públicos** or **fiscales,** public property; **bienes raíces,** real estate; **bienes relictos,** (law) estate (of the deceased); **bienes reservables** or **reservativos,** (law) property inherited under legal provision that it shall subsequently pass on to a specific person or persons under certain circumstances; **bienes semovientes,** (law) livestock property; **en or por b. de,** for the good or benefit of; **hacerle b. a uno,** to do someone good, benefit someone; **hombre de b.,** good, honest or upright man; **no hay mal que por b. no venga,** every cloud has a silver lining. —*adv.* 1. well, properly, correctly. 2. well, successfully. 3. willingly, readily, e.g. *yo b. accedería a eso,* I would willingly agree to that. 4. easily, well e.g. *b. se puede hacer esta labor en un día,* one can easily or well do this work in one day, *b. puedo creer,* I can well *or* easily believe. 5. well, fully, e.g. *b. se sabe que es imposible,* it is well known that it's impossible. 6. very, quite, completely, e.g. *esta piña está b. madura,* this pineapple is quite ripe. 7. much, a great deal, e.g. *b. hemos caminado hoy,* we have walked a great deal today. 8. okay, e.g. *está b.,* okay, it's all right; *ahora b.,* now then. — **b. que,** although; **de b. a mejor,** better and better; **más b.,** rather; **no b.,** as soon as, just as; **o** b., or else, otherwise; **si b.,** although; **tener a b.,** to think or consider it wise; to be kind enough to (do something); **y b.**, well! well then! and so? —*a.* comfortably placed, well-to-do, e.g. *gente b.,* well-to-do people.
bienal, *a.* biennial, occurring every two years. —*m., f.* a biennial event or festival, e.g. *la bienal de Sao Paulo,* Sao Paulo's (art) biennial exhibition.
bienalmente, *adv.* biennially.
bienandante, *a.* lucky, fortunate; prosperous.
bienandanza, *f.* success, good fortune, luck; prosperity.
bienaventuradamente, *adv.* fortunately, happily, prosperously.
bienaventurado, da, *a.* 1. blessed, beatified, enjoying heavenly bliss. 2. lucky, fortunate. —*m., f.* (iron.) simple, naive person.
bienaventuranza, *f.* 1. heavenly bliss, blessedness. 2. prosperity, happiness. 3. (*pl.*) the Beatitudes of Christ's Sermon on the Mount.
bienestar, *m.* well-being, welfare; comfort, material ease.
bienfortunado, da, *a.* fortunate, lucky.
biengranada, *f.* (bot.) goosefoot (Chenopodium botrys).
bienhablado, da, *a.* well-spoken, courteous.
bienhadado, da, *a.* fortunate, lucky.
bienhechor, ra, *a.* charitable, benevolent, kind. —*m., f.* benefactor (*m.*), benefactress (*f.*).
bienhechuría, *f.* (Cuba) improvements made on rented property.
bienintencionadamente, *adv.* with good intentions.
bienintencionado, da, *a.* well-meaning.
bienio, *m.* biennium, a period of two years.
bienllegada, *f.* welcome, e.g. *venimos a darte la b.,* we've come to welcome you.
bienmandado, da, *a.* obedient, submissive, respectful.
bienmesabe, *m.* meringue-like dessert made with beaten egg whites and sugar.
bienoliente, *a.* sweet-smelling, fragrant.
bienquerencia, *m.* good-will, esteem; affection.
bienquerer, *m., var. of* **bienquerencia.**
bienquerer, (*ref. 17*) *tr.v.* to esteem (someone); to be fond of.
bienqueriente, *a.* affectionate, fond.
bienquerré, *ref.* **bienquerer.**
bienquiera, bienquiero, *ref.* **bienquerer.**
bienquise, bienquisiera, bienquisiese, *ref.* **bienquerer.**
bienquistar, *tr.v.* to reconcile, conciliate, make peace between. —*r.v.* to become reconciled or conciliated.
bienquisto, ta, *irr. past part. of* **bienquerer.** —*a.* esteemed, highly regarded, well-liked.
bienteveo, *m.* 1. lookout hut. 2. (ornith.) king-bird.
bienvenido, da, *a.* welcome. —*f.* welcome; safe arrival; **dar la b. a,** to welcome. —*m., f.* welcome (person).
bienvivir, *i.v.* 1. to live well, live in ease and comfort. 2. to live an honest life.
biercol, *m.* (bot.) a variety of heather.
bierzo, *m.* typical cloth made in Bierzo, a region of the province of Leon, Sp.
bies, *m.* 1. slant. 2. (sew.) bias piping. —*adv.* **al b.,** (tex.) slantwise, on the bias.
bifacial, *a.* (bot.) bifacial.
bifario, ria, *a.* (bot.) bifarious.
bifásico, ca, *a.* (elec.) diphase, diphasic, two-phase.
bife, *m.* (Arg., Urug.) 1. steak, beefsteak; **b. ancho,** entrecote; **b. de cuadril,** rumpsteak; **b. de lomo,** fillet steak. 2. slap, punch.
bífero, ra, *a.* (bot.) biferous, bearing fruit twice a year.
bífido, da, *a.* (bot.) bifid.
bifilar, *a.* (elec.) bifilar, two-wire.
bifloro, ra, *a.* (bot.) biflorate, biflorous.
bifluoruro, *m.* (chem.) bifluoride.
bifocal, *a.* (opt.) bifocal.
biforme, *a.* biform, biformed.
bifronte, *a.* bifront, bifrontal, with two faces.
biftec, *m.* (Amer.) beefsteak.
biftequera, *f.* (Chile) steak broiler.
bifurcación, *f.* bifurcation, forking, embranchment, branching.
bifurcado, da, *a.* forked, bifurcate.
bifurcarse, (*ref. 50*) *r.v.* to bifurcate, fork, branch off.
bifurque, *ref.* **bifurcarse.**
biga, *f.* biga, two-horse chariot; (poet.) team of two horses pulling chariot.
bigamia, *f.* 1. bigamy. 2. (law) second marriage of a widow(er).

bígamo, ma, *a.* bigamous. —*m., f.* 1. bigamist. 2. (law) a widow(er) who marries again. 3. person married to a widow(er).
bigardear, *i.v.* (coll.) to lead an aimless existence, loaf around, be a bum.
bigardía, *f.* pretense, simulation, deception, sham.
bigardo, da, *a.* wanton, perverse, licentious; idle, loafing. —*m.* libertine, debauchee, wanton; idler, loafer, bum.
bigardón, na, *a., var. of* **bigardo.**
bígaro, *m.* (zool.) periwinkle, marine snail.
bigarrado, da, *a., var. of* **abigarrado,** variegated, motley, multicolored.
bigato, *m.* ancient Roman silver coin.
bigeminado, da, *a.* bigeminate, double, paired.
bigeminia, *f.* bigeminy, pair.
bigémino, na, *a.* bigeminal, double, paired.
bignonia, *f.* (bot.) bignonia.
bignoniáceo, a, *a.* (bot.) bignoniaceous. —*f.* (*pl.*) Bignoniaceae.
bigorneta, *f.* anvil.
bigornia, *f.* two-beaked anvil. — **los de la b.,** (sl.) gang of ruffians.
bigornio, *m.* (sl.) bully, thug, member of a gang of ruffians.
bigorrella, *f.* sinker, heavy stone used to submerge net when fishing.
bigotazo, *m. aug. of* **bigote,** large mustache.
bigote, *m.* 1. whisker, mustache; (*pl.*) whiskers. 2. (print.) tapered dash. 3. (min.), slag tap (semicircular opening of blast furnace from which slag is taken); (*pl.*) flames (that come out of blast furnace opening); (*pl.*) metal which has filtered into the cracks on the inside of a furnace. 4. (Mex.) croquette. — **no tener malos bigotes,** (coll.) to be good looking (woman); **hombre de bigotes,** (coll.) upright, righteous man; **de b. al ojo,** (coll.) arrogant, ostentatious.
bigotera, *f.* 1. mustache cover (worn in bed). 2. froth (of wine, beer, etc.) left on upper lip after drinking (*gen. in pl.*) 3. ribbons (worn at the breast by women). 4. small folding seat (in carriage). 5. toecap (of shoe). 6. small compasses. — **pegar a uno una b.,** (coll.) to trick, swindle; **tener buenas bigoteras,** (coll.) to be good-looking.
bigotudo, da *a.* mustachioed, thickly mustached.
biguá, *f.* (ornith., Arg.) cormorant.
bigudí, *m.* hair-curler, curling pin.
bija, *f.* 1. (bot.) annatto tree (Bixa orellana); annatto fruit and seed. 2. annatto (dye).
bijirita, *f.* 1. (Cuba, ornith.) a warbler. 2. (Cuba) small paper kite. —*m.* (Cuba) formerly a Cuban of Spanish father; a derog. term for patriot during Cuba's wars of independence.
bijol, *m.* yellowish powder obtained from the annatto seed and used in cooking for coloring and flavoring food.
bikini, *m.* bikini (very brief bathing suit).
bilabiado, da, *a.* (bot.) bilabiate.
bilabial, *a.* (phonet.) bilabial.
bilao, *m.* (Phil. I.) tray made with strips of cane.
bilateral, *a.* bilateral; **simetría b.,** (zool.) bilateral symmetry.
bilbaíno, na, *a.* of or from Bilbao, Spain. —*m., f.* native or inhabitant of Bilbao.
bilenda, *f.* (Dom. Rep.) profit.
biliar, biliario, ria, *a.* biliary; **cálculo b.,** (med.) gallstone; **vesícula biliar,** (anat.) gallbladder.
bilimbín, *m.* (Phil. I., bot.) bilimbi tree.
bilineal, *a.* (geom.) bilinear.
bilingüe, *a.* bilingual, concerning two languages, e.g. *diccionario b.,* bilingual dictionary, *escritor b.,* bilingual writer.
bilingüismo, *m.* bilingualism, bilingual quality or ability.
bilioso, sa, *a.* 1. (med.) bilious. 2. (fig.) ill-tempered, bilious.
bilirrubina, *f.* (biochem.) bilirubin.
bilis, *f.* (med., fig.) bile; **cortar la b.,** to take antibilious medicine; **exaltarse a uno la b.,** (fig.) to get angry or annoyed.
bilítero, ra, *a.* biliteral, two-lettered.
biliverdina, *f.* (biochem.) biliverdin.
billa, *f.* (in billiards) ball pocketed after it has struck another ball; **b. limpia,** the pocketed ball is the player's ball; **b. sucia,** the pocketed ball is not the player's ball.
billalda, *f.* tipcat (children's game).
billar, *m.* 1. billiards (game), pool. 2. billiard saloon or hall, billiard room, pool room. — **b. romano,** pinball (game).
billarda, *f.* 1. tipcat (children's game). 2. (Hond.) lizard trap.
billarista, *m.* billiard player, pool player.
billetado, da, *a.* (her.) billety, billetté, studded with billets.
billetaje, *m.* 1. seating capacity (of theater, bus, etc.). 2. (Cuba, sl.) dough, plenty of money.
billete, *m.* 1. ticket (of bus, theater, etc.); lottery or raffle ticket. 2. bill, banknote, treasury bill. 3. (her.) billet. 4. note, short letter; **b. circular,** tourist stopover ticket, mileage ticket; **b. de banco,** banknote; **b. de ida y vuelta,** roundtrip ticket; **b. kilométrico,** mileage ticket; **b. sencillo** or **de ida,** one-way ticket; **medio b.,** half fare.
billetera, *f.* (Amer.), *var. of* **billetero.**
billetero, *m., f.* 1. wallet, billfold. 2. (Cuba, P. Rico, Mex.) lottery ticket vendor.
billón, *m.* 1. billion, one million millions (G.B.). 2. trillion (U.S.).
billonario, ria, *m., f.* billionaire.
billonésimo, ma, *a., m.* billionth.
bilma, *f.* (Cuba, Chile, Mex.) poultice, medicated bandage.
bilmar, *tr.v.* (Cuba, Chile, Mex.) to apply a poultice.
bilobado, da, *a.* (anat.) bilobate, bilobated, bilobed.
bilobulado, da, *a.* (anat.) bilobate, bilobated, bilobed.
bilocación, *f.* (theol.) bilocation, presence of a person in two different places simultaneously.
bilocarse, (*ref. 50*) *r.v.* 1. to be in two places simultaneously. 2. (Arg.) to go mad.
bilocular, *a.* (biol.) bilocular.
bilogía, *f.* literary work divided in two parts.
bilongo, *m.* (Cuba) witchcraft, sorcery; love potion, philter.
biloque, biloqué, *ref.* **bilocarse.**
biltrotear, *i.v.* (coll.) to gad about.
biltrotera, *f.* (coll.) gadabout, gay bird (sl.), (woman who likes to go out on the town.).
bimano, na, *a.* (zool.) bimanous, two-handed. —*m.* (*pl.*) (zool.) Bimana.
bimanual, *a.* (med.) bimanual.
bimástil, *m.* (Amer., tel.) dipole antenna.
bimba, *f.* 1. (coll.) top hat. 2. (Hond.) tall person.
bimbalete, *m.* 1. (Mex.) well sweep, a primitive type pump for extracting water from shallow wells. 2. (Mex.) round beam or timber. 3. (Mex.) seesaw.
bimbral, *m.* (coll.) place where willows grow.
bimbre, *m.* (coll.) osier, willow, wicker.
bimembre, *a.* having two limbs or parts.
bimensual, *a.* semimonthly, twice a month.
bimestral, *a.* bimonthly, every two months.
bimestre, *m.* 1. two-month period, **bimester.** 2. bimonthly rent, salary or pension. —*a.* bimonthly, bimestrial.
bimetal, *m.* (chem., phys., econ.) **bimetal.**
bimetálico, ca, *a.* (chem., phys., econ.) bimetallic.
bimetalismo, *m.* (chem., phys., econ.) bimetallism.
bimetalista, *a.* (chem., phys., econ.) bimetallistic. —*m., f.* bimetallist.
bimolecular, *a.* (chem.) bimolecular.
bimorfo, fa, *a.* (biol., min.) dimorphic, dimorphous.
bimotor, *a.* bimotored, twin-motor, twin-motored. —*m.* bimotored or twin-motored airplane.
bina, *f.* 1. second plowing or digging. 2. second hoeing.
binación, f. (rel.) celebration of two masses in one day by the same priest.
binadera, *f.* plow; hoe.
binado, a, *a.* (bot.) binate.
binador, *m.* 1. plow; hoe. 2. plower; hoer.
binadura, *f.* 1. second plowing or digging. 2. second hoeing.
binar, *tr.v.* (agr.) to plow over a second time; to hoe (vines) a second time. —*i.v.* (rel.) to celebrate two masses on a feast day (the same priest).
binario, ria, *a.* binary. — **estrella b.,** binary star; **sistema b.,** (biol., math.) binary system.
binazón, *f.* 1. second plowing or digging. 2. second hoeing.
bincha, *f.* (S. Amer.) cloth headband; thick ribbon or heavy kerchief worn around the head.
bingarrote, *m.* (Mex.) a strong liquor made from the maguey plant, such as **pulque.**
binguí, (*pl.* **binguíes**) *m.* (Mex.) drink extracted from the maguey plant.
binocular, *a.* binocular. —*m.* (*pl.*) field glasses, binoculars.
binóculo, *m.* lorgnette, pince-nez; spectacles; (*pl.*) opera or field glasses, binoculars.
binodo, *m.* (rad., metal.) binode.
binomial, binominal, *a.* binomial; **sistema b.** (biol.) binomial system.
binomio, *m.* (math.) binomial; **b. de Newton,** (math.) binomial theorem.
bínubo, ba, *a.* twice-married. —*m., f.* twice-married person.
binucleado, da, *a.* (biol.) binucleate.
binuclear, *a.* (biol.) binuclear.
binza, *f.* shell membrane (of egg); pellicle (of onion); pellicle or thin membrane (of animal).
bioblasto, *m.* (biol.) bioblast.
biocatalizador, *m.* (biochem.) biocatalyst.
bioclimatología, *f.* bioclimatology, the study of the relationship between climate and biological processes.
biodinámica, *f.* biodynamics, the study of the physiological processes of the body.
bioecología, *f.* bioecology, the study of the relationship between ecology and biological processes.
bioelemento, *m.* any chemical element essential to the normal development of a species.
bioensayo, *m.* (biochem.) bio-assay.
biofísica, *f.* (biol.) biophysics.
biogénesis, *f.* (biol.) biogenesis, biogeny.
biogenético, ca, *a.* biogenetic, biogenetical.
biogenia, *f.* biogeny.
biógeno, na, *a.* biogenic, biogenous.
biogeografía, *f.* (biol.) biogeography.
biogeográfico, ca, *a.* (biol.) biogeographic.
biografía, *f.* biography.
biografiado, da, *past part. of* **biografiar.** —*m., f.* subject of a biography.
biografiar, *tr.v.* to write a biography of (a person).
biográfico, ca, *a.* biographical, e.g. *semblanza b.,* biographical sketch.
biógrafo, fa, *m., f.* biographer.

biólisis, *f.* (biol.) biolysis.
biología, *f.* biology, the science that studies life.
biológico, ca, *a.* biological, biologic. — **guerra biológica,** biological warfare.
biologismo, *m.* (sociol.) biologism.
biólogo, *m.* biologist.
biombo, *m.* screen; folding screen.
biomecánica, *f.* (biol.) biomechanics.
biometeorología, *f.* biometeorology.
biometría, *f.* biometry, biometrics, the application of statistics to the solution of biological problems.
biónica, *f.* bionics, a branch of computer science.
bionomía, *f.* bionomy, science of the laws of life.
bionómico, ca, *a.* bionomic, bionomical.
bionte, *m.* (bot.) biont, living organism.
biónico, ca, *a.* (bot.) biontic.
bioplasma, *m.* (physiol.) bioplasm.
biopsia, *f.* (med.) biopsy.
bioquímico, ca, *a.* biochemical. —*m.* biochemist. —*f.* biochemistry.
biosfera, *f.* biosphere.
biosíntesis, *f.* (biochem.) biosynthesis.
biosociología, *f.* (sociol.) biosociology.
biostática, *f.* (biol.) biostatics.
biot, *m.* (phys.) a unit of electric current equal to ten amperes.
biota, *f.* (bot.) biota.
bioterapia, *f.* (biol.) biotherapy.
biótico, ca, *a.* biotic, biotical, caused by living beings.
biotipo, *m.* (biol.) biotype.
biotita, *f.* (min.) biotite.
biouvulado, da, *a.* (biol.) biovular.
bióxido, *m.* (chem.) dioxide; **b. de carbono,** (chem.) carbon dioxide.
bíparo, ra, *a.* (zool., bot.) biparous.
bipartición, *f.* bipartition, division into two parts.
bipartido, da, bipartito, ta, *a.* bipartite, having two parts.
bípede, *a., var. of* **bípedo.**
bípedo, da, *a., m.* (zool.) biped.
bipétalo, *a.* (bot.) bipetalous.
bipinado, da, *a.* (bot.) bipinnate.
biplano, *a., m.* biplane.
bípode, bipié, *m.* bipod, two-legged support.
bipolar, *a.* bipolar, two-pole.
biprima, *f.* (math.) double prime (X").
bipropulsante, *m.* bipropellant, a type of rocket fuel.
BIRF *abbrev. of* **Banco Internacional de Reconstrucción y Fomento,** International Reconstruction and Development Bank.
biribí, *m.* (reg., Sp.) confusion, uproar.
biribís, *m.* 1. type of roulette game 2. roulette board.
biricú, *m.* sword belt.
birimbao, *m.* (mus.) Jew's harp.
birimbí, *a.* (Col.) weak, sickly.
biringo, ga, *a.* (Col.) naked.
biriquí, (*pl.* **biriquíes**) *m.* (Peru) carpenter's brace.
birla, o, *f., m.* (Sp., reg.) bowling pin.
birlar, *tr.v.* 1. to throw (a bowling ball) for a second time from where it stopped. 2. (coll.) to kill or knock down at one blow. 3. (coll.) to attain wealth or promotion by dishonest means. 4. (sl.) to rob; to filch, swipe, lift, steal.
birlesca, *f.* (sl.) gang of thugs.
birlesco, *m.* (sl.) thug, thief.
birlí, (*pl.* birlíes) *m.* 1. (print.) blank space at bottom of printed page. 2. (printer's) earnings from this blank space.
birlibirloque, por arte de b., coll.) as if by magic, by sleight of hand.
birlocha, *f.* kite (toy).
birlocho, *m.* barouche (carriage).
birlón, *m.* jack pin (used in bowling).
birlonga, *f.* a variant of the game of ombre in which the holder of the ace of spades must make the bid; a la b., (coll.) carelessly, sloppily.
Birmania, *f.* Burma.
birmano, na, *a., m., f.* Burmese.
birrectángulo, *a.* (geom.) birectangular.
birrefringencia, *f.* (phys.) birefringence, double refraction.
birrefringente, *a.* (phys.) birefringent, producing double refraction.
birreme, *f.* (mar.) bireme, ancient galley.
birreta, *f.* biretta, cardinal's cap.
birrete, *m.* biretta; (Spanish professors') academic cap; judges' and lawyers' cap; beret, cap; (Chile) three-cornered hat.
birretina, *f.* small cap or beret; hussar's or grenadier's fur cap.
birria, *f.* 1. ridiculous thing, rubbish, non-sense; ridiculously or garishly dressed person. 2. (Amer.) grudge, hatred, aversion; **jugar de b.,** (Amer., coll.) to play apathetically, without interest.
birriñaque, *m.* (Hond.) ill-shaped roll of bread.
birrión, *m.* (Cuba) smudge, blot, esp. left on the face after applying make-up sloppily.
birrotulado, *a.* two-hinged.
bis, *adv.* (mus., print.) bis, twice. —*interj.* (theat.) encore, bis.
bisabuelo, la, *m.* great-grandfather; (*pl.*) great grandparents. —*f.* great-grandmother.
bisagra, *f.* 1. hinge. 2. shoemaker's boxwood polisher. — **b. de paleta** or **ramal,** strap hinge; b. **acodada,** offset hinge; **b. de muelle,** spring hinge; **b. desmontable,** loose-pin butt.
bisanual, *a.* (bot.) biennial (said of plants).
bisanuo, nua, *m., f.* (bot.) biennial.
bisar, *tr.v.* to repeat (song, etc. as an encore).
bisayo, ya, *a., m., f.* Visayan, Bisayan. —*m.* Visayan (language). —*f.* (*pl.*) **B.,** Visayan Islands, Bisayas, in the Philippines.
bisbís, *m.* 1. type of roulette. 2. roulette board.
bisbisar, bisbisear, *tr.v.* to mumble, mutter between the teeth.
bisbiseo, *m.* muttering, mumbling.
biscuit, *m.* biscuit, unglazed pottery after first firing; **porcelana de b.,** Sevres porcelain.
bisecar, (*ref.50*) *tr.v.* (geom.) to bisect, divide (a figure) into two equal parts.
bisección, *f.* (geom.) bisection.
bisector, triz, *a.* bisecting. —*f.* bisector, bisectrix.
bisel, *m.* bevelled edge, bevel, chamfer.
biselado, *past part. of* **biselar.** —*m.* beveling.
biselador, ra, *m.* beveler. —*f.* chamfering tool.
biselar, *tr.v.* to bevel, chamfer.
bisemanal, *a.* semiweekly.
biseque, bisequé, *ref.* **bisecar.**
bisexual, *a., m., f.* bisexual, hermaphrodite.
bisiesto, *a.* bissextile, leap (year). —*m.* leap year, bissextile; **mudar b.** or **de. b.,** (coll.) to change one's ways, turn over a new leaf.
bisilábico, ca, *a., var. of* **bisílabo.**
bisílabo, ba, *a.* bisyllabic, of two syllables.
bisilicato, *m.* (chem.) bisilicate.
bismutina, *f.* (min.) bismuthine, bismuthinite, bismuth glance.
bismutinita, *f.* bismuthinite, native bismuth sulphide.
bismutita, *f.* (min.) bismutite.
bismuto, *m.* (chem.) bismuth.
bisnieto, ta, *m., f.* great-grandchild. —*m.* great-grandson. —*f.* great-granddaughter.
biso, *m.* (zool.) byssus, filament secreted by mollusks.
bisojo, ja, *a.* squint-eyed, cross-eyed, cock-eyed. —*m., f.* squinter, squint-eye.
bisonte, *m.* (zool.) bison, N. American buffalo.
bisoñada, *f.* (coll.) blunder or foolish act due to youth or inexperience.
bisoñé, *m.* toupee, hairpiece.
bisoñería, *f.* (coll.), *var. of* bisoñada.
bisoño, ña, *a.* inexperienced, green; raw, new (recruit). —*m., f.* greenhorn, tenderfoot, inexperienced person; rookie, recruit.
bispón, *m.* roll of oilcloth (used by sword maker).
bistec, biftec, *m.* beefsteak.
bisteque, *m.* (Amer.), *var. of* **bistec.**
bistorta, *f.* (bot.) bistort.
bistre, *m.* (p.) bister, bistre, yellowish-brown pigment.
bistrecha, *f.* advance, advance payment.
bisturí, (*pl.* **bisturíes**) *m.* (surg.) scalpel, bistoury, surgical knife.
bisulco, ca, (zool.) cloven-hoofed, cloven-footed, bisulcate.
bisulfato, *m.* (chem.) bisulfate.
bisulfito, *m.* (chem.) bisulfite.
bisulfuro, *m.* (chem.) bisulfide, disulfide. — **b. de carbono,** (chem.) carbon disulfide.
bisunto, ta, *a.* dirty, greasy.
bisurco, ca, *a.* double-bladed (plow).
bisutería, *f.* imitation jewelry, costume jewelry; bijouterie.
bita, *f.* (mar.) bitt, cleat.
bitácora, *f.* (mar.) binnacle, compass case; **aguja de b.,** compass; **cuaderno de b.,** logbook.
bitadura, *f.* (mar.) cable bitt (turn of the anchor cable laid ready for casting the anchor).
bitango, *m.* kite (toy).
bitar, *tr.v.* (mar.) to bitt, to secure the anchor cable around the bitt.
bitartrato, *m.* (chem.) bitartrate.
bitínico, ca, bitinio, nia, *a.* Bithynian, of Bithynia, ancient region of Asia Minor.
bitneriáceo, a, *a.* (bot.) sterculiaceous. —*f.* (*pl.*) (bot.) sterculiaceae.
bitongo, ga, *a.* (coll.) child-like, infantile; **niño** b., (coll.) big baby, crybaby, spoilt child; **niña b.,** girl or woman who wants to pass for a child.
bitoque, *m.* 1. bung, plug (of barrel). 2. (Amer.) cannula (of syringe). 3. (Mex.) faucet, spigot. 4. (C. Amer.) sewer.
bitor, *m.* (ornith.) bittern.
bítter, *m.* bitters (an ingredient in some cocktails).
bitumen, *m.* (min.) bitumen.
bituminoso, sa, *a.* (min.) bituminous.
bivalencia, *f.* (chem.) bivalence.
bivalente, *a.* (chem.) bivalent.
bivalvo, va, *a.* (zool.) bivalve.
bixáceo, a, bixíneo, a, *a.* (bot.) bixaceous. —*f.* (bot.) (*pl.*) Bixaceae.
biyugado, da, *a.* (bot.) bijugate.
biza, *f.* (ichth.) bonito, tuna.
Bizancio, *m.* Byzantium, ancient name of Istanbul (until the 4th century A. D.).
bizantinismo, *m.* 1. Byzantine style or character. 2. a life of luxury and corruption. 3. artistic over-ornamentation. 4. fondness for pointless or hair-splitting conversations. 5. Byzantine studies.
bizantino, na, *a.* Byzantine, pertaining to the Byzantine Empire or its culture. (fig.) pointless, hair-splitting (discussion). —*m., f.* Byzantine.
bizarramente, *adv.* 1. gallantly, valiantly, courageously. 2. magnanimously, nobly.
bizarrear, *i.v.* to act gallantly or magnanimously.
bizarría, *f.* 1. gallantry, valor, courage. 2. magnanimity, nobility.
bizarro, rra, *a.* 1. valiant, brave, gallant, courageous. 2. magnanimous, noble.

bizarrón, *m.* large candlestick, candelabrum.
bizaza, *f.* leather saddlebag.
bizbirindo, da, *a.* (Mex.) lively, gay.
bizcaitarra, *m.* (Sp.) Basque nationalist; advocate of Basque autonomy.
bizcar, (*ref. 50*) i.v. to squint. —*tr.v.* to wink at.
bizco, ca, *a.* cross-eyed, squint-eyed, cock-eyed; — **dejar a uno b.,** to amaze, astound, leave speechless or goggle-eyed. —*m., f.* squinter, squint-eye, cross-eyed person.
bizcochada, *f.* 1. soup made from hardtack and milk. 2. long slit roll (bread). 3. a dessert made with leftover cake and pudding (somewhat like the English trifle).
bizcochar, *tr.v.* 1. to bake (bread) a second time, to bake hardtack. 2. (cer.) to fire biscuit pottery.
bizcochería, *f.* bakery shop, pastry shop; sweet-shop (G.B.), candy store.
bizcochero, ra, *a.* of or pertaining to pastry. —*m., f.* baker, pastry chef.
bizcocho, *m.* 1. cake; torte; biscuit; pastry. 2. (mas.) plaster. 3. (cer.) biscuit, bisque, unglazed pottery. — **b. borracho,** tipsy cake; **embarcarse con poco b.,** to launch into a business with insufficient means.
bizcochuelo, *m.* sponge cake; hardtack.
bizcorneado, da, *a.* 1. (print.) creased, folded crookedly. 2. squint-eyed, cross-eyed. 3. warped (wood); crooked, misshapen.
bizcornear, *i.v.* to squint.
bizcorneto, ta, *a.* (Amer.) squint-eyed, cross-eyed.
bizcotela, *f.* (cul.) ladyfinger or sponge cake with icing.
bizma, *f.* poultice, cataplasm.
bizmar, *tr.v.* to apply a poultice.
bizna, *f.* (bot.) membrane dividing walnut kernel.
biznaga, *f.* 1. (bot.) bishop's weed. 2. toothpick (made from bishop's weed). 3. (Mex., bot.) bisnaga (Ferocactus hematocanthus).
biznagal, *m.* (bot.) field of bishop's weed.
biznieto, ta, *m., f.* great-grandchild. —*m.* great-grandson. —*f.* great-granddaughter.
bizque, bizqué, *ref.* **bizcar.**
bizquear, *i.v.* (coll.) to squint.
bizquera, *f.* strabismus, squint.
Bk *sym. of* **berkelio,** berkelium (Bk).
blanca, *f.* (numis.) ancient Spanish copper coin. 2. (mus.) half note. — **b. morfea,** (vet.) ringworm, tetter; **estar sin b., no tener b.,** not to have a penny, to be broke.
Blanca Nieve, Blancanieves, *f.* (lit.) Snow White; **B. N. y los Siete Enanitos,** Snow White and the Seven Dwarfs.
blancarte, *m.* (min.) gangue.
blancazo, za, *a.* (coll.) whitish.
blanco, ca, *a.* 1. white (color; race; bread; wine); fair (complexion). 2. (coll.) chicken, cowardly. — **arma b.,** cutting weapon. —*m., f.* 1. white (person). 2. (coll.) coward. —*m.* 1. white (color). 2. blaze, white spot (on coat of an animal). 3. target, butt; (fig.) aim, goal. 4. blank space, blank, gap; intermission; (P. Rico) application, blank, document. 5. (print.) first form. — **b. de titanio,** titanium white; **b. de ballena,** spermaceti; **b. de zinc,** zinc white, zinc oxide; **b. de España, Spanish white, whiting, basic lead carbonate; b. de la uña,** half moon of the nail; **b. del ojo,** white of the eye, sclera; **b. fijo,** stationary target; **calentar al b.,** to make or heat white hot: **dar en el b.,** to hit the target; **en b.,** blank, e.g. *endoso en b.,* blank endorsement; **firma en b.,** blank signature; **en b. y negro,** in black and white; **hacer b.,** to hit the target, make a bull's eye; **quedarse en b.,** to be at a loss, not to understand at all.
blancor, *m.* whiteness.
blancote, ta, *a.* (coll.) yellow (sl.), cowardly. —*m., f.* coward.
blancura, *f.* whiteness; **b. del ojo** (vet.) nebula, spot on the cornea.
blancuzco, ca, *a.* whitish; off-white.
blanda, *f.* (sl.) bed.
blandamente, *adv.* softly, meekly.
blandeador, ra, *a.* softening, convincing, persuasive; ingratiating.
blandear, *tr.v.* 1. to soften, convince, persuade. 2. to brandish. —*i.v., r.v.* to soften, yield, give in, cede.
blandengue, *a.* soft; docile, weak. —*m.* ancient Argentine lancer, frontier guard.
blandenguería, *f.* softness; docility, weakness.
blandicia, *f.* 1. blandishment, flattery. 2. gentleness, softness, blandness.
blandiente, *a.* 1. displayed ostentatiously, brandished; waving. 2. (rare) quivering, trembling, shaking.
blandir, *tr.v.* to brandish, flourish, swing. —*i.v., r.v.* (rare) to quiver, shake, tremble.
blando, da, *a.* 1. soft, tender, pliant, e.g. *b. al tacto,* soft to the touch; flaccid, flabby. 2. soft, feeble, weak, lacking firmness, e.g. *b. de carácter,* weak-willed, of weak character. 3. meek, soft, kind, benign, e.g. *b. de corazón,* soft-hearted. 4. soft, delicate, pampered, coddled. 5. temperate, mild (weather). 6. (mus.) lowered a semitone. — **jabón blando,** soft soap; **tomar los blandos,** (taur.) to plunge a sword into the bull without touching the bone.
blandón, *m.* 1. large wax candle. 2. candelabrum, large candlestick.
blanducho, cha, *a., var. of* **blandujo.**
blandujo, ja, *a.* (coll.) softish.
blandura, *f.* 1. softness; flabbiness, flaccidness. 2. softness, weakness (of character). 3. softness, kindness, gentleness. 4. softness, comfort, ease, luxury. 5. compliment, blandishment, flattering remark. 6. poultice. 7. white cosmetic. 8. (geol.) soft layer (in limestone). 9. mildness (weather).
blandurilla, *f.* cosmetic made from lard and aromatic herbs.
blanduzco, ca, *a.* (coll.) softish.
blanqueación, *f.* whitening; bleaching; whitewashing; blanching (of metals).
blanqueada, *f.* (Mex.), *var. of* **blanqueo.**
blanqueado, *m.* (Chile, Mex.), *var. of* blanqueo.
blanqueador, ra, *a.* whitening; bleaching; whitewashing. —*m., f.* bleach; white-washer.
blanqueadura, *f., var. of* **blanqueo.**
blanqueamiento, *m. var. of* **blanqueo.**
blanquear, *tr.v.* to whiten; to bleach; to whitewash; to blanch, to polish (metals); to wax honeycombs (bees). —*i.v.* to be whitish; to turn white; to turn whitish, to fade.
blanquecedor, *m.* coin blancher or polisher (in the mint).
blanquecer, (*ref. 45*) *tr.v.* to blanch (metals); to whiten; to polish (gold, silver).
blanquecimiento, *m.* blanching (of metals).
blanquecino, na, *a.* whitish; off-white.
blanqueo, *m.* whitening; bleaching; white-washing; blanching (of metals); waxing (honeycomb); fading, turning white or whitish.
blanqueta, *f.* (tex,) ancient coarse woolen fabric.
blanquete, *m.* white cosmetic.
blanquezco, blanquezca, *ref.* **blanquecer.**
blanquición, *f.* blanching (of metals).
blanquillo, lla, *a.* white (bread, flour, wheat). —*m.* 1. white wheat, white flour. 2. (Chile, Peru) white peach. 3. (ichth., Chile) blanquillo. 4. lower trump card (ombre card game). 5. (Mex.) euphemism for egg. — **pino b.,** (bot.) Scotch pine; **soldado b.,** (coll.) line infantry soldier.
blanquimento, *m., var. of* **blanquimiento.**
blanquimiento, *m.* bleaching solution (for fabrics); blanching solution (for metals).
blanquinegro, a, *a.* white and black.
blanquinoso, sa, *a.* whitish; off-white.
blanquizal, *m.* chalk pit.
blanquizar, *m., var. of* **blanquizal.**
blanquizco, ca, *a.* whitish; off-white.
blao, *a., m.* (her.) azure.
blasfemable, *a.* vituperable.
blasfemador, ra, *a.* blasphemous, blaspheming. —*m., f.* blasphemer.
blasfemamente, *adv.* blasphemously.
blasfemante, *a.* blaspheming.
blasfemar, *i.v.* to blaspheme, curse, swear.
blasfematorio, ria, *a.* blasphemous.
blasfemia, *f.* blasphemy; insult, affront.
blasfemo, ma, *a.* blasphemous. —*m., f.* blasphemer.
blasón, *m.* 1. coat of arms, escutcheon. 2. heraldry. 3. armorial bearing device. 4. honor, glory. — **hacer b.,** (fig.) to boast, brag.
blasonado, da, *past part. of* **blasonar. —***a.* illustrious, blue-blooded.
blasonador, ra, *a.* boasting, bragging.
blasonar, *tr.v.* to emblazon. —*i.v.* to boast, brag.
blasonería, *f.* boast, bravado, braggadocio.
blasonista, *m., f.* heraldry expert.
blastema, *m.* (biol.) blastema.
blastocele, *m.* (biol.) blastocele, blastococl, blastocoele.
blastocisto, *m.* (biol.) blastocyst.
blastoderma, *m., var. of* **blastodermo.**
blastodérmico, ca, *a.* blastodermio, blastodermatic.
blastodermo, *m.* (biol.) blastoderm.
blastodisco, *m.* (biol.) blastodisc.
blastogénesis, *f.* (biol.) blastogenesis.
blastómero, *m.* (biol.) blastomere.
blastomiceto, *m.* (bact.) blastomyceto.
blastomicosis, *f.* (bact.) blastomycosis.
blastóporo, *m.* (biol.) blastopore.
blastofera, *f.* (biol.) blastosphere.
blástula, *f.* (biol.) blastula.
blata, *f.* (ento.) cockroach.
blavo, va, *a.* yellowish gray and reddish.
ble, *m.* handball (game).
bledo, *m.* (bot.) blite, goosefoot, pigweed. — **no dársele a uno un b. de una cosa, no importarle a uno un b.,** not to give a hoot about, **no valer un b.,** not to be worth a cent, to be completely insignificant.
blefaritis, *f.* (med.) blepharitis, inflammation of the eyelids.
blefaroplastia, *f.* (surg.) blepharoplasty, plastic surgery performed on the eyelids.
blefaróstato, *m.* (surg.) blepharostat, instrument for keeping eyelids open during eye surgery.
blenda, *f.* (min.) blende, zinc sulfide. — **b. de cinc,** (min.) zinc blende.
blenia, *f.* (ichth.) blenny.
blenoftalmía, *f.* (med.) purulent conjunctivitis.
blenorragia, *f.* (med.) blennorrhagia.
blenorrágico, ca, *a.* (med.) blennorrhagic.
blenorrea, *f.* (med.) blennorrhea.
blinda, *f.* (mil.) blind, curtain.
blindado, da, *past part. of* **blindar. —***a.* armored; **carro b.,** armored car.
blindaje, *m.* (mil., mar.) armor, armor plating; (mil.) blindage; (elec.) shield. — **b. cerrado,** (mil.) interlocking armor; **b. antimagnético,** magnetic screen or shield.
blindar, *tr.v.* to armor, armor-plate; (elec.) to shield.

bloc, block, *m.* pad, block, writing pad.
bloca, *f.* (mil.) stud, boss (on a shield).
blocao, *m.* (mil.) movable blockhouse.
blonda, *f.* silk lace.
blondina, *f.* scalloped strip of silk lace.
blondo, da, *a.* (gal., poet.) blond.
bloque, *m.* 1. block (solid piece of material). 2. bloc, block, group (of political parties, countries, etc.). 3. pad, block, writing pad. 4. (mec.) (cylinder, engine) block. 5. (geol.) block, e.g. *bloques erráticos,* erratic blocks. 6. (elec.) (fuse) block. 7. (print.) block. — **b. de casas,** (C. Amer.) block of houses; **b. del motor,** (auto.) engine block; **en b.,** in bloc, all together; **b. amortiguador,** cushion block; **b. calibrador,** (mec.) gage block; **b. de cilindros,** cylinder block.
bloqueador, ra, *a.* blockading, obstructing. —*m., f.* blockader.
bloquear, *tr.v.* 1. to block, block up; to obstruct, hold up. 2. (mil., mar., pol.) to blockade. 3. (com.) to freeze, block (an account). 4. (print.) to turn (a letter, type slug, etc.) face down. 5. (med.) to block. 6. to brake (car, train, etc.).
bloqueo, *m.* (mil., mar., pol.) blockade. 2. (com.) freezing, blocking (of accounts, funds). 3. (psyc.) blocking, blockage, block. 4. (med.) block, nerve block, block anesthesia. — **b. del corazón,** (med.) heart block; **b. efectivo,** (law) effective blockade; **b. en el papel,** (law) paper blockade (consisting only of declarations); **burlar or violar el b.,** to run the blockade; **forzador de b.,** blockade runner.
bloquera, *f.* (Sp.) concrete-block machine.
bluff, *m.* bluff, sham.
blusa, *f.* blouse, tunic, ladies' shirt.
blusón, *m.* smock.
boa, *f.* (zool.) boa. —*m.* boa, lady's fur or feather stole.
boalaje, *m.* 1. pasture ground (for cattle). 2. (Arg.) tax levied on pasture ground.
boalar, *m.* community herd (of cattle).
boardilla, *f.* attic, garret.
boato, *m.* show, ostentation, show of wealth.
bobada, *f.* foolishness, silliness; foolish remark or act.
bobalías, *m., f.* (coll.) fool, nitwit, idiot.
bobalicón, na, *a.* silly, foolish. —*m., f.* (coll.) fool, idiot, clown.
bobamente, *adv.* foolishly, stupidly.
bobarrón, na, *a., m., f.* (coll.) big fool or idiot.
bobatel, *m.* (coll.) fool, idiot.
bobáticamente, *adv., var. of* **bobamente.**
bobático, ca, *a.* (coll.) foolish, silly, stupid.
bobear, *i.v.* 1. to fool, play the fool. 2. to fool, idle or trifle around.
bobera, *f., var. of* **bobería.**
bobería, *f.* 1. foolishness, foolery; foolish remark or act. 2. trifle, insignificant thing.
bóbilis bóbilis, de b. b., (coll.) free, without effort.
bobillo, *m.* 1. glazed big-bellied jug. 2. lace fichu (worn by women over the shoulders).
bobina, *f.* bobbin, spool, reel, drum; (elec.) coil, bobbin. — **b. apagachispas,** blowout coil; **b. captadora,** (rad.) pickup coil; **b. de chispas,** spark coil; b. **de inducción,** (auto.) ignition coil; **b. de indución,** induction coil; **b. de panal,** honeycomb coil; **b. de reacción** or **de reactancia,** chocking, kicking coil; **b. de regeneración or realimentación,** (elec., rad.) feedback coil; **b. de sintonización,** tuning coil; **b. de voltaje,** (elec.) pressure coil; **b. excitadora,** exciting coil; **b. móvil,** (elec.) moving coil; **b. móvil de altavoz or de la voz,** (rad.) voice coil; **b. térmica,** (tel.) heat coil; **b. vibratoria,** vibrator or trembler coil.
bobinado, *m.* (elec.) winding, coiling.
bobinadora, *f.* winding machine.
bobinar, *tr.v.* to wind, reel, spool; (elec.) to coil.
bobo, ba, *a.* foolish, stupid, dumb, silly; simple, gullible. —*m., f.* fool, nitwit, dolt, ninny, simpleton, dunce. —*m.* 1. ruff, flounce. 2. clown, jester (in comedies and farces). 3. (Cuba) old maid (card game). 4. (Guat., Mex., ichth.) barbel (Joturus globiceps). — **b. de capirote;** blithering or complete idiot; **b. de Coria,** world's greatest fool; **entre bobos anda el juego,** set a thief to catch a thief.
bobón, na, *a.* very foolish, stupid or silly. —*m., f.* fool, nitwit, dolt, simpleton, ninny, booby, chump.
bobote, ta, *a.* foolish, silly. —*m., f.* fool, nitwit, simpleton, ninny, booby, chump.
bobuno, na, *a.* foolish, stupid.
boca, *f.* 1. (anat.) mouth. 2. (zool.) pincer (of crustaceans). 3. mouth (of river, cave, tunnel, etc.), muzzle (of gun, cannon), entrance (of valley, street, etc.), opening (in oven, hearth, etc.), inlet, intake. 4. (fig.) mouth, person (to be fed or maintained). 5. cutting edge (of hoe, chisel), peen (of hammer). 6. flavor, taste (of wines). — **a. b.,** verbally, by word of mouth: **a b. de cañon,** at close range, point blank; **a b. de costal,** freely, without moderation; **a b. de jarro,** drinking without moderation, like a fish; (fig.) point blank, at close range; **a b. de noche,** at nightfall; **a b. llena,** frankly, openly, outspokenly; **abrir la b.,** to whet the appetite; **andar de b. en b.,** to be the talk of the town, to be common knowledge; **a pedir de b.,** exactly as one wants it, according to one's wish; **blando de b.,** sensitive to the bit, tendermouthed (horse); blabber-mouthed (person); **b. abajo,** on one's stomach; **b. arriba,** on one's back; **b. de agua,** hydrant; **b. de aspiración,** air inlet; **b. de desagüe, drain inlet; b. de dragón,** (bot.) snapdragon (Antirrhinum majus); **b. de escorpión,** evil tongue (person); **b. de escotilla,** hatchway; **b. de espuerta,** large mouth; **b. fuego,** firearm, ordnance piece; **b. de gachas,** (coll.) mumbler; (coll.) splutterer; **b. del estómago,** pit of the stomach, (anat.) cardiac opening; **b. de león,** (bot., Cuba) lion's mouth, snapdragon; **b. de expendio,** sales outlet; **b. de lobo,** pitch black, pitch dark; **b. de mina,** pithead; **b. de oro,** eloquent speaker, silver tongue; **b. de riego,** faucet, hydrant; **b. de verdades,** outspoken, frank person; (iron.) liar; **b. rasgada,** large mouth; **b. regañada,** mouth with puckered lip; **buscar a uno la b.,** (coll.) to provoke someone to speak, draw someone out; **cállate la b.,** shut up, shut your mouth; **cerrarle la b. a uno,** to silence someone; **de b. en b.,** from person to person, from mouth to mouth (gossip, news, etc.); **decir lo que se le viene a la b.,** to say whatever comes into one's head; **duro de b.,** insensitive to the bit, hard-mouthed (horse); **en b. cerrada no entran moscas,** silence is golden; **ganarle la b. a uno,** to persuade someone to speak, draw someone out; **hablar uno por b. de ganso,** (coll.) to say what one is told to; **hablar uno por b. de otro,** (coll.) to adopt and express somebody else's opinion; **hacer b.,** (coll.) to whet the appetite; **hacer la b. agua,** to make the mouth water; **meterse en la b. del lobo,** to go into the lion's den, go knowingly into danger; **no abrir uno la b.,** to keep silent (when one should speak); **no decir uno esta b. es mía,** (coll.) not to speak a word, not to say boo; **obedecer de b.,** to pay lip-service to; **quedarse con la b. abierta,** to be astounded, be left openmouthed or speechless; **tapar la b. a,** to silence, stop someone from talking (by bribes, etc.); to silence, squash (someone with arguments); **telón de b.,** (theat.) front curtain; **valiente de b.,** braggart, cardboard hero.
bocabajo, *m.* 1. (Cuba) flogging formerly given to slaves. 2. (P. Rico) sycophant.
bocabarra, *f.* (mar.) socket, bar hole (of a capstan).
bocacalle, *f.* street intersection; narrow street opening into a wider one.
bocacaz, (*pl.* **bocacaces**) *m.* spillway (of dam).
bocacha, *f.* 1. big mouth, blabbermouth. 2. wide-mouthed blunderbuss.
bocací, *m.* (tex.) bocasine, fine buckram.
bocada, *f., var. of* **bocanada.**
bocadear, *tr.v.* to divide into bits or mouthfuls.
bocadillo, *m.* 1. thin linen; narrow ribbon. 2. snack; cocktail canapé, appetizer or tidbit; dainty sandwich. 3. guava dessert; (Cuba, Hond.) coconut or potato dessert. 4. (theat.) bit part.
bocadito, *m.* 1. tidbit, morsel, (Amer.) cocktail canapé, appetizer or tidbit. 2. (Cuba) sandwich. 3. (Cuba) cigarette wrapped in tobacco leaf.
bocado, *m.* 1. mouthful; tidbit; morsel; bite (of food). 2. poison (in food). 3. bit, bridle; (vet.) twitch. 4. (*pl.*) dried preserves. — **b. de Adán,** Adam's apple; **b. sin hueso,** (coll.) pure profit; (coll.) cushy job, sinecure; **buen b.,** (coll.) plum; cushy job; **caro b.,** (coll.) expensive and unsatisfactory item; **con el b. en la boca,** eat and run; **me lo comería a bocados,** (coll.) I could eat it up; **quitarse el b. de la boca por alguno,** to give everything to help somebody.
bocajarro, *m.,* **a b.,** point-blank; unexpectedly.
bocal, *m.* 1. mouth, entrance. 2. (top.) gap. 3. (min.) pit head. 4. (mar.) narrows, strait. 5. (Arg.) diversion dam. 6. widemouthed wine jug (for drawing wine from jars).
bocallave, *m.* keyhole; keyhole plate.
bocamanga, *f.* cuff, wristband.
bocamejora, *f.* (min.) auxiliary shaft.
bocamina, *f.* mine entrance.
bocana, *f.* estuary, inlet.
bocanada, *f.* mouthful (of liquid); puff (of smoke). — **b. de viento,** gust of wind; **b. de gente,** (coll.) crowd, jam or crush of people; **echar bocanadas,** to boast, brag.
bocarrena, *f.* (min.) cavity in stone, lined with crystal.
bocarte, *m.* 1. (min.) crusher, ore-crushing machine, stamp mill. 2. (ichth.) anchory.
bocartear, *tr.v.* to crush (ore).
bocateja, *f.* front tile (of each line of roof tiling).
bocatería, *f.* (Ven.) boasting, bragging.
bocatero, ra, *a.* (Cuba, Hond., Ven.) boastful, bragging. —*m., f.* boaster, braggart.
bocatijera, *f.* carriage pole socket (of forecarriage).
bocatoma, *f.* 1. (Chile) spillway, sluice (of dam). 2. (hydr.) intake.
bocaza, *f.* big mouth. —m. (coll.) blabbermouth, big mouth (person who talks too much).
bocazas, *m.* (coll.) blabbermouth.
bocazo, *m.* fizzle (explosion producing no effect).
bocear, *i.v., var. of* **bocezar.**
bocece, *ref.* **bocezar.**
bocel, *m.* 1. (archit.) torus, rounded convex molding. 2. (carp.) molding plane. — **cuarto b.,** ovolo, quarter round; **medio b.,** half round (molding).
boceladora, *f.* molding plane.
bocelar, *tr.v.* to cut moldings on; to emboss.
bocelete, *m. dim. of* **bocel,** small molding plane.
bocelón, *m. aug. of* **bocel,** large molding plane.
bocera, *f.* 1. smear, stickiness on lips (after eating or drinking). 2. (med.) perleche, soreness of the lips.

boceras, *m.* braggart, mountebank.
boceto, *m.* sketch, outline, model, dummy.
bocezar, (*ref. 53*) *i.v.* to move the lips from side to side (animals).
boche, *m.* 1. (Ven.) blow of one bowl against another. 2. (Ven., coll.) rebuff, slight. 3. (Peru, Chile) fight, quarrel, uproar, tumult, riot. 4. hole in the ground (in game of chuck farthing). 5. (Chile) wheat bran. — **dar b.** or **un b. (a uno),** (Ven.) to give (someone) the cold shoulder or the brush-off.
bochinche, *m.* (Amer.) tumult, uproar; riot.
bochinchero, ra, *a.* rabble-rousing, agitating, troublemaking. —*m., f.* rabblerouser, agitator, troublemaker, gossip.
bochista, *m., f.* good bowler.
bochorno, *m.* 1. embarrassment. 2. suffocating heat; sultriness, stuffiness. 3. flush, redness; blush. — **sentir b.,** to be suffocating, be very hot; **pasar un b.,** to suffer an embarrassment.
bochornoso, sa, *a.* 1. embarrassing. 2. disgraceful, disgusting, scandalous. 3. sultry, suffocating.
bocín, *m.* 1. hubcap of bast matting (on carts). 2. feed pipe (of water wheel). 3. (Col.) stand where the stake is placed (quoit game).
bocina, *f.* 1. (rad.) speaker, loudspeaker. 2. horn (of car, gramophone); foghorn (of ship). 3. conch shell (used as a horn). 4. megaphone. 5. **B.,** (astron.) Little Bear, Ursa Minor, Little Dipper. 6. (mar.) bushing, lining (of a hole). 7. (Col., Chile) ear trumpet. 8. (mus.) horn, trumpet. 9. (Amer.) mouthpiece (of a telephone). 10. (Amer.) hubcap. — **b. exponencial,** (rad.) exponential horn; **b. de bruma,** foghorn.
bocinar, *i.v.* 1. to blow a horn. 2. to speak through a megaphone.
bocinero, *m.* hornblower.
bocio, *m.* (med.) goiter; **b. exoftálmico,** exophthalmic goiter.
bock, *m.* 1. bock beer, traditionally available in early spring. 2. beer mug.
bocón, na, *a.* 1. big-mouthed. 2. (coll.) big-mouthed, bragging, boastful. —*m., f.* 1. (coll.) big-mouthed person, blabber-mouth. 2. big mouth, braggart.
bocoy, *m.* large cask or barrel.
bocudo, da, *a.* big-mouthed.
bocha, *f.* bowl; (*pl.*) bowling; a b., (Urug.) in abundance, galore.
bochar, *tr.v.* 1. to hit and move (a bowl); to bowl. 2. (Ven., coll.) to rebuff, give the brush-off, give the cold shoulder.
bochazo, *m.* blow of one bowl against another.
boda, *f.* 1. wedding, nuptials. 2. (*pl.*) anniversary. — **bodas de diamante, de oro, de plata,** diamond, golden, silver anniversary.
bode, *m.* male goat, billy goat.
bodega, *f.* 1. wine vault or cellar. 2. big vintage, big yield of wine (of certain region). 3. tavern, barroom, taproom. 4. pantry; granary; storehouse, warehouse. 5. (mar.) hold (of a ship). 6. (Amer.) grocer's, grocery store.
bodegaje, *m.* (Amer.) storage charges.
bodegón, *m.* 1. cheap restaurant; tavern, taproom, pub. 2. (p.) still life. — **¿en qué b. hemos comido juntos?** (derog.) why the familiarity?
bodegoncillo, *m.* cheap little restaurant; **b. de puntapié,** mobile food stall.
bodegonear, *i.v.* to go pub crawling (G.B.), go bar hopping.
bodegonero, ra, *m., f.* restaurant keeper, pub keeper (G.B.). —*m.* barman, bartender. —*f.* barmaid.
bodeguero, ra, *m., f.* 1. owner or keeper of wine cellar. 2. (Amer.) grocer.
bodigo, *m.* bread roll presented in church as an offering.
bodijo, *m.* 1. (coll.) unequal match, misalliance. 2. (coll.) quiet wedding, marriage with little ceremony.
bodocal, *a.* black (grape); black grape (vine).
bodocazo, *m.* blow of a pellet (from a crossbow).
bodón, *m.* 1. pond (that dries in the summer). 2. bulrush growth.
bodonal, *m.* (Salv.) 1. muddy ground. 2. rush growth.
bodoque, *m.* 1. clay pellet (shot from a crossbow). 2. lump; (Mex.) bump, lump, swelling. 3. tuft (in embroidery, mattress). 4. blockhead, dimwit, dolt. 5. (Mex.) sloppy job, mess.
bodoquera, *f.* 1. pellet mold (for making clay pellets). 2. cradle (on the string of a crossbow for placing pellets). 3. blowgun (weapon); pea shooter.
bodorrio, *m.* (coll.), *var. of* **bodijo.**
bodrio, *m.* 1. soup formerly given to the poor. 2. poorly seasoned stew. 3. pig's blood and onions (for stuffing blood sausage). 4. (fig.) hodgepodge, jumbled mixture.
bóer, *a., m., f.* Boer, Afrikaner.
boezuelo, *m.* decoy ox (used in patridge hunting).
bofarse, *r.v.* to grow spongy; to sag.
bofe, *m.* lung; (*pl.*) lights (of animals); **echar uno el b. or los bofes,** to work oneself hard; (Amer.) to pant, be out of breath; **ser un b.,** (Cuba, coll.) to be an unpleasant, disagreeable person.
bofena, *f., var. of* **bofe.**
bófeta, *f.* (tex.) tarlatan, thin stiff muslin.
bofetada, *f.* 1. slap. 2. insult, slap in the face. — **dar una b. a uno,** to slap; to insult, slight, snub.
bofetán, *m., var. of* **bófeta.**
bofetón, *m.* 1. hard slap (in the face). 2. (fig.) insult, slight, snub. 3. (theat.) revolving panel, used for quick changes of set.
bofo, fa, *a.* spongy, soft, flabby.
boga, *f.* 1. rowing. 2. (fig.) vogue, fashion, style, e.g. *estar en b.,* to be in vogue or in fashion. 3. (ichth.) bream. — **b. arrancada,** (mar.) quick strong rowing; **b. larga,** (mar.) slow rhythmic rowing. —*m., f.* rower, oar.
bogada, *f.* distance covered in one oar stroke.
bogador, ra, *m., f.* rower (of a boat).
bogante, *a.* rowing.
bogar, (*ref. 51*) *i.v.* to row. —*tr.v.* (min., Chile) to skim (molten metal).
bogavante, *m.* 1. (zool.) lobster (Homarus gammarus). 2. strokesman (of a galley).
bogie, boggie, *m.* bogie, truck.
Bogotá, *f.,* Bogota, capital of Colombia.
bogotano, na, *a.* of or from Bogota, Colombia. —*m., f.* inhabitant or native of Bogota.
bogue, bogué, *ref.* **bogar.**
bohardilla, *f., var. of* **buhardilla.**
bohemia, *f.* 1. Bohemia, bohemian life. 2. **B.,** Bohemia, a region of Central Europe.
bohemiano, na, *a., m., f.* Bohemian (native of Bohemia).
bohémico, ca, *a.* Bohemian (pertaining to Bohemia).
bohemio, mia, *a.* 1. Bohemian (pertaining to the Central European region of Bohemia). 2. (fig.) bohemian (unconventional, artistic, etc.). —*m., f.* 1. Bohemian, native or inhabitant of Bohemia. 2. (fig.) bohemian (unconventional artist or intellectual). —*m.* Bohemian (language).
bohemo, ma, *a., m., f.* Bohemian.
bohena, *f.* 1. lung (of animals). 2. pork-lung sausage.
bohío, *m.* (Car.) hut, cabin (usually made of planks or canes and thatched with palm leaves).
bohordo, *m.* 1. (bot.) cattail reed; scape, stalk. 2. javelin, dart (used in tournaments).
boicot, *m.* boycott; **b. de consumidores;** consumer's strike.
boicoteador, ra, *a.* boycotting. —*m., f.* boycotter.
boicotear, *tr.v.* to boycott.
boicoteo, *m.* boycott, boycotting.
boíl, *m.* ox stable, corral for oxen.
boina, *f.* beret, French or Basque cap.
boiquira, *f.* (Amer.) rattlesnake.
boira, *f.* mist; haze.
boite, *m.* night club, discotheque.
boj, *m.* 1. (bot.) boxwood. 2. boxwood block used by shoemakers. 3. (mar.) *var. of* **bojeo.**
boja, *f.* (bot.) southernwood.
bojar, *tr.v.* 1. to sail around an island. 2. (mar.) to measure the perimeter of (an island or cape). 3. to scrape clean (leather). 4. to smooth (cordovan leather) with a currier's knife. —*i.v.* to measure (miles) in perimeter.
boje, *m.* (bot.) boxwood tree.
bojear, *tr.v.* 1. (mar.) to measure the perimeter of (an island or cape). 2. to sail around an island. —*i.v.* 1. to measure (so many miles) in perimeter.
bojedad, *f.* (Mex.) simpleness, foolishness.
bojedal, *m.* boxwood grove.
bojeo, *m.* (mar.) measuring of the perimeter (of an island or cape).
bojiganga, *f.* (theat.) company of strolling comedians.
bojo, *m.* (mar.) measuring of the perimeter (of an island or cape).
bojote, *m.* (Col., Hond., Ven.) bundle, parcel, package; **estar uno hecho un b.,** (coll.) to be badly dressed.
bojotero, *m.* (Col.) bagasse packer, person who forms bagasse into bundles (to be dumped in the furnace of a sugar mill).
bol, *m.* 1. punch bowl; bowl. 2. fishing net. 3. casting (of a fishing net). 4. ninepin (game). 5. red clay. — **b. arménico** or **de Armenia,** Armenian bole, red clay.
bola, *f.* 1. ball; globe, sphere; pellet; ball bearing; (Amer.) marble, (*pl.*) marbles (game). 2. grand slam (in cards). 3. (mar.) truck, signal disks. 4. shoe polish. 5. (coll.) rumor, lie, hoax. 6. game in which iron balls are thrown, the winner being the player who throws the farthest. 7. (Col.) police car. 8. (Chile) large round kite. 9. (Mex.) turmoil, uproar, quarrel. 10. (Ven.) round tamale. 11. (*pl.*) (Cuba, Chile) kind of croquet (game. 12. (Cuba) rumor, gossip, humbug. — **b. de alcanfor,** moth ball; **b. de billar,** billiard ball; **b. de cristal,** crystal ball (of fortune teller); **b. de nieve,** snowball; (bot.) snowball; **b. negra,** blackball (in voting); **¡dale b.!** (coll.) sock it!; **dar b. a,** to polish, shine; (Amer.) to take notice of, pay attention to; **dejar que ruede** or **dejar rodar la b.,** to let something ride, let things take their course; **no dar pie con b.,** to be unable to do anything right.
bolacha, *f.* (Bol.) ball of crude rubber.
bolada, *f.* 1. cast, throw (of ball or bowl); stroke, shot (in billiards). 2. (artil.) chase (of cannon). 3. small avalanche. 4. (Amer.) lie, hoax, rumor. 5. (Chile) delicacies, goodies, food parcel. 6. (Arg., Ven.) opportunity, piece of luck (in business). — **de b.,** in a row, one after another.
bolado, *m.* 1. fondant made of syrup, egg white and lemon and dissolved in water to make a refreshing drink. 2. (Chile, Hond., Mex.) affair, business. 3. (Mex.) love affair. 4. (Hond.) skillful stroke (in billiards).
bolandista, *m.* Bollandist, a Jesuit hagiographer.
bolaño, *m.* stoneshot (fired from a medieval cannon).

bolardo, *m.* (mar.) bollard, mooring post.
bolazo, *m.* blow with a ball. — **de b.,** (coll.) hurriedly, carelessly.
bolchevique, *a., m., f.* Bolshevik.
bolcheviquismo, *m.* Bolshevism, political doctrine advocating the overthrow of capitalism; Russian communism.
bolchevismo, *m., var. of* **bolcheviquismo.**
bolchevizar, (*ref. 53*) *tr.v.* to Bolshevize.
boldina, *f.* (chem.) boldine, boldin, an alkaloid.
boldo, *m.* 1. (bot.) boldo. 2. (pharm.) medicinal drink made from boldo leaves.
boleada, *f.* (Arg.) deer hunt (using bolas).
boleador, *m.* (Mex.) shoeshiner, bootblack.
boleadoras, *f.* (*pl.*) bola, bolas (hunting sling used by gauchos).
bolear, *tr.v.* 1. to throw a ball; (fig.) to impel. 2. (Arg., Urug.) to lasso or sling with a bolas. 3. (Arg., Urug.) to play a dirty trick on; to confuse, trick, deceive, perplex, entangle. 4. (Amer., sl.) to fail, flunk, plough (in an examination); to blackball, reject, vote against. 5. (Mex.) to polish, shine (shoes). —*i.v.* 1. to bowl; to knock the ball about (in certain games). 2. (coll.) to fib, lie. —*r.v.* 1. to rear and buck, and roll over on its back (a horse). 2. to trip, stumble. 3. (Arg., Urug.) to be confused or perplexed; to be tricked or deceived.
boleco, ca, *a.* (Guat.) drunk.
boleo, *m.* 1. knocking a ball about (in certain games).
bolera, *f.* bowling alley.
bolero, *m.* 1. (mus.) bolero (Spanish dance). 2. bolero (women's jacket). 3. (C. Amer.) top hat. 4. (Peru) cup and ball (toy). —*m., f.* 1. bolero dancer. 2. fibber, liar. —*a.* 1. truant. 2. fibbing, lying. — **el B. de Ravel,** (mus.) Ravel's Bolero.
boleta, *f.* 1. ticket, slip, voucher, warrant; pay voucher, warrant or slip; entrance ticket, pass. 2. (mil.) billet, lodging warrant. 3. (Amer.) certificate, e.g. *b. de sanidad,* health certificate. 4. (Amer.) ballot, voting slip. 5. (Arg.) ticket (given for driving offense). 6. small packet of tobacco. 7. (Chile, Bol.) rough draft of document. — **b. de venta,** sales check; **dar b.,** (coll.) to send (an unpleasant person) packing.
boletar, *tr.v.* to make up small paper packets of (tobacco).
boletería, *f.* (Amer.) ticket office, box office.
boletero, *m.* 1. billeting officer. 2. (Amer.) ticket seller or agent.
boletín, *m.* 1. bulletin, gazette, newsletter. 2. ticket, voucher, warrant. — **b. meteorológico,** weather report.
boleto, *m.* 1. (Amer.) ticket (for train, theater, bus, etc.). 2. (Amer.) lottery ticket. — **b. de ida y vuelta,** round trip ticket; **b. de venta,** sales ticket or slip; promissory sales contract; **medio b.,** half fare.
bolichada, *f.* 1. cast of a dragnet. 2. (coll.) lucky shot or break. — **de una b.,** at one throw, at the same time.
boliche, *m.* 1. jack (in game of bowls); bowling, ninepins; bowling alley. 2. bilboquet, cup and ball game. 3. inferior quality tobacco. 4. small charcoal kiln; lead-melting furnace. 5. (Amer.) cheap-jack shop; small shop; cheap restaurant. 6. (Cuba) meat cut for pot roast. 7. (mar.) small dragnet. 8. small fish. 9. bowline (for small net).
bolichear, *i.v.* (Arg.) to engage in small business transactions.
bolichera, *f.* (Peru) fishing smack, purse seiner.
bolichero, ra, *m., f.* 1. attendant or owner of a bowling alley. 2. (Arg.) retailer, small business man.
bólido, *m.* 1. bolide, fireball; meteor, shooting star. 2. (fig.) anything that is very quick or fast.
bolígrafo, *m.* ball point pen.
bolillo, *m.* 1. bobbin used in lace making. 2. iron pin placed at one end of a pool table. 3. mold for stiffening gauze or lace cuffs; gauze or lace cuff edging. 4. coffin bone (in horse's hoof). 5. (Arg.) rolling pin; (Mex.) bread roll. 6. (*pl.*) bars of candy. 7. (Amer.) (*pl.*) drumsticks.
bolín, *m.* jack (in bowls). — **de b., de bolán,** (coll.) without reflection, thoughtlessly.
bolina, *f.* 1. (mar.) bowline; (mar.) sounding line, lead; (mar.) hammock clew. 2. (mar.) flogging. 3. (mar.) bearing which lies at a distance of 67.5 degrees on either side of the ship's course. 4. (coll.) uproar, pandemonium, row; **echar de b.,** to boast, brag; **ir** or **navegar de b.,** to sail close to the wind, sail close-hauled; **viento de b.,** wind blowing from the direction toward which a boat is sailing.
bolinche, bolindre, *m.* 1. marbles (game). 2. (carp.) knob-like ornament carved on a piece of furniture.
bolineador, ra, *a.* (mar.) sailing well (when close-hauled or close to the wind).
bolinear, *i.v.* (mar.) to sail close to the wind, sail close-hauled.
bolinero, ra, *a.* 1. (mar.) sailing well (when close-hauled or close to the wind). 2. (Chile) quarrelsome, noisy, troublemaking, brawling.
bolisa, *f.* spark, hot cinder.
bolista, *m.* (Mex.) rowdy, brawler, troublemaker.
bolita, *f. dim. of* **bola,** small ball; (Amer., coll.) numbers game, illegal betting.
bolitero, ra, *m., f.* numbers runner.
bolívar, *m.* bolivar, Venezuelan monetary unit.
bolivariano, na, *a.* Bolivarian (relating to Simón Bolívar).
Bolivia, *f.* Bolivia.
boliviano, na, *a., m., f.* Bolivian. —*m.* boliviano, former Bolivian monetary unit.
bolla, *f.* (arch.) tax on the manufacture of playing cards.
bolladura, *f.* 1. dent, unevenness. 2. embossing. 3. bump, bruise.
bollar, *tr.v.* 1. to stamp with a trade mark or name of manufacturer. 2. to emboss.
bollén, *m.* (bot.) rosaceous tree (Kagenekia oblonga).
bollería, *f.* bakery, baker's shop, bun shop.
bollero, ra, *m., f.* 1. baker. 2. bun seller.
bollo, *m.* 1. bun, roll. 2. bulge; boss (in metal) caused by a blow; lump, bump, swelling (on the head). 3. goffer, crimp, ruffle (in dress border or in upholstery). 4. (Col.) tamale; (Sp., reg.) fritter; puffed cruller. 5. (Chile) lump of clay (for making a tile). 6. (Hond.) punch. 7. (Amer., vulg.) the female pudendum. — **b. de relieve,** embossment (on silverware); **b. maimón,** bun; marzipan filled with fruit confectionery.
bollón, *m.* 1. boss, stud, large-headed ornamental nail. 2. button earring. 3. embossment (on beaten silverware). 4. (bot.) bud, shoot.
bollonado, da, *a.* embossed (with ornamental nails), studded.
bolo, *m.* 1. ninepin, (*pl.*) ninepins, bowling. 2. grand slam, clean sweep (in cards). 3. dunce, nitwit, ignoramus. 4. (theat.) second-rate company of traveling actors. 5. (archit.) newel post. 6. (pharm.) large pill. 7. (Phil. I.) type of machete. — **b. alimenticio,** bolus; **b. arménico** or **de Armenia,** Armenian bole; **echar a rodar los bolos,** to stir up trouble, make mischief. —*a.* 1. thickwitted, dumb, ignorant. 2. (C. Amer.) drunk. 2. (Cuba) tailless (birds).
bolómetro, *m.* (phys.) bolometer, instrument that measures radiant energy.
bolón, *m.* 1. (Chile) large cobblestone used in the foundations of a building. 2. (Mex., Cuba) disorderly crowd.
bolonio, *a.* (coll.) ignorant, thickwitted, stupid. —*m.* (coll.) dunce, ignoramus.
boloñes, sa, *a., m., f.* Bolognese, from the Italian city of Bologna.
bolsa, *f.* 1. bag, sack, purse, pouch; pucker (in clothes); (*pl.*) (anat.) scrotum. 2. stock exchange; stock market. 3. wealth, money, fortune. 4. (med.) pocket (of pus); (anat.) bursa, sac. 5. (min.) pocket (of ore). — **alargar uno la b.,** to collect money to meet some big expense; **bajar** or **subir (la** b.), to drop or rise (stock exchange prices); **b. alcista,** bull market; **b. bajista,** bear market; **b. de agua caliente,** hot water bottle; **b. de aire,** (ornith.) air cell (of birds); (aer.) air hole, air pocket, air trap; **b. de comercio,** stock exchange; **b. de corporales,** (ecc.) altar-cloth or corporal container; **b. de dormir,** sleeping bag; **b. de granos,** corn exchange; **b. negra,** black market; b. **de pastor,** (bot.) shepherd's purse; **b. de trabajo,** labor exchange; **b. de valores,** stock exchange; **b. de vapor,** vapor lock; **b. de hielo,** ice pack; **hacer bolsas,** to pucker (clothes); **jugar a la b.,** to buy or sell stocks on margin, speculate on the stock market; **la b. o la vida,** your money or your life; **no abrir fácilmente la b.,** to be tight-fisted.
bolsada, *f.* (min.) pocket, cavity, pocket of rich ore.
bolsear, *tr.v.* 1. (Guat., Hond., Mex.) to pick (someone's) pocket, pick the pocket of. 2. (Chile) to cadge from, sponge on. 3. (Arg., Bol., Peru) to jilt. 4. to pucker, wrinkle.
bolseo, *m.* (Chile) cadging, sponging.
bolsera, *f.* snood, a baglike net formerly used by women to hold up the hair.
bolsería, *f.* 1. bag or purse-making; bag or purse factory or store. 2. collection of bags or purses.
bolsero, *m.* 1. bag maker or seller. 2. (Chile) cadger, sponger.
bolsico, *m.* (Chile) pocket (in clothes).
bolsicón, *m.* (Ecuad., Col.) coarse woolen skirt worn by country women.
bolsicona, *f.* (Ecuad., Col.) woman who wears a **bolsicón.**
bolsillo, *m.* 1. pocket. 2. (fig.) pocket, money, income, fortune, e.g. *cada uno debe vivir de acuerdo a su b.,* everyone ought to live according to his pocket. — **b. del pantalón,** trouser pocket; **b. de parche,** patch pocket; **consultar con el b.,** to examine the state of one's finances; **libro de b.,** pocketbook; paperback, small book; **meterse a uno en el b.,** to win someone's favor or support; **sacarse** or **voltearse los bolsillos,** to turn out one's pockets; **tener en el b.,** to have in one's pocket, hace in one's power or under one's control, to have (someone or something) in the bag.
bolsín, *m.* meeting or meeting-place of stockbrokers after the closing of the market.
bolsiquear, *tr.v.* (Amer.) to search (someone's) pockets, frisk.
bolsista, *m.* stockbroker, member of a stock exchange.
bolso, *m.* 1. handbag, purse. 2. (mar.) billow, bulge (of sails).
bolsón, *m.* 1. *aug. of* **bolsa,** large bag. 2. wooden base (of olive crusher). 3. (mas.) iron brace. 4. (Amer.) school bag. 5. (C. Amer.) dunce, fool. 6. (Bol.) pocket (of ore).
bolsudo, da, *a.* baggy, loose.
bomba, *f.* 1. (mec.) pump. 2. fire engine. 3. (mil.) bomb, shell. 4. lamp globe; (Peru) electric light bulb. 5. (mus.) slide (of trombone, etc.). 6. large

earthenware basin (used to collect overflow of oil and water in oil mills). 7. (coll.) improvised verses. 8. (Amer.) bubble. 9. (Amer.) lie, rumor. 10. (Car.) gas station (U.S.). 11. (sl., Amer.) something great. 12. (Amer.) drunk, drinking bout. 13. (Amer., coll.) attractive woman. 14. (Cuba, Mex.) top hat. 15. (Ecuad.) aerostatic balloon. — **a prueba de bombas,** bombproof; **¡bomba!** (*interj.*) listen! attention! silence! **b. alimenticia** or **de alimentación,** feed pump; b. **al vacío, vacuum pump; b. alternativa,** reciprocating pump; **b. aspirante,** suction pump; **b. atómica.** atomic bomb; **b. cazabobos,** booby-trap bomb; **b. centrífuga,** centrifugal pump; **b. colgante** or **suspendida,** sinking pump; **b. corazón-pulmón,** heart-lung machine; **b. de acción retardada,** time bomb; **b. de aceite,** (auto.) oil pump; **b. de agua,** water pump; **b. de aire,** pump. **b. de carena,** (mar.) bilge pump; **b. de cobalto,** cobalt bomb; **b. de combustible,** fuel pump; **b. contadora,** metering gasoline pump; **b. de dispersión,** cluster bomb; **b. de émbolo,** piston pump; **b. de estribo,** stirrup pump; **b. de mano,** hand pump; (mil.) hand grenade; **b. de neutrones,** neutron bomb; **b. de paso recto,** straightway pump; **b. de sentina,** sump pump, (mar.) bilge pump; **b. de sumidero,** sump pump; **b. de tiempo,** or **de relojería,** time bomb; **b. espiral,** screw pump; **b. fétida,** stink bomb; **b. estomacal,** stomach pump; **b. fumígena,** smoke bomb; **b. H** or **de hidrógeno,** hydrogen bomb, H-bomb; **b. impelente,** force pump; **b. incendiaria,** incendiary bomb; **b. lacrimógena,** tear gas canister; **b. Molotov,** Molotov cocktail; **b. reforzadora,** booster pump; **b. rompemanzanas,** (mil.) blockbuster; b. **rotatoria** or **rotativa,** rotary pump; **b. trampa,** bobby-trap bomb; **b. voladora,** flying or buzz bomb; **caer como una b.,** to fall or come like a bombshell; (Cuba, sl.) to be disagreeable, unpleasant, shocking; **estar echando bombas,** (coll.) to be very hot; **estar en b.,** (Amer.) to be drunk; **pegarse una b.,** (Amer.) to get dead drunk; **ser una b.,** (Peru) to be useless or hopeless, be a dead loss.

bombacáceo, ea, (bot.) *a.* bombacaceous. —*f.* (*pl.*) Bombacaceae.

bombáceo, ea, *a., f.* (*pl.*), *var. of* **bombacáceo.**

bombacha, *f.* (Amer.) short baggy trousers. — **pantalones de b.,** knickers.

bombache, *m.* (Cuba), *var. of* **bombacha.**

bombacho, *a.* baggy, loose-fitting (trousers). —*m.* (*pl.*) baggy trousers.

bombaje, *m.* pumping.

bombarda, *f.* 1. (mil.) bombard, ancient mortar. 2. (arch.) small war vessel (with bomb-throwing mortars); two-masted sailing vessel. 3. (mus.) bombard, bombardon (instrument); bombarde (bass organ stop).

bombardear, *tr.v.* 1. to bombard, shell; to bomb. 2. (phys.) to bombard. — **b. de rebote,** to skip-bomb; **b. en picado** or **picada,** to dive-bomb.

bombardeo, *m.* 1. bombardment, shelling; bombing. 2. (phys.) bombarding. — **b. aéreo,** air raid; **b. a gran** or **poca altura,** high or low altitude bombing; **b. de precisión,** precision bombing; **b. de rebote,** skip bombing; **b. de saturación,** saturation or area bombing; **b. en picada** or **picado,** dive bombing.

bombardero, ra, *a.* bombarding; bombing; **lancha b.,** gunboat. —*m.* 1. bombardier, gunner, artilleryman. 2. bomber (plane and person).

bombardino, *m.* (mus.) saxhorn.

bombardón, *m.* (mus.) bombardon, bass tuba, bass saxhorn.

bombasí, *m.* bombazine, fustian (fabric).

bombástico, ca, *a.* bombastic, inflated, grandiose.

bombazo, *m.* 1. bomb explosion; bomb blast, bomb damage. 2. (Arg., coll.) uncommon occurrence.

bombé, *m.* gig, light two-wheeled one-horse carriage.

bombeado, da, *past part. of* **bombear.** —*a.* curved, convex, arched; warped.

bombeador, *m.* pumpman, pumper.

bombear, *tr.v.* 1. to shell, bomb. 2. to make curved, convex or arched. 3. (Amer.) to pump. 4. (Arg., Urug.) to reconnoiter, scout; to observe, watch, spy on. 5. (Col.) to dismiss, fire (coll.). 6. (Amer.) to fail (an exam). 7. to praise lavishly. —*r.v.* to become curved, convex or arched.

bombeo, *m.* 1. convexity, curve, arching, warping. 2. (Amer.) pumping.

bombera, *f.* (Cuba) insipidity, dullness, inanity; inane remark.

bombero, *m.* 1. fireman. 2. pumper. 3. (Arg., Urug.) scout, spy, reconnoiterer. —*a.* dull, stupid.

bómbice, *m.* (ento.) bombyx, silkworm.

bombilla, *f.* 1. electric light bulb. 2. tube (for drawing off liquids); (Arg., Urug.) small tube for sucking maté out of a gourd. 3. (Mex.) large ladle. 4. (mar.) ship's lamp. 5. lamp chimney. — **b. de luz instantánea,** (photog.) flash bulb.

bombillo, *m.* 1. trap in drainpipe. 2. thief tube. 3. (mar.) hand pump. 4. (Amer.) electric light bulb.

bombín, *m.* (coll.) bowler hat, derby.

bombista, *m., f.* 1. pumpmaker. 2. praiser, bombastic journalist or writer.

bombo, ba, *a.* 1. (coll.) dazed, stunned. 2. (Cuba) lukewarm; tasteless, insipid (said of fruit). —*m.* 1. bass drum; bass drummer. 2. barge, flat-bottomed boat. 3. revolving drum (used in lotteries); leather bag or basket from which numbered billiard balls are drawn by lot by the players. 4. fuss, ballyhoo, noise, fanfare, publicity. — **dar b. a,** (coll.) to make a great fanfare about, praise to the skies; **de b. y** platillos, (coll.) bombastic, showy; **hacer** or **hacerse b.,** to blow one's own trumpet.

bombón, *m.* 1. bonbon (candy). 2. (Phil. I.) bamboo bowl. 3. (Cuba) ladle (for stirring juice in sugar cane mills).

bombona, *f.* demijohn, narrow-necked bottle for storing wine.

bombonaje, *m.* (bot.) jipijapa, a palm-like plant whose leaves are used in the manufacture of Panama hats.

bombonera, *f.* bonbonniere, candy or chocolate box or dish.

bombote, *m.* (Ven.) barge.

bombotó, *m.* (P. Rico, cul.) a coconut pastry.

bonachón, na, *a.* good-natured, genial, easygoing. —*m., f.* good-natured and easygoing person.

bonaerense, *a.* of or from Buenos Aires. *m., f.* inhabitant or native of Buenos Aires.

bonancible, *a.* tranquil, calm, still, serene (sea, wind or weather).

bonanza, *f.* 1. fair weather, calm at sea. 2. (fig.) bonanza, prosperity. 3. (min.) bonanza, rich ore deposit.

bonanzoso, sa, *a.* prosperous, flourishing, thriving.

bonapartismo, *m.* (hist.) Bonapartism, the Bonapartist party.

bonapartista, *a., m., f.* (hist.) Bonapartist.

bonazo, za, *a. aug. of* **bueno,** extremely good; (coll.) good-natured, easygoing.

bondad, *f.* goodness, kindness, kindliness. — **tener la b. de** + *inf.,* to be so kind as to + *inf.,* please + *inf.,* e.g. *tenga la b. de esperar,* would you be so kind as to wait.

bondadosamente, *adv.* kindly; gently.

bondadoso, sa, *a.* kind; good, good-natured, gentle.

bondoso, sa, *a., var. of* **bondadoso.**

boneta, *f.* (mar.) bonnet, additional canvas laced on to sail in moderate winds.

bonetada, *f.* (coll.) raising of hat (in greeting).

bonetazo, *m.* blow with a cap or bonnet.

bonete, *m.* 1. bonnet, cap. 2. (coll.) secular priest. 3. flaring candy dish. 4. (fort.) bonnet, small two-faced outwork at a salient angle. 5. (zool.) bonnet, reticulum, second stomach of ruminants. — **gran b.,** big shot (coll.), important, influential person.

bonetería, *f.* 1. cap-making; cap factory or store. 2. (Amer.) notions store.

bonetero, *m.* 1. cap maker or seller. 2. (bot.) spindle tree.

bonetillo, *m.* hair ornament.

bonetón, *m.* (Chile) game of forfeits.

bonga, *f.* (bot., Phil. I.) areca, palm.

bongo, *m.* (C. Amer.) bungo, bongo, large canoe or dugout; (Amer.) small ferryboat.

bongó, *m.* bongo drum.

bonhomía, *f.* bonhomie, goodfellowship.

boniatal, *m.* (Amer.) field of sweet potatoes.

boniatillo, *m.* (Cuba, cul.) a confection of sweet potatoes.

boniato, *m.* (bot.) sweet potato.

bonico, ca, *a., var. of* **bonito.**

bonificación, *f.* 1. bonus (given to employee to augment salary). 2. (S. Amer.) increased production, rise in production. 3. (com.) discount, reduction.

bonificar, (*ref. 50*) *tr.v.* 1. to increase (production). 2. (com.) to give a discount to.

bonifique, bonifiqué, *ref.* **bonificar.**

bonina, *f.* (bot.) oxeye, ringflower.

bonísimo, ma, *a. super. of* **bueno,** very good, extremely good.

bonítalo, *m.* ichth.) bonito, striped tuna.

bonitamente, *adv.* 1. prettily, attractively. 2. artfully, cunningly.

bonito, *m.* (ichth.) bonito, skipjack, striped tuna.

bonito, ta, *a.* pretty, attractive.

bonitura, *f.* prettiness, loveliness.

bonizal, *m.* cornfield, field of **bonizo.**

bonizo, *m.* type of small-grained, short-stalked corn.

Bonn, *m.* Bonn, capital of West Germany.

bono, *m.* (com.) bond, certificate; voucher, meal ticket. — **b. contribución,** charity raffle ticket; **b. del estado,** government bond; **b. de tesorería,** debenture bond; **b. perpetuo** or **sin vencimiento,** annuity bond.

bonzo, *m.* (rel.) bonze, a Buddhist monk.

boñiga, *f.* cattle dung.

boñigo, *m.* turd, piece of dung.

Bootes, *m.* (astron.) Bootes, a constellation.

boqueada, *f.* gasp. — **dar la última b.,** to give one's dying gasp; **dar las boqueadas** or **estar dando las boqueadas,** to be at death's door; to be about to finish.

boquear, *i.v.* 1. to open one's mouth, gasp. 2. to be in the throes of death. 3. (coll.) to be about to end. —*r.v.* to pronounce, utter; to mouth.

boquera, *f.* 1. sluice in an irrigation ditch. 2. window of a hayloft. 3. (med.) sore, crack (at the corner of the mouth); (vet.) ulcer (in the mouth).

boqueriento, ta, *a.* (Chile) having sores at the corners of the mouth.

boquerón, *m.* 1. large hole, opening or gap. 2. (ichth.) small variety of sardine (Sardinella allecia).

boqueta, *m., f.* (Col., Ven.) harelipped person.

boquete, *m.* gap, narrow entrance; breach, opening, pass.
boqui, *m.* (Chile, bot.) a climbing plant (used in the manufacturing of baskets).
boquiabierto, ta, *a.* gaping, openmouthed; (fig.) fascinated, astonished, agape.
boquiancho, cha, *a.* wide-mouthed.
boquiangosto, ta, *a.* narrow-mouthed.
boquiblando, da, *a.* tender-mouthed.
boquiconejuno, na, *a.* rabbit-mouthed, with a mouth like a rabbit (horse).
boquiduro, ra, *a.* hard-mouthed (animal).
boquiflojo, ja, *a.* (Mex., coll.) talkative, loquacious.
boquifresco, ca, *a.* 1. fresh-mouthed (horse). 2. (coll.) straightforward, outspoken (person).
boquifruncido, da, *a.* pucker-mouthed (horse).
boquihendido, da, *a.* wide-mouthed (horse).
boquihundido, da, *a.* said of a horse with an indented mouth.
boquilla, *f.* 1. *dim. of* **boca.** 2. lower opening of trouser leg. 3. outlet (of irrigation ditch). 4. (mus.) mouthpiece (of musical instrument); cigarette holder, cigar holder; stem, mouthpiece (of pipe); tip (of cigars), cork tip (of cigarette). 5. (carp.) mortise. 6. (mil.) clamp holding forward end of stock of the gun barrel. 7. (mil.) fuse hole (of projectiles). 8. metal ring (at the mouth of scabbard). 9. nozzle (of a hose pipe); burner (of gas jet). — **b. con filtro,** filter tip (cigarette); **b. de collar,** (mec.) ring chuck; **b. de guía,** (mec.) jig bushing; **b. regadera,** sprinkler head; **b. de manguera,** hose nozzle; **b. rociadora,** spray nozzle; **de b.,** (gambling) without putting up the stake money; with no intention of carrying out one's promise.
boquimuelle, *a.* 1. soft-mouthed (horse). 2. (fig.) docile, easily-managed, tractable; gullible, simple.
boquín, *m.* coarse baize (fabric).
boquinatural, *a.* normal-mouthed (horse).
boquinegro, gra, *a.* black-mouthed, black-snouted (animal). —*m.* (zool.) a land snail with a black head and yellowish body.
boquineto, ta, boquinete, ta, (Col., Ven.) *a.* harelipped. —*m.* harelipped person.
boquirrasgado, da, *a.* wide-mouthed.
boquirroto, ta, *a.* 1. wide-mouthed. 2. (coll.) talkative, loquacious, garrulous.
boquirrubio, bia, *a.* 1. (fig.) blabbing, garrulous, indiscreet, talkative. 2. inexperienced, naive, ingenuous, candid. —*m.* (coll.) playboy, dandy.
boquiseco, ca, *a.* dry-mouthed.
boquitorcido, da, *a., var. of* **boquituerto.**
boquituerto, ta, *a.* wry-mouthed (horse).
boracita, *f.* (min.) boracite.
boratado, da, *a.* (chem.) borated. — **talco b.,** (pharm.) medicated powder.
boratera, *f.* (Amer.) borate deposit.
boratero, ra, *a.* (Chile) borate. —*m.* (Chile) borate dealer.
borato, *m.* (chem.) borate.
bórax, *m.* (chem.) borax.
borbollar, *i.v.* to bubble, boil.
borbollear, *i.v., var. of* **borbollar.**
borbolleo, *m.* bubbling, boiling.
borbollón, *m.* bubbling. — **a borbollones** (fig.) impetuously, hastily.
borbollonear, *i.v., var. of* **borbollar.**
Borbón, *m.* (hist.) Bourbon.
borbónico, ca, *a.* (hist.) Bourbon, pertaining to the Bourbons.
borbonismo, *m.* (hist.) Bourbon regime, Bourbonism.
borbor, *m.* bubbling, boiling.
borborigmo, *m.* (med.) borborigmy, bowel sounds.
borboritar, *i.v.* to bubble, boil.
borbotar, *i.v.* 1. to bubble, boil (water). 2. to bubble out, gush out (blood).
borbotear, *i.v., var. of* **borbotar.**
borboteo, *m.* bubbling, boiling, gushing.
borbotón, *m.* bubbling, boiling. — **a borbotones,** in a torrent, in a gush, e.g. *hablar a borbotones,* to speak in a torrent of words, *la sangre salía a borbotones,* the blood flowed out in a torrent, the blood was gushing out.
borceguí, (*pl.* **borceguíes**) *m.* ankle boot, half boot, buskin.
borceguinería, *f.* ankle boot factory or shop.
borceguinero, ra, *m., f.* ankle boot maker or dealer.
borcelana, *f.* 1. (Mex.) chamber pot. 2. wash basin. 3. cup and saucer.
borcellar, *m.* brim, rim (of a cup or jar).
borda, *f.* 1. (mar.) gunwale. 2. (mar.) mainsail (of a galley). 3. hut, cottage. — **arrojar por la b.,** to throw overboard; **b. entrante; por encima de la b.,** (mar.) overside.
bordada, *f.* 1. (mar.) board (course made on one tack). 2. (coll.) pacing to and fro. — **dar bordadas,** (mar.) to tack back and forth; to pace to and fro.
bordado, *past part. of* **bordar.** —*m.* embroidering; embroidery. — **b. a canutillo,** embroidery with beads and bugles; **b. de realce,** raised embroidery.
bordador, ra, *m., f.* embroiderer.
bordadura, *f.* 1. embroidery. 2. (her.) bordure.
bordaje, *m.* (mar.) side planks.
bordar, *tr.v.* 1. to embroider. 2. (fig.) to do (something) with grace and beauty.
borde, *m.* edge, border, side; brim, rim (of a cup, jar, etc.); (mar.) board, side (of a ship). — **al b. de,** on the brink of, on the verge of; **al b. del mar,** on the seashore; **b. de salida,** (aer.) trailing edge.
borde, *a.* 1. wild, uncultivated (plants). 2. bastard, illegitimate. —*m., f.* bastard, illegitimate child.
bordeadora, *f.* (mec.) tube expander, beading tool; flue roller, ridger.
bordear, *tr.v.* 1. to skirt, go round, go round the edge of. 2. to border on, approach, come near to. *i.v.* (mar.) to tack back and forth.
bordejada, *f.* (Amer.) *var. of* **bordada.**
bordejear, *i.v.* (Amer.) *var. of* **bordear.**
bordelés, sa, *a.* of or from Bordeaux, France. —*m., f.* inhabitant or native of Bordeaux. —*f.* wine cask of 225 liters.
bordillo, *m.* curb, margin (of a sidewalk, platform, etc.).
bordinga, *f.* (mar.) reinforcement plank.
bordo, *m.* 1. (mar.) shipboard, side of a ship. 2. (mar.) board (course made on one tack). 3. (Guat., Mex.) dam, dyke. — **a b.,** aboard, on board; **al b.,** alongside (ship); **dar bordos,** (mar.) to tack; **de alto b.,** (mar.) large sea-going (vessel); (fig.) important, top-flight, top-drawer (person, business).
bordón, *m.* 1. Jacob's staff, pilgrim's staff. 2. (poet., mus.) refrain, burden; pet word, pet phrase (continually repeated by someone in conversation). 3. (mus.) bass strings (of guitar, etc.); (mus.) snare (of a drum). 4. (mus.) bourdon (drone bass as, e.g. bagpipes; organ stop). 5. guide, staff, mainstay, support (of a person). 6. (print.) omission, out. 7. (surg.) catgut used to dilate body ducts.
bordoncillo, *m.* pet word, pet phrase.
bordonear, *i.v.* 1. to go along tapping the ground with a staff. 2. to wander around begging. 3. (mus.) to strum on a guitar. 4. (Ven., Peru) to buzz (insects).
bordoneo, *m.* strumming (of a guitar).
bordonería, *f.* wandering, roving, vagrancy.
bordonero, ra, *a.* wandering, vagrant. —*m., f.* tramp, vagabond, vagrant.
bordura, *f.* (her.) bordure.
boreal, *a.* boreal, northern. — **aurora b.,** aurora borealis, northern lights; **hemisferio b.,** (geog.) northern hemisphere.
bóreas, *m.* 1. Boreas, the north wind. 2. (myth.) **B.,** Boreas.
borgoña, *m.* Burgundy, Burgundy wine; **B.,** Burgundy (region of France).
borgoñón, na, *a., m., f.* Burgundian, from Burgundy, France.
borgoñota, *f.* burgonet, an ancient helmet.
boricado, da, *a.* (chem.) containing boric acid.
bórico, *a.* (chem.) boric.
boricua, *m., f. a.* Puerto Rican.
Borinquen, *f.* aboriginal and poetic name of Puerto Rico.
borinqueño, ña, *a., m., f.* Puerto Rican.
borla, *f.* 1. tassel, tuft; tassel on academic cap. 2. (*pl.*) (bot.) amaranth. — **tomar la b.,** to take a doctor's or master's degree.
borlarse, *r.v.* (Amer.) to become a doctor; take a higher degree.
borlilla, *f.* (bot.) anther.
borlón, *m.* 1. large tassel or tuft. 2. (tex.) dimity. 3. (*pl.*) (bot.) amaranth.
borne, *m.* 1. point, tip (of jousting lance). 2. (elec.) binding post, terminal screw, connection terminal. 3. (bot.) a kind of oak tree. —*a.* hard, brittle, splintery (wood).
borneadero, *m.* (mar.) 1. swinging berth. 2. berth of a ship at anchor.
borneadizo, za, *a.* pliant, flexible, easily twisted or warped.
bornear, *tr.v.* 1. to twist, bend, warp. 2. to carve, cut (a column). 3. (archit.) to set in place (building stones). 4. (archit.) to check alignment of (a plank, row of posts, etc.) with the eye. 5. (Mex.) to roll (the ball) so as to knock down as many pins as possible (in bowling). —*i.v.* (mar.) to swing or turn on its moorings (a ship). —*r.v.* to become warped or twisted.
borneo, *m.* 1. bending, warping, twisting. 2. (mar.) twisting at anchor (ship); (mar.) twisting or turning space (space in which ships can turn around). 3. swinging or twisting of the body (in a dance). 4. alignment (with the eye).
borneol, *m.* (chem.) borneol.
borni, (*pl.* **borníes**) *m.* (ornith.) marsh harrier.
bornido, *m.* (sl.) hanged man.
bornizo, *a.* **corcho b.,** cork obtained from the first stripping of cork oak.
boro, *m.* (chem.) boron.
borococo, *m.* (Cuba) muddle, confusion, hurly-burly.
borona, *f.* 1. (bot.) millet; maize, Indian corn. 2. maize bread; (Col., C. Rica, Ven.) bread crumb.
borondanga, *f.* (coll.) heap of junk or rubbish; hodge-podge.
boronía, *f.* stew of tomato, eggplant, squash and red peppers.
boroschi, *m.* (zool.) wild dog (Chrysocion brachyurus).
borosilicato, *m.* (chem.) borosilicate.
borra, *f.* 1. sediment, dregs, lees. 2. yearling ewe. 3. shortest part of the wool. 4. goat's hair. 5. nap, down. 6. fluff (of cotton or dust). 7. livestock tax. 8. (coll.) trash, nonsense, idle chatter.
borra, *f.* (chem.) borax.
borrable, *a.* erasable.
borracha, *f.* wineskin, leather wine bottle.
borrachada, *f.* drunkenness.

borrachear, *i.v.* (coll.) to get drunk frequently, drink a great deal.
borrachera, *f.* 1. drunkenness. 2. drinking bout, spree, binge. 3. (coll.) enthusiasm, fury. — **coger una b.,** to get drunk; **irse de b.,** to go on a spree, go on a binge.
borrachería, *f.* (vulg.) bar, public house, pub.
borrachero, *m.* (bot.) thorn apple, jimson weed.
borrachez, *f.* 1. drunkenness. 2. (fig.) delirium, mental derangement.
borrachín, *m. dim. of* **borracho,** habitual drunkard.
borracho, a, *a.* 1. drunk, tipsy, intoxicated. 2. violet, wine-colored. 3. (fig.) drunk, blind, inflamed (with anger, passion, etc.). 4. Chile) rotten, over-ripe (fruit). — **b. como una cuba,** blind drunk. —*m., f.* drunk, drunken person; drunkard, sot, habitual drunkard. —*m.* small cake soaked in rum.
borrachón, na, *m., f. aug. of* **borracho,** drunkard.
borrachuela, *f.* (bot.) bearded darnel.
borrachuelo, la, *m., f.* drunkard.
borrado, da, *past part. of* **borrar.** —*a.* (Peru) pock-marked.
borrador, *m.* 1. rough copy, rough draft. 2. day book, shopkeeper's blotter. 3. (Amer.) rubber, eraser. — **sacar de b. a** (coll.) to dress up.
borradura, *f.* erasure, deletion.
borragináceo, a, borragíneo, a, *a.* (bot.) boraginaceous. —*f.* (*pl.*) Boraginaceae.
borraj, *m.* chem.) borax.
borraja, *f.* (bot.) borage.
borrajear, *tr.v.* to doodle; to scribble, scrawl.
borrajo, *m.* 1. ember, cinder. 2. pine straw, pine tags, dried pine needles.
borrar, *tr.v.* 1. to rub out, erase; to scratch out, cross out, strike out, delete, expunge. 2. to erase (e.g. thought, memory); (comput.) to zap.
borrasca, *f.* 1. storm, tempest, squall. 2. (fig.) storm, danger. 3. (coll.) orgy, revel. 4. (min., Mex.) lack of ore in mining lode.
borrascoso, sa, *a.* stormy, tempestuous.
borrasquero, ra, *a.* (coll.) rowdy, turbulent, licentious.
borratina, *f.* (Arg., coll.) erasure (esp. of names of candidates from a ballot).
borregada, *f.* flock of yearling sheep.
borregaje, *m.* (Chile) *var. of* **borregada.**
borrego, ga, *m., f.* yearling sheep or lamb. 2. boob, simpleton, gullible person. —*m.* (Cuba, Mex.) rumor, false news.
borreguero, ra, *a.* (land) suitable for pasturing sheep or lambs. —*m., f.* shepherd(ess) in charge of sheep.
borreguil, *a.* lamb-like, sheep-like.
borrén, *m.* joint of the saddle tree and the pad of the saddle, bolster, cantle.
borrica, *f.* 1. she-ass, female donkey. 2. (vulg.) stupid woman. —*a.* (vulg.) ignorant, stupid, dense (woman, girl).
borricada, *f.* 1. herd of asses. 2. donkey ride. 3. (coll.) asinine or stupid remark or action.
borrical, *a.* asinine; stupid.
borrico, *m.* 1. ass, donkey. 2. (carp.) sawhorse, carpenter's bench. 3. (vulg.) fool, dolt, ass. —*a.* (vulg.) stupid, asinine (man, boy).
borricón, *m.* 1. (coll.) drudge, plodder. 2. scaffold horse, large sawhorse. —*a.* drudging, hardworking, toiling.
borricote, *m., a.* (coll.) *var. of* **borricón.**
borrilla, *f.* down, fuzz (on fruit).
borriqueño, ña, *a.* asinine, ass-like.
borriquero, *m.* donkey boy, donkey or ass driver. —*a.* **cardo b.,** (bot.) cotton thistle.
borriquete, *m.* 1. (carp.) sawhorse; carpenter's bench. 2. (mar.) lower foretopsail.
borro, *m.* 1. yearling lamb. 2. sheep tax.
borrominesco, *a.* (archit.) in the style of Boromini and Bernini (Italian architects who influenced seventeenth-century Spanish architecture).
borrón, *m.* 1. ink blot, smudge. 2. blemish, blot. 3. rough draft, rough copy; (p.) preliminary sketch. 4. (*pl.*) (print.) excess of paste (on overlay). — **b. y cuenta nueva,** (fig.) clean slate.
borronear, *tr.v.* to scribble, scrawl; to doodle; to outline.
borroniento, ta, *a.* (Chile) *var. of* **borroso.**
borroso, sa, *a.* muddy, cloudy, turbid (a liquid), full of dregs or sediment; smudgy, smeared, illegible (writing); (fig.) blurred, indistinct (object).
borrumbada, *f.* 1. (coll.) boast, **brag. 2.** ostentatious or extravagant expenditure.
boruca, *f.* uproar, tumult, noise, din.
boruga, *f.* (Cuba) refreshment made of curdled milk and sugar.
borujo, *m.* 1. small lump or ball. 2. oil cake (residue left after extracting oil from olive pips).
borujón, *m., var. of* **burujón.**
boruquiento, ta, *a.* (Mex.) noisy, boisterous, gay.
borusca, *f.* dry fallen leaves; brushwood.
boscaje, *m.* 1. boscage, thicket, copse, grove. 2. (p.) woodland scene, landscape.
boscoso, sa, *a.* wooded, woody; woodland.
Bósforo, *m.* Bosphorus, Bosporus.
bosorola, *f.* (C. Amer.) sediment, dregs.
bosque, *m.* wood, forest. — **b. maderable,** timber forest.
bosquecillo, *m.* thicket, copse.
bosquejado, da, *a.* outlined, sketchy.
bosquejador, ra, *a.* sketching. —*m., f.* sketcher.
bosquejar, *tr.v.* to sketch, outline, draft.
bosquejo, *m.* sketch, outline, draft.
bosquete, *m. dim. of* **bosque,** thicket, copse, tended grove or park.
bosquimán, *m.* Bushman (nomadic hunter of South Africa).
bosta, *f.* horse dung, cow dung.
bostece, bostecé, *ref.* **bostezar.**
bostezador, ra, *a.* yawning. —*m., f.* a person who yawns frequently.
bostezante, *a.* yawning.
bostezar, (*ref. 53*) *i.v. to yawn.*
bostezo, *m.* yawn.
bota, *f.* 1. boot. 2. wineskin, leather wine bottle; cask, wine cask. 3. liquid measure of 516 liters. — **b. de montar,** riding boot; **b. fuerte,** tall wide riding boot; **b. de potro,** (Arg.) riding boot made of the skin of a horse's leg; **estar uno de botas** or **con las botas puestas,** to be ready; **ponerse uno las botas,** (coll.) to become rich, strike it rich; to take advantage of or profit from (a situation, etc.).
botabarro, *m.* (Chile) mudguard, fender.
botada, *f.* 1. launching (of a ship). 2. (Cuba) dismissal, firing.
botadero, *m.* 1. (Chile, Peru) dump, rubbish heap, garbage heap. 2. (Col.) ford.
botado, da, *a.* 1. (Amer.) cheap, given away. 2. (Mex.) drunk. —*m.,* f. foundling waif.
botador, ra, *a.* 1. bucking (horse). 2. (Amer.) wasteful, extravagant, prodigal. —*m.* 1. (mar.) boat pole. 2. (carp.) punch, nail set. 3. (dent.) pelican. 4. (print.) shooting stick for loosening and tightening quoins.
botadura, *f.* (mar.) launching. — **b. de plata,** (Amer.) waste of money.
botafuego, *m.* 1. (artil.) linstock. 2. (coll.) hothead, firebrand, spitfire, quick-tempered person.
botafumeiro, *m.* (coll.) thurible, censer. — manejar el b., (coll.) to flatter, fawn upon.
botaganado, *m.* (ry.) cow-catcher.
botagueña, *f.* (cul.) pork haslet sausage.
botalomo, *m.* bookbinder's tool for shaping back of a book.
botalón, *m.* (mar.) boom; (Col.) hitching post or stake.
botamanga, *f.* (Chile) cuff.
botamen, *m.* pots and jars in a drugstore; water casks aboard a ship.
botana, *f.* 1. patch (on wineskins). 2. plug (in wine barrels). 3. (coll.) plaster (on a wound). 4. scar. 5. (Col., Cuba) leather sheath on cock's spurs. 6. (Mex., Guat.) cocktail canapé, appetizer or tidbit.
botanga, *f.* (mar.) outrigger.
botánica, *f.* 1. botany. 2. (Amer.) store where medicinal herbs are sold.
botánico, ca, *a.* botanical; **jardín b.,** botanical garden. —*m., f.* botanist.
botanista, *m., f.* botanist.
botar, *tr.v.* 1. to throw; to cast, fling, hurl; (Amer.) to throw away. 2. to launch (boat). 3. (mar.) to turn, shift (helm). 4. (Amer.) to dismiss, fire (sl.). 5. (Amer.) to waste, squander. —*i.v.* 1. to bounce, rebound (ball). 2. to jump, bound (person). 3. to prance, caper (horse). —*r.v.* (equit.) to buck.
botaratada, *f.* (coll.) madcap, rash or foolish action.
botarate, *m.* 1. (coll.) madcap, fool. 2. (Amer.) spendthrift.
botarel, *m.* (archit.) abutment, buttress.
botarete, *a.* **arco b.,** (archit.) flying buttress.
botarga, *f.* 1. (arch.) loose breeches, galligaskins. 2. clownish or multicolored costume (worn in carnivals). 3. clown, merry andrew, buffoon. 4. a kind of sausage.
botasilla, *f.* (mil.) boots and saddles, bugle call for the saddling of horses.
botavante, *m.* (mar., arch.) boarding pike.
botavara, *f.* (mar.) gaff, boom. — **b. de cangreja,** gaffsail boom.
bote, *m.* 1. thrust, blow (with lance or spear). 2. bounce (of a ball or person); prance, caper (of a horse); ricochet, rebound (of projectile). 3. chuck farthing hole. 4. pot, jar. 5. (Amer., sl.) jug, jail, clink. 6. (Chile) freezer. — **b. de carnero,** bucking (of a horse); **de b. y voleo,** instantly, immediately, right away; **b. de metralla,** grapeshot canister, case shot.
bote, *m.* rowboat. — **b. de remos,** rowboat; **b. de salvamento, b. salvavidas,** rescue boat, lifesaving boat, lifeboat; **darse el b.** (coll.) to beat it, to abscond. **de b. en b.,** chockfull, packed, completely full.
botecario, *m.* ancient wartime tax.
botella, *f.* 1. bottle. 2. liquid measure of .7563 liters. 3. (Cuba) sinecure, soft job (coll.). — **b. de greda,** (Chile) porous bottle (used for cooling by evaporation); **b. de Leiden,** (phys.) Leyden jar.
botellazo, *m.* blow with a bottle.
botellería, *f.* (Col., Guat., Hond.) refreshments parlor or kiosk, soft drinks bar.
botellero, *m.* 1. bottle manufacterer; bottle dealer. 2. bottle rack; wire basket for bottles. 3. (Mex.) seller of refreshments. —*a.* (Cuba) said of politicians or persons who give out or receive sinecures.
botellón, *m. aug. of* **botella,** big bottle; (Mex.) demijohn.
botequín, *m.* (mar.) scull.
batería, *f.* 1. wineskin shop, shop of a wineskin maker. 2. (mar.) water casks aboard a ship. 3. (Arg., Chile) shoe shop or factory.

botero, *m.* 1. wineskin maker or seller. 2. (Chile) shoemaker, shoe dealer. 3. boatman, skipper. — **Pedro B.,** (coll.) the devil.
botica, *f.* 1. pharmacy, drugstore. 2. medicines. 3. (fig.) ingredient, drug, mixture. 4. store, stall, shop. — **de todo como en b.,** everything under the sun.
boticario, ria, *m., f.* druggist, pharmacist. —*f.* pharmacist's wife.
botija, *f.* 1. short-necked earthen jug or ewer. 2. (Cuba) tin milk jug. 3. (Cuba, bot.) poró-poró tree (Cochlospermun vitifolium). 4. (C. Amer.) buried treasure. 5. (coll., Urug.) child. — **decir b. verde a,** (Col., Cuba) to insult; **estar hecho una b.,** (coll.) to be in a tantrum (a child); to be very fat.
botijero, ra, *m., f.* maker or seller of earthen jars.
botijo, *m.* 1. two-spouted earthen jar with a handle. 2. small plump child. 3. (coll.) chunky fellow.
botijuela, *f.* 1. gratuity, tip. 2. gift given on finishing a transaction.
botilla, *f.* 1. woman's boot. 2. small winebag.
botiller, *m., var. of* **botillero.**
botillería, *f.* 1. refreshment kiosk, soft-drink store, ice cream parlor. 2. (Chile) soft-drink business, liquor or wine business.
botillero, *m.* 1. refreshment kiosk attendant, refreshment seller, ice cream parlor owner. 2. (Mex.) shoe dealer.
botillo, *m.* small wineskin.
botín, *m.* 1. half boot, bootee, high shoe. 2. spat, gaiter. 3. (Chile) sock.
botín, *m.* booty, plunder; spoils of war.
botina, *f.* bootee, ladies' ankle boot.
botinería, *f.* bootmaker's shop; boot shop.
botinero, ra, *a.* black-footed (cattle). —*m.* bootmaker, boot seller.
botiquín, *m.* 1. medicine cabinet or chest; medical kit. 2. (Ven.) retail liquor store.
botito, *m.* man's elastic-sided or buttoned ankle boot.
botivoleo, *m.* (sport.) returning or striking a ball on the bounce.
boto, ta, *a.* 1. blunt, obtuse. 2. (fig.) obtuse, dull, slow on the uptake. —*m.* skin (used to make wineskins).
botocudo, da, *a., m., f.* Botocudo (a member of the Tapuyan tribe of Brazil).
botón, *m.* 1. button (for clothes). 2. knob, handle. 3. bell push. 4. (bot.) bud; gynecium. 5. (archit.) bead, annulet. 6. (fenc.) button, safety guard on sword tip. 7. (Cuba) contemptuous reproach. 8. (mus.) valve button (of wind instrument); (mus.) button (knob in end block to which tailpiece of violin is secured). — **al b.,** (Arg., Chile) in vain; **b. del cebador,** (auto.) choke button; **b. de arranque,** (auto.) starter pedal; (elec.) starting button; **b. de fuego,** (med.) cautery; **b. de mando,** control knob; **b. de oro,** (bot.) creeping crow-foot; **b. de sintonía** or **sintonización,** (rad.) tuning knob.
botonadura, *f.* buttons, set of buttons.
botonar, *i.v.* (Cuba, Chile) to bud.
botonazo, *m.* (fenc.) thrust with a foil.
botoncillo, *m.* (bot.) buttonwood.
botonería, *f.* button factory; button shop.
botonero, ra, *m., f.* button maker; button seller. —*f.* panel of push buttons.
botones, *m.* (coll.) page, bellboy, buttons.
bototo, *m.* 1. (Chile, Ecuad.) gourd or calabash for carrying water. 2. (Chile) clodhopper.
botulina, *f.* (bac.) botulin.
botulismo, *m.* (med.) botulism.
botuto, *m.* 1. (bot.) long hollow stem of the papaw fruit. 2. war trumpet (of the Orinoco River Indians).
bou, *m.* trawling by paired fishing boats.
bóveda, *f.* 1. vault, dome, cupola; arch. 2. vault (vaulted chamber; underground chamber; crypt, burial chamber). 3. (anat.) vault. 4. (fig., poet.) vault or canopy of heaven, sky. — **b. celeste,** vault of heaven, canopy of heaven; sky, firmament; **b. cilíndrica,** (archit.) barrel vault; **b. claustral, b. de aljibe,** (archit.) cloister vault; **b. de crucería,** (archit.) groin vault; **b. de medio punto,** (archit.) semicircular arch; **b. esférica,** (archit.) dome; **b. craneal,** (anat.) cranial vault; **b. de seguridad,** bank vault; **b. en cañón,** (archit.) barrel vault; **b. fingida,** (archit.) fake or imitation vault; **b. palatina,** (anat.) hard palate; **b. por arista,** (archit.) intersection or cross vault; **b. vaida,** (archit.) groined vault.
bovedilla, *f.* 1. (archit.) small vault (between rafters). 2. (mar.) counter. — **subirse uno a las bovedillas,** (coll.) to be (all) up in the air, blow up, lose one's temper.
bóvido, *a.* (zool.) bovid. —*m.* bovid; (*pl.*) Bovidae.
bovino, na, *a., m.* (zool.) bovine.
boxeador, *m.* boxer, pugilist.
boxear, *i.v.* to box.
boxeo, *m.* boxing, pugilism.
boya, *f.* buoy; floating cork (supporting edge of fishing net). — **b. de amarre** or **anclaje,** mooring buoy; **b. de espía,** warping buoy; **b. luminosa,** gas buoy, light buoy; **b. de campana, b. sonora,** (mar.) bell buoy; **b. de salvamento, b. salvavidas,** life buoy; **b. de silbato,** (mar.) whistling buoy; **b. de tambor, b.-túnel, b. cilíndrica,** can buoy; **de buena b.,** thriving, flourishing, enjoying good fortune.
boyada, *f.* herd of oxen.
boyal, *a.* cattle-like.
boyante, *a.* 1. thriving, prosperous, flourishing, enjoying good fortune. 2. (mar.) buoyant, sailing high in the water. 3. (taur.) listless and easily managed (bull).
boyar, *i.v.* to float; (mar.) to be afloat again.
boyazo, *m. aug. of* **buey,** large ox.
boycot, *m.* (Angl.) boycott.
boycotear, *tr.v.* to boycott.
boycoteo, *m.* boycott, boycotting.
boyé, *m.* (Bol.) snake (kept in plantations to destroy vermin).
boyera, *f.* ox pen, ox stable.
boyeriza, *f.* ox pen, ox stable.
boyerizo, *m.* ox driver.
boyero, *m.* 1. ox driver. 2. (astron.) **B.,** Bootes (northern constellation). 3. (ornith.) oriole.
boyezuelo, *m. dim. of* **buey,** small ox.
Boy Scout *m.* Boy Scout.
boyuno, na, *a.* bovine, ox-like.
boza, *f.* (mar.) stopper (lashing for checking and holding cable); (mar.) painter, guesswarp, small boat, mooring line.
bozal, *a.* 1. simple, stupid, doltish, dimwitted. 2. unskilled, inexperienced, green, clumsy. 3. wild, untamed (horse). —*m., f.* 1. (coll.) simpleton, dimwit. 2. (coll.) greenhorn, novice, bungler, duffer. —*m.* 1. muzzle; (calf's) spiked noseband (to prevent it from suckling); ornamental bells (on a halter); (Cuba, Chile, Mex.) halter.
bozalillo, *m.* (Ecuad., Mex.) headstall; halter.
bozo, *m.* down (on upper lip). 2. muzzle, mouth (exterior part of the mouth). 3. halter (for leading horses).
Br *sym. of* **bromo,** bromine (Br).
brabante, *m.* 1. brabant (linen cloth). 2. B., Brabant.
bracamarte *m.* (mil., arch.) broadsword, one-edged sword.
braceada, *f.* swinging of the arms.
braceador, ra, *a.* high-stepping (horse).
braceaje, *m.* 1. coining, minting. 2. (mar.) fathomage, depth.
bracear, *i.v.* 1. to flail or swing one's arms. 2. to make strokes, swim. 3. to struggle vigorously. 4. (equit.) to step high. —*tr.v.* 1. to brace, move by means of braces. 2. (mar.) to measure in fathoms.
braceo, *m.* 1. swinging of the arms. 2. overarm stroke (in swimming). 3. struggling. 4. (mar.) quarter yard.
braceral, *m.* (arch.) brassart (armor).
bracero, a, *a.* throwing, thrown with the hand. —*m.* 1. laborer, day laborer. 2. man who offers his arm as a support. 3. good shot, good marksman.
bracete, *m. dim. of* **brazo,** small arm. — **de b.,** (coll.) arm in arm.
bracil, *m.* (arch.) brassart, arm piece of armor.
bracillo, *m.* cheek (of horse's bit).
bracmán, *m.* (rel.) Brahman.
braco, ca, *a.* snub-nosed. —*m.* pointer, setter (dog). —*m., f.* (coll.) snub-nosed person.
bráctea, *f.* (bot.) bract.
bracteado, da, *a.* (bot.) bracteate.
bracteal, *a.* (bot.) bracteal.
bracteola, *f.* (bot.) bractlet, bracteole.
bracteolado, da, *a.* (bot.) bracteolate.
bradicardia, *f.* (med.) bradycardia, slow action of the heart.
bradilalia, *f.* (med.) bradylalia.
bradipepsia, *f.* (med.) bradypepsy, slow digestion.
bradipo, *m.* (zool.) bradypus, three-toed sloth.
bradita, *f.* (astron.) falling star, dim and slow-moving meteor.
brafonera, *f.* (arch.) rerebrace (piece of armor covering upper arm).
braga, *f.* 1. rope sling (for hoisting barrels, etc.). 2. nappy, diaper. 3. (*pl.*) panties, step-ins; (*pl.*) man's knee breeches; (*pl.*) wide breeches.
bragada, *f.* gaskin, inside of the thigh of some animals.
bragado, da, *a.* 1. with gaskins of a different color from the rest of the body (animal). 2. (coll.) malicious, malignant, trouble-making (person). 3. (coll.) energetic and firm (person).
bragadura, *f.* crotch (part of the body or of trousers).
bragazas, *m.* (coll.) docile, henpecked man. —*a.* docile, easily-managed.
braguero, *m.* 1. truss, support for rupture. 2. (Mex.) bull's girthrope used in bareback riding. 3. (Peru, equit.) martingale. 4. (mar.) breeching (rope securing gun to ship's side). 5. (Chile) baby's swaddling cloth.
bragueta, *f.* fly (of trousers).
braguetazo, *m. aug. of* **bragueta,** big fly (of trousers); **dar b.,** (vulg.) to marry a rich woman.
braguetero, *a.* (coll.) lustful, lecherous, lascivious (man); (Chile) (poor man) who makes a wealthy marriage. —*m.* lecher, libertine.
braguillas, *m.* (fig.) little boy (who has just started wearing trousers); spoilt child.
brahman, *m.* (rel.) Brahman, Brahmin.
brahmánico, ca, *a.* Brahminic, Brahminical.
brahmanismo, *m.* Brahmanism, Brahminism.
brahmín, *m.* Brahmin, Brahman.
brahón, *m.* (arch.) roll or fold in garment encircling upper arm.
brahonera, *f., var. of* **brahón.**
brama, *f.* 1. rut, heat. 2. rut, mating season (of deer, and other animals).
bramadera, *f.* 1. bull-roarer. 2. shepherd's horn. 3. (arch.) rattle (for scaring away animals). 4. (Col., Cuba) vent (of furnace).

bramadero, *m.* 1. tethering post. 2. (hunt.) rutting or mating place (deer and other animals).
bramador, ra, *a.* bellowing. —*m., f.* bellower. —*m.* (sl.) town crier.
bramante, *a.* bellowing; roaring. —*m.* 1. hemp twine; thin string, wrapping cord. 2. brabant (linen cloth).
bramar, *i.v.* to bellow (animals); to bellow, roar, rage, storm (person); to roar, howl (wind, waves etc.).
bramera, *f.* (Chile) vent (of a furnace).
bramido, *m.* bellow, roar (of angry person or savage beasts); roaring, howl (of wind or waves).
bramo, *m.* (sl.) 1. bellow. 2. outcry.
bramón, *m.* (sl.) tattletale, squealer.
bramona, *f.* **soltar la b.,** to break out into insults (gamblers).
bramuras, *f. (pl.)* fierce threats, bravadoes, display of intense anger.
bran de Inglaterra, *m.* (arch.) old Spanish dance.
branca, *f.* point of a horn; **b. ursina,** (bot.) thistle.
brancada, *f.* dragnet, sweep net.
brancal, *m.* frame, (of wagon, carriage).
brandal, *m.* (mar.) sidepiece of a rope ladder; (mar.) backstay.
brandís, *m.* (arch.) overcoat, greatcoat.
branque, *m.* (mar.) stem (of prow).
branquia, *f.* (zool.) gill, branchia.
branquiado, da, *a.* branchiate.
branquial, *a.* branchial.
branquífero, ra, *a.* branchiferous.
branza, *f.* fastening ring (for securing chains of galley slaves).
braquiado, da, *a.* brachiate.
braquial, *a.* brachial.
braquicefálico, ca, *a.* brachycephalic.
braquicéfalo, la, *a.* (anth.) brachycephalic.
braquicranio, nia, *a.* (anth.) brachycranial, brachycranic.
braquidactilia, *f.* brachydactyly.
braquidáctilo, la, *a.* (anat.) brachydactylous.
braquigrafía, *f.* shorthand writing, stenography.
braquiópodo, *a.* (zool.) brachiopod. —*m. (pl.)* (zool.) Brachiopoda.
braquiuro, *a.* (zool.) brachyuran. —*m.* (zool.) brachyuran, *(pl.)* Brachyura.
brasa, *f.* live coal, red-hot coal. — **estar como en brasas, estar en brasas,** to be on tenterhooks, be uneasy; **estar hecho unas brasas,** to be flushed, be red in the face; **pasar como sobre brasas,** to touch very lightly on.
brasero, *m.* 1. brazier, fire-pan. 2. (Mex.) hearth, fireplace.
Brasil, *m.* Brazil.
brasil, *f.* 1. (bot.) brazilwood tree, brasiletto; brazilwood; brazil, Brazil red. 2. (arch.) rouge cosmetic.
brasilado, da, *a.* red, Brazil red.
brasileína, *f.* (chem.) brasilein.
brasileño, ña, *a., m., f.* Brazilian.
brasilero, ra, *a.* (Amer.), *var. of* **brasileño, ña.**
brasilete, *m.* (bot.) brasiletto; brazilwood.
Brasilia, *f.* Brasilia, capital of Brazil.
brasilina, *f.* (chem.) brasilin, brazilin.
brasmología, *f.* science of tides.
brava, *f.* 1. (Cuba) fierce threat. 2. (Cuba) sponging, touch, bite (sl.) (for a loan). — **a la b.,** by force.
bravamente, *adv.* 1. bravely, courageously. 2. cruelly. 3. well, perfectly. 4. copiously, abundantly.
bravata, *f.* 1. fierce threat. 2. boast, brag, bravado.
bravatear, *i.v.* (Chile), *var. of* **bravear.**
braveador, ra, *a.* bullying, blustering, threatening. —*m., f.* threatener, bully.
bravear, *i.v.* to bluster, bully.
bravera, *f.* vent (of a furnace).
bravero, *m.* (Cuba) bully, braggart, blusterer.
braveza, *f.* 1. fierceness, ferocity (of beasts); fury, roughness (of sea or elements). 2. bravery (of persons).
bravío, a, *a.* wild, indomitable, savage; (fig.) wild, uncultivated (plants); (fig.) uncouth, unpolished, uneducated (person). —*m.* fierceness, ferocity (of bulls).
bravo, va, *a.* 1. fierce, ferocious (animals). 2. rough (sea). 3. brave, courageous. 4. fine, excellent. 5. craggy, rough, uneven. 6. angry, irate. 7. (coll.) bullying, boasting, blustering. 8. (coll.) ill-humored, cross-grained. 9. (coll.) sumptuous, magnificent. 10. (coll.) difficult, hard. 11. (Cuba) scheming, ambitious (person). —*interj.* **¡bravo!** well done.
bravocear, *tr.v.* (rare) to encourage. —*i.v.* to bully, bluster.
bravonel, *m.* braggart, bully.
bravosía, *f., var. of* **bravosidad.**
bravosidad, *f.* elegance, charm; arrogance, bravado.
bravoso, sa, *a., var.* of **bravo.**
bravote, *m.* (sl.) bully, boaster.
bravucón, na, *a.* (coll.) boasting, bragging. —*m., f.* boaster, braggart.
bravuconada, *f.* rodomontade, boast, brag.
bravuconería, *f.* boastfulness.
bravura, *f.* 1. fierceness, ferocity (of beasts). 2. courage, bravery, pluck. 3. bravado, bluster. 4. (mus.) bravura.
braza, *f.* 1. (mar.) fathom. 2. (mar.) brace (rope). 3. breast stroke (in swimming).
brazada, *f.* 1. stroke (in swimming and rowing). 2. armful. 3. (Col., Chile, Ven.) fathom. — **b. de espaldas,** backstroke; **b. de pecho,** breast stroke; **b. de piedra,** (Mex.) cubic measure (4.70 cubic meters) used in dealing in stone blocks.
brazado, *m.* armful.
brazaje, *m.* (mar.) fathomage, depth of water in fathoms.
brazal, *m.* 1. brassart (piece of armor); arm band. 2. clasp, handle (of a shield). 3. irrigation ditch. 4. (mar.) headrail.
brazalete, *m.* bracelet; brassart (piece of armor).
brazo, *m.* 1. arm (of body; law; armchair; balance beam, etc.); foreleg (of quadrupeds); branch (of tree, candelabrum, etc.). 2. (fig.) strength, power. 3. *(pl.)* protectors, defenders, patrons, backers. 4. *(pl.)* workmen, hands, laborers. — **a b. partido,** with bare fists; (fig.) tooth and nail; **asidos del b.,** arm in arm; **b. de gitano,** (cul.) jelly roll; **b. de grúa,** boom, jib (crane); stiffleg (derrick); **b. del ancla,** anchor arm; **de mar,** inlet; **b. derecho,** right-hand man; **b. de rio,** branch of a river; **b. de ruptura,** (auto.) breaker arm; **b. lector,** pickup arm; **b. politíco,** political wing; **b. polar,** pole arm (planimeter); **b. volado,** cantilever arm; **con los brazos abiertos,** with open arms; **con los brazos cruzados,** idly, lazily, doing nothing; **cruzarse de brazos,** to be or remain idle; **no dar uno su b. a torcer,** (coll.) to stick to one's guns, remain firm.
brazola, *f.* (mar.) coaming (of hatchways).
brazolargo, *m.* (Amer.) spider monkey.
brazuelo, *m.* 1. *dim. of* **brazo,** small arm. 2. shoulder (of an animal).
brea, *f.* 1. tar, pitch; (mar.) calking pitch. 2. tarpaulin. 3. (Guat.) dough (money). — **b. crasa,** mixture of colophony, tar and galipot; **b. mineral,** asphalt, mineral pitch; **b. seca,** colophony, rosin.
brear, *tr.v.* (coll.) to maltreat; to annoy, vex; (coll.) to make fun of, play tricks on.
brebaje, *m.* beverage, potion; (mar.) grog, drink served to ship's crew.
brebajo, *m., var. of* **brebaje.**
breca, *f.* 1. (ichth.) bleak, blay. 2. (ichth.) sea bream (Pagellus erythrinus).
brecha, *f.* 1. breach, gap; opening, hole. 2. (geol.) breccia. 3. (fig.) impression (on the mind). — **abrir b.,** (mil.) to make a breach; (fig.) to make an impression on; **batir en b.,** (mil.) to breach, batter (wall, rampart) so as to open a breach; **b. generacional,** generation gap; **estar siempre en la b.,** to be prepared, be always on the alert, be on one's guard.
brechación, *f.* (geol.) brecciation.
brechiforme, *a.* brecciated.
brecina, *f.* (bot.) kind of heather.
brécol, *m.* (bot.) broccoli.
brecolera, *f.* (bot.) broccoli.
brega, *f.* 1. fight, scrap, brawl. 2. trick, joke. — **andar a la b.,** to work very hard; **dar b. a,** to play a trick on.
bregar, *(ref. 51) i.v.* to fight, brawl, scrap; to work hard, labor, toil; to struggle (against obstacles). —*tr.v.* to work (dough) with rolling pin.
bregue, bregué, *ref.* **bregar.**
brema, *f.* (ichth.) bream.
bren, *m.* bran (of wheat or other grain).
brenca, *f.* sluice post.
breña, *f.* rugged, uneven or brambly ground.
breñal, *m.* rugged, uneven or brambly region.
breñar, *m., var. of* **breñal.**
breñoso, sa, *a.* craggy, uneven, brambly (ground, region).
breque, *m.* 1. (Amer.) shackle, fetter. 2. (Amer., ry.) hand brake. 3. luggage van. 4. (ichth.) bleak, blay.
brequero, *m.* (Amer., ry.) brakeman.
bresca, *f.* honeycomb.
brescar, *(ref. 50), tr.v.* to cut honeycombs from (beehives).
bresque, bresqué, *ref.* **brescar.**
bretaña, *f.* 1. Brittany, Brittany cloth. 2. (bot.) hyacinth. 3. **B.,** Brittany. — **Gran B.,** Great Britain.
brete, *m.* 1. shackles, fetters. 2. (fig.) tight spot, difficulty. 3. (rare) dungeon. 4. (Arg.) short passageway (for cattle). 5. (P. Rico) a love affair. — **estar en un b.,** to be in difficulties.
bretón, na, *a., m., f.* Breton. —*m.* 1. Breton (language). 2. (bot.) kale; Brussels sprout (plant), *(pl.)* Brussels sprouts (edible green heads).
bretónica, *f., var. of* **betónica.**
breva, *f.* 1. early fig (first annual fruit of the fig tree). 2. early acorn. 3. flat loosely-rolled cigar. 4. windfall, stroke of luck. — **estar más blando que una b.,** (coll.) to be as meek as a lamb.
breval, *a.* early (fig.). —*m.* early-bearing fig tree.
breve, *a.* brief, short; (gram.) short. — **en b.,** shortly, soon; in brief, in short. —*m.* papal brief. —*f.* (mus.) breve.
brevedad, *f.* brevity, briefness, shortness. — **a la mayor b. posible,** as soon as possible.
brevemente, *adv.* briefly, concisely.
brevete, *m.* 1. patent (for an invention); certificate, warrant, brevet. 2. letterhead. 3. memorandum; note. 4. (Peru) driver's license.
breviario, *m.* 1. (ecc.) breviary. 2. breviary, brief summary, compendium. 3. (print.) brevier.
brevipenne, *a.* (zool.) brevipennato. —*f. (pl).* (zool.) Brevipennates.
brezal, *m.* heath, tract of land covered with heather.
brezo, *m.* 1. (bot.) heather, heath. 2. cradle.
briaga, *f.* sling rope, hoisting rope, thick hemp or bass rope.
brial, *m.* (arch.) rich silken skirt; short overskirt (worn by soldiers).
briba, *f.* truancy, idleness, loafing. — **andar a la b.,** to live an idle life, loaf around; **hombre de la b.,** good-for-nothing person.

bribar, *i.v.* to lead a vagabond life.
bribón, na, *a.* 1. lazy, loafing, indolent. 2. roguish, rascally. —*m., f.* 1. idler, loafer, bum. 2. rogue, rascal.
bribonada, *f.* trick, piece of mischief, rascality.
bribonazo, *m.* big scamp or rascal.
bribonear, *i.v.* 1. to loaf, idle, bum around, be a bum. 2. to behave roguishly or mischievously.
bribonería, *f.* 1. idleness, laziness, loafing, idle life. 2. roguery, mischief, rascality.
bribonesco, ca, *a.* knavish, rascally, roguish.
bribonzuelo, *m.* little scamp.
bricbarca, *m.* (mar.) three-masted ship, bark.
brice, bricé, *ref.* **brizar.**
bricho, *m.* gold or silver spangle (used in embroidery).
brida, *f.* 1. bridle. 2. (mec.) flange; splice plate, bar or piece; clamp, dog. 3. (*pl.*) (surg.) fibrous membrane (which forms around edge of wounds or abscesses). — **a la b.,** riding with long stirrups; **a toda b.,** (fig.) at full gallop, at full speed; **b. ciega,** (plumb.) blind flange; blank flange; **b. de acoplamiento,** companion flange; coupling flange; **b. de enchufe,** socket flange; **b. lisa,** blank flange; **b. reductora,** reducing flange.
bridar, *tr.v.* 1. to bridle. 2. (plumb.) to flange.
bridecú, *m.* sword belt.
bridge, *m.* bridge (card game). — **b. contrato,** contract bridge; **b. remate,** auction bridge.
bridón, *m.* 1. horseman riding with long stirrups. 2. small bridle; bridoon. 3. horse with a saddle with stirrups slung low; (poet.) high spirited noble steed.
brigada, *f.* 1. (mil.) brigade; (mil.) squad, group (of soldiers); section (of ship's crew); gang, team (of workmen); team, train (of beasts of burden); fleet (of tractors, etc.). 2. (mil.) sergeant first class, sergeant major. — **b. antiexplosivos** or **de explosivos,** bomb squad; **b. de estupefacientes,** drug squad; **B. de Investigación Criminal,** Federal Bureau of Investigation, FBI.
brigadero, *m.* mule driver, pack driver (attached to army).
brigadier, *m.* 1. (mil., mar.) head cadet (in charge of section). 2. (mil.) brigadier, brigadier general; (mil., arch.) sergeant major, sergeant first class. 3. (mar.) rear admiral; (mar., arch.) corporal.
brigadiera, *f.* (coll.) brigadier's or rear admiral's wife.
brigantina, *f.* brigandine (body armor of scales and armor plates).
brigantino, na, *a.* of or from Corunna, Spain. —*m., f.* native or inhabitant of Corunna.
brigola, *f.* (mil., arch.) battering ram.
Briján, *m.* **saber más que B.,** (coll.) to be very clever and sharp-witted.
brillador, ra, *a.* sparkling, glittering.
brillante, *a.* 1. sparkling, glittering, brilliant, bright, shining. 2. (fig.) brilliant, outstanding. 3. (mus.) brilliant. —*m.* brilliant, diamond.
brillantemente, *adv.* 1. brilliantly, brightly. 2. brilliantly, outstandingly.
brillantez, *f., var. of* **brillo.**
brillantina, *f.* 1. brilliantine, shiny percaline (cloth). 2. metal polish. 3. brilliantine, hair tonic.
brillar, *i.v.* 1. to shine, sparkle, glitter. 2. to shine, stand out, excel. — **no todo lo que brilla es oro,** all that glitters is not gold.
brillazón, *m.* (Arg.) mirage.
brillo, *m.* 1. brilliance, brightness; glitter, shine. 2. splendor, glitter.
brin, *m.* fine canvas; (Amer.) canvas (used for linings and for oil painting).
brincador, ra, *a.* jumping, leaping; skipping.
brincar, (*ref. 50*) *i.v.* 1. to skip, jump, frolic, frisk. 2. (coll.) to fly into a rage. —*tr.v.* 1. to bounce (a child) up and down. 2. (coll.) to skip, omit (something).
brinco, *m.* 1. skip, hop, jump, leap. 2. (arch.) small jewel worn in a lady's headdress. — **b. hidráulico,** hydraulic jump.
brincho, *m.* highest flush (in game of **quinolas**).
brindar, *tr.v.* 1. to offer. 2. to invite. — **b. a +** *inf.,* to invite + *inf.;* **b. a alguien algo,** to offer someone something. —*i.v.* to drink a toast; **b. a** or **por,** to drink a toast to, toast. —*r.v.* to volunteer, offer; **brindarse a +** *inf.,* to offer + *inf.*
brindis, *m.* toast (to one's health).
brinque, brinqué, *ref.* **brincar.**
brinquillo, *m., var. of* **brinquiño.**
brinquiño, *m.* 1. trinket, small piece of jewelry. 2. very small sweet or candy. — **estar** or **ir hecho un b.,** (coll.) to be dressed fit to kill, to be very elegant.
briñón, *m.* (bot.) small and very tasty variety of peach.
brío, *m.* 1. spirit, vigor, enterprise, go. 2. elegance, charm.
briófita, *m.* (bot.) bryophyte.
briol, *m.* (mar.) buntline.
briología, *f.* (bot.) bryology.
brionia, *f.* (bot.) bryony.
briosamente, *adv.* spiritedly, vigorously.
brioso, sa, *a.* spirited, vigorous; enterprising.
briozoo, *m.* (zool.) bryozoan.
briqueta, *f.* briquette (coal brick).
brisa, *f.* 1. breeze, light wind. 2. skin of pressed grapes.
brisca, *f.* 1. card game. 2. the three or ace of the suits which are not trumps in this game and in the game of **tute.**
briscado, da, *past part. of* **briscar.** —*a.* hilo b., silver or gold thread (used in embroidery). —*m.* brocade, silk cloth embroidered with gold or silver thread.
briscar, (*ref. 50*) *tr.v.* to weave or embroider with gold or silver thread.
brisera, *f.* glass shade, lamp chimney (for lamp or lantern).
brisero, *m.* (Col.) *var. of* **brisera.**
brisote, *m.* strong breeze.
brisque, brisqué, *ref.* **briscar.**
bristol, *m.* Bristol board.
brisura, *f.* (her.) label.
británica, *f.* (bot.) American water dock.
británico, ca, *a.* British.
britano, na, *a.* British, pertaining to ancient Britain; English. —*m., f.* Briton.
briza, *f.* (bot.) quaking grass.
brizar, (*ref. 53*) *tr.v.* to rock (a cradle).
brizna, *f.* 1. string, fiber (of bean, etc.). 2. (Ven.) drizzle.
briznar, *i.v.* (Ven.) to drizzle.
briznoso, sa, *a.* stringy, filamented, fibrous.
brizo, *m.* cradle.
broa, *f.* 1. biscuit, cracker. 2. corn bread. 3. (mar.) shallow cove.
broca, *f.* 1. reel, bobbin (used for weaving). 2. drill, drill bit. 3. shoemaker's tack. — **b. de dos puntas,** double-ended drill; **b. buriladora,** router bit; **b. de avellanar,** countersinking bit; **b. de barrena, b. de diamantes,** diamond bit; **b. de trinquete,** ratchet drill; **b. estrellada,** star bit; **b. salomónica,** twist drill.
brocadillo, *m.* light, thin brocade.
brocado, *m.* brocade.
brocal, *m.* 1. curbstone (of boot well). 2. metal ring (at the mouth of a scabbard). 3. mouthpiece (of a wine bag). 4. (mil.) flange (on the mouth of a cannon). 5. (min.) mouth (of a shaft). 6. ornamental steel rim (of a shield).
brocamantón, *m.* (arch.) large jeweled brooch.
brocatel, *m.* brocatel, brocatelle (cloth and marble).
brocato, *m.* (Sp.) gold or silver brocade.
broce, brocé, *ref.* **brozar.**
brocearse, *r.v.* 1. (Amer., min.) to become exhausted (mine). 2. (Amer.) to fall through, fail, fold up (a business).
broceo, *m.* (S. Amer., min.) exhaustion, becoming exhausted (mine).
brocha, *f.* 1. brush, paint brush. 2. loaded dice. — **b. de afeitar,** shaving brush; **pintor de b. gorda,** house painter; (coll.) second-rate painter.
brochada, *f.* brush stroke.
brochado, da, *a.* brocaded (fabric).
brochadura, *f.* hooks and eyes, clasps, set of hooks and eyes or clasps (on coats, capes, etc.).
brochal, *m.* (archit.) header, header beam.
brochazo, *m., var. of* **brochada.**
broche, *m.* clasp, hook and eye, snap; (Chile) spring clip (for papers); (*pl.*) (Ecuad.) cuff links.
brocheta, *f.* (cul.) brochette, skewer.
brochón, *m. aug. of* **brocha,** whitewashing brush.
brocino, *m.* bump, lump, swelling.
brócula, *f.* locksmith's drill.
bróculi, *m.* (bot.) broccoli.
brodete, *m.* (coll.), *var. of* **brodio.**
brodio, *m.* (obs.) soup given to the poor at convents; poorly seasoned stew; hog's blood and onions (for stuffing blood pudding).
brollador, ra, *a.* bubbling, boiling.
brollo, *m.* (Ven.), *var. of* **embrollo,** imbroglio, confusion.
broma, *f.* joke, jest; fun, merriment, gaiety. — **b. pesada,** practical, joke; **bromas aparte,** joking apart; **déjate de bromas,** stop playing around, come on, be serious; **en b.,** as a joke; jokingly; **estar de b.,** to be in a joking mood; **gastar** or **hacer una b. a,** to play a joke on; **tomar en b.,** to take as a joke, not to take seriously.
broma, *f.* (mas.) 1. mixture of gravel, stone and mortar. 2. (zool.) shipworm.
bromal, *m.* (chem.) bromal.
bromar, *tr.v.* to gnaw, bore (shipworm.)
bromato, *m.* (chem.) bromate.
bromatología, *f.* dietetics.
bromatólogo, *m.* dietician, dietitian.
bromazo, *m.* heavy-handed joke, practical joke.
bromear, *i.v., r.v.* to joke, jest.
bromeliáceo, a, *a.* (bot.) bromeliaceous. —*f.* bromeliad; (*pl.*) Bromeliaceae.
bromhídrico, ca, *a.* (chem.) bromhydric, hydrobromic.
bromhidrosis, *f.* (med.) bromidrosis, osmidrosis, fetid sweating.
brómico, ca, *a.* (chem.) bromic.
bromirita, *f.* (min.) bromyrite, native silver bromide.
bromismo, *m.* (med.) bromism.
bromista, *a.* joking, bantering, waggish (person). —*m., f.* joker, wag.
bromito, *m.* (chem.) bromite.
bromo, *m.* 1. (chem.) bromine. 2. (bot.) brome grass.
bromuro, *m.* (chem.) bromide. — **b. de metilo,** (chem.) methyl bromide; **b. de plata,** (chem.) silver bromide; **b. potásico,** (chem.) potassium bromide.
bronca, *f.* 1. (coll.) row, quarrel. 2. (taur., theat.) razz, hiss. — **tenerle b. a,** to have one's knife into, have it in for; **armar b.,** to start a row; **echarle a uno una b.,** to tell someone off; **llevarse una b.,** to be called on the carpet.

broncamente, *adv.* roughly, harshly, gruffly.
bronce, *m.* 1. bronze (alloy, statue). 2. (poet.) cannon, bell, trumpet. 3. (numis.) copper coin. —**b. de aluminio,** aluminum bronze; **b. de campana** or **campanil,** bell metal; **b. de cañón,** gun metal; **b. fosforado,** phosphor bronze; **ser de b.** or **un b.,** (coll.) to be hard and unbending; to be a ceaseless worker, be very strong; **b. amarillo,** brass; **b. cromado,** chromium bronze; **b. duro,** hard bronze, hard or bell metal.
bronceado, da, *past part. of* **broncear.** —*a.* 1. bronze-colored. 2. bronzed, tanned. —*m.* bronzing; suntan, tan.
bronceadura, *f.* bronzing; suntan.
broncear, *tr.v.* 1. to bronze, make bronze-colored. 2. to tan, suntan, bronze. —*r.v.* to get a tan, get suntanned.
broncería, *f.* bronzes, bronze articles, bronze work.
broncíneo, a, *a.* bronze, bronzelike.
broncista, *m.* bronzesmith.
bronco, ca, *a.* 1. coarse, rough. 2. brittle (metals). 3. rasping, harsh (voice or music). 4. (fig.) rough, harsh, gruff (disposition).
bronconeumonía, *f.* (med.) bronchopneumonia.
broncorea, *f.* (med.) bronchorrhea.
broncospia, *f.* (med.) bronchoscopy.
broncoscopio, *m.* (med.) bronchoscope.
broncostenosis, *f.* (med.) bronchostenosis.
bronquear, *tr.v.* (Cuba) to reprimand severely, scold, give a tongue-lashing-(coll.).
bronquedad, *f.* 1. roughness, coarseness. 2. brittleness (of metals). 3. hoarseness, harshness (of voice or music). 4. (fig.) roughness, harshness, gruffness (of disposition).
bronquial, *a.* (med.) bronchial.
bronquiectasia, *f.* (med.) bronchiectasis.
bronquina, *f.* (coll.) scrap, quarrel.
bronquinoso, sa, bronquista, *a.* (Amer.) troublemaking.
bronquio, *m.* (anat.) bronchus, bronchial tube.
bronquíolo, *m.* (anat.) bronchiole.
bronquítico, ca, *a.* (med.) bronchitic.
bronquitis, *f.* (med.) bronchitis.
brontosaurio, brontosaurus, *m.* (paleon.) brontosaurus.
broquel, *m.* 1. buckler, small shield; (fig.) shield, defense. 2. (mar.) boxhauled position (of sails).
broquelarse, *r.v.* to shield oneself, protect oneself.
broquelazo, *m.* blow dealt with a shield or buckler.
broquelero, *m.* 1. shield maker; soldier using a buckler. 2. (fig.) troublemaker, quarrelsome person.
broqueles, *m.* (*pl.*) poling boards.
broquelillo, *m.* small button-shaped earring.
broquelona, *f.* (Bol., ento.) tick.
broquero, *m.* (Sp., mach.) bit dresser.
broqueta, *f.* brochette, skewer.
brota, *f.* bud, shoot, sprout; (Chile) budding, sprouting.
brotadura, *f.* budding, sprouting.
brótano, *m.* (bot.) southernwood.
brotar, *i.v.* 1. to sprout, bud; to send out shoots. 2. to spring, gush, rise (water). 3. (fig.) to break out, erupt (rash, etc.). 4. (fig.) to break out, appear (uprisings, plots, etc.).
brote, *m.* 1. bud, shoot, sprout. 2. outbreak, e.g. *un b. de violencia or viruela,* an outbreak of violence or smallpox.
brótula, *f.* (ichth.) brotulid, blenny.
broza, *f.* 1. brushwood (dead leaves, branches, etc.). 2. refuse, trash, rubbish. 3. undergrowth, underbrush. 4. (fig.) rubbish, nonsense. 5. (print.) printer's brush.
brozador, *m.* (print.) type cleaning table.
brozar, (*ref. 53*) *tr.v.* (print.) to brush, clean (type) with a brush.
broznamente, *adv.* roughly, harshly.
brozno, na, *a., var. of* **bronco.**
brozoso, sa, *a.* 1. brushy; covered with undergrowth. 2. (fig.) full of rubbish.
bruce, brucé, *ref.* **bruzar.**
brucelosis, *f.* (med., vet.) brucellosis.
brucero, *m.* brush and broom maker or seller.
bruces, de b., face downwards, on one's stomach; **echarse de b.,** to lie face downward; **caer de b.,** to fall flat on one's face.
brucina, *f.* (pharm.) brucin, brucine (poisonous alkaloid).
brucita, *f.* (min.) brucite.
brugo, *m.* (ento.) oak larva; plant louse.
bruja, *f.* 1. witch, sorceress. 2. (coll.) witch, old hag, crone. 3. (ornith.) owl. 4. (Cuba, bot.) day lily; atamasco lily. 5. (Cuba, ento.) owlet moth (Erebus odorata). 6. (Cuba) person who dresses up as ghost. —*a.* (coll., Cuba, Mex.) penniless, e.g. *estoy b.,* I'm broke.
brujear, *i.v.* to practice witchcraft.
brujería, *f.* witchcraft, sorcery.
brujesco, ca, *a.* witch-like, magic.
brujidor, *m., var. of* **grujidor,** glazier's nippers or trimmers.
brujidura, *f.* bewitching.
brujilla, *f.* tumbler, roly-poly (a doll on a weighted base).
brujir, *tr.v., var. of* **grujir,** to pare, trim (grass) with nippers.
brujo, *m.* sorcerer, magician, wizard, warlock. —**El Amor Brujo,** The Phantom Lover (a ballet suite by Manuel de Falla, the title in this case applying to an imagined, incorporeal lover).
brujo, ja, *a.* 1. (Chile) false, fraudulent. 2. (Cuba, Mex., P. Rico) impoverished, down and out, broke (coll.). —*m.* pauper, down and out person.
brújula, *f.* 1. magnetic needle. 2. compass (instrument for calculating direction). 3. sight (of a gun). 4. peep hole. 5. (astron.) **B.,** Compasses. —**b. de bolsillo,** pocket compass; **perder la b.,** (fig.) to lose one's touch; **b. de inclinación,** dipping compass; **b. de nonio,** vernier compass; **b. de senos,** sine galvanometer; **b. goniométrica,** radio compass.
brujulear, *tr.v.* 1. to peek and try to guess one's cards in a table game. 2. (coll.) to conjecture, surmise, guess. 3. (coll.) to scheme.
brujuleo, *m.* 1. lifting one's cards gradually in a game, trying to guess them. 2. (coll.) conjecture, surmise, guess. 3. (coll.) finagling, scheming, maneuvering.
brulote, *m.* 1. fire ship. 2. (Bol., Chile) rude word, swear word, curse, e.g. *de cirle a uno un b.,* to swear at or curse somebody. 3. (Arg., Urug.) incendiary manuscript.
bruma, *f.* fog, mist, e.g. *la b. matutina,* the morning fog.
brumador, ra, *a., var. of* **abrumador,** crushing, overwhelming.
brumal, *a.* foggy, misty, e.g. *un otoño b.,* a misty autumn.
brumamiento, *m.* fogging or misting over; fog, mist, e.g. *empezó el b.,* the fog has begun to spread.
brumar, *tr.v., var. of* **abrumar,** to crush, oppress, overwhelm; to weary, annoy.
brumario, *m.* Brumaire, second month of the French Revolutionary calendar.
brumazón, *f. aug. of* **bruma,** thick fog; (coll., G.B.) peasouper.
brumo, *m.* pure white wax (used in the final dipping of church candles).
brumoso, sa, *a.* foggy, misty, hazy, e.g. *lago brumoso,* a misty lake; *tarde brumosa,* a foggy afternoon.
bruno, *m.* black plum tree; black plum.
bruno, na, *a.* dark-colored, black, e.g. *cabellera bruna,* dark tresses; *bigote bruno,* dark mustache.
bruñido, *m., var. of* **bruñidura.**
bruñidor, ra, *a.* polishing, burnishing. —*m., f.* polisher, burnisher. —*m.* polishing or burnishing tool, buffing wheel, buffer.
bruñidura, *f.* polishing, burnishing.
bruñimiento, *m., var. of* **bruñidura.**
bruñir, (*ref. 66*) *tr.v.* 1. to polish, burnish, buff. 2. (coll.) to spruce up, ruffle one's feathers. 3. (Guat.) to annoy, bother.
bruño, *m.* black plum, black plum tree.
brusca, *f.* 1. (Ven.) stinking weed. 2. (Cuba) brushwood, kindling wood. 3. (mar.) camber, roundup, upward curvature of beams (of ship).
bruscamente, *adv.* 1. brusquely, roughly. 2. suddenly, hastily, unexpectedly, e.g. *me empujaron b.,* they pushed me roughly.
bruscate, *m.* stew of sheep's or goat's liver.
brusco, ca, *a.* 1. brusque, rough, abrupt, blunt, e.g. *no seas b.,* don't be so blunt. 2. sudden, quick. —*m.* 1. (bot.) butcher's broom. 2. harvest remains, gleanings, leavings (e.g. grapes too small for picking).
brusela, *f.* (bot.) large periwinkle, cutfinger.
Bruselas, *f.* Brussels, capital of Belgium.
bruselas, *f.* (*pl.*) jeweller's pincers.
bruselense, *a.* of or from Brussels. —*m., f.* inhabitant or native of Brussels.
brusquedad, *f.* 1. brusqueness, abruptness, bluntness. 2. suddenness.
brutal, *a.* 1. brutal, brutish. 2. (fig.) fabulous, stupendous, wonderful, terrific, tremendous; enormous, huge. —*m.* brute, beast.
brutalice, *ref.* **brutalizarse.**
brutalidad, *f.* 1. brutality, savagery, brutishness. 2. (coll.) stupidity, foolishness. 3. (coll.) slew, loads, enormous amount.
brutalizarse, (*ref. 53*) *r.v.* to become brutish.
brutalmente, *adv.* 1. brutally, savagely. 2. (fig.) fabulously, wonderfully.
brutesco, ca, *a., var. of* **grutesco.**
bruteza, *f.* brutishness; roughness, lack of polish.
Bruto, *m.* Brutus, Roman political and military leader who participated in the assassination of Julius Caesar.
bruto, ta, *a.* 1. stupid, boorish, brutish, ignorant, thick (coll.). 2. gross, total, e.g. *peso bruto,* gross weight, *ganancias brutas,* gross profit. 3. brute, e.g. *fuerza bruta,* brute force. 4. rough, uncut, unpolished, e.g. *diamante bruto,* uncut diamond. 5. (coll.) huge, enormous. 6. (Chile) unpedigreed (said of native cock as compared with English bird). —**a la bruta, a lo bruto,** (Amer.) brutally, violently, by force; **en bruto,** (fig.) in the rough, e.g. *diamante en bruto,* diamond in the rough. —*m., f.* ignoramus, blockhead, dolt, boor. —*m.* brute, beast (person; animal).
bruza, *f.* coarse brush, horse brush.
bruzador, *m.* (print.) type cleaning board or table.
bruzar, (*ref. 53*) *tr.v.* 1. (print.) to brush, clean (type) with a brush. 2. to groom (horses).
Bs. As. *abbrev. of* **Buenos Aires,** Buenos Aires.
BTU *abbrev. of* **unidad de calor británica,** British Thermal Unit (B.T.U.)
bu, *m.* (coll.) bugaboo, bogey man; **hacer el b.,** to scare, frighten.
búa, *f.* 1. (med.) bubo, pustule. 2. (med.) (*pl.*) buboes, frambesia, pian (disease).
buarillo, *m., var. of* **buharro.**

buaro, *m.*, *var. of* **buharro.**
buba, *f.* 1. (med.) bubo, pustule. 2. (med.) (*pl.*) buboes, frambesia, pian (disease).
búbalo, la, *m.*, *f.* (zool.) bubalis, bubal.
bubático, ca, *a.* (med.) buboed, having buboes. —*m.*, *f.* buboed person, person suffering from buboes.
bubi, *m.* Bube, Bubi (West African black from the island of Fernando Poo).
bubón, *m.* 1. (med.) pustule, bubo. 2. (med.) (*pl.*) buboes, frambesia, pian (disease).
bubónico, ca, *a.* bubonic; **peste b.,** bubonic plague.
buboso, sa, *a.* buboed. —*m.*, *f.* buboed person, person suffering from buboes.
bucal, *a.* buccal, pertaining to the mouth; higiene b., oral hygiene.
bucanero, *m.* (hist.) buccaneer.
bucare, *m.* (bot.) South American tree used as shade for coffee plants.
Bucarest, *m.* Bucharest, capital of Rumania.
búcaro, *m.* 1. flower vase. 2. fragrant clay. 3. (Hond.) a variety of lily (arum family).
buccino, *m.* (zool.) whelk.
buce, *ref.* **buzar.**
buceador, ra, *m.*, *f.* diver; underwater worker.
bucear, *i.v.* 1. to dive, swim under water; to work as a diver. 2. (fig.) to delve (into), investigate.
bucéfalo, *m.* 1. (coll.) dolt, oaf, blockhead. 2. **B.,** Bucephalus (Alexander the Great's horse).
bucentauro, *m.* (myth.) bucentaur, centaur with the body of a bull.
buceo, *m.* diving; underwater searching.
bucero, ra, *a.* black-nosed (hound). —*m.* black-nosed hound.
buchaca, *f.* 1. pocket, bag; (Cuba, Mex.) billiard-table pocket. 2. (Hond., coll.) jail, jug, clink.
buchada, *f.* mouthful.
buche, *m.* 1. crop, craw, maw; belly, stomach. 2. mouthful. 3. pucker, crease (in clothing). 4. bag (in a tunny fish net). 5. (fig., coll.) bosom. 6. (Ecuad.) top hat. 7. (Mex.) goiter, mumps. 8. (Cuba) bum, tramp, hobo. 9. newborn donkey; suckling donkey. — **ser un b. y plumas,** to be a bluff.
buchería, *f.* (Cuba) rudeness, coarseness.
buchete, *m.* puffed-out cheek.
buchinche, *m.* leaky garret, hovel; (Cuba) low-class tavern, dive.
buchón, na, *a.* 1. pouting (pigeon). 2. (Col.) fat, stout. 3. (Cuba) kind-hearted, good-natured. —*m.*, *f.* (*pl.*) (coll.) kids, children. —*m.* (Ven.) official who makes illicit profits from public office.
bucle, *m.* curl, ringlet, lock of hair.
buco, *m.* 1. male goat, billy goat. 2. opening, hole, gap, aperture.
bucólica, *f.* 1. bucolic (poem). 2. (coll.) meal, food; hunger.
bucólico, ca, *a.* bucolic, e.g. *poema bucólico,* bucolic poem.
bucolismo, *m.* a liking for bucolic poetry.
bucráneo, *m.* (archit.) bucranium.
bucul, *m.* (Guat.) a large dish or bowl made of a gourd or calabash.
Buda, *m.* Buddha, religious philosopher and teacher who lived in India circa 500 B.C.
Budapest, *m.* Budapest, capital of Hungary.
budare, *m.* (Ven.) baking pan (for corn bread).
búdico, ca, *a.* Buddhist, Buddhistic.
budín, *m.* pudding.
budinera, *f.* pudding pan or platter.
budión, *m.* (ichth.) blenny (Blennius pavo).
budismo, *m.* Buddhism.
budista, *a.*, *m.*, *f.* Buddhist.
buen, *a. apocope of* **bueno,** used only before masculine singular nouns and before infinitives which are used as nouns, e.g. *un buen samaritano,* a good Samaritan, *el buen vestir,* proper dressing.
buenaboya, *m.* freeman hired as a galley oarsman.
buenamente, *adv.* 1. easily. 2. voluntarily, willingly, spontaneously.
buenandanza, *f.* success, good fortune, luck, prosperity.
buenastardes, *f. pl.* (Cuba, bot.) four-o'clock.
buenaventura, *f.* good luck; fortune (as told by a fortune teller). — **decirle a uno la b.,** to tell someone his fortune.
buenazo, za, *a.* 1. (coll.) good-natured, kind, easy-going. 2. (coll.) very good, excellent, super.
buenísimo, ma, *a.* (coll.) very good, extremely good.
bueno, na, *a.* 1. good (kind, benevolent; well-behaved; of good quality; excellent; able, clever; tasty, flavorsome; funny, amusing; fit, suitable, appropriate, convenient). 2. good, considerable, big, biggish, high. 3. well, recovered, healthy. 4. wearable, serviceable, usable, in good condition (clothes). 5. simple, ingenuous. — **a las buenas,** voluntarily, willingly; **aceptar lo bueno con lo malo,** to take the good with the bad; **buenos días, buenas noches,** good morning, good evening, night; **a la buena de Dios,** (coll.) without thought or reflection, without any preparation, haphazardly; **¡buena es ésa** or **ésta!** (iron.) this is a fine state of affairs!; **está bueno,** that's enough, stop it; **de buenas a primeras,** suddenly; immediately, right away; **estar de buenas,** to be in a good mood; **lo bueno es,** (iron.) the funny or strange thing is; **por buenas** or **por la buena,** willingly.
bueno, *adv.* well, all right, very well, okay. —*m.* good (mark on an examination).
Buenos Aires, *m.* Buenos Aires, capital of Argentina.
buenpasar, *m.* good or reasonable standard of living.
buey, *m.* 1. ox, bullock. 2. (Mex., fig.) cuckold. 3. (P. Rico) packet, great amount of money. — **b. corneta,** (Arg., Chile, Urug.) one-horned ox; (Arg., Urug.) busybody, meddlesome person; (Bol.) troublemaker, agitator; **b. de agua,** water measure; volume of water (flowing from conduit or spring); (mar.) inrush of water through a porthole; **b. de cabestrillo,** or **de caza,** stalking ox; stalking horse; hunting blind; **b. de marzo,** tax paid in March; **b. marino,** (zool.) sea cow; **b. muerto,** (P. Rico) bargain, windfall; **trabajar como un b.,** to work like an ox or a horse.
bueyada, *f.* (coll.) herd of oxen.
bueyazo, *m.* (coll.) large ox.
bueyecillo, bueyecito, *m.* small ox.
bueyero, *m.* (coll.) ox driver.
bueyezuelo, *m.* small ox.
bueyuno, na, *a.* bovine, ox-like.
bufa, *f.* 1. jest, piece of buffoonery. 2. (her.) lower part of a visor. 3. (Cuba) drunk, drunken spree.
bufado, da, *a.* blown (said of glass blown extremely thin).
bufador, *m.* volcanic crevice (emitting smoke or steam).
bufalada, *f.* (bot.) mezereon.
bufalino, na, *a.* buffalo (pertaining to buffaloes).
búfalo, la, *m.*, *f.* (zool.) buffalo.
bufanda, *f.* scarf, muffler.
búfano, na, *a.* (Cuba, Ven.) spongy, soft.
bufar, *i.v.* 1. to snort (an animal). 2. (coll.) to snort, puff (with anger, exhaustion, etc.). —*r.v.* to bulge, blister (a wall, a painted surface).
bufeo, *m.* (Arg., Peru) porpoise, dolphin.
bufet, *m.* (Amer.) buffet, a self-service, informal meal.
bufete, *m.* writing desk; (fig.) lawyer's office; lawyer's clientele. — **abrir b.,** to set up practice (as a lawyer), open a law office.
bufetillo, *m.* 1. small writing desk. 2. small (lawyer's) office.
bufido, *m.* snort, bellow.
bufo, fa, *a.* buffoonish, clownish, farcical, comic; **opera b.,** comic opera. —*m.* buffoon, clown.
bufón, na, *a.* buffoonish, comic, clownish, farcical. —*m.*, *f.* clown, buffoon.
bufonada, *f.* piece of buffoonery, jest, joke; sarcastic remark.
bufonazo, *m. aug. of* **bufón.**
bufoncillo, *m. dim. of* **bufón.**
bufonear, *i.v.*, *r.v.* to act the buffoon, to joke, jest.
bufonería, *f.*, *var. of* **bufonada.**
bufonesco, ca, *a.* buffoonish, clownish, comical; vulgar, coarse.
bufonice, *ref.* **bufonizar.**
bufonizar, (*ref. 53*) *i.v.* to joke, jest, banter.
bugalla, *f.* gall, oak gall.
buganvilla, *f.* (bot.) bougainvillaea.
bugle, *m.* (mus.) bugle, musical instrument resembling a trumpet.
buglosa, *f.* (bot.) bugloss, oxtongue.
buharda, *f.* 1. dormer window. 2. attic, garret. 3. (fort.) projecting balcony or platform.
buhardilla, *f.* 1. dormer window. 2. attic, garret.
buharro, *m.* (ornith.) scops owl.
buhedal, *m.* (arch.) swampy land.
buhedera, *f.* embrasure, loophole; hole, aperture.
buhedo, *m.* pool or pond which dries up in summer.
buhero, *m.* keeper of hunting owls.
buhído, da, *a.* 1. sharp, keen. 2. grooved; striated.
buhío, *m.*, *var. of* **bohío.**
buho, *m.* 1. (ornith.) eagle owl, horned owl. 2. (coll.) retiring, antisocial person.
buhonería, *f.* peddler's wares; (*pl.*) trinkets, notions, knicknacks.
buhonero, *m.* peddler, hawker.
buitre, *m.* (ornith.) vulture; **gran b. de las Indias,** (ornith.) condor.
buitreada, *f.* (Chile, Peru) vomiting, stomach illness.
buitrear, *i.v.* 1. (Chile, Peru) to vomit, throw up (coll.) 2. (Chile) to hunt vultures.
buitrera, *f.* vulture trap; **estar ya para b.,** to be ready for the vultures, be about to die, be an old wreck.
buitrero, ra, *a.* vulturine. —*m.* vulture hunter.
buitrón, *m.* 1. (osier) fish trap. 2. partridge hunting net. 3. (Amer.) silver-smelting blast furnace. 4. ashpit (of furnace). 5. (hunt.) pit-trap for game.
buja, *f.* (Mex.) *var. of* **buje.**
bujarasol, *m.* reddish variety of fig.
bujarra, *f.* (Ven.) *var. of* **bujarrón.**
bujarrón, *a.* (vulg.) sodomitic, sodomitical —*m.* bugger (vulg.), sodomite.
buje, *m.* axle box, bushing, sleeve; shaft pillow; **b. maestro,** master bushing.
bujeda, *f.*, *var. of* **bujedal.**
bujedal, *m.* boxwood grove or plantation.
bujedo, *m.*, *var. of* **bujedal.**
bujería, *f.* baubles, gewgaws, knicknacks.
bujeta, *f.* 1. wooden box. 2. perfume bottle.
bujía, *f.* 1. candle; candlestick. 2. (phys.) candle, candlepower. 3. (mec.) sparking plug. 4. (med.) bougie. 5. **b. de Hefner,** (phys.) Hefner candle; **bujía-hora,** (phys.) candle hour; **b. decimal,** decimal candle; **b.-pie,** foot-candle.
bujier, *m.* chief of a candle-making workshop.
bujiería, *f.* candle-making workshop or factory; candle-making trade.

bul, *m.* (Cuba) shandy, a refreshing drink made with beer, sugar and lemon.
bula, *f.* 1. (hist., ecc.) bulla (medal worn by a noble Roman youth; leaden seal). 2. papal bull. — **b. de carne,** papal permission to eat meat on fast days; **b. de composición,** dispensation granted by the Commissioner General of the Crusades to persons appropriating property of unverified ownership; **b. de difuntos,** bull permitting application of indulgences to the dead; **b. de lacticinios,** bull allowing ecclesiastics to partake of lactic foods on days when this is forbidden; **echar las bulas (a uno),** to impose a burden on; (coll.) to reprimand severely; **hay bulas para difuntos,** (coll.) there is a way out of everything; **no poder con la b.,** (coll.) to have no strength for anything, be exhausted or pooped.
bulárcama, *f.* (mar.) rider, rib reinforcement in a ship's hull.
bulario, *m.* bullary, collection of papal bulls.
bulbar, *a.* bulbar, pertaining to bulbs.
bulbillo, *m.* (bot.) bulbil.
bulbo, *m.* (bot., anat.) bulb; **b. de la aorta,** (anat.) bulb of the aorta; **b. del ojo,** (anat.) bulb of the eye; **b. dental,** (anat.) bulb of the tooth; **b. piloso,** (anat.) bulb of the hair; **b. raquídeo,** (anat.) bulb of the spinal cord, medulla oblongata; **b. uretral,** (anat.) bulb of the penis or urethra; **b. electrónico,** electron tube; **b. fotoeléctrico,** photo tube, photo-electric tube.
bulboso, sa, *a.* bulbous.
buldog, *m.* (zool.) bulldog.
bulerías, *f.* (*pl.*) lively Andalusian dance and song accompanied by intricate syncopated clapping.
bulero, *m.* (rel., hist.) pardoner, person commissioned with the distribution of indulgences and dispensations.
buleto, *m.* papal brief.
bulevar, *m.* boulevard.
Bulgaria, *f.* Bulgaria.
búlgaro, ra, *a., m., f.* Bulgarian. —*m.* Bulgarian (language).
bulí, (*pl.* **bulíes**) *m.* (Phil. I., bot.) buri, buri palm.
bulimia, *f.* (med.) bulimia, insatiable hunger.
bulímico, ca, *a.* (med.) bulimic, bulimiac.
bulín, *m.* 1. (Peru, sl.) brothel. 2. (Arg.) well-furnished apartment.
bulla, *f.* 1. noise, hubbub, racket (coll.). 2. crowd. 3. (Amer.) fight; argument. — **meter a b.,** (coll.) to interrrupt, obstruct, hinder; **meter b.,** to make a noise, create a racket.
bullado, da, *a.* (Amer.) sensational, much talked about.
bullaje, *m.* crowd, throng.
bullanga, *f.* racket, noise, uproar.
bullanguero, ra, *a.* noisy, rowdy, boisterous. —*m., f.* rowdy, noisy or boisterous person.
bullar, *tr.v.* to mark with a seal (goods, etc.).
bullaranga, *f.* (Amer.) *var. of* **bullanga.**
bullarengue, *m.* 1. (coll.) bustle (of dress). 2. (Cuba) anything false or artificial. 3. (reg., Sp.) a curly hair style.
bullebulle, *m.* (coll.) busybody, nosy person, bustler.
bullente, *a.* boiling.
bullicio, *m.* noise, hubbub, bustle; uproar.
bulliciosamente, *adv.* boisterously, noisily.
bullicioso, sa, *a.* noisy, tumultuous, rowdy; boisterous, restless; lively, merry.
bullidor, ra, *a.* lively, bustling, effervescent.
bullir, (*ref. 65*) *tr.v.* 1. to move, budge. 2 (Amer.) to pester, annoy. —*i.v.* 1. to boil; to bubble. 2. swarm, teem, abound. 3. to bustle about. 4. to happen or occur frequently. 5. (fig.) to stir, budge, show signs of life.
bullón, *m.* 1. ornamental stud (trimming the binding of some large books). 2. puff (in a dress). 3. dye boiling in a cauldron.
bulo, *m.* false rumor or news (circulated for a specific purpose).
bulón, *m.* bolt, (Arg.) machine bolt; **b. de anclaje,** anchor bolt; **b. del émbolo,** (engin.) piston pin; **b. zurdo,** left-hand thread bolt.
bulonar, *tr.v.* (mec.) to bolt.
bulto, *m.* 1. bulk, volume. 2. form, shape. 3. bundle, package; bale; piece of luggage. 4. swelling, bump. 5. bust, statue. 6. pillowcase. 7. (Col., Hond., Mex.) satchel, school bag, briefcase. — **a b.,** as a whole, broadly; wholesale; **buscar a uno el b.,** (coll.) to try to pick a quarrel with someone; **coger a uno el b.,** (coll.) to lay hold of or seize someone; **de b.,** important; **escurrir, guardar or huir el b.,** (coll.) to avoid danger or risk; to evade or get out of responsibility, pass the buck; **poner de b. una cosa,** to call attention to something; **ser de b.,** to be clear or manifest.
bululú, *m.* 1. strolling player (giving solo performance). 2. (Ven.) commotion, racket, uproar, disturbance.
bumerang, *m.* boomerang, a weapong used by Australian aborigines.
buna, *f.* buna (synthetic rubber).
bunga, *f.* 1. (Cuba) small band of few but very active instruments. 2. (Cuba) lie.
bungalow, *m.* (Amer.) bungalow.
buniatal, *m.* sweet potato field or plantation.
buniatillo, *m., var. of* **boniatillo.**
buniato, *m., var. of* **boniato,** sweet potato.
bunio, *m.* 1. bulb or root left for seed. 2. (med.) bunion.
búnker, bunker, *m.* bunker.
buña, *f.* jam or preserves prepared by Araucan Indians from fried or baked fermented potatoes.
buñoleria, *f.* doughnut or cruller shop or bakery.
buñolero, ra, *m., f.* doughnut or cruller maker.
buñuelo, *m.* 1. doughnut, cruller. 2. (coll.) botch, mess, bungle (work, job).
bupresto, *m.* (ento.) buprestid, buprestid beetle.
buque, *m.* 1. ship, vessel, boat. 2. hull (of a ship). 3. capacity, space. — **b. almirante,** flagship; **b. cablero,** cable ship; **b. carguero,** freighter, cargo boat; **b. cisterna or tanque,** tanker; **b. de cruz,** (mar.) square rigger; **b. de guerra,** (mar.) warship; **b. frigorífico,** refrigerator ship; **b. de paletas or ruedas,** paddle steamer; **b. de transporte,** (mar.) transport, troopship; **b. de vapor,** (mar.) steamship, steamer; **b. de vela,** (mar.) sailboat, sailing ship; **b. en lastre,** (mar.) ship in ballast, ship traveling with no cargo; **b. en rosca,** (mar.) newly launched ship with no rigging; **b. escuela,** training ship; **b. gemelo,** sister ship; **b. hospital,** hospital ship; **b. madrina,** mother ship; **b. mercante,** (mar.) merchant ship; merchantman; **b. petrolero,** oil tanker; **b. submarino,** (mar.) submarine; **b. taller,** repair ship.
buqué, *m.* bouquet (of wine, of flowers).
buquenque, *m., f.* (Cuba) *var. of* **alcahuete.**
buraca, *f.* (Bol.) leather bag or pouch.
buraco, *m.* (reg., Sp.) hole, round opening.
burato, *m.* 1. crepe, Canton silk (fabric used during mourning). 2. thin transparent cloak or cape.
burbuja, *f.* bubble.
burbujeante, *a.* bubbling.
burbujear, *i.v.* to bubble.
burbujeo, *m.* the act of bubbling.
burchaca, *f., var. of* **burjaca,** large leather bag.
burche, *f.* tower (for defense).
burda, *f.* (mar.) backstay.
burdamente, *adv.* 1. basely, meanly. 2. coarsely, roughly.
burdégano, *m.* hinny, the offspring of a horse and a female donkey.
burdel, *a.* lustful, libidinous, licentious. —*m.* brothel, whorehouse, cathouse (sl.).
Burdeos, *m.* Bordeaux, city in France.
burdeos, *m.* Bordeaux (wine).
burdo, da, *a.* 1. coarse, rough. 2. mean, base.
burear, *i.v.* (Col.) to have a fine time, to be entertained.
burel, *m.* 1. (her.) bar (whose width is one ninth the length of the shield). —*a.* (taur.) said of a reddish brown bull.
burelado, *a.* (her.) barred (*ref.* **burel**).
burén, *m.* (Car.) flat griddle for toasting or panbroiling.
bureo, *m.* 1. a criminal court for the trial of persons of the royal household. 2. entertainment, amusement.
bureta, *f.* (chem.) burette.
burga, *f.* hot springs, spa.
burgado, *m.* small land snail.
burgalés, sa, *a.* of or from Burgos, Spain. —*m., f.* inhabitant or native of Burgos.
burgo, *m.* small town, borough.
burgomaestre, *m.* burgomaster, mayor (in some cities of Europe).
burgrave, *m.* (hist.) burgrave (hereditary lord of a burg, a title used formerly in Germany).
burgraviato, *m.* burgraviate (office or jurisdiction of a burgrave).
burgueño, ña, *a.* burghal. —*m., f.* burgess, burgher, native of a borough.
burgués, sa, *a.* bourgeois, middle-class. —*m., f.* member of the middle class, bourgeois (*m.*), bourgeoise (*f.*).
burguesía, *f.* bourgeoisie, middle class.
burguesismo, *m.* bourgeois qualities and manners.
burí, *m.* (Phil. I., bot.) buri, buri palm; buntal fiber.
buriel, *a.* dark red, e.g. *mi potro b.,* my dark red colt.
buril, m. 1. burin, graver. 2. (astron.) **B.,** Caelum, Caela Sculptoris. — **b. chaple redondo,** gouge-pointed burin; **b. chaple en forma de escoplo,** chisel-pointed burin.
burilada, *f.* 1. burin stroke or line. 2. sliver of silver used for comparison while assaying. 3. chisel cut.
buriladura, *f.* the act of engraving.
burilar, *tr.v.* to engrave with a burin; to chisel, carve.
burío, *m.* (Hond.) (bot.) tibourbou (Apeiba tibourbou), fibrous tree used to make rope.
burjaca, *f.* pilgrim's or beggar's leather bag (used to carry food and clothing donations).
burla, *f.* 1. gibe, sneer, jeer, scoff; ridicule, mockery, scoffing, gibing; affront, insult. 2. joke, jest. 3. evasion, dodging, eluding; 4. **b. burlando,** (coll.) unawares; quietly, on the quiet, pretending indifference; **de burlas,** not seriously, for fun; **hacer b. de,** to make fun of.
burladero, *m.* 1. (taur.) enclosure in barrier to let bullfighter escape from the bull. 2. safety island, safety zone (in a street).
burlador, ra, *a.* scoffing, sneering, gibing, mocking, ridiculing; joking, jesting. —*m.* 1. Casanova, seducer. 2. conjurer's cup, trick cup (with hidden holes to make the user wet). 3. hidden jet of water (to sprinkle on the unwary). — **El Burlador de Sevilla,** (lit.) Don Juan.
burlar, *tr.v.* 1. to evade, dodge, elude, get past, outwit. 2. to thwart, frustrate, defeat. 3. to deceive, trick. 4. to make fun of, laugh at, mock. —*i.v., r.v.* to make fun, laugh; **b.** or **burlarse de,** to make fun of, mock, laugh at, ridicule; to seduce, deceive (a woman); to evade, to elude.

burlería, *f.* 1. trick, deception. 2. old wives' tale, tall story. 3. derision, ridicule, scorn. — **no me cuentes burlerías,** don't tell me stories.
burlescamente, *adv.* funnily, comically, jocosely.
burlesco, ca, *a.* (coll.) funny, comical, jocose, burlesque.
burlete, *m.* weather stripping applied to doors and windows.
burlisto, ta, *a.* (Hond.) *var. of* **burlón.**
burlón, na, *a.* 1. mocking, gibing, jeering, ridiculing. 2. waggish, joking, bantering. —*m., f.* 1. mocker, giber. 2. wag, joker.
burlonamente, *adv.* mockingly, scoffingly, gibingly.
burlote, *m.* game in which the relatively small bank changes hands (cards, dice, etc.).
buró, *m.* bureau, writing desk; (Mex.) night table, bedside table.
burocracia, *f.* bureaucracy.
burócrata, *m., f.* bureaucrat.
burocrático, ca, *a.* bureaucratic.
burocratismo, *m.* bureaucratism.
burra, *f.* 1. she-ass, jenny ass. 2. stupid woman, simpleton. 3. (coll.) drudge, slave. — **caer uno de su b.,** (coll.) to acknowledge one's mistakes; **írsele a uno la b.,** (coll.) to let the cat out of the bag, let slip (information).
burrada, *f.* 1. drove of donkeys or asses. 2. (fig.) violation of the rules in the card game of burro. 3. (coll.) stupidity, foolishness, stupid or foolish act or remark. 4. (coll.) enormous amount, e.g. *una b. de gente,* a large crowd.
burrajear, *tr.v., var. of* **borrajear,** to scribble, doodle.
burrajo, *m.* dry dung (used as fuel). —*a.* rude, coarse.
burreño, *m., var. of* **burdégano.**
burrero, *m.* drover or owner of asses.
burrillo, *m.* (coll.) religious calendar; notebook.
burrito, ta, *m., f. dim. of* **burro,** small donkey. —*m.* (Mex.) popcorn.
burríon, *m.* (Guat., Hond.) humming bird.
burro, *a.* stupid, assinine. —*m.* 1. donkey, ass. 2. sawbuck, sawhorse. 3. cogwheel (of a silk reel). 4. card game; the loser of every hand in that card game. 5. (coll.) ass, dolt, blockhead, dullard. 6. drudge, plodder, hack. 7. (Mex.) stepladder. 8. (mar.) feed pump. 9. (Col., P. Rico) leapfrog (game). 10. (Mex.) bangs, short hair worn across the forehead. — **b. cargado de letras,** learned ass; **b. de carga,** (coll.) plodder, hack, drudge (man); **caer uno de su b.,** (coll.) to acknowledge one's mistake; **correr b.,** (coll.) to get lost, disappear.
burrumbada, *f., var. of* **barrumbada.**
bursátil, *a.* pertaining to stock exchange transactions.
bursiforme, *a.* (bot., zool.) bursiform.
bursitis, *f.* (med.) bursitis.
burucuyá, *f.* (Arg.) passionflower.
burujo, *m.* 1. ball, lump (of wool, paste, etc.). 2. oil cake, mass of ground olive pips.
burujón, *m.* 1. large lump or mass. 2. bump, swelling, lump. 3. large bundle or heap (of laundry, etc.).
burundanga, *f.* (Cuba) hodgepodge; a collection of worthless items. — **estar en la b.,** (sl., Cuba) to be with it, be in the know.
bus, *m.* (Amer., coll.) bus, autobus.
busaca, *f.* (Col., Ven.) billiard table pocket; (Ven.) bag.
busca, *f.* 1. search; hunt; pursuit. 2. (Cuba, Mex.) perquisite, fringe benefits. 3. hunting dog, hound; beating party (to raise game).
buscabulla, *m., f.* troublemaker.
buscada, *f.* search; hunt; pursuit.
buscador, ra, *a.* searching. —*m., f.* searcher, seeker. —*m.* 1. (astron.) finder (of telescope). 2. (rad.) cat's whisker. 3. **b. de gangas,** bargain hunter. —*f.* (Cuba) streetwalker.
buscaniguas, (*pl.* **buscaniguas**) *m.* (Col., Guat.) squib, cracker, serpent firecracker.
buscapié, *m.* (fig.) hint, insinuation.
buscapiés, (*pl.* **buscapiés**) *m.* squib, cracker (fireworks).
buscapiques, (*pl.* **buscapiques**) *m.* (Perú) *var. of* **buscapiés.**
buscapleitos, (*pl.* **buscapleitos**) *m., f.* (coll.) troublemaker, quarrelsome person.
buscar, (*ref. 50*) *tr.v.* 1. to search for, look for, seek; to call or ask for. 2. (Chile, Mex.) to irritate, provoke. — **buscársela,** (coll.) to hustle, shift about for a living; to ask for it, look for trouble; **b. tres pies al gato,** to look for trouble.
buscarruidos, (*pl.* **buscarruidos**) *m., f.* (coll.) troublemaker. —*m.* (mar., coll.) scout ship, reconnaissance ship.
buscasoles, *a. invar.* (fig.) sun-worshiping (intent upon getting a sun tan).
buscavida, (*pl.* **buscavidas**) *m., f.* 1. (*pl.*) (coll.) busybody, snoop, nosy person, gossipmonger. 2. (coll.) hustler, hard worker.
busco, *m.* 1. sill of sluicegate. 2. (hydr.) gate, lock or miter sill. 3. toe wall.
buscón, na, *a.* 1. searching, seeking. 2. pilfering, cheating, chiseling (coll.). —*m., f.* 1. searcher, seeker. 2. pilferer, cheat, petty thief. —*f.* streetwalker.
busier, *m., var. of* **bujier.**
busilis, *m.* (coll.) root of a difficulty, crux of a matter; **dar en el b.,** to get to the nitty-gritty.
busque, busqué, *ref.* **buscar.**
búsqueda, *f.* search, hunt; research.
busquillo, *m.* (Chile, Peru, coll.) hustler, hard worker.
busto, *m.* 1. bust (sculpture). 2. the bosom or breast, esp. of a woman. — **erguir el b.,** to straighten up.
bustrófedon, *m., adv.* boustrophedon, writing lines alternately from left to right and right to left, imitating the furrows left by plowing.
butaca, *f.* 1. armchair, easy chair. 2. (theat.) orchestra or box seat.
butadieno, *m.* (chem.) butadiene.
butagamba, *f., var. of* **gutagamba.**
butano, *m.* (chem.) butane.
buten, de b., (coll.) first class, topnotch, excellent.
buteno, *m.* (chem.) buteno.
buteonina, *f.* (ornith.) buteonine.
buterola, *f.* dolly, rivet set.
butifarra, *f.* 1. pork sausage. 2. (Peru) sandwich made of a roll with pork, lettuce and spicy onion dressing. 3. (coll.) loose baggy sock or stocking. 4. (coll., Arg.) a wild party.
butifarrero, ra. *m., f.* one who makes or sells pork sausages or sandwiches.
butileno, *m.* (chem.) butylene.
butílico, ca, *a.* butylic.
butilo, *m.* (chem.) butyl.
butiráceo, a, *a.* butyraceous.
butiral, *m.* (chem.) butyral.
butiraldehido, *m.* (chem.) butyraldehyde.
butirato, *m.* (chem.) butyrate.
butírico, ca, *a.* butyric.
butirina, *f.* (chem.) butyrin.
butiro, *m.* (rare) butter.
butirómetro, *m.* butyrometer (device for measuring fat content).
butiroso, sa, *a.* butyraceous, butyrous, greasy.
butomeo, a, butomáceo, a, *a.* (bot.) butomaceous. —*f.* (*pl.*) Butomaceae.
butrino, *m.* (osier) fish trap.
butrón, *m., var. of* **buitrón.**
butuco, ca, *a.* (Hond.) chubby, plump; of good disposition. —*m.* a good Joe (sl.).
buxáceo, a, *a.* (bot.) buxaceous. —*f.* (*pl.*) Buxaceae.
buyador, *m.* brazier.
buyo, *m.* chewing paste or wad of betel leaf, nut and lime; (Phil. I.) betel.
buz, *m.* kiss of respect and reverence; **hacer el b.,** to flatter, butter up.
buzamiento, *m.* (geol., min.) dip, dipping (of stratum).
búzano, *m.* 1. diver. 2. ancient piece of artillery, somewhat like a culverin.
buzar, (*ref. 53*) *i.v.* (geol.) to dip.
buzarda, *f.* (mar.) breasthook, forehook.
buzcorona, *m.* (arch.) blow on the head dealt as a joke by person holding out his hand to be kissed.
buzo, *m.* 1. diver. 2. ancient type of ship.
buzón, *m.* 1. outflow conduit or canal; sewer, drain, gutter. 2. mailbox, letterbox; **b. de sugerencias,** suggestion box. 3. lid, cover; plug, stopper.
buzonera, *f.* gutter in a courtyard.
byroniano, na, *a.* pertaining to Lord Byron, his poetry or his life.

C

C, *f.* c, third letter of the Spanish alphabet; Roman numeral equivalent to one hundred.
C *sym. of* **carbono,** carbon (C).
¡ca¡ *interj., var. of* **¡quiá!** Oh, no! not really! (denoting incredulity or denial).
Ca *sym. of* **calcio,** calcium (Ca).
c.a. *abbrev. of* **corriente alterna,** alternating current (A.C.).
Caaba, *f.* Kaaba or Caaba, the sacred Moslem shrine at Mecca.
cabal, *a.* 1. complete, full, e.g. *un hombre c.,* an honorable man, *en el sentido c. de la palabra,* in the full sense of the word. 2. just, exact (account, weight, etc.). — **no estar en sus cabales,** not to be all there, not to be in one's right mind; **por sus cabales,** completely, fully; at the right price; in the proper order. —*adv.* 1. exactly, precisely. 2. completely, fully.
cabal, *m.* (bot.) (Phil. I.) loganiaceous tree (Fragaea volubilis).
cábala, *f.* 1. cabala (occult rabbinical interpretation of Scripture). 2. divination, occult means of divining. 3. (coll.) cabal, intrigue, secret plotting. 4. (*gen. pl.*) conjecture, supposition.
cabalero, *m.* (Sp.) a second-born son, without right to inheritance of his father's estate.
cabalgada, *f.* 1. band of mounted marauders. 2. (arch.) obligatory cavalry service rendered by vassals. 3. foray, cavalry raid. 4. booty taken in foray.
cabalgador, ra, *m., f.* rider.
cabalgadura, *f.* horse, mount; beast of burden.
cabalgamiento, *m.* (poet.) *var. of* **hipermetria.**
cabalgar, *a.* (Chile) *var. of* **caballar.**
cabalgar, (*ref. 51*) *tr.v.* 1. to ride (a horse). 2. to mount (a gun). 3. to cover (a mare). —*i.v.* 1. to ride horseback, to go horseback riding. 2. to parade on horseback, to ride in a cavalcade.
cabalgata, *f.* procession of riders, cavalcade.
cabalgazón, *f.* covering (of mare by stallion).
cabalgue, cabalgué, *ref.* **cabalgar.**
cabalhuste, *m.* saddle stand.
cabalice, *ref.* **cabalizar.**
cabalidad, *f.* the quality of totality, completion; precision, correctness; integrity.
cabalino, na, *a.* pertaining to a representation of a horse (said of certain fountains).
cabalista, *m.* cabalist; one skilled in the traditions of the cabala.
cabalístico, ca, *a.* cabalistic; (fig.) cryptic, mysterious.
caballa, *f.* (ichth.) mackerel.
caballada, *f.* 1. drove or herd of horses. 2. (Amer.) stupidity, foolishness.
caballaje, *m.* 1. covering (of mare by stallion or she-ass by jackass). 2. covering fee. 3. (mec.) horsepower.
caballar, *a.* pertaining to or resembling horses, equine.
caballazo, *m.* (Chile, Mex.) jolt or trampling with a horse.
caballear, *i.v.* (coll.) to go horseback riding frequently.
caballejo, *m.* 1. *dim. of* **caballo,** small horse, nag. 2. vet.) shoeing-frame.
caballerango, *m.* (Mex.) stableman, horse trainer, head groom.
caballerato, *m.* 1. right of laymen to enjoy ecclesiastical benefices by virtue of Papal dispensation. 2. intermediate rank (between nobility and commoner) of esquire or gentleman granted to Catalonians by the king.
caballerear, *i.v.* to affect the behavior of a gentleman; to put on airs.
caballerescamente, *adv.* in a gentlemanly manner. gallantly.
caballeresco, ca, *a.* 1. gentlemanly, gallant; chivalrous. 2. knightly, chivalric. 3. (of books, tales) concerning knight-errantry.
caballerete, *m.* (coll.) young dandy, young gentleman. fashionable young fellow.
caballería, *f.* 1. mount, horse, mule. 2. (mil.) cavalry. 3. knightly order, knights, e.g. *la C. de Santiago,* the Knights of Santiago; knighthood, rank and privileges of a knight; gentry, nobility, aristocracy of a given region; band or group of knights. 4. chivalrous undertaking, chivalrous behavior. 5. knight's share of booty or of conquered territory; knight's fee, a grant of land made on the condition of maintaining one mounted man-at-arms. 6. land measure (in Spain about 95 acres, in Cuba 33, in P. Rico 194, in Mex. 106). — **andarse uno en caballerías,** to bow and scrape, be excessively polite; **c. andante,** knight-errantry; **c. ligera,** light cavalry; **c. mayor,** horse, mule; **c. menor,** donkey, ass.
caballerito, *m. dim. of* **caballero,** young gentleman, a well-mannered male child.
caballeriza, *f.* 1. stable (building). 2. aggregate of horses or mules belonging to a stable. 3. stable hands, staff of grooms. 4. groom's wife.
caballerizo, *m.* head groom; **c. de campo** or **del rey,** royal equerry; **c. mayor del rey,** Master of the Horse; **primer c. del rey,** immediate assistant to the Master of the Horse.
caballero, ra, *a.* riding, mounted. —*m.* 1. nobleman. 2. knight, cavalier, member of an order of knighthood. 3. gentleman. 4. Sir (respectful form of address). — **armar c. a,** to knight; **c. andante,** knight-errant; **c. cubierto,** grandee who enjoys the privilege of retaining his hat in the king's presence; (coll.) ill-mannered man who does not remove his hat when courtesy requires it; **c. de industria,** swindler, confidence man, knave.
caballerosamente, *adv.* in a gentlemanly manner, gallantly, chivalrously.
caballerosidad, *f.* gentlemanliness, chivalry.
caballeroso, sa, *a.* gentlemanly, chivalrous, gallant.
caballerote, *m.* (coll., derog.) uncouth or loutish gentleman.
caballeta, *f.* (ento.) grasshopper.
caballete, *m.* 1. *dim. of* **caballo,** small horse. 2. (painter's) easel. 3. (archit.) hip, ridge (of roof). 4. rack (instrument of torture). 5. scutching board or table (for dressing hemp or flax). 6. stand for saddles. 7. carpenter's horse, sawbuck, sawhorse; gantry, barrelstand. 8. ridge (between furrows). 9. chimney cowl. 10. bridge (of nose). 11. bird's breastbone. 12. potter's trivet. 13. (min.) (Mex.) mass of barren rock. 14. **C. del pintor,** (astron.) Painter's Easel. — **c. de andamio,** scaffold horse; **c. portapoleas,** crown block.
caballico, *m.* (reg., Sp.) *dim. of* **caballo,** little horse.
caballista, *m.* 1. horseman, expert horseman. 2. expert on horses and horsemanship. 3. highwayman.
caballito, *m.* 1. *dim. of* **caballo,** small horse, pony. 2. hobbyhorse. 3. (*pl.*) game of roulette in which a small horse points to the winning number. 4. (*pl.*) carousel, merry-go-round. 5. (Peru) small boat. — **c. de Bamba,** useless person or thing; **c. del diablo, c. de San Vicente,** (Cuba, Hond., ento.) dragonfly; **c. de totora,** (Amer.) small reed boat. **c. de mar,** sea horse.
caballo, *m.* 1. (zool.) horse. 2. knight (in chess). 3. Spanish playing card bearing picture of a horse. 4. horse, sawbuck, sawhorse. 5. (mec.) horsepower, e.g. *un motor de diez caballos,* a ten-horsepower engine. 6. cross thread on skein. 7. (med.) buboes. 8. (min.) vein of barren rock. 9. (*pl.*) horse troopers, cavalry, horse. 10. (sl.) horse (heroin). — **a c.,** on horseback; **a c. de,** astride, riding on; **a c. regalado, no se le mira el colmillo,** don't look a gift horse in the mouth; **a mata c.,** at full gallop, at breakneck speed; **c. aguililla,** (Amer.) very fast horse; **caballos al eje,** shaft horsepower; **c. blanco,** white knight, angel, financial backer of risky enterprise; **c. dama,** queen's knight (in chess); **c. de agua,** (zool.) hippopotamus, river horse; **c. de aldaba,** horse used on special gala occasions; **c. de batalla,** charger, battle horse; hobby horse; (coll.) bone of contention, crux of controversy; **c. de buena boca,** easy-going person; **c. de carrera,** race horse; **c. de Frisa** or **Frisia,** (mil.) cheval-de-frise; **c. de fuerza,** (mec.) horsepower; **c. de diablo,** (ento.) dragonfly; **c. de mano,** leading horse (on right hand side of coach pole); **c. de mar, c. marino,** (ichth.) sea horse; **c. de montar,** saddle horse; **c. de posta,** posthorse; **c. de silla,** saddle horse; **c. de tiro,** draft horse; **c. de tronco,** pole horse (horse harnessed next to the carriage); **c. de Troya,** (hist.) Trojan Horse; **c. de vapor,** (mec.) horsepower; **c. hora,** (mec.) horsepower hour; **c. métrico,** metric horsepower; **caballos de régimen,** (engin.) horsepower rating; **de a c.,** mounted; **ir a c.,** to go on horseback; **montar a c.,** to ride, go horseback riding.
caballón, *m.* 1. large, clumsy horse. 2. ridge of ploughed land between two furrows; dike, levee.
caballuno, na, *a.* pertaining to a horse, horselike.
cabalmente, *adv.* 1. precisely, exactly. 2. completely, fully.
cabalonga, *f.* (Cuba, Mex., bot.) St. Ignatius bean.
cabanga, *f.* (C. Amer.) sadness, melancholy.
cabaña, *f.* 1. cabin, cottage, hut. 2. flock, herd, drove; drove of grain-carrying horses or mules. 3. (billiards) balk line. 4. pastoral scene. 5. (Arg., Urug.) cattle-breeding ranch.

cabañal, *a.* pertaining to a sheep and cattle path. —*m.* village of huts or cabins.
cabañería, *f.* weekly ration of food allotted to shepherds.
cabañero, ra, *a.* pertaining to a herd of cattle or a drove of mules. —*m.* shepherd; drover.
cabañil, *a.* pertaining to shepherds' huts. —*m.* 1. shepherd, drover. 2. drove of mules, kept for carrying grain.
cabañuelas, *f. pl.* 1. popular weather forecast for next 12 months based on the weather of first 12, 18 or 24 days of January or August. 2. (Bol.) first summer rains. — **fiesta de las Cabañuelas,** feast of Tabernacles.
cabaret, *m.* cabaret, night club.
cabarga, *f.* (Amer.) leather hoof covers for cattle used when crossing the Andes.
cabás, *m.* small shopping basket or bag.
cabdal, *a.* **águila c.,** (ornith.) royal or golden eagle.
cabe, *m.* blow given by one ball to another in a game of croquet. — **c. de pala,** (coll.) unexpected opportunity to achieve a desired objective; **dar un c.,** (coll.) to hurt, damage.
cabe, *prep.* (poet.) nigh to; beside.
cabeceada, *f.* nod, nodding. 2. (Amer.) header (action of heading a soccerball).
cabeceado, *m.* heavy stroke (on the stem of certain letters).
cabeceador, ra, *a.* pertaining to nodding (in drowsiness) or shaking the head (in disapproval); tossing or shaking the head (of horses). —*m.* martingale.
cabeceamiento, *m., var. of* **cabeceo.**
cabecear, *i.v.* 1. to nod (in drowsiness); to shake the head (in disapproval); to shake or toss the head (a horse). 2. to pitch, plunge (a boat); to lurch, sway back and forth (a carriage). 3. to tilt or tip forward (a load). 4. (Chile) to form the head or tip of a cigar. —*tr.v.* 1. (print.) to thicken the stems of certain letters. 2. to fortify new wine with old; to blend wines. 3. (bkb.) to put the headband on a book. 4. to edge or bind (a rug). 5. to revamp the foot of a stocking. 6. (Cuba) to tie together (tobacco leaves). 7. (agr.) to plow the extremities of a parcel of land.
cabeceo, *m.* 1. shaking, tossing, nodding of the head. 2. pitching, plunging (a boat); lurching, swaying (a carriage). 3. tilting forward (a load).
cabecera, *f.* 1. the beginning or principal part of something. 2. headboard (of a bed). 3. head (of a table). 4. source (of a river). 5. capital (of a county, district, region). 6. (print.) head, headline; heading. 7. (bkb.) headband. 8. unploughed ends at either end of a furrow. 9. pillow, bolster. 10. (*pl.*) (print.) quoins. — **asistir or estar a la c. del enfermo,** to tend a bed-ridden person, nurse the sick; **c. de puente,** (mil.) bridgehead; **médico de c.,** bedside doctor, attending physician. —*m.* (min.) foreman (of crew of drillers).
cabecero, *m.* 1. (print.) head or headline writer. 2. (print.) head or headline setter. 3. header beam; cap, lintel; head block. 4. (mas.) header bondstone; yoke of a window frame. — **c. de esclusa,** lock head; **c. de pozo,** manhole head.
cabeciancho, cha, *a.* broad-headed.
cabeciduro, ra, *a.* (Col., Cuba) stubborn, pigheaded.
cabecil, *m.* cloth pad used by porters for relieving pressure of heavy loads carried on the head.
cabecilla, *f.* 1. *dim. of* **cabeza,** small head. 2. closing folds of the paper roll of certain cigarettes. —*m., f.* (coll.) rowdy, roughneck; madcap. —*m.* ringleader, gang leader, rebel leader.
cabellado, da, *a.* chestnut brown, of brownish hue.
cabelladura, *f., var. of* **cabellera.**
cabellar, *i.v.* 1. to grow hair. 2. to wear or put on false hair (as a wig, toupee, switch). —*r.v.* to wear or put on a hairpiece.
cabellera, *f.* 1. hair, head of hair; man. 2. (astron.) coma, tail (of a comet); **c. de Berenice,** (astron.) Coma Berenices.
cabello, *m.* 1. hair (singly and collectively). 2. (bot.) corn silk. — **asirse de un c.,** (coll.) to seize on to anything (to obtain one's ends); **c. de ángel,** (cul.) sweet made with syrup and fibrous part of the pumpkin; (Peru, Arg.) vermicelli; (Amer., bot.) species of clematis; (Chile, Peru) dodder, love vine; **cortar un c. en el aire,** (coll.) to be very bright or keen-witted, be sharp as a needle; **estar colgado de los cabellos,** (coll.) to feel insecure or afraid, be on edge; **estar pendiente de un c.,** (coll.) to hang by a thread, be in imminent danger; **ponérsele a uno los cabellos de punta,** (coll.) to stand on end (one's hair); **traer una cosa por los cabellos,** (coll.) to drag something farfetched (into a talk); **tropezar en un c.,** (coll.) to be deterred by trifles, drown in a teacup.
cabelludo, *a.* 1. hairy, shaggy. 2. (bot.) fibrous, filamentous. — **cuero c.,** scalp.
caber, (*ref. 4*) *i.v.* 1. to fit, to have enough room, be enough room for, e.g. *la multitud no cabía en la plaza,* there was not enough room for the crowd in the square. 2. to be one's duty to, fall to, e.g. *me cabe ir a visitarle,* it is my duty to visit him, *me cupo el honor de ir,* the honor of going fell to me. 3. to be possible, e.g. *todo cabe en la naturaleza,* everything is possible in nature. — **cabe que,** it is fitting that; it is suitable that; it is right or just that; **no cabe duda,** there is no doubt; **no cabe más,** that is the limit; **no c. en sí,** to be arrogant; to be beside oneself (with joy); **todo cabe en él,** he is capable of anything.
cabero, ra, *a.* (obs.) last, ultimate, final.
cabestraje, *m.* 1. halters. 2. payment given to cattle drovers.
cabestrante, *m.* (mar.) capstan.
cabestrar, *tr.v.* to halter. —*i.v.* to hunt or stalk game with a stalking-ox.
cabestrear, *i.v.* to be obedient to the halter, to be led easily by the halter. —*tr.v.* (Amer.) to lead by the halter.
cabestrería, *f.* halter maker's shop.
cabestrero, ra, *a.* (reg.) accustomed to the halter. —*m.* maker of halters.
cabestrillo, *m.* 1. (arm.) sling. 2. chain, necklace.
cabestro, *m.* 1. halter, lead (for cattle, horses). 2. ox leading a herd of bulls.
cabete, *m.* metal tag or tip, aglet (of a lace, etc.).
cabeza, *f.* 1. head (top part of a human or animal body); head (top part of a nail, pin, hammer, etc.); head, end (of bridge, beam); top, summit (of mountain); head, source (of river); top edge (of page); head, vanguard (of procession, army). 2. head, brains, judgment, intelligence. 3. head, person, unit, e.g. *cobró dos pesetas por c.,* he charged two pesetas a head, *un rebaño de cien cabezas,* a herd of a hundred head of cattle. 4. head, life, e.g. *le costó la c.,* it cost him his head or life. 5. head, chief (of clan, etc.). 6. capital (of state or province) 7. bell yoke. 8. (carp.) strip of wood (dovetailed on to head of a board to prevent warping). 9. (Hond.) (min) middlings, tailings (of ore). — **a la c. de,** at the head of; directing, managing, leading; **alzar** or **levantar la c.,** to get on one's feet, get one's head above water, get out of the woods; to get well, recover; **bajar uno la c.,** (coll.) to conform, submit, obey; **buena c. para los números,** a good head for figures; **c. de ajo,** garlic bulb; **c. de clavo,** (archit.) nail-headed or nailhead molding; **c. de chorlito,** (coll.) featherbrain, giddy-headed person; **c. de émbolo,** pistonhead; **c. de esclusa,** (hydr.) lock head; **c. dura,** hard-headed, stubborn person; **c. de familia,** head of the family; **c. de grabación,** recording head (of a tape machine); **c. de hierro,** pigheaded person, mule; **c. de la biela,** (mec.) big end; **C. de la Iglesia,** Head of the Church; **C. del Dragón,** (astron.) Dragon's Head (ascending node); **c. de lectura,** playback head (of a tape recorder); **c. de lobo,** (coll.) something flaunted to attract favor; **c. de Medusa,** (astron.) Medusa's head; **c. de partido,** chief town of a district, county town; **c. de perro,** (bot.) pilewort, lesser celandine; **c. de playa,** (mil.) beachhead; **c. de proceso,** (law) court order for the investigation of a crime; **c. de puente,** (mil.) bridgehead; **c. de tornillo,** screwhead; **c. de toro,** (Cuba, bot.) laurel (Beilschmiedia pendula); **c. de válvula,** valve bonnet; **c. embutida** or **perdida,** (rivets) countersunk head; **c. loca,** harebrained, irresponsible person; **c. reproductora,** playback head (of tape recorder); **c. sonora,** sound head (of movie projector); **c. supresora,** erase head (of tape recorder); **c. vana,** (coll.) addled or tired mind (through fatigue); **calentarse uno la c.,** to become mentally tired; **cargársele a uno la c.,** to feel drowsy or heavy-headed; **dar de c.,** to come down in the world, fall on hard times; **dar en la c. a uno** (coll.) to thwart, to get even with, to oppose someone; **de c.,** head first; on end; (coll.) of course, definitely; **encarjársele a uno en la c. alguna cosa.** (coll.) to get something into one's head, become stubbornly convinced of something; **escarmentar por c. ajena,** to learn from others' mistakes; **henchir a uno la c. con viento,** to flatter, puff up; **ir c. abajo,** (coll.) to go downhill, go to rack and ruin; **írsele a uno la c.,** to lose one's mind, go off one's head; **meter a uno en la c. alguna cosa,** to put something into someone's head; to get or drive something into someone's head; **meter la c.,** to gain admittance, get one's foot inside the door; **meterse de c.,** (coll.) to go head and shoulders into something; **no levantar la c.,** (coll.) to keep one's nose to the grindstone; to keep one's eyes on one's work; not to recover (from an illness, misfortune); **no tener donde volver la c.,** (coll.) to have nowhere to turn or no one to turn to; **pasarle a uno una cosa por la c.,** (coll.) to come into one's head; **perder la c.,** to lose one's head, be at a loss as to what to do; **romperse la c.,** to break one's neck (to get or do something); **quitar a uno algo de la c.,** to make someone change his mind; **romperse uno la c.,** (coll.) to rack one's brains; **sacar la c.,** (coll.) to show up; to speak out, raise one's voice; **sentar la c.,** (coll.) to settle down, come to one's senses; **subirse una cosa a la c.,** to go to one's head (drink, glory); **tener buena or mala c.,** to have a good or bad head (for art, science, etc.); to be able or unable to take (wine, liquor); **tener la c. como una olla de grillos,** (coll.) to be in a dither; **(estar) tocado de la c.,** (coll.) (to be) touched in the head.
cabezada, *f.* 1. butt with the head; blow on the head. 2. nod (of drowsiness or greeting). 3. pitch, plunge (of a ship). 4. headstall, head gear (horse). 5. (bkb.) cord for sewing the headband of a book. 6. instep of a boot. 7. highest part of a plot of land. — **c. de silla,** (Ecuad.) saddlebow, saddletree; **c. potrera,** rope halter; **dar cabezadas,** to nod (in drowsiness); **darse de cabezadas,** (coll.) to knock one's head against the wall with fruitless inquiries.

cabezal, *m.* 1. small head pillow; bolster. 2. narrow mattress. 3. (surg.) compress, pad, bandage. 4. forepart of a carriage. 5. (mec.) headstock (of a lathe). 6. crossbeam, stringer; lintel. 7. (print.) heading, head. — **c. de choque,** (ry.) bumper, bumping post or block; **c. fijo,** (mec.) headstock; **c. giratorio,** (mec.) toolhead; **c. móvil,** tail-stock, poppethead.
cabezalejo, ico, illo, ito, *m. dim. of* **cabezal,** small compress, little pillow or bolster.
cabezalero, ra, *m.* 1. executor (of a will). 2. leader of leaseholders who collects the rents and pays them to the landlord. —*f.* executrix (of a will).
cabezazo, *m.* butt with the head; header (action of heading a soccerball).
cabezo, *m.* 1. high hill; peak, summit (of a mountain); hillock, hummock. 2. collar (of a shirt). 3. (mar.) reef.
cabezón, na, *a.* 1. (coll.) big-headed, large-headed. 2. (coll.) obstinate, stubborn, pigheaded. 3. (Chile) heady (wine). —*m.* 1. large head. 2. tax register or registry. 3. collar, collar-band (of a shirt); head opening (of a garment). 4. (equit.) cavesson. 5. (*pl.*) (Col.) eddies (around a rock in a river). — **c. de serreta,** (equit.) cavesson; **llevar or traer de los cabezones a uno,** (coll.) to drag someone along against his will, lead (one) by the nose.
cabezonada, *f.* (coll.) stubbornness, pigheadedness.
cabezorro, *m.* (coll.) large misshapen head.
cabezota, *a.* stubborn; obstinate. —*f. aug. of* **cabeza,** big head, large head. —*m., f.* 1. (coll.) big-headed or large-headed person. 2. stubborn, obstinate person.
cabezudamente, *adv.* stubbornly, obstinately.
cabezudo, da, *a.* 1. big-headed, large-headed. 2. (coll.) obstinate, pigheaded. 3. (coll.) heady (liquor). —*m.* 1. effigy with outsize head used in carnivals. 2. (ichth.) mullet, striped mullet.
cabezuela, *f.* 1. *dim. of* **cabeza,** small head. 2. coarse flour, middling. 3. sediment (in wine). 4. (bot.) capitulum, head (of a flower). 5. rosebud (from which rose water is made). 6. (bot.) cornflower. —*m., f.* (coll.) madcap, harebrained person.
cabezuelo, *m. dim. of* **cabezo,** small peak or hill.
cabida, *f.* 1. capacity; room, space. 2. expanse; extent. — **dar c. a,** to make room for; **tener c. en,** to be acceptable; to be suitable.
cabido, *past part. of* **caber.** —*a.* having a commandership (knight of the Order of Malta).
cabila, *f.* tribe of Kabyles (tribe of Bedouins or Berbers).
cabildada, *f.* (coll.) hasty or imprudent decision of a town council.
cabildante, *m.* (Amer.) town councilor.
cabildear, *i.v.* to lobby, to maneuver or scheme for votes (in town council, etc.).
cabildeo, *m.* lobbying, political maneuvering.
cabildero, *m.* lobbyist, political schemer.
cabildo, *m.* 1. town hall, town council; town council meeting. 2. (ecc.) cathedral chapter; chapter meeting. 3. chapter (of certain brotherhoods).
cabileño, ña, *a.* pertaining to the Kabyles. —*m.* Kabyle (Algerian or Tunisian Berber, member of a Kabyle).
cabilla, *f.* 1. steel bar, dowel, driftbolt. 2. (mar.) treenail; pintle, belaying pin; spoke (of a ship's steering wheel). — **c. de maniobra,** (mar.) belaying pin; **c. de tensión,** tension dowel.
cabillero, *m.* (mar.) pin rail, pin rack (for belaying pins).
cabillo, *m.* (bot.) stalk, stem.
cabima, *f.* (bot.) cedrela, Spanish cedar (Cedrela angustifolia).
cabimiento, *m.* 1. capacity, space, room. 2. right to a commandery of a knight in the Order of Malta.
cabina, *f.* cabin (of aircraft, of ship); (pilot's) cockpit; cab, cabin (truck driver); (telephone) booth; **c. anticlimática,** (aer.) pressurized cabin; **c. de cambio de agujas, (ry.)** signal box (G.B.), signal tower (U.S.); **c. de control,** control room; **c. de mando,** (aer.) flight deck; **c. de prensa,** press box; **c. de proyección,** projection room; **c. insonorizada,** (rad., tel.) isolation booth; **c. presurizada,** (aer.) pressurized cabin, pressure cabin; **c. telefónica,** telephone box or booth.
cabio, *m.* joist, rafter; trimmer; crosspiece, lintel.
cabizbajo, ja, *a.* crestfallen, downhearted, depressed.
cable, *m.* 1. cable, rope, hawser. 2. (elec.) cable. 3. cable, cable's length (120 fathoms). 4. (coll.) cable, cablegram. — **c. de alzar,** hoisting line; **c. de mando,** operating cable; **c. blindado,** (elec., rad.) screened cable; **c. de cadena,** chain cable; **c. eléctrico,** electric cable; **c. portante,** suspension cable; **c. submarino,** submarine telegraph cable; **echar un c.,** to throw a line, help, give a hand.
cableado, *past part. of* **cablear.** —*m.* (mar.) making into a cable.
cablear, *tr.v.* (mar.) to make into a cable; to twist, to lay.
cablecarril, *m.* cablecar, cableway.
cablegrafiar, *tr.v., i.v.* to cable.
cablegráfico, ca, *a.* pertaining to cablegrams.
cablegrama, *m.* cablegram, cable.
cablero, *m.* cable ship; rigger.
cablerriel, *m.* track cable.
cabo, *m.* 1. end. 2. stub, bit, piece, butt (cigar, etc.). 3. handle, haft, shaft. 4. thread, strand. 5. package, bundle. 6. headland, cape. 7. (cards) lowest card of any suit. 8. leader, boss, chief. 9. place, point, locality. 10. (mar.) rope, cable. 11. (mil.) corporal. 12. (*pl.*) accessories (of clothing). 13. (*pl.*) feet, muzzle and mane (of horse). 14. (*pl.*) main points (of a speech, etc.). — **al c.,** at last, finally, in the end; **al c. de,** at the end of; **al fin y al c.,** after all; at last; **atar cabos,** to put two and two together; **c. blanco,** untarred rope; **C. Bretón,** Cape Breton Island; **c. de año,** anniversary mass for dead person; **c. de barra,** (Mex.) piece of eight (coin); final payment, last coin handed over in settling an account; **C. de Buena Esperanza,** Cape of Good Hope; **c. de cañón,** gunner; **c. de escuadra,** platoon corporal; **c. de fila,** leading soldier in file; **c. de hacha,** ax handle; **C. de Hornos,** Cape Horn; **c. de labor,** tackle rope; **c. de maestranza,** foreman; **c. de mar,** (mar.) petty officer; **c. de pico,** pick handle; **c. de ronda,** patrol leader; **C. Finisterre,** Cape Finisterre; **c. suelto,** (coll.) loose end, unfinished business; **cabos negros** (of women) dark eyes, eyebrows and hair; **C. Verde,** Cape Verde; **dar c. a,** to put the finishing touches to; **de c. a rabo,** (coll.) from beginning to end; **el C.,** Cape Province, Capetown; **llevar a c.,** to carry out, perform, execute; **llevar hasta el c. (una cosa),** to see (something) through to the end, persevere (in something) to the end; **no dejar c. suelto,** to take every precaution, take every measure; **segundo c.,** second-in-command.
cabotaje, *m.* coastal sailing or trading.
cabra, *f.* 1. goat; female goat, she-goat. 2. ballista, ancient military catapult. 3. (zool.) bivalve mollusk. 4. (astron.) **C.,** Capella, star in the constellation Auriga, 5. (Col., Cuba, Ven.) cheating move at dice or dominoes. 6. (Chile) gig, cabriolet, light two-wheeled carriage. 7. (Chile) prop, timber support, carpenter's sawhorse. — **c. de almizcle,** musk deer (Moschus moschiferus); **c. de Angora,** Angora goat; **c. montés,** wild goat, mountain goat; **la c. siempre tira al monte,** the leopard never changes his spots.
cabrahigadura, *f.* caprification, the pollination of cultivated fig trees.
cabrahigal, *m.* grove of wild fig trees.
cabrahigar, (*ref. 51*) *tr.v.* to caprificate, to pollinate cultivated fig trees.
cabrahigo, *m.* caprifig, wild fig tree; wild fig.
cabrahigue, cabrahigué, *ref.* **cabrahigar.**
cabrear, *i.v.* 1. (Chile) to caper, gambol, leap about. 2. (Peru) to dribble (soccerball). —*r.v.* to become suspicious; to be on one's guard, to become irritated or annoyed. —*v.t.* to bother or annoy someone.
cabreo, *m.* 1. (Peru) dribbling (in football). 2. irritation, annoyance.
cabrera, *f.* 1. female goatherd; goatherd's wife. 2. (Arg.) an angry woman.
cabrería, *f.* goat's milk dairy; goat pen.
cabreriza, *f.* goat pen; goatherd's wife.
cabrerizo, za, *a.* goatish, goatlike, pertaining to goats. —*m.* goatherd.
cabrero, *m.* 1. goatherd. 2. (ornith.) kind of finch (Spindalis pretrei). 3. (Arg.) an angry man.
cabrestante, *m.* (mar.) capstan, winch, crab. — **c. corredizo,** (hydr.) traveling gate hoist; **c. manual,** hand-power winch.
cabria, *f.* winch, capstan, derrick, crane. — **c. de aguilón,** jib crane; **c. de vientos,** guy derrick.
cabrial, *m.* rafter.
cabrilla, *f.* 1. sawhorse. 2. (ichth.) cabrilla. 3. (*pl.*) burn marks caused by habitually sitting too near the fire. 4. "ducks and drakes", skipping of a flat stone on water. 5. white horses, white-caps (waves). 6. (*pl*) (astron.) **C.,** Pleiades.
cabrillear, *i.v.* 1. to break into foam, form white horses or whitecaps. 2. to glimmer, twinkle, sparkle.
cabrilleo, *m.* foaming, breaking into foam (sea waves).
cabrina, *f.* goat-skin.
cabrio, *m.* 1. (archit.) joist; plank from three to six yards long. 2. (her.) honor point.
cabrío, a, *a.* goatish, goatlike, goat, of goats. —*m.* herd of goats.
cabriola, *f.* jump, leap, skip; pirouette; caper, capriole (of horse); **dar cabriolas,** to jump, skip, leap; to caper, prance.
cabriolar, *i.v.* to jump, leap, skip; to prance, caper.
cabriolé, *m.* 1. cabriolet, convertible car or coach. 2. short cape without sleeves.
cabriolear, *i.v., var. of* **cabriolar.**
cabrita, *f.* (mil.) ballista, ancient military catapult.
cabritilla, *f.* lambskin, kidskin, e.g. *guantes de c.,* kidskin gloves.
cabrito, *m.* 1. kid, young goat. 2. (Chile) (*pl.*) popcorn.
cabrituno, na, *a.* of kids or young goats.
cabro, *m.* (arch.) billy goat, male goat.
cabrón, *m.* 1. male goat. 2. (coll.) cuckold, one who consents to the adultery of his wife. 3. (Amer., vulg.) bastard, bugger. 4. (Chile, Peru) pimp.
cabronada, *f.* indignity, insult; dirty trick.
cabronzuelo, *m.* 1. *dim. of* **cabrón,** small billy goat. 2. (sl., Sp.) urchin, a pest of a child.
cabruno, na, *a.* goat, goatlike.
cabujón, *m.* 1. cabochon, polished uncut convex gem. 2. ornamental head of nail.
cábula, *f.* (Arg.) trick, ruse, stratagem.
cabulista, *m.* schemer; tricky person.
caburé, *m.* (S. Amer.) gnome owl, pygmy owl.

cabuya, *f.* 1. (bot.) cabuya, giant lily, giant cabuya (Furcraea cabuya). 2. Mauritius hemp, sisal; (mar.) cordage; (Amer.) cord, string; sisal or hemp rope. — **dar c.,** (Amer.) to tie, fasten, bind; **ponerse en la c.,** (S. Amer.) to get the point of; to become fully informed about.
cabuyera, *f.* hammock clews.
cabuyería, *f.* (mar.) cordage, rigging, outfit of ropes or cables.
cabuyo, *m.* (Ecuad.) *var. of* **cabuya.**
caca, *f.* 1. (coll.) human excrement. 2. (coll.) defect, error, misdemeanor. 3. (coll.) filth, dirt. 4. (Mex.), (coll.) luck. — **has hecho c.?,** have you gone to the toilet?, have you pooped?; **me hice c.,** I messed my pants.
cacaguatal, *m.* (Guat.), *var. of* **cacahual.**
cacahual, *m.* cacao plantation.
cacahuate, *m., var. of* **cacahuete.**
cacahuatero, ra, *m., f.* (Mex.) peanut vendor.
cacahué, *m., var. of* **cacahuete.**
cacahuero, *m.* (Amer.) cacao planter, dealer or merchant; cacao plantation hand, loader or screener of cacao or cocoa beans.
cacahuete, *m.* (bot.) peanut (plant and seed).
cacahuey, *m., var of* **cacahuete.**
cacalota, *f.* (Hond.) debt.
cacalote, *m.* 1. (Mex., ornith.) crow (Corvus corux). 2. (C. Amer.) popcorn.
cacao, *m.* 1. (bot.) cacao, cocoa, chocolate tree. 2. cacao or cocoa bean. 3. (cul.) cocoa, chocolate (powder and beverage); **c. ladino,** (Guat.) type of cacao with small beans; **c. mico,** (Hond.) wild cacao. — **no valer un c.,** to be not worth a bean; **pedir c.,** (Amer.) to beg for mercy.
cacaotal, *m., var. of* **cacahual.**
cacaraña, *f.* pockmark. —*a.* (C. Amer.) scribbled, illegible (said of handwriting).
cacarañado, da, *a.* pockmarked, pitted.
cacarañar, *tr.v.* 1. (Guat., Mex.) to pit; to make pockmarked. 2. to scratch; to pinch.
cacaraquear, *i.v.* (imp. u.) *var. of* **cacarear.**
cacaraqueo, *m., var. of* **cacareo.**
cacareador, ra, *a.* 1. crowing, cackling. 2. (coll.) boasting, bragging, crowing.
cacarear, *i.v.* to crow, cackle. —*tr.v.* (coll.) to boast about, brag about, crow over.
cacareo, *m.* 1. crowing, cackling. 2. (coll.) boast, boasting, bragging, crowing.
cacarico, ca, *a.* (C. Amer.) 1. numb. 2. swollen.
cacarizo, za, *a.* (Mex.) pitted, pockmarked.
cacaste, *m.* (C. Rica, Hond.) *var. of* **cacaxtle.**
cacatúa, *f.* cockatoo.
cacaxtle, *m.* (Mex.) pack frame, wooden frame fitted on the shoulders and back to aid in carrying loads.
cacaxtlero, *m.* (Mex.) bearer, porter (who uses a **cacaxtle).**
cace, cacé, *ref.* **cazar.**
cacear, *tr.v.* to stir with a ladle.
caceo, *m.* stirring (with a ladle).
cacera, *f.* irrigation ditch.
cacería, *f.* 1. hunting, hunt. 2. bag, game bagged. 3. (p.) hunting scene; **salir de c.,** to go hunting.
cacerina, *f.* cartridge pouch; (mar.) fuse box formerly carried by gunner.
cacerola, *f.* casserole, stew pot, saucepan.
cacerolada, *f.* contents of a saucepan or casserole.
caceta, *f.* strainer ladle (used by pharmacists).
cacha, *f.* 1. handle plate, cheek (of handle of knife, etc.); handle, handgrip (of knife, revolver), butt (of revolver). 2. buttock (of small game, rabbit, etc.). 3. cheek (of face). 4. (Amer.) horn (of bull). 5. (Amer.) trick, deception. 6. (Bol.) metal spur (on fighting cock). 7. (Bol.) wooden chest or trunk. 8. (Guat.) effort, perseverance. 9. (Pan.) cheek, sauce, impudence, insolence. — **a medias cachas,** (Mex.) tipsy; **de c.,** (Ecuad.) mockingly; **hacer c.,** (Guat.) to try hard, make an effort; (Chile, Peru) to make fun of, mock; **hasta las cachas,** (coll.) up to the hilt, up to one's ears; **sacar c.,** (Peru) to make fun of.
cachaciento, ta, *a.* (Chile) slow, sluggish.
cachaco, *m.* 1. (Col.) dandy, dude. 2. (Peru) policeman, bobby, cop (coll.).
cachada, *f.* 1. blow given by one spinning top to another. 2. (Amer.) goring (by a bull). 3. (Arg., Urug.) mockery.
cachafaz, *m.* (S. Amer.) rascal, scoundrel, rogue.
cachagua, *f.* (Mex.) sewer.
cachalote, *m.* (zool.) sperm whale (Physeta macrocephalos).
cachamarín, *m., var. of* **cachemarín.**
cachampa, *f.* (ichth.) striped mullet.
cachanlagua, *f., var. of* **canchalagua.**
cachano, *m.* (coll.) devil; **llamar a c.,** (coll.) to ask (for something) in vain.
cachaña, *f.* 1. (Chile) small parrot. 2. (Chile) mockery, derision; **hacer c.,** (Chile) to make fun of someone or something.
cachañar *tr.v.* (Chile) to make fun of, mock, ridicule.
cachañero, ra, *a.* (Chile) mocking, scoffing, derisive.
cachapa, *f.* (Ven., cul.) cornbread, corn muffin.
cachar, *tr.v.* 1. to break into pieces; to split (wood). 2. to plow, break up (hilly land). 3. (Amer.) to make fun of, ridicule, tease; to annoy, pester, irritate, plague. 4. (C. Amer.) to get, obtain; (Amer.) to take, seize, take hold of; to take, steal, purloin. 5. (Amer.) to catch (someone doing something). 6. (Amer.) to gore, butt with the horns. 7. (Peru, sl.) to have sexual intercourse with.
cacharpari, *m.* (Peru) farewell party or dance.
cacharpas, *f.* (*pl.*) (Amer.) odds and ends, knickknacks; trappings (of gauchos).
cacharpaya, *f.* (Bol., Peru) *var. of* **cacharpari.**
cacharpearse, *r.v.* (Chile) to dress up, put on one's glad rags or best clothes.
cacharpero, *m.* (Chile) peddler who sells notions and second-hand clothes.
cacharrería, *f.* cheap crockery shop.
cacharrero, *m., f.* one who sells ordinary crockery, dishes, pots, etc.
cacharro, *m.* 1. ordinary crock, pot, saucepan; old piece of earthenware. 2. piece of rubbish or junk, (*pl.*) junk, rubbish; old wreck (any machine which does not work properly). 3. (Col.) bauble, gewgaw. 4. (Car., coll.) jalopy; family automobile. 5. (C. Amer.) jail.
cachava, *f.* 1. boys' game in which a ball is hit into a hole in the ground with a stick; the stick used in such a game. 2. shepherd's staff.
cachavazo, *m.* stroke with the **cachava.**
cachaza, *f.* 1. (coll.) slowness, sluggishness, indifference. 2. raw, uncured rum. 3. first froth on cane juice when boiled.
cachazo, *m.* (Chile, Mex., taur.) goring.
cachazudo, da, *a.* slow, sluggish, indifferent. —*m., f.* sluggard, slowpoke (coll.). —*m.* (Cuba) tobacco worm.
cache, *a.* (Arg.) badly dressed; dowdy; slovenly.
cachear, *tr.v.* 1. search, frisk. 2. (Chile) to gore (bull).
cachemarín, *m.* (mar.) coasting lugger.
cachemir, *m., var. of* **casimir.**
cachemir, ra, *m.* (tex.) cashmere. —*f.* **C.** Kashmir, region in Asia.
cacheo, *m.* search (of a person), frisking.
cachera, *f.* coarse long-napped fabric, baize.
cachería, *f.* 1. (Amer.) small retail shop or business. 2. (Arg.) bad taste (in dress).
cachero, ra, *a.* 1. (C. Amer.) hard-working, diligent, active, assiduous. 2. (Col., C. Rica, Ven.) lying, untruthful, swindling. 3. (Peru) joking, waggish. —*m.* (Amer.) sodomite.
cacheta, *f., var. of* **gacheta,** lever, tooth (of a latch).
cachetada, *f.* (Amer.) a hard slap on the face.
cachete, *m.* 1. cheek, plump cheek. 2. slap, punch. 3. dagger, stiletto.
cachetear, *tr.v.* (Amer.) to slap, cuff hard.
cachetero, *m.* 1. short dagger, stiletto; slaughtering-knife (used on cattle). 2. (taur.) bullfighter who finishes off the bull with a short dagger. 3. (coll.) person who finishes off something or someone.
cachetina, *f.* fisticuffs, fist fight.
cachetón, na, *a.* 1. (Amer.) plump-cheeked. 2. (Mex.) brazen, shameless. 3. (Chile) pretentious.
cachetudo, da, *a.* plump-cheeked.
cachicamo, *m.* (Col., Ven., zool.) armadillo.
cachicán, *m.* 1. farm overseer. 2. (coll.) shrewd person. —*a.* (coll.) astute, shrewd, smart (coll.).
cachicuerno, na, *a.* horn-handled (knife, weapon).
cachicha, *f.* (Hond.) rage, tantrum.
cachidiablo, *m.* (coll.) person who dresses up as the devil for a masquerade.
cachifo, *m.* (Col., Ven.) boy, lad, youngster.
cachifollar, *tr.v.* to humiliate, snub, crush.
cachigordete, ta, *a.* (coll.) *var. of* **cachigordo.**
cachigordo, da, *a.* pudgy, chubby, plump.
cachilo, *m.* (Arg., ornith.) crown sparrow (Zonotrichia capensis).
cachilla, *f.* (Chile) cooked wheat.
cachillada, *f.* litter (animals).
cachimán, *m.* (Arg., bot.) chirimoya, sugar apple, sweetsop (Annona squamosa).
cachimba, *f.* 1. (Amer.) (smoking) pipe. 2. (Arg.) shallow well, hole dug on beach in search for drinking water. 3. (Hond.) empty cartridge shell.
cachimbazo, *m.* (Amer.) 1. gunshot. 2. slap. 3. slug, swig, drink.
cachimbo, *m.* 1. (Amer.) (smoking) pipe. 2. (Cuba) small sugar mill. 3. (Peru, coll.) university freshman; bandsman, amateur or second-rate musician. — **chupar c.,** (Ven.) to smoke a pipe; (Ven., coll.) to suck one's thumb.
cachina, *f.* (Bol.) natural alum.
cachinflín, *m.* (C. Amer.) serpent firecracker.
cachingo, *m.* (Peru, sl.) mediocre musician.
cachipodar, *tr.v.* to cut small branches off tree.
cachipolla, *f.* (ento.) dayfly, May fly.
cachiporra, *f.* 1. club with a large knob. 2. bludgeon (weapon). 3. (Cuba, ornith.) black-necked stilt.
cachiporrazo, *m.* blow with a club, clubbing, bludgeoning.
cachiporrero, *m.* (Chile, coll.) verger; choirmaster.
cachiporro, *m.* club, bludgeon. —*a.* (coll.) puffy-cheeked, chubby-faced.
cachipuco, ca, *a.* (C. Amer.) having one cheek puffier than the other.
cachiri, *m.* (Ven.) fermented Indian drink of cassava or sweet potato.
cachirula, *f.* (Col.) head-shawl or mantilla made of hand-tatted net.
cachirulo, *m.* 1. vessel, pot (esp. for liquor). 2. three-masted schooner or ketch. 3. hair ornament of ribbons and feathers formerly used by women; (coll.) hat. 4. (Mex.) chamois reinforcement (on riding breeches or pants). 5. (sl.) lover, paramour. 6. (*pl.*) baubles, trinkets, junk.
cachivache, *m.* 1. (*pl.*) pots and pans; odds and ends, bits and pieces; junk, trash. 2. a good-for-nothing, unimportant man.

cachivachería, *f.* (Peru) junk; junk shop.
cachivachero, ra, *m., f.* junk peddler.
cachizo, *a.* thick (timber). —*m.* thick timber.
cacho, cha, *a.* bent, turned-down. —*m.* 1. bit, small piece, hunk, chunk. 2. (ichth.) kind of mullet. 3. card game played with half a pack. 4. (Arg., Chile) dice box (for shooting dice). 5. (Amer.) horn (of animal); drinking horn. 6. (Guat.) crescent-shaped roll (bread). 7. (Arg.) bunch of bananas. 8. (Amer.) anecdote, spicy story; (Ven.) joke, jest. 9. (Chile) unsaleable piece of merchandise, dud goods (sl.). — **echar c.,** (Col.) to surpass, outshine; **estar fuera de c.,** (coll.) to be safe or out of danger; **un cacho, un cachito,** a piece, a little, a bit.
cacholas, *f.* (*pl.*) (mar.) cheeks of the masts, hounds.
cachón, *m.* 1. (mar.) breaker wave. 2. (C. Amer., Col.) said of an animal having big horns.
cachondearse, *r.v.* (coll.) 1. to banter, exchange witticisms. 2. to get sexually aroused.
cachondeo, *m.* 1. (vulg.) banter, raillery, joking. 2. (sl., Sp.) the preliminary sex play.
cachondo, da, *a.* in heat, in rut (animals); (human beings).
cachondo, da, *a.* in heat, in rut (animals); lustful (human beings).
cachopín, *m., var. of* **cachupín.**
cachopo, *m.* stump, dry trunk.
cachorrada, *f.* (Ven.) spiteful action or word; surly or snappy remark.
cachorreñas, *f.* (*pl.*) soups made with oil, vinegar, garlic and red pepper.
cachorrillo, *m.* small pistol.
cachorro, rra, *m., f.* pup; whelp; cub. —*m.* small pistol. —*a.* 1. (Cuba) spiteful. 2. (Ven.) surly, snappy.
cachú, *m.* (bot., pharm.) catechu.
cachua, *f.* Indian dance of Peru, and Bolivia.
cachuar, *i.v.* (Peru) to dance the **cachua.**
cachucha, *f.* 1. small boat. 2. cap, woollen cap. 3. solo dance and song of the classic Andalusian school. 4. (Chile, coll.) slap, cuff.
cachuchear, *i.v.* to spoil, indulge, pet; to flatter.
cachuchero, *m.* one who sells caps, notions, odds and ends.
cachucho, *m.* 1. oil measure (one-sixth of a pound). 2. (archery) arrow compartment (in a quiver). 3. pincushion; pin box. 4. small boat. 5. (ichth.) type of snapper (Dentex macrophthalmus); (Amer., ichth.) sea bass (Serranus oculatus).
cachudo, da, *a.* (Chile) cunning, crafty. —*m.* (ornith.) Chilean crested tyrant flycatcher (Culicivora parvutus).
cachuela, *f.* 1. (cul.) stew made with pork offal or rabbit hearts and livers. 2. gizzard, sweetbread (of birds).
cachuelo, *m.* 1. (Peru, coll.) side job, small job, small service or favor. 2. small, edible river fish.
cachumba, *f.* (bot.) saffron-like plant of the Phil. I.
cachumbo, *m.* 1. hard shell of certain fruit (coconut, etc.). 2. (Col.) hair curl, ringlet.
cachunde, *f.* cachou pastilles; catechu (extract).
cachupín, *m.* (derog.) newly-arrived Spanish settler in America.
cachureco, ca, *a.* 1. (Mex.) deformed, crooked. 2. (C. Amer.) conservative.
cacica, *f.* female Indian chief; wife of an Indian chief or a political boss.
cacicato, *m., var. of* **cacicazgo.**
cacicazgo, *m.* 1. chieftaincy, chieftainship, rank or domain of an Indian chief. 2. (coll.) authority or power of a political boss.
cacillo, *m.* small ladle.
cacimba, *f.* 1. shallow well, hole dug on the shore in search for drinking water. 2. pail, bucket.
cacique, *m.* 1. cacique, Indian chieftain; (coll.) political boss, cacique. 2. (ornith.) cacique, any of various tropical orioles.
caciquil, *a.* cacique-like; pertaining to political bossism.
caciquismo, *m.* caciquism, domination by petty chiefs or political bosses, bossism.
cacle, *m.* 1. (Mex.) coarse leather sandal. 2. (Cuba) house slipper.
caco, *m.* 1. thief. 2. (myth.) C., Cacus, a celebrated thief whose hideaway was in the Aventine Hill of Rome. 3. (coll.) coward, poltroon.
cacodilato, *m.* (chem.) cacodylate.
cacodílico, *a.* (chem.) cacodylic.
cacodilo, *m.* (chem.) cacodyl.
cacofonía, *f.* 1. cacophony; monotonous or irritating alliteration. 2. mixture of unharmonious sounds.
cacofónico, ca, *a.* cacophonous, unharmonious.
cacogénesis, cacogenia, *f.* (biol.) cacogenesis.
cacogénica, *f.* (biol.) cacogenics.
cacografía, *f.* cacography, misspelling.
cacomite, *m.* (bot.) tigerflower.
cacomiztle, *m.* (zool.) cacomistle.
cacoquimia, *f.* (med.) cacohymia, cacochymy.
cacoquímico, ca, *a.* (med.) cacochymic. —*m., f.* person suffering from cacochymy.
cacoquimio, mia, *m., f.* pale, melancholy person.
cacorro, *m.* (Col.) effeminate man, pansy (coll.).
cactáceo, a, cácteo, a, *a.* (bot.) cactaceous. —*f.* (*pl.*) (bot.) Cactaceae.
cacto, *m.* (bot.) cactus.
cactus, *m., var. of* **cacto.**
cacumen, *m.* (coll.) acumen, shrewdness, brains, discernment, perspicacity.
cacuminal, *a.* (phonet.) cacuminal.
cacunda, *f.* (Arg.) upper part of the back of a stoop-shouldered person, hump of hump-backed person; (Urug.) hump.
cada, *f.* (bot.) juniper shrub, cade.
cada, *a.* each; every; **c.** + *numeral,* every, e.g. *viene c. cuatro días,* he comes every four days; **c. cual, c. uno,** each one, everyone; **c. vez** or **día** + *comp.,* increasingly, more and more, e.g. *la situación se vuelve c. vez más difícil,* the situation gets increasingly difficult, the situation gets more difficult each day; **c. vez que,** whenever, every time that.
cadahalso, *m.* shed, shack, wooden shelter.
cadalecho, *m.* pallet made with branches.
cadalso, *m.* raised platform, stand; scaffold (for executions).
cadañego, ga, *a.* (bot.) bearing abundant fruit every year.
cadañero, ra, *a.* annual, yearly; lasting one year; giving birth annually.
cadarzo, *m.* floss, coarse outer silk (of the cocoon not used in spinning); outer layers of the cocoon.
cádava, *f.* burnt stump of furze.
cadaval, *m.* place where many burned furze stumps remain standing.
cadáver, *m.* corpse, body; **ladrón de cadáveres,** body snatcher.
cadavérico, ca, *a.* cadaverous.
cadaverina, *f.* (chem.) cadaverine.
cadejo, *m.* 1. tangled hair, tangle, snarl (of hair); small skein (of silk, etc.); cluster of strands (for making tassels, ropes); (Arg.) lock (of hair). 2. (Hond., coll.) imaginary night-haunting animal.
cadena, *f.* 1. chain (connected series of metal or other links used for support, restraint, mechanical transmission, etc.). 2. chain, spar, boom (across river or harbor). 3. (fig.) chain, yoke, shackle, fetter. 4. chain gang. 5. chain (of events, hotels, newspapers, stores, radio stations, atoms, etc.). 6. (archit.) chain course. 7. (archit.) wooden frame (on which masonry is built). 8. (archit.) horizontal fender (over kitchen hearth or range). 9. (elec.) chain, circuit. 10. (Amer.) chain stitch (embroidery, knitting). 11. (tel.) channel. — **c. abierta,** (chem.) open chain; **c. antirrobo,** bicycle lock; **c. de agrimensor,** (surv.) measuring chain; **c. de aisladores,** (phys.) chain insulator; **c. de desintegración,** (phys.) decay chain; **c. de distribución,** (auto.) timing chain; **c. de emisoras,** radio network; **c. de enganche,** (ry) chain coupling; **c. de fondeo,** mooring chain; **c. de mando,** (auto.) drive chain; chain of command; **c. de montaje** or **de ensamblaje,** assembly line; **c. de montañas,** chain of mountains, mountain range; **c. de oruga,** crawler belt; **c. de rocas,** reef, ridge of rock; **c. de seguridad,** safety chain; **c. perpetua,** (law) life imprisonment; **cadenas antideslizantes** or **de rueda,** snow chains; **c. sin fin,** endless chain; **c. transportadora,** chain conveyor; **reacción en c.,** chain reaction.
cadenada, *f.* (top.) length of one chain.
cadencia, *f.* 1. cadence (fall of voice; rhythm or beat of poetry, prose or music; rhythmical movement of dancing; uniform pace in marching). 2. (mus.) cadence (strain concluding musical phrase); cadenza (flourish at the close of movement). — **c. de paso,** (mil.) cadence (marching pace); **c. perfecta,** (mus.) perfect cadence; **c. suspendida,** (mus.) deceptive, false, interrupted or suspended cadence.
cadenciosamente, *adv.* rhythmically, liltingly.
cadencioso, sa, *a.* rhythmical, lilting.
cadenero, *m.* (surveyor's) chainman.
cadeneta, *f.* 1. chain stitch (embroidery, knitting). 2. ornamentation on book headbands.
cadenilla, *f.* small ornamental chain; **c. de tiro,** (elec.) pull chain.
cadente, *a.* 1. crumbling, tottering, in a ruinous state; declining, decaying. 2. rhythmical, lilting.
cadera, *f.* 1. (anat.) hip. 2. (*pl.*) bustle (of dress).
caderillas, *f.* (*pl.*) bustle (of dress).
caderudo, da, *a.* large-hipped, heavy-hipped.
cadetada, *f.* (coll.) prank, lark; antic; **hacer una c.,** to play a joke.
cadete, *m.* (mil.) cadet; (Arg., Bol.) apprentice, office boy. — **hacer el c.,** to play pranks.
cadi, *m.* Ecuadorian ivory palm (Phytelephas macrocarpa).
cadí, *m.* cadi, Mohammedan magistrate.
cadiazgo, *m.* office or rank of a cadi.
cádillar, *m.* place covered with burrs or prickly weeds.
cadillo, *m.* 1. (bot.) hedgehog parsley; (bot.) cocklebur, burdock. 2. (Chile) thistledown, down of other plants. 3. (med.) wart. 4. (tex.) (*pl.*) thrum, warp ends.
cadmía, *f.* (metal.) zinc oxide sublimate; tutty (crude zinc oxide found on flues of smelting furnaces).
cadmiado, *a.* cadmium-plated.
cadmio, *m.* (chem.) cadmium.
Cadmo, *m.* (myth.) Cadmus, founder of Thebes.
cadoce, *m.* (ichth.) goby, gudgeon.
cadoso, cadozo, *m.* whirlpool, eddy.
caducamente, *adv.* feebly, weakly.
caducante, *a.* obsolete; lapsing, expiring.
caducar, (*ref. 50*) *i.v.* 1. to be senile. 2. to become void (a will, law); to lapse, expire (a right, passport); (coll.) to wear out, deteriorate.
caduceo, *m.* (hist., myth.) caduceus, the staff carried by Mercury and Hermes, emblem of commerce and medicine.

caducidad, *f.* 1. (law) caducity, voidance, lapsing, nullity. 2. caducity, senility, decrepitude. — **c. de la instancia,** (law) discontinuance of suit, nonsuit.
caduco, ca, *a.* 1. lapsed, expired, canceled, null and void. 2. old, senile. 3. caducous, perishable, transitory, fleeting.
caduque, *ref.* **caducar.**
caduquez, *f.* caducity, senility.
cadedizo, za, *a.* liable to fall; (bot.) deciduous. —*m.* (Amer.) lean-to.
Caedmon, Cedmon, *m.* Caedmon, first English poet whose name is known (7th century A.D.).
caedura, *f.* (tex.) waste, refuse, loose threads dropping from loom.
caer, (*ref. 5*) *i.v.* 1. to fall; to drop; to tumble, topple. 2. to fall (dynasty, empire, government, etc.; to fall from grace or favor (a person). 3. to fall, drop (prices, value). 4. to fall, come or descend suddenly, e.g. *c. sobre el enemigo,* to fall on the enemy. 5. to be caught, e.g. *ya cayó el asesino,* the murderer has already been caught. 6. to fall due. 7. to get, fall (to one), e.g. *le cayó el premio,* he got or won the prize, *le cayó una fuerte multa,* he got a very stiff fine. 8. to be, be situated, e.g. *la puerta cae a la izquierda,* the door is on the left; to be included, fall, lie (within certain limits, rules, etc.); to occur, fall, be, e.g. *su cumpleaños cae en marzo,* his birthday is in March. 9. to be, be found or considered, e.g. *este tipo me cae sumamente antipático,* I find this fellow extremely unpleasant, *él me cae terriblemente pesado,* I find him a terrible bore, *él les cayó muy bien,* he was very favorably received by them, he made a real hit with them. 10. to draw to a close (day); to set (sun). 11. (coll.) to fall, die (in battle). 12. to become faint (color). 13. to drop (wind). — **ahora caigo,** now I understand, now I get it; **al c. la noche,** at nightfall; **c. bien,** to hang well, fit well, be becoming (clothes); **caerle bien a uno,** to fit one well, suit one, look well on one (clothes), e.g. *el nuevo terno le cae bien,* his new suit fits him well or looks well on him; to please one, e.g. *mi respuesta* or *actitud no le cayó muy bien,* my reply or attitude did not please him very much, he did not like my reply or attitude very much; to agree with (one's stomach), e.g. *la comida china no me cae bien,* Chinese food does not agree with me; **c. de espaldas,** to fall backwards, fall on one's back; **c. de cabeza,** to fall on one's head; **c. del burro,** to recognize one's mistake; **c. del cielo,** to come out of the blue; **c. de pie,** to fall on one's feet, have good luck; **c. de plano,** to fall flat; **c. en desgracia,** to fall into disgrace; **c. en el error,** to fall into the error, make the mistake; **c. en la cuenta,** to catch on, understand, realize, find out; **c. en la emboscada,** to fall into the ambush; **c. en la red,** to fall into the net; **c. en la trampa,** to fall into the trap, fall for the trap; **c. en cama. c. enfermo,** to fall ill or sick; **caerle (a uno) en gracia,** to find pleasant and agreeable, e.g. *me cae en gracia este muchacho,* I find this boy pleasant; **c. mal,** to fit badly, hang badly, be unbecoming (clothes); **caerle mal a uno,** to fit one badly, not to suit or look well on one; to displease or annoy one; to disagree with one's stomach (food); **c. por su propio peso,** to be obvious or self-evident; **caído del nido,** wet behind the ears, inexperienced, ingenuous; **dejar c.,** to drop, let fall; **estar al c.,** to be about to happen. —*r.v.* 1. to fall; to drop. 2. to become depressed, lose heart. 3. to bend, droop, e.g. *las ramas se caían por el peso de la nieve,* the branches were bending with the weight of the snow. — **caérsele (a uno) los anillos,** (coll.) to lose one's social standing, lose one's reputation, go down in people's eyes; **caerse de suyo** or **de sí mismo,** to be obvious or self-evident; **caerse muerto,** to drop dead; **caerse muerto de risa,** to die laughing; **caerse muerto de susto** or **de miedo,** to jump out of one's skin, die of fright; **no tener donde caerse muerto,** to be destitute, be very poor; **haberse caído de un nido,** to be very credulous, be rather simple or stupid.
café, *a.* coffee, coffee-colored. —*m.* 1. coffee (coffee bean, ground coffee bean, beverage); (bot.) coffee tree or plant. 2. cafe, coffee shop. 3. (Amer.) reprimand, telling-off, e.g. *dar un c.,* to tell off, give (someone) a reprimand. 4. (Mex.) annoyance, irritation, displeasure. — **c. cantante,** café chantant, night club, cabaret; **c. con leche,** coffee with milk; **c. descafeinado,** decaffeinated coffee; **c. en grano,** coffee beans; **c. exprés** or **expreso,** espresso; **c. instantáneo,** instant coffee; **c. molido,** ground coffee; **c. negro, puro** or **solo,** black coffee; **c. soluble,** instant coffee; **c. torrado,** roasted coffee. **estar de mal c.,** (C. Amer.) to be in a bad mood, be out of sorts.
cafeína, *f.* (chem.) caffeine.
cafería, *f.* hamlet, village.
cafetal, *m.* coffee plantation.
cafetalero, ra, *a.* pertaining to coffee-growing. —*m., f.* owner of a coffee plantation, coffee grower, coffee planter.
cafetalista, *m., f.* (Cuba) owner of a coffee plantation, coffee grower, coffee planter.
cafetera, *f.* 1. coffee pot, percolator. 2. proprietress of a coffee shop; (woman) coffee seller.
cafetería, *f.* (Amer.) cafeteria, coffee shop, café; (Amer.) retail coffee shop; (Amer.) coffee roasting and grinding factory.
cafetero, ra, *a.* 1. coffee, pertaining to coffee. 2. (coll.) fond of coffee. —*m., f.* coffee picker. —*m.* proprietor of a coffee shop; coffee seller.
cafetín, *m. dim. of* **café,** small coffee shop.
cafeto, *m.* (bot.) coffee tree or plant.
cafetómano, na, *m., f., a.* said of one who habitually drinks coffee or likes to frequent coffee houses.
cafetucho, *m. derog. of* **café,** small or ill-tended coffee shop or café.
cáfila, *f.* (coll.) crowd, flock, multitude.
cafiroleta, *f.* (Cuba) dessert made of sweet potato, grated coconut and sugar.
cafre, *a.* 1. pertaining to the Kaffir, a South African tribe. 2. (fig.) barbarous and cruel. 3. coarse and uncouth. —*m., f.* 1. Kaffir. 2. barbarous and cruel person. 3. oaf, lout, churl.
caftán, *m.* caftan, Moorish robe.
caftén, *m.* (Arg.) brothel owner, pimp.
cafúa, *f.* (Arg.) prison, jail.
cagaaceite, *m.* (ornith.) missel thrush.
cagachín, *m.* 1. (ento.) small red mosquito. 2. (ornith.) small linnet.
cagada, *f.* 1. (vulg.) excrement, shit (vulg.). 2. (vulg) error, mistake.
cagadero, *m.* (vulg.) latrine, lavatory.
cagado, da, *past part. of* **cagar.** —*a.* (vulg.) spiritless, spineless; chicken (coll.), cowardly.
cagafierro, *m.* dross of iron.
cagajón, *m.* horse dung.
cagalaolla, *m.* (coll.) clown, masquerader.
cagalera, *f.* 1. (coll.) diarrhea, excessive loosening of bowels. 2. (Hond., bot.) spiky shrub used for thickset hedges.
cagaluta, *f., var. of* **cagarruta,** droppings (deer, rabbits, etc.).
cagar, (*ref. 51*) *i.v., r.v.* (vulg.) to defecate, evacuate the bowels, shit (vulg.). —*tr.v.* to soil, stain, spoil; to botch up.
cagarrache, *m.* 1. one who washes pips in olive mill. 2. (ornith.) missel thrush.
cagarria, *f.* (bot.) morel.
cagarropa, *m.* (ento.) small red mosquito.
cagarruta, *f.* deer, rabbits or sheep droppings.
cagatinta, *m.* (coll., derog.) office worker, pen-pusher.
cagatorio, *m., var. of* **cagadero.**
cagón, na, *a.* 1. diarrheic, afflicted with diarrhea. 2. (coll.) yellow-livered, cowardly. —*m., f.* 1. one who is afflicted with diarrhea. 2. (coll.) coward, chicken (coll.). 3. (ichth., Cuba) parrot fish. 4. (ornith., Cuba) martineta.
caguama, *f.* (zool.) green turtle; shell (of this turtle).
caguane, *m.* (Cuba, zool.) univalve mollusk similar to strombus.
caguanete, *m.* (Cuba) fluff (of cotton, etc.).
caguaní, *m.* (bot.) ironwood (Sideroxylon foetidissimum).
caguara, *m.* (Cuba, zool.) strombus, univalve mollusk.
caguarero, *m.* (ornith., Cuba) bird of prey (Leptodon wilsoni) which feeds on mollusks.
caguayo, *m.* (Cuba) lizard.
cague, cagué, *ref.* **cagar.**
cagueta, *a.* (coll.) chicken, cowardly.
cagüil, *m.* (ornith.) *var. of* **cahuil.**
cahíz, (*pl.* **cahices**) *m.* (agr.) dry measure of 666 liters.
cahuil, *m.* (ornith., Chile) sea gull (Laurus pipixcan).
cahuín, *m.* (Chile) drunken spree.
caíble, *a.* apt to fall.
caico, *m.* (Cuba) large reef.
caíd, *m.* caid, Moorish official.
caída, *f.* 1. fall; falling; tumble. 2. fall, downfall, collapse (of empire, etc.). 3. slope, gradient; (geol.) dip. 4. fall, hang, way of hanging (of curtain); fold (in curtains or clothes). 5. (Phil. I.) interior gallery overlooking courtyard. 6. (mar.) drop, hoist, depth (of sail). 7. (*pl.*) falling ends of wool; coarse wool (from sheep's rump). 8. (*pl.*) witticisms, witty remarks. — **a la c. de la tarde,** in the late afternoon; **a la c. del sol,** at sunset; **c. de agua,** waterfall; **c. de latiguillo,** (taur.) fall flat on the back (a picador); **c. de ojos,** lowering or dropping of the eyes; **c. de potencial de línea,** (elec.) line drop; La C., (Bib.) the Fall (of Adam); **c. bruta,** (hydr.) gross head; **c. de fricción,** (hydr.) friction drop; **c. pluvial,** (meteorol.) rainfall.
caído, da, *past part. of* **caer.** —*a.* 1. fallen. 2. crestfallen, disheartened, cowed. 3. round, bent (shoulders). —*m.* 1. oblique line (on paper to guide children's writing). 2. (*pl.*) income due. 3. (*pl.*) the fallen (in battle).
caiga, caigo, *ref.* **caer.**
caigua, *f.* (Peru, Arg., bot.) cucurbitaceous plant (Cyclanthera tonduzii) bearing fruits similar to bell peppers; fruit of this plant, served stuffed with meat.
caima, *a.* (Bol.) tasteless, insipid.
caimacán, *m.* 1. Kaimakam, assistant to grand vizier. 2. (Col.) person of authority.
caimán, *m.* 1. (zool.) alligator, caiman. 2. (fig.) fox, cunning person, schemer. 3. (mec.) Stillson wrench. 4. (Mex.) ore chute.
caimanera, *f.* (Cuba) alligator or caiman grounds.
caimiento, *m.* 1. fall, falling. 2. faintness, weakness; depression, lowness (of spirit).
caimital, *m.* place where star-apple trees abound.

caimitillo, *m.* (Cuba, bot.) caimitillo, satinleaf.
caimito, *m.* (C. Amer., bot.) star apple.
Caín, *m.* (Bib.) Cain; **pasar or sufrir las de C.,** to have a terrible time.
caique, *m.* caique, skiff, ketch.
cairel, *m.* 1. toupee, small wig. 2. fringe, trimming; (*pl.*) furbelows, trimmings. 3. silk strands fastening hair of wig. 4. spit-curl. 5. (mar.) rail. 6. (archit.) decoration in Gothic architecture.
cairelar, *tr.v.* to fringe, decorate clothes with fringes.
cairo, *m.* (Cuba) coarse cotton wick.
Cairo, *m.* **El C.,** Cairo, capital of Egypt.
caisimón, *m.* (Cuba) (bot.) wild plant with leaves used medicinally.
caite, *m.* (C. Amer.) coarse leather sandal.
caja, *f.* 1. box, case, chest, casket; safe, strongbox; till, cashbox; coffin; (mec.) housing, casing. 2. body (of car, carriage). 3. (mus.) drum. 4. wooden case (covering some musical instruments such as the piano); resonance box (e.g. of guitar). 5. hole, hollow, groove, notch (in which nut of arbalest fits); (carp.) socket, groove, mortise. 6. cashier's desk or office; cashier; (com.) cash, cash in hand. 7. (coll.) chest, thorax. 8. wooden stand or tripod (on which a brazier is placed). 9. pointer housing (of scales). 10. (gun) stock. 11. well, shaft (of stairs, elevator). 12. distributing post office. 13. office, bureau (for collecting revenue); recruiting office. 14. wings (in theater). 15. (Chile) bed (of river). 16. (bot.) seed box, capsule. 17. (print.) type case. 18. (Chile, min.) salband, selvage, gouge. — **c. alta,** (print.) upper case (for capital letters); **c. ascendente, c. de caballeros, c. de agujas,** (tex.) drop box; **c. baja,** (print.) lower case (for small letters); **c. basculante,** dump body; **c. chica,** petty cash; **c. de acceso,** (elec.) pull box; **c. de aceite** or **grasa,** oil cup or box; **c. de agua,** reservoir, water tank; (ry.) water tank (on tender); **c. de ahorros,** savings bank; **c. de ascensor,** lift or elevator shaft; **c. de bolas,** ball cage, retainer; **c. de cambios** or **velocidades,** gearbox; **c. de caudales,** safe, strongbox; **c. de colores,** paintbox; **c. de chumacera,** journal box, pillow block; axle box; **c.-dique,** cofferdam; **c. de distribución,** (mec.) valve chest; steam chest; **c. de embrague,** (auto.) clutch housing; **c. de empalme,** (elec.) junction box, joint or splice box; **c. fuerte,** safe, strongbox; **c. de fuego,** (mec.) firebox; **c. de fusibles** or **tapones,** (elec.) fuse box; **c. de herramientas,** tool box; **c. de humo,** smoke box (chamber in steam boiler); **c. del cuerpo,** chest; **c. del eje,** axle box; **c. del tambor,** (anat.) middle ear; **c. de mando,** control box; **c. de música,** music box; **c. de Pandora,** Pandora's box; **c. de paso,** (elec.) pull box; **c. de pensiones,** pension fund; **c. de registro,** manhole; **c. de resistencias,** (elec.) resistance box; **c. de rodillos,** roller race; **c. de salida,** (elec.) outlet box; **c. de seguridad,** safe deposit box; **c. de transmisiones,** transmission box; **c. de válvulas** or **de distribución,** (mec.) valve box or chest; **c. de vapor,** steam chest or box; **c. de ventilación,** (min.) air shaft; **c. de viga,** (bldg.) beam pocket; **c. de volteo,** dump body; **c. fuerte,** strongbox, safe; **c. perdida,** (print.) sorts case, back boxes of a type case; type page; **c. postal de ahorros,** postal savings bank; **c. registradora,** till, cash register; **c. y espiga,** (carp.) mortise and tenon.
cajear, *tr.v.* to mortise, recess.
cajel, *a.* **naranja c.,** bitter-sweet orange.
cajera, *f.* 1. woman cashier. 2. (mar.) sheave channel or groove. — **c. de chaveta,** (mec.) keyway, key seat; **c. de lubricación,** oil groove.
cajería, *f.* box shop or factory.
cajero, *m.* 1. box maker. 2. cashier, teller. 3. hawker, peddler.
cajeta, *f.* 1. small box. 2. (C. Rica, Ecuad., Peru) thick-lipped person. 3. snuffbox. 4. (Mex.) a confection set to jell in a wooden box. 5. (mar.) sennit, plaited rope. — **de c.,** (C. Amer., Mex.) excellent, first-class; excellently, very well.
cajete, *m.* (Guat., Mex.) earthenware bowl.
cajetilla, *f.* (cigarette) pack, packet.
cajetín, *m.* 1. small box; ticket box (of streetcar conductor); (print.) box (each individual compartment in a type case). 2. stamp (mark and instrument). 3. (elec.) cleat insulator.
cají, *m.* (ichth., Cuba) porgy.
cajiga, *f.* (bot.) gall oak.
cajigal, *m.* gall oak grove.
cajilla, *f.* (bot.) seed case.
cajista, *m., f.* (print.) typesetter, compositor.
cajo, *m.* (print.) flange (on back of books to fit on the covers).
cajón, *m.* 1. *aug. of* **caja,** large box, case, chest; drawer (in furniture); (mil.) caisson (for munitions). 2. space between shelves. 3. stall, shop, booth. 4. (Amer.) ravine. 5. (archit.) panel, space between columns (in wall). 6. (arch.) (Mex., Peru) mail (coming from Spain in galleons). 7. (Mex., Peru) grocery store. 8. (Peru) drum (made out of a box). 9. (Amer.) coffin. — **c. de sastre,** (coll.) odds and ends, hodgepodge; (coll.) muddle-headed person, muddlehead, jumblehead; **c. neumático,** (engin.) pneumatic caisson; **ser de c. una cosa,** to be common, usual or customary; **c. de embalaje,** packing case; **c. de esqueleto,** crate.
cajonada, *f.* (mar.) crew's lockers.
cajonera, *f.* chest of drawers in vestry (for vestments).
cajonería, *f.* set of drawers (in piece of furniture).
cajonero, *m.* 1. (Mex.) shopkeeper, storekeeper. 2. (min.) cager, onsetter, bottomer.
cajonga, *f.* (Hond.) large corn cake.
cajuela, *f. dim. of* **caja,** small box.
cajuil, *m.* (Dom. Rep., bot.) cashew tree.
cal, *f.* lime; **c. anhidra,** anhydrous lime; **c. blanca,** high-calcium lime; **c. cáustica,** caustic lime; **c. y canto,** stone masonry; **c. hidráulica,** hydraulic lime; **c. muerta,** slaked or hydrated lime; **c. viva,** quicklime.
cala, *f.* 1. plugging, cutting of slice of fruit (to sample it); slice, plug (of fruit for tasting). 2. (med.) suppository. 3. (mas.) test boring (in a wall). 4. (mar.) hold, draft. 5. fishing ground. 6. (med.) probe (instrument to test the depth of a wound). 7. (sl.) hole. 8. cove, small bay, inlet. 9. (bot.) calla lily.
calaba, *m.* calaba, Santa Maria tree (Calophyllum calaba).
calabacear, *tr.v.* 1. (coll.) to fail, flunk (an examination). 2. (coll.) to turn (a suitor) down, to jilt (coll.), give someone the air (sl.). —*r.v.* **calabacearse por,** to break one's back for; **calabacearse por** + *inf.,* to break one's back to + *inf.*
calabacero, ra, *m., f.* pumpkin or marrow seller. —*m.* (bot.) calabash tree (Crescentia cujete). —*f.* (bot.) squash, pumpkin, marrow.
calabacil, *a.* gourd-like (pear).
calabacilla, *f.* (bot.) 1. bitter cucumber. 2. an earring shaped like a pumpkin.
calabacín, *m.* 1. (bot.) squash, vegetable marrow. 2. dolt, pumpkin head.
calabacinate, *m.* marrow or squash stew.
calabacino, *m.* gourd, calabash (used as vessel, bottle or bowl).
calabaza, *f.* 1. (bot.) squash, pumpkin, marrow (plant and fruit). 2. calabash, gourd (used as bowl or bottle). 3. pumpkin head, dullard, dimwit. 4. (mar.) old tub, heavy unseaworthy vessel. — **c. bonetera** or **pastelera,** bonnet-shaped pumpkin; **c. confitera** or **totanera,** pumpkin; **c. vinatera,** bottle gourd; **dar calabazas,** to fail (in examinations), flunk (sl.); to turn (a suitor) down, give someone the air to (sl.).
calabazada, *f.* butt with the head; blow or bump on the head; **darse de calabazadas por,** to break one's back for; **darse de calabazadas por** + *inf.,* to break one's back + *inf.*
calabazar, *m.* squash or pumpkin field.
calabazate, *m.* dried squash preserve; squash peel steeped in honey or molasses.
calabazazo, *m.* knock or blow given with a gourd; (coll.) blow, bump on the head.
calabazo, *m.* 1. squash, pumpkin, marrow. 2. gourd, calabash (used as a bottle or bowl). 3. (Cuba, mus.) instrument made from a gourd. 4. (mar.) old tub, heavy unseaworthy vessel.
calabazon, *m. aug. of* **calabaza,** large squash or pumpkin.
calabobos, *m.* (coll.) continued drizzle, fine, gentle rain.
calabocero, *m.* jailer.
calabozo, *m.* 1. dungeon, cell; jail, calaboose. 2. pruning hook or knife.
calabrés, sa, *a.* Calabrian, from or pertaining or Calabria, a region in Italy.
calabriada, *f.* 1. mixture of white and red wine. 2. hodgepodge, potpourri.
calabriar, *tr.v.* to mix, confuse.
calabrotar, *tr.v.* (mar.) to weave (three strands) into a cable or hawser.
calabrote, *m.* (mar.) cable, hawser.
calacuerda, *f.* (mil.) beat of drums (signal to commence fire).
calada, *f.* 1. soaking, drenching. 2. lowering (of a net into water). 3. swoop, dive (of birds of prey). — **dar una c.,** (coll.) to reprimand someone.
caladero, *m.* place for casting fish nets.
caladio, *m.* (bot.) caladium, an ornamental plant.
caladizo, za, *a.* passing through easily; runny (of liquids).
calado, *m.* 1. (sew.) drawn work, hemstitching. 2. openwork, fretwork. 3. (mar.) draft (of a vessel); (mar.) depth. 4. (*pl.*) deep lace collar. — **c. en plena carga,** (mar.) load draft; **c. máximo,** extreme draft; **c. medio,** mean draft; **c. sin carga,** light draft.
calador, *m.* 1. (mec.) driller, perforator, borer, maker of openwork or fretwork, hemstitcher. 2. (med.) surgeon's probe. 3. (mar.) calking iron, calking chisel. 4. (Arg., Mex.) sampler (for extracting samples from bales).
caladora, *f.* (Ven.) large pirogue, large dugout canoe.
caladre, *f.* (ornith.) calander, a bird of the lark family.
caladura, *f.* plugging, cutting of slice of fruit (for sampling); plug, slice (of fruit for sampling or tasting); boring.
calafate, *m.* (mar.) calker, caulker; shipyard carpenter.
calafateado, *m.* calking, caulking (trade and work).
calafateador, *m.* caulker, calker.
calafateadura, *f.* calking, caulking.
calafatear, *tr.v.* to caulk, calk (ships); to plug, fill up (other joints).
calafateo, *m.* caulking, calking.
calafatería, *f.* caulking, calking.
calafatín, *m.* caulker's or calker's apprentice.
calagozo, *m.* pruning hook or knife.
calagraña, *f.* variety of poor quality grape; small white thin-skinned grape.
calaguala, *f.* (bot.) polypody, medicinal fern (Polypodium calaguala).

calaguasca, *f.* (Col.) raw, uncured brandy.
calahorra, *f.* public office formerly in charge of distributing bread in times of scarcity.
calaíta, *f.* turquoise (stone).
calaje, *m.* (elec.) angular displacement; (tool) setting (angle).
calalú, *m.* 1. (Cuba) pottage made with gumbo. 2. (Cuba, bot.) calalu (plant used as greens). 3. (Salv., bot.) okra, gumbo.
calaluz, (*pl.* **calaluces**) *m.* small vessel used in the East Indies.
calamaco, *m.* calamanco, former type of woolen cloth with a glossy face.
calamar, *m.* (zool.) squid.
calambac, *m.* (bot.) calambac, agalloch (Aquilaria agallocha).
calambre, *m.* cramp; muscular spasm. — **c. de los escritores,** writer's cramp.
calambreña, *f.* (Cuba, bot.) sea grape, woody vine of the buckwheat family (Coccolobis nivea).
calambuco, *m.* 1. (bot.) calaba, Santa Maria tree. (Callophyllum calaba). 2. (Cuba, coll.) a religious zealot.
calamento, *m.* 1. (bot.) calamint. 2. lowering or casting of fishing nets.
calamidad, *f.* calamity, disaster.
calamiforme, *a.* calamiferous, calamiform, quill-like.
calamillera, *f.* pot hook, pot hanger.
calamina, *f.* 1. (min.) calamine. 2. (Peru) corrugated iron. 3. (*pl.*) (Amer.) galvanized corrugated sheets.
calaminar, *a.* pertaining to calamine.
calaminta, *f.* (bot.) calamint.
calamistro, *m.* (archeol.) calamistrum, an ancient curling iron (for hair).
calamita, *f., var. of* **calamite.**
calamita, *f.* loadstone, lodestone, magnetite; compass.
calamite, *f.* small green toad.
calamitosamente, *adv.* calamitously.
calamitoso, sa, *a.* calamitous.
cálamo, *m.* 1. ancient reed flute. 2. (poet.) reed, stalk, stem. 3. (poet.) pen. 4. calamus. 5. (zool.) calamus (barrel or quill or feather). — **c. aromático,** (bot.) calamus, sweet flag root.
calamocano, *a.* 1. (coll.) tipsy, lit-up, merry, slightly drunk. 2. (coll.) doddering.
calamoco, *m.* icicle.
cálamo currente, (lat.) *adv.* hastily, hurriedly.
calamocha, *f.* dull yellow ocher.
calamón, *m.* 1. (ornith.) purple gallinule, sultana (Porphyrio caeruleus). 2. stud, roundheaded nail. 3. stay (supporting the beam in an oil mill). 4. pivot, fulcrum hole (of Roman scales).
calamondín, *m.* (Phil. I., bot.) calamondin.
calamorra, *a.* woolly-faced (sheep). —*f.* (coll.) head.
calamorrada, *f.* butt wih the head; bump (on the head).
calamorrar, *v.t.* to butt with the head.
calamorrazo, *m.* (coll.) bump (on the head).
calamorro, *m.* (Chile) clog, rough coarse shoe.
calandraca, *f.* (mar.) hardtack soup.
calandraco, *m.* (Arg., Col.) rag, tatter.
calandrado, *past part. of* **calandrar.** —*m.* calendering.
calandrajo, *m.* 1. (coll.) tatter, rag. 2. (coll.) dope, fool, sap.
calandrar, *tr.v.* to calender (cloth, paper).
calandria, *f.* 1. calender, machine for calendering cloth. 2. treadmill cage (of a hoisting winch). 3. (ornith.) calander, a type of lark. —*m., f.* (coll.) malingerer, leadswinger, goldbrick (sl.) one who feigns illness to get into hospital.

cálanis, *m.* (bot.) calamus, sweet flag root.
calántica, *f.* miter, mitre, a 15th C. women's headdress like a bishop's miter.
calaña, *f.* 1. character, kind, nature, sort, type. 2. pattern, model. 3. inexpensive reed hand fan.
calañés, *m.* stiff, low-crowned black hat with rolled up brim, formerly worn by Andalusian peasants and still used by Spanish Gypsies and flamenco dancers.
cálao, *m.* (ornith.) hornbill.
calapatillo, *m.* (ento.) grain weevil.
calar, *a.* caucareous, lime, limy. —*m.* limestone quarry.
calar, *tr.v.* 1. to soak, drench; permeate. 2. to pierce, perforate. 3. to hemstitch, make drawn work on (cloth); to cut openwork, fretwork or tracings on (cloth, paper, etc.). 4. to plug, cut a wedge of (fruit for sampling). 5. to jam on, pull (a hat) down on one's head. 6. (mil.) to lower (pike, lance) to the on guard position; (mil.) to fix (bayonets). 7. (coll.) to size up, gauge (a person); (coll.) to grasp, understand, perceive (design or motive). 8. (Col.) to squash, humiliate. 9. (Amer.) to sample, take a sample of. 10. (mar.) to lower, haul down. 11. (mar.) to lower, cast (net). 12. (sl.) to pick (a pocket). 13. (Arg., Urug.) to stare at, watch fixedly. —*i.v.* (mar.) to draw. —*r.v.* 1. to get drenched or soaked; to soak through, seep through. 2. to swoop down on, pounce (birds). 3. to slip in, get in, work one's way in. 4. to pull down or jam (one's hat) on one's head. — **calarse haste los huesos,** to get soaked to the skin; **lo calé,** (sl.) I got his number, I've caught on to what he is up to.
calasancio, cia, *a.* pertaining to religious schools.
cálato, *m.* (archaeol.) calathus, type of wicker basket.
calato, ta, *a.* (Peru, coll.) naked, nude.
calatraveño ña, *a.* of or from Calatrava. —*m., f.* native or inhabitant of Calatava, Spain.
calatravo, va, *a.* of Calatrava (knightly order). —*m.* member of the Order of Calatrava.
calavera, *f.* 1. skull. 2. (ento.) death's head moth (Acherontia atropos). 3. (Mex., auto.) tail light. —*m.* madcap, daredevil; profligate, rake.
calaverada, *f.* (coll.) reckless act, mad escapade.
calaverear, *i.v.* to lead a wild or dissolute life.
calaverilla, ita, *f. dim. of* **calavera,** little skull. —*m.* youth who sows his wild oats.
calavernario, *m.* ossuary, charnel house.
calazo, *m.* (Guat.) blow, knock.
calazón, *f.* (mar.) draft (of a ship).
calca, *f.* 1. (Amer.) granary. 2. a copy; **c. heliográfica,** sun print, blue print.
calcadera, *f.* (arch.) heel.
calcado, *m.* tracing.
calcador, ra, *m., f.* tracer (person who traces). —*m.* tracer (instrument for tracing).
calcamar, *m.* Brazilian sea bird.
calcáneo, *m.* (anat.) calcaneus, **calcaneum.**
calcañal, *m., var. of* **calcañar.**
calcañar, *m.* heel, heel bone.
calcaño, *m., var. of* **calcañar.**
calcañuelo, *m.* disease affecting bees.
calcar, (*ref. 50*) *tr.v.* 1. to trace (drawing). 2. to tread on. 3. to imitate or copy someone slavishly.
calcáreo, rea, *a.* calcareous, limy.
Calcas, *m.* (myth.) Calchas, Greek priest who devised the ruse of the Trojan horse.
calce, *m.* 1. iron rim or tire. 2. extra piece of steel added to the worn blade of a plow, etc. 3. wedge. 4. (Guat., Mex.) foot (of a document).
calce, calcé, *ref.* **calzar.**
calcedonia, *f.* (min.) chalcedony, pearl grey agate.
calceiforme, *a.* (bot.) calceiform.

cálceo, *m.* close-fitting top boot worn by Romans.
calceolaria, *f.* (bot.) calceolaria.
calcés, *m.* (mar.) masthead.
calceta, *f.* 1. stocking. 2. fetter, shackle. — **hacer c.** to knit.
calcetar, *i.v.* to knit stockings or socks.
calcetería, *f.* 1. hosiery, hosiery trade or shop. 2. knitted goods.
calcetero, ra, *m., f.* hosier; stocking maker or mender.
calcetín, *m. dim. of* **calceta,** sock.
calceto, *a.* (Col., C. Rica) feather-legged (fowl). —*m.* feather-legged domestic fowl.
calcetón, *m. aug. of* **calceta,** cloth stocking, legging.
calcha, *f.* 1. (Chile) (*gen. pl.*) tuft of hair (on a horse's fetlock); (Chile) tuft, feathers (which some birds have on the leg). 2. (Arg., Chile) workman's clothing or bedding.
calchon, na, *a.* 1. (Chile) feather-legged (bird). 2. (Chile) having shaggy fetlocks (horses).
calchona, *f.* 1. ghost, bogey-man, goblin, (Chile imaginary and malevolent spirit who frightens travelers. 2. (Chile) witch, hag. 3. (Chile) coach, carriage.
calchudo, da, *a.* (Chile) smart, full of tricks.
cálcico, ca, *a.* (chem.) calcic.
calcícolo, la, *a.* (bot.) calcicolous.
calcicosis, *f.* (med.) calcicosis.
calcídico, *m.* (archaeol.) gallery, corridor.
calcídido, *m.* (ento.) chalcid, chalcidid, (*pl.*) Chalcididae.
calcífero, ra, *a.* calciferous.
calcificación, *f.* calcification.
calcificar, (*ref. 50*) *tr.v.* to calcify.
calcifique, calcifiqué, *ref.* **calcificar.**
calcífugo, ga, *a.* (bot.) calcifugous.
calcillas, *f.* (*pl.*) short, narrow knee-breeches. —*m.* (coll.) 1. coward, mouse, chicken, timid man. 2. a short man.
calcímetro, *m.* calcimeter.
calcina, *f.* a name for concrete.
calcinable, *a.* calcinable.
calcinación, *f.* calcination.
calcinador, ra, *a.* calcinatory. —*m., f.* calciner.
calcinamiento, *m., var. of* **calcinación.**
calcinar, *tr.v.* to calcine.
calcinatorio, *m.* calcinatory, vessel used for calcination.
calcinero, *m.* lime-kiln worker; lime burner.
calcio, *m.* (min.) calcium.
calcita, *f.* (min.) calcite, natural calcium carbonate.
calcitrapa, *f.* (bot.) star thistle.
calco, *m.* tracing, traced copy. — **c. a lápiz,** pencil tracing; **c. heliográfico,** blue-print; **c. litográfico, lithotracing.**
calcografía, *f.* 1. chalcography (engraving on metals); chalcography, copperplate engraving. 2. printing with engraved metal plates; printing shop.
calcografiar, *tr.v.* to print by means of metal plates.
calcográfico, *a.* 1. chalcographic. 2. pertaining to printing by means of metal plates.
calcógrafo, *m.* 1. chalcographer. 2. printer who uses metal plates.
calcomanía, *f.* decalcomania, transfer.
calcopirita, *f.* (min.) chalcopyrite.
calcosina, *f., var. of* **calcosita.**
calcosita, *f.* (min.) chalcocite, copper glance.
calcotipia, *f.* chalcography, copperplate engraving.
calcotriquita, *f.* (min.) copper oxide.
calculable, *a.* calculable.
calculación, *f.* calculation.

calculadamente, *adv.* calculatedly, deliberately.
calculador, a, *a.* calculating. *—f.* calculator; **c. de bolsillo,** pocket calculator.
calcular, *tr.v.* to calculate.
calculatorio, ria, *a.* calculatory, calculative.
calculista, *a.* calculative. *—m., f.* 1. computer, estimating clerk, estimator (one who calculates costs, amounts, etc. for a project). 2. rapid calculator. 3. planner, schemer.
cálculo, *m.* 1. calculation; computation. 2. prudence, thought, sense. 3. (med.) calculus, stone; (*pl.*) (med.) gallstones (disease). 4. (math.) calculus. — **c. biliar,** gallstone; **c. de espacio, c. de la composición,** (print.) castoff; **c. de variaciones,** (math.) calculus of variations; **c. diferencial,** (math.) differential calculus; **c. infinitesimal,** (math.) infinitesimal calculus; **c. integral,** (math.) integral calculus; **c. prudencial,** estimate, approximate calculation; **c. renal,** kidney stone; **c. tipográfico,** (print.) castoff.
calculosis, *f.* (med.) gallstones.
calculoso, sa, *a.* (med.) calculous. *—m., f.* person suffering from gallstones.
Calcuta, *f.* Calcutta, city in India, capital of West Bengal.
calda, *f.* 1. warming, heating. 2. fueling, stoking; batch of fuel. 3. (*pl.*) hot springs.
caldaico, ca, *a.* Chaldean, Chaldaic, of or pertaining to Chaldea, ancient province of Babylonia.
caldaria, *a.* (arch.) **ley c.,** law of trial by ordeal (involving thrusting one's hand into boiling water).
caldario, *m.* caldarium, hot room of the Roman thermae.
caldeado, da, *past part. of* **caldear.** *—a.* heated (tempers, etc.).
caldeamiento, *m.* heating.
caldear, *tr.v.* 1. to heat up, overheat, make red-hot. 2. to make heated (spirits, tempers, atmosphere, passions). *—r.v.* 1. to become overheated, become red hot. 2. to become heated (tempers, spirits, atmosphere, passions). — **c. el ambiente,** to liven things up.
caldén, *m.* (bot.) calden (tree), prosopis algarrobilla.
caldeo, *m.* heating; welding. — **c. a martillo,** hammer welding; **c. de herrero,** blacksmith welding. *—a., m., f.* Chaldean.
caldera, *f.* 1. boiler; caldron, vat, copper; pot; caldronful, vatful; boilerful. 2. kettledrum case. 3. (Arg.) teapot, coffeepot. 4. (her.) artificial figure with raised handles which terminate in serpentine heads. 5. (min.) winze; sump. — **c. acuotubular,** watertube boiler; **c. de jabón,** soap factory; **c. de vapor,** steam boiler; **c. tubular,** tubular boiler; **las calderas de Pedro Botero,** hell; **c. de calefacción,** heating boiler; **c. de hogar contenido,** integral-furnace boiler; **c. de torna-llama,** return-tubular boiler; **c. locomóvil,** portable boiler on wheels.
calderada, *f.* boilerful, potful, copperful, caldronful, kettleful; **c. de pescado,** a fish stew.
calderería, *f.* boilermaking, coppermaking, caldronmaking (trade); boilermaker's, coppermaker's or caldron maker's shop or neighborhood; blacksmith's shop, iron works.
calderero, *m.* 1. boilermaker, coppermaker, potmaker, caldron maker; boiler seller, pot seller, caldron seller. 2. a certain tribe of Spanish Gypsies whose women were sung about for their beauty.
caldereta, *f.* 1. *dim. of* **caldera,** small pot; holy water bowl. 2. fish or lamb stew. 3. (mar.) storm winds blowing from the land.
calderilla, *f.* 1. holy-water vessel. 2. coin (copper, bronze or non-precious metal); change, coopers (G.B.). 3. (bot.) alpine currant (Ribes alpinum).
caldero, *m.* pot, small caldron, cauldron, copper (G.B.).
calderón, *m.* 1. *aug. of* **caldera,** copper, caldron. 2. (math.) symbol denoting a thousand. 3. (gram.) paragraph (symbol). 4. (mus.) pause, fermata. 5. (ichth.) blackfish (Globicephala melas).
calderoniano, na, *a.* (Sp. lit.) Calderonian, pertaining to or characteristic of Pedro Calderón de la Barca or his style.
calderuela, *f.* 1. *dim. of* **caldera,** small pot. 2. dark lantern used by night hunters to drive partridge into the net.
caldibaldo, *m., var. of* **calducho.**
caldillo, *m.* sauce, gravy (of some stews); (Mex., cul.) minced meat in light gravy or broth.
caldo, *m.* 1. broth, bouillon, consommé. 2. dressing, sauce (for salads or gazpacho). 3. juice (of apples, grapes, etc.), (Mex.) sugar cane juice. 4. (Mex., bot.) pot marigold (Calendula officinalis). — **c. de cultivo,** (med.) culture broth; **c. esforzado,** invigorating, strengthening broth; **hacer el c. gordo a,** to make things easy for. smooth the way for.
caldoso, sa, *a.* full of broth. *—adv.* in plenty of sauce.
calducho, *m.* 1. (derog.) thin, poorly seasoned broth. 2. (Chile) day off (from work, school).
calduda, *f.* (Chile) meat pasty, patty turnover filled with meat, gravy, eggs, raisins, olives.
caldudo, da, *a.* full of broth.
cale, *m.* slap, smack.
calé, *m.* 1. (Col., Ecuad., numis.) quarter of a **real,** no longer in use. 2. a Spanish Gypsy. — **la raza c.,** the Gypsy people.
calecer, (*ref. 45*) *i.v.* to get or become hot, heat up.
calecico, *m. dim. of* **cáliz,** small chalice.
caledonio, nia, *a., m., f.* Caledonian, of or pertaining to Caledonia, poetic name for Scotland.
calefacción, *f.* heating, calefaction; heating system; **c. a panel radiante,** radiant heating; **c. a vapor,** vapor or steam heating; **c. central,** central heating; **c. por vapor,** vapor or steam heating.
calefactorio, *m.* calefactory (heated sittingroom in a convent).
caleidoscópico, ca, *a.* kaleidoscopic.
caleidoscopio, *m.* kaleidoscope.
calembé, *m.* (Cuba) loincloth.
calenda, *f.* 1. (rel.) section of the martyrology listing the names and acts of the saints with the dates of their corresponding feast-days. 2. (*pl.*) (Roman and ecclesiastic) calends (the first day of each month). 3. (*pl.*) time, period, epoch; (iron.). — **calendas griegas,** Greek calends, never.
calendar, *tr.v.* to date (letters, documents).
calendario, *m.* calendar, almanac; **c. americano** or **de taco,** desk calendar; **c. de pared,** wall calendar; **c. de Flora,** (bot.) botanical almanac; **c. gregoriano, c. nuevo, c. reformado,** Gregorian calendar; **c. juliano** Julian calendar.
calendarista, *m., f.* person who designs or makes calendars.
calender, *m.* calender, one of a Sufistic order of wandering dervishes.
caléndula, *f.* (bot.) calendula, pot marigold.
calentador, ra, *a.* heating, warming. *—m.* 1. heater; warming pan (for bed). 2. (coll.) very large pocket watch.
calentamiento, *m.* 1. heating, warming. 2. (vet.) inflammation (of hoof or lungs).
calentar, (*ref. 33*) *tr.v.* 1. to heat, heat up; to warm, warm up. 2. to retain (the ball) a moment in the **cesta** (or hand before returning it (in pelota). 3. (coll.) to liven up, give pep to (a business). 4. (coll.) to thrash, beat. 5. (Chile) to annoy, irritate. — **c. al blanco,** to make white-hot; **c. al rojo,** to make red-hot; **c. la silla,** to stay long. *—r.v.* 1. to warm oneself; to get hot, get warm. 2. to get sexually aroused. 3. to get heated or worked up (in arguments). 4. (Amer.) to get annoyed, get angry. — **calentarse a la lumbre,** to warm oneself by the fire.
calentito, ta, *a.* 1. very warm; piping-hot. 2. (coll.) fresh, new, right off the press, the oven, etc.
calentón, *m.* 1. (coll.) warm. 2. (Peru) fit of anger; **darse un c.,** to flare up in a rage; **tener un c.,** (Peru) to get annoyed or angry; (Cuba, sl.) to have hot pants (for someone).
calentura, *f.* 1. temperature, fever; (Chile) tuberculosis. 2. (Cuba) decomposition (of tobacco due to slow fermentation). 3. (Cuba, bot.) type of milkweed (used as an emetic and in making cordage). 4. (Col.) fit of anger. 5. (sl.) sexual desire.
calenturiento, ta, *a.* 1. feverish. 2. (Chile) tuberculous. *—m., f.* person suffering from fever; sexually aroused person.
calenturón, *m.* 1. *aug. of* **calentura,** high fever. 2. (sl.) a strong sexual desire.
calenturoso, sa, *a., var. of* **calenturiento.**
caleño, ña, *a.* calcareous, containing or producing lime.
calepino, *m.* calepin, Latin dictionary.
calera, *f.* 1. limestone quarry; limekiln. 2. fishing smack.
calería, *f.* lime-crushing mill.
calero, ra, *a.* lime, calcareous. *—m.* limestone quarryman; lime burner; lime dealer; limestone quarry.
calés, *m., var. of* **calesa.**
calesa, *f.* 1. calash, light low-wheeled carriage with a leather top or hood. 2. (C. Amer.) meat worm.
calesera, *f.* 1. ornamental jacket worn by Andalusian calash drivers. 2. (*pl.*) a style of Andalusian song made popular by calash drivers in the 19th century.
calesero, *m.* calash driver.
calesín, *m.* light calash drawn by one horse.
calesinero, *m.* driver of a light calash.
calesitas, *f. pl.* (Arg.) merry-go-round.
caleta, *f.* 1. *dim. of* **cala,** cove, small bay; (Amer.) small port. 2. (Ven.) stevedores' or porters' union. — **c. buena,** (Chile, sl.) thief's cache.
caletear, *i.v.* (Amer.) to stop at all ports (ship), stop at every station (train), land at every airport en route (plane).
caletero, *m.* 1. (Amer.) stevedore, porter. 2. plane which lands at every airport en route; milk-train; coaster, ship calling at every port.
caletre, *m.* (coll.) sense, judgement, discernment, brains; **no le cabe en el c.,** he does not understand.
calezca, *ref.* **calecer.**
cali, *m.* (chem.) alkali.
Calibán, *m.* 1. Caliban, in Shakespeare's *The Tempest.* 2. (fig.) a slavish man.
calibeado, da, *a.* (med.) chalybeate.
calibración, *f.* calibration.
calibrador, *m.* calibrator, calipers, gage, caliper gauge. — **c. de cubo,** socket gauge; **c. a cursor,** slide caliper; **c. de alambre,** wire gage; **c. de brocas,** drill gage.
calibraje, *m.* gaging, calibration.
calibrar, *tr.v.* to calibrate, to gage, measure.
calibre, *m.* 1. caliber (of a projectile), bore (of firearm), thickness (of wire), diameter (of tube). 2. size, importance. 3. (coll.) caliber, quality. — **c. de comprobación,** check gauge; **ser de buen**

or **mal c.,** (coll.) to be big or small; to be of good or bad quality; **c. de nonio,** vernier calipers; **c. de profundidad,** depth range.
calicanto, *m.* 1. rubblework, stone masonry. 2. (bot.) allspice. — **de c., (fig.)** strong, firm, solid.
calicata, *f.* (min.) testing pit, prospecting pit (for ascertaining the presence of minerals).
caliche, *m.* 1. pebbly particle (in bricks). 2. bruise (in fruit). 3. flake of lime (of a whitewashed wall). 4. (Bol., Chile, Peru) sodium nitrate; Chile saltpeter; sodium nitrate deposit; caliche, nitrate-bearing rock or gravel; (Peru) heap of soil from which sodium has been extracted.
calichera, *f.* (Bol., Chile, Peru) nitrate field.
caliciflora, *a.* (bot.) calycifloral. —*f.* (*pl.*) family of calycifloral flowers.
caliciforme, *a.* (bot.) calyciform.
calicillo, *m.* (bot.) verticil or whorl of leaves.
calicinal, calicino, na, *a.* (bot.) calycine, calycinal.
calicó, *m.* (tex.) calico, a cotton fabric.
calicud, *f.* (tex.) sheer silk fabric.
caliculado, da, *a.* (bot.) calyculate, having a calycle.
calicular, *a.* (bot.) calycular.
calículo, *m.* (bot.) calycle, epicalyx; (zool.) calyculus, calycle.
calidad, *f.* 1. quality, worth, class, excellence, e.g. *una tela de buena c.,* a good-quality cloth. 2. quality, nobility, rank, e.g. *una dama de c.,* a lady of quality. 3. position, status, capacity, e.g. *su c. de ciudadano,* his status as citizen. 4. importance, seriousness. 5. condition, stipulation (in a contract); regulation, rule (in cards). 6. (log.) quality. 7. nature, character, quality. — **a c. de que,** provided that, on the condition that; **en c. de,** as, in the capacity of, in the position of.
calidez, *f.* (med.) heat, warmth.
cálido, da, *a.* 1. warm, hot (climate, country, etc.) 2. hot, piquant (food). 3. warm, enthusiastic. 4. (p.) warm (color, etc.).
calidoscópico, ca, *a.* kaleidoscopic.
calidoscopio, *m.* kaleidoscope.
calientapiés, *m.* footwarmer.
calientaplatos, (*pl.* **calientaplatos**) *m.* hot plate, plate warmer.
caliente, *a.* 1. warm, hot. 2. (fig.) heated (argument). 3. (p.) warm (colors). — **c. de cascos,** hotheaded, hot-tempered; **en c.,** instantly, at once; **estar c.,** to be sexually aroused.
caliente, caliento, *ref.* **calentar.**
califa, *m.* caliph, head of a Moslem state.
califal, *a.* caliphal, pertaining to the reign or tenure of a caliph.
califato, *m.* caliphate, a state or region governed by a caliph.
califero, ra, *a.* lime-producing, containing lime.
calificable, *a.* describable; qualifiable.
calificación, *f.* 1. assessment, evaluation; grading, rating, classification. 2. marking; mark, grade (in examinations).
calificadamente, *adv.* qualifiedly, competently.
calificado, da, *past part. of* **calificar.** —*a.* 1. qualified, competent. 2. proven, attested.
calificador, ra, *a.* classifying; marking, grading; assessing. —*m.* grader, classifier, person who rates or grades; censor; **c. del Santo Oficio,** censor appointed by the Inquisition.
calificar, (*ref. 50*) *tr.v.* 1. to rate, rank, class, classify, assess. 2. to consider, regard, think of, e.g. *¿cómo calificas a Juan?* what do you think of John? 3. to call, describe, declare, e.g. *lo calificó de incompetente,* he called him incompetent. 4. to mark, grade (examination); to censor, grade (films, plays, etc.). 5. to ennoble, exalt, extol. 6. (gram.) to qualify. —*r.v.* to prove one's noble birth.
calificativo, va, *a.* (gram.) qualifying. —*m.* (gram.) qualifier.
califique, califiqué, *ref.* **calificar.**
californiano, na, *a., m., f.* Californian.
califórnico, ca, *a.* Californian.
californio, *m.* (chem.) californium.
cáliga, *f.* 1. caliga, Roman soldier's sandal. 2. bishop's gaiter.
calígine, *f.* 1. mist, fog; darkness. 2. excessive heat, sultriness.
caliginoso, sa, *a.* 1. caliginous, dark, murky. 2. hot, sultry.
caligrafía, *f.* calligraphy, penmanship, correct or artistic hand writing.
caligrafiar, *tr.v.* to write or inscribe artistically.
caligráfico, ca, *a.* calligraphic, pertaining to handwriting.
calígrafo, *m.* calligrapher, handwriting expert.
calilla, *f.* 1. *dim. of* **cala,** small suppository. 2. (Amer.) pest, nuisance, annoyance.
calima, *f.* 1. haze, mist, fog. 2. (mar.) buoy of strung cork-floats.
calimaco, *m.* (tex.) calamanco (thin woolen fabric with a glossy face).
calimba, *f.* (Cuba) branding iron.
calimbar, *tr.v.* (Cuba) to brand (cattle).
calimbo, *m.* quality, brand, mark.
calimete, *m.* (Dom. Rep.) drinking straw.
calimoso, sa, *a., var. of* **calinoso.**
calimote, *m.* middle cork placed at the mouth of certain fishing nets.
calina, *f.* haze, mist, fog.
calinda, *f.* (Cuba) calinda (African dance).
calinoso, sa, *a.* hazy, misty, foggy.
Calíope, *f.* (myth.) Calliope, the Muse of epical poetry.
calípedes, *m.* (zool.) sloth.
calipedia, *f.* the supposed art of procreating beautiful children.
calipédico, ca, *a.* concerning the supposed art of procreating beautiful children.
calípico, *a.* (astron.) callippic.
calipso, *m.* 1. calypso, a West Indian dance and its music. 2. (myth.) C., Calypso, the sea nymph who fascinated Ulysses. 3. (bot.) calypso (orchid.). 4. asteroid.
caliptra, *f.* (bot.) calyptra.
calisaya, *f.* calisaya bark.
calistenia, *f.* calisthenics, callisthenics.
calisténico, ca, *a.* calisthenic.
calitipia, *f.* (photog.) calotype.
cáliz, (*pl.* **cálices**) *m.* 1. chalice (used for wine in mass). 2. (poet.) chalice, goblet, cup; bitter cup or grief. 3. (bot.) calyx.
caliza, *f.* limestone; **c. hidráulica,** hydraulic limestone; **c. lenta,** dolomite.
calizo, za, *a.* calcareous, limy, containing lime.
calla, *f.* (Chile) trowel, dibble.
callada, *f.* 1. silence, muteness. 2. (mar.) drop, lull (in the wind), calming (of the sea). — **a las calladas, de c.,** (coll.) on the sly, secretly; **dar uno la c. por respuesta,** to keep silent, remain silent (not answering a question).
callada, *f.* dinner at which a dish of tripe is the main or the only course.
calladamente, *adv.* quietly; on the quiet, secretly.
calladito, *adv.* (coll.) very quietly. —*m.* (Chile) popular dance without singing.
callado, da, *past part. of* **callar.** —*a.* 1. silent, quiet, reticent, reserved (person). 2. secret, surreptitious (action).
callamiento, *m.* silencing; falling silent.
callampa, *f.* 1. (Chile, Ecuad., Peru) mushroom. 2. (Chile) felt hat. — **población c.,** (Chile) shanty town.
callana, *f.* 1. dross which can still be refined. 2. (metal.) assayer's crucible. 3. (Amer.) Indian earthenware pan for toasting corn. 4. (Chile) large pocket watch. 5. (Peru) crock, shard.
callandico, to, *adv.* (coll.) on the sly, furtively.
callando, *adv.* on the quiet, furtively.
callantar, *tr.v.* to silence, quiet, hush; (coll.) to quiet; soothe, calm.
callao, *m.* pebble; (Can. I.) flat stretch of land paved with pebbles.
callapo, *m.* 1. (min., Chile) prop, wooden support. 2. (min., Chile) step. 3. (Peru) handbarrow.
callar, *tr.v.* to conceal (a thought, etc.), keep (something) secret; to omit, refrain from stating, pass over. —*i.v.* to be silent, keep silent; to cease or stop speaking, singing, shouting, barking, crowing or making a noise; to shut up; to become quiet, grow silent; **¡calle! ¡calla!** *interj.* (of surprise) how extraordinary! you don't say! what do you know! — **calla callando,** quietly, surreptitiously; **calla y cuez,** stick to the business at hand; **quien calla, otorga,** silence gives consent. —*tr.v.* 1. to be silent; to stop speaking, singing, shouting, barking or making a noise; to shut up; to become quiet, grow silent. 2. to keep (a thing) secret; to omit, pass over. — **callarse la boca,** to shut up; **cállate la boca,** shut up, shut your mouth; **al buen c. llaman Sancho,** silence is golden.
calle, *f.* 1. street, road. 2. village within the jurisdiction of a larger town. 3. row of squares (on chessboard or draftsboard). 4. (print.) hound's tooth, white streak running down printed matter due to accidental juxtaposition of letters. 5. lane (of a runner or swimmer in a race). — **abrir, c.,** to make way, open a path; **azotar calles,** to wander aimlessly about, gad about, walk the streets; **c. ciega,** dead end; **c. de dirección única** or **sentido único** or **una vía** or **un solo sentido,** one-way street; **c. de la amargura,** (coll.) period of difficulties or adversities; **c. mayor,** longest diagonal of draftsboard; main street; **coger la c.,** to leave, go out; **dejar a uno en la c.,** to throw someone out of a job, leave someone destitute; **doblar la c.,** to turn the corner; **echar por la c. de en medio,** to ride roughshod over (to get something); **echar a uno a la c., plantar** or **poner a uno en la c.,** to throw one out of one's house; **echarse a la c.,** to riot, rebel, rise; **estar en la c.,** to be out (i.e. not at home); **hacer c.,** to make way; **poner en la c.,** to dismiss, fire, sack; **quedar** or **quedarse en la c.,** to be left without work, lose one's job.
callear, *tr.v.* to clear the lanes or walks in (a vineyard).
callecalle, *m.* (Chile, bot.) a species of medicinal plant.
calleja, *f.* side street, back street; lane, alley, narrow street.
Calleja, sépase or **ya se verá** or **ya verán quien es C.,** (coll.) I'll show you, you'll see; **cuentos de C.,** Mother Goose's Nursery Rhymes.
callejear, *i.v.* to gad about, gallivant about, be always out of the house.
callejeo, *m.* the action of roaming aimlessly about the streets.
callejero, ra, *a.* 1. fond of going out or of roaming the streets. 2. pertaining to the street, e.g. *vendedor c.,* street vendor. —*m.* list of streets, street guide (in city guidebook, etc.); list of subscribers' addresses (kept by newspaper and magazine distributors).
callejo, *m.* (reg., Sp.) trap, snare.
callejón, *m. aug. of* **calle,** alley, lane; (taur.) space between the barricade of the bull-ring and first row of seats; **c. del eje,** (mar.) shaft tunnel; **c. sin**

salida, (coll.) blind alley, cul-de-sac; deadlock, impasse, stalemate.
callejuela, *f.* 1. *dim. of* **calleja,** side street, back street; lane, alley, narrow street. 2. (coll.) pretext, way out, subterfuge.
callera, *a.* (bot.) **hierba c.,** orpine.
callicida, *m.* corn remover, corn-removing ointment.
callista, *m., f.* pedicurist, chiropodist.
callo, *m.* 1. corn, callosity, callus. 2. heel calk of horseshoe; shoe (for oxen hoofs). 3. (surg.) callus (forming around a bone fracture). 4. (*pl.*) (cul.) tripe.
callón, *m.* (carp.) awl sharpener.
callonca, *a.* 1. half-roasted (chestnut or acorn). 2. blowzy, worldly (woman). 3. (coll.) doddering, feeble (said of old persons).
callosidad, *f.* 1. callosity, hardened skin. 2. (*pl.*) (med.) hardened tissue in some chronic ulcers.
calloso, sa, *a.* callous, corneous; calloused; **cuerpo calloso,** (anat.) callosum, corpus callosum.
calma, *f.* 1. calm, calm weather. 2. lull, letup, slack time (in business, activities, etc.); abatement (of pain). 3. calm, serenity, tranquility, peace. 4. (coll.) sloth, sluggishness, laziness, apathy. — **c. chicha,** (mar.) dead calm; **en c.,** (mar.) dead calm, completely calm; **tener c.,** to keep one's cool (sl.).
calmado, da, *past part. of* **calmar. —*a.*** 1. quiet, calm. 2. soothed, calmed, pacified.
calmante, *a.* soothing; (med.) sedative. —*m.* (med.) sedative.
calmar, *tr.v* to calm, soothe, quiet. —*r.v.* to become calm, calm down. —*i.v.* to grow calm, abate, die down (wind).
calmazo, *m. aug. of* **calma,** (mar.) dead calm.
calmil, *m.* (Mex.) vegetable patch, cultivated piece of land adjacent to a farmer's house.
calmo, ma, *a.* 1. calm. 2. barren, treeless, bare.
calmoso, sa, *a.* 1. calm. 2. (coll.) sluggish, indolent, lazy.
calmuco, ca, *a., m., f.* Kalmuck, pertaining to a people of Western Mongolia.
calmudo, da, *a.* 1. calm. 2. (coll.) sluggish, indolent, lazy.
calnado, *m.* (arch.) padlock.
calo, *m.* (Ecuad.) long, thick cane containing water in the stem.
caló, *m.* 1. the language of the Spanish Gypsies. 2. ruffians' argot.
calobiótica, *f.* art of good living, natural tendency of man to orderly, regular life.
calocéfalo, la, *a.* calocephalous, beautifulheaded.
calófilo, la, *a.* (bot.) calophyllous, beautiful-leafed.
calofriarse, *r.v.* to have a chill.
calofrío, *m., var. of* **escalofrío,** chill.
calografía, *f., var. of* **caligrafía.**
calología, *f.* aesthetics.
calomel, *m.* (pharm.) calomel.
calomelanos, *m.* (*pl.*) (pharm.) calomel.
calón, *m.* 1. rod used to hold mouth of fishing net open. 2. sounding pole, pole for measuring depth of water. 3. (min.) vein full of sand.
calona, *f.* (med.) chalone (endocrine secretion).
calonche, *m.* alcoholic drink made from prickly pear juice and sugar.
calóptero, ra, *a.* (zool.) calopterous, having beautiful wings.
calor, *m.* 1. (phys.) heat. 2. heat, hotness, warmth. 3. heat, warmth, ardor (of feelings, passions, etc.). 4. warmth (of welcome, reception, etc.). 5. thick, heat (of battle, fray, etc.). — **c. animal,** (physiol.) animal heat; **c. canicular,** sultry, suffocating heat; **c. de hígado,** flush, red spots on the cheeks (believed to be caused by liver trouble); **c. específico,** (phys.) specific heat; **c. latente,** (phys.) latent heat; **c. natural,** natural heat of the body; **entrar en c.,** to warm up; **hacer c.,** to be hot (of weather); **tener c.,** to be or feel hot (persons); **tomar con c.,** to carry out with great zeal.
caloría, *f.* (phys.) calorie.
caloriamperímetro, *m.* (elec.) thermal ammeter.
caloricidad, *f.* (physiol.) caloricity.
calórico, ca, *a.* caloric. —*m.* caloric, heat.
calorídoro, *m.* a device used in laundries and dyers' shops to utilize the heat in the vats after the dyes are used up.
calorífero, ra, *a.* heat-producing, giving out heat. —*m.* heating system, heater, radiator; foot warmer. — **c. de aire,** air heater; **c. de vapor,** steam heater, radiator; **c. mural,** wall radiator.
calorificación, *f.* (physiol.) calorification.
calorífico, ca, *a.* calorific.
calorífugo, *a.* heat-resisting; noncombustible.
calorimetría, *f.* (phys.) calorimetry.
calorimétrico, ca, *a.* (phys.) calorimetric, calorimetrical.
calorímetro, *m.* (phys.) calorimeter.
calorimotor, *m.* (phys.) calorimotor.
calorosamente, *adv., var. of* **calurosamente.**
caloroso, sa, *a., var of* **caluroso.**
calosa, *f.* (bot.) callose.
calosfriarse, *r.v.* to have the shivers.
calosfrío, *m.* shiver.
caloso, sa, *a.* porous (paper).
calostro, *m.* colostrum, first milk secreted by mammary glands after birth of the young.
calota, *f.* (med.) plaster cap (medication applied to the head as a treatment for ringworm).
calote, *m.* (Arg.) trick, swindle.
caloteador, ra, *m., f.* (Arg.) thief.
calotear, *tr.v.* (Arg.) to trick, swindle, chisel (sl.).
calotipia, *f.* (photog.) calotype.
caloyo, *m.* 1. newborn lamb or kid. 2. new recruit, recently drafted soldier.
calpamulo, la, *a.* (Mex.) of mixed Indian, black and Chinese ancestry.
calpixque, *m.* (Mex., arch.) foreman in charge of the Indians on an estate; (Mex.) official in charge of collecting taxes from the Indians.
calpul, *m.* 1. (Guat.) meeting, gathering, powwow. 2. (Hond.) mound indicating the site of an aboriginal village.
calque, calqué, *ref.* **calcar.**
calquín, *m.* (ornith., Arg.) medium-sized eagle of the Patagonian Andes.
calseco, ca, *a.* lime-cured.
calta, *f.* (bot.) marsh marigold.
calucha, *f.* (Bol.) inner shell of coconuts, almonds, and other nuts.
caluma, *f.* 1. (Peru) gorge (in the Andes). 2. (Peru) Indian village.
calumet, *m.* calumet, peace pipe.
calumnia, *f.* calumny, slander.
calumniador, ra, *a.* slandering, calumnious. —*m., f.* slanderer, calumniator.
calumniar, *tr.v.* to slander, defame, calumniate.
calumniosamente, *adv.* slanderously, calumniously.
calumnioso, sa, *a.* slanderous, calumnious.
calungo, *m.* (Col.) curly-headed dog.
caluro, *m.* (ornith., C. Amer.) trogon.
calurosamente, *adv.* warmly; enthusiastically.
caluroso, sa, *a.* 1. warm, hot. 2. (fig.) warm, enthusiastic.
calutrón, *m.* (phys.) calutron.
caluyo, *m.* (Bol.) shuffling Indian figure dance.
calva, *f.* 1. bald pate, bald patch; bare or threadbare patch (in fur, felt, carpet, etc.); bare patch (in field, plantation or grove). 2. game consisting of throwing stones at the top part of a piece of wood, without their touching the ground before. — **c. de almete,** top of a helmet.
calvar, *tr.v.* 1. (in the game of **calva**) to hit the top part of a target. 2. to fool, deceive.
calvario, *m.* 1. **C.,** Calvary; Way of the Cross. 2. (coll.) calvary, succession of troubles or sorrows. 3. (coll.) succession of debts chalked up against customer's name by shopkeeper.
calvatrueno, *m.* 1. (coll.) baldness of the whole head. 2. (coll.) madcap, reckless and wild person.
calverizo, za, *a.* having many clearings or open spaces (woods, forest).
calvero, *m.* 1. bare patch, open space, clearing (in a wood or forest). 2. chalk pit.
calvete, *a. dim. of* **calvo,** bald. —*m.* bald man.
calvez, *f., var. of* **calvicie.**
calvicie, *f.* baldness.
calvijar, *m.* 1. bare patch, open space, clearing (in a wood, forest). 2. chalk pit.
calvinismo, *m.* (rel.) Calvinism, the doctrines and religious teaching of John Calvin.
calvinista, *a., m., f.* Calvinist, pertaining to or a follower of the doctrines of John Calvin.
Calvino, *m.* John Calvin, French Protestant reformer.
calvitar, *m.* bare patch, open space, clearing (in wood or forest).
calvo, va, *a.* bald (people); bare, barren (ground); threadbare, worn (cloth). —*m., f.* bald person.
calza, *f.* 1. identification ribbon or band (put on animals). 2. wedge, chock. 3. (coll.) stocking. 4. (*pl.*) breeches, tights, hose. 5. (*pl.*) (sl.) shackles, fetters. 6. (her.) pile. 7. (Col.) tooth filling. — **medias calzas,** knee-stockings; **poner en calzas prietas,** to put in a tight spot; **verse en calzas prietas,** to find oneself in a tight spot or in a fix.
calzacalzón, *m.* longbreeches, galligaskins.
calzada, *f.* wide road, causeway, highway.
calzadera, *f.* 1. thin hemp lace (for tying sandals). 2. chock, block, wedge (to immobilize a wheel).
calzado, da, *past part. of* **calzar. —*a.*** 1. calced, wearing shoes, shod (said of monks who don't belong to a discalced order). 2. feathered to the claws (birds). 3. having legs of different color from the rest of the body (quadrupeds). 4. (her.) piled. —*m.* footwear (boots, shoes, etc.); hosiery (socks, stockings, etc.); **calzado ortopédico,** orthopedic shoes.
calzador, *m.* 1. shoehorn. 2. (Bol.) pencil holder.
calzadura, *f.* 1. the act of putting on shoes; wedging, fitting, supporting. 2. felly, felloe, wooden tire, wooden rim-piece of wheel. — **c. con madera,** (archit.) underpinning.
calzar, (*ref. 53*) *tr.v.* 1. to shoe, put shoes or boots on; to provide with shoes or boots. 2. to wear (certain size of shoe). 3. to wear (spurs, boots, gloves). 4. to wedge, place a wedge under (the legs of furniture or machinery); to chock, put a chock under, scotch (wheel, barrel, etc. to prevent movement). 5. to tip, trim with iron (the worn part of a plowshare); to put the rims on coach wheels. 6. (firearms) to fit (bullets of a given caliber). 7. (coll.) to grasp (mentally), e.g. *él calza poco,* he grasps little, he is rather dim. 8. (Guat.) to bank, hill (plants). 9. (print.) to raise, underlay. 10. (Col.) to fill a tooth. 11. (Arg.) to get, obtain. —*i.v.* **c. bien** or **mal,** to wear well-made or poorly-made shoes, wear good-quality or poor-quality footwear. —*r.v.* 1. to put on (shoes, boots). 2. to wear (spurs, boots, gloves). — **calzarse a alguien,** (coll.) to control or boss someone about; **calzarse algo,** (coll.) to obtain, get.

calzo, *m.* 1. block, chock, wedge; (mar.) stowing chock. 2. (mec.) fulcrum. 3. (mil.) trigger-spring of crossbow. 4. (*pl.*) legs (of a horse).

calzón, *m.* 1. (*used gen. in the pl.*) breeches, trousers, knee-breeches; (Amer.) drawers, knickers, panties, underpants, pants, underdrawers. 2. steeple jack's safety belt. 3. ombre (card game). 4. (Bol.) hot peppery pork stew. 5. (Mex.) sugar cane blight. — **a c. quitado,** (coll.) boldly, without fear or hesitation, openly, brazenly; **amarrarse los calzones,** (coll.) to prepare for action; **calzarse** or **ponerse los calzones,** (coll.) to wear the trousers, be the boss; **calzones cortos,** shorts; **tener bien puestos los calzones, tener muchos calzones,** (coll.) to be a real man.

calzonarias, *f.* (*pl.*) (Col.) braces, suspenders.

calzonazos, *m.* (coll.) softy, weakling.

calzoncillos, *m.* (*pl.*) pants, underpants, drawers, underdrawers.

calzoneras, *f.* (*pl.*) (Mex.) trousers, buttoned on both sides of the legs.

calzoneta, *f.* (Guat.) bathing trunks.

calzonte, *m.* (Amer.) beam of a hut roof.

calzonudo, da, *a.* 1. (Mex.) intrepid, brave. 2. (Arg., Peru) irresolute, stupid.

calzorras, *m.* (coll.) drip, weak, soft fellow.

cama, *f.* 1. bed; bedstead; bed canopy. 2. lair, burrow; straw bed, litter (in stables). 3. floor (of truck or cart). 4. (agr.) part of fruit resting on the ground. 5. (cul.) layer (of meat, vegetables, etc.). 6. litter (of animals). 7. (mar.) hole formed in mud or sand by stranded ship. — **abrir la c.,** to turn down the bed; **caer en c.,** to fall ill, take to one's bed (because of illness); **c. camerote,** bunk bed; **c. de agua,** water bed; **c. de galgos** or **de podencos,** untidy, uncomfortable bed; **c. de matrimonio, c. de dos plazas, c. doble,** double bed; **c. de roca,** (geol.) bedrock, ledge rock; **c. de una plaza, c. simple,** single bed; **c. elástica,** trampoline; **camas gemelas,** twin beds; **c. turca,** studio couch, divan; **estar en c., guardar c.,** to be sick in bed, keep to one's bed (because of illness, etc.); **hacer la c.,** to make the bed; **hacer la c. a uno,** to work secretly against someone; **ir a la c.,** to go to sleep, (fig.) to go to bed with someone, make love.

cama, *f.* 1. (*gen. pl.*) cheek piece, cheek (of bit). 2. (agr.) sheath (of plow). 3. (mec.) felly, felloe, segment of a wheel rim. 4. (*pl.*) gores (inserted into circular capes and skirts to give them flare).

camá, *m.* (ornith., Cuba) a small brown pigeon (Geotrigon caniceps).

camachuelo, *m.* (ornith.) linnet.

camada, *f.* 1. litter, brood (of animals). 2. layer (of sliced potatoes, fruit, etc.). 3. (coll.) gang, band of thieves. 4. (min.) plank flooring (of mine).

camafeo, *m.* cameo.

camagón, *m.* (bot., Phil. I.) camagon, redwood tree bearing edible fruit.

camagua, *a.* (C. Amer.) ripening (corn). —*f.* (bot., Cuba) species of hardwood tree (Wallenia laurifolia).

camahueto, *m.* (Chile) fabulous aquatic animal credited with mysterious powers.

camal, *m.* 1. hemp cord halter. 2. gambrel,stick used by butchers to suspend slaughtered animals, esp. pigs. 3. (Ecuad., Peru) slaughterhouse, abattoir.

camáldula, *f.* (rel.) Order of the Camaldolites (reformed Benedictine order, founded by St. Romuald in 1012).

camaldulense, *a.* (rel.) of the Camaldolites (reformed Benedictine order). —*m.* Camaldolite.

camaleón, *m.* 1.(zool.) chameleon, (Cuba) anoli, anole (Anolis carolinensis). 2. (coll.) chameleon, changeable person. 3. (Bol., zool.) iguana. 4. (C. Rica, ornith.) small North American falcon (Falco sparverus) — **c. mineral,** chameleon mineral, potassium permanganate.

camaleónico, ca, *a.* (fig.) volatile, moody, temperamental (person).

camaleopardo, *m.* (astron.) Chameleon, a southern constellation.

camalero, *m.* (Ecuad., Peru) cattle slaughterer; wholesale butcher or meat dealer.

camalotal, *m.* water hyacinth bed.

camalote, *m.* (bot.) water hyacinth; floating island of water hyacinths.

camama, *f.* (coll.) trick, hoax, fib, lie, rumor.

camambú, *f.* (bot., Arg.) a wild plant with yellow flowers and orange berries (Physolis viscosa).

camamila, *f.* (bot.) camomile.

camanance, *m.* (C. Rica) dimple on the face.

camanchaca, *f.* (Chile, Peru) thick lowlying fog (of the Tarapacá desert).

camándula, *f.* 1. (rel.) Order of the Camaldolites. 2. rosary composed of one or three chaplets of ten beads. 3. (coll.) humbug, trickery, astuteness. — **tener muchas camándulas,** to be full of tricks, be full of humbug or hypocrisy.

camandulear, *i.v.* 1. to be a humbug, be hypocritically devout. 2. (Amer.) to intrigue; gossip.

camandulense, *a., var. of* **camaldulense.**

camandulería, *f.* humbug, hipocritical piety.

camandulero, ra, *a.* (coll.) humbugging, hypocritical. —*m., f.* humbug, hypocrite.

camanonca, *f.* old cloth used for lining clothes.

camao, *m.* (Cuba) small wild pigeon (Geotrigon Caniceps).

cámara, *f.* 1. chamber, compartment. 2. chamber, parlor, drawing room; royal chamber (of palace); (mar.) commander's quarters, cabin or stateroom. 3. loft, hayloft; granary. 4. legislative house, chamber (e.g. deputies). 5. chamber, board, council, association, e.g. *c. de comercio,* chamber of commerce; *c. agrícola,* farm board or council, farmers' association. 6. (anat.) cavity, chamber. 7. chamber, breech (of firearms). 8. inner tube (of tire). 9. (photog.) camera. 10. (artil.) small saluting gun. 11. stool, movement of bowels; (*pl.*) diarrhea. — **a** or **en c. lenta,** slow-motion, in slow motion, e.g. *película a c. lenta,* slow-motion picture, picture in slow motion; **c. alta, c.** baja, upper house, lower house (of parliament); **c. anublada,** (phys.) cloud chamber; **c. ardiente,** chapelle ardente, funeral chamber; **c. cartográfica,** mapping camera; **c. clara,** camera lucida; **c. compensadora,** (com.) clearing house; **c. de aire,** inner tube (of tire); air chamber; **c. de aspiración,** suction chamber; **c. de cajón,** box camera; **c. de carga,** (hydr.) surge tank or chamber; forebay; **c. de combustión,** combustion chamber; **c. de compresión,** compression chamber; **c. de decantación,** settling basin; **c. de diputados,** Chamber of Deputies; House of Representatives; **c. de fuelle, c. plegadiza,** folding camera; **c. de gas,** gas chamber; **c. de horrores,** chamber of horrors; **c. de los Comunes,** House of Commons; **c. de los Lores,** House of Lords; **c. de mando,** control room; **c. de máquinas,** engine room; **c. de niebla,** (phys.) could chamber; **c. de pleno,** (a.c.) plenum chamber; **C. de Representantes,** House of Representatives; **c. de resonancia,** (rad.) echo chamber; **c. de salida,** (hydr.) afterbay; **C. de Senadores,** Senate; **c. de televisión,** telecamera; **c. de turbina,** wheel pit; **c. de vapor,** steam chest or box; **c. fotográfica,** (photog.) camera; **c. frigorífica,** refrigerating chamber, cold-storage chamber; **c. mortuoria,** funeral chamber, chapelle ardente; **c. obscura,** camera obscura; **de c.,** court, royal, e.g. *médico de c.,* royal physician, *pintor de c.,* court painter; chamber, e.g. *música de c.,* chamber music.

camarada, *m.* comrade, chum, **pal.** —*f.* group of comrades or companions.

camaradería, *f.* camaraderie, comradeship, good-fellowship.

camaraje, *m.* granary rent.

camaranchón, *m.* attic, loft, lumber room.

camarera, *f.* waitress (in restaurant); stewardess (on ships or planes); head maid; **c. mayor,** chief lady-in-waiting.

camarería, *f.* 1. job or position of a chief maid, waitress, etc. 2. (arch.) perquisite of the Lord Chamberlain (in Spain).

camarero, *m.* 1. chamberlain; steward (of great house; on plane or ship); waiter (in restaurant). 2. granary keeper. — **c. mayor,** Lord Chamberlain.

camareta, *f.* 1. small room or chamber. 2. (mar.) small cabin, deck cabin, midshipman's cabin. 3. (Amer.) small cannon fired during public festivities.

camareto, *m.* (bot., Cuba) sweet potato.

camarico, *m.* 1. gift, offering (given by American Indians to the priests). 2. (Chile, coll.) favorite haunt. 3. (Chile, coll.) love affair.

camariento, ta, *a.* diarrheic, suffering from diarrhea. —*m.* one who suffers from diarrhea.

camarilla, *f.* camarilla, cabal, clique, power group, coterie (influencing affairs of state).

camarillesco, ca, *a.* cliquish.

camarín, *m.* 1. *dim. of* **cámara,** dressing room, changing room; boudoir; study, private office (of a house). 2. niche or alcove (behind an altar); closet for the jewelry and ornaments of an image.

camarista, *m.* Minister in the King's Council. —*f.* lady-in-waiting to the Queen.

camarlengado, *m.* office of the papal chamberlain.

camarlengato, *m., var. of* **camarlengado.**

camarlengo, *m.* papal chamberlain.

cámaro, *m.* (zool.) prawn, shrimp.

camarógrafo, *m.* (tel., cinem.) cameraman.

camarón, *m.* 1. (zool.) common prawn. 2. (C. Rica) tip, gratuity. — **c. que se duerme se lo lleva la corriente,** keep on your toes or you'll be left behind.

camaronera, *f.* 1. woman who sells prawn or shrimp. 2. prawn or shrimp net.

camaronero, *m.* 1. man who sells prawn or shrimp. 2. shrimp boat. 3. (Peru, ornith.) kingfisher.

camarote, *m.* (mar.) cabin, stateroom, berth.

camarotero, *m.* (mar., Amer.) steward, stateroom attendant.

camarroya, *f.* wild chicory.

camarú, *m.* (Amer., bot.) tree whose bark contains a quinine-like substance.

camasquince, *m., f.* (coll.) meddler, meddlesome person, busybody.

camastra, *f.* (Amer.) cunning, astuteness.

camastrear, *i.v.* (Amer.) to be sly or cunning.

camastro, *m.* (derog.) cot, rough or makeshift bed.

camastrón, na, *m., f. sly,* artful, cunning person. —*a.* sly, cunning, artful.

camastronazo, *m. aug. of* **camastrón.**

camastrónería, *f.* (coll.) slyness, cunning, artfulness.

camba, *f.* 1. cheek piece of a horse's bit. 2. (*pl.*) gores of circular skirt or cape.

cambado, da, *a.* (Arg. Ven.) bowlegged; knock-kneed.
cambalachar, *tr.v., var. of* **cambalachear.**
cambalache, *m.* 1. barter, swapping (of little value). 2. (Arg.) second-hand shop.
cambalachear, *tr.v.* to swap, barter, trade (things of little value).
cambalachero, ra, *m., f.* barterer, swapper.
cambaleo, *m.* musical combo composed of five men and one female vocalist.
cambar, *tr.v.* (Arg., Ven.) to bend, curve.
cambará, *m.* South American tree (Moquinia polymorpha).
cámbaro, *m.* (zool.) crayfish, crawfish.
cambera, *f.* crayfish net.
cambeto, ta, *a.* (Ven.) bowlegged.
cambiable, *a.* changeable, exchangeable.
cambiacorrea, *m.* (mec.) belt shifter.
cambiada, *f.* 1. (equit.) change of gait (of a horse). 2. (mar.) going about (on the other tack).
cambiadiscos, *m.* automatic record changer.
cambiadizo, za, *a.* changeable, variable.
cambiador, ra, *a.* changing; exchanging. *—m., f.* changer; barterer, exchanger. *—m.* 1. changer. 2. (Chile, Mex., ry.) switchman. 3. (Chile) shifting lever (of block and tackle). — **c. automático,** (Arg., Urug.), record changer; **c. de frecuencia,** (rad.) frequency changer.
cambial, *a.* (bot.) cambial.
cambiamano, *m.* railroad switch.
cambiamiento, *m.* change, mutation, variation.
cambiante, *a.* changing; changeable. *—m.* 1. (*gen. pl.*) irridescence, chatoyancy, sheen. money changer.
cambiar, *tr.v.* 1. to change (to convert; to alter; to replace), e.g. *c. una llanta,* to change a tire, *hay que cambiar las reglas,* the rules must be changed, *tienes que c. tus pesetas en dólares,* you have to change your pesetas into dollars. 2. to exchange, swap, e.g. c. *saludos, to exchange greetings, c. impresiones or ideas.* 3. to make a galloping horse change gait. 4.(mar.) to shift (tackle). 5. (mar.) to bring or turn about. — **marcha,** (mec.) to reverse, to change speed. *—i.v.* 1. to change. 2. to change step (a galloping horse). 3. to change, swing around, veer (wind). — **c. de,** to change, *e.g. c. de ropa,* to change one's clothes, *c. de asiento,* to change seats; *c. de idea,* to change one's mind. *—r.v.* 1. to be changed or exchanged. 2. to change, after. 3. to change, swing around, veer (wind). 4. to change, change one's clothes.
cambiario, ria, *a.* pertaining to exchange.
cambiavía, (ry.) *m. switchman; switch;* **c. salta-carril,** jumper switch.
cambiazo, *m. aug. of* **cambio,** big change; fraudulent exchange; **dar el c.,** (coll.) to switch (one thing) fraudulently for another.
cambija, *f.* water tower.
cambil, *m.* (vet.) medicine for dogs.
cambín, *m.* hat-shaped fish trap made of wicker-work.
cambio, *m.* 1. change, alteration. 2. interchange, exchange, e.g. *c. de ideas,* exchange of ideas. 3. exchange, switching (of one thing for another). 4. swinging around, veering, change (of direction of wind, etc.). 5. change, small change (money in small bills or coins). 6. (com.) premium (paid or charged on drafts and bills). 7. (com.) exchange (of one currency for another); exchange rate (of currency exchange). 8. (com.) quotation price (price of stocks and shares, etc.). 9. (ry.) switchpoint. 10. (law) exchange of posts (by two holders of government jobs or ecclesiastical benefices). 11. (auto.) gear, e.g. *caja de cambios,* gearbox. 12. (bot.) cambium. — **c. aéreo,** (ry.) overhead frog; **a c. de,** in exchange for; **c. automático,** (auto.) automatic transmission; **c. cierto,** (econ.) certain exchange; **c. de estado,** (phys.) change of state; **c. de fase,** (rad.) phase shift; **c. de parecer** or **de intenciones,** change of heart; **c. de tope,** (ry.) stub switch; **c. de velocidad,** (auto.) gearshift; **c. de vía,** ry.) switch; turnout; **c. de voz,** change of voice; **c. extranjero,** (econ.) foreign exchange; **c. minuto,** exchange rate (of money); **c. volumétrico,** (chem.) volume change; **en c., on the other hand; whereas; in return, in exchange; en c. de,** instead of; in return for; **letra de c.,** bill of exchange; **libre c.,** free trade; **tipo de c.,** (econ.) exchange rate.
cambista, *m. f.* 1. money broker, money chager, cambist; banker. 2. (Arg., ry.) switchman.
cámbium, *m.* (bot.) cambium.
Camboya, Cambodia, *f. Cambodia.*
camboyano, na, *a., m., f.* Cambodian.
cambray, *m.* (tex.) chambray, light cotton fabric.
cambrayado, da, *a.* chambray-like.
cambrayón, *m.* (tex.) cotton cambric, coarse cambric.
cambriano, na, *a.* 1. (geol.) Cambrian. 2. Cambrian, pertaining to ancient Wales. *—m., f.* Cambrian, native of Cambria or Wales, G.B.
cámbrico, ca, *a., m., f., var. of* **cambriano.**
cambrillón, *m.* (*gen. pl.*) inner leather strip used to build up the sole of a shoe.
cambrón, *m.* (bot.) buckthorn; (bot.) bramble; (*pl.*) Christ's thorn.
cambrona, *f.* (Arg.) rough cotton cloth.
cambronal, *m.* buckthorn or bramble thicket or patch.
cambronera, *f.* (bot.) matrimony vine, boxthorn.
cambroño, *m.* (bot.) broom; hairy cytisus.
cambrún, *m.* (Col.) type of woolen fabric.
cambucha, *f.* (Chile) small kite (toy).
cambucho, *m.* 1. (Chile) paper cone (for holding chocolates etc. or used as headgear). 2. (Chile) waste paper basket, laundry basket. 3. small, dark or unpleasant room. 4. (Chile) straw cover (for bottles). 5. (Chile) small kite (toy).
cambuí, *m.* (Arg., Urug., bot.) tree similar to the guava.
cambuj, *m.* 1. mask. 2. baby's cloth head-covering tied tightly to keep the head straight.
cambujo, ja, *a.* 1. reddish-black (donkey). 2. (Mex.) of mestizo and Chinese descent. 3. (Mex.) having black feathers and dark flesh (said of fowl). *—m., f.* (Mex.) person of mestizo and Chinese descent.
cambullón, *m.* 1. (Peru) swindle, dirty deal. 2. (Chile) political plot, conspiracy. 3. (Col., Mex.) barter, trading in things of little value.
cambur, *m.* (bot.) banana tree, plantain (Musa paradisiaca); **c. criollo,** green variety of plantain; **c.** bartón or **c. topocho, c. titiaro, c. higo, c. amarillo, c. pigmeo,** various small varieties of plantain; **c. manzano,** fine variety of plantain having an apple flavor; **c. morado,** red plantain.
cambute, *m.* (bot.) 1. a leguminous plant. 2. (Cuba, bot.) liana.
cambuto, ta, *a.* (Peru) small and chubby.
camedrio, *m.* (bot.) wall germander.
camedris, *m., var. of* **camedrio.**
camedrita, *m.* germander wine.
camelador, ra, *a.* flattering, cajoling.
camelar, *tr.v.* 1. (coll.) to woo, court. 2. (coll.) to deceive, deceive with flattery. 3. (coll.) to love, desire. 4. (Mex.) to watch, observe.
camelete, *m.* (mil.) large cannon.
camelia, *f.* (bot.) camellia; (Cuba, bot.) corn poppy.
camélidos, *m.* (*pl.*) (zool.) Camelidae.
camelieo, a, *a.* (bot.) theaceous. *—f.* (bot.) (*pl.*) Theaceae.
camelina, *f.* (bot.) gold-of-pleasure.
camella, *f.* 1. bow of yoke. 2. female camel. 3. milk pail. 4. ridge in ploughed land. 5. feeding trough.
camellejo, *m. dim. of* **camello,** small camel.
camellería, *f.* job of camel driver; camel driving.
camellero, *m.* camel driver, cameleer.
camello, *m.* 1. (zool.) camel. 2. (mar.) camel, watertight structure used for lifting boats above the waterline. — **c. pardal,** (zool.) camelopard, giraffe.
camellón, *m.* 1. ridge of furrow. 2. camlet (cloth). 3. drinking trough. 4. bed of flowers.
camelo, *m.* 1. (coll.) flirting, wooing. 2. (coll.) teasing, joking, fun. 3. (coll.) hoax, false rumor. — **dar c. a,** to tease, make fun of; **de c.** sham, bogus.
camelotado, da, *a.* camlet-like (cloth).
camelote, *m.* 1. camlet (cloth). 2. (bot.) a tropical weed. — **c. de aguas,** smooth-surfaced, glossy camlet; **c. de pelo,** cameline, finest camlet.
camelotina, *f.* camlet (cloth).
camelotón, *m.* coarse camlet (cloth).
camena, *f.* (poet.) muse.
camenal, *a.* of the Camenae (muses).
camera, *f.* (Col., zool.) wild black rabbit.
cameralismo, *m.* cameralism.
cameramán, *m.* (cine.) cameraman.
camerino, *m.* (theat.) dressing room.
camero, ra, *a.* large, wide or double bed. *—m., f.* bedmaker, maker of bedroom accessories.
Camerón, Camerún, *m.* Cameroons.
camia, *f.* (bot., Phil. I.) bilimbi (Averrhoa bilimbi).
camibar, *m.* (C. Rica, Nic., bot.) copaiba tree; copaiba balsam.
cámica, *f.* (Chile) slope of roof.
camilo, *a.* pertaining to the Order of St. Camilo de Lelis, a congregation that cares for the sick. *—m.* 1. member of that order. 2. camillus, altar boy in ancient Roman religious ceremonies.
camilucho, cha, *m., f.* (Arg.) Indian day-laborer.
camilla, *f.* 1. chaise longue, couch; stretcher, litter. 2. table with a built-in foot-warmer underneath.
camillero, *m.* stretcher-bearer.
caminada, *f.* (Col.) day's journey.
caminador, ra, *a.* fond of walking, good at walking.
caminante, *a.* walking, traveling. *—m., f.* walker, a person who walks. *—m.* 1. footman or groom who walks in front of master's horse. 2. (ornith., Chile) small brown bird with reddish tail (Geositta cunicularia).
caminar, *i.v.* to walk; to go, travel; **c. derecho,** (coll.) to go straight, act honestly. *—tr.v.* to walk.
caminata, *f.* (coll.) hike, long trek, tiring walk.
caminejo, *m. derog. dim. of* **camino,** small rough road, donkey track.
caminero, ra, *a.* road, e.g. *peón c.,* road worker.
caminí, *m.* best quality Paraguayan maté (Ilex paraguayensis).
camino, *m.* 1. road, path, track; route. 2. trip, journey. 3. way, course, means (to reach, obtain or achieve something). — **abrir c.,** to clear the way; to open the way; to find a way; to pioneer; **a medio c.,** halfway; **c. asendereado,** beaten track; much frequented path or route; **c. carretero, c. carretil,** wagon road; (coll.) commonplace way of doing things, beaten path; **c. carril,** cart track; **c. cubierto,** (fort.) covered or covert way; **c. de abastecimiento,** (mil.) supply route; **c. de cabaña,** cattle or sheep path, break one's routine; **c. vecinal, de herradura,** bridle path; **c. de hierro,** railway; **c. de ruedas,** wagon or

carriage road; **c. de Santiago,** (astron.) Milky Way; **c. de sirga,** towpath; **c. real,** highway, highroad; (fig.) royal road, sure way; **c. trillado,** beaten path, e.g. *salir del c. trillado,* to get off the beaten path, break one's routine; **c. vecinal,** municipal road; **cruzarse en el camino (de alguien),** to get in (someone's) way; to meet by chance; **de c.,** on the way; in passing; traveling (clothes, etc.); **estar en c.,** to be on one's way; **hacer de un c. dos mandados,** to kill two birds with one stone; **hacerse c.,** to make one's way (in career, life, etc.); **ir fuera de c.,** to go astray, be mistaken, go wrong, go off the track; **llevar c. (una cosa),** (coll.) to be correct, be on the right track; **meterle (a uno) por c.,** (coll.) to put (someone) on the right track; **no llevar c.,** (coll.) to be on the wrong track; **partir el c.,** to meet halfway; **ponerse en c.,** to set out, begin one's journey; **quedarse a medio c.,** to stop halfway; **salir al c.,** to be a highwayman; **traer a buen c.,** to put right, put on the right track or path.

camión, *m.* truck, lorry; (Mex.) omnibus, bus; **c. articulado,** semi, semitrailer. **c. blindado** or **acorazado,** armored truck; **c. celular,** patrol wagon; **c. cisterna,** tank truck; **c. de cama plana,** flat truck; **c. de la basura,** garbage truck; **c. de mudanzas,** moving van; **c. de volteo,** dump truck; **c. grúa,** tow truck; **c. mezclador,** (const.) truck mixer; **c. remolcador,** tow truck.

camionada, *f.* truckload.

camionaje, *m.* trucking, trucking service; trucking charge.

camionero, *m.* truck driver, teamster; truck owner or contractor.

camioneta, *f.* light truck or lorry; station wagon.

camisa, *f.* 1. shirt; shift, chemise. 2. husk, thin skin (of fruit, grain or vegetables). 3. (snake's) slough. 4. (mec.) case, casing, jacket. 5. coat of whitewash. 6. (gas) mantle. 7. cover, jacket (of bundle of papers). 8. Chile paper lining (applied as a foundation for wall paper). 9. (fort.) chemise, revetment. 10. (print.) cloth tympan (on impression cylinder of press). — **c. alquitranada, c. de fuego** or **c. embreada,** (mar.) fire chemise; **c. de agua,** (mec.) water jacket; **c. de dormir,** nightshirt; **c. de etiqueta,** dress shirt; **c. de fuerza,** strait jacket; **c. del pistón,** (auto.) piston skirt; **c. de vapor,** steam jacket; **c. negra,** (polit.) blackshirt, fascist (World War II); **dejar a uno sin c.,** (coll.) to ruin a person, leave someone without a shirt on his back; **en c.,** without a dowry (bride); **en mangas de c.,** in shirtsleeves; **jugar uno hasta la c.,** (coll.) to be inordinately fond of gambling; to bet one's shirt; **meterse uno en c. de once varas,** (coll.) to bite off more than one can chew; **no llegarle a uno la c. al cuerpo,** to be extremely anxious, be on tenterhooks.

camisería, *f.* shirt shop or factory, haberdashery.

camisero, ra, *m., f.* shirt maker; shirt dealer, haberdasher.

camiseta, *f.* undershirt, polo shirt.

camisola, *f.* man's dress shirt; ruffled shirt; (Chile) woman's blouse.

camisolín, *m.* dickey, false shirt front.

camisón, *m. aug. of* **camisa,** nightdress, nightshirt; (Amer.) long chemise or camisole; muumuu; (Col., Pan., Ven.) woman's dress.

camisote, *m.* hauberk, long-sleeved coat of mail.

camita, *a., m., f.* Hamite, pertaining to Caucasoid peoples of Africa, such as the Berbers and the Egyptians.

camítico, ca, *a.* Hamitic.

camoatí, *m.* (Arg., Urug., Par.) species of wasp (Polybia Scutellaris); wasps' nest.

camocán, *m.* type of brocade used in the East and Spain in the Middle Ages.

camochar, *tr.v.* (Hond.) to trim, prune (trees, plants).

camomila, *f.* (bot.) camomile.

camón, *m.* 1. portable throne. 2. oriel, glass-enclosed balcony; **c. de vidrios,** glass partition. 3. *aug. of* **cama,** large bed. 4. cheek piece, cheek (of bit). 5. felly, felloe, rim-segment of wheel. 6. (archit.) curb rafter, arched rafter.

camonadura, *f.* (Cuba) wooden rim of cart-wheel.

camoncillo, *m.* taboret, small backless stool.

camorra, *f.* (coll.) quarrel, squabble; **armar c.,** to pick a quarrel; **buscar c.,** to look for trouble.

camorrear, *i.v.* to quarrel.

camorrero, ra, *a., m., f., var. of* **camorrista.**

camorrista, *a.* (coll.) quarrelsome. —*m., f.* quarrelsome person.

camotal, *m.* (Amer.) sweet potato field.

camote, *m.* 1. (Amer., bot.) sweet potato (Ipomea batatas). 2. (Amer.) affection, infatuation, love. 3. (Amer., coll.) lover, mistress. 4. (Amer., coll.) lie, fib. 5. (Mex.) rogue, scoundrel. 6. (El Salv., coll.) welt, weal, bruise. 7. (Ecuad., Mex.) fool, stupid fellow. — **tomar c. a,** (Amer.) to become very fond of, become infatuated with; **tragar c.,** (Mex.) to stammer.

camoteo, *m.* (Arg.) quarrel.

camotear, *i.v.* 1. (Mex.) to wander or roam aimlessly about, to loiter. 2. (Arg.) to pilfer.

camotero, ra, *m., f.* (Mex.) one who sells sweet potatoes.

camotillo, *m.* 1. (Peru) sweet dish made of mashed sweet potato. 2. (Mex.) violet colored wood streaked with black. 3. (El Salv., Guat., Hond.) tumeric. 4. (C. Rica) sago.

campa, *a.* treeless (ground).

campacán, *m.* (bot.) champac, champak.

cámpago, *m.* (archeol.) campagus, Roman boot.

campal, *a.* pertaining to a field or camp; **batalla c.,** pitched battle.

campamento, *m.* 1. encampment, camp. 2. encamping, camping. — **c. de gitanos,** Gypsy camp; (fig.) a messy room; **c. militar,** military camp.

campana, *f.* 1. bell; bell-shaped object. 2. parish church; parish. 3. striking clock. 4. (archit.) bell. 5. curfew. 6. (Amer.) lookout, cover man. — **a c. tañida,** at the sound of the bell; **c. de aire,** (engin.) air chamber, air receiver; **c. de buzo,** diving bell; **c. de chimenea,** funnel of a chimney; **c. de vidrio,** bell jar; **echar las campanas a vuelo,** to proclaim or announce joyfully, set the bells ringing; **por quien dobla la c.,** for whom the bell tolls.

campanada, *f.* 1. stroke of a bell; ringing of a bell. 2. (coll.) scandal, sensational news.

campanario, *m.* bell tower, campanile, belfry; **de c.,** mean, despicable.

campanear, *i.v.* to toll, peal or ring a bell or the bells.

campanela, *f.* 1. dance step consisting of leaping in the air and twirling one foot in a small circle. 2. (mus.) overtone, note plucked on an open guitar string in the middle of a chord.

campaneo, *m.* 1. frequent pealing or ringing of bells. 2. (coll.) mincing step, affected manner of walking, swinging the shoulders and hips.

campanero, *m.* 1. bell founder or maker. 2. bell ringer, bellman. 3. (ornith.) campanero, bellbird.

campaneta, *f. dim. of* **campana,** small bell.

campaniforme, *a.* bell-shaped.

campanil, *m.* belfry, bell tower. —*a.* pertaining to bells; **bronce c.,** bell bronze.

campanilla, *f.* 1. hand bell; doorbell. 2. bubble. 3. (anat.) uvula. 4. (bot.) bellflower; campanilla. 5. tassel (on clothes, draperies, etc.). 6. (Cuba, bot.) liana. 7. (print.) badly-cased letter that falls out on the bedplate. — **c. de invierno,** (bot.) snowdrop; **c. de otoño,** (bot.) autumn snowflake; **c. de primavera,** (bot.) spring snowflake; **de muchas campanillas,** very important, of great importance or distinction.

campanillazo, *m.* loud ringing of a handbell or doorbell.

campanillear, *i.v.* to ring a bell persistently.

campanilleo, *m.* ringing of a bell.

campanillero, *m.* bell ringer (of a handbell).

campano, *m.* cowbell; small hand bell used in convents. 2. (Amer.) tree whose wood resembles mahogany.

campanología, *f.* campanology, the study of bells; the art of bell ringing.

campanólogo, ga, *m., f.* campanologist, expert in bell-making or bell-ringing.

campante, *a.* (coll.) satisfied, pleased with oneself; cheerful, buoyant.

campanudo, da, *a.* 1. bell-like, bell-shaped. 2. resonant, high-sounding (word, language).

campánula, *f.* (bot.) campanula, bellflower.

campanuláceo, a, *a.* (bot.) campanulaceous —*f.* (*pl.*) Campanulaceae.

campanulado, da, *a.* (bot.) campanulate.

campaña, *f.* 1. campaign (military, naval, political, etc.). 2. period of work or activity, working season. 3. champaign, flat, open country. 4. (Amer.) countryside. 5. (her.) champe. 6. (mar.) cruise. — **viveres de c.,** stores, provisions; **c. publicitaria,** publicity campaign.

campañista, *m.* (Chile) shepherd.

campañisto, *m.* (Chile), *var. of* **campañista.**

campañol, *m.* (zool.) field mouse.

campar, *i.v.* 1. to excel, stand out. 2. to camp.

campatedije, *m.* (Mex., coll.) so-and-so (said in lieu of a person's name).

campeada, *f.* sortie, raid, foray.

campeador, *a.* outstandingly brave and noble in the field of battle. —*m.* great and noble warrior; **El Cid Campeador,** (Sp., hist.) the Cid.

campear, *i.v.* 1. to go out to pasture (cattle, etc.); to go on the prowl (wild animals). 2. to turn green (fields). 3. to stand out, excel. 4. (mil.) to campaign, be in the field; to take the field; to reconnoiter. 5. (Arg., Chile, Urug.) to search the countryside (for a person or an animal).

campechana, *f.* 1. (mar.) fantail grating. 2. (Cuba, Mex.) mixed alcoholic drink, cocktail. 3. (Ven.) hammock.

campechanamente, *adv.* in an easygoing or good-humored manner, genially, cheerfully.

campechanía, campechanería, *f.* 1. good humor, heartiness, geniality, cheerfulness. 2. generosity.

campechano, na, *a.* 1. (coll.) good-humored, easygoing, hearty, frank, genial. 2. (coll.) generous, open-handed.

campecico, illo, ito, *m. dim. of* **campo,** small field.

campeche, *m.* (bot.) logwood, campeachy wood.

campeón, *m.* 1. champion; **c. titular,** defending champion. 2. champion or defender of a doctrine or a cause.

campeonato, *m.* championship.

campero, ra, *a.* 1. in the open, unsheltered, sleeping out in the open fields (cattle, etc.). 2. (Amer.) nimble-footed, sure-footed (a wading or climbing animal); (Mex.) gently trotting (of a horse). 3. (Arg., Urug.) skilled in farming, countrywise. 4. (agr.) creeping, having leaves or stems spread out horizontally (plants). —*m.* 1. friar in charge of farm work of monastery. 2. vehicle fit for hard roads.

campesino, na, *a.* country; rural, rustic; peasant (as *a.*). *—m., f.* peasant; country boy (*m.*), country girl (*f.*).
campestre, *a.* pertaining to the country; rural, pastoral. *—m.* old Mexican dance.
campichuelo, *m.* (Arg.) small, grassy field.
campilán, *m.* kampilan, campilan (long straight-edged cutlass broadening towards the point).
campilótropo, pa, *a.* (bot.) campylotropous.
campillo, *m. dim. of* **campo,** small field; common land (outside a village and owned by the community).
campiña, *f.* country, countryside; flat expanse of arable land; **cerrarse uno de c.,** (coll.) to stand firm, stick to one's guns.
campirano, na, *a.* 1. (C. Rica) uncouth, rude, churlish. 2. (Mex.) rural, rustic. 3. (Mex.) skilled in farming; expert in horses. *—m., f.* 1. (Mex.) peasant; countrywoman (*f.*), countryman (*m.*). 2. (Mex.) skilled farmer; horsebreaker, broncobuster.
campista, *m.* 1. camper. 2. (min., Amer.) mine leaseholder. 3. (C. Amer.) cowboy, cattle herder.
campizal, *m.* small area of land partly covered with grass.
campo, *m.* 1. field; country, countryside. 2. background (of paintings, fabrics, flags); (her.) field (of an escutcheon). 3. space, room. 4. field, sphere (of activities, etc.). 5. camp, faction, band, side, e.g. *un oficial del c. carlista,* an officer from the Carlist camp. 6. scope, range. 7. field, (pitch for football, etc.). 8. camp, encampment. 9. (phys.) field (magnetic, etc.). 10. (math.) field. 11. (mil.) field, field of operations. — **a c. abierto,** (dueling) with no boundaries or with no quarter given; **a c. raso,** in the open; **a c. travieso** or **traviesa,** cross-country; **c. abierto,** open country; **c. de Agramante,** bedlam; **c. de aterrizaje,** landing field; **c. de aviación,** airfield; **c. de batalla,** battlefield; battleground; **c. de concentración,** concentration camp; **c. de derivación,** (elec.) shunt field; **c. de entrenamiento,** (mil.) training camp; **c. de fútbol,** soccer field; **c. de fuerzas,** (phys.) field of force; **c. de instrucción,** (mil.) training camp; **c. de internación,** internment camp; **c. del honor,** field of honor (in dueling), field of battle; **c. de minas,** mine field; **c. de parada,** (mil.) parade ground; **c. de racionales,** (math.) the rational number field, the field of rationals; **c. de trabajo,** labor camp; **c. gravitatorio,** (phys.) gravitational field; **c. magnético,** magnetic field; **c. operatorio,** (med.) surgical area; **c. raso,** flat, bare country; **c. regadío,** (agr.) permanently irrigated land; **c. santo,** cementery; **c. vectorial,** (phys.) vector field; **c. visual,** field of vision, visual field; **Campos Elíseos** or **Elisios,** (myth.) Elysian Fields; **dar c. a,** to give free rein to; **de c. y pista,** track-and-field (athletic events); **dejar el c. abierto (or libre),** to leave the field open, withdraw from competition; **hacer c.,** to clear the way, make room; **hacerse al c.,** to flee to the country (fugitives); **ir a c. travieso,** to cut across country; **juntar c.,** (mil.) to strike camp, (fig.) to finish, give up (an undertaking); **profundidad de c.,** (opt., photog.) depth of field; **quedar en el c.,** to be killed (in battle, dueling); **reconocer el c.,** to reconnoiter, explore the ground; **sacar al c. (a uno),** to challenge (to a fight, debate; **salir a c.** or **al c.,** to sally forth, enter into battle.
camposanto, *m.* cemetery.
camuatí, *m.* (Arg., ento.) species of wasp (Polybia scutellaris).
camucha, *f.* (coll.) small messy bed.
camuesa, *f.* (bot.) pippin (apple).
camueso, *m.* 1. (bot.) pippin tree. 2. (coll.) dunce, fool.
camuflaje, *m.* (gal.) camouflage.
camuflar, *tr.v.* (gal.) to camouflage.
camuliano, na, *a.* (Aztec.) ripening (fruit).
camungo, *m.* (Peru, ornith.) chaja, a large variety of crested screamer (Channa torquata).
camuñas, *f.* (*pl.*) seeds (of any kind except wheat, rye and barley). *—m.* goblin, ghost.
camuza, *f., var. of* **gamuza.**
can, *m.* 1. dog. 2. small bronze gun; trigger (of a firearm). 3. (poet.) **C.,** Canis Major. 4. (archit.) modillion; bracket, corbel. — **c. de busca,** retriever, hunting hound; **C. Mayor,** (astron.) Canis Major; **C. Menor,** (astron.) Canis Minor, the Lesser Dog; **quien bien quiere a Beltrán bien quiere a su c.,** love me, love my dog.
can, *m.* Khan, a title given to officials and dignitaries in some eastern countries.
cana, *f.* (*gen. pl.*) gray hair, white hair; **echar una c. al aire,** (coll.) to go on a spree, have fun; **peinar canas,** (coll.) to be old or white-haired; **quitar mil canas a uno,** (coll.) to take a load off one's mind.
cana, *f.* 1. measure equivalent to about 1.68 meters. 2. (Cuba, bot.) a variety of fan palm (Sabal parviflora). 3. (Amer., sl.) jug, clink, jail.
Canaán, *m.* (Bib.) Canaan, the Promised Land (region between the Jordan and the Mediterranean).
canabina, *f.* (chem.) cannabin.
canabíneo, a, *a.* (bot.) cannabinaceous. *—f.* (*pl.*) (bot.) Cannabinaceae, a small family of plants comprising the hop and hemp.
canaca, *m.* 1. (Chile, Peru, derog.) Chink, Jap (derog. name for a person of the yellow race). 2. (Chile) brothel keeper.
canáceo, a, *a.* (bot.) cannaceous. *—f.* (*pl.*) (bot.) Cannaceae.
canaco, ca, *m., f.* Kanaka, South Sea islander.
canacuate, *m.* (Mex.) boa constrictor.
Canadá, *m.* Canada.
canadiense, *a., m., f.* Canadian.
canadillo, *m.* (bot.) joint fir, sphedra.
canadio, *m.* metal from the platinum group.
canal, *m.* 1. canal, waterway, e.g. *c. de Panamá* or *Suez,* Panama or Suez Canal; channel, strait, e.g. *c. de la Mancha,* English Channel. 2. channel, ditch, canal (for carrying water), e.g. *c. de riego* or *desagüe,* irrigation or drainage channel or ditch; flume, race; natural underground channel. 3. channel (deeper part of harbor, river, etc.). 4. canal, duct, conduit, pipe. 5. groove, striation, canal, furrow, e.g. *c. neural,* neural groove, *c. medular,* medullary canal or groove. 6. (rad., tel.) channel. 7. long narrow valley. 8. drinking trough. 9. weaver's comb. 10. gullet, throat. — **c. de agotamiento,** drainage canal; **c. de alambres,** (elec.) wireway; **c. de corriente portadora,** (elec.) carrier channel; **c. de lluvia,** gutter; **c. de radiodifusión,** broadcasting channel; **c. de riego,** irrigation canal; **c. U,** (metal.) channel iron; **c. resinífero,** (bot.) resin canal; **c. torácico,** (anat.) thoracic duct. *—f.* 1. channel; pipe, conduit, tube, duct. 2. gutter tile; gutter. 3. groove, channel, flute (in columns, etc.); groove, pass (of rolling mill). 4. front edge (of book). 5. dressed carcass (carcass cleaned and ready for use). — **abrir en c.,** to slit open from top to bottom; **c. maestro,** main channel or gutter; **en c.,** split open from top to bottom.
canalado, da, *a.* grooved, fluted.
canaladura, *f.* (archit.) flute, groove, flutting.
canaleja, *f. dim. of* **canal,** small channel, hopper, chute (for grain passing through to the mill).
canalera, *f.* roof gutter.
canaleta, *f.* 1. chute; groove, corrugation; roof gutter, eaves trough. 2. (Arg.) street gutter. 3. spout. — **c. de toma en marcha,** (ry.) track pan; **c. plegadiza,** jacknife chute.
canalete, *m.* 1. wide-bladed paddle (of canoe). 2. (mar.) winding frame (for making cables).
canaletear, *i.v.* (Ven., Col.) to row, paddle.
canaleto, *m.* (archit.) cavetto molding.
canalí, *m.* (Cuba) paddle (of a canoe).
canalice, canalicé, *ref.* **canalizar.**
canaliculado, da, *a.* (bot.) canaliculate.
canalículo, *m.* (anat., zool.) canaliculus.
canalizable, *a.* capable of being channelled.
canalización, *f.* 1. canalization, cutting of channels. 2. channeling, confining in a channel. 3. channeling (of water for irrigation); piping (water, gas, electricity for domestic use). 4. pipes, tubing; (elec.) wiring. 5. (Amer.) sewers, drains, sewage system. 6. (fig.) channeling, direction.
canalizar, (*ref. 53*) *tr.v.* 1. to canalize, cut channels in. 2. to channel, confine in a channel (river, stream, etc.). 3. to channel (water for irrigation); to pipe (water, gas, electricity for domestic use). 4. (fig.) to channel, direct.
canalizo, *m.* (mar.) narrow channel (between shoals or islands).
canalla, *f.* (coll.) rabble, riffraff, the canaille. *—m., f.* (coll.) cur, swine, despicable person.
canallada, *f.* low despicable act, lowness, meanness.
canallesco, ca, *a.* low, base, mean, rotten (coll.), despicable.
canalón, *m.* 1. gutter (alongside the eaves of a roof). 2. shovel hat.
canana, *f.* cartridge belt.
cananeo, a, *a., m., f.* Canaanite. *—m.* Canaanite, Canaanite language.
cananga, *f.* (bot.) ilang-ilang.
canapé, *m.* 1. couch, sofa, settee. 2. canapé, appetizer, hors d'oeuvre.
canard, *m.* (gal.) canard, hoax, lie.
Canarias, *f.* (*pl.*) Canaries, Canary Islands.
canaricultor, *m.* canary breeder.
canaricultura, *f.* art of breeding canaries.
canariense, *a.* Canarian, pertaining to the Canary Islands. *—m., f.* Canarian.
canariera, *f.* large canary cage or aviary.
canario, ria, *a.* Canarian. *—m., f.* Canarian, native of the Canary Islands. *—m.* 1. (ornith.) canary. 2. canary, an ancient Spanish dance. 3. (mar.) a kind of lateenrigged vessel used in the Canary Islands. 4. (C. Rica) a yellow-flowered swamp plant, a kind of water primrose. 5. (Chile) generous tipper. — **¡canario!** goodness me! good heavens!
canasta, *f.* 1. basket, hamper. 2. (mar.) bowknot used to hoist a furled sail or flag. 3. basket, goal (in basketball). 4. canasta, bask rummy (card game).
canastada, *f.* basketful.
canastería, *f.* 1. wicker objects. 2. basket factory or shop.
canastero, ra, *m., f.* 1. basket maker or seller. 2. vendor who carries his wares in a basket. 3. baker's boy who takes the bread from the oven to the cooling room. 4. (ornith., Chile) kind of weaver-bird. — **gitano canastero,** Spanish Gypsy of the basketweavers' tribe (famous for their wit and artistic vein).
canastilla, *f.* 1. small wicker basket, work basket, sewing basket. 2. layette, complete clothing outfit for newborn baby. 3. (Arg., P. Rico) hope chest.

canastillero, ra, *m., f.* maker or seller of wicker baskets.
canastillo, *m.* wicker tray.
canastita, *f.* 1. small basket. 2. (ornith., Arg.) snipe, woodcock.
canasto, *m.* narrow-mouthed basket; **¡canastos!** —*interj.* good heavens! Great Scott!
canastro, *m., var. of* **canasto.**
Canberra, *f.* Canberra, capital of Australia.
cancagua, *f.* (Amer.) fine sand (used in making bricks, ovens, and as a cement in construction).
cáncamo, *m.* 1. gum or resin resembling myrrh. 2. (Cuba) ugly, decrepit person. 3. (mar.) ringbolt; eyebolt. — **c. de mar,** large wave, buffet or impact from a large wave; **c. arponado,** ragged bolt; **c. de cuello,** shoulder eyebolt.
cancamurria, *f.* (coll.) melancholy, sadness, doldrums, blue mood, funk.
cancamusa, *f.* (coll.) hocus-pocus, trickery intended to cloak a deception.
cancán, *m.* 1. cancan, Parisian dance. 2. a lacy, flounced skirt or petticoat. 3. (C. Rica, ornith.) a nonspeaking parrot.
cáncana, *f.* 1. dunce's bench (used to punish schoolboys). 2. dark, short-legged spider.
cancaneado, da, *a.* (C. Rica) pockmarked.
cancanear, *i.v.* 1. (coll.) to wander about, loiter around. 2. (Col., Mex., Cuba) to stutter; to fail, stall (a motor).
cancaneo, *m.* 1. (Mex., coll.) stuttering; loitering. 2. (Cuba) noise of a failing motor.
cáncamo, *m.* (coll.) louse.
cancel, *m.* 1. inner door to keep out drafts. 2. wooden partition screen. 3. glass partition in a chapel (enabling the king to attend incognito). 4. (Mex.) folding screen.
cancela, *f.* iron grating, grilled door; iron trellis work.
cancelación, *f.* 1. cancellation; annulment. 2. settlement, payment.
cancelado, da, *a.* (bot.) cancellate.
canceladura, *f., var. of* **cancelación.**
cancelar, *tr.v.* 1. to cancel; to annul. 2. to expunge, wipe out, strike out. 3. to settle, pay, pay off.
cancelaría, *f.* Papal chancery.
cancelariato, *m.* chancellorship or rectorship of a university.
cancelario, *m.* chancellor or rector of a university.
cancelería, *f., var. of* **cancelaría.**
canceloso, sa, *a.* (anat.) cancellous.
cáncer, *m.* 1. (med.) cancer. 2. (astron.) C., Cancer.
canceración, *f.* (med.) canceration.
cancerado, da, *past part. of* **cancerar.** —*a.* 1. cancerous. 2. suffering from cancer. 3. malignant, vicious, evil.
cancerar, *tr.v.* 1. to make cancerous. 2. to consume, destroy, waste away. 3. to reprove, punish. —*r.v.* to contract cancer; to become cancerous, turn cancerous.
cancerbero, *m.* 1. C., (myth.) Cerberus. 2. (fig.) ruthless guardian.
canceriforme, *a.* (med.) cancriform.
cancerígeno, na, *a.* (med.) cancerigenic. —*m.* carcinogen.
cancerología, *f.* cancerology, study of cancer.
cancerólogo, *m.* cancer specialist.
canceroso, sa, *a.* cancerous.
cancha, *f.* 1. (sport.) pitch, ground, field (for football, cricket, baseball); court (for tennis, pelota, etc.); golf links; cockpit (for cock fighting). 2. (S. Amer.) racetrack; open unencumbered place or space. 3. (S. Amer.) fenced yard (for lumber, junk, etc.). 4. (S. Amer.) long wide reach of a river. 5. (Col.) gaming fee (charged by the owner of a gambling house). 6. (Urug.) path, road. 7. (Arg., Chile, Urug.) skill acquired by experience. — **abrir** or **dar c. a uno,** to concede an advantage to; **¡cancha!** (Urug., Arg.) make way!; **c. de césped,** grass court; **estar uno en su c.,** (Chile, Arg., Urug.) to be in one's element, on one's home ground.
cancha, *f.* (S. Amer.) toasted beans or corn; **como c.,** (Peru) in great abundance, in great quantities.
canchada, *a.* (Arg., Par.) toasted.
canchal, *m.* rocky ground, pebbly field.
canchalagua, *f.* (bot.) canchalagua.
canchamina, *f.* (Chile) ore dump separating yard (in a mine).
canchaminero, *m.* (Chile) mineworker employed in the separating yard, separator.
canchar, *tr.v.* (Quech.) 1. (Arg., Par.) to toast; to roast. 2. (Arg.) to play patty cake. —*i.v.* (Peru) to be for hire (person).
canche, *a.* 1. (C. Amer.) blond. 2. (Col.) poorly seasoned (food).
canchear, *i.v.* 1. to clamber over boulders or rocks. 2. (Arg.) to play at fencing with the hands. 3. (Amer.) to shirk or shun work, to goof off (U.S., sl.).
cancheo, *m.* task-shunning.
canchero, ra, *a.* 1. (Arg., Chile, Peru) adroit, skilled, experienced; self-assured, confident. 2. (Peru) scheming wily (priest). 3. (Chile) shiftless, shirking. —*m.* 1. (Amer.) groundsman; owner of a playing field or court. 2. (Chile) scorer, scorekeeper of game.
cancho, *m.* 1. boulder or large rock; (*gen. pl.*) rocky ground. 2. (Chile) tip, gratuity; (Peru) pay, wage.
canchón, *m.* 1. *aug. of* **cancha,** large boulder. 2. (Peru) large yard or corral; (Peru) fenced-in pasture land.
cancilla, *f.* wrought iron gate.
canciller, *m.* 1. chancellor, chief minister of state; high ranking government official. 2. chancellor (chief secretary of an embassy, consulate, etc.). 3. Minister of Foreign Affairs, Secretary of State (U.S.) — **c. del Exchequer,** Chancellor of the Exchequer; **c. mayor de Castilla,** Archbishop of Toledo.
cancillerato, *m.* chancellorship.
cancilleresco, ca, *a.* of a chancellery or chancellor; formal.
cancillería, *f.* 1. chancellorship; chancellery, chancery. 2. Foreign Office (G.B.), State Department (U.S.). — **c. apostólica,** Papal Chancery.
canción, *f.* 1. song; melody of a song. 2. (poet.) canzone, lay, ballad. — **c. de cuna,** lullaby, cradle song; **c. de gesta,** chanson de geste; **c. de trilla,** harvesters song; **volver a la misma c.,** (coll.) to harp on the same theme; **esa es otra c.,** that is another matter.
cancioncica, illa, ita, *f. dim. of* **canción,** canzonet.
cancionero, *m.* anthology, collection of songs and poems.
cancioneta, *f. dim. of* **canción,** lively little song.
cancionista, *m.* composer or singer of popular songs.
canco, *m.* 1. (Chile) clay casserole; flower-pot. 2. (Bol.) buttocks. 3. (coll.) pederast.
cancón, *m.* (coll.) bugaboo, bogeyman.
cancona, *a.* (Chile) broad-hipped (woman). —*f.* broad-hipped woman.
cancriforme, *a.* cancriform.
cancrinita, *f.* (min.) cancrinite.
cancro, *m.* 1. (med.) cancer. 2. (bot.) canker, blight of treebark causing decay.
cancroide, *m.* (med.) cancroid tumor.
cancroideo, dea, *a.* (med.) cancroid, cancerous; (bot.) cankerous.
candado, *m.* 1. padlock. 2. (Col.) goatee. 3. (*pl.*) cavities on either side of the frog in a horse's hoof. — **c. de combinación,** combination padlock, letter-lock; **estar con c.,** to be padlocked; **c. de aldaba,** hasp lock.
candaliza, *f.* (mar.) brail.
cándalo, *m.* dried pine tree branch.
candallero, *m.* (S. Amer.) axle seat shaft bearing (in a winch).
candamo, *m.* old country dance.
candar, *tr.v.* to lock; to shut, lock up.
cande, *a.* **azúcar c.,** sugar candy.
candeal, *a.* **trigo c.,** white wheat (Tritioum campactum) or any similar variety of wheat producing white flour; **pan c.,** white bread (made of white wheat). —*m.* white wheat; white bread.
candeda, *f.* chestnut blossom.
candela, *f.* 1. candle; candlestick. 2. (coll.) fire, heat; light (for a cigarrette). 3. (phys.) candle (unit of luminous intensity). 4. (bot.) chestnut blossom. 5. inclination of the balance needle towards the object weighed. — **acabarse la c.,** to be about to die; **arrimar c.,** (coll.) to beat, thrash; **como unas candelas,** (coll.) beautifully; **dar c.,** (Ven.) to bother, annoy; **en c.,** (mar.) vertical (a ship's mast, etc.); **estar con la c. en la mano,** to be about to die, on the point of death.
candelabro, *m.* 1. candelabrum. 2. (bot.) cereus, candelabra-shaped cactus (Cereus haematurius).
candelada, *f.* 1. bonfire. 2. candles.
candelaria, *f.* 1. Candlemas. 2. (bot.) great mullein; (Peru) mullein flower.
candelecho, *m.* thatch hut (for the watchman of a vineyard).
candeleja, *f.* (Amer.) socket pan of a candlestick.
candelejón, *m.* (Amer.) dunce, fool.
candelerazo, *m.* blow with a candlestick.
candelero, *m.* 1. candlestick; candle maker or seller; oil-lamp; fishing torch. 2. (mil.) wooden frame-work for sandbagging. 3. (mar.) stanchion. — **c. ciego,** (mar.) stanchion without a top ring; **c. de ojo,** (mar.) stanchion with top ring; **estar** or **poner en c.,** to be or place in high office or in a position of great authority; to be or make very popular.
candeleta, *f., var. of* **candaliza.**
candelilla, *f.* 1. *dim. of* **candela,** small candle. 2. (med.) bougie, catheter. 3. (bot.) ament, catkin. 4. (bot.) candelilla. 5. (Cuba) overstitch (sewing). 6. (Cuba) insect (Phtorimea operculella) which attacks the leaf of the tobacco plant. 7. (Amer.) glowworm. 8. (Chile) ignis fatuus, will-o'-the-wisp. — (*gen. in pl.*) **hacerle a uno candelillas los ojos,** to sparkle (the eyes), e.g. *le hacen candelillas los ojos,* his eyes sparkle (from the effects of alcohol).
candelita, *f.* (ornith.) redstart, warbler.
candelizas, *f.* (*pl.*) (mar.) frails.
candelizo, *m.* (coll.) icicle.
candelón, *m.* (Dom. Rep., bot.) a hardwood tree.
candencia, *f.* candescence.
candente, *a.* 1. red-hot, white-hot, candescent. 2. (fig.) burning, important; **cuestión c.,** burning question.
candi, *a.* **azúcar c.,** sugar candy.
candial, *a., var. of* **candeal.**
candidación, *f.* crystallization (of sugar).
cándidamente, *adv.* ingenuously, naively; foolishly.
candidato, ta, *m., f.* candidate.
candidatura, *f.* candidature, candidacy; list of candidates.
candidez, *f.* 1. ingenuousness, simplicity, naiveté; foolishness; silly or foolish remark. 2. whiteness.

cándido, da, *a.* 1. ingenuous, naive, simple, sincere, guileless, foolish. 2. white.
candiel, *m.* eggnog made of white wine, yolk of egg and sugar.
candil, *m.* 1. oil lamp; ancient teapot-shaped oil lamp. 2. surroyal, crown (of an antler); (coll.) peak, cock (of a hat). 3. (coll.) long irregular tuck (in a skirt). 4. (Cuba, ichth.) squirrelfish. 5. (Mex.) chandelier. 6. (*pl.*) (bot.) birthwort. 7. (bot.) wake-robin (Arisarum Vulgare). — **ni buscado con un c.,** (coll.) just right for the job; **poder arder en un c.,** to be very strong (wine), be very trenchant (criticism), be very sharp or clever (person).
candilada, *f.* oil spilt from a lamp, oil stain.
candilazo, *m.* blow with a lamp.
candileja, *f.* 1. oil container (of a lamp); lampion, small rudimentary oil lamp. 2. (*pl.*) (theat.) footlights. 3. (bot.) corn cockle (Agrostemma githago).
candilejo, *m.* 1. *dim. of* **candil,** small hanging oil lamp. 2. (bot.) corn cockle (Agrostemma githago).
candilera, *f.* (bot.) phlomis (Phlomis lychnitis).
candililo, *m.* (*gen. in pl.*) (bot.) wakerobin (Arisarum Vulgare).
candilón, *m. aug. of* **candil,** large hanging oil lamp.
candinga, *f.* 1. (Chile) pestering, annoyance. 2. (Hond.) pretty pickle, fine mess. 3. (Mex.) devil.
candiota, *a., m., f.* Candiot, Cretan. —*f.* barrel; large earthenware wine jar.
candiotera, *f.* wine cellar, wine barrel depository; (collection of) wine casks.
candiotero, *m.* maker or seller of wine barrels.
candombe, *m.* lively dance of South American blacks; dancehall where the **candombe** is danced; the long drum with one drumhead used for beating out the rhythm of the **candombe.**
candonga, *f.* 1. trick, trap; flattery, soft soaping. 2. kidding, teasing, badinage, joking. 3. (coll.) draft mule. 4. (Hond.) navel bandage (to bind newborn baby's navel). 5. (mar.) triangular storm sail on mizzen mast. 6. (*pl.*) (Col.) earrings. — **dar candonga,** to tease, kid.
candongo, ga, *a.* 1. flattering, ingratiating, softsoaping (coll.). 2. malingering, shirking. —*m., f.* 1. flatterer, soft-soaper. 2. malingerer, shirker.
candonguear, *tr.v.* to chaff, tease, kid. —*i.v.* (coll.) to shirk, malinger, artfully avoid work.
candonguero, ra, *a.* (coll.) teasing, kidding, waggish.
candor, *m.* 1. simplicity, innocence, naiveté. 2. candor, whiteness.
candorosamente, *adv.* innocently, simply, naively.
candoroso, sa, *a.* innocent, simple, naive.
candray, *m.* small double-ended boat.
candungo, *m.* 1. (P. Rico) tin tube for protecting documents. 2. (Dom. Rep.) dice box. —*a.* (Peru) funny, comical; silly, stupid.
cané, *m.* card game resembling **monte.**
caneca, *f.* 1. pocket flask, liquor bottle. 2. (Arg.) wooden bucket. 3. (Cuba) liquid measure of 19 liters. 4. (Ecuad.) earthenware water cooling jar.
canecillo, *m.* (archit.) truss, bracket, modillion, corbel (projection supporting a cornice).
caneco, ca, *a.* (Bol.) tipsy, drunk, lit-up, merry. —*m.* glazed earthenware liquor bottle.
canéfora, *f.* canephoros, basket-bearer in early Greek religious festivals, carrying offerings for the gods.
caneicitos, *m.* (*pl.*) (Cuba) fete, outdoor fair.
¡canejo! *interj.* (Arg., coll.) confound it!
canela, *f.* 1. cinnamon (spice); cinnamon bark. 2. (coll.) gem, jewel (anything exquisite). — **¡canela!** good gracious! marvelous!
caneláceo, a, *a.* (bot.) canellaceous. —*f.* (bot.) (*pl.*) Canellaceae.
canelado, da, *a.* cinnamon-colored, cinnamon-flavored.
canelar, *m.* cinnamon plantation.
canelillo, *m.* (C. Rica, bot.) cinnamon tree.
canelina, *f.* essence of white cinnamon.
canelita, *f.* (geol.) a type of meteoric rock.
canelo, la, *a.* cinnamon-colored (said gen. of dogs and horses). —*m.* (bot.) cinnamon tree; (Chile) Winter's bark (Drimys winteri).
canelón, *m.* 1. roof gutter. 2. long, sharp-pointed icicle. 3. tubular braid or trimming (as on epaulets). 4. cinnamon candy. 5. thickest thongs (of the cat-o-nine-tails). 6. (Mex.) blow of one spinning top against another. 7. (Ven.) curl made with a curling iron. 8. (cul.) cannelon, tubular noodle stuffed with a savory filling and cooked in a tomato, meat or cheese sauce, (*pl.*) canneloni, cannelons.
caneo, *m.* cabin, hut.
canequí, *m.* cannequin (fine muslin, woven in India).
canequita, *f.* (Cuba) liquid measure.
canesú, *m.* 1. corset cover. 2. yoke of a shirt or blouse. 3. guimpe.
canevá, *m.* (gal.) canvas, burlap.
caney, *m.* 1. (hist., Antilles) the large hut or cabin occupied by the Indian chiefs. 2. (Antilles) peasant's hut. 3. (Cuba) river bend.
canfeno, *m.* (chem.) camphine, camphene.
canfín, *m.* (C. Rica) petroleum.
canfol, *m.* (chem.) camphol.
canforato, *m.* (chem.) camphorate.
canforero, *m.* (bot.) camphor tree.
canga, *f.* 1. cangue, cang, type of Chinese pillory. 2. (S. Amer.) clayey iron ore.
cangagua, *f.* (Ecuad.) strong type of clay used for making bricks and fired earthenware objects.
cangalla, *m., f.* 1. (Col.) rake, emaciated person or animal. 2. (Arg., Peru) coward, mouse (coll.), runt (sl.). 3. (Arg., Chile) slag, tailings. 4. (Bol.) packsaddle. 5. (Salv.) rag.
cangallar, *tr.v.* 1. (Chile) to steal (ore from a mine). 2. (Chile) to cheat (the tax collector).
cangallero, ra, *a.* (Chile, Peru) 1. one who steals ore or minerals from a mine. 2. (Peru) vendor of inexpensive wares.
cangilón, *m.* 1. large jug or pitcher; scoop (of chain pump), dipping or dredging bucket. 2. stiff, curved pleat of a ruff. 3. drum. 4. (Amer.) rut, cart or wagon rut. 5. (Cuba, Col.) pothole, hole (in road). — **c. basculante,** tip bucket; **c. de arrastre,** dragline bucket.
cangre, *m.* (Cuba) cutting of the yucca root used for planting.
cangreja, *a.* (mar.) fore-and-aft (sail); **vela c.,** fore-and-aft sail.
cangrejada, *f.* 1. (Ecuad.) stupidity. 2. (Peru) perfidy.
cangrejal, *m.* (Arg.) swampy ground infested with black crabs.
cangrejera, *f.* crab nest.
cangrejero, ra, *m., f.* crab fisher, seller or dealer. —*m.* 1. species of heron. 2. (Guat.) dog-like animal which feeds on crabs. 3. (Chile) crab nest.
cangrejo, *m.* 1. (zool.) crayfish; crab. 2. (astron.) **C., Cancer,** the Crab; Crab nebula. 3. kneepiece; elbow-piece (of medieval plate armor). 4. (mar.) gaff. 5. caulking bit. 6. (ry.) handcar, trolley. — **c. azul,** (zool.) blue crab; **c. bayoneta,** (zool.) king crab; **c. de los cocoteros,** (zool.) purse or coconut crab; **c. de mar,** (zool.) green or shore crab; **c. de río,** (zool.) fresh-water crayfish; **c. ermitaño,** (zool.) hermit crab; **c. moro,** (zool., cul.) moro crab.
cangrejuelo, *m. dim. of* **cangrejo,** small crab or crayfish.
cangrena, *f.* (med.) gangrene.
cangrenarse, *r.v.* to become gangrenous, gangrene.
cangrenoso, sa, *a.* gangrenous.
cangrina, *f.* 1. (Cuba, vet.) anthrax. 2. (Col., coll.) discomfort, annoyance.
cangro, *m.* (Amer.) cancer.
cangroso, sa, *a.* (arch.) cancerous.
canguelo, *m.* 1. (coll.) fear. 2. (Ven.) chilliness.
cangüeso, *m.* (ichth.) goby (Gobius niger).
canguil, *m.* (Ecuad.) a variety of small succulent corn; popcorn.
canguro, *m.* (zool.) kangaroo.
cania, *f.* (bot.) type of monoecius nettle.
caníbal, *a., m., f.* 1. cannibal. 2. (fig.) said of a cruel person.
canibalismo, *m.* cannibalism.
canica, *f.* 1. (bot.) Cuban wild cinnamon. 2. marble; (*pl.*) game of marbles.
canicie, *f.* whiteness, greyness (of person's hair).
canícula, *f.* 1. (astron.) **C.,** Dog Star. 2. dog days (hottest days of summer).
canicular, *a.* canicular. —*m.* (*pl.*) the dog days.
caniculario, *m.* dog watcher; dog catcher.
cánido, *m.* (zool.) canid, (*pl.*) Canidae.
canijo, ja, *a.* (coll.) feeble, frail, sickly. —*m., f.* feeble, sickly person, invalid.
canil, *m.* coarse brown bread, dog biscuit.
canilla, *f.* 1. (anat.) long bone (of leg, arm, wing); (Amer., coll.) leg, skinny leg. 2. shuttle, bobbin, spool. 3. stripe, rib (in woven fabrics). 4. spigot, tap, faucet (in barrel). 5. (Peru) dice game. 6. (Amer.) shin bone. — **irse uno de c.,** (coll.) to have diarrhea, be loose-bowelled; (coll.) to prattle, gabble; **tener c.,** (Mex.) to be tough or strong. —*a.* **uva c.,** (bot.) common stonecrop.
canillado, da, *a.* striped, ribbed (with stray threads).
canillar, *tr.v.* to wind on a spool.
canillera, *f.* 1. shin-pad (used in sports); jambeau (on medieval plate armor). 2. (Col.) panic, terror. 3. (Ecuad.) trembling.
canillero, ra, *m., f.* bobbin-maker. —*m.* spigot hole (in cask).
canillita, *m.* (S. Amer.) newsboy, newspaper vendor.
canilludo, da, *a.* (Amer.) long-shanked, long-legged.
canime, *m.* (Col., Peru, bot.) copaiba.
canina, *f.* 1. dog dung. 2. (arch.) dog days.
caninez, *f.* ravenous hunger.
canino, na, *a.* canine; doglike. — **tener hambre c.,** to be ravenously hungry. —*m.* (anat.) canine (tooth).
caniquí, *m.* cannequin (fine muslin woven in India).
canistel, *m.* (Cuba, bot.) canistel, lucuma, eggfruit.
canistro, *m.* (archeol.) rush basket.
canje, *m.* barter, exchange; **c. de prisioneros,** (mil.) exchange of war prisoners.
canjeable, *a.* exchangeable.
canjear, *tr.v.* to exchange.
canjura, *f.* (Hond.) powerful native poison containing copper oxide.
cannabáceo, a, *a.* (bot.) cannabaceous. —*f.* (*pl.*) Cannabaceae.
cannabíneo, a, *a.* (bot.) cannabaceous. —*f.* (*pl.*) Cannabaceae.
cannáceo, a, *a.* (bot.) cannaceous. —*f.* (*pl.*) Cannaceae.
cano, na, *a.* white-haired, grey-haired, hoary; (fig.) ancient, old; (poet.) hoary, snow-white, milky-white.

canoa, *f.* 1. canoe, dugout; (captain's) gig. 2. (Amer.) water conduit or duct; (C. Rica, Chile) gutter (on roof). 3. (Amer.) feeding trough. 4. (Chile) sheath (enclosing the fruit of the Coquito palm). — **c. automóvil,** motor-boat; **sombrero de c.,** shovel hat (worn by clergymen).
canódromo, *m.* dog track, greyhound track, greyhound stadium.
canoero, ra, *m., f.* canoeist; person who owns or works with a canoe.
canon, *m.* 1. canon, precept (of church doctrine, artistic judgment, etc.). 2. (Bib.) canon (list of Biblical books considered genuine); list, catalogue, canon. 3. (ecc.) Canon (part of the Mass beginning with "Te igitur"); canon (book containing this part of the mass). 4. (*pl.*) (ecc.) canon law. 5. (print.) canon (24 point type). 6. (mus.) canon (composition for two or more voices repeating the same melodic phrase). 7. tax; rent; (min.) royalty. 8. aesthetic norm or standard. — **c. conducticio,** rural rent; **c. de arrendamiento,** (law) rental rate; **c. de producción** or **de superficie,** (min.) mining royalty.
canonesa, *f.* canoness.
canónica, *f.* canonical rule, religious life or rule followed by canons.
canonical, *a.* canonical, pertaining to canons.
canónicamente, *adv.* canonically, in accordance with canon law.
canonicato, *m.* canonry (canons collectively), canonicate, canonship.
canonice, canonicé, *ref.* **canonizar.**
canonicidad, *f.* canonicity.
canónico, ca, *a.* canonical.
canóniga, *f.* 1. (coll.) siesta, nap (before a meal). 2. (coll.) drunkenness.
canónigo, *m.* canon, prebendary (a member of a religious group living according to a canon or rule).
canonista, *m.* canonist (an expert in or student of canon law).
canonizable, *a.* worthy of being canonized.
canonización. *f.* canonization.
canonizar, (*ref. 53*) *tr.v.* 1. to canonize (a saint). 2. (fig.) to approve, applaud, praise. 3. (fig.) to certify (something), to codify.
canonjía, *f.* 1. canonry (canons collectively), canonicate, canonship. 2. (coll.) sinecure, soft job.
canope, *m.* (archeol.) canopic vase (an Egyptian urn used to hold the remains of the dead).
Canopo, *m.* (astron.) Canopus (star).
canoro, ra, *a.* 1. canorous, pleasant sounding, melodious, musical (e.g. bird song and the human voice). 2. (fig.) lyrical, melodious, graceful (said of poetry, musical instruments, etc.).
canoso, sa, *a* gray-haired, grizzled, hoary.
canotier, *m.* flat-brimmed straw hat, boater (G.B.)
canquén, *m.* (Chile) species of wild goose.
cansadamente, *adv.* 1. wearily, tiredly. 2. annoyingly, tiresomely.
cansado, da, *past part. of* **cansar.** —*a.* 1. tired, fatigued, weary; exhausted (land); worn (things). 2. bothersome, tiresome, tedious (person).
cansador, ra, *a.* (Amer.) wearisome, tiresome, tiring, exhausting.
cansancio, *m.* fatigue, weariness, lassitude.
cansar, *tr.v.* 1. to tire; to make tired, weary. 2. to exhaust (e.g. land or soil by overtilling). 3. (coll.) to annoy, bore, bother. —*r.v.* to tire, get tired, become tired, weary or exhausted. — **cansarse de** + *inf.*, to get tired of + *ger.*
cansera, *f.* 1. (coll.) annoyance; annoying foible or habit. 2. (Amer., coll.) time lost, wasted effort. 3. (coll., Sp.) fatigue, boredom.
cansino, na, *a.* 1. exhausted by work (said of man or beast). 2. annoying, irritating. 3. slow, slothful.
cansón, na, *m., f.* (Amer.) a person or thing that is tiring or boring.
cantábile, *m.* (mus.) cantabile, flowing majestic passage.
cantable, *a.* (mus.) to be sung slowly. —*m.* 1. (mus.) lyrics, esp. the verse part of a musical comedy. 2. (mus.) cantabile, passage in an easy, flowing manner.
cantábrico, ca, *a.* Cantabrian, pertaining to the coast and regions of the N. of Spain; **mar Cantabrico,** the Bay of Biscay.
cántabro, bra, *a., m., f.* Cantabrian, of Cantabria, a region of Northern Spain; **montes Cántabros,** the Cantabrian mountains.
cantaclaro, ra, *a.* frank, outspoken. —*m.* frank or outspoken person.
cantada, *f.* (mus.) cantata, a composition consisting of vocal solos, choruses, etc.
cantador, ra, *m., f.* singer (of Spanish popular or folk songs).
cantal, *m.* a stone block; stony ground.
cantalear, *i.v.* to warble or coo; to hum or sing softly.
cantaleta, *f.* 1. charivari, a noisy or confused mock serenade. 2. (Amer.) constant nagging or scolding. — **dar c.,** to make fun of; **la misma c.,** the same tune, the same tiring subject, the same old song.
cantaletear, *tr.v.* 1. (Amer.) to harp on, repeat continually. 2. (Amer.) to make fun of, scoff at, or ridicule.
cantalinoso, sa, *a.* stony or rocky (ground).
cantamisano, *m., var. of* **misacantano.**
cantante, *a.* singing. —*m., f.* singer.
cantaor, ra, *m., f.* (coll.) singer, esp. a flamenco singer.
cantar, *m.* 1. song, folk-song. 2. (Chile) bit of gossip. — **c. de gesta,** epic poem; **C. de los Cantares,** (Bib.) Song of Songs; **ése es otro c.,** (coll.) that is another story, that is a horse of a different color, that's another kettle of fish.
cantar, *tr.v.* to sing; to chant; to sing of or about. — **cantarlas claras,** to tell without beating about the bush; to give someone a piece of one's mind. —*i.v.* 1. to sing; to chant. 2. (coll. to squeak, creak, rattle (machinery, vehicles, etc.); to chirp (insects). 3. to bid, to call trump (in cards). 4. (coll.) to confess, (sl.) to sing. 5. (mar.) to whistle an order or command. 6. (mar.) to sing chanteys. 7. (mus.) to play the melody. — **c. de plano,** (coll.) to confess everything, make a full confession; **c. mal y porfiar,** (coll.) to do something badly and persist in doing it.
cántara, *f.* 1. a 1. large, narrow-mouthed pitcher. 2. a liquid measure (32 pints).
cantarada, *f.* a pitcherful.
cantarela, *f.* 1. treble string (on a violin, guitar). 2. (bot.) chanterelle (type of edible mushroom).
cantarera, *f.* shelf for pitchers, jars, etc.
cantarería, *f.* pottery shop, earthenware shop.
cantarero, *m.* potter; dealer in earthenware.
cantárida, *f.* 1. (ento.) blister beetle, Spanish fly, cantharis. 2. (med.) cantharides, cantharidal plaster. 3. cantharides blister (caused by cantharidal plaster).
cantarilla, *f.* unglazed earthenware jug.
cantarillo, *m.* 1. *dim. of* **cántaro,** small jug. 2. (bot.) rock jasmine (Androsace septentrionalis).
cantarín, na, *a.* (coll.) fond of singing, always singing. —*m., f.* singer, professional singer.
cántaro, *m.* 1. pitcher, wine measure (of varying capacity). 2. box, ballot box. 3. (Mex.) bassoon. — **a cántaros,** abundantly, copiously; **estar** or **entrar en c.,** (coll.) to be in the running (for a job); to be proposed (for a job); **llover a cántaros,** (coll.) to rain cats and dogs.
cantata, *f.* (mus.) cantata, choral composition.
cantatriz, (*pl.* **cantatrices**) *f.* chanteuse, songstress.
cantazo, *m.* blow from a stone or rock.
cante, *m.* **c. flamenco** or **c. jondo,** flamenco singing.
canteado, da, *a.* on edge, upright (bricks, stones, etc.).
canteador, ra, *m., f.* (carp.) edger; edging saw; pitching tool. — **c. de acera,** curb tool; **c. en bisel,** bevel edger.
cantear, *tr.v.* 1. to edge, work or plane the edges of (a board, stone, etc.). 2. to place (bricks) on edge or upright. 3. to cut or quarry stone.
cantel, *m.* (mar.) (*gen. pl.*) ends of old ropes put under casks to steady them.
cantera, *f.* 1. (stone) quarry, (clay) pit. 2. talent, ability, capacity (of a person).
cantería, *f.* 1. stonecutting. 2. stonework, masonry. 3. ashlar, piece of dressed or hewn stone.
canterios, *m.* (*pl.*) transverse roof beams.
canterito, *m.* small crust or piece of bread.
cantero, *m.* 1. stonecutter. 2. crust (e.g. of bread). 3. (Amer.) square flowerbed. — **c. de heredad,** (coll.) piece of land that can be worked or cultivated.
canticio, *m.* (coll.) continuous, annoying singing, droning.
cántico, *m.* canticle; song.
cantidad, *f.* quantity; amount, sum (of money); (prosody) quantity (of a syllable). — **c. alzada,** agreed sum; **c. concurrente,** amount required to complete a certain sum; **c. constante,** (math.) constant, constant quantity; **c. de calor,** (phys.) amount of heat; **c. de energía,** (phys.) energy (quantity); **c. de masa,** (phys.) mass (quantity); **c. de movimiento,** (mech.) momentum; **c. negativa,** (math.) negative quantity; **c. positiva,** (math.) positive quantity; **c. variable,** (math.) variable, variable quantity.
cantiga, *f.* (arch.) poem, ballad.
cantil, *m.* 1. cliff; undersea shelf; brink of a precipice. 2. (Guat.) a large snake.
cantilena, *f., var. of* **cantinela.**
cantilever, *m.* (archit., aer.) cantilever.
cantillo, *m.* 1. corner, cornerstone. 2. pebble; jackstone. 3. (*pl.*) jacks, jackstones (game).
cantimpla, *a.* (Arg., Urug.) silly, foolish (person). —*m., f.* fool, simpleton.
cantimplora, *f.* 1. canteen, water bottle. 2. water cooling jar. 3. siphon. 4. (Guat.) mumps. 5. (Col.) powder flask.
cantina, *f.* 1. cafeteria, buffet; canteen, factory lunchroom; (educ.) refectory; (mil.) mess; (Amer.) bar, saloon, tavern. 2. wine cellar. 3. picnic hamper, sandwich box; knapsack.
cantinela, *f.* 1. song, simple ballad. 2. (coll.) same old tune, same old song or subject.
cantinera, *f.* 1. female sutler (woman accompanying troops to sell them provisions and liquor), vivandière. 2. barmaid.
cantinero, *m.* 1. bartender, saloon keeper. 2. servant in charge of wine cellar.
cantiña, *f.* (coll.) popular song, well-known ditty.
cantizal, *m.* stony ground, rough uneven terrain.
canto, *m.* 1. song; chant. 2. singing, art of singing. 3. melody, tune. 4. short heroic poem; canto, stanza of an epic poem; poem, any poetical composition. — **al c. del gallo,** (coll.) at cockcrow, at daybreak; **c. de órgano** or **c. figurado** or **c. mensurable,** (ecc.) cantus mensurabilis, measured music; **c. del cisne,** swansong; **c. gregoriano** or **c. llano,** Gregorian chant, plainsong;

en c. llano, (coll.) in plain language; **ser c. llano una cosa,** (coll.) to be plain sailing; to be plain or unembroidered.

canto, *m.* 1. edge, end, border; corner; back, blunt edge (of sword or knife); front edge (of book). 2. thickness. 3. stone, rock, pebble; stone-throwing game in which he who throws farthest wins. — **a c.,** on the edge, very near; **al c.,** (coll.) next to one, beside one; **c. de pan,** crust of bread; **c. pelado** or **c. rodado,** round, smooth pebble; **darse uno con un c. en el pecho,** (coll.) to thank one's lucky stars; to be grateful; **de c.,** on edge; upright; **c. de corte,** cutting edge; **c. vivo,** square or sharp edge.

cantollanista, *m., f.* plainsong expert.

cantón, *m.* 1. corner (of a building). 2. canton; region, district. 3. (mil.) cantonment. 4. (Hond.) butte, isolated hill. 5. (her.) canton. 6. (Amer.) fine crepe used in dressmaking. — **c. de honor,** (her.) quarter of honor; **c. redondo,** (carp.) a rough round file.

cantonada, *f.* canton (of a building). — **dar c. a uno,** (coll.) to evade someone, give someone the slip.

cantonado, da, *a.* (her.) cantoned, quartered.

cantonal, *a.* cantonal, pertaining to a canton or district. —*m., f.* supporter of cantonalism.

cantonalismo, *m.* cantonalism, political system of dividing a country into almost independent cantons or districts; (fig.) anarchic subdivision of authority in a nation.

cantonalista, *a.* cantonal. —*m., f.* supporter of cantonalism.

cantonar, *tr.v.* (mil.) to canton, quarter (troops).

cantonear, *i.v.* to idle, loaf about, wander or roam aimlessly about.

cantonearse, *r.v.* (coll.) to strut; to flounce, mince, walk in an affected manner.

cantoneo, *m.* (coll.) action of mincing, flouncing, walking in an affected manner.

cantonera, *f.* 1. corner band (reinforcement on the corner of a trunk, etc.), cornerpiece (decorative reinforcement on the corner of a book). 2. corner table. 3. streetwalker, prostitute.

cantonero, ra, *a.* loafing, idling. —*m., f.* loafer, idler. —*m.* (bkb.) cornerpiece; instrument used by book binders for gilding book corners.

cantor, ra, *a.* singing. — **ave c.,** songbird. —*m., f.* 1. singer, songster. 2. poet, bard. —*f.* 1. (coll., Chile) bedpan. 2. (zool.) songbird. (*pl.*) order of song birds.

cantoral, *m.* hymnbook, choir book.

Cantórbery, *m.* Canterbury, city in England, seat of the archbishop of the Church of England.

cantorral, *m.* stony, pebbly ground.

cantoso, sa, *a.* stony, pebbly (ground).

cantú, (*pl.* **cantúes**) *m.* (bot.) cantuta, Inca magic flower.

cantúa, *f.* (Cuba) a candy made of sweet potato, coconut, sesame and sugar.

cantuariense, *a.* Canterburian. —*m., f.* inhabitant or native of Canterbury, city in England.

cantueso, *m.* (bot.) lavender, French lavender.

canturía, *f.* singing exercise; vocal music; musical quality (of a composition); monotonous singing.

canturrear, *i.v.* (coll.) to hum, sing softly.

canturreo, *m.* humming, singing in a low voice.

canturria, *f.* monotonous singing.

canturriar, *i.v.* to hum, sing in a low voice.

cantuta, *f.* (bot.) cantuta, Incaic magic flower.

cánula, *f.* 1. small reed. 2. (med.) cannula; nozzle of a syringe.

canular, *a.* tubular, cannular.

canutero, *m.* 1. case for pins, needles. 2. (Amer.) penhandle.

canutillo, *m.* 1. bugle bead (stitched to tassels and fringes on women's dresses). 2. gold or silver embroidery twist. 3. (zool.) the seminal receptacle of a female lobster. 4. (Cuba, Mex., bot.) hamelia (plant).

canuto, *m.* 1. internode, segment of a cane between two nodes. 2. tube, tubular container. 3. soldier's discharge warrant. 4. sac in which locusts lay their eggs. 5. (C. Amer., Ven.) penhandle. 6. (Mex.) ice cream stick. — **en c.,** in bud.

canuto, *m.* (Chile) Protestant minister or pastor; Protestant.

caña, *f.* 1. cane, reed; stalk, stem; (bot.) giant reed; (Amer.) sugar cane. 2. (anat.) long bone (in the arm or leg). 3. marrow, medula. 4. leg (of boot or stocking). 5. tall, narrow wine glass; wine measure. 6. agrarian measure equal to 2.508 square meters. 7. notch, groove (in the blade of a sword). 8. chase of cannon; tipstock (into which the barrel of a rifle, shotgun, etc. fits). 9. (archit.) shaft of column. 10. glass blower's tube. 11. cannon, shank (of horse's leg). 12. (min.) gallery. 13. (*pl.*) mock war game played on horseback with canes instead of lances. 14. Andalusian folk song. 15. (Col.) boast, brag. 16. (Amer.) uncured brandy or rum. 17. (Col., Ecuad., Ven.) hoax, false news, rumor, lie. — **c. borde,** (bot.) ditch reed; **c. brava,** (bot.) giant or ditch reed; (bot.) (Amer) uva grass; (bot.) huiscoyol (shrubby Central American palm); **c. común,** (bot.) giant or ditch reed; **c. de azúcar,** sugar cane; **c. de Bengala,** (bot.) rattan, rattan palm; **c. de Castilla,** (bot.) giant or ditch reed; (Amer.) uva grass; **c. de columna,** shaft of a column; **c. de cuentas, c. de la India,** (bot.) Indian shot (Canna Indica); **c. de Indias** (bot.) rattan, rattan palm; **c. del ancla,** (mar.) anchor shank; **c. del pulmón.** (anat.) trachea; **c. del timón,** (mar.) tiller; **c. de pescar,** fishing rod; **c. de vaca,** cow's cannon bone; marrow; **c. de volar,** blasting hole; **c. dulce,** sugar cane; **c. espina,** kind of bamboo; **c. melar,** sugar cane; **jugar a uno a las cañas,** to wound someone with sharp pointed canes; **las cañas se vuelven lanzas,** what begins as a joke ends in tragedy.

cañacoro, *m.* (bot.) Indian shot, Indian reed.

cañada, *f.* 1. gulch, gully, ravine. 2. (Amer.) stream; (Amer.) bed of stream. 3. marrow (of cow's shinbone). 4. cattle trail or path. — **c. real,** cattle trail.

cañadilla, *f.* (zool.) edible mollusk (Murex brandaris).

cañadul, *f.* (Col.) sugar cane.

cañaduzal, *m.* (Amer.) sugar cane plantation.

cañafístola, *f., var. of* **cañafístula.**

cañafístula, *f.* (bot.) 1. drumstick tree, canafistula. 2. pods of the drumstick tree.

cañaheja, *f.* (bot.) giant fennel; **c. hedionda,** (bot.) thapsia.

cañaherla, *f., var of* **cañaheja.**

cañahua, *f.* (Peru) Indian millet.

cañahuatal, *m.* guayacan or lignum vitae plantation.

cañahuate, *m.* (Col., bot.) guayacan, lignum vitae (Guayacum officinalis).

cañahueca, *m., f.* (coll.) chatterbox, babbler, gossip.

cañajelga, *f.* (bot.) giant fennel.

cañal, *m.* 1. cane brake, cane thicket; cane plantation. 2. weir, a cane fence or palisade for trapping fish; small channel used for trapping river fish.

cañalieca, *f.* weir, a cane fence or palisade for trapping fish.

cañamar, *m.* hemp field.

cañamazo, *m.* 1. tow, short broken fibers; coarse canvas, burlap; cross-stitch canvas (used for embroidery work). 2. (Cuba, bot.) carpet grass (Axonopus compressus).

cañamelar, *m.* sugar cane plantation.

cañameño, ña, *a.* hempen, made of hemp fiber.

cañamero, ra, *a.* hemp, e.g. *industria cañamera,* hemp industry.

cañamiel, *f.* sugar cane.

cañamiza, *f.* hemp bagasse, hemp waste.

cañamo, *m.* (bot.) hemp, hempfiber, hemp cloth; hemp rope, hemp net, sling; (Amer.) hemp rope. — **c. de Manila,** (bot.) Manila hemp, abaca; **c. embreado,** tarred marline; **c. trenzado,** braided hemp.

cañamón, *m.* hempseed (used principally as bird food).

cañamoncillo, *m.* very fine sand.

cañamonero, ra, *m., f.* hempseed vendor.

cañar, *m., var. of* **cañal.**

cañareja, *f.* (bot.) giant fennel.

cañariego, ga, *a.* droving, drover (applied to men, dogs, or horsemen who accompany migrating herds of sheep); **pellejo c.,** the skin of a sheep that died on the march.

cañarroya, *f.* (bot.) wall pellitory, pellitory.

cañavera, *f.* (bot.) ditch reed, reed-grass.

cañaveral, *m.* canebrake, cane thicket; sugar cane plantation.

cañaverear, *tr.v.* to wound with sharp-pointed canes.

cañavererría, *f.* stall or shop where reeds or canes are sold.

cañaverero, *m.* cane or reed vendor.

cañazo, *m.* 1. blow given with a reed or a cane. 2. (Amer.) sugar cane brandy, raw cane liquor. — **dar c. a uno,** (coll.) to sadden, make sad or pensive; **darse c.,** (coll., Cuba) to get a nasty surprise, be disappointed, be undeceived.

cañedo, *m.* canebrake, cane thicket; sugar cane storehouse.

cañera, *f.* tray with holes for wine glasses.

cañería, *f.* pipe, conduit; piping, pipe line. — **c. bridada,** flanged pipe; **c. de acueducto,** water mains; **c. de carga,** penstock, force main.

cañerla, *f.* (bot.) giant fennel.

cañero, *m.* pipe fitter, steam pipe fitter.

cañero, ra, *a.* pertaining to sugar cane. —*m.* 1. (Col., coll.) liar. 2. (Amer.) sugar cane planter or dealer. 3. (Mex.) sugar cane storehouse.

cañeta, *f.* (bot.) ditch reed, reed-grass.

cañete, *m. dim. of* **caño,** small pipe or tube.

cañí, *m., f* a Spanish Gypsy. —*a.* pertaining to the Spanish Gypsies, their language and culture; **España Cañí,** Spain, Kingdom of the Gypsies.

cañifla, *f.* (C. Rica, Hond.) withered or emaciated arm or leg.

cañihueco, *a.* **trigo c.,** hollow-stemmed wheat.

cañilavado, da, *a.* spindle-legged, spindle-shanked (horse, mule).

cañilla, *f.* (Chile) small cane or stick for winding kite string.

cañillera, *f.* shin guard, shin armor.

cañinque, *a.* (Amer.) feeble, weak, sickly, emaciated.

cañista, *m., f.* hurdler, hurdle maker, man who makes cane frames or hurdles.

cañivano, *a.* **trigo c.,** hollow-stemmed wheat.

cañiza, *a.* grained lengthwise (wood). —*f.* coarse linen.

cañizal, *m., var. of* **cañizar.**

cañizar, *m.* canebrake, cane thicket; sugar cane plantation.

cañizo, *m.* 1. cane frame, hurdle or wattle (used as beds for breeding silk worms). 2. handle of a threshing harrow. 3. frame used in hat making.

caño, *m.* 1. pipe, tube conduit; sewage pipe; drainpipe, gutter; organ pipe. 2. spurt, jet. 3. tap, faucet. 4. wine cellar; cellar for cooling water. 5. (min.) gallery. 6. (mar.) narrow channel, fairway. — **c. de bridas,** flanged pipe; **c. de drenaje,** drain pipe, draintile.
cañocal, *a.* (mar.) easily split or cracked (wood).
cañón, *m.* 1. barrel (of gun); pipe (of organ); tube (of telescope or bellows). 2. (mil.) gun, cannon. 3. quill, hollow stem (of a feather); pinfeather. 4. goffer, flute; fold (in clothes). 5. stubble (of a beard). 6. bridle bit. 7. armpiece of ancient armor. 8. (Col.) tree trunk, bole. 9. canyon, gulch, ravine. 10. (Peru) mountain trail. 11. (Guat.) ugly woman. — **c. antiaéreo,** antiaircraft gun; **c. antitanque,** antitank gun; **c. de campaña,** field gun; **c. de chimenea,** chimney flue; **c. de escobén,** (mar.) hawse pipe; **c. de gran** or **largo alcance,** long-range gun; **c. de plaza** or **sitio,** siege gun or cannon, heavy field gun; **c. de tiro rápido,** quick-firing gun; **c. de torre,** turret gun; **c. lanzacabos,** line-throwing gun; **c. lanzacemento,** cement gun; **c. perforador,** (pet.) perforating gun; **c. obús,** howitzer; **c. rayado,** rifled barrel.
cañonazo, *m.* 1. cannon shot. 2. boom, bang, report (of cannon). 3. injury or damage caused by a cannon shot. 4. (coll.) bombshell, a devastating piece of news. 5. powerful shot (in soccer).
cañoncico, *m., var. of* **cañoncillo.**
cañoncillo, *m.* 1. *dim. of* **cañón,** small cannon. 2. small tube or pipe.
cañonear, *tr.v.* to cannonade, bombard, shell. —*r.v.* to bombard each other.
cañoneo, *m.* the action of cannonading, bombarding, shelling; bombardment, cannonade.
cañonera, *f.* 1. embrasure for cannon; (fort.) gun emplacement; (mar.) gunport. 2. campaign tent. 3. (Amer.) holster for a pistol.
cañonería, *f.* 1. set of organ pipes. 2. artillery. 3. battery of cannons.
cañonero, ra, *a.* (mar.) with mounted cannons, armed (said of a ship). —*f.* (mar.) gunboat.
cañota, *f.* (bot.) ditch reed, reed-grass.
cañucela, *f.* slender cane or reed.
cañuela, *f. dim. of* **caña,** small cane or reed; (bot.) fescue grass. — **c. alta,** (bot.) meadow fescue.
cañutazo, *m.* (coll.) rumor, tale, bit of gossip.
cañutería, *f.* 1. (mus.) set of organ pipes. 2. bugle bead embroidery.
cañutero, *m.* pin or needle case.
cañutillo, *m., var. of* **canutillo.**
cañuto, *m.* 1. tube, pipe. 2. (coll.) tattletale, talebearer. 3. (bot.) internode, segment of a cane or vine between two nodes.
cao, *m.* (Cuba, ornith.) species of carnivorous crow.
caoba, *f.* (bot.) mahogany tree and its wood, e.g. *muebles de c.,* mahogany furniture.
caobana, *f.* (bot.) mahogany tree.
caobilla, *f.* (bot.) shrub of the mahogany family (Trichilia isthmensis).
caobo, *m.* (bot.) mahogany tree.
caolín, *m.* kaolin, china clay, a fine white clay used in making pottery and ceramics.
caolinita, *f.* (min.) kaolinite.
caos, *m.* chaos; confusion, disorder.
caótico, ca, *a.* chaotic.
Cap. *abbrev. of* **Capitán,** Captain (Capt.).
capa, *f.* 1. cape, cloak, mantle; coat, coating (of paint); layer, frosting (of icing); bed, layer (of earth, mortar, etc.); cover, covering; outer leaf, wrapping leaf (of a cigar); (bldg.) course. 2. color of an animal's coat. 3. (zool.) paca. 4. (fig.) cloak, mask, pretext, cover-up, smokescreen (coll.); (coll.) concealer, harborer (of criminals). 5. (coll.) property, fortune. 6. (her.) sparver (tent-like division of an escutcheon). 7. (com.) primage (gratuity paid to ship's captain). 8. (fort.) earth revetment on the slope of a parapet or breastwork. 9. (geol., anat.) stratum. — **andar de c. caída,** (coll.) to be crestfallen, downcast or low (in spirits); to be in poor health; to be down and out (in fortune); **c. aguadera,** rainproof cape; (mar.) tarred canvas around a masthole; **c. aislante** or **aisladora,** (bldg.) waterproofing course; **c. barrera,** (rad.) barrier or blocking layer; **c. consistorial,** (ecc.) bishop's cope, cappa magna; **c. D,** (rad.) D layer; **c. de Heaviside,** Heaviside layer; **c. del cielo,** (fig.) vault or canopy of heaven, firmament; **c. de rey,** (bot.) Joseph's coat **c. E.** (rad.) E layer; **c. freática,** phreatic layer or stratum; ground water, water table; aquifer; **c. gascona,** rainproof cape; **c. inversora,** (astron.) middle zone of the chromosphere; **c. magna,** (ecc.) cappa magna, bishop's cope; **c. pigmentaria,** (anat.) pigmentary layer (of skin); **c. pluvial,** (ecc.) pluvial (officiating cope); **c. rota,** (coll.) secret emissary; **c. torera,** (taur.) bullfighter's cape; **de c. y espada,** cloak-and-dagger (play, book, situation); **defender a c. y espada,** to do the utmost for someone, to stick up for someone; **echar la c. al toro,** (coll.) to intervene on another's behalf; **el que tiene c. escapa,** (coll.) a person with resources can get out of any tight spot; **estar, estarse** or **ponerse a la c.,** (mar.) to lay to; (coll.) to be on the lookout for an opportunity, watch and wait; **hacer a uno la c.,** (coll.) to hide, harbor (someone); **hacer de su c. un sayo,** (coll.) to settle one's own affairs, paddle one's own canoe; **so c. de,** under the pretext or pretense of; **tirar (a uno) de la c.,** (coll.) to warn, caution (someone).
capá, *m.* (bot.) species of West Indian oak used in ship-building.
capacete, *m.* 1. helmet, casque. 2. (Cuba) folding top or hood on a calash-type carriage.
capacidad, *f.* 1. capacity, space, room; extent, area. 2. capacity, ability, talent, capability. 3. (fig.) opportunity, means, capacitance. 4. (phys., elec.) capacitance. 5. (law) capacity, legal qualification or competency. — **c. de corriente** or **de conducción,** (elec.) carrying capacity; **c. de fuego,** firepower; **c. adquisitiva,** purchasing power; **c. asignada,** rated capacity; **c. parásita,** (rad.) stray capacitance; **c. portante,** carrying capacity, bearing power.
capacitación, *f.* training, learning.
capacitador, *m.* (elec.) capacitor, condenser.
capacitancia, *f.* (elec., mech.) capacitance; **c. acústica,** (rad.) acoustic capacitance or compliance; **c. propia,** (rad.) self-capacitance.
capacitar, *tr.v.* 1. to train, equip, qualify. 2. to empower, delegate, commission. —*r.v.* to train oneself to be competent or qualified.
capacitivo, va, *a.* (elec.) capacitive.
capacitor, *m.* (elec.) capacitor, condenser. — **c. filtrador,** (rad.) smoothing capacitor; **c. regulable,** variable capacitor.
capacha, *f.* 1. fruit basket, hamper, or frail woven of willow, hemp, palm, or other fibers. 2. (coll.) Order of St. John of God (who received alms in baskets). 3. (Ecuad., sl.) jail. — **caer en la c.,** (Arg.) to fall into a trap (someone who is fleeing the authorities).
capachada, *f.* (Chile) basketful.
capachero, *m.* porter (who carries his consignment in a basket).
capacho, *m.* 1. frail, basket; pannier; basket lid; (mas.) basket-like burlap or leather hod (for carrying mortar); pressing bag or basket (used in extracting olive oil). 2. (ornith.) night heron (Nycticorax nycticorax). 3. (coll.) monk of the Order of St. John the Divine. 4. (Ven., bot.) edible canna (Canna edulis); canna; arrowroot. 5. (Amer.) bag, knapsack. 6. (Amer.) an old, frayed hat.
capada, *f.* 1. (coll.) contents of a cape or cloak, cloakful. 2. castration.
capadocio, cia, *a., m., f.* Cappadocian, pertaining to, or a native of Cappadocia, a region in Asia Minor.
capador, *m.* gelder, castrator, castrater; gelder's whistle.
capadura, *f.* 1. castration; gelding; castration scar. 2. tobacco leaf of inferior quality used for filler in cigars.
capar, *tr.v.* 1. to castrate, geld. 2. (coll.) to reduce, diminish; to curtail, clip, cut off.
caparazón, *m.* 1. caparison (an ornamented covering for horses); a leather cover to shield horses from the rain; seatcover, saddle-cover; hood, tarpaulin (of carriage). 2. skeleton, carcass (of fowl). 3. (ento.) shell (of crustaceans), integument (of insects). 4. feed bag hung around a horse's neck.
caparídeo, a, caparidáceo, a, *a.* (bot.) capparidaceous. —*f.* (*pl.*) (bot.) Capparidaceae (family).
caparra, *f.* 1. (ento.) louse (of animals). 2. pledged money, deposit, a pledge or partial payment.
caparrilla, *f.* small tick that plagues bees.
caparro, *m.* (Col., Peru, Ven., zool.) white woolly monkey (Lagothrix lagothricha).
caparrón, *m.* (bot.) bud (of a tree).
caparrós, *m., var. of* **caparrosa.**
caparrosa, *f.* (chem.) vitriol, copperas (ferrous sulfate). — **c. azul,** blue or Roman vitriol; **c. blanca,** white vitriol; **c. roja,** red vitriol; **c. verde,** green vitriol.
capataz, (*pl.* **capataces**) *m.* 1. foreman (of factory, road or building gang); overseer (on a farm). 2. steward. 3. leader. — **c. de cultivo,** agriculturist or forester.
capataza, *f.* forewoman; wife of a foreman or farm overseer.
capaz, (*pl.pl.* **capaces**) *a.* 1. able, clever, capable, competent. 2. large, spacious. — **c. de,** capable of; large or big enough to hold, e.g. *una caja c. de diez kilos,* a box big enough to hold ten kilos; **c. para,** qualified for, fit for, apt for.
capazmente, *adv.* 1. spaciously, capaciously. 2. ably, capably, competently.
capazo, *m.* 1. large basket, pannier. 2. blow given with a cloak or cape.
capción, *m.* attraction (of attention, etc.); attainment, winning (of good-will, etc.); (law) seizure, arrest.
capciosamente, *adv.* captiously, trickily, insidiously.
capciosidad, *f.* captiousness, trickiness, trickery.
capcioso, sa, *a.* captious, tricky (said of fallacious or specious words, doctrines, propositions, etc.).
capea, *f.* 1. the challenging of the bull with one's cape. 2. amateur bullfight with young bulls.
capeador, *m.* 1. one who steals someone's cape. 2. capeman, bullfighter who specializes in graceful capework, e.g. *es el mejor c. de la cuadrilla,* he is the best capeman on the team.
capear, *tr.v.* 1. to steal someone's cape. 2. to evade and deceive with lies and pretexts. 3. (taur.) to make cape passes at the bull. 4. (mar.) to lay to; to weather the storm by maneuvering expertly. 5. (Col.) to wave to. — **c. el temporal,** (fig.) to try to get out of a difficult situation.
capeja, *f.* (derog.) skimpy or shabby cloak.

Capela, *f.* (astron.) Capella (star).
capelán, *m.* (ichth.) capelin, a small smeltlike fish used esp. as bait.
capelina, *f.* (surg.) capeline, a cap-shaped bandage for the head.
capellada, *f.* toecap (of a shoe); patch on the uppers of shoes.
capellán, *m.* (ecc.) chaplain; clergyman. — **c. castrense,** army chaplain; **c. de altar,** priest who assists at the mass.
capellanía, *f.* (ecc.) benefice or foundation subject to certain obligations. — **c. laical,** foundation without ecclesiastical intervention.
capellar, *m.* Moorish cloak (used formerly in Spain).
capellina, *f.* 1. capeline, casque (of medieval armor); cavalry soldier wearing a capeline. 2. hood, (worn by peasants). 3. (surg.) capeline (bandage). 4. (metal.) iron or bronze bell (used formerly to cover silver ore when refining by distillation). 5. (metal.) muffle furnace (in silver refining).
capelo, *m.* 1. cardinal's hat, biretta; cardinalate. 2. (her.) crest on a prelate's coat-of-arms. 3. (Amer.) bell jar. — **de doctor,** (Amer.) mortarboard, academic cap.
capeo, *m.* 1. (mar.) weathering (a storm). 2. (taur.) capework. 3. (taur.) bullfight with young bulls; amateur bullfight.
capeón, *m.* (taur.) young or immature bull used in trial passes.
capero, *a.* **tabaco c.,** fine-grade tobacco. —*m.* 1. (ecc.) prelate who carries the cope. 2. hat-and-coat rack or stand.
caperol, *m.* (mar.) head (of any construction piece); (mar.) stemhead, the highest part of the prow of a boat.
caperucear, *tr.v.* to doff or tip one's hat.
caperuceta, *f. dim. of* **caperuza,** small hood or cap.
Caperucita Roja, *f.* Little Red Ridinghood.
caperuza, *f.* 1. pointed hood or cap. 2. (min.) hollow clay cylinder (formerly used in silver refining). 3. cowl, hood (of the chimney); (mec.) hood, cap.
caperuzado, da, *a.* (her.) hooded.
caperuzón, *m.* large hood or pointed cap.
capeta, *f.* short cape or cloak without shoulder cape.
capetonada, *f.* violent vomiting experienced by travelers in tropical zones.
capi, *m.* 1. (Amer., bot.) maize, corn. 2. (Chile, bot.) pod, capsule.
capia, *f.* (Arg., Col., Peru, bot.) variety of sweet maize; (Arg., Col.) corn pudding.
capialce, capialcé, *ref.* **capialzar.**
capialzado, *a.* (archit.) splayed (said of an arch or lintel). —*m.* (archit.) splay, splayed arch.
capialzar, (*ref. 53*) *tr.v.* (archit.) to splay (an archway or lintel).
capialzo, *m.* (archit.) splay, slope (of the intrados of an arch).
capibara, *m.* (Arg., zool.) capybara, waterhog.
capicatí, *m.* (bot.) species of sedge (Killingit adorata) used to make a special liquor in Paraguay.
capichola, *f.* (tex.) ribbed silk fabric.
capicholado, da, *a.* resembling ribbed silk.
capicúa, *m.* 1. (in dominoes) winning move with a piece which can be used at either end. 2. palindrome, word or expression that reads the same backward or forward, e.g. *oro,* gold; *ala,* wing.
capidengue, *m.* shawl or kerchief worn by women as head covering.
capigorra, *m.* (coll.) *var. of* **capigorrón.**
capigorrista, *a., m.* (coll.), *var. of* **capigorrón.**
capigorrón, *m.* 1. (coll.) loafer, tramp, bum (coll.). 2. (coll.) minor cleric (who does not qualify for major orders).
capiguara, *m.* (Amer., zool.) capybara, waterhog.
capiláceo, a. *a.* (bot.) capillaceous.
capilar, *a.* capillary. — **vasos capilares,** (anat.) capillaries (blood vessels). —*m.* (*pl.*) (anat.) capillaries.
capilaridad, *f.* capillarity, capillary attraction.
capilarímetro, *m.* capillarimeter, an instrument for grading the purity of alcohol.
capilla, *f.* 1. hood, cowl. 2. chapel, small church or place of worship; oratory; choir of a church. 3. body of chaplains or priests. 4. (coll.) friar, clergyman. 5. (print.) advance sheet. — **ardiente,** catafalque surrounded by candelabra (for persons lying in state); **c. mayor,** principal part of the church; **estar en capilla,** to be in the death house, be awaiting execution; (coll) to await anxiously (the outcome of something), be on tenterhooks; **estar en c. ardiente,** to lie in state.
capillada, *f.* blow with a hood or cap.
capillejo, *m.* 1. silk skein. 2. small coif or hood formerly worn indoors.
capillera, *f.* small chapel; shrine; chapel-shaped niche.
capillero, *m.* 1. sexton, sacristan (of a chapel); churchwarden. 2. beadle (of a religious society).
capillo, *m.* 1. baby cap or bonnet; hood; baptismal veil or cap (of an infant). 2. toe lining (in shoes). 3. cap of a distaff. 4. rabbit net. 5. cone-shaped bag (for straining wax). 6. cocoon. 7. bud (of flower). 8. inner wrapper or first leaf covering (of a cigar). 9. (mar.) tin or wood binnacle covering (to protect against humidity); (mar.) covering for shroud and shifter ends. 10. colander for wax.
capilludo, da, *a.* 1. hood-like, cowl-like. 2. hooded, cowled, e.g. *monje capilludo,* a hooded monk.
capincho, *m.* (Arg., zool.) capybara, waterhog.
capingo, *m.* (Amer.) short narrow cape.
capipardo, *m.* laborer, artisan.
capirolaza, *m.* (Guat.) slug of liquor.
capirotada, *f.* 1. (cul.) dressing made of herbs, eggs, garlic, etc. 2. (Amer., cul.) native dish of meat, corn, cheese and spices. 3. (Mex., coll.) common grave, pauper's grave.
capirotado, da, *a.* (her.) hooded.
capirotazo, *m.* flip, fillip (with a finger), usually against someone's head.
capirote, *a.* with a head of a different color from the rest of the body (cattle). —*m.* 1. hood (worn by mourners, scholars, etc.). 2. (falconry) leather mask or hood. 3. flip, fillip (with a finger). — **c. de colmena,** beehive cover; **tonto de c.,** prize fool, nitwit, blockhead, sucker (coll., U.S.).
capirotero, *a.* (hunt.) accustomed to a hood (said of a well-trained falcon).
capirucho, *m.* (coll.) hood, cap; paper cone worn on the head; fool's cap.
capisayo, *m.* mantelet; bishop's mantelletta; (Col.) vest, undershirt.
capiscol, *m.* 1. precentor, chanter; choir leader. 2. (sl.) rooster.
capiscolía, *f.* precentorship.
capistro, *m.* (hist.) head armor of Roman battle horses.
capitación, *f.* capitation, per capita tax assessment; poll tax, head tax.
capitado, da, *a.* (bot.) capitate.
capital, *a.* 1. capital (city; punishment). 2. mortal (sins). 3. principal, chief, major; essential, fundamental, most important. 4. (gram.) capital (letter). — **lo c.,** the most important thing. —*m.* (com., econ.) capital; principal; wealth; estate brought to a marriage by the husband. — **c. aventurado,** venture capital; **c. circulante** or **de rotación,** circulating, working capital; **c. disponible** or **realizable,** free capital; **c. fijo,** fixed capital; **c. líquido,** net or liquid capital. —*f.* 1. capital (city). 2. (fort.) capital.
capitaleño, ña, *a.* pertaining to or resident of a capital city.
capitalice, capitalicé, *ref.* **capitalizar.**
capitalidad, *f.* capital status of a town or city; capital area.
capitalino, na, *a.* of the capital. —*m., f.* inhabitant or native of the capital; (fig.) a sophisticated person.
capitalismo, *m.* capitalism.
capitalista, *a.* capitalist, capitalistic. —*m., f.* capitalist.
capitalizable, *a.* capitalizable.
capitalización, *f.* 1. capitalization, conversion into capital. 2. compounding (of interest).
capitalizar, (*ref. 53*) tr.v. 1. to capitalize (convert into capital). 2. to compound, add (interest) to principal.
capitalmente, *adv.* mortally, gravely, seriously.
capitán, *m.* (mil., mar., sport.) captain; leader; chief; foreman; ringleader. — **c. de alto bordo,** (mar.) captain; **c. de bandera,** (mar.) captain of the flagship, flag captain; **c. de corbeta,** (mar.) lieutenant commander; **c. de fragata,** (mar.) commander; **c. de llaves,** (mil., fort.) ordnance officer in charge of an ordnance depot; **c. de mar y guerra,** (mar.) commander or captain of a man-of-war; **c. de navío,** (mar.) captain; **c. de puerto,** (mar.) harbor master; **c. general del ejército,** (mil.) field marshal, commander-in-chief; **c. general de la armada,** (mar.) admiral of the fleet; **c. preboste,** (mil.) provost, provost marshal.
capitana, *f.* 1. (mar.) flagship. 2. (coll.) captain's wife; woman captain or leader.
capitanear, *tr.v.* to captain; to lead, command.
capitanía, *f.* 1. (mil.) captaincy, captainship (post of a captain). 2. (mil.) company (of troops led by a captain). 3. (mar.) port or harbor charges, anchorage. — **c. de puerto,** (mar.) harbor master's office; **c. general,** (mil.) captaincy general (post, offices or jurisdiction of a captain general); (Amer.) (in colonial times) territory governed by a captain general with certain powers independent of viceregal jurisdiction.
capitel, *m.* (archit.) capital (of a column); spire (e.g., of a church).
capitolino, na, *a.* Capitoline, pertaining to the Capitol. —*m.* jewel head or stud (used in ornamentation).
capitolio, *m.* 1. C., Capitol. 2. the temple of Jupiter; (fig.) an elevated and majestic building. 3. (archaeol.) acropolis. — **subir al c.,** (coll.) to triumph, succeed, make the grade (coll.).
capitón, *m.* 1. (ichth.) striped mullet. 2. (Salv.) knock on the head.
capitoné, *a.* quilted, padded (cloth, upholstered furniture, etc.).
capitoso, *a.* 1. strong, heady (wines). 2. (arch.) obstinate, strong-willed.
capítula, *f.* (rel.) passage of Scripture (read at divine service).
capitulación, *f.* 1. capitulation, surrender. 2. agreement, pact. 3. (*pl.*) civil marriage contract. — **c. incondicional,** unconditional surrender.
capitulado, da, *past part. of* **capitular.** —*a.* abridged, condensed.
capitulante, *a.* capitulating.
capitular, *a.* capitular, capitulary (pertaining to a chapter, ecclesiastical or civic). —*m.* capitular, capitulary (member of a chapter, ecclesiastical or civic).

capitular, *i.v.* 1. to capitulate, surrender. 2. to make an agreement or pact, come to terms. 3. (ecc.) to sing prayers (at divine service). —*tr.v.* to charge, impeach; **c. a uno de,** to charge someone with.
capitulario, *m.* (ecc.) book containing passages of Scripture to be read at divine service.
capitularmente, *adv.* in accordance with the rules of a chapter, council or assembly.
capitulear, *i.v.* (Amer.) *var. of* **cabildear.**
capituleo, *m.* (Amer.) *var. of* **cabildeo.**
capítulo, *m.* 1. chapter (of a book or treatise). 2. chapter (assembly of canons, members of a religious order or secular clergy; assembly of a military or knightly order); chapter house, meeting-place of such a chapter. 3. assembly, meeting; municipal council. 4. (ecc.) severe public reprimand (of a member of a religious order before his coummunity). 5. accusation, charge. 6. determination, resolution, resolve. 7. subject, matter. — **c. de culpas,** accusation, charge (against one having held an employment or public office); **capítulos matrimoniales,** marriage articles, marriage contract, civil marriage; **ganar** (or **perder**) **c.,** (coll.) to attain (or not to attain) one's objective (among several competitors); **llamar** (or **traer**) **a c.,** to call to account, bring to task.
capizana, *f.* criniere, upper neckpiece of a horse's armor.
capnomancia, *f.* divination by means of smoke shapes and signs.
capó, *m.* the hood of an automobile engine.
capoc, *m.* kapok.
capolar, *tr.v.* 1. to tear or cut into pieces, chop up. 2. to hash, to mince; to grind into chopped meat. 3. (Sp.) to behead.
capón, *a.* castrated (man or animal), gelded (animal). —*m.* 1. eunuch; gelding; capon (chicken). 2. bundle of vine brushwood. 3. (mar.) anchor stopper at the cathead. — **c. de galera,** (cul.) soup made with bread, oil, vinegar and olives; **c. de leche,** capon fattened in a coop.
capón, *m.* (coll.) rap on the head (given with the knuckles).
capona, *a.* key formerly held by the royal chamberlains. —*f.* epaulet without fringe.
caponar, *tr.v.* (agr.) to tie up (vine branches or shoots in order to facilitate tilling).
caponera, *f.* 1. coop (for fattening capons). 2. (coll.) place where one can get something for nothing; place good for a free meal or hand-out (coll.). 3. (coll.) jail, clink. 4. (fort.) caponiere.
capoquero, *m.* (bot.) kapok tree.
caporal, *m.* 1. chief, boss; foreman, overseer (of workmen). 2. (mil.) corporal. 3. (Amer.) person in charge of herds of cattle.
capota, *f.* 1. (bot.) head of the teasel or fuller's thistle. 2. bonnet (women's headress); bonnet, hood (of a vehicle). 3. (auto.) the folding top of a convertible. 4. short collarless cape; cape without a hood.
capotar, *i.v.* to turn a somersault, turn over (car, plane).
capotazo, *m.* (taur.) flourish with the cape.
capote, *m.* 1. capote, topcoat, cloak; (mil.) greatcoat; (taur.) cape worn in the opening procession. 2. (coll.) frown, scowl. 3. (coll.) blanket of clouds. 4. (Amer.) beating, thrashing. — **para mi c.,** (coll.) to my way of thinking, as I understand it; **c. de brega,** (taur.) working cape; **c. de montar,** short riding cape; **c. de monte,** poncho; **c. de paseo,** (taur.) show cape (the embroidered one worn only during the parade); **dar c.,** (coll.) to make every trick (in cards), clear the deck (coll.); to silence (someone in an argument), squash (coll.); to leave without food (people who come late); (Mex., Chile) to deceive, trick; **de c.,** (Mex.) secretly, surreptitiously; **decirse para su c.,** to mutter into one's beard, mutter under one's breath; **echar un c.,** to come to someone's aid.
capotear, *tr.v.* 1. (taur.) to distract the bull with the cape. 2. to put off, stall. 3. to evade, get out of (responsibilities, obligations). 4. (theat.) to put (a show) on in a hurry, to improvise.
capoteo, *m.* (taur.) capework.
capotera, *f.* 1. (Amer.) clothes hanger or clothes rack. 2. (Amer.) canvas traveling bag open at either end.
capotero, ra, *m., f.* person who makes or sells cloaks.
capotillo, *m.* (Sp.) short double cape copied from Napoleonic days.
capotudo, da, *a.* frowning.
caprario, ria, *a.* goat-like, pertaining to a goat.
capreolado, da, *a.* (bot.) capreolate.
capricho, *m.* 1. caprice, whim. 2. fancy, keen desire, e.g. *tener c. por algo,* to have a fancy for something. 3. caprice (fanciful and imaginative work of art). 4. (mus.) caprice, capriccio. 5. a person, animal, or thing that is the object of a whim or desire.
caprichosamente, *adv.* capriciously, fancifully, whimsically, stubbornly.
caprichoso, sa, *a.* capricious; stubborn.
caprichudo, da, *a.* capricious, whimsical; stubborn.
cáprico, ca, *a.* (chem.) capric (acid).
capricornio, *m.* 1. (astron.) C., Capricorn. 2. (ento.) capricorn beetle.
caprificación, *f.* (bot.) caprification.
caprifoliáceo, a, *a.* (bot.) caprifoliaceous. —*f.* caprifolium; (*pl.*) Caprifoliaceae.
capriforme, *a.* capriform.
caprílico, ca, *a.* (chem.) caprylic.
caprino, na, *a.* goat-like, goatish, caprine, capric.
caprípede, *a.* (poet.) *var. of* **caprípedo.**
caprípedo, da, *a.* goat-footed, split-hoofed.
caproico, ca, *a.* (chem.) caproic (acid).
capsaicina, *f.* (chem.) capsaicin.
cápsula, *f.* 1. (anat., chem., pharm., bot.) capsule. 2. capsule, detachable compartment of airplane or rocket. 3. metal cap or seal (on bottles or flasks). 4. cartridge shell; cap, percussion cap (of bullet, etc.). 5. laboratory dish. — **c. atrabiliaria** or **renal,** (anat.) atrabiliary gland, renal capsule or gland, suprarenal gland; **c. sinovial,** (anat.) synovial capsule; **c. suprarrenal,** (anat.) suprarenal capsule or gland; **c. detonante** or fulminante, exploder, blasting cap.
capsular, *a.* capsular, pertaining to or resembling a capsule.
capsular, *tr.v.* to cap, seal (a bottle) with a stopper.
captación, *f.* 1. understanding, grasp, comprehension (of an idea). 2. reception, pickup (of broadcast), hearing (of sound). 3. winning (of confidence, friendship, admiration, good will). 4. attraction (of attention). 5. (hydr.) impounding, diversion; harnessing (of water power).
captar, *tr.v.* 1. to win (confidence, friendship, good will, admiration); to earn, win (confidence, trust). 2. to capture, attract (attention). 3. to understand, grasp (an idea). 4. to catch, hear; to receive, pick up (broadcast). 5. to capture, depict (e.g. atmosphere, as in a story). 6. to trap, impound (waters); to harness (water power).
captura, *f.* capture, apprehension (e.g. of a criminal).
capturar, *tr.v.* to capture, to arrest or apprehend (e.g. a criminal).
capuana, *f.* (coll.) a spanking, beating, whipping.
capuce, capucé, *ref.* **capuzar.**
capuceta, *f.* ducking, dipping (someone's head in water).
capucha, *f.* 1. hood (of a garment); cowl. 2. circumflex accent.
capuchina, *f.* 1. (bot.) garden nasturtium, Indian cress. 2. portable metal lamp (with a cone-shaped extinguisher). 3. cone-shaped candy or sweet (made from egg yolks and sugar). 4. (print.) set of printing frames joined at the top.
capuchino, na, *a.* 1. Capuchin (monk; order). 2. (Chile) small (fruit). —*m.* 1. Capuchin (monk). 2. (zool.) capuchin (monkey). 3. (ornith.) capuchin (pigeon). 4. (P. Rico) a kind of small paper kite. —*f.* 1. (bot.) garden nasturtium, Indian cress, 2. portable metal lamp (with cone-shaped extinguisher). 3. cone-shaped sweet (made from egg yolks and sugar). 4. (print.) set of printing frames joined at the top. 5. Poor Clare (nun).
capucho, *m.* hood, cowl.
capuchón, *m.* 1. ladies' cloak with hood. 2. prison garment. 3. short domino. — **ponerse el c.** (coll.) to go to jail.
capujar, *tr.v.* 1. (Arg.) to catch (a flying object). 2. (Arg.) to forestall, anticipate (someone's saying something).
Capuleto, *m.* Capulet (a member of the house of Capulet in Shakespeare's *Romeo and Juliet*).
capulí, *m.* (bot.) capulin (Prunus capuli); capulin cherry. 2. (Cuba, bot.) calabur tree, silkwood (Muntingia calabura). 3. (Peru, bot.) cape gooseberry (Physalis peruviana).
capúlido, *m.* 1. limpet (a mollusk). 2. (*pl.*) (zool.) limpet family.
capulín, *m., var. of* **capulí.**
capulina, *f.* 1. (Amer.) capulin cherry. 2. (Cuba, bot.) calabur tree, silkwood (Mutingia calabura). 3. (Mex., ento.) poisonous black spider (Latrodectus curassavienis).
cápulo, *m.* limpet (a kind of mollusk).
capultamal, *m.* (Mex.) a small round cake or tamale made with capulin cherries.
capullo, *m.* 1. cocoon. 2. (bot.) bud, bloom; acorn cup. 3. coarse silk (made from silk of cocoon). 4. (anat.) foreskin, prepuce. 5. bundle of boiled flax.
capuz, (*pl.* **capuces**) *m.* 1. hood, cowl; long mourning cloak; hooded cloak; gala cape or cloak. 2. ducking (someone in water).
capuzar, (*ref. 53*) *tr.v.* 1. to duck (someone). 2. (mar.) to load a boat so that it draws more at the bow.
caquéctico, ca, *a.* (med.) cachectic. —*m., f.* person suffering from cachexia.
caquexia, *f.* 1. (bot.) chlorosis, etiolation. 2. (med.) cachexia, the state of weakness, undernourishment, etc. esp. associated with severe illness.
caqui, *m.* 1. (bot.) kaki, Japanese persimmon (fruit and plant). 2. khaki (cloth and color).
caquino, *m.* (Amer.) guffaw, horselaugh, cackle (*gen. pl.*).
car, *m.* (mar.) lower and thicker end of a lateen yard.
cara, *f.* 1. face (front of the head). 2. countenance, face, look. 3. presence, manner, expression, mien. 4. facade, facing, front (of buildings, etc.). 5. surface; (geom.) face, plane. 6. head, obverse (of coins). 7. base of a sugar-loaf. 8. (agr.) set of incisions (in rubber tree). — **a c. descubierta,** publicly, openly, frankly; **c. o cruz,** heads or tails; **asomar la c.,** to show one's face; **caérsele a uno la c. de vergüenza,** to blush with shame; **c. a c.,** face to face; **c. adelante,** looking or facing forward; **c. de acelga,** surly face; **c. de aleluya,** cheerful, smiling face or look; **c. de**

hereje, ugly look; **c. de juez,** stern face or look; **c. del montón,** (agr.) best and heaviest wheat, grain which falls on windward side when winnowing; **c. de pascua,** (coll.) cheerful, smiling face or look; **c. de perro,** surly, unfriendly face or look; **c. de pocos amigos,** unfriendly, forbidding face; **c. de risa,** cheerful, smiling face or look; **c. de vaqueta,** stiff, hostile look; brazen face; **c. de viernes,** lean sad face or look; **c. de vinagre,** unfriendly, forbidding look or face, vinegary look; **cruzar la c. a,** to slap, whip; **dar c. a,** to face; **dar en c. a,** to throw (something) in someone's face; **dar la c.,** to take the responsibility, be willing to take the consequences; **dar la c. por otro,** to go to someone's defense; to make oneself responsible for someone; **de c.,** face on; in one's face; **echar a c. o cruz,** to toss up for; **echar a la c.** or **en la c. alguna cosa,** to throw something in (someone's face); **en su c.,** to one's face; **guardar la c.,** to hide; **hacer a dos caras,** to do in a two-faced manner; **hacer c. a,** to face, resist; **lavar la c. a uno,** to lick (someone's) boots, fawn upon; **poner buena c. a,** to take well or cheerfully; **poner c. larga,** to make a long face; **poner mala c. a,** to take badly, take unwillingly; **ponérsele roja la cara,** to turn red in the face; **querer algo por su linda c.** to want something without meriting it; **sacar en c.,** to throw in one's face; **sacar la c. por,** to come to the defense of; **saltar a la c.,** to answer back angrily, fly at someone's face; to jump to the eye, be evident; **tener c. de,** to look like, e.g. *tener c. de ladrón,* to look like a thief; **tener c. de corcho, tener c. dura,** to be brazen or shameless; **un c. pálida,** (derog.) a paleface (white man); **verse las caras,** to have it out face to face; **voltear a uno la c.,** to ignore or deliberately fail to recognize one.

cáraba, *f.* caique, a Levantine sailing vessel.

caraba, *f.* festive gathering of rural people; **a c. en bicicleta,** a difficult task, a messy affair.

carabao, *m.* (zool.) carabao, water buffalo.

cárabe, *m.* amber, a fossil resin.

carabela, *f.* caravel, a fast, light sailing ship used esp. in the 16th century; **las carabelas de Colón,** Columbus' caravels.

carabelón, *m.* (mar.) brig, brigantine.

carábido, *m.* (ento.) carabid, a variety of beetle; (*pl.*) Carabidae, family of beetles.

carabina, *f.* 1. carbine. 2. (coll.) chaperon, duenna. — **c. rayada,** rifled carbine; **ser lo mismo que la c. de Ambrosio,** (coll.) to be no good at all, be useless.

carabinazo, *m.* a shot from a carbine; bang, crack, report of a carbine shot; the wound or damage produced by a carbine shot.

carabinero, *m.* 1. carabineer. 2. excise officer, soldier detailed to pursue smugglers. 3. (ichth.) shrimp, prawn. 4. (coll.) grouch. 5. (Chile) policeman. — **carabineros reales,** the Spanish Royal Cavalry Corps.

carablanca, *m.* (zool., Col., C. Rica) whitefaced monkey.

cárabo, *m.* 1. caique, a kind of light skiff. 2. (ento.) carabus, a large ground beetle.

carabritear, *i.v.* to pursue the female (said of the male goat in rut).

caraca, *f.* (Cuba) bun made with cornflour.

caracal, *m.* (zool.) caracal, a species of lynx.

cara-cará, *a.* (Arg.) pertaining to an Indian tribe which formerly inhabited the Parana region. —*m., f.* member of this tribe.

caracará, *m.* (ornith., Arg., Par., Urug.) caracara, a vulture-like hawk of S. Amer.

Caracas, *f.* capital of Venezuela.

caracas, *m.* cacao from Caracas; (Mex.) chocolate.

caracatey, *m.* (ornith., Amer.) night hawk, goatsucker (Chordeiles minor).

caracha, *m., f.* (Chile, Peru, vet.) mange, scabies, itch.

carache, *m., var. of* **caracha.**

carachento, ta, *a.* (S. Amer., vet.) mangy, scabby.

¡caracho! *interj.* damn! an expression of surprise, dismay, anger, etc.

caracho, cha, *a.* violet-colored, purple.

carachoso, sa, *a.* (Peru, vet.) mangy.

carachupa, *f.* (Peru, zool.) opossum.

caracoa, *f.* (Phil. I.) rowboat.

caracol, *m.* 1. snail; (snail) shell. 2. fusee (of a watch). 3. (coll.) curl (of hair). 4. (anat.) cochlea. 5. (equit.) caracole, turn. 6. (*pl.*) Andalusian dance and song. 7. (Mex.) short night-dress; woman's embroidered blouse. — **c. judío,** whiteshelled snail; **hacer caracoles,** to zigzag; **escalera de c.,** spiral staircase.

caracola, *f.* 1. conch (large marine shell). 2. (*pl.*) (reg., Sp.) the lacy flounces of a flamenco dancer's skirt.

caracolada, *f.* (cul.) snail stew.

caracolear, *i.v.* (equit.) to caracole, turn.

caracolejo, *m. dim. of* **caracol,** small snail.

caracoleo, *m.* (equit.) a caracole, caracoling, a turn.

caracolero, ra, *m., f.* snail gatherer, snail vendor.

¡caracoles! *interj.* an exclamation of emphasis or surprise, expressing dismay, anger, admiration, pleasure.

caracolí, *m.* (bot., Col.) carcoli (tree) (Anacardium excelsum).

caracolillo, *m.* 1. a small snail. 2. (bot.) Australian pea (Dolichus lignosus). 3. high quality coffee having small round beans. 4. veined mahogany (Swietenia mahogani). 5. trimming, flounce (on hem of garment).

caracolito, *m. dim. of* **caracol.**

carácter, *m.* 1. character, disposition, nature. 2. character, strength of character. 3. character, personality. 4. trait, feature, characteristic. 5. (Amer.) virtue, quality, *e.g. hombre de gran c.,* man of high moral values. 6. position, capacity, status, e.g. *en su c. de juez,* in his capacity or position as judge. 7. character, letter (of an alphabet); handwriting, hand. 8. impression, mark (of a character). 9. magic symbol, sign. 10. mark, brand, stamp (to distinguish cattle). 11. style (of writing or speaking). 12. (theol.) character, spiritual mark. — **c. anal,** (psyc.) anal character; **c. de imprenta,** type; **c. específico,** (biol.) specific character; **c. oral,** (psyc.) oral character; **de medio c.,** midway between one genre and another; of undefined character (of music, literature).

caracterice, caractericé, *ref.* **caracterizar.**

caracterismo, *m.* characteristics, distinctive nature.

característica, *f.* characteristic, feature, distinctive quality; (math., mech., elec.) characteristic. — **c. anódica,** plate characteristic; **c. de traspaso,** (rad.) transfer characteristic.

característicamente, *adv.* characteristically; remarkably, signally.

característico, ca, *a.* characteristic, typical, distinctive. —*m., f.* (theat.) character actress; character actor.

caracterización, *f.* (theat.) characterization.

caracterizado, da, *past part. of* **caracterizar.** —*a.* outstanding, distinguished, notable.

caracterizar, (*ref. 53*) *tr.v.* 1. to characterize. 2. (theat.) to play (a part) effectively. 3. to distinguish, confer a distinction or honor on. —*r.v.* 1. to be characterized. 2. (theat.) to make up and dress up (for a role).

caracterología, *f.* (psyc.) the study of the character and personality of man.

caracú, (*pl.* **caracúes**) *m.* (Amer.) marrow, marrowbone, used in cooking stews, etc.

caracul, *m.* karakul, caracul, a type of Central Asian sheep; its fur or pelt.

carado, da, *a.* **bien c.,** pleasant-looking, friendly-looking; **mal c.,** ugly-looking; vicious-looking.

caradura, *a.* shameless, brazen. —*m., f.* shameless or brazen person.

caraguatá, *f.* (bot., Amer.) caraguata (plant and fiber).

caraguay, *m.* (zool., Bol.) large lizard (Podinema teguixim).

caraira, *f.* (ornith., Cuba) species of vulture (Cathartes aura jota).

caraja, *f.* (Mex., mar.) gaff sail (used by Veracruz fishermen).

carajo, *m.* (vulg.) prick, dick. —*interj.* (vulg.) damn, blast it, shit, e.g. *no me importa un c.,* I don't give a damn, *vete al c.,* go to hell.

carama, *f.* frost, rime.

caramanchel, *m.* 1. (mar.) hatch cover. 2. hut, shack; garret; (Peru) shed, leanto. 3. (Ecuad.) street vendor's stand. 4. canteen, eating house, restaurant.

caramanchelero, ra, *m., f.* 1. a person who sells food, drinks, etc., in a canteen. 2. (Ecuad.) street vendor, hawker, peddler.

caramanchón, *m.* garret, attic.

caramañola *f.* (Chile, Arg.) *var. of* **caramayola.**

caramayola, *f.* (Chile) soldier's canteen, water flask.

caramba, *f.* ancient adornment for women's hair.

¡caramba! *interj.* gracious! an expression of surprise, dismay, anger, aversion, etc.

carambanado, da, *a.* frozen; turned into an icicle.

carámbano, *m.* icicle.

carambillo, *m.* (bot.) saltwort, a source of barilla, a crude soda ash.

carambola, *f.* 1. carom, cannon (in billiards). 2. (coll.) two-fold result from a single act, killing two birds with one stone. 3. (coll.) trick, hoax. 4. chance. — **por c.,** (coll.) indirectly; by chance, by luck.

carambola, *f.* (bot.) carambola, Chinese gooseberry (fruit of the carambola tree).

carambolear, *tr.v.* to carom (in billiards).

carambolero, ra, *m., f.* (Arg., Chile), *var. of* **carambolista.**

carambolista, *m., f.* a billiard player who is an expert carom shooter.

carambolo, *m.* (bot.) carambola tree; the Chinese gooseberry tree.

caramel, *m.* (ichth.) atherine (Atherina hepsetus) a variety of Mediterranean sardine.

caramelice, caramelicé, *ref.* **caramelizar.**

caramelización, *f.* caramelization.

caramelizar, (*ref. 53*) *tr.v.* (cul.) to cover with caramel.

caramelo, *m.* (cul.) caramel; candy. — **¡de c.!** (coll.) fine! excellent!

caramente, *adv.* 1. expensively, costly. 2. dearly, truly, sincerely. 3. (law) solemnly (swear, declare, etc.).

caramera, *f.* (Ven.) set of uneven teeth.

caramida, *f.* (min.) lodestone.

caramilla, *f.* (min.) calamine.

caramillar, *m.* ground where saltwort abounds, saltwort patch or field.

caramilleras, *f.* (*pl.*) pot-hook.

caramillo, *m.* 1. shawm, small shrill flute; pipe, Pandean pipe. 2. (bot.) saltwort (Salsola soda). 3. untidy heap. 4. gossip, mischief. — **armar** or **levantar un c.,** to spread gossip, make mischief.

caramilloso, sa, *a.* 1. (coll.) touchy, peevish, snappy. 2. (coll.) finicky, fastidious, fussy.
caramujo, *m.* barnacle.
caramuzal, *m.* caramoussal, a Turkish or Moorish merchant ship of the 18th century.
carancho, *m.* (ornith., Arg., Bol., Urug.) caracara, carrion hawk; (Peru) horned owl.
carandaí, caranday, *m.* (bot., Arg., Par.) carnauba, wax palm.
caranegra, *f.* (Arg.) black-faced sheep. —*m.* (Col., C. Rica, Ven.) black-faced monkey (of the Atheles genus).
caranga, *f.* (ento., Amer.) louse.
carángano, *m.* (ento., Amer.) louse.
carantamaula, *f.* 1. (coll.) frightening mask; (coll.) scarecrow. 2. ugly-looking person.
carantoña, *f.* 1. (coll.) frightening mask. 2. (coll.) painted-up old hag. 3. (*pl.*) weedling, cajolery, flattery. — **hacer carantoñas,** to wheedle, soft-soap, cajole.
carantoñero, ra, *m., f.* (coll.) wheedler, cajoler, flatterer.
caraña, *m.* caranna, caranna gum; (bot.) species of bursera (Protium carana).
caráota, *f.* (bot., Ven.) kidney bean, French bean.
carapa, *f.* (bot., Amer.) crab wood (Garapa guianensis).
carapacho, *m.* shell, carapace; (cul., Cuba) shellfish cooked in the shell.
carapato, *m.* castor oil.
¡carape! *interj.* an expression of surprise, dismay, anger, aversion, etc.
carapucho, *m.* (Peru) type of grass whose seeds cause drunkenness.
carapulca, *f.* (cul., Peru) stew made of meat, potato and red pepper.
caraqueño, ña, *a.* of or from Caracas. —*m., f.* native or inhabitant of Caracas.
carasol, *m.* sun terrace, sun porch, sun deck, sun parlor, solarium.
carate, *m.* (med.) carate, caraate, pinta, spots on the skin caused by treponema carateum.
caratea, *f.* (med., Col., Ecuad., Ven.) tropical form of scrofula.
carato, *m.* (P. Rico, Ven.) a drink made of rice or ground corn, pineapple or soursop juice with sugar and water.
carátula, *f.* 1. mask. 2. (fig.) the theatrical profession, the theater. 3. (Amer.) title page (of book).
caratulado, da, *a.* masked, wearing a mask.
caratulero, ra, *m., f.* maker or vendor of masks.
caraú, (*pl.* **caraúes**) *m.* (Arg., Par., ornith.) species of crane (Aramus scolopaceius carau).
caravana, *f.* 1. caravan, company of traders, camel train; expedition against pirates and Moors (by knights of Malta); (coll.) excursion group. 2. (Cuba) bird trap. 3. (Hond., Mex.) courtesy, politeness. 4. (*pl.*) (Arg., Bol., Chile) earrings. 5. (Amer.) excessive flattery.
caravanero, *m.* caravaneer, caravan leader.
caravasar, *m.* caravanserai, caravansary, inn where caravans rest at night.
caray, *m.* tortoise; tortoise shell.
¡caray! *interj.* damn! an expression of surprise, dismay, anger, aversion, etc.
carayá, *m.* (Arg., Col.) alouatte, the howling monkey (Alouatta caraya).
carayaca, *m.* (Ven.) *var. of* **carayá.**
carbamato, *m.* (chem.) carbamate.
carbámico, ca, *a.* (chem.) carbamic.
carbamida, *f.* (chem.) carbamide, urea.
cárbaso, *m.* 1. fine linen; linen garment. 2. (poet.) sail (of a ship).
carbinol, *m.* (chem.) carbinol.
carbodinamita, *f.* (chem.) carbodynamite.
carbohidrato, *m.* (chem.) carbohydrate.
carbol, *m.* (chem.) phenol.
carbólico, *a.* (chem.) carbolic, phenolic.
carbolíneo, *m.* carbolineum (a wood preserver).
carbón, *m.* 1. coal; charcoal; carbon. 2. carbon pencil, charcoal. 3. dead ember or cinder. 4. (agr.) smut, charcoal rot. 5. (elec.) carbon (of arc lamp). — **c. activado,** activated carbon; **c. animal,** charcoal black, bone black; **c. de arranque,** calcined root black; **c. bituminoso,** bituminous coal; **c. de canutillo,** charcoal made of the thin branches of some trees; **c. de forja, c. para fragua,** blacksmith coal; **c. de gas** or **retorta,** gas carbon; **c. de piedra, c. mineral,** coal; **c. vegetal, de palo** or **de leña,** charcoal; **papel c.,** carbon paper.
carbonada, *f.* 1. load of coal put into a furnace. 2. (cul.) broiled minced meat; sweet fritter; (Arg., Chile, Peru) meat stew with rice, pumpkin, potatoes and corn.
carbonado, *m.* carbon diamond, black diamond, carbonado.
carbonalla, *f.* mortar used to construct the hearth of a reverberatory furnace.
carbonar, *t.v.* to char; to make into charcoal. —*r.v.* to become carbonized or charred.
carbonario, a, *a.* Carbonarist, said of certain secret societies, established in France and Italy for revolutionary ends. —*m., f.* Carbonaro, a member of such a society; (*pl.*) Carbonari.
carbonarismo, *m.* Carbonarism, the political doctrines or beliefs of the Carbonari.
carbonatado, da, *a.* (chem.) to carbonated.
carbonatar, *tr.v* (chem.) to carbonate. —*r.v* to become carbonated.
carbonato, *m.* (chem.) carbonate. — **c. de calcio** or **cal,** calcium carbonate; **c. de potasio,** potassium carbonate; **c. sódico,** sodium carbonate; **c. sódico anhidro,** soda ash, anhydrous sodium carbonate.
carboncillo, *m.* 1. fine coal, slack. 2. carbon pencil, charcoal (for drawing). 3. charcoal rot, smut (a plant disease, esp. of cereal grasses such as wheat). 4. black sand. — **dibujo al c.,** charcoal sketch.
carbonear, *tr.v.* to make into charcoal.
carboneo, *m.* charcoal making or burning.
carbonera, *f.* 1. charcoal kiln, wood pile covered with clay for making charcoal. 2. coal bunker, coalbin; (Amer., ry.) tender. 3. woman who sells charcoal or coal. 4. (Amer.) coal mine. 5. (mar.) main topmast staysail.
carbonería, *f.* coal shop, coal yard; charcoal store or shop.
carbonero, ra, *a.* pertaining to coal or charcoal. —*m., f.* one who makes or sells charcoal.
carbonice, carbonicé, *ref.* **carbonizar.**
carbónico, ca, *a.* (chem.) carbonic.
carbónidos, *m.* (*pl.*) (chem.) substances containing carbon.
carbonífero, ra, *a.* carboniferous, coalbearing; (geol.) Carboniferous (period). —*m.* (geol.) Carboniferous.
carbonilla, *f.* coal dust, slack; granulated coke; cinders.
carbonilo, *m.* (chem.) carbonyl.
carbonio, *m.* (phys.) carbonium.
carbonita, *f.* carbonite (blasting explosive; mineral coke).
carbonización, *f.* carbonization.
carbonizar, (*ref. 53*) *tr.v.* to carbonize; to burn, char. —*r.v.* to become carbonized.
carbono, *m.* (chem.) carbon.
carbonómetro, *m.* (engin.) carbonometer.
carbonoso, sa, *a.* carbonous, carbonaceous, that contains or is similar to carbon, coal, or charcoal.
carborundo, *m.* carborundum.
carboxilasa, *f.* (biochem.) carboxylase.
carboxilo, *m.* (chem.) carboxyl.
carboxillo, *m.* (chem.) carboxyl.
carbuncal, *a.* carbuncular, pertaining to or resembling a carbuncle.
carbunclo, *m.* 1. carbuncle, garnet, ruby. 2. (vet.) anthrax, carbuncle; (med.) carbuncle.
carbunco, *m.* 1. (vet.) anthrax, carbuncle, disease of cattle; (med.) carbuncle. 2. (ento., C. Rica) firefly or fire beetle (Pyrophorus noctilucus). — **c. sintomático,** symptomatic anthrax, blackleg, infectious disease of cattle and sheep.
carbuncosis, *f.* (med.) carbuncular infection.
carbuncoso, sa, *a.* carbuncular.
carbúnculo, *m.* carbuncle, ruby.
carburación, *f.* carburetion, carburation, carburization.
carburador, *m.* carburetor. — **c. inyector,** jet or injection carburetor; **c. pulverizador,** spray carburetor.
carburante, *a.* containing a hydrocarbon. —*m.* fuel (such as gasoline, etc.).
carburar, *tr.v.* (chem.) to carburet, carburize, carburate. —*i.v.* (Guat.) to strut, swagger.
carburina, *f.* carbon sulfide (used in drycleaning and dyeing).
carburo, *m.* (chem.) carbide. — **c. de calcio, (chem.) calcium carbide; c. cementado,** cemented carbide.
carca, *a., m., f.* (derog.) Carlist, a supporter of Don Carlos, a pretender to the throne of Spain; by extension, a person who is a reactionary. —*f.* (Amer.) pot in which **chica,** a native beer, is cooked or fermented.
carcahuesal, *m.* (Col.) swamp, marsh, marshy land.
carcaj, *m.* quiver (for arrows); holster or socket (on a crossbelt supporting the cross in processions); (Amer.) leather rifle case (on a saddle).
carcajada, *f.* bellow, guffaw, horselaugh; outburst of laughter.
carcajear, *i.v., r.v.* to guffaw, laugh heartily.
carcamal, *m.* (coll.) old decrepit person, old wreck.
carcamán, *a.* (Cuba) low-class (foreigner), despicable (person). —*m., f.* 1. (Amer.) pretentious, self-important person. 2. (Amer.) low-class foreigner. 3. (Amer.) decrepit old person, old wreck. —*m.* (mar.) old tub, heavy unseaworthy ship.
cárcamo, *m., var. of* **cárcavo.**
carcañal, *m.* heel (of the foot).
carcasa, *f.* 1. a certain kind of incendiary bomb. 2. (Amer.) inner tube of a pneumatic tire. 3. casing, framework. — **c. de motor,** (elec.) motor frame.
cárcava, *f.* 1. gully; 2. hole, pit, ditch; grave. 3. (mil.) enclosure.
carcavina, *f., var. of* **cárcava.**
cárcavo, *m.* cavity or socket in which the journal of a water mill wheel turns.
carcavón, *m. aug. of* **cárcava,** ditch, gully.
carcavuezo, *m.* deep pit.
carcax, *m., var. of* **carcaj.**
carcax, *m.* metal anklet, bracelet, or armlet.
carcayú, *m.* (zool.) carcajou.
carcaza, *f., var. of* **carcaj.**
cárcel, *f.* 1. prison, jail. 2. runner, groove (on which a sluice gate moves). 3. (carp.) clamp, wooden vise; (print.) bail (in a platen press).
carcelaje, *m.* jailer's fee paid by convicts upon their release from prison; forced detention (not necessarily in a prison).
carcelario, ria, *a.* pertaining or relative to a prison or jail.

carcelera, *f.* a type of plaintive Andalusian folk song in which the lyrics tell of the hardships of prison life.
carcelería, *f.* 1. forced detention (not necessarily in a prison). 2. bail. — **guardar c.,** to be forced to stay within certain limits.
carcelero, ra, *a.* pertaining to a prison or jail. —*m., f.* jailer; warden.
carcinógeno, *m.* (med.) carcinogen.
carcinología, *f.* carcinology, study of crustaceans.
carcinológico, ca, *a.* carcinological.
carcinoma, *m.* (med.) carcinoma, cancer.
carcinomatosis, *f.* (med.) carcinomatosis.
carcinomatoso, sa, *a.* (med.) carcinomatous.
carcocha, *f.* (Peru) jalopy, old car.
cárcola, *f.* treadle of a loom.
carcoma, *f.* 1. (ento.) wood borer. 2. wood dust (left by wood borer). 3. worry, preoccupation, anxiety. 4. drain (on income); spendthrift.
carcomer, *tr.v.* to gnaw (wood borers); to eat away, consume (one's health, good spirits, etc.), to undermine. —*r.v.* to become worm-eaten; to decay (teeth).
carcunda, *a., m., f.* (derog.), Carlist, *var. of* **carca.**
carda, *f.* 1. (tex.) carding (of cloth); card, teasel (instrument for carding). 2. (bot.) teasel. 3. (coll.) severe reprimand, scolding. 4. (mar.) a small galley. — **dar una c.,** to give (someone) a dressing-down or a scolding; to reprimand severely; **todos somos de la c.,** we are all in the same boat.
cardada, *f.* (tex.) cardful, amount of wool carded at one time.
cardador, ra, *m., f.* (tex.) carder, person who cards wool. —*m.* (ento.) kind of myriapod or millipede.
cardadura, *f.* action of carding (wool or cloth).
cardal, *m.* thistle patch.
cardamina, *f.* (bot.) pepper cress, peppergrass.
cardamomo, *m.* (bot.) cardamom.
cardán, *m.* (mech.) Cardan joint, universal joint. — **junta c.,** Cardan joint, universal joint.
cardánico, ca, *a.* (mec.) Cardan, e.g. *junta cardánica,* Cardan joint.
cardar, *tr.v.* (tex.) to card; to raise the nap on, teasel.
cardario, *m.* (ichth.) species of ray whose body is covered with sharp spines.
cardelina, *f.* (ornith.) goldfinch, a variety of linnet.
cardenal, *m.* 1. (ecc.) cardinal. 2. (ornith.) cardinal, cardinal bird. 3. (Chile) geranium. 4. weal, welt, wale.
cardenalato, *m.* cardinalate, cardinalship.
cardenalicio, cia, *a.* (ecc.) pertaining to a cardinal.
cardencha, *f.* 1. (bot.) teasel. 2. card (for wool or cloth).
cardenchal, *m.* teasel patch.
cardenilla, *f.* a variety of small, purplish, late-ripening grape.
cardenillo, *m.* 1. (chem.) verdigris. 2. (p.) verdigris.
cárdeno, na, *a.* 1. purplish, violet, livid. 2. greyish (bull). 3. opaline (water).
cardería, *f.* (tex.) carding room.
cardíaca, *f.* (bot.) motherwort.
cardiáceo, a, *a.* heart-shaped.
cardíaco, ca, *a.* (med.) cardiac, heart. —*m., f.* cardiac, sufferer from heart disease.
cardialgia, *f.* (med.) cardialgia.
cardiálgico, ca, *a.* (med.) cardialgic.
cardiar, *tr.v.* (Ven.) to ream.
cardias, *m.* (anat.) cardia, cardiac orifice between the stomach and esophagus.
cardillar, *m.* golden thistle patch.
cardillo, *m.* 1. (bot.) golden thistle. 2. (Mex.) glint, gleam, flashing reflection of the sun's rays (e.g. by a mirror).
cardinal, *a.* cardinal, principal, fundamental; cardinal (number, point).
cardinas, *f.* (*pl.*) (archit.) thistle leaf decorations.
cardiografía, *f.* (med.) cardiography.
cardiógrafo, *m.* (med.) cardiograph.
cardiograma, *m.* (med.) cardiogram.
cardiología, *f.* (med.) cardiology.
cardiólogo, *m.* (med.) cardiologist.
cardiópata, *a.* (med.) suffering from a heart disease. —*m., f.* person suffering from a heart disease.
cardiopatía, (med.) *f.* cardiopathy.
cardiovascular, *a.* (anat.) cardiovascular, of the heart and blood vessels as a unified body system.
cardítico, ca, *a.* (med.) carditic, of or relative to the heart.
carditis, *f.* (med.) carditis.
cardizal, *m.* thistle patch.
cardo, *m.* 1. (bot.) thistle. 2. (fig.) a fierce or unruly person. — **c. ajonjero** or **aljonjero,** carline thistle; **c. borriqueño, borriquero** or **yesquero,** cotton thistle; **c. corredor** or **estelado,** field eryngo; **c. de Maria, lechar** or **mariano,** milk thistle; **c. estrellado,** star thistle; **c. huso,** woolly carthamus.
cardón, *m.* 1. (bot.) teasel; (Peru, Ven.) thistle. 2. (tex.) carding (of cloth). 3. (Amer.) giant cactus.
Cardona, más listo que C., (coll.) sharp as a needle, smart as a whip.
cardonal, *m.* (Amer.) place abounding in thistles.
cardoncillo, *m.* (bot.) milk thistle.
carducha, *f.* (tex.) heavy iron card (for carding wool, etc.).
cardume, *m., var. of* **cardumen.**
cardumen, *m.* 1. school, shoal (of fish). 2. (Chile) abundance, slew (coll.), great quantity, lot.
carduzador, ra, *m., f.* (tex.) carder.
carduzal, *m.* thistle patch.
carduzar, (*ref. 53*) *tr.v.* (tex.) to card; to raise the nap on (cloth); to comb (fibers).
careador, *m.* (Dom. Rep.) a man who handles a fighting cock during a cockfight.
carear, *tr.v.* 1. (law) to confront, bring face to face (witnesses, criminals, etc.). 2. to lead, drive, tend (cattle). 3. to give final cleansing to (sugar loaf). 4. to match, compare (two things). —*i.v.* to face; **c. a,** to face, look towards. —*r.v.* to meet (for discussion); to meet face to face, face one another.
carecer, (*ref. 45*) *i.v* to lack. — **c. de,** to lack, want, be in need (of).
careciente, *a.* lacking, wanting.
carecimiento, *m.* lack, want, need.
carel, *m.* border, rim (of a plate or other vessel); upper edge (of ship's hull).
carena, *f.* 1. part of the vessel under water. 2. (mar.) careening, careen (repairing of a ship). 3. mocking, banter. — **dar c.,** (mar.) to careen; **dar c. a uno,** (coll.) to mock, make fun of.
carenadura, *f.* (mar.) action of careening, careenage, repairing of a ship.
carenaje, *m.* (mar., aer.) ship repair; careenage.
carenar, *tr.v.* (mar.) to careen, repair, clean and caulk. — **c. de firme,** to careen completely.
carencia, *f.* lack, want, deficiency.
carenero, *m.* (mar.) dry dock, careenage, careening place.
carenote, *m.* (mar.) careening prop (for supporting a dry-docked ship).
carente, *a.* lacking, devoid. — **c. de,** lacking, devoid of.
careo, *m.* 1. confrontation (of witnesses, etc.); meeting; matching, comparison. 2. (Amer.) the action of cockfighting.
carero, ra, *a.* (coll.) said of a merchant who charges high prices.
carestía, *f.* lack, shortage, paucity, scarcity, dearth. — **c. de la vida,** high cost of living.
careta, *f.* mask; fencer's mask. — **quitarle la c. a,** to unmask; **c. antigás,** gas mask; **c. de soldador,** welding mask.
careto, ta, *a.* white-faced (cattle and horses).
carey, *m.* 1. (zool.) hawksbill turtle (Eretmochis imbricata); tortoise shell. 2. (bot., Cuba) rough-leaved liana; shrub yielding tortoise shell-like wood.
carezca, carezco, *ref.* **carecer.**
carga, *f.* 1. loading; load; cargo, freight. 2. load (particular measure of certain articles). 3. liability, obligation; load, burden, worry, care (on the mind). 4. tax, duty, tribute. 5. (mil.) charge (of a bullet, shell, etc.); nozzle of a powder flask. 6. (mil.) charge, attack. 7. (elec.) charge; (elec.) load. 8. (vet.) poultice. 9. refill (for ball point pen). — **a c. cerrada,** without thought or reflexion; at once, immediately; **a cargas,** abundantly, in thousands; **buque de c., freighter,** cargo boat; **c. abierta,** (mil.) bayonet or sword charge in open formation; **c. aérea,** airfreight; **c. a granel,** bulk cargo; **c. alar,** (aer.) wing loading or load; **c. balanceada** or **dividida,** (elec.) balanced load; **c. bruta,** dead tonnage; **c. cerrada,** (mil.) bayonet or sword charge in close formation; (coll.) severe or harsh reprimand; **c. concejil,** obligatory municipal or local tax or service; **c. de barreno,** blasting charge; **c. de bombas,** bomb load; **c. de caballería,** cavalry charge; **c. de demolición** or **destrucción,** demolition charge; **c. de flexión,** (engin.) beam loading; **c. de petral,** head-on charge; **c. de profundidad,** depth charge; **c. de la prueba,** burden of proof; **c. de rueda,** wheel load; **c. de velocidad, c. dinámica,** (hydr.) dynamic head; **c. espacial** or **de espacio** (elec.) space charge; **c. fija or muerta** dead load; **c. fundamental,** (elec.) base load; **c. mayor,** load suitable for a mule or pack horse; **c. menor,** load suitable for an ass or donkey; **c. neta,** cargo deadweight tonnage; **c. por unidad,** unit load; **c. real,** land or property tax; **c. viva** or **móvil,** (archit., engin.) live load; **llevar la c. de una cosa,** to be responsible for something; **quedarse con la c. en las costillas,** to be left holding the bag; **volver a la c.,** to persist in an undertaking, to keep at it; to harp on the same subject.
cargadas, *f.* card game.
cargadera, *f.* 1. (mar.) downhaul, brail, inhaul. 2. (Col.) (*pl.*) suspenders (accessory to hold up trousers).
cargadero, *m.* 1. loading platform, loading or freight station, wharf. 2. (archit.) lintel.
cargadilla, *f.* (coll.) accrued interest (on a debt).
cargado, da, *past part. of* **cargar.** —*a.* 1. sultry (weather). 2. about to give birth, said of sheep and, in some places, of other females, including women. 3. strong (coffee, tea). 4. (her.) inescutcheoned, emblazoned. —*m.* step in Spanish dancing.
cargador, *m.* 1. loader, porter, stevedore. 2. shipper. 3. pitchfork. 4. (artil.) rammer, ramrod. 5. loader, one who loads the gun. 6. magazine (of rifle, etc.). 7. (Guat.) noisy rocket. 8. (Chile) shoot left in pruning to support the weight of the new fruit. — **c. de acumuladores,** battery charger; **c. de cartuchos,** cartridge clip; **c. portátil,** wagon leader, portable conveyor; **c. sacudidor,** shaking skip loader.
cargamento, *m.* load; cargo.
cargante, *a.* bothering, annoying.

cargar, (*ref. 51*) *tr.v* 1. to load (truck, ship, etc. with cargo, merchandise); (fig.) to load (with jewels, ornaments, etc.), load or weigh down, burden (with obligations, tasks). 2. to load (gun, rifle with shells or bullets, camera with film, kiln with ceramics, etc.); to put a refill in (a ball point pen); to charge (an electric battery); to stoke (a furnace). 3. to place or to put (blame) on, e.g. *le cargaron toda la culpa,* they placed all the blame on him; to accuse of, charge with, e.g. *le cargaron el delito a él,* they accused him of the crime. 4. to put or to place (responsibility) on, entrust (responsibility) to. 5. to impose (taxes) on. 6. to raise, increase (taxes). 7. (mil.) to charge, attack. 8. to eat, drink (too much). 9. (Amer.) to carry, take. 10. (com.) to charge (to an account). 11. to clew up, furl (sails). 12. to annoy, weary, tire. 13. to beat, play a higher card than. 14. to increase one's stake on. 15. (Amer.) to wear. — **c. con** or **de,** to load with; to overload with, burden with; **c. de cadenas,** to put in irons; **c. la mano a,** to be very severe with; **cargarle en cuenta** or **a su cuenta,** to charge to one's account; **cargar con el muerto,** to be left holding the bag; **c. uno su cruz,** to bear one's cross. —*i.v.* 1. to load. 2. to veer, turn, e.g. *cargó la tempestad hacia el oeste,* the storm veered towards the west. 3. to incline, lean; to rest, e.g. *carga sobre dos columnas,* it rests on two columns. 4. to fall (accent on certain syllables). 5. to crop well, produce a great deal (fruit trees, etc.). 6. to pack, crowd. — **c. con,** to carry, take, take away; to steal, walk off with; to take upon oneself, shoulder, be responsible for, e.g. *él carga con todo,* he is responsible for everything, *yo cargo con la responsabilidad,* I'll take the responsibility; **c. sobre,** to rest on; to fall on, devolve on; to pester, importune. —*r.v.* 1. to become overcast, become cloudy. 2. to turn, veer (wind). 3. to become bored or annoyed. 4. to rest, lean, incline. 5. (coll.) to kill, liquidate, bump off; to eliminate, get rid of; to break. — **cargarse de,** to have much or many, have a great number of; to be overloaded with; to fill, become filled with (e.g. tears); **cargársela,** to take the blame, e.g. él se la cargó por todos, he took the blame for everyone.

cargareme, *m.* receipt, deposit voucher.

cargazón, *f.* 1. load; cargo. 2. bank of heavy clouds, heavy, overcast sky. 3. heaviness (heavy feeling of the head, stomach, etc.). 4. (Arg.) contraption, awkward piece of machinery. 5. (Chile) heavy crop or load of fruit.

cargo, *m.* 1. post, office, position; task, duty. 2. charge, accusation. 3. charge, direction, management, care, control. 4. loading; load, weight, burden; (bldg.) load of stones (1/3 of cubic meter); load, batch (of grapes or olives to be pressed). 5. (com.) debit, sum of amounts due. 6. (Chile) certificate affixed to the foot of documents in law courts acknowledging date and hour of receipt. — **a c. de,** in charge of; **c. concejil** or **de la república,** compulsory public office; **c. de conciencia,** burden on the conscience, sense of guilt, remorse; **hacer c. a uno de,** to accuse of, charge one with; **hacerse c. de,** to make oneself responsible for, take charge of, take over, take on; to understand, grasp, realize.

cargosear, *tr.v.* (Chile) to annoy, bother, pester, importune.

cargoso, sa, *a.* burdensome, onerous; bothersome, annoying, tiresome.

cargue, cargué, *ref.* **cargar.**

carguero, ra, *a.* freight, cargo (train, ship, etc.); of burden (animal). —*m.* 1. carrier (a person). 2. (Amer.) beast of burden. 3. cargo boat.

carguío, *m.* load; cargo, freight.

cari, *a.* (Arg., Chile) beige-colored. —*m.* (cul.) curry.

caria, *f.* (archit.) shaft (of a column).

cariacedo, da, *a.* sour-faced, surly, bad-tempered.

cariaco, *m.* 1. (Cuba) popular dance. 2. (Ecuad.) fermented drink of cane-syrup, cassava and potatoes.

cariacontecido, da, *a.* (coll.) crestfallen; glum; dejected, worried.

cariacuchillado, da, *a.* scar-faced.

cariado, da, *a.* (med.) carious, decayed (bones, teeth).

cariadura, *f.* (med.) caries, decay (of bones, teeth).

cariaguileño, ña, *a.* aquiline-featured, hawk-faced.

carialegre, *a.* bright-faced, smiling, cheerful.

carialzado, da, *a.* proud-looking, holding his (her) head high.

cariampollado, da, *a., var. of* **cariampollar.**

cariampollar, *a.* chubby-cheeked, plump-cheeked.

cariancho, cha, *a.* broad-faced.

cariaquito, *m.* (bot.) garden variety of verbena.

cariar, (*ref. 54*) *tr.v.* (med.) to cause to decay, produce caries in. —*r.v.* to decay, become decayed.

cariátide, *f.* (archit.) caryatid, a supporting column in the form of a female figure.

caríbal, *a., m., f.* cannibal.

Caribdis, *m.* (hist.) Charybdis, a whirlpool on the Sicilian side of the Straits of Messina, formerly feared by mariners.

caribe, *a.* Caribbean. —*m., f.* Carib. —*m.* 1. Carib (language). 2. C., Caribbean (sea). 3. savage, cruel and inhuman person. 4. (ichth.) caribe, piranha, man-eating fish.

caribello, *a.* having a white-spotted forehead (said of a bull).

cariblanca, *m.* (zool., Col., C. Rica) whitefaced monkey (of the Cebidae family).

cariblanco, *m.* (zool., C. Rica) white-lipped peccary (Tayassu peccari).

caribú, (*pl.* **caribúes**) *m.* (zool.) caribou.

carica, *f.* a variety of kidney bean.

caricari, *m.* (ornith.) Audubon's caracara, a large hawk resembling a vulture.

caricato, *m.* 1. (mus.) basso buffo (bass who sings comic roles in opera). 2. (Amer.) caricature.

caricatura, *f.* caricature; cartoon.

caricaturar, *tr.v., var. of* **caricaturizar.**

caricaturesco, ca, *a.* pertaining to caricature.

caricaturice, caricaturicé, *ref.* **caricaturizar.**

caricaturista, *m., f.* caricaturist, cartoonist.

caricaturizar, (*ref. 53*) *tr.v.* to caricature.

carichato, ta, *a.* flat-faced, flat-featured.

caricia, *f.* caress, blandishment, petting.

cariciosamente, *adv.* caressingly.

caricioso, sa, *a.* affectionate.

caricuerdo, a, *a.* said of a person who looks well composed, controlled or stable.

caridad, *f.* 1. charity; alms. 2. light refreshment (served at religious festivals or wakes and funerals). 3. (Mex.) prison food. 4. (mar.) spare anchor. 5. charity (form of address used in some religious orders). — **la c. comienza por la casa,** charity begins at home.

caridelantero, ra, *a.* (coll.) bold, forward, brazen, impudent.

caridoliente, *a.* mournful, woebegone, glum.

cariedón, *m.* (ento.) nut weevil.

carientismo, *m.* (rhet.) delicate irony.

caries, *f.* 1. (med.) caries, tooth decay. 2. (agr.) wheat smut, bunt.

carifresco, *a.* (Cuba, P. Rico) brazen, shameless.

carifruncido, da, *a.* (coll.) with wrinkled brow, frowning.

carigordo, da, *a.* (coll.) fat-faced, chubby-faced.

cariharto, ta, *a.* round-faced.

carilampiño, ña, *a.* smooth-faced, beardless, said of adult males with little or no beard.

carilargo, ga, *a.* 1. (coll.) long-faced. 2. (Amer., coll.) disgusted, annoyed.

carilimpio, pia, *a.* (Amer.) brazen, shameless.

carilla, *f.* 1. beekeeper's wire mask. 2. page, side of a book leaf or a sheet of paper.

carilleno, na, *a.* (coll.) plump-faced, full-faced.

carillo, lla, *a.* dear, beloved, darling. —*m., f.* beloved, darling, lover (esp. in pastoral poetry).

carillón, *m.* (mus.) carillon.

carilucio, cia, *a.* (coll.) shiny-faced.

carimba, *f.* (Peru, arch.) brand, ídentification mark put on slaves.

carimbo, *m.* (Bol.) branding iron for cattle.

carina, *f.* (anat., zool., bot.) carina.

carincho, *m.* (Amer.) stew made with meat, potatoes and green peppers.

carinegro, gra, *a.* dark, swarthy (complexioned).

carininfo, fa, *a.* effeminate-looking.

cariñana, *f.* (arch.) wimple-like woman's headdress.

cariñar, *i.v.* (Arg.) to feel blue, melancholy; to feel nostalgic.

cariñena, *m.* aromatic sweet wine produced in Saragossa, Spain.

cariño, *m.* love, affection, fondness; devotion; loving care (in one's work); (*pl.*) endearments, words of affection; **cariños a,** (give my) love to.

cariñosamente, *adv.* affectionately, lovingly.

cariñoso, sa, *a.* affectionate, loving.

carioca, *a.* pertaining to Rio de Janeiro, Brazil. —*m., f.* (coll.) native of Rio de Janeiro.

cariocar, *m.* (bot.) souari nut tree.

cariocinesis, *f.* (biol.) karyokinesis, mitosis.

cariofiláceo, a, *a.* (bot.) caryophyllaceous. —*f.* (*pl.*) Caryophyllaceae.

cariofileo, a, *a., f.* (bot.) *var. of* **cariofiláceo.**

cariofilina, *f.* (chem.) caryophyllin.

cariolinfa, *f.* (physiol.) karyolymph.

cariología, *f.* (physiol.) karyology.

cariomitoma, *m.* (biol.) karyomitome.

carioplasma, *m.* (biol.) karyoplasm.

cariópside, *f.* (bot.) caryopsis.

carioquinesis, *f.* (biol.) karyokinesis, mitosis.

cariosistemática, *f.* (biol.) karyosystematics.

cariosoma, *m.* (biol.) karyosome.

cariotina, *f.* (biol.) karyotin.

cariparejo, ja, *a.* (coll.) poker-faced (coll.); inscrutable.

caripelado, *m.* (Col., zool.) a species of monkey.

carirraído, da, *a.* (coll.) brazen-faced, brazen, bold, forward.

carirredondo, da, *a.* (coll.) round-faced.

carisea, *f.* (tex.) jersey, a light woolen fabric with a cotton warp.

cariseto, *m.* (tex.) coarse woolen fabric.

carisma, *m.* 1. (rel.) charisma, a divinely inspired gift or power. 2. (polit.) a hypnotic quality in leadership arousing love and devotion in the people.

carismático, ca, *a.* charismatic, pertaining to charisma, e.g. *un lider c.,* a charismatic leader.

carisquis, *m.* (bot., Phil. I.) species of acacia (Acacia julibrissin).

carita, *f.* 1. little face (a diminutive or a term of endearment). 2. (Dom. Rep., coll.) an uninvited guest. 3. (bot.) black-eyed pea. 4. (bot.) mesquite. — **dar** or **hacer c.,** (Amer.) to smile back (a flirting woman).

caritán, *m.* (Phil. I.) man who collects palm juice (for making tuba liquor).

caritativamente, *adv.* charitably.

caritativo, va, *a.* charitable.
carite, *m.* (ichth., Cuba) a variety of large swordfish (Scomberomorus maculatus).
cariucho, *m.* (cul., Ecuad.) a stew of meat, potatoes and green peppers.
cariz, *m.* look, aspect; prospect.
carla, *f.* (tex.) East Indian painted fabric.
carlanca, *f.* 1. mastiff's spiked collar; (Ecuad.) stick fixed to an animal's collar to prevent it from getting through fences. 2. (coll.) (*gen. pl.*) trick, ruse. 3. (C. Rica, Col.) shackle. 4. (Hond.) bother, annoyance; pest, nuisance. — **tener muchas carlancas,** to be very crafty or cunning.
carlancón, na, *m., f.* tricky, cunning, crafty person.—*a.* cunning, crafty, sly, tricky.
carlanga, *f.* (Mex.) tatter, rag.
carlear, *i.v.* to pant, gasp.
carleta, *f.* 1. rough file (for filing and shaping iron). 2. (min.) slate from Angers, France.
carlín, *m.* (numis.) carlin, a Spanish silver coin of the time of Charles V.
carlina, *a.,* **angélica c.,** (bot.) angelica, carline thistle.
carlinga, *f.* 1. compartment, area used by passengers and crew of an airplane. 2. (mar.) mast step (base opening into which mast fits).
carlismo, *m.* (polit.) Carlism, the movement supporting the Bourbon pretender to the throne of Spain.
carlista, *a., m., f.* (polit.) Carlist.
carlita, *f.* (opt.) reading glasses or lenses.
Carlomagno, *m.* (hist.) Charlemagne, king and emperor of much of western Europe (742-814).
carlota, *f.* (cul.) charlotte, a succulent dessert made with sponge cake; **c. rusa,** charlotte russe, charlotte with whipped cream and glazed fruit.
carlovingio, gia, *a.* pertaining to Charlemagne, his time or his dynasty.
carmañola, *f.* 1. carmagnole (jacket). 2. carmagnole, a popular song of the French Revolution.
carmel, *m.* (bot.) a variety of plantain.
carmelina, *f.* wool obtained from the second shearing of the vicuña.
carmelita, *a.* 1. (rel.) Carmelite. 2. (Cuba, Chile) brown (color). —*m., f.* (rel.) Carmelite. —*f.* (bot.) nasturtium flower (used in salads).
carmelitano, na, *a.* (rel.) Carmelite.
Carmelo, Monte C., (Bib.) Mount Carmel.
carmen, *m.* 1. (rel.) Carmelite Order, Order of Our Lady of Mount Carmel. 2. (Sp., reg.) typical villa of Granada. 3. poetic composition; verse.
carmenador, *m.* 1. comb. 2. comber, carder.
carmenadura, *f.* combing, carding.
carmenar, *tr.v.* 1. to comb, disentangle; to card. 2. (coll.) to pull (someone's) hair, pull the hair of. 3. (coll.) to fleece, swindle, rob.
carmentales, *f. pl.* Carmentalia, ancient Roman festivities in honor of the goddess Carmenta.
carmes, *m., var. of* **quermes.**
carmesí, *a.* crimson, red, scarlet. —*m.* 1. crimson. 2. cochineal or kermes powder. 3. crimson silk (fabric).
carmesita, *f.* (min.) silicate of iron and aluminum oxide.
carmín, *m.* 1. carmine (dye). 2. carmine, crimson. 3. (bot.) pokeweed. 4. (bot.) mallow rose.
carminar, *tr.v.* (arch.) to expel.
carminativo, va, *a., m.* (med.) carminative.
carmíneo, a, *a.* carmine; rosy.
carminita, *f.* (min.) carminite.
carminoso, sa, *a.* carmine-hued; rosy.
carnación, *f.* (her.) carnation, flesh-colored tint.
carnada, *f.* bait; (coll.) snare, trap; **c. viva,** live bait.
carnadura, *f.* musculature; muscularity, robustness; fleshiness.
carnaje, *m.* 1. salt beef, jerked meat. 2. (arch.) carnage.
carnal, *a.* 1. carnal. 2. sensual, lustful. 3. (fig.) worldly. 4. related by blood, e.g. *primo c.,* full cousin, first cousin. —*m.* (ecc.) non-Lenten period.
carnalidad, *f.* carnality, lustfulness.
carnalita, *f.* (min.) carnallite.
carnalmente, *adv.* carnally; lustfully.
carnauba, *f.* (bot.) carnauba, a variety of Brazilian palm that yields a commercially valuable hard wax.
carnaval, *m.* 1. carnival; (*pl.*) Mardi gras. 2. (coll.) a noisy gathering or meeting. 3. a travesty. — **baile de c.,** costume party, masked ball.
carnavalada, *f.* carnival joke, lark, bit of fun.
carnavalesco, ca, *a.* pertaining to carnival.
carnaza, *f.* 1. fleshy side of hide or skin. 2. bait. 3. (coll.) corpulence. 4. (Amer., coll.) scapegoat, fall guy. — **echar a uno de c.,** to put the blame on, make a scapegoat of.
carnazón, *f.* inflammation of a wound.
carne, *f.* 1. meat; flesh; pulp (of fruit). 2. flesh (in opposition to spirit). — **c. blanca,** white meat; **c. cediza,** tainted meat; **c. de cañon,** cannon fodder; **c. de gallina,** (bot.) white rot in wood; (coll.) goose pimples; **c. de membrillo,** (cul.) quince preserve or jelly; **c. de res,** (Amer.) beef; **c. de sábado,** offal, giblets; **c. de su c.,** one's own flesh and blood; **c. de vaca,** beef; **c. fiambre,** cold meat; **c. magra,** lean meat; **c. mollar,** lean, boneless meat, filet; **c. sin hueso,** (coll.) a sinecure, plum, cinch, an easy job; **c. vacuna,** beef; **c. viva,** (med.) raw flesh, quick; **criar, cobrar** or **echar carnes,** to put on weight; **en carnes,** naked, in the raw; **en c. viva,** raw, without skin; (fig.) in a sore spot; **hombre de c. y hueso,** man of flesh and blood, truly human person; **no ser ni c. ni pescado,** to be neither fish nor fowl; **poner uno toda la c. en el asador,** (coll.) to risk everything on one stake, put all one's eggs in one basket; **ser uña y c.,** to be hand and glove, to be intimate friends.
carné, *m.* 1. appointment book. 2. identification document, identity card.
carneada, *f.* 1. (Amer.) slaughtering, butchering of animals. 2. slaughterhouse, abattoir.
carnear, *tr.v.* 1. (Amer.) to slaughter, butcher animals. 2. (Chile) to trick, take in, skin (sl.). 3. (Mex.) to knife to death.
carnecilla, *f.* wart, fleshy outgrowth.
cárneo, a, *a.* (arch.) fleshy.
carnerada, *f.* flock of sheep.
carneraje, *m.* tax on sheep.
carnereamiento, *m.* penalty imposed for damage caused by trespassing sheep.
carnerear, *tr.v.* to slaughter cattle or sheep as penalty for damage caused by them.
carnerero, *m.* shepherd.
carneril, *a.* pertaining to sheep; **dehesa c.,** sheep pasture.
carnero, *m.* 1. (zool.) sheep; ram. 2. (cul.) mutton. 3. (Amer., fig.) sheep, lamb (timid or easily led person). 4. (astrol.) the sign of Aries. — **c. de la sierra or de la tierra,** (Arg., coll.) llama, alpaca, guanaco or vicuña; **c. del Cabo,** (ornith.) albatross; **c. de simiente,** breeding ram; **c. llano,** wether, castrated ram; **c. marino,** (zool.) seal; **c. verde,** mutton stew prepared with parsley and other ingredients; **no hay tales carneros,** (coll.) there is no such thing, it is not true; nonsense.
carnero, *m.* 1. burial ground, charnel. 2. charnel house; family vault. — **cantar para el c.,** (Arg.) to die; **mandar al c.,** to kill.
carneruno, na, *a.* pertaining to sheep; sheeplike.
carnestolendas, *f. pl.* carnival, Mardi gras; Shrovetide.
carnet, *m.* identity card, identification papers.
carnicería, *f.* 1. butcher's shop, meat market; **c. de caballo,** horse butcher shop. 2. (Ecuad.) slaughterhouse. 3. butchery, slaughter, carnage.
carnicero, ra, *a.* 1. carnivorous, meat-eating. 2. cruel, bloodthirsty, sanguinary. 3. fattening (pasture). 4. fond of meat. —*m., f.* butcher. —*m.* (zool.) carnivore; (*pl.*) Carnivora.
cárnico, ca, *a.* pertaining to meat (industry, etc.).
carnicol, *m.* toe of cloven-footed animal.
carnificación, *f.* (med.) carnification (process of turning to flesh).
carnificarse, (*ref. 50*) *r.v.* (med.) to carnify, turn into flesh.
carnífice, *m.* 1. fire (term used by alchemists). 2. (arch.) executioner.
carnifique, carnifiqué, *ref.* **carnificarse.**
carniforme, *a.* fleshlike, carniform.
carnina, *f.* (chem.) carnine, a substance derived from meat extracts and from yeast.
carniola, *f.* (min.) carnelian.
carniseco, ca, *a.* lean, scrawny, scraggy.
carnívoro, ra, *a.* carnivorous (animal, plant). —*m.* (zool.) carnivore; (*pl.*) Carnivora.
carniza, *f.* (coll.) meat scraps, waste meat fed to animals, offal; (coll.) carrion.
carnosidad, *f.* 1. carnosity, fleshy excrescence. 2. corpulence, fleshiness.
carnoso, sa, *a.* 1. meaty, fleshy, meat-like, fleshlike; (bot.) pulpy, carnose. 2. fleshy, having lots of flesh. 3. full of marrow.
carnotita, *f.* (min.) carnotite.
carnudo, da, *a.* fleshy, meaty.
carnuz, *m.* (Sp.) *var. of* **carroña.**
carnuza, *f.* (derog.) poor quality meat.
caro, ra, *a.* 1. dear, expensive, costly. 2. beloved, dear. — **c. mitad,** better half, one's spouse. —*m.* (Cuba) dish made of crab roe and manioc or cassava.
caro, *adv.* dearly, expensively, e.g., *él vende muy c.,* he sells his things very expensively or at very high prices. — **¡te costará c.!** you'll pay for that!
caroba, *f.* (Arg., bot.) carob tree, caroba tree (Bignonia antisyphilitica).
caroca, *f.* 1. decorations hung in the streets for certain festivals. 2. farce, burlesque, satirical play. 3. (coll.) hypocritically flattering or cajoling remark, blandishment; (*pl.*) cajolery, wheedling, soft-soaping. — **hacer carocas,** to cajole, flatter.
carocha, *f.* eggs (of bees and other insects).
carochar, *tr.v.* (ento.) to lay eggs.
carola, *f.* carol, old round dance accompanied by song.
carolingio, gia, *a., var. of* **carlovingio.**
carolino, na, *a.* (hist.) of or pertaining to the reign of various kings called Charles or Carlos. —*m., f.* native or inhabitant of the Caroline Islands or the Carolinas (states of the U.S.).
cárolus, *m.* (numis.) carolus, a coin used in Spain during the time of Charles V.
caromomia, *f.* mummified human flesh (formerly valued for medicinal purposes).
Carón, Caronte, *m.* (myth.) Charon, the boatman who ferried the souls of the dead across the river Styx to Hades.
carón, na, *a.* 1. (Amer.) fat-faced. 2. (Col.) brazen, impudent.
carona, *f.* 1. saddle padding (used to protect the horse). 2. part of horse's back upon which saddle rests.
caroñoso, sa, *a.* saddle-galled (horse).
caroquero, ra, *a.* flattering, wheedling, cajoling. —*m., f.* flatterer, cajoler.

carosiero, ra, *m.* (bot.) a Brazilian palm with apple-like fruit. —*f.* fruit of that tree.
carosis, *f.* (med.) deep stupor (accompanied by complete insensibility).
caroteno, *m.* (biochem.) carotene, an organic pigment.
carotenoide, *a.* (biochem.) carotenoide.
carótida, *f.* (anat.) carotid (arteries).
carotina, *f.* (chem.) carotene, an organic pigment.
carozo, *m.* 1. corn cob. 2. stone, pit (of fruits).
carpa, *f.* 1. (ichth.) carp. 2. tent, awning; (Mex.) carnival, circus, e.g. *gente de c.,* carnival folk. 3. a bunch of grapes.
carpanel, *a.* (archit.) **arco c.,** basket-handle arch.
carpanta, *f.* 1. (coll.) rabid hunger. 2. (Mex.) happy crowd (of people), gang (of rowdies or roughnecks). 3. (Sp.) laxity; laziness.
Cárpatos, *m. pl.* Carpathian Mountains.
carpe, *m.* (bot.) hornbeam, yoke elm.
carpedal, *m.* hornbeam grove, yoke elm grove.
carpelado, da, *a.* (bot.) carpellate.
carpelar, *a.* (bot.) carpellary.
carpelo, *m.* (bot.) carpel.
carpeta, *f.* 1. table cover. 2. briefcase; folder, letter file. 3. (com.) docket, bill, voucher. 4. (Amer.) desk (office, hotel and school), e.g. *c. del hotel,* front desk of a hotel. 5. (Arg., Urug.) baize covering gambling tables.
Carpetania, la, *f.* ancient region of central Spain.
carpetano, na, *a.* of or pertaining to la Carpetania; **la playa carpetana,** the shores of the Manzanares (i.e. Madrid). —*m., f.* native or inhabitant of la Carpetania; (fig.) Madrilenian.
carpetazo, *m.* **dar c.,** to shelve, pigeonhole, lay aside; to consider (a matter) closed.
carpiano, na, *a.* (anat.) carpal, pertaining to the wrist.
carpidor, *m.* (Amer.) hoe, rake.
carpincho, *m.* (Amer., zool.) capybara, a large S. American rodent.
carpintear, *i.v.* to work as carpenter, carpenter; (coll.) to do carpentering as a hobby.
carpintera, *a.* **abeja c.,** (ento.) carpenter bee.
carpintería, *f.* 1. carpentry, carpentering. 2. carpenter's shop. — **c. mecánica,** millwork; **c. de obra,** structural carpentry.
carpinteril, *a.* of or pertaining to a carpenter.
carpintero, *m.* 1. carpenter. 2. (ento.) carpenter bee. 3. (ornith.) woodpecker. — **c. adermador,** timberman; **c. armador,** erecting carpenter; **c. de obra de afuera, c. de armar,** framer, carpenter who makes house-frames; **c. de blanco,** cabinet maker; **c. de carretas, c. de prieto,** cartwright; **c. de navío** or **ribera,** shipwright; **maestro c.,** foreman, master carpenter; **pájaro c.,** (ornith.) woodpecker.
carpir, *tr.v.* 1. to scratch, graze. 2. to stun. 3. (Amer.) to weed, rake, hoe. —*r.v.* 1. to be scratched or grazed, scratch oneself; to hurt oneself. 2. to be stunned.
carpo, *m.* (anat.) carpus.
carpobálsamo, *m.* (bot.) fruit of the balm of Gilead tree.
carpófago, ga, *a.* carpophagous, fruit-eating.
carpóforo, *m.* (bot.) carpophore.
carpogonio, *m.* (bot.) carpogonium.
carpología, *f.* (bot.) carpology, the study of the structure of fruits and seeds.
carpóspora, *f.* (bot.) carpospore.
carquerol, *m.* any of several fixtures on a velvet loom to which the treadle cords are attached.
carquesa, *f.* carquaise (heated chamber or arch of an annealing furnace).
carquexia, *f.* (bot.) variety of Canary broom (Genista sphaero).
carraca, *f.* 1. (mar.) carrack, galleon; (derog.) old tub, hulk (old and slow ship). 2. shipyard (in particular the one in Cádiz, Sp.). 3. rattle (a percussion instrument or a child's toy). 4. (mec.) ratchet. 5. (Col.) jawbone.
carraco, ca, *a.* old, decrepit. —*m., f.* old, decrepit person. —*m.* (Col., ornith.) Audubon's Caracara; (C. Rica) small wild duck.
Carracuca, estar más perdido que C., to be caught in a hopeless predicament.
carrada, *f.* cartload, carload.
carral, *m.* wine barrel or drum (used for transporting over long distances).
carraleja, *f.* (ento.) oil beetle (Meloe proscarabeus).
carralero, *m.* wine barrel-maker.
carrampla, *f.* (Ecuad.) destitution, absolute poverty.
carramplón, *m.* 1. (Col.) nail (used in shoemaking). 2. (Col.) typical musical instrument. 3. (Col., Mex.) a type of musket.
carranca, *f.* mastiff's spiked collar.
carranchoso, sa, *a.* (Amer.) rough, uncouth.
carranza, *f.* spike of mastiff's collar.
carraña, *f.* (Sp.) 1. ire, anger. 2. a volatile or hot-tempered person.
carrao, *m.* 1. (Ven., ornith.) crane-like bird (Aramus vociferus). 2. (*pl.*) (Col., Cuba) rough, thicksoled shoes.
carraón, *m.* einkorn wheat.
carrasca, *f.* 1. (bot.) holm oak, holly oak. 2. (Col., Ven.) a rasping musical instrument played by folk bands.
carrascal, *m.* holm oak grove.
carrascalejo, *m. dim. of* **carrascal, small** holm oak.
carrasco, *m.* (bot.) *var. of* **carrasca.**
carrascoso, sa, *a.* (land) abounding in holm oaks.
carraspada, *f.* negus, watered wine and spices.
carraspear, *i.v.* to be hoarse, suffer from hoarseness of the throat.
carraspeño, ña, *a.* hoarse (voice).
carraspeo, *m.* the act of clearing one's throat; hoarseness.
carraspera, *f.* (coll.) hoarseness (of throat).
carraspique, *m.* (bot.) candytuft (Iberis umbellata).
carrasposa, *f.* (Col., bot.) a rough-leaved plant (Calea aspera).
carrasposo, sa, *a.* 1. chronically hoarse. 2. (Col., Ven.) rough, prickly. —*m., f.* person with a chronically hoarse throat.
carrasquear, *i.v.* to crackle or crunch something between the teeth.
carrasqueño, ña, *a.* (coll.) rough; hard. —*m.* holm oak.
carrasquera, *f.* holm oak grove.
carrejo, *m.* corridor, passage, hallway.
carrendilla, *f.* (Chile) row, string; **de c.,** habitually; by heart; automatically.
carrera, *f.* 1. race; run; running. 2. race track or course; course, trajectory, path (of sun or star); highway, high road; road, street; route, run (of procession, shipping line, etc.). 3. line, row (of trees, etc.); course (of bricks). 4. ladder; run (in stockings). 5. parting (of hair). 6. career, profession. 7. life, life span. 8. stroke (of piston). 9. (archit.) girder, joist, rafter. 10. quick short steps forward, bending the body (in Spanish and flamenco dancing). 11. (mus.) run, a rapid passage of an octave up or down the scale. 12. (*pl.*) (horse, motorcar, etc.) races; racing. — **a c. abierta** or **tendida,** at top speed; **a la c.,** at a run, running; quickly, fast, in a rush; **c. a campo traviesa,** cross-country race; **c. armamentista** or **de armamentos,** arms or armaments race; **c. ascendente,** (mec.) upstroke (piston); **c. de admisión,** (mec.) intake stroke; **c. de baquetas,** gauntlet (punishment); **c. de compresión,** (engin.) compression stroke; **c. de encendido,** (auto.) ignition stroke; **c. de escape,** (mec.) exhaust stroke; **c. descendente,** (mec.) stroke; **c. de expulsión,** (mec.) scavenging stroke; **c. de fondo,** long-distance race; **carreras de galgos,** greyhound racing; **c. de Indias,** (hist.) trade between Spain and South America; **c. de la válvula,** (mec.) valve travel; **c. de medio fondo,** middle-distance race; **c. de obstáculos,** obstacle race; **c. de regreso** or **retroceso,** (mec.) return stroke; **c. de relevos** or **postas,** relay race; **c. de resistencia,** endurance race; **c. de vallas,** hurdle race; **c. de velocidad,** sprint; **c. motriz,** (engin.) working or power stroke; **c. pedestre,** footrace; **dar c. a,** to pay for (a person's studies); **de c.,** career, e.g. *diplomático de c.,* carrer diplomat; **en c.,** in the running; **entrar en** or **por c.,** to get on the right track; **fuera de c.,** out of the running; **hacer c. de,** to take up the career of; to be successful as; **no poder hacer c. con uno,** to be unable to bring (someone) to reason.
carrerilla, *f.* 1. two quick short steps forward, bending the body (in Spanish dances). 2. (mus.) run (rapid passage up or down an octave). —*adv.* (coll.) **de c.,** from memory, by heart; (to do a thing) rapidly.
carrerista, *m., f.* 1. bettor, racing fan. 2. racing cyclist, racer. —*m.* outrider, servant on horseback attending a carriage.
carrero, *m.* carter, cart driver, teamster.
carreta, *f.* cart, wagon; **c. de mano,** (Ven.) wheelbarrow.
carretada, *f.* 1. cartload, wagonload. 2. (Mex.) a weight measure. 3. (coll.) load, slew, great amount. — **a carretadas,** (coll.) by the wagonload, in scores, copiously, abundantly.
carretaje, *m.* carting, cartage.
carretal, *m.* (bldg.) rough-hewn ashlar.
carrete, *m.* reel (of film, etc.), spool, bobbin; fishing-reel; (elec.) coil. — **c. de encendido,** (auto.) ignition coil; **c. de inducción,** (elec.) induction coil; **dar c.,** to reel off, play out (fishing line); **dar c. a uno,** (coll.) to keep someone dangling; **revelar un c.,** to develop a roll (of film).
carretear, *tr.v.* 1. to cart, convey by wagon or cart. 2. to drive (a wagon or cart). —*i.v.* (Cuba) to shriek, chatter loudly (parakeets, parrots). —*r.v.* to pull unevenly (oxen, mules).
carretel, *m.* spool, reel; (mar.) log reel, spunyarn winch. — **c. de hilo,** spool of thread.
carretela, *f.* 1. calash, shallow carriage with four seats and folding top. 2. (Chile) bus; public coach.
carreteo, *m.* (avia.) taxiing.
carretera, *f.* highway; public road. — **c. de cuatro vías,** four-lane highway; **c. de vía libre,** express highway, expressway.
carretería, *f.* 1. cartwright's workshop. 2. cartmaking, wagonmaking. 3. carting, transporting. 4. (group of) carts or wagons. 5. (mus.) 17th century dance.
carreteril, *a.* pertaining to carters or teamsters.
carretero, *a.* wagon, carriage. —*m.* 1. cart-wright, cart maker. 2. carter, teamster, driver (of carts and wagons). — **jurar como un c.,** to swear like a trooper.
carretil, *a.* pertaining to carts and wagons.
carretilla, *f.* 1. wheelbarrow, small cart. 2. go-cart; baby's walker (for learning to walk). 3. squib, a kind of firecracker. 4. small wheel used to cut pastry. 5. (Arg., Chile) jawbone. 6. (Arg.) burr. — **de c.,** (coll.) mechanically, by rote, by heart; **c. de equipaje,** baggage truck; **c. de**

mano, hand or warehouse truck; **c. eléctrica,** (elec.) electric squib.
carretillada, *f.* cartload, wheelbarrowload.
carretillero, *m.* (bldg.) wheelbarrow man; (Arg., Urug.) carter, cart driver; (min.) trammer.
carretillo, *m.* pulley (on braid-making looms).
carretón, *m.* 1. small cart; portable grindstone and treadle (mounted on a cart); go-cart; child's walker; (Amer.) large dray or cart. 2. (Hond., Guat., P. Rico) spool (of thread). — **c. de lámpara,** church lamp pulley (for raising and lowering a lamp).
carretonada, *f.* cartload, wagonload.
carretonaje, *m.* (Chile) cartage, drayage.
carretoncillo, *m.* 1. *dim. of* **carretón,** small cart. 2. toboggan, sled.
carretonero, *m.* 1. cartdriver, drayman. 2. (Col., bot.) clover.
carric, *m.* overcoat with shoulder cape, fashionable in the early 19th century.
carricera, *f.* (bot.) plume grass.
carricoche, *m.* covered cart or wagon; (derog.) decrepit carriage, rattle-trap (coll.).
carricuba, *f.* watering cart, sprinkling van.
carriego, *m.* 1. osier fishing trap. 2. large basket (for bleaching flax-yarn).
carriel, *m.* (Col., Ecuad., Ven.) muleteer's belt pouch; (C. Rica) handbag, reticule; (C. Rica, Ven.) valise, travelling-bag.
carril, *m.* 1. track, rut, groove (of a wheel); narrow road, lane. 2. furrow. 3. (ry.) rail. 4. (Chile, coll.) train. — **c. americano,** trail; **c. conductor,** (ry.) contact rail; **c. contraaguja,** stock rail; **c. de cremallera** or **dentado,** rack rail; **c. de cambio** or **aguja,** switch rail; **c. maestro,** running rail; **c. único,** monorail.
carrilada, *f.* track, rut (of a wheel).
carrilano, *m.* 1. (Chile, Arg.) railroad worker. 2. (Chile, coll.) thief, brigand.
carrilera, *f.* 1. track, rut (of wheel); lane of a highway. 2. (Cuba, ry.) track; railroad siding. 3. (Col., bldg.) crosstie timber foundation. — **c. de grúa,** crane runway; **c. de oruga,** crawler tread; **c. decauville,** narrow-gage track.
carrilete, *m.* ancient surgical instrument.
carrillada, *f.* 1. jowl fat of a hog. 2. (*pl.*) chattering of the teeth (from cold). 3. (arch.) slap in the face.
carrillera, *f.* 1. jaw (of an animal). 2. (mil.) chin strap (on helmets).
carrillo, *m.* 1. cheek. 2. hoisting-tackle, pulley. — **comer a dos carrillos,** (coll.) to eat voraciously, gorge (oneself); (coll.) to have two sources of income or several lucrative jobs; to run with the hare and hunt with the hounds.
carrilludo, da, *a.* plump-cheeked, chubby-cheeked.
carriño, *m.* (artil.) limber (of a gun carriage).
carriola, *f.* 1. trundle bed. 2. cariole, small three-wheeled carriage formerly used by royalty. 3. a long roller skate with three small wheels used by children.
carriquí, *m.* (Col., ornith.) green jay (Xanthoura yucas).
carrizada, *f.* (mar.) row of casks towed over the water.
carrizal, *m.* field of reeds.
carrizo, *m.* (bot.) ditch reed.
carro, *m.* 1. cart, wagon, truck; chariot, car; (Amer.) car, motorcar, automobile; (Amer., ry.) car, van, wagon; (Amer.) tramcar, trolley car. 2. wagonload, cartload. 3. running gear (of a car, cart, carriage). 4. (print.) bed, carriage of a press. 5. (mec.) carriage (e.g. of a typewriter). 6. (astron.) C., Ursa Major. 7. (mil.) tank. 8. (Ven.) cheat, swindler; swindle. 9. (Cuba, sl.) attractive woman. — **c. alegórico,** float (in a parade); **c. blindado,** (mil.) armored car; **c. cisterna** or **tanque,** tank car or lorry; **c. correo,** (ry.) mail car or van; **c. de asalto,** (mil.) heavy tank; **c. basculador,** dump car; **c. de basura,** garbage truck; **c. de carga,** (ry.) freight car, goods truck; **c. de combate,** (mil.) combat car; **c. de mudanzas,** removal van, moving van; **c. de oro,** fine iridescent woolen fabric; **c. de plataforma,** (ry.) flatcar; **c. de remolque,** trailer; **c. de volteo,** dump car; **c. de riego,** street sprinkler; **c. de serie,** stock car; **c. falcado,** scythed war chariot; **c. frigorífico,** refrigerator car or truck; **c. fuerte,** dray; **c. fúnebre,** hearse; **c. ganadero,** (ry.) cattle car; **C. Mayor,** (astron.) Great Bear, Big Dipper, Ursa Major (constellation); **C. Menor,** (astron.) Little Dipper, Ursa Minor (constellation); **c. remolcado,** trailer; **c.-soporte,** lathe saddle; **c. tanque,** (ry.) tank car; **c. triunfal,** triumphal car, float (used in processions, festivals); **c. urbano,** (Amer.) trolley car, streetcar; **cogerle a uno el c.,** (coll.) to be unlucky, meet with adversity; to be thwarted; **parar a alguien el c.,** to calm someone down; **tirar el c.,** to do all the work; **untar el c.,** (coll.) to bribe, grease the palm.
carrobomba, *f.* (Chile) fire engine.
carrocería, *f.* 1. carriage shop or workshop. 2. (auto.) body, coachwork. — **c. de volteo,** dump body.
carrocero, *a.* carriage, coach. —*m.* 1. carriage or coach builder. 2. (Sp.) wheel-wright.
carrocha, *f.* eggs (of insects).
carrochar, *i.v.* to lay eggs (insects).
carrocín, *m.* gig (carriage).
carromatero, *m.* drayman, carter.
carromato, *m.* 1. covered wagon. 2. (derog.) old automobile.
carrón, *m.* hodful of bricks (brick-load carried by one man).
carronada, *f.* (artil.) carronade, an obsolete type of light cannon.
carroña, *f.* carrion.
carroñar, *tr.v.* to infect with scab or mange (sheep).
carroño, ña, *a.* 1. putrefied, putrid, rotten. 2. (said of a rooster) not good for cock-fighting. 3. (Col.) cowardly. —*m.* coward.
carroñoso, sa, *a.* foul-smelling, fetid.
carroza, *f.* 1. large coach or carriage. 2. float, decorated vehicle for parades, etc. 3. (Amer.) hearse. 4. (mar.) awning.
carruaje, *m.* 1. coach, carriage. 2. caravan of coaches.
carruajero, *m.* 1. coachman. 2. (Amer.) coach builder.
carruata, *f.* (bot.) sisal, sisal hemp.
carruca, *f.* (hist.) ancient Roman carriage.
carrucha, *f.* pulley.
carrucho, *m.* (derog.) broken-down vehicle, rattle-trap.
carruco, *m.* 1. (derog.) cart. 2. small cart. 3. hodful of roof tiles.
carrujado, da, *a.* crinkled, wrinkled. —*m.* shirring, gathering (silk, velvet, etc.).
carrujo, *m.* tree top.
carrusel, *m.* carrousel, merry-go-round.
carta, *f.* 1. letter, epistle. 2. charter, constitution; ordinance, decree. 3. (law) writ. 4. chart, map. 5. playing card. 6. menu. — **a. c. cabal,** thoroughly, fully, in every respect; **c. abierta,** open letter; public royal mandate or decree; letter of credit for unlimited amount; **c. acordada,** court warning; **c. aérea, airmail letter; c. blanca,** carte blanche, full powers, free rein; **c. certificada,** certified or registered letter; **c. colorimétrica,** color chart; **c. credencial,** (dipl.) credentials; letter of credence; **c. de amparo, de encomienda, de seguro,** royal safe-conduct; **c. de ciudadanía,** naturalization papers; **c. de comisión, (law) letter of commission, warrant; c. de contramarca,** letter of marque and reprisal; **c. de crédito,** (com.) letter of credit; **c. de creencia,** credentials; **c. de derechos,** bill of rights; **c. de dote,** (law) document detailing wife's dowry; **c. de emplazamiento,** (law) summons, citation, subpoena; **c. de espera** or **moratoria,** (law) moratorium (extension granted to a debtor); **c. de examen,** diploma, license (to practice a trade or profession); **c. de fletamento,** (mar.) charter party; **c. de gracia,** (law) reversion of sale contract; **c. de guia,** safe-conduct, travel permit; **c. de hermandad,** (ecc.) title of admittance as member of a religious community; **c. de hidalguía, c. ejecutoria, c. ejecutoria de hidalguía,** letter patent of nobility; **c. de legos,** (law) writ of inhibition (whereby an ecclesiastical judge is inhibited by a high court of justice from intervening in purely lay proceedings); **c. de libre,** (law) guardian's discharge (letter of discharge of a legal guardian when a minor becomes of age); **c. del tiempo,** (meteorol.) weather chart; **c. de marca,** (mar.) letter of marque; **c. de marear,** sea chart, ocean chart; **c. de navegación,** navigation chart; **c. de pago,** receipt (for payment) **c. de pésame,** letter of condolence; **c. de porte,** (com.) way-bill; **c. de presentación, c. de recomendación,** letter of introduction; **c. de Urías,** (coll.) trick; trap; **c. de vecindad,** certificate of residence; **c. de venta,** bill of sale; **c. de vuelo,** flight plan; **c. falsa,** low playing card (in card games); **c. familiar,** personal letter; **c. forera,** judicial writ; court permission to bring suit within the period of one year; **c. geográfica,** map; **C. Magna,** (hist.) Magna Charta; **c. meteorológica,** weather chart; **c. nocturna,** night letter (telegram); **c. orden,** mandatory letter; **c. pastoral,** (ecc.) pastoral or episcopal letter; **c. pécora,** document on parchment; **c. planialtimétrica,** (top.) contour map; **c. postal,** (Amer.) post card; **c. puebla,** settlers' title deed, certificate of settlers' rights; **c. receptoria,** warrant of investigation (document granting authority for judicial investigation); **c. telegrama,** day letter (telegram); **c. urgente,** special-delivery letter; **c. verde,** green card; **c. vista,** (in some card games) a card which may be looked at before being chosen; **despachar, echar** or **poner una c.,** to post a letter; **echar las cartas,** to read one's fortune with cards; **enseñar las cartas,** (coll.) to show one's hand; **entregar uno la c.,** (coll.) to spill the beans, let the cat out of the bag; **hablen cartas y callen barbas,** (coll.) it is no use arguing against written proof; **jugar a cartas vistas,** (coll.) to act on inside information; to bet on a certainty; to put or lay one's cards on the table; **jugar a la mala c.,** (fig.) to back the wrong horse; **no ver c.,** to have a bad hand, have bad cards; **poner las cartas sobre la mesa,** (coll.) to put one's cards on the table; **tomar cartas en,** (coll.) to intervene or take part in.
cartabón, *m.* 1. drawing triangle or set square. 2. shoemaker's size stick. 3. (top.) octagonal prism used as surveyor's cross. 4. (archit.) angle formed by two slopes of a roof. — **c. con transportador,** protractor triangle; **c. dilatable,** (Sp.) bevel protractor; protractor triangle.
cartagenero, ra, *a.* of or from Cartagena, Spain or Colombia. —*m., f.* inhabitant or native of Cartagena.

cartaginense, *a., m., f.* (hist.) Carthaginian (from the ancient Phoenician city).
cartaginés, sa, *a., m., f.* Carthaginian.
Cartago, *f.* (hist.) Carthage, ancient Phoenician colony in N. Africa.
cártama, *f., var. of* **cártamo.**
cártamo, *m.* (bot.) safflower (Carthamus tinctorius).
cartapacio, *m.* 1. satchel, children's schoolbag, children's folder (for papers). 2. memorandum book, notebook, exercise book. 3. portfolio.
cartapel, *m.* paper containing useless notes or information.
cartazo, *m.* (coll.) strong letter of censure.
carteado, da, *a.* without side bets (card games).
cartear, *i.v.* to sound out by playing low cards (in card games). *—r.v.* to correspond, write letters to one another.
cartel, *m.* 1. poster; placard; handbill; alphabet chart, reading chart (in schools). 2. lampoon, pasquinade. 3. cartel, challenge to combat. 4. sardine fishing net. 5. (econ.) cartel, trust. — **tener c.,** (coll.) to have an established reputation.
cartela, *f.* 1. writing tablet, card, wooden tablet. 2. (archit.) modillion, console, bracket; iron stay for supporting a balcony. 3. (her.) billet, a rectangular emblem. — **c. atiesadora,** tilting bracket; tangery bracket.
cartelado, da, *a.* (her.) emblazoned with billets.
cartelera, *f.* 1. billboard. 2. entertainment listing (in a newspaper).
cartelero, ra, *a.* of box-office attraction (said of an artist or show). *—m.* bill-sticker, billposter, a person who posts playbills, advertisements, etc.
cartelito, *m.* sign.
cartelón, *m.* show bill, poster, placard; chart.
carteo, *m.* correspondence, exchange of letters.
cárter, *m.* (mec.) housing, casing, cover; (auto.) crank case. — **c. de engranajes,** (auto.) gearbox.
cartera, *f.* 1. pocketbook, wallet; (lady's) handbag; portfolio, letter case. 2. pocket flap. 3. portfolio, office of a cabinet minister, e.g. *ministro sin c.,* minister without portfolio. 4. (com.) portfolio (list of assets owned).
cartería, *f.* 1. postman's job. 2. (post office) sorting room.
carterista, *m.* pickpocket; purse snatcher; petty thief.
cartero, *m.* postman, mailman.
cartesianismo, *m.* (philos.) Cartesianism, philosophy of Descartes.
cartesiano, na, *a., m., f.* (philos.) Cartesian.
carteta, *f.* lansquenet (card game).
cartilágine, *m.* (anat.) cartilage.
cartilagíneo, a, *a.* (anat.) cartilaginous.
cartilaginoso, sa, *a.* (anat.) cartilaginous.
cartílago, *m.* (anat.) cartilage.
cartilla, *f.* 1. reading primer. 2. booklet, leaflet, short treatise. 3. book, card, e.g. *c. de racionamiento,* ration book, *c. de ahorros,* savings book, *c. militar,* military service book; identity card; good conduct or health certificate. 4. clergyman's certificate of ordination. 5. church calendar. — **leerle a uno la c.,** to lecture, reprimand severely; **no estar en la c.,** to be out of the ordinary; **no saber la c.,** to be an ignoramus.
cartillero, ra, *a.* (coll.) hackneyed, frequently performed (plays); ham (actors).
Cartismo, *m.* (hist.) Chartism, the doctrines of a group of 19th century English reformers.
Cartista, *m., f.* (hist.) Chartist.
cartivana, *f.* (bkb.) hinge.
cartografía, *f.* cartography, chartography, map making; set of maps. — **c. aérea,** aerial photographic surveying, airplane mapping.
cartografiar, *tr.v.* to survey, make maps.
cartográfico, ca, *a.* cartographic, cartographical.
cartógrafo, *m.* map maker, cartographer or chartographer.
cartograma, *m.* cartogram, a map giving graphical statistics.
cartolas, *f. (pl.) var. of* **artolas.**
cartomancia, *f.* cartomancy, fortune telling by cards.
cartomántico, ca, *a.* pertaining to cartomancy. *—m., f.* fortune teller, card reader.
cartometría, *f.* the measuring of distances on maps.
cartométrico, ca, *a.* pertaining to the measuring of distances on maps.
cartómetro, *m.* curvimeter, chartometer (instrument for measuring traced lines on charts or maps).
cartón, *m.* 1. cardboard, pasteboard; carton, cardboard box. 2. metal ornament imitating leaves. 3. (p.) cartoon (design or study which serves as a model for transferring or copying). 4. (archit.) brace, bracket, corbel. — **c. de paja,** strawboard; **c. piedra,** papier-mâché; **c. yeso,** plasterboard.
cartonaje, *m.* cardboard articles or products.
cartoné, *m.* **en c.,** (bkb.) bound in hard covers.
cartonería, *f.* cardboard factory or shop.
cartonero, ra, *a.* cardboard. *—m., f.* cardboard or pasteboard-maker or seller.
cartoteca, *f.* map file.
cartuchera, *f.* cartridge box or pouch; cartridge belt.
cartucho, *m.* 1. cartridge. 2. roll of coins. 3. paper cone. 4. (Cuba) brown paper bag. — **c. de dinamita,** dynamite stick; **c. de perdigones,** trick, catchpenny; **quemar uno el último c.,** (coll.) to use up one's last resource, play one's last trick.
cartuja, *f.* 1. (rel.) Carthusian convent or monastery, charterhouse. 2. (rel.) **C.,** Carthusian Order.
cartujano, na, *a.* (rel.) Carthusian. *—m.* Carthusian, Carthusian monk.
cartujo, *m.* 1. (rel.) Carthusian, Carthusian monk. 2. (coll.) recluse, uncommunicative person.
cartulario, *m.* chartulary (register book of title deeds or charters; archivist).
cartulina, *f.* bristol board; fine, smooth cardboard. — **c. común,** millboard; **c. de porcelana,** coated cardboard.
cartusana, *f.* rickrack, wavy-edged braid.
caruata, *f.* (Ven., bot.) agave.
carúncula, *f.* (anat., zool.) caruncle. — **c. lagrimal,** (anat.) lachrymal caruncle.
carunculado, da, *a.* (anat.) carunculated, carunculate.
caruncular, *a.* (anat.) caruncular, carunculate.
carurú, *m.* (bot.) pigweed (used for making bleach).
caruto, *m.* (bot.) caruto, genipap.
carvajal, *m.* oak grove or wood.
carvajo, *m.* (bot.) oak tree.
carvallar, *m., var. of* **carvajal.**
carvalledo, *m., var. of* **carvajal.**
carvallo, *m.* (bot.) oak tree.
carvi, *m.* caraway seed.
cas, *f.* house (used only in popular speech).
casa, *f.* 1. house, dwelling; home. 2. house, family, household. 3. house, family, line, dynasty. 4. business establishment or firm. 5. square (on the chess or draught board). 6. semi-circle (in backgammon). 7. balk line (in billiards). 8. estate, property. — **a la c.,** home, e.g. *regresó a la c.,* he went home; **c. abierta,** house and office combined; open-fronted shop or store; **C. Blanca,** White House; **c. celeste,** (astrol.) house, each one of the twelve divisions of the celestial arch; **c. central,** home or central office; **c. consistorial,** town or city hall; **c. cuna,** children's home; **c. de aseo,** day hostel; **c. de banca, bank or banking house; c. de baños,** bathhouse, public baths; **c. de beneficencia,** children's home; **c. de bombas,** pump house; **c. de calderas,** boilerhouse; **c. de cambio,** money exchange office; **c. de campo,** country house; **c. de citas,** brothel; house of assignation; **c. de comercio,** business firm; **c. de comidas,** eatery, modest restaurant, chophouse; **c. de conversación,** 17th century gambling house or casino; **c. de corrección,** reformatory, reform school; **c. de correos,** post office; **c. de departamentos,** apartment house; **c. de Dios,** house of God, church; **c. de distribución,** (elec.) switch house; **c. de empeños,** pawnshop; **c. de expósitos,** foundling home; **c. de huéspedes,** (arch.) boarding house; **c. de juego,** gambling house; **c. de labor** or **de labranza,** farmhouse; **c. de locos** or **orates,** madhouse, insane asylum; (coll.) madhouse, noisy, riotous house; **c. del Señor,** house of God, church; **c. de mancebía,** brothel; **c. de máquinas,** engine room; **c. de maternidad,** maternity hospital; **c. de moneda,** mint; **c. de muñecas,** doll house; **c. de placer,** summer or holiday house; **c. de postas,** post house or inn; **c. de préstamos,** pawnshop; **c. de pupilos,** boarding house for students; **c. de salud,** clinic, private hospital; **c. de socorro,** first aid post or hospital; **c. de tía,** (coll.) jail; **c. de tócame Roque,** (theat.) very full and badly run house; **c. de tolerancia,** brothel; **c. de trueno,** rowdy house; **c. de vecindad,** tenement building; **c. discográfica,** record company; **c. editorial,** publishing firm; **c. embrujada,** haunted house; **c. fuerte,** fortress; rich or powerful family; **c. matriz,** main office; **c. modelo,** model home, sample house (of a development); **c. mortuoria,** house where someone has recently died; **c. pública,** brothel; **c. real,** royal palace; royal family, royal house; **c. robada,** poorly furnished house; **c. rodante,** mobile home, trailer; caravan; **c. santa,** house of the Holy Sepulchre in Jerusalem; **c. solar,** solar home; **c. solariega,** ancestral home, manor house; **caérsele a uno la c. encima,** (coll.) to be crushed or overwhelmed with trouble; **echar la c. por la ventana,** (coll.) to spend lavishly, blow one's money; **empezar la c. por el tejado,** to put the cart before the horse; **en c.,** at home; **estar de c.,** to be simply or plainly dressed; **estrenar la c.,** to have a housewarming; **levantar la c.,** (coll.) to move, move house; **paga cuatrocientas pesetas de casa,** she pays four hundred pesetas rent; **poner c.,** to make a home, set up house; **ser de la c.,** to be like one of the family; **ser uno de su c.,** to be a homebody.
casabe, *m.* 1. (cul.) cassava bread. 2. (ichth.) amberfish.
casabillo, *m.* (Cuba) white mole (on the skin).
casaca, *f.* 1. jacket; long coat. 2. (coll.) matrimony, wedding. — **volver la c.,** to be a turncoat, change sides; **cambia-casaca,** turncoat.
casación, *f.* (law) cassation, abrogation, annulment.
casacón, *m.* greatcoat, overcoat.
casadero, ra, *a.* marriageable; of marriageable age.
casado, da, *past part. of* **casar.** *—m., f.* married person. *—m.* (print.) imposition (folding the pages so that the numbers run consecutively).
casaisaco, *m.* (Cuba, bot.) bromeliad.
casal, *m.* 1. country house. 2. (Arg., Urug.) pair (of animals, male and female).
casalicio, *m.* house, building.

casamata, *f.* (mil.) casemate, an armored enclosure with openings for guns.
casamentero, ra, *a.* matchmaking. —*m., f.* matchmaker, marriage broker.
casamiento, *m.* marriage, wedding.
casampulga, *f.* (Salv., Hond.) poisonous spider with a red abdomen.
Casandra, *f.* 1. (myth.) Cassandra, daughter of Hecuba, to whom Apollo gave prophetic power. 2. a person whose warnings are ignored. 3. (astron.) asteroid.
casapuerta, *f.* porch; entrance hall; vestibule.
casaquilla, *f.* short jacket.
casar, *m.* hamlet, small cluster of houses.
casar, *tr.v.* (law) to abrogate, rescind, annul, cancel; to quash (a sentence).
casar, *r.v.* to marry, get married; **antes que te cases, mira lo que haces,** look before you leap; **casarse con,** to get married to; **casarse en segundas nupcias,** to remarry. —*tr.v.* 1. to marry, join in wedlock; (coll.) to marry off (a daughter). 2. to match (colors, furniture, etc.). —*i.v.* 1. to marry. 2. to match; **c. con,** to get married to.
casariego, ga, *a., var. of* **casero, ra.**
casarón, *m., aug. of* **casa,** large house; a big dilapidated house.
casatienda, *f.* store or shop and house combined.
casbah, *f.* casbah, kasbah, in N. Africa, a fortress; the old quarter of a city.
casca, *f.* 1. bagasse of pressed grapes. 2. tanning bark. 3. cake made of marzipan and lemon or sweet potato with coating of sugar. 4. peel, rind, shell.
cascabel, *m.* 1. small bell, sleigh bell, jingle bell, hawk bell. 2. cascabel, a round projection behind the breech of a muzzle-loading cannon. — **de c. gordo,** cheap, trashy (literary or artistic work); **poner el c. al gato,** to bell the cat, do a risky or daring deed; **ser alegre como un c.,** to be happy as a lark; **serpiente de c.,** rattlesnake.
cascabela, *f.* (C. Rica, zool.) rattlesnake.
cascabelada, *f.* 1. noisy festival. 2. (coll.), scatterbrained remark or action.
cascabelear, *tr.v.* 1. (coll.) to induce, encourage, egg on, goad, stir up (into doing something). —*i.v.* 1. to jingle (bells). 2. to act in a scatterbrained manner.
cascabelero, ra, *a.* (coll.) scatterbrained, featherbrained. —*m.* 1. baby's rattle. 2. scatterbrain.
cascabelillo, *m. dim. of* **cascabel, small** round dark purple plum.
cascabillo, *m.* 1. small bell. 2. husk (of wheat or barley). 3. acorn cup.
cascaciruelas, *m., f.* (coll.) contemptible, good-for-nothing person.
cascada, *f.* cascade, waterfall; **en c.,** (elec.) cascade, e.g. *acoplamiento* or *conexión en c.,* (elec.) cascade rectifier circuit, *amplificación en c.,* cascade amplification, *tubo de rayos X en c.,* (elec.) cascade tube. —*a.* flat, weak, broken (voice).
cascado, da, *past part. of* **cascar.** —*a.* (coll.) worn-out, spent, exhausted.
cascadura, *f.* breaking, cracking, splitting; broken shell or pieces.
cascajal, *m., var. of* **cascajar.**
cascajar, *m.* 1. gravel pit. 2. dump for grape bagasse.
cascajera, *f.* gravelly, shingly or rubbly ground.
cascajero, *m.* 1. (Col.) gravel pit. 2. (Col.) abandoned mine.
cascajo, *m.* 1. gravel, shingle. 2. nuts (almonds, walnuts, etc.). 3. (coll.) broken piece of crockery or glassware; junk, rubbish; discarded old furniture. 4. (coll.) copper coin. — **estar hecho un c.,** to be worn out, be an old wreck.
cascajoso, sa, *a.* gravelly, shingly.
cascalbo, *a.* **pino c.,** (bot.) Austrian pine (Pinus nigra); **trigo c.,** a sub-variety of durum wheat (Triticum durum).
cascamajar, *tr.v.* to break or crush; to crack by pounding.
cascamiento, *m.* breaking, cracking, crushing, splitting.
cascante, *a.* breaking, cracking, splitting.
cascanueces, *m.* 1. nutcracker. 2. (ornith.) nutcracker, 3. (coll.) madcap, harebrained young man.
cascapiñones, *m.* pine-nut cracker (implement); person who shells pine nuts.
cascar, *(ref. 50) tr.v.* 1. to break, crack, split. 2. (coll.) to hit, beat, pummel. 3. (coll.) to break, ruin (one's health). —*r.v.* 1. to break, crack, split. 2. to fall ill. —*i.v.* (coll.) to chatter, prattle.
cáscara, *f.* shell (of nuts or eggs); peel, skin, rind (of fruit); rind (of cheese); husk, hull (of grains); (Amer.) bark (trees). — **c. sagrada,** (pharm.) cascara sagrada, a laxative; **¡cáscaras!** good heavens!; **ser de c. amarga,** (coll.) to be a troublemaker.
cascarada, *f.* (sl.) quarrel, uproar.
cascarañado, da, *a.* (Cuba, P. Rico) pockmarked.
cascarazo, *m.* 1. (P. Rico, Col.) heavy blow. 2. (P. Rico) large gulp or drink of liquor.
cascarela, *f.* lansquenet (card game).
cascarilla, *f. dim. of* **cáscara.** — 1. (pharm.) cascarilla, cascarilla bark, sweetwood bark; cinchona, Jesuit's bark, Peruvian bark. 2. husk. 3. lamina, thin layer, foil (of metal). 4. powdered eggshell formerly used as a cosmetic. 5. toasted cacao husk used for making hot drinks.
cascarillal, *m.* (Peru) cinchona (tree) grove or plantation.
cascarillero, ra, *m., f.* gatherer or vendor of cinchona. —*m.* cinchona tree.
cascarillina, *f.* (chem.) cinchonine, the bitter principle of cinchona.
cascarillo, *m.* (bot., S. Amer.) cinchona tree, medicinal tree from which cascarilla bark and quinine are obtained.
cascarón, *m.* 1. *aug. of* **cáscara.** 2. thick shell, peel. or rind; eggshell (esp. the broken shell). 3. trick in lansquenet (card game). 4. (archit.) calotte, a vault whose surface covers one quarter of the area of a sphere. 5. (Urug.) kind of cork oak. — **aún no haber salido del c.,** to be wet behind the ears, be inexperienced; **c. de nuez,** cockleshell, boat too small for its purpose.
cascarrabias, *m., f.* (coll.) grouch, crab, sourpuss, bad-tempered person.
cascarria, *f.* spatter of mud (on clothing).
cascarrina, *f., var. of* **granizo.**
cascarrojas, *m. pl.* insects, worms, vermin (plaguing ships).
cascarrón, na, *a.* (coll.) rough, harsh, uncouth. —*m.* (mar.) strong wind (necessitating shortening of sail).
cascarudo, da, *a.* thick-shelled, thick-skinned, having a thick peel or rind.
cascaruleta, *f.* 1. (bot.) type of Andalusian wheat. 2. (coll.) rattling of teeth.
casco, *m.* 1. helmet, headpiece. 2. hoof. 3. (mar.) hull; hulk (of old ship). 4. cask, barrel, keg, bottle. 5. fleshy layers (of onion). 6. skull, cranium; (*pl.*) cow's head, sheep's head; (*pl.*) (coll.) head (of a person). 7. shard, potsherd, fragment of broken glass or pottery. 8. (med.) ringworm cap. 9. crown (of hat). 10. saddletree. 11. area, limits, e.g. *dentro del c. de Londres,* within the London area. 12. (Amer.) slice (of fruit) e.g. *c. de guayaba,* (cul.) guava shell. 13. (Phil. I.) casco, flat-bottomed boat. — **abajar el c.,** (vet.) to pare down the hoof; **alegre** or **ligero de cascos,** (coll.) harebrained, featherbrained, flighty; **c. de buzo,** diver's helmet; **c. de cartucho,** cartridge case; **c. de casa,** skeleton or shell of a building; **c. de población,** buildings of a town; **c. de soldador,** welder's helmet; **cortar a c.,** to prune right back; **lavar el c.** or **los cascos a,** (coll.) to flatter, soft-soap (coll.); **levantar de cascos a,** (coll.) to egg on, goad on (with false hopes); **metérsele a uno en los cascos alguna idea,** to get something into one's head; **romper a uno el c.,** to break someone's head, crown someone (coll.); to bore, tire (with irrelevant chatter); **romperse uno los cascos,** (coll.) to beat one's brains out (studying or trying to find something out); **sentar los cascos,** to settle down, become more sensible and prudent.
cascol, *m.* resin of a Guianan tree (used in the manufacture of black sealing-wax).
cascote, *m.* debris, rubble.
cascudo, da, *a.* big-hoofed (animal).
cascué, *m.* (ichth.) a species of sturgeon which inhabits the Nile.
caseación, *f.* curdling, caseation (of milk).
caseico, ca, *a.* caseic; **ácido c.,** (chem.) caseic acid.
caseificación, *f.* caseation, conversion into cheese; (med.) caseation, necrosis.
caseificar, *(ref. 50) tr.v.* to casefy, transform into casein (milk).
caseifique, caseifiqué, *ref.* **caseificar.**
caseína, *f.* (chem.) casein, a milk protein.
caseinógeno, *m.* (biochem.) caseinogen, a milk protein.
cáseo, a, *a,* caseous; cheesy. —*m.* curd.
caseosa, *f.* (biochem.) caseose, a by-product of digestion.
caseoso, sa, *a.* caseous; cheesy, cheeselike.
caseramente, *adv.* plainly, informally, without ceremony.
casería, *f.* 1. country house and its outbuildings. 2. housekeeping. 3. (Chile) customers.
caserillo, *m.* homespun (cloth).
caserío, *m.* 1. hamlet, group of houses; country house and its outbuildings. 2. (P. Rico) housing project.
caserna, *f.* (mil.) bomb-proof bunker.
casero, ra, *a.* home-loving, simple, homely, homespun (people); family-like, homely, e.g. *reunión c.,* a family or informal gathering; house, e.g. *mi ropa c.,* my house clothes; homemade; domestic (animals); **estar muy c. (una mujer),** to be wearing plain house clothes (a woman). —*m., f.* 1. landlord, landlady. 2. caretaker. 3. (Amer.) customer. 4. (Amer.) stall-keeper, shopkeeper.
caserón, *m. aug. of* **casa,** mansion; large broken down house.
caseta, *f.* 1. beach-hut, beach cabin. 2. sentry box. 3. kennel. 4. kiosk (at a fair); booth. 5. small house, hut. — **c. de derrota,** (mar.) chart room, chart house; **c. de peaje,** tollbooth; **c. telefónica,** telephone booth.
casetón, *m.* (archit.) caisson, coffer (of ceiling).
casi, *adv.* almost, nearly, close to; **c. que** or **c. c.,** very nearly, e.g. *c. c. me caigo,* I almost fell; **c. nada,** hardly or scarcely anything; **c. nunca,** hardly or scarcely ever.
casia, *f.* (bot.) cassia.
casicontrato, *m.* (law) quasi-contract.
casida, *f.* (poet.) qasida, Arabian or Persian love poem.
casidulina, *f.* (zool.) cassidulina, microscopic sub-order of sea urchins.
casilla, *f.* 1. lodge, cabin (game keeper's); hut (watchman's); box (of keeper or sentry); (theat.) box-office. 2. post office box; pigeon-hole (for

letters, documents). 3. square (of chessboard). 4. box, square (of form); square, column (of ruled paper). 5. compartment, division (of a box). 6. (Cuba) bird trap. 7. (Ecuad.) toilet, water closet. 8. locker; 9. (Arg.) bathhouse. 10. (Cuba) boxcar. 11. (coll.) lockup, jail. **c. postal,** (Amer.) P.O. box; **c. telefónica,** telephone booth or box; **sacar a uno de sus casillas,** (coll.) to change a person's way of living; to infuriate someone; **salir uno de sus casillas,** (coll.) to lose one's temper, blow one's top, fly off the handle.

casiller, *m.* (arch.) a palace attendant.

casillero, *m.* 1. shelf or desk with pigeonholes. 2. filing cabinet. 3. (sport.) scoreboard.

casimba, *f.* (Amer.) well; spring.

casimir, *m.* (tex.) cashmere, cassimere, fine woolen cloth.

casimiro, ra, *a.* (Amer., coll.) one-eyed, with one eye (person); cross-eyed, squint-eyed.

casimpulga, *f.* (Nic.) a poisonous spider with short legs and a red abdomen.

casina, *f.* 1. yaupon, a species of holly (Ilex vomitoria). 2. drink made from the leaves of this shrub as a substitute for tea.

casineta, *f.* (Amer.) woolen cloth used for lining.

casinete, *m.* (Arg., Chile, Hond.) cashmere of inferior quality; (Ecuad., Ven.) cheap inferior cloth.

casinita, *f.* (min.) hyalophane, baryta feldspar.

casino, *m.* casino, club, clubhouse; public resort; **c. de juego,** gambling casino; **c. militar,** army club.

Casio, *m.* (hist.) Cassius, Roman general who conspired against Caesar. — **púrpura de** C., purple of Cassius, a purple pigment.

Casiopea, *f.* 1. (myth.) Cassiopeia, the wife of Cepheus and mother of Andromeda. 2. (astron.) Cassiopeia, a northern constellation.

casis, *f.* 1. (bot.) black currant, cassis (Ribes nigrum). 2. (zool.) queen conch.

casitéridos, *m., pl.* (chem.) group of elements comprising tin, antimony, zinc and cadmium.

casiterita, *f.* (min.) cassiterite.

casmodia, *f.* (med.) spasmodic yawning.

casné, *m.* (Mex.) silk muffler.

caso, *m.* 1. case, event, circumstance; happening, occasion. 2. case, affair, question. 3., (med., gram., law) case. — **a c. hecho,** deliberately; on purpose; assured of success; **caer uno en mal c.,** (coll.) to incur disapproval; fall into disrepute; **c. de conciencia,** question of conscience; **c. de honra,** question of honor; **c. de menos valer,** discrediting action; **c. de prueba,** (law) test case; **c. fortuito,** act of God; **c. perdido,** hopeless case; **c. que +** *subj.*, **dado el c. que +** *subj.*, if + *subj.*, e.g. *dado el c. que venga,* if he should come, should he come; **de c. pensado,** on purpose, deliberately; **del c.,** appropriate, pertinent, e.g. *tomar las medidas del c.,* to take the appropriate measures; **en c. de,** in the event of, in the case of; **en c. de que,** see **dado el c. que; en el mejor** or **peor de los casos,** at best or worst; **en todo c.,** in any cse, at any rate, anyway, anyhow; **estar uno en el c.,** to be familiar with the case (fact or subject), be in the know; **hablar al c.,** to speak pertinently or to the point; **hacer al c.,** to bear on the subject, (coll.) to be pertinent; to be suitable; **hacer c. a uno,** to take notice of, heed; **hacer c. omiso de,** to ignore, pay no attention to, take no notice of; **no venir al c.,** to be irrelevant, have nothing to do with the question; **poner por c.,** to take as an example; **ser c. negado,** (coll.) to be almost an impossibility; **ser del c.,** (coll.) to be pertinent or to the point; **vamos al c.,** (coll.) let us come to the point, let's get down to brass tacks; **venir al c.,** to bear on the subject, be pertinent, be relevant; **verse en el c. de,** to find oneself obliged to.

casón, *m. aug. of* **casa,** large house.

casona, *f.* a large house; the house of a feudal lord.

casorio, *m.* (coll.) hasty marriage; simple or unostentatious wedding.

caspa, *f.* 1. dandruff, scurf. 2. (med.) **scurf** (scales). 3. patina (of copper).

caspaletear, *i.v.* (Col.) to get furious, get impatient, lose patience.

caspera, *f.* fine tooth comb.

caspete, *m.* (Col.) stew; daily ration, chow (sl.).

caspicias, *f. pl.* (coll.) leftovers; dregs.

caspio, pia, *a.* Caspian. —*m.* C., Caspian, Caspian Sea.

caspiroleta, *f.* (Ecuad., Chile, Peru) hot punch made of milk, eggs, spirits, cinnamon and sugar.

¡cáspita! *interj.* wow! gee! holy cow! (expressing surprise, befuddlement or admiration.)

casposo, sa, *a.* scurfy, full of dandruff.

casque, casqué, *ref.* **cascar.**

casquería, *f.* 1. tripe shop. 2. tinware.

casquero, *m.* 1. tripe vendor. 2. place where pine kernels are cracked (to be used for confectionery).

casquetada, *f.* (rare) *var. of* **calaverada.**

casquetazo, *m.* butt or blow with the head.

casquete, *m.* 1. helmet, casque; calotte, skull cap, cap. 2. (med.) ringworm cap. 3. wiglet. — **c. esférico,** (geom.) one-base spherical segment; **c. de la válvula,** (auto.) valve bonnet.

casquiacopado, da, *a.* cup-hoofed (horse).

casquiblando, da, *a.* soft-hoofed (horse).

casquiderramado, da, *a.* flat-hoofed, broad-hoofed (horse).

casquijo, *m.* gravel, ballast, broken stone.

casquilucio, cia, *a., var. of* **casquivano.**

casquilla, *f.* 1. (beekeeping) the covering of queen bee cells. 2. (*pl.*) silver weights used by jewelers.

casquillo, *m.* 1. ferrule, socket, sleeve (ring or cap around tool handle to prevent splitting). 2. iron arrowhead. 3. metal part of cardboard cartridge case; empty cartridge (of a bullet). 4. (Peru, Ven.) horseshoe. 5. (Hond.) hat lining. 6. pipe cap. 7. (min.) blasting cap, exploder. — **c. de bayoneta,** bayonet-socket base (lamp); **c. escariador,** reaming shell (drill); **c. partido,** (mec.) split bushing.

casquimuleño, na, *a.* (horse) having small cylindrical hoofs like a mule.

casquín, *m.* (C. Amer.) blow on the head.

casquite, *a.* (Ven.) sourish (drink); (fig.) sour-tempered, ill-tempered.

casquivano, na, *a.* (coll.) feather-brained, scatter-brained.

cassette (*or* **cassete**), 1. cassette, audio cassette; **en c.,** taped, recorded, audiotaped. 2. (Esp.) cassette player. 3. (Esp.) cassette recorder.

casta, *f.* breed (of animals), lineage (of persons); caste (of society); ilk, kind, class (of things). — **cruzar las castas,** to cross-breed; **de c. le viene al galgo,** like father, like son.

castálidas, *f. pl.* (myth.) Castalides, the Muses.

castalio, lia, *a.* Castalian, pertaining to the Muses.

castamente, *adv.* chastely, modestly.

castaña, *f.* 1. chestnut (fruit). 2. demijohn, carboy, round-shaped bottle. 3. bun, chignon (hair arrangement). 4. (Cuba) journal bearing of the roller of a sugar cane mill. 5. (Mex.) keg, small barrel. — **c. apilada, pilonga, maya,** dried chestnut; **c. regoldana,** wild chestnut; **dar a uno la c.,** to play a trick on; **dar a uno para castañas,** to threaten someone with punishment; **sacar las castañas del fuego,** to pull the chestnuts out of the fire.

castañal, *m., var. of* **castañar.**

castañar, *m.* grove of chestnut trees.

castañeda, *f., var. of* **castañar.**

castañero, ra, *m., f.* chestnut vendor. —*m.* (ornith.) turtle dove (Streptopelia turtur).

castañeta, *f.* 1. (mus.) castanet. 2. finger snap. 3. (ichth.) castagnole, pomfret (Brama, raii). 4. bow (on bullfighter's pigtail).

castañetada, *f., var. of* **castañetazo.**

castañetazo, *m.* clack of a castanet, snap (sound of fingersnap); sound of a chestnut bursting in the fire; cracking (of one's joints).

castañeteado, *m.* clacking of castanet.

castañetear, *i.v.* 1. to play the castanets. 2. to chatter (teeth). 3. to crack (the knees, when walking). 4. to squawk (male partridge). —*tr.v.* to click (the fingers).

castañeteo, *m.* clacking (of castanets); chattering (of the teeth); cracking (of the knees).

castaño, ña, *a.* chestnut, brown or hazel (colored). —*m.* (bot.) chestnut (tree and wood); chestnut (color). — **c. de Indias,** (bot.) horse chestnut (Aesculus hippocastanum); **c. regoldano,** wild chestnut (Castanopsis philippinensis); **pasar de c. obscuro,** (coll.) to be too much, go too far, be the limit.

castañola, *f.* (ichth.) castagnole, pomfret (Brama raii).

castañuela, *f.* 1. castanet. 2. (bot.) species of sedge (Cyperus rotundus). — **estar uno como unas castañuelas,** (coll.) to be in a very gay mood.

castañuelo, la, *a.* chestnut (color of horse).

castellán, *m.* castellan, governor or warden of a castle or fort.

castellana, *f.* 1. chatelaine (the mistress of a castle; the wife of a castellan). 2. woman native of Castile, Spain. 3. (poet.) stanza of four octosyllabic verses. — **c. de oro,** an old Spanish coin.

castellanamente, *adv.* in the Castilian manner; (coll.) properly, nobly.

castellanía, *f.* independent district having its own laws.

castellanice, castellanicé, *ref.* **castellanizar.**

castellanismo, *m.* Castilianism, word or idiom peculiar to Castile.

castellanizar, (*ref.* 53) *tr.v.* to hispanicize, adapt (a foreign word) to Spanish usage.

castellano, na, *a.* Castilian, of or pertaining to the province of Castile, Sp.; **a la castellana,** in the Castilian fashion; **gallina castellana,** (Chile) grey chicken with red specks. —*m.* 1. Castilian, native of Castile. 2. Spanish, Castilian (the standard form of the Spanish language). 3. an old Spanish gold coin. 4. pikeman, man-at-arms. 5. castellan, warden of a castle.

castellar, *m.* (bot.) St. John's wort.

casticidad, *f.* purity (of language).

casticismo, *m.* purity, purism (of language, national customs, fashions, etc.).

casticista, *m.* purist (language).

castidad, *f.* chastity; celibacy.

castigación, *f., var. of* **castigo.**

castigadera, *f.* thong for tying the clapper of a bell.

castigador, ra, *a.* 1. punishing, punitive, chastising. 2. (coll.) coquettish, philandering. —*m., f.* punisher, chastiser. —*m.* (coll.) ladykiller. —*f.* vamp, flirt.

castigar, (*ref.* 51) *tr.v.* 1. to punish, chastise, castigate; to mortify (the flesh). 2. to polish, correct (style). 3. (fig.) to reduce, cut down (expenses, a budget, etc.). 4. (fig.) to flirt; to tease (sexually).

castigo, *m.* 1. punishment, chastisement; penalty. 2. (fig.) correction, polishing (of writings or proofs). — **c. corporal,** corporal punishment; **ser de c. una cosa,** to be arduous or hard (to accomplish or do).

castigue, castigué, *ref.* **castigar.**
castila, (Phil. I.) Spanish (person). —*m., f.* Spaniard. —*m.* Spanish (language).
Castilla, *f.* Castile, a province of Spain; **¡Ancha Castilla!** full steam ahead!
castilla, *f.* (text., Amer.) wool coating.
castillado, da, *a.* (her.) castellated, provided or dotted with castles (a shield).
castillaje, *m.* (arch.) toll paid to cross the domain of a castle.
castillejo, *m.* 1. *dim. of* **castillo,** small castle. 2. go-cart, walker (for teaching children to walk). 3. (bldg.) scaffolding, trestlework. 4. children's game, played with nuts, entailing knocking down a pile of nuts. 5. frame beam (of a hand loom).
castillería, *f.* (arch.) toll paid to cross the domain of a castle.
castillete, *m.* 1. *dim. of* **castillo,** small castle. 2. scaffold; trestle bent. 3. frame horse; gallows frame. 4. oil derrick. 5. (min.) headframe. — **c. de transmisión,** transmission tower.
castillo, *m.* 1. castle. 2. load (of a cart). 3. (mar.) forecastle; forecastle deck. — **c. de popa,** (mar.) poop deck; **c. de proa,** (mar.) foredeck; **castillos en el aire,** (coll.) castles in the air or in Spain; **castillos de naipes,** house of cards; **hacer castillos en el aire,** (coll.) to build castles in the air; **hacer uno castillos de naipes,** to build on sand or on a flimsy foundation.
castilluelo, *m. dim. of* **castillo,** small castle.
castina, *f.* (min.) flux.
castizamente, *adv.* with purity (of style, choice of words, etc.).
castizo, za, *a.* 1. of good breed. 2. pure (style); typical (customs, manners). 3. very prolific. —*m., f.* (Mex.) quadroon, offspring of a mestizo and a Spaniard.
casto, ta, *a.* pure, chaste, virginal.
castor, *m.* 1. (zool.) beaver. 2. beaver skin or pelt; beaver cloth, castor.
Cástor, *m.* (astron., myth.) Castor, one of the stars of the constellation Gemini. — **C. y Pólux,** Castor and Pollux; St. Elmo's fire; (astron.) Gemini (the constellation).
castora, *f.* high-crowned hat.
castorcillo, *m.* serge, a twilled worsted fabric.
castoreño, *a.* felt, beaverskin (hat).
castóreo, *m.* (pharm.) castoreum, castor oil.
castorina, *f.* 1. castor, heavy type of broadcloth. 2. (chem.) castorin, oil extracted from castoreum.
castra, *f.* 1. castration, gelding, emasculation. 2. (hort.) pruning. 3. extraction of honeycombs. 4. season when animals are castrated. 5. pruning season.
castración, *f.* 1. castration, gelding, emasculation. 2. (hort.) pruning. 3. extraction of honeycombs.
castradera, *f.* iron tool for extracting honeycombs.
castrado, *m.* eunuch; gelding.
castrador, *m.* 1. castrator, gelder. 2. gelder's whistle.
castradura, *f.* 1. castration. 2. scar left by castration.
castrametación, *f.* (mil.) castrametation, laying out of a military camp.
castrapuercas, *m.* gelder's whistle.
castrapuercos, *m., var. of* **castrapuercas.**
castrar, *tr.v.* 1. to castrate, geld, spay. 2. to dry (wounds). 3. (hort.) to prune. 4. to extract honeycombs. 5. to thin out (grain field). 6. (fig.) to weaken, enervate. —*r.v.* to dry up (wounds).
castrazón, *f.* extraction of honeycombs; season for the extraction of honeycombs.
castrense, *a.* pertaining or relative to the military.
castro, *m.* 1. a children's game similar to hopscotch. 2. (Sp.) castle; hillock with castle in ruins. 3. *var. of* **castrazón.**
castrón, *m.* castrated goat; (Cuba) castrated pig.
cástula, *f.* (hist.) long tunic worn by Roman women.
casual, *a.* 1. accidental, fortuitous, chance. 2. casual. 3. occasional.
casualidad, *f.* chance; coincidence; fortuity. — **dar** la **c. que,** to just happen, e.g. *da la c. que,* it just happens that; **por c.,** by chance.
casualismo, *m.* (philos.) casualism, the doctrine that attributes all events to chance.
casualista, *m., f.* (philos.) casualist, an expounder of casualism.
casualmente, *adv.* 1. by chance, accidentally, coincidentally. 2. (Amer.) precisely, exactly; e.g. *c. ahora mismo,* precisely at this moment.
casuáridos, *m.* (ornith.) Casuaridae, family of the cassowaries.
casuarina, *f.* (bot.) casuarina, beef-wood, she-oak.
casuario, *m.* (ornith.) cassowary.
casuca, *f., var. of* **casucha.**
casucha, *f.* (derog.) hut, hovel, decrepit cottage.
casucho, *m., var. of* **casucha.**
casuismo, *m.* (philos., theol.) casuistry, casuistic doctrine.
casuista, *a.* (philos., theol.) casuistic, casuistical. —*m., f.* casuist.
casuística, *f.* (theol., philos.) casuistry, doctrine dealing with conscience and moral right.
casuístico, ca, *a.* (theol., philos.) casuistical, casuistic.
casulla, *f.* 1. (ecc.) chasuble. 2. (Hond.) grain of rice with husk.
casullero, *m.* chasuble-maker, vestmentmaker.
cata, *f.* 1. sampling, tasting, trying; sample. 2. (Col., Mex., min.) trial pit. 3. (Col.) hidden or secret thing. 4. prospecting, exploration (of ground for mining). 5. (Amer., ornith.) parrot, parakeet. — **dar c.,** to examine, look at; to search for; **darse c. de (una cosa),** to see, notice, become aware of (something).
catabólico, ca, *a.* (biol.) catabolic.
catabolismo, *m.* (biol.) catabolism.
catabre, *m.* (Col.) gourd used to carry seed grain.
catabro, *m.* (Col.), *var. of* **catabre.**
catacaldos, *m., f.* (col.) dabbler, dilettante; fickle person who takes on many things but never finishes them; busybody, meddler.
cataclástico, *a.* (geol.) cataclastic.
cataclismo, *m.* cataclysm; catastrophe.
catacresis, *f.* (rhet.) catachresis.
catacumbas, *f.* (*pl.*) catacombs.
catacústica, *f.* (phys.) catacoustics.
catadióptrico, ca, *a.* (phys.) catadioptric.
catador, ra, *m., f.* taster, sampler. —*f.* earth auger, any tool for exploring the ground.
catádromo, ma, *a.* (ichth.) catadromous.
catadura, *f.* 1. tasting, sampling; trying. 2. (coll.) appearance, face, aspect, e.g. *un tipo de mala c.,* mean-looking fellow.
catafalco, *m.* 1. catafalque. 2. scaffold, platform.
cataforesis, *f.* (chem.) cataphoresis.
catajarria, *f.* (Ven.) series, string.
catalán, na, *a., m., f.* Catalan, Catalonian, from the Spanish region of Catalonia. —*m.* Catalan (language).
catalanismo, *m.* 1. political party and doctrine favoring Catalonian autonomy. 2. word or idiom peculiar to the Catalan language.
catalanista, *m., f.* (Sp.) Catalanist, a supporter of Catalonian autonomy.
catalasa, *f.* (chem.) catalase.
cataldo, *m.* (mar.) bonnet of jib or foresail.
cataléctico, *a.* (poet.) catalectic.
catalecto, *m.* (poet.) catalectic verse.
catalejo, *m.* (opt.) telescope; spyglass.
catalepsia, *f.* (med.) catalepsy.
cataléptico, ca, *a., m., f.* (med.) cataleptic.
catalicón, *m.* (pharm.) a laxative made of senna, rhubarb and tamarind.
catalina, *a.* **rueda c.,** escapement wheel (of a watch).
catalineta, *f.* (Cuba, ichth.) catalufa.
catálisis, *f.* (chem.) catalysis.
catalítico, ca, *a.* (chem.) catalytic.
catalizador, *m.* (chem.) catalyst.
catalnica, *f.* (coll., ornith.) parakeet.
catalogación, *f.* cataloging, cataloguing.
catalogador, ra, *a.* cataloging, cataloguing. —*m., f.* cataloger, cataloguer.
catalogar, (*ref. 51*) *tr.v.* to catalog (ue), list.
catálogo, *m.* catalog(ue).
catalogue, catalogué, *ref.* **catalogar.**
catalpa, *f.* (bot.) catalpa (Catalpa bignonoides).
catalufa, *f.* 1. thick, plushlike wool cloth used for carpeting. 2. (Cuba, ichth.) catalufa.
cataluja, *f.* (Cuba, ichth.) catalufa.
Cataluña, *f.* Catalonia, region in N.E. Spain.
catamenia, *f.* (physiol.) catamenia, menses.
catamenial, *a.* (physiol.) catamenial.
catán, *m.* cutlass, scimitar.
catana, *f.* 1. cutlass, scimitar; (Arg., Chile, derog.) large old sabre. 2. (Cuba) heavy, rough, shapeless thing. 3. (Ven.) blue-green parakeet (Conurus hoffmanis). 4. (Peru) stroke, blow. 5. (Arg., Urug.) short machete. 6. (Amer.) small boat, skiff.
catanga, *f.* 1. (Arg., ento.) scarabeus (Scarrabeus sacer). 2. (Col.) fishing basket, fish trap. 3. (Bol.) small fruit cart.
catante, *a.* observing, viewing; gauging.
cataplasia, *f.* (biol.) cataplasia.
cataplasma, *f.* 1. (med.) cataplasma, poultice. 2. (coll.) bore, boring person.
cataplexia, *f.* (med.) cataplexy; apoplexy.
¡cataplum! *interj.* plop! bang! crash! (the sound of something falling).
catapulta, *f.* catapult.
catar, *tr.v.* 1. to sample, taste, test, try. 2. to look at, examine, investigate, inspect. 3. to extract (honeycombs from a beehive). 4. to look at, observe. 5. to look for, search for.
cataraña, *f.* 1. (ornith.) species of heron. 2. (zool.) a kind of lizard of the W. Indies.
catarata, *f.* 1. waterfall, cataract; (*pl.*) falls. 2. (med.) cataract. 3. (*pl.*) heavy rainladen clouds. — **tener uno c.,** (coll.) to be blind (with passion or ignorance); **las cataratas del Niágara,** Niagara Falls.
catarinita, *f.* 1. (Mex., ornith.) parakeet. 2. (Mex., ento.) red beetle.
cátaros, *m.* (*pl.*) (rel.) cathari, catharists.
catarral, *a.* (med.) catarrhal, pertaining to a cold or catarrh.
catarribera, *m.* 1. falconer. 2. (coll.) lawyer appointed to investigate administrative irregularities.
catarro, *m.* (med.) catarrh; head cold.
catarrocas, *f.* (geol.) cataclastic rocks.
catarroso, sa, *a.* (med.) catarrhal.
catarsis, *f.* 1. catharsis, purification. 2. (med.) catharsis, purgation (esp. of the bowels). 3. (psyc.) catharsis, a technique used to relieve tension and anxiety; the result of this process.
catártico, ca, *a.* (med., pharm.) cathartic, laxative. —*m.* laxative.
catasalsas, *m., f.* meddler, busybody; dabbler, dilettante.
catascopio, *m.* (mar., arch.) scout (ship).
catástasis, *f.* (rhet.) catastasis, the climax of the action of a play.

catastral, *a.* cadastral, landed-property.
catastro, *m.* cadastre, the registry of quantity, value and ownership of real estate (used in assessing taxes).
catástrofe, *f.* 1. catastrophe. 2. (fig.) catastrophe, something of poor quality or badly done, e.g. *el estreno fue una c.,* (coll.) opening night was a failure.
catastrófico, ca, *a.* catastrophic, catastrophical.
catata, *f.* (bot.) large yellow maté.
catatán, *m.* (Chile, coll.) physical punishment.
catatar, *tr.v.* (Amer.) to bewitch, enchant.
catatá, *a.* (Cuba) fatuous, foolish, insignificant (person). *—m., f.* (Cuba) fool, pipsqueak.
catatipia, *f.* (photog.) contact catalysis.
catatonía, *f.* (med.) catatonia.
catauro, *m.* (Antilles) palmetto basket.
cataviento, *m.* (mar.) dogvane.
catavino, *m.* wine taster's cup.
catavinos, *m.* 1. wine taster or connoisseur. 2. (coll.) drunkard.
cate, *m.* 1. blow, slap in the face. 2. a failing grade in school examinations.
cateador, *m.* 1. (min.) prospector. 2. (min.) miner's pick, prospector's pick.
catear, *tr.v.* 1. to seek, search for. 2. (coll.) to fail, flunk (an examination). 3. (Arg., Chile, Peru) to prospect for (minerals). 4. (Mex.) to break into, search (someone's house). 5. (Arg., Chile) to spy on, watch.
catecismo, *m.* (rel.) catechism, the book of Christian doctrine.
catecú, *m.* (med., pharm.) catechu, a powerful astringent.
catecúmeno, na, *m., f.* (rel.) catechumen, a convert to Christianity.
cátedra, *f.* 1. (professorial) chair, professorship. 2. professor's chair. 3. classroom, lecture room. 4. lecturer's desk. 5. subject taught by a professor. 6. cathedra (episcopal dignity or see). — **c. del espíritu santo,** the pulpit; **c. de San Pedro,** the Holy See; **poner c.,** to pontificate; **ser la c.,** (Cuba, coll.) to be very knowledgeable in a subject.
catedral, *a., f.* cathedral.
catedralicio, cia, *a.* cathedral, pertaining to a cathedral.
catedralidad, *f.* (rel.) status of a cathedral.
catedrática, *f.* female professor (of a university); (coll.) wife of a professor.
catedrático, *m.* 1. professor (of a university). 2. (ecc.) cathedraticum, annual sum paid to support a bishop.
categorema, *m.* (log.) categorem, name.
categoría, *f.* category; class, condition, position (of person); **hombre de c.,** man of position.
categóricamente, *adv.* categorically, absolutely.
categórico, ca, *a.* categorical, absolute.
categorismo, *m.* categorical system.
categorización, *f.* categorization.
categorizar, (*ref. 53*) *tr.v.* to categorize.
catela, *f.* (arch.) gold or silver chain (used by the Romans as jewelry).
catenaria, *a., f.* (geom.) catenary.
catenular, *a.* chain-like, catenate, catenulate.
cateo, *m.* (Amer.) prospecting (for minerals).
catequesis, *f., var. of* **catequismo.**
catequice, catequicé, *ref.* **catequizar.**
catequismo, *m.* (rel.) catechism (religious or other instruction by means of questions and answers).
catequista, *m., f.* (rel.) catechist.
catequístico, ca, *a.* catechistic, catechistical.
catequizador, ra, *m., f.* catechizer; persuader.
catequizante, *a.* catechizing; persuading.
catequizar, (*ref. 53*) *tr.v.* to catechize; to persuade, win over, prevail upon.
cateramba, *f.* (bot.) colocynth, African bitter apple (Citrullus colocynthis).
cateresis, *f.* (med.) weakness, debilitation.
caterético, ca, *a.* (med.) caustic.
caterva, *f.* (derog.) mob, crowd; horde; heap, pile, stack (of things).
catervarios, *m.* (*pl.*) (hist.) team of Roman gladiators.
catete, *m.* 1. (Chile, coll.) the devil. 2. (Chile, cul.) pork-broth porridge.
catéter, *m.* (surg.) catheter.
cateterismo, *m.* (surg.) catheterization, exploratory examination with a catheter.
cateterizar, (*ref. 53*) *tr.v.* (surg.) to catheterize.
cateto, ta, *m., f.* villager, rustic; (coll.) yokel, boor, oaf; dunce. *—m.* (geom.) leg of a right-angled triangle.
catetómetro, *m.* (phys.) cathetometer.
catexis, *f.* (psyc.) cathexis.
catey, *m.* 1. (Cuba, ornith.) a small parrot. 2. (W. Indies, bot.) species of palm-tree (Acrocomea aculeata).
catgut, *m.* (Angl., surg.) catgut.
catibía, *f.* (Amer.) grated yucca or cassava root; **comer c.,** (Cuba) to waste time; to talk nonsense.
catibo, *m.* (Cuba, zool.) a small water snake.
catigua, *f.* (Arg., bot.) species of Argentinian trichilia tree (Trichilia catigua).
Catilina, *m.* Catiline, Roman politician who conspired against the Senate.
catilinaria, *a.* Catilinarian (said of Cicero's speeches against Catiline). *—f.* one of Cicero's Catilinarian speeches; (coll.) philippic, diatribe, severe criticism or denunciation.
catimarón, *m.* (mar.) catamaran.
catimbao, *m.* 1. (Chile, Peru) effigy, puppet (brought out during Corpus Christi processions). 2. (Chile) ridiculously dressed person, freak. 3. (Chile) clown. 4. (Peru) pudgy, chubby person.
catimia, *f.* (min.) gold or silver vein.
catín, *m.* (metal.) copper-refining crucible.
catinga, *f.* 1. (S. Amer.) stench, unpleasant odor of certain animals and plants; smell of human sweat. 2. a stunted type of forest, esp. in Brazil. 3. (Chile, derog.) landlubber.
catingoso, sa, *a.* (Arg.) foul-smelling, ill-smelling.
catingudo, da, *a.* (S. Amer.) stinking.
catino, *m.* (min.) small crucible for molten metal.
catión, *m.* (phys.) cation, positive ion.
catiónico, ca, *a.* (phys.) cationic.
catire, *a.* (S. Amer.) blond, red haired. 2. said of the offspring of mulatto and white parents.
catirrinos, *m.* (*pl.*) Catarrhine, suborder of Asian and African monkeys.
catita, *f.* (Arg., Bol., Chile) species of parakeet.
catite, *m.* 1. loaf of highly refined sugar. 2. cone-shaped Andalusian hat. 3. light slap, cuff. 4. (Mex.) silk fabric. — **dar c.,** (coll.) to hit, beat; to humiliate.
catitear, *i.v.* 1. (Arg.) to nod the head (said of old people). 2. (coll.) to be short of money.
cativí, *f.* (Hond., med.) type of herpes.
cativo, *m.* (C. Rica, bot.) species of acacia (Prioria copaifera).
cato, *m.* 1. catechu (substance extracted from a species of Acacia catechu). 2. (Mex.) blow, thump. 3. (Bol.) agrarian measure.
catoche, *m.* (Mex., coll.) ill-temper, sulkiness.
catódico, ca, *a.* (phys.) cathodic.
cátodo, *m.* (phys.) cathode.
catodógrafo, *m.* cathodograph, radiograph.
católicamente, *adv.* catholically (according to Catholic doctrine).
catolice, catolicé, *ref.* **catolizar.**
catolicidad, *f.* 1. catholicity (universality). 2. Catholicism (as a religious group or doctrine).
catolicísimo, ma, *a. super. of* **católico,** extremely catholic.
catolicismo, *m.* Catholicism (faith, practice, adherence to the Catholic Church).
católico, ca, *a.* 1. catholic, universal. 2. Catholic, professing or pertaining to the Catholic faith. 3. true, infallible. 4. (coll.) healthy, sound, perfect, e.g. *no estar muy c.,* to be out of sorts, feel unwell. *—m., f.* Catholic.
catolicón, *m.* (pharm.) a cathartic made of senna, rhubarb and tamarind.
catolito, *m.* (elec.) catholyte.
catolizar, (*ref. 53*) *tr.v.* to catholicize (to convert to the Catholic faith).
catón, *m.* 1. (hist.) C., Cato. 2. (fig.) severe censor or critic. 3. child's primer, first reader.
catoniano, na, *a.* Catonian, severe.
catonismo, *m.* Catoism, severity.
catonizar, (*ref. 53*) *i.v.* to censure severely, be a severe critic.
catóptrica, *f.* (opt.) catoptrics.
catóptrico, ca, *a.* (opt.) catoptric, of or pertaining to mirrors or reflected images.
catoptromancia, *f.* divination by the use of mirrors.
catoptroscopia, *f.* (med.) use of light-reflecting objects in medical examinations.
catorce, *a.* fourteen; fourteenth. *—m.* fourteen; fourteenth, e.g. *Catorce de Julio,* the fourteenth of July (Bastille Day).
catorcena, *f.* group of fourteen units.
catorceno, na, *a.* fourteenth; fourteen-year-old.
catorrazo, *m.* (Mex.) a severe blow.
catorro, *m.* (Mex.) a blow and its effect.
catorzal, *m.* timber beam 14 ft. long by 8 in. wide and 6 in. thick.
catorzavo, va, *a. fourteenth. —m., f.* the fourteenth.
catraca, *f.* 1. (Mex.) species of pheasant. 2. (Arg.) ratchet, toothed wheel.
catracho, cha, *a., m., f.* (C. Amer., coll.) Honduran.
catre, *m.* small bedstead, camp bed, cot. — **c. clínico,** (Chile) hospital cot; **c. de balsa,** (Arg.) raft; **c. de tijera,** camp bed; **c. de viento,** (Amer.) canvas cot.
catrecillo, *m.* folding chair or stool.
catricofre, *m.* box containing a folding bed and its bedding to be put out of the way when not in use.
catrín, *m.* (Mex.) dandy. *—a.* conceited, foppish.
catrintre, *m.* 1. (Chile) cottage cheese. 2. (Chile, coll.) shabby person, pauper.
Catulo, *m.* (hist.) Catullus, Roman lyric poet.
caturra, *f.* (ornith., Chile) small parrot or parakeet.
catuto, *m.* (Chile) bread made with mashed cooked wheat.
catzo, *m.* (Ecuad., ento.) species of bumblebee.
cauba, *f.* (bot., Arg.) variety of spiny senna tree (Bauhinia pruinosa).
caúca, *f.* (Bol.) 1. wheatflour cake. 2. (Col., Ecuad.) grass grown for forage.
caucáseo, a, *a.* Caucasian (pertaining to the Caucasus).
caucasiano, na, *a., var. of* **caucáseo.**
caucásico, ca, *a.* Caucasian (applied to the white race).
Cáucaso, *m.* Caucasus, Caucasus Mountains.
caucau, *m.* (Peru) a highly seasoned stew made of potatoes, tripe and vegetables.
cauce, *m.* river-bed; ditch, trench.
caucel, *m.* (C. Rica, Hond., zool.) American wild-cat.

caucha, *f.* (Chile, bot.) species of thistle used as an antidote for poisonous spider bite.
cauchal, *m.* grove of rubber trees, rubber plantation.
cauchau, *m.* (Chile, bot.) myrtle tree berry.
cauchera, *f.* rubber-yielding plant.
cauchero, ra, *a.* rubber (pertaining to rubber or the rubber industry). —*m.* rubber planter or plantation worker.
cauchil, *m.* small basin or reservoir of water.
caucho, *m.* 1. rubber, rubber latex, India rubber. 2. (Col.) waterproof cape, oilskin. — **c. esponjoso,** foam rubber; **c. vulcanizado,** vulcanized rubber.
cauchotado, *a.* (Arg.) rubberized, waterproofed.
cauchotar, *tr.v.* to treat with rubber.
cauchotina, *f.* (chem.) caoutchoucin, caoutchouc oil, rubber oil (used in tanneries).
caución, *m.* caution, precaution; caveat; (law) pledge, surety, guaranty; bail. — **bajo c.,** (law) on bail; **c. de indemnidad** or **c. personal,** (law) bond of indemnity.
caucionar, *tr.v.* 1. (law) to bond; to pledge, guarantee. 2. to caution, warn against (danger, misfortune, evil, etc.).
cauda, *f.* (ecc.) train of a bishop's robe.
caudado, da, *a.* (zool., her.) caudate, caudated, having a tail or an appendage resembling a tail.
caudal, *a.* 1. (zool.) caudal, pertaining to a tail. 2. carrying or holding a lot of water. —*m.* 1. wealth, fortune, property. 2. flow, volume (of running water). 3. (fig.) abundance, plenty, large quantity. — **c. relicto,** (law) estate of the deceased; **hacer c. de,** to esteem, hold in high regard; **redondear uno su c.,** to add to one's wealth or get rid of debts; **c. crítico,** (hydr.) critical flow.
caudalejo, *m. dim. of* **caudal,** small fortune, respectable or tidy sum of money.
caudalosamente, *adv.* abundantly, copiously.
caudaloso, sa *a.* 1. abundant, plentiful (a river, lake, waterfall). 2. opulent, wealthy, rich.
caudatario, *m.* 1. (ecc.) clergyman who carries the train of an officiating bishop's robe. 2. (coll.) flatterer, apple-polisher (coll., U.S.).
caudato, ta, *a.* (zool., her.) *var. of* **caudado.**
caudatrémula, *f.* (ornith.) white wagtail (Motacilla alba).
caudillaje, *m.* leadership, rule by a caudillo; (Amer.) caciquism, domination by political bosses; (Chile) tyranny, despotism.
caudillismo, *m., var. of* **caudillaje.**
caudillo, *m.* caudillo, chief, leader, commander.
caudimano, *a.* (zool.) having a prehensile tail.
caudón, *m.* (ornith.) European shrike, butcher-bird (Lanius excubitor).
caula, *f.* (Chile, Hond.) trick, deception, ruse.
caulescente, *a.* (bot.) caulescent, having a stem visible above the ground.
caulícolo, *m., var. of* **caulículo.**
caulículo, *m.* (archit.) caulicole, cauliculus.
caulífero, ra, *a.* (bot.) cauligenous, borne upon the stem.
cauliforme, *a.* cauliform, stem-like.
caulote, *m.* (bot., Hond.) a variety of mulberry-tree.
cauno, *m.* (ornith.) a crested screamer (Chauna torquata).
cauque, *m.* 1. (ichth., Chile) a species of large silversides or grey mullet. 2. (Chile, coll.) smart, alert person, livewire (coll.).
cauri, *m.* (ichth.) cowrie (Cypraca moneta).
cauro, *m.* northwest wind.
causa, *f.* 1. cause, origin of an effect, motive or reason for acting. 2. movement or doctrine a person supports. 3. (law) trial. — **a c. de,** because of; **acriminar la c.,** (law) to aggravate an action; **arrastrar la c.,** (law) to bring a case to a higher court; **c. eficiente,** (philos.) efficient cause; **c. final,** (philos.) final cause; **c. impulsiva, c. motiva,** (philos.) motivation, impelling motive; **c. instrumental,** (law) test or leading case; **c. onerosa,** (law) valuable consideration, onerous consideration; **c. primera,** (philos.) first cause, prime mover; **c. pública,** commonweal, public welfare; **causas mayores,** (canon law) cases judged solely by the Apostolic See; **conocer de una c.,** (law) to judge a case; **dar la c. por conclusa,** (law) to close a case; **hacer c.,** (law) to bring action; **hacer c. común,** to make common cause with; **hacer uno la c. de otro,** to support another person's case or cause; **salir a la c.** de, (law) to take up someone's case.
causa, *f.* 1. (Chile, coll.) snack (between meals). 2. (Peru, cul.) cold mashed potato entree with chili, boiled eggs and olives. — **echar una c.,** (Chile) to take a snack.
causador, ra, *a.* causing, causative. —*m., f.* agent, originator.
causahabiente, *m.* (law) assignee.
causal, *a.* (gram.) causative, causal (conjunction). —*f.* cause, motive, reason.
causalidad, *f.* cause, origin; (philos.) causality, law of cause and effect.
causante, *a.* causing, originating, causative. —*m., f.* one who causes, originator; (law) principal, constituent.
causar, *tr.v.* 1. to cause, produce, occasion. 2. (Sp.) to sue.
causativo, va, *a.* causative.
causear, *i.v.* (Chile) to have a snack or bite (between meals). —*tr.v.* 1. (Chile) to eat. 2. to defeat, outdo.
causeo, *m.* (Chile) snack, bite.
causía, *f.* wide-brimmed felt hat, used in ancient Greece and Rome.
causídica, *f.* (archit.) center of a cruciform nave (of a church).
causídico, ca, *a.* (law) causidical, forensic. —*m.* lawyer, counselor, advocate.
causón, *m.* high fever of short duration.
cáusticamente, *adv.* caustically, mordantly, scathingly.
causticar, (*ref.* 50) *tr.v.* to make caustic, to causticize.
causticidad, *f.* causticity; (fig.) mordancy, mordacity.
cáustico, ca, *a.* (chem.) caustic; (fig.) caustic, scathing, mordant, sharp-tongued. —*m.* (chem.) caustic (medicament); (med.) blistering plaster. —*f.* (phys., math.) caustic.
caustique, caustiqué, *ref.* **causticar.**
causuelo, *m.* (Nic., zool.) American wildcat.
cautamente, *adv.* cautiously, warily.
cautela, *f.* caution, prudence, wariness; astuteness; guile, wile, cleverness, cunning, craftiness. — **absolver a c.,** (ecc.) to absolve when there is doubt.
cautelar, *tr.v.* to prevent, avoid, forestall. —*r.v.* to take precautions against.
cautelosamente, *adv.* cautiously; warily; stealthily.
cauteloso, sa, *a.* cautious, careful, wary.
cauterice, cautericé, *ref.* **cauterizar.**
cauterio, *m.* cauterization; (surg.) cautery, cauterizing agent; (fig.) cure, remedy, corrective. — **c. actual,** (surg.) cautery, searing iron; **c. potential,** (surg.) caustic, cauterizing chemical.
cauterización, *f.* (med.) cauterization; (fig.) a difficult but salutary solution.
cauterizador, ra, *a. (med.) cauterizing.* —*m.* (med.) cautery, cauterizing agent; cauterizer.
cauterizante, *a.* cauterizing.
cauterizar, (*ref.* 53) tr.v. 1. to cauterize. 2. (fig.) to eradicate, extirpate. 3. (fig.) to reproach severely; to blame.
cautín, *m.* soldering iron.
cautivador, ra, *a.* captivating, winsome, charming.
cautivante, *a.* captivating, fascinating.
cautivar, *tr.v.* 1. to capture, to take prisoner. 2. (fig.) to captivate, charm, enthrall.
cautiverio, *m.* the state of being in captivity.
cautividad, *f.* captivity; prison.
cautivo, va, *a.* captive; imprisoned.
cauto, ta, *a.* cautious, prudent, wary, circumspect.
cauza, *f.* box for silkworm eggs.
cava, *f.* 1. (agr.) digging and banking of vines. 2. wine cellar, esp. in a royal palace; butler's pantry. 3. (mil.) moat.
cava, *f.* (anat.) vena cava.
cavacote, *m.* (agr.) mound of earth used as a landmark.
cavadizo, za, *a.* 1. dug out of a pit (said of sand, earth, etc.). 2. soft, loose, easily dug.
cavador, ra, *m., f.* digger, excavator; *c. de zanjas,* trench machine, ditch digger.
cavadura, *f.* digging, excavation.
cavalillo, *m.* (agr.) irrigation ditch or canal dividing two estates.
caván, *m.* (Phil. I.) large liquid measure.
cavar, *tr.v.* to dig, excavate. —*i.v.* to delve into, study or probe deeply into some subject.
cavatina, *f.* (mus.) cavatina, short simple aria.
cavazón, *f.* digging, excavation.
cávea, *f.* (archeol.) 1. Roman cage or cave for birds and other animals. 2. row of seats for spectators on the steps of Roman theatres and circus arenas.
cavedio, *m.* (archeol.) courtyard in Roman houses.
caverna, *f.* 1. cave; cavern. 2. (med.) cavity.
cavernario, ria, *a.* pertaining to caves; cavernous; (fig.) backward, uncultured.
cavernícola, *a.* 1. cave-dwelling, living in caves. 2. (coll., fig.) reactionary, having backward social and political attitudes.
cavernidad, *f., var. of* **cavernosidad.**
cavernosidad, *f.* natural cave, cavern.
cavernoso, sa, *a.* cavernous; cavern-like.
cavero, *m.* (agr.) ditch digger.
caveto, *m.* (archit.) cavetto, concave molding whose profile is the quadrant of a circle.
caví, *m.* (Peru) an edible root.
cavia, *f.* (agr.) circular excavation around a tree trunk (to retain water).
cavia, *m.* (zool.) guinea pig.
cavial, *m., var. of* **caviar.**
caviar, *m.* caviar, caviare; sturgeon roe.
cavicornios, *m.* (*pl.*) (zool.) Cavicorns, family of hollow-horned animals.
cavidad, *f.* cavity.
cavilación, *f.* brooding, fretting.
cavilar, *i.v.* to brood, fret. —*tr.v.* to reflect upon.
cavilosamente, *adv.* with excessive caution; ponderingly.
cavilosidad, *f.* suspicion, mistrust; apprehension.
caviloso, sa, *a.* 1. suspicious, mistrustful. 2. (Col.) fastidious; quarrelsome. 3. (C. Rica) gossipy, talebearing, acting as an informer against someone.
cavío, *m.* digging.
cavitación, *f.* cavitation.
cay, *m.* (zool., Arg.) a type of Capuchin monkey (Cebus paraguayanus).
cayada, *f.* shepherd's staff.
cayadilla, *f.* fire-rake (of a blacksmith's forge).
cayado, *m.* shepherd's hook, crook, staff; bishop's crosier.

cayajabo, *m.* (bot., C. Amer.) jack bean (Canavalia cubrensis or Canavalia nitida).
cayama, *f.* ornith., Cuba) species of fish-eating bird.
cayán, *m.* (Phil. I.) bamboo awning.
cayana, *f.* (Amer.) pot used by Indians for grinding or toasting wheat or corn.
cayanco, *m.* (Hond., med.) hot poultice made of herbs.
cayapear, *i.v.* (Ven.) to gang up on and attack a person.
cayapona, *f.* (Amer.) a plant from which a strong laxative is extracted.
cayarí, *m.* (Cuba) a type of small red crab.
cayaya, *f.* 1. (bot., Cuba) wild shrub bearing fruit similar to pepper. 2. (ornith., Guat.) gallinaceous bird of the genus Ortalis.
cayendo, *ref.* **caer.**
cayente, *a.* falling, dropping.
cayeputi, *m.* (bot.) cajuput tree; paperbark tree (Melanenia leucodendron).
cayera, cayese, cayó, *ref.* **caer.**
cayo, *m.* key, islet; **C. Hueso,** Key West; **Cayos de la Florida,** Florida Keys.
cayote, *m.* (bot.) *var. of* **chayote,** a pear-shaped fruit of the cucumber family (Sechium edule). — **cidra c.,** a variety of watermelon.
cayuco, ca, *m., f.* 1. (Cuba) large-headed person. 2. obstinate person. —*m.* (Amer.) Indian canoe used for fishing.
cayuela, *f.* a kind of blue-colored limestone.
cayumbo, *m.* (bot.) a type of liana that grows in rivers and marshes.
cayutana, *f.* (bot.) a kind of rue.
caz, (*pl.* caces) *m.* ditch, trench, irrigation canal.
caza, *f.* 1. hunting; hunt, chase. 2. (wild) game; bag (animals caught). 3. (coll.) pursuit plane. — **c. a chorro,** jet-fighter; **c. de brujas,** witch hunt; **c. de cabezas,** head-hunting; **c. del hombre,** manhunt; **c. del tesoro,** treasure hunt; **c. del zorro,** fox hunt; **c. mayor,** big game; **c. menor,** small game; **c. submarina,** underwater fishing; **ir** or **andar a c. de,** to go hunting for, to be in search of; **ir** or **andar a c. de gangas,** (coll.) to be on the look-out for a soft job, easy pickings or a bargain; **dar c.,** to give chase, pursue; to ferret out (a job, secret); **espantar uno la c.,** (coll.) to spoil one's prospects from haste or ill-advised methods; **levantar uno la c.,** (coll.) to give the game away, to let the cat out of the bag.
caza, *f.* (arch.) gauze-like lawn or muslin.
cazabe, *m.* (Amer.) cassava bread or cake.
cazabombardero, *m.* fighter bomber (airplane).
cazaclavos, *m.* (mec.) nail-lifter; claw bar.
cazadero, *m.* hunting ground.
cazador, ra, *a.* 1. hunting, predatory (animal). 2. (coll.) proselytizing (person). —*m.* 1. hunter. 2. (mil.) chasseur. — **c. de alforja,** trapper, hunter who uses dogs, snares, etc. but not firearms; **c. de autógrafos,** autograph hunter; **c. de cabezas,** headhunter; **c. de dotes,** dowry hunter; **c. de pieles,** trapper; **c. furtivo,** poacher; **c. mayor,** royal huntsman. —*f.* huntress.
cazadora, *f.* (tail.) hunting jacket.
cazadora, *f.* (ornith., C. Rica) yellow warbler (Dendroica aestiva).
cazaguate, *m.* (bot., Mex.) morning glory.
cazalla, *f.* (Sp.) a popular crude brandy.
cazamoscas, *m.* (ornith.) flycatcher.
cazar, (*ref. 53*) *tr.v.* 1. to hunt; to chase, to track down; 2. to catch. 3. to land, (coll.) get, attain (something difficult). 4. (mar.) to tally, haul in (a sail).
cazarete, *m.* one of the parts of the dragnet.
cazarra, *f.* a type of wooden feed trough used for sheep.
cazarro, *m.* hollowed-out tree trunk.
cazasubmarino, *m.* submarine chaser.
cazata, *f.* hunting; hunt.
cazatorpedero, *m.* (mar.) torpedo boat destroyer.
cazcalear, *i.v.* (coll.) to scurry or bustle about (pretending to be at work).
cazcarria, *f.* (*gen. pl.*) splattered mud dried and caked on one's clothes.
cazcarriento, ta, *a.* mud-splashed, splattered with mud.
cazcorvo, va, *a.* bow-legged (said of a horse).
cazo, *m.* 1. ladle, dipper. 2. blunt edge of a knife. 3. glue pot. 4. melting pan. — **c. de fundidor,** casting ladle, founder's scoop.
cazolada, *f.* panful, potful.
cazoleja, *f. dim. of* **cazuela,** pan; (mil.) pan (of a gunlock).
cazolero, *m.* man who likes to meddle in women's housework.
cazoleta, *f.* 1. *dim. of* **cazuela,** small pan or pot; bowl (of a smoking pipe); (mil.) pan (of a gunlock). 2. kind of perfume; incense burner. 3. guard (of a sword). 4. boss (of a shield).
cazoletear, *i.v.* to meddle.
cazoletero, *m.* man who meddles in woman's work.
cazolón, *m. aug. of* **cazuela,** large casserole, pot.
cazón, *m.* (ichth.) smooth dogfish (Mustelis canis); dogfish, small shark. 2. (arch.) muscavado sugar.
cazonal, *m.* 1. tackle for catching dogfish; strong net (for catching dogfish and for deep-sea fishing). 2. (coll.) very difficult situation, mess.
cazonete, *m.* (mar.) toggle.
cazudo, da, *a.* 1. having a large, heavy guard (swords). 2. having a thick, blunt edge (knives).
cazuela, *f.* 1. (cul.) casserole (container); casserole full; casserole, dish prepared in a casserole. 2. (theat.) gallery; (theat., arch.) gallery for women. 3. (Chile, cul.) national dish made of meat, chicken, corn and vegetables and highly seasoned with red pepper. 4. (print.) composing stick (for several lines). — **c. carnicera,** large casserole; **c. de mariscos,** shellfish stew.
cazumbrar, *tr.v.* to calk (wine casks) with oakum.
cazumbre, *m.* oakum, hempen calking (for wine casks).
cazumbrón, *m.* cooper, wine-cask maker or repairer.
cazuñar, *tr.v.* (C. Amer.) to steal.
cazurria, *f.* reticence, taciturnity.
cazurro, rra, *a.* (coll.) taciturn, reserved, reticent, sulky, sullen. —*m., f.* taciturn person.
cazuz, (*pl.* **cazuces**) *m.* (bot.) ivy.
CC *abbrev. of* **centímetro cúbico,** cubic centimeter (cc).
C.C. *abbrev. of* **corriente continua,** direct current (DC).
c/c *abbrev. of* **cuenta corriente,** current account.
CD *abbrev. of* **cuerpo diplomático,** diplomatic corps (CD).
Cd *sym. of* **cadmio,** cadmium (Cd).
C.D. *abbrev. of* **corriente directa,** direct current (DC).
C. de J. *abbrev. of* **Compañía de Jesús,** Society of Jesus.
ce, *f.* (name of the letter "c"); **ce por be** or **ce por ce,** word by word, in great detail; **por ce o por be,** (coll.) by hook or by crook, in one way or another.
¡ce! *interj.* psst!
Ce *sym. of* **cerio,** cerium (Ce).
cea, *f.* (anat.) hip bone.
CEA *abbrev. of* **Comisión de Energía Atómica,** Atomic Energy Commission (AEC).
ceanoto, *m.* (bot.) New Jersey tea (Ceanothus americanus).
cearina, *f.* (med.) cearin.
ceática, *f.* (med.) sciatica.
ceba, *f.* 1. special feed to fatten animals rapidly. 2. (fig.) stoking (of a furnace).
cebada, *f.* (bot.) barley; **c. perlada,** pearl barley.
cebadal, *m.* barley field.
cebadar, *tr.v.* to feed barley to (animals).
cebadazo, za, *a.* pertaining to barley, e.g. *paja c.,* barley straw.
cebadera, *f.* 1. nose bag, feed bag; barley bin. 2. (mar.) sprit sail. 3. (min.) furnace charger.
cebadero, *m.* 1. barley dealer. 2. stable boy. 3. mule carrying the feed for a mule-train; bell mule, lead mule (of a mule train).
cebadero, *m.* 1. falconer, hawk trainer. 2. feeding place (for animals). 3. bait set out for game. 4. painting depicting domestic fowl at feeding time. 5. (min.) opening through which a furnace is fed.
cebadilla, *f.* 1. (bot.) long-spiked wild barley. 2. (bot.) sabadilla (seeds); (bot.) hellebore, root of white hellebore (used in making snuff and insecticides), sneezewort (bot., coll.), prickly oxeye.
cebadina, *f.* (chem.) sabadine.
cebado, da, *past part. of* **cebar.** —*a.* maneating (said of a wild beast which has tasted human flesh and is therefore more dangerous).
cebado, *m.* priming; feeding; **c. automático,** (mec.) self-priming.
cebador, *m.* 1. one who fattens animals. 2. (mil.) powder horn, powder flask.
cebadura, *f.* 1. flattening (of domestic animals). 2. (Arg.) the preparing of maté, a popular beverage; the amount of dried maté leaves used in the preparation of the beverage; the dried leaves after maté has been prepared (further usable as fertilizer).
cebar, *tr.v.* 1. to feed, fatten (animals). 2. to bait (a fishbook). 3. (fig.) to feed, stoke, fuel (a light, fire, furnace, etc.). 4. to prime (a firearm). 5. to start up (a machine). 6. to remagnetize, build up (magnetism). 7. (fig.) to excite, incite (a passion). 8. to drive in (a nail, a screw). 9. to light (a rocket or fireworks). —*i.v.* to peentrate, embed itself, hold fast (a nail, screw). —*r.v.* to rage (a disease or an epidemic).
cebellina, *a.* zibeline, pertaining to the sable. — **marta cebellina,** Russian sable.
cebero, *m.* large basket used to hold feed for animals.
cebiche, *m.* (cul., Peru) national dish of raw fish marinated in lemon juice.
cebil, *m.* (bot.) cebil, a leguminous South American tree valued for its lumber, its bark rich in tannic acid and its leaves (used as forage).
cebipero, cebipiro, *m.* (bot.) Brazilian tree having an astringent bark and used as a cure for rheumatism.
cebo, *m.* 1. fodder, fattening feed. 2. bait (for fishing). 3. primer, primer charge (in fireamrs); (min.) charge (for furnaces). 4. (coll.) fuel (to kindle passion, etc.). 5. inducement, lure, bait (to attract someone). — **c. de gelatina,** gelatin primer; **c. fulminante,** blasting cap, exploder.
cebo, *m.* (zool.) red guenon of E. Africa.
cebolla, *f.* 1. onion; bulb. 2. heart or core of a tree. 3. timber with distended layers. 4. oil receptacle (of a lamp). 5. (mec.) strainer, screen (in water pipes). 6. (mec.) strainer for a foot valve. 7. (C. Amer., coll.) authority, command, e.g. *agarrar la c.,* to grab the reins, take over, take command. — **c. albarrana,** (bot.) squill (Urigenia scilla); **c. escalonia,** (bot.) shallot, scallion.
cebollada, *f.* (cul.) onion stew.
cebollana, *f.* (bot.) chives.

cebollar, *m.* onion patch.
cebollero, ra, *m., f.* one who sells onions.
cebolleta, *f.* (bot.) variety of onion (Allium fistulosum); spring onion; (Cuba, bot.) kind of chufa or edible sedge.
cebollino, *m.* (agr.) onion seedling; onion seed; chives. — **escardar cebollinos,** (coll.) to waste time on trifles; **váyase Ud. a escardar cebollinos,** (coll.) go jump in the lake.
cebollita, *m.* (Arg., coll.) child from four to twelve years old.
cebollón, *m. aug. of* **cebolla,** large onion.
cebollón, na, *m., f.* (Chile, coll.) old bachelor; old maid.
cebolludo, da, *a.* 1. having or growing from a bulb. 2. rude, rough-mannered (person). 3. thick-set, stocky (person).
cebón, na, *a.* fattened. —*m.* hog, pig.
ceboncillo, *m. dim. of* **cebón,** fatling, a young animal fattened before being slaughtered.
ceborrincha, *f.* (bot.) wild onion.
cebra, *f.* (zool.) zebra.
cebrado, da, *a.* zebrine (said of a horse or other animal having zebra-like striation or bands).
cebratana, *f., var. of* **cerbatana,** blowgun.
cebruno, na, *a., var. of* **cervuno,** bay, bayard (reddish-brown horse).
cebú, (*pl.* **cebúes**) *m.* (zool.) zebu, Asiatic ox.
ceburro, *a.* said of a variety of white, first quality wheat, flour or bread.
ceca, *f.* 1. mint (place where money is coined). 2. coin (in Morocco). — **de la Ceca a la Meca,** (coll.) from pillar to post, hither and thither, hither and yon.
CECA *abbrev. of* **Comunidad Europea del Carbón y del Acero,** European Coal and Steel Community.
ceceante, *a.* lisping (speech).
cecear, *i.v.* to lisp; to pronounce the "s" sound as a "th".
ceceo, *m.* lisp; pronouncing "s" like "th".
ceceoso, sa, *a.* lisping. —*m., f.* lisper.
cecesmil, *m.* (Hond.) a plot of land planted with early tender corn.
cecí, *m.* (Cuba, ichth.) porgy, yellow grunt.
cecial, *m.* dried and cured hake or other similar fish.
cecidia, *f.* cecidium, nutgall (of oak or other tree).
Cecilia, *f.* (rel.) Saint Cecilia, patroness of music.
cecina, *f.* cured meat (corned, dried, smoked or hung); (Arg.) charqui, jerked beef or other meat.
cecinar, *tr.v.* to cure meat (by salting, drying, hanging or smoking).
cecografía, *f.* method of writing used by the blind.
cecógrafo, *m.* device used by the blind to write.
cécubo, *m.* famous wine of ancient Rome (made in the village of Cecubo, Campania).
cechero, *m.* (hunt.) stalker.
ceda, *f.* bristle.
cedacear, *i.v.* to diminish, dim, cloud (vision).
cedacería, *f.* sieve factory or shop.
cedacero, *m.* person who makes or sells sieves.
cedacillo, *m.* 1. *dim. of* **cedazo,** small sieve. 2. (bot.) quaking grass, lady's-hair.
cedazo, *m.* sieve; large fishing net; screen. — **c. eléctrico,** electric bolter; **c. vibrante,** vibrating screen.
cedazuelo, *m. dim. of* **cedazo,** small sieve or strainer.
cedente, *a.* ceding, granting, yielding; deferring; transferring, conveying.
ceder, *tr.v.* to cede, hand over, convey, yield, transfer; to relinquish, abandon, leave. —*i.v.* to decrease, lessen, diminish. — **c. a,** to yield to, submit to, give in to, surrender to; **c. en,** to slacken, e.g. *ceder en su empeño,* to slacken in one's efforts.
cedilla, *f.* (gram.) cedilla.
cedizo, za, *a.* tainted, spoiled (food).
cedo, *adv.* (Sp., arch.) at once, right away, immediately.
cedoaria, *f.* (bot.) zedoary (Curcuma zedoaria); **c. amarilla,** turmeric (Curcuma longa); **c. larga,** long zedoary.
cedra, *f.* (arch.) cithara, zither, ancient Greek stringed instrument of the lyre type.
cedras, *f.* (*pl.*) shepherd's leather bags or knapsacks.
cedreleón, *m.* cedar oil; cedar resin (used in ancient times).
cedreno, *m.* (chem.) cedrene.
cedria, *f.* resin from the cedar.
cédride, *f.* cedar cone.
cedrino, na, *a.* pertaining to the cedar.
cedrito, *m.* drink made with sweet wine and cedar resin.
cedro, *m.* (bot.) cedar. — **c. amargo or blanco,** (C. Rica) white cedar (Cedrus thyoides), (Cedrela Mexicana); **c. colorado,** red cedar (Juniperus virginiana); **c. de España,** savin, (Spanish Juniper), (Juniperus Sabina); **c. de la India,** deodar (Cedrus deodora); **c. de Singapur,** toon (tree) (Toona serrata); **c. del Líbano,** cedar of Lebanon; **c. dulce,** (C. Rica) cedrela.
cedróleo, *m.* (chem.) cedar oil.
cedrón, *m.* (bot.) cedron (Simaba cedron).
cédula, *f.* slip (of paper); document, card, certificate. — **c. ante diem,** schedule, summons to a meeting; **c. de cambio,** (arch.) draft, bill of exchange; **c. de identidad,** identity card or papers; **c. de vecindad,** identity card, identification papers; **c. en blanco,** application blank or form; blank check; **c. personal,** identity card, identification papers; **c. real,** royal letters patent; **c. testamentaria,** (law) codicil (of a will); **dar c. de vida,** (coll.) to spare one's life; **echar cédulas,** to draw or cast lots.
cedulaje, *m.* fee paid formerly for royal letters patent.
cedulario, *m.* collection of royal letters patent.
cedulón, *m.* 1. (coll.) *aug. of* **cédula.** 2. decree, edict, proclamation (posted in public places). 3. (fig.) pasquinade, lampoon.
CEE *abbrev. of* **Comunidad Económica Europea,** European Economic Community (EEC).
cefalalgia, *f.* (med.) cephalalgia, headache.
cefalálgico, ca, *a.* (med.) relating to a headache or cephalalgia.
cefalea, *f.* migraine, violent headache.
cefálico, ca, *a.* (zool.) cephalic.
cefalina, *f.* (biochem.) cephalin.
cefalitis, *f.* (med.) encephalitis.
cefalización, *f.* (zool.) cephalization.
céfalo, *m.* 1. (ichth.) striped mullet. 2. (myth.) C., Cephalus, son of Hermes.
cefalocordado, da, *a.* (zool.) cephalochordal. —*m.* (zool.) cephalochord, (*pl.*) Cephalochorda, Cephalochordata.
cefalometría, *f.* (anth.) cephalometry.
cefalópodo, da, *a.* (zool.) cephalopodan, cephalopod. —*m.* (zool.) cephalopod; (*pl*) Cephalopoda.
cefalorraquídeo, a, *a.* (anat.) cephalorachidian.
cefalotórax, *m.* (zool.) cephalothorax.
cefear, *i.v.* (Sp.) to root (a hog).
cefeida, *f.* (astron.) cepheid.
Cefeo, *m.* (astron.) Cepheus.
céfiro, *m.* 1. zephyrus, west wind; zephyr, gentle breeze; zephyr (cloth). 2. (myth.) C., Zephyr, son of the Dawn.
cefo, *m.* (zool.) red guenon of E. Africa (Cercepithecus cephus).
cegador, ra, *a.* blinding, dazzling.
cegajo, *m.* two-year-old billy goat.
cegajoso, sa, *a.* bleary-eyed.
cegar, (*ref. 67*) *tr.v.* 1. to blind. 2. to fill in (a well), block up (a pipe), wall up or seal up (a door), block (a path). —*i.v.* to go or grow blind, lose one's sight. —*r.v.* to be blinded (by passion, etc.).
cegarra, *a., m., f.* (coll.) *var. of* **cegato.**
cegarrita, *a.* (coll.) squinting (from near-sightedness). —*m., f.* squinter, one who squints; **a ojos cegarritas,** (coll.) squintingly, askance.
cegato, ta, *a.* (coll.) short-sighted, near-sighted; dim-sighted, poor-sighted. —*m., f.* poor-sighted person.
cegatón, na, *a.* (Amer., coll.) short-sighted, near-sighted.
cegatoso, sa, *a.* bleary-eyed. —*m., f.* bleary-eyed person.
cegesimal, *a.* (phys.) centimeter-gram-second, applied to a system of measurement in which the fundamental units are the centimeter, gram, and second.
cegrí, *m.* a member of the Zegris (family of Moors of Granada, rivals of the Abencerrajes); **cegries y abencerrajes,** (coll.) Montagues and Capulets.
cegué, *ref.* **cegar.**
ceguedad, *f.* 1. blindness. 2. ignorance. 3. (fig.) hallucination.
ceguera, *f.* 1. blindness; type of ophthalmia. 2. (fig.) obfuscation.
ceiba, *f.* 1. (bot.) ceiba tree, silk-cotton tree. 2. (bot.) sea moss, alga.
ceibal, *m.* ceiba or ceibo tree grove.
ceibo, *m.* ceibo, ceibo tree (Erythrina cristagalli), silk-cotton tree.
ceibón, *m.* (Cuba) a species of tall-growing ceiba tree.
Ceilán, *m.* Ceylon.
ceilanés, nesa, *a.* of or pertaining to Ceylon. —*m., f.* native of that country.
ceína, *f.* (chem.) zein, zeine (a prolamin obtained from Indian corn).
ceisatita, *f.* (min.) variety of opal.
ceja, *f.* 1. brow, eyebrow. 2. projection; edge, border; flange, rim. 3. cap or circle of clouds (surrounding a hill). 4. brow, summit, top (of a hill or mountain). 5. (Amer.) narrow road, path. 6. (mus.) nut (ridge at upper end of stringed instruments); (mus.) capotasto (adjustable clamp on guitar to change pitch). — **dar a uno entre c. y c.,** to tell someone to his face; **fruncir las cejas,** to knit one's brow, frown; **hasta las cejas,** up to one's eyebrows; **quemarse uno las cejas,** to burn the midnight oil; **tener a uno entre c. y c.,** to dislike someone, to have it in for someone; **tener algo entre c. y c.,** to have something fixed in one's head.
cejadero, *m.* back strap (of a carriage harness).
cejador, *m., var. of* **cejadero.**
cejar, *i.v.* to move backwards, back up; to draw back; to withdraw (from an undertaking).
ceje, *m.* a medicinal plant used to treat skin rashes.
cejijunto, ta, *a.* thick-browed, beetle-browed; (fig.) frowning, scowling.
cejilla, *f.* (mus.) capotasto (adjustable clamp on a guitar to change pitch).
cejo, *m.* 1. morning mist rising from rivers at sunrise. 2. cord of esparto grass.
cejudo, da, *a.* thick-browed, bushy-browed, beetle-browed.
cejuela, *f.* 1. *dim. of* **ceja,** thin or small eyebrow. 2. narrow edging or binding. 3. (mus.) capotasto (of a guitar).
cejunto, ta, *a., var. of* **cejijunto.**
cela, *f.* (archit.) cella, naos (of Roman and Greek temples).

celacanto, *m.* (ichth.) coelacanth.
celada, *f.* 1. sallet (medieval helmet). 2. medieval cavalryman who wore a sallet. 3. part of the key of a crossbow or ballista. — **c. borgoñata,** sallet without a visor.
celada, *f.* ambush, ambuscade; (fig.) snare, (booby) trap, trick; e.g. *caer en una celada,* to fall into a trap, be tricked.
celadamente, *adv.* secretively, furtively, stealthily.
CELADE *abbrev. of* **Centro Latinoamericano de Demografía,** Latin American Population Study Center.
celador, ra, *a.* watchful, vigilant. —*m., f.* 1. constable, policeman, policewoman. 2. custodian, curator, watchman, caretaker, warden. — **ladrones y celadores,** cops and robbers.
celaduría, *f.* job or headquarters of a watchman or caretaker.
celaje, *m.* 1. (*pl.*) of varicolored clouds; streaks; (mar.) clouds. 2. skylight (window). 3. (fig.) presage, sign, indication. — **correr como un c.,** to run like the wind.
celajería, *f.* (mar.) scud.
celambre, *f.* jealousy.
celán, *m.* (ichth.) a species of herring.
celandés, sa, *a.* of or from Zeeland (Netherlands). —*m., f.* Zeelander, native of Zeeland.
Celáneo, *m.* (astron., myth.) Celaeno (one of the Pleiades).
celante, *a.* said of a Franciscan friar who observes a strict rule of poverty (i.e. a Capuchin friar).
celar, *tr.v.* 1. to see to (the observance of laws). 2. to supervise, superintend, watch, keep a watch on, keep a sharp eye on; to be jealously watchful of (a loved one). —*i.v.* **c. por,** to watch out for, take care of.
celar, *tr.v.* 1. to cover, conceal, hide. 2. to engrave; to carve; to sculpt.
celastráceo, a, celastríneo, a, *a.* (bot.) celastraceous. —*f.* celastraceous tree; (*pl.*) Celastraceae (family).
celastro, *m.* (bot.) Hottentot cherry.
celda, *f.* cell (in a convent, prison or beehives). — **c. acolchada,** padded cell; **c. seca,** (elec.) dry cell; **c. fotoeléctrica,** photoelectric cell.
celdilla, *f.* 1. cellule; cell (of insect hives). 2. (fig.) niche (in a wall). 3. (bot.) cell, theca, anther cell.
celebérrimo, ma, *a. super. of* **célebre,** most famous, illustrious.
Célebes, *m.* Celebes, islands of Indonesia (Indonesian name: Sulawesi).
celebración, *f.* 1. celebration. 2. praise.
celebrador, ra, *a.* celebrating; extolling, praising. —*m., f.* one who celebrates, celebrator; one who praises.
celebrante, *a.* celebrating; officiating. —*m.* (ecc.) celebrant (priest); participant in any celebration.
celebrar, *tr.v.* 1. to celebrate (church festival, anniversary, etc.) 2. to celebrate, say (mass). 3. to extol, praise, applaud. 4. to venerate, respect; to accept or look upon with pleasure or approval. 5. to enter into, make (an agreement). 6. to hold (a meeting). —*i.v.* to say or celebrate mass.
célebre, *a.* 1. celebrated, famous, renowned; notable. 2. (coll.) witty, funny. 3. (coll.) eccentric, strange. 4. (Amer., coll.) pretty (woman).
celecanto, *m.* (ichth.) coelacanth.
célebremente, *adv.* eminently; famously; with pageantry or solemnity.
celebridad, *f.* 1. renown, fame; eminence. 2. pomp, magnificence, pageantry. 3. celebrity (famous person).
celemín, *m.* old Castilian measure for land and grain thereof.
celeminear, *i.v.* (Sp.) to go from one place to another.
celenterado, da, *a.* (zool.) coelenterate. —*m.* (zool.) coelenterate, (*pl.*) Coelenterata.
celenterios, *m.* (*pl.*) (zool.) Coelenterata.
celeque, *a.* (Salv., Hond.) tender (fruit).
celera, *f.* (coll.) jealousy.
célere, *a.* prompt, quick, rapid, swift. —*m.* one of the select 300 knights of ancient Roman nobility. —*f.* (*pl.*) (myth.) the hours.
celeridad, *f.* celerity, rapidity, quickness; promptness.
celerífero, ra, *a.* rapid (transit).
celerímetro, *m.* speedometer.
celescopio, *m.* (phys.) coelioscope, abdominoscope.
celesta, *f.* (mus.) celesta.
celeste, *a.* 1. celestial, heavenly. 2. sky-blue, celestial blue. 3. Celestial (Empire), (same as Chinese Empire). 4. (mus.) muting, soft (pedal) — **cuerpo c.,** heavenly body. —*m.* 1. sky blue. 2. (mus.) celeste, voix celeste (organ stop).
celestial, *a.* 1. celestial, heavenly, divine. 2. (iron.) silly, idiotic, foolish, fatuous.
celestialmente, *adv.* celestially, divinely; (fig.) perfectly, excellently, admirably.
celestina, *f.* (min.) celestite.
celestina, *f.* procuress, bawd, madam (of a brothel).
celestinesco, ca, *a.* pertaining or relating to a pimp or procuress.
celestino, na, *a.* Celestine, Benedictine (said of a monk of the religious order founded by Pope Celestine V or pertaining to this order). —*m.* Celestine, Benedictine (monk).
celfo, *m.* (zool.) red guenon of E. Africa.
celia, *f.* fermented wheat beverage of ancient Spain.
celíaca, *f.* (med.) celiac disease, chylous diarrhea.
celíaco, ca, *a.* (anat.) celiac, abdominal, intestinal; **arteria celíaca,** celiac artery. —*m., f.* (med.) person suffering from celiac disease.
celibato, *m.* celibacy; (coll.) bachelor.
celibatario, *m., var. of* **célibe.**
célibe, *a.* celibate, unmarried. —*m., f.* celibate, single person, bachelor, spinster.
célico, ca, *a.* (poet.) celestial, heavenly, divine.
celícola, *m.* one who dwells in heaven.
celidonato, *m.* (chem.) chelidonate.
celidonia, *f.* (bot.) celandine, swallowwort (Chelidonium majus). — **c. menor,** pilewort, lesser celandine.
celidónico, ca, *a.* (chem.) chelidonic.
celinda, *f.* (bot.) syringa, mock orange.
celindrate, *m.* stew seasoned with coriander.
celo, *m.* 1. zeal; ardor, fervor, devotion. 2. sedulousness, earnestness. 3. jealousy, envy; (*pl.*) jealousy, suspicions. 4. heat, rut (of animals). — **dar celos,** to make jealous; **en c.,** in rut, in heat; **tener celos,** to be jealous.
celofán, *m.* cellophane.
celoidina, *f.* (photog.) celloidin.
celoma, *m.* (anat., zool.) coelom, coelome, celom.
celomado, da, *a.* (zool.) coelomate, coelomatous. —*m.* (zool.) coelomate, (*pl.*) Coelomata.
celosa, *f.* (Cuba) shrub of the verbena family (Duranta repens).
celosamente, *adv.* 1. zealously; devotedly. 2. jealously, mistrustfully; enviously.
celosía, *f.* 1. latticed window or shutter; latticework. 2. jealousy. — **mirar por c.,** to feel jealousy; **c. de ventilación,** louver.
celoso, sa, *a.* 1. jealous; envious; mistrustful, suspicious. 2. zealous, earnest. 3. (mar.) crank, easily capsized.
celotipia, *f.* jealousy, jealous passion.
celsitud, *f.* greatness, grandeur, loftiness; excellence; Highness (title).
celta, *a.* Celtic. —*m., f.* Celt. —*m.* Celtic (language).
celtibérico, ca, celtiberio, ria, celtíbero, ra, celtibero, ra, *a., m., f.* Celtiberian, pertaining to the Spanish race and culture resulting from the mixture of Iberians and Celts in N.E. Spain during Roman times.
céltico, ca, *a.* Celtic, pertaining to the Celts.
celtídeo, a, *a.* (bot.) ulmaceous. —*f.* (*pl.*) Ulmaceae.
celtista, *m., f.* Celticist, one who studies the history or language of the Celts.
celtohispánico, ca, *a.* Celto - Spanish, pertaining to the Celtic civilization in Spain.
celtohispano, na, *a., var. of* **celtohispánico.**
célula, *f.* 1. (biol., elec., polit.) cell. 2. (aer.) airframe. — **c. embrionaria** or **germen,** germ cell; **c. fotoeléctrica,** photoelectric cell; **c. fotoemisora,** phototube; **c. nerviosa,** nerve cell; **c. pigmentaria,** pigment cell; **c. polar,** polar body, cell or globule; **c. talofido,** (rad.) thalofide cell.
celulado, da, *a.* celled, formed by or containing cells.
celular, *a.* 1. (bot., zool.) cellular (tissue, etc.). 2. (law) (said of prisons) having individual cells. — **coche c.,** Black Maria, paddy wagon, police ambulance.
celulario, ria, *a.* cellular, composed of many cells.
celulasa, *f.* (biochem.) cellulase.
celulitis, *f.* (med.) cellulitis.
celuloide, *m.* celluloid.
celulosa, *f.* (chem.) cellulose; **c. de etilo,** (chem.) ethyl cellulose; **c. regenerada,** (chem.) regenerated cellulose.
celulósico, ca, *a.* cellulosic.
celuloso, sa, *a.* cellular, cellulated (having many cells).
cellar, *a.* **hierro c.,** iron manufactured in strips (for use as cask hoops in cooperage, etc.).
cellenco, ca, *a.* (coll.) decrepit, senile.
cellerizo, *m.* majordomo of a monastery (in some religious orders).
cellisca, *f.* sleet storm, rain storm.
cellisquear, *i.v.* to sleet.
cello, *m.* hoop (of a cask, barrel, bucket, etc.).
címbalo, *m.* (mus.) cembalo, harpsicord.
cementación, *f.* (metal.) cementation.
cementadora, *f.* 1. (Sp.) cement gun. 2. (Ecuad.) cementing equipment.
cementar, *tr.v.* (metal.) to cement (to modify the composition of a solid by heating it in contact with a powder).
cementerial, *a.* cemeterial, pertaining to a cemetery.
cementerio, *m.* cemetery, graveyard, burial ground.
cementita, *f.* (metal.) cementite.
cemento, *m.* (bldg., min., metal., dent.) cement; **c. armado,** reinforced concrete; **c. de goma,** rubber cement; **c. de Portland,** Portland cement; **c. real,** mixture of clay, blue vitriol and marine salt used formerly in gold refining.
cementoso, sa, *a.* cement-like.
cempoal, *m.* (Mex.) Indian carnation.
cena, *f.* dinner, evening meal; supper; **c. de gala,** banquet; **c. de negocios,** business dinner; **c. espectáculo,** dinner with live entertainment; **la c. de Baltazar,** Belshazzar's Feast; **la última c.,** the Last Supper.
cenaoscuras, *m., f.* 1. (coll.) recluse; an unsociable or shy person. 2. (coll.) miser, skinflint.
cenáculo, *m.* 1. cenacle (room where Christ and His apostles had the Last Supper). 2. (fig.) reunion, dinner.
cenacho, *m.* large wicker basket.
cenadero, *m.* supper-room; garden bower, arbor.
cenador, ra, *a.* pertaining to dinner. —*m., f.* diner; person who has eaten excessively at dinner. —*m.* bower, arbor; loggia or gallery around the patio of houses in Granada.

cenaduría, *f.* (Mex.) inn, tavern.
cenagal, *m.* quagmire, morass; (coll.) fix, difficult situation; **estar metido en un c.,** to be in a fix, be in a difficult situation.
cenagoso, sa, *a.* muddy, miry.
cenal, *m.* (mar.) topgallant rig of a felucca.
cenancle, *m.* (Mex.) ear of corn.
cenar, *i.v.* to dine, sup, have supper. *—tr.v.* to dine on, sup on.
cenata, *f.* (Col., Cuba) abundant and convivial supper party.
cenca, *f.* (Peru) crest (of a bird).
cencapa, *f.* (Peru) headstall of the halter of a llama.
cenceño, ña, *a.* thin, lean, slender (persons, animals, plants).
cencerra, *f., var. of* **cencerro.**
cencerrada, *f.,* (coll.) noisy serenade of bells, horns, etc. on a widower's second wedding night.
cencerrear, *i.v.* 1. to jingle, clang (cowbells). 2. (coll.) to strum, thrum, twang. 3. to play discordantly. 4. (coll.) to rattle, squeak, creak (locks, bolts, doors).
cencerreo, *a.* jingling, clanging (of cowbells); strumming, twanging (a musical instrument); rattling, squeaking, creaking.
cencerro, *m.* cowbell, bell (worn by animals); **a cencerros tapados,** with muffled bells; quietly, stealthily; **c. zumbón,** bell worn by leading cow.
cencerrón, *m.* bunch of small grapes left on the vine.
cencido, da, *a.* untilled (soil).
cencro, *m.* a Brazilian serpent.
cencuate, *m.* (Mex.) poisonous, variegated snake (Pityphis deppel).
cencha, *f.* crossbar, crosspiece (for the legs of a sofa, bed, etc.).
cendal, *m.* 1. (tex.) sendal (a sheer silk or linen fabric). 2. (ecc.) humeral veil. 3. barbs (of a feather). 4. (mar.) xebec, Moorish three-masted vessel.
cendalí, *a.* (tex.) resembling sendal.
cendolilla, *f.* giddy young girl, flapper (coll.).
cendra, *f.* (metal.) bone ash (used in refining gold and silver).
cendrada, *f.* bone ash; layer of ash in a furnace (in silver refining).
cendradilla, *f.* (metal.) small furnace for refining precious metals.
cendrado, da, *past part. of* **cendrar.** *—a.* pure, refined.
cendrar, *tr.v.* to purify, refine.
cendrazo, *m.* (metal.) cupel residue (adhering to silver before it is weighed).
cenefa, *f.* 1. edging, border, trimming; flounce; valance. 2.(ecc.) central piece of a chasuble. 3. (archit.) ornamental border or frieze. 4. (mar.) side canvasses or curtain of an awning.
cenestesia, *f.* (psyc.) coenesthesia, the undifferentiated complex of organic sensation; vital sense.
cenestésico, ca, *a.* (psyc.) coenesthetic.
cenete, *a.* of or pertaining to the Berber tribe of Zenecha. *—m., f.* Zenecha tribesman.
cení, *m.* (metal.) latten, latten brass, fine brass or bronze.
cenia, *f.* 1. noria, water-wheel. 2. Moroccan garden or orchard irrigated by a noria.
cenicero, *m.* 1. ashpit, ashpan (of a furnace or kitchen stove). 2. ashtray.
cenícero, *m., var. of* **cenízaro.**
cenicienta, *f.* Cinderella.
ceniciento, ta, *a.* ashen, ashy, ash-colored.
cenicilla, *f.* (bot.) oidium (genus of fungi causing powdery mildew).
cenismo, *m.* mixture of dialects.
cenit, *m.* (astron.) zenith; (fig.) peak, culmination, eg. *en el c. de su gloria,* at the peak of his fame.
cenital, *a.* (astron.) zenithal.
ceniza, *f.* 1. ash, ashes, cinders. 2. (bot.) cidium. 3. (*pl.*) ashes, human remains. 4. (p.) priming (of ash and glue for canvases). — **c. azul or azules,** mixture of copper sulfate with an arsenical combination; **c. volcánicas,** volcanic ash; **de color c.,** ash-colored; **reducir algo a cenizas,** (fig.) to destroy, ruin something; **Miércoles de ceniza,** Ash Wednesday; **tomar uno la c.,** to have one's forehead marked with ashes on the first day of Lent.
cenizal, *m.* ashpit.
cenízaro, *m.* (C. Rica) Saman rain tree.
cenizo, za, *a.* ashen, ashy, ash-colored. *—m.* 1. (bot.) white goosefoot, pigweed. 2. (bot.) oidium. 3. (coll.) wet blanket, party pooper.
cenizoso, sa, *a.* 1. ashy (covered with ashes). 2. ashen, ash-colored.
cenobial, *a.* cenobitical, monasterial.
cenobio, *m.* monastery, convent.
cenobita, *m., f.* cenobite; monk, nun.
cenobítico, ca, *a.* cenobitic, monastic.
cenobitismo, *m.* cenobitism, monasticism.
cenogénesis, *f.* (biol.) cenogenesis.
cenogenético, ca, *a.* (biol.) cenogenetic.
cenojil, *m.* garter.
cenopegias, *f. pl.* (rel.) Feast of Tabernacles (commemorative of the dwellings of the Israelites while wandering in the wilderness).
cenotafio, *m.* cenotaph, monument honoring a dead person.
cenote, *m.* cenote, natural underground reservoir.
cenozoico, ca, *a.* (geol.) Cenozoic.
censal, *a.* census, of a census.
censar, *tr.v.* (Amer.) to take a census of.
censatario, *m.* 1. (law) pledger, pledgeor, one bound by a living pledge. 2. taxpayer. 3. lessee. 4. one who pays an annuity out of his estate.
censido, da, *a.* (law) pledged.
censo, *m.* 1. census (of population, etc.); official register of citizens having the right to vote. 2. head-tax, tribute (paid by ancient Romans); tax. 3. (ecc.) annual stipend (paid formerly by some churches to their prelates). 4. (law) living pledge, contract whereby an estate is pledged to payment of an annuity as interest on a loan (without transfer of title). — **fundar un c.,** to obtain an income through mortgage; **levantar el c.,** to take the census; **ser un c.,** (coll.) to be a constant source of expenditure or annoyance; to be a burden, be a drain.
censontle, censontli, *m.* (Mex.) mocking bird.
censor, *m.* 1. censor; carper, critic, censorious person. 2. proctor (enforcing compliance with regulations in colleges, etc.).
censoría, *f.* censorship.
censorino, na, *a., var. of* **censorio.**
censorio, ria, *a.* censorial.
censual, *a.* censual (pertaining to a census); pertaining to a pledge or an annuity.
censualista, *m.* pledgee; lessor; annuitant, one receiving the product from a living pledge.
censuario, *m., var. of* **censatario.**
censura, *f.* 1. censorship, post of censor. 2. censorship, censoring, e.g. *la c. es muy estricta,* the censorship is very strict. 3. censure, condemnation, criticism. 4. (ecc.) censure.
censurable, *a.* censurable, reprehensible.
censurador, ra, *a.* censorious; condemnatory; critical. *—m., f.* censurer, critic.
censurante, *a.* censuring; condemning; criticizing.
censurar, *tr.v.* to censure, criticize, condemn; to judge.
censurista, *m., f.* faultfinder, carping critic.
cent. *abbrev. of* **centavo,** cent (c).
centalla, *f.* spark (from burning coal).
centaura, *f.* (bot.) centaury.
centaurea, *f., var. of* **centaura.**
centaureo, a, *a.* (bot.) gentianaceous. *—f.* gentian; (*pl.*) Gentianaceae.
centaurina, *f.* (chem.) bitter extract of the thistle.
centauro, *m.* 1. (myth.) centaur. 2. (astron.) C., Centaurus (constellation).
centavo, va, *a.* centesimal, hundredth. *—m.* one-hundredth; (Amer.) cent (coin).
centella, *f.* 1. spark (of flint or fire; of love, etc.); streak (of lightning). 2. (Chile) crowfoot. — **echar rayos y centellas,** (coll.) to blow up, hit the ceiling, get furious.
centellador, ra, *a.* scintillating, sparkling, twinkling.
centellante, *a., var. of* **centelleante.**
centellar, *i.v., var. of* **centellear.**
centelleante, *a.* sparkling; twinkling; flickering.
centellear, *i.v.* to sparkle, twinkle, scintillate; to shimmer; to flicker.
centelleo, *m.* sparkle, twinkle; sparkling, twinkling; flickering (of a fire, light); glimmer, shimmer (of a fabric, waves, etc.).
centellero, *m., var. of* **centillero.**
centellón, *m. aug. of* **centella,** large spark; flash.
centén, *m.* Spanish gold coin worth 25 pesetas (formerly 100 reales).
centena, *f.* (math.) one hundred (as a unit).
centenada, *f.* a hundred; **a centenadas,** (coll.) by the hundred, in hundreds.
centenal, *m.* one hundred (as a unit).
centenal, *m.* (agr.) rye field.
centenar, *m.* 1. one hundred. 2. centenary (celebration and anniversary). — **a centenares,** fig.) in hundreds, by the hundred.
centenar, *m.* rye field.
centenario, ria, *a.* centennial, centenary, of or pertaining to a period of 100 years; centenarian. *—m., f.* centenarian, a person 100 years old. *—m.* centenary, centennial, a 100th anniversary or its celebration.
centenaza, *a.* rye. *—f.* rye straw.
centenero, ra, *a.* suitable for rye cultivation (said of soil).
centeno, *m.* (bot.) rye.
centeno, na, *a.* hundredth.
centenoso, sa, *a.* containing much rye.
centesimal, *a.* centesimal, hundredth, of or divided into hundredths.
centésimo, ma, *a., m.* hundredth.
centiárea, *f.* centiare, square meter (surface measure).
centibara, *f.* (meteorol.) centibar.
centiestéreo, *m.* centistere, a unit of volume equal to one-hundreth of a cubic meter.
centígrado, da, *a.* centigrade.
centigramo, *m.* centigram.
centil, *m.* centile.
centilitro, *m.* centiliter.
centiloquio, *m.* work divided into a hundred sections or chapters.
centillero, *m.* seven-branched candelabrum (used in the exhibition of the blessed sacrament).
centímano, *a.* (myth.) hundred-handed (mythological giants).
centímetro, *m.* 1. centimeter. 2. (coll.) tape measure; **c.-gramo-segundo,** centimeter-gram-second.
céntimo, ma, *a.* hundredth (part). *—m.* hundredth; cent, centime (coin worth a one hundredth part of a monetary unit).
centinela, *m., f.* 1. (mil.) sentry, guard. 2. (coll.) observer, watchful person; scout. — **c. de vista,** prisoner's guard; **c. perdida,** (mil.) advance

guard, scout; **estar de c., hacer c.,** to be on guard, be on sentry duty.
centinodia, *f.* (bot.) knotgrass (Polygonum aviculare).
centípedo, *m.* (zool.) centipede.
centiplicado, da, *a.* centuplicated, hundredfold.
centipoise, *m.* centipoise, unit of viscosity measure.
centipondio, *m.* quintal, hundredweight.
centolla, *f.* (zool.) spider crab.
centollo, *m., var. of* **centolla.**
centón, *m.* 1. patchwork quilt, crazy quilt. 2. (mil.) coarse gun-cover (used formerly on artillery). 3. (fig.) cento (literary composition formed of selections from other writers).
centonar, *tr.v.* 1. to heap or pile together haphazardly. 2. (fig.) to compose (literary works) by using quotes or selections from other writers.
centrado, da, *past part. of* **centrar.** *—a.* centered (said of a precision instrument or machine part).
centrador, ra, *m.* centralizer, centering device. *—f.* spotting tool. — **c. fijo,** (mach.) steady rest.
centraje, *m.* centering; **de propio c.,** self-centering.
central, *a.* central; centered, centric. *—f.* 1. head office, central office, headquarters. 2. mother house (of a religious order). 3. (elec.) powerhouse. 4. (telephone) exchange. *—m.* (Cuba, Dom. Rep., P. Rico) sugar mill. — **c. azucarera,** sugar mill; **c. de correos,** central Post Office; **c. de teléfonos, or telefónica,** central, telephone exchange; **c. generadora,** electric power plant; **c. hidroeléctrica,** hydroelectric power station; **c. nuclear,** nuclear power plant; **c. sindical,** labor union; **c. térmica,** steam power plant.
centralice, centralicé, *ref.* **centralizar.**
centralidad, *f.* centrality.
centralismo, *m.* centralism (doctrine, system).
centralista, *a., m., f.* centralist (advocate of centralism).
centralita, *f.* telephone exchange.
centralización, *f.* centralization.
centralizador, ra, *a.* centralizing. *—m., f.* centralizer.
centralizar, (*ref. 53*) *tr.v.* to centralize. *—r.v.* to become centralized.
centralmente, *adv.* centrally.
centrar, *tr.v.* 1. to center. 2. to focus, center (rays, shots on a definite spot). 3. to align the centers of. 4. to hit dead center. 5. (carp.) to true. *—i.v.* to be the center of.
céntrico, ca, *a.* central, centric.
centrifugación, *f.* centrifugation.
centrifugador, ra, *a.* centrifugal (machine). *—f.* centrifugal machinery, centrifuge.
centrífugo, ga, *a.* centrifugal.
centrina, *f.* (ichth.) sea spider.
centrino, *m.* (ichth.) species of selachian (Oxynctus centrina).
centríolo, *m.* (biol.) centriole.
centrípeto, ta, *a.* centripetal.
centrisco, *m.* (ichth.) bellows fish, trumpet fish (Centriscus scolopax).
centrista, *m., f.* (polit.) centrist, member of a center party.
centro, *m.* 1. center. 2. headquarters. 3. club, center. 4. object, goal, center (of one's desires). 5. (fenc.) point of balance. 6. long dress made of coarse fabric and worn by Ecuadorean Indian women. 7. (Cuba) three-piece suit. 8. (Mex., Hond.) waistcoat. — **c. comercial,** shopping mall; **c. de atracción** or **gravitación,** (astron.) center of attraction; **c. de flotabilidad,** center of buoyancy; **c. de foniatría,** speech clinc; **c. de gravedad,** (phys.) center of gravity; **c. delantero,** center forward (in soccer); **c. de la vista,** center of vision; **c. de masa** or **inercia,** (phys.) center of mass; **c. de mesa,** table center, centerpiece; **c. demográfico** or **de población,** center of population; **c. de rotación,** center of gyration; **c. espacial,** space center; **c. geométrico,** geometric center; **c. nervioso,** (anat.) nerve center; **c. turístico,** tourist center; **de c. a c.,** (mec., auto.) center to center; **estar uno en su c.,** (coll.) to be in one's element.
Centroamérica, *f.* Central America.
centroamericano, na, *a., m., f.* Central American.
centrobárico, ca, *a.* (mec.) centrobaric.
centroeuropeo, a, *a., m., f.* central European.
centroide, *m.* centroid.
centromedio, *m.* center half (in soccer).
centrómero, *m.* (biol.) centromere.
centrosfera, *f.* (biol., geol.) centrosphere.
centrosoma, *m.* (biol.) centrosome.
centunviral, *m.* (hist.) 1. pertaining to a centumvir. 2. a member of a Roman Court (centumvirate) of about one hundred judges or jurors chosen to try civil suits.
centunvirato, *m.* (hist.) centumvirate, council of the centumvirs.
centunviro, *m.* (hist.) centumvir, member of a tribunal of one hundred members (in ancient Rome).
centuplicar, (*ref. 50*) *tr.v.* to centuplicate, centuple. *—r.v.* to become centuplicated.
centuplique, centupliqué, *ref.* **centuplicar.**
céntuplo, pla, *a.* centuple, hundredfold. *—m.* hundredfold.
centuria, *f.* 1. century. 2. century (division of 100 men in a Roman legion).
centurión, *m.* (hist.) centurion, commanding officer in ancient Rome.
centurionazgo, *m.* (hist.) centurionship, office of a centurion.
cenzalino, na, *a.* (ento.) pertaining to the mosquito.
cénzalo, *m.* (ento.) mosquito.
cenzaya, *f.* (reg., Sp.) nursemaid, nurserymaid; baby sitter.
cenzonte, *m.* (Hond., Mex., ornith.) mockingbird.
ceñideras, *f.* (*pl.*) apron worn by farm laborers and coal shovelers.
ceñido, da, *past part. of* **ceñir.** *—a.* 1. sparing, thrifty. 2. tight, close-fitting. 3. narrow-waisted, wasp-waisted.
ceñidor, *m.* belt, girdle, sash, waist band.
ceñidura, *f.* 1. girdling, encirclement. 2. restraint.
ceñiglo, *m.* (bot.) white goosefoot (Chenopodium album).
ceñir, (*ref. 41*) *tr.v.* 1. to gird, engirdle; to encircle, circle, surround; to enclose. 2. to fit tight or closely (clothes). 3. to hem in, restrain. 4. to abbreviate, shorten, reduce, lessen. — **c. el viento,** (mar.) to sail close to the wind, haul the wind. *—r.v.* 1. to be sparing, moderate or restrained (in one's expenditures, words, acts). 2. to adjust oneself to (work, an occupation). — **ceñirse a,** to adhere to; to get close to; **ceñirse en las palabras** or **gestos,** to be restrained in one's speech or gestures; **c. espada,** to wear a sword; **ceñirse en sus gastos,** to cut one's expenses; **ceñirse la corona,** to ascend the throne.
ceño, *m.* ring, hoop, band, circlet; (vet.) coronary cushion (on a horse's hoof).
ceño, *m.* frown, scowl, glower; threatening aspect, (of the clouds, sea, etc.)
ceñoso, sa, *a.* (vet.) ridged, with a ridgelike swelling on the hoof.
ceñoso, sa, *a., var. of* **ceñudo.**
ceñudo, da, *a.* frowning, scowling, glowering; angry, menacing.
ceo, *m.* (ichth.) John Dory fish (Zeus faber).
ceolita, *f.* (min.) zeolite.
cepa, *f.* 1. (bot.) rootstalk, underground stem base; (agr.) grapevine stock; grapevine; (bot.) stump, stub; root (of an animal's tail, horns, etc.). 2. nucleus of cloud formation. 3. stock, origin (of family lineage). 4. (archit.) pier of an arch or bridge. 5. (Hond.) group of trees or plants having a common root. 6. (Mex.) large pit or hole. — **c. virgen,** (bot.) vine-like plant; **de buena c.,** (fig.) of good stock, of good family; **de pura c.,** genuine, authentic.
cepacaballo, *m.* (bot.) cardoon.
cepadgo, *m.* (formerly) fee paid by prisoner in stocks.
CEPAL *abbrev. of* **Comisión Económica para América Latina,** Economic Commission for Latin America.
cepeda, *f.* land overgrown with shrubs and undergrowth (whose stumps are used for making charcoal).
cepejón, *m.* (bot.) 1. thick root growing from the tree trunk. 2. thick end of a broken branch.
cepellón, *m.* (agr.) clod of earth left on roots of plants when they are transplanted.
cepera, *f., var. of* **cepeda.**
cepilladora, *f.* planer, plane; jointer.
cepilladura, *f.* (carp.) planing; wood shavings.
cepillar, *tr.v.* (carp.) to plane, make smooth, to brush; (coll.) to polish.
cepillazo, (Amer.) adulation; flattery.
cepillo, *m.* 1. brush. 2. (carp.) plane. 3. poor box, alms box, collection bag or basket. 4. (Amer.) flatterer. — **c. bocel,** (carp.) fluting plane; **c. de achaflanar,** bevel plane; **c. biselador,** chamfer plane; **c. dentado,** toothing plane; **c. de ranurar,** grooving plane; **c. para la ropa,** clothesbrush; **c. para las uñas,** nailbrush; **c. de dientes,** toothbrush; **c. rebajador,** sash plane; **c. mecánico,** planer, jointer; **c. universal,** jointing plane.
cepita, *f.* (min.) type of agate consisting of concentric layers.
cepo, *m.* 1. bough, branch (of a tree); cutoff branch of a tree. 2. base, stock (of an anvil); handle (of a tool). 3. pillory, stocks (punishment). 4. reel (for winding silk). 5. wood or metal animal trap. 6. poor box, alms box. 7. clamp (for newspapers, etc.). 8. (artil.) stock (of a field gun). 9. (archit.) pile.
cepo, *m.* (zool.) red guenon of E. Africa, (Cercopithecus cephus).
cepola, *f.* (ichth.) ribbonfish (Cepola rubescens).
cepón, *m. aug. of* **cepa,** grapevine stock.
ceporro, *m.* 1. old vinestock (used for firewood). 2. (fig.) rough, uncouth man, boor, oaf.
cepote, *m.* (mil.) iron clamp to secure trigger guard (on rifles).
ceprén, *m.* lever, crowbar.
ceptí, *a.* of or from Ceuta (Morocco).
cequí, *m.* sequin (ancient gold coin).
cequia, *f., var. of* **acequia.**
cequión, *m.* (Chile) large ditch or canal.
cera, *f.* 1. wax (of insects, plants); beeswax. 2. candle wax. 3. (*pl.*) honeycomb (of bees). — **c. aleda,** bee glue, propolis; **c. amarilla,** yellow wax (wax recently separated from the honey); **c. blanca,** bleached wax; **c. de los oídos,** earwax, cerumen; **c. de lustrar,** floor polish; **c. toral,** unbleached wax; **c. vana,** wax in empty honeycombs; **ser uno como la c.,** (coll.) to be pliable, docile.
ceracate, *f.* (min.) yellow agate.
ceráceo, a, *a.* ceraceous, waxy.

cerachates, *f.* (*pl.*) wax stones.
ceración, *f.* (metal.) smelting, fusion (of metals).
cerafolio, *m.* (bot.) common chervil.
ceragallo, *f.* (C. Rica, bot.) herbaceous perennial of the lobelia family.
cerambícido, da, *a., m., f.* (zool.) cerambycid, pertaining to a variety of beetle.
cerámica, *f.* 1. ceramics, pottery (art). 2. (archeol.) ceramography, study of ceramics.
cerámico, ca, *a.* ceramic, pertaining to ceramics.
ceramista, *m., f.* ceramist, maker of ceramics.
ceramita, *f.* kind of precious stone; brick stronger than granite.
cerapez, *f.* shoemaker's wax.
cerargirita, *f.* cerargyrite, horn silver, native silver chloride.
cerasiote, *m.* (pharm.) a purgative containing cherry juice.
cerasita, *f.* (min.) feldspar of aluminum silicate and magnesium.
cerasta, cerastas, *f.* (zool.) cerastes, horned viper (Cerastes cornutus).
ceraste, cerastes, *m., var. of* **cerasta.**
cerástide, *m.* (ento.) night-flying moth.
ceratias, *m.* (astron.) double-tailed comet.
cerato, *m.* (pharm.) cerate; **c. de galeno,** cerate mixed with attar of roses; **c. de saturno,** cerate mixed with attar of roses and white lead; **c. simple,** simple or basic cerate.
ceratódido, *m.* (ichth.) ceratodus, (*pl.*) Ceratodidae.
ceraunia, *f.* oriental jade (ancient name of jasper or flint).
ceraunomancia, *f.* divination by thunderstorm.
ceraunómetro, *m.* (phys.) instrument for measuring the intensity of lightning.
cerbatana, *f.* 1. blow gun; pea-shooter. 2. ear-trumpet. 3. small culverin. — **hablar uno por c.,** (coll.) to speak through an intermediary or spokesman.
cerbero, *m.* 1. *var. of* **cancerbero.** 2. (bot.) variety of poisonous shrub (Cerbera odallam).
cerca, *f.* 1. fence, wall. 2. (mil.) square (formation). — **c. alambrada,** wire fence.
cerca, *adv.* near, nearby, close by; **cerca de,** near, close to; approximately, nearly; to, at the court of, e.g. *embajador c. de la corte de St. James,* ambassador at the Court of St. James; **de c.,** at close quarters, from a short distance. —*m.* (*pl.*) foreground (of a picture); **tener buen** or **mal cerca,** to look good or bad at close quarters.
cercado, *m.* enclosure, fenced or walled-in garden; fence, wall; (Peru) district. — **c. eslabonado,** chain-link fencing.
cercador, ra, *a.* fencing; surrounding. —*m.* 1. hedger, one who fences or encloses. 2. (metal.) iron graver (tool).
cercamiento, *m.* fencing, enclosing, walling-in.
cercanamente, *adv.* shortly, soon, in a little while (time); close by, at a short distance.
cercanía, *f.* proximity, nearness; neighborhood, vicinity, environs (*gen. pl.*).
cercano, na, *a.* near, close.
cercar, (*ref. 50*) tr.v. 1. to fence, wall-in, enclose. 2. (mil.) to circumvallate; (mil.) to besiege, lay siege to. 3. (fig.) to surround, crowd around.
cercaria, *f.* (zool.) cercaria.
cercén, cercen, *adv.* **a cercén,** completely, entirely; all-round; to the roots.
cercenador, ra, *a.* curtailing; cutting; clipping; paring. —*m., f.* trimmer, cutter; curtailer.
cercenadura, *f.* cutting, clipping; paring; cuttings, parings; curtailment, reduction.
cercenamiento, *m., var. of* **cercenadura.**
cercenar, *tr.v.* to cut off, cut away; to pare, cut around; to reduce, curtail (expenses, etc.).
cercera, *f.* 1. cold northerly wind. 2. air tube, window (for ventilation).
cerceta, *f.* 1. (ornith.) garganey. 2. (*pl.*) fawn's first growth of antlers.
cercha, *f.* 1. (bldg.) truss (of an arch or vault). 2. (archit.) flexible rule for measuring curved surfaces. 3. (mas.) curved template (for shaping ashlar). 4. (carp.) segment (of a circular table, etc.). 5. (mar.) outer rim (of a steering wheel or helm). 6. (Cuba) rod, rib (supporting carriage hood or mosquito net).
cerchar, *tr.v.* (agr.) to layer (vines).
cerchón, *m.* (archit.) truss, ribbed framework (of an arch or a vault).
cerciorar, *tr.v., r.v.* 1. to assure. 2. to ascertain, to find out. — **cerciorarse de,** to ascertain, to make sure.
cerco, *m.* 1. fence, wall; edge, border. 2. ring, circle; witch's circle; (astron.) ring, halo. 3. gyration. 4. hoop (of a cask); rim (of a wheel). 5. frame (of a door, etc.). 6. (mil.) siege. 7. (Hond.) quickset hedge. — **alzar el c.,** (mil.) to raise the siege; **poner c.,** (mil.) to besiege, lay siege.
cercopiteco, *m.* (zool.) cercopithecus (monkey).
cercote, *m.* seine (fishing-net).
cerda, *f.* 1. horsehair; bristle. 2. sow. 3. (vet.) carbuncle (on a hog's neck). 4. (agr.) new-mown wheat. 5. (agr.) bundle of uncombed flax.
cerdamen, *m.* bundle of bristles.
cerdear, *i.v.* 1. to become weak in the forelegs (horses or wounded bulls). 2. to screech (a stringed instrument). 3. (coll.) to refuse obstinately (to do something), look for excuses (for not doing it). 4. (Arg.) to cut a horse's mane.
Cerdeña, *f.* (geog.) Sardinia.
cerdo, *m.* pig, hog; pork meat; (coll.) dirty, rude man. — **chuleta de c.,** pork chop.
cerdoso, sa, *a.* bristly.
cerdudo, da, *a.* 1. bristly, hirsute. 2. (fig.) hairy (man).
cereal, *a.* cereal, cerealian; of or pertaining to the goddess Ceres. —*m.* cereal (plant, grain). —*f. pl.* festival in honor of Ceres.
cerealina, *f.* (chem.) nitrogenous substance found in bran.
cerealista, *a.* cereal (pertaining to the cereal production).
cerebelo, *m.* (anat.) cerebellum.
cerebración, *f.* cerebration.
cerebral, *a.* 1. (anat.) cerebral. 2. (fig.) cerebral, intellectually inclined.
cerebrina, *f.* (pharm.) cerebrin.
cerebro, *m.* (anat.) brain, cerebrum; (fig.) head, brain, mind, intellectual capacity, e.g., *él es un cerebro,* he is a brain. — **c. electrónico,** electronic brain; **c. medio,** (anat.) midbrain; **c. posterior,** (anat.) after brain; **lavado de c.,** brain washing.
cerebroespinal, *a.* (anat.) cerebrospinal.
cerebrósida, *f.* (biochem.) cerebroside.
cereceda, *f.* 1. cherry orchard. 2. (sl.) chain of prisoners.
cerecilla, *f.* (bot.) cherry pepper (Capsioum baccatum).
ceremonia, *f.* 1. ceremony; rite. 2. ceremony, pomp, display, ostentation, show; ceremoniousness, formality, protocol; affected compliment. — **con c.,** ceremoniously, formally, with pomp, in style; **guardar c.,** to observe the formalities; (*pl.*) **maestro de ceremonias,** master of ceremonies, emcee.
ceremonial, *a.* ceremonial, ceremonious. —*m.* 1. ceremonial. 2. book of ceremonies to be observed on public occasions.
ceremonialmente, *adv., var. of* **ceremoniosamente.**
ceremoniáticamente, *adv.* according to ceremony.
ceremoniático, ca, *a.* pertaining to ceremony.
ceremoniero, ra, *a.* (derog.) punctilious, ceremonious.
ceremoniosamente, *adv.* ceremoniously, formally; punctiliously.
ceremonioso, sa, *a.* ceremonious, formal, punctilious.
cereño, ña, *a.* wax-colored (dogs).
céreo, a, *a.* waxen, waxy.
cerería, *f.* candle maker's shop.
cerero, *m.* candle maker; **c. mayor,** royal chandler.
Ceres, *m.* (myth.) Ceres, Roman goddess of harvest; (astron.) Ceres (asteroid).
ceresina, *f.* cherry-tree gum (or gum extracted from other varieties of the genus Prunus).
cerezo, *m.* (bot.) cherry tree; cherry wood; (Amer.) chaparro, dwarf evergreen oak. — **c. de los hotentotes,** (bot.) Hottentot cherry; **c. silvestre,** (bot.) dogwood.
cérico, ca, *a.* ceric, containing cerium.
cérido, *m.* (chem.) cerium metal.
cerífero, ra, *a.* ceriferous, containing wax.
cerífica, *a.* **pintura c.,** encaustic painting done with multicolored wax.
ceriflor, *f.* (bot.) honeywort, honeyflower.
cerilla, *f.* 1. wax taper, wax match. 2. wax cosmetic. 3. (anat.) cerumen, earwax.
cerillero, ra, *m., f.* match vendor. —*f.* matchbox.
cerillo, *m.* 1. long taper; matchstick. 2. (Cuba, bot.) variety of soapberry tree (Hypalate trifoliate).
cerina, *f.* 1. cerin (from cork tree). 2. (min.) cerium silicate. 3. (chem.) substance obtained from white wax.
cerio, *m.* (min.) cerium.
ceriolario, *m.* (archeol.) candelabrum used by ancient Romans.
cerita, *f.* (min.) cerite.
cerito, *m.* (C. Rica, bot.) small shrub bearing wax-like flowers.
cermeña, *f.* (bot.) wild pear (fruit).
cermeño, *m.* 1. (bot.) wild pear (Pyrus communis). 2. (coll.) lout, uncouth and coarse person.
cerna, *f.* core of a tree.
cernada, *f.* 1. leached ashes. 2. size, priming (of canvases for tempera painting). 3. (vet.) poultice (of ashes, etc.).
cernadero, *m.* 1. leach of coarse cloth (used in laundering). 2. linen or silk fabric formerly used to make cape collars.
cernaja, *f.* a strip of fringe added to ox harness to keep flies away.
cerne, *a.* strong, solid (esp. wood). —*m.* heart (of a tree).
cernedera, *f.* wooden frame to support sieves (in bolting).
cernedero, *m.* 1. flour sifter's apron. 2. sifting or bolting room (for flour).
cernedor, ra, *m., f.* sifter, bolter. —*m.* sieve.
cerneja, *f.* (*gen. pl.*) (vet.) fetlock of a horse.
cernejudo, da, *a.* (vet.) having thick fetlocks (of a horse).
cerner, (*ref. 30*) *tr.v.* 1. to sift, bolt. 2. (fig.) to scan, keep watch on. 3. (fig.) to sift, clarify, revise (one's thoughts and actions). —*i.v.* 1. (agr.) to begin to bloom or blossom (flowers). 2. to drizzle. —*r.v.* 1. to hover (birds); to be imminent, to threaten (storm, evil). 2. to walk swaying one's hips.
cernícalo, *m.* 1. (ornith.) kestrel, sparrow hawk. 2. (coll.) boor, lout. — **coger uno un c.,** to get tipsy or drunk. —*a.* (coll.) crude, loutish.
cernidillo, *m.* 1. drizzle. 2. (fig.) mincing gait.
cernido, *m.* sifting of flour; flour sifted and ready to be made into dough.

cernidura, *f.* sifting; (*pl.*) residue, dregs of flour after sifting.
cernir, (*ref. 31*) *tr.v* to sift.
cerno, *m.* heart or core of hardwood.
cero, *m.* zero; **c. absoluto,** (phys.) absolute zero; **ser un c. a la izquierda,** (coll.) to be useless, be a nonentity.
ceroferario, *m.* (ecc.) candle bearer.
cerógrafo, *m.* (archeol.) seal ring used by ancient Romans to seal coffers.
ceroleína, *f.* (chem.) one of the three components of beeswax.
cerollo, lla, *a.* reaped when green and tender (wheat).
ceroma, *f.* (archeol.) oil and wax ointment used by wrestlers in ancient Rome.
ceromancía, ceromancia, *f.* ceromancy (divination by wax dropped in water).
ceromático, ca, *a.* (pharm.) containing oil and wax.
ceromiel, *m.* (med.) ointment of wax and honey formerly applied to ulcers and wounds.
cerón, *m.* residue of honey-comb wax, dross of wax.
ceronero, *m.* one who trades in honeycomb wax.
ceroplástica, *f.* ceroplastics, wax modeling.
cerorrinco, *m.* (ornith.) American hawk-like bird of prey.
ceroso, sa, *a.* 1. waxy, wax-like; soft as wax. 2. (Mex.) soft (boiled eggs).
cerote, *m.* 1. shoemaker's wax. 2. (Bol.) wax taper. 3. (coll.) fear. — (Amer.) **estar hecho un c.,** to look grubby and unkempt, to look a mess.
cerotear, *tr.v.* to wax (cobbler's thread). —*i.v.* (Chile) to drip (wax).
cerotero, *m.* felt for smearing pitch on fireworks.
cerótico, ca, *a.* (chem.) cerotic.
ceroto, *m.* (pharm.) cerate.
cerque, cerqué, *ref.* **cercar.**
cerquillo, *m.* 1. fringe (of a monk's tonsure). 2. welt (of a shoe). 3. (Amer.) fringe, bangs (of hair).
cerquita, *adv.* (coll.) close, very near, at a short distance.
cerracatín, na, *m., f.* miser, tightwad, skinflint.
cerrada, *f.* section of the hide covering the animal's backbone.
cerradero, ra, *a.* closing, shutting. —*m.* 1. (mec.) catch, staple (of a bolt). 2. clasp, drawstrings (of a bag).
cerradizo, za, *a.* closable, that can be closed, shut or fastened (e.g. a door).
cerrado, da, *past part. of* **cerrar.** —*a.* 1. incomprehensible, obscure. 2. gloomy, overcast (sky). 3. thick (beard). 4. (coll.) quiet, silent, reserved. 5. (coll.) with a heavy local accent. 6. (phonet.) closed. 7. (coll.) stupid, dense, dim, e.g. *c. de mollera,* stupid. 8. (coll.) obstinate, inflexible. —*m.* fenced-in garden or property.
cerrador, ra, *a.* closing, locking. —*m.* bolt, bar, hasp, clasp; device for closing.
cerradura, *f.* 1. locking, shutting, closing. 2. lock. — **c. de combinación,** combination lock; **c. de cilindros,** cylinder lock; **c. de golpe** or **de golpe y porrazo,** spring lock.
cerraja, *f.* 1. lock. 2. (bot.) corn sow thistle (Sonchus arvensis).
cerrajear, *i.v.* to work as a locksmith.
cerrajería, *f.* locksmith's trade; locksmith's shop, hardware shop.
cerrajero, *m.* locksmith.
cerrajón, *m.* steep, craggy hill.
cerramiento, *m.* 1. closing, shutting (action); closure, occlusion. 2. fence; partition. 3. stopper, plug. 4. (bldg.) partition wall. 5. (archit.) roof. — **c. de razones,** (law) conclusion of a pleading.
cerrar, (*ref. 29*) *tr.v.* 1. to close; to shut; to lock, bolt, latch. 2. to finish, conclude, terminate. 3. to block, close (road, path, etc.). 4. to swerve in front of (when driving). 5. to block up, fill in, stop up (hole, etc.). 6. to seal (envelope). 7. to close, dissolve (parliament). 8. to bring up the rear of (a march or procession). 9. to enclose, surround, fence in. 10. to cut off, switch off (water, electricity). 11. to give up practice of (a profession), e.g. *c. el bufete,* to give up practicing law, to retire from professional activities; **c. con llave,** to lock up. —*i.v.* 1. to shut, close. 2. to become even (horse's teeth); **c. en falso,** not to catch (door, lock). — **al c. la noche,** in the dead of night. —*r.v.* 1. to close. 2. to heal, close. 3. (mil.) to close ranks (troops). 4. (coll.) to be determined, stand firm (in opinions, objectives); — **cerrarse en falso,** to heal only superficially; **cerrársele a uno todas las puertas,** to find all avenues closed.
cerrazón, *f.* 1. blanket of storm clouds. 2. (Col.) spur (of a mountain range). 3. (Amer.) fog. 4. (fig.) obstinacy; hardheadedness.
cerrejón, *m.* small hill, hillock.
cerrería, *f.* (coll.) laxity, license.
cerreta, *f.* (mar.) wale (each of the wales from the stemhead to the cathead of a vessel).
cerrevedijón, *m.* large tuft of tangled hair or wool.
cerril, *a.* 1. rough, uneven (ground). 2. wild. untamed (cattle, horses). 3. (coll.) rough, uncouth. 4. obstinate; bullheaded.
cerrilla, *f.* mill (screw press for milling coins).
cerrillar, *tr.v.* to mill, flute (coins).
cerrillo, *m.* 1. (bot.) grama grass. 2. (*pl.*) milling dies or collars (for milling coins).
cerrilmente, *adv.* brusquely, roughly, rudely.
cerrión, *m.* icicle (on water pipes, roof gutters).
cerro, *m.* 1. hill, hillock. 2. neck (of animal). 3. backbone. 4. batch of combed flax or hemp. — **echar uno por esos cerros,** (coll.) to go astray; **echar** or **irse por los cerros de Ubeda,** (coll., fig.) to digress, wander (in conversation); to get off the track; **en c.,** bareback.
cerrojazo, *m.* **dar c.,** to shoot a bolt roughly or abruptly; to dissolve (parliament) suddenly.
cerrojillo, to, *m.* 1. (ornith.) coal titmouse (Parus ater). 2. bolt, latch.
cerrojo, *m.* bolt, latch; **c. de embutir,** mortise bolt, flush bolt; **c. de seguridad,** safety bolt; **c. de resorte,** spring bolt; **c. dormido,** dead bolt.
cerrón, *m.* rough burlap; hemp, oakum.
cerruma, *f.* (zool.) pastern (of a horse).
certamen, *m.* 1. contest, competition (esp. literary). 2. literary debate.
certeneja, *f.* 1. pit dug in a riverbed. 2. (Mex.) small, deep waterhole.
certeramente, *adv.* unerringly, accurately.
certero, ra, *a.* 1. well-aimed, accurate; good (shot). 2. knowledgeable, well-informed; sure, certain. — **es un tirador c.,** he is a good shot.
certeza, *f.* certainty; **tener la c.,** to be certain or sure.
certidumbre, *f., var. of* **certeza.**
certificable, *a.* certifiable.
certificación, *f.* certification, attestation; certificate; registering (of mail).
certificado, *past part. of* **certificar.** —*a.* registered (mail). —*m.* certificate; **c. de acciones,** (com.) certificate of stock; **c. de adeudo,** (com.) certificate of indebtedness; **c. de defunción,** death certificate.
certificador, ra, *a.* certifying. —*m., f.* certifier.
certificar, (*ref. 50*) *tr.v.* to certify, attest, affirm; to register (mail); (law) to certify, attest.
certificatorio, ria, *a.* certificatory, certifying.
certifique, certifiqué, *ref.* **certificar.**
certinidad, *f., var. of* **certeza.**
certísimo, ma, *a. super. of* **cierto,** most certain.
certitud, *f., var. of* **certeza.**
cerúleo, a, *a.* cerulean, azure (sky, sea).
cerulina, *f.* (chem.) soluble indigo blue (dye).
ceruma, *f. var. of* **cerruma.**
cerumen, *m.* cerumen, earwax.
cerusa, *f.* (chem.) ceruse, white lead.
cerusita, *f.* (min.) cerussite.
cerval, *a.* cervine, deerlike; **miedo c.,** great fear.
cervantino, na, cervantesco, ca, cervántico, ca, *a.* pertaining to Cervantes.
cervantismo, *m.* influence of Cervantes.
cervantista, *m., f.* Cervantes scholar or specialist.
cervantófilo, la, *a.* pertaining to one who admires or collects the works of Cervantes.
cervario, ria, *a.* cervine, deer-like.
cervatica, *f.* (ento.) locust (Locusta vinidissima).
cervatillo, *m.* (zool.) musk deer (Moschus moschiferous).
cervato, *m.* (zool.) fawn.
cerveceo, *m.* beer fermentation.
cervecería, *f.* brewery; public house (G.B.), beer saloon (U.S.).
cervecero, ra, *m., f.* brewer, beer dealer or vendor.
cerveza, *f.* beer; **c. al grifo** or **a presión** or **de barril** or **c. tirada,** draft beer; **c. clara,** light bear; **c. de marzo,** bock beer; **c. doble,** strong beer; **c. floja,** small beer; **c. negra** or **parda,** dark beer; **c. reposada** or **de conserva** or **rubia,** lager beer.
cervicabra, *f.* (zool.) species of antelope (from India).
cervical, *a.* (anat.) cervical.
cervicitis, *f.* (med.) cervicitis.
cervicular, *a.* cervical.
cérvidos, *m.* (*pl.*) (zool.) Cervidae (deer family).
cervigón, *m., var. of* **cerviguillo.**
cervigudo, da, *a.* thick-necked, bullnecked (coll.); obstinate, stubborn, pig-headed.
cerviguillo, *m.* thick nape, thick neck.
cervillera, *f.* sallet with beaver (medieval armor).
cervino, na, *a.* cervine, deer-like.
cerviz, (*pl.* **cervices**) *f.* cervix, back of the neck, nape; **bajar or doblar uno la c.,** to submit, humble oneself; **levantar la c.,** to put on airs, become arrogant; **ser de dura c.,** to be headstrong.
cervuno, na, *a.* 1. (zool.) cervine, deer-like. 2. bay, bay-colored (horse). 3. made of deerskin, deerskin (as *a.*).
cesación, *f.* cessation, ceasing, discontinuance; **c. a divinis,** canonical suspension of religious services in a desecrated church.
cesamiento, *m., var. of* **cesación.**
cesante, *a.* unemployed, jobless, laid off. —*m., f.* dismissed public employee (with or without a pension); unemployed person.
cesantía, *f.* unemployment; pension (of a dismissed public employee); temporary suspension (of a public employee).
cesar, *i.v.* to cease, stop, come to an end; to abandon, give up, e.g. *c. en sus propósitos,* to abandon one's intentions. — **c. de** + *inf.,* to stop + *ger.*
cesáreo, a, *a.* 1. Caesarean, imperial. 2. (med.) Caesarean. —*f.* (med.) Caesarean (operation).
cesariano, na, *a.* Caesarean (pertaining to Julius Caesar). —*m., f.* follower of Julius Caesar.
cesarismo, *m.* Caesarism, autocracy.
cesarista, *m.* Caesarist, advocate of autocracy.
cese, *m.* 1. cease, ceasing. 2. document ordering cessation of payment of a public employee's salary. — **c. de fuego,** ceasefire.
cesible, *a.* (law) transferable.

cesio, *m.* (metal.) cesium.
cesión, *f.* cession, transfer; **c. con prioridades,** (law) preferential assignment; **c. de bienes,** (law) cessic bonorum; **c. gratuita,** (law) voluntary conveyance.
cesionario, ria, *m., f.* (law) cessionary, transferee.
cesionista, *m., f.* (com.) transferrer, assigner.
cesonario, ria, *m., f., var. of* **cesionario.**
césped, *m.* 1. lawn; grass, turf, turf sod (segment of lawn). 2. bark growing over pruned part of vine.
céspede, *m., var. of* **césped.**
cespedera, *f.* field from which grass sods are taken.
cespitar, *i.v.* to hesitate, waver, vacillate.
cespitoso, sa, *a.* (bot.) cespitose, matted.
cesta, *f.* 1. basket, hamper. 2. scoop-like racket used in the game of jai-alai. — **c. de merienda,** lunch basket; **llevar la c.,** (coll., fig.) to procure, to pimp.
cestada, *f.* basketful.
cestería, *f.* basket factory or shop; basketry.
cestero, ra, *m., f.* basket maker or vendor.
cestiario, *m.* Roman gladiator who fought with a cestus.
cesto, *m.* basket; **c. de papeles,** wastepaper basket; **coger agua en un c.,** to labor in vain; **estar hecho un c.,** (coll.) to be drunk or sleepy.
cesto, *m.* cestus (hand guards used by boxers).
cestodo, da, *a.* (zool.) cestode, cestoid. —*m.* cestode; (*pl.*) Cestoda.
cestón, *m.* 1. large basket. 2. (mil.) corbeil, gabion.
cestonada, *f.* (mil.) defensive work using gabions.
cesura, *f.* (poet.) caesura, cesura, pause in poetry.
ceta, *f., var. of* **zeta.**
cetáceo, a, *a.* (zool.) cetacean. —*m.* cetacian; (*pl.*) Cetacea.
cetano, *m.* (chem.) cetane.
cetaria, *f.* fish-hatchery.
cetario, *m.* breeding ground (of marine mammals).
cético, ca, *a.* (chem.) cetic (said of an acid extracted from cetin).
cetil, *m.* ancient Portuguese coin.
cetilato, *m.* (chem.) derivative of cetyl.
cetilo, *m.* (chem.) cetyl.
cetina, *f.* cetin.
cetís, *m.* ancient Portuguese coin.
cetona, *f.* (chem.) ketone.
cetonia, *f.* (ento.) sap chafer; **c. dorada** (ento.), rose chafer.
cetónico, ca, *a.* ketone (body).
cetosa, *f.* (chem.) ketose.
cetra, *f.* (hist.) leather shield.
cetrarina, *f.* (chem.) cetrarin.
cetrería, *f.* falconry.
cetrero, *m.* 1. falconer. 2. (ecc.) verger (official who carries a verge).
cetrino, na, *a.* 1. sallow (complexion). 2. melancholy (mood). 3. greenish yellow, citrine, citron-like.
cetro, *m.* 1. scepter; staff; (ecc.) rod, verge; perch (in a bird cage). 2. (fig.) reign, rule (of a prince); (fig.) sovereignty. — **empuñar el c.,** to begin to reign; **c. de locuras,** jester's stick.
ceugma, *f.* (rhet.) *var. of* **zeugma.**
ceutí, *a.* of or from Ceuta, North Africa. —*m., f.* native or inhabitant of Ceuta. —*m.* ancient coin of Ceuta.
cevadina, *f.* (chem.) sabadine.
Cf *sym. of* **californio,** californium (Cf).
C F I *abbrev. of* **Corporación Financiera Internacional,** International Finance Corporation (I F C).
cg. *abbrev. of* **centigramo,** centigram (cg., cgm.).
C G T *abbrev. of* **Confederación General de Trabajadores,** General Workers' Union.
cha, *m.* (Amer., Phil. I.) tea.
chabacanada, *f., var. of* **chabacanería.**
chabacanamente, *adv.* 1. cheaply, shoddily; clumsily, crudely. 2. tastelessly, in poor or bad taste.
chabacanear, *i.v.* to work shoddily or carelessly.
chabacanería, *f.* 1. lack of taste, tastelessness. 2. cheapness, shoddiness.
chabacano, na, *a.* 1. tasteless, lacking in taste. 2. cheap, shoddy, poorly made. —*m.* 1. (Mex.) a species of apricot tree. 2. (Phil. I.) patois of Spanish and a regional Philippine dialect.
chabela, *f.* 1. (Bol.) drink made of wine and grain spirits. 2. (Arg.) best friend (said by children).
chabola, *f.* (Sp.) hut, hovel; **las chabolas,** shantytown.
chabuc, *m.* chabouk, chabuk (whip).
chaca, *f.* (Chile) edible shellfish.
chacal, *m.* jackal.
chacalín, *m.* (Hond., zool.) prawn, shrimp.
chacana, *f.* (Ecuad.) 1. stretcher, litter. 2. (Peru) storeroom for fruit.
chacanear, *tr.v.* (Chile) to spur on, goad on.
chácara, *f.* 1. (Amer.) *var. of* **chacra,** small farm. 2. (Ven.) large leather bag worn strapped across the back and chest.
chacarear, *i.v.* (Arg.) to farm, be a farmer.
chacarería, *f.* 1. (Chile) group of small farms. 2. (Chile, Peru, Ecuad.) farming.
chacarero, ra, *m., f.* 1. (Arg., Chile, Urug.) farmer. 2. (Col.) quack, unlicensed practitioner of medicine.
chacarona, *f.* (Can. I., ichth.) dentex (Dentex maroccanus); cured fish.
chacarrachaca, *f.* (coll.) racket, hullabaloo, row.
chacate, *m.* (Mex., bot.) chacate.
chace, chacé, *ref.* **chazar.**
chacera, *f.* (Col.) tray used by vendors of fruit, candy, etc.
chacha, *f.* 1. *abbrev. of* **muchacha,** girl, lass, youngster. 2. nursemaid.
chachá, *m.* 1. (Cuba) a musical instrument. 2. (Guat.) gizzard of fowl.
chachacaste, *m.* (C. Amer.) brandy.
chachaco, ca, *a.* pock-marked.
chachachá, *m.* cha-cha-cha, cha-cha, popular Latin American dance similar to the mambo.
chachagua, *m.* (*pl.*) (Nic.) twins.
chachahuate, *m.* (Guat.) breastband strapped around a horse for bareback riding.
chachalaca, *f.* 1. (Mex., ornith.) chachalaca (Ortalis vetula macalli). 2. (Mex.) chatterbox.
cháchara, *f.* 1. (coll.) prattle, chatter, babble; idle talk. 2. (*pl.*) trinkets, baubles, gewgaws.
chacharear, *i.v.* to chatter, prattle, babble.
chacharería, *f.* (Amer.) collection of trinkets or trifles.
chacharero, ra, *a.* prattling, talkative, garrulous. —*m., f.* 1. prattler, chatterbox, chatterer. 2. peddler of trinkets.
chacharita, *f.* (zool.) collared peccary (Pecari tayacu).
chacharón, na, *a.* talkative, garrulous. —*m., f.* chatterbox, chatterer.
chacho, *m.* 1. *abbrev. of* **muchacho,** boy, lad. 2. (C. Amer.) twin. 3. (Mex.) servant.
chacina, *f.* dried and salted beef; spiced pork used in sausage.
chacinería, *f.* 1. delicatessen, sausage shop. 2. sausage-making, preparation of pressed meats.
chacinero, ra, *m., f.* maker or seller of dried beef or spiced pork.
chacma, *m.* (zool.) chacma.
chaco, *m.* 1. (Amer.) hunt, hunting. 2. (Bol., Par.) **C.,** large bordering region. 3. (Bol.) plantation; small farm; field marked off for exploration. 4. (Ven., arch.) alligator trap.
chacó, *m.* shako, tall cylindrical hat or helmet worn by the light cavalry.
chacolí, *m.* chacoli, light dry wine of Northern Spain.
chacolotear, *i.v.* to clatter (a loose horseshoe).
chacoloteo, *m.* clattering (of a horseshoe).
chacón, *m.* (Phil. I.) a large lizard.
chacona, *f.* (mus.) chaconne, ancient dance of Spanish origin.
chaconada, *f.* jaconet, a light, thin, cotton fabric.
chaconero, ra, *m., f.* person who used to compose chaconnes.
chacota, *f.* banter, joking, kidding; boisterousness, brouhaha, hullabaloo. — **echar una cosa a ch.,** (coll.) to heckle, make a hullabaloo (so that something can't be heard); **hacer una ch. de una cosa,** (coll.) make fun of or ridicule something.
chacote, *m.* (Bol.) long sharp dagger.
chacotear, *i.v.* to kid, joke, jest; to make a lot of noise.
chacoteo, *m.* joking, jesting, kidding.
chacotero, ra, *a.* (coll.) joking, waggish, jesting. —*m., f.* joker, tease, wisecracker; boisterous or rowdy person.
chacra, *f.* (Amer.) small farm; **helársele a uno la ch.,** (Chile) to fail in an undertaking; to suffer misfortune.
chacta, *f.* (Peru) inferior alcohol distilled from sugarcane.
chacuaco, ca, *a.* (Amer.) crude, coarse, ugly. —*m.* 1. (min.) low blast furnace. 2. (C. Amer.) poorly made cigarette; (Mex., Salv.) cigarette butt. 3. (Dom. Rep., Urug.) boor, country bumpkin.
chacual, *m.* (Mex.) pelota or jai alai basket.
chacualear, *i.v.* (Mex.) *var. of* **chacolotear.**
Chad, *m.* the republic of Chad.
chafaldete, *m.* (mar.) clew line.
chafaldita, *f.* (coll.) joke, jest, banter.
chafalditero, ra, *a.* joking, jesting, bantering. —*m., f.* (coll.) joker, banterer.
chafallar, *tr.v.* (coll.) to botch up, mend or do shoddily.
chafallo, *m.* (coll.) shoddy repair, clumsy mending or patching.
chafallón, na, *a.* shoddy, careless. —*m., f.* shoddy workman. botcher.
chafalmejas, *m., f.* (coll.) dauber, poor painter.
chafalonía, *f.* old, useless silver objects (for melting down).
chafalote, *m.* 1. (Bol.) slow, clumsy horse. 2. (Arg.) uncouth, ill-mannered person.
chafandín, *m.* emptyheaded or silly snob.
chafar, *tr.v.* 1. to beat down, flatten. 2. to crease, crumple, rumple (clothes). 3. (fig., coll.) to squash, squelch (someone) in conversation. —*r.v.* to become flattened.
chafariz, (*pl.* **chafarices**) *m.* top of a monumental fountain where the jets are situated.
chafarote, *m.* 1. short wide cutlass; long thin sabre or sword. 2. (Arg., Col.) crude person. 3. (Guat.) uncouth person of military rank.
chafarraño, *m.* (Can. I.) corn cake.
chafarrinada, *f.* spot, stain, blot.
chafarrinar, *tr.v.* to stain, spot, blot.
chafarrinón, *m.* spot, stain; **echar uno un ch.,** (coll.) to commit a faux pas; (coll.) to disgrace the family name.
chafe, *m.* (Arg., Urug., sl.) cop, policeman.
chafirro, *m.* (Mex., C. Rica) knife, machete.
chaflán, *m.* chamfer, bevel, cant.
chaflanado, da, *a.* (archit.) canted.
chaflanador, *m.* beveling tool.
chaflanar, *tr.v.* to chamfer, bevel.
chagolla, *f.* 1. (Mex.) false or very worn coin. 2. anything contemptible. — **de ch.,** for nothing, free.

chagra, *m.* 1. (Ecuad.) peasant; boor, country hick (sl.). 2. (Col.) small rural property.
chagrillo, *m.* (Ecuad.) shower of flower petals strewn in street processions; **hacer ch.,** to spill, scramble something.
chagrín, *m.* tooled leather.
chagua, *f.* (Col.) band, gang; **en ch.,** traditional system of cooperative labor, esp. to transport heavy objects.
chagual, *m.* (Arg., Chile, Peru, bot.) caraguata (Bromelia argentina).
chaguala, *f.* 1. (Col.) metal ornament worn by Indians; nose ring. 2. (Ven.) scrap metal. 3. (Col.) scar. 4. (Mex.) old shoe; slipper; down-at-the-heels shoe.
chagualón, *m.* (Col., bot.) incense tree (Camiphora boswellia).
chaguar, *tr.v.* 1. (Arg.) to wring, wring out (wet clothes, etc.). 2. (Ven.) to clear land while the soil is wet. 3. (Arg.) to milk (cattle). 4. (Col.) the act of twisting the yarn in blanket-weaving.
cháguar, *m.* 1. (S. Amer.) fiber cord used to spin a top. 2. (Peru) hemp rope.
chaguarama, *m.* (C. Amer., bot.) royal palm (Roystonea regia).
chaguarazo, *m.* (Arg., Urug.) 1. whiplash. 2. insult; vulgar and antagonizing remark.
chagüite, chahuite, *m.* 1. (C. Amer.) bog, swamp, morass. 2. (C. Amer.) seedbed in humid soil.
chahuistle, *f.* (Mex., bot.) wheat rust, bunt.
chaina, *f.* (Mex.) 1. Indian flute. 2. (Peru) linnet, goldfinch.
chair, *m.* inner side of a skin or hide.
chaira, *f.* 1. cobbler's knife. 2. steel knife sharpener.
chajá, *m.* (Arg., ornith.) chaja, crested screamer (Chauna torquata).
chajal, *m.* (Ecuad., Guat.) Indian in the service of a parish priest.
chajuán, *m.* (Col.) heat wave, stifling heat.
chal, *m.* stole, shawl.
chala, *f.* 1. (Chile, Peru) corn husk. 2. (Arg., coll.) dough, money.
chalaco, ca, *m., f.* (Peru) 1. person born in Callao, Peru. 2. a kind of straw hat.
chalado, da, *a.* distraught, addle-brained, muddled; **ch. por,** crazy about (someone or something).
chalala, *f.* (Chile) simple sandal worn by peasants.
chalán, na, *a.* pertaining to horse-dealing or trading. —*m.* 1. sharp horse dealer or trader. 2. (Peru) horse trainer, broncho buster. 3. (Mex.) one who collects fares on rural buses. —*f.* flat-bottomed boat, barge.
chalanear, *i.v.* to make a shrewd trade. —*tr.v.* 1. to break or train (horses). 2. (Arg., fig.) to ride (a person) mortifying him verbally. 3. (C. Amer.) to play a joke on.
chalaneo, *m.* trading; (Peru) horsebreaking.
chalanería, *f.* tricks, sales technique (used by horse traders).
chalanesco, ca, *a.* (derog.) tricky, astute, clever, shrewd.
chalarse, *r.v.* to go mad, lose one's head. — **ch. por,** to fall hopelessly in love with, lose one's head over.
chalate, *m.* (Mex.) small, lean horse.
¡chalay! *interj.* (Arg.) exclamation indicating that something smells delicious.
chalaza, *f.* chalaza, each of two filaments holding the egg yolk in place inside the shell.
chalcha, *f.* (Chile) double chin.
chalchihuite, *m.* 1. (Mex., C. Rica) emerald in the rough. 2. (*pl.*) (C. Amer.) baubles, trinkets, gewgaws.
chalchudo, da, *a.* (Chile) chubby-cheeked.
chalé, *m., var. of* **chalet.**
chaleco, *m.* waistcoat, vest.
chalequero, ra, *m., f.* waistcoat-maker, vest-maker.
chalet, *m.* chalet, summer house, Swiss-style cottage.
chalí, *m.* challis (cloth), mohair, delaine.
chalina, *f.* 1. (Amer.) narrow shawl. 2. cravat, scarf.
chalón, *m.* (Arg., Urug., Chile) large, warm shawl.
chalona, *f.* (Bol., Peru, Arg.) jerked or salted mutton.
chalote, *m.* (bot.) shallot.
chaludo, da, *a.* (Arg.) well-heeled, wealthy, well-off.
chalupa, *f.* 1. sloop, shallop; launch, long boat; (Mex.) canoe for two persons. 2. (Mex.) corn tortilla fried and filled with chopped meat, lettuce, cheese, etc.
chama, *f.* (coll.) exchange, barter, trade.
chamaco, ca, *m., f.* (Mex.) kid, youngster.
chamada, *f.* 1. brushwood. 2. (coll.) streak of bad luck.
chamagoso, sa, *a.* (Mex.) dirty, unkempt; low, vulgar.
chamagua, *f.* (Mex.) field of corn beginning to ripen.
chamal, *m.* (Arg., Chile) blanket worn by the Araucan Indians in lieu of trousers.
chamanto, *m.* (Chile) multicolored woolen cape or cloak.
chamar, *tr.v.* (coll.) to exchange, barter.
chámara, *f., var. of* **chamarasca.**
chamarasca, *f.* brushwood; brushwood fire, quick blaze kindled with brushwood.
chamarilear, *tr.v.* to barter, exchange.
chamarilero, ra, *m., f.* junk dealer, junkman.
chamarillero, ra, *m., f.* 1. dealer in secondhand merchandise. 2. gambler.
chamarillón, na, *m., f.* person who plays cards poorly.
chamariz, (*pl.* **chamarices**) *m.* (ornith.) greenfinch.
chamarón, *m.* (ornith.) long-tailed titmouse.
chamarra, *f.* 1. coarse cloth jacket; (Mex.) sheepskin jacket. 2. (C. Amer., Ven.) wool blanket worn as a wrap during the day and used as bedcover at night. 3. (C. Amer.) trick, cheat.
chamarreta, *f.* short, loose sports jacket.
chamarro, *m.* (C. Amer., Mex.) coarse woolen shawl or blanket.
chamba, *f.* (coll.) 1. fluke, piece of luck, lucky break. 2. (col.) wide, deep ditch. 3. (Mex., coll.) job, employment. 4. (Arg., Ecuad.) turf. 5. (Bol., min.) bluish grey sulfate of zinc.
chambado, *m.* (Arg., Chile) drinking vessel made of horn.
chambear, *i.v.* 1. (Col., Ecuad.) to go through the grasslands, across the turf. 2. (Ecuad.) to fill in land with sod. 3. (Mex., coll.) to work, to do a job. —*tr.v.* 1. (Col.) to plant grass. 2. (Mex.) to swap, exchange.
chambelán, *m.* chamberlain, royal attendant; high official.
chamberga, *f.* long, loose cassock.
chambergo, *a.* of or pertaining to the Shomberg regiment of guards serving Charles II in Spain. —*m.* broad-brimmed soft hat.
chamberines, *m.* (*pl.*) (Mex.) flashy ornaments, trinkets, tinsel.
chambilla, *f.* (archit.) stone wall supporting an iron fence.
chambo, *m.* (Mex.) exchange of grain for other goods.
chambón, na, *a.* (coll.) awkward, clumsy (in a game); unskillful, incompetent, butterfingered, fumblefisted; undeservingly lucky. —*m., f.* bungler; botcher; greenhorn.
chambonada, *f.* 1. (coll.) foolish mistake, bungle or blunder. 2. (coll.) undeserved piece of luck.
chambonear, *i.v.* (Amer.) to make foolish mistakes; to bungle, botch.
chamborote, *a.* 1. (Ecuad.) said of long white pepper. 2. (Ecuad., Guat., fig.) said of long-nosed person.
chambra, *f.* 1. short loose blouse or jacket worn by women at home. 2. (Dom. Rep.) safety pin. — **de ch.,** by chance.
chambrana, *f.* 1. (archit.) wooden or stone frame around doors. 2. (Ven.) uproar, noise.
chambuque, *m.* (Col.) way of lassoing cattle; **echar ch.,** to lasso.
chamburgo, *m.* (Col.) stagnant water; puddle, pool.
chamelicos, *m.* (*pl.*) 1. (Chile, Peru) old, worn clothing; discardable household utensils. 2. (Col.) tawdry ornaments or frills of dress.
chamelote, *m.* camlet, strong cloth, waterproof material.
chamelotón, *m.* ordinary, coarse camlet.
chamerluco, *m.* close-fitting jacket with a collar (formerly worn by women).
chamicado, da, *a.* (Chile, Peru) silent, taciturn; suffering from a hangover.
chamical, *m.* (Arg., Peru, Ecuad.) place where **chamico** is plentiful.
chamicera, *f.* stretch of burnt woodland.
chamicero, ra, *a.* pertaining to burnt wood.
chamico, *m.* (bot.) thorn apple, Jimson weed. — **dar ch. a,** to bewitch, seduce.
chamiza, *f.* 1. (bot.) chamiso, chamise, wild cane used for thatching. 2. brushwood used as kindling.
chamizar, *tr.v.* to thatch or cover with wild cane.
chamizo, *m.* 1. half-burnt tree or log. 2. thatched hut. 3. (coll.) den, hangout.
chamorra, *f.* (coll.) shorn head, shaved head.
chamorro, rra, *a.* shorn, clipped; beardless (wheat). —*m., f.* person with shorn or shaved head.
champa, *f.* 1. (Chile, Peru) clod of earth, sod, piece of turf. 2. (Chile, Peru) ball, clump, cluster, tangle, ravel, snarl. 3. (C. Amer.) primitive hut or shelter.
champaca, *f.* (bot.) champak, an East Indian tree (Michelia champaca).
champán, *m.* 1. sampan (river boat, flatbottomed barge). 2. champagne.
champanera, *f.* 1. (Mex.) team of draft animals belonging to a farm hand who hires out.
champaña, *m.* champagne.
champañazo, *m.* (Chile) champagne party.
champañizar, (*ref. 53*) *tr.v.* to make (wine) sparkling.
champar, *tr.v.* 1. (coll.) to say unpleasant things to. 2. to remind of a favor.
champí, *m.* (Arg.) a tiny insect (Trox suberosus); **hacerse uno el ch.,** (coll.) to play possum; to play dumb.
champiñón, *m.* mushroom.
champola, *f.* (Cuba) a kind of milkshake made with the pulp of some tropical fruit; **c. de guanabana,** custard-apple shake.
champú, *m.* (Angl.) shampoo.
champurrado, *past part. of* **champurrar.** —*m.* 1. mixture of liquors. 2. (Mex.) chocolate-flavored atole (cornmeal drink). 3. (Amer.) hodgepodge, anything scrambled.
champurrar, *tr.v.* (coll.) to mix (liquors).

champurrear, *tr.v., var. of* **chapurrear.**
champuz, *m.* (Ecuad., Peru) cornmeal mush flavored with orange juice and sugar.
chamuchina, *f.* 1. (Amer.) crowd, rabble; group of children. 2. (Ecuad., Ven.) fight, quarrel. 3. (Par.) meat grilled over charcoal embers.
chamullar, *i.v.* (coll.) to talk, speak.
chamuscado, da, *past part. of* **chamuscar.** *a.* 1. (coll.) infected, tainted (with vice or passion). 2. singed, scorched.
chamuscar, (*ref. 50*) *tr.v.* 1. to singe, sear, scorch. 2. (Mex.) to sell cheaply. —*r.v.* 1. to singe, scorch, become singed. 2. (Col.) to get furious.
chamusco, *m., var. of* **chamusquina.**
chamusque, chamusqué, *ref.* **chamuscar.**
chamusquina, *f.* 1. singe, scorch; singeing, scorching. 2. (coll.) quarrel, dispute. — **oler a ch.,** (coll.) to look like a fight, look nasty (when a quarrel becomes heated); to smell of heresy (declarations of faith).
chamusquino, na, *a.* (Ecuad.) vulgar; unaesthetic; in poor taste.
chan, *m.* (Salv., Guat.) sage seed. 2. (C. Amer.) refreshing drink made with lemon, water, sage seed and sugar.
chana, *f.* (Hond.) winning hand in a card game.
chanada, *f.* (coll.) trick, ruse.
chanate, *m.* (Mex.) blackbird.
chanca, *f.* 1. (Bol.) hash made with rabbit or chicken and peppers. 2. (Peru, Chile) threshing, beating.
chancacazo, *m.* 1. (Chile) *aug. of* **chanca,** severe beating, kicking. 2. (Peru) stoning.
chancada, *f.* 1. (Amer.) crude brown sugar in blocks. 2. (Ecuad.) toasted corn or wheat, ground and mixed with honey.
chancadora, *f.* (Chile) crusher, crushing machine, grinder; machine for crushing metals.
chancar, (*ref. 50*) *tr.v.* 1. (Chile, Peru, C. Amer.) to crush, grind. 2. (C. Amer., Chile, Peru) to mistreat, beat up. 3. (Chile, Ecuad.) to do something poorly or half-way.
chancay, *m.* (Peru) sponge cake or sweet bread.
chance, *m.* (Amer.) chance, opportunity, possibility.
chancear, *i.v., r.v.* to joke, jest, fool.
chancero, ra, *a.* merry, jocose. —*m., f.* joker, jester, banterer.
chancha, *f.* 1. (Amer.) sow, female pig. 2. (Arg.) pod, string bean. 3. (Col., sl.) trap, mouth. — **hacer la ch.,** (Chile) to play hookey, miss classes in school.
cháncharras máncharras, *f.* (*pl.*) excuses, pretexts (for not doing something); **no andemos en ch. m.,** let's not beat about the bush.
chanchería, *f.* (Arg., Chile) pork butcher shop, sausage shop.
chanchira, *f.* (Col.) rag, ragged clothes.
chanchiriento, ta, *a.* (Col.) ragged.
chancho, cha, *a.* (Amer.) dirty, filthy. —*m.* (Amer.) hog, pig. — **botar el ch.,** (Peru, vulg.) to fart, break wind; **hacer un ch.,** (Chile, vulg.) to belch; (S. Amer.) **quedar como ch.,** to let someone down, fall down on an obligation; (S. Amer.) **ser (dos personas) como chanchos,** to be close friends.
chanchullero, ra, *a.* crooked, swindling. —*m., f.* crook, swindler, racketeer (coll.).
chanchullo, *m.* (coll.) swindle, racket, crooked dealing; graft, political corruption. — **andar en chanchullos,** to be up to some crooked business; to practice graft, be in on the take (sl.).
chanciller, *m.* chancellor.
chancillería, *f.* 1. chancery (court). 2. chancellor's fees and post.
chancla, *f.* 1. old shoe worn down at the heels. 2. slipper.
chancleta, *f.* 1. slipper, house shoe. 2. (S. Amer., derog.) newborn girl. —*m., f.* (coll.) washout, useless person, nincompoop. — **largar la ch.,** (Cuba, coll.) to kick the bucket, to die.
chancletear, *i.v.* to go around in slippers; to shuffle about, dragging one's shoes or slippers.
chancleteo, *m.* clatter, patter of slippers.
chancletero, ra, chancletudo, da, *a.* (Amer.) low-born; low class.
chanclo, *m.* clog, wooden-soled or thick, leather-soled overshoe; galosh, overshoe, rubber.
chancón, *m.* (Peru) grind, bookworm, unusually dedicated student.
chancro, *m.* (med.) chancre, venereal or syphilitic ulcer.
chancroide, *f.* (med.) chancroid.
chancroso, sa, *a.* chancrous.
chancuar, *tr.v., var. of* **chancar,** (Arg.) to grind, crush.
chancuco, *m.* (Col.) smuggled tobacco.
chanda, *f.* (Col.) itch, mange.
chaneca, *f.* (Bol., coll.) braid, plait.
chanfaina, *f.* stew made of liver and lungs.
chanfle, *m.* 1. (Mex.) chamfer, bevel, cant. 2. (Arg.) cop, policeman.
chanflear, *tr.v.* to bevel.
chanflón, na, *a.* 1. rough, crude, rude, coarse. 2. said of a person trying to pass himself off as something he is not. —*m.* 1. ancient copper coin. 2. (Sp.) children's game.
changa, *f.* 1. (Cuba) joke, jest. 2. unimportant business deal or barter. 3. (Arg.) the job of portering.
changador, *m.* (Arg., Chile) porter, carrier.
changalla, *f.* (Chile) variety of shrimp.
changamé, *m.* (ornith.) a Panamanian species of thrush.
chango, ga, *a.* 1. (Mex.) clever, bright. 2. (P. Rico) said of one who likes to joke. 3. (Chile) dull, tedious, boring. —*m., f.* 1. (Mex.) young person. 2. (Mex.) monkey. 3. (Arg., Urug.) child, kid. — **estar ch.,** (Mex., P. Rico, Dom. Rep.) to be plentiful and cheap; **ponerse ch.,** (Mex.) to take precautions, be on guard, get smart.
Changó, *m.* (Cuba) principal deity in the African lore of the Antilles, often identified with Saint Barbara.
changote, *m.* (metal.) billet, bloom.
changuear, *i.v.* (Col., Cuba, P. Rico) to joke, jest.
changuero, ra, *a.* 1. (Col., Cuba, P. Rico) jocose, sportive, merry. 2. (Arg.) said of an animal or vehicle that makes short trips.
changüí, *m.* 1. (coll.) hoax, joke, trick. 2. (Cuba) a country dance. — **dar ch. a,** to play a trick on.
changuito, *m. dim. of* **chango,** (Mex.) little monkey.
chano, chano, *adv.* (coll.) slowly, step by step.
chanque, chanqué, *ref.* **chancar.**
chanquete, *m.* (S. Sp.) a small, succulent fish eaten fried as an appetizer.
chantado, *m.* wall or fence built of flagstone.
chantaje, *m.* blackmail.
chantajista, *m., f.* blackmailer.
chantar, *tr.v.* 1. to put on (clothes). 2. to stick in, thrust in, drive in (something). 3. to say (something) straight to someone's face. 4. to fence off (a property). 5. to pave with flagstones.
chantillí, *m.* whipped cream.
chanto, *m.* (Sp.) trunk, branch, stone (stuck vertically into the ground); stone block (used in making fences and pavement).
chantre, *m.* cantor, precentor (leading singer in a cathedral).
chantría, *f.* precentorship, office of cantor.
chanza, *f.* joke, fun, jest. — **de ch.,** in fun.
chanzoneta, *f.* 1. carol, chansonette, little song. 2. (coll.) joke, jest.
chanzonetero, *m.* writer of chansonettes or carols, chansonnier.
chaña, *f.* (Chile, coll.) scrimmage, skirmish, struggle.
chañaca, *f.* 1. (Chile) itch, mange, skin disease. 2. discredit, ill fame. — **hacer ch.,** to break into small pieces.
chañar, (Amer.) variety of tree.
chaño, *m.* (Chile) coarse wool blanket.
chapa, *f.* 1. sheet (of metal, wood), plate; (carp.) veneer (layer of wood). 2. (Cuba) license plate (of an automobile). 3. (S. Amer.) shingle (of a doctor, lawyer, etc.). 4. rouge; blush. 5. (coll.) good sense, good judgment, e.g. *hombre de ch.,* sensible or judicious man. 6. (*pl.*) game of tossing two coins in the air. 7. (Amer.) lock. 8. (Ecuad., sl.) policeman. 9. (Peru) rosy cheek. 10. (auto.) body work. 11. (Col.) key ring. 12. bottle cap. — **ch. metálica,** sheet metal.
chapadamente, *adv.* (arch.) perfectly.
chapadanza, *f.* 1. joke, banter. 2. (Col.) disorder, confusion.
chapado, da, *past part. of* chapar. —*a.* 1. red-cheeked. 2. covered with metal sheets or sheeting; veneered. — **ch. a la antigua,** (coll.) old-fashioned. —*f.* a slap in the face.
chapalear, *i.v.* 1. to splash, splatter. 2. to rattle.
chapaleo, *m.* 1. splash, splatter. 2. (Ven.) clicking noise made by a loose spur or horseshoe.
chapaleta, *f.* valve (of a hydraulic pump); flap, cap, clapper.
chapaleteo, *m.* lapping (of waves); patter (of rain).
chapaneco, ca, *a.* (Mex., coll.) short, stubby (person).
chapapote, *m.* (Amer.) Trinidad asphalt, mineral tar.
chapar, *tr.v.* 1. to cover, to plate with silver or gold; to veneer. 2. to fit, set (tiles, etc.). 3. to say something disagreeable. — **le chapó un no como una casa,** he said no quite definitely.
chaparra, *f.* 1. (bot.) kermes oak. 2. (arch.) broad, low carriage.
chaparrada, *f., var. of* **chaparrón,** downpour, heavy shower.
chaparral, *m.* grove of dwarf oaks.
chaparrazo, *m.* (Hond., Ven.) *var. of* **chaparrón.**
chaparrear, *i.v.* to rain heavily, pour.
chaparreras, *f.* (*pl.*) (Mex.) chaps, openseated leather garment worn over cowboy's ordinary trousers as a protection for the legs.
chaparro, *m.* 1. dwarf or scrub oak; (C. Amer.) chaparro (Curatella americana). 2. short, stubby person. 3. (Mex.) kid, child.
chaparrón, *m.* heavy rain of short duration, downpour, shower.
chapatal, *m.* quagmire, bog, swamp.
chape, *m.* 1. (Col., Chile) tress, braid, plait (of hair). 2. (Chile, zool.) slug, snail.
chapeado, da, *past part. of* **chapear.** —*a.* 1. covered with metal sheets or sheeting; veneered. 2. (Amer.) said of someone with high coloring. —*m.* veneering; veneer.
chapear, *tr.v.* 1. to cover with metal sheets or sheeting. 2. (carp.) to veneer. 3. (Cuba) to clear (the ground) with a machete. —*i.v.* to rattle (a loose horseshoe).
chapecar, (*ref. 50*) *tr.v.* (Chile) to **braid.** plait (hair); (Chile) to string (onions, etc.).
chapelete, *m.* formerly used bonnet or head cover.
chapeo, *m.* (coll.) hat.
chapeque, chapequé, *ref.* **chapecar.**
chapera, *f.* (bldg.) ramp made of planks and used in lieu of stairs during construction.

chapería, *f.* ornamental sheets, sheeting or veneer.
chaperón, na, *m.* 1. hood, cowl. 2. (archit.) wooden support, gutter. —*m., f.* chaperone.
chaperonado, da, *a.* (her.) hooded, capped.
chapeta, *f.* 1. rosy cheek. 2. small metal plate.
chapetón, na, *a.* 1. (Amer.) newly arrived from Europe. 2. (Amer.) inexperienced, unskillful. 3. (Arg.) boastful, bragging. —*m. f.* (Amer.) newly arrived Spanish immigrant. —*m.* 1. (Amer.) downpour, shower. 2. (Peru) newcomer's illness (on arrival from Europe). — **pasar el ch.,** (coll.) to emerge from a danger or difficulty.
chapetonada, *f.* 1. (Peru) illness suffered by newly arrived Europeans. 2. (Amer.) inexperience, behavior of a greenhorn. 3. (Peru) itching skin eruption, rash. 4. (Dom. Rep.) cloudburst.
chapín, *a.* (Col., Hond.) bowlegged; having crooked feet (person).
chapín, na, *m., f.* (C. Amer. coll.) person born in Guatemala. 2. (Col., Guat., Hond.) youngster. —*m.* 1. (ichth.) trunkfish. 2. woman's shoe with a cork sole, clog.
chapinazo, *m.* blow with a clog or patten.
chapinería, *f.* job or trade of clog-maker; shop where clogs are made; stall or store where clogs are sold.
chapinero, *m.* person who makes or sells clogs or pattens.
chapinete, *m.* (archit.) wooden beam which forms part of a wooden frame.
chapino, na, *a.* (Arg. coll.) bowlegged.
chápiro, *m.* (coll.) expression conveying anger. — **por vida del ch., ¡voto al ch.!** confound it!
chapisca, *f.* (C. Rica) corn harvest.
chapista, *m.* sheet-metal worker.
chapistería, *f.* sheet-metal work; **taller de ch.,** auto shop, garage, repair shop (for bodywork).
chapistero, *m.* sheet-metal worker; tinker.
chapitel, *m.* 1. spire (of a tower); capital (of a column). 2. pivot (of a magnetic needle).
chaple, *m.* graver, burin, tool used by sculptors and engravers.
chapó, *m.* game of billiards for four players.
chapodar, *tr.v.* to prune, trim, lop, clip (a tree); (fig.) to cut down, reduce.
chapodo, *m.* branch trimmed from a tree; lopping.
chapola, *f.* (Col.) butterfly, moth.
chapolear, *i.v.* (Col., fig.) to flit from flower to flower; to be fickle and capricious in love.
chapolero, ra, *a.* (Col.) said of a fickle person.
chapón, *m.* large ink stain, ink blot.
chapona, *f.* 1. loose house jacket or blouse. 2. (Sp.) barber's smock.
chapopote, *m.* (Mex.) Trinidad asphalt.
chaposo, sa, *a.* (Bol., Peru) thick-bearded and rosy-cheeked.
chapotazo, *m.* (Arg.) a splash of water thrown by someone's cupped hands.
chapote, *m.* (Mex., Guat.) a type of wax formerly chewed to clean, whiten, and strengthen teeth.
chapotear, *tr.v.* to moisten, wet, dampen (with a wet sponge or cloth). —*i.v.* to splash water with the feet or hands.
chapoteo, *m.* splash, splatter.
chapuce, chapucé, *ref.* **chapuzar.**
chapuceador, ra, *m., f.* blunderer, blunderhead.
chapucear, *tr.v.* to do hurriedly and in a slapdash manner; (coll.) to do in a slipshod manner, to botch, bungle.
chapuceramente, *adv.* in a slipshod manner, shoddily, carelessly; fumblingly, clumsily.
chapucería, *f.* 1. botch, shoddy or slipshod piece of work; shoddiness, shoddy work. 2. fib, lie.
chapucero, ra, *a.* 1. shoddy, slipshod (work or person). 2. rough, unpolished, clumsy, rude. —*m., f.* 1. bungler, sloppy, careless worker. 2. blacksmith who forges simple objects such as nails, trivets, etc.
chapul, *m.* (Col.) dragonfly.
chapulín, *m.* 1. (Amer.) locust, large grasshopper. 2. (C. Amer.) small child, tot.
chapurrado, *past part. of* **chapurrar.** —*m.* cocktail; (Cuba) drink made of water, plums, sugar and cloves boiled together.
chapurrar, chapurrear, *tr.v.* 1. to speak (a foreign language) poorly or with difficulty, e.g. *yo chapurro el francés,* I speak a little French. 2. to mix (drinks).
chapuz, (*pl.* **chapuces**) *m.* 1. trifle. 2. slipshod or clumsy work. 3. (mar.) spar. 4. ducking, the act of pushing someone briefly under water. — **dar ch.,** to duck.
chapuza, *f.* slipshod work; unimportant work or job.
chapuzar, (*ref. 53*) *tr.v.* to duck (someone) under water. —*i.v., r.v.* to duck or take a quick dip under water.
chapuzón, *m.* duck, ducking.
chaqué, *m* morning coat, cut-away coat.
chaqueño, ña, *a.* of or from the Chaco, a region of S. Amer. between Argentina, Bolivia and Paraguay.
chaqueta, *f.* jacket; **c. de fumar,** smoking jacket; **ch. salvavidas,** life jacket; **ch. cazadora,** hunting jacket.
chaquete, *m.* backgammon (a table game).
chaquetear, *i.v.* 1. to be afraid, draw back; to run away, flee. 2. to change sides, become a turncoat; to change one's opinion, to renege.
chaquetilla, *f.* short jacket, bolero; **ch. torera,** bullfighter's jacket.
chaquetón, *m. aug. of* **chaqueta,** overcoat.
chaquiñán, *m.* (Ecuad.) path, short-cut.
chaquira, *f.* 1. glass bead, mock-pearl (sold by Spaniards to Peruvian Indians). 2. (Mex., Col.) embroidery beads or spangles.
chara, *f.* (Arg., Chile) ostrich fledgling.
charabán, *m.* charabanc, coach.
charada, *f.* charade.
charadrio, *m.* (ornith.) stone curlew, thick-knee (Burhinus cedicnemus).
charal, *m.* (Mex.) a lake fish.
charamusca, *f.* 1. (*pl.*) brushwood, firewood. 2. (Mex.) candy or taffy twist or spiral.
charamusquero, ra, *m., f.* (Mex.) vendor of candy twists.
charanga, *f.* 1. (mus.) brass band; fanfare. 2. (Mex., Cuba, C. Rica) a family party, a small but festive gathering.
charango, *m.* a kind of five-stringed bandore or guitar used by Peruvian Indians.
charanguero, ra, *a.* slipshod, shoddy, careless. —*m., f.* 1. bungler, slipshod person. 2. (reg., S. Amer.) peddler. 3. (reg., S. Amer.) small boat used in trading along the coast.
charapa, *f.* (Peru, zool.) small edible tortoise.
charape, *m.* (Mex.) fermented beverage made with agave juice, corn, honey, cloves and cinnamon.
charca, *f.* pool, pond, basin.
charcal, *m.* marshy land, land full of puddles of water.
charco, *m.* pool, pond, puddle; **pasar uno el ch.,** (coll.) to cross the ocean.
charcón, na, *a.* (Arg.) lean, thin (person, animal). —*m.* (Arg.) animal (esp. cattle).
charla, *f.* 1. (coll.) chat, conversation, prattle; lecture, talk. 2. (ornith.) missel thrush (Turdus viscivorus).
charlador, ra, *a.* garrulous, talkative, (coll.) prattling. —*m., f.* chatterbox, chatterer, prattler.
charladuría, *f.* prattle, chatter; gossip.
charlante, *a.* (coll.) prattling, garrulous, talkative.
charlatín, na, *m., f.* (coll.) gossip, prattler.
charlar, *i.v.* to chat, converse, talk; to chatter, prattle.
charlatán, na, *a.* 1. garrulous, talkative, chattering; gossiping. 2. phoney (coll.), swindling. —*m., f.* 1. charlatan, fast talker, quack, swindler, mountebank. 2. prattler, chatterbox; gossip, gossip-monger.
charlatanear, *i.v., var. of* **charlar.**
charlatanería, *f.* 1. loquacity, garrulity, talkativeness. 2. quackery.
charlatanismo, *m.* 1. garrulity, loquacity; charlatanism. 2. quackery.
charlear, *i.v.* to croak (a frog).
charlón, na, *a.* (Ecuad.) garrulous, talkative. —*m., f.* chatterbox.
charlotear, *i.v.* to chatter, prattle.
charloteo, *m.* chat, conversation; chatter, prattle; gossip.
charneca, *f.* (bot.) mastic tree.
charnecal, *m.* plantation or grove of mastic trees.
charnela, *f.* hinge (of a window, door; of a bivalve shell); buckle chape; knuckle.
charneta, *f.* (coll.), *var. of* **charnela.**
charnical, *m., var. of* **charnecal.**
charniegos, *m.* (*pl.*) (coll.) shackles, fetters.
charol, *m.* 1. varnish, lacquer, japan. 2. patent leather (of shoes). — **darse charol,** to blow one's own trumpet; to put on airs.
charola, *f.* 1. (Mex., Arg.) tray. 2. (Amer.) large ugly eye.
charolado, da, *past part. of* **charolar.** —*a.* glossy, shiny; enameled, varnished, japanned. —*m.* (Amer.) varnishing; varnished surface.
charolador, *m., var. of* **charolista.**
charolar, *tr.v.* to varnish, japan, lacquer, enamel.
charolista, *m.* varnisher, japanner, lacquerer.
charpa, *f.* 1. pistol belt; bandoleer. 2. (med., anat.) sling.
charpar, *tr.v.* to scarp; to lap.
charque, *m.* (Arg., Mex.) jerked beef (meat).
charquear, *tr.v.* 1. (Amer.) to jerk (beef, or other meat). 2. (Arg.) to slash, cut (a person) to pieces, kill. 3. (Amer.) to malign, vilify. 4. (Arg.) to grip the bridle of (a bucking horse) in order not to fall.
charquecillo, *m.* (Peru) dried and salted conger eel or moray.
charquetal, *m.* marsh, land full of puddles.
charqui, *m.* (Amer.) charqui, jerked meat, meat cut in strips and dried in the sun.
charquicán, *m.* (Bol., Chile, Peru) stew made with jerked meat, potatoes, beans and other ingredients, seasoned with peppers.
charquillo, *m. dim. of* **charco,** small pool or puddle.
charra, *f.* (Hond.) 1. broad-brimmed hat. 2. (Ecuad.) itch, mange.
charrada, *f.* 1. coarseness, uncouthness. 2. Castilian peasant dance. 3. gaudiness, tawdriness, bad taste.
charramente, *adv.* uncouthly; gaudily, tawdrily.
charrán, *a.* scoundrelly, knavish, roguish. —*m.* scoundrel, rogue.
charranada, *f.* a scoundrelly or knavish act or remark.
charranear, *i.v.* to lead a scoundrel's life, be a rascal.
charranería, *f.* roguery, knavery.
charrasca, *f.* 1. (coll.) dangling sword; jack knife; generic term for knives. 2. (Nic.) overcooked meat.
charrasco, *m.* (coll., hum.) dangling sword (too large for its user and therefore dragging and bumping at every step).

charrería, *f.* gaudy or tawdry dress or ornament.
charretera, *f.* 1. (mil.) epaulet, epaulette. 2. decorative garter; garter buckle. 3. shoulder pad worn by water carriers.
charro, rra, *a.* 1. of or pertaining to a Castilian peasant. 2. uncouth, coarse, rustic. 3. flashy, gaudy, garish. 4. (Mex.) skilled at horseback riding. 5. (Mex.) picturesque. *—m., f.* 1. Castilian peasant. 2. boor, uncouth person. *—m.* (Mex.) expert horseman; cowboy.
charrúa, *m., f.* Indian of a tribe of nomads who roamed over an extensive area including most of Uruguay and parts of Brazil and Argentina. *—a.* 1. of or pertaining to that tribe. 2. said of Uruguay and Uruguayans.
charuto, *m.* (S. Amer., reg.) cheroot, cigar wrapped in corn husk; ordinary cigarette.
chasca, *f.* 1. brushwood. 2. (Amer.) matted or tangled hair.
chascada, *f.* (Hond.) gratuity, tip.
chascar, (*ref. 50*) *i.v.* 1. to crack, crackle. 2. to cluck one's tongue. *—tr.v. to crunch, grind between the teeth (food).*
chascarrillo, *m.* joke, witty anecdote, spicy tale.
chascás, *m.* schapska, a type of helmet.
chasco, *m.* trick, ruse; disappointment. — **dar ch.,** to disappoint, fail (someone); **llevarse un ch.,** to be disappointed.
chascón, na, *a.* 1. (Bol., Chile) entangled, matted, dishevelled; (Arg.) bushy-haired. 2. (Bol.) dull, awkward.
chasconear, *tr.v.* (Chile) to entangle; to pull (someone's hair). *—r.v.* to pull or tear (one's own hair).
chasis, *m.* 1. chassis, framework (of a car). 2. (photog.) plateholder.
chasponazo, *m.* nick caused by a grazing bullet.
chasque, chasqué, *ref.* **chascar.**
chasquear, *tr.v.* 1. to play a practical joke on. 2. to crack (a whip). 3. to snap (one's fingers). 4. to break, fail to keep (a promise). 5. (Col.) to champ (the bit); (fig.) to resist. *—i.v.* 1. to crackle (dry wood). 2. (Amer.) to chatter (teeth). *—r.v.* to be thwarted or frustrated; to come to naught.
chasqui, *m.* (S. Amer., hist.) Indian courier or messenger.
chasquido, *m.* crack (of a whip); snap, crackle; cracking sound (of something breaking).
chata, *f.* 1. bedpan. 2. scow, barge, flat car.
chatarra, *f.* scarp iron; iron scoria or slag; junk.
chatarrería, *f.* junk shop or yard.
chatarrero, ra, *m., f.* junk dealer, scrap-iron dealer.
chatasca, *f., var. of* **charquicán.**
chatedad, *f.* flatness.
chato, ta, *a.* 1. flat-nosed, pug-nosed, snub-nosed. 2. blunt. 3. flat; short, low. 4. (Amer.) without lofty purposes. 5. (Amer.) humdrum, commonplace. *—m.* 1. a small, thick, straight-up wine glass. 2. (coll., Sp.) any alcoholic drink taken with friends. *—m., f.* (coll.) darling, baby (coll.). — **dejar ch.,** (Amer.) to defeat, humiliate; (Mex.) to deceive; **quedarse ch.,** (Amer.) to fail at an undertaking.
chatón, *m.* large precious stone mounted in its setting.
chatre, *a.* (Amer.) richly decked out, elegant, all dressed up.
chatungo, ga, *a.* (coll.) *var.* of **chato,** darling.
chaucha, *f.* 1. (S. Amer.) new potato. 2. (Arg.) string bean, haricot. 3. (Peru, Cuba) food, meal. 4. (S. Amer.) small coin; money. 5. (Ecuad.) small profits, modest stipend. *—a.* (Arg.) poor; without charm.
chauchau, *m.* (Chile, Peru, sl.) food; hash.
chauche, *m.* red varnish or paint.
chauchera, *f.* (Chile) coin purse.
chaúl, *m.* Chinese silk.
chauvinismo, *m.* chauvinism.
chauvinista, *a., m., f.* chauvinist.
chauz, (*pl.* **chauces**) *m.* constable (among the Arabs).
chaval, la, *m.* (Sp.) lad, youngster, young lad. *—f.* lass.
chavalería, *f.* (coll., Sp.) children.
chavalongo, *m.* (Chile, imp. u.) typhoid.
chavasca, *f.* brushwood.
chavea, *m.* (coll.) lad, boy.
chaveta, *f.* 1. forelock, key, cotter, split pin, linchpin. 2. (Peru) cobbler's knife, knife. — **perder uno la chaveta,** (coll.) to go crazy, go off one's rocker.
chavo, *m.* 1. copper (any of various coins). 2. (Mex.) 350 square meters. — **chavos,** (coll.) money; **ni un c. prieto,** (P. Rico) not a red cent.
chaya, *f.* (Amer.) Mardi gras or carnival tricks and pranks; (*pl.*) confetti, streamers, etc.
chayotada, *f.* (Guat.) stupidity, foolishness.
chayote, *m.* (bot.) 1. chayote (plant and fruit). 2. (Hond.) coward. 3. (C. Amer.) incompetent person.
chayotera, *f.* chayote plant.
chaza, *f.* 1. stopping the ball in a game of pelota; mark or point where the ball stops. 2. (mar.) space between two gun ports. 3. (Ecuad.) place where windows are located in a wall. 4. (Peru) warehouse for small cargo on the docks of a port.
chazador, *m.* person who stops the ball (in pelota); marker, scorer.
chazar, (*ref. 53*) *tr.v.* 1. to stop (the ball) before it reaches the winning line (in pelota); to mark (the spot where the ball stopped). 2. (Ecuad.) to rein (a horse) suddenly.
che, *interj.* (Arg.) hey, Mack! listen, man! (a colloquial exclamation calling attention or expressing surprise, which originates from the Valencian dialect).
checo, ca, *a., m.,* Czechoslovakian. *—m.* the Slavic language of the Czechs.
checoeslovaco, ca, checoslovaco, ca, *a., m., f.* Czechoslovakian.
cheche, *m.* (Cuba) braggart, bragger.
chécheres, *m.* (*pl.*) (Amer.) odds and ends, bits and pieces, trinkets.
cheira, *f., var. of* **chaira.**
chejche, *a.* (Quech.) 1. (Peru) grey. 2. (Arg.) yellowish (animals). 3. discolored. 4. motley, e.g. *gallina ch.,* speckled hen.
cheje, *m.* (El Salv., Hond.) link of chain.
chele, *m.* 1. (C. Amer.) white-haired man; alien who is not Spanish. 2. (C. Amer.) rheum of the eyes.
chelear, *tr.v.* (C. Amer.) to whiten. *—i.v.* to become rheumy (the eyes).
cheles, *m.* (Mex.) (*pl.*) Mayan Indians who lived in Tihoo, near Mérida, Yucatan.
chelín, *m.* shilling (coin).
chelo, *a.* (Mex.) blond, white-haired. *—m.* (Mex., reg.) peon, farm hand.
chemulco, *m.* (Dom. Rep.) man's wool suit.
chen, *m., f.* Indian of a tribe of Mayans who originally lived in and around Campeche and Yucatan. *—a.* of or pertaining to these Indians.
chencha, *a.* (Mex.) lazy, loafing.
chepa, *f.* (coll.) hump, hunch (on the back); **de chepa,** (Col.) by chance; **las tres chepas,** (Chile) stars of the Orion constellation.
chépica, *f.* (Chile) grama grass.
cheque, *m.* check, cheque, sight draft; **c. a fecha,** postdated check; **c. comida,** meal ticket; **ch. de caja** or **gerencia bancaria,** cashier's check; **cheques de viaje** or **viajeros,** travelers checks; **c. en blanco,** blank check; **c. sin fondos,** bad check.
chequear, *tr.v.* (Amer.) 1. to check, inspect, examine. 2. to verify. 3. to check (with a checkmark). 4. (Amer.) to check baggage.
chequén, *m.* (Chile) a variety of myrtle.
chequeo, *m.* (Amer.) check, check-up, examination.
chercha, *f.* 1. (Hond.) noise, uproar. 2. (Ven.) joke, jest.
cherchar, *i.v.* (Ven.) to joke, jest, make fun of someone or something.
cherna, *f.* (ichth.) grouper; giant bass (Serranus gigas).
cherva, *f.* (bot.) castor-oil plant.
chesche, *a., var. of* **chejche.**
cheuque, *m.* (Chile) flamingo, a long-legged bird.
cheurón, *m.* (her.) chevron.
cheuto, ta, *a.* (Chile) hare-lipped.
chévere, *a.* (Cuba, P. Rico, sl.) terrific, great. *—m.* braggart.
cheviot, *m.* a woolen fabric with a coarse twill weave made from the wool of cheviot sheep.
chía, *f.* 1. short black mourning hood; hood or cowl worn as mark of nobility. 2. (bot.) chia, a species of sage. 3. (Mex.) beverage made from sage seeds, lemon juice, and sugar.
chibalete, *m.* (print.) composing stand, frame or cabinet.
chibcha, *a.* of or pertaining to the **Chibchas,** an extinct tribe of Indians of a highly advanced culture, who lived on the central plateau of Colombia. *—m.* language of the Chibchas. *—m., f.* member of that tribe.
chibiguazú, *m.* (zool.) ocelot.
chibolo, *m.* (Ecuad.) small round body, mass; bump, bruise.
chiborra, *f.* fool or clown who follows street processions, parades, etc.
chibuquí, *m.* chibouk, chibouque, a long Turkish pipe.
chic, *a.* (fr.) chic, elegant, smart (attire).
chica, *f.* 1. girl. 2. (Arg., Urug.) wad or plug of chewing tobacco. 3. (Cuba) an old Afro-Spanish dance formerly performed by the slaves.
chicada, *f.* 1. group of sickly lambs separated from the rest of the flock and allowed to graze on better pasture. 2. childish remark or act.
chicalote, *m.* (bot.) chicalote, prickly poppy, argemone.
chicana, *f.* (gal., Amer.) chicanery, cunning, subterfuge.
chicanear, *i.v.* (gal., Amer.) to be cunning, subtly tricky.
chicanero, ra, *a.* 1. (Amer.) cunning, tricky. 2. (Ecuad.) stingy.
chicano, na, *a.* of or pertaining to Mexican-Americans born in the S.W. of the U.S. *—m., f.* person of Mexican extraction, born and living in the U.S.
chicarrón, na, *a.* grown-up (child). *—m.* big, strapping boy. *—f.* big, strapping boy. *—f.* big, strapping girl.
chicha, *f.* 1. chicha, any of various alcoholic beverages made by fermenting corn, grape, cane sugar, pineapple, etc. 2. non-alcoholic beverage, e.g. *ch. de uva,* (Arg., Peru) grape juice drink. 3. (coll.) meat. 4. (Arg.) blood (said by children), e.g. *te voy a sacar la ch.,* I'm going to bloody your nose. — **estar de ch.,** (C. Amer.) to be ill humored; **estar ch.** (algo), (Mex.) to be pleasont; to be amusing; **estar como ch.,** (Col.) to be plentiful; **estar en ch. (alguien),** (Bol.) to be drunk; **estar en ch. (algo),** (Bol.) to bubble or

foam; **estar hecho una ch.,** (Ecuad.) to be very dirty; **de ch. y nabo,** insignificant, of little importance; **ni ch. ni limonada** (coll.) neither fish nor fowl; **sacar la ch. a algo o alguien,** to take the greatest possible advantage of something or someone, to make someone work hard or suffer; **calma ch.,** dead calm.

chícharo, *m.* (bot.) pea; **potage de chícharos,** pea soup.

chicharra, *f.* 1. cicada, harvest fly. 2. kazoo (toy). 3. chatterbox, talkative woman. — **cantar la ch.,** (coll.) to be very hot; **hablar como una ch.,** to be loquacious, talk like a parrot.

chicharrar, *tr.v.* 1. to sizzle, fry too much; to scorch, heat excessively. 2. (Bol., Cuba, Chile) to squash, crush. —*r.v.* to wilt, wither (from the heat).

chicharrear, *i.v.* to chirp or creak (a cricket).

chicharrero, ra, *m., f.* person who makes or sells kazoos. —*m.* oven, very hot place.

chicharro, *m.* 1. cracklings (crisp pork fat). 2. (ichth.) caranx (Trachurus trachurus); horse mackerel.

chicharrón, *m.* 1. cracklings, crisp pork rind, (Peru) roast pork; over-roasted meat. 2. (coll.) person with a very dark suntan.

chichas, *f.* (*pl.*) (C. Rica) bosom, breasts of a woman.

chiche, *m.* 1. (Arg.) toy. 2. (Arg., Chile) trinket, imitation jewel. 3. (Guat., Mex.) breast of a wet-nurse. 4. (Ecuad.) meat (in baby talk). 5. (Amer.) skillful person. 6. (Amer.) comfortable, well decorated, small shop or house. 7. gift presented on anniversary occasions. 8. (Peru) a certain spice. —*a.* (C. Amer.) easy, comfortable. —*adv.* (C. Amer.) very easily.

chichear, *i.v.* to hiss.

chicheo, *m.* hissing, hiss.

chichería, *f.* shop or saloon where chicha is sold.

chichero, ra, *m., f.* person who sells, makes or drinks chicha.

chichi, *f.* 1. (Guat., Mex., coll.) wet nurse. 2. (Mex.) breast. 3. (Arg.) nipple of the female breast.

chichí, *m.* (Arg.) littoral of the Parana River.

chichicaste, *m.* (C. Amer.) nettle (Urtica baccifera), the fibers of which are used in cordage.

chichicuilote, *m.* (Mex.) Baird's sandpiper (Pisobia bairdii), a wading bird.

chichigua, *f.* 1. (Amer., vulg.) wet nurse. 2. (Col., sl.) petty gambling.

chichilasa, *f.* 1. (Mex.) small, malignant red ant (Formica rufa). 2. (coll., Mex.) spitfire, beautiful but very spirited woman.

chichilo, *m.* (zool., Bol.) pinche (Leontocebus cedipus), South American tamarin, a small long-tailed monkey.

chichimeca, *m., f.* Indian of a nomadic group belonging to the Otomi linguistic stock. —*a.* of or pertaining to these Indians.

chichirimico, *m.* 1. (Peru, Ecuad.) children's game played by hiding an object. 2. (Ecuad.) card game.

chichirimoche, *m.* much, e.g. *de noche chichirimoche, de mañana chichirinada,* rich at night, poor in the morning; happy this moment, sad the next; one thing one minute and another the next.

chichirinada, *f.* nothing.

chichisbear, *tr.v.* to court, to woo.

chichisbeo, *m.* 1. flattery, gifts and gallant acts of courtship. 2. ardent admirer or suitor. 3. flirtation.

chichito, *m.* 1. (coll.) small child. 2. (coll.) Spanish American.

chicho, *m.* curl; spitcurl on the forehead or cheek.

chichoca, *f.* (Arg.) flour milled from corn.

chicholo, *m.* (Arg.) a sweetmeat, wrapped in a corn leaf.

chichón, na, *a.* 1. (C. Amer.) easy, presenting no difficulty. 2. (S. Amer.) teasing, joke-playing. —*m.* bump, swelling (on the head, bruise. —*f.* (Guat.) woman with a well developed bosom.

chichoncito, illo, *m. dim. of* **chichón,** small swelling or bump.

chichonear, *i.v.* (S. Amer.) to make or play jokes.

chichonera, *f.* 1. padded cap (to protect a child's head from bumps). 2. (Col.) disorder in the street; brawl, row.

chichota, *f.* 1. iota, fraction; **sin faltar ch.,** without missing an iota. 2. (C. Amer., coll.) big tit (vulg.), large breast.

chichurro, *m.* stock or broth made by boiling sausages.

chicle, *m.* 1. chicle (gum). 2. (Amer.) chewing gum.

chiclear, *i.v.* (Mex.) to chew gum.

chico, ca, *a.* little, small, minute, e.g. *este vaso es muy chico,* this glass is very small. —*m.* 1. boy, youngster, lad, young fellow, chap. 2. a measure of wine (168 milliliters). — **chico con grande,** the big mixed with the small, all included, without missing anything. —*f.* little girl; (coll.) girl, lass, young woman. — **mi chica,** my girl, my fiancée; my daughter.

chicoco, ca, *m., f.* (Chile) a small but husky and healthy youngster (said as an endearment).

chicolear, *i.v., r.v.* (Amer.) to enjoy oneself; to play like a child. —*tr.v.* (coll.) to pay compliments to (a woman).

chicoleo, *m.* 1. compliment (to a woman). 2. (Arg.) childish play or behavior. — **no andarse con ch.,** to act or behave seriously.

chicolongo, *m.* (Cuba) game played by aiming marbles or coins at a small hole.

chícora, *f.* (Ven.) earth-digging tool.

chicoria, *f.* (bot.) chicory.

chicoriáceo, a, *a.* (bot.) cichoriaceous. —*f.* (*pl.*) Cichoriaceae.

chicorro, ra, *m., f.* (coll.) a healthy, husky youngster.

chicorrotico, ca, *a. dim. of* **chico,** little, very small.

chicorrotín, na, *a.* small, little. —*m., f.* small child, tot.

chicotazo, *m.* 1. whiplash, blow with a whip. 2. (Dom. Rep.) a drink or swig of alcohol.

chicote, ta, *m.* (coll.) strong, strapping lad. —*f.* robust young girl. —*m.* 1. (coll.) cigar, cigarette butt. 2. (Amer.) whip. 3. (mar.) end of a rope or cable. 4. (Peru) wire, electric cord.

chicotear, *tr.v.* 1. (Amer.) to flog, whip. 2. (Amer.) to kill. 3. (Col.) to break to bits. 4. (Ven.) to fight. —*r.v.* 1. (Chile) to discipline oneself. 2. (Dom. Rep.) to get drunk.

chicozapote, *m.* (bot.) sapodilla (Achras zapota).

chicuaco, ca, *a.* (Ven.) silly, imbecilic.

chicuelo, la, *a. dim. of* **chico,** youngster.

chifla, *f.* 1. hissing, cat call, whistling (in protest); whistle. 2. paring knife, crescent-shaped knife (used by leather workers). 3. (Mex.) bad humor.

chiflacayote, *m.* (bot.) a large variety of pumpkin.

chifladera, *f.* whistle.

chiflado, da, *past part. of* **chiflar.** —*a.* (coll.) crazy, mad, nuts, madly in love. —*m., f.* nut, loon (crazy person).

chifladura, *f.* 1. craziness, madness, wild idea. 2. whistling; hissing.

chiflar, *i.v.* to blow a whistle; to whistle. —*tr.v.* 1. to jeer, hiss at, boo. 2. (coll.) to gulp down, drink quickly. —*r.v.* (coll.) to go batty or crazy. — **chiflárselas,** (C. Amer.) to die.

chiflar, *tr.v.* to pare or trim (leather).

chiflato, *m.* whistle.

chifle, *m.* 1. whistle; bird call, decoy whistle. 2. horn; (mil., hunt.) powder horn. 3. (Amer.) horn used as a flask to carry water. 3. (Peru, Ecuad.) banana or plantain chip. 4. (Peru) dish made with pork, corn and bananas. — **dejarle a alguien al ch.,** to leave someone unprovided for; **estar al ch.,** (C. Amer.) to be exposed to a disagreeable experience.

chiflete, *m.* whistle (instrument).

chiflido, *m.* whistle (sound).

chiflo, *m.* act of whistling.

chiflón, *m.* 1. (Amer.) draught (of air). 2. (Mex.) waterspout, jet. 3. (Mex., Chile, min.) caving in (of loose rock). — **ch. de agua,** water jet; **ch. de arena,** sand blast.

chigrero, *m.* (Ecuad.) peddler, hawker.

chigua, *f.* 1. (Chile) large basket (made of rope, cane, leather or bark). 2. (Chile) simple cradle. 3. (Arg.) big stomach or belly.

chigualo, *m.* (Ecuad.) game in which poems are recited by moonlight.

chiguar, *tr.v.* (Arg.) 1. to tug (a rope). 2. to pull (someone's hair). —*r.v.* to braid one's own hair.

chigüil, *m.* (Ecuad.) dough made of corn meal, butter, eggs and cheese cooked in a corn leaf.

chihuahua, *m.* (Ecuad.) holiday fireworks in the shape of a human body. —*m., f.* very small, short-haired dog common in Mexico. —*interj.* (Mex.) expression of surprise or emphasis.

chijete, *a.* (Chile) joking, wisecracking, spicy-talking (esp. said of women).

chilaba, *f.* Moorish hooded cloak or long loose robe.

chilacayote, *m.* (bot.) chilacayote (gourd plant or fruit).

chilacoa, *f.* (Col., ornith.) a kind of woodcock, partridge.

chilanco, *m.* pool left on the shore by a river.

chilaquil, *m.* 1. (Mex.) old dirty hat. 2. (*pl.*) (Mex.) casserole dish made of chopped tortilla and chili sauce with meat or cheese.

chilaquila, *f.* (Guat.) tortilla stuffed with cheese, herbs and peppers.

chilar, *m.* chili or pepper patch, chili field.

chilate, *m.* (C. Amer.) drink made of red pepper, corn and cocoa.

chilatole, *m.* (Mex.) corn, peppers and pork stew.

chilcano, *m.* (Peru) stew made of fish, onions, oranges and peppers; soup made with a fish head.

chilchote, *m.* (Mex., bot.) a variety of very hot chili.

chilco, *m.* (Chile, bot.) wild fuchsia.

Chile, *m.* Chile.

chile, *m.* 1. (bot., C. and S. Amer.) chile, all varieties of red, green or bell peppers. 2. (C. Amer.) hoax, lie. 3. (Col.) fish net. — **estar hecho un ch.,** (Mex., Nic.) to be enraged; **parecer ch. relleno,** to be dressed in ragged clothing.

chilenismo, *m.* word or idiom peculiar to Chileans.

chileno, na, *a., m., f.* Chilean.

chileño, ña, *a., m., f., var. of* **chileno.**

chilero, ra, *m., f.* (Mex., derog.) grocer. 2. (C. Amer.) serving dish for chile.

chilillo, *m.* (C. Amer.) whip; switch.

chilindrina, *f.* 1. (coll.) trifle, bagatelle. 2. (coll.) anecdote, joke, funny story. 3. (coll.) banter, raillery.

chilindrinero, ra, *a.* (coll.) bantering, lively joking. —*m., f.* joker, comic, storyteller.

chilindrón, *m.* 1. (cul.) a special marinade and preparation for meats. 2. a card game.

chilinguear, *tr.v.* (Col.) to swing.

chilla, *f.* 1. decoy call (for foxes, rabbits, hares, etc.). 2. (carp.) thin board or plank (of inferior quality wood), clapboard. 3. (Chile) small fox.

4. (Arg.) long, bristly hair of certain animals; bristly human hair. 5. (Mex.) upper balconies of a theatre. 6. (Mex.) poverty.
chillado, *m.* (carp.) roof of lathing and shingles or clapboard.
chillador, ra, *a.* screaming, shrieking. —*m., f.* screamer, shrieker.
chillante, *a.* screeching, shrieking.
chillar, *i.v.* 1. to scream, shriek, screech; to squeak, creak (wheels). 2. to sizzle, hiss (bacon, etc.). 3. to call (with a decoy whistle or horn). 4. (p.) to be ill-matched or poorly mixed. —*r.v.* 1. (C. Amer.) to become ashamed. 2. (Amer.) to become annoyed, to take offense.
chillera, *f.* 1. (mar.) iron stow bar (to stow ammunition. 2. (*pl.*) (mar.) rowlocks.
chillería, *f.* screaming, screeching, shrieking; reprimand, dressing-down.
chillido, *m.* scream, screech, shriek.
chillo, *m.* 1. (carp.) thin board, clapboard. 2. (C. Amer.) debt. 3. (P. Rico) ordinary person. 4. (Ecuad.) angry demand by a group. 5. (Ecuad.) state of annoyance or resentment.
chillo, lla, *a.* (Peru) dark black (skin, race).
chillón, *m.* lath nail, shingle nail; **c. real,** large lath nail, spike.
chillón, na, *a.* 1. (coll.) strident, harsh, shrill; shrieking; bawling, screaming. 2. (fig.) flashy, gaudy, clashing (colors).
chillonazo, *m.* (C. Rica) humiliation, shame.
chilmole, *m.* (Mex.) a tomato, onion and pepper sauce, similar to the vinaigrette.
chilote, *m.* (Mex.) 1. drink made of chili and pulque. 2. (Mex.) ear of young, tender corn.
chilpe, *m.* 1. (Ecuad.) agave leaf; (Ecuad.) dried corn leaf. 2. (*pl.*) (Chile) rags, shreds, tatters.
chiltipiquín, *m.* (bot.) hot chili (plant and fruit).
chiltote, *m.* (Guat., ornith.) Baltimore oriole (Icterus Baltimore).
chimachima, *m.* (Arg., ornith.) chimachima, a species of caracara.
chimal, *m.* (Mex.) tousled hair.
chimango, *m.* (Arg., ornith.) chimango, a species of caracara.
chimar, *tr.v.* (C. Amer., fig.) to annoy, irritate.
chimbador, *m.* (Peru) person expert in fording or crossing rivers.
chimbo, *m.* (S. Amer.) dessert made with sugar, almonds and egg yolks.
chimbombera, *f.* (Ven., coll.) pernicious anemia.
chimenea, *f.* 1. chimney; funnel (of ship); fireplace, hearth; kitchen-range. 2. (mil.) inner casing (in the breech of firearms). 3. (theat.) wooden channel (where counterweights for moving scenery slide up and down). 4. (min.) opening, shaft. — **caerle a uno una cosa por la ch.,** (coll.) to have a windfall, fall into one's lap; **ch. de aire,** (min.) air shaft; **ch. francesa,** mantelpiece.
chimiscol, *m.* (C. Rica) sugar-cane brandy.
chimiscolear, *i.v.* (Mex.) to gossip.
chimó, *m.* (Ven.) plug of tobacco and hydrous carbonate of soda chewed by Indians.
chimojo, *m.* (Cuba) antispasmodic made of tobacco, banana peel, sage and other ingredients.
chimolero, ra, *m., f.* (Mex., derog.) innkeeper, tavern owner.
chimpancé, *m.* (zool.) chimpanzee.
china, *f.* 1. pebble, small stone. 2. game of shutting one's hands and guessing which one contains the pebble. 3. (coll.) money. — **poner chinas a uno,** (coll.) to put obstacles in one's way; **tocarle a uno la ch.,** to be in luck, have luck; to win; **tropezar uno en una ch.,** (coll.) to stumble over trifles.
china, *f.* 1. (bot.) chinaroot. 2. china porcelain; Chinese silk, linen or cotton fabric. 3. (P. Rico) orange. 4. (Amer.) Indian maid; good looking girl or woman. 5. (Guat., Salv.) child's nurse.
chinaca, *f.* (Mex.) poor people.
chinama, *f.* (Guat.) hut, hovel, shanty.
chinamitla, *f.* (Mex.) small thatch-roofed hut.
chinampa, *f.* (Mex.) small garden tract; (*pl.*) floating gardens in the canals and lagoons in Xochimilco, Mexico City, famous for producing flowers and fruit.
chinampear, *i.v.* (Mex.) to run away (a fighting cock).
chinampero, ra, *m., f.* cultivator of **chinampas** of floating orchards.
chinana, *f.* 1. (Mex.) suppository. 2. (Mex.) nuisance, bother, annoyance.
chinanta, *f.* (Phil. I.) weight of about 6.326 kilos or 14 pounds.
chinapo, *m.* (Mex.) obsidian, volcanic stone.
chinar, *tr.v.* to pave with pebbles.
chinarro, *m.* large pebble.
chinata, *f.* (Cuba) small round stone; marble used in a game similar to penny-pitching.
chinateado, *m.* (metal.) stratum or layer of pebbles.
chinazo, *m.* large stone, large pebble. 2. blow with a pebble.
chincapino, *m.* (bot.) chinquapin.
chinchal, *m.* (Cuba, P. Rico) small tobacco vendor's stall or shop; small, poor shop or stall.
chinchar, *tr.v.* 1. (coll.) to annoy, irritate, bother. 2. to kill.
chincharrazo, *m.* (coll.) blow with the flat part of a sword; slap.
chincharrero, *m.* 1. bug pit, place swarming with bedbugs. 2. (Amer.) small fishing smack.
chinche, *f.* 1. (ento.) bedbug, bug. 2. thumb tack. 3. (coll.) bore, boring person; pest, nuisance; disagreeable person. — **caer** or **morir como chinches,** (coll.) to die like flies.
chinchel, *m.* (Chile) tavern, barroom.
chinchemolle, *m.* (Chile, ento.) ill-smelling beetle or roach.
chinchero, *m.* bug-trap.
chincheta, *f.* thumb-tack.
chinchibí, *m.* (C. Amer., Bol., Peru) fermented drink flavored with ginger.
chinchilla, *f.* (zool.) chinchilla (animal and fur).
chinchimén, *m.* (Chile, zool.) sea otter (Lutra felina).
chinchín, *m.* 1. (coll.) sound of music. 2. (Cuba) drizzle, light rain. 3. (bot.) evergreen shrub (Azara microphylla). 4. (Amer.) baby's rattle made of silver. 5. (Dom. Rep.) mite, speck, bit. 6. (Mex., mus.) finger cymbals (used by flamenco dancers).
chinchintor, *m.* (Hond., zool.) poisonous viper.
chinchona, *f.* quinine.
chinchorrazo, *m.* 1. (Col., P. Rico, Ven.) slap with a sword or something flat. 2. (Dom. Rep.) swig of alcohol.
chinchorrear, *tr.v.* (Col.) to fish with a net. —*i.v.* to swing in a hammock.
chinchorrería, *f.* 1. (coll.) tiresomeness, tediousness. 2. (coll.) gossip, tale, rumor.
chinchorrero, *a.* (coll.) gossiping, tale-spreading. —*m., f.* gossip, gossipmonger.
chinchorro, *m.* 1. small dragnet. 2. (mar.) very small rowboat. 3. (Ven.) hammock (used by Indians). 4. (P. Rico, Dom. Rep.) poor shop. 5. (C. Rica) cluster of shacks; shabby rooms for rent. 6. (Mex.) small drove of pack animals; small herd.
chinchoso, sa, *a.* (coll.) tiresome, boring, tedious.
chinchulines, *m.* (*pl.*) (Arg.) barbecued tripe.
chinchurria, *f.* 1. (Ven.) offal. 2. (Ven., vulg.) whore.
chincol, *m.* (Amer.) crown sparrow (Zonotrichia capensis).
chincual, *m.* (Mex.) measles.
chincualear, *i.v.* (Mex.) to carouse around, go out on the town.
chincualero, ra, *m.* (Mex.) person who carouses or goes out on the town.
chiné, *a.* chiné, mottled patterned (fabric).
chinear, *tr.v.* 1. (C. Amer.) to carry in one's arms, or on one's back. 2. (C. Amer.) to pamper.
chinela, *f.* slipper, mule, house shoe; clog, chopine.
chinelazo, *m.* blow given with a slipper or a clog.
chinelón, *m.* large slipper or overshoe; (Ven.) high shoe.
chinero, *a.* (Chile, Ecuad., coll.) said of a man known to seduce country girls. —*m.* china cabinet or cupboard.
chinesco, ca, *a.* Chinese; **a la chinesca,** in the Chinese way. —*m.* (mus.) pavillon chinois, Chinese crescent, Chinese pavilion (instrument used in military bands); bells.
chinga, *f.* 1. (C. Rica) cigar or cigarette butt. 2. (C. Rica) money paid to the owner of a gambling room. 3. (Hond.) jest, banter. 4. (Ven.) drunkenness. 5. (Pan.) gambling. 6. (Ven.) negligible amount of something. 7. (C. Rica) skinny, ugly mare. 8. (Mex.) drubbing or thrashing. 9. (Col.) men's bathing trunks. 10. (Guat., El Salv.) rehearsal of a cockfight.
chingado, da, *a.* 1. (Peru) failed, unsuccessful. 2. (Arg.) crooked, lop-sided.
chingana, *f.* 1. (Amer.) low class barroom with a dance floor. 2. (S. Amer.) noisy party with drinking and singing. 3. (Bol.) cave, well or underground tunnel.
chinganear, *i.v.* (Amer.) to go on a binge or drunk, go on a spree.
chingar, (*ref. 51*) *tr.v.* 1. (coll.) to drink frequently. 2. (Guat.) to train (fighting cocks). 3. (Ven.) to hang and carry (an object) over the shoulder. 4. (C. Rica) to cut off (the tail of an animal). 5. (Mex., C. Amer., sl.) to annoy, bother, molest; to injure, harm, oppress. 6. to fuck (vulg.), have sexual intercourse with. —*r.v.* 1. (coll.) to get drunk. 2. (Amer.) to fail, miscarry; not to explode (fireworks).
chingo, ga, *a.* 1. (Cuba, coll.) small, little, tiny. 2. (C. Rica) large-tailed (animal). 3. (Amer.) short (clothing). 4. (Amer.) in underwear (a person). 5. (Amer.) pug-nosed, flat-nosed. —*m., f.* 1. (Amer.) pug-nosed person. 2. (Pan.) trousers worn by rural workers. 3. (*pl.*) (C. Amer.) underwear. — **estar uno ch. por algo,** to want something very badly; **quedarse uno ch.,** to be left naked; **tener ch. a alguien,** to make a fool of someone.
chingolo, *m.* (Arg., ornith.) crown sparrow (Zonotrichia capensis).
chingón, na, *m., f.* (Mex., C. Amer., vulg.) nuisance, rotter, bastard; bugger, fucker (vulg.).
chingue, *m.* (Chile, zool.) skunk.
chingue, chingué, *ref.* **chingar.**
chinguero, *m.* (C. Rica) gambler.
chinguillo, *m.* 1. (Amer.) basket in which fish is carried; basket strapped on to the back of a wagon to increase its capacity. 2. simple cradle used by the poor.
chinguirito, *m.* (Cuba, Mex.) inferior quality rum; a swig or nip.
chino, na, *a.* Chinese. —*m.* Chinese; Chinese (language); (*pl.*) the Chinese. —*f.* Chinese woman.
chino, na, *a., m., f.* half-breed, vulgar name for a person of mixed racial extraction, esp. American Indian.

chino, *m.* 1. (Amer.) servant. 2. (Amer., coll.) honey, pet, darling (term of endearment). 3. (Chile) Indian.
chinófilo, la, *m., f.* sinophile.
chinonga, *f.* (Arg., derog.) half-breed; servant of poor appearance.
chinuk, *a., m., f.* Chinook. —*m.* Chinook (language).
chipá, *m.* 1. (Bol., Col., Chile) fruit basket. 2. (Arg., coll.) jail, prison.
chipá, *m.* (Arg.) manioc or corn cake.
chipaco, *m.* (Arg.) bran cake. — **cara de ch.** (Bol.) sad, listless face.
chipe, *m.* 1. (Chile, Ven.) the smallest sum that can be bet at a gaming table. 2. (Guat.) a woman's last son. —*a.* weakened by poor nursing (a baby).
chipé, *f.* truth, goodness. — **de chipé,** (coll.) excellent, first-rate.
chipén, *f.* activity, bustle, turmoil. — **de c.,** (coll.) excellent, first-rate.
chipi, *m., f.* 1. weaned baby. 2. crying child.
chipiar, *tr.v.* (Guat., coll.) to annoy, irritate, bother.
chipichape, *m.* (coll.) blow; uproar, turmoil, fight.
chipichipi, *m.* (Mex.) drizzle, light rain.
chipil, *m., f.* (Mex.) cry-baby; teething baby.
chipilo, *m.* (Bol.) banana or plantain chip, banana fritter.
chipión, *m.* (C. Amer.) telling off (coll.), reprimand.
chipirón, *m.* (zool.) squid, variety of cuttlefish.
chipojo, *m.* (Cuba, zool.) chameleon.
chiporra, *f.* (Guat., Hond.) tumor on the head.
chipote, *m.* (Amer.) slap, blow; (C. Amer.) children's game involving handslapping.
chipotear, *tr.v.* (C. Amer.) to slap; cuff, buffet.
Chipre, *m.* Cyprus.
chipriota, te, *a., m., f.* Cypriot, of or pertaining to the island of Cyprus.
chiqueadores, *m.* (*pl.*) (Mex.) 1. discs of turtle shell worn as jewelry by women. 2. (C. Amer.) small paper plasters applied to the forehead to relieve headache.
chiquear, *tr.v.* 1. (Cuba, Mex.) to pet, fondle; to ask for caresses. 2. (Peru) to confront, check. —*r.v.* 1. (Mex.) to play hard to get. 2. (C. Amer.) to walk with a twisting movement; to strut.
chiqueo, *m.* 1. (Cuba, Mex., P. Rico) endearment, flattery. 2. (C. Amer.) twisting of the body.
chiquerear, *tr.v.* (Ecuad.) to herd (cattle) into corrals or stalls.
chiquero, *m.* 1. pigsty. 2. chicken yard. 3. (taur.) bull pen. 4. goat hut or pen.
chiquichaque, *m.* 1. sawer, sawyer. 2. noise produced by the jaws when chewing.
chiquilicuatro, *m.* (coll.) busybody, meddler.
chiquilín, na, *m., f., var. of* **chiquillo.**
chiquillada, *f.* childish or infantile remark or action.
chiquillería, *f.* (coll.) flock of noisy children.
chiquillo, lla, *m., f.* child; rowdy youngster; (Sp., sl.) darling, beloved.
chiquirín, *m.* (Guat.) a type of cicada (Odopea imbellis).
chiquirritico, ca, llo, lla, to, ta, *a.* (coll.) *dim. of* **chico,** tiny, weeny, very small.
chiquirritín, na, *a.* (coll.) *dim. of* **chiquitín,** tiny. —*m., f.* tiny baby, tot.
chiquisá, *f.* (Amer.) hornet.
chiquitín, na, *a.* (coll.) *dim. of* **chiquito,** tiny, weeny. —*m., f.* tiny baby, tot.
chiquito, ta, *a.* (coll.) *dim. of* **chico,** tiny, weeny, very little, very small. —*m., f.* infant, tot, kiddy; **andarse uno en or con chiquitas,** (coll.) to dilly dally, beat about the bush, be evasive; **hacerse uno el ch.,** to conceal one's knowledge or capabilities.
chiquitura, *f.* 1. (Arg.) smallness. 2. (C. Amer.) childishness.
chira, *f.* 1. (C. Rica) banana skin. 2. (coll.) shred, tatter. 3. (Salv.) ulcer, sore, wound.
chirajera, *f.* (C. Amer.) big stack of dishes, pots and pans.
chirajo, *m.* (C. Amer.) pots and pans; utensils; rags.
chirapa, *f.* 1. (Amer.) rag, tatter. 2. (Peru) rain while the sun is shining. 3. (Bol.) woman employed in a menial job in a mine.
chiraposo, sa, *a.* 1. (Amer.) tattered, ragged. —*m., f.* person dressed in tatters.
chirca, *f.* 1. (C. Rica) cigarette butt. 2. (C. Rica) thin, worn out horse.
chircal, *m.* (Col.) tile works or factory.
chircaleño, chircalero, *m.* (Col.) tile maker, brick maker, potter.
chircate, *m.* (Col.) skirt of coarse material.
chiribico, *m.* 1. (Cuba, ichth.) small, purple, elliptical fish with very small head and eyes (Pomacanthus paru). 2. (Cuba) fried pastry strips.
chiribita, *f.* 1. spark (*gen. pl.*). 2. (bot.) daisy. 3. (*pl.*) (coll.) spots (before the eye). — **echar uno chiribitas,** (coll.) to fume with anger; **hacer chiribitas los ojos,** (coll.) to see spots before the eyes.
chiribital, *m.* (Col.) uncultivated land.
chiribitil, *m.* garret; narrow cubbyhole or corner; (coll.) tiny room.
chiricatana, *m.* (Ecuad.) poncho of coarse material.
chirigaita, *f.* a variety of Spanish melon.
chirigota, *f.* (coll.) joke, quip, jest.
chirigotero, ra, *a.* joking, bantering, gay, merry.
chirimbolo, *m.* (coll.) tool, implement, gadget, utensil; vessel; (*pl.*) pots and pans; tools, gear.
chirimía, *f.* (mus.) shawm, flageolet. —*m.* flageolet player.
chirimoya, *f.* (bot.) cherimoya (fruit), custard apple.
chirimoyo, *m.* (bot.) cherimoya tree, custard apple tree.
chirinada, *f.* (Arg.) failure.
chiringa, *f.* (Cuba, P. Rico) a small kite. —*interj.* (Cuba) expression of disapproval or annoyance.
chiringo, *m.* (Mex.) fragment, piece, bit.
chirinola, *f.* 1. game similar to ninepins. 2. trifle, bagatelle. 3. (Col.) fight, scrap. — **no me entretengo en chirinolas,** I don't waste time in trifles.
chiripa, *f.* 1. fluke (in billiards). 2. (P. Rico) bit, mite. 3. (P. Rico) gratuity. 4. (P. Rico) small business. 5. (coll.) lucky chance, piece of luck, fluke. — **de** or **por ch.,** by a fluke, by a piece of luck.
chiripá, *m.* (Arg., Urug.) the gaucho's dress trousers, made of an embroidered worsted shawl with a corner drawn between the legs over lace pantaloons.
chiripazo, *m.* fluke, piece of luck. — **de** or **por puro ch.,** by a complete fluke, by a pure piece of luck.
chiripear, *tr.v.* to win (points) by a fluke (in billiards).
chiripero, *m.* lucky player, billiard player who wins more by fluke than by skill; lucky person.
chirivía, *f.* 1. (bot.) parsnip. 2. (ornith.) wagtail.
chirivisco, *m.* (Guat.) dried-up bramble thicket.
chirla, *f.* (zool.) mussel.
chirlador, ra, *a.* (zool.) prattling, jabbering. —*m., f.* prattler, inveterate talker.
chirlar, *i.v.* (coll.) to jabber, prattle, chatter noisily and incessantly.
chirlata, *f.* (coll.) cheap gambling room.
chirlazo, *m., var. of* **chirlo.**
chirle, *a.* (coll.) insipid, tasteless. —*m.* droppings of sheep or goats; **agua ch.,** tasteless, tepid drink.
chirlear, *tr.v.* (Amer.) to wound, knife.
chirlería, *f.* much prattle and chatter.
chirlo, *m.* long slash or scar on the face.
chirlomirlo, *m.* 1. tidbit, insubstantial food. 2. refrain (of a children's song).
chirmol, *m.* (Guat.) sauce prepared with chili, tomato and onion.
chirolazo, *m.* (C. Amer.) drink or swig of alcohol.
chirona, *f.* (coll.) jail, prison, calaboose, jug, hoosegow.
chiros, *m.* (*pl.*) (Col.) rags, tatters.
chiroso, sa, *a.* 1. (C. Amer., Col.) dirty, slovenly, unkempt. 2. (C. Amer., Col.) despicable.
chirota, *m.* (Hond., coll.) tomboy, mannish woman.
chirote, *m.* 1. (Ecuad., Peru, ornith.) a kind of linnet. 2. (Peru) lout, dolt, fool.
chirraca, *f.* 1. (C. Amer.) resin, incense. 2. flattery, adulation. — **saltarse la ch.,** to jump on someone's shoulders.
chirriadero, ra, *a., var. of* **chirriador.**
chirriador, ra, *a.* 1. sizzling, hissing. 2. creaking, squeaking. 3. shrieking. 4. (coll.) discordant, out of tune.
chirriar, *i.v.* 1. to sizzle, spatter (bacon, etc.). 2. to creak, squeak. 3. to screech, shriek (birds). 4. (coll.) to sing out of tune. 5. (Col.) to go on a spree.
chirrido, *m.* 1. screeching, chirping, cheeping (of crickets, etc.). 2. creaking, squeaking (of wheels, etc.). 3. shriek (of birds). 4. hiss, sizzling.
chirringo, *m.* (Col.) small boy.
chirrío, *m., var. of* **chirrido.**
chirrión, *m.* 1. creaking cart, e.g. *el ch. de la basura,* the garbage truck (cart, etc.). 2. (Amer.) heavy leather whip.
chirrionero, *m.* garbage cart driver; scavenger.
chirrisco, ca, *a.* 1. (C. Amer., Ven.) very small. 2. (Mex.) skirt-chasing (said of men, esp. old men.).
chirula, *f.* (mus.) small Basque flute, played with the right hand while the left beats a drum.
chirulí, (*pl.* **chirulíes**) *m.* (Ven.) bird of the Tanager family, allied to the finches, whose song seems to repeat the syllables of its name.
chirulio, *m.* (Hond.) dish prepared with scrambled eggs, corn, chili, annato and salt.
chirumbela, *f., var. of* **churumbela.** 1. type of flageolet. 2. tube for drinking maté.
chirumen, *m.* (coll.) acumen, common sense, good judgment.
chirusa, chiruza, *f.* (Amer.) common, ignorant young woman.
¡chis! *interj.* hush! quiet! silence.
chiscarra, *f.* (min.) soft crumbly limestone.
chischás, *m.* clashing of swords.
chischís, *m.* (Amer.) drizzle of rain.
chischisco, *m.* (Arg.) scramble.
chiscón, *m.* small room, garret.
chisgarabís, *m.* (coll.) busybody, meddler.
chisgo, *m.* (Mex., coll.) charm, elegance.
chisgua, *f.* (Col.) knapsack, rucksack.
chisguete, *m.* 1. short draft of wine. 2. (coll.) jet, squirt, spurt (of liquid). 3. tube (of ointment, etc.). — **echar un ch.,** to take a short drink.
chismar, *i.v., var. of* **chismear.**
chisme, *m.* 1. piece of gossip, rumor, story; (*pl.*) gossip, tittle-tattle. 2. (coll.) trifle, knickknack; (*pl.*) odds and ends; lumber, junk.
chismear, *i.v.* to gossip.
chismería, *f.* gossip, tittle-tattle, gossiping.
chismero, ra, *a., m., f., var. of* **chismoso.**

chismografía, *f.* (coll.) gossip; fondness for gossip.
chismorrear, *i.v.* (coll.) *var. of* **chismear.**
chismorreo, *m.* (coll.) gossip, tittle-tattle, gossiping.
chismoso, sa, gossiping, tattling. —*m., f.* gossip, gossipmonger.
chismoteo, *m.* habitual gossiping.
chispa, *f.* 1. spark. 2. diamond chip. 3. sprinkle, drop (of rain). 4. bit, morsel, mite, particle, drop, e.g. *no le dieron ni una ch. de pan,* they did not give him even a morsel of bread. 5. wit, sparkle; brightness, intelligence. 6. (coll.) drunkenness, tipsiness. 7. two-wheeled horsedrawn cart. 8. (Guat., derog.) success. —*a.* (Mex.) amusing. — **ch. eléctrica,** electric spark; **ch. piloto,** pilot spark; **¡chispas!** good heavens!; **dar chispas,** to be bright, be intelligent and alert; **echar uno chispas,** to flare up; to fume with anger; **ser uno una ch.,** to be very lively or sharp-witted, be a live wire; **tener ch.,** to be witty.
chisparse, *r.v.* to get tipsy, get drunk.
chispazo, *m.* 1. flying spark. 2. spark burn. 3. flare-up (brief event indicating more serious ones later). 4. piece of gossip; (*pl.*) gossip; **ir con** or **dar el ch.,** to carry tales.
chispeante, *a.* sparkling; (fig.) brilliant, sharp, ingenious (imagination).
chispear, *i.v.* 1. to throw out sparks, spark; to sparkle, scintillate. 2. (coll.) to drizzle.
chispero, *m.* 1. blacksmith. 2. (hist., Sp.) low-brow dandy or braggart, typical of Madrid in the early 19th century. 3. (Col., Dom. Rep.) person who spreads false rumors. 4. (Dom. Rep.) revolver, pistol.
chispo, pa, *a.* (coll.) tipsy, tight, drunk. —*m.* (coll.) short drink.
chispoleto, ta, *a.* bright, clever, sharpwitted.
chisporrotear, *i.v.* to splutter, spit, throw out sparks (boiling oil or fat).
chisporroteo, *m.* spluttering, spitting (from boiling oil or fat, etc.).
chisposo, sa, *a.* sparking, spluttering.
chisque, *m., var. of* **chisquero.**
chisquero, *m.* 1. leather pouch attached to the belt. 2. cigarette lighter.
chistar, *i.v.* to speak (*gen. in negative*). — **sin ch. ni mistar,** without a single word, without uttering a word.
chiste, *m.* joke, jest, witticism; amusing remark or incident, funny thing. — **caer en el ch.,** (coll.) to get the joke; to get the point; **ch. colorado** or **verde,** off-color joke; **dar uno en el ch.,** (coll.) to spot the trouble, guess right; **hacer ch. de una cosa,** to make a joke of something.
chistera, *f.* 1. fish basket. 2. jai alai basket. 3. (coll.) top hat, silk hat.
chistido, *m.* (Arg.) whistle, hiss.
chistosamente, *adv.* humorously, amusingly, comically, wittily.
chistoso, sa, *a.* funny, humorous, witty, amusing.
chita, *f.* 1. anklebone. 2. game consisting of throwing stones at an upright anklebone or piece of wood. 3. (Mex.) small finemesh net. — **a la ch. callando,** (coll.) silently; stealthily, on the quiet; **dar en la ch.,** to hit the nail on the head.
chitar, *i.v., var. of* **chistar,** to speak.
chite, *m.* (Col.) Saint-John's wort.
chiticalla, *m., f.* 1. (coll.) discreet person. 2. secret.
chiticallando, *adv.* (coll.) discreetly, quietly, stealthily.
chito, *m.* game consisting of throwing stones at an upright anklebone or piece of wood; piece of wood on which the stakes are placed in the game of **chito.** — **irse a ch.,** (coll.) to lead a debauched life.
¡chito! *interj.* (coll.) hush! quiet! shush!
¡chitón! *interj., var. of* **chito.**
chitón, *m.* (zool.) chiton (mollusk).
chiva, *f.* 1. (Amer.) blanket, coverlet. 2. (Ven.) net-bag. 3. (Amer.) goatee, beard; **chivas,** belongings; junk; secondhand clothes.
chivarras, *f.* (*pl.*) (Mex.) goatskin breeches.
chivarro, rra, *m., f.* kid more than one but less than two years old.
chivata, *f.* shepherd's staff.
chivato, *m.* 1. kid between six months and one year old. 2. (coll.) informer, tattletale.
chivetero, *m.* fold for kids (goats).
chivillo, *m.* (Peru) cacique, species of oriole (Cassicus or Cacicus palliatus).
chivital, *m., var. of* **chivetero.**
chivo, *m.* receptacle for olive oil lees.
chivo, va, *m., f.* kid (young goat), goat; **ch. expiatorio,** scapegoat.
¡cho! *interj.* whoa!
chocante, *a.* 1. shocking, offensive; vulgarly witty. 2. (Mex.) annoying, irritating, vexatious.
chocar, (*ref. 50*) *i.v.* 1. to collide, crash, strike, hit. 2. to fight, to clash, meet (in combat). 3. to irritate, annoy, provoke. 4. to surprise, shock, astonish, amaze. 5. (coll.) to displease, e.g. *me choca esta fruta,* I dislike this fruit; **chocarla,** (col.) to shake hands. —*tr.v.* to crash (one's car).
chocarrear, *i.v.* to tell dirty jokes, make ribald remarks.
chocarrería, *f.* coarse joke; ribaldry.
chocarrero, ra, *a.* coarse, vulgar, indecent. —*m., f.* vulgar comic, person who tells dirty jokes.
chocha, *f.* 1. (ornith.) woodcock; **ch. de mar** (ichth.) shrimpfish. 2. (vulg., Amer.) vulva.
chochaperdiz, (*pl.* **chochaperdices**) *f.* woodcock.
chochear, *i.v.* 1. to be in one's dotage, be doddering. 2. (coll.) to dote (on).
chochera, *f., var. of* **chochez.**
chochez, *f.* 1. dotage, senility. 2. doting, excessive fondness towards a child.
chocho, *m.* 1. (bot.) lupine seed. 2. cinnamon candy; (*pl.*) candy to keep a child quiet.
chocho, cha, *a.* 1. doting, very fond, delighted. 2. doddering (because of age). — **estar ch.,** to behave like a doddering old fool about someone or something.
chochocol, *m.* (Mex.) large earthen jar.
choclar, *i.v.* to drive a ball through a hoop (in croquet).
choclo, *m.* 1. clog, galosh. 2. (Amer.) corncob, ear of corn.
choclón, na, *a.* slovenly, poorly dressed. —*m.* (in croquet) driving of the ball through a hoop.
choco, *m.* small cuttlefish.
choco, *a.* 1. (Bol.) dark-red. 2. (Col.) swarthy, dark-complexioned. 3. (Chile) fuzzy-haired. 4. (Chile) tail-less; one-legged; one-eared. 5. (Guat., Hond.) one-eyed. —*m.* 1. (Bol.) top hat. 2. (Chile) tree stump.
chocolate, *m.* chocolate. — **chocolates surtidos,** assorted chocolates.
chocolatera, *f.* chocolate pot.
chocolatería, *f.* chocolate factory or shop.
chocolatero, ra, *a.* fond of chocolate. —*m., f.* chocolate maker or seller.
chócolo, *m.* 1. (Col.) corncob. 2. (Col.) children's game in which coins are aimed at a small hole in the ground.
chofe, *m.* (*gen. pl.*) lungs, liver, gizzard, etc. as an economical and nutritive food.
chofer, *m.* driver, chauffeur.
chofeta, *f.* fire pan (for lighting cigars).
chofista, *m.* name formerly used for a penniless student (who presumably subsisted on **chofe**).
chola, *f.* (coll.), *var. of* **cholla.**
cholga, *f.* (Chile) small mussel.
cholla, *f.* (coll.) head; mind, brain.
cholo, la, *a., m., f.* (Bol., Peru) mestizo.
choloque, *m.* (Amer.) (bot.) soapberry.
chomba, *f.* (Chile) woman's sweater; (Peru) large earthen vessel.
chompa, *f.* 1. (Amer.) hand drill. 2. (Ven.) iron bar. 3. (S. Amer.) sweater.
chonco, *m.* (C. Rica, coll.) stump (of an amputated limb).
chongo, *m.* 1. (Mex.) chignon; (Guat.) curl (of hair). 2. (Mex.) joke, jest. — **ch. zamorano,** a famous Mexican confection.
chonguearse, *r.v.* (Mex., coll.) to joke, jest, banter.
chonta, *f.* (Amer., bot.) tucuma (Astrocaryum chonta).
chontaduro, *m.* (Ecuad.) (species of) palm (Guilielma speciosa).
chontal, *m.* a field or grove of **chonta.**
chopa, *f.* (ichth.) chopa, rudderfish (Spondyliosoma cantharus).
chopa, *f.* (mar.) top-gallant peep.
chopal, *m., var. of* **chopera.**
chopalera, *f., var. of* **chopera.**
chope, *m.* 1. (Chile) hoe; oyster rake. 2. punch, blow.
chopear, *i.v.* (Chile) to punch, strike with the fist.
chopera, *f.* poplar grove.
chopo, *m.* Lombardy or black poplar.
chopo, *m.* (coll.) rifle.
choque, *m.* 1. crash, collision; clash, dispute, quarrel; (mil.) clash, skirmish, brush. 2. shock. — **ch. eléctrico,** electric shock; **ch. nervioso,** nervous shock; **ch. de agua** or **ariete,** (hydr.) water hammer.
choque, choqué, *ref.* **chocar.**
choquezuela, *f.* knee-cap, patella.
chorcha, *f.* (ornith.) woodcock.
chordón, *m.* raspberry bush; raspberry (fruit), raspberry jam.
chorear, *r.v.* (Chile, coll.) to grumble, moan (coll.). mutter discontentedly.
chorear, *tr.v.* (Peru) to swipe, whip, snitch, pinch, steal.
choreo, *m.* (Peru) pinching, stealing.
choricera, *f.* sausage machine.
choricería, *f.* sausage store or shop.
choricero, ra, *m., f.* 1. sausage maker or seller. 2. (Cuba, coll.) bungler, shoddy worker.
chorillo, *m.* (Peru) mill for coarse fabrics.
chorizo, *m.* 1. sausage (gen. pork). 2. ropewalker's pole. 3. (Col.) fool. 4. (Cuba, coll.) a shoddy job.
chorla, *f.* (Col., ornith.) sandgrouse.
chorlito, *m.* 1. (ornith.) golden plover, grey plover, curlew. 2. (coll.) harebrained person, scatterbrain. — **¡cabeza de ch.!** scatterbrain!
chorlo, *m.* 1. (min.) tourmaline, schorl. 2. (min.) aluminum silicate. 3. (Col.) great-great-grandchild.
choro, *m.* (Chile, Peru) large mussel.
choro, *m.* (coll.) thief.
chorote, *m.* (Col.) unglazed chocolate pot; (Cuba) any thick beverage; (Ven.) a beverage of chocolate, water and brown sugar.
choroy, *m.* (Chile) small parrot.
chorreado, da, *past part. of* **chorrear.** —*a.* 1. having dark, vertical stripes (cattle). 2. (Amer.) dirty, stained. 3. (Ecuad.) wet, soaked.
chorreadura, *f.* spouting, spurting, gushing; dripping; stain (from dripping liquid).
chorrear, *i.v.* to gush, spurt, spout; to drip; to trickle.
chorreo, *m.* spouting, spurting, gushing, dripping; trickle.

chorrera, *f.* 1. spout (from which liquid trickles). 2. channel, gully, mark (left by liquid). 3. rapids (of river). 4. jabot, shirt frill. 5. ornamental pendant for badges, stars, etc.
chorretada, *f.* (coll.) spurt, jet, squirt; extra portion served as good measure. — **hablar a chorretadas,** (coll.) to speak nineteen to the dozen, speak hurriedly.
chorrillo, *m.* (coll.) constant flow or stream — **irse por el ch.,** to follow the crowd, swim with the current; **irse por el ch. de hacer una cosa,** to make a habit of doing something; **sembrar a ch.,** to sow while plowing; **tomar el ch. de hacer una cosa,** to get into the habit of doing something.
chorro, *m.* spout, jet, spurt (of liquid); stream, shower (of small articles such as grain). — **avión a ch.,** jet, jet-plane; **a chorros,** (coll.) abundantly, in floods; **ch. de voz,** a blasting voice; **hablar a chorros,** to speak nineteen to the dozen, speak hurriedly; **soltar el ch.,** (coll.) to burst into laughter; **ch. contraído,** (hydr.) vena contracta.
chorroborro, *m.* (derog., fig.) an avalanche of useless objects.
chorrón, *m.* dressed hemp.
chortal, *m.* pool or small lake fed by spring.
chotacabras, *f.* (ornith.) goatsucker, nightjar.
chote, *m.* (bot., Cuba) chayote, a variety of calabash.
chotear, *tr.v.* to make fun of, mock, jeer at.
choteo, *m.* chaffing; jeering, mocking.
chotis, *m.* schottische, a popular dance in Europe at the beginning of the century.
choto, ta, *m., f.* suckling calf or kid.
chotuno, na, *a.* suckling, unweaned (kid or lamb); thin, sickly (lamb). — **oler a chotuno,** to smell like a goat, be smelly.
chova, *f.* (ornith.) chough, jackdaw; (ornith.) hooded crow.
choz, (*pl.* **choces**) *f.* shock, surprise. — **de ch.,** suddenly.
choza, *f.* hut; hovel, humble dwelling; cabin, shanty.
chozno, na, *m., f.* great-great-great grandchild.
chozo, *m.* small hut; hovel.
chozpar, *i.v.* to gambol, frisk, caper (lambs, kids, etc.).
chozpo, *m.* gambol, frisk, caper.
chozpón, na, *a.* frisky, capering.
chozuela, *f. dim. of* **choza,** small hut; hovel.
chual, *m.* (bot.) goosefoot or pigweed.
chuascle, *m.* (Mex.) trap (for hunting).
chubarba, *f.* (bot.) stonecrop, a plant of the genus sedum.
chubasco, *m.* 1. cloudburst, downpour, squall, shower; (mar.) threatening storm cloud. 2. setback, temporary upset.
chubascoso, *a.* squally.
chubasquería, *f.* (mar.) blanket of storm clouds.
chubasquero, *m.* (reg.) raincoat.
chuca, *f.* hollow side of bone (in game of knucklebones).
chucán, na, *a.* (Guat.) ribald, coarse, vulgarly witty.
chucanear, *i.v.* (Guat.) to joke, jest.
chúcaro, ra, *a.* (Amer.) wild, untamed, skittish (mules, horses or bulls).
chuce, chucé, *ref.* **chuzar.**
chucero, *m.* pikeman.
chucha, *f.* 1. (coll.) bitch. 2. (zoll., Col.) opossum. 3. (coll.) drunken spree, drunk. 4. (coll.) laziness, indolence. 5. (Chile, Peru, vulg.) cunt (vulg.). —*interj.* shoo! off! begone! (to frighten a dog away).
chuchazo, *m.* (Cuba, Ven.) whiplash, lash of the whip.
chuchear, *i.v.* 1. to whisper. 2. (hunt.) to trap, ensnare, catch.
chuchería, *f.* 1. trinket, trifle, bauble. 2. tasty tidbit, snack. 3. (hunt.) trapping; small game.
chuchero, ra, *a.* using traps and decoys (huntsman). —*m.* 1. (Col.) peddler, hawker. 2. (Cuba, ry.) switchtender. 3. (Cuba) a vulgar, flashy dresser.
chucho, *m.* 1. (ornith.) pygmy owl, gnome owl (Glaucidium nanum). 2. (Chile, Arg.) the shivers; malaria fever, ague. 3. (coll.) dog. 4. (Cuba) electric switch. 5. (ornith., S. Amer.) small herringlike fish. 6. (Cuba) needle, prick. 7. (ichth., Cuba) (species of) sting-ray. 8. (Cuba. Ven.) whip. —*interj.* shoo! go away! (said to a dog).
chuchoca, *f.* (S. Amer.) corn toasted, pounded and cooked into meal.
chuchumeco, *m.* (derog.) little runt.
chucua, *f.* (Col.) marsh, swamp, bog.
chucuru, *m.* (Ecuad., zool.) (species of) weasel.
chucuto, ta, *a.* (Ven.) bobtail, docked-tail (dog).
chueca, *f.* 1. stump (of a tree). 2. (anat.) ball of socket-joint. 3. a type of hockey ball; kind of hockey. 4. (coll.) joke, trick.
chueco, ca, *a.* (S. Amer.) bowlegged; (Mex.) crooked, bent.
chueta, *m., f.* (hist.) Chueta (descendant of Christianized Jews).
chufa, *f.* (bot.) chufa, a sedge (cyperus esculentus). — **echar chufas,** (coll.) to act the bully, bully.
chufar, *i.v., r.v.* to mock, taunt, jeer.
chufería, *f.* place where chufa orgeat is made or sold.
chufero, ra, *m., f.* chufa seller.
chufeta, *f.* fire pan (for lighting cigars).
chufeta, *f.* (coll.) joke, jest.
chufla, *f.* joke, jest.
chufleta, *f.* (coll.) joke, jest.
chufletear, *i.v.* (coll.) to joke, jest, banter.
chufletero, ra, *a.* (coll.) amusing, joking, jesting, bantering. —*m., f.* joker, banterer.
chula, *f.* 1. fruit of the night-blooming cereus or prickly pear. 2. a pretty, sassy girl.
chulada, *f.* 1. coarseness, vulgarity. 2. wagishness, roguishness, lightheartedness; waggish or lighthearted remark or action.
chulama, mo, *f.* (sl.) girl. —*m.* (sl.) boy.
chulapo, pa, *m., f.* a swaggering swain or belle of the lower sections of Madrid.
chulear, *tr.v.* to banter, kid, make fun of wittily.
chulería, *f.* 1. charm, sparkle, waggishness, lightheartedness. 2. the boisterous rabble (Madrid).
chulesco, *a.* smart, natty, flashy.
chuleta, *f.* 1. (cul.) veal cutlet, pork or mutton chop. 2. (carp.) filling. 3. (coll.) slap. 4. (coll.) mutton chops, whiskers, sideburns.
chullo, lla, *a.* (Ecuad.) odd, single item of a pair (glove, shoe, etc.).
chulo, la, *a.* 1. lighthearted, roguish. 2. smart, natty, flashy. 3. (Amer.) pretty, good-looking. —*m.* 1. gay and lively person. 2. smart person, natty dresser (among the lower sections of Madrid). 3. butcher's helper. 4. (taur.) bull-fighter's assistant. 5. pimp.
chumacera, *f.* 1. (mec.) axle bearing, journal bearing, bearing. 2. (mar.) oarlock; (mar.) strip of wood to which the oarlock is fixed. — **ch. partida,** split bearing; **ch. recalentada,** hotbox, hot bearing.
chumarse, *r.v.* (Arg.) to get drunk.
chumbe, *m.* (Col., Peru) girdle, belt (to hold up skirt).
chumbera, *f.* (bot.) prickly pear, nopal.
chumbo, ba, *a.* (bot.) prickly (pear).
chumpipe, *m.* (Guat.) turkey.
chuncaca, *f.* (C. Amer.) *var. of* **chancaca,** brown sugar.
chuncho, cha, *a.* (Peru) bashful, shy. —*m.* 1. (Peru) savage jungle Indian. 2. (bot.) (Peru) calendula, pot marigold. 3. (Hond.) anything (equivalent to U.S. whatchamacallit or thingamajig).
chunga, *f.* (coll.) joke, jest. — **estar de ch.,** to be in a joking mood; **tomar en ch.,** to take as a joke.
chunga, *f.* (S. Amer., ornith.) a cranelike bird, Burmeister's seriema, (chunga burmeisteri).
chungarse, (*ref. 51*) *r.v., var. of* **chunguearse.**
chungue, chungué, *ref.* **chungarse.**
chunguearse, *r.v.* to joke with one another.
chuño, *m.* (S. Amer.) potato starch; frozen dried potato.
chupa, *f.* frock, long underjacket. — **ponerle a uno como ch. de dómine.** (coll.) to give someone a severe dressing down; to wipe the floor with, leave squashed and abashed.
chupa, *f.* (Phil. I.) grain measure (0.37 liter); liquid measure (0.735 liter).
chupada, *f.* suck, sucking.
chupaderito, *m.* teething ring. — **andarse con** or **en chupaderitos,** to employ ineffective means for the task.
chupadero, ra, *a.* sucking. —*m.* teething ring.
chupado, da, *past part. of* **chupar.** —*a.* (coll.) emaciated, lean, thin.
chupador, ra, *a.* sucking. —*m., f.* sucker. —*m.* 1. teething ring. 2. (Amer.) heavy drinker. 3. strainer for foot valve. 4. (lab.) nipple. 5. swab.
chupadorcito, *m.* **andarse con** or **en chupadorcitos,** to use ineffective means for the task.
chupadura, *f.* sucking, suck.
chupaflor, *m.* (ornith., Mex.) humming bird.
chupamirto, *m.* (ornith., Mex.) humming bird.
chupar, *tr.v.* 1. to suck; to absorb. 2. (coll.) to eat away (someone's worldly goods or inheritance), to sponge on someone. 3. (Amer.) to drink. —*i.v.* to suck. —*r.v.* to waste away, become emaciated.
chupatintas, *m.* (coll.) penpusher, petty clerk.
chupativo, va, *a.* sucking; absorbent.
chupe, *m.* (Chile) stew of fresh fish or clams, bread, eggs, cheese, tomato, potato, etc.
chupeta, *f.* 1. *dim. of* **chupa,** short frock, short jacket. 2. nipple, pacifier. 3. (mar.) roundhouse.
chupete, *m.* 1. nipple (of nursing bottle); baby's comforter, pacifier. 2. (Amer.) lollipop. — **ser de ch.,** to be exquisite or delicious.
chupetear, *tr.v.* to suck gently from time to time.
chupeteo, *m.* gentle sucking.
chupetín, *m.* tight doublet, under jacket, jerkin.
chupetón, *m.* strong suck.
chupín, *m.* short doublet or under jacket.
chupinazo, *m.* 1. mortar-firing in firework displays. 2. (coll.) powerful shot (in soccer).
chupón, na, *a.* 1. sucking. 2. (coll.) swindling. —*m., f.* (coll.) swindler. —*m.* 1. down (not fully-formed feather). 2. (bot.) shoot (which debilitates the tree). 3. (mec.) piston (of suction pump). 4. (Amer.) baby's comforter, pacifier. 5. plunger (to fix a drain).
chupóptero, *m.* (coll.) parasite, holder of a sinecure.
chuquisa, *f.* prostitute.
churana, *f.* (S. Amer.) quiver (for arrows).
churcha, *f.* (zool., Amer.) opossum.
churco, *m.* (bot.) wood sorrel (Oxalis gigantea).
churdón, *m.* raspberry, raspberry plant; concentrated raspberry syrup.
churla, *f., var. of* **churlo.**
churlo, *m.* tightly closed container for spices and other aromatics.

churo, *m.* 1. (Ecuad.) lock of hair. 2. (Ecuad., zool.) snail.
churra, *f.* (ornith.) sandgrouse.
churrasco, *m.* (S. Amer.) grilled steak, broiled steak; grilling or broiling steak.
churre, *m.* 1. thick, dirty fat. 2. (coll.) grime, ingrained dirt, grease, filth.
churrea, *f.* (ornith.) California grouse.
churrería, *f.* place where fritters or crullers are fried or sold.
churrero, ra, *m., f.* fritter or cruller maker or seller.
churretada, *f.* large dirty spot; mass of dirty spots (on the body).
churrete, *m.* dirty spot or mark (on one's body).
churretoso, sa, *a.* dirty, soiled.
churriana, *f.* (vulg.) whore, strumpet.
churrías, *f.* (*pl.*) (coll., Amer.) diarrhea.
churriburri, *m.* 1. (coll.) ruffian, tough; band of toughs; confusion, noise, uproar. 2. ragamuffin.
churriento, ta, *a.* full of dirty marks or spots.
churrigueresco, ca, *a.* (archit.) churrigueresque, baroque; highly ornamented, florid.
churriguerismo, *m.* (archit.) churriguerism, excessive ornamentation.
churriguerista, *m.* (archit.) churriguerist, architect who adopts a churrigueresque, baroque or highly ornamental style (after the Spanish architect José Churriguera, 1650-1723).
churrillero, ra, *a., m., var. of* **churrullero.**
churro, *m.* 1. (cul.) fritter, cruller. 2. (coll.) botch-up, slipshod piece of work.
churro, rra, *a.* 1. coarse (of wool); coarse wooled (sheep). 2. (Peru) handsome, attractive. —*m., f.* 1. coarse wool sheep. 2. (Arg., Mex.) handsome person.
churruchada, *f.* spoonful.
churrullero, ra, *a.* garrulous, talkative, jabbering. —*m., f.* chatterbox, jabberer.
churruscar, (*ref. 50*) *tr.v.* (cul.) to burn. —*r.v.* to get burnt.
churrusco, *m.* burnt piece of toast.
churrusque, churrusqué, *ref.* **churruscar.**
churumbel, *m.* child, boy (in Spanish Gypsy dialect).
churumbela, *f.* 1. (mus.) (species of) flageolet. 2. (S. Amer.) silver tube for drinking maté.
churumen, *m.* (coll.) *var. of* **chirumen.**
churumo, *m.* (coll.) juice; **poco ch.,** not much juice, money or sense.
¡chus! *interj.* here, doggie! — **no decir chus ni mus,** not to say a word.
chuscada, *f.* witty, waggish or roguish remark.
chuscamente, *adv.* wittily, roguishly.
chusco, ca, *a.* 1. witty, roguish. 2. (Peru) mongrel (dog). 3. (Peru) unrefined (person, manners). —*m., f.* wit. —*m.* piece or crumb of bread.
chusma, *f.* rabble, mob; (arch.) crew of galley slaves.
chusmaje, *m.* (Amer.) rabble, riff-raff, mob.
chuspa, *f.* (S. Amer., Quech.) knapsack, bag.
chusque, *m.* (bot., Col.) (species of) bamboo (Chusquea scandens).
chusquisa, *f.* (Chile, Peru) prostitute.
chut, *m.* shot (in soccer).
chutar, *tr.v.* to shoot (in soccer).
chuva, *f.* (zool., Peru) spider monkey (Ateles variegates).
chuza, *f.* (Mex.) strike (in bowling); knocking down all pins with one ball.
chuzar, (*ref. 53*) *tr.v.* (Col.) to prick, wound.
chuzazo, *m.* pike wound, thrust with a pointed weapon.
chuznieto, ta, *m., f.* great-great-great-grandchild.
chuzo, *m.* 1. pike. 2. (Cuba) horsewhip. 3. (Peru, Chile) shoe. — **caer, llover** or **nevar chuzos,** to rain cats and dogs; to hail or snow heavily.
chuzón, na, *a.* astute, sharp, sagacious; witty. —*m., f.* sharp, sagacious person; wit. —*m.* clown, jester.
chuzonada, *f.* coarse joke.
chuzonería, *f.* joke, jest, banter or kidding.
cía, *f.* (anat.) hip bone.
Cía., cía. *abbrev. of* **compañía,** company (Co.).
ciaboga, *f.* (mar.) putting about (of a row-boat, steamer); **hacer c.,** to make a commotion.
cianamida, *f.* (chem.) cyanamide, cyanamid.
cianato, *m.* (chem.) cyanate.
cianea, *f.* (min.) lazulite.
cianhídrico, *a.* (chem.) hydrocyanic, prussic (acid).
cianí, *m.* low carat African gold coin.
ciánico, ca, *a.* (chem.) cyanic (acid).
cianina, *f.* (chem.) cyanine.
cianita, *f.* (chem.) cyanite.
cianoblamina, *f.* (med.) cyanocobalamin.
cianocobalamina, *f.* (med.) cyanocobalamin.
cianógeno, *m.* (chem.) cyanogen.
cianosis, *f.* (med.) cyanosis.
cianótico, ca, *a.* (med.) cyanotic.
cianotipia, *f.* blueprinting.
cianotipo, *m.* cyanotype, blueprint.
cianuración, *f.* (metal.) cyanide process.
cianúrico, ca, *a.* (chem.) cyanuric.
cianuro, *m.* (chem.) cyanide; **c. de potasio,** potassium cyanide; **c. de sodio,** sodium cyanide.
CIAP *abbrev. of* **Comité Interamericano de la Alianza para el Progreso,** Inter-American Committee of the Alliance for Progress.
ciar, (*ref. 54*) *i.v.* 1. to go backwards, back up. 2. (mar.) to put about, turn round. 3. (fig.) to back out (of a business deal); to slacken or cede (in one's demands, etc.).
ciática, *f.* (med.) sciatica; lumbago.
ciático, ca, *a.* sciatic.
ciato, *m.* (archaeol.) cyathus, kyathos (ancient cup or ladle used by Romans).
cibal, *a.* cibarious.
cibario, ria, *a.* said of Roman food laws.
cibeleo, a, *a.* (poet.) of the goddess Cybele.
Cibeles, *f.* (myth.) Cybele, goddess of the Earth.
cibera, *f.* quantity of wheat put into mill hopper; grain used for fodder; residue of pressed fruit.
cibernética, *f.* cybernetics.
cibiaca, *f.* litter, stretcher.
cibica, *f.* 1. iron clout (on upper side of axletree). 2. (mar.) cramp, clamp, staple.
cibicón, *m. aug. of* **cibica,** large iron clout.
cíbola, *f.* (zool.) female bison.
cíbolo, *m.* (zool.) bison.
ciborio, *m.* 1. (archit.) ciborium. 2. (archeol.) ancient Greek or Roman drinking cup.
cibucán, *m.* (Cuba, Ven.) large basket.
cibui, *m.* (Peru, bot.) cedar.
cica, *f.* (bot.) cycad.
cicadáceas, *f.* (*pl.*) cycadaceae.
cicádeo, a, *a.* like a cicada.
cicádidos, *m.* (*pl.*) (zool.) Cicadidae.
cicatear, *i.v.* (coll.) to act meanly or stingily.
cicatería, *f.* niggardliness, stinginess, meanness.
cicatero, ra, *a.* niggardly, miserly, stingy, mean. —*m., f.* miser, skinflint, mean person.
cicateruelo, la, *a., m., f. dim. of* **cicatero,** stingy or mean little runt.
cicatricera, *f.* nurse (formerly called so in the Spanish Army).
cicatrícula, *f.* cicatricle.
cicatriz, (*pl.* **cicatrices**), *f.* 1. scar, cicatrix, cicatrice. 2. (fig.) unpleasant impression remaining on the mind.
cicatrización, *f.* cicatrization.
cicatrizal, *a.* cicatricial.
cicatrizante, *a.* cicatrizing, cicatrizant. —*m.* cicatrizant, healing agent.
cicatrizar, (*ref. 53*) *tr.v., i.v., r.v.* to cicatrize, heal.
cicatrizativo, va, *a.* cicatrizing, cicatrisive, cicatrizant.
cicera, *f.* (bot.) kind of chick-pea.
cicércula, cicercha, *f., vars. of* **almorta.**
cícero, *m.* 1. (print.) pica. 2. (print.) unit of measurement equal to 12 points or 4.5 mm.
cicerón, *m.* 1. (fig.) eloquent person. 2. C., Cicero, Roman statesman and orator.
cicerone, *m.* cicerone, guide.
ciceroniano, na, *a.* Ciceronian.
cicindela, *f.* (ento.) tiger beetle (Cicindela campestris).
cicindélidos, *m. pl.* (ento.) Cicindelidae.
ciclada, *f.* long, bell-shaped gown formerly used by women.
ciclaje, *m.* (elec.), (Chile) frequency.
ciclamina, *f.* (chem.) cyclamin.
ciclamino, *m.* (bot.) cyclamen.
ciclamor, *m.* (bot.) Judas tree (Cercis siliquastrum).
ciclán, *a.* having one testicle. —*m.* lamb or young goat with undeveloped testicles.
ciclar, *tr.v.* to polish, burnish (precious stones).
ciclatón, *m.* cyclas (tunic or mantle worn in the Middle Ages).
cíclico, ca, *a.* cyclic, cyclical.
ciclismo, *m.* cycling (sport); **c. en pista,** track cycling.
ciclista, *m., f.* cyclist, bicycle rider.
ciclo, *m.* 1. cycle. 2. (Amer.) levels of academic studies, e.g. *c. primario,* elementary studies, *c. universitario,* university studies. 3. series of cultural events, e.g. *c. de conferencias,* series of conferences. — **c. decemnoval, decemnovario** or **lunar,** lunar cycle, Metonic cycle; **c. menstrual,** menstrual cycle; **c. pascual,** Paschal cycle, Dyonisian period; **c. solar,** cycle of the sun, cycle of Sundays, solar cycle.
cicloidal, *a.* (geom.) cycloidal.
cicloide, *f.* (geom.) cycloid. —*a.* (psyc.) pertaining to a cyclothymic person.
cicloideo, a, *a., var. of* **cicloidal.**
cicloinversor, *m.* (elec.) cycloinverter.
ciclometría, *f.* cyclometry.
ciclométrico, ca, *a.* cyclometric.
ciclómetro, *m.* cyclometer.
ciclón, *m.* cyclone.
ciclonal, *a.* cyclonal, cyclonic.
ciclónico, ca, *a.* cyclonic, cyclonical.
cíclope, *m.* (myth.) Cyclops.
ciclópeo, a, *a.* Cyclopean; (fig.) huge, gigantic, colossal.
ciclópico, ca, *a., var. of* **ciclópeo.**
cicloplejía, *f.* (med.) cycloplegia.
ciclopropano, *m.* (chem.) cyclopropane.
ciclorama, *m.* cyclorama.
ciclosis, *f.* (physiol.) cyclosis.
ciclostilo, *m.* cyclostyle.
ciclóstomo, ma, *a.* (zool.) cyclostome, cyclostomate, cyclostomatous. —*m., f.* (zool.) cyclostome, (*pl.*) Cyclostomata.
ciclotimia, *f.* (psyc.) cyclothymia.
ciclotímico, ca, *a.* (psyc.) cyclothymic.
ciclótomo, *a.* (math.) cyclotomic.
ciclotrón, *m.* (phys.) cyclotron.
cicuta, *f.* (bot.) hemlock, poison hemlock (Conium maculatum); hemlock (poison); **c. menor,** (bot.) poison parsley.
cicutina, *f.* (chem.) coniine.
Cid, *m.* 1. (arch.) lord, sire (title). 2. (fig.) strong and courageous man. — **el C.** or **el C. Campeador,** the Cid, Rodrigo Díaz de Vivar, Spanish hero of the 11th century.

cidiano, na, *a.* pertaining to the **Cid.**
cidra, *f.* (bot.) citron (fruit).
cidracayote, *f.* (bot.) American gourd or calabash.
cidrada, *f.* (cul.) candied citron; citron preserve.
cidral, *m.* plantation of citron trees; citron tree.
cidrato, *m.* (bot.) citrus fruit (of the azamboere tree).
cidrayota, *m.* (bot., S. Amer.) winter squash.
cidrera, *f., var. of* **cidro.**
cidria, *f., var. of* **cedria.**
cidro, *m.* (bot.) citron tree (Citrus medica).
cidronela, *f.* (bot.) citronella, balm, garden balm (Melissa officinalis).
ciegamente, *adv.* blindly.
ciegayernos, *m.* (coll.) showy, worthless thing, humbug.
ciego, ga, *a.* 1. blind. 2. choked-up, blocked-up (pipe, conduit). 3. (fig.) blind, blinded, e.g. *c. de ira,* blind with rage, *c. de amor,* blinded by love, *c. de celos,* blinded by jealousy, blind with jealousy. — **a ciegas,** blindly, in the dark; blind, e.g. *vuelo a ciegas,* (aer.) blind flying; (coll.) unthinkingly, without due thought or reflection; **más c. que un topo,** as blind as a bat. —*m.* 1. black pudding. 2. (anat.) caecum, blind gut. —*m., f.* blind person.
ciego, ciegue, *ref.* **cegar.**
cieguecico, ca, llo, lla, to, ta, *a., m., f. dim. of* **ciego.**
cieguezuelo, la, *a., m., f. dim. of* **ciego.**
cielito, *m.* 1. (Arg.) gaucho tune and round dance. 2. dearest, darling.
cielo, *m.* 1. sky, firmament. 2. climate; weather. 3. heaven, paradise, glory, bliss. 4. (fig.) canopy (of a bed). 5. top, roof (of a car, etc.); ceiling. — **a c. abierto** or **descubierto,** in the open; **bajado del c.,** (coll.), prodigious, excellent, perfect; **caer del c.,** to be sent from heaven, be a godsend; **cerrarse el c.,** to cloud over, become overcast; **c. de la boca,** palate, roof of the mouth; **c. raso,** ceiling (of a house); **clamar al c.,** to cry out to heaven (in protest); **el c. se vino abajo,** it rained cats and dogs; all hell broke out; **encapotarse el c.,** to cloud over, become overcast; **escupir al c.,** (coll.) to have one's own unkind remarks backfire; **juntársele a uno c. y tierra,** to be in a terrible predicament; **llovido del c.,** (coll.) heaven-sent, god-sent (opportune, lucky); **medio c.,** (astron.) meridian; (astrol.) midheaven; **mover c. y tierra,** (coll.) to move heaven and earth, to do all in one's power; **poner el grito en el c.,** to raise the roof, complain aloud; **ver uno el c. abierto,** (coll.) to see a way out (of a difficulty); **poner en** or **por el c.,** to praise to the skies.
ciempiés, *m.* 1. (ento.) centipede. 2. (coll.) incoherent nonsense.
cien, *a.* one hundred (always used before a noun instead of **ciento**).
ciénaga, *f.* swamp, marsh, morass, bog.
ciencia, *f.* science; erudition, knowledge, learning; art, skill; certainty. — **a** or **de c. cierta,** with complete certainty, beyond a shadow of doubt; **a c. y paciencia,** on sufferance, with someone's permission or leave; **c. ficción,** science fiction; **ciencias exactas,** exact sciences; **ciencias naturales,** natural sciences; **ciencias ocultas,** occult sciences; **Ciencias Políticas,** Political Science.
cienmilésimo, ma, *a.* hundred thousandth. —*m.* one hundred thousandth.
cienmilímetro, *m.* one hundredth part of a millimeter.
cienmilmillonésimo, ma, *a.* hundred thousand millionth. —*m.* one hundred thousand millionth.
cienmillonésimo, ma, *a.* hundred millionth. —*m.* one hundred millionth.
cieno, *m.* mud, slime, mire.
cienoso, sa, *a.* muddy.
ciensayos, *m.* legendary bird of multicolored plumage.
científicamente, *adv.* scientifically.
cientificismo, *m.* scientism.
científico, ca, *a.* scientific. —*m., f.* scientist.
ciento, *a.* one hundred; **el número c.,** the number one hundred. —*m.* 1. hundred (figure, quantity). 2. (*pl.*) card game for two (won by scoring 100 points). — **por c.,** per cent, by the hundred; **por cientos,** by the hundreds, in large numbers.
cientopiés, *m., var. of* **ciempiés.**
cierna, *f.* (bot.) anther (of wheat, a vine, etc.).
cierna, cierno, *ref.* **cerner, cernir.**
cierne, *m.* blossoming, budding; **en cierne,** in bud; in its infancy; in its inception, in embryo.
cierre, *m.* 1. closure; closing, shutting, locking, sealing. 2. shut-down, lock-out (of factory, mine). 3. fastener, clasp, snap; lock, seal. — **c. del cojinete,** bearing seal; **c. hermético,** hermetic seal; **c. hidráulico,** water seal; **c. metálico,** folding iron shutter; **c. relámpago,** zipper, zip fastener.
cierre, cierro, *ref.* **cerrar.**
cierro, *m.* 1. closure; shutting, closing. 2. (Amer.) wall, fence. 3. (Amer.) envelope. — **c. de cristales,** closed porch, bay window, oriel window.
ciertamente, *adv.* certainly, surely.
cierto, ta, *a.* 1. certain, definite. 2. true, e.g. *es cierto que nunca ha mentido,* it is true that he has never lied. 3. certain, sure, convinced, e.g. *estoy cierto de que no vendrá,* I'm certain he won't come. 4. certain (used indefinitely), e.g. *c. día,* a certain day. 5. certain, some, e.g. *ciertos hombres,* some men. — **lo c. es que,** the truth is that.
cierto, *adv.* certainly, truly. — **por c.,** by the way, incidentally; certainly.
cierva, *f.* (zool.) hind (female deer).
ciervo, *m.* (zool.) stag, hart; **c. volante,** stag beetle (Lucanus servus).
cierzas *f.* (*pl.*) (agr.) new vine shoots (after pruning), tendrils.
cierzo, *m.* cold north wind.
CIES *abbrev. of* **Consejo Interamericano Económico y Social,** Inter-American Economic and Social Council.
cifela, *m.* (bot.) cyphella fungus.
cifosis, *f.* (med.) kyphosis, curvature of the spine.
cifra, *f.* 1. figure, number, numerical character. 2. cipher, code, cryptogram. 3. monogram, device, emblem. 4. sum total. 5. contraction, abbreviation. 6. music written with numbers. —*adv.* **en c.,** mysteriously, obscurely; briefly, concisely.
cifradamente, *adv.* briefly, succinctly, in a few words.
cifrado, da, *past part. of* **cifrar.** —*a.* coded, in cipher, in code.
cifrar, *tr.v.* 1. to cipher, code, put into code. 2. (fig.) to summarize, reduce, condense. — **c. en,** to focus or center (one's ambition) on; to place (one's hopes) on; to base (one's happiness) on. —*r.v.* to be summarized or condensed.
cigala, *f.* 1. (zool.) an edible crustacean. 2. (mar.) twine coil covering anchor or grapnel rings.
cigarra, *f.* (ento.) cicada, grasshopper; **c. de mar,** (zool.) sea crayfish.
cigarral, *m.* (Sp.) fenced fruit garden (in outskirts of a city).
cigarrera, *f.* 1. woman cigarette maker or seller. 2. cigar box, cigar cabinet, cigar or cigarette case.
cigarrería, *f.* 1. (Amer.) tobacconist's, cigarette shop. 2. cigar or cigarette factory.
cigarrero, ra, *m.* tobacconist; cigarette or cigar maker or seller.
cigarrillo, *m.* cigarette.
cigarro, *m.* cigar, cigarette; **c. puro,** cigar.
cigarrón, *m. aug. of* **cigarra,** (ento.) large cicada.
cigofiláceo, a, cigofileo, a, *a.* (bot.) zygophyllaceous. —*f.* (bot.) zygophyllaceous plant; (*pl.*) Zygophyllaceae.
cigoma, *m.* (anat.) zygoma.
cigomático, ca, *a.* (anat.) zygomatic.
cigomorfismo, *m.* (bot.) zygomorphism.
cigomorfo, fa, *a.* (biol.) zygomorphic, zygomorphous.
cigoñal, *m.* 1. well sweep, picotah, shadoof. 2. (fort.) beam (for raising a drawbridge).
cigoñino, *m.* young stork, stork chick.
cigoñuela, *f.* (ornith.) black-winged stilt (Himantopus himanthopus).
cigoto, *m.* (biol.) zygote; egg.
cigua, *f.* 1. (C. Amer., bot.) a variety of greenheart or Nectandra tree (Nectandra cigua). 2. (Cuba) sea-snail, whelk.
ciguapa, *f.* 1. (Car.) blue-billed owl-like bird. 2. (C. Rica) sapotaceous tree (Vitellaria salicifolium).
ciguaraya, *f.* (Cuba) common name of a medicinal plant.
ciguatarse, *r.v.* (med.) to get ciguatera or fish poisoning.
ciguatera, *f.* (med., Amer.) fish poisoning, ciguatera.
ciguato, ta, *a.* suffering from ciguatera or fish poisoning. —*m., f.* one suffering from ciguatera; (Amer., coll.) idiot, dumb; (fig.) pale, anemic.
cigüeña, *f.* 1. (ornith.) stork. 2. yoke of a bell. 3. (mec.) crank, winch. 4. (Car.) a small, hand-operated railroad car. — **pie de c.,** (bot.) stork-bill; **pintar la c.,** (coll.) to pose, show off.
cigüeñal, *m.* 1. (mec.) crank, crankshaft; (mec.) double crank (of crankshaft). 2. sweep (of a well). 3. hoisting chain beam (of drawbridge). — **c. equilibrado** or **de compensación,** balanced crankshaft; **c. de cuatro codos,** two-throw crankshaft; **c. voladizo,** overhanging crankshaft.
cigüeño, *m.* 1. male stork. 2. (coll.) tall, gangling man.
cigüeñuela, *f.* (mec.) small crank, hand crank; **c. de la caña del timón,** (mar.) gooseneck of the tiller.
cigüete, *f.* (bot.) variety of white-grape.
cija, *f.* 1. stall, stable (for sheep); hay barn. 2. (reg.) dungeon.
cilampa, *f.* (C. Amer.) drizzle (rain).
cilanco, *m.* pool (left by a receding river).
cilantro, *m.* (bot.) coriander.
cilia, *m.* (anat.) cilium.
ciliado, da, *a.* ciliate, ciliated. —*m.* (zool.) ciliate, (*pl.*) Ciliata.
ciliar, *a.* ciliary, pertaining to eyelashes or eyebrows.
cilicio, *m.* 1. hair shirt. 2. cilice (garment of haircloth or iron spikes worn by penitents). 3. (mil.) coarse canvas (used as a gun-cover).
cilindrada, *f.* 1. (mec.) cylinder capacity. 2. each of the movements of the cylinder.
cilindrado, *past part. of* **cilindrar.** —*m.* calendering, pressing, rolling.
cilindrar, *tr.v.* to calender, press (paper, cloth); to roll (road).
cilíndrico, ca, *a.* cylindrical.
cilindro, *m.* (geom., mec.) cylinder; (print.) roller; **c. compresor,** road roller; **c. de escarchar,** silver-smith's rolls; **c. estriado,** fluted cylinder; **c. maestro,** (auto.) master cylinder (brake); **c. sacanúcleos,** core barrel (drill).
cilindroeje, *m.* (anat.) axis cylinder.
cilindroide, *m.* (math.) cylindroid.
cilla, *f.* 1. granary. 2. tax (revenue).

cillerero, *m.* cellarer (steward of certain monasteries).
cillería, *f.* cellarer's office.
cilleriza, *f.* cellaress (nun directing convent housekeeping).
cillerízo, *m.* granary keeper.
cillero, *m.* 1. granary keeper (for produce collected as tithes). 2. granary, barn; storehouse, storeroom, pantry, cellar.
cima, *f.* 1. top, summit (of a tree, mountain); (fig.) height, pinnacle, apex. 2. (bot.) cyme; (bot.) stalk. — **dar c. a una cosa,** to put the finishing touch to; **mirar una cosa por c.,** (coll.) to glance cursorily at (something); **por c.,** on high, high above; superficially, cursorily.
cimacio, *m.* (archit.) cyma, ogee.
cimarrón, na, *a.* 1. (Amer.) runaway, fugitive. 2. (fig.) wild, unruly. 3. (Amer.) wild (animal, plant, etc.). —*m.* 1. (Amer.) fugitive slave. 2. (Amer.) lazy sailor. 3. (Arg.) unsweetened maté.
cimarronada, *f.* (Amer.) herd of wild animals.
cimarronear, *i.v.* 1. (hist.) to run away (a slave). 2. (Urug., Arg.) to drink unsweetened maté.
cimasa, *f.* (biochem.) zymase.
cimba, *f.* 1. (Bol.) hair braid (worn by blacks). 2. (archeol.) Roman river boat.
cimbado, *m.* (Bol.) braided whip.
cimbalaria, *f.* (bot.) Kenilworth ivy (Cymbalaria muralis).
cimbalero, *m.* (mus.) cymbal player, cymbalist.
cimbalillo, *m.* small bell.
cimbalista, *m.* (mus.) cymbalist.
címbalo, *m.* (mus.) cymbal.
cimbanillo, *m., var. of* **cimbalillo.**
címbara, *f.* short, broad scythe (for cutting bramble).
cimbel, *m.* 1. rope (to tie decoy pigeons). 2. decoy pigeon or duck, call bird.
cimboga, *f.* citron (fruit).
cimborio, *m., var. of* **cimborrio.**
cimborrio, *m.* (archit.) cupola, dome; (archit.) base or lantern of a cupola.
cimbra, *f.* 1. (archit.) centering (of an arch); (archit.) intrados (of an arch or vault). 2. (S. Amer.) bird trap. 3. (mar.) curvature (of timbers of a vessel's hull). — **plena c.,** semi-circular curvature.
cimbrado, *m.* quick twist of the waist (in Spanish dances).
cimbrar, *tr.v.* 1. to bend; to sway, swing. 2. (coll.) to beat, thrash. 3. to vibrate, shake; to brandish. 4. (archit.) to put the centering in (an arch). —*r.v.* to bend, buckle; to sway; to shake. —*i.v.* (Amer.) to change direction suddenly.
cimbre, *m.* underground gallery or passage.
cimbreante, *a.* flexible, pliant, supple; swaying, swinging.
cimbrear, *tr.v., r.v., var. of* **cimbrar.**
cimbreño, ña, *a.* flexible, pliant; willowy, tall and graceful.
cimbreo, *m.* bending, flexing; swinging, swishing; swaying; vibrating, shaking.
cimbria, *f.* (archit.) fillet.
címbrico, ca, *a.* (hist.) Cimbrian (pertaining to the Cimbri), Cimbric.
cimbro, bra, *a.* (hist.) Cimbrian. —*m., f.* Cimbrian (one of the Cimbri). —*m.* Cimbrian (language).
cimbrón, *m.* 1. (Amer.) violent pull or jerk. 2. (Ecuad.) sharp sudden pain.
cimbronazo, *m.* 1. blow with the flat of the sword. 2. (Amer.) shudder. 3. (Ven.) earthquake. 4. (Amer.) violent pull or jerk.
cimeno, *m.* (chem.) cymene.
cimentación, *f.* foundation; construction; establishment, consolidation.
cimentado, *past part. of* **cimentar.** —*m.* (metal.) refinement of gold (with powdered brick and vinegar).
cimentador, ra, *a.* founding, establishing; cementing, consolidating. —*m., f.* founder, creator; consolidator.
cimentar, (*ref. 29*) *tr.v.* 1. to lay the foundations of (a building, society); to lay down, establish (principles, basis); to foster, consolidate (peace). 2. (metal.) to refine (gold).
cimera, *f.* crest.
cimerio, ria, *a., m., f.* (myth.) Cimmerian.
cimero, ra, *a.* top, topmost.
cimiente, cimiento, *ref.* **cimentar.**
cimiento, *m.* 1. (bldg.) foundation, substructure. 2. root, origin, cause (of a vice). 3. (*pl.*) basis, fundamentals (of a branch of knowledge); (*pl.*) (bldg.) foundations. — **echar los cimientos,** to lay the foundations.
cimillo, *m.* flexible stick to which a decoy bird is tied.
cimitarra, *f.* scimitar.
cimo, *m.* (med.) zyme.
cimofana, *f.* (min.) cymophane.
cimogénesis, *f.* (biochem.) zymogenesis.
cimógeno, na, *a.* (bac.) zymogenic.
cimógrafo, *m.* kymograph.
cimólisis, *f.* (biochem.) zymolysis.
cimología, *f.* (med.) zymology.
cimómetro, *m.* 1. (rad., elec.) cymometer, instrument for measuring electromagnetic waves. 2. (biochem.) zymometer, instrument for measuring the degree of fermentation.
cimorra, *f.* (vet.) glanders.
cimorro, *m.* church tower.
cimoscopio, *m.* (elec.) cymoscope.
cimosis, *f.* zymosis.
cimoso, sa, *a.* (bot.) cymose.
cimótico, ca, *a.* zymotic.
cimpa, *f.* (Peru) braid of hair; rope of esparto grass.
cimurgia, *f.* (chem.) zymurgy.
cina, *f.* (Ecuad.) species of grass.
cinabrino, na, *a.* cinnabarine.
cinabrio, *m.* (min.) cinnabar; vermilion (color).
cinamato, *m.* (chem.) cinnamate.
cinámico, ca, *a.* cinnamic, cinnamonic (pertaining to cinnamon).
cinamomo, *m.* (bot.) chinaberry tree, bead tree, azederach.
cinc, *m.* (*pl.* **cines**) (metal.) zinc.
cinca, *f.* infraction in the game of ninepins.
cincado, da, *a.* galvanized, zinc-plated, zinc coated.
cincar, *tr.v.* to galvanize.
cincato, *m.* (chem.) zincate.
cincel, *m.* chisel; drove; graver, burin. — **c.** desbastador, drove chisel, boaster, boasting chisel.
cincelado, *past part. of* **cincelar.** —*m., var. of* **cinceladura.**
cincelador, *m.* chiseler, engraver, carver.
cinceladura, *f.* chiseling, engraving, carving.
cincelar, *tr.v.* to chisel, engrave, carve, sculpt.
cincha, *f.* girth, cinch; **c. de brida,** saddle girth; **c. de jineta,** side-saddle cinch; **c. maestra,** surcingle; **ir** or **venir rompiendo cinchas,** (coll.) to ride at breakneck speed; **a revienta c.,** reluctantly.
cinchada, *f.* (Amer.) 1. *var. of* **cinchadura.** 2. game consisting of testing the strength of two groups of persons or animals.
cinchadura, *f.* girthing, cinching.
cinchar, *tr.v.* to cinch, cinch-up, girth (a horse). -*i.v.* 1. (Amer.) to work hard. 2. to make great efforts to obtain desired results. 3. (Amer.) to pull a heavy object with a horse.
cinchazo, *m.* (C. Rica, Hond.) blow of a sword.
cinchera, *f.* girth place (girth part of a horse); (vet.) girth sore.
cincho, *m.* 1. girdle, belt; belly-band (on persons). 2. stomacher, corselet. 3. (Amer.) cinch, iron hoop (of a barrel); iron rim (of a wheel); iron stave, grappling ring. 4. cheese mold. 5. (archit.) projecting rib of an arch. 6. (vet.) coronary cushion (on a horse's hoof). 7. (Mex.) girth, cinch (of a horse).
cinchuela, *f. dim. of* **cincha,** narrow strip, belt or strap.
cíncico, ca, *a.* (chem.) zincous.
cincífero, ra, *a.* zinciferous.
cincita, *f.* (min.) zincite, red zinc ore.
cinco, *a.* five; fifth. —*m.* 1. five; five; fifth. 2. (Ven.) five-stringed guitar. 3. (Amer.) five-stringed guitar. 3. (Amer.) five-cent piece. — **decir (a uno) cuantas son c.,** to give (someone) a piece of one's mind; **saber cuantas son c.,** to know the score.
cincoenrama, *f.* (bot.) common cinquefoil, five-finger, five-leaf.
cincograbado, *m.* zincograph (an engraving in zinc).
cincogrbador, *m.* zincographer.
cincografía, *f.* zincography (art of engraving in zinc).
cincográfico, ca, *a.* zincographical, zincographic.
cincolina, *f.* (chem.) quinidine, quinidin.
cincomesino, na. *a.* 1. five months old. 2. born during the fifth month of pregnancy.
cincona, *f.* (bot.) cinchona.
cinconina, *f.* (chem.) cinchonine.
cincuenta, *a., m.* fifty, fiftieth.
cincuentavo, va, *a., m.* one-fiftieth (part); fiftieth.
cincuentena, *f.* fifty (collection of fifty articles).
cincuentenario, ria, *a.* fiftieth (anniversary); fifty-year-old. —*m.* fiftieth anniversary.
cincuenteno, na, *a.* fiftieth.
cincuentín, *m.* old Spanish silver coin worth 50 reales.
cincuentón, na, *a.* fifty-year-old. —*m., f.* quinquagenarian.
cine, *m.* (coll.) cinema; movies, pictures; movie theater; cinematography. — **c.de verano,** drive-in movie; **parlante or sonoro,** talkies (coll.), talking pictures; **c. mudo,** silent movies; **estrella de c.,** movie star; **hacer c.,** to make films (acting, directing, etc.).
cineasta, *m.* film producer or maker; movie star.
cincgética, *f.* (hunt.) cynegetics.
cinegético, ca, *a.* cynegetic, cynegetical.
cinema, *m.* cinema.
cinemascopio, *m.* cinemascope, a process of motion picture production.
cinemateca, *f.* film library.
cinemático, ca, *a.* (phys.) kinematic. —*f.* (phys.) kinematics.
cinematografía, *f.* cinematography.
cinematográfico, ca, *a.* cinematographic.
cinematógrafo, *m.* 1. cinematograph, moving picture projector. 2. movie theater.
cineol, *m.* (chem.) cineole.
cineración, *f.* incineration.
cinerama, *m.* cinerama.
cineraria, *f.* (bot.) cineraria.
cinerario, ria, *a.* cinerary; pertaining to or containing human ashes. — **urna cineraria,** cinerary urn.
cinéreo, a, *a.* ashy, cinereous; ashen, ashcolored.
cinericio, cia, *a.* ashen, ashy; ash-like.
cinescopio, *m.* (tel.) kinescope.
cinesia, cinesis, *f.* (med.) kinesitherapy, kinesiatrics.

cinesiología, *f.* (med.) kinesiology.
cinesiterapia, *f.* kinesitherapy.
cinestesia, *f.* (physiol.) kinesthesia, kinesthesis.
cinestésico, ca, *a.* (physiol.) kinesthetic.
cinético, ca, *a.* (phys.) kinetic. —*f.* (phys.) kinetics.
cinetoscopio, *m.* kinetoscope.
cingalés, sa, *a., m., f.* Ceylonese, Singhalese.
cíngaro, ra, *a., m., f.* gypsy.
cingiberáceo, a, *a.* (bot.) zingiberaceous. —*f. pl.* Zingiberaceae.
cinglado, *past part. of* **cinglar.** —*m.* (metal.) puddling, blooming.
cinglar, *tr.v.* (metal.) to puddle, bloom (iron.).
cinglar, *tr.v.* (mar.) to scull, propel by means of an oar in the stern.
cingleta, *f.* rope to drag up a fishing net.
cíngulo, *m.* (ecc.) cingulum; (mil.) **sash** (insignia).
cínicamente, *adv.* cynically.
cínico, ca, *a.* cynical; shameless, impudent; satirical. —*m., f.* cynic.
cínife, *m.* mosquito, gnat.
cinismo, *m.* cynicism; shamelessness; wantonness, impudence.
cinocéfalo, *m.* (zool.) cynocephalus, baboon.
cinódromo, *m.* dog track, greyhound track.
cinoglosa, *f.* (bot.) hound's tongue (Cynoglossum officinale).
Cinosura, *f.* (astron.) Cynosure, Ursa Minor.
cinquén, *m.* ancient Spanish coin.
cinqueño, *m.* card game played by five people.
cinquero, *m.* zinc worker.
cinquina, *f.* five-number lottery ticket, five numbers drawn (in a lottery), keno (in lotto).
cinta, *f.* (ichth.) ribbonfish.
cinta, *f.* 1. ribbon; tape; band, strip, sash. 2. (surv.) measuring tape. 3. hempen tuna fishing net. 4. curb (of a sidewalk). 5. film, picture. 6. (archit.) fillet, listel; (archit.) scroll. 7. (her.) bend, bar. 8. (Cuba, bldg.) joining strip (on roofing-boards). 9. (mas.) first layer of floor-bricks laid against the wall. 10. (bot.) ribbon grass (Phalaris arundinacea). 11. (vet.) coronet (of a hoof). 12. (*pl.*) (mar.) wales, bends. — **c. adhesiva,** adhesive tape; **c. aisladora,** insulating tape; **c. cinematográfica,** motion picture film; **c. correctora,** correction tape; **c. de embrague,** clutch band; **c. de freno,** (auto.) brake band or lining; **c. de máquina,** typewriter ribbon; **c. de medir,** measuring tape; **c. de teleimpresora,** ticker tape; **c. de transporte,** conveyor belt; **c. durex** or **pegante** or **scotch,** Scotch tape; **c. magnética or magnetofónica,** magnetic tape, recording tape; **c. métrica,** tape measure. —*adv.* **en c.,** under subjection.
cintagorda, *f.* strong outer tuna fishing net.
cintajo, *m. derog. of* **cinta.**
cintar, *tr.v.* (archit.) to ornament with fillets or friezes.
cintarazo, *m.* stroke with the flat of a sword.
cintarear, *tr.v.* (coll.) to strike with the flat of a sword.
cinteado, da, *a.* ribboned, beribboned.
cintería, *f.* ribbons, ribboning; ribbon shop or trade.
cintero, ra, *m., f.* ribbon seller or maker. —*m.* (women's) ornamented belt or girdle; rope, halter; cable.
cinteta, *f.* fishing net (used in the Mediterranean).
cintilar, *tr.v.* to sparkle, twinkle.
cintilla, *f. dim. of* **cinta.**
cintillo, *m.* 1. ornamented hat or head band. 2. (jewel.) circlet ring.
cinto, ta, *irr. past part. of* **ceñir.** —*a.* girt, girdled, encircled. —*m.* 1. belt, girdle. 2. waist, waistline. 3. (Arg., ichth.) species of small red tuna.
cintra, *f.* (archit curve)of an arch or vault).
cintrado, da, *a.* (archit.) arched, curved.
cintrel, *m.* (mas.) rule, line (to determine the angle of the bricks in an arch).
cintura, *f.* 1. waist, waistline. 2. corselet, girdle. 3. (archit.) chimney throat. 4. (mar.) rigging knot. — **meter en c.,** to discipline, control, bring a person to his senses.
cinturón, *m.* 1. belt; sword belt; sash. 2. belt, cordon, line (of mountains, forts, etc.). — **c. de Orión,** (astron.) Orion's belt; **c. de salvamento,** life belt; **c. de seguridad,** safety belt.
cinzolín, *a.* reddish-violet, fuchsia (color).
ciña, ciño, *ref.* **ceñir.**
cipariso, *m.* (poet.) cypress.
cipayo, *m.* 1. sepoy. 2. (Cuba, P. Rico, derog.) name given to natives who joined the Spanish army. 3. (Arg., derog.) politician at the service of foreign interests.
cipe, *a.* (Amer.) weak, emaciated (infant). —*m.* (Salv.) resin.
cipera, *f.* (archit.) support for the base of a lantern or ridge turret (on roof joist).
ciperáceo, a, *a.* (bot.) cyperaceous. —*f. pl.* (bot.) Cyperaceae (family).
cipo, *m.* 1. cippus, gravestone; milestone, milepost; signpost; boundary stone. 2. (Col.) large piece, chunk.
cipolino, na, *a.* cipolin (as *a.*). —*m.* cipolin marble.
cipote, *a.* 1. (Col.) silly, foolish. 2. (Guat.) fat, plump, pudgy. —*m., f.* (Salv., Hond.) youngster, imp, rascal.
ciprés, *m.* (bot.) cypress. 2. (Mex.) (ecc.) main altar.
cipresal, *m.* cypress grove or plantation.
cipresillo, *m.* (bot.) lavender cotton (Santolina chamaecyparissus).
cipresino, na, *a.* cypress (as a.), made of cypress; cypress-like.
ciprínido, da, *a., m.,* (ichth.) cyprinid.
ciprino, na, *a., var. of* **ciprio.**
ciprinodonte, *m.* (zool.) cyprinodont.
ciprinoideo, a, *a.* (ichth.) cyprinoid.
ciprio, pria, *a., m., f.* Cypriot, Ciprian (of the island of Cyprus).
cipriota, *m., f.* Cypriot, Cyprian, native of Cyprus.
cipripedio, *m.* (bot.) cypripedium.
ciquiricata, *f.* (coll.) obsequiousness, flattery.
ciquitroque, *m.* (cul.) stew of tomatoes and peppers.
circasiano, na, *a., m., f.* Circassian (of Circassia, in the N.W. Caucasus).
circe, *f.* 1. wily, deceitful woman. 2. (myth.) **C.,** Circe, the enchantress in Homer's Odyssey.
circense, *a.* Circensian (relating to the Roman Circus).
circinado, da, *a.* (bot.) circinate.
circo, *m.* 1. circus. 2. amphitheatre. 3. (geol.) cirque (natural rocky amphitheatre).
circón, *m.* (min.) zircon.
circona, *f.* (chem.) zirconia (zirconium dioxide).
circonio, *m.* (chem.) zirconium.
circuición, *f.* (encirclement, encompassment.
circuir, (*ref.* 48) *tr.v.* to surround.
circuito, *m.* 1. perimeter, circumference, circuit, periphery. 2. circuit, circular movement. 3. racecourse, racetrack (for horses); track, racing track (for cars, motorcycles). 4. network (of roads, railways, radio). 5. (elec.) circuit. 6. tour, excursion, trip. — **c. abierto,** (elec.) open circuit; **c. abierto, (elec.)** open circuit; **c. activador,** (rad.) trigger circuit; **c. cerrado,** (elec.) closed circuit; **c. combinado,** (elec.) compound circuit; **c. de absorción,** (rad.) tank circuit; **c. de reflexión,** (rad.) reflex circuit; **c. de rejilla,** (rad.) grid circuit; **c. derivado,** (elec.) shunt circuit; **c. de vía,** track circuit; **c. de voltaje,** (elec.) pressure circuit; **c. en contrafase, simétrico** or **equilibrado,** push-pull circuit; **c. impreso,** (rad.) printed circuit; **c. inducido,** (elec.) secondary circuit; **c. inductor,** primary circuit; **circuitos acoplados** or **de sintonía simultánea,** (rad.) gauged circuits; **corto c.,** (elec.) short circuit; **cortar el c.,** to break the circuit.
circulación, *f.* 1. circulation (currency, blood, etc.) 2. traffic (of vehicles, people); **parar la c.,** to stop the traffic.
circulador, *m.* circulator.
circulante, *a.* circulating, circulatory. —*m.* currency; **expansión del c.,** (econ.) currency expansion.
circular, *a.* circular. —*f.* circular, circular letter. —*tr.v., i.v.* to circulate, to move, to travel, to keep moving.
circularmente, *adv.* circularly.
circulatorio, ria, *a.* circulatory.
círculo, *m.* 1. circle, circumference, ring. 2. (social) club, circle, group. — **c. acimutal,** (mar.) azimuth circle; **c. de declinación,** (astron.) declination center, nour circle; **c. de reflexión,** (astron., mar.) reflecting circle; **c. horario,** (astron.) hour circle; **c. mamario,** (anat.) areola (of a nipple); **c. máximo,** (geom.) great circle; **c. menor,** (geom.) small circle; **c. meridiano,** astron.) meridian circle; **c. mural,** (astron.) vertical circle; **c. polar,** (astron., geog.) polar circle; **c. polar antártico,** (geog.) antarctic circle; **c. polar ártico, (geog.) arctic circle; c. repetidor,** (surv.) repeating instrument; **c. taquimétrico,** stadia circle; **c. vicioso,** vicious circle; (log.) circle, argument in a circle.
circumcirca, *adv.* (coll.) about, around, thereabout; almost, nearly.
circumpolar, *a.* circumpolar.
circuncidante, *a.* circumcising.
circuncidar, *tr.v.* to circumcise; (fig.) to trim, cut down, modify, curtail.
circuncisión, *f.* circumcision; (rel.) Feast of the Circumcision (January 1st).
circunciso, *irr. past part. of* **circuncidar.** —*a.* circumcised. —*m., f.* (fig.) Jew, Moor, Berber; (*pl.*) the circumcised.
circundante, *a.* encircling, surrounding, encompassing.
circundar, *tr.v.* to encircle, surround, encompass.
circunferencia, *f.* (geom.) circumference.
circunferencial, *a.* circumferential.
circunferencialmente, *adv.* in circumference.
circunferente, *a.* circumscribing, limiting.
circunferir, (*ref.* 42) *tr.v.* to circumscribe, limit, confine.
circunfiera, circunfiero, *ref.* **circunferir.**
circunfiriendo, circunfiriera, circunfiriese, *ref.* **circunferir.**
circunflejo, *a.* (gram., anat.) circumflex. —*m.* circumflex accent.
circunfuso, sa, *a.* circumfused.
circunlocución, *f.* (rhet.) periphrasis, circumlocution.
circunloquio, *m.* circumlocution, circumvolution.
circunnavegación, *f.* circumnavigation.
circunnavegante, *a.* circumnavigating. —*m., f.* circumnavigator.
circunnavegar, (*ref.* 51) *tr.v.* to circumnavigate, go around.
circunnavegue, circunnavegué, *ref.* **circunnavegar.**
circunscribir, *irr. past part.:* **circunscrito.** —*tr.v.* to circumscribe, limit, confine, restrict; (geom.) to circumscribe. —*r.v.* to restrict or limit oneself.

circunscripción, *f.* 1. circumscription; limitation, restriction. 2. district, territory (administrative, military, electoral, ecclesiastical).
circunscripto, ta, *a., var. of* **circunscrito.**
circunscrito, ta, *irr. past part. of* **circunscribir.** —*a.* (geom.) circumscriptive.
circunsolar, *a.* circumsolar.
circunspección, *f.* circumspection; caution, prudence, discretion; decorum, propriety, sobriety.
circunspecto, ta, *a.* circumspect; prudent, discreet; decorous, proper, dignified.
circunstancia, *f.* circumstance; **bajo las circunstancias,** under the circumstances; **c. agravante,** (law) aggravating circumstance: **c. atenuante,** (law) extenuating circumstance; **c. eximente,** (law) exculpatory or exonerating circumstance; en **circunstancias apremiadas,** in reduced circumstances; **en las actuales circunstancias,** under the present circumstances; **estar a la altura de las circunstancias,** to be equal to the occasion; **ponerse a la altura de las circunstancias,** to rise to the occasion.
circunstanciadamente, *adv.* minutely, in detail, precisely.
circunstanciado, da, *a.* detailed, minute.
circunstancial, *a.* circumstantial.
circunstante, *a.* surrounding; standing nearby, attending, present. —*m., f.* bystander, onlooker, spectator.
circunvalación, *f.* (mil.) circumvallation.
circunvalar, *tr.v.* to surround, encircle; (mil.) to circumvallate.
circunvecino, na, *a.* adjacent, contiguous, neighboring, close, near.
circunvolar, (*ref. 33*) *tr.v.* to fly around, circumaviate.
circunvolución, *f.* circumvolution; convolution, coil. — **circunvoluciones de los intestinos,** convolutions of the intestines; **c. cerebral,** (anat.) cerebral convolution.
circunvuele, circunvuelo, *ref.* **circunvolar.**
circunyacente, *a.* circumjacent, surrounding.
cirenaico, ca, *a.* (hist.) Cyrenaic, pertaining to Cyrene or Cyrenaic philosophy. —*m., f.* Cyrenaic, native of Cyrene or follower of Cyrenaic philosophy. —*f.* C., Cyrenaica, Cirenaica.
cireneo, *a., m., f.* (hist.) Cyrenaic, native of Cyrene.
cirial, *m.* (ecc.) processional candlestick.
cirigallo, lla, *m., f.* person who appears busy but accomplishes nothing.
cirílico, ca, *a.* Cyrillic, pertaining to the Slavic alphabet.
cirineo, *m.* (coll.) assistant, helper, man Friday.
cirio, *m.* 1. long wax candle. 2. (Cuba) (bot.) pine-like tree valued for its hard yellow wood and ornamental foliage (Xilopia obtusifolia); (Amer.) (bot.) saguaro cactus.
cirolero, *m.* plum tree.
cirquero, ra, *n.* (Amer.) 1. acrobat. 2. circus manager. 3. (sl.) overly energetic dancer, musician, actor.
cirrípedo, *a.* (zool.) cirripedial, cirripede (relating to barnacles). —*m.* cirripede barnacle, (*pl.*) Cirripedia (order).
cirro, *m.* 1. (med.) scirrhus (tumor). 2. (meteorol., bot., zool.) cirrus.
cirrocúmulo, *m.* (meteorol.) cirrocumulus, cumulocirrus.
cirroestrato, *m.* (meteorol.) cirrostratus.
cirrópodos, *m. pl.* (zool.) Cirripeds, Cirripodia (degenerate marine crustaceans, free-swimming as larvae but parasites as adults).
cirrosis, *f.* (med.) cirrhosis.
cirroso, sa, *a.* cirrose, cirrous.
cirrótico, ca, *a.* (med.) cirrhotic.
ciruela, *f.* plum; prune. — **c. amacena or damascena,** damson plum; **c. claudia, c. verbal,** greengage; **c. de fraile,** elongated species of green plum; **c. de yema,** yellow plum; **c. pasa,** dry plum, prune.
ciruelillo, *m.* (Amer.) protaceous tree with scarlet flowers and fine wood (Embothrium coccineum).
ciruelo, *m.* 1. plum tree. 2. (coll.) fool, incompetent clown. — **c. amarillo, c. campechano,** (Cuba, bot.) mountain plum (Zimenes Americano).
cirugía, *f.* surgery; **c. con laser,** laser surgery; **c. estética** or **plástica,** plastic surgery; **c. menor** or **ministrante,** minor surgery.
cirujano, na, *f.* surgeon; **c. dentista,** dental surgeon.
cisalpino, na, *a.* cisalpine (between Rome and the Alps).
cisandino, na, *a.* cisandine (on this side of the Andes).
cisca, *f.* (bot.) common reedgrass.
ciscar, (*ref. 50*) *tr.v.* (coll.) to soil, smear, make dirty. —*r.v.* to defecate, evacuate the bowels.
cisco, *m.* 1. slack (coal). 2. (coll.) hubbub, uproar, rumpus; wrangle, squabble. — **hacer c.,** to tear to pieces, smash into smithereens; **meter c.,** to cause a rumpus.
ciscón, *m.* ash and cinders (left in a coal furnace).
cisión, *f.* incision.
cisípedo, *a.* (zool.) digitate, having toes.
cisma, *m., f.* schism; discord, dissension.
cismáticamente, *adv.* schismatically.
cismático, ca, *a.* 1. schismatic. 2. (Col.) finicky, prudish. —*m., f.* gossip.
cismontano, na, *a.* cismontane.
Cisne, *m.* (astron.) Swan, Cygnus.
cisne, *m.* swan; (poet.) swan (great poet or musician); **canto del c.,** swan song; **cuello de c.,** graceful, slender neck.
cisoide, *m.* (geom.) cissoid.
cisoria, *a.* carving; **arte c.,** art of carving.
cispadano, na, *a.* cispadane (on the Rome side of the river Po).
cisque, cisqué, *ref.* **ciscar.**
cisquera, *f.* slack-shed.
cisquero, *m.* 1. slack maker or dealer. 2. pounce bag (for stencilling).
cistáceo, cea, *a.* (bot.) cistaceous.
cistectomía, *f.* (surg.) cystectomy.
cisteína, *f.* (chem.) cysteine.
cistel, *m., var. of* **cister.**
cister, *m.* (ecc.) Cistercian Order.
cisterciense, *a.* (rel.) Cistercian, a member of a monastic order founded in France under Benedictine rule.
cistercosis, *f.* (med., vet.) cysticercosis.
cisterna, *f.* cistern, reservoir, water-tank.
cisticerco, *m.* (med., vet.) cysticercus, bladderworm.
cisticercoide, *a., m.* (zool.) cysticercoid, a larval tapeworm.
cisticercosis, *f.* (med.) cysticercosis.
cístico, ca, *a.* cystic. —*m.* (med.) cystic duct.
cistina, *f.* (chem.) cystine.
cistíneo, a, *a.* (bot.) cistaceous. —*f.* (bot.) cistus or rockrose; (*pl.*) Cistaceae, rockrose family.
cistitis, *f.* (med.) cystitis, inflammation of the bladder.
cisto, *m.* (bot.) cistus, rockrose.
cistocarpo, *m.* (bot.) cystocarp.
cistocele, *f.* (med.) cystocele.
cistoide, *a., m.* (med., paleon.) cystoid.
cistolito, *m.* (bot., med.) cystolith.
cistoma, *m.* (med.) cystoma.
cistoscopio, *m.* (surg.) cystoscope.
cistotomía, *f.* (surg.) cystotomy.
cistótomo, *m.* (surg.) cystotome.
cisura, *f.* incision, scission, fissure.
cita, *f.* 1. appointment, engagement; rendezvous, date (coll.). 2. quotation, quote (coll.); reference. — **casa de citas,** brothel, house of assignation; **c. previa,** by appointment; **darse c.,** to make an engagement (with one another).
citable, *a.* worthy of being quoted.
citación, *f.* citation, quotation, reference; (law) citation, summons, subpoena; **c. de evicción,** (law) eviction notice; **c. de remate,** (law) notice of public sale.
citado, da, *past part. of* **citar.** —*a.* mentioned; **arriba citado,** above-mentioned.
citador, ra, *a.* citing; quoting; summoning. —*m., f.* citer; quoter; summoner.
Citano, na, *m., f., var. of* **Zutano,** (coll.) so and so, Tom, Dick and Harry.
citar, *tr.v.* 1. to make an appointment or engagement with (on business); to make an engagement or date with, date (socially). 2. to quote, cite, refer to. 3. (taur.) to incite (the bull) to attack. 4. (law) to cite, summon.
cítara, *f.* zither, a musical instrument.
citara, *f.* 1. (mas.) single stretcher bond wall. 2. (mil.) flanks, troops on the flanks.
citarilla, *f. dim. of* **citara,** thin partition wall; **c. sardinel,** (archit.) thin partition wall of a stretcher or diagonal bond.
citarista, *m., f.* zither player.
citarón, *m.* (mass.) foundation base.
citasa, *f.* (biochem.) cytase.
citatorio, ria, *a.* (law) citatory, summoning. —*f.* citation, summons.
citereo, a, *a.* (myth., poet.) Cytherean, pertaining to the goddess Aphrodite and her presumed birthplace.
citerior, *a.* hither, hithermost, nearer.
citisina, *f.* (chem.) cytisine.
cítiso, *m.* (bot.) cytisus, plant of the pea family.
citoblasto, *m.* (biol.) cytoblast.
citocinesis, *f.* (biol.) cytokinesis.
citocromo, *m.* (biochem.) cytochrome.
citodiagnosis, *f.* (med.) cytodiagnosis.
citofagia, *f.* (biol.) cytophagy.
citogenética, *f.* (biol.) cytogenetics.
citola, *f.* millclapper, millclack.
citolisina, *f.* (biochem.) cytolysin.
citólisis, *f.* (physiol.) cytolysis.
citolítico, ca, *a.* (biochem.) cytolytic.
citología, *f.* (biol.) cytology.
citológico, ca, *a.* (biol.) cytological, cytologic.
citólogo, *m.* (biol.) cytologist.
citoplasma, *m.* (bot., zool.) cytoplasm.
citoplasmático, ca, *a.* cytoplasmic.
citoplástico, ca, *a.* (biol.) cytoplastic.
citoplastina, *f.* (biol.) cytoplast.
citoquímica, *f.* (biochem.) cytochemistry.
citote, *m.* (coll.) ultimatum, threat (forcing someone to do something).
citotrópico, ca, *a.* (med.) cytotropic.
citramontano, na, *a.* cismontane, on this side of the mountains.
citrato, *m.* (chem.) citrate.
cítrico, ca, *a.* (chem.) citric.
citrina, *f.* (chem.) citrin, lemon oil.
citrino, *m.* (min.) citrine.
citrón, *m.* lemon.
citronelol, *m.* (chem.) citronellol.
ciudad, *f.* 1. city, town. 2. town council, civic body. — **c. natal,** birthplace, native town, hometown; **C. del Vaticano,** Vatican City; **C. de México,** Mexico City; **c. dormitorio,** bedroom community; **c. sanitaria,** hospital complex; **c. universitaria,** university campus; **la c. del oso y madroño,** Madrid.

ciudadanía, *f.* 1. citizenship. 2. people, citizens.
ciudadano, na, *a.* civic; of or pertaining to the city, urban. —*m., f.* citizen; burgher.
ciudadela, *f.* citadel, fortress.
civeta, *f.* (zool.) civet (cat).
civeto, *m.* civet (perfume).
cívico, ca, *a.* civic; patriotic.
civil, *a.* 1. civil, civilian. 2. civil, polite, sociable. 3. (law) civil (of citizens' rights), e.g. *ley c.*, civil law. — **derechos civiles,** civil rights; **guerra c.,** civil war. —*m.* (coll.) member of the Spanish Civil Guard. —*m., f.* civilian.
civilice, civilicé, *ref.* **civilizar.**
civilidad, *f.* civility, sociability, courtesy, urbanity.
civilista, *a.* specializing in civil law. —*m.* 1. authority or expert in civil law. 2. (Amer.) antimilitarist.
civilización, *f.* civilization.
civilizado, da, *past part, of* **civilizar.** —*a.* civilized, educated.
civilizador, ra, *a.* civilizing. —*m., f.* civilizer.
civilizar, (*ref.* *53*) *tr.v.* to civilize. —*r.v.* to become civilized.
civilmente, *adv.* civilly, courteously
civismo, *m.* civic conscience, patriotism.
cizalla, *f.* 1. shears, clippers; (paper or metal) guillotine. 2. metal clippings, chips or shavings. — **c. de guillotina,** guillotine shears; **c. para chapa,** sheetmetal shear.
cizallar, *tr.v.* to shear, clip, cut, trim.
cizallas, *f. pl. var. of* **cizalla.**
cizaña, *f.* 1. (bot.) bearded darnel, darnel (weed). 2. (coll.) corrupting vice. 3. (coll.) harmful influence. 4. (coll.) discord, dissension. — **meter** or **sembrar c.,** to sow discord; **separar la c. del buen grano,** to separate the chaff from the grain.
cizañador, ra, *a.* trouble-making, mischief-making, agitating. —*m., f.* trouble-maker, mischief-maker.
cizañar, *tr.v.* to sow discord, create enmity.
cizañero, ra, *a., m., f., var. of* **cizañador.**
cl. *abbrev. of* **centilitro,** centiliter (cl.).
Cl *sym. of* **cloro,** chlorine (Cl).
c/l *abbrev. of* **curso legal,** legal tender.
clac, (*pl.* **claques**) *m.* opera hat; collapsible hat.
claco, *m.* (Mex.) ancient copper coin.
clacota, *f.* (Mex.) boil, pimple.
cladóceros, *m. pl.* (zool.) Cladocera.
cladodio, *m.* (bot.) cladode, cladophyll.
clamar, *i.v.* to clamor, cry out, implore, wail; **c. al cielo,** to cry out to heaven (in protest).
clámide, *f.* chlamys (ancient Greek riding mantle).
clamidóspora, *f.* (bot.) chlamydospore.
clamor, *m.* clamor, outcry, clangor, uproar; wail, lamentation; knell, toll for the dead.
clamoreada, *f.* clamor, outcry, wailing; toll for the dead.
clamorear, *tr.v.* to clamor, wail, cry out insistently. —*i.v.* to toll the death knell.
clamoreo, *m.* clamoring; (coll.) beseeching, pleading.
clamoroso, sa, *a.* clamorous, wailing.
clan, *m.* clan.
clandestinamente, *adv.* clandestinely, secretly.
clandestinidad, *f.* clandestinity, secrecy.
clandestinista, *m.,f.* (Amer.) liquor smuggler or runner.
clandestino, na, a. clandestine, secret.
clanga, *f.* (ornith.) solan goose (Sula bassana).
clangor, *m.* (poet.) clarion, blare of the trumpet; clangor.
claque, *f.* (coll.) claque (hired applauders in a theatre).
claqueta, *f.* (cine.) clap-stick.
clara, *f.* 1. white of egg. 2. faulty, thinly-woven patch in textiles; bald patch (in hair); brief clearing-up or break in rainy weather.
claraboya, *f.* skylight; **c. de bóveda,** vault light.
claramente, *adv.* clearly, distinctly, plainly.
clarar, *tr.v., var. of* **aclarar,** to make clear, explain, clarify.
clarea, *f.* an aromatic beverage made with wine, honey and spices.
clarear, *tr.v.* 1. to make lighter, lighten (a color). 2. (Mex.) to shoot through. —*i.v.* to dawn, get light. —*r.v.* 1. to be transparent. 2. (coll.) to give oneself away, disclose one's plans involuntarily.
clarecer, (*ref.* *45*) *i.v.* to dawn.
clarens, *m.* clarence (carriage).
clareo, *m.* clearing (of trees).
clarete, *a., m.* claret, rosé wine.
clareza, *f., var. of* **claridad.**
claridad, *f.* 1. clarity, clearness, distinctness; brightness. 2. splendor, radiance. 3. esteem, fame. 4. (*pl.*) simple truths, plain language. — **c. de la vista** or **de los ojos,** clear-sightedness, perspicacity.
claridoso, sa, *a.* (Mex.) frank, blunt, plain-spoken, outspoken.
clarificación, *f.* clarification; refining, purifying; illumination.
clarificadora, *f.* clarifier, vessel used in clarifying sugar.
clarificar, (*ref.* *50*) *tr.v.* 1. to clarify (an idea, liquid). 2. to illuminate; light up.
clarificativo, va, *a.* clarifying.
clarífico, ca, *a.* (rare) resplendent, radiant, shining.
clarifique, clarifiqué, *ref.* **clarificar.**
clarimente, *m.* cosmetic lotion formerly used by women.
clarimento, *m.* brightness, brilliance (of paint).
clarín, *m.* 1. (mus.) clarion; bugle; clarion (organ stop or register); clarionist, bugler. 2. fine cambric (fabric). 3. (Chile) sweet pea. — **c. de la selva,** (ornith.) American species of grey thrush (Myadestes unicolor).
clarinada, *f.* 1. clarion or bugle call. 2. (coll.) inappropriate remark, foolish or stupid remark.
clarinero, *m.* bugler.
clarinete, *m.* (mus.) clarinet; clarinetist, clarinet player.
clarinetista, *m., f.* (mus.) clarinetist.
clarión, *m.* white crayon, chalk.
clarioncillo, *m.* pastel, crayon.
clarisa, *a.* (rel.) Clarist (of the Franciscan nuns). —*f.* Clare, Poor Clare (nun).
clarísimo, ma, *a. super. of* **claro,** perfectly clear, very clear; most perceptive (said of a thinker).
clarividencia, *f.* clear-sightedness, perspicacity, discernment; clairvoyance.
clarividente, *a.* clairvoyant.
claro, ra, *a.* 1. clear (cloudless; limpid, crystalline; distinct; lucid, intelligible; evident, obvious). 2. bright, light (room with much light). 3. straightforward, candid. 4. thin (liquids; hair, fabrics). 5. light (colors). 6. sharp, acute (mind). 7. illustrious, famous. 8. (vet.) splay-legged (horse). — **a las claras,** openly, publicly; evident; **claro como el agua,** as plain as the nose on your face; **por lo claro,** clearly, in a clear manner.
claro, *adv.* 1. clearly. 2. of course, naturally. — **c. está, c. que sí,** yes, of course; **c. que no,** of course not. —*m.* 1. pause, break (in speech); gap, space (in writing, crowd); clearing, opening (in a wood). 2. (bldg.) skylight; (*pl.*) windows, openings (to admit light). 3. (p.) light (in a painting). 4. (Amer.) break (in rain). — **c. de luna,** moonlight; **poner** or **sacar en c.,** to clear up, elucidate, make clear, explain.
claror, *m.* resplendence, radiance, luminosity, brightness.
claroscuro, *m.* (p.) 1. chiaroscuro; contrast of light and shadows in a painting. 2. a monochromatic design.
clarucho, cha, *a.* (derog.) weak, watery (said of coffee, wine, etc.).
clase, *f.* 1. class, type, kind. 2. class, rank of society. 3. class, lesson. 4. classroom. 5. class, form. 6. (*pl.*) (mil.) non-commissioned officers. — **c. alta,** upper class; **c. baja,** lower class; **c. media,** middle class; **c. obrera,** working class; **de c.,** distinguished, notable; non-commissioned; **de primera, segunda c.,** first-class, second-class; **lucha de clases,** class struggle; **toda c. de,** all kinds of.
clásicamente, *adv.* classically.
clasicismo, *m.* classicism.
clasicista, *a., m., f.* classicist.
clásico, ca, *a.* 1. classic; classical. 2. notable, outstanding. 3. (coll.) typical, characteristic. —*m.* 1. classic (as in art work of enduring excellence). 2. classicist.
clasificable, *a.* classifiable.
clasificación, *f.* classification.
clasificador, ra, *a.* classifying; classificatory. —*m., f.* classifier, sorter —*m.* filing-cabinet. — **c. de cedazo,** screen classifier.
clasificar, (*ref.* *50*) *tr.v.* to classify; to sort out. —*r.v.* to qualify, classify (in sports).
clasifique, clasifiqué, *ref.* **clasificar.**
clasista, *a.* discriminating. —*m., f.* advocate of class discrimination.
clasmatocito, *m.* (biol.) clasmatocyte.
clástico, ca, *a.* (geol.) clastic.
claudia, *a.* greengage (plum).
claudicación, *f.* 1. the act of giving up, abandoning or failing in an endeavor. 2. lameness, claudication.
claudicante, *a.* 1. limping, hobbling. 2. (fig.) said of a person who gives up easily.
claudicar, (*ref.* *50*) *i.v.* 1. to limp, hobble. 2. to abandon one's duties; to give up or back down.
claudique, claudiqué, *ref.* **claudicar.**
claustra, *f.* cloister; gallery, arcade.
claustral, *a.* cloistral, monastic; cloistered. —*m., f.* cloistered or claustral nun or monk.
claustrillo, *m.* small assembly hall (of a university).
claustro, *m.* 1. cloister; monastic state. 2. university council. — **c. de profesores,** body of professors, faculty; **claustro materno,** the womb.
claustrofobia, *f.* (psyc.) claustrophobia, abnormal fear of confined places.
cláusula, *f.* clause, article (of law, treaty); (gram.) sentence; phrase. — **c. compuesta,** (gram.) complex sentence; **c. consecutiva,** (gram.) consecutive clause; **c. penal,** (law) penalty clause, forfeit clause; **c. resolutoria,** (law) defeasance clause; **c. simple,** (gram.) simple sentence.
clausulado, da, *a.* disconnected, disjointed (style). —*m.* series of clauses or articles.
clausular, *tr.v.* to close, finish (sentence, speech).
clausura, *f.* 1. (monastic) confinement, reclusion; monastic life; inner recess (of monastery or convent). 2. closing session (of congress or a convention); (Amer.) closing (of bank or port); (Amer.) commencement, closing ceremony (of school).
clausurar, *tr.v.* 1. to close, bring to a close (a meeting, etc.). 2. to block (a road); to plug (a pipe); to wall-up, close up (a door, etc.).
clava, *f.* 1. club, cudgel. 2. (mar.) scupper.
clavadizo, za, *a.* studded, nail-studded.
clavado, da, *past part of* **clavar.** —*a.* 1. nail-studded. 2. fixed; stuck, stopped (clock); sharp, on the dot, e.g. *a las tres clavadas,* at three

o'clock sharp. — **c. para,** perfect for, ideal for (a post, a purpose); **este saco te queda clavado,** this jacket fits you perfectly.
clavadura *f.* piercing of a horse's hoof (when shoeing).
claval, *a.* (anat.) said of the juncture of two bones, where one penetrates the other.
clavar, *tr.v.* 1. to nail; to knock or drive in (a nail, pin). 2. to fix, fasten (with a pin). 3. to pierce, prick, spike; to accloy (pierce a horse's hoof when shoeing); (mil.) to spike (guns). 4. to set (a jewel). 5. (coll.) to fix, *e.g. clavó los ojos en ella,* he fixed his eyes on her. 6. (coll.) to stop, *e.g. le dejó clavado,* he stopped him dead.
clavario, ria, *m., f.* keeper of the keys (of a knightly order).
clavazón, *f.* set or assortment of nails.
clave, *a.* key, e.g. *hombre c.,* key man, *palabra c.,* key word. —*m.* clavichord, clavecin. —*f.* 1. key (to a code, mystery, etc.); code. 2. preface (of a book). 3. (archit.) keystone (of an arch). 4. (mus.) clef. 5. (mus.) (*pl.*) clavés, percussion instrument used in the folkloric music of the Antilles. — **c. de cifra,** cipher key; **c. de fa,** (mus.) base clef; **c. de sol,** (mus.) treble clef; **echar la c.,** to close a speech, transaction, etc.
clavecín, *m.* (mus.) harpsichord, cembalo.
clavel, *m.* (bot.) carnation, pink; **c. coronado,** (bot.) common garden pink (Dianthus plumarius); **c. de China,** (bot.) China pink; **c. de las Indias,** (bot.) French marigold; **c. del Japón,** (bot.) sweet Williams (Dianthus barbatus); **c. doble** or **reventón,** (bot.) double carnation, clove pink.
clavelito, *m.* (bot.) pink.
clavelón, *m.* (bot.) marigold.
clavellina, *f.* 1. (bot.) pink. 2. (artil.) vent plug (stopping powder from entering priming hole). — **c. de pluma,** (bot.) garden pink.
claveque, *m.* rock crystal.
clavera, *f.* 1. nail head mold (for forming nail heads); nail hole. 2. (Sp.) boundary line.
clavería, *f.* 1. rank of keeper of the keys (in knightly orders). 2. (arch., ecc.) the communal administration of a cathedral's treasury.
clavero, *m.* (bot.) clove tree (Eugenia aromatica).
clavero, ra, *m., f.* janitor, caretaker; turnkey (of a prison); treasurer. —*m.* keeper of the keys (in some military orders).
claveta, *f.* peg, wooden pin.
clavete, *m.* 1. tack. 2. (mus.) plectrum.
clavetear, *tr.v.* 1. to stud (with ornamental nails). 2. to tip, put metal tags or ferrules on (laces, ribbons). 3. (coll.) to finish up, wind up (a transaction).
clavicembalista, *m.* (mus.) harpsichord player.
clavicémbalo, *m.* (mus.) harpsichord.
clavicímbano, *m., var. of* **clavicémbalo.**
clavicordio, *m.* (mus.) clavichord.
clavicornio, nia, *a.* (zool., ento.) clavicorn. —*m.* (zool., ento.) clavicorn, (*pl.*) Clavicornia.
clavícula, *f.* (anat.) clavicle, collar bone.
claviculado, da, *a.* (zool., anat.) claviculate.
clavicular, *a.* clavicular.
clavija, *f.* 1. peg (of a musical instrument, telephone switchboard). 2. plug, bung (of a cask). 3. (mec.) pin, pintle, axletree pin (of a wheel); (carp.) peg, dowel, dowel pin; treenail. — **apretarle a uno las clavijas,** (coll.) to put the screws on (someone); **c. maestra,** fore axletree pintle (of a carriage); **c. de contacto,** (elec.) plug.
clavijero, *m.* 1. (mus.) pegbox (of guitar, etc.); wrest plank (of pianos, etc.). 2. peg, hook (for clothes). 3. (agr.) clevis (of a plough).
clavillo, to, *m.* 1. pin (of a hinge, scissors, fan); (mus.) pin (regulating the tension of piano strings). 2. clove (spice).
claviórgano, *m.* (mus.) string organ.
clavo, *m.* 1. nail. 2. hard corn (on a toe). 3. (med.) tent (lint wad to keep a wound open). 4. (cul.) clove (spice). 5. migraine, splitting headache; stab of pain, acute grief or pain. 6. (med.) head (of a boil). 7. (Amer.) unsaleable goods. — **agarrarse uno a** or **de un c. ardiendo,** to clutch at straws (use any means to get out of difficulty); **clavar un c. con la cabeza,** (coll.) to be stubborn as a mule; **c. baladí,** horseshoe nail; **c. calamón,** upholsterer's nail; **c. chanflón,** coarsely finished nail; **c. chillón,** small finishing nail; **c. de chilla,** long lath nail (for roofing); **c. de listonaje,** lath nail; **c. de rosca,** round-headed screw; **c. de roseta,** rosette head ornamental nail; **c. estaca,** large spike; **c. hechizo,** large horseshoe nail (on draft horses); **c. pasado,** (vet.) pastern tumor (spreading from one side to the other); **c. rielero,** track spike; **c. romano,** nail with ornamented screw-top head, picture nail; **c. tachuela,** tack; **c. trabal,** finishing nail (for beams); **dar uno en el c.,** (coll.) to hit the nail on the head, to guess right; **dar una en el c. y ciento en la herradura,** (coll.) to be more often wrong that right; **hacer c.,** (mas.) to build solidly or firmly (a construction, road); **por un c. se pierde la herradura,** penny wise pound foolish; **remachar uno el c.,** (coll.) to add error to error; to drive a point home (in argument); **sacarse el c.,** to get one's own back, get one's revenge; **ser de c. pasado,** (coll.) to be obvious, evident or self-evident; **un c. saca otro c.,** (coll.) one grief cures another.
claxon, *m.* horn, hooter (of automobile).
claxonazo, *m.* hoot (G.B.) or honk on a horn.
clazol, *m.* (Mex.) bagasse (of sugar cane).
cleistógamo, a, *a.* (bot.) cleistogamic, cleistogamous.
clemátide, *f.* (bot.) clematis, traveller's-joy, virgin's bower.
clemencia, *f.* clemency, mercy.
clemente, *a.* 1. clement, merciful. 2. benign, calm (weather).
clementemente, *adv.* mercifully, clemently.
clementina, *f.* (ecc.) each of the Clementine Decretals, (*pl.*) (ecc.) Clementine Decretals.
Cleopatra, *f.* Cleopatra, queen of Egypt, mistress of Julius Caesar and Mark Antony.
clepsidra, *f.* clepsydra, water-clock.
cleptomanía, *f.* kleptomania, cleptomania.
cleptomaníaco, ca, *a.* kleptomaniac.
cleptómano, na, *a., m., f.* kleptomaniac.
clerecía, *f.* clergy; priesthood.
clerical, *a.* clerical, pertaining to the clergy.
clericalismo, *m.* clericalism, clerical influence.
clericalmente, *adv.* clerically, according to the rules of the clergy.
clericato, *m.* priesthood, clericate.
clericatura, *f.* priesthood, clericate.
clerigalla, *f.* (derog.) clergy.
clérigo, *m.* clergyman, minister, priest; cleric; (arch.) scholar, clerk; **c. de corona,** cleric who has received only the first tonsure; **c. de misa,** priest.
clériguicia, *f.* (derog.) clergy.
cleriguillo, *m. dim. of* **clérigo,** petty clergyman (a derog. term).
clerizón, *m.* (ecc.) chorister, acolyte.
clerizonte, *m.* fake priest; (coll.) poorly dressed or rough-mannered priest.
clero, *m.* clergy; **c. regular,** regular clergy (monastic); **c. secular,** secular clergy (non-monastic).
clerofobia, *f.* hatred of the clergy.
clerófobo, ba, *a.* clergy-hating. —*m., f.* clergy hater.
cleuasmo, *m.* (rhet.) figure of speech in which the speaker attributes his good actions to another or another's bad actions to himself.
clíbano, *m.* (archeol.) a type of cuirass worn by ancient Persians.
cliché, *m.* 1. (print.) cliché, plate. 2. cliché, hackneyed or trite phrase or idea.
cliente, *m., f.* 1. client, customer. 2. client (Roman history), a plebeian who was under the protection of a patrician.
clientela, *f.* clientele; patients, practice (of doctors); protection, patronage.
clima, *m.* 1. climate; clime, zone, region; (geog.) climatic zone. 2. (fig.) milieu, ambiance.
climaterapia, *f.* climatotherapy.
climatérico, ca, *a.* climacteric; critical; (coll.) dangerous; **estar uno c.,** (coll.) to be in a bad humor.
climático, ca, *a.* climatic.
climatización, *f.* air conditioning.
climatología, *f.* climatology, the study of climate and weather.
climatológico, ca, *a.* climatologic, climatological.
clímax, *m.* climax.
clin, *f., var. of* **crin.**
clínica, *f.* clinic; private hospital; clinic, practical medical instruction.
clínico, ca, *a.* clinical (pertaining to a clinic). —*m.* physician.
clinómetro, *m.* clinometer, slope level, angle meter.
clinopodio, *m.* (bot.) wild basil.
clip, *m.* (Angl.) paper clip.
clípeo, *m.* 1. (archaeol.) clipeus (ancient Roman shield). 2. (ento.) clypeus.
clíper, *m.* (mar., aer.) clipper.
clisado, *past part, of* **clisar.** —*m.* (print.) stereotypy, stereotype, stereotyping.
clisar, *tr.v.* (print.) to stereotype.
clisé, *m.* (print.) cliché, stereotype plate.
clistel, *m., var. of* **clister.**
clistelera, *f.* (formerly) nurse who administers enemas.
clister, *m.* (med.) clyster, enema.
clisterice, clistericé, *ref.* **clisterizar.**
clisterizar, (*ref. 53*) *tr.v.* (med.) to clyster, administer an enema to.
clistrón, *m.* (phys.) klystron.
clitelo, *m.* (zool.) clitellum.
Clitemnestra, *f.* (myth.) Clytemnestra, Clytaemnestra, wife of Agamemnon.
clitómetro, *m.* (top.) clinometer.
clitorídeo, a, *a.* (anat.) clitoric, clitoral.
clítoris, *m.* (anat.) clitoris.
clivaje, *m.* (geol.) cleavage, stratification; **c. de disyunción,** fracture cleavage; **c. de flujo,** flow cleavage.
clivoso, sa, *a.* (poet.) sloping.
clo, *m.* cluck, cackle of a hen.
cloaca, *f.* sewer (drain); (zool.) cloaca. — **c. pluvial,** storm sewer.
cloasma, *f.* (med.) chloasma.
clocar, (*ref. 69*) *i.v.* to cluck, cackle (a hen).
Cloe, *f.* Chloe, lover of Daphnis in an old Greek pastoral romance of the 3rd century.
clon, clona, *m., f.* (biol.) clone.
clónico, ca, *a.* (med.) clonic.
clonismo, *m.* (med.) clonism.
clono, clonus, *m.* (med.) clonus, clonos.
cloque, *m.* (mar.) boat-hook; gaff (used in tuna fishing).
cloquear, *i.v.* to cluck, cackle (a brooding hen).
cloquear, *tr.v.* to gaff (tuna fish).
cloqueo, *m.* clucking, cackling (a brooding hen).

cloquera, *f.* broodiness (of a hen, etc.).
cloquero, *m.* one who uses a gaff (in tuna fishing).
cloración, *f.* (chem.) chlorination.
clorado, da, *a.* (chem.) chloro.
clorador, *m.* (chem.) chlorinator.
cloral, *m.* (chem., med.) chloral, chloral hydrate.
cloralosa, *f.* (chem.) chloralose.
cloramina, *f.* (chem.) cloramine.
clorar, *tr.v.* to chlorinate.
clorato, *m.* (chem.) chlorate; **c. de potasio,** (chem.) potassium chlorate; **c. de sodio,** (chem.) sodium chlorate.
clorela, *f.* (bot.) chlorella.
clorhidrato, *m.* (chem.) hydrochloride.
clorhídrico, ca, *a.* (chem.) hydrochloric.
clorhidrina, *f.* (chem.) chlorohydrin.
clórico, ca, *a.* (chem.) chloric.
clorideas, *f. pl.* (bot.) Chloranthaceae.
clorímetro, *m.* chlorimeter.
clorinación, *f.* chlorination.
clorinar, *tr.v.* (chem.) to chlorinate.
clorita, *f.* (min.) chlorite.
clorítico, ca, *a.* (geol.) chloritic.
clorito, *m.* (chem.) chlorite.
cloro, *m.* (chem.) chlorine.
cloroamoníaco, *m.* (chem.) chloramine.
clorobenceno, *m.* (chem.) chlorobenzene.
clorocresol, *m.* (chem.) chlorocresol.
clorodina, *f.* (chem.) chlorodyne.
clorofenol, *m.* (chem.) chlorophenol.
clorofila, *f.* (bot.) chlorophyll.
clorofilasa, *f.* (chem.) chlorophyllase.
clorofílico, ca, *a.* (bot.) chlorophyllose, chlorophyllous.
clorofilo, la, *a.* (bot.) chlorophyllous (having green or yellow-green leaves).
cloroformice, cloroformicé, *ref.* **cloroformizar.**
clorofórmico, ca, *a.* chloroformic.
cloroformizar, (*ref. 53*) *tr.v.* (med.) to chloroform.
cloroformo, *m.* (chem.) chloroform.
clorometría, *f.* chlorometry.
clorómetro, *m.* (chem.) chlorometer.
cloromicetina, *f.* (pharm.) chloromycetin.
cloropicrina, *f.* (chem.) chloropicrin.
cloroplasto, *m.* (bot.) chloroplast.
cloropreno, *m.* (chem.) chloroprene.
cloroquina, *f.* (pharm.) chloroquinine.
clorosis, *f.* (med.) chlorosis.
cloroso, sa, *a.* (chem.) chlorous.
clorotetraciclina, *f.* (pharm.) chlortetracycline.
clorotiacida, *f.* (pharm.) chlorothiazide.
clorótico, ca, *a.* chlorotic. —*m., f.* patient suffering from chlorosis.
clorpromasina, *f.* (pharm.) chlorpromazine.
clorurar, *tr.v.* to transform into chloride.
cloruro, *m.* (chem.) chloride; **c. aúrico,** gold chloride; **c. cálcico** or **de calcio,** calcium chloride; **c. de amonio,** ammonium chloride; **c. de cal,** chloride of lime; **c. de cinc,** zinc chloride; **c. de etilo,** ethyl chloride; **c. de potasio,** potassium chloride; **c. de sodio, c. sódico,** sodium chloride, common salt; **c. de vinilo,** vinyl chloride; **c. mercúrico,** mercury or mercuric chloride.
Cloto, *f.* (myth.) Clotho, one of the three Fates.
club, *m.* (Angl.) club.
clubista, *m.* clubman, club member.
clueco, ca, *a.* 1. broody (said of an incubating hen, etc.). 2. (coll.) decrepit (person). —*f.* brooder (hen).
clupeido, *m.* (ichth.) clupeid, (*pl.*) Clupeidae.
cm. *abbrev. of* **centímetro,** centimeter (cm.).
Cm *sym. of* **curio,** curium (Cm).
C.M.B., c.m.b. *abbrev. of* **cuyas manos beso,** your humble servant.
Cnosos, *m.* Knossos, capital of ancient Crete, center of Minoan civilization.
coa, *f.* 1. (Amer.) sharp wooden rod formerly used by American Indians to till the soil; (Mex.) primitive hoe. 2. (Chile) prison slang.
coacción, *f.* coercion, compulsion, constraint, coaction; (law) duress.
coaccionar, *tr.v.* to force, coerce, compel.
coacervación, *f.* piling, heaping, gathering together.
coacervar, *tr.v.* to pile up, heap up, gather together.
coacreedor, ra, *m., f.* joint creditor.
coactar, *tr.v.* to force, compel, coerce, constrain.
coactible, *a.* coercible.
coactivo, va, *a.* coercive, coercing, compelling, coactive.
coacusado, da, *a.* (law) jointly accused. —*m., f.* (law) codefendant.
coacusar, *v.t.* (law) to accuse jointly.
coadjutor, ra, *m.* coadjutor, assistant, helper.
coadjutoría, *f.* coadjutorship.
coadministrador, *m.* (ecc.) coadjutor bishop.
coadquisición, *f.* joint acquisition.
coadunación, *f.* coadunation; uniting, mixing, combining; mixture, combination, union.
coadunamiento, *m., var. of* **coadunación.**
coadunar, *tr.v.* to coadunate, combine, mix, unite.
coadyutor, *m., var. of* **coadjutor.**
coadyutorio, ria, *a.* coadjutant, assisting.
coadyuvador, ra, *m., f.* collaborator, cooperator.
coadyuvante, *a.* cooperating, collaborating. —*m., f.* (law) state's attorney.
coadyuvar, *tr.v.* to help, cooperate with, collaborate with.
coagente, *m.* co-agent, co-party, cooperator.
coagulable, *a.* coagulable.
coagulación, *f.* coagulation (blood); clotting, curdling (milk).
coagulado, da, *a.* coagulated, clotted.
coagulador, ra, *a.* coagulant, coagulative.
coagulante, *a.* coagulating.
coagular, *tr.v., r.v.* to coagulate (blood); to clot; to curdle (milk).
coagulasa, *f.* (chem.) coagulase.
coagulativo, va, *a.* coagulative.
coagulina, *f.* (chem.) coagulin.
coágulo, *m.* clot, coagulum; coagulation.
coaguloso, sa, *a.* coagulating, clotting; coagulated.
coaita, *f.* (zool.) coaita, spider monkey (Ateles paniscus).
coala, *m.* (zool.) koala.
coalbacea, *m., f.* coexecutor.
coalescencia, *f.* (med.) coalescence.
coalición, *f.* coalition, alliance.
coalicionista, *m.* coalitionist.
coaltar, *m.* (Sp.) tar, pitch.
coaltitud, *f.* coaltitude, zenith distance.
coalla, *f.* (ornith.) woodcock (Scolopax rusticola).
coana, *f.* (anat.) choana.
coapóstol, *m.* fellow apostle, fellow missionary; co-propagator, coadvocate (of a cause or doctrine).
coaptación, *f.* (surg.) coaptation.
coarcho, *m.* line connecting circular net to the seine anchor (in tuna fishing).
coarmador, *m.* part owner of a ship.
coarrendador, ra, *m., f.* joint lessor.
coarrendatario, ria, *m., f.* joint tenant.
coartación, *f.* 1. limitation, restriction. 2. (ecc.) obligation to become an ordained priest within a certain period after obtaining a church benefice.
coartada, *f.* (law) alibi; **probar una c.,** to establish or provide an alibi.
coartado, da, *past part. of* **coartar.** —*a.* **esclavo c.,** slave who is to be freed under certain conditions.
coartador, ra, *a.* limiting, restrictive. —*m., f.* restrainer.
coartar, *tr.v.* to limit, restrict, curtail.
coartífice, *m., f.* collaborator.
coate, ta, *a., var. of* **cuate,** (Mex.) twin; similar, alike.
coatí, *m.* (zool.) coati.
coautor, ra, *m., f.* coauthor.
coaxial, coaxil, *a.* (engin.) coaxial.
coba, *f.* 1. (coll.) amusing fib, tall tale; yarn. 2. (coll.) flattery, cajolery. — **dar c.,** (coll.) to flatter, soft-soap (coll.).
coba, *f.* (Morocco) Sultan's tent; (Morocco) sanctuary, holy man's tomb; (Morocco, archit.) dome or domed structure.
cobáltico, ca, *a.* (chem.) cobaltic.
cobaltífero, ra, *a.* cobalt-bearing.
cobaltina, *f.* (min.) cobaltite, cobaltine.
cobalto, *m.* (min.) cobalt; **azul de c.,** cobalt blue; **c. arseniatado,** (min.) cobalt bloom.
cobaltocre, *m.* (min.) cobalt bloom.
cobaltoso, sa, *a.* (chem.) containing cobalt.
cobarcho, *m.* seine, large net equipped with floats and weights (used in tuna fishing).
cobarde, *a.* 1. cowardly, faint-hearted. 2. (fig.) dim, weak (eyesight). —*m., f.* coward.
cobardear, *i.v.* to be a coward, act the coward, show cowardice.
cobardemente, *adv.* in a cowardly manner.
cobardía, *f.* cowardice.
cobaya, cobayo, *m.* (zool.) Guinea pig.
cobea, *f.* (C. Amer., bot.) cathedral bells, cup-and-saucer vine (Cobaea scandens).
cobeligerante, *m., f.* cobelligerent (allied countries fighting a common enemy).
cobertera, *f.* 1. lid, cover, top (of pots and pans). 2. procuress, madam (coll.). 3. (*pl.*) two middle feathers of a hawk's tail.
cobertizo, *m.* lean-to, shed; **c. de fletes,** (ry.) freight shed.
cobertor, *m.* bedspread, bedcover.
cobertura, *f.* 1. cover, covering. 2. ceremony in which a grandee received his title from the king (signified by his putting on his hat in the king's presence).
cobez, (*pl.* **cobeces**) *m.* (ornith.) species of hawk.
cobija, *f.* 1. (bldg.) ridge tile. 2. cover, covering. 3. short shawl. 4. covert (of a bird's plumage). 5. (*pl.*) bedclothes.
cobijador, ra, *a.* covering, sheltering, protective. —*m., f.* one who covers or shelters; front, cover-up man.
cobijamiento, *m.* covering; sheltering; lodging.
cobijar, *tr.v.* to cover; to cover up; to shelter; to lodge. —*r.v.* to take shelter or lodging; to cover oneself.
cobijera, *f.* 1. procurer, gossip. 2. (arch.) chambermaid.
cobijo, *m.* covering; shelter, protection; lodging.
cobijón, *m.* (Col.) leather cover (for a packhorse's load).
cobista, *m.* (coll.) flatterer, apple-polisher (U.S., coll.), soft-soaper (coll.).
cobla, *f.* 1. ballad. 2. sardana band (in Catalonia).
cobo, *m.* 1. (Cuba, zool.) gigantic snail (Virgus latro). 2. (C. Rica) blanket.
cobra, *f.* 1. rope (to yoke oxen). 2. team of mares (trained for threshing wheat).
cobra, *f.* 1. (zool.) cobra; **c. de capuchón,** (zool.) hooded cobra. 2. (hunt.) retrieval.
cobrable, *a., var. of* **cobradero.**
cobradero, ra, *a.* collectable; retrievable.
cobrador, *m.* bill-collector, tax collector; bus conductor.
cobranza, *f.* 1. collection, collecting (of money, bills, etc.). 2. cashing (a check). 3. (hunt.) retrieval.

cobrar, *tr.v.* 1. to collect. 2. to recuperate, retrieve, get back. 3. to charge. 4. to cash (a check). 5. to win (affection). 6. to acquire (reputation, fame, etc.). 7. to make (an enemy). 8. to feel (hatred). 9. to gain, pluck up (spirit, courage), take (heart). 10. to obtain (credit). 11. (hunt.) to retrieve. 12. to tighten, tauten (rope). — **c. afición a,** to become fond of; to get to like; **c. ánimo,** take courage; **c. fuerza,** to win or get support; to get strong. —*r.v.* to recuperate, recover, revive.

cobratorio, ria, *a.* pertaining to collection.

cobre, *m.* copper; set of copper pots and pans; (*pl.*) (mus.) brass (instruments of orchestra). — **batir uno el c.,** (coll.) to work with energy, buckle down to work; **batirse el c.,** (coll.) to rake in the shekels working very hard; (coll.) to discuss heatedly; **c. amarillo,** (min.) copper pyrites, chalcopyrite; **c. del cátodo,** (metal.) cathode copper; **c. piritoso,** copper pyrites; **c. quemado,** copper sulphate; **c. verde,** malachite; **mostrar el c.,** to show one's unpleasant side; **quedarse sin un c.,** (Peru) to be broke.

cobre, *m.* brace of dried hake or haddock.

cobreado, da, *a.* copper-plated.

cobreño, ña, *a.* copper.

cobrizo, za, *a.* cupreous, cupriferous; copper, copper-colored.

cobro, *m.* collection, collecting (of money); recovery; cashing (a check); **poner c. en una cosa,** to try hard to get or collect something; to be careful or cautious; **poner en c.,** to put in a safe place; **ponerse uno en c.,** to take refuge, seek safety.

coca, *f.* 1. (bot.) coca (shrub); coca leaf. 2. berry; **c. de Levante,** (bot.) Indian berry tree.

coca, *f.* 1. portion of hair on either side of the part. 2. (mar.) knot, snarl, kink (in rope). 3. (mar.) small medieval sailing vessel. 4. (coll.) head. 5. (coll.) rap on the head (with the knuckles). 6. (Col.) eggshell, skin (of fruit). — **de c.,** (Mex., coll.) gratis, free.

cocacho, *m.* (Arg., Ecuad., Peru) rap on the head with the knuckles.

cocada, *f.* (cul.) macaroon, grated coconut sweetmeat; (cul., Bol., Col., Ecuad.) kind of nougat.

cocador, ra, *a.* 1. (coll.) wheedling, cajoling, coaxing. 2. (coll.) flirting. —*m., f.* 1. (coll.) wheedler, waxer, cajoler. 2. flirt.

cocaína, *f.* cocaine.

cocainismo. *m.* cocainism.

cocainizar, (*ref.* 53) *tr.v.* to cocainize.

cocainómano, na, *a.* addicted to cocaine.

cocal, *m.* 1. (Peru) coca plantation. 2. (Amer.) coconut grove.

cocán, *m.* (Peru) breast (of fowl), white meat.

cocar, (*ref.* 50) *tr.v.* 1. (coll.) to wheedle, coax, cajole. 2. (coll.) to flirt with, make eyes at.

cocarar, *tr.v.* to supply with coca leaves.

cocaví, *m.* (C. Rica) provisions carried on a trip.

coccídido, da, *a.* (zool.) coccidial, coccidian. —*m. pl.* Coccidia.

coccidioidomicosis, coccidioidosis, *f.* (med.) coccidioidomycosis.

coccidiosis, *f.* (med.) coccidiosis.

cóccidos, *m. pl.* (ento.) Coccidae.

coccígeo, a, *a.* (anat.) coccygeal, caudal.

coccinélidos, *m. pl.* (ento.) Coccinelidae, the ladybug family.

coccíneo, a, *a.* dark, purplish red.

cocción, *f.* cooking; baking; boiling; fermenting.

cóccix, *m.* (anat., zool.) coccyx.

cóccus, *m.* (bac.) coccus.

coceador, ra, *a.* kicking (said of a quadruped).

coceadura, *f.* kick, kicking (by an animal).

coceamiento, *m., var. of* **coceadura.**

cocear, *i.v.* to kick (animal); (coll.) to resist, oppose, kick against.

cocedero, ra, *a.* easily cooked, baked or boiled. —*m.* kitchen; fermenting room (for wine).

cocedizo, za, *a.* easily cooked, boiled or baked.

cocedor, *m.* 1. workman in charge of boiling and condensing (certain products). 2. workman in charge of making must syrup (for fortifying wine). 3. boiling room, kitchen.

cocedura, *f., var. of* **cocción.**

cocer, (*ref.* 75) *tr.v.* 1. to cook; to boil: bake (bread, bricks). 2. to fire (ceramics, bricks, etc.). 3. to digest. 4. (med.) to maturate, suppurate. — **ser dura de c. y peor de comer,** to be a hard nut to crack. —*i.v.* 1. to boil. 2. to brew, ferment. 3. to ret (flax). —*r.v.* (fig.) to suffer long and intense pain; **cocerse en su propia salsa,** to stew in one's own juice.

coces, *pl. of* **coz,** kick; **dar c.,** to kick (when done by a quadruped).

cocha, *f.* 1. (metal.) water tank (adjoining the main buddle or washing tank). 2. (coll.) pigsty, hovel. 3. (Peru) large open space, pampa. 4. (Chile, Ecuad.) pond, pool, puddle.

cochada, *f.* (Col.) cooking; baking.

cochambre, *m.* (coll.) greasy, dirty object; (coll.) filth, filthiness.

cochambrería, *f.* (coll.) filthy rubbish.

cochambrero, ra, *a.* (coll.) *var. of* **cochambroso.**

cochambroso, sa, *a.* (coll.) filthy, dirty, grimy. —*m., f.* filthy, messy person, slut (*f.*), slob (*m.*) (coll.).

cocharro, *m.* wood or stone cup.

cochastro, *m.* wild boar suckling.

cochayuyo, *m.* (Peru, Chile, bot.) brown alga, rockweed (Durvillea utilis).

coche, *m.* 1. coach, carriage. 2. automobile, car. 3. pram, perambulator. 4. (ry.) carriage, coach, car. — **c. bomba,** car bomb; **c. cama,** (ry.) sleeping car; **c. celular,** Black Maria, paddy wagon; **c. comedor,** (ry.) dining or restaurant car; **c. de alquiler,** cab, hack; taxi; **c. de bomberas,** fire engine; **c. de camino,** inter-town or city coach; **c. de carreras,** racing car; **c. de colleras,** mule-drawn coach; **c. de correos,** (ry.) mail car or van; **c. de equipajes,** (ry.) luggage or baggage van or car; **c. de plaza, c. de punto,** public service taxi or coach; hack, hackney; **c. deportivo,** sports car; **c. de rúa,** city coach; **c. familiar,** station wagon; **c. fumador,** (ry.) smoking car or carriage; **c. fúnebre** or **mortuorio,** hearse; **c. mirador,** (ry.) observation car; **c. parado,** (coll.) balcony or window giving out to a busy thoroughfare; **c. patrulla,** squad car, prowl car; **c. radio-patrulla,** radio patrol car; **c. salón,** (ry.) chair car; **ir en el c. de San Fernando,** (coll.) to go on foot, go on shank's mare.

coche, *m.* (reg., Sp.) pig, hog.

cochear, *i.v.* to drive a coach. —*i.v., r.v.* to go driving.

cochera, *f.* carriage-house; coach-driver's wife. —*a.* **puerta cochera,** carriage entranceway.

cocherada, *f.* (Mex.) indecent expression or remark.

cocheril, *a.* (coll.) pertaining to coaches or coach men, e.g. *traje c.,* coachman's outfit.

cochero, *m.* 1. coachman. 2. (astron.) **C.,** Auriga, the Charioteer (constellation). — **c. de punto,** hack-driver.

cochero, ra, *a.* (cul.) easily cooked or baked.

cocherón, *m.* large carriage-house.

cochevira, *f.* lard.

cochevís, *f.* (ornith.) species of horned lark (Galerida cristata).

cochi, *m.* call used for hogs (in certain provinces of Spain and Chile).

cochifrito, *m.* (cul.) well-seasoned fricassee of kid or lamb.

cochigato, *m.* a long-legged Mexican bird.

cochina, *f.* (zool.) sow.

cochinada, *f.* (coll.) dirt, filth; (coll.) mean or base action; dirty trick (coll.), filthy business.

cochinamente, *adv.* dirtily, filthily; grossly; (coll.) basely, meanly, shabbily.

cochinata, *f.* (mar.) rider.

Cochinchina, *f.* 1. Cochin China, former region of Indochina, now part of Vietnam. 2. (fig., coll.) antipodes, the ends of the earth.

cochinería, *f.* (coll.) foulness, filthiness; (coll.) coarseness, grossness; meanness; dirty trick, filthy business.

cochinero, ra, *a.* fit for hogs (said of inferior foodstuffs given to swine). — **trote c.** (coll.), light, quick trot of an animal.

cochinilla, *f.* 1. (ento.) cochineal insect; cochineal (dye). 2. wood louse. — **c. de humedad,** pill bug; **c. de San antón,** (ento.) ladybird (Coccinella septem-punctuata).

cochinillo, *m.* suckling pig.

cochino, na, *a.* 1. filthy, dirty, slovenly. 2. mean, stingy. —*m., f.* (coll.) miser, tightwad, skinflint. —*m.* 1. pig, hog; pig, slob (coll.), dirty person. 2. (Cuba, ichth.) triggerfish. — **c. chino,** hairless hog; **c. de monte,** wild hog, wild boar. —*f.* sow; slut, slovenly woman.

cochiquera, *f.* (coll.) *var.* of **cochitril.**

cochite hervite, *adv.* (coll.) helter-skelter, in slapdash manner. —*m.* (coll.) excitable, impetuous person, madcap.

cochitril, *m.* (coll.) dirty hovel, pigsty.

cochizo, *m.* (min.) richest part of a mine.

cocho, cha, *irr. past part. of* **cocer.** —*a.* 1. cooked. 2. dirty, filthy. 3. (Col.) raw. —*m.* 1. pig. 2. (Chile, cul.) custard or pudding made with toasted flour. —*f.* sow.

cochura, *f.* 1. cooking, baking; boiling. 2. batch of dough (for bread).

cochurero, *m.* (min.) furnace tender or stoker (in a quicksilver refinery).

cochurra, *f.* (Cuba, cul.) guava dessert.

cocido, da, *past part. of* **cocer.** —*a.* cooked, boiled, baked. — **estar uno c. en (una cosa),** to be well versed or experienced in (something); to be steeped in (a subject). —*m.* stew; **c. madrileño,** Spanish boiled dinner.

cociente, *m.* (math.) quotient; **c. intelectual,** intelligence quotient.

cocimiento, *m.* 1. cooking; baking; boiling. 2. fermenting. 3. infusion, brew. 4. soaking, steeping (given to woolen materials prior to dyeing). 5. firing (of ceramics, bricks, etc.).

cocina, *f.* 1. kitchen. 2. (kitchen) cooker, stove, range. 3. (cul.) potage of vegetable; (cul.) broth, soup. 4. cooking, cuisine. — **c. rodante,** (mil.) rolling kitchen; **c. francesa,** French cuisine.

cocinar, *tr.v.* to cook; (Col.) to bake. —*i.v.* (coll.) to meddle (in other people's affairs).

cocinería, *f.* (Chile) cheap eating house.

cocinero, ra, *m., f.* cook. — **haber sido cocinero antes que fraile,** to be well qualified, have practical knowledge of a subject.

cocinilla, *m.* (coll.) meddler, busybody (esp. in domestic affairs and woman's work).

cocinilla, ta, *f.* portable stove, camp-stove; heating stove.

cóclea, *f.* 1. Archimedean screw. 2. (anat.) cochlea.

coclear, *a.* (anat.) cochlear.

coclear, *m.* weight measure equivalent to half a drachm.

coclearia, *f.* (bot.) scurvy grass (Cochlearia officinalis).

coco, *m.* 1. (bot.) coconut palm, coconut tree; coconut (fruit); coconut shell. 2. (coll.) nut, head. 3. (bac.) coccus. 4. (ento.) mealy bug, scale bug. 5. cheap muslin or percale. 6. East Indian berry (used in making rosaries). 7. (Cuba, ornith.) white ibis. — **c. de Levante,** Indian berry tree (Anamirta cocculus); **c. rojo,** (Cuba, ornith.) scarlet ibis; **c. prieto,** (Cuba, ornith.) black ibis.
coco, *m.* 1. bogeyman, spook. 2. (coll.) grimace, face (coll.). — **hacer cocos,** (coll.) to coax, cajole; to make a fuss over someone; (coll.) to flirt, make eyes at; **parecer un c., ser un c.,** (coll.) to be very ugly, look a fright (coll.).
cocó, *m.* (Cuba) whitish earth or gravel (used in masonry and concrete-mixing).
cocobacilar, *a.* (bac.) coccobacillary.
cocobacilo, *m.* (bac.) coccobacillus.
cocobálsamo, *m.* (bot.) fruit of the balsam poplar or balm of Gilead.
cocobolo, *m.* (bot.) Cuban cocobolo tree (Dalbergia retusa); granadilla wood (of the cocobolo tree).
cocodrilo, *m.* (zool.) crocodile, alligator.
cocol, *m.* (Mex., cul.) diamond-shaped bread roll.
cocolera, *f.* (Mex., ornith.) species of turtle dove.
cocolero, *m.* (Mex.) baker or seller of bread rolls (cocoles).
cocolía, *f.* (Mex.) antipathy, aversion, dislike; ill-will.
cocoliche, *m.* (Arg.) pidgin Spanish of Italian immigrants; (Arg., derog.) Italian.
cocoliste, *m.* (Mex.) any epidemic disease; (Mex.) typhoid fever.
cócora, *m., f.* (coll.) nuisance, pest, plague. —*a.* annoying, vexatious, bothersome.
cocoso, sa, *a.* worm-eaten, grub-infested.
cocotal, *m.* coconut plantation; clump of coconut trees.
cocote, *m., var. of* **cogote,** (coll.) occiput (base of the skull).
cocotero, *m.* coconut palm.
coctel, cóctel, *m.* cocktail (drink); cocktail party; **c. atómico,** (med.) atomic cocktail; **c. Molotov,** Molotov cocktail.
coctelera, *f.* cocktail mixer or shaker.
cocui, *m.* (Ven., bot.) agave, maguey.
cocuiza, *f.* (Mex., Ven.) maguey rope.
cocuma, *f.* (Peru, cul.) baked corn on the cob.
cocuy, *m., var. of* **cocuyo.**
cocuyo, *m.* 1. (ento.) fire beetle (Pyrophorus noctilocus). 2. (Cuba, bot.) Bumelia tree (Bumelia nigra). — **c. ciego,** (Cuba, ento.) species of black fire beetle (Zophobas morio).
coda, *f.* 1. (mus.) coda; final repetition (of a piece of music). 2. (carp.) wedge in a mitre joint.
codadura, *f.* rooted layer (of a grapevine).
codal, *a.* 1. elbow, elbow-shaped. 2. one cubit long. —*m.* 1. elbow-piece of armor. 2. thick wax candle one cubit long. 3. layer (of a grapevine). 4. (archit.) shore, prop; (archit.) crossbeam. 5. (carp., mas.) frame, handle (of a saw or a mason's level). 6. (carp.) square. 7. (min.) brick arch (in a mine gallery).
codaste, *m.* (mar.) sternpost.
codazo, *m.* jog, nudge (with the elbow).
codeador, ra, *a.* (Amer., coll.) sponging, cadging. —*m., f.* cadger, sponger (coll.).
codear, *i.v.* to elbow, jostle, jog, nudge. —*tr.v.* (Amer., coll.) to cadge, sponge, wheedle (something out of someone). —*r.v.* **c. con,** (coll.) to be on equal terms with, rub elbows with, hobnob with.
codeína, *f.* (chem., pharm.) codeine.
codelincuencia, *f.* co-delinquency, complicity.
codelincuente, *a.* co-delinquent. —*m., f.* accomplice.
codemandado, *m.* (law) codefendant.
codena, *f.* (tex.) degree of resistance of the weave.
codeo, *m.* 1. elbowing, jostling, nudging. 2. (Amer., coll.) cadging, sponging.
codera, *f.* 1. rash or scab on the elbow. 2. elbow patch. 3. (mar.) stern fast.
codesera, *f.* (bot.) field or plantation of bean-trefoil.
codeso, *m.* (bot.) type of cytisus.
codeudor, ra, *m., f.* joint debtor.
códice, *m.* 1. codex, manuscript, book. 2. (ecc.) part of the missal or breviary containing the office for a diocese or congregation.
codicia, *f.* greed, cupidity, covetousness.
codiciable, *a.* desirable, covetable.
codiciador, ra, *a.* coveting, grasping, greedy. —*m., f.* coveter.
codiciante, *a., var. of* **codiciador.**
codiciar, *tr.v.* to covet, crave for, desire.
codicilar, *a.* codicillary.
codicilo, *m.* codicil.
codiciosamente, *adv.* covetously, greedily.
codicioso, sa, *a.* 1. greedy, covetous. 2. (coll.) hard-working, industrious, eager, anxious. 3. berserk (*bull*). — **c. de,** greedy for.
codificación, *f.* codification.
codificador, ra, *a.* codifying.
codificar, (*ref. 50*) *tr.v.* to codify.
codifique, codifiqué, *ref.* **codificar.**
código, *m.* code (of laws, regulation, ethics, etc.); **c. barrado** or **de barras,** bar code; **c. civil,** civil law; **c. de comercio,** commercial law; **c. del honor,** code of honor; **c. de señales,** (mar.) signal code; **c. genético,** genetic code; **c. militar,** military law; **c. morse,** Morse Code; **c. napoleónico,** Napoleonic Code; **c. penal,** penal code; **c. postal,** zipcode; **c. territorial,** (tel. area code; **c. telegráfico,** telegraph code.
codillera, *f.* (vet.) tumor on the elbow of a horse or mule.
codillo, *m.* 1. elbow or forearm of quadrupeds. 2. snag, stump of a cut branch on a tree. 3. elbow pipe. 4. (equit.) stirrup. 5. (mar.) either end of the keel from which rises the stem and sternpost. — **jugársela uno de c. a otro,** (coll.) to trick, outwit; **tirar a uno al c.,** (coll.) to try to ruin someone.
codirección, *f.* co-management; co-direction.
codirector, ra, *m., f.* co-director; co-manager.
codo, *m.* 1. (anat.) elbow. 2. (mec.) elbow pipe. 3. cubit (measure). — **alzar el c., empinar el c.,** (coll.) to drink excessively, tipple; **beber de codos,** (coll.) to savor a drink by slow sips, drink at leisure; **c. a c.,** on the same level; together, shoulder to shoulder; **c. común, c. geométrico,** linear measure of half a yard; **c. con c.,** (coll.) close together, shoulder to shoulder; **c. en U,** U bend, return bend; **comerse los codos de hambre,** (coll.) to be poverty-stricken, be destitute; **dar de c.,** to nudge; (coll.) to rebuff, spurn, refuse; **estar metido hasta los codos (en algo),** (coll.) to be up to one's neck (in something); **hablar por los codos,** (coll.) to chatter incessantly, talk someone's ear off.
codón, *m.* leather covering for a horse's tail.
codoñate, *m.* (cul.) quince jelly.
codorniz, (*pl.* **codornices**) *f.* (ornith.) quail; **rey de codornices,** (ornith.) water rail (Railus aquaticus).
coeducación, *f.* coeducation.
coeducacional, *a.* coeducational.
coeficiencia, *f.* coefficiency.
coeficiente, *a.* coefficient. —*m.* (math.) coefficient; **c. de cargamento,** load factor; **c. de dilatación,** (phys.) coefficient of expansion; **c. de fricción,** (phys.) coefficient of friction; **c. de ionización,** (chem., phys.) ionization constant; **c. de retardo,** (hydr.) coefficient of retardation; drag coefficient; **c. dieléctrico,** (elec.) dielectric constant; **c. diferencial,** (math.) differential coefficient.
coencausado, *m.* (law) codefendant.
coendú, (*pl.* **coendúes**) *m.* (Amer.) coendou (prehensile-tailed porcupine).
coenzima, *f.* (med.) coenzyme.
coepíscopo, *m.* co-bishop.
coercer, (*ref. 56*) *tr.v.* to restrain, restrict, curb.
coercibilidad, *f.* (phys.) compressibility.
coercible, *a.* restrainable, repressible.
coerción, *f.* (law) restriction, repression.
coercitivo, va, *a.* restrictive, restraining.
coerza, coerzo, *ref.* **coercer.**
coesencial, *a.* coessential.
coetáneo, nea, *a.* coetaneous, contemporary. —*m., f.* contemporary.
coeternidad, *f.* (theol.) coeternity.
coeterno, na, *a.* (theol.) coeternal.
coevo, va, *a.* coeval, coetaneous.
coexistencia, *f.* coexistence.
coexistente, *a.* coexistent.
coexistir, *i.v.* to coexist.
coextenderse, (*ref. 30*) *r.v.* to coextend.
coextienda, coextiendo, *ref.* **coextenderse.**
cofa, *f.* (mar.) top of the lower mast; c. para el vigía, crow's nest.
cofactor, *m.* (math.) cofactor.
cofásico, ca, *a.* cophasal.
cofia, *f.* 1. coif (lady's headwear; padded skull-cap of helmet); hair net. 2. (bot.) husk, seed coat.
cofiador, *m.* (law) joint guarantor, cosurety, cobail.
cofín, *m.* basket, fruit basket.
cofosis, *f.* (med.) complete deafness.
cofrada, *f.* member sister (of a sisterhood).
cofrade, *m., f.* member (of a brotherhood, sisterhood, confraternity, association, society or trade union). —*m.* brother (of a confraternity). —*f.* sister (of a sisterhood).
cofradía, *f.* brotherhood, confraternity; sisterhood; association, society, trade union, guild.
cofre, *m.* 1. chest, trunk, coffer. 2. (ichth.) boxfish, trunkfish. 3. (print.) chase for the imposing stone.
cofrecico, illo, ito, *m. dim. of* **cofre,** small trunk or box.
cofrero, *m.* one who makes or sells chests or trunks.
cofto, ta, *a.* Coptic. —*m., f.* Copt. —*m.* Coptic (language).
cogedera, *f.* 1. rod for gathering esparto grass. 2. box for catching swarming bees. 3. fruit-picker's pole.
cogedero, ra, *a.* ripe or ready for picking (fruit, etc.). —*m.* handle.
cogedizo, za, *a.* easy to pick or gather.
cogedor, ra, *a.* catching; picking, gathering. —*m.* dustpan; ash or coal shovel.
cogedura, *f.* catching; picking, gathering.
cogegotas, *m.* drip pan.
coger, (*ref. 57*) *tr.v.* 1. to catch; to seize, grasp; to take, take hold of; to pick, gather (fruit, etc.). 2. to occupy, take, cover (space). 3. to hold, contain, have room for. 4. to absorb, soak up. 5. (taur.) to gore, horn. 6. to catch, come upon, surprise; to find, discover. 7. to catch up with, overtake. 8. to catch, get (cold, etc.). 9. (Arg., Mex.) to fuck (vulg.), have sexual intercourse with. 10. to take (by the hand). —*i.v.* 1. to fit, go in, have room. 2. to decide, resolve, e.g. *cogí y salí,* I up and went. —*r.v.* to get, catch; to take, take for oneself.

cogida, *f.* 1. (coll.) goring, horning (by a bull). 2. (coll.) harvest, pick, harvesting, gathering, picking.
cogido, *m.* fold, pleat (in a dress, curtain, etc.).
cogienda, *f.* (Col.) harvest, crop.
cogitabundo, da, *a.* pensive, meditative.
cogitación, *f.* cogitation, reflection, meditation.
cogitar, *tr.v.* to cogitate, reflect, meditate, ponder.
cogitativo, va, *a.* cogitative.
cognación, *f.* cognation, blood relationship (through the female line); relationship.
cognado, da, *a.* (gram.) cognate. —*m., f.* cognate, blood relative.
cognaticio, cia, *a.* cognatic.
cognición, *f.* cognition; knowledge.
cognomento, *m.* agnomen, cognomen.
cognoscible, *a.* cognoscible, cognizable, knowable.
cognoscitivo, va, *a.* cognitive, knowing.
cogollero, *m.* (Cuba) tobacco weevil.
cogollo, *m.* 1. heart (of a lettuce, cabbage, etc.). 2. bud, shoot. 3. top of a pine lopped off when using the tree for timber. 4. (Arg.) large cricket (insect). 5. (Mex.) sugar-cane top. 6. (Col.) outcrop (of a mine). 7. (Chile) praise, compliment.
cogombrillo, *m., var. of* **cohombrillo.**
cogombro, *m., var. of* **cohombro.**
cogón, *m.* (bot.) cogon, grass of the Phil. I. used for roof thatching (Imperata cylindrica koenigii).
cogonal, *m.* field covered with cogon.
cogorza, *f.* (coll.) drinking bout, jag, binge.
cogotazo, *m.* blow on the back of the neck.
cogote, *m.* 1. nape, back of the neck. 2. crest, panache (of a helmet). — **ser uno tieso de c.,** to be arrogant, conceited or stuck-up.
cogotera, *f.* havelock, protective flap for the neck (against the sun); sun-shade for horse's head.
cogotillo, *m.* curved iron strip on the fore shaft of a cart or coach.
cogotudo, da, *a.* bull-necked, thick-necked; (coll.) stuck-up. —*m.* (Amer.) wealthy or influential person.
cogucho, *m.* (Cuba) inferior quality sugar.
cóguil, *m.* (Chile) fruit of the **coguilera.**
coguilera, *f.* (Chile) Chilean climbing plant.
cogujada, *f.* (ornith.) crested lark (Galerida cristata).
cogujón, *m.* corner (of a mattress, bolster, pillow or sack).
cogulla, *f.* monk's cowled habit.
cogullada, *f.* pig's dewlap.
cohabitación, *f.* cohabitation.
cohabitar, *i.v.* to cohabit.
cohecha, *f.* (agr.) final tilling or plowing (of fallow land).
cohechador, ra, *a.* bribing. —*m., f.* briber, fixer (sl.).
cohechar, *tr.v.* 1. (agr.) to give the final tilling or plowing to (fallow land before sowing). 2. to bribe.
cohecho, *m.* 1. bribery, bribing. 2. (agr.) time for final tilling before sowing.
cohen, *m.* sorcerer, witch-doctor; procurer, pimp. —*f.* sorceress, witch; procuress.
coheredar, *tr.v.* to coinherit, inherit jointly.
coheredero, ra, *m.* coheir, joint heir. —*f.* coheiress, joint heiress.
coherencia, *f.* coherence; (phys.) cohesion.
coherente, *a.* coherent.
cohesión, *f.* cohesion.
cohesivo, va, *a.* cohesive.
cohesor, *m.* (rad.) coherer.
cohete, *m.* 1. rocket; skyrocket. 2. (Mex.) blasthole. — **al c.,** (Arg., coll.) in vain; **c. a la Congreve** or **c. de guerra,** (artil.) Congreve rocket; **c. balístico intercontinental,** intercontinental ballistic missile; **c. chispero,** shower rocket; **c. de señales,** signal rocket; **c. sonda,** sounding rocket; **c. tronador,** detonating rocket (fireworks).
cohetería, *f.* rocketry.
cohetero, *m.* pyrotechnist, manufacturer of rockets or fireworks.
cohibición, *f.* restriction, restraint.
cohibir, *tr.v.* to restrain, curb, check.
cohobación, *f.* (chem.) redistillation.
cohobar, *tr.v.* (chem.) to redistil.
cohobo, *m.* deerskin; (Ecuad., Peru) deer.
cohollo, *m., var. of* **cogollo.**
cohombral, *m.* cucumber field or bed.
cohombrillo, *m.* (bot.) small cucumber, gherkin; **c. amargo,** squirting cucumber (Ecballium elaterium).
cohombro, *m.* 1. (bot.) cucumber. 2. (cul.) cucumber-shaped fritter. — **c. de mar,** (zool.) sea cucumber.
cohonestación, *f.* specious justification, whitewashing (coll.).
cohonestar, *tr.v.* to gloss over, whitewash (coll.).
cohorte, *f.* cohort.
coicoy, *m.* (Chile) small toad with four protuberances on its back (Cystognathus briboni).
coihué, *m.* (Chile, bot.) coigue, coehue, (Chilean evergreen used for thatching) (Nothofagus dombeyi).
coima, *f.* 1. concubine. 2. fee paid to gambling-house owner. 3. (Amer.) bribe.
coime, *f.* gambling-house owner or keeper; billiard-room attendant.
coimero, *m.* 1. gambling-house owner or keeper. 2. (Amer.) bribe taker.
coincidencia, *f.* coincidence.
coincidente, *a.* coincident, coinciding, coindental.
coincidir, *i.v.* to coincide; to agree; to arrive simultaneously.
coinquilinato, *m.* cotenancy.
coinquilino, na, *m., f.* cotenant, joint tenant.
coinquinar, *tr.v.* to stain, soil. —*r.v.* to tarnish or lose one's reputation.
cointeresado, da, *a.* jointly interested. —*m., f.* associate, partner, sharer; jointly interested party.
coipo, *m.* (Arg., Chile. zool.) coupu, coypou (kind of beaver) (Myocaster coypus).
coirón, *m.* (Bol., Chile, Peru, bot.) broom sedge (Andropogon argenteus).
coironal, *m.* field covered with broom sedge.
coito, *m.* coitus, sexual intercourse; **c. interrupto,** coitus interruptus.
coja, *f.* (coll.) strumpet, whore.
coja, *ref.* **coger.**
cojal, *m.* carder's apron.
cojate, *m.* (Cuba, bot.) amomum (Amomum thyrsoideum erectum).
cojatillo, *m.* (Cuba, bot.) wild amomum.
cojear, *i.v.* 1. to limp, hobble; to wobble (table, chair, etc.). 2. (coll.) to slip, stumble, act immorally. 3. (coll.) to suffer (from a physical defect). — **saber de qué pie cojea,** to know someone's weaknesses.
cojera, *f.* lameness, limp.
cojijo, *m.* 1. bug, grub, insect. 2. vexation, discontent, peevishness.
cojijoso, sa, *a.* peevish, irritable.
cojín, *m.* cushion, pillow; hassock; (mar.) bolster, fender; **c. de aire,** air cushion.
cojinete, *m.* 1. small cushion. 2. (ry.) chair, socket or clutch securing rail to sleeper. 3. (mec.) die (for threading). 4. (mec.) bearing, pillow lock, bolster. 5. (print.) roller clamp. — **c. de bolas** or **bolillas,** ball bearing; **c. de bolas con adaptador,** adapter-type ball bearing; **c. de collares,** collar bearing; **c. de rodillos,** roller bearing; **c. de manguito,** sleeve bearing; **c. de roscar,** die for threading; screw plate; **c. de terraja,** die for threading.
cojinúa, *f.* (Cuba, Mex., ichth.) cavalla.
cojitranco, ca, *a.* (derog.) restless, mischievous (said of a cripple). —*m., f.* restless, mischievous cripple.
cojo, ja, *a.* lame; crippled; wobbly (chair, table); game (leg); feeble, lame (excuse, reasoning). — **no ser c. ni manco,** to be experienced. —*m., f.* cripple; lame person.
cojo, *ref.* coger.
cojobo, *m.* (Cuba, bot.) red quebracho.
cojolite, *m.* (Mex., ornith.) species of pheasant (Penelope purpurescens).
cojones, *m. pl.* (vulg.) balls, (vulg.) testicles.
cojudo, da, *a.* uncastrated, unspayed (animal).
cojuelo, ela, *m., f. dim. of* **cojo,** a small lame person; crippled child.
cok, *m.* coke (coal); **c. de retorta,** gas coke.
col, *f.* cabbage; **c. de Bruselas,** Brussels sprouts; **c. morada,** red cabbage.
cola, *f.* 1. tail (of an animal), extremity; appendage. 2. end; tail end (of piece of cloth); tail (of coat, aeroplane, comet, etc.); train (of a gown). 3. queue, line (of people). 4. (archit.) tailing, inner joint (of a stone or beam in a wall). 5. (fort.) rear (of a trench or fortification). 6. (fort.) entrance (to a bastion). 7. (mus.) prolonged note (on the last syllable of a song). — **a. c. de milano,** ornamented in dovetail style; **a la c.,** at the end, last, behind; **apearse por la c.,** (coll.) to make a silly remark; **c. de caballo,** (bot.) horsetail, scouring rush; ponytail (hair style); **c. de Dragón,** (astron.) Dragon's tail; **c. del León,** (astron.) Denebola (star); **c. de martillo,** peen of a hammer; **c. de milano** or **de pato,** (carp.) dovetail tenon; **c. de zorra,** (bot.) foxtail; **formar** or **hacer c.,** to form a queue or line, line up, queue up; **hacer bajar la c. a uno,** (fig., coll.) to humiliate someone; **llevar uno c.** or la c., to be last (in examination results); **ser uno arrimado a la c.** or **hacia la c.,** (coll.) to be dim-witted; **tener** or **traer c. (una cosa),** to bring or cause serious consequences.
cola, *f.* 1. glue. 2. (bot.) kola nut. — **c. de boca,** solid glue pastille (for sticking paper, etc.); **c. de carpintero,** wood glue; **c. de pescado,** isinglass, fish gelatin; fish glue; **c. de retal,** (p.) size (for preparing canvases).
colaboración, *f.* collaboration; cooperation; contribution (to a newspaper, etc.).
colaboracionista, *m., f.* collaborator, esp. the person who collaborates with a political or military adversary.
colaborador, ra, *m.,f.* collaborator; partner, colleague; contributor (to a magazine).
colaborar, *i.v.* to collaborate; to cooperate, contribute.
colación, *f.* 1. light meal, collation, snack. 2. (ecc.) collation (bestowal of clerical benefice; conference of monks). 3. (ecc.) parish lands. 4. conferring, granting (university degree). 5. comparison. — **c. de bienes,** (law) collation, hodgepodge (of inheritance); **hacer c.,** to have a snack; **sacar uno a c.,** (coll.) to mention, make mention of; **traer a c.,** (coll.) to produce as proofs or reasons; (coll.) to bring in irrelevantly (in a speech or conversation); **traer a c. y partición (una cosa),** (law) include in a collation (an inheritance).
colacionar *tr.v.* 1. to compare, collate. 2. (ecc.) to collate, to bestow an ecclesiastical benefice on. 3. (law) to bring into collation (an inheritance).
colactáneo, a, *m., f.* foster brother, foster sister (having been nursed by the same female).

colada, *f.* 1. wash; bleaching (of laundry); bleach, bleaching solution; bleached laundry. 2. straining, filtering. 3. cattle trail, road (between pastures); mountain pass, defile, narrow gorge. 4.(metal.) tapping (of molten metal in blast furnace). — **estar en la misma c.,** to be in the same boat, be in the same boat, be in the same situation; **meter en la c.,** (coll.) to involve, get mixed up in; **salir en la c.,** to come to light, come out in the wash; **todo saldrá en la c.,** you'll pay for it (used as a threat).
colada, *f.* (fig.) good sword or swordsman (origin: one of El Cid's fine swords).
coladera, *f.* 1. strainer, colander. 2. (Amer.) drain.
coladero, *m.* 1. colander, strainer, filter. 2. narrow trail or pass. 3. (min.) hole for dumping ore (from one mine level to another).
coladizo, za, *a.* passing through easily; able to permeate easily (liquids).
colador, *m.* (ecc.) collator (bestower of a collation).
colador, *m.* 1. strainer, colander. 2. (print.) leach tub.
coladora, *f.* bleacher, bleaching woman; bleaching machine.
coladura, *f.* 1. straining; filtering. 2. (coll.) lies, fibs; lying, fibbing. 3. (*pl.*) wax dregs.
colágeno, na, *a.* (biochem.) collagenous. —*f.* (biochem.) collagen.
colagogo, *ga,* a. (med.) cholagogue, cholagogic (provoking discharge of bile).
colaina, *f.* split or damage in timber.
colambre, *f.* (tanning) pelts, skins, peltry.
colana, *f.* (coll.) drink.
colanilla, *f.* small latch, sash bolt (of a window or door).
colaña, *f.* low partition wall.
colapez, *f.* isinglass, fish gelatin or glue.
colapiscis, *f., var. of* **colapez.**
colapso, *m.* (med.) collapse, prostration.
colapsoterapia, *f.* (med.) collapse therapy.
colar, (*ref.* 33) *tr.v.* 1. to strain, filter, percolate. 2. to bleach. 3. (coll.) to pass off (something false for genuine). 4. to cast (iron). 5. (rel.) to collate, bestow (a benefice). —*i.v.* 1. to squeeze, pass, wriggle (through). 2. to leak; to filter; to ooze. 3. to come in, blow in (air through a crack). 4. to drink wine. — **no c. una cosa,** (coll.) to be unconvincing, e.g. *su historia no me cuela,* his story does not convince me. —*r.v.* 1. to slip in, sneak in, gate-crash (coll.). 2. to leak; to filter; to ooze. 3. (coll.) to tell lies, fib. 4. to slip, make a slip, put one's foot in it.
colateral, *a.* collateral; lateral, side. —*m., f.* collateral (applied to relatives not of direct descent).
colatitud, *f.* (astron.) colatitude.
colativo, va, *a.* (ecc.) collative (held by collation).
colativo, va, *a.* cleansing.
colayo, *m.* (ichth.) edible kind of dogfish.
colbac, *m.* calpack, Turkish cap.
colcha, *f.* bedspread, counterpane; quilt.
colchado, da, *past part. of* **colchar.** —*a.* quilted.
colchadura, *f.* quilting.
colchar, *tr.v.* to quilt.
colchar, *tr.v.* (mar.) to lay (strands of rope).
colchero, ra, *m., f.* quilt maker; quilt seller.
cólchico, *m.* (bot.) colchicum.
colchón, *m.* mattress; **c. de aire,** air mattress; **c. de muelles,** spring mattress; **c. de plumas,** feather mattress; **c. de viento,** air mattress; **c. de agua,** waterfilled mattress, water bed.
colchoncillo, *m. dim. of* **colchón,** small mattress.
colchonera, *a.* tufting (needle).
colchonería, *f.* 1. wool shop. 2. mattress and pillow shop.
colchonero, ra, *m., f.* mattress maker or seller.
colchoneta, *f.* bunk mattress, light mattress, long, narrow mattress.
colcótar, *m.* (chem.) red pigmentation used in paint, obtained through powdered iron peroxide.
coleada, *f.* 1. flick, switch (of tail by cows, horses, etc.); wag (of tail by dog); swish (of fish's tail). 2. (Ven.) the act of throwing a bull down by its tail.
coleador, ra, *a.* tail-wagging, tail-switching, tail-flicking (animal). —*m., f.* bull fighter or cattle herder who throws down a bull by twisting its tail.
coleadura, *f.* tail-wagging, tail-switching or flicking.
colear, *tr.v.* 1. to wag (tail). 2. to hold (a bull) by the tail; (Amer.) to throw (a bull) by pulling its tail. 3. (Col., coll.) to annoy, bother. 4. (Guat.) to follow, tail. 5. (Chile) to fail (in an examination). —*i.v.* to move, swish or wag its tail. — **colea todavía (un asunto),** the matter is not yet settled.
colección, *f.* collection (of stamps, etc.), aggregation, accumulation; gathering, array; anthology.
coleccionador, ra, *m., f.* collector (of stamps, etc.).
coleccionar, *tr.v.* to collect; to form a collection (of stamps, paintings, etc.).
coleccionista, *m., f., var. of* **coleccionador.**
colecistectomía, *f.* (med.) cholecystectomy.
colecistitis, *f.* (med.) cholecystitis, inflammation of the gallbladder.
colecta, *f.* 1. (charity) collection, community or charity drive; collection (money collected in church); tax collection. 2. (ecc.) collect (of Mass). 3. congregation, gathering (of people in church).
colectación, *f.* collection (of money).
colectar, *tr.v.* to collect (money; literary works into one edition).
colecticio, cia, *a.* 1. raw, untrained, inexperienced (troop of soldiers). 2. omnibus (edition of author's works); compilatory.
colectivamente, *adv.* collectively; in common, jointly.
colectividad, *f.* community, group (of people); the whole; collectivity; collective ownership.
colectivismo, *m.* collectivism.
colectivista, *a.* collectivist, collectivistic. —*m., f.* collectivist.
colectivización, *f.* collectivization.
colectivizar, (*ref.* 53) *tr.v.* to collectivize.
colectivo, va, *a.* collective; communal, common, joint. —*m.* 1. (gram.) collective (noun). 2. (Arg., Peru) jitney, passenger vehicle smaller than a bus. 3. (Peru) collection of money (contributed by friends for newlyweds, people's birthdays, wedding anniversaries, etc.).
colectomía, *f.* (med.) colectomy.
colector, ra, *a.* collecting. —*m.* 1. collector (of taxes, of collection in church), gatherer. 2. (elec.) collector, commutator. 3. drainage ditch; main sewage channel. — **c. cloacal,** main sewer; **c. centrífugo,** centrifugal collector; **c. de aceite,** (auto.) drip pan; **c. de desagüe,** main soil pipe, house drain, sewer.
colecturía, *f.* collectorship (office of tax collector or of a priest who takes the collection); tax office.
colédoco, *m.* (anat.) choledochus, common bile duct.
colega, *m., f.* colleague, coworker, fellow member, associate; opposite number, counterpart; (coll.) buddy.
colegatario, *m.* (law) colegatary, colegatee; coinheritor.
colegiación, *f.* association; membership of an association.
colegiadamente, *adv.* in a group or community.
colegiado, da, *past part. of* **colegiarse.** —*a.* collegiate.
colegial, *a.* 1. of or pertaining to school. 2. (ecc.) collegiate. —*m.* 1. schoolboy, pupil, student; scholarship student; (coll.) shy, inexperienced youth, greenhorn (coll.). 2. (Chile, ornith.) red and black bird living along river banks and lakes. — **c. capellán,** monitor, student in charge of a school chapel.
colegiala, *f.* schoolgirl.
colegialmente, *adv., var. of* **colegiadamente.**
colegiarse, *r.v.* to form an association; to join a group of members of a given profession or class.
colegiata, *f.* collegiate church.
colegiatura, *f.* scholarship.
colegio, *m.* 1. school, college, academy. 2. college, association (of professionals); (ecc.) college (e.g. of cardinals). — **c. apostólico,** college of the Apostles; **c. de cardenales,** College of Cardinals; **c. electoral,** electoral college.
colegir, (*ref.* 76) *tr.v.* 1. to gather together, collect. 2. to deduce, infer, gather.
colegislador, ra, *a.* colegislative.
colemanita, *f.* (min.) colemanite.
colémbolo, *m.* (ento.) collembolan, (*pl.*) Collembola.
colemia, *f.* (med.) cholemia, cholaemia, abnormal presence of bile in the blood.
colendo, *a.* feast (day).
colénquima, *f.* (bot.) collenchyma.
coleo, *m., var. of* **coleadura.**
coleóptero, ra, (ento.) *a.* coleopterous, coleopteral. —*m.* coleopteran, beetle; (*pl.*) Coleoptera.
coleóptilo, *m.* (bot.) coleoptile.
coleorriza, *f.* (bot.) coleorhiza.
colera, *f.* ornament on a horse's tail.
cólera, *f.* 1. anger, rage, fury. 2. (med.) bile, choler. 3. gummed white buckram (cloth). — **cortar la c.,** to take something to cure biliousness; (coll.) to have a snack; **cortar la c. a uno,** to check (someone's) anger; to calm down, pacify, soothe; **dar c.,** to annoy, anger; **montar en c.,** to get angry or furious; **tomar c.,** to lose one's temper. —*m.* (med., vet.) cholera; **c. asiático,** Asiatic cholera; **c. esporádico,** sporadic European or summer cholera; **c. de gallinas,** chicken cholera; **c. morbo,** cholera morbus.
colérico, ca, *a.* 1. choleric, irascible, bad-tempered. 2. (med.) cholera, of cholera, choleraic, e.g. *síntomas coléricos,* symptoms of cholera. 3. (med.) stricken with cholera. —*m., f.* 1. bad-tempered person. 2. cholera patient, person stricken with cholera.
coleriforme, *a.* (med.) resembling cholera.
colerina, *f.* (med.) cholerine.
colesterina, *f.* (med.) cholesterin, cholesterol.
colesterol, *m.* (biochem.) cholesterol.
coleta, *f.* 1. pigtail, queue. 2. postscript. 3. burlap, canvas. — **media c.,** short pigtail; **cortarse la c.,** (taur.) to give up bullfighting; (coll.) to give up a habit or hobby; **tener** or **traer c.,** to have serious consequences.
coletazo, *m.* blow with the tail.
coletero, *m.* one who makes or sells leather jerkins or doublets.
coletilla, *f.* 1. pigtail, queue (of hair). 2. postscript.
coletillo, *m.* sleeveless jacket; small doublet, jerkin.
coleto, *m.* 1. deerskin jerkin. 2. body (of a person). 3. oneself, e.g. *dije para mi c.,* I said to myself. 4. (Col.) insolence. — **echarse una cosa al c.,** (coll.) to eat up, drink up; (coll.) to read something from beginning to end.

coletón, *m.* (Ven.) sackcloth, burlap.
coletudo, da, *a.* (Col.) brazen, cheeky, insolent.
colgadero, ra, *a.* hangable, able to be hung; fit for keeping, storable (fruit, meat, etc.). *—m.* hook, peg; ring (for hook).
colgadizo, za, *a.* hanging, suspended. *—m.* lean-to; (Cuba, Dom. Rep.) porch roof.
colgado, da, *past part. of* **colgar.** *—a.* 1. uncertain, undecided, pending. 2. (coll.) let down, disappointed, e.g. *dejar c.,* to let down, to leave in the lurch.
colgador, *m.* 1. (print.) peel. 2. clothes hook or peg; clothes hanger.
colgadura, *f.* hanging, drapery, tapestry.
colgajo, *m.* 1. tatter, rag. 2. bunch (of fruit hung up for keeping). 3. (surg.) flap (of skin used to cover a wound).
colgamiento, *m.* hanging; act of hanging.
colgandejo, *m.* (Col.) tatter, rag.
colgandero, ra, *a., var. of* **colgante.**
colgante, *a.* hanging, pendent; dangling. *—m.* 1. drop (of a chandelier); pendant (jewel). 2. (archit.) pendant, boss, festoon. 3. (mec.) hanger. 4. (carp.) kingpost.
colgar, (*ref. 72*) *tr.v.* 1. to hang, hang up, suspend. 2. to drape (with hangings). 2. to hang, put to death by hanging. 3. to blame, put the blame on. *—i.v.* 1. to hang; to be suspended; to dangle, hang loose. 2. to depend on, hang on (someone's decision). 3. to attribute to; make responsible for. — **c. los hábitos,** to doff the cassock; **c. el sable,** to retire; to give up a fight or a quest.
colgué, *ref.* **colgar.**
colibacilo, *m.* (med.) colon bacillus.
colibacilosis, *f.* (med.) colibacillosis.
coliblanco, ca, *a.* white-tailed, having a white tail.
colibrí, *m.* (ornith.) humming bird, colibri.
cólica, *f.* mild colic.
colicano, na, *a.* grey-tailed, having a grey tail.
colíche, *m.* (coll.) open house (party).
cólico, ca, *a.* (chem.) cholic acid.
cólico, ca, *a.* (anat., med.) colic, colonic, of or pertaining to the colon; **arteria cólica,** (anat.) colic artery; **dolor cólico,** (med.) colic, tormina (intestinal pain). *—m.* (med.) colic; **c. cerrado,** (med.) colic aggravated by persistent constipation; **c. de los pintores,** (med.) painters' colic; **c. de plomo,** (med.) lead colic; **c. hepático,** (med.) hepatic spasm (due to gallbladder stones); **c. miserere,** (med.) intestinal occlusion; **c. nefrítico** or **renal,** (med.) nephritic spasm (due to kidney stones).
colicoli, *m.* (Chile, ento.) horsefly, gadfly.
colicuación, *f.* 1. melting, fusion. 2. (med.) colliquation, wasting away through loss of liquids in the body.
colicuante, *a.* fusing; colliquant, colliquative; dissolving.
colicuar, (*ref. 55*) *tr.v.* to colliquate; to dissolve, to fuse, melt together (several substances). *—r.v.* to melt, fuse.
colicuativo, va, *a.* (med.) colliquative; profuse or excessive (said of discharges).
colicuecer, (*ref. 45*) *tr.v., var. of* **colicuar.**
colicuezca, colicuezco, *ref.* **colicuecer.**
coliflor, *f.* (bot.) cauliflower.
coliforme, *a.* (med.) coliform.
coligación, *f.* colligation, coalition, union, amalgamation; connection, tie, link, alliance.
coligado, da, *past part. of* **coligarse.** *—a.* associated, united. *—m., f.* leaguer, covenanter.
coligadura, *f., var. of* **coligación.**
coligamiento, *m., var. of* **coligación.**
coligarse, *r.v.* to unite, amalgamate, join; to associate (with others).
coligue, coligué, *ref.* **coligar.**
coligüe, *m.* (Arg., Chile, bot.) gramineous leafy creeper used as fodder; its seeds are used to make soup.
colijo, colija, *ref.* **colegir.**
colilarga, *f.* (Chile, ornith.) scissor-tailed fly-catcher.
colilla, *f.* 1. cigarette end, cigar or cigarette butt. 2. waist-to-hem train (used formerly on women's cloaks).
colillero, ra, *m., f.* one who picks up cigar or cigarette butts.
colimación, *f.* (phys.) collimation.
colimador, *m.* (phys.) collimator.
colimbo, *m.* (ornith.) grebe.
colín, *a.* short tailed, bobtailed (horse). *—m.* (Mex., ornith.) colin, American quail or bobwhite.
colina, *f.* 1. hill, knoll. 2. (bot.) cabbage seed; cabbage patch. 3. (chem.) choline, cholin.
colinabo, *m.* (bot.) kohlrabi; turnip; young cabbage.
colincho, cha, *a.* (Amer.) tailless, without a tail.
colindante, *a.* adjoining, adjacent, contiguous; neighboring, e.g. *propiedad c.,* adjacent property.
colindar, *i.v.* to adjoin, border, be contiguous (with), abut.
colineación, *f.* (math.) collineation.
colineal, *a.* collinear.
colinérgico, ca, *a.* (physiol.) choloidic.
colinesterasa, *f.* (biol.) cholinesterase.
colineta, *f.* 1. attractively arranged plate of sweets. 2. bouquet of flowers.
colino, *m.* cabbage seed; cabbage nursery (for producing seedlings).
colipava, *a.* fan-tailed, fan-tail, said of a type of dove.
colirio, *m.* (med.) collyrium, eyewash, eye drops.
colirrojo, *m.* (ornith.) redstart.
colisa, *f.* (mar.) swivel gun; swivel gun platform.
coliseo, *m.* coliseum; arena, a large theatre.
colisión, *f.* collision; bump, bruise; abrasion; clash, conflict (of ideas, etc.).
colitigante, *m., f.* (law) co-litigant, joint litigant.
colitis, *f.* (med.) colitis.
coliza, *f.* (mar.) *var. of* **colisa.**
colmadamente, *adv.* abundantly, lavishly; generously.
colmado, da, *past part. of* **colmar.** *—a.* full, filled, replete; heaped, overflowing. *—m.* 1. restaurant specializing in certain food. 2. (P. Rico) grocery store.
colmar, *tr.v.* to fill, fill up, fill to the brim, fill to overflowing; to heap (food on a plate); to lavish, heap, shower (with gifts, etc.).
colmatación, *f.* filling; earth fill; silting up.
colmena, *f.* 1. beehive. 2. (fig.) a crowded, noisy place.
colmenar, *m.* apiary.
colmenero, ra, *m., f.* beekeeper, apiarist. *—m.* (Mex.) honey bear.
colmenilla, *f.* (bot.) morel mushroom.
colmillada, *f., var. of* **colmillazo.**
colmillar, *a.* pertaining to the eyeteeth or to fangs.
colmillazo, *m.* 1. large eyetooth or fang. 2. wound or bite caused by a tusk or fang.
colmillejo, *m. dim. of* **colmillo,** small eyetooth or fang.
colmillo, *m.* canine tooth, eyetooth; fang (of a dog, wild animal), tusk (of a boar, walrus, elephant); **enseñar uno los colmillos,** (coll.) to show one's teeth, look fierce; **escupir uno por el c.,** (coll.) to swagger, bluster, talk big (feign courage); **tener uno el c. retorcido,** (coll.) to be sharp, shrewd or canny.
colmilludo, da, *a.* 1. large tusked or fanged, having large or prominent canine teeth. 2. (coll.) sharp, shrewd, canny.
colmo, *m.* 1. overflow (contents rising above the brim and overflowing from a container). 2. height, limit, culmination, e.g. *el c. de la mala crianza,* the height of rudeness, *el c. de la estupidez,* the height of stupidity. 3. (coll.) end, limit, last straw. — **eso es el c.,** this is the end or limit, this is the last straw; **llenar al c.,** to fill to the brim; **para c. de males,** to cap it all, to make things worse.
colmo, *m.* straw thatching; thatched roof.
colmo, ma, *a.* full; filled; heaped; overflowing, brimming.
colobo, *m.* (zool.) colobus (monkey) (Colobus candidus).
colocación, *f.* 1. placing, putting, situating; place, situation, location; position. 2. arrangement, distribution, placement. 3. job, position, post, situation, employment.
colocar, (*ref. 50*) *tr.v.* to place, put (in place); to situate, locate; to station; to place or settle (a person in a job). *—r.v.* to place or station oneself (in place); to get a job (in, with).
colocasia, *f.* (bot.) taro, colocasia, Egyptian bean.
colocho, *m.* 1. (C. Rica) shaving (of wood or metal). 2. (C. Rica) curl, ringlet (of hair).
colocolo, *m.* (Chile) 1. mythological animal. 2. wild cat.
colocutor, ra, *m., f.* co-speaker, speaker; one of the speakers in a dialogue.
colodión, *m.* (chem.) collodion.
colodra, *f.* 1. milking pail or bucket. 2. wooden wine pail (for measuring). 3. drinking horn. — **ser uno una c.,** to be a heavy drinker.
colodrazgo, *m.* wine tax or duty.
colodrillo, *m.* back of the head, nape.
colofón, *m.* (print.) colophon.
colofonia, *f.* colophony, rosin.
colofonita, *f.* (min.) colophonite.
cologüina, *f.* (Guat.) variety of chicken.
coloidal, *a.* (chem.) colloidal.
coloide, *m.* (chem.) colloid.
coloideo, a, *a.* (chem.) colloidal.
Colombia, *f.* Colombia.
colombiano, na, *a., m., f.* Colombian.
colombino, na, *a.* Columbian, pertaining to or in reference to Columbus, e.g. *escultura precolombina,* pre-Columbian sculpture.
colombo, *m.* (bot.) calumba (Jatcorhiza palmata).
colombófilo, la, *a.* pertaining to pigeon breeding. *—m., f.* pigeon breeder.
colon, *m.* 1. (med.) colon. 2. (gram.) main clause in a compound sentence. 3. (gram.) colon, semicolon. — **c. imperfecto,** (gram.) subordinate or dependent clause; **c. perfecto,** (gram.) simple sentence, main clause; **c. transverso,** (anat.) transverse colon.
colón, *m.* monetary units of Costa Rica and El Salvador.
Colón, *m.* Columbus; **Cristóbal C.,** Christopher Columbus, discoverer of America.
colonato, *m.* colonization (system).
colonche, *m.* (Mex.) fermented drink made from juice of prickly pear and sugar.
colonia, *f.* 1. colony, settlement; (biol., bac.) colony. 2. (Cuba) sugarcane plantation. 3. smooth silk ribbon about one inch wide. 4. housing development. — **media c.,** narrow silk ribbon; **C. del Cabo,** Cape Colony.
colonia, *f.* 1. cologne, eau-de-cologne. 2. (Cuba, bot.) alpinia (Alpinia nutans). 3. C., Cologne, a city in Germany.
coloniaje, *m.* (Amer.) colonial period, control of an underdeveloped people by a foreign power.

colonial, *a.* colonial; (com.) colonial, overseas, from the colonies (merchandise).
colonialismo, *m.* colonialism, the system or policy by which a world power keeps foreign colonies, esp. to exploit them economically.
colonialista, *m.* colonialist.
colonice, colonicé, *ref.* **colonizar.**
colónico, ca, *a.* (anat.) colonic.
colonista, *m.* colonialist.
colonización, *f.* colonization, settlement.
colonizador, ra, *a.* colonizing, settling, settler (as *a.*). —*m., f.* colonizer, settler.
colonizar, (*ref. 53*) *tr.v.* to colonize, settle; to establish a colony or settlement.
colono, *m.* colonist, settler; tenant farmer.
coloque, coloqué, *ref.* **colocar.**
coloquial, *a.* 1. colloquial, pertaining to conversation. 2. (philol.) peculiar to the language used in common conversation.
coloquio, *m.* colloquy, discourse, conversation; (lit.) dialogue.
coloquíntida, *f.* (bot.) colocynth, bitter apple, bitter cucumber (Citrullus colocynthis).
color, *m.* 1. color; hue; coloring (of painting); rouge (cosmetic). 2. pretext, motive, reason. 3. character, coloring (of style, of opinions, etc.). 4. side, party, faction, color. 5. flush (in poker). — **c. complementario,** complementary color; **c. básico, elemental, fundamental or simple,** primary color; **c. del espectro solar** or del iris, (phys.) spectrum color; **c. firme,** fast color, **c. quebrado,** faded color; **colores nacionales,** flag colors, national colors; **dar c.** or **colores,** to paint; **de c.,** colored (clothing); colored, dark, black (person, race); **mudar uno de c.,** to blush, blanch; to change color (the face); **pintar una cosa con negros colores,** to be pessimistic, to take a dim, dark or gloomy view of things; **ponerse uno de mil colores,** to flush (with anger, shame); to blush; **robar el c.,** to make fade or look faded; **sacarle los colores a la cara,** to make blush; **so c. de,** under the pretext or excuse of; **subido de c.,** risqué (joke, etc.); **tomar c.,** to ripen (fruit, vegetables); (fig.) to take shape, shape up, mature (projects, etc.); **ver las cosas de c. de rosa,** (coll.) to see things through rose-colored glasses. —*f.* color, hue.
coloración, *f.* coloration, coloring; **c. defensiva,** (biol.) protective coloration; **c. de Gram,** (bac.) Gram's method.
colorado, da, *past part. of* **colorar.** —*a.* 1. colored; reddish, red, ruddy. 2. (fig.) risqué (story). 3. (fig.) specious, plausible. — **ponerse c.,** to blush.
coloradote, ta, *a.* (coll.) red-faced, ruddy complexioned; flushed.
colorante, *a.* coloring, dying, tinting. —*m.* coloring matter.
colorar, *tr.v.* to color, give color to; to paint; to tinge; to dye, tint (clothes, hair, etc.).
colorativo, va, *a.* colorific.
colorear, *tr.v.* 1. to color, tint. 2. (fig.) to gloss over, varnish (a lie, etc.). 3. to give specious excuses for, justify (a bad action, etc.). —*i.v.* to redden, go red, turn red; to ripen (fruit).
colorete, *m.* rouge (cosmetic).
colorido, *m.* 1. coloring; color, e.g. *las flores dan mucho c. a la casa,* flowers give a lot of color to the house; rouge (cosmetic). 2. false appearance.
colorífico, ca, *a.* (phys.) colorific, able to give color or tint.
colorimetría, *f.* (chem.) colorimetry.
colorímetro, *m.* (chem.) colorimeter.
colorín, *m.* 1. (ornith.) red linnet (Carduelis carduelis). 2. (*gen. pl.*) bright, vivid color.
colorinche, *m.* (Amer.) gaudy colors, gaudy combination of colors.
colorir, (*ref. 78*) *tr.v.* to color; (fig.) to gloss over, justify, give specious excuses for. —*i.v.* to become colored.
colorismo, *m.* (p.) tendency to emphasize color over drawing; (lit.) tendency to overload style with adjectives and superlatives; floridity (of style).
colorista, *a.* (p.) coloristic. —*m., f.* (p.) colorist; (fig., lit.) vigorous, vivid or colorful writer.
colosal, *a.* colossal, gigantic, tremendous, huge (size or quality); (fig.) colossal, fantastic.
coloso, *m.* 1. (hist.) Colossus (of Rhodes). 2. (fig.) colossus, giant.
colostomía, *f.* (med.) colostomy.
colote, *m.* (Mex.) cylindrical basket.
colotipia, *f.* (print.) collotype.
colpa, *f.* (metal.) colcothar used to treat silver.
colpotomía, *f.* (surg.) colpotomy, incision in the vagina.
colquicina, *f.* (pharm.) colchicine.
cólquico, *m.* (bot.) autumn crocus.
colúbrido, *m.* (zool.) coluber, (*pl.*) Colubridae.
coludir, *i.v.* (law) to collude, work in collusion.
columbario, *m.* (archeol.) columbarium, a set of recesses in ancient Roman cemeteries where burial urns were placed.
columbeta, *f.* somersault.
columbino, na, *a.* 1. columbine, dovelike. 2. (fig.) ingenuous, artless, naive. —*m.* garnet, pigeon blood (color).
columbio, *m.* (chem.) columbium.
columbita, *f.* (min.) columbite.
columbrar, *tr.v.* 1. to perceive or descry at a distance, see from afar. 2. (fig.) to guess, surmise, conjecture, discern.
columbres, *m.* (*pl.*) (sl.) the eyes.
columbrete, *m.* islet (offering shelter to ships).
columelar, *a.* canine (tooth). —*m.* canine tooth.
columna, *f.* 1. column (in writing; of troops or ships). 2. (archit.) column, pillar, pilaster. 3. pile, tower (of things). 4. (fig.) pillar, support, prop. — **c. adosada,** (archit.) engaged column; **c. aislada, exenta** or **suelta,** detached column (not attached to wall); **c. ática** or **cuadrada,** attic or square-based column; **c. barométrica,** (phys.) barometric pressure column; **c. blindada,** armored column; **c. cerrada,** (mil.) close column; **c. compuesta,** (archit.) composite column; **c. de agua, c. de celosía,** latticed column; **c. de fraccionamiento,** (chem.) fractionating tower, water column; **c. de dirección,** (auto.) steering column; **c. embebida, c. entregada,** embedded or engaged column or pilaster; **c. entorchada, c. salomónica,** spiral column; **c. rostrada** or **rostral,** rostral column; **c. termométrica,** (phys.) thermometric pressure column; **c. vertebral,** (med.) spine, spinal column; **c. zunchada,** (bldg.) tied column; **Columnas de Hércules,** Pillars of Hercules; **quinta c.,** (polit.) fifth column.
columnar, *a.* (geol., miner.) columnar.
columnario, ria, *a.* columnar (applied to Spanish-American silver coins bearing an emblem of two columns).
columnata, *f.* colonnade, columns.
columnista, *m.* (jour.) columnist.
columpiar, *tr.v.* to swing, push on a swing. —*r.v.* to swing (on a swing); (coll.) to sway, swing (one's body when walking); to sway, rock (e.g. an unstable table).
columpio, *m.* swing, suspended seat.
coluro, *m.* (astron.) colure.
colusión, *f.* (law) collusion.
colusor, *m.* (law) colluder.
colusoriamente, *adv.* collusively, fraudulently.
colusorio, ria, *a.* (law) collusive.
colutorio, *m.* (med.) collutory, gargle.
coluvial, *a.* (geol.) colluvial.
coluvie, *f.* 1. gang of hoodlums. 2. (fig.) sink, cesspool (of vice, filth).
colza, *f.* (bot.) colza, rape (Brassica napus).
colla, *f.* 1. gorget (of armor). 2. fish trap, consisting of baskets in a line. 3. pair of hunting dogs on a leash.
colla, *f.* 1. (Phil. I.) storm blowing from the southwest. 2. (mar.) final layer of oakum used in calking.
colla, *a.* (Bol.) Andean (native). —*m., f.* native of the Andean plateau.
collación, *f.* collation, light meal, snack.
collada, *f.* 1. mountain pass. 2. (mar.) long blowing wind.
colladía, *f.* range of small hills.
collado, *m.* small hill; mountain pass.
collalba, *f.* wooden mallet, utilized in gardening.
collar, *m.* 1. necklace. 2. ornamental chain. 3. collar (of dog, etc.). 4. ring of feathers (on the neck of some birds). 5. (her.) ornament surrounding a coat of arms. 6. (mec.) ring, flange, collar.
collareja, *f.* 1. (Col., C. Rica, ornith.) blue-colored wild pigeon (Chloroenas albicollis). 2. (C. Rica, Mex., zool.) weasel.
collarejo, *m. dim. of* **collar.**
collarín, *m.* 1. *dim. of* **collar;** collar, stock, dog collar (worn by clergy); necklet; narrow collar (on jackets). 2. ring of a bob fuse. 3. (mec.) sleeve, tube.
collarino, *m.* (archit.) annulet; lower part of capital between the astragal and the shaft of a column.
collazo, *m.* farmhand, farm laborer (who is given land to work for himself); serf.
colleja, *f.* (bot.) corn salad.
collejas, *f.* (*pl.*) thin nerves in sheep's neck.
collera, *f.* 1. padded horse collar (to keep the harness from chafing the neck). 2. (fig.) chain of convicts. 3. (Peru) street gang. 4. (Arg., Chile) (*pl.*) cuff links.— **c. de yeguas,** team of mares.
collerón, *m. aug. of* **collera,** large collar; strong and light fancy collar for carriage horses.
colleta, *f.* (bot.) a species of small cabbage.
colliguay, *m.* (Chile, bot.) euphorbiaceous shrub which gives a pleasant smell when burnt; the juice of its root was used by Indians to poison their arrows.
collón, na, *a.* (coll.) cowardly, timid. —*m., f.* coward, poltroon.
collonada, *f.* (coll.) cowardice, cowardly act.
collonería, *f.* (coll.) cowardice.
coma, *f.* 1. (gram.) comma; **c. decimal,** decimal point. 2. miserere, small boss or bracket under choir seat, to act as support for a person standing. 3. (mus.) inaudible interval between a sharp and a flat tone. — **con puntos y comas, sin faltar una c.,** (coll.) without omitting a single detail.
coma, *m.* (med.) coma.
comadrazgo, *m.* relationship between the mother of a child and its godmother.
comadre, *f.* 1. midwife. 2. name by which the mother of a child and its godmother call each other; name used by father and godfather of a child with respect to its godmother. 3. (coll.) procuress. 4. (coll.) woman friend (of another woman).
comadrear, *i.v.* (coll.) to gossip, talk idly.
comadreja, *f.* (zool.) weasel.
comadreo, *m.* (coll.) gossip, tattle, tittle-tattle (coll.); gossiping, tattling, tale-bearing.
comadrería, *f.* (coll.) gossip.

comadrero, ra, *a.* gossiping, talebearing (person). —*m., f.* gossip, gossipmonger, tattler.
comadrón, *m.* obstetrician, accoucheur.
comadrona, *f.* midwife.
comal, *m.* flat clay dish used in Mexico for cooking tortillas or corn cakes.
comalia, *f.* (vet.) generalized dropsy (of animals, esp. cattle).
comalido, da, *a.* sickly, unhealthy.
comanche, *a., m., f.* Comanche (a tribe of N. American Indians). —*m.* Comanche (language).
comandado, da, *a.* (mil.) officered.
comandancia, *f.* command (position of commander); district and troops under his command, headquarters.
comandanta, *f.* 1. (coll.) commander's wife. 2. (mar.) (formerly) flagship.
comandante, *m.* (mil.) commander; commanding officer; major; **c. de armas,** commandant (of a military post or camp); **c. de barco,** captain, commander (of a warship); **c. en jefe, c. general,** commander in chief, admiral in chief; **c. mayor,** paymaster general.
comandar, *tr.v.* (mil.) to command, have command of; to govern.
comandita, *f.* (com.) limited partnership; **sociedad en c.,** company made up of active and silent partners; silent partnership.
comanditar, *tr.v.* (com.) to finance (an enterprise, without assuming liabilities of management).
comanditario, ria, *a.* silent (partner, partnership); with active and silent partners (a company). —*m., f.* silent partner in a company.
comando, *m.* 1. (mil.) commando, assault group or unit. 2. (mil.) command. 3. (tech.) control. — **c. aéreo,** air command.
comarca, *f.* region, district, province, territory.
comarcal, *a.* regional, of or pertaining to a district.
comarcano, na, *a.* neighboring, nearby, bordering (towns, land, etc.).
comarcar, (*ref. 50*) *i.v.* to border (on), adjoin, touch (countries, towns, etc.). —*tr.v.* to plant trees in straight lines or avenues.
comarque, comarqué, *ref.* **comarcar.**
comatoso, sa, *a.* (med.) comatose.
comba, *f.* 1. curvature, curving, bend; warp (of wood). 2. rope-skipping (game); skipping rope. 3. (Peru) muckle hammer (for spalling stones). — **hacer combas,** (coll.) to sway or swing one's hips (when walking).
combadura, *f.* warping, bending, curving.
combar, *tr.v.* to bend (wood, metal). —*r.v.* to warp, bend, sag; to become bent or warped.
combate, *m.* combat, fight; battle; (fig.) struggle, conflict, battle (mental, emotional).
combatible, *a.* combatable, conquerable.
combatidor, *m.* combatant; fighter; contender.
combatiente, *a.* combatant, contending. —*m.* combatant, soldier.
combatir, *i.v.* to fight, battle (with, against); (fig.) to combat, fight against. —*tr.v.* 1. to combat, fight. 2. to assail, strike, beat upon (said of the wind, sea). 3. to agitate, shake, convulse. —*r.v.* to fight one another; (fig.) to oppose (one another).
combatividad, *f.* combativeness, pugnacity.
combeneficiado, *m.* (ecc.) co-beneficiary, joint beneficiary of a church benefice.
combés, *m.* 1. open space. 2. (mar.) waist (a ship's upper deck).
combina, *f.* (coll.) plan, conspiracy.
combinable, *a.* combinable.
combinación, *f.* 1. combination; (chem.) compound; group of words beginning with the same letters (in a dictionary); combination (woman's underwear). 2. measure, step.
combinar, *tr.v.* 1. to combine; to unite, join; (chem.) to compound. 2. to work out, arrange (a project). —*r.v.* to combine; (chem.) to coalesce, combine.
combinatorio, ria, *a.* combining; combinative, uniting; (math.) combinatorial.
combleza, *f.* mistress, concubine (of a married man).
comblezo, *m.* lover (man who lives with another's wife).
combo, ba, *a.* bent, warped, curved. —*m.* 1. wood or stone base for wine casks. 2. (Chile, Peru) sledge hammer. 3. (Chile) punch, blow with the fist. 4. (Car.) combo, small musical group.
comboso, sa, *a.* bent, warped, curved.
combretáceo, a, *a.* (bot.) combretaceous. —*f.* combretaceous plant; (*pl.*) Combretaceae.
comburente, *a.* (phys.) causing combustion. —*m.* combustive agent.
combustibilidad, *f.* combustibility.
combustible, *a.* combustible. —*m.* fuel; **c. tipo,** reference fuel; **c. nuclear,** nuclear fuel.
combustión, *f.* combustion; **c. espontánea,** (phys.) spontaneous combustion; (med.) burning of body fat (due to excessive use of alcohol); **c. fumívora,** (engin.) smokeless combustion; **c. retardada,** (engin.) afterburning.
combusto, ta, *a.* burned.
combustóleo, *m.* fuel oil.
comebolas, *m., f.* (Cuba) sucker (U.S., coll.) excessively gullible person.
comedero, ra, *a.* edible, eatable. —*m.* 1. feeding trough, feed box or container (for birds). 2. dining-room. 3. (Mex., Cuba) haunt, hang-out (coll.), place frequented by someone. — **limpiarle a uno el c.,** (coll.) to deprive someone of his job or livelihood.
comedia, *f.* 1. comedy, farce; play, drama; theatre. 2. (fig.) sham, pretense, play-acting. — **c. de capa y espada,** cloak-and-dagger play; **c. de costumbres,** comedy of manners, drawing-room comedy; **c. de enredo,** comedy of situation, comedy of intrigue; **c. de figurón,** 17th century Spanish satire (satirical play); **c. de magia,** play with spectacular effects; **c. heroica,** heroic drama; **hacer uno la c.,** (coll.) to pretend, act, play-act.
comediante, ta, *m.* 1. actor; comedian. 2. hypocrite. —*f.* 1. actress; comedienne. 2. hypocrite.
comediar, *tr.v.* 1. to average. 2. to divide equally.
comedidamente, *adv.* courteously, politely, discreetly, with moderation.
comedido, da, *past part. of* **comedirse.** —*a.* polite, civil, courteous; discreet, prudent.
comedimiento, *m.* courtesy, politeness, urbanity; thoughtfulness, consideration.
comedio, *m.* 1. center, middle (of a country or a place). 2. interval (between two periods of time).
comediógrafo, *m.* dramatist, playwright.
comedión, *m.* long, tedious comedy.
comedirse, (*ref. 39*) *r.v.* 1. to be moderate, be controlled; to control or moderate oneself. 2. to be willing, offer oneself.
comedón, *m.* (med.) blackhead, comedo.
comedor, ra, *a.* gluttonous, greedy. —*m.* dining room; restaurant; (ry.) restaurant-car; diner.
comején, *m.* (ento.) termite.
comejenera, *f.* 1. termite nest. 2. (Ven., coll.) den (of thieves or vice).
comencé, *ref.* **comenzar.**
comendador, *m.* 1. commander (of a military order); knight commander (member of an honorary order). 2. (ecc.) prelate (of certain orders). — **c. mayor,** rank below that of grand master (in certain military orders).
comendadora, *f.* mother superior (in some convents); nun (of certain ancient orders).
comendatario, *m.* (ecc.) commendator, cleric who holds a benefice in commendam.
comendaticio, cia, *a.* (ecc.) commendatory (letter from a prelate).
comendatorio, ria, *a.* commendatory, of recommendation, e.g. *carta c.,* letter of recommendation.
comendero, *m.* commendator, holder of a fief or crown benefice.
comensal, *m., f.* 1. dependent, member of a household; retainer. 2. commensal, table companion, fellow diner.
comensalía, *f.* fellowship of members of a household, fellowship of table companions, commensality.
comentador, ra, *m., f.* 1. commentator, annotator. 2. malicious gossip, evil tongue (person).
comentar, *tr.v.* 1. (coll.) to comment, make comments on, talk about. 2. to write a review of a book, play, etc.; to write a comentary on, annotate. —*i.v.* to make comments, comment.
comentario, *m.* annotation, comment, gloss; remark, commentary, gloss; (coll.) comment, criticism; (*pl.*) commentaries, historical memoirs; (*pl.*) malicious or evil gossip.
comentarista, *m., f.* commentator.
comento, *m.* 1. comment, annotation, explanatory note; commentary, gloss. 2. lie, falsehood.
comenzante, *a.* beginning, starting, commencing. —*m., f.* beginner.
comenzar, (*ref. 68*) *tr.v., i.v.* to begin, start, commence; **c. a** + *inf.,* to begin to + *inf.*
comer, *m.* food; **quitárselo uno de su c.,** (coll.) to deprive oneself (of something) for the benefit of others.
comer, *tr.v.* 1. to eat, to dine. 2. to gnaw at (remorse, grief); to corrode, eat into (rust); to wear away, eat away (water on stone). 3. to use; consume (fuel). 4. to fade, make fade (colors). 5. to cause to itch, itch. — **dar de c.,** to feed; **sin comerlo ni beberlo,** (coll.) without having anything to do with it. —*i.v.* to eat; to dine; **c. a dos carrillos,** to gorge or stuff oneself; **c. con los ojos,** to have eyes bigger than one's stomach; **c. y callar,** (coll.) beggars can't be choosers; **ser de buen c.,** (coll.) to be a big or hearty eater; **tener qué c.,** to have enough to eat. —*r.v.* 1. to eat up, finish up, eat (food) completely. 2. to waste, squander, use up. 3. to take (a piece in chess, checkers). 4. to skip, skim over (passage in a book). 5. to swallow, pronounce indistinctly. — **comerse (una cosa) a la otra,** (coll.) to beat or surpass completely, put in the shade; **comerse (una cosa) con los ojos,** to devour (something) with the eyes; **comerse unos a otros,** (coll.) to be at each other's throats, be at loggerheads; **comerse vivo a uno,** (coll.) to skin someone alive, scalp someone; (Peru) to run rings around, outwit, outsmart, dupe.
comerciable, *a.* 1. marketable. 2. (fig.) affable, amiable, sociable (person).
comercial, *a.* commercial, of or pertaining to business; shopping, e.g. *centro c.,* shopping center.
comercialismo, *m.* commercialism.
comercialización, *f.* commercialization.
comercializar, (*ref. 53*) *tr.v.* to commercialize.
comercialmente, *adv.* commercially.
comerciante, *a.* trading, of or pertaining to business. —*m., f.* merchant, trader, dealer, businessman; **c. comisionista,** commission merchant.
comerciar, *i.v.* to trade, deal, traffic; to commerce, do business (with); (fig.) to deal (with), have intercourse or dealings (with people).

comercio, *m.* 1. trade, business, commerce; business, business world, businessmen; business section (of a town); shop, commercial establishment. 2. intercourse, dealings (between two countries); illicit sexual relations or intercourse. 3. a card game. — **bolsa de c.,** stock exchange; **c. carnal,** sexual intercourse; **c. de cabotaje,** (mar.) coastal trade; **c. exterior,** foreign trade; **c. interior,** home trade, domestic commerce.

comestible, *a.* edible, eatable. —*m., f.* (*gen. pl.*) food, foodstuff; provisions.

cometa, *m.* (astron.) comet; **c. barbato,** bearded comet; **c. caudato,** caudate comet; **c. corniforme,** corniform comet; **c. crinito,** crinite comet; **c. periódico,** periodic comet. —*f.* 1. kite. 2. comet (a card game).

cometario, ria, *a.* (astron.) cometary, of or pertaining to a comet.

cometedor, ra, *a.* perpetrating, committing. —*m., f.* perpetrator, offender.

cometer, *tr.v.* 1. to entrust, charge (with). 2. to commit, perpetrate. 3. to use (figures of speech). 4. (com.) to commission, give an agency or a franchise.

cometido, *past part. of* **cometer.** —*m.* assignment, commission, duty; moral obligation.

comezón, *f.* 1. itch, itching. 2. (fig.) itch (coll.), longing, desire.

comible, *a.* (coll.) edible, eatable, passable.

cómicamente, *adv.* comically, funnily, amusingly.

comicastro, *m.* second-rate actor, ham actor.

comicial, *a.* comitial.

comicidad, *f.* comicalness, funniness, the quality of being comical.

comicios, *m.* (*pl.*) comitia (of ancient Romans); (polit.) elections, polls, voting.

cómico, ca, *a.* comic, comical, funny, amusing. —*m.* comedian; actor; player; **c. de la legua,** strolling player or actor. —*f.* comedienne; actress.

comida, *f.* food, nourishment; meal, fare; feed; dinner, banquet. — **cambiar la c.,** to vomit, throw up, be sick; **c. corrida,** (Amer.) table d'hote; **cama y c.,** bed and board.

comidilla, *f.* 1. favorite pastime, pet hobby. 2. (coll.) talk, common talk (subject of gossip), e.g. *su conducta es la c. del pueblo,* her behavior is the talk of the town.

comido, da, *past part. of* **comer.** —*a.* **fed,** having eaten or dined; **c. de,** eaten by, e.g. *c. de comején,* termite-eaten; **c. por servido,** hand-to-mouth wages; **c. y bebido,** (coll.) maintained, supported, kept; **estar c. y bebido,** to have wined and dined; **sin haberla c. ni bebido,** (coll.) without having anything to do with it.

comience, comienzo, *ref.* **comenzar.**

comienzo, *m.* beginning, start; **dar c.,** to begin.

comigo, (arch.) *var. of* **conmigo.**

comilitón, *m.* comrade-in-arms, fellow soldier.

comilitona, *f.* feast, blowout (coll.), big meal, splendid repast.

comillas, *f.* (*pl.*) quotation marks; **abran c.,** open quotation marks, quote; **cierren c.,** close quotation marks, unquote; **entre c.,** in quotation marks, quote.

comilón, na, *a.* hearty eating. —*m., f.* gourmand, big eater, hearty eater, glutton.

comilona, *f.* (coll.) feast, spread, blowout (coll.), splendid meal.

cominear, *i.v.* to fuss like an old woman.

comineria, *f.* (*gen. pl.*) fussiness; meticulosity, punctiliousness; hair-splitting (in conversation).

cominero, *a.* (coll.) fussy. —*m.* fusser, fussy man, old woman (coll.).

cominillo, *m.* 1. (bot.) darnel (Lolium temulentum). 2. (Chile) itch, itching. 3. (Chile, Arg., coll.) perplexity, uneasiness.

comino, *m.* (bot.) cumin (Cuminium cyminum); cumin seed; **c. rústico,** (bot.) lasewort; **importarle a uno un c.,** not to care, not to give a damn; **no vale un c.,** (coll.) it is not worth a fig, pin or straw.

comiquear, *i.v.* to act in amateur theatricals, put on amateur shows, play charades.

comiquería, *f.* (coll.) group of second-rate actors.

comisar, *tr.v.* to confiscate.

comisaria, *f.* (coll.) wife of a commissioner, a chief of police or commissar.

comisaría, *f.* commissariat, the post of commissioner or commissar; office or headquarters of a commissioner or commissar; (Amer.) police station, police headquarters.

comisariato, *m., var. of* **comisaría.**

comisario, *m.* commissioner; commissary, commissar; sheriff; (Amer.) chief of police, police inspector; **c. de entrada, hospital receptionist; c. de guerra,** (mil.) commissary general; **c. general,** (mil.) chief of ordnance; **c. ordenador,** (mil.) quartermaster general.

comiscar, (*ref. 50*) *tr.v.* to nibble, peck at (food).

comisión, *f.* 1. commission, committee. 2. (com.) commission, percentage (paid to agent). 3. commission, assignment; mandate, order; task, errand. 4. perpetration, committing. 5. (Mex.) (type of) policeman. — **c. mercantil,** (com.) agency contract, contract appointing agent; commission, percentage (paid to agent.); **c. mixta,** joint committee; **c. permanente,** standing committee.

comisionado, da, *past part. of* **comisionar. —*a.*** commissioned, empowered, charged with. —*m., f.* commissioner; representative; proxy agent; member (of a committee, etc.); **c. de apremio,** tax collector, tax enforcement officer.

comisionar, *tr.v.* to commission, charge, entrust; to empower, appoint, authorize.

comisionista, *m., f.* agent, representative, commission agent.

comiso, *m.* (law) confiscation (of illegal goods); seizure, attachment; (law) confiscated goods.

comisorio, ria, *a.* (law) valid or binding for a specified time.

comisque, comisqué, *ref.* **comiscar.**

comisquear, *tr.v.* to nibble, peck at (food).

comistión, *f.* mixture, melange.

comistrajo, *m.* (coll.) mess, hodgepodge, (of food).

comisura, *f.* (anat.) commissure, juncture, union; **c. de los labios,** corners of the mouth.

comital, *a.* pertaining to a count.

comité, *m.* committee, commission; **c. de redacción,** editorial board; **c. de trabajadores,** workers' committee; **c. ejecutivo,** executive committee.

comitente, *a.* commissioning, entrusting. —*m., f.* one who commissions, client; committent.

comitiva, *f.* retinue, suite, party, group.

cómitre, *m.* (arch., mar.) galley-slave driver; (mar.) sea captain under admiral's orders.

como, *adv.* 1. as, e.g. *tan blanco c. la nieve,* as white as snow. 2. like, e.g. *un hombre c. él no debe estar libre,* a man like him should not be free. 3. as if, as though, *e.g. se quedó c. muerto,* he remained as though dead. 4. as, in the manner of, in the position of, e.g. *él asistió a la boda c. testigo,* he attended the wedding as a witness. 5. something like, about, approximately, e.g. *había c. mil personas en la plaza,* there were about one thousand people in the square. — **c. que,** as if, as though; **c. no sea para,** unless to, except to; **c. quien dice,** (Amer.) so to speak; **c. quiera que,** however, in whatever way; since, inasmuch as; **c. sea,** in any way whatever, in whatever way possible; **la manera c.,** the way that, the way in which.

cómo, *adv.* (**como** carries a written accent in direct and indirect questions) 1. how, e.g. *¿c. te sientes?* how do you feel?, *no sé c. agradecerle,* I don't know how to thank you. 2. what, e.g. *¿c. dijiste?* what did you say. 3. why, *¿c. no te fuiste con él?* why didn't you go with him? — **el c. y el cuándo,** the means and the opportunity. —*interj.* (**como** carries a written accent in interjections) how!; what!; what did you say!; **¡c. así!** how is it possible!; **¡c. no!** of course; how else.

como, *conj.* 1. as, since, because, e.g. *c. no había llegado a las seis, me fui a la casa,* since he had not arrived by six o'clock, I went home. 2. if, e.g. *c. no te enmiendes, dejaremos de ser amigos,* if you don't change your ways, our friendship will end.

cómoda, *f.* chest of drawers, bureau.

comodable, *a.* (law) loanable, lendable.

cómodamente, *adv.* comfortably; easily, with ease; conveniently.

comodante, *m., f.* (law) bailor or lender in a commodatum; one who lends freely for a specified period of time.

comodatario, ria, *m., f.* (law) bailee or receiver in a commodatum.

comodato, *m.* (law) commodate, commodatum; contract of loan and restitution.

comodidad, *f.* 1. comfortableness; comfort. 2. facility; convenience. 3. interest, advantage, profit. 4. leisure, ease. 5. (*pl.*) comforts, creature comforts.

comodín, *m.* 1. wild card. 2. all-purpose gadget. 3. (coll.) weak excuse.

comodista, *a., var. of* **comodón.**

cómodo, da, *a.* 1. comfortable, commodious. 2. easy, relaxed. 3. handy, convenient.

comodón, na, *a.* comfort-loving (person).

comodoro, *m.* (mar.) commodore.

compacidad, *f., var. of* **compactibilidad.**

compact, compact disc, *m.* compact disc, CD; compact disc player, CD player.

compactación, *f.* compressing, compression, making compact; compacting, consolidating.

compactar, *tr.v.* to compress, make compact.

compactibilidad, *f.* compactness.

compacto, ta, *a.* compact; tight, dense (crowd); close-grained (wood); close (weave); (print.) closely printed; (print.) thin (type).

compadecer, (*ref. 45*) *tr.v.* to sympathize with, commiserate with, feel sorry for, pity. —*r.v.* to go together, harmonize; **compadecerse de,** to feel sorry for, pity.

compadezca, compadezco, *ref.* **compadecer.**

compadraje, *m.* clique, group, ring, cabal.

compadrar, *i.v.* 1. to become associated with a person by being a godparent to his child. 2. to become great friends. — **c. con,** to get along well with, hit it off with.

compadrazgo, *m.* 1. compaternity, relationship between parents and godparents of a child. 2. clique, ring, group, cabal.

compadre, *m.* 1. godfather or father (in relation with one another). 2. (coll.) intimate friend, old boy (coll.), buddy (U.S., coll.).

compadrería, *f.* friendship, fellowship, chumminess (coll.).

compaginación, *f.* 1. arrangement, harmony; putting in order. 2. (print.) paging, collation, putting in order (of printed sheets).

compaginador, ra, *m.* (print.) pager, collator. —*m., f.* arranger, adjuster.

compaginar, *tr.v.* to arrange in order (sheets of paper); (print.) to page up, to collate, put (pages) in order. —*r.v.* to conform, fit.

companage, *m.* snack, cold meats or cheese eaten with bread.
compango, *m., var. of* **companage.**
compaña, *f.* 1. group, crowd, troupe, retinue. 2. companion; company.
compañerismo, *m.* comradeship, camaraderie, fellowship, companionship.
compañero, ra, *m., f.* 1. companion, friend, pal; workmate, associate. 2. counterpart, twin (of two things which are alike). — **c. de armas,** comrade-in-arms; **c. de colegio,** schoolmate, schoolfriend; **c. de trabajo,** fellow worker, workmate; **c. de viaje,** fellow traveler.
compañía, *f.* company, companionship; (mil., com., theat.) company; **c. anónima,** (com.) stock company; **c. comanditaria,** (com.) silent partnership; **C. de Jesús,** Society of Jesus; **c. del ahorcado,** (coll.) unreliable friend; **c. de la legua,** company of strolling players; **c. de seguros,** insurance company; **c. fiduciaria,** trust company; **c. propietaria,** (com.) closed corporation; **c. regular colectiva,** co-partnership; **dama de c.,** lady companion; **hacer c. a,** to keep (someone) company.
comparabilidad, *f.* comparability.
comparable, *a.* comparable.
comparación, *f.* comparison; (rhet.) simile; (gram.) comparison; **correr la c.,** to be proportionate (said of things being compared).
comparado, da, *past part. of* **comparar.** —*a.* comparative.
comparador, *m.* (phys.) comparator.
comparanza, *f.* comparison.
comparar, *tr.v.* to compare; to check; to collate.
comparativamente, *adv.* comparatively.
comparativo, va, *a.* comparative.
comparecencia, *f.* (law) appearance, (personally or in writing before a judge).
comparecer, (*ref. 45*) *i.v.* (law) to appear in court.
compareciente, *m., f.* (law) appearing party, person appearing in court.
comparendo, *m.* (law) summons.
comparezca, comparezco, *ref.* **comparecer.**
comparición, *f.* (law) appearance; summons.
comparsa, *f.* (theat.) chorus, extras; costumed group (dressed alike at carnival time). —*m., f.* extra, member of the chorus.
comparte, *m., f.* (law) partner (in business); accomplice (in a crime).
compartidor, ra, *m., f.* partner, co-owner.
compartimiento, *m.* 1. distribution, division. 2. enclosure; compartment (of a train, plane, etc.). — **c. de bombas,** bomb bay; **c. estanco,** (mar.) watertight compartment.
compartir, *tr.v.* to share; to divide.
comparto, *m.* (Col.) tax, contribution.
compás, *m.* 1. compass, pair of compasses (for drawing curves); dividers; calipers. 2. compass (for ascertaining directions). 3. territory surrounding a monastery and belonging to it. 4. church atrium. 5. springs (of a coach hood). 6. size. 7. rule (of life), standard, pattern. 8. (astron.) C., Circinus. 9. (fenc.) movement, change of posture. 10. (mus.) tempo, rhythm; time, measure; beat, motion of a conductor's arm marking the rhythm. — **a c.,** in step; **al c. de,** in step with; to the rhythm of; **c. binario.** (mus.) duple time; **c. de agrimensor,** surveyor's compass; **c. de arco,** quadrant compass; **c. de calibres,** inside calipers, caliper compass (calipers measuring distances inside cylinders, bottles, etc.); **c. de cuadrante,** quadrant compass; **c. de dos por cuatro,** (mus.) quadruple time or measure; **c. de espera,** (mus.) bar rest, rest lasting one bar; (coll.) short pause; **c. de espesores** or **de gruesos,** calipers, outside calipers; **c. de exterior,** outside calipers; **c. de precisión.** hair compass, hairspring dividers; **c. de proporción,** proportional compass; **c. de punta seca,** dividers; **c. deslizante** or **de vara,** beam compass; **c. de trazar,** draftsman's compass; **c. de reducción,** proportional dividers; **c. de tres piernas,** triangular compass; **c. extraño,** (fenc.) retreating step made with the left foot; **c. mixto,** (fenc.) step composed of two other basic steps; **c. oblicuo,** (fenc.) side step; **c. recto,** (fenc.) forward step made with the right foot; **fuera de c.,** out of step; **ir con el c. en la mano,** (coll.) to act prudently and carefully; **llevar el c.,** (coll.) to conduct, beat time; **perder el c.,** to lose step, get out of step.
compasadamente, *adv.* carefully, prudently, sensibly.
compasado, da, *past part. of* **compasar.** —*a.* moderate, prudent, sensible.
compasar, *tr.v.* 1. to measure with a compass. 2. to apportion exactly (time, expenses). 3. (mus.) to divide into bars.
compasible, *a.* pitiable, compassionate.
compasillo, *m.* (mus.) four-four time.
compasión, *f.* compassion, mercy, pity, sympathy.
compasionado, da, *a.* passionate, impassioned, ardent, fervent.
compasivamente, *adv.* compassionately, pityingly.
compasivo, va, *a.* compassionate; sympathetic, merciful.
compaternidad, *f.* compaternity, relationship between a godfather and the parents of a child.
compatibilidad, *f.* compatibility.
compatible, *a.* compatible.
compatiblemente, *adv.* compatibly.
compatricio, cia, *m., f., var. of* **compatriota.**
compatriota, *m., f.* compatriot, fellow-citizen. —*m.* countryman, fellow countryman. —*f.* fellow countrywoman.
compatrón, *m., var. of* **compatrono.**
compatronato, *m.* rights and attributes of a joint employer.
compatrono, na, *m., f.* joint employer,
compeler, *tr.v.* to compel, constrain, force, oblige.
compendiador, ra, *a.* summarizing, synoptic, outlining. —*m., f.* summarizer, person who makes a compendium or synopsis.
compendiar, *tr.v.* to summarize, condense, to abridge.
compendiariamente, *adv., var. of* **compendiosamente.**
compendice, compendicé, *ref.* **compendizar.**
compendio, *m.* outline, compendium, synopsis, digest, abstract; resumé; **en c.,** in short, briefly, in a few words.
compendiosamente, *adv.* in a few words, concisely, briefly.
compendioso, sa, *a.* compendious, synoptic, brief, concise.
compendista, *m.* author of an outline or compendium; summarizer, synoptist.
compendizar, (*ref. 53*) *tr.v., var. of* **compendiar.**
compenetración, *f.* compenetration, interpenetration.
compenetrarse, *r.v.* 1. to compenetrate, interpenetrate. 2. to have the same ideas. — **c. en,** to enter fully into; **c. con,** to acquaint oneself fully with; to become thoroughly aware and informed about.
compensable, *a.* compensable, entitled to compensation.
compensación, *f.* compensation, balancing; recompense; **c. de brújula,** compass compensation.
compensador, ra, *a.* compensating, compensative, balancing. —*m.* compensator; compensating pendulum (of a clock); **c. de arranque,** (elec.) starting compensator; **c. elevador,** (elec.) balancer-booster.
compensar, *tr.v.* to compensate; indemnify; to make amends for, make up for. —*r.v.* to compensate oneself; to be compensated.
compensativo, va, *a., var. of* **compensatorio.**
compensatorio, ria, *a.* compensatory, compensative.
competencia, *f.* 1. competition, rivalry. 2. responsibility, obligation. 3. competence, aptitude, fitness. 4. (law) competence, jurisdiction cognizance, legal authority. — **a c.,** competitively, in competition with one another; **de c.,** competitive.
competente, *a.* competent, qualified, apt, capable; (law) competent, legally qualified or authorized; adequate, appropriate, suitable, sufficient.
competentemente, *adv.* competently; adequately, suitably.
competer, *i.v.* 1. to be one's business, concern or duty. 2. to behave, be incumbent on (one), be up to or fall to (one).
competición, *f.* competition, rivalry.
competidor, ra, *a.* competitive, competing, contesting; rival. —*m., f.* competitor; contestant, contender; opponent, rival.
competir, (*ref. 39*) *i.v.* 1. to compete, contest, vie, contend (with someone for something). 2. to match, be on a par. —*r.v.* to compete, compete with one another.
competitivo, va, *a.* competitive (prices).
compilación, *f.* compilation, collection.
compilador, ra, *a.* compiling. —*m., f.* compiler; collector.
compilar, *tr.v.* to compile, anthologize; to gather, collect (literary works).
compilatorio, ria, *a.* compilatory, pertaining to compilation.
compinche, *m., f.* (coll.) bosom friend, pal, chum, buddy.
compita, *ref.* **competir.**
compitales, *f.* (*pl.*) (hist.) Compitalia, Laralia (ancient Roman festival).
compitiendo, compitiera, compitiese, *ref.* competir.
compito, *ref.* **competir.**
complacedero, ra, *a. var. of* **complaciente.**
complacedor, ra, *a.* pleasing, accommodating, agreeable.
complacencia, *f.* pleasure, satisfaction; compliance, complacency; **tener la c. de presentar,** to have the pleasure of presenting.
complacer, (*ref. 13*) *tr.v.* to please, humor; accommodate, gratify. —*r.v.* to be pleased, take pleasure in; to like or enjoy (doing something); **complacerse con, en** or **de,** to take pleasure in.
complacido, da, *past part. of* **complacer.** —*a.* satisfied, content; **c. de sí,** complacent, smug.
complaciente, *a.* obliging, complaisant, accommodating; agreeable, affable, eager to please.
complacimiento, *m., var. of* **complacencia.**
complazca, complazco, complazgo, *ref.* complacer.
complejidad, *f.* complexity, intricacy.
complejo, ja, *a.* complex, intricate; (gram.) complex (sentence); (math.) compound (number). —*m.* complex; **c. de culpa,** guilt complex; **c. de Edipo,** Oedipus complex; **c. de Electra,** Electra complex; **c. de inferioridad,** inferiority complex; **c. deportivo,** sports complex; **c. fundamental,** (geol.) basal complex; **c. hotelero,** hotel complex; **c. industrial,** industrial complex; **c.**

turístico, tourist resort; **c. vitamínico,** vitamin complex.
complementar, *tr.v.* to complement, complete.
complementario, ria, *a.* complementary.
complemento, *m.* complement; (geom.) complement (angle or arc); (gram.) object, complement; **c. directo,** (gram.) direct object; **c. indirecto,** indirect object.
completamente, *adv.* completely, entirely, absolutely, fully; perfectly.
completar, *tr.v.* to complete; to finish, consummate; to perfect.
completas, *f.* (*pl.*) (ecc.) compline.
completivo, va, *a.* completive, complemental, complementary, completing.
completo, ta, *a.* complete, perfect; completed, finished, perfected; full (bus, etc.); **por c.,** completely.
complexidad, *f., var. of* **complejidad.**
complexión, *f.* 1. (physiol.) build, physique; constitution. 2. character, nature, temperament. 3. (rhet.) emphasis given to a sentence by repetition of the word commencing and ending several successive phrases. — **de c. gruesa,** stocky, hefty.
complexionado, da, *a.* **bien c.,** well-built; robust, strong; **mal c.,** weakly-built; weak, frail.
complexional, *a.* (physiol.) constitutional.
complexo, xa, *a., var. of* **complejo.**
complicación, *f.* complication.
complicado, da, *past part. of* **complicar. —***a.* complicated; complex, intricate; (fig.) difficult.
complicar, (*ref. 50*) *tr.v.* 1. complicate, make complicated or involved. 2. to involve (in difficulties, etc.). —*r.v.* 1. to become complicated or involved. 2. to become involved, embroiled or mixed up (in).
cómplice, *m., f.* accomplice, accessory; (coll.) partner in crime; **c. encubridor,** (law) accessory after the fact; **c. instigador,** (law) accessory before the fact.
complicidad, *f.* complicity, abetment.
complique, compliqué, *ref.* **complicar.**
complot, *m.* (coll.) frame-up; intrigue, scheme; (coll.) plot, conspiracy, complot.
complotar, *i.v.* to plot, conspire.
compluvio, *m.* (archeol.) compluvium.
compón, *m.* (her.) each of the squares of alternate tinctures of a componé bearing (on an escutcheon).
componado, da, *a.* (her.) componé.
componedor, ra, *m., f.* 1. arbitrator, referee, peacemaker. 2. dresser, adorner. 3. repairer, mender, fixer. 4. composer. —*m.* 1. (print.) composing stick. 2. (Chile) bonesetter. — **amigable c.,** (law) referee, arbitrator (chosen by litigants); **muchos componedores descomponen a la novia,** too many cooks spoil the broth.
componenda, *f.* 1. fee paid for indulgences. 2. doubtful compromise or agreement or deal; settlement.
componente, *a., m.* component.
componer, (*ref. 15*) *tr.v.* 1. to compose, form, make up; to constitute, compound, prepare. 2. to season, fortify (wine). 3. to tidy up, put in order, arrange; to fix (one's hair); to make beautiful, adorn, decorate. 4. to repair, mend, fix; restore, brace; (coll.) to settle (stomach), fortify, strengthen (health). 5. to settle, adjust (differences); to reconcile (persons). 6. to compose, create, produce (music, art, literature); to write. 7. (print.) to make up, compose, set (type). 8. (Arg.) to train (a gamecock or racehorse). —*i.v.* to compose, write (poetry, music). —*r.v.* 1. to be composed (of), be made up (of). 2. to bedeck or array oneself, dress up. 3. to settle one's differences, be reconciled. — **componérselas,** to manage for oneself, to get by.
componga, compongo, *ref.* **componer.**
componible, *a.* arrangeable, reconcilable, fixable.
comporta, *f.* 1. large basket (used in grape harvesting). 2. (Peru) mold (used in solidifying refined sulphur).
comportable, *a.* endurable, tolerable, bearable.
comportamiento, *m.* conduct, behavior, deportment.
comportar, *tr.v.* (fig.) to bear, tolerate, suffer, endure. —*r.v.* to behave (oneself), act, conduct oneself properly.
comporte, *m.* 1. conduct, behavior. 2. bearing, deportment; manner, carriage.
comportero, ra, *m., f.* maker or seller of grape baskets.
comportilla, *f. dim. of* **comporta,** small basket.
composición, *f.* 1. (mus., lit) composition. 2. settlement, agreement, adjustment. 3. restraint, moderation. 4. (gram.) combination, compounding (of basic words with prefixes).
compositivo, va, *a.* (gram.) combining (of prefixes).
compositor, ra, *m., f.* (mus.) composer.
compostura, *f.* 1. composition, make-up, formation, structure. 2. repair, repairing, mending. 3. tidiness, neatness, trimness, smartness. 4. treatment (given to materials, wines, etc.). 5. settlement, arrangement, adjustment, agreement. 6. moderation, sedateness, sobriety, circumspection. — **en c.,** under repair; **tener mucha c.,** to be very neat or smart.
compota, *f.* (cul.) compote, preserve; stewed fruit; (Cuba) pureed baby food.
compotera, *f.* compote bowl for stewed fruit.
compra, *f.* purchase, buy (coll.); purchasing; buying; shopping; marketing; **hacer** or **ir de compras,** to go shopping.
comprable, *a.* purchasable.
comprachilla, *f.* (Guat.) species of blackbird.
compradillo, *m., var. of* **comprado** (card game).
compradizo, za, *a.* purchasable.
comprado, *past part. of* **comprar. —***a.* bought, purchased. —*m.* card game with four players, similar to ombre.
comprador, ra, *a.* purchasing, buying. —*m., f.* purchaser, buyer, shopper.
comprante, *a., m., f., var. of* **comprador.**
comprar, *tr.v.* 1. to buy, purchase. 2. (fig.) to bribe, buy, buy off. — **c. a fardo cerrado,** to buy a pig in a poke (coll.).
compraventa, *f.* (com.) contract of purchase and sale.
cómpreda, *f.* (arch.) *var. of* **compra.**
comprehensivo, va. *a., var. of* **comprensivo.**
comprendedor, ra, *a.* understanding; encompassing.
comprender, *tr.v.* 1. to understand, comprehend. 2. to comprise, include, embrace, comprehend.
comprensibilidad, *f.* comprehensibility; understanding.
comprensible, *a.* comprehensible, intelligible, understanding.
comprensión, *f.* 1. comprehension, understanding. 2. (log.) intension (aspects comprised in an idea).
comprensividad, *f.* understanding.
comprensivo, va, *a.* understanding, comprehensive, comprehending; comprehensive (embracing or including).
comprenso, sa, *irr. past part. of* **comprender.**
comprensor, ra, *a.* 1. inclusive, embracing, comprising, encompassing. 2. (theol.) blessed (enjoying heavenly bliss). —*m., f.* (theol.) blessed soul (in heaven).
compresa, *f.* (med.) compress; **c. fría,** cold pack; **c. higiénica,** sanitary napkin.
compresbítero, *m.* (ecc.) fellow ordinand.
compresibilidad, *f.* compressibility.
compresible, *a.* compressible, condensable.
compresímetro, *m.* compression gage.
compresión, *f.* compression; (gram.) syneresis; **c. compuesta,** (bridge) combined squeeze; **c. de la imagen,** (tel.) picture compression.
compresivo, va, *a.* compressive; (fig.) restrictive, repressive.
compreso, sa, *irr. past part. of* **comprimir.**
compresor, ra, *a.* compressive, compressing. —*m.* compressor; **c. de aire,** air compressor; **c. centrífugo,** centrifugal compressor.
comprimario, ria, *m., f.* (theat.) singer of supporting roles.
comprimente, *a.* compressing; constricting; repressing, restraining, restricting.
comprimible, *a.* compressible; constrictable; condensable, repressible.
comprimido, da, *past part. of* **comprimir. —***a.* compressed, condensed, e.g. *aire c.,* compressed air; flattened. —*m.* tablet, pastille, pill.
comprimir, *tr.v.* to compress, condense; constrict; to repress, restrain.
comprobable, *a.* provable, verifiable, ascertainable.
comprobación, *f.* verification, check, proof, substantiation.
comprobador, *m.* checker; tester.
comprobante, *a.* verifying, substantiating, proving. —*m.* proof, evidence; voucher, check; **c. de venta,** sales check.
comprobar, (*ref. 33*) *tr.v.* to verify, check; to prove, confirm, substantiate.
comprobatorio, ria, *a.* proving, attesting, verifying, confirming.
comprefesor, ra, *m., f.* colleague, fellow-professional.
comprometedor, ra, *a.* compromising, jeopardising. —*m., f.* something or someone that compromises or jeopardizes.
comprometer, *tr.v.* 1. to compromise, place in a compromising situation (tarnishing one's reputation). 2. to bind, pledge, place under an obligation. 3. (law) to submit to arbitration, entrust to a third party. —*r.v.* 1. to compromise oneself. 2. to commit, bind or pledge oneself; to become involved; to make oneself responsible for. 3. to become engaged or betrothed. 4. to make an engagement or appointment. — **comprometerse a** + *inf.,* to pledge oneself, promise to + *inf.*
comprometimiento, *m.* 1. implication, involvement, predicament, embarrassment (in compromising situation). 2. pledge, promise. 3. obligation.
compromisario, *a.* arbitrating, mediating. —*m.* 1. arbitrator, mediator, umpire, referee. 2. candidate, delegate.
compromiso, *m.* 1. pledge, commitment, promise. 2. engagement (to be married). 3. appointment; engagement, date (coll.). 4. compromising situation, predicament, embarrassment. 5. (law) compromise, arbitration, agreement. 6. delegation, deputation (elected to make an appointment to office).
compromisorio, ria, *a.* of or pertaining to a compromise.
comprovincial, *a.* (ecc.) comprovincial (said of a co-bishop of an archiepiscopal province or diocese).
comprovinciano, na, *m., f.* fellow provincial (of the same province).
compruebe, compruebo, *ref.* **comprobar.**

compuerta, *f.* 1. lock, sluice, floodgate; door hatch, half door; door curtain on old-fashioned coaches. 2. (arch.) scapular bearing a knight's badge or cross. — **c. basculante,** tilting gate; **c. de marea,** tide gate, floodgate; **c. de esclusa,** sluice gate; lock gate; **c. de toma,** (hydr.) intake gate; **c. rodante** or **de rodillos** (hydr.) roller gate; **c. estranguladora,** (a.c.) throttling damper.
compuestamente, *adv.* with composure, in an orderly manner.
compuesto, ta, *irr. past part. of* **componer** —*a.* 1. compound, composite. 2. moderate, sober, circumspect. 3. (bot.) composite (plant). 4. (gram.) compound (word). 5. (archit.) composite. —*m.* (chem.) compound. — **c. aditivo,** (chem.) additive compound or product; **c. de soldar,** soldering paste; **c. cuaternario de amonio,** (chem.) quaternary ammonium compound. —*f.* (bot.) composite (plant); (*pl.*) Compositae.
compulsa, *f.* 1. comparison, collation (of documents). 2. (law) authenticated copy of a document submitted for comparison.
compulsación, *f.* comparison, collation (of documents).
compulsar, *tr.v.* 1. to collate, compare (documents). 2. (law) to make verbatim or authentic copies (of a document). 3. (Amer.) to compel.
compulsión, *f.* compulsion.
compulsivo, va, *a.* compelling, compulsive.
compulso, sa, *irr. past part. of* **compeler.**
compulsorio, ria, *a.* **orden c.,** (law) order allowing copies (of documents) to be made. —*f.* (law) order allowing copies (of documents) to be made.
compunción, *f.* compunction, remorse; pity, distress, sorrow (over another's misfortune).
compungido, da, *past part. of* **compungir.** —*a.* sorrowful, distressed, upset.
compungir, (*ref. 62*) *tr.v.* to move to tears, sorrow or compunction. —*r.v.* to feel compunction or remorse (for one's sins); to be distressed (by), be unhappy (over).
compungivo, va, *a.* pricking, stinging.
compunja, compunjo, *ref.* **compungir.**
compurgación, *f.* (law) compurgation.
compurgador, *m.* compurgator, one swearing the innocence of another.
compurgar, (*ref. 51*) *tr.v.* 1. to try by compurgation. 2. (Mex.) to finish serving (period in prison).
compurgue, compurgué, *ref.* **compurgar.**
compuse, compusiera, compusiese, *ref.* **componer.**
computable *a.* — **esos años no son computables para,** those years do not count toward.
computación, *f.* computing; **curso de c.,** computer course.
computacional *a.* computer, computational.
computadora, *f.* **computador** *m.,* computer; **c. central,** central computer; **c. de a bordo,** onboard computer; **c. de mesa,** desktop computer; **c. doméstica,** home computer; **c. portátil,** laptop computer.
computadorización, *f.* computerization.
computadorizado, da, *a.* computerized.
computadorizar, *tr.v.* to computerize.
computar, *reflex.v.* to count, e.g. *esos años no se computan,* those years do not count.
computerización, computarización, *f.* computerization.
computerizado, computarizado, da, *a.* computerized.
computerizar, computarizar, *tr.v.* to computerize.
computista, *m., f.* computer programer.
cómputo, *m.* computation, calculation; count, counting; estimate; **c. eclesiástico,** ecclesiastical computation to determine the date of movable feasts.
comto, ta, *a.* (rare) precious, over-refined (language, style or manner).
comulación, *f., var. of* **acumulación,** accumulation.
comulgante, *a.* (ecc.) communicant, communicating. —*m., f.* (ecc.) communicant (one who receives Holy Communion).
comulgar, (*ref. 51*) *tr.v.* to administer Holy Communion to. —*i.v.* 1. to take communion, receive Holy Communion. 2. to commune; to have a close rapport with. — **c. con ruedas de molino,** (coll.) to be gullible, be easily taken in.
comulgatorio, *m.* Communion rail; (in nuns' cloisters) small window through which Holy Communion is administered.
comulgue, comulgué, *ref.* **comulgar.**
común, *a.* 1. common, held in common, public, e.g. *bienes comunes,* common property. 2. shared, common, e.g. *con baño c.,* with shared bathroom. 3. usual, ordinary, common, e.g. *precio c.,* usual price. 4. well-known, familiar, common, e.g. *es c. a todos,* it is familiar to everyone. 5. common, vulgar. 6. (gram.) common, e.g. *nombre c.,* common noun. — **c. de dos,** (gram.) common (gender); **c. de tres,** (Lat. gram.) common (adjectives); **sentido c.,** common sense. —*m.* 1. people, population; the community, general public. 2. toilet, water-closet, lavatory. 3. (Mex.) buttocks. — **el c. de las gentes,** the majority of the people; **en c.,** in common, collectively; **por lo c.,** generally, commonly, usually, ordinarily.
comuna, *f.* 1. commune; **la C.,** the Commune, the revolutionary French governments of 1792 and 1871. 2. organization and house shared by a group of compatible people, usually young rebels (U.S.).
comunal, *a.* communal. —*m.* the community.
comunalmente, *adv.* in common, communally.
comunero, ra, *a.* popular, pleasing. —*m., f.* 1. (hist., Sp.) member of the party that rose against Charles I. 2. part-owner, joint owner. 3. (*pl.*) towns with common pasture land. 4. (Peru) member of a village community.
comunicabilidad, *f.* communicability.
comunicable, *a.* communicable, impartable; communicative, sociable, friendly, affable.
comunicación, *f.* communication; connection; official communiqué; rhetorical question; (*pl.*) communications, system of communications (mail, telegraph, telephone).
comunicado, *past part. of* **comunicar.** —*m.* communiqué; public letter or statement, letter to the editor; **c. de prensa,** press release.
comunicador, ra, *a.* communicating, connecting (of doors, etc.).
comunicante, *a., m., f.* communicating.
comunicar, (*ref. 50*) *tr.v.* to communicate; to send, pass on; to impart, to make known; to inform, transmit. —*r.v.* to communicate, communicate with one another.
comunicativo, va, *a.* communicative, affable; infectious (laughter, smile, etc.).
comunicatorias, *a.* (*pl.*) (ecc.) testimonial (letters, given formerly).
comunicatorio, ria, *a.* communicatory.
comunidad, *f.* 1. community, group (of people; of interests); (village) commune, community. 2. (arch.) (*pl.*) people's uprisings in Castile during the reign of Charles. I. — **C. Británica de Naciones,** British Commonwealth; **c. lingüística,** speech community; **de c.,** in common, jointly.
comunión, *f.* 1. communion; union, fellowship. 2. communion, intimate mutual understanding. 3. (ecc.) (Holy) Communion; the Holy Sacrament.
comunique, comuniqué, *ref.* **comunicar.**
comunismo, *m.* Communism.
comunista, *a.* communist, communistic. —*m., f.* Communist.
comúnmente, *adv.* usually, generally, ordinarily; frequently, often.
comuña, *f.* wheat mixed with rye.
comuñas, *f. pl.* any grain but wheat, rye or barley; seeds.
con, *prep.* 1. with. 2. although, in spite of. — **c.** + *inf.,* by + *ger.,* e.g. *c. pagar la cuenta se libró de un pleito,* by paying the bill he avoided a lawsuit; **c. que,** and so, then it, e.g. *c. que fuiste tú quien me mandó el regalo,* so it was you who sent me the gift; **c. tal que,** provided that, so long as; **estar c.** —*n.,* to have + *n.,* e.g. *estar c. fiebre,* to have a temperature.
conación, *f.* (psyc.) conation.
conacho, *m.* (Peru, min.) mortar formerly used for crushing gold or silver ores.
conativo, va, *a.* (psyc.) conative.
conato, *m.* attempt; endeavor, effort, try; (psyc.) conatus.
conca, *f.* 1. shell, snail shell. 2. (sl.) soup bowl.
concadenar, *tr.v.* (fig.) to concatenate, link, join together.
concambio, *m.* exchange.
concanónigo, *m.* (ecc.) fellow canon, joint canon (in the same church).
concatedralidad, *f.* title of cathedral if conferred on a church in conjunction with an already existing cathedral; joint relationship of two cathedrals, whereby the canons of one may sit in the choir of the other.
concatenación, *f.* 1. concatenation, linking. 2. (rhet.) anadiplosis, epanastrophe, repetition, for effect, of the last word of a clause as the first word of the next.
concatenar, *tr.v., var. of* **concadenar.**
concausa, *f.* joint cause, joint origin.
cóncava, *f.* a hollow, a cavity.
concavidad, *f.* concavity, hollowness.
cóncavo, va, *a,* concave. —*m.* 1. concavity, concave surface. 2. (min.) free space left around the mouth of a mine shaft to provide space for operation of the drill.
concavoconvexo, a, *a.* concavo-convex.
concebible, *a,* conceivable.
concebimiento, *m.* conception.
concebir, (*ref. 39*) *i.v.* 1. to conceive, become pregnant. 2. to conceive, imagine. —*tr.v.* 1. to conceive (an idea; a baby). 2. to take (a liking to someone or something). 3. to write, express, e.g. *una carta concebida en términos enérgicos,* a letter written in strong language.
concedente, *a.* conceding, granting. —*m., f.* conceder, granter.
conceder, *tr.v.* 1. to concede, admit, grant, bestow; to give. 2. to agree about.
concedido, da, *a.* conceded, granted.
concejal, *m.* councillor, alderman, councilman.
concejala, *f.* wife of a councillor; female councillor, councilwoman.
concejalía, *f.* councillorship, dignity or office of councillor.
concejeramente, *adv.* openly, publicly.
concejero, ra, *a.* open, public. —*m.* (Amer.) councilman.
concejil, *a.* council, pertaining to a council, common, public; (arch.) sent into the armed services by a council.
concejo, *m.* 1. town-council, board of aldermen; council-house, town hall; towncouncil, meeting. 2. (rare) foundling. — **c. abierto,** full council,

public council; **c. de la Mesta,** yearly meeting of cattlebreeders and shepherds.
concento, *m.* (mus.) harmonious singing.
concentrabilidad, *f.* ability to concentrate.
concentrable, *a.* capable of being concentrated.
concentración, *f.* concentration.
concentrado, da, *past part. of* **concentrar.** —*a.* 1. centered, placed at the center of something. 2. concentrated (alcohol). 3. withdrawn, uncommunicative, introspective (character).
concentrador, ra, *a.* concentrative, concentrating.
concentrar, *tr.v.* 1. to concentrate; to focus, center. 2. (chem.) to make concentrated, make a concentrated solution of. 3. to control, restrain (anger). —*r.v.* 1. to become concentrated. 2. to be focussed, centered. 3. to withdraw into oneself, become withdrawn or introspective.
concentricidad, *f.* concentricity.
concéntrico, ca, *a.* (geom.) concentric.
concentuoso, sa, *a.* harmonious.
concepción, *f.* conception, act of conceiving; (ecc.) feast of the Immaculate Conception. — **la Inmaculada C.** or **la Purísima C.,** (theol.) the Immaculate Conception.
concepcionista, *a., f.* (ecc.) Conceptionist (said of a nun belonging to the third Franciscan Order of the Immaculate Conception).
conceptáculo, *m.* (bot.) conceptacle.
conceptear, *i.v.* to use ingenious or clever expressions, make puns or witty remarks.
conceptible, *a.* conceivable.
conceptismo, *m.* (lit.) conceptism (literary style of 17th century Spain characterized by conceits and puns).
conceptista, *a.* conceptist, full of conceits or puns, euphuistic. —*m., f.* conceptist writer, writer employing many conceits and puns.
conceptivo, va, *a.* capable of conceiving.
concepto, *m.* 1. concept, idea. 2. conceit, witticism, pun. 3. opinion, judgment, esteem. — **en todo c.,** in every respect; **formar un c.,** to form an idea of; **por c. de,** on account of; **¿en qué concepto?** from what point of view? **por ningún concepto,** not on any terms, by no means.
conceptual, *a.* conceptual.
conceptualismo, *m.* (philos.) conceptualism.
conceptualista, *a.* (philos.) conceptualistic. —*m., f.* (philos.) conceptualist.
conceptuar, (*ref. 55*) *tr.v.* to consider, regard, deem, think, believe, e.g. *estar conceptuado de* or *por rico,* to be considered or thought rich.
conceptuosamente, *adv.* 1. pithily; epigrammatically, sententiously. 2. using conceits and word play, wittily.
conceptuosidad, *f.* pithiness, sententiousness, epigrammatism.
conceptuoso, sa, *a.* 1. pithy, meaty, epigrammatic. 2. full of conceits and word play.
concernencia, *f.* relationship, relation.
concerniente, *a.* concerning; relating or applicable (to); **en lo c. a,** in or with regard to, as for.
concernir, (*ref. 31*) *tr.v.* to concern; relate to, belong to. —*i.v.* to belong, be pertinent.
concertadamente, *adv.* 1. in an orderly manner; harmoniously. 2. by previous agreement or appointment.
concertado, da, *past part. of* **concertar.** —*a.* concerted, arranged (e.g. a marriage).
concertador, ra, *a.* arranging. —*m., f.* arranger. — **c. de privilegios,** person who issues royal grants or privileges.
concertante, *a.* (mus.) 1. concerted, arranged for two or more voices or instruments. 2. contracting (parties in a contract or deal). —*m.* (mus.) arrangement for two or more voices.
concertar, (*ref. 29*) *tr.v.* 1. to arrange, agree upon, fix (etc.); to make (peace, a business deal, etc.). 2. to bring together, reconcile, unite; to harmonize. 3. to coordinate (e.g. the arrival of a plane with the departure of a train). 4. (gram.) to make (nouns and adjectives) agree. 5. (hunt.) to rouse (the game). —*i.v.* to agree; (gram.) to agree. —*r.v.* to become reconciled, come to an agreement; to unite, join together.
concertina, *f.* (mus.) concertina, musical instrument that resembles an accordeon but has buttons rather than a keyboard.
concertino, *m.* (mus.) first violin, leader (of orchestra), concertmaster.
concertista, *m., f.* player, performer, concert pianist, violinist or singer.
concesible, *a.* grantable, concedable.
concesión, *f.* 1. concession; grant (e.g. by a government). 2. (rhet.) epistrophe.
concesionario, *m.* (law) concessionaire, one receiving a concession.
concesivo, va, *a.* 1. concessive; 2. concessible, grantable.
concha, *f.* 1. shell; (zool.) oyster; scallop; tortoise shell. 2. (theat.) prompt box. 3. (mar.) closed bay, cove. 4. millstone. 5. insignia, badge (worn by members of a knightly order). 6. (anat.) concha (of the ear). 7. (Arg., Chile, Urug., vulg.) cunt (vulg.). 8. (Guat.) egg shell. 9. (Col., Ven.) sluggishness. 10. (Peru) crude hearth (for cooking) made of three rocks. 11. (mar.) a bay, sometimes shallow, well protected by land. — **c. de perla,** mother-of-pearl; **meterse uno en su c.,** to withdraw into one's shell; **salir de su c.,** to come out of one's shell; **tener c.,** (Ecuad., Peru, coll.) **to be fresh.**
conchabado, da, *past part. of* **conchabar.**
conchabanza, *f.* 1. comfort, comfortable position. 2. (coll.) ganging-up, banding together, conspiracy, plotting, plot.
conchabar, *tr.v.* to join, unite. 2. to mix first class wool with second class. 3. (Amer.) to hire. —*r.v.* 1. to gang, band or join together. 2. (Amer.) to be hired.
conchabero, ra, *m., f.* pieceworker, hired hand.
conchabo, *m.* 1. domestic service, menial job; any job or work for hire or pay. 2. (Arg., hum.) any place of employment; any employment. 3. (Chile) barter, exchange.
conchado, da, *a.* conchiferous, crustaceous, with a shell.
conchal, *a.* superior quality, first class (said of silk spun from selected cocoons).
conchar, *tr.v.* (Ecuad.) to drink to the last drop. —*i.v.* 1. to drink the cheapest liquor. 2. (Dom. Rep.) to drive a cheap rattle-trap taxi.
conchero, *m.* conchiferous or shelly deposit (prehistoric deposit of shells, mollusks, fish).
conchesta, *f.* (Sp., reg.) snowdrift.
conchífero, ra, *a.* (geol.) conchiferous.
conchil, *m.* (zool.) species of non-spinose murex or rock shell.
conchilla, ita, *dim. of* **concha.**
concho, cha, *a.* 1. (Ecuad.) amber or fawncolored, tan. 2. (Peru) dark red. 3. (Chile) bottom, end (as *a.*).
concho, *m.* 1. sediment, dregs. 2. (*pl.*) (Amer.) left-overs (of food). 3. (C. Rica) simple rural inhabitant. 4. (Dom. Rep.) cheap, rattle-trap taxi. 5. (Ecuad.) corn husk. — **hasta el c.,** (Amer.) to the finish; **irse al c.,** (Chile) to sink; **c. primo,** (Dom. Rep.) symbol of the Dominican people.
conchudo, da, *a.* 1. conchiferous, shellbearing (animal). 2. (coll.) reserved, cautious. 3. (coll.) cunning, crafty, wily, shrewd. 4. (Amer., coll.) idiotic; sluggish. 5. (Ecuad., Mex., Peru) fresh, brazen (person). 6. (P. Rico) obstinate; reckless.
conchuela, *f.* 1. *dim. of* **concha,** small shell. 2. (mar.) seabed strewn with broken seashells.
concia, *f.* (hunt.) private preserve, private hunting ground (private part of the woods where trespassing is forbidden); forest reserves or reservation.
conciba, concibo, *ref.* **concebir.**
concibiendo, concibiera, concibiese, *ref.* concebir.
conciencia, *f.* 1. conscience, moral awareness, integrity, scruples; conscientiousness, reliability. 2. consciousness, awareness. — **a c.,** conscientiously, honestly; **acusar a uno la c.,** to have pangs, twinges of conscience, feel guilty, e.g. *la c. me está acusando,* my conscience is bothering me; **ancho de c.,** morally lax; **cagar uno la c.,** to burden one's conscience; **c. doble,** (psyc.) double consciousness; **c. limpia,** clear conscience; **c. sucia,** guilty conscience; **descargar uno la c.,** to ease one's conscience; to unburden one's conscience, confess (one's sins); **en c.,** in all conscience; according to one's conscience; **estrecho de c.,** strict, uncompromising; **libertad de c.,** freedom of thought; **hombre de c.,** man of integrity; **hombre sin c.,** unscrupulous man.
concienzudamente, *adv.* conscientiously.
concienzudo, da, *a.* conscientious, scrupulous, thorough, painstaking; high-principled.
concierna, concierne, *ref.* **concernir.**
concierte, concierto, *ref.* **concertar.**
concierto, *m.* 1. concert, harmony. 2. agreement, contract, arrangement, settlement. 3. (mus.) concert (performance); concerto (composition). — **de c.,** in concert, together, in agreement; **piano de c.,** concert grand.
conciliable, *a.* reconcilable.
conciliábulo, *m.* 1. conciliabule, conventicle. 2. clandestine meeting. 3. unlawful assembly.
conciliación, *f.* 1. reconciliation, conciliation, settlement (of disputes). 2. compatibility, affinity; concordance, harmony; agreement. 3. (fig.) favor, protection.
conciliador, ra, *a.* conciliatory, conciliative, reconciling.
conciliar, *a.* council, pertaining to councils. —*m., f.* council member.
conciliar, *tr.v.* 1. to conciliate, reconcile; to win or earn the good will of. 2. (rare) to earn the hatred of. —*r.v.* to win or earn good will. — **c. el sueño,** to induce sleep.
conciliativo, va, *a.* conciliative, reconciling. —*m.* conciliator, reconciler.
conciliatorio, ria, *a.* conciliatory, reconciliatory.
concilio, *m.* council; council decrees. — **c. ecuménico,** (ecc.) ecumenical council.
concino, na, *a.* (rare, lit.) concinnous, elegant (style).
concíón, *f.* (rare) sermon.
concionador, ra, *m., f.* preacher, public speaker.
concisamente, *adv.* concisely, succinctly; briefly.
concisión, *f.* conciseness, succinctness.
conciso, sa, *a.* concise, succinct.
concitación, *f.* instigation, incitement, provocation.
concitador, ra, *a.* instigating, inciting, provoking. —*m., f.* instigator, inciter, provoker, agitator.
concitar, *tr.v.* to agitate, stir up, incite.
concitativo, va, *a.* inciting, agitating, provoking.
conciudadano, na, *m., f.* fellow citizen, fellow townsman. —*m.* countryman. —*f.* countrywoman.
conclave, *m., var. of* **cónclave.**
cónclave, *m.* conclave, meeting of cardinals to elect the pope; (fig.) any meeting of importance.

conclavista, *m.* (ecc.) conclavist (ecclesiastic attendant of a cardinal at a conclave).
concluir, (*ref. 48*) *tr.v.* 1. to conclude, finish, end, close (e.g. a business deal). 2. to conclude, deduce. 3. to convince. 4. to put the finishing touches to (a work of art). 5. (law) to sum up. 6. (fenc.) to disarm (the adversary) by catching his sword by the hilt. —*i.v., r.v.* to finish, end. — **c. de** + *inf.*, to finish + *ger.*, e.g. *c. de pintar el cuadro,* to finish painting the picture.
conclusion, *f.* conclusion, end; (law) (*gen. pl.*) summing up. — **en c.,** in conclusion, finally, to conclude.
conclusivo, va, *a.* conclusive, final.
concluso, sa, *irr. past part. of* **concluir.** —*a.* (law) closed (case) pending sentence.
concluya, concluyendo, concluyera, concluyese, concluyo, *ref.* **concluir.**
concluyente, *a.* conclusive, convincing, unequivocal. — **argumento c.,** convincing argument; **hablar en términos concluyentes,** to speak in unequivocal terms.
concluyentemente, *adv.* conclusively.
concofrade, *m.* fellow member of a brotherhood or confraternity.
concoide, *a.* conchoidal. —*f.* (geom.) conchoid.
concoideo, a, *a.* conchoidal.
concolega, *m.* shoolmate.
concomerse, *r.v.* (coll.) 1. to wriggle one's back and shoulders, to shrug. 2. (fig.) to fidget; to itch, squirm, burn (with impatience, etc.); to be gnawed or eaten up (with envy); to be consumed (with pain, grief).
concomimiento, *m.* (coll.) wriggling; itch, itching; fidgeting, squirming; gnawing.
concomio, *m., var. of* **concomimiento.**
concomitancia, *f.* concomitance, accompaniment; coexistence.
concomitante, *a.* concomitant, accompanying.
concomitar, *tr.v.* to accompany, go together with.
concón, *m.* (ornith., Chile) barn owl (Strix alueo).
concordable, *a.* conciliable, reconcilable; concordant, consistent; conformable.
concordablemente, *adv.* concordantly, conformably, in accordance.
concordación, *f.* coordination; combination; conformity.
concordador, ra, *a.* coordinating; conciliating; appeasing, pacifying; harmonizing. —*m., f.* coordinator, conciliator, moderator, pacifier, peacemaker.
concordancia, *f.* agreement, concordance; (gram.) agreement; (mus.) harmony; (*pl.*) concordance (alphabetical index of the principal words in a book).
concordante, *a.* concordant, agreeing.
concordar, (*ref. 33*) *tr.v.* to conciliate, reconcile, bring to an agreement; to harmonize; to make tally or agree; (gram.) to make agree. —*i.v.* to agree, tally, to be congenial, be in agreement; (gram.) to agree.
concordata, *f., var. of* **concordato.**
concordatario, ria, *a.* concordat, pertaining to a concordat.
concordativo, va, *a.* conciliating, reconciling.
concordato, *m.* (ecc.) concordat, an agreement between a pope and a government with regard to the interests of the church.
concorde, *a.* in agreement.
concordemente, *adv.* in agreement, by mutual consent.
concordia, *f.* 1. concord, harmony, accord; settlement, agreement. 2. double finger ring. — **de c.,** jointly, by common consent.
concorpóreo, a, *a.* (theol.) one with Christ (said of a communicant who receives Holy Communion worthily).
concreado, da, *a.* innate, inborn, inherent.
concreción, *f.* concretion; (med.) stone, calculus, e.g. *c. biliaria,* gallstone.
concrecionar, *i.v., r.v.* to form into concretions, concrete.
concrescencia, *f.* (bot.) concrescence.
concretamente, *adv.* concretely, specifically.
concretar, *tr.v.* 1. to make concrete, make real, realize, make come true. 2. to make more concrete, explicit, clear or precise, explain. —*r.v.* to limit or confine oneself.
concreto, ta, *a.* concrete, specific; dense; thick; **en concreto,** succinctly, in short, briefly. —*m.* 1. concretion. 2. (Amer., bldg.) concrete.
concubina, *f.* concubine, mistress; (law) common law wife.
concubinario, *m.* concubinary, person who has a concubine or mistress.
concubinato, *m.* concubinage, hetairism; (law) common law marriage.
concúbito, *m.* coitus, concubitus.
concuerda, por c., verbatim, faithful to the original manuscript.
concuerda, concuerde, *ref.* **concordar.**
conculcación, *f.* 1. treading on, trampling (with the feet). 2. trampling on, infringement, infraction or violation (of rights, laws, etc.).
conculcador, ra, *a.* trampling; transgressing, infringing, violating.
conculcar, (*ref. 50*) *tr.v.* 1. to trample, tread under foot. 2. to infringe on (rights); violate, break (rules, etc.).
conculque, conculqué, *ref.* **conculcar.**
concuna, *f.* (Col.) species of wild pigeon (Columba palumbus).
concuñado, da, *m., f.* spouse of one's own spouse's brother or sister.
concuño, ña, *m., f.* (Amer.), *var. of* **concuñado.**
concupiscencia, *f.* 1. concupiscence, lust (esp. sexual), carnality. 2. avarice, greed.
concupiscente, *a.* 1. concupiscent, lustful, carnal. 2. greedy, avaricious.
concupiscible, *a.* concupiscible, desirable; sensual, voluptuous, sensuous.
concurrencia, *f.* 1. crowd, gathering, assembly, audience, attendance. 2. concurrence, coincidence. 3. competition, rivalry. 4. assistance, help.
concurrente, *a.* 1. concurrent, coinciding (in time). 2. attending, in attendance. 3. contending, competing. —*m., f.* 1. person in attendance. 2. competitor.
concurrido, da, *past part. of* **concurrir.** —*a.* well attended, full of people, crowded.
concurrir, *i.v.* 1. to meet, assemble, gather; to attend, be present. 2. to concur, agree. 3. to compete, contend. 4. to coincide (in time). — **c. a,** to be present at, attend; to compete, take part in; **c. en,** to agree with, concur with.
concursado, *m.* (law) debtor (declared as such by bankruptcy law).
concursante, *m., f.* competitor, participant; candidate (in an examination for a public post); contestant.
concursar, *tr.v.* (law) to declare insolvent or bankrupt. —*i.v.* to take part or be a candidate in an examination for a public post.
concurso, *m.* 1. concourse, assembly, gathering, crowd, congregation. 2. concurrence, simultaneous happening. 3. aid, assistance, cooperation. 4. exhibition (with prizes). 5. contest, competition. 6. licitation, bidding (to obtain a contract). — **c. de acreedores,** meeting of creditors, bankruptcy proceedings; **c. de belleza,** beauty contest; **c. hípico,** horse show; **fuera de c.,** out of the running; **presentarse a c.,** to enter a contest.
concusión, *f.* 1. concussion. 2. extortion.
concusionario, ria, *a.* concussive, shaking. —*m., f.* extortionist, extortioner.
condado, *m.* earldom, countship (dignity, jurisdiction or possessions of an earl or count); county, shire (land held by a count or earl).
condal, *a.* of or pertaining to an earl or count.
conde, *m.* 1. count, earl. 2. gypsy chief. 3. (Sp., reg.) overseer. — **C. de Barcelona,** one of the titles of the king of Spain.
condecente, *a.* suitable, fit, appropriate, proper.
condecir, (*ref. 7*) *i.v.* to fit, go with, harmonize with, match.
condecoración, *f.* decoration, medal, badge; bestowal of decorations, decoration ceremony.
condecorar, *tr.v.* to decorate (with honors, medals, etc.); to invest (with), bestow (on).
condena, *f.* (law) sentence; **c. condicional,** suspended sentence; **cumplir una c.,** to serve a sentence; **c. judicial,** (law) conviction.
condenable, *a.* condemnable; blamable, censurable, reprehensible.
condenación, *f.* condemnation; (rel.) damnation; (law) judgment, sentence, conviction.
condenado, da, *past part. of* **condenar.** —*a.* 1. reprobate; (fig.) perverse, wicked, vicious. 2. (Chile) astute, shrewd. —*m., f.* convict, criminal; reprobate; wretch.
condenador, ra, *a.* condemnatory, incriminating, condemning; censuring, denouncing, disapproving. —*m., f.* condemner.
condenar, *tr.v.* 1. to condemn; to sentence. 2. to condemn, censure, denounce. 3. to seal up, board up (a room, door, window). — **le condenaron por ladrón,** they sentenced him for theft. —*r.v.* 1. to condemn oneself. 2. to be damned, suffer eternal damnation.
condenatorio, ria, *a.* condemnatory.
condensabilidad, *f.* condensability.
condensable, *a.* condensable.
condensación, *f.* condensation.
condensado, *m.* condensate.
condensador, ra, *a.* condensing, condenser (as *a.*). —*m.* condenser. — **c. a vacío,** vacuum condenser; **c. de acoplamiento,** (rad.) coupling condenser; **c. de filtro,** (rad.) filter capacitor; **c. de fuerzas,** (mec.) accumulator; **c. de paso** or **derivación,** (elec.) by-pass condenser; **c. de rejilla,** (rad.) grid condenser; **c. de sintonía,** (rad.) tuning condenser; **c. de un paso,** single-flow condenser; **c. eléctrico,** (elec.) condenser, capacitor, storage battery; **c. múltiple,** gang condenser; **c. patrón,** standard capacitor; **c. rotatorio** or **sincrónico,** (elec.) rotatory or synchronous condenser; **c. variable,** (rad.) variable condenser.
condensante, *a.* condensing.
condensar, *tr.v.* to condense, compress; (fig.) to abridge. —*r.v.* to be condensed, to thicken.
condensativo, va, *a.* condensing.
condenso, sa, *irr. past part. of* **condensar.**
condesa, *f.* countess.
condesar, *tr.v.* to save, economize.
condescendencia, *f.* condescension; complaisance, indulgence, tolerance.
condescender, (*ref. 30*) *i.v.* to agree; to accede, acquiesce, yield; **c. a** or **en,** to be gracious enough to, be pleasant or nice enough to, be kind enough to, e.g. *el rey condescendió a darme la mano,* the king was gracious enough to shake my hand; to agree to e.g. *el escritor famoso condescendió a venir a darnos una conferencia,* the famous writer agreed to give us a lecture; to accede to, yield, e.g. *c. a sus ruegos,* to yield to one's requests.

condescendiente, *a.* complaisant, obliging, indulgent, tolerant, acquiescent, easy-going.
condescienda, condesciendo, *ref.* **condescender.**
condesil, *a.* (hum.) of a count or earl.
condestable, *m.* 1. (arch.) constable, Lord High Constable. 2. (mar.) artillery sergeant.
condestablesa, *f.* wife of a Lord High Constable.
condestablía, *f.* constableship.
condice, condiciendo, *ref.* **condecir.**
condicíon, *f.* 1. condition, state. 2. condition, stipulation, proviso. 3. social status, position or rank. 4. character, nature, disposition. 5. (*pl.*) ability, aptitude, talent. 6. (*pl.*) conditions, circumstances. — **a c. de** or **bajo la c. de que,** on condition that, under the condition that; **c. callada** or **tácita,** (law) implicit or implied condition; **c. casual,** (law) contingent condition; **c. imposible de derecho,** (law) condition contrary to law; **c. imposible de hecho,** (law) physically impossible condition; **c. resolutoria,** (law) resolutory condition, defeasance; **condiciones atmosféricas,** weather conditions; **condiciones de entrega,** terms of delivery; **condiciones de pago,** terms of payment; **condiciones de venta,** conditions of sale; **de c.,** of importance or rank (a person); **de c. que,** in such a way that; **en condiciones de navegabilidad,** airworthy; seaworthy; **quebrarle a uno la c.,** to take someone down a peg; **tener condiciones,** to be qualified or well equipped (for a job, a task).
condicionado, da, *past part. of* **condicionar.** —*a.* conditional. — **trabajo mal c.,** work under bad conditions; **c. a,** subject to, conditioned by.
condicional, *a.* conditional.
condicionalmente, *adv.* conditionally, provisionally.
condicionamiento, *a.* (tex.) analysis, testing (of fibers).
condicionar, *i.v.* to agree, fit, suit. —*tr.v.* 1. to condition; to prepare. 2. (tex.) to analize, test (fibers).
condiga, condigo, *ref.* **condecir.**
condignamente, *adv.* correspondingly, fittingly.
condigno, na, *a.* fitting, corresponding, condign, e.g. *la pena es condigna del delito,* the penalty fits the crime.
condije, condijera, codijese, *ref.* **condecir.**
condilar, *a.* (anat.) condylar.
cóndilo, *m.* (anat.) condyle (joint).
condiloideo, a, *a.* (anat.) condyloid.
condiloma, *m.* (med.) condyloma.
condimentación, *f.* condimenting, seasoning.
condimentar, *tr.v.* to season, flavor.
condimento, *m.* condiment, seasoning.
condiré, *ref.* **condecir.**
condiscípulo, la, *m., f.* fellow student, schoolmate, schoolfellow, condisciple.
condolecerse, (*ref. 45*) *r.v., var. of* **condolerse.**
condolencia, *f.* condolence, commiseration.
condolerse, (*ref. 34*) *r.v.* to condole, to sympathize, feel sorry, feel pity. — **c. de** or **por,** to sympathize with, feel sorry or pity for.
condolezca, condolezco, *ref.* **condolecerse.**
condominio, *m.* (law) joint ownership; condominium.
condómino, *m., f.* (law) joint owner.
condón, *m.* condom, contraceptive.
condonación, *f.* condoning, forgiving, pardoning, remission.
condonante, *a.* condoning, pardoning, forgiving, remitting.
condonar, *tr.v.* to condone, pardon, excuse, forgive; to release from (a debt).
cóndor, *m.* 1. (ornith.) condor. 2. (Col., Chile, num.) a gold coin.
condotiero, *m.* (Ital.) condottiere, mercenary soldier.
condrila, *f.* (bot.) gum succory (Chondrilla juncea).
condrín, *m.* (Phil. I.) unit of weight for precious metals.
condrioma, *m.* (biol.) chondriome.
condriosoma, *m.* (biol.) chondriosome.
condrito, *m.* (astron., geol.) chondrite.
condrocráneo, *m.* (anat.) chondrocranium.
condrografía, *f.* (anat.) decription of cartilages.
condrología, *f.* (anat.) chondrology, the sum of knowledge of the cartilages.
condroma, *m.* (med.) chondroma.
condropterigio, gia, *m., a.* (ichth.) chondropterygian. —*m., pl.* chondropterygii.
cóndrulo, *m.* (astron., geol.) chondrule.
conducción, *f.* 1. transportation, conveyance. 2. (auto.) driving; (auto.) drive, e.g. *c. por la izquierda* or *derecha,* left-hand or right-hand driving. 3. pipes, piping, pipeline. 4. (phys.) conduction. 5. agreement (on prices or salaries). — **c. de calor,** (engin.) thermal conduction; **c. de tiro,** (artil.) fire control; **c. electrolítica,** (chem.) electrolytic conduction.
conducencia, *f., var. of* **conducción.**
conducente, *a.* conducive, leading.
conducir, (*ref. 47*) *tr.v.* 1. to carry, transport, convey. 2. to lead, guide. 3. to drive (a wagon, car). 4. to lead, command (an army). 5. to direct, conduct, manage (a business, etc.). 6. to fix, stipulate (prices, salaries). —*i.v.* to lead, go. —*r.v.* behave, act, conduct oneself.
conducta, *f.* 1. conduct, behavior. 2. guidance; convoy; anything transported in a convoy. 3. management (of a business); government (of a state). 4. wage paid by a village to a rural doctor. 5. contingent of new recruits joining a regiment. — **mejorar de c.,** to mend one's ways, to improve one's conduct.
conductancia, *f.* (engin.) conductance. — **c. anódica,** (rad.) plate conductance; **c. electródica,** (rad.) electrode or grid or plate conductance; **c. molar,** (chem.) molar conductance, molecular conductivity.
conductero, *m.* leader of a convoy.
conductibilidad, *f.* conductivity.
conductible, *a.* conveyable, conductible.
conductividad, *f.* conductivity. — **c. magnética,** (elec.) magnetic conductivity; permeability; **c. molecular,** (chem.) molecular conductivity, permeability; **c. térmica,** (engin.) thermal conductivity.
conductivo, va, *a.* conductive, conducive, conducing.
conducto, *m.* channel, conduit, pipe; (anat.) duct, canal; (fig.) channels, mediation, agency; **c. alimenticio,** alimentary canal; **c. auditivo,** ear canal; **c. biliar,** (anat.) bile duct; **c. de desagüe,** sewer, drain; **c. de humo,** flue; **c. deferente,** (anat.) emissary duct (in testicles); **c. hepático,** (anat.) bile duct, hepatic duct; **c. portacable,** (elec.) cable duct; **c. surtidor,** supply pipe; **por c. de,** through, by means of.
conductor, ra, *a.* conducting. —*m.* 1. driver (of an omnibus, etc.). 2. (phys.) conductor (of electricity, heat, etc.). 3. (law) tenant (of a house). 4. (Amer.) conductor, e.g. *c. de orquesta,* orchestra conductor. — **c. a tierra,** ground wire, grounding conductor; **c. de entrada,** (elec.) lead-in wire; **c. de gusano,** screw conveyor; **conductores de compensación,** (elec.) compensatory leads.
conducho, *m.* food, provisions; food exacted from vassals by their lords.
conduela, conduelo, *ref.* **condolerse.**
condueño, ña, *m., f.* joint owner, co-owner.
conduerma, *f.* (Ven.) drowsiness, sluggishness.
conduje, condujese, condujera, *ref.* **conducir.**
condumio, *m.* 1. (coll.) food eaten with bread; abundance of food. 2. (Mex.) kind of nougat.
conduplicación, *f.* (rhet.) reduplication, repetition of the last word of a sentence at the beginning of the next.
conduplicado, da, *a.* (bot.) conduplicate.
condurango, *m.* (Ecuad., bot.) condurango (Marsdenia condurango).
condutal, *m.* gutter.
conduzca, conduzco, *ref.* **conducir.**
conectador, *m.* (elec.) connector; (mech.) connecting rod, coupling.
conectar, *tr.v.* to connect; to couple; to plug in.
conectivo, va, *a.* connective, connecting; coupling.
conector, *m.* connector; **c. a tierra,** (elec.) grounding connector; **c. de bridas,** flanged connector; **c. en cruz,** cross connector; **c. en T,** T connector.
coneja, *f.* doe rabbit; **ser una c.,** (coll.) to be fertile as a rabbit.
conejal, *m., var. of* **conejar.**
conejar, *m.* rabbit warren or farm.
conejera, *f.* 1. rabbit warren, hutch, rabbit burrow; rabbitry, place where rabbits are bred. 2. long narrow cave. 3. (coll.) den (of vice), dive, hangout (for the underworld). 4. (fig.) overcrowded room.
conejero, ra, *a.* rabbit-hunting (dog). —*m., f.* rabbit breeder; rabbit seller.
conejillo, *m. dim. of* **conejo,** bunny, little rabbit. — **c. de Indias,** guinea pig.
conejo, *m.* rabbit; **el c. ido, el consejo venido,** it's no good locking the stable door after the horse has bolted.
conejuelo, *m. dim. of* **conejo,** bunny rabbit.
conejuno, na, *a.* of or pertaining to a rabbit, rabbit-like. —*f.* rabbit fur.
conexidades, *f.* (*pl.*) appurtenances, adjuncts.
conexión, *f.* 1. connection. 2. (*pl.*) connections, friends. — **c. de estrella,** (elec.) Y connection; **c. de trompeta,** (auto.) banjo connection; **c. en cascada,** (elec.) cascade rectifier circuit; **c. en tríangulo** or **de delta,** (elec.) delta connection; **c. perfecta a tierra,** (elec., rad.) dead ground.
conexionar, *tr.v.* to connect, join, link.
conexionarse, *r.v.* to make social or commercial connections; to get in touch or contact with.
conexivo, va, *a.* connective.
conexo, xa, *a.* connected, related; (law) linked (crimes which should be dealt with in the same case).
confabulación, *f.* 1. conspiracy, collusion, plot; scheming, plotting, conspiring, conniving. 2. conference, discussion.
confabulador, ra, *m., f.* 1. schemer, plotter, conniver. 2. (arch.) narrator of fables. 3. participant in a conference or discussion.
confabular, *i.v.* to discuss, confer. —*r.v.* to plot, scheme, collude, connive.
confalón, *m.* gonfalon, standard, banner, flag.
confalonier, *m., var. of* **confaloniero.**
confaloniero, *m.* gonfalonier, standard bearer.
confarreación, *f.* confarreation (the highest form of marriage among the ancient Romans).
confección, *f.* 1. making (of a dress); workmanship, manufacture, confection. 2. (pharm.) confection, concoction. 3. ready-made suit or dress.
confeccionador, ra, *a.* making, manufacturing. —*m., f.* maker, confectioner, manufacturer.
confeccionar, *tr.v.* to make, prepare; to make (a dress); (pharm.) to confect, compound (prescriptions).

confector, *m.* gladiator.
confederación, *f.* confederation, alliance, league, federation.
confederado, da, *past part. of* **confederar.** —*a.* confederate, confederated, allied. —*m., f.* confederate, ally.
confederar, *tr.v., r.v.* to confederate, ally.
confederativo, va, *a.* confederative.
conferencia, *f.* 1. lecture, talk. 2. conference; discussion; meeting, assembly. 3. **c. interurbana,** long-distance telephone call; **c. a cobro revertido,** collect call; **c. persona a persona,** person-to-person call. — **c. de prensa,** press conference; **c. en la cima** or **cumbre,** summit conference.
conferenciante, *m., f.* lecturer, speaker.
conferenciar, *i.v.* to confer, hold a discussion.
conferencista, *m., f.* (Amer.) *var. of* **conferenciante.**
conferir, (*ref.42*) *tr.v.* 1. to confer, award, bestow, grant. 2. to compare. 3. to attribute. —*i.v.* to confer, consult, talk (with).
confesa, *f.* widow who became a nun.
confesable, *a.* able to be confessed, admittable.
confesado, da, *past part. of* **confesar.** —*m., f.* (coll.) penitent.
confesante, *a.* confessing. —*m., f.* (law) plaintiff or defendant who makes a declaration in court.
confesar, (*ref. 29*) *tr.v.* 1. to confess, acknowledge. 2. (ecc.) to hear confession (a priest). — **c. uno de plano,** to make a clean breast of. —*r.v.* to confess; (ecc.) to make confession, confess one's sins; **confesarse a Dios,** to confess to God; **confesarse con su confesor,** to confess one's sins to one's confessor; **confesarse de sus culpas,** to confess one's faults.
confesión, *f.* 1. confession; admission (of guilt, sins, etc.). 2. faith, avowal. 3. (law) testimony, declaration. — **escuchar c.,** to confess, to hear a parishioner's confession (a priest).
confesional, *a.* confessional, confessionary. —*m., f.* member of a confession (religious faith).
confesionario, *m.* (ecc.) confessional (box); (ecc.) confessional procedure (in a book, etc.).
confesionista, *a., m., f.* Lutheran, Confessionist.
confeso, sa, *a.* 1. (law) self-confessed, self-convicted. 2. converted (said of a Jew). —*m., f.* converted Jew. —*m.* (ecc.) lay brother. —*f.* widow who has become a nun.
confesonario, *m.* confessional booth.
confesor *m.* (ecc.) confessor (father); (rel.) confessor, believer (Christian confessing faith at the time of persecution); **c. de manga ancha,** lenient father confessor.
confesorio, *m., var. of* **confesonario.**
confesuría, *f.* confessorship.
confeti, *m.* confetti.
confiable, *a.* trustworthy, reliable, dependable.
confiadamente, *adv.* confidently, with assurance, trustingly.
confiado, da, *past part. of* **confiar.** —*a.* 1. trustful, confident, unsuspicious, trusting. 2. self-confident, cocksure, presumptuous. — **c. en sí mismo,** self-confident.
confiador, *a.* trusting. —*m.* (law) co-guarantor.
confianza, *f.* 1. confidence, trust, reliance, faith. 2. self-confidence, assurance. 3. familiarity, informality. 4. presumptuousness, cocksureness. 5. private agreement (between traders, etc.). — **abuso de c.,** breach of faith; **c. en sí mismo,** self-confidence; **de c.,** intimate, close (friend); trustworthy, reliable; **en c.,** in confidence, confidentially; **estar en c.,** (coll.) to be informal, unceremonious.
confianzudo, da, *a.* (coll.) fresh, bold, overfamiliar.
confiar, (*ref. 51*) *tr.v.* to entrust; **c. a** or **en,** to entrust to. —*i.v., r.v.* to trust, have faith or confidence; **c. en** or **de,** to trust in.
confidencia, *f.* confidence, secret or confidential information.
confidencial, *a.* confidential.
confidencialmente, *adv.* confidentially.
confidente, ta, *a.* faithful, sure, trusty, trustworthy. —*m., f.* 1. confidant, advisor (*m.*), confidante (*f.*). 2. spy, secret agent, informer. —*m.* sofa for two, loveseat.
confidentemente, *adv.* confidentially; faithfully.
confiera, confiero, *ref.* **conferir.**
confiese, confieso, *ref.* **confesar.**
configuración, *f.* configuration, shape, form.
configurar, *tr.v.* to form, shape. —*r.v.* to be or become shaped or formed.
confín, *a.* bordering, adjoining. —*m.* boundary, frontier, limit; (*pl.*) confines; horizon.
confinación, *f., var. of* **confinamiento.**
confinado, da, *past part. of* **confinar.** —*a.* deported, exiled. —*m.* paroled convict, deported convict.
confinamiento, *m.* 1. bordering, adjoining; adjacence, contiguousness. 2. deportation, exile; confinement to a certain area while on parole.
confinante, *a.* bordering, adjoining, abutting.
confinar, *tr.v.* 1. to confine, imprison, incarcerate. 2. to banish, exile, deport; e.g. *c. al cuartel,* to confine to barracks. —*i.v.* to border, adjoin, e.g. *confinar con,* to border on. —*r.v.* to shut oneself up, seclude oneself.
confingir, (*ref. 62*) *tr.v.* (pharm.) to compound or mix with a liquid (to form a mass).
confinja, confinjo, *ref.* **confingir.**
confiriendo, confiriera, confiriese, confirió, *ref.* **conferir.**
confirmación, *f.* confirmation, affirmation, corroboration; (rel.) confirmation (sacrament).
confirmadamente, *adv.* assuredly, firmly; with approval.
confirmador, ra, *a.* confirmatory, confirmative, confirming. —*m., f.* confirmer.
confirmando, da, *m., f.* (rel.) confirmand (candidate for confirmation).
confirmante, *a.* confirming. —*m., f.* confirmer, corroborator.
confirmar, *tr.v.* to confirm, corroborate, verify; to strengthen, support, ratify; (rel.) to confirm.
confirmativo, va, *a., var. of* **confirmatorio.**
confirmatorio, ria, *a.* confirmatory, confirmative.
confiscable, *a.* confiscable.
confiscación, *f.* confiscation, forfeiture.
confiscado, da, *past part. of* **confiscar.** —*a.* (Ven., coll.) roguish, devilish.
confiscador, ra, *m., f.* confiscator.
confiscar, (*ref. 50*) *tr.v.* to confiscate.
confisgado, da, *a.* (C. Amer.) roguish, devilish.
confisque, confisqué, *ref.* **confiscar.**
confitado, da, *past part. of* **confitar.** —*a.* 1. candied, sugar-coated, sugared, crystallized (fruit, nuts). 2. (coll.) hopeful, confident.
confitar, *tr.v.* 1. to coat with sugar; to candy, crystallize (fruits, nuts); to preserve, stew in syrup. 2. (fig.) to mollify, smooth, sweeten.
confite, *m.* candy, bonbon, sweet; **estar a partir de un c.** or **morder en un c.,** to be hand in glove, to be intimate.
confitente, *a.* self-confessed, self-convicted.
confiteor, *m.* (ecc.) confiteor; (fig.) frank or public confession of a fault or error.
confitera, *f.* dish or box to hold candy or bonbons.
confitería, *f.* candy shop, sweet shop; confectionery, confectioner's factory or shop; (Arg.) pastry shop; café, tearoom.
confitero, ra, *m., f.* confectioner, person who makes or sells candy. —*m.* candy or bonbon jar.
confitico, llo, to, *m.* small, delicate embroidery on coverlets.
confitura, *f.* confiture, candied or crystallized fruit, sweetmeat, preserve.
conflación, *f.* (metal.) melting, fusing (of solids).
conflagración, *f.* 1. conflagration, fire, blaze. 2. (fig.) conflagration, outbreak, uprising, revolt.
conflagrar, *tr.v.* to burn, set on fire, ignite.
conflátil, *a.* fusible, meltable, smeltable.
conflictivo, va, *a.* conflictive, full of conflict.
conflicto, *m.* conflict, quarrel, dispute; discord, strife; (fig.) conflict, struggle, antagonism, anguish (mental, moral).
confluencia, *f.* confluence.
confluente, *a.* confluent; convergent. —*m.* confluence (of rivers); junction.
confluir, (*ref. 48*) *i.v.* to converge, join, come together (rivers, roads); to converge, meet, assemble (people).
confluya, confluye, confluyera, confluyese, *ref.* **confluir.**
conformación, *f.* 1. build, physique. 2. conformation, formation, structure.
conformador, *m.* 1. shaper. 2. hat block, shoe mold.
conformante, *a.* (math.) conformal.
conformar, *tr.v.* to form, shape, to block (a hat). 2. to adjust, adapt. —*i.v.* to agree, be in agreement; to conform, become adapted or adjusted. —*r.v.* to resign oneself; to conform, to comply; become adjusted; to content oneself; to agree. — **conformarse con,** to conform to; to resign oneself to; to content oneself with.
conforme, *a.* 1. in agreement, agreeing. 2. in order, O.K. (coll.). 3. agreed, e.g. *estamos conformes en este punto,* we are agreed on this point. 4. similar, alike. 5. resigned, patient. — **c. a,** in accordance with; **c. con,** in agreement with, resigned to; **¿conforme?** do you agree, are you in agreement? —*conj.* as soon as, e.g. *c. amanezca,* as soon as dawn breaks. —*m.* written endorsement or approval (of a document).
conformemente, *adv.* in agreement.
conformidad, *f.* 1. agreement; harmony, concord; conformity. 2. similarity, resemblance. 3. symmetry, proportion. 4. patience, forbearance, resignation. — **de c.** or **en c.,** in agreement; **estar en c.,** to be in agreement.
conformismo, *m.* conformism.
conformista, *a., m., f.* conformist (in the Church of England).
confort, *m.* comfort, well-being.
confortable, *a.* comfortable; comforting, consoling, cheering.
confortablemente, *adv.* comfortably.
confortación, *f.* comforting, the act of cheering; comfort, solace, consolation, encouragement.
confortador, ra, *a.* comforting, consoling, solacing, soothing; strengthening, invigorating. —*m., f.* comforter, consoler, soother.
confortamiento, *m., var. of* **confortación.**
confortante, *a.* comforting, consoling; cheering; invigorating, strengthening. —*m.* 1. mitten. 2. comforter. 3. invigorating drink, tonic.
confortar, *tr.v.* to comfort, solace, console; to cheer, encourage; to strengthen, invigorate.
confortativo, va, *a.* comforting, consoling. —*m.* 1. comfort, solace, consolation. 2. tonic, invigorating drink.
conforte, *m.* comfort, solace, strengthening, invigorating.
confracción, *f.* fracture, fracturing, breaking.
confraternal, *a.* confraternal.

confraternar, *i.v.* to be or become good friends.
confraternice, confraternicé, *ref.* **confraternizar.**
confraternidad, *f.* confraternity, brotherhood; fellowship, close friendship.
confraternizar, (*ref. 53*) *i.v.* to fraternize, become intimate friends.
confricación, *f.* friction, rubbing; scouring, scraping.
confricar, (*ref. 50*) *tr.v.* to rub.
confrique, confriqué, *ref.* **confricar.**
confrontación, *f.* 1. confrontation; facing, confronting. 2. comparison. 3. affinity, mutual sympathy, propinquity.
confrontante, *a.* confronting; comparing.
confrontar, *tr.v.* to confront, bring face to face; to collate; to compare. —*i.v.* to border; **c. con,** border on. —*r.v.* (fig.) to get along with, agree in sentiments and opinions.
confucianismo, *m.* Confucianism (the ethical system based on the teachings of Confucius).
confucianista, *a., m., f., var. of* **confuciano.**
confuciano, na, *a.* Confucian. —*m., f.* Confucianist.
Confucio, *m.* Confucius (Chinese philosopher and teacher).
confulgencia, *f.* brilliance, radiance, effulgence.
confundible, *a.* confusing, mistakable.
confundimiento, *m.* confusion, bewilderment, perplexity.
confundir, *tr.v.* 1. to mix up, disorder, disarrange, jumble together, muddle up; to blend, mix. 2. to mistake, e.g. *c. por,* to mistake for. 3. to confuse, muddle up, perplex. 4. to convince, confound (in an argument). 5. to disconcert, embarrass, make uncomfortable. —*r.v.* 1. to mix, blend, fuse, mingle (e.g. with a crowd). 2. to be muddled or jumbled up (things). 3. to make a mistake. 4. to be confused, muddled or perplexed.
confusamente, *adv.* 1. confusedly; in confusion; in disorder; helter-skelter. 2. indistinctly, hazily.
confusión, *f.* 1. confusion, disorder, muddle, mess. 2. confusion, perplexity. 3. haziness, lack of clarity (in style). 4. embarrassment, humiliation. — **c. de lenguas,** (Bib.) confusion of tongues.
confusionar, *tr.v. to* confuse, bewilder.
confusionismo, *m.* confusion of ideas.
confuso, sa, *irr. past part. of* **confundir.** —*a.* 1. confused; mixed up, jumbled. 2. obscure; blurred, hazy, unintelligible, indistinct. 3. (fig.) perplexed, confused, perturbed, doubtful, disconcerted.
confutación, *f.* confutation, disproof.
confutador, ra, *a.* confuting. —*m., f.* confuter.
confutar, *tr.v.* to confute, disprove, refute.
confutatorio, ria, *a.* confuting, confutative.
conga, *f.* 1. (Cuba) large grey or reddish rodent larger than a rat. 2. (Col.) large poisonous ant. 3. (Cuba) a popular dance of African origin and its music; a large African drum essential to that dance.
congal, *m.* (Mex.) bordello, whorehouse.
congelable, *a.* 1. freezable. 2. congealable.
congelación, *f.* 1. freezing. 2. congealment.
congelador, ra, *a.* freezing, refrigerating. —*m., f.* freezer, icebox; freezing compartment in a refrigerator.
congelamiento, *m., var. of* **congelación.**
congelante, *a.* freezing, refrigerant.
congelar, *tr.v.* 1. to congeal. 2. to freeze. 3. (econ.) to fix (prices or wages) at a given level. —*r.v.* 1. to congeal or be congealed. 2. to freeze, get or become frozen.
congelativo, va, *a.* freezing.
congénere, *a.* congeneric, congenerous. — *m.* fellow. —*f.* (fig.) sister.
congenérico, ca, *a.* congeneric, of like kind.
congenial, *a.* congenial, of kindred temperament.
congenialidad, *f.* congeniality.
congeniar, *i.v.* to be compatible or congenial; to get along together.
congénito, ta, *a.* congenital, connate.
congerie, *f.* congeries, heap, pile.
congestión, *f.* congestion.
congestionado, da, *a.* congested; (med.) congested.
congestionar, *tr.v.* to congest, make congested. —*r.v.* to become congested, congest.
congestivo, va, *a.* (med.) congestive.
congiario, *m.* (hist.) congiary, gift from the Roman emperor to the people.
congio, *m.* congius (ancient Roman liquid measure).
conglobación, *f.* conglobation, heap, heaping up; (fig.) conglomeration (of words, ideas, etc.).
conglobar, *tr.v.* to conglobate, conglobe, heap together. —*r.v.* to become conglobated or heaped up.
conglomeración, *f. conglomeration, agglomeration.*
conglomerado, da, *past part. of* **conglomerar.** —*a.* conglomerate. —*m.* conglomerate. — **c. de granito,** granolithic (floor); **c. fundamental,** (geol.) basal conglomerate.
conglomerante, *a.* bonding or adhesive material such as cement, plaster, etc.
conglomerar, *tr.v., r.v.,* to conglomerate.
conglutinación, *f.* conglutination, gluing together.
conglutinador, *m.* coalescer.
conglutinante, *a.* conglutinating, conglutinant. —*m.* conglutinator.
conglutinar, *tr.v., r.v.,* to conglutinate, cement, unite, join.
conglutinativo, va, *a.* conglutinative, viscous, conglutinating. —*m.* conglutinator.
conglutinoso, sa, *a.* conglutinative, adhesive (agent).
Congo, *m.* Congo. — **Rupública del Congo,** Republic of Congo (Brazzaville); **República Democrática del Congo,** Democratic Republic of Congo (Kinshasa).
congo, ga, *m., f.* 1. (Cuba, coll.) person of the black race. 2. (Peru) short, chubby person. —*m.* 1. (Mex., coll.) the femur of a pig. 2. (C. Rica, Salv.) howling monkey (Alouatta pallista). 3. (Amer.) second crop tobacco leaf.
congoja, *f.* anguish, affliction, distress, anxiety, sorrow, grief.
congojar, *tr.v., r.v., var. of* **acongojar.**
congojosamente, *adv.* painfully, distressfully.
congojoso, sa, *a.* 1. distressing, afflictive. 2. in anguish, anguished, distressed, extremely upset.
congoleño, ña, *a., m., f.* Congoese, Congolese.
congolés, lesa, *a.* of or pertaining to the Congo. —*m., f.* person born in the Congo.
cóngolo, *m.* 1. (Col.) fishing net. 2. dish made from a gourd.
congorocho, *m.* (Ven.) kind of centipede inhabiting marshy places.
congosto, *m.* canyon, defile, narrow pass.
congraciador, ra, *a.* ingratiating; obsequious, flattering, fawning.
congraciamiento, *m.* ingratiation, flattery, fawning, obsequiousness.
congraciar, *tr.v.* to adulate, flatter.
congraciarse, *r.v.* to ingratiate oneself, curry favor; **congraciarse con,** to ingratiate oneself or curry favor with.
congratulación, *m.* congratulation.
congratulador, ra, *m., f.* congratulant, congratulator.
congratular, *tr.v.* to congratulate; **c. de** or **por,** to congratulate on or for. —*r.v.* to congratulate oneself; rejoice.
congratulatorio, ria, *a.* congratulatory, congratulating.
congregación, *f.* 1. congregation, meeting, gathering, assembly. 2. brotherhood, confraternity. 3. congregation (committee of cardinals; religious order). — **c. de los** fieles, a meeting of parishioners.
congregacionalismo, *m.* (rel.) Congregationalism.
congregacionalista, *m., f.* (rel.) Congregationalist.
congregacionista, *m., f.* (imp. u.) *var. of* **congregante.**
congregante, ta, *m., f.* member of a congregation, fraternity or brotherhood.
congregar, (*ref. 51*) *tr.v., r.v.* to congregate, assemble.
congregue, congregué, *ref.* **congregar.**
congresal, *m.* (Amer.), *var. of* **congresista.**
congresista, *m., f.* member of a congress or convention.
congreso, *m.* 1. congress; convention. 2. congress, national legislative body; congress building.
congrio, *m.* (ichth.) conger eel.
congrua, *f.* (ecc.) income which an ordinand must possess in order to be ordained.
congruamente, *adv., var. of* **congruentemente.**
congruencia, *f.* 1. congruence, congruity, aptness, fitness. 2. (law) cohesion, coherence. 3. (math.) congruence.
congruente, *a.* congruent, congruous; fitting, apt; (math.) congruent.
congruentemente, *adv.* congruently, congruously, aptly.
congruidad, *f.* congruity, congruence, fitness, aptness.
congruo, grua, *a.* congruous.
conhortar, *tr.v.* (arch.) to console, comfort, solace.
conicidad, *f.* (geom.) conicity.
conicina, *f.* (chem.) coiine.
cónico, ca, *a.* conical, conic.
conídico, ca, *a.* (bot.) conidial.
conidio, *m.* (bot.) conidium.
conidióforo, *m.* (bot.) conidiophore.
conífero, ra, *a.* (bot.) coniferous, conebearing. —*f.* (bot.) conifer, (*pl.*) Coniferae.
coniforme, *a.* coniform, cone-shaped.
conio, *m.* (bot.) conium.
conirrostro, tra, *a.* (ornith.) conirostral. —*m. pl.* (ornith.) Conirostres.
conivalvo, va, *a.* (zool.) cone-shelled, spiral-shelled.
coniza, *f.* (bot.) inula (Inula coniza), a medicinal herb.
conj. *abbrev. of* **conjunción,** conjunction (conj.).
conjetura, *f.* conjecture, surmise, supposition.
conjeturable, *a.* conjecturable, surmisable.
conjeturador, ra, *a.* conjecturing, surmising, guessing.
conjetural, *a.* conjectural.
conjeturalmente, *adv.* conjecturally, by guess.
conjeturar, *tr.v.* to conjecture, surmise, guess.
conjuez, (*pl.* **conjueces**) *m.* co-judge, joint judge.
conjugable, *a.* able to be conjugated.
conjugación, *f.* (gram., biol.) conjugation.
conjugado, da, *past part. of* **conjugar.** —*a.* (math.) conjugate.
conjugar, (*ref. 51*) *tr.v.* 1. (gram.) to conjugate. 2. to conjugate, to join, to fuse.
conjugue, conjugué, *ref.* **conjugar.**
conjunción, *f.* (astron., astrol., gram.) conjunction, union, junction.

conjuntamente, *adv.* jointly, together.
conjuntiva, *f.* (anat.) conjunctiva (membrane of the eye).
conjuntival, *a.* (anat.) conjunctival.
conjuntivitis, *f.* (med.) conjunctivitis.
conjuntivo, va, *a.* conjunctive, joining; (gram.) conjunctive.
conjunto, ta, *a.* joined, joint, linked; related, allied, connected. —*m.* 1. whole, entirety. 2. set (of clothes), two-piece suit. 3. (mus.) ensemble, band (of musicians). — **c. motriz,** (engin., Arg.) power plant; **c. residencial,** condominium; **de c.,** general, united; **en c.,** as a whole; **en su c.,** in its entirety.
conjura, *f.* conspiracy, plot (gen. against the ruler or the state).
conjuración, *f., var. of* **conjura.**
conjurado, da, *past part. of* **conjurar.** —*a.* plotting, conspiring. —*m., f.* plotter, conspirator.
conjurador, ra, *m., f.* 1. plotter, conspirator. 2. conjurer.
conjuramentar, *tr.v.* to administer an oath, swear in. —*r.v.* to take the oath, bind oneself by oath.
conjurante, *a.* plotting, conspiring. —*m., f.* plotter, conspirator.
conjurar, *i.v.* 1. to swear, pledge oneself. 2. to conspire, plot. —*tr.v.* 1. to swear in (e.g. a witness). 2. to entreat, implore, beseech. 3. (ecc.) to exorcise. 4. to avoid, prevent. —*r.v.* to take an oath, pledge oneself.
conjuro, *m.* 1. exorcism. 2. incantation. 3. entreaty.
conllevador, ra, *a.* 1. helpful, assisting. 2. patient. —*m., f.* helper, assistant.
conllevar, *tr.v.* 1. to aid, assist. 2. to tolerate, put up with (coll.), bear patiently, endure.
conmemorable, *a.* memorable.
conmemoración, *f.* commemoration, remembrance.
conmemorar, *tr.v.* to commemorate, remember solemnly; celebrate.
conmemorativo, va, *a.* commemorative, memorial.
conmemoratorio, ria, *a.* commemorative.
conmensal, *m.* messmate, table companion, fellow boarder.
conmesalía, *f.* eating together.
conmesurabilidad, *f.* commensurability.
conmensurable, *a.* commensurate; commensurable, proportional.
conmensuración, *f.* commensuration.
conmensurar, *tr.v.* to measure proportionately, to make commensurate.
conmensurativo, va, *a.* helping to measure proportionately, making commensurate.
conmigo, *pron.* with me, with myself.
conmilitón, *m.* fellow soldier, companion-at-arms, comrade.
conminación, *f.* commination, threat, menace.
conminar, *tr.v.* to threaten, menace; (law) to warn.
conminativo, va, *a.* threatening, menacing.
conminatorio, ria, *a.* comminatory, threatening. —*f.* theatening order; threat.
conminuta, *a.* (surg.) comminuted (fracture).
conmiseración, *f.* commiseration.
conmistión, *f.* commixture, mixture.
conmisto, ta, *a.* mixed, blended, mingled.
conmistura, *f.* commixture, mixture.
conmixtión, *f.* commixture, mixture.
conmixto, ta, *a.* mixed, blended.
conmoción, *f.* 1. commotion, unrest, upheaval; disturbance. 2. shock. 3. tremor (of the earth). — **c. cerebral,** (med.) concussion of the brain.
conmonitorio, *m.* 1. record, report. 2. (law) admonitory note from a superior judge to a lower one.
conmoración, *f.* (rhet.) repetition, elaboration.
conmovedor, ra, *a.* 1. moving, touching; pathetic, sad. 2. disturbing, disquieting; stirring, exciting.
conmover, (*ref. 34*) *tr.v.* to dusturb, trouble, disquiet; to move, touch. —*r.v.* to be moved to pity, be touched.
conmovido, da, *a.* moved, touched; stirred, excited.
conmueva, conmuevo, *ref.* **conmover.**
conmuta, *f.* (Chile, Ecuad., Peru) exchange, barter.
conmutabilidad, *f.* commutability; exchangeability.
conmutable, *a.* exchangeable; commutable; (law) commutable.
conmutación, *f.* 1. commutation, exchange. 2. (rhet.) punning, word play. — **c. de pena,** (law) commutation (of a sentence).
conmutador, ra, *a.* commuting. —*m.* (elec.) commutator; transfer or change-over switch; **c. de banda** or **ondas,** (rad.) band switch; **c. de dos** or **tres direcciones,** two-way or three-way switch; **c. de cuchillas,** knife switch; **c. de polos,** reversing switch; **c. reductor,** (auto.) dimmer switch.
conmutar, *tr.v.* 1. to commute (a sentence). 2. to change, exchange. 3. (elec.) to commutate (to turn or direct a current).
conmutativo, va, *a.* commutative, exchangeable.
conmutatriz, (*pl.* **conmutatrices**) *f.* (elec.) converter, instrument used for converting alternate current to continuous current and viceversa.
connato, ta, *a.* connate, born at the same time (as someone else).
connatural, *a.* connatural, instinctive, inborn, innate, inherent.
connaturalice, connaturalicé, *ref.* **connaturalizar.**
connaturalización, *f.* acclimatization, adaptation.
connaturalizar, (*ref. 53.*) *tr.v.* to acclimatize, adapt. —*r.v.* to acclimatize, adapt or accustom oneself.
connaturalmente, *adv.* naturally, instinctively.
connivencia, *f.* connivance.
connivente, *a.* conniving; (bot.) connivent (said of leaves or parts of a plant which tend to grow towards each other).
connotación, *f.* 1. connotation, implication. 2. remote relationship.
connotado, da, *past past. of* **connotar.** —*a.* (Amer.) renowned, famous. —*m.* remote relationship.
connotante, *a.* connoting.
connotar, *tr.v.* to connote, imply.
connotativo, va, *a.* (gram.) connotative.
connovicio, cia, *m., f.* fellow novice.
connubial, *a.* matrimonial, connubial.
connubio, *m.* matrimony, marriage.
connumerar, *tr.v.* to enumerate, mention, cite.
cono, *m.* (bot., geom.) cone; **c. circular,** (geom.) circular cone (cone with circular base). — **c. de sombra or de penumbra,** (astron.) umbral cone; umbra; **c. de viento,** wind sock; **c. dispersor,** (hydr.) diffusing cone; **c. oblicuo,** (geom.) oblique cone; **c. recto,** (geom.) right cone; **c. truncado,** (geom.) truncated cone.
conocedor, ra, *a.* knowing, expert. —*m., f.* connoisseur; expert.
conocencia, *f.* 1. (coll.) knowledge. 2. (law) confession.
conocer, (*ref. 45*) *tr.v.* 1. to know, be acquainted with (a person); to meet, get to know, become acquainted with; to know (a subject which needs considerable study). 2. to perceive; to tell, distinguish. 3. to confess, recognize. 4. to know carnally, have carnal knowledge of. — **c. de nombre,** to know by name; **c. de vista,** to know by sight. —*i.v.* **c. en** or **de,** to understand, know. —*r.v.* to know one another, be or become acquainted; to know oneself.
conocible, *a.* cognizable, knowable.
conocidamente, *adv.* clearly, distinctly.
conocido, da, *past part. of* **conocer.** —*a.* well-known, distinguished, illustrious. —*m., f.* acquaintance.
conocimiento, *m.* 1. knowledge. 2. understanding, intelligence, sense, reason. 3. consciousness. 4. acquaintance. 5. (com.) bill of lading, document held by ship's captain listing the cargo aboard. 6. (com.) proof of identity. 7. (*pl.*) knowledge; learning. — **c. corrido** or **directo,** through bill of lading; **c. de embarque,** (com.) bill of lading; **c. limpio** or **sin tacha,** (com.) clean bill of lading; **perder el c.,** to lose consciousness; **poner en c. de,** to inform, let know; **recobrar el c.,** to regain consciousness; **venir uno en c. de una cosa,** (coll.) to hear about, get to know.
conoidal, *a.* (geom.) conoidal, conoid.
conoide, *m.* (geom.) conoid.
conoideo, a, *a.* coloidal, conical, cone-shaped.
conopeo, *m.* ciborium, canopy (over the shrine in which the Eucharist is kept).
conopial, *a.* (archit.) ogee arch.
conoto, *m.* (Ven.) sparrow.
conque, *conj.* so, then, well, e.g. *conque no te gusta trabajar,* so you don't like to work! —*m.* 1. (coll.) condition. 2. (Amer.) wherewithal, money.
conquián, *m.* conquian (card game).
conquibus, *m.* (coll.) money.
conquiforme, *a.* conch-shaped, shell-shaped.
conquiliología, *f.* (zool.) conchology.
conquiliólogo, ga, *m., f.* (zool.) conchologist.
conquiolina, *f.* (biochem.) conchiolin.
conquista, *f.* 1. conquest, the act of conquering. 2. person, country, etc. conquered by force. 3. (coll.) success in love; seduction. 4. **La C.,** (hist.) the conquest of America (by Spain).
conquistable, *a.* conquerable; (fig.) attainable, accessible, achievable.
conquistador, ra, *a.* conquering. —*m., f.* conqueror.
conquistadores, *m. pl.* (hist.) Spanish conquerors of the New World in the 16th century.
conquistar, *tr.v.* 1. to conquer. 2. to win; to win over (to one's way of thinking). 3. to attain or achieve through a lot of effort, e.g. *c. una posición social elevada,* conquer a high social position.
conrear, *tr.v.* 1. to prepare (something). 2. to oil (wool). 3. (agr.) to plow a second time.
conreinar, *i.v.* to reign jointly.
conreo, *m.* 1. preparation. 2. oiling (wool). 3. plowing for the second time.
consabido, da, *a.* abovementioned, aforesaid, said; well-known.
consabidor, ra, *a.* said of one who shares some information with others.
consagrable, *a.* consecratory.
consagración, *f.* consecration.
consagrado, da, *past part. of* **consagrar.** —*a.* sacred; devoted, given (to study, sports, etc.). 2. (coll.) famous, renowned, e.g. *un artista c.,* a consummate artist.
consagrante, *a.* consecrating. —*m., f.* consecrator.
consagrar, *tr.v.* 1. to consecrate, hallow, sanctify. 2. to deify, apotheosize. 3. to devote, dedicate (to God, study, etc.). 4. to erect a monument to. 5. to authorize or codify (a new meaning of a word). —*r.v.* 1. to devote or dedicate oneself. 2. (coll.) to become famous or renowned.

consanguíneo, a, *a.* consanguineous; agnate (said of children of the same father but different mothers). *—m., f.* blood relation, kinsman, kinswoman.
consanguinidad, *f.* consanguinity, kinship, blood relationship.
consciencia, *f.* (psyc.) conscience.
consciente, *a.* 1. (physically) conscious. 2. conscious, aware. 3. conscientious, reliable.
conscientemente, *adv.* 1. consciously. 2. conscientiously.
conscripción, *f.* (Amer.) conscription, recruiting, military draft.
conscripto, ta, *m., f.* (Amer.) conscript, recruit, draftee.
consecución, *f.* obtaining, acquisition, attainment.
consecuencia, *f.* 1. consequence. 2. consistency. — **en c.,** accordingly, therefore; **guardar c,** to remain consistent; **por c.,** consequently; **ser de c.,** to be important; **tener** or traer **consecuencias,** to have or bring consequences; **traer a c. una cosa,** to bring (something) into consideration.
consecuente, *a.* 1. consequent, consecutive. 2. consistent. *—m.* (log., math.) consequent.
consecuentemente, *adv.* consequently, therefore, in consequence.
consecutivamente, *adv.* consecutively, successively.
consecutivo, va, *a.* consecutive; successive. — **c. a,** resulting from.
conseguimiento, *m.* attainment, obtaining.
conseguir, (*ref. 77*) *tr.v.* to obtain, attain, get (coll.); **c.** + *inf.*, to succeed in + *ger.*, manage to + *inf.*
conseja, *f.* 1. tale, fable, fairy story. 2. conciliabule, clandestine meeting.
consejero, ra, *a.* advisory. *—m., f.* 1. counselor, adviser. 2. councillor, councilman (*m.*), councilwoman (*f.*). *—m.* 1. minister (of a government council). 2. (fig.) warning, lesson (from an unpleasant experience).
consejo, *m.* 1. counsel, advice. 2. council; council house. — **c. de Estado,** council of state; **c. de familia,** (law) board of guardians (of a minor, etc.); **c. de guerra,** court-martial; Council of War; **c. de Indias,** Council of the Indies, in charge of Spain's possessions abroad; **c. de instrucción pública,** Ministry of Education; **c. de Ministros,** Cabinet (of Ministers); **c. de sanidad,** board of health, health board; **c. de Seguridad,** Security Council.
consenso, *m.* consensus, general assent or consent.
consensual, *a.* (law) consensual.
consentido, da, *a.* 1. said of a cuckolded husband. 2. spoiled, pampered, coddled.
consentidor, ra, *a.* 1. acquiescent, acquiescing. 2. (coll.) pampering, spoiling. *—m., f.* 1. acquiescent person. 2. (coll.) pamperer, spoiler (of children).
consentimiento, *m.* consent, compliance, acquiescence.
consentir, (*ref. 42*) *tr.v.* 1. to consent to, agree to; to permit, tolerate, allow. 2. to spoil, pamper; to indulge, be indulgent with. 3. to believe, think. *—i.v.* 1. to consent, assent. 2. to become weak or loose, crack. — **c. en,** to consent to, agree to; **c. a** or **con,** to be indulgent with, indulge, suffer, tolerate. *—r.v.* to begin to break, crack or split.
conserje, *m.* concierge, janitor, porter.
conserjería, *f.* concierge's, porter's, or janitor's desk or office; reception desk (of a hotel); post of concierge, porter or janitor.
conserva, *f.* 1. (cul.) conserve, preserve; candied fruit; preserved food; pickles. 2. (mar.) convoy. — **c. de carne,** canned or tinned meat; **c. de legumbres,** canned or tinned vegetables; **conservas alimenticias,** canned or tinned foods.
conservación, *f.* preservation, conservation; keeping; upkeep, maintenance, care; **c. de la energía,** (phys.) conservation of energy; **c. de la masa,** (phys.) conservation of mass; **c. de sí mismo, c. propia,** self-preservation; **c. de suelos,** soil conservation.
conservador, ra, *a.* conserving, preservative; (polit.) conservative. — **juez c.,** ecclesiastic appointed to defend ecclesiastical rights and property in a certain area. *—m., f.* 1. preserver, keeper; warden, custodian, curator (of a museum, etc.). 2. (polit.) conservative.
conservaduría, *f.* post of custodian, curatorship; curator's or custodian's office.
conservadurismo, *m.* conservatism, reaction against social or liberal changes in politics and life.
conservante, *a.* conserving, preserving.
conservar, *tr.v.* 1. to preserve, maintain, conserve; to keep (friends, secrets, etc.). 2. to preserve, pickle, can. *—r.v.* 1. to be preserved. 2. to reserve, keep, keep for oneself. 3. to take care of one's health, stay young.
conservatismo, *m.* (Amer.) conservatism.
conservativo, va, *a.* preservative (agent).
conservatoría, *f.* the post of keeper, warden, custodian, curator.
conservatorio, ria, *a.* conservatory. *—m.* conservatory, conservatoire (school of art, science, music).
conservería, *f.* pickling, preserving; canning (skill, process).
conservero, ra, *a.* preserving, canning. *—m., f.* canner, person who preserves food.
considerable, *a.* considerable; worthy of consideration; powerful, important (person, group); substantial, big, e.g. *un éxito c.,* considerable success.
considerablemente, *adv.* considerably, substantially, greatly.
consideración, *f.* 1. consideration, deliberation. 2. consideration, deference. 3. reason, motive. — **bajo** or **en c.,** under consideration; **en c. a,** in consideration of; **ser de c. (una cosa),** to be important, of consequence or worthy of consideration; **tomar en c.,** to take into consideration or account.
consideradamente, *adv.* considerately, deferentially; thoughtfully, judiciously.
considerado, da, *past part. of* **considerar.** *—a.* 1. considerate, thoughtful. 2. respected, highly regarded. 3. prudent, judicious.
considerando, *m.* (law) whereas, legal reason, clause of a law or proclamation.
considerar, *tr.v.* 1. to consider; to think. 2. to treat with respect or consideration. *—r.v.* to consider or believe oneself; to be considered, e.g. *él se considera un genio,* he considers himself a genius.
consienta, consiento, *ref.* **consentir.**
consiervo, *m.* serf or slave belonging to the same master, fellow slave.
consiga, *ref.* **conseguir.**
consigna, *f.* 1. slogan, watchword, rallying cry; order, instruction (pol., econ.). 2. baggage check.
consignación, *f.* 1. consignment. 2. deposit (of money). — **en c.,** (com.) on consignment.
consignador, *m.* (com.) consignor, depositor.
consignar, *tr.v.* 1. to consign, send, transmit. 2. to deposit, put in storage (goods); (com.) to consign, deposit (money). 3. to set apart, assign. 4. to consign, transfer (income from an estate in settlement of a debt). 5. to state, set or write down. 6. (law) to deposit in trust.
consignatario, *m.* 1. (com.) consignee (agent receiving a consignment). 2. (law) creditor who administers an estate in consignation until a debt is paid. 3. (law) consignatary (person receiving deposited money).
consigo, with him, with her, with them; with himself, with herself, with themselves; **hablar c. mismo,** to talk to oneself; **no llevar dinero c.,** to carry no money with one; **no tenerlas todas c.,** to have one's doubts, not to be sure.
consigo, *ref.* **conseguir.**
consiguiendo, *ref.* **conseguir.**
consiguiente, *a.* consequent, resulting, issuing; **c. a,** resulting from; **por c.,** consequently. *—m.* (rhet.) consequent (syllogism).
consiguientemente, *adv.* consequently.
consiguiera, consiguiese, *ref.* **conseguir.**
consiliario, ria, *m., f.* counselor, advisor; consultant, advisor.
consintiendo, *ref.* **consentir.**
consintiente, *a.* consentient, agreeing.
consintiera, consintiese, consintió, *ref.* **consentir.**
consistencia, *f.* consistency, consistence; durability, stability, solidity.
consistente, *a.* consistent; (Amer.) consequent, corresponding.
consistir, *i.v.* to consist; to be composed; **c. en,** to consist in; to be composed of, consist of.
consistorial, *a.* (ecc.) consistorial. *—m.* (ecc.) member of a consistory.
consistorialmente, *adv.* (ecc.) by consistorial decision.
consistorio, *m.* (ecc.) consistory; council (of Roman Emperors); town council; town hall; **c. divino,** God's judgment seat or throne.
consocio, cia, *m., f.* fellow partner, co-partner; fellow member (of a club).
consola, *f.* console table.
consolable, *a.* consolable.
consolablemente, *adv.* consolingly, comfortingly, soothingly.
consolación, *f.* 1. consolation, comfort, solace. 2. fine, penalty (in cards).
consolado, da, *past part. of* **consolar.** *—a.* consoled, comforted.
consolador, ra, *a.* consoling, comforting, solacing. *—m., f.* comforter, consoler.
consolante, *a.* consoling, comforting, solacing.
consolar, (*ref. 33*) *tr.v.* to console, comfort, solace. *—r.v.* to console or comfort oneself.
consolativo, va, *a., var. of* **consolador.**
consolatorio, ria, *a.* consolatory, consoling.
consólida, *f.* (bot.) common comfrey; **c. real,** larkspur.
consolidación, *f.* consolidation.
consolidado, da, *past part. of* **consolidar.** *—a.* consolidated.
consolidar, *tr.v.* 1. to consolidate; to strengthen, make firm or strong. 2. to fund (a floating debt). 3. to put together, repair. *—r.v.* 1. to become consolidated. 2. (law) to combine, merge, consolidate (property under one control).
consolidativo, va, *a.* consolidative, consolidating.
consomé, *m.* (cul.) consommé, clear soup, broth.
consonancia, *f.* 1. (mus.) harmony, consonance. 2. assonance, consonance, rhyme (in words); (rhet.) unnecessary use of assonance.
consonante, *a.* consonantal; harmonious, consonant; rhyming, assonantic. *—m.* assonantic sound, rhyming word. *—f.* consonant (letter).
consonantemente, *adv.* consonantly; concordantly, harmoniously.

consonantización, *f.* the action of converting a vowel into a consonant.
consonantizar, *tr.v.* to convert a vowel into a consonant, e.g. the *u* of *Paulo* into the *b* of *Pablo.*
consonar, (*ref. 33*) *i.v.* 1. (mus.) to harmonize, be in harmony. 2. to rhyme (by assonance). 3. to agree, be harmonious, harmonize.
cónsone, *a.* consonant, harmonious. —*m.* (mus.) chord.
cónsono, na, *a.* consonant, harmonious; (mus.) harmonious.
consorcio, *m.* 1. consortium, association, partnership. 2. consortium, marital fellowship.
consorte, *m., f.* 1. consort, spouse; partner, associate. 2. (*pl.*) (law) co-litigants (in a lawsuit); (law) accomplices. — **Príncipe c.,** Prince Consort.
conspicuo, cua, *a.* outstanding, prominent; illustrious, famous, eminent.
conspiración, *f.* conspiracy, plot.
conspirado, da, *past part. of* **conspirar.** —*m.* conspirator, plotter.
conspirador, ra, *m., f.* conspirator, plotter.
conspirar, *i.v.* to conspire, plot; to convene or agree to act against someone or something.
constancia, *f.* 1. constancy, perseverance, steadfastness. 2. certainty. 3. evidence, proof.
constante, *a.* 1. constant, steadfast; persevering. 2. durable, lasting. 3. faithful, loyal. 4. (math.) constant. 5. verifying, substantiating. —*f.* 1. (phys., math.) constant. 2. constant feature or factor. — **c. capilar,** capillary potential; **c. de la gravitación,** (phys.) gravitational constant.
constantemente, *adv.* constantly; steadfastly, perseveringly; undoubtedly, certainly.
Constantinopla, *f.* Constantinople, former name of Istanbul.
constar, *i.v.* 1. to be clear, obvious or evident. 2. to have the proper meter and accent (a poem). 3. to be recorded or registered. — **c. de,** to be composed of, consist of.
constatación, *f.* (imp. u.) substantiation, verification, proof.
constatar, *tr.v.* (gal.) to verify, prove, confirm.
constelación, *f.* 1. (astron., astrol.) constellation. 2. climate, temperature.
constelado, da, *past part. of* **constelar.** —*a.* starry, starstudded; (fig.) studded.
constelar, *tr.v.* (gal.) to cover, fill, stud.
consternación, *f.* consternation, panic; distress.
consternar, *tr.v.* to disturb greatly, disquiet, dismay, consternate. —*r.v.* to be greatly disturbed or disquieted.
constipación, *f.* cold, head cold; **c. de vientre,** constipation.
constipado, *past part. of* **constipar.** —*m.* head cold, e.g. *pesqué un c.,* I caught a cold.
constipar, *tr.v.* 1. to give a cold, cause to catch cold. 2. to contract, close up, obstruct the pores (preventing perspiration). —*r.v.* to catch a cold.
constipativo, va, *a.* (arch.) liable to produce or cause a cold.
constitución, *f.* 1. constitution (of the body; system of laws). 2. (chem.) composition, structure. 3. establishment, setting-up, constitution. 4. state (of affairs), condition. — **c. apostólica,** (ecc.) papal decree, bull rescript or brief; **c. atmosférica,** atmospheric condition (as it influences living beings); **c. pontificia,** bull, papal letter (of general interest).
constitucional, *a.* constitutional. —*m.* (polit.) constitutionalist.
constitucionalismo, *m.* constitutionalism, adherence to a constitutional form of government.
constitucionalmente, *adv.* constitutionally.
constituidor, ra, *a.* constitutive.
constituir, (*ref. 48*) *tr.v.* 1. to constitute; to compose, make up. 2. to establish, set up, form, create (a ruling, institution, company). — **c. en,** to place under, e.g. *c. en obligación,* to place under an obligation; **c. en apuro,** to put in a difficult situation; **c. en un puesto,** to place in a position or post. —*r.v.* to be established, set up or created; **c. en,** to assume the position of, set oneself up as, e.g. *se constituyó en juez,* he set himself up as judge.
constitutivo, va, *a.* constituent, component. —*m.* component part.
constituya, constituyendo, *ref.* **constituir.**
constituyente, *a.* constituent, component. —*m.* constituent; component. —*f.* (*pl.*) Cortes convened to reform the Spanish Constitution.
constituyera, constituyese, constituyo, *ref.* **constituir.**
constreñidamente, *adv.* forcibly, by force.
constreñimiento, *m.* constraint, compulsion, obligation.
constreñir, (*ref. 41*) *tr.v.* to constrain, compel, force, oblige; (med.) to constipate, bind, make costive.
constricción, *f.* constriction, contraction, constringency.
constrictivo, va, *a.* 1. constraining, compelling. 2. (med.) astringent, binding, constricting.
constrictor, ra *a.* contrictive, constricting, contracting; (med.) astringent, constrictive. —*m.* (med.) astringent.
constringente, *a.* constringent, constraining, binding.
constriña, constriñendo, constriñera, constriñese, constriño, *ref.* **constreñir.**
construcción, *f.* construction; **c. esquemática,** skeleton construction; **c. naval,** shipbuilding; **edificio en c.,** building under construction.
constructivo, va, *a.* constructive.
constructor, ra, *a.* of or pertaining to construction, e.g. *compañia constructora,* construction company. —*m., f.* constructor, builder; **c. naval** or **de buques,** shipbuilder.
construir, (*ref. 48*) *tr.v.* 1. to construct, build, form. 2. (gram.) to construct; analyze, interpret.
construya, construyendo, construyera, construyese, construyo, *ref.* **construir.**
constuprador, *m.* debaucher, corrupter, defiler.
constuprar, *tr.v.* to defile, corrupt.
consubstanciación, *f.* (theol.) consubstantiation.
consubstancial, *a.* consubstantial, having the same substance.
consubstancialidad, *f.* consubstantiality.
consuegrar, *i.v.* become joint parents-in-law (relationship between the parents of the bride and the groom).
consuegro, ra, *m., f.* father or mother-in-law of one's offspring in relation to oneself.
consuelda, *f.* (bot.) common comfrey; **c. menor,** (bot.) tuberous comfrey (Symphytum tuberosum); **c. roja,** (bot.) cinquefoil, potentilla, tormentilla.
consuele, consuelo, *ref.* **consolar.**
consuelo, *m.* consolation, comfort, relief; joy, delight. — **sin c.,** inconsolable; unrelenting.
consuena, consuene, *ref.* **consonar.**
consueta, *f.* 1. rule (of an ecclesiastical chapter). 2. (*pl.*) prayers in commemoration of the saints, sung at vespers and laudes on certain days. 3. (theat.) prompter.
consuetudinario, ria, *a.* customary, generally practiced; confirmed, inveterate, e.g. *un bebedor c.,* a confirmed drinker.
cónsul, *m.* consul; **c. general,** consul general.
cónsula, *f.* (coll.) wife of a consul.
consulado, *m.* consulship (office of consul, term of office); consulate (residence); **c. general,** consulate general.
consular, *a.* consular; **factura c.,** consular invoice.
consulesa, *f.* (coll.) wife of a consul.
consulta, *f.* 1. opinion, judgment; proposal, recommendation (sent to king by ministers). 2. consultation (with doctor, lawyer, etc; between doctors or lawyers, etc.). — **hacer una c.,** to ask for advice; (med.) to consult (a doctor).
consultable, *a.* worthy or in need of deliberation.
consultación, *f.* consultation, conference; deliberation.
consultante, *a.* consultant, consulting.
consultar, *tr.v.* 1. to consult; to look up, consult (dictionary). 2. to discuss, talk over, deliberate about. 3. to advise, present proposals or recommendations to. — **c. con la almohada,** to think over, to sleep on. —*i.v.* to consult.
consultivo, va, *a.* consultative; advisory.
consultor, ra, *a.* consulting, advisory, consultative. —*m., f.* 1. consultant (professional called in for advice). 2. advisor, counselor.
consultorio, *m.* 1. consulting room, doctor's office or clinic, dispensary. 2. information bureau. 3. (journ., tel.) answers to questions.
consumación, *f.* 1. consummation; completion, termination. 2. extinction, destruction. — **la c. de los hechos,** the end of the affair.
consumadamente, *adv.* consummately, completely, perfectly.
consumado, da, *past part. of* **consumar.** —*a.* consummate, perfect, complete, e.g. *un artista consumado,* a consummate artist. —*m.* rich meat broth, consommé.
consumador, ra, *a.* consummating. —*m., f.* consummator.
consumar, *tr.v.* to consummate; (law) to complete (a contract, etc.).
consumativo, va, *a.* consummative, completing.
consumero, *m.* 1. exciseman. 2. coastguard (looking out for smugglers).
consumible, *a.* consumable.
consumición, *f.* 1. consumption. 2. destruction. 3. wasting away (of the body).
consumido, da, *past part. of* **consumir.** —*a.* (coll.) 1. emaciated, thin, worn out. 2. fretful, over-ansious, worrisome, e.g. *c. de curiosidad,* consumed with curiosity.
consumidor, ra, *a.* consuming. —*m., f.* consumer (of goods, food, drink, etc.).
consumimiento, *m.* 1. consumption. 2. destruction. 3. wasting away (the body).
consumir, *tr.v.* 1. to consume; to eat; to use up. 2. to waste or eat away (the body, funds, etc.). 3. to take the Eucharist (the priest). 4. to afflict, eat away, gnaw at (grief). —*r.v.* 1. to be consumed; to be used up. 2. to waste away. 3. to be afflicted, pine (with grief). 4. (cul.) to boil away, evaporate (water, soup, etc.).
consumo, *m.* 1. consumption. 2. (*pl.*) (hist.) octroi, municipal or excise tax on food brought into town for sale.
consunción, *f.* 1. consumption. 2. destruction. 3. wasting away (the body); (med.) consumption.
consuno, de c., jointly, together, by mutual agreement or consent.
consuntivo, va, *a.* consuming.
consunto, ta, *irr. past part. of* **consumir.**
consustancial, *a.* (theol.) consubstantial.
consustancialidad, *f.* (theol.) consubstantiality.
contabilidad, *f.* 1. accountancy, accounting. 2. countability, computability. — **c. de costos,** cost accounting.
contabilizar, (*ref. 53*) *tr.v.* (acc.) to enter, record or register in accounts or books.

contable, *a.* countable, computable. —*m.* accountant; bookkeeper.
contacto, *m.* 1. contact. 2. (auto.) ignition. — **c. de inversión,** (elec.) reverse contact; **c. de tope,** (elec.) butt contact; **ponerse en c.,** to get in contact or in touch with.
contactor, *m.* (elec.) contactor.
contadero, ra, *a.* countable, (which may or should be counted, e.g. days counted from a certain date). —*m.* narrow passage where cattle are counted.
contado, da, *past part. of* **contar.** —*a.* 1. rare, uncommon. 2. specific, set. 3. numbered, e.g. *sus días están contados,* his days are numbered. — **al contado,** cash, in cash; **de contado,** at once, immediately.
contador, ra, *a.* counting. —*m., f.* accountant, bookkeeper; paymaster, cashier, purser; (law) auditor; **c. de costos,** cost accountant; **c. público diplomado,** certified public accountant, chartered accountant. —*m.* 1. counter, desk; desk with pigeon-holes. 2. meter (for gas, water, electricity). 3. counter, counting device (e.g. for counting number of people going through turnstile). —*f.* cash register. — **c. de centelleo,** (phys.) scintillation counter, scintillometer; **c. de corriente,** (hydr.) current meter; (elec.) ampere-hour meter; **c. de estacionamiento,** (auto.) parking meter; **c. de flujo,** (aer.) flowmeter; **c. de tiempo,** timing device; **c. de reloj,** (elec.) clock meter; **c. Geiger,** Geiger counter; **c. kilométrico,** odometer, device to measure distance traversed.
contaduría, *f.* 1. accountancy. 2. accountant's office. 3. post of accountant, auditorship. 4. (theat.) booking office. 5. (Ecuad.) pawnshop. — **c. del ejército,** army paymaster's office; **c. de provincia,** provincial office of internal revenue.
contagiar, *tr.v.* to give or spread (a disease) by contagion; to infect with, transmit (enthusiasm, hate, etc.); to give or spread (bad habits). —*r.v.* to be caught up by (hate, enthusiasm, etc.); to get, develop (bad habits); **se contagió con mi entusiasmo,** he was caught up by or infected with my enthusiasm; **contagiarse de una enfermedad,** to catch a disease.
contagio, *m.* 1. contagion, spreading (of disease); (fig.) contamination, corruption (caused by bad example or indoctrination); (fig.) communication, transmission (of a good or bad quality). 2. contagious disease; contagious germ.
contagión, *f.* (rare) *var. of* **contagio.**
contagiosidad, *f.* contagion, contagiousness.
contagioso, sa, *a.* contagious, catching.
contal, *m.* string of counting beads.
contaminación, *f.* contamination; infection; pollution, corruption; defilement; soiling, befouling.
contaminado, da, *past part. of* **contaminar.** —*a.* corrupted, polluted, contaminated.
contaminador, ra, *a.* contaminating, infecting; polluting, corrupting; defiling; befouling. —*m.* contaminant, pollutant.
contaminante, *a.* contaminating. —*m.* pollutant.
contaminar, *tr.v.* 1. to contaminate, infect. 2. to corrupt, alter (a text). 3. to soil, stain, make dirty. 4. to corrupt, pervert (morals). 5. to pollute. —*r.v.* to be contaminated; to be corrupted.
contante, *a.* counting; cash (money), e.g. *dinero c. y sonante,* cash, ready money.
contar, (*ref. 33*) *tr.v.* 1. to count. 2. to tell, relate, recount. 3. to have, e.g. *él cuenta con muchos amigos,* he has many friends. 4. to count, consider, include, rate, class. — **c. por hecha una cosa,** to consider something as good as done. —*i.v.* to count; **c. con,** to count on, rely on, depend on; to think, bargain for, e.g. *no conté con que podia llover,* I hadn't thought it would rain.
contario, *m.* (archit.) bead molding.
contemperante, *a.* tempering; pacifying.
contemperar, *tr.v.* to moderate, to temper.
contemplación, *f.* 1. contemplation, meditation. 2. obsequiousness, fawning, codling.
contemplador, ra, *a.* contemplative; meditative. —*m., f.* contemplator, meditator.
contemplar, *tr.v.* 1. to contemplate; to meditate, reflect or ponder on; to look at, study (a view, picture, etc.) 2. to be pleasant towards, treat indulgently, coddle.
contemplativamente, *adv.* contemplatively, meditatively.
contemplativo, va, *a.* 1. contemplative, meditative. 2. attentive, obliging, indulgent, coddling.
contemporaneidad, *f.* contemporaneity, contemporaneousness.
contemporáneo, a, *a., m., f.* contemporary, coeval, coetaneous.
contemporice, contemporicé, *ref.* **contemporizar.**
contemporización, *f.* temporization, compromise.
contemporizador, ra, *a.* temporizing. —*m., f.* temporizer; one who acquiesces (for the sake of peace).
contemporizar, (*ref. 53*) *i.v.* to temporize, to comply, to acquiesce.
contén, *m.* curb (of sidewalk).
contención, *f.* 1. retaining, blocking, damming, e.g. *un muro de c.,* a retaining wall. 2. competition, contest. 3. (law) dispute.
contencioso, sa, *a.* contentious, quarrelsome; (law) contentious.
contendedor, *m., var. of* **contendiente.**
contender, (*ref. 30*) *i.v.* to contend, fight; to compete; (fig.) to argue, discuss, dispute.
contendiente, *a.* contending. —*m., f.* contender, opponent, antagonist; rival; disputant, litigant.
contendor, *m., var. of* **contendiente.**
contenedor, *a.* containing; retaining, restraining, damming.
contenencia, *f.* 1. gliding (of birds). 2. hesitation step (in Spanish dancing).
contener, (*ref. 23.*) *tr.v.* 1. to contain, hold. 2. to restrain, hold back, check, curb. — **c. la risa,** to keep a straight face. —*r.v.* to contain oneself, check oneself, hold oneself back.
contenga, contengo, *ref.* **contener.**
contenible, *a.* containable.
contenido, da, *past part, of* **contener.** —*a.* controlled, restrained, moderate, temperate, circumspect. —*m.* contents; content, subject matter (of a book).
conteniente, *a.* containing, holding, comprising.
contenta, *f.* 1. treat, present. 2. (Amer.) cum laude university degree. 3. (com.) endorsement. 4. (mar.) good conduct and capability certificate. 5. (law, Amer.) document of release or discharge (of a debt, given by creditor).
contentadizo, za, *a.* easily pleased; amenable, easy-going. — **mal c.** hard to please.
contentamiento, *m.* 1. contentment, happiness, joy. 2. acquiescence, compliance.
contentar, *tr.v.* 1. to please, gratify, satisfy. 2. (com.) to endorse. —*r.v.* to be content or pleased; to content oneself (with something). — **ser (uno) de buen c.,** to be easily pleased; **ser (uno) de mal c.,** to be hard to please.
contentible, *a.* contemptible, despicable.
contentivo, va, *a.* containing, restraining, holding. — **apósito c.,** (surg.) binding bandage (over swab or compress); **vendaje c.,** binding bandage.
contento, ta, *a.* happy, joyful, gay; content, satisfied. —*m.* happiness, gladness, joy; contentment, satisfaction; **a c.,** to one's liking or satisfaction; **no caber uno de c.,** to be beside oneself with joy or happiness; **ser (uno) de buen c.,** to be easily pleased; **ser (uno) de mal c.,** to be hard to please.
contera, *f.* 1. ferrule, metal cap (on cane, umbrella. etc.); chape (of a scabbard). 2. (mil.) cascabel (projection behind breech of cannon). 3. (poet) refrain; last three lines of a sextain. 4. (fig.) end, ending, finishing touch. — **echar la c.,** (coll.) to conclude, finish; **por c.,** to end with, finally.
contérmino, na, *a.* adjoining, contiguous (territory or town).
contero, *m.* (archit.) bead molding.
conterráneo, a, *a.* from the same country. —*m., f.* fellow countryman (*m.*), countrywoman (*f.*).
contertuliano, na, *m., f.* fellow member of social or literary circle.
contertulio, lia, *m., f.* (coll.) *var. of* **contertuliano.**
contesta, *f.* (Mex., Pan., coll.) conversation; reply, retort.
contestable, *a.* 1. contestable, debatable. disputable. 2. answerable.
contestación, *f.* 1. answer, reply. 2. argument, dispute. — **c. a la demanda,** (law) plea, allegation (defendant's answer to plaintiff's accusations).
contestar, *tr.v.* 1. to answer, reply to. 2. to corroborate, confirm, affirm. 3. to contest, impugn, refute, deny. — **c. el timbre, el teléfono, la puerta,** answer the bell, the telephone, the door. —*i.v.* 1. to answer. 2. to agree, accord.
conteste, *a.* (law) confirming evidence given by another witness.
contexto, *m.* 1. context (passage in a book). 2. interweaving, intermixture.
contextuar, (*ref. 55*) *tr.v.* to prove by use of quotations.
contextura, *f.* 1. contexture, structure, composition. 2. (fig.) build, frame (of body), e.g. *es un hombre de c. fuerte,* he is a man of strong build.
contezuelo, *m.* (derog.) short story.
conticinio, *m.* dead of night.
contienda, *f.* fight, battle; dispute, quarrel; contest, competition.
contienda, contiendo, *ref.* **contender.**
contiene, *ref.* **contener.**
contignación, *f.* (archit.) floorboards, laths (of ceiling), framework.
contigo, *pron.* with you, e.g. *iré contigo al cine,* I'll go with you to the movies.
contiguamente, *adv.* contiguously, adjacently.
contigüidad, *f.* contiguity, contiguousness.
contiguo, gua, *a.* contiguous, adjoining, adjacent.
contimás, *adv.* (obs.) the more, e.g. *contimás me pidas, menos te daré,* the more you ask for, the less you'll get.
continencia, *f.* 1. continence, moderation, abstinence. 2. graceful curtsy in dancing.
continental, *a.* continental, pertaining to a continent. —*m.* public office; letter or notice from a public office.
continente, *a.* containing; restraining; continent. —*m.* 1. container. 2. countenance, mien, bearing, air. 3. (geog.) continent.
continentemente, *adv.* continently, chastely, with moderation.
contingencia, *f.* contingency; risk, hazard.
contingente, *a.* contingent. —*m.* 1. contingency, possibility. 2. contribution, share, quota; (com.) quota (import, export or production). 3. contingent (of troops, children, etc.).
contingentemente, *adv.* by chance, fortuitously, accidentally.

contingible, *a.* possible, liable to happen.
continuación, *f.* continuation, sequel; continuance; prolongation; **a c.,** following, next.
continuadamente, *adv., var. of* **continuamente.**
continuado, da, *a.* continued.
continuador, ra, *a.* continuing. *—m., f.* continuer, follower.
continuamente, *adv.* continuously.
continuar, (*ref. 55*) *tr.v.* to continue, carry on. *—i.v.* to continue, persist, carry on; to endure, remain. — **c.** + *ger.,* to go on + *ger.,* e.g. *c. hablando,* to go on talking.
continuativo, va, *a.* continuative.
continuidad, *f.* continuity; **solución de c.** interruption, break.
continuo, nua, *a.* 1. continuous, prolonged, uninterrupted; persevering, steady. 2. (mec.) endless. — **a la continua, de continuo,** continually, all the time. *—m.* 1. continuum. 2. (formerly) member of the royal guard. *—adv.* continually, all the time.
contómetro, *m.* comptometer, a calculating machine.
contonearse, *r.v.* to walk provocatively swaying one's shoulders or hips.
contoneo, *m.* swaying, provocative gait or walk.
contorcerse, (*ref. 74*) *r.v.* to contort or twist oneself, writhe; to distort one's features, grimace.
contorción, contorsión, *f.* contortion, writhing.
contornado, da, *past part. of* **contornar.** *—a.* (her.) contourné.
contornar, *tr.v., var. of* **contornear.**
contorneado, da, *past part. of* **contornear.** *—a.* shapely.
contornear, *tr.v.* 1. to go round or around (a place). 2. (p.) to sketch or draw the outline, contour or profile of.
contorneo, *m.* 1. going round or around. 2. (p.) sketching, outlining.
contorno, *m.* 1. (p.) contour, outline. 2. (numis.) rim (of a coin). 3. (*pl.*) surroundings, environs, outskirts. — **en c.,** around.
contorsión, *f.* contortion, writhing, spasmodic twisting; grimace, grotesque gesture.
contorsionarse, *r.v.* to contort oneself, writhe, make contortions.
contorsionista, *m., f.* contortionist (circus performer).
contra, *prep.* against; in opposition to, contrary to, counter to; opposite, facing; toward; **c. viento y marea,** against all odds. *—m.* 1. con, opposing vote, reason, etc. 2. (mus.) organ pedal; (*pl.*) bassoon organ stops *—f.* 1. (coll.) difficulty, opposition. 2. (fenc.) counter, circular parry. 3. (Amer.) freebie (sl.), something extra or free of charge. — **engañar la c.,** (fenc.) to foil a counter with a pretended thrust; **hacer a uno la c.,** to oppose or cross one; **hacer la c., ir a la c.,** (cards) to be the main opponent in ombre; **ir en c.,** to go against, disagree with (someone or something); **el pro y el c.,** the pro and the con; **llevar la c.,** to contradict, oppose or thwart.
contraabertura, *f.* (surg.) contrafissure, counteropening.
contraacusación, *f.* counteraccusation.
contraaletas, *f.* (*pl.*) (mar.) counter-fashion pieces (the outermost timbers on both sides of the ship's stern).
contraalisios, *m.* antitrade winds.
contraalmirante, *m.* (mar.) rear-admiral.
contraamantillos, *f. pl.* (mar.) counterbraces.
contraamura, *f.* (mar.) preventer tack.
contraantena, *f.* (rad.) counterpoise.
contraaproches, *m. pl.* counterapproach.
contraarmadura, *f.* (archit.) false lower and gentler slope or pitch of a double pitch roof, built in when the upper slope is too steep.
contraarmiños, *m. pl.* (her.) counterermine (black field with silver spots).
contraatacar, (*ref. 50*) *tr.v.* to counterattack.
contraataguía, *f.* (engin.) reinforcing cofferdam.
contraataque, *m.* (mil.) counterattack.
contraaviso, *m.* counter notice, countermanding notice.
contrabajo, *m.* (mus.) contrabass, double bass; (sl.) bull fiddle; contrabass horn; contrabassist (player); deepbass, basso profundo (voice, singer).
contrabajón, *m.* (mus.) double bassoon, contrabassoon.
contrabajonista, *m.* (mus.) double bassoon player.
contrabalancear, *tr.v.* to counterpoise, counterweight; (fig.) to counterbalance, make up for.
contrabalanza, *f.* counterbalance, counterweight; contrast.
contrabandado, *a.* (her.) counterchanged.
contrabandear, *i.v.* to smuggle.
contrabandista, *m.* smuggler, contrabandist.
contrabando, *m.* contraband; smuggled goods; smuggling. — **de c.,** illegally.
contrabarrado, da, *a.* (her.) counterbarred.
contrabarrera, *f.* second row of seats in the bullring.
contrabasa, *f.* (archit.) plinth, pedestal.
contrabatería, *f.* (mil.) counterbattery.
contrabatir, *tr.v.* (mil.) to fire back on.
contrabitas, *f.* (*pl.*) (mar.) standards of the bitts.
contrabloqueo, *m.* counter blockade.
contrabocel, *m.* (archit.) cavetto.
contrabolina, *f.* (mar.) preventer bowline.
contrabovedilla, *f.* (mar.) second counter, upper counter.
contrabracear, *tr.v.* (mar.) to counterbrace.
contrabraceo, *m.* (mar.) counterbracing.
contrabranque, *m.* (mar.) stemson, apron.
contrabraza, *f.* (mar.) preventer brace.
contrabrazola, *f.* (mar.) headledge.
contracaja, *f.* (print.) upper box of a type case (for seldom used type).
contracalcar, *tr.v.* to trace from the reverse side in order to obtain a back view of the original.
contracambiada, *f.* (equit.) changing of the horse's forefoot; change of gait.
contracambio, *m.* exchange; (com.) re-exchange; (fig.) compensation.
contracanal, *m.* by-channel, branch channel, leading from or to another one.
contracandela, *f.* (Amer.) backfire, fire break (burning of an area to halt forest fire).
contracarril, *m.* (ry.) guard rail, safety rail, wing rail.
contracarta, *f.* (law) counterdeed (countering a former contract).
contracción, *f.* 1. contraction, shrinking. 2. (gram.) contraction; synaeresis. — **c. de la vena fluida,** (phys.) natural thinning out of liquid or gas stream going out through a narrow outlet.
contracebadera, *f.* (mar.) sprit-topsail.
contracédula, *f.* counter order.
contracepción, *f.* (neol.) contraception.
contraceptivo, va, *a., m.* contraceptive.
contracercos, *m.* (*pl.*) door and window trim.
contracielo, *m.* (min., Mex.) raise, upraise; **c. ventilador,** ventilation raise.
contracifra, *f.* cipher, key; code.
contracimiento, *m.* wall or paving to protect a foundation.
contracircuito, *m.* (elec.) circuit breaker.
contraclave, *f.* (archit.) voussoir next to keystone.
contracodaste, *m.* (mar.) inner sternpost.
contracorriente, *f.* (elec., geog., mar.) countercurrent.
contracosta, *f.* other side or opposite coast.
contractibilidad, *f.* contractibility.
contráctil, *a.* contractile.
contractilidad, *f.* contractility.
contractivo, va, *a.* contractive, contractile.
contracto, ta, *irr. past part. of* **contraer.**
contractual, *a.* contractual, stipulated by contract.
contractura, *f.* (med.) contracture.
contracuartelado, da, *a.* (her.) counterchanged.
contracuerdas, *f. pl.* (mar.) outward deck planks.
contracurva, *f.* (ry.) reverse curve.
contrachoque, *m.* bumper, buffer.
contradancista, *m., f.* dancer who leads the cotillion.
contradanza, *f.* country dance, contredance, cotillion, quadrille.
contradecir, (*ref. 7*) *tr.v.* to contradict, oppose. *—r.v.* to contradict oneself.
contrademanda, *f.* (law, com.) counterclaim.
contrademandar, *tr.v., i.v.* to counterclaim.
contraderivación, *f.* (elec.) back shunt.
contradicción, *f.* contradiction; opposition.
contradice, contradiciendo, *ref.* **contradecir.**
contradictor, ra, *a.* contradictory. *—m., f.* contradicter, contradictor.
contradictoria, *f.* (log.) contradictory proposition.
contradictoriamente, *adv.* contradictorily.
contradictorio, ria, *a.* contradictory.
contradicho, cha, *irr. past part. of* **contradecir.**
contradiga, contradigo, *ref.* **contradecir.**
contradije, contradijera, contradijese, *ref.* **contradecir.**
contradique, *m.* counterdike, a second dike.
contradiré, *ref.* **contradecir.**
contradriza, *f.* (mar.) second halliard.
contradurmiente, *m.* (mar.) clamp.
contraeje, *m.* (mec.) countershaft.
contraelectromotriz, *a.* (elec.) counterelectromotive.
contraemboscada, *f.* counter-ambush.
contraembozo, *m.* (dressm.) cape-facing.
contraempuje, *m.* (engin.) counterthrust.
contraendosar, *tr.v.* to reindorse.
contraensayo, *m.* (engin.) check analysis.
contraenvite, *m.* bluff call (in card games).
contraer, (*ref. 24*) *tr.v.* 1. to contract, reduce, shrink. 2. to join, draw together; to tighten. 3. to contract, catch (illness); to get, acquire, fall into (a habit); to incur (a debt). 4. to assume, take on (an obligation) to enter into, make (an agreement, engagement). 5. to shorten, condense (a speech); (gram.) to contract, shorten (words). — **c. amistad,** to make friends; **c. deudas,** to get into debt; **c. matrimonio,** to marry, get married. *—r.v.* to contract or become contracted (a muscle, nerve, etc.).
contraescarpa, *f.* (fort.) counterscarp.
contraescota, *f.* (mar.) preventer sheet.
contraescotín, *m.* (mar.) preventer, topsail sheet.
contraescritura, *f.* (law) counterdeed (countering a former contract).
contraespionaje, *m.* counterespionage.
contraestay, *m.* (mar.) preventer stay.
contraexplosión, *f.* (auto.) backfire.
contrafacción, *f.* (arch.) counterfeit, forgery, imitation, fake.
contrafagot, *m.* (mus.) contrafagotto.
contrafajado, da, *a.* (her.) counterfessed.
contrafallar, *tr.v.* to overtrump (in card games).
contrafallo, *m.* overtrumping.
contrafianza, *f.* indemnity bond.
contrafibra, *f.* cross grain.
contrafigura, *f.* (theat.) counterpart, double (of an actor).

contrafilo, *m.* back edge blade (on the blade point of a dagger, broadsword, etc.).
contrafilón, *m.* (min.) counterlode, countervein.
contrafirma, *f.* 1. (law) inhibition of a prior decree. 2. counter signature.
contraflecha, *f.* (mec.) camber.
contraflorado, da, *a.* (her.) counterflory, counterfleury.
contraflujo, *m.* reverse current, counter-current, counterflow, eddy.
contrafoque, *m.* (mar.) foretop staysail.
contrafoso, *m.* 1. (theat.) second cellar or basement under stage. 2. (fort.) avantfosse or outer ditch.
contrafuero, *m.* infringement or violation of a charter, privilege or municipal law.
contrafuerte, *m.* 1. saddlestrap (for securing girth or cinch). 2. heel reinforcement (of a shoe). 3. (archit.) buttress, counterfort. 4. (fort.) fort opposite another fort. 5. (geol.) secondary mountain range, ridge, spur.
contrafuga, *f.* (mus.) counterfugue.
contragolpe, *m.* 1. counter, counter blow. 2. (med.) contrecoup (reaction in a part of the body other than that which has suffered a contusion). 3. (engin.) reverse or back stroke of a piston.
contragradiente, *f.* (bldg.) reverse grade.
contraguardia, *f.* (fort.) counterguard.
contraguerrilla, *f.* anti-guerrilla troops.
contraguía, *f.* the left front mule in a team.
contrahacedor, ra, *a.* 1. imitating, imitative; plagiarizing. 2. falsifying, forging, faking. 3. dissembling, feigning. —*m., f.* 1. imitator, copier; mimic. 2. counterfeiter, faker. 3. plagiarist.
contrahacer, (*ref. 10*) *tr.v.* 1. to imitate, copy. 2. to forge, counterfeit, fake. 3. to plagiarize, pirate (ideas, literary works, etc.). 4. (fig.) to feign, simulate, dissemble. —*r.v.* to pretend, feign.
contrahaga, contrahago, *ref.* **contrahacer.**
contraharé, contraharía, *ref.* **contrahacer.**
contrahaz, (*pl.* **contrahaces**) *f.* wrong side (of a fabric, etc.).
contrahecho, cha, *irr. past part. of* **contrahacer.** —*a.* 1. deformed, humpbacked. 2. counterfeit, spurious. —*m., f.* hunchback, deformed person.
contrahechura, *f.* 1. counterfeit, forgery, fake. 2. plagiarism. 3. imitation, copy.
contrahice, contrahiciera, contrahiciese, *ref.* **contrahacer.**
contrahierba, *f.* 1. (S. Amer., bot) contrayerva. 2. any medicament containing the root of the contrayerva. 3. (fig.) antidote, preventive.
contrahilera, *f.* 1. (archit.) auxiliary ridgepiece. 2. (mil.) auxiliary line of defense.
contrahilo, *adv.* **a contrahilo,** across the grain (of a fabric).
contrahoradar, *tr.v.* (carp.) to bore on the opposite side.
contrahuella, *f.* (archit.) riser (of a staircase).
contraiga, contraigo, *ref.* **contraer.**
contraincendios, *a.* fireproof, fire-resisting; pertaining to fire fighting.
contraindicación, *f.* (med.) contraindication.
contraindicante, *m.* (med.) contraindicant.
contraindicar, (*ref. 50*) *tr.v.* (med.) to contraindicate.
contraindique, contraindiqué, *ref.* **contraindicar.**
contrairritación, *f.* (med.) counterirritation.
contrairritante, *m.* (med.) counterirritant.
contraje, contrajese, contrajera, *ref.* **contraer.**
contralecho, a c., *adv.* (archit.) laid perpendicularly, crossbond.
contralizos, *m. pl.* (tex.) rods for moving leashes.
contralmirante, *m.* (mar.) rear-admiral.
contralor, *m.* comptroller (royal household, fiscal, army, etc.), inspector.
contraloría, *f.* comptrollership.
contralto, *m.* (mus.) contralto (voice). —*m., f.* (mus.) contralto (male or female singer).
contraluz, (*pl.* **contraluces**) *f.* view (of things) seen against the light; **a c.,** (photog.) backlighted.
contramaestre, *m.* foreman, overseer; (mar.) boatswain, chief petty officer (enforcing orders issued by captain); **c. de muralla,** dockside busybody (civilian who loiters about the docks criticizing nautical operations); **segundo c.,** (mar.) boatswain's mate.
contramalla, *f.* 1. outer wide-meshed net (in double net fishing). 2. space within a small-meshed net.
contramalladura, *f., var. of* **contramalla.**
contramallar, *tr.v.* to make wide-meshed nets.
contramandar, *tr.v.* to countermand, to cancel a previously given order.
contramandato, *m.* counterorder, countermand.
contramangas, *f.* (*pl.*) oversleeves (formerly used to cover shirt or blouse sleeves).
contramaniobra, *f.* countermaneuver.
contramanivela, *f.* (mec.) drag link.
contramano, *adv.* **a c.,** in the wrong direction; against the traffic.
contramarca, *f.* 1. countermark; customs duty; right to impose a customs duty; customs duty mark or seal. 2. (numis.) mark on re-minted coins or medals, countermark.
contramarcar, (*ref. 50*) *tr.v.* to countermark; to mark with a customs seal.
contramarco, *m.* (carp.) frame of a French window.
contramarcha, *f.* 1. countermarch, marching back, backtracking. 2. (mil., mar.) evolution, change of front, change of course. 3. (mec.) reverse gear. 4. part of a loom.
contramarchar, *i.v.* (mil.) to countermarch; to backtrack, walk back (over same ground).
contramarea, *f.* (mar.) opposing tide, counter tide.
contramarque, contramarqué, *ref.* **contramarcar.**
contramartillo, *m.* (mec., bldg.) dolly, bucker.
contramatar, *tr.v.* to hit hard, thump. —*r.v.* (Mex.) to repent.
contramatriz, *f.* (mec.) top die.
contramesana, *f.* (mar.) mizzenmast.
contramina, *f.* 1. (mil.) countermine, underground gallery. 2. (min.) communicating tunnel between two mines. 3. (fig.) countermove, counterplot, counter-stroke.
contraminar, *tr.v.* (mil.) to countermine; to counter, countermine (someone else's plans).
contramuelle, *m.* (mec.) counter-spring, duplicate spring.
contramuralla, *f.* (fort.) low rampart, countermure.
contramuro, *m., var. of* **contramuralla.**
contranatural, *a.* unnatural.
contranota, *f.* (law) counterresolution, counterproposal (of a public official with regard to a subordinate's report).
contraofensiva, *f.* (mil.) counteroffensive.
contraorden, *f.* counterorder, countermand.
contrapalado, da, *a.* (her.) counterpaly.
contrapalanquín, *m.* (mar.) preventer clewgarnet.
contrapar, *m.* (archit.) common rafter, roof rafter (in a gabled or tiled roof).
contraparte, *f.* counterpart.
contrapartida, *f.* (acc.) cross entry (in double-entry bookkeeping).
contrapás, *m.* 1. figure or step in country dancing. 2. a popular dance in some parts of Catalonia.
contrapasamiento, *m.* change of sides, changing over (to the opposite band or party).
contrapasar, *i.v.* to change sides, join the opposite party.
contrapaso, *m.* 1. step in an opposite direction, back step. 2. (mus.) second part (in canon singing).
contrapear, *tr.v.* (carp.) to glue or cement layers of wood together (with the grains of adjacent layers at right angles).
contrapechar, *tr.v.* (arch.) to ride one's horse straight at the chest of another horse.
contrapelo, *adv.* **a c.,** against the natural direction, against the grain (of fur, hair, pile, etc.), the wrong way, e.g. *acariciar un gato a c.,* to stroke a cat the wrong way; (fig.) contrary to normal practice; violently, forcibly; against one's will, unwillingly.
contrapendiente, *f.* 1. reverse grade, acclivity. 2. (Sp., Arg.) downgrade following an upgrade.
contrapesar, *tr.v.* to counterbalance, counterpoise; to counterweight; (fig.) to counteract, offset, compensate, make up for.
contrapeso, *m.* 1. counterweight, counterbalance, counterpoise. 2. makeweight (thrown into a scale to make up weight). 3. counterbalance, curb, check. 4. ropewalker's pole. 5. (numis.) re-minted coin. 6. (Chile) restlessness.
contrapeste, *m.* remedy against the plague.
contrapilastra, *f.* 1. (archit.) counterpilaster, counterpillar. 2. (carp.) wood weatherstrip, draught excluder (around doors, windows).
contrapiso, *m.* 1. subgloor. 2. (Arg., bldg.) subgrade.
contraplacado, *m.* plywood.
contraplancha, *f.* (engin.) splice plate; (mec.) backing strip.
contrapóliza, *f.* insurance policy which cancels the previous one.
contrapondré, contrapondría, *ref.* **contraponer.**
contraponedor, ra, *a.* 1. comparing; contrasting. 2. opposing. —*m., f.* 1. confronter, opposer. 2. one who compares.
contraponer, (*ref. 15*) *tr.v.* to compare, contrast; to oppose, set or pit against. —*r.v.* to oppose, set or pit oneself against.
contraponga, contrapongo, *ref.* **contraponer.**
contraportada, *f.* back page; **c. del disco,** flip side.
contraposición, *f.* contraposition. opposition; comparison.
contrapozo, *m.* (fort.) fougasse (in a countermine).
contrapresa, *f.* (hydr.) downstream cofferdam; stilling-pool weir.
contrapresión, *f.* back pressure.
contraprincipio, *m.* assertion contrary to an established principle.
contraproducente, *a.* self-defeating, counterproductive.
contrapromesa, *f.* withdrawal of a promise.
contraproposición, *f.* counterproposition.
contrapropósito, *m.* cross-purpose.
contraproyecto, *m.* counter-project, counterplan.
contraprueba, *m.* 1. counterevidence. 2. (print.) second proof.
contrapuerta, *f.* hall door (between a hall and the rest of the house); storm door; (fort.) second or interior gate.
contrapuesto, ta, *irr. past part. of* **contraponer.**
contrapunce, contrapuncé, *ref.* **contrapunzar.**
contrapunción, *f.* (med.) counteropening.

contrapuntante, *m.* (mus.) contrapuntist (singer).
contrapuntarse, *r.v.* to quarrel, wrangle.
contrapuntear, *tr.v.* 1. to sing in counterpoint. 2. to be sarcastic towards, taunt. —*r.v.* 1. to quarrel, wrangle. 2. to become piqued or annoyed.
contrapuntista, *m.* (mus.) contrapuntist, contrapuntalist (composer).
contrapunto, *m.* (mus.) counterpoint.
contrapunzar, (*ref. 53*) *tr.v.* to punch or drive in (with a punch).
contrapunzón, *m.* 1. punch for driving in nails. 2. punch of a stamping die. 3. gunsmith's countermark on guns.
contrapuse, contrapusiera, contrapusiese, *ref.* **contraponer.**
contraquerella, *f.* (law) cross action, crosscomplaint.
contraquilla, *f.* (mar.) false keel.
contrariamente, *adv.* **c. a,** contrary to.
contrariar, (*ref. 54*) *tr.v.* 1. to oppose, go against. 2. to contradict. 3. to annoy, vex. 4. to hinder, impede, obstruct.
contrariedad, *f.* 1. obstacle, impediment, hindrance, setback. 2. annoyance, vexation. 3. reversal, upset.
contrario, ria, *a.* 1. contrary; opposite. 2. unfavorable, adverse, bad (luck, conditions, etc.). 3. harmful, bad (for the health). — **al** or **por el contrario,** on the contrary; **de lo contrario,** otherwise, if not; **lo contrario,** the opposite, e.g. *no dijo eso sino lo contrario,* he did not say that but the opposite; **llevar la contraria,** to contradict, oppose, go counter to. —*m., f.* opponent, rival, competitor.
contrarrasante, *m.* (top.) adverse grade.
contrarraya, *f.* crosshatching line (in engraving).
contrarreclamación, *f.* counterclaim.
Contrarreforma, *f.* (rel.) Counter-Reformation.
contrarregistro, *m.* control register (check of fiscal or excise revenue accounts).
contrarreguera, *f.* (agr.) oblique auxiliary irrigation ditch (to distribute water evenly).
contrarréplica, *f.* retort, rejoinder, riposte; (law) rejoinder, document in which defendant replies to plaintiff's charges.
contrarrestar, *tr.v.* 1. to counteract, check, stop, block, thwart, resist, oppose. 2. to hit the ball back (to the wall) from the service line (in jai-alai).
contrarresto, *m.* 1. counteraction; checking, blocking. 2. player who returns the ball from the service line (in game of jai-alai).
contrarrevolución, *m.* counterrevolution.
contrarrevolucionario, ria, *m., f., a.* counterrevolutionary.
contrarriel, *m.* (ry.) guardrail, wing rail.
contrarroda, *f.* (mar.) stemson.
contrarronda, *f.* (mil.) counterround.
contrarrotura, *f.* (vet.) plaster, poultice (to heal a wound).
contrasalida, *f.* (mil.) countersally.
contrasalva, *f.* (artil.) counter salute, return salvo.
contraseguro, *m.* retrievable premium insurance, premium deposit insurance.
contrasellar, *tr.v.* to counterseal.
contrasello, *m.* counterseal (superimposed on first seal); mark of counterseal.
contrasentido, *m.* 1. antilogy, contradiction. 2. mistranslation, misinterpretation. 3. stupidity, piece of nonsense.
contraseña, *f.* 1. countersign, secret sign; (mil.) countersign, password; (mil.) parole (watchword given only to officers of the guard and of the day). 2. countersign (customs mark). — **c. de salida,** readmission ticket (so as to return to a theatre after the intermission).
contrastable, *a.* contrastable.
contrastador, ra, *a., m., f.* contrasting.
contrastante, *a.* contrasting.
contrastar, *tr.v.* 1. to resist, face, stand up to. 2. to assay (coins); to assay and seal (weights and measures). —*i.v.* to contrast, differ, place in opposition to.
contraste, *m.* 1. contrast. 2. resistance, opposition. 3. public assayer (of the mint); public assaying office, public inspector of weights and measures; public weighing of raw silk. 4. (coll.) controversy, quarrel. 5. (mar.) sudden change in the wind (to the opposite direction).
contrata, *f.* 1. contract. 2. (theat.) engagement.
contratación, *f.* 1. making of a contract. 2. contracting; hiring, engagement. 3. trade, commerce, business enterprise.
contrataladro, *m.* (mec.) counterbore.
contratalud, *m.* counterslope; (top.) foreslope.
contratante, *a.* contracting. —*m., f.* contracting party; contractor, hirer.
contratapa, *f.* 1. auxiliary top or cover. 2. back cover of a book.
contratar, *tr.v.* 1. to contract; to hire, engage. 2. to make a contract for.
contratensión, *f.* (elec.) counter-electromotive force.
contratiempo, *m.* 1.contretemps, setback, mishap, inconvenience. 2. (mus.) syncopation. — **a c.,** in syncopated time.
contratiro, *m.* 1. back draft. 2. (min.) auxiliary shaft.
contratista, *m., f.* contractor; **c. de edificación, building contractor.**
contrato, *m.* contract; agreement enforceable by law; **c. a la gruesa, c. a riesgo marítimo, c. de cambio marítimo,** (mar., law) respondentia; **c. a. título gratuito,** (law) gratuitous contract; **c. de alquiler,** rental agreement, lease; **c. de compraventa or compra y venta,** (com.) contract of purchase, contract of purchase and sale, bill of sale; **c. de fletamiento.** (com.) charter party.
contratope, *m.* rear stop, back bumper.
contratorpedero, *m.* (mar.) torpedo-boat destroyer.
contratrancaniles, *m. pl.* (mar.) inner waterways.
contratreta, *f.* counterplot, counterstroke, countertrick.
contratrinchera, *f.* (fort.) counterapproaches.
contratuerca, *f.* lock nut, jam nut.
contravalación, *f.* (fort.) contravallation, countervallation.
contravalar, *tr.v.* (fort.) to construct a contravallation in front of.
contravalor, *m.* (com.) countervalue, equivalent.
contravapor, *m.* (mec.) back pressure steam, e.g. *dar c.,* to reverse steam (in a locomotive).
contravástago, *m.* (mec.) piston tail rod.
contravención, *f.* contravention, infringement, infraction, breach, violation.
contraveneno, *m.* 1. antidote. 2. (fig.) precaution, antidote, remedy.
contravenga, contravengo, *ref.* **contravenir.**
contravenir, (*ref. 26*) *tr.v.* to contravene, infringe, violate (a law).
contraventana, *f.* storm window; window shutter.
contraventor, ra, *a.* contravening, infringing, violating. —*m., f.* contravener, infringer, violator.
contraventura, *f.* misfortune.
contraverado, da, *a.* (her.) countervair, countervary.
contraveros, *m. pl.* (her.) countervairs.
contravidriera, *f.* storm window (second window used in very cold climates).
contravidrio, *m.* glazing molding.
contraviene, *ref.* **contravenir.**
contraviento, *a.* wind bracing. —*m.* 1. (archit.) windbrace. 2. (carp.) straining piece.
contravine, contraviniendo, contraviniera, contraviniese, *ref.* **contravenir.**
contravisita, *f.* second visit (made to verify results of a previous one).
contravoluta, *f.* (archit.) secondary volute or scroll.
contrayendo, *ref.* **contraer.**
contrayente, *a.* contracting (marriage partner). —*m., f.* contracting party (in a marriage).
contrecho, cha, *a.* crippled, maimed.
contrete, *m.* (Ecuad.) prop, support, stay.
contribución, *f.* contribution; levy; tax; **c. directa,** direct tax; **c. de guerra,** war tax or levy; **c. indirecta,** indirect tax; **c. de sangre,** military service; **c. territorial,** land tax.
contribuidor, ra, *a.* contributing, contributory. —*m., f.* contributor.
contribuir, (*ref. 48*) *tr.v.* to contribute. —*i.v.* to contribute.
contribulado, da, *a.* afflicted, troubled, grieved.
contributario, ria, *m., f.* fellow contributor or taxpayer.
contributivo, va, *a.* contributive.
contribuya, contribuyendo, *ref.* **contribuir.**
contribuyente, *a.* contributing, contributory. —*m., f.* contributor; taxpayer.
contribuyera, contribuyese, contribuyo, *ref.* **contribuir.**
contrición, *f.* contrition, contriteness, repentance.
contrín, *m.* (Phil. I.) unit of weight (0.39 grs.)
contrincante, *m.* fellow candidate (for a chair, professorship, etc.); competitor, rival, opponent; opposite number.
contristar, *tr.v.* to sadden, make unhappy. —*r.v.* to become sad or unhappy.
contrito, ta, *a.* contrite, repentant, penitent.
control, *m.* 1. control, direction; inspection, checking; control point. 2. examination. 3. control, restraint. — **bajo su c.,** under one's control; **c. de la natalidad,** birth control; **c. de precios,** price control; **c. de tono,** (rad.) tone control; **c. de vuelo,** flight control; **c. remoto,** remote control; **c. sobre si mismo,** self-control; **fuera de c.,** out of control; **puesto de c.,** control point.
controlar, *tr.v.* 1. to inspect, check, examine. 2. to control, govern.
contróler, *m.* (elec.) controller (on electric car or locomotive).
controversia, *f.* controversy, dispute; argument, debate.
controversista, *m.* controversialist, disputant, disputer, debater.
controvertible, *a.* controvertible, debatable.
controvertir, (*ref. 31*) *i.v.* to controvert, argue, discuss. —*tr.v.* to discuss.
controvierta, controvierto, *ref.* **controvertir.**
controvirtiendo, controvirtiera, controvirtió, *ref.* **controvertir.**
contubernio, *m.* 1. cohabitation; concubinage. 2. (coll.) collusion, complicity, connivence.
contuerza, contuerzo, *ref.* **contorcerse.**
contumacia, *f.* 1. contumacy, obduracy. 2. (law) contumacy, default, non-appearance.
contumaz, (*pl.* **contumaces**) *a.* 1. contumacious, stubborn, obdurate, 2. germ-carrying, disease-spreading. 3. inveterate. 4. (law) contumacious, defaulting. —*m., f.* (law) defaulter, person guilty of contumacy or non-appearance.
contumazmente, *adv.* contumaciously, stubbornly, obstinately.
contumelia, *f.* contumely, insult, abuse.

contumelioso, sa, *a.* contumelious, insulting, abusive.
contundente, *a.* 1. contusive, bruising. 2. (coll.) conclusive, overwhelming, forcible (evidence, argument, etc.).
contundir, *tr.v.* to bruise, bump, batter. *—r.v.* to bruise or bump oneself.
conturbación, *f.* uneasiness, anxiety, perturbation.
conturbado, da, *past part. of* **conturbar.** *—a.* uneasy, anxious, perturbed, disturbed.
conturbador, ra, *a.* perturbing, disturbing, upsetting. *—m., f.* perturber, disturber, upsetter.
conturbar, *tr.v.* to perturb, disturb, disquiet, make uneasy. *—r.v.* to become perturbed, disturbed or uneasy.
conturbativo, va, *a.* perturbing, disturbing, disquieting, upsetting.
contusión, *f.* contusion, bruise.
contusionar, *tr.v.* (imp. u.), *var. of* **contundir.**
contuso, sa, *a.* bruised, contused. *—m., f.* person with contusions.
contutor, *m.* co-guardian.
contuve, contuviera, contuviese, *ref.* **contener.**
conuco, *m.* (Cuba, obs.) plot of land granted to slaves for cultivation. 2. (Amer.) small farm.
convalecencia, *f.* 1. convalescence. 2. sanatorium, rest home.
convalecer, (*ref. 45*) *i.v.* to convalesce; to recover.
convaleciente, *a.* convalescent. *—m., f.* convalescent (patient).
convalezco, convalezca, *ref.* **convalecer.**
convalidación, *f.* confirmation, revalidation.
convalidar, *tr.v.* (law) to confirm.
convección, *f.* (phys.) convection.
convecino, na, *a.* near, adjacent, contiguous; neighboring. *—m., f.* neighbor.
convector, *m.* (elec., engin.) convector.
convelerse, *r.v.* (med.) to twitch (muscles), to contract.
convencedor, ra, *a.* convincing; persuasive. *—m., f.* convincer.
convencer, (*ref. 56*) *tr.v.* to convince. *—r.v.* to become convinced.
convencible, *a.* convincible.
convencimiento, *m.* conviction; convincing.
convención, *f.* 1. agreement, pact, contract. 2. conformity, harmony. 3. national assembly. 4. convention (political).
convencional, *a.* conventional, set, established; contractual. *—m.* member of an assembly, delegate.
convencionalismo, *m.* conventionalism, convention, conventionality, standard rule or custom.
convencionalmente, *adv.* conventionally.
convenga, convengo, *ref.* **convenir.**
convenible, *a.* easy-going (coll.), docile, compliant; reasonable, fair, moderate (price).
convenido, da, *past part. of* **convenir.** *—a.* agreed upon.
conveniencia, *f.* 1. convenience, comfort; profit, advantage. 2. harmony, agreement, conformity, pact. 3. place, position (in domestic service). 4. (*pl.*) perquisites, emoluments (given to domestic servants). 5. (*pl.*) assets, income property.
convenienciero, ra, *a.* selfish, self-centered, thinking only of one's own convenience.
conveniente, *a.* 1. convenient. 2. advantageous, profitable. 3. worthwhile. 4. advisable. 5. suitable, fit, right. 6. proper, correct (behavior).
convenientemente, *adv.* conveniently; profitably, suitably.
convenio, *m.* agreement, covenant, pact; (com.) settlement.
convenir, (*ref.26*) *i.v.* 1. to be advisable; to suit; to be convenient; to be profitable, worthwhile or advantageous. 2. to agree, concur. 3. to correspond, belong. *—r.v.* to agree, come to an agreement; **convenirse a, en** or **con,** to agree to, to agree with.
conventico, *m., var. of* **conventillo.**
conventícula, *f., var. of* **conventículo.**
conventículo, *m.* conventicle, secret or illicit meeting.
conventillo, *m.* (Arg., Chile) tenement house.
convento, *m.* convent; monastery.
conventual, *a.* conventual, monastic. *—m.* conventual (member of a convent); Conventual (a Franciscan friar).
conventualidad, *f.* 1. convent or monastery life, communal life. 2. assignment of monk or nun to a monastery or convent.
conventualmente, *adv.* conventually, monastically.
convenza, convenzo, *ref.* **convencer.**
convergencia, *f.* convergence, convergency.
convergente, *a.* convergent, converging.
converger, (*ref. 62*) *i.v., var. of* **convergir.**
convergir, (*ref. 62*) *i.v.* to converge, meet (at a given point); (fig.) to concur, agree (opinions, etc.); to join, unite (towards a given end).
converja, converjo, *ref.* **convergir, converger.**
conversa, *f.* (coll.) chat, talk.
conversable, *a.* affable, friendly, sociable, approachable.
conversación, *f.* 1. conversation; chat. 2. assembly, meeting. 3. illicit intercourse or dealings.— **dirigir la c. a,** to direct oneself to a person, address someone specifically (in a conversation); **sacar uno la c.,** to bring up or introduce a subject for discussion; **trabar c.,** to start a conversation.
conversador, ra, *a.* talkative; **él es poco c.,** he does not talk much. *—m., f.* talker, conversationalist.
conversar, *i.v.* 1. to converse, chat, talk. 2. to live together. 3. to deal, have dealings (with). 4. (mil.) to wheel, change front.
conversión, *f.* 1. conversion. 2. (mil.) wheel; wheeling, changing front. 3. (rhet.) epistrophe, concluding two or more clauses with the same word or phrase.
conversivo, va, *a.* conversive, having the ability to convert or change.
converso, sa, *irr. past part. of* **convertir.** *—a.* converted. *—m., f.* convert. *—m.* (ecc.) lay brother (in some orders).
conversón, na, *a.* (Col., coll.) talkative, garrulous.
conversor, ra, *m., f.* converter.
convertibilidad, *f.* convertibility.
convertible, *a.* convertible, changeable, transformable. *—m.* (auto.) convertible.
convertidor, *m.* converter; **c. de frecuencia,** (elec.) frequency changer or converter; **c. sincrónico** or **rotativo,** (elec.) synchronous converter; **c. de onda,** (rad.) wave converter.
convertir, (*ref. 42*) *tr.v.* to convert; to change; to turn. *—r.v.* to become converted; to turn into.
convexidad, *f.* convexity.
convexo, xa, *a.* convex.
convexocóncavo, va, *a.* convexo-concave.
convicción, *f.* conviction, certainty.
convicto, ta, *irr. past. part. of* **convencer.** *—a.* convicted, guilty. *—m., f.* convict.
convictor, *m.* boarder (in certain colleges or religious communities).
convictorio, *m.* students' quarters (in Jesuit colleges).
convidada, *f.* treat (to a drink); **pagar una convidada,** to stand a treat, stand a drink.
convidado, da, *past part. of* **convidar.** *—m., f.* guest; **como el convidado de piedra,** mute, quiet, grave.
convidador, ra, *a.* inviting. *—m., f* host.
convidante, *a.* inviting. *—m., f.* host, hostess, one who extends an invitation.
convidar, *tr.v.* to invite, to treat; to allure, entice; induce, cause. — **c. a** + *inf.*, to invite to + *inf.;* **c. a una copa,** to offer a drink.
conviene, *ref.* **convenir.**
convierta, convierto, *ref.* **convertir.**
convincente, *a.* convincing.
convincentemente, *adv.* convincingly.
convine, conviniendo, conviniera, conviniese, *ref.* **convenir.**
convirtiendo, convirtiera, convirtiese, *ref.* **convertir.**
convite, *m.* invitation; party, treat, feast.
convival, *a.* convivial, festive.
convivencia, *f.* living together, cohabitation.
conviviente, *a.* living together. *—m., f.* person who cohabits with another.
convivir, *i.v* to cohabit, live together.
convocación *f., convocation, convoking.*
convocador, ra, *a.* convoking, summoning. *—m., f.* convoker, convener.
convocar, (*ref. 50*) *tr.v.* 1. to convoke, call together, convene, summon. 2. to acclaim.
convocatoria, *f.* summons; edict; notice of a meeting.
convocatorio, ria, *a.* summoning, convoking.
convoluto, ta, *a.* convolute.
convolvuláceo, a, *a.* (bot.) convolvulaceous. *—f.* convolvulus; (*pl.*) Convolvulaceae.
convólvulo, *m.* 1. (zool.) vine fretter, vinegrub. 2. (bot.) convolvulus.
convoque, convoqué, *ref.* **convocar.**
convoy, *m.* 1. convoy, escort, guard; (coll.) retinue, following. 2. cruet stand (for oil and vinegar).
convoyante, *a.* convoying, escorting.
convoyar, *tr.v.* to convoy, escort, guard.
convulsión, *f.* 1. convulsion. 2. (social) upheaval, (political) agitation. 3. (seismic) movement.
convulsionar, *tr.v.* 1. (med.) to convulse. 2. disturb violently.
convulsionario, ria, *a.* convulsionary, suffering convulsions.
convulsivo, va, *a.* convulsive; (med.) whooping (cough).
convulso, sa, *a.* convulsed.
conyúdice, *m., var. of* **conjuez.**
conyugal, *a.* conjugal, connubial.
conyugalmente, *adv.* conjugally, connubially.
cónyuge, *m., f.* spouse, consort; (*pl.*) married couple.
conyugicida, *m., f.* person who kills his spouse.
conyugicidio, *m.* killing of one spouse by the other.
coñac, *m.* cognac, brandy.
coño, *m.* (vulg.) cunt; **¡c.!** (vulg.) damn it! fuck it!
coolí, *m.* coolie, cooly.
cooperación, *f.* cooperating, cooperation.
cooperador, ra, *a.* cooperative. *—m., f.* cooperator.
cooperante, *a.* cooperating.
cooperar, *i.v.* to cooperate.
cooperario, *m.* cooperator.
cooperativo, va, *a.* cooperative. *—f.* cooperative society; **cooperativa de construcción,** building society.
coopositor, ra, *m., f* candidate (for a position to be awarded by competition).
coordenado, da, *a.* (math.) coordinate. *—f.* coordinate; **coordenada cartesiana,** Cartesian coordinate; **coordenada polar,** (math.) polar

coordinate; **coordenada rectangular,** geom.) rectangular coordinate.
coordinación, *f.* coordination.
coordinadamente, *adv.* coordinately.
coordinado, da, *a.* (math.), *var. of* **coordenado.**
coordinador, ra, *a.* coordinating, coordinative. —*m., f.* coordinator.
coordinamiento, *m., var. of* **coordinación.**
coordinar, *tr.v.* to coordinate.
coordinativo, va,, *a.* coordinative, coordinating.
copa, *f.* 1. wineglass, goblet, stemmed glass; (fig.) drink, cocktail; glassful. 2. treetop, crown (of a tree); crown (of a hat). 3. gill, liquid unit of 126 milliliters. 4. cup-shaped brazier. 5. each card of the suit of **copas** (in Spanish cards); (*pl.*) one of the suits in Spanish cards represented by a goblet. 6. cup (in sporting events). 7. (astron.) the Cup, the Constellation Crater. 8. drink. 9. (*pl.*) bosses (rings of a bridle bit). — **c. de helado, c. helada,** ice cream sundae; **c. del horno,** roof of a furnace; **c. de succión,** suction cup; **c. graduada,** measuring cup or glass; **irse uno de copas,** (coll.) to break wind; **echar por copas,** (Amer.) to exaggerate; **tomar una c.,** to have an alcoholic drink.
copada, *f.* (ornith.) crested lark.
copado, da, *past part. of* **copar.** —*a.* topped, e.g. *un arbol bien copado,* a bushy-topped tree.
copador, *m.* mallet (for bending iron, copper, tin, etc.).
copaiba, *f.* (bot.) copaifera, copaiba; copaiba balsam, copaiba; **c. de la India,** copaiba resin or balsam.
copaína, *f.* (chem.) copaene.
copal, *m.* copal (resin).
copalillo, *m.* (Cuba, bot.) species of chaste tree (Vitex rigens); (Hond.) courbaril (Hymenaea courbaril).
copaljocal, copaljocote, *m.* a Mexican tree resembling a cherry tree.
cópano, *m.* (arch.) small ship.
copante, *m.* (Hond.) stepping stone.
copaquira, *f.* (Chile, Peru) copper sulfate, blue vitriol.
copar, *f.* copartnership, joint partnership; co-participation.
copartícipe, *m., f.* copartner, joint partner; co-participant.
copayero, *m.* (bot.) copaifera, copaiba.
copaza, *f. aug. of* **copa,** a large stemmed glass.
copazo, *m. aug. of* **copo,** large snowflake.
cope, *m.* closely woven portion of a fishing net.
copé, *m.* a kind of naphtha.
copear, *i.v.* to sell drinks by the glassful; to drink, tipple, take a nip.
copec, *m.,* kopeck (Russian coin).
copeisillo, *m.* (bot.) pitch apple (Clusia rosea).
copela, *f.* (metal.) cupel.
copelación, *f.* (metal.) cupellation.
copelar, *tr.v.* (metal.) to cupel.
Copenhague, *m.* Copenhagen, capital of Denmark.
copeo, *m.* selling of drinks by the glassful; drinking, tippling.
copépodo, da, *m., a.* (zool.) copepod.
copera, *f.* cupboard, cabinet for glasses, china closet.
copernicano, na, *a., m.* Copernican, pertaining to Copernicus or his theories.
Copérnico, *m.* Copernicus, Polish astronomer of the 16th century.
copero, *m.* cupbearer; glassware cabinet or cupboard; **c. mayor de la reina** or del rey, King's or Queen's cupbearer.
copete, *m.* 1. tuft (of flax for spinning). 2. crest, crown (of a bird), forelock (of a horse). 3. quiff, forelock (of a person). 4. toupee, hairpiece. 5. top, headpiece (of furniture, mirrors). 6. tongue (of a shoe). 7. topping (on ice cream, sherbet). 8. summit, top. 9. (coll.) presumption, arrogance, snobbishness. — **tener mucho c.,** to be arrogant, be snobbish; **de alto c.,** highborn, well-bred; important.
copetín, *m.* (coll.) drink, cocktail.
copetinera, *f.* (coll.) bar-girl; girl who serves drinks in a nightclub.
copetón, na, *a.* 1. (Col.) merry, lit-up, slightly drunk. 2. (Amer.) arrogant. —*f.* (Mex.) a well-dressed woman.
copetón, *m.* (Col., ornith.) crested sparrow.
copetuda, *f.* 1. (ornith.) skylark (Alauda arvensis). 2. (Cuba, bot.) marigold.
copetudo, da, *a.* 1. crested, tufted, crowned. 2. (coll.) conceited, snobbish, arrogant.
copey, *m.* (bot.) copei, pitch apple (Clusia rosea).
copia, *f.* 1. copy; duplicate; imitation; (mus.) score transcript; living image, exact likeness. 2. (gram.) grammatical summary (at end of a grammar book). 3. abundance, plenty, profusion. — **c. al carbón,** carbon copy; **c. heliográfica,** blueprint, sun print; **c. en limpio,** fair copy; **c. por contacto,** (photog.) contact print.
copiador, ra, *a.* copying. —*m., f.* copier, copyist, transcriber. —*m.* letter-file, letter-book. —*f.* copying machine; (mach.) copying lathe.
copiante, *a.* copying. —*m., f.* copier, copyist, transcriber.
copiar, *tr.v.* 1. to copy; to copy down, take down, (speech, notes, etc.). 2. to imitate, to mimic, to ape.
copihue, *m.* (Chile, bot.) lapageria (Lapageria rosea), vine of the lily family.
copilador, ra, *a., var. of* **compilador,** compiling. —*m., f.* compiler.
copilar, *tr.v., var. of* **compilar,** to compile, to collect.
copilla, *f.* 1. small brazier for lighting cigars. 2. small cup.
copiloto, *m.* (aer.) copilot; (auto.) co-driver.
copina, *m.* (Mex.) whole skin (of an animal).
copinar, *tr.v.* to skin (an animal), to remove the pelt in one piece.
copinol, *m.* (Guat., bot.) courbaril (Hymenaea courbaril).
copiosamente, *adv.* copiously, abundantly.
copiosidad, *f.* copiousness, abundance, plenty, profusion.
copioso, sa, *a.* copious, abundant, plentiful; profuse.
copista, *m., f.* copyist, copier, transcriber.
copita, *f. dim. of* **copa,** small glass or drink.
copito, *m. dim. of* **copo,** small snowflake.
copla, *f.* 1. verse, stanza, strophe; popular song, ballad; (*pl.*) (coll.) verse, poetry. 2. pair, couple. — **c. de arte mayor,** stanza of eight Alexandrines; **c. de pie quebrado,** stanza of eight lines; **coplas de Calaínos,** (coll.) irrelevancies, irrelevant remarks; **c. de ciego,** doggerel, jingle; **andar en coplas,** (coll.) to be common knowledge, be the talk of the town.
coplanar, coplanario, *a.* (geom.) **coplanar,** in the same plane.
coplear, *i.v.* to compose or recite verses; to compose or sing songs or ballads.
copleja, *f.* (derog.) insignificant ditty or doggerel.
coplería, *f.* verses; ballads, songs; balladry.
coplero, ra, *m., f.* ballad seller; poetaster.
coplica, illa, ita, *f. dim. of* **copla,** little verse or popular couplet.
coplista, *m., var. of* **coplero.**
copo, *m.* 1. flake, e.g. *c. de nieve,* snowflake. 2. tuft, bunch (of wool, flax, etc., ready for spinning). 3. clot, coagulation. 4. bottom of a purseseine; catch or haul with a purseseine. 5. the act of matching the bank with a bet (gambling), banco.
copolimerizar, (*ref. 53*) *tr.v.* to copolymerize.
copón, *m.* 1. *aug. of* **copa,** large goblet. 2. (ecc.) ciborium, pyx (Eucharistic vessel).
coposesión, *f.* joint possession.
coposesor, ra, *m., f.* joint possessor, co-owner, joint owner.
coposo, sa, *a., var. of* **copado.**
copra, *f.* copra, cocoanut meat.
coprofagia, *f.* coprophagy.
coprófago, ga, *a.* (zool.) coprophagous, scavenging, dung-eating.
coprolito, *m.* (paleon.) coprolite; (**physiol.**) coprolith.
copropiedad, *f.* joint ownership; property held in common.
copropietario, ria, *m., f.* coproprietor, joint owner.
cóptico, ca, *a., var. of* **copto.**
copto, ta, *a.* Coptic. —*m., f.* Copt. —*m.* Coptic (ancient language or Egypt language).
copucha, *f.* (Chile) bladder (inflatable rubber or skin bag); **hacer copuchas,** (Chile) to puff one's cheeks.
copudo, da, *a.* tufted, bushy, thick-topped.
cópula, *f.* 1. coupling, union, connection, link. 2. copulation, coition, sexual intercourse. 3. (gram., log., anat.) copula. 4. (archit.) cupola, dome.
copularse, *r.v.* to copulate, have sexual intercourse.
copulativamente, *adv.* copulatively, jointly.
copulativo, va, *a.* copulative, joining, uniting together.
coque, *m.* (min.) coke.
coque, coqué, *ref.* **cocar.**
coqueluche, *f.* (gal.) whooping cough.
coquera, *f.* 1. head of a top (toy). **2. small** hole in a stone. 3. coke bin.
coquero, ra, *m., f.* (Bol.) one who sells or is addicted to coca leaves.
coqueta, *a.* coquettish, flirtatious. —*f.* 1. coquette, flirt. 2. small loaf or roll of bread. 3. (coll.) dressing table, cosmetic shelf.
coquetear, *i.v.* to flirt; **c. con,** to flirt with, make eyes at.
coqueteo, *m.* flirting, flirtation.
coquetería, *f.* 1. coquetry, coquettishness; flirtation, flirting. 2. artificiality, affectation (in dress or manners).
coquetismo, *m., var. of* **coquetería.**
coquetón, na, *a.* (coll.) attractive, pretty, coquettish, cute (coll.). —*m.* lady-killer (coll.). —*f.* coquette; vamp.
coquetonamente, *adv.* coquettishly, flirtatiously.
coquificar, *tr.v., var. of* **coquizar.**
coquillo, *m.* 1. small bead. 2. (Cuba) fine white cotton fabric, muslin.
coquimbo, *m.* (Amer.) burrowing owl, (speotyto cunicularia).
coquina, *f.* (zool., Sp.) a small, succulent shellfish which abounds in the Andalusian coast; cockle (Donax).
coquinero, ra, *m., f.* (Sp.) one who sells coquinas or cockles on the shell; (fig.) a brazen, witty wanton (in Andalusian lore).
coquipelado, da, *a.* (P. Rico) with head closely shaven.
coquito, *m.* 1. face, grimace (to make a baby smile). 2. (ornith.) species of turtledove (Streptopelia turtur). 3. (bot.) coquito palm (Jubaea spectabilis).
coquizar, (*ref. 53*) *tr.v.* to coke, convert into (coal) coke.

Cor. *abbrev. of* **Epístola de San Pablo a los Corintios,** Corinthians (Cor.).
cora, *f.* regíon, district (among the Arabs).
cora, *f.* (Peru, bot.) darnel, bearded darnel (Lolium temulentum).
coracán, *m.* (bot.) annual bluegrass (**Poa** annua).
coráceo, a, *a., var. of* **coriáceo.**
coracero, *m.* 1. cuirassier. 2. (coll.) strong black cigar (of poor quality).
coracilla, *f. dim. of* **coraza,** small coat of mail.
coracina, *f.* shirt of scale mail (armor).
coracoides, *a.* (zool.) coracoid.
coracora, *f.* (Phil. I.) coasting vessel.
coracha, *f.* leather bag (for transporting tobacco, cocoa, etc.).
corada, *f.* entrails, haslet (of an animal).
corago, *m.* choragus, (in Greek drama) the leader of the chorus.
coraje, *m.* courage, bravery; fortitude, mettle; spunk, spirit; anger, temper.
corajina, *f.* (coll.) fit of anger.
corajoso, sa, *a.* angry, wrathful, annoyed.
corajudo, da, *a.* 1. brave. 2. irascible, irritable.
coral, *m.* 1. (zool., jewel.) coral. 2. (bot., Cuba) coral tree, coral bean tree; (*pl.*) coral beads (of coral bean tree). 3. (*pl.*) comb and wattle, caruncle (of turkey). — **fino como un c.** o **más fino que un c.,** shrewd, astute; sharp as a needle. —*f.* (zool.) coral snake.
coral, *a.* choral. —*m.* (mus.) chorale.
coralarios, *m.* (*pl.*) (zool.) Anthozoa.
coralero, ra, *m., f.* one who works with or sells coral or coral objects.
coralífero, ra, *a.* coralliferous.
coralígeno, na, *a.* coralligenous.
coralillo, *m.* coral snake (Micrurus corallinus).
coralina, *f.* 1. (bot., zool.) coralline (calcareous alga; any coral-like animal). 2. (chem.) coralline, corallin (sodium salt of surin).
coralino, na, *a.* corralline, coralloid, pertaining to or resembling coral.
coralito, *m.* (Col.) coral plant (Russelia equisetiformis).
corambre, *f.* pelts, hides, skins, peltry; skin (receptacle for liquids); **alzar c.,** to hang up skins to dry (in tanning).
corambrero, *m.* dealer in skins and hides.
Corán, *m.* (rel.) Koran, sacred book of the Moslems.
corana, *f.* (Chile) (type of) sickle.
coránico, ca, *a.* Koranic, pertaining to the Koran.
coranvobis, *m.* (coll.) solemn, portly person.
corasí, *m.* (Chile) red-headed mosquito.
coraza, *f.* 1. breastplate, cuirass, **armor;** (mar.) armor plate (of a ship). 2. (zool.) cuirass shell, carapace (of a turtle). — **c. reticulada,** (elec.) basket-weave armor; **c. trabada,** interlocking armor.
coraznada, *f.* 1. heart, core (of pine tree). 2. (cul.) heart fricassé.
corazón, *m.* 1. (anat.) heart. 2. spirit, courage, heart. 3. kindness, benevolence, heart. 4. heart, core, center. 5. heart (card.). — **abrir el c. a uno,** to give heart to, encourage; **anunciarle** or **decirle una cosa el c.,** to have a presentiment of something; **atravesar el c.,** to move with pity or compassion; **blando de c.,** soft-hearted; **con el c. en la mano,** frankly, openly, sincerely; **c. de Carlos,** (astron.) Charles's Wain; **c. de León,** (astron.) Regulus; **de c.,** heartily, sincerely, openly; **darle a uno un vuelco el c.,** to have one's heart skip a beat; **helársele el c.,** (one's heart) to miss a beat, stand still; **no caberle el c. en el pecho,** to boil with anger; to have one's heart beating wildly (with emotions); to be distraught with grief; **no tener c.,** to be heartless, have no heart; **hacer de tripas c.,** to pluck up courage; **tener el c. en la boca,** to be scared, excited; in suspense.
corazonada, *f.* 1. impulse; presentiment, hunch. 2. (coll.) offal, entrails.
corazoncillo, *m.* (bot.) variety of St. John's-wort (Hypericum perforatum).
corbachada, *f.* whiplash.
corbacho, *m.* cowhide whip.
corbata, *f.* 1. tie, necktie; cravat, neck-scarf. 2. sash, streamer (fastened to a banner). 3. ribbon (used as insignia). 4. shot (in billiards) in which the ball is shot around the opponent's ball bouncing off two cushions. — **c. de lazo** or **mariposa,** bow tie. —*m.* 1. layman, non-professional man. 2. unqualified advisor (i.e. not lawyer) in royal courts.
corbatería, *f.* necktie or tie shop.
corbatero, ra, *m., f.* necktie or tie seller or maker.
corbatín, *m.* bow tie; **irse** or **salirse por el c.,** (coll.) to be scrawny and long necked.
corbato, *m.* cooler, cooling bath (for the coil of a still).
corbe, *m.* (arch.) measurement by the basketful.
corbeta, *f.* (mar.) corvette.
corbona, *f.* basket.
Córcega, *f.* Corsica, French island in the Mediterranean.
corcel, *m.* steed, charger (horse).
corcesca, *f.* (arch.) halberd with two barbs.
corcha, *f.* 1. cork. 2. cork bucket (for keeping wine cool). 3. beehive. 4. (mar.) laying of a rope.
corchapín, *m.* (mar.) ancient sailboat.
corchar, *tr.v.* 1. (mar.) to lay (strands of rope). 2. (Col.) to fail an examination, to flunk (coll.) 3. to stop a bottle with a cork.
corche, *m.* cork-soled sandal.
corchea, *f.* (mus.) quaver.
corchera, *f.* wine cooler made of laminated cork.
corchero, ra, *a.* pertaining to cork, e.g. *industria corchera,* the cork industry.
corchero, *m.* worker who strips cork trees.
corcheta, *f.* eye (of a hook, snap fastener or clasp).
corchete, *m.* 1. hook and eye, clasp; hook (of hook and eye). 2. (carp.) bench stop or hook. 3. (mus., print.) brace, bracket; (print.) overrun (words written above line due to lack of space). 4. (coll.) constable, catchpole.
corcho, *m.* 1. cork, cork bark; cork, bottle-stopper; cork bucket (for keeping wine cool); cork box (for certain food-stuffs); cork mat; cork-soled sandal. 2. beehive. — **c. bornizo** or **c. virgen,** first bark of cork tree; **c. segundero,** second bark of cork tree; **estar c.,** (Col.) to be ignorant of something; **hacer el c.,** (Chile) to dissapear rapidly.
¡córcholis! *interj.* gracious! what do you know!
corchoso, sa, *a.* cork-like.
corchotaponero, ra, *a.* related to the industry that makes corks and bottle stoppers.
corcino, *m.* (zool.) small roe deer (Capreolus capreolus).
corcor, *m.* (C. Amer., P. Rico) gurgle (of liquid passing down throat).
corcova, *f.* hunch, hump (on the back).
corcovado, da, *past part. of* **corcovar.** —*a.* humpbacked, hunchbacked. —*m., f.* hunchback, humpback.
corcovar, *tr.v.* to curve, bend.
corcovear, *i.v.* to buck, curvet (a horse).
corcoveta, *f. dim. of* **corcova,** small hump; (coll.) hunchback (person).
corcovo, *m.* 1. bucking, curvet (of a horse); leap, spring. 2. curvature, crookedness.
corcuncho, cha, *a.* (C. Amer.) hunchbacked.
corcusido, *past part. of* **corcusir.** —*m.* shoddy stitching, poor needlework; shoddy patch.
corcusir, *tr.v.* to mend, sew or darn shoddily.
corda, *f.* **estar a la c.,** (mar.) to be close hauled or lying-to.
cordado, da, *a.* 1. (her.) with the strings of a musical instrument in different colored enamel. 2. (zool.) chordate. —*m.* (zool.) chordate, (*pl.*) chordates. —*f.* group of mountain climbers tied together by the same rope.
cordaje, *m.* 1. (mar.) cordage, rigging. 2. (mus.) complete set of guitar strings.
cordal, *m.* (mus.) tailpiece (on string instruments).
cordal, *a.* **muela cordal,** wisdom tooth.
cordato, ta, *a.* judicious, prudent, sensible.
cordel, *m.* 1. cord, thin rope, twine. 2. length of five paces. 3. cattle path. 4. (Cuba) agrarian measure. — **a c.,** in a straight line; **a hurta c.,** causing the top to spin in mid-air (in a game of tops); treacherously, stealthily, on the sly; **c. de merinas,** narrow cattle path.
cordelado, da, *past part. of* **cordelar.** —*a.* corded (ribbon).
cordelar, *tr.v.* to measure; to demarcate, mark limits of.
cordelazo, *m.* a lash given with a length of rope.
cordelejo, *m.* 1. *dim. of* **cordel,** narrow or small cord. 2. (coll.) teasing, leg-pulling, e.g. *dar c. a,* to tease, chaff, make fun of.
cordelería, *f.* 1. cord or rope-making trade; rope or cord maker's shop; ropes, cordage. 2. (mar.) rigging.
cordelero, ra, *m., f.* rope or cord maker or seller.
cordelillo, *m. dim. of* **cordel,** narrow or small cord. — **dar c.,** to flatter or cajole.
cordellate, *m.* twill, ribbed or corded wool cloth.
cordera, *f.* ewe lamb; (fig.) lamb (meek, docile woman).
corderaje, *m.* (Chile) large flock of sheep or lambs.
cordería, *f.* cordage, ropes.
corderilla, *f. dim. of* **cordera,** ewe lamb.
corderillo, *m.* dressed lambskin.
corderina, *f.* lambskin.
corderino, na, *a.* pertaining to a lamb.
cordero, *m.* lamb; dressed lambskin; (fig.) lamb, sheep (meek, docile man); **c. mueso,** small-eared lamb; **c. pascual,** (rel.) paschal lamb; **c. recental,** suckling lamb; **c. rencoso,** lamb with undescended testicle; **el C. de Dios** or **el C. Divino,** the Lamb of God.
corderuela, *f. dim. of* **cordera,** small ewe lamb.
corderuelo, *m. dim. of* **cordero,** baby lamb.
corderuna, *f.* lambskin.
cordezuela, *f. dim. of* **cuerda,** thin cord.
cordíaco, ca, *a.* (med.) cardiac.
cordial, *a.* 1. stimulating (beverage). 2. cordial, friendly. —*m.* cordial, tonic. — **dedo c.,** forefinger.
cordialidad, *f.* cordiality, warmth, affection.
cordialmente, *adv.* cordially, warmly.
cordierita, *f.* (min.) cordierite.
cordiforme, *a.* cordiform, cordate, heart-shaped.
cordilla, *f.* new-born tunny fish or tuna.
cordilla, *f.* sheep tripe (used as cat food).
cordillera, *f.* cordillera, mountain range.
cordillerano, na, *a.* corlilleran. — **perdiz c.** (ornith., Chile) Andean partridge.
cordita, *f.* (chem.) cordite.
córdoba, *m.* monetary unit of Nicaragua.
cordobán, *m.* cordovan, Spanish leather; tanned goatskin.
cordobana, andar a la c., (coll.) to go around stark naked.
cordobanero, *m.* one who tans cordovan leather.

cordobés, sa, *a., m., f.* Cordovan of or from Córdoba, Spain.
cordón, *m.* 1. cord, cordon (for tying clothes); (decorative) braid, cord; girdle (of a monk's habit); (elec.) cord, flex; (mar.) strand (of rope). 2. (archit.) cordon, stringcourse. 3. cordon, ring (of police, soldiers, etc.). 4. (vet.) white stripe (on a horse's head). 5. (mil.) (*pl.*) aiguillettes. 6. (Arg.) curb (of sidewalk or pavement). — **c. sanitario,** sanitary cordon; **c. umbilical,** umbilical cord; **cordones de zapatos,** shoe laces.
cordonazo, *m.* lash given with a rope or cord. — **c. de San Francisco,** (mar.) first equinoctial storm in Autumn.
cordoncillo, *m.* 1. rib, wale, cord (on fabrics such as corduroy). 2. milling (on coins).
cordonería, *f.* 1. cord-making; cordage, cords; cord-maker's shop. 2. passementerie trade; passementerie, fringes, braids; passementerie shop.
cordonero, ra, *m., f.* 1. cord maker. 2. passementerie worker, maker of trimming braid. —*m.* (mar.) rigging maker.
cordura, *f.* prudence, good sense, judiciousness, wisdom.
corea, *f.* 1. dance accompanied by singing. 2. (med.) chorea, St. Vitus' dance.
Corea, *f.* Korea; **C. del Norte,** North Korea; **C. del Sur,** South Korea.
coreano, na, *a., m., f.* Korean (of or from Korea).
corear, *tr.v.* 1. to compose (music) for choral singing; to accompany (music) with a chorus. 2. to echo meekly (someone else's) opinion. 3. (fig.) to acclaim, applaud.
corecico, llo, *m., var. of* **corezuelo.**
corega, *m.* choragus, choregus, patron or sponsor of a chorus of dancers or singers in ancient Greece.
corego, *m., var. of* **corega.**
coreico, ca, *a.* (med.) choreic.
coreo, *m.* (poet.) trochee, foot in Latin verse.
coreo, *m.* interplay or interweaving of choruses in choral singing.
coreografía, *f.* choreography, art of creating dances and ballets.
coreográfico, ca, *a.* choreographic.
coreógrafo, *m.* choreographer.
corepíscopo, *m.* prelate substituting for a bishop.
corete, *m.* 1. piece of leather used by harnessmakers to cover nailheads. 2. kidskin used for polishing sculpture.
corezuelo, *m.* 1. *dim. of* **cuero,** small hide. 2. suckling pig, skin of a roast suckling pig.
Corfú, *m.* Corfu, one of the Ionian Islands off the N.W. coast of Greece.
cori, *m.* (bot.) a variety of St. John's wort (Hypericum perforatum).
corí, *m.* (zool.) restless cavy, guinea pig (Cavia porcellus).
Coria, bobo de C. (coll.) proverbial fool, jackass.
coriáceo, a, *a.* coriaceous, leather-like.
coriámbico, ca, *a., m.* (poet.) choriambic (verse).
coriambo, *m.* (poet.) choriamb.
coriana, *f.* (Col.) blanket, rug.
coribante, *m.* (myth.) Corybant (mythical attendant of Cybele).
corídalo, *m.* (bot.) corydalis.
corifeo, *m.* coryphaeus (leader of the chorus in Greek drama); (fig.) leader (of a party or faction, etc.).
coriláceo, *a.* (bot.) corylaceous. —*f.* (bot.) corylaceous plant; (*pl.*) Corylaceae.
corimbo, *m.* (bot.) corymb.
corindón, *m.* (min.) corundum.
coríntico, ca, *a., var. of* **corintio.**
corintio, tia, *a., m., f.* 1. Corinthian, native of Corinth, Greece. 2. pertaining to the city of that name. 3. pertaining to a style of Greek architecture.
corinto, *m.* 1. **C.,** Corinth, a city of Greece. 2. color of prunes from Corinth. —*a.* deep red, purplish.
Coriolano, *m.* Coriolanus, a tragedy by Shakespeare based on the legend of Gaius Marcius Coriolanus, a Roman general of the 5th century.
corion, *m.* (zool.) chorion.
corisco, ca, *a.* (Ven.) furious, enraged.
corista, *m.* 1. (ecc.) choir priest. 2. member of the chorus. —*f.* (female) member of the chorus; (theat.) chorus girl.
corito, ta, *a.* 1. naked. 2. (fig.) pusillanimous, timid. —*m.* (Sp., reg.) mountain dweller; wine carrier.
coriza, *f.* 1. leather sandal. 2. (med.) coryza, head cold.
corla, *f.* gold varnish.
corlador, ra, *m., f.* one who treats silver with gold varnish.
corladura, *f.* gold-colored varnish (for gilding silver).
corlar, *tr.v.* to coat (silver) with gold varnish.
corleador, ra, *m., f., var. of* **corlador, ra.**
corlear, *tr.v., var. of* **corlar.**
corma, *f.* 1. wood shackle, stocks (for fettering people), wooden hobble (for animals). 2. hindrance, burden, millstone.
cormofita, *f.* (bot.) cormophyte, (*pl.*) Cormophyta.
cormorán, *m.* (ornith.) cormorant.
cornac, *m., var. of* **cornaca.**
cornaca, *m.* mahout (elephant tamer, keeper and driver).
cornáceo, a, *a.* (bot.) cornaceous. —*f.* (bot.) (*pl.*) Cornaceae.
cornada, *f.* 1. butt, horn thrust (of an animal). 2. (fenc.) upward thrust. 3. (taur.) goring.
cornadillo, *m. dim. of* **cornado,** small copper coin; **emplear** or **poner uno su c.,** (coll.) to put in or add one's share, to contribute towards a given end.
cornado, *m.* ancient Spanish coin; **no valer un c.,** (coll.) to be worthless or useless.
cornadura, *f., var. of* **cornamenta.**
cornal, *m.* rope, strap or yoke (gen. for oxen).
cornalina, *f.* (min.) carnelian, cornelian.
cornalón, *a.* long-horned (gen. applied to fighting bulls).
cornamenta, *f.* horns (of animals).
cornamusa, *f.* 1. (mus.) horn; bagpipe. 2. (mar.) cleat. 3. (metal.) retort used formerly to sublimate certain metals.
cornatillo, *m.* horn-shaped olive.
córnea, *f.* (anat.) cornea; **c. opaca,** (anat.) sclera; **c. transparente,** cornea.
corneador, ra, *a.* butting (animal).
corneana, *f.* (geol.) hornfels.
cornear, *tr.v.* to butt (with the horns); to gore, e.g. *lo cornearon,* (taur.) he was gored.
cornecillo, cico, to, *m. dim. of* **cuerno,** little horn.
corneja, *f.* (ornith.) hooded crow (Corvus cornix); variety of hawk owl.
cornejal, *m.* dogwood grove.
cornejo, *m.* (bot.) dogwood tree.
cornelina, *f., var. of* **cornalina.**
córneo, a, *a.* horny, horn-like; (bot.) cornaceous. —*f.* dogwood tree, cornaceous plant; (*pl.*) Cornaceae (family), dogwood family.
córner, *m.* (Angl., Amer.) 1. each one of the angles of a field of soccer, hockey, etc. 2. a corner shot (in certain ball games).
cornerina, *f., var. of* **cornalina.**
cornero, *m.* crust (of bread).
corneta, *f.* 1. cornet, bugle; shepherd's horn. 2. (mil.) cavalry standard or pennant. 3. (mil.) cornet, cavalry company. — **c. acústica,** ear trumpet; **c. de monte,** hunting horn; **c. de posta,** post horn. —*m.* cornettist, bugler; (mil.) cornet, officer carrying the standard.
cornete, *m.* 1. *dim. of* **cuerno,** small horn. 2. (anat.) turbinal bone or cartilage.
cornetilla, *f.* (bot.) a variety of gourd-shaped hot pepper.
cornetín, *m.* 1. cornet. 2. cornetist.
corneto, ta, *a.* (Amer.) 1. knock-kneed, bow-legged. 2. crooked-horned (cattle).
cornezuelo, *m.* 1. *dim. of* **cuerno,** small horn. 2. (agr., med.) ergot. 3. (vet.) deer-horn tissue separator (for separating blood vessels and tissues). 4. (bot.) long pointed olive; horn-shaped olive.
corniabierto, ta, *a.* (taur.) with horns set wide apart.
cornial, *a.* horn-shaped.
corniapretado, da, *a.* (taur.) with close-set horns.
cornicabra, *f.* (bot.) 1. terebinth tree. 2. a variety of long, pointed olive. 3. wild fig tree.
cornicorto, ta, *a.* short-horned.
corniculado, da, *a.* (bot.) corniculate.
corniforme, *a.* corniform, horn-shaped.
cornigacho, cha, *a.* with horns tilted downward.
cornígero, ra, *a.* (poet.) cornigerous, horned.
cornija, *f.* archit.) cornice.
cornijal, *m.* 1. corner (of a mattress, building, etc.). 2. lavabo (towel used by the priest during communion service).
cornijamento, *m.* (archit.), *var. of* **cornisamento.**
cornijamiento, *m.* (archit.), *var. of* **cornisamento.**
cornijón, *m.* 1. (archit.) entablature. 2. outer corner (of a building or wall).
cornil, *m., var. of* **cornal.**
corniola, *f., var. of* **cornalina.**
cornisa, *f.* (archit.) cornice.
cornisamento, *m.* (archit.) entablature.
cornisamiento, *m.* (archit.), *var. of* **cornisamento.**
cornisón, *m., var. of* **cornijón.**
corniveleto, ta, *a.* straight-horned (cattle).
cornizo, *m.* (bot.), *var. of* **cornejo.**
corno, *m.* 1. (bot.) dogwood tree. 2. (mus.) horn. — **c. inglés,** (mus.) English horn.
Cornualles, *m.* Cornwall, county in the S.W. tip of England.
cornucopia, *f.* 1. cornucopia, horn of plenty. 2. gilt mirror with candelabra.
cornudilla, *f.* (ichth.) hammerhead (shark).
cornudo, da, *a.* 1. horned. 2. (coll.) cuckolded. —*m.* cuckold; **tras de c., apaleado,** (coll.) this adds insult to injury.
cornúpeta, *a.* (poet., numis.) cornupete, charging, attacking animal or representation thereof. —*m.* (coll.) bull; attacking animal.
cornúpeto, *m.* (coll.) fighting bull; representation of an attacking animal.
cornuto, *a.* (log.) **argumento c.,** dilemma.
coro, *m.* 1. choir (body of singers; part of the church where the choir sings; division of angels). 2. chorus (composition for several voices). 3. (theat.) chorus (in Greek and Elizabethan theater, etc.). 4. (ecc.) singing and reciting of the canonical hours. 5. each side of the choir (in a church). — **a c.,** in a chorus, in unison; **hacer c. a,** to join, back up, support (someone in his opinions); **de c.,** by memory or rote.
Coro, *m.* (poet.) Caurus, northwest wind.
corocero, ra, *a.* (P. Rico) mean, miserly, tight-fisted.
corocha, *f.* 1. (arch.) long, loose jacket. 2. (ento.) larva of grapevine flea beetle.

corografía, *f.* chorography, the geographic description of a country, the mapping of a region.
corográfico, ca, *a.* chorographic, pertaining to the geographic description or the mapping of a country.
corógrafo, *m.* chorographer.
coroideo, dea, *a.* (anat.) choroid (membrane).
coroides, *f.* (anat.) choroid membrane, choroid coat.
corojito, ta, *a.* (Cuba) chubby, fat.
corojo, *m.* (bot.) cohune palm, corozo palm; **c. de Guinea,** African oil palm.
corola, *f.* (bot.) corolla.
corolario, *m.* corollary; deduction, inference.
coroliflora, *a.* (bot.) corollifloral. —*f.* corollifloral plant; (*pl.*) Corolliflorae.
corona, *f.* 1. crown, coronet, diadem. 2. crown (of olives), garland; (funeral) wreath. 3. halo, nimbus (on a heavenly being). 4. (anat., bot., astron., elec., archit.) corona. 5. crown (of the head, a tooth). 6. tonsure (of a monk). 7. crown, royal power; crown, kingdom. 8. honor, glory. 9. crest, top (of a hill, etc.). 10. crowning touch, finishing touch. 11. (fort.) crownwork. 12. crown (coin). 13. rosary of seven decades. 14. (mec.) washer. 15. (geom.) annulus. 16. (mar.) pendant (cable). 17. ring, rim (of wheel). — **abrir la c.,** (ecc.) to tonsure; **ceñir** or **ceñirse la c.,** to ascend the throne, begin to reign; **c. austral,** (astron.) Corona Australis; **c. boreal,** (astron.) Corona Borealis; **c. de laurel,** crown of laurels; **c. del casco,** (vet.) coronet (lower part of a horse's pastern); **c. dentada,** crown wheel; **c. de rey** or **real,** (bot.) a variety of yellow globe daisy; **c. funeraria** or **de flores,** funeral wreath; **c. imperial,** (bot.) crown imperial (Fritillaria imperialis).
coronación, *f.* 1. coronation, crowning. 2. crowning, culmination. 3. (archit.) crown, coping, copestone. 4. promotion (in chess). crowning (in checkers).
coronado, *past part. of* **coronar.** —*m.* tonsured cleric.
coronal, *a.* (anat.) frontal (bone). —*m.* frontal bone.
coronamento, *m., var. of* **coronamiento.**
coronamiento, *m.* 1. crowning, culmination. 2. (archit.) crown, coping, copestone. 3. (mar.) taffrail.
coronar, *tr.v.* 1. to crown (a sovereign). 2. to finish, crown. 3. to crown (in checkers) promote (in chess). —*r.v.* 1. to crown oneself. 2. to become covered (with flowers). 3. (med.) to crown (the head of the fetus at childbirth).
coronaria, *f.* crown wheel, second wheel (of a watch).
coronario, ria, *a.* crown, coronal, coronary; fine (gold); (bot.) crown-shaped; (anat.) coronary.
corondel, *m.* 1. (print.) reglet, lead column rule. 2. (print.) (*pl.*) vertical watermark lines.
coronel, *m.* 1. (mil.) colonel. 2. (Cuba) large kite.
coronel, *m.* 1. (archit.) cyma, cymatium. 2. (her.) crown.
coronela, *a.* pertaining to a colonel. —*f.* colonel's wife.
coronelato, *m., var. of* **coronelía.**
coronelía, *f.* 1. colonelship. 2. (obs., mil.) regiment.
corónide, *f.* crowning, culmination.
coronilla, *f.* crown (of the head); **andar** or **bailar de c.,** (coll.) to work hard and conscientiously, keep hard at it; **dar de c.,** (coll.) to bump one's head on the ground; **estar (uno) hasta la c.,** to be fed up, sick of or tired of something.
coronio, *m.* (astron.) coronium (substance found in the solar corona and unknown on earth).
coronta, *f.* (Amer.) corncob.
corosol, *m.* (bot.) a variety of custard-apple tree.
corotos, *m.* (*pl.*) (Ven., coll.) household utensils, odds and ends.
coroza, *f.* 1. cone-shaped cap worn formerly as punishment. 2. hooded straw cape.
corozo, *m.* (bot.) cohune palm, corozo palm; cohune nut.
corpa, *f.* (min.) lump of crude ore.
corpachón, *m., var. of* **corpanchón.**
corpanchón, *m.* (coll.) *aug. of* **cuerpo,** big bulky body; carcass of fowl.
corpazo, *m.* (coll.) *aug. of* **cuerpo,** large, ungainly body.
corpecico, llo, to, *m.* 1. *dim. of* **cuerpo,** small or slight body. 2. sleeveless doublet, waistcoat; sleeveless waist or bodice.
corpiño, *m.* 1. *dim. of* **cuerpo,** little body. 2. bodice, waist. 3. brassiere.
corporación, *f.* corporation; association, group; (Car.) stock company.
corporal, *a.* corporal. —*m.* (ecc.) corporal (cloth used in the Eucharist).
corporalidad, *f.* corporality.
corporalmente, *adv.* corporally, bodily, physically.
corporativamente, *adv.* corporately.
corporativo, va, *a.* corporate, corporative.
corporeidad, *f.* corporeity.
corpóreo, rea, *a.* corporeal, physical, material; corporal, bodily.
corpudo, da, *a., var. of* **corpulento.**
corpulencia, *f.* corpulence.
corpulento, ta, *a.* corpulent; bulky, thickset, stocky.
corpus, *m.* (ecc.) Corpus Christi.
corpuscular, *a.* (anat., philos.) corpuscular.
corpusculista, *m., f.* (philos.) corpuscularian.
corpúsculo, *m.* corpuscle; **c. de inclusión,** (med.) inclusion body; **c. táctil,** (anat.) tactile corpuscle.
corración, *f.* (geol.) corrasion.
corral, *m.* 1. yard; corral, enclosure; stockyard, pen, fold. 2. (arch.) open-air theater. 3. fish weir (fence built in a river or sea to catch fish). — **c. de madera,** timber yard; **c. de vacas,** (coll.) pigsty, dump, dirty untidy place; **hacer corrales,** (coll) to be absent (from classes).
corralero, ra, *a.* pertaining to a yard or corral. —*m., f.* 1. person in charge of loading and receiving cattle in trains, ships or trucks. 2. person who dries and sells manure.
corraliza, *f.* yard, court.
corralón, *m.* yard.
correa, *f.* 1. belt (clothing); machine part. 2. dog leash. 3. flexibility; fluidity. 4. (archit.) purlin. 5. (*pl.*) duster made of leather straps. — **besar uno c.,** (coll.) to humble oneself; **c. articulada,** link or chair belt; **c. conductora,** belt conveyor; **c. cruzada** or **en cruz,** (mec.) crossed belt; **c. de seguridad,** (aer.) safety bolt; **c. de transmisión** or **transmisora,** drive belt, transmission belt; **c. de ventilador,** (auto., mec.) fan belt; **c. dentada,** cog belt; **c. en cuña,** V belt; **c. sin fin,** endless belt; **c. transportadora,** conveyor belt; **tener uno c.,** (coll.) to be able to take a joke; to be tough or strong; to have a vivid personality.
correaje, *m.* belting, belts; **c. de cuero,** rawhide belting.
correal, *m.* deerskin (used for making clothes).
correar, *tr.v.* (tex.) to dress and soften wool fabric or fibres.
correazo, *m.* lash given with a leather strap.
correcalles, *m.* (coll.) loafer, loiterer, good-for-nothing.
corrección, *f.* 1. correction, adjustment. 2. reprimand, reproof; punishment, chastisement. 3. correctness, propriety, decorum. — **c. de pruebas** or **galeradas,** (print.) proofreading; **c. disciplinaria,** corrective punishment.
correccional, *a.* correctional; corrective. —*m.* reformatory, reform school.
correccionalismo, *m.* correctional penal system; system based on reform and correction rather than punishment.
correccionalista, *m.* correctionalist, advocate of a correctional penal system.
correctamente, *adv.* correctly, properly.
correctibilidad, *f.* quality of being correctable, rectifiable.
correctivo, va, *a.* corrective (medicament, agent, etc.); correctional. —*m.* corrective, corrective agent or measure; punishment.
correcto, ta, *irr. past part. of* **corregir.** —*a.* correct, proper.
corrector, ra, *a.* correcting; corrective. —*m.* 1. corrector; (print.) proofreader. 2. superior, abbot (in certain monasteries). — **c. de pruebas** or **galeradas,** (print.) proofreader.
correndentor, ra, *a.* co-redeeming. —*m., f.* co-redeemer.
corredera, *f.* 1. runner, groove, track (of sliding doors, etc.); runner, rail (of a curtain fixture); sliding section (of a lattice window). 2. upper grinding stone (of a mill). 3. (ento.) cockroach. 4. street road. 5. (coll.) procuress. 6. (artil.) recoil platform. 7. (mar.) log (apparatus measuring ship's speed); (mar.) log line; log reel. 8. (mec.) slide valve (of steam cylinders). 9. racetrack. — **de c.,** sliding (doors, etc.).
corredero, *m.* 1. (Mex.) racetrack. 2. (Mex.) dried-up riverbed. 3. (Ven.) favorite haunt, favorite place.
corredizo, za, *a.* sliding (doors); slip (knot). —*m.* groove, runner.
corredor, ra, *a.* 1. running; racing; race, e.g. *caballo c.,* racehorse. 2. (zool.) ratite —*m., f.* runner. — **c. de coches,** racing driver; **c. de fondo,** long-distance runner.; **c. de vallas,** hurdler. —*m.* 1. (com.) broker, agent. 2. (mil.) scout, raider, skirmisher. 3. corridor, passage; (fort.) covered way. — **c. de apuestas,** bookmaker, bookie; **c. de cambio,** (com.) exchange broker; **c. de comercio,** (com.) stock-broker; **c. de la muerte,** death row; **c. de lonja or de mercaderías,** sales agent, salesman; **c. de oreja,** exchange broker; (coll.) talebearer; (coll.) pimp, procurer; **c. de seguros,** insurance broker; **c. intérprete de buques,** (law) licensed shipping agent. —*f.* (*pl.*) (zool.) Ratitae, ratite family.
corredura, *f.* overflow (of liquids).
correduría, *f.* 1. brokerage; broker's office or commision. 2. (law) fine, mulct. — **c. de finca,** real estate business.
correería, *f.* shop where belts or straps are made and or sold.
correero, ra, *m., f.* person who makes or sells belts or straps.
corregencia, *f.* co-regency, temporary joint rule.
corregente, *a., m., f.* co-regent.
corregibilidad, *f.* corrigibility, reformability.
corregible, *a.* rectifiable, that can be corrected or ammended.
corregidor, ra, *a.* correcting. —*m.* corregidor (Spanish magistrate); mayor appointed by the king.
corregidora, *f.* wife of a **corregidor.**
corregimiento, *m.* dignity, jurisdiction or office of a corregidor.
corregir, (*ref.* 76) *tr.v.* 1. to correct; to modify, moderate. 2. (Cuba) to evacuate (the bowels). — **c. pruebas** or **galeradas,** (print.) to proofread galleys.

correhuela, *f.* 1. *dim. of* **correa,** small or narrow strap. 2. (bot.) bindweed (Convulvulus arvensis); (bot.) knotgrass (Polygonum aviculare). 3. child's game played with a stick and looped strap.

correinado, *m.* co-reign, joint rule.

correinante, *a.* co-reigning, jointly ruling.

correjel, *m.* thick flexible leather.

correlación, *f.* correlation, analogy.

correlacionar, *tr.v.* to correlate, relate.

correlativamente, *adv.* correlatively.

correlativo, va, *a.* correlative.

correligionario, ria, *m., f.* coreligionist, (of the same religious or political beliefs); (coll.) collegue, coworker.

correlón, na, *a.* (Amer.) 1. running. 2. cowardly, afraid.

correncia, *f.* 1. (coll.) diarrhea, looseness of the bowels. 2. shyness, bashfulness. 3. verbosity.

correndilla, *f.* (coll.) short run, dash.

correntada, *f.* (Amer.) place in a river where the current is strongest.

correntía, *f.* (coll.) looseness of the bowels, diarrhea.

correntío, *a.* running (liquids); (coll.) light, agile.

correntón, na, *a* 1. gadding, sociable, fond of company; playful, jesting, gay. 2. (Col., P. Rico) strong (current of water).

correntoso, sa, *a.* (Amer.) swift, rapid (river, current).

correo, *m.* 1. post, mail. 2. (*gen. pl.*) postal service, mail service. 3. (com.) correspondence, e.g. *leer el c.,* to read the correspondence. 4. post office, *e.g. echar la carta al c.,* to deposit the letter in the mailbox. 5. courier, runner. — **a vuelta de c.,** by return mail; **c. certificado,** registered mail; **c. aéreo,** airmail; **c. de gabinete,** official courier; **c. de malas nuevas,** (coll.) one who enjoys bringing bad news; **c. electrónico,** electronic mail; **c. urgente,** special delivery; **lista de c.,** general delivery.

correo, *m.* (law) accomplice, joint culprit.

correón, *m. aug. of* **correa,** large strap, supporting brace.

correoso, sa, *a.* flexible, elastic, easily bent; (fig.) tough, rubbery, leathery (said of bread of other food).

correr, *i.v.* 1. to run, race. 2. to flow, run (rivers, liquid, etc.). 2. to blow (wind, etc.). 4. to go, stretch, extend, run (road, range of mountains). 5. to pass by, elapse (period of time). 6. to fall due (payment). 7. to go through (documents, etc.). 8. to be valid, accepted (currency). 9. (mar.) to run before the wind. — **c. a,** to sell at, be priced at; **a todo c.,** at full speed; **a todo turbio c.** or **a turbio c.,** however bad things may seem; **c. a.** + *inf.,* to run to, hasten to + *inf.* **c. con ,** to be responsible for, e.g. *yo corro con los gastos de la casa,* I'm responsible for the household expenses; **c. la voz,** to be rumored; **c. por,** to be chargeable to, e.g. *eso corre por mi cuenta,* this is chargeable to me; to be responsible for, e.g. *eso corre por mi cuenta,* I'll settle, arrange or be responsible for this; **que corre, current** (month). *—tr.v.* 1. to race (horse, car). 2. to tip (scales). 3. to slide, shift (furniture); to draw (curtains); to shoot (a bolt), e.g. *c. el pestillo,* to bolt, shoot the bolt. 4. to untie (knot). 5. to run (danger, risk, etc.); to experience, undergo, seek, e.g. *se fue a c. aventuras,* he went to seek adventure. 6. to travel around. 7. to raid. 8. to be engaged or employed in the sale of, be dedicated to the sale of. 9. (coll.) to embarrass, confuse, squelch (coll.). 10. (coll.) or miss (classes), be absent from (the office). 12. (Mex.) to throw (someone) out. 13. (Amer.) to fire (someone) from a job (coll.) — **correrla,** (coll.) to live it up, go on a spree; **c. mundo,** to see the world, get experience; **c. olas,** to ride the surf, surf-ride. *—r.v.* 1. to slide or slip easily. 2. to run (wax, etc.). 3. (coll.) to become embarrassed or confused. 4. (Sp., vulg.) **correrse,** to have an orgasm. 5. (coll.) to go far, overdo it; (coll.) to offer too much (for something). 6. (coll.) to get away from, e.g. *me le corrí,* I got away from him.

correría, *f.* 1. raid, foray, incursion. 2. short trip, excursion.

correspondencia, *f.* 1. correspondence, relationship. 2. correspondence; mail, post. 3. contact, communication.

corresponder, *i.v.* 1. to repay, return (a favor). 2. to belong to, fall to; to be up to, be one's turn to; to concern. 3. to fit, match, go together. *—r.v.* 1. to correspond, write to one another. 2. to love each other. 3. to communicate.

correspondiente, *a.* 1. corresponding, respective; agreeable, suitable. *—m., f.* correspondent.

correspondientemente, *adv.* correspondingly; appropriately, suitably, fittingly.

corresponsal, *m., f.* correspondent.

corresponsalía, *f.* the job or assignment of correspondent of a news service or newspaper.

corretaje, *m.* brokerage; broker's fee or commission.

correteada, *f.* (Chile) the action of running, chasing or pursuing.

corretear, *i.v.* (coll.) to run arround, run about. *—tr.v.* (Amer.) to follow, pursue, chase.

correteo, *m.* running around, running about; playing rough (rowdy children).

corretora, *f.* nun in charge of directing the choir.

correvedile, *m., var. of* **correveidile.**

correveidile, *m., f.* 1. (coll.) gossip, gossipmonger. 2. (coll.) pimp, go-between, procurer.

correverás, *m.* mechanical toy (operated by a hidden spring).

corrida, *f.* 1. bullfight. 2. race, run, sprint. — **de c.,** quickly.

corridamente, *adv.* easily, freely, fluently.

corrido, da, *past part. of* **correr.** *—a.* 1. in excess (a weight or measurement). 2. embarrassed, abashed, squashed. 3. worldly, experienced. 4. cursive (writing). 5. fully grown. 6. in sequence, in a row. *—m.* 1. lean-to, projecting roof (running around a corral). 2. (archit.) unbroken section (in a building). 3. (*pl.*) accrued interest.

corriente, *a.* 1. running (water). 2. current, present (weeks, months, years). 3. current (account in a bank). 4. common, usual, commonplace, standard; cheap, ordinary, common. 5. easy, flowing, fluid (literary style). — **c. y moliente,** (coll.) usual, normal, commonplace; on the dot, punctual (payments). *—f.* current (of water, electricity); (fig.) current, course, drift (e.g. of national affairs). — **c.** abajo, downstream; **c. arriba,** upstream; **c. alterna,** (elec.) alternating current; **c. avanzada** or **en adelanto,** (elec.) leading current; **c. conductiva** or **de conducción,** (elec.) conduction current; **c. continua,** (elec.) direct or continuous current; **c. cruzada,** crosscurrent; **c. de carga,** (elec.) charging current; **c. de Foucault,** (elec.) Foucault current; **C. del Golfo,** Gulf Stream; **c. de placa,** (elec.) plate current; **c. de régimen,** (elec.) operating current; **c. de rejilla,** (rad.) grid current; **c. de retorno,** (elec.) return circuit; **c. de saturación,** (elec., rad.) saturation current; **c. directa,** direct current (d.c.); **c. específica,** (elec.) current density; **c. freática,** subsurface flow, watertable stream; **c. en triángulo,** (elec.) delta current; **c. inversa,** (elec.) reverse current; **c. parásita,** (elec.) eddy current; **c. primaria** or **inductora,** (elec.) primary current; **dejarse llevar de la c.,** (coll.) to drift with the tide (of public opinion), follow the herd; **ir** or **navegar contra la c.,** to swim against the tide, go against public opinion; **irse con** or **tras la c.,** to follow the herd, go along with the tide (of public opinion); **tomar la c. desde la fuente,** to trace the stream to its source, get to the bottom of things, find out the real reason. *—m.* the current month; **al c.,** up to date; right on time, on the dot payments); **estar al c.,** to be fully aware of, be informed, up-to-date on, be au courant, be abreast (of news, etc.); **poner al c.,** to bring up-to-date on.

corrientemente, *adv.* 1. usually, ordinarily. 2. fluently, easily.

corrigendo, da, *m., f.* inmate of a reformatory or penitentiary.

corrija, corrijo, *ref.* **corregir.**

corrillero, ra, *a.* troublemaking, agitating.

corrillo, *m.* huddle, small circle or group, clique.

corrimiento, *m.* 1. running. 2. melting. 3. watery discharge, secretion (of the eyes, etc.). 4. running sore. 5. landslide. 6. embarrassment, shyness. 7. (agr.) blight (of grapevine). 8. (Amer.) rheumatism.

corrincho, *m.* gang of hoodlums, riff-raff.

corrivación, *f.* impolding, joining (of streams for irrigation purposes).

corro, *m.* 1. circle, group (of talkers); ring, circle. 2. game of ring-around-a-rosy. — **echar en c.,** to sound public opinion; **hacer c.,** to clear a space (of people); **hacer c. aparte,** (coll.) to follow another party; to create a new party or faction.

corroboración, *f.* corroboration, confirmation; strengthening, fortifying.

corroborante, *a.* corroborating, confirming; (med.) corroborant, invigorating (medicine). *—m.* (med.) corroborant, corroborative, tonic.

corroborar, *tr.v.* to strengthen, fortify; to corroborate, support, back up.

corroborativo, va, *a.* corroborative, confirmatory.

corrobra, *f.* treat or party given to the participants in a sale or auction.

corroer, (*ref.19*) *tr.v.* to corrode, eat away; (fig.) to consume, eat away, corrode (grief or remorse). *—r.v.* to become corroded or eaten away.

corrompedor, ra, *a., m., f., var. of* **corruptor.**

corromper, *tr.v.* 1. to corrupt; to seduce; to pervert; to vitiate, pollute. 2. to rot, putrefy, spoil (food). 3. to bribe, suborn. 4. (coll.) to disturb, upset. *—r.v.* 1. to become corrupted or perverted. 2. to rot, go bad or rotten. 3. to degenerate, be vitiated (language, customs). *—i.v.* to smell bad.

corrompidamente, *adv.* corruptly, pervertedly.

corroncha, *f.* (Hond., imp. u.) shell.

corroncho, *m.* (Col., ichth.) small river fish (Hypostomus aburrensis).

corronchoso, sa, *a.* (Col.) rough, rude, uncouth.

corrosible, *a.* easily corroded.

corrosión, *f.* corrosion.

corrosivo, va, *a.* corrosive.

corroyente, *a.* corrosive, corroding.

corrugación, *f.* corrugation.

corrugar, *tr.v.* to corrugate. — **cartón corrugado,** corrugated cardboard.

corrulla, *f.* (mar.) storeroom (for rigging).

corrumpente, *a.* corrupting, perverting; (coll.) annoying, disturbing.

corrupción, *f.* 1. corruption; perversion; seduction. 2. rotting, putrefaction. 3. bribery, bribing. 4. alteration (of a manuscript). 5. vitiation, pollution (of language, customs, air, etc.).

corruptamente, *adv.* corruptly.
corruptela, *f.* corruption; bad habit, vice.
corruptibilidad, *f.* corruptibility; ability to rot or go bad.
corruptible, *a.* corruptible; pervertible; able to rot or go bad.
corruptivo, va, *a.* corrupting, corruptive; putrefactive, causing to rot.
corrupto, ta, *irr. past part. of* **corromper.** —*a.* corrupt.
corruptor, ra, *a.* corrupting, corruptive. —*m., f.* corrupter, perverter; seducer.
corrusco, *m.* (coll.) crust, dry broken piece of bread.
corsa, *f.* (Can. I.) dray, cart (for heavy loads).
corsaco, *m.* (zool.) corsac.
corsario, ria, *m., f.* (hist.) corsair, privateer.
corsé, *m.* corset, corselet.
corsear, *i.v.* (mar.) to privateer.
corsetería, *f.* corset factory or shop.
corsetero, ra, *m., f.* person who designs, makes or sells corsets and ladies' foundations.
corso, *m.* (mar.) privateering; (Amer.) parade. — **ir** or **salir a c.,** to go privateering.
corso, sa, *a., m., f.* Corsican, native of Corsica.
corta, *f.* felling (of trees); cutting (of sugar cane, etc.).
cortaalambre, *m.* wire cutter, nippers.
cortabolsas, (*pl.* **cortabolsas**) *m., f.* (coll.) cutpurse, pickpocket, petty thief.
cortacable, *m.* cable cutter (tool and operator).
cortacadena, *m.* chain cutter (tool and person).
cortacallos, (*pl.* **cortacallos**) *m.* corn parer, corn cutter (tool).
cortacigarros, (*pl.* **cortacigarros**) *m.* cigar cutter (tool).
cortacircuitos, (*pl.* **cortacircuitos**) *m.* (elec.) circuit breaker, fuse. — **c. de fusible,** fuse cutout; **c. térmico,** thermal cutout.
cortacorriente, *m.* (elec.) current breaker, switch.
cortada, *past part. of* **cortar.** —*a.* sour, e.g. *leche c.,* sour milk.
cortadera, *f.* 1. blacksmith's chisel; apiarist's knife. 2. (Amer., bot.) bulrush with sharp leaves.
cortadillo, lla, *a.* (numis.) octagonal, noncircular (coin). —*m.* 1. tumbler (glass). 2. measure for liquids (about a gill). 3. (sl.) trick (at cards). — **echar cortadillos,** (coll.) to speak mincingly or affectedly; (coll.) to drink glasses of wine.
cortado, da, *past part. of* **cortar.** —*a.* 1. proportioned, exactly fitting. 2. (mus., lit.) choppy. 3. (her.) party, parted, one half of shield or figure painted with a different enamel from the other half. —*m.* 1. small glass. 2. capriole, caper, leap (in dancing).
cortador, ra, *a.* cutting; slicing. —*m.* 1. cutter (in tailoring, shoemaking, etc.); butcher; carver. 2. (anat.) incisor (tooth). —*f.* cutter, chisel.
cortadura, *f.* 1. cutting; cut, incision, slit, gash, slash. 2. mountain pass, defile, gorge. 3. clipping, cut-out (of paper). 4. (fort.) parapet (with merlons). 5. (min.) station, widening where a gallery reaches the main shaft. 6. (*pl.*) cuttings, scraps, shreds (left over).
cortafiambres, *m.* meat slicer.
cortafrío, *m.* cold chisel; **c. ranurador,** grooving chisel.
cortafuego, *m.* (agr.) fireguard, clear space left to prevent fire from spreading; (bldg.) fire wall, fireproof well.
cortalápices, (*pl.* **cortalápices**) *m.* pencil sharpener.
cortamente, *adv.* scantily, sparingly.
cortante, *a.* cutting, sharp. —*m.* butcher; butcher's knife or cleaver.
cortapicos, (*pl.* **cortapicos**) *m.* (ento.) earwig. — **cortapicos y callares,** children should be seen and not heard.
cortapiés, (*pl.* **cortapiés**) *m.* (coll.) slash or knife-thrust aimed at the legs.
cortapisa, *f.* 1. (dressm.) band, trimming. 2. wit, grace, charm. 3. (coll.) red tape, e.g. *¡qué tanta c.!* what a lot of red tape! 4. (*pl.*) restraints, restrictions; conditions.
cortaplumas, (*pl.* **cortaplumas**) *m.* pen-knife.
cortapuros, (*pl.* **cortapuros**) *m.* cigar cutter.
cortar, *tr.v.* 1. to cut; to cleave, sever; to gash, slash, slit; to hew, chop (wood). 2. to cut out (a dress, clipping). 3. to whittle (quill). 4. to remove honeycombs (from beehives). 5. to cut (a pack of cards); to cut water (a ship). 6. to cut off, disconnect (electricity, water, etc.). 7. to cut, cut down, reduce (expenses, speech, a play, etc.). 8. to break off, interrupt (a conversation). 9. to cut short, stop, check, curb, impede (a course of events, etc.). 10. to cut through, pierce. 11. to arbitrate, decide (a business dispute). 12. to curdle, turn sour. 13. (mil.) to cut off (an army). 14. (Amer.) to take a shortcut. — **c. bien,** to pronounce distinctly or clearly; to read (verse) well; **c. mal,** to pronounce indistinctly; to read (verse) poorly; **c. de,** to separate or divide from. —*i.v.* 1. to cut; to be sharp (a knife). 2. (coll.) to gossip, talk about someone behind his back. — **c. por el camino más corto,** to take a short cut; **c. por lo sano,** (coll.) to settle the matter quickly and decisively. —*r.v.* 1. to curdle (milk, etc.). 2. to split (a fabric or garment) along the folds. 3. to crack or become chapped from the cold (hands). 4. to become embarrassed, confused or flustered. 5. to turn shy.
cortarroscas, *f.* threading machine.
cortatubos, *m.* pipe cutter; tube cutter.
cortaviento, *m.* windscreen, windshield (of a vehicle).
corte, *m.* 1. cut; cutting; whittling (of a quill). 2. (dressm.) cutting; cut, fit (of a dress); (mil.) cutting shop (for uniforms). 3. felling (trees), cutting (sugar cane). 4. length, piece (of cloth). 5. cutting edge, edge (of knife); edge (of a book). 6. (archit.) vertical section of a building. 7. arbitration. — **c. alemán,** crew cut; **c. de cuentas,** (com.) closing of accounts (without notice to one's creditors); **c. de pelo,** haircut; **c. transversal,** cross section; **c. al sesgo,** bias cut.
corte, *f.* 1. court (residence; body of courtiers). 2. entourage, suite, retinue. 3. yard, courtyard. 4. stable; sheepfold. 5. Supreme Court; (Amer.) court (of justice). 6. (*pl.*) (Sp.) **C.,** Cortes. — **c. de sucesiones,** court of probate; **hacer la c.,** to woo or court (said of lovers).
cortedad, *f.* 1. shortness, scarcity, paucity; lack, dearth (of education, talent). 2. timidity, shyness, bashfulness.
cortejador, ra, *a.* courting, wooing. —*m., f.* courter, wooer; suitor (man).
cortejante, *a.* courting; wooing, attending; escorting, accompanying. —*m.* gallant, beau.
cortejar, *tr.v.* 1. to woo, court. 2. to escort, accompany. 3. to wait upon, attend, serve.
cortejo, *m.* 1. court, courting, wooing; courtship. 2. escorting, attendance. 3. retinue, escort, entourage; cortege. 4. gift, present. 5. (coll.) lover, beau.
cortés, *a.* courteous, polite, gallant, gracious.
cortesanamente, *adv.* courteously, politely, attentively, gallantly.
cortesanazo, za, *a.* affected, courteous, fawning, mealy-mouthed.
cortesanía, *f.* courtesy, politeness, attentiveness, gallantry.
cortesano, na, *a.* court, courtlike; courtly. —*m., f.* courtier, royal attendant.
cortesía, *f.* 1. courtesy, politeness; attentiveness, gallantry. 2. gift; grace, favor. 3. formal ending of a letter. 4. days of grace (allowed for paying a debt). 5. title (form of address). 6. (print.) blank page or space (between chapters). 7. bow, curtsy.
cortésmente, *adv.* courteously, politely, attentively.
corteza, *f.* 1. bark (of a tree); skin, peel (of a fruit); crust (of bread); rind (of cheese); (anat., bot.) cortex. 2. (fig.) surface, outward appearance. 3. uncouthness, crudeness, boorishness. — **c. peruviana,** (bot.) cinchona.
corteza, *f.* (ornith.) sandgrouse (Pterocles orientalis).
cortezón, *m. aug. of* **corteza,** thick bark (of a tree).
cortezudo, da, *a.* 1. thick-barked. 2. uncouth, boorish.
cortezuela, *f. dim. of* **corteza,** thin bark (of a tree).
cortical, *a.* cortical, pertaining to the bark or the outer skin.
corticina, *f.* (biochem.) cortin.
corticoide, corticosteroide, *m.* (biochem.) corticosteroid.
corticoso, sa, *a.* (bot.) corticose, corticous.
corticosterona, *f.* (biochem.) corticosterone.
corticotrofina, corticotropina, *f.* (physiol.) corticotrophin, corticotropin.
cortijada, *f.* group of outbuildings (belonging to a grange or farm); group of granges or farms.
cortijero, ra, *m., f.* farmer, granger. —*m.* foreman of a farm or grange.
cortijo, *m.* farm, grange; (Sp.) a country home. — **alborotar el c.,** (coll.) to cause a commotion; (coll.) to animate or induce people to attend some festivity.
cortil, *m.* yard, courtyard; corral.
cortina, *f.* 1. curtain; drapery, hanging; screen, covering; (fort.) curtain. 2. royal dais (in chapel). 3. fenced-in field. 4. (coll.) dregs of wine (left in glasses). — **c. de bambú,** (polit.) Bamboo Curtain; **c. de ducha,** shower curtain; **c. de enrollar,** blind; **c. de hierro,** (polit.) Iron Curtain; **c. de humo,** smokescreen; **c. de muelle,** sustaining wall (of a dike), breakwater; **c. musical,** theme song; **correr la c.,** to unveil, uncover; to pass over, conceal, hide; **dormir a cortinas verdes,** (coll.) to sleep in the open.
cortina, *f.* (biochem.) cortin.
cortinaje, *m.* curtains, draperies, hangings.
cortinal, *m.* fenced-in field.
cortinilla, *f.* small curtain (for keeping out the sunlight).
cortinón, *m. aug. of* **cortina,** large curtain, portiere.
cortisona, *f.* (med.) cortisone.
corto, ta, *a.* 1. short. 2. scarce, scant. 3. short, short of the mark (a bullet or ball, etc.). 4. shy, timid, bashful. 5. dull, stupid, dim-witted, e.g. *c. de luces,* dim-witted, dull. — **a la c. o a la larga,** sooner or later, in the end; **c. de oído,** hard of hearing; **c. de vista,** short-sighted; **c. de aliento,** short of breath; **quedarse c.,** to be lost for words; to fall short of.
cortocircuito, *m.* (elec.) short circuit.
cortón, *m.* (ento.) mole cricket.
corúa, *f.* (Cuba, ornith.) species of cormorant.
coruja, *f.* (ornith.) barn owl.
corulla, *f.* (mar.) stowage space (for rigging).
coruña, *f.* coarse linen woven in Corunna, Spain.
coruñés, sa, *a.* of or from Corunna, Northern Spain. —*m., f.* inhabitant or native of Corunna.
coruscante, *a.* gleaming, shining, sparkling.
coruscar, (*ref. 50*) *i.v.* (poet.) to gleam, sparkle, shine.

corusco, ca, *a.* (poet.) sparkling, gleaming.
corusque, corusqué, *ref.* **coruscar.**
corva, *f.* 1. (anat.) ham, back of knee. 2. upper wing coverts (of a falcon). 3. (vet.) tumor on the inner side of the hock (of a horse).
corvadura, *f.* bend; curvature; (archit.) arch or curve (of a vault).
corval, *a.* long said of a certain type of olive.
corvato, *m.* young crow, crow fledgling.
corvaza, *f.* (vet.) tumor on the outer hock.
corvecito, *m. dim. of* **cuervo,** small crow, young crow.
corvejón, *m.* (ornith.) cormorant.
corvejón, *m.* hock, hock joint.
corvejos *m.* (*pl.*) (vet.) hock.
corveta, *f.* (equit.) curvet, jump in which all four legs of the horse are off the ground for an instant.
corvetear, *i.v.* (equit.) to curvet.
córvidos, *m.* (*pl.*) (ornith.) Corvidae.
corvillo, *m.* 1. a kind of sickle with a hooked point. 2. (Sp., reg.) a type of basket. — **miércoles c.,** Ash Wednesday.
corvina, *f.* (ichth.) corbina, corvina.
corvinera, *f.* corvina fishing net.
corvino, na, *a.* corvine; crowlike.
corvo, va, *a.* curved, arched, bent. —*m.* 1. hook, drag. 2. (ichth.) corvina, corbina.
corza, *f.* (zool.) doe.
corzo, *m.* (zool.) deer.
corzuelo, *m.* unhusked wheat left over after threshing.
cosa, *f.* 1. thing; something; (negatively) anything, nothing, e.g. *no vale cosa,* it it not worth anything, it is worth nothing; (law) thing, object. 2. affair, business; matter. — **a c. hecha,** successfully; **ante todas cosas,** above all, before anything else; **como quien no quiere la c.,** (coll.) offhandedly, diffidently, pretending indifference; **como si tal c.,** (coll.) as though nothing had happened; **c. de,** (coll.) about, more or less, something like; **c. del otro mundo,** (coll.) something extraordinary or unusual; **c. de oír,** something worth hearing; **c. de reír,** laughing matter; **c. de ver,** something worth seeing, quite a sight; **c. hecha,** fait accompli; **c. no vista** or **nunca vista,** (coll.) something hitherto unseen, unheard-of event or thing; **c. perdida,** hopeless case; **¡qué c. rara!** what a strange thing; **c. y c.,** riddle, enigma; **es una c. seria,** it's a serious matter; **poquita c.,** (coll.) insignificant person, squirt, runt, pipsqueak; **ni c. parecida, ni c. que lo valga,** nor anything like it; **no decir c. con c.,** to be incoherent, talk incoherently; **no es gran c.,** it's nothing to write home about, it's not very extraordinary; **no hay c. con c.,** nothing is in its right place, the place is in a shambles; **no hay tal c.,** there is no such thing, it is false or untrue; **no hacer c. a derechas,** to do nothing right, do everything wrong; **no sea c. que,** lest, or it may be that (expression indicating caution), e.g. *no digas eso, no sea c. que te arrepientas,* don't say that, lest you regret it; **no ser c. del otro mundo,** (coll.) to be nothing extraordinary; **no tener uno c. suya,** to be generous or openhanded, keep nothing for oneself; **otra c.,** something else; **otra c. es con guitarra,** (coll.) you'll be whistling (or dancing) to a different tune (said to one who is bragging about something he will not be able to do in a given situation); **¿qué cosa?** what? what did you say? what's that?; **ser algo c. de uno,** to be one's own business, e.g. *es c. suya,* that's his affair, that's his business.
cosaco, ca, *a.* Cossack. —*m., f.* Cossack.
cosario, ria, *a.* 1. pertaining to a carrier. 2. frequented. —*m.* 1. carrier, expressman. 2. professional hunter, huntsman.
coscacho, *m.* (Amer.) slap or punch on the head.
coscarse, (*ref. 50*) *r.v.* to shrug one's shoulders.
coscoja, *f.* 1. (bot.) kermes oak; dried oak leaf. 2. small metal tube or roller on a buckle to facilitate the smooth running of a strap).
coscojal, *m.* oak grove or thicket.
coscojar, *m., var. of* **coscojal.**
coscojero, ra, *a.* (Arg., Urug., equit.) said of a horse that is champing continually.
coscojita, *f.* hopscotch (game).
coscojo, *m.* 1. (bot.) kermes gall. 2. (*pl.*) chain of a horse's bridle.
coscolina, *f.* (Mex.) loose woman, tramp.
coscomate, *m.* (Mex.) closed clay repository for corn.
coscón, na, *a.* (coll.) crafty, cunning, wily, astute. —*m., f.* wily person, smart alec (coll.).
coscoroba, *f.* (Arg., Chile, ornith.) small short-necked swan.
coscorrón, *m.* 1. knock on the head. 2. crust of bread; crunchy, crispy crouton.
cosec. *abbrev. of* **cosecante,** cosecant (cosec. csc.).
cosecante, *f.* (math.) cosecant.
cosecha, *f.* harvest, crop; harvest season; (fig.) crop, bunch, stack. — **de la propia c.,** of one's own creation or invention.
cosechar, *i.v., tr.v.* to harvest, reap.
cosechero, ra, *m., f.* harvester, reaper.
cosedura, *f. (dressm.) seam.*
coselete, *m.* 1. corslet, corselet (armor). 2. (ento.) thorax (of insects).
coseno, *m.* (math.) cosine; **c. verso,** coversed sine.
coser, *tr.v.* to sew; to mend; to join together; **estar cosido a,** to be stuck to, be closely attached to. —*i.v.* to sew, do needlework; **ser (una cosa) c. y cantar,** (coll.) to be very easy, be child's play or a cinch (coll.); **c. a puñaladas,** to stab repeatedly.
cosetada, *f.* run, sprint.
cosible, *m.* sewable.
cósico, *a.* (math.) **número c.,** number having the exact power of another number.
cosicosa, *f.* (coll.) enigma, riddle.
cosido, *past part. of* **coser.** —*m.* sewing; needlework. — **c. de la cama,** bed coverings, (coverlet, top sheet and blanket, sometimes sewn together).
cosidura, *f.* (mar.) lashings.
cosignatario, a, *m., f.* cosignatory, cosigner.
cosijo, *m.* 1. bug (insect). 2. annoyance, irritation.
cosijoso, sa, *a.* (Mex.) peevish, querulous, grumbly.
cosita, *f. dim. of* **cosa,** small thing, trifle.
cosmético, ca, *a., m.* cosmetic.
cosmetología, *f.* cosmetology.
cosmetólogo, a, *m., f.* cosmetologist.
cósmico, ca, *a.* cosmic.
cosmogonía, *f.* cosmogony, the study of the formation of the universe.
cosmogónico, ca, *a.* cosmogonic.
cosmografía, *f.* cosmography, descriptive astronomy.
cosmográfico, ca, *a.* cosmographic.
cosmógrafo, *m.* cosmographer.
cosmología, *f.* cosmology, the metaphysical study of the formation of the universe.
cosmológico, ca, *a.* cosmological.
cosmólogo, *m.* cosmologist.
cosmonauta, *m., f.* cosmonaut, astronaut.
cosmonáutico, ca, *a.* cosmonautic. —*f.* cosmonautics.
cosmopolita, *a., m.* cosmopolitan.
cosmopolitismo, *m.* cosmopolitanism.
cosmorama, *m.* cosmorama, a visual rendition of the most important sights and events of the universe.
cosmos, *m.* cosmos, the universe; the world.
cosmotrón, *m.* cosmotron.
cosmovisión, *f.* Weltanschauung, a conception of the world from a specific viewpoint.
coso, *m.* 1. arena (for bullfighting and other public festivals). 2. main street. 3. (ento.) woodborer.
cospe, *m.* (carp.) 1. groove (produced by hewing or sawing). 2. chop, hack.
cospel, *m.* (numis.) blank coin (before minting).
cosque, *m.* (coll.) knock or rap on the head.
cosquillar, *tr.v., var. of* **cosquillear.**
cosquillas, *f.* (*pl.*) tickling; **buscarle a uno las cosquillas,** (coll.) to annoy, tease; **hacerle a uno cosquillas una cosa,** (coll.) to tickle; to tickle one's fancy or curiosity; (coll.) to cause one to be suspicious or wary; **tener malas cosquillas,** (coll.) to be touchy, bad-tempered.
cosquillear, *tr.v.* to tickle; to itch or prickle.
cosquillejas, *f.* (*pl.*) *dim. of* **cosquillas,** tickling.
cosquilleo, *m.* tickle, tickling; prickling; tingling; itching.
cosquilloso, sa, *a.* ticklish; touchy.
costa, *f.* cost, price; living allowance (paid to a worker); (*pl.*) (law) costs, fees; **a c. de,** at the cost of, by dint of; **a toda c.,** at all costs.
costa, *f.* 1. coast. 2. cobbler's polishing tool. — **barajar la c.,** (mar.) to hug the shore, sail close to the shore; **C. de Marfil,** Ivory Coast; **C. de Oro,** Gold Coast; **no hay moros en la c.,** the coast is clear.
costado, *m.* 1. side, (mil.) flank. 2. (*pl.*) lines (of parentage). — **dar el c.,** (mar.) to turn broadside on.
costal, *a.* costal, pertaining to the ribs. —*m.* 1. sack, bag. 2. braces (for frames of adobe walls. — **eso es harina de otro c.,** (coll.) that's a horse of a different color; **no parecer c. de paja,** (coll.) to look attractive; **vaciar uno el c.,** (coll.) to tell everything; to unburden oneself to someone.
costalada, *f.* bump, bang (caused by a fall on the side or back).
costalazo, *m., var. of* **costalada.**
costalejo, *m. dim. of* **costal,** small sack.
costana, *f.* 1. steep road, steep slope. 2. (mar.) rib (of a ship).
costanera, *f.* 1. slope. 2. (*pl.*) (archit.) rafters.
costanero, ra, *a.* 1. sloping, steep. 2. coastal, coast.
costanilla, *f.* very steep road.
costar, (*ref. 33*) *i.v.* 1. to cost. 2. to be difficult, e.g. *le cuesta mucho a uno confesar sus defectos,* it takes a lot (it's difficult) to admit to one's faults, *me costó mucho trabajo convencerle,* it took me a lot (it was difficult) to convince him. — **c. un ojo de la cara,** to cost a fortune; **cuesta trabajo creerlo,** it's hard to believe it. —*r.v.* **costarse el dinero,** to spend a lot of money.
Costa Rica, *f.* Costa Rica.
costarricense, *a., m., f.* Costa Rican.
costarriqueño, na, *a., m., f.* Costa Rican.
coste, *m.* cost, price. — **a c. y costas, at** cost price; without profit.
costear, *tr.v.* 1. to pay for. 2. (Peru) to make fun of. 3. (mar.) to hug (the coast), sail close to (the shore). —*r.v.* to pay for itself.
costeño, ña, *a., var. of* **costanero, (Amer.)** of or pertaining to the coast or shore.
costera, *f.* 1. side (of a bale, etc.); wrapping sheet protecting the paper ream. 2. slope (of a hill). 3. coast. 4. (mar.) fishing season.
costero, ra, *a.* coastal. —*m.* 1. first plank of timber (sawed lengthwise). 2. (min.) side wall of a high furnace; (min.) side face of an ore deposit.
costezuela, *f. dim. of* **cuesta,** small slope.

costil, *a.* costal, pertaining to the ribs.
costilla, *f.* 1. rib (of a body, ship, arch, leaf); chop, cutlet. 2. (coll.) wealth, fortune, property. 3. rung (of a chair); stave (of a barrel); bar, rod. 4. (coll.) wife, one's better half. 5. (*pl.*) (coll.) back. — **c. falsa,** false rib; **c. flotante,** (anat.) floating rib; **c. verdadera,** (anat.) true rib; **medirle a uno las costillas,** to give someone a beating; **pasearle a uno las costillas,** to kick or trample someone; **reír a costillas de uno,** (Amer.) to laugh at someone's expense.
costillaje, *m.* (coll.), *var. of* **costillar.**
costillar, *m.* ribs; ribbing; frame of a ship.
costiller, *m.* (arch.) royal equerry.
costilludo, da, *a.* (coll.) broad-shouldered well-built.
costino, na, *a.* (bot.) costus.
costo, *m.* cost, price; **al c.,** at cost price; **c. de la vida,** cost of living; **c., seguro y flete,** cost, insurance and freight (c.i.f.).
costo, *m.* (bot.) sawwort, costusroot; **c. hortense,** (bot.) costmary.
costosamente, *adv.* expensively, at great cost, extravagantly.
costoso, sa, *a.* costly, expensive; (fig.) costly, grievous.
costra, *f.* 1. crust, scale. 2. scab (of a wound). 3. biscuit given to galley slaves. 4. snuff (of a candlewick). — **c. de azúcar,** sugar residue or crust (in boilers), caldron coating; **c. de herrumbre,** rust scale; **c. láctea,** (med.) infantile eczema.
costrada, *f.* sugar-coated pie or pastry.
costroso, sa, *a.* crusty; scabby.
costumbre, *f.* 1. custom; practice; habit; (*pl.*) mores, customs (of a nation, etc.). 2. menstruation. — **de c. or por c.,** usually; **tener por c.,** to be in the habit of.
costumbrismo, *m.* literary style that gives particular attention to description of typical regional or national customs.
costumbrista, *a.* folkloric, pertaining to an artist or writer who specializes in depicting regional customs and manners.
costura, *f.* sewing, needlework; seam; (mar.) seam; **meter a uno en c.,** (coll.) to make someone see reason, calm down, restrain; **saber de toda c.,** (coll.) to be worldly wise; **sentar las costuras,** (dressm.) to press a seam; **sentar a uno las costuras,** (coll.) to give someone one a beating; to punish, chastise, reprimand; **c. de soldadura,** welded seam.
costurera, *f.* seamstress.
costurero, *m.* sewing table, cabinet or basket; sewing room.
costurón, *m.* 1. *aug. of* **costura,** large seam; (derog.) untidy rough seam. 2. (fig.) prominent scar.
cota, *f.* 1. habergeon, hauberk, coat of armor; tabard. 2. (fort.) palisade, stockade. 3. callous hide (on a boar's back). 4. quota, share. 5. (top.) contour elevation reading; elevation. — **c. de altura** or **de nivel,** (top.) elevation; **c. de comparación,** datum; **c. de referencia,** datum plane, datum; **c. de malla,** coat of mail.
cotación, *f.* elevation.
cotana, *f.* mortise hole; mortise chisel.
cotangente, *f.* (geom.) cotangent.
cotanza, *f.* (tex.) thin linen fabric.
cotardía, *f.* lined jacket or waistcoat (used in Spain in the Middle Ages).
cotarra, *f.* slope, bank of a ravine.
cotarrera, *f.* (coll.) gossip, gossipmonger.
cotarro, *m.* 1. night shelter (for vagrants), flophouse (U.S., sl.) 2. bank (of a ravine). — **alborotar el c.,** (coll.) to cause or stir up trouble; **andar de c. en c.,** (coll.) to flit around from place to place, fritter time away in idle visiting.
cotejable, *a.* comparable.
cotejamiento, *m.* checking, comparing.
cotejar, *tr.v.* to compare, to check; to reconcile facts or information.
cotejo, *m.* checking; comparison, collation; **c. de letras,** (law) expert comparison of handwriting (to prove authenticity).
coterna, *f.* (Col., coll.) gnat.
coterráneo, a, *a.* of the same land or country.
cotí, *m.* ticking (mattress material).
cotice, coticé, *ref.* **cotizar.**
cotidianamente, *adv.* daily, everyday.
cotidiano, na, *a.* daily.
cotila, *f.* cotyla, bone socket.
cotiledón, *m.* (bot.) cotyledon.
cotiledóneo, a, *a.* (bot.) cotyledonous. —*f.* (*pl.*) Cotyledon (family).
cotilla, *f.* 1. corset, stays. 2. (fig.) gossip, gossipmonger.
cotillear, *i.v.* (coll.) to gossip.
cotillero, ra, *m., f.* 1. corset maker or seller. 2. (fig.) gossiper.
cotillo, *m.* head (of a hammer or other tool).
cotillón, *m.* cotillion (dance).
cotín, *m.* 1. back stroke (given to a ball). 2. (Amer.) ticking (mattress material).
cotinga, *m.* (Amer., ornith.) Cotinga (genus).
cotiza, *f.* (her.) cotise.
cotiza, *f.* (Ven.) peasant's sandal. — **ponerse uno las cotizas,** to hide oneself, take shelter.
cotizable, *a.* quotable, priceable.
cotización, *f.* quotation, quoting (of price); current price.
cotizado, da, *a.* (her.) cotised.
cotizado, da, *past part. of* **cotizar.** —*a.* (coll.) popular (person); greatly sought after (goods).
cotizar, (*ref. 53*) *tr.v.* to quote (prices); to price, set a price on, value; to call out (current prices) in a stock exchange; (Ven.) to distinguish.
coto, *m.* 1. enclosed land. 2. boundary stone, landmark. 3. end, stop, limit. — **c. redondo,** group of neighboring estates belonging to one owner; **poner c. a,** to put a stop or an end to.
coto, *m.* 1. price, tariff, rate. 2. price-fixing agreement. 3. lineal measurement of about half a palm. 4. billiard game in which one party must win three times successively to win the game.
coto, *m.* 1. (Amer.) goiter. 2. (zool.) howling monkey. 3. (ichth.) miller's thumb.
cotomono, *m.* (Peru, zool.) stentor, howling monkey.
cotón, *m.* (tex.) printed cotton fabric.
cotona, *f.* 1. (Chile, Peru) coarse cotton undershirt. 2. (Mex.) jacket. 3. (P. Rico) nightgown.
cotonada, *f.* cotton or linen fabric with woven-in, raised design.
cotoncillo, *m.* button on a painter's maul-stick (small ball of wool or cotton).
cotonía, *f.* (tex.) coarse white dimity.
cotorra, *f.* 1. (ornith.) cockatoo; parrot, parrakeet; magpie. 2. (coll.) chatterbox, parrot.
cotorrear, *i.v.* (coll.) to chatter, prattle, babble.
cotorreo, *m.* (coll.) chattering, babbling, prattle.
cotorrera, *f.* 1. (ornith.) female cockatoo. 2. (coll.) chatterbox, prattler, babbler.
cotorrón, na, *a.* said of people past their prime but still affecting youthful manners and attire.
cototo, *m.* (Arg., Chile) bump, lump, bruise.
cotovía, *f.* (ornith.) crested lark (Alauda cristata).
cotral, *a., var. of* **cutral.**
cotúa, *f.* (ornith.) cormorant.
cotudo, da, *a.* hairy; fuzzy; fluffy.
cotudo, da, *a.* (*Amer.*) goitrous (afflicted with goiter).
cotufa, *f.* 1. (bot.) Jerusalem artichoke (Heliantus tuberosus). 2. delicacy, tidbit. — **pedir cotufas en el golfo,** (coll.) to ask for the moon.
cotunita, *f.* (geol.) cotunite, native lead chloride.
coturno, *m.* cothurnus. — **calzar el c.,** to use high flown language; **de c. alto,** of high rank.
cotutor, *m.* co-guardian.
cotuza, *f.* (Salv., Guat., zool.) agouti (rodent).
coulomb, *m.* (phys.) coulomb.
covacha, *f.* 1. small cave, grotto. 2. (Mex.) cubbyhole under the stairs. 3. (Ecuad.) shop selling farm products. 4. (Bol.) adobe bench (in inns).
covachuela, *f.* 1. *dim. of* **covacha,** grotto. 2. (coll.) ministerial office; (coll.) public office. 3. small shop (situated in church cellars).
covachuelista, *m.* (coll.) government clerk.
covachuelo, *m.* (coll.), *var. of* **covachuelista.**
covadera, *f.* (Chile, Peru) natural guano deposit.
covalencia, *f.* (chem.) covalence, covalency.
covalente, *a.* (chem.) covalent.
covanilla, *f., var. of* **covanillo.**
covanillo, *m. dim. of* **cuévano,** small grape basket (carried on the back).
covariante, *a.* (math.) covariant.
covezuela, *f. dim. of* **cueva,** small cave.
coxal, *a.* (anat.) coxal (pertaining to coxa or hip joint).
coxalgia, *f.* (med.) coxalgia.
coxálgico, *a.* coxalgic.
coxcojilla, ta, *f.* form of hopscotch (children's game).
coxis, *m.* (anat.) coccyx.
coy, *m.* (mar.) hammock.
coya, *f.* wife of the Inca, empress or princess (title used by ancient Peruvians).
coyol, *m.* (bot., Amer.) cohune palm (Attalea cohune); cohune nut.
coyolar, *m* (Guat., Mex.) plantation of cohune palms.
coyote, *m.* 1. (zool.) coyote, prairie wolf. 2. (Mex.) stockbroker.
coyotear, *i.v.* to operate as a stockbroker.
coyotero, ra, *a., m.* (Amer.) coyote-hunting (dog). —*f.* (coyote) trap.
coyunda, *f.* 1. strap for yoking oxen. 2. lace (for sandals). 3. marriage tie. 4. subjection, domination, yoke.
coyuntero, *m.* farmer who yokes his ox with another's to make a team.
coyuntura, *f.* 1. joint, articulation. 2. occasion, opportunity; **hablar uno por las coyunturas,** (coll.) to talk one's head off.
coyuyo, *m.* (Arg., ento.) large cicada.
coz,)*pl.* **coces**) *f.* 1. kick. 2. kick, recoil (of a gun). 3. butt (of a rifle). 4. backwash (of a ship). 5. thicker end (of a piece of timber); (mar.) base of a topmast. 6. (coll.) insult, rude remark or reply, grossness. — **mandar a coces,** to order someone about rudely or roughly; **soltar uno una c.,** (coll.) to answer rudely; **tirar coces,** (coll.) to rebel, resist authority.
cps *abbrev. of* **ciclos por segundo,** cycles per second (cps, c/s).
Cr *sym. of* **cromio,** chromium (Cr).
crabrón, *m.* hornet, large wasp.
crac, *m.* (com.) bankruptcy, failure.
cramponado, da, *a.* (her.) cramponnée.
cran, *m.* (print.) nick on type (to indicate correct position on the composing stick).
craneal, *a.* cranial, skull.
craneano, na, *a., var. of* **craneal.**
cráneo, *m.* cranium, skull; **tener seco** or **secársele a uno el c.,** (coll.) to be or go crazy.
craneología, *f.* craniology (science of determining the intellectual and emotional tendencies of a person by studying the shape of his brain).

craneológico, ca, *a.* craniological.
craneólogo, *m.* craniologist.
craneometría, *f.* craniometry.
craneómetro, *m.* craniometer.
craniado, da, *a., m* (zool.) craniate.
craniano, na, *a., var. of* **craneal.**
crápula, *f.* inebriation, intoxication, drunkenness, crapulence; (coll.) dissipation, debauchery, licentiousness.
crapuloso, sa, *a.* intemperate, drunken, crapulous; (coll.) dissolute, dissipated, debauched, licentious.
craquear, *tr.v.* to crack (petroleum).
craqueo, *m.* cracking (of petroleum).
crasamente, *adv.* crassly, ignorantly, stupidly.
crascitar, *i.v.* to croak, caw (as a crow).
crasedad, *f.* (arch.) *var. of* **crasitud.**
crasiento, ta, *a.* greasy.
crasitud, *f.* body fat, adipose tissue.
craso, sa, *a.* 1. fat, greasy. 2. thick, dense (oil). 3. crass, gross, flagrant, inexcusable (error, ignorance, etc.). —*m.* fat, fatness.
crasuláceo, a, *a.* (bot.) crassulaceous. —*f.* crassula (crassulaceous plant); (*pl.*) Crassulaceae (family).
cráter, *m.* 1. crater, mouth of a volcano. 2. (astron.) C., Crateris, Crater, the Cup (constellation).
crátera, *f.* (archeol.) krater, crater, Greek or Roman amphora.
crateriforme, *a.* with the form of a crater, crater-shaped.
cratícula, *f.* 1. (ecc.) small window or grille through which nuns receive Holy Communion. 2. (phys.) diffraction grating.
craza, *f.* crucible (to melt gold and silver for coins).
crazada, *f.* (metal.) cupelled silver ready for alloying.
crea, *f.* semi-fine linen.
creable, *a.* creatable.
creación, *f.* 1. (lit., fig.) creation. 2. C., the world.
creador, ra, *a.* (coll.) creative (artist, mind, etc.). —*m.* Creator, God. —*m., f.* creator.
crear, *tr.v.* to create, to establish, to institute; to design, invent.
creatina, *f.* (biochem.) creatine.
creatinina, *f.* (biochem.) creatinine.
creativo, va, *a.* creative.
crecal, *m.* (her.) device in the form of a candelabrum or branched candlestick.
crecedero, ra, *a.* growing; allowing for growth, able to be lengthened (clothes).
crecer, (*ref. 45*) *i.v.* to grow; to increase; to augment, to wax (the moon); to swell (a river). — **ver c. la hierba,** (coll.) to be very sharp, be very bright or intelligent. —*r.v.* to become important, rise or come up in the world; to become self-important, high and mighty, swell-headed.
creces, *f.* (*pl.*) 1. increase; excess, extra. 2. interest in kind paid by a farmer who borrows from a public granary. 3. signs of growth (in a child). — **con c.,** with interest.
crecida, *f.* freshet, swelling (of a river or stream).
crecidamente, *adv.* amply, abundantly, fully, plentifully, in excess.
crecido, da, *past part. of* **crecer.** —*a.* (coll.) big, large, numerous. —*m.* (*pl.*) added stitches (in knitting).
creciente, *a.* growing; increasing. —*m.* (her.) crescent. —*f.* freshet, swelling (of a river). — **c. de la luna,** waxing of the moon; **c. del mar,** rising tide, flood tide.
crecimiento, *m.* growth, growing; increase; swelling (of a river).
credencia, *f.* 1. (ecc.) credence. 2. (arch.) credence, wine sideboard.
credencial, *a.* credential, accrediting. —*f.* credential letter; (*pl.*) credentials, credential letters, letters of credence.
credenciero, *m.* winetaster, in charge of the royal credence.
credibilidad, *f.* credibility.
crediticio, cia, *a.* pertaining to public or private credit.
crédito, *m.* 1. (com.) credit; letter of credit. 2. belief, credence. 3. reputation, name, authority, standing. — **a c.,** on credit; **abrir un c. a uno,** to grant or extend credit to someone; **c. abierto** or **en blanco,** open credit; **c. de vivienda, c. hipotecario,** mortgage; **c. en cuenta corriente,** overdraft protection; **c. global** or **rotativo,** (com.) revolving credit; **dar a c.,** to lend (money) on credit; **dar c.,** to believe; **sentar** or **tener sentado el c.,** to establish or enjoy a good reputation.
credo, *m.* 1. (rel.) creed. 2. beliefs, credo, creed. — con **el c. en la boca,** with one's heart in one's mouth; **en un c.,** in a jiffy, in a wink; **que canta el c.,** (coll.) fantastic, extraordinary, unbelievable, e.g. *dice cada mentira que canta el c.,* he tells the most fantastic lies.
crédulamente, *adv.* credulously, gullibly.
credulidad, *f.* credulity, credulousness, gullibility.
crédulo, la, *a.* credulous; gullible.
creederas, *f.* (*pl.*) (coll.) gullibility, e.g. *tener buenas, grandes,* or *bravas creederas,* to be very gullible.
creedero, ra, *a.* credible, believable, verisimilar.
creedor, ra, *a., var. of* **crédulo.**
creencia, *f.* belief, creed.
creer, (*ref. 60*) *tr.v.* to believe; to think, believe. — **ya lo creo,** of course, naturally, I should think so. —*i.v.* to believe. — **ver es c.,** seeing is believing. —*r.v.* to believe; to think or regard oneself to be. — **¿qué te crees?** who do you think you are?
crehuela, *f.* coarse lining material.
creíble, *a.* credible, believable.
creíblemente, *adv.* probably, possibly.
creído, da, *a.* (Amer.) 1. conceited, vain, foppish. 2. credulous, trusting.
crema, *f.* 1. cream. 2. face cream. 3. (gram.) diaresis. — **la c.,** the cream, flower, elite; **c. agria** or **ácida,** sour cream; **c. bronceadora,** suntan lotion; **c. chantilly,** whipped cream; **c. de afeitar,** shaving cream.
cremación, *f.* cremation, incineration.
cremallera, *f.* 1. (mec.) rack, toothed bar. 2. zipper. — **c. doble de dientes alternados,** (ry.) Abt rack; **c. reguladora,** control rack.
crematística, *f.* political economy.
crematístico, ca, *a.* pertaining to political economy.
crematorio, ria, *a.* cremating, incinerating; **horno c.,** crematory.
cremento, *m.* increase.
cremería, *f.* (Arg.) creamery, dairy.
cremómetro, *m.* creamometer, cream gauge.
cremonés, sa, *a.* of or from Cremona. —*m., f.* native of Cremona, city in Italy (famous for its fine violin makers).
crémor, *m.* (chem.) cream of tartar. — **c. tártaro,** (chem.) cream of tartar.
cremoso, sa, *a.* creamy.
crencha, *f.* parting (of hair); each side of parted hair.
crenchar, *tr.v.* to part the hair.
crenulado, da, *a.* (bot.) crenulate.
Creón, *m.* (myth.) Creon, Antigone's uncle and the one who condemned her to be buried alive.
creosol, *m.* (chem.) creosol.
creosota, *f.* (chem.) creosote.
creosotado, da, *past part. of* **creosotar.** —*a.* containing creosote.
creosotar, *tr.v.* to creosote (lumber).
crepé, *m.* (imp. u.) wig, toupée.
crepitación, *f.* crepitation, crackling; (med.) crepitation.
crepitante, *a.* crepitating, crackling.
crepitar, *i.v.* to crepitate, crackle.
crepuscular, *a.* crepuscular, twilight.
crepusculino, na, *a., var. of* **crepuscular.**
crepúsculo, *m.* twilight, dusk, dawn.
crequeté, *m.* (Cuba, ornith.) night-hawk (Chordeiles minor).
cresa, *f.* maggot, larva (of two-winged insects); flyblow; egg of the queen bee.
cresílico, ca, *a.* (chem.) cresylic.
creso, *m.* 1. Croesus, wealthy person. 2. (hist.) **C.,** Croesus, last king of Lydia, known for his generosity.
cresol, *m.* (chem.) cresol.
crespilla, *f.* (bot.) morel.
crespillo, *m.* (Hond., bot.) clematis.
crespina, *f.* coif, hairnet, hair cap.
crespo, pa, *a.* 1. curly, kinky (hair); curled (leaves). 2. (coll.) obscure, complicated (style, speech). 3. (coll.) huffy, testy, irritated, vexed. —*m.* curl, ringlet (of hair).
crespón, *m.* (tex.) crepe, crape; **c. de luto, c. fúnebre,** crape; mourning band.
cresta, *f.* 1. crest (of a bird or a wave). 2. comb (of a cock). 3. summit, top, peak. — **c. de gallo,** (bot.) cockscomb, yellow rattle; **alzar** or **levantar la c.,** (coll.) to put one's nose in the air, show arrogance; **dar en la c. a uno,** (coll.) to cut someone short, squelch someone (coll.).
crestado, da, *a.* crested, tufted.
crestería, *f.* (archit.) cresting (on a building); (fort.) battlements; (fort.) merlons, crenellation.
crestomatía, *f.* chrestomathy, collection of writings.
crestón, *m.* 1. *aug. of* **cresta,** large crest; crest (of a helmet). 2. (min.) outcrop.
crestudo, da, *a.* 1. big-crested. 2. (coll.) haughty, high and mighty.
creta, *f.* crumbly, chalky lime.
Creta, *f.* Crete, Greek island in the Mediterranean, center of the Minoan civilization in pre-Hellenic history.
cretáceo, a, *a.* cretaceous; (geol.) Cretaceous (period).
cretense, *a., m., f.* Cretan, of or pertaining to the island of Crete; a native of Crete.
crético, ca, *a.* Cretan. —*m.* (poet.) amphimacer, three-syllabled foot (long, short, long).
cretinismo, *m.* (med.) cretinism.
cretino, na, *a.* (med.) cretinous. —*m., f.* (fig.) cretin, imbecile.
cretona, *f.* (tex.) cretonne.
creyendo, *ref.* **creer.**
creyente, *a.* believing. —*m., f.* believer.
creyera, creyó, *ref.* **creer.**
creyón, *m.* (gal.) crayon; charcoal pencil; **c. de labios,** lipstick.
crezca, crezco, *ref.* **crecer.**
crezneja, *f., var. of* **crizneja.**
cría, *f.* 1. breeding; rearing, raising, nursing. 2. offspring, litter, brood, young (of animals).
criada, *f.* 1. female servant, maid. 2. (fig.) paddle (for beating clothes in washing).
criadero, ra, *a.* prolific, fruitful, fecund. —*m.* 1. nursery (for trees, plants). 2. breeding place; fish hatchery; rabbit warren; stud farm; stock farm. 3. (min.) bed, seam, vein.
criadilla, *f.* 1. testicle of an animal; (*pl.*) (cul.) lamb fry. 2. round roll of bread. — **c. de mar,** (zool.) polyp; **c. de tierra,** (bot.) truffle.

criado, da, *past part. of* **criar.** —*a.* brought up, bred, behaved, e.g. *bien* or *mal criado,* well or badly brought up, well or ill bred; well or badly behaved. —*m.* servant. —*f.* maid servant; **salirle a uno la criada respondona,** (coll.) to turn out to be no bargain at all.

criador, ra, *a.* nourishing, nutritive; fruitful (land). —*m.* Creator (God). —*m., f.* 1. breeder. 2. viniculturist, vine grower. —*f.* wet-nurse.

criaduelo, la, *m., f. dim. of* **criado, da,** young or minor servant.

criamiento, *m.* 1. renovation, preservation. 2. the act of breeding and tending.

criandera, *f.* (Amer.) wet nurse.

crianestesia, *f.* (med.) cryanesthesia.

crianza, *f.* 1. nursing, nurturing; lactation period. 2. breeding, manners; **buena c.,** good breeding, good manners.

criar, (*ref. 54*) *tr.v.* 1. to raise, bring up, rear. 2. to breed, raise (animals); to produce (crops); to engender, beget. 3. to nurse, suckle; to nourish, feed. 4. to create; to institute, establish; to set up (a business). 5. to grow or flourish (in a certain climate or milieu), e.g. *las trufas se crían bajo tierra,* truffles are grown underground. — **cría cuervos y te sacarán los ojos,** mind that you don't lavish your gifts upon the ungrateful; **Dios los cría y ellos se juntan,** birds of a feather flock together.

criatura, *f.* 1. creature. 2. infant, baby, child. 3. foetus. — **c. abortiva,** (law) unborn child; **ser uno una criatura,** (coll.) to be young or tender in years; to be childish, act like a child.

criba, *f.* sieve, screen, riddle; **estar una cosa hecha una c.,** to be riddled with holes; **c. corrediza,** traveling screen; **c. hidráulica,** (min.) jig; **c. lavadora,** scrubbing or washing screen.

cribado, *past part. of* **cribar.** —*m.* sieving, sifting, riddling, screening.

cribador, ra, *a.* screening, sieving. —*m., f.* screener, sifter.

cribar, *tr.v.* to sieve, screen; to bolt (grain).

cribelo, *m.* (zool.) cribellum.

cribo, *m., var. of* **criba.**

cric, *m.* (mec.) jack (hoist); **c. de tornillo,** screw jack, jackscrew; **c. hidráulico,** hydraulic jack.

crica, *f.* (vulg., P. Rico) female sexual organs.

cricétido, *m.* (zool.) cricetid.

cricoides, *a.* (med.) cricoid. —*m.* cricoid cartilage (of the larynx).

cricquet, *m., var. of* **criquet.**

crimen, *m.* crime, criminal offense, felony.

criminación, *f.* accusation, charge, incrimination, crimination.

criminal, *a.* criminal; delinquent. —*m., f.* criminal, felon, delinquent; **c. de guerra,** war criminal.

criminalidad, *f.* criminality; crime, e.g. *el índice de c.,* the crime rate.

criminalista, *m., f.* criminologist, penologist, criminalist; criminal lawyer.

criminalmente, *adv.* criminally.

criminar, *tr.v.* to accuse, charge, incriminate, criminate; (coll.) to censure, criticize.

criminología, *f.* criminology, penology.

criminológico, ca, *a.* criminological.

criminólogo, ga, *m., f.* criminologist.

criminoso, sa, *a.* criminal. —*m., f.* criminal, delinquent.

crimno, *m.* coarse wheat flour, wheat meal.

crimoterapia, *f.* (med.) crymotherapy.

crin, *f.* (*gen. pl.*) mane (of animals); horsehair. — **c. vegetal,** vegetable hair or horsehair; **tenerse uno a las crines,** (coll.) to hold on (to one's position, etc.).

crinado, da, *past part. of* **crinar.** —*a.* (poet.) maned, long-haired.

crinífero, ra, *a.* mane-bearing.

crinito, ta, *a.* crinite, hairy; tufted.

crinoideo, dea, *a.* (zool.) crinoid, flower-shaped.

crinolina, *f.* 1. crinoline; buckram, stiffening material. 2. hoop skirt; stiff petticoat.

crío, *m.* (coll.) nursing baby, sucking infant, nurseling.

criofílico, ca, *a.* cryophilic.

criogenia, *f.* (phys.) cryogenics, cryogeny, science that studies the effect of very low temperatures on the properties of matter.

criógeno, na, *a.* (chem.) cryogenic. —*m.* cryogen, freezing mixture.

criohidrato, *m.* (chem.) cryohydrate.

criolita, *f.* (min.) cryolite.

criollismo, *m.* (Amer.) an expression or custom typical of the New World.

criollo, lla, *a., m., f.* 1. Creole. 2. said of the American born of European parents. —*a.* (coll., Amer.) native, domestic, homey.

criómetro, *m.* (phys.) cryometer, a thermometer for measuring very low temperatures.

crioscopia, *f.* (phys.) cryoscopy.

crióstato, *m.* (phys.) cryostat.

crioterapia, *f.* (med.) crymotherapy, cryotherapy.

cripta, *f.* crypt; vault, undercroft; (anat.) crypt, glandular cavity.

criptoanálisis, *m.* cryptoanalysis, the study of secret writing.

criptoclástico, ca, *a.* (geol.) cryptoclastic.

criptocristalino, na, *a.* (phys., chem.) cryptocrystalline.

criptófita, *f.* (bot.) cryptophyte.

criptógamo, ma, *a.* (bot.) cryptogamio, cryptogamous. —*f.* (*pl.*) Cryptogams (family).

criptogénico, ca, *a.* cryptogenic, of obscure or unknown origin.

criptografía, *f.* cryptography, the study of codes and other secret writing.

criptográfico, ca, *a.* cryptographic, cryptographical, pertaining to codes and other secret writing.

criptógrafo, *m.* 1. cryptographer, cryptographist, person who specializes in decoding secret writing. 2. (tel.) scrambler.

criptograma, *m.* cryptograph, cryptogram, message in cipher or code.

criptón, *m.* (chem.) krypton.

criptorquidia, *f.* (med.) cryptorchidism, cryptorchism.

criptozoito, *m.* (med.) cryptozoite.

criquet, *m.* (sport.) cricket.

cris, *m.* creese, kris (dagger).

crisálida, *f.* (zool.) chrysalis, pupa.

crisantema, *f., var. of* **crisantemo.**

crisantemo, *m.* (bot.) chrysanthemun.

criselefantino, na, *a.* chryselephantine, said of certain objects made in ancient Greece, usually overlaid with gold and ivory.

crisis, *f.* 1. crisis, grave turn of events. 2. judgment, conclusion (after careful consideration of a matter). — **c. de energía,** energy crisis; **c. de vivienda,** housing shortage. — **c. ministerial,** cabinet crisis; **c. nerviosa,** nervous breakdown.

crisma, *m., f.* (ecc.) chrism, consecrated oil. —*f.* head; **romperle a uno la c.,** (coll.) to brain someone, break someone's head.

crismal, *m.* (ecc.) chrismatory.

crismar, *tr.v.* (obs.) to baptize or confirm.

crismera, *f.* (ecc.) chrismatory (cruet or vessel where the crism is kept).

crisneja, *f., var. of* **crizneja.**

crisoberilo, *m.* (min.) chrysoberyl.

crisol, *m.* crucible; (metal) crucible, hearth (of a smelting furnace).

crisolada, *f.* contents of a crucible.

crisolar, *tr.v.* to smelt, refine (in a crucible).

crisolito, *m.* (min.) chrysolite; **c. de los volcanes,** chrysolite, olivine, peridot; **c. oriental,** yellow topaz.

crisomélidos, *m.* (*pl.*) (ento.) Chrysomelidae.

crisopacio, *m., var. of* **crisoprasa.**

crisopeya, *f.* alchemy.

crisopo, *m.* (ento.) lacewing.

crisoprasa, *f.* (min.) chrysoprase, green chalcedony.

crisotilo, *m.* (min.) chrysotile.

crispadura, *f.* twitching (of a muscle); convulsion, contraction; (fig.) nerve-wracking.

crispamiento, *m., var. of* **crispadura.**

crispar, *tr.v.* to contract, convulse, make twitch; (coll.) to put on edge (the nerves); to tremble (the voice). —*r.v.* to twitch, contract. — **se me crisparon los nervios,** it put my nerves on edge.

crispatura, *f., var. of* **crispadura.**

crispir, *tr.v.* to marble, spatter with paint to give the appearance of marble.

crista, *f.* (her.) crest (of helmet).

cristal, *m.* 1. (chem., min.) crystal. 2. crystal, crystal glass; ornament of crystal; pane of glass. 3. (fig.) looking-glass, mirror. 4. (poet.) water. 5. lens. — **c. armado,** wire glass; **c. de roca,** rock crystal; **c. de seguridad,** safety glass; **c. esmerilado,** ground glass; **c. estriado,** ribbed glass; **c. hilado,** spun glass; **c. irrompible,** safety or nonshattering glass; **c. tallado,** cut glass.

cristalera, *f.* 1. sideboard, cupboard; glass cabinet. 2. glass door.

cristalería, *f.* glassware factory or shop; glassware, crystalware.

cristalice, cristalicé, *ref.* **cristalizar.**

cristalífero, ra, *a.* crystalliferous.

cristalinidad, *f.* crystallinity.

cristalino, na, *a.* crystalline; pellucid, limpid, clear. —*m.* (anat.) crystalline lens.

cristalítico, ca, *a.* (min.) crystallitic.

cristalito, *m.* (min.) crystallite.

cristalizable, *a.* crystallizable.

cristalización, *f.* crystallization.

cristalizador, *m.* crystallizer (a vessel used in laboratory processes).

cristalizar, (*ref. 53*) *tr.v., i.v., r.v.* to crystallize.

cristalografía, *f.* (min.) crystallography, the study of the form and properties of crystals.

cristalográfico, ca, *a.* crystallographical.

cristalógrafo, fa, *m., f.* crystallographer, person who studies and classifies crystals and their properties.

cristaloide, *m.* (chem.) crystalloid.

cristaloideo, a, *a.* crystalloidal.

cristalomancia, *f.* divination (reading) using a mirror.

cristalosa, *f.* (med.) crystallose.

cristel, *m.* clyster, enema.

cristianamente, *adv.* in a Christian manner.

cristianar, *tr.v.* (coll.) to baptize, christen.

cristiandad, *f.* Christendom.

cristianesco, ca, *a.* said of Moorish works of art, customs, etc. when they imitate or resemble Spanish styles.

cristianice, cristianicé, *ref.* **cristianizar.**

cristianísimo, ma, *a.* most Christian (his most Christian French Majesty).

cristianismo, *f.* 1. Christianity. 2. christening, baptism.

cristianización, *f.* Christianization.

cristianizar, (*ref. 53*) *tr.v.* to convert to Christianity, Christianize.

cristiano, na, *a.* Christian. —*m., f.* Christian. —*m.* 1. fellow man; (coll.) living soul, person, e.g. *no había un c. en la calle,* there was not a living

soul in the street. 2. (hum.) Spanish (language). 3. (coll.) watery wine. — **c. nuevo,** recently baptized adult; **hablar uno en c.,** (coll.) to speak in common language or in plain terms.
cristino, na, *a., m., f.* (hist., Sp.) partisan of doña Isabel II against the Pretender.
Cristo, *m.* 1. Christ. 2. crucifix, image of Christ crucified. — **a mal c. mucha sangre,** the sensational always covers up bad workmanship (said of cheap works of art or literature); **como a un santo c. un par de pistolas,** (coll.) it's like dungarees on a duchess (indicating the incongruousness of one thing with another); **donde C. dio las tres voces,** (coll.) far away, at the end of the earth; **ni C. que lo fundó,** absolutely not (when denying the truth of an observation or existence of something); **ni por un c.,** (coll.) by no means, not for the world; **sacar el c.,** (coll.) to try to bully or badger into (doing something).
cristofué, *m.* (ornith.) tyrant flycatcher (Pitangus sulphuratus bolivianus).
cristus, *m.* christcross, cross printed at the beginning of the alphabet; alphabet. — **estar uno en el c.,** to be in the early stages, be just starting; **no saber uno el c.,** to be very ignorant.
crisuela, *f.* dripping-pan of an oil lamp.
criterio, *m.* criterion; judgment, discernment.
crítica, *f.* 1. criticism; critique, critical examination, e.g. *C. de la Razón Pura,* Critique of Pure Reason. 2. criticism, censure; gossip.
criticable, *a.* censurable.
criticador, ra, *a.* critical, criticizing. —*m., f.* criticizer, critic, censurer.
criticalidad, *f.* (chem.) criticality.
críticamente, *adv.* critically.
criticar, (*ref. 50*) *tr.v.* to criticize, judge; to censure, criticize.
criticastro, *m.* criticaster, an incompetent critic (in literature and journalism).
criticismo, *m.* Kantianism, critical philosophy.
crítico, ca, *a.* 1. critical, decisive; acute (moment, situation, illness). 2. (Amer.) carping, faultfinding. —*m.* critic; reviewer; (coll.) pedant.
criticón, na, *a.* faultfinding, carping. —*m., f.* criticaster, faultfinder.
critique, critiqué, *ref.* **criticar.**
critiqueo, *m.* gossip, gossiping.
critiquizar, (*ref. 53*) *tr.v.* (coll.) to criticize excessively.
crizneja, *f.* plait of hair, braid; rope or plait of osiers or rushes.
Croacia, *f.* Croatia, a republic of Yugoslavia.
croar, *i.v.* to croak, to make a croaking sound.
croata, *a., m., f.* Croatian, Croat.
crocante, *m.* roast almond caramel; peanut brittle; nougat.
croceína, *f.* (chem.) crocein.
crocetina, *f.* (chem.) crocetin.
crocino, na, *a.* crocus, crocus-like; of or pertaining to saffron.
crocitar, *i.v.* to crow.
croco, *m.* (bot.) crocus (saffron).
crocodilo, *m.* (zool.) crocodile.
crocoíta, *f.* (min.) crocoite.
croché, *m.* crochet needle; crochet (needlework).
crochet, *m.* crochet (needlework).
crol, *m.* crawl (swimming stroke).
cromado, *past part. of* **cromar.** —*a.* chromium-plated. —*m.* chromium-plating, chroming.
cromar, *tr.v.* to chromium-plate, chrome.
cromatar, *tr.v.* to chromate.
cromático, ca, *a.* chromatic. —*m.* (mus.) chromatic, chromatic semitone. —*f.* chromatics, the study of colors.
cromátide, *m.* (biol.) chromatid.
cromatina, *f.* (biol.) chromatin.
cromatismo, *m.* (opt., biol., bot.) chromatism, chromaticity; (mus.) chromaticism.
cromato, *m.* (chem.) chromate.
cromatóforo, *m.* (biol.) chromatophore.
cromatólisis, *f.* (med.) chromatolysis.
cromatolítico, ca, *a.* (med.) chromatolytic.
cromatología, *f.* chromatics, the study of colors.
cromatoplasma, *m.* (biol.) chromoplasm.
cromel, *m.* (metal.) chromel (alloy).
crómico, ca, *a.* (chem.) chromic.
cromita, *f.* (min.) chromite.
cromo, *m.* (metal.) chrome, chromium.
cromofotografía, *f.* color photography.
cromógeno, na, *a.* chromogenous (producing color); chromogenic (pertaining to chromogen). —*m.* (chem.) chromogen (substance which, by contact with the air, becomes a coloring matter).
cromolitografía, *f.* (print.) chromolithography.
cromolitografiar, *tr.v.* (print.) to print by means of chromolithography.
cromolitográfico, ca, *a.* (print.) chromolithographic.
cromolitógrafo, *m.* (print.) chromolithographer.
cromómero, *m.* (biol.) chromomere.
cromómetro, *m.* (engin.) chromometer.
cromonema, *m.* (biol.) chromonema.
cromoníquel, *m.* (metal.) chrome-nickel (steel).
cromoplástida, *f.* (biol.) chromoplast.
cromoplasto, *m.* (biol.) chromoplast.
cromoproteína, *f.* (biol.) chromoprotein.
cromosfera, *f.* (astron.) chromosphere.
cromoso, sa, *a.* (chem.) chromous.
cromosoma, *m.* (biol.) chromosome; **c. X,** (biol.) X chromosome.
cromotipia, *f.* (print.) chromotypy, color printing; chromotype, color print.
cromotipografía, *f.* (print.) chromotypography, art of color printing; color print.
cromotipográfico, ca, *a.* (print.) chromotypographic.
cronaxia, *f.* (med.) chronaxie.
crónica, *f.* 1. chronicle, history. 2. feature article (journalism).
crónicamente, *adv.* chronically, habitually, recurrently.
cronicidad, *f.* the quality or condition of being chronic.
cronicismo, *m.* (med.) chronic condition.
crónico, ca, *a.* chronic, habitual, recurrent, e.g. *tos crónica,* chronic cough.
cronicón, *m.* short chronicle, brief narration.
cronista, *m., f.* chronicler, historian; feature writer (journalism).
cronístico, ca, *a.* of or pertaining to a chronicle or a history.
crónlech, *m.* (archeol.) cromlech, dolmen.
cronografía, *f., var. of* **cronología.**
cronógrafo, *m.* chronograph; stopwatch; chronographer, chronologist.
cronograma, *m.* chronogram, a certain type of inscription.
cronología, *f.* chronology, the science of measuring time in fixed periods; the order of occurrence of events; a list of dates in proper sequence.
cronológicamente, *adv.* chronologically.
cronológico, ca, *a.* chronologic, chronological.
cronologista, *m.* chronologist, chronologer.
cronólogo, *m.* chronologist, chronologer.
cronometrador, ra, *m., f.* (sport.) time-keeper.
cronometraje, *m.* timing.
cronometrar, *tr.v.* to time or measure with a chronometer.
cronometría, *f.* chronometry, the exact measuring of time.
cronométrico, ca, *a.* chronometric, pertaining to chronometry.
cronometrista, *m.* person who makes chronometers.
cronómetro, *m.* chronometer. — **c. atómico,** (phys.) atomic clock.
Cronos, *m.* (myth.) Cronus, Time, father of the gods.
cronoscopio, *m.* (phys.) chronoscope.
cronotrón, *m.* chronotron.
croquet, *m.* croquet (game).
croqueta, *f.* (cul.) croquette, fritter.
croquis, *m.* sketch, rough draft.
croscitar, *i.v.* to crow.
crótalo, *m.* 1. (zool.) rattlesnake. 2. (poet.) castanet; Egyptian finger cymbal (a small percussion instrument similar to the castanet).
crotón, *m.* (bot.) croton, castor oil plant.
crotorar, *i.v.* to cry, rattle (like a stork).
croupier, *m.* a person in charge of a gambling table, roulette, or other casino games.
cruce, *m.* crossing; crossroad; **c. a nivel** or de vía, grade crossing; **c. en trébol,** clover-leaf intersection; **c. inferior,** undergrade crossing; **c. superior,** overhead crossing.
cruce, crucé, *ref.* **cruzar.**
cruceño, ña, *a., m., f.* native of or belonging to villages in Spain or Latin America called Cruz, Cruces or Santa Cruz.
crucera, *f.* withers of a horse.
crucería, *f.* (archit.) Gothic fan vaulting, fan tracery vaulting.
crucero, *a.* (archit.) **arco c.,** cross vault. —*m.* 1. (ecc.) crucifer, crossbearer. 2. crossroads; railroad crossing. 3. (archit.) transept. 4. (astron.) Southern Cross. 5. (carp.) batten, crosspiece. 6. (print.) crossbar (of a chase); fold (in a folded sheet of paper). 7. (mar.) cruiser (ship); cruise; cruising. 8. (geol.) cleavage. — **c. de bolsillo, pocket** battleship; **velocidad de c.,** cruising speed.
cruceta, *f.* 1. intersection, crosspiece (in trelliswork). 2. cross-stitch (in embroidery). 3. (mar.) crosstree.
crucial, *a.* 1. crucial, critical, decisive. 2. cruciform, cross-shaped.
cruciata, *f.* (bot.) crosswort.
cruciferario, *m.* (ecc.) crucifer, cross-bearer (in religious processions).
crucífero, ra, *a.* (poet.) cruciate, cruciferous (bearing or marked with a cross); (bot.) cruciferous (plant). —*m.* (ecc.) crucifer, cross-bearer. —*f.* (bot.) crucifer (cruciferous plant); (*pl.*) (bot.) Cruciferas.
crucificado, da, *past part. of* **crucificar.** —*a. crucified;* **el Crucificado,** the Crucified, Christ.
crucificar, (*ref. 50*) *tr.v.* to crucify, torture; (fig.) to criticize mordantly.
crucifijo, *m.* crucifix.
crucifique, crucifiqué, *ref.* **crucificar.**
crucifixión, *f.* crucifixion.
crucifixor, *m.* crucifier.
cruciforme, *a.* cruciform, cross-shaped.
crucígero, ra, *a.* (poet.) cruciate (marked with or bearing a cross).
crucigrama, *m.* crossword puzzle.
crucillo, *m.* pushpin (children's game).
crudamente, *adv.* harshly, roughly, rudely, severely.
crudelísimo, ma, *a.* very cruel, inhuman, merciless.
crudeza, *f.* 1. crudeness, coarseness, grossness. 2. rawness (of food); unripeness (of fruit). 3. roughness, severity, harshness. 4. (coll.) bravado, affected courage. 5. (*pl.*) undigested food.

crudillo, *m.* (tail.) unbleached linen (used as lining and stiffening).
crudo, da, *a.* 1. raw (food), unripe, green (fruit). 2. crude; coarse, gross. 3. indigestible (food); uncured (food, leather); untreated (material); raw (silk); unbleached (linen). 4. cruel, harsh, rough. 5. raw, severe, harsh (weather). 6. (coll.) crucial, decisive, critical (moment). 7. (coll.) blustering, boastful, full of bravado. —*m.* (surg.) unripe, hard (said of an abscess). —*f.* 1. hard (water). 2. (Mex.) hangover, morning after.
cruel, *a.* 1. cruel. 2. intense (cold). 3. agonizing (pain). 4. bloody, violent (battle). 5. hard, cruel (blow).
crueldad, *f.* cruelty.
cruelmente, *adv.* cruelly, brutally.
cruentamente, *adv.* bloodily, with bloodshed.
cruento, ta, *a.* bloody; **lucha cruenta,** hard and bloody fight.
crujía, *f.* 1. corridor, passage; (mar.) midship gangway; railed aisle leading from choir to altar. 2. hospital ward. 3. (archit.) bay (space between two walls, etc.). — **c. de piezas,** row of rooms; **pasar** or **sufrir una c.,** to go through a bad or rough time.
crujidero, ra, *a.* crackling; creaking; rustling.
crujido, *past part. of* **crujir.** —*m.* 1. creak, crackle, crackling; rustle. 2. flaw in sword blade. — **dar c.,** to crackle, crack noisily.
crujiente, *a.* crackling; creaking; rustling.
crujir, *i.v.* to creak (wood, doors, etc.); to crackle (burning wood, etc.); to rustle (a fabric, leaves); to rattle, grind (teeth).
crúor, *m.* (obs.) coloring in blood; blood clot, cruor; (poet.) blood.
crup, *m.* (med.) diptheria, croup.
crupal, *a.* (med.) croupy, croupous (cough, respiration).
crupié, *m., var. of* **croupier.**
crural, *a.* (anat.) crural, femoral.
crustáceo, a, *a.* crustaceous, scabby; (zool.) crustaceous, crustacean, shell-bearing. —*m.* (zool.) crustacean; (*pl.*) Crustaceae.
crústula, *f.* small piece of bark, thin bark.
cruz, (*pl.* **cruces**) *f.* 1. cross. 2. tails (reverse of a coin). 3. withers (of an animal). 4. top of a tree-trunk where horizontal branches begin. 5. each of the two supporting arms in a beehive (to support honeycombs). 6. (print.) dagger, obelisk. 7. (fig.) cross, burden, trial, affliction. 8. **C.,** (astron.) Crux, Southern Cross. 9. (her.) cross, crosslet (bearing on a shield). 10. (mar.) center of a sail yard or spar; (mar.) throat (of an anchor). 11. (min.) wall separating the hearth of a Spanish blast furnace. 12. (*pl.*) spokes (of a flour mill wheel). — **a c. y escuadra,** (carp.) in mortise and tenon joints; **andar con las cruces a cuestas,** to pray for something earnestly; **cargar su c.,** to bear one's cross; **c. decusata,** decussate or X-shaped cross; **c. de Jerusalem,** (bot.) scarlet lychnis (Lychnis chalcedonica); **c. del ancla,** anchor throat; **C. del Cisne,** (astron.) Northern Cross; **C. de Malta,** Maltese Cross; **C. de San Andrés,** Saint Andrew's Cross; (carp.) X-shaped beams; **c. doble,** (print.) double dagger; **c. flordelisada,** (her.) cross-fleury; **c. gamada,** swastika; **c. geométrica,** (astron.) cross-staff (ancient sextant); **c. potenzada,** cross potent; **c. reticular,** (opt.) cross hairs; **Gran C.,** Grand Cross (in knightly orders); **c. y raya,** (coll.) no more of this! this is the end!; **en c.,** with extended arms; cross, e.g. *conectar en c.,* cross connector; (her.) crossed; **fallo en c.,** crossruff (in whist); **hacerse uno cruces,** to be amazed or surprised; **trasquilar a cruces a uno,** (coll.) to cut one's hair unevenly.
cruzada, *f.* 1. crusade; Tribunal of the Crusades. 2. (coll.) campaign, drive. 3. crossroads, intersection.
cruzado, da, *past part. of* **cruzar.** —*a.* 1. crossed. 2. transverse. 3. twilled (material). 4. crusader, crusading (knight). 5. crossbred (animal). 6. (her.) crossed, cross surmounted. 7. (com.) crossed (check). —*m.* 1. crusader (knight). 2. ancient Castilian coin (varying in value according to period); crusado, Portuguese silver coin. 3. (mus.) plucking of first and third strings followed by plucking of second string (in guitar playing). 4. cross-forming pattern (in dancing).
cruzamen, *m.* (mar.) square or width (of a sail).
cruzamiento, *m.* 1. investment with a cross insignia. 2. crossing, crossbreeding, interbreeding (of animals). 3. crossing, intersecting.
cruzar, (*ref. 53*) *tr.v.* 1. to cross (one's legs, a road, a check, etc.). 2. to invest with a cross (a knight of an order of chivalry). 3. to cross, crossbreed (animals). 4. (mar.) to cruise around (a given area, as in blockading, convoying, etc.). — **c. palabras con,** to have words with, have a quarrel with; **cruzarle a uno la cara,** to slap one in the face. —*r.v.* 1. to take the cross, enlist in a crusade. 2. to cross or pass one another. 3. to get in the way, intercept, bar. 4. to pile up, tangle up (business affairs or papers). 5. (geom.) to cross or pass without touching (of two lines in space). 6. (vet.) to cross the legs in walking (a horse). — **cruzarse de brazos,** to remain inactive or idle, to refrain from helping or taking some action.
Cs *sym. of* **cesio,** cesium (Cs).
cta. *abbrev. of* **cuenta,** account (acc.).
cta. de *abbrev. of* **cuenta de,** account of (a/o).
cte. *abbrev. of* **corriente,** instant (inst.).
ctenóforo, ra, *a.* (zool.) ctenophoran. —*m.* (zool.) ctenophoran, ctenophore, (*pl.*) Ctenophora.
cu, *m.* name given by the Conquistadores to Mexican temples.
Cu *sym. of* **cobre,** copper, cuprum (Cu).
c/u *abbrev. of* **cada uno,** each (ea.).
cuaba, *f.* (Cuba) Jamaica rosewood (Amyris balsamifera).
cuacar, (*ref. 50*) *tr.v.* (Col., P. Rico) to please (gen. in negative sentence), e.g. *eso que dices no me cuaca,* I do not like what you say.
cuácara, *f.* (Col.) frock coat; (Chile) blouse, jacket.
cuaco, *m.* 1. (Mex., Dom. Rep.) nag, scrawny horse. 2. cassava flour, yucca root flour.
cuaderna, *f.* 1. double fours (in backgammon). 2. ancient Spanish coin. 3. (mar.) frame (of a hull); rib (of a frame); **c. de armar,** main ribs or timber (of ship's frame); **c. maestra,** midship frame.
cuadernal, *m.* (mar.) block, block and tackle.
cuadernalete, *m.* (mar.) short, double block.
cuadernillo, *m.* 1. quinternion (set of five folded sheets of paper). 2. (ecc.) ecclesiastical calendar.
cuaderno, *m.* 1. exercise book, notebook 2. (coll.) pack of playing cards. 3. (print.) quarto (set of four folded sheets of papers). — **c. de bitácora** (mar.) logbook.
cuadra, *f.* 1. large hall or room; ward (in hospital); dormitory (in barracks, prison, etc.). 2. stable. 3. quarter of a mile. 4. (Amer.) block, square (of houses); block (distance between streets). 5. (mar.) quarter, width of beam (at quarter length of ship from either end).
cuadrada, *f.* (mus.) breve.
cuadradamente, *adv.* exactly, perfectly, precisely.
cuadradillo, *m.* 1. gusset (of a shirt sleeve). 2. square ruler (for drawing lines). 3. lump of sugar, sugar cube.
cuadrado, da, *past part. of* **cuadrar.** —*a.* 1. square. 2. (coll.) complete, perfect. 3. (Col.) elegant, graceful. —*m.* 1. square. 2. square ruler. 3. clock (on a stocking). 4. gusset (of a shirt sleeve). 5. (math.) square (of a number). 6. (astrol.) quartile, square (aspect). 7. (print.) quadrat, quad. 8. mold (for minting). — **c. de las refracciones,** refraction quadrant (for sundials); **c. geométrica,** (math.) geometrical quadrant; **c. mágico,** magic square; **c. perfecto,** (math.) perfect square; **de c.,** (coll.) perfectly; face to face (in fencing); **dejar a uno de c.,** (coll.) to strike home, hit where it hurts most; **mover de c.,** (archit.) to rest on a horizontal surface.
cuadragenario, ria, *a.* quadragenarian, forty-year old.
cuadragésima, *f.* Lent, Quadragesima.
cuadragesimal, *a.* Lenten, quadragesimal.
cuadragésimo, ma, *a.* fortieth. —*m.* one-fortieth (part).
cuadral, *m.* (archit.) angle brace, truss.
cuadrangular, *a.* quadrangular, tetragonal, four-cornered. —*m.* home run (in baseball).
cuadrángulo, la, *a.* quadrangular. —*m.* quadrangle.
cuadrantal, *m.* quadrantal (ancient Roman liquid measure).
cuadrante, *m.* 1. quadrant (quarter of a circle; instrument for measuring angles); Roman coin. 2. (law) quarter of an inheritance. 3. (archit.) angle-brace, truss. 4. sundial. 5. (Mex.) sacristy. — **c. azimutal,** azimuth dial; **c. de reducción,** (mar.) log bearings (on a nautical chart); **c. de reflexión,** Hadley's quadrant, reflecting quadrant; **c. oscilante,** Stephenson link.
cuadrar, *tr.v.* 1. to make square, square, form into a square. 2. (math., geom., carp.) to square. 3. to please, suit; to satisfy, seem correct or right. —*i.v.* 1. to agree, tally (with), match, fit. 2. (Amer.) to suit, become (clothes). —*r.v.* 1. to stand at attention; to stand square; to stand firm (horse). 2. (coll.) to become suddenly serious; to take a firm stand. 3. (Col.) to park a car.
cuadrático, ca, *a.* (math.) quadratic, quadric.
cuadratín, *m.* (print.) quadrat, quad.
cuadratura, *f.* squaring; (astron.) quadrature; **c. del círculo,** squaring the circle.
cuadrete, *m. dim. of* **cuadro,** small square.
cuádrica, *f.* (math.) quadric.
cuadricenal, *a.* done every forty years.
cuadriceps, *a.* (anat.) quadricipital. —*m.* (anat.) quadriceps.
cuadriciclo, *m.* quadricycle.
cuadrícula, *f.* quadrille; grillage; grid squares. — **c. de azimuth,** azimuth grid; c. de perspectiva, perspective grid.
cuadriculación, *f.* graticulation.
cuadriculado, da, *a.* cross-sectioned, squared, marked with intersecting lines to form squares.
cuadricular, *a.* squared, quadrille (paper).
cuadricular, *tr.v.* to divide into squares, to square (paper).
cuadrienal, *a.* quadrennial, lasting four years; occurring every four years.
cuadrienio, *m.* quadrennium, four-year period; **c. legal,** (law) period following majority of age, cessation of incapacity or absence (of a person).
cuadrífido, da, *a.* (bot.) quadrifid.
cuadrifoliado, da, *a.* (bot.) quadrifoliate, four-leafed.
cuadrifolio, lia, *a.* quadrifoliate, four-leafed.
cuadrifolioliado, da, *a.* (bot.) quadrifoliolate.
cuadriforme, *a.* quadriform, four-faced.
cuadriga, *f.* quadriga (Roman chariot); team of four horses in one front line.

cuadrigémino, na, *a.* (anat.) quadrigeminal.
cuadrigentésimo, ma, *a.* four hundredth.
cuadriguero, *m.* charioteer (of a quadriga).
cuadril, *m.* haunch bone; haunch (of a horse); hip.
cuadrilátero, ra, *a., m.* quadrilateral.
cuadriliteral, *a.* quadriliteral, four-lettered (word).
cuadrilítero, ra, *a., var. of* **cuadriliteral.**
cuadrilla, *f.* 1. gang, crew (of workers); band, gang (of criminals); team (of contestants); (taur.) cuadrilla (of a matador); posse. 2. quadrille, a square dance of French origin.
cuadrillazo, *m.* (Chile) group attack or assault against one person.
cuadrillero, *m.* foreman (of a gang of workers); leader (of a gang of criminals); captain (of a team of contestants); member of a posse; (Phil. I.) rural policeman.
cuadrillo, *m.* quarrel, arrow; a square-headed missile formerly used in crossbows.
cuadrilobulado, da, *a.* four-lobed.
cuadrilongo, ga, *a.* rectangular, oblong. —*m.* rectangle, oblong; (mil.) rectangular formation (of troops).
cuadrimestre, *a.* pertaining to a four- month period. —*m.* period of four months.
cuadrinieto, ta, *m.* great-great-grandson. —*f.* great-great-granddaughter.
cuadrinomio, *m.* (math.) quadrinomial.
cuadripartido, da, *a.* quadripartite, divided into four parts.
cuadriplicado, da, *a.* quadrupled.
cuadriplicar, (*ref. 50*) *tr.v.* to quadruplicate.
cuadriplique, cuadripliqué, *ref.* **cuadriplicar.**
cuadrípolo, *m.* (phys.) quadrupole.
cuadrisílabo, ba, *a.* quadrisyllabic. —*m. quadrisyllable.*
cuadrivalente, *a.* (chem.) quadrivalent.
cuadrivio, *m.* 1. crossroads. 2. quadrivium (liberal arts). 3. (arch.) the unity of the four mathematical arts (arithmetic, music, geometry, and astronomy).
cuadrivista, *m.* quadrivium scholar.
cuadríyugo, *m.* four-horse carriage.
cuadro, ra, *a.* square. —*m.* 1. square, rectangle. 2. painting, picture; sight, scene, picture. 3. description, picture. 4. table, statistical chart, tabulation. 5. flower bed or patch. 6. (theat.) scene; tableau. 7. frame (of a picture, bicycle). 8. (astrol.) quartile aspect. 9. (print.) platen. 10. (mil.) square (formation); (mil.) cadre, officers of a regiment. 11. board, panel (of controls). — **a cuadros,** checkered, plaid (material); **c. al óleo,** oil painting; **c. anunciador,** indicator board; **c. comparado,** (acc., com.) comparative statement; **c. conmutador, c. de conmutadores,** (elec., tel.) switchboard; **c. de distribución,** (elc., tel.) switchboard; **c. de fusibles,** (elec.) fuseboard; **c. de gobierno,** control board or panel; **c. de mandos,** control panel; **c. de señales, signal panel or board; c. sinóptico,** synoptic table or chart; **c. vivo,** (theat.) tableau vivant; **en c.,** square; **estar** or **quedar en c.,** to be destitute or down and out; to be left with a command and no troops.
cuadropea, *f., var. of* **cuatropea.**
cuadrúmano, na, *a.* (zool.) quadrumanous. —*m.* quadrumane, (*pl.*) Quadrumana.
cuadrupedal, *a.* quadrupedal, four-footed.
cuadrupedante, *a.* (poet.), *var. of* **cuadrúpedo.**
cuadrúpede, *a., var. of* **cuadrúpedo.**
cuadrúpedo, *a.* quadruped, quadrupedal. —*m.* quadruped.
cuádruple, *a.* quadruple, four-fold.
cuádruplex, *m.* (tel.) quadruplex system.
cuadruplicación, *f.* quadruplication.
cuadruplicar, (*ref. 50*) *tr.v.* to quadruple, quadruplicate.
cuadruplique, cuadrupliqué, *ref.* **cuadruplicar.**
cuádruplo, pla, *a., m.* quadruple.
cuaima, *f.* (Ven.) a poisonous snake; (fig.) a dangerous and wily person.
cuajada, *f.* curd (of milk); cottage cheese.
cuajadillo, *m.* fine compact embroidery work (on silk).
cuajado, da, *past part. of* **cuajar.** —*a.* (coll.) dumbfounded, astonished; fast asleep. — **leche cuajada,** (cul.) junket; yogurt. —*m.* type of mincemeat.
cuajadura, *f.* curdling (of milk; setting, jelling (gelatine); solidifying; coagulation.
cuajaleche, *m.* (bot.) cleavers, catchweed, goose-grass.
cuajamiento, *m.* coagulation.
cuajar, *tr.v.* 1. to curdle (milk); to jell, set (gelatine); to coagulate; to solidify. 2. to ornament excessively. —*i.v.* 1. to turn or work out well, be successful, succeed. 2. to please, like, e.g. *Juan no me cuaja mucho,* I don't like John very much. 3. (Mex.) to prattle aimlessly. —*r.v.* 1. to curdle; to jell, set; to coagulate; to solidify. 2. to turn or work out well, be successful. 3. to fill up, get filled. —*m.* (zool.) abomasum, fourth stomach (of a ruminant).
cuajarón, *m.* clot, coagulum, grume.
cuajicote, *m.* (Mex., ento.) carpenter bee.
cuajilote, *m.* (Mex.) tree of the genus Parmentiera (Parmentiera edulis).
cuajiote, *m.* (C. Amer.) gum-producing poisonous tree of the Anacardiaceae (sumac) family (Pseudosmodinguin perniciosum).
cuajo, *m.* 1. rennet. 2. curd. 3. (zool.) abomasum. 4. (coll.) patience, calmness; slowness, sluggishness. 5. (Mex.) idle chatter. 6. (Mex.) recess, break (in schools). 7. (Mex.) fib, rumor, hoax, piece of gossip. 8. (Cuba) solidifying of cane juice. — **de c.,** by the roots; **ensanchar el c.,** to have patience, be patient; **tener buen** or **mucho c.,** to be very patient; to be sluggish or slow; **volverse el c.,** to throw up its milk (a baby).
cuakerismo, *m.* Quakerism.
cuákero, ra, *m., f.* Quaker.
cual, *rel. pron.* which; who, e.g. *Antonio, el cual salió ayer de Madrid,* Anthony, who left Madrid yesterday; as, such as, e.g. *le detuvieron sucesos imprevistos, lo cual ocurre a menudo,* unforeseen circumstances detained him, as often happens; **cada cual,** each one, **tal para cual,** a perfect pair or couple; **por lo cual,** because of which. —*adv. as, such as;* **cual . . . tal,** like . . . like, just as . . . so, e.g. *cual el padre, tal el hijo,* like father, like son; **cual es Pedro, tal es Juan,** just as Peter is, so is John; **tal cual,** just as, exactly as, in the same manner as.
cuál, *a.* which, e.g. *¿en cuál caja está?* which box is it in? *interrog. pron.,* which, which one, e.g. *¿cuál de los dos te gusta más?* which of the two do you like best? —*dubitative pron.,* which, which one, what, e.g. *ignoro cuál de los dos será elegido,* I do not know which of the two will be elected; *ignoro cuál será el resultado final,* I do not know what the final result will be. —*indef. pron.,* some, e.g. *tengo muchos sombreros, cuales nuevos, cuales viejos.* —*adv.* how. e.g. ¡cuál feliz sería ella contigo! how happy she would be with you!
cualesquier, *indef. pron. pl. of* **cualquier.**
cualesquiera, *indef. pron. pl. of* **cualquiera.**
cualidad, *f.* quality, virtue, good feature.
cualitativo, va, *a.* qualitative.
cualquier, *a.* (used only before a noun) any, e.g. c. *niño,* any child.
cualquiera, *indef. pron.* anyone; either, e.g. *c. de los dos,* either of the two, either one. —*rel. pron.* whoever; whatever, e.g. *voy a devolver todos los regalos que me envíe, cualesquiera que sean,* I'm going to return all the presents he sends me, whatever they are. —*a.* (*used after the noun*) any; just any sort or kind of, e.g. *no vamos a alquilar una casa c.,* we're not going to rent just any house, *es un hombre c.,* he's no one in particular. —*m.* nobody, a nonentity; **ser un c.,** to be a nobody.
cuan, *adv.* how; *cuan . . . tan,* as . . . as, e.g. *se irguió c. alto era,* he rose to his full height; (accented in questions and exclamations), e.g. *¡cuán bella era!* how beautiful she was!
cuando, *conj.* 1. when. 2. though, even though; e.g. *no faltaría a la verdad aún c. le fuera en ello la vida,* he would not lie though his life depended on it. 3. since, if, e.g. *c. tú lo dices, verdad será,* since you say so, it must be true. 4. sometimes, e.g. *de vez en cuando con motivo, de vez en cuando sin él,* sometimes with a reason, sometimes without it. — **cuando lo de,** at the time of, in the case of; **c. más,** at the most; **c. menos,** at least; **c. mucho,** at the most; **c. no,** if not, otherwise; **c. quiera que,** whenever; **de c. en c., de vez en c.,** from time to time; **hasta c.,** until such time.
cuándo, *interrog. adv.* when? e.g. *¿de cuándo acá?* since when? —*m.* when, e.g. *el c. y el cómo,* the when and the how.
cuantía, *f.* 1. quantity, amount. 2. importance, distinction, worth; **de mayor or de menor c.,** of major importance, or of minor importance (person or thing).
cuantiar, *tr.v.* to value, appraise, estimate (an estate, etc.).
cuántico, ca, *a.* (phys.) quantum; **teoría cuántica,** quantum theory.
cuantidad, *f.* quantity (used mostly in philosophy and mathematics).
cuantificación, *f.* (phys.) quantization.
cuantificar, *tr.v.* (phys.) to quantize.
cuantimás, *adv.* (coll.) all the more so.
cuantiosamente, *adv.* copiously, abundantly.
cuantioso, sa, *a.* considerable, large, substantial (fortune, etc.); copious, abundant; numerous.
cuantitativo, va, *a.* quantitative.
cuanto, ta, *a., rel. pron.* as much as, everything, all, e.g. *le dio cuanto tenía,* he gave him everything he had; whatever, e.g. *le daba c. quería,* he would give her whatever (or as much as) she wanted; **cuantos,** as many as, all those who; **unos cuantos,** a few.
cuanto, *adv.* as, as much as, e.g. *tanto vales c. tienes,* you are worth as much as you own; the more, the greater, e.g. *c. mayor la virtud, mayor el premio,* the greater the virtue, the greater the reward; **c. a,** as to, as regards; **c. antes,** or **c. más antes,** as soon as possible; **c. más** or **c. y más,** how much more so, all the more so, even more so; **c. más que** or **c. y más que,** all the more so as, even more so as; **c. más . . . tanto más,** the more . . . the more; **c. quiera,** although, even though; **en c.,** as soon as; while; **en c. a,** as to, in regard to; **por c.,** inasmuch as, insofar as.
cuánto, ta, *a. rel. pron.,* how much, how many, e.g. *¡cuántos infelices!* how many unfortunate beings!; what, e.g. *¡cuánta majestad!* what majesty!; **por cuánto,** not for anything, under no circumstances, e.g. *por cuánto dejaría Juan de ir al teatro,* not for anything would John miss

going to the theatre. —*adv.* how long; how, e.g. *dile c. me alegro de oírlo,* tell him how glad I am to hear it.
cuanto, *m.* (phys.) quantum; **c. de luz,** (phys.) light quantum.
cuantómetro, *m.* (phys.) quantometer.
cuaquerismo, *m.* Quakerism.
cuáquero, ra, *m., f.* Quaker.
cuarango, *m.* (bot., Peru) species of Cinchona (Cinchona condaminea).
cuarcífero, ra, *a.* (geol.) quartziferous.
cuarcita, *f.* (min.) quartzite.
cuarcítico, ca, *a.* (geol.) quartzitic.
cuarenta, *a., m.* forty; **cantar a uno las c.,** (coll.) to give someone a piece of one's mind.
cuarentavo, va, *a., m.* fortieth.
cuarentena, *f.* 1. forty, two score; forty days, months, years. 2. Lent. 3. quarantine. — **poner** or *pasar en cuarentena,* to quarantine, put in quarantine; to suspend judgment; to question (the truth of something).
cuarentón, na, *a.* forty-year-old (person); in his forties (said of a person). —*m., f.* forty-year-old.
cuaresma, *f.* Lent, Quadragesima; collection of Lent sermons.
cuaresmal, *a.* Lenten, quadragesimal.
cuaresmario, *m.* collection of Lent sermons.
cuarta, *f.* 1. fourth (part); quarter. 2. one-fourth of a **vara** (Spanish yard). 3. sequence of four cards of same suit. 4. piece of timber (of varying lengths). 5. (Mex.) quirt, short horsewhip. 6. (astron.) quadrant (of Zodiac circle). 7. (mar.) rhumb, point (of a compass). 8. (mil. quarter of a company. 9. (mus.) fourth.
cuartago, *m.* small horse; pony.
cuartal, *m.* a fourth of a loaf of bread; quarter, dry measure.
cuartán, *m.* (Sp.) grain measure; oil measure.
cuartana, *f.* (med.) quartan, ague, fever recurring every four days.
cuartanal, *a.* quartan, intermittent fever.
cuartanario, ria, *a.* suffering from quartan (fever).
cuartar, *tr.v.* (agr.) to plow (ground) for the fourth time.
cuartazo, *m.* (Mex.) blow with a whip, whiplash.
cuartazos, *m.* slob (coll.), fat, lazy, unkempt man.
cuartear, *tr.v.* 1. to quarter, divide into four parts; to divide into pieces. 2. to bid a fourth more for (at public auctions). 3. to zig-zag along (a vehicle). 4. (Mex.) to whip repeatedly (with a horse whip). —*i.v.* (taur.) to dodge (the bull's horns. —*r.v.* 1. to split, crack (a wall or roof, etc.). 2. (taur.) to dodge (bull's horns). 3. (Mex.) to fail to keep, break (a promise).
cuartel, *m.* 1. quarter, fourth. 2. quarter, district, zone, ward (of a city). 3. lot (of land). 4. flowerbed. 5. (poet.) quatrain. 6. (her.) compartment, canton, division (of an escutcheon); (her.) quarters. 7. (mar.) hatch cover. 8. (mil.) barracks, quarters. 9. quarter (clemency to a conquered enemy, etc.). 10. (mil.) tax paid by the people for quartering of troops. — **c. general,** (mil.) general headquarters; **no dar c.** to give no quarter, be utterly ruthless; **franco c.,** (her.) chief dexter canton; **estar de c.,** (mil.) to be unassigned (said of officers).
cuartelada, *f.* (Amer.) mutiny, military uprising, putsch; antimutiny committee of officers.
cuartelado, *past part. of* **cuartelar.** —*m.* quartered shield.
cuartelar, *tr.v.* 1. (her.) to quarter. 2. (agr.), (Méx.) to divide with elevated ridges for irrigation.
cuartelazo, *m.* (Amer.) mutiny, military uprising. putsch.
cuartelero, ra, *a.* pertaining to military barracks. —*m.* 1. (mil.) orderly who guards and cleans the billet or barrack room. 2. (mar.) sailor in charge of luggage.
cuartelesco, ca, *a.* (Amer.), *var. of* **cuartelero.**
cuartelillo, *m.* billet, barracks.
cuarteo, *m.* 1. crack, split, fissure. 2. dodge, swerve, side-step; dodging, side-stepping. — **al c.,** (taur.) dodging.
cuartera, *f.* 1. (Sp.) beam measuring 8 inches in breadth and depth and 15 feet in length. 2. dry measure of approximately 70 liters.
cuartería, *f.* (Amer.) dilapidated rooming house.
cuarterola, *f.* 1. quarter cask; measurement equivalent to 129 liters. 2. (Chile) firearm slightly shorter than a carbine.
cuarterón, na, *a.* of mulatto and Spanish parentage. —*m., f.* quadroon. —*m.* 1. quarter, quartern, fourth; quarter of a pound. 2. window shutter; door panel.
cuarteta, *f.* octosyllabic quatrain.
cuartete, *m., var. of* **cuarteto.**
cuarteto, *m.* 1. (poet.) hendecasyllabic quatrain. 2. (mus.) quarter. — **c. de cuerdas,** string quartet.
cuártico, ca, *a.* (math.) quartic.
cuartil, *m.* (statistics) quartile.
cuartilla, *f.* (print.) page of copy; (*pl.*) copy, pages of a manuscript.
cuartilla, *f.* 1. (vet.) pastern. 2. measure of capacity of 13.87 liters; liquid measure of 4.033 liters; 2.8125 kilos (weight).
cuartillero, *m.* (print.) copyboy, employee whose job it is to collect copy and take it to the editor's office.
cuartillo, *m.* 1. measure of capacity of 1.156 milliliters; liquid measure of .504 liters. 2. (numis.) quarter of a **real.**
cuartilludo, da, *a.* (vet.) having long pasterns (horse).
cuartito, *m. dim. of* **cuarto,** small room.
cuartizo, *m.* plank or length of wood (of various lengths).
cuarto, *a.* fourth; quarter. —*m.* 1. fourth. 2. quarter (of an hour; of a body; fourth part of a dress). 3. living quarters; room, chamber. 4. line, branch (of family through each of one's grandparents). 5. (vet.) crack (in horse's hoof). 6. lot, plot (of land sold for pasture). 7. (mil.) picket, squad (of troops on sentry watch); watch (time on sentry). 8. (numis.) 3 centimes (of a Spanish peseta). 9. (*pl.*) (coll.) money, capital. — **c. de baño,** bathroom; **c. de conversión,** (fenc.) quarter wheel; **c. de costura,** sewing room; **c. creciente,** first quarter (of moon); **c. de culebrina,** (mil.) small cannon; **c. delantero,** (vet.) forequarter; **c. de luna,** (astron.) quarter, fourth of lunar period; **c. de máquinas,** engine room; **c. de tono,** (mus.) quarter tone; **c. menguante,** last quarter (of the moon); **c. oscuro,** (photog.) darkroom; **c. tocador,** powder room; **c. trasero,** (vet.) hindquarter; **c. vigilante,** (mil.) squad on the alert; **cuatro cuartos,** twopence, very little (money), e.g. *lo compró por cuatro cuartos,* he bought it for a song; **c. y comida,** room and board; **de tres al c.,** of very little value, of no account; **echar uno su c. a espadas,** to put one's oar in, butt in, interrupt; **el c. falso de noche pasa,** anything goes under cover of dark; **en c.,** (print.) quarto (edition); **en c. mayor** or *prolongado,* (print.) quarto (edition) on fine paper; **en c. menor,** quarto (edition) on ordinary paper; **estar uno sin c.** or **no tener un c.,** (coll.) to be broke, not to have a bean; **hacer cuartos (un pollo),** to cut (a chicken) into quarters; **tener uno buenos cuartos,** (coll.) to be strong, be well-built.
cuartogénito, ta, *a.* born fourth in the family. —*m., f.* fourth child, fourth-born (in the family).
cuartón, *m.* 1. (carp.) length or plank of wood. 2. (agr.) square field or patch. 3. liquid measure.
cuartucho, *m.* dingy room or hovel.
cuarzo, *m.* (min.) quartz; **c. ahumado,** cairngorm, smoky quartz; **c. hialino,** rock crystal.
cuarzoso, sa, *a.* containing quartz.
cuasar, cuásar, *m.* quasar.
cuascle, *m.* (Mex.) horse blanket.
cuasi, *adv.* almost, quasi.
cuasia, *f.* (bot.) quassia wood, bitterwood.
cuasicontrato, *m.* (law) quasi contract.
cuasidelito, *m.* (law) quasi delict (unintentional offense).
cuasimodo, *m.* Quasimodo, first Sunday after Easter.
cuasina, *f.* (chem., pharm.) quassin.
cuasipúblico, ca, *a.* quasi-public.
cuate, ta, *a.* (Mex.) twin. —*m., f.* 1. (Mex.) twin. 2. buddy, pal, friend.
cuatepín, *m.* (Mex., coll.) slap.
cuatequil, *m.* (Mex.) maize.
cuaterna, *f.* quatern, combination of four numbers (in a lottery).
cuaternario, ria, *a.* quaternary, having four parts; (geol.) Quaternary. —*m.* quaternary; (geol.) Quaternary.
cuaternio, cuaternión, *m.* (math.) quaternion, tetrad.
cuaterno, na, *a.* (geol., chem.) quaternary.
cuatezón, na, *a.* (Mex.) hornless (ox or sheep).
cuatí, *m.* (zool., Arg., Col.) coati, animal like a raccoon or civet, with a long, flexible snout.
cuatorvirato, *m.* quatuorvirate, government by four equal powers.
cuatorviro, *m.* quatuorvir, each one of the four Roman magistrates who presided over the government of a city.
cuatralbo, ba, *a.* (vet.) white-quartered. —*m.* one in charge of four galleys.
cuatratuo, tua, *a.* of mulatto and Spanish parents, quadroon.
cuatreño, ña, *a.* four-year old (young bull or heifer).
cuatrero, *a.* horse thief, cattle rustler.
cuatricromía, *f.* (print.) four-color reproduction.
cuatriduano, *a.* four-day, four-day-old.
cuatrienio, *m.* quadrennium, period of four years.
cuatrifilar, *a.* (elec.) four-wire.
cuatrilingüe, *a.* quadrilingual.
cuatrillo, *m.* card game similar to ombre but played by four people.
cuatrillón, *m.* quadrillion.
cuatrimestre, *a.* four-month. —*m.* period of four months.
cuatrimotor, *m.* four-engine plane.
cuatrinca, *f.* foursome, group of four (people or things); (in the game of bezique) four of a kind.
cuatrisílabo, ba, *a.* four-syllable (as *a.*), four-syllabled. —*m.* four-syllable word.
cuatro, *a.* four; fourth. —*m.* 1. four; fourth. 2. person with the vote of four persons. 3. (mus.) quartet. 4. (in hopscotch) square in the middle. 5. (Ven.) small four-stringed guitar. 6. (sl.) horse; **c. de menor,** (sl.) ass, donkey; **más de c.,** quite a few.
cuatrocentista, *m.* quattrocentist, Italian artist of the fifteenth century.
cuatrocientos, tas, *a., m.* four hundred.
cuatrodoblar, *tr.v.* to quadruple, quadruplicate.
cuatropea, *f.* sales tax formerly paid in public markets upon the purchase of horses and cattle.
cuatropeado, *m.* a change of step in certain dances.
cuatropeo, *m.* (imp. u.) nag, pony, hack.

cuatrotanto, *m.* quadruple, quantity multiplied by four.
cuba, *f.* 1. vat, barrel, cask, tub; vatful, tubful. 2. (coll.) tub, pot-belly, very stout person. 3. (coll.) sot, drunkard. 4. (metal.) stack (of blast furnace). — **calar las cubas,** to measure the depth of wine vat (to assess taxes on wine); **estar hecho una c.,** to be drunk as a vat.
Cuba, *f.* Cuba.
cubación, *f.* (math.) cubing.
cubaje, *m.* volume, cubical contents; capacity.
cubanicú, *m.* (bot., Cuba) coca (Erythoxylon minutifolium).
cubanismo, *m.* Cubanism, Cuban word, expression or custom.
cubanizar, (*ref. 53*) *tr.v.* to Cubanize.
cubano, na, *a., m., f.* Cuban.
cubeba, *f.* (bot.) cubeb (Piper cubeba).
cubera, *f.* (ichth.) snapper, pargo (Lutjanus latidus).
cubería, *f.* coopering, barrel-making; coopery, cooperage; cooper's workshop.
cubero, *m.* cooper; one who makes or sells pails or buckets.
cubertura, *f.* cover, covering.
cubeta, *f.* 1. small vat, tub, or cask; bucket, pail. 2. (chem.) tray, dish; (photog.) developing tray; ice-tray (for ice cubes). 3. (mus.) pedestal of harp. 4. (phys.) mercury cistern in barometer. 5. (Mex.) top hat. — **c. del carburador,** (mec.) float chamber; **c. del termómetro,** bulb (of a thermometer).
cubetada, *f.* bucketful.
cubeto, *m.* small wooden tub or vat.
cúbica, *f.* (tex.) shalloon, a lightweight twilled fabric.
cubicación, *f.* (math.) cubing; cubic measurement, measurement of volume.
cubicaje, *m.* volume, cubical contents, cubage, displacement; capacity.
cubicar, (*ref. 50*) *tr.v.* 1. (math.) to cube. 2. (geom.) to measure volume or capacity of a body. 3. (min.) to block out.
cúbico, ca, *a.* cubic.
cubiculario, *m.* royal valet.
cubículo, *m.* cubicle, alcove, cubbyhole (U.S.).
cubichete, *m.* 1. (artil.) gun apron. 2. (mar.) waterboard, (stopping water from entering the half deck).
cubierta, *f.* 1. cover; envelope (of letter); wrapping. 2. (archit.) roof. 3. (mar.) deck. 4. (fig.) excuse, pretext. — **c. de arqueo,** (mar.) tonnage deck; **c. de batería,** (mar.) gun deck; **c. de lona,** tarpaulin, canvas cover; **c. de paseo,** (mar.) promenade deck; **c. de popa,** (mar.) afterdeck; **c. de tubería,** pipe insulation.
cubiertamente, *adv.* covertly, secretly.
cubierto, ta, *irr. past part. of* **cubrir.** —*m.* 1. cover (plate, napkin, etc. laid before each person at table); tray or plate with a napkin for serving bread and biscuits; cover charge. 2. fixed menu meal in a restaurant. 3. (bldg.) roof, roofing. 4. shelter, cover. — **a c. de,** under cover of; **bajo c.,** under cover.
cubijar, *tr.v., var. of* **cobijar,** to cover up. —*r.v.* to take shelter.
cubil, *m.* 1. lair, den. 2. bed of a river.
cubilar, *m.* (animal) lair; sheepfold.
cubilar, *i.v.* to gather in the sheepfold for the night.
cubilete, *m.* 1. dicebox (for shooting dice); juggler's cup; beer glass; (cul.) copper baking mold. 2. (cul.) dish of meat (stewed in this mold); (cul.) pie (baked in this mold). 3. (Col.) high hat.
cubiletear, *i.v.* 1. to juggle. 2. (fig.) to scheme, juggle.
cubileteo, *m.* 1. juggling. 2. (fig.) scheming, juggling.
cubiletero, *m.* 1. crapshooter. 2. (cul.) copper baking mold.
cubilote, *m.* (metal.) cupola (furnace for re-melting strained iron).
cubilla, *f., var. of* **cubillo.**
cubillo, *m.* 1. (ento.) oil beetle (Meloe proscarabeus). 2. watercooler. 3. (theat.) each of two small boxes on either side of the stage, under the best boxes.
cubique, cubiqué, *ref.* **cubicar.**
cubismo, *m.* (p.) cubism, a school of painting characterized by geometric forms.
cubista, *a., m., f.* (p.) cubist.
cubital, *a.* (anat.) cubital, pertaining to the cubitus; cubital, measuring one cubit.
cúbito, *m.* (anat.) cubitus, largest bone of the forearm.
cubo, *m.* 1. pail, bucket. 2. hub (of wheel). 3. socket (in chandelier); (mil.) socket (for bayonet or halberd blade). 4. barrel (of watch spring). 5. water tank (for collecting water in water mills). 6. circular tower (in fortress).
cubo, *m.* (math., geom., archit.) cube.
cubocubo, *m.* (math.) 9th power of a number.
cuboides, *a.* (anat.) cuboid (said of a bone of the foot). —*m.* cuboid, cuboid bone.
cubre, *m.* blanket, cover.
cubreasiento, *m.* seat cover.
cubrecadena, *m.* bicycle chainguard.
cubrecama, *f.* bedcover, bedspread, quilt.
cubrecorsé, *m.* undergarment worn over the corset.
cubrefuego, *m.* (mil.) curfew.
cubrejunta, *m.* splice plate, butt strap, fishplate, scab; edge or seam strip; joint runner.
cubrenuca, *f.* havelock, neck-cover, neckguard (for a military cap).
cubreobjeto, *m.* (bact.) cover glass, slide (for covering exhibits for use in a microscope).
cubrepán, *m.* fire shovel used by shepherds.
cubrición, *f.* (vet.) covering, coupling, mating.
cubriente, *a.* covering.
cubrimiento, *m.* 1. covering, hiding. 2. roofing.
cubrir, *irr. past part.:* **cubierto.** —*tr.v.* 1. to cover; to envelop, cloak, shroud. 2. to disguise. 3. (bldg.) to roof, put the roof on. 4. (vet.) to cover, serve, mate with. 5. (mil.) to cover, defend. 6. (com.) to meet, cover (expenses). —*r.v.* 1. to cover oneself; to become covered. 2. to put one's hat on. 3. to take formal possession of his rank (a grandee by donning his hat in the King's presence). 4. (mil.) to defend one's position with difficulty. 5. to cross its legs in cantering (a horse). 6. (com.) to cover (a debt).
cuca, *f.* 1. (bot.) chufa, sedge (Cyperus esculentus). 2. (ento.) caterpillar. 3. (coll.) woman given to gambling. — **mala c.,** evil or malicious person.
cucalón, *m.* (Chile) busybody.
cucambé, *m.* (Col., Ven.) hide-and-seek game.
cucamonas, *f.* (*pl.*) (fig.) wheedling, cajoling.
cucaña, *f.* 1. greased pole (made slippery with soap or with grease and climbed so as to obtain the prize at the top); climbing the greased pole (sport). 2. (coll.) cinch, windfall.
cucañero, ra, *a.* smart, clever (at obtaining things without effort). —*m., f.* smartalec.
cucar, (*ref. 50*) *tr.v.* 1. to wink. 2. to mock, make fun of. 3. (among hunters) to let one another know of the approach of game. 4. (coll.) to provoke, excite. —*i.v.* to bolt, rush off (cattle when bitten by fleas).
cucaracha, *f.* (ento.) cockroach; cochineal insect.
cucarachera, *f.* cockroach trap; cockroach nest.
cucarda, *f.* 1. cockade, rosette. 2. bridle ornament. 3. (mec.) toothed finishing hammer (used by stonemasons).
cucarro, *a.* name given to children dressed as priests; worldly (priest).
cucarrón, *m.* (Col.) beetle.
cucayo, *m.* (Bol., Ecuad.) food, provisions (for journey).
cucha, *f.* (Peru), *var. of* **laguna,** lagoon.
cuchar, *tr.v.* to fertilize with a mixture of manure and compost.
cuchar, *f.* 1. spoon, tablespoon. 2. (arch.) an ancient grain measure.
cuchara, *f.* 1. spoon; ladle, dipper. 2. (artil.) curved shovel used for putting gunpowder in cannons. 3. (mar.) scoop for bailing boats. — **c. de albañil,** trowel; **c. de fundición,** casting ladle; **c. de postre,** dessert spoon; **c. de sopa,** soup spoon; **media c.,** (coll.) mediocre person; **meter uno su c.,** (coll.) to meddle, butt in, interfere.
cucharada, *f.* spoonful; **meter uno su c.,** to meddle, interfere, butt in, put one's two cents in (coll.).
cucharal, *m.* spoon bag formerly used by shepherds.
cucharear, *tr.v.* to spoon out, ladle out. —*i.v.* 1. to stir. 2. to meddle, interfere.
cucharero, ra, *m., f.* person who makes or sells spoons. —*m.* spoon rack.
cuchareta, *f.* 1. *dim. of* **cuchara,** small spoon. 2. type of Andalusian wheat. 3. liver inflammation (in sheep). 4. (ornith. (Amer.) spoonbill (any of many wading birds).
cucharetear, *i.v.* 1. (coll.) to stir (with a spoon). 2. (coll.) to interfere, poke one's nose into other people's business.
cucharetero, ra, *m., f.* person who makes or sells spoons. —*m.* 1. spoon rack. 2. (coll.) frill (of a petticoat).
cucharilla, *f.* 1. *dim. of* **cuchara,** little spoon, teaspoon. 2. liver disease (in pigs). 3. iron rod with flat bent end used for gathering dust from drilled hole.
cucharita, *f. dim. of* **cuchara,** teaspoon.
cucharón, *m.* big spoon, serving spoon, scoop, ladle; **c. de almeja** or **de mordazas,** clamshell bucket; **c. de descarga por debajo,** drop-bottom bucket; **c. de draga,** dredge dipper; dragline bucket; **c. de pala,** shovel dipper; **c. de quijadas,** grab bucket; **c. excavador,** digging bucket; **c. volcador,** dump bucket; **despacharse uno con el c.,** to pocket or snatch the biggest part for oneself.
cucharro, *m.* (mar.) harpings, timbers used during construction of ship to hold the frames.
cuché, *a.* sleek or coated (paper used for printing quality magazines).
cuchí, *m., var. of* **cochino.**
cuchichear, *i.v.* to whisper.
cuchicheo, *m.* whisper, whispering.
cuchichiar, *i.v.* to call like a partridge.
cuchilla, *f.* 1. knife, chopping tool (with a broad blade); razor blade; (Amer.) pocket knife; knife-blade; (poet.) sword; (arch.) halberd. 2. ragged mountain. — **c. de arado,** colter; **c. de interruptor,** (elec.) switch blade.
cuchillada, *f.* 1. stroke, slash, thrust, stab (with knife, sword, etc.); gash, wound (with a knife). 2. ornamental slashes (in a dress). 3. quarrel, dispute. — **dar c.,** (theat.) to steal the show.
cuchillar, *a.* knife-like; pertaining to knives.
cuchilleja, *f. dim. of* **cuchilla,** small knife or blade.
cuchillejo, *m.* (derog.) *dim. of* **cuchillo,** small knife.
cuchillería, *f.* cutlery, knifemaking; knife or cutler's shop; street where knife makers or cutlers live.

cuchillero, *m.* 1. cutler, knife maker. 2. iron band or ring; cleat, wedge. 3. (Amer.) troublemaker, brawler.
cuchillo, *m.* 1. knife. 2. godet, gore (triangular piece of cloth inserted in garments or sails). 3. heel (of a stocking). 4. force, authority, power. 5. (mar.) triangular sail. 6. (archit.) frame (supporting roofing, bridge, etc.). 7. (ornith.) each of six feathers of falcon's wing following the first one. — **c. bayoneta,** bayonet; **c. de armadura,** (archit.) scissors truss; **c. de monte,** hunting knife; **c. de resorte,** flickknife, switchblade, switchblade knife; **c. mangorrero,** rough, badly forged knife; **c.-serrucho,** saw knife; **pasar a c.,** to put to death, put to the sword.
cuchipanda, *f.* (coll.) festive meal enjoyed by a group of people.
cuchitril, *m.* hole, den, very small dismal room.
cucho, *m.* fertilizing mixture of manure and compost.
cucho, cha, *a.* (Mex.) snub-nosed, flat-nosed. —*m.* 1. (Chile) cat. 2. (C. Amer.) hunchback. 3. (Col.) hole, den, hovel.
cuchubal, *m.* (C. Amer.) racket, scheme, shady deal.
cuchuco, *m.* (Col.) pork and barley soup.
cuchuchear, *i.v.* to whisper; to spread gossip.
cuchufleta, *f.* joke, jest.
cuchufletero, ra, *a.* joking, wisecracking (coll.). —*m.* joker, tease, wiseacre.
cuchugo, *m.* (Col., Ecuad.) saddlebag.
cuchumbo, *m.* 1. (C. Amer.) funnel. 2. (C. Amer.) bucket. 3. dice box.
cuchuvo, *m.* (S. Amer.) saddlebag.
cuclillas, en c., squatting, crouching; sitting on one's haunches.
cuclillo, *m.* 1. (ornith.) cuckoo. 2. (fig.) cuckold. — **reloj de c.,** cuckoo clock.
cuco, ca, *a.* 1. (coll.) pretty, nice, neat. 2. clever, smart. —*m., f.* expert, wizard, smart fellow. —*m.* 1. (ento.) caterpillar. 2. (ornith.) cuckoo. 3. card game. 4. (coll.) gambler. 5. ghost, phantom, bogeyman (coll.).
cucú, *m.* cuckoo, cuckooing (call of the cuckoo).
cucuche, a c., (C. Amer.) astride, astraddle.
cucufato, *m.* (Bol., Peru) prude, bigot.
cucuiza, *f.* (Mex., Ven.) sisal, sisal fiber (made of agave).
cucular, *a.* cucullate, hood-shaped.
cuculí, (*pl.* **cuculíes**) *m., f.* (Chile, Peru) small grey dove with bright blue circles around the eyes, easily domesticated (Columbia neloda).
cuculiforme, *a.* cuculiform, pertaining to cuckoos.
cuculla, *f.* hood, cowl, monk's scapular.
cucuma, *m.* (Col.) bread made from a yucca-like root.
cucúrbita, *f.* retort (chemical instrument).
cucurbitáceo, a, *a.* (bot.) cucurbitaceous. —*f.* (*pl.*) (bot.) Cucurbitaceae, plants of the gourd family.
cucurucho, *m.* paper cone.
cucuyo, *m., var. of* **cocuyo.**
cudria, *f.* tressed rope (used to tie baskets together).
cudú, *m.* koodoo (African antelope).
cuébano, *m., var. of* **cuévano,** basket, hamper.
cueca, *f.* popular dance of Chile.
cuece, *ref.* **cocer.**
cuele, cuelo, *ref.* **colar.**
cuélebre, *m.* dragon.
cuelga, *f.* 1. bunch of fruit. 2. birthday present.
cuelgacapas, *m.* coatrack, coat-tree.
cuelgasombreros, *m.* hatrack.
cuelgo, cuelgue, *ref.* **colgar.**
cuellicorto, ta, *a.* short-necked.
cuellierguido, da, *a.* stiff-necked.
cuellilargo, ga, *a.* long-necked.
cuello, *m.,* 1. neck; collar (of a shirt; adornment around the neck); (clergyman's) stock. 2. neck (of a bottle; thinnest part of certain objects). 3. leaf stalk (of onion, etc.). — **c. acanalado, alechugado, escarolado,** Elizabethan (fluted) collar; **c. alto** or **arrollado,** turtleneck; **c. de Venturi,** (engin.) Venturi throat; **c. duro,** stiff collar (of a shirt); **c. ortopédico,** surgical collar, cervical collar; **c. romano,** dog collar; **levantar uno el c.,** (coll.) to raise one's head (after misfortune); **estar con la soga al c.,** to be in imminent danger; to be in a fix.
cuelmo, *m.* candlewood, torch.
cuenca, *f.* 1. wooden bowl. 2. (eye) socket. 3. (geol.) valley; basin, drainage area, watershed. — **c. hidrográfica,** (geol.) watershed, drainage area.
cuenco, *m.* earthen bowl; hollowness.
cuenda, *f.* thread (to tie a skein together); **por la c. se devana la madeja,** the simple way is the best.
cuenta, *f.* 1. counting, calculation, reckoning, count. 2. (com.) account; bill, check. 3. account, answer, report, e.g. *no doy c. a nadie de mi conducta,* I am not accountable to anyone for my conduct. 4. responsibility, care. 5. bead (of rosary). — **abrir c.,** to open an account; **a buena c.,** on account; upon someone else's word; **a fin de cuentas,** after all, all things considered; **ajustar cuentas,** (coll.) to settle accounts; **caer uno en la c.,** (coll.) to realize, understand; to find out about; **cerrar la c.,** to close the account; **con c. y razón,** punctually; (fig.) carefully, cautiously; **correr por la misma c.,** to be one and the same thing; to be included in the same account; **cubrir la c.,** to balance accounts; **c. abierta,** open account; **c. acreedora,** account with credit balance, account payable; **c. al descubierto,** short account (on stock exchange); **c. bancaria,** bank account; **c. conjunta** or **mancomunada,** joint account; **c. corriente,** current account; **c. de adelantos,** drawing account; **c. de ahorros,** savings account; **c. en caja,** cash account; **c. de capital,** capital account; **c. de compra-venta,** trading account; **c. de crédito,** credit account; **c. de depósito,** deposit account; **c. de ganancias y pérdidas,** profit and loss account; **c. de la vieja,** counting on one's fingers, simple way of counting; **c. de registro,** trust account; **c. deudora,** account with a debit balance, account receivable; **c. en participación,** temporary partnership; **c. girada,** account rendered; **c. patrimonial,** capital account; **c. por cobrar,** account receivable; **c. por pagar,** account payable; **c. regresiva,** count-down; **c. sin movimiento,** inactive account; **cuentas del Gran Capitán,** exorbitant and fictitious accounts; **cuentas galanes,** dreams, castles in the air; **c. y razón conserva** or **sustenta amistad,** (coll.) short reckoning makes long friends; **dar uno buena** or **mala c. de su persona,** (coll.) to give a good or bad account of oneself; **dar c. de,** to tell of, recount; **dar c. de una cosa,** (coll.) to finish off, destroy (a thing); **dar uno en la c.,** to realize, become aware of; **dar cuentas de,** to give an explanation or account of; **darse c. de,** to realize, become aware of; **de c.,** important, of importance (person); **de c. y riesgo de uno,** at one's responsibility and risk; **echar cuentas** or **la cuenta,** to work out the account; **echar** or **hacer uno la c. sin la huéspeda,** (coll.) to count one's chickens before they are hatched; **en resumidas cuentas,** in short, in a word; in brief; **entrar una cosa en c.,** to be pertinent, have to do with, enter into account; **entrar uno en cuentas consigo,** (coll.) to think matters over, to weigh things up; **estar fuera de c.,** to have completed the nine months of pregnancy; **estemos a cuentas,** let's settle this; **girar la c.,** to make out and send the bill to the debtor; **hacerse uno c.** or **la c.,** to pretend, make believe; **llevar cuentas** or **las cuentas,** to keep the accounts or books; **llevar la c. de,** to keep account of; **no hacer c. de una cosa,** to consider of no account; **no querer uno cuentas con otro,** not to want to do business with another person; **no tener c. con una cosa,** to have nothing to do with something; **pedir cuentas a,** to ask for an explanation; **perder la c.,** to lose count of; to forget (through length of time); **poner en c.,** to take into consideration; **por la c.,** by all accounts, apparently; **por mi c.,** in my opinion; **por su propia c.,** on one's own account; under one's own steam; **rendir cuentas de,** to give an explanation or account of; **saldar la c. con alguien,** to settle or square accounts with someone; **salirle a c.,** to be worth one's while, come out winning, stand to gain; **tener en c.,** to keep or bear in mind; **tomar en c.,** to take into account; **vamos a cuentas,** (coll.) let's settle this.
cuentacacao, *f.* (Hond.) slightly poisonous spider which leaves a rash on human skin.
cuentacorrentista, *m., f.* (com.) owner of a current account.
cuentadante, *a., m., f.* trustee.
cuentagotas (*pl.* **cuentagotas**) *m.* eyedropper, medicine dropper.
cuentahílos, (*pl.* **cuetahílos**) *m.* threadcounter (microscope used to count the number of threads in a fabric).
cuentakilómetros, (*pl.* **cuentakilómetros**) *m.* mileage recorder, odometer.
cuentamillas, *m.* speedometer.
cuentapasos, (*pl.* **cuentapasos**) *m.* pedometer.
cuente, *ref.* **contar.**
cuentear, *i.v.* (C. Amer.) to gossip.
cuentero, ra, *a.* gossipy. —*m., f.* gossip, gossipmonger.
cuentezuela, *f.* (derog.) *dim. of* **cuenta,** small bead.
cuentista, *a.* (coll.) gossipy. —*m., f.* short story writer, story-teller; gossip, gossipmonger.
cuento, *m.* 1. story, tale. 2. counting, reckoning. 3. (coll.) gossip, tittle-tattle. 4. (coll.) disagreement. 5. (math.) million. — **c. de cuentos,** (coll.) complicated story; **c. de fantasmas,** ghost story; **c. de hadas,** fairy tale; **c. de horno,** popular story; **c. del tío,** confidence trick or story; **c. de viejas,** old wives' tale, tall story; **c. largo,** long story; **cuentos de Calleja,** Mother Goose's Nursery Rhymes; **el c. de nunca acabar,** (coll.) endless business; **degollar el c.,** (coll.) to butt in, interrupt rudely; **dejarse de cuentos,** (coll.) to come to the point; **despachurrar, destripar a uno el c.,** (coll.) to give a story away, interrupt a story; to frustrate; **ése es el c.,** (coll.) this is the gist of it; **estar uno en el c.,** (coll.) to be well informed; **no querer uno cuentos con serranos,** not to look for a quarrel; **ser mucho c.,** (coll.) to be important, be very useful; **sin c.,** (coll.) infinite, countless; **traer a c.,** (coll.) to mention, bring in, introduce (subject into a conversation); **va de c.,** (coll.) it is said, the story goes; **venir a c.,** to be relevant; to be useful, to come in handy; **venirle a uno con cuentos,** to bother someone with trifles.
cuento, *m.* 1. tip (of a tool or weapon). 2. prop, support. 3. joint (of bird's wing).

cuento, *ref.* **contar.**
cuentón, na, *a.* gossipmongering, gossipy. *—m., f.* gossip.
cuera, *f.* (arch.) leather jacket.
cuerazo, *m.* (Ecuad.) lash, whiplash.
cuerda, *f.* 1. cord, rope, twine. 2. spring (of a watch). 3. (arch.) fuse (for cannons, etc.). 4. chain gang, chain of prisoners. 5. mountain range. 6. (Cuba, P. Rico, Sp.) an ancient land measure. 7. (mus.) string (of violin, etc.); (mus.) voice (bass, tenor, alto, soprano); (mus.) voice range. 8. (geom.) chord. 9. (topog.) measuring chain. 10. (archit.) spring line, starting point of arch or vault. 11. (anat.) vocal chord, cord. (*pl.*) tendons. 12. (mar.) (*pl.*) deck strakes. — **aflojar la c.,** to take a breather, take a rest; to slacken discipline; **andar en la c. floja,** (coll.) to be in a delicate or difficult situation, do the balancing act; **apretar hasta que salte la c.,** to overtax (one's) patience; **apretar la c.,** to tighten up discipline, be more severe; **calar la c.,** to light the fuse; **c. de saltar,** skipping rope; **c. falsa,** (mus.) string out of tune; **c. floja,** tight-rope; **c. guía** or **freno,** trail rope; **c. sin fin,** spliced rope or cable; **cuerdas vocales,** (anat.) vocal chords; **dar c.,** to prolong, draw out; **dar c. a uno,** to get someone started (on a favorite subject of conversation); **dar c. al reloj,** to wind a clock or watch; **de c. automática,** self-winding; **echar una c.,** (top.) to measure (land) roughly or superficially; **la c. está tirante,** the rules are being strictly enforced; **no ser uno de la c. de otro,** not to be of the same opinion; **por debajo de c.,** secretly; **tener la c. tirante,** to be severe; **tirar de la c. a uno,** (coll.) to restrain, hold back; **tirar de la c. para todos o para ninguno,** to be impartial, accord equal treatment to all; **tocar en la c. sensible,** to touch (someone's) soft or sensitive spot.
cuerdamente, *adv.* prudently, wisely, sensibly.
cuerdezuela, *f.* small rope.
cuerdo, da, *a.* sane; sensible, wise, prudent (person).
cuereada, *f.* 1. (C. Amer.) tanning season (leather). 2. (Amer.) thrashing, beating.
cuerear, *tr.v.* 1. (C. Amer.) to tan (leather). 2. (Amer.) to beat, thrash.
cuerezuelo, *m.* 1. small hide. 2. suckling pig.
cueriza, *f.* (Amer.) thrashing, beating, spanking.
cuerna, *f.* 1. drinking horn. 2. antlers, horns (of any animal). 3. hunting horn.
cuérnago, *m.* riverbed.
cuernezuelo, *m.* small horn, cornicle.
cuernito, *m.* (Amer.) croissant, crescent-shaped bun.
cuerno, *m.* 1. horn (of animals); horn (substance); feeler, antenna (of insects). 2. (mus.) horn. 3. side (of certain objects); (mil.) flank. 4. tip, horn (of half moon). — **c. de la abundancia,** cornucopia, horn of plenty; **c. de Amón,** ammonite; **c. de caza,** hunting horn; **en los cuernos del toro,** (coll.) in imminent danger; **estar de c. con uno,** (coll.) to be at odds or angry with someone; **levantar a uno hasta los cuernos de la luna,** to praise to the skies, overpraise; **no valer un c.,** to be worth little or nothing; **poner los cuernos a,** to be unfaithful to, cuckold; **ponerse de c. con,** to get angry with; **saber a c. quemado,** (coll.) to cause dismay, disgust or displeasure; **sobre c. penitencia,** (coll.) to add insult to injury; **¡vete al c.¡** go to the devil!
cuero, *m.* skin, hide, pelt; leather; wine skin; **c. cabelludo,** scalp; **c. curtido al cromo,** chrome leather; **c. en verde,** rawhide, untanned hide or skin; **c. exterior,** (anat.) cuticle, epidermis; **c. interior,** (anat.) cutis; **dejar a uno en c.,** to ruin, leave without a penny; **en cueros** or **en cueros vivos,** stark naked; **entre c. y carne,** under the skin, intimately; **estar uno hecho un c.,** (coll.) to be completely drunk; **romperse el c.,** (Col.) to work very hard, work one's fingers to the bone; **dar c.,** spank (a child).
cuerpear, *i.v.* (Arg.) to swerve, dodge; to avoid, get out of (duty, etc.).
cuerpo, *m.* 1. body; trunk, torso; bodice; figure, build, e.g. *ella tiene buen c.,* she has a good figure. 2. body, particle of matter; substance, matter. 3. volume, book. 4. body (of laws, of writings, of people, etc.); corps (diplomatic, military, ballet). 5. thickness (of fabrics, liquids, etc.). 6. size. 7. corpse, body. 8. part, unit, component (of cupboard, of building, etc.). 9. (geom.) body, three-dimensional figure. 10. (print.) body, size (of type). — **a c. de rey, (estar or vivir),** (to live) like a king; **a c. descubierto,** without shelter or cover; patently, manifestly; **c. a c.,** hand to hand (combat); **c. calloso,** (anat.) corpus callosum; **c. cetónico,** (chem., physiol.) ketone body; **c. compuesto,** (chem.) compound; **c. de baile,** corps of ballet; **c. de bomba,** barrel, cylinder (of suction pump); **c. de bomberos,** fire department; **c. de caballo,** (mil.) length of horse's body; **c. de ejército,** (mil.) army corps; **c. de émbolo,** (mec.) piston barrel; **c. de guardia,** guard, guard post; **c. de iglesia,** main body of church; **c. de delito,** (law) corpus delicti; **c. de paz,** peace corps; **c. de saneamiento,** (mil.) sanitary corps; **c. diplomático,** diplomatic corps; **c. expedicionario,** expeditionary force; **c. facultativo,** body of experts; **c. legal,** body of laws; **c. muerto,** (mar.) mooring buoy; **c. polar,** (biol.) polar body, cell or globule; **c. simple,** (chem.) element, simple substance; **c. sin alma,** lifeless person, wet blanket; **c. tiroides,** (anat.) thyroid; **c. volante,** (mil.) flying column; **dar uno con el c. en tierra,** (coll.) to fall on the ground; **dar c.,** thicken (a liquid); **dar de c.,** to have a bowel movement; **de c. entero,** full-length (mirror, portrait); **de medio c.,** half-length (portrait); **echar uno el c. fuera,** to avoid difficulties or obligations; **en c.,** in shirt sleeves; in a body, en masse; **en c. y en alma,** (coll.) completely, entirely; **estar de c. presente,** to be on view, lie in state (a corpse); to be present, in person; **falsear el c.,** to duck, dodge; **hacer del c.,** to have a bowel movement; **huir** or **hurtar el c.,** to duck, dodge (a blow); **no quedarse uno con nada en el c.,** to say everything, get everything off one's chest; **pedirle a uno el c.,** to crave or long for something; **quedarse con una cosa en el c.,** to leave something unsaid, not to say everything; **tomar c.,** to increase, grow; to thicken (consistency); **volverle a uno el alma al c.,** to recover (from fright or shock).
cuérrago, *m.* riverbed.
cuerudo, da, *a.* 1. (Amer.) slow, sluggish (horse). 2. (C. Amer.) brazen, shameless (person).
cuerva, *f.* (ornith.) female rook, a European bird similar to the American crow.
cuervo, *m.* 1. (ornith.) crow; raven (Corvus corax). 2. C., (astron.) Corvus. — **c. marino,** (ornith.) cormorant; **c. merendero,** (ornith.) rook; **c. negro,** (Amer.) loan shark; **no puede ser el c. más negro que las alas,** (coll.) nothing worse than this can happen; **tomar la del c.,** (coll.) to scram.
cuesco, *m.* 1. stone, pit (of fruit). 2. millstone (of an oil mill). 3. (vulg.) noisy fart. 4. (Mex.) large lump of mineral. 5. (min.) dross.
cuesquillo, *m. dim. of* **cuesco,** small stone or pit (of fruit).
cuesta, *f.* slope, gradient; **a cuestas,** on one's shoulders or back; (fig.) (to take) upon oneself; **c. abajo,** downhill; **c. arriba,** uphill; **c. de enero,** (coll.) difficult financial phase or period; **hacérsele c. arriba una cosa,** to find something difficult or tiring; **echarse a cuestas (una cosa),** to take (something) on, undertake, make oneself responsible for; **ir c. abajo,** to degenerate, decline, go downhill; **llevar uno a cuestas,** (coll.) to shoulder or take someone else's obligations upon oneself.
cuesta, *f., var. of* **cuestación.**
cuesta, *ref.* **costar.**
cuestación, *f.* collection, petition (for charity).
cueste, *ref.* **costar.**
cuestero, ra, *m., f.* person who collects alms.
cuestezuela, *f. dim. of* **cuesta,** small slope.
cuestión, *f.* 1. question, matter; affair, business; dispute, quarrel, controversy. 2. point, issue (under discussion). 3. (math.) problem. — **c. batallona,** (coll.) very vexing question, moot point; **c. candente,** burning question; **c. de competencia,** (law) question of legal precedence; **c. de confianza,** plea for a vote of confidence; **c. de gabinete,** affair of state; very important matter; **c. determinada,** (math.) problem with one or a definite number of solutions; **c. diminuta,** (math.) problem with an infinite number of solutions; **en c.,** under discussion, in question; **es c. de unas horas,** it's a matter of a few hours.
cuestionable, *a.* questionable, dubious.
cuestionar, *tr.v.* to debate, discuss, dispute.
cuestionario, *m.* questionnaire.
cuesto, *m.* hillock, low hill.
cuestor, *m.* 1. quaestor (Roman official). 2. collector of gifts (for charity).
cuestuario, ria, *a., var. of* **cuestoso.**
cuestuoso, sa, *a.* lucrative, productive, profitable.
cuestura, *f.* questorship.
cuete, *a.* (Mex.) drunk. *—m.* 1. (Mex.) slice of rump (of beef). 2. (Guat., Mex., Peru) pistol. 3. (Mex.) drunk, drunken spree; drunk, drunk person.
cuetearse, *r.v.* (Col.) to go off, blow up.
cueto, *m.* crag, inaccesible peak, craggy mountain top; fortified peak.
cueva, *f.* cave, grotto; cellar, basement; **c. de ladrones,** (coll.) thieves' den.
cuévano, *m.* large basket, hamper; small straw basket strapped to the back (used to transport provisions or for carrying children).
cuevero, *m.* cave, grotto or basement digger.
cueza, cuezo, *ref.* **cocer.**
cuezo, *m.* mortar mixing trough, hod; **meter uno el cuezo,** (coll.) to butt into (a conversation), get mixed up in.
cúfico, ca, *a.* kufic (applied to early Arabic alphabet).
cugujada, *f.* (ornith.) crested lark (Calerida cristata).
cugulla, *f., var. of* **cogulla,** cowl.
cuicacoche, *f.* (ornith., Mex.) song bird (Harphorynchus longirostris).
cuico, ca, *a.* (Ecuad., Cuba) thin, skinny. *—m., f.* 1. (Amer., derog.) foreigner. 2. (Arg.) mestizo. *—m.* Mex., derog.) policeman, cop (sl.). *—f.* (Dom. Rep., P. Rico) skip rope (game).
cuida, *f.* older girl who looks after younger schoolmates.
cuidado, *m.* 1. care; caution. 2. care, charge. 3. anxiety, care, concern, worry. — **con c.,** carefully; to be cautious or apprehensive; **c. con,** look out for, beware of; **correr una cosa al c. de uno,** to be responsible for something; **¡cuidado!** careful! be careful!; **c. conmigo,** keep out of my

way, beware; **de c.,** seriously ill; **perder c.,** not to worry; **salir de su c. (una mujer),** to give birth; **tener c.,** to be careful, cautious.
cuidador, ra, *a.* careful, cautious. —*m., f.* 1. caretaker. 2. trainer. 3. (Arg.) nurse. —*f.* (Mex.) governess; baby sitter.
cuidadosamente, *adv.* carefully, cautiously; warily.
cuidadoso, sa, *a.* careful; vigilant; attentive (to details).
cuidaniños, *m. f.* (Amer.) baby sitter.
cuidar, *tr.v.* to look after, take care of. —*i.v.* (with **de**) to look after, take care of. —*r.v.* to look after or take care of oneself; **cuidarse de,** to care about, worry about (e.g. what people say); to take care to, be careful about.
cuido, *m.* care, minding, attention.
cuidoso, sa, *a., var., of* **cuidadoso.**
cuija, *f.* 1. (Mex.) small thin lizard. 2. (Mex.) thin ugly woman.
cuino, *m.* swine, pig.
cuita, *f.* grief, anxiety, affliction, care; **contar sus cuitas,** to tell one's troubles.
cuitadamente, *adv.* anxiously, worriedly, distressfully.
cuitado, da, *a.* anxious, worried, distressed; spiritless, timid.
cuitamiento, *m.* timidity, spiritlessness.
cuja, *f.* 1. bucket socket, holder (on the saddle, to hold the lance or the flag staff). 2. bedstead.
cuje, *m.* (Cuba) 1. horizontal supports for drying tobacco. 2. withe; tough, flexible twig.
cuji, (*pl.* **cujíes**) *m.* (Ven., bot.) huisache, sponge tree (Acacia farnesiana).
cujisal, *m.* (Ven.) huisache grove.
cujón, *m.* corner (of a mattress or cushion).
culada, *f.* blow with the buttocks or behind.
culantrillo, *m.* (bot.) maidenhair fern.
culantro, *m.* (bot.) coriander (Coriandrum satirum).
culata, *f.* 1. haunch, buttock (of a horse). 2. butt (of a firearm); breech (of a gun). 3. (fig.) rear end. 4. (mec.) head (of a cylinder). 5. (elec.) armature, keeper. — **salir el tiro por la c.,** to backfire, to boomerang.
culatazo, *m.* 1. blow with a rifle or pistol butt. 2. kick (of a firearm).
culateo, *m.* recoil, kick (of a firearm).
culcusido, *m., var. of* **corcusido,** careless stitching.
culebra, *f.* 1. (zool) small snake. 2. coil, spiral (of a still). 3. winding passage (dug by larvae in cork). 4. (coll.) trick, practical joke, jocose jostling. 5. sudden disturbance 6. (mar.) cable, line. — **Culebra y Nube,** (astron.) Ophiuchus; **hacer c.,** to slither along like a snake, wind, zigzag.
culebrazo, *m.* practical joke, trick.
culebrear, *i.v.* to slither like a snake, to zigzag.
culebreo, *m.* winding, weaving, zigzaging, slithering like a snake.
culebrilla, *f.* 1. (med.) ringworm. 2. (bot.) green dragon (Dracunculus vulgaris). 3. split, fissure (in gun barrel). 4. (zool.) amphibaena. — **c. de agua,** water snake.
culebrina, *f.* 1. (mil.) culverin. 2. luminous electric meteor (resembling a wavy line).
culebrón, *m.* 1. *aug. of* **culebra,** large snake. 2. (coll.) smart fellow, crafty, astute fellow; (coll.) scheming woman, snake-in-the-grass, evil woman.
culera, *f.* 1. stains left in children's diapers. 2. patch on the seat of the pants.
culero, ra, *a.* lazy, slothful. — m. 1. child's diaper. 2. (vet.) excrescence which forms on tails of certain birds.
culícido, *m.* (ento.) culicid, (*pl.*) Culicidae.
culinario, ria, *a.* culinary, pertaining to cooking or cuisine.
culinegro, gra, *a.* (coll.) black-bottomed.
culipandear, *v.i.* (Cuba, vulg.) 1. to walk swaying the behind. 2. to come and go, flutter about. 3. to deceive, evade.
culminación, *f.* culmination; (astron.) culmination (highest point of a heavenly body above the horizon).
culminante, *a.* culminating; highest (point of a mountain); (fig.) outstanding; (astron.) culminating (position).
culminar, *i.v.* 1. to culminate. 2. (astron.) to reach highest altitude.
culo, *m.* 1. seat, behind, backside (coll.), bottom (of people) (coll.); ass (vulg.); (anat.) anus; rump (of beasts). 2. end (of anything); bottom (of glass). 3. dregs (of liquid in a glass). 4. flat side of knucklebone (in game of knucklebones). — **c. de mal asiento,** (coll.) fidgety breeches, restless person; **c. de pollo,** (coll.) pucker, bulge, wrinkle (in clothing); **c. de botella,** (coll.) imitation precious stone.
culombio, *m.* (phys.) coulomb.
culón, na, *a.* broad in the beam (coll.), with a fat backside. —*m.* (coll.) disabled soldier.
culote, *m.* 1. *aug. of* **culo.** 2. (mil.) rear, base (projectile, cartridge).
culpa, *f.* fault, blame; guilt; **c. jurídica,** guilt; **c.** lata, (law) culpa lata, gross negligence; **c. leve,** (law) culpa levis, negligence; **echar la c. a alguien,** to blame someone; **tener la c. de,** to be guilty of.
culpabilidad, *f.* guilt.
culpable, *a.* guilty, culpable, to blame, blamable. —*m., f.* culprit.
culpablemente, *a.* culpably.
culpación, *f.* blaming, inculpation.
culpadamente, *adv.* culpably.
culpado, da, *past part. of* **culpar.** —*a.* guilty. —*m., f.* culprit.
culpar, *tr.v.* to blame; to accuse; to censure, criticise. —*r.v.* to blame oneself, take the blame.
culpeo, *m.* (Chile) species of large fox.
culposo, sa, *a.* culpable.
cultalatiniparla, *f.* (hum.) euphuistic or affected style of speech.
cultamente, *adv.* with refinement, in a cultured manner; (fig.) affectedly.
cultedad, *f.* (hum.) affected elegance of style.
culteranismo, *m.* (lit.) euphuism, preciosity.
culterano, na, *a.* (lit.) euphuistic, precious (literary style). —*m., f.* (lit.) euphuistic writer.
cultería, *f.* (hum.) affected elegance of style.
cultero, ra, *a.* (hum.) euphuistic (style). —*m., f.* euphuistic writer.
cultiparlar, *i.v.* to speak in a euphuistic manner.
cultiparlista, *a.* euphuistic, precious. —*m., f.* euphuistic speaker, one who speaks in a euphuistic manner.
cultismo, *m.* euphuism, preciosity; learned word, word taken from Latin or Greek.
cultivable, *a.* cultivatable, arable.
cultivación, *f.* cultivation.
cultivado, da, *a.* 1. cultured, refined. 2. tilled, sown.
cultivador, ra, *a.* cultivating. —*m., f.* cultivator.
cultivar, *tr.v.* 1. to cultivate (land, friendship, etc.). 2. to develop, cultivate (memory, talents); to dedicate oneself to, cultivate (the arts, etc.). 3. (biol.) to culture.
cultivo, *m.* cultivation. — **caldo de c.,** (biol.) culture broth.
culto, ta, *a.* 1. cultivated (plants, etc.). 2. cultured, refined, cultivated (people). 3. learned, erudite. 4. euphuistic, precious. 5. learned (word, taken from Greek or Latin). —*m.* 1. cult; religion 2. worship; respect; homage. 3. ritual. — **c. a la personalidad,** personality cult; **c. de dulía,** worship given to the angels and saints; **c. de hiperdulía,** worship given to the Virgin Mary; **c. de latría,** worship given to God; **c. externo,** external ritual; **c. indebido,** superstitious or unreligious ritual; **c. interno,** personal worship (faith, etc); **c. superfluo,** empty ritual.
cultor, ra, *a.* worshiping. —*m., f.* worshiper.
cultual, *a.* cultist; ritualistic.
cultura, *f.* 1. culture, knowledge; refinement, good breeding or manners. 2. civilization, culture, e.g. *la c. hispánica,* Hispanic culture.
cultural, *a.* cultural, intellectual (endeavor).
culturar, *tr.v.* to cultivate.
cuma, *f.* 1. (Amer.) godmother. 2. (Hond.) long knife.
cumárico, ca, *a.* (chem.) coumarie.
cumarina, *f.* (chem.) coumarin.
cumarona, *f.* (chem.) coumarone.
cumarú, *m.* (bot.) tonka bean tree.
cumba, *f.* (Hond.) large vessel (made from a gourd).
cumbancha, *f.* (Cuba, Dom. Rep.) noisy party.
cumbanchar, *i.v.* (Cuba, Dom. Rep.) to go on a spree, have a party.
cumbanchero, ra, *a.* (Cuba, Dom. Rep.) gay, merry, fond of merry making.
cumbarí, *m.* (bot., Arg.) hot red pepper or chili.
cumbé, *m.* (Amer.) negro dance and its accompanying music.
cumbo, *m.* (Hond.) gourd or vessel with a narrow mouth; (Salv.) gourd with a square mouth.
cumbre, *f.* summit, crest, top; (fig.) height, acme, pinnacle; **cita en la c.,** (polit.) summit meeting.
cumbrera, *f.* 1. (bldg.) ridgepole, ridge-piece. 2. (carp.) a very large beam. 3. lintel. 4. summit, top.
cúmel, *m.* kümmel (liqueur).
cumiche, *a.* (C. Amer.) baby (of the family).
cumínico, *a.* (chem.) cumic.
cuminol, *m.* (chem.) cuminol, cumaldehyde.
cumpa, *m.* (Amer., coll.) comrade, friend, buddy.
cúmplase, *m.* 1. official confirmation (of public appointment). 2. (Amer.) presidential approval or consent for the implementation of a law.
cumpleaños, *m.* birthday.
cumplidamente, *adv.* completely, entirely.
cumplidero, ra, *a.* 1. expiring (by a certain date). 2. convenient, suitable.
cumplido, da, *past part. of* cumplir. —*a.* 1. complete; perfect. 2. full, ample (clothes). 3. courteous, polite, correct. 4. (Peru) responsible, trustworthy, reliable (always fulfilling obligations). —*m.* (mark of) courtesy, politeness.
cumplidor, ra, *a.* reliable, trustworthy.
cumplimentar, *tr.v.* 1. to congratulate. 2. to pay a courtesy call. 3. (law) to carry out, execute.
cumplimentero, ra, *a.* (coll.) obsequious, full of compliments.
cumplimiento, *m.* 1. fulfillment, performance, carrying out. 2. expiration (date). 3. courtesy, politeness, formality. 4. token offer. 5. perfection. — **de or por c.,** out of courtesy.
cumplir, *tr.v.* 1. to carry out, perform, execute (orders, instructions); to fulfill, keep (promise, wish, etc.). 2. to be (so many years) old, reach (so many years of age). 3. to help, aid. — **c. años,** to have one's birthday; **c. la palabra,** to keep one's word; **c. una condena,** to serve a prison term. —*i.v.* 1. to fulfill one's obligations. 2. to finish one's military service. 3. to expire (period of time); to fall due for payment (draft). 4. to be advisable or convenient. — **c. con,** to

fulfill one's obligations to (someone); to fulfill (one's obligations); **c. (uno) por (otro),** to pay respects for someone else; **por c.,** as a mere formality or courtesy. —*r.v.* to come true, be fulfilled.
cumquibus, *m.* (coll.) wherewithal, money, cash.
cumucho, *m.* (Chile) crowd; swarm.
cumulador, ra, *a.* accumulating.
cumular, *tr.v.* to accumulate.
cumulativo, a, *a.* cumulative.
cúmulo, *m.* 1. heap. 2. (meteorol.) cumulus, set of rounded masses of clouds. 3. (fig.) crowd, great quantity or number. — **c. estelar,** (astron.) galaxy.
cumulonimbo, *m.* (meteorol.) cumulonimbus.
cumulostrato, *m.* (meteorol.) cumulostratus.
cuna, *f.* 1. cradle. 2. foundling hospital. 3. improvised rustic bridge. 4. (fig.) birthplace. 5. (fig.) lineage, origin, birth. 6. (vet.) space between cow's horns. 7. (mar.) stocks (for shipbuilding).
cunaguaro, *m.* (zool., Ven.) coelot.
cunar, *tr.v.* to rock (the cradle).
cunasiri, *m.* Peruvian aromatic tree.
cuncuna, *f.* 1. (ornith., Chile) wild pigeon, any of a variety of Columbae. 2. (ento.) (Chile) bagworm (Oiketicus kirbii).
cunchos, *m. pl.* (Col.) sediment.
cunda, *m.* (Cuba, Peru) jokester merry, happy-go-lucky person.
cundido, *past part. of* **cundir.** —*m.* any food that can be eaten between bread slices, e.g. cheese, fruit jam, etc.
cundir, *i.v.* 1. to spread (oil, liquid; news). 2. to swell (rice, beans). 3. to increase, multiply.
cunear, *tr.v.* to rock (the cradle). —*r.v.* (coll.) to rock, sway, swing, move from side to side.
cuneiforme, *a.* 1. cuneiform, wedge-shaped (said of writing characters used in ancient civilizations of Persia and Assyria). 2. (bot.) cuneate, wedge-shaped (leaves and petals).
cúneo, *m.* 1. cuneus, space between vomitories; entrance between banks of seats in theatres and amphitheatres of ancient Rome. 2. (mil.) wedge (formation of troops designed to divide enemy troops).
cuneo, *m.* rocking, swaying.
cunera, *f.* woman who used to baby-sit for royal infants in a palace.
cunero, ra, *a.* 1. foundling. 2. alien (said of a candidate supported by the government to constituency where he is a stranger). 3. (taur.) (bull) of unknown stock. —*m., f.* foundling.
cuneta, *f.* ditch, gutter; curb.
cuneteadora, *f.* ditcher, ditch digger.
cunicultor, ra, *a.* rabbit-breeding. —*m., f.* rabbit-breeder.
cunicultura, *f.* rabbit breeding.
cunita, *f.* cat's cradle (children's game).
cuña, *f.* 1. wedge; quoin. 2. pyramid-shaped paving stone. 3. (anat.) cuneiform (bone of the tarsus). 4. help, useful or helpful person, e.g. *ser una buena c.,* to be a great help (to someone). — **c. del colector,** (elec.) commutator bar.
cuñadía, *f.* relationship between brothers-in-law or sisters-in-law, affinity, relationship through marriage.
cuñado, da, *m.* brother-in-law. —*f.* sister-in-law.
cuñar, *tr.v.* to coin, mint.
cuñete, *m.* keg, firkin, small barrel; **c. de pólvora, powder keg.**
cuño, *m,* 1. mold (for coins, medals, etc.); impression (from the mold); (fig.) impression mark. 2. (mil.) wedge (formation of troops).
cuociente, *m.* (math.) quotient.
cuodlibetal, *a., var. of* **cuodlibético.**
cuodlibético, ca, *a.* quodlibetic.
cuodlibeto, *m.* 1. quodlibet, scholastic debate. 2. (coll.) sarcastic remark.
cuota, *f.* 1. payment (on installment plan contract); fee (for school), subscription (to a club). 2. quota, share, part.
cuotidiano, na, *a.* daily.
cupé, *m.* coupé (car and carriage).
cupe, *ref.* **caber.**
cupido, *m.* 1. (myth.) C., Cupid, god of love. 2. (fig.) a young Casanova, a gallant swain.
cupiera, cupiese, *ref.* **caber.**
cupilca, *f.* (Chile) thin pudding made with toasted flour and wine or cider.
cuplé, *m.* popular song, ditty.
cupletista, *f.* singer of popular songs.
cupo, *m.* quota, share; (Amer.) room, space; (Méx.) jail; (Méx.) seating capacity; **cupos** (Amer.) vacancies, rooms for rent.
cupón, *m.* (com.) coupon. — **c. federal,** food stamp; **c. obsequio,** gift certificate; **c. respuesta,** (postal) reply coupon; **talonario de cupones,** book of coupons.
cupresíneas, *f.* (*pl.*) (bot.) Cypress family.
cupresino, na, *a.* (poet.) of or pertaining to the cypress tree.
cúprico, ca, *a.* (chem.) cupric, pertaining to copper.
cuprífero, ra, *a.* (min.) cupriferous.
cuprita, *f.* (min.) cuprite.
cuproaluminio, *m.* (metal.) duralumin.
cuproníquel, *m.* 1. cupronickel, nickel-bronze. 2. ancient Spanish coin.
cuproso, sa, *a.* (chem.) cuprous.
cúpula, *f.* 1. dome, cupola. 2. (bot.) cupule, cup-shaped involucre. 3. (mar.) turret of monitor (heavily armored vessel with one or more revolving turrets). — **c. de vapor** or **caldera,** steam dome.
cupulífero, ra, *a.* (bot.) cupuliferous. —*f.* cupuliferous tree; (*pl.*) Cupuliferae.
cupulino, *m.* (archit.) lantern, small cupola on top of another.
cuque, cuqué, *ref.* **cucar.**
cuquear, *tr.v.* (Cuba) to prod, goad, provoke.
cuquería, *f.* astuteness, craftiness.
cuquero, *m.* rogue, rascal.
cuquillo, *m.* (ornith.) cuckoo.
cura, *m.* parish priest, vicar; (coll.) priest. — **c. de almas,** parish priest; **c. de misa y olla,** ignorant priest; **c. ecónomo,** substitute parish priest; **c. párroco,** parish priest. —*f.* cure, treatment; **alargar la c.,** to prolong (some business) for one's own profit; **c. de almas,** care of souls; **encarecer uno la c.,** to exaggerate one's efforts (in order to obtain praise or profit); **no tener c.,** (coll.) to be incorrigible; **ponerse uno en c.,** to undergo treatment, begin a treatment or cure.
curable, *a.* curable.
curaca, *m.* (Amer.) chief, headman (of village); boss, chief (controlling a district of the country).
curación, *f.* cure, treatment.
curadillo, *m.* (ichth.) codfish.
curado, da, *past part. of* **curar.** —*a.* hardened, strengthened. —*m.* curing; **c. al agua,** (bldg.) water curing.
curador, ra, *a.* curing, healing. —*m., f.* 1. caretaker, curator (of a museum). 2. healer, curer. 3. (law) tutor, guardian (of a child or invalid). 4. curer (of fish, meat, etc.); dresser (of skins); bleacher (of linen). — **c. ad hoc,** (law) guardian of an invalid or lunatic; **c. ad lítem,** (law) guardian of a minor.
curaduría, *f.* tutorship, guardianship; **c. ejemplar,** guardianship of a lunatic.
curagua, *f.* (S. Amer.) a type of coarse, hard-grained corn or maize.
curalotodo, *m.* cure-all.
curalle, *m.* morsel of food dipped in medication, which hunters used to give to their falcons.
curandería, *f.* quackery, witch medicine.
curandero, ra, *m., f.* quack; witch doctor.
curanto, *m.* (Chile) typical stew of meat and sea-food barbecued on heated stones.
curar, *tr.v.* 1. to cure; to nurse, treat (a patient); to heal; to dress (a sore or wound). 2. to prepare; to cure, salt, smoke (meat or fish); to dress, tan (skins or furs); to season, dry (wood); to bleach (linen). 3. (fig.) to restore, heal (the soul); (fig.) to remedy (an evil). — **c. en salud,** to cure before the illness takes a hold. —*i.v.* to get well, to recover. —*r.v.* 1. to recover; to undergo treatment; to cure oneself. 2. (Chile) to get drunk.
curare, *m.* curare, powerful vegetable poison used by some primitive tribes to make poison arrows.
curarina, *f.* (chem.) curarine.
curasao, *m.* Curacao, an orange-flavored liqueur.
curatela, *f., var. of* **curaduría.**
curativa, *f.* (med.) remedy, curative, cure.
curativo, va, *a.* curative.
curato, *m.* (ecc.) curacy; parish.
curazao, *m.* 1. C., Curaçao, largest island of the Dutch Antilles. 2. curaçao, orange-flavored liqueur.
curazoleño, ña, *a.* of or from the island of Curaçao. —*m., f.* native or inhabitant of Curaçao.
curbana, *f.* (bot., Cuba) tree-bearing bark that can be used as cinnamon.
curbaril, *m.* (bot., C. Amer.) courbaril, locust tree (Hymenea curbaril).
curculio, *m.* (zool.) curculio.
cúrcuma, *f.* 1. curcuma, turmeric (used in cooking and dyeing). 2. curcumin (resinous substance present in turmeric).
curcuncho, cha, *a.* (Amer.) hunchbacked.
curcusí, *m.* (ento., Bol.) fire beetle (Pyrophorous noctilicus).
curcusilla, *f.* (anat.) coccyx uropygium, tail bone (in birds).
curda, *f.* (coll.) drunkenness, drunk.
curdo, da, *a.* Kurdish, pertaining to a region in S.W. Asia. —*m., f.* Kurd.
cureña, *f.* (mil.) gun-carriage; gun-stock (in the rough); stock (of a cross-bow); **a c. rasa,** (mil.) without parapet or breastwork; (coll.) defenseless; out in the open; without the slightest cover.
cureñaje, *m.* gun carriages.
curesca, *f.* nap residue (of wool) left on carding machine after carding.
curetaje, *m.* (surg.) curettage.
curetuí, *m.* (Arg., ornith.) antshrike.
curí, *m.* 1. (bot.) a coniferous tree, whose cones are edible. 2. (Amer., zool.) guinea pig.
curia, *f.* 1. curia (political subdivision of Roman tribe; senate house, senate). 2. tribunal, court; bar (body of lawyers, judges, etc.). 3. (ecc.) Curia, Curia Romana.
curial, *a.* curial. —*m.* 1. lawyer, attorney; court clerk. 2. member of the Curia Romana.
curialesco, ca, *a.* (derog.) legalistic; priestlike, clerical (style, subtlety, etc.).
curiana, *f.* (ento.) cockroach.
curiara, *f.* curiara (dugout canoe).
curibay, *m.* (Arg., bot.) (species of) pine with medicinal fruit.
curiche, *m.* 1. (Bol.) swamp, lagoon. 2. (Chile) dark or black person.
curie, *m.* (phys.) curie.
curiel, *m.* (Cuba, zool.) guinea pig (Cavia porcellus).

curio, *m.* (chem.) curium.
curiosamente, *adv.* 1. curiously. 2. carefully, neatly; painstakingly.
curiosear, *i.v.* to pry, investigate; to snoop (coll.).
curioseo, *m.* the act of prying or snooping.
curiosidad, *f.* 1. curiosity, inquisitiveness. 2. cleanliness, neatness; care, carefulness. 3. curio, a rare object, a small trinket.
curioso, sa, *a.* 1. curious, inquisitive. 2. clean, neat; careful. *—m., f.* busybody, snooper.
curiquingue, *m.* (Ecuad., ornith.) **caracara.**
curita, *f.* (min.) curite.
curricán, *m.* fishing tackle with only one hook.
currículum vitae, *m.* (Lat.) résumé, curriculum vitae.
currinche, *m.* cub reporter.
curro, rra, *a.* (coll.) handsome, goodlooking. *—m., f.* (Cuba, Mex.) an Andalusian emigré, a southern Spaniard living in America.
curruca, *f.* (ornith.) whitethroat (Sylvia curruca).
currutaco, ca, *a.* (coll.) foppish, dandyish. *—m., f.* dandy, fop, dude.
cursado, da, *past part. of* **cursar.** *—a.* skilled, versed (in a certain field).
cursante, *m.* (Amer.) student. *—a.* frequenting; assiduous.
cursar, *tr.v.* 1. to frequent, haunt. 2. to study, follow, attend (a course of studies). 3. to attend to, transmit, expedite (a petition, legal matter). 4. to do assiduously.
cursería, *f., var. of* **cursilería.**
cursi, *a.* (coll.) affected; tasteless; showy, gaudy, cheap. *—m., f.* (coll.) person who lacks taste.
cursilería, *f.* 1. vulgarity; cheapness, flashiness. 2. (coll.) group of flashy or vulgar persons.
cursillista, *m., f.* student.
cursillo, *m.* short course (of studies or lectures).
cursivo, va, *a.* cursive, running (writing). *—f.* script.
curso, *m.* 1. course (of river; of time; of studies; textbook); direction. 2. movement, flow; run, route, current. 3. (*pl.*) diarrhea. 4. circulation, e.g. *monedas en c.,* coins in circulation. 5. currency, tender, e.g. *c. legal,* legal tender. — **c. de la corriente,** (mar.) current's flow; **c. de repaso,** refresher course; **c. por correspondencia,** correspondence course.
cursómetro, *m.* (ry.) speedometer.
cursor, *m.* 1. courier. 2. (mec.) slide (to cover an aperture). — **c. de procesiones,** (ecc.) marshal of religious processions; **c. portaherramienta,** toolslide; **c. transversal,** cross slide.
cursoripedo, da, *a.* (ornith.) cursorial.
curtación, *f.* (astron.) curtation.
curtido, da, *past part. of* **curtir.** *a.* 1. tanned, curried (leather). 2. experienced accustomed. 3. weatherbeaten, sunburned, roughened. *—m.* 1. bark (of trees). 2. (*pl.*) tanned leather. — **c. al cromo,** chrome-tanned.
curtidor, ra, *m., f.* tanner (worker).
curtidura, *f.* tanning, currying (of leather).
curtiduría, *f.* tannery.
curtiembre, *f.* tanning; (Amer.) tannery
curtiente, *a.* curing, tanning (substance). *—m.* tanning agent.
curtimiento, *m.* tanning, curing.
curtir, *tr.v.* 1. to tan (hides; the skin). 2. to harden, toughen, inure (to hardships). *—r.v.* 1. to become sun-tanned, weather-beaten. 2. to become hardened or toughened.
curto, corto, ta, *a.* dock-tailed.
curtosis, *f.* (statistics) kurtosis.
curú, (*pl.* **curúes**) *m.* (Peru) moth larva.
curubo, *m.* (Col., bot.) passion flower.
curuca, *f.* (ornith.) barn owl.
curucú, *m.* 1. (ornith.) quetzal (Pharomacrus mosinmo). 2. (med.) disease caused by the bite of certain S. Amer. snakes.
curuguá, *m.* (Arg., bot.) mucuna (Mucuna odorifera).
curuja, *f.* (ornith.) barn owl.
curul, *a.* curule, aedile, an official in charge of public works (in ancient Rome); the chair he occupied.
curunda, *f.* (Ecuad.) stripped corn cob.
curupay, *m.* (Arg., bot.) curupay, angico (Piptademia macrocarpa).
caruro, *m.* (Chile, zool.) cururo, species of field mice. *—a.* (Chile) dark, dark-skinned.
curva, *f.* 1. curve, curvature; bend. 2. (mar.) knee. — **c. acampanada,** bell-shaped curve; **c. cerrada,** sharp curve; **c. de bao,** (mar.) beam knee; **c. de enlace,** (ry.) connecting curve; **c. de frecuencias acumuladas,** (statistics) frequency curve; **c. de nivel,** (top.) contour line; **c. inversa,** (ry.) reverse curve; **c. isóbata, (top.) depth contour; c. isócora,** (phys.) isochor, isochore; **c. sedástica, (statistics) sedastic curve; c. sinusoidal,** (math.) sine curve; **c. suave,** easy curve.
curvación, *f.* curvature; bend.
curvar, *tr.v., r.v.* to curve, bend.
curvatura, *f.* curvature; bend, bending.
curvear, *i.v.* to curve.
curvidad, *f., var. of* **curvatura.**
curvidad. *f., var. of* curvatura.
curvilíneo, a, *a.* 1. (geom.) curvilinear. 2. curvaceous, shapely (said of a woman).
curvo, va, *a.* curved, crooked, bent. *—m.* (reg., Sp.) fenced pasture ground.
cusca, *f.* (Mex.) prostitute.
cuscungo, *m.* (Ecuad., ornith.) horned owl.
cuscurro, *m.* crust of bread.
cuscuta, *f.* (bot.) dodder.
cusir, *tr.v., var. of* **corcusir,** (coll.) to sew clumsily, sew shoddily.
cusita, *a., m., f.* (linguistics) Cushitic, Cushite.
cusma, *f.* (Peru, Ecuad.) *var. of* **cuzma.**
cuspa, *f.* (Ven., bot.) cusparia bark tree (Cusparia trifoliata).
cuspe, *m.* (Chile, Col.) spinning top.
cuspi, *m.* 1. (Col.) spinning top. 2. (Col.) short noisy person.
cuspidado, da, *a.* (bot.) cuspate, cuspated, cusped, cuspidate, cuspidated.
cúspide, *f.* 1. peak, summit (of mountain). 2. (geom.) apex (of angle).
cuspídeo, a, *a.* (bot.) cuspate, cuspated, cusped, cuspidate, cuspidated.
custodia, *f.* 1. custody; care; guard (guarding a prisoner), safe-keeping. 2. (ecc.) monstrance; tabernacle (receptacle for holding the Holy Eucharist).
custodiar, *tr.v.* to guard, watch, take care of.
custodio, *a.* guardian; **ángel c.,** guardian angel. *—m.* guardian, custodian.
cusubé, *m.* (Cuba) sweet made of yucca starch, sugar, water and sometimes eggs, rolled into a small ball; (coll.) a term of endearment for a small child or a petite girl.
cusumbe, *m.* (Ecuad., zoll.) coati.
cusumbo, *m.* (Col., zool.) coati.
cususa, *f.* (C. Amer.) crude, uncured rum.
cutacha, *f.* (Hond.) long straight knife.
cutama, *f.* 1. (Chile) dullard, oaf, dimwit. 2. (Chile) bag or sack full of odds and ends.
cutáneo, a, *a.* cutaneous, pertaining to the skin.
cutara, *f.* (Cuba, Mex., C. Rica) cheap, simple bedroom slipper or shoe worn by country people.
cutarra, *f.* (Hond.) *var. of* **cutara.**
cúter, *m.* (mar.) cutter.
cutete, *m.* (Guat., zool.) lizard (Lacerta basilicum).
cutí, *m.* (tex.) ticking (for pillowcases, etc.).
cutícula, *f.* (anat.) cuticle, epidermis; pellicle, thin skin.
cuticular, *a.* cuticular.
cutina, *f.* (biochem.) cutin.
cutio, *m.* (obs.) manual labor.
cutir, *tr.v.* to knock, strike (against something).
cutirreacción, *f.* (med.) skin test.
cutis, *m.* skin, cutis, complexion.
cuto, ta, *a.* (C. Amer.) maimed, missing a limb (person).
cutral, *a.* old, worn out (ox or cow), destined for the slaughterhouse.
cutre, *a.* (coll.) stingy, mean. *—m.* miser, mean person.
cutusa, *f.* (ornith., Col.) variety of turtledove (Chaemepelia rufipennis).
cuy, *m.* (Amer., zool.) guinea pig (Cavia porcellus).
cuyabra, *f.* (Col.) gourd (vessel.)
cuyo, ya, *rel. pron.* whose; of which; of whom, e.g. *este es el paciente de cuyo caso te hablé,* this is the patient of whose case I spoke to you.
cuyují, *m.* (Cuba) a very hard and crumbly type of flint stone.
cuzco, *m.* small yapping dog.
cuzcuz (*pl.* **cuzcuces**) *m., var. of* **alcuzcuz.**
cuzma, *f.* (Ecuad., Peru) sleeveless wool shirt worn by the Indians.
CV *abbrev. of* **caballo de vapor,** horsepower (hp).
C y F *abbrev. of* **costo y flete,** cost and freight (CAF, C and F, CF).
C y S *abbrev. of* **costo y seguro,** cost and insurance (CI).
czar, *m.* Czar, Russian emperor.
czarevitz, *m.* Czarevitch, eldest son of a Czar.
czariano, na, *a.* czarist, pertaining to czarism or the Czar.
czarina, *f.* Czarina, wife of the Czar or Empress of Russia.

D

D, *f.* d, fourth letter of the Spanish alphabet.
D. *abbrev. of* 1. **Don,** Mister (Mr., Esq.). 2. **debe,** debit.
Da. *abbrev. of* **Doña,** Mistress, Miss (Mrs., Miss).
dable, *a.* possible, feasible.
daca, (coll.) give me, hand over; **andar en toma y d.,** (coll.) to argue, quarrel, discuss; **toma y d.,** give-and-take.
da capo, (mus.) da capo, from the beginning.
dacha, *f.* dacha (*Russian country home*)
dacio, cia, *a., m., f.* Dacian. —*f.* **D.,** Dacia, ancient kingdom in Europe. —*m.* tribute, tax.
dación, *f.* (law) giving, handing over.
dacrón, *m.* (tex.) Dacron, a synthetic, wrinkle-resistant fiber (trademark).
dactilado, da, *a.* finger-shaped.
dactilar, *a.* digital, pertaining to the fingers. —**cartera d.,** (Amer.) driver's license.
dactílico, ca, *a.* (poet.) dactylic.
dactiliología, *f.* (archeol.) dactyliology, study of finger-rings and their precious stones.
dactilión, *m.* (mus.) dactylion, device for developing dexterity in piano players.
dáctilo, *m.* (poet.) dactyl.
dactilografía, *f.* typewriting.
dactilográfico, ca, *a.* pertaining to typewriting.
dactilógrafo, fa, *m., f.* typist. —*f.* typewriter.
dactilolalia, *f.* dactylology, talking with fingers (as done by deafmutes).
dactilología, *f.* dactylology, finger language.
dactiloscopia, *f.* dactyloscopy, study of finger-prints.
dactiloscópico, ca, *a.* dactyloscopic, pertaining to finger-prints.
dadaísmo, *m.* Dadaism, a movement from 1916 to 1922 in painting, sculpture and literature.
dadaísta, *m., f.* Dadaist, follower of Dada (in art, literature).
dádiva, *f.* present, gift; grant, contribution.
dadivado, da, *past part. of* **dadivar.** —*a.* (rare) bribed, bought.
dadivar, *tr.v.* to give a present to, endow, make a gift to.
dadivosamente, *adv.* bountifully, generously, liberally.
dadivosidad, *f.* bountifulness, generosity, liberality.
dadivoso, sa, *a.* bountiful, generous, liberal.
dado, *m.* 1. die, (*pl.*) dice. 2. (archit.) pedestal, dado (of column). 3. (mec.) block (supporting axle, etc.). 4. (mil.) case-shot, grape-shot. 5. (mar.) stud, iron brace across link of chain (as reinforcement). — **cargar los dados,** to load the dice; **según salga el d.,** (coll.) better wait and see how things turn out; **correr el d.,** (coll.) to be in luck; **d. deflector,** (hydr.) baffle piers or blocks; **dados cargados,** loaded dice; **dar** o **echar el d.,** (coll.) to trick, play one false.
dado, da, *past part. of* **dar.** — **d. que,** as long as, provided that, given that; **dado a lo,** according to, judging by.
dador, ra, *a.* giving. —*m., f.* giver; bearer (of a letter, a gift, a message); (com.) drawer (of a bill of exchange).
Dafne, *f.* 1. (myth.) Daphne, nymph who escaped from Apollo by becoming a laurel tree. **2. d.,** a variety of small shrubs and their fragrant blossoms.
Dafnis, *f.* (myth.) Daphnis; **D. y Cloe,** Daphnis and Chloe, lovers in a Greek pastoral romance.
daga, *f.* 1. line of bricks (in a kiln). 2. dagger, poniard. — **llegar a las dagas,** to reach a critical or crucial point.
dagame, *m.* (Cuba, bot.) dagame (Calycophyllus candisissimus).
dagón, *m. aug. of* **daga,** large dagger.
daguerrotipar, *tr.v.* (photog.) to daguerreotype, to make photographs by an early method using a plate of chemically treated metal or glass.
daguerrotipia, *f.* (photog.) daguerreotyping, daguerreotypy, an early method of photography.
daguerrotipo, *m.* daguerreotype.
dahír, *m.* (in Morocco) carte blanche of Sultan; caliph's decree published by high commissioner.
Dahomey, *m.* Dahomey, country in West Africa.
dahomeyano, na, *a., m., f.* Dahoman, pertaining to or from Dahomey.
daifa, *f.* concubine, mistress.
daimio, *m.* daimio (Japanese feudal lord).
dajao, *m.* (Cuba, ichth.) fresh water mullet (Agonostomus monticola).
dala, *f.* (mar.) pump dale.
dalaga, *f.* (Phil. I.) maid, maiden, virgin.
¡dale! *interj.* expressing displeasure at someone's obstinacy.
dalia, *f.* (bot.) dahlia.
Dalila, *f.* (Bib.) Delilah, Samson's mistress who betrayed him.
dalla, *f., var. of* **dalle.**
dallador, *m.* mower, scytheman, person who reaps with a scythe.
dalle, *m.* scythe.
dálmata, *a., m., f.* 1. Dalmatian, from or pertaining to Dalmatia, a region in Yugoslavia. 2. Dalmatian, a breed of dog with spotted pelt, formerly called coach dog or firehouse dog.
dálmatica, *f.* dalmatic, vestment worn by the Romans, still used by priests in some ceremonies.
dalmático, ca, *a., m., f.* 1. Dalmatian. —*m.* Dalmatian (language).
daltoniano, na, *a.* Daltonian, color blind. —*m., f.* person suffering from color blindness.
daltonismo, *m.* (med.) Daltonism, color blindness.
dama, *f.* 1. dame, lady, mistress, lady-in-waiting; lady's maid; leading lady (in a play); concubine, mistress. 2. king (at draughts or checkers), queen (at chess). 3. ancient Spanish dance. 4. mound of earth left in excavation. 5. (*pl.*) checkers, draughts. — **d. cortesana,** courtesan; **d. de compañía,** lady-in-waiting; **d. de honor,** maid of honor, matron of honor; bridesmaid; **d. de noche,** (bot.) morning glory (Ipomoea alba); **d. joven,** (theat.) juvenile lead, ingénue; **d. secreta,** advantage given to one player in draughts, which allows him to take one of his opponent's pieces when he wishes to; **ser una d.,** to be a lady; **ser (una mujer) muy d.,** to be ladylike; **soplar uno la d. a otro,** to huff, take the opponent's figure (in game of draughts); to steal someone's girl.
dama, *f.* 1. (metal.) dam (of blast furnace). 2. (zool.) fallow deer.
damaceno, na, *a., m., f.* native or inhabitant of the city of Damascus (capital of Syria); pertaining to the city of Damascus.
damajuana, *f.* demijohn, a large earthenware or glass bottle, gen. with a narrow neck and wicker casing.
damascado, da, *a.* damask-like, ornamented, printed or engraved in arabesque design.
damasceno, na, *a., m., f.* 1. Damascene, of or pertaining to Damascus. 2. damson, plum.
damasco, *m.* 1. (tex.) damask. 2. (bot.) damson plum; damson (fruit).
Damasco, *m.* Damascus, capital of Syria.
damasina, *f.* (tex.) damassin, light damask.
damasquillo, *m.* (tex.) damassin, light damask.
damasquina, *f.* (bot.) French marigold (Tagetes patula).
damasquinado, da, *past part. of* **damasquinar.** —*a.* damascened, damascene. —*m.* damascene, damascene work (tooling or inlay on metal, leather).
damasquinar, *tr.v.* to damascene (to tool or engrave arabesque design on leather or metal).
damasquino, na, *a.* Damascene (referring to Damascus and its people).
damería, *f.* finickiness, prudishness, excessive delicacy.
damisela, *f.* young lady; debutante.
damnación, *f.* damnation, condemnation.
damnificado, da, *past part. of* **damnificar.** —*a.* damaged, injured. —*m., f.* victim of an accident or disaster.
damnificador, ra, *a.* producing damage, injury or distress.
damnificar, (*ref. 50) tr.v.* to damage, hurt, injure.
damnifique, damnifiqué, *ref.* **damnificar.**
Damocles, *m.* (myth.) Damocles, a courtier of ancient Syracuse who was seated under a sword hanging by a single hair to give him a lesson in the perils of a ruler's life; **espada de D.,** sword of Damocles, any imminent danger.
Dánae, *f.* (myth.) Danae, mother of Perseus.
Danaides, *f.* (*pl.*) (myth.) Danaides, Danaidae, the fifty daughters of Danaus, king of Argos.
dance, dancé, *ref.* **danzar.**
danchado, da, *a.* (her.) dentate, indented.
dáncing, *m.* (Amer.) dance hall.
dandi, *m.* dandy, fop.
dandismo, *m.* dandyism, foppishness.
danés, sa, *a.* Danish. —*m., f.* Dane. —*m.* Danish (language); **gran d.,** (zool.) Great Dane.
dango, *m.* (ornith.) gannet (gooselike, webfooted sea bird).
dánico, ca, *a.* Danish, of or pertaining to Denmark.
danta, *f.* (zool.) tapir.
dante, *m.* (zool.) tapir, elk, antelope. —*m., f.* giver. —*a.* giving. — **D.,** Dante Alighieri, medieval Italian poet, author of *The Divine Comedy.*
dantellado, da, *a.* dentated, serrated.

DEF

dantesco, ca, *a.* Dantesque, pertaining to the poet Dante or to his outstanding work, *The Divine Comedy;* by extension, anything terrifying or recalling hell.
dantista, *m.* Dantean, expert on the works of Dante.
danto, *m.* (C. Amer., ornith.) umbrella bird (Cephalopterus glabricolis).
danubiano, na, *a.* Danubian, pertaining to the river Danube.
Danubio, *m.* Danube, a river flowing from Germany eastward into the Black Sea.
danza, *f.* 1. dance; dancing; habanera (Cuban dance). 2. (coll.) shady or dubious business, enterprise, project or affair. 3. quarrel, dispute. — **andar** or **estar en la d.,** to be involved or mixed up in some affair; **d. de arcos,** arcade; **d. de cintas,** Maypole dance; **d. de espadas,** sword dance; quarrel, dispute; **d. del vientre,** belly dance. **d. prima,** ancient Spanish dance; **baja d.,** allemande, low German dance; **meterle a uno en la d.,** to involve someone in an affair.
danzador, ra, *a.* dancing. —*m., f.* dancer.
danzante, *m., f.* 1. dancer. 2. (coll.) hustler, sharp operator (in business). 3. (coll.) fidgety person, jack-in-the-box, busy-body, meddler.
danzar, (*ref. 53*) *tr.v.* to dance. —*i.v.* 1. to dance; move quickly. 2. (coll.) to meddle, interfere.
danzarín, na, *m., f.* 1. dancer. 2. (coll.) meddler, busybody.
danzón, *m.* a popular Cuban dance derived from the habanera.
dañable, *a.,* harmful, damaging, hurtful; reprehensible.
dañado, da, *past part. of* **dañar.** —*a.* 1. bad, perverse, vicious, corrupt. 2. damaged; spoiled (fruit or vegetables). 3. (Can. I.) leprous. —*m., f.* reprobate, vicious person.
dañador, ra, *a.* harmful, damaging, injurious. —*m., f.* damager, spoiler.
dañar, *tr.v.* to damage; to injure, harm, hurt; to spoil. —*r.v.* to become damaged or injured; to spoil.
dañino, na, *a.* harmful, damaging, injurious; destructive.
daño, *m.* 1. damage; harm, injury. 2. (com.) discount. — **d. emergente,** (law) detriment, damage; **daños punitivos,** (law) vindictive damages; **daños y perjuicios,** damages; **hacerse d.,** to hurt oneself; **sin d. de barras,** without danger for anyone.
dañosamente, *adv.* harmfully, injuriously.
dañoso, sa, *a.* harmful, injurious, damaging.
dar, (*ref. 6*) *tr.v.* 1. to give; to produce, bear (fruit, etc.). 2. to deal (cards). 3. to convey, communicate, send (condolences). 4. to deliver, give (blows). 5. (a clock) to strike (the hour). 6. to mean, signify, e.g. *a mí me da lo mismo,* it's all the same to me. 7. (fig.) to tell, presage, e.g. *me da el corazón que,* my heart tells me that. — **ahí me las den todas,** (coll.) I don't give a darn; **d. barreno,** (mar.) to scuttle (a ship); **d. brincos** or **saltos,** to jump up and down; **d. contramarcha,** to reverse gear; **d. fondo,** to anchor; **d. gusto,** to please, make happy; **d. la mano,** to shake hands; **d. por,** to declare, e.g. *el juez le dio por inocente,* the judge declared him innocent; to consider, regard, e.g. *d. por hecha una cosa,* to consider something accomplished; **d. por hecho que,** to take for granted that; **d. (algo) por bien empleado,** to consider something worth the trouble; **d. por concluso,** (law) to consider or declare a case closed; **d. por muerto,** to consider dead; to think (one) dead; **d. prestado,** to lend; **d. que hablar,** to give grounds for criticism; **d. que hacer,** to cause (someone) trouble; **d. que pensar,** to give grounds for suspicion; to make (one) think; **d. que sentir,** to hurt (someone's) feelings; **dársela a uno,** (coll.) to make a fool of someone, trick or hoax someone; **d. un abrazo,** to embrace; **d. un bofetón,** to slap, hit; **d. y tomar,** to discuss, e.g. *en esto hay mucho que d. y tomar,* there is much to discuss about this matter; (equit.) to tighten and loosen the reins; **donde las dan, las toman,** if one sows evil, one will reap it; **han dado las cinco,** it's five o'clock. —*i.v.* 1. to strike (a clock). 2. to catch, get, e.g. *le dio un resfrío,* he caught cold; to have, e.g. *le dio un ataque de corazón,* he had a heart attack; to get into, e.g. *le dio un ataque de furia,* he got into a fury. 3. to arise, occur, e.g. *si da el caso,* if the circumstance should arise. — **¡dale!** get away with you; come along, hurry up; keep it up, you're on the right track; **d. a,** to face, give on to, e.g. *mi ventana da a la plaza,* my window faces the square; **d. con,** to find; to meet; **d. consigo en,** to go, e.g. *di conmigo en París,* I went to Paris; to fall, e.g. *di conmigo en el suelo,* I fell on the ground; to make or cause to fall, knock down, e.g. *di con él en la tierra,* I made him fall or knocked him to the ground; **d. de,** to paint, coat, e.g. *d. de barniz,* to varnish; **d. de beber,** to give (someone) something to drink; **d. de bofetones,** to slap, hit; **d. de comer,** to feed, give (someone) something to eat; **d. de espaldas,** to fall on one's back; **d. de palos,** to administer a thrashing; **d. de sí,** to stretch, give; **d. en,** to hit or strike on, e.g. *darle a uno en la cabeza,* to hit someone on the head; to hit, e.g. *él dio en el blanco,* he hit the target; to get, e.g. *dio en el chiste,* he got the joke; **d. en duro,** to meet resistance; **d. en vacío** or **vago,** to be unsuccessful, fail (in doing something); **d. sobre uno,** to attack someone; **d. tras uno,** to pursue or chase someone; **de donde diere,** at random, without reflection. —*r.v.* 1. to give of oneself. 2. to surrender; to give in. 3. to grow, be fruitful, e.g. *las patatas se dan bien aquí,* potatoes grow well here. 4. to stop, fall (game being hunted). — **darse a,** to devote oneself to (study, etc.); give oneself up to (drinking, vice, etc.); **darse a buenas,** to yield, give in; **darse a conocer,** to get a name for oneself; to reveal one's character; **darse a entender,** to make oneself understood; **darse contra,** to hit oneself against; **dárselas de,** to pose as; to boast or brag of being; **dársele a uno algo, mucho** or **poco,** to care a lot, very much or little about something; **darse por,** to consider or think oneself; **darse por aludido,** to take it personally; **darse por ofendido,** to take offense, feel offended; **darse por vencido,** to surrender, give up; **no dársele a uno nada,** (coll.) not to matter to one at all.
dardabasí, *m.* (ornith.) hawk, kite.
Dardanelos, *m.* (*pl.*) Dardanelles, strait joining the Sea of Marmara and the Aegean Sea.
dardanio, nia, *a.* (hist.) Dardanian, Dardan, Trojan.
dárdano, na, *a., m., f.* (hist.) Dardan, Dardanian, Trojan.
dardo, *m.* 1. dart, arrow. 2. (fig.) satirical remark, cutting remark. 3. (ichth.) dace, bleak.
dares y tomares, (coll.) give and take; quarrels, discussions, disputes, arguments; **andar en d. y t.,** to argue, discuss, quarrel.
Darío, *m.* (hist.) Darius, king of Persia, defeated by the Greeks at Marathon.
dársena, *f.* dock, inner harbor.
darviniano, na, *a.* Darwinian, pertaining to Darwin's theory of evolution.
darvinismo, *m.* Darwinism, Darwin's theory of evolution which holds that all species of life develop from earlier forms.
darvinista, *a., m., f.* Darwinist, pertaining to the theories of Darwin; follower of Darwin's theories.
dasocracia, *f.* forestry, the science of forestry.
dasocrático, ca, *a.* of or pertaining to forestry.
dasonomía, *f.* forestry, the science of forestry.
dasonómico, ca, *a.* pertaining to forestry.
data, *f.* 1. date. 2. (com.) data, items (of an account). 3. outlet (of reservoir). — **de larga d.,** of long ago, very ancient.
datar, *tr.v.* 1. to date. 2. (com.) to credit. 3. to check, to collect information on. —*i.v.* to date; **d. de,** to date from. —*r.v.* (com.) to be entered in the account.
dataría, *f.* (ecc.) datary, curial office.
datario, *m.* (ecc.) datary, curial officer.
dátil, *m.* 1. (bot.) date (fruit). 2. (zool.) date mussel, piddock. 3. (*pl.*) (coll.) fingers. — **d. de mar,** (zool.) date mussel, piddock.
datilado, da, *a.* date-colored; datelike, date-shaped.
datilera, ro, *a.* pertaining to dates (fruit). —*f.* (bot.) date palm.
datismo, *m.* (rhet.) excessive metonymy, excessive use of synonyms.
dativo, va, *a., m.* (gram.) dative.
dato, *m.* 1. fact, datum, piece of information, (*pl.*) data, information, facts. 2. document.
dato, *m.* high rank title among certain Moslem people.
datura, *f.* (bot.) datura.
daturina, *f.* (pharm.) alkaloid extracted from the thorn apple.
dauco, *m.* (bot.) bishop's weed; (bot.) wild carrot.
davalar, *i.v.* (mar.) to drift.
davídico, ca, *a.* Davidic, pertaining to King David, his poetry or psalms.
davina, *f.* miner's safety lamp.
dayak, *m., f.* 1. Dayak, Dyak, a member of an aboriginal tribe of Borneo. 2. the Indonesian language of this people.
daza, *f.* (bot.) sorghum; panic grass.
de, *prep.* 1. (indicating possession) of, 's, s', e.g. *la casa de mi padre,* my father's house, *la paciencia de Job,* the patience of Job. 2. (indicating manner) on, e.g. *de pie,* on one's feet, standing; in, e.g. *vestirse de prestado,* to dress in borrowed clothes, *de una manera muy desagradable,* in a very unpleasant way. 3. (indicating direction or origin) from, e.g. *vengo de Málaga,* I come from Malaga. 4. (indicating composition) of, made of, e.g. *vestido de seda,* silk dress. 5. (indicating contents) of, e.g. *vaso de agua,* glass of water. 6. of (indicating quality), e.g. *hombre de valor,* man of courage. 7. in, with (wearing), e.g. *el hombre del traje azul,* the man in the blue suit. 8. about, on, e.g. *¿habla Ud. de mis asuntos?* are you talking about my affairs?; *libro de cocina,* cook book. 9. for, to (with infinitives), e.g. *es hora de actuar,* it is time to act. 10. as, e.g. *ella trabaja de cocinera,* she works as a cook. 11. (indicating time) at, in, by, e.g. *de noche,* at night, *de día,* by day. 12. than (when used with numerals), e.g. *tiene más de cincuenta años,* he's older than fifty. 13. (used to strengthen adjectives), e.g. *el bueno de Pedro,* that good Peter, good old Peter. 14. (used to express pity or sorrow), e.g. *ay de mí,* woe is me, wretched me. 15. (for expressing purpose), e.g. *hoja de afeitar,* razor blade. 16. (expressing cause) through, out of, because; for, e.g. *lo hizo de miedo,* he did it out of fear. — **de ... en,** from ... to, by, after, in

serial order, e.g. *de casa en casa,* from house to house, *de uno en uno,* one by one.
dea, *f.* (poet.) goddess.
deambular, *i.v.* to wander aimlessly, roam about; to stroll.
deambulatorio, *m.* (archit.) ambulatory, apse aisle (in a church).
deán, *m.* (ecc.) dean.
deanato, *m.* deanship, deanery.
deanazgo, *m., var. of* **deanato.**
debacle, *m.* (fr.) catastrophe, disaster, debacle.
debajero, *m.* (Ecuad.) underskirt worn by the Indians.
debajo, *adv.* underneath, below; **d. de,** under, underneath, below.
debate, *m.* debate; dispute, controversy, fight.
debatir, *tr.v.* to debate, argue, discuss; to fight, struggle.
debe, *m.* (com.) debit.
debelación, *f.* conquest, victory in war.
debelador, ra, *a.* conquering, victorious. —*m., f.* conqueror, victor.
debelar, *tr.v.* to conquer, subdue; to defeat the adversary.
deber, *m.* 1. duty, chores, daily drudge; obligation. 2. debt. 3. exercise, piece of school work or homework.
deber, *tr.v.* to owe; **no d. nada (una cosa) a otra,** (coll.) to be equal (two things). —*aux. v.* **d. +** *inf.* to have to, must, ought, should (expressing obligation or moral duty), e.g. *un buen hijo debe obedecer a sus padres,* a good son ought to obey his parents; **d. de +** *inf.,* must (expressing conjecture), e.g. *debe de hacer frío afuera,* it must be cold outside.
debidamente, *adv.* duly, properly, well done, as it should be.
debido, da, *past part. of* **deber.** —*a.* due, proper; **como es debido,** (coll.) as it should be; **d. a,** due to, because of.
débil, *a.* weak, feeble; vulnerable, e.g. *la carne es d.,* the flesh is weak (vulnerable, corruptible).
debilidad, *f.* weakness, debility; weakness, liking, inclination (towards someone or something), vulnerability, e.g. *el dulce es mi d.,* sweets are my undoing.
debilitación, *f.* debilitation, weakening; weakness.
debilitadamente, *adv.* weakly, feebly.
debilitante, *a.* weakening, debilitating.
debilitar, *tr.v.* to weaken, debilitate, enervate. —*r.v.* to become weak or feeble.
débilmente, *adv.* weakly, feebly.
débito, *m.* (com.) debit.
debó, *m.* scraper (for dressing skins).
debocar, (*ref. 50*) *i.v.* (Arg.) to vomit.
deboque, deboqué, *ref.* **debocar.**
debut, *m.* (fr.) 1. debut; initiation. 2. (theat.) first performance, opening.
debutante *a.* **una tenista d.,** a newcomer to tennis. —*m., f.* 1. newcomer, performer or player making his or her first public appearance. 2. debutante; **baile de debutantes,** coming-out party.
debutar, *i.v.* to make one's debut; (theat.) to open (a play, a season).
decaamperio, *m.* (elec.) deca-ampere.
década, *f.* decade; group of ten days or years; ten volumes.
decadencia, *f.* decadence, decline; **d. del imperio romano,** the decline of the Roman Empire; **estar en d.,** to be on the decline.
decadente, *a.* decadent.
decadentismo, *m.* decadence, decadentism, literary movement of the decadents.
decadentista, *a., m., f.* (lit.) decadentist, member of a late 19th century literary movement tending towards the artificial and abnormal.
decaedro, *m.* (geom.) decahedron.
decaer, (*ref. 5*) *i.v.* 1. to decay; to weaken, sink, fail, fade, decline. 2. (mar.) to drift off course.
decagonal, *a.* (geom.) decagonal.
decágono, na, *a.* (geom.) decagonal, having ten angles. —*m.* (geom.) decagon.
decagramo, *m.* decagram (weight measure), ten grams.
decaído, da, *past part. of* **decaer.** —*a.* weak, languid, run-down; depressed, discouraged.
decaiga, decaigo, *ref.* **decaer.**
decaimiento, *m.* decadence, decline; weakness; languor; discouragement.
decalaje, *m.* (aer.) stagger.
decalcificación, *f., var. of* **descalcificación,** (med.) decalcification.
decalescencia, *f.* (phys.) decalescence.
decalitro, *m.* decaliter (liquid measure amounting to ten liters).
decálogo, *m.* (rel.) Decalogue, The Ten Commandments.
decalvación, *f.* (obs.) the action of shaving.
decalvar, *tr.v.* (obs.) to shave.
decámero, ra, *a.* (bot.) decamerous.
decámetro, *m.* decameter, a measure of length equal to ten meters.
decampar, *i.v.* to decamp, strike or break camp.
decanato, *m.* deanship (post of university dean); deanery (post and residence of university dean); (ecc.) deanery.
decania, *f.* property or church belonging to a monastery.
decano, *m.* 1. dean (of a university, etc.); (fig.) doyen, dean, senior member of a group. 2. senior, oldest member of an organization or a body, e.g. *d. del cuerpo diplomático,* the dean of the diplomatic corps.
decantación, *f.* decanting, decantation, pouring off.
decantador, *m.* settling tank, catch basin, silt basin.
decantar, *tr.v.* 1. to exaggerate, aggrandize, praise. 2. to decant, to pour off.
decapante, *a.* pickling, stripping, rust-removing. —*m.* pickle, stripper, rust-removing agent.
decapar, *tr.v.* to pickle, strip, remove rust from.
decapitación, *f.* decapitation, beheading.
decapitar, *tr.v.* to decapitate, behead.
decápodo, *a.* (zool.) decapod. —*m.* (zool.) decapod; (*pl.*) Decapoda.
decarbonatador, *m.* (mec.) decarbonator.
decarbonatar, *tr.v.* (mec.) to decarbonate.
decarbonizar, *tr.v.* (mec.) to decarbonize.
decarburación, *f.* (mec.) decarburation, decarbonization.
decárea, *f.* decare, a unit of surface measure equal to ten ares (.2471 acre).
decasílabo, ba, *a.* decasyllabic, ten-syllable. —*m.* decasyllable.
decastéreo, *m.* decastere, a measure of volume equal to ten cubic meters.
decayendo, decayera, decayese, decayó, *ref.* decaer.
deceleración, *f.* 1. deceleration, slowing down, retardation. 2. (phys.) negative acceleration.
decemnovenal, *a.* lasting nineteen years; (astron.) lunar, Metonic (cycle).
decemnovenario, ria, *a., var. of* **decemnovenal.**
decena, *f.* ten (group of ten); (mus.) tenth.
decenal, *a.* 1. decennial, lasting ten years. 2. something that occurs every ten years.
decenar, *m.* squad or crew of ten.
decenario, ria, *a.* pertaining to ten, decennial. —*m.* 1. decade, decennium. 2. rosary with ten beads.
decencia, *f.* decency, honesty; cleanliness, tidiness; dignity, propriety.
decenio, *m.* decade, decennium, ten-year period.
deceno, na, *a.* tenth.
decentar, (*ref. 29*) *tr.v.* 1. to cut off the first slice of, begin, start (cutting or using). 2. (fig.) to begin to deteriorate or decline (in health). —*r.v.* to get bedsores.
decente, *a.* decent, honest; respectable; honorable; clean, tidy.
decentemente, *adv.* decently; honorably; cleanly, tidily.
decenvir, *m., var. of* **decenviro.**
decenviral, *a.* (polit.) decemviral, pertaining to a decemvirate.
decenvirato, *m.* (polit.) 1. decemvirate, a body of ten magistrates. 2. the position or term of such a group.
decenviro, *m.* (polit.) 1. decemvir, a member of a council of ten magistrates in ancient Rome. 2. a member of any ruling group of ten.
decepción, *f.* 1. disappointment, disillusion, disenchantment. 2. deception, deceiving.
decepcionado, da, *a.* disillusioned, disappointed, disenchanted.
decepcionar, *tr.v.* to disappoint, disillusion, disenchant.
deceso, *m.* decease, death.
dechado, *m.* 1. pattern, sample; sampler (in embroidery). 2. (fig.) standard, example, model. — **d. de virtudes,** model of virtues.
deciamperio, *m.* (elec.) deciampere.
deciárea, *f.* deciare, a surface measure equal to one-tenth are (10 square meters or 11.96 square yards).
decibel, decibelio, *m.* (phys.) decibel.
decible, *a.* expressible, explicable, utterable, mentionable.
decidero, ra, *a.* proper, able to be told or said; mentionable, speakable.
decididamente, *adv.* decisively, resolutely; (imp. u.) definitely, certainly.
decidido, da, *past part. of* **decidir.** —*a.* determined, resolute, bold.
decidir, *tr.v.* to decide; to settle, resolve. —*i.v.* to decide, determine. —*r.v.* to decide; to make up one's mind; **decidirse a,** to decide to.
decidor, ra, *a.* witty, fluent (in talking). —*m., f.* fluent speaker, wit.
deciente, deciento, *ref.* **decentar.**
decigramo, *m.* decigram, a weight measure equal to one tenth of a gram.
decilitro, *m.* deciliter, a liquid measure equal to one-tenth liter.
décima, *f.* 1. tenth. 2. (mus.) Cuban country ballad. 3. Spanish stanza of ten octo-syllabic lines. 4. tenth of a degree (on a thermometer).
decimacuarta, *a.* fourteenth (in the *f.* form, e.g. *la d. niña,* the fourteenth girl).
decimal, *a.* decimal; pertaining to tithes or the 10% tax paid to the king. —*m.* decimal; **d. periódico,** (math.) circulating decimal.
decimalmente, *adv.* decimally.
decimanona, *a.* nineteenth (in the *f.* form).
decimanovena, *f.* (mus.) nineteenth, organ stop sounding pitches two octaves and a fifth above the keys used.
decímetro, *m.* decimeter.
décimo, ma, *a.* tenth. —*m.* 1. tenth. 2. tenth part of lottery ticket. 3. (Col., Mex., Ecuad.) ten-cent silver coin.
decimoctavo, va, *a.* eighteenth.
decimocuarto, ta, *a.* fourteenth.
decimonono, na, *a.* nineteenth.
decimonoveno, na, *a.* nineteenth.

decimoquinto, ta, *a.* fifteenth.
decimoséptimo, ma, *a.* seventeenth.
decimosexto, ta, *a.* sixteenth.
decimotercero, ra, *a.* thirteenth.
decimotercio, cia, *a.* thirteenth.
deciocheno, na, *a.* eighteenth.
decir, *m.* saying; **decires de la gente,** talk, gossip, rumors (unfavorable); **es un d.,** it is a mere saying.
decir, (*ref. 7*) *tr.v.* 1. to say; to tell. 2. to give, express (opinion, etc.). 3. to show, portray, express. — **como quien dice,** (coll.) as it were, so to speak; **como quien no dice nada,** (coll.) it's no light matter, it's no trifle; **como si dijéramos,** (coll.) so to speak; **d. a uno cuántas son cinco,** (coll.) to give someone a piece of one's mind; **d. (de) nones,** to deny; **d. a uno de una hasta ciento,** (coll.) to tell someone exactly what is what, speak one's mind freely; **d. uno entre** or **para sí,** to say to oneself; **d. lo que se le viene a la boca,** to say whatever comes into one's head; **d. y hacer** (fig.), to do very quickly; **dícese,** that is to say; **diga,** what can I do for you?; **¡digo!** attention, listen, stop; **digo yo,** says I (sl.); **dizque,** (coll.) it is said, they do say; **el qué dirán,** what people may say, public opinion; **¿lo he de d. cantado y rezado?** how many times shall I repeat it?; **mejor dicho,** to put it more exactly; in other words; **no d. uno malo ni bueno,** (coll.) to give no reply; **no d. ni pío,** (coll.) not to say a word; **no d. de sentir,** to keep silent; to acquiesce; **no digamos,** (coll.) not quite, but very nearly; **por mejor d.,** to put it more exactly; **que digamos,** (coll.) to speak of, e.g. *no llueve mucho que digamos,* it is not raining much; **según el d. general,** by all accounts. —*i.v.* **d. bien a,** to suit, go well on; **d. mal a,** not to suit, not to go well on; **¡no me digas!** you don't say!
decisión, *f.* 1. decision, ruling, resolution; verdict, judgment. 2. decision, resolution, resoluteness, determination. — **d. dividida,** split decision.
decisivamente, *adv.* decisively, resolutely.
decisivo, va, *a.* decisive, conclusive.
decisorio, *a.* (law) decisory, decisive.
decistéreo, *m.* decistere, one-tenth of a cubic meter.
declamación, *f.* declamation, harangue, oration, speech.
declamador, ra, *a.* declaiming. —*m., f.* declaimer, orator, reciter.
declamar, *tr.v., i.v.* to declaim, recite.
declamatorio, ria, *a.* declamatory, oratorical, bombastic.
declarable, *a.* declarable.
declaración, *f.* 1. declaration, statement; (law) deposition, statement; manifestation, deposition, affidavit. 2. call (in bridge). — **d. de aduana,** customs declaration; **d. de derechos,** bill of rights; **D. de la Independencia,** Declaration of Independence; **d. de la renta, d. del impuesto sobre la renta,** income tax return; **d. jurada,** affidavit, sworn statement; **d. de quiebra,** declaration of bankruptcy.
declaradamente, *adv.* manifestly, clearly, avowedly.
declarado, da, *past part. of* **declarar.** —*a.* (Amer.) ostensible; **enemigo (a) d.,** professed enemy.
declarador, ra, *a.* declaring. —*m., f.* declarer, deponent.
declarante, *a.* declaring. —*m., f.* (law) declarant (one who makes a deposition or statement), deponent, witness.
declarar, *tr.v.* to declare; to make known; (law) to pronounce, find, testify, decide. —*i.v.* to make a statement, depose. —*r.v.* 1. to declare oneself. 2. to show itself, make itself known (an illness). 3. to break out (a fire); to come up (wind). — **declararse a,** to unbosom oneself to, open one's heart to; **declararse a favor de,** to declare oneself in favor of; **declararse por,** to declare one's support for.
declarativo, va, *a.* declaratory, assertive.
declaratorio, ria, *a.* declaratory.
declinable, *a.* (gram.) declinable.
declinación, *f.* 1. decline, decay. 2. descent, decline. 3. (astron., top.) declination. 4. (gram.) declension; (gram.) inflection, declining (of noun, adjective, etc.). — **d. de la aguja, d. magnética,** magnetic declination, declination of magnetic needle or compass; **no saber uno las declinaciones,** (fig., coll.) to be ignorant.
declinante, *a.* declining; (top.) inclined.
declinar, *tr.v.* 1. (gram.) to decline, inflect. 2. to decline, refuse. —*i.v.* 1. to decay; to fail, get weak, decline (health, sight), to diminish or abate; to deteriorate. 2. to draw to an end (day); to go down (sun). 3. to fall from (virtue into vice). 4. to lean downwards or sideways.
declinatoria, *f.* (law) declinatory plea.
declinatorio, *m.* declination compass.
declinómetro, *m.* declinometer.
declive, *m.* slope, declivity, drop, fall; **en d.,** sloping, slanting downwards.
declividad, *f., var. of* **declive.**
declivio, *m., var. of* **declive.**
declorinación, *f.* (chem.) dechlorination.
decocción, *f.* 1. decoction. 2. (med.) amputation.
decohesión, *f.* (rad.) decohesion.
decohesor, *m.* (rad.) decoherer.
decoloración, *f.* discoloration, decoloration; bleaching; fading.
decolorante, *m.* decolorant. —*a.* decolorizing.
decolorar, *tr.v.* to decolorize, discolor, bleach. —*r.v.* to lose its color, fade.
decomisar, *tr.v.* to confiscate, seize.
decomiso, *m.* (law) seizure, confiscation; confiscated goods, seizure.
decoración, *f.* 1. decoration, ornaments; interior appointments; (theat.) scenery, decor, setting, props.; **d. de interiores,** interior decoration. 2. memorization, the act of learning by heart.
decorado, da, *past part. of* **decorar.** —*m.* 1. decoration, ornaments; (theat.) scenery, decor, setting. 2. memorization, learning by heart.
decorador, ra, *a.* decorating, ornamental. —*m., f.* decorator, interior or set designer.
decorar, *tr.v.* 1. to decorate, adorn, embellish. 2. to decorate, bestow honors on, honor. 3. to memorize, learn by heart, recite.
decorativo, va, *a.* decorative, ornamental; handsome-looking (said of a girl).
decoro, *m.* 1. decorum, propriety. 2. respect, deference. 3. purity, chastity. 4. honor, self-respect.
decorosamente, *adv.* decorously.
decoroso, sa, *a.* decorous, dignified; becoming, proper, seemly.
decrecer, (*ref. 45*) *i.v.* to decrease, diminish, dwindle, decline.
decreciente, *a.* diminishing, decreasing, declining.
decrecimiento, *m.* decrease, dwindling, diminution.
decremento, *m., var. of* **disminución,** decrease, dwindling.
decrepitación, *f.* decrepitation, crackling due to great heat.
decrepitante, *a.* 1. crackling. 2. (chem.) decrepitant.
decrepitar, *tr.v., i.v.* to decrepitate, to expose to a high heat; to decrepitate, to crackle.
decrépito, ta, *a.* decrepit, aged, in disrepair, worn down due to old age or long use (person or thing).
decrepitud, *f.* decrepitude; dotage, senility, old age.
decrescendo, *adv., m.* (mus.) decrescendo, diminuendo.
decretal, *a.* (ecc.) decretal, pertaining to papal decrees. —*f.* decretal (papal decree clarifying doubt on a particular question); (*pl.*) decretals (collection of these decrees).
decretalista, *m.* decretalist, one who interprets papal decrees.
decretar, *tr.v.* to decree; to resolve, decide; (law) to give judgment on.
decretero, *m.* 1. list of decrees. 2. (law) list of names of the accused.
decretista, *m.* (ecc.) decretist, expert on canon law.
decreto, *m.* decree; **d. condicional,** (law) decree nisi (in divorce case); **D. de Graciano,** Gratian Decree, book of canon law; d. ley, decree-law.
decretorio, *a.* (med.) critical; **día d.,** critical day (of an illness).
decrezca, decrezco, *ref.* **decrecer.**
decúbito, *m.* decubitus, reclining position; d. lateral, lateral decubitus; **d. supino,** dorsal decubitus.
decumbente, *a.* decumbent, lying down (due to sickness).
decuplar, *tr.v., var.* of **decuplicar.**
decuplicar, (*ref. 50*) *tr.v.* to decuple, make tenfold, multiply by ten.
decuplique, decupliqué, *ref.* **decuplicar.**
décuplo, pla, *a., m.* decuple, tenfold.
decuria, *f.* 1. decury (Roman History). 2. class of ten students.
decuriato, *m.* member of a class of ten students.
decurión, *m.* 1. decurion (Roman History). 2. monitor or student in charge of the rest of the class.
decurionato, *m.* decurionate; body of decurions.
decurrente, *a.* (bot.) decurrent, extending downward.
decursas, *f.* (*pl.*) (law) arrears of rents.
decurso, *m.* course, movement, lapse (of time).
decurvado, da, *a.* (bot.) decurved.
decusación, *f.* decussation, in intersection forming an X.
decusado, da, *a., var. of* **decuso.**
decuso, sa, *a.* (bot.) decussate, with pairs of opposite shoots at right angles to pair below, X-shaped.
dedada, *f.* thimbleful, pinch drop; **dar a uno una d. de miel,** (coll.) to keep one's hopes up.
dedal, *m.* thimble; thumb-stall or protecting pad used by workers.
dedalera, *f.* (bot.) digitalis, foxglove.
dédalo, *m.* 1. (fig.) labyrinth, entanglement, confusion. 2. **D.,** (myth.) Daedalus, builder of the Labyrinth in Crete, and of wings used by him and his son Icarus to escape from the Labyrinth.
dedeo, *m.* (mus.) dexterity, agility of fingers (in playing an instrument).
dedicaión, *f.* 1. dedication, consecration, devotion, perseverance. 2. dedicatory inscription.
dedicante, *a.* dedicating.
dedicar, (*ref. 50*) *tr.v.* 1. to dedicate, devote. 2. to address or inscribe (a literary work, etc.). —*r.v.* to devote or dedicate oneself (to).
dedicativo, va, *a.* dedicatory.
dedicatoria, *f.* dedicatory, inscription, dedication (passage dedicating a book to a person).
dedicatorio, ria, *a.* dedicatory.
dedición, *f.* unconditional surrender.
dedignar, *tr.v.* to disdain, despise.
dedil, *m.* fingerstall, thumbstall.

dedillo, *m.* small finger; **al d.,** (coll.) perfectly, thoroughly; **saber al d.,** to have (a subject) at one's fingertips, know (it) perfectly, to know by heart.
dedique, dediqué, *ref.* **dedicar.**
dedo, *m.* 1. finger; toe. 2. measurement of about 18 mm.; measurement of ten stitches (in knitting); finger, finger's breadth (portion measuring a finger). — **a dos dedos de,** within an ace of; **alzar uno el d.,** to raise an objection; **atar uno bien su d.,** to take due precautions in regard to one's own interests; **contar con los dedos,** to count on one's fingers; **chuparse uno los dedos,** to take relish or great enjoyment; **d. anular,** ring finger; **d. auricular** or **meñique,** little finger; **d. cordial, de en medio** or **del corazón,** middle finger; **d. gordo,** big toe, **d. pulgar,** thumb, **d. índice,** index finger; **d. médico,** ring finger; **el d. de Dios,** (fig.) God's hand; **mamarse** or **chuparse el d.,** to be stupid or foolish; **meterle a uno los dedos,** (coll.) to pump someone (for information); **morderse los dedos,** to bite one's fingers out of anger or frustration; **poner uno el d. en la llaga,** to put one's finger on the sore spot or source of the trouble; **poner (a uno) los cinco dedos en la cara,** to slap or hit in the face; **ponerse uno el d. en la boca,** to hold one's tongue, be quiet; **señalar a uno con el d.,** to accuse, to put the finger on (someone); **ser uno el d. malo,** to be the scapegoat or whipping boy; **tener dos dedos de frente,** to be sensible or intelligent.
dedolar, (*ref. 33*) *tr.v.* (surg.) to cut obliquely.
deducción, *f.* 1. deduction; conclusion, inference. 2. drawing or taking off (e.g. water). 3. (mus.) diatonic sequence or progression.
deducible, *a.* deductible; deducible; inferable.
deduciente, *a.* deducing, inferring.
deducir, (*ref. 47*) *tr.v.* 1. to deduce, infer, conclude. 2. to deduct, subtract. 3. (law) to allege.
deductivo, va, *a.* deductive.
deduele, deduelo, *ref.* **dedolar.**
deduje, dedujera, dedujese, *ref.* **deducir.**
deduzca, deduzco, *ref.* **deducir.**
defalcar, (*ref. 50*) *tr.v., var. of* **desfalcar.**
defalque, defalqué, *ref.* **defalcar.**
defasaje, *m.* (elec.) phase shift, dephasing.
defasar, *tr.v.* (elec.) to dephase.
defecación, *f.* defecation; purification; bowel movement.
defecar, (*ref. 50*) *tr.v.* to purify; to defecate. —*i.v.* to defecate.
defección, *f.* defection, desertion; apostasy.
defectibilidad, *f.* defectiveness.
defectible, *a.* imperfect; defective, faulty.
defectillo, *m. dim. of* **defecto,** slight fault or defect.
defectivo, va, *a.* defective, faulty; (gram.) defective. —*m.* (gram.) defective (verb).
defecto, *m.* 1. defect, fault, imperfection. 2. absence, lack. 3. (*pl.*) (print.) sheets left over or lacking in an edition. — **en d. de,** in the absence of.
defectuosamente, *adv.* defectively, deficiently, faultily.
defectuoso, sa, *a.* defective, imperfect, faulty.
defendedero, ra, *a.* defensible.
defendedor, ra, *a., var. of* **defensor.** —*m., f.* defender, protector.
defender, (*ref. 30*) *tr.v.* 1. to defend, protect; (law) to defend. 2. to stop, impede, delay. —*r.v.* to defend or protect oneself.
defendible, *a.* defensible.
defendido, da, *past part. of* **defender.** —*a.* defended. —*m., f.* defendant.
defenecer, *tr.v.* (com.) to close (an account).
defenecimiento, *m.* (com.) settlement.
defensa, *f.* 1. defense; protection; (law) defense. 2. (*pl.*) (mil.) defenses, fortifications. 3. (*pl.*) (mar.) fender, skids. 4. (sport) back (in football). 5. (auto., Amer.) bumper.— **d. pasiva,** (mil.) static defense; **d. propia, legítima d.,** (law) self-defense.
defensión, *f.* shelter, safeguard, defense.
defensiva, *f.* defensive, defensive position; **estar** or **ponerse a la defensiva,** to be or put oneself on the defensive.
defensivo, va, *a.* defensive, protective. —*m.* 1. defense, protection, safeguard. 2. (med.) wet compress.
defensor, ra, *a.* defending; defensive, protective. —*m., f.* defender, protector. —*m.* (law) counsel for the defense, defense counsel.
defensoría, *f.* (law) post of defense counsel.
defensorio, *m.* defense, plea; manifesto; written apology in defense or satisfaction of a person or thing.
defeque, defequé, *ref.* **defecar.**
deferencia, *f.* deference; courtesy.
deferente, *a.* 1. deferential; respectful, courteous, polite. 2. (anat.) deferent.
deferido, da, *past part. of* **deferir.** —*a.* (law) decisory or decisive (oath).
deferir, (*ref. 42*) *i.v.* to defer, yield. —*tr.v.* to delegate, give part of (power or jurisdiction to another body).
defervescencia, *f.* (med.) defervescence.
deficiencia, *f.* deficiency, lack; fault, defect.
deficiente, *a.* deficient, faulty, imperfect.
déficit, *m.* (com.) deficit, shortage.
defienda, defiendo, *ref.* **defender.**
defiera, defiero, *ref.* **deferir.**
definible, *a.* definable.
definición, *f.* 1. definition. 2. (opt.) definition. 3. (ecc.) decision, definition (solution of problems by a legitimate authority). 4. (*pl.*) rules, statutes (military orders).
definido, da, *past part. of* **definir.** —*a.* defined; (gram.) definite (article). —*m.* definition.
definidor, ra, *a.* defining. —*m., f.* definer. —*m.* definitor (in certain religious orders, a member of the governing council).
definir, *tr.v.* 1. to define (words). 2. to decide, determine, resolve (problems). 3. (p.) to complete, finish (a work in all its details).
definitivamente, *adv.* definitively, decisively.
definitivo, va, *a.* definitive, final; **en definitiva,** then, so, finally, e.g. *¿en d. vamos o no?* are we going then, or not?
definitorio, ria, *a.* defining. —*m.* (ecc.) chapter of definitors; meeting or assembly of definitors; assembly room, council hall (for meetings of definitors).
defiriendo, defiriera, defiriese, defirió, *ref.* **deferir.**
deflación, *f.* deflation.
deflacionista, *a.* deflationary.
deflagración, *f.* deflagration, sudden burst of flames without explosion.
deflagrador, ra, *a.* deflagrating. —*m.* (phys.) electric exploder (for detonating blasting charge).
deflagrar, *i.v.* to deflagrate, burn with sudden and sparkling combustion; to flash.
deflector, *m.* baffle, deflector.
deflegmar, *tr.v.* (chem.) to dephlegmate, rectify.
deflexión, *f.* deflection.
deflexo, a, *a.* (bot.) deflexed.
deflujo, *m.* (med.) defluxion.
defluxión, *f.* (med.) defluxion.
defoliación, *f.* defoliation, loss of leaves.
deformación, *f.* 1. deformation; distortion. 2. (mec.) strain. — **d. lindera or de límite,** (geol.) boundary deformation.
deformado, da, *past part. of* **deformar.** —*a.* deformed.
deformador, ra, *a.* deforming. —*m., f.* deformer.
deformar, *tr.v.* deform.—*r.v.* to become deformed.
deformatorio, ria, *a.* deforming.
deforme, *a.* deformed; ugly, misshapen, distorted, disfigured.
deformemente, *adv.* deformedly, distortedly.
deformidad, *f.* deformity; ugliness; (fig.) perversion.
defraudación, *f.* defrauding; cheating; swindle.
defraudador, ra, *a.* defrauding; cheating. —*m., f.* defrauder; swindler, cheater.
defraudar, *tr.v.* 1. to defraud, deprive, cheat. 2. (fig.) to disappoint, thwart (one's hopes). 3. (fig.) to disturb, spoil (one's sleep). 4. to block out (light).
defuera, *adv.* outside, externally; **por d.,** on the outside, outwardly.
defunción, *f.* death, decease, demise.
degausaje, *m.* (mar.) degaussing.
degeneración, *f.* degeneration, degeneracy; (med.) degeneration, deterioration (of tissue); **d. amiloidea,** (med.) amyloid degeneration.
degenerado, da, *past part. of* **degenerar.** —*a., m., f.* degenerate.
degenerante, *a.* degenerating, deteriorating.
degenerar, *i.v.* to degenerate.
degenerativo, va, *a.* degenerative.
deglución, *f.* deglutition, swallowing.
deglutir, *tr.v., i.v.* to swallow.
degollación, *f.* decollation, beheading.
degolladero, *m.* 1. windpipe. 2. slaughterhouse. 3. scaffold (for execution). 4. (theat., arch.) barrier between seats of the stalls and the pit. — **llevar a uno al d.,** (coll.) to expose somebody to danger.
degollado, da, *past part. of* **degollar.** —*m.* (dressm.) décolleté, low-necked dress. — **mirar con ojos de carnero d.,** to have a lovesick or innocent look.
degollador, ra, *a.* throat-cutting, beheading. —*m.* executioner, beheader.
degolladura, *f.* 1. the act of cutting someone's throat. 2. (dressm.) low neck. 3. (archit.) shaft (of balustrade, etc.). 4. (bldg.) joint (between two bricks).
degollamiento, *m., var. of* **degollación.**
degollante, *a.* (coll.) stupid, foolish; tiring, annoying, bothersome. —*m., f.* (coll.) bore, pest, nuisance, fool.
degollar, (*ref. 33*) *tr.v.* 1. to behead, decapitate; to cut the throat or neck of. 2. (dressm.) to cut (the neck) low. 3. (fig.) to destroy, ruin. 4. (theat.) to perform poorly, murder (a play or part). 5. (taur.) to kill (the bull) with several thrusts. 6. (fig., coll.) to bore, tire, annoy. 7. (mar.) to slash (a sail) with a knife (to save a vessel in an emergency).
degollina, *f.* (coll.) slaughter, butchery, mass murder.
degradación, *f.* 1. degradation, humiliation; depravity. 2. (mil.) degradation, demotion, lowering in rank. 3. (p.) gradation, progressive diminution (of figures according to perspective); (p.) toning down (of colors, of light). — **d. canónica,** degradation, defrocking of a priest; **d. real** or **actual,** (law) official demotion or lowering in rank.
degradado, da, *past part. of* **degradar.** —*a.* **ortografía degradada,** (geom.) linear perspective.
degradante, *a.* degrading.
degradar, *tr.v.* 1. to demote, degrade, reduce in rank. 2. to degrade, humiliate, lower, debase. 3. (p.) to tone down (colors). —*r.v.* to become debased; to degrade or lower oneself.

degredo, *m.* (Ven.) isolation hospital (for people with contagious diseases).
degu, *m.* (Chile) rat, rodent.
degüelle, degüello, *ref.* **degollar.**
degüello, *m.* 1. beheading, decapitation, decollation, throat-cutting; slaughter, butchery. 2. narrow part, neck. — **entrar a d.,** (mil.) to enter and slaughter (the population); **tirar a d.,** (fig., coll.) to endeavor to harm (someone); **tocar a d.,** (mil.) to sound the charge.
degustación, *f.* the action of tasting.
degustar, *tr.v.* to taste, to sample (foods, etc.).
dehesa, *f.* pasture land, grazing ground.
dehesar, *tr.v., var. of* **adehesar.**
dehesero, *m.* keeper of pasture ground; cowhand.
dehiscencia, *f.* (bot.) dehiscence.
dehiscente, *a.* (bot.) dehiscent.
deicida, *a.* deicidal. —*m., f.* deicide, the killer of a god.
deicidio, *m.* deicide, the killing of a god.
deidad, *f.* deity, divinity; god, goddess.
deificación, *f.* deification.
deificar, (*ref. 50*) *tr.v.* 1. to deify. 2. (fig.) to glorify, exalt, to praise lavishly. —*r.v.* to unite with God (the soul in mystic philosophy).
deífico, ca, *a.* deific, godly, divine.
deifique, deifiqué, *ref.* **deificar.**
deiforme, *a.* godlike, deiform.
deípara, *a.* deiparous, applied only to the Virgin Mary, mother of God.
deísmo, *m.* (rel.) deism, 17th and 18th century rational belief that God created the world and its natural laws but takes no part in its functioning.
deísta, *a.* (rel.) deistic, pertaining to deism. —*m., f.* deist, one who believes in deism.
deja, *f.* (carp.) ridge, projection (between two cuts or notches).
dejación, *f.* relinquishment, abandonment; (law) assignment.
dejada, *f.* relinquishment, abandonment.
dejadez, *f.* slovenliness, untidiness, sluttishness; negligence, neglect, laziness.
dejado, da, *past part. of* **dejar.** —*a.* 1. slovenly, untidy, unkempt; lazy, negligent. 2. depressed, dejected, listless, low-spirited. — **d. de la mano de Dios,** utterly abandoned or forsaken.
dejamiento, *m.* 1. abandonment, relinquishment. 2. neglicence, slovenliness, laziness. 3. listlessness, languor; depression. 4. indifference, coolness, estrangement.
dejar, *tr.v.* 1. to leave (something or someone behind one), e.g. *dejó instrucciones detalladas,* he left detailed instructions, *la dejé en la estación,* I left her at the station. 2. to leave, bequeath, e.g. *me dejó una fortuna enorme,* he left me an enormous fortune. 3. to leave; to abandon, desert; to go away from. 4. to let, allow, permit. 5. to yield, produce (e.g. a profit). 6. to leave, entrust, e.g. *dejé el negocio al cuidado de mi hermano,* I left the business in the care of my brother. 7. to name, designate, appoint, e.g. *te dejó por heredero,* he named or designated you his heir. 8. to lend. 9. to consider, regard, e.g. *d. a uno por loco,* to consider someone a madman. 10. to leave, let be, e.g. *d. en paz, d. tranquilo,* to leave in peace, leave alone. — **d.** + *inf.,* to let + *inf.,* allow + *inf.,* permit + *inf.,* e.g. *no la deja salir,* he does not let her come out, he does not allow or permit her to come out; to let be + *past part.,* e.g. *dejó oír la voz,* he let his voice be heard; **d. atrás,** to leave behind; to surpass, outdo; ¡deja! let it go, never mind; ¡déjame! let me be, leave me alone; **d. caer,** to drop, let fall; **d. escrito** or **dicho,** to leave word, leave a note or message; **d. saber,** (Amer.) to let know; **d. en cueros,** to leave naked; **d. por** or que + *inf.,* to leave to be + *past part.,* e.g. *d. mucho por hacer,* to leave much to be done, *deja mucho que desear,* it leaves much to be desired. —*i.v.* to stop; **d. de** + *inf.,* to stop or cease + *ger.,* e.g. *ella dejó de llorar,* she stopped crying; to fail to + *inf.,* e.g. *no dejes de venir,* do not fail to come; **d. de existir,** to die, pass away. —*r.v.* 1. to neglect oneself, become slovenly or careless, let oneself go. 2. to let or allow oneself. 3. to become dispirited, discouraged or despondent, lose heart. 4. to give oneself (up to), abandon oneself (to); **dejarse** + *inf.,* to let or allow oneself + *inf.;* to let or allow oneself be + *past part.,* e.g. *dejarse querer,* to let oneself be loved; **dejarse caer,** to drop a hint, hint; to drop in, drop by unexpectedly; **dejarse de** + *inf.,* to stop + *ger.,* e.g. *déjate de gritar* or *llorar,* stop shouting or crying; **dejarse de** + *n.,* to stop + *ger.,* put aside + *n.,* e.g. *déjate de chistes,* stop joking, *déjate de cuentos,* let's have no more of your stories; **dejarse llevar de,** to let oneself be carried by; **dejarse rogar,** to make oneself hard to get; **no dejarse ensillar,** not to allow oneself to be bossed about or stepped upon.
dejativo, va, *a.* lazy, indolent.
deje, *m.* (coll.) accent, inflection, lilt, e.g. *él tiene un d. andaluz,* he has an Andalusian inflection.
dejillo, *m.* 1. aftertaste, savor (of foods, etc.). 2. accent (of a region).
dejo, *m.* 1. accent, lilt (of certain region; of someone speaking a foreign language). 2. abandonment, relinquishment. 3. end, termination. 4. drop, descent (in voice). 5. laziness, indolence, negligence. 6. aftertaste (of food or beverage).
de jure, de jure, legitimate; **gobierno de jure,** legally constituted government.
del, *contraction of* **de** *and* **el,** e.g. *las penas del artista,* the tribulations of the artist.
delación, *f.* accusation, delation, denunciation.
delaminación, *f.* (biol.) delamination.
delantal, *m.* apron, pinafore.
delante, *adv.* before, in front, ahead. — **d. de,** in front of; in the presence of; opposite; **d. de mí,** in front of me, in front of him, her, them.
delantera, *f.* 1. front, front part (of anything). 2. front row (in theater, circus). 3. front edge (of book). 4. boundary line (of village, estate, etc.). 5. lead, headway (over someone in a race); advantage. 6. (*pl.*) leggings. — **coger** or **tomar la d.,** to take the lead, get ahead; to anticipate, beat (someone) to (doing something).
delantero, ra, *a.* front, fore, first; leading (horse of a team). —*m.* 1. postilion. 2. forward (in certain games).
delatable, *a.* accusable, blamable.
delatante, *a.* accusing, denouncing. —*m., f.* informer.
delatar, *tr.v.* to denounce, inform on, accuse.
delator, ra, *a.* informing, accusing, denouncing. —*m.* informer, accuser, denouncer.
dele, *m.* (print.) dele, mark of deletion, delete.
deleble, *a.* erasable, removable.
delectación, *f.* delectation, delight, pleasure.
delegación, *f.* delegation (delegating of power; group of delegates); delegate's office; delegate's commission, proxy; **d. de hacienda,** local income-tax office.
delegado, da, *past part. of* **delegar.** —*m., f.* delegate; representative, proxy.
delegante, *a.* delegating; constituent.
delegar, (*ref. 51*) *tr.v.* to delegate.
delegatorio, ria, *a.* delegatory, pertaining to or holding delegated authority.
delegue, delegué, *ref.* **delegar.**
deleitable, *a.* delectable, delightful; delicious.
deleitablemente, *adv.* delightfully, delectably.
deleitación, *f.* delectation, delight, pleasure.
deleitamiento, *m., var. of* **delectación.**
deleitante, *a.* delightful, delectable.
deleitar, *tr.v.* to delight, please, enchant. —*r.v.* **deleitarse en** or **con,** to delight in, take great pleasure in, enjoy (something) very much; **deleitarse en** + *inf.,* to delight in + *ger.,* e.g. *me deleito en contemplar esa escultura,* I delight in looking at that sculpture.
deleite, *m.* delight, pleasure, delectation.
deleitosamente, *adv.* delightfully.
deleitoso, sa, *a.* delightful.
deletéreo, a, *a.* deleterious, poisonous, noxious.
deletreador, ra, *a.* spelling. —*m., f.* speller.
deletrear, *tr.v.* 1. to spell, e.g. *¿cómo se deletrea tu nombre?* how does one spell your name? 2. (fig.) to decipher, interpret.
deletreo, *m.* spelling.
deleznable, *a.* 1. crumbly; slippery. 2. (fig.) frail, weak, unstable. 3. perishable; fragile.
deleznarse, *r.v.* to slide, slip; to crumble or disintegrate.
délfico, ca, *a.* (hist., myth.) Delphic, Delphian, pertaining to the city or the oracle of Delphi.
delfín, *m.* 1. (zool.) dolphin. 2. (astron.) **D.,** Delphinus, Dolphin. 3. dauphin, former title given to the eldest son of the king of France.
delfina, *f.* dauphiness, dauphine, wife of the dauphin of France (the crown prince).
Delfos, *m.* Delphi, ancient city in Greece.
delga, *f.* (elec.) commutator bar.
delgadamente, *adv.* delicately, thinly; (fig.) sharply, acutely, subtly; discreetly.
delgadez, *f.* slimness, slenderness, thinness, leanness.
delgado, da, *a.* 1. slim, slender; thin, lean. 2. delicate. 3. (agr.) poor, thin, exhausted (soil). 4. (fig.) acute, sharp, subtle. —*m.* 1. (mar.) dead-rising (each of the vertical frames in the run of a ship). 2. (*pl.*) flanks (of animals).
delgaducho, cha, *a.* thinnish, lanky, lean.
deliberación, *f.* deliberation.
deliberadamente, *adv.* deliberately, on purpose.
deliberado, da, *past part. of* **deliberar.** —*a.* intentional, voluntary, on purpose.
deliberante, *a.* deliberating, deliberative.
deliberar, *i.v.* to deliberate, meditate, ponder; to discuss, confer; d. **sobre,** to consider, deliberate over. —*tr.v.* to decide, resolve; to determine.
deliberativo, va, *a.* deliberative.
delicadamente, *adv.* delicately.
delicadez, *f.* 1. weakness, frailty. 2. sensitiveness; touchiness. 3. laziness, indolence.
delicadeza, *f.* 1. fineness, daintiness, delicateness (of lace, tracery, etc.). 2. softness, gentleness (of character); sensitivity, sensibility (of nature). 3. politeness, tact, urbanity. 4. scrupulousness, exactness. 5. weakness, frailty.
delicado, da, *a.* 1. delicate, gentle. 2. fine, exquisite, delicate (features; piece of work). 3. fragile, delicate, easily broken. 4. frail, delicate, sickly. 5. difficult, ticklish, delicate (question). 6. tender, delicious (meat, etc.). 7. subtle, sharp, ingenious (remark). 8. touchy, sensitive (of character); difficult (to please). 9. scrupulous, very exact.
delicaducho, cha, *a.* sickly, weak, ailing (person).
delicia, *f.* delight; pleasure.
deliciosamente, *adv.* delightfully; deliciously.
delicioso, sa, *a.* delightful; delicious.
delictivo, va, *a.* criminal, delinquent.
delictuoso, sa, *a., var. of* **delictivo.**

delicuescencia, *f.* (chem.) deliquescence.
delicuescente, *a.* (chem.) deliquescent.
delimitación, *f.* delimitation, demarcation.
delimitar, *tr.v.* to delimit, fix or mark limits of.
delinca, delinco, *ref.* **delinquir.**
delincuencia, *f.* delinquency; **d. juvenil,** juvenile delinquency.
delincuente, *a.* criminal, offender, delinquent. —*m., f.* criminal, delinquent; **d. primario,** first offender.
delineación, *f.* delineation, drawing, sketch, draft.
delineador, ra, *a.* delineating, tracing, drawing. —*m., f.* delineator; draftsman, designer.
delineamiento, *m., var. of* **delineación.**
delineante, *a.* delineating, drawing. —*m.* draftsman; delineator.
delinear, *tr.v.* to delineate, draw, sketch, design.
delinquimiento, *m.* delinquency, guilt; transgression, violation of the law.
delinquir, (*ref. 64*) *i.v.* to violate or break the law; to be delinquent, to transgress.
deliquio, *m.* faint, swoon; ecstasy, rapture.
delirante, *a.* delirious.
delirar, *i.v.* 1. to be delirious, suffer from delirium. 2. (fig.) to talk nonsense, behave madly or absurdly; to rave or rant.
delirio, *m.* 1. delirium. 2. (fig.) delirium, craze, rapture, e.g. *tengo d. contigo,* I am crazy about you. 3. (coll.) nonsense, rubbish. — **d. de grandeza,** delusions of grandeur.
delírium tremens, *m.* (med.) delirium tremens.
delitescencia, *f.* 1. (med.) delitescency, delitescence, sudden disappearance of an infection. 2. (chem.) loss of water through crystallization.
delito, *m.* crime, offense, felony; misdemeanor; transgression. — **d. común,** (law) common law crime; **d. consumado,** (law) consummated crime; **d. de lesa majestad,** lese-majesty, high treason; **d. flagrante,** flagrant crime (one detected in the act); **d. político,** political offense; **d. de incendio,** (law) arson.
della, llo, (arch.) *contr. of* **de ella, de ello,** hers, its, his, etc.
delta, *f.* delta, fourth letter in the Greek alphabet. —*m.* (geog.) delta.
deltaico, ca, *a.* deltaic, having a triangular shape; pertaining to a delta.
deltoideo, a, *a.* deltoid, triangular.
deltoides, *a.* deltoid, triangular; (anat.) deltoid. —*m.* (anat.) deltoid.
deludir, *tr.v.* to delude, deceive.
delusivo, va, *a.* delusive, deceptive, fallacious.
delusor, ra, *a.* delusive, deceptive. —*m., f.* deceiver, deluder.
delusoriamente, *adv.* delusively, deceptively.
delusorio, ria, *a.* delusive, deceptive, fallacious.
demacración, *f.* emaciation.
demacrado, da, *past part. of* **demacrarse.** —*a.* emaciated, pale, worn-out.
demacrar, *tr.v.* to emaciate, make lean, waste. —*r.v.* to become emaciated or wasted, waste away.
demagogia, *f.* demagogy, methods or practices of attempting to gain power by persuasive, emotional appeals.
demagógico, ca, *a.* demagogic.
demagogo, *m.* demagogue. —*a.* demagogic.
demanda, *f.* 1. demand; claim. 2. (com.) order (for goods). 3. (law) writ; claim; suit, complaint. 4. appeal, request (for help, money, etc.); alms, money (requested by church); image used in requesting alms. 5. question. 6. search, quest. 7. enterprise. — **contestar uno la d.,** (law) to oppose the claim; **d. máxima,** (elec.) peak load; **d. por daños y perjuicios,** (law) claim for damages; **demandas y respuestas,** haggling negotiations; **ir en d. de una persona** or **cosa,** to go in search of, search for; **ley de oferta y d.,** law of supply and demand; **salir uno a la d.,** (law) to oppose an action or a decision; (fig.) to oppose (someone); to defend (something).
demandadero, ra, *m., f.* messenger (in a monastery or prison). —*m.* errand boy. —*f.* errand girl.
demandado, da, *past part. of* **demandar.** —*m., f.* (law) defendant.
demandador, ra, *m., f.* 1. (law) plaintiff, claimant. 2. alms-collector.
demandante, *m., f.* (com., law) plaintiff, claimant.
demandar, *tr.v.* 1. to demand. 2. to long for, crave for. 3. to ask (a question). 4. (law) to claim against, file a suit against.
demarcación, *f.* demarcation, marking out of boundaries; marked out territory.
demarcador, ra, *a.* demarcating, dividing. —*m., f.* demarcator, boundary maker, surveyor.
demarcar, (*ref. 50*) *tr.v.* to demarcate, delimit, establish limits (of a state, territory, etc.).
demarque, demarqué, *ref.* **demarcar.**
demás, *a.* other, rest of the, e.g. *la d. gente,* the rest of the people, the other people; **lo d.,** the rest; **los d.,** the others, the rest; **y d.,** and the rest, etcetera, e.g. *Juan y d.,* John and the rest, John, etc. —*adv.* moreover, besides; **por d.,** in vain, uselessly; too, excessively; **por lo d.,** as for the rest, otherwise, apart from this.
demasía, *f.* 1. excess, surplus. 2. boldness, audacity. 3. insolence, rudeness. 4. evil, wickedness, iniquity. 5. (min.) space between two claims, no-man's land. — **en d.,** excessively, too much.
demasiadamente, *adv.* excessively, too much, too.
demasiado, da, *a.* too much, excessive. —*adv.* too; too much; excessively.
demasiarse, (*ref. 54*) *r.v.* to exceed oneself, go beyond oneself.
demediar, *tr.v.* 1. to divide in halves. 2. to accomplish half of (a journey); to come to the middle of (one's lifetime). —*r.v.* to divide in half.
demencia, *f.* madness, insanity; (med.) dementia; **d. precoz,** dementia praecox.
dementar, *tr.v.* to drive mad, craze. —*r.v.* to become mad, crazy, insane.
demente, *a.* demented, crazy, mad, insane. —*m.* madman. —*f.* madwoman.
demergido, da, *a.* dejected, spiritless.
demeritar, *tr.v., i.v.* (Amer.) to demerit.
demérito, *m.* demerit, unworthiness.
demeritorio, ria, *a.* unworthy, undeserving.
demisión, *f.* submission, humility.
demiurgo, *m.* (philos.) Demiurge.
democracia, *f.* democracy.
demócrata, *a.* democratic. —*m., f.* democrat.
democráticamente, *adv.* democratically.
democratice, democraticé, *ref.* **democratizar.**
democrático, ca, *a.* democratic; (fig.) popular, unencumbered, e.g. *una costumbre muy d.,* a very popular custom.
democratización, *f.* democratization.
democratizar, (*ref. 53*) *tr.v.* to make democratic, democratize. —*r.v.* to become democratic.
demodulación, *f.* (rad.) demodulation.
demografía, *f.* demography, population study.
demográfico, ca, *a.* demographical.
demógrafo, *m.* demographer.
demoledor, ra, *a.* destructive, demolishing. —*m., f.* demolisher. —*f.* wrecker; demolition tool.
demoler, (*ref. 34*) *tr.v.* to demolish, destroy, pull down, dismantle.
demolición, *f.* demolition, destruction.
demonche, *m.* (coll.) demon, devil.
demoníaco, ca, *a.* demoniacal, devilish, demonic; possessed by the devil. —*m., f.* demoniac, person possessed by the devil.
demonio, *m.* demon, devil; evil spirit, supernatural being. — **demonio! ¡demonios!** the deuce!; **estudiar uno con el d.,** (coll.) to show great tendency for evil; to be full of devilishness; **tener uno el d. en el cuerpo,** to have the devil in one.
demoniomanía, *f., var. of* **demonomanía.**
demonismo, *m.* demonism.
demonólatra, *m., f.* demonolater, worshipper of demons.
demonolatría, *f.* demonolatry, worship of demons.
demonología, *f.* demonology, study of demons.
demonomancia, *f.* divination with the help of demons.
demonomanía, *f.* demonomania, demonopathy, mania of a person who believes himself possessed by demons.
demontre, *m.* (coll.) devil, demon. — **¡d.!** the deuce! damn!
demoñejo, *m.* demon, devil, little devil.
demoñuelo, *m., var. of* **demoñejo.**
demora, *f.* 1. delay. 2. (Amer., arch.) eight-month period during which the Indians had to work in the mines in lieu of paying taxes. 3. (mar.) bearing.
demorar, *tr.v.* to delay, retard. —*i.v.* 1. to stay, remain, tarry. 2. (mar.) to bear. — **d. mucho** or **poco,** to take long or not to take long.
demorón, na, *a.* (coll.) slow. —*m., f.* (coll.) slow poke, slow person.
demoroso, sa, *a.* (Arg., Chile) slow, sluggish.
demóstenes, *m.* 1. (coll.) eloquent speakcr. 2. D., Demosthenes.
demostino, na, *a.* Demosthenic, pertaining to Demosthenes.
demostrable, *a.* demonstrable, capable of being shown or proved.
demostrablemente, *adv.* demonstrably.
demostración, *f.* demonstration, show, proof; (Amer.) public demonstration.
demostrador, ra, *a.* demonstrating. —*m., f.* demonstrator.
demostrar, (*ref. 33*) *tr.v.* to demonstrate, show; to prove; to make evident.
demostrativamente, *adv.* clearly, demonstratively.
demostrativo, va, *a.* demonstrative; (gram.) demonstrative. —*m.* (gram.) demonstrative (pronoun, adjective).
demótico, ca, *a.* demotic, pertaining to the popular form of ancient Egyptian writing.
demudación, *f.* change, alteration.
demudamiento, *m., var. of* **demudación.**
demudar, *tr.v.* to change; to alter; disguise. —*r.v.* to change suddenly (one's color, expression, humor, etc.); to become suddenly disturbed or agitated.
demuela, demuelo, *ref.* **demoler.**
demuestre, demuestro, *ref.* **demostrar.**
demulcente, *a., m.* (med.) demulcent, emollient.
demulsionar, demulsificar, desemulsionar, *tr.v.* (chem.) to demulsify.
denantes, *adv.* before.
denario, ria, *a.* denary. —*m.* denarius; ancient Roman coin.
dendriforme, *a.* dendriform, tree-shaped.
dendrita, *f.* 1. (min., geol.) dendrite. 2. tree fossil.
dendrítico, ca, *a.* (geol., bot.) dentritic.
dendrocronología, *f.* (geol., bot.) dendrochronology.
dendrografía, *f.* (geol., bot.) dendrography.
dendrográfico, ca, *a.* (geol., bot.) dendrographic.
dendroide, *a., var. of* **dendroideo.**
dendroideo, a, *a.* dendroid, resembling a tree; arborescent.

dendrología, *f.* dendrology, the scientific study of trees.
dendrológico, ca, *a.* (bot.) dendrological.
dendrómetro, *m.* dendrometer, instrument for taking the measurements of a tree.
denegación, *f.* denegation; refusal, denial.
denegar, (*ref. 67*) *tr.v.* to refuse, deny.
denegatorio, ria, *a.* negatory; pertaining to a negation.
denegrecer, (*ref. 45*) *tr.v.* to blacken, darken. —*r.v.* to become or turn dark, cloud over; to turn black.
denegrezca, denegrezco, *ref.* **denegrecer.**
denegrido, da, *past part. of* **denegrir.** —*a.* blackish.
denegrir, *tr.v., r.v., var. of* **denegrecer.**
denegué, *ref.* **denegar.**
dengoso, sa, *a.* affected, fastidious, finicky; modest or prudish.
dengue, *m.* 1. affectedness, affected fastidiousness or modesty. 2. woman's cape with long points crossing in front and tying at the back. 3. (med.) dengue, dengue fever, break-bone fever. 4. (Col.) affected gait. 5. (Chile, bot.) marvel of Peru. 6. (Sp., reg.) devil, evil spirit.
denguear, *i.v.* to be fastidious, be fussy.
denguero, ra, *a., var. of* **dengoso.**
deniego, deniegue, *ref.* **denegar.**
denigración, *f.* defamation, denigration, slander, revilement.
denigrante, *a.* denigratory, slanderous, defamatory, calumnious, abusive. —*m., f.* defamer, reviler, denigrator, slanderer.
denigrar, *tr.v.* to denigrate, slander, defame, revile.
denigrativamente, *adv.* calumniously, abusively, insultingly.
denigrativo, va, *a.* denigratory, abusive, defamatory, calumnious.
denodadamente, *adv.* boldly, intrepidly, daringly, resolutely.
denodado, da, *a.* bold, intrepid, daring, audacious, brave.
denominación, *f.* denomination, designation, title.
denominadamente, *adv.* clearly, distinctly.
denominado, da, *past part. of* **denominar.** —*a.* (math.) denominate.
denominador, ra, *a.* denominating. —*m., f.* denominator. —*m.* (math.) denominator, divisor; **hacer desaparecer los denominadores,** (math.) to eliminate fractions.
denominar, *tr.v.* to name, indicate (by name); to denominate, designate.
denominativo, va, *a.* denominative; (gram.) denominative. —*m.* (gram.) denominative (verb).
denostada, *f.* insult, affront.
denostadamente, *adv.* insultingly, abusively, ignominiously.
denostador, ra, *a.* insulting, abusive. —*m., f.* insulter, abuser.
denostar, (*ref. 33*) *tr.v.* to insult, abuse.
denostosamente, *adv., var. of* **denostadamente.**
denotación, *f.* denotation, indication, meaning.
denotar, *tr.v.* to denote; to indicate; to mean.
denotativo, va, *a.* denotative, denotive.
densamente, *adv.* densely.
densidad, *f.* density; denseness; compactness; (phys.) density. — **d. absoluta,** (phys.) true specific gravity; **d. de corriente,** (elec.) current density; **d. de radiacion,** (phys.) radiant flux.
densificación, *f.* (phys.) densification.
densificar, (*ref. 50*) *tr.v.* to make dense, to thicken. —*r.v.* to become dense, thick.
densifique, densifiqué, *ref.* **densificar.**
densimetría, *f.* densimetry, measurement of density.
densímetro, *m.* (phys.) densimeter, hydrometer.
densitómetro, *m.* (photog., cine.) densitometer.
denso, sa, *a.* 1. dense; thick; compact, closely packed (crowd). 2. (fig.) obcure, confused.
dentado, da, *past part. of* **dentar.** —*a.* 1. toothed; dentate, denticulate, dentated; serrated. 2. (her.) crenellated, decorated with notches or indentations.
dentadura, *f.* set of teeth, denture; **d. postiza,** false teeth.
dental, *a.* dental; (phonet.) dental. —*f.* (phonet.) dental, dental consonant. —*m.* (agr.) moldboard, plowshare bed; tooth of a threshing machine; **hilo d.,** dental floss.
dentalización, *f.* (phonet.) dentalization.
dentar, (*ref. 29*) *tr.v.* to tooth, provide with teeth; to serrate, indent. —*i.v.* to teethe, cut teeth.
dentario, ria, *a.* dental, pertaining to the teeth.
dentecillo, *m. dim. of* **diente,** small tooth.
dentejón, *m.* yoke (for oxen).
dentellada, *f.* snap of the jaws or teeth; bite; mark or wound made by the teeth. — **a dentelladas,** with the teeth, biting.
dentellado, da, *past part. of* **dentellar.** —*a.* 1. toothed, denticulate, dentate, serrated, provided with teeth. 2. toothlike. 3. bitten, wounded, marked with tooth wounds. 4. (her.) dentelated, dentellated, surrounded by small nicks or indentations.
dentellar, *i.v.* to chatter (teeth).
dentellear, *tr.v.* to nibble; to bite.
dentellón, *m.* 1. tooth (of a lock). 2. (archit.) dentil, denticle. 3. (bldg.) tooth (of teething), any of the bricks left protruding from a wall to allow subsequent extension.
dentera, *f.* 1. unpleasant tingling in the teeth. 2. (fig.) envy; (fig.) vehement desire or longing. — **dar a uno d.,** to put one's teeth on edge; to make one desire or long for (something).
dentezuelo, *m. dim. of* **diente,** small tooth.
dentición, *f.* 1. dentition, cutting of teeth, teething; teething period. 2. (zool.) dentition, kind and number of teeth characteristic of a species.
denticulación, *f.* (zool.) denticulation, mass of very small toothlike projections.
denticulado, da, *a.* denticulate, having dentils.
denticular, *a.* dentate, tooth-shaped.
dentículo, *m.* (archit.) dentil, small ornamental notches on upper part of Ionic (or other) frieze.
dentífrico, ca, *a.* of tooth (paste, powder, etc.). —*m.* dentifrice, tooth paste.
dentina, *f.* (anat.) dentine, dentin.
dentirrostro, tra, *a.* (ornith.) dentirostral. —*m.* (ornith.) (*pl.*) Dentirostres.
dentista, *a.* dental. —*m., f.* dentist; **cirujano d.,** dental surgeon.
dentistería, *f.* (Ecuad.) 1. denstistry. 2. dentist's office.
dentivano, na, *a.* having long wide teeth (horse).
dentolabial, *a.* (phonet.) dentilabial.
dentón, na, *a.* with long uneven teeth. —*m.* (ichth.) dentex.
dentrambos, bas, *contraction of* **de entrambos** *and* **de entrambas.**
dentro, *adv.* inside, within; **d. de,** inside; within, in; **d. de poco,** soon, shortly, in a short while; **d. o fuera,** yes or no! make up your mind!
dentrodera, *f.* (Col.) servant, cleaning woman.
dentudo, da, *a.* with long, prominent teeth.
dentuzo, za, *a.* (Cuba) *var. of* **dentudo.**
denudacion, *f.* (bot., geol.) denudation.
denudar, *tr.v.* (bot., geol.) to denude, lay bare. —*r.v.* to be denuded.
denuedo, *m.* boldness, courage.
denueste, denuesto, *ref.* **denostar.**
denuesto, *m.* insult, affront; abuse.
denuncia, *f.* 1. announcement, declaration. 2. accusation, denunciation; reporting (of theft, etc. the police) e.g. *hice una d. sobre el robo de mi cartera,* I reported the theft of my wallet. — **d. falsa,** (law) false accusation.
denunciación, *f.* accusation, denunciation.
denunciador, ra, *a.* denouncing, denunciatory. —*m., f.* denouncer, accuser.
denunciante, *m., f.* 1. denouncer, informer. 2. (law) plaintiff. 3. claimant (of a mine).
denunciar, *tr.v.* 1. to denounce, censure. 2. to denounce, accuse; to report (a crime to the police). 3. to proclaim, announce; to foretell. 4. (min.) to register one's claim (to a mine). 5. (dipl.) to denounce, give notice of the termination of a treaty.
denunciatorio, ria, *a.* denunciatory, threatening, accusing.
denuncio, *m.* 1. (min.) denouncement, registering of a claim to a mine; application for mining concession. 2. (Amer.) denunciation, denouncement.
deodara, *m.* (bot.) deodar, East Indian cedar tree.
Deo gracias, *m.* Deo gratias, a greeting; (coll.) a humble attitude.
deontología, *f.* deontology, the theory of duty and moral obligation.
Deo volente, *m.* (coll.) Deo volente, God willing.
dep. *abbrev. of* **departamento,** department (dep., dept.).
deparar, *tr.v.* to supply, provide; to present, furnish.
departamental, *a.* departmental, pertaining to a department.
departamento, *m.* 1. department, section; province, district (into which a country is divided). 2. branch; department (of government; of a shop). 3. compartment (of a box, train). 4. apartment, flat (in apartment building). — **d. de bienes raíces,** real estate department; **d. de mercería,** notions counter (in a department store).
departidor, ra, *a., m., f.* speaker, talker, converser.
departir, *i.v.* to converse, speak, talk.
depauperación, *f.* 1. impoverishment. 2. (med.) weakening, exhaustion.
depauperar, *tr.v.* 1. to impoverish. 2. (med.) to weaken, exhaust. —*r.v.* to become weak, exhausted.
dependencia, *f.* 1. dependence, dependance, reliance. 2. branch; branch office. 3. business, agency. 4. relationship; friendship. 5. employees. 6. (*pl.*) accessories.
depender, *i.v.* to depend; to be subject to.
dependiente, ta, *a.* dependent, subordinate. —*m., f.* employee, shop assistant, clerk.
depilación, *f.* depilation.
depilar, *tr.v., r.v.* to depilate, remove hair.
depilatorio, ria, *a., m.* depilatory.
deplorable, *a.* deplorable, lamentable, regrettable.
deplorablemente, *adv.* deplorably, miserably, wretchedly.
deplorar, *tr.v.* to deplore, lament, grieve over or for.
depondré, depondría, *ref.* **deponer.**
deponente, *a., m.* (gram.) deponent (verb).
deponer, (*ref. 15*) *tr.v.* 1. to lay aside, put aside. 2. to depose, deprive of office. 3. (law) to testify. 4. to lower, bring down. —*i.v.* 1. to defecate, evacuate the bowels. 2. (Mex.) to vomit.
deponga, depongo, *ref.* **deponer.**
depopulador, ra, *a.* devastating, destructive. —*m., f.* devastator, destroyer.
deportación, *f.* deportation, banishment.
deportante, *var. of* **deportista.**

deportar, *tr.v.* to deport, exile, banish.
deporte, *m.* sport; recreation, amusement.
deportismo, *m.* sport, sports, sportiveness.
deportista, *m.,* sportsman. —*f.* sportswoman.
deportivamente, *adv.* sportively, sportingly.
deportividad, *f.* sportsmanship.
deportivo, va, *a.* sporting, sportive, sporty; sports, e.g. *club d.,* sports club.
deportoso, sa, *a.* amusing.
deposición, *f.* 1. deposal, deposition, declaration; removal from office. 2. bowel movement, defecation. 3. (law) deposition, testimony under oath. — **d. electrolítica,** (chem.) electrodeposition.
depositador, ra, *a.* depositing. —*m., f.* depositor.
depositante, *m., f.* depositor.
depositar, *tr.v.* 1. to deposit; to entrust; to put, place. 2. (law) to place (a person) where he is free of restraint; to confine, keep. 3. to place (a body) in a receiving vault. —*r.v.* to settle, be precipitated; (chem.) to deposit.
depositaría, *f.* depository; treasury; post of treasurer; **d. general,** post of public treasurer.
depositario, ria, *a.* pertaining to a deposit. —*m., f.* depositary, trustee, keeper (of a deposit). —*m.* public treasurer.
depósito, *m.* 1. deposit; depository. 2. storeroom; warehouse, storehouse; depot. 3. deposit, down payment. 4. (mil.) depot. 5. (geol.) deposit; sediment, accumulation. — **d. a la vista,** (com.) demand deposit; **d. compresor,** pressure tank; **d. de agua,** reservoir, water tank; **d. de cadaveres,** morgue, **d. de equipajes,** checkroom, left-luggage office (G.B.); **d. de gasolina,** gas tank; **d. de locomotoras,** (ry.) roundhouse; **d. de municiones,** ammunition dump; **d. de suministros,** (mil.) supply depot; **d. disponible,** (com.) demand deposit; **d. indistinto,** (com.) joint deposit.
depravación, *f.* depravation, depravity.
depravadamente, *adv.* depravedly.
depravado, da, *past part. of* **depravar.** —*a.* depraved, perverted, corrupted. —*m., f.* depraved person, degenerate.
depravador, ra, *a., m.* depraving. —*m., f.* depraver, corrupter.
depravar, *tr.v.* to harm, damage; to deprave, corrupt. —*r.v.* to be harmed; to become depraved or corrupted.
deprecación, *f.* petition, entreaty.
deprecante, *a.* beseeching, imploring. —*m., f.* suppliant, beseecher, implorer.
deprecar, (*ref. 50*) *tr.v.* to beg, implore, beseech.
deprecativo, va, *a.* deprecatory, deprecative; supplicating, imploring.
deprecatorio, ria, *a., var. of* **deprecativo.**
depreciación, *f.* depreciation, decrease in value; **d. de línea simplista** or **recta,** (econ.) straight-line depreciation.
depreciar, *tr.v.* to depreciate, lower the value of.
depredación, *f.* 1. depredation, ravaging, plundering, pillaging. 2. embezzlement, malversation.
depredador, ra, *m., f.* plunderer, pillager.
depredar, *tr.v.* to depredate, plunder, pillage.
depreque, deprequé, *ref.* **deprecar.**
depresión, *f.* 1. depression; lowering; hollow. 2. (psyc.) depression; sadness. 3. (Amer.) depression, economic crisis. — **d. barométrica,** (meteorol.) depression, low; **d. de horizonte,** (mar.) dip, dip of the horizon.
depresivo, va, *a.* depressing, depressive.
depresomotor, ra, *a.* (med.) depressomotor.
depresor, ra, *a.* depressant. —*m., f.* depressant; (anat.) depressor.
deprimente, *a.* depressing, depressive.
deprimido, da, *past part. of* **deprimir.** —*a.* depressed, sad.
deprimir, *tr.v.* 1. (psyc.) to depress. 2. to compress; to press in; to press down. 3. to lower (column of mercury in barometer; prices). 4. to humiliate, squash (someone). —*r.v.* 1. to become or get depressed (mentally). 2. to become compressed. 3. to fall (column of mercury; prices). 4. to be humiliated. 5. to dip, be lower (a line in relation to others).
De Profundis, *m.* De Profundis, funeral psalm.
depuesto, ta, *irr. past part. of* **deponer.**
depurable, *a.* purifiable.
depuración, *f.* depuration, purification, cleansing.
depurador, ra, *a.* depurating, purificatory, purifying. —*m.* purifier, depurator (purifying machine); **d. centrífugo,** (chem.) centrifugal cleaner.
depurar, *tr.v.* to depurate, purify, cleanse; to purge. —*r.v.* to become purified or cleansed.
depurativo, va, *a., m.* (med.) depurative.
depuratorio, ria, *a.* depuratory, purifying, cleansing.
depusiera, depusiese, depuse, *ref.* **deponer.**
deputar, *tr.v., var. of* **diputar.**
deque, *adv.* (coll.) when, after, on.
derecera, *f., var. of* **derechera.**
derechamente, *adv.* 1. directly, straight. 2. (fig.) wisely, justly. 3. honestly, properly. 4. (fig.) clearly, openly.
derechazo, *m.* right, blow with the right hand (in boxing).
derechero, ra, *a.* just, right, honest, correct. —*m.* tax collector, clerk in charge of collecting fees. —*f.* straight path, short cut.
derechismo, *m.* (polit.) rightism, principles of the right wing.
derechista, *m., f.* (polit.) rightist, right-winger, reactionary.
derecho, cha, *a.* 1. right; right-hand. 2. straight; upright. 3. correct, appropriate. — **a derecha,** on the right-hand side; **a derechas,** correctly, properly; **a las derechas,** honestly, correctly, in an honest manner. —*f.* 1. right hand; right side, right hand side. 2. (polit.) the right, conservative, traditionalist party, the right wing. — **a la d.,** to the right; (mil.) right turn. —*m.* 1. right. 2. law; laws. 3. path, road. 4. right side (of cloth, etc.). 5. (*pl.*) duties, taxes; fees, charges. — **de d.,** by right; **d. administrativo,** administrative law; **d. a no sufrir necesidad,** freedom from want; **d. a vivir sin temor,** freedom from fear; **d. canónico,** canon law; **d. civil** or **común,** civil law; **d. comparado,** comparative law of jurisprudence; **d. consuetudinario,** customary law, common law (established by custom and precedent); **d. criminal,** criminal law; **d. de acrecer,** right of accession; **d. de asilo,** right of asylum; **d. de dominio privado,** right of property; **d. de gentes,** international law; **d. de guardarse de publicidad,** right of privacy; **d. de matrícula,** registration fee; **d. de pataleo,** (coll.) right to grumble or complain; **d. de pernada,** droit du seigneur; **d. de regalía,** tax on manufactured tobacco; **d. de registro,** right of search; **d. de reproducción,** copyright; **d. de reunion,** right of assembly; **d. de vivir,** right to live; **d. divino,** Divine Right; **d. eclesiástico,** canon law; **d. empresarial,** business law; **d. escrito,** statute law, written law; **d. internacional,** international law; **d. mercantil,** business law; **d. natural,** natural right, natural law; **d. no escrito,** unwritten or common law; **d. patentario,** patent law; **d. penal,** penal law, criminal law; **d. político,** constitutional law; **d. positivo,** statute or positive law; **d. privado,** private law; **d. procesal,** procedural law; **d. público,** public law; **derechos adquiridos,** (law) vested rights; **derechos aduaneros** or **de importación,** customs duties; **derechos civiles,** civil rights; **derechos conyugales,** conjugal rights; **derechos consulares,** consular fees; **derechos de aduana,** customs duties; **derechos de almacenaje,** storage or warehouse charges; **derechos de anclaje,** anchorage dues; **derechos de autor,** copyright; royalties; **derechos de ejecución,** performance rights (of actors, opera singers, ballet dancers, etc.); **derechos de entrada,** import duties; **derechos del hombre,** rights of man; **derechos de muelle,** wharfage, dockage; **derechos de puerto,** harbor dues; **derechos humanos,** human rights; **derechos particulares** or **de individuo,** private rights; **no hay d.,** it's not fair, it's not right; **por d. propio,** in his or its own right; **según d.,** by rights.
derechura, *f.* straightness, rightness; **en d.,** straight, directly; immediately, right away.
deriva, *f.* drift, deviation off course. — **ir a la d.,** (mar., fig.) to drift.
derivación, *f.* 1. derivation. 2. deduction, inference. 3. leading off, taking off (e.g. water). 4. (elec.) leakage, loss (of electricity due to dampness); shunt, shunt connection. 5. (gram., med., math.) derivation. — **de d.,** (elec.) shunt (field); **d. central,** (elec.) central tap; **d. maestra,** (elec.) master service.
derivado, da, *past part. of* **derivar.** —*a.* (elec.) shunt (circuit). —*f.* (math.) derivative.
derivar, *i.v.* 1. to derive, come from. 2. to drift, go off course. —*tr.v.* 1. (gram.) to derive. 2. to lead, conduct; to guide. —*r.v.* to derive from, come from.
derivativo, va, *a.* (gram., med.) derivative. —*m.* (med.) derivative, agent producing derivation.
derivo, *m.* origin, source.
derivómetro, *m.* (aer.) drift meter.
dermalgia, *f.* (med.) skin neuralgia.
dermáptero, ra, *a., m.* (ento.) dermapteran.
dermatitis, *f.* (med.) dermatitis.
dermatófito, *m.* (med.) dermatophyte.
dermatoideo, a, *a.* dermatoid, resembling skin.
dermatología, *f.* (med.) dermatology.
dermatológico, ca, *a.* (med.) dermatological, dermatologic.
dermatólogo, ga, *m., f.* (med.) dermatologist.
dermatoma, *m.* (physiol.) dermatome.
dermatosis, *f.* (med.) dermatosis.
dermesto, *m.* (ento.) larder beetle (Dermestes lardarius).
dérmico, ca, *a.* dermic, dermal, cutaneous.
dermis, *f.* (anat.) derma, dermis.
dermitis, *f.* (med.) dermatitis.
dermóptero, ra, *a.* (zool.) dermopterous. —*m.* (zool.) dermopteran.
dermotropo, a, *a.* (med.) dermotropic.
derogación, *f.* 1. derogation, abolition, repeal. 2. decrease, deterioration.
derogar, (*ref. 51*) *tr.v.* 1. to derogate, abolish, repeal; to destroy; to reform. 2. to lower in esteem; disparage.
derogatorio, ria, *a.* 1. (law) repealing, annulling. 2. derogatory, pejorative.
derogue, derogué, *ref.* **derogar.**
derrabadura, *f.* (vet.) wound left by docking the tail of an animal.
derrabar, *tr.v.* (vet.) to dock, clip (animal's tail).
derrama, *f.* apportionment, distribution of tax; temporary or extraordinary contribution or tax.
derramadamente, *adv.* profusely, liberally; indiscriminately, carelessly.
derramadero, *m.* drain, sink, dump.

derramado, da, *past part. of* **derramar.** —*a.* wasteful, prodigal.
derramador, ra, *a.* prodigal. —*m., f.* waster.
derramadura, *f., var. of* **derramamiento.**
derramamiento, *m.* 1. spilling. 2. dispersion, scattering; spreading. 3. overflow. — **d. de sangre,** bloodshed.
derramaplaceres, *m.* (coll.) killjoy, spoilsport.
derramar, *tr.v.* 1. to spill; to pour out. 2. to scatter, spread. 3. to apportion (taxes). 4. (fig.) to publish, spread, divulge (news). —*r.v.* 1. to scatter, spread. 2. to spill. 3. to run over, overflow.
derramasolaces, *m., f.* (coll.) killjoy, spoilsport.
derrame, *m.* 1. spilling. 2. dispersion, scattering. 3. spreading. 4. overflow; leakage; liquid or grain spill. 5. (archit.) chamfer, splay. 6. slope, declivity. 7. outlet (of a gorge). 8. (mar.) leakage of wind (through boltropes). 9. (med.) extravasation, effusion.
derramo, *m.* (archit.) splay, chamfer, slope, bevel.
derrapar, *i.v.* (Mex.) to slip, slide, skid.
derraspado, da, *a.* **trigo derraspado,** stubpointed, small and flat eared corn, with soft grain and scant husk.
derredor, *m.* circumference, periphery; **al** or **en d.,** around; **por todo el d.,** all around.
derrelicto, ta, *irr. past part. of* **derrelinquir.** —*m.* (mar.) derelict, abandoned ship or person.
derrelinca, derrelinco, *ref.* **derrelinquir.**
derrelinquir, (*ref. 64*) *tr.v.* to relinquish, abandon, forsake.
derrenegar, (*ref. 67*) *i.v.* (coll.) **d. de,** to abhor, detest, abominate.
derrenegué, *ref.* **derrenegar.**
derrengado, da, *past part. of* **derrengar.** —*a.* 1. lame. 2. bent, crooked. 3. exhausted (after much movement).
derrengadura, *f.* spraining or lesion of hips, spine or ribs; crookedness.
derrengar, (*ref. 67*) *tr.v.* 1. to sprain or injure severely the hip, spine or ribs of. 2. to bend, make bent. —*r.v.* 1. to twist or injure severely one's hip, spine or ribs. 2. to become bent or crooked.
derrengué, *ref.* **derrengar.**
derreniego, *m.* (coll.) curse, oath.
derreniego, derreniegue, *ref.* **derrenegar.**
derretido, da, *past part. of* **derretir.** —*a.* (coll.) madly in love, enamored. —*m.* concrete.
derretimiento, *m.* 1. melting, thaw. 2. (fig.) passionate love.
derretir, (*ref. 39*) *tr.v.* 1. to melt, liquefy, dissolve. 2. (fig.) to spend, squander, waste (fortune, property). 3. (coll.) to change (money to pay in gambling). —*r.v.* 1. to melt, dissolve. 2. to fall passionately in love; (fig.) to be consumed with love; (coll.) to fall in love easily. 3. (coll.) to be impatient or restless.
derribado, da, *past part. of* **derribar.** —*a.* lowrumped (horse).
derribador, *m.* 1. overthrower. 2. feller; horseman who knocks down cows or bulls with a goad stick.
derribar, *tr.v.* 1. to knock down (a person); to tear down, demolish (house, a wall); to shoot down (a plane); to overthrow (a goverment or leader from power); to throw to the ground (a bull, a horse). 2. to humiliate, humble. —*r.v.* to throw oneself to the ground; to fall down.
derribo, *m.* demolition; (*pl.*) debris, rubble.
derriengo, derriengue, *ref.* **derrengar.**
derrisco, *m.* deep ravine.
derrita, derritiendo, derritiera, derritiese, derritió, derrito, *ref.* **derretir.**
derrocadero, *m.* rocky precipice, craggy mountaintop.
derrocamiento, *m.* 1. demolition; hurtling. 2. (polit.) overthrow.
derrocar, *tr.v.* 1. to hurtle, throw, cast. 2. to demolish, knock down. 3. to overthrow, bring down (from power). 4. to enervate, weaken. —*r.v.* to hurl oneself.
derrochador, ra, *a.* wasteful, squandering. —*m., f.* spendthrift, squanderer.
derrochar, *tr.v.* to waste, squander.
derroche, *m.* waste, squandering, extravagance.
derronchar, *tr.v.* (arch.) to fight, combat.
derroqué, *ref.* **derrocar.**
derrostrarse, *r.v.* to become disfigured (face).
derrota, *f.* 1. (mil.) defeat, rout. 2. path, track. 3. (mar.) ship's course. 4. permission for cattle to graze in harvested fields. — **seguir la d.,** (mil.) to rout, pursue and harass the enemy.
derrotado, da, *past part. of* **derrotar.**
derrotar, *tr.v.* 1. to defeat, beat (an army); to rout, put to flight. 2. to ruin, spoil (clothes, furniture; health). —*r.v.* (mar.) to drift or be driven off course.
derrote, *m.* (taur.) thrust with the horns.
derrotero, *m.* 1. (mar.) course, route; collection of charts. 2. (fig.) means, ways, methods (to achieve something).
derrotismo, *m.* defeatism.
derrotista, *a., m., f.* defeatist.
derrubiar, *tr.v.* to wash away, erode, undermine (river banks). —*r.v.* to become undermined, eroded or washed away.
derrubio, *m.* erosion, undermining, washing away; alluvium, alluvion, soil deposited by water; **d. glacial,** (geol.) glacial drift.
derrueco, derrueque, *ref.* **derrocar.**
derruir, (*ref. 48*) *tr.v.* to demolish, destroy, pull down (a building).
derrumbadero, *m.* 1. precipice, crag. 2. (fig.) danger, hazard, risk.
derrumbamiento, *m.* 1. demolition, tearing down. 2. (min.) cave-in; landslide.
derrumbar, *tr.v.* 1. to hurl, cast. 2. to tear down, demolish. —*r.v.* 1. to fall down; to plunge, fall. 2. (min.) to cave in, collapse. 3. (Amer.) to fail.
derrumbe, *m.* 1. precipice, crag. 2. (min.) cavein; landslide. 3. tumbling down, collapse.
derrumbo, *m.* precipice, crag.
derruya, derruyo, *ref.* **derruir.**
derviche, *m.* dervish, a Muslim monk.
desabarrancar, (*ref. 50*) *tr.v.* to pull out, draw, drag or extricate from a gully, ditch or swamp; (fig.) to rescue (from difficulties).
desabarranque, desabarranqué, *ref.* **desabarrancar.**
desabastecer, (*ref. 45*) *tr.v.* to deprive of provisions.
desabastezca, desabastesco, *ref.* **desabastecer.**
desabejar, *tr.v.* to remove bees from (a hive).
desabillé, *m.* (gal.) pegnoir, negligee.
desabollador, *m.* dent remover (device).
desabollar, *tr.v.* to remove dents from, flatten.
desabonarse, *r.v.* to discontinue a subscription.
desabono, *m.* 1. discontinuance or withdrawal of a subscription. 2. damage, harm (done to someone by malicious gossip).
desabor, *m.* insipidness, tastelessness.
desabordarse, *r.v.* (mar.) to get clear (two ships) after a collision or fouling.
desaborido, da, *a.* insipid, tasteless; (coll.) dull, inane, vapid, spiritless, insipid.
desabotonar, *tr.v.* to unbutton. —*r.v.* to unbutton one's clothes. —*i.v.* to bloom, blossom, burst into flower.
desabridamente, *adv.* 1. insipidly, tastelessly. 2. gruffly, disagreeably, rudely; unpleasantly.
desabrido, da, *a.* 1. insipid, tasteless; unsavory; unpleasant, disagreeable (food). 2. unsettled, inclement (weather). 3. (fig.) disagreeable, rude, sharp, gruff, surly (in behavior).
desabrigadamente, *adv.* without covering or shelter.
desabrigado, da, *past part. of* **desabrigar.** —*a.* unsheltered, uncovered, exposed; shelterless, harborless; without support, destitute, abandoned.
desabrigar, (*ref. 51*) *tr.v.* to uncover; to undress, remove clothing of; to deprive of shelter or covering. —*r.v.* to undress, take off one's clothing or covering.
desabrigo, *m.* 1. uncovering. 2. lack of shelter, clothing or covering. 3. (fig.) destitution, abandonment, desertion.
desabrigue, desabrigué, *ref.* **desabrigar.**
desabrimiento, *m.* 1. tastelessness, insipidness, insipidity; unpleasantness (of taste). 2. (fig.) rudeness, gruffness, sharpness, unpleasantness. 3. (fig.) disagreeableness, unpleasantness. 4. violent recoil (in firearms).
desabrir, *tr.v.* 1. to make tasteless or insipid (food). 2. (fig.) to vex, harass, annoy. —*r.v.* to feel vexed, annoyed or upset.
desabrochar, *tr.v.* 1. to unfasten, unbutton, unclasp, undo (clothing). 2. to reveal, disclose. 3. (fig.) to open. —*r.v.* to unbotton, unfasten or undo one's clothing; **desabrocharse con,** to unbosom oneself or open one's heart to.
desabsorción, *f.* (phys.) desorption.
desacalorarse, *r.v.* to cool off.
desacatadamente, *adv.* disrespectfully; irreverently.
desacatado, da, *past part. of* **desacatar.**
desacatador, ra, *a.* disrespectful; irreverent. —*m., f.* disrespectful person.
desacatamiento, *m., var. of* **desacato.**
desacatar, *tr.v.* to treat disrespectfully or irreverently. —*r.v.* to behave disrespectfully or irreverently.
desacato, *m.* disrespect, irreverence; (law) contempt; **d. al tribunal,** (law) contempt of court.
desacedar, *tr.v.* to remove or eliminate acidity, sourness, harshness or roughness.
desaceitado, da, *a.* unoiled, in need of being oiled.
desaceitar, *tr.v.* to remove oil and grease from.
desacelerar, *tr.v.* (phys.) to decelerate.
desacerar, *tr.v.* to wear out the steel of (a tool). —*r.v.* to lose its steel surface.
desacerbar, *tr.v.* to temper, assuage, sweeten; to remove sourness of.
desacertadamente, *adv.* wrongly, mistakenly, erroneously, misguidedly.
desacertado, da, *past part. of* **desacertar.** —*a.* wrong, misguided, mistaken.
desacertar, (*ref. 29*) *i.v.* to err, be wrong, make a mistake, commit an error; to act wrongly, misguidedly or unwisely.
desacidificar, (*ref. 50*) *tr.v.* to remove, eliminate or neutralize acidity of.
desacidifique, desacidifiqué, *ref.* **desacidificar.**
desacierte, desacierto, *ref.* **desacertar.**
desacierto, *m.* error, mistake, blunder; unwise or misguided statement or act.
desacobardar, *tr.v.* to allay the fears of, inspire courage in, reassure.
desacomedido, da, *a.* unobliging.
desacomodadamente, *adv.* inconveniently.
desacomodado, da, *past part. of* **desacomodar.** —*a.* 1. inconvenient, troublesome. 2. poor, impecunious. 3. unemployed, without employment.

desacomodamiento, *m.* inconvenience, trouble.
desacomodar, *tr.v.* 1. to inconvenience, bother. 2. to dismiss, discharge (from employment). *—r.v.* to lose one's job, be dismissed.
desacomodo, *m.* discharge, dismissal (from employment); loss of employment; unemployment.
desacompañamiento, *m.* lack of company, loneliness.
desacompañar, *tr.v.* to leave the company of, abandon, leave alone.
desaconsejadamente, *adv.* ill-advisedly, unwisely, imprudently.
desaconsejado, da, *past part. of* **desaconsejar.** *—a.* ill-advised, imprudent, capricious. *—m., f.* imprudent or capricious person.
desaconsejar, *tr.v.* to dissuade.
desacoplar, *tr.v.* to uncouple, disconnect, disengage.
desacordadamente, *adv.* discordantly, inharmoniously.
desacordado, da, *past part. of* **desacordar.** *—a.* (p.) discordant, clashing, inharmonious (colors); out of proportion, lacking perspective.
desacordante, *a.* discordant.
desacordar, (*ref. 33*) *tr.v.* to put out of tune. *—r.v.* 1. to become forgetful, lose one's memory. 2. to get out of tune.
desacorde, *a.* discordant, inharmonious; (fig.) incongruous.
desacorralar, *tr.v.* 1. to let (cattle) out of an enclosure. 2. (taur.) to bring the bull out into the open or the arena.
desacostumbradamente, *adv.* unusually.
desacostumbrado, da, *past part. of* **desacostumbrar.** *—a.* unusual.
desacostumbrar, *tr.v.* to disaccustom, make (someone) lose the custom of. *—r.v.* to get out of, lose the habit or custom.
desacotar, *tr.v.* 1. to lay open (pastures), unfence; to remove or take down fences of. 2. to lift the restrictions on. 3. to reject, refuse. *—i.v.* to withdraw from an agreement or deal.
desacoto, *m.* 1. laying open, unfencing (field or pasture). 2. lifting of restrictions.
desacreditado, da, *past part. of* **desacreditar.** *—a.* discredited, disgraced.
desacreditar, *tr.v.* to discredit, bring discredit on, disgrace.
desactivar, *tr.v.* to deactivate.
desacuerde, desacuerdo, *ref.* **desacordar.**
desacuerdo, *m.* 1. discord, disagreement; disconformity. 2. error, blunder, mistake. 3. forgetfulness, forgetting. 4. mental derangement.
desacuñador, *m.* (print.) shooting stick.
desachirarse, *r.v.* (Col.) to clear, brighten up (sky).
desadaptado, da, *a.* maladapted, maladaptive.
desaderece, desaderecé, *ref.* **desaderezar.**
desaderezar, (*ref. 53*) *tr.v.* to disarrange, ruffle. *—r.v.* to become disarranged, untidy or ruffled.
desadeudar, *tr.v.* to free from debt. *—r.v.* to get out of debt, pay one's debts.
desadorar, *tr.v.* to cease to worship.
desadormecer, (*ref. 45*) *tr.v.* 1. to wake, rouse. 2. (fig.) to clear (one's head). 3. to free or relieve from numbness. *—r.v.* 1. to wake up. 2. to become wide-awake or clearheaded. 3. to get free from numbness.
desadormezca, desadormezco, *ref.* **desadormecer.**
desadornar, *tr.v.* to remove, divest or strip of ornaments or decorations.
desadorno, *m.* lack of ornaments or decorations, bareness.
desadvertidamente, *adv.* inadvertently.
desadvertido, da, *past part. of* **desadvertir.** *—a.* inadvertent, unaware, inattentive.
desadvertimiento, *m.* inadvertence.
desadvertir, (*ref. 42*) *tr.v.* to fail to notice, be unaware of.
desadvierta, desadvierto, *ref.* **desadvertir.**
desadvirtiendo, desadvirtiera, desadvirtiese, desadvirtió, *ref.* **desadvertir.**
desafección, *f.* ill-will; disaffection; dislike.
desafecto, ta, *a.* disaffected; opposed. *—m.* ill-will, dislike; disaffection.
desaferrar, (*ref. 29*) *tr.v.* 1. to loosen, unfasten; to let go. 2. to unfurl. 3. (fig.) to make a person change his mind or alter his opinion. 4. (mar.) to weigh anchor. *—r.v.* 1. to loosen or let go one's hold. 2. to change one's mind or alter one's opinion.
desafiadero, *m.* dueling ground.
desafiador, ra, *a.* challenging; defiant. *—m., f.* challenger.
desafiar, (*ref. 54*) *tr.v.* to challenge, dare, defy; to oppose, rival, compete with.
desafición, *f.* dislike, lack of fondness.
desaficionar, *tr.v.* to destroy or kill interest, liking or fondness (for anything); to cause to dislike. *—r.v.* (with **de**) to lose one's liking or fondness (for).
desafierre, desafierro, *ref.* **desaferrar.**
desafilar, *tr.v.* to blunt. *—r.v.* to become blunt.
desafinación, *f.* dissonance, the condition of being out of tune, off-key.
desafinadamente, *adv.* out of tune, dissonantly, off-key.
desafinar, *i.v.* 1. to be, play or sing out of tune. 2. (fig.) to speak indiscreetly, make an unfortunate remark. *—r.v.* to get out of tune.
desafío, *m.* challenge; defiance; rivalry, competition.
desaforadamente, *adv.* 1. to excess, excessively. 2. rowdily; lawlessly. 3. imprudently, rudely, insolently.
desaforado, da, *past part. of* **desaforar.** *—a.* 1. lawless; disorderly, wild; illegal, unlawful. 2. impudent, insolent. 3. huge, excessive.
desaforar, (*ref. 33*) *tr.v.* 1. to violate or encroach upon one's privileges. 2. to deprive of rights or privileges. *—r.v.* to forget oneself; to act wildly or lawlessly.
desaforo, *m.* (Cuba) impulse, rage, fury.
desaforrar, *tr.v.* to remove the lining of.
desafortunado, da, *a.* unfortunate, unlucky, unhappy.
desafuere, desafuero, *ref.* **desaforar.**
desafuero, *m.* 1. lawlessness, outrage, excess; infraction of law, crime. 2. (law) privation of privileges.
desagarrar, *tr.v.* (coll.) to release, let go.
desagraciado, da, *past part. of* **desgraciar.** *—a.* 1. plain, ugly. 2. artless, prosaic (person); dull, lifeless (work of art); lacking life or spark. 3. unfortunate, unhappy. 4. (Car.) shameless, uncouth.
desagraciar, *tr.v.* 1. to make ungraceful, deprive of beauty or charm, make ugly. 2. (Car.) to deflower a girl.
desagradable, *a.* disagreeable, displeasing, unpleasant.
desagradablemente, *adv.* disagreeably, unpleasantly.
desagradar, *i.v.* to displease; to cause displeasure or unpleasantness to.
desagradecer, (*ref. 45*) *tr.v.* to be ungrateful; to be unappreciative.
desagradecidamente, *adv.* ungratefully.
desagradecido, da, *past part. of* **desagradecer.** *—a.* ungrateful. *—m., f.* ingrate, ungrateful person.
desagradecimiento, *m.* ungratefulness, ingratitude.
desagradezca, desagradezco, *ref.* **desagradecer.**
desagrado, *m.* displeasure, discontent.
desagraviar, *tr.v.* to put to rights, make amends for, to apologize to; to indemnify or compensate for. *—r.v.* to obtain satisfaction or compensation.
desagravio, *m.* amends, satisfaction; indemnification, compensation. — **hacer algo en d. de,** to do something in amends for.
desagregación, *f.* disintegration, segregation, separation.
desagregado, da, *a.* (phys.) disintegrated.
desagregar, (*ref. 51*) *tr.v., r.v.* to separate, segregate.
desagregue, desagregué, *ref.* **desagregar.**
desaguable, *a.* drainable.
desaguace, desaguacé, *ref.* **desaguazar.**
desaguadero, *m.* drain, ditch, outlet; (fig.) drain (on one's resources).
desaguador, *m.* drain, outlet, ditch.
desaguar, (*ref. 52*) *tr.v.* 1. to drain, empty of water, draw off water from. 2. (fig.) to dissipate, drain, consume. *—i.v.* to flow, empty itself (river into sea). *—r.v.* to vomit; to empty the bowels.
desaguazar, (*ref. 53*) *tr.v.* to drain, to empty of water.
desagüe, *m.* drain, outlet; drainage, draining, sewerage; **d. de azotea,** roof drain; **d. superficial,** surface drainage.
desaguisadamente, *adv.* unlawfully, unjustly, wrongly, unreasonably.
desaguisado, da, *a.* unlawful, wrongful, outrageous. *—m.* offense, outrage; (Amer.) mess, disorder.
desaherrojar, *tr.v.* to unfetter, unshackle. *—r.v.* to get out of one's shackles or fetters.
desahijar, *tr.v.* to separate offspring from (e.g. a dam). *—r.v.* to swarm (bees).
desahitarse, *r.v.* to cure oneself of indigestion.
desahogadamente, *adv.* 1. insolently, impudently, brazenly. 2. comfortably, easily. 3. relaxedly.
desahogado, da, *past part. of* **desahogar.** *—a.* 1. insolent, impudent, brazen. 2. spacious, roomy, clear (not crowded or cluttered). 3. well-to-do, comfortable.
desahogar, (*ref. 51*) *tr.v.* 1. to comfort, console, lend a hand to; to alleviate, relieve. 2. to give vent to (feelings). *—r.v.* 1. to unbosom oneself, unburden one's troubles, confide (in). 2. to give vent to one's feelings. 3. to relax, make oneself comfortable, take things easy. 4. to get clear of debt, pay one's debts. 5. to speak one's mind (to), give a piece of one's mind (to).
desahogo, *m.* 1. alleviation, relief. 2. vent (for feelings). 3. ease, comfort. 4. rest, relaxation, well-being. 5. freedom, frankness. — **vivir con d.,** to live comfortably.
desahogue, desahogué, *ref.* **desahogar.**
desahuciadamente, *adv.* without hope, hopelessly, despairingly.
desahuciado, da, *past part. of* **desahuciar.** *—a.* hopeless (a patient); dispossessed (a tenant).
desahuciar, *tr.v.* 1. to deprive of hope; to lose hope for (recovery of the sick). 2. to evict, dispossess (a tenant).
desahucio, *m.* eviction, dispossession of a tenant.
desahumado, da, *past part. of* **desahumar.** *—a.* vapid, flat, weak, lifeless (liquor).
desahumar, *tr.v.* to dispel smoke from, to rid of smoke.

desainadura, *f.* (vet.) liquefaction or loss of fat or fatty tissue (disease of horses due to overwork).
desainar, *tr.v.* 1. to cause to lose fat, cause loss of fat in. 2. to remove thickness or substance of. 3. (in falconry) to debilitate the goshawk during moult by curtailing food and purging. —*r.v.* 1. to lose fat. 2. to lose it's substance.
desairadamente, *adv.* ungracefully, unattractively, awkwardly.
desairado, da, *past part. of* **desairar.** —*a.* 1. ungraceful, unattractive. 2. unsuccessful.
desairar, *tr.v.* 1. to slight, snub, rebuff, ignore, disregard. 2. to value (something) lightly.
desaire, *m.* 1. ungracefulness, unattractiveness, awkwardness. 2. slight, snub, rebuff. — **sufrir un d.,** to meet with a rebuff.
desaislarse, *r.v.* to come out of isolation or seclusion.
desajustar, *tr.v.* to disarrange, to put out of order. —*r.v.* 1. to withdraw from, fail to fulfill (an agreement). 2. to get out of order, break down.
desajuste, *m.* maladjustment; break down, getting out of order; breaking of or withdrawal from a contract.
desalabanza, *f.* disparagement, belittlement; vituperation.
desalabar, *tr.v.* to disparage, belittle; to vituperate.
desalabear, *tr.v.* (carp. to flatten or straighten (warped board); (carp.) to plane level or flat.
desalabeo, *m.* (carp.) leveling, flattening, straightening.
desaladamente, *adv.* 1. hastily, hurriedly, swiftly. 2. anxiously, eagerly, desirously.
desalado, da, *past part. of* **desalar.** —*a.* 1. hasty, hurried. 2. anxious, eager.
desalagar, (*(ref. 51*) *tr.v.* to dry, drain, dry up.
desalague, desalagué, *ref.* **desalagar.**
desalar, *tr.v.* 1. to desalt, remove salt from. 2. to remove or clip wings of. —*r.v.* to run, rush. — **desalarse por** + *inf.*, to crave, be anxious or eager to + *inf.*
desalbardar, *tr.v.* to remove the pack saddle from.
desalentadamente, *adv.* 1. dispiritedly. 2. feebly, faintly.
desalentador, ra, *a.* discouraging, disheartening, e.g. *noticias desalentadoras,* disheartening news.
desalentar, (*ref. 29*) *tr.v.* 1. to make breathless, put out of breath. 2. (fig.) to dishearten, discourage, dispirit. —*r.v.* to get disheartened, discouraged or dispirited.
desalfombrar, *tr.v.* to remove the carpets from.
desalforjar, *tr.v.* to take (something) out of a saddlebag. —*r.v.* (coll. to loosen one's clothing (for comfort).
desalhajar, *tr.v.* to strip (a room) of furniture and equipment.
desaliente, desaliento, *ref.* **desalentar.**
desaliento, *m.* 1. discouragement, dejection, dismay. 2. faintness, weakness, languor.
desalineación, *f.* disalignment.
desalineado, da, *past part. of* **desalinear.** —*a.* disaligned, out-of-line; untrue.
desalinear, *tr.v.* to disalign. —*r.v.* to get out of alignment, get out of line.
desaliñadamente, *adv.* in a slovenly manner, slatternly, untidily; dirtily.
desaliñado, da, *past part. of* **desaliñar.** —*a.* slovenly, untidy; dirty, shabby.
desaliñar, *tr.v.* to disarrange, disorder; to make dirty; to make untidy. —*r.v.* to become disarranged, untidy or dirty.
desaliño, *m.* 1. slovenliness, untidiness; shabbiness, dirtiness; (fig.) neglect, carelessness. 2. (*pl.*) very long earrings.
desalivar, *i.v., r.v.* to salivate profusely.
desalmadamente, *adv.* heartlessly, inhumanly, cruelly, mercilessly, pitilessly.
desalmado, da, *past part. of* **desalmar.** —*a.* heartless, inhuman, cruel, merciless, pitiless, cold-blooded.
desalmamiento, *m.* heartlessness, inhumanity, cruelty, mercilessness.
desalmar, *tr.v.* 1. to weaken, debilitate. 2. to disturb, upset. —*r.v.* 1. to become weak or faint. 2. to become disturbed or upset. — **desalmarse por,** to crave or long for.
desalmenado, da, *a.* without merlons (battlement).
desalmidonar, *tr.v.* to unstarch, remove starch from.
desalojado, da *past part. of* **desalojar.** —*a.* evicted, dispossessed, displaced, e.g. *inquilino desalojado,* evicted tenant.
desalojamiento, *m.* dislodgment, displacement, disposal; eviction, ejection.
desalojar, *tr.v.* 1. to dislodge, displace. 2. to evict, eject, dispossess. —*i.v.* to move out of, leave, quit, evacuate (a room or house).
desalojo, *m., var. of* **desalojamiento.**
desalquilado, da, *past part. of* **desalquilar.** —*a.* vacant, unrented.
desalquilar, *tr.v.* to vacate, leave (rented premises).
desalterar, *tr.v.* to calm, quiet, soothe.
desalumbradamente, *adv.* unsteadily, unsurely, dazedly.
desalumbrado, da, *a.* dazzled; unsure, unsteady, bewildered, dazed.
desalumbramiento, *m.* blindness; unsureness, lack of judgment.
desamable, *a.* unlovely, unlovable, unworthy of love.
desamador, ra, *a.* hating. —*m., f.* loather, hater.
desamar, *tr.v.* to cease to love; to detest, dislike.
desamarrar, *tr.v.* to untie, unbind, unlash; (mar.) to cast off, unmoor; (fig.) to separate, part, unloose. —*r.v.* to come untied or loose.
desamartelar, *tr.v.* to destroy or kill (someone's) love or affection. —*r.v.* to turn cold or indifferent.
desamasado, da, *a.* undone, disunited.
desamigado, da, *a.* estranged (friends).
desamistarse, *r.v.* to become enemies; to quarrel, fall out; to become estranged.
desamoblar, (*ref. 33*) *tr.v.* to strip of furniture (a room, a house).
desamoldar, *tr.v.* to misshape, make (something) lose its shape; (fig.) to throw out of proportion; to disfigure.
desamor, *m.* lack of love; indifference; enmity.
desamoradamente, *adv.* lovelessly, coldly, indifferently.
desamorado, da, *past part. of* **desamorar.** —*a.* loveless, unloving, cold.
desamorar, *tr.v.* to lose the love of; to cause (someone) to lose his love for. —*r.v.* to cease loving.
desamoroso, sa, *a.* loveless, unloving, cold, indifferent.
desamorrar, *tr.v.* 1. (coll.) to liven (someone) up, buck up (coll.), cheer up. 2. to draw (someone) into the conversation.
desamortice, desamorticé, *ref.* **desamortizar.**
desamortizable, *a.* (law) disentailable.
desamortización, *f.* (law) disentailment; freeing from mortmain.
desamortizador, ra, *a.* (law) disentailing. —*m., f.* disentailer.
desamortizar, (*ref. 53*) *tr.v.* (law) to disentail, free from mortmain.
desamotinarse, *r.v.* to withdraw from a mutiny.
desamparadamente, *adv.* without protection.
desamparado, da, *a,* abandoned, forlorn; helpless.
desamparador, ra, *a.* abandoning, forsaking. —*m., f.* forsaker, deserter, abandoner.
desamparar, *tr.v.* to abandon, forsake; to quit, leave; (law) to relinquish, give up.
desamparo, *m.* abandonment, helplessness; desertion; (law) dereliction.
desamueblado, da, *past part. of* **desamueblar.** —*a.* unfurnished (room, house).
desamueblar, *tr.v.* to strip of furniture (a room or a house).
desanclar, *tr.v., var. of* **desancorar.**
desancorar, *tr.v.* (mar.) to weigh the anchor of. —*i.v.* to weigh anchor.
desandar, (*ref. 1*) *tr.v.* to go back (over the road traveled); to retrace (one's steps), e.g. *d. lo andado,* to retrace one's steps.
desandrajado, da, *a.* ragged, tattered, shabby.
desanduviera, desanduviese, desanduvo, *ref.* **desandar.**
desangramiento, *m.* profuse bleeding, loss of blood.
desangrar, *tr.v.* 1. to bleed copiously. 2. to drain, empty (lake, tank). 3. (fig.) to bleed, impoverish, consume (someone's fortune). —*r.v.* to bleed profusely, lose a lot of blood; to bleed to death.
desanidar, *i.v.* to leave the nest (birds). —*tr.v.* (fig.) to dislodge from a hiding-place.
desanimación, *f.* (Amer.) tediousness; listlessness; apathy.
desanimadamente, *adv.* dispiritedly, spiritlessly, dejectedly.
desanimado, da, *a.* lifeless, discouraged; (Amer.) dull (party, etc.).
desanimar, *tr.v.* to discourage, dishearten, daunt. —*r.v.* to get discouraged.
desánimo, *m.* dispiritedness, faintheartedness, discouragement.
desanublar, *tr.v.* (fig.) to brighten, make clear. —*r.v.* to clear, become bright (sky).
desanudar, *tr.v.* to untie (a knot, a bow); (fig.) to clarify, elucidate, disentangle.
desañudadura, *f.* untying; (fig.) clarification, elucidation, disentanglement.
desañudar, *tr.v., var. of* **desanudar.**
desaojadera, *f.* female charm dispeller; curer of the evil eye.
desaojar, *tr.v.* to cure of the evil eye, dispel the evil eye from.
desapacibilidad, *f.* unpleasantness, disagreeableness.
desapacible, *a.* unpleasant, disagreeable.
desapaciblemente, *adv.* unpleasantly, disagreeably.
desapadrinar, *tr.v.* 1. to disapprove of. 2. to withdraw support from.
desapañar, *tr.v.* to disarrange, disarray, make untidy.
desaparear, *tr.v.* to separate (a pair), to break (a set).
desaparecer, (*ref. 45*) *tr.v.* to make disappear. —*i.v., r.v.* to disappear, vanish.
desaparecimiento, *m., var. of* **desaparición.**
desaparejar, *tr.v.* 1. to unharness, remove the harness of. 2. (mar.) to unrig; to strip or dismantle (a ship). —*r.v.* to become unharnessed.
desaparezca, desaparezco, *ref.* **desaparecer.**
desaparición, *f.* disappearance, vanishing.
desaparroquiar, *tr.v.* 1. to remove from a parish. 2. take away customers from. —*r.v.* 1. to lose one's parish. 2. to lose customers.
desapasionadamente, *adv.* dispassionately, impartially.

desapasionado, da, *past part. of* **desapasionar.** —*a.* dispassionate, impartial.
desapasionar, *tr.v.* to take away love or fondness for (a person or thing). —*r.v.* (with **de**) to overcome one's passion (for), lose one's passion, love or fondness (for).
desapegar, (*ref. 51*) *tr.v.* to unstick; to detach, separate. —*r.v.* 1. to come unstuck or apart. 2. (fig.) to lose one's love or fondness for (a person or thing); to become indifferent to.
desapego, *m.* coolness, indifference, coldness; lack of affection or fondness.
desapegue, desapegué, *ref.* **desapegar.**
desapercibidamente, *adv.* 1. unpreparedly, without warning. 2. without being noticed. 3. (Amer.) inadvertently.
desapercibido, da, *a.* 1. unprepared, unprovided, unready. 2. unnoticed, e.g. *pasar d.,* to be unnoticed. 3. (Amer.) inadverted, inattentive.
desapercibimiento, *m.* unpreparedness, unreadiness.
desapernar, *tr.v.* to loosen or remove bolts.
desapestar, *tr.v.* to disinfect, to remove odors from.
desapiadadamente, *adv., var. of* **despiadadamente,** mercilessly, pitilessly, cruelly.
desapiadado, da, *a., var. of* **despiadado,** merciless, pitiless, coldblooded, cruel.
desapiolar, *tr.v.* to untie trussed small game.
desaplacible, *a.* disagreeable, unpleasant.
desaplicación, *f.* lack of application, indolence, laziness, carelessness.
desaplicadamente, *adv.* without application, indolently.
desaplicado, da, *past part. of* **desaplicar.** —*a.* indolent, lazy, not diligent or industrious. —*m., f.* lazybones, idler.
desaplicar, (*ref. 50*) *tr.v.* to make lazy or neglectful. —*r.v.* to become lazy or neglectful.
desaplique, desapliqué, *ref.* **desaplicar.**
desaplomar, *tr.v.* (mas.) to make lean to one side. —*r.v.* to lean to one side, get out of plumb.
desapoderadamente, *adv.* impetuously, wildly, violently
desapoderado, da, *a.* impetuous, headlong, ungovernable; wild, violent.
desapoderamiento, *m.* 1. dispossession; privation of power or authority. 2. unruliness, wildness.
desapoderar, *tr.v.* to dispossess; to remove power from, deprive of power. —*r.v.* to become dispossessed, lose one's possessions.
desapolillar, *tr.v.* to rid of moths; (fig.) to dust, air. —*r.v.* (coll.) to clear oneself of cobwebs, give oneself an airing.
desaporcar, (*ref. 50*) *tr.v.* (agr.) to remove banked-up earth from (around plants).
desaporque, desaporqué, *ref.* **desaporcar.**
desaposentar, *tr.v.* 1. to turn out or evict from a room or house. 2. to drive away, send away.
desaposesionar, *tr.v.* to dispossess.
desapoyar, *tr.v.* to withdraw support from; to remove the props or support from.
desapreciar, *tr.v.* to underestimate; to think little of.
desaprender, *tr.v.* to unlearn, to forget what one has learned.
desaprensar, *tr.v.* 1. to raise nap or pile on (cloth), take the gloss off. 2. (fig.) to extricate.
desaprensión, *f.* indifference, insouciance, neglect, lack of conscientiousness.
desaprensivo, va, *a.* unconscientious, neglectful.
desapretar, (*ref. 29*) *tr.v.* to loosen. —*r.v.* to become loose.
desapriete, desaprieto, *ref.* **desapretar.**
desaprisionar, *tr.v.* to release, set free.
desaprobación, *f.* disapproval.
desaprobar, (*ref. 33*) *tr.v.* to disapprove of, condemn.
desapropiación, *f., var. of* **desapropiamiento.**
desapropiamiento, *m.* giving up, cession, surrender (of one's property).
desapropiarse, *r.v.* to give up, surrender, cede, divest oneself (of one's property).
desapropio, *m., var. of* **desapropiamiento.**
desaprovechadamente, *adv.* unprofitably.
desaprovechado, da, *past part. of* **desaprovechar.** —*a.* idle, lazy, indifferent to profiting from advantages; unprofitable (said of activities or business). —*m., f.* idle or lazy person.
desaprovechamiento, *m.* waste, ill-use, misuse (of opportunities); lack of progress, backwardness.
desaprovechar, *tr.v.* to waste, misuse (opportunities, etc.). —*i.v.* to lose ground, go backwards (in studies, etc.).
desapruebe, desapruebo, *ref.* **desaprobar.**
desapuntalar, *tr.v.* to remove supports or props from (a building).
desapuntar, *tr.v.* 1. (dressm.) to unstitch, undo the stitches of. 2. to make lose aim; to put out of aim.
desaquellarse, *r.v.* (coll.) to get discouraged, become disheartened.
desarbolar, *tr.v.* 1. (mar.) to dismast, strip (a ship) of masts. 2. to clear of trees.
desarbolo, *m.* (mar.) stripping (a ship) of its masts.
desarenar, *tr.v.* to clear of sand, remove sand from.
desareno, *m.* removal or clearing of sand.
desarmable, *a.* collapsible, dismountable.
desarmador, *m.* (mil.) hammer (of a gun).
desarmadura, *f., var. of* **desarme.**
desarmamiento, *m., var. of* **desarme.**
desarmar, *tr.v.* 1. to disarm, divest of arms. 2. to dismount; to take apart, take to pieces (machines). 3. to discharge, disband (troops). 4. (mar.) to dismantle and lay up (a ship). 5. to soften, assuage, lessen, temper (anger, evil). 6. (taur.) to make a bull butt in the air. —*r.v.* 1. to disarm, divest oneself of arms. 2. to come to pieces, fall to pieces.
desarme, *m.* disarmament, disarming.
desarraigar, (*ref. 51*) *tr.v.* 1. to uproot (a plant, a person or idea); to extirpate. 2. to eradicate, get rid of (vice, habit, etc.). 3. to make (someone) give up an opinion. 4. to banish, expel. —*r.v.* 1. to become uprooted. 2. to be eradicated.
desarraigo, *m.* uprooting, eradication.
desarraigue, desarraigué, *ref.* **desarraigar.**
desarrancarse, (*ref. 50*) *r.v.* to abandon, withdraw from (an association).
desarranque, desarranqué, *ref.* **desarrancarse.**
desarrapado, da, *a.* torn and tattered, ragged.
desarreboce, desarrebocé, *ref.* **desarrebozar.**
desarrebozadamente, *adv.* openly, clearly.
desarrebozar, (*ref. 53*) *tr.v.* 1. to uncover, unveil; to disclose, reveal. 2. (fig.) to manifest, evince, make clear. —*r.v.* 1. to be uncovered or unveiled; to be disclosed or revealed. 2. (fig.) to be made manifest or clear.
desarrebujar, *tr.v.* 1. to disentangle, unwind, uncoil, unravel. 2. to loosen, unfasten (one's clothes). 3. (fig.) to explain, clarify, elucidate. —*r.v.* to loosen or unfasten one's clothes.
desarregladamente, *adv.* untidily; unmethodically.
desarreglado, da, *past part. of* **desarreglar.** —*a.* 1. untidy, disorderly, slovenly. 2. immoderate, intemperate. 3. out of order (machine).
desarreglar, *tr.v.* 1. to disarrange; make untidy. 2. to put out of order (machine). —*r.v.* 1. to break down, get out of order. 2. to get untidy or disarranged.
desarreglo, *m.* muddle, mess, confusion; disorder, disturbance.
desarrendar, (*ref. 29*) *tr.v.* 1. to unbridle (a horse). 2. to stop renting; to terminate the lease of. —*r.v.* to shake off bridle (said of a horse).
desarrevolver, (*ref. 34*) *tr.v.* to disentangle, unravel, clear up.
desarrevuelva, desarrevuelvo, *ref.* **desarrevolver.**
desarriende, desarriendo, *ref.* **desarrendar.**
desarrimar, *tr.v.* 1. to separate, move away from. 2. to dissuade.
desarrimo, *m.* lack of support.
desarrollable, *a.* developable, able to be developed.
desarrollado, da, *past part. of* **desarrollar.** —*a.* developed, expanded, e.g. *país desarrollado,* developed country.
desarrollar, *tr.v.* 1. to develop; to promote, expand. 2. to unroll, unfurl, unwind. 3. to expound, explain (a theory); (math.) to set forth and work out (a problem). 4. (archit.) to draw (a building) in all its cross sections. —*r.v.* to develop; to be developed; to develop oneself, to grow. 2. to unwind, unfurl. 3. to take place, develop.
desarrollo, *m.* 1. development, growth, expansion. 2. unrolling, unwinding. 3. exposition (of a theory); (math.) working out (of a problem).
desarropar, *tr.v.* to undress, disrobe. —*r.v.* to get undressed or uncovered.
desarrugadura, *f.* unwrinkling, smoothing out of wrinkles.
desarrugar, (*ref. 51*) *tr.v.* 1. to unwrinkle, smooth out wrinkles of, make smooth. 2. (fig.) to mollify, to bring out of ill-humor.
desarrugue, desarrugué, *ref.* **desarrugar.**
desarrumar, *tr.v.* (mar.) to unload (cargo); to break out (the hold).
desarticulación, *f.* disarticulation.
desarticulado, da, *past part. of* **desarticular.** —*a.* disjointed; inarticulate.
desarticular, *tr.v.* 1. to disarticulate, disjoint (bones). 2. (fig.) to disassemble (a machine). —*r.v.* to become disarticulated, disarticulate, disjointed.
desartillar, *tr.v.* to take guns from (ship or fort).
desarzonar, *tr.v.* to throw from the saddle, unhorse.
desasado, da, *a.* handleless, without handles.
desaseadamente, *adv.* untidily, dirtily.
desaseado, da, *past part. of* **desasear.** —*a.* untidy, dirty, slovenly.
desasear, *tr.v.* to make dirty, slovenly or untidy.
desasegurar, *tr.v.* 1. to make unsure; to unbrace, loosen, make insecure or unsteady. 2. (com.) to cancel the insurance on.
desasentar, (*ref. 29*) *tr.v.* to move; to remove. —*i.v.* (fig.) to displease. —*r.v.* to rise from one's seat, to stand up.
desaseo, *m.* untidiness, slovenliness; dirtiness, uncleanliness.
desasga, desasgo, *ref.* **desasir.**
desasiente, desasiento, *ref.* **desasentar.**
desasimiento, *m.* 1. letting loose; letting go. 2. disinterestedness, generosity.
desasimilación, *f.* (physiol.) disassimilation.
desasir, (*ref. 2*) *tr.v.* to let go, let loose. —*r.v.* to get free of, disengage oneself, get loose; **desasirse de,** to give away.
desasistir, *tr.v.* to abandon, forsake.
desasnar, *tr.v.* (coll.) to refine, make refined. —*r.v.* to become refined, acquire good manners.
desasociable, *a.* unsociable.
desasociar, *tr.v.* to separate, disassociate.

desasosegadamente, *adv.* restlessly, anxiously.
desasosegar, (*ref. 67*) *tr.v.* to make restless, uneasy or anxious; to disturb, upset.
desasosegué, *ref.* **desasosegar.**
desasosiego, *m.* restlessness, anxiety, uneasiness.
desasosiego, desasosiegue, *ref.* **desasosegar.**
desastradamente, *adv.* 1. untidily, sloppily, carelessly. 2. unfortunately, unluckily.
desastrado, da, *a.* 1. untidy, slovenly, dirty, slatternly. 2. unfortunate, wretched, unlucky. *—m., f.* sloven, shabbily dressed person.
desastre, *m.* disaster; catastrophe.
desastrosamente, *adv.* disastrously.
desastroso, sa, *a.* disastrous; unfortunate.
desatacar, (*ref. 50*) *tr.v.* 1. to unfasten (buttons, clamps, etc.). 2. (mil.) to draw the ramrod from (firearms). *—r.v.* 1. to become unfastened. 2. to undo one's trousers.
desatadamente, *adv.* freely, unrestrainedly.
desatado, da, *past part. of* **desatar.** *—a.* untied, loose, unfastened.
desatador, ra, *a.* untying. *—m., f.* a person or thing that unties.
desatadura, *f.* 1. untying, undoing. 2. letting loose. 3. unraveling, solving.
desatalentado, da, *a.* puzzled, disconcerted.
desatancar, (*ref. 50*) *tr.v.* to unblock, clear the obstruction in (pipe). *—r.v.* to get out of the mud or a rut.
desatanque, desatanqué, *ref.* **desatancar.**
desataque, desataqué, *ref.* **desatacar.**
desatar, *tr.v.* 1. to untie, undo. 2. to liquefy, melt. 3. to unravel, solve. 4. to let loose. *—r.v.* 1. to become unlaced or undone. 2. to stop feeling self-conscious, make oneself at home. 3. to let oneself go, act unrestrainedly. 4. to talk excessively. 5. to break loose (storm, passion, etc.).
desatascar, (*ref. 50*) *tr.v.* 1. to pull out of a rut or the mud. 2. to unblock, clear the obstruction from. 3. (fig.) to get (someone) out of difficulties. *—r.v.* to get out of a rut or the mud.
desatasque, desatasqué, *ref.* **desatascar.**
desataviar, (*ref. 54*) *tr.v.* to divest of ornaments or clothing.
desatavío, *m.* disarray, untidiness (in dress).
desate, *m.* 1. flood (of words). 2. letting loose (action). — **d. de vientre,** looseness of the bowels, diarrhea.
desatención, *f.* 1. inattention, disregard, lack of attention. 2. discourtesy, disrespect, rudeness.
desatender, (*ref. 30*) *tr.v.* 1. to ignore, disregard. 2. to neglect, not to comply with, leave unfulfilled (one's duties).
desatentadamente, *adv.* wildly, rashly, unwisely, injudiciously.
desatentado, da, *past part. of* **desatentar.** *—a.* 1. wild, rash, unwise, injudicious. 2. excessive, severe. *—m., f.* madcap, imprudent person.
desatentamente, *adv.* uncivilly, impolitely.
desatentar, (*ref. 29*) *tr.v.* 1. to make lose one's sense of security. 2. to confuse, befuddle, bewilder. *—r.v.* 1. to become insecure. 2. to become confused or bewildered.
desatento, ta, *a.* inattentive; discourteous, impolite. *—m., f.* discourteous, impolite person.
desaterrar, *tr.v.* (Amer.) to clear of rubble or earth.
desatesorar, *tr.v.* to spend the treasure of.
desatibar, *tr.v.* (min.) to clear of rubble or earth.
desatienda, desatiendo, *ref.* **desatender.**
desatiente, desatiento, *ref.* **desatentar.**
desatiento, *m.* 1. restlessness, uneasiness. 2. (med.) loss of touch.
desatierre, *m.* (Amer.) rubbish or rubble dump.
desatinadamente, *adv.* wildly, rashly, without thinking; foolishly, stupidly.
desatinado, da, *past part. of* **desatinar.** *—a.* 1. rash, imprudent, unwise. 2. wild, unruly, disorderly, crazy. 3. foolish, stupid. *—m., f.* madcap, fool.
desatinar, *tr.v.* to confuse, befuddle, bewilder. *—i.v.* 1. to talk nonsense; to act crazily. 2. to get confused, befuddled or bewildered.
desatino, *m.* folly, foolishness, stupidity; tactless or foolish remark or act.
desatolondrar, *tr.v.* to bring a person to his senses. *—r.v.* to come to one's senses.
desatollar, *tr.v.* to pull out of the mud or a rut. *—r.v.* to get out of the mud or a rut.
desatontarse, *r.v.* to come to, recover one's senses; (fig.) to wake up.
desatorar, *tr.v.* 1. to unblock, unclog, clear 2. (min.) to clear of debris or rubble. 3. (mar.) to break out, unload.
desatornillar, *tr.v.* to unscrew.
desatracar, (*ref. 50*) *tr.v.* (mar.) to move away (one boat from another or from the pier). *—r.v.* (mar.) to move off, push off. *—i.v.* (mar.) to sheer away from the coast.
desatraer, (*ref. 24*) *tr.v.* to separate, disjoin.
desatraiga, desatraigo, *ref.* **desatraer.**
desatraillar, *tr.v.* to unleash (gen. said of dogs).
desatraje, desatrajera, desatrajese, *ref.* **desatraer.**
desatrampar, *tr.v.* to unblock, unclog, clear of obstruction (pipe or conduit).
desatrancar, (*ref. 50*) *tr.v.* 1. to unbar, unbolt. 2. to unclog, unblock, clear of obstruction (well, conduit, pipe).
desatranque, desatranqué, *ref.* **desatrancar.**
desatraque, desatraqué, *ref.* **desatracar.**
desatrayendo, *ref.* **desatraer.**
desatufarse, *r.v.* 1. to clear one's head. 2. to cool off (after a fit of anger).
desaturdir, *tr.v.* to bring to, bring out of a daze or stupor.
desautorice, desautoricé, *ref.* **desautorizar.**
desautoridad, *f.* lack of authority.
desautorización, *f.* privation of authority; disallowance.
desautorizadamente, *adv.* without authorization.
desautorizado, da, *past part. of* **desautorizar.** *—a.* unauthorized, without authority.
desautorizar, (*ref. 53*) *tr.v.* to deprive of authority; to disallow, withdraw permission for.
desavahado, da, *past part. of* **desavahar.** *—a.* clear, free from mist and smoke.
desavahamiento, *m.* airing; cooling off.
desavahar, *tr.v.* 1. to cool off, let cool. 2. to air, ventilate. *—r.v.* to relax, take things easy, enjoy oneself.
desavecindado, da, *past part. of* **desavecindarse.** *—a.* unpopulated, deserted (house or place).
desavecindarse, *r.v.* to move away from the neighborhood.
desavendré, desavendría, *ref.* **desavenir.**
desavenencia, *f.* discord, enmity, disagreement.
desavenga, desavengo, *ref.* **desavenir.**
desavenido, da, *past part. of* **desavenir.** *—a.* incompatible.
desavenir, (*ref. 26*) *tr.v.* to bring discord between; to make hostile. *—r.v.* to disagree, quarrel, fall out (friends).
desaventajadamente, *adv.* disadvantageously, at a disadvantage.
desaventajado, da, *a.* disadvantageous, disadvantaged.
desaventura, *f.* (rare) misfortune.
desaviar, (*ref. 54*) *tr.v.* 1. to deprive or leave without necessary equipment. 2. to lead astray, to mislead. *—r.v.* 1. to be left without or deprived of necessary equipment. 2. to go astray.
desavine, *ref.* **desavenir.**
desaviniendo, desaviniera, desaviniese, *ref.* **desavenir.**
desavío, *m.* 1. misleading, leading astray. 2. lack of equipment.
desavisado, da, *past part. of* **desavisar.** *—a.* uninformed, unaware.
desavisar, *tr.v.* to contradict or revoke (a previous notice, information, etc.); to countermand.
desayudar, *tr.v.* to hinder, impede, hamper.
desayunado, da, *past part. of* **desayunar.** *—a.* having breakfasted.
desayunar, *i.v.* (imp. u.) *var. of* **desayunarse.**
desayunarse, *r.v.* 1. to have breakfast. 2. (fig.) to receive the first news of.
desayuno, *m.* breakfast.
desazogar, (*ref. 51*) *tr.v.* to remove the quicksilver from.
desazogue, desazogué, *ref.* **desazogar.**
desazón, *f.* 1. tastelessness, insipidity. 2. (agr.) unfitness (of soil) for cultivation. 3. irritation, annoyance. 4. indisposition, upset, uneasiness.
desazonado, da, *past part. of* **desazonar.** *—a.* 1. (agr.) unfit for cultivation (soil). 2. (fig.) unwell, indisposed; uneasy, restless.
desazonar, *tr.v.* 1. (cul.) to make tasteless; to spoil the taste of. 2. (fig.) to annoy, irritate. *—r.v.* 1. to become annoyed, irritated or upset. 2. to feel indisposed or restless.
desazufrar, *tr.v.* (chem.) to desulfurize.
desbabar, *i.v., r.v.* to drivel, slaver. *—tr.v.* (cul.) to clean snails of slime.
desbagar, (*ref. 51*) *tr.v.* to extract linseed from its capsule.
desbague, desbagué, *ref.* **desbagar.**
desbancar, (*ref. 50*) *tr.v.* 1. to clear of benches. 2. (in cards) to win the bank from. 3. to replace (someone) in the affections of another.
desbandada, *f.* rout, disorderly flight; **a la d.,** helter-skelter, in great confusion.
desbandarse, *r.v.* 1. to scatter or flee in disorder; to disperse. 2. to withdraw (from), leave. 3. (mil.) to desert.
desbanque, desbanqué, *ref.* **desbancar.**
desbañado, *a.* (hunt.) not watered (said of a falcon on the days of the hunt).
desbarahúste, *m., var. of* **desbarajuste.**
desbarahustar, *tr.v., var. of* **desbarajustar.**
desbarajustar, *tr.v.* to throw into disorder or confusion; to disarrange.
desbarajuste, *m.* disorder, confusion.
desbaratadamente, *adv.* in a disorderly way; confusedly, incoherently (said of speaking).
desbaratado, da, *past part. of* **desbaratar.** *—a.* (coll.) wrecked, broken; wild, unruly. *—m., f.* (coll.) debauchee; wreck, ruin (person).
desbaratador, ra, *a.* wrecking, destroying. *—m., f.* wrecker, destroyer.
desbaratamiento, *m.* wrecking, upsetting; thwarting, frustration.
desbaratar, *tr.v.* 1. to wreck, ruin. 2. to squander, misspend, waste (money, etc.). 3. to thwart, frustrate, hinder. 4. (mil.) to disperse, rout, throw into confusion (the enemy). *—i.v.* to act crazily; to talk nonsense. *—r.v.* 1. to be wrecked or ruined. 2. to be squandered. 3. to talk or act wildly or unreasonably.
desbarate, *m.* 1. wrecking, ruin. 2. squandering. 3. (mil.) dispersion, routing. 4. (med.) diarrhea, loose bowels. 5. thwarting, frustration. 6. nonsense, foolishness.
desbarato, *m., var. of* **desbarate.**
desbarbado, da, *past part. of* **desbarbar.** *—a.* (derog.) pertaining to a young man or woman; beardless.

desbarbar, *tr.v.* to trim; (coll.) to shave. —*r.v.* (coll.) to shave.
desbarbillar, *tr.v.* (agr.) to cut off rootlets, to prune, to trim, cut back.
desbardar, *tr.v.* to remove thatch from (top of fence walls).
desbarnizar, *tr.v.* to remove varnish or shellac.
desbarrancadero, *m.* (Amer.) precipice; ravine.
desbarrar, *i.v.* 1. to hurl an iron bar as far as possible. 2. to slip away, steal away. 3. to talk nonsense, to make a mistake, act foolishly.
desbarretar, *tr.v.* to unbar, take bars down from.
desbarrigado, da, *past part. of* **desbarrigar.** —*a.* having a small abdomen; small-bellied.
desbarrigar, (*ref. 51*) *tr.v.* 1. (coll.) to wound or hurt (someone) in the abdomen. 2. to rip a person's abdomen open.
desbarrigue, desbarrigué, *ref.* **desbarrigar.**
desbarro, *m.* 1. slip, blunder, mistake; nonsense. 2. slipping or stealing away.
desbastador, *m.* dressing tool, dressing plane, chisel or file.
desbastadura, *f.* trimming, planing, dressing.
desbastar, *tr.v.* 1. to wear out, weaken. 2. to plane; to smooth, trim. 3. to refine, educate and polish. —*r.v.* to become refined, acquire good manners.
desbaste, *m.* 1. wear and tear. 2. planing; rough dressing. — **estar en d.,** to be prepared roughly, be roughly dressed.
desbastecido, da, *a.* without provisions.
desbautice, desbauticé, *ref.* **desbautizarse.**
desbautizarse, (*ref. 53*) *r.v.* (coll.) to lose one's temper, fly into a temper.
desbazadero, *m.* wet and slippery place.
desbeber, *i.v.* (coll.) to urinate.
desbecerrar, *tr.v.* to wean (a calf).
desblanquecido, da, *a.* whitish.
desblanquiñado, da, *a., var. of* **desblanquecido.**
desbloquear, *tr.v.* (com.) to unfreeze, unblock (credit).
desbloqueo, *m.* (com.) unfreezing, unblocking (credit, consignments, etc.).
desbocadamente, *adv.* unrestrainedly; unashamedly, brazenly.
desbocado, da, *past part. of* **desbocar.** —*a.* 1. broken-lipped or mouthed (jar, jug). 2. nicked (cutting edge of tool). 3. (mil.) widemouthed (gun). 4. (coll.) foul-mouthed, coarse. 5. runaway, bolting (horse). —*m., f.* foul-mouthed or coarse person, foul mouth.
desbocamiento, *m.* 1. bolting, running-away (of a horse). 2. coarse, insulting language; abuse, insults.
desbocar, (*ref. 50*) *tr.v.* to break the mouth or spout of (a vessel). —*i.v.* 1. to lead (one street into another). 2. to flow or empty (river into sea). —*r.v.* 1. to bolt, run away (horse). 2. (fig.) to break into a stream of abuse.
desbonetarse, *r.v.* to remove one's bonnet.
desboque, desboqué, *ref.* **desbocar.**
desboquillar, *tr.v.* to break the mouth-piece of; to remove the nozzle from.
desbordamiento, *m.* 1. overflowing. 2. violence, lack of restraint.
desbordante, *a.* overflowing; uncontainable, unrestrainable.
desbordar, *i.v.* to overflow; to run over. —*r.v.* 1. to overflow; to run over. 2. to be beside oneself, e.g. *me desbordé de alegría,* I was beside myself with joy.
desbornice, desbornicé, *ref.* **desbornizar.**
desbornizar, (*ref. 53*) *tr.v.* to remove bark from a cork tree.
desboronar, *tr.v., r.v., var. of* **desmoronar.**
desborradora, *f.* (tex.) burler, worker who removes the knots or burls in cloth.
desborrar, *tr.v.* (tex.) to burl, remove the knots or burls from cloth.
desboscar, *tr.v.* (agr., Chile, Mex.) to clear of plants, to defoliate.
desbotonar, *tr.v.* (Cuba, Peru) 1. to remove buds from tobacco plants. 2. (Amer.) to unbutton (clothing).
desbrace, desbracé, *ref.* **desbrazarse.**
desbragado, *a.* (coll.) without breeches; ragged, destitute. —*m.* bum.
desbraguetado, *a.* (coll.) with fly-buttons undone.
desbravador, *m.* broncobuster, one who tames wild horses.
desbravar, *tr.v.* to tame, break in (horse or mules). —*i.v., r.v.* 1. to become less wild (said of beasts). 2. to abate, calm down (the sea, storm, rage, anger). 3. to lose strength (spirits).
desbravecer, (*ref. 45*) *i.v., r.v.* 1. to become less wild (beasts). 2. to abate, grow calmer (the sea, storm, rage, anger). 3. to lose strength (spirits).
desbravezca, desbravezco, *ref.* **desbravecer.**
desbrazarse, (*ref. 53*) *r.v.* to stretch one's arms violently; to swing one's arms violently.
desbrevarse, *r.v.* to lose vitality or strength.
desbridamiento, *m.* (surg.) debridement, removal of lacerated or contaminated tissue.
desbridar, *tr.v.* 1. (surg.) to debride, practice debridement on. 2. to unbridle, remove the bridle from.
desbriznar, *tr.v.* 1. to cut into little pieces; (cul.) to mince, shred (meat, vegetables). 2. (cul.) to remove the fibers from string-beans. 3. (bot.) to remove stigmas from (saffron flower).
desbroce, *m., var. of* **desbrozo.**
desbroce, desbrocé, *ref.* **desbrozar.**
desbrozar, (*ref. 53*) *tr.v.* to clear of brushwood.
desbrozo, *m.* rubbish, brushwood, clipped branches; clearing away of brushwood or rubbish.
desbruar, (*ref. 55*) *tr.v.* (tex.) to remove oil from cloth (before fulling).
desbrujar, *tr.v., var. of* **desmoronar.**
desbuchar, *tr.v.* 1. to disgorge (said of birds). 2. to disclose, tell, sing (sl.). 3. to remove the fat from. 4. to ease (a falcon's) maw; to purge (a falcon's) stomach.
desbulla, *f.* oyster shell.
desbullador, *m.* oyster fork.
desbullar, *tr.v.* to open (oysters); to remove (oysters) from their shells.
descabal, *a.* imperfect, incomplete; damaged.
descabalamiento, *m.* making incomplete or imperfect; diminution, impairment.
descabalar, *tr.v.* to make incomplete or imperfect; to remove part of. —*r.v.* to become incomplete or imperfect.
descabalgadura, *f.* dismounting (from a horse).
descabalgar, (*ref. 51*) *i.v.* to dismount (from a horse). —*tr.v.* (artil.) to dismount (a gun from its carriage); to put (a gun) out of action by destroying the gun carriage. —*r.v.* (artil.) to be put out of action (a gun).
descabalgue, descabalgué, *ref.* **descabalgar.**
descabece, descabecé, *ref.* **descabezar.**
descabelladamente, *adv.* rashly, wildly, crazily, haphazardly.
descabellado, da, *past part. of* **descabellar.** —*a.* rash, wild; disordered; disheveled; absurd, illogical, preposterous.
descabellar, *tr.v.* 1. to ruffle or disarrange (the hair). 2. (taur.) to kill (the bull) with one thrust of the sword in the neck. —*r.v.* to become disheveled.
descabello, *m.* (taur.) the killing of the bull with one thrust of the sword in the neck.
descabestrar, *tr.v.* to free an animal's leg caught in the bridle.
descabezadamente, *tr.v., var. of* **descabelladamente.**
descabezado, da, *past part. of* **descabezar.** —*a.* rash, wild, injudicious. —*m., f.* madcap, rash or wild person.
descabezamiento, *m.* beheading; cutting-off top (of trees, posts, etc.).
descabezar, (*ref. 53*) *tr.v.* 1. to behead, decapitate; to remove the head or top of. 2. (coll.) to begin to make headway, surmount (difficulties). 3. (mil.) to surmount (an obstacle). 4. (mil.) to move (front ranks) to new position. — **d. el sueño,** to have forty winks, have a nap. —*i.v.* to border (on), abut. —*r.v.* 1. to rack one's brains. 2. (agr.) to shed grain (cereals, ears of corn, etc.).
descabritar, *tr.v.* to wean (kids); to separate (the kids from the goats).
descabullirse, (*ref. 65*) *r.v.* 1. to slip out, steal away, sneak out. 2. to evade, avoid.
descachalandrado, da, *a.* (S. Amer.) sloppy, untidy, slovenly.
descachar, *tr.v.* (Amer.) *var. of* **descornar.**
descacharrado, da, *a.* (Guat., Hond.) slovenly, untidy, dirty, ragged.
descachazar, (*ref. 53*) *tr.v.* (Cuba, Ecuad., P. Rico) to remove scum from (sugar cane juice).
descaderar, *tr.v.* to dislocate or sprain (someone's) hip. —*r.v.* to dislocate or sprain one's hip.
descadillador, ra, *m., f.* worker who cuts off the warp ends or thrums (from woolen cloth).
descadillar, *tr.v.* to cut off the warp end or thrums (from woolen cloth).
descaecer, (*ref. 45*) *i.v.* to decline, decay; to languish, droop; to decrease.
descaecimiento, *m.* weakness; debilitation, decline, decay; languishing, defection; despondency.
descaer, *i.v., var. of* **decaer.**
descaezca, descaezco, *ref.* **descaecer.**
descafeinado, da, *a.* decaffeinated, containing no caffeine.
descafilar, *tr.v.* (bldg.) to smooth (bricks, flagstones, tiles).
descaimiento, *m., var. of* **descaecimiento.**
descalabace, descalabacé, *ref.* **descalabazarse.**
descalabazarse, (*ref. 53*) *r.v.* (coll.) to rack one's brains.
descalabrado, da, *past part. of* **descalabrar.** —*a.* 1. wounded in the head. 2. unsuccessful, losing, e.g. *salir d.,* to come out badly, come out losing (from a deal, etc.). —*m., f.* loser, unsuccessful person.
descalabradura, *f.* 1. head wound; head scar. 2. (Cuba) misfortune, setback.
descalabrar, *tr.v.* to wound in the head; to wound, hurt, injure; (fig.) to damage, harm. —*r.v.* to hurt or wound oneself in the head.
descalabro, *m.* setback; misfortune, calamity.
descalandrajar, *tr.v.* to rip or tear to tatters or rags.
descalcador, *m.* 1. (mar.) ravehook. 2. (carp.) claw.
descalcar, (*ref. 50*) *tr.v.* (mar.) to extract oakum from the seams.
descalce, *m.* undermining.
descalce, descalcé, *ref.* **descalzar.**
descalcez, *f.* barefootedness, lack of shoes.
descalcificación, *f.* (med.) decalcification.
descalificación, *f.* disqualification.
descalificado, da, *a.* disqualified.
descalificar, (*ref. 50*) *tr.v.* to disqualify; to take power or authority from.
descalifique, descalifiqué, *ref.* **descalificar.**

descalostrado, da, *a.* having passed the colostrum stage (a baby).
descalque, descalqué, *ref.* **descalcar.**
descalzar, (*ref. 53*) *tr.v.* 1. to take off or remove footwear. 2. to undermine, dig under. 3. to remove the wedge or block from. —*r.v.* 1. to take off or remove one's footwear. 2. to lose a shoe or shoes (a horse). 3. to become discalced (a monk, nun).
descalzo, za, *irr. past part. of* **descalzar.** —*a.* 1. barefooted, shoeless, unshod. 2. (rel.) discalced. 3. (fig.) naked, ragged, poor. —*m., f.* discalced (monk or nun).
descamación, *f.* (med.) desquamation, peeling off (skin, scales).
descamador, *m.* scaler.
descamarse, *r.v.* to desquamate, lose one's skin, scales.
descambiar, *tr.v.* to change back (something already exchanged); to cancel an exchange.
descaminadamente, *adv.* misguidedly, wrongly; on the wrong track.
descaminado, da, *past part. of* **descaminar.** —*a.* misguided, mistaken; ill-advised.
descaminar, *tr.v.* 1. to mislead, misguide. 2. to lead astray, tempt, entice. 3. to bring in, smuggle (contraband). —*r.v.* to go astray, to lose one's way.
descamino, *m.* 1. misguidance, leading astray; going astray. 2. error, blunder. 3. contraband, smuggled goods. 4. foolishness, stupid remark, nonsense.
descamisado, da, *a.* (coll.) shirtless; poor, shabby, ragged. —*m., f.* 1. ragamuffin, tatterdemalion; pauper. 2. (Arg.) a member of the proletariat, any worker.
descampado, da, *a.* free, open, clear. —*m.* clear place, clear open site; **en d.,** in the open country.
descampar, *tr.v.* to clear (land or place of brush or rubbish).
descansadamente, *adv.* restfully, quietly, leisurely.
descansadero, *m.* resting place.
descansado, da, *past part. of* **descansar.** —*a.* restful, quiet; relaxed, rested, refreshed.
descansar, *tr.v.* 1. to aid. 2. to rest, lean, to set down on. —*i.v.* 1. to rest; to relax, repose; to lie fallow, rest (land). 2. to rest, lean. 3. to lie (buried).— **descansarse en,** to trust, have confidence in.
descansillo, *m.* landing (of a staircase).
descanso, *m.* 1. rest, repose, relief, consolation. 2. landing (of a staircase). 3. seat, support. 4. (mil.) parade rest.
descantar, *tr.v.* to clear of stones.
descantear, *tr.v.* to chamfer, splay; to smooth off, round off (stones).
descanterar, *tr.v.* to remove or cut the crust off; to remove the corners or edges of (gen. said of bread).
descantillar, *tr.v.* 1. to break the edges or corners of; to bevel the edges of; to spall, chip off. 2. to deduct, subtract.
descantillón, *m., var of* **escantillón.**
descantonar, *tr.v., var. of* **descantillar.**
descañar, *tr.v.* to break the stem of (wheat or other plants).
descañonar, *tr.v.* 1. to pluck out the pinfeathers of a bird. 2. to shave close. 3. (coll.) to fleece, skin (someone) out of his money.
descaperuce, descaperucé, *ref.* **descaperuzar.**
descaperuzar, (*ref. 53*) *tr.v., r.v.* to take the hood from, unhood, uncowl.
descaperuzo, *m.* taking off the hood, unhooding.
descapillar, *tr.v.* to remove the cape from. —*r.v.* to remove or take off one's cape.
descapirotar, *tr.v.* to remove the hood or cape from. —*r.v.* to take off one's hood or cape.
descapotable, *a., m.* (auto.) convertible.
descapotar, *tr.v.* to roll back the top of (a convertible car).
descaradamente, *adv.* brazenly, shamelessly, impudently, insolently.
descarado, da, *past part. of* **descararse.** —*a.* shameless, brazen, impudent, insolent. —*m., f.* scoundrel, rogue.
descaramiento, *m.* shamelessness, brazenness, insolence, impudence.
descararse, *r.v.* to behave impudently, brazenly, insolently or shamelessly; to be saucy.
descarbonación, *f.* decarbonation.
descarbonatar, *tr.v.* (chem.) to decarbonate, remove carbonic acid from.
descarbonizar, (*ref. 53*) *tr.v* to decarbonize.
descarburación, *f.* decarbonation.
descarburar, *tr.v.* to decarbonize.
descarcañalar, *tr.v.* to tread down the heel of (a shoe).
descarga, *f.* 1. unloading. 2. unburdening. 3. (mil.) discharge; volley; firing. 4. (elec.) discharge. 5. (archit.) reduction of weight (to prevent collapse of construction). — **d. espontánea,** (elec.) self-discharge.
descargadas, *a.* (*pl.*) (her.) defamed, dishonored (coat of arms).
descargadero, *m.* wharf, unloading place, pier.
descargador, *m.* 1. porter, stevedore. 2. (mil.) wad-hook.
descargadura, *f.* the bone without the meat (after the butcher bones a cut).
descargar, (*ref. 51*) *tr.v.* 1. to unload, take off (cargo). 2. to unburden, ease (the conscience). 3. to bone (a cut of meat). 4. (mil.) to shoot, fire, discharge. 5. (mil.) to unload. 6. (elec.) to discharge. 7. to give or deal violently (blows). 8. (fig.) to free (from an obligation). —*i.v.* 1. to flow, empty (river into sea). 2. to burst with rain (a cloud). —*r.v.* 1. to resign, quit. 2. to unburden oneself. — **descargarse de,** to free oneself of (an obligation); to clear oneself of (a charge); **descargarse de algo en alguien,** to unload something on someone.
descargo, *m.* 1. unloading. 2. (com.) entry (in ledger of credit or debit). 3. excuse; (law) plea (of defendant), evidence favorable to the defendant. 4. **release** (from an obligation, debt). 5. (law) acquittal (from a charge).
descargue, *m.* unloading (of freight).
descargue, descargué, *ref.* **descargar.**
descariñarse, *r.v.* to lose one's affection or love for; to become indifferent to.
descariño, *m.* coolness, indifference, lack of affection.
descarnada, *f.* (coll.) death.
descarnadamente, *adv.* frankly, plainly; without coating the pill.
descarnado, da, *past part. of* **descarnar.** —*a.* lean, thin; bare, unadorned.
descarnador, *m.* 1. (dent.) scraper, instrument for removing flesh from a tooth. 2. hide scraper (tanning).
descarnadura, *f.* removal of flesh.
descarnar, *tr.v.* 1. to remove the flesh from; to scrape flesh from. 2. to wear away, corrode; to wash away; to lay bare, remove covering from. 3. (fig.) to remove from earthly things, to disembody. —*r.v.* 1. to lose flesh, become emaciated. 2. to become washed or worn away. 3. to spend or consume one's fortune.
descaro, *m.* brazenness, insolence, impudence, effrontery, boldness.
descarozado, *m.* (Arg., Chile) pitted peach left in the sun to dry.
descarozar, (*ref. 53*) *tr.v.* (Arg.) to pit, stone, remove stones or pits from (fruit).
descarriamiento, *m., var. of* **descarrío.**
descarriar, (*ref. 54*) *tr.v.* 1. to misguide, lead astray. 2. to separate (certain number of animals) from flock or herd. —*r.v.* to get lost; to go astray, to choose the wrong path, lead a dissipated life.
descarriladura, *f., var. of* **descarrilamiento.**
descarrilamiento, *m.* derailment; (fig.) the act of going astray in life.
descarrilar, *i.v.* to get derailed, run or go off the rails; (fig.) to go astray.
descarrillar, *tr.v.* to break the jaws of, to slap someone.
descarrío, *m.* leading astray; going astray; losing one's way, getting lost; (fig.) choosing the wrong path in life.
descartar, *tr.v.* to discard; to put aside, eliminate. —*r.v.* 1. to discard. 2. to get out (of), evade, excuse oneself (from doing something).
descarte, *m.* 1. discarding (of cards); discard (cards discarded). 2. excuse, pretext, shirking, subterfuge.
descartuchar, *tr.v.* (Chile) to deflower a girl. —*r.v.* (Chile) to have sexual intercourse for the first time (a man).
descasamiento, *m.* annulment of marriage.
descasar, *tr.v.* 1. to separate (unmarried couples living together); to annul the marriage of. 2. to disturb, disarrange. 3. (print.) to change the position of pages of a sheet (in order to arrange them correctly). —*r.v.* 1. to become separated. 2. to become disarranged, get disturbed.
descascar, (*ref. 50*) *tr.v.* to shell, peel. —*r.v.* 1. to break into pieces. 2. to boast, brag; to talk nonsense.
descascarar, *tr.v.* to shell, peel. —*r.v.* to peel, lose its peel or shell; to peel off (paint, etc.).
descascarillado, *past part. of* **descascarillar.** —*m.* peeling; peeling off, flaking off (paint, etc.).
descascarillar, *tr.v.* to peel. —*r.v.* to peel; to peel off, flake off (paint, etc.).
descaspar, *tr.v.* 1. to clean off dandruff. 2. to scrape off (a half-dressed hide, in the tanning process).
descasque, *m.* stripping of bark, decortication (esp. of cork trees).
descasque, descasqué, *ref.* **descascar.**
descastado, da, *past part. of* **descastar.** —*a.* showing lack of affection; cold, indifferent to affection. —*m., f.* person showing little love or affection for his family.
descastar, *tr.v.* to exterminate, eliminate (animals).
descatolice, descatolicé, *ref.* **descatolizar.**
descatolizar, (*ref. 53*) *tr.v.* to induce (a person or a people) to abandon Catholicism. —*r.v.* to abandon Catholicism.
descaudalado, da, *a.* ruined, penniless, bankrupt.
descebar, *tr.v.* (mil.) to unprime (firearms).
descendencia, *f.* descendants; origin, ancestry, lineage.
descendente, *a.* 1. descending. 2. said of the train going from the interior to the coast. 3. (mar.) ebb (tide).
descender, (*ref. 30*) *i.v.* 1. to go down, descend; to flow or run down. 2. to descend, derive (e.g. from noble origin). 3. to come, derive, emanate, spring (one thing from another). —*tr.v.* 1. to bring down, lower. 2. to descend, go down.
descendiente *a.* descending. —*m., f.* descendant, offspring.
descendimiento, *m.* descent, lowering, bringing down.

descensión, *f.* descension, descent; decline.
descenso, *m.* 1. descent; descending; fall. 2. (med.) descent, descensus, prolapse. 3. demotion; (mil.) degradation.
descentrado, da, *past part. of* **descentrar.** —*a.* off-center.
descentralice, descentralicé, *ref.* **descentralizar.**
descentralización, *f.* decentralization.
descentralizador, ra, *a.* decentralizing.
descentralizar, (*ref. 53*) *tr.v.* to decentralize.
descentrar, *tr.v.* to put off-center. —*r.v.* to become off-center, out of plumb.
desceñido, da, *past part. of* **desceñir.** —*a.* loose, loose-fitting.
desceñidura, *f.* ungirding, unbelting.
desceñir, (*ref. 41*) *tr.v.* to unbelt, ungird, take off (someone's) belt, girdle, crown. —*r.v.* to take off, e.g. *se desciñó la corona,* he took off his crown, (fig.) he abdicated.
descepar, *tr.v.* 1. to uproot, pull up by the roots. 2. to eradicate; to wipe out, exterminate. 3. (mar.) to remove the stocks from an anchor.
descerar, *tr.v.* to remove the empty combs from a beehive.
descercado, da, *past part. of* **descercar.** —*a.* open, unfenced.
descercador, *m.* (mil.) one who forces the enemy to raise a siege, one who does away with a wall or fence.
descercar, (*ref. 50*) *tr.v.* 1. to destroy, knock down, demolish (a fence, wall, etc.). 2. (mil.) to raise or lift the siege of.
descerco, *m.* the raising of a siege.
descerece, descerecé, *ref.* **descerezar.**
descerezar, (*ref. 53*) *tr.v.* to pulp (coffee beans).
descerque, descerqué, *ref.* **descercar.**
descerrajado, da, *past part. of* **descerrajar.** —*a.* (coll.) perverse, corrupt, wicked.
descerrajadura, *f.* the act of removing or breaking a lock.
descerrajar, *tr.v.* 1. to remove, break off or force the lock of. 2. to fire, discharge a shot.
descerrar, (*ref. 29*) *tr.v.* to open, unlock, unbolt; to discharge a gun.
descerrumarse, *r.v.* (vet.) to wrench the pastern joint (a horse).
descervigamiento, *m.* twisting the neck (of an animal).
descervigar, (*ref. 51*) *tr.v.* to twist or wrench the neck of (an animal).
descervigue, descervigué, *ref.* **descervigar.**
deschalar, *tr.v.* (Arg.) to remove the husk from corn.
descharchar, *tr.v.* (C. Amer., Angl.) to discharge, dismiss from employment.
deschavetado, da, *a.* (Amer., coll.) crazy, mad, off one's rocker.
deschavetarse, *r.v.* (coll.) to go crazy, to go off one's rocker, go mad.
deschuponar, *tr.v.* (agr.) to strip (a tree) of its shoots.
descienda, desciendo, *ref.* **descender.**
descifrable, *a.* decipherable, interpretable.
descifrador, ra, *m., f.* decipherer.
descifrar, *tr.v.* to decipher; to make out the meaning of.
descimbramiento, *m.* (archit.) the act of removing the centers (of a building).
descimbrar, *tr.v.* (archit.) to remove the centering from.
descimentar, *tr.v.* to demolish or destroy the foundations of.
descinchar, *tr.v.* to ungirth, uncinch (a horse).
descinto, ta, *irr. past part. of* **desceñir.**
desciña, desciñendo, desciñera, desciñese, desciño, desciñó, *ref.* **desceñir.**
descivilizar, *tr.v.* to make uncivilized. —*r.v.* to become uncivilized.
desclasificar, *tr.v.* to declassify.
desclavador, *m.* (carp.) claw bar, nail puller, claw wrench.
desclavar, *tr.v.* 1. to remove or take out the nails from. 2. to unfasten, unpeg. 3. (fig.) to remove, dismount (jewels from setting).
desclorurar, *tr.v.* to remove the sodium chloride or salt from.
descoagulable, *a.* able to be dissolved, soluble, liquefiable.
descoagulante, *a.* liquefying, dissolving; clot-dissolving.
descoagular, *tr.v., r.v.* to liquefy, dissolve (a clot).
descobajar, *tr.v.* to remove the stalk from bunches of grapes.
descobijar, *tr.v.* to discover, reveal; to uncover, unclothe. —*r.v.* to undress, to become uncovered.
descocadamente, *a.* brazenly, impudently.
descocado, da, *past part. of* **descocar.** —*a.* bold-faced, brazen, impudent. —*m., f.* brazen person.
descocar, (*ref. 50*) *tr.v.* to clean or rid (trees) of insects.
descocarse, *r.v.* to be impudent, brazen, or petulant; to take too many liberties.
descocedura, *f.* digestion.
descocer, (*ref. 75*) *tr.v.* to digest.
descoco, *m.* (coll.) brazenness, boldness, impudence, insolence.
descochollado, da, *a.* (Chile) 1. ragged. 2. vicious, evil, base. 3. bad-tempered.
descoger, (*ref. 57*) *tr.v.* to unfold, extend, spread.
descogollar, *tr.v.* to strip (trees) of shoots; to remove the hearts from (vegetables).
descogotado, da, *past part. of* **descogotar.** —*a.* with the back of the neck exposed; with the back of the head shaven.
descogotar, *tr.v.* (hunt.) to cut off the antlers of (a deer).
descohesión, *f.* decohesion.
descohesor, *m.* (elec.) decoherer.
descoja, descojo, *ref.* **descoger.**
descolada, *f.* (Mex.) slight, discourtesy, oversight, rudeness.
descolar, *tr.v.* 1. to cut off or dock the tail of. 2. to cut off the fag end of (a piece of cloth). 3. (Mex.) to slight, to show contempt for.
descolchar, *tr.v.* (mar.) to untwist (a cable). —*r.v.* to become untwisted.
descolgar, (*ref. 72*) *tr.v.* 1. to take down; to let down, lower. 2. to remove the hangings from. —*r.v.* 1. to go down, descend. 2. to slide or slip down; to let oneself down. 3. (coll.) to do (something) suddenly and unexpectedly. 4. (coll.) to show up or appear unexpectedly. — **descolgarse con,** to blurt out, come out with.
descolgué, *ref.* **descolgar.**
descoligado, da, *a.* unfederated, independent, unassociated, non-unionized, unattached.
descolladamente, *adv.* haughtily, loftily.
descollamiento, *m., var. of* **descuello.**
descollante, *a.* prominent, outstanding.
descollar, (*ref. 33*) *i.v., r.v.* to stand out, excel; to protrude, be visible or prominent.
descolmar, *tr.v.* 1. to level, take off the overflow (of a measure). 2. to diminish.
descolmillar, *tr.v.* to pull out, extract or break the tusks or fangs of.
descolocado, da, *a.* unemployed, without work or a job.
descolón, *m.* (Mex.) slight, insult, affront.
descolorado, da, *past part. of* **descolorar.** —*a.* colorless, faded.
descoloramiento, *m.* discoloration; bleaching; fading.
descolorante, *a.* bleaching, discoloring. —*m.* bleach, whitening agent.
descolorar, *tr.v.* to discolor; bleach; to fade. —*tr.v.* to become faded; to become bleached.
descolorido, da, *past part. of* **descolorir.** —*a.* colorless, faded; whitened, bleached.
descolorimiento, *m.* fading, bleaching, discoloration; paleness.
descolorir, *tr.v.* to fade, bleach, discolor.
descombrar, *tr.v.* to disencumber; to clear, to remove (obstacles, debris, etc.).
descombro, *m.* disencumbering; clearing, cleaning-up.
descomedidamente, *adv.* 1. immoderately, to excess. 2. rudely, impolitely.
descomedido, da, *past part. of* **descomedirse.** —*a.* 1. excessive, immoderate. 2. rude, impolite.
descomedimiento, *m.* rudeness, discourtesy.
descomedirse, (*ref. 39*) *r.v.* to be rude, discourteous or impolite.
descomer, *i.v.* (coll.) to defecate.
descomida, descomidiendo, descomidiera, descomidiese, descomidió, descomido, *ref.* **descomedirse.**
descomodidad, *f.* discomfort; inconvenience.
descompadrar, *tr.v.* (coll.) to estrange, make enemies of (friends). —*i.v.* (coll.) to fall out, disagree (friends), break up one's friendship (with).
descompaginar, *tr.v.* to upset, disarrange, disrupt. —*r.v.* to fall to pieces.
descompás, *m.* excess, lack of proportion or moderation.
descompasadamente, *adv.* 1. immoderately, to excess. 2. rudely, impolitely.
descompasado, da, *past part. of* **descompasarse.** —*a.* 1. immoderate, excessive. 2. rude, impolite.
descompasarse, *r.v.* to be rude, discourteous or impolite.
descompensación, *f.* (med.) decompensation.
descompondré, descompondría, *ref.* descomponer.
descomponer, (*ref. 15*) *tr.v.* 1. to disarrange, disturb, disrupt, upset the order of. 2. to decompose, decompound, break up (substance into components). 3. to decompose, cause to rot or decay. 4. to alienate (friends), upset, break up (a friendship). 5. (phys.) to change, transform (one energy into another). 6. (math.) to break (a number) down (into factors, etc.). —*r.v.* 1. to become disarranged or disturbed. 2. to decompose, decay, putrefy, rot. 3. to decline, go to pieces (health). 4. to change for the worse, become inclement (weather). 5. (Amer.) to break down, get out of order (machine). 6. to dislocate (arm, leg, etc.). — **descomponerse con alguien,** to get angry with someone, fall out with someone.
descomponga, descompongo, *ref.* **descomponer.**
descomponible, *a.* decomposable (matter).
descomposición, *f.* 1. decomposition, decay. 2. disorder, disarrangement. 3. (chem.) decomposition, breaking up (of compounds into components). 4. distortion (of the features). 5. breakdown, failure (of machine).
descompostura, *f.* 1. disarrangement, disturbance, disorder. 2. slovenliness, dirtiness, untidiness. 3. (fig.) rudeness, impoliteness, insolence, impudence. 4. failure, breakdown (of a machine).
descompresión, *f.* decompression.
descompresor, *m.* decompressor.

descomprimir, *tr.v.* to decompress.
descompuestamente, *adv.* impudently, insolently, discourteously, rudely.
descompuesto, ta, *past part. of* **descomponer.** —*a.* 1. rude, impolite; out of temper. 2. (mec.) out of order. 3. (meterorol.) gusty, boisterous.
descompuse, descompusiera, descompusiese, *ref.* **descomponer.**
descomulgado, da, *past part. of* **descomulgar.** —*a.* perverse, wicked. —*m., f.* wicked person.
descomulgador, *m.* excommunicator.
descomulgar, (*ref. 51*) *tr.v.* to excommunicate.
descomulgue, descomulgué, *ref.* **descomulgar.**
descomunal, *a.* extraordinary, enormous, uncommon, monstrous, colossal.
descomunalmente, *adv.* excessively, immoderately, extraordinarily.
descomunión, *f.* excommunication.
desconceptuar, (*ref. 53*) *tr.v.* to discredit. —*r.v.* to become discredited.
desconcertadamente, *adv.* disconcertedly; confusedly, in a disorderly manner.
desconcertado, da, *past part. of* **desconcertar.** —*a.* disorderly, wild, lawless, unruly.
desconcertador, ra, *a.* disconcerting. —*m.* disturber.
desconcertadura, *f.* disturbance; confusion; unruliness.
desconcertante, *a.* disconcerting; puzzling, bewildering.
desconcertar, (*ref. 29*) *tr.v.* 1. to disconcert, surprise, baffle. 2. to put out of order; to disarrange, disturb, disrupt. 3. to dislocate. —*r.v.* 1. to get disarranged or untidy; to get out of order. 2. to get dislocated (bone). 3. to be disconcerted or baffled. 4. to fall out, disagree (friends). 5. to become upset or annoyed.
desconchabar, *tr.v.* (Amer.) to dislocate a joint.
desconchado, *past part. of* **desconchar.** —*m.* part of a wall which has lost its facing, scaly area of a wall; chipped part (on porcelain).
desconchar, *tr.v.* to strip off a surface or facing of. —*r.v.* to flake, peel, chip off (surface of wall).
desconchinflado, da, *past part. of* **desconchinflar.** —*a.* (Cuba, Mex., C. Amer.) out of order, disarranged, disheveled.
desconchinflar, *tr.v.* (Mex., Cuba) to disarrange, break, put out of order.
desconchón, *m.* chip, flake (fallen from wall facing).
desconcierte, desconcierto, *ref.* **desconcertar.**
desconcierto, *m.* 1. disconcert; confusion, perplexity, bewilderment. 2. disharmony, disorder. 3. unruliness, wildness, rashness, disorderliness; lack of control or moderation. 4. dislocation (of bone). 5. breakdown, failure (of machine). 6. (fig.) diarrhea, looseness of bowels.
desconcordia, *f.* discord, disagreement.
desconectar, *tr.v.* to disconnect; (elec.) unplug. —*r.v.* to become disconnected.
desconfiadamente, *adv.* mistrustfully, mistrustingly, distrustfully, suspiciously; diffidently.
desconfiado, da, *past part. of* **desconfiar.** —*a.* distrusting, distrustful, suspicious; diffident.
desconfianza, *f.* distrust, mistrust, suspicion; diffidence.
desconfiar, (*ref. 54*) *i.v.* (with **de**) to distrust; to doubt; to suspect; to lack confidence.
desconformar, *i.v.* (with **en**) to disagree, differ. —*r.v.* not to fit together, not suit one another; to clash.
desconforme, *a., var. of* **disconforme.**
desconformidad, *f., var. of* **disconformidad.**
descongelación, *f.* defrosting, thawing.
descongelador, *m.* defroster, thawer, deicer.
descongelar, *tr.v.* to defrost; to unfreeze, to thaw.
descongestión, *f.* relieving of a congestion.
descongestionar *tr.v.* 1. to relieve the congestion of. 2. (Amer.) to disperse (crowd, traffic, etc.). 3. to organize, arrange, set in order (a multitude of persons or things).
desconocer, (*ref. 45*) *tr.v.* 1. to have forgotten; to not know, be ignorant of. 2. to disown, disclaim, disavow. 3. to fail to recognize. 4. to ignore, pass by, pretend not to know.
desconocidamente, *adv.* ungratefully; ignorantly, unknowingly.
desconocido, da, *past part. of* **desconocer.** —*a.* 1. ungrateful. 2. unknown; unrecognizable; greatly changed. —*m., f.* 1. ungrateful person. 2. stranger, newcomer, unknown person.
desconocimiento, *m.* 1. ignorance, disregard. 2. ingratitude, ungratefulness.
desconozca, desconozco, *ref.* **desconocer.**
desconsentir, (*ref. 42*) *tr.v.* to disapprove, not to consent to; to reject.
desconsideración, *f.* inconsiderateness, disregard.
desconsideradamente, *adv.* inconsiderately, rashly.
desconsiderado, da, *past part. of* **desconsiderar.** —*a.* rash, inconsiderate, thoughtless. —*m., f.* thoughtless person.
desconsiderar, *tr.v.* to be inconsiderate or thoughtless towards.
desconsienta, desconsiento, *ref.* **desconsentir.**
desconsintiendo, desconsintiera, desconsintiese, desconsintió, *ref.* **desconsentir.**
desconsolación, *f.* disconsolateness, disconsolation, grief, sorrow.
desconsoladamente, *adv.* disconsolately, sorrowfully, tearfully.
desconsolado, da, *past part. of* **desconsolar.** —*a.* disconsolate, dejected, miserable; discouraged.
desconsolador, ra, *a.* distressing, heart-breaking; discouraging.
desconsolar, (*ref. 33*) *tr.v.* to distress, afflict. —*r.v.* to mourn, grieve, sorrow; to lose heart.
desconsuele, desconsuelo, *ref.* **desconsolar.**
desconsuelo, *m.* 1. grief, distress, sorrow, desolation, disconsolateness. 2. weakness (of stomach).
descontable, *a.* (com.) discountable.
descontagiar, *tr.v.* to disinfect, purify.
descontaminación, *f.* decontamination.
descontaminar, *tr.v.* to decontaminate; to disinfect.
descontar, (*ref. 33*) *tr.v.* 1. to discount; to rebate, give a rebate on. 2. to deduct, take away. 3. (fig.) to disregard; to lessen or diminish (someone's merit or importance). 4. to take for granted. —**dar por descontado,** to take for granted; **estar descontado que,** to be taken for granted or certain that.
descontentadizo, za, *a.* easily displeased; fastidious, difficult to please, faultfinding.
descontentamiento, *m.* discontent, discontentedness, displeasure; disagreement (between friends).
descontentar, *tr.v.* to make discontent, displease. —*r.v.* to become discontented or displeased.
descontento, ta, *past part. of* **descontentar.** —*a.* discontent, dissatisfied, displeased; uneasy. —*m.* displeasure, discontentedness, dissatisfaction; uneasiness.
descontinuación, *f.* discontinuance, discontinuation, cessation.
descontinuar, (*ref. 55*) *tr.v.* to discontinue, cease, leave off, suspend.
descontinuo, nua, *a.* discontinuous, discontinued.
desconvenga, desconvengo, *ref.* **desconvenir.**
desconvenible, *a.* incongruous, discordant; disproportionate.
desconveniencia, *f.* inconvenience, disadvantage; (fig.) handicap.
desconveniente, *a.* inconvenient; incongruous, discordant.
desconvenir, (*ref. 26*) *i.v.* 1. to disagree, not to concur. 2. to be dissimilar; to be disproportionate, not to fit or match. —*r.v.* to disagree.
desconversable, *a.* disagreeable, unsociable; retiring.
desconvidar, *tr.v.* to cancel an invitation to; to rescind an offer or promise to.
desconvine, desconviniendo, desconviniera, desconviniese, *ref.* **desconvenir.**
descopar, *tr.v.* to trim (a treetop), to lop off the top (of a tree).
descoque, descoqué, *ref.* **descocar.**
descorazonadamente, *adv.* dejectedly, dispiritedly.
descorazonamiento, *m.* dejection, dispiritedness; discouragement; depression.
descorazonar, *tr.v.* 1. to dishearten, discourage. 2. to tear out the heart of. —*r.v.* to get discouraged or disheartened.
descorchador, *m.* 1. corkscrew. 2. one who draws the cork.
descorchar, *tr.v.* 1. to cut cork from (cork tree). 2. to break open (the beehive) in order to remove the honey. 3. to uncork, draw the cork from. 4. to break open (a chest or trunk).
descorche, *m.* the act of stripping a cork tree.
descordar, (*ref. 33*) *tr.v.* 1. (mus.) to unstring (an instrument). 2. (taur.) to kill (the bull) instantly by stabbing in the back of the neck with the sword.
descorderar, *tr.v.* to separate the lambs from the ewes.
descornar, (*ref. 33*) *tr.v.* to remove the horns from, dehorn. —*r.v.* (coll.) to rack one's brains.
descoronar, *tr.v.* 1. to remove the crown from, decrown. 2. to lower the empty wine casks (from the tiers).
descorrear, *i.v.* to shed the skin covering the horns (a deer) in the growing process.
descorregido, da, *a.* disarranged, uncorrected; defective.
descorrer, *tr.v.* 1. to run back over (ground already covered). 2. to draw (curtains), to unbolt (door). —*r.v., i.v.* to flow (liquids).
descorrimiento, *m.* flowing.
descortece, descortecé, *ref.* **descortezar.**
descortés, *a.* impolite, discourteous, ill-mannered, rude. —*m., f.* rude person.
descortesía, *f.* discourtesy, impoliteness.
descortésmente, *adv.* discourteously, impolitely, rudely.
descortezador, *m.* 1. (mec.) decorticator (instrument for removing bark). 2. bark-cutter (workman who strips off bark).
descortezadura, *f.* bark (cut from tree); peeled part (of tree).
descortezamiento, *m.* removal of bark, decortication.
descortezar, (*ref. 53*) *tr.v.* 1. to strip the bark from, decorticate; to remove the crust from bread, to hull or shell fruit. 2. (coll.) to refine, make refined, polish the manners of. —*r.v.* (coll.) to become civilized or refined.
descortezo, *m.* removal of bark, decortication (of trees).
descortinar, *tr.v.* (mil.) to demolish the curtain or bastion of.

descosedura, *f.* rip in a seam, part of seam which has become unstitched.
descoser, *tr.v.* 1. to unstitch, cut the stitches or seams of. 2. (mar.) to unlash. —*r.v.* 1. to let out, blurt out (a secret), e.g. *no d. los labios,* to keep silent. 2. (coll.) to fart (vulg.).
descosidamente, *adv.* excessively; immoderately; incoherently.
descosido, da, *past part. of* **descoser.** —*a.* 1. indiscreet, blabbing. 2. disorderly. 3. immoderate, wild, excessive. —*m.* unstitched seam. — **como un d.,** immoderately, to excess; **beber como un d.,** to drink like a fish; **reír como un d.,** to laugh one's head off.
descostarse, *r.v.* to draw away, move away.
descostillar, *tr.v.* to pound or hit on the ribs. —*r.v.* 1. to fall flat on the ground. 2. to break one's ribs.
descostrar, *tr.v.* to remove the crust from.
descotar, *tr.v.* to cut low in the neck. —*r.v.* to wear a low-cut neckline.
descote, *m.* décolletage, low-cut neckline.
descoyuntamiento, *m.* 1. dislocation. 2. exhaustion.
descoyuntar, *tr.v.* 1. to dislocate (bones). 2. to vex, annoy. —*r.v.* to become dislocated (one's bones); **d. de risa,** to split one's sides with laughter.
descoyunto, *m., var. of* **descoyuntamiento.**
descrecencia, *f.* decrease; diminishing.
descrecer, (*ref. 45*) *i.v.* to decrease, diminish; subside.
descrecimiento, *m.* decrease; reduction; the act of diminishing in size or volume.
descrédito, *m.* discredit, disrepute.
descreencia, *f.* disbelief, unbelief.
descreer, (*ref. 60*) *tr.v.* 1. to disbelieve. 2. to disregard, ignore; to deny due recognition to something. 3. to disown.
descreídamente, *adv.* disbelievingly, incredulously.
descreído, da, *past part. of* **descreer.** —*a.* unbelieving, disbelieving. —*m., f.* unbeliever, disbeliever, infidel.
descreimiento, *m.* disbelief, unbelief, lack of faith.
descremar, *tr.v.* (Amer.) to skim milk.
descrestadera, *f.* (Col.) swindle, deception.
descrestar, *tr.v.* 1. to remove the crest or comb from. 2. (Col.) to swindle, deceive, take in.
descreyendo, descreyera, descreyese, descreyó, *ref.* **descreer.**
descrezca, descrezco, *ref.* **descrecer.**
descriarse, (*ref. 54*) *r.v.* to get worse; to become spoiled.
describible, *a.* describable.
describir, *tr.v.* to describe; to delineate; **d. un círculo,** to describe a circle.
descripción, *f.* 1. description. 2. (law) inventory.
descriptible, *a.* describable.
descriptivo, va, *a.* descriptive; **geometría descriptiva,** descriptive geometry.
descripto, ta, *irr. past part. of* **describir.**
descriptor, ra, *a.* descriptive. —*m., f.* describer.
descrismar, *tr.v.* 1. (rel.) to remove the chrism from. 2. (coll.) to give (someone) a blow on the head. —*r.v.* 1. (coll.) to lose one's patience or temper. 2. (coll.) to rack one's brains.
descristianar, *tr.v.* (rel.) to remove the chrism. 2. to give (someone) a blow on the head.
descristianice, descristianicé, *ref.* **descristianizar.**
descristianizar, (*ref. 53*) *tr.v.* to dechristianize; to make unchristian.
descrito, ta, *irr. past part. of* **describir.**
descruce, descrucé, *ref.* **descruzar.**
descruzar, (*ref. 53*) *tr.v.* to uncross.
descuadernar, *tr.v.* 1. to unbind, take the binding from, take to pieces. 2. to confuse, bewilder. —*r.v.* to fall to pieces, lose its binding.
descuadrillado, da, *past part. of* **descuadrillarse.** —*a.* separated from the lines, from a gang or troupe. —*m.* (vet.) sprain in the haunch.
descuadrillarse, *r.v.* to sprain (its haunches).
descuajar, *tr.v.* 1. to liquefy, dissolve. 2. (coll.) to dishearten, discourage. 3. (agr.) to uproot, pull up by the roots. —*r.v.* to dissolve, liquefy.
descuajaringado, da, *past part. of* **descuajaringarse.** —*a.* 1. (Amer.) disarranged, fallen to pieces; jumbled. 2. (Arg., Par.) slovenly, untidy.
descuajaringarse, (*ref. 51*) *r.v.* (coll.) to get exhausted, be pooped (sl.); to fall to pieces.
descuajaringue, descuajaringué, *ref.* **descuajaringarse.**
descuaje, *m.* (agr.) *var. of* **descuajo.**
descuajo, *m.* (agr.) uprooting.
descuartice, descuarticé, *ref.* **descuartizar.**
descuartizamiento, *m.* quartering, breaking or cutting into pieces; carving.
descuartizar, (*ref. 53*) *tr.v.* to quarter, cut into quarters; to divide into pieces; (coll.) to cut apart; to carve.
descubierta, *f.* 1. tart, open pie. 2. (mar.) reconnoitering at dawn and dusk (by patrol ships). 3. (mar.) morning and evening inspection of the rigging (on board ship). 4. (mil.) reconnaissance, scouting mission. — **a la d.,** openly; out in the open, without shelter.
descubiertamente, *adv.* openly, clearly.
descubierto, ta, *irr. past part. of* **descubrir.** —*a.* bare, uncovered, bareheaded; exposed, unprotected. —*m.* 1. (ecc.) exposition (of the sacrament). 2. (com.) deficit. — **al d.,** (com.) short; openly; **en d.,** (com.) overdrawn, uncovered; **en todo lo d.,** in the whole wide world; **girar en d.,** (com.) to overdraw; **giro en d.,** overdraft.
descubridero, *m.* lookout, lookout post.
descubridor, ra, *a.* discovering; reconnaissance; reconnoitering (ship). —*m., f.* discoverer, finder. —*m.* 1. (mil.) scout, reconnoiter. 2. the scouting ship in a fleet or an armada.
descubrimiento, *m.* discovery, disclosure, find, e.g. *el d. de América,* the discovery of the New World.
descubrir, *tr.v.* 1. to discover; to find out. 2. to uncover; to reveal, expose to view, bring to light. 3. to make out, be able to see. 4. (mil.) to reconnoiter. —*r.v.* 1. to remove one's hat, cap, etc. 2. to make one's presence known.
descuelgo, descuelgue, *ref.* **descolgar.**
descuelle, descuello, *ref.* **descollar.**
descuello, *m.* 1. excessive height or stature, hugeness, loftiness. 2. superiority, pre-eminence. 3. haughtiness, arrogance.
descuente, descuento, *ref.* **descontar.**
descuento, *m.* discount; reduction; rebate; allowance.
descuerar, *tr.v.* to skin, remove the skin from.
descuerde, descuerdo, *ref.* **descordar.**
descuernacabras, *m.* cold north wind.
descuerne, descuerno, *ref.* **descornar.**
descuerno, *m.* (coll.) insult, slight, affront.
descueza, descuezo, *ref.* **descocer.**
descuida, *imper. of* **descuidar,** don't worry.
descuidadamente, *adv.* carelessly, thoughtlessly.
descuidado, da, *past part. of* **descuidar.** —*a.* 1. careless, negligent, thoughtless. 2. untidy, slovenly. 3. unprepared, off guard. 4. neglected, abandoned, unattended.
descuidar, *tr.v.* 1. to neglect, forget, abandon, not attend to. 2. to make careless or negligent, divert (someone's) attention from (his duty), put off guard. 3. to free of a care or obligation. —*i.v.* 1. to be negligent or careless. 2. not to bother or worry. — **d. de,** to neglect, forget. —*r.v.* 1. to be negligent or careless. 2. not to take care of oneself. — **descuidarse de,** to neglect, forget about, not bother about.
descuidero, ra, *a., m., f.* pickpocket.
descuido, *m.* 1. carelessness, negligence, neglect; forgetfulness, remissness, thoughtlessness. 2. slip, lack of attention — **al d.** or **al d. y con cuidado,** with affected carelessness; **con d.,** carelessly; **en un d.,** when least expected, suddenly.
descuitado, da, *a.* untroubled, carefree.
descular, *tr.v.* to break the bottom of (box, jar).
descumbrado, da, *a.* flat (land).
descurtir, *tr.v.* to bleach, whiten (tanned leather).
desdar, *tr.v.* to unwind, to turn in the opposite direction.
desde, *prep.* from; since; after; **d. ahora,** from now on; **d. entonces,** from that time on, since then; **d. hace,** for, e.g. *d. hace muchos años,* for many years; **d. luego,** immediately; of course, naturally; **d. que,** since; as soon as; **d. ya,** (Amer.) right now.
desdecir, (*ref. 3*) *i.v.* (with de) 1. to degenerate, decline, go to seed. 2. to be unworthy (of), not live up (to). 3. to differ, not match. 4. to change, be different; to change face. —*r.v.* (with **de**) 1. to retract, take back, withdraw. 2. to contradict oneself, say the opposite.
desdén, *m.* disdain, disdainfulness, scorn; **al desdén,** with affected carelessness.
desdentado, da, *past part. of* **desdentar.** —*a.* 1. toothless. 2. (zool.) edentate. —*m.* (zool.) edentate; (*pl.*) Edentata.
desdentar, (*ref. 29*) *tr.v.* to pull, extract teeth from; to leave (someone) without teeth.
desdeñable, *a.* contemptible, despicable.
desdeñadamente, *adv.* disdainfully.
desdeñador, ra, *a.* disdainful, underestimating, depreciating. —*m., f.* scorner, disdainer.
desdeñar, *tr.v.* to treat disdainfully, disdain, scorn. —*r.v.* to be disdainful.
desdeñosamente, *adv.* disdainfully.
desdeñoso, sa, *a.* disdainful, scornful, contemptuous.
desdevanar, *tr.v.* to unwind, unreel. —*r.v.* to become unwound.
desdibujado, da, *past part. of* **desdibujarse.** —*a.* faultily drawn; defective, disproportionate.
desdibujarse. *r.v.* to fade, lose its outline.
desdicha, *f.* disgrace, affliction, misfortune; poverty, need, indigence.
desdichadamente, *adv.* unfortunately.
desdichado, da, *a.* 1. unfortunate, ill-starred. 2. wretched, pitiful, miserable. 3. spiritless, timid. —*m., f.* (coll.) poor wretch, poor devil.
desdicho, cha, *irr. past part. of* **desdecir.**
desdiciendo, *ref.* **desdecir.**
desdiente, desdiento, *ref.* **desdentar.**
desdiga, desdigo, *ref.* **desdecir.**
desdije, desdijera, desdijese, *ref.* **desdecir.**
desdoblamiento, *m.* 1. unfolding, spreading out. 2. (fig.) exposition, explanation, elucidation.
desdoblar, *tr.v., r.v.* 1. to unfold, spread open. 2. to split, break down (into component parts).
desdonado, da, *a.* 1. ungraceful, awkward, clumsy. 2. tactless.
desdorar, *tr.v.* to ungild; to tarnish, sully (virtue, reputation or good name). —*r.v.* 1. to lose its gilt finish. 2. to be sullied or tarnished.
desdoro, *m.* tarnishing; stain, blemish, blot (on reputation).
desdoroso, sa, *a.* indecorous, harmful (to reputation).

deseable, *a.* desirable.
deseablemente, *adv.* desirably.
deseador, ra, *a.* desirous. —*m., f.* desirer, wisher.
desear, *tr.v.* to desire, long for, want, wish; **d.** + *inf.*, to wish, desire to, e.g. *deseo viajar en agosto,* I wish to travel in August.
desecación, *f.* desiccation, exsiccation, drying.
desecado, da, *a.* dry, desiccated.
desecador, ra, *a.* desiccating, drying. —*m.* drier, dehydrator; (chem.) desiccator; (tex.) drying room.
desecamiento, *m., var. of* **desecación.**
desecante, *a.* desiccating, drying. —*m.* desiccant, drying agent.
desecar, (*ref. 50*) *tr.v.* to dry, desiccate. —*r.v.* to become desiccated.
desecativo, va, *a.* desiccative, desiccatory, exsiccant, drying.
desechable, *a.* throw-away, discardable, disposable.
desechadamente, *adv.* vilely, despicably.
desechar, *tr.v.* 1. to reject, cast aside (advice); to exclude. 2. to scorn, be disdainful of. 3. to throw off, get rid of (fear, worry); to discard, throw away or out (old clothes). 4. to reprove, censure.
desecho, *m.* 1. remainder, waste, residue; refuse, debris; cast-off (clothing, etc.). 2. contempt, disdain.
desedificación, *f.* (fig.) bad example.
desedificar, (*ref. 50*) *tr.v.* to set a bad example to; to exert an evil influence on.
desegregación, *f.* desegregation.
desegregar, *tr.v.* to desegregate.
deselectrice, deselectricé, *ref.* **deselectrizar.**
deselectrización, *f.* (elec.) discharging.
deselectrizar, (*ref. 53*) *tr.v.* to discharge (e.g. a battery).
desellar, *tr.v.* to unseal, remove the seal from (letters, packages, etc.).
desembalaje, *m.* unpacking, opening of boxes, bales, freight containers.
desembalar, *tr.v.* to unpack, open large containers.
desembaldosar, *tr.v.* to untile, unpave, remove the tiles from.
desemballestar, *i.v.* to get ready to swoop down (a falcon).
desembanastar, *tr.v.* 1. to take out of a basket. 2. to chatter, prattle or babble about. 3. to draw (a sword). —*r.v.* 1. (coll.) to break out or get free (a caged animal). 2. (coll.) to alight (from a carriage).
desembarace, desembaracé, *ref.* **desembarazar.**
desembarazadamente, *adv.* freely, without hindrance.
desembarazado, da, *past part. of* **desembarazar.** —*a.* free, clear, unhampered, unrestrained, unencumbered.
desembarazar, (*ref. 53*) *tr.v.* to clear or free of obstacles, disencumber; to ease or loosen. —*r.v.* to free oneself (of obstacles or difficulties).
desembarazo, *m.* freedom, lack of restraint; naturalness, ease.
desembarcadero, *m.* wharf, landing stage, quay, pier.
desembarcar, (*ref. 50*) *tr.v.* to disembark; to unload, put ashore. —*i.v.* 1. to disembark, go ashore. 2. to end in a landing (stairs). 3. (mar.) to leave, quit (a sailor) the crew. 4. (coll.) to alight (from a carriage). —*r.v.* 1. to disembark, go ashore. 2. (coll.) to be delivered of a child.
desembarco, *m.* 1. (mil.) landing (of troops); landing, disembarkation. 2. landing (of a staircase.)
desembargadamente, *adv.* freely, without impediment.
desembargador, *m.* privy councillor in Portugal.
desembargar, (*ref. 51*) *tr.v.* to remove or clear away restrictions from; (law) to raise the embargo or order of seizure from.
desembargo, *m.* (law) raising of an embargo or order of seizure.
desembargue, desembargué, *ref.* **desembargar.**
desembarque, *m.* debarkation, landing; unloading (of a shipment).
desembarque, desembarqué, *ref.* **desembarcar.**
desembarrancar, (*ref. 50*) *tr.v.* to pull (a foundered ship) off a reef or sandbank. —*i.v.* to get free of a reef.
desembarranque, desembarranqué, *ref.* **desembarrancar.**
desembarrar, *tr.v.* to clean, clear of mud.
desembaular, *tr.v.* 1. to take out of a trunk, bag, box, etc. 2. to unbosom (one's troubles to).
desembebecerse, (*ref. 45*) *r.v.* to recover (from one's shock, worry, etc.).
desembebezca, desembebezco, *ref.* **desembebecerse.**
desembelesarse, *r.v.* to recover from one's amazement or ecstasy.
desemblantado, da, *past part. of* **desemblantarse.** —*a.* with a frightened or worried look.
desemblantarse, *r.v.* to look frightened, afraid or worried.
desembocadero, *m.* entrance, outlet (of one street into another); mouth, outlet (of a river).
desembocadura, *f.* mouth, outlet (of river); entrance, outlet (of one street into another).
desembocar, (*ref. 50*) *i.v.* 1. to empty, flow (river into sea). 2. to lead, go (one street into another). 3. to end in, result in.
desemboce, desembocé, *ref.* **desembozar.**
desembojadera, *f.* female worker who removes silk cocoons from the southernwood.
desembojar, *tr.v.* to remove (silk cocoons) from the southernwood.
desembolsable, *a.* that can be taken from a bag, purse; (fig.) disbursable.
desembolsar, *tr.v.* 1. to take out from a purse or bag. 2. to disburse, pay.
desembolso, *m.* disbursement, payment; expenditure, outlay (of money).
desemboque, *m., var. of* **desembocadero.**
desemboque, desemboqué, *ref.* **desembocar.**
desemborrachar, *tr.v.* to sober up, make sober. —*r.v.* to sober up, become sober.
desemboscarse, (*ref. 50*) *r.v.* 1. to emerge from the woods. 2. to escape or get out of an ambush.
desembosque, desembosqué, *ref.* **desemboscarse.**
desembotar, *tr.v.* 1. to make sharp, sharpen (a blunt edge). 2. to wake up, rouse (the senses, the spirit).
desembozar, (*ref. 53*) *tr.v.* to uncover the face of, to unmask, reveal, expose. —*r.v.* to show or uncover one's face; to come to light, be revealed or unmasked.
desembozo, *m.* uncovering; unmasking, revealing.
desembrace, desembracé, *ref.* **desembrazar.**
desembragar, (*ref. 51*) *tr.v.* (mec.) to declutch, disengage (gears of a motor).
desembrague, *m.* declutching, disengagement (of gears).
desembrague, desembragué, *ref.* **desembragar.**
desembravecer, (*ref. 45*) *tr.v.* to tame, domesticate; to calm. —*r.v.* to become tame or domesticated; to become calm.
desembravecimiento, *m.* taming, domestication.
desembravezca, desembravezco, *ref.* **desembravecer.**
desembrazar, (*ref. 53*) *tr.v.* 1. to take or remove (something) from one's arm. 2. to hurl, throw, cast.
desembriagar, (*ref. 51*) *tr.v., r.v.* to sober up.
desembriague, desembriagué, *ref.* **desembriagar.**
desembridar, *tr.v.* to unbridle, remove the bridle from.
desembroce, desembrocé, *ref.* **desembrozar.**
desembrollar, *tr.v.* 1. (coll.) to untangle, unravel, disentangle. 2. clarify, clear up (a misunderstanding, etc.).
desembrozar, (*ref. 53*) *tr.v., var. of* **desbrozar.**
desembrujar, *tr.v.* to remove a spell from.
desembuchar, *tr.v.* 1. to disgorge (birds). 2. (coll.) to disclose or tell everything about, spill the beans (coll.).
desemejablemente, *adv.* dissimilarly.
desemejante, *a.* different, dissimilar, unlike.
desemejantemente, *adv.* dissimilarly, differently.
desemejanza, *f.* unlikeness, dissimilarity, difference.
desemejar, *i.v.* to be dissimilar, unlike or different. —*tr.v.* to disfigure.
desempacar, (*ref. 50*) *tr.v.* to unpack.
desempacarse, (*ref. 50*) *r.v.* to calm down, grow calm.
desempachar, *tr.v.* to relieve of indigestion. —*r.v.* 1. to cure oneself of indigestion. 2. (coll.) to become graceful, agile, vivacious.
desempacho, *m.* (fig.) ease, calmness, nerve (coll.).
desempalagar, (*ref. 51*) *tr.v.* 1. to restore the appetite to; to rid of nausea. 2. to clear (a mill) of stagnant water. —*r.v.* to get back one's appetite.
desempalague, desempalagué, *ref.* **desempalagar.**
desempañar, *tr.v.* 1. to clean, polish, remove blur from (glass). 2. to unswathe, unswaddle, remove diapers from (a child).
desempapelar, *tr.v.* 1. to unwrap. 2. to remove wallpaper from; to remove posters, advertisements or notices from.
desempaque, *m.* unpacking.
desempaque, desempaqué, *ref.* **desempacar.**
desempaquetar, *tr.v.* to unpack, take out of a packet, unwrap.
desemparejar, *tr.v.* to make uneven, unmatch. —*r.v.* to become uneven.
desemparentado, da, *a.* without relatives.
desemparvar, *tr.v.* to heap up (mown wheat).
desempastado, da, *a.* (Amer.) unbound (book).
desempastar, *tr.v.* (Amer.) to take the cover off (books); to take the filling out of (tooth).
desempatar, *tr.v.* to break a tie between; to disjoint; to make uneven.
desempavonar, *tr.v.* (metal.) to remove the bluing or bronzing from (iron, steel).
desempedrador, *m.* person who removes the paving (as of a street).
desempedrar, (*ref. 29*) *tr.v.* 1. to remove pavement or cobblestones from; to remove stone from (a wall, the street). 2. (coll.) to rush along, walk the streets in a great hurry.
desempegar, (*ref. 51*) *tr.v.* 1. to remove pitch (resin) from. 2. to unglue.
desempegue, desempegué, *ref.* **desempegar.**
desempeñado, da, *past part. of* **desempeñar.** —*a.* free from debt.
desempeñamiento, *m.* (arch.), *var. of* **desempeño.**
desempeñar, *tr.v.* 1. to redeem, recover (pawned goods). 2. to free from debt. 3. to rescue or pull out of a difficulty. 4. to fulfill, carry out; to fill

(an office, a function); to hold (a position). 5. (theat.) to play, act, perform (a part). *—r.v.* 1. to free oneself or get out of debt. 2. to get out of difficulties. 3. (taur.) to dismount from the horse and fight the bull on foot.
desempeño, *m.* 1. redeeming (of something pawned). 2. fulfillment, performance, carrying out (of duties). 3. (theat.) acting, playing, performance (of a part).
desempeorarse, *r.v.* to recover, recuperate; to regain (health).
desemperece, desemperecé, *ref.* **desemperezar.**
desemperezar, (*ref. 53*) *i.v., r.v.* to throw off one's laziness, become active.
desempernar, *tr.v.* to unbolt, to remove bolts from.
desempiedre, desempiedro, *ref.* **desempedrar.**
desempleado, da, *a.* unemployed. *—m., f.* unemployed person.
desempleo, *m.* (Amer.) unemployment; **d. en masa,** mass unemployment.
desemplomar, *tr.v.* to remove the leaden seal from.
desemplumar, *tr.v.* to pluck, take the feathers out of.
desempobrecer, *tr.v.* to relieve poverty or misery.
desempoce, desempocé, *ref.* **desempozar.**
desempolvadura, *f.* dusting, removal of dust.
desempolvar, *tr.v.* to dust, remove dust from, free from dust or powder. *—r.v.* (Mex.) to brush up (on an old skill).
desempolvoradura, *f.* dusting, removal of dust.
desempolvorar, *tr.v., var. of* **desempolvar.**
desemponzoñar, *tr.v.* to free or rid of poison.
desempotrar, *tr.v.* to pull out, to remove the support of.
desempulgadura, *f.* unstringing (of a crossbow).
desempulgar, (*ref. 51*) *tr.v.* to unstring (a crossbow).
desempulgue, desempulgué, *ref.* **desempulgar.**
desenalbardar, *tr.v.* to unsaddle, remove pack and saddle from.
desenamorar, *tr.v.* to destroy the love or affection of. *—r.v.* to lose one's love or affection (for).
desenastar, *tr.v.* to remove the handle or haft from tools or stock from weapons.
desencabalgar, (*ref. 51*) *tr.v.* (artil.) to dismount a cannon.
desencabalgue, desencabalgué, *ref.* **desencabalgar.**
desencabestrar, *tr.v.* to disentangle (horse's leg) from the halter or the bridle.
desencadenamiento, *m.* the act of unchaining; letting loose.
desencadenar, *tr.v.* to unchain, unshackle, unfetter; to let loose, to free, liberate. *—r.v.* to break loose; to run wild; **desencadenarse (una tormenta),** to break out (a storm).
desencajadura, *f.* disconnection, break (in a chain).
desencajamiento, *m.* 1. disconnection, taking apart, disassembly. 2. distortion or blanching (of the face because of illness or anger).
desencajar, *tr.v.* 1. to take apart, disconnect, disjoin. 2. to remove, take out or off. *—r.v.* 1. to come apart, become disconnected. 2. to become contorted or distorted (the face with anger); to become sickly-looking (through illness).
desencaje, *m., var. of* **desencajamiento.**
desencajonamiento, *m.* unboxing.
desencajonar, *tr.v.* to uncrate, unpack; to take out of a box; (fig.) to find something long lost in a drawer.
desencalabrinar, *tr.v.* to free of dizziness. *—r.v.* to get one's balance back, recover from dizziness.
desencalcar, (*ref. 50*) *tr.v.* to loosen or dissolve (caked matter).
desencalque, desencalqué, *ref.* **desencalcar.**
desencallar, *tr.v.* (mar.) to free a ship from a shoal or a reef.
desencaminar, *tr.v.* 1. to lead astray, misdirect, misguide. 2. to dissuade from.
desencantado, da, *a.* (Amer.) disillusioned, disenchanted, disappointed.
desencantamiento, *m.* disenchantment; disillusionment.
desencantar, *tr.v.* to disenchant; to disillusion. *—r.v.* to become disenchanted; to become disillusioned.
desencantaración, *f.* 1. drawing (of lots); balloting. 2. withdrawal of a name from a list of candidates.
desencantarar, *tr.v.* 1. to draw (lots) from a ballot box. 2. to withdraw (a name from list of candidates).
desencanto, *m.* disenchantment; disillusionment.
desencapillar, *tr.v.* (mar.) to unrig, remove the rigging from.
desencapotadura, *f.* uncloaking; removing the cloak; revelation.
desencapotar, *tr.v.* 1. to uncloak, remove a cape or cloak from; (coll.) to uncloak, reveal. 2. to make a horse raise its head. *—r.v.* 1. to remove one's cloak. 2. to become clear (sky). 3. to calm down, grow calm.
desencaprichar, *tr.v.* to dissuade from a caprice or whim. *—r.v.* to forget or rid oneself of a caprice or whim.
desencarcelar, *tr.v.* to free (from prison); set at liberty.
desencarecer, (*ref. 45*) *tr.v.* to cheapen, lower the price of.
desencarezca, desencarezco, *ref.* **desencarecer.**
desencargar, (*ref. 51*) *tr.v.* 1. to remove from a post or employment. 2. to revoke a request. 3. to cancel an order (of goods, etc.).
desencargue, desencargué, *ref.* **desencargar.**
desencarnar, *tr.v.* 1. to remove meat from. 2. to lose fondness or liking for (something), grow tired of.
desencartonar, *tr.v.* to remove the cardboard from.
desencastillar, *tr.v.* 1. to eject from a castle. 2. to reveal; to bring to light. *—r.v.* to come to light, be revealed.
desencepar, *tr.v.* (mar.) to clear anchor.
desencerrar, (*ref. 29*) *tr.v.* 1. to free, liberate (from confinement). 2. to open, unclose, unlock. 3. to reveal, unearth, bring to light.
desencierre, desencierro, *ref.* **desencerrar.**
desencintar, *tr.v.* 1. to remove the ribbons from. 2. to remove the curbing from (a pavement).
desenclavar, *tr.v.* 1. to unnail, draw out the nails from. 2. (fig.) to remove violently from, to yank out.
desenclavijar, *tr.v.* 1. to unpeg, remove the pins or pegs from (musical instrument). 2. to loosen, untie, disconnect, take away.
desencoger, (*ref. 57*) *tr.v.* to unfold, spread out. *—r.v.* to lose one's timidity or reserve.
desencogimiento, *m.* 1. unfolding, spreading out. 2. ease, naturalness, self-assurance.
desencoja, desencojo, *ref.* **desencoger.**
desencoladura, *f.* ungluing.
desencolar, *tr.v.* to unglue, unstick, make loose, loosen. *—r.v.* to become unglued or unstuck; to come loose.
desencolerice, desencolericé, *ref.* **desencolerizar.**
desencolerizar, (*ref. 53*) *tr.v.* to pacify, calm, soothe (a person). *—r.v.* to calm down (from anger).
desenconamiento, *m.* 1. allaying or relieving of inflammation. 2. pacification, soothing; calmness, calm (after anger).
desenconar, *tr.v.* 1. (med.) to disinflame, relieve the inflammation of. 2. to soothe, pacify; to restrain, control (one's temper). *—r.v.* 1. to become smooth. 2. (med.) to become disinflamed, become less inflamed. 3. to calm down, grow calm; to control one's temper, cool off, quiet down.
desencono, *m.* 1. allaying or relieving of inflammation. 2. soothing, pacification; calmness, calm (after anger). 3. restraining; restraint, control (of anger).
desencordar, (*ref. 33*) *tr.v.* to unstring (gen. said of a musical instrument).
desencordelar, *tr.v.* to remove the strings or cords from.
desencorvar, *tr.v.* to straighten, unbend, make straight.
desencovar, *tr.v.* to take out of a cave; to drive out of a cave (a wild animal).
desencrespar, *tr.v.* to uncurl, unfrizzle (hair, etc.).
desencuadernado, da, *past part. of* **desencuadernar.** *—m.* (fig., coll.) pack of cards.
desencuadernar, *tr.v.* to unbind (a book). *—r.v.* to become unbound, come to pieces.
desencuerde, desencuerdo, *ref.* **desencordar.**
desenchufar, *tr.v.* to disconnect, unplug.
desendemoniar, *tr.v.* to exorcise, drive out an evil spirit from.
desendiablar, *tr.v., var. of* **desendemoniar.**
desendiosar, *tr.v.* to bring down off one's pedestal, bring down to earth, to knock (someone) down a peg.
desenfadadamente, *adv.* with ease, with self-assurance, confidently, boldly.
desenfadaderas, *f.* (*pl.*) (coll.) resourcefulness; **tener d.,** to be resourceful.
desenfadado, da, *past part. of* **desenfadar.** *—a.* 1. confident, self-assured, natural, easy (way of acting, etc.). 2. wide, spacious (place).
desenfadar, *tr.v.* to soothe, pacify, calm, placate. *—r.v.* to calm down, cool off (coll.).
desenfado, *m.* 1. naturalness, confidence, assurance, ease (in demeanor). 2. diversion, relaxation.
desenfaldar, *tr.v.* to untuck, let down, lower (the hem of a skirt, the train of a dress, etc.).
desenfardar, *tr.v.* to unpack, untie, undo (bundles, bales, etc.).
desenfardelar, *tr.v., var. of* **desenfardar.**
desenfilado, da, *past part. of* **desenfilar.** *—a.* (mil.) under cover from fire. *—f.* (fort.) defilading.
desenfilamiento, *m.* (fort.) defilading.
desenfilar, *tr.v.* (mil., mar.) to cover from enemy fire, defilade. *—r.v.* to be covered from enemy fire, be defiladed.
desenfoque, *m.* incorrect focusing, the condition of being out of focus.
desenfrailar, *tr.v.* to top (a tree). *—i.v.* to leave the cloister, cease to be a monk. 2. (coll.) to become free, be emancipated, overcome subjection or oppression. 3. (coll.) to take time off (from work), take a vacation.
desenfrenadamente, *adv.* wildly, without restraint, unrestrainedly, licentiously.
desenfrenado, da, *past part. of* **desenfrenar.** *—a.* unrestrained, unruly, wild, uncontrolled, licentious, wanton.
desenfrenamiento, *m.* lack of restraint, unrestraint; wildness, unruliness; wantonness.

desenfrenar, *tr.v.* to unbridle (horses). —*r.v.* 1. to surrender or abandon oneself (to vice); to unbridle one's passions. 2. to break loose (a storm, passion, etc.).
desenfreno, *m.* (fig.) unrestraint, unruliness, wildness; wantonness, license; **d. de vientre,** (med.) uncontrollable diarrhea.
desenfundar, *tr.v.* to unsheath, remove the covering from.
desenfurecer, (*ref. 45*) *tr.v.* to soothe, pacify, calm. —*r.v.* to calm down, cool off.
desenfurezca, desenfurezco, *ref.* **desenfurecer.**
desenganchar, *tr.v.* to unhook, detach, disengage, unfasten, to uncouple (dogs); unhitch, unharness (horses). —*r.v.* to become disengaged, detached, unhooked, unfastened.
desengañadamente, *adv.* 1. openly, ingenuously, sincerely. 2. (coll.) badly, poorly.
desengañado, da, *past part. of* **desengañar.** —*a.* disillusioned, disabused.
desengañador, ra, *a.* disillusioning; undeceiving. —*m., f.* disillusioner.
desengañar, *tr.v.* 1. to undeceive, make (someone) realize the truth, make (someone) aware of his error. 2. to disillusion. —*r.v.* to become undeceived, realize the truth.
desengañilar, *tr.v.* to free (someone) from being throttled.
desengaño, *m.* 1. realization of the truth; disillusion, disillusionment. 2. home truth, plain truth, reproach. 3. (*pl.*) lessons learned from experience.
desengarce, desengarcé, *ref.* **desengarzar.**
desengargolar, *tr.v.* (Col.) to untangle.
desengarrafar, *tr.v.* to let go, release one's grip on.
desengarzar, (*ref. 53*) *tr.v.* 1. to unlink, unhook, unclasp. 2. to remove (a jewel) from its setting. —*r.v.* to become unlinked or unhooked.
desengastar, *tr.v.* to remove from its setting (a jewel, a precious stone).
desengomar, *tr.v.* to unstick, unglue, ungum; to unsize (silk).
desengoznar, *tr.v.* 1. to unhinge, remove the hinges from. 2. to throw out of gear. —*r.v.* to contort one's body (in certain movements or dances).
desengranar, *tr.v.* to disengage (e.g. two cogged wheels); to disconnect, uncouple.
desengrane, *m.* disengaging of gears.
desengrasar, *tr.v.* to remove the fat or grease from. —*i.v.* 1. (coll.) to lose weight, get thin. 2. to remove the taste of fat by eating fruit, olives, dessert, etc. 3. (fig.) to have a change; change one's job.
desengrase, *m.* removal of grease.
desengraso, *m.* (Col.) sweet, dessert.
desengrilletar, *tr.v.* (mar.) to knock a link out of (a chain).
desengrosar, (*ref. 33*) *tr.v.* to make thin. —*i.v.* to become or grow thin.
desengrudamiento, *m.* removal of paste.
desengrudar, *tr.v.* to remove or scrape the paste from.
desengruese, desengrueso, *ref.* **desengrosar.**
desenhebrar, *tr.v.* to unthread (a needle).
desenhetrar, *tr.v.* to untangle, unravel (hair).
desenhornar, *tr.v.* to remove from the oven.
desenjaece, desenjaecé, *ref.* **desenjaezar.**
desenjaezar, (*ref. 53*) *tr.v.* to unharness a horse.
desenjalmar, *tr.v.* to unsaddle, unload, remove the packsaddle or other burden from (a horse, mule, etc.).
desenjaular, *tr.v.* 1. to uncage, set free. 2. (coll.) to let out of jail.
desenlabonar, *tr.v., var. of* **deseslabonar.**
desenlace, *m.* denouement, conclusion, end (of a play); outcome, result.
desenlace, desenlacé, *ref.* **desenlazar.**
desenladrillar, *tr.v.* to remove bricks from, dig or rip bricks out of.
desenlatar, *tr.v.* (Amer.) to remove from a can.
desenlazamiento, *m.* 1. untying, unlacing, undoing. 2. settlement, solution. 3. denouement, conclusion (of a play, a problem, etc.).
desenlazar, (*ref. 53*) *tr.v.* 1. to unlace, undo, untie. 2. to settle, resolve (a difficulty). 3. to unravel (the plot of a play). —*r.v.* 1. to become untied or loose. 2. to develop, unfold, reach a denouement, e.g. *esta comedia se desenlaza ridículamente,* this play has a ridiculous denouement.
desenlodar, *tr.v.* to clean or remove mud from.
desenlosar, *tr.v.* to remove flagstones from.
desenlutado, da, *past part. of* **desenlutar.** —*a.* having come out of mourning.
desenlutar, *tr.v.* to make (someone) give up mourning. —*r.v.* to come out of mourning.
desenmallar, *tr.v.* to remove (fish) from a net.
desenmarañado, *a.* disentangled, unraveled, clarified.
desenmarañar, *tr.v.* to untangle, disentangle; unravel; (fig.) to clear up, clarify, elucidate.
desenmascaradamente, *adv.* unashamedly, openly, boldly.
desenmascarado, da, *past part. of* **desenmascarar.** —*a.* unmasked; exposed.
desenmascarar, *tr.v.* to unmask; (fig.) to reveal, expose, unmask. —*r.v.* to unmask, take off one's mask.
desenmohecer, (*ref. 45*) *tr.v.* to remove rust from, to remove mold from, rid of mildew.
desenmohezca, desenmohezco, *ref.* **desenmohecer.**
desenmudecer, (*ref. 45*) *tr.v.* to rid of a speech impediment. —*i.v.* 1. to rid oneself of a speech impediment. 2. (fig.) to break a long silence.
desenmudezca, desenmudezco, *ref.* **desenmudecer.**
desenojado, da, *past part. of* **desenojar.** —*a.* soothed; pacified, calmed.
desenojar, *tr.v.* to soothe, calm, pacify. —*r.v.* 1. to become calm, calm down, cool off. 2. to amuse oneself, relax, rest.
desenojo, *m.* calmness, calm (after anger).
desenojoso, sa, *a.* soothing, calming, pacifying.
desenredado, da, *past part, of* **desenredar.** —*a.* disentangled, extricated; explained, clarified.
desenredar, *tr.v.* to disentangle, untangle, unravel; (fig.) to put in order, clear up. —*r.v.* to extricate oneself (from difficulties), disentangle or disinvolve oneself (from difficulties).
desenredo, *m.* disentanglement, unraveling; clearing up; disinvolvement, extrication (from difficulties); denouement.
desenrice, desenricé, *ref.* **desenrizar.**
desenrizar, (*ref. 53*) *tr.v.* to uncurl.
desenrollar, *tr.v.* to unroll, unwind. —*r.v.* to become unwound.
desenronar, *tr.v.* to remove debris from.
desenroscar, *tr.v.* (Amer.) to unscrew, to untwine, unwind, untwist.
desenrudecer, (*ref. 45*) *tr.v.* to civilize, educate, refine. —*r.v.* to become refined, educated or civilized.
desenrudezca, desenrudezco, *ref.* **desenrudecer.**
desensabanar, *tr.v.* (coll.) to take sheets off (a bed).
desensamblar, *tr.v.* to disassemble, take apart, take to pieces.
desensañar, *tr.v.* to soothe, pacify, appease. —*r.v.* to be soothed, appeased, pacified.
desensartar, *tr.v.* to unthread; to unstring.
desensebar, *tr.v.* to strip of fat. —*i.v.* 1. to have a change, vary (one's occupation). 2. to remove the taste of fat. 3. to get thin.
desenseñar, *tr.v.* to re-educate, teach correctly.
desensibilizador, *m.* (photog.) desensitizer.
desensibilizante, *m.* (med., physiol.) desensitizer.
desensibilizar, (*ref. 53*) *tr.v.* (med., physiol., photog.) to desensitize.
desensillado, da, *past part. of* **desensillar.** —*a.* unsaddled; unseated.
desensillar, *tr.v.* to unsaddle.
desensoberbecer, (*ref. 45*) *tr.v.* to make humble, to humble. —*r.v.* to become humble.
desensortijado, da, *a.* 1. straight, uncurled (hair). 2. dislocated, displaced (bone).
desentablar, *tr.v.* 1. to rip up planking or boards from. 2. to disarrange, throw into disorder or confusion. 3. to break up (a friendship), break off (a business deal).
desentalingar, (*ref. 51*) *tr.v.* (mar.) to unbend, unfasten (a cable from an anchor ring).
desentalingue, desentalingué, *ref.* **desentalingar.**
desentarimar, *tr.v.* to remove boarding, parquet flooring or planking from.
desentechar, *tr.v.* (Amer.) to tear the ceiling off.
desentenderse, (*ref. 30*) *r.v.* to feign ignorance, pretend not to understand or know. — **d. de,** to feign ignorance of; to take no part in, have nothing to do with.
desentendido, da, *past part. of* **desentender.** —*a.* ignorant, unmindful; **hacerse el d.,** (coll.) to pretend not to notice.
desenterrado, da, *a.* disinterred; disentombed.
desenterrador, *m.* exhumer, person who disinters or digs up.
desenterramiento, *m.* 1. disinterment, exhumation; unearthing. 2. remembering, recalling.
desenterrar, (*ref. 29*) *tr.v.* to disinter, exhume; to dig up, unearth. 2. (fig.) to remember, recall; to expose.
desentienda, desentiendo, *ref.* **desentenderse.**
desentierramuertos, *m., f.* (coll.) defamer of the dead.
desentierre, desentierro, *ref* **desenterrar.**
desentoldar, *tr.v.* 1. to strip the awnings off, remove the awnings from. 2. to strip of ornaments. —*r.v.* (Mex.) to clear up (the sky).
desentonación, *f.* dissonance, tunelessness.
desentonadamente, *adv.* out of tune, dissonantly, tunelessly, inharmoniously.
desentonado, da, *past part. of* **desentonar.** —*a.* tone-deaf.
desentonamiento, *m., var. of* **desentono.**
desentonar, *tr.v.* to humble, humiliate. —*i.v.* 1. to be out of tune, sing or play out of tune; to be inharmonious. 2. to say things out of place; to be out of place; to be unsuitable, to stand out awkwardly. —*r.v.* to talk loudly and disrespectfully.
desentono, *m.* 1. dissonance, lack of musicality. 2. harshness, loudness (of voice). 3. awkwardness (of speech or manners).
desentornillar, *tr.v.* to unscrew.
desentorpecer, (*ref. 45*) *tr.v.* 1. to rid of numbness, bring back to life, revive (a foot or an arm). 2. to make lively, alert or intelligent. 3. to clear the way for, get (something) out of the path of, to make things easier for. —*r.v.* 1. to come back to life. 2. to become lively or bright again.
desentorpezca, desentorpezco, *ref.* **desentorpecer.**
desentrampar, *tr.v.* (coll.) to release from debt. —*r.v.* (coll.) to get out of hock, to pay one's debts.

desentrañamiento, *m.* giving one's all for love.
desentrañar, *tr.v.* 1. to disembowel; to remove the entrails from. 2. to get to the bottom of (a matter). *—r.v.* to give one's all for love.
desentrenado, da, *past part. of* **desentrenarse.** *—a.* out of training.
desentrenarse, *r.v.* to get out of training.
desentristecer, *tr.v.* to allay (someone's) sadness; to confort, to cheer up.
desentronice, desentronicé, *ref.* **desentronizar.**
desentronizar, (*ref. 53*) *tr.v.* to dethrone; (fig.) to depose, overthrow.
desentumecer, (*ref. 45*) *tr.v.* to rid of numbness, revive, bring back to life. *—r.v.* to come back to life (numbed limbs).
desentumecimiento, *m.* recovery from numbness.
desentumezca, desentumezco, *ref.* **desentumecer.**
desentumir, *tr.v., var of* **desentumecer.**
desenvainar, *tr.v.* 1. to draw, unsheathe (a sword, etc.). 2. to show (claws). 3. (coll.) to uncover, expose, reveal.
desenvelejar, *tr.v.* (mar.) to strip of sails.
desenvendar, *tr.v.* to unbandage, remove bandages from.
desenvenenar, *tr.v.* to extract or remove poison from.
desenvergar, (*ref. 51*) *tr.v.* (mar.) to untie, unbend (sails) from the yards.
desenvergue, desenvergué, *ref.* **desenvergar.**
desenviolar, *tr.v.* to purify (a desecrated place).
desenvoltura, *f.* 1. assurance, confidence, ease, naturalness. 2. boldness, forwardness. 3. eloquence, facility (in speaking).
desenvolvedor, ra, *a.* investigating. *—m., f.* investigator.
desenvolver, (*ref. 34*) *tr.v.* 1. to unroll, unwrap. 2. to disentangle, unravel, clear up. 3. to develop, expand. 4. to expound (a theory). *—r.v.* 1. to become unwrapped or unrolled. 2. to grow, develop, expand, evolve. 3. to lose one's timidity, become assured or confident. 4. (coll.) to get oneself out of (a jam).
desenvolvimiento, *m.* 1. unwrapping, unfolding. 2. development, expansion. 3. clearing up, disentanglement, unraveling. 4. exposition (of a theory). 5. escape (from a difficult situation).
desenvueltamente, *adv.* 1. with assurance or confidence, easily, naturally. 2. expediently. 3. eloquently.
desenvuelto, ta, *irr. past part. of* **desenvolver.** *—a.* 1. confident, assured, easy, natural (in manner). 2. forward, bold. 3. eloquent, quick (in speech).
desenvuelva, desenvuelvo, *ref.* **desenvolver.**
desenyesar, *tr.v.* to remove plaster from.
desenzarce, desenzarcé, *ref.* **desenzarzar.**
desenzarzar, (*ref. 53*) *tr.v.* 1. to extricate or disentangle from brambles. 2. (fig.) to separate and calm down (persons fighting). *—r.v.* 1. to extricate oneself from brambles. 2. to calm down, cool off.
deseo, *m.* desire, wish; appetite; sexual urge. — **coger a d. una cosa,** to achieve or attain one's dearest wish; **morirse uno de d.,** (fig.) to be dying with desire.
deseoso, sa, *a.* desirous; anxious.
deseque, desequé, *ref.* **desecar.**
desequido, da, *a.* dried out, dehydrated.
desequilibrado, da, *past part. of* **desequilibrar.** *—a.* unbalanced; (fig.) mentally unbalanced.
desequilibrar, *tr.v.* 1. to throw off balance. 2. to unbalance mentally. *—r.v.* 1. to lose one's balance. 2. to become mentally unbalanced.
desequilibrio, *m.* 1. lack of equilibrium. 2. (fig.) unbalanced mental condition.
deserción, *f.* desertion, abandonment; (law) forfeiture.
deserrado, da, *a.* unerring, free of error.
desertar, *tr.v.* to desert, abandon (one's country, ranks, cause); (law) to abandon (a case). *—r.v.* to desert. — **d. a,** to go over to; **d. de,** to desert from.
desértico, ca, *a.* desert-like, deserted; unpopulated.
desertor, ra, *m., f.* deserter; forsaker; fugitive.
deservicio, *m.* disservice, ill turn.
deservidor, *m.* one who does a disservice; one who abandons duty.
deservir, (*ref. 39*) *tr.v.* to serve ill, to do a disservice to; to fail to do (one's duty).
desescamar, *tr.v.* to remove scales from.
desescarchador, *m.* defroster (device); **d. del parabrisas,** (aut.) windshield defroster.
desescombrar, *tr.v.* to clear of rubble; to remove rubbish from.
deseslabonar, *tr.v.* to unlink, disconnect (links of a chain).
desespaldar, *tr.v.* to break or wrench the back of. *—r.v.* to wrench or break one's back.
desespañolice, desespañolicé, *ref.* **desespañolizar.**
desespañolizar, (*ref. 53*) *tr.v.* to obliterate from objects or persons the condition of being Spanish.
desesperación, *f.* desperation, anger, passion, fury; **ser una d.,** (coll.) to be unbearable.
desesperadamente, *adv.* desperately; hopelessly.
desesperado, da, *past part. of* **desesperar.** *—a.* desperate; hopeless. *—m., f.* desperate person.
desesperance, desesperancé, *ref.* **desesperanzar.**
desesperante, *a.* maddening, infuriating, causing despair.
desesperanza, *f.* despair, desperation, hopelessness.
desesperanzar, (*ref. 53*) *tr.v.* to deprive of hope, discourage. *—i.v.* to despair; to get or become discouraged.
desesperar, *tr.v.* 1. to exasperate, infuriate. 2. to deprive of hope, discourage. *—i.v.* to lose hope, to despair. *—r.v.* 1. to become or get desperate, despair; to lose hope. 2. to become or get exasperated.
desespero, *m.* (Amer.) despair; impatience; hopelessness.
desestancar, (*ref. 50*) *tr.v.* 1. (com.) to raise the monopoly on. 2. to open, release (water held back, etc.).
desestanco, *m.* 1. freeing, releasing (waters, etc.). 2. abolition of a monopoly.
desestanque, desestanqué, *ref.* **desestancar.**
desestañar, *tr.v.* to remove tin from, to unsolder. *—r.v.* to lose its tin coating.
desesterar, *tr.v.* to remove the rush mat from (a room, etc.).
desestero, *m.* removal of rush mats; season in which floor mats are removed and stored away.
desestima, *f., var. of* **desestimación.**
desestimación, *f.* lack of esteem, disesteem, disrespect.
desestimador, ra, *a.* disesteeming, contemptuous, despising. *—m., f.* ingrate; despiser.
desestimar, *tr.v.* 1. to think little of, hold in low esteem, disesteem. 2. to reject, refuse.
desexualización, *f.* (med.) desexualization.
desfacedor, *m., f.* (arch.) undoer, e.g. *d. de entuertos,* (coll.) avenger of wrongs.
desfacer, *tr.v.* (arch.), *var. of* **deshacer,** to undo, e.g. *d. entuertos,* to undo or to right wrongs.
desfachatadamente, *adv.* brazenly, insolently, impudently.
desfachatado, da, *a.* (coll.) brazen, shameless; boldfaced, barefaced; impudent, insolent.
desfachatez, *f.* brazenness, shamelessness; insolence.
desfajar, *tr.v.* to ungird, unbind, remove a girdle from. *—r.v.* to remove one's girdle, unbind oneself.
desfalcador, ra, *a.* embezzling. *—m., f.* embezzler, defaulter.
desfalcar, (*ref. 50*) *tr.v.* 1. to embezzle. 2. to remove a part of. 3. to bring (someone) down (from power or favor).
desfalco, *m.* 1. embezzlement; defalcation. 2. removal, taking away.
desfalque, desfalqué, *ref.* **desfalcar.**
desfallecer, (*ref. 45*) *tr.v.* to weaken, make weak. *—i.v.* to weaken, become weak; to faint, to swoon.
desfallecido, da, *past part. of* **desfallecer.** *—a.* faint; languid; spent, weak, e.g. *d. de hambre,* famished.
desfalleciente, *a.* weakening, debilitating.
desfallecimiento, *m.* weakness, debilitation; fainting, swooning.
desfallezca, desfallezco, *ref.* **desfallecer.**
desfamar, *tr.v.* to defame.
desfavorable, *a.* unfavorable, contrary; harmful.
desfavorablemente, *adv.* unfavorably.
desfavorecedor, ra, *a.* disesteeming, disfavoring *—m., f.* person who does a disfavor.
desfavorecer, (*ref. 45*) *tr.v.* 1. to disfavor, slight, hold (a person) in low esteem. 2. to contradict, oppose.
desfavorezca, desfavorezco, *ref.* **desfavorecer.**
desfecho, *past part. of* **desfacer.**
desfibrado, *m.* removal of fibers.
desfibradora, *f.* fiber-removing machine.
desfibrar, *tr.v.* to remove fibers from.
desfiguración, *f.* 1. defiguration, defacement. 2. camouflage; alteration.
desfigurado, da, *past part. of* **desfigurar.** *—a.* 1. disfigured, deformed, misshapen. 2. defaced. 3. disguised; distorted, misrepresented (e.g. the truth, the facts).
desfiguramiento, *m., var. of* **desfiguración.**
desfigurar, *tr.v.* 1. to disfigure; to deform, misshape. 2. to deface, make illegible. 3. to disguise; to distort, misrepresent (e.g. the facts, the truth). *—r.v.* to become disfigured or deformed (through accident); to become distorted (by anger).
desfijar, *tr.v.* to remove, pull off.
desfilachar, *tr.v., var. of* **deshilachar.**
desfilada, *f.* (mil.) single file.
desfiladero, *m.* defile, narrow pass; rocky, steep mountain path.
desfilar, *i.v.* to defile, parade by, march in review, march in single file; (coll.) file in, file out, file by.
desfile, *m.* parade, march; procession.
desflecar, (*ref. 50*) *tr.v.* to remove the fringe or border from. *—r.v.* to become unraveled or threadbare.
desflemar, *i.v.* to cough up phlegm. *—tr.v.* (chem.) to dephlegmate, rectify (spirits).
desfleque, desflequé, *ref.* **desflecar.**
desflocar, (*ref. 69*) *tr.v., var. of* **desflecar.**
desfloqué, *ref.* **desflocar.**
desfloración, *f.* defloration, deflowering; rape, sexual violation.
desfloramiento, *m., var. of* **desfloración.**
desflorar, *tr.v.* 1. to deflower, violate, rape. 2. to pull the flowers off. 3. to treat superficially. *—r.v.* to lose its patina or finish.

desflorecer, (*ref. 45*) *i.v., r.v.* to lose its flowers, to wither.
desflorecido, da, *a.* having lost its flowers; wilted, withered.
desflorecimiento, *m.* loss of flowers, withering; loss of patina or finish.
desflorezca, desflorezco, *ref.* **desflorecer.**
desflueco, desflueque, *ref.* **desflocar.**
desfogar, (*ref. 51*) *tr.v.* 1. to make a vent or an opening in (something) in order to allow fire to escape. 2. to slake (lime). 3. to give vent to, give free rein to (anger). —*i.v.* to break (a storm). —*r.v.* to give vent or free rein to one's passion or anger, (coll.) to let off steam.
desfogonar, *tr.v.* to break or remove the touchhole of (cannons and guns). —*r.v.* to burst (the touchhole of a gun).
desfogue, *m.* 1. vent. 2. venting, giving vent to (ire, passion, etc.).
desfogue, desfogué, *ref.* **desfogar.**
desfollonar, *tr.v.* to prune, strip off leaves and shoots.
desfondar, *tr.v.* 1. to break or break off the bottom of; (mar.) to damage or fracture the bottom, bilge. 2. (agr.) to loosen, plow or dig deeply. —*r.v.* to have its bottom broken, lose its bottom; (mar.) to have its bottom fractured or damaged, to bilge.
desfonde, *m.* 1. deep plowing. 2. the action of breaking the bottom (of a bottle, a ship, etc.).
desformado, da, *past part. of* **desformar. —***a.* disfigured, deformed.
desformar, *tr.v.* to deform, misshape, disfigure.
desfortalecer, (*ref. 45*) *tr.v.* to demolish (a fortress); to remove the garrison from (a fortress).
desfortalezca, desfortalezco, *ref.* **desfortalecer.**
desfrenamiento, *m.* (fig.) *var. of* **desenfreno.**
desfrenar, *tr.v., r.v., var. of* **desenfrenar.**
desfruncir, (*ref. 61*) *tr.v.* to unfold, unfurl, spread out.
desfrunza, desfrunzo, *ref.* **desfruncir.**
desfrutar, *tr.v.* to pick the green fruit from (a tree).
desga, *f.* very large wooden trough.
desgaire, *m.* 1. carelessness, slovenliness; affected carelessness. 2. contemptuous gesture. — **al d.,** carelessly, with affected carelessness; contemptuously.
desgajadura, *f.* ripping off, tearing off (of a branch).
desgajar, *tr.v.* to rip or tear off (a branch); to rip or tear apart or to pieces. —*r.v.* to come apart, come loose, break off; to break away or loose; to become disjointed.
desgaje, *m.* ripping or tearing apart; tearing off.
desgalgadero, *m.* steep and rugged slope, rocky precipice.
desgalgar, (*ref. 51*) *tr.v.* to hurl, cast or throw headlong. —*r.v.* to throw oneself headlong.
desgalgue, desgalgué, *ref.* **desgalgar.**
desgalichado, da, *a.* (coll.) untidy, unkempt, ungainly.
desgalillarse, *r.v.* (Amer.) to yell or scream at the top of one's voice.
desgana, *f.* 1. lack of appetite. 2. unwillingness, reluctance. — **con d.,** reluctantly, unwillingly; without zest or appetite.
desganado, da, *past part. of* **desganar. —***a.* 1. unwilling, indifferent. 2. not hungry.
desganar, *tr.v.* to take away the desire to do or the interest in (something). —*r.v.* to lose one's appetite; to lose interest in, grow tired of doing (something).
desganchar, *tr.v.* to lop off branches from.
desgano, *m.* 1. reluctance, unwillingness. 2. lack of appetite. — **con d.,** reluctantly; without zest or enthusiasm.
desgañifarse, *r.v.* (coll.) *var. of* **desgañitarse.**
desgañitarse, *r.v.* (coll.) to scream or yell at the top of one's voice.
desgañotar, *tr.v.* (Amer.) to kill by cutting the windpipe of or by dislocating the cervical vertebra of (birds, etc.).
desgarbado, da, *a.* ungainly, awkward, inelegant, lacking poise and presence.
desgarbo, *m.* (Amer.) lack of grace.
desgargantarse, *r.v.* (coll.) to scream or yell at the top of one's voice.
desgargolar, *tr.v.* 1. to ripple (flax), remove seeds from (flax). 2. (carp.) take (a piece of wood) out of a notch or groove.
desgaritar, *i.v.* to lose the way. —*r.v.* 1. to lose the way; to get lost, go astray, stray (from the fold). 2. to give up, abandon (an idea, a project).
desgarradamente, *adv.* brazenly, boldly, shamelessly, insolently, barefacedly.
desgarrado, da, *past part. of* **desgarrar. —***a.* 1. torn, rent, ripped, broken. 2. dissolute; impudent, shameless.
desgarrador, ra, *a.* 1. tearing. 2. heartrending. 3. blood-curdling, frightening.
desgarradura, *f.* tear, rent, split, rip, laceration.
desgarramiento, *m.* tearing, rending, splitting, ripping; rip, tear, rent.
desgarrar, *tr.v.* 1. to tear, rip, split; to rend, break (someone's heart, etc.). 2. to cough hard to raise (phlegm). —*r.v.* 1. to tear, rend, split. 2. to break away, leave the company of others.
desgarro, *m.* 1. split, rip, rent, tear, laceration. 2. shamelessness, brazenness, impudence, boldness; swaggering, boastfulness. 3. (Amer.) sputum.
desgarrón, *m.* large tear, rip or split (in clothes); shred, tatter (of torn clothing).
desgasificador, *m.* (chem.) deaerator.
desgastado, da, *past part. of* **desgastar. —***a.* (coll.) worn-out, weakened.
desgastador, ra, *a.* wearing, consuming, weakening.
desgastamiento, *m.* extravagance, prodigality, waste.
desgastar, *tr.v.* to wear away; to wear out; to weaken. —*r.v.* to wear away; to wear out; to become weak, lose one's vigor or strength.
desgaste, *m.* wear and tear; wearing away; wearing out; erosion.
desgatar, *tr.v.* (agr.) to weed.
desgausamiento, *m.* degaussing (a ship, to protect it from mines).
desgaznatarse, *r.v.* (coll.) to yell or scream at the top of one's voice.
desglosable, *a.* detachable.
desglosar, *tr.v.* 1. to remove footnotes or marginal comments from (a manuscript). 2. to detach, rip out, tear off (pages or sheets).
desglose, *m.* removal of footnotes or marginal comments; removal (of sheets or pages).
desgobernado, da, *past part. of* **desgobernar. —***a.* undisciplined, unbridled, unrestrained.
desgobernadura, *f.* (vet.) dislocation, displacement (of bones).
desgobernar, (*ref. 29*) *tr.v.* 1. to misgovern, mismanage. 2. to dislocate (bones). 3. (mar.) to be careless or negligent in control of (the tiller). —*r.v.* to contort one's limbs (in certain dances, etc.).
desgobierne, desgobierno, *ref.* **desgobernar.**
desgobierno, *m.* 1. disorder, confusion, misgovernment, mismanagement. 2. (vet.) dislocation, displacement (of bones).
desgolletar, *tr.v.* 1. to break the neck off (a vase, etc.). 2. to loosen or take off the clothing around (the neck).
desgomar, *tr.v.* to ungum, unsize (silk).
desgonzar, (*ref. 53*) *tr.v.* 1. to unhinge, remove the hinges from. 2. to disturb, upset, throw into confusion or disorder. —*r.v.* to be thrown into confusion or disorder.
desgorrarse, *r.v.* to remove one's hat, cap, etc.
desgoznar, *tr.v.* to unhinge, remove hinges from. —*r.v.* to contort one's limbs (in certain movements).
desgracia, *f.* 1. misfortune; misshap; disgrace, disfavor, displeasure. 2. roughness, uncouthness. 3. clumsiness, awkwardness, lack of charm, poise or presence. — **caer en d.,** (coll.) to fall into disgrace; **por d.,** unfortunately.
desgraciadamente, *adv.* unfortunately.
desgraciado, da, *past part. of* **desgraciar. —***a.* 1. unfortunate; unlucky. 2. clumsy, awkward, graceless, lacking poise or presence. 3. disagreeable, unpleasant. —*m., f.* (coll.) 1. mean or disagreeable person, rotter. 2. wretch; crook, despicable person; (Cuba) son of a bitch (vulg.).
desgraciar, *tr.v.* 1. to displease, annoy. 2. to spoil, ruin, impede the growth of. 3. to deflower or seduce a girl. —*r.v.* 1. to spoil; to be spoiled or ruined, fail to develop, to degenerate. 2. to fall out (with a friend), fall into disfavor (with). 3. to fail, be unsuccessful (a business, etc.). 4. (S. Amer.) to wound or kill someone.
desgramar, *tr.v.* to remove or pull up the grass from.
desgranadera, *f.* grape-picker.
desgranado, da, *past part. of* **desgranar. —***a.* with some teeth broken (cogwheel).
desgranador, ra, *a.* shelling, threshing. —*m., f.* threshing machine, shelling machine; person who shells or threshes.
desgranamiento, *m.* (artil.) grooves formed on the venthole of a narrow-barreled cannon.
desgranar, *tr.v.* 1. to remove the grain from (corn) or grapes from (a bunch). 2. (artil.) to grade or classify (powder). —*r.v.* 1. to lose its grain (corn), lose its grapes (bunch, cluster). 2. to wear away (the vent hole of a cannon). 3. to become unstrung (beads).
desgrance, desgrancé, *ref.* **desgranzar.**
desgrane, *m.* husking, shelling, threshing (grain); unstringing (beads).
desgranzar, (*ref. 53*) *tr.v.* 1. to separate chaff from. 2. (p.) to give the first grinding to (colors).
desgrasar, *tr.v.* to remove grease from.
desgrase, *m.* removal of grease.
desgravación, *f.* lowering of duties or taxes.
desgravar, *tr.v.* to lower duties or taxes on.
desgreñado, da, *past part. of* **desgreñar. —***a.* disheveled, rumpled, unkempt.
desgreñar, *tr.v.* to dishevel, make untidy (hair). —*r.v.* 1. to become disheveled or untidy. 2. to quarrel heatedly.
desguace, *m.* 1. (mar.) breaking up (a ship). 2. rough dressing (of lumber).
desguace, desguacé, *ref.* **desguazar.**
desguanzar, (*ref. 53*) *tr.v.* (Mex.) to tire out, exhaust. —*r.v.* 1. (Mex.) to get tired or exhausted. 2. (Amer.) to fall to pieces.
desguanzo, *m.* (Mex.) exhaustion, tiredness.
desguañangado, da, *a.* (Chile) sloppy, carelessly dressed.
desguañangar, *tr.v.* (Amer., sl.) to damage, break; to take apart, loosen. —*r.v.* (P. Rico, sl.) to lose heart.
desguardo, *m.* (Arg.) talisman.
desguarnecer, (*ref. 45*) *tr.v.* 1. to remove or strip off trimmings or adornments from; to dismantle, strip down, remove parts from (a machine). 2. to unharness, remove the harness from. 3. to

disarm (an opponent); to remove the garrison from (a fort).
desguarnir, *tr.v.* (mar.) to unwind (rope) from a capstan, remove (rope) from a pulley-wheel.
desguazar, (*ref. 53*) *tr.v.* 1. (carp.) to rough-dress, hew. 2. (mar.) to break up, take to pieces, dismantle (a ship). 3. (Cuba, Mex., Ven.) to destroy; to shatter.
desguince, *m.* 1. knife used for cutting rags in a paper-mill. 2. dodging, swerve (of the body).
desguince, desguincé, *ref.* **desguinzar.**
desguindar, *tr.v.* (mar.) to lower. —*r.v.* to slip down, slide down.
desguinzar, (*ref. 53*) *tr.v.* to cut (rags) with a knife (in the paper-mill).
deshabitado, da, *past part. of* **deshabitar.** —*a.* uninhabited, unoccupied.
deshabitar, *tr.v.* 1. to leave, vacate, abandon (a house, etc.). 2. to depopulate, kill or scatter the inhabitants of (a city, zone, etc.).
deshabituación, *f.* disaccustoming; losing the habit; disuse.
deshabituar, (*ref. 55*) *tr.v.* to disaccustom, make one lose the habit. —*r.v.* to lose the habit, get out of the habit.
deshacedor, ra, *a.* undoing. —*m., f.* undoer; **d. de agravios,** undoer of wrongs, revenger of wrongs.
deshacer, (*ref. 10*) *tr.v.* 1. to undo. 2. to destroy. 3. to take apart; cut to pieces. 4. to break, violate (a treaty). 5. to wear away, weaken, wear out. 6. to vanquish, rout, put to flight. 7. to dissolve, liquefy. —*r.v.* 1. to fall to pieces. 2. to wear away, wear out. 3. to dissolve, liquefy. 4. to be ruined, go to rack and ruin. 5. to upset oneself, go to pieces (with worry, etc.). 6. to disappear, vanish. 7. to work like a slave. 8. to get deformed or misshapen. 9. to grow thin and weak. — **deshacerse de,** to get rid of; **deshacerse en,** to dissolve into (compliments, tears, etc.).
deshaga, deshago, *ref.* **deshacer.**
deshaldo, *m.* spring trimming of honeycombs.
deshambrido, da, *a.* ravenous, starving, famished.
desharé, desharía, *ref.* **deshacer.**
desharrapado, da, *a.* ragged, shabby. —*m., f.* ragamuffin, beggar, bum (coll.).
desharrapamiento, *m.* misery, poverty, penury.
deshebillar, *tr.v.* to unbuckle.
deshebrar, *tr.v.* 1. to undo, unravel (cloth). 2. to cut in very thin pieces, tear to shreds.
deshecha, *f.* 1. sham, pretense. 2. polite farewell. 3. short song to end a poem. 4. counter step in Spanish dancing. 5. exit, prompt departure. — **hacer uno la d.,** to feign, pretend.
deshechizar, (*ref. 53*) *tr.v.* to break the spell on, remove the spell from.
deshechizo, *m.* breaking off a magic spell.
deshecho, cha, *irr. past part. of* **deshacer.** —*a.* 1. strong, violent (rain, storm). 2. exhausted, tired out (coll.). 3. dissolved, well-mixed.
deshelador, *m.* defroster.
deshelar, (*ref. 29*) *tr.v., r.v.* to melt, thaw; to defrost.
desherbar, (*ref. 29*) *tr.v.* to weed, to rid of weeds.
desheredación, *f.* disinheritance, disinheriting.
desheredado, da, *past part. of* **desheredar.** —*a.* disinherited.
desheredamiento, *m., var. of* **desheredación.**
desheredar, *tr.v.* to disinherit, deprive of an inheritance. —*r.v.* to disgrace or dishonor one's family; to degenerate.
deshermanar, *tr.v.* (fig.) to make unlike or different. —*r.v.* to forsake a brother, to reject brotherly love.
desherradura, *f.* (vet.) footsoreness, soreness on the hoof of an unshod horse.
desherrar, (*ref. 29*) *tr.v.* 1. to unshackle, unfetter. 2. to remove the shoes from (a horse). —*r.v.* 1. to free oneself from one's fetters or shackles. 2. to lose its shoe, kick off its shoe (a horse).
desherrumbramiento, *m.* removal of rust.
desherrumbrar, *tr.v.* to remove rust from.
deshice, *ref.* **deshacer.**
deshiciera, deshiciese, *ref.* **deshacer.**
deshidratación, *f.* dehydration.
deshidratador, *m.* dehydrator.
deshidratar, *tr.v.* (chem.) to dehydrate. —*r.v.* to become dehydrated.
deshidrogenación, *f.* (chem.) dehydrogenation, dehydrogenization.
deshidrogenar, *tr.v.* (chem.) to dehydrogenate, dehydrogenize.
deshidrogenasa, *f.* (biochem.) dehydrogenase.
deshiele, deshielo, *ref.* **deshelar.**
deshielo, *m.* thaw (of snow or ice); melting, defrosting.
deshierba, *f.* weeding.
deshierbe, deshierbo, *ref.* **desherbar**
deshierre, deshierro, *ref.* **desherrar**
deshijar, *tr.v.* 1. (Cuba) to remove suckers from (a plant). 2. to separate the offspring from the mother.
deshilachar, *tr.v.* to remove threads from (a piece of cloth). —*r.v.* to become frayed.
deshilado, da, *past part. of* **deshilar.** —*a.* in single file. — **a la deshilada,** in single file; secretly. —*m.* (*pl.*) hemstitch, openwork (embroidery).
deshiladura, *f.* drawing threads; unraveling the borders (of cloth); preparation of the fabric for hemstitching or openwork embroidery.
deshilar, *tr.v.* 1. to draw threads from; to undo or unravel the edges of (cloth) in order to make a fringe. 2. to distract (a swarm of bees) and lead them to a new hive. 3. to shred (meat). —*i.v.* to grow thin.
deshilo, *m.* distracting (bees) and leading them to a new hive.
deshilvanado, da, *past part. of* **deshilvanar.** —*a.* (fig.) disjointed, disconnected, incoherent, desultory (talks, thoughts).
deshilvanar, *tr.v.* (tail.) to remove the tacks from; to remove basting threads from.
deshincadura, *f.* removal, pulling out, drawing out (something nailed or fixed).
deshincar, (*ref. 50*) *tr.v.* to draw out, remove, pull out.
deshinchadura, *f.* act of reducing a swelling; subsiding of a swelling.
deshinchar, *tr.v.* 1. to reduce or relieve the swelling of. 2. to soothe, calm, pacify (anger). —*r.v.* 1. to go down (a swelling). 2. (fig.) to become deflated, lose one's arrogance or presumption.
deshinchazón, *f.* reduction or subsiding of a swelling.
deshinque, deshinqué, *ref.* **deshincar.**
deshipnotizar, (*ref. 53*) *tr.v.* to free from the effects or influence of hypnosis.
deshipotecar, (*ref. 50*) *tr.v.* to free from or cancel a mortgage on.
deshipoteque, deshipotequé, *ref.* **deshipotecar.**
deshojado, da, *past part. of* **deshojar.** —*a.* defoliated, leafless, denudated, denuded.
deshojador, ra, *a.* leaf-stripping (from a tree). —*m., f.* stripper of leaves, leaf-picker.
deshojadura, *f.* stripping of leaves or petals; defoliation.
deshojar, *tr.v.* to defoliate; to strip or remove the leaves from; to remove the petals from. —*r.v.* to lose its leaves or petals.
deshoje, *m.* fall or shedding of leaves.
deshollejar, *tr.v.* to peel, remove the skin from (a fruit or vegetable).
deshollinadera, *f.* chimney-sweep's brush.
deshollinado, da, *past part. of* **deshollinar.** —*a.* soot-free, swept clean (a chimney).
deshollinador, ra, *a.* 1. chimney-sweeping, soot-sweeping. 2. (coll.) curious, inquisitive. —*m., f.* 1. chimney sweep. 2. (coll.) snoopy or inquisitive person. —*m.* any chimney-sweeping brush or appliance; long-handled brush (for cleaning away soot).
deshollinar, *tr.v.* 1. to sweep (chimneys); to clean off soot. 2. (coll.) to scrutinize, examine attentively, look searchingly at.
deshonestamente, *adv.* 1. dishonestly, untruthfully. 2. indecently, improperly, immodestly.
deshonestarse, *r.v.* to lose one's sobriety of behavior; to become immodest or indecent.
deshonestidad, *f.* 1. dishonesty, untruthfulness. 2. immodesty, indecency, impropriety, lewdness; improper or indecent act or remark.
deshonesto, ta, *a.* 1. dishonest, untruthful. 2. immodest, improper, indecent, lewd.
deshonor, *m.* dishonor, disgrace; affront, insult.
deshonorar, *tr.v.* to dishonor, disgrace; to deprive of dignity, office or employment. —*r.v.* to become dishonored or disgraced.
deshonra, *f.* dishonor, disgrace; dishonorable act.
deshonrabuenos, *m., f.* 1. (coll.) slanderer. 2. (coll.) black sheep, ne'er-do-well, good-for-nothing.
deshonradamente, *adv.* dishonorably, disgracefully, shamefully.
deshonrador, ra, *a.* dishonorable, disgraceful. —*m., f.* dishonorer, disgracer.
deshonrar, *tr.v.* 1. to dishonor, disgrace. 2. to seduce, rape. 3. to despise, scorn; to insult, affront.
deshonrible, *a.* (coll.) contemptible, despicable. —*m., f.* despicable person, scoundrel.
deshonrosamente, *adv.* dishonorably, disgracefully, shamefully.
deshonroso, sa, *a.* dishonorable, disgraceful, shameful.
deshora, *f.* inconvenient time. — **a d.,** or **a deshoras,** at an inconvenient time, inopportunely, at the wrong moment; suddenly, unexpectedly.
deshornar, *tr.v.* to take out of the oven.
deshospedamiento, *m.* inhospitality; refusal of lodgings.
deshuesado, da, *past part. of* **deshuesar.** —*a.* pitted (fruit); boned (meat).
deshuesadora, *f.* pitter (instrument for removing stones from fruit, etc.).
deshuesar, *tr.v.* to bone (meat, fish); to remove the pits from (fruit).
deshuese, deshueso, *ref.* **desosar.**
deshumanización, *f.* dehumanization.
deshumanizar, (*ref. 53*) *tr.v.* to dehumanize.
deshumano, na, *a.* inhuman.
deshumedecer, (*ref. 45*) *tr.v.* to dry out, dehumidify. —*r.v.* to dry out, be dehumidified.
deshumedezca, deshumedezco, *ref.* **deshumedecer.**
desiderable, *a.* desirable.
desiderativo, va, *a.* desiderative, denoting desire.
desiderátum, *m.* desideratum, anything needed or wanted.
desidia, *f.* laziness, indolence; negligence.
desidiosamente, *adv.* lazily, idly, indolently.
desidioso, sa, *a.* idle, lazy, indolent. —*m., f.* idler, lazy person.
desierto, ta, *a.* 1. deserted, uninhabited, empty. 2. without contestants or bidders (a contest or an auction) —*m.* desert, wasteland, wilderness.

— **predicar en d.,** (coll.) to preach to the winds (to no effect).
designable, *a.* designable.
designación, *f.* designation; appointment.
designado, da, *past part. of* **designar.** —*a.* designated, assigned, planned; appointed, indicated, specified.
designar, *tr.v.* 1. to plan (e.g. work). 2. to designate (something) for a special purpose; to assign (someone) to a particular function or position.
designio, *m.* design, plan, intention.
desigual, *a.* 1. unequal. 2. rugged, broken, uneven (land). 3. rough. 4. (fig.) arduous, difficult. 5. (fig.) changeable, unstable (weather, etc.).
desigualar, *tr.v.* to make unequal. —*r.v.* to get ahead, advance, get a head start; to excell.
desigualdad, *f.* 1. inequality, disparity. 2. unevenness, roughness, ruggedness (of terrain). 3. (math.) sign of inequality.
desigualmente, *adv.* unequally, differently; with a handicap or disparity.
desilusión, *f.* disillusion, disillusionment; realization of the truth; disappointment.
desilusionar, *tr.v.* to disillusion, disenchant; to disappoint. —*r.v.* to become disillusioned; to be disappointed, lose one's illusions.
desimaginar, *tr.v.* to obliterate, blot out (an image from the mind).
desimanación, *f.* demagnetization, demagnetizing.
desimanar, *tr.v.* to demagnetize. —*r.v.* to become demagnetized, lose its magnetism.
desimantación, *f.* demagnetization.
desimantado, da, *past part. of* **desimantar.** —*a.* demagnetized.
desimantar, *tr.v.* to demagnetize. —*r.v.* to become demagnetized, lose its magnetism.
desimpondré, desimpondría, *ref.* **desimponer.**
desimponer, (*ref. 15*) *tr.v.* (print.) to remove the imposition from (the form).
desimponga, desimpongo, *ref.* **desimponer.**
desimpresionar, *tr.v.* to undeceive, disabuse. —*r.v.* to become undeceived or disabused.
desimpuse, *ref.* **desimponer.**
desimpusiera, desimpusiese, *ref.* **desimponer.**
desinclinar, *tr.v.* to disincline, to make unwilling. —*r.v.* to become disinclined, become unwilling.
desincorporar, *tr.v., r.v.* to separate, disunite, divide, break up.
desincrustante, *m., a.* boiler compound or fluid (to prevent the formation of scale).
desincrustar, *tr.v.* to descale, remove the scale from (boilers, etc.).
desinencia, *f.* (gram.) desinence, ending, termination (of words); way of ending sentences.
desinencial, *a.* desinential.
desinfartar, *tr.v.* (med.) to dissolve an infarct or a blood clot. —*r.v.* to have a blood clot or infarct dissolved.
desinfección, *f.* disinfection, disinfecting.
desinfectado, da, *past part. of* **desinfectar.** —*a.* disinfected.
desinfectante, *a.* disinfectant, disinfecting. —*m.* disinfectant.
desinfectar, *tr.v.* to disinfect. —*r.v.* to become disinfected.
desinficionamiento, *m.* disinfection.
desinficionar, *tr.v., r.v., var. of* **desinfectar.**
desinflación, *f.* deflation.
desinflamación, *f.* reduction or subsiding of inflammation; cure or loss of inflammation.
desinflamar, *tr.v.* to cure or reduce inflammation from. —*r.v.* to become less inflamed, lose its inflammation (a wound).
desinflar, *tr.v.* to deflate, remove air from, collapse. —*r.v.* to become deflated.
desinsaculación, *f.* drawing of names (e.g. to choose jurors).
desinsacular, *tr.v.* to draw from a box, sack, or other receptacle (the names of jurors, etc.).
desinsectación, *f.* fumigation, ridding of insects.
desinsectar, *tr.v.* to fumigate; rid of insects, parasites or vermin.
desintegrable, *a.* fissionable.
desintegración, *f.* disintegration; decay; **d. atómica,** atomic fission; **d. térmica,** (phys.) thermal fission.
desintegrador, *m.* disintegrator; **d. catalítico,** catalytic cracker (of petroleum).
desintegrar, *tr.v., r.v.* to disintegrate, decompose; (phys.) to disintegrate, decay.
desinterés, *m.* disinterestedness, altruism, selflessness.
desinteresadamente, *adv.* disinterestedly, altruistically.
desinteresado, da, *past part. of* **desinteresarse.** —*a.* disinterested, altruistic.
desinteresarse, *r.v.* to become disinterested, lose one's interest (for, in).
desintestinar, *tr.v.* to disembowel, eviscerate.
desintonizar, *tr.v.* (rad.) to be off beam (the dial).
desintoxicación, *f.* detoxification.
desintoxicar, (*ref. 50*) *tr.v.* to detoxicate, detoxify.
desinvernar, (*ref. 29*) *i.v.* (mil.) to leave winter quarters (troops).
desinvierne, desinvierno, *ref.* **desinvernar.**
desirva, desirvo, *ref.* **deservir.**
desirviendo, desirviera, desirviese, desirvió, *ref.* **deservir.**
desistencia, *f., var. of* **desistimiento.**
desistimiento, *m.* desistance; (law) waiving (of a right).
desistir, *i.v.* (law) to desist, to waive a right. — **desistir de,** to desist from, stop, give up, e.g. *d. de un intento,* to desist from trying.
desjarretadera, *f.* hamstringing knife (for hocking cattle).
desjarretar, *tr.v.* 1. to hamstring, cripple an animal by cutting its hamstring. 2. (coll.) to weaken, debilitate.
desjarrete, *m.* hamstringing, hocking.
desjugar, (*ref. 51*) *tr.v.* to extract juice from. —*r.v.* to become juiceless or dry, lose its juice.
desjuiciado, da, *a.* injudicious, showing poor judgment; senseless.
desjuntamiento, *m.* separation, coming apart, disjunction.
desjuntar, *tr.v.* to separate, divide, pull apart, disjoint. —*r.v.* to come apart, separate.
deslabonar, *tr.v.* 1. to unlink, disconnect or break the links of. 2. to take apart, take to pieces; to disjoin, disconnect. 3. to destroy, ruin, upset (a project). —*r.v.* 1. to become disconnected; to come apart or to pieces. 2. to fail, be upset (a project). 3. to withdraw or break away (from someone's company).
deslace, deslacé, *ref.* **deslazar.**
desladrillar, *tr.v.* to remove bricks or floor-tiles from.
deslamar, *tr.v.* to remove mud from.
deslastrar, *tr.v.* (mar.) to remove ballast from.
deslatar, *tr.v.* to remove the laths from.
deslavace, deslavacé, *ref.* **deslavazar.**
deslavado, da, *past part. of* **deslavar.** —*a.* (fig.) brazen, bold; shameless, impudent. —*m., f.* brazen person.
deslavadura, *f.* light wash or washing, rinse; fading, weakening.
deslavar, *tr.v.* 1. to wash lightly, rinse. 2. to weaken, fade, wear out (clothes) by washing. 3. to take away (quality, color, strength, etc.).
deslavazar, (*ref. 53*) *tr.v., var of* **deslavar.**
deslave, *m.* (Amer.) alluvion, landslide, avalanche.
deslayo, *adv.* **en d.,** in single file, one after another.
deslazamiento, *m., var. of* **desenlazamiento.**
deslazar, (*ref. 53*) *tr.v., var. of* **desenlazar.**
desleal, *a.* disloyal, faithless.
deslealmente, *adv.* disloyally, treacherously.
deslealtad, *f.* disloyalty, treachery, faithlessness.
deslechugador, ra, *a.* pruning; weeding. —*m., f.* pruner; weeder (of vineyards).
deslechugar, (*ref. 51*) *tr.v.* (agr.) to prune, clip off leaves or shoots from; (agr.) to weed, rid of weeds (vineyards).
deslechuguillar, *tr.v.* (agr.) *var. of* **deslechugar.**
desleidura, *f., var. of* **desleimiento.**
desleimiento, *m.* dissolving, dilution; melting.
desleír, (*ref. 40*) *tr.v.* 1. to dissolve, liquefy, melt; mix. 2. (fig.) to dilute, weaken (ideas or speech) by excess of words. —*r.v.* to become mixed or diluted.
deslendrar, (*ref. 29*) *tr.v.* to remove nits from, delouse.
deslenguado, da, *past part. of* **deslenguar.** —*a.* 1. foulmouthed, coarse, vulgar, scurrilous. 2. garrulous, talkative.
deslenguamiento, *m.* (coll.) coarseness, foulmouthedness; foul language.
deslenguar, (*ref. 52*) *tr.v.* to cut out or remove the tongue from. —*r.v.* to let forth a string of insults or oaths, break into foul language, talk coarsely or vulgarly; to talk excessively, blab, prattle.
desleyera, desleyese, desleyó, *ref.* **desleír.**
deslía, deslío, *ref.* **desleír.**
desliar, (*ref. 54*) *tr.v.* 1. to untie, undo. 2. to separate lees from (wine). —*r.v.* to become loose (a bundle).
deslice, deslicé, *ref.* **deslizar.**
desliendre, desliendro, *ref.* **deslendrar.**
desligadura, *f.* untying, loosening; unraveling, disentanglement; disjunction.
desligar, (*ref. 51*) *tr.v.* to untie, unfasten, undo, unbind. 2. to disentangle, unravel. 3. to absolve from (ecclesiastical censure); to free, excuse (from an obligation). 4. (mus.) to play staccato. —*r.v.* 1. to become unfastened, undone or loose. 2. to be resolved or settled.
desligue, desligué, *ref.* **desligar.**
deslindador, *m.* surveyor, one who sets boundaries.
deslindamiento, *m., var. of* **deslinde.**
deslindar, *tr.v.* 1. to delimit, delimitate, determine the limits of. 2. (fig.) to clear up, define, elucidate.
deslinde, *m.* 1. delimitation, setting of boundaries, demarcation. 2. (fig.) elucidation, clearing up.
desliñar, *tr.v.* (tex.) to remove stray threads from.
deslío, *m.* separating the dregs or lees from must or new wine.
desliz, (*pl.* **deslices**) *m.* 1. slipping; sliding. 2. slip, mistake, false step, slip, pecadillo. 3. portion of quicksilver lost in the smelting of silver.
deslizable, *a.* said of something that can slip, slide or glide.
deslizadero, ra, *a.* slippery. —*m.* slide, slippery place.
deslizadizo, za, *a.* slippery.
deslizador, *m.* (aer.) glider.
deslizamiento, *m.* slip; sliding, slipping, gliding.
deslizante, *a.* sliding, slipping, gliding.
deslizar, (*ref. 53*) *tr.v.* 1. to slide. 2. to let slip, let out (a secret). —*i.v.* to slide; to slip. —*r.v.* 1. to slide, slither; to glide. 2. to slip away, sneak away. 3. to slip out (a remark). 4. to slip, slide, skid (into a vice). — **deslizarse por,** to slide down.

desloar, *tr.v.* to abuse, revile.
deslomadura, *f.* 1. back-breaking. 2. (vet.) disease of the loin muscles in certain quadrupeds.
deslomar, *tr.v.* to break or injure the back of, to strain the loins of. —*r.v.* 1. to break or injure one's back. 2. (coll.) to break one's back by working.
deslucidamente, *adv.* ungracefully, awkwardly; poorly, badly.
deslucido, da, *past part. of* **deslucir.** —*a.* dull, lackluster, dreary, tedious; dowdy, inelegant, undistinguished; **quedar d.,** to make a poor impression (after a speech, a performance, etc.).
deslucimiento, *m.* lack of charm or distinction; gracelessness, awkwardness; dullness, dowdiness.
deslucir, (*ref. 46*) *tr.v.* 1. to tarnish; to spoil. 2. to discredit. 3. to deprive of charm, grace, distinction; to be unbecoming to. —*r.v.* 1. to become tarnished or dull. 2. to become discredited.
deslumbrado, da, *a.* dazzled; overwhelmed, bewildered.
deslumbrador, ra, *a.* dazzling, brilliant, glaring; overwhelming, bewildering.
deslumbramiento, *m.* 1. dazzling, blinding (by glaring light). 2. confusion (of mind), bewilderment, bafflement; (fig.) blindness.
deslumbrante, *a.* 1. brilliant, dazzling, glaring. 2. overwhelming, bewildering.
deslumbrar, *tr.v.* 1. to dazzle, blind. 2. to overwhelm, bewilder, baffle. —*r.v.* to be dazzled, overwhelmed or bewildered.
deslustrador, ra, *a.* tarnishing, dimming; discrediting. —*m., f.* tarnisher, person or something that removes sheen or gloss.
deslustrar, *tr.v.* 1. to tarnish, dim, make dull. 2. to tarnish the reputation of, discredit.
deslustre, *m.* 1. dullness, dimness, opaqueness; dimming, dulling. 2. (fig.) discredit, loss of prestige.
deslustroso, sa, *a.* inelegant; unbecoming.
desluzca, desluzco, *ref.* **deslucir.**
desmadejado, da, *past part. of* **desmadejar.** —*a.* run-down, lifeless, weak.
desmadejamiento, *m.* listlessness, languor; enervation, lack of vitality or vigor.
desmadejar, *tr.v.* to enervate, make listless. —*r.v.* to become listless or enervated.
desmadrado, da, *past part. of* **desmadrar.** —*a.* abandoned by or separated from its mother (said of an animal).
desmadrar, *tr.v.* to wean, separate (an animal) from its mother.
desmagnetizar, *tr.v.* to demagnetize.
desmajolar, (*ref. 33*) *tr.v.* 1. to pull up young grapevines from. 2. to untie, loosen the laces of (a shoe).
desmajuele, desmajuelo, *ref.* **desmajolar.**
desmalazado, da, *a.* 1. lax, careless, negligent. 2. dejected, downhearted, dispirited.
desmalezar, *tr.v.* (Amer.) to weed; to clear the land of underbrush or thickets.
desmallador, ra, *m., f.* one who breaks, rips or undoes nets or meshes.
desmalladura, *f.* undoing, breaking or cutting of the meshes (of a net).
desmallar, *tr.v.* to cut, undo or destroy the meshes of (a net or a stocking). —*r.v.* to have its meshes cut or undone.
desmamar, *tr.v.* to wean.
desmamonar, *tr.v.* to remove suckers from (a plant).
desmamparar, *tr.v.* to forsake, abandon, leave unprovided for or unprotected.
desmán, *m.* 1. excess, disorderliness, unruliness. 2. misfortune, mishap. 3. (zool.) desman.
desmanarse, *r.v.* to stray from the flock or herd.
desmanchar, *tr.v.* (Amer.) to remove spots from, take the stains out of (clothing).
desmandado, da, *past part. of* **desmandar.** —*a.* disobedient, impudent, intractable, out of hand.
desmandamiento, *m.* 1. revoking. 2. rudeness, impudence, excess.
desmandar, *tr.v.* to countermand, rescind, revoke, repeal, void (an order); to revoke, annul (a legacy). —*r.v.* 1. to be rude, disrespectful or impudent. 2. to withdraw, separate oneself (from the group, flock, etc.); to stray from the flock or herd. 3. (P. Rico) to get a head start. — **no te desmandes,** take it easy, don't lose your head.
desmanear, *tr.v.* to unhobble, unfetter (a horse, mule, etc.). —*r.v.* to get free from its hobble.
desmangar, (*ref. 51*) *tr.v.* to remove the handle from. —*r.v.* to lose its handle (a tool).
desmangue, desmangué, *ref.* **desmangar.**
desmaniguar, *tr.v.* (Cuba, P. Rico) to clear of vines, trees, thickets. —*r.v.* (Cuba, coll.) to get the hayseed out of one's hair, to give up or get rid of one's rural habits.
desmanotado, da, *a.* (coll.) clumsy, awkward. —*m., f.* awkward person, bungler.
desmanquillar, *i.v.* (Ecuad.) 1. to brush a horse. 2. to fail repeatedly.
desmantecado, da, *a.* free of fat or lard.
desmantecar, (*ref. 50*) *tr.v.* to remove fat or lard from.
desmantelado, da, *past part. of* **desmantelar.** —*a.* 1. dismantled, disassembled. 2. dilapidated, falling apart, in ruins.
desmantelamiento, *m.* the act of dismantling or disassembling.
desmantelar, *tr.v.* 1. to demolish, dismantle, knock down (the walls of a fort). 2. to abandon, vacate (a house); to strip of furniture (a house). 3. (mar.) to unmast, dismast; to unrig, strip of rigging.
desmanteque, desmantequé, *ref.* **desmantecar.**
desmaña, *f.* clumsiness, awkwardness; indolence.
desmañadamente, *adv.* clumsily, awkwardly; lazily.
desmañado, da, *a.* 1. clumsy, awkward, maladroit. 2. lazy, slothful, indolent, idle. —*m., f.* 1. clumsy or awkward person, bungler. 2. idler.
desmaño, *m.* neglectfulness, carelessness, negligence.
desmarañar, *tr.v.* to disentangle, unravel.
desmarcar, (*ref. 50*) *tr.v.* to efface, remove markers. —*r.v.* to evade an adversary (in football).
desmarojador, ra, *m., f.* person who removes parasites, dead leaves, or branches (from trees).
desmarojar, *tr.v.* to rid (trees) of parasites, dead leaves or branches.
desmarrido, da, *a.* 1. languid, listless, melancholy, dejected. 2. exhausted, spent.
desmatar, *tr.v.* to clear of shrubs, underbrush, thickets.
desmayadamente, *adv.* faintly, weakly.
desmayado, da, *past part. of* **desmayar.** —*a.* lifeless, wan, faint, weak (colors); lifeless, languid, exhausted; discouraged, disheartened.
desmayar, *tr.v.* to dismay, distress. —*i.v.* to lose heart or courage, be disheartened. —*r.v.* to faint, swoon.
desmayo, *m.* 1. fainting, faint, swoon. 2. dismay, discouragement. 3. (bot.) weeping-willow.
desmazalado, da, *a.* weak, lifeless, languid; (fig.) dejected, dispirited.
desmechado, da, *a.* (Amer.) wild, ruffled, tousled (hair).
desmedidamente, *adv.* excessively, immoderately; disproportionately.
desmedido, da, *past part. of* **desmedirse.** —*a.* excessive, immoderate, disproportionate.
desmedirse, (*ref. 39*) *r.v.* to forget oneself; to overstep; to be disrespectful, rude, or impudent.
desmedra, *f., var. of* **desmedro.**
desmedrado, da, *past part. of* **desmedrar.** —*a.* wasted, emaciated; deteriorated.
desmedrar, *tr.v.* to damage, impair. —*r.v.* to deteriorate, be impaired or damaged. —*i.v.* to decline, to deteriorate.
desmedro, *m.* deterioration; decline; damage, impairment.
desmejora, *f.* deterioration, impairment.
desmejoramiento, *m.* deterioration, impairment, decline.
desmejorar, *tr.v.* to impair, damage. —*r.v.* 1. to deteriorate, be impaired or damaged. 2. to get worse, decline in health. —*i.v.* to get worse, decline in health.
desmelancolice, desmelancolicé, *ref.* **desmelancolizar.**
desmelancolizar, (*ref. 53*) *tr.v.* to cheer up, enliven. —*r.v.* to become lively.
desmelar, (*ref. 29*) *tr.v.* to remove honey from (a beehive).
desmelenado, da, *a.* disheveled, with untidy, tousled hair.
desmelenar, *tr.v.* to dishevel, ruffle the hair of (a person). —*r.v.* to become disheveled, tousled, ruffled.
desmembración, *f.* dismemberment, amputation.
desmembrador, ra, *a.* dismembering. —*m., f.* one who dismembers.
desmembrar, (*ref. 29*) *tr.v.* to dismember; to divide or cut into pieces; (surg.) to amputate. — **d. de,** to separate from; to cut from. —*r.v.* to become dismembered or divided; **desmembrarse de,** to secede, break away from.
desmemoria, *f.* poor memory, forgetfulness.
desmemoriado, da, *past part. of* **desmemoriarse.** —*a.* forgetful, absent-minded; having little or no memory; amnesic. —*m., f.* forgetful person, scatterbrain; person suffering from amnesia.
desmemoriarse, *r.v.* to become forgetful; lose one's memory.
desmenguado, da, *a.* diminished, lessened, depleted.
desmenguar, (*ref. 52*) *tr.v.* to lessen, diminish.
desmentida, *f.* 1. denial; contradiction. 2. disproof, refutation.
desmentido, *m.* 1. denial, contradiction. 2. disproof, refutation.
desmentidor, ra, *a.* denying. —*m., f.* 1. person who denies or contradicts. 2. person who refutes or disproves.
desmentir, (*ref. 42*) *tr.v.* 1. to prove false, disprove, prove to the contrary. 2. to deny. 3. to conceal, cover up. 4. to act contrary to the best expected of (one's birth, profession, character). —*i.v.* to deviate, stray away, get out of line.
desmenuce, desmenucé, *ref.* **desmenuzar.**
desmenuzable, *a.* crumbly, shreddable, easy to break into pieces or to crumble.
desmenuzador, ra, *a.* scrutinizing, investigating. —*m., f.* investigator, scrutinizer.
desmenuzamiento, *m.* crumbling, shredding, breaking into pieces.
desmenuzar, (*ref. 53*) *tr.v.* to crumble, shred, break into pieces; to mill, sift; (fig.) to tear to pieces, analyze minutely. —*r.v.* to crumble, break to pieces.
desmeollamiento, *m.* removal of marrow.
desmeollar, *tr.v.* to remove marrow from.
desmerecedor, ra, *a.* unworthy, undeserving.

desmerecer, (*ref. 45*) *tr.v.* 1. to be unworthy of; to be undeserving of. 2. to mar, spoil. *—i.v.* to decline in value, depreciate; to be inferior (to), to compare unfavorably (with).
desmerecimiento, *m.* demerit, unworthiness.
desmerezca, desmerezco, *ref.* **desmerecer.**
desmesura, *f.* excess, lack of restraint or moderation.
desmesuradamente, *adv.* excessively, unrestrainedly, inordinately, immoderately, disproportionately.
desmesurado, da, *past part. of* **desmesurar.** *—a.* 1. excessive, inordinate, unrestrained. 2. forward, impudent, insolent, bold.
desmesurar, *tr.v.* to put in disorder, disarray; disturb, upset. *—r.v.* to be rude or impolite, forget oneself; to be insolent, to go too far (coll.).
desmida, desmido, *ref.* **desmedirse.**
desmidia, *f.* (bot.) desmid.
desmidiendo, desmidiera, desmidiese, desmidió, *ref.* **desmedirse.**
desmiele, desmielo, *ref.* **desmelar.**
desmielinación, *f.* (med.) demyelination, destruction of the myelin sheath of nerves.
desmiembre, desmiembro, *ref.* **desmembrar.**
desmienta, desmiento, *ref.* **dementir.**
desmigajar, *tr.v.* to crumble. *—r.v.* to crumble, break into pieces.
desmigar, (*ref. 51*) *tr.v.* to crumble (bread).
desmigue, desmigué, *ref.* **desmigar.**
desmilitarización, *f.* demilitarization.
desmilitarizar, (*ref. 53*) *tr.v.* to demilitarize.
desmineralización, *f.* (med.) demineralization (loss of mineral substances).
desmintiendo, desmintiera, desmintiese, *ref.* **desmentir.**
desmintió, *ref.* **desmentir.**
desmirado, da, *a.* (Mex.) hasty, reckless, without circumspection.
desmirriado, da, *a.* (coll.) 1. skinny, thin, emaciated; run-down (coll.). 2. exhausted.
desmocha, *f., var. of* **desmoche.**
desmochadura, *f., var. of* **desmoche.**
desmochar, *tr.v.* to top, lop off the top of (a tree, bush, etc.); to dehorn, cut the horns of (a bull); to cut (a literary work, musical composition, etc.).
desmoche, *m.* 1. topping, lopping off the top (of a tree); dehorning (of a bull); cutting (of a literary work). 2. (coll.) series of dismissals, pruning of the staff (in an office, etc.).
desmocho, *m.* heap of clippings (of a tree).
desmodulación, *f.* (rad.) demodulation, detection.
desmodulador, *m.* (tel., rad.) scrambler, demodulator, detector.
desmodular, *tr.v.* (tel., rad.) to scramble, demodulate, detect.
desmogar, (*ref. 51*) *i.v.* to cast horns (said of deer).
desmogue, *m.* casting of horns (of deer).
desmogue, *ref.* **desmogar.**
desmoide, *a.* (anat.) desmoid, having the appearance or characteristics of a ligament.
desmolado, da, *a.* toothless, having no molars or grinders.
desmoldamiento, *m.* removal of a casting from the mold.
desmoldar, *tr.v.* to take out of its mold.
desmolde, *m., ref.* **desmoldamiento.**
desmoler, (*ref. 37*) *tr.v.* to wear out, corrode, eat away.
desmonetice, desmoneticé, *ref.* **desmonetizar.**
desmonetización, *f.* demonetization, conversion (of coins) into bullion.
desmonetizar, (*ref. 53*) *tr.v.* to demonetize, to convert (coins) into bullion. *—r.v.* to depreciate, lose value (stocks).

desmonta, *f., var. of* **desmonte.**
desmontable, *a.* dismountable, demountable; easy to disassemble or take apart.
desmontado, da, *past part. of* **desmontar.** *—a.* 1. unmounted, dismounted. 2. (mec.) knocked down. 3. cleared of trees (land).
desmontador, *m.* 1. (auto.) tire remover. 2. person who clears wooded land.
desmontadura, *f.* 1. demounting, dismounting, alighting. 2. clearing of shrubbery, cutting or felling of trees.
desmontaje, *m.* (mec.) dismantling, disassembly.
desmontar, *tr.v.* 1. to alight from, dismount from; to unhorse, knock (someone) from his horse; to dismount (section of cavalry). 2. to dismantle, dismount, take to pieces; to demolish, knock down. 3. to clear of trees or shrubs. 4. to scatter (a pile of wood or dirt); to level (ground). 5. (artil.) to uncock. 6. (artil.) to knock out (an enemy gun). *—r.v., i.v.* to dismount (from a horse).
desmonte, *m.* 1. clearing or felling of trees. 2. leveling (of land). 3. felled trees, cut shrubs. 4. clearing, cleared land. 5. (*pl.*) (min.) discarded ore or rock.
desmoñar, *tr.v.* (coll.) to undo a bun or knot of hair.
desmoralice, desmoralicé, *ref.* **desmoralizar.**
desmoralización, *f.* demoralization, corruption.
desmoralizado, da, *past part. of* **desmoralizar.** *—a.* demoralized, corrupted, depraved.
desmoralizador, ra, *a.* demoralizing. *—m., f.* demoralizer.
desmoralizar, (*ref. 53*) *tr.v.* 1. to corrupt, deprave. 2. to demoralize, dishearten. *—r.v.* 1. to become corrupt or depraved. 2. to become demoralized.
desmorecerse, (*ref. 45*) *r.v.* 1. to be seized (with passion); to burst (with laughter); to be overcome (with pain); (Amer.) to gasp (from crying). 2. (Cuba, Dom. Rep., Ven.) to become discouraged. 3. (Mex., Peru) to be extremely eager.
desmorezca, desmorezco, *ref.* **desmorecerse.**
desmoronadizo, za, *a.* crumbly; liable to crumble, lacking solidity.
desmoronamiento, *m.* 1. crumbling, decaying. 2. (fig.) breakdown (of morals, discipline, spirit, etc.).
desmoronar, *tr.v.* 1. to cause to decay, wear away. 2. to crumble, break to pieces. *—r.v.* to disintegrate, decay; to crumble, fall to pieces; to collapse; to decline, decrease, come to naught.
desmostar, *tr.v.* to separate must from the grapes. *—i.v.* to ferment.
desmostarse, *r.v.* to lose their must (grapes).
desmotadera, *f.* 1. burler (woman). 2. (tex.) burling machine. 3. (Amer.) cotton gin.
desmotador, ra, *m., f.* burler, workman who removes knots or threads from cloth. *—f.* 1. (tex.) burling machine. 2. (Amer.) cotton gin.
desmotar, *tr.v.* 1. to burl (wool or cloth), remove the knots or threads from. 2. (Amer.) to gin (cotton).
desmote, *m.* 1. (tex.) burling. 2. (Amer.) ginning.
desmovilización, *f.* demobilization.
desmovilizar, (*ref. 53*) *tr.v.* to demobilize.
desmuela, desmuelo, *ref.* **desmoler.**
desmugrar, *tr.v.* to remove or strip grease from cloth (in textile mills).
desmullendo, *ref.* **desmullir.**
desmullera, desmullese, desmulló, *ref.* **desmullir.**
desmullir, (*ref. 65*) *tr.v.* to make unresilient or hard, take the softness or fluffiness out of.
desmuración, *f.* extermination of rats and mice.
desmurador, *m.* mouser cat.
desnacionalización, *f.* denationalization.

desnacionalizar, (*ref. 53*) *tr.v.* to denationalize.
desnarigado, da, *past part. of* **desnarigar.** *—a.* small-nosed. *—m., f.* small-nosed person.
desnarigar, (*ref. 51*) *tr.v.* to cut off the nose of.
desnarigue, desnarigué, *ref.* **desnarigar.**
desnatadora, *f.* separator, skimmer (for removing the cream of milk).
desnatar, *tr.v.* 1. to skim, remove the cream of (milk); (min.) to remove the scoria or slag from. 2. to take the cream of, pick the best of.
desnaturalice, desnaturalicé, *ref.* **desnaturalizar.**
desnaturalización, *f.* 1. expatriation; denaturalization, privation of civic rights. 2. changing, disfigurement, perversion. 3. denaturing, denaturization (e.g. of alcohol).
desnaturalizado, da, *past part. of* **desnaturalizar.** *—a.* 1. unnatural, cruel, wicked. 2. denatured, denaturized (e.g. alcohol).
desnaturalizante, *m.* (chem.) denaturant.
desnaturalizar, (*ref. 53*) *tr.v.* 1. to denaturalize, divest of citizenship; to banish, expatriate. 2. to denature, change, pervert, corrupt. 3. to denature, denaturize (e.g. alcohol). *—r.v.* to become denaturalized, lose one's citizenship; to be banished.
desnazificación, *f.* (pol.) denazification.
desnazificar, (*ref. 50*) *tr.v.* (pol.) to denazify.
desnecesario, ria, *a.* (rare) unnecessary.
desnegamiento, *m.* (rare) 1. contradiction, denial. 2. retraction, recantation.
desnegar, (*ref. 67*) *tr.v.* (rare) to contradict.*—r.v.* to retract, recant, take back a statement.
desnegué, *ref.* **desnegar.**
desnervar, *tr.v.* to enervate, weaken.
desnevado, da, *past part. of* **desnevar.***—a.* cleared of snow; snowless (said of a place usually snow-covered).
desnevar, (*ref. 29*) *i.v.* to thaw, melt (snow).
desniego, desniegue, *ref.* **desnegar.**
desnieve, *m.* thawing, thaw.
desnieve, desnievo, *ref.* **desnevar.**
desnitrificación, *f.* denitrification, removal of nitrates.
desnitrificar, (*ref. 50*) *tr.v.* to denitrify, remove nitrates.
desnivel, *m.* unevenness (of landscape); depression, drop, fall (in level or surface).**—d. bruto,** (hydr.) gross head; d. útil, (hydr.) useful head.
desnivelación, *f.* unleveling, making unlevel; unevenness; difference in elevation.
desnivelar, *tr.v.* to make uneven; to tilt, tip; to throw out of balance (a budget, an organization).*—r.v.* to become tilted; to be thrown out of balance (a budget, an organization).
desnucar, (*ref. 50*) *tr.v.* to break the neck of.*—r.v.* to break one's neck, e.g. *casi me desnuqué,* I almost broke my neck.
desnuclearización, *f.* denuclearizatic.
desnudador, ra, *a.* denuding, stripping.*—m., f.* one who denudes.
desnudamente, *adv.* nakedly; openly, clearly, without concealment.
desnudamiento, *m.* undressing, stripping; denuding, denudation.
desnudar, *tr.v.* 1. to undress, to strip; denude, lay bare. 2. (mar.) to unrig.*—r.v.* to strip, undress.**—desnudarse de,** to free oneself of, get rid of (vices, habits).
desnudez, *f.* nakedness, nudity, bareness.
desnudismo, *m.* nudism; streaking.
desnudista, *m., f.* nudist; streaker.*—f.* stripteaser.
desnudo, da, *a.* 1. naked, nude, undressed; bare. 2. (fig.) dispossessed, destitute. 3. naked, plain, clear, manifest (e.g. truth).**—desnudo de,** lacking, without (merit, virtue); **d. de la cintura**

para arriba, stripped to the waist.—*m.* (p.) nude.
desnuque, desnuqué, *ref.* **desnucar.**
desnutrición, *f.* (med.) malnutrition.
desnutrido, da, *past part. of* **desnutrir.**—*a.* (coll.) emaciated.
desnutrirse, *r.v.* to become undernourished.
desobedecer, (*ref. 45*) *tr.v.* to disobey.
desobedezca, desobedezco, *ref.* **desobedecer.**
desobediencia, *f.* disobedience.
desobediente, *a.* disobedient.
desobligado, da, *past part. of* **desobligar.**—*a.* 1. offensive, disobliging, antagonistic. 2. released from an obligation.
desobligar, (*ref. 51*) *tr.v.* 1. to free, release (from duty). 2. to estrange; to alienate (a person's good will).
desobligue, desobligué, *ref.* **desobligar.**
desobstrucción, *f.* removal of obstruction or obstacles.
desobstruir, (*ref. 48*) *tr.v.* remove an obstruction from; to clear.
desobstruya, desobstruyo, *ref.* **desobstruir.**
desocasionado, da, *a.* out of place; inopportune.
desocupación, *f.* unemployment; idleness.
desocupadamente, *adv.* freely, easily, without obstruction.
desocupado, da, *past part. of* **desocupar.**—*a.* 1. vacant, empty. 2. unemployed, out of work. 3. idle, unoccupied.—*m., f.* unemployed person.
desocupar, *tr.v.* to clear (a space); to empty (a container); to vacate.—*r.v.* 1. to finish (one's work, etc.). 2. (Arg., Par.) to give birth.
desodorante, *a., m.* deodorant, deodorizer.
desodorizar, (*ref. 53*) *tr.v.* to deodorize.
desoiga, desoigo, *ref.* **desoír.**
desoír, (*ref. 12*) *tr.v.* to ignore, pay no attention to, not to heed.
desojar, *tr.v.* to break the eye of (a needle).—*r.v.* 1. to have the eye broken (a needle). 2. (fig.) to look hard, strain one's eyes; to hunt high and low.
desolación, *f.* desolation; grief, distress.
desolado, da, *past part. of* **desolar.**—*a.* disconsolate, desolate.
desolador, ra, *a.* 1. desolating, destructive. 2. distressing, aggrieving.
desolar, (*ref. 33*) *tr.v.* to desolate, destroy, lay waste.—*r.v.* (fig.) to be grieved or distressed.
desoldar, (*ref. 33*) *tr.v.* to unsolder.—*r.v.* to become unsoldered; to break apart.
desolidarizarse, (*ref. 53*) *r.v.* to break with, break away from, withdraw one's support from.
desolladamente, *adv.* (coll.) impudently, brazenly, boldly, insolently.
desolladero, *m.* skinning room (in a slaughterhouse or abattoir).
desollado, da, *past part. of* **desollar.**—*a.* (coll.) impudent, brazen.—*m., f.* (coll.) impudent person.
desollador, ra, *a.* 1. skinning. 2. (coll., fig.) exorbitant, high-priced.—*m., f.* 1. skinner. 2. (coll.) fleecer, cut-throat, (person who charges high prices).—*m.* (ornith.) butcherbird.
desolladura, *f.* 1. skinning, flaying. 2. fleecing (charging exorbitant prices). 3. graze, scratch.
desollar, (*ref. 33*) *tr.v.* 1. to skin, flay. 2. (fig.) to injure, harm.—**d. a uno vivo,** (coll.) to skin alive, fleece or charge someone an exorbitant price; (coll.) to tear to pieces, flay, criticize bitterly.
desollón, *m.* (coll.) graze, scratch.
desonce, *m.* taking away one or two ounces from poundweight.
desonce, desoncé, *ref.* **desonzar.**
desonzar, (*ref. 53*) *tr.v.* 1. to take away one or two ounces from (a poundweight). 2. (rare) to defame, slander, revile.
desopilación, *f.* (med.) deoppilation, treatment for oppilation.
desopilar, *tr.v.* (med.) 1. to deoppilate, free from obstructions. 2. to make (a person) laugh.—*r.v.* 1. (med.) to be treated for oppilation; to be cured of oppilation. 2. to split one's sides with laughter.
desopilativo, va, *a., m.* (med.) deoppilative, deobstruent.
desopinado, da, *past part. of* **desopinar.**—*a.* discredited.
desopinar, *tr.v.* to discredit, defame.
desopresión, *f.* freedom, delivery from oppression.
desoprimir, *tr.v.* to free, deliver from oppression.
desorbitado, da, *a.* 1. (Amer.) out of proportion (e.g. prices). 2. (Amer., coll.) pop-eyed, beside oneself (from an emotion).
desorbitar, *tr.v.* 1. to take out of orbit. 2. to give too much importance to.—*r.v.* to get out of orbit; (fig.) to get out of one's usual routine or rut.
desorden, *m.* disorder, confusion, jumble; turmoil, disturbance, riot.
desordenación, *f., var. of* **desorden.**
desordenadamente, *adv.* in a disorderly way; confusedly.
desordenado, da, *past part. of* **desordenar.**—*a.* disorderly; unruly, wild, lawless.
desordenamiento, *m., var. of* **desorden.**
desordenar, *tr.v.* to disarrange, disorder, make untidy; to throw into confusion or disorder.—*r.v.* 1. to become disarranged or untidy. 2. to forget oneself, be impolite or rude. 3. to be out of order, to become unmanageable.
desorejado, da, *past part. of* **desorejar.**—*a.* 1. (coll.) infamous, abject, despicable. 2. (Peru, coll.) tone-deaf, having no ear for music. 3. (Chile) without handles. 4. (Cuba) lavish, wasteful.
desorejamiento, *m.* cutting or cropping off of ears.
desorejar, *tr.v.* to cut off (a person's) ears (ancient punishment); to crop off the ears (as done to certain breeds of dogs e.g. boxers, Great Danes, etc.).
desorganice, desorganicé, *ref.* **desorganizar.**
desorganización, *f.* disorganization.
desorganizadamente, *adv.* in a disorganized or disorderly way.
desorganizador, ra, *a.* disorganizing.—*m., f.* disorganizer.
desorganizar, (*ref. 53*)*tr.v.* to disorganize; disarrange, disperse, break up; confuse.—*r.v.* to become disorganized, confused; to disband, disperse.
desorientación, *f.* 1. leading astray, disorientation; loss of bearings. 2. confusion.
desorientado, da, *past part. of* **desorientar.**—*a.* disoriented; said of one who has lost his bearings or way; confused, misled.
desorientador, ra, *a.* confusing, misleading.
desorientamiento, *m., var. of* **desorientación.**
desorientar, *tr.v.* 1. to make (a person) lose his bearings, to lead astray. 2. to confuse, mislead.—*r.v.* 1. to lose one's bearings or way. 2. to become confused.
desorillar, *tr.v.* (dressm.) to cut selvages from (cloth); (print.) to cut edges from (paper).
desornamentado, da, *a.* stripped of ornaments.
desortijado, da, *past part. of* **desortijar.**—*a.* (vet.) sprained, dislocated.
desortijar, *tr.v.* (agr.) to hoe, weed for the first time (new plants).
desosar, (*ref. 36*) *tr.v.* to bone, remove the bones from (fowl); to stone, remove pits or stones from (fruit).
desovar, *i.v.* to spawn (fishes); to oviposit (insects).
desove, *m.* spawning; spawning season; oviposition.
desovillar, *tr.v.* to unwind, unravel (spools); to unravel, disentangle, solve (a mystery, difficulty, etc.).—*r.v.* to be unraveled, cleared up or solved (a mystery, etc.).
desoxicorticosterona, *f.* (biochem.) deoxycorticosterone.
desoxidable, *a.* deoxidizable.
desoxidación, *f.* deoxidation, descaling.—**d. por flameo con soplete multichorros,** flame descaling (plates).
desoxidado, *a., m.* deoxidized, descaled; killed, deadmelted (steels); **d. con boro,** borodeoxidized; **d. mecánicamente,** mechanically descaled.
desoxidante, *a.* deoxidizing.—*m.* deoxidizer, deoxidant.
desoxidar, *tr.v.* to deoxidize, remove the oxygen from; to remove rust from (metal).—*r.v.* to lose its oxygen.
desoxigenación, *f.* (chem.) deoxygenation, deoxidation.
desoxigenante, *a.* deoxygenating; deoxidizing.—*m.* deoxidizer.
desoxigenar, *tr.v.* to deoxygenate; deoxygenize.—*r.v.* to lose its oxygen.
desoyendo, desoyera, desoyese, desoyó, *ref.* **desoír.**
despabiladeras, *f.* (*pl.*) (candle) snuffers.
despabilado, da, *past part. of* **desopabilar.**—*a.* alert; (fig.) clever, smart.
despabilador, ra, *m., f.* snuffer.—*m.* candle snuffer.
despabiladura, *f.* snuff (of a wick).
despabilar, *tr.v.* 1. to remove the snuff from, trim (a candlewick). 2. to use or go through quickly, squander (a meal, an inheritance). 3. to filch, pilfer, steal. 4. to sharpen (a person's) wits, liven up. 5. (coll.) to kill.—*r.v.* 1. to wake up, rouse oneself; to sharpen one's wits, become alert. 2. (Cuba, coll.) to go away, leave.—**¡despabílate!** wake up! get going!
despachaderas, *f.* (*pl.*) 1. surly reply. 2. efficiency, briskness (in handling business); resourcefulness.
despachado, da, *past part. of* **despachar.**—*a.* 1. efficient, brisk, resourceful. 2. (coll.) brazen, impudent, bold, insolent.
despachador, ra, *a.* efficient, brisk, quick.—*m.* 1. expediter, person who dispatches; **d. de almacén,** warehouse dispatcher. 2. (min., Amer.) excavator.
despachante, *m.* (Arg.) clerk, employee; **d. de aduana,** customs agent.
despachar, *tr.v.* 1. to dispatch, send off (a letter, message). 2. to settle (business). 3. (coll.) to wait on or help (customers). 4. (coll.) to dismiss (from employment). 5. (coll.) to kill, polish off. 6. to clear (merchandise going through customs).—*i.v.* 1. to hurry. 2. (coll.) to give birth.—*r.v.* 1. to get rid (of). 2. to hurry. 3. (coll.) to give birth. 4. (vulg.) to kill. 5. to be sold. 6. (coll.) to speak one's mind, e.g. *me despaché con el jefe,* I told the boss off.
despachero, ra, *m., f.* (Chile) storekeeper.
despacho, *m.* 1. dispatch, sending off, shipping. 2. dismissal (from employment). 3. study; office, depot, bureau; shop, department in a store. 4. official message, dispatch; telegram, cable, telephone message. 5. warrant, commission (given

to an agent in charge of a business). 6. (law) official writ.—**d. de aduana,** customs' clearance; **d. de boletos or billetes,** ticket office; **d. de autobuses,** bus depot; **d. de equipajes,** baggage baggage room; **tener buen d.,** to be prompt and efficient.

despachurrado, da, *past part. of* **despachurrar.**—*a.* squashed, crushed, smashed.—**dejar a uno d.,** to leave one dumb-founded.

despachurramiento, *m.* squashing, crushing.

despachurrar, *tr.v.* 1. to squash, smash, crush. 2. (coll.) to muddle up (a story, an explanation). 3. (coll.) to squelch a person in an argument; to disconcert with a clever repartee.

despachurro, *m.* squashing, crushing, smashing; (coll.) mangling, butchering; squelching.

despacio, *adv.* 1. slowly, little by little; gently, carefully, leisurely.—*interj.* easy! easy does it! take it easy!

despacioso, sa, *a.* slow, phlegmatic, sluggish.

despacito, *adv.* (coll.) very slowly, inch by inch.—*interj.* (coll.) gently! carefully!; **d. se va lejos,** he who walks slowly gets farther.

despajador, ra, *a.* winnowing.—*m., f.* winnower, one who winnows (grain).

despajadura, *f.* winnowing; sifting.

despajar, *tr.v.* 1. to winnow, separate the chaff from (the wheat). 2. (min.) to sift (ore).

despajo, *m.* winnowing or cleaning grain.

despaldar, *tr.v., r.v.* to break or dislocate the back or the shoulder of.

despaldilladura, *f.* breaking or dislocation of an animal's back or shoulder.

despaldillar, *tr.v.* to break or dislocate (an animal's) shoulder.—*r.v.* to dislocate or break its shoulder (an animal).

despaletillar, *tr.v.* 1. to break or dislocate an animal's shoulder. 2. (coll.) to pound or pummel on the back.—*r.v.* to break or dislocate its shoulder (an animal).

despalillado, da, *a.* stripped of stems and veins (tobacco leaves).—*m.* removal of stems (from raisins, grapes, tobacco leaves).

despalillador, ra, *m., f.* one who removes veins and stems from tobacco leaves.

despalillar, *tr.v.* 1. to remove veins and stems from (tobacco leaves); to remove stems from (raisins, grapes). 2. (P. Rico, sl.) to kill.

despalmador, *m.* 1. (mar.) careening place, dry dock, dockyard. 2. (vet.) hoofparing knife.

despalmadura, *f.* 1. (mar.) careening, calking, paying the bottom. 2. paring a horse's hoof; (*pl.*) parings from a horse's hooves.

despalmar, *tr.v.* 1. (mar.) to careen, grave, calk, clean the bottom of (a ship). 2. to pare (a horse's hooves). 3. (carp.) to chamfer, bevel. 4. to pull up (grass).

despalme, *m.* 1. (vet.) paring of a horse's hooves. 2. hatchet-blow to fell a tree.

despampanador, ra, *m., f.* (agr.) pruner or trimmer of vines (one who cuts off suckers and shoots).

despampanadura, *f.* (agr.) pruning, trimming (of vines).

despampanante, *a.* astounding, astonishing, stunning, e.g. *¡estás despampanante!* (coll.) you look stunning!

despampanar, *tr.v.* 1. (agr.) to prune, cut or trim the shoots or suckers from. 2. (coll.) to amaze, astound, astonish, confuse, bewilder. 3. to squash, burst.—*i.v.* (coll.) to let off steam by saying what one thinks.—*r.v.* (coll.) to be badly bruised or hurt from a fall, e.g. *me caí y me despampané,* I fell and hurt myself.

despampanillar, *tr.v.* (agr.) to prune, trim (vines).

despampano, *m.* (agr.), *var. of* **despampanadura.**

despamplonar, *tr.v.* (agr.) to remove shoots from very close-growing plants.—*r.v.* to sprain one's hand.

despancar, (*ref. 50*) *tr.v.* (Arg., Bol., Peru) to husk corn.

despancijar, *tr.v., r.v., var. of* **despanzurrar.**

despanzurrar, *tr.v.* (coll.) to rip open the belly of.

despapar, *i.v.* (equit.) to carry the head too high (said of horses).

despapucho, *m.* (Peru) nonsense, foolishness, stupidity.

desparecer, (*ref. 45*) *i.v., r.v.* to disappear, vanish.—*tr.v.* to hide, conceal.

desparedar, *tr.v.* to demolish the walls of (a building).

desparejar, *tr.v.* to make unequal, uneven; to break up a pair of.—*r.v.* to become uneven.

desparejo, ja, *a.* odd, uneven, not matching.

desparezca, desparezco, *ref.* **desparecer.**

desparpajado, da, *past part. of* **desparpajar.**—*a.* 1. brisk, alert; confident, assured. 2. petulant, garrulous.

desparpajar, *tr.v.* 1. to throw into disorder, spoil, ruin. 2. (C. Rica, Hond., Mex.) to scatter, spread.—*i.v.* to prattle, chatter, babble.—*r.v.* 1. to talk one's head off. 2. (Hond., P. Rico) to awaken, to wake up.

desparpajo, *m.* 1. (coll.) ease, confidence, assurance; pertness (in actions and speech). 2. (Guat., Hond., coll.) untidiness, disorder, confusion.

desparramado, da, *past part. of* **desparramar.**—*a.* wide-open, scattered, spread.

desparramador, ra, *a.* scattering, sprinkling, spreading, dispersing; squandering, wasteful.—*m., f.* spendthrift, waster, prodigal.

desparramamiento, *m.* scattering, sprinkling, spreading; squandering, extravagance.

desparramar, *tr.v.* 1. to scatter, sprinkle, spread, disseminate. 2. to squander, lavish (a fortune), e.g. *él desparramó su herencia,* he squandered his inheritance. 3. (Arg.) to dilute, thin out.—*r.v.* 1. to scatter, spread, be dispersed. 2. to be dissipated, lead a carefree, frivolous life.

desparramo, *m.* 1. (Amer.) scattering, sprinkling, spreading; dispersion, scattering, disorderly flight. 2. (Chile) disorder, confusion.

desparrancarse, (*ref. 50*) *r.v., var. of* **esparrancarse.**

desparranque, desparranqué, *ref.* **desparrancarse.**

despartidor, ra, *a.* 1. separating, dividing. 2. peacemaking.—*m., f.* 1. separator, divider. 2. pacificator.

despartimiento, *m.* 1. separation, division. 2. peacemaking, reconciliation.

departir, *tr.v.* 1. to separate, divide. 2. to make peace between or among, reconcile.

desparvar, *tr.v.* (agr.) to pile up (threshed grain) prior to winnowing; to undo the sheaves and spread the stalks.

despasar, *tr.v.* 1. to remove (a ribbon, rope, cord) from. 2. (mar.) to unsling; to fleet, unreeve, shift.

despatarrada, *f.* (coll.) splits, high kicks (a step in certain Spanish and Basque dances); **hacer la d.,** to lie on the ground pretending to be hurt, to feign illness or exhaustion.

despatarrar, *tr.v.* 1. (coll.) to open (the legs) wide. 2. to amaze, horrify, astound.—*r.v.* 1. (coll.) to open one's legs wide. 2. (coll.) to be amazed, horrified. 3. to fall on the ground with legs wide apart; to straddle.—**despatarrarse de risa,** to split with laughter.

despatillado, *m.* (carp.) tenon.

despatillar, *tr.v.* 1. (carp.) to mortise, tenon. 2. to shave off the whiskers of.—*r.v.* to shave off one's whiskers.

despaturrar, *i.v.* (Col., Chile, Ven.), *var. of* **despatarrar.**

despavesaderas, *f.* (*pl.*) candle snuffers.

despavesadura, *f.* snuffing (of a candle).

despavesar, *tr.v.* 1. to remove the snuff from, trim (a candlewick). 2. to blow the ash from (embers).

despavonar, *tr.v.* to remove the blue from (iron, steel).—*r.v.* to lose its blue glaze (iron, steel).

despavoridamente, *adv.* terrifiedly, seized with fear.

despavorido, da, *past part. of* **despavorir.**—*a.* terrified, horrified, aghast.

despavorir, *i.v.* to be afraid, to be terrified.—*r.v.* to be seized with fear.

despeadura, *f.* footsoreness; (vet.) founder.

despeamiento, *m., var. of* **despeadura.**

despearse, *r.v.* to injure one's feet (by excessive walking); to become bruised (a horse's hooves).

despece, despecé, *ref.* **despezar.**

despechadamente, *adv.* vindictively, spitefully.

despechado, da, *past part. of* **despechar.**—*a.* peeved; spiteful, vindictive; resentful.

despechamiento, *m., var. of* **despecho.**

despechar, *tr.v.* 1. to disgust, make indignant or resentful. 2. to wean (a child).—*r.v.* to become peevish, disgusted, resentful, indignant.

despecho, *m.* 1. spite, wrath. 2. displeasure; peevishness; indignation. 3. dejection, despair. 4. grudge, ill-will. 5. (Chile) weaning.—**a d. de,** in spite of, in defiance of; **por d.,** out of spite.

despechugadura, *f.* 1. removal of the breast (from a fowl). 2. uncovering one's breast.

despechugar, (*ref. 51*) *tr.v.* to cut the breast (of a fowl).—*r.v.* (coll.) to go bare breasted, to show the breast.

despechugue, despechugué, *ref.* **despechugar.**

despectivamente, *adv.* derogatorily, depreciatorily, disparagingly, contemptuously.

despectivo, va, *a.* depreciatory, derogatory, disparaging, contemptuous; (gram.) pejorative.

despedace, despedacé, *ref.* **despedazar.**

despedazador, ra, *a.* 1. tearing, mangling, shredding. 2. (fig.) destroying, ruining.—*m., f.* lacerator, mangler; dissector.

despedazamiento, *m.* 1. breaking, tearing or falling to pieces. 2. (fig.) ruin, destruction.

despedazar, (*ref. 53*) *tr.v.* 1. to break or tear to pieces, mangle, shred. 2. to ruin, injure, damage. 3. to break (someone's heart); to torment.—*r.v.* 1. to fall or break to pieces. 2. to be ruined. 3. to be broken (into pieces).

despedida, *f.* 1. farewell, leave-taking, parting. 2. dismissal, discharge. 3. final couplet of certain popular songs.

despedido, da, *past part. of* **despedir.**—*a.* 1. discharged, dismissed. 2. discharged, thrown off, e.g. *salió d. del caballo,* he was thrown off the horse.

despedimiento, *m.* 1. farewell, leave-taking. 2. dismissal, discharge.

despedir, (*ref. 39*) *tr.v.* 1. to hurl, cast, throw, fling, dart. 2. to dismiss, fire, discharge. 3. to dismiss, get rid of (an idea, etc.). 4. to give off, exhale; to give out, radiate, emit. 5. to say good-bye to, see off, escort to the door, 6. to send away, send packing.—*r.v.* to say goodbye, bid farewell.—**despedirse a la francesa,** to take French leave; to go off or leave without a word; **despedirse de,** to say good-bye to, one's leave of; **d. el duelo,** to deliver the funeral oration.

despedrar, *tr.v., var. of* **despedregar.**

despedregar, (*ref. 51*) *tr.v.* to remove the rocks or stones from, to clear a place of rubble.

despedregue, despedregué, *ref.* **despedregar.**

despegable, *a.* detachable, that can be unglued or disjoined.

despegadamente, *adv.* coldy, coolly, indifferently, unconcernedly.
despegado, da, *past part. of* **despegar.**—*a.* (coll.) unpleasant, disagreeable, surly; unaffectionate.
despegadura, *f.* unsticking, ungluing, undoing, opening (of a letter); detaching, separating.
despegamiento, *m.* coolness, coldness, indifference; moroseness.
despegar, (*ref.* 51) *tr.v.* 1. to unstick, unglue; to detach, disjoin, to separate; to open (a letter). 2. (Mex.) to unharness.—*i.v.* to take off (an airplane).—**d. los labios,** to speak.—*r.v.* 1. to come unstuck, come apart. 2. to take off (an airplane). 3. to withdraw one's affection, to grow indifferent.
despego, *m., var. of* **desapego,** coldness, coolness, indifference; (coll.) ingratitude, gruffness.
despegue, *m.* 1. take-off (of an aeroplane). 2. blast-off (of a rocket).—**dd. vertical,** lift-off; **d. con ayuda de cohetes,** jet-assisted take-off.
despegue, despegué, *ref.* **despegar.**
despeinado, da, *a.* uncombed; disheveled.
despeinar, *tr.v.* to disarrange the hair of.—*r.v.* to become uncombed or disarranged.
despejadamente, *adv.* confidently, naturally; clear-sightedly; readily, freely, smartly.
despejado, da, *past part. of* **despejar.**—*a.* 1. confident, assured (in behavior), vivacious. 2. clear, penetrating (mind); serene. 3. spacious, wide, large. 4. clear, cloudless (sky); clear, unobstructed (vision, panorama).
despejar, *tr.v.* 1. to clear away; to disoccupy, vacate, clear (a space). 2. to explain, clarify. 3. (math.) to resolve, solve.—*r.v.* 1. to become confident and assured. 2. to relax, amuse oneself. 3. to clear (the sky). 4. to abate (fever).
despejo, *m.* 1. clearing, disoccupying. 2. confidence, ease, assurance, naturalness (of behavior). 3. clear-sightedness, lucidity.—**ángulo de d.,** clearance angle.
despellejadura, *f.* 1. skinning, flaying. 2. graze, scratch. 3. (fig.) slandering, maligning.
despellejar, *tr.v.* 1. to skin, flay. 2. (fig.) to slander, malign, speak ill of.
despelotarse, *r.v.* (coll.) to become robust, hefty.
despelucar, (*ref.* 50) *tr.v.* (Col., Chile, Hond.) *var. of* **despeluzar.**
despeluce, despelucé, *ref.* **despeluzar.**
despeluque, despeluqué, *ref.* **despelucar.**
despeluzamiento, *m.* 1. disheveling, ruffling, mussing (of hair); untidiness (of hair). 2. standing on end (hair).
despeluzar, (*ref.* 53) *tr.v.* 1. to rumple, dishevel, muss, entangle (hair). 2. to make (hair) stand on end. 3. (Cuba) to skin, fleece, leave without a penny.—*r.v.* 1. to become rumpled or disheveled (hair). 2. to stand on end (hair); to become terrified.
despeluznante, *a.* horrifying, terrifying, making the hair stand on end.
despeluznar, *tr.v., r.v., var. of* **despeluzar.**
despenador, ra, *a.* consoling, solacing.—*m., f.* consoler; one who relieves pains or sorrow.
despenar, *tr.v.* 1. to console, solace; to relieve from pain. 2. to finish (someone) off, kill. 3. (Chile) to make desperate, deprive of hope.
despendedor, ra, *a.* spendthrift, wasteful, prodigal, lavish.—*m., f.* spendthrift, wastrel, squanderer.
despender, *tr.v.* to squander, waste (money, time); to misspend.
despenolar, *tr.v.* (mar.) to break the yard arms off.
despensa, *f.* 1. larder, pantry, storeroom; provisions; daily ration of provisions. 2. steward, butler; post of steward or butler, stewardship. 3. yearly contract for fodder. 4. (Mex.) strong room (in a mine, for precious metals). 5. (mar.) steward's room.
despensería, *f.* stewardship, post of butler.
despensero, ra, *m., f.* 1. steward butler, caterer, 2. dispenser, distributor.
despeñadamente, *adv.* rashly, precipitately, impetuously, boldly, audaciously.
despeñadero, ra, *a.* precipitous, steep, headlong; dangerous, hazardous.—*m.* 1. precipice, crag. 2. risk, danger, hazard.
despeñadizo, za, *a.* precipitous, steep; glib, slippery.
despeñamiento, *m., var. of* **despeño.**
despeñar, *tr.v.* to hurl, cast, throw. —*r.v.* to throw oneself, hurl oneself; to fall or plunge headlong; to throw oneself headlong (into a vice).—*i.v.* to lead a licentious life.
despeño, *m.* 1. hurling or casting from a height; headlong plunge or fall. 2. diarrhea. 3. (fig.) ruin, fall, failure; loss of credit or fortune.
despeo, *f.* footsoreness; (vet.) founder.
despepitadora, *f.* seed separator; corer, stoner; **d. de algodón,** cotton gin.
despepitar, *tr.v.* to remove pits or seeds from (fruit); to gin (cotton).
despepitarse, *r.v.* to rant, rave, scream, shout; to act or speak rashly.—**d. uno por algo,** (coll.) to be crazy about, to long for, to be itching to.
despercudido, da, *past part. of* **despercudir.**—*a.* (Amer.) alert, smart, awake.
despercudir, *tr.v.* 1. to cleanse or wash what is soiled or stained. 2. (Amer.) to liven up, make smart, wise up.—*r.v.* (Amer.) to become smart and alert.
desperdiciadamente, *adv.* wastefully, profusely.
desperdiciado, da, *past part. of* **desperdiciar.**—*a.* squandered, wasted.
desperdiciador, ra, *a.* wasteful, squandering.—*m., f.* waster, squanderer, spendthrift, lavisher.
desperdiciar, *tr.v.* to waste, squander, misspend; to lose, to miss (an opportunity, etc.), e.g. *desperdicié la ocasión,* I missed the chance.
desperdicio, *m.* 1. waste, squandering, wasting. 2. waste, offal, poor or useless parts, e.g. *esta carne no tiene d.,* this meat has no waste (all of it is good to eat). 3. (*pl.*) leftovers, remains, garbage. —**desperdicios industriales,** industrial wastes.
desperdigamiento, *m.* scattering, separating, dispersion.
desperdigar, (*ref.* 51) *tr.v.* to scatter, separate, disperse.—*r.v.* to become scattered, separated or dispersed.
desperdigue, desperdigué, *ref.* **desperdigar.**
desperece, desperecé, *ref.* **desperezarse.**
desperecerse, (*ref.* 45) *r.v.* to become consumed with a yearning, longing or desire (for something).
desperezarse, (*ref.* 53) *r.v.* to stretch oneself, to stretch out, to shake off drowsiness.
desperezca, desperezco, *ref.* **desperecerse.**
desperezo, *m.* stretching (of the limbs); the act of waking up fully, of shaking off drowsiness.
desperfeccionar, *tr.v.* (Amer., coll.) to damage, impair, spoil.—*i.v.* to deteriorate.
desperfecto, *m.* slight damage; blemish, flaw; imperfection; wear and tear.
desperfilar, *tr.v.* 1. (rare, p.) to soften the outlines of. 2. (mil.) to camouflage.—*r.v.* to lose the pose of a profile; to become disarranged.
despernado, da, *past part. of* **despernar.**—*a.* (fig.) worn out (from walking), fatigued, footsore, weary, tired out.
despernancarse, (*ref.* 50) *r.v.* (Amer.) to spread or open one's legs wide, to straddle ungracefully.
despernanque, despernanqué, *ref.* **despernancarse.**
despernar, (*ref.* 29) *tr.v.* to injure or cut off the legs of.—*r.v.* to injure or lose one's legs.
despertador, ra, *a.* awakening, arousing.—*m., f.* one who wakes people up.—*m.* 1. alarm clock. 2. mechanism which warns lamp-lighters that fuel is low. 3. (fig.) warning, hint, admonition.
despertamiento, *m.* awakening, waking up.
despertar, (*ref.* 29) *tr.v.* 1. to wake up, rouse from sleep. 2. to awaken, arouse (suspicions, interest). 3. to recall, bring (to one's memory). 4. to whet (the appetite).—*i.v.* 1. to wake up. 2. to wise up, become more alert.—*r.v.* to wake up; to revive.
despesar, *m.* displeasure, annoyance, dislike.
despestañar, *tr.v.* to pluck out the eyelashes of.—*r.v.* 1. to pluck one's eyelashes. 2. to hunt high and low (for something). 3. (Arg.) to study very hard, burn the midnight oil. 4. to look intently, to stare.
despezar, (*ref.* 53) *tr.v.* 1. to diminish; to bevel; to taper (tubes so that they fit one into another). 2. (archit.) to divide (a wall, arch, etc.) into its component parts.
despezo, *m.* 1. tapering (of a tube, pipe, etc.). 2. (archit.) division (of a wall or an arch) into component parts. 3. beveled edge of cut stone (dovetailed on to other stone). 4. (carp.) block of wood.
despezonar, *tr.v.* 1. to remove the nipple or umbo from (a lemon, lime, etc.). 2. to divide, separate.—*r.v.* to come off (said of an umbo, nipple, end of an axle, spindle, etc.).
despezuñarse, *r.v.* 1. to become useless (the hoof of an animal). 2. (Col., Chile, Hond.) to walk very quickly. 3. (Col., Chile, Hond.) to exert oneself greatly. 4. (Amer.) to be very eager (to do something); to long for.
despiadadamente, *adv.* pitilessly, inhumanly, mercilessly.
despiadado, da, *a.* pitiless, inhuman, merciless.
despicar, (*ref.* 50) *tr.v.* to satisfy, give satisfaction to.—*r.v.* 1. to get satisfaction, revenge. 2. to break its beak (a bird).
despichar, *tr.v.* 1. to expel, exhale, give off, exude (a smell or moisture). 2. to separate grape clusters (prior to pressing them for wine). 3. (Col., Chile) to crush, squash.—*i.v.* (coll.) to waste away, die.
despidida, despidiendo, despidiera, despidiese, despidió, despido, *ref.* **despedir.**
despidida, *f.* (reg.) passage for water, gutter.
despidiente, *m.* (bldg.) board separating a scaffold from a wall under construction.—**d. de agua,** flushing.
despido, *m.* discharge, dismissal, layoff.
despierne, despierno, *ref.* **despernar.**
despiertamente, *adv.* ingeniously, cleverly; alertly, vividly.
despierte, despierto, *ref.* **despertar.**
despierto, ta, *irr. past part. of* **despertar.**—*a.* (fig.) 1. watchful, alert, alive. 2. diligent, lively. 3. smart, clever, clearsighted.
despiezar, (*ref.* 53) *tr.v.* (archit.) to divide (a wall or an arch) into its component parts.
despiezo, *m.* (archit.) division (of walls or an arch) into component parts; joining or fitting of stones.
despigmentación, *f.* depigmentation.
despilaramiento, *m.* (S. Amer.) the act of removing props (from a mine).
despilarar, *tr.v.* (S. Amer.) to remove the props from (mines).
despilfarradamente, *adv.* wastefully, extravagantly.

despilfarrado, da, *past part. of* **despilfarrar.**—*a.* 1. wasteful, squandering, extravagant; wasted, squandered. 2. shabby, ragged. 3. (C. Rica) thin, spread out.—*m., f.* 1. squanderer, waster. 2. ragamuffin, scarecrow, shabby person.
despilfarrador, ra, *a.* wasteful, squandering, extravagant.—*m., f.* squanderer, wastrel, prodigal.
despilfarrar, *tr.v.* to squander, waste, consume.—*r.v.* (coll.) to squander, misspend a large quantity of money.
despilfarro, *m.* 1. waste, extravagance; squandering, wastefulness, lavishness. 2. spoiling, ruining (of clothes, etc.) through neglect. 3. mismanagement, maladministration.
despimpollar, *tr.v.* (agr.) to prune, trim (vines) of new shoots and unwanted growth.
despince, despincé, *ref.* **despinzar.**
despinces, *m.* (*pl.*) burling tweezers, tweezers for removing the burls or knots from cloth.
despinochar, *tr.v.* to remove the husk from, to husk (ears of corn).
despintar, *tr.v.* 1. to erase; blot, blur, smear. 2. (fig.) to disfigure, to change; to spoil.—*i.v.* to degenerate.—*r.v.* 1. to become blurred, faded or bleached. 2. to forget, e.g. *se me despintó de la memoria,* it has faded from my memory; I have forgotten it.
despinte, *m.* (Chile, min.) low grade mineral.
despinzadera, *f.* (woman) burler; burling instrument.
despinzado, *past part. of* **despinzar.**—*m.* burling, removal of burls or knots (from cloth).
despinzador, ra, *a.* burling (operator, machine, instrument).
despinzar, (*ref. 53*) *tr.v.* to burl (cloth).
despinzas, *f. (pl.)* burling tweezers, burling iron.
despiojador, *m.* delousing instrument, delouser (method); **peine d.,** delousing comb.
despiojar, *tr.v.* 1. to delouse. 2. (coll.) to free from poverty, elevate. —*r.v.* 1. to become deloused; to delouse oneself. 2. to rise from one's poverty.
despique, *m.* satisfaction; revenge, vengeance.
despique, despiqué, *ref.* **despicar.**
despistado, da, *a.* (coll.) insecure, lost, adrift, up the wrong tree (coll.).
despistar, *tr.v.* to lead astray, mislead; to put off the scent.—*r.v.* to lose one's way, go astray; to lose the scent.
despitorrado, *a.* (taur.) with broken horns (said of a fighting bull).
despizcar, (*ref. 50*) *tr.v.* to break or grind into small pieces; to shred, cut into small pieces.—*r.v.* 1. to become shredded. 2. (fig.) to tear oneself to pieces (trying to do something), to exert oneself.
despizque, despizqué, *ref.* **despizcar.**
desplace, desplacé, *ref.* **desplazar.**
desplacer, (*ref. 13*) *tr.v.* to displease, annoy., —*m.* displeasure, annoyance.
desplanchar, *tr.v.* to rumple, crease, wrinkle.—*r.v.* to become rumpled, crumpled, or creased.
desplantación, *f.* uprooting.
desplantador, ra, *a.* uprooting.—*m.* (agr.) trowel for uprooting plants.
desplantar, *tr.v.* 1. to uproot (a plant). 2. to turn or deviate from the vertical.—*r.v.* 1. to turn from the vertical. 2. (dance, fenc.) to lose onc's erect posture.
desplante, *m.* 1. (dance, fenc.) oblique posture. 2. arrogant or defiant remark or action; brazenness, insolence, impudence, boldness. 3. a sudden stance of defiance during a pause in flamenco dancing.
desplatación, *j.* separation of silver (from another metal).
desplatado, da, *past part. of* **desplatar.**—*a.* (coll.) penniless, broke.
desplatar, *tr.v.* to remove or separate the silver from (another metal).
desplate, *m.* removal of silver.
desplayado, *m.* 1. (Arg.) strip of sand left by ebb tide. 2. (Arg.) clearing (in the woods).
desplayar, *i.v.* to ebb (the tide); to recede from the shore.
desplaye, *m.* (Chile) ebbing (of the tide).
desplazamiento, *m.* 1. displacement; removal; shifting (from one place to another). 2. (mar.) displacement.—**d. cargado,** loaded displacement; **d. de frecuencia** (rad.) frequency drift.
desplazar, (*ref. 53*) *tr.v.* 1. (mar.) to displace. 2. to move, shift (from one place to another). 3. (mil.) to force the enemy out (from a position, etc.).—*r.v.* to be moved or shifted.
desplazca, desplazco, *ref.* **desplacer.**
desplegador, *m.* (auto.) tire spreader.
desplegadura, *f.* 1. unfolding, spreading. 2. elucidation, exploration.
desplegar, (*ref. 67*) *tr.v.* 1. to unfold, spread out; to unfurl. 2. to explain, clarify, elucidate. 3. to display, show, manifest. 4. (mil.) to deploy, spread out.—**d. la bandera,** to unfurl the flag.—*r.v.* 1. to unfold, spread; to unfurl. 2. (mil.) to deploy, spread out.
desplegué, *ref.* **desplegar.**
despleguetear, *tr.v.* (agr.) to remove tendrils from (young plants).
despliego, despliegue, *ref.* **desplegar.**
despliegue, *m.* 1. (mil.) deployment, spreading out. 2. unfurling; unfolding, spreading out.
desplomar, *tr.v.* 1. to cause (something) to lean or lose its vertical position. 2. (Ven.) to scold, reprove.—*r.v.* 1. to lose its vertical position, lean; to collapse, get out of plumb, topple over, tumble down. 2. (fig.) to fall down; (fig.) to collapse, faint.
desplome, *m.* 1. leaning; collapse; fainting; downfall, fall (of a dynasty, etc.). 2. (archit.) overhang.—**en d.,** overhanging.
desplomo, *m.* 1. leaning (of a building). 2. (Ven.) scolding, reproof.
desplumado, da, *past part. of* **desplumar.**—*a.* (coll.) despoiled, stripped of one's property, money, etc.
desplumadura, *f.* plucking (of a bird).
desplumar, *tr.v.* 1. to pluck (a bird). 2. (coll.) to fleece, skin, leave without money.—*r.v.* to moult, lose its feathers.
desplume, *m., var. of* **desplumadura.**
despoblación, *f.* depopulation, lack of population.
despoblado, *m.* desert, wilderness, deserted, uninhabited place.
despoblador, ra, *a.* depopulating, ravaging, despoiling.—*m., f.* ravager, despoiler.
despoblar, (*ref. 33*) *tr.v.* 1. to depopulate. 2. to strip, deprive of, despoil. 3. to lay waste, ravage, turn into wilderness. 4. (min.) to understaff a mine.—*r.v.* to become depopulated; to become deserted.
despoetice, despoeticé, *ref.* **despoetizar.**
despoetizar, (*ref. 53*) *tr.v.* to make prosaic, deprive of its poetry or poetic character.
despojador, ra, *a.* despoiling, plundering, ravaging, pillaging.—*m., f.* plunderer, pillager, ravager.
despojar, *tr.v.* 1. to strip; to rob; to despoil; (coll.) to fleece. 2. to deprive, dispossess.—*r.v.* 1. to take off, strip, divest oneself (of clothes). 2. to give away, give up, relinquish, forsake.
despojo, *m.* 1. stripping; robbing; despoiling, plundering, ravaging; booty, spoils, plunder. 2. dispossession. 3. victim, prey. 4. (*gen. pl.*) offal (of a slaughtered animal); giblets (of fowl). 5. (*pl.*) leftovers, leavings (of food). 6. (*pl.*) low grade minerals. 7. (*pl.*) (bldg.) useful rubble. 8. (*pl.*) mortal remains (of a body), corpse. 9. slough, cast-off serpent's skin.
despolarice, despolaricé, *ref.* **despolarizar.**
despolarización, *f.* (phys.) depolarization.
despolarizador, ra, *a.* (phys.) depolarizing. —*m.* depolarizer.—**despolarizador anódico,** anodic depolarizer.
despolarizar, (*ref. 53*) *tr.v.* (phys.) to depolarize.
despolvar, *tr.v.* to dust, remove the dust or powder from.
despolvorear, *tr.v.* 1. to dust, remove or shake the dust from. 2. to thrust away, dismiss. 3. (Amer., arch.) to sprinkle.
despolvoreo, *m.* dusting; sprinkling.
despopularice, despopularicé, *ref.* **despopularizar.**
despopularizar, (*ref. 53*) *tr.v.* to make unpopular.—*r.v.* to lose popularity, become unpopular.
desporrondingarse, (*ref. 51*) *r.v.* (Col., Guat., coll.) to blow or squander one's money; to be extravagant.
desportilladura, *f.* chip in a bottle neck or the top of a jug.
desportillar, *tr.v.* to chip, break off a chip of (a jug, a bottle, etc.); to chip off the edge or the corners.—*r.v.* to become chipped.
desposado, da, *a.* 1. newlywed. 2. handcuffed. —*m., f.* 1. newlywed. 2. handcuffed person.
desposando, da, *m., f.* person about to be married, betrothed; bride (*f.*), bridegroom (*m.*).
desposar, *tr.v.* to wed, marry, to perform a marriage.—*r.v.* to get married, wed, marry; to get or become engaged.
desposeedor, ra, *a.* dispossessing.—*m., f.* dispossessor.
desposeer, (*ref. 60*) *tr.v.* to dispossess, to divest, to oust.—*r.v.* to renounce, give up (one's possessions).
desposeimiento, *m.* dispossession.
desposeyendo, desposeyera, desposeyese, desposeyó, *ref.* **desposeer.**
desposorios, *m.* (*pl.*) betrothal; nuptial vows, marriage vows.
despostar, *tr.v.* (Arg., Chile, Ecuad.) to cut up (a slaughtered animal).
desposte, *m.* (Chile) cutting up (of slaughtered animals).
despostillar, *tr.v.* (Mex.) *var. of* **desportillar.**
déspota, *m.* despot, autocrat, tyrant.
despóticamente, *adv.* despotically, autocratically, tyrannically.
despótico, ca, *a.* despotic, autocratic, tyrannical.
despotismo, *m.* despotism, tyranny, absolutism.
despotizar, (*ref. 53*) *tr.v.* (Arg., Peru) to tyrannize; to oppress, govern or treat tyrannically.
despotricar, (*ref. 50*) *i.v.* (coll.) to rant, rave, rail.
despotrique, *m.* ranting, raving.
despotrique, despotriqué, *ref.* **despotricar.**
despreciable, *a.* 1. despicable, contemptible, abject. 2. worthless, insignificant, paltry.
despreciador, ra, *a.* despising, scorning.—*m., f.* despiser, scorner.
despreciar, *tr.v.* to despise, scorn, look down on; to disdain, to slight, reject, rebuff.
despreciativamente, *adv.* scornfully, contemptuously, disdainfully.
despreciativo, va, *a.* contemptuous, disdainful, scornful.
desprecio, *m.* contempt, scorn, disdain, disregard.
desprender, *tr.v.* 1. to let loose, loosen, detach, release; to untie. 2. to let fly or loose (bolts of lighting), to give off (vapors, gases); to shoot

(sparks).—*r.v.* 1. to come loose (from), come away (from), become detached (from), to come off. 2. to shoot out (sparks, bolts of lightning); to be given off (vapors, gases). 3. to get rid of; to give away. 4. to issue (from); to be deduced or inferred (from).— **desprenderse de,** to give away, divest oneself of (one's property); to be inferred from, be seen in; to come off of.

desprendido, da, *past part. of* **desprender.**—*a.* disinterested, unselfish; altruistic.

desprendimiento, *m.* 1. loosening, coming loose; detaching, detachment; liberation, giving off (of vapors, gases). 2. landslide, slip. 3. (med.) detachment. 4. (min.) spontaneous liberation (of firedamp). 5. indifference, coolness. 6. generosity, altruism, disinterestedness. 7. (art.) Descent from the Cross.—**d.s ecundario,** (rad.) secondary emission; **d. termiónico,** (rad.) thermionic emission, Edison effect.

desprensar, *tr.v.* (print.) to remove from the press.

despreocupación, *f.* 1. unconcern, nonchalance. 2. unconventionality. 3. impartiality, lack of bias. 4. absentmindedness.

despreocupado, da, *past part. of* **despreocuparse.**—*a.* 1. unworried, unconcerned, carefree, happy-go-lucky, nonchalant. 2. unconventional. 3. absentminded. 4. untidy, carelessly dressed. 5. impartial, unbiased, without preconceived notions.

despreocuparse, *r.v.* 1. to put aside or forget one's cares or worries. 2. to become careless or negligent.—**d. de,** not to pay attention to; to neglect or forget.

despresar, *tr.v.* (Chile) to carve (a fowl).

desprestigiado, da, *past part. of* **desprestigiar.**—*a.* in bad repute; having lost one's prestige or reputation; suddenly scorned, unpopular.

desprestigiar, *tr.v.* 1. to cause (a person or thing) to lose prestige. 2. to run down (coll.), slander, speak ill of.—*r.v.* to lose one's good name, reputation or prestige.

desprestigio, *m.* loss of reputation, discredit; loss of prestige or popularity.

desprevención, *f.* unpreparedness, improvidence, lack of caution.

desprevenidamente, *adv.* improvidently, unexpectedly, unpreparedly, off one's guard.

desprevenido, da, *a.* unprepared, unready.—**coger a alguien desprevenido,** to catch someone off guard.

desproporción, *f.* disproportion, lack of proportion, order or symmetry; disparity.

desproporcionadamente, *adv.* disproportionately.

desproporcionado, da, *past part. of* **desproporcionar.**—*a.* disproportionate, unsymmetrical; oversize, out of proportion.

desproporcionar, *tr.v.* to disproportion, mismatch, deprive of symmetry.

despropositado, da, *a.* absurb, senseless, ridiculous.

despropósito, *m.* absurdity, nonsense; senselessness, oddity.

desproveer, (*ref. 60*) *tr.v.* to deprive of provisions; to deprive of necessities.

desproveídamente, *adv.* unpreparedly, off one's guard, unexpectedly, improvidently.

desproveído, da, *past part. of* **desproveer.**—*a.* unprovided for; unprepared.

desproveyendo, desproveyera, desproveyese, desproveyó, *ref.* **desproveer.**

desprovisto, ta, *irr. past part. of* **desproveer.**—*a.* lacking, devoid of, destitute.

despueble, *m.* depopulation, lack of population.

despueble, despueblo, *ref.* **despoblar.**

despueblo, *m., var. of* **despueble.**

después, *adv.* after, afterwards; later; then; **d. de,** after; next to, after; **d. de todo,** after all, when all is said and done; **d. de usted,** after you (sir, madam).

despulgar, (*ref. 51*) *tr.v.* to remove fleas from.

despulir, *tr.v.* to frost, tarnish; to grind (glass).

despulmonarse, *r.v.* to exhaust or wear oneself out, become exhausted.

despulpado, *m.* the removal of pulp (from fruit); extracting of pulp.

despulpador, *m.* pulp-removing machine.

despulpar, *tr.v.* to remove or extract pulp from (fruit).

despulsamiento, *m.* the act of suffering a deep shock.

despulsar, *tr.v.* to put into a state of shock.—*r.v.* to suffer a deep shock (through an accident).—**despulsarse por,** to long for, want or desire eagerly; (Mex.) to work very hard for.

despumación, *f.* skimming (of liquids); removal of scum.

despumadera, *f.* skimmer, skimming spoon.

despumar, *tr.v.* to skim liquids.

despuntador, *m.* (min.) ore separator; ore crusher.

despuntadura, *f.* blunting, breaking of the point.

despuntar, *tr.v.* 1. to blunt, break or knock off the point of. 2. to cut away the dry combs of (a beehive). 3. (mar.) to sail around, double (a cape). —*i.v.* 1. to sprout, bud, come through, begin to grow. 2. to begin to dawn, break (the day). 3. to excel. 4. to manifest wit or cleverness. —*r.v.* to break its point or tip.—**d. el día, d. el alba, d. la aurora,** to dawn, to rise (the sun), to break (the day).

despunte, *m.* 1. blunting, breaking of a point. 2. (Arg., Chile) cuttings, twigs (of a tree).

desque, *adv.* (poet., coll.) *contr. of* **desde** *and* **que,** since.

desquebrajar, *tr.v.* to crack, split.

desquejar, *tr.v.* (agr.) to pluck up shoots near the root of a plant.

desqueje, *m.* taking cuttings, slipping, plucking up shoots.

desquerer, (*ref. 17*) *tr.v.* to cease to love or like, to lose affection for.

desquerré, desquerría, *ref.* **desquerer.**

desquiciador, ra, *a.* unhinging; unsettling, upsetting; disruptive. —*m., f.* one who unhinges, unsettles.

desquiciamiento, *m.* (fig.) perturbation or mental unhinging (of a person).

desquiciar, *tr.v.* 1. to unhinge, to disjoint, disconnect. 2. to upset; undermine, unsettle, disturb; to unhinge, make unstable (mentally). 3. to deprive (someone) of favor or standing. —*r.v.* 1. to come off its hinges (a door) or out of its frame (a window). 2. to become unstable, lose one's reason. 3. to become upset, disturbed or unsettled. 4. to come loose, become disconnected.

desquicio, *m.* (Arg.), *var. of* **desquiciamiento.**

desquiera, desquiero, *ref.* **desquerer.**

desquijaramiento, *m.* the act of breaking the jaws.

desquijarar, *tr.v.* to break the jaws of.—*r.v.* to break one's jaws; (mar.) to break the cheek of a block.—**desquijararse de risa,** to roar with laughter.

desquijerar, *tr.v.* (carp.) to tenon.

desquilatar, *tr.v.* 1. (fig.) to lessen the intrinsic value of. 2. to lower the standard or diminish the intrinsic value of (precious metal).

desquise, desquisiera, desquisiese, *ref.* **desquerer.**

desquitarse, *r.v.* **d. de,** to win back, recoup, recover; to make up for (e.g. a long time without food); to avenge oneself or get satisfaction for, get even with.

desquite, *m.* 1. recovery, recouping; revenge, retaliation; compensation. 2. (sport) return match.

desrabar, *tr.v., var. of* **desrabotar.**

desrabotar, *tr.v.* to cut off the tails of (gen. said of sheep).

desramar, *tr.v.* to cut off the branches of; to prune.

desrancharse, *r.v.* 1. to leave, go away. 2. to get out of a mess (coll.). 3. (mil.) to separate, disperse (groups of soldiers).

desraspado, *a.* **trigo d.,** stub-pointed, small and flat-eared corn with soft grain and little husk.

desraspar, *tr.v.* to remove the stems from (grapes).

desrastrojar, *tr.v.* (agr.) to remove the stubble from.

desratice, desraticé, *ref.* **desratizar.**

desratización, *f.* rat-extermination.

desratizar, (*ref. 53*) *tr.v.* to rid of rats; to exterminate rats in (shops, ships, houses, etc.).

desrayar, *tr.v.* (agr.) to dig drainage ditches in a sown field.

desrazonable, *a.* (coll.) unreasonable; irrational, absurd.

desregladamente, *adv.* in a disorderly manner, irregularly.

desreglado, da, *past part. of* **desreglar.**—*a.* disorderly, irregular.

desreglar, *tr.v.* to upset, disarrange.—*r.v.*to be ungovernable.

desrelingar, (*ref. 51*) *tr.v.* (mar.) to remove the bolt-ropes from (sails).

desrelingue, desrelingué, *ref.* **desrelingar.**

desreputación, *f.* (coll.) disgrace, discredit, dishonor, disrepute.

desrice, desricé, *ref.* **desrizar.**

desrielar, *i.v.* (Bol., Chile) to become derailed, run off the rails.

desriñonar, *tr.v.* to strain or wrench the hip or the spine of.—*r.v.* to wrench one's hip or spine.

desriscar, (*ref. 50*) *tr.v.* to hurl or fling from a precipice.—*r.v.* to fall from a precipice; to throw oneself from a precipice.

desrisque, desrisqué, *ref.* **desriscar.**

desrizar, (*ref. 53*) *tr.v.* to uncurl; (mar.) to unfurl (sails).—*r.v.* to become uncurled or straight (hair); to become unfurled, unfurl.

desroblar, *tr.v.* to unbend or straighten (the bent end of a nail); to unclinch, to remove rivets from.

destacable, *a.* outstanding, remarkable.

destacado, da, *past part. of* **destacar.**—*a.* outstanding, prominent; marked, striking.

destacamento, *m.* (mil.) detachment, detail; post, station; **d. de fajina,** (mil.) fatigue detail.

destacar, (*ref. 50*) *tr.v.* 1. to underline, emphasize. 2. (art) to emphasize, make stand out, highlight. 3. (mil.) to detail, assign.—*i.v.* 1. to stand out, project. 2. (art.) to stand out, be highlighted.—*r.v.* to be outstanding or prominent; to excel.

destace, destacé, *ref.* **destazar.**

destaconar, *tr.v.* to wear out the heels of (shoes, etc.).

destachonar, *tr.v.* to take out the tacks from.

destajador, *m.* smith's hammer.

destajar, *tr.v.* 1. to settle, specify (conditions). 2. to do work by the job or the task. 3. to cut (a deck of cards). 4. (Ecuad., Mex., Peru) to cut up, carve into pieces.

destajero, ra, *m., f., var. of* **destajista.**

destajista, *m., f.* pieceworker, task worker, jobber.

destajo, *m.* 1. piecework; job, job of work. 2. (coll.) roughly, at a guess; in bulk.—**a. d.,** by the piece; diligently, earnestly; **hablar a d.,** to talk excessively.

destalonar, *tr.v.* 1. to remove or wear out the heel of. 2. to remove the receipt or coupon from. 3. (vet.) to level (a horse's hoof).—*r.v.* to wear away (the heel); to lose one's heel.

destallar, *tr.v.* to prune, remove the useless stems or branches from plants.
destanteo, *m.* (Mex.) confusion.
destapada, *f.* (cul.) tart, open pie.
destapadura, *f.* uncovering, uncorking; revelation.
destapar, *tr.v.* 1. to uncover; to take the lid off; to uncork (a bottle); to unplug. 2. (fig.) to discover. 3. (P. Rico) to slap.—*i.v.* (Mex.) to flee (on horseback); (Mex.) to bolt (a horse); (Mex.) to start to run.—*r.v.* to uncover oneself, throw off the covers (in bed).
destapiado, *m.* place where mud walls have been knocked down; unwalled place.
destapiar, *tr.v.* to pull down walls of.
destaponar, *tr.v.* to unplug, unstop; to uncork.
destaque, destaqué, *ref.* **destacar.**
destarar, *tr.v.* (com.)to deduct the tare from.
destartalado, da, *a.* untidy, shabby, ramshackle, poorly furnished.
destartalo, *m.* (coll.) disorder, mess, untidiness.
destazador, *m.* cutter, carver (of slaughtered animals).
destazar, (*ref. 53*) *tr.v.* to cut up (a carcass).
destechadura, *f.* unroofing, removal of the roof.
destechar, *tr.v.* to unroof, remove the roof from.
destejar, *tr.v.* 1. to remove tiles from. 2. to leave defenseless.
destejer, *tr.v.* 1. to unravel, undo, unweave (cloth), unbraid. 2. to upset, disrupt, undo. —*r.v.* 1. to be unraveled or undone. 2. to be upset or disrupted.
destellar, *i.v.* to twinkle, sparkle, flash; to scintillate.
destello, *m.* sparkle, twinkle; beam; flash; scintillation.
destempladamente, *adv.* intemperately, immoderately; irregularly, unevenly.
destemplado, da, *past part. of* **destemplar.**—*a.* 1. immoderate, intemperate. 2. loud, strident, noisy (shouts). 3. dissonant, off-tune (instrument). 4. irregular, uneven (pulse). 5. (p.) inharmonious.
destemplanza, *f.* 1. harshness, severity, inclemency (of climate); instability, changeability, variability (of weather). 2. lack of moderation, intemperance, excess, immoderateness (in speech, actions, etc.). 3. (med.) irregularity, unevenness (of pulse). 4. (med.) distemper, indisposition, illness.
destemplar, *tr.v.* 1. to disturb the order or harmony of. 2. (mus.) to put out of tune. 3. to steep, put in an infusion.—*r.v.* 1. to get out of tune. 2. to lose temper (metals). 3. to become irregular (pulse). 4. to lose control of oneself and be rude. 5. (Amer.) to have one's teeth on edge. 6. (Amer.) to feel sick, feverish.
destemple, *m.* 1. dissonance (of a musical instrument), disharmony. 2. slight indisposition (of health). 3. (fig.) discomposure, disorder, confusion. 4. intemperance, lack of moderation. 5. untempering, lack of temper.
destentar, (*ref. 29*) *tr.v.* to dissuade from temptation.
desteñir, (*ref. 41*) *tr.v., iv., r.v.* to fade; to discolor, to change or lose its original color.
desternerar, *tr.v.* (Arg., Chile, P. Rico) to wean (young calves).
desternillarse, *r.v.* to tear or dislocate a cartilage.—**d. de risa,** to split one's sides with laughter.
desterradero, *m.* (fig.) remote secluded place; out-of-the-way part of a town.
desterrado, da, *past part. of* **desterrar.**—*a.* banished, outcast.—*m., f.* exile, outcast.
desterrar, (*ref. 29*) *tr.v.* 1. to exile, banish; to deport. 2. to remove earth from (the roots). 3. (fig.) to drive away, get rid of.
desterronador, ra, *m., f.* (mach.) stubble plow, clod-crushing harrow.
desterronamiento, *m.* breaking up of clods (in a field); breaking up (earth).
desterronar, *tr.v.* to break up clods in (a field), break up earth in (a field).
destetadera, *f.* weaning device placed on the udders to stop calves from suckling.
destetar, *tr.v.* 1. to wean.—*r.v.* to break away from an old habit or custom.
destete, *m.* weaning.
desteto, *m.* group of weaned calves; stable or place for newly weaned mules.
destiempo, *adv.* a d., inopportunely, unseasonably, untimely; out of turn.
destiento, *m.* surprise, start; commotion.
destierre, *m.* (min.)removal of earth from ore, cleaning ore, sluicing.
destierre, destierro, *ref.* **desterrar.**
destierro, *m.* exile, banishment; deportation; land or place where an exile lives; remote place, lands end, the wilds.
destilable, *a.* distillable.
destilación, *f.* 1. distillation, filtration. 2. (med.) defluxion, flow of humors.—**d. fraccionada,** fractioned distillation; **d. del. agua salada,** saline water conversion; **d. extractiva,** extractive destillation; **d. por comprensión,** compression destillation.
destiladera, *f.* 1. still, alembic. 2. water filter.
destilado, *m.* (chem.) distillate.
destilador, ra, *a.* distilling; filtering.—*m., f.* distiller.—*m.* 1. water filter. 2. still, alembic.
destilar, *tr.v.* to distil; to filter; to drip with, exude, ooze with.—*i.v.* to trickle drop by drop; to exude, ooze.—*r.v.* to filter.
destilatorio, ria, *a.* distilling, distillatory.—*m.* distillery; still, alembic.
destilería, *f.* distillery.
destinación, *f.* 1. assignment. 2. destination.
destinado, da, *past part. of* **destinar.**—*a.* appointed (to); destined (for); addressed (to).—**estar d. a,** to be bound to, to be destined to or for.
destinar, *tr.v.* 1. to destine; to allot (money); to designate; to assign (a person to a place or employment). 2. (mar.) to station ships.
destinatario, ria, *m.,f.* addressee; consignee.
destino, *m.* 1. destiny; fate; doom, fortune, future. 2. destination. 3. post, job; place of employment.—**con d. a,** bound for.
destiña, destiño, *ref.* **desteñir.**
destiñar, *tr.v.* to remove the honeyless part of the comb from a beehive.
destiñendo, destiñera, destiñese, *ref.* desteñir.
destiño, *m.* honeyless part of combs.
destiranizado, da, *a.* liberated, freed from tyranny.
destitución, *f.* 1. destitution, dereliction, abandonment. 2. dismissal, discharge (from employment or office).
destituíble, *a.* dismissable, removable.
destituir, (*ref. 48*) *tr.v.* 1. to discharge, dismiss, remove from (a post, an employment, an office). 2. to deprive (of something); to make destitute.
destitulado, da, *a.* without title, deprived of title.
destituya, destituyendo, destituyera, destituyese, destituyo, *ref.* **destituir.**
destocar, (*ref. 50*) *tr.v.* to bare (someone's head), remove the headgear, hat or scarf from, to uncoif.—*r.v.* to bare one's head; to remove one's scarf or hat.
destoconar, *tr.v.* (Ven.) to blunt or cut down the horns (of a bull, a cow).
destoque, destoqué, *ref.* **destocar.**
destorcedura, *f.* untwisting, untwining, uncurling.
destorcer, *tr.v.* 1. to untwist, undo, unwind, untwine. 2. (fig.) to straighten out, rectify.—*r.v.* 1. to become untwisted; to unwind. 2. (mar.) to drift, get off the course.
destorlongado, da, *a.* (Mex.) wild, unruly, disorderly; extravagant, spend-thrift.
destornillado, da, *past part. of* **destornillar.**—*a.* (fig.) harebrained, crazy, rash, brainless.—*m., f.* madcap.
destornillador, *m.* screwdriver, turnscrew (G.B.).
destornillamiento, *m.* 1. unscrewing. 2. (fig.) recklessness; wild, rash behavior.
destornillar, *tr.v.* to unscrew.—*r.v.* 1. to become unscrewed. 2. (fig.) to lose one's head, to act recklessly.
destorrentado, da, *a.* (C. Amer.) wild, unruly, disorderly; confused.
destorrentarse, *r.v.* (C. Amer.) to lose one's head, to become confused.
destoserse, *r.v.* to feign a cough (before speaking or as a cue); to clear the throat.
destostarse, *r.v.* to lose one's suntan.
destrabar, *tr.v.* 1. to untie, unbind, unfetter. 2. to clear the obstructions from. 3. to detach, disconnect, separate.—*r.v.* to become untied or unbound.
destrabazón, *m.* untying, unbinding, detachment, separation.
destraillar, *tr.v.* to unleash (dogs).
destral, *m.* hatchet, small axe.
destraleja, *f.* small hatchet.
destralero, *m.* person who makes or sells hatchets.
destramar, *tr.v.* 1. to unweave, unwarp. 2. to discover or defeat a plot.
destrancador, *m.* plunger.
destrancar, (*ref. 50*) *tr.v., var. of* **desatrancar.**
destranque, destranqué, *ref.* **destrancar.**
destrejar, *i.v.* to act expertly, to work with skill.
destrence, destrencé, *ref.* **destrenzar.**
destrenzar, (*ref. 53*) *tr.v.* to unbraid, unplait; to undo a tress of.—*r.v.* to unplait one's hair.
destreza, *f.* skill, dexterity, adroitness, expertness, deftness, skillfulness, mastery, nimbleness.
destrice, destricé, *ref.* **destrizar.**
destrincar, (*ref. 50*) *tr.v.* (mar.) to unfasten, unlash.—*r.v.* (mar.) to become undone, loose or unfastened.
destrinque, destrinqué, *ref.* **destrincar.**
destripacuentos, *m., f.* (coll.) inopportune interrupter of a speaker.
destripador, ra, *a.* disemboweling.—*m., f.* disemboweler, ripper.—**el. d. de Londres,** Jack the Ripper.
destripamiento, *m.* disemboweling.
destripar, *tr.v.* 1. to disembowel, eviscerate; to remove the stuffing from (e.g. a pillow). 2. to crush, squash. 3. (coll.) to interrupt, spoil by revealing the end (of a story).—*r.v.* (Mex., coll.) to abandon one's studies.
destripaterrones, *m.* (coll.) clod-hopper, harrower; day laborer; country bumpkin.
destripular, *tr.v.* to discharge the crew of (a vessel).
destrísimo, ma, *a.* very skillful or dexterous, masterly.
destriunfar, *tr.v.* to draw out all the trumps (in a card game).
destrizar, (*ref. 53*) *tr.v.* to tear into strips, to break into pieces, to crumble, mince, shred.—*r.v.* to become grieved or heartbroken, to be overcome with grief.
destrocar, (*ref. 69*) *tr.v.* to change back; to call off (a barter).
destroce, destrocé, *ref.* **destrozar.**
destrón, *m.* blind man's guide.

destronamiento, *m.* dethroning, dethronement; (fig.) overthrow.
destronar, *tr.v.* to dethrone, depose; (fig.) to overthrow, bring down (from power).
destroncamiento, *m.* 1. lopping off (of branches, twigs, etc. of trees); 2. (fig.) ruination, exhaustion.
destroncar, (*ref. 50*) *tr.v.* 1. to chop or cut down, fell. 2. to maim, mutilate, destroy; to dislocate. 3. to ruin (someone). 4. to exhaust. 5. (Mex., Chile) to uproot; to tread underfoot.—*r.v.* 1. to maim or cripple oneself. 2. to get exhausted or tired out.
destronque, *m.* (Chile, Mex.) uprooting.
destronque, destronqué, *ref.* **destroncar.**
destroqué, *ref.* **destrocar.**
destroyer, *m.* (mar., Angl.) destroyer.
destrozador, ra, *a.* destructive.—*m., f.* destroyer, mangler.
destrozar, (*ref. 53*) *tr.v.* 1. to destroy; to mangle, break to pieces; to rip; to ruin, wreck, smash. 2. to shatter (someone's spirit or morale). 3. (mil.) to annihilate, wipe out (sl.). 4. to squander, waste, blow (coll.).
destrozo, *m.* damage; destruction, havoc, ruin, defeat, massacre.
destrozón, na, *a.* (coll.) destructive.—*m., f.* destructive person, vandal.
destrucción, *f.* destruction; damage, havoc; extinction.
destructibilidad, *f.* destructibility.
destructible, *a.* destructible, destroyable.
destructivamente, *adv.* destructively.
destructividad, *f.* destructiveness.
destructivo, va, *a.* destructive, wasteful.
destructor, ra, *a.* destructive, destroying.—*m.* 1. (mar.) destroyer. 2. destroyer, destructor; harasser.
destrueco, destrueque, *m.* changing back (of things exchanged); reversal of a barter.
destrueco, destrueque, *ref.* **destrocar.**
destruíble, *a.* destroyable, destructible.
destruidor, ra, *a.* destructive.—*m., f.* destroyer, destructor, devastator.
destruir, (*ref. 48*) *tr.v.* to destroy; to ruin, waste, exterminate, extirpate. (fig.) to squander, waste (one's fortune).—*r.v.* (math.) to cancel each other out.
destruya, destruyendo, *ref.* destruir.
destruyente, *a.* destructive, destroying; exterminating.
destruyera, destruyese, destruyo, *ref.* **destruir.**
destuerza, destuerzo, *ref.* **destorcer.**
destusar, *tr.v.* (Amer.) to remove husks from corn.
destutanarse, *r.v.* (Col.) to break one's neck; to fret.
desubstanciar, *tr.v. var. of* **desustanciar.**
desucación, *f.* extraction of juice.
desucar, (*ref. 50*) *tr.v.* to extract the juice from.
desudación, *f.* drying or wiping off the sweat.
desudar, *tr.v.* to wipe the seat off (someone, something).
desuelde, desueldo, *ref.* **desoldar.**
desuele, desuelo, *ref.* **desolar.**
desuellacaras, *m.* (coll.) clumsy barber.—*m., f.* (coll.) impudent, shameless person.
desuelle, desuello, *ref.* **desollar.**
desuello, *m.* 1. flaying, skinning, fleecing. 2. impudence, insolence, brazenness.—**es un d.,** it's highway robbery, it's exorbitant (price).
desuerar, *tr.v.* to remove the serum from, to drain (whey).
desulfuración, *f.* (chem.) desulfurization.
desulfurar, *tr.v.* (chem.) to desulfurize.
desuncir, (*ref. 61*) *tr.v.* to unyoke.
desunidamente, *adv.* disunitedly, severally, separately.
desunido, da, *past part. of* **desunir.**—*a.* disunited, separated; (fig.) estranged, disaffected.
desunión, *f.* 1. disunion, separation, disjunction. 2. (fig.) discord, dissension, disagreement, disaffection.
desunir, *tr.v.* to disunite; to separate, disconnect; to estrange, to cause discord.—*r.v.* to separate; to become disconnected or separated; to fall or break apart.
desunza, desunzo, *ref.* **desuncir.**
desuñar, *tr.v* 1. to tear out the nails or claws of. 2. to pull up the old roots from.—*r.v.* 1. to work one's fingers to the bone. 2. to indulge in vice and dissipation.
desuñir, (*ref. 66*) *tr.v.* (Arg.) to unyoke.
desuque, desuqué, *ref.* **desucar.**
desurcar, (*ref. 50*) *tr.v.* to remove or undo the furrows from.
desurdir, *tr.v.* 1. to unweave (cloth); to undo the warp of, unravel. 2. to thwart, frustrate (a plot, intrigue); to upset, stop, intercept.
desurque, desurqué, *ref.* **desurcar.**
desusadamente, *adv.* contrary to custom, out of use, unusually.
desusado, da, *past part. of* **desusar.**—*a.* 1. obsolete, archaic. 2. unaccustomed.
desusar, *tr.v.* to discontinue the use of.—*r.v.* to become obsolete or unused, go out of use.
desuso, *m.* disuse, obsolescence.
desustanciar, *tr.v.* to weaken; to dilute; to enervate; to deprive of strength or substance.—*r.v.* to become weak; to become thin or diluted.
desvahar, *tr.v.* (agr.) to remove withered parts from (a plant).
desvaído, da, *a.* 1. lanky, clumsy, awkward, gaunt. 2. dull, faded (color).
desvainadura, *f.* shelling, husking.
desvainar, *tr.v.* to shell, remove from pod (peas, beans); to shuck, to husk.
desvalido, da, *a.* destitute; helpless; unprotected.
desvalijador, *m.* robber, thief; highwayman.
desvalijamiento, *m.* robbery; rifling; stick-up (sl.).
desvalijar, *tr.v.* to steal contents of (a bag or valise); (fig.) to rob, swindle, to stick up (sl.).
desvalijo, *m., var. of* **desvalijamiento.**
desvalimiento, *m.* destitution, abandonment; helplessness, dereliction, want, need.
desvalorar, *tr.v.* to discredit; depreciate, devalue.
desvalorice, desvaloricé, *ref.* **desvalorizar.**
desvalorización, *f.* devaluation, depreciation.
desvalorizar, (*ref. 53*) *tr.v.* to devalue, lessen the value of. —*r.v.* to lose its value, to depreciate.
desván, *m.* garret, attic, loft; **d. gatero** or **perdido,** uninhabitable garret, cock loft.
desvanecedor, ra, *a.* evaporating; disappearing, vanishing; diffusing. —*m.* (photog.) mask; diffuser.
desvanecer, (*ref. 45*) *tr.v.* 1. to make vanish or disappear; to soften or diffuse; to banish, drive away, dismiss (fears, ideas, suspicions). 2. to make vain or presumptuous. 3. to make dizzy. 4. (photog.) to mask. —*r.v.* 1. to disappear, vanish; to evaporate (spirits, wines). 2. to become insipid. 3. to become vain or presumptuous. 4. to become dizzy, to faint or swoon.
desvanecidamente, *adv.* vainly, presumptuously, haughtily.
desvanecido, da, *past part. of* **desvanecer.** —*a.* haughty, vain, presumptuous, arrogant.
desvanecimiento, *m.* 1. faintness, dizziness; dizzy spell, fainting fit. 2. vanity, arrogance, pride, presumption. 3. fading, fade out, disappearence.
desvanezca, desvanezco, *ref.* **desvanecer.**
desvarar, *tr.v.* 1. to slip, slide. 2. (mar.) to refloat (a ship that was grounded). —*r.v.* to slip, slide, skid.
desvariadamente, *adv.* wildly, crazily; nonsensically, foolishly.
desvariado, da, *past part. of* **desvariar.** —*a.* 1. delirious, raving, wild, crazy. 2. nonsensical, absurd; disorderly, irregular. 3. long and crooked (branches of a tree).
desvariar, (*ref. 54*) *i.v.* to be delirious, talk nonsense, rave, rant; to dote.
desvarío, *m.* 1. delirium, madness. 2. wildness, craziness; nonsense, stupidity, wild remark or act; (*pl.*) ravings, e.g. *los desvarios de una mente enjerma,* the ravings of a sick mind. 3. (fig.) monstrosity. 4. caprice, whim.
desvasar, *tr.v.* (Arg.) to pare a hoof of (a horse).
desvastigar, (*ref. 51*) *tr.v.* to prune, cut away useless branches from.
desvastigue, desvastigué, *ref.* **desvastigar.**
desvatado, da, *a.* (elec.) wattless.
desvece, desvecé, *ref.* **desvezar.**
desvedar, *tr.v.* to raise or revoke the prohibition or restriction on.
desveladamente, *adv.* watchfully; anxiously; sleeplessly, restlessly; vigilantly.
desvelado, da, *past part. of* **desvelar.** —*a.* wakeful, sleepless; watchful, careful; anxious, worried, fearful.
desvelamiento, *m., var. of* **desvelo.**
desvelar, *tr.v.* to keep awake. —*r.v.* to stay awake; to have a sleepless night. — **desvelarse por,** to be anxious about, be watchful for.
desvelo, *m.* 1. wakefulness, sleeplessness, restlessness; watchfulness, vigilance. 2. anxiety, concern; care, solicitude.
desvenar, *tr.v.* 1. to remove the veins from (meat; tobacco leaves); (min.) to extract (ore) from veins. 2. (equit.) to raise the port (of a bit).
desvencijado, da, *past part. of* **desvencijar.** —*a.* broken-down, rickety, loose-jointed.
desvencijar, *tr.v.* to loosen, pull apart, divide, break, weaken. —*r.v.* 1. to go to rack and ruin. 2. (coll.) to be exhausted; to relax.
desvendar, *tr.v.* to unbandage, take off a bandage from. —*r.v.* to become unbandaged.
desveno, *m.* port, tongue groove (of a horse's bit).
desventaja, *f.* disadvantage, drawback, handicap, loss, disfavor.
desventajosamente, *adv.* disadvantageously, unprofitably.
desventajoso, sa, *a.* disadvantageous, unfavorable; unprofitable, detrimental.
desventar, (*ref. 29*) *tr.v.* to vent; let the air out of.
desventura, *f.* misfortune, bad luck, misadventure, calamity; misery.
desventuradamente, *adv.* unfortunately, unhappily.
desventurado, da, *a.* 1. unfortunate, unlucky, unhappy, miserable. 2. spiritless, fainthearted, timid, pusillanimous. —*m., f.* 1. poor wretch or devil. 2. weakling, poor fish.
desvergoncé, *ref.* **desvergonzarse.**
desvergonzadamente, *adv.* impudently, shamelessly, brazenly.
desvergonzado, da, *past part. of* **desvergonzarse.** —*a.* shameless, brazen, immodest; insolent, impudent, cheeky.
desvergonzarse, (*ref. 71*) *r.v.* to be disrespectful, rude or insolent.
desvergüence, desvergüenzo, *ref.* **desvergonzarse.**
desvergüenza, *f.* 1. impudence, insolence; shamelessness, brazenness. 2. oath, insolent remark. 3. (Cuba) obscenity.

desvestir, (*ref. 39*) *tr.v., r.v.* to undress, strip.
desvezar, *tr.v.* (agr.) to cut the young shoots of vines near the roots.
desviación, *f.* 1. deviation; diversion, deflection. 2. oblique or slanting position (of a pendulum, arm, etc.). 3. (med.) extravasation. 4. (med.) deviation, change of position (of organs, bones). 5. deviation, deflection (of compass needle). — **d. electromagnética,** (rad.) electromagnetic deflection; d. **magnética,** (rad.) magnetic deviation.
desviadero, *m.* railway switch, siding, side-track.
desviado, da, *past part. of* **desviar. —***a.* off the track, askew.
desviador, ra, *a.* diverting, deviating; deflecting. —*m.* shifter. — **d. de correa,** belt shifter.
desviamiento, *m.* (arch.), *var. of* **desvío.**
desviar, (*ref. 54*) *tr.v.* 1. to divert; to lead off, lead away; to turn away; to dissuade; to deflect. 2. (fenc.) to parry. —*r.v.* 1. to turn off, go off; to branch off; to swerve; to deviate (from a doctrine). 2. to abandon, give up (an idea). — **d. la mirada,** to look away, to avoid someone's eyes.
desviejar, *tr.v.* to separate old sheep from (the flock).
desviente, desviento, *ref.* **desventar.**
desvincular, *tr.v.* 1. (law) to free from mortmain. 2. to separate, to estrange (a person) from his family or other ties. — **desvincularse de,** to lose contact with or get out of touch with.
desvío, *m.* 1. diversion; deviation; turning off; deflection. 2. detour; branch road, by-pass. 3. (ry.) siding. 4. coolness, coldness, indifference. 5. (bldg.) cross-piece in a scaffolding platform to keep it from swinging to and fro. — **d. de atajo,** (ry.) catch siding; **d. de la brújula,** compass error; **d. de frecuencia,** (rad.) frequency drift; **d. muerto,** (ry.) stub track.
desvirar, *tr.v.* 1. to pare off the rough edges of a shoesole; to trim the edges of a book. 2. (mar.) to reverse the capstan.
desvirgar, (*ref. 51*) *tr.v.* to deflower (a virgin).
desvirtuar, (*ref. 55*) *tr.v.* 1. to change, adulterate, to lessen the value, merit or quality of. 2. to make insipid or vapid. 3. to weaken.
desvitrificar, (*ref. 50*) *tr.v.* to devitrify; to make (glass) opaque.
desvitrifique, desvitrifiqué, *ref.* **desvitrificar.**
desvivirse, *r.v.* (with **por**) to be eager (to), be dying (to), (coll.) be anxious (to), to manifest a great desire to please somebody.
desvolcanarse, *r.v.* (Col.) to collapse, tumble down.
desvolvedor, *m.* nut wrench.
desvolver, (*ref 34*) *tr.v.* 1. to alter, change (the shape). 2. to plow, till (land).
desvuelto, ta, *irr. past part. of* **desvolver.**
desvuelva, desvuelvo, *ref.* **desvolver.**
desyemar, *tr.v.* 1. (agr.) to remove buds from. 2. to separate the yolk from the white of an egg.
desyerbador, ra, *a.* weeding, grubbing. —*m., f.* weeder.
desyerbar, *tr.v.* to weed, to grub up.
desyugar, (*ref. 51*) *tr.v.* to unyoke (oxen).
desyugue, desyugué, *ref.* **desyugar.**
deszocar, (*ref. 50*) *tr.v.* 1. to maim, injure or hurt (someone) in the foot. 2. (archit.) to remove the socle of (a column). —*r.v. to maim, injure or hurt one's foot.*
deszoque, deszoqué, *ref.* **deszocar.**
deszulacar, (*ref. 50*) *tr.v.* to remove the packing stuff or pitch from.
deszulaque, deszulaqué, *ref.* **deszulacar.**
deszumar, *tr.v.* to extract the juice from. —*r.v.* to lose its juice.

detal, detall, *m.* 1. (com.) retail. 2. (mil.) disbursement accounts (in military establishments). — **al d.,** retail.
detalladamente, *adv.* in detail.
detallar, *tr.v.* to relate in detail; to specify in detail, itemize, enumerate.
detalle, *m.* 1. detail, particular, specification. 2. (Amer.) retail.
detallista, *m., f.* 1. (com.) retailer. 2. (art.) artist who highlights the details surrounding his subject.
detasa, *f.* (ry.) rebate on freight charges.
detección, *f.* detection, monitoring, sensing; **d audible** audible detection; **d. de defectos,** defect detection; **d. de fugas,** leakage finding; **d. de la criticidad,** (nuclear reactor) criticality detection; **d. microquímica,** microchemical detection; **d. de submarinos,** submarine detection.
detective, *m.* (Angl.) detective.
detector, *m.* 1. (phys.) detector; locator, finder, monitor, scanner. 2. sensor, sensing. — **d. amplificador,** amplifying detector; **d. de correlación cruzada,** cross-correlation detector; **d. de incendios,** smoke detector; **d. de mentiras,** lie detector; **d. de metales,** metal detector; **d. de minas,** mine detector; **d. de polaridad,** polarity detector; **d. de objectos metálicos,** metal detector; **d. submarino,** underwater detector.
detención, *f.* 1. detention; stop, halt, standstill; deadlock. 2. delay. 3. detention, arrest. 4. (mar.) demurrage, arrest, embargo (of a ship). — **d. domiciliaria,** house arrest; **d. preventiva,** police custody.
detendré, detendría, *ref.* detener.
detenedor, ra, *a.* detaining; stopping. —*m., f.* detainer; stopper; arrester; check, catch.
detenencia, *f., var. of* **detención.**
detener, (*ref. 23*) *tr.v.* 1. to stop, halt, detain. 2. to arrest, detain. 3. to keep, retain. 4. (mar.) to embargo. —*r.v.* to stop, halt; to linger, pause, tarry.
detenga, detengo, *ref.* **detener.**
detenidamente, *adv.* thoroughly, minutely, in detail; cautiously.
detenido, da, *past part. of* **detener. —***a.* 1. minute, thorough. 2. fainthearted, timid, spiritless. 3. niggardly, sparing; parsimonious. 4. dilatory. —*m., f.* person under arrest.
detenimiento, *m., var. of* **detención.**
detentación, *f.* (law) deforcement; withholding (an estate, etc.) from its rightful owner.
detentador, *m.* (law) deforciant.
detentar, *tr.v.* (law) to detain, retain, to keep unlawfully.
detente, *m.* a painted or embroidered image of a saint carried in the bosom against danger or attack; any amulet or talisman carried for that purpose.
detergente, *a.* detergent, detersive. —*m.* detergent.
deterger, (*ref. 57*) *tr.v.* (med.) to deterge; to absterge; to cleanse (an ulcer or a wound).
deterior, *a.* (rare) inferior, worse.
deterioración, *f.* deterioration, damage, impairment, wear and tear.
deteriorado, da, *past part. of* **deteriorar. —***a.* (coll.) worn-out, beat-up.
deteriorar, *tr.v.* to damage, impair, wear out, spoil. —*r.v.* to deteriorate; to be damaged, impaired, worn out.
deterioro, *m.* deterioration; damage, impairment, wear and tear.
deterja, deterjo, *ref.* **deterger.**
determinable, *a.* determinable, ascertainable.
determinación, *f.* 1. determination. 2. fixing, specifying. 3. resolution; decision, conclusion. 4. determination, resolve, courage, firmness.

determinadamente, *adv.* 1. determinately, resolutely, definitively. 2. specifically, expressly.
determinado, da, *past part. of* **determinar. —***a.* 1. bold, firm, determined, resolute. 2. definite, specific. 3. fixed (lock). 4. (gram.) definite. 5. (math.) having a definite or limited number of solutions.
determinante, *a.* 1. determining. 2. (gram.) governing (verb). —*m.* (biol., math., philol.) determinant.
determinar, *tr.v.* 1. to determine. 2. to fix, specify, to appoint, assign (a time, a place, etc.). 3. to distinguish, make out, discern. 4. to decide, convince, e.g. *esto me determinó a ayudarle,* this decided me to help him. 5. to decide, e.g. *determiné marcharme,* I decided to leave. 6. (law) to settle, decide, judge. —*r.v.* to decide, make up one's mind.
determinativo, va, *a.* determinative.
determinismo, *m.* (philos.) determinism.
determinista, *a.* pertaining to determinism. —*m., f.* determinist.
detersión, *f.* (med.) detersion, cleansing.
detersivo, va, *a.* detersive, detergent; cleansing.
detersorio, ria, *a.* detersive, detergent, cleansing (agent). —*m.* detergent, detersive.
detestable, *a.* detestable, abominable, hateful, loathsome.
detestablemente, *adv.* detestably, abominably.
detestación, *f.* detestation, abomination, abhorrence, horror, hatred.
detestar, *tr.v.* to detest, hate, loathe.
detienebuey, *m.* (bot.) common restharrow (Ononis spinosa).
detonación, *f.* detonation; blast, explosion; **d. nuclear,** nuclear detonation.
detonador, *m.* detonator; **d. eléctrico,** exploder.
detonante, *a.* detonating, detonative.
detonar, *i.v.* to detonate; to explode.
detorsión, *f.* (med.) twisting of a muscle, nerve or ligament; distortion.
detracción, *f.* 1. detraction, calumny, slander, defamation. 2. taking away, withdrawal.
detractar, *tr.v.* to detract, slander, defame, decry.
detractor, ra, *a.* detracting, slanderous, defamatory. —*m., f.* detractor, slanderer.
detraer, (*ref. 24*) *tr.v.* 1. to slander, defame, decry, detract. 2. to take away, remove, withdraw.
detraiga, detraigo, *ref.* **detraer.**
detraje, detrajera, detrajese, *ref.* **detraer.**
detrás, *adv.* behind, in or at the rear; after; **d. de,** behind; behind (someone's) back, in (someone's) absence; **por d.,** behind (someone's) back, in (someone's) absence.
detrayendo, *ref.* **detraer.**
detrición, *f.* detrition, wearing away.
detrimento, *m.* detriment, damage, harm, injury; **con d. de,** with detriment to.
detrítico, ca, *a.* (geol.) detrital, detritic.
detrito, *m.* 1. (geol.) detritus, loose fragment of rock disintegration, a product of disintegration or wearing away. 2. (med.) detritus. 3. detritus; rubbish. — **d. de la roza,** bug dust, slotting (mines); **d. del sondeo,** cuttings; **d. radioactivo,** radioactive waste.
detritus, *m., var. of* **detrito.**
detuve, detuviera, detuviese, *ref.* **detener.**
deuda, *f.* 1. debt. 2. trespass, offense, sin. — **d. consolidada,** funded debt; **d. externa,** foreign debt; **d. flotante,** floating debt; **deudas incobrables,** bad debts; **d. pública,** national debt; **deudas privilegiadas,** (law) preferential debts; **d. de honor,** debt of honor; **perdónanos nuestras deudas,** (Bib.) forgive us our debts.
deudo, da, *m., f.* relative, kinsman, kinswoman (*f.*). —*m.* relationship, kinship.

deudor, ra, *a.* indebted; debit; **e.g.** *lado deudor,* debit side (of an account). —*m., f.* debtor; **d. hipotecario,** mortgager; **d. moroso,** delinquent (in payment).
deuteranopia, *f.* (med.) deuteranopia, color blindness marked by confusion of purplish red and green.
deuterio, *m.* (chem.) deuterium, heavy water.
deuterión, *f.* (chem.) deuteron.
deuterogamia, *f.* deuterogamia, deuterogamy.
deuterógamo, ma, *m., f.* deuterogamist.
deuterón, *m.* (phys.) deuteron.
Deuteronomio, *m.* (Bib.) Deuteronomy.
deuteropatía, *f.* (med.) deuteropathy.
deuteruro, *m.* (chem.) deuteride.
deutón, *m.* (chem.) deuton, deuteron.
deutoplasma, *m.* (biol.) deutoplasm.
deutoplasmático, ca, *a.* (biol.) deutoplasmic.
deutóxido, *m.* (chem.) deutoxide.
devalar, *i.v.* (mar.) to drift off course.
devaluación, *f.* devaluation.
devaluado, da, *a.* devaluated.
devaluar, (*ref. 53*) *tr.v.* to devaluate (currency).
devanadera, *f.* 1. bobbin, reel, spool. 2. winding frame. 3. (mar.) log-reel. 4. (theat.) mechanism for revolving sets.
devanado, *m.* 1. (elec.) winding. 2. spooling, reeling. — **d. de anillo,** (elec.) ring winding; **d. del inducido,** (mec.) armature winding; **d. en derivación,** (elec.) shunt winding; **d. ondulado** or **en espiral,** (elec.) wave winding.
devanador, ra, *a.* winding, reeling. —*m.* winder, core, spool, reel; (Amer.) winding frame; **devanador de lanzadera,** shuttle winder.
Devanagari, *m.* Devanagari, the Sanscrit alphabet.
devanar, *tr.v.* to wind, reel. —*r.v.* (Cuba, Mex.) to double up with pain or laughter; **devanarse los sesos,** (coll.) to rack one's brains.
devaneador, ra, *a.* raving, delirious.
devanear, *i.v.* to rave; talk nonsense.
devaneo, *m.* 1. delirium, madness; nonsense. 2. dissipation, idle pastime. 3. flirtation.
devantal, *m., var. of* **delantal.**
devastación, *f.* devastation, destruction, desolation, havoc, ruin, waste.
devastador, ra, *a.* devastating, destructive. —*m., f.* destroyer, devastator, desolator; harasser.
devastar, *tr.v.* to devastate, lay waste, ravage, ruin.
devendrá, devendría, devenga, *ref.* **devenir.**
devengado, da, *past part. of* **devengar.** —*a.* earned, due (salaries); accrued (interests). —*m.* (*pl.*) amounts due, salaries or interests due.
devengar, (*ref. 51*) *tr.v.* to produce (interest); to have (salary, interests) due; to receive, be entitled to (an allowance).
devengo, *m.* amount due.
devengue, *ref.* **devengar.**
devenir, (*ref. 26*) *i.v.* 1. to happen, to come about. 2. (philos.) to become.
deviación, *f., var. of* **desviación.**
deviniendo, deviniera, deviniese, devino, *ref.* **devenir.**
devisa, *f.* ancient patrimony which was inherited by brothers as co-heirs.
devisar, *tr.v.* (Mex.) 1. to stop, check, impede. 2. to descry at a distance.
devisero, *m.* nobleman who possessed a patrimony.
devoción, *f.* 1. devotion, devoutness, piety. 2. loyalty, strong affection, attachment.
devocionario, *m.* prayer book.
devolución, *f.* 1. return. 2. refund, repayment. 3. restoration, restitution. 3. (law) devolution.
devolutivo, va, *a.* (law) returnable, restorable, restitutive.
devolutorio, ria, *a., var. of* **devolutivo.**
devolver, (*ref. 34*) *tr.v.* 1. to return, give back, send back; to restore; to refund. 2. (coll.) to throw or bring up, vomit. —*r.v.* (Amer.) to return, go or come back.
devoniano, na, *a.* (geol.) Devonian, period in the Paleozoic Era.
devónico, ca, *a., var. of* **devoniano.**
devorado, da, *past part. of* **devorar.** —*a.* devoured, afflicted with, consumed by, e.g. *devorado por la fiebre,* consumed by fever.
devorador, ra, *a.* ravenous, voracious. —*m., f.* devourer.
devorante, *a.* ravenous, voracious.
devorar, *tr.v.* 1. to devour, swallow up, gobble. 2. to squander, waste. 3. to ruin, destroy. 4. to consume, devour (flames, passion, etc.).
devotamente, *adv.* devoutly, devotedly.
devotería, *f.* sanctimoniousness, hypocritical devotion, false piety.
devoto, ta, *a.* 1. devout, pious. 2. revered, venerable (shrine, image). 3. devoted, attached; loyal. — **d. de,** devoted to, very fond of. —*m., f.* devotee (of a saint or a person).
devuelto, ta, *irr. past part. of* **devolver.**
devuelva, devuelvo, *ref.* **devolver.**
dexiocardia, *f.* (med.) dexiocardia, deviation of the heart to the right.
dexiotrópico, ca, *a.* dexiotropic, situated on the right, turning to the right.
dexteridad, *f.* dexterity, skillfulness.
dextran, *m.* (chem.) dextran, white amorphous gum.
dextrano, *m.* (chem.) dextran.
dextrina, *f.* (chem.) dextrine, the gummy or soluble matter present in starch globules.
dextro, *m.* church precincts which granted the right of sanctuary.
dextrógiro, ra, *a.* (phys.) dextrogyrate; dextrogyrous. —*m.* dextrorotatory.
dextroglucosa, *f.* (chem.) dextroglucose.
dextrorrotatorio, ria, *a.* dextrorotatory, dextrogyrous.
dextrorso, sa, *a.* (bot.) dextrorse, rising from right to left, as a spiral line, a helix or a climbing plant.
dextrórsum, *adv.* towards the right.
dextrosa, *f.* dextrose.
dextrotrópico, ca, *a.* dextrotropic, turning to the right.
dey, *m.* dey, title of the ancient rulers of Tunis, Algiers and Tripoli; Turkish governor of Algiers.
deyección, *f.* 1. (geol.) ejecta. 2. (med.) dejection (of faeces); (*pl.*) dejecta, stool.
deyectar, *i.v.* (med.) to deject (excrement, stools, faeces).
deyector, *m.* device for preventing crusty formations in boilers.
dezmable, *a.* tithable, taxable, subject to tithes.
dezmar, *tr.v., var. of* **diezmar.**
dezmatorio, *m.* place where tithes were collected; tithing, a territory allocated to a church for the collection of tithes.
dezmeño, ña, *a., var. of* **dezmero.**
dezmería, *f.* tithe land.
dezmero, ra, *a.* tithing, pertaining to tithe. —*m., f.* tither.
dezocar, (*ref. 50*) *tr.v.* (Chile) to dislocate the hand of. —*r.v.* to dislocate one's hand.
dg. *abbrev. of* **decigramo,** decigram (dg.).
di, *ref.* dar, decir.
dia, *m.* 1. day; daylight, daytime. 2. birthday. 3. sunshine. — **abrir el d.,** to dawn; to clear up (the weather); **a días,** now and then; **al d. siguiente,** (on) the next or following day; **alcanzar a uno en días,** to outlive someone; **al d.,** up to date; **poner al d.,** to bring up to date; **al otro d.,** (on) the following day; **antes del d.,** at dawn; **a tantos días fecha** or **vista,** (com.) to be paid on the date stated; **buenos días** or **buen d.,** good morning, good day; **cada tercer d.,** every other day; **cerrarse el d.,** to become overcast; **¡cualquier d.!** (iron.) like hell! I should say not! **dar los buenos días a otro,** to say good morning; **dar los días a otro,** to wish someone a happy birthday; **de cada d.,** daily; **de d.,** by day; **de d. a d.,** soon, at any moment; **de d. en d.,** from day to day **del d.,** in fashion, fashionable; fresh today; **de medio d.,** part-time; **despuntar el d.,** to dawn; **de un d. a otro,** at any moment, soon, any time now; **d. de ajuste de cuentas,** day of reckoning; **d. de año nuevo,** New Year's Day; **d. de asueto,** day off, holiday; **d. de ayuno,** fast day; **d. de campo,** day in the country; (coll.) day of rest; **d. de ceniza,** Ash Wednesday; **d. de entresemana,** weekday; **d. de guardar** or **precepto,** holy day of obligation (to go to mass); **d. del juicio,** Judgment Day, doomsday; (fig.) the very last moment or hour, never; **d. de la expiación,** Day of Atonement; **d. de la raza,** Columbus or Discovery Day; **d. de las madres,** Mother's Day; **d. de los enamorados, el d. de San Valentín,** Valentine's Day; **d. de los inocentes,** December 28, day of practical jokes equivalent to April Fool's Day; **d. de los muertos, d. de los fieles difuntos,** All Souls' Day; **d. de mucho, víspera de nada,** life is full of ups and downs; **d. de pescado,** (ecc.) fish day; **d. de Reyes,** Twelfth Night, Epiphany; **d. de todos los Santos,** All Saint's Day; **d. de trabajo,** working day; **d. de viernes** or **vigilia,** (ecc.) fish day; **d. entre semana,** weekday; **d. feriado,** bank holiday (when courts and banks are closed); **d. festivo,** public holiday; **d. hábil, d. laborable,** working day; **d. lectivo,** school day; **d. libre,** free day; **d. por medio,** every other day; **d. puente,** working day between two holidays; **d. sandwich,** the *día puente* taken as a vacation; **días de gracia,** days of grace (for payment of a debt); **d. útil,** working day; **el d. de Año Nuevo,** New Year's Day; **el d. de la Hispanidad, el d. de la raza,** Columbus Day; **el d. de juicio final,** Judgment Day; **el d. de los difuntos, el d. de los muertos,** All Soul's Day; **el d. menos pensado,** one of these days; **el mejor d.,** (iron.) some unlucky day; **el otro d.,** the other day; **en pleno d.,** in full daylight; **en su d.,** in due time; **entrado en días,** advanced in years; **estar al d.,** to be up to date (on affairs, on a subject); **hoy d.** or **hoy en d.,** nowadays; **medio d. de asueto,** half-holiday; **no pasar un d. por uno,** (coll.) not to look a day older; **oscurecerse el d.,** to become overcast; **otro d.,** some other day; **tener (uno) días,** to have one's days, be changeable; **todo el santo d.,** all day long; **un buen d.,** one fine day; **un d. sí y otro no,** now and then; **vivir al d.,** to live from hand to mouth.
diabasa, *f.* (min.) diabase.
diabásico, *a.* (geol.) diabasic.
diabaso, *m.* (zool.) species of horsefly.
diabetes, *f.* (med.) diabetes.
diabético, ca, *a., m., f.* (med.) diabetic.
diabetis, *f., var. of* **diabetes.**
diabeto, *m.* automatic flushing cistern.
diabla, *f.* 1. (coll.) demoness, she-devil. 2. (tex.) carding machine, carder. 3. (theat.) battery of footlights. — **a la d.,** carelessly, any old way; **cosido a la d.,** bound in paper (book).
diablear, *i.v.* (coll.) to play pranks, be up to mischief.

diablejo, *m. dim. of* **diablo,** little devil.
diablería, *f.* devilment, mischief; prank.
diablesa, *f.* (coll.) demoness, she-devil.
diablesco, ca, *a.* devilish.
diablillo, *m.* 1. *dim. of* **diablo,** little devil, imp, young rascal; person disguised as a devil; (coll.) scheming imp. 2. (*pl.*) (coll.) short hairs at the back of the neck.
diablito, *m.* 1. *dim. of* **diablo,** little devil, imp. 2. (Cuba) Negro clown, African ritual dancer.
diablo, *m.* 1. devil, Satan, demon. 2. crosspatch, bad-tempered person. 3. imp, rascal, rogue, little devil, scamp. 4. schemer, astute person. 5. ugly person, ogre. 6. (in billiards) the rest. 7. carding machine. 8. (Chile) ox-cart, dray. 9. (Chile) claw, nail puller. — **andar el d. suelto,** to be in an uproar, restless, troublesome (a town, etc.); **así paga el d. a quien le sirve,** that's what one gets for trying to help; **como el d.,** like the devil, very much, exceedingly, e.g. *esto duele como el d.,* this hurts like the devil; **¡con mil diablos!** damn! blast it!; **mandar al d. a una persona,** to send someone to hell; **darle a uno diablos azules,** to see pink elephants; **del d., de los diablos, de los mil diablos, de todos los diablos,** (coll.) a hell of a, e.g. *un ruido de los mil diablos,* a hell of a noise; **d. cojuelo,** schemer, cunning person; **d. marino,** (ichth.) scorpene; **¡diablos!** (coll.) damn it! confound it!; **diablos azules,** delirium tremens; **donde el d. dio las tres voces,** at the end of nowhere, very far and out of the way; **donde el d. perdió el poncho,** (Arg., Chile) in hell and beyond; **había una de todos los diablos,** (coll.) there was a tremendous rumpus or shindy; **irse como alma que lleva el d.,** to go or leave hastily; **llevarse el d. una cosa,** to turn out badly, fizzle, fall through; **más sabe el d. por viejo que por d.,** experience and age is what counts; **¡pobre d.!** poor devil!; **¡qué diablos!** what the devil!; **tener el d. en el cuerpo,** to have an itch, a restless, mischievous desire; **tirar el d. de la manta,** to let the cat out of the bag.
diablura, *f.* deviltry, devilment, piece of mischief, wild prank.
diabólicamente, *adv.* diabolically, devilishly.
diabólico, ca, *a.* diabolical, devilish.
diabolín, *m.* chocolate drop wrapped in a piece of paper containing a proverb.
diábolo, *m.* diabolo (game).
diacatolicón, *m.* (pharm.) diacatholicon, purgative electuary.
diacáustico, ca, *a., m.* (phys.) diacaustic.
diácido, *m.* (chem.) diacid.
diacinesis, *f.* (biol.) diakinesis.
diacinético, ca, *a.* (biol.) diakinetic.
diacitrón, *m.* candied citron or lemon peel.
diacodión, *m.* (pharm.) diacodion, poppy syrup, formerly used as a narcotic.
diaconado, *m., var. of* **diaconato.**
diaconal, *a.* diaconal, of or pertaining to deacons.
diaconar, *i.v.* to act as deacon.
diaconato, *m.* diaconate, deaconship.
diaconía, *f.* district under deacon's jurisdiction; diaconia, deaconry, hospice or chapel under a deacon.
diaconisa, *f.* deaconess.
diácono, *m.* deacon.
diacrítico, ca, *a.* 1. (gram.) diacritical. 2. (med.) diagnostic.
diactínico, ca, *a.* (phys.) diactinic.
diactinismo, *m.* (phys.) diactinism.
diacústica, *f.* diacoustics.
díada, *f.* (chem.) dyad.
diadelfo, fa, *a.* (bot.) diadelphous; diadelph.
diadema, *f.* diadem; tiara, crown; halo.
diademado, da, *a.* (her.) diademed.
diado, *a., contr. of* **día dado,** fixed, appointed (day).
diadoco, *m.* (hist.) heir apparent to Greek throne; (*pl.*) Diadochi, successors of Alexander the Great.
diafanice, diafanicé, *ref.* **diafanizar.**
diafanidad, *f.* diaphaneity, diaphanousness, translucency, transparency.
diafanizar, (*ref. 53*) *tr.v.* to make diaphanous, transparent, translucent.
diáfano, na, *a.* diaphanous, transparent, translucent; clear; (fig.) lucid, limpid.
diafisario, ria, *a.* (anat., biol.) diaphysial, diaphyseal.
diáfisis, *f.* (anat., biol.) diaphysis.
diaforesis, *f.* (med.) diaphoresis, perspiration.
diaforético, ca, *a.* (med.) diaphoretic, inducing perspiration. —*m.* diaphoretic.
diafragma, *m.* 1. (anat., mec.) diaphragm. 2. diaphragm, contraceptive device. — **d. iris,** (photog.) iris diaphragm.
diafragmar, *tr.v.* (photog.) to diaphragm, graduate the diaphragm of.
diafragmático, ca, *a.* diaphragmatic.
diagnosis, *f.* (med.) diagnosis; (bot., zool.) diagnosis, a concise technical description of a species or group.
diagnosta, *m., f.* diagnostician.
diagnosticar, (*ref. 50*) *tr.v.* to diagnose.
diagnóstico, ca, *a.* (med.) diagnostic. —*m.* diagnosis, the result of diagnosing; diagnostic symptoms (of an illness).
diagnostique, diagnostiqué, *ref.* **diagnosticar.**
diagonal, *a.* diagonal; oblique. —*f.* 1. (geom.) diagonal. 2. (tex.) diagonal, diagonal cloth. 3. stay; guy wire. — **d. en barra,** (her.) bend sinister.
diagonalmente, *adv.* diagonally, obliquely.
diagráfico, *a.* diagraphic.
diágrafo, *m.* diagraph, an instrument for enlarging or reducing sketches during tracing.
diagrama, *m.* diagram; **d. estereográfico,** (geol.) block diagram; **d. logarítmico,** (math.) logarithmic plot; **d. vectorial,** vector diagram.
dial, *a.* daily. —*m.* 1. radio dial. 2. (*pl.*) diary, journal; ephemeris.
diálaga, *f.* (min.) diallage (pyroxene).
dialectal, *a.* dialectal, pertaining to a dialect.
dialectalismo, *m.* dialecticism.
dialéctica, *f.* dialectics, dialectic.
dialéctico, ca, *a.* dialectic, dialectical; pertaining to dialectics. —*m.* dialectician.
dialecto, *m.* dialect; (philol.) dialect, branch language (developed from a root language).
dialectología, *f.* dialectology, science or study of dialects.
dialice, dialicé, *ref.* **dializar.**
dialipétalo, la, *a.* (bot.) dialypetalous.
dialisépalo, la, *a.* (bot.) dialysepalous.
diálisis, *f.* (chem.) dialysis, separation of parts.
dializador, *a.* dialytic. —*m.* (chem. dialyzer.
dializar, (*ref. 53*) *tr.v.* (chem.) to dialyze.
dialogal, *a.* dialogistic, colloquial.
dialogar, (*ref. 51*) *i.v.* to speak in dialogue; to converse. —*tr.v.* to write in dialogue form.
dialogice, dialogicé, *ref.* **dialogizar.**
dialogismo, *m.* (rhet.) dialogism.
dialogístico, ca, *a.* dialogistic; colloquial.
dialogizar, (*ref. 53*) *i.v., var. of.* **dialogar.**
diálogo, *m.* dialogue.
dialogue, dialogué, *ref.* **dialogar.**
dialoguista, *m.,* dialogist, dialoguer (writer of dialogues).
dialtea, *f.* (pharm.) marsh mallow ointment.
diamagnético, ca, *a., m.* (phys.) diamagnetic.
diamagnetismo, *m.* (phys.) diamagnetism.
diamantado, da, *a.* diamond-like, diamond-studded.
diamantar, *tr.v.* to give (something) a diamond-like lustre.
diamante, *m.* 1. diamond; glazier's diamond. 2. miner's lamp. 3. diamond (suit of cards). 4. (mil.) piece of ordnance. — **d. brillante,** cut diamond; **d. defectuoso,** lasque; **d. del ancla,** anchor crown; **d. en bruto,** uncut diamond; diamond in the rough (person with great yet uncultivated qualities); **d. rebolludo,** round uncut diamond; **d. rosa,** rose-cut diamond; **d. tabla,** square-cut diamond.
diamantífero, *a.* diamantiferous; containing diamonds.
diamantino, na, *a.* pertaining to diamonds; (made) of diamonds; diamond-like, diamantine; (poet.) adamantine, unbreakable, hard.
diamantista, *m.* diamond cutter; diamond merchant.
diamela, *f.* (bot.) Arabian jasmine.
diametral, *a.* diametrical, diametric; (geom., min., mec.) diametric, diametral.
diametralmente, *adv.* diametrically; **d. opuesto,** totally opposed.
diámetro, *m.* (geom.) diameter; **d. aparente,** (astron.) apparent diameter; **d. conjugado,** (geom.) conjugate diameter; **d. interior,** (mec.) internal diameter; caliper, bore; **d. máximo,** major or outside diameter (of screw); full diameter (of nut).
diamida, *f.* (biochem.) diamide.
diana, *f.* 1. (mil.) reveille. 2. (mil.) bull's eye (in target). 3. (poet.) the moon. 4. **D.,** (myth.) Diana, goddess of the moon and of hunting.
dianche, *m.* (coll.) *var. of* **diantre.**
diandro, dra, *a.* (bot.) diandrous, diandrian.
dianoético, ca, *a.* (philos.) dianoetic.
diantre, *m.* (coll.) devil. —*interj.* darn! blast it!
diapalma, *f.* (pharm.) diapalma (desiccant lead plaster).
diapasón, *m.* (mus.) diapason; standard of pitch; finger board (e.g. of violin); tuning fork. — **d. alto,** concert pitch; **d. bajo,** international pitch; **d. de concierto,** concert pitch; **d. normal,** normal, French or international pitch; **subir** or **bajar el d.,** (coll.) to raise or lower one's tone of voice.
diapédesis, *f.* (med.) diapedesis.
diapente, *m.* (mus.) perfect fifth.
diapófisis. *f.* (anat., zool.) diapophysis.
diapositiva, *f.* (photog.) diapositive, slide; plate; lantern slide.
diaprea, *f.* (bot.) small round plum.
diapreado, da, *a.* (her.) variegated.
diápsido, a, *a.* (paleon.) diapsid, diapsidan. —*m.* diapsid, diapsidan, (*pl.*) Diapsida.
diaquenio, *m.* (bot.) diachaenium; two-seeded fruit.
diaquilón, *m.* (pharm.) diachylon; plaster.
diariamente, *adv.* daily.
diario, ria, *a.* daily. —*m.* 1. dairy. 2. newspaper, daily; **d. de la mañana,** morning paper; **d. de la noche,** evening paper; **d. hablado,** news program; **d. matutino** or **matinal,** morning paper; **d. vespertino,** evening paper. 3. daily expenses. 4. (com.) journal, daybook; **d. de a bordo, d. de navegación,** (mar.) log, logbook; **d. de sesiones,** legislative record (equivalent to the Congressional Record). —*adv.* daily; **a d.,** every day; **de d.,** everyday (e.g. everyday clothes); every day, daily.

diarismo, *m.* (Amer.) journalism.
diarista, *m.* 1. diarist. 2. (Amer.) journalist, reporter.
diarquía, *f.* diarchy.
diarrea, *f.* (med.) diarrhea.
diarreico, ca, *a.* (med.) diarrheic, diarrheal.
diárrico, *a., var. of* **diarreico.**
diartrosis, *f.* (anat.) diarthrosis.
diascopia, *f.* (med.) radioscopic examination; radioscopic test or testing.
diascordio, *m.* (pharm.) diascordium.
diasén, *m.* (pharm.) senna purgative.
diáspero, *m., var. of* **diaspro.**
diáspora, *f.* dispersion; **D.,** (hist.) the dispersion of the Jews in the 2nd century A.D.
diásporo, *m.* (min.) diaspore.
diaspro, *m.* kind of jasper; d. **sanguino,** heliotrope, bloodstone.
diastasa, *f.* (chem.) diastase.
diastasis, *f.* (med.) diastasis; luxation.
diastático, ca, *a.* (chem.) diastatic.
diastema, *m.* (anat., med.) diastema; (geol.) diastem.
diáster, *m.* (biol.) diaster.
diástilo, *m.* (archit.) diastyle.
diástole, *f.* (physiol., poet.) diastole.
diastólico, ca, *a.* (physiol., poet.) diastolic.
diastrofia, *f.* (med.) dislocation; sprain.
diastrofismo, *m.* (geol.) diastrophism.
diatérmano, na, *a.* (phys.) diathermanous.
diatermia, *f.* (med.) diathermy.
diatérmico, ca, *a.* (phys.) diathermic.
diatesarón, *m.* (mus.) diatessaron, perfect fourth.
diatésico, ca, *a.* (med.) diathetic.
diátesis, *f.* (med.) diathesis.
diatomáceo, a, *a.* (bot.) diatomaceous.
diatomea, *f.* (bot.) diatom.
diatómico, ca, *a.* (chem.) diatomic.
diatomita, *f.* (min.) diatomite.
diatónicamente, *adv.* diatonically.
diatónico, ca, *a.* (mus.) diatonic.
diatriba, *f.* diatribe.
diatrópico, ca, *a.* (bot.) diatropic.
diatropismo, *m.* (bot.) diatropism.
diazina, *f.* (chem.) diazine.
dibásico, ca, *a.* (chem.) dibasic.
dibranquiado, da, *a.* (zool.) dibranchiate. —*m.* (zool.) dibranchiate, (*pl.*) Dibranchia, Dibranchiata.
dibujador, ra, *a.* (rare) sketching, drawing, delineating. —*m., f.* sketches, draftsman.
dibujante, *a.* sketching, drawing. —*m., f.* sketcher, draftsman.
dibujar, *tr.v.* to sketch, draw; to describe vividly; sketch, outline. —*r.v.* 1. to be outlined, to stand out. 2. to be revealed, to take form.
dibujo, *m.* drawing, sketch; pattern, design; (fig.) description; portrayal. — **d. geométrico,** geometrical drawing; **d. esquemático,** schematic drawing; **d. del natural,** (p.) sketching from live model; **dibujos animados,** animated cartoons; **no meterse uno en dibujos,** to keep to the business at hand, attend to one's business.
dic. *abbrev. of* **diciembre,** December (Dec.); **dícese,** that is to say (i.e.).
dicacidad, *f.* biting wit, banter, sauciness.
dicasio, *m.* (bot.) dichasium.
dicaz, (*pl.* **dicaces**) *a.* bitingly or caustically witty; sharp, keen, sarcastic.
dicción, *f.* 1. diction, enunciation, pronunciation. 2. diction, style.
diccionario, *m.* dictionary; **d. de ideas afines** or **d. de sinónimos** or **d. ideológico,** thesaurus; **d. bilingue,** bilingual dictionary; **d. de uso,** dictionary of usage; **d. enciclopédico,** encyclopedic dictionary; **d. etimológico,** etymological dictionary.
diccionarista, *m., f.* lexicographer.
dicente, *a.* saying, uttering. —*m., f.* sayer, utterer.
dicentra, *f.* (bot.) dicentra.
díceres, *m.* (*pl.*) rumors.
dicha, *f.* happiness, bliss; good luck, good fortune; **a** or **por d.,** by luck, by chance; **nunca es tarde si la d. es buena,** no wait is too long for happiness.
dicharachero, ra, *a.* (coll.) racy, witty, spicy, full of amusing observations.
dicharacho, *m.* (coll.) spicy remark, amusing observation; slang or idiomatic expression.
dichero, ra, *a.* (coll., reg.) witty, amusing (conversationalist).
dicho, cha, *irr. past part. of* **decir.** —*m.* 1. saying, adage, proverb; witticism, amusing remark, wisecrack. 2. (*pl.*) marriage vows. 3. (coll.) slang or vulgar expression. 4. (law) declaration, statement (made by witness). — **a estar por lo d.,** as far as it goes; **d. de las gentes,** public opinion; talk, rumors; **del d. al hecho hay un gran trecho,** there's many a slip twixt the cup and the lip; **d. y hecho,** no sooner said than done; **lo d., d.,** I meant what I said.
dichosamente, *adv.* happily, luckily, fortunately.
dichoso, sa, *a.* 1. happy, blissful; lucky, fortunate. 2. (coll., iron.) blessed, tiresome, annoying.
diciembre, *m.* December.
diciendo, *ref.* **decir.**
diciente, *a.* saying, uttering.
diclamídeo, a, *a.* (bot.) dichlamydeous.
dicogamia, *f.* (bot.) dichogamy.
dicógamo, ma, *a.* (bot.) dichogamous.
dicotiledón, *a.* (bot.) dicotyledonous. —*m.* dicotyledon; (*pl.*) Dicotyledoneae.
dicotiledóneo, a, *a.* dicotyledoneous (plant). —*f.* dicotyledon; (*pl.*) Dicotyledoneae.
dicotomía, *f.* (biol., astron., psyc., log.) dichotomy.
dicotómico, ca, *a.* dichotomic.
dicótomo, ma, *a.* dichotomous.
dicroico, ca, *a.* (phys.) dichroic.
dicroísmo, *m.* (phys.) dichroism.
dicroíta, *f.* (min.) dichroite.
dicromático, ca, *a.* dichromatic..
dicromatismo, *m.* (phys.) dichromatism, dichroism.
dicromato, *m.* (chem.) dichromate. — **d. de sodio,** (chem.) sodium dichromate.
dicromatopsia, *f.* (physiol.) dichromatopsia, dichromatism.
dicroscopio, *m.* (phys.) dichrooscope, dichroscope.
dicrotismo, *m.* (med.) dicrotism.
dicroto, ta, *a.* (med.) dicrotic.
dictado, *past part. of* **dictar.** —*m.* 1. title (of nobility). 2. dictation. 3. (*pl.*) dictates (of one's conscience). — **escribir al d.,** to take dictation.
dictador, *m.* dictator.
dictadura, *f.* dictatorship.
dictáfono, *m.* dictaphone (trademark), dictating machine.
dictamen, *m.* opinion, judgment; suggestion, advice, e.g. *tomar d. de un hermano,* to take a brother's advice.
dictaminador, ra, *a.* adjudicating, judging.
dictaminar, *i.v.* 1. to express one's opinion. 2. to pronounce judgment; to render a decision.
díctamo, *m.* 1. (bot.) dittany. 2. (Cuba, bot.) variety of spurge (Pedilanthus tethimaloides). — **d. blanco,** (bot.) fraxinella, garden dittany; **d. crético,** marjoram.
dictar, *tr.v.* 1. to dictate; prescribe, command. 2. (law) to pronounce (sentence). 3. (fig.) to suggest, direct, prompt. 4. (Amer.) to give a course of studies; lecture. — **d. una conferencia,** to give a lecture; **d. una carta,** to dictate a letter.
dictatorial, *a.* dictatorial; imperious, overbearing.
dictatorialmente, *adv.* dictatorially, imperiously.
dictatorio, ria, *a.* dictatorial, pertaining to a dictator.
dicterio, *m.* insult, taunt, stern reproach.
dictógrafo, *m.* dictograph (trademark); recording instrument.
dicumarol, *m.* (med.) dicoumarol, dicoumarin.
didáctica, *f.* didactics.
didácticamente, *adv.* didactically.
didáctico, ca, *a.* didactic, didactical, preceptive.
didáctilo, la, *a.* didactylous, two-fingered.
didascálico, ca, *a.* (rare) *var. of* **didáctico.**
didelfo, fa, *a.* (zool.) didelphian. —*m.* (zool.) didelphian, didelph; (*pl.*) Didelphia (animals like the opossum and the kangaroo).
didímeo, a, *a.* (poet.) pertaining to Apollo.
didimio, *m.* (metal.) didymium.
dídimo, ma, *a.* (bot., zool.) didymous. —*m.* (zool.) testicle.
didracma, *m.* (numis.) didrachma, ancient Hebrew coin worth a quarter of an ounce of silver.
diecinueve, *a.* nineteen, nineteenth. —*m.* nineteen; nineteenth (in dates).
diecinueveavo, va, *a.* nineteenth. —*m.* ninteenth, nineteenth part.
dieciochavo, va, *a.* eighteenth. —*m.* eighteenth, eighteenth part.
dieciocheno, na, *a.* eighteenth. —*m.* 1. (numis.) coin minted in Valencia during the Austrian dynasty. 2. (tex.) a closely woven fabric.
dieciochismo, *m.* spirit, character, manners and style of the eighteenth century.
dieciochista, *a.* pertaining to the eighteenth century. —*m., f.* eighteenth-century specialist.
dieciocho, *a.* eighteen; eighteenth. —*m.* eighteen; eighteenth (in dates).
dieciséis, *a.* sixteen; sixteenth. —*m.* sixteen; sixteenth (in dates).
dieciseisavo, va, *a.* sixteenth. —*m.* sixteenth, sixteenth part; **en dieciseisavo,** (print.) sextodecimo.
dieciseiseno, na, *a., var. of* **decimosexto.**
diecisiete, a. seventeen; seventeenth. —*m.* seventeen; seventeenth (in dates).
diecisieteavo, va, *a.* seventeenth. —*m.* seventeenth, seventeenth part.
diedro, dra, *a.* (geom.) dihedral. —*m.* dihedral angle.
diego, *m.* (bot.) four-o'clock (Mirabilis jalapa).
dieldrin, *m.* (chem.) dieldrin.
dieléctrico, ca, *a.* (phys.) dielectric.
diencéfalo, *m.* (anat.) interbrain.
diente, *m.* 1. (anat.) tooth; fang, tusk; (ornith.) temium (cutting edge on bird's bill). 2. (archit.) toothing. 3. (mec.) tooth (of saw, rake, file), cog (of wheel); prong, tine (of fork). 4. (print.) imprint, punch through; printing fault caused by the print on the first form not being matched with the print on the second impression. — **aguzar uno los dientes,** to whet one's appetite; **alargársele a uno los dientes,** to have one's teeth set on edge; to long (for something); **a regañadientes,** reluctantly, unwillingly; **crujirle a uno los dientes,** to grind one's teeth (with impatience or pain); **dar uno d. con d.,** to shiver, have one's teeth chattering (with cold or fear); **de dientes afuera,** insincerely; **d. de ajo,** clove of garlic; **d. de leche,** milk tooth; **d. de león,** dandelion; **d. de lobo,** (jewel) burnisher; very long nail, spike; **d. de muerto,** (bot.) blue vetch (Vicia cracca); **d. de perro,** (mec.) chisel; (sculp.) dented chisel; (dressm.) uneven sewing; (archit.) dogtooth; (bot.) dogtooth violet; **d. incisivo,** (anat.) incisor; **d. molar,** (anat.) molar;

d. permanente, (anat.) permanent tooth; **enseñar** or **mostrar uno los dientes,** to bare one's teeth (menacingly); **estar a d.,** to be hungry; **haberle nacido** or **salido los dientes a uno (haciendo una cosa),** to have been born (doing something); **hablar uno entre dientes,** to mumble; to grumble; **hincar uno el d.,** to get one's hands on, collar, appropriate; to get one's teeth into (a problem); **meterle d.,** (Arg., Chile) to get one's teeth into (a subject); **pelar el d.,** (coll., Amer.) to smile flirtatiously; (Mex., P. Rico, Ven.) to butter up, to flatter; **rechinar los dientes,** to gnash one's teeth (with rage or fury); **tener uno buen d.,** to have a big appetite, like one's food; **tomar** or **traer a uno entre dientes,** (coll.) to be hostile to someone; to run someone down, speak ill of.

diente, diento, *ref.* **dentar.**

dientecico, illo, ito, *m. dim. of* **diente.**

dientimellado, da, *a.* jagged-toothed, with nicked teeth.

dientudo, da, *a.* with long, uneven, or protruding teeth.

diera, *ref.* **dar.**

diéresis, *f.* (rhet., surg.) diaeresis.

dieron, diese, *ref.* **dar.**

diesel, *m.* diesel (engine).

diesi, *f.* (mus.) diesis, the Pythagorean semitone; (mus.) sharp.

diestra, *f.* right hand; support; **juntar d. con d.,** to join forces.

diestramente, *adv.* dexterously, skillfully, deftly.

diestro, tra, *a.* 1. right. 2. dexterous, skillful, deft; shrewd, sharp, experienced (in business). *—m.* 1. swordsman. 2. (taur.) bull-fighter, matador. 3. halter, bridle. — **a d. y siniestro,** right and left; slapdash, helter-skelter. *—f.* right hand.

dieta, *f.* 1. diet, regulated or prescribed meals. 2. (coll.) fast, fasting. 3. conference, congress. 4. (*gen. pl.*) daily expense allowance. 5. (*pl.*) pay, salary, (given to public official while carrying out public commission). 6. (law) ten-league journey. — **d. láctea,** milk diet; **d. hídrica,** or **líquida,** liquid diet. **estar a d.,** to be on a diet.

dietario, *m.* family account book; memorandum book.

dietética, *f.* (med.) dietetics.

dietético, ca, *a.* dietary, dietetic.

dietilestilbestrol, *m.* (biochem.) diethylstilbestrol.

dietista, *m. f.* dietitian, dietician, nutritionist.

diez, (*pl.* **dieces**) *a.* ten; tenth. *—m.* 1. ten; tenth (in dates). 2. decade (of the rosary); larger bead placed between decades of the rosary. — **d. de bolos,** (in bowling) pin standing alone in front of ninepins; **d. de últimas,** (cards) ten points going to the one who makes the last trick; **hacer las d. de últimas,** (coll.) to be left with nothing, get nothing; **las d. de la mañana,** ten o'clock in the morning.

diezmal, *a.* pertaining to tithe; decimal; tenth.

diezmar, *tr.v.* 1. to decimate. 2. to pay the tithe to (church). 3. to punish one delinquent in ten. 4. (fig.) to decimate, ravage, destroy.

diezmero, ra, *m., f.* one who pays tithes; tithe collector.

diezmesino, na, *a.* ten-month old.

diezmilésimo, ma, *a.* ten-thousandth. *—m.* ten-thousandth, each of ten thousand equal parts.

diezmilímetro, *m.* one tenth of a millimeter.

diezmillo, *m.* (Mex.) filet, loin, sirloin.

diezmillonésimo, ma, *a.* ten-millionth. *—m.* ten-millionth, ten-millionth part.

diezmilmillonésimo, ma, *a.* ten-thousand-millionth. *—m.* ten-thousand-millionth, ten-thousand-millionth part.

diezmo, *m.* tithe; tenth part.

difamación, *f.* defamation, slander, (law) libel, e.g. *entablar un juicio por d.,* to institute a libel suit.

difamador, ra, *a.* defamatory, slanderous. *—m., f.* defamer, slanderer, libeler.

difamante, *a.* defamatory, slanderous, libeling.

difamar, *tr.v.* to defame, slander, calumniate; to discredit.

difamatorio, ria, *a.* defamatory, slanderous, libelous.

difarreación, *f.* (hist.) diffarreation, Roman divorce.

difásico, ca, *a.* (elec.) diphase, diphasic.

difenilamina, *f.* (chem.) diphenylamine.

difenilo, *m.* (chem.) diphenyl.

diferencia, *f.* 1. difference, variation, dissimilarity. 2. disagreement, difference of opinion; controversy. 3. (log.) differentia. 4. (math.) difference. — **a. d. de,** unlike; **d. de potencial,** (phys.) difference of potential; **partir la d.,** to split the difference.

diferenciación, *f.* differentiation.

diferencial, *a.* differential. *—f.* (math.) differential. *—m.* (mec.) differential gear, differential.

diferenciar, *tr.v.* 1. to differentiate, distinguish. 2. to change or vary the use of. 3. (math.) to differentiate (an expression or equation). *—i.v.* to differ, disagree. *—r.v.* 1. to differ, be different or unlike; to become differentiated. 2. to distinguish oneself. 3. (biol.) to differentiate.

diferendo, *m.* (Chile) quarrel, difference, dispute.

diferente, *a.* different, dissimilar. *—adv.* in a different way, differently.

diferentemente, *adv.* differently, in a different way; diversely.

diferido, da, *past part. of* diferir. *—a.* deferred, delayed; **en d.,** (rad., tel.) prerecorded.

diferir, (*ref. 42*) *tr.v.* to defer, delay, postpone, put off. *—i.v.* to differ,, be different.

dificercal, *a.* (zool.) diphycercal.

difícil, *a.* 1. difficult, hard; arduous, e.g. *d. de hacer,* difficult to do. 2. difficult, hard to please.

difícilmente, *adv.* difficulty, with difficulty.

dificultad, *f.* 1. difficulty, obstacle, impediment. 2. objection (to an opinion).

dificultador, ra, *a.* difficult, troublemaking; pessimistic. *—m., f.* obstructor, person who puts obstacles in the way; pessimist.

dificultar, *tr.v.* to impede, hamper, render difficult; to obstruct, hinder. *—i.v.* to consider unlikely.

dificultosamente, *adv.* with difficulty.

dificultoso, sa, *a.* 1. difficult, hard, laborious. 2. (coll.) strange, ugly. 3. difficult, troublemaking.

difidación, *f.* diffidation, declaration of war; public statement justifying such a declaration.

difidencia, *f.* mistrust, distrust, diffidence.

difidente, *a.* mistrustful, distrusting, diffident.

difiera, difiero, *ref.* **diferir.**

difiléctico, ca, *a.* (biol.) diphyletic.

dífilo, la, *a.* (bot.) diphyllous; having two leaves.

difiriendo, difiera difiriese, difirió, *ref.* **diferir.**

difluencia, *f.* diffluence.

difluente, *a.* diffluent, deliquescent; flowing away.

difluir, (*ref. 48*) *i.v.* to flow in all directions; to spread, extend; shed.

difluya, difluye, *ref.* **difluir.**

difosgeno, *m.* (chem.) diphosgene.

difracción, *f.* (phys., opt.) diffraction.

difractar, *tr.v.* (phys.) to diffract. *—r.v.* to become diffracted.

difrangente, *a.* diffractive, diffrangible.

difteria, *f.* (med.) diphtheria.

diftérico, ca, *a.* diphtherial, diphtheritic. diphtheric.

difteritis, *f.* (med.) diphtheritis.

difumar, *tr.v., r.v., var. of* **esfumar.**

difuminar, tr.v. (p.) to stump, tone colors with a stump.

difumino, *m.* (p.) stump.

difundido, da, *past part. of* **difundir.** *—a.* diffused, widespread, scattered, widely-known.

difundidor, ra, *a.* diffusing, disseminating. *—m., f.* diffuser, disseminator.

difundir, *tr.v.* to diffuse; to disseminate, spread; to divulge, publish, make known; (rad.) to broadcast. *—r.v.* to spread, extend.

difunto, ta, *a.* deceased, dead; late; defunct; **d. de taberna,** dead drunk. *—m., f.* deceased, dead person; corpse; **mi difunto,** (coll.) my late husband; **día de los difuntos,** All Soul's Day; **los Difuntos,** All Soul's Day.

difusamente, *adv.* diffusely, diffusedly.

difusibilidad, *f.* (phys.) diffusibility.

difusible, *a.* diffusible.

difusión, *f.* 1. diffusion, spreading, propagation. 2. diffusiveness, prolixity (of style). 3. (phys.) diffusion. 4. (rad.) broadcasting.

difusivo, va, *a.* diffusive.

difuso, sa, *irr. past part. of* **difundir.** *—a.* 1. diffuse, wordy (style). 2. hazy, blurred (outlines). 3. diffused (light). 4. vague, obscure (concepts). 5. broad, wide, extended.

difusor, ra, *a.* diffusing, spreading. *—m.* diffuser (sugar manufacturing). *—f.* (rad.) broadcasting station.

diga, *ref.* **decir.**

digástrico, ca, *a.* (anat.) digastric.

digénesis *f.* (biol.) digenesis.

digenético, ca, *a.* (biol.) digenetic.

digerible, *a.* digestible.

digerir, (*ref. 42*) *tr.v.* 1. to digest. 2. (fig.) to bear, suffer, endure. 3. (fig.) to consider, assimilate. 4. (chem.) to digest, soften (by heat).

digestibilidad, *f.* digestibility.

digestible, *a.* digestible.

digestión, *f.* 1. digestion. 2. (chem.) softening.

digestivo, va, *a.* digestive. *—m.* digestive; (surg.) suppurative.

digesto, *m.* digest, compendium; **D.,** Digest, Pandects (compendium of Roman laws).

digestor, *m.* digester (apparatus).

digiera, digiero, *ref.* **digerir.**

digiriendo, digiriera, digiriese, digirió, *ref.* **digerir.**

digitación, *f.* (mus.) fingering.

digitado, da, *a.* digitate; (zool., bot.) digitate.

digital, *a.* digital, pertaining to fingers. *—f.* 1. (bot.) digitalis, foxglove. 2. (pharm.) digitalis. — **huella d.,** fingerprint.

digitalina, *f.* (chem.) digitalin.

digitalismo, *m.* (med.) digitalism.

digitalización, *f.* (med.) digitalization.

digitalizar, (*ref. 53*) *tr.v.* to digitalize.

digitiforme, *a.* digitiform, fingershaped.

digitígrado, da, *a.* (zool.) digitigrade.

dígito, *a.* digital. *—m.* (math., astron.) digit.

digitoxina, *f.* (chem.) digitoxin.

diglifo, *m.* (archit.) diglyph.

dignación, *f.* condescension; accommodation.

dignamente, *adv.* with dignity; worthily.

dignarse, *r.v.* to deign, vouchsafe, condescend; **d. a,** to deign to.

dignatario, *m.* dignitary.

dignidad, *f.* 1. dignity, honor, moral esteem; dignified bearing, e.g. *hablar con d.,* to speak with dignity. 2. rank, office, position, e.g. *d. de obispo,* the rank of bishop.

dignificación, *f.* dignification.

dignificante, *a.* dignifying.

dignificar, (*ref. 50*) *tr.v.* to dignify; to honor.
dignifique, dignifiqué, *ref.* **dignificar.**
digno, na, *a.* meritorious, deserving; honorable, dignified; **d. de,** worthy of, deserving.
digo, *ref.* **decir.**
digrama, *m.* (phonet.) digraph.
digresión, *f.* digression, deviation.
digresivo, va, *a.* digressive.
dihíbrido, da, *a.* (biol.) dihybrid.
dihidrotaquisterol, *m.* (biochem.) dihydrotachysterol.
dihueñe, dihueñi, *m.* (Chile, bot.) species of edible fungus.
dije, *m.* 1. trinket, charm; amulet; locket. 2. (coll.) jewel (person), e.g. *nuestra cocinera es un d.,* our cook is a jewel. 3. (coll.) beautifully attired person. 4. a person of sterling qualities. 5. (*pl.*) boasts, bravado, braggadocio.
dije, dijera, dijese, *ref.* **decir.**
dilaceración, *f.* laceration, dilaceration.
dilacerar, *tr.v.* 1. to dilacerate, tear asunder. 2. (fig.) to harm, hurt (honor, pride, etc.).
dilación, *f.* delay, detention, procrastination.
dilantina, *f.* (chem.) dilantin.
dilapidación, *f.* squandering, dissipation, waste.
dilapidado, da, *past part. of* **dilapidar.** —*a.* squandered, wasted (e.g. fortune, time, talent).
dilapidador, ra, *a.* squandering, dissipating. —*m., f.* sqaunderer, wastrel, prodigal.
dilapidar, *tr.v.* to dilapidate; to squander, waste, dissipate.
dilatabilidad, *f.* dilatability, expansibility.
dilatable, *a.* dilatable, expansible.
dilatación, *f.* 1. dilation, expansion, distention. 2. calmness, serenity, tranquility (in grief). 3. (surg.) dilatation (of cavity, ducts, etc.). 4. (phys.) expansion. 5. diffuseness, prolixity.
dilatadamente, *adv.* 1. dilatedly. 2. (Amer.) with delay. 3. slowly, long-windedly.
dilatado, da, *past part. of* **dilatar.** —*a.* 1. extensive, vast. 2. extended, expanded, widened. 3. (Amer.) delayed, deferred.
dilatador, ra, *a.* dilating, expanding. —*m.* (surg.) dilator.
dilatar, *tr.v.* 1. to dilate, expand, widen, enlarge. 2. to postpone, defer. 3. to spread, extend. —*r.v.* 1. to dilate, expand. 2. to be postponed or deferred. 3. to spread. 4. to be diffuse (in a talk). 5. to tarry, linger. —*i.v.* to tarry, linger, be a long time.
dilatativo, va, *a.* dilative.
dilatorio, ria, *a.* (law) dilatory, delaying, (law) said of a move meant to delay court action. —*f.* (*gen. used in pl.*) delay, waste of time.
dilección, *f.* pure love, sincere affection.
dilecto, ta, *a.* beloved; loved.
dilema, *m.* dilemma.
dilemático, *a.* dilemmatic.
diletante, *a.* dilettante; superficial or amateurish. —*m., f.* dilettante, a dabbler in art, music, literature, etc.
diletantismo, *m.* dilettantism.
diligencia, *f.* 1. diligence; industriousness; care. 2. speed, briskness, rapidity. 3. diligence, stagecoach. 4. (coll.) task, job, errand, piece of business. 5. (law) proceedings. 6. effort. 7. step, démarche. — **diligencias de la casa,** household chores; **hacer una d.,** to do a task or an errand; to evacuate the bowels; **hacer sus diligencias,** to make every effort (to get something).
diligenciar, *tr.v.* 1. to take the necessary steps to (accomplish something). 2. (law) to deal with, handle. 3. to hasten, to further.
diligenciero, *m.* agent, representative.
diligente, *a.* 1. diligent; careful; industrious. 2. quick, speedy, prompt, swift.
diligentemente, *adv.* diligently, assiduously; swiftly.
dille, *m.* (Chile) cicada.
dilogía, *f.* ambiguity, double sense.
dilucidación, *f.* elucidation, explanation, explication.
dilucidador, ra, *a.* explanatory. —*m., f.* elucidator, interpreter.
dilucidar, *tr.v.* to elucidate, explain.
dilucidario, *m.* explanatory note or writing.
dilución, *f.* dilution.
dilúculo, *m.* dawn; the sixth part of the night.
diluente, *a.* diluent, diluting, solvent.
diluir, (*ref. 48*) *tr.v.* to dilute; to dissolve, weaken. —*r.v.* to be dissolved; to be diluted or weakened.
diluvial, *a.* 1. diluvial, diluvian (pertaining to a flood). 2. (geol.) produced by a flood. —*m.* diluvium, diluvial deposits.
diluviano, na, *a.* (Bib.) diluvian, diluvial (pertaining to the Flood).
diluviar, *i.v.* to pour with rain.
diluvio, *m.* 1. flood, deluge, inundation; overflow. 2. (coll.) abundance. — **el D.,** the Flood.
diluya, diluyendo, *ref.* **diluir.**
diluyente, *a.* diluting, diluent.
diluyo, *ref.* **diluir.**
dimanación, *f.* springing, flowing, issuing (from).
dimanante, *a.* springing, originating, flowing (from).
dimanar, *i.v.* to spring from, flow, have its source; to proceed from, originate in, be due to, e.g. *su éxito dimana de su belleza,* her success is due to her beauty.
dimensión, *f.* (geom.) dimension, magnitude, capacity; size, measure, bulk; extent; **cuarta d.,** fourth dimension.
dimensional, *a.* dimensional.
dímero, *a.* (bot., zool.) dimerous, bipartite.
dimes, (coll.) disputes, quarrels, arguments; **andar en d. y diretes,** to quarrel or squabble.
dimetálico, ca, *a.* (chem.) dimetallic.
dímetro, *m.* (poet.) dimeter, a verse of two measures.
dimiario, *a.* (zool.) dimyarian, dimyaric.
dimicado, *m.* (Arg.) openwork (embroidery).
dimidiar, *tr.v.* (rare) to halve, to divide in two parts.
diminución, *f.* diminution, reduction, tapering, lessening.
diminuir, (*ref. 48*) *tr.v., r.v.* to diminish, lessen, reduce; abate; taper.
diminutamente, *adv.* minutely, in smallest measure or quantity, diminutively.
diminutivamente, *adv.* (gram.) diminutively.
diminutivo, va, *a.* diminishing; (gram.) diminutive. —*m.* (gram.) diminutive.
diminuto, ta, *a.* diminutive, small, little, minute. 2. petite. — **submarino diminuto,** midget submarine.
diminuya, diminuyendo, diminuyo, *ref.* **diminuir.**
dimisión, *f.* resignation (of office, membership, etc).
dimisionario, ria, *a.* resigning. —*m., f.* resigner, person resigning (from office, a job, a club, etc.).
dimisorias, *f.* (*pl.*) 1. (ecc.) dimissorials, dimissory letters. 2. sudden or unceremonious mismissal, discharge, firing.
dimitente, *a.* resigning. —*m., f.* resigner, person resigning (from a job, a club, etc.).
dimitir, *tr.v.* to resign, give up, relinquish.
dimorfismo, *m.* (min.) dimorphism.
dimorfo, fa, *a.* (min.) dimorphic, dimorphous.
din, *m.* (coll.) dough, money, cash.
dina, *f.* (phys.) dyne.
dinacho, *m.* (bot., Chile) gunnera (Gunnera chilensis).
Dinamarca, *f.* Denmark.
dinamarqués, sa, *a.* Danish. —*m., f.* Dane. —*m.* Danish (language).
dinámetro, *m.* (opt.) dynameter.
dinamia, *f.* (mec.) kilogram-meter, unit of energy expended to raise one kilogram through one meter.
dinámica, *f.* (mec.) dynamics.
dinámico, ca, *a.* 1. (phys.) dynamic. 2. dynamic, energetic, vigorous, forceful.
dinamismo, *m.* 1. dynamism. 2. the quality of being energetic, vigorous, forceful.
dinamista, *a.* dynamistic. —*m., f.* dynamist.
dinamita, *f.* dynamite.
dinamitar, *tr.v.* to dynamite, to blast.
dinamitazo, *m.* explosion, dynamite blast.
dinamitero, ra, *m., f.* dynamiter.
dínamo, *f.* (phys.) dynamo; **d. motor,** motor generator.
dinamoeléctrico, ca, *a.* dynamoelectric, dynamoelectrical.
dinamometría, *f.* dynamometry.
dinamométrico, ca, *a.* dynamometric, dynamometrical.
dinamómetro, *m.* (mec.) dynamometer.
dinamotor, *m.* (elec.) dynamotor.
dinar, *m.* (numis.) dinar, monetary unit of Yugoslavia and several nations in N. Africa and the Middle East.
dinasta, *m.* dynast, sovereign, monarch.
dinastía, *f.* dynasty, sovereignty.
dinástico, ca, *a.* dynastic, dynastical.
dinastismo, *m.* adherence or loyalty to a dynasty.
dinastrón, *m.* (elec.) dynatron.
dinerada, *f.* 1. fortune, large sum of money. 2. an old silver coin.
dineral, *m.* 1. fortune, great sum of money. 2. set of weights for checking the weight of coins. — **d. de quilates,** set of weights used by jewelers for valuing pearls and precious stones.
dinerillo, *m.* 1. copper coin (used formerly). 2. (coll.) small quantity of money, e.g. *yo tengo mis dinerillos,* I have my (small) savings.
dinero, *m.* 1. money; wealth, fortune. 2. silver and copper coin (used in Castille in the 16th century); ancient Peruvian silver coin; penny. 3. weight of 1.20 grams (used for silver). — **botar d.,** to squander, misspend money; **d. al contado,** ready cash, ready money; **d. caliente,** hot (illegal) money; **d. contante y sonante,** ready cash, ready money; **d. de bolsillo,** pocket money; **d. efectivo** or **en efectivo,** cash; **d. llama d.,** money makes money; **d. negro** or **sucio,** undeclared income; **d. suelto,** small change; **hacer d.,** (coll.) to make money; **los dineros del sacristán cantando se vienen y cantando se van,** easy come, easy go; **persona de d.,** rich person, person of means; **poderoso caballero es Don D.,** money is powerful.
dineroso, sa, *a.* rich, moneyed, wealthy.
dineruelo, *m. dim. of* **dinero,** small coin, change, copper.
dingo, *m.* dingo, Australian dog.
dingolondango, *m.* (coll.) caressing, petting, spoiling; **hacer dingolondangos,** to pet, spoil; to caress.
dinodo, *m.* (rad.) dynode, electron mirror.
dinoflagelado, *m.* (biol.) dinoflagellate, (*pl.*) Dinoflagellata.
dinornis, *m.* (paleon.) dinornis.
dinosaurio, *m.* (paleon.) dinosaur.
dinoterio, *m.* (paleon.) dinothere, dinotherium.
dintel, *m.* (archit.) lintel; (imp. u.) threshold.
dintelar, *tr.v.* to build a lintel on, provide with a lintel; to build in the shape of a lintel.

dintorno, *m.* (archit., p.) outline, delineation.
dió, diste, *ref.* **dar.**
diocesano, na, *a., m.* diocesan, pertaining to a diocese.
diócesi, diócesis, *f.* (ecc.) diocese.
diodo, *m.* (rad.) diode.
Diógenes, *m.* Diogenes, cynic philosopher of Athens.
Diomedes, *m.* (myth.) Diomedes, Greek warrior who helped steal the statue of Athena.
dionea, *f.* (bot.) Venus Venus' flytrap.
dionisia, *f.* (min.) bloodstone, dionise (kind of precious stone, reputed to prevent drunkenness when dissolved in water).
dionisíacas, *f.* (*pl.*) Dionysia, Greek festivals in honor of Dionysius, from which Greek drama originated.
dionisíaco, ca, *a.* Dionysiac, Dionysian, pertaining to Dionysius or Bacchus.
Dionisio, *m.* Dionysius; **D. el Exiguo, D. el Menor,** Dionysius Exiguus; **D. el Areopagita,** Dionysius the Areopagite.
Dionisos, *m.* (myth.) Dionysius, Greek god of wine and revelry (Bacchus in Roman mythology).
diópsido, *m.* (min.) diopside.
dioptasa, *f.* (min.) dioptase.
dioptómetro, *m.* (opt.) dioptometer.
dioptra, *f.* (opt.) diopter, alidade; sight (of a quadrant, etc.).
dioptría, *f.* (opt.) diopter, unit used to measure the strength of a lens.
dióptrica, *f.* (opt.) dioptrics, part of optics dealing with refractive power.
dióptrico, ca, *a.* (opt.) dioptric, dioptrical; refractive.
diorama, *m.* (p.) diorama.
diorámico, ca, *a.* (p.) dioramic.
diorita, *f.* (geol.) diorite.
Dios, *m.* God; **d.,** god; idol; **D. Hombre,** (theol.) Jesus Christ; **¡a d.!** good-bye!; **¡a D. mi dinero!,** (coll.) another thing gone down the drain (i.e. lost); **a la buena de D.,** (coll.) without any preparations or provisions; haphazardly; **a la de D. es Cristo,** (to do a thing) haphazardly without thinking; **¡anda con D.!** God be with you, farewell; **¡auí de D.!** so help me God; may God be my witness¡; **¡bendito sea D.!** my God! it's God's will; **clamar a D.,** (fig.) to cry out to the skies (a manifest injustice or mistake); **como D. le da a uno a entender,** as well as possible, to the best of one's ability; **como D. manda,** as it should be; **de D.,** (coll.) abundantly; **dejar D. de su mano a uno,** to go completely off one's rocker, to lose one's senses (fig.); **de menos nos hizo D.,** however bad or impossible it may seem (we must not abandon hope of achieving our object); **digan, que de D. dijeron,** (coll.) let them say what they please, I don't care; **D. aprieta pero no ahoga,** don't give up hope, God will save you in the end; **D. da el frío según la ropa,** God helps according to one's needs; **D. dirá,** God will decide; **D. los cría y ellos se juntan,** (coll.) birds of a feather flock together; **D. mediante,** God willing; **¡D. mío!** goodness gracious!; **a D. rogando y con el mazo dando,** while you pray for a miracle do what you can to help yourself; **D. sabe,** goodness only knows, only God knows; **D. te ayude,** bless you; **D. y ayuda,** (coll.) (to need) God and all his angels; **estar con D.,** to be in Heaven; **irse uno con D.,** to leave, take one's leave; to go off angrily; **la de D. es Cristo,** quarrel, dispute; shindy, rumpus, uproar; **llamar D. a uno por un camino,** (coll.) to have a vocation for something; **recibir uno a D.,** to take Holy Communion; **tener D. a uno de su mano,** to be under God's care or protection; **¡válgame D.!** goodness gracious me! (in surprise and displeasure); God preserve me; **vaya con D.,** good-bye, may God go with you; **¡vaya por D.!** it's God's will; **vaya usted con D.,** (iron.) get away with you, no thank you very much (rejecting something); **venga D. y véalo,** God is my witness; **venir D. a ver a uno,** to have a windfall or unexpected piece of luck; **¡voto a D.!** oh God! my God!
diosa, *f.* goddess.
dioscóreo, a, *a.* (bot.) dioscoreaceous. *—f.* (*pl.*) (bot.) Dioscoreaceae.
diostedé, *m.* (ornith., S. Amer.) kind of toucan (Rhanphastos ariel).
diotelismo, *m.* (theol.) Dyothelism.
dióxido, *m.* (chem.) dioxide; **d. carbónico,** carbon dioxide; **d. de titanio,** titanium dioxide.
dipétalo, la, *a.* (bot.) dipetalous, having two petals.
diplejía, *f.* (med.) diplegia.
diplobácilo, *m.* (med.) diplobacillus.
diploblástico, ca, *a.* (biol.) diploblastic.
diplodoco, *m.* (zool.) diplodocus.
diploe, *m.* (anat.) diploe.
diploico, ca, *a.* (anat.) diploic.
diploide, *a.* (biol.) diploid.
diploma, *m.* diploma, charter, certificate; bull, license, title.
diplomacia, *f.* 1. diplomacy (conducting of negotiations between countries). 2. diplomacy, tact. 3. diplomatic service, foreign service, e.g. *entrar en la d.,* to enter the diplomatic service. — **d. del dólar,** dollar diplomacy.
diplomado, da, *a.* (Gal.) having a diploma, having an academic degree.
diplomar, *tr.v.* to give a diploma to. *—r.v.* to receive a diploma; to graduate.
diplómata, *m.* (imp. u.) diplomat.
diplomáticamente, *adv.* diplomatically.
diplomático, ca, *a.* diplomatic; tactful. *—m.,f.* diplomat. *—f.* diplomatics, branch of paleography dealing with documents, charters, bulls, diplomas, etc.; diplomatics, diplomacy.
diplopía, *f.* (med.) diplopia (double vision).
diplópodo, da, *a.* (zool.) diplopodous. *—m.* diplopod; (*pl.*) Diplopoda.
dipneo, a, *a.* (zool.) dipneumonous; having two respiratory organs; Dipnoan.
dipodia, *f.* dipody, measure consisting of two metrical feet.
dipolar, *a.* (phys.) dipolar, having two poles.
dipolo, *m.* (phys., chem., rad.) dipole.
dipsáceo, a, *a.* (bot.) dipsacaceous. *—f.* (bot.) dipsacaceous plant; (*pl.*) (bot.) Dipsacaceae.
dipsomanía, *f.* dipsomania, alcoholism.
dipsomaníaco, ca, *a., m., f.* dipsomaniac, alcoholic.
dipsómano, na, *a., m., f., var. of* **dipsomaníaco.**
díptero, ra, *a.* (archit.) dipteral, with a double peristyle or colonnade; (sculp.) having two wings; (zool.) dipterous, two-winged. *—m.* (ento.) dipteron; (*pl.*) (ento.) Diptera.
dipterocárpeo, a, *a.* (bot.) dipterocarpaceous. *—f.* (bot.) dipterocarp, any plant of the genus Diptorocarpaceae; (*pl.*) (bot.) Dipterocarpaceae.
díptico, ca, *m., f.* 1. diptych, two-leaved writing tablet (*gen. pl.*). 2. diptych, picture or series of pictures painted on two hinged tablets.
diptongación, *f.* (gram.) diphthongization.
diptongar, (*ref. 51*) *tr.v.* (gram.) to diphthongize.
diptongo, *m.* (gram.) diphthong.
diptongue, diptongué, *ref.* **diptongar.**
diputación, *f.* 1. deputation, delegation, committee. 2. post of congressman (U.S.), Member of Parliament (G.B.), or of the Spanish Cortes.
diputado, da, *past part. of* **diputar.** *—m., f.* representative, delegate, deputy; congressman, congresswoman (U.S.); member of parliament (G.B.); **d. a Cortes,** congressman, member of the Spanish Parliament; **d. provincial,** district deputy.
diputador, ra, *a., m., f.* constituent.
diputar, *tr.v.* to deputize, appoint as one's representative; to assign; to designate, empower, delegate.
dique, *m.* 1. dike, dam; mound, bank. 2. jetty, dock. 3. (fig.) check, barrier. 4. (geol.) dike, outcrop of sterile rock. — **d. de carena,** dry dock; **d. de contención,** dam dike; **d. de marea,** wet dock; **d. de retardo,** (hydr.) current retard; **d. flotante,** floating dock; **d. seco,** dry dock.
dirceo, a, *a.* (hist., lit.) Theban, of Thebes (Egypt).
diré, diría, *ref.* **decir.**
dirección, *f.* 1. direction, management, managing. 2. direction, course, route, way; trend, tendency. 3. guidance, direction; instruction; command. 4. board of directors, management. 5. directorship, post of manager or director; director's or manager's office. 6. address (of domicile, etc.). 7. (geol.) strike. 8. (auto.) steering; steering gear or mechanism. — **d. de tiro,** (mar., mil.) fire control; **d. general,** head office, headquarters; inertial guidance; **d. postal,** post-office address; **d. equivocada,** wrong address.
directamente, *adv.* directly, in a straight manner, line or direction, e.g. *vete d. a casa,* go straight home.
directivo, va, *a.* directive, managing. *—f.* 1. board of directors, management. 2. directive, general instruction.
directo, ta, *a.* direct; straight; straight through (train); (gram.) direct; **transmitir en d.,** (tel.) to broadcast live.
director, ra, *a.* directing, guiding; managing, governing; (geom.) director; **círculo director,** (geom.) director circle; **plano director,** (geom.) director plane, directrix. *—m.* director, manager (of a firm, business); headmaster, principal (of a school); conductor (of an orchestra); editor (of a newspaper); producer (of a play), director (of a film); **d. de escena, d. escénico,** (theat.) stage manager; **d. de fuego,** (mil, mar.) fire controller; **d. espiritual,** spiritual advisor; **d. general,** director general; **d. visitante,** (mus.) guest conductor. *—f.* directress, manageress; headmistress, principal (of a school).
directoral, *a.* directorial.
directorio, ria, *a.* directory, directive, directorial. *—m.* 1. directory (containing addresses etc.). 2. manual, e.g. *d. de navegación,* sailing manual. 3. (ecc.) directory (containing directions for worship). 4. directorate, governing body.
Directorio, *m.* Directory, Directoire; the executive body in the First Republic of France; the neoclassical style of that period.
directriz, (*pl.* **directrices**) *f.* (geom.) directriz. *—a.* (geom.) director.
dirhem, *m.* 1. dirhem, dirham, derham, Arabian silver coin used in the Middles Ages. 2. monetary unit in Morocco.
dirigente, *a.* directing, leading, governing. *—m.* leader; manager; **clase d.,** ruling class.
dirigible, *a., m.* 1. dirigible, manageable. 2. (avia.) dirigible, blimp.
dirigir, (*ref. 62*) *tr.v.* 1. to direct. 2. to manage (a business); to lead, head. 3. to guide (a person) with advice. 4. to steer (a boat), drive (a car). 5. to address, direct (a letter). 6. to dedicate (a work). 7. (mus.) to conduct. — **d. la palabra a,** to address, speak to.

dirigirse, (*ref.* 62) *r.v.* (with a) 1. to go to, make one's way to. 2. to address, speak to; to write to, e.g. *d. a un extraño,* to address (speak or write to) a stranger.
dirigismo, *m.* state control of the economy.
dirija, dirijo, *ref.* **dirigir.**
dirimente, *a.* dissolving, annulling.
dirimible, *a.* annullable, dissolvable.
dirimir, *tr.v.* 1. to dissolve, annul, declare void, e.g. *d. un matrimonio,* to annul a marriage. 2. to settle (a dispute).
disanto, *m. contr. of* **día santo,** church holy day.
disartria, *f.* (med.) dysarthria, difficulty in the articulation of words.
discantar, *tr.v.* 1. to sing, chant. 2. (mus.) to descant, sing in counterpoint or in descant. 3. to compose, recite (verses). 4. (fig.) to comment on.
discante, *m.* 1. small guitar. 2. musical concert, especially of string instruments. 3. (Peru, coll.) folly, craziness.
discantus, *m.* (mus.) descant, counterpoint.
discar, *tr.v.* to dial (a telephone number).
disceptación, *f.* (rare) argument, controversy, dispute, debate; discussion.
disceptar, *i.v.* (rare) to discept, argue, debate.
discernible, *a.* discernible, perceptible.
discernidor, ra, *a.* discerning. —*m., f.* discerner.
discerniente, *a.* discerning; discriminating.
discernimiento, *m.* 1. discernment, perception; judgment. 2. (law) appointment of a guardian; commitment.
discernir, (*ref.* 31) *tr.v.* 1. to distinguish, discern. 2. (law) to appoint (someone) as guardian; trustee, etc.
discierna, discierno, *ref.* **discernir.**
disciplina, *f.* 1. discipline. 2. teaching, instruction. 3. systematic training; rule of conduct; order. 4. scourge, cat-o-nine-tails.
disciplinable, *a.* disciplinable.
disciplinadamente, *adv.* with discipline, with order.
disciplinado, da, *past part. of* **disciplinar.** —*a.* 1. disciplined, trained. 2. (fig.) variegated, streaked (flowers).
disciplinal, *a.* disciplinal, disciplinary.
disciplinante, *m., f.* flagellant, penitent (in religious processions).
disciplinar, *tr.v.* 1. to discipline, subject to discipline, control. 2. to teach, instruct, train. 3. to whip, scourge. —*r.v.* to discipline oneself.
disciplinario, ria, *a.* disciplinary, corrective.
disciplinazo, *m.* whiplash, lash.
discipulado, *m.* 1. discipleship. 2. teaching; instruction. 3. disciples, students, body of disciples.
discipular, *a.* discipular, pertaining to a disciple.
discípulo, la, *m., f.* disciple, pupil, student; disciple, follower (of a doctrine).
disco, *m.* 1. disk, disc. 2. (sport.) discus, quoit. 3. phonograph or gramophone record, disc, record. 4. (astron., bot., anat.) disk, disc. — **d. compacto** or **digital,** compact disc, CD; compact disc player, CD player; **d. cromático,** (opt.) color disk; **d. de arranque,** boot disk; **d. de larga duración,** album, LP; **d. de mando del embrague,** (auto.) clutch-driving disk; **d. de señales,** (ry.) semaphore, signal disc; **d. duro,** hard disk; **d. fijo,** fixed disk; **d. flexible,** or **floppy,** floppy disk; **d. germinativo,** (biol.) germinal disc; **d. motor,** (auto.) driving disk; **d. óptico,** (anat.) optic disk; video disk; **d. rígido,** hard disk; **d. sencillo,** single; **lanzamiento del d.,** throwing the discus; **d. volador,** flying saucer; **poner un d.,** (Amer.) to play a record; (fig.) make a long repetitious speech; **cambia el d.,** (sl.) change the subject.
discóbolo, *m.* (sport.) discobolus, discus thrower.
discófilo, *m.* discophile.
discográfico, ca, *a.* record (e.g. *shop*).
discoidal, *a.* discoidal, discoid, disk-shaped.
discoide, discoideo, a, *a.* (bot.) discoid.
díscolo, la, *a.* wayward, ungovernable, intractable, disobedient.
discoloro, ra, *a.* (bot.) of two or more colors.
disconforme, *a.* disagreeing.
disconformidad, *f.* difference, disparity, nonconformity.
discontinuación, *f.* discontinuance, discontinuation.
discontinuar, (*ref.* 55) *tr.v.* to discontinue, cease.
discontinuidad, *f.* discontinuance.
discontinuo, nua, *a.* discontinuous.
disconvenga, disconvengo, *ref.* **disconvenir.**
disconveniencia, *f.* 1. inconvenience. 2. incongruity.
disconveniente, *a.* 1. inconvenient. 2. incongruous, discordant.
disconvenir, (*ref.* 26) *i.v.* 1. to disagree, differ. 2. not to match; to be dissimilar; to be disproportionate.
disconvine, *ref.* **disconvenir.**
disconviniendo, disconviniera, disconviniense, *ref.* **disconvenir.**
discordancia, *f.* discordance, disagreement, opposition.
discordante, *a.* discordant, disagreeing.
discordar, (*ref.* 33) *i.v.* 1. to differ, disagree. 2. (mus.) to be out of tune.
discorde, *a.* 1. in disagreement, opposed, of different opinions. 2. (mus.) out of tune, discordant, dissonant.
discordia, *f.* 1. discord, disagreement, dissension. 2. (law) variance.
discoteca, *f.* 1. record library; record collection. 2. discothéque. 3. record cabinet. 4. record shop.
discrasia, *f.* (med.) dyscrasia.
discreción, *f.* 1. discretion; tact, good judgment, prudence. 2. sharpness of mind, sagacity. — **a d.,** at one's discretion; optionally; (mil.) unconditionally.
discrecional, *a.* discretionary; optional.
discrecionalmente, *adv.* discretionally; optionally.
discrepancia, *f.* discrepancy; difference, dissent, disagreement.
discrepante, *a.* discrepant, discordant; disagreeing, different.
discrepar, *i.v.* to differ; to disagree; **d. de,** to disagree with.
discretamente, *adv.* discreetly, with prudence.
discretear, *i.v.* to affect discretion.
discreteo, *m.* affected discretion.
discreto, ta, *a.* 1. discreet; prudent, circumspect. 2. moderate; inconspicuous. 3. (med., math.) discrete, composed of distinct parts. 4. (coll.) passable, not bad, fairly good. — **a lo d.,** at one's discretion; discreetly. —*m., f.* adviser, counsellor (to the superior in a religious community).
discretorio, *m.* body of counsellors (in some religious communities); meeting place of counsellors.
discrimen, *m.* 1. difference; discrimination. 2. (rare) hazard, risk, peril.
discriminación, *f.* discrimination.
discriminador, ra, *a.* discriminating, discriminative. —*m., f.* discriminator.
discriminar, *tr.v.* to distinguish, discriminate.
discriminatorio, ria, *a.* (Amer.) discriminatory.
discromía, *f.* (med.) dyschroa, discoloration of the skin.
discuerde, discuerdo, *ref.* **discordar.**
disculpa, *f.* excuse, apology; **pedir disculpas,** to apologize, ask (someone's) pardon.
disculpable, *a.* excusable, pardonable.
disculpablemente, *adv.* excusably, pardonably.
disculpadamente, *adv.* excusably.
disculpar, *tr.v.* to excuse, pardon. —*r.v.* to apologize; **disculparse con (alguien),** to apologize to, make excuses to (someone); **disculparse de (algo),** to apologize for (something).
discurrir, *i.v.* 1. to roam, ramble. 2. to reflect on or ponder; to talk about. —*tr.v.* to invent, devise, think up; to conjecture.
discursante, *a.* discoursing, lecturing. —*m., f.* lecturer, speaker.
discursar, *tr.v.* to discourse on, lecture on.
discursear, *i.v.* (derog., iron.) to make a speech, to harangue.
discursista, *m., f.* windbag, idle talker; (iron.) speechmaker.
discursivo, va, *a.* discursive, reflective, meditative, thoughtful.
discurso, *m.* 1. discourse, speech. 2. (gram.) speech, e.g. *d. directo,* direct speech; *las partes del d.,* the parts of speech. 3. treatise, essay. 4. reasoning power; discourse; (act of) reasoning; meditation. 5. course, flow (of time). — **d. de sobremesa,** after-dinner speech.
discusión, *f.* discussion; argument, dispute; **sin d.,** without question.
discusivo, va, *a.* (med.) resolvent, discussive.
discutible, *a.* debatable, disputable; moot.
discutidor, ra, *a.* argumentative, arguing. —*m., f.* arguer.
discutir, *tr.v.* to discuss; to argue over or about. —*i.v.* to discuss; to argue; **d. sobre,** to discuss; to argue over.
disecable, *a.* dissectible.
disecación, *f., var. of* **disección.**
disecador, *m.* dissector.
disecar, (*ref.* 50) *tr.v.* 1. to dissect, anatomize (a cadaver, etc.). 2. to stuff (dead animals). 3. to preserve and mount (plants) for study.
disección, *f.* 1. dissection, anatomy. 2. preservation and mounting (of plants for study). 3. stuffing (of dead animals).
disecea, *f.* (med.) dysacousia, defective hearing.
disector, *m.* dissector.
diseminación, *f.* dissemination; spreading, scattering.
diseminador, ra, *a.* disseminating, spreading. —*m., f.* disseminator, spreader.
diseminar, *tr.v.* to disseminate, spread. —*r.v.* to scatter, disperse; to spread, become disseminated.
disemínulo, *m.* (bot.) disseminule.
disensión, *f.* dissension, disagreement, discord, strife; dispute, argument.
disenso, *m.* dissent, disagreement; **mutuo d.,** (law) rescission.
disentería, *f.* (med.) dysentery.
disentérico, ca, *a.* dysenteric.
disentimiento, *m.* dissent, disagreement.
disentir, (*ref.* 42) *i.v.* to disagree, differ, dissent; **d. de,** to disagree with.
diseñador, ra, *m., f.* designer (of fashions, etc.); delineator, sketcher.
diseñar, *tr.v.* to design (create); to draw, sketch, outline.
diseño, *m.* 1. design, drawing, sketch. 2. outline, sketch; portrayal, description.
disépalo, la, *a.* (bot.) disepalous, having two sepals or divisions of the calyx.

disepimento, *m.* (paleon.) dissepiment.
diseque, disequé, *ref.* **disecar.**
disertación, *f.* dissertation, discourse, disquisition, speech. 2. essay, thesis, dissertation.
disertador, ra, *a.* disquisitive. —*m., f.* expounder; speaker, discourser.
disertante, *a.* discoursing, expounding. —*m., f.* dissertator, discourser, speaker.
disertar, *i.v.* to discourse, expound; discuss; **d. acerca de,** to discourse on.
diserto, ta, *a.* eloquent, fluent.
disestesia, *f.* (med.) dysesthesia, dysaesthesia, impairment of any of the senses.
disfagia, *f.* (med.) dysphagia, difficulty in swallowing.
disfamación, *f.* defamation, calumny, slander.
disfamar, *tr.v.* to defame, calumniate, slander; to discredit.
disfamatorio, ria, *a.* (rare) defamatory, slanderous.
disfasia, *f.* (med.) dysphasia, impairment or loss of ability to use or understand language.
disfavor, *m.* disfavor, loss of favor; slight, snub, rebuff.
disfonía, *f.* (med.) dysphonia.
disforia, *f.* (psyc.) dysphoria.
disformar, *tr.v., var. of* **deformar.**
disforme, *a.* 1. deformed; shapeless. 2. hideous, ugly. 3. huge, enormous; **error d.,** (fig.) enormous mistake.
disformidad, *f.* 1. deformity; shapelessness. 2. hugeness.
disfrace, disfracé, *ref.* **disfrazar.**
disfraz, (*pl.* **disfraces**) *m.* disguise, fancy dress; costume, mask; (fig.) dissimulation, dissembling; **baile de disfraces,** masked ball.
disfrazar, (*ref. 53*) *tr.v.* to disguise, to cloak, disguise (feeling). —*r.v.* to dress for a masquerade, to disguise oneself.
disfrutar, *tr.v.* to enjoy; to reap the benefits of; to receive (income). —*r.v.* **d. de,** to enjoy; to receive (income). — **d. con,** to enjoy; to have a good time with.
disfrute, *m.* enjoyment (of a benefit); use; benefit.
disfumar, *tr.v., var. of* **esfumar.**
disfumino, *m., var. of* **esfumino.**
disfunción, *f.* (med.) dysfunction.
disgenesia, *f.* (biol.) dysgenesis; dysgenics.
disgregable, *a.* separable.
disgregación, *f.* disintegration; dispersion; separation.
disgregador, ra, *a.* disintegratory. —*m., f.* disintegrator.
disgregante, *a.* disintegrating. —*m., f.* disintegrator.
disgregar, (*ref. 51*) *tr.v.* to break up; to disunite, separate; to disperse (a crowd); to break to pieces. —*r.v.* to disintegrate, break to pieces; to disperse, break up (a crowd).
disgregativo, va, *a.* disintegrating, disintegrative.
disgregue, disgregué, *ref.* **disgregar.**
disgustadamente, *adv.* with displeasure.
disgustado, da, *past part. of* **disgustar.** —*a.* displeased, annoyed, peevish; glum, sad.
disgustar, *tr.v.* to displease, annoy; to dislike, e.g. *me disgusta que vengas,* I dislike your coming. —*r.v.* to be displeased or annoyed; to fall out; **disgustarse con alguien,** to fall out with, to be annoyed or displeased with someone. — **disgustarse de algo,** to get annoyed at something.
disgusto, *m.* 1. annoyance, irritation, vexation, anger. 2. quarrel, disagreement, tiff (coll.) 3. sorrow, chagrin. 4. distastefulness (of food). — **a d., against** one's will, unwillingly.
disgustoso, sa, *a.* unpleasant, disagreeable; annoying, vexatious.
disidencia, *f.* dissidence, disagreement.
disidente, *a.* dissenting. —*m., f.* dissenter, dissident, dissentient.
disidir, *i.v.* to dissent.
disienta, disiento, *ref.* **disentir.**
disílabo, ba, *a.* dissyllabic. —*m.* dissyllable.
disímbolo, la, *a.* (Mex.) dissimilar, unlike, different.
disimetría, *f.* asymmetry.
disimétrico, ca, *a.* asymmetrical.
disímil, *a.* dissimilar, unlike, different.
disimilación, *f.* (phonet.) dissimilation.
disimilar, *tr.v., r.v.* to dissimilate. —*a.* dissimilar.
disimilitud, *f.* dissimilarity, unlikeness, dissimilitude.
disimulable, *a.* excusable, pardonable.
disimulación, *f.* dissimulation, dissembling; pretense.
disimuladamente, *adv.* dissemblingly, furtively, slyly.
disimulado, da, *past part. of* **disimular.** —*a.* hypocritical, underhanded, sly, furtive, dissembling. —*m., f.* dissimulator, dissembler, hypocrite.
disimulador, ra, *a.* dissimulating, simulating, dissembling. —*m., f.* dissimulator, dissembler.
disimular, *tr.v.* 1. to dissemble; to pretend, feign. 2. to mask, disguise, cloak; to cover up, conceal. 3. to pardon, excuse; to tolerate, overlook. —*i.v.* to dissemble.
disimulo, *m.* 1. dissimulation, dissembling, pretense, feigning. 2. tolerance, indulgence.
disintiendo, disintiera, disintiese, disintió, *ref.* **disentir.**
disipable, *a.* dispersable, easily scattered or wasted.
disipación, *f.* 1. dissipation, dispersion, scattering, breaking up. 2. squandering, wasting (of a fortune). 3. (fig.) dissipation, dissoluteness, profligacy, pleasure-seeking.
disipadamente, *adv.* dissolutely, dissipatedly; wastefully.
disipado, da, *past part. of* **disipar.** —*a.* dissipated, pleasure-seeking, dissolute; wasteful, spendthrift. —*m., f.* spendthrift, wastrel; debauchee.
disipador, ra, *a.* prodigal, squandering. —*m., f.* spendthrift, wastrel, squanderer.
disipante, *a.* dissipating; squandering.
disipar, *tr.v.* to dissipate, to disperse, break up, scatter, dispel; to squander, waste, spend recklessly. —*r.v.* 1. to disappear, vanish, evanesce; to evaporate. 2. (fig.) to vanish (a dream, suspicion, etc.).
dislacerar, *tr.v., var. of* **dilacerar.**
dislalia, *f.* (med.) dyslalia, difficulty in articulating.
dislate, *m.* nonsense, absurdity.
dislocación, *f.* dislocation.
dislocadura, *f., var. of* **dislocación.**
dislocar, (*ref. 50*) *tr.v.* to dislocate, put out of joint. —*r.v.* to dislocate (one's arm, etc.); to become dislocated.
disloque, *m.* (coll.) tops, the best, top-notch.
disloque, disloqué, *ref.* **dislocar.**
dismembración, *f., var. of* **desmembración.**
dismenorrea, *f.* (med.) dysmenorrhea.
disminución, *f.* 1. diminution, deduction, decrease. 2. decline, weakening. 3. (archit.) diminution, taper. 4. (vet.) disease in the hooves of cattle. — **ir en d.,** to decline, go into a decline (health, credit).
disminuir, (*ref. 48*) *tr.v.* to diminish, reduce, decrease, lessen. —*r.v., i.v.* to diminish, lessen, dwindle; to grow shorter (the day).
disminuya, disminuyendo, disminuyo, *ref.* **disminuir.**
disnea, *f.* (med.) dyspnea, difficult or labored respiration.
disneico, ca, *a.* (med.) dyspneic, dyspneal.
disociable, *a.* separable, dissociable.
disociación, *f.* dissociation, separation.
disociador, ra, *a.* dissociative; (coll.) disruptive (person).
disociar, *tr.v., r.v.* to dissociate, separate.
disolubilidad, *f.* dissolubility; solubility.
disoluble, *a.* dissoluble.
disolución, *f.* 1. dissolution (of a substance; of a partnership; of government); disintegration, breaking up (of society, a family, etc.); liquidation (of a company). 2. dissoluteness, dissipation. 3. (chem.) solution.
disolutamente, *adv.* dissolutely.
disolutivo, va, *a.* dissolvent.
disoluto, *a.* dissolute, dissipated, licentious, profligate.
disolvente, *a., m.* dissolvent, solvent.
disolver, (*ref. 34*) *tr.v.* 1. to dissolve (a solid, parliament, a marriage). 2. to destroy, break up. 3. to resolve, settle. 4. to liquidate (a company). —*r.v.* 1. to dissolve. 2. to break up.
disón, *m.* (mus.) dissonance, discord.
disonancia, *f.* dissonance, discord; disagreement; (mus.) dissonance.
disonante, *a.* 1. dissonant, discordant; unsuitable. 2. (mus.) dissonant, inharmonious.
disonar, (*ref. 33*) *i.v.* to be out of tune; to be discordant; to disagree.
dísono, na, *a., var. of* **disonante.**
disosmia, *f.* (med.) dyschromatepsia, poor color discrimination.
dispar, *a.* unequal, unlike, different; unmatched.
disparada, *f.* (Amer.) sudden flight, bolting, darting, shooting off; **a la d.,** at full speed; **tomar la d.,** to dash off.
disparadamente, *adv.* suddenly, hastily, precipitously and violently.
disparadero, *m.* trigger. — **poner a uno en el d.,** to drive one to distraction.
disparador, *m.* 1. shooter, firer. 2. trigger. 3. escapement (of a watch). 4. release (of a camera). 5. (mar.) anchor-tripper. — **poner en el d.,** (coll.) to drive to distraction.
disparar, *tr.v.* 1. to shoot, fire. 2. to hurl, let fly, throw with violence. —*i.v.* 1. (coll.) to talk nonsense. 2. (Amer.) to bolt, dart off. 3. (Mex.) to be a big spender, squander money. —*r.v.* 1. to go off (firearm). 2. to bolt, dash off blindly. 3. to become furious, lose one's patience. — **dispararse con,** to fly off the handle at, get furious with.
disparatadamente, *adv.* absurdly, foolishly, nonsensically; blunderingly.
disparatado, da, *past part. of* **disparatar.** —*a.* 1. absurd, foolish, silly, nonsensical, senseless; crazy, wild; mad. 2. (coll.) enormous, tremendous, huge.
disparatador, ra, *a.* wild; foolish, absurd, blundering, nonsensical. —*m., f.* fool, one who talks nonsense.
disparatar, *i.v.* 1. to talk nonsense. 2. to act absurdly, to blunder.
disparate, *m.* 1. foolish remark, (*pl.*) nonsense, balderdash, poppycock, tommyrot. 2. wild, madcap idea or action. 3. (Arg., coll.) enormous amount, exorbitant price. 4. (Ecuad.) insignificant, worthless object.
disparatero, ra, *a.* (Amer.) *var. of* **disparatador.**
disparatorio, *m.* bunch of nonsense; a speech or literary work abounding in absurdities.
disparejo, *a.* uneven; unequal; different, disparate.
disparidad, *f.* disparity, difference, dissimilarity, inequality.

disparo, *m.* 1. shot; discharge. 2. (fig.) absurdity, nonsense, foolishness. — **d. de ensayo,** trial shot.
dispendio, *m.* waste, squandering; excessive expenditure.
dispendiosamente, *adv.* extravagantly, wastefully.
dispendioso, sa, *a.* expensive, costly; extravagant, wasteful.
dispensa, *f.* dispensation, exemption, privilege; certificate of dispensation or exemption.
dispensable, *a.* dispensable; excusable, pardonable.
dispensación, *f.* dispensation; exemption; certificate of dispensation or exemption.
dispensador, ra, *a.* 1. dispensing, exempting; pardoning. 2. distributing. —*m., f.* dispenser; distributor.
dispensar, *tr.v.* 1. to dispense, grant, confer, bestow. 2. to exempt, excuse, e.g. *d. a uno de asistir,* to excuse from attending. 3. to excuse, forgive, pardon, e.g. *dispénseme* or *dispense,* forgive me, pardon me, excuse me. —*r.v.* to excuse oneself (from doing something).
dispensaría, *f.* (Chile, Peru) dispensary.
dispensario, *m.* dispensary; consulting room, clinic.
dispepsia, *f.* (med.) dyspepsia.
dispéptico, ca, *a.* dyspeptic.
dispersar, *tr.v.* 1. to disperse, scatter. 2. (mil.) to put to flight, rout. 3. (mil.) to deploy. —*r.v.* to disperse, scatter, (mil.) to spread out, to deploy.
dispersión, *f.* dispersion; **d. magnética,** (elec.) magnetic leakage; **d. nuclear,** (phys.) nuclear scattering; **d. retrógrada,** (phys.) backscatter, backscattering.
dispersivo, va, *a.* dispersive.
disperso, sa, *a.* 1. spread out, dispersed, scattered. 2. (obs.) unattached (soldier).
displazca, displazco, *ref.* **displacer.**
displicencia, *f.* coolness, indifference, aloofness; faintheartedness, lack of spirit.
displicente, *a.* unpleasant, disagreeable; peevish; indifferent, aloof.
dispondré, dispondría, *ref.* **disponer.**
disponedor, ra, *a.* arranging, disposing. —*m., f.* arranger, disposer.
disponer, (*ref. 15*) *tr.v.* 1. to dispose, arrange. 2. to form up, line up (troops, ships). 3. to give instructions for. 4. to get ready, prepare. —*i.v.* to dispose; **d. de,** to dispose of; to make use of; to have at one's disposal, have, possess; to make one's will on (one's property). —*r.v.* 1. to get ready, prepare oneself; to get ready to die, make one's will. 2. to form up, line up. — **disponerse a marchar,** to get ready to go.
disponga, dispongo, *ref.* **disponer.**
disponibilidad, *f.* availability, amount of money available (*gen. pl.*); availability for service.
disponible, *a.* available, on hand; ready for service, on call.
disposición, *f.* 1. arrangement. 2. disposal. 3. formation, forming up, lining up. 4. aptitude, talent, bent, leaning. 5. state of health. 6. disposition, nature, character. 7. decree, order, decision, resolution. 8. measure, proportion, disposition. 9. (archit.) lay-out. 10. organization (of a literary work). — **a la d. de,** at the disposal of; **estar en d.,** to be ready; **la última d.,** the last will and testament.
dispositivamente, *adv.* dispositively.
dispositivo, va, *a.* dispositive. —*m.* device, contrivance, mechanism, gadget. — **d. alimentador,** feeding device; **d. calibrador,** calibrating device; **d. de lanzamiento,** launcher; **d. de seguridad,** safety device.
disprosio, *m.* (chem.) dysprosium.
dispuesto, ta, *irr. past part. of* **disponer.** —*a.* 1. graceful, spruce, elegant, comely. 2. capable, able, smart. — **bien d.,** well, in good health; favorable, well-disposed; **mal d.,** ill, indisposed; unfavorable, ill-disposed; **estar d. a,** to be ready to, be prepared to.
dispuse, dispusiera, dispusiese, *ref.* **disponer.**
disputa, *f.* dispute, argument, controversy, debate; squabble, quarrel. — **sin d.,** indisputably, indubitably.
disputable, *a.* disputable, debatable, moot.
disputador, ra, *a.* argumentative, disputant. —*m., f.* argumentative person, disputant.
disputante, *a.* disputing, debating; quarreling; contending.
disputar, *tr.v.* 1. to dispute; to debate, discuss; to argue or squabble over. 2. to compete for, contend for. —*i.v.* to argue, quarrel; to debate; **d. acerca de** or **sobre,** to argue about.
disputativamente, *adv.* disputatively, by dispute.
disquería, *f.* record store.
disquero, ra, *a.* disk, record.
disquete, disquette, *m.* diskette, floppy disk.
disquetera, *f.* disk drive.
disquisición, *f.* disquisition.
distancia, *f.* distance; difference; (fig.) disparity. — **d. de enfoque,** (photog.) focal length; **a d.,** at a distance; **acortar las distancias,** to meet halfway; **d. de medio fondo,** middle distance (in athletics); **d. polar,** (astron.) polar distance; **llamada de larga d.,** long distance call.
distanciado, da, *past part. of* **distanciar.** —*a.* 1. left behind. 2. set apart, put at a distance. 3. given an inferior placing due to an infringement (a horse in a race).
distanciamiento, *m.* remoteness.
distanciar, *tr.v.* 1. to put or place at a distance; to separate. 2. (in horse-racing) to award an inferior placing as a penalty for an infringement. —*r.v.* to keep oneself apart (from friends, etc.).
distante, *a.* distant, far, remote; (mar.) off.
distantemente, *adv.* distantly, remotely.
distar, *i.v.* 1. to be a certain distance. 2. to be different. — **d. de,** to be (away) from, e.g. *su casa dista dos cuadras de aquí,* his house is three blocks (away) from here; **dista mucho de ser perfecto,** it is far from being perfect.
distender, (*ref. 30*) *tr.v.* to distend; (med.) to distend, swell. —*i.v.* (med.) to become distended, swollen.
distensible, *a.* (med.) distensible.
distensión, *f.* distension, distention, expansion; **d. internacional,** détente.
dístico, ca, *a.* (bot.) distichous. —*m.* (poet.) distich, couplet.
distienda, distiende, *ref.* **distender.**
distinción, *f.* 1. distinction, elegance, manners. 2. honor, privilege, prerogative. 3. seeing, making out (a far off object). 4. deference, consideration, respect. 5. clarity, clearness. — **a d. de,** unlike, as distinct from, in contrast to.
distinga, distingo, *ref.* **distinguir.**
distingo, *m.* 1. distinction. 2. restriction, qualification.
distinguible, *a.* distinguishable.
distinguido, da, *past part. of* **distinguir.** —*a.* distinguished, prominent, outstanding, famous, illustrious.
distinguir, (*ref. 63*) *tr.v.* 1. to distinguish. 2. to tell or see the difference between. 3. to make out, see (something) in the distance. 4. to characterize. 5. to honor, bestow a distinction on. 6. to favor, show preference for. —*r.v.* to distinguish oneself, excel.
distintamente, *adv.* 1. distinctly. 2. clearly, differently.
distintivo, va, *a.* distinctive, distinguishing, characteristic. —*m.* 1. distinctive or distinguishing mark or feature, characteristic. 2. badge, insignia. 3. colors (of a racing stable).
distinto, ta, *a.* 1. different, distinct, unlike. 2. distinct, clear.
distocia, *f.* (med.) dystocia.
distócico, ca, *a.* (med.) dystocial.
dístomo, *a., m.* (zool.) distomatous.
distorsión, *f.* distortion.
distracción, *f.* 1. distraction. 2. inattentiveness, daydreaming, inattention. 3. diversion, amusement, entertainment; pastime. — **por d.,** through an oversight; as a pastime.
distraer, (*ref. 24*) *tr.v.* 1. to distract (attention), divert (thoughts); to divert from, turn away from. 2. to divert, amuse, entertain, cheer. 3. to lead astray. 4. to embezzle, misappropriate. —*r.v.* 1. to amuse oneself. 2. to alter one's purpose or intention. 3. to let one's mind wander, be inattentive, be distracted.
distraídamente, *adv.* absent-mindedly.
distraído, da, *past part. of* **distraer.** —*a.* 1. absent-minded; inattentive. 2. profligate, dissolute, pleasure-seeking. 3. (Chile, Mex.) ragged, slovenly, dirty. —*m., f.* 1. absent-minded person. 2. rake, libertine, profligate.
distraiga, distraigo, *ref.* **distraer.**
distraimiento, *m., var. of* **distracción.**
distraje, distrajera, distrajese, *ref.* **distraer.**
distrayendo, *ref.* **distraer.**
distribución, *f.* 1. distribution, apportionment, allotment. 2. supply system (network of pipes carrying gas, water or electricity). 3. (print., mec.) distribution. — **d. de tierras,** land distribution.
distribuidor, ra, *a.* distributive, distributing, apportioning. —*m., f.* distributor. —*m.* 1. (auto., tel.) distributor. 2. slide valve (in a steam engine). 3. (agr.) fertilizer spreader. — **d. automático,** slot machine.
distribuir, (*ref. 48*) *tr.v.* 1. to distribute; to apportion, allot, allocate. 2. (print.) to distribute, return type to the type case. —*r.v.* to be distributed.
distributivamente, *adv.* distributively.
distributivo, va, *a.* distributive.
distributor, ra, *a.* distributing. —*m., f.* distributor.
distribuya, distribuyendo, *ref.* **distribuir.**
distribuyente, *a.* distributing, distributive.
distribuyera, distribuyese, distribuyo, *ref.* **distribuir.**
distrito, *m.* district, precinct, ward, region; **d. rojo,** red-light district.
distrofia, *f.* (med., biol.) dystrophy, distrophia.
distrófico, ca, *a.* (med.) dystrophic.
disturbar, *tr.v.* to disturb.
disturbio, *m.* disturbance, commotion.
disuadir, *tr.v.* to dissuade.
disuasión, *f.* dissuasion.
disuasivo, va, *a.* dissuasive.
disuelto, ta, *irr. past part. of* **disolver.**
disuelva, disuelvo, *ref.* **disolver.**
disuena, disuene, *ref.* **disonar.**
disuria, *f.* (med.) dysuria.
disúrico, ca, *a.* (med.) dysuric.
disyunción, *f.* 1. disjunction. 2. (gram.) disjunctive particle.
disyunta, *f.* (mus., obs.) disjunct motion.
disyuntiva, *f.* disjunctive, dilemma, alternative.
disyuntivamente, *adv.* disjunctively; separately.
disyuntivo, va, *a.* disjunctive.

disyuntor, *m.* (elec.) circuit breaker.
dita, *f.* 1. bond, guarantee, surety; guarantor, surety, bondsman, bond (person who guarantees payment). 2. (Chile, C. Amer., Mex.) debt.
ditá, *m.* (bot., Phil. I.) dita (Alstonia scholaris).
ditaína, *f.* ditamine, a febrifuge extracted from the dita bark.
diteísmo, *m.* ditheism, belief in two supreme gods; dualism.
diteísta, *a.* ditheistic. —*m., f.* ditheist.
ditiónico, ca, *a.* (chem.) dithionic.
ditirámbico, ca, *a.* dithyrambic.
ditirambo, *m.* dithyramb; (fig.) exaggerated eulogy.
dítono, *m.* (mus.) ditone.
diuca, *f.* (Arg., Chile, ornith.) variety of finch. —*m.* (Arg., Chile, coll.) teacher's pet, favorite.
diuresis, *f.* (med.) diuresis.
diurético, ca, *m., a.* (med.) diuretic.
diurno, na, *a.* diurnal, daily; (bot.) diurnal. —*m.* (ecc.) diurnal.
diuturnidad, *f.* diuturnity, long duration.
diuturno, na, *a.* lengthy, long, lasting a long time.
diva, *f.* 1. diva, prima donna. 2. (poet.) goddess.
divagación, *f.* wandering, rambling, digression.
divagador, ra, *a.* digressive, wandering. —*m. f.* wanderer, digressor.
divagar, (*ref. 51*) *i.v.* to wander, ramble, digress; to wander, roam.
diván, *m.* 1. divan, turkish council and its assembly hall. 2. divan, low couch. 3. divan, a collection of Oriental or Arab (style) poems by one author.
divergencia, *f.* divergence; disagreement.
divergente, *a.* divergent, diverging.
divergir, (*ref. 62*) *i.v.* to diverge; (fig.) to disagree, differ (opinions, etc.).
diverja, diverjo, *ref.* **divergir.**
diversamente, *adv.* differently.
diversidad, *f.* 1. diversity, difference; dissimilarity. 2. abundance. 3. variety, assortment.
diversificación, *f.* diversification.
diversificar, (*ref. 50*) *tr.v.* to diversify.
diversifique, diversifiqué, *ref.* **diversificar.**
diversiforme, *a.* diversiform.
diversión, *f.* diversion; entertainment, amusement; (mil.) diversion.
diversivo, va, *a.* (med.) divertive.
diverso, sa, *a.* 1. different, distinct, diverse. 2. (*pl.*) various, several, many.
divertículo, *m.* (biol.) diverticulum.
diverticulosis, *f.* (med.) diverticulosis.
divertido, da, *past part. of* **divertir.** —*a.* 1. amusing, diverting, entertaining. 2. merry, gay, funny, good-humored. 3. (Amer.) drunk, lit-up (coll.).
divertimiento, *m.* diversion, amusement; distraction; (mus.) divertimento; (ballet, theat.) divertissement.
divertir, (*ref. 42*) *tr.v.* 1. to divert, distract (attention). 2. to amuse, entertain. 3. (med.) to draw away (a body fluid). 4. (mil.) to divert. —*r.v.* 1. to be diverted or distracted. 2. to amuse or entertain oneself, have a good time.
dividendo, *m.* (math., com.) dividend.
divididero, ra, *a.* divisible.
dividir, *tr.v.* 1. to divide. 2. to split; distribute. 3. (fig.) to separate, disunite (by provoking discord). —*r.v.* to divide; to separate from.
dividiví, (*pl.* **dividivíes**) *m.* (bot.) dividivi.
dividuo, dua, *a.* (law) divisible.
divierta, divierto, *ref.* **divertir.**
divierta, *f.* (Guat., Mex.) a dance or party among simple folk.
divieso, *m.* (med.) boil, furuncle.
divinación, *f., var. of* **adivinación.**
divinal, *a.* (poet.) divine.
divinamente, *adv.* divinely; (fig.) admirably, perfectly.
divinativo, va, *a.* divinatory.
divinatorio, ria, *a.* divinatory; divining, e.g. *una varilla divinatoria,* a divining rod.
divinice, divinicé, *ref.* **divinizar.**
divinidad, *f.* 1. divinity, deity, godhead. 2. heathen deity. 3. god, goddess. 4. very beautiful person or thing.
divinización, *f.* deification; glorification.
divinizar, (*ref. 53*) *tr.v.* 1. to deify. 2. to sanctify, make sacred. 3. (fig.) to glorify, praise excessively.
divino, na, *a.* divine, godlike; (fig.) divine, heavenly, marvelous.
divisa, *f.* 1. (*gen. pl.*) foreign currency. 2. badge, emblem, insignia; (her.) motto. 3. (law) devise. 4. (taur.) owner's colors.
divisar, *tr.v.* 1. to descry, see, perceive. 2. (her.) to vary (an escutcheon) by adding new devices.
divisibilidad, *f.* divisibility.
divisible, *a.* divisible.
división, *f.* 1. division, dividing, distribution. 2. (fig.) division, discord, disagreement. 3. (math., mar., mil., log.) division. 4. dash, hyphen. 5. (rhet.) organized distribution of points under discussion. 6. quarter, section. — **d. administrativa** or **territorial,** administrative region; **d. continental,** (geol.) continental divide; **d. de poderes,** separation of powers.
divisional, *a.* divisional.
divisionario, ria, *a.* divisional; **moneda divisionaria,** currency equivalent to an exact fraction of the legal tender unit.
divisionismo, *m.* (p.) divisionism.
divisivo, va, *a.* divisive.
diviso, sa, *irr. past part. of* **dividir.** —*a.* divided, disunited, split.
divisor, ra, *a.* dividing; (math.) factorial. —*m.* divider; (math.) divisor; factor. — **d. común,** common divisor; **d. de tensión,** (elec.) voltage divider; **máximo d. común,** (math.) greatest common divisor.
divisorio, ria, *a.* dividing, separating. —*f.* (geol.) divide. —*m.* (print.) copyholder.
divo, va, *a.* 1. (poet.) divine. 2. leading (opera singer). —*m.* god, deity. —*m., f.* leading singer (in opera). —*f.* goddess.
divorciar, *tr.v.* to divorce; to separate. —*r.v.* to get divorced, divorce.
divorcio, *m.* 1. divorce; separation. 2. (Col.) women's jail.
divulgable, *a.* disclosable, revealable.
divulgación, *f.* disclosure, revelation; publication, spreading (of news, information, etc.).
divulgador, ra, *a.* disclosing, revealing. —*m., f.* discloser, revealer, divulger.
divulgar, (*ref. 51*) *tr.v.* to divulge, make known, reveal, disclose. —*r.v.* to become known.
divulgue, divulgué, *ref.* **divulgar.**
diyambo, *m.* (poet.) diiamb.
diz, *contr. of* **dice** or **dícese,** it is said, or they say.
dizque, *contr. of* **dicen que,** they say that. —*m.* rumor. —*a.* supposed. —*adv.* supposedly.
dl. *abbrev. of* **decilitro,** deciliter (dl.).
Dl. *abbrev. of* **decalitro,** decaliter (dkl.)
dm. *abbrev. of* **decímetro,** decimeter (dm.).
Dm. *abbrev. of* **decámetro,** decameter (dkm.).
Dm. *abbrev. of* **Dios mediante,** God willing.
do, *m.* (mus.) do, first note in diatonic scale; **d. de pecho,** highest note reached by a tenor voice; (coll.) supreme effort (made to achieve something).
do, *adv.* (poet.) *var. of* **donde.**
dobla, *f.* 1. old Spanish coin (worth 10 pesetas). 2. (coll.) doubling (of stake). 3. (Chile, min.) right to one day's free mining. 4. (Chile, coll.) free meal, free share.
dobladamente, *adv.* 1. doubly. 2. underhandedly, deceitfully.
dobladas, *f.* (*pl.*) (Cuba) death knell.
dobladilla, *f.* an old card game; **a la d.,** doubly, repeatedly.
dobladillar, *tr.v.* to hem, put a hem or border on.
dobladillo, *m.* 1. hem, border. 2. strong yarn used for knitting hose or socks.
doblado, da, *past part. of* **doblar.** —*a.* 1. bent. 2. two-faced, underhanded, double-dealing. 3. short and stocky, thickset (person). 4. uneven, broken (land). — **d. al fuego** or **en caliente,** heat-bent; **d. en frío,** (tech.) bent cold. —*m.* (tex.) measure of the fold.
doblador, *m.* 1. doubler, bender, folder. 2. (rad.) doubler. 3. (Guat.) corn husk (used to roll tobacco into cigarettes).
dobladura, *f.* 1. fold; crease. 2. reserve horse (taken along by cavalrymen).
doblaje, *m.* dubbing (of film).
doblamiento, *m.* doubling; bending; folding.
doblar, *tr.v.* 1. to double. 2. to fold. 3. to bend. 4. to turn (a corner); to pass the top of (a hill); (mar.) to double, round (a cape). 5. (cine.) to dub (a motion picture). 6. to persuade (someone) to change his mind. 7. to cause great sorrow or sadness to. 8. to knock (an opponent's ball) to the other end of the table (in billiards). 9. to irrigate twice. 10. (com.) to postpone (a stock market transaction). 11. (Mex., coll.) to shoot down. —*i.v.* 1. to fold. 2. to toll, ring (bells). 3. to yield, give in. 4. (theat.) to double, play two roles. 5. to celebrate mass twice (in one day). 6. (taur.) to collapse, fall down dead (bull). —*r.v.* 1. to fold. 2. to bend, bend down. 3. to yield, give in. 4. to become uneven and broken (land). — **se dobló de risa,** he doubled up with laughter.
doble, *a.* 1. double; twofold, duplicate. 2. thick, heavy (cloth). 3. thickset, stocky. 4. (chem.) binary. 5. two-faced, underhanded, double-dealing. —*m.* 1. double. 2. tolling, death knell. 3. fold, crease. 4. step in a Spanish dance. 5. (com.) short term stock market operation and money earned or lost in it. 6. (com.) extension of maturity date and money paid for this extension. 7. double, stand in (in a play or film). 8. (mas.) second row of tiles. — **a tres dobles y un repique,** (Amer.) broke, down and out, penniless; **d. agente,** double agent; **d. barba,** (coll.) double chin; **d. contabilidad,** double-entry bookkeeping; **d. fondo,** false bottom; **d. juego,** double dealing; **d. nacionalidad,** dual nationality; **d. personalidad,** split personality; **d. tracción,** four-wheel drive; **d. ve** or **d. u** letter **W; d. escuadra,** T square; **d. I, I beam;** cross. —*adv.* doubly; **al d.,** doubly.
doblegable, *a.* pliant, malleable, easily folded.
doblegadizo, za, *a.* pliant, flexible.
doblegar, (*ref. 51*) *tr.v.* 1. to bend, flex. 2. to brandish. 3. to make or force (someone) to change his mind or behavior; to subject or bend to one's will. —*r.v.* 1. to bend. 2. to yield, give in, change one's mind or behavior.
doblegue, doblegué, *ref.* **doblegar.**
doblemano, *f.* (mus.) mechanism in an organ.
doblemente, *adv.* 1. doubly. 2. underhandedly, deceitfully.
doblero, *m.* 1. (carp.) piece of wood or timber. 2. (Sp.) old Mallorcan coin.
doblete, *a.* of medium thickness (cloth). —*m.* 1. doublet, imitation gem. 2. (philol.) doublet. 3. stroke in a game of billiards.
doblez, (*pl.* **dobleces**) *m.* 1. fold; crease. 2. duplicity, double-dealing, underhandedness.
doblilla, *f.* old Spanish gold coin.

doblón, *m.* doubloon; **d. de a ocho,** piece of eight; **d. de oro,** doubloon; **d. de vaca,** tripe; **escupir doblones,** (coll.) to make a show of one's wealth, throw one's money about.
doblonada, *f.* fortune, large sum of money; **echar doblanadas,** to exaggerate one's wealth.
doc. *abbrev. of* **docena,** dozen (doz., dz.),
doca, *f.* (bot.) fig marigold (Mesembrianthenum equilaterale).
doce, *a.* twelve; twelfth. —*m.* twelve; twelfth (in dates). —*f.* **las doce,** twelve o'clock.
doceañista, *a., m., f.* (hist.) partisan of the Spanish Constitution of 1812.
docena, *f.* dozen. — **d. del fraile,** baker's dozen; **meterse uno en d. con otros,** (coll.) to butt into a conversation conducted by one's superiors; **no entrar uno en d. con otros,** to be diffferent from others; **por d.,** by the dozen.
docenal, *a.* able to be divided in or sold by the dozen.
docenario, ria, *a.* composed of twelve, containing one dozen units.
docencia, *f.* teaching, instruction.
doceno, na, *a.* twelfth; made of twelve hundred threads (cloth).
docente, *a.* teaching; of education, educational; **personal d.,** teaching staff; **centros docentes,** centers of education.
doceta, *a.* (philos., relig.) Docetic. —*m., f.* Docetist.
docetismo, *m.* (philos., relig.) Docetism.
docientos, *a., var. of* **doscientos,** two- hundred.
dócil, *a.* 1. docile, tractable, obedient. 2. ductile, flexible, malleable (metal), easily worked (stone).
docilidad, *f.* docility, flexibility.
docilitar, *tr.v.* to make docile, tame or tractable; to make malleable or ductile. —*r.v.* to become docile, tractable or malleable.
dócilmente, *adv.* docilely, with docility; obediently.
docimasia, docimástica, *f.* (min., med.) docimasy.
docimástico, ca, *a.* docimastic, docimastical.
dock, *m.* 1. (Amer.) dock, quay, wharf. 2. storehouse, warehouse.
Doct. *abbrev. of* **Doctor,** Doctor (Dr.).
doctamente, *adv.* learnedly, eruditely.
doctitud, *f.* (obs.) erudition.
docto, ta, *a.* learned, erudite, expert.
doctor, ra, *m., f.* 1. (coll.) physician. 2. academician, holder of a doctor's degree; professor. 3. (Amer.) title given to lawyers and magistrates. —*f.* (coll.) doctor's wife; bluestocking, erudite woman.
doctorado, *m.* doctorate, studies required for a doctorate; complete knowledge (of a certain subject).
doctoral, *a.* doctoral.
doctoramiento, *m.* the act of conferring or receiving a doctor's degree.
doctorando, da, *m., f.* person close to receiving a doctor's degree.
doctorar, *tr.v.* to confer a doctor's degree on. —*r.v.* to receive a doctor's degree.
doctrina, *f.* 1. doctrine, teaching. 2. knowledge, learning. 3. sermon preaching the gospel. 4. (Amer.) collative curateship. 5. (Amer., hist.) Indian community converted to Christianity but lacking a parish.
doctrinador, ra, *a.* teaching, instructing. —*m., f.* teacher, instructor.
doctrinal, *a.* doctrinal. —*m.* book of doctrines or rules; catechism.
doctrinante, *a.* teaching, instructing.
doctrinar, *tr.v.* to teach, instruct.
doctrinario, ria, *a.* doctrinarian; doctrinal. —*m., f.* doctrinaire.
doctrinarismo, *m.* (pol.) doctrinairism.
doctrinero, *m.* 1. one who teaches the Christian doctrine. 2. (Amer., hist.) priest in charge of an Indian parish.
doctrino, *m.* orphan studying under a charity grant.
documentación, *f.* documentation; documents.
documentado, da, *past part. of* **documentar.** —*a.* 1. well documented, possessing the required documents. 2. well read, well informed; versed in a certain subject.
documental, *a.* documental. —*m.* (cine.) documentary.
documentalmente, *adv.* documentally, with the required documents.
documentar, *tr.v.* 1. to prove with documents, document. 2. to inform about. —*r.v.* to inform oneself about something.
documento, *m.* document; **d. a la vista,** sight bill or draft; **d. comercial,** commercial paper.
dodecaedro, *m.* (geom.) dodecahedron.
dodecafónico, ca, *a.* (mus.) dodecaphonic, twelve-tone.
dodecafonismo, *m.* (mus.) dodecaphonism.
dodecágono, na, *a.* (geom.) dodecagonal. —*m.* (geom.) dodecagon.
Dodecaneso, *m.* Dodecanese, group of twelve Greek islands in the Aegean (capital Rhodes).
dodecasílabo, ba, *a., m.* dodecasyllabic.
dodrante, *m.* (hist.) three quarters of a Roman inheritance.
dogal, *m.* halter rope; noose, hangman's rope; slipknot; **estar con el d. a la garganta,** (coll.) to be in a tight spot, have a sword hanging over one's head, have one's neck in a noose.
dogaresa, *f.* (Ital., hist.) doge's wife.
dogma, *m.* (pol., philos., relig.) dogma.
dogmáticamente, *adv.* dogmatically.
dogmatice, dogmaticé, *ref.* **dogmatizar.**
dogmático, ca, *a.* dogmatic. —*m.* (philos.) philosopher of dogmatic school of philosophy.
dogmatismo, *m.* (philos., relig.) dogmatism; dogma, doctrines (of a religion).
dogmatista, *m.* dogmatist, propounder of new doctrines.
dogmatizador, *m., var. of* **dogmatizante.**
dogmatizante, *a.* dogmatizing. —*m., f.* dogmatizer; dogmatist, propounder of new doctrines.
dogmatizar, (*ref. 53*) *tr.v.* to teach or propound as dogma; to affirm dogmatically. —*i.v.* to dogmatize.
dogo, ga, *m., f.* bulldog (dog).
dogre, *m.* (mar.) dogger, ketch-like fishing boat.
doladera, *a.* cooper's (adze). —*f.* cooper's adze.
dolador, *m.* stonecutter; hewer (of wood).
doladura, *f.* shavings, splinters (of wood); chips (of stone).
dolaje, *m.* wine absorbed by a vat.
dolamas, *f.* (*pl.*) aches, pains; (vet.) hidden pains (of horses).
dolames, *m.* (*pl.*) (vet.) hidden pains (of horses).
dolar, (*ref. 33*) *tr.v.* to hew (wood); to cut (stone).
dólar, *m.* dollar, U.S. monetary unit.
dolce, *a.* (mus.) dolce.
dolencia, *f.* ache, pain; illness, disease, ailment.
doler, (*ref. 34*) *i.v.* to hurt, ache; to pain, grieve; **me duele la cabeza,** my head aches, I have a headache. —*r.v.* to repent, be sorry; to regret, be distressed; to sympathize, pity; to complain, whine; **ahí duele** or **le duele,** (coll.) you have hit the nail on the head, that is the weak spot; **dolerse de sus pecados,** to repent for one's sins; **dolerse de su propia ignorancia,** to be distressed at one's own ignorance; **dolerse de su situación,** to sympathize with someone's situation; **no dolerle a uno prendas,** (coll.) to be generous, be open-handed.
dolerita, *f.* (min.) dolerite.
dolicocefalia, *f.* (anth.) dolichocephaly.
dolicocefálico, ca, *a.* (anth.) dolichocephalic.
dolicocéfalo, la, *a.* dolichocephalic, dolichocephalous.
doliente, *a.* 1. ailing, sick, ill. 2. sorrowful, sad, afflicted. —*m.* 1. mourner. 2. sick person.
dolmán, *m.* dolman, military jacket.
dolmen, *m.* (archeol.) dolmen, cromlech.
dolménico, ca, *a.* (archeol.) dolmenic.
dolo, *m.* 1. fraud, deception, deceit; (law) dolus, fraud. 2. (law) premeditation, intent. — **d. bueno,** (law) dolus bonus, justifiable deceit; **d. malo,** (law) dolus malus, fraud.
dolobre, *m.* stone hammer.
dolomía, *f.* (min.) dolomite.
dolomita, *f., var. of* **dolomía.**
Dolomitas, *f.* (*pl.*) Dolomites, a division of the E. Alps (N. Italy).
dolomítico, ca, *a.* (geol.) dolomitic.
dolor, *m.* 1. pain, ache. 2. grief; sadness, sorrow. 3. contrition, regret. — **d. de cabeza,** headache; **d. de corazón,** (fig.) contrition, sorrow for sins committed; **d. de viudo** or **viuda,** (coll.) quick sharp pain; **d. sordo,** dull nagging pain; **estar con dolores,** to be in labor; **dolores del parto,** labor pains.
dolora, *f.* (poet.) short, dramatic poem of philosophical content (a genre created by the popular Spanish poet, Ramón Campoamor).
dolorido, da, *a.* painful, sore, aching; pained, anguishing, grieved. —*m.* (obs.) chief mourner.
Dolorosa, *f.* (ecc.) an image of Our Lady of Sorrows; (fig., Sp.) a beautiful but grieving woman.
dolorosamente, *adv.* painfully; regrettably, lamentably.
doloroso, sa, *a.* painful, pitiful, moving.
dolosamente, *adv.* deceptively, deceitfully; (law) fraudulently.
doloso, sa, *a.* deceptive, deceitful, fraudulent.
dom, *m.* (ecc.) dom, title of respect given to Carthusian and Benedictine monks.
dom. *abbrev. of* **domingo,** Sunday (Sun.).
doma, *f.* taming, breaking-in (of horse); (fig.) control, repression (of passions, etc.).
domable, *a.* tamable; controllable; conquerable.
domador, ra, *m., f.* tamer, one who tames wild beast (in a circus); horsebreaker, bronco buster; **d. de leones,** lion tamer; **d. de fieras,** tamer of wild beasts.
domadura, *f.* taming (wild animals); breaking-in (of horses).
domar, *tr.v.* to tame (wild animals); to break in (horses); (fig.) to tame, overcome, control, conquer, master.
dombo, *m.* (archit.) dome, cupola.
domellar, *tr.v., var. of* **domeñar.**
domeñable, *a.* tamable, subduable; tractable.
domeñar, *tr.v.* to tame; to subdue, master.
domesticable, *a.* tameable, capable of domestication.
domesticación, *f.* domestication.
domesticar, (*ref. 50*) *tr.v.* 1. to tame, domesticate (wild animals), break in (horses). 2. (fig.) to educate, make gentle, refine (a person). —*r.v.* to become tame, refined or well-mannered.
domesticidad, *f.* domesticity.
doméstico, ca, *a.* domestic, pertaining to the home or homeland. —*m., f.* dometic, household servant.
domestique, domestiqué, *ref.* **domesticar.**
domestiquez, domestiqueza, *f.* (rare) tameness.

domiciliar, *tr.v.* 1. to domicile. 2. (Mex.) to address (a letter). —*r.v.* to settle, dwell, take up residence.
domiciliario, ria, *a.* domiciliary; carried out or given in the home. —*m., f.* resident, tenant.
domicilio, *m.* domicile; residence, house, home; **a d.,** delivered to the house or home; in the house or home (said of services, etc.); **adquirir** or **contraer d.,** to settle, take up residence; **d. social,** (law, com.) corporate domicile or premises.
dominación, *f.* 1. domination; dominion, authority, power, rule. 2. (mil.) commanding position or ground. 3. (*pl.*) (theol.) dominations, fourth choir of angels.
dominador, ra, *a.* dominating; domineering, overbearing. —*m., f.* dominator; domineering person.
dominante, *a.* 1. domineering, dominating, overbearing, dictatorial. 2. dominant, prevailing, chief; principal; (astrol.) dominant. —*f.* (mus.) dominant, fifth note of the scale.
dominar, *tr.v.* 1. to dominate; to rule, have sway over. 2. to master, control, repress (passions). 3. to have or acquire a thorough knowledge of, master (science or art). —*i.v.* to stand out above (a mountain, tall building, etc.). —*r.v.* to control oneself. — **d. las pasiones,** to control one's passions; **d. un idioma,** to know a language thoroughly; **d. el panorama,** to stand out above the surroundings.
dominativo, va, *a., var. of* **dominante.**
dominatriz, (*pl.* **dominatrices**) *a.* (rare), *var. of* **dominadora.**
dómine, *m.* (coll.) dominie, teacher of Latin grammar; (derog.) pompous pedant.
domingada, *f.* party or festival taking place on a Sunday.
domingo, *m.* Sunday; **d. de Adviento,** Advent Sunday; **d. de Cuasimodo,** Quasimodo, Low Sunday; **d. de Pascua** or **Resurrección,** Easter Sunday; **d. de Pentescostés,** Whitsunday, Pentecost; **d. de Piñata,** first Sunday of Lent; **d. de Ramos,** Palm Sunday; **d. de Resurrección,** Easter Sunday; **guardar el d.,** to keep the Sabbath; **hacer d.,** to take a holiday; **salir con un** or **su d. siete,** to make a silly or uncalled-for remark; **ser (algo) un d. siete** or **Juan Domingo siete,** (Arg.) to bring unexpected disaster to a business or undertaking.
dominguejo, *m.* 1. *var. of* **dominguillo.** 2. (Chile, Peru, Ven.) a nobody. 3. (Chile, Peru, arch.) scarecrow.
dominguero, ra, *a.* pertaining to Sunday (clothes).
dominguillo, *m.* roly-poly, tumbler, schmo, weighted doll; **traer a uno como** or **hecho un d.,** to boss or order one about.
domínica, *f.* (ecc.) Sunday; Gospel, Epistle, etc. corresponding to each Sunday.
dominical, *a.* 1. dominical, pertaining to Sunday. 2. feudal (tax). 3. proprietary (rights). —*f.* Sunday function at a university.
dominicano, na, *a.* 1. Dominican (priest). 2. Dominican, of or pertaining to the Dominican Republic. —*m., f.* Dominican, native of the Dominican Republic.
dominico, ca, *a.* Dominican, of the Dominican Order. —*m.* Dominican (priest).
domínico, *a.* (Amer., imp. u.), *var. of* **dominico.**
dominio, *m.* 1. dominion, power. 2. dominion, domain, territorial possession (*gen. pl.*). 3. control, e.g. *d. sobre sí mismo,* self-control. 4. (law) ownership; **d. directo,** (law) legal ownership; **d. eminente,** (law) eminent domain, dominium eminens; **d. público,** (law) public domain, public property; state property; **d. útil,** (law) useful ownership, usufruct; **ser del d. público,** to be common knowledge; to be in the public domain (intellectual property).
dominó, *m.* 1. dominoes (game). 2. domino, loose hooded cloak worn to conceal identity at masquerades.
domo, *m.* (archit.) dome; cupola.
dompedro, *m.* 1. (bot.) four o'clock. 2. (coll.) chamber pot.
don, *m.* 1. present, gift. 2. gift, talent, knack, natural ability; faculty; **d. de gentes,** charm, winning ways; **d. de hablar,** eloquence, gift of gab (sl.); **d. de lenguas,** ability for languages; **d. de errar,** (coll.) knack for doing things wrong.
don, *m.* Don, title of respect prefixed to Christian names; **d. Cómodo,** (coll.) sybarite, one fond of his creature comforts; **d. Diego,** (bot.) four-o-clock; **D. Juan,** Don Juan, Casanova, ladykiller; **Don Quijote,** Don Quixote.
dona, *f.* 1. (rare) lady, woman. 2. (Chile) gift, bequest; (*pl.*) bridegroom's presents to the bride. 3. (C. Amer., P. Rico, Angl.) doughnut.
donación, *f.* donation, gift, grant.
donadío, *m.* property derived from royal grants.
donado, da, *past part. of* **donar.** —*m.* (ecc.) lay brother. —*f.* lay sister.
donador, ra, *a.* bestowing, donating. —*m., f.* donor, giver.
donaire, *m.* grace, charm; poise, dash, verve, élan.
donairoso, sa, *a.* graceful, poised; dashing.
donante, *a.* donating, giving. —*m., f.* donor, giver; **d. de sangre,** blood donor.
donar, *tr.v.* to donate, bestow, grant, give.
donatario, *m.* donee, recipient of a gift, donation or grant.
donatismo, *m.* (rel.) Donatism.
donatista, *a., m., f.* (rel.) Donatist.
donativo, *m.* donation, gift, grant.
doncel, *m.* 1. (arch.) bachelor, young nobleman attending knight; page of honor. 2. virgin male. —*a.* smooth, sweet (said of wines, etc.).
doncella, *f.* 1. maiden, maid, virgin; lady's maid. 2. (ichth.) (species of) blenny. 3. (Peru) sensitive plant (Mimosa pudica).
doncelleja, *f.* (arch.) young maiden, young female servant.
doncellería, *f.* (coll.) *var. of* **doncellez.**
doncellez, *f.* maidenhead, virginity.
doncellica, ita, *f. dim. of* **doncella,** young maid, girl.
doncellueca, *f.* (coll.) old maid, spinster.
doncelluela, *f.* young maiden.
donde, *adv.* (accented in questions, i.e. **dónde**) where; in which, where; (Amer.) at or in the house, office or shop of, e.g. *está d. los Gómez,* he is at the Gómez' house, *se fue d. el médico,* he went to the doctor's. — **de d.,** from where; from what, by which, on which grounds; **¿de dónde?** from where? from what? on what grounds?; **d. no,** if not, otherwise; **por d.,** whereby, by (means of) which; **¿por dónde?** which way?
dondequiera, *adv.* wherever, anywhere; **d. que,** wherever; **por d.,** everywhere, in every place.
dondiego, *m.* (bot.) four o'clock (Mirabilis jalapa); **d. de día,** morning glory; **d. de noche,** marvel of Peru.
dongón, *m.* (bot., Phil. I.) dungen (Terretia sylvateia), a tree producing very hard wood used in shipbuilding.
donguindo, *m.* (bot.) a variety of pear tree.
donillero, *m.* (coll.) card-sharp, trickster, gambler's come-on.
donjuán, *m.* (bot.) *var. of* **dondiego.**
donjuanesco, ca, *a.* like Don Juan or Casanova, philandering.
donjuanismo, *m.* characteristics of a Don Juan or a Casanova.
donosamente, *adv.* gracefully, elegantly; with great élan, naturalness or assurance.
donosidad, *f., var. of* **donosura.**
donoso, sa, *a.* elegant, graceful, assured, poised.
donosura, *f.* elegance, gracefulness, assurance, naturalness, élan, poise.
doña, *f.* title of respect used before a woman's Christian name (gen. given to married women and widows); **Doña Ana,** Dona Anna; **la Doña,** (Amer., coll.) the lady of the house, the boss, the woman in charge.
doñear, *i.v.* (coll.) to spend much time with women, to be at ease with women.
doñegal, *a., var. of* **doñigal.**
doñigal, *a.* (bot.) a variety of red fig.
dopado, da, *a.* (Amer.) doped, drugged.
dopar, *tr.v.* (Amer.) to dope, to administer a drug.
doquier, doquiera, *adv.* wherever, anywhere; **por d.,** everywhere.
dorada, *f.* 1. (ichth.) gilthead. 2. (Cuba, ento.) venomous fly.
doradilla, *f.* 1. (ichth.) gilthead. 2. (bot.) scale fern.
doradillo, lla, *a.* (Arg., C. Rica) honey-colored (horse). —*m.* 1. fine brass-wire. 2. (ornith.) white wagtail.
dorado, da, *past part. of* **dorar.** —*a.* golden (color; age, period), gilded; (cul.) golden brown; (Cuba) honey-colored (horse). —*m.* 1. (ichth.) dorado. 2. gilding (act of gilding). 3. gilt, gilding (on furniture, etc.). 4. **D.** or **Pez D.,** (astron.) Dorado, the Swordfish.
dorador, ra, *m., f.* gilder.
doradura, *f.* gilding.
doral, *m.* (ornith.) fly-catcher.
dorar, *tr.v.* 1. to gild, cover with gold leaf. 2. (fig.) to gild, disguise (an unpleasant fact). 3. (cul.) to brown, fry golden brown. —*r.v.* 1. (cul.) to brown, turn or become brown. 2. (poet., fig.) to take on a gold tint, become golden.— **d. la píldora,** (coll.) to make (facts or news) easy to swallow.
dórico, ca, *a.* (hist., archit.) Doric.
Dórida, *f.* (hist.) Doris, mountainous region of Greece, believed to be the home of the Dorians.
dorio, ria, *a., m., f.* (hist.) Dorian.
Doris, *f.* (myth.) Doris, mother of the Nereids.
dormán, *m.* (mil.) dolman, hussar's jacket.
dormida, *f.* dormant stage (of a silk-worm); a lair (for animals), roost (for birds); night's sleep; (C. Rica, Chile), night's lodging, place to sleep overnight.
dormidera, *f.* 1. (bot.) garden poppy. 2. (Cuba) sensitive plant. 3. (*pl.*) (coll.) facility for falling asleep, e.g. *tener buenas dormideras,* to fall asleep easily.
dormidero, ra, *a.* soporific. —*m.* temporary place of rest for sheep and cattle.
dormido, da, *past part. of* **dormir.** —*a.* asleep; sleepy, e.g. *está un poco d.,* he's rather sleepy; dull, slow; **mal d.,** sleeping restlessly; **quedar d.,** to fall asleep; **quedarse d.,** to oversleep; to fall asleep.
dormidor, ra, *a.* sleepy, sleepy-headed. —*m., f.* sleepy-head, one who sleeps too much.
dormiente, *a., var. of* **durmiente.**
dormilón, na, *a.* (coll.) sleepy, sleepy-headed. —*m., f.* (coll.) sleepy-head, one who sleeps too much. —*m.* (ornith.) (Amer.) goatsucker, nightjar.
dormilona, *f.* 1. easy chair for taking a nap; head rest on an armchair. 2. (*pl.*) pearl or diamond earrings. 3. (Amer.) sensitive plant. 4. (Ven.) nightgown.

dormir, (*ref. 38*) *i.v.* 1. to sleep. 2. to rest, grow calm. 3. to neglect one's affairs. 4. to spin evenly (a top). 5. to be left in the pack (a card). **d. a pierna suelta,** to sleep soundly; **d. como una piedra,** to sleep like a log. —*tr.v.* 1. to lull to sleep, put to sleep. 2. (Arg., coll.) to knock (a person) out or unconscious by a punch in the nose. — **d. la mona,** to sleep off a hangover; **d. la siesta,** to take an afternoon nap. —*r.v.* 1. to fall asleep, go to sleep. 2. to get pins and needles, go to sleep (a foot or a hand). 3. to neglect one's affairs. 4. (mar.) to heel or lean over excessively (due to a strong wind). 5. (mar.) to be sluggish (a compass needle weak in magnetism). — **dormirse en los laureles,** to rest on one's laurels.
dormirlas, *m.* hide-and-seek (game).
dormitar, *i.v.* to doze, be drowsy.
dormitivo, va, *a., m.* (med.) soporific.
dormitorio, *m.* bedroom; dormitory.
dornajo, *m.* 1. small trough; tray, pan. 2. (Can. I.) manger (for feeding horses).
dornillero, *m.* person who makes or sells troughs or wooden tubs.
dornillo, *m.* trough; wooden tub or bowl.
dorsal, *a.* dorsal, pertaining to the back; **espina d.,** dorsal spine; **aleta d.,** (ichth.) dorsal fin.
dorso, *m.* dorsum, back; **al d.,** on the back (e.g. of a check); **el d. de la mano,** the back of the hand.
dos, *a.* two. —*m.* two; second (in dates); (cards) two, deuce; **a. d.,** (in a game of pelota) thirty points each; en **un d. por tres,** (coll.) quickly, in a wink; **d. y d.,** (Amer.) amble, ambling gait (of a horse); **en un d. por tres,** (coll.) in a jiffy, in no time at all, in a wink; **como que d. y d. son cuatro,** an evident truth; **los d.,** both; **entre los d.,** between you and me; **estar en tres y d.,** to have only one alternative.
dosaje, *m.* dosage; portion.
dosalbo, ba, *a.* with two white feet (a horse).
dosañal, *a.* two-year old, biennial.
doscientos, tas, *a., m., f.* two hundred, two-hundredth.
dosel, *m.* canopy; dossal, dosser; portiere, curtain.
doselera, *f.* valance, drapery (of a canopy).
doselete, *m.* (archit.) canopy.
dosificación, *f.* (pharm., med.) dosage.
dosificadamente, *adv.* proportionately.
dosificar, (*ref. 50*) *tr.v.* 1. to dose, measure out the doses of. 2. (chem.) to analyze.
dosifique, dosifiqué, *ref.* **dosificar.**
dosillo, *m.* a card game for two persons.
dosimetría, *f.* dosimetry, measurement of doses.
dosimétrico, ca, *a.* dosimetric.
dosis, *f.* dose (of medicine); amount, dose, portion.
dotación, *f.* 1. endowment, bequest; dowry; endowing, bequeathing. 2. complement, crew (of a ship); (aer.) crew; staff, personnel (of an office). 3. (Cuba, hist.) slave work force of an estate or a plantation.
dotado, da, *past part. of* **dotar.** —*a.* endowed, gifted; **d. de,** endowed with.
dotador, ra, *m., f.* endower, giver, donor.
dotal, *a.* dotal, pertaining to or related to dot or dowry.
dotante, *a.* endowing, giving, bequeathing. —*m., f.* endower, giver.
dotar, *tr.v.* 1. to endow; to bequeath; to give a dowry to. 2. to furnish, provide; to equip (a ship, office, etc.); to staff (an office); to man (a ship). 3. to assign a wage to (someone). — **d. de,** to furnish or provide with; to endow with.
dote, *m.* 1. dowry. 2. stock of counters (held by each player in card games). —*f.* 1. dowry. 2. gift, talent, endowment (*gen. in pl.*), e.g. *d. de mando,* leadership ability.

dovela, *f.* 1. (archit.) voussoir, wedge-shaped stone used in arches and vaults. 2. (mas.) face of interior and exterior curves of an arch.
dovelaje, *m.* voussoirs (of an arch).
dovelar, *tr.v.* (mas.) to cut (stones) into voussoirs.
doy, *ref.* **dar.**
dozavado, da, *a.* twelve-sided, dodecagonal; containing twelve parts.
dozavo, va, *a., m.* twelfth. — **en d.,** (print.) duodecimo, twelvemo.
Dr. *abbrev. of* **Doctor,** Doctor (Dr.).
Dra. *abbrev. of* **Doctora** (f.) Doctor (Dr.).
draba, *f.* (bot.) whitlow grass, draba.
dracma, *f.* 1. drachm, drachma (coin). 2. dram; drachm (weight); **d. líquida,** fluidram, fluid dram.
Dracón, *m.* (hist.) Draco, Athenian statesman.
draconiano, na, *a.* Draconian, cruel, severe.
dracúnculo, *m.* (zool.) dracunculus, nematode parasite.
draga, *f.* dredger; dredge. — **d. cavadora,** dragline excavator; **d. de cucharón de mordazas, d. de balde,** clamshell dredge.
dragado, *past part. of* **dragar.** —*m.* dredging.
dragaje, *m.* dredging.
dragaminas, *m.* (mar.) mine sweeper.
dragante, *m.* (her.) dragon's head with open jaws biting or swallowing something.
dragar, (*ref. 51*) *tr.* to dredge.
drago, *m.* (bot.) dragon tree.
dragomán, *m.* dragoman, interpreter, tourist guide.
dragón, *m.* 1. dragon (legendary animal). 2. (zool.) dragon, flying dragon, species of lizard. 3. (bot.) snapdragon (Antirrhinum majus). 4. (vet.) kind of leucoma (on the pupil of an animal's eye). 5. (mil.) dragoon. 6. (metal.) feed opening (of a furnace). 7. (astron.) **D.,** Dragon, Draco. — **d. marino,** (ichth.) greater weever.
dragona, *f.* 1. dragoness, female dragon. 2. (mil.) shoulder knot. 3. (Chile, Mex.) sword fastener. 4. (Mex.) man's cape with collar and hood.
dragonadas, *f.* (*pl.*) 1. (hist.) dragonnade. 2. persecution involving raid by troops.
dragoncillo, *m.* 1. *dim. of* **dragón,** small dragon. 2. dragon, antique firearm. 3. (bot.) tarragon, herb used for seasoning. 4. (*pl.*) (bot.) snapdragon.
dragonear, *i.v.* (Amer.) to manipulate; to boast; **d. de,** to pass oneself off as, pretend to be.
dragonete, *m.* (her.) *var. of* **dragante.**
dragonites, *f.* draconites, fabulous stone said to be in the heads of dragons.
dragontea, *f.* (bot.) green dragon (Dracunculus vulgaris).
dragontino, na, *a.* dragonish, dragon-like, dracontine.
drague, dragué, *ref.* **dragar.**
drama, *m.* 1. (theat.) drama, tragedy. 2. tragic occurrence, catastrophe.
dramamina, *f.* (pharm.) dramamine.
dramática, *f.* dramatic art, dramaturgy; playwriting.
dramáticamente, *adv.* dramatically.
dramatice, dramaticé, *ref.* **dramatizar.**
dramático, ca, *a.* dramatic, moving. —*m., f.* dramatist; dramatic actor; (fig.) affected, artificial person.
dramatismo, *m.* drama, dramatic character or atmosphere (e.g. of a scene or situation).
dramatizable, *a.* said of a literary work or an event which can be adapted for the theatre.
dramatización, *f.* dramatization; (theat., cine.) adaptation, libretto.
dramatizar, (*ref. 53*) *tr.v.* to dramatize.

dramaturgia, *f.* dramaturgy, dramatic art; playwriting.
dramaturgo, *m.* dramatist, playwright.
dramón, *m.* (coll.) blood and thunder melodrama; (coll.) domestic tragedy.
draque, *m.* (Amer.) liquor made of water, brandy, sugar and nutmeg.
drástico, ca, *a.* drastic; (med.) drastic, strongly purgative. —*m.* drastic (purgative).
dravidiano, na, *a., m., f.* Dravidian, pertaining to an ancient people of S. India and N. Ceylon.
dravídico, ca, *a.* Dravidic.
drenaje, *m.* drainage; (surg.) drainage.
drenar, *tr.v.* to drain.
dría, driada, dríade, *f.* (myth.) dryad, wood-nymph.
driblar, *tr.v., i.v.* (sport.) to dribble.
drice, dricé, *ref.* **drizar.**
dril, *m.* (tex.) drill, coarse twilled linen.
drimirríceo, a, *a.* (bot.) zingiberaceous. —*f.* (bot.) zingiberaceous plant; (*pl.*) Zingiberacea.
drino, *m.* (zool.) green tree (a poisonous snake).
driza, *f.* (mar.) halyard.
drizar, (*ref. 53*) *tr.v.* (mar.) to hoist up the yards.
droga, *f.* 1. drug, medicine. 2. fib, lie; trick. 3. nuisance, bother. 4. (Amer.) bad debt. — **mandar a uno a la d.,** to tell someone to go jump in the lake.
drogado, da, *past part. of* **drogar.** —*a.* doped. —*m.* doping.
drogar, (*ref. 51*) *tr.v.* to drug, to dope.
drogmán, *m., var. of* **dragomán.**
drogue, drogué, *ref.* **drogar.**
droguería, *f.* drug trade; drug manufacture; drug store.
droguero, ra, *m., f.* 1. druggist. 2. (Chile, Mex., Peru) swindler, cheat.
droguete, *m.* drugget, striped woolen fabric.
drogui, *m.* (Arg., Urug.) habitual drunkard.
droguista, *m., f.* 1. druggist. 2. (fig.) swindler, trickster; impostor.
drolático, *a.* 1. droll. 2. ribald, spicy.
dromedario, *m.* (zool.) dromedary, North-African one-humped camel.
dropacismo, *m.* a kind of depilatory cream.
drope, *m.* (coll.) cur, cad, a despicable person.
drosera, *f.* (bot.) sundew.
drosófila, *f.* (ento.) drosophila.
drosómetro, *m.* (phys.) drosometer, instrument for measuring the quantity of dew.
druida, *m.* (hist.) druid.
druídico, ca, *a.* druidic, druidical, pertaining to the ancient Celtic culture of the Druids.
druidismo, *m.* (hist., philos.) druidism.
drupa, *f.* (bot.) drupe, stone fruit.
drupáceo, a, *a.* (bot.) drupaceous.
drusa, *f.* (min.) druse.
druso, sa, *a.* Drusian, Drusean. —*m., f.* Druse, member of a secret sect of Moslems based in the Middle East.
dúa, *f.* 1. (obs.) obligatory service (in defense work). 2. (min.) gang, team (of workers).
dual, *a., m.* (gram.) dual.
dualidad, *f.* 1. duality. 2. (chem.) faculty of some substances to crystallize into two different geometrical figures.
dualismo, *m.* (philos.) dualism.
dualista, *a.* dualistic. —*m., f.* dualist.
dualístico, ca, *a.* dualistic.
duba, *f.* earth wall, earth enclosure.
dubio, *m.* (law) doubt.
dubitable, *a.* dubious, doubtful, questionable.
dubitación, *f.* dubitation, doubt; (rhet.) rhetorical question.
dubitativamente, *adv.* doubtfully, dubitatively.

dubitativo, va, *a.* doubtful; (gram.) dubitative.
dublé, *m.* gold or silver plating.
ducado, *m.* 1. dukedom; duchy. 2. ducat, gold coin.
ducal, *a.* ducal, pertaining to a duke or a dukedom.
duce, *m.* (hist.) chief, leader in ancient Rome; **Il D.,** Benito Mussolini.
ducentésimo, ma, *a., m.* two-hundredth.
ducha, *f.* 1. shower; douche; (med.) irrigation, jet of water applied to a part of body for medicinal purpose. 2. (tex.) stripe (in cloth).
duchar, *tr.v.* to give a shower to; to douche. —*r.v.* to take a shower; to douche.
ducho, cha, *a.* skillful, expert, experienced.
dúctil, *a.* ductile, yielding, malleable; (fig.) easy-going; easy to handle, manageable.
ductilidad, *f.* ductility.
ductivo, va, *a.* conducive.
ductor, *m.* 1. guide, conductor. 2. (surg.) probe.
dúctulo, *m.* (anat.) ductule.
duda, *f.* doubt, qualm, misgiving; **entrar en dudas,** to begin to have doubts; **sin d.,** without doubt, indubitably.
dudable, *a.* doubtful, dubious.
dudar, *tr.v., i.v.* to doubt, to hesitate. — **d. de,** to distrust, question; **no lo dudo,** I don't doubt it.
dudosamente, *aav.* doubtfully, dubiously.
dudoso, sa, *a.* doubtful, dubious; questionable; hesitant.
duela, *f.* 1. stave (of a cask, barrel, pail, etc.). 2. (zool.) liver fluke, parasitic worm.
duela, *ref.* **doler.**
duelaje, *m.* wine absorbed by the barrel.
duele, *ref.* **doler.**
duelista, *m.* duelist, dueler.
duelo, *m.* 1. duel, e.g. *batirse a d.,* to fight a duel. 2. grief, sorrow, pain, affliction; mourning, bereavement; mourners, mourning party. 3. (*pl.*) troubles, trials, tribulations. — **d. a muerte,** a fight to the end; **estar de d.,** to be in mourning.
duelo, *ref.* **doler.**
duenario, *m.* two-days' religious exercise.
duende, *m.* 1. elf, goblin, fairy, genie; ghost. 2. charm, charisma. 3. (fig., Sp.) an ineffable, enchanting quality present in some people and certain works of art and literature; **tener d.,** to have "it".
duendo, da, *a.* tame, domesticated.
dueña, *f.* 1. owner, proprietress, landlady. 2. lady, mistress (of the house); matron, lady, married woman. 3. duenna, chaperone.
dueñesco, ca, *a.* (coll.) duenna-like, chaperone-like.
dueño, *m.* owner, proprietor, landlord; master (of the house); **d. de sí mismo,** master of oneself, cool-headed person; **hacerse uno d. de una cosa,** (coll.) to learn a thing thoroughly, acquire a thorough knowledge of, master something; to take possession of; **ser d. de,** to own, be the owner of; **ser uno d.,** or **muy d. de hacer una cosa,** to be at liberty or free to do a thing; **mi d.,** (coll.) my master, my beloved.
duerma, *ref.* **dormir.**
duermevela, *m.* (coll.) doze, light sleep; restless sleep, broken sleep.
duermo, *ref.* **dormir.**
duerna, *f.* trough, bowl.
duerno, *m.* (print.) double sheet.
duetista, *m., f.* (mus.) duettist, one who sings or composes duets.
dueto, *m.* (mus.) duet.
dugo, *m.* (C. Amer.) help, aid, assistance.
dugongo, *m.* (zool.) dugong.
dula, *f.* 1. each of the plots of land irrigated by the same ditch. 2. common pasture ground. 3. common herd (of cattle grazing on the same pasture).
dulcamara, *f.* (bot.) bittersweet.
dulce, *a.* 1. sweet. 2. fresh (water). 3. sweet, mild, gentle (character). 4. soft, ductile (metals). 5. (p.) softly and delicately colored. —*m.* 1. sweet, candy. 2. sweet, dessert. 3. preserves, preserved fruit. 4. (C. Amer.) brown sugar leaf. — **a nadie le amarga un d.,** (coll.) don't refuse a gift; **d. de fruta,** preserved fruit; **agua d.,** spring or river water.
dulcedumbre, *f.* sweetness, softness.
dulcémele, *m.* (mus.) dulcimer.
dulcemente, *adv.* sweetly, softly.
dulcera, *f.* dish for preserves, dessert or sweets.
dulcería, *f.* sweetshop, confectioner's shop.
dulcero, ra, *a.* sweet-toothed, fond of sweets; **ser d.,** to have a sweet tooth. —*m., f.* confectioner; **maestro d.,** chief confectioner or baker.
dulcificación, *f.* sweetening; soothing, mollification, dulcification.
dulcificante, *a.* sweetening; appeasing, soothing. —*m.* sweetening (agent), sweetener.
dulcificar, (*ref. 50*) *tr.v.* 1. to sweeten. 2. (fig.) to mollify, appease, soothe, dulcify. —*r.v.* to become sweetened.
dulcifique, dulcifiqué, *ref.* **dulcificar.**
dulcinea, *f.* 1. (coll.) beloved, woman of one's dreams. 2. ideal.
dulcísono, na, *a.* (poet.) sweet-sounding.
dulero, *m.* herdsman, shepherd; guardian of a common pasture.
dulía, *f.* (relig.) dulia, worship of angels and saints.
dulimán, *m.* dolman, Turkish robe.
dulzaina, *f.* 1. (mus.) flageolet, small flute. 2. (derog.) large quantity of sweets or dessert.
dulzaino, na, *a.* (coll.) excessively sweet; too rich.
dulzamara, *f.* (bot.) bittersweet.
dulzarrón, na, *a.* (coll.) too sweet, oversweet, cloying.
dulzón, na, *a.* (Amer.) sweetish; (fig.) pleasant.
dulzor, *m.* sweetness.
dulzura, *f.* 1. sweetness. 2. mildness (of climate). 3. sweetness, mildness, gentleness (of character). 4. endearment, affectionate remark or observation.
dulzurar, *tr.v.* (chem.) to remove the salt from.
duma, *f.* (hist.) Duma, the parliament of Czarist Russia.
dumdum, *a.* (mil.) dumdum (bullet).
dumping, *m.* (econ., Amer.) dumping.
duna, *f.* (geol.) dune.
dundo, da, *a.* (C. Amer., Col.) stupid, foolish, silly.
dunita, *f.* dunnite (explosive).
Duns Escoto, (hist.) Duns Scotus, Scottish philosopher and theologian of the 13th century.
dúo, *m.* (mus.) duo, duet.
duodecimal, *a.* duodecimal.
duodécimo, ma, *a., m.* twelfth.
duodécuplo, pla, *a., m.* duodecuple, duodenary.
duodenal, *a.* (anat.) duodenal.
duodenario, ria, *a.* lasting twelve days.
duodenitis, *f.* (med.) duodenitis.
duodeno, na, *a.* twelfth. —*m.* (anat.) duodenum.
duomesino, na, *a.* of two months.
dupla, *f.* extra dish served in school refectories on certain days.
dupleta, *f.* daily double (wager on the results of two horse races).
dúplex, *m.* 1. (metal.) duplex process. 2. (rad., tel.) duplex system, duplex telegraphy.
dúplica, *f.* (law) defendant's rejoinder.
duplicación, *f.* duplication.
duplicadamente, *adv.* doubly.
duplicado, *past part. of* **duplicar.** —*m.* duplicate; **por d.,** in duplicate.
duplicador, ra, *a.* duplicating, doubling. —*m.* duplicator; **d. de voltaje,** (rad.) voltage doubler. —*f.* duplicator, copying machine.
duplicar, (*ref. 50*) *tr.v.* 1. to duplicate; to double. 2. (law) to rejoin, reply. —*r.v.* to be duplicated; to be doubled.
duplicata, *f.* duplicate, double.
duplicativo, va, *a.* duplicative.
duplicatura, *f., var. of* **dobladura.**
dúplice, *a.* 1. double, duplex. 2. (ecc.) having both nuns and monks (convent or monastery).
duplicidad, *f.* 1. duplicity, double-dealing, falseness. 2. duplication, doubling.
duplique, dupliqué, *ref.* **duplicar.**
duplo, pla, *a., m.* double, duple, duplicate.
duque, *m.* 1. duke. 2. (coll.) fold in a mantilla. — **d. de alba,** (mar.) clump of piles used for mooring; **D. de Hierro,** Iron Duke (Duke of Wellington); **gran duque,** (ornith.) grand duke, variety of owl.
duquecito, *m. dim. of* **duque,** young or little duke.
duquesa, *f.* duchess.
durabilidad, *f.* durability; permanence.
durable, *a.* durable, lasting.
duración, *f.* duration; **de larga d.,** long-playing (record).
duraderamente, *adv.* durably, lastingly.
duradero, ra, *a.* durable, lasting.
duraluminio, *m.* duralumin.
duramadre, duramáter, *f.* (anat.) dura mater.
duramen, *m.* (bot.) duramen.
duramente, *adv.* harshly, rigorously; **tratar d.,** to treat harshly.
durante, *prep.* during; for (a length of time).
durar, *i.v.* 1. to last, endure; to remain, e.g. *aún duran en pie las pirámides de Egipto,* the pyramids of Egypt still remain standing; *la ropa me dura mucho,* clothes last me a long time.
duraznero, *m.* (bot.) peach tree.
duraznilla, *f.* (bot.) peach (fruit.)
duraznillo, *m.* 1. (bot.) a variety of plant resembling a peach tree. 2. (Arg., bot.) species of solanum (Solanum glaucum).
durazno, *m.* (bot.) peach tree; peach (fruit.).
Durero, *m.* Durer (Albrecht), German painter and wood engraver of the 16th century.
dureza, *f.* 1. hardness. 2. toughness, strength. 3. harshness, severity, cruelty. 4. obstinacy, stubbornness. 5. meanness. 6. roughness, uncouthness. 7. (med.) callosity, hardness (of skin). — **d. de corazón,** hardheartedness; **d. de vientre,** constipation.
durillo, *m.* 1. (bot.) laurustine (Viburnum tinus). 2. (bot.) dogwood tree.
durina, *f.* (vet.) dourine.
durmiendo, *ref.* **dormir.**
durmiente, *a.* sleeping, dormant. —*m., f.* sleeper; **la bella d.,** Sleeping Beauty. —*m.* 1. girder, rafter, crossbeam. 2. (mar.) shelfpiece. 3. (Amer., ry.) sleeper, tie.
durmiera, durmiese, durmió, *ref.* **dormir.**
duro, ra, *a.* 1. hard; firm, solid. 2. tough, resilient, strong. 3. cruel, hard; severe, harsh. 4. unbearable, offensive. 5. obstinate, stubborn. 6. mean, stingy (coll.), ungenerous. 7. rough, uncouth. 8. (Mex.) drunk, tipsy. 9. (sculp., p.) crude. — **d. de corazon,** hard-hearted; **d. de oído,** hard of hearing; **más da el d. que el desnudo,** even a miser gives more than a pauper; **tener la cabeza dura,** to be hard headed or stubborn; **tomar las duras con las maduras,** to take the bad with the good or the rough with the smooth; **a duras penas,** with difficulty, hardly. —*m.* five-peseta coin. —*adv.* hard, with force, violently.
duunvir, *m.* (hist.) duumvir, magistrate (in ancient Rome).
duunviral, *a.* (hist.) duumviral.
duunvirato, *m.* (hist., pol.) duumvirate, government by two.
duunviro, *m., var. of* **duunvir.**
dux, *m.* (Ital., hist.) doge.
duz, *a.* (coll.) sweet.
Dy *sym. of* **disprosio,** dysprosium (Dy).

E

E, *f.* e, fifth letter of the Spanish alphabet.
e, *conj.* and (used instead of **y** before words beginning with *i* or *hi,* e.g. *padre e hijo*).
E. *abbrev. of* **este,** East (E).
¡ea! *interj.* come along! (exclamation of encouragement or incitement).
ebanista, *m.* cabinetmaker; woodworker.
ebanistería, *f.* 1. cabinet maker's workshop. 2. cabinet-making, cabinet work.
ébano, *m.* (bot.) ebony, ebony wood.
ebenáceo, a, *a.* (bot.) ebenaceous. —*f.* (*pl.*) (bot.) Ebenaceae.
ebionita, *a.* (rel.) Ebionitic. —*m., f.* Ebionite.
ebonita, *f.* ebonite.
eborario, ria, *a.* made of ivory (said only of sculptures).
ebracteado, da, *a.* (bot.) ebracteate, ebracteated.
ebrancado, da, *a.* (her., gal.) with cut branches.
ebriedad, *f.* drunkenness, inebriation.
ebrio, bria, *a.* 1. drunk, inebriated, intoxicated, tipsy. 2. (fig.) blind (e.g. with passion or anger). —*m., f.* drunk.
ebrioso, sa, *a.* easily intoxicated; fond of drinking. —*m., f.* drunkard, drinker.
ebullición, *f.* boiling; ebullition; bubbling, effervescence; ferment, agitation; **punto de e.,** boiling point.
ebullómetro, *m.* (phys.) instrument that registers the boiling point.
ebulloscopio, *m.* (phys.) ebullioscope, ebulliometer.
eburnación, *f.* (med.) eburnation.
ebúrneo, a, *a.* ivory-like, made of ivory.
ecarté, *m.* ecarté (card game).
eccehomo, *m.* 1. (rel.) Ecce Homo. 2. poor wretch, person who inspires pity.
eccema, *f.* (med.) eczema.
eccematoso, sa, *a.* (med.) eczematous.
eccoprótico, *m.* (med.) light purgative.
ecdisis, *f.* (zool.) ecdysis.
ecesis, *f.* (biol.) ecesis.
echacantos, *m.* (coll.) empty-headed, good-for-nothing.
echacorvear, *tr.v.* to pimp, pander, procure.
echacorvería, *f.* (coll.) pimping, pandering, procuring.
echacuervos, *m.* 1. pimp, pander, procurer. 2. swindler, cheat, impostor.
echada, *f.* 1. throw, cast. 2. man's length (on the ground). 3. (Arg., Mex.) boast, fib, bluff.
echadero, *m.* (coll.) pad; resting place, place of repose.
echadillo, lla, *a., m., f.* foundling.
echadizo, za, *a.* 1. sent surreptitiously to spy or spread rumors. 2. subtly spread around. 3. waste, useless, discarded. 4. foundling, abandoned. —*m., f.* 1. spy. 2. foundling. 3. debris, refuse.
echado, da, *past part. of* **echar.** —*a.* lying down; indolent, lazy. —*m.* (min.) dip in a vein.
echador, ra, *a.* 1. throwing, casting, hurling. 2. (Mex.) boasting, bragging. —*m., f.* braggart, boaster, person who exaggerates.
echadura, *f.* 1. brooding, hatching, setting (of hens). 2. (*pl.*) chaff, siftings, winnowing. — **e. de pollos,** brood of chicks.
echamiento, *m.* throwing, pitching, casting, hurling; ejection, expulsion.
echapellas, *m.* wool-soaker.
echaperros, *m.* (arch.) beadle who drives dogs away from the church.
echar, *tr.v.* 1. to throw, cast, pitch, toss, fling; to throw out or away; to dump. 2. to shed (blood); to shoot out, emit (sparks); to give off, exude, exhale (an odor). 3. to throw out, eject, expel; to dismiss, discharge (from a post). 4. to pour (a liquid); to spread (e.g. butter); to put on, apply (an ointment, lotion, etc.). 5. to mate (animals). 6. to play, to deal (cards). 7. to make (a speech); to preach (a sermon); to recite (verses). 8. (coll.) to smoke (a cigarette). 9. to sentence (to prison, etc.). 10. to attribute, ascribe, e.g. *¿qué edad le echas?* how old do you think he is? 11. to present, bring, e.g. *¿te crees un campeón? bueno, te voy a e. un gallo,* so you think you're a champion, well I'll bring you a tough nut to crack. 12. to grow, put out, e.g. *e. raíces,* to grow roots, take root, send out roots, *echar los dientes,* to cut or grow teeth, *e. pelo,* to grow hair. 13. to take, eat, drink, e.g. *e. un bocado* or *un trago,* to take a bite to eat or a drink. 14. to lock, bolt, e.g. *e. llave* or *cerrojo a la puerta,* to lock or bolt the door. 15. to make, e.g. *e. cálculos* or *cuentas,* to reckon, calculate, work out. 16. to utter, say, e.g. *e. bravatas,* to boast, brag, *e. maldiciones,* to curse. 17. to get, acquire, develop, e.g. *e. carnes,* to put on flesh or weight, *e. barriga,* to develop a paunch or a stomach. — **e. abajo,** to demolish, knock down; to raze, destroy; **e. al mar,** to jettison (cargo); **e. (un niño) al mundo,** to bring (a child) into the world; **e. a perder,** to spoil, ruin; to lead astray, corrupt; **e. a pique,** to sink, wreck, scuttle; **e. a perder,** to ruin, to spoil; **e. a volar,** to make public, publish; **e. de menos,** to miss, notice the absence of; to miss, pine for; **e. el asunto a pares y nones,** to decide a matter by playing odds and evens; **e. el cuerpo atrás** or **a un lado,** to lean backwards or to one side; **e. en cara,** to throw in someone's face, to flaunt; **echarla de,** to pose as; to boast of being; **echarlas,** (Chile) to run away, scram (coll.); **echarlo a juego,** to take (something) as a joke or in fun; **echarlo todo a rodar,** to ruin, spoil; to blow up (in anger); **e. mano a.** to lay hands on, to grab, seize; **e. por largo,** to consider in detail; **e. por mayor, por arrobas** or **por quintales,** to exaggerate; **e. rayos, centellas** or **chispas,** to fume with anger; **e. suertes,** to draw lots. —*i.v.* to grow, sprout; **e. a,** to begin, to start, e.g. *e. a reír,* to burst out laughing, *e. a correr,* to break into a run, begin running, *e. a rodar,* to set rolling; **e. a la lotería** or **una rifa,** to gamble in a lottery, enter a raffle; **e. de comer,** to give (animals) something to eat; **e. de ver,** to notice; **e. por,** to take up, go into (a profession), e.g. *e. por la iglesia,* to enter or go into the church; to go, e.g. *e. por la izquierda,* to bear to the left, *e. por el atajo,* to go by or take a short cut, *e. por el camino,* to go down the road. —*r.v.* 1. to throw oneself. 2. to lie down, stretch out. 3. to brood, set (a hen). 4. to calm down (a wind). 5. to apply oneself, e.g. *echarse a pensar,* to begin thinking. 6. to take, eat, drink. — **echarse a dormir,** to lie down to sleep; to neglect one's things; **echarse a la vida,** to become a prostitute; **echarse a perder,** to spoil, become spoiled; to go to the dogs, go astray; **echarse atrás,** to lean backwards; to retract (from), back out (of); **echárselas de,** to pose as; to boast of being; **echarse sobre,** to rush at, fall upon.
echarpe, *f.* stole, scarf.
echazón, *m.* throwing; (mar.) jettison.
echona, *f.* (Arg., Chile) sickle, billhook.
Ecl. *abbrev. of* **Eclesiastés,** Ecclesiastes (Eccles.).
eclampsia, *f.* (med.) eclampsia, spasm.
eclecticismo, *m.* (philos.) eclecticism.
ecléctico, ca, *a., m., f.* eclectic.
Eclesiastés, *m.* (Bibl.) Ecclesiastes.
eclesiásticamente, *adv.* ecclesiastically.
eclesiastice, *ref.* **eclesiastizar.**
eclesiástico, ca, *a.* ecclesiastical, ecclesiastic. —*m.* 1. ecclesiastic, clergyman, priest. 2. **E.,** (Bibl.) Ecclesiasticus.
eclesiastizar, (*ref. 53*) *tr.v.* to transfer to ecclesiastical use or possession.
Ecli. *abbrev. of* **Eclesiástico,** Ecclesiasticus (Ecclus.).
eclímetro, *m.* (top.) clinometer.
eclipsable, *a.* eclipsable, that can be eclipsed.
eclipsar, *tr.v.* (astron.) to eclipse; (fig.) to eclipse, outshine, overshadow, obscure. —*r.v.* to be eclipsed, to disappear; to vanish from the limelight.
eclipse, *m.* (astron., fig.) eclipse; disappearance; **e. parcial,** partial eclipse; **e. total,** total eclipse.
eclipsis, *f.* (gram.) ellipsis.
eclíptica, *f.* (astron.) ecliptic.
eclíptico, *a.* (astron.) ecliptic, ecliptical.
eclisa, *f.* (ry.) fishplate; **e. cantonera** or **de ángulo,** angle bar.
écloga, *f.* eclogue, short pastoral poem.
eclógico, ca, *a.* (poet.) pertaining to an eclogue (bucolic verse).
eclosión, *f.* 1. budding (of a plant); birth. 2. appearance.
eco, *m.* echo; distant sound; repetition of words (in a song or poem); **tener e.,** to catch on, become popular; to be sonorous.
ecocidio, *m.* ecocide.
ecoico, ca, *a.* echoic, pertaining to an echo.
ecolalia, *f.* (med.) echolalia.
ecología, *f.* ecology, the science dealing with an organism in relation to its environment.
ecológico, ca, *a.* ecologic, ecological.
ecólogo, ga, *m., f.* ecologist.
economato, *m.* 1. trusteeship, guardianship; post of ecclesiastical administrator. 2. commissary; cooperative store (e.g. in an army camp).
economía, *f.* 1. economy. 2. thrift, thriftiness, frugality; scantiness. 3. want, poverty. 4. (*pl.*) savings. 5. prudent administration. 6. (ciencia que trata de la producción, distribución y consumo de las riquezas) economics. — **e. doméstica,**

home economics, household management; **e. política,** political economy, economics.
económicamente, *adv.* economically; cheaply, inexpensively.
economice, economicé, *ref.* **economizar.**
económico, ca, *a.* 1. economic (pertaining to economics and economy). 2. economical, money-saving; inexpensive; thrifty, frugal. 3. mean, stingy, (coll.) niggardly.
economista, *m.* economist.
economizar, (*ref. 53*) *tr.v.* to economize, to save; to spare (for future use).
ecónomo, *a.* acting (priest). —*m.* 1. ecclesiastical administrator. 2. trustee, guardian (of an estate); curator. 3. acting priest.
ECOSOC *abbrev. of* **Consejo Económico y Social de las Naciones Unidas,** United Nations Economic and Social Council (UNESCO).
ecrina, *a.* **glándula e.,** (physiol.) eccrine gland.
ecrinología, *f.* (physiol.) eccrinology.
ectasia, *f.* (med.) ectasia, dilation of an organ.
ectima, *f.* (med.) ecthyma.
ectoblástico, ca, *a.* (biol.) ectoblastic.
ectoblasto, *m.* (biol.) ectoblast.
ectodermo, *m.* (anat.) ectoderm.
ectógeno, na, *a.* (bac.) ectogenic, ectogenous.
ectómero, *m.* (biol.) ectomere.
ectomorfia, *f.* (anth.) ectomorphy.
ectomórfico, ca, *a.* (anth.) ectomorphic.
ectópago, *m.* (med.) Siamese twin.
ectoparásito, *m.* ectoparasite, a parasite which lives on the surface of another organism, e.g. the flea.
ectopia, *f.* (med.) ectopia.
ectoplasma, *m.* (biol.) ectoplasm.
ectosarco, *m.* (biol.) ectosarc.
ectropión, *m.* (med.) ectropion.
ecuable, *a.* (mec.) uniform (motion), equable.
ecuación, *f.* (math., chem., astron.) equation; **e. cuadrática** or **de segundo grado,** quadratic equation; **e. de primer grado,** simple equation; **e. diferencial,** differential equation; **e. lineal,** linear equation; **e. de tiempo,** equation of time.
ecuador, *m.* 1. equator. 2. **E.,** Ecuador (the country).
ecuánime, *a.* equable, calm, serene, composed; even-tempered.
ecuanimidad, *f.* equanimity, composure, calmness, even temper.
ecuatorial, *a.* equatorial. —*m.* equatorial (telescope).
ecuatoriano, na, *a., m., f.* Ecuadoran, Ecuadorean, Ecuadorian.
ecuestre, *a.* equestrian, on horseback, mounted.
ecumene, *m.* the inhabited and cultivated part of the planet earth.
ecumenicidad, *f.* ecumenicity, universality.
ecuménico, ca, *a.* ecumenical, universal.
ecuóreo, rea, *a.* (poet.) aequoreal, pertaining to the sea.
eczema, *m.* (med.) eczema.
eczematoso, sa, *a.* eczematous.
edad, *f.* age; era, epoch, time; **de e.,** elderly, getting on in years; mature; **de cierta e., de e. avanzada,** advanced in years; **e. antigua,** ancient times; **e. avanzada,** old age; **e. crítica,** menopause, change of life; **e. de bronce,** Bronze Age; **e. de hierro,** Iron Age; **e. del espacio,** space age; **e. de oro,** golden age; **e. de piedra,** Stone Age; **e. escolar,** school age; **e. madura,** maturity; **e. media,** Middle Ages; **e. mental,** mental age; **e. provecta,** maturity; **e. temprana,** youth; **e. viril,** prime of life; **llegar a la mayoría de e.,** to come of age; **mayor de e.** of age; adult; **menor de e.,** under age; minor.
edáfico, ca, *a.* edaphic; soil-like.
edafología, *f.* edaphology, pedology.
edafólogo, *m.* pedologist, soil expert.
Edda, *f.* (lit.) Edda, compendium of ancient Scandinavian literature and mythology.
edecán, *m.* (mil.) aide-de-camp.
edelweiss, *m.* (bot.) edelweiss.
edema, *m.* (med.) edema, oedema.
edematoso, sa, *a.* edematous, edematose.
Edén, *m.* (Bibl., fig.) Eden, paradise.
edénico, ca, *a.* Edenic.
edentado, da, *a.* edentate. —*m.* (zool.) edentate, (*pl.*) Edentata.
edición, *f.* publication; edition, issue; **e. abreviada,** abridged edition; **e. de bolsillo,** pocket edition; **e. diamante,** diamond edition, edition in diamond print; **e. escolar,** school edition; **e. príncipe,** first edition; **segunda e.,** (fig.) spit and image, double (of a person).
edicto, *m.* edict, proclamation.
edículo, *m.* small building, shrine, niche.
edificación, *f.* construction, building; edification.
edificador, ra, *a.* 1. constructing, building. 2. edifying, constructive, instructive. —*m., f.* builder, constructor.
edificante, *a.* edifying, instructive.
edificar, (*ref. 50*) *tr.v.* 1. to construct, build, erect. 2. to edify, instruct, improve.
edificativo, va, *a.* edifying, instructive; exemplary.
edificatorio, ria, *a.* building, constructing.
edificio, *m.* building, edifice, structure, e.g. *e. rascacielos,* skyscraper; **bajo e.,** on the inside, indoors.
edifique, edifiqué, *ref.* **edificar.**
edil, *m.* aedile, edile, Roman magistrate in charge of public works; town councillor, alderman.
edila, *f.* female member of a council or municipality.
edilicio, cia, *a.* civic, municipal; aedilian, edilic, of or pertaining to an edile.
edilidad, *f.* aedileship; councillorship.
Edimburgo, *m.* Edinburgh, capital of Scotland.
Edipo, *m.* (myth.) Oedipus; **complejo de E.,** Oedipus complex.
editar, *tr.v.* to publish.
editor, ra, *a.* publishing. —*m., f.* publisher, editor; **e. responsable,** responsible editor, person legally responsible for publications.
editorial, *a.* publishing; editorial. —*m.* editorial. —*f.* publishing company or house.
editorialista, *m.* (jour.) editorial writer.
edrar, *tr.v.* (agr.) to dig around (vines) a second time
edredón, *m.* (Gal.) eiderdown (feather); eiderdown, feather quilt.
educable, *a.* educable.
educación, *f.* education, training, instruction; good manners, good breeding; **buena e.,** good manners **e. a distancia,** correspondence courses; **e. especial,** special education (for children with problems that interfere with their education); **e. física,** physical education or training; **e. general básica, e. primaria,** primary education; **e. preescolar,** preschool education; **e. privada,** private education; **e. secundaria,** secondary education; **e. sexual,** sex education; **e. superior,** higher education; **mala e.,** bad manners.
educacional, *a.* (neol.) educational.
educado, da, *past part. of* **educar.** —*a.* well-mannered, polite.
educador, ra, *a.* educating; instructing. —*m., f.* teacher, educator.
educando, da, *m., f.* student, pupil, disciple.
educar, (*ref. 50*) *tr.v.* to educate; to instruct, teach, train; to rear, bring up.
educativo, va, *a.* educational, educative.
educción, *f.* eduction; deduction.
educir, (*ref. 47*) *tr.v.* to educe, bring out, elicit, extract.
eduje, edujera, edujese, *ref.* **educir.**
edulcoración, *f.* (pharm.) sweetening.
edulcorar, *tr.v.* (pharm.) to sweeten, to make more palatable or pleasant.
eduque, eduqué, *ref.* **educar.**
eduzca, eduzco, *ref.* **educir.**
EE. UU. A. *abbrev. of* **Estados Unidos de América,** United States of America (USA).
efebo, *m.* ephebe, ephebus, youth, adolescent.
efectismo, *m.* (art., lit.) striving for effect.
efectista, *a.* fond of effects, showy, flashy, sensational. —*m., f.* flashy writer, composer, etc., one fond of effects.
efectivamente, *adv.* in effect, really, actually, indeed, in fact; effectually.
efectividad, *f.* effectiveness.
efectivo, va, *a.* effective; real, actual. —*m.* cash; **en e.,** in cash; **e. en caja,** (acc.) cash in hand; **premio en e.,** cash prize.
efecto, *m.* 1. effect, result. 2. end, effect, purpose. 3. article of merchandise. 4. commercial or negotiable paper. 5. spin (given to a ball in tennis, cricket, etc.). 6. effect, impression (on the mind). 7. (elec., mec.) effect. 8. (*pl.*) **effects,** goods, chattels, movable property; (*pl.*) merchandise, goods. — **darle e. a,** to put spin on (a ball); **de doble e.,** (mec.) double-acting; **de simple e.,** (mec.) single-acting **e. cambiario,** bill of exchange; **e. comercial,** commercial paper; **e. de borde,** (rad.) fringe effect; **e. invernadero,** greenhouse effect; **e. óptico,** optical illusion; **e. postal,** postage stamp; **e. secundario,** side effect; **e. termoeléctrico,** thermoelectric effect, thermocurrent; **efectos bancarios,** bank paper; **efectos de consumo,** consumer goods; **efectos públicos,** government bonds or securities; **efectos sonoros,** sound effects; **e. Volta,** (phys.) Volta effect; **con** or **en e.,** in effect, as a matter of fact, really, actually; **hacer e.,** to have an effect; to take effect; **llevar a** or **poner en e.,** to put into effect, carry out; **surtir e.,** to have the desired effect.
efector, *m.* (physiol.) effector.
efectuación, *f.* carrying out, accomplishment, performance, realization.
efectuar, (*ref. 55*) *tr.v.* to carry out, effect, perform; to produce, bring about, to realize. —*r.v.* to take place, be carried out.
efedrina, *f.* (pharm.) ephedrine.
efélide, *f.* freckle; (med.) ephelis.
efémera, *f.* (med.) ephemeral fever, one-day fever.
efeméride, *f.* anniversary; (*pl.*) ephemerides, e.g. *las efemérides del día,* anniversaries of events that took place on that day in history; (*pl.*) diary, journal.
efendi, *m.* effendi, a Turkish title of respect.
eferente, *a.* (anat.) efferent, bearing away.
efervescencia, *f.* effervescence; agitation, excitement, bubbling over.
efervescente, *a.* effervescent, agitated, bubbling.
efesino, na, efesio, sia, *a., m., f.* Ephesian.
Éfeso, *m.* Ephesus, ancient Greek city; site of a large temple of Artemis.
efialtes, *f.* (med.) nightmare.
eficacia, *f.* efficacy, efficaciousness, effectiveness.
eficaz, (*pl.* **eficaces**) *a.* efficacious, effective.
eficazmente, *adv.* efficaciously, effectively.
eficiencia, *f.* efficiency.
eficiente, *a.* efficient.
eficientemente, *adv.* efficiently.
efigie, *f.* 1. effigy, image. 2. (fig.) personification.

efímera, *f.* (zool.) May fly, ephemerid.
efímero, ra, *a.* ephemeral, shortlived; (med.) ephemeral (fever).
eflorecerse, (*ref. 45*) *r.v.* (chem.) to effloresce, change to a powder from loss of water or crystallization.
eflorescencia, *f.* (med., chem.) efflorescence.
eflorescente, *a.* efflorescent.
eflorezca, *ref.* **eflorecerse.**
efluvio, *m.* exhalation, emanation; (elec.) effluvium, discharge; (fig.) radiation, expression.
efod, *m.* ephod, official garment of the Jewish high priest.
éforo, *m.* (hist.) ephor, one of the five Spartan magistrates.
efugio, *m.* evasion, subterfuge, shift.
efundir, *tr.v.* (rare) to effuse, pour, spill.
efusión, *f.* effusion; (fig.) effusion, effusiveness; **e. de sangre,** bloodshed, spilling of blood.
efusivo, va, *a.* effusive; warm, expressive.
efuso, sa, *past part. of* **efundir.** —*a.* effused.
egeo, *a.* (hist., geog.) Aegean. —*m.* **E.** Aegean (sea).
egida, égida, *f.* (myth., fig.) aegis, shield, protection, defense; **bajo la e. de,** under the protection or sponsorhip of.
egílope, *f.* (bot.) wild cat, egilops, aegilops.
egipán, *m.* (myth.) Pan, satyr.
egipciaco, ca, *a., m., f., var. of* **egipcio.**
egipciano, na, *a., m., f., var. of* **egipcio.**
egipcio, cia, *a., m., f.* Egyptian. —*m.* Egyptian (language).
Egipto, *m.* Egypt.
egiptología, *f.* Egyptology, the study of ancient Egyptian life, art and culture.
egiptológico, ca, *a.* Egyptological.
egiptólogo, ga, *m., f.* Egyptologist.
égira, *f.* hegira, hejira, flight of Mohammed from Mecca.
Egisto, *m.* (myth.) Aegisthus, son of Thyestes and lover of Clytemnestra.
eglantina, *f.* (bot.) eglantine.
égloga, *f.* eclogue, pastoral poem.
ego, *m.* (philos., psyc.) ego, the self.
egocéntrico, ca, *a.* egocentric.
egocentrismo, *m.* egocentrism, selfishness.
egoísmo, *m.* egoism, selfishness; self-love.
egoísta, *a.* selfish, egoistical, egoistic; self-centered. —*m., f.* egoist.
egoístamente, *adv.* egoistically.
egoistón, na, *a.* (coll.) completely or utterly self-centered.
ególatra, *a.* self-worshiping, egolatrous, narcissistic.
egolatría, *f.* self-worship, self-idolatry, narcissism.
egolátrico, ca, *a.* self-worshiping.
egotismo, *m.* egotism.
egotista, *a.* egotistic. —*m., f.* egotist.
egregiamente, *adv.* egregiously, illustriously, eminently.
egregio, gia, *a.* distinguished, eminent, egregious, illustrious.
egrena, *f.* iron clamp.
egresar, *i.v.* (Amer.) to leave (school or college) at the termination of studies; to leave, go away.
egreso, *m.* 1. (Amer.) departure. 2. (com.) expenditure, expense, debit. 3. (Amer.) graduation.
egrisador, *m.* box for diamond dust.
egrisar, *tr.v.* to polish diamonds.
¡eh! *interj.* eh! ah! here!
eidero, *m.* (ornith.) eider duck.
eidético, ca, *a.* (psyc.) eidetic.
einstenio, *m.* (chem.) einsteinium.
eirá, *m.* (zool., Arg., Par.) grey fox (Chrysocio brachyrus).

ej. *abbrev. of* **ejemplo,** example (ex.).
eje, *m.* 1. axis. 2. (mec.) axle, shaft, spindle. 3. crux, main point, fundamental idea. 4. (geom.) axis. — **de e. a e.,** (mec., auto.) center to center; **e. cardán** or **cardánico,** (auto.) cardan shaft; **e. de transmisión,** drive shaft, propeller shaft; **e. loco,** idler shaft; **e. magnético,** (geophys.) magnetic axis; **e. mayor,** (geom.) major axis (of the ellipse); **e. menor,** (geom.) minor axis (of the ellipse); **e. motor** or **motriz,** (mec.) drive shaft; **e. óptico,** optical axis; **e. polar,** polar axis; **e. sísmico,** (geophys.) seismic axis; **e. trasero,** rear axle.
ejecución, *f.* 1. execution. 2. performance; completion. 3. (law) attachment, distraint, seizure and sale of property to pay a debt.
ejecutable, *a.* 1. executable; feasible, workable, practicable, performable. 2. (law) suable for debt, distrainable, attachable, liable.
ejecutado, da, *past part. of* **ejecutar.** —*a.* executed.
ejecutante, *m. f.* 1. executant, performer. 2. (law) distrainor.
ejecutar, *tr.v.* to execute; to perform, carry out; (law) to attach, distrain, seize and sell (property) to pay a debt.
ejecutivamente, *adv.* 1. promptly, efficiently. 2. executively, by executive means.
ejecutivo, va, *a.* 1. executive, executory. 2. prompt, quick, efficient. —*m* executive (administrative branch of government); administrator. —*f.* administrative committee.
ejecutor, ra, *a.* performing; executing. —*m., f.* executor; performer; **ejecutor de la justicia,** executioner; **ejecutor testamentario,** executor (of a will); **ejecutora testamentaria,** executrix. —*m.* executive officer.
ejecutoria, *f.* 1. legal patent of nobility, pedigree. 2. ennobling action, noble quality. 3. gift, ability, endowment, distinction. 4. (law) final judgement; (law) writ of execution (of a judgement).
ejecutoría, *f.* executorship, office or post of executor.
ejecutorial, *a.* (law) pertaining to writs of execution passed by an ecclesiastical tribunal.
ejecutoriar, *tr.v.* 1. to make final and conclusive (a judgment). 2. (fig.) to confirm, establish the truth of. —*r.v.* to become final and conclusive (a judgment).
ejecutorio, ria, *a.* (law) executory.
¡ejem! *interj.* exclamation used to call attention or make a pause in conversation.
ejemplar, *a.* exemplary. —*m.* 1. model, pattern, prototype. 2. copy, reproduction. 3. specimen, sample. 4. example, warning. 5. precedent. — **sin ejemplar,** unique, unprecedented.
ejemplarice, ejemplaricé, *ref.* **ejemplarizar.**
ejemplaridad, *f.* exemplariness; outstanding quality.
ejemplarizar, (*ref. 53*) *tr.v.* to set a good example to, serve as an example to.
ejemplarmente, *adv.* exemplarily, edifyingly.
ejemplificación, *f.* exemplification, illustration.
ejemplificar, (*ref. 50*) *tr.v.* to exemplify, illustrate.
ejemplifique, ejemplifiqué, *ref.* **ejemplificar.**
ejemplo, *m.* example; instance; **dar e.,** to set an example; **hacer un e. de,** to make an example of; **por e.,** for example, for instance; **sentar e.,** to give or set an example; **sin e.,** unprecedented, unique.
ejercer, (*ref. 56*) *tr.v.* 1. to practice (a profession). 2. to exercise (one's rights). —*i.v.* to practice a profession.
ejercicio, *m.* 1. exercise; drill, activity. 2. practice, practicing (of a profession). 3. fiscal year. 4. test (for office, etc.). 5. (mil.) drill. — **e. de tiro,** rifle practice; **e. de tiro táctico,** (mil.) combat firing; **ejercicios antiaéreos,** air-raid drill; **ejercicios de soltura,** loosening-up exercises; **en e.,** acting, in charge; **hacer e.,** to exercise; (mil.) to drill.
ejercitación, *f.* exercise; practice.
ejercitante, *m., f.* 1. exercitant, person engaged in spiritual exercises. 2. candidate (for office).
ejercitar, *tr.v.* to exercise, to practice; to train. —*r.v.* to train; to practice.
ejército, *m.* army.
ejerza, ejerzo, *ref.* **ejercer.**
ejido, *m.* common land; common threshing land, public grazing pasture.
ejión, *m.* (archit.) bracket, purlin, corbel piece.
ejote, *m.* 1. (Mex.) young and tender string bean. 2. (Guat.) large stitch.
el, *m. def. art.* the.
él, *m. pers. pron.* he.
elaboración, *f.* 1. manufacture, making. 2. working (of metal, wood, etc.). 3. (physiol.) elaboration (of food).
elaborado, da, *past part. of* **elaborar.** —*a.* wrought, manufactured.
elaborador, ra, *a.* manufacturing, elaborating.
elaborar, *tr.v.* 1. to manufacture, make. 2. to work (wood, metals, etc.). 3. to elaborate, work out (e.g. a plan). 4. (physiol.) to elaborate, digest (food).
elación, *f.* 1. magnanimity, nobility, generosity. 2. elevation, exaltation (of spirit). 3. arrogance, haughtiness; grandeur. 4. pomposity (of style).
elamí, *m.* (mus.) elamí.
elamita, *a.* Elamite, Elamitic, of or pertaining to an ancient kingdom of S. W. Asia. —*m., f.* Elamite.
elan, *m.* (Gal.) élan, vigor, animation, drive.
elápido, *m.* (zool.) elapid.
elasmobranquio, *a., m.* (ichth.) elasmobranch.
elástica, *f.* vest, undershirt, tee shirt.
elasticidad, *f.* elasticity.
elástico, ca, *a.* elastic, flexible. —*m.* 1. elastic, elastic band. 2. stockinet vest. 3. (*pl.*) suspenders.
elastina, *f.* (biochem.) elastin.
elastómero, *m.* (chem.) elastomer.
elaterina, *f.* (chem.) elaterin.
elaterio, *m.* (bot.) squirting cucumber.
elaterita, *f.* (min.) elaterite.
elayómetro, *m.* oleometer (instrument for measuring the density of oil).
elche, *m.* apostate, renegade (from the Christian religion).
eleagnáceo, a, *a.* (bot.) elaeagnaceous. —*f.* (*pl.*) (bot.) Elaeagnaceae.
eleático, ca, *a.* (philos.) *m., f.* Eleatic.
eleatismo, *m.* (philos.) Eleaticism.
eleborastro, *m.* (bot.) helleboraster.
eléboro, *m.* (bot.) hellebore; **e. blanco,** (bot.) white hellebore; **e. negro,** (bot.) Christmas rose.
elección, *f.* 1. election; choice. 2. (*pl.*) (pol.) election.
eleccionario, *a.* (Amer.) electoral.
electivo, va, *a.* elective.
electo, ta, *irr. past part. of* **elegir.** —*a.* elect, chosen. —*m., f.* elect, elected, chosen or appointed person.
elector, ra, *a.* electing. —*m., f.* elector, voter. —*m.* elector (German Prince).
electorado, *m.* electorate.
electoral, *a.* electoral.
electorero, *m.* electioneer, political hustler.
Electra, *f.* Electra; **complejo de E.,** (psyc.) Electra complex.
electrice, electricé, *ref.* **electrizar.**
electricidad, *f.* electricity; **e. dinámica,** dynamic or voltaic electricity; **e. estática,** static electricity.

electricista, *m., f.* electrician.
eléctrico, ca, *a.* electric, electrical.
electrificación, *f.* electrification.
electrificar, (*ref. 50*) *tr.v.* to electrify.
electrifique, electrifiqué, *ref.* **electrificar.**
electriz, (*pl.* **electrices**) *f.* electress, wife of an elector in the old German Empire.
electrizable, *a.* electrifiable.
electrización, *f.* electrification.
electrizador, ra, *a.* electrifying. —*m., f.* electrifier.
electrizante, *a.* electrifying; highly stimulating, vivacious, able to animate; (fig.) dizzying.
electrizar, (*ref. 53*) *tr.v.* (elec., fig.) to electrify. —*r.v.* to become electrified.
electro, *m.* 1. amber. 2. electrum, natural pale yellow alloy of gold and silver.
electroacústica, *f.* (phys.) electroacoustics.
electroafinidad, *f.* electroaffinity.
electroanálisis, *m.* (chem.) electroanalysis.
electroanestesia, *f.* (med.) anesthesia produced by electric current.
electrobomba, *f.* electropump.
electrocaldera, *f.* electric boiler.
electrocardiografía, *f.* electrocardiography.
electrocardiógrafo, *m.* electrocardiograph.
electrocardiograma, *m.* electrocardiogram.
electrochapeado, *m.* (chem.) electro-plating.
electrochoque, *m.* (med.) electroshock therapy.
electrocinético, ca, *a.* (phys.) electrokinetic. —*f.* electrokinetics.
electrocirugía, *f.* electrosurgery.
electrocoagulación, *f.* (med.) electrocoagulation.
electrocución, *f.* electrocution.
electrocutar, *tr.v.* to electrocute. —*r.v.* to be electrocuted.
electrodeposición, *f.* (chem.) electro-plating.
electrodepósito, *m.* (chem.) electrodeposit.
electrodinámica, *f.* (phys.) electrodynamics.
electrodinámico, ca, *a.* electrodynamic, electrodynamical.
electrodinamómetro, *m.* (engin.) electrodynamometer.
electrodo, *m.* (phys.) electrode; **e. de calomelanos,** (chem.) calomel electrode; **e. de placa,** plate electrode; **e. de tierra,** grounding electrode.
electrodoméstico, ca, *a.* electric-appliance. —*m.* electric appliance.
electroencefalografía, *f.* (med.) electroencephalography.
electroencefalógrafo, *m.* (med.) electroencephalograph.
electroencefalograma, *m.* electroencephalogram.
electroestática, *f.* electrostatics.
electroestático, ca, *a.* (phys.) electrostatic.
electrófono, *m.* electric phonograph.
electroforesis, *f.* (chem., phys.) electrophoresis.
electroforo, *m.* (phys.) electrophorus.
electrogalvanizar, *tr.v.* to electrogalvanize.
electrógeno, na, *a.* (phys.) generating electricity. —*m.* electric generator.
electrograbado, *m.* electrogravure.
electrógrafo, *m.* (phys.) electrograph.
electroimán, *m.* (phys., engin.) electromagnet.
electrolice, electrolicé, *ref.* **electrolizar.**
electrólisis, *f.* (chem.) electrolysis.
electrolítico, ca, *a.* (chem.) electrolytic, electrolytical.
electrólito, *m.* (phys., chem.) electrolyte.
electrolización, *f.* electrolyzation.
electrolizador, ra, *a.* electrolyzing. —*m.* electrolyzer.
electrolizar, (*ref. 53*) *tr.v.* (phys., chem.) to electrolyze.
electromagnético, ca, *a.* electromagnetic.
electromagnetismo, *m.* electromagnetism.
electromecánico, ca, *a.* electromechanical. —*f.* electromechanics.
electrometalurgia, *f.* (chem.) electrometallurgy.
electrometría, *f.* (phys.) electrometry.
electrométrico, ca, *a.* electrometric.
electrómetro, *m.* (phys.) electrometer.
electromotor, ra, *a.* electromotive. —*m.* electromotor, electric motor.
electromotriz, (*pl.* **electromotrices**) *a.* electromotive.
electrón, *m.* (phys.) electron.
electronegativo, va, *a.* (phys., chem.) electronegative.
electrónico, ca, *a.* (phys., engin.) electronic. —*f.* electronics.
electronografía, *f.* (print.) electronography.
electroplastia, *f.* (chem.) electro-plating.
electropositivo, va, *a.* (phys., chem.) electropositive.
electropropulsión, *f.* (phys., engin.) electric drive.
electropuntura, *f.* (med.) electropuncture.
electroquímica, *f.* (chem.) electrochemistry.
electroquímico, ca, *a.* electrochemical.
electroscopio, *m.* (phys.) electroscope.
electrosiderurgia, *f.* electrometallurgy.
electrostático, ca, *a.* electrostatic. —*f.* electrostatics.
electrotecnia, *f.* electrical engineering, electrotechnics.
electrotécnico, ca, *a.* electrotechnical.
electroterapeuta, *m., f.* (med.) electrotherapist.
electroterapia, *f.* (med.) electrotherapy.
electrotérmico, ca, *a.* (phys.) electrothermal, electrothermic.
electrotipia, *f.* (print.) electrotypy.
electrotípico, ca, *a.* (print.) electrotypic.
electrotipo, *m.* (print.) electrotype.
electrotónico, ca, *a.* (physiol.) electrotonic.
electrótono, *m.* (physiol.) electrotonus.
electrovalencia, *f.* (phys., chem.) electrovalency, electrovalence.
electuario, *m.* (pharm.) electuary.
elefancía, *f.* (med.) elephantiasis.
elefancíaco, ca, *a., m., f.* (med.) elephantiac.
elefanta, *f.* (zool.) female elephant.
elefante, ta, *m., f.* elephant; **e. blanco,** (fig.) white elephant; **e. marino,** (zool.) elephant seal; **sacarse la rifa del e.,** to acquire or receive something which is more trouble than it is worth.
elefantiasis, *f.* (med.) elephantiasis.
elefantino, na, *a.* elephantine, of or pertaining to elephants.
elefantón, *m.* (Hond., med.) elephantiasis.
elegancia, *f.* elegance, taste, style, grace.
elegante, *a.* elegant; stylish, modish; gallant, tasteful, fine.
elegantemente, *adv.* elegantly; neatly, stylishly, fashionably.
elegantón, na, *a.* (coll.) very elegant or smart, well groomed; fashionable.
elegía, *f.* (poet.) elegy, mournful composition or poem written as a lament for the dead.
elegíaco, ca, *a.* (poet.) elegiac; mournful, sad.
elegibilidad, *f.* eligibility.
elegible, *a.* eligible, suitable.
elegido, da, *past part. of* **elegir.** —*a., m., f.* elect, chosen.
elegir, (*ref. 76*) *tr.v.* to elect; to choose, select, pick.
elego, ga, *a.* mournful, plaintive, sorrowful.
elementado, da, *a.* (Col., Chile) absentminded, careless.
elemental, *a.* elemental, fundamental; elementary; obvious; **color e.,** primary color; **escuela e.,** primary school.
elementalmente, *adv.* elementally; elementarily.
elementarse, *r.v.* (Chile) to become muddled or confused.
elemento, *m.* 1. element, ingredient. 2. (chem., math., philos.) element. 3. (elec.) element; cell. 4. medium, natural habitat, element. 5. basic principle or factor. 6. (Amer.) dimwit, dullard, boob. 7. (*pl.*) rudiments, elements (of a science or art). 8. (*pl.*) resources, means. — **e. secundario,** (elec.) secondary cell; **estar en su e.,** to be in one's element.
elemí, *m.* (chem.) elemi, fragant oleoresin obtained from tropical trees.
elenco, *m.* 1. catalogue, list, table. 2. (theat.) company, members of a company; cast (of a play); (sport) team. 3. (philos.) elenchus.
eleópteno, *m.* (chem.) eleoptene.
elepé, *m.* album, LP.
eleusino, na, *a.* (hist.) Eleusinian; **misterios eleusinos,** Eleusinian mysteries (in honor of Demeter and Persephone, in the ancient Greek city of Eleusis).
elevación, *f.* 1. elevation, raising (someone to a dignity or high position); ascent. 2. (astron., archit., artil.) elevation. 3. height, rise (in the ground). 4. (moral) loftiness. 5. (ecc.) Elevation (of the host). 6. raising, building (of a monument). 7. rapture, ecstasy. 8. (math.) raising, involution (to a power). — **e. frontal** or **del frente,** front elevation; **e. lateral,** side elevation; **e. posterior,** rear elevation.
elevadamente, *adv.* loftily.
elevado, da, *past part. of* **elevar.** —*a.* 1. high; towering, tall. 2. exalted, majestic, grand; lofty, sublime.
elevador, ra, *a.* elevating. —*m.* 1. (med.) elevator. 2. (Amer.) elevator, hoist, lift. — **e. de granos,** grain elevator; **e. de leva y rodillo,** cam-and-roller hoist; **e. de voltaje,** (elec.) booster transformer.
elevamiento, *m.* elevation; rapture, ecstasy.
elevar, *tr.v.* 1. to raise, lift, hoist, heave. 2. to raise, elevate (someone) to a dignity. 3. to promote, raise (to a higher position in a firm). 4. (math.) to raise (to a power). —*r.v.* 1. to rise; to raise oneself. 2. to be transported (in ecstasy). 3. to become vain or conceited. — **e. al cuadrado,** (math.) to square; **e. a una potencia.** (math.) to raise to a power.
elfo, *m.* elf.
elidir, *tr.v.* 1. (phonet., gram.) to elide, omit, slur over (a vowel or syllable) in order to form a liaison between two words. 2. to elide, eliminate, nullify, suppress, weaken.
elige, *ref.* **elegir.**
eligiendo, eligiera, eligiese, eligió, *ref.* **elegir.**
elija, *ref.* **elegir.**
elijación, *f.* (pharm.) seething, steeping.
elijar, *tr.v.* (pharm.) to seethe, boil, steep (herbs, etc.).
elijo, *ref.* **elegir.**
eliminación, *f.* elimination; disposal; **e. de basura,** garbage disposal.
eliminador, ra, *a.* eliminating. —*m., f.* eliminator.
eliminar, *tr.v.* 1. to eliminate. 2. to remove, strike out, to leave out.
eliminatorio, ria, *a.* eliminating. —*f.* (sport.) preliminary (to eliminate contestants or teams); preliminary round; heat (in athletics).
elipse, *f.* (geom.) ellipse.
elipsis, *f.* (gram.) ellipsis.
elipsógrafo, *m.* ellipsograph.
elipsoidal, *a.* (geom.) ellipsoidal.
elipsoide, *m.* (geom.) ellipsoid.
elípticamente, *adv.* elliptically.

elipticidad, *f.* ellipticity.
elíptico, ca, *a.* (geom., gram.) elliptic, elliptical.
elíseo, a, elisio, sia, *a.* Elysian, happy, blissful. — **Campos Elíseos,** (myth.) Elysian fields, residence of the gods.
elisión, *f.* (gram.) elision.
elite, *m.* (Gal.) élite, the selected few, the best.
élitro, *m.* (ento.) elytron, elytrum, wing cover.
elíxir, elixir, *m.* elixir.
elocución, *f.* elocution.
elocuencia, *f.* eloquence.
elocuente, *a.* eloquent.
elocuentemente, *adv.* eloquently.
elogiable, *a.* praiseworthy, worthy of praise.
elogiador, ra, *a.* eulogistic. —*m., f.* eulogist, encomiast.
elogiar, *tr.v.* to praise, extol, laud; to eulogize.
elogio, *m.* praise, eulogy; panegyric.
elogioso, sa, *a.* eulogistic, laudatory.
elongación, *f.* (astron., med.) elongation.
elotada, *f.* (Mex.) meal of green corn.
elote, *m.* ear of tender corn; **pagar los elotes,** (coll., C. Rica, Hond.) to get the blame, be the scape-goat.
El Salvador, *m.* El Salvador.
elucidación, *f.* elucidation, explanation.
elucidar, *tr.v.* to elucidate, explain, to clear up.
elucubración, *f.* lucubration; intensive, laborious study.
eludible, *a.* eludible, avoidable.
eludir, *tr.v.* to elude; to avoid; to evade.
eluviación, *f.* (geol.) eluviation.
eluvio, *m.* (geol.) eluvium.
elzeviriano, na, *a.* Elzevir, Elzevirian, pertaining to the famous Dutch publishing house (1583-1680) or to its modern influences on type design and book production.
elzevirio, *m.* (print.) Elzevir.
ella, *third pers. sing. f. pron.* she, her, e.g. *¿es e. su hermana?* is she your sister?
ellas, *third pers. pl. f. pron.* they, them, e.g. *e. son mis hermanas,* they are my sisters.
ello, *neut. pers. pron.* it, e.g. *e. es obvio,* it is obvious.
ellos, *third pers. pl. m. pron.* they, them e.g. *a e. se debe,* it is because of them, *e. son mis hermanos,* they are my brothers.
EM *abbrev. of* **Estado Mayor,** General Staff (G.S.).
emaciación, *f.* (med.) emaciation.
emanación, *f.* emanation, effluvium.
emanante, *a.* emanating; issuing.
emanantismo, *m.* (philos.) emanationism.
emanantista, *a., m., f.* (philos.) emanationist.
emanar, *i.v.* to emanate, proceed or arise from.
emancipación, *f.* emancipation.
emancipador, ra, *a.* emancipating. —*m., f.* emancipator, liberator.
emancipar, *tr.v.* to emancipate, free, liberate. —*r.v.* to become emancipated, freed or liberated; to emancipate or free oneself.
emasculación, *f.* emasculation, castration.
emascular, *tr.v.* to emasculate, castrate.
embabiamiento, *m.* (coll.) fascination, captivation, enthrallment, absentmindedness, woolgathering.
embabucar, (*ref. 50*) *tr.v.* to deceive, trick, mislead, delude.
embabuque, embabuqué, *ref.* **embabucar.**
embace, embacé, *ref.* **embazar.**
embachar, *tr.v.* to pen (sheep for shearing).
embadurnador, ra, *a.* smearing, daubing. —*m., f.* smearer, dauber.
embadurnar, *tr.v.* to smear, daub. —*r.v.* to become smeared.
embaición, *f.* deception, tricking, swindling, flimflam (slang).
embaidor, ra, *a.* deceptive, misleading. —*m., f.* deceiver, trickster, cheat, swindler, impostor.
embaimiento, *a.* deception, delusion.
embaír, (*ref. 78*) *tr.v.* to deceive, trick, mislead, delude.
embajada, *f.* 1. embassy; ambassadorship. 2. message, commission. 3. impertinent suggestion or demand.
embajador, *m.* 1. ambassador. 2. (fig.) envoy, messenger, emissary. 3. (coll.) go-between.
embajadora, *f.* 1. ambassadress; ambassador's wife. 2. (coll.) messenger, emissary.
embalado, da, *past part. of* **embalar.** —*a.* like a shot, at full speed. — **el carro se fue e.,** the car went off like a shot.
embalador, *m.* packer.
embaladura, *f.* (Chile) packing, crating, baling.
embalaje, *m.* packing, crating, baling; packing expenses.
embalar, *tr.v.* to pack, crate, bale. —*i.v.* 1. to beat the water to drive fish into the nets. 2. (sport.) to sprint. 3. (S. Amer.) to step on the gas, put on speed. —*r.v.* 1. to race (a motor). 2. to let oneself be carried away by a passion, etc.
embaldosado, *past part. of* **embaldosar.** —*m.* tiling.
embaldosadura, *f.* tiling.
embaldosar, *tr.v.* to tile.
emballenado, *m.* whalebone framework.
emballenador, ra, *m., f.* person who stiffens (clothing or other articles) with whalebone stays; corset-maker.
emballenar, *tr.v.* to stiffen with whalebone stays.
emballestado, da, *past part. of* **emballestarse.** —*a.* (vet.) with a crooked fetlock. —*m.* (vet.) bending of the fetlock joint.
emballestadura, *f.* (vet.) bending of the fetlock joint.
emballestarse, *r.v.* to get ready to fire a crossbow.
embalsadero, *m.* swamp, marshy land, slough, rain pool.
embalsamador, ra, *a.* embalming. —*m., f.* embalmer.
embalsamamiento, *m.* embalming.
embalsamar, *tr.v.* 1. to embalm. 2. to perfume. —*r.v.* to become aromatic or fragrant.
embalsar, *tr.v.* 1. to put (something) on a raft. 2. (mar.) to sling, hoist. 3. to dam up. —*r.v.* to be dammed up.
embalse, *m.* 1. damming, damming up; dammed up waters. 2. (mar.) slinging. — **e. regulador,** regulating reservoir; **e. retardador,** retarding basin or reservoir.
embalumar, *tr.v.* to load with large bulky objects. —*r.v.* to overload oneself, burden oneself (with too much work).
embanastar, *tr.v.* 1. to put into a basket. 2. (fig.) to crowd in, squeeze in. —*r.v.* to crowd or squeeze together.
embancarse, (*ref. 50*) *r.v.* 1. (Mex., metal.) to stick to the walls of a furnace. 2. (Chile, Ecuad.) to silt up, become blocked (river). 3. (mar.) to run aground.
embanderar, *tr.v.* to decorate with flags and pennants.
embanquetar, *tr.v.* (Mex.) to put sidewalks or pavements on.
embarace, embaracé, *ref.* **embarazar.**
embarazadamente, *adv.* with difficulty, awkwardly.
embarazada, *a.* pregnant. —*f.* pregnant woman.
embarazador, ra, *a.* embarrassing, awkward.
embarazar, (*ref. 53*) *tr.v.* 1. to hamper, impede, hold up, (coll.) to blunder; to embarrass or burden. 2. to make pregnant. —*r.v.* 1. to be hampered or impeded. 2. to become pregnant.
embarazo, *m.* 1. obstacle, impediment, difficulty, interference, obstruction. 2. pregnancy. 3. shyness, bashfulness; embarrasment, awkwardness.
embarazosamente, *adv.* with difficulty, awkwardly, cumbersomely.
embarazoso, sa, *a.* 1. embarrassing. 2. inconvenient. 3. cumbersome, obstructive. 4. difficult.
embarbascarse, (*ref. 50*) *r.v.* 1. to become entangled in the roots (a plow). 2. (fig.) to become confused or entangled. 3. to run into difficulties (a business).
embarbasque, embarbasqué, *ref.* **embarbascarse.**
embarbecer, (*ref. 45*) *i.v.* to grow a beard.
embarbezca, embarbezco, *ref.* **embarbecer.**
embarbillado, *m.* (carp.) rabbeting; rabbet joint.
embarbillar, *tr.v.* (carp.) to rabbet.
embarcación, *f.* 1. (mar.) ship, boat, vessel. 2. embarkation. — **e. de desembarco,** (mil.) landing craft; **e. menor,** small craft.
embarcadero, *m.* 1. quay, landing stage, pier; dock, wharf. 2. (ry.) platform.
embarcador, *m.* shipper, loader, freighter.
embarcar, (*ref. 50*) *tr.v.* 1. to load; to embark, put (people) aboard. 2. to ship, send (merchandise). 3. to embark (on an enterprise). —*r.v.* 1. to embark, go aboard. 2. to embark (on an enterprise). 3. to be entangled (in a lawsuit).
embarco, *m.* embarkation, sailing, shipping.
embardar, *tr.v.* to thatch (roofs, walls, etc.).
embargable, *a.* (law) subject to embargo.
embargador, *m.* one who applies an embargo.
embargante, *a.* obstructing, impeding; arresting, restraining. — **no embargante,** nevertheless, notwithstanding.
embargar, (*ref. 51*) *tr.v.* 1. to obstruct, impede, hamper, hold up. 2. to paralyze. 3. (law) to embargo, place an embargo on.
embargo, *m.* 1. indigestion. 2. (law) embargo, sequestration, seizure. — **sin embargo,** notwithstanding, nevertheless; in spite of (the fact).
embargue, embargué, *ref.* **embargar.**
embarnizadura, *f.* 1. varnish (coat of varnish). 2. varnishing (action).
embarnizar, (*ref. 53*) *tr.v.* to varnish.
embarque, *m.* shipment (of cargo); loading (of cargo).
embarque, embarqué, *ref.* **embarcar.**
embarrada, *f.* (Chile, Arg.) blunder; stupidity, foolishness, stupid act.
embarradilla, *f.* (Mex.) sweet pastry or pie.
embarrado, *past part. of* **embarrar.** —*m.* plaster, mud plaster (for walls).
embarrador, ra, *a.* 1. staining, bedaubing. 2. (fig.) mischief-making, intriguing, lying. —*m., f.* 1. mischief-maker, liar, intriguer. 2. plasterer.
embarradura, *f.* smearing, splattering with mud; muddy spot or stain.
embarrancar, (*ref. 50*) *tr.v.* to put aground. —*i.v.* 1. to run or go aground. 2. to get bogged down (in difficulties). 3. to get stuck (in mud). 4. to run into a ditch. —*r.v.* 1. to run into a ditch. 2. to get stuck (in mud).
embarranque, embarranqué, *ref.* **embarrancar.**
embarrar, *tr.v.* 1. to splash with mud; to smear or stain with mud; to smear, bedaub, stain. 2. to pry up with a lever. 3. (Mex.) to involve in a shady business affair. 4. to flush (a partridge) into the tree tops. —*r.v.* 1. to become splashed, smeared or stained with mud; to become smeared or stained. 2. to flush into the tree tops.
embarrialarse, *r.v.* (C. Amer.) to get muddy, get covered with mud.
embarrilado, *m.* barreling, putting into barrels.

embarrilador, *m.* person who packs or fills barrels.
embarrilar, *tr.v.* to barrel, put in barrels.
embarrizarse, *r.v.* to get muddy, get covered with mud.
embarrotar, *tr.v.* to bar, strengthen with bars.
embarullador, ra, *a.* muddling. —*m., f.* 1. muddler. 2. careless or shoddy worker.
embarullar, *tr.v.* 1. to jumble or mix together in a muddle. 2. to do hastily or carelessly.
embasamiento, *m.* (archit.) foundation (of a building).
embastar, *tr.v.* 1. to fix (material) on an embroidering frame. 2. to stitch; to baste, to tack. 3. to harness with a packsaddle.
embaste, *m.* (dressm.) basting; stitching.
embastecer, (*ref.* 45) *i.v.* to get fat. —*r.v.* to become gross or coarse.
embastezca, embastezco, *ref.* **embastecer.**
embate, *m.* 1. pounding, dashing (of the waves). 2. sudden attack or rush (at the enemy). 3. soft cool sea breeze. — **embates de la fortuna,** reverses of fortune.
embaucador, ra, *a.* deceiving; swindling, bamboozling, cheating. —*m., f.* trickster, swindler, bamboozler, cheater.
embaucamiento, *m.* swindling, tricking, cheating.
embaucar, (*ref.* 50) *tr.v.* to deceive, cheat, trick, swindle, bamboozle.
embaulado, da, *past part. of* **embaular.** —*a.* packed, crammed.
embaular, *tr.v.* 1. to pack in a trunk. 2. (coll.) to cram (food).
embauque, embauqué, *ref.* **embaucar.**
embausamiento, *m.* amazement, astonishment.
embayarse, *r.v.* (Ecuad.) to become angry, get annoyed.
embazadura, *f.* 1. brown dye. 2. (fig.) astonishment, amazement.
embazar, (*ref.* 53) *tr.v.* 1. to dye brown. 2. to stop, obstruct, impede. 3. (fig.) to amaze, astonish. —*i.v.* (fig.) to be amazed or astonished. —*r.v.* 1. to become tired or bored. 2. to become bloated.
embazarse, (*ref.* 53) *r.v.* (cards) to make tricks.
embebecer, (*ref.* 45) *tr.v.* to amuse, divert. —*r.v.* to be fascinated, enthralled or absorbed.
embebecidamente, *adv.* fascinatedly, captivatedly; enthralled.
embebecimiento, *m.* fascination, captivation, enthrallment.
embebedor, ra, *a.* imbibing. —*m., f.* imbiber.
embeber, *tr.v.* 1. to absorb; to soak up. 2. to contain, enclose. 3. to take or gather in, shorten (e.g. skirt). 4. to soak, steep. 5. to insert, fit in; to embed. 6. to incorporate, add. —*i.v.* to shrink. —*r.v.* 1. to be absorbed, fascinated or enthralled. 2. to soak or steep oneself (in a subject).
embebezca, embebezco, *ref.* **embebecer.**
embebido, da, *past part. of* **embeber.** —*a.* (archit.) **columna embebida,** imbedded column.
embecadura, *f.* (archit.) spandrel.
embelecador, ra, *a.* deceptive, tricky. —*m., f.* trickster, duper, cheat, deceiver, impostor.
embelecamiento, *m.* tricking, deception; trick, fraud, swindle.
embelecar, (*ref.* 50) *tr.v.* to deceive, trick, hoodwink, dupe, swindle.
embeleco, *m.* 1. fraud, trick, deception. 2. (coll.) bore, nuisance, pest.
embeleñar, *tr.v.* 1. to drug with henbane; to drug, stupefy. 2. to captivate, fascinate, enthrall.
embeleque, embelequé, *ref.* **embelecar.**
embelesamiento, *m.* captivation, rapture, ecstasy, enchantment, fascination, enthrallment.
embelesar, *tr.v.* to fascinate, enthrall, captivate, enrapture, enchant. —*r.v.* to be captivated, enthralled, fascinated, enraptured or enchanted.
embeleso, *m.* 1. captivation, enchantment, rapture, enthrallment, fascination; delight, joy, enchanting thing. 2. (Cuba, bot.) leadwort (Plumbago europea).
embellaquecerse, (*ref.* 45) *r.v.* to become sly or cunning, become a rogue or scoundrel.
embellaquezca, embellaquezco, *ref.* **embellaquecerse.**
embellecer, (*ref.* 45) *tr.v.* to beautify, make beautiful, to adorn, to embellish.
embellecimiento, *m.* beautification, embellishment.
embellezca, embellezco, *ref.* **embellecer.**
embermejar, *tr.v., r.v., i.v., var. of* **embermejecer.**
embermejecer, (*ref.* 45) *tr.v.* 1. to make or dye red. 2. to make (someone) embarrassed, make (someone) blush. —*i.v.* to turn red or reddish. —*r.v.* to blush; to get red.
embermejezca, embermejezco, *ref.* **embermejecer.**
emberrenchinarse, emberrincharse, *r.v.* (coll.) to fly into a tantrum or rage.
embestida, *f.* 1. attack, assault, onslaught; charge (of a bull). 2. (coll.) touch (for money), pestering (for money or about business).
embestidor, ra, *a.* charging (bull); attacking. —*m.* (coll.) sponger.
embestidura, *f., var. of* **embestida.**
embestir, (*ref.* 39) *tr.v.* 1. to attack, assail, assault; to charge (a bull). 2. (coll.) to pester (about business or with requests for money), touch for money. —*i.v.* (coll.) to attack, to rush.
embetunar, *tr.v.* 1. to black, blacken, cover with boot polish. 2. to cover with pitch or tar.
embicadura, *f.* 1. (mar.) steering straight for land. 2. (mar.) luffing.
embicar, (*ref.* 50) *i.v.* (mar.) to steer straight for land. —*tr.v.* 1. (Cuba) to succeed in inserting something (in a hole). 2. (mar.) to top (the yards) with a sign of mourning. 3. (mar.) to luff.
embijado, da, *past part. of* **embijar.** —*a.* (Mex.) uneven.
embijar, *tr.v.* 1. to paint with annatto, paint vermilion. 2. (Hond., Mex.) to make dirty, soil, stain.
embije, *m.* reddening, painting vermilion.
embique, embiqué, *ref.* **embicar.**
embista, embisto, *ref.* **embestir.**
embistiendo, embistiera, embistiese, embistió, *ref.* **embestir.**
embizcar, (*ref.* 50) *i.v., r.v.* to become cross-eyed.
embizque, embizqué, *ref.* **embizcar.**
emblandecer, (*ref.* 45) *tr.v.* to soften, mollify. —*r.v.* to become soft, to be moved by pity.
emblandezca, emblandezco, *ref.* **emblandecer.**
emblanquecer, (*ref.* 45) *tr.v.* to whiten, bleach, make white. —*r.v.* to become white or bleached.
emblanquecimiento, *m.* whitening, bleaching, blanching.
emblanquezca, emblanquezco, *ref.* **emblanquecer.**
emblema, *m.* emblem, symbol; device.
emblemáticamente, *adv.* emblematically, symbolically.
emblemático, ca, *a.* emblematic, symbolic.
embobamiento, *m.* stupefaction, enthrallment, captivation.
embobar, *tr.v.* to stupefy, fascinate, enthrall, captivate. —*r.v.* to be stupefied, enthralled, enchanted or captivated.
embobecer, (*ref.* 45) *tr.v.* to stultify, make foolish, vapid or inane. —*r.v.* to become stultified, foolish or inane.
embobecimiento, *m.* stultification, stupefaction.
embobezca, embobezco, *ref.* **embobecer.**
embobinar, *tr.v.* to wind.
embocadero, *m.* mouth, outlet, narrow channel.
embocado, da, *past part. of* **embocar.** —*a.* smooth (wine).
embocadura, *f.* 1. mouthpiece (of a musical instrument; of a horse's bit). 2. taste (of wine). 3. mouth, navigable reaches (of a river). 4. (theat.) proscenium arch. — **tomar la e.,** to begin to play (a wind instrument) with skill; (coll.) to overcome the initial difficulties (of anything).
embocar, (*ref.* 50) *tr.v.* 1. to put in the mouth. 2. to pass (a ball or lance) through a hoop or ring. 3. to hole (a golf ball, a billiard ball). 4. to make (a person) swallow, make (someone) believe (incorrect news). 5. (coll.) to gorge, gulp down, cram down (food). 6. to begin, undertake (a business enterprise, project). 7. (coll.) to throw. —*r.v.* to enter, go into (a narrow place).
emboce, embocé, *ref.* **embozar.**
embocinado, da, *a.* trumpet-shaped, funnel-shaped.
embochinchar, *tr.v.* to agitate, stir up, arouse, excite, aggravate.
embodegar, (*ref.* 51) *tr.v.* to store, put in storage (in a warehouse or cellar).
embodegue, embodegué, *ref.* **embodegar.**
embojar, *tr.v.* to place branches in silkworm sheds, to prepare the sheds for the cocoons.
embojo, *m.* 1. branches (for silkworms). 2. placing branches in silkworm sheds.
embolada, *f.* stroke (of a piston).
embolado, *past part. of* **embolar.** —*m.* 1. (theat.) minor role. 2. bull with wooden balls on the tips of its horns (as a protection). 3. (coll.) trick, deception. 4. (coll.) a mess of trouble.
embolar, *tr.v.* 1. to cap the bull's horns with wooden balls (as a protection). 2. to shine or polish (shoes). 3. to size (for gilding).
embolectomía, *f.* (med.) embolectomy.
embolia, *f.* (med.) embolism; (med.) embolus, clot.
embolismador, ra, *a.* detracting, disparaging. —*m., f.* disparager, detractor.
embolismal, *a.* embolismic (said of time added to regularize a calendar).
embolismar, *tr.v.* 1. (coll.) to gossip or spread tales about. 2. (Chile) to incite, agitate.
embolismático, ca, *a.* confused, unintelligible, tangled, obscure.
embolismo, *m.* 1. embolism, intercalation (of time). 2. confusion, muddle. 3. (coll.) lie, falsehood, gossip.
émbolo, *m.* (mec.) piston; plunger; **e. de tronco,** (mec.) trunk piston.
embolsar, *tr.v.* 1. to pocket; to put in one's purse. 2. to pocket, make, earn. 3. to reimburse.
embolsicar, *tr.v.* to pocket, put in one's pocket or purse.
embolso, *m.* pocketing; putting in one's purse.
embonada, *f.* (mar.) sheathing (of a vessel).
embonar, *tr.v.* 1. to improve, repair. 2. (mar.) to sheathe (a vessel to broaden its beam). 3. (Cuba, Mex.) to fit, suit, become. 4. (Amer.) to fertilize.
embono, *m.* (mar.) sheathing, lining, doubling (of a ship).
emboñigar, (*ref.* 51) *tr.v.* to smear or plaster with cow-dung.
emboque, *m.* 1. passage through a narrow place. 2. (coll.) deception, trick, hoax. 3. (Chile) cup and ball (game).
emboque, emboqué, *ref.* **embocar.**
emboquillar, *tr.v.* 1. to put a tip on a cigarette. 2. (min.) to make the entrance or aperture (of a blast hole); to make the entrance (of a mine gallery or tunnel).

embornal, *m.* (mar.) scupper hole.
emborrace, emborracé, *ref.* **emborrazar.**
emborrachador, ra, *a.* intoxicating, inebriating.
emborrachamiento, *m.* (coll.) drunkenness, intoxication.
emborrachar, *tr.v.* to intoxicate, get or make drunk; to make drowsy. —*r.v.* to get drunk; to mix, run (colors) due to humidity.
emborrar, *tr.v.* 1. to stuff, pad (chairs, pack-saddles, etc.). 2. to card wool a second time. 3. (coll.) to cram down, gorge, gulp down.
emborrascar, (*ref. 50*) *tr.v.* to irritate, annoy, provoke, enrage. —*r.v.* 1. to become stormy (weather). 2. to fail, go on the rocks, go to rack and ruin. 3. (Arg., Hond., Mex.) to become exhausted (a mine).
emborrasque, emborrasqué, *ref.* **emborrascar.**
emborrazamiento, *m.* (cul.) covering with batter; basting fowl while roasting.
emborrazar, (*ref. 53*) *tr.v.* (cul.) to cover with batter; to baste or lard (a fowl) while roasting.
emborricarse, (*ref. 50*) *r.v.* 1. to be stunned or bewildered. 2. (coll.) to fall madly in love.
emborrice, *ref.* **emborrizar.**
emborrique, emborriqué, *ref.* **emborricarse.**
emborrizar, (*ref. 53*) *tr.v.* (tex.) to card (wool) for the first time.
emborronador, ra, *a.* smudging, blotting; scribbling.
emborronar, *tr.v.* to cover (paper) with blots or smudges; (coll.) to scribble.
emborrullarse, *r.v.* (coll.) to quarrel noisily, wrangle.
emboscada, *f.* 1. ambush, ambuscade. 2. trap, trick, stratagem.
emboscadura, *f.* ambush, ambuscade; ambushing, waylaying.
emboscar, (*ref. 50*) *tr.v.* to place in ambush, ambush. —*r.v.* 1. to lie in ambush, ambush; to hide in the woods. 2. (fig.) to find a comfortable or easy job in order to avoid a more difficult or hard one.
embosque, embosqué, *ref.* **emboscar.**
embosquecer, (*ref. 45*) *i.v.* to become wooded (park, area, land).
embostar, *tr.v.* 1. to fertilize with dung. 2. (Arg., Ven.) to plaster with earth mixed with dung.
embotado, da, *past part. of* **embotar.** —*a.* 1. (Chile) black-footed (cattle). 2. blunt, dull.
embotador, ra, *a.* blunting; enervating, dulling. —*m., f.* person who blunts swords, etc.
embotadura, *f.* bluntness, dullness (of weapons).
embotamiento, *m.* blunting (of weapons); enervating, dulling, e.g. *e. de los sentidos,* dulling of the senses, drowsiness.
embotar, *tr.v.* 1. to blunt. 2. to enervate, weaken, dull, make drowsy. 3. to put (something) in a jar or container. —*r.v.* 1. to become blunt (an edge). 2. to become dull, drowsy. 3. (coll.) to put on one's boots.
embotellado, *past part. of* **embotellar.** —*a.* prepared (speech, etc.); crammed (studies, etc.). —*m.* bottling (of wine, soft drinks, beer, etc.).
embotellador, ra, *m., f.* bottler. —*f.* bottling machine. —*a.* bottling.
embotellamiento, *m.* 1. bottling. 2. (coll.) traffic jam, bottleneck.
embotellar, *tr.v.* 1. to bottle (liquids). 2. (fig.) to bottle up (enemy ships in a port). 3. (fig.) to corner (a person); to paralyze (a business deal).
emboticar, (*ref. 50*) *tr.v.* (Chile) to overdose with medicine.—*r.v.* (Chile) to overdose oneself with medicines.
embotijar, *tr.v.* 1. to put or keep in jugs. 2. to put a layer of jugs under (flooring) to keep out dampness. —*r.v.* 1. (coll.) to swell up, become swollen. 2. (coll.) to fly into a rage, get furious.
embovedar, *tr.v.* to arch, vault; to build an arch over.
embozadamente, *adv.* in a veiled manner, disguisedly (manner of saying something); in secret, secretly, on the sly.
embozado, da, *past part. of* **embozar.** —*a.* muffled, masked, with the face covered. —*m., f.* person whose face is covered.
embozalar, *tr.v.* to muzzle, put a muzzle on.
embozar, (*ref. 53*) *tr.v.* 1. to mask, muffle, cover (the lower part of the face) with a cloak. 2. to disguise, mask, cloak (one's intentions or plans). 3. to muzzle (an animal). —*r.v.* to cover one's face.
embozo, *m.* 1. muffler, part of a cloak covering the lower part of the face. 2. (*pl.*) lining on the edge of a cloak or cape. 3. upper hem or fold of the sheet. 4. dissimulation, concealment (of one's intentions); **quitarse el e.,** to make one's intentions known, come out into the open; **sin e.,** frankly, openly.
embracé, embrace, *ref.* **embrazar.**
embracilado, da, *a.* (coll.) constantly carried in the arms (children).
embragar, (*ref. 51*) *tr.v.* 1. (mar.) to sling, tie with ropes (for hoisting). 2. (mec.) to engage, connect; (auto.) to engage the clutch of a motor.
embrague, *m.* clutch; throwing in the clutch; coupling; **e. cónico,** cone clutch; **e. de discos,** plate clutch; **e. de fricción,** friction clutch; **e. de garras,** claw clutch, dog clutch; **e. de mordaza** or **quijadas,** jaw clutch; **e. espiral,** coil clutch; **e. seco,** dry clutch.
embrague, embragué, *ref.* **embragar.**
embravecer, (*ref. 45*) *tr.v.* to infuriate, enrage. —*i.v.* to become strong, revive (plants). —*r.v.* 1. to become furious or angry. 2. to become rough (the sea); **embravecerse con** or **contra,** to get furious at.
embravecimiento, *m.* fury, anger, rage.
embravezca, embravezco, *ref.* **embravecer.**
embrazadura, *f.* 1. grasping or taking up (a shield). 2. grasp, handle (of a shield).
embrazar, (*ref. 53*) *tr.v.* to clasp; to grasp, take up (a shield).
embreado, da, *past part. of* **embrear.** —*m.* tarring. —*a.* tarred.
embreadura, *f.* pitching, tarring, covering with pitch or tar.
embrear, *tr.v.* to tar, pitch, cover with tar or pitch.
embregarse, (*ref. 51*) *r.v.* to wrangle, quarrel, get into a quarrel.
embregue, embregué, *ref.* **embregarse.**
embreñarse, *r.v.* to hide among brambles.
embriagado, da, *past part. of* **embriagar.** —*a.* drunk, intoxicated.
embriagador, ra, *a.* intoxicating, heady, e.g. *un perfume e.,* a heady scent.
embriagante, *a.* intoxicating, heady.
embriagar, (*ref. 51*) *tr.v.* 1. to intoxicate, make tipsy or drunk. 2. to enrapture, transport. —*r.v.* 1. to become intoxicated or drunk. 2. to be enraptured or transported.
embriague, embriagué, *ref.* **embriagar.**
embriaguez, *f.* intoxication, drunkenness; (fig.) rapture, transport, ecstasy.
embridar, *tr.v.* to put a bridle on, bridle (a horse); to make (a horse) hold its head well.
embriófita, *f.* (bot.) embryophyte, (*pl.*) Embryophyta.
embriogenia, *f.* (biol.) embryogeny.
embriogénico, ca, *a.* (biol.) embryogenic.
embriología, *f.* (biol.) embryology.
embriológico, ca, *a.* (biol.) embryologic, embryological.
embriólogo, ga, *m., f.* embryologist.
embrión, *m.* (biol.) embryo.
embrionado, da, *a.* (bot.) embryonated.
embrionario, ria, *a.* (biol.) embryonic.
embroca, *f.* poultice, cataplasm.
embrocación, *f.* 1. (med.) embrocation. 2. poultice, cataplasm.
embrocar, (*ref. 50*) *tr.v.* 1. to empty (one container into another). 2. to place upside down. 3. to wind (thread) on a reel. 4. to nail, tack (soles of shoes). 5. (taur.) to catch (the bullfighter) between the horns. —*i.v.* (Mex.) to put a garment over one's head. —*r.v.* to come out poorly (from a deal).
embrochado, da, *a.* embroidered in gold or silver threads.
embrochalar, *tr.v.* (archit.) to support (a beam) with a header beam, crosspiece or stay.
embrolla, *f.* (coll.) *var. of* **embrollo.**
embrolladamente, *adv.* confusedly, in a muddled manner.
embrollador, ra, *a.* 1. confusing, muddling. 2. embroiling, troublemaking. —*m., f.* troublemaker.
embrollar, *tr.v.* to mix up, muddle, confuse, complicate, entangle, embroil. —*r.v.* to become muddled or mixed up.
embrollo, *m.* 1. muddle, tangle, confusion, mess. 2. difficult situation. 3. trick, lie, deception.
embrollón, na, *a., m., f.* (coll.) *var. of* **embrollador.**
embrolloso, sa, *a.* (coll.) embroiling, troublemaking, causing confusion.
embromado, da, *past part. of* **embromar.** —*a.* 1. vexed, annoyed. 2. (Amer.) said of someone going through a difficult situation. 3. (Amer.) ill, sick. 4. (Amer.) penniless, broke. 5. (mar.) misty, hazy, foggy.
embromador, ra, *a.* bantering, chaffing. —*m., f.* joker, banterer, chaffer.
embromar, *tr.v.* 1. to tease, banter at, chaff. 2. to cheat, trick, hoodwink. 3. (Chile, Mex.) to hold up, detain. 4. (Amer.) to annoy, vex. 5. (Arg., Chile, P. Rico) to harm, damage. 6. (mar.) to chinse. —*i.v.* to loiter, dally. —*r.v.* 1. to loiter, dally. 2. to become damaged.
embroque, embroqué, *ref.* **embrocar.**
embroquelarse, *r.v.* to shield oneself.
embroquetar, *tr.v.* to skewer (the legs of fowls) before broiling.
embrosquilar, *tr.v.* to put (cattle) into a fold.
embrujamiento, *m.* bewitchment.
embrujar, *tr.v.* to bewitch.
embrutecedor, ra, *a.* brutalizing, dehumanizing.
embrutecer, (*ref. 45*) *tr.v.* to brutalize, stupefy, stultify. —*r.v.* to become brutalized or irrational.
embrutecimiento, *m.* brutalization.
embuchado, *past part. of* **embuchar.** —*m.* 1. pork sausage. 2. (fig.) blind, screen, cover-up (to conceal other activities). 3. (coll.) feigned anger or annoyance. 4. (fig., theat.) impromptu joke or gag (not in the script). 5. (fig.) fraudulent voting. 6. (Cuba) indigestion (of fowls).
embuchar, *tr.v.* to stuff with minced meat (a sausage); to cram the maw (of birds); (coll.) to stuff, cram down, gorge (food).
embudador, ra, *m., f.* one who funnels.
embudar, *tr.v.* 1. to funnel into. 2. (fig.) to trick, ensnare. 3. to make (game) enter an enclosure (by means of a narrowing fence).
embudista, *a.* (fig.) tricking; intriguing. —*m., f.* trickster, deceiver.
embudo, *m.* 1. funnel. 2. (fig.) trick, trap. — **ley del e.,** (fig., coll.) unequal law, one-sided agreement.
embullador, ra, *a.* animating, exciting.

embullar, *tr.v.* to animate, excite, make merry. —*r.v.* to become excited or merry. —*i.v.* (Amer.) to make merry.
embullo, *m.* (Amer.) noise, gaiety, revelry; (Cuba) excitement, anticipation.
emburujar, *tr.v.* 1. (coll.) to make lumpy. 2. (fig.) to jumble or muddle; (Cuba) to confuse, mix up. —*r.v.* 1. to become lumpy. 2. (Amer.) to wrap oneself up.
embuste, *m.* 1. trick, fraud, deception, hoax; lie, fib. 2. (*pl.*) baubles, trinkets.
embustear, *i.v.* to lie, fib.
embustería, *f.* (coll.) trick; deception.
embustero, ra, *a.* lying, fibbing. —*m., f.* liar, fibber (coll.).
embustidor, ra, *a.* lying.
embustir, *i.v.* (rare) to tell lies, lie.
embutidera, *f.* (mec.) rivet set (a cupped tool for forming a head on a rivet).
embutido, da, *past part. of* **embutir. —***m.* 1. inlay, marquetry. 2. sausage. 3. lace trimming.
embutidura, *f.* (mar.) worming.
embutir, *tr.v.* 1. to inlay. 2. to pack tightly, stuff; to cram into a small space; to stuff, cram (with food). 3. to drive in (knowledge). —*r.v.* to gorge, stuff oneself.
emelga, *f., var. of* **amelga.**
emenagogo, *a.* (med.) emmenagogic. —*m.* emmenagogue.
emergencia, *f.* 1. emergency, accident. 2. emergence, appearance.
emergente, *a.* emergent, resulting, issuing.
emerger, (*ref. 57*) *i.v.* to emerge, come to the surface.
emeritense, *a.* from or of Merida, Spain. —*m., f.* native of Merida.
emérito, ta, *a.* emeritus, retired. —*m.* emeritus, Roman veteran honorably discharged after completing his service.
emerja, emerjo, *ref.* **emerger.**
emersión, *f.* (astron.) emersion, reappearance (of a celestial body after an eclipse).
emético, ca, *a.* (med.) emetic. —*m.* emetic (agent which causes vomiting).
emetina, *f.* (pharm.) emetine.
emétrope, *a.* emmetropic, said of normal vision.
emetropía, *f.* (med.) emmetropia, normal vision.
emídidos, *m.* (*pl.*) (zool.) Emydidae (subfamily of cholonians, fresh-water tortoises, terrapins).
emienda, *f.* (obs.) *var. of* **enmienda,** amendment, correction.
emigración, *f.* emigration; migration; **e.** golondrina, short period emigration.
emigrado, da, *past part. of* **emigrar. —***m., f.* emigrant, emigré.
emigrante, *a.* emigrating; migrating. —*m.* emigrant, emigré.
emigrar, *i.v.* to emigrate; to go and live abroad; to migrate (birds, animals).
emigratorio, ria, *a.* migratory.
eminencia, *f.* 1. eminence. 2. height, rise, hill. 3. Eminence (title). 4. eminent figure. — **con e., eminently.**
eminencial, *a.* (philos.) virtual, potential (having the power to produce effects by its influence rather than by actual connection).
eminencialmente, *adv.* (philos.) virtually, potentially.
eminente, *a.* 1. eminent, outstanding, prominent. 2. high, lofty, eminent.
eminentemente, *adv.* 1. eminently, excellently. 2. (philos.) virtually.
eminentísimo, ma, *a.* most eminent.
emir, *m.* amir, emir; Moslem prince or leader.
emisario, ria, *m., f.* emissary; envoy, agent.
emisión, *f.* 1. emission. 2. issue (stock, public bonds, etc.). 3. (rad.) broadcast. — **e. espectral,** (opt.) spectral emission; **e. secundaria,** (rad.) secondary emission.
emisividad, *f.* (phys.) emissivity.
emisor, ra, *a.* emitting; broadcasting. —*m.* radio transmitter. —*f.* broadcasting station.
emitir, *tr.v.* 1. to emit, send forth, e.g. *e. un suspiro,* to give a sigh. 2. to issue (money). 3. to give, express (an opinion). 4. (radio, tel.) to broadcast.
emoción, *f.* 1. emotion, feeling. 2. excitement, thrill.
emocional, *a.* emotional.
emocionante, *a.* 1. touching, moving. 2. exciting, thrilling.
emocionar, *tr.v.* to move, touch. —*r.v.* to be moved, touched, thrilled.
emoliente, *a., m.* (med.) emollient.
emolumento, *m.* emolument.
emotividad, *f.* emotionality.
emotivo, va, *a.* 1. emotive, causing emotion. 2. emotional, sensitive to emotion.
empacador, ra, *a.* packing, crating, baling. —*m.* packer, crater, baler. —*f.* packing or crating machine.
empacamiento, *m.* 1. (Amer.) balking (of a horse). 2. obstinacy, hard-headedness.
empacar, (*ref. 50*) *tr.v.* to pack, crate, bale.
empacarse, (*ref. 50*) *r.v.* 1. to become stubborn, stand firm, dig one's heels in, persist. 2. (fig.) to get rattled or flustered, be put off (from what one was doing). 3. (Amer.) to halk (animals).
empachadamente, *adv.* awkwardly, clumsily.
empachado, da, *past part. of* **empachar. —***a.* awkward, clumsy.
empachar, *tr.v.* 1. to hinder, obstruct, impede. 2. to give indigestion to. 3. to disguise, cloak. —*r.v.* 1. to get indigestion, to become surfeited. 2. to become embarrassed, rattled or flustered.
empacho, *m.* 1. shyness, bashfulness. 2. surfeit; indigestion, flatulence. — **sin e.,** without embarrassment or ceremony.
empachoso, sa, *a.* 1. shameful, embarrasing. 2. indigestible, causing indigestion.
empacón, na, *a.* 1. (Amer.) stubborn. 2. (Amer.) balky (animal).
empadrarse, *r.v.* to become excessively fond of one's parents (a child).
empadronado, da, *m., f.* registered voter.
empadronador, *m.* census-taker.
empadronamiento, *m.* census; census-taking; tax list.
empadronar, *tr.v.* to take a census of; to register in a census or a taxpayers list.
empajada, *f.* fodder; mixture of hay and bran fed to horses.
empajar, *tr.v.* 1. to cover or stuff with straw. 2. (Chile, Col.) to thatch. 3. (Amer.) to mix clay with straw (for making adobe bricks). —*r.v.* 1. (Chile) to bear much stalk and little grain (cereal plants). 2. (Cuba, P. Rico) to fill oneself with tidbits. 3. (Mex.) to make a good profit.
empajolar, *tr.v.* to smoke, cure (wine boots and barrels).
empalagamiento, *m.* 1. surfeit; cloying. 2. (fig.) annoyance, irritation.
empalagar, (*ref. 51*) *tr.v.* 1. to surfeit, pall, cloy. 2. (fig.) to bore, irritate, tire. —*r.v.* 1. to become surfeited. 2. to be bored or tired.
empalago, *m.* 1. surfeit; cloying. 2. annoyance, irritation.
empalagoso, sa, *a.* 1. cloying, sickly (food), too sweet or syrupy. 2. (fig.) annoying, bothersome, tiresome (person). —*m., f.* bothersome person, bore, pest, nuisance.
empalague, empalagué, *ref.* **empalagar.**
empalamiento, *m.* impalement, impaling.
empalar, *tr.v.* to impale. —*r.v.* 1. (Chile) to indulge in one's whims, persist. 2. (Chile) to become stiff or numb (limbs).
empaliada, *f.* bunting, balcony hangings and ceremonial decorations.
empaliar, *tr.v.* to decorate with streamers, banners, bunting.
empalicar, (*ref. 50*) *tr.v.* to cajole, wheedle.
empalice, empalicé, *ref.* **empalizar.**
empalidecer, (*ref. 45*) *i.v.* to pale, become pale.
empalidezca, empalidezco, *ref.* **empalidecer.**
empalizada, *f.* fence, palisade; stockade.
empalizar, (*ref. 53*) *tr.v.* to fence, fence in.
empalletado, *m.* (mar.) collision mat (fastened to the side of a boat).
empalmadura, *f., var. of* **empalme.**
empalmar, *tr.v.* to join, couple; to splice; (fig.) to combine. —*i.v.* 1. to join. 2. to follow, succeed. —*r.v.* 1. to join, meet. 2. to connect (two trains, buses, etc.). 3. to conceal (a knife) between one's palm and sleeve.
empalme, *m.* joining, coupling; joint; splice; combination; junction (between roads or railways); connection (between two trains, buses).
empalomado, *m.* (hydraul.) loose-stone damming wall.
empalomadura, *f.* (mar.) cord tying the boltrope to the sail.
empalomar, *tr.v.* (mar.) to sew (the boltrope to the sail).
empamparse, *r.v.* (Amer.) to get lost in the pampas.
empampirolado, da, *a.* (coll.) boastful, vain.
empanada, *f.* 1. turnover pie or pastry. 2. fraud, deception, intrigue.
empanadilla, *f. dim. of* **empanada,** small turnover, pie or pastry.
empanado, da, *past part. of* **empanar. —***a.* 1. breaded, dipped in a batter. 2. without direct light or ventilation. —*m.* room without direct light or ventillation.
empanar, *tr.v.* 1. to bread or dip in a batter; to dip in breadcrumbs. 2. (agr.) to sow (wheat). —*r.v.* (agr.) to be choked (land that has been too closely sowed).
empandar, *tr.v.* to bend, warp. —*r.v.* to become bent or warped; to sag.
empandillar, *tr.v.* 1. (coll.) to slip (a card) under another in order to cheat. 2. to hoodwink, trick.
empanizar, *tr.v.* to cover with breadcrumbs, crackermeal, etc.
empantanar, *tr.v.* 1. to swamp, flood. 2. to obstruct, hold up. —*r.v.* 1. to become swamped. 2. to get bogged down; to be obstructed or held up.
empanzarse, *r.v.* to get surfeited with food or drink.
empañado, da, *a.* 1. swaddled. 2. dim, foggy (glass, crystal). 3. (fig.) sullied, soiled; blemished, stained.
empañadura, *f.* swaddling; swaddling clothes (of an infant).
empañar, *tr.v.* 1. to swaddle. 2. to cloud, mist, blur, dim, e.g. *se me empañaron los ojos,* my eyes became blurred (with tears).
empañetar, *tr.v.* (Amer.) to plaster, parget.
empañicar, (*ref. 50*) *tr.v.* (mar.) to hand, furl (a sail).
empañique, empañiqué, *ref.* **empañicar.**
empapado, da, *past part. of* **empapar. —***a.* (fig.) well informed, knowledgeable.
empapamiento, *m.* soaking, dousing; sogginess.
empapar, *tr.v.* 1. to soak; to drench, saturate. 2. to soak up, absorb. —*r.v.* (coll.) to fill oneself, gorge oneself; **empaparse de,** to become soaked

with; to get to know completely, become completely conversant in.
empapelado, *past part. of* **empapelar.** —*m.* papering (of a room, trunk); paper (used in papering).
empapelador, ra, *m., f.* paper-hanger, paperer.
empapelar, *tr.v.* 1. to paper, to line with paper; to wrap in paper. 2. (coll.) to bring legal proceedings against.
empapirotar, *tr.v., r.v.* to dress up elaborately.
empapuce, empapucé, *ref.* **empapuzar.**
empapuciar, *tr.v., var. of* **empapujar.**
empapujar, *tr.v.* to stuff, cram (with food).
empapuzar, (*ref.* 53) *tr.v., var. of* **empapujar.**
empaque, *m.* 1. packing, packing cloth, wrapping paper. 2. air, mien, appearance. 3. affected seriousness. 4. (Amer.) nerve, cheek, brazenness, impudence. 5. (Amer.) bloat, air (in cattle).
empaque, empaqué, *ref.* **empacar.**
empaquetado, da, *past part. of* **empaquetar.** —*a.* (Amer.) elaborately dressed, all decked out.
empaquetador, ra, *m., f.* packer, wrapper.
empaquetadura, *f.* (mec.) packing, gasket. —**e. laminar,** (mec.) sheet packing; **e. metálica,** metallic packing.
empaquetar, *tr.v.* 1. to pack, wrap, parcel up, bale. 2. (fig.) to stuff, pack (people into a small space). 3. (Chile) to stuff (with filling). 4. (Amer.) to dress up.
emparamado, da, *past part. of* **emparamarse.** —*a.* (Amer.) shivering with cold; (fig.) frozen.
emparamarse, *r.v.* (Col., Ven.) 1. to freeze to death. 2. to tremble or shiver because of exposure to extreme cold.
emparamentar, *tr.v.* to bedeck, adorn.
emparchar, *tr.v.* to dress (a wounded or sick person) with plaster patches.
empardar, *tr.v.* (Arg.) to draw, tie.
emparedado, da, *past. part. of* **emparedar.** —*a.* confined; withdrawn. —*m., f.* recluse. —*m.* sandwich; any food inserted between layers of bread.
emparedamiento, *m.* 1. immurement, confinement; confining. 2. hermitage, cloister.
emparedar, *tr.v.* to confine (a person); to wall in, immure; to hide (something) between walls.
emparejado, da, *past part. of* **emparejar.** —*a.* leveled, even; matched, coupled.
emparejador, ra, *m., f.* leveler, smoother, matcher, fitter; plane.
emparejadura, *f.* 1. smoothing, leveling. 2. matching, pairing.
emparejamiento, *m.* 1. matching, pairing. 2. smoothing, leveling.
emparejar, *tr.v.* 1. to match, pair off. 2. to make (a surface) level, level; to level off, smooth (land). 3. to push (doors) to, close (without locking). —*i.v.* to catch up (with); to match. —*r.v.* to pair off, form pairs.
emparentado, da, *past part. of* **emparentar.** —*a.* related by marriage.
emparentar, (*ref.* 29) *i.v.* to become related by marriage.
empariente, empariento, *ref.* **emparentar.**
emparrado, *past part. of* **emparrar.** —*m.* 1. vine arbor, bower; trellis, arbor frame. 2. (coll.) hair combed from the side upwards (to cover a partially bald head).
emparrar, *tr.v.* to make into a vine arbor or bower.
emparrillado, *past part. of* **emparrillar.** —*m.* grillage (framework of timber or steel crossbeams as a foundation for building on marshy land).
emparrillar, *tr.v.* 1. to broil on a grill. 2. (archit.) to strengthen with a grillage.
emparvar, *tr.v.* to lay (grain) for threshing.
empastada, *f.* (Chile) pasture, grass.
empastado, da, *a.* said of a book bound with a hard cover (made of cloth, leather, cardboard, etc.).
empastador, ra, *a.* impasting. —*m.* 1. (p.) impasting-brush. 2. (p.) painter who applies paint thickly. 3. (Amer., print.) bookbinder.
empastar, *tr.v.* 1. to cover with paste. 2. (print.) to bind with hard covers. 3. to fill a tooth. 4. (p.) to impaste, apply colors thickly (to a canvas). 5. (Amer.) to turn into pasture (land). —*r.v.* (Chile) to become overgrown with weeds.
empaste, *m.* 1. binding (a book) in hard covers. 2. filling (of a tooth). 3. (p.) impasto. 4. (p.) blending (of colors). 5. (Arg., vet.) meteorism.
empastelamiento, *m.* (print.) pi, pieing.
empastelar, *tr.v.* 1. (coll.) to arrange or settle hastily and unfairly. 2. (print.) to pie. —*r.v.* (print.) to become pied or disarranged.
empatadera, *f.* (coll.) impediment, suspension.
empatar, *tr.v.* 1. to equal, to match. 2. (Amer.) to couple, join; to splice. 3. to impede, hold up. —*i.v.* 1. to tie, be equal. 2. (Amer.) to join. —*r.v.* to tie, be equal.
empate, *m.* 1. the action of equaling, splicing, joining. 2. tie (sports).
empatía, *f.* (psyc.) empathy.
empatillar, *tr.v.* to join, splice.
empavar, *tr.v.* 1. (Peru) to pull (someone's) leg, tease, kid. 2. (Ecuad.) to irritate, annoy. —*r.v.* 1. to become embarrassed. 2. to become annoyed or irritated.
empavesada, *f.* 1. defensive wall made with pavises or shields. 2. (mar.) canvas dressing for ships; (mar.) canvas covering for hammocks and cots.
empavesado, da, *past part. of* **empavesar.** —*a.* armed with shields, protected, shielded. —*m.* 1. soldier armed with a shield. 2. (mar.) ship's dressing or bunting.
empavesar, *tr.v.* (mar.) to decorate with bunting, dress (a ship); to veil (a public monument or statue before inauguration).
empavonar, *tr.v.* 1. to blue (paint) iron or steel in order to protect it. 2. (Amer.) to grease.
empecatado, da, *a.* 1. incorrigible, devilish. 2. unlucky, ill-starred, unfortunate.
empecé, *ref.* **empezar.**
empecedero, ra, *a.* harmful, damaging.
empecer, (*ref.* 45) *tr.v.* to harm, hurt, damage. —*i.v.* to obstruct, impede.
empecible, *a., var. of* **empecedero.**
empecimiento, *m.* harm, damage; obstacle.
empecinado, da, *past part. of* **empecinarse.** —*a.* obstinate, stubborn. —*m.* pitch manufacturer or dealer.
empecinamiento, *m.* obstinacy, stubbornness.
empecinar, *tr.v.* to smear or cover with pitch.
empecinarse, *r.v.* to become obstinate, stubborn or persistent.
empedernido, da, *past part. of* **empedernir.** —*a.* 1. insensible. 2. hard-hearted. 3. diehard, e.g. *un conservador e.*, a diehard conservative; inveterate (smoker, drinker); hardened (criminal); confirmed (bachelor).
empedernir, (*ref.* 78) *tr.v.* to harden, indurate. —*r.v.* to harden, become hard, insensitive or hard-hearted.
empedrado, da, *past part. of* **empedrar.** —*a.* 1. mottled, spotted (horse). 2. (fig.) flecked with clouds (the sky). —*m.* paving; stone pavement.
empedrador, *m.* stone paver.
empedramiento, *m.* stone paving.
empedrar, (*ref.* 29) *tr.v.* 1. to pave with stones. 2. (fig.) to dot, sprinkle, cover, pepper, strew.
empega, *f.* 1. pitch. 2. pitch mark made on cattle or sheep.
empegado, *past part. of* **empegar.** —*m.* tarpaulin.
empegadura, *f.* coat of pitch.
empegar, (*ref.* 51) *tr.v.* 1. to coat with pitch. 2. to mark (cattle or sheep) with pitch.
empego, *m.* marking (cattle or sheep) with pitch.
empegue, empegué, *ref.* **empegar.**
empeguntar, *tr.v.* to mark (cattle or sheep) with pitch.
empeine, *m.* 1. (anat.) groin. 2. instep (of a foot); vamp (of a boot). 3. (med.) impetigo; ringworm. 4. (bot.) liverwort, hepatica.
empeinoso, sa, *a.* pustulous, pimply; impetiginous; infected with ringworm.
empelar, *i.v.* 1. to grow hair. 2. match (horses of similar color).
empelazgarse, (*ref.* 51) *r.v.* (coll.) to quarrel, get into a quarrel or a row.
empelazgue, empelazgué, *ref.* **empelazgarse.**
empelechar, *tr.v.* to cover or line with marble; to dress with marble.
empella, *f.* 1. vamp (of a shoe). 2. (Amer.) pork fat.
empellar, *tr.v.* to push, shove, jostle.
empellejar, *tr.v.* to cover or line with skins.
empeller, (*ref.* 58) *tr.v., var of* **empellar.**
empellita, *f.* (Cuba) pork crackling; fatback rind.
empellón, *m.* shove, push; **a empellones,** (coll.) pushing violently.
empelotarse, *r.v.* 1. (coll.) to get into a row or quarrel. 2. (Mex.) to fall passionately in love, become infatuated; to conceive an urge or longing (for something or someone). 3. (Amer.) to strip, undress completely.
empeltre, *m.* side graft; sapling.
empenachado, da, *past part. of* **empenachar.** —*a.* plumed, tufted.
empenachar, *tr.v.* to decorate with plumes or tufts.
empenta, *f.* prop, support, stay.
empentar, *tr.v.* (min.) to stay, prop (sides of a mine) evenly.
empeñadamente, *adv.* persistently, tenaciously; strenuously, hard.
empeñado, da, *past part. of* **empeñar.** —*a.* heated, excited (discussion); persisting, determined.
empeñaduría, *f.* (Amer.) pawnshop.
empeñar, *tr.v.* 1. to pawn. 2. to oblige, compel, constrain. 3. to begin (a battle, dispute, etc.). —*r.v.* 1. to go into debt. 2. to insist, persist. —**empeñarse en,** to be bent on; to engage in (a battle); **empeñarse por** or **con,** to intercede for; **e. hasta la camisa,** to risk losing one's shirt (in a venture).
empeñero, ra, *m., f.* (Mex.) pawnbroker.
empeño, *m.* 1. pledge, pawn. 2. obligation. 3. involvement, commitment. 4. determination, tenacity, persistence. 5. patron, supporter. 6. (coll.) pull, influence. 7. (Mex.) pawnshop. —**casa de empeños,** pawnshop; **con e.,** tenaciously, with great perseverance, with determination; **en e.,** in pawn, in hock; as a pledge; **tener e.,** to want, desire; to be eager or persistent.
empeñoso, sa, *a.* (Amer.) persistent, tenacious.
empeoramiento, *m.* deterioration, worsening.
empeorar, *tr.v.* to impair, make worse. —*i.v.* to become worse (sickness, situation, etc.); to deteriorate. —*r.v.* to get worse, to worsen.
empequeñecer, (*ref.* 45) *tr.v.* to reduce, diminish, make smaller; to belittle.
empequeñecimiento, *m.* reduction, diminution, belittling.
empequeñezca, empequeñezco, *ref.* **empequeñecer.**
emperador, *m.* 1 emperor. 2. (Cuba, ichth.) swordfish (Xiphias gladius).

emperatriz, (*pl.* **emperatrices**) *f.* empress.
emperchado, *m.* fence made with green to worsen.
emperchar, *tr.v.* to hang up, put on a hanger. —*r.v.* to become caught in a snare (game).
empercudir, *tr.v.* (Cuba) to stain, soil (clothing) by careless washing.
emperdigar, (*ref.* *51*) *tr.v.*, *var. of* **perdigar,** to prepare meat for cooking.
emperece, emperecé, *ref.* **emperezar.**
emperejilar, *tr.v.* (coll.) to doll up or dress someone up. —*r.v.* (coll.) to doll oneself up, dress oneself up, e.g. *los domingos yo me emperejilo,* I get all dolled up on Sundays.
emperezar, (*ref.* *53*) *r.v.*, *i.v.* to become lazy or indolent. —*tr.v.* (fig.) to obstruct, delay, retard.
empergaminado, da, *past part. of* **empergaminar.** —*a.* bound in parchment; (fig.) formal, stiff (said of a person).
empergaminar, *tr.v.* to bind (books) in parchment.
empericarse, (*ref.* *50*) *r.v.* 1. (Col.) to get drunk or tipsy. 2. (Mex.) to climb; to get on top; to rise (in social position). 3. (Mex.) to blush.
emperifolliar, *tr.v.*, *r.v.*, *var. of* **emperejilar.**
emperique, emperiqué, *ref.* **empericarse.**
emperlar, *tr.v.* to impearl. —*r.v.* to adorn oneself with pearls; (fig.) to get all dolled up.
empernar, *tr.v.* to nail, bolt, screw, fasten with pins or pegs.
empero, *conj.* but; nevertheless, however, yet, notwithstanding.
emperrada, *f.* 1. ombre (card game). 2. fit of stubborn anger.
emperramiento, *m.* stubbornness, obstinacy; anger, ire.
emperrarse, *r.v.* (coll.) 1. to be or get stubborn or obstinate, stand one's ground. 2. to persist. 3. to get angry, e.g. *me emperré con ella,* I got mad at her. — **e. en +** *inf.*, (coll.) to try subbornly to + *inf.*
empertigar, (*ref.* *51*) *tr.v.* (Chile) to yoke oxen.
empertigue, empertigué, *ref.* **empertigar.**
empesador, *m.* brush or broom of reeds used by weavers to smooth and trim warp.
empetatar, *tr.v.* (Guat., Mex., Peru) to cover (a floor) with rush mats.
empetro, *m.* (bot.) samphire (Crithmum maritimum).
empezar, (*ref.* *68*) *tr.v.*, *i.v.* to begin, commence; to start. — **e. por,** to begin by; **e. la casa por el tejado,** to put the cart before the horse.
empezca, empezco, *ref.* **empecer.**
empicarse, (*ref.* *50*) *r.v.* to become overfond, become too attached or infatuated.
empicharse, *r.v.* (Ven.) to go bad, to become rotten.
empicotadura, *f.* the act of pillorying.
empicotar, *tr.v.* to pillory, put in the stocks.
empiece, *m.* (coll.) beginning, start, initiation.
empiece, *ref.* **empezar.**
empiedre, empiedro, *ref.* **empedrar.**
empiello, empielle, *ref.* **empellar.**
empiema, *m.* (med.) empyema.
empiezo, *m.* (Amer.) beginning, start.
empiezo, *ref.* **empezar.**
empilar, *tr.v.* to pile up, put in a pile.
empilonar, *tr.v.* (Cuba) to pile up (dried tobacco leaves).
empiluchar, *tr.v.* (Chile) to strip.
empinada, irse a la e., (equit.) to rear on the hind legs (horse).
empinado, da, *past part. of* **empinar.** —*a.* very high, elevated; steep; (coll.) stuck up, conceited.
empinador, ra, *m.*, *f.* (coll.) drunk, drunkard.
empinadura, *f.*, *var. of* **empinamiento.**
empinamiento, *m.* elevation, erection, raising.
empinar, *tr.v.* 1. to raise, elevate. 2. to tilt (a bottle); **e. el codo,** to drink heavily. —*i.v.* to drink a great deal. —*r.v.* 1. to stand on tiptoe; to rear on the hind legs. 2. to tower, rise high (building, tower, etc.). 3. (aer.) to zoom. 4. to climb, climb up.
empingorotado, da, *past part. of* **empingorotar.** —*a.* parvenu; snobbish, stuckup (coll.). —*m.*, *f.* parvenu, nouveau riche.
empingorotar, *tr.v.* to put (an object) on top of another. —*r.v.* 1. to climb on top of something. 2. (coll.) to become haughty or stuck-up.
empino, *m.* (archit.) apex of a vaulted arch.
empiñonado, *m.* candy made of piñón seeds.
empiolar, *tr.v.* (obs.) to tie by the legs; to arrest.
empipada, *f.* (Chile, Ecuad.) satiety, surfeit, (coll.) bellyful.
empiparse, *i.v.* (Chile, Ecuad.) to gorge oneself, to guzzle.
empique, empiqué, *ref.* **empicarse.**
empíreo, a, *a.* empyreal; (fig.) heavenly, sublime. —*m.* empyrean, celestial.
empireuma, *m.* (chem.) empyreuma.
empireumático, ca, *a.* (chem.) empyreumatic.
empíricamente, *adv.* empirically, by experience rather than by theory.
empírico, ca, *a.* empirical, empiric, based on experience rather than on theory. —*m.*, *f.* empiricist.
empirismo, *m.* empiricism.
empitonar, *tr.v.* (taur.) to gore the bullfighter with the horns.
empizarrado, *past part. of* **empizarrar.** —*m.* slate roof.
empizarrar, *tr.v.* to slate, roof with slates.
emplace, emplacé, *ref.* **emplazar.**
emplantillar, *tr.v.* (Chile) to fill in (wall foundations) with rubble.
emplastadura, *f.* 1. application of a plaster or plasters. 2. make-up; application of cosmetics (to the face).
emplastamiento, *m.*, *var. of* **emplastadura.**
emplastar, *tr.v.* 1. to apply a plaster to. 2. to make up (with cosmetics). 3. (coll.) to hamper, hold up, obstruct (a business deal). —*r.v.* 1. to make up (one's face). 2. to get smeared or covered.
emplastecer, (*ref.* *45*) *tr.v.* (p.) to smooth (a surface).
emplastezca, emplastezco, *ref.* **emplastecer.**
emplástico, ca, *a.* 1. sticky. 2. (med.) suppurative.
emplasto, *m.* 1. poultice, plaster. 2. (coll.) unsatisfactory settlement or compromise. 3. weakling, sickly person. 4. (Amer., coll.) annoying person. 5. (Amer.) patch; gob.
emplástrico, ca, *a.* 1. sticky. 2. (med.) suppurative.
emplazador, *m.* (law) summoner, one who summons.
emplazamiento, *m.* 1. summons; summoning. 2. site, location, position.
emplazar, (*ref.* *53*) *tr.v.* 1. to summon; to challenge or call upon (someone) to make a statement on an issue. 2. (hunt.) to reconnoiter and set out posts in (an area). 3. to place, situate, put, locate.
empleable, *a.* employable.
empleado, da, *past part. of* **emplear.** —*m.*, *f.* employee; **empleada de hogar,** female servant, housemaid; **e. de ventanilla,** windowman.
empleador, ra, *m.*, *f.* employer.
emplear, *tr.v.* to employ, engage, hire; to use; to spend. —*r.v.* to get a job; **emplearse de,** to get a job as; **empleársele bien a uno,** to get what one deserves.
empleita, *f.* plait of esparto or bass-weed (used in making hats, etc.).
empleitero, ra, *m.*, f. person who sells or makes plaits of esparto or bass-weed.
emplenta, *f.* section of a mud or adobe wall (made in one session).
empleo, *m.* employment; job, post, occupation; profession; **pleno e.,** full employment.
empleomanía, *f.* 1. mania for holding public office. 2. employees, personnel.
emplomado, *past part. of* **emplomar.** —*m.* lead roof; leading, leadwork (in windows).
emplomador, ra, *m.*, *f.* leadworker, plumber.
emplomadura, *f.* leadwork, leading (of windows); lead covering, lead (used in leading).
emplomar, *tr.v.* 1. to cover with lead; to lead, fix (windows) with lead. 2. to fix a lead seal on. 3. (Amer.) to fill (a tooth).
emplumar, *tr.v.* 1. to feather, tar and feather. 2. to decorate with feathers. 3. (Cuba, Guat., coll.) to trick, deceive, hoodwink. 4. (Ecuad., Ven.) to send to jail or into exile. 5. (Hond.) to give a beating, beat. — **emplumarlas,** (Chile) to beat it, run away. —*i.v.* 1. to fledge. 2. (Amer.) to flee, take flight.
emplumecer, (*ref.* *45*) *i.v.* to fledge, to grow feathers.
emplumezca, *ref.* **emplumecer.**
empobrecer, (*ref.* *45*) *tr.v.* to impoverish. —*i.v.*, *r.v.* to become poor or impoverished; to become exhausted (land).
empobrecimiento, *m.* impoverishment.
empoce, empocé, *ref.* **empozar.**
empodrecer, (*ref.* *45*) *i.v.*, *r.v.* to rot, putrefy; to be impaired; to spoil, be spoiled.
empodrezca, *ref.* **empodrecer.**
empoltronarse, (*ref.* *45*) *r.v.* (rare) to become idle, sluggish or lazy.
empolvado, da, *a.* (Mex.) rusty, out of practice.
empolvar, *tr.v.* to powder, dust or sprinkle with powder. —*r.v.* to powder oneself; (Mex.) to get out of practice, get rusty; (Dom. Rep.) to run away, to beat it (coll.).
empolvoramiento, *m.* powdering; dusting with powder.
empolvorar, *tr.v.* to powder; to dust or sprinkle with powder.
empolvorice, *ref.* **empolvorizar.**
empolvorizar, (*ref.* *53*) *tr.v.* to powder; to dust or sprinkle with powder.
empollador, ra, *m.*, *f.* hatcher; incubator.
empolladura, *f.* brood of bees.
empollar, *tr.v.* to hatch, brood. —*r.v.* 1. to breed (bees); 2. (coll.) to study hard; to brood, dwell (on a subject). —*i.v.* to breed (bees).
empollón, na, *m.*, *f.* (derog.) grind (student who studies with uncommon dedication).
emponchado, da, *a.* 1. (Amer.) wearing a poncho. 2. (fig.) (Arg., Peru) suspicious.
emponcharse, *r.v.* (Amer.) to wrap one-self in a poncho.
emponzoñador, ra, *a.* poisonous, venomous; (fig.) damaging, harmful. —*m.*, *f.* poisoner.
emponzoñamiento, *m.* poisoning.
emponzoñar, *tr.v.* 1. to poison. 2. to damage, harm, hurt; to ruin, spoil.
empopada, *f.* (mar.) sailing before the wind.
empopar, *i.v.* 1. (mar.) to be very low at the stern. 2. to sail before the wind.
emporcar, (*ref.* *69*) *tr.v.* to soil, dirty. —*r.v.* to get dirty or filthy.
emporio, *m.* emporium, mart, market; center.
emporqué, *ref.* **emporcar.**
empotramiento, *m.* embedding; fixture built into a wall.
empotrar, *tr.v.* 1. to embed, fix in, build in. 2. to put (beehives) in a hole in the ground. 3. to make flush.

empotrerar, *tr.v.* 1. (Amer.) to turn (an estate) into a cattle farm. 2. (Amer.) to put (cattle) out to graze or pasture.
empozar, (*ref. 53*) *tr.v.* 1. to put or throw in a well. 2. to soak, ret (flax). —*i.v.* (Amer.) to form puddles, stagnate (said of water). —*r.v.* 1. to be thrown into a well. 2. (coll.) to be pigeon-holed or shelved (said of documents).
empradice, *ref.* **empradizar.**
empradizar, (*ref. 53*) *tr.v.* to turn into a meadow or pasture land. —*r.v.* to become pasture land.
emprendedor, ra, *a.* enterprising, plucky.
emprender, *tr.v.* to set about, begin, undertake. — **e. a bofetadas con,** to set about, attack; **emprenderla con,** to quarrel with; **emprenderla para,** to set out for.
empreñar, *tr.v.* to impregnate, make pregnant. —*r.v.* to become pregnant.
empresa, *f.* 1. enterprise, undertaking. 2. firm, business, company, management. 3. device, legend, motto. 4. design, intenion, undertaking. — **e. de servicios públicos,** public utility; **e. filial,** subsidiary company; **e. mecenas,** sponsors (of an event); **e. privada,** private enterprise; **e. tiburón,** raider; **e. unipersonal,** self-employed person.
empresarial, *a.* business; managerial —*f.* (*pl.*) business studies.
empresario, ria, *m., f.* contractor; manager; theatre manager, impresario; promoter. — **e. de pompas fúnebres,** funeral director; **e. de publicidad,** advertising man.
emprestar, *tr.v.* (imp. u.) to lend; (rare) to borrow.
empréstito, *m.* loan; **e. de guerra,** war loan; **e. forzoso,** (econ.) forced loan; **e. público,** government loan.
emprima, *f.* first fruit; (*pl.*) first products or fruits.
emprimado, *past part. of* **emprimar.** —*m.* second carding (of wool).
emprimar, *tr.v.* 1. to give a second carding to (wool). 2. (coll.) to take advantage of (an inexperienced person), dupe. 3. (p.) to prime (canvas).
empringar, (*ref. 51*) *tr.v., var. of* **pringar.**
empringue, empringué, *ref.* **empringar.**
empuchar, *tr.v.* to bleach (yarn), dip (skeins) in lye.
empuerco, empuerque, *ref.* **emporcar.**
empujada, *f.* (Amer.) push, shove.
empujador, ra, *a.* pushing. —*m., f.* pusher, jostler.
empujar, *tr.v.* 1. to push, shove. 2. (fig.) to dismiss, remove (a person) from a position or job. 3. (fig.) to press, bring pressure on.
empuje, *m.* 1. shove, push. 2. thrust. e. drive, push. 4. (fig.) energy, enterprise.
empujón, *m.* 1. push, shove, thrust. 2. (fig.) help, e.g. *dame un e.,* give me a hand, a push. 3. rapid progress (in work). — **a empujones,** by fits and starts, in jerks; roughly, brusquely.
empulgadura, *f.* nocking, notching (of a crossbow).
empulgar, (*ref. 51*) *tr.v.* 1. to tighten (the string of a crossbow ready for firing). 2. to fill with fleas.
empulgue, empulgué, *ref.* **empulgar.**
empulguera, *f.* 1. notch, nock (of a cross-bow, arbalest). 2. (*pl.*) thumbscrew, an instrument of torture.
empuntar, *tr.v.* 1. (Col.) to put a point on. 2. to guide or direct towards. — **empuntarlas,** (Col.) to scram, beat it.
empuñador, ra, *a.* grasping, clutching.
empuñadura, *f.* 1. sword hilt. 2. (fig., coll.) beginning of a story (such as "Once upon a time"). 3. handle (of a cane, an umbrella).
empuñar, *tr.v.* 1. to grip, grasp, clutch. 2. to brandish (a weapon, etc.). 3. (fig.) to obtain (a job).
empuñidura, *f.* (mar.) oaring, head-oaring.
empurpurado, da, *a.* dressed in purple.
empurrar, *tr.v.* (Par.) to fornicate. —*r.v.* (C. Amer.) to get annoyed or irritated.
emputecer, (*ref. 45*) *tr.v.* to prostitute, corrupt.
emulación, *f.* emulation; desire to equal or surpass.
emulador, ra, *a.* emulating. —*m., f.* emulator, competitor, rival.
emular, *tr.v., r.v.* to emulate, to try to equal or surpass.
emulgente, *a.* (anat.) emulgent (arteries and veins taking blood to the kidney).
émulo, la, *a.* emulating. —*m., f.* emulator, competitor.
emulsificar, *tr.v.* to emulsify.
emulsión, *f.* (pharm.) emulsion.
emulsionable, *a.* emulsifiable, emulsible.
emulsionador, *m.* emulsifier.
emulsionamiento, *m.* emulsification.
emulsionar, *tr.v.* to emulsify.
emulsivo, va, *a.* (pharm.) emulsive.
emulsor, *m.* emulsifier (device).
emunción, *f.* (med.) excretion.
emuntorio, *m.* 1. (med.) emunctory. 2. (*pl.*) secretory glands.
en, *prep.* 1. in, e.g., *está en Madrid,* he is in Madrid; *en noviembre,* in November. 2. on, e.g. *en la mesa,* on the table; *nunca en domingo,* never on Sunday. 3. at, e.g. *en el cine,* at the cinema, *esto sucedió en Navidad,* this happened at Christmas. 4. by, e.g. *le conocí en el andar,* I recognized him by his walk. 5. into, e.g. *convertir en algo útil,* to turn into something useful. 6. to, e.g. *convertirse en polvo,* to turn to dust. 7. upon, e.g. *en llegando,* upon arriving.
enaceitar, *tr.v.* to oil, grease. —*r.v.* to become oily.
enacerar, *tr.v.* 1. to steel (to harden). 2. (fig.) to strengthen, harden.
enaciado, *m.* (hist.) subject of the Spanish kings linked to the Saracens by ties of friendship and common interest.
enagua, *f.* (*gen. in pl.*) underskirt, slip, petticoat; skirts.
enaguace, enaguacé, *ref.* **enaguazar.**
enaguachar, *tr.v.* 1. to flood, soak, overfill with water. 2. to bloat (the stomach) with water. —*r.v.* to become bloated with water or fresh fruit.
enaguar, (*ref. 52*) *tr.v.* to flood, soak, overfill with water.
enaguazar, (*ref. 53*) *tr.v.* to flood (land). —*r.v.* to become flooded (land).
enagüillas, *f.* (*pl.*) *dim. of* **enaguas,** short petticoat, kilt; short skirt.
enajenable, *a.* alienable, transferable.
enajenación, *f.* 1. alienation. 2. transferring (of property). 3. absence of mind, distraction; rapture, ecstasy. — **e. mental,** mental derangement, madness.
enajenador, ra, *m., f.* alienor, transferrer (of property).
enajenamiento, *m., var. of* **enajenación.**
enajenar, *tr.v.* 1. to alienate, transfer, sell, give away. 2. to make someone lose his self-control; to drive to distraction; to transport, enrapture; to paralyze. 3. to alienate (a friend). —*r.v.* 1. to be transported (by joy); to be beside oneself (with anger); to be paralyzed (with fear). 2. to become estranged (friends).
enálage, *f.* (gram.) enallage.
enalbar, *tr.v.* (metal.) to make white hot.
enalbardar, *tr.v.* 1. to saddle. 2. to cover with batter, bread. 3. to lard, cover (roasting fowl) with bacon.
enalmagrado, da, *past part. of* **enalmagrar.** —*a.* (fig.) despicable, vile.
enalmagrar, *tr.v.* to stain with red ochre.
enalmenar, *tr.v.* to provide with battlements.
enaltecer, (*ref. 45*) *tr.v.* to extol, praise.
enaltecimiento, *m.* extolling, praise, exaltation.
enaltezca, enaltezco, *ref.* **enaltecer.**
enamarillecer, (*ref. 45*) *i.v., r.v.* to turn yellow.
enamarillezca, *ref.* **enamarillecer.**
enamoradamente, *adv.* lovingly, affectionately; passionately.
enamoradizo, za, *a.* inclined to fall in love, easily infatuated.
enamorado, da, *past part. of* **enamorar.** —*a.* in love; easily infatuated (person); **e. de,** in love with, enamored of. —*m.* boyfriend, sweetheart; lover (of the arts, etc.); (*pl.*) sweethearts. —*f.* girlfriend, sweetheart.
enamorador, ra, *a.* wooing, courting. —*m., f.* wooer, beau, suitor.
enamoramiento, *m.* love affair; wooing, courting; the act of being or falling in love.
enamorar, *tr.v.* to enamor, inspire love in; to flirt with, woo, court. —*r.v.* to fall in love; **enamorarse de,** to fall in love with.
enamoricarse, (*ref. 50*) *r.v.* (coll.) to become infatuated with.
enamorique, enamoriqué, *ref.* **enamoricarse.**
enamoriscarse, (*ref. 50*) *r.v., var. of* **enamoricarse.**
enancarse, (*ref. 50*) *r.v.* (Amer.) 1. to ride on a horse's haunches. 2. (Mex.) to rear up (a horse).
enanchar, *tr.v.* (coll.) to widen, enlarge, loosen.
enangostar, *tr.v.* to narrow, make narrower. —*r.v.* to narrow, become narrow.
enanismo, *m.* (med.) manism, dwarfism.
enanito, ta, *a. dim. of* **enano.** —*m., f.* little dwarf, midget.
enano, na, *a.* small, minute, little, dwarfish. —*m., f.* dwarf.
enante, *f.* (bot.) water fennel (Oenanthe phellandrium).
enántico, ca, *a.* enanthic, of or pertaining to wine.
enantiomorfo, *m.* (chem.) enantiomorph.
enarbolado, *past part. of* **enarbolar.** —*m.* framework, structure (of a tower or dome).
enarbolar, *tr.v.* to hoist, raise. —*r.v.* 1. to rear up on its hind legs (a horse). 2. to become angry, get furious.
enarcar, (*ref. 50*) *tr.v.* 1. to bend, arch. 2. to hoop (barrels, etc.). —*r.v.* 1. to bend, arch. 2. to shrink, become smaller. 3. (Mex.) to rear (a horse).
enardecedor, ra, *a.* fiery, provocative, inflammatory.
enardecer, (*ref. 45*) *tr.v.* (fig.) to kindle, fire, inflame. —*r.v.* 1. to get worked up or excited. 2. to become inflamed (a sore).
enardecimiento, *m.* exciting, firing, inflaming; excitement; inflammation.
enardezca, enardezco, *ref.* **enardecer.**
enarenación, *f.* coat of plaster (on a wall) before painting; priming.
enarenado, da, *a.* sandy. —*m.* gravel path.
enarenar, *tr.v.* 1. to sand, cover with sand. 2. (min.) to mix fine sand with silver ore to induce amalgamation. —*r.v.* 1. to become covered with sand. 2. (mar.) to run aground.
enarmonar, *tr.v.* to set or place upright. —*r.v.* to rear on its back legs (a horse).
enarmónico, *a.* (mus.) enharmonic.
enarque, enarqué, *ref.* **enarcar.**
enartar, *tr.v.* (arch.) to put a spell upon, charm, bewitch (with magic).
enartrosis, *f.* (anat.) enarthrosis.
enastado, da, *past part. of* **enastar.** —*a.* horned.
enastar, *tr.v.* to put a handle or a shaft on an.
enastillar, *tr.v.* to put a handle (on a tool) or a shaft (on an arrow).

encabador, *m.* (Col.) penholder.
encabalgamiento, *m.* 1. (mil.) gun carriage. 2. (poet.) enjambment.
encabalgante, *a.* resting (said of a beam resting on a joist, etc.).
encabalgar, (*ref. 51*) *i.v.* to rest or lean upon something. —*tr.v.* to provide with horses.
encabalgue, encabalgué, *ref.* **encabalgar.**
encaballado, *past part. of* **encaballar.** —*m.* (print.) pieing, jumbling of lines, letters and spaces.
encaballadura, *f.* (mas.) overlapping.
encaballar, *tr.v.* 1. to place overlapping, overlap; to imbricate (tiles). 2. (print.) to pie, jumble (lines, letters and spaces). —*i.v.* to overlap; to rest on something. —*r.v.* (print.) to become pied or jumbled.
encabar, *tr.v.* to helve (provide tools with handles).
encabece, encabecé, *ref.* **encabezar.**
encabellecerse, (*ref. 45*) *r.v.* to grow hair, let one's hair grow.
encabellezca, *ref.* **encabellecerse.**
encabestradura, *f.* (vet.) halter blister (on the pastern).
encabestrar, *tr.v.* 1. to halter, put a halter on; to make obey or follow the halter. 2. (fig.) to persuade, induce, lead. —*r.v.* to become tangled up in the halter (a horse).
encabezadora, *f.* (mec.) heading machine; **e. de pernos,** (mec.) bolt-heading machine.
encabezadura, *f.* (carp.) scarfing, heading.
encabezamiento, *m.* 1. registering, inscribing; census-taking. 2. tax-roll; tax-rate. 3. heading (of a will); caption, headline (of a newspaper).
encabezar, (*ref. 53*) *tr.v.* 1. to draw up (a list). 2. to register, inscribe, enroll. 3. to put the title on (a book or document) or headline on (a newspaper). 4. to fortify, top up (wine). 5. (Amer.) to head, lead. 6. (carp.) to scarf, join. —*r.v.* 1. to agree, come to terms (on a payment). 2. to put up with (one evil in order to avoid a worse one).
encabillar, *tr.v.* (mar.) to scotch, pin, bolt.
encabrahigar, (*ref. 51*) *tr.v.* (agr.) to caprificate.
encabriar, *tr.v.* to put up rafters for (the roof).
encabritarse, *r.v.* 1. to rear (a horse). 2. to pitch or lurch upward (a ship, car or plane). 3. to become furious.
encabronar, *tr.v.* (Col., Cuba) to make furious. —*r.v.* to become furious.
encabuyar, *tr.v.* (Amer.) to tie up with a cord or a line.
encachado, *past part. of* **encachar.** —*m.* concrete lining (of a sewer or a canal).
encachar, *tr.v.* 1. to line (a canal or a sewer) with concrete. 2. to helve (a knife). 3. (Amer.) to lower the head (a bull) before charging.
encachilarse, *r.v.* (Arg.) to get furious.
encachorrarse, *r.v.* (Cuba) to be obstinate, to become stubborn; to become obsessedly infatuated.
encadenación, *f., var. of* **encadenamiento.**
encadenado, da, *past part. of* **encadenar.** —*a.* (poet.) linked (said of poetry which repeats last verse of a stanza or last words of a verse at the beginning of the next stanza or verse). —*m.* (archit.) buttress, reinforcement.
encadenadura, *f., var. of* **encadenamiento.**
encadenamiento, *m.* chaining, enchainment; concatenation; linking, connection.
encadenar, *tr.v.* to chain, put in chains; to connect, link, join; (bldg.) to brace; (bldg.) to buttress; (mas.) to bond. —*r.v.* to be linked together.
encajador, *m.* 1. enchaser; enchasing tool. 2. person who enchases or inserts.
encajadura, *f.* 1. inserting, enclosing; enchasing; insertion, enclosure. 2. socket, groove.
encajar, *tr.v.* 1. to put in, insert; to fit in; to fit (e.g. a ring on a finger); to push in, force in. 2. to push shut (the lid of a trunk). 3. to slip in (a remark, hint); to tell (a story). 4. (coll.) to deal, give (a blow); to hit with, e.g. *le encajé un tintero en la cabeza,* I hit him on the head with an inkwell. 5. (coll.) to make hear, buttonhole with (a harangue). 6. (coll.) to pass off on, foist off on, palm off on. 7. (carp.) to rabbet. —*i.v.* 1. to close or shut properly. 2. to fit, go together (colors, design); **e. en,** to fit (a door into a frame); to be appropriate or fitting (a phrase in a speech). —*r.v.* 1. to squeeze in. 2. (coll.) to put on (a garment). 3. (coll.) to push in, intrude, butt in.
encaje, *m.* 1. (tex.) lace. 2. inserting; enclosing; enchasing. 3. socket, groove; (carp.) furrow. 4. inlaid work. 5. (*pl.*) (her.) interlinking triangles. 6. (com.) cash reserve. — **e. bancario,** bank reserves to cover obligations; **e. de bolillos,** bone lace; **e. de Bruselas,** duchess lace.
encajerarse, *r.v.* (mar.) to get fouled (guys, lines, stays, etc.).
encajero, ra, *m., f.* laceworker, lacemaker, laceseller.
encajetar, *tr.v.* to put, insert, enchase.
encajetillar, *tr.v.* to put (tobacco or cigarettes) into packages or packs.
encajonado, da, *past part. of* **encajonar.** —*m.* cofferdam; (archit.) boxing work (in which earth is pressed down in frames to form walls, etc.).
encajonamiento, *m.* 1. packing, boxing, encasement, packaging. 2. narrowing (of a river) between steep, rocky banks.
encajonar, *tr.v.* 1. to box, encase, crate. 2. to squeeze in. 3. (bldg.) to box (cement). 4. (archit.) to buttress, reinforce. —*r.v.* 1. to flow through a narrow ravine (a river). 2. to squeeze in.
encalabernarse, *r.v.* (coll., Cuba) to become obstinate, balk, dig one's heels in.
encalaboce, encalabocé, *ref.* **encalabozar.**
encalabozar, (*ref. 53*) *tr.v.* (coll.) to lock up, put in a dungeon or cell.
encalabrinado, da, *past part. of* **encalabrinar.** —*a.* obstinate, stubborn.
encalabrinamiento, *m.* intoxication, overcoming; dizziness; excitement, irritation.
encalabrinar, *tr.v.* 1. to excite, irritate. 2. to make dizzy, overcome, intoxicate (an odor, a wine). —*r.v.* 1. to become dizzy or intoxicated. 2. (coll.) to get set on something, get something into one's head. 3. (coll.) to become stubbornly enamored or infatuated.
encalada, *f.* metal piece in a harness.
encalado, *m.* whitewashing, whitening.
encalador, ra, *m., f.* whitewasher. —*m.* lime vat (for skinning hides).
encaladura, *f.* whitewashing, whitening.
encalambrarse, *r.v.* (Amer.) to become numb (limbs).
encalamocar, (*ref. 50*) *tr.v.* (Col., Ven.) to stupefy, stun. —*r.v.* to be stupefied or stunned.
encalar, *tr.v.* 1. to whitewash. 2. to lime, sprinkle with lime. 3. to place in a cove or canyon.
encalladero, *m.* sand bank, reef, shoal.
encalladura, *f.* running aground, grounding, stranding.
encallar, *i.v.* 1. (mar.) to run aground. 2. (fig.) to founder, get bogged down in difficulties (business, enterprise). —*r.v.* to harden (due to an interruption in cooking).
encallecer, (*ref. 45*) *i.v.* to develop corns, harden (skin). —*r.v.* 1. to become calloused. 2. (fig.) to become hardened (to work or vice).
encallejonar, *tr.v.* to lead or force through a narrow alley or passage. —*r.v.* to go through a narrow alley or passage.
encallezca, encallezco, *ref.* **encallecer.**
encalmadura, *f.* (vet.) a disease (of horses) caused by overheating.
encalmarse, *r.v.* 1 (vet.) to become overheated (horses). 2. to calm down (wind).
encalostrarse, *r.v.* to become sick from sucking colostrum or first milk (newborn infant).
encalvecer, (*ref. 45*) *i.v.* to become bald.
encalvezca, encalvezco, *ref.* **encalvecer.**
encamación, *f.* (min.) propping, stull.
encamado, *past part. of* **encamar.** —*m.* drooping (of corn).
encamar, *tr.v.* 1. to spread out, lay out on the floor. 2. (min.) to fill up with straw. —*r.v.* 1. to go or take to bed. 2. to hide, couch (game). 3. to droop, to be beaten down by rain or wind (corn).
encamarar, *tr.v.* to store (grain) in a granary.
encambijar, *tr.v.* to store and distribute (water) by means of raised tanks.
encambrar, *tr.v., var. of* **encamarar.**
encambronar, *tr.v.* 1. to hedge or surround with brambles. 2. to strengthen with iron.
encaminadura, *f., var. of* **encaminamiento.**
encaminamiento, *m.* the action of directing; guiding.
encaminar, *tr.v.* to direct; to guide, put on the right road. —*r.v.* to make for, set out for (a place); to be on the way to.
encamisada, *f.* 1. (mil.) camisado, night attack. 2. night masquerade.
encamisar, *tr.v.* 1. to put a shirt on. 2. to put covers on; to wrap. 3. (fig.) to disguise. —*r.v.* 1. to put on a shirt. 2. (mil.) to disguise for a camisado.
encamonado, da, *a.* (archit.) supported with a cane frame.
encamotarse, *r.v.* coll., Amer.) to fall in love.
encampanado, da, *past part. of* **encampanar.** —*a.* bell shaped; **dejar a uno encampanado,** (coll., Mex., P. Rico) to leave in the lurch, leave high and dry.
encampanar, *tr.v.* 1. (P. Rico, Ven.) to elevate, raise. 2. (Mex., coll.) to leave (someone) in the lurch. 3. (P. Rico, Ven.) to send away. —*r.v.* 1. (coll.) to brag or boast. 2. (Peru) to become involved or complicated. 3. (taur.) to raise its head defiantly (the bull). 4. (Col., coll.) to fall in love. 5. (Ven.) to withdraw, retire. 6. (Mex.) to get into a jam.
encanalar, *tr.v.* to pipe, channel; to convey (through pipes, conduits, etc.).
encanalice, encanalicé, *ref.* **encanalizar.**
encanalizar, (*ref. 53*) *tr.v., var. of* **encanalar.**
encanallamiento, *m.* degeneracy, corruption.
encanallar, *tr.v.* to corrupt, debase, deprave. —*r.v.* to become degenerate, corrupted or depraved.
encanar, *tr.v.* (Arg.) to put in prison, jail.
encanarse, *r.v.* to become stiff (an infant, from laughing or crying).
encanastar, *tr.v.* to put into baskets.
encancerarse, *r.v.* to become cancerous.
encandecer, (*ref. 45*) *tr.v.* to make incandescent.
encandelar, *i.v.* to blossom (trees). —*tr.v.* (Cuba) to be angry. —*r.v.* (Cuba) to become angry, annoyed.
encandelillar, *tr.v.* 1. (dressm.) to overstitch. 2. (Chile, Hond.) to blind, dazzle. —*r.v.* to become blinded or dazzled.
encandezca, co, *ref.* **encandecer.**
encandiladera, *f.* (coll.) procuress.
encandilado, da, *past part. of* **encandilar.** —*a.* (coll.) erect, tall. — **sombrero encandilado,** cocked hat.
encandilador, ra, *a.* (rare) blinding, dazzling. —*f.* (coll.) procuress.
encandilar, *tr.v.* 1. to blind, dazzle; (fig.) to dazzle, delude. 2. (coll.) to poke, rake (a fire). —*r.v.* to become bloodshot (eyes).

encanecer, *(ref. 45) i.v.* 1. to grow greyhaired. 2. to grow moldy. 3. to age, get old. *—r.v.* to become moldy. *—tr.v.* to turn grey.
encanezca, encanezco, *ref.* **encanecer.**
encanijado, da, *past part. of* **encanijar.** *—a.* (Ecuad.) numb, frozen.
encanijamiento, *m.* weakening, emaciation.
encanijar, *tr.v.* to weaken, emaciate, make weak and sickly (gen. said of children). *—r.v.* to become weak and sickly.
encanillar, *tr.v.* to wind on a spool (thread).
encantación, *f., var. of* **encantamiento.**
encantado, da, *past part. of* **encantar.** *—a.* 1. delighted, enchanted. 2. (coll.) absent-minded. 3. (coll.) haunted (a house), e.g. *palacio encantado,* haunted palace.
encantador, ra, *a.* captivating, enchanting, charming; delightful. *—m., f.* charmer; **e. de serpientes,** snake charmer. *—m.* sorcerer, magician. *—f.* sorceress; enchantress.
encantamiento, *m.* enchantment; sorcery, bewitchment, witchcraft.
encantar, *tr.v.* to cast a spell on, enchant, bewitch; to enchant, delight, charm, fascinate.
encantarar, *tr.v.* to put into a pitcher or ballot box.
encante, *m.* auction, public sale; auction rooms.
encanto, *m.* 1. enchantment, bewitchment; charm. 2. fascination, delight. 3. *(pl.)* natural talents or personal charms.
encantorio, *m.* (coll.) *var. of* **encantamiento.**
encantusar, *tr.v.* (coll.) to coax, wheedle; to trick, hoodwink.
encanutar, *tr.v.* 1. to flute, shape like a tube. 2. to put in a tube. 3. to tip (cigarettes). *—r.v.* to become tube-shaped.
encañado, da, *past part. of* **encañar.** *—m.* 1. water conduit, pipeline. 2. trellis of reeds or cane. *—f.* gorge, ravine.
encañador, ra, *m., f.* silk-winder, spool winder.
encañadura, *f.* stalks of rye used as stuffing in straw beds and packsaddles.
encañar, *tr.v.* 1. to channel (water); to drain (by means of ditches and channels). 2. to stake (plants); to wind on a spool (silk, etc.). 3. to stack (wood) for charring. *—i.v.* to form stalks (cereals).
encañice, encañicé, *ref.* **encañizar.**
encañizada, *f.* 1. weir, reed fence for catching fish. 2. trellis of cane reeds (for plants).
encañizar, *(ref. 53) tr.v.* to put up reed frames; to cover with reed frames (newly laid plaster).
encañonar, *tr.v.* 1. to channel; to pipe. 2. (tex.) to wind, spool. 3. (hunt.) to point, aim (a gun) at. 4. (dressm.) to flute, goffer. 5. (bkb.) to inset. *—i.v.* to fledge, begin to grow feathers.
encañutar, *tr.v.* (arch.) to flute.
encapacetado, da, *a.* helmeted, casqued, morioned (wearing a helmet).
encapachadura, *f.* bags or baskets of olives piled up for pressing.
encapachar, *tr.v.* to put in a basket or bag.
encapado, da, *past part. of* **encapar.** *—a.* (min.) underground (said of a seam which does not rise to the surface).
encapar, *tr.v.* to cloak, cover with a cape. *—r.v.* to put on a cloak.
encapazar, *(ref. 53) tr.v., var. of* **encapachar.**
encaperuce, encaperucé, *ref.* **encaperuzar.**
encaperuzado, da, *a.* hooded.
encaperuzar, *(ref. 53) tr.v.* to hood, cover with a hood. *—r.v.* to put a hood on.
encapillado, da, *past part. of* **encapillar.** *—m.* prisoner in death row.
encapilladura, *f.* hooding of the falcon.
encapillar, *tr.v.* 1. to hood (a falcon). 2. (mar.) to rig (the yards). 3. (min.) to open a new gallery in. *—r.v.* 1. (coll.) to put on (clothes) over the head. 2. (mar.) (wave) to buffet and flood (deck). 3. (mar.) to mount, go on top of, hook up to.
encapirotar, *tr.v.* to hood (a falcon).
encapotadura, *f.* frown, scowl.
encapotamiento, *m., var. of* **encapotadura.**
encapotar, *tr.v.* to cover with a cloak, cloak. *—r.v.* 1. to frown, glower; to become cloudy, cloud over. 2. to lower the head (horses). 3. (Cuba, P. Rico) to be sick or listless (birds).
encapricharse, *r.v.* to take it into one's head (to); to take a fancy (to; for); to become infatuated (with).
encapsular, *tr.v.* to encapsulate, capsule.
encapuce, encapucé, *ref.* **encapuzar.**
encapuchado, da, *past part. of* **encapuchar.** *—a.* hooded, cowled.
encapuchar, *tr.v.* to hood, cover with a hood. *—r.v.* to put one's hood on.
encapullado, da, *a.* bud-like, closed like a bud.
encapuzar, *(ref. 53) tr.v.* to hood, cover with a hood. *—r.v.* to put on one's hood.
encarado, da, *past part. of* **encarar.** *—a.* faced, featured. — **bien e.,** well-featured, good-looking; **mal e.,** ugly-looking.
encaramar, *tr.v.* 1. to raise, lift up, elevate. 2. (coll.) to praise, extol. 3. (coll.) to elevate, raise, promote. *—r.v.* to climb; to climb or get to the top, attain a high position; to perch (a bird).
encaramiento, *m.* facing; aiming.
encarar, *r.v., i.v.* to face, confront. *—tr.v.* to aim, point.
encaratularse, *r.v.* to put on a mask, mask oneself.
encarcavinar, *tr.v.* to bury; to suffocate or choke with a foul smell or odor.
encarcelación, *f.* imprisonment, incarceration.
encarcelador, ra, *a.* imprisoning, incarcerating.
encarcelamiento, *m., var. of* **encarcelación.**
encarcelar, *tr.v.* 1. to imprison, incarcerate. 2. (bldg.) to imbed, embed; (carp.) to clamp.
encarecedor, ra, *a.* praising, extolling. *—m., f.* praiser, extoller.
encarecer, *(ref. 45) tr.v.* to raise the price of; (coll.) to praise excessively; to recommend strongly. *—r.v.* to become more expensive.
encarecidamente, *adv.* earnestly, insistently; eagerly.
encarecimiento, *m.* 1. rise in price. 2. praising, praise; recommendation. — **con e.,** earnestly, insistently.
encarezca, encarezco, *ref.* **encarecer.**
encargado, da, *past part. of* **encargar.** *—a.* commissioned. *—m., f.* representative, agent; foreman; person in charge; superintendent; manager; **e. de negocios,** chargé d'affaires.
encargar, *(ref. 51) tr.v.* 1. to entrust, put in charge (of). 2. to recommend, advise. 3. to ask, request; to ask or request (someone) to bring or buy (something); to order (goods); **e. a alguien que + subj.,** to ask someone to + *inf.;* to entrust someone with + *ger.;* **e. a,** to order (goods) from. *—r.v.* to take charge (of), put oneself in charge (of), make oneself responsible (for); **encargarse de + inf.,** to take charge of or make oneself responsible for + *ger.*
encargo, *m.* 1. errand, task, job; assignment. 2. (com.) order (for goods). 3. post, employment. 4. request. — **como hecho de e.,** as if made to order.
encargue, encargué, *ref.* **encargar.**
encariñado, da, *a.* endearing.
encariñamiento, *m.* endearment, affection.
encariñar, *tr.v.* to inspire affection or love; endear; to make fond (of). *—r.v.* to become fond; **encariñarse con,** to become fond of.
encarna, *f.* (hunt.) blooding of the hounds.
encarnación, *f.* 1. incarnation. 2. (theol.) Incarnation. 3. (fig.) personification. 4. (p.) flesh color. — **e. de paletilla,** (p.) mat finish flesh color; **e. de pulimento,** polished finish flesh color.
encarnadino, na, *a.* incarnadine.
encarnado, da, *past part. of* **encarnar.** *—a.* flesh-colored, pink; red. *—m.* pink, flesh color.
encarnadura, *f.* 1. healing properties (of flesh). 2. flesh wound. 3. (hunt.) feeding on the entrails of game (hounds).
encarnamiento, *m.* healing process (of a wound).
encarnar, *tr.v.* 1. to embody, personify (an idea, a doctrine). 2. to bait (a fishing line). 3. (hunt.) to blood (the hounds). 4. (p.) to give flesh color tint to. *—i.v.* 1. to be incarnated, become flesh. 2. to heal over (a wound). 3. to pierce or penetrate the flesh. 4. to make a strong impression (on). 5. (hunt.) to eat the entrails of game (the hounds). *—r.v.* to join, mix.
encarnativo, va, *a.* (med.) healing, incarnative. *—m.* healing agent.
encarne, *m.* (hunt.) blooding, first feeding of entrails given to the hounds.
encarnecer, *(ref. 45) i.v.* to put on weight or flesh.
encarnezca, encarnezco, *ref.* **encarnecer.**
encarnice, encarnicé, *ref.* **encarnizar.**
encarnizadamente, *adv.* cruelly, savagely.
encarnizado, da, *past part. of* **encarnizar.** *—a.* 1. bloodshot. 2. bloody (battle); hard-fought (debate, polemic); cruel, pitiless (person).
encarnizamiento, *m.* 1. eating or gorging meat (hungry animals). 2. (fig.) bloodthirstiness, extreme cruelty.
encarnizar, *(ref. 53) tr.v.* 1. to blood (hounds). 2. to anger, infuriate, set (against). *—r.v.* 1. to gorge on meat (hounds). 2. to fight bitterly or bloodily. — **encarnizarse contra,** to get angry or furious with, be set against; **encarnizarse en,** to glut one's fury on.
encaro, *m.* 1. facing, confronting. 2. aiming (a gun); aim. 3. blunderbuss. 4. cheek rest (on a gunstock).
encarpetar, *tr.v.* to file away, put in a file or portfolio; (Amer.) to shelve, pigeonhole (papers).
encarrilar, *tr.v.* 1. to direct, guide. 2. to put back on the track. 3. to put on the right track. *—r.v.* to get fouled up, slip and get stuck (a rope on a pulley).
encarrillar, *tr.v., var. of* **encarrilar.**
encarroñar, *tr.v.* to rot, make rot. *—r.v.* to rot, go rotten.
encarrujado, da, *past part. of* **encarrujarse.** *—a.* wrinkled; gathered; curled, corrugated. *—m.* shirring, gathering.
encarrujar, *tr.v.* to wrinkle, kink, twist; to gather (a dress). *—r.v.* to become twisted or wrinkled.
encartación, *f.* enrollment under a charter; recognition of vassalage; village under vassalage; lands held under a charter.
encartamiento, *m.* 1. proscription. 2. judicial dispatch containing a sentence. 3. enrollment under a charter.
encartar, *tr.v.* 1. to proscribe, outlaw. 2. to summon, call. 3. to register, enroll. 4. to include. 5. to lead a suit which can be followed. *—i.v.* to be opportune. *—r.v.* to be forced to follow suit (in a card game).
encarte, *m.* 1. playing a suit which can be followed. 2. order of cards at the end of a hand.
encartonador, ra, *m., f.* (bkb.) bookbinder.
encartonar, *tr.v.* to cover with cardboard; to bind (books) with cardboard.
encartuchar, *tr.v.* (Col., Ecuad., P. Rico) to roll into a cone. *—r.v.* to roll or become rolled into a cone.

encasar, *tr.v.* (med.) to set (a bone).
encascabelar, *tr.v.* to decorate with jingle bells. —*r.v.* to adorn oneself with jingle bells.
encascotar, *tr.v.* to fill with rubble; to reinforce with rubble.
encasillable, *a.* able to be pigeonholed.
encasillado, *past part. of* **encasillar.** —*m.* 1. set of pigeonholes, pigeonholes. 2. list of government-supported candidates.
encasillar, *tr.v.* 1. to pigeonhole; to classify, sort out. 2. to assign (a candidate) to a voting district.
encasquetar, *tr.v.* 1. to pull (a hat) tightly down on (one's head). 2. (fig.) to convince of, force (an idea, opinion) on. 3. to force on, make someone hear. —*r.v.* 1. to pull (a hat) tightly down on (one's head). 2. to get it into one's head, e.g. *se le encasquetó la idea de viajar,* he got it into his head to travel.
encasquillador, *m.* (Amer.) farrier, blacksmith.
encasquillar, *tr.v.* (Amer.) to shoe (a horse). —*r.v.* 1. to stick, get stuck, become jammed (an automatic pistol). 2. (Cuba, coll.) to become afraid, get frightened.
encastar, *tr.v.* to improve by cross-breeding. —*i.v.* to breed.
encastillado, da, *past part. of* **encastillar.** —*a.* 1. haughty, proud, arrogant. 2. castled, castellated.
encastillamiento, *m.* 1. fortifying with castles, fortification. 2. withdrawal to a castle, stronghold or crag. 3. stacking (wood). 4. scaffolding. 5. persistence in an idea.
encastillar, *tr.v.* 1. to fortify with castles. 2. to pile, stack (wood). 3. to build a scaffold (for building). 4. to make queen-cells in (beehives). —*r.v.* 1. to retreat to a stronghold or fortress; to defend oneself in a castle; to take refuge. 2. (fig.) to persist; to be obstinate or unyielding.
encastrar, *tr.v.* 1. (mec.) to mesh, engage, fit together (two wheels). 2. to insert, fit in; to chase.
encastre, *m.* (mec.) fitting, embedding. — **e. giratorio,** swivel socket.
encatarrado, da, *a.* (obs.) having a cold or catarrh.
encatrado, *m.* (Arg., Chile) scaffold.
encatusar, *tr.v.* 1. to inveigle, coax, wheedle. 2. to trick, hoodwink.
encauce, encaucé, *ref.* **encauzar.**
encauchado, *past part. of* **encauchar.** —*m.* (Amer.) rubber-lined fabric; rubber-lined poncho.
encauchar, *tr.v.* to line, face or cover with rubber.
encausar, *tr.v.* (law) to prosecute, bring legal proceedings against.
encauste, *m.* 1. red ink (used formerly by emperors). 2. (p.) encaustic. — **pintura al e.,** encaustic painting.
encáustico, ca, *a.* (p.) encaustic. —*m.* mixture of turpentine and wax used as a protective coating against dampness.
encausto, *m., var. of* **encauste.**
encauzamiento, *m.* channeling; guiding, directing, leading.
encauzar, (*ref. 53*) *tr.v.* to channel, to guide, direct, lead.
encavarse, *r.v.* to hide, hide in a cave or burrow.
encebadamiento, *m.* (vet.) surfeit, bloat, flatulence (in horses, caused by over-drinking after meals).
encebadar, *tr.v.* to feed too much wheat and give bloat to (horses). —*r.v.* to become sick from bloat or flatulence (a horse).
encebollado, *past part. of* **encebollar.** —*a.* (Sp., coll.) obstinately in love; obfuscated. —*m.* stew heavily seasoned with onions.
encebollar, *tr.v.* to season heavily with onions.
encefálico, ca, *a.* (biol.) encephalic.
encefalítico, ca, *a.* (med.) encephalitic.
encefalitis, *f.* (med.) encephalitis, inflammation of the brain; **e. letárgica,** sleeping sickness, encephalitis lethargica.
encéfalo, *m.* (anat.) encephalon, brain.
encefalografía, *f.* (med.) encephalography.
encefalógrafo, *m.* (med.) encephalograph.
encefalograma, *m.* (med.) encephalogram.
encefaloideo, dea, *a.* (biol.) encephaloid.
encefaloma, *m.* (med.) encephaloma.
encefalomielitis, *f.* (vet., med.) encephalomyelitis.
encefalopatía, *f.* (med.) encephalopathy.
Encélade, *m.* (astron.) Enceladus.
encelajarse, *r.v.* to become covered with multicolored clouds (the sky).
encelamiento, *m.* jealousy, jealousness.
encelar, *tr.v.* to provoke or excite jealousy in, make jealous. —*r.v.* 1. to become jealous. 2. to rut, be in heat (animals).
enceldamiento, *m.* imprisoning in a cell.
enceldar, *tr.v.* to put in a cell, to imprison or incarcerate.
encella, *f.* cheese hoop, cheesemold.
encellar, *tr.v.* to mold cheese or curds.
encenadas, *f, pl.* dried brush, kindling.
encenagado, da, *past part. of* **encenagarse.** —*a.* muddy, stained or filled with mud.
encenagamiento, *m.* wallowing in mud; wallowing (in vice).
encenagarse, (*ref. 51*) *r.v.* to wallow in mud; to wallow (in vice).
encenague, encenagué, *ref.* **encenagarse.**
encencerrado, da, *a.* carrying a wether bell.
encendajas, *f.* (*pl.*) kindling wood.
encendedor, ra, *a.* lighting. —*m.* lighter; **e. de bolsillo,** cigarette-lighter.
encender, (*ref. 30*) *tr.v.* 1. to light, ignite, kindle. 2. to turn on, switch on (a light). 3. to set afire or on fire, to put the torch to. 4. to burn (the tongue) with pepper. 5. to cause, start (war). 6. to inflame, provoke (anger). —*r.v.* 1. to blush. 2. to flare up (in anger). 3. to break out, begin (a war, a conflagration).
encendidamente, *adv.* ardently, vividly, fiercely, with fire or passion.
encendido, da, *past part. of* **encender.** —*a.* bright (colors); red, inflamed. —*m.* (auto.) ignition; **e. por acumulador,** battery ignition; **e. por compresión,** compression ignition; **punto de e.,** flash point.
encendimiento, *m.* burning; fury, fierceness (of anger); ardor, vehemence (of passions).
encendrar, *tr.v.* to purify, refine (metals), to smelt.
encenice, encenicé, *ref.* **encenizar.**
encenizar, (*ref. 53*) *tr.v.* to cover with ashes. —*r.v.* to become covered with ashes.
encentador, ra, *a.* beginning, starting.
encentadura, *f.* beginning, start.
encentamiento, *m., var. of* **encentadura.**
encentar, *tr.v.* to begin to cut the first slice of. —*r.v.* to get bedsores.
encentrar, *tr.v., var. of* **centrar,** to center.
encepador, *m.* gunstocker.
encepadura, *f.* (carp.) tie-joint.
encepar, *tr.v.* 1. to put (a person) in the stocks. 2. to stock (a gun, an anchor). 3. (carp.) to join with ties. —*i.v.* to take deep root (plants). —*r.v.* 1. to take deep root (plants). 2. (mar.) to foul (said of the anchor).
encepe, *m.* taking deep root.
encerado, da, *past part. of* **encerar.** —*a.* wax-colored. —*m.* 1. oilcloth, oilskin; tarpaulin. 2. blackboard. 3. wax surface (of a floor or furniture). 4. wax plaster.
encerador, ra, *m., f.* floor waxer or polisher. —*f.* polishing machine.
enceramiento, *m.* waxing, polishing.
encerar, *tr.v.* 1. to wax. 2. to stain with wax (e.g. candle drippings). 3. (bldg.) to thicken (mortar). —*r.v., i.v.* to ripen, turn yellow (wheat, corn).
encernadar, *tr.v.* to cover with ashes (left after lixiviation).
encerotar, *tr.v.* to wax (thread).
encerradero, *m.* pen, sty or corral, fold; (taur.) bull pen.
encerrador, ra, *a.* penning in; locking up. —*m.* one who pens or locks up stock.
encerradura, *f., var. of* **encerramiento.**
encerramiento, *m.* 1. locking up, confining, confinement. 2. enclosure; jail, prison. 3. retreat, retirement (to a monastery).
encerrar, (*ref. 29*) *tr.v.* 1. to shut or lock in, lock up; to enclose. 2. to hold, contain. 3. (in checkers) to mate. —*r.v.* to shut oneself up, confine oneself, go into seclusion.
encerrona, *f.* 1. (coll.) voluntary retreat or seclusion. 2. (in dominoes) finishing a game when one's opponents hold many points. 3. (taur.) private bullfight. 4. (fig.) trap. — **hacer la e.,** to go into voluntary retreat or seclusion.
encespedar, *tr.v.* to turf, cover with turf or sod.
encestar, *tr.v.* 1. to put in a basket. 2. (coll., rare) to floor (an opponent).
encetadura, *f.* start, beginning.
encetar, *tr.v.* to start, begin (using something).
enchalecar, (*ref. 50*) *tr.v.* (Amer.) to strip naked.
enchancletar, *tr.v.* 1. to slip on (shoes). 2. to scuff or drag (one's shoes) like slippers. —*r.v.* to slip on one's shoes or slippers.
enchapado, *past part. of* **enchapar.** —*m.* veneering, plating, overlay.
enchapar, *tr.v.* to veneer, plate, overlay.
enchapinado, da, *a.* (bldg.) built on an arch or vault.
encharcada, *f.* puddle, pond, pool.
encharcamiento, *m.* 1. swamping, flooding.
encharcar, (*ref. 50*) *tr.v.* 1. to flood (land). 2. to bloat (the stomach) with water. —*r.v.* 1. to become flooded or swamped. 2. to wallow (in vice).
encharque, encharqué, *ref.* **encharcar.**
enchicharse, *r.v.* 1. (Amer.) to become drunk with chicha (fermented liquor). 2. (Amer., fig.) to become angry.
enchilada, *f.* (Mex., Guat.) corn pancake filled with meat, chicken, etc. and green or red pepper sauce.
enchilado, *past part. of* **enchilar.** —*m.* (Cuba) shellfish stew with red or green pepper, tomatoes and onion.
enchilar, *tr.v.* (C. Rica, Cuba, Mex.) to season with red pepper; (Mex.) to irritate, annoy; (C. Rica) to play a joke on. —*r.v.* (Mex.) to get irritated or annoyed.
enchinar, *tr.v.* 1. to cobble (a street) with pebbles. 2. (Mex.) to curl (hair).
enchinarrar, *tr.v.* to cobble (a street) with pebbles.
enchiquerar, *tr.v.* 1. to put into a pen, pen (a bull). 2. (coll.) to put in jail.
enchironar, *tr.v.* (coll.) to put in jail.
enchispar, *tr.v.* (Amer.) to make drunk. —*r.v.* (Amer.) to get drunk.
enchivarse, *r.v.* (Col., Ecuad.) to get into a rage, fly into a tantrum.
enchuchar, *tr.v.* (Cuba) to switch, turn the switch off; to switch on.
enchuecar, (*ref. 50*) *tr.v., r.v.* (Chile, Mex., coll.) to twist, bend, make or become crooked.
enchufado, da, *a.* (coll.) knowing the right people; **a. con,** getting on well with. *m., f.* person holding a post or position through influence.

enchufar, *tr.v.* 1. to connect (two pipes); (elec.) to plug in, connect. 2. to combine, merge (two businesses). 3. to join. 4. (Peru) to foist (something) off on (someone). 5. (coll.) to pull strings for, to use one's influence on behalf of. —*r.v.* (derog.) to get a sinecure or cushy job (coll.).
enchufe, *m.* 1. plugging in. 2. male joint (of pipe fitting into another pipe); joint, connection (between two pipes). 3. (elec.) plug, socket. 4. (coll.) sinecure. — **e. abierto,** open socket; **e. cerrado,** closed socket; **e. fusible,** fuse plug; **e. y cordón,** bell-and-spigot; **e. y espiga,** bell-and-spigot.
enchufista, *m., f.* (derog., coll.) sinecurist, person who holds various sinecures.
enchuletar, *tr.v.* (carp.) to stuff or fill with wood chips.
encía, *f.* (anat.) gum (of the mouth).
encíclica, *f.* encyclical, encyclical letter.
enciclopedia, *f.* 1. encyclopedia, encyclopaedia. 2. Encyclopedia, writings of the Encyclopedists (of the French Enlightenment).
enciclopédico, ca, *a.* encyclopedic, encyclopedical.
enciclopedismo, *m.* Encyclopedism.
enciclopedista, *m., f.* encyclopedist, person who compiles or helps compile an encyclopedia.
encienda, enciendo, *ref.* **encender.**
enciente, enciento, *ref.* **encentar.**
encierra, *f.* 1. (Chile) enclosure of stock in an abattoir. 2. (Chile) winter pastures.
encierre, encierro, *ref.* **encerrar.**
encierro, *m.* 1. shutting or locking up, confinement; enclosure. 2. retreat, retirement, seclusion. 3. narrow prison. 4. (taur.) penning (of bulls), driving (the bulls) into a pen.
encima, *adv.* 1. above; overhead; at the top; upstairs. 2. on top of one, e.g. *he tenido un montón de clientes e. toda la mañana,* I have had a crowd of customers on top of me all morning. 3. in addition; moreover, besides. 4. on or with me, you, him, her, us or them, e.g. *no tengo una peseta e.,* I don't have one peseta on me. — **echarse e.,** to take upon oneself; **e. de,** on; on top of; above; in addition to; **pasar por e. de alguien,** to go over someone's head; **por e.,** over; overhead; superficially; **por e. de,** above, over; in spite of; without paying attention to; **quitar de e.,** to free or rid of, rid oneself of; **venir e.,** to come at (as in anger); to come down on (as to correct, punish or reprimand).
encimar, *tr.v.* 1. to put on top. 2. to raise high. 3. to add to (one's bet). 4. (Col., Peru) to add, throw in. —*i.v.* (Chile) to reach the top or summit. *r.v.* to rise above (something else).
encimero, ra, *a.* top, above.
encina, *f.* (bot.) oak (tree and wood).
encinal, *m., var. of* **encinar.**
encinar, *m.* oak grove.
encino, *m.* (bot.) oak (tree).
encinta, *a.* pregnant, with child, in a family way (coll.).
encintado, *past part. of* **encintar.** —*m.* 1. beribboning. 2. curb (of the pavement).
encintar, *tr.v.* 1. to beribbon. 2. (agr.) to put a bridle on (a young bull). 3. to rim with a curbstone. 4. (mar.) to put wales on (ship). 5. (rare) to make pregnant. —*r.v.* to become pregnant.
encismar, *tr.v.* to cause disagreement or discord among.
enciso, *m.* land where ewes pasture after giving birth.
encisto, *m.* encysted tumor.
encizañador, ra, *a.* troublemaking. —*m., f.* troublemaker.
encizañar, *tr.v.* to cause trouble, disagreement or discord.
enclaustrar, *tr.v.* 1. to put in a cloister, cloister. 2. (fig.) to hide, conceal; to obscure.
enclavación, *f.* nailing, nailing down, fixing.
enclavado, da, *past part. of* **enclavar.** —*a.* joined (to), fixed (to), embedded (in). —*m.* enclave.
enclavadura, *f.* 1. wound (on a horse's foot because of poor shoeing). 2. (carp.) groove, embedding.
enclavar, *tr.v.* 1. to nail, nail down. 2. to wound (a horse's foot, when shoeing). 3. to pierce. 4. (coll.) to trick, deceive, cheat. 5. to place, to determine the position of.
enclavijar, *tr.v.* 1. to peg, join with pegs. 2. to peg, put pegs on (a string instrument).
enclenque, *a.* weak, feeble, sickly.
énclisis, *f.* (gram.) enclisis.
enclítico, ca, *a.* (gram.) enclitic. —*f.* (gram.) enclitic, enclitic word or particle.
enclocar, (*ref.* 69) *i.v., r.v.* to become broody (a hen).
encloquecer, (*ref.* 45) *i.v., var. of* **enclocar.**
encloquezca, *ref.* **encloquecer.**
enclueque, *ref.* **enclocar.**
encobar, *i.v., r.v.* to brood, sit on eggs (said of a hen).
encobertado, da, *a.* covered with a quilt.
encobijar, *tr.v.* to cover; to shelter.
encobrado, da, *past part. of* **encobrar.** —*a.* containing copper; copper-colored, copper-clad.
encobrar, *tr.v.* 1. to cover or coat with copper. 2. (Chile) to tie (an animal's bridle) to the trunk of a tree or to secure (it) with a heavy stone.
encochado, da, *a.* carriage-bound, car-bound (said of one who travels often in a car or carriage).
encoclar, (*ref.* 33) *i.v., r.v., var. of* **enclocar.**
encocorar, *tr.v.* (coll.) to annoy, irritate or vex. —*r.v.* (coll.) to get mad, annoyed, vexed or irritated.
encocrar, *i.v., r.v., var. of* **enclocar.**
encodillarse, *r.v.* to hide in an inaccessible corner of the burrow (rabbit, skunk, etc.).
encofrado, *past part. of* **encofrar.** —*m.* 1. (bldg.) plank molding (for a cornice). 2. (fort.) planking, timbering (to hold up the sides of a gallery). 3. (min.) planked gallery (of a mine).
encofrar, *tr.v.* 1. (min.) to plank, timber (sides of a mine gallery). 2. (bldg.) to build a plank molding for.
encoger, (*ref.* 57) *tr.v.* 1. to shrink (material); to contract. 2. to shrug (shoulders). 3. to bend (elbow; leg), pull in (one's legs). 4. to intimidate, frighten; to make timid. —*i.v.* to shrink; to contract. —*r.v.* 1. to shrink; to contract. 2. to feel timid, shy or bashful. — **encogerse de hombros,** to shrug one's shoulders.
encogidamente, *adv.* timidly, bashfully.
encogido, da, *past part. of* **encoger.** —*a.* timid, bashful, retiring, awkward. —*m., f.* timid person.
encogimiento, *m.* 1. shrinking; contracting. 2. timidity, shyness, bashfulness, awkwardness. 3. shrug, shrugging (of shoulders).
encogollarse, *r.v.* to go to the top of a tree (in a certain game).
encohetar, *tr.v.* (taur.) to excite the bull with firecrackers. —*r.v.* (C. Rica) to get angry or furious.
encoja, *ref.* **encoger.**
encojar, *tr.v.* to lame, cripple. —*r.v.* 1. (coll.) to become ill; to feign illness. 2. to malinger. 3. to become lame or crippled.
encojo, *ref.* **encoger.**
encolado, da, *past part. of* **encolar.** —*a.* (Chile, Mex.) dandified, natty, dapper. —*m.* 1. clarification (of wine). 2. priming, sizing; gluing.
encoladura, *f.* 1. sticking, gluing. 2. priming, sizing. 3. clarification (of wine).
encolamiento, *m.* 1. gluing, sticking. 2. priming, sizing. 3. clarification (of wine).
encolar, *tr.v.* 1. to glue, stick. 2. to clarify (wine). 3. to prime, size (a canvas).
encolerice, encolericé, *ref.* **encolerizar.**
encolerizar, (*ref.* 53) *tr.v.* to anger. —*r.v.* to become angry.
encomendable, *a.* commendable.
encomendado, *past part. of* **encomendar.** —*m.* (mil.) knight-commander's assistant; subordinate.
encomendamiento, *m.* commission, charge, task.
encomendar, (*ref.* 29) *tr.v.* 1. to entrust, commend, commit. 2. to make a knight-commander. —*i.v.* to become a knight-commander. —*r.v.* 1. to commit, entrust or commend oneself. 2. to send one's regards (to someone).
encomendero, *m.* 1. commissioner, agent; one entrusted with an official job or mission. 2. (hist.) Spanish colonist who was granted Indian laborers by royal decree.
encomiador, ra, *a.* eulogistic, encomiastic. —*m., f.* praiser, encomiast, eulogizer.
encomiar, *tr.v.* to praise, eulogize, extol.
encomiasta, *m.* panegyrist, eulogizer, praiser.
encomiástico, ca, *a.* encomiastic, eulogistic, complimentary.
encomienda, *f.* 1. commandership, mission, commission. 2. commandery, district under knight-commander's jurisdiction. 3. knight-commander's cross. 4. Indian village and inhabitants (granted to Spanish colonists by royal decree). 5. (Amer.) postal package. 6. task, job, commission. 7. praise, commendation. 8. protection, patronage, sponsorship. 9. (*pl.*) regards, compliments.
encomiende, encomiendo, *ref.* **encomendar.**
encomio, *m.* encomium, commendation, praise, eulogy.
encomioso, sa, *a.* (Chile) encomiastic, eulogistic, praising.
encompadrar, *i.v.* 1. (coll.) to become related to someone as godfather or godmother to his child. 2. to become very friendly.
enconadura, *f.* inflammation (of a wound).
enconamiento, 1. inflammation (of a wound). 2. enmity, rancor, hate.
enconar, *tr.v.* 1. to make sore, inflame, irritate (a wound). 2. to load (the conscience) with feelings of guilt. 3. to irritate, anger, annoy. —*r.v.* 1. to rankle, fester (a wound); to become inflamed or red. 2. to load one's conscience with feelings of guilt. 3. to get annoyed or angry.
enconcharse, *r.v.* (Col., P. Rico) to withdraw into one's shell, retire from society.
encondroma, *m.* (med.) chondroma.
enconfitar, *tr.v.* (cul.) to candy, coat with crystallized sugar.
encono, *m.* 1. rancor, enmity, ill-will. 2. (Chile) inflammation, soreness.
enconoso, sa, *a.* 1. rancorous, splenetic, nasty, irascible, crabby. 2. sore, sensitive, inflamed (a wound).
enconrear, *tr.v., var. of* **conrear.**
encontradamente, *adv.* opposite one another, facing each other, contrarily.
encontradizo, za, *a.* popping up all over the place, appearing everywhere. — **hacerse uno el e.,** to pretend to meet someone by chance.
encontrado, da, *past part. of* **encontrar.** —*a.* 1. facing or opposite one another. 2. diametrically opposed or different, contrary.
encontrar, (*ref.* 33) *tr.v.* 1. to meet, encounter. 2. to find, come across. —*i.v.* to meet. —*r.v.* 1. to meet. 2. to find oneself. 3. to fall out, become

enemies. 4. to differ, disagree, be opposed (opinions, ideas). 5. to concur, coincide, be the same or alike (emotions, character). — **encontrarse con,** to meet, come across.
encontronazo, encontrón, *m.* crash, collision, e.g. *los dos coches se dieron un e.,* the two cars collided with one another; clash, e.g. *tuve un e. con ella,* I had a disagreement with her.
encopetado, da, *past part. of* **encopetar.** —*a.* 1. arrogant, haughty, high and mighty, presumptuous. 2. (coll.) of noble descent, of ancient lineage. 3. crested, high-swept. —*m.* (archit.) cathetus or vertical height of a roof.
encopetar, *tr.v.* 1. to sweep (the hair) high up in front. 2. to raise on high. —*r.v.* 1. to rise high over the forehead (the hair). 2. to rise. 3. (fig.) to become conceited or vain.
encorachar, *tr.v.* to put into a leather bag.
encorajar, *tr.v.* to encourage, put heart into. —*r.v.* to get incensed or angry, fly into a fury.
encorajinarse, *r.v.* (coll.) to get angry, fly into a rage.
encorar, (*ref. 33*) *tr.v.* 1. to cover with leather; to encase or wrap in leather. 2. to cause (wounds) to grow new skin. —*r.v., i.v.* to grow new skin, heal (wounds).
encorazado, da, *a.* 1. wearing cuirass. 2. covered with or wrapped in leather.
encorchador, ra, *m., f.* one who corks bottles. —*f.* corking machine.
encorchar, *tr.v.* 1. to hive (bees). 2. to cork (bottles).
encorchetar, *tr.v.* 1. to put hook and eye clasps on (clothes). 2. to fasten with clasps, fasten with hooks and eyes. 3. (bldg.) to fasten with clamps, clamp (stones).
encordadura, *f.* (mus.) the set of strings (of an instrument).
encordar, (*ref. 33*) *tr.v.* 1. (mus.) to string, put strings on (a string instrument). 2. to bind with a cord.
encordelado, da, *a.* corded, stringed, tied with twine or string.
encordelar, *tr.v.* 1. to tie or bind with cord. 2. to ornament with braid and gimp.
encordonado, da, *past part. of* **encordonar.** —*a.* decorated with braid and gimp.
encordonador, ra, *m., f.* stringer, corder.
encordonar, *tr.v.* 1. to bind with cords. 2. to tie with laces or cords (e.g. shoes).
encorecer, (*ref. 45*) *tr.v.* to cause (wounds) to grow new skin. —*i.v.* to grow skin, heal (wounds).
encorezca, *ref.* **encorecer.**
encoriación, *f.* healing (of a wound).
encornado, da, *a.* horned. — **bien e.,** with well-shaped horns; **mal e.,** with badly shaped horns.
encornadura, *f.* horns; shape or position of the horns (of bulls); set of horns.
encornudar, *tr.v.* to cuckold. —*i.v.* to grow horns.
encorozar, (*ref. 53*) *tr.v.* 1. to make (a criminal) wear the **coroza** (cone-shaped hat with drawings indicating the wearer's crime). 2. (Amer.) to smooth, make level (a wall).
encorralar, *tr.v.* to pen, to corral (cattle).
encorrear, *tr.v.* to fasten (cattle) with straps.
encorselar, *tr.v., r.v.* (Arg., P. Rico, Can. I.) *var. of* **encorsetar.**
encorsetar, *tr.v.* to corset, put a corset on. —*r.v.* to put on a corset; to bind oneself up tightly.
encortinar, *tr.v.* to provide with curtains, curtain.
encorvada, *f.* 1. stooping, bending down. 2. grotesque dance. — **hacer la e.,** to feign illness (in order to avoid doing a disagreeable task).
encorvadura, *f.* curve, bend; bending, curving, crookedness.
encorvamiento, *m., var. of* **encorvadura.**
encorvar, *tr.v.* to bend, curve. —*r.v.* 1. to bend down, stoop. 2. (equit.) to buck. 3. to favor, be partial (towards), show inclination or preference (for).
encostalar, *tr.v.* to put into sacks.
encostarse, *r.v.* (mar.) to hug the coast.
encostillado, *m.* (min.) lagging, strengthening for pit props.
encostradura, *f.* 1. (archit.) incrustation (of marble, etc.). 2. whitewashing. 3. crust.
encostrar, *tr.v.* to coat, cover with a coating; to incrust; to put a crust on (a pie). —*i.v., r.v.* to form a crust; to become incrusted.
encovadura, *f.* putting (something) in a hole or cave; locking away; hiding.
encovar, (*ref. 33*)*tr.v.* 1. to put in a cave or hole. 2. to conceal, hide. —*r.v.* to hide, conceal oneself.
encrasar, *tr.v.* 1. to thicken. 2. to fertilize. —*r.v.* 1. to become thick. 2. become more fertile (soil).
encrespado, da, *past part. of* **encrespar.** —*a.* 1. curly (hair). 2. rough (sea). —*m.* curling (of hair); curl.
encrespador, ra, *a.* curling. —*m.* curler, curling tongs, curling iron.
encrespadura, *f.* curling (of hair); curl.
encrespamiento, *m.* curling (of hair); curl.
encrespar, *tr.v.* 1. to curl. 2. to make (hair) stand on end. 3. to enrage, excite, agitate. 4. to stir up, make rough (the sea). —*r.v.* 1. to curl, become curled. 2. to stand on end (hair). 3. to become enraged, excited or agitated. 4. to become rough (the sea). 5. to become complicated or difficult.
encrestado, da, *past part. of* **encrestarse.** —*a.* (fig.) proud, haughty, arrogant.
encrestarse, *r.v.* to stiffen its crest (a bird).
encrucijada, *f.* 1. crossroads. 2. (fig.) opportunity for trapping a person; ambush. 3. (fig.) dilemma.
encrudecer, (*ref. 45*) *tr.v.* 1. to make rough or raw. 2. (fig.) to irritate, exasperate, annoy. —*r.v.* 1. to become harsh or severe (weather). 2. to become irritated or exasperated.
encrudecimiento, *m.* irritation, rawness; worsening.
encrudezca, encrudezco, *ref.* **encrudecer.**
encrueceler, (*ref. 45*) *tr.v.* to incite to cruelty. —*r.v.* to become cruel.
encruelezca, encruelezco, *ref.* **encruelecer.**
encuadernable, *a.* able to be bound (a book).
encuadernación, *f.* bookbinding (the art and the product).
encuadernador, ra, *m., f.* bookbinder. —*m.* clip, pin (to fix papers together).
encuadernar, *tr.v.* to bind (books).
encuadramiento, encuadre, *m.* focussing (on an object) in photography.
encuadrar, *tr.v.* 1. to frame, to square; to fit into a frame, to square up. 2. (fig.) to fit in, insert. 3. (fig.) to surround.
encuartar, *tr.v.* 1. to reckon the excess or extra charge on. 2. to hitch an extra draft horse or oxen to. —*r.v.* (Mex.) to get into difficulties, get into a fix.
encuarte, *m.* 1. extra draft horse or yoke of oxen (for dragging uphill). 2. extra charge (on wood or stone) when pieces exceed certain dimensions.
encuartero, *m.* person taking care of an extra horse or yoke of oxen.
encubar, *tr.v.* 1. to vat, pour into a vat, to cask or barrel. 2. (min.) to shore up (a mine shaft).
encubertar, (*ref. 29*) *tr.v.* to cover with silks or tapestry; to caparison, trap (a horse). —*r.v.* to put on armor.
encubierta, *f.* fraud, deceit.
encubiertamente, *adv.* secretly, deceitfully; fraudulently, deceptively.
encubierto, ta, *irr. past part. of* **encubrir.**
encubridizo, za, *a.* concealable, easily hidden.
encubridor, ra, *a.* concealing. —*m.* concealer, go-between; harborer (of a criminal); (law) accessory after the fact.
encubrimiento, *m.* concealment; (law) complicity.
encubrir, *irr. past part. of* **encubierto.** —*tr.v.* to conceal, hide; to harbor (a criminal). — **ayudar y.e.,** to aid and abet.
encuentre, encuentro, *ref.* **encontrar.**
encuentro, *m.* 1. encounter; meeting; collision; (mil.) clash, skirmish. 2. match, game (of soccer, etc.). 3. ramming, butting (between two rams). 4. fall of two cards or dice of equal value. 5. (billiards) shot, carom. 6. (archit.) angle (formed by two crossing rafters); nook, niche. 7. (zool.) armpit; (*pl.*) wing joint (of birds); (*pl.*) shoulder joint (of quadrupeds). 8. (*pl.*) (tex.) temples (of a loom). 9. (*pl.*) (print.) spaces, blanks (for printing different colored letters) — **e. amistoso,** friendly match or game; **ir al e. de uno,** to go out to meet someone; **salirle a uno al e.,** to go out to meet or receive someone; to oppose or face someone; to anticipate or forestall someone; to beat someone to it.
encuerar, *tr.v., r.v.* (Mex., Cuba) to strip, undress.
encuerde, encuerdo, *ref.* **encordar.**
encuere, encuero, *ref.* **encorar.**
encuesta, *f.* 1. inquiry, investigation. 2. survey, poll (of public opinion).
encuestador, dora, *m.f.* pollster.
encuestar, *tr.v.* to poll.
encuevar, *tr.v., r.v., var. of* **encovar.**
encueve, encuevo, *ref.* **encovar.**
encuitarse, *r.v.* to grieve, sorrow, anguish.
enculatar, *tr.v.* to cover (a beehive) with an upturned basket or earthenware jar.
encumbradamente, *adv.* haughtily, arrogantly.
encumbrado, da, *past part. of* **encumbrar.** —*a.* tall, high; lofty, stately.
encumbramiento, *m.* 1. raising. 2. height, elevation. 3. exaltation; eminence, prominence.
encumbrar, *tr.v.* 1. to raise. 2. to climb to the top of (the summit). 3. to exalt, honor. —*r.v.* 1. to rise. 2. to become proud or haughty. 3. to tower, rise. 4. to be exalted or honored.
encunar, *tr.v.* 1. to put (an infant) in the cradle. 2. (taur.) to catch between its horns.
encurdelarse, *r.v.* to get drunk.
encureñar, *tr.v.* to put on a gun-carriage.
encurtido, *past part. of* **encurtir.** —*m.* (cul.) pickled fruit or vegetable.
encurtir, *tr.v.* to pickle, to preserve in vinegar.
ende, *adv.* **por e.,** therefore, consequently, e.g. *es bonita y por e. envidiada,* she is beautiful, consequently she is envied.
endeble, *a.* weak, feeble, frail; thin, flimsy; weak, poor, bad.
endeblez, *f.* weakness, frailness, feebleness; thinness, flimsiness.
endeblucho, cha, *a.* (coll.) weakly, sickly, lifeless.
endécada, *f.* period of eleven years.
endecágono, na, *a.* (geom.) hendecagonal. —*m.* (geom.) hendecagon, undecagon, an eleven-sided polygon.
endecasílabo, ba, *a.* hendecasyllabic. —*m.* hendecasyllabic verse.
endecha, *f.* 1. dirge, mournful song, plaintive melody. 2. assonanted hexasyllabic or heptasyllabic quatrain; **e. endecasílaba** or real, quatrain consisting of three heptasyllabic lines and one hendecasyllabic which assonates with the second line.

endechadera, *f.* hired mourner, professional mourner.
endechar, *tr.v.* to accompany with a dirge. —*r.v.* to mourn, lament, sorrow, grieve.
endehesar, *tr.v.* to pasture, put cattle out to pasture.
endejas, *f.* (*pl.*) (mas.) toothings.
endemia, *f.* (med.) endemic, endemic illness.
endemicidad, *f.* (med.) endemicity.
endémico, ca, *a.* (med.) endemic.
endemoniado, da, *past part. of* **endemoniar.** —*a.* possessed by the devil; (coll.) devilish, fiendish. —*m., f.* possessed person.
endemoniar, *tr.v.* 1. to possess with the devil. 2. (coll.) to enrage, infuriate. —*r.v.* to get furious, fly into a rage.
endenantes, *adv.* 1. (coll.) before. 2. (Amer.) a while ago.
endentado, da, *past part. of* **endentar.** —*a.* (her.) indented, serrated.
endentar, (*reg. 29*) *tr.v.* 1. to engage, gear, mesh. 2. to tooth, key, serrate, notch.
endentecer, (*ref. 45*) *i.v.* to teethe, grow teeth, cut teeth.
endentezca, *ref.* **endentecer.**
enderece, enderecé, *ref.* **enderezar.**
enderezadamente, *adv.* honestly, uprightly, rightly.
enderezado, da, *past part. of* **enderezar.** —*a.* favorable, opportune, fitting, suitable.
enderezador, ra, *a.* straightening. —*m., f.* good manager; righter; straightener (of affairs). —*m.* 1. (elec.) rectifier. 2. (mec.) straightener.
enderezamiento, *m.* straightening; rectification.
enderezar, (*ref. 53*) *tr.v.* 1. to straighten; to put or stand up straight. 2. to correct, rectify. 3. to direct (one's efforts towards getting something). 4. to straighten out, put in order. 5. to correct, punish. 6. (elec.) to convert into direct current, rectify. —*i.v.* to make or go straight (for somewhere). —*r.v.* 1. to become straight. 2. to stand up straight, straighten up. 3. to make straight (for). 4. to be directed (towards getting something).
endérmico, ca, *a.* (med.) endermic.
endeudarse, *r.v.* 1. to get or go into debt. 2. to recognize an obligation.
endevotado, da, *a.* 1. very devout, pious. 2. devoted (to), fond (of).
endiablada, *f.* masquerade in which people are disguised as devils.
endiabladamente, *adv.* devilishly; abominably.
endiablado, da, *past part. of* **endiablar.** —*a.* 1. devilish; fiendish. 2. ugly, repulsive. 3. perverse, wicked. 4. fiendishly difficult or complicated.
endiablar, *tr.v.* to pervert, corrupt. —*r.v.* to be furious.
endíadis, *f.* (rhet.) hendiadys.
endibia, *f.* (bot.) endive.
endiente, endiento, *ref.* **endentar.**
endilgador, ra, *a.* (coll.) directing. —*m., f.* 1. (coll.) director, guide. 2. pander, pimp.
endilgar, (*ref. 51*) *tr.v.* 1. (coll.) to send, direct. 2. to guide, help. 3. to foist (something unwanted or unpleasant) off on.
endilgue, endilgué, *ref.* **endilgar.**
Endimión, *m.* (myth.) Endymion, young shepherd loved by Selene, condemned by Jupiter to eternal youth.
endino na, *a.* (coll.) perverse, wicked.
endiosamiento, *m.* 1. haughtiness, conceit, arrogance, pride. 2. abstraction, absorption.
endiosar, *tr.v.* to deify. —*r.v.* 1. to become conceited, arrogant or haughty. 2. to be transported, abstracted or absorbed. 3. to be elated (e.g. with pride).
enditarse, *r.v.* (Amer.) to go or get into debt.
endivia, *f.* endive.
endobiótico, ca, *a.* (bot.) endobiotic.
endoblado, da, *past part. of* **endoblar.** —*a.* suckling with two ewes.
endoblar, *tr.v.* to make two ewes feed one lamb.
endoblástico, ca, *a.* (biol.) endoblastic.
endoblasto, *m.* (biol.) endoblast.
endoble, *m.* (min.) double wages (of miners and smelting workers).
endocardíaco, ca, *a.* (anat.) endocardial.
endocardio, *m.* (anat.) endocardium.
endocarditis, *f.* (med.) endocarditis.
endocarpio, *m.* (bot.) endocarp.
endoclinal, *a.* (geol.) endoclinal. —*m.* endocline.
endocráneo, *m.* (anat., ento.) endocranium.
endocrino, na, *a.* (physiol.) endocrine.
endocrinología, *f.* (physiol.) endocrinology.
endodermis, *f.* (bot.) endodermis.
endodermo, *m.* 1. (bot.) endodermis. 2. (zool.) endoderm.
endodoncia, *f.* (dent.) endodontia.
endoenzima, *f.* (biochem.) endoenzyme.
endoesquelético, ca, *a.* (anat.) endoskeletal.
endoesqueleto, *m.* (anat.) endoskeleton.
endofasia, *f.* (psyc.) endophasia, internal speech; thoughts with no external vocalization.
endófito, *m.* (bot.) endophyte, entophyte.
endogamia, *f.* (biol.) endogamy, inbreeding.
endogénesis, *f.* (biol.) endogeny.
endogenia, *f.* (biol.) endogeny.
endógeno, na, *a.* (anat.) endogenous.
endolinfa, *f.* (anat.) endolymph.
endometritis, *f.* (med.) endometritis.
endomingado, da, *past part. of* **endomingarse.** —*a.* dolled up (in Sunday best); well-dressed.
endomingarse, (*ref. 51*) *r.v.* to put on one's Sunday best, dress up.
endomixis, *f.* (biol.) endomixis.
endomorfía, *f.* (min., anth.) endomorphy.
endomórfico, ca, *a.* endomorphic.
endomorfismo, *m.* (geol.) endomorphism.
endomorfo, fa, *a.* (min., anth.) endomorphic.
endoparásito, *m.* endoparasite.
endoplasma, *m.* (biol.) endoplasm.
endopodito, *m.* (zool.) endopodite.
endorsar, *tr.v.* to indorse, endorse (a draft, check, etc.).
endorso, *m.* (com.) endorsement.
endosable, *a.* endorsable.
endosante, *a.* endorsing. —*m., f.* endorser.
endosar, *tr.v.* 1. to endorse (a check). 2. to pass on to, foist off on (someone).
endosarco, *m.* (biol.) endosarc.
endosatario, ria, *m., f.* endorsee, person in whose favor a bill or check is endorsed.
endoscopio, *m.* (surg.) endoscope.
endose, *m.* move in ombre when principal player or principal opponent causes the third player to take a second trick.
endoselado, da, *a.* canopied.
endoselar, *tr.v.* to canopy, hang with a canopy.
endosmómetro, *m.* (phys.) endosmometer.
endosmosis, *f.* (phys.) endosmosis.
endosmótico, ca, *a.* (phys.) endosmotic.
endoso, *m.* *endorsement.* — **e. en blanco,** blank endorsement.
endosperma, *m.* (bot.) endosperm.
endospérmeo, mea, *a.* (bot.) endospermous.
endóspora, *f.* (bot.) endospore.
endospórico, ca, *a.* (bot.) endosporic.
endosternito, *m.* (ento.) endosternite.
endostio, *m.* (anat.) endosteum.
endostosis, *f.* (med.) endostosis.
endotecio, *m.* (bot.) endothecium.
endotelial, *a.* (anat.) endothelial.
endotelio, *m.* (med.) endothelium.
endotelioma, *m.* (med.) endothelioma.
endoteloide, *a.* (anat.) endotheloid.
endotérmico, ca, *a.* (chem.) endothermic.
endotóxico, ca, *a.* (bac.) endotoxic.
endotoxina, *f.* (bac.) endotoxin.
endovenoso, sa, *a.* endovenous, intravenous.
endozoico, ca, *a.* (bot.) endozoic.
endriago, *m.* (myth.) fabled monster, part man, part beast.
endrina, *f.* (bot.) sloe (fruit).
endrinal, *m.* thicket of sloe trees.
endrino, na, *a.* sloe-colored, bluish black. —*m.* (bot.) sloe, blackthorn (tree).
endrogarse, (*ref. 51*) *r.v.* 1. to take drugs, become addicted to drugs. 2. (Guat., Mex., Peru) to go into debt, get into debt.
endulce, endulcé, *ref.* **endulzar.**
endulzadura, *f.* sweetening.
endulzar, (*ref. 53*) *tr.v.* 1. to sweeten. 2. (fig.) to soften, make bearable, ease. 3. (p.) (rare) to blur, dim (outlines of paintings). —*r.v.* 1. to become sweet. 2. (fig.) to become bearable or easier.
endurador, ra, *a.* niggardly, stingy, mean. —*m., f.* miser, skinflint, tightwad.
endurar, *tr.v.* 1. to harden. 2. to endure, put up with, tolerate. 3. to postpone, put off. 4. to save, be thrifty with. —*r.v.* to become hard, harden.
endurecer, (*ref. 45*) *tr.v.* 1. to harden, make hard. 2. to toughen up, make hardy or tough. —*i.v.* to become hard or cruel. —*r.v.* 1. to harden, become hard. 2. to become hardy or tough.
endurecidamente, *adv.* tenaciously, stubbornly.
endurecido, da, *past part. of* **endurecer.** —*a.* hardened; hard, hardhearted; experienced.
endurecimiento, *m.* 1. hardening. 2. hardness. 3. (fig.) obstinacy, stubbornness, tenacity. — **e. de las arterias,** (med.) hardening of the arteries.
endurezca, endurezco, *ref.* **endurecer.**
ene, *f.* en (name of the letter "n"); **e. de palo,** (coll.) gallows; **ser de e. una cosa,** (coll.) to be inevitable. —*a.* x, e.g. *eso costará e. pesetas,* that will cost x pesetas.
E.N.E. *abbrev. of* **estenordeste,** (mar.) east-north-east (ENE).
enea, *f.* 1. (bot.) cattail, bulrush. 2. (Cuba) any flexible tree bark.
eneaedro, *m.* (geom.) enneagon, nonagon, a nine-sided polygon.
eneágono, na, *a.* (geom.) enneagonal, nine-sided. —*m.* (geom.) nonagon, enneagon.
eneal, *m.* patch of cattail or bulrushes.
Eneas, *m.* (myth.) Aeneas, Trojan prince, hero of Virgil's *Aeneid.*
eneasílabo, ba, *a.* enneasyllabic, nine-syllabled. —*m.* enneasyllabic verse.
enebral, *m.* patch or thicket of juniper trees.
enebrina, *f.* juniper berry.
enebro, *m.* (bot.) juniper tree; juniper wood.
enechado, da, *a.* foundling, abandoned (newborn child). —*m., f.* foundling.
Eneida, *f.* (lit.) Aeneid, epic poem by Virgil concerning the adventures of Aeneas, a Trojan prince who fought against the Greeks.
enejar, *tr.v.* to put an axle on; to place the axle on.
eneldo, *m.* (bot.) dill.
enema, *f.* (med.) enema.
enemiga, *f.* enmity, animosity, antagonism, ill will.
enemigamente, *adv.* antagonistically, hostilely.
enemigo, ga, *a.* enemy; **e. de,** hostile to. —*m., f.* enemy, foe, adversary. —*m.* 1. enemy (in a war). 2. devil. — **e. jurado,** sworn enemy; **e. malo,** devil.
enemistad, *f.* enmity, antagonism.

enemistar, *tr.v.* to make enemies of, antagonize. —*r.v.* to become enemies; to fall out (with); **enemistarse con,** to fall out with; to become an enemy of.
éneo, a, *a.* (poet.) brazen, of brass or copper.
eneolítico, ca, *a.* Aeneolithic.
energesis, *f.* (bot.) energesis.
energético, ca, *a.* (phys.) pertaining or relative to energy. —*f.* (phys.) energetics.
energía, *f.* 1. energy, power. 2. efficacy, effectiveness. 3. (phys.) energy. — **e. atómica,** atomic energy; **e. calórica,** heat energy; **e. cinética,** kinetic energy; **e. de enlace,** (phys., chem.) binding energy; **e. eléctrica,** electric power; **e. hidráulica,** waterpower; **e. mecánica,** mechanical energy; **e. nuclear,** nuclear energy; **e. potencial,** potential energy; **e. radiante,** radiant energy; **e. térmica,** steam-generated power.
enérgicamente, *adv.* energetically, vigorously.
enérgico, ca, *a.* energetic, vigorous, lively.
enérgida, *f.* (bot.) energid.
energúmeno, na, *m., f.* energumen, one possessed by an evil spirit; (fig.) wild impulsive person.
enerizar, (*ref. 53*) *tr.v., r.v.* (rare) *var. of* **erizar.**
enero, *m.* January.
enervación, *f.* 1. enervation; weakening. 2. effeminacy.
enervador, ra, *a.* enervating.
enervamiento, *m.* 1. enervation; weakening. 2. effeminacy.
enervante, *a.* enervating, weakening.
enervar, *tr.v.* 1. to enervate, weaken, debilitate. 2. (fig.) to weaken, decrease the strength or force of (arguments, etc.). —*r.v.* 1. to become enervated or debilitated. 2. to lose its force, be weakened (an argument).
enésimo, ma, *a.* nth (undetermined number of times); (math.) nth. — **por la enésima vez, vete a la cama,** for the nth time, go to bed.
enfadadizo, za, *a.* irritable, peevish, irascible, touchy.
enfadamiento, *m.* anger, annoyance, irritation.
enfadar, *tr.v.* to annoy, anger, make angry, irritate. —*r.v.* to get annoyed or angry; **enfadarse por** or **de algo,** to get angry about something; **enfadarse con** or **contra alguien,** to get angry with someone.
enfado, *m.* 1. annoyance; irritation, anger. 2. drudgery, grinding work.
enfadosamente, *adv.* angrily.
enfadoso, sa, *a.* annoying, irritating.
enfaenado, da, *a.* working busily; carried away, immersed in hard work.
enfaldado, *a.* (coll.) involved with women; running after women.
enfaldador, *m.* large pin (used to hold up a skirt).
enfaldar, *tr.v.* to clip off lower branches of (a tree). —*r.v.* to tuck or gather up one's skirt.
enfaldo, *m.* tucked up skirt or dress; hollow in a tucked up skirt (used for carrying things).
enfangar, (*ref. 51*) *tr.v.* to make muddy. —*r.v.* 1. to get muddy. 2. (coll.) to take part in a shady (coll.) or dirty business. 3. to sink into or wallow in vice, give oneself up to sensual pleasures.
enfangue, enfangué, *ref.* **enfangar.**
enfardar, *tr.v.* to pack, bale, crate.
enfardelador, *m.* packer, baler.
enfardeladura, *f.* packing, baling.
enfardelar, *tr.v.* to bundle, pack into bundles; to pack, bale, embale.
énfasis, *m., f.* emphasis, stress (gen. *m.*). —*m.* exaggeration, affectation (in tone of voice, expression or gesture).
enfáticamente, *adv.* emphatically.
enfático, ca, *a.* emphatic.
enfatizar, (*ref. 53*) *tr.v.* to emphasize.
enfermar, *i.v., r.v.* to fall ill. —*tr.v.* to make ill; (fig.) to weaken, debilitate, enervate.
enfermedad, *f.* illness, sickness, malady; disease. — **e. contagiosa,** contagious disease; **e. del legionario,** Legionnaires' disease; **e. del sueño,** sleeping sickness; **e. de Parkinson,** Parkinson's disease; **e. de transmisión sexual,** sexually transmitted disease; **e. hereditaria,** hereditary disease; **e. infantil,** childhood disease; **e. mental,** mental illness; **e. nervosa,** nervous disorder; **e. por carencia, e. por deficiencia,** deficiency disease; **e. profesional,** occupational disease; **e. venérea,** venereal disease.
enfermería, *f.* 1. infirmary, hospital, (mar.) sick bay (of a ship). 2. patients of a hospital.
enfermero, ra, *m., f.* nurse; **e. graduada (do),** registered nurse; **e. auxiliar,** nurse's aide.
enfermizo, za, *a.* sickly, weakly (person); unhealthy (climate, passion).
enfermo, ma, *a.* sick, ill, sickly, weakly; **caer e.,** *to fall ill;* **estar e.,** to be ill or sick; **ser e.,** to be an invalid. —*m., f.* sick person, invalid; patient. —*m.* sick man. —*f.* sick woman.
enfermoso, sa, *a.* (Col., Ecuad., Hond., Mex.) sickly, weakly; indisposed.
enfermucho, cha, *a.* sickly, weakly.
enfervorice, enfervoricé, *ref.* **enfervorizar.**
enfervorizador, ra, *a.* animating, rousing, encouraging. —*m., f.* encourager, animator, rouser.
enfervorizar, (*ref. 53*) *tr.v.* to animate, encourage; to arouse, incite. —*r.v.* to become animated; to get aroused or worked up.
enfeudación, *f.* 1. enfeoffment, infeudation. 2. enfeoffment, title of enfeoffment or infeudation.
enfeudar, *tr.v.* to enfeoff, give in vassalage.
enfielar, *tr.v.* to balance (scales).
enfierecerse, (*ref. 45*) *r.v.* (rare) to become furious.
enfierezca, *ref.* **enfierecerse.**
enfiestarse, *r.v.* (Amer.) to have a good time, let one's hair down.
enfilado, da, *past part. of* **enfilar.** —*a.* (her.) enfiled.
enfilar, *tr.v.* 1. to place in a line or row. 2. to direct (e.g. one's eyes). 3. to go down or along (e.g. the street). 4. to string (pearls). 5. (mil.) to enfilade, rake with fire. 6. to follow (a certain direction). — **e. derecho,** to stay on the straight and narrow.
enfisema, *m.* (med.) emphysema.
enfisematoso, sa, (med.) emphysematous.
enfistolar, *tr.v., r.v.* (med.) to turn into a fistula.
enfiteusis, *f.* (law) emphyteusis.
enfiteuta, *m., f.* (law) emphyteuta, holder of land by emphyteusis.
enfitéutico, ca, *a.* (law) emphyteutic.
enflacar, (*ref. 50*) *i.v.* to grow or become thin.
enflaquecer, (*ref. 45*) *tr.v.* 1. to make thin or lean, wear away. 2. to weaken, debilitate. —*i.v.* 1. to grow or become thin. 2. to flag, diminish (will, spirits), to lose heart, get discouraged. —*r.v.* to grow thin.
enflaquecimiento, *m.* 1. loss of weight. 2. weakening. 3. flagging (of spirits).
enflaquezca, enflaquezco, *ref.* **enflaquecer.**
enflautado, da, *past part. of* **enflautar.** —*a.* bombastic, pompous. —*f.* (Hond., Peru) vulgar or stupid remark.
enflautador, ra, *a.* swindling, cheating. —*m., f.* swindler, cheat. —*m.* pimp. —*f.* procuress, madam.
enflautar, *tr.v.* 1. to inflate, blow up. 2. (coll.) to procure. 3. (coll.) to cheat, deceive. 4. (Col., Guat., Mex.) to force (a thing) upon.
enflechado, da, *a.* loaded, with arrow ready (said of a bow).
enflorar, *tr.v.* to adorn with flowers.
enflorecer, (*ref. 45*) *i.v.* to bloom, blossom, flower.
enfocar, (*ref. 50*) *tr.v.* 1. to focus. 2. to reduce (a subject) to its fundamentals.
enfoque, *m.* focussing, putting into focus; focus.
enfoque, enfoqué, *ref.* **enfocar.**
enfosado, *m.* (vet.) *var. of* **encebadamiento.**
enfoscado, *past part. of* **enfoscar.** —*m.* (mas.) filling up (holes), plastering.
enfoscar, (*ref. 50*) *tr.v.* (mas.) to fill up (holes, cavities, etc.); to plaster (a wall). —*r.v.* 1. to become surly or gruff. 2. to become deeply involved, plunge in up to the hilt (e.g. in a business). 3. to become covered with clouds, cloud over.
enfosque, enfosqué, *ref.* **enfoscar.**
enfrailar, *tr.v.* to make into a monk or friar. —*i.v., r.v.* to become a monk or friar.
enfranje, *m.* (Chile) *var. of* **enfranque.**
enfranque, *m.* shank, narrow part of the sole beneath the instep.
enfranquecer, (*ref. 45*) *tr.v.* to free, release, liberate.
enfranquezca, *ref.* **enfranquecer.**
enfrascamiento, *m.* entanglement, involvement.
enfrascar, (*ref. 50*) *tr.v.* to bottle, put into bottles.
enfrascarse, (*ref. 50*) *r.v.* 1. to become entangled or involved (in). 2. to devote oneself (to).
enfrasque, enfrasqué, *ref.* **enfrascar.**
enfrenador, ra, *a.* bridling, restraining. —*m., f.* person who restrains or bridles horses.
enfrenamiento, *m.* (fig.) bridling, checking, curbing.
enfrenar, *tr.v.* 1. to curb, bridle, rein in (horse). 2. to train (a horse) to obey the bridle. 3. to brake, apply the brakes to (a train, etc.). 4. (fig.) to check, restrain (passions). —*r.v.* to check or restrain one's passions.
enfrentar, *tr.v.* 1. to confront, bring face to face. 2. to face, confront (a danger, etc.). —*i.v.* to meet or come face to face. —*r.v.* 1. to meet or come face to face. 2. to face. — **enfrentarse con la realidad,** to face reality.
enfrente, *adv.* in front, opposite; **e. de,** opposite; in front of; against, in opposition to.
enfriadera, *f.* cooler, cooling jug.
enfriadero, *m.* cooling place; cold storage.
enfriador, ra, *a.* cooling. —*m.* cooling place.
enfriamiento, *m.* 1. cooling, refrigeration. 2. chill, cold. — **e. atmosférico,** atmospheric cooling.
enfriar, — (*ref. 54*) *tr.v.* to chill, cool; **e. por aire,** to air-cool. —*i.v.* to cool down; to turn cold. —*r.v.* to become cold or cool; to turn cold; to cool down or off; to catch cold.
enfrontar, *tr.v.* to confront, face. —*i.v.* **e. con,** to face, confront.
enfroscarse, (*ref. 50*) *r.v.* to become entangled or involved (in).
enfullar, *tr.v.* (coll.) to cheat (in card games).
enfullinarse, *r.v.* (Chile, Mex.) to get annoyed, peeved or angry.
enfunchar, *tr.v.* (Cuba) to annoy, make angry. —*r.v.* to become annoyed, take offense.
enfundadura, *f.* sheathing, covering, casing.
enfundar, *tr.v.* 1. to put in a case; to sheathe. 2. to fill, stuff.
enfuñarse, *r.v.* (Cuba) to become angry.
enfurecer, (*ref. 45*) *tr.v.* to infuriate, make furious. —*r.v.* 1. to become infuriated or furious. 2. (fig.) to become rough or stormy (the sea).
enfurecimiento, *m.* infuriation.
enfurezca, enfurezco, *ref.* **enfurecer.**
enfurruñamiento, *m.* anger.

enfurruñarse, *r.v.* (coll.) to get angry, ratty or peeved.
enfurruscarse, (*ref. 50*) *r.v.* (Chile, coll.) *var. of* **enfurruñarse.**
enfurtido, *past part. of* **enfurtir.** —*m.* (tex.) fulling.
enfurtir, *tr.v.* 1. (tex.) to full (cloth). 2. to cake, press together (felt). —*r.v.* to become caked or pressed together (nap of felt or velvet).
engabanado, da, *a.* wearing an overcoat.
engace, *m.* 1. setting (of precious stones). 2. (fig.) link, connection.
engace, engacé, *ref.* **engazar.**
engafar, *tr.v.* 1. to pull back the string of (a crossbow). 2. to apply the safety catch to (a gun). 3. to hook, catch hold of (with hooks).
engaitador, ra, *a.* 1. (coll.) bamboozling, tricking. 2. coaxing, wheedling.
engaitar, *tr.v.* 1. (coll.) to bamboozle, trick, deceive. 2. to coax, wheedle.
engalabernar, *tr.v.* (carp.) to join, connect; to assemble.
engalanado, da, *past part. of* **engalanar.** —*a.* bedecked, adorned.
engalanar, *tr.v.* to adorn, decorate, deck. —*r.v.* to adorn or decorate oneself.
engalgar, (*ref. 51*) *tr.v.* 1. to scotch (a wheel). 2. (mar.) to back (an anchor).
engalgue, engalgué, *ref.* **engalgar.**
engallado, da, *past part. of* **engallarse.** —*a.* 1. erect, upright. 2. proud, arrogant.
engallador, *m.* overcheck rein (to make the horse hold its head up).
engalladura, *f., var. of* **galladura.**
engallarse, *r.v.* 1. to draw oneself up haughtily. 2. to hold its head up straight (a horse).
enganchador, ra, *a.* hooking. —*m., f.* hooker, one who hooks something.
enganchamiento, *m., var. of* **enganche.**
enganchar, *tr.v.* 1. to hook, catch with a hook. 2. to hang on a hook. 3. to couple, connect; to hitch, hitch up. 4. to hook, inveigle, ensnare; (mil.) to entice into enlisting. 5. (taur.) to hook (on a horn) and toss. —*i.v.* to get caught (on a hook). —*r.v.* 1. to get caught or hooked up. 2. (mil.) to enlist, join up.
enganche, *m.* 1. coupling; hooking; hitching. 2. hook; clasp. 3. (ry.) coupling, coupler. 4. trap; inveiglement. 5. (mil.) enlistment. — **e. para remolque,** towing hitch; trailer hitch; **e. universal,** universal hitch.
engandujo, *m.* twisted, hanging thread of a fringe.
engañabobos, (*pl.* **engañabobos**) *m., f.* (coll.) trickster, swindler. —*m.* trick, swindle.
engañadizo, za, *a.* gullible, credulous, easily deceived.
engañado, da, *past part. of* **engañar.** —*a.* mistaken; deceived.
engañador, ra, *a.* deceiving, deceptive. —*m., f.* deceiver, trickster.
engañamundo, engañamundos, (*pl.* **engañamundos**) *m., var. of* **engañador.**
engañanecios, (*pl.* **engañanecios**) *m.* trickster, swindler.
engañante, *a.* deceiving, deceptive.
engañapastores, *m.* (ornith.) wagtail.
engañar, *tr.v.* 1. to deceive, cheat, trick, fool; to cuckold. 2. to while away (time); to ward or stave off (hunger, sleep). 3. to make more appetizing. 4. to entice, inveigle. —*r.v.* to deceive oneself; to be mistaken.
engañifa, *f.* (coll.) trick, fraud, swindle, hoax.
engaño, *m.* 1. trick, swindle, hoax, fraud; deception, deceptiveness, illusoriness, fallaciousness. 2. mistake, misunderstanding. 3. article of fishing tackle. 4. (taur.) working cape. — **e. de sí mismo,** self-deceit, self-deception; **llamarse uno a e.,** to withdraw from a contract alleging fraud; **salir del e.,** to realize one's mistake, see things as they are.
engañosamente, *adv.* deceptively, fraudulently, fallaciously.
engañoso, sa, *a.* deceptive, illusory, fallacious, misleading, false; artful.
engarabatar, *tr.v.* (coll.) to hook on to, catch hold of with a hook. —*r.v.* (coll.) to become hook-like or crooked.
engarabitar, *i.v., r.v.* 1. to climb, go up. 2. to become hook-like or crooked. 3. to become numb (with the cold).
engaratusar, *tr.v.* (Amer.) 1. to cajole, coax, wheedle; to inveigle, beguile. 2. to trick, take (someone) in.
engarbado, da, *past part. of* **engarbarse.** —*a.* held up by the top of another tree (said of a felled tree); perched on the top of a tree (said of a bird).
engarbarse, *r.v.* to perch up high (birds).
engarbullar, *tr.v.* (coll.) to confuse, muddle, entangle.
engarce, *m.* 1. linking, joining; stringing together. 2. (jewel) setting, mounting.
engarce, engarcé, *ref.* **engarzar.**
engargantadura, *f., var. of* **engargante.**
engargantar, *tr.v.* to put (something) into the throat. —*i.v.* 1. to put one's foot all the way into the stirrup. 2. (mec.) to mesh, engage. —*r.v.* to thrust one's foot into the stirrup.
engargante, *m.* (mec.) engaging, meshing.
engargolado, *past part. of* **engargolar.** —*m.* groove for sliding doors; (carp.) tongue and groove joint, male and female joint.
engargolar, *tr.v.* to fit together, join, connect.
engaritar, *tr.v.* 1. to furnish with turrets or sentry boxes. 2. (coll.) to trick, deceive, bamboozle.
engarnio, *m.* (coll.) good-for-nothing, ne'er-do-well.
engarrafador, ra, *a.* grabbing, seizing.
engarrafar, *tr.v.* (coll.) to grab, seize tightly.
engarrar, *tr.v.* to seize, grab, snatch; to take hold of, take.
engarriar, *i.v., r.v.* to climb.
engarro, *m.* seizing, grabbing, snatching.
engarrotar, *tr.v.* 1. to garrote. 2. to squeeze tightly. 3. to bind tightly. 4. (Arg.) to make numb. —*r.v.* to grow stiff or numb with cold, e.g. *se me engarrotaron los dedos,* my fingers became stiff and numb.
engarzador, ra, *a.* 1. linking, connecting. 2. (jewel.) mounting, setting. —*m., f.* 1. one who strings beads, pearls, etc. 2. (jewel.) setter, mounter.
engarzadura, *f., var. of* **engarce.**
engarzar, (*ref. 53*) *tr.v.* 1. to link, join, connect; to string together. 2. to curl (hair). 3. (jewel.) to set, mount.
engastado, da, *past part. of* **engastar.** —*a.* (jewel.) set or mounted as a precious stone.
engastador, ra, *a.* setting. —*m., f.* (jewel.) setter, mounter.
engastadura, *f., var. of* **engaste.**
engastar, *tr.v.* (jewel.) to set, mount, enchase.
engaste, *m.* 1. (jewel.) setting, mounting; bezel, groove holding a gem. 2. pearl flat on one side and round on the other.
engatado, da, *past part. of* **engatar.** —*a.* light-fingered, thievish, accustomed to steal.
engatar, *tr.v.* (coll.) to trick, deceive, bamboozle.
engatillado, da, *past part. of* **engatillar.** —*a.* (vet.) with a high thick neck. —*m.* (mec.) lock-seaming; (archit.) clamping, cramping, joining with clamps.
engatillar, *tr.v.* (mec.) to lock-seam, join by means of lock-seams (sheets of metal); (archit.) to clamp, cramp.
engatusador, ra, *a.* inveigling, beguiling; cajoling, coaxing. —*m., f.* 1. inveigler, beguiler, cajoler. 2. trickster, swindler.
engatusamiento, *m.* 1. inveigling, beguiling; cajoling. 2. tricking, swindling.
engatusar, *tr.v.* 1. to inveigle, beguile; to cajole, wheedle. 2. to trick, swindle, take (someone) in.
engaviar, *tr.v., r.v.* to climb, mount.
engavillada, *f.* a clump or grouping of wheat sheaves.
engavillar, *tr.v., var. of* **agavillar.**
engazamiento, *m.* 1. linking, joining; stringing together. 2. (jewel.) setting, mounting.
engazar, (*ref. 53*) *tr.v.* 1. to link, join, connect; to string together. 2. to curl (hair). 3. (jewel.) to mount, set. 4. (tex.) to dye (in the cloth). 5. (mar.) to strap down (blocks).
engendrable, *a.* that which may be engendered or begotten.
engendrador, ra, *a.* begetting, engendering. —*m.* begetter, engenderer.
engendramiento, *m.* begetting, engendering.
engendrante, *a.* begetting, generating.
engendrar, *tr.v.* to beget, engender; to create, produce, generate; to cause. —*r.v.* (fig.) to be engendered; to be created or caused.
engendro, *m.* 1. foetus. 2. monster, abortion; stunt, runt (child born malformed). 3. botch, mess, poorly worked out idea or plan. — **mal e.,** unruly youth, troublemaker.
engeridor, *m.* grafting knife.
engestado, da, *a., var. of* agestado.
engibar, *tr.v.* to make hunched. —*r.v.* to become hunched up, hunch up.
englandado, englantado, *a.* (her.) acorned, charged with acorns (oak tree on a shield).
englobado, da, *past part. of* **englobar.** —*a.* enclosed or included within a group.
englobar, *tr.v.* to include.
engolado, da, *a.* 1. with a gorget (of armor); with a neck piece or ruff (a woman's dress). 2. deep-throated (voice). 3. hoarse, raspy; choked. 4. pompous, affected (speech). 5. (fig.) fatuous, haughty, conceited.
engolamiento, *m.* 1. way of speaking in a deep-throated, husky voice. 2. pomposity in speech and attitude.
engolfar, *r.v. i.v.* to put out to sea. —*r.v.* 1. to put out to sea. 2. to become deeply involved; to become deeply absorbed; to let oneself go.
engolillado, da, *past part. of* **engolillarse.** —*a.* 1. wearing a ruff or gorget. 2. proud of clinging to old customs.
engolillarse, *r.v.* (Cuba) to go into debt.
engollamiento, *m.* vanity, conceit, haughtiness, pride.
engolletado, da, *past part. of* **engolletarse.** —*a.* (coll.) stuck-up, proud, haughty, vain or conceited.
engolletarse, *r.v.* (coll.) to become proud, vain or conceited.
engolondrinar, *tr.v.* to make conceited or vain. —*r.v.* 1. to become conceited or vain. 2. to become superficially infatuated, fall lightly in love.
engolosinador, ra, *a.* tempting, enticing, alluring.
engolosinar, *tr.v.* to tempt, entice, lure. —*r.v.* to take a liking to, get fond of, get a taste for; **e. con el juego,** to take a liking to gambling.
engomado, da, *past part. of* **engomar.** —*a.* 1. starchy, stiff (cloth). 2. (Chile) smart, spruce, all dressed up.

engomadura, *f.* gumming; sizing, treating (cloth) with size; propolization (first coating of wax given to hives by bees).
engomar, *tr.v.* to glue, gum (paper); to size, treat with size.
engorar, (*ref. 35*) *tr.v.* to addle, make addled. —*r.v., i.v.* to addle, become addled.
engorda, *f.* 1. (Chile, Mex.) fattening. 2. (Chile, Mex.) herd of cattle fattened for slaughter.
engordadero, *m.* fattening barn or sty; fattening season; fattening fodder.
engordador, ra, *a.* fattening. —*m., f.* one who fattens livestock.
engordar, *tr.v.* to fatten. —*i.v.* 1. to grow or get fat, put on weight. 2. (coll.) to get rich.
engorde, *m.* fattening (of cattle).
engorrar, *tr.v.* (Ven.) to irritate, bother, annoy. —*r.v.* to be caught on a hook.
engorro, *m.* obstacle, nuisance, bother; embarrassment.
engorroso, sa, *a.* annoying, troublesome, embarrassing.
engoznar, *tr.v.* to hinge, fix with a hinge; to place a hinge on (door, lid, etc.).
engrama, *m.* (biol., psyc.) engram.
engrampar, *tr.v.* to staple (papers, etc.).
engranado, da, *past part. of* **engranar.** —*a.* geared, in gear.
engranaje, *m.* 1. engagement, engaging (of gears). 2. (mec.) gearing, gears, gear wheels. 3. (fig.) connection, link, interlocking (of ideas, circumstances). — **desplazador de engranajes,** (mec.) gear-shift, gear change; **e. con tornillo sin fin,** (mec.) screw or worm gear; **e. de corona,** (mec.) crown wheel; **e. de transmisión,** (mec.) transmission gear; **e. de velocidad regulable,** (mec.) variable speed gear; **e. diferencial,** (mec.) differential gear; **e. en bisel,** (mec.) bevel gear; **e. fresado** or **tallado,** (mec.) out gear; **e. impulsor** or **transmisor,** (mec.) drive gear; **engranajes planetarios,** (mec.) planet differential or gear, planetary gear; **rueda de e.,** (mec.) gearwheel.
engranamiento, *m.* (mec.) enmeshing, enmeshment.
engranar, *i.v.* 1. (mec.) to engage, connect. 2. to link, connect, interlock. —*tr.v.* to join, connect, link, to put into gear.
engrandar, *tr.v.* to enlarge, amplify, augment. —*r.v.* to grow bigger or larger.
engrandecer, (*ref. 45*) *tr.v.* 1. to increase, enlarge, amplify, augment. 2. to enhance, heighten; to praise, extol; to exaggerate, magnify; (fig.) to exalt, elevate. —*r.v.* to become exalted.
engrandecimiento, *m.* 1. increase, enlargement, amplification. 2. enhancement; exaggeration, magnification; exaltation, elevation.
engrandezca, engrandezco, *ref.* **engrandecer.**
engrane, *m.* gear; meshing; cog, cogwheel.
engranerar, *tr.v.* to store or put (grain) in a granary.
engranujarse, *r.v.* 1. to become pimply or covered with pimples. 2. to become a rascal or rogue.
engrapadora, *f.* stapler.
engrapar, *tr.v.* 1. to clamp, cramp. 2. to staple.
engrasación, *f.* greasing, oiling, lubrication.
engrasado, da, *past part. of* **engrasar.** —*a.* greased, oiled, lubricated —*m.* lubrication, greasing.
engrasador, *m.* grease cup; grease gun; oiler, lubricator.
engrasar, *tr.v.* 1. to grease, oil, lubricate; to smear with fat or grease. 2. (tex.) to dress (cloth). 3. to manure, fertilize. —*r.v.* 1. to get smeared with grease or fat, get greasy. 2. (Mex.) to get lead poisoning.
engrase, *m.* greasing, oiling, lubrication; lubricant, lubricating agent. — **e. por goteo,** (auto.) drip feed.
engravar, *tr.v.* to cover with gravel or pebbles.
engravecer, *tr.v.* to make heavy. —*r.v.* to become heavy.
engredar, *r.v.* to treat with clay or chalk.
engreído, da, *past part. of* **engreír.** —*a.* spoiled, conceited, stuck-up.
engreimiento, *m.* conceit, vanity, pretentiousness.
engreír, (*ref. 40*) *tr.v.* 1. to make conceited, swollen-headed or vain. 2. to make fond (of). 3. (Amer.) to spoil, pamper, indulge. —*r.v.* 1. to become conceited or vain. 2. to become or grow fond (of). 3. (Amer.) to become spoiled or pampered. — **engreírse en algo,** to become fond of or take a liking to something.
engreñado, da, *a.* disheveled, rumpled, tousled.
engrescar, *tr.v.* 1. to incite or goad into fighting. 2. to make merry, stir to merriment. —*r.v.* 1. to pick a quarrel, get into a fight. 2. to join in the fun.
engrifar, *tr.v.* to curl, crimp; to make (hair) stand on end. —*r.v.* 1. to curl, crimp up; to stand on end (hair). 2. to rear (a horse), e.g. *se engrifó el caballo,* the horse reared up.
engrillar, *tr.v.* 1. to shackle, fetter, put in irons. 2. (P. Rico, Ven.) to lower or drop the head (a horse).
engrilletar, *tr.v.* (mar.) to shackle (two lengths of chain).
engringarse, (*ref. 51*) *r.v.* (coll.) to adopt or imitate the manners and habits of foreigners (esp. Americans and Englishmen).
engringue, engringué, *ref.* **engringarse.**
engrosamiento, *m.* broadening, thickening; increase, enlargement.
engrosar, (*ref. 33*) *tr.v.* 1. to make thick, thicken, broaden. 2. to increase, augment, swell (the membership of an organization). —*i.v.* to put on weight or flesh.
engrudador, ra, *m., f.* paster. —*m.* pasting-brush.
engrudamiento, *m.* pasting.
engrudar, *tr.v.* to paste. —*r.v.* to form into a paste, take the consistency of paste.
engrudo, *m.* paste (for sticking).
engruesar, *i.v., var. of* **engrosar.**
engruese, engrueso, *ref.* **engrosar.**
engrumecerse, (*ref. 45*) *r.v.* to clot, coagulate; to curdle.
engrumezca, *ref.* **engrumecerse.**
enguachinar, *tr.v.* to flood. —*r.v.* 1. to become flooded. 2. (Col.) to become vulgar.
engualdrapar, *tr.v* to caparison, put the trappings on (a horse).
enguantar, *tr.v.* to glove. —*r.v.* to put on gloves.
enguatar, *tr.v.* to line with wadding; to quilt.
enguedejado, da, *a.* in long tresses; long-haired; (coll.) finicky about one's hair; proud of one's hair.
enguera, enguere, *ref.* **engorar.**
enguichado, da, *a.* (her.) said of a horn or trumpet hanging from a cord or strap.
enguijarrado, *m.* cobble paving.
enguijarrar, *tr.v.* to pave with cobbles or cobblestones.
enguillar, *tr.v.* (mar.) to reinforce rope by winding cord around it.
enguillotarse, *r.v.* (coll.) to be engrossed or absorbed (in).
enguirnaldar, *tr.v.* to decorate with garlands; to enwreathe; to bedeck.
enguizgar, (*ref. 51*) *tr.v.* to incite, excite, urge on.
enguizgue, enguizgué, *ref.* **enguizgar.**
engullidor, ra, *m., f.* gulper, bolter (of food); glutton.
engullir, (*ref. 65*) *tr.v.* to gulp down, bolt, gobble (food).
engurrio, *m.* sadness, melancholy.
engurruñar, *tr.v* to wrinkle. —*r.v.* 1. to wrinkle up, become wrinkled. 2. (coll.) to be melancholy or sorrowful (like a bird in moult).
engurruñir, (*ref. 66*) *tr.v.* to wrinkle.
enhacinar, *tr.v.* to stack, put in a pile or heap, pile up.
enharinar, *tr.v.* to flour, cover with flour. —*r.v.* to get covered with flour.
enhastiar, *tr.v.* to bore, weary, annoy; to cloy, glut, satiate. —*r.v.* to get bored or weary; to become glutted or sated.
enhastillar, *tr.v.* to put (arrows) in the quiver.
enhatijar, *tr.v.* to cover (the mouth of a beehive) with netting or bassweed.
enhebillar, *tr.v.* to put a buckle on (a strap).
enhebrar, *tr.v.* to thread (a needle); to string (beads); to string together; **e. una mentira tras otra,** to tell a string of lies, tell a pack of lies.
enhenar, *tr.v.* to cover with hay.
enherbolar, *tr.v.* to poison with herbs.
enhestador, *m.* raiser; hoister.
enhestar, (*ref. 29*) *tr.v.* 1. to hoist, raise aloft. 2. to set upright or erect. —*r.v.* 1. to stand upright or erect. 2. to rise up.
enhielar, *tr.v.* to mix with bile or gall, make bitter.
enhiesto, ta, *irr. past part. of* **enhestar.** —*a.* upright, erect, straight.
enhilado, da, *past part. of* **enhilar.** —*a.* in line, in order; well coordinated.
enhilar, *tr.v.* 1. to thread (a needle); to string (beads). 2. (fig.) to put in order, marshal (ideas); to direct, guide. 3. to line up. —*i.v.* to direct oneself (towards), set out (for).
enhorabuena, *f.* congratulations, felicitation; approval; **dar la e.,** to congratulate. —*adv.* luckily, fortunately; welcome, e.g. *llegaste e.,* fortunately, you have arrived.
enhoramala, *adv.* unfortunately; with disapproval. — **¡e. entré en tu casa!** damn the moment I entered your house!; **mandar a una persona e.,** to send a person to the devil.
enhorcar, (*ref. 50*) *tr.v.* to string (onions or garlic).
enhornar, *tr.v.* to put into an oven.
enhorque, enhorqué, *ref.* **enhorcar.**
enhorquetar, *tr.v.* (Amer.) to place astride or astraddle. —*r.v.* to place oneself astride, sit astride.
enhuecar, (*ref. 50*) *tr.v., var. of* **ahuecar.**
enhueque, enhuequé, *ref.* **enhue car.**
enhuerar, *tr.v.* to addle, make addled. —*i.v., r.v.* to addle, become addled.
enigma, *m.* enigma, puzzle, riddle.
enigmáticamente, *adv.* enigmatically.
enigmático, ca, *a.* enigmatic, enigmatical.
enigmatista, *m., f.* enigmatist, one who talks in riddles.
enjabonado, da, *past part. of* **enjabonar.** —*a.* (Cuba) grey, mottled, piebald. —*m.* soaping, washing with soap.
enjabonadura, *f.* soaping, washing.
enjabonar, *tr.v.* 1. to soap, wash with soap. 2. (coll.) to soft-soap, flatter. 3. (coll.) to upbraid, reprimand, reprove.
enjaece, enjaecé, *ref.* **enjaezar.**
enjaezar, (*ref. 53*) *tr.v.* to harness, put trappings on.
enjaguadura, *f., var. of* **enjuagadura.**
enjaguar, (*ref. 52*) *tr.v., var. of* **enjuagar.**
enjagüe, *m.* 1. adjudication in favor of a ship's creditors. 2. (Amer.) rinsing, rinse.
enjalbegado, *past part. of* **enjalbegar.** —*m.* whitewashing.
enjalbegador, ra, *a.* whitewashing. —*m., f.* whitewasher.

enjalbegadura, *f.* whitewashing.
enjalbegar, (*ref. 51*) *tr.v.* to whitewash. —*tr.v., r.v.* to make up, put on make-up.
enjalbegue, enjalbegué, *ref.* **enjalbegar.**
enjalma, *f.* light packsaddle.
enjalmar, *tr.v.* to put a packsaddle on. —*i.v.* to make packsaddles.
enjalmero, *m.* person who makes or sells packsaddles.
enjambradera, *f.* capping or wax covering of the queen bee's cell; queen bee; bee that by its buzzing gives signal for swarming.
enjambradero, *m.* swarming place (of bees).
enjambrar, *tr.v.* 1. to collect (bees) into a swarm. 2. to take a swarm from (a hive). —*i.v.* 1. to swarm. 2. (fig.) to multiply abundantly, increase greatly.
enjambrazón, *f.* swarming (of bees).
enjambre, *m.* swarm (of bees); crowd, bevy, multitude.
enjaquimar, *tr.v.* to put a halter or headstall on.
enjarciar, *tr.v.* to rig (a ship).
enjardinar, *tr.v.* to trim (trees) as in a garden.
enjaretado, *past part. of* **enjaretar.** —*m.* wooden grating or latticework.
enjaretar, *tr.v.* 1. to pass or run a string through (e.g. a hem). 2. to reel or rattle off (verses, words, etc.). 3. to rush through, do (something) in a rush. 4. (coll.) to foist (something unpleasant) on (someone). 5. (Mex., Ven., coll.) to include, insert.
enjaular, *tr.v.* 1. to put in a cage, to cage. 2. (coll.) to imprison, confine.
enjebar, *tr.v.* 1. to steep in lye or bleach (cloth) before dyeing. 2. to whiten with a thin coat of plaster.
enjebe, *m.* 1. alum. 2. lye, bleach. 3. bleaching (of cloth) prior to dyeing.
enjergar, (*ref. 51*) *tr.v.* (coll.) to start and direct (a business).
enjergue, enjergué, *ref.* **enjergar.**
enjertación, *f.* grafting; budding; insertion.
enjertal, *m.* nursery of grafted fruit trees.
enjertar, *tr.v., var. of* **injertar,** to graft.
enjerto, ta, *irr. past part. of* **enjertar.** —*m.* 1. grafted plant. 2. (fig.) mixture, conglomeration.
enjicar, (*ref. 50*) *tr.v.* (Cuba) to affix cords to (a hammock).
enjordonar, *tr.v.* (rare) to rejuvenate.
enjorguinarse, *r.v.* to become a sorcerer.
enjoyado, da, *past part. of* **enjoyar.** —*a.* (arch.) bejeweled.
enjoyar, *tr.v.* to bejewel; (fig.) to adorn, embellish, beautify; to set with precious stones.
enjoyelado, da, *a.* wrought into jewels (gold or silver); bejeweled.
enjoyelador, *m.* setter (of precious stones), jeweler.
enjuagadientes, *m.* (coll.) mouthwash.
enjuagadura, *f.* rinsing, rinse; wash, rinse, rinsing liquid.
enjuagar, (*ref. 51*) *tr.v.* to rinse. —*r.v.* to rinse, rinse out.
enjuagatorio, *m.* 1. act of rinsing. 2. finger bowl. 3. mouthwash.
enjuague, *m.* 1. rinsing, rinse. 2. rinsing water, wash, rinse. 3. pitcher, washbowl (for rinsing in). 4. plot, scheme, stratagem.
enjuague, enjuagué, *ref.* **enjuagar.**
enjugador, ra, *a.* drying. —*m.* drier; clothes drier, clotheshorse.
enjugar, (*ref. 51*) *tr.v.* 1. to dry; to wipe, wipe away. 2. (fig.) to wipe out, settle, pay (a debt). —*r.v.* 1. to become lean or thin. 2. to dry, wipe, wipe away. — **enjugarse las lágrimas,** to wipe away or dry one's tears; **enjugarse las manos,** to wipe or dry one's hands.
enjugue, enjugué, *ref.* **enjugar.**
enjuiciable, *a.* indictable, chargeable.
enjuiciamiento, *m.* 1. judgment, judging. 2. (law) trial. 3. (law) suit. 4. prosecution. 5. (law) procedure.
enjuiciar, *tr.v.* 1. (fig.) to examine, consider. 2. (law) to file or bring a suit or action against, to prosecute. 3. (law) to pass judgment on. 4. (law) to try (a case).
enjulio, *m.* warp beam (of a loom), warp rod.
enjullo, *m., var. of* **enjulio.**
enjuncar, (*ref. 50*) *tr.v.* 1. to cover with rushes. 2. (mar.) to lash with rush ropes (a sail); to unlash the gaskets (of a sail) and lash with rope-yarn.
enjundia, *f.* 1. ovary fat (of a fowl); fat, grease (of animals). 2. (lit., fig.) essence, substance. 3. vigor, energy, spirit. 4. innate temperament or character. — **un tema de mucha e.,** a subject of much substance.
enjundioso, sa, *a.* 1. fatty. 2. substantial. 3. vigorous, forceful. — **un caldo e.,** a rich broth.
enjunque, *m.* (mar.) kentledge, pig-iron ballast; kentledge-laying.
enjunque, enjunqué, *ref.* **enjuncar.**
enjuta, *f.* 1. (archit.) spandrel. 2. (archit.) pendentive.
enjutar, *tr.v.* 1. to dry (plaster, etc.) 2. (archit.) to fill up (spandrels). —*r.v.* to become dry, dry out.
enjutez, *f.* dryness.
enjuto, ta, *irr. past part. of* **enjugar.** —*a.* lean, thin, dry; **e. de carnes,** lean. —*m.* 1. (*pl.*) brushwood. 2. (*pl.*) tidbits, cocktail snacks.
enlabiador, ra, *a.* deceiving. —*m., f.* deceiver, bamboozler (coll.).
enlabiar, *tr.v.* 1. to bring one's lips to, press one's lips against. 2. to take in, deceive, trick, bamboozle (coll.).
enlabio, *m.* deception, bamboozling; enticement by cunning words.
enlace, *m.* 1. linking; union, connection, link, liaison. 2. (ry.) junction, connection (between two trains). 3. relationship; wedding, marriage. 4. mediator, intermediary, link. — **e. covalente,** (phys.) covalent bond.
enlace, enlacé, *ref.* **enlazar.**
enlaciar, *tr.v.* 1. to make flaccid, languid or limp. 2. to wither. —*r.v.* 1. to become flaccid, languid or limp. 2. to wither.
enladrillado, *past part. of* **enladrillar.** —*m.* brick paving or pavement, brick work.
enladrillador, *m.* bricklayer.
enladrilladura, *f.* brick pavement or paving.
enladrillar, *tr.v.* to lay a brick pavement, to pave with bricks.
enlagunar, *tr.v.* to flood, to turn into a pond. —*r.v.* to become flooded.
enlajar, *tr.v.* (Ven.) to pave with tiles or flagstones.
enlamar, *tr.v.* to cover with silt, mud or slime.
enlanado, da, *a.* covered in wool, full of wool.
enlardar, *tr.v.* (cul.) to baste, to lard (a meat roast).
enlatar, *tr.v.* 1. to can. 2. to roof with tin.
enlazable, *a.* connectable, linkable, joinable.
enlazador, ra, *a.* linking, connecting, uniting. —*m., f.* connector, binder.
enlazadura, *f.* 1. lacing. 2. binding, linking, coupling.
enlazamiento, *m., var. of* **enlace.**
enlazar, (*ref. 53*) *tr.v.* 1. to join, connect, link. 2. to lasso (an animal). 3. to lace, enlace, tie with cords or ribbons. —*r.v.* 1. to join, connect, link up, interlock; to be linked or connected. 2. (fig.) to marry, get married; to become related by marriage.
enlechar, *tr.v.* (mas.) to grout, fill (cracks in ceilings or foundations) with grout (a thin mortar or plaster).
enlechuguillado, da, *a.* (arch.) wearing a ruff.
enlegajar, *tr.v.* to gather into a file, into a docket (papers).
enlegamar, *tr.v.* 1. to fertilize with silt. 2. to spatter with slime or mud. 3. to reclaim (swampy land) by silting.
enlejiar, *tr.v.* 1. to steep in lye or bleach. 2. (chem.) to dissolve (an alkali) in water.
enlencé, *ref.* **enlenzar.**
enlenzar, (*ref. 68*) *tr.v.* to strengthen with strips of linen.
enlerdar, *tr.v.* to make torpid or dull.
enlice, enlicé, *ref.* **enlizar.**
enlience, enlienzo, *ref.* **enlenzar.**
enligar, (*ref. 51*) *tr.v.* to smear with birdlime. —*r.v.* to be trapped in birdlime (a bird).
enligue, enligué, *ref.* **enligar.**
enlistonado, *past part. of* **enlistonar.** —*m.* (carp.) laths, lathing.
enlistonar, *tr.v.* to lath.
enlizar, (*ref. 53*) *tr.v.* to add leases or leashes to (a loom).
enllantar, *tr.v.* to put a tire on (a wheel), to rim (a wheel).
enllentecer, (*ref. 45*) *tr.v., r.v.* to soften, to blandish.
enllentezca, enllentezco, *ref.* **enllentecer.**
enllocar, (*ref. 50*) *i.v., r.v., var. of* **enclocar.**
enlloque, enllocar, *ref.* **enllocar.**
enlobreguecer, (*ref. 45*) *tr.v.* to make dark, darken. —*r.v.* to get dark.
enlobreguezca, *ref.* **enlobreguecer.**
enlodadura, *f.* muddy stains; muddying, the act of daubing or filling with mud.
enlodamiento, *m., var. of* **enlodadura.**
enlodar, *tr.v.* 1. to muddy, spatter with mud. 2. to plaster (a wall) with mud. 3. (fig.) to besmirch, defame, throw mud at. 4. (min.) to lute or seal with a cement of clay (sides of a mine). —*r.v.* 1. to get muddied, get covered with mud. 2. (fig.) to be defamed.
enloquecedor, ra, *a.* maddening.
enloquecer, (*ref. 45*) *tr.v.* 1. to drive insane, to madden. 2. (fig.) to enchant, delight, adore, e.g. *esta música me enloquece,* I adore this music. —*i.v.* 1. to go mad or crazy, become demented. 2. to become barren, bear fruit irregularly (trees).
enloquecimiento, *m.* madness, insanity; the process of going mad.
enloquezca, enloquezco, *ref.* **enloquecer.**
enlosado, *past part. of* **enlosar.** —*m.* tiling, tiled floor, flagged pavement.
enlosador, *m.* tiler, tile layer, paver.
enlosar, *tr.v.* to tile, pave with tiles or flags.
enlozanarse, *r.v.* to be or become luxuriant; to exude health and vitality.
enlucido, da, *past part. of* **enlucir.** —*a.* whitewashed; plastered. —*m.* coat of plaster, plaster, plastering.
enlucidor, *m.* plasterer.
enlucimiento, *m.* plastering, pargeting; polishing, scouring (of metals).
enlucir, (*ref. 46*) *tr.v.* 1. to plaster, parget, whitewash. 2. to polish, burnish.
enlustrecer, (*ref. 45*) *tr.v.* to shine, polish, brighten.
enlustrezca, enlustrezco, *ref.* **enlustrecer.**
enlutar, *tr.v.* 1. to cast into mourning. 2. (fig.) to make dark, darken, to veil. 3. (fig.) to sadden. —*r.v.* 1. to dress in mourning, go into mourning. 2. to get dark.
enluzca, enluzco, *ref.* **enlucir.**
enmadejar, *tr.v.* (Chile) to wind into a skein.

enmaderación, *f.* 1. woodwork, timbering, planking, boarding; wainscoting. 2. (min.) propping, pit props.
enmaderado, *past part. of* **enmaderar.** *—m., var. of* **enmaderamiento.**
enmaderamiento, *m.* woodwork, timbering, planking, boarding, wainscoting, paneling.
enmaderar, *tr.v.* to plank, timber, board, cover with timber; to roof or floor with timber.
enmadrarse, *r.v.* to become excessively fond of one's mother, become a mamma's boy.
enmagrecer, (*ref. 45*) *tr.v.* to make thin or lean. *—i.v., r.v.* to grow thin, lean or skinny, to lose weight.
enmagrezca, enmagrezco, *ref.* **enmagrecer.**
enmalecerse, enmalezarse, (*ref. 45*) *r.v.* to become covered with weeds or undergrowth.
enmalezca, enmalezco, *ref.* **enmalecer.**
enmallarse, *r.v.* to get caught in the meshes of a net (a fish).
enmalle, *m.* gill net.
enmangar, (*ref. 51*) *tr.v.* to put a handle or haft on, haft.
enmangue, enmangué, *ref.* **enmangar.**
enmaniguarse, (*ref. 52*) *r.v.* 1. (Cuba) to become covered with undergrowth, become jungle. 2. (Cuba) to get used to country life.
enmantar, *tr.v.* to cover with a blanket. *—r.v.* 1. to cover oneself with a blanket. 2. (fig.) to become sad and melancholy.
enmarañador, ra, *a.* entangling, puzzling, perplexing. *—m., f.* entangler, bungler.
enmarañamiento, *m.* 1. entangling, entanglement. 2. confusion, complication.
enmarañar, *tr.v.* 1. to tangle up, entangle. 2. (fig.) to confuse, make complicated or involved; complicate. *—r.v.* 1. to get tangled up, become entangled. 2. (fig.) to become confused or complicated.
enmararse, *r.v.* (mar.) to sail out into the open sea.
enmaridar, *i.v., r.v.* to get married (a woman), to take a husband.
enmarillecerse, (*ref. 45*) *r.v.* to turn faded and yellow.
enmarillezca, *ref.* **enmarillecerse.**
enmaromar, *tr.v.* to rope, tie with a rope.
enmascarado, da, *past part. of* **enmascarar.** *—m., f.* masked guest at a masquerade ball; masked participant in a carnival.
enmascaramiento, *m.* camouflage.
enmascarar, *tr.v.* to mask; (fig.) to disguise. *—r.v.* to put on a mask, mask or disguise oneself.
enmasillar, *tr.v.* to putty, to caulk, to cement.
enmatarse, *r.v.* to hide in the bushes.
enmelar, (*ref. 29*) *tr.v.* 1. to smear with honey; to add honey to; (fig.) to sweeten, make pleasant. *—i.v.* to make honey (bees).
enmendable, *a.* emendable, amendable, rectifiable.
enmendación, *f.* emendation, correction, rectification.
enmendador, ra, *a.* corrective, emendatory. *—m., f.* corrector, amender, reviser.
enmendadura, *f.* correction, emendation.
enmendatura, *f.* (Col., Chile, P. Rico) correction, emendation.
enmendar, (*ref. 29*) *tr.v.* 1. to emend, amend; reform, correct; to make amends for, compensate, redress. 2. (law) to revise (a judgment). 3. (mar.) to alter (a course). *—r.v.* to mend one's ways, lead a new life.
enmiele, enmielo, *ref.* **enmelar.**
enmienda, *f.* 1. emendation, correction, rectification. 2. compensation, redress, amends. 3. amendment, change (in laws, plans, etc.).
enmiende, enmiendo, *ref.* **enmendar.**
enmohecer, (*ref. 45*) *tr.v.* 1. to make moldy, mildewy or musty. 2. to rust, make rusty. 3. to dull, make rusty (memory). *—r.v.* 1. to become moldy, mildewy or musty. 2. to go rusty.
enmohecido, da, *past part. of* **enmohecer.** *—a.* rusty, moldy.
enmohecimiento, *m.* 1. rusting; rustiness. 2. moldiness, mildew.
enmohezca, *ref.* **enmohecer.**
enmollecer, (*ref. 45*) *tr.v., r.v.* to soften, to mollify.
enmollezca, enmollezco, *ref.* **enmollecer.**
enmonarse, *r.v.* (Amer.) to get drunk.
enmondar, *tr.v.* to burl, free of knots or loose threads.
enmontarse, *r.v.* (C. Amer., Col.) to become covered with undergrowth, to turn into a wilderness.
enmordace, enmordacé, *ref.* **enmordazar.**
enmordazar, (*ref. 53*) *var. of* **amordazar.**
enmostar, *tr.v.* to stain with must or grape juice. *—r.v.* to get or be stained with must or grape juice.
enmudecer, (*ref. 45*) *tr.v.* to silence, hush. *—i.v.* to be or keep silent; to be or become speechless.
enmudecimiento, *m.* silencing; silence; speechlessness.
enmudezca, enmudezco, *ref.* enmudecer.
enmuescar, *tr.v.* to notch, mortise.
enmugrar, *tr.v., var. of* **enmugrecer.**
enmugrecer, (*ref. 45*) *tr.v.* to make dirty or grimy; to dirty or soil.
enmugrezca, *ref.* **enmugrecer.**
enmustiar, *tr.v., r.v.* (rare) to wither.
ennegrecer, (*ref. 45*) *tr.v.* to blacken, make black. *—r.v.* 1. to turn black. 2. (fig.) to become dark or cloudy.
ennegrecimiento, *m.* blackening; turning black, the act of darkening or obscuring.
ennegrezca, *ref.* **ennegrecer.**
ennoblecedor, ra, *a.* ennobling.
ennoblecer, (*ref. 45*) *tr.v.* to ennoble; (fig.) to adorn, embellish. *—r.v.* to become ennobled.
ennoblecimiento, *m.* ennobling, ennoblement.
ennoblezca, ennoblezco, *ref.* **ennoblecer.**
ennudecer, (*ref. 45*) *i.v.* 1. to stop growing, become stunted. 2. to become knotted.
ennudezca, *ref.* **ennudecer.**
enodio, *m.* staggard (deer between 3 and 5 years old); fawn.
enojada, *f.* (coll., Mex.) anger.
enojadizo, za, *a.* quick-tempered, touchy, irascible, easily annoyed, fretful, peevish.
enojar, *tr.v.* to vex, make angry; to annoy, irritate, put out. *—r.v.* 1. to get angry; to get annoyed, irritated or put out. 2. (rare) to become rough (the sea), become violent or strong (the wind). — **enojarse con** or **contra una persona,** to get annoyed or angry with someone; **enojarse de algo,** to get angry or annoyed with or at something; **enojarse de +** *inf.*, to get angry or annoyed at + *ger.*, e.g. *se enojó de verme allí,* he got annoyed at seeing me there.
enojo, *m.* anger, annoyance, irritation; bother; trouble, work (*gen. in pl.*).
enojón, na, *a.* (Mex., Chile) quick-tempered, touchy, irritable.
enojosamente, *adv.* angrily, crossly.
enojoso, sa, *a.* annoying, irritating, vexatious, troublesome.
enol, *m.* (chem.) enol.
enólico, ca, *a.* (chem.) enolic.
enología, *f.* oenology, study of wines, the art of wine-making.
enológico, ca, *a.* oenological.
enólogo, *m.* oenologist.
enomel, *m.* (hist.) oenomel.
enometría, *f.* wine alcoholometry.
enómetro, *m.* wine alcoholometer.
enorgullecer, (*ref. 45*) *tr.v.* to make proud. *—r.v.* to be proud, pride oneself; to swell with pride; **enorgullecerse de algo,** to be proud of or pride oneself on something.
enorgullecido, da, *past part. of* **enorgullecer.** *—a.* proud; haughty, arrogant.
enorgullecimiento, *m.* 1. feeling or sense of pride. 2. arrogance, haughtiness.
enorgullezca, enorgullezco, *ref.* **enorgullecer.**
enorme, *a.* enormous, huge, vast; (fig.) grave, serious; (coll.) terrible, terrific.
enormemente, *adv.* enormously, greatly.
enormidad, *f.* 1. enormity, hugeness, vastness. 2. enormity, monstrousness, excessive wickedness. 3. (fig.) folly, stupidity.
enormísimo, ma, *a. super. of* **enorme,** most enormous; hugest.
enostosis, *f.* (med.) enostosis, bony tumor.
enotecnia, *f.* art of wine making.
enotécnico, ca, *a.* pertaining to wine making.
enquecle, *ref.* **encoclar.**
enquiciar, *tr.v.* 1. to put (a door) on hinges, put (a window) in a frame. 2. (fig.) to put in order, set right; to settle, make stable. *—r.v.* to become settled or stable.
enquillotrar, *tr.v.* to make conceited. *—r.v.* 1. to become conceited. 2. (coll.) to fall in love.
enquiridión, *m.* enchiridion, handbook, manual.
enquistado, da, *past part. of* **enquistar.** *—a.* 1. (med.) cyst-like. 2. (fig.) embedded, enchased.
enquistar, *r.v.* (med.) to encyst, form a cyst.
enrabar, *tr.v.* 1. to back (a truck) into a convenient place for loading. 2. to lash down (cargo at the end of the truck).
enrabiar, *tr.v.* to make angry, enrage. *—r.v.* to get angry or enraged.
enracimarse, *r.v.* to form into clusters.
enraice, *ref.* **enraizar.**
enraizar, (*ref. 53*) *i.v.* to grow roots; to take root.
enralecer, (*ref. 45*) *i.v.* to grow thin (e.g. hair).
enramada, *f.* 1. bower, arbor, grove. 2. decoration made with branches.
enramado, *past part. of* **enramar.** *—m.* (mar.) frames (of a ship).
enramar, *tr.v.* 1. to interweave (branches), to embower; to decorate with branches. 2. (mar.) to set up (frames of a ship). *—i.v.* to grow branches. *—r.v.* to hide between the branches.
enramblar, *tr.v.* (tex.) to tenter (cloth).
enrame, *m.* interweaving of branches, act of embowering.
enranciar, *tr.v.* to make rancid. *—r.v.* to become rancid or stale.
enrarecer, (*ref. 45*) *tr.v.* 1. to thin, rarefy (a gas). 2. to make scarce. *—i.v.* to become scarce. *—r.v.* 1. to become thin or rarefied. 2. to become scarce.
enrarecido, *past part. of* **enrarecer.** *—a.* rarefied.
enrarecimiento, *m.* thinning, rarefying; scarcity.
enrarezca, *ref.* enrarecer.
enrasado, *past part. of* **enrasar.** *—m.* (bldg.) filling of a spandrel.
enrasar, *tr.v.* (bldg.) to make level or even, to smooth, plane; to level up, grade. *—i.v.* 1. (bldg.) to be even or level. 2. (phys.) to become level (liquids).
enrase, *m.* (bldg.) leveling, grading; leveling course.
enrasillar, *tr.v.* (bldg.) to floor with hollow bricks.
enratonarse, *r.v.* (coll.) to be ill from eating mice (said of cats).
enrayar, *tr.v.* 1. to put spokes in, spoke (a wheel). 2. to scotch (a wheel) with a spoke.

enredadera, *a.* (bot.) climbing, trailing. —*f.* (bot.) climbing plant, creeper, vine; bindweed (Polygonus convulvulus). — **e. de campanillas,** (bot.) morning glory (Ipomoea violacea).
enredado, da, *past part. of* **enredar.** —*a.* entangled, matted, involved.
enredador, ra, *a.* 1. entangling. 2. (coll.) gossipmongering. 3. mischief-making. —*m., f.* gossip, tattler, meddler, busy-body; mischief-maker.
enredar, *tr.v.* 1. to entangle, tangle; to complicate, make complicated. 2. to cause trouble between. 3. to involve, mix (someone) up in, compromise (in difficulties). 4. to net; to spread nets or snares for (birds). —*i.v.* to cause trouble, get into mischief, be mischievous (said esp. of children). —*r.v.* 1. to get entangled; to get tangled up. 2. to become complicated; to become involved. 3. (coll.) to have an affair. — **enredarse en algo,** to get mixed up or involved in something; to get tangled up (with something); **enredarse con alguien,** to get mixed up with someone; to have a love affair with someone.
enredijo, *m.* (coll.) mess, trouble, tangle.
enredista, *a.* (Amer.) mischief-making; gossipmongering. —*m., f.* mischief-maker; busybody, gossipmonger.
enredo, *m.* 1. tangle, snarl (in wool). 2. mess, trouble, complicated situation. 3. mischievous story or piece of gossip. 4. mischief, mischievousness. 5. (fig.) plot (of a play, etc.). 6. (*pl.*) goods and chattels, pots and pans.
enredoso, sa, *a.* 1. complicated, difficult, involved. 2. (Chile, Mex.) mischief-making, gossipmongering.
enrehojar, *tr.v.* to turn wax into sheets (in order to bleach it).
enrejado, *past part. of* **enrejar.** —*m.* 1. grating, lattice; railings; trellis, grill work. 2. open work embroidery.
enrejadura, *f.* (vet.) wound the plough-share sometimes causes in the foot of a horse or an ox.
enrejalar, *tr.v.* (bldg.) to lay (bricks) in crisscross tiers.
enrejar, *tr.v.* 1. to put railings around (property, real estate); to put a grating or lattice on (a window). 2. to stack (planks of wood) crisscross in order to air them.
enrejar, *tr.v.* 1. (agr.) to put a blade in (a plough). 2. to cut (a horse's or an ox's foot) with a ploughshare. 3. (Hond.) to tie (a calf) to the leg of a cow about to be milked.
enrevesado, da, *a.* 1. unruly, frisky, mischievous. 2. obscure, difficult (to understand), nonsensical.
enriado, *past part. of* **enriar.** —*m.* soaking, retting (linen, hemp, etc.).
enriador, ra, *m., f.* soaker, retter (of linen, hemp, etc.).
enriamiento, *m.* soaking, retting (of linen).
enriar, (*ref.* 54) *tr.v.* to soak, ret (linen or hemp); to steep, submerge.
enrice, enricé, *ref.* **enrizar.**
enrielar, *tr.v.* 1. to make into ingots or bars; to pour into ingot molds. 2. (Amer.) to lay rails on. 3. (Amer.) to put back on the rails. 4. (Amer.) to guide, direct.
enripiar, *tr.v.* (mas.) to fill with gravel or rubble.
enriquecedor, ra, *a.* enriching, wealth-producing.
enriquecer, (*ref.* 45) *tr.v.* 1. to enrich, make wealthy. 2. (fig.) to enrich, enhance, adorn. —*i.v., r.v.* 1. to get rich, become rich or wealthy. 2. to prosper, e.g. *enriqueció en pocos años,* he became wealthy in a few years.
enriquecimiento, *m.* enriching, enrichment; enhancement.
enriquezca, enriquezco, *ref.* **enriquecer.**
enriscado, da, *past part. of* enriscar. —*a.* craggy, rugged.
enriscamiento, *m.* 1. taking shelter among cliffs. 2. the act of raising or lifting.
enriscar, (*ref.* 50) *tr.v.* to raise, lift.—*r.v.* to take refuge among cliffs and rocks.
enrisque, enrisqué, *ref.* **enriscar.**
enristrar, *tr.v.* 1. to couch (a lance); to tilt (a lance). 2. (fig.) to go straight towards. 3. to overcome (a difficulty). 4. to string (onions, etc.).
enristre, *m.* couching (of a lance); tilting (of a lance).
enrizamiento, *m.* curling, waving (of hair).
enrizar, (*ref.* 53) *tr.v.* to curl, wave (hair). —*r.v.* to curl, become curly or wavy.
enrocar, (*ref.* 50) *tr.v. & i.v.* (in chess) to castle; (in croquet) to roquet. —*r.v.* to get tangled on the rocks (at the bottom of the sea).
enrocar, (*ref.* 69) *tr.v.* to put (wool or linen) on the distaff.
enrodelado, da, *a.* armed with a round shield.
enrodrigar, (*ref.* 51) **enrodrigonar,** *tr.v.* (agr.) to stake, prop up (vines) with stakes.
enrojar, *tr.v.* 1. to redden, make red. 2. to heat up (an oven). —*r.v.* to redden, get or turn red.
enrojecer, (*ref.* 45) *tr.v.* 1. to make redhot. 2. to redden, make red. —*i.v.* to blush, get red. —*r.v.* 1. to redden, get or turn red. 2. to blush, get red. 3. to become red-hot.
enrojecimiento, *m.* reddening; blushing.
enrojezca, enrojezco, *ref.* **enrojecer.**
enrolamiento, *m.* enlistment; enrollment.
enrolar, *tr.v., r.v.* to sign on, to enlist.
enrollado, *past part. of* **enrollar.** —*m.* 1. volute. 2. (cul.) swiss roll.
enrollamiento, *m.* winding; **e. en derivación,** (elec.) shunt winding.
enrollar, *tr.v.* 1. to wind, coil, wrap, roll up, form into a roll. 2. to cobble, pave with cobble stones.
enromar, *tr.v.* to blunt, dull (a point or an edge).
enrona, *f.* refuse, debris, rubbish.
enronar, *tr.v.* to throw rubbish in (a backyard, etc.).
enronquecer, (*ref.* 45) *tr.v.* to make hoarse. —*r.v.* to become hoarse.
enronquecimiento, *m.* hoarseness.
enronquezca, enronquezco, *ref.* **enronquecer.**
enroñar, *tr.v.* 1. to cover with scabs. 2. to rust, make (something) rusty. —*r.v.* to rust, get rusty.
enroque, *m.* castling (of a king) in chess.
enroqué, *ref.* **enrocar.**
enroscadamente, *adv.* as a coil or a spiral.
enroscadura, *f.* coiling, twisting; coil, twist, curlicue.
enroscar, (*ref.* 50) *tr.v.* 1. to curl, twist, twine. 2. to screw in. —*r.v.* to curl, twist, coil.
enrosque, enrosqué, *ref.* **enroscar.**
enrostrar, *tr.v.* to reproach, upbraid, throw in one's face.
enrubiador, ra, *a.* bleaching (said esp. of hair).
enrubiar, *tr.v.* to bleach, dye blond (the hair). —*r.v.* to turn blond.
enrubio, *m.* bleaching (the hair); hair bleach.
enrudecer, (*ref.* 45) *tr.v.* to roughen; to dull, stultify (person's wits). —*r.v.* to become dull or stultified.
enrudezca, enrudezco, *ref.* **enrudecer.**
enrueco, enrueque, *ref.* **enrocar.**
enruede, enruedo, *ref.* **enrodar.**
enruinecer, (*ref.* 45) *i.v.* to become mean, low or vile.
enruinezca, enruinezco, *ref.* **enruinecer.**
enrular, *tr.v.* (Amer.) to curl or wave.
ensabanada, *f., var. of* **encamisada.**
ensabanado, da, *past part. of* **ensabanar.** —*a.* (taur.) with a white body and black head and feet (said of a bull). —*m.* (mas.) white plaster coating (applied to a wall before whitewashing).
ensabanar, *tr.v.* 1. to cover with a sheet, sheet. 2. (mas.) to give (a wall) a coat of plaster (before painting).
ensacador, ra, *m., f.* sacker, bagger. —*f.* bagging machine.
ensacar, (*ref.* 50) *tr.v.* to put into a bag or sack.
ensaimada, *f.* (Sp.) a rich, light pastry roll or breakfast bun.
ensalada, *f.* 1. salad. 2. (fig.) mess, confusion, hodge-podge; medley. 3. (Cuba) julep, sweet drink with lemon, pineapple and mint. — **e. de fruta,** fruit salad.
ensaladera, *f.* salad bowl or dish.
ensaladilla, *f.* 1. (cul.) type of Russian salad. 2. assortment of sweetmeats. 3. (jewel.) different-colored stones, set in a jewel. 4. miscellany, medley.
ensalce, ensalcé, *ref.* **ensalzar.**
ensalivar, *tr.v.* to moisten or wet with saliva. —*r.v.* to become moistened or wet with saliva.
ensalmador, ra, *m., f.* bone-setter; healer, quack.
ensalmar, *tr.v.* to set (bones); to heal by incantations or homemade medicines.
ensalmista, *m., f., a.* medicine man, quack, charlatan.
ensalmo, *m.* curing by incantation and herbal medicines; **por e.,** very quickly, as if by magic.
ensalobrarse, *r.v.* to become salty or briny.
ensalzador, ra, *a.* exalting; praising, extolling. —*m., f.* praiser, exalter.
ensalzamiento, *m.* exaltation; praise.
ensalzar, (*ref.* 53) *tr.v.* 1. to exalt, glorify; to magnify. 2. to praise, extol. —*r.v.* to praise oneself, to boast.
ensamblado, *past part. of* ensamblar. —*m.* (carp.) joinery, joinery work.
ensamblador, *m.* (carp.) joiner; assembler.
ensambladura, *f.* 1. joining, coupling, connecting; assembling. 2. joint, union. — **e. a. cola de milano,** dovetail joint; **e. de caja y espiga,** mortise and tenon joint; **e. de lengüeta,** tongue and groove joint; **e. en bisel,** bevel joint.
ensamblaje, *m.* 1. joining, connecting, coupling; assembling. 2. joint, union.
ensamblar, *tr.v.* 1. to join, couple, connect; to scarf; to assemble. 2. (carp.) to joint; **e. a cola de milano,** to dovetail.
ensamble, *m., var. of* **ensambladura.**
ensancha, *f.* extension, widening; **dar ensanchas,** (fig.) to give time to recover; to give too much liberty.
ensanchador, ra, *a.* stretching, expanding, widening. —*m.* glove-stretcher; expander, reamer; widener; (pet.) enlarger. — **e. de neumáticos,** (auto.) tire spreader.
ensanchamiento, *m.* widening, extension, broadening, expansion, enlargement.
ensanchar, *tr.v.* to widen, broaden, extend, expand, dilate; to stretch. —*r.v., i.v.* (fig.) to assume an air of self-importance.
ensanche, *m.* 1. extension, widening, expansion, enlargement, broadening. 2. tuck of material (left inside a garment for later enlargement). 3. expansion area (of a town). — **e. de banda,** (rad.) band spread; **e. de faja,** (rad.) band spread.
ensandecer, (*ref.* 45) *i.v.* to become simple or feeble-minded.
ensangrentamiento, *m.* staining or covering with blood.
ensangrentar, (*ref.* 29) *tr.v.* to stain with blood. —*r.v.* 1. to become stained with blood. 2. (fig.) to fly into a fury, get heated or annoyed (in an argument); **ensangrentarse con** or **contra,** to become cruel to or towards.
ensangriente, ensangriento, *ref.* **ensangrentar.**

ensañamiento, *m.* extreme cruelty; (law) aggravated brutality.
ensañar, *tr.v.* to infuriate, enrage. —*r.v.* to vent or glut one's cruelty; **ensañarse en,** to glut one's cruelty on; **ensañarse con** or **contra,** to become cruel to or towards.
ensaque, ensaqué, *ref.* **ensacar.**
ensarmentar, *tr.v.* to layer (vines).
ensarnecer, (*ref. 45*) *i.v.* to itch all over.
ensarnezca, ensarnezco, *ref.* **ensarnecer.**
ensartar, *tr.v.* 1. to string (beads); to thread (a needle). 2. to pierce, run through, penetrate. 3. (fig.) to rattle off, reel off (lies, etc.). 4. (Amer.) to foist or palm (something) off on. —*r.v.* (Amer.) to get stuck with.
ensarte, *m.* (Peru) racket, swindle.
ensay, *m.* assaying, testing (of metals).
ensayador, ra, *m., f.* 1. rehearser. 2. assayer.
ensayalarse, *r.v.* to put on a sackcloth.
ensayar, *tr.v.* 1. to test, try. 2. to teach, train. 3. to rehearse. 4. to test, assay (metals). —*r.v.* to practice, rehearse.
ensaye, *m.* assaying, testing (of metals).
ensayismo, *m.* art of essay-writing.
ensayista, *m., f.* essayist.
ensayo, *m.* 1. trial, test. 2. rehearsal; practice. 3. essay (literary composition). 4. assaying, testing; analysis. — **e. biológico,** bioassay; **e. general,** (theat.) dress rehearsal.
ensebar, *tr.v.* to grease, smear with grease or fat.
enseguida, *adv.* at once, inmediately.
enselvado, da, *past part. of* **enselvar.** —*a.* woody, thickly wooded.
enselvar, *tr.v.* to ambush. —*r.v.* 1. to hide in the woods. 2. to become wooded.
ensenada, *f.* cove, inlet, small bay.
ensenado, da, *past part, of* **ensenar.** —*a.* breast-shaped; having the shape of a cove.
ensenar, *tr.v.* 1. to hide (something) in one's bosom. 2. (mar.) to sail (a ship) into a bay.
enseña, *f.* insignia, badge; flag, pennant, standard.
enseñable, *a.* teachable.
enseñado, da, *past part. of* **enseñar.** —*a.* 1. well educated, well-mannered; **mal e.,** badly brought up, badly trained. 2. accustomed.
enseñador, ra, *a.* teaching.
enseñamiento, *m.* teaching; education.
enseñanza, *f.* 1. teaching; education; doctrine. 2. example, lesson. 3. (*pl.*) teachings, doctrine, principles. —**e. a distancia,** correspondence courses; **e. media** or **secundaria,** high school, secondary education; **e. primaria,** primary education; **e. programada,** programmed learning; **e. superior,** higher or university education; **e. universitaria,** university education; **primera e.,** primary education; **segunda e.,** high or secondary school education.
enseñar, *tr.v.* to teach; to show; to point out, indicate; **enseñar a** + *inf.,* to teach to + *inf.;* to teach or show how to +*inf.* —*r.v.* to teach or accustom oneself.
enseñoramiento, *m.* seizure, taking possession.
enseñorearse, *r.v.* to take possession; **enseñorearse de,** to take possession of.
enserar, *tr.v.* to cover with esparto matting.
enseres, *m.* (*pl.*) household goods, utensils, implements, gear, equipment; **e. de pescar,** fishing tackle.
enseriarse, *r.v.* (Amer.) to become serious.
ensiforme, *a.* (bot.) ensiform, sword-shaped.
ensilaje, *m.* ensilage, storage in a silo.
ensilar, *tr.v.* to store in a silo, ensile.
ensillada, *f.* saddle, ridge between two hills or mountains.
ensillado, da, *past part. of* **ensillar.** —*a.* saddle-backed (said of a horse).
ensilladura, *f.* 1. saddling. 2. part of a horse's back where the saddle is placed. 3. lumbar curve (in a vertebral column).
ensillar, *tr.v.* to saddle.
ensilvecerse, (*ref. 45*) *r.v.* to become wooded or forested.
ensilvezca, *ref.* **ensilvecerse.**
ensimismado, da, *past part. of* **ensimismarse.** —*a.* 1. deep in thought, pensive. 2. (S. Amer.) conceited, vain.
ensimismamiento, *m.* absorption in thought.
ensimismarse, *r.v.* 1. to become lost or absorbed in thought. 2. (S. Amer.) to become conceited or vain.
ensoberbecer, (*ref. 45*) *tr.v.* to make arrogant or proud. —*r.v.* 1. to become arrogant or proud. 2. to become rough (the sea).
ensoberbecimiento, *m.* pride, arrogance, haughtiness.
ensoberbezca, ensoberbezco, *ref.* **ensoberbecer.**
ensogar, (*ref. 51*) *tr.v.* 1. to rope, tie with a rope. 2. to bind or cover with rope.
ensogue, ensogué, *ref.* **ensogar.**
ensolerar, *tr.v.* to place (beehives) on a wooden base.
ensolver, (*ref. 34*) *tr.v.* 1. to include. 2. to reduce, condense, abridge. 3. (med.) to dissipate, resolve (a tumor inflammation).
ensombrecer, (*ref. 45*) *tr.v.* to darken; to dim. —*r.v.* to become sad or melancholy.
ensombrezca, ensombrezco, *ref.* **ensombrecer.**
ensoñador, ra, *a.* dreamy; enchanting. —*m., f.* dreamer.
ensopar, *tr.v.* 1. to soak, steep. 2. to drench, dunk. —*r.v.* to get soaked or drenched.
ensordecedor, ra, *a.* deafening.
ensordecer, (*ref. 45*) *tr.v.* 1. to deafen, make deaf. 2. (phonet.) to unvoice, make unvoiced. —*i.v.* 1. to become or go deaf. 2. to become silent, to not answer.
ensordecimiento, *m.* deafening; going deaf; deafness.
ensordezca, ensordezco, *ref.* **ensordecer.**
ensortijamiento, *m.* curling, crimping; curls, ringlets, curlicue, kink.
ensortijar, *tr.v.* 1. to curl, form ringlets in, to kink. 2. to put an iron ring in, ring (an animal's nose). —*r.v.* to become curly, wavy or kinky.
ensotarse, *r.v.* to enter a grove or thicket.
ensuciador, ra, *a.* dirtying, staining, soiling.
ensuciamiento, *m.* dirtying, soiling, staining; polluting.
ensuciar, *tr.v.* 1. to dirty, stain, soil, smear; pollute; defile. 2. to stain, smirch, discredit (someone's reputation); **ensuciarla,** to make a mess of something, botch something up. —*i.v.* to have a bowel movement. —*r.v.* 1. to become or get dirty or soiled; to wet oneself. 2. (coll.) to dishonor oneself. 3. to wet or soil (one's bed or clothing).
ensuelva, ensuelvo, *ref.* **ensolver.**
ensueño, *m.* dream; daydream, reverie; illusion, fantasy.
ensullo, *m.* (tex.) warp beam (of a loom).
entabacarse, (*ref. 50*) *r.v.* to smoke excessively.
entabicar, (*ref. 50*) *tr.v.* (Amer.) to wall up, board up.
entablación, *f.* 1. boarding up; planks, boards, planking. 2. beginning, starting (of a conversation, negotiations, etc.). 3. filing, bringing (of a legal action). 4. registering (of church annals, etc.) on tablets.
entablado, *past part. of* **entablar.** —*m.* 1. platform. 2. flooring, floorboards.
entabladura, *f.* boarding, planking; timbering; boards, planks.
entablamento, *m.* (archit.) entablature.
entablar, *tr.v.* 1. to board, board up, cover with boards. 2. (surg.) to splint, fasten with splints. 3. to set up (chessmen or checkers) on board. 4. to bring, file (a suit or legal action). 5. to start, begin (fight, conversation, etc.); to prepare. 6. to write on tablets (in the church). 7. (Arg.) to train (cattle) to rove in a herd. — **e. juicio a,** to file a suit against; **e. un reclamo,** to file a claim. —*r.v.* 1. settle into a definite direction (the wind). 2. to resist turning its head (a horse). 3. (Arg.) to graze in a herd.
entable, *m.* 1. boarding, boards. 2. position of the men or pieces in a game of chess or checkers. 3. (Col.) business, position, employment.
entablerarse, *r.v.* (taur.) to stay close to the barrier (the bull).
entablillar, *tr.v.* (surg.) to splint, fasten with splints.
entado, *a.* (her.) enté, grafted; **e. en punta,** enté en point (Fr.), having, on the base, a concave triangle pointing upward.
entalamadura, *f.* cane awning (over a carriage).
entalamar, *tr.v.* to cover with an awning.
entalegar, (*ref. 51*) *tr.v.* 1. to put into a pouch or bag. 2. to save, hoard (money).
entalingar, (*ref. 51*) *tr.v.* (mar.) to clinch (a cable) to the anchor ring.
entalingue, entalingué, *ref.* **entalingar.**
entallable, *a.* able to be carved; able to be fitted (clothes).
entallador, *m.* carver, sculptor; engraver.
entalladura, *f.* 1. carving, sculpting; engraving. 2. incision (to remove resin). 3. (carp.) mortise, notch, groove (to make a joint).
entallamiento, *m., var. of* **entalladura.**
entallar, *tr.v.* 1. to carve, sculpture; to engrave. 2. to tap, make an incision in (a tree) to extract resin. 3. to notch, groove, make a cut in (wood) to make a joint. 4. to fit or adjust (a garment). —*i.v.* to fit well (a garment).
entallecer, (*ref. 45*) *i.v., r.v.* to grow shoots, sprout.
entallezca, *ref.* **entallecer.**
entallo, *m.* carving, work of sculpture; engraving.
entalonar, *i.v.* to grow new shoots.
entalpía, *f.* enthalpy, a thermodynamic function.
entamar, *tr.v.* to cover with fluff. —*r.v.* to become covered with fluff.
entapar, *tr.v.* (Chile) to bind (a book).
entapetado, da, *a.* covered with a table-cloth or rug.
entapice, entapicé, *ref.* **entapizar.**
entapizar, (*ref. 53*) *tr.v.* 1. to tapestry, hang with tapestries; to upholster (furniture). 2. (fig.) to cover, deck, adorn.
entapujar, *tr.v.* (coll.) to cover; (fig.) to cover up, cloak (the truth). —*r.v.* to become covered.
entarascar, (*ref. 50*) *tr.v., r.v.* (coll.) to overdress.
entarasque, entarasqué, *ref.* **entarascar.**
entarimado, *past part. of* **entarimar.** —*m.* (carp.) flooring, floorboards; parquet (floors).
entarimador, *m.* (carp.) one who lays floorboards.
entarimar, *tr.v.* to cover with floorboards.
entarquinamiento, *m.* fertilizing with silt or slime.
entarquinar, *tr.v.* 1. to fertilize with silt. 2. to make muddy, spatter with mud. 3. to reclaim (bogland) with silt.
entarugado, *past part. of* **entarugar.** —*m.* paving of wooden blocks.
entarugar, (*ref. 51*) *tr.v.* to pave with wooden blocks.
entarugue, entarugué, *ref.* **entarugar.**
éntasis, *f.* (archit.) entasis.
ente, *m.* entity, being; (coll.) queer character.

enteco, ca, *a.* sickly, weak, thin.
entechar, *tr.v.* (Chile) to roof.
entejar, *tr.v.* (Col.) to tile, cover with tiles.
entelarañado, da, *a.* full of or covered with cobwebs.
entelequia, *f.* (philos.) entelechy.
entelerido, da, *a.* 1. numb with cold or fright. 2. (Amer.) sickly, weakly, thin.
entena, *f.* (mar.) lateen yard; long beam.
entenado, da, *m., f.* stepchild. —*m.* stepson. —*f.* stepdaughter.
entenallas, *f.* (mec.) pincers; handvise.
entendederas, *f., pl.* (coll.) intellect, understanding, mind, brains; **tener buenas** or **malas e.,** to be bright or dull (intellectually).
entendedor, ra, *a.* understanding. —*m., f.* one who understands; **al buen e., pocas palabras,** a word to the wise is sufficient.
entender, (*ref. 30*) *tr.v.* 1. to understand. 2. to think, consider. 3. to intend, want. —*i.v.* to understand; **e. de,** to understand, e.g. *él no entiende de niños,* he doesn't understand children; to have a knowledge of; to have a thorough knowledge of; **e. en,** to have a knowledge of; to deal with, be in charge of. —*r.v.* 1. to understand or know oneself. 2. to be meant. 3. to have one's reasons (for doing something), e.g. *yo me entiendo,* I have my reasons. 4. to come to an agreement; to understand one another. 5. to have secret relations with one another; **entenderse con,** to get along with, to come to an agreement with, to have an affair with; to apply or refer to, e.g. *esa ley no se entiende conmigo,* this law does not apply to me. —*m.* opinion; **a mi e.,** to my way of thinking, as I see it.
entendidamente, *adv.* knowingly; cleverly, intelligently.
entendido, da, *past part. of* **entender.** —*a.* informed, expert, instructed, learned, experienced; **no darse por e.,** to pretend not to understand, turn a deaf ear to. —*m.* expert, connoisseur.
entendimiento, *m.* understanding, comprehension; mind, (human) reason.
entenebrecer, (*ref. 45*) *tr.v.* to darken, make dark. —*r.v.* to become dark.
entenebrezca, *ref.* **entenebrecer.**
entente, *f.* entente, pact, agreement; harmony between persons or states.
enterado, da, *past part. of* **enterar.** —*a.* 1. informed, well-informed, posted, up-to-date. 2. (Chile) conceited, proud, haughty.
enteralgia, *f.* (med.) enteralgia, acute intestinal pain.
enteramente, *adv.* completely, wholly, fully, entirely.
enterar, *tr.v.* 1. to inform, acquaint. 2. (Arg., Chile) to complete (a sum of money). 3. (Col., C. Rica, Hond., Mex.) to pay. —*r.v.* to find out, come to know; **enterarse de,** to find out about, get to know about.
entercarse, (*ref. 50*) *r.v.* to become obstinate or stubborn.
enterciar, *tr.v.* (Cuba, Mex.) to pack tobacco in bales.
entereza, *f.* 1. entirety, completeness. 2. (fig.) integrity, uprightness, honesty. 3. (fig.) fortitude, firmness, courage. 4. (fig.) strictness (in obedience to discipline).
entérico, ca, *a.* (med.) enteric.
enterísimo, ma, *a. super. of* **entero,** most complete; firmest (of character).
enteritis, *f.* (med.) enteritis.
enterizo, za, *a.* whole, entire; in one piece.
enternecedor, ra, *a.* touching, moving.
enternecer, (*ref. 45*) *tr.v.* to make tender, soften; to move, to touch. —*r.v.* to soften, be moved or touched.
enternecidamente, *adv.* tenderly, compassionately.
enternecido, da, *a.* moved, touched.
enternecimiento, *m.* compassion, pity.
enternezca, enternezco, *ref.* **enternecer.**
entero, *a.* 1. whole, entire, complete. 2. (coll.) honest, upright. 3. just, straight. 4. robust, strong, sound, healthy. 5. steadfast, loyal, constant. 6. (math.) whole. 7. uncastrated (animal). 8. pure, uncorrupted, virginal. 9. thick, strong (cloth). —*m.* 1. (math.) integer, whole number. 2. (Amer.) payment. —**por entero,** completely, entirely.
enterocelíaco, ca, *a.* (med.) enterocoelic.
enterocelo, *m.* (med.) enterocoele, enterocoel.
enterocinasa, *f.* (biochem.) enterokinase.
enterococo, *m.* (med.) enterococcus.
enterocolitis, *f.* (med.) enterocolitis.
enterogastrona, *f.* (physiol.) enterogastrone.
enterohepatitis, *f.* (med.) enterohepatitis.
enterología, *f.* (med.) enterology.
enterólogo, *m.* (med.) enterologist.
enteron, *m.* (anat.) enteron.
enteroquinasa, *f.* (biochem.) enterokinase.
enterostomía, *f.* (med.) enterostomy.
enterotomía, *f.* (surg.) enterotomy.
enterque, enterqué, *ref.* **entercarse.**
enterrador, *m.* 1. gravedigger, sexton. 2. (ento.) sexton-beetle, burying beetle.
enterramiento, *m.* 1. interment, burial. 2. tomb, grave.
enterrar, (*ref. 29*) *tr.v.* 1. to bury, inter. 2. (fig.) to outlive, bury (one's relatives). 3. to hide, bury. 4. to forget, abandon, bury. 5. to drive in (a nail, etc.). —*r.v.* 1. to bury oneself, withdraw, retire (to a remote place). 2. to be driven in, embed itself. — **enterrarse en vida,** to retire from society, to take up a monastic life.
enterratorio, *m.* (Arg., Chile) Indian cemetery.
enterronar, *tr.v.* to cover with clods of earth.
entesamiento, *m.* tautness.
entesar, (*ref. 29*) *tr.v.* 1. to strengthen. 2. to tauten, tighten, stretch.
entestado, da, *a.* stubborn, obstinate.
entético, ca, *a.* (med.) enthetic.
entibación, *f.* (min.) propping, shoring; props, shores.
entibador, *m.* (min.) timberman, shorer, worker who puts in pit props.
entibar, *tr.v.* (min.) to prop, shore. —*i.v.* to rest (on).
entibiadero, *m.* cooler, cooling space or room.
entibiar, *tr.v.* 1. to make lukewarm or tepid. 2. (fig.) to temper, moderate (passions, etc.). —*r.v.* to cool down, slacken, relax.
entibo, *m.* 1. (min.) timber (for props). 2. (archit.) buttress, abutment. 3. foundation, prop, stay, support.
entidad, *f.* 1. entity. 2. essence, substance, entity. 3. importance, consequence. 4. body, organization, company; **e. comercial,** business firm.
entienda, entiendo, *ref.* entender.
entierre, entierro, *ref.* **enterrar.**
entierro, *m.* 1. burial, funeral, interment. 2. tomb, grave. 3. funeral procession. 4. (coll.) buried treasure. — **Santo Entierro,** Good Friday procession.
entiesar, *tr.v.* to stiffen, make stiff.
entiese, entieso, *ref.* **entesar.**
entigrecerse, (*ref. 45*) *r.v.* (fig.) to become furious, get angry.
entigrezca, entigrezco, *ref.* **entigrecerse.**
entilar, *tr.v.* (Hond.) to blacken.
entimema, *m.* (philos.) enthymeme.
entimemático, ca, *a.* (philos.) enthymematical, pertaining to enthymeme.
entinar, *tr.v.* to place in a tub or vat.
entintado, *a.* inked (in). —*m.* inking.
entintador, ra, *a.* inking.
entintar, *tr.v.* to ink, stain or color with ink; to color, tint, dye.
entisar, *tr.v.* (Cuba) to cover with a net or a rope (a jar or bottle).
entizar, (*ref. 53*) *tr.v.* (Amer.) to chalk, put chalk on (a billiard cue).
entiznar, *tr.v.* to soil or stain with soot; to stain, soil; to besmirch, stain (a reputation), to revile, defame.
entoblasto, *m.* (biol.) entoblast.
entoldado, *past part. of* **entoldar.** —*m.* covering with an awning; awnings, tents.
entoldamiento, *m.* covering with an awning; awnings, tents.
entoldar, *tr.v.* to cover with an awning; to tapestry, deck, adorn with tapestries. —*r.v.* 1. to cloud over (the sky). 2. (fig.) to become conceited or vain.
entomatado, da, *a.* cooked with tomatoes, e.g. *langosta entomatada,* lobster in tomato sauce.
entomizar, (*ref. 53*) *tr.v.* (carp.) to tie (timbers) with bast ropes so that plaster will stick to them.
entomófago, ga, *a.* (zool.) entomophagous, insectivorous.
entomófilo, la, *a.* interested in insects; (bot.) entomophilous, fertilized by means of insects.
entomología, *f.* entomology.
entomológico, ca, *a.* entomological.
entomólogo, *m.* entomologist.
entomostráceo, cea, *a., m.* (zool.) entomostracan.
entompeatada, *f.* (Mex., coll.) deception, trick, swindle.
entompeatar, *tr.v.* (Mex., coll.) to trick, deceive.
entonación, *f.* 1. intonation; intoning, modulation; (phonet.) intonation. 2. arrogance, haughtiness, presumption. 3. blowing the bellows of an organ.
entonadera, *f.* blow lever of an organ.
entonado, da, *past part. of* **entonar.** —*a.* 1. harmonious. 2. (fig.) arrogant, haughty, high-toned. 3. (photog.) process of toning.
entonador, ra, *m., f.* 1. person who sings in tune. 2. (photog.) toner, harmonizer. 3. organ blower.
entonamiento, *m.* intonation.
entonar, *tr.v.* 1. to intone. 2. to sing (something) in tune. 3. (mus.) to work the bellows of (an organ). 4. to tone up (the body), to invigorate. 5. (p.) to harmonize (colors). —*r.v.* to put on airs, be or become full of oneself, be or become arrogant.
entonatorio, *m.* chant book (book containing chants sung by church choir); book of sacred music.
entonces, *adv.* then; in that case; **¿e.?** so?; **de e. acá,** since then; **hasta e.,** up to then; **por e.,** at that time; **pues e.,** well then. —*m.* that time; **en aquel e.,** at that time; **en ese e.,** (Amer.) at that time.
entonelar, *tr.v.* to put in casks or barrels.
entongar, (*ref. 51*) *tr.v.* to pile up, stack.
entongue, entongué, *ref.* **entongar.**
entono, *m.* 1. intoning, intonation. 2. arrogance, haughtiness.
entontar, *tr.v.* 1. (Amer.) to stupefy, stultify. 2. to make stupid or foolish. —*r.v.* to be stupefied or stultified.
entontecer, (*ref. 45*) *tr.v.* 1. to make silly, stupid or foolish. 2. to stultify. —*i.v., r.v.* 1. to become silly or foolish. 2. to become stultified.

entontecimiento, *m.* stultification, foolishness, stupidity.

entontezca, entontezco, *ref.* **entontecer.**

entoprocto, *m.* (zool.) entoproct.

entorchado, *past part. of* **entorchar.** *—m.* 1. bullion fringe, gold braid embroidery on gala uniforms. 2. (mus.) bass strings.

entorchar, *tr.v.* 1. to bind with gold or silver cord. 2. to twist or tie (several candles) together to form a torch. 3. to cover a string by winding a wire around it.

entorilar, *tr.v.* (taur.) to put (a bull) in the stall or pen.

entornar, *tr.v.* 1. to half-close. 2. to tilt (a saucepan). *—r.v.* to be upset (a saucepan). — **e. los ojos,** to half-close the eyes; **e. la puerta,** to set the door ajar.

entornillar, *tr.v.* 1. to twist or make into the form of a screw or spiral. 2. to thread (a screw).

entorpecedor, ra, *a.* numbing, deadening.

entorpecer, (*ref. 45*) *tr.v.* 1. to make slow or torpid. 2. to befuddle, confuse, cloud, deaden (the mind or intelligence). 3. to hamper, delay. 4. to jam, make (a lock, etc.) stick. *—r.v.* 1. to become slow or torpid. 2. to become clouded or befuddled (the mind). 3. to be delayed or hampered. 4. to get stuck (e.g. a lock). — **e. el camino,** to obstruct the way.

entorpecimiento, *m.* 1. dulling, deadening, befuddling (of the mind); torpor, deadness. 2. delay. 3. sticking (of a lock).

entorpezca, entorpezco, *ref.* **entorpecer.**

entortadura, *f.* bending; crookedness.

entortar, (*ref. 33*) *tr.v.* 1. to make crooked. 2. to make blind in one eye. *—r.v.* to become crooked.

entosigar, (*ref. 51*) *tr.v.* to poison.

entosigue, entosigué, *ref.* **entosigar.**

entozoario, *m.* (zool.) entozoan.

entozoico, ca, *a.* (zool.) entozoic, entozoal.

entrada, *f.* 1. entrance; vestibule; entrance hall, foyer. 2. entry, entrance, ingress. 3. admission (into an official body as member). 4. opportunity, opening. 5. gate (at a football match, etc.); audience, house (number attending theater, etc.). 6. gate or box-office takings; (com.) earnings, cash receipts. 7. admission ticket. 8. beginning (of a speech, book, etc.); first days (of a year, month, season). 9. intimacy, friendship. — **tener e. en,** to be on intimate terms with. 10. (mar.) leak. 11. hand (in cards). 12. privilege of entering (adjacent palace rooms). 13. (cul.) entrée. 14. (*pl.*) hairline receding at the temples. 15. invasion (by an enemy), encroachment. 16. (archit.) end of a beam embedded in concrete. 17. (min.) shift (period of work). 18. (mus., theat.) entry, entrance. 19. (Mex., Cuba) sudden attack, beating. 20. down payment. — **dar e. a,** to admit, let in; **e. de aire,** (aer., auto.) air intake; **e. de pavana,** ridiculous or impertinent remark or proposal made in all gravity; **e. general,** (theat.) standing room; **e. por salida,** (com.) entry made in the debit and credit side of an account; (fig.) a business in which the advantages and disadvantages are equal; (coll.) short visit; >**mucha e.,** (theat.) good house, big audience.

entrado, da, *past part. of* **entrar.** *—a.* (Chile) meddling, meddlesome. — **e. en años,** advanced in years; **muy e.,** far along in, e.g. *muy e. marzo,* far along in March.

entrador, ra, *a.* 1. (C. Rica, Mex., Ven.) daring, venturesome. 2. (Chile) intruding, forward (person).

entramado, *m.* (carp.) wooden framework, baywork.

entramar, *tr.v.* (carp.) to build a framework for.

entrambos, bas, *a., pron.* (*pl.*) both.

entrampar, *tr.v.* 1. to trap, ensnare. 2. to trick, deceive. 3. to confuse, entangle, complicate. 4. to involve in debt. *—r.v.* 1. to get into difficulties. 2. (coll.) to fall or go into debt.

entrante, *a.* 1. next, coming (week, month, etc.). 2. (geom., fort.) re-entering, re-entrant. 3. (archit.) recessed. 4. (mar.) incoming, rising (tide). 5. (mil.) incoming, relief (guard). *—m.* (archit.) recess, niche.

entraña, *f., var. of* **entrañas.**

entrañable, *a.* intimate, very affectionate, close; deep (affection).

entrañablemente, *adv.* very affectionately or lovingly.

entrañar, *tr.v.* 1. to bury deep. 2. to carry within, contain, involve. *—r.v.* 1. to be buried or entombed. 2. to become deeply attached (to someone).

entrañas, *f.* (*pl.*) 1. entrails, innards. 2. center, middle. 3. will power. 4. nature, disposition, idiosyncrasy. 5. innermost recess. — **de buenas entrañas,** good-hearted, good-natured; **sin entrañas,** pitiless; **e. mías,** my beloved, my love.

entrapace, *ref.* **entrapazar.**

entrapada, *f.* sturdy red fabric often used in upholstery.

entrapajar, *tr.v.* to wrap or bandage in rags. *—r.v.* 1. to wrap in rags. 2. to get dirty and dusty.

entrapar, *tr.v.* 1. to powder (one's hair). 2. (agr.) to fertilize (plants) with rags. *—r.v.* 1. to become covered with dust or dirt. 2. to become blunt (a knife).

entrapazar, (*ref. 53*) *i.v.* to cheat, swindle.

entrar, *i.v.* 1. to enter, go in. 2. to fit (a hat, garment). 3. to fit, go (something into something else). 4 to attack; to charge (a bull). 5. to begin, start (seasons; books, speeches, etc.). 6. to be the bidder in cards, contracting to make a certain number of tricks. 7. to be included or counted (in a group). 8. to go (into), be used (in), (material in a garment, ingredients in a cake, etc.). 9. (mus.) to come in (at the correct moment in a score). *—tr.v.* 1. to bring or to put inside (things). 2. to invade, attack, storm. 3. to hit, attack. 4. to influence, get at (coll.). 5. (mar.) to overhaul, overtake. — **no entrarle a uno,** (coll.) to dislike, e.g. *no me entra ese libro,* I don't like this book; to be unable to learn, e.g. *no me entran las matemáticas,* I cannot learn mathematics; **e. a,** to enter, go into (a room, etc.); **e. en,** to enter, go in; to go in or into, fit into; to have access to, be admitted in; to adopt, take up (customs); to take part in; **e. en calor,** to warm up; **e. en dudas,** to begin to have one's doubts; **e. en función,** to go into operation; **e. en huelga,** to go on strike; **e. en órbita,** to go into orbit; **e. en pormenores,** to go into details; **e. en recelo,** to begin to be suspicious or afraid; **e. en vigencia,** to come into force; **e. en vigor,** to take effect. *—r.v.* to enter, sneak in stealthily.

entre, *prep.* between; among, amongst, amid, amidst; **e. tanto,** in the interim, meanwhile; **pensar e. sí,** to think to oneself; **e. tú y yo,** between you and me, confidentially.

entreabierto, ta, *irr. past part. of* **entreabrir.** *—a.* ajar, half-opened, e.g. *la puerta está e.,* the door is ajar.

entreabrir, *tr.v.* to open slightly, to set ajar. *—r.v.* to open slightly, to be ajar.

entreacto, *m.* 1. entr'acte, intermission. 2. small cigar.

entreancho, cha, *a.* of medium width.

entrecalle, *f.* (archit.) space or groove between two moldings.

entrecanal, *f.* (archit.) fillet (between two grooves or flutings).

entrecano, na, *a.* greying (hair or beard).

entrecasco, *m., var. of* **entrecorteza.**

entrecava, *f.* shallow digging.

entrecavar, *tr.v.* to dig shallowly or superficially.

entrecejo, *m.* 1. space between the eyebrows. 2. frown.

entrecerca, *f.* space between two fences.

entrecerrar, (*ref. 29*) *tr.v.* to half-close.

entrechocarse, (*ref. 50*) *r.v.* to collide.

entrechoque, *ref.* **entrechocarse.**

entrecinta, *f.* (archit.) collar beam.

entreclaro, ra, *a.* lightish, clearish.

entrecogedura, *f.* catching, capture; forcing, compelling.

entrecoger, (*ref. 57*) *tr.v.* 1. to trap, catch. 2. (fig.) to press, compel, force (by arguments or threats). 3. to intercept.

entrecoja, entrecojo, *ref.* **entrecoger.**

entrecomillado, da, *a.* in quotes. *—m.* quote, quotation.

entrecomillar, *tr.v.* to put in quotes, in quotation marks.

entrecoro, *m.* chancel.

entrecortado, da, *past part. of* **entrecortar.** *—a.* intermittent; broken (sobs, voice); labored (breathing).

entrecortadura, *f.* partial cut.

entrecortadamente, *adv.* falteringly.

entrecortar, *tr.v.* to cut something without severing it.

entrecorteza, *f.* ingrown bark (defect in timber caused by two branches having grown together and a piece of bark staying inside the wood).

entrecote, *m.* sirloin, loin.

entrecriarse, (*ref. 54*) *r.v.* to grow among other plants.

entrecruce, *ref.* **entrecruzar.**

entrecruzar, (*ref. 53*) *tr.v.* to intercross; to interweave. *—r.v.* to become intercrossed; to interweave; to intercross.

entrecubierta, entrecubiertas, *f.* (*pl.*) (mar.) between decks.

entrecuesto, *m.* backbone; sirloin, loin.

entredecir, (*ref. 3*) *tr.v.* to prohibit; to interdict; (ecc.) to prohibit the use of the sacraments.

entrediciendo, *ref.* **entredecir.**

entredicho, cha, *past part. of* **entredecir.** *—a.* interdicted, prohibited. *—m.* interdiction, prohibition; (ecc.) interdict, debarment from use of the sacraments.

entredigo, entredije, entredijera, entredijese, *ref.* **entredecir.**

entredoble, *a.* of medium thickness (cloth).

entredós, *m.* 1. (sew.) lace insert. 2. (bldg.) built-in cupboard between two windows. 3. (print.) long primer.

entrefilete, *m.* short extra item (inserted in newspaper), filler.

entrefino, na, *a.* of medium quality, middling good (coll.).

entreforro, *m.* (dressm.) interlining.

entrega, *f.* 1. delivery; handing over; surrender. 2. installment, fascicle, serial division (of a book). 3. (archit.) part of a beam or embedded stone. — **pago contra e., e. contra reembolso,** cash on delivery (C.O.D.).

entregadero, ra, *a.* (com.) deliverable.

entregado, da, *past part. of* **entregar.** *—a.* (archit.) embedded.

entregador, ra, *a.* delivering. *—m., f.* deliverer.

entregamiento, *m.* delivery; handing over, surrender.

entregar, (*ref. 51*) *tr.v.* 1. to deliver; to hand over, surrender. 2. (archit.) to embed, fix. — **entregarla,** (coll.) to die. —*r.v.* 1. to give oneself up, surrender; to give in. 2. to devote or dedicate oneself, give oneself up. — **entregarse a,** to devote oneself wholly to; to surrender oneself to.
entregue, entregué, *ref.* **entregar.**
entreguismo, *m.* (Amer.) policy of conceding the exploitation of mineral wealth and the operation of essential services to foreign companies.
entreguista, *m.* (Amer.) person who advocates conceding the exploitation of mineral wealth and the operation of essential services to foreign companies.
entrehierro, *m.* (elec.) air gap.
entrejuntar, *tr.v.* to join (the panels to the frame), to assemble, fit together (panels and frames).
entrelace, entrelacé, *ref.* **entrelazar.**
entrelargo, ga, *a.* longish, quite or rather long.
entrelazamiento, *m.* interweaving, interlacing, intertwining.
entrelazar, (*ref. 53*) *tr.v.* to interweave, interlace, intertwine; to braid.
entrelinear, *tr.v.* to write between the lines.
entreliño, *m.* space between rows of trees or vines.
entrelistado, da, *a.* striped (cloth); variegated.
entrelucir, (*ref. 46*) *i.v.* to show or shine through.
entreluzca, *ref.* **entrelucir.**
entremediar, *tr.v.* to place between.
entremedias, *adv.* in between, half-way. — **e. de,** between; in the middle of; in the midst of.
entremés, *m.* 1. appetizer, antipasto, hors d'oeuvres, side dish, entremets. 2. (theat.) one-act farce (presented between acts of a play).
entremesear, *tr.v.* 1. to act in a one-act comedy or farce. 2. (fig.) to intersperse (a serious conversation) with jokes and asides.
entremesil, *a.* said of a one-act farce.
entremesista, *m., f.* writer or player of one-act farces or comedies.
entremeter, *tr.v.* to insert, place between. —*r.v.* to meddle, intrude; to butt in, meddle.
entremetido, da, *past part. of* **entremeter.** —*a.* meddlesome, intruding. —*m., f.* meddler, busybody, intruder, go-between.
entremetimiento, *m.* 1. meddling, intruding, meddlesomeness. 2. insertion, interposition.
entremezcladura, *f.* intermingling, intermixing, intermixture.
entremezclar, *tr.v.* to intermingle, intermix.
entremiche, *m.* (mar.) end of a beam (between waterway and shelfpiece).
entremiso, *m.* cheese shelf (for draining whey from cheese).
entremorir, (*ref. 38*) *i.v.* to flicker, splutter, burn out (a candle), to die out.
entremuera, *ref.* **entremorir.**
entremuriera, entremuriese, entremurió, *ref.* **entremorir.**
entrenador, *m.* trainer, coach.
entrenamiento, *m.* training, coaching.
entrenar, *tr.v., r.v.* to train.
entrencar, (*ref. 50*) *tr.v.* to put rods into (a beehive) to hold up the honeycombs.
entrence, entrencé, *ref.* **entrenzar.**
entrenque, entrenqué, *ref.* **entrencar.**
entrenudo, *m.* (bot.) internode.
entrenzar, (*ref. 53*) *tr.v.* to braid, plait, entwine.
entreoiga, entreoigo, *ref.* **entreoír.**
entreoír, (*ref. 12*) *tr.v.* to half-hear, hear vaguely or indistinctly.
entreordinario, ria, *a.* middling, fair (coll.).
entreoscuro, ra, *a.* semi-dark, darkish.
entreoyendo, entreoyera, entreoyese, *ref.* **entreoír.**
entreoyó, *ref.* **entreoír.**
entrepalmadura, *f.* (vet.) suppurating sore (on a horse's foot) caused by a blow.
entrepanes, *m.* (*pl.*) fallow land or fields.
entrepañado, da, *a.* composed of panels.
entrepaño, *m.* (archit.) panel, bay (space between two pillars); (carp.) panel (of a door or a window); shelf (of a cupboard).
entreparecerse, (*ref. 45*) *r.v.* to show through.
entreparezca, entreparezco, *ref.* **entreparecer.**
entrepaso, *m.* rack pace (of a horse).
entrepechuga, *f.* flesh or meat on the wishbone (of fowl).
entrepeines, *m.* (*pl.*) wool waste left in combs (after the removal of the worsted).
entrepelado, da, *a.* piebald, pied (horse); variegated.
entrepelar, *i.v.* to be pied or piebald.
entrepernar, (*ref. 29*) *i.v.* to put one's legs between someone else's legs.
entrepiernas, *f.* (*pl.*) 1. innerside of thighs, crotch. 2. patches on the crotch of trousers or pants. 3. (Chile) bathing trunks.
entrepierne, entrepierno, *ref.* **entrepernar.**
entrepiso, *m.* 1. mezzanine. 2. (min.) space between galleries.
entrépito, ta, *a.* (Ven.) meddlesome, meddling.
entreplano, *m.* (aer.) gap.
entrepretado, da, *a.* (vet.) with an injured breast or shoulder.
entrepuentes, *m.* (*pl.*) (mar.) between decks.
entrepunce, entrepuncé, *ref.* **entrepunzar.**
entrepunzadura, *f.* intermittent shooting pain.
entrepunzar, (*ref. 53*) *tr.v.* to cause (one) intermittent shooting pains.
entrerraído, da, *a.* shabby, partly wornout.
entrerrenglón, *m.* interline.
entrerrenglonadura, *f.* writing between the lines, interlineation.
entrerrenglonar, *tr.v.* to write between the lines, interlineate.
entrerrieles, *m., var. of* **entrevía.**
entrerrosca, *f.* (mec.) nipple.
entresaca, *f.* 1. thinning out (of plants, hair). 2. selection, culling, picking out.
entresacadura, *f., var. of* **entresaca.**
entresacar, (*ref. 50*) *tr.v.* 1. to select, cull, pick out. 2. to thin out (trees, plants); to thin (hair).
entresaque, entresaqué, *ref.* **entresacar.**
entresijo, *m.* 1. (anat.) mesentery. 2. (fig.) secret. — **tener muchos entresijos,** to have many difficulties; (fig.) to be careful or cautious.
entresuelo, *m.* mezzanine, entresol.
entresurco, *m.* (agr.) space between furrows.
entretalla, entretalladura, *f.* bas-relief.
entretallar, *tr.v.* 1. to carve in bas-relief; to carve, engrave. 2. to do openwork on (cloth). 3. to impede, obstruct, stop. —*r.v.* to fit together or in.
entretanto, *adv.* meanwhile, in the meantime. —*m.* meanwhile, meantime.
entretecho, *m.* (Chile, Arg.) garret, attic, loft.
entretejedor, ra, *a.* interweaving, interknitting.
entretejedura, *f.* interweaving, intertexture.
entretejer, *tr.v.* to interweave, intertwine; to mix, mingle, variegate. — **e. con,** to weave into, e.g. *e. citas con el texto,* to weave quotations into the text.
entretejimiento, *m.* interweaving, intertexture.
entretela, *f.* 1. (dressm.) interlining, buckram. 2. (*pl.*) (coll.) innermost being or self.
entretelar, *tr.v.* 1. (dressm.) to interline, interface. 2. (Mex.) to press out (folds in newsprint).
entretención, *f.* (Amer.) entertainment, amusement, pastime.
entretendré, entretendría, *ref.* **entretener.**
entretenedor, ra, *a.,* entertaining, amusing. —*m., f.* entertainer.
entretener, (*ref. 23*) *tr.v.* 1. to entertain, amuse, divert. 2. to make bearable, allay (pain), stave off (hunger), while away (the time). 3. to protract, delay (a business deal); to delay, put off, keep waiting (a person). —*r.v.* 1. to be amused, amuse oneself. 2. to delay, dally. 3. to be held up, be delayed. — **entretenerse en** + *inf.,* to amuse oneself + *ger.*
entretenga, entretengo, *ref.* **entretener.**
entretenida, dar a uno la e., to put someone off with excuses.
entretenido, da, *past part. of* **entretener.** —*a.* 1. amusing, entertaining, pleasant. 2. (her.) interwoven, interlaced. —*m.* apprentice (on very small wages).
entretenimiento, *m.* 1. entertainment; amusement, game, pastime. 2. maintenance, conservation.
entretiempo, *m.* spring or autumn, the in-between season; **traje de e.,** suit or dress suitable for both spring and fall wear.
entretuve, entretuviera, entretuviese, *ref.* **entretener.**
entreuntar, *tr.v.* to oil, grease or paint lightly; to anoint slightly.
entrevenarse, *r.v.* to enter or diffuse through the veins.
entreventana, *f.* pier, space between two windows.
entrever, (*ref. 27*) *tr.v.* 1. to descry, see vaguely; to catch a glimpse of. 2. to guess, conjure, surmise.
entreverado, da, *past part. of* **entreverar.** —*a* intermixed; both fat and lean (said of meat). —*m.* (Ven.) mutton seasoned with salt and vinegar and roasted on a spit.
entreverar, *tr.v.* to intermingle, mix. —*r.v.* 1. (Arg.) to mix together helter-skelter, get jumbled together. 2. (Arg.) to clash in hand-to-hand battle (cavalry).
entrevero, *m.* 1. (Arg.) mingling, mixing. 2. (Arg., Chile) jumble, confusion, disorder. 3. (Arg.) hand-to-hand cavalry combat.
entreví, *ref.* **entrever.**
entrevía, *f.* (ry.) gauge or gage; **e. ancha,** broad or wide gauge; **e. angosta,** narrow gauge; **e. normal,** standard gauge.
entreviera, entreviese, entrevió, *ref.* **entrever.**
entrevista, *f.* interview; meeting, conference; **e. de prensa,** press conference.
entrevistador, ra, *m., f.* interviewer.
entrevistar, *tr.v.* to interview.
entrevistarse, *r.v.* to have a meeting or an interview; **e. con,** to interview, have an interview with.
entrevuelta, *f.* (agr.) short furrow used to straighten main furrow in field.
entripado, da, *past part. of* **entriparse.** —*a.* 1. in the intestines or belly. 2. not cleaned, not eviscerated (dead animal). —*m.* 1. stomachache. 2. (coll.) disguised anger or displeasure.
entriparse, *r.v.* (Col., Ecuad., vulg.) to get angry or annoyed.
entristecedor, ra, *a.* saddening, sad.
entristecer, (*ref. 45*) *tr.v.* to sadden, make unhappy; to grieve, afflict. —*r.v.* to become sad, melancholy or unhappy.
entristecimiento, *m.* saddening; sadness, unhappiness, mournfulness; dejection.
entristezca, entristezco, *ref.* **entristecer.**
entrojar, *tr.v.* to store (grain) in granary; to garner grain.
entrometer, *tr.v., var. of* **entremeter.**
entrometido, da, *a., var. of* **entremetido.**

entrometimiento, *m.* intermeddling; intrusion.
entromparse, *r.v.* 1. (Amer.) to get angry or annoyed. 2. (coll.) to get drunk.
entronar, *tr.v.* to enthrone.
entroncamiento, *m.* 1. relationship (between two people). 2. (Amer.) connection, junction (between two bus routes, etc.).
entroncar, (*ref. 50*) *tr.v.* 1. to show the relationship between (two persons). 2. (Mex.) to mate horses of the same color. —*i.v.* 1. to be related, to become related. 2. (Amer.) to connect, link up, form a junction (e.g. two bus routes).
entronerar, *tr.v.* (billiards) to pocket (a ball). —*r.v.* to fall into a pocket.
entronice, entronicé, *ref.* **entronizar.**
entronización, *f.* 1. enthroning, enthronement. 2. exaltation.
entronizar, (*ref. 53*) *tr.v.* 1. to enthrone. 2. to exalt; to put in a high position. —*r.v.* to put on airs, become arrogant.
entronque, *m.* 1. cognation, connection, blood relationship. 2. railway junction.
entronque, *ref.* **entroncar.**
entropía, *f.* (phys.) entropy.
entropillar, *tr.v.* (Arg.) to train (horses) to run in herds.
entropión, *m.* (med.) entropion.
entruchada, *f.* (coll.) plot, intrigue; underhanded affair, trick, deception.
entruchado, da, *past part. of* **entruchar.** —*m.* (coll.) plot, intrigue, trick.
entruchar, *tr.v.* to lure, entice, to trick into (doing something).
entruchón, na, *a.* (coll.) plotting, intriguing (person). —*m., f.* plotter, intriguer, schemer.
entrujar, *tr.v.* 1. to store (olives) in bins; to store (grain) in a granary. 2. to pocket, put away.
entubar, *tr.v.* to put into tubes; to outfit with a casing.
entuerte, entuerto, *ref.* **entortar.**
entuerto, *m.* 1. offense, wrong, injustice. 2. (*pl.*) afterpains (of birth).
entullecer, (*ref. 45*) *tr.v.* to stop, check, obstruct. —*i.v., r.v.* to become crippled or paralyzed.
entullezca, entullezco, *ref.* **entullecer.**
entumecer, (*ref. 45*) *tr.v.* to numb, make numb. —*r.v.* 1. to go or become numb. 2. (fig.) to become swollen (river), surge (sea).
entumecimiento, *m.* 1. numbness, torpor. 2. swelling (of river), swell (of sea).
entumezca, entumezco, *ref.* **entumecer.**
entumirse, *r.v.* to go to sleep, become torpid or numb (a limb) through inaction.
entunarse, *r.v.* (Amer.) to be pricked by a thorn.
entunicar, (*ref. 50*) *tr.v.* 1. to plaster (for fresco painting). 2. to put a tunic on.
entunique, *ref.* **entunicar.**
entupir, *tr.v.* 1. to block, obstruct, clog, stop up. 2. to squeeze, compress, tighten. —*r.v.* to become blocked, obstructed or clogged up.
enturbiamiento, *m.* 1. muddiness. 2. confusion, disorder.
enturbiar, *tr.v.* 1. to muddle, to make muddy or cloudy. 2. (fig.) to disturb, obscure, confuse. —*r.v.* 1. to become muddy. 2. to become disarranged.
entusarse, *r.v.* (Ecuad.) to get sulky.
entusiasmar, *tr.v.* to make enthusiastic, to enrapture; to encourage. —*r.v.* to become enthusiastic; to become encouraged.
entusiasmo, *m.* 1. enthusiasm, fervor. 2. (divine or poetic) inspiration.
entusiasta, *a.* enthusiastic, fervorous. —*m., f.* enthusiast, fan, e.g. *un e. del ajedrez,* a chess fan.
entusiástico, ca, *a.* enthusiastic.
entutumarse, *r.v.* (Col.) to become confused or mixed up.
enucleación, *f.* (surg.) enucleation.
enuclear, *tr.v.* (surg.) to enucleate.
énula campana, *f.* (bot.) inula, elecampane.
enumeración, *f.* enumeration.
enumerador, ra, *a.* enumerating, enumerative. —*m., f.* enumerator.
enumerar, *tr.v.* to enumerate.
enumerativo, va, *a.* enumerative.
enunciación, *f.* enunciation, declaration, statement.
enunciado, *past part. of* **enunciar.** —*m., var. of* **enunciación.**
enunciar, *tr.v.* to state, enunciate (an idea).
enunciativo, va, *a.* enunciative.
envainador, ra, *a.* sheathing.
envainar, *tr.v.* to sheathe (e.g. a sword); to enclose, encase, sheathe.
envalentonamiento, *m.* encouragement; boldness, daring.
envalentonar, *tr.v.* to encourage, to inspirit, to embolden. —*r.v.* 1. to pluck up courage, become bold. 2. to become boastful; (Amer.) to brag and strut.
envalijar, *tr.v.* to pack or put in a suitcase or valise.
envanecer, (*ref. 45*) *tr.v.* to make conceited, vain or arrogant. —*r.v.* 1. to become vain, conceited or arrogant. 2. (Chile) to wither or rot (crops). — **envanecerse con, de** or **por,** to become conceited or vain with or about.
envanecimiento, *m.* vanity, conceit, arrogance.
envanezca, envanezco, *ref.* **envanecer.**
envaramiento, *m.* numbness, stiffness.
envarar, *tr.v.* to benumb, make stiff or torpid. —*r.v.* to go to sleep, become numb or stiff.
envarbascar, (*ref. 50*) *tr.v.* to poison (water) with mullein (in order to stun the fish).
envarbasque, envarbasqué, *ref.* **envarbascar.**
envaronar, *i.v.* to grow strong, become robust and virile.
envasado, da, *past part. of* **envasar.** —*a.* packed; **e. al vacío,** vacuum-packed.
envasador, ra, *a.* bottling, packing, canning, tinning. —*m., f.* packer; bottler, filler. —*m.* large funnel.
envasar, *tr.v.* 1. to bottle, barrel, cask (liquid); to pack, tin, can (solids); to sack (grain); to put into any vessel or container. 2. to drink to excess. 3. to push, poke, plunge (sword, etc.) into.
envase, *m.* 1. packing, bottling, canning, tinning, filling. 2. container, bottle, jar, can, tin, package.
envedijarse, *r.v.* 1. to become tangled. 2. (coll.) to get into a quarrel or fight; to wrangle.
envegarse, *r.v.* (Chile) to become sodden or swampy.
envejecer, (*ref. 45*) *tr.v.* to age, make old. *a.* 1. old, aged; worn out by suffering. 2. (fig.) tried, experienced; accustomed habituated.
envejecido, da, *past part. of* **envejecer.** —*a.* 1. old, aged; worn out by suffering. 2. (fig.) tried, experienced; accustomed, habituated.
envejecimiento, *m.* aging; age, oldness.
envejezca, envejezco, *ref.* **envejecer.**
envendar, *tr.v., var. of* **vendar.**
envenenado, da, *past part. of* **envenenar.** —*a.* poisoned; embittered, enraged. —*m., f.* a bitter, vengeful person.
envenenador, ra, *a.* poisonous. —*m., f.* poisoner.
envenenamiento, *m.* poisoning.
envenenar, *tr.v.* 1. to poison, envenom. 2. to interpret maliciously. 3. to make bitter (someone's life, existence, etc.). —*r.v.* 1. to poison oneself. 2. to become bitter.
enverar, *i.v.* to begin to ripen, to begin to show color (said of fruit).
enverdecer, (*ref. 45*) *i.v.* to turn green; become green again.
enverdezca, *ref.* **enverdecer.**
envergadura, *f.* 1. (mar.) breadth (of sails). 2. wingspan, wingspread (of a bird or a plane). 3. importance, prestige, e.g, *un plan de gran e.,* a plan of major importance.
envergar, (*ref. 51*) *tr.v.* (mar.) to bend (the sails), to fasten (sails) to the yards.
envergue, *m.* (mar.) sail rope, roband, robbin.
envergue, envergué, *ref.* **envergar.**
enverjado, *m.* grating, lattice, grillwork.
envero, *m.* golden red (said of ripening fruit); a type of golden red grape.
envés, *m.* wrong side; the back (of something having two sides).
envesado, da, *a.* 1. showing the wrong side. 2. said of the flashy, polished or finished side of a hide, e.g. *cabritilla e.,* polished kidskin.
envestidura, *f., var. of* **investidura.**
envestir, (*ref. 39*) *tr.v., var. of* **investir.**
enviada, *f.* sending; consignment, shipment.
enviadizo, za, *a.* sent, regularly sent; fit or equipped to be sent.
enviado, *past part. of* enviar. —*m.* envoy, messenger, delegate; **e. extraordinario,** envoy extraordinary; **e. de prensa,** (jour.) special correspondent.
enviajado, da, *a.* (archit.) sloping, sloped, oblique.
enviar, (*ref. 54*) *tr.v.* to send; to dispatch, ship, mail, forward; convey, transmit; **e. a. +** *inf.,* to send to + *inf.;* **e. a paseo,** to send someone packing; **e. un parte,** (jour.) to file a dispatch.
enviciador, ra, *a.* addicting, corrupting; habit-forming.
enviciamiento, *m.* 1. corruption, vitiation. 2. addiction.
enviciar, *tr.v.* to corrupt, vitiate, spoil. —*i.v.* to grow much foliage and little fruit. —*r.v.* to become addicted or overfond; **enviciarse con** or **en,** to become addicted to, to develop a habit of.
envidada, *f.* side bet; making of side bet (in gambling).
envidador, ra, *m., f.* one who makes a side bet (in cards); challenger.
envidar, *tr.v.* (in cards) to make a side bet with (on top of bets already made); **e. en** or **de falso,** to offer grudgingly (hoping not to be accepted). —*i.v.* to bid, bet.
envidia, *f.* envy; desire to emulate.
envidiable, *a.* enviable, eliciting envy, e.g. *él tiene una posición e.,* he has an enviable position.
envidiar, *tr.v.* to envy; to covet.
envidioso, sa, *a.* envious, jealous. —*m.* envious man. —*f.* envious woman.
envigado, *past part. of* **envigar.** —*m.* rafters, beams.
envigar, (*ref. 51*) *tr.v.* to install the rafters or beams in. —*i.v.* to install rafters or beams.
envigorice, envigoricé, *ref.* **envigorizar.**
envigorizar, (*ref. 53*) *tr.v., var. of* **vigorizar.**
envigue, envigué, *ref.* **envigar.**
envilecedor, ra, *a.* debasing, degrading.
envilecer, (*ref. 45*) *tr.v.* to debase, degrade, vilify. —*r.v.* to become degraded, low or despicable; to degrade or debase oneself.
envilecimiento, *m.* debasement, degradation, vilification.
envilezca, envilezco, *ref.* **envilecer.**
envinado, da, *past part. of* envinar. —*a.* (Mex.) wine-colored; with a slight taste of wine.
envinagrar, *tr.v.* to add vinegar to, e.g. *e. la ensalada,* to put vinegar on the salad.
envinar, *tr.v.* to mix wine with (water).

envío, *m.* sending, dispatching, shipping; remittance, shipment, consignment.
envión, *m.* push, shove.
envirar, *tr.v.* to fasten (a beehive) with wooden nails.
envirotado, da, *a.* arrogant, stuck-up, full of airs.
enviscamiento, *m.* smearing with birdlime.
enviscar, (*ref. 50*) *tr.v.* 1. to smear with birdlime. 2. to incite, provoke. —*r.v.* to get stuck to the birdlime, get caught in birdlime.
envisque, envisqué, *ref.* **enviscar.**
envite, *m.* 1. side bet made on top of bets already laid; stake at cards. 2. offer, invitation. 3. push, shove. — **al primar e.,** at the first sign, right off, at once.
enviudar, *i.v.* to become a widower or a widow.
envolatado, da, *a.* (Col.) busy.
envoltijo, *m.* 1. cover, wrapping, wrapper. (Ecuad.) bundle.
envoltorio, *m.* 1. bundle. 2. (tex.) knot (flaw in woolen fabric), defective woof.
envoltura, *f.* 1. swaddling clothes (also used in *pl.*). 2. cover, wrapping, wrapper, envelope; sheath. 3. (bot.) involucre. — **e. del eje,** (auto.) axle housing.
envolvedero, *m., var. of* **envolvedor.**
envolvedor, *m., f.* wrapper (person). —*m.* 1. cover, wrapping, wrapper. 2. changing table (for changing a baby).
envolvente, *a.* covering, wrapping, cushioning.
envolver, (*ref. 34*) *tr.v.* 1. to wrap, pack, make into a bundle; to cover; to swaddle. 2. to wind (thread, etc.). 3. to run circles around, tie up, floor (an opponent in argument). 4. (mil.) to surround. 5. to implicate, involve. —*r.v.* 1. to become or get involved, implicated. 2. to have an affair. 3. to engage (in combat).
envolvimiento, *m.* 1. wrapping, envelopment. 2. involvement, entanglement. 3. (mil.) encirclement. — **e. vertical,** (mil.) vertical envelopment.
envuelto, ta, *irr. past part. of* **envolver.** —*a.* wrapped. —*m.* (Mex., cul.) rolled and filled tortilla. —*f.* (*pl.*) swaddling clothes.
envuelva, envuelvo, *ref.* **envolver.**
enyerbarse, *r.v.* 1. (Cuba, Chile, P. Rico) to become covered with grass. 2. (Mex.) to get bewitched (by sorcery). 3. (P. Rico) to become intoxicated with marihuana.
enyesado, *past part. of* **enyesar.** —*m.* 1. plasterwork, plastering. 2. treatment of wine with gypsum, to clarify it and make it stronger.
enyesadura, *f.* plastering.
enyesar, *tr.v.* 1. to plaster, fill with plaster, to apply chalk to; to whitewash. 2. to treat with gypsum. 3. (surg.) to plaster, put in a plaster cast.
enyetar, *tr.v.* (Arg., sl.) to give bad luck to.
enyugar, (*ref. 51*) *tr.v.* to yoke. —*r.v.* (fig.) to get married.
enyugue, enyugué, *ref.* **enyugar.**
enzainarse, *r.v.* 1. to look askance, sideways or out of the corner of one's eye. 2. to become untrustworthy or deceitful.
enzamarrado, da, *a.* wearing a sheepskin jacket; wearing chaps.
enzarce, enzarcé, *ref.* **enzarzar.**
enzarzar, (*ref. 53*) *tr.v.* 1. to cover with brambles. 2. (fig.) to cause trouble between, alienate. 3. to place wattles or hurdles for (silkworms). —*r.v.* 1. to get entangled in brambles or underbrush. 2. to become involved in difficulties. 3. to get involved in (a dispute or quarrel).
enzima, *f.* (chem.) enzyme.
enzimático, ca, *a.* (biochem.) enzymatic, enzymic.
enzimología, *f.* (biochem.) enzymology.
enzocar, (*ref. 50*) *tr.v.* (Chile) to put in, insert.
enzolvar, *tr.v.* (Mex.) to clog, stop up. —*r.v.* to become clogged up.
enzootia, *f.* (vet.) enzootic.
enzoótico, ca, *a.* (vet.) enzootic.
enzoquetar, *tr.v.* to place wooden blocks in (timber framework).
enzunchar, *tr.v.* to bind with hoops or iron bands.
enzurdecer, (*ref. 45*) *i.v.* to become lefthanded.
enzurdezca, enzurdezco, *ref.* **enzurdecer.**
enzurice, enzuricé, *ref.* **enzurizar.**
enzurizar, (*ref. 53*) *tr.v.* to incite, to sow discord among, cause trouble between.
enzurromar, *tr.v.* 1. to put in a bag, to bag. 2. (coll.) to put in, enclose.
eoceno, *a., m.* (geol.) Eocene.
eólico, ca, *a.* 1. (hist.) Aeolian, pertaining to Aeolia, ancient region in Asia Minor. 2. (geol., geog.) aeolian, formed by the winds. —*m.* Aeolic dialect.
eolio, lia, *a.* Aeolian, pertaining to Aeolia or to Aeolus, god of the winds; **arpa eolia,** Aeolian harp. —*m., f.* Aeolian, native of Aeolia, an ancient region in Asia Minor.
eolípilo, *m.* aeolipile, eolipile, an ancient prototypal steam engine.
eolítico, ca, *a.* (geol.) eolithic.
eolito, *m.* eolith, primitive stone implement.
Eolo, *m.* (myth.) Aeolus, the god of the winds.
eón, *m.* aeon, eon, a long period of time, eternity.
eosina, *f.* (chem.) eosin.
eosinófilo, la, *a.* (biol.) eosinophilic.
eozoico, ca, *a.* (geol.) eozoic.
epacta, *f.* 1. (astron.) epact. 2. liturgical calendar.
epactilla, *f.* annual liturgical calendar.
epanadiplosis, *f.* (rhet.) epanadiplosis.
epanáfora, *f.* (rhet.) anaphora.
epanalepsis, *f.* (rhet.) epanadiplosis.
epanástrofe, *f.* (rhet.) epanastrophe.
epanortosis, *f.* (rhet.) epanorthosis.
eparca, *m.* (hist., rel.) eparch.
eparquía, *f.* (hist.) eparchy, an administrative subdivision in Greece.
epazote, *m.* (Mex., bot.) Mexican tea.
E.P.D. *abbrev. of* **en paz descanse,** rest in peace (R.I.P.).
epencéfalo, *m.* (anat.) epencephalon.
epéndimo, *m.* (anat.) ependyma.
epéntesis, *f.* (gram.) epenthesis.
epentético, ca, *a.* (gram.) epenthetic.
eperlano, *m.* (ichth.) smelt.
epexégesis, *f.* epexegesis, the addition of an explanation or clarification to a text.
epiblasto, *m.* (anat.) epiblast.
épica, *f.* epic poetry; the poetic narrative of a heroic deed or a national struggle.
epicáliz, *m.* (bot.) epicalyx.
épicamente, *adv.* epically.
epicanto, *m.* (anat.) epicanthus.
epicardio, *m.* (anat.) epicardium.
epicarpio, *a.* (bot.) epicarp.
epicedio, *m.* epicedium, funeral ode.
epiceno, *a.* epicene, belonging to both genders.
epicentral, *a.* (geol.) epicentral.
epicentro, *m.* (geol.) epicenter.
epiceyo, *m.* epicedium, a funeral hymn or ode.
epicíclico, ca, *a.* (astron.) epicyclic.
epiciclo, *m.* (astron.) epicycle.
epicicloide, *f.* (geom.) epicycloid.
épico, ca, *a.* epic, pertaining to epic poetry; heroic.
epicóndilo, *m.* (anat.) epicondyle.
epicótilo, *m.* (bot.) epicotyl.
epicraneal, *a.* (med.) epicranial.
epicrítico, ca, *a.* (physiol., psyc.) epicritic.
epicureísmo, *m.* (philos.) Epicureanism; epicureanism, epicurism; sensualism.
epicúreo, a, *a.* (philos.) Epicurean, pertaining to Epicurus or his teachings; epicurean, pleasure-loving. —*m., f.* (philos.) Epicurean; epicurean, lover of pleasure.
Epicuro, *m.* Epicurus, Greek philosopher founder of Epicureanism.
epidemia, *f.* (med.) epidemic.
epidemial, *a., var. of* **epidémico.**
epidémico, ca, *a.* epidemic.
epidemiología, *f.* epidemiology.
epidemiólogo, *m.* (med.) epidemiologist.
epidendro, *m.* (bot.) epidendrum, epidendron.
epidérmico, ca, *a.* epidermal, epidermic.
epidermis, *f.* (anat.) epidermis, outer skin.
epidermoide, *a.* epidermoid, epidermoidal.
epidiascopio, *m.* (photog.) epidiascope, opaque projector.
epidídimo, *m.* (anat.) epididymis.
epidota, *f.* (min.) epidote.
epifanía, *f.* (ecc.) Epiphany; Twelfth Night.
epifenomenismo, *m.* (philos.) epiphenomenalism.
epifenómeno, *m.* (med., philos.) epiphenomenon.
epífisis, *f.* (anat.) epiphysis.
epifito, ta, *a.* (bot.) epiphytic. —*f.* (bot.) epiphyte.
epifitótico, ca, *a.* (bot.) epiphytotic.
epifonema, *f.* (rhet.) epiphonema.
epifora, *f.* (med.) epiphora.
epigástrico, ca, *a.* (anat.) epigastric.
epigastrio, *a.* (anat.) epigastrium.
epigénesis, *f.* (biol., geol.) epigenesis.
epigenético, ca, *a.* (geol.) epigenetic.
epigénico, ca, *a.* (geol.) epigene.
epigeo, a, *a.* (bot.) epigeal, epigean, epigeous.
epigino, na, *a.* (bot.) epigynous.
epiglosis, *f.* (ento.) epipharynx, epiglottis.
epiglótico, ca, *a.* (anat.) epiglottal, epiglottic.
epiglotis, *f.* (anat., zool.) epiglottis.
epígono, *m.* epigone, successor, follower.
epígrafe, *m.* epigraph, inscription; quotation.
epigrafía, *f.* epigraphy, the study of inscriptions.
epigráfico, ca, *a.* epigraphic.
epigrafista, *m., f.* epigraphist.
epigrama, *m.* epigram; witty, pointed statement, poem or inscription.
epigramatario, ria, *a.* epigrammatic. —*m.* 1. epigrammatist; composer of epigrams. 2. collection of epigrams.
epigramático, ca, *a.* epigrammatic. —*m.* epigrammatist.
epigramatista, epigramista, *m.* epigrammatist.
epilepsia, *f.* (med.) epilepsy.
epiléptico, ca, *a., m., f.* (med.) epileptic.
epileptiforme, *a.* (med.) epileptiform.
epileptoide, *a.* (med.) epileptoid.
epilogación, *f.* epilogue.
epilogal, *a.* epilogic, compendious, summary.
epilogar, (*ref. 51*) *tr.v.* to summarize, recapitulate, sum up.
epilogismo, *m.* (astron.) computation.
epílogo, *m.* 1. epilogue. 2. (fig.) compendium, brief summary, recapitulation. 3. (rhet.) peroration.
epilogue, epilogué, *ref.* **epilogar.**
epimisio, *m.* (anat.) epimysium.
epímone, *f.* (rhet.) repetition of a word or sentence in order to emphasize the meaning.
epimorfosis, *f.* (med.) epimorphosis.
epinastia, *f.* (bot.) epinasty.
epinástico, ca, *a.* (bot.) epinastic.
epinefrina, *f.* (biol.) epinephrine, epinephrin.
epineurio, *m.* (anat.) epineurium.
epineuro, *m.* (anat.) epineurium.
epinicio, *m.* epinicion, triumphal ode.
epipaleolítico, ca, *a.* (paleon.) Epipaleolithic.
epiplón, *m.* (anat.) epiploon, omentum.

epiquerema, *m.* (log.) epicheirema.
epiqueya, *f.* interpretation of law, according to circumstances.
episcopado, *m.* episcopacy, episcopate, bishopric.
episcopal, *a.* 1. episcopal (pertaining to bishops). 2. Episcopal (pertaining to the Protestant Episcopal Church).
episcopalismo, *m.* episcopalism (theory that supreme authority of church resides in the bishops).
episcopalista, *m., f.* 1. partisan of episcopalism. 2. Episcopalian (member of Protestant Episcopal Church).
episcopologio, *m.* chronological list of bishops.
episódicamente, *adv.* episodically.
episódico, ca, *a.* episodic, episodical.
episodio, *m.* episode, digression (from the main narrative); incidental narrative.
epispástico, ca, *a., m.* epispastic, causing blisters; blistering agent.
epistasia, *f.* (med.) epistasis, epistasy.
epistasis, *f.* (med.) epistasis, epistasy.
epistaxis, *f.* (med.) epistaxis, nasal hemorrhage.
epistemología, *f.* (philos.) epistemology.
epistemológico, ca, *a.* (philos.) epistemological.
epistemólogo, *m.* (philos.) epistemologist.
episternón, *m.* (anat.) episternum.
epistilo, *m.* (archit.) epistyle.
epístola, *f.* epistle, letter; (bib.) Epistle.
epistolar, *a.* 1. (lit.) epistolary, composed as a series of letters. 2. of or pertaining to letter-writing.
epistolario, *m.* 1. (ecc.) epistolary. 2. volume of letters.
epistolero, *m.* epistler.
epistolio, *m., var. of* **epistolario.**
epistológrafo, fa, *m., f.* epistolographer, epistolographist.
epístrofe, *f.* (rhet.) epistrophe.
epitafio, *m.* epitaph; an inscription engraved on a tombstone.
epitalámico, ca, *a.* of or pertaining to the epithalamium or the nuptial song.
epitalamio, *m.* epithalamium, nuptial song.
epítasis, *f.* (theat.) epitasis, the part of a play, esp. classic drama, between the exposition and the denouement.
epitelial, *a.* (anat.) epithelial.
epitelio, *m.* (anat.) epithelium.
epitelioide, *a.* (anat.) epithelioid.
epitelioma, *f.* (med.) epithelioma.
epítema, *f.* (med.) epithem.
epíteto, *m.* epithet.
epítima, *f.* (med.) epithem; (fig.) solace, relief, consolation.
epitimar, *tr.v.* (med.) to apply epithem to.
epítimo, *m.* (bot.) clover dodder, epithyme.
epitomadamente, *adv.* precisely, briefly, concisely.
epitomador, ra, *a.* epitomizing. —*m., f.* epitomist, writer of epitomes.
epitomar, *tr.v.* to epitomize, abridge, summarize.
epítome, *m.* epitome, summary, compendium.
epítrito, *m.* (poet.) epitrite.
epitrope, *f.* (rhet.) epitrope.
epizoario, *m.* (vet.) epizoon.
epizoico, ca, *a.* (zool.) epizoic.
epizootia, *f.* (vet.) epizootic, epizootic disease.
epizoótico, ca, *a.* (vet.) epizootic.
época, *f.* epoch, era, age; time; **é. cenozoica,** (geol.) Cenozoic age; **é. geológica,** geologic age; **é. glacial,** ice age; **é. mesozoica,** Mesozoic age; **é. paleozoica,** (geol.) Paleozoic age; **e. victoriana,** Victorian age; **hacer é.,** to make history, to open a new era; **traje de é.,** period costume.
epoda, *f.,* **epodo,** *m.* (poet.) epode.
epónimo, ma, *a.* eponymous, eponymic. —*m.* eponym.
epopeya, *f.* (poet.) epic poem; epopee.
epoxia, *f.* (chem.) epoxy.
epóxido, *m.* (chem.) epoxide.
epsomita, *f.* epsomite, Epsom salt.
épulis, *m.* (med.) epulis, gum tumor.
epulón, *m.* gourmand, epicurean.
equiángulo, la, *a.* (geom.) equiangular.
equidad, *f.* 1. equity, fairness, impartiality. 2. (law) equity, natural law. 3. equanimity, equitableness (of character). 4. reasonableness, moderateness (of prices, contract conditions).
equidiferencia, *f.* (math.) equidifference; arithmetical progression.
equidimensional, *a.* of equal dimensions.
equidistancia, *f.* equidistance.
equidistante, *a.* equidistant, equally distant.
equidistar, *i.v.* to be equidistant.
equidna, *m.* (zool.) echidna.
équido, *a., m.* (zool.) equine.
equilátero, ra, *a.* (geom.) equilateral.
equilibrado, da, *past part. of* **equilibrar.** —*a.* well-balanced, stable (of character).
equilibrar, *tr.v.* to balance, equilibrate, counterpoise. —*r.v.* to balance.
equilibrio, *m.* 1. equilibrium, balance. 2. counterbalance, counterpoise. — **e. de poder,** (polit.) balance of power; **e. dinámico,** dynamic balance; **perder el e.,** to lose one's balance.
equilibrista, *m., f.* tight-rope walker, equilibrist, aerealist.
equimolecular, *a.* (phys.) equimolecular.
equimosis, *f.* (med.) ecchymosis.
equino, na, *a.* equine. —*m.* 1. (archit.) echinus. 2. (ichth.) sea urchin.
equinoccial, *a. (astron.) equinoctial.* —*f.* (astron.) equinoctial line.
equinoccio, *m.* (astron.) equinox; **e. vernal,** (astron.) vernal equinox.
equinococo, *m.* (bact.) echinococcus, larva of tapeworm.
equinococosis, *f.* (med.) echinococcosis.
equinodermo, *a.* (zool.) echinodermatous. —*m.* (zool.) echinoderm; (*pl.*) Echinodermata.
equinoideo, a, *a., m.* (zool.) echinoid.
equinulado, da, *a.* echinulate.
equipado, da, *past part. of* **equipar.** —*a.* furnished, provided, equipped.
equipaje, *m.* 1. luggage, baggage; equipment. 2. (mar.) crew. — **exceso de e.,** excess baggage or luggage; **e. de mano,** hand baggage, carry-on luggage.
equipal, *m.* (Mex.) rustic chair.
equipar, *tr.v.* 1. to equip, outfit; furnish. 2. (mar.) to provision (ship).
equiparable, *a.* comparable, matchable.
equiparación, *f.* comparing, collation, matching, balancing.
equiparar, *tr.v.* to compare, match, make equal, balance; to collate.
equipo, *m.* 1. equipment; appurtenances, instruments. 2. outfit, uniform, trappings. 3. crew, team (of workers); (sport) team. — **e. de alta fidelidad,** hi-fi system; **e. de música,** sound system; **e. de novia,** trousseau; **e. de reparación,** repair squad; **e. de serie,** standard fittings; **e. de sonido,** sound system; **e. móvil,** outside broadcsting unit; **e. quirúrgico,** surgical instruments; **e. rodante,** (ry.) rolling stock.
equipolado, *a.* (her.) checkered.
equipolencia, *f.* (log.) equipollence, equality of power.
equipolente, *a.* (log.) equipollent.
equiponderancia, *f.* equipoise, equiponderance.
equiponderante, *a.* equiponderant, evenly balanced.
equiponderar, *tr.v.* to equiponderate, be equal in weight.
equipotencial, *a.* (phys.) equipotential, having the same potential at every point.
equis, *f.* ex (name of the letter "x"). —*a.* certain, e.g. *necesito una cantidad e.,* I need a certain quantity.
equisetáceo, a, *a.* (bot.) equisetaceous. —*f.* (*pl.*) Equisetaceae.
equiseto, *m.* (bot.) equisetum.
equitación, *f.* equitation, horseback riding.
equitativamente, *adv.* equitably, fairly.
equitativo, va, *a.* equitable, fair, just, reasonable.
équite, *m.* Roman citizen of the military class.
equivalencia, *f.* equivalence, equivalent.
equivalente, *a., m.* equivalent, tantamount.
equivalentemente, *adv.* equivalently.
equivaler, (*ref. 25*) *i.v.* to equal, be equal or equivalent to; to amount to.
equivalga, *ref.* **equivaler.**
equivocación, *f.* mistake, error, blunder.
equivocadamente, *adv.* mistakenly, erroneously.
equivocado, da, *past part. of* **equivocar.** —*a.* wrong, incorrect, mistaken, erroneous; **número e.,** wrong number.
equívocamente, *adv.* equivocally, ambiguously.
equivocar, (*ref. 50*) *tr.v.* mistake. —*i.v.* to equivocate, prevaricate. —*r.v.* to be mistaken, make a mistake; to blunder; **e. con,** to mistake, to take one thing for another.
equívoco, ca, *a.* equivocal, ambiguous. —*m.* equivoque; ambiguity; (Amer., arch.) mistake, error.
equivoque, equivoqué, *ref.* **equivocar.**
equivoquista, *m.* equivocator (one who uses many ambiguities); quibbler; punster.
Er *sym. of* **erbio,** erbium (Er).
era, *f.* era, age, epoch; **e. atómica,** atomic age; **e. común, cristiana** or **de Cristo,** Christian era; **e. espacial** or **de exploración espacial,** space age; **e. glacial,** ice age.
era, *f.* 1. (agr.) threshing floor. 2. vegetable garden, flower bed. 3. (min., bldg.) working yard (for washing minerals; for preparing cement, etc.). 4. (Bol.) vessel where chicha is left to ferment.
era, éramos, *ref.* **ser.**
eral, *m.* young ox or bull (not yet two years old).
erar, *tr.v.* (agr.) to mark out (vegetable patches or flower beds), to lay out (a garden patch).
erario, *m.* national or public funds, exchequer, public treasury.
erasmiano, na, *a., m., f.* (phonet.) Erasmian (following Erasmus' system of Greek pronunciation).
Erasmo, *m.* Erasmus, Dutch scholar and humanist of the 16th century.
Erato, *m.* (myth.) Erato, the muse of lyric poetry.
erbio, *m.* (min.) erbium.
Erebo, *m.* (myth.) Erebus, underworld through which the dead passed before entering Hades.
erección, *f.* 1. erection, raising, building. 2. establishment, founding. 3. (physiol.) erection.
eréctil, *a.* erectile.
erectilidad, *f.* erectility.
erector, ra, *a.* erecting. —*m., f.* **erector, builder; founder.**
eremita, *m.* eremite, hermit; recluse.
eremítico, ca, *a.* eremitic, solitary, hermit-like.
eremitorio, *m.* place with one or more hermitages.
erepsina, *f.* (biochem.) erepsin.
eretísmico, ca, *a.* (med.) erethismic.
eretismo, *m.* (med.) erethism.
ergástula, *f.,* **ergástulo,** *m.* ergastulum (prison for slaves).

ergio, *m.* (phys.) erg, ergon.
ergo, *conj.* (Lat.) ergo, therefore.
ergógrafo, *m.* (med.) ergograph.
ergómetro, *m.* (med.) ergometer.
ergonovina, *f.* (pharm.) ergonovine.
ergosterina, *f.* (chem.) ergosterol.
ergosterol, *m.* (chem.) ergosterol.
ergotamina, *f.* (pharm.) ergotamine.
ergoterapeuta, *m., f.* occupational therapist.
ergoterapia, *f.* occupational therapy.
ergotice, ergoticé, *ref.* **ergotizar.**
ergótico, ca, *a.* (chem.) ergotic.
ergotina, *f.* (pharm.) ergotin.
ergotismo, *m.* 1. (philos.) sophistry. 2. (med.) ergotism.
ergotista, *a.* (philos.) sophistic, arguing, debating. —*m., f.* (philos.) sophist.
ergotizante, *a.* sophistic.
ergotizar, (*ref. 53*) *i.v.* (philos.) to argue or debate fallaciously.
erguen, *m.* (bot.) argan tree.
erguido, da, *past part. of* **erguir.** —*a.* erect; puffed up with pride.
erguimiento, *m.* erection, straightening up.
erguir, (*ref. 44*) *tr.v.* to raise (head), straighten (neck); **e. el busto,** to straighten up. —*r.v.* 1. to stand or sit erect. 2. to straighten (oneself) up. 3. (fig.) to become vain, proud or conceited.
erial, *a.* (agr.) uncultivated, unplowed, untilled (ground). —*m.* (agr.) untilled land.
eriazo, *a.* (agr.) *var. of* **erial.**
ericáceo, a, *a.* (bot.) ericaceous. —*f.* (*pl.*) (bot.) Ericaceae, heath family.
erice, ericé, *ref.* **erizar.**
Eridano, *m.* (astron., myth.) Eridanus.
erigir, (*ref. 62*) *tr.v.* to erect, build, construct; **e. (algo** or **alguien) en,** to raise up (thing, person) to the status of, set (person) up as. —*r.v.* to establish oneself, set oneself up, e.g. *se erigió en juez,* he set himself up as judge.
erija, erijo, *ref.* **erigir.**
Erín, *m.* Erin, ancient and poetic name for Ireland.
erina, *f.* (surg.) forceps.
eringe, *f.* (bot.) eryngo.
Erinias, *f.* (*pl.*) (myth.) Erinyes, the Furies.
erío, a, *a.* (agr.) uncultivated, untilled, unplowed (land).
erisipela, *f.* (med.) erysipelas.
erisipelar, *tr.v.* (med.) to cause erysipelas. —*r.v.* to get erysipelas.
erisipelatoso, sa, *a.* (med.) erysipelatous, erysipelatoid.
erístico, ca, *a.* (philos.) eristic, sophistical.
eritema, *f.* (med.) erythema; **e. solar,** erythema solare, erythema caused by sunburn.
eritreo, a, *a.* Eritrean (of or relating to the Red Sea). —*m.* **E.,** Erythraean main, the Red Sea. —*f.* **E.,** Eritrea, province of Ethiopia.
eritrina, *f.* (min.) erythrite, cobalt bloom.
eritrismo, *m.* (anat., zool.) erythrism, unusual redness of pigmentation.
eritrita, *f.* (chem.) erythritol.
eritroblasto, *m.* (anat.) erythroblast.
eritrocito, *m.* (physiol.) erythrocyte, red corpuscle.
eritrocitómetro, *m.* (med.) erythrocytometer.
eritromicina, *f.* (med.) erythromycin.
eritrón, *m.* (physiol.) erythron.
eritropoyesis, *f.* (physiol.) erythropoiesis.
eritrosina, *f.* (chem.) erythrosin, erythrosine.
eritroxíleo, a, *a.* (bot.) erythroxylaceous. —*f.* erythroxylaceous plant; (*pl.*) Erythroxylaceae.
erizado, da, *past part. of* **erizar.** —*a.* bristly, spiky, spiny; full, bristling, e.g. *un negocio erizado de dificultades,* a business bristling with difficulties.
erizamiento, *m.* bristling, setting on end (e.g. hair, from anger, fear, etc.).
erizar, (*ref. 53*) *r.v.* to bristle; to stand on end (hair); to get goose-pimples (coll.); to stick out; (fig., rare) to become uneasy or ill at ease. —*tr.v.* to bristle, make stand on end, set on end (hair, etc.).
erizo, *m.* 1. (zool.) hedgehog. 2. (bot.) tibourbou. 3. (bot.) bur (of chestnuts, etc.). 4. (ichth.) globefish, puffer. 5. (coll.) crosspatch, bad-tempered person. 6. sprocket wheel, rag wheel. — **e. de mar,** (ichth.) sea urchin, echinus.
erizón, *m.* (bot.) blue genista.
ermita, *f.* hermitage.
ermitaño, ña, *m., f.* hermit. —*m.* (ichth.) hermit crab.
ermitorio, *m.* place with one or more hermitages.
ermunio, *m.* (arch.) one exempt from service or tribute.
erogación, *f.* distribution (of property, wealth); (Amer.) donation, alms.
erogar, (*ref. 51*) *tr.v.* 1. to distribute (wealth or property). 2. (imp. u., Mex.) to cause, originate. 3. (Amer.) to donate, to contribute (money to a cause, etc.).
erogatorio, *m.* pipe for drawing liquids.
erógeno, na, *a.* (psyc.) erogenous, erogenic.
erogue, erogué, *ref.* **erogar.**
Eros, *m.* (myth.) Eros, the god of love.
erosión, *f.* erosion; wearing away.
erosionar, *tr.v.* to erode.
erosivo, va, *a.* erosive.
erotema, *f.* (rhet.) rhetorical question.
eróticamente, *adv.* erotically.
erótico, ca, *a.* erotic, of or arousing sexual feelings or desire.
erotismo, *m.* erotism, sensuality.
erotomanía, *f.* (med.) erotomania, eroticomania.
erotómano, na, *a.* (med.) erotomaniac.
errabundo, da, *a.* errant, wandering.
errada, *f.* miss (in the game of billiards).
erradamente, *adv.* mistakenly, erroneously.
erradicación, *f.* eradication; uprooting, extermination.
erradicar, (*ref. 50*) *tr.v.* to eradicate, tear up by the roots.
erradique, erradiqué, *ref.* **erradicar.**
erradizo, za, *a.* errant, wandering.
errado, da, *past part. of* **errar.** —*a.* mistaken, erring, erroneous.
erraj, *m.* coal made from crushed olive stones.
errante, *a.* wandering, roving, nomadic, rambling.
errar, (*ref. 32*) *tr.v.* to miss (target, vocation); to fail (in one's duty). —*i.v.* 1. to rove, wander, roam; to wander, stray (thoughts). 2. to make a mistake, to err. —*r.v.* to **err,** be mistaken, make a mistake.
errata, *f.* (print.) erratum, misprint, typographical error; **fe de erratas,** list of errata.
errático, ca, *a.* 1. vagabond, wandering. 2. (med., geol.) erratic.
errátil, *a.* erratic, fickle, changeable, wavering; unpredictable.
erre, *f.* Spanish name for the double "r"; **e. que e.,** (coll.) stubbornly, persistently.
errona, *f.* (Chile) miss (by player in a game).
erróneamente, *adv.* erroneously, mistakenly.
erróneo, *a.* erroneous, mistaken.
error, *m.* error; misconception; mistake; **e. craso,** crass error; **e. de curso,** tracking error (of a phonograph record); **e. de derecho,** legal error; **e. de hecho,** factual error; **e. de imprenta** or **tipográfico,** misprint, printer's error. **e. de la brújula,** compass error; **e. tabular,** standard error (in ballistics).
erubescencia, *f.* blush, erubescence.
erubescente, *a.* blushing, red; erubescent.
eructación, *f.* belching, eructation.
eructar, *i.v.* to eructate, belch, burp (coll.).
eructo, *m.* belch, burp, eructation.
erudición, *f.* erudition, learning, scholarship.
eruditamente, *adv.* eruditely, learnedly.
erudito, ta, *a.* erudite, learned, scholarly. —*m., f.* scholar; **e. a la violeta,** dilettante.
eruginoso, sa, *a.* rusty, rusted; musty.
erupción, *f.* eruption (of a volcano, etc.); bursting; (med.) eruption, rash.
eruptivo, va, *a.* eruptive.
erutación, *f., var. of* **eructación.**
erutar, *iv., var. of* **eructar.**
eruto, *m., var. of* **eructo.**
ervato, *m.* (bot.) hog's fennel (Peucedanum officinale).
ervilla, *f.* (bot.) carob, carob bean tree, algarroba; spring vetch (Vicia sativa).
esa, ésa, *f., a., pron.* that, that one, that thing, e.g. *ésa es barata,* that is a cheap one, *no me vengas con ésa,* don't give me that stuff, don't tell me that, *en una de ésas,* one of these times, when you least expect it, *me gusta esa chica,* I like that girl.
esbarar, *i.v.* to slip, slide.
esbatimentante, *a.* (p.) casting a shadow.
esbatimentar, *tr.v.* (p.) to draw a shadow on. —*i.v.* (p.) to cast a shadow.
esbatimento, *m.* (p.) shadow, shade (in a painting or drawing).
esbeltez, esbelteza, *f.* gracefulness, slenderness, litheness.
esbelto, ta, *a.* svelte, graceful, lithe, slender, slim.
esbirro, *m.* 1. constable, bailiff, police officer. 2. (coll.) henchman; underling.
esboce, esbocé, *ref.* **esbozar.**
esbozar, (*ref. 53*) *tr.v.* to sketch; to outline.
esbozo, *m.* sketch, outline; rough draft.
escabechado, da, *past part. of* **escabechar.** —*a.* (coll.) painted up, with dyed hair.
escabechar, *tr.v.* 1. (cul.) to pickle, marinate (fish, meat). 2. (coll.) to dye (grey hair). 3. (coll.) to stab to death. 4. (coll) to fail, flunk (a pupil in an exam.).
escabeche, *m.* 1. (cul.) marinade of oil, vinegar, herbs and spices (to preserve fish, meat, etc.); pickled fish. 2. (coll.) dye for grey hair. 3. (Chile) pickle.
escabechina, *f.* (coll.) havoc, destruction.
escabel, *m.* footstool; stool; small bench; (coll.) stepping stone, foothold (to gain ambitious ends).
escabiosa, *f.* 1. (bot.) scabious. 2. (Col., Cuba) variety of figwort (Capriaria biflora).
escabioso, sa, *a.* (med.) scabious.
escabro, *m.* (vet.) scab, mange (of sheep); scaly bark (disease of tree bark or vines).
escabrosamente, *adv.* roughly, ruggedly; harshly.
escabrosidad, *f.* roughness, ruggedness, cragginess; (fig.) harshness, hardness, asperity.
escabroso, sa, *a.* rough, rugged, craggy (of terrain); hard, harsh (character); scabrous, risqué, salacious (of a novel).
escabuche, *f.* small weeding hoe.
escabullarse, *r.v.* (Amer.) *var. of* **escabullirse.**
escabullimiento, *m.* sneaking out, evasion, slipping away.
escabullirse, (*ref. 65*) *r.v.* to slip (from, through or out); to slither out; to sneak away, to escape.
escacado, da, *a.* (her.) checkered.
escachalandrado, da, *a.* (C. Amer., Col.) untidy, slovenly, dirty.
escachar, *tr.v.* (coll.) to crack; to crush, squash; (imp. u.) to break. —*r.v.* (coll.) to get smashed; to crash, collide.

escacharrar, *tr.v.* to break (crockery); (fig.) to spoil, damage, ruin. —*r.v.* to become broken (of crockery); (fig.) to become damaged or spoilt.
escachifollar, *tr.v.* to humiliate, shame.
escafandro, dra, *m., f.* diver's suit, diving suit; **escafandra autónoma,** scuba; **escafandra espacial,** space suit.
escafilar, *tr.v.* to trim (used bricks or tiles).
escafoides, *a.* (anat.) scaphoid (bone).
escajo, *m.* wasteland, uncultivated land.
escala, *f.* 1. scale; ladder, stepladder. 2. port of call, stopping point, e.g. *el barco hizo e. en Vigo,* the steamer called (made a call) at Vigo. 3. (mil.) register, list. — **e. cerrada,** (mil.) promotion list according to seniority; **e. de calado,** (mar.) draft gauge; **e. cromática,** chromatic scale; **e. de cuerda,** rope ladder; **e. de mar y de tierra,** (mar.) general navy register of men on active and home service; **e. de popa** or **portalón,** (mar.) accommodation ladder; **e. de reserva,** register or list of reserves (military or naval); **e. de valores,** set of values; **e. de viento,** (mar.) rope ladder; **e. diatónica,** (mus.) diatonic scale; **e. franca,** (com.) free port; **e. gráfica,** graphic scale; **e. móvil,** sliding scale; **en gran e.,** on a large scale; ambitiously; **e. real,** royal flush; **e. salarial,** salary or wage scale; **e. telescópica,** extending ladder.
escalable, *a.* scalable, climbable.
escalaborne, *m.* smooth piece of wood (for making gunstock).
escalabrar, *tr.v., var. of* **descalabrar,** to wound on the head.
escalada, *f.* scaling, climbing; **e. en roca,** rock climbing.
escalado, da, *past part. of* **escalar.** —*a.* split (said of fish split for salting).
escalador, ra, *a.* scaling, climbing. —*m., f.* 1. climber, mountain climber. 2. (sl.) housebreaker.
escalafón, *m.* list, roll, register, roster (listing qualifications, seniority, rank, etc.).
escalamiento, *m.* scaling, climbing.
escálamo, *m.* (mar.) rowlock, oarlock, thole (also **escalamera**).
escalar, *tr.v.* 1. (arch., mil.) to escalade (enter using ladders); to break in or into, enter by force. 2. to scale, climb, ascend. 3. to open a sluice or water gate. 4. to split (fish, fowl, etc.) for salting or curing. —*i.v.* (fig.) to rise, climb (by dubious means). —*a.* (math.) scalar.
escaldado, da, *past part. of* **escaldar.** —*a.* 1. (coll.) wary, suspicious. 2. (fig.) lewd, loose (woman).
escaldadura, *f.* 1. scald, scalding. 2. (baby's) diaper or nappy rash.
escaldar, *tr.v.* 1. to scald, burn (with hot liquid). 2. to make red hot (as iron). —*r.v.* 1. to get scalded, burned. 2. to get diaper rash.
escaldo, *m.* skald (ancient Scandinavian writer of epics).
escaleno, *a.* (geom.) scalene.
escalentamiento, *m.* (vet.) inflammation of the feet of animals (or horses' hoofs).
escalera, *f.* 1. ladder; stairs, staircase. 2. sequence, ladder (in cards); straight (in poker). 3. framework of a cart; sides of a cart. 4. (coll.) uneven line or cut (of a bad haircut). — **de e. abajo,** (coll.) menial, downstairs (said of servants); **e. de caracol** or **de husillo,** or **espiral,** spiral staircase; **e. de color** or **real,** royal flush; **e. de emergencia,** emergency stairs; **e. de escapulario,** (min.) hand ladder on the inside of the well; **e. de incendios,** fire escape; **e. de mano,** hand ladder; **e. de servicio,** service stairs; **e. de tierra** or **doble,** stepladder; **e. mecánica,** escalator; **e. telescópica** or **extensible,** aerial ladder.
escalerilla, *f.* 1. small stepladder. 2. sequence of three cards. 3. (vet.) speculum (instrument used to open and explore a horse's mouth). — **en e.,** irregularly arranged.
escalerón, *m.* large ladder (for climbing trees).
escaleta, *f.* a frame for lifting cars or carriages; a kind of jack.
escalfado, da, *past part. of* **escalfar.** —*a.* 1. blistered (said of badly plastered walls). 2. poached (egg).
escalfador, *m.* 1. barber's metal pitcher (for heating water); chafing dish. 2. painter's torch (for removing paint).
escalfar, *tr.v.* 1. to poach (eggs, fish). 2. to burn and blister (bread). —*r.v.* to become burned and blistered (bread).
escalfarote, *m.* boot with double lining to keep the feet warm.
escalfeta, *f.* chafing dish, dish warmer; small brazier.
escalinata, *f.* (archit.) perron, front steps (of a building); grand staircase.
escalio, *m.* uncultivated or abandoned land.
escalla, *m.* (bot.) short-stemmed wheat.
escalmo, *m.* 1. (mar.) thole, tholepin, row-lock. 2. (mec.) wooden wedge (to raise or tighten machine parts).
escalo, *m.* scaling, climbing, ascent; breaking in (to steal); breaking into or out of a closed place.
escalofriado, da, *a.* cold, chilly, chilled, shivering.
escalofrío, *m.* shiver, shudder, chill; **sentir escalofríos de miedo,** (coll.) to shudder from fear, to go hot and cold with fear.
escalón, *m.* 1. step, stair (of staircase), rung (of ladder); rung, step (in career, in promotion); stepping-stone (to obtain something). 2. (mil.) echelon. — **en escalones,** unevenly (cut or shaped).
escalona, *f.* (bot.) shallot.
escalonamiento, *m.* putting or arranging at regular intervals; (mil.) echeloning.
escalonar, *tr.v.* to put or arrange at regular intervals; to post or station at regular intervals; (mil.) to echelon.
escalonia, *f., var. of* **escaloña.**
escaloña *f.* (bot.) shallot, scallion.
escalope, *m.* (cul.) scaloppini; breaded and fried cut of beef, veal or pork.
escalpar, *tr.v.* to scalp, to cut or tear the scalp from.
escalpe, escalpo, *m.* (U.S., hist.) scalp (of the enemy shown for trophy or bounty).
escalpelo, *m.* (surg.) scalpel.
escalplo, *m.* tanner's knife.
escama, *f.* 1. (ichth., zool.) scale; flake, (anything resembling a scale). 2. (coll.) resentment; (coll.) suspicion, mistrust; **tener escamas,** (coll.) to be astute or shrewd.
escamado, da, *past part. of* **escamar.** —*m., f.* scalloped embroidery. —*a.* (coll.) wary, cautious, suspicious.
escamadura, *f.* 1. scaling (of fish). 2. scalloping (of embroidery). 3. a wary or suspicious feeling or mood.
escamar, *tr.v.* 1. to scale (fish). 2. to scallop (embroidery); to fashion scales on (as in metal work, carving, etc.). 3. (coll.) to make suspicious, mistrustful or wary. —*i.v.* to scallop, fashion in scales. —*r.v.* to become suspicious, mistrustful or wary.
escamel, *m.* sword-maker's anvil.
escamocho, cha, *m., f.* left-overs (of food).
escamón, na, *a.* suspicious, mistrustful, wary.
escamonda, *f.* pruning (of trees).
escamondadura, *f.* pruned-off branches.
escamondar, *tr.v.* to prune (trees); (fig.) to prune, trim, cut away (something superfluous); to clean, cleanse.
escamondo, *m.* pruning; clearing of trees.
escamonea, *f.* (bot., pharm.) scammony (cathartic rosin).
escamoneado, da, *past part. of* **escamonearse.** —*a.* with or containing scammony.
escamonearse, *r.v.* (coll.) to become suspicious or wary.
escamosidad, *f.* scaliness.
escamoso, sa, *a.* scaly, squamous.
escamotar, *tr.v., var. of* **escamotear.**
escamoteador, ra, *a.* juggling. —*m., f.* 1. juggler. 2. (coll.) filcher, pickpocket.
escamotear, *tr.v.* to make disappear (by sleight of hand); (coll.) to filch, swipe, lift, steal; to swindle, get something by artful means.
escamoteo, *m.* 1. sleight of hand. 2. (coll.) filching, lifting, swiping.
escampada, *f.* (coll.) bright period (on a rainy day); subsiding rain.
escampado, da, *past part. of* **escampar.** —*a.* clear, open (space, field); uncluttered.
escampar, *tr.v.* to clear (a place); to unclutter. —*i.v.* 1. to stop raining, clear up (weather). 2. (fig.) to cease making an effort. 3. (Col.) to get out of the rain. — **¡ya escampa!,** (coll.) cut it out!.
escampavía, *f.* (mar.) scout (vessel); coast guard cutter.
escampo, *m.* clearing, clearing out, uncluttering.
escamudo, da, *a.* scaly, full of scales.
escamujar, *tr.v.* to prune (a tree).
escamujo, *m.* lopped-off olive branch; pruning season (of olive trees).
escancia, *f.* the act of pouring or serving wine.
escanciador, ra, *m., f.* wine server, wine steward, cupbearer.
escanciano, *m.* wine steward, wine server.
escanciar, *tr.v.* to pour, serve (wine). —*i.v.* to drink wine, e.g. *e. la copa,* to drink to the dregs.
escanda, *f.* (bot.) spelt wheat (Triticum spelta).
escandalar, *m.* (mar.) compass room (in a galley).
escandalera, *f.* (coll.) commotion, rumpus, disturbance.
encandalice, escandalicé, *ref.* **escandalizar.**
escandalizador, ra, *a.* scandalizing, shocking. —*m., f.* scandalizer; troublemaker.
escandalizar, (*ref. 53*) *r.v.* to scandalize, shock, offend. —*r.v.* to become shocked or scandalized; to be annoyed or offended.
escandallar, *tr.v.* 1. (mar.) to sound. 2. to sample, try (to ascertain quality). 3. to assess price of (merchandise).
escandallo, *m.* 1. (mar.) sounding-lead. 2. experiment, trial. 3. (com.) pricing (of goods).
escándalo, *m.* 1. scandal, offense; licentiousness. 2. rumpus, commotion, disturbance, noise. 3. awe, astonishment.
escandalosa, *f.* (mar.) gaff, top sail; **echar la e.,** (coll.) to talk abusively to.
escandalosamente, *adv.* scandalously, disgracefully, shockingly, shamefully.
escandaloso, sa, *a.* 1. scandalous, disgraceful, shocking. 2. noisy, rowdy, turbulent.
escandelar, escandelarete, *m.* (mar.) compass room.
escandia, *f.* (bot.) spelt (wheat).
escandina, *f.* (min.) scandium oxide.
Escandinavia, *f.* Scandinavia.
escandinavo, va, *a., m., f.* Scandinavian.
escandio, *m.* (chem.) scandium.
escandir, *tr.v.* (poet.) to scan (verse).
escansión, *f.* (poet.) scansion.
escantillar, *tr.v.* to gauge, find the exact measurement of; to measure from a point or line; to take the pattern of.

escantillón, *m.* template, templet, pattern.
escaña, *f.* (bot.) spelt (wheat).
escaño, *m.* 1. seat (in parliament or congress); bench. 2. (mar.) sheer-rail.
escañuelo, *m.* footstool.
escapado, da, *a.* escaped, loose. —*m., f.* escapee; fugitive. —*f.* escape, flight; escapade; **darse una e.,** (coll.) to slip out on some errand; to go on a spree.
escapamiento, *m.* escape, flight, fleeing.
escapar, *tr.v.* 1. to make (a horse) gallop, run hard. 2. to save, free. —*i.v.* to escape, flee, run away; to slip out. —*r.v.* 1. to escape, flee, run away; to slip out. 2. to escape, leak (gas, water). — **escapársele a uno una cosa,** to miss, not notice, not see; **se me escapó la lengua,** I said it without thinking; **se me escapó la risa,** I couldn't control my laughter; **se escaparon de la cárcel,** they escaped from jail.
escaparate, *m.* 1. shop window, display window. 2. glass case, display cabinet. 3. (Amer.) wardrobe, closet.
escaparatista, *m., f.* window dresser.
escapatoria, *f.* escape, flight; (coll.) way out, excuse, evasion, subterfuge; loophole.
escape, *m.* 1. escape; flight. 2. leak (of gas, water). 3. escapement (of watch). 4. exhaust, exhaust pipe. — **a e.,** at breakneck speed; **e. de áncora,** anchor escapement (of watch); **tubo de e.,** exhaust pipe.
escapífero, a, *a.* (bot.) scapose.
escapiforme, *a.* (bot.) scapiform.
escapismo, *m.* (psyc.) escapism.
escapista, *a.* escapist.
escapo, *m.* 1. (archit.) scape, shaft of column. 2. (bot.) scape.
escapolita, *f.* (min.) scapolite.
escápula, *f.* (anat.) scapula, shoulder blade.
escapular, *tr.v.* (mar.) to round (a cape), clear (a reef or other obstacle). —*a.* (anat.) scapular.
escapulario, *m.* (ecc.) scapular, scapulary.
escaque, *m.* square (on a chessboard, coat of arms); (*pl.*) chess (game).
escaqueado, da, *a.* checkered.
escara, *f.* (med.) eschar, scab, crust, slough.
escarabajear, *tr.v.* (coll.) to worry, bother, annoy. —*i.v.* 1. to crawl about. 2. to scribble, scrawl, doodle.
escarabajeo, *m.* 1. harassment, worry. 2. scrawling, scribbling, doodling.
escarabajo, *m.* 1. (ento.) scarab, black beetle; scarabaeus. 2. (fig.) flaw (in metal or fabric). 3. (coll.) runt, midget. 4. (artil.) small hole in cannon. 5. (coll.) (*pl.*) scrawl, scribble. — **e. de resorte,** (ento.) click beetle.
escarabajuelo, *m.* (ento.) flea beetle, vine beetle (Altica ampelophaga).
escarabeido, da, *a., m.* (ento.) scarabaeid.
escarabeino, na, *a., m.* (ento.) scarabaean.
escaramuce, escaramucé, *ref.* **escaramuzar.**
escaramucear, *i.v.* to engage in a skirmish, to skirmish.
escaramujo, *m.* 1. (bot.) dog rose. 2. (zool.) goose barnacle (Mitella polymerus). 3. (Cuba) evil eye, spell.
escaramuza, *f.* skirmish; quarrel, dispute.
escaramuzador, *m.* skirmisher, quarreler.
escaramuzar, (*ref. 53*) *i.v.* 1. to skirmish, engage in a skirmish. 2. to turn from one side to another (horse).
escarapela, *f.* 1. badge, cockade, emblem or trimming (worn on the hat or helmet). 2. dispute, wrangle, quarrel, free-for-all.
escarapelar, *i.v.* 1. to wrangle, quarrel, fight, argue. 2. (Amer.) to shell, peel. 3. (Col.) to rumple, crease. —*r.v.* (Mex., Peru) to get goose flesh.
escarbadero, *m.* place where animals scrape or dig the ground.
escarbadientes, *m.* toothpick.
escarbador, ra, *a.* scratching, scraping. —*m.* scratcher, scraper.
escarbadura, *f.* scraping, scratch, digging.
escarbaorejas, *m.* earpick.
escarbar, *tr.v.* 1. to scratch, scrape, dig (the ground); to paw (the ground). 2. to pick (teeth, ears). 3. to poke, rake (a fire). 4. (fig.) to dig up, investigate, unearth (a secret).
escarbillos, *m.* (*pl.*) cinders.
escarbo, *m.* scratching, scraping, digging.
escarcear, *i.v.* (Arg., Ven.) to caracole, curvet (a horse).
escarcela, *f.* 1. belt pouch; (hunt.) game bag. 2. hairnet, coif. 3. (arch.) cuisse (of armor).
escarceo, *m.* 1. (mar.) choppiness (of the sea). 2. (fig.) digression, circumlocution. 3. (*pl.*) caracoles, caracolling, curvetting (of a horse).
escarcha, *f.* frost, hoarfrost, rime.
escarchada, *f.* (bot.) ice plant (Mesembryanthemum crystallynum).
escarchado, da, *past part. of* **escarchar.** —*a.* frosted, frosty. —*m.* gold or silver frostwork, frost-like embroidery in gold or silver.
escarchador, ra, *a.* frosting. —*m.* freezing tool.
escarchar, *tr.v.* 1. to ice, freeze; to frost (a cake); to frost, give (a surface) the appearance of frost. 2. to dilute (potter's clay). 3. to make sugar crystallize on an anis branch (in a bottle of brandy). —*i.v.* to become frosty, get frosty; to become covered with frost.
escarche, *m.* 1. *var. of* **escarcha.** 2. frost-work.
escarcho, *m.* (ichth.) gurnard red surmullet (Trigla lyra).
escarcina, *f.* cutlass, short curved sword.
escarcinazo, *m.* blow with a cutlass.
escarcuñar, *tr.v., var. of* **escudriñar.**
escarda, *f.* the action and effect of weeding; weeding hoe.
escardadera, *f.* 1. weeder (woman). 2. weeding hoe.
escardador, ra, *m., f.* weeder (person).
escardadura, *f.* weeding.
escardamiento, *m.* weeding.
escardar, *tr.v.* 1. to weed, weed out. 2. to weed out, remove, take out (bad from good).
escardilla, *f.* small weeding hoe.
escardillar, *tr.v., var. of* **escardar.**
escardillo, *m.* 1. small weeding hoe. 2. thistledown. 3. sparkle, reflection (of a shiny object in the dark).
escariador, *m.* (mec.) reamer.
escariar, *tr.v.* (mec.) to ream.
escarice, escaricé, *ref.* **escarizar.**
escarificación. *f.* (surg.) scarification.
escarificador, *m.* 1. (agr.) harrow, scarifier. 2. (surg.) scarificator, scarifier. — **e. de discos,** (agr.) disk harrow.
escarificar, (*ref. 50*) *tr.v.* 1. (agr., surg.) to scarify. 2. (surg.) to remove slough or a scab from.
escarifique, escarifiqué, *ref.* **escarificar.**
escarioso, sa, *a.* (bot.) scarious.
escarizar, (*ref. 53*) *tr.v.* (surg.) to remove the slough or scab from.
escarlador, *m.* comb polisher (in comb manufacture).
escarlata, *f.* 1. scarlet (color). 2. scarlet cloth; fine cloth. 3. (med.) scarlet fever.
escarlatina, *f.* 1. red woolen cloth. 2. (med.) scarlet fever, scarlatina.
escarlatiniforme, *a.* (med.) similar to scarlatina.
escarlatinoide, *a.* (med.) scarlatinoid.
escarmenador, *m.* (tex.) teaseller, carder, comb for wool.
escarmenar, *tr.v.* 1. to comb, disentangle (hair, yarn). 2. (fig.) to punish, give a dressing-down. 3. (fig.) to cheat, swindle a little at a time. 4. (min.) to pick out (the ore from the waste).
escarmentado, da, *past part. of* **escarmentar.** —*a.* taught by punishment or experience.
escarmentar, (*ref. 29*) *tr.v.* to correct severely, punish, chastise. —*i.v.* **e. en cabeza** ajena, to learn from another's mistakes.
escarmiente, escarmiento, *ref.* **escarmentar.**
escarmiento, *m.* warning, lesson (gained from punishment or experience), e.g. *que te sirva de e.,* let it be a lesson to you.
escarnecedor, ra, *a.* derisive, scoffing, ridiculing. —*m., f.* derider, ridiculer, scoffer.
escarnecer, (*ref. 45*) *tr.v.* to ridicule, deride, mock, jeer at.
escarnecidamente, *adv.* scoffingly, mockingly, derisively.
escarnecimiento, *m., var. of* **escarnio.**
escarnezca, escarnezco, *ref.* **escarnecer.**
escarnio, *m.* derision, mocking; scoff, jeer.
escaro, ra, *m.* (ichth.) scarus, parrot fish (Scarus cretensis). —*a.* having crooked feet or ankles.
escarola, *f.* 1. (bot.) endive. 2. ruffled collar, ruff.
escarolado, da, *past part. of* **escarolar.** —*a.* curled, frilled, ruffled.
escarolar, *tr.v.* to curl, frill, ruffle.
escarótico, ca, *a.* (surg.) escharotic, cauterizing, caustic.
escarpa, *f.* 1. scarp, rough slope. 2. (mil.) scarp, escarpment.
escarpado, da, *past part. of* **escarpar.** —*a.* steep; craggy, rugged.
escarpadura, *f.* scarp, rugged slope.
escarpar, *tr.v.* 1. (carp., sculp.) to rasp, scrape. 2. to escarp, slope.
escarpe, *m.* 1. scarp, escarpment, ragged slope. 2. (carp.) scarf, scarf joint. 3. solleret (of armor).
escarpelo, *m.* 1. (surg.) scalpel. 2. (carp., sculp.) rasp.
escarpia, *f.* hooked nail, tenterhook, spike.
escarpiador, *m.* clamp, fastener (for water pipes).
escarpidor, *m.* large-toothed comb.
escarpín, *m.* 1. thin-soled open shoe, pump. 2. spat, short cloth gaiter. 3. (Amer.) sock, bobby sock. 4. (Amer.) (*pl.*) baby's booties.
escarpión, en e., in the form of or shaped like a tenterhook.
escarramanado, da, *a.* ruffianly, bullying, lawless.
escarrancharse, *r.v.* (Cuba, Ven.) to spread one's legs wide.
escarza, *f.* (vet.) sore (on a horse's hoof).
escarzano, *a.* (archit.) segmental (arch.).
escarzar, (*ref. 53*) *tr.v.* 1. to bend (a stick) into an arc by means of cords. 2. to remove (damaged honeycombs from the beehive).
escarzo, *m.* 1. dirty honeycomb; removal of dirty honeycombs; season when such honeycombs are removed. 2. floss (of silk). 3. punk, bracket fungus.
escasamente, *adv.* 1. scantily, scarcely. 2. barely; hardly.
escasear, *tr.v.* 1. to give sparingly or reluctantly, skimp; to reduce, decrease, be sparing (of, with), save. 2. (mas., carp.) to bevel, cut at an angle. —*i.v.* to be or become scarce or rare, e.g. *las fresas escasean en enero,* strawberries are scarce in January.
escasero, ra, *a., m., f.* (coll.) scarce, hard to get.
escasez, (*pl.* **escaseces**) *f.* 1. scarcity, lack, dearth, shortage. 2. miserliness, meagerness, niggardliness, stinginess (coll.). 3. poverty, want, need.
escaso, sa, *a.* 1. scarce, short, limited; scanty, scant, meager. 2. mean, niggardly, miserly; frugal, skimpy.

escatimado, da, *past part. of* **escatimar.** —*a.* little, meager, skimpy.
escatimar, *tr.v.* 1. to skimp, scrimp, give sparingly. 2. (rare) to use (words) incorrectly.
escatimosamente, *adv.* cunningly, craftily.
escatimoso, sa, *a.* cunning, crafty, malicious.
escatofagia, *f.* (zool., med.) coprophagy, eating of excrement.
escatófago, ga, *a.* (zool.) coprophagous, scatophagous.
escatófilo, la, *a.* (ento.) coprophilous.
escatol, *m.* (chem.) skatole, skatol.
escatología, *f.* 1. (theol.) eschatology (doctrine of death, resurrection, etc.). 2. scatology (the study of feces).
escatológico, ca, *a.* 1. (theol.) eschatological. 2. scatologic.
escaupil, *m.* 1. quilted battle tunic used by ancient Mexicans. 2. (C. Rica) hunter's bag.
escaut, *m., f.* (Amer.) boy or girl scout.
escavanar, *tr.v.* (agr.) to hoe, loosen the soil (in weeding).
escayola, *f.* scagliola; stucco, plaster.
escena, *f.* 1. scene, scenery. 2. stage (of theater). 3. theater, stage, acting (as a profession). 4. drama, theater (literary genre). 5. sight, view. 6. (fig.) scene, episode. — **desaparecer de e.,** to disappear from the scene; to die; **e. retrospectiva,** flashback (in film); **hacer una e.,** to make a scene; **poner en e.,** to stage, present (a play); **puesta en e.,** (theat.) staging; **director de e.,** stage director.
escenario, *m.* 1. (theat.) stage, scenery. 2. (fig.) setting, background. 3. (fig.) the center of attention. — **e. giratorio,** (theat.) revolving stage.
escénico, ca, *a.* scenic, (pertaining to the stage or stage effects); **arte e.,** acting, drama, dramatic art, e.g. *escuela de arte e.,* school of dramatic art; **efectos escénicos,** stage effects.
escenificación, *f.* staging, dramatization, adaptation (of literary work) for the stage.
escenificar, (*ref. 50*) *tr.v.* to stage, adapt for the stage, dramatize.
escenifique, escenifiqué, *ref.* **escenificar.**
escenografía, *f.* scenography.
escenográficamente, *adv.* scenographically.
escenográfico, ca, *a.* scenographic.
escenógrafo, *m.* (theat.) scenographer, set designer.
escepticismo, *m.* skepticism, scepticism.
escéptico, ca, *a.* skeptical, sceptical. —*m., f.* skeptic, sceptic.
esciente, *a.* knowing.
escifozoario, *m.* (zool.) scyphozoan.
escila, *f.* 1. (bot.) squill, sea onion (Urginea maritima). 2. **E.,** Scylla. — **entre E. y Caribdis,** (fig.) between Scylla and Charibdis, between two evils.
escíncidos, *m.* (*pl.*) (zool.) Scincidae.
escinco, *m.* (zool.) skink; adda.
escindir, *tr.v.* to divide, split, separate.
escintilación, *f.* (astron.) scintillation.
escintilar, *i.v.* to scintillate; to sparkle, twinkle.
escirro, *m.* (med.) scirrhus, tumor.
escirroso, sa, *a.* (med.) scirrhous.
escisión, *f.* 1. division, splitting, cleavage, schism. 2. (med.) excision, cutting out. — **e. nuclear,** (phys.) nuclear fission.
escita, *a., m., f.* Scythian.
escítico, ca, *a.* Scythian.
esciúrido, da, *a.* (zool.) sciuroid.
esclarea, *f.* (bot.) clary, clary sage.
esclarecedor, ra, *a.* enlightening, illuminating; elucidating. —*m., f.* enlightener; elucidator.
esclarecer, (*ref. 45*) *tr.v.* 1. to lighten, illuminate, brighten. 2. (fig.) to clarify, make clear, elucidate. 3. (fig.) to make famous or eminent. —*i.v.* to dawn, get light.
esclarecidamente, *adv.* illustriously, eminently.
esclarecido, da, *past part. of* **esclarecer.** —*a.* outstanding, eminent, distinguished, renowned, illustrious.
esclarecimiento, *m.* 1. clearing up (of a crime); explanation, elucidation. 2. illumination. 3. ennoblement.
esclarezca, esclarezco, *ref.* **esclarecer.**
esclavice, esclavicé, *ref.* **esclavizar.**
esclavina, *f.* shoulder cape (of a coat or cloak); pelerine, tippet.
esclavista, *a.* pro-slavery. —*m., f.* advocate of slavery.
esclavitud, *f.* 1. slavery, servitude. 2. religious brotherhood or congregation. 3. (fig.) slavery, domination.
esclavizar, (*ref. 53*) *tr.v.* 1. to enslave; to make a slave of (someone). 2. to dominate, subjugate; drive hard.
esclavo, va, *a.* enslaved; (fig.) subjected, dominated. —*m., f.* 1. slave. 2. member of a religious brotherhood or congregation. — **e. ladino,** slave with more than one year of slavery. —*f.* bangle, slave bracelet.
esclavonía, *f.* (Chile) religious brotherhood or congregation.
esclavonio, nia, *a.* (geog.) Slavonian, Slavonic (of or from Slavonia). —*m., f.* Slavonian, Slav.
esclerénquima, *m.* (bot., biol.) sclerenchyma.
escleriasis, *f.* (med.) scleriasis.
escleritis, *f.* (med.) scleritis.
esclerodermia, *f.* (med.) scleroderma (a disease of the skin).
escleroftalmia, *f.* (med.) escleropthalmia.
escleroma, *m.* (med.) scleroma; sclerosis.
esclerómetro, *m.* (min.) sclerometer.
esclerósico, ca, *a.* (med.) pertaining to sclerosis.
esclerosis, *f.* (med.) sclerosis; a hardening of body tissues or parts. — **e. múltiple,** multiple sclerosis.
escleroso, sa, *a.* pertaining to sclerosis; sclerotic.
esclerótico, ca, *a.* sclerotic. —*f.* (anat.) sclera, sclerotic.
esclerotitis, *f.* (med.) sclerotitis.
esclerotomía, *f.* (surg.) sclerotomy.
esclusa, *f.* lock, sluice; floodgate, milldam.
escoa, *f.* point of greatest curvature (of a ship's rib).
escoba, *f.* broom; (bot.) broom; **e. amarga,** (bot., Cuba) bastard feverfew; **e. amargosa,** (bot., Hond.) canchalagua (Centaurium chilensis).
escobada, *f.* sweep, stroke (with a broom); light sweeping, quick sweep.
escobadera, *f.* sweeper, sweeping-woman.
escobajo, *m.* 1. old broom. 2. stalk of a bunch of grapes (after fruit has been removed).
escobar, *tr.v.* to sweep (with a broom). —*m.* (bot.) broom field or thicket.
escobazar, (*ref. 53*) *tr.v.* to sprinkle with a wet broom or branch.
escobazo, *m.* blow given with a broom; sweeping stroke, sweep (with a broom). — **echar (a uno) a escobazos,** (fig.) to kick out (someone).
escobero, ra, *m., f.* broom maker or vendor. —*f.* (bot.) Spanish broom.
escobeta, *f.* 1. small brush. 2. (Mex.) tuft of hair on an old turkey's neck.
escobetear, *tr.v.* (Mex.) to sweep (with a broom).
escobilla, *f.* 1. brush. 2. gold or silver sweepings. 3. (elec.) brush (of a dynamo). 4. (bot.) teasel, wild teasel (plant and bur). 5. (bot.) heather, heath. 6. (Cuba, Chile) tuft of hair on turkey's neck. — **e. amarga,** (C. Rica) garden cress; **e. positiva,** (elec.) positive brush.
escobillado, *past part. of* **escobillar.** —*m.* (Arg., Chile) quick tapping (of feet in certain dances).
escobillar, *tr.v.* 1. to brush. 2. (Amer.) to tap the feet (in certain dances).
escobilleo, *m.* (Arg., Chile) quick tapping (of feet in certain dances).
escobillón, *m.* 1. (artil.) swab. 2. large broom.
escobina, *f.* sawdust (produced by drilling); filings (of metal).
escobo, *m.* thick brushwood; brambles, briers.
escobón, *m.* 1. *aug. of* **escoba,** long-handled broom, short-handled broom, chimney sweeper's brush. 2. (bot.) broom.
escocedura, *f.* inflammation, irritation (of skin), burning itch.
escocer, (*ref. 75*) *tr.v.* to annoy, vex. —*i.v.* to smart, sting. —*r.v.* 1. (fig.) to be sorry. 2. to become red, inflamed or irritated.
escocés, sa, *a.* 1. Scottish, Scots, Scotch. 2. plaid (material). —*m., f.* Scot (native). —*m.* 1. Scotsman. 2. Scotch plaid (cloth). 3. Scotch, Scottish (language). —*f.* Scotswoman.
escocia, *f.* 1. (ichth.) codfish. 2. (archit.) scotia.
Escocia, *f.* Scotland.
escocimiento, *m.* burning, smarting, stinging, chafing.
escoda, *f.* (mas.) bricklayer's or stonecutter's hammer.
escodadero, *m.* (hunt.) place where stags rub the velvet from their horns.
escodar, *tr.v.* 1. to hew, cut (stones). 2. (hunt.) to shake the antlers to free them of velvet.
escofia, *f.* coif, cap.
escofiar, *tr.v.* to put a coif on. —*r.v.* to put a coif on one's head.
escofieta, *f.* gauze coif (formerly worn by women); hairnet; (Cuba) baby's bonnet.
escofina, *f.* coarse file, rasp; **e. de ajustar,** wood rasp.
escofinar, *tr.v.* to rasp, file.
escogedor, ra, *a.* choosing, selecting. —*m., f.* chooser, picker, selector.
escoger, (*ref. 57*) *tr.v.* to choose, select, pick.
escogida, *f.* 1. (Amer.) grading, sorting (of tobacco). 2. (Cuba) tobacco grading or sorting room.
escogidamente, *adv.* discerningly, discriminatingly, aptly; selectively; perfectly, excellently.
escogido, da, *past part. of* **escoger.** —*a.* selected, chosen; select, choice.
escogiente, *a.* choosing, selecting.
escogimiento, *m.* choice, selection; choosing.
escoja, escojo, *ref.* **escoger.**
escolanía, *f.* (Sp.) body of trainee acolytes or choir scholars.
escolano, *m.* (formerly) trainee acolyte; choir scholar (in certain Spanish monasteries).
escolapio, pia, *a.* of or pertaining to the Scuole Pie (religious schools in Rome). —*m.* Piarist (cleric). —*f.* Piarist (nun). —*m., f.* student of the Scuole Pie.
escolar, *a.* scholastic, pertaining to a student or school. —*m., f.* scholar, pupil, student.
escolar, (*ref. 33*) *i.v., r.v.* to squeeze through.
escolaridad, *f.* (school) courses, curriculum.
escolariego, ga, *a.* scholarly, pertaining to scholars or students.
escolástica, *f., var. of* **escolasticismo.**
escolásticamente, *adv.* scholastically.
escolasticismo, *m.* scholasticism; (philos., rel.) Scholasticism.
escolástico, ca, *a.* scholastic, academic; (philos.) Scholastic. —*m.* (philos.) Schoolman, Scholastic.
escolecita, *f.* (min.) scolecite.
escoleta, *f.* (Mex.) amateur music band.
escólex, *m.* (zool.) scolex, head of a tapeworm.

escoliador, ra, *m., f.* scholiast, commentator, annotator.
escoliar, *tr.v.* to annotate, explain, comment on.
escoliasta, *m., var. of* **escoliador.**
escolimado, da, *a.* (coll.) delicate, weak, puny, rickety, sickly.
escolimoso, sa, *a.* (coll.) crabby, peevish, disagreeable.
escolio, *m.* scholium, comment, annotation.
escoliosis, *f.* (med.) scoliosis, lateral curvature of spine.
escollar, *i.v.* (Arg.) to hit a reef, run aground on a reef. 2. (Arg., Chile) to fail, come to grief (a project).
escollera, *f.* breakwater, jetty.
escollo, *m.* 1. reef. 2. (fig.) danger, pitfall; obstacle, difficulty.
escolopendra, *f.* 1. (zool.) scolopendrid, centipede. 2. (bot.) hart's-tongue fern. 3. irridescent green marine annelid.
escolta, *f.* escort; convoy, guard.
escoltar, *tr.v.* to escort; to convoy.
escombra, *f.* clearing, cleaning; sweeping.
escombrar, *tr.v.* 1. to clear of rubble or obstacles, clear. 2. to clear, sweep. 3. to remove the bad raisins from (the cluster).
escombrera, *f.* 1. dump, rubble heap. 2. rubble, debris.
escombro, *m.* 1. small inferior raisin. 2. (*pl.*) rubble, debris; (min.) deads. 3. (ichth.) mackerel.
escomendrijo, *m.* (coll.) small puny person, runt.
escomerse, *r.v.* to wear away, erode.
esconce, *m.* corner, angle.
esconce, esconcé, *ref.* **esconzar.**
escondedero, *m.* hiding or lurking place.
esconder, *tr.v.* to hide, conceal. *r.v.* to hide, hide oneself. — **tirar la piedra y e. la mano,** to be a hypocrite.
escondidamente, *adv.* secretly, on the sly.
escondidas, *f.* (*pl.*) (Amer.) hide-and-seek; **a e.,** secretly.
escondidillas, a e., on the sly.
escondido, *m.* hiding; (Amer.) hide-and-seek.
escondimiento, *m.* hiding, concealment.
escondite, *m.* 1. hide-and-seek. 2. hiding place; hideaway. — **jugar al e.,** to play hide-and-seek.
escondrijo, *m.* hiding place; hideaway, hideout.
esconzado, da, *past part. of* **esconzar.** —*a.* angular, cornered, having corners.
esconzar, (*ref.* 53) *tr.v.* to corner, provide with corners or angles.
escopeta, *f.* shotgun, rifle. — **e. de aire** or **aire comprimido** or **viento,** air gun, air rifle; **e. de dos cañones,** double-barreled shotgun; **e. negra,** professional hunter; **e. recortada** or **de cañones recortados; como una e.,** (fig.) like a shot, quickly.
escopetar, *tr.v.* (min.) to remove earth from (gold mine).
escopetazo, *m.* 1. gunshot, rifle shot; gunshot wound. 2. (fig.) sudden bad news.
escopetear, *tr.v.* to shoot at with a rifle or shotgun. —*r.v.* (fig., coll.) to shower each other (with), exchange (insults, compliments).
escopeteo, *m.* gunshot fire.
escopetería, *f.* riflemen, troops armed with rifles. 2. volley of gunshots.
escopetero, *m.* 1. rifleman, musketeer. 2. gunsmith, gun maker or seller. 3. huntsman.
escopetilla, *f. dim. of* **escopeta;** small gun; small cannon.
escopetón, *m. aug. of* **escopeta,** large gun or rifle; large unwieldy rifle.
escopladura, escopleadura, *f.* cut, groove (carved in wood with a chisel).
escoplear, *tr.v.* (carp.) to chisel, notch.
escoplillo, ito, *m. dim. of* **escoplo,** small chisel.
escoplo, *m.* (carp.) chisel; **e. de cantera,** (mas.) stonecutter's chisel.
escopolamina, *f.* (chem.) scopolamine, scopolamin.
escora, *f.* 1. (mar.) line running through widest point of curvature. 2. (mar.) shore, prop (in shipbuilding). 3. (mar.) list, heel.
escorar, *tr.v.* (mar.) to shore or prop up. —*i.v.* 1. (mar.) to list, heel. 2. (mar.) to reach low tide. —*r.v.* (Cuba, Hond.) to seek shelter, take shelter (behind something).
escorbútico, *a.* scorbutic.
escorbuto, *m.* (med.) scurvy.
escorce, escorcé, *ref.* **escorzar.**
escorchapín, *m.* ancient sailing vessel.
escorchar, *tr.v.* to skin, flay.
escordio, *m.* (bot.) water germander (Teucrium scordium).
escoria, *f.* 1. scoria, slag, scum, dross (of molten metal). 2. scoria, volcanic ash or cinders. 3. (fig.) trash, muck; dregs, scum, e.g. *e. de la humanidad,* scum of the earth. — **e. de cemento,** cement clinker; **e. de fundición,** slag.
escoriáceo, a, *a.* (min.) scoriaceous.
escoriación, *f.* skinning, flaying.
escorial, *m.* slag heap or dump; heap of slag.
escoriar, *tr.v.* to skin, flay.
escorificación, *f.* (chem.) scorification.
escorificar, *tr.v.* 1. (chem.) to scorify. 2. (metal.) to reduce to scoria.
escoriforme, *a.* scoriform.
escorpena, escorpera, *f. var. of* **escorpina.**
escorpina, *f.* (ichth.) (species of) scorpene, hogfish (Scorpaena porcus).
Escorpio, *m.* (astron.) Scorpio.
escorpioide, *a.* (bot.) scorpioid. —*f.* (bot.) variety of coronilla (Coronilla scorpioidea).
escorpión, *m.* 1. (ento.) scorpion. 2. (ichth.) scorpion fish. 3. military catapult, form of ancient ballister. 4. scorpion, cat-o-nine tails with metal points. 5. (astron., astrol.) **E.,** Scorpio.
escorpionídeo, dea, *a., m., f.* (zool.) scorpaenoid.
escorrozo, *m.* (coll.) enjoyment, pleasure.
escorzado, *past part. of* **escorzar.** —*m., var. of* **es-corzo.**
escorzar, (*ref.* 53) *tr.v.* 1. (p.) to foreshorten. 2. to reduce, to abridge.
escorzo, *m.* (p.) foreshortening; foreshortened figure.
escorzón, *m.* (zool.) toad (Ceratophrys ornata).
escorzonera, *f.* (bot.) black salsify, viper's grass.
escoscar, (*ref.* 50) *tr.v.* 1. to remove dandruff from. 2. to shell (nuts). —*r.v.* to shrug one's shoulders.
escosque, escosqué, *ref.* **escoscar.**
escota, *f.* (mar.) sheet.
escotado, *past part. of* **escotar.** —*m., var. of* **escotadura.**
escotadura, *f.* 1. neckline, neck (of a garment). 2. armhole (of ancient armor). 3. (theat.) large trap door (of stage).
escotar, *tr.v.* 1. to cut (to fit or shape). 2. to drain. 3. to pay one's share of (a common expenditure).
escote, *m.* 1. neck, neckline; low or décolleté neck or neckline. 2. breast showing above neckline. 3. lace collar or frill. 4. share, quota; **ir al e.,** to go Dutch.
escotero, ra, *a.* 1. travelling light, untrammeled; free. 2. (mar.) unaccompanied, (said of a vessel sailing alone).
escotilla, *f.* (mar.) hatchway.
escotillón, *m.* 1. trap door. 2. (mar.) scuttle. 3. (theat.) stage trap.
escotín, *m.* (mar.) topsail sheet.
escotismo, *m.* (philos.) Scotism (doctrine of Scotus).
escotista, *a., m., f.* Scotist.
escotoma, *m.* (med.) scotoma.
escotomía, *f.* (med.) scotomy.
escozor, *m.* 1. burning, smarting, stinging; itching. 2. sorrow, grief.
escriba, *m.* scribe (teacher of Jewish law).
escribanía, *f.* 1. court clerkship, office of court clerk. 2. office or profession of a notary. 3. writing desk. 4. writing materials.
escribanil, *a.* notarial; pertaining to a notary or clerk.
escribano, na, *m.* 1. notary. 2. court clerk. 3. judge's secretary. 4. amanuensis, clerk. 5. expert in penmanship, penman. — **e. del agua,** (ento.) whirligig beetle (Gyrinus natator). —*f.* wife of a notary or court clerk; notary, court clerk; (Arg.) lady notary.
escribido, da, (imp. u.) *a.* derog. used only in the idiom: **leído y escribido,** (coll.) half-educated (person posing as learned).
escribidor, ra, *m., f.* (coll.) poor writer, scribbler.
escribiente, *m., f.* amanuensis, clerk, scribe, scrivener.
escribir, *tr.v.* to write. —*r.v.* to enroll, enlist (in); to communicate with (others) in writing. — **máquina de e.,** typewriter; **papel de e.,** writing paper (stationery).
escriño, *m.* straw basket (for carrying bran or chaff of grain); casket, coffer, jewel box.
escripia, *f.* fisherman's reed basket.
escrita, *f.* (ichth.) mottled skate.
escritilla, *f.* (*pl.*) (cul.) lamb's fries.
escrito, ta, *irr. past part. of* **escribir.** —*m.* 1. writing, document, manuscript. 2. (*pl.*) writings, works (of an author). 3. (law) writ; brief; plea, pleading; petition, application. — **e. de calificación,** (law) indictment; **e. de conclusión** or **de conclusiones,** (law) brief, conclusion of plea; **por e.,** in writing.
escritor, ra, *m.* writer, author; journalist. —*f.* authoress, writer; journalist.
escritorcillo, lla, *dim. of* **escritor.** —*m., f.* scribbler, would-be writer.
escritorio, *m.* 1. writing desk. 2. study, office. 3. jewel cabinet.
escritorzuelo, la, *m., f.* (derog.) mediocre writer.
escritura, *f.* 1. writing. 2. handwriting, penmanship. 3. document; (law) deed; instrument; contract, indenture. 4. (literary) work, writing. — **e. de propiedad,** (law) title deed.
Escritura, *f.* (Bib.) Scripture; the Bible (*gen. in pl.*). — **la Sagrada E.,** Holy Writ, Holy Scripture.
escriturar, *tr.v.* (law) to notarize, execute by deed.
escriturario, a, *a.* (law) notarial. —*m.* scripturist, one who explains the Scriptures.
escrófula, *f.* (med.) scrofula.
escrofularia, *f.* (bot.) figwort.
escrofulariáceo, a, *a.* (bot.) scrophulariaceous. —*f.* (bot.) Scrophularia; (*pl.*) Scrophulariaceae.
escrofulismo, *m.* (med.) scrofulism.
escrofuloso, sa, *a.* (med.) scrofulous.
escrotal, *a.* (med.) scrotal.
escroto, *m.* (anat.) scrotum.
escrupulice, escrupulicé, *ref.* **escrupulizar.**
escrupulillo, *m.* pellet or little ball (inside a jingle bell or rattle).
escrupulizar, (*ref.* 53) *i.v.* to have scruples, qualms, misgivings.
escrúpulo, *m.* 1. scruple; misgiving, qualm. 2. conscientiousness, scrupulousness. 3. pebble (which gets into the shoe). 4. (astron.) minute.

5. (pharm.) scruple (ancient weight). — **e. de monja,** puerile foolish misgiving; **no tener escrúpulos,** to have no scruples, be unscrupulous.

escrupulosamente, *adv.* scrupulously, thoroughly, carefully; conscientiously.

escrupulosidad, *f.* scrupulousness, thoroughness, carefulness; conscientiousness.

escrupuloso, sa, *a.* scrupulous, thorough, careful, punctilious; conscientious, responsible; exact, precise.

escrutador, ra, *a.* scrutinizing, examining; (fig.) searching (look). —*m., f.* inspector (of electoral votes); examiner.

escrutar, *tr.v.* to scrutinize, examine, inspect; to count, make a scrutiny of (electoral votes).

escrutinio, *m.* scrutiny, careful examination; scrutiny (of electoral votes), counting of votes.

escrutiñador, ra, *m., f.* scrutinizer, examiner, investigator.

escuadra, *f.* 1. (drawing) triangle, set square; carpenter's square. 2. (carp.) corner brace, angle iron. 3. (mil.) squad (of soldiers); post of squad corporal. 4. squad, gang, crew (of workers). 5. (mar.) squadron. 6. (carp.) scantling. — **a e.,** at right angles; **e. ajustable,** caliper square; **e. de agrimensor,** cross staff; **e. falsa,** bevel square; **e. sutil,** light coast guard fleet.

escuadración, *f.* squaring.

escuadrador, *m.* squaring tool.

escuadrar, *tr.v.* (mas., carp.) to square.

escuadreo, *m.* squaring (finding the number of areal units in a given area); quadrature.

escuadría, *f.* scantling (of timber); **square.**

escuadrilla, *f.* squadron of small ships; (air) squadron.

escuadro, *m.* (ichth.) mottled skate.

escuadrón, *m.* (mil.) squadron (of cavalry).

escuadronar, *tr.v.* (mil.) to squadron, form into squadrons.

escuadroncete, *m. dim. of* **escuadrón,** troop, small squadron (of cavalry).

escuadronista, *m.* (mil.) cavalry tactician.

escualidez, *f.* 1. squalor, filth. 2. gauntness, emaciation.

escuálido, da, *a.* 1. squalid, filthy. 2. emaciated, thin; of languid appearance.

escualo, *m.* (ichth.) spiny dogfish; shark.

escualoideo, a, *a.* (ichth.) squaloid.

escualor, *m., var. of* **escualidez.**

escucha, *f.* 1. listening; **e. telefónica,** wire tap. 2. (mil.) scout, sentry. 3. locutory chaperone (in convents). 4. maid who sleeps outside her mistress' room to be within call. 5. King's listening window (in council chamber). 6. (*pl.*) (fort.) small radial galleries running along the glacis.

escuchador, ra, *a.* listening.

escuchante, *a.* listening.

escuchar, *tr.v.* to listen to; to pay attention to, attend to. —*i.v.* to listen. —*r.v.* to speak or recite with affected slowness.

escuchimizado, da, *a.* very thin and weak, frail, puny.

escudar, *tr.v.* to shield; to protect, defend. —*r.v.* to shield or protect oneself.

escuderaje, *m.* service of a page or squire.

escuderear, *tr.v.* to serve as squire or page to, attend, wait on.

escuderete, *m. dim. of* **escudero,** young squire or page.

escudería, *f.* squireship (service of a knight's squire).

escuderil, *a.* of or pertaining to a squire or page.

escuderilmente, *adv.* in the manner of a squire or page.

escudero, ra, *a.* of or pertaining to a squire or page. —*m.* 1. squire, shield bearer; attendant (of distinguished person); lady's page. 2. nobleman. 3. shield maker. 4. (hunt.) young boar which accompanies an older one. — **e. de pie,** royal messenger.

escuderón, *m.* (derog.) boaster, bluffer; vain, pretentious person.

escudete, *m.* 1. small shield. 2. escutcheon (of a keyhole). 3. (dressm.) gusset. 4. round spot or blemish (on green olives). 5. (bot.) European water lily.

escudilla, *f.* wide bowl; large coffee cup.

escudillar, *tr.v.* 1. to serve into bowls or deep plates. 2. to pour (boiling broth over bread). 3. to control, manage, run.

escudillo, *m.* 1. *dim. of* **escudo,** small shield. 2. gold coin.

escudo, *m.* 1. shield; (her.) escutcheon, coat-of-arms. 2. (artil.) shield, sideplate (of light artillery). 3. monetary unit of Chile and Portugal. 4. escutcheon (of a keyhole). 5. bandage (on a vein incision). 6. (astron.) meteor. 7. (fig.) protection, shield. 8. (mar.) backboard (of a boat seat). 9. (hunt.) shoulder of a wild boar. — **e. acuartelado,** (her.) quartered coat-of-arms; **e. de armas,** (her.) coat-of-arms.

escudriñable, *a.* investigable, capable of being scrutinized.

escudriñador, ra, *a.* scrutinizing, investigating; prying. —*m., f.* scrutinizer; prier.

escudriñamiento, *m.* scrutiny, investigation, search.

escudriñar, *tr.v.* to scrutinize, examine, investigate.

escuela, *f.* 1. school (in all senses). 2. doctrine or system. 3. style, method. — **e. de conductores** or **choferes** or **manejo,** driving school; **e. de equitación,** riding school or academy; **e. de verano,** summer school; **e. impresionista,** (mus., p., lit.) impressionist school; **e. militar,** military academy; **e. naval,** naval academy; **e. nocturna,** night school; **e. normal,** teachers' training college, normal school; **e. por correspondencia,** correspondence school; **e. primaria,** elementary or primary school, grammar school; **e. pública,** public school (U.S.); **e. secundaria,** secondary school (G.B.); high school (U.S.); **e. vocacional,** vocational school.

escuelante, *m.* (Col., Mex., Ven.) schoolboy.

escuelero, ra, *m., f.* (Amer., vulg.) school-teacher.

escuerzo, *m.* 1. (zool.) toad. 2. (coll.) thin, physically weak person.

escuetamente, *adv.* plainly, simply.

escueto, ta, *a.* 1. plain, simple, direct; unadorned. 2. free, unencumbered.

escueza, escuezo, *ref.* **escocer.**

escuintle, *m.* (Mex., derog.) urchin, ragamuffin.

esculapio, *m.* 1. (rare) Aesculapian; (coll.) physician, doctor. 2. **E.,** (myth.) Aesculapius, Roman god of medicine.

esculcar, (*ref. 50*) *tr.v.* 1. to spy on, watch. 2. (Amer.) to search (a person).

escullador, *m.* dipper (for oil).

escullirse, (*ref. 65*) *r.v.* to slip or sneak away.

esculpidor, ra, *m., f.* sculptor; engraver.

esculpir, *tr.v.* to sculpture; to engrave.

esculque, esculqué, *ref.* **esculcar.**

escultor, ra, *m.* sculptor. —*f.* sculptress.

escultórico, ca, *a.* sculptural.

escultura, *f.* sculpture; carved, chiseled or modeled piece of artwork.

escultural, *a.* sculptural; statuesque.

esculturar, *tr.v.* to sculpture.

escuna, *f.* (mar.) schooner.

escupidera, *f.* spittoon; (Arg., Chile, Ecuad.) urinal, chamber pot.

escupidero, *m.* 1. spitting place. 2. difficult situation in which one is open to public scorn.

escupido, da, *past part. of* **escupir.** —*m.* spittle, sputum.

escupidor, ra, *a.* frequently spitting. —*m., f.* spitter. —*m.* 1. (Ecuad., P. Rico) spittoon. 2. (Col.) round mat. 3. (Hond., Mex.) fireworks.

escupidura, *f.* 1. spit, spittle, saliva. 2. lip sore (due to high fever).

escupir, *tr.v.* 1. to spit, spit out; to spew forth bullets (a gun). 2. to cast aside scornfully. 3. to come out in (sores). 4. to give off, exude. —*i.v.* to spit. — **e. a uno,** (fig.) to insult someone.

escupitajo, escupitina, escupitinajo, *m.* (coll.) spit, spittle.

escupo, *m.* spit, spittle.

escurana, *f.* (Amer.) darkness (preceding a storm).

escurar, *tr.v.* (tex.) to scour (cloth) before fulling.

escurialense, *a.* pertaining to the Spanish town and monastery of El Escorial.

escurra, *m.* rogue, rascal, scoundrel.

escurreplatos, *m.* draining rack (for dishes).

escurribanda, *f.* 1. (coll.) pretext, excuse, way out. 2. (coll.) diarrhea. 3. (coll.) running, discharge (of a sore). 4. (coll.) beating.

escurrideras, *f.* (*pl.*) (Mex., Guat.) excess irrigation water.

escurridero, *m.* drainboard, draining board, plate rack (on kitchen sink); (min.) drainpipe, outlet; (photog.) drying rack (for photographic plates).

escurridizo, za, *a.* slippery. — **hacerse uno escurridizo,** (fig., coll.) to sneak away.

escurrido, da, *past part. of* **escurrir.** —*a.* 1. narrow-hipped. 2. wearing a tight-fitting skirt. 3. (Mex., P. Rico) cowed, shamed, abashed.

escurridor, *m.* colander; draining rack (for dishes or bottles); (photog.) drying rack for plates.

escurriduras, *f.* (*pl.*) lees, dregs; **llegar uno a las e.,** to get to the bottom of the barrel, come to the end.

escurrimbres, *f.* (*pl.*) *var. of* **escurriduras.**

escurrimiento, *m.* 1. draining; dripping. 2. (fig.) sneaking out.

escurrir, *tr.v.* to drain. —*i.v.* 1. to drip, trickle, ooze. 2. to slip, slide; to be slippery. —*r.v.* 1. to drain. 2. to drip, trickle, ooze. 3. to slip, slide. 4. to escape, slip or sneak out. 5. (coll.) to go too far, say too much. 6. (coll.) to offer too much. — **escurrirse entre las manos,** to slip between one's hands.

escusado, *m., var. of* **excusado,** toilet, water closet, w.c.

escusalí, *m.* small apron.

escutiforme, *a.* scutiform; (bot., zool.) scutate.

esdrujulice, esdrujulicé, *ref.* **esdrujulizar.**

esdrujulizar, (*ref. 53*) *tr.v.* (gram.) to proparoxytone, accentuate on the antepenultimate syllable.

esdrújulo, la, *a.* (gram.) proparoxytonic, accented on the antepenultimate syllable (of a word). —*m.* (gram.) proparoxytone.

ese, *f.* 1. ess (name of the letter "s"). 2. shaped link (of chain). 3. (mus.) sound hole (in violin). — (*pl.*) **andar** or **ir haciendo eses,** (coll.) to reel or sway from one side to another; to zig-zag, walk as a drunkard.

ESE *abbrev. of* **estesudeste,** east-southeast (ESE).

ese, esa, (*pl.* **esos, esas**) *dem. a.* that. — **ese hombre,** that man; **esa mujer,** that woman; **esos muchachos,** those boys; **esas niñas,** those girls.

ése, ésa, (*pl.* **ésos, ésas**) *dem. pron.* that one; there. — (*pl.*) **¡conque ésas tenemos!** so that's it! so that's what it's about!; **ésa,** your town, there (i.e. reference to the town to which one is going or

writing, e.g. *llegaré a ésa dentro de ocho días,* I shall arrive there or in your town in a week); **ni por ésas ni por esotras,** by no means whatsoever.
esecilla, *f.* 1. *dim. of* **ese,** little ess. **2. metal** hook (to fasten on buttons, etc.).
esencia, *f.* 1. essence; being; entity. **2.** (chem.) essence oil; a perfume, fragrance. — **e. mineral,** mineral oil or spirits; **quinta e.,** quintessence.
esencial, *a.* essential; **ser e.,** to be indispensable or essential.
esencialmente, *adv.* essentially.
esenio, *a.* Essenian. —*m., f.* Essene, member of an ancient Hebraic sect.
eserina, *f.* (chem.) eserine.
esfacelación, *f.* (med.) sphacelation.
esfacelado, da, *a.* (med.) sphacelate.
esfacelarse, *r.v.* (med.) to sphacelate, become gangrenous (a tissue).
esfacelo, *m.* (med.) sphacelus, gangrenous tissue.
esfagníneo, nea, *a.* (bot.) sphagnous, sphagneous. —*f.* (bot.) sphagnum.
esfalerita, *f.* (min.) sphalerite.
esfena, *f.* (min.) sphene, sphena.
esfenoidal, *a.* (anat.) sphenoidal; pertaining to the sphenoid bone.
esfenoides, *a., m.* (anat.) sphenoid (bone).
esfera, *f.* 1. sphere (range of action, knowledge, influence; social position, rank). 2. (geom.) sphere. 3. heavens, sphere. 4. dial (e.g. of a clock). — **e. armilar,** (geog.) armillary sphere; or globe; **e. celeste,** celestial sphere; **e. de influencia,** sphere of influence; **e. recta,** (astron.) right sphere; **e. terráquea** o **terrestre,** (geog.) globe, the earth; **e. social,** social stratum.
esferal, *a.* (rare) spherical.
esfericidad, *f.* (geom.) sphericity.
esférico, ca, *a.* (geom.) spherical.
esferográfica, *f.* (Arg.) ball-point pen.
esferoidal, *a.* (geom.) spheroidal.
esferoide, *m.* (geom.) spheroid.
esferómetro, *m.* spherometer.
esfígmico, ca, *a.* (physiol.) sphygmic.
esfigmógrafo, *m.* (physiol.) sphygmograph.
esfigmomanómetro, *m.* (physiol.) sphygmomanometer.
esfigmómetro, *m.* (med.) sphygmometer.
esfinge, *f.* 1. sphinx. 2. (fig.) enigmatic person. 3. (ento.) lawkmoth. — **ser** or **parecer una e.,** to be sphinxlike or enigmatic.
esfíngido, da, *a.* sphinxlike. —*m.* (ento.) sphingid; (*pl.*) Sphingidae.
esfínter, *m.* (anat.) sphincter, ring-like muscle closing a natural orifice in the body.
esforcé, *ref.* **esforzar.**
esforrocinar, *tr.v.* (agr.) to remove the runners from (vine).
esforrocino, *m.* (agr.) new runner (of vines).
esforzadamente, *adv.* vigorously; bravely.
esforzado, da, *past part. of* **esforzar.** —*a.* brave, spirited, vigorous.
esforzador, ra, *a.* encouraging; strengthening. —*m., f.* encourager; strengthener.
esforzar, (*ref. 70*) *tr.v.* to strengthen; to encourage. —*i.v.* to gain courage. —*r.v.* to strive, make an effort; **esforzarse a, en** or **por +** *inf.,* to strive to + *inf.,* e.g. *esforzarse por salir bien,* to strive to do well.
esfuerce, esfuerzo, *ref.* **esforzar.**
esfuerzo, *m.* 1. effort. 2. vigor, spirit, courage. 3. endeavor. — **e. admisible,** (engin.) safe or allowable stress; **e. de ruptura,** breaking stress; **e. de trabajo,** working stress; **e. tractor,** tensile stress; tractive effort.
esfumación, *f.* (p.) stumping.
esfumado, da, *past part. of* **esfumar.** —*a.* (p.) sfumato.
esfumar, *tr.v.* (p.) to stump; (p.) to tone down (colors in order to achieve an effect of vagueness and distance). —*r.v.* (fig.) to vanish, disappear.
esfuminar, *tr.v.* (p.) to stump.
esfumino, *m.* (p.) stump, cylinder of rolled paper with conical ends, used for shading crayon or pencil strokes.
esgarrar, *tr.v.* to try to cough up (phlegm). —*i.v.* to cough hard (trying to bring up phlegm).
esgrafiado, *m.* (p.) graffito.
esgrafiar, *tr.v.* (p.) to decorate with graffito.
esgrima, *f.* (art of) fencing.
esgrimidor, *m.* swordsman, fencer, fencing master.
esgrimidura, *f.* (act of) fencing.
esgrimir, *tr.v.* 1. to wield (a weapon). 2. to use, put forward, wield (arguments, accusations). —*i.v.* to fence.
esgrimista, *m., f.* (Amer.) swordsman, fencer; (coll., Chile) sponger.
esguace, esguacé, *ref.* **esguazar.**
esguazable, *a.* fordable (river, brook, etc.).
esguazar, (*ref. 53*) *tr.v.* to ford (a shallow body of water).
esguazo, *m.* fording; ford.
esgucio, *m.* (archit.) cavetto; molding.
esguín, *m.* (ichth.) parr, smolt, young salmon before it enters the sea.
esguince, *m.* 1. dodge, feint. 2. frown, disdainful gesture. 3. twist, sprain (of joint).
esguízaro, ra, *a., m., f.* Swiss. — **pobre esguízaro,** (coll.) poor and helpless man or boy.
eslabón, *m.* 1. link. 2. knife-sharpening steel. 3. steel (for striking sparks from flint). 4. (ento.) black scorpion. 5. (vet.) bog spavin, bone spavin. — **e. interruptor,** (elec.) disconnecting link; **e. perdido,** missing link.
eslabonado, da, *a.* chained, concatenate.
eslabonador, ra, *a.* linking, interlinking, connecting.
eslabonamiento, *m.* linking, interlinking, connection.
eslabonar, *tr.v.* to link; (fig.) to string together, join, interlink, connect. —*r.v.* to link up, link together.
eslavismo, *m.* Slavism (culture, interests, characteristics of the Slavic people).
eslavo, va, *a.* Slav, Slavonic. —*m., f.* Slav, Slavonian. —*m.* Slavonic, Slavic language.
eslinga, *f.* (mar.) sling; **e. de cadena,** chain sling.
eslizón, *m.* (zool.) seps (Seps chalcides).
eslora, *f.* (mar.) length (of ships); (*pl.*) (mar.) binding strakes (of the deck); **e. de flotación,** waterline length; **e. total,** over-all length.
eslovaco, ca, *a., m., f.* Slovak, Slovakian.
esloveno, na, *a., m., f.* Slovenian, Slovene, pertaining to Slovenia, a Yugoslavian republic.
esmaltador, ra, *m., f.* enameler, enamelist.
esmaltadura, *f.* the action and effect of enameling; enamel work.
esmaltar, *tr.v.* 1. to enamel. 2. (fig.) to color, adorn. 3. (fig.) to grace, to enhance.
esmalte, *m.* 1. enamel (vitreous varnish; object painted with enamel); enameling, enamel work. 2. (p.) smalt, cobalt blue. 3. (her.) color, tincture. 4. (anat.) enamel (of teeth). 5. (fig.) luster, splendor. — **e. para uñas,** nail polish.
esmaltín, *m.* smalt, cobalt blue; brilliant blue pigment.
esmaltina, *f.* (min.) smaltine, smaltite.
esméctico, ca, *a.* (min.) smetic, detergent.
esmeradamente, *adv.* very carefully, meticulously or painstakingly.
esmerado, da, *past part. of* **esmerar.** —*a.* very careful, meticulous, painstaking.
esmerador, *m.* polisher (of metals or gems).
esmeralda, *f.* emerald.
esmeraldino, na, *a.* emerald-like (in color).
esmerar, *tr.v.* to polish. —*r.v.* to be meticulous or painstaking, take great pains (in one's work).
esmerejón, *m.* 1. (ornith.) merlin. 2. (mil.) small caliber gun.
esmeril, *m.* 1. emery. 2. small artillery gun. — **papel de e.,** sandpaper.
esmerilador, ra, *a.* grinding. —*m., f.* grinder, polisher.
esmerilar, *tr.v.* to polish with emery; to grind.
esmerilazo, *m.* shot from an **esmeril** (small artillery gun).
esmero, *m.* painstaking care, meticulousness.
esmilaceo, a, *a.* (bot.) smilacaceous (plant). —*f.* (*pl.*) Smilaceae, smilax family.
esmirnio, *m.* (bot.) smallage, wild celery.
esmirriado, da, *a.* emaciated, thin.
esmitsonita, *f.* (min.) smithsonite.
esmoladera, *f.* grindstone, whetstone.
esmoquin, *m.* dinner jacket, men's evening dress, tuxedo.
esmorecer, (*ref. 45*) *i.v., r.v.* (reg., Amer.) to faint, weaken, lose one's breath.
esmuciarse, *r.v.* to slip (from the hands, etc.).
esnob, *a.* snobbish, snobby. —*m., f.* snob.
esnobismo, *m.* snobbishness, snobbery.
eso, *dem. neut. pron.* that; the same. — **a e. de las ocho,** about or around eight o'clock; **e. mismo,** exactly; **por e.,** therefore; **por e. es que,** that's why.
esofágico, ca, *a.* (anat.) esophageal.
esófago, *m.* (anat.) esophagus.
esópico, ca, *a.* Aesopian, Aesopic, pertaining to Aesop or his fables.
Esopo, *m.* Aesop, Greek author, famous for his fables.
esotérico, ca, *a.* 1. esoteric. 2. (philos.) esoteric doctrine. 3. confidential, private.
esotro, esotra, *dem. pron.* that other one. —*a.* that other.
espabiladeras, *f.* (*pl.*) snuffers (for candles).
espabilado, da, *past part. of* **espabilar.** —*a.* (coll.) aware, smart, intelligent. —*f.* (Col.) a blinking of the eyes.
espabilar, *tr.v.* to snuff (candle). —*i.v.* (Col.) to blink. —*r.v.* to wake up.
espaciador, *m.* 1. (print.) space band. 2. spacer, space bar (typewriter).
espacial, *a.* 1. spatial. 2. space (as *a.*). — **viaje e.,** space travel.
espaciar, *tr.v.* to space out; to spread; (print.) to space. —*r.v.* 1. to expatiate, write or speak at length. 2. (fig.) to relax, enjoy oneself.
espacio, *m.* 1. space, room, area. 2. space, period (of time). 3. (mus.) interval. 4. delay, slowness. 5. (print.) space. — **e. aéreo,** airspace; **e. de cuña,** (print.) space band; **e. exterior** or **sideral,** outer space; **el e.,** space; **e. muerto,** (mil.) dead space; **era del e.,** Space Age; **e. vital,** living space, lebensraum; **espacios abiertos,** open spaces; **espacios verdes,** green spaces.
espaciosamente, *adv.* slowly, unhurriedly.
espaciosidad, *f.* spaciousness, capacity.
espacioso, sa, *a.* 1. spacious, roomy, ample. 2. slow, deliberate, unhurried.
espaciotemporal, *a.* spatiotemporal, spacetime (existing in both space and time).
espachurrar, *tr.v.* to squash, crush.
espada, *f.* 1. sword, rapier; swordsman. 2. spade (card); (*pl.*) spades (suit); ace of spades. 3. (ichth.) swordfish. 4. (geom.) vertical height of a segment of a circle. — **danza de espadas,** sword dance; **colgar la e.,** to retire, resign, give

up (a job); **entre la e. y la pared,** between the devil and the deep blue sea; **e. blanca,** ordinary sword; **e. de Damocles,** sword of Damocles, constant menace; **e. de dos filos,** (fig.) double-edged sword, boomerang; **e. de Orión,** (astron.) Orion's sword; **e. negra,** (fenc.) foil; **salir uno con su media e.,** (coll.) to stick one's nose (into a conversation). *—m.* 1. matador, bullfighter; **primer e.,** principal bullfighter. 2. (fig.) ace, exceptional person.

espadachín, *m.* 1. good swordsman or fencer. 2. bully, braggart.

espadador, ra, *m., f.* one who brakes (hemp or flax).

espadaña, *f.* 1. (bot.) cattail, reed mace. 2. bell gable, belfry.

espadañada, *f.* 1. gush, spout (of blood or water through the mouth); spewing, regurgitation.

espadañal, *m.* marsh where reed mace or cattails grow.

espadañar, *tr.v.* to open, fan out (tail feathers).

espadar, *tr.v.* to brake, swingle, crush (hemp or flax).

espadante, *m.* (ichth.) swordfish.

espadería, *f.* swordmaker's shop; sword shop.

espadero, *m.* swordmaker; sword seller; blades-mith.

espádice, *m.* (bot.) spadix.

espadíceo, a, *a.* (bot.) spadiceous.

espadilla, *f.* 1. *dim. of* **espada,** small sword. 2. insignia of the order of Santiago. 3. swingle, hemp brake. 4. (mar.) scull, oar used as rudder. 5. ace of spades. 6. cue, rod (billiards). 7. ornamental hairpin. 8. (mar.) provisional helm or tiller.

espadillado, *past part. of* **espadillar.** *—m.* braking, crushing (of hemp or flax).

espadillar, *tr.v., var. of* **espadar.**

espadillazo, *m.* loss of the ace of spades (in certain card games); bad luck at cards.

espadín, *m.* dress sword, rapier.

espadón, *m.* 1. *aug. of* **espada,** broadsword. 2. (coll.) brass hat, high-ranking soldier; important person. 3. castrated man, eunuch.

espadrapo, *m., var. of* **esparadrapo,** bandage, court plaster.

espagírica, *f.* the art of purifying metals.

espagírico, ca, *a.* pertaining to the art of purifying metals.

espahí, *m.* 1. spahi, Turkish cavalryman. 2. native cavalryman (of the former French army in Algeria).

espalda, *f.* 1. (anat.) back (*also in pl.*). 2. back part, back (of a house, chair, etc.). 3. (*pl.*) bodyguard. 4. (mil.) rearguard. 5. (Ecuad.) fate, destiny. — **dar or volver la e.,** to turn one's back, to turn away; **echarse sobre las espaldas,** to take on one's shoulders, (fig.) to bear a burden; **e. con e.,** back to back; **e. mojada,** (derog.) wetback; **tener uno buenas espaldas,** to be tough or resistant; **tener guardadas las espaldas,** to be well protected.

espaldar, *m.* 1. back (of body; of chair); back piece, back plate (of cuirass). 2. trellis, espalier (for plants). 3. (zool.) upper part of shell (of reptiles). 4. (*pl.*) tapestry hangings (in the manner of a frieze).

espaldarazo, *m.* 1. blow on the back. 2. accolade. 3. (fig.) backing, support, help (to people or ideas). 3. (taur.) the sponsoring (ceremony) of a bullfighter upon reaching the grade of matador.

espaldarcete, *m.* upper part of back plate (of coat of armor).

espaldarón, *m.* back plate, back piece (of a cuirass).

espaldear, *tr.v.* (mar.) to poop, break against the stern of.

espalder, *m.* stern rower (in a galley).

espaldera, *f.* trellis, espalier (for plants); wall behind the espalier.

espaldilla *f.* 1. (anat.) shoulder blade. 2. back pieces (of a jerkin or jacket). 3. shoulder (of lamb, pig, etc.). 4. (taur.) the shoulder blades of the bull.

espalditendido, da, *a.* (coll.) stretched out or lying on one's back.

espaldón, na, *a.* (Col.) broad-shouldered or backed. *—m.* 1. (carp.) tenon. 2. dam, barrier (to check flow of water or soil). 3. (fort.) barricade.

espaldonarse, *r.v.* (mil.) to take cover (from enemy fire) behind a natural shelter.

espaldudo, da, *a.* broad-shouldered, broad-backed.

espalera, *f.* espalier, trellis.

espalmador, *m.* hoof-paring knife.

espalmadura, *f.* hoof parings.

espalmar, *tr.v.* to pare (horses') hooves.

espalto, *m.* (p.) dark glaze, dark-colored paint.

espantable, *a.* frightening; frightful, dreadful.

espantablemente, *adv.* terrifyingly, frighteningly.

espantada, *f.* 1. terror, fright, fear. 2. bolting, sudden flight (of an animal). 3. sudden stop or halt (from fear).

espantadizo, za, *a.* easily frightened, scary (coll.), jumpy.

espantador, ra, *a.* 1. frightening, terrifying. 2. (Col., Arg., Guat.) easily frightened.

espantagustos, *m.* (*pl.*) killjoy, spoilsport, wet-blanket (coll.), party pooper.

espantajo, *m.* 1. scarecrow. 2. frightening object. 3. (coll.) obnoxious person, pest (coll.). 4. fright (coll.), hag.

espantalobos, *m.* (*pl.*) (bot.) bladder senna (Colutea arborescens).

espantamoscas, *m.* (*pl.*) fly trap; device for trapping flies.

espantanublados, *m.* (*pl.*) (coll.) 1. vagabond, beggar. 2. meddler, busybody.

espantapájaros, *m.* (*pl.*) scarecrow.

espantapastores, *m.* (*pl.*) (bot.) meadow saffron, autumn crocus.

espantar, *tr.v.* 1. to frighten, scare. 2. to frighten or scare away; to drive or shoo away. *—r.v.* 1. to be frightened, scared or alarmed. 2. to be astonished or amazed (at).

espantavillanos, *m.* (coll.) gaudy trinket of low value.

espante, *m.* panic (caused by stampeding cattle).

espanto, *m.* 1. terror, fright, panic, consternation. 2. awe, astonishment, wonder. 3. menace, threat. 4. illness caused by fright, shock. 5. (Amer.) spook, ghost, apparition. — **estar curado de e.,** to be experienced.

espantosamente, *adv.* frightfully; terrifyingly, frighteningly.

espantoso, sa, *a.* 1. frightening, horrifying, terrifying; frightful, dreadful. 2. astounding, amazing.

España, *f.* Spain.

español, la, *a.* Spanish. *—m., f.* Spaniard. *—m.* Spanish (language). — **a la española,** in the Spanish manner.

españolado, da, *a.* Spanish-like; pertaining to the customs of Spain. *—f.* (gen. derog.) bogusly Spanish (act, work, etc.).

españolar, *tr.v., r.v., var. of* **españolizar.**

españolería, *f., var. of* **españolada.**

españoleta, *f.* ancient Spanish dance.

españolice, *ref.* **españolizar.**

españolismo, *m.* 1. love of Spain, love of things Spanish. 2. Hispanicism, Spanish idiom. 3. Spanish character or essence.

españolista, *a.* Hispanist, Hispanophile.

españolización, *f.* Hispanization.

españolizado, da, *past part. of* **españolizar.** *—a.* Spanish-looking.

españolizar, (*ref. 53*) *tr.v.* to Hispanize. *—r.v.* to adopt the manners or customs of Spain.

esparadrapo, *m.* sticking plaster, adhesive tape, bandage, court plaster.

esparaván, *m.* 1. (ornith.) sparrow hawk. 2. (vet.) spavin.

esparavel, *m.* 1. casting net (for fishing). 2. (mas.) mortarboard; hod.

esparceta, *f.* (bot.) (variety of) sainfoin (Onobrychis sativa).

esparciata, *a., m., f.* Spartan.

esparcidamente, *adv.* separately, sparsely.

esparcido, da, *past part. of* **esparcir.** *—a.* 1. scattered, disseminated; spread out. 2. (fig.) merry, gay, amusing, entertaining, jovial.

esparcidor, ra, *a.* scattering; spreading. *—m., f.* scatterer; spreader.

esparcimiento, *m.* 1. scattering; spreading. 2. relaxation, recreation. 3. frankness, openness; friendliness; joviality, gaiety.

esparcir, (*ref. 61*) *tr.v.* 1. to spread, to scatter. 2. to relax, divert. *—r.v.* 1. to spread; to be scattered. 2. to relax, take things easy, have a good time.

esparragado, da, *a.* pertaining to the asparagus. *—m.* asparagus stew.

esparragador, ra, *m., f.* asparagus grower or picker.

esparragamiento, *m.* asparagus cultivation or picking.

esparragar, (*ref. 51*) *i.v.* to grow, tend or pick asparagus.

espárrago, *m.* 1. (bot.) asparagus (plant and edible shoot). 2. peg ladder. 3. awning pole. 4. metal bell pull. — **e. perico,** extra large asparagus; **mandar (a uno) a freír espárragos,** (coll.) to tell (someone) to go jump in the lake.

esparragón, *m.* corded silk cloth.

esparraguero, ra, *m., f.* asparagus grower, picker or seller. *—f.* asparagus plant, field and bed; asparagus plate.

esparraguina, *f.* (min.) asparagin.

esparrancado, da, *past part. of* **esparrancarse.** *—a.* straddling, with legs spread apart; widely separated, far apart.

esparrancarse, (*ref. 50*) *r.v.* (coll.) to spread one's legs wide apart.

esparranque, esparranqué, *ref.* **esparrancarse.**

Espartaco, *m.* Spartacus, Thracian gladiator, leader of a slave revolt in Rome.

espartal, *m.* field of esparto grass.

espartano, na, *a.* 1. Spartan, pertaining to Sparta, a city in ancient Greece. 2. (coll.) stoical, frugal, severe. *—m., f.* Spartan.

esparteína, *f.* (chem.) sparteine.

esparteña, *f.* espadrille, rope-soled sandal.

espartería, *f.* making of esparto articles; workshop where esparto articles are made.

espartero, ra, *m., f.* maker and seller of esparto articles.

espartilla, *f.* rolled mop of rush or esparto (for grooming horses).

espartillo, *m. dim. of* **esparto,** esparto smeared with birdlime (to snare birds); (Amer.) graminaceous plant used for fodder.

espartizal, *m.* esparto field.

esparto, *m.* (bot.) esparto, esparto grass.

esparver, *m.* (ornith.) hawk, sparrow hawk.
esparza, esparzo, *ref.* **esparcir.**
espasmo, *m.* (med.) spasm.
espasmódico, ca, *a.* (med.) spasmodic.
espástico, ca, *a.* (med.) spastic, spasmodic.
espata, *f.* (bot.) spathe.
espatarrada, *f.* (coll.) spreading legs wide apart (in dancing).
espatarrarse, *r.v.* to fall with one's legs wide apart; to straddle.
espático, ca, *a.* (min.) spathic, foliated.
espato, *m.* (min.) spar. — **e. calizo,** (min.) calcspar; **e. de Islandia,** (min.) Iceland spar; **e. flúor,** (min.) fluorspar; fluorite; **e. pesado,** (min.) barite, heavy spar.
espátula, *f.* 1. spatula; (p.) palette knife. 2. (ornith.) common spoonbill (Platalea leucorodia).
espatulado, da, *a.* spatular; (bot.) spatulate.
espaviento, *m., var. of* **aspaviento,** fuss, excitement, exaggerated panic; **no hagas tanto e.,** don't make such a fuss.
espavorice, espavoricé, *ref.* **espavorizarse.**
espavorido, da, *a.* terrified, panic-stricken.
espay, *m.* spahi, spahee.
especería, *f., var. of* **especiería.**
especia, *f.* 1. spice, aromatic herbs. 2. (*pl.*) desserts (served formerly with wine at the end of a meal).
especiado, da, *a.* spicy, well-seasoned.
especial, *a.* 1. special, especial. 2. particular, specific. — **en e.,** specially; **entrega e.,** special delivery.
especialice, especialicé, *ref.* **especializar.**
especialidad, *f.* speciality, specialty; major field of studies or interest.
especialista, *a.* specialist, specialistic. —*m., f.* specialist.
especialización, *f.* specialization.
especializado, da, *a., m., f.* specialist, expert.
especializar, (*ref. 53*) *i.v., r.v.* to specialize.
especialmente, *adv.* specially, particularly, especially.
especiar, *tr.v.* to spice, season.
especie, *f.* 1. species. 2. type, kind, sort, variety. 3. image, species. 4. case; affair, matter; incident, event. 5. piece of news, rumor; subject. 6. pretext, appearance. 7. (fenc.) feint. 8. (zool.) species. — **en e.,** in kind (i.e. not in money); **escapársele a uno una e.,** to let something slip indiscreetly; **especies sacramentales,** (ecc.) species (of Eucharist); **soltar una e.,** to send out a feeler (to sound someone out); to spread a rumor.
especiería, *f.* spices; spice trade or shop; grocery store.
especiero, ra, *m., f.* spice merchant. —*m.* spice box.
especificación, *f.* specification. — **e. modelo,** standard specification.
especificadamente, *adv.* specifically.
especificar, (*ref. 50*) *tr.v.* to specify; itemize; to state, define.
especificativo, va, *a.* specific, specifying.
específico, ca, *a.* specific; definite. *m.* (med.) specific, specific remedy; patent medicine.
especifique, especifiqué, *ref.* **especificar.**
espécimen, *m.* specimen; sample.
especioso, sa, *a.* 1. beautiful, neat, perfect. 2. (fig.) specious, deceptive.
especiota, *f.* (coll.) hoax, cock-and-bull story.
espectable, *a.* notable, distinguished; conspicuous.
espectacular, *a.* spectacular; showy.
espectáculo, *m.* 1. spectacle, sight. 2. show, performance (in theater, etc.). 3. exhibition, spectacle, scandal. — **dar un e.,** to be or present quite a sight.
espectador, ra, *a.* observing, watching. —*m., f.* spectator, onlooker; (*pl.*) audience.
espectral, *a.* ghostly, spooky; (phys.) spectral.
espectro, *m.* 1. specter, ghost, spook. 2. (phys.) spectrum. — **e. continuo,** (phys.) continuous spectrum; **e. de absorción,** (phys.) absorption spectrum; **e. de bandas,** (phys.) band spectrum; **e. de emisión,** (phys.) emission spectrum.
espectrofotómetro, *m.* (opt.) spectrophotometer.
espectrografía, *f.* (phys.) spectrography.
espectrógrafo, *m.* (phys.) spectrograph. — **e. de masa,** (phys.) mass spectograph.
espectrograma, *m.* (phys.) spectrogram.
espectroheliógrafo, *m.* (astron.) spectroheliograph.
espectroheliograma, *m.* (astr.) spectroheliogram.
espectrohelioscopio, *m.* (astron., phys.) spectrohelioscope.
espectrometría, *f.* (phys.) spectrometry.
espectrómetro, *m.* (phys.) spectrometer.
espectroscopia, *f.* (phys.) spectroscopy.
espectroscópico, ca, *a.* (phys.) spectroscopic, spectroscopical.
espectroscopio, *m.* (phys.) spectroscope.
especulación, *f.* 1. (com.) speculation, venture; risky trading. 2. study, observation, contemplation. 3. scheme.
especulador, ra, *a.* speculatory. —*m., f.* speculator.
especular, *tr.v.* 1. to view, inspect, scrutinize. 2. to ponder, speculate on. —*i.v.* to speculate; (com.) to speculate. —*a.* specular, relating to a mirror.
especulativa, *f.* 1. (philos.) human faculty of speculation, ability to reason. 2. understanding.
especulativamente, *adv.* speculatively.
especulativo, va, *a.* speculative; meditative, thoughtful, reflective.
espéculo, *m.* (med.) speculum.
espejado, da, *past part. of* **espejar.** —*a.* 1. limpid, clear. 2. mirror-like, reflecting light or images.
espejar, *tr.v.* to clear, disencumber. —*r.v.* to be reflected.
espejear, *i.v.* to shine, gleam, glint, glitter, sparkle; to reflect (as a mirror).
espejeo, *m., var. of* **espejismo.**
espejera, *f.* (Cuba, vet.) sore or wound caused by the harness or the spur.
espejería, *f.* mirror shop.
espejero, ra, *m., f.* mirror maker or vendor.
espejismo, *m.* mirage, optical illusion; (fig.) illusion, figment of the imagination.
espejo, *m.* 1. mirror, looking glass. 2. mirror-like surface. 3. model, example (e.g. of virtue). 4. (archit.) ovoid ornament (fitted in a molding). 5. (*pl.*) whorl of hair (on horse's chest). — **e. de cuerpo entero,** full-length mirror; **e. lateral,** wing mirror; **e. retrovisor,** (auto.) rearview mirror, driving mirror; **e. ustorio,** burning glass; **mirarse en uno como en un e.,** to be very fond of; **mírate en ese e.,** let that be an example to you.
espejuela, *f.* (equit.) bar, curb (of a bit); **e. abierta,** bar of a snaffle bit; **e. cerrada,** bar of a bar bit.
espejuelo, *m.* 1. (min.) selenite; sheet of talc mica. 2. skylight, window (with selenite panes). 3. mirror-studded piece of wood to decoy larks. 4. glint, sheen (on cut wood). 5. (cul.) candied citron or squash. 6. waste matter accumulating in honeycombs. 7. (vet.) callosity (developed by an animal embryo during gestation). 8. (vet.) chestnut (horny excrescence on the inner side of a horse's leg). 9. (*pl.*) glasses, spectacles; lenses.
espeleología, *f.* speleology, the study of caves, caverns and grottos.
espeleólogo, *m.* speleologist, spelunker.
espelta, *f.* (bot.) spelt (a cereal).
espélteo, a, *a.* of or pertaining to spelt (wheat).
espelucar, (*ref. 50*) *tr.v.* 1. (Arg., Col., P. Rico). 2. to muss, ruffle (hair). 3. to make (hair) stand on end. —*r.v.* 1. to become mussed or ruffled. 2. stand on end (hair).
espeluce, espelucé, *ref.* **espeluzar.**
espelunca, *f.* cave, grotto, cavern.
espeluzar, (*ref. 53*) *tr.v.* 1. to muss, ruffle (hair). 2. to make (the hair) stand on end. —*r.v.* 1. to become mussed or ruffled. 2. to stand on end (hair).
espeluznamiento, *m.* disheveling, mussing.
espeluznante, *a.* hair-raising, horrifying, terrifying.
espeluznar, *tr.v.* 1. to ruffle (hair, pile of cloth, etc.). 2. to make (the hair) stand on end. —*r.v.* 1. to become ruffled (hair). 2. to stand on end (hair).
espeluzno, *m.* 1. (coll.) tremor, shiver, chill. 2. (Mex.) chills with fever.
espeque, *m.* 1. handspike, lever. 2. stay, prop (of a wall).
espera, *f.* 1. wait, waiting; expectation, expectancy. 2. (law) adjournment, respite. 3. (mus.) pause, rest, interval. 4. restraint, prudence. 5. (carp.) notch. 6. (mil.) ancient piece of ordnance. — **sala de e.,** waiting room; **un compás de e.,** (mus.) a bar's rest; **en e. de,** awaiting, expecting; **cazar a e.,** (hunt.) to lie in wait for game; **quien e. desespera,** he who waits ends up losing his patience.
esperador, ra, *a.* expectant, hoping.
esperance, esperancé, *ref.* **esperanzar.**
esperantista, *m., f.* Esperantist, advocate of Esperanto.
esperanto, *m.* Esperanto, an artificial language for international use, based on words common to the principal European languages.
esperanza, *f.* hope; expectation; prospects. — **dar e.,** to encourage, give hope; **no hay e.,** there is no hope, the case is hopeless.
esperanzado, da, *past part. of* **esperanzar.** —*a.* hopeful, full of hope or expectations; encouraged.
esperanzar, (*ref. 53*) *tr.v.* to make hopeful, give hope, to encourage.
esperar, *tr.v.* 1. to hope; to hope for. 2. to expect, to look for. 3. to wait for; to await; to be in store, e.g. *mala noche nos espera,* a bad night awaits us or is in store for us. —*i.v.* 1. to wait. 2. to hope. 3. to expect (a baby). — **e. en,** to put one's faith in, pin one's hopes on; **e. levantado,** to wait up for; **e. sentado,** to have a long wait in store, wait until the cows come home.
esperece, esperecé *ref.* **esperezarse.**
esperezarse, (*ref. 53*) *r.v.* to stretch (one's limbs), to stretch oneself (in order to become fully awake, alert).
esperezo, *m.* the act of stretching the limbs (in order to become fully awake or alert).
esperiego, ga, *a.* sour (said of a type of apple).
esperma, *f.* 1. (biol.) sperm, semen. 2. **e. de ballena,** (zool., chem.) spermaceti, whale oil.
espermacio, *m.* (bot.) spermatium.
espermáfita, *f.* (bot.) spermatophyte.
espermagonio, *m.* (bot.) spermagonium.
espermaticida, *a.* spermicidal. —*m.* spermicide.
espermático, ca, *a.* spermatic, seminal.
espermátide, *m.* (biol.) spermatid.
espermatocida, *a.* spermatocidal, spermacidal.
espermatocito, *m.* (biol.) spermatocyte.
espermatófita, *f.* (bot.) spermatophyte.

espermatóforo, *m.* (zool.) spermatophore.
espermatogénesis, *f.* (med.) spermatogenesis, spermatogeny.
espermatogonio, *m.* (zool.) spermatogonium.
espermatología, *f.* (biol., bot.) spermatology.
espermatorrea, *f.* (med.) spermatorrhea.
espermatozoario, *m., var. of* **espermatozoide.**
espermatozoide, *m.* (zool.) spermatozoon; (bot., zool.) spermatozoid.
espermatozoo, *m.* spermatozoon.
espermicida, *a.* spermicidal. *—m.* spermicide.
espermiducto, *m.* spermatic duct.
espermina, *f.* (biochem.) spermine, spermin.
espermiogénesis, *f.* (med.) spermiogenesis.
espermófilo, *m.* (zool.) spermophile.
espermogonia, *f.* (bot.) spermogonium, spermatogonium.
espernada, *f.* end link (of a chain).
espernancarse, *r.v.* (Amer.) to straddle, sit with the legs wide apart.
esperón, *m.* 1. (mar.) ram (of a warship). 2. (coll.) long wait.
esperonte, *m.* (fort.) ravelin.
esperpento, *m.* 1. (coll.) fright (ugly person or thing). 2. (coll.) rubbish, rot, nonsense, absurdity. 3. folly, foolishness.
esperriaca, *f.* last pressing of the grapes.
esperrilita, *f.* (min.) sperrylite.
espesamiento, *m.* (reg.) coagulation, thickening of a liquid.
espesar, *m.* densest part of a forest.
espesar, *tr.v.* 1. to thicken, condense, coagulate, curdle. 2. to mass, assemble. 3. to knit closer; to make dense. *—r.v.* 1. to grow or become thicker (a tree, a forest). 2. to become thicker or condensed. — **e. la salsa,** to thicken the sauce.
espesartino, na, *f.* (min.) spessartite.
espesativo, va, *a.* thickening.
espeso, sa, *a.* 1. thick, dense. 2. thick, compact. 3. dirty, unkempt.
espesor, *m.* thickness (of a board, etc.); density (of oil, etc.).
espesura, *f.* 1. thickness, density; closeness. 2. thicket, luxuriant growth. 3. abundant hair, thick mane. 4. (fig.) slovenliness, dirt.
espetaperro, *adv.* precipitately; **a e.,** like a bat out of hell, at breakneck speed.
espetar, *tr.v.* 1. to skewer, spit; to pierce, transfix. 2. to spring a surprise upon someone; to cause someone annoyance or surprise. *—r.v.* 1. to become solemn and stiff. 2. (coll.) to ensconce oneself in a position of dignity or pride.
espetera, *f.* 1. kitchen rack; kitchen ware. 2. (fig.) woman's breasts. 3. (C. Amer.) pretext, excuse.
espetón, *m.* 1. skewer, spit. 2. iron prong, fire poker (for a furnace). 3. large pin. 4. jab, poke, blow given with a spit. 5. (ichth.) pipefish, needlefish.
espía, *m., f.* spy; **e. doble,** double agent, spy who works for both sides. *—f.* 1. stay, guide line. 2. (mar.) warping; warp, warping line; **dar** o **tender una e.,** to run out a warp.
espiado, da, *past part. of* **espiar.** *—a.* fastened with stays.
espiar, (*ref. 54*) *tr.v.* to spy upon. *—i.v.* to spy. *—i.v., r.v.* (mar.) to warp.
espibia, *f.* (vet.) *var. of* **espibio.**
espibio, espibión, *m.* (vet.) sprain in the nape (of a horse).
espica, *f.* (med.) spica.
espicanardi, *f.* (bot.) *var. of* **espicanardo.**
espicanardo, *m.* (bot.) spikenard.
espiciforme, *a.* spiciform, shaped like a spike.
espícula, *f.* (zool.) spicule.
espichar, *tr.v.* 1. to prick (with a pin). 2. (Chile, Peru) to put a tap or a spigot on. *—i.v.* (coll.) to kick the bucket, to give up the ghost; to die. *—r.v.* 1. (Guat.) to become cowardly or frightened. 2. (Mex.) to become ashamed. 3. (Col.) to become empty, drained, deflated.
espiche, *m.* 1. sharp-pointed weapon, meat-pit, spike. 2. plug, bung, spigot.
espichón, *m.* prick, stab; wound made with a sharp instrument or weapon.
espiga, *f.* 1. (bot.) spike, ear, tassel (of corn, wheat, etc.); (bot.) shoot, spray, sprig. 2. tang (of knife, sword, file, etc.; part of blade fitting into the handle). 3. (carp.) tenon, tongue. 4. (carp.) peg, wooden pin; brad. 5. wedge-end (of a step of a spiral staircase). 6. clapper, tongue (of a bell). 7. fuse, detonator. 8. (mar.) masthead. 9. (mar.) gunter sail. 10. pin (passing through the eye of a hinge). — **e. roscada,** dowel screw.
espigadera, *f.* gleaner.
espigadilla, *f.* (bot.) sabadilla.
espigado, da, *past part. of* **espigar.** *—a.* 1. spiky; (bot.) spicate. 2. ripe (plants). 3. (fig.) tall, slim, slender, svelte.
espigador, ra, *m., f.* gleaner.
espigar, (*ref. 51*) *tr.v.* 1. to glean (corn); to cull (from books). 2. (carp.) to tenon, dovetail. *—i.v.* to tassel (cereals). *—r.v.* 1. to go to seed (plants). 2. to grow tall, to grow up; to become tall and slender (said of youngsters).
espigo, *m.* tang (of a knife, file, etc.).
espigón, *m.* 1. goad (for animals); point (of a sharp instrument). 2. sharp ear or spike; ear, spike. 3. tall barren peak; butte. 4. breakwater; pier.
espigue, espigué, *ref.* **espigar.**
espiguear, *i.v.* (Mex.) to swish the tail up and down (a horse).
espigueo, *m.* gleaning; gleaning season.
espiguilla, *f.* 1. (bot.) spikelet. 2. narrow edging or fringe. 3. flower of the poplar. 4. (bot.) spear grass.
espín, *m.* (mil.) square (battle formation); **puerco e.,** porcupine.
espina, *f.* 1. thorn, thistle (of a plant); splinter (of wood); fishbone. 2. (anat.) spine; (anat.) apophysis. 3. (hist.) spina, low wall making a longitudinal division in the arena of a circus. 4. apprehension, suspicion. — **e. blanca,** (bot.) cotton thistle; **e. de cruz,** (Arg., Peru, bot.) anchor plant; **e. de pescado,** (tex.) herringbone (design); **e. dorsal,** (anat.) spine; **e. santa,** (bot.) Christ's thorn; **dar mala e.,** to cause suspicion or apprehension; **estar en espinas,** to be on tenterhooks.
espinaca, *f.* (bot.) spinach.
espinadura, *f.* prick, pricking with a thorn.
espinal, *a.* (anat.) spinal, dorsal.
espinapez, *m.* 1. (carp.) herringbone work. 2. (fig.) difficulty, trouble.
espinar, *m.* 1. place covered with thorn bushes. 2. (fig.) difficulty, trouble, e.g. *ahí está el e.,* therein lies the trouble.
espinar, *tr.v.* 1. to prick. 2. (agr.) to surround (new trees) with prickly branches for protection). 3. (mil.) to form (troops) into squares (ancient military combat formation). 4. (fig.) to nettle, hurt (with an unkind remark). *—i.v.* to prick. *—r.v.* 1. to be pricked. 2. (fig.) to be nettled or hurt (by an unkind remark).
espinazo, *m.* 1. backbone, spine. 2. (archit.) keystone (of an arch or vault). — **doblar el e.,** (coll.) to bend over backwards, grovel, be servile.
espinel, *m.* boulter (fishing line with many hooks attached), trotline.
espinela, *f.* 1. (poet.) octosyllabic ten-line stanza. 2. (min.) spinel.
espíneo, a, *a.* of thorns, made of thorns.
espinera, *f.* (bot.) hawthorn.
espineta, *f.* (mus.) spinet.
espingarda, *f.* 1. espingole, long-barreled musket; type of cannon, springal (used by the Moors). 2. (coll.) tall, gangling person.
espingardada, *f.* musket or cannon shot wound.
espingardería, *f.* company of Moorish musketeers; muskets.
espingardero, *m.* Moorish musketeer.*espinilla, f.* 1. (anat.) shinbone. 2. blackhead (pimple on the face). 3. small thorn.
espinillera, *f.* jambeau, greave (shin guard of armor); shin pad (of workers or sportsmen).
espino, *m.* (bot.) hawthorn; **e. artificial,** barbed wire; **e. cerval,** purging buckthorn; **e. negro,** buckthorn.
espinochar, *tr.v.* to husk (corn).
espinosismo, *m.* Spinozism (philosophy of Benedict de Spinoza).
espinosista, *a.* Spinozistic. *—m., f.* Spinozist, advocate of the philosophy of Spinoza.
espinoso, sa, *a.* 1. thorny, spiny. 2. (fig.) difficult, dangerous, ticklish (situation, etc.).
espinudo, da, *a.* (Chile) *var. of* **espinoso.**
espinzar, *tr.v.* to burl.
espiocha, *f.* pickaxe.
espión, *m.* spy.
espionaje, *m.* espionage, spying.
espionar, *tr.v.* to spy.
espira, *f.* 1. (archit.) surbase. 2. (geom.) helix, spiral. 3. (geom.) spire, turn (in a spiral). 4. (zool.) whorl (of a shell).
espiración, *f.* exhalation, expiration; breathing, respiration.
espiráculo, *m.* (zool.) spiracle.
espirador, ra, *a.* expiratory (muscles for breathing).
espiral, *a.* spiral, winding, helical. *—f.* 1. spiral. 2. balance spring, hairspring (in a watch).
espirante, *a.* exhaling, breathing out, respiring.
espirar, *tr.v.* 1. to breathe out, exhale. 2. to encourage, animate, give heart to. 3. (theol.) to infuse with a divine spirit. *—i.v.* 1. to breathe; to breathe out. 2. (poet.) to blow softly (the wind).
espirativo, va, *a.* 1. (theol.) able to create by spiration. 2. (theol.) infusing a divine spirit (in a person).
espirea, *f.* (bot.) spiraea.
espirema, *m.* (biol.) spireme.
espiriforme, *a.* spiry, like a coil or a spiral.
espirilo, *m.* (bac.) spirillum.
espiritado, da, *past part. of* **espiritar.** *—a.* (coll.) skeleton-like, extremely thin (person).
espiritar, *tr.v.* 1. (coll.) to annoy, enrage; (coll.) to agitate, disturb. 2. (rare) to possess with devils. *—r.v.* to become agitated; to fret; be disturbed.
espiritismo, *m.* spiritualism, spiritism.
espiritista, *a.* spiritualistic, spiritistic. *—m., f.* spiritualist.
espiritosamente, *adv.* spiritedly, lively.
espiritoso, sa, *a.* 1. spirited, lively. 2. spiritous, alcoholic (said of beverages).
espíritu, *m.* 1. spirit; soul; temper, disposition. 2. courage, valor, spirit; vitality, energy. 3. breathing (in ancient Greek). 4. (ecc.) gift, e.g. *e. de profecía,* gift of prophecy. 5. (chem.) essence, spirit (distilled from substances). 6. (*pl.*) ghosts, apparitions. — **e. adiaforético,** (chem.) methyl alcohol; **e. de contradicción,** contradictory disposition, e.g. *tener e. de contradicción,* to be contrary, like to contradict; **e. de cuerpo,** esprit de corps; **e. de equipo,** team spirit; **e. de las aguas,** water sprite; **e. de sal,** spirit of salt (hydrochloric acid); **e. de vino,** alcohol, spirit of wine; **e. maligno,** the devil; **E. Santo,** Holy Spirit, Holy Ghost.

espiritual, *a.* spiritual, pertaining to the spirit, non-corporeal.
espiritualice, *ref.* **espiritualizar.**
espiritualidad, *f.* spirituality, incorporeity.
espiritualismo, *m.* (philos.) spiritualism, idealism (as opposed to materialism).
espiritualista, *a.* (philos.) spiritualistic; non-materialistic. —*m., f.* (philos.) spiritualist, idealist.
espiritualizar, (*ref. 53*) *tr.v.* to spiritualize; to etherealize; to purify, to refine.
espiritualmente, *adv.* spiritually; ethereally.
espirituoso, sa, *a., var. of* **espiritoso.**
espíritusanto, *m.* (C. Rica, Nic.) species of orchid (Peristeria alata).
espirogira, *f.* (bot.) spirogyra.
espirógrafo, *m.* (physiol.) spirograph, instrument for recording the movement of breathing.
espiroidal, *a.* spiroid, spiral in shape.
espirómetro, *m.* spirometer, pulmometer.
espiroqueta, *f.* (bac.) spirochete.
espiroquetosis, *f.* spirochetosis, spirochaetosis.
espírula, *f.* (zool.) spirula.
espita, *f.* 1. palm (measurement). 2. tap (of a barrel), faucet, spout, spigot. 3. (coll.) drunkard, tippler.
espitar, *tr.v.* to tap, put a faucet on.
espito, *m.* (print., bkb.) peel (T-shaped stick on which wet paper is hung to dry).
espláchnico, ca, *a.* (anat.) splanchnic, visceral.
esplacnología, *f.* (anat.) splanchnology.
esplendente, *a.* (poet.) shining, glittering, resplendent, dazzling.
esplender, *i.v.* (poet.) to shine, glitter; to dazzle.
espléndidamente, *adv.* 1. splendidly, with lavish generosity. 2. magnificently.
esplendidez, *f.* 1. largess, generosity, liberality. 2. splendor, magnificence.
espléndido, da, *a.* 1. splendid, magnificent, grand. 2. generous, liberal. 3. sumptuous; resplendent, glittering, shining.
esplendor, *m.* 1. splendor, magnificence. 2. radiancy. 3. noble quality or nature.
esplendorosamente, *adv.* splendorously, resplendently, radiantly.
esplendoroso, sa, *a.* resplendent, magnificent, radiant.
esplénico, ca, *a.* splenic, splenetic. —*m.* (anat.) splenius muscle.
esplenio, *m.* (anat.) splenius (muscle).
esplenitis, *f.* (med.) splenitis, inflammation of the spleen.
esplenomegalia, *f.* (med.) splenomegaly.
esplenotomía, *f.* (surg.) splenotomy.
espliego, *m.* lavender (flower and dried seeds).
esplín, *m.* spleen, melancholy; the blues (coll.).
esplique, *m.* bird snare.
espolada, *f.* prick with a spur; **e. de vino,** (coll.) slug or shot of wine.
espolazo, *m., aug. of* **espolada,** violent jab with a spur.
espoleadura, *f.* spurgall, wound made by a spur.
espolear *tr.v.* to spur (a horse); to urge, incite, instigate, encourage (a person or animal).
espoleta, *f.* 1. wishbone. 2. fuse, fuze (of bomb, charge); **e. de barreno,** blasting fuse; **e. de doble efecto,** combination fuse; **e. de percusión,** percussion fuse; **e. de proximidad,** proximity fuse; **e. de radioproximidad,** proximity fuse; **e. de retardo,** delay fuse; **e. de tiempo,** time fuse.
espolín, *m.* 1. spur (fixed to the boot). 2. (bot.) feather grass. 3. small shuttle (for weaving flower patterns into brocade). 4. flowered silk cloth, flowered brocade.
espolinar, *tr.v.* to brocade with flowers.
espolio, *m.* (ecc.) spolium, property left by a prelate.
espolique, *m.* running footman.
espolista, *m.* 1. running footman. 2. (ecc.) tenant of spolium property.
espolón, *m.* 1. spur (of a fowl); fetlock (of a horse). 2. (archit.) buttress. 3. dike, mole; breakwater, groyne, jetty; pier, esplanade. 4. (mar.) ram (of a warship or galley). 5. cutwater (of a ship or bridge). 6. spur, ridge (of a mountain). 7. (coll.) chilblain.
espolonado, da, *a.* (ornith.) spiked, spicate. —*f.* sudden cavalry attack.
espolonazo, *m.* thrust with the spurs.
espolvorear, *tr.v.* 1. to dust, brush the dust from. 2. to sprinkle, shake powder over (something); to dust, sprinkle (something) with powder.
espolvorizar, (*ref. 53*) *tr.v.* to sprinkle, shake powder over (something).
espondaico, ca, *a.* (poet.) spondaic.
espondeo, *m.* (poet.) spondee.
espóndil, espóndilo, *m.* (anat.) spondyl, spondyle, vertebra.
espondilitis, *f.* (med.) spondylitis, inflammation of the vertebrae.
espondilosis, *f.* (med.) spondylosis.
espongiario, *m.* (zool.) sponge.
espongina, *f.* (biochem.) spongin.
esponja, *f.* 1. sponge. 2. (coll.) leech, sponger. 3. (Amer.) drunkard, drunk. 4. (chem.) sponge (i.e. platinum). — **tirar la e.,** to throw in the towel.
esponjado, da, *past part. of* **esponjar.** —*m.* mixture of beaten egg whites, sugar and lemon juice (used to sweeten and soften drinking water); meringue, fondant. —*a.* (fig.) puffed up (a person).
esponjadura, *f.* 1. sponginess; fluffiness; fluffing up. 2. (artil.) flaw in cast metal.
esponjamiento, *m.* (Arg.) *var. of* **esponjadura.**
esponjar, *tr.v.* to make fluffy, make spongy; to fluff up. —*r.v.* 1. to become fluffy or spongy. 2. to become puffed up, conceited. 3. to put on weight and glow with health.
esponjera, *f.* sponge rack, sponge holder.
esponjilla, ita, uela, *f. dim. of* **esponja,** small sponge.
esponjosidad, *f.* sponginess.
esponjoso, sa, *a.* spongy; porous and light in weight.
esponsales, *m.* (*pl.*) betrothal, engagement; espousal, nuptials.
esponsalicio, cia, *a.* of betrothal (as *a.*), nuptial.
espontáneamente, *adv.* spontaneously, without premeditation.
espontanearse, *r.v.* to open up, reveal one's intimate feelings.
espontaneidad, *f.* spontaneity, unpremeditated act or behavior.
espontáneo, a, *a.* spontaneous, unpremeditated.
espontón, *m.* spontoon, ancient type of lance.
espontonada, *f.* salute made with a spontoon; lance blow; blow given with a spontoon.
espora, *f.* (bot.) spore.
esporádico, ca, *a.* sporadic, irregular; isolated (occurrence).
esporangio, *m.* (bot.) sporangium.
esporangióforo, *m.* (bot.) sporangiophore.
esporidio, *m.* (bot.) sporidium.
esporífero, ra, *a.* (bot.) sporiferous, having spores.
esporo, *m., var. of* **espora.**
esporocarpio, *m.* (bot.) sporocarp.
esporocarpo, *m.* (bot.) *var. of* **esporocarpio.**
esporocisto, *m.* (zool.) sporocyst.
esporófilo, *m.* (bot.) sporophyll, sporophyl.
esporófito, *m.* (bot.) sporophyte.
esporóforo, *m.* (bot.) sporophore.
esporogénesis, *f.* (biol.) sporogenesis.
esporogenia, *f.* (biol.) sporogeny.
esporogonio, *m.* (bot.) sporogonium.
esporonto, *m.* (zool.) sporont.
esporozoario, *m.* (zool.) sporozoan.
esporozoito, *m.* (zool.) sporozoite.
esporrondingarse, *var. of* **desporrondingarse.** —*r.v.* 1. (C. Amer., Col.) to spend lavishly, go on a spending spree. 2. (C. Amer., Col.) to fall to pieces.
esportada, *f.* basketful; fruit basket.
esportear, *tr.v.* to transport in baskets.
esportilla, *f. dim. of* **espuerta,** small basket.
esportillero, *m.* carrier, porter, errand-boy.
esportillo, *m.* esparto grass basket.
esportón, *m.* large basket.
esportonada, *f.* basketful.
espórula, *f.* (biol.) sporule.
esporulación, *f.* (biol.) sporulation.
esporular, *i.v.* (biol.) to sporulate.
esposado, da, *past part. of* **esposar.** —*a.* 1. handcuffed. 2. newlywed. —*m., f.* newlywed.
esposar, *tr.v.* to handcuff, shackle.
esposas, *f.* (*pl.*) handcuffs, manacles, shackles.
esposo, sa, *m., f.* husband (*m.*), consort, wife (*f.*), spouse. —*f.* prelate's ring.
espuela, *f.* 1. spur. 2. (fig.) spur, incentive, stimulus. 3. spur (of fowl). 4. (Arg., Chile) wishbone (of fowl). — **calzar e.,** to be a knight; **correr la e.,** to spur deeply; to reprehend severely; **dar de e.** or **de espuelas,** to spur; **e. de caballero,** (bot.) field larkspur; **estar con or tener las espuelas calzadas,** to be about to start a journey; **poner espuelas a (alguien),** to incite, urge on, goad on.
espuerta, *f.* two-handled basket; **a espuertas,** abundantly, by the basketful.
espulgador, ra, *m., f.* delouser.
espulgar, (*ref. 51*) *tr.v.* 1. to delouse, remove fleas from. 2. to examine minutely, scrutinize. —*r.v.* to delouse oneself, rid oneself of fleas.
espulgo, *m.* 1. delousing, ridding of fleas. 2. scrutiny, meticulous examination.
espulgue, espulgué, *ref.* **espulgar.**
espuma, *f.* 1. foam, froth, spume; lather; scum. 2. (coll.) cream, flower, pick, élite. — **crecer como e.,** (coll.) to shoot up, grow quickly; to grow rapidly prosperous; **e. de caucho,** foam rubber; **e. de mar,** sea foam; **e. de mar,** (min.) meerschaum, sepiolite; **e. de nitro,** (min.) saltpeter.
espumadera, *f.* skimmer, skimming spoon, slotted spoon.
espumador, ra, *m., f.* skimmer, person who removes froth, foam or scum.
espumaje, *m.* frothiness, foaminess.
espumajear, *i.v.* to foam or froth at the mouth.
espumajo, *m., var. of* **espumarajo.**
espumajoso, sa, *a.* foamy, frothy; scummy.
espumante, *a.* sparkling, bubbly (wine); frothing, foaming.
espumar, *tr.v.* to skim, remove froth, foam or scum from. —*i.v.* 1. to froth, foam. 2. (fig.) to shoot up, grow rapidly.
espumarajo, *m.* foam, froth (from the mouth).
espúmeo, a, *a.* foamy, frothy, spumous, spumy; scummy.
espumero, *m.* salina, salt pond or lake (where salt water collects for crystallization).
espumilla, *f.* 1. (cul.) sheer crepe. 2. (Ecuad., Hond.) meringue.
espumillón, *m.* (tex.) heavy grosgrain or faille.
espumosidad, *f.* frothiness, foaminess.
espumoso, sa, *a.* frothy, foamy, spumous; lathery (soap).

espundia, *f.* 1. (vet.) cancerous ulcer. 2. (S. Amer.) elephantiasis.
espurio, ria, *a.* 1. spurious, false. 2. bastard, illegitimate. 3. adulterated.
espurrear, espurriar, *tr.v.* to sprinkle with spit.
esputar, *tr.v.* to spit, expectorate.
esputo, *m.* sputum, spittle, spit, saliva.
esq. *abbrev. of* **esquina,** corner.
esquebrajar, *tr.v., r.v.* to crack, split, fracture; to cleave.
esquejar, *tr.v.* (agr.) to make cuttings or slips from.
esqueje, *m.* (agr.) cutting, slip (for planting).
esquela, *f.* note, short letter; printed card, invitation, notice or announcement; **e. de defunción,** obituary note, notice or card; **e. amatoria,** love letter.
esqueletado, da, *a.* very thin, emaciated, gaunt, skeleton-like.
esquelético, ca, *a.* skeletal; (coll.) very thin, emaciated, gaunt, skeleton-like, wasted.
esqueleto, *m.* 1. skeleton. 2. (fig.) skeleton, framework; sketch, outline. 3. (fig.) extremely thin person. 4. (Amer.) form, blank, application form.
esquema, *m.* plan, outline, sketch, diagram; table, tabulation; (philos.) schema. — **e. alámbrico,** (elec.) wiring diagram.
esquemáticamente, *adv.* schematically, diagrammatically, in outline.
esquematice, esquematicé, *ref.* **esquematizar.**
esquemático, ca, *a.* schematic, diagrammatic.
esquematismo, *m.* schematism; diagrams, sketches (illustrating a book).
esquematizar, (*ref. 53*) *tr.v.* to schematize; to outline; sketch; to make a diagram or draft of.
esquena, *f.* spine, backbone (of fishes).
esquenanto, *m.* (bot.) camel grass.
esquero, *m.* small leather pouch or bag.
esquí, (*pl.* **esquís**) *m.* ski; **e. alpino,** downhill skiing; **e. náutico** or **acuático,** water skiing; **e. nórdico** or **de fondo,** cross-country skiing; **hacer e. acuático,** to water-ski.
esquiador, ra, *m., f.* skier.
esquiar, (*ref. 54*) *i.v.* to ski.
esquiascopia, *f.* (med.) skiascopy.
esquiciar, *tr.v.* (p., rare) to begin to sketch or outline.
esquicio, *m.* sketch, outline, rough draft.
esquifada, *f.* 1. skiff load, cargo carried by a small row boat or skiff. 2. vault of a cistern.
esquifar, *tr.v.* (mar.) to fit out or man (a ship); to provision (a ship); to provide a boat with oars.
esquifazón, *m.* (mar.) oars of a galley; crew of oarsmen.
esquife, *m.* 1. (mar.) skiff, rowboat. 2. (archit.) cylindrical vault.
esquila, *f.* 1. round cow bell; small bell. 2. shearing (of sheep).
esquila, *f.* 1. (zool.) shrimp, prawn. 2. (ento.) whirligig beetle (Gyrinus natator). 3. (bot.) squill (Urginea maritima); **e. de agua,** (ichth.) mantis prawn (Squilla mantis).
esquilador, ra, *a.* sheep-shearing. —*m., f.* sheepshearer. —*f.* sheepshearer, sheep-shearing machine.
esquilar, *tr.v.* to shear (sheep), clip, crop (hair of other animals).
esquileo, *m.* shearing; shearing shed; shearing season.
esquilimoso, sa, *a.* (coll.) finicky, fastidious, squeamish.
esquilmar, *tr.v.* 1. to harvest, reap, gather in (crops). 2. to exhaust, impoverish, tire out (soil, plants, crops). 3. (fig.) to impoverish; to swindle, cheat, exploit.
esquilmo, *m.* 1. harvest, crops, farm produce. 2. farm by-products and compatible activities. 3, (fig.) harvest. 4. (Mex.) farm scrapings.
Esquilo, *m.* (lit.) Aeschylus, one of the great playwrights of ancient Greece.
esquilón, *m.* large round cowbell; large bell.
esquimal, *a.* of or pertaining to the Eskimos. —*m., f.* Eskimo, member of a group of native North American people.
esquina, *f.* corner; **a la vuelta de la e.,** around the corner; **estar en e. uno con otro,** to be in disagreement or on bad terms with one another; **hacer e.,** to be on the corner (a building); to form a corner (two streets).
esquinado, da, *past part. of* **esquinar.** —*a.* 1. having corners, angular. 2. unsociable, intractable, withdrawn.
esquinadura, *f.* angularity, unsociability.
esquinal, *m.* angle iron; iron knee; corner plate.
esquinante, esquinanto, *m.* (bot.) camel grass.
esquinar, *tr.v.* 1. to form a corner with. 2. to place at an angle. 3. (carp.) to square. —*i.v.* to form a corner (with). —*r.v.* **esquinarse con,** to fall out with, quarrel with.
esquinazo, *m.* 1. (coll.) corner. 2. (Chile, coll.) serenade. — **dar e.,** (coll.) to leave (someone) in the lurch, leave (someone) flat, stand (someone) up; to evade, give the slip (to someone).
esquince, esquincé, *ref.* **esquinzar.**
esquinco, *m.* (zool.) skink, lizard.
esquinela, *f.* greave, jambeau (of armor).
esquinero, ra, *a.* (Amer.) on the corner. —*f.* (Amer.) corner (piece of furniture); corner cupboard.
esquinudo, da, *a.* angular, sharp-cornered.
esquinzador, *m.* shredding room (in a paper mill), rag engine.
esquinzar, (*ref. 53*) *tr.v.* to shred rags (in a paper mill).
esquiraza, *f.* ancient square-rigged vessel.
esquirla, *f.* splinter (of a bone).
esquirol, *m.* 1. strikebreaker, blackleg, scab. 2. (Sp., reg.) squirrel.
esquisto, *m.* (min.) schist, slate; **e. petrolífero,** oil shale.
esquistoso, sa, *a.* schistose, slaty; foliated.
esquistosomiasis, *f.* (med., vet.) schistosomiasis.
esquitar, *tr.v.* to pardon, cancel or remit a debt.
esquite, *m.* (C. Rica, Hond., Mex.) popcorn.
esquivar, *tr.v.* to avoid, evade; to side-step, dodge, duck. —*r.v.* to withdraw, excuse oneself (from doing something).
esquivez, *f.* aloofness, coolness, disdain; unsociability, unfriendliness.
esquivo, va, *a.* unsociable, unfriendly; aloof, distant, disdainful.
esquizado, da, *a.* mottled (marble).
esquizocárpico, ca, *a.* (bot.) schizocarpic.
esquizocarpo, *m.* (bot.) schizocarp.
esquizófita, *f.* (bot.) schizophyte.
esquizofrenia, *f.* (psyc.) schizophrenia.
esquizofrénico, ca, *a.* schizophrenic. —*m., f.* schizophrenic, schizophrene.
esquizogénesis, *f.* (biol.) schizogenesis.
esquizogonia, *f.* (biol.) schizogony.
esquizoide, *a.* (psyc.) schizoid.
esquizoidia, *f.* (psyc.) schizoidism.
esquizomiceta, *f.* (bot.) schizomycete; (*pl.*) Schizomycetes.
esquizomicosis, *f.* (med.) schizomycosis.
esquizópodo, *m.* (zool.) schizopod, (*pl.*) Schizopoda.
esquizotimia, *f.* (psyc.) schizothymia.
estabilice, estabilicé, *ref.* **estabilizar.**
estabilidad, *f.* stability, steadiness, firmness; constancy.
estabilísimo, ma, *a. super. of* **estable,** very stable, firm or steady.
estabilización, *f.* stabilization.
estabilizador, ra, *a.* stabilizing. —*m., f.* stabilizer (person). —*m.* stabilizer. — **e. vertical,** (aer.) vertical stabilizer.
estabilizar, (*ref. 53*) *tr.v.* to stabilize, make stable or firm.
estable, *a.* stable, firm, steadfast.
establear, *tr.v.* to accustom (cattle) to a stable. —*r.v.* to become accustomed to being confined to a stable.
establecedor, ra, *a.* establishing; founding, instituting. —*m., f.* establisher, founder, institutor.
establecer, (*ref. 45*) *tr.v.* 1. to establish; to found, institute; to set up. 2. to establish, state, decree. —*r.v.* 1. to take up residence. 2. to set oneself up in business.
estableciente, *a.* establishing.
establecimiento, *m.* 1. establishment, foundation. 2. establishment store; premises, locale. 3. establishment, statute, decree. 4. settlement, colony. — **e. de las mareas,** (mar.) time of spring tide; **e. de puerto,** (mar.) vulgar or common establishment.
establemente, *adv.* stably, firmly.
establero, *m.* stableboy, groom, stableman.
establezca, establezco, *ref.* **establecer.**
establo, *m.* 1. stable. 2. (astron.) **E.,** the Crib, Praesepe; **establos de Augías,** (myth.) Augean Stables.
estabulación, *f.* stabling, keeping and raising livestock in a stable.
estabular, *tr.v.* to stable; to raise or keep livestock in stables.
estaca, *f.* 1. stake, post, picket; cudgel, club. 2. (agr.) cutting, stem cutting. 3. (carp.) spike, nail. 4. (Arg., Chile) mining concession. 5. (Chile) spur (of fowl).
estacada, *f.* 1. stockade, palisade; paling fence. 2. dueling field. — **dejar a alguien en la e.,** (coll.) to leave someone in the lurch; **quedarse en la e.,** to be beaten; to fail, be unsuccessful.
estacado, *m.* arena, jousting ground, dueling site.
estacadura, *f.* stakes (of a truck or cart).
estacar, (*ref. 50*) *tr.v.* 1. to tether to a stake. 2. to enclose, fence in. 3. to stake out boundaries of. 4. (Amer.) to fasten down with stakes. —*r.v.* 1. (fig.) to stand stock-still. 2. to become stiff as a ramrod. 3. (Col., C. Rica) to prick oneself. 4. (Ecuad.) to balk, become unruly (a horse).
estacazo, *m.* 1. blow given with a stake. 2. (fig.) blow, setback.
estación, *f.* 1. season, period of time. 2. station (train, telegraph, radio); stop, stopping-off point (in the course of a journey). 3. stay, stop, sojourn. 4. (ecc.) station (of the cross). 5. (rare) state, condition, position. 6. (astron.) stationary point. 7. (bot.) station, natural habitat. 8. (top.) observation point. — **e. de lluvias,** rainy season; **e. de mercancías,** (ry.) freight station; **e. de esquí,** ski resort; **e. de invierno** or **invernal,** winter resort; **e. depuradora (de aguas residuales),** sewage plant; **e. de seguimiento,** tracking station; **e. de servicio,** service station; **e. de taxis,** hack stand, taxi stand; **e. espacial,** space station; **e. e. ferroviaria,** railway station; **e. meteorológica,** weather station; **e. orbital,** orbital space station; **e. termal,** thermal spa; **e. terminal** or **término,** terminus; **e. transmisora,** (rad.) sending or broadcasting station.
estacional, *a.* seasonal; (astron.) stationary.
estacionamiento, *m.* stationing, posting, settling; parking (of a car).
estacionar, *tr.v.* 1. to station, post, place; to assign or appoint (someone) to a place or position. 2. to park (a car). 3. to mate sheep. —*r.v.* to station

or place oneself; to settle oneself; to remain stationary.

estacionario, ria, *a.* stationary; fixed, stable; (astron.) stationary (planet). —*m.* (arch., Sp.) bookseller.

estacionero, ra, *m., f.* person who frequently prays at the Stations of the Cross.

estacionómetro, *m.* (P. Rico) parking meter.

estacte, *f.* essence or oil of myrrh.

estacha, *f.* harpoon cable or line; (mar.) hawser, cable, line.

estada, *f.* stay, stop, sojourn, residence.

estadal, *m.* 1. lineal measurement (of about 3 meters). 2. length of waxed wick. 3. blessed ribbon worn around the neck.

estadero, *m.* royal land surveyor (for the division of land).

estadía, *f.* 1. stay, sojourn, stop. 2. sitting, session (of an artist's model). 3. (com.) demurrage (delay of a boat in unloading; the cost of such delay).

estadia, *f.* (surv.) stadia.

estadio, *m.* 1. stadium; racecourse. 2. furlong (measurement). 3. phase, stage.

estadiómetro, *m.* (phys.) stadiometer.

estadista, *m.* 1. statesman. 2. statistician.

estadística, *f.* statistics.

estadístico, ca, *a.* statistical.

estadizo, za, *a.* stagnant (water); motionless (air).

estado, *m.* 1. condition, state (of health, mind, etc.). 2. status (social, legal, economic, governmental); rank, class, estate. 3. state, nation, country; government. 4. statement, report, account. — **en e. (interesante),** pregnant, in the family way; **e. benefactor** or **de bienestar,** welfare state; **e. civil,** marital status; **e. ciudad,** city state; **e. crítico,** (phys.) critical state; **e. de alarma,** (mil.) state of emergency; **e. de ánimo,** state of mind; **e. de cosas,** state of affairs; **e. de cuenta,** (com.) statement; **e. de derecho,** democracy; **e. de emergencia** or **excepción** state of emergency; **e. de guerra,** state of war; **e. de prevención,** state of alert; **e. de sitio,** martial law; **e. general, e. llano,** commons, common people, commonalty; **e. honesto,** maidenhood, virginity; **e. libre asociado,** commonwealth; **e. mayor,** (mil.) staff; **e. mayor general,** (mil.) general staff; **e. sólido** (phys., elec.) solid state; **Estados Pontificios,** Papal States; **e. tapón,** buffer state; **e. totalitario,** police state; **en buen e.,** in good shape.

Estados Unidos de América, *m.* (*pl.*) United States of America.

Estados Unidos Mexicanos, *m.* (*pl.*) United States of Mexico.

estafa, *f.* 1. swindle, deceit, trick, confidence trick. 2. (equit.) stirrup.

estafador, ra, *m., f.* swindler, crook, con man.

estafar, *tr.v.* to swindle; (law) to defraud.

estafermo, *m.* 1. revolving figure or dummy armed with a stick (used as a target by horsemen, who endeavored to wound it without being hit). 2. gawk, boob (sl.). 3. fright, ridiculously dressed person.

estafeta, *f.* 1. post office. 2. post, runner, courier, mail-carrier. 3. (dipl.) courier.

estafetero, *m.* postmaster; postman.

estafetil, *a.* pertaining to the post, post office, or couriers.

estafilococia, *f.* (med.) staphylococcia.

estafilococo, *m.* (med.) staphylococcus.

estafiloma, *m.* (med.) staphyloma.

estafilorrafia, *f.* (med.) staphylorrhaphy, staphyloraphy.

estafilotomía, *f.* (med.) staphylotomy.

estafisagria, *f.* (bot.) stavesacre.

estagnación, *f.* (Amer.) stagnation; paralyzation, cessation (of business, etc).

estajero, *m., var. of* **estajista.**

estajista, *m.* pieceworker, jobber, task worker.

estajo, *m.* piecework; job, work assignment, freelance job.

estala, *f.* 1. stable. 2. (mar.) port of call; seaport.

estalación, *f.* class, station (in society); rank; order.

estalactita, *f.* (geol.) stalactite.

estalactítico, ca, *a.* stalactic, stalactitic.

estalagmita, *f.* (geol.) stalagmite.

estalagmítico, ca, *a.* stalagmitic.

estalladora, *f.* blasting machine.

estallante, *a.* bursting, exploding.

estallar, *i.v.* 1. explode, burst. 2. to crack (a whip). 3. to break out (an epidemic, a revolution, a fire). 4. to break loose (one's fury or anger). 5. to blow up, blow one's top (with anger).

estallido, *m.* 1. explosion, crack, report (of firearms). 2. crack (of a whip). 3. outburst. — **e. de guerra,** outbreak of war.

estallo, *m., var. of* **estallido.**

estambrar, *tr.v.* (tex.) to spin (wool) into worsted yarn.

estambre, *m.* 1. (tex.) worsted; worsted yarn. 2. (bot.) stamen.

Estambul, *m.* Istanbul, port and city in Turkey.

estamenara, *f.* (mar.) futtock.

estamental, *a.* pertaining to the estates composing the Cortes of Aragon.

estamento, *m.* 1. estate, each of the estates which composed the Cortes of Aragon (nobility, clergy and commons). 2. state, class.

estameña, *f.* (tex.) estamene, etamine, serge.

estameñete, *m.* (tex.) kind of estamene.

estaminado, da, *a.* (bot.) staminate.

estaminal, *a.* (bot.) staminal.

estamíneo, a, *a.* (bot.) stamineous.

estaminífero, ra, *a.* (bot.) staminiferous.

estaminodio, *m.* (bot.) staminodium, staminode.

estampa, *f.* 1. illustration, engraving, print. 2. looks, appearance, aspect. 3. card with an illustration, illustrated religious text (used for first communions, etc.). 4. press, printing, e.g. *dar una obra a la e.,* to send a work to be printed. 5. footprint. — **tener mala e.,** to be ugly and disagreeable looking; **la e. de la herejía,** a hideous countenance or appearance.

estampación, *f.* printing, engraving; stamping; **e. en seco,** (bkb.) blind tooling.

estampado, da, *a.* (tex.) stamped, embossed (fabric). —*m.* 1. (tex.) print, cotton print. 2. impression, stamping. 3. printing, engraving.

estampador, *m.* engraver; printer, one who makes prints.

estampadora, *f.* stamping machine.

estampar, *tr.v.* 1. to stamp (a design in metal). 2. to print, engrave. 3. to print (e.g. one's footstep in the sand). 4. (coll.) to dash, slam, throw (against something). 5. to stamp, impress, engrave (on one's mind). 6. to imprint (a kiss).

estampería, *f.* engraver's shop, print shop or business; shop where illustrated religious texts are sold.

estampero, *m.* engraver, person who makes or sells prints.

estampida, *f.* 1. crash, explosion, report (of a gun). 2. (Amer.) stampede (of cattle). 3. (fig.) sudden departure.

estampido, *m.* crash, explosion, report (of gun); **e. sónico,** sonic boom.

estampilla, *f.* 1. rubber stamp, signet, seal. 2. (Amer.) postage stamp. 3. small print; illustrated religious text.

estampillado, *past part. of* **estampillar.** —*m.* stamping, marking.

estampillar, *tr.v.* to stamp; to mark with a rubber stamp.

estampita, *f. dim. of* **estampa,** small illustration, print.

estancación, *f.* 1. standstill; deadlock; coming to a standstill, paralyzation. 2. state monopoly.

estancado, *a.* stagnant.

estancamiento, *m., var. of* **estancación.**

estancar, (*ref. 50*) *tr.v.* 1. to dam up, stanch, stem (a current of water). 2. (com.) to corner (a market); convert (a business or industry) into a monopoly, esp. a state-controlled monopoly. 3. to hold up (a document); to bring (a business deal) to a standstill. 4. (mar.) to fother (a leak). —*r.v.* 1. to become dammed up; become stagnant, stagnate. 2. to be paralyzed, held up; to come to a standstill. 3. to stick in the stomach.

estancia, *f.* 1. stay, sojourn. 2. room; sitting-room. 3. each day (spent in a hospital); cost of a day (in a hospital). 4. (poet.) stanza. 5. (Arg., Chile) ranch; (Cuba, Ven.) country house. 6. (Ven., W. Indies) truck farm.

estanciero, *m.* (Amer.) owner of a farmstead; rancher, ranch overseer; small farmer.

estanco, *a.* (mar.) watertight, leakproof, seaworthy. —*m.* 1. monopoly, state monopoly, state store (where controlled goods are sold). 2. (fig.) archives. 3. (Ecuad.) spirits or liquor store.

estándar, *m., a.* standard.

estandarización, *f.* standardization.

estandardizar, (*ref. 53*) *tr.v* to standarize.

estandarte, *m.* standard, banner, colors, flag.

estangurria, *f.* (med.) strangury; catheter.

estannato, *m.* (chem.) stannate.

estánnico, ca, *a.* (chem.) stannic.

estannita, *m.* (min.) stannite.

estannoso, sa, *a.* (chem.) stannous.

estanque, *m.* pool, pond; reservoir, basin; dam.

estanque, estanqué, *ref.* **estancar.**

estanquero, *m.* retailer of government controlled goods (such as tobacco, etc.); cigar store clerk or keeper, tobacconist.

estanquero, ra, estanquillero, ra, *m., f.* shopkeeper, storekeeper (in a state controlled store).

estanquidad, *f.* watertightness.

estanquillero, ra, *m., f.* tobacconist.

estanquillo, *m.* 1. state store (where controlled goods are sold). 2. tobacconist's shop. 3. (Mex.) small dirty shop. 4. (Ecuad.) pub, bar.

estanquito, *m. dim. of* **estanco,** small pond, pool.

estantal, *m.* (archit.) buttress, abutment.

estantalar, *tr.v.* (archit.) to buttress, strengthen with abutments.

estante, *a.* extant, existing, being; fixed, permanent. —*m.* 1. shelving, set of shelves, shelves; bookcase. 2. leg (of a machine stand). 3. (Amer.) timber post or pillar (supporting a house). 4. (mar.) (*pl.*) posts (for lashing rigging to).

estantería, *f.* shelves, shelving, bookcase.

estantigua, *f.* 1. hobgoblin, ghost; procession of phantoms and hobgoblins. 2. (coll.) fright, scarecrow; poorly dressed and ungainly person.

estantío, a, *a.* 1. stationary, standing still. 2. sluggish, slow, spiritless.

estañado, da, *a.* tin-plated.

estañador, *m.* tinman, tinsmith, tin plater; pewterer.

estañadura, *f.* tinning, plating or coating with tin; tin plating.

estañar, *tr.v.* 1. to plate with tin, to tin. 2. to solder with tin.

estañero, *m.* tinsmith, tinman; dealer in tin articles.

estañífero, *a.* (geol.) bearing tin.

estaño, *m.* tin.
estañoso, sa, *a.* (chem.) stannous.
estapedio, *m.* (anat.) stapedius.
estaque, estaqué, *ref.* **estacar.**
estaquero, *m.* 1. hole (for rungs in a ladder or stakes in a cart). 2. (hunt.) year-old buck or doe.
estaquilla, *f.* peg, pin, tack; spike, long nail; wooden pin.
estaquillador, *m.* shoemaker's pegging awl.
estaquillar, *tr.v.* 1. to peg, fasten with pegs. 2. (agr.) to plant with cuttings.
estar, (*ref. 8*) *i.v., r.v.* to be, to exist. 1. to be in a place, e.g. *estamos en casa,* we are home; *el niño está en el colegio,* the child is in school; *ella está presente,* she is present. 2. to be in a mood, state or condition, e.g. *estoy enfermo,* I am ill; *no estés triste,* don't be sad; *el plato está roto,* the dish is broken; *el tiempo está malo,* the weather is foul; *todo está perdido,* all is lost. 3. to be in a place or position, e.g. *estamos de pie,* we are standing (on our feet); *la torre de Pisa está inclinada,* the tower of Pisa is (in a) leaning (position); *estás a mi izquierda,* you are on my left. 4. to be about to, engaged in, disposed or ready to, e.g. *estoy a punto de capitular,* I am about to capitulate; *estamos pintando la casa,* we are painting the house; *hoy estoy de enfermera,* today I am (doing the job of) a nurse; *estoy para servirte,* I am ready to serve you. — **estar a,** to be priced at, to cost, e.g. *están a un dólar la libra,* they (now) cost one dollar a pound; to be ready or agreeable to, e.g. *estoy a lo que digan,* I am ready to do what they say; to be doing, be occupied in, e.g. *estaba a eso cuando llamaste,* I was doing that (precisely) when you called; **¿a cuántos estamos?** what date is today? e.g. *estamos a primero de junio,* it's the first of June; **estar a lo que salte,** to be ready to take advantage of an opportunity; **estar al caer,** to be about to happen, to be due; **estar a matarse,** to be deadly enemies, to be at sword's point; **estar a oscuras,** to be in the dark, be uninformed or unaware of; **estarle a uno bien empleado,** to serve one right, to get one's comeuppance. — **está bien,** it's all right, it's okay; **estar bien a uno,** to suit one well, to fit one properly (or not), e.g. *esa chaqueta no te está bien,* that jacket doesn't fit you; **estar bien con,** to be on good terms with. — **estar con,** to have, e.g. *el niño está con fiebre,* the child has a fever; to be have, e.g. *estar con novio,* to have a boyfriend, to be engaged; *estar con una amiga,* to be staying or living with a friend; *estar contigo* (*con ustedes*), to be with you, be in agreement with you; *estar con candado,* to be padlocked (to be in seclusion); *estar con cólera,* to be angry; *estar con ganas de,* to be in the mood for, to want to; *estar con prisa,* to be in a hurry. — **estar de +** *n.,* to be + *ger.,* e.g. *estar de caza,* to be hunting; *estar de viaje,* to be traveling; *estar de mudanza,* to be moving (to a new house); **estar de +** *n.,* to be in + *n.,* e.g. *estar de fiesta,* to be at a party, in a party mood, on holiday; *estar de buen humor,* to be in a good mood, in good humor; **estar de +** *n.,* to be working or employed as, e.g. *estar de cocinera,* to be working (or acting) as a cook; **estar de más;** to be superfluous or redundant, to bc in the way, to be a supernumerary; **estar de pie,** to be on one's feet, to be standing. — **estar en,** to consist of, to lie in, c.g. *en eso está el problema,* therein lies the problem (of the key thereof); **estar en (mí, ti, ustedes, nosotros,** etc.), to be up to or to behoove or concern (me, you, they, we, etc.), e.g. *estaba en mí el haberlo hecho,* it was up to me to do it; *está en ti terminarlo,* it behooves you to put an end to it; **estar en una cosa,** to be informed about, to understand, be up to an event; **estar en jauja,** to be in a fine position, to be living it up; **estar en paz,** to be at peace, to have made up (after a fight); **estar en todo,** to have a finger in every pie, to be aware of everything, not to miss a trick. — **estar hecho un** or **una,** to have changed or turned into, e.g. *estás hecho una facha,* you look a sight; *estoy hecha una furia,* I am in a fury, I am furious. — **estar mal,** to be ill, be badly off, in a bad situation, to be wrong or mistaken; **estar mal con,** to be on bad terms with, to be in hot water with. — **estar para +** *n.,* to be in the mood or disposition for, e.g. *no estoy para bromas,* I'm in no mood for jokes; *estar para el gato,* to be a wreck, to be on one's last legs. — **estar por,** to be for, in favor of, on the side of, to champion (this or that person or cause); **e. por +** *inf.,* to remain to be done, e.g. *el postre está por hacer,* the dessert remains to be made; to be about to, e.g. *estoy por salir,* I'm about to go out, to leave. — **estar sin,** to be without, e.g. *estoy sin un centavo,* I am without a cent; *estoy sin trabajo,* I am unemployed, I don't have a job; *están sin esperanzas,* they are without hope. — **están verdes,** that's out of the question, impossible; those grapes are green (wish I could have them). — **estar viendo,** to see, to be aware, e.g. *estoy viendo venir el caos,* I see the chaos coming. — **¿estás? ¿estamos?** do you see it? are you with it? do you get it? —*r.v.* to be (as *aux.v.*) e.g. *estarse muriendo o estar muriéndose,* to be dying; *estar hasta tarde o estarse hasta tarde,* to stay late; *estarse callado,* to remain quiet or silent; *estarse parado,* to stay or remain standing. —*aux.v.* to be, e.g. *él está leyendo,* he is reading.
estarcido, *past part. of* **estarcir.** —*m.* stencil, outline.
estarcir, (*ref. 61*) *tr.v.* to stencil, to trace outlines.
estarna, *f.* (ornith.) grey partridge.
estarza, estarzo, *ref.* **estarcir.**
estasis, *f.* (med.) stasis.
estatal, *a.* of or pertaining to the state.
estática, *f.* (mec.) statics.
estático, ca, *a.* 1. static, still. 2. (mec.) static. 3. ecstatic, in ecstasy. 4. speechless, transfixed.
estatificar, (*ref. 50*) *tr.v.* to nationalize.
estatismo, *m.* (polit.) 1. statism. 2. immobility, static state.
estatocisto, *m.* (zool.) statocyst.
estatolito, *m.* (zool.) statolith.
estator, *m.* (mec., elec.) stator.
estatorreactor, *a., m.* (aer.) ramjet, athodyd.
estatoscopio, *m.* (phys., aer.) statoscope.
estatua, *f.* statue; **quedarse** or **estar hecho una e.,** to be rooted to the ground, to stand aghast.
estatuar, (*ref. 55*) *tr.v.* to decorate with statues.
estatuario, ria, *a., m., f.* statuary. —*m.* statuary, sculptor of statues. —*f.* statuary, sculpture.
estatúder, *m.* (hist.) stadholder, stadtholder, high executive and judicial office in the Netherlands.
estatuderato, *m.* stadholdership, stadholderate.
estatuido, da, *a.* statutory.
estatuir, (*ref. 48*) *tr.v.* 1. to establish. 2. to demonstrate, prove (a theory). 3. ordain, enact.
estatura, *f.* stature, height (of a person).
estatutario, ria, *a.* statutory.
estatuto, *m.* statute, ordinance, rule; law; **e. formal,** (law) formal statute; **e. personal,** (law) personal statute.
estatuya, estatuyendo, estatuyo, *ref.* **estatuir.**
estaurolita, *f.* (min.) staurolite.
estauroscopio, *m.* (min.) stauroscope.
estay, *m.* (mar.) stay; **e. mayor,** (mar.) mainstay.
este, *m.* east, orient; east wind.
este, esta, (*pl.* **estos, estas**) *dem. a.* this.
éste, ésta, (*pl.* **éstos, éstas**) *dem. pron.* this one; the latter. — **en éstas,** at this moment; meanwhile.
esteapsina, *f.* (biochem.) steapsin.
estearato, *m.* (chem.) stearate.
esteárico, ca, *a.* (chem.) stearic.
estearina, *f.* (chem.) stearin.
estearopteno, *m.* (chem.) stearoptene.
esteatita, *f.* (min.) steatite; French chalk.
esteatólisis, *f.* (med.) steatolysis.
esteatoma, *m.* (med.) steatoma, fatty tumor.
esteatopigia, *f.* (anat., med.) steatopygia, accumulation of fatty tissue in the buttocks.
esteatorrea, *f.* (med.) steatorrhea.
esteba, *f.* 1. (bot.) meadow spear grass. 2. (mar.) steeve (spar used for stowing bales of wool, etc.).
estebar, *tr.v.* to put (cloth) in the dyekettle. —*m.* place where spear grass grows.
estece, estecé, *ref.* **estezar.**
estefanote, *m.* (Ven., Peru, bot.) stephanotis.
estegomia, *f.* (ento.) yellow fever mosquito.
estegosauro, *m.* (paleon.) stegosaurus.
estela, *f.* 1. wake (of a ship), trail (of a comet, etc.). 2. (bot.) lady's mantle. 3. (archit.) stele. — **e. de condensación,** (aer.) contrail.
estelar, *a.* stellar, sidereal.
estelaria, *f.* (bot.) lady's mantle.
estelárido, da, *a., m., f.* (zool.) asteroidean. —*m., pl.* Asteroidea, starfishes.
estelífero, ra, *a.* (poet.) starry, star-studded.
esteliforme, *a.* stelliform, star-shaped.
estelión, *m.* 1. (zool.) stellion, tarente. 2. toadstone.
estelionato, *m.* (law) stellionate.
estelón, *m.* toadstone.
estemple, *m.* (min.) stemple, prop.
estenia, *f.* (med.) sthenia.
esténico, ca, *a.* (med.) sthenic.
estenio, *m.* (phys.) sthene.
estenocardia, *f.* (med.) stenocardia, angina pectoris.
estenófago, ga, *a.* (zool.) stenophagous.
estenografía, *f.* stenography, shorthand.
estenografiar, (*ref. 54*) *tr.v.* to stenograph, to write in shorthand.
estenográficamente, *adv.* stenographically, in shorthand.
estenográfico, ca, *a.* stenographic, stenographical.
estenógrafo, fa, *m., f.* stenographer.
estenordeste, *m.* 1. east-northeast. 2. east-northeaster, east-northeast wind.
estenosis, *f.* (med.) stenosis.
estenotérmico, ca, *a.* (med.) stenothermal.
estenotermo, a, *a.* (med.) stenothermal.
estenotipia, *f.* stenotype, keyboard machine that prints shorthand symbols.
estentóreo, a, *a.* stentorian, loud (voice).
estepa, *f.* 1. steppe, barren plain. 2. (bot.) rockrose. — **e. blanca,** white-leaved rockrose.
estepar, *m.* place where rockrose abounds.
estepario, ria, *a.* of or pertaining to a steppe.
estepero, ra, *a.* producing rockrose (said of soil). —*m., f.* rockrose seller. —*m.* place covered with rockrose (part of a house).
estepilla, *f.* (bot.) white-leaved rockrose.
estequiología, *f.* (physiol.) stoichiology, stoicheiology, stoechilogy.
estequiometría, *f.* (chem.) stoichiometry, stoicheiometry, stoechiometry.
éster, *m.* (chem.) ester.
estera, *f.* rush-matting, straw mat.

esteral, *m.* (Arg.) estuary, inlet.
esterar, *tr.v.* to cover with matting. —*i.v.* (coll.) to dress in winter clothes (ahead of the season).
esterasa, *f.* (biochem.) esterase.
estercoladura, *f.* **estercolamiento,** *m.* (agr.) manuring.
estercolar, *m.* dung or manure heap.
estercolar, *tr.v.* to manure, fertilize with manure. —*i.v.* to defecate (animals).
estercolero, *m.* dung collector; dung heap.
estercolizo, za, *a.* dung-like, dungy.
estercóreo, a, *a.* stercoraceous, stercoral.
estercuelo, *m.* manuring, muck-spreading.
esterculiáceo, a, *a.* (bot.) sterculiaceous.
estéreo, *m.* stere, cubic meter (of firewood).
estereóbato, *m.* (archit.) stereobate.
estereocromía, *f.* (art.) stereochromy, a process of mural painting.
estereocrómico, ca, *a.* (art.) stereochromic.
estereofónico, ca, *a.* (rad., elec.) stereophonic; (coll.) stereo.
estereografía, *f.* (art., geom.) stereography.
estereográfico, ca, *a.* (art., geom.) stereographic.
estereógrafo, *m.* (art., geom.) stereographer.
estereograma, *m.* (photo.) stereogram.
estereoisomería, *f.* (chem.) stereoisomerism.
estereoisómero, ra, *a.* (chem.) stereoisomeric. —*m.* stereoisomer.
estereometría, *f.* (geom.) stereometry.
estereométrico, ca, *a.* (geom.) stereometric.
estereóptico, *m.* (photo.) stereopticon.
estereoquímica, *f.* stereochemistry.
estereorradián, *m.* (geom.) stereoradian.
estereoscopía, *f.* (photo.) stereoscopy.
estereoscópico, ca, *a.* (photo.) stereoscopic.
estereosónico, *a.* (rad.) stereosonic.
estereotaxis, *f.* (biol.) stereotaxis.
estereotipa, *f., var. of* **estereotipia.**
estereotipado, da, *past part. of* **estereotipar.** —*a.* stereotyped.
estereotipador, *m.* (print.) stereotypist, stereotyper.
estereotipar, *tr.v.* (print.) to stereotype.
estereotipia, *f.* 1. (print.) stereotypy, stereotypography; stereotypist's shop; stereotype (block). 2. (med.) stereotype.
estereotípico, ca, *a.* (print., fig) stereotypic.
estereotipo, *m.* (print., fig.) stereotype.
estereotomía, *f.* (min., archit., art) stereotomy, stonecutting.
estereotropismo, *m.* (biol.) stereotropism.
esterería, *f.* shop where rush matting is made or sold.
esterero, *m.* maker of rush mats; layer of rush mats or matting.
estéril, *a.* 1. sterile, barren; fruitless. 2. lean, poor (harvest, season, year). 3. futile, unfruitful (discussion).
esterilice, esterilicé, *ref.* **esterilizar.**
esterilidad, *f.* 1. sterility, barrenness, infertility. 2. leanness, scarcity, unfruitfulness (of crops). 3. futility (of discussion).
esterilización, *f.* sterilization.
esterilizador, ra, *a.* sterilizing. —*m., f.* sterilizer.
esterilizar, (*ref. 53*) *tr.v.* to sterilize.
esterilla, *f.* 1. *dim. of* **estera,** rush mat. 2. gold or silver braid. 3. straw plait. 4. (C. Rica, Chile, Ecuad.) embroidery canvas. 5. (Arg.) canework (for backs and seats of chairs).
esterlín, *m.* (tex.) bocasine, fine buckram.
esterlina, *a.* 1. (G.B.) sterling (pound). 2. sterling (silver).
esternocostal, *a.* (anat.) sternocostal.
esternón, *m.* (anat.) sternum, breastbone.
estero, *m.* 1. tideland; inlet. 2. (Arg.) marshy or swampy land. 3. (Chile) stream. 4. (Ven.) pond, pool. 5. covering with or laying of rush mats; time for covering with or laying of rush mats.
esteroide, *m.* (chem.) steroid.
esterol, *m.* (biol.) sterol.
esteroscopio, *m.* (photo.) estereoscope.
esterquero, esterquilinio, *m.* dung heap, dunghill.
estertor, *m.* death rattle, rasping breath (of the dying); (med.) stertor.
estertoroso, sa, *a.* stertorous, rasping, labored (breathing).
estesia, *f.* (med.) esthesia.
estesiómetro, *m.* (med., psyc.) esthesiometer.
estesudeste, *m.* east-southeast; east-southeaster, east-southeast wind.
esteta, *m.* aesthete.
estética, *f.* (art, philos.) aesthetics.
estéticamente, *adv.* aesthetically.
esteticismo, *m.* (philos.) aestheticism.
estético, ca, *a.* aesthetic; artistic. —*m.* aesthetician, aesthete.
estetoscopia, *f.* (med.) stethoscopy.
estetoscopio, *m.* (med.) stethoscope.
esteva, *f.* 1. plow-handle. 2. reach (of a wagon); perch of a carriage.
estevado, *a.* bowlegged.
estevón, *m., var. of* **esteva.**
estezado, *past part. of* **estezar.** —*m.* dressed deerskin.
estezar, (*ref. 53*) *tr.v.* to dress (skins).
estiaje, *m.* low water (in the dry season); period of low water; low watermark.
estiba, *f.* 1. (mil.) rammer. 2. place where wool is compressed. 3. (mar.) stowage, stowing (of cargo or ballast). 4. (mar.) cargo; ballast.
estibador, *m.* stevedore, longshoreman.
estibar, *tr.v.* 1. to pack tightly. 2. (mar.) to stow, load. 3. to compress wool.
estibia, *f.* (vet.) sprain in the neck.
estibina, *f.* (chem.) stibine.
estibinita, *f.* (min.) stibnite.
estibio, *m.* (chem.) stibium, antimony.
esticometría, *f.* (poet.) stichometry.
esticomitia, *f.* (rhet.) stichomythia.
estiércol, *m.* dung, manure; (fig.) filth.
estigio, gia, *a.* (myth.) Stygian, of or characteristic of the river Styx encircling Hades; (fig.) infernal, hellish.
estigma, *m.* 1. (bot., zool., med.) stigma. 2. disgrace, affront. 3. brand, birthmark, stigma; mark of infamy. 4. (rel.) stigmata (in the body of Christ).
estigmasterol, *m.* (chem.) stigmasterol.
estigmatice, estigmaticé, *ref.* **estigmatizar.**
estigmático, ca, *a.* (bot.) stigmatic, stigmatical.
estigmatismo, *m.* (ophthal.) stigmatism.
estigmatizado, *m.* stigmatist.
estigmatizador, *a.* stigmatizing. —*m., f.* stigmatizer.
estigmatizar, (*ref. 53*) *tr.v.* 1. to stigmatize. 2. to brand. 3. to affront. 4. (theol.) to cause stigmata to appear.
estilar, *i.v., r.v.* to be in fashion, to be the custom, e.g. *no se estila llevar pieles en verano,* it's not customary to wear furs in summer. —*tr.v.* to draw up (a document). —*tr.v., i.v.* (Amer.) to drip, to distill.
estilbeno, *m.* (chem.) stilbene.
estilbestrol, *m.* (biochem.) stilbestrol, stilboestrol.
estilete, *m.* 1. stylet, style, graver, needle. 2. style, gnomon (of a sundial). 3. stiletto. 4. (med.) probe, stylet.
estilice, estilicé, *ref.* **estilizar.**
estilicidio, *m.* dripping, distillation, drop-by-drop issuing (of a liquid).
estiliforme, *a.* styliform, in the shape of a stylus.
estilismo, *m.* tendency to exaggerate a literary style.
estilista, *m., f.* stylist, master of style.
estilística, *f.* stylistics.
estilístico, ca, *a.* stylistic.
estilita, *a.* (ecc., hist.) stylitic, pertaining to a sect of Christian mystics who lived on the tops of pillars. —*m.* stylite, pillarist.
estilización, *f.* stylization.
estilizado, da, *a.* stylized; (Amer.) slender, lithe.
estilizar, (*ref. 53*) *tr.v.* to stylize, to characterize by stressing certain features.
estilo, *m.* 1. style (in all senses). 2. vogue, fashion. 3. stylus, style (writing instrument). — **al e. de,** in the style of; **e. antiguo,** old style; **e. braza,** breaststroke; **e. de vida,** way of life, lifestyle; **e. directo,** direct speech; **e. indirecto,** indirect speech; **e. libre,** freestyle; **e. mariposa,** butterfly swimming stroke; **e. pecho,** breaststroke; **por el e.,** like that, e.g. *algo por el e.,* something like that.
estilóbato, *m.* (archit.) stylobate, pedestal, a continuous base for a row of columns.
estilográfico, ca, *a.* stylographic (pen or writing). —*f.* fountain pen.
estiloideo, dea, *a.* (anat.) styloid.
estilolito, *m.* (geol.) stylolite.
estilopodio, *m.* (bot.) stylopodium.
estiloso, sa, *a.* (Guat.) vain, proud.
estima, *f.* 1. esteem, respect. 2. (mar.) dead reckoning. — **tener en poca e. a,** to hold in little esteem, have little respect for.
estimabilidad, *f.* estimableness, worthiness.
estimabilísimo, ma, *a. super. of* **estimable,** most estimable, most worthy.
estimable, *a.* 1. worthy of esteem or respect, estimable. 2. calculable, computable.
estimación, *f.* 1. esteem, apreciation, regard, respect. 2. appraisal, valuation, estimate. — **e. propia,** self-respect.
estimador, ra, *a.* appreciative. —*m., f.* appraiser.
estimar, *tr.v.* 1. to estimate. 2. to value. 3. to esteem, respect. 4. to think, consider. —*r.v.* to have a high opinion of oneself or one another.
estimativa, *f.* 1. judgment (faculty to judge). 2. instinct (in animals).
estimulación, *f.* the action and effect of stimulating; (med.) stimulation.
estimulador, ra, *a.* stimulating.
estimulante, *a.* stimulating. —*m.* stimulant.
estimular, *tr.v.* to stimulate; to encourage, spur, urge; to animate. — **e. al estudio,** to encourage to study.
estímulo, *m.* 1. stimulus. 2. (fig.) inducement, incentive. 3. (med.) stimulus.
estingo, *m.* (zool.) skink.
estío, *m.* (poet.) summer.
estiomenar, *tr.v.* (med.) to ulcerate.
estiómeno, *m.* (med.) ulceration; (med.) esthiomeno, estiomenus, lupus of the vulva.
estipendial, *a.* stipendiary, pertaining to a stipend.
estipendiar, *tr.v.* to give a stipend to.
estipendiario, ria, *a., m., f.* stipendiary.
estipendio, *a.* stipend; salary, wages.
estípite, *m.* 1. (archit.) pilastor in the shape of a truncated inverted pyramid. 2. (bot.) stipe, stalk.
estipticar, (*ref. 50*) *tr.v.* (med.) to astringe, bind; to clot.
estipticidad, *f.* (med.) stypticity; astringency.
estíptico, ca, *a.* 1. astringent (taste). 2. costive, constipated. 3. (fig.) mean, miserly, stingy. 4. (med.) styptic; astringent.
estiptique, estiptiqué, *ref.* **estipticar.**
estiptiquez, *f.* (Arg., Col.) constipation.
estípula, *f.* (bot.) stipule.
estipulación, *f.* stipulation.
estipulante, *a.* stipulating.

estipular, *tr.v., i.v.* to stipulate.
estipuliáceo, a, *a.* (bot.) stipular.
estique, *m.* (sculp.) toothed chisel.
estiquirín, *m.* (Hond.) horned owl.
estira, *f.* currier's knife.
estiracáceo, cea, *a.* (bot.) styracaceous. —*f.* styracaceous plant; (*pl.*) Styracaceae.
estirace, estiracé, *ref.* **estirazar.**
estiradamente, *adv.* 1. (fig.) hardly, scarcely. 2. (coll.) violently, forcibly.
estirado, da, *past part. of* **estirar.** —*a.* 1. fastidiously or formally dressed. 2. (fig.) haughty, arrogant. 3. (fig.) tight, stingy, mean. — **e. en frío,** hard-drawn.
estirador, *m.* (p.) drawing frame.
estirajar, *tr.v.* (coll.) *var. of* **estirar.**
estirajón, *m.* (coll.) *var. of* **estirón.**
estiramiento, *m.* 1. stretching. 2. (Chile) arrogance, haughtiness.
estirar, *tr.v.* 1. to stretch; to draw (wire). 2. to iron lightly. 3. (fig.) to stretch (money). 4. (Arg., Peru) to kill. —*r.v.* to stretch, stretch oneself. — **e. la pata,** (sl.) to kick the bucket; to die.
estirazar, (*ref.* 53) *tr.v.* (coll.) *var. of* **estirar.**
estireno, *m.* (chem.) styrene.
estirón, *m.* 1. strong pull, wrench, jerk, yank. 2. rapid growth.
estirpe, *f.* stock, family, lineage, ancestry; (law.) heirs, successors.
estirpicultura, *f.* stirpiculture.
estítico, ca, *a., var. of* **estíptico.**
estitiquez, *f.* (Amer.) constipation.
estivada, *f.* uncultivated land, the brushwood of which is dug up and burned.
estival, *a.* estival, pertaining to summer.
estivo, va, *a., var. of* **estival.**
esto, *dem. pron. neut.* this.— **en e.,** at this moment; meanwhile; **e. es,** that is, that is to say; **con e.,** herewith; **por e. es que,** that is why.
estocada, *f.* 1. thrust (of a sword), stab. 2. wound, stab.
estocafís, *m.* smoked codfish.
estocástico, ca, *a.* stochastic.
estofa, *f.* 1. (rare) embroidered silk material. 2. (fig.) kind, class, type.
estofado, da, *past part. of* **estofar.** —*a.* ornamented, adorned. —*m.* 1. quilting. 2. agraffito. 3. stew.
estofador, ra, *m., f.* quilter.
estofar, *tr.v.* 1. to quilt. 2. to distemper (burnished gold). 3. to do agraffito work on. 4. to size (wood before gilding). 5. to stew. 6. to adorn.
estofo, *m.* 1. quilting. 2. agraffito. 3. sizing.
estoicamente, *adv.* stoically.
estoicidad, *f.* imperturbability; stoicism.
estoicismo, *m.* (philos.) Stoicism; (fig.) stoicism.
estoico, ca, *a.* (philos.) Stoic; (fig.) stoic, stoical. —*m., f.* (philos.) Stoic; (fig.) stoic.
estola, *f.* stole, a long shawl.
estolidez, *f.* dullness, stupidity, dimwittedness (coll.).
estólido, da, *a.* dull, stupid, dimwitted (coll.).
estolón, *m.* 1. (ecc.) deacon's stole. 2. (bot.) stolon.
estoma, *m.* (bot.) stoma.
estomacal, *a.* stomachic; pertaining to the stomach. —*m.* (med.) stomachic.
estomagante, *a.* 1. bloating. 2. (fig.) annoying, irritating.
estomagar, (*ref.* 51) *tr.v.* 1. to give indigestion, bloat. 2. (fig.) to vex, irritate, annoy; to bore, disgust.
estómago, *m.* stomach; **hacer buen** or **mal e.,** to please or displease; **hacer uno e. a una cosa,** to resolve, to stomach or endure (something unpleasant); **quedar a uno algo en el e.,** to hold something back, not say all; **revolver el e.,** to turn or upset the stomach; **tener buen** or **mucho e.,** to be thickskinned; to be able to bear.
estomague, *ref.* **estomagar.**
estomaguero, *m.* baby's bellyband, stomacher.
estomatical, *a., var. of* **estomacal.**
estomático, ca, *a.* stomatic, pertaining to the mouth.
estomaticón, *m.* (med.) stomach plaster.
estomatitis, *f.* (med.) stomatitis, inflammation of the mouth.
estomatología, *f.* (med.) stomatology.
estomatópodo, *m.* (zool.) stomatopod.
estonio, nia, *a., m., f.* Estonian. —*m.* Estonian (language). —*f.* **E.,** Estonia.
estopa, *f.* 1. tow; burlap, tow cloth. 2. (mar.) oakum. — **e. de acero,** steel wool; **e. de algodón,** cotton waste.
estopada, *f.* piece of tow for spinning.
estopeño, ña, *a.* pertaining to a tow; made of tow.
estopera, *f.* (mec.) stuffing box.
estoperol, *m.* 1. (mar.) clout nail; tack, thumbtack. 2. (mar.) tow wick.
estopilla, *f.* finer part of tow; cheesecloth; cambric, lawn.
estopín, *m.* (artil.) priming tube, primer (of a cannon).
estopón, *m.* coarse tow; burlap, sackcloth.
estopor, *m.* (mar.) stopper (of anchor chain).
estoposo, sa, *a.* pertaining to a tow; towy; towlike, towy, fibrous.
estoque, *m.* 1. rapier; sword. 2. (bot.) gladiolus, sword lily. — **bastón de e.,** sword cane; **e. real,** royal sword symbolic of power and justice.
estoqueador, *m.* (taur.) matador.
estoquear, *tr.v.* to stab with a sword or rapier.
estoqueo, *m.* stabbing, thrusting.
estoquillo, *m.* (Chile) marsh sedge, bulrush (Soirpus riparius).
estor, *m.* curtain; blind, shade (for windows).
estora, *f.* matting attached to sides of cart.
estoraque, *m.* (bot.) storax (tree and resin); e. líquido, American storax.
estorbador, ra, *a.* obstructing; hindering; hampering. —*m., f.* obstructor; hinderer.
estorbar, *tr.v.* 1. to obstruct, block; to hinder, hamper, impede. 2. to annoy, bother, be in the way.
estorbo, *m.* 1. obstacle, obstruction; hindrance; stumbling block. 2. bother, nuisance, annoyance.
estorboso, sa, *a.* 1. obstructing, hindering, hampering. 2. bothersome, burdensome, annoying.
estornija, *f.* 1. (mec.) washer (of an axle). 2. a children's game.
estornino, *m.* (ornith.) starling.
estornudar, *i.v.* to sneeze.
estornudo, *m.* sneeze.
estornutatorio, a, *a.* sternutatory, sneeze-inducing; **polvo e.,** sneezing powder.
estotro, tra, *dem. pron.* this other.
estovar, *tr.v.* to cook in butter or oil over a slow fire; to sauté.
estoy, *ref.* **estar.**
estrabismo, *m.* (opt.) strabismus.
estrabotomía, *f.* (med.) strabotomy.
estracilla, *f.* 1. rag, tatter. 2. grey coarse paper.
estrada, *f.* road, highway; **batir la e.,** (mil.) to reconnoiter; **e. encubierta,** (mil.) covert way.
estradiota, *f.* long spear or lance.
estradivario, *m.* (mus.) Stradivarius (a fine make of violin).
estrado, *m.* 1. dais, raised platform. 2. drawing room furniture; drawing room. 3. baker's table. 4. (*pl.*) court rooms. — **citar para estrados,** (law) to subpoena; **hacer estrados,** (law) to hold court.
estrafalariamente, *adv.* 1. (coll.) outlandishly, bizarrely. 2. untidily, carelessly.
estrafalario, ria, *a.* 1. (coll.) outlandish, bizarre, eccentric. 2. slovenly, sloppy, untidy. —*m., f.* eccentric, outlandish character, screwball (sl.).
estragadamente, *adv.* disorderly, sloppily.
estragado, da, *past part. of* **estragar.** —*a.* 1. in disorder, sloppy. 2. corrupted, depraved, vitiated.
estragador, ra, *a.* 1. corrupting, pervading. 2. ravaging, devastating.
estragamiento, *m.* 1. ravage, devastation. 2. (lit., fig.) disruption, chaos.
estragar, (*ref.* 51) *tr.v.* 1. to disrupt; to vitiate. 2. to ravage, devastate. —*r.v.* to become spoiled or ruined.
estrago, *m.* (*gen. in pl.*) devastation, desolation, destruction, damage, havoc.
estragón, *m.* (bot.) tarragon.
estrague, estragué, *ref.* **estragar.**
estrambote, *m.* (poet.) additional couplet or triplet.
estrambóticamente, *adv.* (coll.) outlandishly, bizarrely.
estrambótico, ca, *a.* (coll.) outlandish, bizarre, queer, eccentric.
estramonio, *m.* (bot.) stramonium, Jimson weed, thorn apple.
estrangol, *m.* (vet.) inflammation of horse's tongue caused by bit.
estrangul, *m.* (mus.) mouthpiece (of a wind instrument).
estrangulación, *f.* strangling, strangulation; (surg.) strangulation.
estrangulador, ra, *a.* strangulating, strangling. —*m.* (auto.) choke. —*m., f.* strangler; **e. manual,** (mec.) hand throttle.
estrangular, *tr.v.* 1. to strangle, throttle. 2. (surg.) to strangulate. 3. (auto.) to choke. —*r.v.* 1. to strangle oneself. 2. (surg.) to become strangulated.
estranguria, *f.* (med.) strangury, painful discharge of urine.
estrapalucio, *m.* (coll.) clatter, crash (sound of breakage); racket, hullabaloo, pandemonium.
estraperlista, *m., f.* black marketeer.
estraperlo, *m.* 1. (coll.) black market; black market price, illegal surcharge. 2. (coll.) scheme, racket (gen. for making money). — **de e.,** (coll.) on the black market.
estrás, *m.* imitation jewelry; paste, strass.
Estrasburgo, *m.* Strasbourg.
estratagema, *f.* 1. stratagem; trick, ruse, scheme. 2. craftiness.
estratega, *m., f.* strategist.
estrategia, *f.* 1. strategy. 2. astuteness. 3. (Amer.) craftiness.
estratégicamente, *adv.* strategically.
estratégico, ca, *a.* strategic. —*m.* strategist.
estratego, *m.* strategist.
estratificación, *f.* (geol.) stratification.
estratificado, da, *a.* stratified.
estratificar, (*ref.* 50) *tr.v., r.v.* (geol.) to stratify.
estratifique, *ref.* **estratificar.**
estratiforme, *a.* stratiform.
estratigrafía, *f.* (geol.) stratigraphy.
estrato, *m.* stratum, layer; (geol., anat., biol.) stratum; (meteorol.) stratus. — **e. cristalino,** (geol.) quartziferous stratum; **estratos superiores de la sociedad,** upper strata of society.
estratocúmulo, *m.* (meteorol.) stratocumulus.
estratósfera, *f.* (meteorol.) stratosphere.
estrave, *m.* (mar.) stem (of keel).
estraza, *f.* rag, shred, tatter (of cloth). — **papel de e.,** rag paper (for wrapping).

estrechamente, *adv.* 1. tightly; narrowly. 2. closely; intimately. 3. strictly, rigorously. 4. frugally, austerely, scantily.
estrechamiento, *m.* 1. narrowing; tightening. 2. shaking (of hands). 3. coming closer together, rapprochement.
estrechar, *tr.v.* 1. to tighten, to narrow, reduce. 2. to take in, make narrower (clothes). 3. to press, harass, harry (enemy, etc.); to reduce to difficult straits. 4. to force, compel, oblige. — **e. a uno en los brazos,** to hug or embrace someone; **e. la mano a,** to shake hands with. —*r.v.* 1. to squeeze up, squash together (on seat). 2. to come closer together, become close or closer (relationships). 3. to cut down expenses. 4. to embrace, hug. — **estrecharse en los gastos,** to cut down one's expenses; **estrecharse las manos,** to shake hands.
estrechez, *f.* 1. narrowness; tightness. 2. shortage. 3. closeness, intimacy. 4. (fig.) trouble, difficulty, strait, jam. 5. (fig.) severity, austerity; (fig.) poverty, need, want. 6. (med.) stricture.
estrecho, cha, *a.* 1. narrow; tight. 2. close, intimate (relationship). 3. strict, rigid, severe. 4. mean, niggardly, mean-spirited. 5. tight (coll.), stingy (coll.), mean. —*m.* 1. (geog.) strait. 2. difficulty, jam. 3. (*pl.*) partners (at Twelfth-night revels). — **E. de Gibraltar,** Strait of Gibraltar; **E. de Magallanes,** Strait of Magellan.
estrechón, *m.* 1. (mar.) flapping (of sails). 2. jerk; pitching (of ship). — **e. de manos,** firm handshake.
estrechura, *f.* 1. narrowness. 2. closeness, intimacy. 3. strait, jam, difficulty. 4. austerity, severity.
estregadera, *f.* 1. scrubbing brush. 2. shoescraper.
estregadero, *m.* 1. place where animals rub themselves. 2. place for scrubbing or washing clothes.
estregadura, *f.* rubbing; scouring, scrubbing.
estregamiento, *m., var. of* **estregadura.**
estregar, (*ref. 51*) *tr.v.* to rub; to scrub, scour.
estregón, *m.* hard rub or scrub.
estregué, *ref.* **estregar.**
estrella, *f.* 1. star (heavenly body; spot on horse's head; leading actor or actress; outstanding person). 2. fate, destiny, star. 3. wheel, star wheel (of silk spinning wheel). 4. kind of canvas. 5. (fort.) star fort. 6. (*pl.*) star-shaped noodles. — **campar con su e.,** to be lucky or fortunate; **e. de mar,** (zool.) starfish; **e. errante** or **errática,** (astron.) planet; **e. fija,** (astron.) fixed star; **e. fugaz,** shooting star; **e. polar,** (astron.) pole star; **nacer con** or **tener buena e.,** to be born under a lucky star, be lucky; **poner sobre las estrellas,** to praise excessively; **querer contar las estrellas,** to reach for the moon; **ver estrellas,** (coll.) to see stars, feel sharp pain.
estrellada, *f.* (bot.) starwort, lady's mantle.
estrelladera, *f.* spatula for fried eggs.
estrelladero, *m.* (cul.) egg pan.
estrellado, da, *past part. of* **estrellar.** —*a.* 1. star-shaped, stellate. 2. starry, star-studded. 3. starred (as a horse). 4. (cul.) fried (egg).
estrellamar, *f.* 1. (zool.) starfish. 2. (bot.) hartshorn, hartshorn plantain.
estrellar, *tr.v.* 1. to spangle or cover with stars. 2. (coll.) to smash, dash (against). 3. to fry (eggs). —*r.v.* 1. to become starry or filled with stars. 2. (coll.) to crash, smash. 3. to fail, go on the rocks (a project, etc.). —*a.* stellar, stellated.
estrellera, *f.* (mar.) main tackle.
estrellería, *f.* astrology.
estrellero, ra, *a.* which tosses its head (a horse).
estrellón, *m.* 1. large star. 2. star-shaped firework. 3. (Amer.) crash, collision.

estremecedor, ra, *a.* terrifying, frightening; touching, shocking.
estremecer, (*ref. 45*) *tr.v.* to shake, make tremble; to stagger, shock, astound. —*r.v.* to shake, tremble, quake, quiver (with fear); to shiver, tremble (with the cold).
estremecimiento, *m.* shaking, quaking; shudder, shuddering.
estremezca, estremezco, *ref.* **estremecer.**
estrena, *f.* 1. gift, present. 2. (rare) inauguration, first use.
estrenar, *tr.v.* to use or to do for the first time; to inaugurate; to present for the first time (a film or play); to be the first occupant of; **e. la casa,** to have a housewarming. —*r.v.* to start, commence; to make one's first appearance or debut; to make one's first sale of the day; to open (play, film).
estreno, *m.* premiere, first performance; debut, inauguration.
estrenque, *m.* strong rope.
estrenuidad, *f.* strength, force, vigor; enterprise.*estrenuo, nua, a.* strenuous, strong; vigorous, enterprising.
estreñido, da, *past part. of* **estreñir.** —*a.* 1. constipated. 2. mean, stingy, niggardly, avaricious.
estreñimiento, *m.* constipation.
estreñir, (*ref. 41*) *tr.v.* to constipate, make constipated. —*r.v.* to become constipated.
estrepada, *f.* 1. pull (on a rope or with oars). 2. (mar.) thrust (of a boat driving ahead).
estrépito, *m.* 1. clamor, din, deafening, noise. 2. (fig.) ostentation, show.
estrepitosamente, *adv.* 1. noisily, deafeningly. 2. ostentatiously.
estrepitoso, sa, *a.* 1. noisy, deafening, boisterous, clamorous. 2. ostentatious, showy.
estreptobacilo, *m.* (med.) streptobacillus.
estreptococia, *f.* (med.) streptococcic infection.
estreptococo, *m.* (med.) streptococcus.
estreptolisina, *f.* (biochem.) streptolysin.
estreptomicina, *f.* (pharm.) streptomycin.
estreptoquinasa, *f.* (biochem.) streptokinase.
estreptotricina, *f.* (biochem.) streptothricin.
estría, *f.* (archit.) stria, flute; groove.
estriación, *f.* striation, striature.
estriado, da, *a.* striated, fluted, ribbed; serrated.
estriar, (*ref. 54*) *tr.v.* (archit.) to striate, flute, groove. —*r.v.* to become grooved.
estribación, *f.* (geog.) spur (of mountain range).
estribadero, *m.* prop, stay, support.
estribar, *i.v.* to rest (on), lie (on); to depend (on), be based (on).
estribera, *f.* 1. stirrup (of a saddle); (Arg.) stirrup leather or strap. 2. running board (of a car).
estribería, *f.* stirrup factory or shop.
estriberón, *m.* 1. stepping-stone. 2. (mil.) causeway, temporary road.
estribillo, *m.* refrain, ditty, chorus; pet word or expression.
estribo, *m.* 1. stirrup. 2. step, foot-board (of carriage); running-board (of car). 3. projection at the base of bull-ring barrier (to help bullfighter to jump the barrier). 4. iron ring (on head of an arbalest). 5. (fig.) basis, foundation, support. 6. (carp.) clamp, brace, stirrup. 7. (archit.) buttress, abutment (at base of bridge). 8. (geog.) spur (of mountain range). 9. (anat.) stirrup bone, stapes. — **perder los estribos,** to lose one's temper, lose control of oneself.
estribor, *m.* (mar.) starboard.
estribote, *m.* old poetic form employing a refrain.
estricnina, *f.* (chem.) strychnine.
estricnismo, *m.* (med.) strychninism.
estricote, *m.* (Ven.) disorderly licentious life. — **al e.,** hither and thither; on the go.

estrictamente, *adv.* strictly.
estrictez, *f.* (Amer.) strictness, severity.
estricto, ta, *a.* strict, severe; rigorous. — **dieta estricta,** rigorous diet.
estridencia, *f.* stridence, shrillness.
estridente, *a.* strident, shrill; (poet.) clamorous, noisy.
estridor, *m.* stridence, shrillness.
estridular, *i.v.* to screech, stridulate.
estriduloso, sa, *a.* (med.) stridulatory, stridulous.
estriego, estriegue, *ref.* **estregar.**
estrige, *f.* (ornith.) screech owl.
estrigilación, *f.* (med.) strigilation, massaging with a strigil.
estrilar, estrillar, *i.v.* (Arg., sl.) to be furious, be angry, be in a rage.
estrilo, estrillo, *m.* (Arg.) anger, fury.
estrinque, *m.* (mar.) *var. of* **estrenque.**
estriña, estriñendo, estriñera, estriñese, estriño, *ref.* **estreñir.**
estro, *m.* 1. inspiration, afflatus (of artists). 2. (vet.) oestrus, heat, rut (period of sexual stimulus in female animals). 3. (ento.) botfly; (bot.) larva of botfly.
estrobiláceo, a, *a.* (bot.) strobilaceous.
estróbilo, *m.* (zool.) strobila.
estrobo, *m.* (mar.) grommet, becket; strap, sling.
estroboscopio, *m.* stroboscope.
estrofa, *f.* strophe, stanza; verse.
estrofantina, *f.* (chem.) strophantin.
estrófico, ca, *a.* strophic, divided into strophes.
estrófulo, *m.* (med.) strophulus.
estrógeno, na, *a.* (biochem.) estrogenic. —*m.* (biochem.) estrogen.
estroma, *f.* 1. (anat.) stroma, connective tissue. 2. tapestry.
estrombo, *m.* (zool.) strombus.
estromeyerita, *f.* (min.) stromeyerite.
estromo, *m.* (bot.) stroma.
estrona, *f.* (biochem.) estrone, a female sex hormone.
estronciana, *f.* (chem.) strontia.
estroncianita, *f.* (min.) strontianite.
estroncio, *m.* (chem.) strontium; **e. radiactivo,** (chem.) radiostrontium.
estróngilo, *m.* (vet.) strongyle.
estrongiloidosis, *f.* (vet.) strongylosis.
estropajear, *tr.v.* rub down, scrub (a wall).
estropajeo, *m.* rubbing down, scrubbing (walls).
estropajo, *m.* 1. (bot.) luffa, dishcloth gourd (Luffa cilindrica). 2. esparto brush; rag, mop, dishcloth. 3. (fig.) worthless person; useless thing, trinket. — **tratar a uno como un e.,** to treat someone like a doormat.
estropajosamente, *adv.* (coll.) stammeringly, stutteringly.
estropajoso, sa, *a.* 1. (coll.) stammering, stuttering. 2. untidy, slovenly, unkempt. 3. (coll.) coarse, fibrous; tough (meat).
estropear, *tr.v.* 1. spoil, ruin; to wound, hurt, cripple. 2. to mishandle, mistreat. 3. (mas.) to mix (mortar) a second time. —*r.v.* to be ruined or spoiled; to be hurt or crippled.
estropeo, *m.* injury, damage; mishandling, mistreatment.
estropicio, *m.* 1. (coll.) breakage, crash. 2. noisy disturbance, hullabaloo.
estructura, *f.* structure, order, method.
estructuración, *f.* construction, organization.
estructural, *a.* structural.
estructurar, *tr.v.* to construct, organize.
estruendo, *m.* 1. clamor, noise, clatter, uproar. 2. ostentation, show.
estruendosamente, *adv.* thunderously, noisily, deafeningly.

estruendoso, sa, *a.* deafening, clamorous, noisy.
estrujador, ra, *a.* squeezing, crushing. —*m.* crusher, squeezer.
estrujadura, *f.* pressing, squeezing, crushing.
estrujamiento, *m., var. of* **estrujadura.**
estrujar, *tr.v.* 1. to squeeze, press; to crush, wring. 2. (coll.) to exhaust, oppress, drain (a people).
estrujón, *m.* last pressing (of grapes); (coll.) pressing, squeezing, crushing.
estruma, *f.* (med.) struma.
estrumoso, sa, *a.* strumous.
estuación, *f.* flood-tide.
estuante, *a.* hot, boiling, scorching.
Estuardo, *m.* (hist.) Stuart.
estuario, *m.* estuary.
estucado, *m.* stuccowork.
estucador, *m.* stucco-plasterer.
estucar, (*ref.* *50*) *tr.v.* to stucco, plaster with stucco.
estuchado, da, *a.* wrapped in paper.
estuche, *m.* 1. case, box, casket (for jewelry); sheath, etui (for scissors, etc.). 2. set (of instruments). 3. medium size comb. 4. combination of certain cards. — **e. de pinturas,** paintbox; **ser uno un e.,** (coll.) to be a clever or handy person.
estuchista, *m.* maker of cases or boxes.
estuco, *m.* stucco.
estucurú, *m.* (C. Rica, ornith.) large owl.
estudiado, da, *past part. of* **estudiar.** —*a.* affected, studied, feigned.
estudiador, ra, *a.* (coll.) studious.
estudiantado, *m.* pupils, student body.
estudiante, *m., f.* student; pupil. — **e. de intercambio,** exchange student.
estudiantil, *a.* pertaining to students or studies. — **huelga e.,** student strike.
estudiantino, na, *a.* pertaining to students. —*f.* strolling student band (playing for its own amusement or to collect money); carnival group dressed in old student dress.
estudiantón, *m.* (derog.) plodder, grind, studious but slow scholar.
estudiantuelo, la, *m., f.* (derog.) student.
estudiar, *tr.v.* 1. to study. 2. to read, memorize. 3. to think, mediate; to investigate. 4. (p.) to copy. —*i.v.* to study.
estudio, *m.* 1. study. 2. study, study-room; studio (film, radio, artist's). 3. (fig.) diligence, application. 4. (p.) sketch, study. 5. (mus.) etude, study. 6. (*pl.*) education, schooling. — **dar estudios a alguien,** to support someone during his studies; **e. de grabación,** recording studio; **e. de los mercados,** (econ.) market research; **e. fotográfico,** photographic studio; **e. jurídico,** lawyer's office.
estudiosamente, *adv.* studiously.
estudiosidad, *f.* studiousness.
estudioso, sa, *a.* studious.
estufa, *f.* 1. stove, heater, foot-heater. 2. greenhouse, hothouse, conservatory. 3. drying chamber; sweating-room. — **e. de desinfección,** sterilizer.
estufador, *m.* stew-pan.
estufero, *m., var. of* **estufista.**
estufilla, *f.* hand muff; foot-stove, foot warmer.
estufista, *m., f.* stove-maker; stove repairer; stove seller.
estultamente, *adv.* foolishly, stupidly.
estulticia, *f.* foolishness, stupidity, silliness.
estulto, ta, *a.* foolish, silly.
estuosidad, *f.* burning, excessive heat, feverishness (as from sunburn).
estuoso, sa, *a.* (poet.) hot, ardent, burning.
estupefacción, *f.* stupefaction, astonishment.
estupefaciente, *a.* stupefacient. —*m.* stupefacient, narcotic (as morphine, cocaine).
estupefactivo, va, *a.* stupefying, stupefactive.
estupefacto, ta, *a.* stupefied, astonished, thunderstruck.
estupendamente, *adv.* stupendously.
estupendo, da, *a.* stupendous, wonderful, marvelous.
estúpidamente, *adv.* stupidly.
estupidez, *f.* stupidity, stupid remark or action.
estúpido, da, *a.* stupid, foolish; dull, dim-witted. —*m., f.* idiot, fool.
estupor, *m.* 1. (med.) stupor, lethargy, torpor. 2. (fig.) stupefaction, amazement, astonishment.
estuprador, *m.* rapist, violator.
estuprar, *tr.v.* to rape, violate.
estupro, *m.* (law) defloration (of a minor); rape, violation.
estuque, *m.* stucco.
estuque, estuqué, *ref.* **estucar.**
estuqueria, *f.* stuccowork.
estuquista, *m.* stucco-worker.
esturar, *tr.v.* to overcook; to parch, scorch.
esturgar, (*ref.* *51*) *tr.v.* to fettle (pottery).
esturgue, esturgué, *ref.* **esturgar.**
esturión, *m.* (ornith.) sturgeon; (*pl.*) Acipenseridae, sturgeon family.
estuve, estuviera, estuviese, *ref.* **estar.**
ésula, *f.* (bot.) sun spurge.
esvarar, *i.v., r.v.* to slip.
esvarón, *m.* slip.
esviaje, *m.* (archit.) skew, slope.
eta, *f.* eta, seventh letter of Greek alphabet.
etalaje, *m.* bosh (of a blast furnace).
etano, *m.* (chem.) ethane.
etapa, *f.* 1. stage, step, era, epoch; leg, hop (of race, etc.). 2. (mil.) field ration. 3. (mil.) stop (in march). — **de una e.,** (aer.) single-stage (rocket).
etcétera, *f.* et cetera.
éter, *m.* 1. (chem., phys.) ether. 2. (poet.) sky, heavens, space. — **é. etílico,** (chem.) ethyl ether.
etéreo, a, *a.* 1. ethereal, heavenly. 2. (chem.) ethereal, pertaining to ether.
eterice, etericé, *ref.* **eterizar.**
eterificación, *f.* (chem.) etherification.
eterificar, (*ref.* *50*) *tr.v.* (chem.) to etherify.
eterismo, *m.* etherism.
eterización, *f.* (med.) etherization.
eterizar, (*ref.* *53*) *tr.v.* (med.) to etherize; (chem.) to combine with ether.
eternal, *a., var. of* **eterno.**
eternalmente, *adv., var. of* **eternamente.**
eternamente, *adv.* eternally, perpetually, everlastingly.
eternice, eternicé, *ref.* **eternizar.**
eternidad, *f.* eternity, perpetuity.
eternizable, *a.* worthy of perpetuation.
eternizar, (*ref.* *53*) *tr.v.* 1. to eternize, perpetuate; to prolong indefinitely or interminably. 2. (fig.) to immortalize. —*r.v.* to last an eternity.
eterno, na, *a.* eternal, everlasting, unending.
eteromanía, *f.* etheromania.
etesio, *a.* etesian, periodical (winds). —*m.* etesian wind.
ética, *f.* ethics.
ético, ca, *a.* 1. ethical. 2. (med.) consumptive, phthisical. —*m., f.* ethicist, ethician.
etilamina, *f.* (chem.) ethylamine.
etileno, *m.* (chem.) ethylene, ethene.
etílico, ca, *a.* ethylic.
etilo, *m.* (chem.) ethyl.
étimo, *m., var. of* **etimología.**
etimología, *f.* etymology.
etimológicamente, *adv.* etymologically.
etimologice, etimologicé, *ref.* **etimologizar.**
etimológico, ca, *a.* etymological, etymologic.
etimologista, *m., f.* etymologist.
etimologizar, (*ref.* *53*) *tr.v.* to etymologize, formulate the etymology of.
etimólogo, ga, *m., f.* etymologist.
etiología, *f.* (philos., med.) etiology, aetiology (investigation of causes).
etiológico, ca, *a.* etiological, aetiological.
etíope, *a., m., f.* Ethiopian. —*m.* (chem.) artificial mixture used to prepare vermillion.
Etiopía, *f.* Ethiopia.
etiópico, ca, *a.* Ethiopian, Ethiopic.
etiópide, *f.* (bot.) clary.
etiopio, pia, *a., m., f.* Ethiopian, Ethiopic.
etiqueta, *f.* 1. etiquette, ceremony, formality, protocol. 2. tag, label. — **traje de e.,** evening dress, formal dress.
etiquetero, ra, *a.* ceremonious, punctilious.
etiquez, *f.* (med.) consumption.
etites, *f.* (min.) eaglestone.
etmoidal, *a.* (anat.) ethmoidal, ethmoid.
etmoides, *a., m.* (anat.) ethmoid bone.
etnarca, *m.* (hist.) ethnarch (in ancient Greece).
etnarquía, *f.* (hist.) ethnarchy.
etneo, a, *a.* Etnean, pertaining to Mount Etna.
étnico, ca, *a.* 1. ethnic, ethnical. 2. (gram.) gentilic.
etnocentrismo, *m.* (psyc.) ethnocentrism.
etnogenia, *f.* (anth.) ethnogeny.
etnografía, *f.* (anth.) ethnography.
etnográfico, ca, *a.* ethnographical, ethnographic.
etnógrafo, *m.* ethnographer.
etnología, *f.* (anth.) ethnology.
etnológico, ca, *a.* ethnological, ethnologic.
etnólogo, *m.* ethnologist.
etología, *f.* (biol.) ethology.
etopeya, *f.* ethopoeia, description of the character, habits, beliefs, etc., of an individual.
etrusco, ca, *a., m., f.* Etruscan. —*m.* Etruscan (language).
etusa, *f.* (bot.) hemlock.
Eu *sym. of* **europio,** europium (Eu).
E.U. *abbrev. of* **Estados Unidos,** United States (U.S.).
E.U.A. *abbrev. of* **Estados Unidos de América,** United States of America (U S A).
euboico, ca, *a.* Euboean, Euboic.
eubolia, *f.* discretion in speaking.
eucaína, *f.* (chem., pharm.) eucaine.
eucalipto, *m.* (bot.) eucalyptus.
eucaliptol, *m.* (chem., pharm.) eucalyptole, eucalyptol.
eucaristía, *f.* (ecc.) Eucharist.
eucarístico, ca, *a.* Eucharistic, Eucharistical.
euclasa, *f.* (min.) euclase.
Euclides, *m.* (hist.) Euclid, greek mathematician.
euclidiano, na, *a.* Euclidean.
eucologio, *m.* (ecc.) euchology.
eucósmido, *m.* (ento.) codling moth.
eucrasia, *f.* (med.) normal health.
eucromatina, *f.* (biol.) euchrotin.
eudemonía, *f.* (philos.) eudaemonia.
eudemonismo, *f.* (philos.) eudaemonism.
eudiometría, *f.* (chem.) eudiometry.
eudiómetro, *m.* (phys.) eudiometer.
eufemismo, *m.* euphemism.
eufemístico, ca, *a.* euphemistic, euphemistical.
eufonía, *f.* euphony.
eufónico, ca, *a.* euphonic, euphonical.
eufonizar, (*ref.* *53*) *tr.v.* to euphonize.
euforbiáceo, a, *a.* (bot.) euphorbiaceous. —*f.* (*pl.*) Euphorbiaceae.
euforbio, *m.* 1. (bot.) African or Moroccan spurge (Euphorbia resinifera). 2. (pharm.) euphorbium (brownish resin).
euforia, *f.* 1. euphoria, feeling of well-being. 2. resistance to disease and adversity.
eufórico, ca, *a.* euphoric.

eufótida, *f.* (geol.) euphotide.
eufrasia, *f.* (bot.) eyebright, euphrasy (Euphrasia officinalis).
Eufrates, *m.* Euphrates, river of S. W. Asia.
eufuismo, *m.* euphuism.
eugenesia, *f.* eugenics.
eugenésico, ca, *a.* eugenic, eugenical.
eugenol, *m.* (chem.) eugenol.
euglena, *f.* (zool.) euglena.
eulogia, *f.* (rel.) eulogia.
eumórfico, ca, *a.* (anth.) eumorphic.
eunuco, *m.* eunuch.
eunuquismo, *m.* eunuchism.
eupatorio, *m.* (bot.) eupatorium, boneset.
eupátrida, *m.* (hist.) eupatrid.
eupepsia, *f.* (med.) eupepsia, good digestion.
eupéptico, ca, *a., m., f.* (med.) eupeptic.
eupnea, *f.* (physiol.) eupnea, eupnoea.
Eurasia, *f.* Eurasia.
eurasio, a, eurasiático, ca, *a., m., f.* Eurasian.
EURATOM, *abbrev. of* **Comunidad Europea de Energía Atómica,** European Atomic Energy Community (EURATOM).
eureka, *interj.* eureka! (I found it).
Eurídice, *f.* (myth.) Eurydice, wife of Orpheus.
Eurípides, *m.* (hist., lit.) Euripides, Greek dramatist.
euriptérido, *m.* (paleon.) eurypterid.
euritmia, *f.* eurythmy.
eurítmico, ca, *a.* eurythmic.
euro, *m.* Eurus, east wind; **e. noto,** (poet.) southeast wind.
Europa, *f.* 1. (myth.) Europe. 2. Europe.
europeice, *ref.* **europeizar.**
europeísta, *m., f.* supporter of European unity and hegemony.
europeizar, (*ref. 53*) *tr.v.* to Europeanize.
europeo, a, *a., m., f.* European.
europio, *m.* (chem.) europium.
euscalduna, *a., m.* Basque (language).
éuscaro, ra, éusquero, ra, *a.* Basque (language). —*m.* Basque (language).
eustático, ca, *a.* (geog., geol.) eustatic.
éustilo, *a., m.* (archit.) eustyle.
eutanasia, *f.* euthanasia.
eutéctico, ca, *a., m.* (phys.) eutectic.
eutectoide, *a., m.* (chem.) eutectoid.
euténica, *f.* euthenics.
eutiquianismo, *m.* Eutychianism, doctrine of Eutyches.
eutiquiano, na, *a., m., f.* Eutychian.
eutrapelia, *f.* moderation (in pleasure); innocent or simple pastime or pleasure; jolliness, lightheartedness.
eutrapélico, ca, *a.* moderate, temperate.
eutrofia, *f.* eutrophy.
eutrófico, ca, *a.* eutrophic.
eutropelia, *f., var. of* **eutrapelia.**
eutropélico, ca, *a., var. of* **eutrapélico.**
euxenita, *f.* (min.) euxenite.
ev. *abbrev. of* **electrovoltio,** electron volt (ev).
evacuación, *f.* evacuation.
evacuador, *m.* 1. evacuator. 2. (hydr.) wasteway, escape; spillway.
evacuante, *a.* emetic, diuretic. —*m.* evacuant.
evacuar, (*ref. 55*) *tr.v.* 1. to evacuate; to vacate, empty, disoccupy, leave vacant. 2. to drain (a wound). 3. to carry out, perform.
evacuativo, va, *a.* (med.) evacuative. —*m.* purge, purgative, evacuant.
evacuatorio, ria, *a.* (med.) evacuative. —*m.* public convenience or lavatory.
evadir, *tr.v.* to evade, elude, dodge; to avoid. —*r.v.* to evade; to escape.
evagación, *f.* digression, wandering (of thoughts).
evaluación, *f.* evaluation.
evaluador, ra, *a.* evaluating.
evaluar, (*ref. 55*) *tr.v.* to evaluate, assess.
evanescente, *a.* evanescent, disappearing.
evangeliario, *m.* gospel book.
evangélicamente, *adv.* evangelically, according to the gospel.
evangelice, evangelicé, *ref.* **evangelizar.**
evangélico, ca, *a.* evangelical, evangelic.
evangelio, *m.* 1. gospel, evangel. 2. Christianity. 3. gospel, undisputable truth. — **decir el e.,** to tell the gospel truth. 4. (*pl.*) Gospel-booklet with relics, worn by children.
evangelismo, *m.* (rel.) evangelism.
evangelista, *m.* 1. evangelist (writer of any of the Four Gospels); gospeler, singer of the gospel. 2. (Mex.) amanuensis, public clerk.
evangelistero, *m.* gospeler, singer of the gospel.
evangelización, *f.* evangelization.
evangelizador, ra, *a.* evangelizing. —*m.* evangelist, evangelizer.
evangelizar, (*ref. 53*) *tr.v.* to evangelize, preach the gospel to.
evaporable, *a.* evaporable.
evaporación, *f.* evaporation.
evaporador, ra, *a.* evaporating. —*m., f.* evaporator.
evaporar, *tr.v.* to evaporate. —*r.v.* to evaporate; (fig.) to vanish, evaporate.
evaporatorio, ria, *a.* (med.) evaporative.
evaporice, *ref.* **evaporizar.**
evaporizar, (*ref. 53*) *tr.v., i.v., r.v.* to vaporize.
evaporómetro, *m.* (phys.) evaporimeter.
evasión, *f.* 1. escape; evasion, avoidance. 2. pretext, excuse, evasion. — **e. fiscal** or **de impuestos,** tax evasion.
evasivamente, *adv.* evasively.
evasiva, *f.* pretext, excuse, evasion.
evasivo, va, *a.* evasive.
evasor, ra, *a.* evading, eluding.
evección, *f.* (astron.) evection, inequality of moon's motion in its orbit.
evento, *m.* chance event or occurrence, contingency, happening.
eventual, *a.* accidental, contingent, unexpected, fortuitous; incidental (expenses, income).
eventualidad, *f.* eventuality, contingency.
eventualmente, *adv.* fortuitously, by chance; occasionally, from time to time; irregularly.
eversión, *f.* 1. destruction, desolation, devastation. 2. (med.) eversion.
evicción, *f.* (law) eviction, dispossession.
evidencia, *f.* 1. absolute certainty. 2. (Amer.) evidence, proof. — **poner en e.,** to give (someone) away, to show (someone) is lying; **ponerse en e.,** to give oneself away, to show that one is lying; **quedar en e.,** to be proved, to be found out.
evidenciar, *tr.v.* to make evident, clear; to prove.
evidente, *a.* evident; clear, patent, manifest, obvious.
evidentemente, *adv.* evidently, obviously, plainly.
evitable, *a.* avoidable, evitable.
evitación, *f.* avoidance.
evitar, *tr.v.* to avoid, evade, dodge (coll.), shun.
eviterno, na, *a.* everlasting, unending.
evo, *m.* 1. (theol., poet.) eternity, aeon. 2. age, e.g. *el medioevo,* the Middle Ages.
evocable, *a.* evocable.
evocación, *f.* evocation, evoking.
evocador, ra, *a.* evocative, evocatory.
evocar, (*ref. 50*) *tr.v.* 1. to evoke, recall. 2. to call up (spirits of the dead).
evolución, *f.* 1. evolution, gradual development. 2. (mil., mar.) evolution, maneuver.
evolucionar, *i.v.* 1. to evolve, develop. 2. (mil., mar.) to maneuver, perform evolutions or maneuvers.
evolucionario, *a.* evolutionary.
evolucionismo, *m.* evolutionism.
evolucionista, *a.* evolutionary, evolutionistic. —*m., f.* evolutionist.
evolutivo, va, *a.* evolutive, evolutional, evolutionary.
evolvente, *a.* (geom.) evolvent.
evónimo, *m.* (bot.) spindle tree (Enonymus europaeus).
evoque, evoqué, *ref.* **evocar.**
evulsión, *f.* (med.) evulsion, extraction.
ex-, *pre.* ex, out, out of, off; formerly.
ex abrupto, *adv.* (Lat.) abruptly, violently.
exabrupto, *m.* rebuff, brusque remark.
exaccion, *f.* exaction, levying (of taxes); extortion.
exacerbación, *f.* exacerbation, aggravation.
exacerbar, *tr.v.* to exacerbate, aggravate; to irritate, annoy. —*r.v.* to be exacerbated or aggravated; to become irritated or annoyed.
exactamente, *adv.* exactly.
exactitud, *f.* accuracy, exactness, exactitude.
exacto, ta, *a.* exact, accurate; correct, right, loyal, punctual. —*adv.* (coll.) exactly, quite.
exactor, *m.* tax-collector.
exaedro, *m.* (geom.) hexahedron.
exageración, *f.* exaggeration.
exageradamente, *adv.* exaggeratedly.
exagerador, ra, *a.* exaggerating. —*m., f.* exaggerator.
exagerante, *a.* exaggerating.
exagerar, *tr.v.* to exaggerate.
exagerativamente, *adv.* exaggeratedly.
exagerativo, va, *a.* exaggerative, exaggeratory.
exagonal, *a.* hexagonal.
exágono, *m.* hexagon. —*a.* hexagonal.
exaltación, *f.* exaltation, glorification; elevation, raising; stimulation (of senses).
exaltado, da, *past part. of* **exaltar.** —*a.* hotheaded, excited. —*m., f.* 1. hothead. 2. visionary; zealot.
exaltamiento, *m.* 1. exaltation. 2. elevation (to office).
exaltar, *tr.v.* to exalt, glorify; to praise, extol. —*r.v.* to get excited, worked up (coll.).
examen, *m.* examination; interrogatory; inspection, search; survey. — **dar un e.,** to take an examination; **e. de ingreso,** entrance examination; **e. de testigos,** (law) interrogation of witnesses; **e. libre,** free investigation (using no other criterion than one's reasoning).
examinador, ra, *m., f.* examiner.
examinando, da, *m., f.* examinee.
examinante, *a.* examining.
examinar, *tr.v.* to examine; to inspect, investigate, search; to question. —*r.v.* (with de) to take an examination in.
exangüe, *a.* 1. exsanguine, anemic, bloodless. 2. (fig.) weak, pooped (sl.). 3. (fig.) dead.
exanimación, *f.* lifelessness.
exánime, *a.* lifeless; (fig.) extremely weak, faint.
exantema, *m.* (med.) exanthema, rash.
exantemático, ca, *a.* (med.) exanthematic, exanthematous.
exaración, *f.* (geol.) glacial erosion.
exarca, *m.* exarch (viceroy of Byzantine Emperor, deputy to a patriarch).
exarcado, *m.* exarchate, office or province of an exarch.
exarco, *m., var. of* **exarca.**
exárico, *m.* Moorish tenant or serf.
exasperación, *f.* exasperation, irritation.
exasperante, *a.* exasperating.

exasperar, *tr.v.* to exasperate, irritate; to aggravate, irritate (pain). —*r.v.* to become exasperated; to get worse (pain).
excandecencia, *f.* anger, exasperation.
excandecer, (*ref. 45*) *tr.v.* to infuriate, anger. —*r.v.* to become furious or angry.
excandezca, excandezco, *ref.* **excandecer.**
excarcelable, *a.* releasable.
excarcelación, *f.* (law) freeing, releasing.
excarcelar, *tr.v.* (law) to set free, release.
ex cáthedra, *adv.* ex cathedra, authoritatively, with authority.
excava, *f.* (agr.) removal of soil from around plants.
excavación, *f.* excavation.
excavador, ra, *a.* excavating, digging. —*m., f.* excavator, digger. —*f.* excavator, machine for excavating earth, steam shovel.
excavar, *tr.v.* to excavate, dig; (agr.) to remove soil from. — **e. en escalones,** (min.) to stope.
excedencia, *f.* excess, superfluity; redundancy.
excedente, *a.* excessive; superfluous, surplus; supernumerary, redundant. —*m.* surplus.
exceder, *tr.v.* to surpass; to exceed, go beyond. —*r.v.* to excel oneself, surpass oneself, go beyond oneself; to go too far, to overstep the mark (of what is permissible).
excelencia, *f.* 1. excellence. 2. E., Excellency (title); **por e.,** par excellence.
excelente, *a.* excellent. —*m.* an ancient Spanish gold coin.
excelentemente, *adv.* excellently.
excelentísimo, ma, *a. super. of* **excelente,** most excellent.
excelsamente, *adv.* sublimely, highly.
excelsitud, *f.* sublimeness, loftiness.
excelso, sa, *a.* sublime, elevated, exalted; lofty. — **el Excelso,** the Almighty (God).
excéntricamente, *adv.* eccentrically.
excentricidad, *f.* 1. eccentricity. 2. eccentric or queer remark. 3. (geom.) eccentricity.
excéntrico, ca, *a.* 1. eccentric, eccentrical, queer, odd. 2. (geom.) eccentric, abaxial. —*m.* circus performer, clown. —*f.* (mec.) eccentric (wheel).
excepción, *f.* exception; (law) demurrer, exception.
excepcional, *a.* exceptional; unusual.
excepcionar, *tr.v.* (law) to lodge a demurrer or exception, object against.
exceptivo, va, *a.* exceptive.
excepto, *adv.* except, excepting, save, apart from.
exceptuación, *f.* excluding, exclusion.
exceptuado, da, *past part. of* **exceptuar.** —*a.* exclusive, excluded.
exceptuar, (*ref. 55*) *tr.v.* exclude, leave out, except; to exempt.
excerpta, excerta, *f.* excerpt, extract.
excesivamente, *adv.* excessively.
excesivo, va, *a.* excessive, exorbitant.
exceso, *m.* 1. excess. 2. (com.) surplus. — **en e.,** to excess, excessively; **e. de peso** or **de equipaje,** excess weight or luggage; **e. de velocidad,** speeding, e.g. *le arrestaron por e. de velocidad,* they arrested him for speeding.
excipiente, *m.* (pharm.) excipient.
excisión, *f.* (surg.) excision.
excitabilidad, *f.* excitability, excitableness.
excitable, *a.* excitable.
excitación, *f.* 1. excitment, excitation. 2. stimulation; incitement. — **e. propia,** (elec.) self-excitation.
excitador, ra, *a.* excitatory; stimulating. —*m.* (elec.) exciter.
excitante, *a.* exciting, excitant; stimulating. —*m.* stimulant.
excitar, *tr.v.* to excite; to stimulate; to incite, stir up. —*r.v.* to become excited.
excitativo, va, *a.* exciting, excitative.
excitatriz, *f.* (elec.) exciter.
exclamación, *f.* exclamation.
exclamar, *tr.v.* to exclaim.
exclamativo, va, *a.* exclamatory.
exclamatorio, ria, *a.* exclamatory.
exclaustración, *f.* secularization (of monks or nuns).
exclaustrado, da, *past part. of* **exclaustrar.** —*m., f.* secularized monk or nun.
exclaustrar, *tr.v.* to secularize (monks, nuns).
excluible, *a.* excludable.
excluidor, ra, *a.* excluding, that which excludes.
excluir, (*ref. 48*) *tr.v.* to exclude; to expel, eject, throw out; to reject, deny admission.
exclusión, *f.* 1. exclusion, denying admission, rejection.
exclusiva, *f.* 1. rejection. 2. sole or exclusive right.
exclusivamente, *adv.* exclusively, only.
exclusive, *adv.* exclusively, excluding, not including.
exclusivismo, *m.* exclusivism, blind adherence to one idea (opposite of eclecticism).
exclusivista, *a., m., f.* exclusivist.
exclusivo, va, *a.* exclusive.
excluso, sa, *irr. past part. of* **excluir.**
Excma., Excmo. *abbrev. of* **Excelentísima, Excelentísimo,** Most Excellent.
excogitable, *a.* imaginable, conceivable; devisable.
excogitar, *tr.v.* to excogitate, meditate, think out, deduce; to devise.
excomulgado, da, *past part. of* **excomulgar.** —*a.* 1. excommunicated. 2. (coll.) accursed, wicked, perverse. —*m., f.* excommunicated person, excommunicant.
excomulgador, *m.* excommunicator.
excomulgar, (*ref. 51*) *tr.v.* to excommunicate; to anathematize.
excomulgue, excomulgué, *ref.* **excomulgar.**
excomunión, *f.* excommunication. — **e. mayor,** anathema, active and passive deprivation of sacraments; **e. menor,** passive deprivation of sacraments.
excoriación, *f.* excoriation.
excoriar, *tr.v.* to chafe, excoriate. —*r.v.* to be chafed or worn away; to be rubbed raw.
excrecencia, *f.* excrescence, excrescency.
excreción, *f.* excretion.
excremental, *a.* excremental.
excrementar, *tr.v.* to excrete.
excrementicio, cia, *a.* excremental; waste, e.g. *residuous e.,* waste products (of body).
excremento, *m.* excrement.
excrementoso, sa, *a.* excremental, excrementitious (applied to food which produces more waste products than others).
excrescencia, *f., var. of* **excrecencia.**
excretar, *i.v.* to excrete.
excreto, ta, *a.* excreted.
excretorio, ria, *a.* (zool.) excretory, excretive.
exculpación, *f.* exculpation, exoneration.
exculpar, *tr.v. to* exculpate, exonerate. —*r.v.* to be exculpated or exonerated.
excursión, *f.* 1. excursion, outing, pleasure trip. 2. raid, incursion.
excursionista, *m., f.* excursionist.
excusa, *f.* 1. excuse. 2. (law) demurrer, exception. 3. frail, hamper.
excusabaraja, *f.* wickerwork hamper or basket.
excusable, *a.* excusable, pardonable.
excusación, *f., var. of* **excusa.**
excusadamente, *adv.* unnecessarily, needlessly.
excusado, da, *past part. of* **excusar.** —*a.* 1. exempt (from taxes). 2. unnecessary, needless. 3. reserved, private. — **meterse en la renta del e.,** to meddle in other people's business. —*m.* outhouse, water closet, toilet, lavatory.
excusador, ra, *a.* excusing, exonerating. —*m.* substitute, stand-in.
excusalí, *m.* small apron, pinafore.
excusar, *tr.v.* 1. to excuse, exculpate. 2. to avoid, prevent. 3. to refuse to do or make. 4. to exempt from, excuse from. —*r.v.* 1. to apologize; to excuse oneself. 2. (with de) to refuse to, to decline to.
excusión, *f.* (law) excussion, attachment, legal seizure.
exea, *m.* (mil.) scout.
execrable, *a.* execrable, abominable.
execración, *f.* execration, cursing; (ecc.) desecration, profanation.
execrador, ra, *a.* execrating. —*m., f.* execrator.
execrando, da, *a.* execrable.
execrar, *tr.v.* 1. to execrate, curse, damn, anathematize. 2. to abhor, detest; to reprove severely.
execrativo, va, *a.* execrative.
execratorio, ria, *a.* execratory, execrative.
exedra, *f.* (archit.) exedra, an open portico-like room furnished with seats, used in ancient Greece for conversation.
exégesis, *f.* exegesis, explanation, interpretation (esp. of a religious text).
exegeta, *m.* exegete, interpreter of the Holy Scriptures or of literary texts.
exegético, ca, *a.* exegetic, exegetical, explanatory, expository; (law) expository.
exención, *f.* exemption, privilege, immunity.
exencionar, *tr.v.* to exempt, to free or excuse from.
exentamente, *adv.* 1. freely. 2. simply, clearly, frankly, sincerely.
exentar, *tr.v.* to exempt, free (from), excuse (from); to absolve, acquit. —*r.v.* to excuse, exempt or except oneself.
exento, ta, *a.* 1. free, exempt, privileged; disengaged. 2. open, clear, unobstructed.
exequátur, *m.* exequatur (a document recognizing the validity of papal bulls or the authority of a foreign consul).
exequial, *a.* (Chile) exequial, funeral.
exequias, *f.* (*pl.*) exequies, funeral rites, obsequies.
exequible, *a.* attainable, achievable.
exergo, *m.* (numis.) exergue.
exfoliación, *f.* exfoliation; (med.) desquamation, exfoliation, scaling or peeling off.
exfoliador, ra, *a.* loose-leaf (folder, jotter, calendar). —*m.* (neol.) tear-off calendar pad, desk calendar pad; (Chile) loose-leaf jotting pad; (Peru) loose-leaf folder or file.
exfoliar, *tr.v.* to exfoliate. —*r.v.* to exfoliate, desquamate, peel off in scales.
exhalación, *f.* 1. exhalation. 2. shooting star; flash, streak, bolt (of lightning). 3. fume, vapor.
exhalador, ra, *a.* exhaling. —*m.* exhaler.
exhalar, *tr.v.* 1. to exhale, breathe out; to emit. 2. to heave (sighs), utter (a complaint). —*r.v.* 1. (fig.) to long (for), crave (for). 2. to run swiftly.
exhaustivo, va, *a.* exhausting, exhaustive.
exhausto, ta, *a.* exhausted, empty, drained.
exheredación, *f.* disinheritance.
exheredar, *tr.v.* to disinherit.
exhibición, *f.* exhibition, exposition, show, display; **e. aeronáutica,** air show; **e. de pinturas,** art show; **e. impúdica,** (law) indecent exposure.
exhibicionismo, *m.* exhibitionism; showing-off.
exhibicionista, *m., f.* exhibitionist, show-off.
exhibir, *tr.v.* 1. to exhibit, show, display. 2. (Mex.) to pay (a quantity of money). 3. (law) to present (documents).
exhortación, *f.* 1. exhortation. 2. warning, admonition.

exhortador, ra, *a.* exhortative, exhorting. *—m., f.* exhorter.
exhortar, *tr.v.* to exhort; to warn; to excite or arouse with words.
exhortatorio, ria, *a.* exhortatory.
exhorto, *m.* (law) letters rogatory, letters requisitory.
exhumación, *f.* exhumation, disinterment.
exhumador, ra, *a.* exhuming. *—m., f.* exhumer.
exhumar, *tr.v.* to exhume, disinter; (fig.) to dig up, uncover.
exigencia, *f.* exigency, demand; requirement, e.g. *las exigencias del buen gusto,* the requirements of good taste.
exigente, *a.* demanding, exigent, exacting; (fig.) severe, inflexible, e.g. *un jefe muy e.,* a very demanding boss.
exigible, *a.* exigible, payable on demand; requirable.
exigidero, ra, *a., var. of* **exigible.**
exigir, (*ref. 62*) *tr.v.* to demand; to exact (taxes, money, etc.); to require; to urge.
exigüidad, *f.* exiguity, exiguousness, scantiness, meagerness, smallness.
exiguo, gua, *a.* exiguous, scarce, scanty, meager.
exija, exijo, *ref.* **exigir.**
exilado, *m., var. of* **exiliado.**
exilar, *tr.v., r.v., var. of* **exiliar.**
exiliado, da, *a.* exiled, banished. *—m., f.* exile, expatriate, refugee.
exiliar, *tr.v.* to exile; to expatriate, to banish. *—r.v.* to be exiled; become an expatriate.
exilio, *m.* exile, banishment, expatriation.
eximente, *a.* exempting, exonerating.
eximio, mia, *a.* famous, eminent; most excellent, e.g. *la eximia actriz,* the famous actress, *un ejemplo eximio,* a paramount example.
eximir, *tr.v.* to exempt, free, exonerate; to excuse or clear from; to except, to privilege. *—r.v.* to be exempted or freed.
exinanición, *f.* inanition, exhaustion; weakness, lack of vigor.
exinanido, da, *a.* (rare) exhausted, weak, debilitated, feeble.
existencia, *f.* 1. existence; life, being. 2. (*pl.*) stocks or goods (on hand, etc.). — **en existencia,** in stock, on hand (stock); **existencias disponibles,** (com.) stock in hand; **existencias en demasía,** (com., acc.) surplus stock; **renovar las existencias,** to restock.
existencial, *a.* existential.
existencialismo, *m.* (philos.) existentialism.
existencialista, *m., f., a.* existentialist.
existente, *a.* 1. existing, extant, existent; living. 2. in circulation; (com.) on hand; in stock.
existimación, *f.* estimation, opinion.
existimar, *tr.v.* to estimate, form an opinion of, judge.
existir, *i.v.* to exist; to be.
éxito, *m.* 1. outcome, result, end. 2. success; felicity, accomplishment; hit. — **tener e.,** to be successful; **e. de prestigio,** succès d'estime (critical acclaim); **e. de taquilla,** box office success.
exitoso, sa, *a.* (Amer.) successful, effective, felicitous.
ex libris, *m.* ex libris, bookplate.
exocarpio, *m.* (bot.) exocarp.
exocarpo, *m.* (bot.) exocarp.
exocrino, na, *a.* (anat.) exocrine.
exodermis, *f.* (bot.) exodermis.
exodermo, *m.* (biol.) exoderm, ectoderm.
éxodo, *m.* (Bib.) Exodus; (fig.) exodus, emigration, mass departure.
exodoncia, *f.* (med.) exodontia.
exoenzima, *f.* (biochem.) exoenzyme.
exoérgico, ca, *a.* (chem.) exoergic.
exoesqueleto, *m.* (zool.) exoskeleton.
exoftalmía, *f.* (med.) exophthalmos (abnormal protrusion of the eyeball).
exoftálmico, ca, *a.* (med.) exophthalmic.
exoftalmos, *m., var. of* **exoftalmía.**
exogamia, *f.* 1. (anth.) exogamy, the custom of marrying outside one's own tribe, clan, etc. 2. (bot.) cross-pollination.
exógeno, na, *a.* (anat.) exogenous.
exoneración, *f.* exoneration; discharge; exemption.
exonerar, *tr.v.* 1. to exonerate, exculpate, absolve (of blame). 2. to exempt, discharge, free from (obligation). 3. to evacuate, relieve (the bowels). 4. to dismiss, discharge; remove (from a post).
exonerativo, va, *a.* exonerative.
exorable, *a.* exorable, moved by entreaty, merciful.
exorar, *tr.v.* to beg, beseech, entreat.
exorbitancia, *f.* exorbitance, exorbitancy, excess, excessiveness.
exorbitante, *a.* exorbitant, excessive, enormous, e.g. *precios exorbitantes,* exorbitant prices.
exorbitantemente, *adv.* exorbitantly.
exorcice, exorcicé, *ref.* **exorcizar.**
exorcismo, *m.* exorcism.
exorcista, *m.* exorciser, exorcist.
exorcistado, *m.* (ecc.) order of exorciser.
exorcizante, *a.* exorcising.
exorcizar, (*ref. 53*) *tr.v.* to exorcise, to drive evil spirits away by ritual prayers, incantations, etc.
exordio, *m.* exordium, introduction, preamble.
exornación, *f.* embellishment, adornment, ornamentation.
exornar, *tr.v.* to embellish, adorn, ornament.
exosfera, *f.* (astron.) exosphere.
exósmosis, *f.* (phys.) exosmosis.
exosmótico, ca, *a.* (phys.) exosmotic.
exospora, *f.* (biol.) exospore.
exotérico, ca, *a.* exoteric, public, common.
exotérmico, ca, *a.* (chem.) exothermic.
exotermo, ma, *a.* (chem.) exothermic.
exoticidad, *f.* exoticism, exotism.
exótico, ca, *a.* exotic; strange, alien, foreign; bizarre, extravagant. *—f.* (Mex.) burlesque dancer.
exotiquez, *f.* exoticism, exotism.
exotismo, *m.* exoticism, exotism.
exotoxina, *f.* (biochem.) exotoxin.
expandir, *tr.v., r.v.* to expand, extend; dilate, blow up.
expansibilidad, *f.* (phys.) expansibility.
expansible, *a.* (phys.) expansible.
expansión, *f.* 1. expansion; spreading. 2. rest, relaxation, e.g. *un rato de e.,* a few moments of relaxation. — **e. del circulante,** (econ.) currency expansion.
expansionarse, *r.v.* 1. to relax, rest. 2. to be sociable or communicative.
expansionismo, *m.* (com., polit.) expansionism.
expansionista, *a.* (polit.) expansionist, expansionistic. *—m., f.* expansionist, one who advocates expansionistic policies.
expansivo, va, *a.* 1. expansile (capable of expanding). 2. expansive, sociable, affable, communicative.
expatriación, *f.* expatriation, migration.
expatriado, da, *a., m., f.* expatriate, exile.
expatriarse, *r.v.* to go into exile, leave one's country. *—tr.v.* to expatriate, banish, exile.
expectable, *a.* worthy, reputable, notable, eminent, prominent; creditable.
expectación, *f.* expectation, expectancy; suspense; anticipation. — **de e.,** worthy, reputable, notable.
expectante, *a.* expectant; (law) abeyant.
expectativa, *f.* expectation, hope, expectancy; estar **en** or **a la e. de,** to be in the hope of, hope for; **e. de vida,** life expectancy.
expectoración, *f.* expectoration; sputum.
expectorante, *a.* expectorant. *—m.* (med.) expectorant, cough medicine.
expectorar, *tr.v.* to expectorate, spit out; cough.
expedición, *f.* 1. expedition, journey, trek. 2. dispatch, shipping, sending. 3. shipment. 4. promptness, speed, expeditiousness. 5. (rel.) pontifical brevet or bull.
expedicionario, ria, *a.* expeditionary. *—m., f.* member of an expedition.
expedicionero, *m.* (rel.) emissary delivering papal bulls.
expedidor, ra, *m., f.* forwarding agent, dispatcher, shipper, sender.
expediente, *m.* 1. expedient, means, way. 2. reason, motive. 3. promptness, efficiency (in management of a business). 4. dossier, records, file. 5. (law) action, proceeding. 6. supplies, provisions. — **formar e. a,** to impeach (a public official).
expedienteo, *m.* 1. (law) processing of documents. 2. red tape, (coll.) excessive bureaucracy.
expedir, (*ref. 39*) *tr.v.* 1. to expedite, hasten, facilitate. 2. to send, ship, dispatch. 3. to issue (a document, law, decree, etc.).
expeditamente, *adv.* expeditiously, quickly.
expeditar, *tr.v.* (Amer.) to leave ready; to deal with, carry out.
expeditivo, va, *a.* expeditious, prompt, speedy.
expedito, ta, *a.* ready, free, clear; expeditious, quick.
expelente, *a.* expellant.
expeler, *tr.v.* to expel, eject.
expendedor, ra, *a.* spending. *—m., f.* vendor, seller, dealer, retailer; (theat.) ticket agent; **e. de moneda falsa,** circulator of counterfeit money.
expendeduría, *f.* retail shop (of tobacco and other officially controlled goods).
expender, *tr.v.* 1. to sell, retail; to sell on commission. 2. to spend, lay out (money). 3. (law) to pass, circulate (counterfeit money).
expendición, *f.* retailing, retail selling; distribution.
expendio, *m.* 1. expenditure, expense, outlay. 2. (Amer.) retailing, retail selling. 3. (Mex.) retail shop, e.g. *e. de tabaco,* cigarette stand.
expensar, *tr.v.* (Amer.) to defray the expense of.
expensas, *f.* (*pl.*) expenses, expenditures; charges; (law.) costs (of a lawsuit); **a e. de,** at the expense of.
experiencia, *f.* 1. experience, practice, knowledge. 2. experience, event, e.g. *fue una e. inolvidable,* it was an unforgettable experience. 3. experiment, trial.
experimentación, *f.* experimentation, scientific research, experiment; test, trial.
experimentado, da, *past part. of* **experimentar.** *—a.* experienced, expert, practiced, trained (for the job).
experimentador, ra, *a.* experimenting. *—m., f.* experimenter, researcher, tester.
experimental, *a.* experimental, pertaining to a trial, test or tryout; **teatro e.,** experimental theatre.
experimentalismo, *m.* (philos.) experimentalism.
experimentalmente, *adv.* experimentally, as a trial or tryout.
experimentar, *tr.v.* 1. to experience, go through; to undergo; to suffer, feel, e.g. *e. mareos,* to feel seasick, dizzy or nauseous. 2. to test, try out. *—i.v.* to experiment; **e. en,** to experiment on.

experimento, *m.* experiment, test, trial.
expertamente, *adv.* expertly, skillfully; cunningly, artfully.
experticia, *f.* (Ven.) expertise, skill.
experto, ta, *a.* expert, skillful, deft, knowledgeable. —*m.* expert, specialist.
expiación, *f.* expiation, atonement; reparation.
expiar, (*ref. 54*) *tr.v.* 1. to expiate, atone for. 2. to serve (a sentence). 3. (fig.) to purify (a desecrated temple, etc.).
expiativo, va, *a.* expiative, expiatory.
expiatorio, ria, *a.* expiatory, atoning.
expida, expidiendo, expidiera, expidiese, expidió, expido, *ref.* expedir.
expillo, *m.* (bot.) feverfew.
expiración, *f.* 1. expiration; end; death. 2. (com.) termination, cancellation.
expirante, *a.* expiring.
expirar, *i.v.* to expire, die; (fig.) to expire, finish, end.
explanación, *f.* 1. leveling, smoothing. 2. explanation, elucidation.
explanada, *f.* esplanade; (mil.) esplanade, glacis; (artil.) platform (for guns).
explanar, *tr.v.* 1. to level, smoothe, grade (terrain). 2. (fig.) to explain, interpret, elucidate, clear up.
explantación, *f.* (med.) explantation.
explayada, *a.* (her.) displayed, with wings outspread (an eagle).
explayamiento, *m.* 1. outing; relaxing diversion. 2. the act of dwelling upon a subject.
explayar, *tr.v.* to extend, spread out, enlarge. —*r.v.* 1. to extend, spread out. 2. to expatiate, speak at length. — **explayarse con,** to unbosom oneself to, open one's heart to; **explayarse sobre,** to speak at length, elaborate or expatiate on.
expletivo, va, *a.* (phonet.) expletive.
explicable, *a.* explicable, explainable.
explicablemente, *adv.* explicably.
explicación, *f.* explanation, exposition; interpretation. — **pedir explicaciones,** to ask for an explanation.
explicaderas, *f.* (*pl.*) (coll.) ease in making oneself understood.
explicador, ra, *m., f.* explainer, commentator.
explicar, (*ref. 50*) *tr.v.* 1. to explain; to expound, set forth, elucidate, interpret. 2. to give (a lesson). 3. to lecture on. —*i.v.* to lecture. —*r.v.* 1. to explain oneself, express oneself. 2. to understand, see, e.g. *ahora me explico por qué,* now I understand why. 3. to be explained.
explicativo, va, *a.* explanatory; **nota e.,** note of explanation.
explícitamente, *adv.* explicitly, clearly.
explícito, ta, *a.* explicit, clear, distinctly expressed.
explique, expliqué, *ref.* **explicar.**
explorable, *a.* explorable.
exploración, *f.* 1. exploration, trial, attempt. 2. (mil.) scouting, reconnoitering. 3. (tel.) scanning.
explorador, ra, *a.* 1. exploring. 2. (mil.) scouting. 3. (tel.) scanning. —*m.* 1. explorer. 2. boy scout. 3. (mil.) scout.
explorar, *tr.v.* 1. to explore, investigate, examine. 2. (mil.) to scout, reconnoiter. 3. (tel.) to scan. 4. (med.) to probe.
exploratorio, ria, *a.* 1. exploratory. 2. (med.) probing. —*m.* (med.) probe.
explosión, *f.* 1. explosion; outburst, blast, detonation. 2. (phonet.) explosion; **e. demográfica,** population explosion; **e. por contacto,** (min.) contact fire; **e. sónica,** (aer.) sonic boom.
explosionar, *tr.v.* to explode, make explode. —*r.v.* to explode, blow up.
explosivo, va, *a.* explosive. —*m.* explosive; bomb. —*f.* (phonet.) explosive (consonant).
explosor, *m.* 1. (artil., mil.) exploder. 2. (rad.) oscillator.
explotable, *a.* 1. exploitable. 2. workable, operable. 3. (min.) minable.
explotación, *f.* 1. exploitation, development. 2. working (of a mine). 3. running, operation. 3. plant, installation, works. 4. (pol.) economic enslavement of an underprivileged people or an underdeveloped nation.
explotador, ra, *a.* 1. exploiting. 2. running, operating. —*m., f.* 1. exploiter. 2. plunderer; (Amer.) pimp.
explotar, *tr.v.* 1. to exploit, plunder. 2. to run, operate (a factory, railway, etc.). 3. to work (a mine, etc.). —*i.v.* to explode, blow up.
exployada, *a.* (her.) displayed, with wings outstretched (an eagle).
expoliación, *f.* pillaging, plundering, spoliation; pillage, plunder.
expoliador, ra, *a.* pillaging, despoiling, plundering. —*m., f.* pillager, despoiler, plunderer, spoliator.
expoliar, *tr.v.* to despoil, pillage, plunder, loot, sack.
expolición, *f.* (rhet.) repetition in different forms.
exponencial, *a.* (math.) exponential.
exponente, *a.* explanatory, expository. —*m., f.* exponent, expounder. —*m.* (math.) exponent.
exponer, (*ref. 15*) *tr.v.* 1. to expose, to put in danger, jeopardize. 2. to expose, show, exhibit. 3. to explain, expound. 4. to abandon (a child). —*r.v.* to take a chance, run a risk, to imperil or endanger oneself.
exponga, expongo, *ref.* **exponer.**
exportable, *a.* exportable, fit for shipping.
exportación, *f.* export, exportation; exported goods, ideas, styles, etc.
exportador, ra, *a.* exporting. —*m., f.* exporter, shipper.
exportar, *tr.v.* to export, to ship or send abroad.
exposición, *f.* 1. exposition (expounding of ideas; interpretation). 2. exhibition, fair, exposition. 3. exposure (to danger, etc.). 4. (lit., mus.) exposition. 5. (photog.) exposure. 5. abandonment, exposition (of a child). — **e. canina,** dog show; **e. de escultura,** sculpture exhibition; **e. de flores,** flower show; **e. comercial,** trade fair; **e. ganadera,** cattle show; **e. industrial,** trade fair; **e. universal,** world's fair.
exposímetro, *m.* (photog.) exposure meter.
expositivo, va, *a.* expositive, expository; explanatory.
expósito, ta, *a.* abandoned. —*m., f.* foundling, abandoned child.
expositor, ra, *a.* expository. —*m., f.* 1. expounder, expositor; exponent. 2. exhibitor. —*m.* interpreter, exegete (of the Bible).
expremijo, *m.* cheese-draining shelf (for draining the whey from cheese).
exprés, *a.* express (train). —*m.* 1. express train. 2. transport company.
expresado, da, *a., m., f.* abovementioned, aforesaid.
expresamente, *adv.* 1. expressly, specifically, e.g. *esto fue hecho e. para ti,* this was made expressly for you. 2. explicitly, clearly. 3. rapidly, swiftly.
expresar, *tr.v.* 1. to express. 2. to show, manifest. 3. to depict, represent, express (an idea, etc.). —*r.v.* to express oneself.
expresión, *f.* 1. expression, statement, declaration. 2. gesture, facial expression. 3. expression, idiom, utterance, phrase. 4. squeezing. 5. (pharm.) extract. 6. (math.) expression, formula. 7. (*pl.*) regards, greetings; gesture of esteem. — **e. idiomática,** idiomatic expression.
expresionismo, *m.* (art.) expressionism.
expresionista, *a., m., f.* expressionist; **pintura e.,** expressionist painting.
expresivamente, *adv.* expressively.
expresivo, va, *a.* expressive; demonstrative, affectionate.
expreso, sa, *a.* express, exact, precise; definite, clear; direct (train, etc.). —*m.* express (train, etc.); **e. aéreo,** air express.
exprimidera, *f.* **exprimidero,** *m.* fruit-squeezer, juicer.
exprimido, da, *past part. of* **exprimir.** —*a.* squeezed dry.
exprimir, *tr.v.* 1. to squeeze, squeeze or press out; to wring, wring out. 2. to express vividly.
ex profeso, *adv.* on purpose, expressly, specifically.
expropiación, *f.* expropriation; dispossession.
expropiador, ra, *a.* expropriating. —*m., f.* expropriator.
expropiar, *tr.v.* to expropriate.
expuesto, ta, *irr. past part. of* **exponer.** —*a.* 1. dangerous, hazardous. 2. liable, exposed. 3. on display, on exhibition.
expugnable, *a.* (mil.) expugnable, pregnable, assailable.
expugnación, *f.* (mil.) the act of taking by storm.
expugnador, ra, *a.* (mil.) storming. —*m.* (mil.) assaulter, stormer.
expugnar, *tr.v.* (mil.) to take by storm.
expulsar, *tr.v.* to expel, eject, throw out, drive out; e.g. *lo expulsaron del colegio,* he was expelled from school.
expulsión, *f.* 1. expulsion, expelling, ejection. 2. (fenc.) disarming thrust.
expulsivo, va, *a., m.* expellant (medicine); expulsive.
expulso, sa, *irr. past part. of* **expeler.**
expulsor, ra, *a.* ejecting, expelling. —*m.* ejector. — **e. de cartuchos,** cartridge ejector.
expurgación, *f.* expurgation, purification; (coll.) purge (of officials, employees, etc.).
expurgador, ra, *m., f.* expurgator.
expurgar, (*ref. 51*) *tr.v.* to expurge, expunge; to cleanse, purify; to amend, to correct.
expurgatorio, ria, *a.* expurgating, expurgatory, cleansing, purifying. —*m.* index (of books prohibited by the Roman Catholic Church).
expurgo, *m.* expurgation, purification.
expurgue, expurgué, *ref.* **expurgar.**
expuse, expusiera, expusiese, *ref.* **exponer.**
exquisitamente, *adv.* exquisitely.
exquisitez, *f.* exquisiteness; perfection, excellence.
exquisito, ta, *a.* exquisite, perfect; delicious.
éxtasi, *m., var. of* **éxtasis.**
extasiado, da, *a.* enrapt.
extasiarse, *r.v.* to become ecstatic or enraptured, go into a rapture.
éxtasis, *m.* 1. ecstasy, rapture, transport. 2. (med.) retardation of the normal pulse.
extático, ca, *a.* ecstatic, enraptured, transported.
extatismo, *m.* state of ecstasy.
extemporal, *a.* untimely, inopportune, inconvenient.
extemporáneamente, *adv.* inopportunely, inconveniently.
extemporáneo, a, *a.* untimely, inopportune, inconvenient.
extender, (*ref. 30*) *tr.v.* 1. to extend, expand, enlarge, stretch. 2. to spread out (hay, paint). 3. to give, stretch out (one's hand). 4. to spread out, unfold (a blanket, etc.). 5. to spread, propagate (a

doctrine). 6. to draw up (a document). 7. (cul.) to roll (pastry). —*r.v.* 1. to extend, stretch. 2. to last (a period of time). 3. to wander on, expatiate (in talking or explaining). 4. to spread (an epidemic, a doctrine).
extendidamente, *adv.* extensively; in detail; profoundly.
extendido, da, *a.* 1. extensive, prolonged. 2. extended, elongated, stretched out. 3. general, widespread.
extensamente, *adv.* extensively, in detail.
extensibilidad, *f.* extensibility.
extensible, *a.* extensible, extensile.
extensión, *f.* 1. extension; size, extent, expanse; duration, length (of time); extension, range (of word or idea). 2. (Amer.) an additional line (of a telephone). — **en toda la e. de la palabra,** in every sense of the word.
extensivamente, *adv.* extensively, amply, widely.
extensivo, va, *a.* extensive, widespread; broad, wide, e.g. *el sentido e. de la palabra,* the broad sense of the word.
extenso, sa, *irr. past part. of* **extender.** —*a.* spatious, vast; extensive; **por e.,** extensively, in detail.
extensómetro, *m.* extensometer, an instrument for measuring minute degrees of expansion and contraction (e.g. of metals).
extensor, ra, *a.* extending (muscle). —*m.* 1. extensor (muscle). 2. chest-expander.
extenuación, *f.* 1. debilitation, emaciation; wasting, weakening. 2. (rhet.) litotes.
extenuar, (*ref. 55*) *tr.v.* to debilitate, extenuate; to diminish, weaken. —*r.v.* to become weak or debilitated, to languish, lose strength.
extenuativo, va, *a.* weakening, emaciating.
exterior, *a.* exterior, outer, external; foreign (trade, etc.). —*m.* 1. exterior, outside; appearance, aspect. 2. foreign countries, abroad; **comercio e.,** foreign trade.
exteriorice, exteriorice, *ref.* **exteriorizar.**
exterioridad, *f.* 1. exterior, outside; appearance, aspect; outward appearance. 2. (*pl.*) pomp, show, ostentation.
exteriorización, *f.* manifestation, expression, externalization.
exteriorizar, (*ref. 53*) *tr.v.* to express, externalize, show. —*r.v.* to unbosom oneself, to reveal one's feelings.
exteriormente, *adv.* externally, outwardly.
exterminable, *a.* exterminable, eradicable.
exterminación, *f.* extermination, eradication.
exterminador, ra, *a.* exterminating, eradicating. —*m., f.* exterminator, eradicator.
exterminar, *tr.v.* 1. to exterminate, eradicate; to tear up, root out. 2. (fig.) to devastate, lay waste, destroy, raze.
exterminio, *m.* 1. extermination, eradication. 2. (fig.) devastation, destruction, ruin.
externado, *m.* day-student school or college.
externamente, *adv.* externally, outwardly.
externar, *tr.v.* (Amer.) to express, manifest.
externo, na, *a.* external, exterior, outward. —*m., f.* day pupil.
exteroceptivo, va, *a.* (physiol.) exteroceptive.
exteroceptor, *m.* (physiol.) exteroceptor.
ex testamento, *adv.* by will or testament.
extienda, extiendo, *ref.* **extender.**
extinción, *f.* 1. extinction, suppression; obliteration, abolition. 2. quenching, extinguishing, extinguishment.
extinga, extingo, *ref.* **extinguir.**
extinguible, *a.* extinguishable.
extinguido, da, *a.* extinct; extinguished.
extinguidor, *m.* (Chile) fire extinguisher.
extinguir, (*ref. 63*) *tr.v.* 1. to extinguish, put out; to quench. 2. to wipe out, annihilate; to suppress, destroy, extirpate. —*r.v.* 1. to go out (a light, fire). 2. to fade (a sound). 3. to become extinct.
extintivo, *a.* extinctive; (law) extinguishing.
extinto, ta, *a.* extinguished; extinct; late, deceased. —*m., f.* (Amer.) dead person.
extintor, *m.* (fire) extinguisher.
extirpable, *a.* eradicable; uprootable.
extirpación, *f.* extirpation; eradication, uprooting.
extirpador, ra, *a.* extirpative; eradicating, uprooting. —*m., f.* extirpator. —*m.* (agr.) cultivator.
extirpar, *tr.v.* to uproot, extirpate; (fig.) to eradicate, eliminate, destroy.
extorno, *m.* rebate on an insurance policy (due to adjustment of a policy).
extorsión, *f.* 1. extortion; exaction; overcharge. 2. damage, injury, harm.
extorsionar, *tr.v.* to extort.
extorsionista, *m., f.* extortioner, extortionist.
extra, *a.* remarkable, extraordinary. —*prep.* besides. —*m.* tip, gratuity.
extracción, *f.* 1. extraction, drawing, removal. 2. extraction, origin, lineage, descent. 3. (math.) extraction (of root). 4. drawing of numbers in a lottery.
extracorriente, *f.* (elec.) extracurrent.
extracta, *f.* (law) true copy, extract.
extractador, ra, *a.* abstracting, condensing. —*m., f.* summarizer, abstracter (one who makes an abstract or summary).
extractar, *tr.v.* to abstract, summarize; to epitomize; to abridge.
extracto, *m.* 1. summary, abstract, resumé. 2. (chem., pharm.) extract. — **e. amargo,** (chem.) bitter principle; **e. de malta,** malt extract; **e. de Saturno,** (chem.) lead acetate; **e. tebaico,** opium extract.
extractor, ra, *m., f.* extractor. —*m.* extractor (instrument).
extracurricular, *a.* extracurricular.
extradición, *f.* (law) extradition.
extraditar, *tr.v.* (Amer.) to extradite.
extradós, *m.* (arch.) extrados.
extraer, (*ref. 24*) *tr.v.* 1. to extract, take out; to remove. 2. (chem., math.) to extract. 3. (law) to take a copy of.
extragaláctico, ca, *a.* (astron.) extragalactic.
extraiga, extraigo, *ref.* **extraer.**
extraje, extrajera, extrajese, *ref.* **extraer.**
extrajudicial, *a.* (law) extrajudicial.
extrajudicialmente, *adv.* extrajudicially.
extralimitación, *f.* overstepping of authority, abuse of facilities or authority.
extralimitarse, *r.v.* to abuse (authority); to overstep the mark, go too far.
extramundano, na, *a.* extramundane, out of this world.
extramuros, *adv.* outside the town or city; outside.
extranjería, *f.* 1. status as an alien. 2. the quality of being foreign.
extranjerice, extranjericé, *ref.* **extranjerizar.**
extranjerismo, *m.* 1. foreignism (foreign word in Spanish). 2. xenomania, fondness for foreign things.
extranjerizar, (*ref. 53*) *tr.v.* to introduce foreign customs into (a country). —*r.v.* to adopt foreign customs.
extranjero, ra, *a.* foreign, alien. —*m., f.* foreigner, alien. —*m.* abroad, foreign countries; **del e.,** from abroad; **por** or **en el e.,** abroad.
extranjía, *f.* (coll.) alienism (state of being an alien); **de e.,** (coll.) foreign, alien; (coll.) strange, unexpected.
extranjis, de e., (coll.) foreign, alien; (coll.) strange, unexpected; (coll.) secretly.
extranuclear, *a.* (biol.) extranuclear.
extraña, *f.* (bot.) China aster (Callistephus chinensis).
extrañación, *f.* exile, banishment; expulsion.
extrañamente, *adv.* strangely, oddly, queerly, puzzlingly.
extrañamiento, *f.* 1. estrangement, alienation. 2. exile, banishment. 3. surprise, wonderment.
extrañar, *tr.v.* 1. to surprise. 2. to find strange. 3. to miss, pine for. 4. to exile, banish. —*i.v.* to feel strange. —*r.v.* 1. (with de) to be surprised (at); to wonder, to be puzzled. 2. to go into exile; to go into retirement.
extrañez, extrañeza, *f.* (rare) 1. strangeness, oddness, queerness. 2. disagreement, estrangement, alienation. 3. surprise, wonder.
extraño, ña, *a.* 1. strange, odd, peculiar, queer, puzzling. 2. foreign, alien; **e. a,** unconnected with, alien to. —*m., f.* stranger; foreigner. —*m.* sudden movement of fear or surprise; **hacer un e. (un caballo),** to shy suddenly.
extraoficial, *a.* unofficial, non-official.
extraoficialmente, *adv.* unofficially.
extraordinariamente, *adv.* extraordinarily.
extraordinario, ria, *a.* extraordinary; uncommon, rare, odd. —*m.* 1. special courier. 2. extra dish at a meal. 3. special edition (of a newspaper or a magazine).
extrapolación, *f.* extrapolation.
extrapolar, *tr.v.* to extrapolate.
extrarradio, *m.* outskirts, suburb; administrative area reaching beyond the fringes of a town.
extrasensorial, *a.* extrasensory.
extrasístole, *f.* (med.) extrasystole.
extratémpora, *f.* (ecc.) dispensation to receive Holy Orders at times other than those fixed by the Church.
extraterritorial, *a.* extraterritorial.
extraterritorialidad, *f.* extraterritoriality (exemption from local laws, as sometimes granted to diplomatic representatives).
extrauterino, na, *a.* (med.) extrauterine.
extravagancia, *f.* 1. oddness, craziness, extravaganza, wildness, folly. 2. (*pl.*) nonsense, stupid remarks. — **decir extravagancias,** to talk nonsense, talk wildly.
extravagante, *a.* bizarre, odd, strange, eccentric. —*m., f.* bizarre person. —*f.* (*pl.*) (ecc.) Extravagants, Extravagantes.
extravasación, *f.* (physiol.) extravasation.
extravasarse, *r.v., i.v.* to extravasate, overflow, exude.
extravenar, *tr.v.* to cause (blood) to flow from the veins; (fig.) to displace. —*r.v.* to flow from the veins.
extraversión, *f.* extroversion, extraversion.
extravertido, *m.* (psyc.) extrovert, extravert.
extraviado, da, *past part. of* **extraviar.** —*a.* 1. lost; gone astray, missing, mislaid. 2. wild, unruly; crazy. 3. unfrequented, out of the way (places).
extraviar, (*ref. 54*) *tr.v.* 1. to lead astray, mislead, misguide. 2. to mislay, misplace, lose. —*r.v.* 1. to get lost or mislaid. 2. to go astray, err.
extravío, *m.* 1. wandering off (e.g. the road), going astray, losing one's way. 2. loss, misplacement, mislaying. 3. deviation, aberration, misconduct. 4. irregularity, disorder, error.
extrayendo, *ref.* **extraer.**
extrema, *f.* 1. (coll.) end, final moment (of life). 2. extreme unction.
extremadamente, *adv.* extremely, exceedingly.
extremado, da, *past part. of* **extremar.** —*a.* very great, consummate, extreme, excessive.
extremamente, *adv.* extremely, very, exceedingly.
extremar, *tr.v.* 1. to carry to an extreme (e.g. a punishment). 2. (vet.) to wean. —*i.v.* to take great pains, do one's utmost.

extremaunción, *f.* (ecc.) extreme unction.
extremeño, ña, *a.* 1. Extremenian, of or from Extremadura, Spain. 2. frontier (as *a.*). —*m., f.* 1. Extremenian. 2. frontier dweller.
extremidad, *f.* extremity; end, tip; brink, border, edge. —(*pl.*) (anat.) extremities; **la última e.,** the last moment.
extremismo, *m.* extremism.
extremista, *a., m., f.* extremist.
extremo, ma, *a.* extreme; last, terminal; furthest; far; **E. Oriente,** Far East. —*m.* 1. extreme; end, tip, limit. 2. great care, meticulousness. — **con, de** or **por e.,** excessively, extremely; **de e. a e.,** from beginning to end; from one extreme to another; **hacer extremos,** to gush, effuse, be effusive; **pasar de un e. a otro,** to go from one extreme to another.
extremoso, sa, *a.* 1. extreme, excessive, immoderate, vehement. 2. demonstrative, effusive, gushing.
extrínsecamente, *adv.* extrinsically.
extrínseco, ca, *a.* extrinsic, outward, external.
extrorso, sa, *a.* (bot.) extrorse.
extroversión, *f.* (psych., med.) extroversion.
extrovertido, da, *a., m., f.* (phych.) extrovert.
extrusión, *f.* extrusion.
exuberancia, *f.* exuberance; abundance.
exuberante, *a.* exuberant; luxuriant; overabundant.
exudación, *f.* exudation; sweating, perspiration.
exudado, *past part. of* **exudar.** —*m.* (med.) exudate (exuded matter).
exudar, *tr.v., i.v.* to exude, ooze out.
exulceración, *f.* (med.) ulceration, chafing.
exulcerar, *tr.v.* (med.) to ulcerate, chafe. —*r.v.* (med.) to become ulcerated or chafed.
exultación, *f.* exultation, boundless joy.
exultar, *i.v.* to exult, to rejoice.
exutorio, *m.* (med.) issue, artificial ulcer (to provoke the discharge of pus).
exvoto, *m.* ex-voto, votive offering.
eyaculación, *f.* (med., physiol.) ejaculation; ejection.
eyacular, *tr.v.* to ejaculate, eject (liquids) from the body.
eyección, *m.* ejection; extraction.
eyectar, *tr.v.* to eject.
eyector, *m.* ejector.
ezquerdear, *i.v.* 1. to lean to the left (of a wall). 2. to stray from the right or the correct path or norm.

F

F, *f.* f, sixth letter of the Spanish alphabet, interchangeable with h in the word **fierro** (iron).
f. *abbrev. of* **femenino,** feminine (f., fem.).
F *sym. of* **fluor,** fluorine (F).
fa, *m.* (mus.) fa, fourth note of the diatonic scale.
fab., FAB., *abbrev. of* **franco a bordo,** free on board (F. O. B., f. o. b.); free on steamer.
fabáceo, a, *a.* (bot.) fabaceous, of the legume family.
fabada, *f.* bean and bacon soup (typical dish of Asturias, Spain).
fabiano, *m.* Fabian, pertaining to the Fabian Society of English socialists of the late 19th century.
fabla, *f.* imitation of Old Spanish.
fabordón, *m.* (mus.) faux-bourdon.
fábrica, *f.* 1. factory, plant, works. 2. manufacture, making. 3. building, construction. 4. masonry, brick and mortar. 5. church building funds. 6. fabrication, invention (e.g. of lies). — **a precios de fábrica,** at manufacturer's prices; **f. de montaje,** assembly plant; **marca de f.,** trademark.
fabricación, *f.* manufacture, making, fabrication, construction. — **f. en serie,** mass production; **f. soldada,** welded construction.
fabricado, da, *a.* manufactured, fabricated. — **f. de encargo,** custom-engineered, custom-built; **f. en serie,** mass-produced.
fabricador, ra, *m., f.* 1. manufacturer, maker. 2. inventor (of lies), schemer. 3. (mar.) constructor.
fabricante, *m.* manufacturer, maker, producer, processor. — **f. de acero,** steel manufacturer; **f. de juguetes,** toymaker.
fabricar, (*ref. 50*) *tr.v.* 1. to manufacture, make. 2. to construct, build. 3. to work (e.g. silver). 4. to fabricate, invent (e.g. lies).
fabricoide, *m.* Fabrikoid (trademark), fabric imitating leather.
fabril, *a.* manufacturing; pertaining to factories or workmen.
fabrique, fabriqué, *ref.* **fabricar.**
fabriquero, *m.* 1. manufacturer. 2. church-warden.
fabuco, *m.* (bot.) beechnut, beech-mast.
fábula, *f.* 1. fable; tale, story, legend, fairy tale. 2. rumor, talk, gossip. 3. lie, fictitious story. 4. plot, story (of epic poem, etc.). 5. mythology. — **las Fábulas de Esopo,** Aesop's Fables.
fabulador, *m.* fabulist, writer of fables or mythological tales.
fabulario, *m.* collection of fables, book of fables.
fabulesco, ca, *a.* (lit.) of the fable, e.g. *el género f.,* the genre of the fable.
fabulista, *m., f.* fabulist, writer of fables.
fabulosamente, *adv.* 1. fabulously; enormously. 2. fictitiously, falsely.
fabulosidad, *f.* fabulousness.
fabuloso, sa, *a.* 1. fabulous, enormous, legendary, extraordinary. 2. false, fictitious; incredible.
faca, *f.* long curved jackknife; cutlass.
facción, *f.* 1. faction, party; gang, band. 2. battle. 3. (mil.) duty, e.g. *estar de f.,* to be on duty. 4. (*pl.*) features (of face), e.g. *lindas facciones,* beautiful features. 5. (law) **f. de testamento,** faculty of testating.
faccionario, ria, *a.* partisan, factional.
faccioso, sa, *a.* factious, troublemaking; rebellious, mutinous. —*m., f.* member of a faction; rebel; troublemaker, agitator, partisan.
facer, *tr.v.* (obs.) *ref.* **hacer,** to make, to do (term used in old Spanish literature).
facera, *f., var. of* **acera,** row of houses on either side of a street.
faceta, *f.* 1. facet (of a gem); bezel. 2. (fig.) side, aspect, facet.
facetado, da, *a.* faceted. —*f.* (Mex.) a poor joke.
facetar, facetear, *i.v.* to facet; to cut or bezel a stone.
facha, *f.* (coll.) 1. appearance, look, mien, aspect. 2. (coll.) ridiculous dress or get-up. — **ponerse en f.,** (mar.) to lie to, come almost to a standstill; (coll.) to get ready. — **¡qué fachas tienes!** you look a sight!
fachada, *f.* 1. facade, front, frontage (of a building). 2. facade, front, appearance, look (of someone or something). 3. title page (of a book); frontispiece.
fachado, da, *a.* (coll.) **bien** or **mal f.,** good or bad-looking.
fachear, *i.v.* (mar.) to lie to, to heave, to back (the sails).
fachenda, *f.* (coll.) vanity, conceit, showing-off. —*m., f.* boaster, show-off, conceited person.
fachendear, *i.v.* (coll.) to show off, brag, boast.
fachendista, fachendón, na, fachendoso, sa, *a.* boastful, showing-off, vain. —*m., f.* show-off, boaster, conceited person.
fachinal, *m.* (Amer.) marshland, marsh.
fachosear, *i.v.* (Mex.) to boast, brag, show off.
fachoso, sa, *a.* 1. (coll.) ridiculous looking. 2. (Mex.) boastful, conceited. 3. (Chile, Peru) handsome.
facial, *a.* 1. facial; pertaining to the face. 2. intuitive. — **valor f.,** face value (of stamp, etc.); **ángulo f.,** profile; facial angle.
facialmente, *adv.* intuitively.
facies, *f.* (med., biol.) facies, characteristic appearance.
fácil, *a.* 1. easy. 2. possible, probable. 3. docile, easily managed, pliant. 4. loose, of easy virtue. 5. facile; light. — **f. de +** *inf.,* easy to + *inf.,* e.g. *ser f. de entender,* to be easy to understand. —*adv.* easily.
facilidad, *f.* 1. facility, ease, easiness. 2. ability, facility (e.g. for languages). 3. opportunity, chance. 4. convenience, opportunity. — **dar facilidades,** to facilitate, make easy, help; **grandes facilidades (de pago),** easy terms (of payment).
facilillo, lla, *a.* (iron.) *dim. of* **fácil,** very easy, e.g. *eso es f.,* that is rather easy.
facilitación, *f.* facilitation.
facilitar, *tr.v.* 1. to facilitate, expedite; to make easy. 2. to supply, provide, furnish, e.g. *f. datos al juez,* to supply the judge with facts.
facilitón, na, *a., m., f.* (coll.) one who boasts of finding everything easy to cope with or to solve; boaster, braggart.
fácilmente, *adv.* easily, without difficulty; deftly.
facineroso, sa, *a.* wicked; delinquent, criminal. —*m., f.* wicked person. —*m.* delinquent, criminal; villain, scoundrel.
facistol, *m.* 1. lectern, choir desk. 2. (Cuba, Ven.) vain, conceited person.
facón, *m.* (Arg.) large knife (formerly used by the gauchos).
facsímil, facsímile, *m.* facsimile, exact copy, duplicate, faithful reproduction.
factible, *a.* feasible, practicable, workable; achievable.
facticio, cia, *a.* factitious, artificial.
factitivo, va, *a.* (gram.) factitive.
factor, *m.* 1. factor, cause, element. 2. factor, commission merchant, agent. 3. (mil.) victualler. 4. (ry.) freight clerk, dispatcher. 5. (math., biol., physiol.) factor. — **f. común,** (math.) common factor; **f. de amplitud,** (elec.) peak factor; **f. de carga,** (elec.) load factor; **f. de potencia,** (elec.) power factor; **f. integrante,** (math.) integrating factor; **f. primo,** (math.) prime factor; **f. Rh,** Rh factor; **f. de acumulación,** (nuclear physics) build-up; **f. de corrección,** correcting factor.
factoraje, *m.* 1. agency, commission merchant's office. 2. factorage, post and business of a commission merchant.
factoría, *f.* 1. agency, commission merchant's office. 2. factorage, post and business of a commission merchant. 3. factory, overseas trading post. 4. factory, works, plant; repair shop. 5. (Ecuad., Peru) foundry. — **f. de devanados,** winding factory; **f. carboquímica,** coal-synthesis plant.
factorial, *f.* (math.) factorial.
factótum, *m.* 1. (coll.) factotum, man of all work; righthand man. 2. (coll.) busybody.
factura, *f.* 1. (com.) invoice, bill. 2. (fig.) style, brand, imprint, e.g. *de pura factura picassiana,* of unmistakable Picassian imprint. — **f. original,** original invoice.
facturación, *f.* billing, invoicing; consignment of goods.
facturadora, *f.* billing machine.
facturar, *tr.v.* 1. (com.) to invoice, bill. 2. (ry.) to check (baggage, goods).
fácula, *f.* (astron.) facula.
faculta, *f.* (Ven.) midwife.
facultad, *f.* 1. faculty. 2. power, authority, right. 3. gift, ability. 4. faculty (of a school or university). 5. (med.) strength.
facultar, *tr.v.* to authorize, empower; to commission.
facultativo, va, *a.* optional. —*m.* (med.) doctor, surgeon. — **prescripción facultativa,** doctor's orders or prescription.
facundia, *f.* fluency (of speech), eloquence.
facundo, da, *a.* fluent (in speech), eloquent.
fada, *f.* 1. fairy, witch, enchantress. 2. a variety of small sweet apple.
fading, *m.* (rad.) fading.
fado, *m.* (mus.) Portuguese folk song and dance.
faena, *f.* 1. task, job; work, labor, toil; (*pl.*) chores; (Ecuad., agr.) morning work; (Guat., Mex.) extra work, overtime. 2. (taur.) series of passes (in third part of bullfight, before the kill). 3. (coll.) dirty trick. — **faenas de la casa,** household chores.

faenar, *tr.v.* (Arg.) to slaughter (cattle).
faenero, *m.* (Chile) field hand, field worker; (Amer.) farmhand.
faetón, *m.* 1. phaeton, light horse-drawn carriage. 2. (myth.) **F.,** Phaethon, Phaeton.
fafarrachero, ra, *a.* (Amer.) boastful, vain.
Fafner, Fafnir, *m.* (myth.) Fafnir, Nordic giant who guarded the Nibelung treasure.
fagáceo, a, *a.* (bot.) fagaceous.
fagedeno, *m.* (med.) phagedena, phagedaena.
fagocitario, a, *a.* (biol.) phagocytic.
fagocítico, ca, *a.* (biol.) phagocytic.
fagocito, *m.* (med.) phagocyte.
fagocitosis, *f.* (physiol.) phagocytosis.
fagot, *m.* (mus.) bassoon, fagotto; bassoonist.
fagotista, *m.* (mus.) bassoonist, bassoon player.
Fahrenheit, *a.* Fahrenheit (degrees temperature). — **escala F.,** Fahrenheit scale.
fainada, *f.* (Cuba) rude remark, boorishness.
faino, na, *a.* (Cuba) simple, foolish, unmannerly; rude.
faique, *m.* (Ecuad., Peru, bot.) (species of) acacia (Acacia tortuosa).
faisán, *m.* (ornith.) pheasant.
faisana, *f.* (ornith.) hen pheasant.
faisanería, *f.* enclosure for pheasants.
faisanero, ra, *m., f.* pheasant breeder, keeper or seller.
faja, *f.* 1. sash, belt, girdle; cummerbund (worn with dinner jacket); girdle (woman's undergarment); sash (as insignia); wrapper (for mailing printed matter); bandage. 2. strip (of land); (geog.) zone. 3. (rad.) band. 4. (archit.) fascia, flat band. 5. (archit.) plaster border (around a window, etc.). 6. (her.) fesse. — **f. de frecuencia,** (rad.) frequency band; (med.) **f. abdominal,** abdominal supporter; **f. pantalón,** pantie girdle (woman's undergarment).
fajada, *f.* (Amer.) attack, assault, fight, e.g. *se dieron una f. de película,* they had a whale of a fight.
fajado, da, *past part. of* **fajar.** —*m.* (min.) timber used for making props or floors. —*a.* sashed; whipped, assaulted.
fajadura, *f.* 1. bandaging; swathing, swaddling; wrapping, parceling. 2. (mar.) tarred cordage protecting undersea cables.
fajamiento, *m.* wrapping; bandaging; swaddling.
fajar, *tr.v.* 1. to bind, wrap; to bandage; to swaddle (a child). 2. (Amer.) to give deliver (blows, etc.). 3. (vulg., Cuba) to make advances to a woman. —*r.v.* to put a sash or girdle on; to wrap or bind oneself up. — **fajarse con,** to fight with.
fajardo, *m.* patty, meat pie, vol-au-vent.
faje, *m.* (Mex.) (coll.) hug; (*pl.*) petting.
fajeado, da, *a.* striped, banded.
fajero, *m.* 1. umbilical bandage. 2. wide belt, sash.
fajilla, *f.* (Amer.) wrapper, paper band (for mailing printed matter).
fajín, *m.* small sash or band; sash (as insignia); (Sp., mil.) general's sash.
fajina, *f.* 1. (agr.) rick (of sheaves); kindling, fagot of brushwood; (fort.) fascine, bundle of sticks. 2. job, task, chore; (Cuba) extra work, overtime. 3. (mil.) bugle call for end of duties; call to quarters. — **destacamento de f.,** (mil.) fatigue detail; **meter f.,** to jabber, prattle; **ropa de f.,** work clothes; **servicio de f.,** (mil.) fatigue duty; **uniforme de f.,** fatigues.
fajinada, *f.* (fort.) fascine, revetment or fortification.
fajo, *m.* 1. sheaf; bundle. 2. (*pl.*) baby's swaddling clothes.
fajol, *m.* (bot.) buckwheat.
fajón, *m. aug. of* **faja,** large sash or belt; (archit.) plaster border (around doors and windows).
fajuela, *f.* thin sash or belt.
falacia, *f.* falsehood; falseness, deceit; fraud; (log.) fallacy.
falange, *f.* 1. phalanx (in all senses). 2. **F.,** Falange (Spanish political party).
falangero, *m.* (zool.) phalanger.
falangeta, *f.* (anat.) third phalanx of finger.
falangia, *f.* (ento.) daddy-longlegs, harvestman.
falangiano, na, *a.* (anat.) phalangeal.
falangina, *f.* (anat.) second phalanx.
falangio, *m.* (ento.) daddy-longlegs, harvestman; phalangium.
falangista, *m., f.* (pol.) Falangist, member of the Falange.
falansteriano, na, *a.* phalansterian, pertaining to a large, common dwelling or to a socialist community.
falansterio, *m.* phalanstery, a type of socialist community; any large common dwelling.
falárica, *f.* javelin; dart.
falaris, *f.* (ornith.) European coot, scoter.
falaropo, *m.* (ornith.) phalarope.
falaz, (*pl.* **falaces**) *a.* false, fallacious, deceitful, deceptive; treacherous.
falazmente, *adv.* fallaciously, falsely, deceitfully.
falbalá, *m.* 1. flounce, frill, furbelow. 2. flap on the skirt of a jacket or a coat.
falca, *f.* 1. warp (in timber). 2. (mar.) washboard. 3. wedge. 4. (Col.) extra rim (put on vats). 5. (Arg., Bol.) small still.
falcado, da, *a.* falcated, curved, hooked, in the shape of a scythe, sickle-shaped; falcated (said of ancient war chariots whose wheels had been fitted with protruding knives).
falce, *f.* sickle; falchion (broad curved sword or knife).
falcidia, *a.* (law) Falcidian. —*f.* Falcidian portion (equal to one fourth of the inheritance).
falciforme, *a.* falciform, sickle-shaped.
falcinelo, *m.* (ornith.) eastern glossy ibis.
falcirrostro, tra, *a.* (ornith.) curved beak, sickle-shaped beak.
falcón, *m.* 1. falcon; ancient small cannon. 2. (Cuba, ornith.) a species of falcon.
falconete, *m.* falconet (small cannon).
falcónidos, *m.* (*pl.*) (ornith.) species of predatory birds such as falcons and eagles.
falda, *f.* 1. skirt; petticoat. 2. flap, fold. 3. brassard (shoulder armor); skirt (of armor). 4. plate, skirt, brisket (of beef). 5. lap. 6. foothill (of mountain). 7. (*pl.*) (coll.) skirts, women. — **aficionado a las faldas,** woman chaser, Casanova.
faldamenta, *f.* skirt (of dress); long baggy skirt; flap.
faldamento, *m., var. of* **faldamenta.**
faldar, *m.* skirt of tasses (in armor).
faldear, *tr.v.* to skirt (a hill).
faldellín, *m.* 1. short skirt; underskirt, petticoat. 2. elaborate garment worn by infants during the baptismal ceremony.
faldeo, *m.* (Chile) mountain slopes; (Arg.) foothills.
faldero, ra, *a.* 1. pertaining to the skirt. 2. lap (dog). 3. (fig.) fond of being among women. — **perro f.,** lap dog.
faldeta, *f.* 1. drape (temporarily covering props backstage). 2. *dim. of* **falda,** small skirt. — **en faldetas,** (coll.) half-dressed, in shirttails.
faldicorto, ta, *a.* short-skirted.
faldilla, *f.* (mec.) flap, flange; skirt (pistons); **f. de mamparo,** bulkhead flange.
faldillas, *f.* (*pl.*) 1. coattails. 2. *dim. of* falda, skirt.
faldistorio, *m.* faldstool, bishop's folding stool or chair.
faldón, *m.* 1. shirttail, coattail; tail, skirt (of garment); flap. 2. top millstone (to give weight). 3. (archit.) triangular slope (of roof); tympanum, gable. 4. side walls and lintel (of chimney). 5. flap of a saddle. — **asirse** or **agarrarse a los faldones de alguno,** to seek someone's help or protection.
faldriquera, *f., var. of* **faltriquera.**
faldulario, *m.* (coll.) long trailing clothes.
falena, *f.* (ento.) geometrid, species of moth.
falencia, *f.* 1. illusion, error, mistake, misstatement. 2. (Amer., com.) bankruptcy, failure.
falerno, *m.* Falernian (famous wine of ancient Rome).
falibilidad, *f.* fallibility.
falible, *a.* fallible, subject to error or failure.
fálico, ca, *a.* phallic, pertaining to the phallus.
falimiento, *m.* (rare) falsehood, lie, untruth, deceit.
falla, *f.* 1. fault, defect, imperfection, deficiency; failure. 2. (tex.) faille. 3. (Mex.) baby's bonnet. 4. (geol.) slide, fault, break, dislocation. 5. (Sp.) (*pl.*) Valencia's fire festivals in the spring.
fallada, *f.* trumping, ruff (at cards).
fallador, ra, *m., f.* trumper, ruffing (at cards).
fallanca, *f.* (archit.) flashing (deflecting rain from window or door).
fallar, *tr.v.* (law) to judge, pass judgment on. —*i.v.* (law) to judge, rule, find.
fallar, *tr.v.* to trump, ruff; **f. en cruz,** to crossruff (in bridge). —*i.v.* 1. to trump, ruff. 2. to fail, be unsuccessful, be deficient. 3. to break, give way, e.g. *la cuerda falló,* the rope gave way. 4. to work or function defectively, not to work or function properly, e.g. *el motor está fallando,* the motor is not working properly; to stop working or functioning.
falleba, *f.* latch, bolt, door or window fastener; **f. de salida de emergencia,** fire-exit bolt, exit bolt.
fallecedero, ra, *a.* that may die, expire, fail; perishable, exhaustible.
fallecer, (*ref. 45*) *i.v.* 1. to die, expire. 2. to run out, fail.
falleciente, *a.* dying, expiring.
fallecimiento, *m.* death, decease, demise.
fallezca, fallezco, *ref.* **fallecer.**
fallido, da, *past part. of* **fallir.** —*a.* 1. frustrated, disappointed; unsuccessful. 2. bankrupt, insolvent. 3. uncollectable (debt).
fallir, *i.v.* 1. to run out, fail. 2. (Ven.) to go bankrupt.
fallo, lla, *a.* 1. lacking a card of the suit played. 2. (Chile) weak, faint. —*m.* 1. verdict, decision, ruling judgment, e.g. *dar el f.,* to judge, rule, pronounce the verdict. 2. error, fault; mistake, mixup; breakdown; failure. 3. lack of a card of the suit played. — **f. cardíaco,** heart failure; **f. condicional,** (law) decree nisi (in a divorce case); **f. de deficiencia,** (law) deficiency judgment; **f. fotográfico,** (sport.) photo finish; **f. humano,** human error.
falo, *m.* phallus, penis.
falondres, *adv.* **de f.,** (Cuba, Ven., mar.) suddenly, violently.
Falopio, trompa de F., (anat.) Fallopian tube.
falordía, *f.* fable, story, fairy tale.
falsa, *f.* 1. guide lines. 2. (mus.) dissonance. 3. garret.
falsabraga, *f.* (fort.) low outer rampart.
falsada, *f.* uneven swoop or flight (of a bird).
falsamente, *adv.* falsely, deceitfully.
falsar, *tr.v.* to bluff with (a card in ombre).
falsario, ria, *a.* falsifying, counterfeiting. —*m., f.* falsifier, counterfeiter, misrepresenter, liar; impostor, swindler.
falsarregla, *f.* 1. bevel, bevel square. 2. (Peru, Ven.) lined paper (to go under a sheet or a page to serve as a guide).
falseador, ra, *a.* falsifying; lying. —*m., f.* falsifier, misrepresenter; liar; forger, counterfeiter.

falseamiento, *m.* falsification; misrepresentation, counterfeiting, forgery.
falsear, *tr.v.* 1. to falsify; to misrepresent; to counterfeit, adulterate, forge. 2. to bluff with (a card at ombre). 3. to pick (a lock). 4. to break, pierce, penetrate. 5. (archit.) to bevel, slant, incline. —*i.v.* 1. to bend; to sag; to lose strength; to grow thin (fabric). 2. (mus.) to be out of tune.
falsedad, *f.* falsehood, falsity, deceit; lie, untruth, fib, fiction, fable.
falseo, *m.* (archit.) bevel, slant; beveling, slanting.
falseta, *f.* (mus.) flourish (on guitar).
falsete, *m.* 1. plug, spigot. 2. small door. 3. (mus.) falsetto (voice).
falsía, *f.* duplicity, falseness, falsity.
falsificable, *a.* falsifiable, forgeable.
falsificación, *f.* falsification; forging, counterfeiting; forgery, counterfeit, fake.
falsificado, da, *past part. of* **falsificar.** —*a.* forged; counterfeited; faked.
falsificador, ra, *a.* falsifying; forging, counterfeiting; faking. —*m., f.* falsifier; forger, counterfeiter; faker.
falsificar, (*ref. 50*) *tr.v.* to falsify; to forge, counterfeit (money); to fake, adulterate.
falsifique, falsifiqué, *ref.* **falsificar.**
falsilla, *f.* lined paper (to place under the page as guide).
falso, sa, *a.* 1. false, untrue, incorrect. 2. false, fake, mock, dummy, not real or genuine, counterfeit (money), imitation (jewelry). 3. false, treacherous, deceitful. 4. vicious, balky (horse). 5. inexact, defective, false (weights). 6. awkward, wrong (movement). 7. (Nic.) cowardly. —*m.* 1. reinforcement, lining, facing, hem (of a dress). 2. (mec.) dummy, mock. — **cerrar en f.,** to shut incorrectly; to heal only superficially; **eco f.,** (radar) indirect echo; **en f.,** deceptively, falsely; without proper support; **f. alarma,** false alarm; **f. flete,** (mar.) dead freight; **f. testimonio,** (law) false testimony; **larguero f.,** false spar (aeroplane wing); **modelo f.,** reverse mold; **puerta f.,** back or side door.
falta, *f.* 1. lack, want, absence, shortage. 2. absence (from school). 3. error, mistake, e.g. *f. de ortografía,* spelling mistake; fault (in tennis, pelota), e.g. *f. de pie,* foot fault. 4. fault, failing, shortcoming, defect. 5. misdeed, misdemeanor, breach, e.g. *grave f. contra los buenos modales,* a serious breach of good manners; (law) fault, misdemeanor. 6. weight deficiency (of coin). 7. (med.) absence of catamenia (in pregnant women). 8. (mec.) failure, fault, shortage. — **a f. de,** or **por f. de,** for want of, for lack of; **a f. de pan buenas son tortas,** half a loaf is better than none; **f. de ortografía,** spelling mistake; **f. de pago,** (com.) default of payment; **hacer f.,** to be wanted, be necessary; to be lacking, be missing; **hacerle f. a uno (alguna cosa),** to need (something); **sin f.,** without fail; **f. de aislamiento,** insulating fault; **f. de circularidad,** circularity lack; **f. de contraste,** (photog.) flatness; **f. de corriente,** (elec.) current failure; **f. de excitación,** (elec.) lack of drive.
faltante, *a.* missing, lacking, wanting.
faltar, *i.v.* 1. to be missing, be lacking, be wanting; to be deficient, to fall short; to be absent. 2. to fail, not to function or work. 3. to fail to keep, do, fulfil, carry out or tell, not to keep, do, fulfil, carry out or tell, e.g. *f. a su palabra,* to fail to keep one's word, not to keep one's word, *f. a su deber,* to fail to do one's duty, not to do one's duty, *f. a su lealtad,* to fail to be loyal, *f. a la verdad,* to fail to tell the truth, not to tell the truth. 4. to insult, be rude, be disrespectful, e.g. *faltarle a alguien,* to be rude to someone, insult someone. 5. to lack, be short of, e.g. *me falta un capítulo para completar mi novela,* I am one chapter short of completing my novel; **f. +** *inf.*, to remain to be + *past part.*, e.g. *faltaba escribir dos cartas,* two letters remained to be written. — **f. a una cita,** to break an appointment, to fail to keep an appointment; **f. a la clase,** to cut class, be absent from class; **faltarle a uno,** not to have; to need, be in need of; to be out of; to be short of; **f. para,** to be (so many minutes, hours, etc.) to, e.g. *faltan dos minutos para las seis,* it is two minutes to six; **¡no faltaba más!** that's the limit! that's the last straw! of course!; **poco faltó para que** + *subj.*, nearly, e.g. *poco faltó para que se fueran a las manos,* they nearly came to blows; **faltarle el respeto a uno,** to be rude to, insult, be disrespectful to.
falte, *m.* (Chile) peddler, hawker.
falto, ta, *a.* 1. short, lacking, wanting; devoid. 2. short, incomplete (weight or measurement); defective, deficient. — **f. de,** lacking, short of, e.g. *mi pluma está falta de tinta,* my fountain pen lacks ink; **f. de aliento,** out of breath.
faltón, na, *a.* 1. (coll.) unreliable, dilatory, defaulting; remiss in one's duties. 2. (Cuba) disrespectful.
faltoso, sa, *a.* 1. incomplete. 2. (C. Amer., Mex.) disrespectful, rude. 3. (Col.) quarrelsome.
faltriquera, *f.* 1. pocket; purse, handbag. 2. (theat.) each of two small boxes on either side of the stage.
falúa, *f.* (mar.) tender, small boat, gig.
falucho, *m.* 1. (mar.) felucca, lateener. 2. (Arg.) cocked hat, bicorne.
fama, *f.* 1. fame, renown. 2. reputation, name; glory, prestige. 3. rumor, report. — **tener f.,** to be famous; **mala f.,** bad name or reputation; **unos tienen la f. y otros cardan la lana,** some do all the work and others get the glory.
famélico, ca, *a.* starving, famished; ravenous; emaciated, thin and pale.
familia, *f.* family; household; kin, clan. — **en f.,** en famille; **de buena f.,** wellborn; **f. de acogida,** foster family; **f. extensa,** extended family; **f. monoparental,** single-parent family; **f. nuclear,** nuclear family; **f. numerosa,** large family.
familiar, *a.* 1. familiar, pertaining to a family; domestic. 2. common, colloquial, frequent; well known. 3. plain, unceremonious, homelike. —*m.* 1. relation, member of the family. 2. intimate friend, companion. 3. servant. 4. (ecc.) familiar (servant of the clergy). 5. familiar spirit, demon. 6. (*pl.*) attendants, suite. — **lazos familiares,** family ties; **estilo f.,** colloquial style.
familiarice, familiaricé, *ref.* **familiarizar.**
familiaridad, *f.* familiarity, intimacy, acquaintance.
familiarizado, da, *a.* familiarized, conversant; accustomed, habituated.
familiarizar, (*ref. 53*) *tr.v.* to familiarize, to make popular or well known. —*r.v.* to become or get familiar; to become accustomed, to habituate oneself. — **familiarizarse con,** to familiarize oneself with, become or get familiar with.
familiarmente, *adv.* familiarly.
familiatura, *f.* 1. post of familiar (officer of the Inquisition). 2. post of a college servant.
familión, *m., aug. of* **familia,** large family.
famosamente, *adv.* famously; excellently.
famoso, sa, *a.* 1. famous, renowned, celebrated; notorious. 2. (coll.) excellent, first-rate; enormous, extraordinary, remarkable.
famular, *a.* domestic, famulary, pertaining to the servants.
famulato, famulicio, *m.* 1. post of servant, servantship. 2. servants (of a household).
fámulo, la, *m.* famulus, (coll.) servant. —*f.* (coll.) maid, maidservant.
fanal, *m.* 1. beacon; lighthouse; lantern. 2. glass chimney, candle screen; bell glass. — **f. de arrumbamiento,** (aer.) bearing projector; **f. de luz intermitente,** (mar.) bug; **buque f.,** (mar.) lightship.
fanáticamente, *adv.* fanatically.
fanatice, fanaticé, *ref.* **fanatizar.**
fanático, ca, *a.* fanatical, fanatic. —*m., f.* zealot; fanatic; fan, e.g. *un f. del fútbol,* a soccer fan.
fanatismo, *m.* fanaticism.
fanatizador, ra, *m., f.* person who spreads fanaticism.
fanatizar, (*ref. 53*) *tr.v.* to make fanatical. —*r.v.* to become fanatical.
fandango, *m.* 1. fandango, Spanish regional dance and its music. 2. (coll.) row, racket; brawl, fight.
fandanguero, ra, *a.* fond of dancing and parties. —*m., f.* dancing fan, person fond of dancing.
fandanguillo, *m.* (mus.) one of the principal classical forms of flamenco singing.
fandulario, *m., var. of* **faldulario.**
faneca, *f.* (ichth.) bib.
fanega, *f.* fanega, measure of capacity (1.6 bushels in Spain). — **f. de tierra,** (agr.) measure (1.59 acres).
fanegada, *f., var. of* **fanega de tierra. — a fanegadas,** (fig., coll.) abundantly, plentifully, in great abundance.
fanerófita, *f.* (bot.) phanerophyte.
fanerógamo, ma, *a.* (bot.) phanerogamous. —*m.* (bot.) phanerogam.
fanfarrear, *i.v., var. of* **fanfarronear.**
fanfarria, *f.* 1. (coll.) swagger, bluster, bragging, boasting. 2. (mus.) fanfare. 3. (mus.) band.
fanfarrón, na, *a.* 1. (coll.) bragging, blustering, boasting. 2. (coll.) flashy, showy. —*m., f.* (coll.) braggart, blusterer, boaster. — **trigo fanfarrón,** a variety of wheat.
fanfarronada, *f.* bluster, swagger, fanfaronade; boast, brag. — **decir** or **echar fanfarronadas,** to boast, brag.
fanfarronear, *i.v.* to boast, brag, bluster, bully.
fanfarronería, *f.* fanfaronade, bluster, swagger, bragging, boasting.
fanfarronesca, *f., var. of* **fanfarronería.**
fanfurriña, *f.* (coll.) fit of anger, pettishness.
fangal, fangar, *m.* mudhole, quagmire, bog, slough, swamp.
fango, *m.* mud, mire, slush, silt, slime.
fangosidad, *f.* muddiness, slushiness.
fangoso, sa, *a.* muddy, miry, slushy.
fanguero, *m.* (Cuba, P. Rico, Mex.) quagmire, bog.
fano, *m.* fane, temple (among the pagans).
fantaseador, ra, *a.* daydreaming, fanciful. —*m., f.* daydreamer.
fantasear, *i.v.* to daydream, to fancy. —*tr.v.* to imagine, dream of.
fantasía, *f.* 1. imagination, fancy, fantasy. 2. fantasy, dream, illusory image. 3. story, fiction. 4. (coll.) vanity, conceit, presumption. 5. whim, caprice. 6. (mus.) fantasia, fantasy. 7. (*pl.*) costume jewelry. — **de f.,** fancy work, gaily colored; **joyas de f.,** imitation jewelry; **punto de f.,** (mar.) dead reckoning.
fantasioso, sa, *a.* (coll.) vain, conceited.
fantasma, *m.* 1. ghost, phantom, apparition. 2. vision, illusion. 3. (fig.) conceited person. 4. (tel.) ghost. —*f.* scarecrow. — **los fantasmas del pasado,** (fig.) the phantoms of things past; **f. magnético,** (phys.) magnetic phantom.
fantasmagoría, *f.* 1. phantasmagoria; optical illusion. 2. the use of extraordinary effects in art, theatre, literature, etc.

fantasmagórico, ca, *a.* phantasmagoric.
fantasmal, *a.* ghostly, spectral.
fantasmón, na, *a.* (coll.) very conceited or vain. —*m.* (coll.) stuffed shirt.
fantásticamente, *adv.* fantastically.
fantástico, ca, *a.* 1. fantastic, imaginary; unreal. 2. (coll.) magnificent, wonderful. 3. (Arg.) capricious, whimsical, fanciful.
fantochada, *f.* stupid or ridiculous action.
fantoche, *m.* 1. puppet, marionette. 2. popinjay, ridiculous person, nincompoop.
fañado, da, *a.* one year old (animal).
fañoso, sa, *a.* (Amer.) *var. of* **gangoso.**
FAO *abbrev. of* **Organización de las Naciones Unidas para la Agricultura y la Alimentación,** Food and Agricultural Organization of the United Nations (FAO).
faquín, *m.* porter, carrier, bearer; laborer.
faquir, *m.* fakir, Moslem mystic.
fara, *f.* 1. (Col.) opossum. 2. (zool.) species of African snake.
farachar, *tr.v.* to beat (hemp).
farad, *m.* (elec.) farad.
faraday, *m.* (elec.) faraday, unit of quantity.
faradio, *m.* (elec.) farad, unit of capacity.
farádico, ca, *a.* (elec.) faradic.
faradización, *f.* (med.) faradization.
faradizar, *tr.v.* (med.) to faradize.
faralá, *f.* ruffle, flounce, frill; (coll.) fussy frill, excessively ornate frill or flounce.
farallón, *m.* 1. out-jutting rock, cliff, headland. 2. (min.) outcrop. 3. (Peru, Bol.) crest of a mountain.
faramalla, *a.* bamboozling, swindling, deceiving. —*f.* 1. (coll.) bamboozling talk or patter, cajolery. 2. (coll.) flashy but worthless article. —*m., f.* bamboozler, deceiver, cheat, swindler, cajoler.
faramallear, *i.v.* (Amer.) *var. of* **farolear.**
faramallero, ra, *a.* (coll.) bamboozling, deceiving, swindling; cajoling. —*m., f.* (coll.) bamboozler, deceiver, swindler, cheat; charlatan.
faramallón, na, *a., m., f., var. of* **faramallero.**
farándula, *f.* 1. show business; (arch.) acting, theater (profession). 2. (arch.) company of wandering actors. 3. (coll.) bamboozling talk or patter; show, ostentation. 4. (mus.) farandole.
farandulear, *i.v.* (coll.) to show off, boast, brag.
farandulero, ra, *m., f.* wandering player or actor. 2. (coll.) bamboozler, swindler; tattler, busybody.
farandúlico, ca, *a.* pertaining to show business or actors.
faraón, *m.* 1. Pharaoh, title given to the rulers of ancient Egypt. 2. pharaoh, a card game.
faraónico, ca, *a.* Pharaonic, pertaining to the Pharaoh or his rule.
faraute, *m.* 1. courier, messenger. 2. (king's) herald. 3. (coll.) busybody. 4. (theat., arch.) actor who recites the prologue of a play.
farda, *f.* 1. (hist.) tax levied on Jews and Moors. 2. bundle of clothing. 3. (carp.) mortise, groove, notch.
fardacho, *m.* (zool.) lizard.
fardaje, *m., var. of* **fardería.**
fardar, *tr.v.* to supply or furnish with clothes.
fardel, *m.* 1. bag, knapsack, sack. 2. bundle, parcel. 3. (coll.) slob, slovenly person, e.g. *¡vas hecho un f.!* you look like a bum!
fardería, *f.* collection of bundles or parcels.
fardo, *m.* bale, bundle, parcel; **a f. cerrado,** to swallow a story lock, stock and barrel; **comprar a f. cerrado,** to buy a pig in a poke.
farellón, *m., var. of* **farallón.**
farfalá, *f.* ruffle, flounce, frill, furbellow.
farfallear, *i.v.* (reg.) to stutter, stammer.
farfalloso, sa, *a.* stammering, stuttering.
farfante, farfantón, na, *a.* (coll.) boastful, garrulous. —*m.* (coll.) garrulous boaster, babbler.
farfantonada, farfantonería, *f.* (coll.) boast, brag.
fárfara, *f.* 1. skin, pellicle (of eggshell). 2. (bot.) coltsfoot. — **en f.,** without an eggshell (said of an egg with a skin but no shell); (fig.) half-done, unfinished.
farfolla, *f.* 1. corn husk. 2. flashy, eyecatching but worthless thing.
farfulla, *a.* gabbling, jabbering. —*f.* gabbling, jabbering. —*m., f.* gabbler, jabberer.
farfulladamente, *adv.* hurriedly, hastily, carelessly.
farfullador, ra, *a.* 1. gabbling, jabbering. 2. hasty, slipshod, shoddy. —*m., f.* 1. gabbler. 2. slipshod or shoddy worker.
farfullar, *tr.v., i.v.* 1. to gabble. 2. to do hastily, do shoddily or in a slipshod manner.
farfullero, ra, *a., m., f., var. of* **farfullador.**
fargallón, na, *a.* 1. (coll.) hasty, slipshod. 2. (coll.) slovenly, untidy. —*m., f.* 1. (coll.) hasty slipshod worker. 2. (coll.) slob, slovenly person.
farillón, *m., var. of* **farallón.**
farináceo, a, *a.* farinaceous, mealy.
farinetas, *f.* (*pl.*) (reg., Sp.) porridge, pap.
faringe, *m.* (anat.) pharynx.
faríngeo, a, *a.* (med.) pharyngeal.
faringitis, *f.* (med.) pharyngitis.
faringología, *f.* (med.) pharyngology.
faringoscopia, *f.* (med.) pharyngoscopy.
faringoscopio, *m.* (med.) pharyngoscope.
fariña, *f.* 1. (Arg.) cassava flour. 2. (Sp., reg.) corn cake, cornbread.
farisaicamente, *adv.* pharisaically, hypocritically.
farisaico, ca, *a.* 1. Pharisaical, Pharisaic. 2. pharisaical, pharisaic, hypocritical.
farisaísmo, *m.* 1. Pharisaism (doctrines, etc., of Pharisees). 2. pharisaism (pharisaical attitude, etc.).
fariseísmo, *m.* 1. Pharisaism. 2. pharisaism, hypocrisy.
fariseo, *m.* 1. (Bib.) Pharisee. 2. hypocrite, pharisee. 3. (coll.) mean, malicious person.
farmacéutico, ca, *a.* pharmaceutical. —*m.* pharmacist, pharmaceutist, druggist, apothecary.
farmacia, *f.* 1. pharmacy, pharmaceutics. 2. pharmaceutical profession. 3. drugstore (U.S.), chemist's, chemist's shop (G.B.), pharmacy.
fármaco, *m.* medicine, medication.
farmacognosia, *f.* pharmacognosy, science that deals with medicinal products obtained from natural sources.
farmacología, *f.* pharmacology, the study of the preparation and application of drugs and medicines.
farmacológico, ca, *a.* pharmacological.
farmacólogo, ga, *m., f.* pharmacist, druggist, pharmacologist.
farmacopea, *f.* pharmacopoeia, prescription or formula book.
farmacópola, *m.* (coll.) pharmacist, druggist, apothecary, chemist.
farmacopólico, ca, *a.* (coll.) pharmaceutical, pharmaceutic.
faro, *m.* 1. lighthouse; beacon. 2. (auto.) headlight, headlamp. 3. (fig.) guiding light, beacon. — **f. aéreo,** air beacon; **f. radar,** radar beacon; **f. de aterrizaje,** landing-direction light (airports).
farol, *m.* 1. lamp, light; street-lamp; lantern. 2. cresset, torch holder. 3. (coll.) show-off, bragger, boaster. 4. (coll.) bluff (in cards). 5. (taur.) cape flourish. — **f. de situación,** (mar.) navigation lantern; **f. del cambio de vía,** switch lamp; **echar faroles,** to boast or bluff; **adelante con los faroles,** right on! keep up the good work!
farola, *f.* large street lamp (with several arms); traffic light; lighthouse, beacon; large lantern.
farolazo, *m.* 1. blow given with lantern. 2. (Amer., coll.) nip, swig, drink (of liquor).
farolear, *i.v.* (coll.) to show off, brag, boast.
faroleo, *m.* (coll.) boasting, bragging, showing-off.
farolería, *f.* 1. lamp or lantern shop. 2. boasting, bragging.
farolero, ra, *a.* (coll.) vain, conceited; bragging, boastful. —*m., f.* (coll.) boaster, show-off. —*m.* 1. lantern maker or vendor. 2. lamplighter.
farolillo, *m.* 1. *dim. of* **farol,** small lamp. 2. (bot.) Canterbury bell. 3. (bot.) balloon vine; heartseed.
farolón, *a.* vain, conceited, boastful. —*m., f.* (coll.) boaster, show-off (coll.). —*m.* large lamp or lantern.
Faros, *m.* 1. Pharos, island near Alexandria. 2. famous lighthouse of this island, one of the Seven Wonders of the World.
farota, *f.* (coll.) hussy, jezebel, brazen woman.
farotón, na, *m., f.* (coll.) brazen or cheeky person. —*a.* brazen, impudent, cheeky.
farpa, *f.* each of the points of a pinked or serrated edge.
farpado, da, *a.* scalloped, pinked, notched.
farra, *f.* 1. (ichth.) lavaret, a kind of salmon. 2. (Amer.) spree, party, revelry, binge.
fárrago, *m.* farrago, hodgepodge, jumble, medley.
farragoso, sa, *a.* confused, disorderly.
farraguista, *m., f.* muddlehead, fuddleheaded person.
farrear, *i.v.* (Amer.) to go on a spree or a binge; to paint the town red.
farro, *m.* coarsely-ground peeled barley (after soaking); variety of spelt wheat.
farruco, ca, *a.* (coll.) brave, bold, fearless. —*m., f.* Galician or Asturian who has just left his region. —*f.* (mus.) a variety of flamenco rhythm in song and dance.
farruto, ta, *a.* (Chile) sickly, weak, puny.
farsa, *f.* 1. (theat.) farce. 2. company of comedy actors. 3. poor play, farcical melodrama. 4. farce, sham.
Farsalia, *f.* (hist.) Pharsalia, a district in ancient Thessaly, where Caesar defeated Pompeii; Lucan's famous poem on that theme.
farsanta, *f.* farce actress.
farsante, *a.* hypocritical, fake. —*m., f.* fraud, fake, charlatan, sham. —*m.* farce actor, farceur.
farsear, *i.v.* (Chile) to jest, joke, banter.
farseto, *m.* quilted jacket (formerly worn under armor).
farsista, *m., f.* author of farces, farceur.
fas, por f. o por nefas, (coll.) rightly or wrongly, with or without reason.
fascal, *m.* (agr.) stack, rick, shock.
fasces, *f.* (*pl.*) (hist.) fasces, bundle of rods; symbol of authority in ancient Rome and fascist Italy.
fascia, *f.* (anat.) fascia.
fasciación, *f.* (bot.) fasciation.
fasciado, da, *a.* 1. (zool.) fasciate, fasciated, striped. 2. (bot.) fasciate, flat.
fasciculación, *f.* (anat.) fasciculation.
fasciculado, da, *a.* (bot., anat.) fasciculate, fascicled, fasciated.
fascicular, *a.* (bot.) fascicular.
fascículo, *m.* 1. fascicle, fasciculus (of a book). 2. (bot.) fascicle. 3. (anat.) fasciculus.
fascinación, *f.* fascination, enchantment, bewitchment; allure.
fascinador, ra, *a.* fascinating, charming, bewitching, spell-binding. —*m., f.* charmer.

fascinante, *a.* fascinating, charming, bewitching, alluring.
fascinar, *tr.v.* 1. to fascinate, bewitch, enchant. 2. to deceive.
fascismo, *m.* 1. (pol.) fascism (fascist doctrine and movement in general). 2. **F.,** Fascism (Italian Fascist movement and doctrine).
fascista, *a., m., f.* fascist (relating to fascism in general).
fase, *f.* 1. phase, stage. 2. phase, aspect, view. 3. (astron., phys., elec., chem.) phase. — **f. amplificadora,** gain stage; **f. de amplificación modulada,** modulated amplification stage; **f. de contraveta** (geol.) dyke phase; **f. de estado líquido,** (plastics) treacle stage; **f. de elaboración,** processing step; **f. diploide,** (biol.) diplophase; **f. partida** or **dividida,** (elec.) split phase.
fásoles, *m.* (*pl.*) (bot.) beans, haricots.
fastial, *m.* (archit.) copestone (of a building).
fastidiado, da, *past part. of* **fastdiar.** —*a.* 1. weary, disgusted; annoyed, upset. 2. (coll.) broke (ruined); broken (out of order).
fastidiar, *tr.v.* 1. to annoy, irritate, vex; to pester, bother. 2. to tire, bore, weary. 3. to make sick, upset. 4. to inconvenience, cause inconvenience to. —*r.v.* 1. to get annoyed, irritated or vexed. 2. to be inconvenienced.
fastidio, *m.* 1. annoyance, irritation; bother, nuisance. 2. weariness, boredom, tediousness, ennui. 3. repugnance, revulsion.
fastidiosamente, *adv.* annoyingly, irritatingly, tediously, irritably.
fastidioso, sa, *a.* 1. annoying, irritating, vexing, bothersome, tedious, irksome. 2. sickening. 3. annoyed, irritated.
fastigio, *m.* 1. top, apex, tip; pinnacle, acme, summit. 2. (archit.) fastigium.
fasto, ta, *a.* auspicious, happy, good (day or event). —*m.* luxury, pomp, splendor, magnificence.
fastos, *m.* (*pl.*) 1. fasti (Roman calendar). 2. annals, chronicles.
fastosamente, *adv., var. of* **fastuosamente.**
fastoso, sa, *a., var. of* **fastuoso.**
fastuosamente, *adv.* lavishly, luxuriously, showily, magnificently, with great pomp and splendor.
fastuoso, sa, *a.* ostentatious, lavish, luxurious.
fatal, *a.* 1. fatal, fateful, unavoidable. 2. fatal, deadly, mortal. 3. unlucky, unfortunate. 4. wicked, bad, destructive.
fatalidad, *f.* 1. fate, destiny. 2. fatality, death. 3. misfortune, calamity.
fatalismo, *m.* (philos.) fatalism.
fatalista, *a.* fatalistic. —*m., f.* (philos.) fatalist.
fatalmente, *adv.* 1. fatally, fatefully. 2. inevitably, unavoidably. 3. unfortunately, unluckily, unhappily. 4. very badly.
fatamorgana, *f.* fatamorgana, mirage.
fatídicamente, *adv.* fatidically, prophetically; ominously.
fatídico, ca, *a.* fatidic, fateful; prophetic; ominous.
fatiga, *f.* 1. fatigue, tiredness, weariness. 2. shortness of breath, hard breathing. 3. (mec., agr., physiol.) fatigue. 4. (*pl.*) nausea, sickness. 5. (*pl.*) difficulties, irritations, trouble, bother. — **f. de combate,** combat fatigue; **f. nerviosa,** (med.) strain; **f. visual,** eyestrain.
fatigadamente, *adv.* 1. wearily, tiredly; with difficulty. 2. pantingly, with shortness of breath.
fatigado, da, *past part. of* **fatigar.** —*a.* fatigued, tired, wearied, worn out.
fatigador, ra, *a.* tiring, annoying, irritating.
fatigante, *a., var. of* **fatigoso.**
fatigar, (*ref. 51*) *tr.v.* 1. to tire, fatigue, exhaust. 2. to annoy, irritate, vex; to bore. —*r.v.* to tire, get tired.
fatigosamente, *adv.* 1. wearily, tiredly. 2. heavily, laboriously (breathing). 3. tediously, tiresomely.
fatigoso, sa, *a.* 1. fatiguing, tiring, wearying. 2. fatigued, tired, weary. 3. annoying, irritating, tiresome; boring. 4. hard, labored (breathing).
fatigue, fatigué, *ref.* **fatigar.**
fatimí, fatimita, *a.* Fatimid, descended from Fatima, Mohammed's daughter. —*m., f.* Fatimid, Fatimite, any Fatimid ruler or descendant.
fatuidad, *f.* 1. fatuity, fatuousness, foolishness. 2. fatuous remark. 3. conceit, vanity.
fatuo, a, *a.* 1. fatuous, foolish. 2. conceited, vain. —*m., f.* 1. fool, fathead. 2. conceited fool. — **fuego fatuo,** will-o'-the-wisp.
faucal, *a.* (anat.) faucal.
fauces, *f.* (*pl.*) (anat.) fauces, gullet.
fauna, *f.* fauna, animal life. **f. abisal,** abyssal fauna, deep-sea fauna; **f. del suelo,** soil fauna.
fauno, *m.* (myth.) faun; **F.,** Faunus, Roman demigod of agriculture.
faurestina, *f.* (Cuba, bot.) lebbek, East Indian walnut.
fausto, ta, *a.* fortunate, happy, lucky, auspicious. —*m.* pomp, splendor, magnificence, ostentation; luxury.
faustoso, sa, *a., var. of* **fastuoso.**
fautor, ra, *m., f.* abetter, helper, countenancer, supporter.
fautoría, *f.* aid, assistance, help; support.
fauvismo, *m.* (art.) fauvism, French movement and school of painting started at the beginning of this century by a group of masters which included Matisse, Duty, Rouault, etc.
faveolado, da, *a.* (bot.) faveolate; alveolate, honeycombed.
favila, *f.* (poet.) ember.
favo, *m.* (med.) favus, a disease of the skin.
favonio, *m.* (poet.) zephyr, west wind.
favor, *m.* 1. favor, good turn, kindness, help, aid. 2. favor, grace; protection, patronage. 3. compliment, love token. — **a f. de,** in favor of; with the aid of; by means of; **en f. de,** in favor of; **hazme** or **hágame el f. de,** be kind or good enough to; **por f.,** please; **tener a alguien** or **algo a su f.,** to have someone or something in one's favor.
favorable, *a.* favorable; propitious, desirable, advantageous.
favorablemente, *adv.* favorably.
favorecedor, ra, *a.* becoming, enhancing, e.g. *un vestido f.,* a becoming dress. —*m., f.* favorer, helper.
favorecer, (*ref. 45*) *tr.v.* 1. to favor; to support, back. 2. to help, aid. 3. to do (someone) a favor; to grant, bestow on (prize, privilege). —*r.v.* **favorecerse de,** to avail oneself of someone's support or help.
favorecido, da, *past part. of* **favorecer.** —*a.* favored, helped, backed.
favoreciente, *a.* favoring; helping, assisting.
favorezca, favorezco, *ref.* **favorecer.**
favoritismo, *m.* favoritism, nepotism.
favorito, ta, *a., m., f.* favorite; pet, darling.
fax, *m.* fax; **mandar un f.,** to send a fax; **mandaselo por f.,** send it to him by fax, fax it to him.
faxear, *tr.v.* to fax, to send (something) by fax.
faya, *f.* (tex.) faille, ribbed silk.
fayalita, *f.* (min.) fayalite.
fayanca, *f.* unstable posture; **de f.,** (fig.) negligently, carelessly.
faz, (*pl.* **faces**) *f.* 1. face. 2. obverse (of coin). 3. (archit.) front. 4. (tex.) side, e.g. *tela de doble f.,* fabric with two sides, reversible fabric — **a primera f.,** at first sight; **f. a. f.,** face to face; **en f. y en paz,** publicly and peacefully.
FBI, *m.* FBI.
F.C., f.c. *abbrev. of* **ferrocarril,** railway (ry.).
fe, *f.* 1. faith; confidence, trust; belief, credence. 2. faith, religion. 3. confirmation, attestation, testimony. 4. certificate, testimonial. 5. fidelity, faithfulness. — **a buena f.,** certainly, undoubtedly; **a f.,** in truth, truly; **a f. mía,** on my word of honor; **dar f.,** to attest, certify, authenticate, confirm; **de buena f.,** in good faith; **de mala f.,** in bad faith; **f. de bautismo,** baptismal certificate; **f. de erratas,** (print.) list of errata, errata; **f. de la tierra,** face of the earth; **f. de nacimiento,** birth certificate; **f. de vida,** (law) identity credentials; **f. pública,** (law) legal authority (of a public official to authenticate documents); **hacer f.,** to be valid, be sufficient proof; **tener f. en,** to believe in, to have faith or confidence in.
Fe *sym. of* **hierro,** ferrum (Fe).
fealdad, *f.* 1. ugliness, hideousness, homeliness. 2. (fig.) torpidness, dishonesty, foulness.
feamente, *adv.* uglily; indecorously.
feb. *abbrev. of* **febrero,** February (Feb.).
Febe, *f.* 1. (astron., myth.) Phoebe, one of the satellites of the planet Saturn; goddess of the moon. 2. (poet.) the moon.
febeo, a, *a.* (poet.) Phoebean, pertaining to the sun.
feblaje, *m.* (numis.) deficiency in weight or sterling fineness (of a coin).
feble, *a.* 1. feeble, weak, faint. 2. (numis.) deficent in weight or sterling fineness.
feblemente, *adv.* feebly, weakly.
Febo, *m.* 1. (myth.) Phoebus, one of the names of Apollo, the god of the sun. 2. (poet.) the sun.
febrero, *m.* February.
febricitante, *a.* (med.) feverish.
febrícula, *f.* slight fever.
febrífugo, ga, *a.* (med.) febrifugal. —*m.* (med.) febrifuge.
febril, *a.* febrile, feverish; (fig.) anxious, restless.
febrilmente, *adv.* feverishly.
fecal, *a.* (med.) faecal.
fecalito, *m.* (med.) fecalith.
fecha, *f.* 1. date. 2. day. 3. date, moment, time, e.g. *hasta la f.,* to date, up to this moment, till now. — **a estas fechas,** by now, by this time; **f. de caducidad,** (med.) expiration date; **f. de consumo preferente,** best-before date; **f. de vencimiento,** due date, maturity date (of a note or bill); **hasta la f.,** to date; **¿qué f. es hoy?** what is the date today?
fechación, *f.* dating.
fechador, *m.* (Chile, Mex.) postmark; (Chile, Guat., Mex.) date stamp.
fechar, *tr.v.* to date (a letter, a bill, etc.).
fecho, cha, *past part. of* **facer.** —*a.* done, executed, issued (used only on legal documents). —*m.* note on legal documents to show that they have been executed.
fechoría, *f.* misdeed, villainy; misdemeanor.
fechuría, *f., var. of* **fechoría.**
fecial, *m.* 1. (hist.) herald who announced war or peace in ancient Rome. 2. (*pl.*) fetiales, priestly board in Rome which conducted diplomatic negotiations.
fécula, *f.* starch, fecula.
feculencia, *f.* feculence, lees, dregs.
feculento, ta, *a.* 1. feculent, fecal, foul with impurities. 2. containing starch.
feculoso, sa, *var. of* **feculento.**
fecundable, *a.* fertile, able to be fertilized or fecundated.
fecundación, *f.* fecundation, fertilization.
fecundador, ra, *a.* fecundating, fertilizing.
fecundamente, *adv.* fruitfully, fertilely.
fecundante, *a.* fecundating, fertilizing.

fecundar, *tr.v.* to fecundate, inseminate, impregnate, fertilize; to make fruitful.
fecundativo, va, *a.* fecundative, fecundating, fertilizing.
fecundice, fecundicé, *ref.* **fecundizar.**
fecundidad, *f.* fecundity, fruitfulness, fertility; productiveness; abundance.
fecundización, *f.* fertilization, fecundation.
fecundizador, ra, *a.* fertilizing, fecundating.
fecundizante, *a.* fertilizing, fecundating.
fecundizar, (*ref. 53*) *tr.v.* to fertilize, fecundate, make fruitful or fertile; to impregnate, inseminate.
fecundo, da, *a.* fecund, fertile, fruitful, prolific; abundant, copious.
fedatario, *m.* public official authorized to attest documents.
federación, *f.* federation, confederation.
federal, *a.* federal. —*m., f.* federalist, federal.
federalismo, *m.* federalism.
federalista, *a., m., f.* federalist.
federalización, *f.* federalization.
federar, *tr.v., r.v.* to federate, confederate.
federativo, va, *a.* federative.
Fedra, *f.* (myth.) Phaedra, Theseus' wife.
feérico, ca, *a.* (poet.) fairy-like, fantastic.
fefaút, *m.* (mus.) Lydian mode (in early church music).
féferes, *m. pl.* (Amer.) household goods, tools; knicknacks, bric-a-brac, trinkets, paraphernalia.
fehaciente, *a.* convincing; authentic; (law) attesting, certifying.
felá, fellah, *m.* fellah, peasant, laborer (in Egypt and other Arab nations).
felatorismo, *m.* fellatio.
feldespático, ca, *a.* (min.) feldspathic.
feldespato, *m.* (min.) feldspar.
feldmariscal, *m.* (mil.) field marshall (in certain European countries).
felice, *a.* (poet.) happy.
felicidad, *f.* 1. happiness, felicity, blissfulness. 2. prosperity, success, good luck, good fortune.
felicitación, *f.* congratulations, felicitation, compliments.
felicitar, *tr.v.* 1. to congratulate, felicitate, compliment. 2. to wish (someone) good luck. —*r.v.* to congratulate oneself.
félido, *m.* (zool.) felid; (*pl.*) Felidae.
feligrés, sa, *m., f.* parishioner, church member.
feligresía, *f.* parish (inhabitants and territory), parishoners; rural parish.
felino, na, *a.* (zool., fig.) feline. —*m.* (zool.) feline, felid.
feliz, (*pl.* **felices**) *a.* happy; felicitous; fortunate; lucky.
felizmente, *adv.* fortunately, luckily; happily, successfully.
felodermis, *f.* (bot.) phelloderm.
felodermo, *m.* (bot.) phelloderm.
felogénico, ca, *a.* (bot.) phellogenic.
felógeno, na, *a.* (bot.) phellogenic. —*m.* (bot.) phellogen.
felón, na, *a.* treacherous, perfidious, villainous, base. —*m., f.* villain, wicked person, scoundrel.
felonía, *f.* perfidy, treachery, disloyalty; villainy, base action.
felpa, *f.* 1. (tex.) plush. 2. (coll.) beating. 3. sharp reprimand.
felpado, da, *a.* plushy; shaggy; nappy.
felpar, *tr.v.* 1. to cover with plush. 2. (poet.) to carpet. —*r.v.* (fig., poet.) to become carpeted or covered.
felpilla, *f.* chenille, glossy cord used in trimming dresses and furniture.
felposo, sa, *a.* plushy, velvety; plush-covered.
felpudo, da, *a.* plushy, velvety, downy. —*m.* rug, mat.
felsita, *m.* (min.) felsite.
felús, *m.* (Morocco) small change, coins, coppers.
fem. *abbrev. of* **fuerza electromotriz,** electromotive force.
femenil, *a.* feminine, womanly, womanlike, womanish.
femenilmente, *adv.* effeminately, womanishly.
femenino, na, *a.* feminine; female; **el sexo f.,** the female sex.
fementidamente, *adv.* falsely, perfidiously, treacherously.
fementido, da, *a.* perfidious, false, treacherous; unfaithful, truthless.
fémina, *f.* (coll.) woman, female.
femineidad, *f.* 1. femininity. 2. (law) quality of property belonging to or inheritable by a woman.
feminela, *f.* (artil.) piece of sheepskin (formerly used for cleaning cannons).
femíneo, *a.* feminine, womanly.
feminidad, *f.* femininity.
feminismo, *m.* feminism, principle of the equality of women; movement to win rights for women.
feminista, *a., m., f.* feminist, advocate of feminism.
femoral, *a.* (anat.) femoral.
fémur, *m.* (anat.) femur, thigh-bone.
fenacaína, *f.* (pharm.) phenacaine.
fenacetina, *f.* (pharm.) phenacetin, phenacetine.
fenacina, *f.* (chem.) phenazine.
fenacita, *f.* (min.) phenacite.
fenantreno, *m.* (chem.) phenanthrene.
fenaquistoscopio, *m.* (phys.) phenakistoscope.
fenaquita, *f.* (min.) phenacite.
fenda, *f.* slit, cleavage along wood grain; **fendas de desecación,** drying cracks (timber); **fendas de heladura,** frost cracks (timber); **fendas de merma,** drying cracks (timber).
fendi, *m.* effendi, a Turkish title of respect.
fendiente, *m.* gash, deep cut or wound.
fenecer, (*ref. 45*) *tr.v.* to finish, conclude, to close, to terminate. —*i.v.* to die; to end; to perish.
fenecimiento, *m.* finishing, ending; termination; death; close, finish, end.
fenestración, *f.* (archit., surg.) fenestration.
fenestrado, da, *a.* fenestrate.
fenetidina, *f.* (chem.) phenetidine, phenetidin.
fenetol, *m.* (chem.) phenetole, phenetol.
fenezca, fenezco, *ref.* **fenecer.**
feniano, *a., m.* (hist.) Fenian, pertaining to legendary heroes of ancient Ireland; a member of a former Irish association pledged to fight English rule.
fenicado, da, *past part. of* **fenicar.** —*a.* (chem.) containing carbolic acid.
fenicar, (*ref. 50*) *tr.v.* (chem.) to carbolize, add carbolic acid to.
fenice, *a., m., f.* (poet.) Phoenician.
fenicio, cia, *a., m., f.* Phoenician. —*f.* **F.,** Phoenicia, the ancient region of city-states on the E. Mediterranean.
fénico, *a.* (chem.) carbolic, phenic; **ácido f.,** phenol, carbolic acid.
fenilacético, ca, *a.* phenylacetic.
fenilamina, *f.* (chem.) phenylamine.
fenileno, *m.* (chem.) phenylene.
fenílico, ca, *a.* (chem.) phenylic.
fenilo, *m.* (chem.) phenyl.
Fénix, *m.* 1. (myth., astron.) Phoenix. 2. **f.,** phoenix, a person of distinction, a prodigy. 3. (bot.) a species of palm. — **el ave F.,** Phoenix, Egyptian mythical bird, symbol of immortality.
fenobarbital, *m.* (pharm.) phenobarbital.
fenocristal, *m.* (geol.) phenocryst.
fenogreco, *m.* (bot.) fenugreek.
fenol, *m.* (chem.) phenol, carbolic acid.
fenolato, *m.* (chem.) phenolate.
fenolftaleína, *f.* (chem.) phenolphthalein.
fenólico, ca, *a.* (chem.) phenolic. —*f.* (chem.) phenolic.
fenología, *f.* (biol.) phenology.
fenomenal, *a.* phenomenal; (fig.) phenomenal, remarkable, exceptional, extraordinary.
fenomenalismo, *m.* (philos.) phenomenalism.
fenomenalista, *a.* phenomenalist, phenomenalistic. —*m., f.* phenomenalist.
fenoménico, ca, *a.* phenomenal.
fenomenismo, *m.* (philos.) phenomenalism.
fenómeno, *m.* 1. phenomenon. 2. (coll.) monster, freak. 3. prodigy; colossus. — **f. acústico transitorio,** acoustical transient; **f. de estricción,** pinch phenomenon; **f. de sigmatizante,** sigmatizing phenomenon (steels); **f. termodependiente,** temperature-dependent phenomenon.
fenomenología, *f.* (philos.) phenomenology.
fenotípico, ca, *a.* (biol.) phenotypic.
fenotipo, *m.* (biol.) phenotype.
feo, a, *a.* ugly, homely; improper, heinous; serious, alarming. —*adv.* bad, e.g. *oler feo,* to smell bad. —*m.* (coll.) slight. — **hacer un f. a uno,** to slight someone; **tocarle a uno bailar con la más fea,** to end up with the short end of the stick; **la suerte de la fea la bonita la desea,** the pretty wish they had the luck of the homely.
feote, ta, *a. aug. of* **feo,** very ugly.
feracidad, *f.* fertility, fecundity, fruitfulness (of land).
feral, *a.* (obs.) brutal, cruel, bloodthirsty.
feraz, (*pl.* **feraces**) *a.* fertile, fruitful; abundant, plentiful.
ferecracio, *a., m.* (poet.) Pherecratic (verse).
féretro, *m.* bier, coffin.
feria, *f.* 1. fair, bazaar, public festivity; commercial exhibition. 2. market place. 3. rest, repose; day off, public holiday. 4. (Mex.) change, loose money. 5. (C. Rica, Salv.) tip. 6. (*pl.*) gifts, presents. — **dar ferias,** to make a gift to.
feriado, da, *past part. of* **feriar.** —*a.* **día feriado,** legal holiday.
ferial, *a.* pertaining to fairs; fair. —*m.* market, fairground.
feriante, *a.* attending the fair. —*m., f.* trader at fairs; fairgoer, someone attending a fair or participating in it.
feriar, *tr.v.* 1. to buy at the fair, to sell; to barter. 2. to give presents to, make a gift to. —*i.v.* to suspend work; to take some days off.
ferino, na, *a.* fierce, wild, savage, ferocious. — **tos ferina,** (med.) whooping cough.
fermata, *f.* 1. (mus.) trill, flourish, cadenza. 2. (mus.) pause, hold.
fermentable, *a.* fermentable.
fermentación, *f.* fermentation. — **f. ácida,** acid fermentation; **f. amoniacal,** ammoniacal fermentation; **f. termógena,** (phys.) thermogenic fermentation.
fermentado, da, *past part. of* **fermentar.** —*a.* fermented; leavened.
fermentante, *a.* fermenting.
fermentar, *i.v.* 1. to ferment. 2. (fig.) to be excited or agitated. —*tr.v.* to cause fermentation.
fermentativo, va, *a.* fermentative.
fermento, *m.* ferment, agent producing fermentation; leavening; (chem.) enzyme. — **f. orgánico,** organic ferment; **f. químico,** chemical ferment.
fermio, *m.* (chem.) fermium.
fernambuco, palo de f., *m.* (bot.) Pernambuco wood, dyewood of Brazil.
fernandina, *f.* (tex.) a certain kind of linen fabric no longer used.

feroce, *a.* (poet.) ferocious, fierce.
ferocidad, *f.* ferociousness, ferocity, fierceness, savageness.
feróstico, ca, *a.* 1. (coll.) unruly, wilful; irritable. 2. (coll.) terribly ugly, hideous.
feroz, *a.* ferocious, savage, cruel, fierce; (fig.) ravenous, e.g. *tengo un hambre f.,* I am ravenously hungry.
ferozmente, *adv.* ferociously, fiercely.
ferra, *f.* (ichth.) lavaret (Coregonus lavaretus), a variety of salmon.
ferrada, *f.* iron-knobbed club; mace.
ferrado, da, *a.* iron-plated, ferrate, bound or shod with iron. *—m.* land measure of between 4 and 6 ares; corn measure between 13 and 16 liters.
ferrar, (*ref. 29*) *tr.v.* to trim or plate with iron.
ferrato, *m.* (chem.) ferrate.
ferreña, *a.* 1. hard and dry (walnut). 2. (reg., Sp.) (*pl.*) castanets.
férreo, a, *a.* 1. iron, made of iron; ferrous, containing iron. 2. tough, strong; harsh, stern, severe. — **constitución férrea,** iron-like or tough constitution; **vía férrea,** railway, railroad; **voluntad férrea,** a will of iron.
ferrería, *f.* ironworks, foundry, forge.
ferreruelo, *m.* short cape with a plain collar.
ferrete, *m.* 1. copper sulphate (used in dyeing). 2. iron stamp, marking iron.
ferretear, *tr.v.* 1. to trim or cover with iron. 2. to mark with an iron stamp. 3. to work with iron.
ferretería, *f.* 1. iron works, foundry. 2. hardware; hardware store.
ferretero, ra, *m., f.* ironmonger; hardware dealer.
ferricianhídrico, ca, *a.* (chem.) ferricyanic.
ferricianógeno, *m.* (chem.) ferricyanogen.
ferricianuro, *m.* (chem.) ferricyanide.
férrico, ca, *a.* (chem.) ferric; containing iron.
ferrífero, ra, *a.* ferriferous, iron-bearing.
ferrificarse, (*ref. 50*) *r.v.* (min.) to turn into iron; to be converted into iron.
ferrita, *f.* (min.) ferrite. — **f. delta,** (metal.) delta ferrite.
ferrizo, za, *a.* ferrous; of iron.
ferro, *m.* (mar.) anchor.
ferrobús, *m.* train of two railcars.
ferrocalcita, *f.* (min.) ferrocalcite.
ferrocarril, *m.* railway, railroad; **f. aéreo,** aerial railway; **f. de cable,** cable railway; **f. de cremallera,** rack railway; **f. de vapor,** steam railroad; **f. eléctrico,** electric railroad; **f. elevado,** elevated railroad; **f. funicular,** cable railroad; **f. subterráneo,** subway, underground railway.
ferrocarrilero, ra, *a.* (Amer.) *var. of* **ferroviario.**
ferrocerio, *m.* ferrocerium.
ferrociánico, ca, *a.* (chem.) ferrocyanic.
ferrocianógeno, *m.* (chem.) ferrocyanogen.
ferrocianuro, *m.* (chem.) ferrocyanide.
ferrocromo, *m.* (chem.) ferrochrome, ferrochromium.
ferromagnesiano, na, *a.* (min.) ferromagnesian.
ferromagnético, ca, *a.* (phys.) ferromagnetic.
ferromagnetismo, *m.* ferromagnetism.
ferromanganeso, *m.* (min.) ferromanganese.
ferrón, *m.* ironworker, ironmonger.
ferroprusiato, *m.* (chem.) ferroprussiate.
ferrosilicio, *m.* (min.) ferrosilicon.
ferroso, sa, *a.* (chem.) ferrous.
ferrotipo, *m.* (photog.) tintype, ferrotype.
ferrovía, *f.* railway, railroad.
ferrovial, *a., var. of* **ferroviario.**
ferroviario, ria, *a.* pertaining to railroads or railways. *—m., f.* railroad employee.
ferrugiento, ta, *a.* iron, of iron; iron-like; containing iron.
ferrugíneo, a, *a., var. of* **ferruginoso.**
ferruginoso, sa, *a.* ferruginous, containing iron.
fértil, *a.* fertile, fruitful; plentiful, fecund, productive.
fertilice, fertilicé, *ref.* **fertilizar.**
fertilidad, *f.* fertility, fruitfulness; productiveness; abundance.
fertilizable, *a.* fertilizable.
fertilización, *f.* fertilization; impregnation; **f. cruzada,** cross-fertilization.
fertilizador, ra, *a.* fertilizing.
fertilizante, *a.* fertilizing. *—m.* fertilizer; **f. completo,** (agr.) complete fertilizer.
fertilizar, (*ref. 53*) *tr.v.* to fertilize, make fruitful or productive; to enrich.
fértilmente, *adv.* fertilely, fruitfully.
férula, *f.* 1. ferule, rod, ruler (for punishment). 2. (bot.) giant fennel. 3. (surg.) splint. — **estar (uno) bajo la f. de otro,** (fig.) to be under someone's thumb.
feruláceo, a, *a.* ferulaceous.
fervencia, *f.* boiling alive (ancient form of execution).
ferventísimo, ma, *a. aug. of* **ferviente,** very fervent; very pious.
férvido, da, *a.* fervid; ardent, impassioned.
ferviente, *a.* fervent, ardent; earnest, intensely pious or devoted to a doctrine, a person, an activity.
fervientemente, *adv.* fervently, earnestly.
fervor, *m.* 1. fervor, violent heat. 2. fervidness, zeal, eagerness, ardor.
fervorice, fervoricé, *ref.* **fervorizar.**
fervorín, *m.* short prayer (*gen. in pl.*).
fervorizar, (*ref. 53*) *tr.v.* to inspire; encourage, to incite, inflame. *—r.v.* to become fervent or inspired.
fervorosamente, *adv.* fervently.
fervoroso, sa, *a.* 1. fervent; earnest; enthusiastic. 2. pious, religious.
festejador, ra, *a.* entertaining. *—m., f.* entertainer, host, hostess.
festejante, *a.* entertaining, feasting; hospitable.
festejar, *tr.v.* 1. to fete, entertain, feast; to celebrate. 2. to court, woo. 3. (Mex.) to whip, beat. *—r.v.* to enjoy oneself, have a good time.
festejo, *m.* 1. feast, entertainment, banquet; (Amer.) rowdy celebration or party. 2. courting, wooing. 3. (*pl.*) public festivities.
festero, ra, *m., f.* 1. director of music in a church. 2. party-goer, one who likes parties.
festín, *m.* party, feast, banquet.
festinación, *f.* speed, hurry, haste.
festinar, *tr.v.* (Amer.) to hurry up, hasten, precipitate, accelerate.
festival, *m.* festival, a series of performances celebrating a given art, artist or creator; **f. de cine,** film festival; **f. de Bayreuth,** Bayreuth festival.
festivamente, *adv.* festively, gaily.
festividad, *f.* 1. festivity, celebration, holiday. 2. (ecc.) feast day, holy day. 3. gaiety, humor, merrymaking.
festivo, va, *a.* 1. witty, humorous, funny. 2. festive, gay, joyful. 3. feast, holy (day in the church). *—m.* holiday. — **día festivo,** holiday; **traje festivo,** gala dress.
festón, *m.* 1. festoon, garland, wreath. 2. scallops, ornamental edging. 3. (archit.) festoon.
festonar, *tr.v., var. of* **festonear.**
festoneado, da, *past part. of* **festonear.** *—a.* festooned; scalloped.
festonear, *tr.v* to festoon; to border with ornamental or scalloped edges.
fetación, *f.* gestation; fetation, fetal development.
fetal, *a.* foetal, fetal.
fetén, *a.* (reg., Sp.) sincere, authentic, truthful.
fetiche, *m.* fetish; idol.
fetichismo, *m.* 1. fetishism; idolatry. 2. (med.) fetishism, fetichism.
fetichista, *a.* fetishistic. *—m., f.* **fetishist.**
feticida, *a.* feticidal. *—m., f.* one who commits feticide.
feticidio, *m.* feticide.
fetidez, *f.* stench, stink, fetidness.
fétido, da, *a.* fetid, stinking.
fetiquismo, *m.* (imp. u.) *var. of* **fetichismo.**
feto, *m.* (anat.) foetus, fetus.
fetor, *m.* stench.
feúco, ca, feúcho, cha, *a.* (coll.) ugly.
feudal, *a.* feudal, feudalistic.
feudalidad, *f.* feudality.
feudalismo, *m.* feudalism.
feudar, *tr.v.* to pay tithes or tribute to.
feudatario, ria, *a., m.* feudatory.
feudista, *m.* (law) feudist, expert on feudal law.
feudo, *m.* 1. feud, fief, fee (contract by which feudal lord granted land to vassals; the lands thus granted). 2. tribute, tithe (paid by vassal to lord). 3. fealty (allegiance paid by vassal to lord). — **f. franco,** (law) freehold.
fez, (*pl.* **feces**) *m.* fez, oriental hat, formerly the Turkish national headdress.
FF. CC. *abbrev. of* **ferrocarriles,** railways.
fiable, *a.* trustworthy, reliable.
fiacre, *m.* fiacre, hackney coach, hack-carriage; cab, taxi.
fiado, *past part. of* **fiar.** — **al f.,** on trust, on credit; **comprar al f.,** to buy on credit; **dar f.,** to sell on credit.
fiador, ra, *m., f.* bailsman; guarantor, security, surety, bondsman; **salir f. por otro,** to go bail for someone *—m.* 1. fastener; safety strap (for holding sword secure); fastening cord (round neck, securing a cloak); chin-strap (of hat). 2. (mec.) catch (immobilizing any mechanism); latch, catch, tumbler (of lock); safety catch, sear (of rifle). 3. (bldg.) gutter-hooks (sustaining gutter). 4. (coll.) (boys') buttocks.
fiambrar, *tr.v.* to prepare (food) to be eaten cold; to prepare cold cuts.
fiambre, *a.* 1. cold (meat or food). 2. (fig.) stale (piece of news). *—m.* cold meat, cold food.
fiambrera, *f.* 1. lunch case or basket. 2. lunch pail (for transporting cooked food); set of pans one on top of another (for transporting cooked food). 3. (Arg.) food cabinet, ice-box.
fiambrería, *f.* delicatessen; shop where cold-cuts and cold food are sold.
fiambrero, ra, *m., f.* maker or seller of cold meats and other foods.
fianza, *f.* deposit, guarantee, guaranty, bond, pledging, bail, commitment. — **bajo f.,** on bail; **f. corporativa,** corporate bond; **f. de apelación,** appeal bond; **f. de ejecución,** (contracts) performance bond; **en libertad bajo f.,** free on bail.
fiar, (*ref. 54*) *tr.v.* 1. to guarantee; to go surety or bail for. 2. to sell on credit. 3. to entrust; to confide. *—i.v.* to trust; **f. en,** to trust in. *—r.v.* **fiarse de, a** or **en,** to trust.
fiasco, *m.* fiasco, failure.
fiat, *m.* 1. fiat, a decree; a command to do something. 2. (law) a short order or warrant.
fibra, *f.* 1. thread, fiber; (tex.) staple; grain, streak. 2. strength, stamina, vigor. — **f. acrílica,** acrylic fiber; **f. animal,** animal fiber; **f. artificial,** artificial or man-made fiber; **f. de vidrio** or **cristal,** fiberglass; **f. metálica,** steel wool; **f. óptica,** optical fiber; **f. vegetal,** vegetable fiber.
fibriforme, *a.* fibriform.
fibrilación, *f.* (anat., med.) fibrillation.
fibrilado, da, *a.* fibrillated.

fibrilar, *a.* (anat.) fibrilar.
fibriloso, sa, *a.* (anat., bot.) fibrillose.
fibrilla, *f.* (anat., bot.) fibril.
fibrina, *f.* (chem.) fibrin.
fibrinógeno, na, *a.* (biochem.) fibrinogenous, fibrinogenic. —*m.* (biochem.) fibrinogen.
fibrinolisina, *f.* (biochem.) fibrinolysin.
fibrinólisis, *f.* (biochem.) fibrinolysis.
fibrinoso, sa, *a.* fibrinous.
fibroblástico, ca, *a.* (biol.) fibroblastic.
fibroblasto, *m.* (biol.) fibroblast.
fibrocartilaginoso, sa, *a.* (anat.) fibrocartilaginous.
fibrocartílago, *m.* (anat.) fibrocartilage.
fibrocemento, *m.* asbestos cement, fibrocement.
fibrocito, *m.* (med.) fibrocyte.
fibroide, *a., m.* (med.) fibroid.
fibroideo, a, *a.* fibroid.
fibroína, *f.* (biochem.) fibroin.
fibroma, *m.* (med.) fibroma.
fibrosis, *f.* (med.) fibrosis; **f. cística** or **pancreática,** cystic fibrosis.
fibrositis, *f.* (med.) fibrositis.
fibroso, sa, *a.* fibrous.
fibrótico, ca, *a.* (med.) fibrotic.
fibrovascular, *a.* (bot.) fibrovascular.
fíbula, *f.* 1. (med.) fibula, the outer and lesser bone of the leg. 2. (arch.) clasp or buckle.
ficción, *f.* fiction, invention; (lit., law) fiction. — **f. científica,** science fiction; **f. de derecho** or **legal,** legal fiction; falsehood.
ficcioso, sa, *a.* (Amer.) feigning.
fice, *m.* (ichth.) hake.
ficha, *f.* 1. counter, chip (used in gambling, games); token (used instead of money); domino (piece). 2. filing or index card. 3. (elec.) plug. 4. (Chile) check, bill; — **f. antropométrica,** anthropometric chart; **f. dactiloscópica,** fingerprint record; **f. de registro,** data card; **f. médica,** medical records; **f. perforada,** punch card; **f. policial,** police record; **f. técnica,** technical specifications. **ser una buena f.,** (Arg.) to be a sly fox.
fichar, *tr.v.* 1. to make a dossier on (someone). 2. to register by means of counters. 3. (coll.) to blacklist. 4. to play a domino. —*i.v.* 1. to sign up; **f. por,** to sign up with. 2. to clock in, to punch the timeclock.
fichero, *m.* filing cabinet; index-card system, filing-card system, card-catalog.
fichú, (*pl.* **fichúes**) *m.* fichu, neckerchief.
ficoideo, a, *a.* (bot.) ficoid. —*f.* (bot.) ficoid (plant); (*pl.*) Ficoideae (family).
ficología, *f.* (bot.) phycology.
ficomiceta, *f.* (bot.) phycomycete.
ficomicetos, *m.* (*pl.*) (bot.) Phycomyces.
ficticio, cia, *a.* fictitious; false.
fidecomiso, *m., var. of* **fideicomiso.**
fidedigno, na, *a.* trustworthy, reliable, creditable.
fideero, ra, *m., f.* noodles or spaghetti maker or dealer.
fideicomisario, ria, *a., m., f.* (law) fideicommissary, fideicommissioner; fiduciary, trustee.
fideicomiso, *m.* (law) fideicommissum, trusteeship.
fideísmo, *m.* (philos.) fideism.
fidelidad, *f.* 1. faithfulness, fidelity. 2. exactness, accuracy, precision. — **alta f.,** high fidelity.
fidelismo, *m.* (pol.) partiality to Fidel Castro.
fideo, *m.* 1. (*pl.*) noodles, vermicelli. 2. (coll.) rake, skinny person.
Fidias, *m.* (hist.) Phidias, famous sculptor of ancient Greece.
fiduciario, ria, *a., m., f.* fiduciary.
fiebre, *f.* 1. (med.) fever, high temperature, e.g. *está con f.,* he has a fever or temperature. 2. (med.) fever (febrile disease). 3. (fig.) fever, excitement. — **f. aftosa,** (vet.) aphthous fever or foot-and-mouth disease; **f. amarilla,** (med.) yellow fever; **f. cerebral,** (med.) brain fever; **f. continua,** (med.) continued fever; **f. cuartana,** (med.) quartan, quartan fever; **f. de leche, de los avenales** or **del parto,** (vet.) milk fever (in cows, etc.); **f. de los pantanos,** (med.) swamp fever; **f. del heno,** (med.) hay fever; **f. de Malta,** (med.) Malta fever; **f. intermitente,** (med.) intermittent fever; **f. láctea,** (med.) milk fever (in mothers); **f. palúdica,** (med.) malarial fever, swamp fever; **f. paratifoidea,** (med.) paratyphoid fever; **f. puerperal,** (med.) puerperal fever; **f. recurrente,** (med.) recurrent fever; **f. reumática,** (med.) rheumatic fever; **f. tifoidea,** (med.) typhoid fever; **f. terciana,** (med.) tertian, tertian fever; **f. uterina,** nymphomania.
fiel, *a.* 1. faithful, loyal. 2. faithful, exact, accurate. —*m.* 1. public inspector; inspector of weights and measures. 2. pointer (of scales). 3. pin (holding scissor blades together). 4. (*pl.*) faithful (adherents to a doctrine or religious belief). — **f. de romana,** official inspector of weights in slaughterhouse.
fielato, *m.* 1. inspectorship, post of inspector. 2. office of inspector. 3. octroi (office collecting tax on consumer goods at entrance of a town).
fielazgo, *m., var. of* **fielato.**
fielmente, *adv.* faithfully, loyally.
fieltrar, *tr.v.* to render like felt.
fieltro, *m.* felt; felt hat, cape or rug.
fiera, *f.* 1. wild animal or beast. 2. wild beast, brute, fiend (person). 3. (taur.) bull. 4. wizard, fiend, very astute person, e.g. *es una f. para los negocios,* he is a wizard at business, *es una f. para el golf,* he is a wizard at golf.
fierabrás, *m.* 1. (coll.) devil, fiend, brute, bully. 2. (coll.) imp, scamp, very mischievous child.
fieramente, *adv.* fiercely, savagely, ferociously.
fiereza, *f.* 1. fierceness, ferocity. 2. deformity, ugliness.
fiero, ra, *a.* 1. ferocious, savage, fierce. 2. huge, tremendous, enormous. 3. terrifying, terrible. 4. rough, rude, uncouth, unsociable. 5. ugly. —*m.* threat, boast. — **echar fieros,** to threaten.
fierra, *f.* horseshoe; (Mex.) branding.
fierro, *m.* (arch.) iron.
fiesta, *f.* 1. (ecc.) feast, holy day. 2. holiday, e.g. *fiestas nacionales* or *patrias,* national holidays. 3. party, festivity, celebration, e.g. *f. de cumpleaños,* birthday party. — **aguar la f.,** to spoil the party or fun; to be a kill-joy; **estar de f.,** to be celebrating; **f. de guardar,** day of obligation; **f. de precento,** (ecc.) holy day of obligation; **f. de respeto,** (ecc.) holy day of obligation; **f. fija,** fixed feast; **f. movible,** (ecc.) movable feast; **hacerle fiestas a,** to softsoap, to cajole; **no estar para fiestas,** not to be in the mood for jokes; **se acabó la f.,** (coll.) the party's over, the fun's finished (i.e. let's get back to work).
fiestero, ra, *a.* fond of parties.
fifí, *m.* (Amer.) dandy, dude.
fifiriche, *a.* (C. Rica, Mex., Salv.) weak, thin, feeble. —*m.* (C. Rica, Mex.) dandy, dude.
fígaro, *m.* 1. barber, hairdresser. 2. short jacket.
figle, *m.* (mus.) ophicleide, a wind instrument.
figón, *m.* eating house, chophouse, tavern, inn.
figonero, ra, *m., f.* keeper of a chophouse or eating house.
figueral, *m.* fig tree orchard or garden.
figuerense, *a.* of or from Figueras, Spain. —*m., f.* native or inhabitant of Figueras.
figulino, na, *a.* figuline, of or like clay or terra cotta.
figura, *f.* 1. figure, form, shape. 2. face, aspect, countenance. 3. face card. 4. musical note. 5. character (in a play). 6. figure (in dancing). 7. gesture, grimace. 8. (gram., rhet.) figure. 9. (log.) syllogistic figure. 10. (geom.) figure, diagram. — **f. de dicción,** (rhet.) figure of speech. —*m.* pompous fellow or person. —*m., f.* freak, scarecrow (person).
figurable, *a.* imaginable.
figuración, *f.* 1. representation, figuration, depiction; symbol; (theat.) mock or imitation door, window, etc. (not real or usable). 2. imagination; idea, notion. 3. (Arg.) role in society. 4. (Amer.) prominent place in society, e.g. *tener mucha f.,* to appear a lot in the public eye, figure a great deal in the news.
figuradamente, *adv.* figuratively.
figurado, da, *past part. of* **figurar,** *a.* 1. figurative (language, style). 2. (mus.) figurate. 3. (math.) figurate. 4. transcribed (*pronunciation*).
figurante, ta, *m., f.* (theat.) extra, figurant (*m.*), figurante (*f.*).
figurar, *tr.v.* 1. to depict, represent, draw, outline, figure. 2. to feign. —*i.v.* to figure, be, appear. —*r.v.* to figure, imagine, fancy.
figurativamente, *adv.* figuratively.
figurativo, va, *a.* figurative.
figurería, *f.* grimace, face.
figurero, ra, *a.* grimacing. —*m., f.* 1. grimacer. 2. maker or seller of figurines or statuettes.
figurilla, *m., f.* (coll.) little runt, small insignificant person.
figurín, *m.* 1. dummy model. 2. fashion plate, dude, dandy.
figurón, *m.* 1. (coll.) pretentious nobody. 2. central character (in 17th century Spanish satire). — **f. de proa,** (mar.) figurehead.
fija, *f.* 1. hinge. 2. trowel. 3. (Amer.) sure thing, sure winner (in horseracing, business, etc.).
fijación, *f.* fixing; (chem., psyc.) fixation. — **f. de complemento,** (bac.) complement fixation; **f. del nitrógeno,** (chem.) nitrogen fixation.
fijado, *past part. of* **fijar.** —*m.* (photog.) fixing.
fijador, *a.* fixing. —*m.* 1. (mas.) pointer, workman who points joints. 2. installer of doors and windows. 3. (photog.) fixer, fixing solution. 4. (p.) fixative, fixing liquid (for charcoal or crayon paintings). 5. hair spray.
fijamente, *adv.* fixedly, attentively.
fijante, *a.* (artil.) high (shot).
fijar, *tr.v.* 1. to fix; to stick, paste, glue; to pin; to fasten; to secure; to post (bills). 2. to fix, establish (one's residence). 3. to fix, set, specify (prices, sense of word, date or time of meeting, etc.). 4. to fix, fasten (one's eyes or attention on something). 5. to spread mortar between (bricks). 6. to hinge, install (doors, windows). 7. (photog., chem.) to fix. —*r.v.* 1. to become fixed. 2. to pay attention, notice. 3. to decide, resolve. — **fijarse en,** to pay attention to, notice; **fíjate,** just imagine, just fancy.
fijativo, *m.* (photog.) fixative, fixer, fixing solution.
fijeza, *f.* fixedness, firmness, stability; steadfastness; fastness (of colors); **mirar con f.,** to stare at, look fixedly at.
fijo, ja, *a.* 1. fixed; stationary. 2. set, definite, e.g. *no es nada fijo,* it's nothing definite. 3. fast (color). 4. intent, fixed (look). 5. (chem.) fixed. — **de fijo,** certainly, without doubt; **idea fija,** fixed idea.
fijo, *adv.* certainly, without doubt; **mirar f.,** to stare, look at fixedly or intently.
fil, *m.* official inspector of weights in slaughterhouses. — **f. derecho,** leapfrog.
fila, *f.* line, row, tier; file; rank. — **en f.,** in a line, in a row; **en filas,** on active service; **f. india,** single or Indian file; **ponerse en f.,** to line up;

romper filas (mil.), to break ranks; **salir de las filas,** to rise from the ranks.
filacteria, *f.* (rel.) phylactery.
Filadelfia, *f.* (U.S.) Philadelphia.
filadelfo, fa, *a.* (bot.) of the genus Philadelphus. —*f.* (*pl.*) (bot.) Philadelphus (genus).
filadiz, *m.* floss silk.
filagrama, *f.* wire mold for a watermark.
filamento, *m.* filament.
filamentoso, sa, *a.* filamentous.
filandria, *f.* (zool.) filander (intestinal worm).
filantropía, *f.* philanthropy.
filantrópico, ca, *a.* philanthropic, philanthropical.
filántropo, *m.* philanthropist.
filar, *tr.v.* (mar.) to case out, pay out (as rope).
filaria, *f.* (zool.) filaria, a parasitic worm.
filariasis, filariosis, *f.* (med.) filariosis.
filarmonía, *f.* love of music or harmony.
filarmónico, ca, *a., m., f.* philharmonic.
filástica, *f.* (mar.) rope yarn, rope strands.
filatelia, *f.* philately, stamp collecting.
filatélico, ca, *a.* philatelic.
filatelista, *m., f.* philatelist, stamp collector.
filatería, *f.* 1. fast talk, swindler's patter. 2. verbosity, wordiness.
filatero, ra, *a.* 1. verbose, wordy. 2. fast talking, slick-tongued. —*m., f.* 1. windbag (sl.), verbose speaker. 2. fast or slick talker.
filatura, *f.* spinning mill; spinning.
filderretor, *m.* kind of flannel.
filelí, *m.* very fine flannel.
fileno, na, *a.* (coll.) delicate, effeminate.
filera, *f.* rows of nets with fish traps.
filete, *m.* 1. (cul.) filet, fillet (of fish or meat). 2. (archit., her., bkb.) fillet. 3. (dressm.) reinforcement of hem or border. 4. small roasting spit. 5. thread (of screw). 6. (mar.) esparto cord or rope. 7. (equit.) snaffle-bit. 8. (print.) metal rule of one or more traces used to separate or enclose parts of printed matter; lines separating columns of print. — **gastar muchos filetes,** to use flowery language.
fileteado, da, *a.* (mec.) threaded.
filetear, *tr.v.* 1. (print., dressm.) to fillet, decorate with fillets. 2. (bkb.) to tool. 3. to thread (a screw).
filetón, *m.* thick bullion, twisted cord fringe (used in embroidery).
filfa, *f.* lie, fib, tale.
filheleno, na, *a., m., f.* philhellene, partial to Greek history and culture.
filiación, *f.* 1. filiation; connection, relationship. 2. personal data or description; (mil.) record card (of each soldier).
filial, *a.* filial. —*f.* branch office, subsidiary.
filialmente, *adv.* filially.
filiar, *tr.v.* to take the personal data of. —*r.v.* to join up; to join (the army).
filibote, *m.* flyboat, light broad-beamed vessel.
filibusterismo, *m.* 1. party claiming independence for Spain's overseas possessions. 2. *f.* filibusterism, freebootery.
filibustero, *m.* 1. filibuster, freebooter. 2. patriot working for the emancipation of Spain's overseas possessions.
filicida, *a.* filicidal. —*m., f.* filicide, parent who kills his child.
filicidio, *m.* filicide, killing of a child by his parent.
filiforme, *a.* filiform, thread-like.
filigrana, *f.* 1. filigree. 2. watermark. 3. delicate fine piece of work. 4. (Cuba, bot.) (variety of) lantana (Lantana odorata).
fililí, *m.* (coll.) fineness, delicacy.
filipéndula, *f.* (bot.) meadowsweet, (variety of) spiraea (Spiraea filipendula).
filipense, *a., m., f.* (hist., relig.) Phillipian.
filípica, *f.* 1. **F.,** Phillipic (e.g. of Demosthenes or Cicero). 2. phillipic, violent criticism.
filipichín, *m.* printed moreen, a strong woollen fabric.
filipina, *f.* (Cuba) duck-cloth jacket (worn by men).
Filipinas, *f.* (*pl.*) Philippines, Philippine Islands.
filipinismo, *m.* 1. word or expression used by the Filipinos. 2. affection or fondness for the Philipines.
filipino, na, *a.* Philipine, Filipino. —*m., f.* Filipino, inhabitant of the Philipines.
Filipo, *m.* Philip (as Philip the Second of Macedonia).
filis, *f.* 1. (poet.) charm, delicacy, grace. 2. small earthenware doll, trinket, charm.
filisteo, a, *a., m.* (Bib., fig.) Phillistine. —*a.* (fig.) tall, corpulent person.
fillos, *m.* (*pl.*) leaf-shaped fritter.
film, *m.* (photog., cine.) film; **f. transparente,** ClingWrap (TM), SaranWrap (TM).
filmación, *f.* (cine.) filming, shooting.
filmar, *tr.v.* to film (a motion picture, etc.); to shoot (a scene).
filme, *m.* film; motion picture, movie.
fílmico, ca, *a.* movie, film.
filmina, *f.* slide.
filmografía, *f.* movies, films.
filmoteca, *f.* film library.
filo, *m.* 1. cutting edge (of knife). 2. ridge, dividing line. — **f. del viento,** (mar.) direction of the wind; **f. rabioso,** poorly sharpened edge; **dar f.** or **sacar el f.,** to sharpen; (fig.) to incite, stir up, arouse; **darse un f. a la lengua,** to speak behind someone's back.
filocladio, *m.* (bot.) phylloclade, phylloclad, phyllocladium.
filodio, *m.* (bot.) phyllode.
filófago, ga, *a.* (zool.) phyllophagous.
filogénesis, *f.* (biol.) phylogeny, phylogenesis.
filogenético, ca, *a.* phylogenic, phylogenetic.
filogenia, *f.* (biol.) phylogeny, phylogenesis.
filogénico, ca, *a.* phylogenic, phylogenetic.
filoginia, *f.* philogyny, love or fondness for women.
filógino, na, *a.* philogynous.
filoideo, a, *a.* (bot.) phylloid, phylloidal, phylloideous.
filología, *f.* philology.
filológica, *f., var. of* **filología.**
filológicamente, *adv.* philologically.
filológico, ca, *a.* philological.
filólogo, *m.* philologist.
filoma, *m.* (bot.) phyllome.
filomanía, *f.* (bot.) phyllomania.
filomela, filomena, *f.* (poet.) nightingale, philomel.
filón, *m.* 1. (min.) vein, lode seam. 2. (fig.) gold mine, very profitable business.
filonio, *m.* (pharm.) calmative electuary.
filopodio, *m.* (biol.) phyllopodium.
filópodo, da, *a.* (zool.) phyllopod, phyllopodan. —*m.* (zool.) phyllopod, phyllopodan, (*pl.*) Phyllopoda.
filopos, *m.* (*pl.*) cloth fences to drive game into the required position for hunters.
filoseda, *f.* wool and silk cloth; silk and cotton cloth.
filoso, sa, *a.* (Amer.) sharp, sharp-edged.
filosofador, ra, *a.* philosophizing. —*m., f.* philosophizer.
filosofal, *a.* **piedra f.,** philosopher's stone.
filosofar, *i.v.* to philosophize.
filosofastro, *m.* philosophaster, dabbler in philosophy.
filosofía, *f.* philosophy.
filosóficamente, *adv.* philosophically.
filosófico, ca, *a.* philosophic, philosophical.
filosofismo, *m.* philosophism, spurious philosophy, sophistry.
filósofo, fa, *a.* philosophic; pseudo-philosophical. —*m.* philosopher.
filotáctico, ca, *a.* (bot.) phyllotactic.
filotaxia, *f.* (bot.) phyllotaxy, phyllotaxis.
filotaxis, *f.* (bot.) phyllotaxy, phyllotaxis.
filote, *m.* (Col.) corn silk.
filoxera, *f.* 1. (bot.) phylloxera (Dactylosphaera vitifoli). 2. (coll.) drunkenness; drunken spree.
filtración, *f.* 1. filtration. 2. (coll.) leaking away (of money).
filtrador, ra, *a.* filtering. —*m., f.* filterer. —*m.* filter.
filtrable, *a.* filterable, filtrable.
filtrar, *tr.v., i.v.* to filter. —*r.v.* 1. to filter. 2. to disappear, filter away, dwindle (money, goods, etc.).
filtro, *m.* 1. filter; (opt., photog., elec.) filter. 2. love potion, philter. — **f. acustico** or **de frecuencias,** acoustic or frequency filter; **f. cromofotográfico,** (print.) color screen; **f. de amor,** love potion; **f. de banda.** (rad.) band pass filter; **f. de paso alto,** (rad., elec.) high-pass filter; **f. de paso bajo,** (rad.) low-pass filter; **f. pasa-altos,** (rad., elec.) high-pass filter; **f.-prensa,** filter press; **f. solar,** sunscreen.
filudo, da, *a.* (Amer.) sharp (said of knife).
filum, *m.* (biol.) phylum.
filustre, *m.* (coll.) elegance.
filván, *m.* featheredge (of recently sharpened knife).
fimbria, *f.* 1. border (of a skirt); fringe (used as adornment). 2. (anat.) fimbria.
fimbriado, da, *a.* (bot., zool.) fimbriated, fimbriate.
fimo, *m.* dung, manure.
fimosis, *f.* (med.) phimosis.
fin, *m.* 1. end, finish. 2. aim, purpose; object, goal. — **a f. de** + *inf.,* in order to + *inf.,* with the object of + *ger.,* e.g. *a f. de llegar temprano,* in order to arrive early; **a f. de que** + *subj.,* in order that + *subj.;* **a fines de,** at the end of (a period of time); **al f.,** at last, finally, eventually; **al f. y al cabo, al f. y a la postre,** in the end, when all is said and done; **dar f.,** to finish; to die; **dar f. a,** to destroy, finish off; **en** or **por f.,** finally; after all; in short, in brief; **f. de año,** New Year's Eve; **f. de fiesta,** grand finale; **f. de semana,** week end; **poner f. a,** to stop, put an end to; **sin f.,** endless; innumerable; **un sin f. de,** no end of.
finado, da, *past part. of* **finar.** —*m., f.* deceased, dead person.
final, *a.* final, last, ultimate. —*m.* end; finish, (mus.) finale; **al f. de,** at the end of; **f. feliz,** happy ending (of film, etc.). —*f.* (sport.) finals (of competition); **cuartos de f.,** quarter finals; **semi-finales,** semi-finals.
finalice, finalicé, *ref.* **finalizar.**
finalidad, *f.* aim, purpose, object.
finalista, *m.* (philos., sport) finalist.
finalizar, (*ref. 53*) *tr.v., i.v.* to conclude, finish.
finalmente, *adv.* finally.
finamente, *adv.* courteously, exquisitely.
finamiento, *m.* death.
financiación, *f.* (Amer.) financing.
financiamiento, *m.* financing.
financiar, *tr.v.* to finance.
financista, *m.* (Amer.) financier.
finanzas, *f.* (*pl.*) 1. finance, e.g. *experto en f.,* finance expert. 2. finances, e.g. *las f. de esta compañía están muy mal,* the finances of this company are in very bad shape.

finar, *i.v.* to die, pass away. —*r.v.* to long for, desire, yearn for.
finca, *f.* 1. property, piece of property. 2. (Amer.) farm. — **f. cafetera,** coffee plantation; **f. mala,** (coll.) bad lot, bad egg; **f. raíz,** real estate; **f. rústica,** plot of land.
fincar, (*ref. 50*) *tr.v.* (Arg., Col., Mex.) to place, e.g. *fincó muchas esperanzas en su hijo,* he placed many hopes in his son. —*i..v* 1. to buy real estate. 2. to reside, rest. —*r.v.* to buy real estate.
finchado, da, *a.* vain, conceited, swell-headed.
fincharse, *r.v.* to become conceited or swell-headed.
finés, sa, *a.* Finnish, Finnic, of Finland. —*m., f.* Finn. —*m.* Finnish (language).
fineza, *f.* 1. fineness; excellence. 2. courtesy, kindness, kindly act or word. 3. gift.
fingidamente, *adv.* feignedly.
fingido, da, *past part. of* **fingir.** —*a.* 1. feigned. 2. deceptive, false, sham.
fingidor, ra, *a.* deceptive, false. —*m., f.* fake, sham.
fingimiento, *m.* pretense, pretending, feigning.
fingir, (*ref. 62*) *tr.v.* to pretend, feign; **f.** —*inf.,* to pretend to + *inf.* —*r.v.* to pretend to be.
finible, *a.* finishable, endable.
finiquitar, *tr.v.* 1. to close (an account). 2. to end, conclude, wind up.
finiquito, *m.* closing of an account. — **dar f.,** to close; to finish, wind up.
finir, *i.v.* (arch.) to end, finish.
finítimo, ma, *a.* bordering, neighboring, near, contiguous.
finito, ta, *a.* finite.
finja, finjo, *ref.* **fingir.**
finlandés, sa, *a.* Finnish, of Finland. —*m., f.* Finn. —*m.* Finnish (language).
Finlandia, *f.* Finland.
fino, na, *a.* 1. fine. 2. thin, slender; sheer (fabric). 3. fine-featured. 4. refined, polite, urbane. 5. astute, cunning, shrewd. 7. swift, sharp, slender (sailing craft).
finolis, *a.* (coll.) pedantic, excessively refined.
finque, finqué, *ref.* **fincar.**
finquero, *m.* farm owner.
finta, *f.* 1. feint, fake threat. 2. (fenc.) feint. 3. an ancient tax.
finura, *f.* 1. fineness, excellence. 2. courtesy, urbanity, good breeding.
finústico, ca, *a.* (derog., coll.) over-polite, effusively polite.
fiñana, *m.* black-bearded wheat.
fiofío, *m.* (Chile, ornith.) tyrant flycatcher (Elaenia parvirrostris).
fiordo, *m.* fiord.
fiorituras, *f., pl.* (ital.) adornments, flourishes.
fique, *m.* (Amer.) pita fiber.
firma, *f.* 1. signature. 2. (act of) signing. 3. (com.) firm, business; name of a firm. — **buena f.,** person with good credit; **dar f. en blanco a otro,** to give someone carte blanche or complete freedom (to act); **dar la f. a otro,** to empower someone to represent one; **f. en blanco,** blank signature; **mala f.,** person without credit; **media f.,** surname signature; **llevar la f. de otro,** to represent someone in business affairs.
firmal, *m.* antique brooch.
firmamento, *m.* firmament.
firmán, *m.* firman, royal decree.
firmante, *m., f.* signer, signatory.
firmar, *tr.v.* to sign; **firmado y sellado por,** under the hand and seal of.
firme, *a.* 1. firm, steady, stable. 2. firm, steadfast, resolute, unswerving, staunch. 3. steady (wind). 4. firm, steady (market). — **color f.,** fast color; **de f.,** definitely, firmly; steadfastly, staunchly; **en f.,** (com.) on a firm basis; **estar f. con,** (Peru) to be going steady with; **¡firmes!,** (mil.) attention!; **mantenerse f.,** to stand firm; **ponerse f.,** to stand firm; **tierra f.,** terra firma. —*adv.* firmly. —*m.* foundation, bed (for laying cement or for road laying).
firmemente, *adv.* firmly.
firmeza, *f.* firmness; stability, steadiness; steadfastness, constancy, courage.
firmón, na, *a.* said of a professional who will sign anything, e.g. *abogado f.,* shyster lawyer, pettifogging lawyer.
firulete, *m.* 1. (Amer.) cheap adornment. 2. (Sp.) much twisting and turning (as in dancing, etc.).
fiscal, *a.* treasury; fiscal. —*m.* 1. treasurer. 2. district attorney (U.S.), public prosecutor (G.B.). 3. snooper, informer. 4. (Bol., Peru) churchwarden, lay assistant (of parish priest).
fiscalía, *f.* office of public prosecutor or district attorney; office of treasurer.
fiscalice, fiscalicé, *ref.* **fiscalizar.**
fiscalización, *f.* 1. investigation, inspection; prying, snooping. 2. control, supervision. 3. criticism, censure.
fiscalizador, ra, *a.* prying, investigating, inspecting, e.g. *tiene un afán fiscalizador,* he loves to investigate or pry.
fiscalizar, (*ref. 53*) *tr.v.* 1. to investigate, inspect, pry into; to superintend, supervise. 2. to censure, criticize.
fisco, *m.* exchequer, national treasury, public treasury.
fisga, *f.* 1. fishgig, leister, three pronged harpoon (for fishing). 2. banter, raillery. 3. (Guat., Mex.) banderilla (in bullfighting). — **hacer f. de,** to make fun of.
fisgador, ra, *a.* prying, snooping. —*m., f.* pryer, snooper; harpooner; banterer.
fisgar, (*ref. 51*) *tr.v.* 1. to snoop on, pry on. 2. to harpoon, spear, fish with a fish-gig. —*i.v., r.v.* to make fun of, mock.
fisgón, na, *a.* 1. snooping, prying, meddlesome. 2. bantering. —*m., f.* 1. snooper, busybody, meddler. 2. banterer, jester.
fisgonear, *tr.v.* to pry or snoop constantly or habitually.
fisgoneo, *m.* constant prying.
fisgue, fisgué, *ref.* **fisgar.**
física, *f.* physics.
fisicalismo, *m.* (philos.) physicalism.
físicamente, *adv.* 1. physically, bodily.
físico, ca, *a.* 1. physical. 2. (Cuba, Mex.) finnicky, delicate. —*m.* 1. physicist. 2. physique, appearance, looks.
fisicomatemático, ca, *a.* physicomathematical.
fisicoquímico, ca, *a.* physicochemical. —*f.* physical chemistry.
fisil, *a.* fissile, that can be split.
fisiocracia, *f.* physiocracy, eighteenth century French economic theory.
fisiócrata, *m., f.* physiocrat.
fisiocrático, ca, *a.* physiocratic.
fisiografía, *f.* physiography.
fisiográfico, ca, *a.* physiographic.
fisiógrafo, *m.* physiographer.
fisiología, *f.* physiology.
fisiológicamente, *adv.* physiologically.
fisiológico, ca, *m.* physiological, physiologic.
fisiólogo, *m.* physiologist.
fisión, *f.* fission. — **f. nuclear,** nuclear fission.
fisionable, *a.* fissionable.
fisionar, *tr.v.* to split an atom.
fisionomía, *f.* physiognomy, face; countenance.
fisioterapia, *f.* (med.) physiotherapy.
fisiparidad, *f.* (biol.) fissiparousness, fissiparity.
fisíparo, ra, *a.* (biol.) fissiparous.
fisípedo, da, *a.* clovenhoofed; (zool.) fissiped. —*m.* (zool.) fissiped; (*pl.*) Fissipedia.
fisirrostro, tra, *a.* fissirostral. —*m.* (*pl.*) Fissirostres.
fisonomía, *f.* physiognomy.
fisonómico, ca, *a.* physiognomical, physiognomic.
fisonomista, *m., f.* physiognomist.
fisónomo, *m., var. of* **fisionomista.**
fisostigmina, *f.* (chem.) physostigmine, physostigmin.
fistol, *m.* 1. (sl.) astute and shrewd person, sharp operator (sl.). 2. (Mex.) tie pin.
fistra, *f.* (bot.) bishop's weed (Ammus majus).
fístula, *f.* 1. (med.) fistula. 2. pipe, tube, conduit. 3. pipe, flute, fistula.
fistular, *a.* (med.) fistulous, fistular. —*tr.v.* (med.) to make fistulous.
fistulina, *f.* (bot.) fistulina.
fistuloso, sa, *a.* fistulous, fistular.
fisura, *f.* (med., anat., min.) fissure.
fitina, *f.* (biochem., pharm.) phytin.
fitófago, ga, *a.* (zool.) phytophagous. —*m.* (zool.) phytophagan; (*pl.*) Phytophaga.
fitoflagelado, *m.* (zool.) phytoflagellate.
fitogenesia, *f.* (bot.) phytogenesis, phytogeny.
fitogenético, ca, *a.* phytogenetic, phytogenetical.
fitógeno, na, *a.* phytogenic, phytogenous.
fitogeografía, *f.* (bot.) phytogeography.
fitografía, *f.* (bot.) phytography, descriptive botany.
fitográfico, ca, *a.* phytographic, phytographical.
fitógrafo, *m.* phytographer, phytographist.
fitohormona, *f.* (chem.) phytohormone.
fitolacáceo, cea, *a.* (bot.) phytolaccaceous. —*f.* (bot.) Phytolaccaceae.
fitolita, *f.* (geol.) phytolite, phytolith.
fitología, *f.* phytology, botany.
fitológico, ca, *a.* phytologic, phytological.
fiton, *m.* (bot.) phyton.
fitopatología, *f.* phytopathology, plant pathology.
fitoplancton, *m.* (bot.) phytoplankton.
fitosociología, *f.* (bot.) phytosociology.
fitosociológico, ca, *a.* phytosociologic, phytosociological.
fitosociólogo, *m.* phytosociologist.
fitosterina, *f.* (chem.) phytosterol.
fitosterol, *m.* (chem.) phytosterol.
fitotomía, *f.* phytotomy, vegetable anatomy.
fitotoxina, *f.* phytotoxin.
flabelado, da, *a.* (zool.) flabellate, fanshaped.
flabelicornio, *a.* (zool.) having flabellate or fan-shaped antennae.
flabelífero, ra, *a.* flabellum-bearing, fan-bearing. —*m.* flabellum-bearer, fan-bearer.
flabeliforme, *a.* flabelliform, fan-shaped.
flabelo, *m.* (ecc.) flabellum, large long-handled fan (used exclusively by the Pope).
flacamente, *adv.* weakly, feebly.
flaccidez, *f.* flaccidity, flaccidness; flabbiness.
fláccido, da, *a.* flaccid; flabby, soft.
flaco, ca, *a.* thin, lean; (fig.) weak, feeble. —*m.* weak spot (of a person's character).
flacuchento, ta, *a.* (Amer.) skinny.
flacucho, cha, *a.* (derog.) skinny.
flacura, *f.* thinness, leanness.
flagelación, *f.* flagellation, whipping, scourging.
flagelador, ra, *a.* whipping, flagellant. —*m., f.* flagellator.
flagelante, *m.* 1. flagellant (person who whips himself in penitence). 2. (rel.) **F.,** Flagellant (member of heretic sect believing flagellation more effective than confession).

flagelantismo, *m.* flagellantism.
flagelar, *tr.v.* 1. to flagellate, whip. 2. to vituperate, revile.
flagelo, *m.* 1. scourge, whip; calamity. 2. (zool.) flagellum.
flagicioso, sa, *a.* flagitious, vicious.
flagrancia, *f.* flagrancy; great heat, great blaze.
flagrante, *a.* 1. (poet.) flagrant, blazing, flaming. 2. occurring at the very moment. — **en f.,** in the act, redhanded.
flagrar, *i.v.* (poet.) to blaze, flame.
flama, *f.* 1. flame; reflection or reverberation of flames. 2. (mil.) plume (of helmet).
flamante, *a.* 1. bright, brilliant. 2. new, brand new.
flamear, *i.v.* 1. to blaze, flame. 2. to wave, flutter (as a sail). —*tr.v.* to sterilize (by burning in alcohol).
flamen, (*pl.*) **flamines,** *m.* (hist.) flamen, a Roman priest.
flamenco, ca, *a.* 1. Flemish. 2. flamenco (music, dancing, singing). 3. showy, flashy. 4. (C. Amer.) thin, slender. —*m., f.* 1. Fleming; (*pl.*) the Flemish. 2. showy or flashy dresser. —*f.* buxom wench. —*m.* 1. Flemish (language). 2. (ornith.) flamingo.
flamenquería, *f.* showiness, flashiness; rakishness.
flamenquilla, *f.* 1. small platter. 2. (bot.) marigold.
flamenquismo, *m.* 1. fondness for Andalusian customs. 2. flashiness, showiness, ostentation.
flámeo, *a.* flamelike. —*m.* ancient fire-colored bridal veil.
flamero, *m.* torch-holder, cresset.
flamígero, ra, *a.* (poet.) flaming, blazing.
flámula, *f.* pennant.
flan, *m.* 1. (cul.) baked custard, flan. 2. flan, planchet, blank (piece of metal for minting).
flanco, *m.* flank, side; (mil., fort., mar., mec.) flank.
Flandes, *m.* Flanders.
flanear, *i.v.* (Gal.) to wander idly around, loaf around.
flanero, *m.* custard mold.
flanqueado, da, *past part. of* **flanquear.** —*a.* 1. flanked; defended, protected. 2. (her.) flanched. — **f. de,** flanked or defended by.
flanqueador, ra, *a.* flanking. —*m.* (mil.) flanker.
flanqueante, *a.* flanking.
flanquear, *tr.v.* to flank; to defend, protect.
flanqueo, *m.* flanking.
flanquís, *m.* (her.) saltorel (diminutive, saltier).
flaquear, *i.v.* to weaken; to become weak; to lose heart or spirit.
flaquera, *f.* languor, lassitude, feebleness, weakness.
flaqueza, *f.* 1. thinness, leanness, skinniness (coll.) 2. weakness (moral and physical).
flash, *m.* 1. (photog.) flash lamp. 2. flash, news flash.
flashback, *m.* (cine.) flashback.
flato, *m.* 1. flatus, wind or gas in stomach. 2. (Amer.) sadness, gloom, melancholy.
flatoso, sa, *a.* flatulent.
flatulencia, *f.* flatulence, flatulency.
flatulento, ta, *a.* flatulent.
flatuoso, sa, *a., var. of* **flatoso.**
flauta, *f.* (mus.) flute. — **f. dulce,** recorder; **f. travesera,** Boehm and German flute. —*m.* flautist, flutist.
flautado, da, *a.* flutelike. —*m.* flute (organ stop).
flauteado, da, *a.* flutelike.
flautero, *m.* flute-maker.
flautillo, *m.* (mus.) shawm; high-pitched flute.
flautín, *m.* piccolo; piccolo player.
flautista, *m., f.* flautist, flutist.
flavina, *f.* (biochem.) flavin.
flavo, va, *a.* honey-colored, fallow.
flavona, *f.* (chem.) flavone.
flavonol, *m.* (chem.) flavonol.
flavoproteína, *f.* (biochem.) flavoprotein.
flavopurpurina, *f.* (biochem.) flavopurpurin.
flébil, *a.* (poet.) mournful, lamentable, sad.
flebítico, ca, *a.* phlebitic.
flebitis, *f.* (med.) phlebitis, inflammation of the veins.
flebotomía, *f.* (med.) phlebotomy, blood-letting.
flebotomiano, *m.* phlebotomist, bloodletter.
flecha, *f.* 1. arrow. 2. (fort., archit.) **fleche,** a slender spire. 3. (geom.) height (of arc); rise (of arch). 4. pole (of a wagon). 5. (mec.) shaft, axle. 6. (astron.) **F.,** the Arrow. — **la f. del parto,** a Parthian shot.
flechador, *m.* archer.
flechadura, *f.* (mar.) ratlines.
flechar, *tr.v.* 1. to draw and load (a bow). 2. to strike, wound or kill with an arrow. 3. to strike or smite with love, infatuate. 4. (Mex.) to bet without fear (in gambling).
flechaste, *m.* (mar.) ratline.
flechazo, *m.* 1. arrow shot; arrow wound. 2. sudden love, infatuation.
flechera, *f.* (Ven.) light fast war canoe.
flechería, *f.* shower of arrows; stock or supply of arrows.
flechero, *m.* archer; arrow maker.
fleco, *m.* 1. fringe, flounce. 2. bangs (of hair). 3. frayed-border (of cloth).
flegmasía, *f.* (med.) phlegmasia, inflammation.
flegmonoso, sa, *a.* (med.) phlegmonous.
fleje, *m.* 1. iron hoop, iron strap, iron band. 2. bed spring; long strip of iron forming a bed spring.
flema, *f.* 1. phlegm (humor; spittle). 2. phlegm; calmness, coolness; sluggishness, slowness.
flemático, ca, *a.* phlegmatic, phlegmatical.
fleme, *m.* (vet.) fleam (lancet for blood-letting).
flemón, *m.* (med.) phlegmon; gumboil.
flemonoso, sa, *a.* phlegmonous.
flemoso, sa, *a.* phlegmy.
flemudo, da, *a.* phlegmatic, calm. —*m., f.* phlegmatic person.
fleo, *m.* (bot.) timothy (grass with long cylindrical spikes).
flequezuelo, *m. dim. of* **fleco,** narrow fringe.
flequillo, *m. dim. of* **fleco,** bang, fringe (of hair).
fleta, *f.* (Amer.) whipping (given a child).
fletador, *m.* charterer, freighter.
fletamento, *m.* chartering, freightage; freight charter.
fletante, *m.* (com.) shipowner or representative (in a freight charter).
fletar, *tr.v.* 1. to charter (a ship). 2. to load (merchandise). 3. (Amer.) to hire (animals, wagons, etc.). 4. (Chile, Peru) to let fly or go (blows, insults, etc.). 5. (Guat.) to rub. —*r.v.* 1. (Cuba, Mex.) to depart suddenly, beat it (coll.). 2. (Arg.) to gate-crash (attend uninvited).
flete, *m.* 1. freight, cargo. 2. freight, freightage, freight charge. 3. (Amer.) charter or hiring fee. — **f. falso,** dead freight; **f. pagado,** (com.) freight prepaid.
flexibilidad, *f.* flexibility.
flexible, *a.* flexible. —*m.* 1. (elec.) electric wire, flexible cord. 2. soft felt hat.
flexión, *f.* 1. flection. 2. (gram.) inflection.
flexional, *a.* (gram.) inflectional.
flexor, ra, *a.* flexing; flexor (muscle). —*m.* flexor, flexor muscle.
flexuoso, sa, *a.* flexuous, bending, wavering.
flexura, *f.* fold, flexure, bend.
flictena, *f.* (med.) phlyctena, bulla, small blister.
flicténula, *f.* (med.) phlyctenule.
flirt, *m.* 1. fling. 2. boyfriend; girlfriend.
flirtear, *i.v.* to flirt.
flirteo, *m.* flirting.
flocadura, *f.* fringe trimming.
flocoso, sa, *a.* floccose.
floculación, *f.* (phys., chem.) flocculation.
floculado, da, *a.* (phys., chem.) flocculate.
floculento, ta, *a.* flocculent.
flóculo, *m.* (anat., astron.) flocculus.
floema, *m.* (bot.) phloem.
flogístico, ca, *a.* (med., chem.) phlogistic.
flogisto, *m.* (chem.) phlogiston.
flogopita, *f.* (min.) phlogopite.
flogosis, *f.* (med.) phlogosis.
flojamente, *adv.* laxly, carelessly, slovenly.
flojear, *i.v.* 1. to idle, work carelessly. 2. to weaken, to slacken, grow weak.
flojedad, *f.* 1. looseness, slackness. 2. idleness, laziness; carelessness, slackness. 3. weakness.
flojel, *m.* nap, fluff (of cloth); down, fluff (of feathers).
flojera, *f.* 1. idleness, laziness; carelessness, slackness. 2. weakness; unwillingness, e.g. *me da f. ir allá,* I can't be bothered to go there; **qué f. me da,** I don't feel like going, doing it, etc.
flojo, ja, *a.* 1. lazy, idle, indolent. 2. loose, slack. 3. weak; languid. 4. light (wind). —*m., f.* (coll.) slacker, lazybones.
floqueado, da, *a.* fringed, decorated with a fringe.
flor, *f.* 1. flower; blossom. 2. flower, cream elite. 3. prime (of life). 4. down (of fruit). 5. (metal.) grain (produced by immersion of white hot metal in water). 6. flowers (of wine, beer, etc.). 7. (chem.) flowers (of sulfur, etc.). 8. virginity. 9. (*pl.*) compliments, bouquets (to a woman). 10. type of card game; cheating trick (in cards). 11. grain (of leather). 12. menstrual discharge. 13. (Chile) cloud, white spot (on finger nail). — **a f. de agua,** on or near the water's surface; **a f. de la tierra,** on or near the earth's surface; **caer en f.,** to die in one's youth; **dar (uno) en la f.,** to get or acquire the knack (of doing something); **de mi f.,** (coll.) excellent, magnificent; **decir** or **echar flores,** to compliment, flirt with; **en f.,** in blossom, flowering; in the prime; **f. de amor,** (bot.) amaranth; **f. de azahar,** orange blossom; lemon blossom; **f. de cinc,** (min.) zinc bloom; **f. de la canela,** (coll.) the best, the flower; **f. de la edad,** bloom of youth; **f. de la maravilla,** (bot.) (species of) iris; **f. de la Trinidad,** (bot.) pansy; **f. de la vida,** prime of life; **f. del embudo,** (bot.) calla lily; **f. de lis,** (her.) fleur-de-lis; (bot.) jacobean lily; **f. de Pascua,** poinsettia; **f. desnuda,** achlamydeous flower without calyx or corolla; **f. perfecta,** perfect flower; **f. y nata,** (coll.) the cream of the crop; **flores cordiales,** sudorific herbal infusion; **flores de cantueso,** (coll.) trifles; (min.) cobalt bloom; **flores de maíz,** popcorn; **flores de muerto,** (bot.) marigold; **flores de trapo,** artificial flowers.
flora, *f.* flora; **f. y fauna,** flora and fauna.
floración, *f.* (bot.) flowering, florescence.
floral, *a.* floral.
florales, *a.* **fiestas f.,** (hist.) Floralia (in honor of Flora, goddess of flowers); **juegos f.,** Floral Games.
florar, *i.v.* to flower, bloom.
florcita, *f.* (Amer.) small flower; **andar de f.,** (Amer.) to wander aimlessly, to loaf.
flordelisado, da, *past part. of* **flordelisar.** —*a.* (her.) fleury, charged with fleur-de-lis.
flordelisar, *tr.v.* (her.) to adorn with fleur-de-lis.
floreado, da, *past part. of* **florear.** —*a.* made with superfine flour.
floreal, *m.* (hist.) Floreal (eighth month of French Revolutionary calendar).

florear, *tr.v.* 1. to decorate with flowers. 2. to bolt, sift out the finest part of (flour). 3. to stack (cards) for cheating. —*i.v.* 1. to brandish a sword. 2. to play an arpeggio (on a guitar). 3. to pay compliments. 4. to pick the best. 5. (Amer.) to flower, blossom.
florecedor, ra, *a.* blooming, flowering, blossoming.
florecer, (*ref. 45*) *i.v.* 1. to flower, blossom, bloom. 2. to flourish, prosper. —*r.v.* to become moldy or mildewy.
floreciente, *a.* 1. flowering, blossoming. 2. flourishing, prosperous.
florecimiento, *m.* flowering, blossoming, blooming.
Florencia, *f.* Florence, city in Italy.
florentín, florentino, na, *a., m., f.* Florentine.
florentísimo, ma, *a.* very flourishing or prosperous.
florería, *f.* florist's, flower shop.
florero, *m.* 1. idle chatter; bright but empty remark. 2. brandishing, flourish (of sword). 3. flourish (of hands in air, in Spanish dancing). 4. arpeggio (on the guitar).
florero, ra, *a.* flattering; jesting, joking. —*m., f.* florist. —*m.* 1. flower vase, jardiniere, flower stand. 2. (p.) flower piece, painting of cut flowers.
florescencia, *f.* 1. (bot.) florescence, flowering. 2. (med., chem.) efflorescence.
floresta, *f.* 1. wood, grove, forest; pleasant countryside. 2. collection; anthology.
florestero, *m.* forester, forest guard, keeper.
floreta, *f.* 1. leather border (on the edge of a girth). 2. flourish (in Spanish dance).
floretazo, *m.* rapier thrust or blow.
florete, *a.* superfine (sugar, etc.). —*m.* 1. fleuret-fencing. 2. foil, fleuret, rapier. 3. superfine cotton cloth.
floretear, *tr.v.* to flower, adorn with flowers. —*i.v.* to fence.
floreteo, *m.* foil fencing.
floretista, *m.* expert foil fencer.
florezca, florezco, *ref.* **florecer.**
floricultor, ra, *m., f.* floriculturist.
floricultura, *f.* floriculture.
floridamente, *adv.* (fig.) elegantly, gracefully, with a flourish.
floridano, na, *a., m., f.* Floridian.
floridez, *f.* floridity, floweriness (of style).
florido, da, *a.* 1. full of or covered with flowers. 2. ornate, florid (signature). 3. choice, select. 4. florid, flowery, ornate (style).
floridzina, *f.* (chem.) phlorizin, phlorhizin, phloridzin.
florífero, ra, *a.* (poet.) *var. of* **florígero.**
florígeno, na, *a.* (bot.) florigenic.
florígero, ra, *a.* floriferous.
florilegio, *m.* anthology, selection.
florín *m.* florin (Dutch coin).
floripondio, *m.* 1. (bot.) floripondio (Datura candida). 2. gaudy flower print (in fabrics, etc.).
florista, *m., f.* florist; maker and seller of artificial flowers.
floristería, *f.* (Amer.) florist, flower shop.
florístico, ca, *a.* floristic. —*f.* floristics.
florizina, *f.* (chem.) phlorizin, phlorhizin, phloridzin.
florlisar, *tr.v., var. of* **flordelisar.**
florón, *m.* 1. *aug. of* **flor,** large flower. 2. (archit.) fleuron, finial, rosette (flower ornament).
flósculo, *m.* (bot.) floscule, floret.
flota, *f.* 1. fleet. 2. (coll.) swarm, crowd, throng. 3. (Col.) brag, boast. — **f. aérea,** airfleet.
flotable, *a.* floatable.
flotación *f.* flotation, floating. — **línea de f.,** waterline, flotation line.
flotador, ra, *a.* floating. —*m.* float. — **f. de bola,** ball float.
flotadura, *f.* flotation, floating.
flotamiento, *m.* flotation, floating.
flotante, *a.* 1. floating. 2. (Col., Chile) bragging, boastful.
flotar, *i.v.* to float.
flote, *m.* floating. — **a f.,** afloat; **mantenerse a f.,** to keep one's head above water; **poner a f.,** to re-float; **ponerse a f.,** to get out of difficulties.
flotilla, *f.* flotilla, fleet of small vessels.
fluctuación, *f.* 1. fluctuation. 2. (fig.) vacillation, hesitation, wavering. 3. (med.) fluctuation.
fluctuante, *a.* fluctuating.
fluctuar, (*ref. 55*) *i.v.* 1. to fluctuate. 2. to rise and fall, bob up and down (i.e. on the waves). 3. to waver, vacillate. 4. to be in danger.
fluctuoso, sa, *a.* 1. fluctuating. 2. wavering, indecisive.
fluencia, *f.* 1. flowing. 2. source, spring.
fluente, *a.* flowing.
fluidal, *a.* (geol., min.) fluidal.
fluidez, *f.* 1. fluidity. 2. fluency (of style or language).
fluidificar, (*ref. 50*) *tr.v.* to fluidize.
fluidizar, (*ref. 53*) *tr.v.* to fluidize.
fluido, da, *a.* 1. fluid. 2. (fig.) fluent, flowing (style, language). —*m.* fluid; **f. de cortar,** cutting fluid; **f. motor or operante,** (mec.) working fluid; **fluidos elásticos,** (phys.) gaseous bodies.
fluir, (*ref. 48*) *i.v.* to flow.
flujo, *m.* 1. flow, flowing. 2. flow, discharge. 3. (mar.) rise, flow (of tide). 4. (chem., metal., phys., math.) flux. — **f. blanco,** (med.) leukorrhea; **f. de caja,** cash flow; **f. del mar,** rising tide; **f. de palabras,** flood of words; **f. de sangre,** hemorrhage; **f. de vientre,** diarrhea, loose bowels; **f. luminoso,** (phys.) luminous flux; **f. magnético, (phys.)** magnetic flux; **f. menstrual,** menstrual flow; **f. y reflujo,** ebb and flow, rise and fall.
fluminense, *a.* pertaining to Rio de Janeiro. *m., f.* inhabitant of Rio de Janeiro.
flúor, *m.* 1. (chem.) fluorine. 2. (chem.) flux.
fluoración, *f.* (chem.) fluorination.
fluoresceína, *f.* (chem.) fluorescein.
fluorescencia, *f.* fluorescence.
fluorescente, *a.* fluorescent.
fluorhídrico, *a.* (chem.) hydrofluoric.
fluórico, ca, *a.* (chem.) fluoric.
fluorina, fluorita, *f.* (min.) fluorite, fluor, fluorspar.
fluorización, *f.* (chem.) fluorization.
fluorizar, (*ref. 53*) *tr.v.* to fluoridate.
fluorocarburo, *m.* (chem.) fluorocarbon.
fluorografía, *f.* fluorography.
fluorómetro, *m.* (phys.) fluorometer, fluorimeter.
fluoroscopía, *f.* (med.) fluoroscopy.
fluoroscopio, *m.* (med.) fluoroscope.
fluorosis, *f.* (med.) fluorosis.
fluoruro, *m.* (chem.) fluoride.
fluvial, *a.* 1. river (as *a.*). 2. (geol., bot.) fluvial.
fluviógrafo, *m.* (hydr.) fluviograph.
fluviomarino, na, *a.* (geol.) fluviomarine.
fluviómetro, *m.* fluviometer, fluviograph.
flux, *m.* 1. flush (in cards). 2. (Amer.) suit (of clothes). — **f. de cuatro naipes,** four flush; hacer **uno f.,** to blow all one's money and be in debt; **tener f.,** (Amer.) to be lucky.
fluxión, *f.* 1. (med., math.) fluxion. 2. (dent.) swelling, abscess. 3. (med.) congestion. 4. head cold. — **f. pulmonar,** (med.) congestion of the lungs.
fluya, fluye, *ref.* **fluir.**
F.M.I. *abbrev. of* **Fondo Monetario Internacional,** International Monetary Fund (I. M. F.).
¡fo! *interj.* exclamation of disgust elicited by unpleasant odors.
fobia, *f.* phobia, aversion, dislike.
Fobos, *m.* (astron.) Phobos.
foca, *f.* (zool.) seal.
focal, *a.* (phys., geom.) focal.
foceifiza, *f.* kind of Arab mosaic (made of colored glass).
focha, *f.* (ornith.) European coot, bald coot.
focino, *m.* elephant goad.
foco, *m.* 1. center, focal point, focus. 2. (phys., geom., opt., med.) focus. 3. electric light bulb. — **f. incandescente,** incandescent lamp; **f. real,** real focus; **f. virtual,** virtual focus; **profundidad de f.,** (opt.) depth of focus.
fóculo, *m.* small fireplace or hearth.
fodolí, (*pl.* **fodolíes**) *a.* meddlesome.
fodongo, ga, *a.* (Mex.) dirty, filthy.
foete, *m.* (Amer.) *var. of* **fuete,** whip.
fofadal, *m.* (Arg.) quaking bog.
fofo, fa, *a.* spongy, soft.
fogaje, *m.* 1. hearth money (ancient tax). 2. (phys., geom., opt., med.) focus. 3. (Amer.) stifling or sultry heat. 4. (Ecuad.) blaze. 5. (P. Rico) blush, flush.
fogarada, *f.* sudden blaze, flare.
fogarata, *f.* (coll.) bonfire, blaze.
fogaril, *m.* cresset, iron basket containing combustible material and used as a torch.
fogarizar, (*ref. 53*) *tr.v.* to light bonfires.
fogata, *f.* 1. bonfire, blaze. 2. (mil.) fougasse, small hole charged with powder for clearing obstacles.
fogón, *m.* 1. kitchen range, cooking stove. 2. (mil.) touchhole, vent (of gun). 3. firebox (of furnace). 4. (Amer.) fire, bonfire. 5. (Arg.) group of people round a fire.
fogonadura, *f.* (mar.) mast-hole.
fogonazo, *m.* powder flash.
fogonero, *m.* stoker, fireman.
fogosidad, *f.* fieriness, vehemence, ardor, impetuosity.
fogoso, sa, *a.* fiery, impetuous, vehement; spirited (horse).
foguear, *tr.v.* 1. (mil.) to scale (a gun). 2. (mil.) to accustom to gunfire. 3. to toughen, strengthen. 4. (vet.) to cauterize.
fogueo, *m.* accustoming to gunfire. — **de f.** dummy, e.g. *bala de f.,* dummy or blank bullet, *pistola de f.,* pistol shooting dummy bullets.
foguero, *m.* (Ven.) pyrotechnist, pyrotechnician.
foguezuelo, *m. dim. of* **fuego,** small fire.
foguista, *m.* (Arg.) stoker, fireman.
foja, *f.* 1. (law) leaf (of documents of a law case). 2. (ornith.) European coot, bald coot.
folgo, *m.* foot-warming bag.
foliáceo, a, *a.* (bot.) foliaceous.
foliación, *f.* 1. foliation, numbering the leaves of a book; (print.) folios, page numbers. 2. (archit., geol.) foliation. 3. (bot.) foliation, frondescence, breaking into leaf.
foliado, da, *a.* (bot.) foliose, foliated, folious.
foliar, *tr.v.* (print.) to foliate, folio, number the leaves of.
foliatura. *f., var. of* **foliación.**
fólico, *a.* (chem.) folic.
folicular, *a.* (bot.) follicular.
foliculario, *m.* (derog.) pamphleteer, hack journalist.
foliculina, *f.* (med.) folliculin.
folículo, *m.* (bot., anat.) follicle.
folijones, *m.* (*pl.*) old Castilian dance.
folio, *m.* 1. folio, leaf (of book). 2. (acc.) folio. 3. (print.) page number, folio; running head; fly (four-page section carrying late news). — **de**

a f., enormous, very big, monumental; **en f.,** foliosized; **f. atlántico,** atlas, atlas folio; **f. de Descartes,** folium of Descartes; **f. índico,** Indian leaf; **f. verso** or **vuelto,** (print.) verso.
foliolado, da, *a.* (bot.) foliolate.
folíolo, *m.* (bot.) foliole.
folklore, *m.* folklore.
folklórico, ca, *a.* folkloric.
folklorista, *m., f.* folklorist.
folla, *f.* 1. hodgepodge, jumble. 2. variety show. 3. disorderly joust.
follada, *f.* pie of puff pastry.
follado, *past part. of* **follar.** —*m.* (*pl.*) baggy trousers.
follador, *m.* bellows-man, bellows-operator, worker who operates the bellows.
follaje, *m.* 1. foliage. 2. adornment of intertwined leaves. 3. tasteless and overdone decoration. 4. verbiage, wordiness, verbosity.
follar, (*ref. 33*) *tr.v.* to blow with bellows. —*r.v.* to fart noiselessly.
follar, *tr.v.* to foliate, form into leaves.
follero, *m.* bellows maker or seller.
folletero, *m., var. of* **follero.**
folletín, *m.* serial story (in a newspaper).
folletinesco, ca, *a.* complicated, exciting (as a serial story).
folletinista, *m., f.* serial-writer.
folletista, *m., f.* pamphleteer, writer of booklets or brochures.
folleto, *m.* pamphlet, booklet, brochure.
follisca, *f.* (Col., Ven.) row, quarrel, fight.
follón, na, *a.* 1. lazy, idle. 2. cowardly, worthless. —*m., f.* 1. loafer, idler. 2. good-for-nothing, ne'er-do-well. —*m.* 1. noiseless rocket. 2. root (of tree). 3. row, quarrel, rumpus, fight, squabble; noise, shouting, uproar.
foluz, (*pl.* **foluces**) *f.* ancient copper coin.
fomentación, *f.* (med.) fomentation.
fomentador, ra, *a.* fomenting; promoting. —*m., f.* 1. fomenter, causer, instigator. 2. promoter.
fomentar, *tr.v.* 1. to foment, arouse, excite. 2. to foster, encourage, promote. 3. to sit and hatch (hen). 4. (med.) to foment, apply fomentations to.
fomento, *m.* 1. fomentation. 2. fostering, promotion, furtherance, development; encouragement. 3. warmth. 4. fuel. 5. (med.) fomentation. — **Ministerio de F.,** Ministry of Economic Development.
fon, *m.* (phys.) phon, a unit for measuring the intensity of sound.
fonación, *f.* (phonet.) phonation, vocalization.
fonas, *f.* (*pl.*) (sew.) gussets, gores.
fonda, *f.* inn; restaurant, eating house.
fondable, *a.* fit for anchoring.
fondac, (*pl.* **fondaques**) *m.* fonduk, fondouk, fonduck, fondaco (an inn or mercantile headquarters for foreign traders).
fondado, da, *a.* reinforced in the heads (said of barrels).
fondeadero, *m.* anchorage place, anchoring ground.
fondeado, da, *past part. of* **fondear.** —*a.* (Amer.) wealthy, well-heeled.
fondear, *tr.v.* 1. to sound (the depth of water). 2. to search (a ship for contraband). 3. to examine closely. —*i.v.* to anchor, cast anchor; **estar fondeado,** to ride at anchor. —*r.v.* (Amer.) to get rich.
fondeo, *m.* 1. anchoring, casting anchor. 2. searching (a vessel).
fondero, ra, *m., f.* (Amer.) innkeeper.
fondillón, *m.* 1. lees, dregs (of a cask of liquor). 2. a certain type of crude Spanish wine.
fondillos, *m.* (*pl.*) seat of trousers; (Cuba, coll.) the buttocks.
fondista, *m., f.* 1. innkeeper. 2. long distance runner.
fondo, *m.* 1. bottom; bed (of the sea, etc.). 2. rear, back, further end. 3. depth (e.g. of a house); thickness (of a diamond). 4. background (e.g. of a picture). 5. fund, collection of money. 6. store, fund (e.g. of virtues, knowledge, etc.). 7. (jour.) leading article. 8. fundamentals, basic ideas, essence; content, subject matter. 9. character, disposition. 10. batch, lot, collection (of books coming into a library). 11. petticoat, slip, underskirt. 12. head (of a barrel). 13. (Amer.) cauldron, boiler. 14. (mar.) bottom (of a ship). 15. (*pl.*) funds, capital (money). 16. (mar.) (*pl.*) bottom (of a ship). — **a f.,** perfectly, completely, thoroughly; **bajos fondos,** underworld district (of a town), skid row; **dar f.,** (mar.) to cast or drop anchor; to finish, end; **de f.,** main, leading, e.g. *plato de f.,* main dish; **artículo de f.,** (jour.) leading article; long-distance, e.g. *corredor de f.,* long-distance runner; **corredor de medio f.,** middle-distance runner; **doble f.,** (mar.) double bottom; **echar a f.,** (mar.) to sink; **en f.,** abreast, e.g. *de cuatro en f.,* four abreast; **en el f.,** at heart, deep-down; basically; **estar en fondos,** to be in funds, have money available, have ready cash; **f. de amortización,** sinking fund; **f. de comercio,** goodwill; **f. de contingencia or previsión,** (com.) contingency fund; **f. de garantía de depósitos,** deposit guarantee fund; **f. de inversion,** investment fund; **f. de pensiones,** pension fund; **f. de reptiles,** slush fund; **f. de reserva,** reserve fund; **F. Monetario Internacional,** International Monetary Fund; **f. vitalicio,** life annuity; **irse a f.,** to sink, founder, go down (a ship); **tener buen f.,** to be good at heart; **tener mal f.,** to be basically bad.
fondón, na, *a.* (coll., derog.) flabby, fat. —*m.* 1. dregs, lees (in a cask of liquor). 2. background of velvet or brocade.
fondonga, *f.* (Ven.) big-bellied cow or mare.
fonducho, *m.* cheap and poor class eating house, beanery.
fonébol, *m.* trebuchet, military catapult.
fonema, *m.* (phonet.) phoneme.
fonemático, ca, *a.* phonemic. —*f.* phonemics.
fonémico, ca, *a.* phonemic. —*f.* phonemics.
fonendoscopio, *m.* (med.) phonendoscope.
fonética, *f.* phonetics.
fonético, ca, *a.* phonctic.
fonetismo, *m.* phoneticism.
fonetista, *m., f.* phonetist, phonetician.
foniatría, *f,* speech therapy. speech correction, phoniatrics.
fonfón, *m.* (Cuba) whipping, flogging.
fónica, *f.* phonics.
fónico, ca, *a.* phonic, pertaining to voice or sound.
fonil, *m.* funnel (for wine casks).
fonio, *m.* (phys.) phon, unit of sound.
fonje, *a.* soft, spongy, fluffy.
fono, *m.* (Chile) 1. telephone receiver. 2. telephone number.
fonoautográfico, ca, *a.* phonoautographic.
fonoautógrafo, *m.* (phys.) phonoautograph.
fonocaptor, *m.* (elec.) phonograph or record player pickup.
fonóforo, *m.* (elec.) phonophore, phonopore.
fonografía, *f.* phonography, the recording of sound by phonograph.
fonográfico, ca, *a.* phonographic.
fonógrafo, *m.* phonograph (record player).
fonograma, *m.* phonogram, symbol representing a word, syllable or sound.
fonolita, *f.* (min.) phonolite, perlite.
fonología, *f.* phonology.
fonológico, ca, *a.* phonological.
fonólogo, *m.* phonologist.
fonometría, *f.* phonometry.
fonométrico, ca, *a.* phonometric.
fonómetro, *m.* phonometer.
fonón, *m.* (phys.) phonon.
fonoscopio, *m.* (phys.) phonoscope.
fonoteca, *f.* music library.
fonotipia, *f.* phonotypy.
fonotípico, ca, *a.* phonotypic, phonotypical.
fonotipo, *m.* phonotype.
fonsadera, *f.* 1. (obs.) military service in time of war. 2. (Sp.) war tax.
fonsado, *m.* 1. (formerly) military service (in time of war). 2. digging of a foss or ditch.
fontal, *a.* fontal, original, main, principal.
fontana, *f.* (poet.) fountain, water jet, spring.
fontanal, *a.* fontal. —*m.* spring; place abounding in springs; source of spring water.
fontanar, *m.* spring (of water).
fontanela, *f.* (anat.) fontanel.
fontanería, *f.* plumbing; water supply system; water department.
fontanero, ra, *a.* fountain. —*m.* plumber.
fontegí, *m.* a type of wheat.
fontezuela, *f. dim. of* **fuente,** small spring or fountain.
fontículo, *m.* (med.) fonticulus, issue, artificial ulcer (for draining off pus).
foque, *m.* 1. (mar.) jib. 2. (coll.) high wing collar, piccadilly. — **f. balón,** (mar.) balloon sail.
forado, *m.* (Amer.) hole (in a wall).
forajido, da, *m., f.* outlaw, renegade, bandit; fugitive from justice.
foral, *a.* (law) statutory.
foralmente, *adv.* judicially.
foramen, *m.* hole, opening; hole in the nether stone of a mill; (anat.) foramen.
foraminado, da, *a.* (anat., zool., bot.) foraminate.
foraminal, *a.* (bot.) foraminal.
foraminífero, *a.* (zool.) foraminifer.
foráneo, a, *a.* foreign, alien.
forastero, ra, *a.* outside; foreign, alien. —*m., f.* stranger, newcomer, outsider.
forbante, *m.* freebooter, plunderer.
forcaz, (*pl.* **forcaces**) *a.* having two poles (a cart).
forcé, *ref.* **forzar.**
forcejar, forcejear, *i.v.* to struggle, **strive;** (fig.) to resist tenaciously.
forcejo, forcejeo, *m.* struggle, struggling, strife.
forcejón, *m.* violent effort, struggle or strife.
forcejudo, da, *a.* strong, tough.
fórceps, *m.* (surg.) forceps.
forchina, *f.* fork-like weapon.
forense, *m.* forensic, legal.
forense, *a.* (rare) *var. of* **forastero.**
forero, ra, *a.* statutory. —*m.* leaseholder, lessee.
forestación, *f.* forestation.
forestal, *a.* pertaining to forests or forestry.
forfícula, *f.* (zool.) earwig.
forillo, *m.* (theat.) small backdrop.
forja, *f.* 1. silversmith's forge. 2. iron foundry, iron works. 3. forging, making. 4. (mas.) mortar.
forjado, *past part. of* **forjar.** —*m.* (archit.) framework.
forjador, ra, *a.* forging. —*m.* forger; marker; blacksmith; iron master; goldbeater.
forjadura, *f.* forging, making.
forjar, *tr.v.* 1. to forge, shape, hammer into shape. 2. to forge, make, form. 3. (mas.) to plaster roughly. 4. (mas.) to fill in (spaces between beams) with hollow bricks. 5. to fabricate, concoct, invent (stories, lies, etc.). — **f. ilusiones,** to build castles in the air, delude oneself.

forlón, *m.* four-seater coach.
forma, *f.* 1. form; shape. 2. way, manner. 3. (print.) format, size of a book. 4. (print.) form, type form. 5. (lit.) form, style. 6. (ecc.) host (for communion). 7. (ecc.) formula, words of a ritual. 8. (archit.) arch (of a groined vault). — **dar f. a,** to shape, form; to carry out, perform; **de f. que,** in such a way that; **en buena f.,** in good form; in good shape; **en debida f.,** in the correct manner or way; in form; in good shape; **en f.,** in form; in good shape (said of athletes, performers, etc.).
formable, *a.* formable.
formación, *f.* 1. formation; (mil., geol.) formation. 2. bullion, twisted cord (for gold embroidery). 3. (print.) makeup. — **f. cerrada,** (mil.) close formation; **f. vocacional,** vocational training.
formador, ra, *a.* forming. —*m., f.* former.
formaje, *m.* cheese mold or vat; (Mex.) sugar mold.
formal, *a.* 1. formal 2. serious; quiet; settled. 3. correct, formal, sedate. 4. reliable, punctual. 5. express, definite.
formaldehído, *m.* (chem.) formaldehyde.
formalete, *m.* (archit.) round arch.
formalice, formalicé, *ref.* **formalizar.**
formalidad, *f.* 1. formality. 2. seriousness, solemnity. 3. reliability, punctuality. 4. correctness, propriety, formality; sedateness. 5. requirement, established procedure, requisite, red tape (coll.).
formalina, *f.* (chem.) formalin.
formalismo, *m.* 1. formalism. 2. red tape (coll.).
formalista, *a.* formalistic. —*m., f.* formalist.
formalizar, (*ref.* 53) *tr.v.* 1. to formalize. 2. to legalize, make legal. 3. to settle, confirm. —*r.v.* to become serious or earnest. — **f. un compromiso,** to make it legal (to become officially engaged or married).
formalmente, *adv.* formally; seriously, reliably.
formalote, *a.* (coll.) serious, earnest (gen. said of a young man).
formante, *a.* forming, formative.
formar, *tr.v.* 1. to form. 2. to shape, fashion. 3. to educate, bring up. 4. to pick out (the edges of embroidery work) with cord. —*i.v.* 1. to form (in a procession, etc.). 2. (Mex., print.) to make up forms. —*r.v.* to form; to develop, grow. — **f. parte de,** to be part or member of; **f. fila,** to form into a line.
formativo, va, *a.* formative, e.g. *los años formativos,* the formative years.
formato, *m.* (print.) format.
formatriz, (*pl.* **formatrices**), *a., var. of* **formadora.**
formejar, *tr.v.* 1. (mar.) to trim (the hold). 2. to clear (the ship).
formeno, *m.* (chem.) formene.
formero, *m.* (archit.) arch (of a groined vault).
formiato, *m.* (chem.) formate, salt of formic acid.
formica, *m.* or *f.,* **fórmica,** *f.* Formica (TM).
formicante, *a.* 1. (med.) weak and rapid (pulse). 2. slow, sluggish.
fórmico, *a.* (chem.) formic.
formidable, *a.* formidable; terrific, tremendous, enormous.
formidoloso, sa, *a.* (rare) timorous, timid; horrible, frightening.
formilo, *m.* (chem.) formyl.
formillón, *m.* hat block.
formol, *m.* (chem.) formol.
formón, *m.* 1. chisel. 2. punch for cutting circular objects. — **f. acodado** or **de media caña,** bent gouge.
fórmula, *f.* 1. formula, prescription; recipe. 2. method, pattern; (fig.) solution, **e.g.** *f. mágica,* panacea; **es pura f.,** it's mere formality; **f. de estructura,** (phys.) structural formula; **f. rígida,** hard and fast rule; **por f.,** as a matter of form.
formular, *tr.v.* 1. to formulate. 2. to prescribe. 3. to express, show, e.g. *f. una pregunta,* to pose a question. —*a.* formulary, pertaining to a formula.
formulario, ria, *a.* formulistic; conventional, formal. —*m.* 1. formulary, collection of formulas. 2. form, blank, application, questionnaire.
formulismo, *m.* formulism; red tape.
formulista, *a.* formulistic. —*m., f.* formulist.
fornáceo, a, *a.* (poet.) furnacelike.
fornalla, *f.* (Cuba) ashpan (of a furnace).
fornecino, na, *a.* illegitimate, bastard.
fornelo, *m.* small brazier.
fornicación, *f.* fornication.
fornicador, ra, *a.* fornicating. —*m.* fornicator. —*f.* fornicatrix.
fornicar, (*ref.* 50) *i.v.* to fornicate.
fornicario, ria, *a.* fornicating. —*m.,* fornicator. —*f.* fornicatrix.
fornicio, *m.* fornication.
fornido, da, *a.* husky, strong, robust, stout.
fornique, forniqué, *ref.* **fornicar.**
fornitura, *f.* 1. (print.) type melted to complete a font. 2. (*pl.*) (mil.) cartridge belt.
fórnix, *m.* (anat., bot.) fornix.
foro, *m.* 1. forum. 2. tribunal, court; bar, legal profession. 3. back, rear (of a stage). 4. lease, rent; lease, contract.
forondo, da, *a.* (Chile) pompous, self-satisfied.
forrado, da, *past part. of* **forrar.** —*a.* (Amer., coll.) wealthy, well-heeled.
forraje, *m.* 1. forage, fodder. 2. foraging. 3. hodgepodge, farrago.
forrajeador, *m.* forager, soldier collecting forage.
forrajear, *i.v.* to forage; to collect forage or fodder.
forrajera, *f.* 1. forager's rope and net. 2. sash or braid (on a cavalryman's dress uniform).
forrajero, ra, *a.* pertaining to forage or fodder.
forrar, *tr.v.* to line, put lining in (a dress, a case, etc.); to cover (e.g. a book, furniture). —*r.v.* (coll.) to stuff oneself.
forro, *m.* 1. lining, backing; cover, covering. 2. (mar.) planking, sheathing. — **f. del embrague,** (auto.) clutch lining; **f. del freno,** (auto.) brake lining; **ni por el f.,** (coll.) not in the slightest.
forsitia, *f.* (bot.) forsythia.
fortachón, na, *a.* (coll.) husky, tough, powerful, strong.
fortalecedor, ra, *a.* fortifying; invigorating; encouraging.
fortalecer, (*ref.* 45) *tr.v.* 1. to fortify, strengthen. 2. to corroborate. 3. to encourage, assist, support, e.g. *f. un argumento con datos,* to back up an argument with facts.
fortalecimiento, *m.* fortification, strengthening; fortifications, defenses.
fortaleza, *f.* 1. fortress, stronghold. 2. fortitude. 3. strength, vigor. 4. (*pl.*) minute cracks (in a blade). — **f. volante,** (aer., mil.) flying fortress; **la F.,** the executive mansion of Puerto Rico.
fortalezca, fortalezco, *ref.* **fortalecer.**
forte, *m.* (mus.) forte (loud passage). —*adv.* (mus.) forte, loudly. —*interj.* (mar.) avast!
fortepiano, *m.* (mus., obs.) pianoforte, piano.
fortezuelo, la, *dim. of* **fuerte.** —*a.* not very strong. —*m.* small fort.
fortificable *a.* fortifiable.
fortificación, *f.* fortification; **f. de campaña,** field fortification.
fortificador, ra, *a.* fortifying; strengthening.
fortificante, *a.* fortifying; strengthening. —*m.* tonic.
fortificar, (*ref.* 50) *tr.v.* to strengthen; to fortify.
fortifique, fortifiqué, *ref.* **fortificar.**
fortín, *m.* fortlet, small fort.
fortísimo, ma, *a. super. of* **fuerte,** very strong. —*adv.* (mus.) fortissimo.
fortuitamente, *adv.* fortuitously, accidentally, by chance.
fortuito, ta, *a.* fortuitous, accidental.
fortuna, *f.* 1. fortune, fate. 2. luck, fortune; good luck or fortune. 3. fortune, riches, wealth. 4. tempest, storm. — **por f.,** luckily; **probar f.,** to try one's luck; **soplar la f. a uno,** to be lucky.
fortunón, *m.* 1. a stroke of luck. 2. large fortune.
fortunoso, sa, *a.* (Guat.) fortunate, lucky; happy.
forúnculo, *m.* (med.) furuncle, boil.
forzadamente, *adv.* 1. forcibly, by force. 2. forcedly, artificially.
forzado, da, *past part. of* **forzar.** —*a.* 1. hard (labor). 2. forced, strained, artificial (laugh, smile, etc.). —*m.* galley slave.
forzador, *m.* violator, ravisher; forcer; **f. de bloqueo,** blockade-runner.
forzal, *m.* ridge of a comb (into which teeth fit); the main part of a comb.
forzamiento, *m.* the act of forcing or violating; (coll.) rape.
forzar, (*ref.* 70) *tr.v.* 1. to force, break through (a door). 2. to violate, rape, ravish. 3. to take by storm or assault. 4. to force, compel; **f. a que** + *subj.,* to force (someone) to + *inf.* —*r.v.* to force oneself; **forzarse a** + *inf.,* to force oneself + *inf.*
forzosa, *f.* (coll.) compulsion; **ponerle a uno la f.,** to compel someone to do something.
forzosamente, *adv.* 1. unavoidably, inevitably. 2. forcibly, by force.
forzoso, sa, *a.* 1. inevitable, unavoidable. 2. forced, compelled; obligatory, compulsory. — **aterrizaje forzoso,** forced landing.
forzudamente, *adv.* forcefully, powerfully, strongly.
forzudo, da, *a.* strong, powerful; brawny.
fosa, *f.* 1. grave, pit, tomb. 2. (anat.) fossa, cavity. 3. depression, dip (in the terrain); hollow (in the surface of a bone). — **f. común,** potter's field, common grave; **f. marina,** marine basin; **f. nasal,** nostril; **f. navicular,** (anat.) fossa navicularis; **f. oceánica,** ocean basin; **f. séptica,** septic tank.
fosado, *past part. of* **fosar.** —*m.* **(fort.)** foss, moat, trench.
fosal, *m.* cemetery, burial ground.
fosar, *tr.v.* to dig a foss, trench or moat around.
fosca, *f.* 1. haze, mist, fog. 2. jungle, wild growth.
fosco, ca, *a.* 1. gruff, surly, unsociable. 2. dark, swarthy (skin); gloomy, dark (atmosphere or horizon).
fosfatado, da, *past part. of* **fosfatar.** —*a.* phosphatized.
fosfatar, *tr.v.* to phosphatize.
fosfatasa, *f.* (med.) phosphatase.
fosfático, ca, *a.* (chem.) phosphatic.
fosfátido, *m.* (biochem.) phosphatide.
fosfato, *m.* (chem.) phosphate; **f. cálcico,** (chem.) calcium phosphate.
fosfaturia, *f.* (med.) phosphaturia.
fosfeno, *m.* (physiol.) phosphene.
fosfina, *f.* (chem.) phosphine, phosphin.
fosfito, *m.* (chem.) phosphite.
fosfocreatina, *f.* (biochem.) phosphocreatine, phosphocreatin.
fosfolípido, *m.* (biochem.) phospholipide, phospholipid.
fosfolipina, *f.* (biochem.) phospholipide, phospholipid.
fosfonio, *m.* (chem.) phosphonium.
fosfoproteína, *f.* (biochem.) phosphoprotein.

fosforado, da, *a.* (chem.) phosphorated, phosphoretted.
fosforar, *i.v.* to phosphorate.
fosforecer, (*ref. 45*) *i.v.* to phosphoresce.
fosforera, *f.* match box.
fosforero, ra, *m., f.* person who sells matches. *—f.* box that keeps matches.
fosforescencia, *f.* phosphorescence, luminescence.
fosforescente, *a.* phosphorescent, luminous; **pintura f.,** luminous paint.
fosforescer, (*ref. 45*) *i.v.* to phosphoresce.
fosforezca, fosforezco, *ref.* **fosforecer.**
fosfórico, ca, *a.* (chem.) phosphoric.
fosforilación, *f.* (chem.) phosphorylation.
fosforilasa, *f.* (biochem.) phosphorylase.
fosforismo, *m.* (med.) phosphorism.
fosforita, *f.* (min.) phosphorite.
fósforo, *m.* 1. (chem.) phosphorus. 2. match. 3. (astron.) F., morning star. — **f. de seguridad,** safety match.
fosforólisis, *f.* (physiol.) phosphorolysis.
fosforoscopio, *m.* (phys.) phosphoroscope.
fosforoso, sa, *a.* (chem.) phosphorous.
fosfuro, *m.* (chem.) phosphide.
fosgenita, *f.* (min.) phosgenite.
fosgeno, *m.* (chem.) phosgene.
fósil, *a.* fossil; old, antiquated. *—m.* fossil; (fig.) fossil.
fosilífero, ra, *a.* fossiliferous.
fosilización, *f.* fossilization.
fosilizado, da, *past part. of* **fosilizarse.** *—a.* fossilized.
fosilizarse, (*ref. 53*) *r.v.* to fossilize, become fossilized.
fosique, *m.* snuff bottle (with a perforated top for inhaling).
foso, *m.* 1. pit, hole, fosse. 2. pit, space underneath the stage (of a theater); **f. de orquesta** or **orquestal,** orchestra pit. 3. service pit (of a garage). 4. (fort.) moat, fosse. — **f. séptico,** septic tank.
fot, *m.* (phys.) phot, unit of illumination.
fótico, ca, *a.* photic, pertaining to light.
fotingo, *m.* (Amer.) old car, jalopy.
fotinia, *f.* (bot.) photinia.
fotio, *m.* (phys.) phot, unit of light.
foto, *f.* photo, photograph; **f. de carnet** or **pasaporte,** passport photo.
fotoactínico, ca, *a.* photoactinic.
fotoactivación, *f.* photoactivation.
fotoactivo, va, *a.* (phys.) photoactive.
fotoautótrofo, fa, *a.* (bot.) photoautotrophic.
fotobiótico, ca, *a.* photobiotic.
fotocalco, *m.* photoprint.
fotocátodo, *m.* (phys.) photocathode.
fotocélula, *f.* (elec.) photocell, photoelectric cell.
fotocincografía, *f.* photozincography.
fotocinesis, *f.* (physiol.) photokinesis.
fotocinético, ca, *a.* (physiol.) photokinetic.
fotocomposición, *f.* (print.) phototypesetting.
fotoconductibilidad, *f.* (phys.) photoconductivity.
fotoconductivo, va, *a.* photoconductive.
fotocopia, *f.* photocopy.
fotocopiadora, *f.* photocopier, Xerox machine.
fotocopiar, *tr.v.* to make photocopies of.
fotocorriente, *f.* (phys.) photocurrent.
fotocromía, *f.* photochromy, color photography.
fotocronógrafo, *m.* photochronograph, a device for recording the exact time of an event.
fotodesintegración, *f.* (phys.) photodisintegration.
fotodinámico, ca, *a.* photodynamic. *—f.* photodynamics.
fotoduplicación, *f.* photoduplication.
fotoelectricidad, *f.* photoelectricity.
fotoeléctrico, ca, *a.* photoelectric.
fotoelectrón, *m.* (phys.) photoelectron.
fotoemisión, *f.* (phys.) photoemission.
fotoemisor, ra, *a.* photoemissive.
fotoemulsión, *f.* (phys.) photoemulsion.
fotófilo, la, *a.* (bot.) photophilic.
fotofísico, ca, *a.* photophysic.
fotofisión, *f.* photofission.
fotofluorografía, *f.* (med.) photofluorography.
fotofluorograma, *m.* (med.) photofluorogram.
fotofobia, *f.* (med.) photophobia, abnormal fear of or sensitivity to light.
fotófobo, ba, *a.* photophobic. *—m., f.* photophobic person, one who is abnormally sensitive to light.
fotófono, *m.* (phys.) photophone.
fotogénico, ca, *a.* photogenic.
fotógeno, na, *a.* (bot.) photogenic, producing or generating light, phosphorescent.
fotograbado, *m.* photoengraving, photogravure.
fotograbador, *m.* photoengraver.
fotograbar, *tr.v.* to photoengrave.
fotografía, *f.* 1. photograph, photo, picture. 2. photography (art, process, hobby). 3. photographer's studio. — **f. aérea,** aerial photography; **f. en colores,** color photography; **f. estereoscópica,** stereophotography; **f. tamaño carnet,** wallet-size photo.
fotografiar, (*ref. 54*) *tr.v.* 1. to photograph. 2. to describe vividly.
fotográficamente, *adv.* photographically.
fotográfico, ca, *a.* photographic.
fotógrafo, *m.* photographer.
fotograma, *m.* (photog.) photogram.
fotogrametría, *f.* (photog.) photogrammetry.
fotogramétrico, ca, *a.* photogrammetric.
fotoheliógrafo, *m.* (astron.) photoheliograph.
fotoionización, *f.* (phys.) photoionization.
fotólisis, *f.* (phys.) photolysis.
fotolito, *m.* photolith.
fotolitografia, *f.* 1. photolithography. 2. photolithograph.
fotolitografiar, (*ref. 54*) *tr.v.* to photolithograph, photolith.
fotolitográfico, ca, *a.* photolithographic.
fotología, *f.* optics, photology.
fotomapa, *m.* photomap.
fotomecánico, ca, *a.* photomechanical.
fotometría, *f.* photometry, the branch of optics dealing with the measuring of light.
fotométrico, ca, *a.* photometric.
fotómetro, *m.* (phys., photog.) photometer.
fotomicrografía, *f.* photomicrography, the art of photographing through a microscope.
fotomicroscopio, *m.* (photog.) photomicroscope.
fotomontaje, *m.* photomontage.
fotomultiplicador, *m.* (phys.) photomultiplier.
fotomural, *m.* photomural, a very large photograph used as a mural or wall covering.
fotón, *m.* (phys.) photon.
fotopartícula, *f.* (phys.) photoparticle.
fotoperiodicidad, *f.* (physiol., bot.) photoperiodism.
fotoperíodo, *m.* (physiol., bot.) photoperiod.
fotopía, *f.* (physiol.) photopia.
fotoplaca, *f.* photoplate.
fotoprotón, *m.* (phys.) photoproton.
fotoquímico, ca, *a.* photochemical. *—f.* photochemistry.
fotorrelieve, *m.* photorelief.
fotorreproducción, *f.* photoreproduction.
fotosensibilización, *f.* photosensitization.
fotosensible, *a.* photosensitive.
fotosensitivo, va, *a.* photosensitive.
fotosensitizar, (*ref. 53*) *tr.v.* to photosensitize.
fotosfera, *f.* (astron.) photosphere.
fotosíntesis, *f.* (bot.) photosynthesis.
fotosintético, ca, *a.* photosynthetic.
fotospectroscopio, *m.* photospectroscope.
fotostatar, *tr.v.* to photostat.
fotostático, ca, *a.* photostatic.
fotostato, *m.* photostat.
fototáctico, ca, *a.* (bot.) phototactic.
fototactismo, *m.* (biol.) phototactism, phototaxis.
fototaxia, *f.* (bot.) phototaxy, phototaxis.
fototaxis, *f.* (biol.) phototaxis, phototaxy.
fototelefonía, *f.* phototelephony.
fototelegrafía, *f.* phototelegraphy.
fototelegráfico, ca, *a.* phototelegraphical.
fototerapia, *f.* (med.) phototherapy, phototherapeutics.
fototerápico, ca, *a.* phototherapeutical.
fototipia, *f.* 1. phototypy. 2. phototype.
fototípico, ca, *a.* phototypic.
fototipo, *m.* phototype.
fototipografía, *f.* phototypography.
fototipográfico, ca, *a.* phototypographic.
fototonía, *f.* (physiol.) phototonus.
fototopografía, *f.* phototopography.
fototopográfico, ca, *a.* phototopographic.
fototropismo, *m.* (biol.) phototropism.
fotovoltaico, ca, *a.* photovoltaic.
fotozincografía, *f.* (print.) photozincography.
fotuto, *m.* (Cuba) claxon, horn or trumpet; (Ven.) Indian flute.
fourierismo, *m.* Fourierism, the social doctrines of F. M. C. Fourier (1772-1837).
fóvea, *f.* (anat.) fovea, a small fossa.
fovéola, *f.* (anat.) foveola, foveole.
foveolar, *a.* (anat., bot.) foveolar.
foya, *f.* ovenload of charcoal.
foyer, *m.* foyer, lobby.
frac, (*pl.* **fracs, fraques**) *m.* tails, swallow-tail coat.
fracasado, da, *past part. of* **fracasar.** *—a.* unsuccessful. *—m., f.* failure.
fracasar, *i.v.* 1. to fail, be unsuccessful. 2. to break to pieces.
fracaso, *m.* 1. failure, downfall, ruin. 2. crash, noise.
fracción, *f.* fraction, fragment. — **f. continua,** (math.) continued fraction; **f. decimal,** (math.) decimal fraction; **f. impropia,** (math.) improper fraction; **f. propia,** (math.) proper fraction; **f. simple,** (math.) simple fraction.
fraccionable, *a.* fractionable; divisible.
fraccionado, da, *past part. of* **fraccionar.** *—a.* fractional.
fraccionamiento, *m.* breaking up; fractionization; division; (chem.) fractionation.
fraccionar, *tr.v.* to break up, divide into fractions; to fractionize, fraction; (chem.) to fractionate. *—r.v.* to break up, split, divide.
fraccionario, ria, *a.* fractional.
fractura, *f.* fracture, break; (geol., surg.) fracture; **f. cerrada** or **simple,** (surg.) closed or simple fracture; **f. complicada** or abierta, (surg.) compound fracture; **f. con impacto,** (surg.) impacted fracture; **f. conminuta,** (surg.) comminuted fracture; **f. de fatiga,** stress fracture; **f. en gradas,** (geol.) step fault.
fracturar, *tr.v., r.v.* to fracture, break, rupture.
fraga, *f.* 1. bramble thicket, brambly land. 2. waste wood taken off when timber is roughdressed. 3. (bot.) raspberry.
fragancia, *f.* 1. fragrance, perfume, scent; bouquet (of wine). 2. (coll.) good name, good reputation (of a person).
fragante, *a.* 1. fragrant, sweet-smelling. 2. flagrant. — **en f.,** in the act.
fragaria, *f.* (bot.) strawberry.

fragata, *f.* (mar.) frigate; **f. ligera,** (mar.) corvette.
frágil, *a.* 1. fragile, easily broken, brittle. 2. frail, delicate (in health). 3. weak, lax (morally). 4. (Mex., imp. u.) poor.
fragilidad, *f.* 1. fragileness, fragility. 2. frailty, weakness (moral and physical).
frágilmente, *adv.* fragilely; frailly; weakly; delicately.
fragmentación, *f.* fragmentation.
fragmentar, *tr.v.* to fragment, break or divide into fragments or pieces. —*r.v.* to fragment, break or crumble into fragments.
fragmentario, a, *a.* fragmentary.
fragmento, *m.* fragment, piece, part; (mus., lit.) excerpt, passage.
fragor, *m.* din, uproar, clamor, noise, clangor, clash, e.g. *en el f. de la batalla,* in the din of battle.
fragoroso, sa, *a.* booming, crashing, thundering.
fragosidad, *f.* 1. ruggedness, roughness (of terrain). 2. thickness, denseness (of a forest). 3. rough or rugged terrain or path; cragginess.
fragoso, sa, *a.* 1. rugged, rough; brambly, covered by undergrowth. 2. thundering, booming, crashing, noisy.
fragrante, *a., var. of* **fragante.**
fragua, *f.* forge, smithy's furnace; **sangrar la f.,** (fig.) to let slag run out of a furnace.
fraguado, *past part. of* **fraguar.** —*m.* (mas.) hardening, setting (of plaster).
fraguador, ra, *a.* plotting, planning. —*m., f.* plotter, planner, schemer.
fraguar, (*ref. 52*) *tr.v.* 1. to forge (iron). 2. to think up, devise, contrive (a pretext, lies, etc.); to forge, plan, hatch, scheme, plot (a revolution, etc.). —*i.v.* (mas.) to set, harden (plaster).
fragura, *f., var. of* **fragosidad.**
frailada, *f.* (coll.) unseemly behavior of a friar or a monk.
fraile, *m.* 1. friar, monk; (Amer.) priest, cleric. 2. tuck (a hem of a dress). 3. hood (of a hearth or fireplace). 4. (print.) friar (white or pale patch on a page). 5. (Cuba) residue of cane juice. — **f. de misa y olla,** an uncultured, uneducated cleric.
frailecillo, *m.* 1. *dim. of* **fraile,** little friar. 2. (ornith.) lapwing; (ornith.) Atlantic puffin. 3. each of the two screw pins which secure a spindle (in silk spinning). 4. (Cuba, bot.) croton tree (Croton lobatus).
frailecito, *m.* 1. little friar. 2. children's toy in the shape of a friar's head.
frailengo, ga, fraileño, ña, *a.* (coll.) pertaining to monks or friars.
frailería, *f.* (coll.) monks, friars; priests in general.
frailero, ra, *a.* 1. of a friar or monk. 2. fond of priests, pious.
frailesco, ca, *a.* (coll.) pertaining to monks or friars.
frailía, *f.* regular clergy.
fraillillos, *m.* (*pl.*) (bot.) wake-robin.
frailote, *m. aug. of* **fraile,** fat or stout monk or friar.
frailuco, *m.* (derog.) unimportant monk or friar, a minor priest.
frailuno, na, *a.* (derog.) pertaining to friars and priests.
frambesia, *f.* (med.) frambesia, yaws.
frambuesa, *f.* raspberry (fruit).
frambueso, *m.* (bot.) raspberry, raspberry bush.
frámea, *f.* javelin (used by ancient Germanic tribes).
francachela, *f.* (coll.) banquet, feast, blowout, spree; **ir de f.,** to go out on a spree, go out on the town.
francalete, *m.* a buckled leather strap.
francamente, *adv.* frankly, openly, freely.
francés, sa, *a.* French; **a la francesa,** in the French manner; **despedirse or marcharse a la f.,** to take French leave. —*m.* 1. Frenchman. 2. French (language). —*f.* Frenchwoman.
francesada, *f.* 1. (hist.) French invasion of Spain in 1808. 2. typically French act or remark.
francesilla, *f.* 1. (bot.) Asiatic crowfoot, turban buttercup (Ranunculus asiaticus). 2. (bot.) (species of) damson plum. 3. (cul.) French roll (bread).
Francfort, *m.* Frankfort; **F. del Meno,** Frankfort on the Main; **F. del Oder,** Frankfort on the Oder.
Francia, *f.* France.
francio, *m.* (chem.) francium.
franciscano, na, *a.* 1. Franciscan. 2. greyish brown. —*m., f.* Franciscan (nun or monk).
francisco, ca, *a., m.* Franciscan.
francmasón, na, *m., f.* Freemason, Mason.
francmasonería, *f.* Freemasonry.
franco, ca, *a.* 1. frank, candid. 2. generous, liberal, open-handed. 3. free, unimpeded, unencumbered. 4. exempt, free (of cost, taxes, duties). 5. free (port). 6. (com.) free, e.g. *f. a bordo,* F.O.B., free on board, *f. de porte,* postpaid, *f. en almacén,* ex warehouse, *f. en vagón,* free on rail. 7. Frankish (people, language). 8. Franco, e.g. *Sociedad Franco-Portuguesa,* Franco-Portuguese Society; **f. de servicio,** (S. Amer.) off duty; **lengua franca,** lingua franca. —*m.* 1. Frankish (language). 2. Franc (monetary unit of France, Switzerland, Belgium). 3. tax-free days (at a fair). 4. (coll.) postage stamp.
francoalemán, na, *a.* Franco-German.
francocuartel, *m.* (her.) chief dexter canton (of an escutcheon).
francófilo, la, *a., m., f.* Francophile (fond of all things French).
francófobo, ba, *a., m., f.* Francophobe (averse to all things French).
francófono, na, *a.* French-speaking. —*m., f.* French speaker.
francolín, *m.* (ornith.) black partridge, francolin.
francolino, na, *a.* (Chile, Ecuad.) tailless (chicken).
francote, ta, *a.* very frank, open, straightforward, forthright.
francotirador, *m.* sniper.
franchote, ta, franchute, ta, *m., f.* (derog.) Frenchy, Frenchified person.
franela, *f.* flannel (cloth).
frange, *m.* (her.) quarter, section, division (of an escutcheon divided by two intersecting diagonals).
frangente, *a.* frangent. —*m.* mishap, accident, disaster.
frangible, *a.* frangible, brittle, breakable.
frangir, (*ref. 62*) *tr.v.* to break into pieces, break up.
frangle, *m.* (her.) narrow fesse.
frangollar, *tr.v.* (coll.) to do hurriedly and in a slapdash manner.
frangollo, *m.* 1. porridge, mash; cattle feed of chopped vegetables or crushed grain; (Canar. I.) maize cooked with milk; (Cuba, P. Rico) dessert made with mashed green bananas; (Mex.) poorly cooked food or meal; (Arg., Chile) mashed corn, wheat or maize. 2. (Peru) jumble, hodgepodge, mixture. 3. (Arg.) botched or sloppy job, poor workmanship.
frangollón, na, *a.* (Amer.) bungling, careless, sloppy (person).
frangote, *m.* (com.) bale (larger or smaller than the normal-sized bale).
frángula, *f.* (bot.) berry-bearing alder.
franja, *f.* 1. fringe, border; stripe, band, braid. 2. strip (of land).
franjar, franjear, *tr.v.* to fringe, border, trim with braid or stripes.
franklinita, *f.* (min.) franklinite.
franqueable, *a.* breachable, surmountable.
franqueadora, *f.* postage meter.
franqueamiento, *m., var. of* **franqueo.**
franquear, *tr.v.* 1. to free, exempt (from taxes, duties, etc.). 2. to clear, free (the way). 3. to stamp, affix a stamp to, frank (a letter). 4. to free, enfranchise (a slave). 5. to cross, pass through. 6. to grant or give freely. —*r.v.* 1. to yield, acquiesce. 2. to unbosom oneself. — **franquearse a** or **con,** to unbosom oneself or open one's heart to.
franqueniáceo, a, *a.* (bot.) frankeniaceous. —*f.* (bot.) Frankeniaceae.
franqueo, *m.* 1. postage (mailing charge). 2. stamping, franking (of a letter). 3. enfranchisement, liberation, freeing (of a slave).
franqueza, *f.* 1. frankness, openness. 2. liberality, generosity. 3. freedom, exemption.
franquía, *f.* (mar.) free lane or passage, maneuverable position, sea room; **en f.,** (mar.) in a maneuverable position (for leaving port); (coll.) free to act; **estar en f.,** (mar.) to be in a free lane or maneuverable position, have sea room; **ganar f., ponerse en f.,** (mar.) to get into a free lane or maneuverable position.
franquicia, *f.* franchise, exemption, grant; tax exemption; (com.) franchise; **f. postal,** franking privilege.
fraque, *m.* tails, swallow-tailed coat.
frasca, *f.* 1. brushwood, dry leaves and twigs. 2. (Mex.) noisy or boisterous party.
frasco, *m.* bottle, vial, flask; powder flask; **f. cuentagotas,** dropping bottle.
frase, *f.* 1. phrase, idiom; sentence. 2. phrasing, phraseology, style. — **f. hecha,** set expression; **f. musical,** (mus.) phrase; **f. proverbial,** proverb, saying; **f. sacramental,** standard form, phrasing or phraseology.
frasear, *tr.v.* to phrase.
fraseología, *f.* 1. phraseology, phrasing; literary style. 2. verbosity.
fraseológico, ca, *a.* phraseological.
frasquera, *f.* bottle case or box, liquor case.
frasqueta, *f.* (print.) frisket.
frasquete, frasquillo, ito, *m.* small flask or vial.
Frasquito, *m.* Frank (proper name).
fratás, *m.* (mas.) plastering trowel.
fratasar, *tr.v.* to smooth out (plaster) with a plastering trowel.
fraterna, *f.* severe reprimand, dressingdown.
fraternal, *a.* fraternal, brotherly.
fraternalmente, *adv.* fraternally, in a brotherly manner.
fraternice, fraternicé, *ref.* **fraternizar.**
fraternidad, *f.* fraternity, brotherhood.
fraternizar, (*ref. 53*) *i.v.* to fraternize.
fraterno, na, *a.* fraternal, brotherly.
fratría, *f.* (hist.) phratry, clan or subdivision of a tribe in ancient Greece.
fratricida, *a.* fratricidal. —*m., f.* fratricide (murderer of a brother).
fratricidio, *m.* fratricide (murder of a brother).
fraude, *m.* fraud.
fraudulencia, *f.* (rare) fraud, fraudulence.
fraudulentamente, *adv.* fraudulently.
fraudulento, ta, *a.* fraudulent, deceitful.
fraustina, *f.* wooden head or stand used for combing wigs and headdresses.
fray, *m.* Fra, Brother (used before the name of clergy of certain religious orders), e.g. *Fray Luis de León,* Spanish clergyman and poet of the 16th century.

frazada, *f.* blanket, bed throw.
frazadero, *m.* person who makes blankets.
freático, ca, *a.* phreatic, subsurface.
frecuencia, *f.* frequency; **con f.,** frequently; **corriente de alta f.,** high frequency current; **f. crítica,** (rad.) cutoff frequency; (phys.) threshold frequency; **f. de funcionamiento,** (rad.) operating frequency; **f. heterodina, de pulsación** or **del latido,** (rad.) beat frequency; **f. intermedia,** (rad.) intermediate frequency; **f. modulada,** (rad.) FM; **f. patrón,** (rad.) standard frequency; **f. ultraelevada,** (elec.) ultrahigh frequency; **f. ultrasónica,** ultrasonic frequency; **f. visual,** (t.v.) video frequency.
frecuencímetro, *m.* (elec.) frequency meter.
frecuentación, *f.* frequenting.
frecuentador, ra, *a.* frequenting. —*m., f.* frequenter.
frecuentar, *tr.v.* to frequent, visit often; to repeat, do again and again.
frecuentativo, *a.* (gram.) frequentative. —*m.* frequentative verb (denoting repeated action).
frecuente, *a.* frequent, repeated; habitual, persistent; usual, common.
frecuentemente, *adv.* frequently, often, repeatedly.
fregadera, *f.* (Amer.) nuisance, bother.
fregadero, *m.* kitchen sink; basin.
fregado, da, *past part. of* **fregar.** —*a.* 1. (Amer.) annoying, irritating, tiresome. 2. (Amer.) penniless; in trouble. 3. (Mex.) cunning, artful, sly. —*m.* 1. scrubbing. 2. (coll.) difficulty, mess; squabble, quarrel, fight, rumpus, row; dirty or shady business.
fregador, *m.* sink; dish mop, scrubbing brush.
fregadura, *f.* 1. scrubbing; rubbing. 2. (Amer.) nuisance, bore, annoyance, bother.
fregajo, *m.* mop, scrubbing brush, fiber swab.
fregamiento, *m.* rubbing, friction.
fregar, (*ref. 67*) *tr.v.* 1. to scrub, scour; to wash (dishes); (mar.) to mop, swab. 2. (coll.) to irritate, annoy, bother. —*r.v.* 1. (coll.) to become annoyed or vexed. 2. (Amer., coll.) to come to grief, be in trouble, get into a fix.
fregatina, *f.* (Chile) nuisance, bother, annoyance.
fregatriz, (*pl.* **fregatrices**) **fregona,** *f.* scullery maid, kitchen maid, dishwasher.
fregonil, *a.* pertaining to a scullery maid; (coll.) wench-like.
fregotear, *tr.v.* (coll.) to scrub or scour hastily.
fregoteo, *m.* hasty scrubbing.
fregué, *ref.* **fregar.**
freidura, *f.* frying; pan braising.
freiduría, *f.* fried-fish shop.
freila, *f.* nun attached to certain military orders; lay sister.
freile, *m.* lay brother; priest attached to a military order.
freír, *irr. past part.* **frito** (*ref. 40*) *tr.v.* 1. to fry. 2. to vex, annoy. — **estar frito,** (fig.) to be done for; **al f. será el reír,** he who laughs last, laughs best. —*r.v.* to fry; to be baking, be boiling hot.
freira, *f., var. of* **freila.**
freire, *m., var. of* **freile.**
freiría, *f.* lay brotherhood; group of lay brothers.
fréjol, *m.* (bot.) haricot bean.
frémito, *m.* roar, bellow.
frenaje, *m.* braking; **f. de regeneración** or **recuperación,** regenerative braking; **f. reostático,** resistance braking.
frenar, *tr.v.* to restrain, curb, hold back; to bridle; to brake, apply the brakes to, slow down (by applying brakes). —*i.v.* to brake.
frenería, *f.* brake and lining shop; harness and bridle shop.
frenero, *m.* 1. bit and bridle maker or dealer. 2. brakeman.
frenesí, *m.* frenzy; delirious excitement, rapture, e.g. *tengo f. por la música,* I am crazy about music.
frenéticamente, *adv.* frenetically, frenziedly, wildly.
frenético, ca, *a.* frenetic, frenzied, frantic; furious, wild.
frénico, ca, *a.* (med.) phrenic.
frenillar, *tr.v.* (mar.) to lash, tie; to bridle (oars).
frenillo, *m.* 1. (anat.) frenum, bridle. 2. muzzle (for animals). 3. (C. Amer., Cuba) kite string. 4. (mar.) cable, fox, bobstay. — **no tener f. en la lengua,** (coll.) to be outspoken, say what one thinks.
frenitis, *f.* (med.) phrenitis.
freno, *m.* 1. bit (of harness). 2. brake (of a car, etc.). 3. check, restraint, curb. — **f. acodado,** snaffle bit; **f. de almohadillas,** block brake; **f. de cono,** cone brake; **f. de emergencia,** emergency brake; **f. de fricción,** friction brake; **f. de mano** or **manual,** hand brake; **f. de plato** or **discos,** disk brake; **f. de servicio** or **pedal,** service brake; **f. neumático,** air brake; **frenos asistidos,** power brakes; **frenos de aire,** air brakes; **frenos de disco,** disc brakes; **frenos de tambor,** drum brakes; **frenos hidráulicos,** hydraulic brakes; **f. sobre carril,** track brake; **tascar el f.,** to champ at the bit.
frenología, *f.* phrenology, study of character based on the configurations of the skull.
frenológico, ca, *a.* phrenological.
frenólogo, *m.* phrenologist.
frenópata, *m.* (med.) phrenopathologist, alienist.
frenopatía, *f.* 1. phrenopathy, medical science dealing with mental disease. 2. any mental disease or disorder.
frental, *a.* (anat.) frontal, of the forehead.
frentazo, *m.* (Mex.) rejection, rebuff.
frente, *f.* 1. forehead, brow. 2. front, front part. 3. (fig.) face, countenance; head. — **arrugar la f.,** (coll.) to frown, knit one's brow; **con la f. levantada,** calmly, boldly, with head held high; **de f.,** without hesitation; straight ahead (direction); **f. a,** in front of; in comparison with; **f. a f.,** face to face; **f. calzada,** low forehead; **f. de la onda,** (phys.) wave front; **f. por f.,** opposite. —*m.* 1. (fort.) front, face (of a bastion). 2. (polit.) front (e.g. united front). 3. (mil.) front rank. 4. (mil.) front, front line. 5. (meteorol.) front. — **al f., del f.,** (com.) carried forward (to the next page); **en f.,** in front, opposite, e.g. *en f. mío,* in front of me; **f. de batalla,** (mil.) firing line, battlefront; **f. frío,** (meteorol.) cold front; **f. polar,** (meteorol.) polar front; **f. único,** (polit.) united front; **hacer f. a,** to face, confront. —*m., f.* front (of a building); obverse (of a coin etc.). —*adv.* opposite, in front of; **f. a,** facing, opposite.
frentero, *m.* pad to protect a child's forehead.
frentón, na, *a.* having a large forehead, large-browed.
freo, *m.* (mar.) strait, narrow channel.
freón, *m.* (chem.) freon.
fresa, *f.* 1. (bot.) strawberry. 2. (mec.) drill, milling tool, bit, reamer.
fresada, *f.* dish prepared with flour, milk and butter.
fresado, *past part. of* **fresar.** —*m.* milling; reaming; drilling.
fresadora, *f.* milling machine.
fresal, *m.* strawberry patch.
fresar, *tr.v.* 1. to mill, ream, drill. 2. to decorate with friezes.
fresca, *f.* 1 cool air, fresh air, early morning breeze. 2. blunt remark, piece of one's mind, e.g. *decir a uno cuatro frescas,* to give someone a piece of one's mind.
frescachón, na, *a.* robust, ruddy, buxom; **viento frescachón,** brisk wind, fresh breeze.
frescal, *a.* slightly salted (fish).
frescales, *m., f.* (coll.) fresh or cheeky person.
frescamente, *adv.* 1. freshly, recently, lately. 2. (fig.) impertinently, coolly, bluntly.
fresco, ca, *a.* 1. fresh, cool. 2. fresh, new; cottage (cheese); newly laid, fresh (eggs). 3. ruddy, plump, buxom. 4. serene, cool, calm. 5. (coll.) fresh, bold, cheeky, forward, impertinent, brazen. 6. cool, light (cloth). —*m.* 1. coolness, freshness; fresh wind. 2. fresh fish; fresh bacon. 3. (p.) fresco. 4. (Amer.) cold drink. — **al f.,** in the open air, in the fresh air; **quedar uno f.,** (coll.) to fail, be disappointed.
frescor, *m.* 1. freshness. 2. (p.) pinkness (of flesh tones).
frescote, ta, *a.* (coll.) ruddy, healthy, rosy-cheeked.
frescura, *f.* 1. freshness, coolness. 2. luxuriant verdure or foliage. 3. impertinence, boldness, cheek, impertinent reply, piece of insolence. 4. unconcern, negligence, carelessness. 5. equanimity, serenity.
fresera, *f.* (bot.) strawberry plant.
fresero, ra, *m., f.* strawberry seller.
fresnal, *a.* pertaining to ash trees.
fresneda, *f.* ash tree grove.
fresnillo, *m.* (bot.) white fraxinella (Dictamus albus).
fresno, *m.* (bot.) ash tree (Fraxinus excelsior); ash (wood).
fresón, *m.* (bot.) Chilean strawberry (Fragaria chiloensis).
fresquecito, ta, *a.* (coll.) *dim. of* **fresco,** cool, nice and fresh. —*m.* cool breeze.
fresquedal, *m.* green spot, land which remains green during dry season.
fresquera, *f.* food safe, food cabinet (with mesh or screen sides to keep food cool).
fresquería, *f.* (S. Amer.) ice cream parlor, soda fountain.
fresquero, ra, *m., f.* fresh fish vendor.
fresquilla, *f.* (bot.) kind of peach.
fresquillo, *a., var. of* **fresquito.**
fresquista, *m.* painter of frescoes.
fresquito, ta, *dim. of* **fresco.** —*a.* 1. cool, coolish. 2. new, just made. 3. cool fresh air.
freudianismo, *m.* (psyc.) Freudianism.
freudiano, na, *a., m., f.* Freudian.
frey, *m.* Brother, Fra (appelation used by members of religious military orders).
frez, freza, *f.* dung, excrement.
freza, *f.* 1. spawning (of fishes); spawning season; trail, trench (left by spawning fish); spawn. 2. feeding period of silk worms during each mutation. 3. (hunt.) hole left by rooting animals.
frezada, *f.* blanket.
frezar, (*ref. 53*) *i.v.* to excrete (animals); to eject droppings of grubs from the hive. —*tr.v.* to clean out the hive (bees).
frezar, (*ref. 53*) *i.v.* 1. to spawn. 2. to rub against the sea-bed while spawning (fishes). 3. to feed (silkworms). 4. (hunt.) to root or scratch the ground (animals).
friabilidad, *f.* friability, brittleness.
friable, *a.* friable, brittle.
frialdad, *f.* 1. coldness, coolness. 2. (sexual) frigidity. 3. (fig.) indifference, unconcern, lack of interest.
fríamente, *adv.* 1. coldly, coolly. 2. flatly, dully, colorlessly.

friático, ca, *a.* 1. susceptible to the cold. 2. silly, awkward, foolish.
frica, *f.* (Chile) beating, whipping.
fricación, *f.* rubbing, friction.
fricandó, *m.* (cul.) fricandeau, a French type stew.
fricar, (*ref. 50*) *tr.v.* to rub.
fricasé, *m.* (cul.) fricassee.
fricativo, va, *a., f.* (phonet.) fricative.
fricción, *f.* 1. rub, rubbing; massage; (mec.) friction. 2. friction, discord.
friccionar, *tr.v.* to rub; to massage.
friega, *f.* 1. massage, rubbing. 2. (Col., C. Rica) annoyance, bother, nuisance. 3. (Chile) beating, whipping.
friego, friegue, *ref.* **fregar.**
friendo, friera, *ref.* **freír.**
friera, *f.* chilblain.
friese, *ref.* **freír.**
friga, *f.* (myth.) Frigga.
frigidez, *f.* coldness, frigidity; (med.) frigidity, lack of sexual desire.
frígido, da, *a.* cold, frigid.
frigio, gia, *a., m., f.* (hist.) Phrygian.
frigorífero, *m.* (Amer.) *var. of* **frigorífico.**
frigorífico, ca, *a.* refrigerating, refrigerator, freezing. —*m.* refrigerator; cold-storage plant; refrigerator ship; (ry.) refrigerator van or car.
frijol, *m.* dry bean. — **f. negro,** black bean; **f. colorado,** kidney bean.
frijolar, *m.* bean field.
frimario, *m.* Frimaire (third month of French Revolutionary calendar).
fringilago, *m.* (ornith.) great titmouse.
fringílidos, *m.* (*pl.*) (ornith.) Fringillidae.
frío, a, *a.* 1. cold, frigid. 2. (fig.) cold, cool (reception, reply, welcome, etc.). 3. (sexually) frigid, cold. 4. (fig.) dull, flat, colorless, insipid. — **en f.,** hard-, e.g. *estirado en f.,* hard-drawn; **quedarse f.,** to be left speechless or dumbfounded. —*m.* cold, coldness; **hacer f.,** to be cold (weather); **no darle a uno f. ni calor,** to leave one indifferent; **tener f.,** to be cold (a person); **fríos,** (Amer.) malaria.
frío, frió, fría, *ref.* **freír.**
friolento, ta, *a.* susceptible to the cold.
friolera, *f.* 1. trifle, trinket, bauble. 2. (iron.) of no importance, only, e.g. *ella tiene la f. de cien años,* she's only a hundred years old.
friolero, ra, *a.* 1. susceptible to the cold. 2. (iron.) of great importance.
frión, na, *a.* dull, insipid, colorless.
frisa, *f.* 1. frieze, woolen fabric. 2. (Arg., Chile) friz, nap (of material). 3. (fort.) fraise. 4. (mar.) weatherstripping.
frisado, *past part. of* **frisar.** —*m.* frizzed silk fabric.
frisador, ra, *m., f.* friezer, frizzler, person employed in frizzing cloth.
frisadura, *f.* frizzing, frizzling, friezing (of cloth).
frisar, *tr.v.* 1. to frizz, frizzle, frieze (cloth). 2. to rub. 3. to line, pack (with rubber, leather or cloth to ensure the tight shutting of openings). —*i.v.* 1. to get along, agree. 2. to approach, border, draw near. — **f. en,** to border on, approach.
frisio, sia, *a., m., f.* (hist.) Frisian. —*f.* **F.,** Friesland.
friso, *m.* (archit.) frieze; wainscot, dado.
frísol, *m.* (bot.) bean.
frisón, na, *a., m., f.* Frisian. —*m.* Frisian (language).
frisuelo, *m.* 1. (bot.) small bean. 2. (*pl.*) fritters, crullers.
frita, *f.* 1. (cer.) ferretto, frit. 2. (Cuba) hamburger sandwich.
fritada, *f.* fry (dish of anything fried).
fritado, *past part. of* **fritar.** —*m.* fritting.
fritanga, *f.* fry (dish of anything fried, especially in a great amount of fat).
fritar, *tr.v.* (cer.) to frit.
fritillas, *f.* (*pl.*) fritters, crullers, pancakes.
frito, ta, *past part. of* **freír.** —*a.* fried; **estar f.,** (coll.) to be sunk, be done for. —*m.* 1. fry (dish of anything fried). 2. (Ven.) daily food. —*f.* frit.
fritura, *f.* fry (dish of anything fried); (*pl.*) fritters.
friura, *f.* (reg., Ven.) coldness, coolness.
frívolamente, *adv.* frivolously.
frivolidad, *f.* frivolity, frivolousness.
frivolité, *f.* tatting, fancy handwork.
frívolo, la, *a.* frivolous.
friz, (*pl.* **frices**) *f.* beech tree blossom.
fronda, *f.* 1. (bot.) frond, leaf, shoot. 2. grove. 3. (*pl.*) frondage, foliage. 4. (surg.) sling-shaped bandage, sling.
fronde, *m.* (bot.) frond (of a fern).
frondífero, ra, *a.* frondescent, leafy, luxuriant.
frondio, dia, *a.* (Col., Mex.) dirty, unkempt, ill-humored.
frondosidad, *f.* abundance of foliage.
frondoso, sa, *a.* leafy, abounding in leaves or trees; luxuriant.
frontal, *a.* frontal; **ataque f.,** frontal attack; **hueso f.,** (anat.) frontal, frontal bone. —*m.* 1. frontal, frontlet. 2. (ecc.) (altar) frontal. 3. (anat.) frontal. 4. (Amer.) front (band of bridle, crossing the forehead). 5. (archit.) beam, girder.
frontalera, *f.* 1. front (band or bridle, crossing the forehead); yoke pad (of oxen's yoke). 2. altar frontal trimmings; altar frontal container.
frontalete, *m. dim. of* **frontal,** small altar frontal.
frontera, *f.* 1. frontier. 2. front, frontage; front wall. 3. reinforcing binder (in a wickerwork basket). 4. (mas.) board used to support the mold of a mudwall.
fronterizo, za, *a.* 1. frontier, border. 2. facing, opposite. — **f. a,** opposite, facing.
frontero, ra, *a.* facing, opposite. —*m.* 1. child's frontlet or brow band. 2. frontier commander.
frontil, *m.* yoke pad (of ox).
frontín, *m.* 1. (Mex.) blow on the head. 2. (Cuba) headstall (of bridle).
frontino, na, *a.* marked on the face or forehead (said of animals).
frontis, *m.* frontispiece, facade.
frontispicio, *m.* 1. frontispiece (of a book, etc.) 2. (coll.) face. 3. (archit.) frontispiece, facade; pediment, gable.
frontogénesis, *f.* (meteorol.) frontogenesis.
frontólisis, *f.* (meteorol.) frontolysis.
frontón, *m.* 1. (archit.) pediment; gable. 2. main wall (in pelota court); pelota court. 3. (min.) part of wall of a seam. 4. cliff, rocky promontory.
frontudo, da, *a.* big-browed.
frotación, *f.* rubbing.
frotador, ra, *a.* rubbing. —*m., f.* rubber, one who rubs.
frotadura, *f.* rubbing; friction.
frotamiento, *m.* rubbing; friction.
frotante, *a.* rubbing.
frotar, *tr.v.* to rub.—*r.v.* to rub, rub together.
frote, *m.* rubbing, friction.
frotis, *m.* (bac.) smear; **f. sanguíneo,** (med.) blood smear.
fructidor, *m.* Fructidor (twelfth month of French Revolutionary calendar).
fructíferamente, *adv.* fruitfully.
fructífero, ra, *a.* fructiferous, fruit bearing; (lit., fig.) fruitful.
fructificación, *f.* fructification.
fructificador, ra, *a.* fructifying.
fructificar, (*ref. 50*) *i.v* to fructify, bear fruit; (fig.) to be productive or fruitful.
fructifique, fructifiqué, *ref.* **fructificar.**
fructosa, *f.* (chem.) fructose.
fructuario, ria, *a.* (law) usufructuary.
fructuosamente, *adv.* fruitfully; profitably.
fructuoso, sa, *a.* fruitful; profitable.
fruente, *a.* enjoying.
frufrú, *m.* (tex.) froufrou.
frugal, *a.* frugal.
frugalidad, *f.* frugality.
frugalmente, *adv.* frugally.
frugífero, ra, *a.* (poet.) fructiferous, fruit-bearing.
frugívoro, ra, *a.* frugivorous, fruit-eating.
fruición, *f.* fruition, pleasure, enjoyment, satisfaction; gloating enjoyment or pleasure.
fruir, (*ref. 48*) *i.v* to enjoy what one has achieved or obtained.
fruitivo, va, *a.* enjoyable, pleasurable.
frumentario, ria, *a.* frumentaceous, made of or resembling grain. —*m.* (arch.) Roman officer in charge of wheat shipment for the army.
frumenticio, cia, *a.* frumentaceous.
frunce, *m.* (dressm.) pleat; shirr, gather.
fruncido, da, *past part. of* **fruncir.** —*a.* 1. (sew.) shirred, gathered. 2. (coll.,Amer.) squeamish, affected (person).
fruncidor, ra, *m., f.* shirrer, pleater.
fruncimiento, *m.* 1. (dressm.) shirring, gathering; pleating. 2. trick, pretense.
fruncir, (*ref. 61*) *tr.v.* 1. to knit (eyebrows); to purse (lips). 2. (dressm.) to shirr, gather, pleat. 3. to contract, reduce; to wrinkle, pucker. 4. to conceal, disguise (truth). —*r.v.* to affect modesty.
frunza, frunzo, *ref.* **fruncir.**
fruslera, *f.* brass scrapings or filings.
fruslería, *f.* 1. trifle, trinket. 2. (coll.) triviality; inanity, inane remark.
fruslero, ra, *a.* trifling, trivial, frivolous.
frustración, *f.* frustration, disappointment.
frustráneo, a, *a.* useless, vain, ineffectual, nugatory.
frustrar, *tr.v.* to frustrate, thwart, defeat. —*r.v.* to be frustrated, or thwarted, come to nothing, be a failure.
frustratorio, ria, *a.* frustrating, frustrative.
frustro, tra, *a.* (archeol.) blurred, indistinct (usually said of coins, inscriptions, etc.).
frústulo, *m.* (bot., paleon.) frustule.
fruta, *f.* 1. fruit (edible fruits). 2. fruit, product, result. **f. del tiempo,** fruit eaten in season; **f. de sartén,** fritters, crullers, pancakes, etc.; **f. nueva,** novelty, innovation; **f. prohibida,** forbidden fruit; **frutas secas,** dried fruit; nuts.
frutaje, *m.* (p.) painting of fruit and flowers.
frutal, *a.* pertaining to fruit, fruit-like. —*m.* fruit tree; orchard.
frutar, *i.v.* to bear fruit.
frutecer, (*ref. 45*) *i.v.* (poet.) to bear fruit.
frutería, *f.* fruit shop.
frutero, ra, *a.* fruit (as *a.*). —*m., f.* fruiterer, fruit seller. —*m.* fruit dish or plate; embroidered fruit cover; painting of fruit; basket of imitation fruit.
frutescente, *a.* (bot.) frutescent.
frutezca, *ref.* **frutecer.**
frútice, *m.* (bot.) shrub, frutex.
fruticoso, sa, *a.* (bot.) fruticose.
fruticuloso, sa, *a.* (bot.) fruticose; fruticulose.
fruticultura, *f.* (bot.) fruitgrowing, cultivation of fruit trees.
frutilla, *f.* 1. rosary bead. 2. (Arg., Chile) (bot.) (species of) strawberry. — **f. del campo,** (Chile) Chilean strawberry (Fragaria chiloensis).
frutillar, *m.* (Chile) strawberry field.
frutillero, *m.* (Chile) strawberry seller.
fruto, *m.* 1. fruit (result, product). 2. (bot.) fruit (as part or name of a plant). 3. (*pl.*) fruits; products, commodities. — **dar f.,** to bear fruit; **f. de bendición,** legitimate child; **frutos civiles,** (law) civil

benefits; **frutos en especie,** fungibles, fungible goods; **frutos secos,** nuts and dried fruit; **sacar f.,** to derive or get benefit.

fruya, fruyo, *ref.* **fruir.**

ftaleína, *f.* (chem.) phthalein.

ftálico, ca, *a.* (chem.) phthalic.

ftiriasis, *f.* (med.) phthiriasis.

fu, *interj.* 1. spit or hiss (of a cat). 2. phoo, phoey (expression of contempt). — **hacer f.** or **f. como el gato,** (coll.) to dart off, run away; **ni f. ni fa,** (coll.) neither good nor bad, indifferent, mediocre.

fúcar, *m.* rich man, nabob, Croesus.

fucilar, *i.v.* (poet.) to flash (sheet-lightning); to sparkle, shine.

fucilazo, *m.* sheet lightning, heat lightning.

fuco, *m.* (bot.) fucus, seaweed.

fucsia, *f.* (bot.) fuchsia.

fucsina, *f.* (chem.) fuchsin, fuchsine.

fue, *ref.* **ir; ser.**

fuego, *m.* 1. fire. 2. light (for cigarette, etc.), e.g. *¿tienes f. por favor?* could you give me a light please? 3. signal light or beacon. 4. fire, firing, discharge (of firearms). 5. hearth, home. 6. rash, skin eruption. 7. fire, ardor, fervor; violence. 8. (fort.) flank. 9. (vet.) cautery, cauterization. — **a f. lento,** slowly, little by little; (cul.) on a low flame, in a slow oven, at a low heat; **a sangre y f.,** mercilessly, with fire and sword; violently; **apagar los fuegos,** (mil.) to silence enemy fire; (coll.) to squash or get the better of (someone) in an argument; to take the wind out of (someone's) sails; **arma de f.,** firearm; **atizar el f.,** to stir up trouble; **donde f. se hace, humo sale,** where there is smoke, there is fire; **entre dos fuegos,** between two fires; **estar hecho un f.,** to be seething with anger; to be very worked up; **f. cruzado,** (mil.) cross fire; **f. de apoyo,** (mil.) supporting fire; **f. de cortina,** (mil.) curtain fire; curtain of fire; **f. defensivo,** (mil.) defensive fire; **f. de protección,** (mil.) covering fire; **f. de San Antón** or **San Marcial,** (med.) St. Anthony's fire; **f. de Santelmo,** St. Elmo's fire, corposant; **f. entrecruzado,** (mil.) interlocking fire; **f. fatuo,** ignis fatuus, will-o'-the-wisp; **f. graneado,** (mil.) drumfire, incessant fire; **f. griego,** Greek fire; **f. real,** live ammunition; **fuegos artificiales,** fireworks; **hacer f.,** to fire, shoot; **huir del f. y dar en las brasas,** to jump from the frying-pan into the fire; **jugar con f.,** to play with fire; **levantar f.,** to stir up trouble; **pegar f. a,** to set afire; **poner** or **meter a sangre y f.,** to put to the sword, devastate, destroy; **romper el f.,** to open fire; to start a quarrel or fight. —*interj.* **¡fuego!** fire!

fueguecillo, fueguecito, fueguezuelo, *m. dim. of* **fuego,** small fire.

fueguino, na, *a., m., f.* Fuegian, pertaining to Tierra del Fuego.

fuellar, *m.* colored talcum powder (used for adornment of candles or wax tapers).

fuelle, *m.* 1. bellows; wind bag (of bagpipes). 2. pucker, crease, fold (in dress). 3. folding hood (of carriage). 4. expansible side (of purse, wallet, etc.). 5. clouds over mountains. 6. (coll.) gossipmonger, tattle-tale.

fuente, *f.* 1. spring (of water); fountain. 2. waterspout, tap; water supply system. 3. source, fount; origin. 4. font, baptismal font. 5. dish, platter; dishful. 6. (vet.) gaskin. 7. (med.) issue, artificial ulcer (made to draw out pus). — **beber en buenas fuentes,** to get knowledge or information from reliable sources; **f. cuasiestelar de radio,** quasi-stellar radio source; **f. de beber,** drinking fountain; **f. de energía C,** (rad.) C power supply; **F. de Juventud,** (hist., philos.) Fountain of Youth; **f. de los deseos,** wishing well; **f. de soda,** soda fountain.

fuentezuela, *f. dim. of* **fuente,** small spring; small fountain.

fuer, *m. apocope of* **fuero.** —*adv.* **a f. de,** as a, in the manner of, e.g. *a fuer de noble,* as a nobleman.

fuera, *adv.* outside; out; **de f.,** outside; **estar f. de casa,** to be out; **estar f. de sí,** to be beside oneself (with anger, joy, grief); **f. de,** outside, outside of; except for, apart from; in addition to; **f. de propósito,** inopportune, untimely; **f. de que,** aside from the fact that; **por f.,** on the outside. —*interj.* **¡fuera!** get out!; take off (article of clothing).

fuera, *ref.* **ir; ser.**

fuerarropa, *interj.* **hacer f.,** a command used to order prisoners to disrobe.

fuerce, *ref.* **forzar.**

fuerista, *m., f.* specialist in law; vigorous defender of **fueros** (provincial or state autonomy, civil rights, etc.).

fuero, *m.* 1. law, statute. 2. jurisdiction, power. 3. code of laws. 4. state or provincial privilege, exemption. 5. (*pl.*) (coll.) arrogance, presumption. — **f. de la conciencia,** conscience, heart of hearts; **f. interno** or **interior,** conscience; **a f.,** according to custom; **de f.,** (law) de jure.

fuerte, *a.* 1. strong. 2. robust, vigorous. 3. hard (as diamond). 4. rough, craggy. 5. strongly fortified. 6. silver (coin); overweight (coin). 7. extremely harsh or severe. 8. very good, well-versed, proficient (in a subject). 9. (gram.) strong (verb). — **la pelicula era muy f.,** the film was very powerful. —*m.* 1. fort, fortress. 2. forte, strong point. —*adv.* strongly, copiously, high.

fuertemente, *adv.* 1. (to hit or squeeze) hard. 2. (to speak) loudly, vehemently, passionately. 3. tremendously, greatly (of rising prices). 4. (to punish) severely. 5. closely (guarded).

fuerza, *f.* 1. strength; power, might; vigor, robustness. 2. force, violence, compulsion. 3. rape, violation. 4. stronghold, fortress; fortifications. 5. (mec.) force; power. 6. force, body (of police, firemen, etc.); (*pl.*) (mil.) forces, e.g. *fuerzas armadas,* armed forces. 7. (tail.) interlining. 8. (fenc.) upper third of a sword including the hilt. — **a f. de,** by dint of; by means of, because of; **a la f., por f.,** by force, forcibly; of necessity, perforce; **a viva f.,** by bodily force; **cobrar fuerzas,** to recover one's strength; **f. aceleratriz,** accelerating force; **f. aérea,** air force; **f. animal,** animal power; **f. armada,** army; **f. bruta,** brute force; **f. capilar,** (phys.) capillary attraction; **f. centrifuga,** (phys.) centrifugal force; **f. centrípeta,** (phys.) centripetal force; **f. de gravedad,** (phys.) force of gravity; gravitational force; **f. de inercia,** (phys.) force of inertia; **f. de sustentación,** lift; **f. de tareas,** taskforce; **f. de trabajo,** workforce; **f. de voluntad,** willpower; **f. disuasoria** or **de disuasión,** deterrent; **f. electromotriz,** (mec.) electromotive force; **f. hidráulica,** waterpower, hydraulic power; **f. mayor,** act of God, unforeseen circumstances, force majeure; **f. motriz,** motive power; **f. policial,** or **pública,** police force; **f. retardatriz,** deceleration; police force; **f. viva,** (phys.) actual or kinetic energy; **fuerzas del orden** or **de orden público,** police; **fuerzas paralelas,** (phys.) parallel forces; **fuerzas vivas,** industry, commerce and banking; **sacar uno fuerzas de flaqueza,** to make a tremendous effort (to do something); **ser f.,** to be necessary, imperative or obligatory.

fuerzo, *ref.* **forzar.**

fuese, *ref.* **ir; ser.**

fuetazo, *m.* (Amer.) lash, whiplash.

fuete, *m.* (Amer.) whip.

fufú, *m.* (Cuba, cul.) dish made of mashed plantains and pork rind.

fuga, *f.* 1. flight, escape, runaway; elopement. 2. leak, leakage. 3. (mus.) fugue. — **f. de cerebros,** (Chile) brain drain; **f. de consonantes** or **vocales,** word game where consonants or vowels are replaced by dots; **poner en f.,** to put to flight; **se dio a la f.,** he (she) escaped.

fugacidad, *f.* fugacity, brevity; evanescence.

fugada, *f.* gust (of wind).

fugarse, (*ref.* 51) *r.v.* to flee, run away, escape.

fugaz, (*pl.* **fugaces**) *a.* fleeting, brief, short, transitory, evanescent; volatile (perfume). — **estrella f.,** shooting star; **amor f.,** infatuation.

fugazmente, *adv.* fleetingly, briefly.

fugitivo, va, *a.* passing; brief, transitory, momentary. —*m., f.* fugitive, runaway, escapee.

fugue, fugué, *ref.* **fugarse.**

fuguillas, *m.* (coll.) fast worker, live wire.

fui, *ref.* **ir; ser.**

fuina, *f.* (zool.) stone marten, beech marten.

ful, *a.* (sl.) sham, false.

fulano, na, *m., f.* so-and-so; chap, bloke, fellow. — **f. de tal,** so-and-so, John Doe, Jane Doe; **F., Zutano, Mengano,** the butcher, the baker, the candlestick maker; Tom, Dick and Harry.

fular, *m.* (tex.) foulard, flexible silk material.

fulastre, *a.* (coll.) rough, careless, shoddy, slipshod.

fulcro, *m.* (mec.) fulcrum.

fulero, ra, *a.* 1. (coll.) useless, poor, unsatisfactory. 2. untruthful.

fulgente, fúlgido, da, *a.* brilliant, shining, fulgent, flashing.

fulgir, (*ref.* 62) *i.v.* to flash, sparkle, glitter.

fulgor, *m.* brilliance, brightness; splendor.

fulguración, *f.* flash, flashing; (med.) lightning stroke.

fulgurante, *a.* flashing, fulgurant, resplendent.

fulgurar, *i.v.* to flash, fulgurate; to sparkle.

fulgurezca, *ref.* **fulgurecer.**

fulgurita, *f.* (geol.) fulgurite, vitrified crust produced by fusion of rock due to lightning.

fulguroso, sa, *a.* flashing, fulgurant, fulgurous.

fúlica, *f.* (ornith.) coot.

fuliginoso, sa, *a.* fuliginous, sooty, blackened.

fulja, *ref.* **fulgir.**

fullear, *i.v.* to cheat.

fullería, *f.* cheating (at cards); trick; guile, astuteness.

fullero, ra, *a.* cheating, deceiving. —*m.* card sharp, cheat.

fullona, *f.* (coll.) row, quarrel.

fulminación, *f.* fulmination; thundering, explosion.

fulminador, ra, *a.* fulminating. —*m., f.* fulminator.

fulminante, *a.* 1. fulminating. 2. (med.) fulminating, galloping, sudden. 3. (chem.) fulminating. —*m.* 1. (chem.) fulminating powder, fulminate. 2. (artil.) cap, percussion cap (of bullet, of child's pistol).

fulminar, *tr.v.* 1. to strike or kill with lightning; (fig.) to strike, wound, censure (e.g. with a glance). 2. to throw, hurl. 3. to thunder, fulminate (threats). —*i.v.* to explode, fulminate.

fulminato, *m.* (chem.) fulminate.

fulminatriz, *a., var. of* **fulminadora.**

fulmíneo, a, *a.* fulmineous.

fulmínico, ca, *a.* (chem.) fulminic.

fulminoso, sa, *a.* fulminatory.

fumable, *a.* smokable, good to smoke.

fumada, *f.* puff of smoke.
fumadero, *m.* smoking-room, smoking compartment. — **f. de opio,** (fig.) licentious place, den of iniquity.
fumador, ra, *a.* smoking. —*m., f.* smoker.
fumante, *a.* smoking.
fumar, *tr.v., i.v.* to smoke. —*r.v.* 1. (fig.) to squander, spend, e.g. *me fumé el sueldo,* I squandered my salary. 2. (fig.) to miss, dodge (a class) (G.B.), be absent from (the office).
fumarada, *f.* 1. puff (of smoke). 2. amount of tobacco held in a pipe.
fumaria, *f.* (bot.) fumitory.
fumárico, *a.* (chem.) fumaric (acid).
fumarilo, *m.* (chem.) fumaryl.
fumarina, *m.* (chem.) fumarine.
fumarola, *f.* (geol.) fumarole.
fumífero, ra, *a.* (poet.) smoking, fumiferous.
fumífugo, ga, *a.* smoke-spraying.
fumigación, *f.* fumigation.
fumigador, ra, *m., f.* fumigator (person). —*m.* fumigator (instrument).
fumigar, (*ref. 51*) *tr.v.* to fumigate.
fumigatorio, ria, *a.* fumigatory. —*m.* perfume atomizer.
fumigue, fumigué, *ref.* **fumigar.**
fumista, *m.* stove maker, dealer or repairman; heating pipe plumber.
fumistería, *f.* stove works, heating pipe shop.
fumívoro, ra, *a.* smokeless, smoke-absorbing.
fumorola, *f.* (geol.) fumarole.
fumosidad, *f.* smokiness.
fumoso, sa, *a.* smoky, fumy.
funambulesco, ca, *a.* funambulatory; pertaining to tight-rope walking.
funámbulo, la, *m., f.* funambulist, tight-rope walker.
función, *f.* 1. function; operation. 2. function, ceremony; show, performance. 3. (math.) function. 4. (mil.) action. — **entrar en f.,** to go into action; **entrar en funciones,** to take office, begin duties; **f. benéfica,** benefit performance; **f. continua** or **continuada,** continuous performance; **f. de medianoche** or **de noche** or **de trasnoche,** late show; **f. doble,** double feature; **f. gramatical,** part of speech; **f. periódica,** (math.) periodic function; **f. vectorial,** (engin.) vector function.
funcional, *a.* functional, operating.
funcionalismo, *m.* functionalism.
funcionamiento, *m.* functioning, working, operation.
funcionar, *i.v.* to function, work, run, act; **no funciona** (señal) out of order.
funcionario, *m.* official, functionary.
funda, *f.* case, cover; sheath. — **f. de almohada,** pillowcase, pillowslip.
fundación, *f.* foundation; endowment; establishment, founding; beginning, origin.
fundadamente, *adv.* with good reason, having proof or evidence.
fundador, ra, *a.* founding. —*m., f.* founder. — **el f. de la casa,** the founder of the firm.
fundamental, *a.* fundamental, essential, basic.
fundamentalismo, *m.* (rel.) fundamentalism.
fundamentalista, *a., m., f.* (rel.) fundamentalist.
fundamentalmente, *adv.* fundamentally, in principle.
fundamentar, *tr.v.* 1. to lay the foundations of. 2. (fig.) to make firm, establish.
fundamento, *m.* 1. foundation; basis. 2. grounds, reason. 3. seriousness, reliability. 4. (tex.) weft, woof.
fundar, *tr.v.* 1. to found (institution, city, empire). 2. to base, ground, found (opinions). —*r.v.* to be founded. — **fundarse, en,** to base one's opinion on.

fundente, *a.* (chem.) fusing. —*m.* 1. (chem.) flux. 2. (med.) resolvent (medicine to disperse inflammatory lesions). — **f. para soldar,** soldering flux.
fundería, *f.* foundry, smelting plant.
fundible, *a.* fusible.
fundibulario, *m.* (hist.) Roman soldier who operated the trebuchet.
fundíbulo, *m.* trebuchet, ancient military catapult.
fundición, *f.* 1. melting; smelting. 2. casting, founding. 3. foundry, ironworks. 4. cast iron. 5. (print.) font of type. — **f. en arena seca,** dry casting; **f. gris,** (metal) gray iron.
fúndico, ca, *a.* (anat.) fundic.
fundido, da, *past part. of* **fundir.** —*a.* 1. cast, e.g. *hierro f.,* cast iron. 2. (Amer., sl.) penniless, broke; worn-out, exhausted.
fundidor, *m.* 1. founder, foundryman; smelter. 2. caster.
fundillos, *m.* (*pl.*) *var. of* **fondillos.**
fundir, *tr.v.* 1. to melt; to smelt. 2. to cast, found. 3. (Amer., coll.) to annoy, irritate. —*r.v.* 1. to melt. 2. to fuse, join, unite, merge. 3. (Amer., coll.) to be ruined, bankrupt; worn-out. 4. to blow (fuse, electric lamp, bulb).
fundo, *m.* country estate, farm.
fundón, *m.* 1. (Col.) woman's riding habit or skirt. 2. (Chile) large cover or sheath.
fúnebre, *a.* funeral; funereal, gloomy. — **pompas fúnebres,** funeral rites; **marcha f.,** funeral march.
fúnebremente, *adv.* funereally, gloomily.
funeral, *a.* funeral. —*m.* funeral, (*pl.*) funeral.
funerala, *adv.* (mil.) **a la f.,** with weapons pointed downward (in honor of the dead).
funerario, ria, *a.* funeral. —*m.* undertaker, mortician. —*f.* funeral parlor, undertaker's establishment, undertaking business.
funéreo, a, *a.* (poet.) funereal, dismal, gloomy.
funes, meterse a f., (Col.) to meddle, interfere.
funestamente, *adv.* fatally; unfortunately.
funestar, *tr.v.* to profane, defile, blemish.
funesto, ta, *a.* fatal, ill-fated; unfortunate, mournful.
fungible, *a.* (law) fungible.
fungicida, *a.* fungicidal. —*m.* fungicide.
fungiforme, *a.* fungiform, mushroom-shaped.
fungir, (*ref. 62*) *i.v.* (Amer.) to act, function (in some capacity). — **f. de,** to act or function as surrogate.
fungo, *m.* (med.) fungus.
fungoideo, a, *a.* fungoid, characteristic of a fungus.
fungosidad, *f.* (med.) fungosity.
fungoso, sa, *a.* fungous.
funguino, na, *a.* (bot.) fungal.
funiculado, da, *a.* funiculate, attached by a cord, cable, stem, trunk.
funicular, *a.* funicular. —*m.* cable car.
funículo, *m.* 1. (bot., zool., anat.) funiculus. 2. (archit.) cable moulding.
funja, funjo, *ref.* **fungir.**
fuñido, da, *a.* (Cuba) weak, sickly, puny.
fuñique, *a.* 1. clumsy, awkward, incompetent. 2. fussy, overly particular.
furare, *m.* (Chile, ornith.) thrush.
furcia, *f.* (coll.) girl, doll, chick.
fúrcula, *f.* (anat.) furcula.
furente, *a.* (poet.) furious, irate, raging.
fúrfura, *f.* (med.) furfur.
furfuráceo, a, *a.* furfuraceous.
furfural, *m.* (chem.) furfural.
furfurol, *m.* (chem.) furfural.
furgón, *m.* van, wagon; (ry.) luggage van, baggage car, boxcar; freight car; **f. de cola,** (ry.) caboose.

furgoneta, *f.* truck, van, delivery van or truck.
furia, *f.* 1. fury, rage, anger; violent or angry person; violence, fierceness; frenzy, enthusiasm. 2. (myth.) **F.,** Fury.
furibundo, da, *a.* furious, irate, enraged.
furiente, *a., var. of* **furente.**
furierismo, *m.* (philos.) Fourierism, pertaining to the social principles of Fourier.
furierista, *a.* Fourieristic. —*m., f.* Fourierist.
furiosamente, *adv.* furiously, frantically.
furioso, sa, *a.* furious, raving; (fig.) tremendous, excessive.
furlón, *m.* ancient lightweight carriage.
furo, ra, *a.* shy, bashful. —*m.* (Cuba) hole or opening (at bottom of sugar loaf mold).
furor, *m.* furor, rage. — **hacer f.,** to be the rage; **f. uterino,** (med.) nymphomania; **tener f. por,** to be a fan of.
furriel, furrier, *m.* 1. (mil.) fourier, quartermaster. 2. manager of the royal stables.
furriela, furriera, *f.* stewardship, office of steward of royal household.
furris, *a.* (coll.) shoddy, badly made or done.
furruco, *m.* (Ven.) type of small sonorous drum.
furrusca, *f.* (Col.) row, dispute, commotion, quarrel, squabble.
furtivamente, *adv.* furtively, stealthily.
furtivo, va, *a.* furtive.
furuminga, *f.* (Chile) muddle, jumble, tangle, confusion.
furuncular, *a.* (med.) furuncular.
furúnculo, *m.* (med.) furuncle, boil.
furunculosis, *f.* (med.) furunculosis.
furunculoso, sa, *a.* (med.) furunculous.
fusa, *f.* (mus.) demisemiquaver.
fusado, da, *a.* (her.) spindly, charged with fusils.
fusca, *f.* (ornith.) black duck, black scoter.
fuscina, *f.* (biochem.) fuscin.
fusco, ca, *a.* dark, fuscous, dusky.
fuselado, da, *m.* (aer.) fairing, streamlining. —*a.* streamlined.
fuselaje, *m.* (aer.) fuselage.
fusente, *a.* receding (tide).
fusibilidad, *f.* fusibility.
fusible, *a.* fusible. —*m.* (elec.) fuse. — **f. de cinta,** (elec.) strip fuse.
fusiforme, *a.* fusiform, spindle-shaped.
fúsil, *a.* fusible.
fusil, *m.* (mil.) rifle, gun. — **f. ametrallador,** submachine gun.
fusilamiento, *m.* shooting, execution.
fusilar, *tr.v.* 1. to shoot, execute by shooting. 2. (coll.) to plagiarize.
fusilazo, *m.* 1. rifle shot, shot. 2. sheet lightning.
fusilería, *f.* 1. rifles, guns. 2. fusiliers, riflemen.
fusilero, ra, *a.* rifle, gun. —*m.* fusilier, rifleman.
fusión, *f.* fusion; (fig.) amalgamation, merging, union; melting. — **f. de empresas,** (com.) merger; **f. nuclear,** (phys.) nuclear fusion.
fusionar, *tr.v., r.v.* to combine, merge, amalgamate, unite.
fusionismo, *m.* (pol.) fusionism, coalition.
fusionista, *a., m., f.* (pol.) fusionist.
fusique, *m.* snuff bottle.
fuslina, *f.* smelting works, smeltry.
fusor, *m.* smelting ladle, smelting vessel.
fusta, *f.* 1. brushwood, twigs. 2. coachman's whip. 3. woolen cloth. 4. lateen-rigged vessel.
fustal, fustán, *m.* 1. (tex.) fustian. 2. (Amer.) cotton petticoat.
fustanero, *m.* 1. fustian maker. 2. (Amer., arch.) petticoat maker.
fustaño, *m., var. of* **fustán.**
fuste, *m.* 1. wood, timber. 2. pole; shaft (of lance). 3. (archit.) fust, shaft of a column. 4. (*pl.*) bows (of saddletree). 5. (poet.) saddle. 6. importance,

substance. 7. essence, purport, fundamental idea (of speech, etc.). — **hombre de poco f.,** a man of little import.
fustete, *m.* (bot.) fustet, smoke tree (Cotinus coggyria).
fustigación, *f.* 1. whipping. 2. severe censure.
fustigador, ra, *a.* whipping. —*m., f.* 1. whipper. 2. censurer.
fustigante, *a.* whipping, flaying.
fustigar, (*ref. 51*) *tr.v.* 1. to whip. 2. (fig.) to censure, lash out against.
fustigue, fustigué, *ref.* **fustigar.**
fútbol, *m.* football, soccer.
futbolista, *m.* footballer (G.B.), soccer player.
futbolístico, ca, *a.* of or pertaining to football.
futearse, *r.v.* (Col.) to go rotten or bad, to get spoiled (esp. potatoes).
futesa, *f.* trifle, gewgaw, bauble, bagatelle.
fútil, *a.* futile, trivial, unimportant.
futilidad, *f.* futility.
futraque, *m.* 1. (coll., rare) frock-coat. 2. dandy; panty-waist.
futre, *m.* (Amer.) dandy, dude; fashionably-dressed man.
futura, *f.* 1. reversion (right of future possession of an estate or post when vacant). 2. (coll.) fiancée, intended bride.
futurable, *a.* possible future, e.g. *Colin Powell es un futurable presidente de los EE.UU.,* Colin Powell is a possible future president of the U.S.
futurario, ria, *a.* reversionary.
futurismo, *m.* (art.) futurism.
futurista, *m.* (art.) futurist, futuristic.
futuro, ra, *a.* future. —*m.* 1. future. 2. (coll.) future husband, fiancé. 3. (gram.) future. 4. (*pl.*) (com.) futures. — **f. perfecto,** (gram.) future perfect.

G

G, *f.* g, seventh letter of the Spanish alphabet.
g., *abbrev. of* **gravedad,** acceleration of gravity (g.).
g., *abbrev. of* **gramo,** gram (g.).
Ga *sym. of* **galio,** gallium (Ga).
gabachada, *f.* (Sp., derog.) 1. improper action. 2. foreign word.
gabacho, cha, *a.* 1. Pyrenean. 2. (coll., derog.) Frenchified, French. —*m., f.* 1. Pyrenean. 2. (coll., derog.) Frenchman. —*m.* (coll.) Gallicized Spanish.
gabán, *m.* overcoat.
gabanearse, *r.v.* (C. Amer.) to take, make off with.
gabardina, *f.* 1. gabardine; raincoat. 2. (tex.) twill.
gabarra, *f.* (mar.) barge, freight boat.
gabarrero, *m.* (mar.) bargeman.
gabarro, *m.* 1. (min.) nodule. 2. (tex.) flaw (in cloth). 3. (bldg.) filling (to fill faults in masonry). 4. (vet.) roup. 5. nuisance, bother. 6. mistake (in accounts). 7. (vet.) tumor in horse's foot.
gabazo, *m., var. of* **bagazo.**
gabela, *f.* 1. tax. 2. (fig.) burden, load. 3. (Amer.) advantage. 4. (Col.) mold to form adobes (unfired bricks).
gabinete, *m.* 1. study, studio; small reception room; boudoir. 2. cabinet (furniture). 3. cabinet (of government). 4. room, laboratory. — **g. de física** or **química,** physics or chemistry laboratory; **g. de historia natural,** natural history room; **g. de imagen,** public relations office; **g. del baño,** toilet; **g. de prensa,** press office; **de g.,** theoretical; **g. fantasma,** shadow cabinet; **g. fiscal,** tax consultant's office; **trabajo de g.,** desk work (as opposed to field work).
gablete, *m.* (archit.) gable.
gabrieles, *m.* (*pl.*) (coll.) cooked chickpeas.
gacel, *m.* (zool.) male gazelle.
gacela, *f.* 1. (zool.) gazelle. 2. (fig., poet.) graceful, slender girl.
gaceta, *f.* 1. gazette. 2. (coll.) gossip, gossip-monger. 3. *f.* (cer.) sagger (fire clay box for firing delicate pieces). — **mentir más que la g.,** (coll.) to lie like nobody's business.
gacetera, *f.* woman newspaper seller.
gacetero, *m.* gazetteer (arch.); newspaperman, reporter; news vendor.
gacetilla, *f.* 1. gossip or personal column. 2. short news item. 3. (coll.) newsmonger, gossip.
gacetillero, *m.* gossip columnist; minor journalist.
gacetista, *m.* 1. avid newspaper reader. 2. newsmonger, gossip.
gacha, *f.* 1. soft watery paste. 2. (Col., Ven.) bowl. 3. (*pl.*) porridge, gruel.
gachapanda, a la g., (Col.) in silence, quietly, on the quiet.
gaché, gachó, *m.* a non-gypsy (term used by Spanish gypsies).
gacheta, *f.* 1. thin watery paste. 2. sticking paste. 3. spring lever of latch; notch (in latch).
gachí, *f.* a girl (to a Spanish gypsy).
gacho, cha, *a.* turned or curved down; slouch (hat); with turned or curved down horns; with head held into chest (a horse); **a gachas,** on all fours. —*m.* (Amer.) slouch hat.
gachón, na, *a.* 1. (coll.) pleasant, charming. agreeable. 2. spoiled, pampered.
gachonada, *f.* charm, pleasantness; charming gesture.
gachonería, *f.* grace, charm, attractiveness, pleasantness.
gachumbo, *m.* (Amer.) fruit shell (used for making cups, etc.).
gachupín, pina, *m., f.* (C. Amer., Mex.) Spanish settler in America.
gádido, da, *a.* (ichth.) gadoid. —*m.* (ichth.) gadid.
gaditano, na, *a.* of or pertaining to Cadiz, Spain. —*m., f.* inhabitant of Cadiz.
gadolinio, *m.* (chem.) gadolinium.
gadolinita, *f.* (min.) gadolinite.
gaélico, ca, *a., m.* Gaelic (languages).
gafa, *f.* 1. cramp, clamp; hook. **2. gaffle** (hook for bending crossbow). 3. (*pl.*) (mar.) can hooks. 4. (*pl.*) spectacles; bows (curved sidepieces of spectacles looping over ears). — **gafas bifocales,** bifocals; **gafas de bucear,** diving goggles; **gafas de cerca** or **de leer,** reading glasses; **gafas de esquiar,** skiing goggles; **gafas de sol,** sunglasses; **gafas graduadas,** prescription glasses; **gafas oscuras** or **negras,** dark glasses.
gafar, *tr.v.* 1. to hook, snatch with the claws. 2. to join with cramps, clamp. 3. to jinx.
gafe, *m.* (coll.) bad luck; jinx, person or thing that brings bad luck.
gafedad, *f.* (med.) claw hand; anesthetic leprosy.
gafete, *m.* hook and eye clasp.
gafo, fa, *a.* 1. claw-handed; suffering from anesthetic leprosy. 2. (Col., P. Rico, C. Rica) footsore.
gag, *m.* (gal.) comic situation.
gagá, *a.* gaga (sl.), crazy, doting, foolish.
gago, ga, *a.* (Amer.) stammering, stuttering.
gaguear, *i.v.* (Amer.) to stammer, stutter.
gaguera, *f.* stammer, stutter.
gahnita, *f.* (min.) gahnite.
gaicano, *m.* (ichth.) remora.
gaita, *f.* 1. (mus.) bagpipes, bagpipe. 2. (mus.) flageolet. 3. (type of) barrel organ. 4. (coll.) neck. 5. hard or cumbersome task. — **alargar** or **sacar la g.,** to stick one's neck out; **g. gallega,** bagpipes.
gaitería, *f.* colorful and gaudy dress.
gaitero, ra, *a.* 1. (coll.) waggish, skittish, clownish. 2. gaudy, loud, flamboyant (dress). —*m., f.* buffoon, wag. —*m.* bagpiper.
gaje, *m.* wages, salary (gen. in *pl.*); **gajes del oficio** (coll.), part and parcel of a job, unpleasant features of a job; **son gajes del oficio,** it's all in a day's work.
gajo, *m.* 1. branch (of tree); offshoot stem (of grapevine); bunch (of fruit). 2. section, slice, division (of an orange). 3. prong, tine (of pitchfork). 4. spur (of a mountain range). 5. (bot.) lobe (of leaf). 6. (C. Amer.) lock of hair.
gajoso, sa, *a.* branched, branchy; pronged.
gal, *m.* (phys.) gal.
gala, *f.* 1. festive dress, formal, full dress. 2. grace, charm, elegance. 3. pride, jewel, flower, choice part. 4. (Cuba, Mex.) tip, gratuity. 5. (*pl.*) regalia, finery, trappings. 6. (*pl.*) wedding gifts. — **G. de Francia,** (bot.) balsam apple (Balsamina momordica); **de g.,** full dress (uniform); **hacer g. de,** to glory in, take pride in.
galabardera, *f.* (bot.) dog rose (Rosa canina).
galactagogo, ga, *a.* (med.) galactagogue.
galáctico, ca, *a.* (astron.) galactic.
galactita, galactites, *f.* (min.) galactite.
galactófago, ga, *a.* galactophagous (feeding on milk). —*m., f.* galactophagist.
galactómetro, *m.* galactometer, instrument to measure the density of milk.
galactopoyesis, *f.* (physiol.) galactopoiesis.
galactopoyético, ca, *a* (physiol.) galactopoietic.
galactosa, *f.* (chem.) galactose.
galactósido, *m.* (chem.) galactoside.
galafate, *m.* 1. artful, cunning thief. 2. (coll.) porter, carrier.
galaico, ca, *a.* Galician.
galamero, ra, *a.* sweet toothed; greedy, gluttonous.
galán, *a., m.* elegant fellow; actor; gallant, lover, beau. — **g. de día,** (Cuba, bot.) day jessamine (Cestrum diurnum); **g. de noche,** (Cuba, bot.) night jessamine (Cestrum nocturnum); (C. Rica, bot.) cactus with large white flowers which open at night; **g. joven,** juvenile lead; **primer g.,** (theat.) leading man; **segundo g.,** second lead.
galanamente, *adv.* elegantly, smartly; gracefully.
galancete, *m.* juvenile lead.
galanga, *f.* (bot.) galingale, galangal (Cyperus longus); galingale; aromatic rhizome of this plant.
galano, na, *a.* 1. smart, elegant, spruce (in dress). 2. graceful, elegant (style). 3. (C. Rica) luxuriant, beautiful (of plants). 4. (Cuba, Chile) dappled, mottled (cattle).
galante, *a.* 1. gallant, courteous, well mannered, polite. 2. flirtatious. —**mujer de vida g.,** courtesan.
galanteador, *m.* gallant, beau, Don Juan, flirt.
galantear, *tr.v.* to woo, court; to make eyes at; (fig.) to court (someone's) favor.
galantemente, *adv.* gallantly, courteously.
galanteo, *m.* wooing, courting, flirting.
galantería, *f.* 1. gallantry, courtesy, politeness. 2. elegance, grace, charm. 3. liberality, generosity.
galantina, *f.* (cul.) galantine.
galanura, *f.* elegance, grace, charm.
galapagar, *m.* place where tortoises abound.
galápago, *m.* 1. (zool.) giant turtle. 2. (agr.) moldboard (of plow). 3. flat pulley. 4. cleat, clamp. 5. mold for tiles. 6. (metal.) pig, ingot. 7. (mas.) centering frame. 8. (mas.) facing, revetment (to retain walls of mine). 9. (mas.) coat of mortar (applied to salient angles in tiling). 10. (med.) strip of bandage with split or forked ends. 11. (equit.) English saddle, light saddle; (Hond., Ven.) sidesaddle, ladies' saddle. 12. (mil.) testudo, mantelet. 13. (vet.) soft foot (disease).
galapaguera, *f.* aquarium or tank in which live turtles are kept.
galapo, *m.* laying top (in rope making).
galardón, *m.* guerdon, reward, recompense.
galardonador, ra, *m., f.* rewarder. —*a.* rewarding, recompensing.

galardonar, *tr.v.* to reward, recompense.
Galatea, *f.* (myth., lit.) Galatea.
galatites, *f.* (min.) galactite.
galato, *m.* (chem.) gallate.
galaxia, *f.* 1. (astron.) galaxy, Milky Way. 2. (min.) galactite.
galayo, *f.* crag, cliff.
galbana, *f.* (coll.) laziness, sloth, indolence.
galbanado, da, *a.* brownish, galbanum-colored.
galbanero, ra, *a.* (coll.) lazy, slothful, indolent.
gálbano, *m.* (pharm.) galbanum.
galbanoso, sa, *a.* (coll.) lazy, shiftless, indolent, idle.
gálbula, *f.* (bot.) galbulus, cone of cypress.
galdosiano, na, *a.* pertaining to Benito Pérez Galdós, the Spanish writer.
galdrufa, *f.* spinning top.
gálea, *f.* 1. galea, Roman helmet. 2. (bot., zool.) galea.
galeado, da, *a.* (bot.) galeate.
galeato, *a.* defensive (of preface defending the work).
galeaza, *f.* (mar.) galleass, large galley.
galega, *f.* (bot.) goat's rue.
galeína, *f.* (chem.) gallein.
galembo, *m.* (Col., Ven., ornith.) turkey-buzzard.
galena, *f.* (min.) galena, native lead sulfide.
galénico, ca, *a.* Galenic. —*f.* (pharm.) galenical (medicinal preparation).
galenismo, *m.* (hist., med.) Galenism.
galenista, *m., f.* Galenist.
galeno, *m.* 1. (coll.) doctor, physician. 2. G., Galen.
galeno, na, *a.* soft, gentle (wind, breeze, etc.).
gáleo, *m.* (ichth.) dogfish; swordfish.
galeón, *m.* (mar.) galleon.
galeota, *f.* galiot, small galley.
galeote, *m.* galley slave.
galeoto, *m.* (lit.) pimp, procurer (from El Gran Galeoto, by José Echegaray).
galera, *f.* 1. (mar., print.) galley. 2. covered wagon. 3. woman's prison. 4. large ward (in hospital). 5. (carp.) jack plane. 6. (min.) line of reverberatory furnaces. 7. (zool.) type of prawn. 8. (math.) vertical line drawn between the dividend and divisor. 9. (Hond., Mex.) lean-to, shed. 10. (Arg., Urug., Chile) top hat. 11. (*pl.*) galleys (punishment). — **condenar a galeras,** to sentence to the galleys.
galerada, *f.* 1. wagonload. 2. (print.) galley, galley-proof. — **corregir galeradas,** (print.) to proof-read.
galerero, *m.* owner or mule driver of covered wagon.
galería, *f.* 1. gallery; balcony; corridor, passage; (min., fort., mar., theat.) gallery. 2. (coll.) public, gallery. 3. curtain rod. — **g. comercial,** shopping mall; **g. de alimentación,** indoor food market; **g. de arte,** art gallery; **g. de tiro,** shooting gallery; **hablar para la g.,** (coll.) to play to the gallery.
galerín, *m.* (print.) galley.
galerita, *f.* (ornith.) crested lark (Galerita cristata).
galerna, *f.* **galerno,** *m.* sudden blast of N.W. wind.
galerón, *m.* 1. (S. Amer.) popular song; folk song. 2. (C. Rica, Salv.) shed, leanto. 3. (Mex.) large room.
galés, sa, *a.* Welsh. —*m.* 1. Welshman; (*pl.*) (the) Welsh. 2. Welsh (language). —*f.* Welsh woman.
Gales, *m.* Wales.
galfarro, *m.* bum, loafer, layabout.
galga, *f.* 1. large stone, rolling stone; millstone for grinding olives. 2. (Hond.) yellow ant. 3. rash, mange. 4. shoe ribbon (attaching woman's shoe to ankle).
galga, *f.* 1. hub brake, wagon brake. 2. stretcher, bier (used to carry coffin in burial of the poor). 3. (mar.) anchor back, reinforcing anchor or rope (to reinforce dropped anchor in bad weather). 4. (*pl.*) (min.) props supporting the drum of a winch or windlass.
galgo, ga, *m., f.* greyhound; **g. inglés,** whippet; **g. ruso,** borzoi. —*a.* (Col.) 1. sweet-toothed. 2. avid, eager.
galguear, *i.v.* (C. Amer., Arg.) to want, desire.
galgueño, ña, *a.* greyhound-like.
galguero, *m.* greyhound keeper. —*a.* pertaining to greyhounds.
galguesco, ca, *a., var. of* **galgueño.**
gálgulo, *m.* (ornith.) blue-tailed magpie (Pica cooki).
Galia, *f.* Gaul.
galianos, *m.* (*pl.*) shepherd's cake.
galibar, *tr.v.* (mar.) to template, mark off with a template.
gálibo, *m.* 1. template, pattern; (ry.) gabarit; (mar.) template, gauge. 2. (archit.) perfect proportion (of a column). 3. (fig.) elegance.
galicado, da, *a.* Frenchified, full of galicisms (in style, words, etc.).
galicanismo, *m.* (ecc.) Gallicanism.
galicano, na, *a.* 1. (ecc.) Gallican. 2. Frenchified, full of gallicisms.
Galicia, *f.* Galicia, region of Spain.
galiciano, na, *a.* (arch.) Galician.
galicismo, *m.* gallicism.
galicista, *a.* gallicizing. —*m., f.* gallicizer, user of gallicisms.
gálico, ca, *a.* 1. Gallic, French. 2. (chem.) gallic. —*m.* (med.) syphilis.
galicoso, sa, *a., m., f.* syphilitic.
galilea, *f.* galilee (porch or chapel of church, esp. the part occupied by burial vaults).
galilea, *f.* (in the Greek church) time between Resurrection and Ascension.
galileano, na, *a., m., f.* Galilean.
galileo, a, *a., m., f.* Galilean. —*f.* **G.,** Galilee.
Galileo, *m.* Galileo; **transformación de G.,** (phys.) Galilean transformation.
galillo, *m.* 1. (anat.) uvula, pendent fleshy part of soft palate. 2. (coll.) gullet, throat; strident voice.
galimatías, *m.* (coll.) rigamarole, obscure or involved explanation or talk.
galináceo, a, *a., f.* (zool.), *var. of* **gallináceo.**
galio, *m.* (bot.) galium, bedstraw (Galium album).
galio, *m.* (chem.) gallium.
galiparla, *f.* abundance of gallicisms in speech or language.
galiparlante, *a., var. of* **galiparlista.**
galiparlista, *m.* gallicizer, user of gallicisms.
galipodio, *m.* galipot, gallipot (resin).
galipote, *m.* (mar.) caulking pitch.
galizabra, *f.* (mar.) lateen-rigged vessel.
galla, *f.* cowlick on horse's chest.
galladura, *f.* cicatricle, tread (of egg).
gallarda, *f.* 1. galliard, French dance and music of the 16th century. 2. (print.) a size of type.
gallardamente, *adv.* gallantly; charmingly, with self-assurance.
gallardear, *i.v., r.v.* to behave with self-assurance, ease or grace.
gallardete, *m.* pennant, streamer.
gallardetón, *m.* (mar.) broad, double-tailed pennant.
gallardía, *f.* 1. elegance, charm, self-assurance. 2. gallantry, bravery. 3. generosity, magnanimity, nobleness.
gallardo, da, *a.* 1. elegant, graceful, self-assured, charming. 2. gallant, valiant, spirited. 3. generous, noble, magnanimous.
gallareta, *f.* (ornith.) European coot, bald coot.
gallarón, *m.* (ornith.) little bustard.
gallaruza, *f.* hooded cloak.
gallear, *tr.v.* to tread, cover (of cock). —*i.v.* 1. (coll.) to shout and threaten. 2. (coll.) to stand out, excel. 3. (metal.) to develop rough spots (due to rapid cooling of metal).
gallegada, *f.* 1. crowd of Galicians (collectively). 2. Galician idiom. 3. Galician dance.
gallego, ga, *a.* Galician. —*m., f.* 1. Galician. 2. (Amer., derog.) Spanish immigrant. —*m.* Galician (dialect).
galleguismo, *m.* Galician idiom.
galleo, *m.* (metal.) flaw, rough spot (produced by too rapid cooling of metals).
gallera, *f.* 1. coop for fighting cocks. 2. cockpit, pit for cockfights. 3. cage for fighting cocks.
gallería, *f.* 1. (Cuba) breeding farm for fighting cocks. 2. cockpit.
gallero, *a.* (Amer.) fond of cockfighting. —*m.* 1. (Amer.) gamecock breeder. 2. (Amer.) cockfighting enthusiast.
galleta, *f.* 1. biscuit, cracker; ship biscuit, hardtack. 2. (coll.) slap. 3. kind of anthracite. 4. (Amer.) coarse brown bread. 5. small pitcher. 6. (Arg.) maté gourd.
galletería, *f.* biscuit shop.
galletero, *m.* 1. biscuit barrel, biscuit tin, cookie or cracker jar. 2. biscuit-maker.
gallillo, *m., var. of* galillo.
gallina, *f.* hen, chicken. — **echar una g.,** to put a brooding hen to hatch; **g. ciega,** blindman's buff; **g. clueca,** mother hen; **g. de agua,** (ornith.) water hen, European coot, bald coot; **g. de Guinea,** (ornith.) Guinea hen, Guinea fowl; **g. en corral ajeno,** (coll.) fish out of water; **g. ponedora,** laying hen. —*m., f.* coward, chicken-hearted person.
gallináceo, a, *a.* (zool.) gallinaceous. —*f.* (*pl.*) (zool.) Gallinaceae.
gallinaza, *f.* (ornith.) turkey buzzard.
gallinazo, *m.* (ornith.) turkey buzzard.
gallinejas, *f.* (*pl.*) (cul.) fried chicken giblets.
gallinería, *f.* 1. chicken shop or market. 2. flock of hens. 3. cowardice, chicken-heartedness.
gallinero, ra, *a.* (hunt.) fed on chickens (birds of prey). —*m., f.* poultry dealer. —*m.* 1. hencoop, henhouse; hens (on farm); poultry basket. 2. (theat.) top gallery, top balcony, paradise (sl.). 3. madhouse, bedlam.
gallineta, *f.* 1. (ornith.) European coot. 2. (ornith.) woodcock. 3. (Arg., Col., Chile, Ven.) Guinea hen.
gallinita, *f.* small chicken. — **g. ciega,** blindman's buff.
gallipato, *m.* (zool.) salamandrid (Pleurodeles waltlii).
gallipava, *f.* large hen.
gallipavo, *m.* 1. turkey. 2. (cool.) wrong note (in singing).
gallístico, ca, *a.* pertaining to gamecocks or cockfighting.
gallito, *m.* 1. somebody, important person. 2. cock of the walk, boaster, bragger. 3. (Col.) dart. 4. (Amer.) aggressive or quarrelsome person. — **g. del rey,** (ichth.) blenny (Blennius pavo).
gallo, *m.* 1. cock, rooster. 2. (ichth.) dory. 3. (coll.) aging man, oldtimer. 4. (archit.) ridgepole. 5. pinwheel (toy). 6. (coll.) false note. 7. (coll.) boss. 8. (Amer.) spittle, phlegm. 9. (Col.) shuttlecock. 10. (Amer.) brave man. 11. (Arg.) past master; (Chile) hose truck; 12. (Col.) dart, arrow; 13. (Peru) bedpan; 14. (Mex.) serenade; 15. (Mex.) offcast piece of clothing; 16. (Coll.) cock of the walk. — **alzar or levantar uno el g.,** (coll.) to speak haughtily, be arrogant; **en menos que canta un g.,** (coll.) in a jiffy, in the

winking of an eye; **entre gallos y medianoche,** at an inconvenient time, without warning; **g. de pelea** or **de riña,** game cock; **g. de roca,** (ornith.) cock of the rock; **g. silvestre,** (ornith.) capercaillie; **misa del g.,** midnight mass; **peso g.,** bantam weight (in boxing).
gallocresta, *f.* (bot.) wild sage, vervain sage.
gallofa, *f.* 1. food given to pilgrims. 2. greens, vegetables (for salad or soup). 3. rumor, gossip, idle talk. 4. (ecc.) liturgical calendar.
gallofero, ra, gallofo, fa, *a.* idle, lazy, loafing. —*m., f.* tramp, vagabond, bum, loafer.
gallón, *m.* 1. (archit.) echinus, egg-and-leaf ornament (of Ionic and other orders); egg and leaf on silver cutlery. 2. (mar.) last frame of prow. 3. sod, turf.
gallonada, *f.* turf wall.
gallote, ta, *a.* (C. Rica, Mex.) cocky, pert, self-assured.
galludo, *m.* (Cuba) a kind of shark.
galo, la, *a.* Gallic. —*m., f.* Gaul. —*m.* Gaulish (language); **G.,** Gallus.
galocha, *f.* galosh; clog, wooden shoe.
galochero, *m.* maker or seller of galoshes.
galófilo, la, *a., m., f.* Francophile, Gallophile.
galofobia, *f.* Francophobia.
galófobo, ba, *a., m., f.* Francophobe, Gallophobe.
galón, *m.* 1. gallon (liquid measure). — **g. inglés,** imperial gallon. 2. galloon, braid. 3. (mil.) stripe, decoration.
galoneador, ra, *m., f.* person who makes or applies galloons or braids.
galoneadura, *f.* trimming, braiding.
galonear, *tr.v.* to braid, trim with braid.
galonero, ra, *m., f.* braid or galloon maker.
galonista, *m.* outstanding student at military academy wearing corporal's stripes as reward.
galop, *m.* **galopa,** *f.* galop, gallopade (lively dance).
galopada, *f.* gallop.
galopante, *a.* galloping, acute; (med.) galloping.
galopar, *i.v.* to gallop; to go at a gallop.
galope, *m.* gallop; **a** or **de g.,** at a gallop; very fast or quickly.
galopeado, da, *past part. of* **galopear.** —*a.* hastily done. —*m.* (coll.) slapping, buffeting, punching.
galopear, *i.v., var. of* **galopar.**
galopillo, *m.* scullion, kitchen boy.
galopín, *m.* 1. ragamuffin. 2. scoundrel, rascal. 3. (coll.) wise guy, smart alec. 4. (mar.) cabin boy. — **g. de cocina,** scullion, kitchen boy.
galopinada, *f.* rascality, roguishness, knavery.
galopo, *m.* rascal, scoundrel, rogue.
galpón, *m.* 1. (S Amer, W. Indies) open shed. 2. (Col.) tile works. 3. (Amer.), (hist.) slave quarters. — **g. de cargas,** (ry.) freight or goods shed; **g. de locomotoras,** (ry.) engine house.
galucha, *f.* (Amer.) gallop (gait of a horse).
galuchar, *i.v.* (Amer.) to gallop (horses).
galvanice, galvanicé, *ref.* **galvanizar.**
galvánico, ca, *a.* (phys.) galvanic.
galvanismo, *m.* (phys.) galvanism.
galvanización, *f.* galvanization.
galvanizar, (*ref. 53*) *tr.v.* to galvanize.
galvano, *m.* (print.) electrotype, electrotype plate.
galvanocauterio, *m.* (med.) galvanocautery.
galvanocirugía, *f.* (med.) galvanosurgery.
galvanometría, *f.* galvanometry.
galvanométrico, ca, *a.* galvanometric.
galvanómetro, *m.* (phys.) galvanometer. — **g. de cuerda,** string galvanometer.
galvanoplastia, *f.* (phys.) galvanoplasty, electroplating; (print.) electrotyping.
galvanoplástica, *f.* galvanoplastics.
galvanoplástico, ca, *a.* galvanoplastic.
galvanoscopia, *f.* galvanoscopy.
galvanoscopio, *m.* galvanoscope.
galvanotaxis, *f.* (bot.) galvanotaxis.
galvanotermia, *f.* (med.) galvanothermy.
galvanotipia, *f.* electrotypy, electrotyping.
galvanotipo, *m.* electrotype.
galvanotropismo, *m.* galvanotropism.**gama,** *f.* 1. (zool.) doe, female fallow deer. 2. (mus., fig.) gamut. — **g. dinámica,** dynamic range (of sound).
gamada, *a.* **cruz g.,** gammadion, swastika. —*f.* gammadion, swastika.
gamarra, *f.* martingale (of horse's harness); check strap.
gamarza, *f.* (bot.) African rue.
gamba, *f.* (zool.) prawn, shrimp.
gambado, da, *a.* (Car.) bowlegged.
gambaj, *m., var. of* **gambax.**
gambalo, *m.* (arch.) linen fabric.
gambalúa, *m.* (coll.) tall, lanky, slovenly fellow; good-for-nothing.
gámbaro, *m.* (ichth.) prawn, shrimp.
gambax, *m.* acton (jacket of quilted cotton worn under coat of mail).
gamberro, rra, *a.* dissolute, licentious. —*m., f.* libertine.
gambesina, *f.* **gambesón,** *m.* gambeson (jacket of quilted cotton worn under coat of mail).
gambeta, *f.* 1. caper, prance; cross step (in dancing). 2. (Amer.) dodge, duck, feint. 3. (Arg., Urug.) evasion.
gambetear, *i.v.* to cross-step, do cross steps (in dancing); to prance.
gambeto, *m.* 1. quilted greatcoat. 2. children's bonnet, cap.
gambir, *m.* (bot., pharm.) gambier (catechu).
gambito, *m.* gambit (a chess opening).
gamboa, *f.* (bot.) (variety of) quince.
gambota, *f.* (mar.) counter timber.
gamella, *f.* bow (of yoke).
gamella, *f.* feed trough; large wooden tub.
gamellón, *m.* big trough, big trough for treading grapes.
gameta, *m., f.* (biol., bot.) gamete.
gametangio, *m.* (bot.) gametangium.
gamético, ca, *a.* (biol., bot.) gametic.
gameto, *m.* (biol.) gamete.
gametocito, *m.* (biol.) gametocyte.
gametofita, *f.* **gametofito,** *m.* (bot.) gametophyte.
gametóforo, *m.* (bot.) gametophore.
gametogenia, gametogénesis, *f.* (biol.) gametogenesis.
gamezno, *m.* young or small deer.
gámico, ca, *a.* gamic.
gamitar, *i.v.* to bell (a deer); to make a deer call.
gamitido, *m.* bell, call of deer.
gamma, *f.* gamma (third letter of Greek alphabet; weight).
gamo, *m.* (zool.) buck, male fallow deer.
gamófilo, la, *a.* (bot.) gamophyllous.
gamogénesis, *f.* (biol.) gamogenesis.
gamogenético, ca, *a.* gamogenetic.
gamón, *m.* (bot.) asphodel, liliaceous plant (Asphodelus albus).
gamonal, *m.* 1. asphodel field. 2. (Amer.) boss, chief, large landowner.
gamonalismo, *m.* exploitation of natives by large landowners.
gamonita, *f., var. of* **gamón.**
gamonito, *m.* (bot.) shoot, sucker, rootlet.
gamonoso, sa, *a.* full of asphodels.
gamopétalo, la, *a.* (bot.) gamopetalous.
gamosépalo, la, *a.* (bot.) gamosepalous.
gamuno, na, *a.* buck (skin); shammy.
gamuza, *f.* 1. (zool.) chamois. 2. chamois, shammy leather; suede.
gamuzado, da, *a.* chamois-colored, buff-colored.
gamuzón, *m. aug. of* **gamuza,** coarse chamois or suede.
gana, *f.* 1. desire, wish; hunger, longing. 2. mind, intention. — **darle a uno la g.** or **la real g. de** + *inf.,* to feel like + *ger.;* **de buena g.,** willingly, readily; **de g.,** energetically, zealously, willingly; **de mala g.,** unwillingly; **tener ganas de** + *inf.,* to want to + *inf.;* to have a mind to + *inf.; e.g. tengo ganas de ir al servicio,* I need to go to the bathroom; **tenerle ganas a (uno),** (coll.) to have it in for (someone).
ganadería, *f.* 1. cattle, livestock. 2. cattle ranch or farm. 3. cattle raising, cattle breeding, cattle trade.
ganadero, ra, *a.* cattle (as *a.*). —*m., f.* cattle dealer; cattle breeder. —*m.* cattleman, drover.
ganado, *m.* 1. livestock, cattle. 2. flock, herd, drove; colony (of bees); flock (of people). — **g. bovino,** cattle; **g. bravo,** untamed livestock; **g. caballar,** horses; **g. cabrío,** goats; **g. de cerda,** pigs, hogs; **g. en pie,** cattle on the hoof; **g. equino,** horses; **g. lanar,** sheep; **g. mayor,** cows, oxen, horses, mules; **g. menor,** sheep, goats; **g. moreno,** pigs, hogs; **g. ovejuno,** sheep; **g. porcino,** pigs, hogs; **g. vacuno,** cattle, cows, oxen.
ganador, ra, *a.* winning. —*m., f.* 1. winner. 2. earner.
ganancia, *f.* 1. profit, gain; advantage. (*pl.*) winnings (at cards, etc.). 2. (Amer.) extra, bonus, something added for good measure. — **g. bruta,** gross profit; **g. de capital,** capital gains; **g. líquida** or **neta,** net profit; **ganancias por realizar,** paper profits; **ganancias y pérdidas,** profit and loss.
ganancial, *a.* pertaining to earnings or profit; **bienes gananciales,** joint property, property of a couple acquired after marriage.
ganancioso, sa, *a.* profitable; gaining, winning. —*m., f.* winner; gainer.
ganapán, *m.* 1. porter, carrier, drudge. 2. (coll.) rude, coarse man.
ganapierde, *m., f.* giveaway (in checkers and other games); losing game.
ganar, *tr.v.* 1. to earn, get (a wage). 2. to win (game, battle, etc.; honor, favor). 3. to win (someone) over, win (someone's) support. 4. to reach, get to, arrive at. 5. to beat, be better than, *e.g. te gano en latín,* I am better than you in Latin. 6. to take. — **g. a,** to beat (someone in a game; army in battle); to defeat; **g. a alguien al ajedrez,** to beat someone in or at chess; **ganarle a uno la boca,** to persuade someone to talk, draw someone out; **g. peso,** to put on weight. —*i.v.* 1. to earn, get (good or bad) wage. 2. to win, be the winner. 3. to improve, rise, go up. —*r.v.* 1. to win (e.g. favor, support). 2. to earn. 3. (Arg., Chile) to hide, take refuge. — **ganarse la vida,** to earn one's living, **ganarse el pan** or **el sustento,** to earn one's daily bread or sustenance.
ganchero, *m.* raftsman (one who guides logs down a river or stream).
ganchete, a medio g., (coll.) half, half-done; **de medio g.,** carelessly, shoddily, sloppily; awkwardly, on the edge (when sitting).
ganchillo, *m.* 1. *dim of* **gancho,** crochet needle. 2. crochet work.
gancho, *m.* 1. hook; (shepherd's) crook. 2. stub (of broken off branch). 3. (coll.) coaxer, cajoler, enticer; (coll.) pimp, procurer. 4. (coll.) loop (in writing). 5. (Amer.) hairpin. 6. (Ecuad.) lady's saddle. 7. (coll.) B-girl (in dance halls). — **echar a (uno) el g.,** to trap, entice; **g. de nodriza,** (Col.) safety pin; **hacer g.,** (Arg., Chile) to help;

tener su g., to have one's attraction, be attractive.
ganchoso, sa, *a.* hooked, hook-like; curved.
ganchudo, da, *a.* hook-shaped.
gándara, *f.* lowland, low wasteland; wilderness.
gandaya, *f.* 1. loafing, idleness, laziness. 2. cap, net. — **andar a la g.,** to loaf, to idle.
gandido, da, *a.* (Amer.) gluttonous.
gandinga, *f.* 1. (Car.) offal stew. 2. (min.) fine washed ore. — **¡no tienes g.!** (Cuba) you are shameless!
gandujado, *past part. of* **gandujar.** —*m.* (dressm.) accordion pleating.
gandujar, *tr.v.* to pleat, shirr, gather.
gandul, la, *a.* (coll.) lazy, idle. —*m., f.* loafer, idler. —*m.* (bot.) pigeon pea.
gandulear, *i.v.* to idle, loaf around.
gandulería, *f.* idleness, loafing, laziness.
gandumbas, *a.* (coll.) idle, slothful, lazy. —*m., f.* idler, loafer.
ganeta, *f.* (zool.) genet.
ganforro, rra, *m., f.* scoundrel, ruffian, rogue.
ganga, *f.* 1. (ornith.) pin-tailed sandgrouse. 2. (Cuba, ornith.) tattler (Totanus longiouda).
ganga, *f.* 1. (min.) gangue, gang, worthless matter accompanying minerals. 2. bargain. — **buscador de gangas,** bargain hunter. 3. (gal., Amer.) gang (of ruffians, delinquents, etc.).
gangarilla, *f.* small company of traveling comedians or actors.
gangliado, da, *a.* (anat.) gangliated.
gangliectomía, *f.* (surg.) ganglionectomy.
ganglio, *m.* (anat.) ganglion; (med.) ganglion, small hard tumor.
ganglionar, *a.* (anat.) ganglionic.
ganglionectomía, *f.* (surg.) ganglionectomy.
gangocho, *m.* (Chile, Ecuad.) burlap.
gangolina, *f.* (Arg.) noise, uproar, racket, row.
gangosear, *i.v., var. of* **ganguear.**
gangoseo, *m.* (Arg., Col.) *var. of* **gangueo.**
gangosidad, *f.* nasal quality (in speech).
gangoso, sa, *a.* nasal, twangy (manner of speaking, voice).
gangrena, *f.* (med.) gangrene; (bot.) disease which corrodes tree tissues.
gangrenado, da, *past part. of* **gangrenarse.** —*a.* gangrenous.
gangrenarse, *r.v.* to become gangrenous.
gangrenoso, sa, *a.* gangrenous.
gángster, *m.* gangster.
ganguear, *i.v.* to speak with a nasal twang, talk through one's nose.
gangueo, *m.* (nasal) twang.
ganguero, ra, *m., f.* bargain hunter. —*a.* said of a person who looks for easy jobs.
gánguil, *m.* 1. (mar.) fishing boat with double row and lateen sail; mud lighter, dump scow (for dumping dredged mud). 2. fine-meshed trawl net.
Ganimedes, *m.* (myth., astron.) Ganymede, Ganymedes.
ganoideo, a, *a., m.* (ichth.) ganoid.
ganosamente, *adv.* desirously, eagerly.
ganoso, sa, *a.* desirous (of), eager (to).
gansada, *f.* (coll.) stupidity, inanity, senseless remark.
gansarón, *m.* 1. (ornith.) goose (Anser cinereus). 2. (fig.) lanky, gawky man.
gansear, *i.v.* (coll.) to say or do stupid, inane things.
ganso, sa, *a.* sloppy, indolent; foolish, dim, dull. —*m., f.* slow, silly person. —*m.* 1. (ornith.) gander, goose. 2. (arch.) schoolteacher. — **g. bravo,** wild goose.
ganta, *f.* (Phil. I.) liquid measure equivalent to three liters.
gante, *m.* crude, rough linen.
gantés, sa, *a.* pertaining to Ghent, Belgium. —*m., f.* native of Ghent.
ganzúa, *f.* 1. picklock (thief, instrument). 2. (coll.) wheedler, pumper (wheedling out secrets).
gañán, *m.* 1. farm laborer, farmhand. 2. hefty, rustic person.
gañanía, *f.* 1. gang of farm laborers. 2. farm laborers' hostel or living quarters.
gañido, *past part. of* **gañir.** —*m.* yelping, howling.
gañiles, *m.* 1. (*pl.*) larynx (of animals). 2. gills (of tuna fish).
gañir, (*ref. 66*) *i.v.* to yelp, howl (dogs, etc.); to croak, caw, (birds); (coll.) to wheeze (person).
gañón, *m.* (coll.) gullet.
gañote, *m.* (coll.) gullet; **de g.,** (coll.) free, gratis, for nothing.
gañotear, *i.v.* (coll.) to go for nothing, go without paying.
gaón, *m.* (mar.) paddle (used in certain small boats).
garabatada, *f.* hooking, catching hold of (with hook).
garabatear, *i.v.* 1. to hook, catch with a hook. 2. to scribble. —*tr.v.* 1. to scribble. 2. (coll.) to beat about the bush.
garabateo, *m.* hooking; scribbling, doodling.
garabato, *m.* 1. hook, grapnel; grappling iron. 2. weeding hoe; plow with a double beam (able to be drawn by one horse). 3. (Amer.) pitchfork. 4. thin cord (for tying flax). 5. scribble, scrawl. 6. (*pl.*) extravagant hand gestures.
garabatoso, sa, *a.* full of scribbles.
garabito, *m.* market stall (seat).
garage, *m.* garage; **g. de dos plazas,** two-car garage.
garagista, *m.* garage man, garage attendant.
garama, *f.* 1. (in Morocco) tax; collective fine (paid by tribes for theft committed in their territory). 2. gifts, presents.
garambana, *f.* 1. gaudiness, tawdry trimming. 2. (*pl.*) (coll.) impertinent gestures; grimaces, smirks. 3. (*pl.*) (coll.) scrawl, scribbling.
garambullo, *m.* (Mex., bot.) cactus plant (Lophocereus schotti).
garandumba, *f.* 1. (S. Amer.) large river raft. 2. (Arg.) tall, hefty woman.
garante, *m., f.* (law, com.) bondsman, warrantor, guarantor. —*a.* responsible, e.g. *ser g. de,* to be responsible for.
garantía, *f.* guarantee, guaranty, security; **garantías constitucionales,** civil rights, constitutional guarantees.
garantice, garanticé, *ref.* **garantizar.**
garantir, (*ref. 78*) *tr.v.* to guarantee, answer, vouch for.
garantizador, ra, *a.* guaranteeing.
garantizar, (*ref. 53*) *tr.v.* to guarantee, vouch, answer for.
garañón, *m.* stud jackass; stud camel; (Amer.) studhorse, stallion; (Canar. I.) stud goat.
garapacho, *m.* 1. *var. of* **carapacho.** 2. cork or wooden bowl.
garapiña, *f.* 1. frozen particles (of certain liquids); frozen cream. 2. scalloped galloon or braid. 3. (Car., Mex.) drink made with fermented pineapple juice.
garapiñar, *tr.v.* 1. to freeze (liquid). 2. to candy, coat with sugar. — **almendras garapiñadas,** candied almonds.
garapiñera, *f.* ice-box, ice-cream freezer.
garapita, *f.* small closely-woven fishing net.
garapito, *m.* (ento.) water bug.
garapullo, *m.* dart; shuttlecock.
garata, *f.* (coll.) fight, scuffle.
garatura, *f.* scraper (used in tanning).
garatusa, *f.* 1. (coll.) caress, compliment, e.g. *hacer garatusas,* to wheedle, coax. 2. (fenc.) thrust at face or chest. 3. a card game.
garay, *m.* (Phil. I.) type of lighter or scow.
garbanceo, *m.* (coll.) daily meal, sustenance.
garbancero, ra, *a.* pertaining to chickpea. —*m., f.* 1. chickpea dealer, chickpea vendor. 2. (Mex.) young servant.
garbancillo, *m.* (Ven.) leguminous bush with fruit that resembles chickpea (Astragalus garbancillo).
garbanzal, *m.* chickpea field.
garbanzo, *m.* (bot.) chickpea; **por un garbanzo no se descompone la olla,** (coll.) one voice of dissent does not change the issue.
garbanzuelo, *m.* 1. *dim. of* **garbanzo.** 2. (vet.) spavin.
garbar, *tr.v.* (agr.) to sheave, sheaf.
garbear, *i.v.* 1. to put on airs (of grandeur, dignity, elegance). 2. (coll.) to cheat. 3. to shift for oneself, make out as best one can.
garbera, *f.* (agr.) shock (of sheaves).
garbías, *m.* (*pl.*) dish prepared with herbs, cheese, lard, flour and eggs.
garbillador, ra, *a.* sieving, sifting, riddling. —*m., f.* siever, sifter, riddler.
garbillar, *tr.v.* to sieve, sift, riddle.
garbillo, *m.* 1. grain, sieve. 2. chaff, grain husks. 3. (min.) riddle, sieve. 4. (min.) riddled ore.
garbín, *m.* (arch.) net coif.
garbino, *m.* Southwest wind.
garbo, *m.* 1. fine, proud and assured bearing; elegant bearing; dash, elegance, grace, charm. 2. magnanimity, generosity.
gárboli, *m.* (Cuba) (game of) hide-and-seek.
garbón, *m.* (ornith.) male partridge.
garbosamente, *adv.* gracefully, elegantly, generously.
garboso, sa, *a.* 1. graceful, elegant, charming. 2. generous.
garbullo, *m.* hubbub, noisy crowd, melée.
garceta, *f.* 1. (ornith.) lesser egret (Egretta garceta). 2. side block (of hair). 3. (*pl.*) sprouting horns or antlers (of deer).
gardenia, *f.* (bot.) gardenia.
gardingo, *m.* member of Visigoth court below duke and count.
garduja, *f.* (min.) slag (from mercury mines).
garduña, *f.* (zool.) stone marten.
garduño, ña, *m., f.* thief, pickpocket.
garete, ir al or **irse al g.,** (mar.) to be adrift, drift.
garfa, *f.* claw. — **echar la g.,** to seize (something) with the claws.
garfada, *f.* seizing (with the claws).
garfear, *i.v.* to hook, catch hold of or seize with a hook.
garfiada, *f., var. of* **garfada.**
garfio, *m.* grappling iron, hook, grapple, drag hook, gaff; **garfios de trepar,** climbing irons.
gargajeada, *f.* expectoration, spitting out of phlegm.
gargajear, *i.v.* to expectorate, spit out phlegm.
gargajeo, *m.* expectoration, spitting out of phlegm.
gargajiento, ta, *a., var. of* **gargajoso.**
gargajo, *m.* phlegm, spit.
gargajoso, sa, *a.* continually spitting, expectorating or hawking.
gargal, *m.* (Chile, bot.) gall nut (of the oak).
garganchón, *m.* gullet, windpipe.
garganta, *f.* 1. throat; (anat.) esophagus, gullet. 2. (fig.) gorge, canyon, ravine. 3. (fig.) neck (of bottle). 4. (fig.) curvature of plow connecting moldboard and beam. 5. (archit.) gorgerin, necking (of columns). 6. (fort.) loophole, embrasure. — **g. de polea,** gorge or groove (of pulley); **tener buena g.,** to have a fine singing voice.

gargantada, *f.* spit, sputum.
gargantear, *i.v.* 1. to warble, trill, quaver. 2. (mar.) to strap a deadeye.
garganteo, *m.* trilling, warbling, quavering.
gargantil, *m.* groove in barber's basin (to fit the neck into).
gargantilla, *f.* 1. necklace; beads (of necklace). 2. (Phil. I.) water jug.
gargantón, *m.* 1. large necklace. 2. (Mex.) halter.
gárgara, *f.* gargling; (*gen. in pl.*) (Amer.) gargle (liquid used for gargling); **hacer gárgaras,** to gargle.
gargarear, *i.v.* (Chile, Peru) to gargle.
gargarice, gargaricé, *ref.* **gargarizar.**
gargarismo, *m.* gargling, gargle; gargle (liquid used for gargling).
gargarizar, (*ref. 53*) *i.v.* to gargle.
gárgaro, *m.* (Cuba, Ven.) (game of) hide-and-seek.
gargavero, *m.* 1. gullet, windpipe. 2. musical instrument composed of two flutes with one single mouthpiece.
gárgol, *a.* rotten, addled (eggs). —*m.* (carp.) groove, mortise.
gárgola, *f.* 1. (archit.) gargoyle. 2. (bot.) linseed capsule.
garguero, gargüero, *m.* gullet; windpipe, trachea.
garibaldina, *f.* (Italian hist.) garibaldi (red blouse worn by Garibaldi and his partisans).
garifo, fa, *a.* natty, spruce, smart, neat, tidy.
gariofilea, *f.* (bot.) gillyflower, wild carnation.
garita, *f.* 1. sentry box; porter's lodge. 2. lavatory, water closet. 3. (Mex.) city gate. — **g. de peaje,** tollbooth; **g. de señales,** (ry.) signal tower (U.S.), signal box (G.B.).
garitero, *m.* 1. owner of gaming house, master of a gambling den. 2. gambler.
garito, *m.* 1. gaming house, gambling den. 2. winnings (at gambling), gambling profits.
garla, *f.* (coll.) chatter, prattle, talk.
garlador, ra, *a.* chattering, prattling. —*m., f.* chatter, prattler.
garlancha, *f.* (Col.) shovel, spade.
garlante, *a.* chattering, prattling.
garlar, *i.v.* (coll.) to chatter, prattle, converse.
garlero, ra, *a.* (Col.) talkative, garrulous.
garlido, *m.* (rare) chirping (of crickets); screeching (of wheels).
garlito, *m.* fish trap, fish snare; (coll.) trap, snare. — **coger a uno en el g.,** (coll.) to catch someone in the act.
garlocha, *f.* 1. *var. of* **garrocha.** 2. (taur.) spear, lance (of picador); goad-stick.
garlopa, *f.* (carp.) large plane (for smoothing wood already planed).
garma, *f.* steep ravine, sharp slope.
garnacha, *f.* 1. gown, robe (of judge, don). 2. troupe of strolling players. 3. (Mex.) thick tortilla. 4. grenache, purple grape, wine made from same; non-alcoholic cool drink.
garnica, *f.* (Bol.) very hot pepper.
garniel, *m.* leather pouch; (Ecuad., Mex.) leather case.
garnierita, *f.* (min.) garnierite.
garo, *m.* dish prepared by Romans by marinating entrails of certain fish.
garoso, sa, *a.* (Ven., Col.) hungry, ravenous; greedy, gluttonous.
garpa, *f.* bunch of grapes.
garra, *f.* 1. claw, talon. 2. human hand. 3. (mar.) hook of harpoon. 4. (Amer.) edge of hide (where it is fixed for stretching); (Amer.) dried, withered piece of leather. 5. (Col.) leather bag. 6. (Amer.) (*pl.*) rags, tatters. — **caer en las garras de,** to fall into the clutches or under the power of.
garrafa, *f.* carafe, decanter.
garrafal, *a.* 1. large and sweet (cherries and trees producing these cherries). 2. (coll.) enormous, tremendous, whopping, great.
garrafiñar, *tr.v.* (coll.) to wrench away, snatch away.
garrafón, *m.* demijohn.
garrama, *f.* 1. tax or tribute paid by Mohammedans. 2. (coll.) fraud, robbery, swindle.
garramar, *tr.v.* (coll.) to steal, pinch (coll.), lift (coll.).
garrancha *f.* 1. (bot.) spathe, **spadix.** 2. (coll.) sword. 3. (Col.) hook.
garranchada, garranchazo, *m.* wound made by a hook or a branch.
garrancho, *m.* branch (torn from tree).
garranchuelo, *m.* (bot.) crab grass (Digitaria sanguinalis).
garrapata, *f.* 1. (ento.) tick, chigger. 2. (coll., mil.) hack, jade, worn-out, disabled horse.
garrapatear, *i.v.* to scribble, scrawl; to doodle.
garrapatero, *m.* (Col., Ecuad., ornith.) ani.
garrapato, *m.* pothook, scribbled letter; (*pl.*) scribbling, scribble, scrawl; doodling.
garrapatoso, sa, *a.* untidy, scribbled, scrawled (handwriting).
garrapiñado, da, *past part. of* **garrapiñar.** —*a.* sugar-coated (almonds).
garrapiñar, *tr.v.* to wrench away, snatch away.
garrapiñera, *f., var. of* **garapiñera.**
garrar, *i.v.* (mar.) to drag the anchor.
garrasí, (*pl.* **garrasíes**) *m.* (Ven.) cowboys' breeches or chaps.
garrear, *i.v.* (mar.) to drag the anchor.
garrideza, *f.* (arch.) elegance, smartness.
garrido, da, *past part. of* **garrir.** —*a.* elegant, smart, spruce.
garrir, *i.v.* to squawk (parrot).
garroba, *f.* carob, algarroba (Vicia monantha).
garrobal, *m.* plantation or clump of carob bean trees.
garrobilla, *f.* chips of carob tree used for tanning leather.
garrobo, *m.* (C. Amer.) tropical lizard (Lacerta horrida).
garrocha, *f.* 1. (taur.) lance, spear (used by picador); goad-stick. 2. (sport.) pole (for vaulting).
garrochada, *f.* prick with the goad-stick.
garrochar, *tr.v.* (taur.) to weaken or wound (the bull) with a lance.
garrochazo, *m.* wound or thrust inflicted with lance.
garrocheador, ra, *m., f.* 1. goader, lancebearer. 2. (sport.) pole-vaulter.
garrochear, *tr.v., var. of* **garrochar.**
garrochista, *m.* (taur.) picador, person who lowers bull's head with a lance. —*m., f.* pole-vaulter.
garrochón, *m.* (taur.) spear, lance (used by mounted bullfighter).
garrofa, *f.* (bot.) carob bean.
garrofal, *a.* large and sweet (cherries and trees producing them). —*m.* plantation or clump of carob bean trees.
garrón, *m.* 1. talon, claw (of bird); paw of rabbits. 2. branch (cut from tree).
garrotal, *m.* olive tree plantation grown from cuttings.
garrotazo, *m.* blow given with a club or cudgel.
garrote, *m.* 1. club, stick, cudgel. 2. (med.) tourniquet. 3. garrote (instrument for administering capital punishment). 4. (mar.) turning fid (for tightening a cable). 5. (bot.) cutting or scion. 6. break (in a line); sag, bulge (in a wall); bend, twist (in a tube). 7. (Mex.) brake (of a coach).
garrotear, *tr.v.* (Ecuad., Chile, Peru) to beat with a stick, cudgel, club.
garrotero, *m.* 1. (Chile, Peru) attacker, bully. 2. (Mex., ry.) brakeman. —*a.* (Cuba, Chile) mean, tightfisted, stingy.
garrotillo, *m.* (med.) croup, laryngeal diphtheria.
garrotín, *m.* Spanish gypsy dance (popular at the turn of the century).
garrubia, *f.* (bot.) seed of common vetch.
garrucha, *f.* pulley, block. — **g. diferencial de cadena,** chain block.
garrucho, *m.* (mar.) grommet, cringle.
garruchuela, *f.* (mar.) small grommet.
garrudo, da, *a.* 1. strong-clawed. 2. (Mex.) muscular, brawny.
garrulador, ra, *a.* garrulous, talkative; noisy (wind); chirpy (bird).
garrulería, *f.* chatter, prattle, blather.
garrulidad, *f.* garrulousness.
gárrulo, la, *a.* garrulous, talkative; noisy (wind); chirpy (bird).
garúa, *f.* (Amer.) drizzle, fine misty rain.
garuar, (*ref. 55*) *i.v.* (Amer.) to drizzle.
garujo, *m.* concrete, mortar.
garulla, *f.* 1. loose grapes. 2. (coll.) rabble, mob, crowd.
garullada, *f.* (coll.) rabble, crowd, mob.
garvier, *m.* small leather pouch.
garvín, *m.* hair net, snood.
garza, *f.* (ornith.) heron; **g. real,** (ornith.) gray heron (Ardea cinerea).
garzo, za, *a.* bluish. —*m.* (bot.) agaric. — **ojos garzos,** (poet.) blue eyes.
garzón, *m.* 1. lad, boy, stripling, youth; male child. 2. (Ven., ornith.) great white heron (Casmeradius albus).
garzota, *f.* 1. (ornith.) night heron (Nycticorax nycticorax). 2. plumage, crest.
garzul, *m.* a variety of wheat.
gas, *m.* 1. gas, fumes, emanation, vapor, (coal) gas. 2. (gal., coll.) gasoline. — **g. amonéaco,** ammonia gas; **g. de agua,** (chem.) water gas; **g. de alumbrado,** illuminating gas; **g. de carbón** or **de hulla,** coal gas; **g. hilarante,** laughing gas; **g. inerte,** inert gas; **g. lacrimógeno,** tear gas; **g. licuado,** liquified gas; **g. mostaza,** mustard gas; **g. neurotóxico** or **nervioso,** nerve gas; **g. pobre,** producer gas; **g. tóxico,** (mil.) poison gas.
gasa, *f.* 1. gauze (very sheer cloth; medical gauze). 2. crepe, mourning band.
gascón, na, *a., m., f.* Gascon, of Gascony, France.
gasconada, *f.* gasconade, bravado, boast.
gasconés, sa, *a., m., f.* Gascon (appl. to the people of Gascony).
gaseiforme, *a.* gaseous, gasiform.
gaseoso, sa, *a.* gaseous. —*f.* fizzy drink.
gasfitero, *m.* plumber; gas fitter.
gasificable, *a.* gasifiable.
gasificación, *f.* gasification.
gasificar, (*ref. 50*) *tr.v.* (chem.) to gasify.
gasifique, gasifiqué, *ref.* **gasificar.**
gasiforme, *a.* gasiform.
gasista, *m.* gas fitter.
gasné, *m.* (Mex.) handkerchief.
gasoducto, *m.* gas pipe.
gasógeno, *m.* 1. gas generator. 2. mixture of water and benzine.
gasoleno, *m., var. of* **gasolina.**
gasóleo, *m* gas oil (used in Diesel engines).
gasolina, *f.* gasoline. (U.S.), petrol (G.B.). — **g. de alto octanaje,** high-octane gasoline; **g. normal,** regular gasoline; **g. sin plomo,** unleaded gasoline; **g. super,** high-test gasoline;
gasolinera, *f.* 1. motor boat. 2. gas station, filling station.
gasómetro, *m.* 1. gasometer. 2. gasholder, gasometer.

gasón, *m.* 1. plaster rubble. 2. clod of earth. 3. grass, sod.
gastable, *a.* expendable.
gastadero, *m.* (coll.) waste, wasting. — **g. de tiempo,** waste of time.
gastado, da, *past part. of* **gastar.** —*a.* 1. wornout, shabby; threadbare. 2. exhausted. 3. worn, blurred.
gastador, ra, *a.* wasteful, extravagant, prodigal. —*m., f.* waster, spendthrift. —*m.* 1. convict condemned to hard labor. 2. (mil.) pioneer, sapper.
gastamiento, *m.* wearing out; wasting away, consumption.
gastar, *tr.v.* 1. to spend. 2. to waste, squander. 3. to wear out (clothes). 4. to use up, exhaust, consume. 5. to devastate, lay waste. 6. to digest. 7. to spoil, ruin. 8. to have or use habitually. 9. to wear, sport; to use; to have, possess. —*r.v.* to be used up; to wear out; to waste away; to become exhausted. — **g. bromas,** to joke habitually; **g. bromas con,** to tease about.
gasterópodo, *a.* (zool.) gastropodous. —*m.* (zool.) gastropod; (*pl.*) Gastropoda.
gasterosteo, *m.* (icth.) stickleback.
gasto, *m.* 1. expense, expenditure, outlay; spending, waste. 2. (phys.) volume of flow. — **g. de capital,** capital expenditure; **g. deficitario,** (econ.) deficit spending; **gastos corrientes,** running expenses; **gastos de correo,** postage; **gastos de envío,** postage and handling; **gastos de explotación,** operating costs; **gastos de mantenimiento,** maintenance costs; **gastos de operación,** (com.) operating expenses; **gastos de representación,** entertainment allowance; **gastos de viaje,** travel expenses; **gastos generales** or **fijos** or **estructurales,** overhead; **libre de gastos a bordo,** free-on-board.
gastoso, sa, *a.* wasteful, extravagant, prodigal.
gastral, *a.* (anat.) gastral.
gastralgia, *f.* (med.) gastralgia, stomach pains.
gastrálgico, ca, *a.* (med.) gastralgic.
gastrectomía, *f.* (med.) gastrectomy.
gastricismo, *m.* (med.) gastricism.
gástrico, ca, *a.* (med.) gastric.
gastrina, *f.* (biochem.) gastrin.
gastritis, *m.* (med.) gastritis.
gastrocelo, *m.* (anat.) gastrocoel, gastrocoele.
gastrocólico, ca, *a.* (physiol.) gastrocolic.
gastroenteritis, *f.* (med.) gastroenteritis.
gastroenterología, *f.* (med.) gastroenterology.
gastroenterólogo, *m.* (med.) gastroenterologist.
gastrogénico, ca, *a.* (med.) gastrogenic.
gastrointestinal, *a.* (med.) gastrointestinal.
gastromanía, *f.* gluttony.
gastronomía, *f.* gastronomy, the art of good eating; epicurism.
gastronómico, ca, *a.* gastronomic, gastronomical.
gastrónomo, *m.* gastronome, gastronomist.
gastroscopia, *f.* (med.) gastroscopy.
gastroscopio, *m.* (med.) gastroscope.
gastrotomía, *f.* (surg.) gastrotomy.
gastrotrico, *m.* (zool.) gastrotrichan.
gastrovascular, *a.* gastrovascular.
gástrula, *f.* (biol.) gastrula.
gastrulación, *f.* (biol.) gastrulation.
gata, *f.* 1. female cat, tabby, kitty. 2. (bot.) restharrow (Ononis spinosa). 3. low-hanging mountain cloud. 4. girl of Madrid. 5. (Cuba, ichth.) gata. 6. (Chile) crank. 7. (S. Amer., mec.) jack. 8. (mil.) cat, cat house or castle. 9. (Mex.) servant girl. — **a gatas,** on all fours; **g. parida,** (coll.) thin, emaciated woman or girl.
gatada, *f.* 1. cat-like act. 2. sudden turn (of the hare when closely pursued). 3. (coll.) dirty trick, mean trick.
gattalón, na, *a.* rascally, scoundrelly. —*m., f.* rascal, scoundrel.
gatatumba, *f.* (coll.) feigned sympathy, respect or emotion.
gatazo, *m.* 1. *aug. of* **gato,** large cat. 2. confidence trick, swindle.
gateado, da, *past part. of* **gatear.** —*a.* 1. cat-like, feline. 2. grained, striped (wood, etc.). —*m.* 1. creeping, crawling; climbing. 2. (bot.) gateado (American hard wood).
gateamiento, *m.* crawling, creeping; climbing.
gatear, *i.v.* to crawl, creep; to climb. —*tr.v.* 1. (coll.) to scratch, claw. 2. (coll.) to steal, pinch. 3. (Mex.) to make advances to the maids or servant girls.
gatera, *f.* 1. cathole. 2. (mar.) hawsehole, cathole. 3. thief. —*m.* rogue, rascal, scamp.
gatería, *f.* 1. (coll.) cats, swarm of cats. 2. (coll.) gang of young rowdies. 3. (coll.) sham humility, wheedling, cajolery.
gatero, ra, *a.* inhabited or frequented by cats. —*m., f.* cat dealer; cat lover.
gatesco, ca, *a.* (coll.), *var. of* **gatuno.**
gatillazo, *m.* click of the hammer of a gunlock.
gatillo, *m.* 1. trigger; firingpin, hammer. 2. dentist's forceps. 3. (coll.) petty thief. 4. nape (of certain quadrupeds).
gato, *m.* 1. cat, tomcat, tom. 2. moneybag; money in moneybag. 3. (mec.) jack, lifting jack. 4. (mil.) gun-searcher. 5. (coll.) petty thief, filcher. 6. (coll.) wise guy, shrewd astute fellow. 7. (coll.) man of Madrid. 8. (coll.) senior cadet (in military academy). 9. (carp.) clamp, vise. — **buscar tres pies al g.,** to look for trouble; **cuatro gatos,** a few, one or two people; **dar g. por liebre,** to gyp, swindle; **de noche todos los gatos son pardos,** everything is permissible at night; **g. con botas,** Puss in Boots; **g. de algalia,** (zool.) civet cat; **g. de Angora,** (zool.) Angora cat; **g. de arena,** (mec.) sand jack; **g. de vía,** (ry.) track jack; **g. hidráulico,** hydraulic jack; **g. montés,** (zool.) wildcat; **g. persa,** (zool.) Persian cat; **g. siamés,** (zool.) Siamese cat; **g. encerrado,** (coll.) something fishy; **llevar el g. al agua,** (coll.) to overcome a difficulty; to take a chance or risk.
gatuna, *f., var. of* **gatuña.**
gatuno, na, *a.* catlike, feline.
gatuña, *f.* (bot.) restharrow, cammock, (Ononis spinosa).
gatuperio, *m.* 1. hodgepodge. 2. (coll.) scheme, conspiracy, intrigue; fraud.
gauchada, *f.* 1. (Arg., Urug.) smart piece of work. 2. (Arg., Peru) good turn, favor. — **hazme una g.,** do me a favor (like a good gaucho).
gauchaje, *m.* (Arg., Urug.) group of gauchos.
gauchesco, ca, *a.* gaucho-like.
gaucho, cha, *a.* 1. gaucho. 2. (Arg., Urug.) shrewd, astute, sly. 3. (Arg.) rude, uncouth. —*m.* 1. gaucho. 2. (Arg., Urug.) expert horseman.
gaudeamus, *m.* (coll.) joy, festivity. — **andar de g.,** to merry-make or celebrate.
gaulteria, *f.* (bot.) gaultheria.
gauss, *m.* (phys.) gauss.
gavanza, *f.* (bot.) dog rose (flower).
gavanzo, *m.* (bot.) dog rose (plant).
gavera, *f.* 1. (Col., Mex., Ven.) brick or tile-mold. 2. (Peru) mold for adobe walls; wall. 3. (Col.) wooden cooling vat for sugarcane syrup.
gaveta, *f.* drawer (of a desk etc.).
gavia, *f.* 1. (mar.) topsail; main topsail; top, crow's nest. 2. drainage or boundary ditch. 3. cage formerly used for madmen. 4. seagull, gull. 5. (min.) gang of laborers who pass loads from hand to hand.
gavial, *m.* (zool.) gavial, a species of crocodile.
gaviar, *i.v.* (Amer.) to tassel (corn).
gaviero, *m.* (mar.) ship's lookout, mastman, topman; **g. de proa,** foretopman.
gavieta, *f.* (mar.) mizzenmast or bowsprit; crow's nest.
gaviete, *m.* (mar.) cathead.
gavilán *m.* 1. (ornith.) sparrow hawk. 2. hair stroke, flourish (in writing). 3. (either) side of pen nib. 4. quillon (of sword). 5. plowstaff paddle or blade. 6. (mar.) grappling iron. 7. thistle flower. 8. (Amer.) ingrown nail.
gavilancillo, *m.* point of an artichoke leaf.
gavilla, *f.* 1. sheaf; small bundle. 2. (fig.) gang (e.g. of toughs). — **una g. de ladrones,** a gang of thieves.
gavillar, *tr.v.* to bind into sheaves.
gavillero, *m.* 1. row of sheaves; stacking place for sheaves. 2. (Chile) laborer loading sheaves on cart.
gavina, *f.* seagull, gull.
gavión, *m.* 1. (fort., hydr., engin.) gabion. 2. hat with broad brim and high crown.
gaviota, *f.* seagull, gull.
gavota, *f.* gavotte, gavot (French dance and music).
gay, *a,* 1. gay, bright, cheerful; **el g. saber,** poetics. 2. gay, homosexual. —*m.* gay man, gay. —*f.* gay woman, lesbian.
gaya, *f.* 1. colored stripe; triumphal sash (awarded to the victors). 2. (ornith.) magpie.
gayado, da, *past part. of* **gayar.** —*a.* striped.
gayadura, *f.* decorative stripes, colored striping.
gayar, *tr.v.* to decorate or trim anything with colored stripes.
gayata, *f.* shepherd's crook.
gayo, ya, *a.* gay, bright (colors, etc.). — **gaya ciencia,** poetry.
gayola, *f.* cage; (coll.) jail, can, jug.
gayomba, *f.* (bot.) Spanish broom (Spartium junceum).
gayuba, *f.* (bot.) bearberry.
gaza, *f.* loop (on a rope, a bow, etc.); (mar.) splice, noose; strap, loop.
gazafatón, *m.* (coll.) *var. of* **gazapatón.**
gazapa, *f.* (coll.) lie, fib.
gazapatón, *m.* (coll.) stupid remark; fluff (in speech).
gazapera, *f.* 1. rabbit warren. 2. (coll.) gang (e.g. of toughs). 3. (coll.) quarrel, brawl, row, wrangle, squabble.
gazapina, *f.* 1. (coll.) gang (e.g. of crooks). 2. quarrel, brawl.
gazapo, *m.* 1. coney, young rabbit. 2. (coll.) astute fellow. 3. (coll.) lie. 4. (coll.) slip, error (in writing or speech).
gazapón, *m.* 1. gambling house or den. 2. gambling profits.
gazmiar, (*ref. 54*) *tr.v.* 1. to relish, smell with relish. 2. to nibble (tidbits of food being cooked). —*r.v.* (coll. to complain.
gazmol, *m.* pustule on the tongue or roof of the mouth of birds of prey.
gazmoñada, *f.* prudishness; prudery; hypocrisy, affected devotion.
gazmoñería, *f., var. of* **gazmoñada.**
gazmoñero, ra, *a.* prudish, priggish; hypocritical, affectedly devout. —*m., f.* prude, prig.
gazmoño, ña, *a., var. of* **gazmoñero.**
gaznápiro, ra, *a.* simple, foolish. —*m., f.* simpleton, fool; booby (sl.).
gaznar, *i.v., var. of* **graznar.**
gaznatada, *f.* blow on the throat; (Hond., Mex., Ven.) punch.
gaznatazo, *m., var. of* **gaznatada.**
gaznate, *m.* 1. gullet, throttle, windpipe. 2. fritter. 3. (Mex.) sweet made with pineapple and coconut. — **remojar el g.,** to wet one's whistle, have a drink.

gaznatón, *m.* 1. slap; blow. 2. fritter.
gazofia, *f.* swill, hogwash, refuse.
gazofilacio, *m.* gazophylacium, treasury (in the Temple of Jerusalem).
gazpachero, ra, *m., f.* maker of gazpacho.
gazpacho, *m.* gazpacho, soup prepared with oil, tomatoes, vinegar, salt, garlic, onions and bread and served cold.
gazuza, *f.* (coll.) hunger.
gazuzo, za, *a.* (Chile) hungry.
Gd *sym. of* **gadolinio,** gadolinium (Gd).
Ge *sym. of* **germanio,** germanium (Ge).
Ge, Gea, *f.* (myth.) Gaea, Gaia, Ge, Greek goddess of the earth.
gea, *f.* 1. mineral wealth of a region. 2. treatise describing minerals of a region.
geato, *m.* (chem.) humato.
geco, *m.* (zool.) gecko.
gecónidos, *m.* (*pl.*) (zool.) Gekkonidae.
gehena, *m.* Gehenna, hell; (hist.) **G.,** Gehenna, Jewish heroine among the Berbers.
géiser, *m.* geyser.
geiserita, *f.* (min.) geyserite.
gelación, *f.* (chem.) gelation.
gelatina, *f.* gelatine; (cul.) gelatin (used for making jelly); (cul.) jelly. — **g. explosiva,** gelatin dynamite.
gelatinoso, sa, *a.* gelatinous.
geldre, *m.* (bot.) guelder rose.
gelfe, *m.* black slave.
gélido, da, *a.* (poet.) gelid, icy cold, frigid.
gelsemina, *f.* (bot.) gelsemium.
gelsemio, *m.* (bot.) gelsemium.
gema, *f.* 1. gem, precious stone. 2. (carp.) wane. 3. (bot.) gemma, bud.
gemación, *f.* (bot.) gemmation.
gemebundo, da, *a.* groaning, moaning or wailing loudly.
gemela, *f.* (bot.) Arabian jazmine.
gemelíforo, ra, *a.* (bot.) geminiflorous.
gemelo, la, *a., m., f.* twin. —*m.* 1. cuff link. 2. (anat.) gemellus. 3. (*pl.*) binoculars. 4. (*pl.*) (astron.) **G.,** Gemini. 5. (*pl.*) (carp.) strengthening slats. — **gemelos de campaña** or **campo,** field glasses; **gemelos de teatro,** opera glasses.
gemido, *past part. of* **gemir.** —*m.* groan, moan, wail.
gemidor, ra, *a.* groaning, moaning, wailing.
geminación, *f.* (rhet.) gemination.
geminado, da, *past part. of* **geminar.**
geminar, *tr.v.* to geminate.
gemínifloro, ra, *a.* geminiflorous.
Géminis, *m.* 1. (astron.) **G.,** Gemini. 2. (pharm.) plaster of white lead and wax.
gemíparo, ra, *a.* (bot.) gemmiparous.
gemiquear, *i.v.* (Chile, reg.) to whine, blubber.
gemiqueo, *m.* (Chile) whining, blubbering.
gemir, (*ref. 39*) *i.v.* to groan, moan, wail; to howl.
gémula, *f.* (bot., zool.) gemmule.
gemulación, *f.* (bot.) gemmulation.
gen, *m.* (biol.) gene.
Gén. *abbrev. of* **Génesis,** Genesis (Gen.).
genciana, *f.* (bot.) gentian.
gencianáceo, cea, *a.* gentianaceous. —*f.* (*pl.*) Gentianaceae.
gendarme, *m.* gendarme; policeman, guard.
gendarmería, *f.* gendarmery; body of guards.
genealogía, *f.* genealogy.
genealógico, ca, *a.* genealogical.
genealogista, *m.* genealogist.
generable, *a.* generable, that can be generated.
generación, *f.* 1. generation; descendents, offspring, progeny. 2. (mec.) generation.
generador, ra, *a.* generating, generative. —*m., f.* begetter, generator, engenderer. —*m.* (mec., elec.) generator; **g. de gas,** gas generator; **g. de señales,** (rad.) signal generator.
general, *a.* 1. general. 2. common, usual. 3. widely read, highly educated. —*m.* (mil., ecc.) general. — **en g.** or **por lo g.,** in general, generally, usually; **g. de brigada,** brigadier (G.B.), brigadier general (U.S.); **g. de división,** major general; **g. en jefe,** general-in-chief; **generales,** personal data.
generala, *f.* 1. general's wife. 2. (mil.) call to arms.
generalato, *m.* (mil., ecc.) generalship; generals of the army.
generalice, generalicé, *ref.* **generalizar.**
generalidad, *f.* 1. generality, general statement. 2. majority, bulk. 3. (Sp., hist.) **G.,** Catalan legislative assembly.
generalísimo, *m.* generalissimo, commander in chief.
generalización, *f.* generalization.
generalizador, ra, *a.* generalizing.
generalizar, (*ref. 53*) *tr.v.* 1. to make general or common, generalize. 2. to generalize, derive a general principle from; to generalize on, make generalizations on. —*i.v.* to generalize. —*r.v.* to become general or generalized.
generalmente, *adv.* generally.
generar, *tr.v.* to generate, produce; (mec.) to generate.
generativo, va, *a.* generative.
generatriz, (*pl.* **generatrices**) generating. —*a.* (geom.) generatrix.
genéricamente, *adv.* generically.
genérico, ca, *a.* 1. generic; (gram.) common (noun). 2. (gram.) indicating gender.
género, *m.* 1. kind, sort, type. 2. way, manner. 3. (biol.) genus. 4. (tex.) cloth, material, fabric; **géneros de pieza,** piece goods, yard goods. 5. (p., lit.) genre. 6. (gram.) gender. 7. (*pl.*) (com.) goods, merchandise. — **de g.,** (lit., p.) genre, e.g. *pintor de g.,* genre painter; **g. chico,** (theat.) farces, variety, vaudeville; **g. humano,** humanity, human race; **g. novelístico,** the novel (as genre).
generosamente, *adv.* generously.
generosidad, *f.* 1. generosity, liberality. 2. magnanimity; nobility. 3. valor, courage.
generoso, sa, *a.* 1. generous, liberal. 2. magnanimous, noble. 3. excellent, fine. 4. generous, full-bodied (wine). 5. high-born, noble.
genesíaco, ca, *a.* genetic (in the Bible).
genésico, ca, *a.* genesic, generative.
génesis, *m.* **G.,** Genesis, first book of the Pentateuch. —*f.* genesis, beginning.
genética, *f.* genetics, the branch of biology that studies inheritance.
geneticista, *m., f.* geneticist.
genético, ca, *a.* genetic.
genetista, *m., f.* geneticist.
genetlíaca, *f.* (astrol.) genethlialogy.
genetlíaco, ca, *a.* genethlialogical, genethlialogic. —*m.* genethliac, one who makes horoscopes.
Gengis Kan, *m.* Genghis Khan, Mongol conqueror.
genial, *a.* 1. brilliant, inspired. 2. (coll.) agreeable, pleasant; genial, affable. 3. typical, characteristic (of someone's character).
genialidad, *f.* 1. peculiarity (of character). 2. a genial word or deed.
genialmente, *adv.* brilliantly, cleverly, with inspiration.
geniazo, *m. aug. of* **genio,** (coll.) violent temper.
geniculación, *f.* (biol.) geniculation, knee-like joint or bend.
geniculado, da, *a.* (bot., zool.) geniculate.
genio, *m.* 1. genius. 2. temper, temperament; character, disposition. 3. ability, talent. 4. spirit, energy. 5. genie, pagan spirit. 6. (p.) angel, heavenly figure (in painting). — **corto de g.,** shy, timid; **persona de mal g.,** bad-tempered person; **g. y figura,** creative and personal image of a person (artist, politician, etc.).
genista, *f.* (bot.) genista, broom (Genista sphaerocarpa).
genital, *a.* genital. —*m.* (*pl.*) genitals.
genitivo, va, *a., m.* (gram.) genitive (case).
genitor, *m.* begetter, engenderer.
genitourinario, ria, *a.* (anat.) genitourinary.
genízaro, ra, *a.* (Mex.) half-breed.
genízaro, *var. of* **jenízaro,** turkish infantryman.
genocidio, *m.* genocide, the systematic extermination of a group of people.
genol, *m.* (mar.) futtock.
genoma, *m.* (biol.) genome, genom.
genospecie, *f.* (biol.) genospecies.
genotipo, *m.* (biol.) genotype.
Génova, *f.* Genoa, N. Italian city.
genovés, sa, *a., m., f.* Genoese.
gens, *f.* gens (in Roman history).
gente, *f.* 1. people; nation. 2. (mar.) crew; (mil.) troops, men. 3. (coll.) people, folks, family. 4. (*pl.*) (Bib.) gentiles. 5. (Amer.) decent or respectable folk. — **buena g.,** (Amer.) good sort of people, e.g. *él es buena g.,* he's a good guy; **g. bien,** upper class, the well-to-do; **g. de barrio,** common people; **g. de bien,** respectable folk; **g. de coleta,** bullfighters; **g. de color,** colored people; **g. de escalera abajo,** (coll.) underlings, underdogs; **g. de vida airada,** libertines, prostitutes, pimps; **g. del bronce,** (coll.) happy-go-lucky people; **g. de mar,** seamen, sailors; **g. de medio pelo,** lower middle class; **g. de paz,** friend (reply to "who goes there?"); **g. de pelo** or **pelusa,** the well-off, the rich; **g. de toda broza,** tramps, bums; **g. de trato,** tradesmen, businessmen; **g. de traza,** responsible reliable people; **g. forzada,** convicts; **g. gorda,** (coll.) people of position; **g. menuda,** (coll.) children, kiddies; **g. perdida,** bums, tramps; crooks, the underworld; **hacer g.,** to recruit men; to gather people together; **ser g.,** (Amer.) to be decent or respectable.
gentecilla, *f. dim. of* **gente,** (derog.) the rabble, the mob.
gentil, *a.* 1. kind, pleasant, agreeable. 2. polite, genteel. 3. gallant, spirited, charming. 4. tremendous, great. 5. (Bib.) gentile. —*m., f.* (Bib.) gentile; heathen.
gentileza, *f.* 1. gallantry, courtesy. 2. kindness, pleasantness. 3. elegance, refinement; show, dash. 4. ease, self-confidence, self-assurance.
gentilhombre, *m.* 1. gentleman-in-waiting; messenger to the king. 2. (as a form of address) my good sir! kind sir! 3. handsome fellow. — **g. de cámara,** gentleman-in-waiting.
gentilice, gentilicé, *ref.* **gentilizar.**
gentilicio, cia, *a.* gentile (denoting a people, nation or family). — **nombre g.,** gentile noun, gentilic. —*m.* gentile, gentilic (adjective or noun).
gentílico, ca, *a.* gentile; heathen.
gentilidad, *f.* heathendom.
gentilismo, *m., var. of* **gentilidad.**
gentilizar, (*ref. 53*) *tr.v.* to make heathen, heathenize. —*i.v.* to practice heathen rites.
gentilmente, *adv.* kindly, pleasantly, courteously.
gentío, *m.* crowd, mob, multitude.
gentualla, gentuza, *f.* (derog.) rabble, mob.
genuflexión, *f.* bow, genuflexion, genuflection.
genuino, na, *a.* genuine; legitimate.
génuli, *m.* (min.) orpiment.
geocéntrico, ca, *a.* geocentric, having the Earth as its center.
geocronología, *f.* (geol.) geochronology.

geocronológico, ca, *a.* (geol.) geochronological.
geocronometría, *f.* (geol.) geochronometry.
geocronométrico, ca, *a.* (geol.) geochronometrical.
geoda, *f.* (geol.) geode.
geodesia, *f.* (geol.) geodesy.
geodésico, ca, *a.* geodesic.
geodesta, *m.* (geol.) geodesist.
geodinámico, ca, *a.* (geol.) geodynamic, geodynamical. —*f.* geodynamics.
geofagia, *f.* geophagy.
geófago, ga, *a.* geophagous. —*m., f.* geophagist.
geofísica, *f.* geophysics.
geofísico, ca, *a.* geophysical.
geófito, *f.* (bot.) geophyte.
geogenia, *f.* (geol.) geogony.
geogénico, ca, *a.* geogonic, geogonical.
geognosia, *f.* (geol.) geognosy.
geognosta, *m.* geognost, geognosy expert.
geognóstico, ca, *a.* geognostical.
geogonía, *f., var. of* **geogenia.**
geogónico, ca, *a.* geogonic, geogonical.
geografía, *f.* geography. — **g. física,** physical geography.
geográficamente, *adv.* geographically.
geográfico, ca, *a.* geographic, geographical.
geógrafo, *m.* geographer.
geoide, *m.* geoid, shape of the earth.
geología, *f.* geology.
geológico, ca, *a.* geological.
geólogo, *m.* geologist.
geomagnético, ca, *a.* geomagnetic.
geomagnetismo, *m.* geomagnetism.
geomancia, *f.* geomancy, divination by an examination of lines formed in a handful of earth.
geomántico, ca, *a.* geomantic. —*m.* geomancer.
geómetra, *m.* geometrician, geometer.
geometral, *a., var. of* **geométrico.**
geometría, *f.* geometry. — **g. analítica,** analytical geometry; **g. del espacio,** solid geometry; **g. descriptiva,** descriptive geometry; **g. plana,** plane geometry; **g. proyectiva,** projective geometry.
geométricamente, *adv.* geometrically.
geométrico, ca, *a.* geometric, geometrical; (fig.) exact, mathematical.
geométrido, *m.* (ento.) geometrid; (*pl.*) Geometridae.
geomorfía, *f.* (geol.) geomorphy.
geomórfico, ca, *a.* geomorphic.
geomorfología, *f.* (geol.) geomorphology.
geonomía, *f.* (geol.) geonomy.
geonómico, ca, *a.* geonomic.
geopolítico, ca, *a.* geopolitic, geopolitical. —*f.* geopolitics.
geoponía, geopónica, *f.* geoponics, agriculture.
geopónico, ca, *a.* geoponic, agricultural.
geoquímico, ca, *f.* geochemistry. —*a.* geochemical.
georama, *m.* georama.
georgiano, *a., m., f.* Georgian.
geórgica, co, *a.* georgic, said of a poem dealing with a pastoral or bucolic subject.
geoscopia, *f.* geoscopy.
geosinclinal, (geol.) *a.* geosynclinal. —*m.* geosyncline, geosynclinal.
geostático, ca, *a.* geostatic. —*f.* geostatics.
geostrófico, ca, *a.* (meteorol.) geostrophic.
geotáctico, ca, *a.* geotactic.
geotaxis, *f.* (biol.) geotaxis.
geotaxismo, *m.* (biol.) geotaxis.
geotectónico, ca, *a.* (geol.) geotectonic.
geotérmico, ca, *a.* geothermic.
geotrópico, ca, *a.* (biol.) geotropic.
geotropismo, *m.* (bot.) geotropism, the movement or growth of a living organism in response to the force of gravity.
geraniáceo, a, *a.* (bot.) geraniaceous. —*f.* (*pl.*) (bot.) Geraniaceae.
geranio, *m.* (bot.) geranium. — **g. de malva,** nutmeg geranium; **g. de rosa,** rose geranium.
geraniol, *m.* (chem.) geraniol.
gerbo, *m.* (zool.) gerbil, gerbille.
gerencia, *f.* 1. management; managership, post of manager. 2. manager's office.
gerente, *m.* (com.) manager.
geriatra, *m., f.* geriatrician, doctor whose specialty is treating the aged.
geriatría, *f.* (med.) geriatrics.
gericaya, *f.* (Mex.) custard.
gerifalte, *m.* 1. (ornith.) gyrfalcon, gerfalcon. 2. (mil.) gerfalcon, small caliber culverin. — **como un g.,** in grand style, in lordly fashion.
germán, *a., var. of* **germano.**
germanesco, ca, *a.* pertaining to slang.
germanía, *f.* 1. thieves' slang, gypsies' slang. 2. concubinage.
germanice, *ref.* **germanizar.**
germánico, ca, *a.* Germanic. —*m.* 1. Germanic (language). **2. G.,** Germanicus.
germanio, *m.* (chem.) germanium.
germanismo, *m.* Germanism, a typically German word or expression.
germanización, *f.* germanization.
germanizar, (*ref. 53*) *tr.v.* to germanize. —*r.v.* to become germanized.
germano, na, *a., m., f.* German. —*m.* brother-German.
germanófilo, la, *a., m., f.* Germanophile.
germanofobia, *f.* Germanophobia.
germanófobo, ba, *a.* Germanophobic. —*m., f.* Germanophobe.
germen, *m.* (bact., biol., fig.) germ; **g. plasma,** (biol.) germ plasm, germ plasma.
germicida, *a.* germicidal. —*m.* germicide, germ killer.
germinación, *f.* germination, sprouting.
germinador, ra, *a.* germinating. —*m.* germinator.
germinal, *a.* germinal. —*m.* Germinal, seventh month of the French Revolutionary calendar.
germinante, *a.* germinating, sprouting.
germinar, *i.v.* to germinate, sprout.
germinativo, va, *a.* germinative.
geromorfismo, *m.* (biol., med.) gerontomorphosis.
gerontocracia, *f.* gerontocracy, government by old men.
gerontología, *f.* (med.) gerontology.
gerontólogo, *m.* (med.) gerontologist.
gerundense, *a.* of or pertaining to Gerona, Spain. —*m., f.* native of Gerona.
gerundiada, *f.* (coll.) bombastic expression, meaningless expression.
gerundiano, na, *a.* (coll.) bombastic, empty, pompous.
gerundio, *m.* (gram.) 1. present participle (part of a verb with the same form as the Latin gerund; it is used to form the progressive tenses in Spanish, e.g. *estaba corriendo,* he was running, and in the ablative absolute construction, e.g. *reinando Isabel se descubrió América.* America was discovered when Isabel was reigning). 2. gerund (in reference to Latin).
gerundio, *m.* (coll.) bombastic writer or speaker.
gerusía, *f.* Gerousia, Gerusia.
gesta, *f.* exploit, epic poem or narrative. — **cantar de g.,** chanson de geste.
gestación, *f.* (med.) gestation; (fig.) time or period during which something is conceived, planned, etc.
gestaltismo, *m.* Gestalt psychology.
gestatorio, ria, *a.* gestatorial (chair).
gestear, *i.v.* to gesticulate, gesture; to grimace, make faces.
gestero, ra, *a.* inclined to grimace; gesticulative.
gesticulación, *f.* grimacing; gesticulation.
gesticular, *i.v.* to grimace, make faces; to gesticulate, gesture.
gesticuloso, sa, *a.* grimacing; gesticulatory.
gestión, *f.* 1. step, measure; arrangement. 2. management. — **hacer gestiones,** to take steps, negotiate.
gestionar, *tr.v.* to negotiate; to arrange for; to take steps to.
gesto, *m.* 1. face, grimace, look, expression. 2. gesture; gesticulation. 3. face. 4. gesture, action, e.g. *es un lindo g.,* it is a very nice gesture. — **estar de buen** or **mal g.,** to be in a good or bad temper or mood; **hacer gestos,** to grimace, make faces; to gesture, gesticulate; **hacer gestos a,** to look askance or disdainfully at; **poner g.,** to look annoyed.
gestor, ra, *a.* (com.) negotiating. —*m., f.* negotiator. —*m.* manager. — **g. de negocios,** business representative or manager.
gestudo, da, *a.* scowling, cross-looking. —*m., f.* cross-looking person.
Getsemaní, *m.* (Bib.) Gethsemane.
géyser, *m.* (geol.) geyser.
geyserita, *f.* (min.) geyserite.
Ghana, *f.* Ghana, African republic.
ghanés, nesa, *m., f., a.* Ghanaian.
ghetto, *m.* ghetto.
giba, *f.* 1. hump. 2. (coll.) bother, nuisance.
gibado, da, *past part. of* **gibar.** —*a.* hunched, bent.
gibar, *tr.v.* 1. to bend, curve. 2. (coll.) to bother, annoy.
gibelino, na, *a., m.* (hist.) Ghibelline.
gibón, *m.* (zool.) gibbon.
gibosidad, *f.* gibbosity, hump-like protuberance.
giboso, sa, *a.* gibbous, humpbacked.
Gibraltar, *f.* (Rock of) Gibraltar.
gibraltareño, ña, *a.* Gibraltar (as. *a.*) —*m., f.* native of Gibraltar.
giga, *f.* ancient dance and music.
giganta, *f.* 1. giantess. 2. (bot.) sunflower.
gigante, *a.* gigantic, giant, huge. —*m.* 1. giant. 2. giant figure (in carnival parades).
gigantea, *f.* (bot.) sunflower.
giganteo, a, *a.* (rare) giant, gigantic.
gigantesco, ca, *a.* gigantic, huge.
gigantez, *f.* gigantic size.
gigantilla, *f.* 1. large-headed figure (in carnival). 2. short fat woman.
gigantismo, *m.* (med.) gigantism, giantism.
gigantón, na, *m., f. aug. of* **gigante,** huge giant or giantess. —*m.* 1. large cardboard figure (in carnival parade). 2. (bot.) large purple dahlia (Dahlia variabilis).
gígolo, *m.* (fr.) gigolo, pimp.
gigote, *m.* (cul.) fricassee; minced meat stew, hash. — **hacer g. (una cosa),** to smash to smithereens.
gijonense, *a., var. of* **gijonés.**
gijonés, sa, *a.* of or pertaining to Gijón, Spain. —*m., f.* native of Gijón.
gilí, *a.* (coll.) silly, foolish, stupid.
gilvo, va, *a.* honey-colored.
gima, *ref.* **gemir.**
gimiendo, gimiera, gimiese, gimió, *ref.* **gemir.**
gimnasia, *f.* gymnastics.
gimnasiarca, *m.* (hist.) gymnasiarch.
gimnasio, *m.* 1. gymnasium. 2. gymnasium, secondary school.
gimnasta, *m.* gymnast; athlete.
gimnástica, *f.* gymnastics; athletics.
gimnástico, ca, *a.* gymnastic; athletic.
gímnico, ca, *a.* pertaining to athletic contests.

gimnosofía, *f.* gymnosophy.
gimnosofista, *m.* gymnosophist, a member of an ancient Hindu sect.
gimnospermo, ma, *a.* (bot.) gymnospermous. —*f.* (bot.) gymnosperm.
gimnospora, *f.* (biol.) gymnospore.
gimnoto, *m.* (ichth.) electric eel.
gimo, *ref.* **gemir.**
gimoteador, ra, *a.* whining.
gimotear, *i.v.* (coll.) to whine.
gimoteo, *m.* (coll.) whining, whine.
ginandra, *f.* (bot.) gynandrous.
ginandria, *f.* (biol.) gynandry.
ginandrismo, *m.* (biol.) gynandry.
ginandro, dra, *a.* gynandrous.
ginandromorfismo, *m.* (biol.) gynandromorphism.
ginandromorfo, fa, *a.* (biol.) gynandromorphic. —*m.* (biol.) gynandromorph.
ginantropía, *f.* (biol.) gynandry.
ginebra, *f.* 1. confusion, disorder, bedlam. 2. uproar, din. 3. crude form of xylophone.
ginebra, *f.* gin (liquor).
Ginebra, *f.* 1. Geneva, city in Switzerland. 2. (lit.) Guinevere.
ginebrada, *f.* (cul.) pastry with cream filling.
ginebrés, sa, *a., var. of* **ginebrino.**
ginebrino, na, *a., m., f.* Genevan, Genevese, from the city of Geneva.
gineceo, *m.* 1. (bot.) gyneceum, gynaeceum, gynoecium. 2. (arch.) gynaeceum (the women's quarters in a Greek house).
ginecocracia, *f.* gynecocracy, petticoat rule, government by women.
ginecoide, *a.* (med.) gynecoid.
ginecología, *f.* (med.) gynecology.
ginecológico, ca, *a.* gynecological.
ginecólogo, *m.* (med.) gynecologist.
ginesta, *f.* (bot.) genista, broom (Genista sphaerocarpa).
gineta, *f.* (zool.) genet.
gingidio, *m.* (bot.) bishop's weed (Ammi viznaga).
gingival, *a.* gingival, pertaining to the gums.
gingivitis, *f.* (med.) gingivitis, an infection of the gums.
gínglimo, *m.* (anat.) ginglymus.
giniatría, *f.* (med.) gyniatrics.
ginofórico, ca, *a.* (bot.) gynophoric.
ginóforo, *m.* (bot.) gynophore.
ginseng, *m.* (bot.) ginseng.
giobertita, *f.* (min.) magnesium carbonate.
gipsífero, ra, gypsiferous.
gipsófila, *m.* (bot.) gypsophila, baby's breath.
gira, *f.* tour; excursion.
girada, *f.* (dancing) pirouette, turn.
girado, *m.* (com.) drawee.
girador, ora, *m., f.* (com.) drawer.
giralda, *f.* vane, weathercock (in human or animal shape).
giraldete, *m.* (ecc.) sleeveless rochet or surplice.
giraldilla, *f.* 1. popular Asturian dance. 2. (taur.) a pass with the sword.
girándula, *f.* 1. girandole, pinwheel. 2. revolving jet of water.
girante, *a.* revolving, turning, spinning, rotating.
girar, *tr.v.* (com.) to write out, draw (a check). —*i.v.* 1. to turn round, spin round; to revolve, gyrate, rotate. 2. to revolve (a conversation round a subject). 3. to turn, veer. 4. to trade, do business. — **g. contra,** to draw on, write a check against.
girasol, *m.* 1. (bot.) sunflower. 2. (fig.) sycophant, favorite.
giratorio, ria, *a.* revolving; gyratory. —*m.* revolving bookcase.
girino, *m.* (ento.) whirligig beetle.
giro, *m.* 1. turn; spinning, turning; gyration, rotation, revolution. 2. turn (of phrase; in conversation or events). 3. boast, threat, brag. 4. gash, slash; scar (on face). 5. (com.) draft; bill of exchange, money order. 6. (com.) turnover, business. 7. (com.) line of business. — **g. a la vista,** (com.) demand bill, demand draft; **g. bancario,** bank draft; **g. de cambio a plazo,** (com.) time draft or note; **g. de favor or cortesía,** accommodation paper; **g. postal,** (com.) post-office order, money order.
giro, ra, *a.* (Amer., reg.) streaked with yellow (a cock's plumage).
giroestabilizador, *m.* (aer., mar.) gyrostabilizer.
giroflé, *m.* (bot.) clove tree.
girofrecuencia, *f.* (phys.) gyrofrequency.
girola, *f.* (archit.) apse aisle, retrochoir.
giromagnético, ca, *a.* (phys.) gyromagnetic.
girómetro, *m.* (phys.) gyrometer.
Gironda, *f.* Gironde (French river). — **la G.,** (hist.) the Gironde (political party).
girondino, na, *a., m.* (hist.) Girondist.
giroscópico, ca, *a.* gyroscopic.
giroscopio, *m.* (phys.) gyroscope.
girostático, ca, *a.* (phys.) gyrostatic. —*f.* (phys.) gyrostatics.
giróstato, *m.* (phys.) gyrostat.
giróvago, ga, *a.* vagabond; wandering (esp. a monk not subject to rule and going from one monastery to another). —*m., f.* vagabond; wanderer.
gis, *m.* chalk, white crayon; (Col.) slate pencil.
giste, *m.* head (on beer), froth.
gitanada, *f.* 1. (derog.) gypsy-like action. 2. (fig.) flattery, wheedling, cajolery.
gitanamente, *adv.* (fig.) with flattery or cajolery.
gitanear, *i.v.* (fig.) to flatter, cajole, softsoap.
gitanería, *f.* 1. (coll.) flattery, cajolery. 2. gypsies, band of gypsies. 3. gypsyism, gypsy-like turn of speech.
gitanesco, ca, *a.* gypsy-like.
gitanismo, *m.* 1. gypsy life, gypsy ways. 2. gypsies, group of gypsies.
gitano, na, *a.* 1. gypsy. 2. (rare) Egyptian. 3. (fig.) charming, winning. —*m., f.* 1. gypsy. 2. (rare) Egyptian. 3. (fig.) charmer.
glabro, bra, *a.* bald; beardless, glabrous.
glaciación, *f.* (geol.) glaciation.
glacial, *a.* 1. icy, freezing. 2. (geog.) glacial. 3. (fig.) cold, indifferent, cool, unfriendly.
glacialmente, *adv.* icily, coldly.
glaciar, *m.* (geol.) glacier.
glaciario, ria, *a.* (geol.) glacial. — **período g.,** glacial era.
glaciarismo, *m.* glaciology, study of glaciers.
glacifluvial, *a.* (geol.) glaciofluvial.
glaciología, *f.* glaciology.
glacis, *m.* (mil.) glacis, sloping embankment.
gladiado, da, *a.* (bot.) gladiate.
gladiador, *m.* gladiator.
gladiatorio, ria, *a.* gladiatorial.
gladio, *m.* 1. (bot.) cattail, reed mace. 2. (zool.) gladius.
gladiolo, *m.* (bot.) gladiolus.
glande, *m.* (anat.) glans penis.
glandífero, ra, glandígero, ra, *a.* (bot.) glandiferous, acorn-bearing.
glándula, *f.* (anat., bot.) gland. — **g. carotidea,** carotid gland; **g. de secreción interna, g. endocrina,** endocrine gland; **g. lagrimal,** lacrimal gland; **g. mamaria,** mammary gland; **g. pineal,** pineal gland; **g. pituitaria,** pituitary gland; **g. prostática,** prostate gland; **g. sebacea,** sebaceous gland; **g. sudoripara,** sweat gland; **g. suprarrenal,** adrenal gland; **g. tiroidea,** thyroid gland.
glandular, *a.* glandular.
glanduloso, sa, *a.* glandulous.
glasé, *m.* (tex.) glacé silk, very shiny taffeta.
glaseado, da, *past part. of* **glasear.** —*a.* shiny, glossy.
glasear, *tr.v.* 1. to calender (paper). 2. to glacé (fruit, fabrics, etc.).
glasto, *m.* (bot.) woad (Isatis tinctoria).
glauberita, *f.* (min.) glauberite.
glaucio, *m.* (bot.) horn poppy.
glauco, ca, *a.* light green. —*m.* (**zool.**) glaucus, sea slug.
Glauco, *m.* (myth.) Glaucus, son of Sisyphus.
glaucoma, *m.* (med.) glaucoma.
glaucomatoso, sa, *a.* (med.) glaucomatous.
glauconita, *f.* (min.) glauconite.
gleba, *f.* sod, glebe.
glena, *f.* (anat.) depression or cavity (in bone).
glenoideo, a, *a.* (anat.) glenoid.
glera, *f.* gravel pit.
gliadina, *f.* (chem.) gliadin.
glicerato, *m.* (chem.) glycerate.
glicérico, ca, (chem.) *a.* glyceric.
glicérido, *m.* (chem.) glyceride.
glicerilo, *m.* (chem.) glyceryl.
glicerina, *f.* (chem.) glycerine.
glicerinar, *tr.v.* to glycerinate.
glicerol, *m.* (chem.) glycerol.
glicerosa, *f.* (chem.) glyceraldehyde.
glicina, *f.* 1. (bot.) wisteria. 2. (chem.) glycine.
glicocola, *f.* (chem.) glycine.
glicogénesis, *f.* (physiol.) glycogenesis.
glicogenia, *f.* (physiol.) glycogenesis.
glicogénico, ca, *a.* glycogenic.
glicógeno, *m.* (chem.) glycogen.
glicol, *m.* (chem.) glycol.
glicólico, ca, *a.* (chem.) glycolic.
glicólisis, *f.* (biochem.) glycolysis.
gliconio, *a., m.* glyconic (verse).
glicoproteína, *f.* (biochem.) glycoprotein.
glicósido, *m.* (chem.) glycoside.
glicosuria, *f.* (med.) glycosuria.
glifo, *m.* (archit.) glyph.
glioma, *m.* (med.) glioma.
glíptica, *f.* glyptics, the art of engraving on gems, coins, medals, etc.
gliptodonte, *m.* (paleon.) glyptodont.
gliptografía, *f.* glyptography.
gliptógrafo, *m.* glyptographer; engraver.
gliptología, *f.* glyptography.
gliptólogo, *m.* glyptographer; engraver.
global, *a.* 1. global. 2. lump, e.g. *cantidad g.,* lump sum.
globina, *f.* (biochem.) globin.
globo, *m.* 1. globe. 2. balloon. 3. round lamp shade. — **en g.,** as a whole; **g. aerostático,** aerostat, balloon; **g. cautivo,** captive balloon; **g. celeste,** celestial globe; **g. de barrera,** barrage balloon; **g. dirigible,** airship, dirigible; **g. ocular,** eyeball; **g. radiosonda,** radio balloon; **g. sonda,** sounding balloon; **g. terráqueo** or **terrestre,** earth, terrestrial globe; globe (round map of the world).
globoso, *a.* globoid, globose.
globular, *a.* globular.
globulariáceo, a, *a.* (bot.) globulariaceous. —*f.* (*pl.*) (bot.) Globulariaceae.
globulífero, ra, *a.* (anat.) globuliferous.
globulina, *f.* globulin. — **g. gamma,** (physiol.) gamma globulin.
glóbulo, *m.* 1. globule. 2. (bot.) globule. 3. (anat.) corpuscle (of blood). — **g. blanco,** white corpuscle; **g. rojo,** red corpuscle.
globuloso, sa, *a.* globulous, globulose.
glomerular, *a.* (biol.) glomerular.

glomérulo, *m.* (anat., zool.) glomerulus; (bot.) glomerule.
glomerulonefritis, *f.* (med.) glomerulonephritis.
gloquidio, *m.* (bot., zool.) glochidium.
gloria, *f.* 1. glory. 2. heavenly bliss; heaven, glory. 3. delight, bliss. 4. glory, fame. 5. (*pl.*) glory (representation of heaven). — **estar en la g.,** to be very happy; to be dead, be in heaven; **estar en sus glorias,** to be in one's glory, element or seventh heaven; **ganar la g.,** to die, go to heaven; **oler a g.,** to smell wonderfully or gloriously; **saber a g.,** to taste delicious. —*m.* (ecc.) Gloria.
gloriar, (*ref. 54*) *tr.v.* to glorify. —*r.v.* 1. to boast, brag. 2. to glory, exult. 3. to be proud, take pride. — **gloriarse de,** to boast or brag about; to be proud of, take pride in; **gloriarse en,** to glory in (e.g. the Lord).
glorieta, *f.* 1. gazebo. 2. arbor, bower. 3. square, plaza.
glorificable, *a.* glorifiable.
glorificación, *f.* glorification.
glorificador, ra, *a.* glorifying. —*m., f.* glorifier.
glorificante, *a.* glorifying.
glorificar, (*ref. 50*) *tr.v.* to glorify. —*r.v.* to glory, exult.
glorifique, glorifiqué, *ref.* **glorificar.**
gloriosamente, *adv.* gloriously.
glorioso, sa, *a.* 1. glorious. 2. vainglorious, boastful.
glosa, *f.* 1. gloss, commentary. 2. (com.) footnote. 3. (poet.) gloss. 4. (mus.) variation (on a theme).
glosador, ra, *a.* glossing, glossatorial. —*m., f.* commentator, glosser.
glosar, *tr.v.* 1. to gloss, annotate. 2. to censure, criticize, gloss.
glosario, *m.* glossary; vocabulary, list.
glose, *m.* glossing, annotating.
glosectomía, *f.* (surg.) glossectomy.
glosilla, *f.* 1. small glossary. 2. (print.) minion type.
glosis, *f.* (zool.) glossa.
glositis, *f.* (med.) glossitis.
glosofaríngeo, a, *a.* (anat.) glossopharyngeal.
glosopeda, *f.* (vet.) foot-and-mouth disease.
glossina, *f.* (ento.) glossina.
glótico, ca, *a.* (anat., phonet.) glottal.
glotis, *f.* (anat.) glottis.
glotitis, *f.* (med.) glossitis.
glotológico, ca, *a.* glottologic, glottological.
glotón, na, *a.* gluttonous; greedy. —*m., f.* glutton, epicure. —*m.* (zool.) glutton.
glotonamente, *adv.* gluttonously; greedily.
glotonear, *i.v.* to gormandize, devour, eat gluttonously.
glotonería, *f.* gluttony; greed.
gloxínea, *f.* (bot.) gloxinia.
glucina, *f.* (chem.) glucina.
glucinio, *m.* (chem.) glucinium.
glucogenia, *f.* (physiol.) glycogeny.
glucogénico, ca, *a.* (chem.) glycogenic.
glucómetro, *m.* (chem.) glucometer, hydrometer for determining the sugar content of a liquid.
gluconato, *m.* (chem.) gluconate.
glucoproteína, *f.* (chem.) glycoprotein.
glucosa, *f.* (chem.) glucose.
glucósido, *m.* (chem.) glucoside.
glucosuria, *f.* (med.) glycosuria.
glucosúrico, ca, *a.* (med.) glucosuric.
gluma, *f.* (bot.) glume, gluma.
glumáceo, a, *a.* (bot.) glumaceous.
glutamato, *m.* (chem.) glutamate.
glutamina, *f.* (chem.) glutamine.
gluten, *m.* gluten; colloid; glue.
glutenoideo, a, *a.* glutenous.
glúteo, a, *a.* (anat.) gluteal.
glutinosidad, *f.* glutinousness, glutinosity.
glutinoso, sa, *a.* glutinous, viscid, sticky.
gnático, ca, *a.* (anat.) gnathic.
gnatio, *m.* (anth.) gnathion.
gneis, *m.* (min.) gneiss, a kind of a rock.
gneísico, ca, *a.* gneissic.
gnetáceo, a, *a.* (bot.) gnetaceous. —*f.* (*pl.*) (bot.) Gnetaceae.
gnómico, ca, *a.* gnomic. —*m.* gnomic poet.
gnomo, *m.* gnome.
gnomon, *m.* 1. gnomon, sundial. 2. stonecutter's triangle or squarer. — **g. movible,** bevel square.
gnomónica, *f.* gnomonics, the measurement of time by sundials.
gnomónico, ca, *a.* gnomonic, gnomonical.
gnosis, *f.* (metaph.) gnosis, knowledge.
gnosticismo, *m.* (philos.) Gnosticism, a philosophical system stressing intuitive knowledge in spiritual matters.
gnóstico, ca, *a., m., f.* Gnostic.
gnu, *m.* (zool.) gnu, wildebeest.
goa, *f.* (metal.) 1. pig (iron), bloom. 2. (agr.) dibble.
gobernable, *a.* governable; manageable.
gobernación, *f.* 1. government; governing. 2. G., Department of the Interior (U.S.), Home Office (G.B.).
gobernador, ra, *a.* governing. —*m.* governor.
gobernadora, *f.* governor's wife; woman governor.
gobernadorcillo, *m.* (Phil. I.) minor judge.
gobernalle, *m.* (mar.) rudder, helm.
gobernante, *a.* governing, ruling. — **clase g.,** the ruling class. —*m., f.* ruler. —*m.* (coll.) self-appointed boss.
gobernar, (*ref. 29*) *tr.v.* 1. to govern, rule. 2. to steer (boat), lead (procession, dance); to guide, direct. —*i.v.* 1. to govern. 2. (mar.) to steer, obey the helm.
gobernativo, va, *a.* governmental.
gobernoso, sa, *a.* (coll.) orderly, systematic, methodical.
góbido, *m.* (ichth.) gobioid.
gobierna, *f.* weather vane.
gobierne, *ref.* **gobernar.**
gobiernista, *a.* (Amer.) government, governmental.
gobierno, *ref.* **gobernar.**
gobierno, *m.* 1. government. 2. rule. 3. governorship (post of governor; length of governor's rule). 4. governmental district. 5. government house; governor's office. 6. (mar.) rudder, helm; steering. 7. management, direction; guidance. — **para su g.,** for your information; **servir de g.,** to serve as a guide, model or warning; **g. interino** or **en funciones,** caretaker government.
gobio, *m.* (ichth.) gudgeon.
goce, *m.* 1. enjoyment, pleasure. 2. benefit.
goce, gocé, *ref.* **gozar.**
gocete, *m.* armpit guard (in ancient armor).
gocho, cha, *m., f.* (coll.) pig, swine, hog. —*f.* (coll.) sow.
godesco, ca, godible, *a.* gay, merry, cheerful, jovial, genial.
godo, da, *a.* 1. Gothic. 2. (Amer., derog.) Spanish. —*m., f.* 1. Goth. 2. (Amer., derog.) Spaniard. — **hacerse de los godos,** to boast of nobility.
gofio, *m.* 1. (Can. I., Amer.) roasted corn meal. 2. (Ven.) sweet cake made with corn meal. — **comer g.,** (Amer.) to be a fool.
gofo, fa, *a.* 1. stupid, oafish, crude, coarse. 2. (art.) dwarf figure.
gol, *m.* (Angl.) goal (in football).
gola, *f.* 1. gullet, throat. 2. (mil.) gorget (neck guard of armor; officer's ornamental neck plate). 3. gorget, ruff. 4. (archit.) gula. 5. (fort.) gorge. 6. channel (into a port, etc.).
goldre, *m.* quiver (for arrows).
goleada, *f.* tremendous margin of victory (in soccer, basketball, etc.).
golear, *tr.v.* to score many goals against, to slaughter (U.S., sl.), beat hollow (G.B.).
goleta, *f.* (mar.) schooner.
golf, *m.* (sport.) golf; **jugador de g.,** golfer.
golfán, *m.* (bot.) water lily.
golfante, *a.* scoundrelly, shameless. —*m., f.* scoundrel, rogue.
golfear, *i.v.* to live like a street urchin; to waste time.
golfería, *f.* 1. gang of street urchins. 2. vandalism.
golfillo, *m.* 1. *dim. of* **golfo,** small **gulf. 2.** urchin.
golfín, *m.* (ichth.) dolphin.
golfo, fa, *a.* mean, ugly, nasty. —*m., f.* (reg., Madrid) urchin, ragamuffin. —*f.* prostitute.
golfo, *m.* gulf; bay. — **G. de Bengala, Bay** of Bengal; **G. de Gascuña** or **Vizcaya,** Bay of Biscay; **G. Pérsico,** Persian Gulf.
Gólgota, *m.* (Bib.) Golgotha.
goliardesco, ca, *a.* goliardic.
goliardo, da, *a.* 1. intemperate, immoderate. 2. gluttonous, gormandizing. —*m.* goliard.
Goliat, *m.* (Bib.) Goliath, giant Philistine warrior slain by David.
golilla, *f.* 1. gorget, ruff; magistrate's stock or collar. 2. (mec.) washer. 3. (bldg.) pipe flange; sleeve, collar (joining pipes). 4. (Bol., Arg., Urug.) gaucho's scarf. 5. (Amer.) ruff (of a cock). —*m.* (arch.) magistrate.
golillero, ra, *m., f.* gorget or ruff maker.
gollería, *f.* 1. delicacy, delicious tidbit. 2. (*pl.*) extras, privileges, favors.
golletazo, *m.* 1. blow on the neck of a bottle (to open it). 2. sudden end (given to some difficult business). 3. (taur.) sword thrust through the bull's neck down into the chest.
gollete, *m.* 1. gullet, throat. 2. neck (of a bottle). 3. neckband (of some religious habits). — **estar hasta el g.,** to be fed up, be sick to death; to be full (of food).
gollizno, gollizo, *m.* gully (of river).
golondrina, *f.* 1. (ornith.) swallow. 2. (ichth.) sapphirine gurnard, swallow fish. 3. (C. Rica, Hond.) spurge (Euphorbia maculata).
golondrinera, *f.* (bot.) swallowwort, celandine.
golondrino, *m.* 1. male swallow. 2. (ichth.) sapphire gurnard, swallow fish. 3. wanderer. 4. (med.) boil under the armpit.
golondro, *m.* longing, yearning, desire, fancy (for). **campar de g.,** (coll.) to be a sponger or para site.
golosamente, *adv.* 1. with relish. 2. greedily.
golosear, *i.v.* to nibble at tidbits, be constantly eating tidbits or delicacies.
golosina, *f.* 1. delicacy, tidbit. 2. desire, fancy, appetite. 3. a luxury.— **g. en barra,** candy bar.
golosinar, golosinear, *i.v.* to nibble at tidbits, be constantly eating tidbits or delicacies.
goloso, sa, *a.* 1. sweet-toothed. 2. greedy, gluttonous. 3. appetizing, delicious. — **ser g.,** to have a sweet tooth. —*m., f.* gourmand.
golpazo, *m.* great blow or knock.
golpe, *m.* 1. blow, knock, hit; bump, bang. 2. crowd (of people); gush (of water); blast (of music); gust (of wind). 3. blow (of misfortune). 4. heartbeat. 5. spring bolt (of lock). 6. bunch of seedlings (in one hole); hole in which seedlings are planted. 7. shot, stroke (in billiards). 8. pocket flap. 9. trimming (on dress). 10. surprise. 11. wit, wittiness. 12. high spot (in a comedy). 13. successful bet. 14. (Mex.) sledge hammer. — **a g.,** in bunches (of seedlings planted thus); **a. golpes,** with blows; sporadically, in fits and

starts, intermittently; **a. g. seguro,** with certainty; **dar el g.** to strike, hit; **dar g. (una cosa),** to cause a surprise; **de g.,** suddenly, all of a sudden; **de g. y porrazo,** (coll.) without thought, in a rush, helter skelter; **de un g.,** at one stroke; **g. de compresión,** (mec.) compression stroke; **g. de estado,** coup d'état; **g. de expulsión,** (mec.) exhaust stroke; **g. de suerte,** or **fortuna,** stroke of luck; **g. de glotis** (phonet.) glottal stop; **g. de gracia,** coup de grace, death blow; **g. de mar,** (mar.) huge wave; **g. de mano,** sudden attack; **g. de pechos,** great grief, beating of the breast; **g. de tijera,** scissors kick (in swimming); **g. de timón,** change of direction; **g. de vista,** glance, look; **g. eléctrico,** electric shock; **g. en vano,** miss; unsuccessful attempt; **g. maestro,** masterstroke; **no dar g.,** not to do a stroke of work, be very lazy.

golpeadero, *m.* continual beating or banging.

golpeador, ra, *a.* striking, knocking, hitting, beating. —*m., f.* striker, beater, hitter, knocker.

golpeadura, *f.* 1. blow, knock, hit. 2. hitting, knocking.

golpear, *tr.v., i.v.* to hit, strike, bang, knock; to pound.

golpeo, *m., var. of* **golpeadura.**

golpete, *m.* door stop (to keep door open).

golpetear, *tr.v., i.v.* to pound, hammer, pommel.

golpeteo, *m.* pounding, hammering, pommeling.

golpista, *m. f.* (S. Amer.) coupist (person who attempts a coup d'état).

golpiza, *f.* (Amer.) beating, thrashing.

goma, *f.* 1. rubber. 2. (sticking) gum, glue. 3. rubber band. 4. (med.) gumma. 5. (Amer.) hangover.— **estar de g.,** (Amer.) to have a hangover; **g. adragante,** tragacanth; **g. arábiga,** gum arabic; **g. de borrar,** eraser, rubber; **g. de mascar,** chewing gum; **g. de pegar,** glue; **g. dos,** plastic explosive; **g. elástica,** rubber; **g. esponjosa,** sponge rubber; **g. espumosa,** or **espuma,** foam rubber; **g. guta,** gamboge; **g. laca,** shellac, lacquer.

gomecillo, *m.* (coll.) blind man's guide.

gomero, ra, *a.* of or pertaining to rubber or gum. —*m.* 1. (Amer.) rubber planter; worker on rubber plantation. 2. (bot.) rubber plant.

gomia, *f.* 1. snake-like monster. 2. bogeyman. 3. (coll.) glutton, gormandizer. 4. (coll.) waster, devourer, drain, consumer.

gomista, *m., f.* dealer in gum or rubber.

Gomorra, *f.* (Bib.) Gomorrah, Gomorrha.

gomorresina, *f.* gum resin.

gomosería, *f.* foppishness, foppery, dandyism.

gomosidad, *f.* gumminess, viscosity.

gomosis, *f.* (bot.) gummosis.

gomoso, sa, *a.* 1. gummy, viscous. 2. (med.) gummatous (suffering from gummas). —*m., f.* (med.) syphilitic suffering from gummas. —*m.* fop, dandy.

gónada, *f.* (anat.) gonad.

gonadotrófico, ca, *a.* (biochem.) gonadotrophic.

gonadotrópico, ca, *a.* (biochem.) gonadotrophic.

gonaducto, *m.* (biol.) gonophore.

gonce, *m.* hinge.

góndola, *f.* gondola.

gondolero, *m.* gondolier.

gonela, *f.* (arch.) silk or leather tunic.

gonfalón, *m.* flag, banner, standard.

gonfaloniero, *m.* flag bearer, standard bearer.

gonfosis, *f.* (anat.) gomphosis.

gong, *m.* (mus.) gong, bell, alarm.

gongorice, *ref.* **gongorizar.**

gongorino, na, *a.* Gongoristic; euphuistic. —*m., f.* Gongorist; euphuist.

gongorismo, *m.* Gongorism; euphuism, precious language.

gongorista, *m., f.* (poet.) euphuist.

gongorizar, (*ref. 53*) *i.v.* to copy the style of Gongora; to write or speak Gongoristically or euphuistically or in a precious language.

gonia, *m.* (biol.) gonium.

gonidio, *m.* (bot.) gonidium.

gonio, *m.* (anth.) gonion.

goniometría, *f.* goniometry, the measurement of angles.

goniométrico, ca, *a.* goniometric, goniometrical.

goniómetro, *m.* goniometer, instrument for measuring angles.

gonión, *m.* (anth.) gonion.

gonocito, *m.* (biol.) gonocyte.

gonococo, *m.* (bact.) gonococcus.

gonóforo, *m.* (bot., zool.) gonophore.

gonoporo, *m.* (zool.) gonopore.

gonorrea, *f.* (med.) gonorrhea.

gonorreico, ca, *a.* gonorrheal.

gorbión, *m., var. of* **gurbión.**

gorda, *f.* (Mex.) corn omelet; **se armó la g.,** (coll.) there was a big hullabaloo.

gordal, *a.* fat, fleshy, thick.

gordana, *f.* beef lard.

gordiano, na, *a.* Gordian; intricate, complicated. — **nudo gordiano,** Gordian knot.

gordiflón, na, gordinflón, na, *a.* (coll.) tubby, chubby, fleshy. —*m., f.* fatty, tubby.

gordo, da, *a.* 1. fat, corpulent, stout, plump. 2. fat (meat). 3. thick, coarse (cloth). —*m.* 1. lottery, prize. 2. fat (of meat). —**algo g.,** great news or event; **el g.,** first prize (of lottery); **caer g,** to be annoying, disagreeable; **sacarse el g.,** (coll.) to hit the jack pot.

gordolobo, *m.* (bot.) great mullein.

gordura, *f.* 1. fat, grease. 2. fatness, corpulence, plumpness, stoutness.

gorfe, *m.* deep hole in a river forming a whirlpool or eddy.

gorga, *f.* hawk's food.

gorgojarse, *r.v., var. of* **agorgojarse.**

gorgojo, *m.* 1. (ento.) grub, mite, weevil. 2. (coll.) tiny person, midget.

gorgojoso, sa, *a.* weevil or grub-ridden.

gorgón, *m.* (Col.) concrete.

Gorgona, *f.* (myth.) Gorgon, evil Greek deity.

gorgóneo, a, *a.* Gorgon, Gorgonian.

gorgónido, *a., m.* (zool.) gorgonian.

gorgor, *m.* gurgling, gurgle.

gorgorear, *i.v.* (Chile, reg.) to trill, quiver (voice).

gorgoreta, *f.* (Phil. I.) water cooling jar.

gorgorita, *f.* 1. small bubble. 2. (coll.) trill.

gorgoritear, *i.v.* (coll.) to trill, quaver (voice).

gorgorito, *m.* (coll.) trill, quaver (of voice).

górgoro, *m.* (Amer.) bubble.

gorgorotada, *f.* gulp (of liquor).

gorgoteo, *m.* gurgling, gurgle.

gorgotero, *m.* peddler, hawker.

gorguera, *f.* 1. ruff. 2. gorget, neck guard (of armor). 3. (bot.) involucre.

gorguz, (*pl.* **gorguces**), *m.* 1. short spear or lance. 2. long pole for picking pine cones. 3. (Mex.) point (of lance or goad).

gorigori, *m.* (coll.) funeral dirge.

gorila, *m.* (zool.) gorilla.

gorja, *f.* gorge, throat, gullet. — **estar uno de g.,** (coll.) to be in a festive or gay mood.

gorjal, *m.* 1. collar (of priest). 2. gorget, neck guard (of armor).

gorjeador, ra, *a.* warbling, trilling; gurgling.

gorjear, *i.v.* to warble, trill. —*r.v.* to gurgle (baby).

gorjeo, *m.* warble, trill; warbling; gurgling (of baby).

gormar, *tr.v.* to vomit, spew.

gorra, *f.* cap; bonnet; (mil.) busby; **g. de baño,** bathing cap, shower cap; **g. de marinero,** sailor's hat; **g. de vasco,** beret. —*m.* parasite, sponger. — **andar de g.,** to sponge, cadge; **comer de g.,** to sponge or cadge a meal or food; **de g.,** at someone else's expense; **vivir de g.,** to live parasitically, be a parasite, cadger or sponger.

gorrada, *f.* salute or greeting made by raising one's hat.

gorrear, *i. v.* to live parasitically, sponge.

gorrería, *f.* cap or bonnet shop or makers.

gorrero, ra, *m., f.* cap or bonnet maker. —*m.* parasite, sponger.

gorretada, *f.* salute or greeting made by raising one's hat.

gorrete, *m.* small cap or bonnet.

gorrín, *m.* suckling pig, piglet.

gorrinería, *f.* 1. filth, dirt. 2. (coll.) vulgarity, coarseness.

gorrino, na, *m., f.* suckling pig, piglet; pig, swine. 2. pig, slovenly person.

gorríon, *m.* (ornith.) house sparrow.

gorrionera, *f.* (coll.) thieves' den.

gorrista, *a.* sponging, cadging. —*m. f.* sponger, cadger.

gorro, *m.* cap; bonnet. — **apretarse el g.,** (Amer.) to get ready to run away, prepare for flight; **g. de baño,** bathing cap, shower cap; **g. de cocinero,** chef's hat; **g. de dormir,** nightcap; **g. de ducha,** shower cap; **g. frigio,** Phrygian cap; liberty cap; **poner el g. a,** to annoy, pester; (coll.) to cuckold (one's spouse).

gorrón, *m.* 1. round smooth pebble. 2. bacon rind. 3. (mec.) gudgeon, male pivot.

gorrón, na, *a.* sponging, cadging. —*m., f.* cadger, sponger. —*m.* libertine, ne'er-do-well. —*f.* (coll.) prostitute.

gorronal, *m.* land covered with pebbles or gravel.

gorronear, *i. v.* to live as a sponger or cadger, be a parasite; to cadge, sponge.

gorronería, *f.* sponging, cadging.

gorullo, *m.* lump, wad (e.g. of wool or paper).

gosipol, *m.* (chem.) gossypol.

gota, *f.* 1. drop (of liquid). 2. (med.) gout. 3. (archit.) gutta. — **g. a g.,** very gradual; **g. caduca** or **coral,** (med.) epilepsy; **gotas,** (med.) drops; **gotas nasales,** nose drops; **g. serena,** (med.) amaurosis; **sudar la g. gorda,** to sweat blood, work very hard (for something); **ser como dos gotas de agua,** to be like two peas in a pod, to be the spitting image of someone.

goteado, da, *past part. of* **gotear.** —*a.* spotted, stained with spots.

gotear, *i.v.* 1. to drip. 2. to drizzle. 3. to give in driblets.

goteo, *m.* dripping.

gotera, *f.* 1. dripping, drips. 2. leak. 3. gutter (of roof). 4. drip mark. 5. tree disease caused by infiltration of water into trunk. 5. valance (of a canopy). 6. (*pl.*) aches and pains. — **es una g.,** it's a constant source of trouble.

gotero, *m.* (Amer.) dropper, medicine dropper.

goterón, *m.* 1. large raindrop. 2. (archit.) throating, groove, water channel.

gótico, ca, *a.* 1. Gothic (civilization; art; script). 2. noble, illustrious. — **escritura gótica,** Gothic script. —*m.* Gothic (language, art style); **g. flamígero,** flamboyant Gothic; **g. tardío,** late Gothic. —*f.* Gothic script. — **niño g.,** a precocious and petulant child.

gotón, na, *a., m., f.* Goth.

gotoso, sa, *a.* gouty. —*m., f.* person who suffers from gout.

goyesco, ca, *a.* in the style of Goya.

gozar, (*ref. 53*) *tr.v.* 1. to enjoy, possess, have. 2. to have sexual intercourse with. —*i.v.* to enjoy oneself; **g. con,** to be happy or glad about; to take pleasure in; **g. de,** to enjoy, possess, have.

gozne, *m.* hinge (of doors, windows, etc.).
gozo, *m.* 1. joy, delight, pleasure. 2. (fig.) blaze. 3. (*pl.*) poems in praise of the Virgin or the saints.
gozosamente, *adv.* joyfully.
gozoso, sa, *a.* joyful, rejoicing.
gozque, *m.* little yapper (dog).
gozquejo, *m. dim. of* **gosque.**
gr. *abbrev. of* **gramo,** gram (gr).
grabación, *f.* recording, taping (of music, etc.); cutting (of gramophone record); recording, tape (on which music, etc. is recorded).
grabado, *past part. of* **grabar.** —*a.* recorded, on tape. —*m.* engraving (art process); engraving, print, cut. — **g. al agua fuerte,** etching; **g. a punta seca,** dry point; **g. en cobre,** copperplate; **g. en hueco,** intaglio; **g. en madera,** woodcut; **g. en relieve,** embossing.
grabador, ra, *a.* recording. —*m., f.* engraver. —*m., f.* recorder. — **g. de cassettes,** cassette recorder; **g. de cinta,** tape recorder.
grabadura, *f.* engraving; etching, incision.
grabar, *tr.v.* 1. to engrave. 2. to record (music); to cut (a record); **g. en cassette,** to tape, to audiotape; **g. en video,** to videotape. 3. (fig.) to engrave (in the memory). —*r.v.* (fig.) to become engraved (in the memory).
grabazón, *f.* sculptured adornment; engraved ornament.
gracejada, *f.* (Amer.) clowning, joking, jesting, buffoonery.
gracejar, *i.v.* 1. to write or speak wittily. 2. to tell jokes, joke, jest.
gracejo, *m.* wit, lightness, winsomeness; grace; (Guat.) joker, buffoon, clown.
gracia, *f.* 1. charm, gracefulness, lightness of manner; pleasantness, affability, agreeableness. 2. wittiness, wit; witticism, witty remark; funniness. 3. (ecc.) grace (of God). 4. forgiveness, grace, pardon (of a king). 5. favor; grace. 6. Grace, e.g. *Su Gracia, el Arzobispo,* His Grace, the Archbishop. 7. point, sense, e.g. *no veo la g. de ir tan temprano.* I don't see the point of going so early. 8. name. 9. (*pl.*) (myth.) Graces. — **caer de la g. de,** to fall from favor or grace; **caer en g.,** to please, be pleasing; **dar en la g. de** + *inf.,* to keep on + *ger.,* e.g. *dar en la g. de decir,* to keep on saying, harp on; **dar gracias,** to thank, say thank you; **de g.,** gratis, free; **en g. que,** considering, taking into consideration that; **estar en g.,** to be in favor; to be in a state of grace; **g. de niño,** cuteness; **gracias,** thanks, thank you; **gracias a,** thanks to, owing to; **gracias a Dios,** thank God; **hacer g.,** to please, be pleasing; **no estar de g.** or **para gracias,** to be in no mood for jokes; **tener g.,** to be funny, e.g. *eso no tiene nada de g.,* this is not at all funny.
graciable, *a.* 1. gracious, affable, amiable, good-natured. 2. easily granted.
grácil, *a.* gracile, fine, slender, thin.
graciola, *f.* (bot.) hedge hyssop.
graciosamente, *adv.* 1. gracefully; amusingly, funnily. 2. graciously, kindly, affably. 3. free, gratis.
graciosidad, *f.* 1. gracefulness, beauty. 2. gratuitousness.
gracioso, sa, *a.* 1. charming, vivacious, lively; attractive, pretty; graceful. 2. funny, amusing; witty. 3. free, gratis, gratuitous. —*m., f.* gracioso, comic, comedian (comic character in Spanish plays).
grada, *f.* 1. step (of a staircase). 2. bleachers, tier of seats, gradin; tiers of seats. 3. (mar.) slip (sloping plane on which a boat is built or repaired).
grada, *f.* 1. (ecc.) locutory, speaking grille or grating (in a convent). 2. (agr.) harrow. — **g. de cota,** brush harrow; **g. de dientes,** peg-tooth harrow; **g. de dientes flexibles,** spring-tooth harrow; **g. de discos,** disk harrow.
gradación, *f.* 1. gradation. 2. (mus.) gradation. 3. (rhet.) climax, gradation (series of propositions each more forceful than the one before).
gradado, da, *past part. of* **gradar.** —*a.* with gradins or steps.
gradar, *tr.v.* (agr.) to harrow, to break with the harrow.
gradecilla, *f.* 1. *dim. of* **grada,** small step. 2. (archit.) astragal, ring between shaft and capital.
gradeo, *m.* (agr.) harrowing.
gradería, *f.* steps; rows or tiers of seats, bleachers; gradins.
gradiente, *m.* (math., meteorol.) gradient, declivity. —*f.* (Amer.) gradient, slope.
gradilla, *f.* 1. portable stepladder, small seat or step. 2. brick, mold.
gradinar, *tr.v.* (art.) to chisel with a graver.
gradíolo, *m.* (bot.) gladiolus.
grado, *m.* 1. step. 2. degree, grade (relative quantity, intensity, seriousness, etc.). 3. (math., gram., mus.) degree. 4. (mil.) rank. 5. (educ.) degree, academic title. 6. (educ.) grade, class, form. 7. degree (on a thermometer or compass). 8. degree (of kinship). 9. (*pl.*) (ecc.) minor orders. — **de g. en g.,** by degrees; **de g. único,** single-stage (turbine); **en alto g.,** to a great extent; **en g. superlativo,** in the highest degree; **en menor g.,** to a lesser extent; **en sumo g.,** exceedingly, extremely; **hasta tal g.,** to such an extent.
grado, *m.* will, liking; **mal de mi, tu,** etc. **g.,** against my, your, etc. wishes; **de or de buen g.,** willingly; **de mal** or **sin g.,** unwillingly; **de su g.,** willingly; **de su mal g.,** unwillingly; **ser en g. de uno,** to please someone, be to someone's liking.
graduable, *a.* that can be graduated or regulated, adjustable.
graduación, *f.* 1. graduation. 2. commencement exercises. 3. alcoholic strength. 4. (mil.) rank.
graduado, da, *past part. of* **graduar.** —*a.* (mil.) brevet. —*m., f.* graduate.
graduador, *m.* graduator; gauge, gauger.
gradual, *a.* gradual, by degrees. —*m.* (ecc.) gradual, response sung at mass.
gradualmente, *adv.* gradually, step by step.
graduando, da, *m., f.* candidate for a degree.
graduar, (*ref. 55*) *tr.v.* 1. to graduate. 2. to grade; to appraise, compare, classify, gauge. 3. to measure (e.g. the density of milk). 4. to graduate, mark in degrees. 5. (educ.) to graduate, confer a degree on. — **g. de,** (educ.) to graduate as; (mil.) to give the rank of; **g. de** or **por,** to grade or rate as (good, bad, etc.). —*r.v.* to graduate; to be graduated; **graduarse de,** to graduate as, be graduated as.
graffiti, *m.* graffiti.
gráficamente, *adv.* graphically; vividly.
gráfico, ca, *a.* 1. graphic, graphical. 2. graphic, vivid, clear. —*f., m.* graph; diagram.
gráfila, grafila, *f.* border, edge (of a coin).
grafio, *m.* graver (used for graffito work).
grafioles, *m.* (*pl.*) S-shaped fritters.
grafismo, *m.* graphics; **g. electrónico,** electronic graphics; **g. por computadora,** computer graphics.
grafitación, *f.* graphitization.
grafitar, *tr.v.* to graphitize.
grafítico, ca, *a.* graphitic.
grafitización, *f.* graphitization.
grafitizar, (*ref. 53*) *tr.v.* to graphitize.
grafito, *m.* 1. (min.) graphite, plumbago. 2. (archeol.) graffito.
grafófono, *m.* Graphophone, trademark for an early type of phonograph.
grafología, *f.* graphology, the study of handwriting as a clue to character and personality.
grafólogo, *m.* graphologist, a person who analyzes handwriting.
grafomanía, *f.* graphomania, mania for scribbling or writing.
grafómano, na, *a.* graphomaniacal. —*m., f.* graphomaniac.
grafómetro, *m.* (top.) graphometer, an instrument for measuring angles; circumferentor.
grafomotor, *m.* (med.) graphomotor.
gragea, *f.* sprinkles, multicolored candy granules used for decorating cakes.
graja, *f.* (ornith.) (female) rook, crow.
grajal, *a.* pertaining to crows, ravens or magpies.
grajear, *i. v.* to caw (crows); to gurgle (infants); to chatter (magpies).
grajero, ra, *a.* frequented by crows. —*f.* rookery.
grajo, *m.* 1. (ornith.) rook, crow, jackdaw. 2. (rare) prattler, chatterbox, charlatan. 3. (Amer.) body odor.
grajuelo, *m. dim. of* **grajo,** small rook, small jackdaw.
grajuno, na, *a.* crow-like.
Gral. *abbrev. of* **General,** General (Gen.).
gralario, *a.* grallatorial, wading (said of birds).
grama, *f.* (bot.) grama grass, Bermuda grass, conch grass. — **g. de olor,** (bot.) vernal grass.
gramal, *m.* field of Bermuda grass; turf.
gramalla, *f.* long gown; coat of mail.
gramallera, *f.* pot hook (in a fireplace).
gramalote, *m.* (bot., Col., Ecuad., Peru) yard grass; fodder crop.
gramar, *tr.v.* to knead.
gramática, *f.* 1. grammar. 2. grammar book. — **g. parda,** (coll.) astuteness, cunning.
gramatical, *a.* grammatical; correct.
gramaticalmente, *adv.* grammatically; correctly.
gramático, ca, *a.* grammatical. —*m.* grammarian.
gramatiquear, *i.v.* (coll., derog.) to go in for grammatical hairsplitting or subtleties.
gramatiquería, *f.* (coll., derog.) grammatical hairsplitting.
gramicidina, *f.* (med.) gramicidin.
gramil, *m.* (carp.) gauge, marking gauge.
gramilla, *f.* 1. (Arg., bot.) grass lawn. 2. bed of the hemp-brake.
gramíneo, nea, *a.* (bot.) gramineous, grassy.
gramínívoro, ra, *a.* grass-eating.
gramnegativo, va, *a.* (bac.) gram-negative.
gramo, *m.* gram, gramme (unit of weight in the metrical system).
gramófono, *m.* gramophone, record player, phonograph (Amer.).
gramómetro, *m.* (print.) type gauge.
gramoso, sa, *a.* pertaining to Bermuda grass; producing Bermuda grass.
grampa, *f.* staple, clamp, cramp; hook for carrying weights. — **g. a cadena,** (mec.) chain vise.
Grampianos, *m.* (*pl.*) **los G.,** the Grampians, a mountain range in Central Scotland.
grampositivo, va, *a.* (bac.) gram-positive.
gran, *a.* grand, great, large (*short form of* **grande**, *used before nouns in the singular);* **el g. capital,** big business; **g. angular,** wide-angle lens; **g. danés,** Great Dane; **G. Depresión,** Great Depression; **g. duque,** grand duke; **G. Guerra,** Great War; **g. maestro internacional,** international grand master; **g. ópera,** grand opera; **g. poeta,** great poet; **G. Premio,** Grand Prix; **g. público,** the general public; **g. simpático,** sympathetic nervous system; **g. superficie,** large supermarket; **g. cantidad,** large quantity.
grana, *f.* 1. (agr.) seeding, seeding time; seed. 2. (coll.) urchin, ragamuffin.

grana, *f.* 1. (ento.) grain, cochineal, kermes insect. 2. kermes, kermes berry. 3. scarlet (color). 4. fine scarlet cloth. 5. seed, seeding. — **g. del Paraíso,** (bot.) cardamon; **ponerse como una g.,** to blush to the ears.
granada, *f.* 1. (bot.) pomegranate (fruit). 2. (mil.) grenade, shell. — **g. de fogueo,** dummy grenade; **g. de mano,** hand grenade.
granadal, *m.* pomegranate orchard.
granadera, *f.* hand-grenade pouch.
granadero, *m.* 1. (mil.) grenadier. 2. (coll.) tall man.
granadilla, *f.* 1. (bot.) passionflower (Passiflora coerulea). 2. (bot.) (Amer.) passionflower (plant; Passiflora edulis); granadilla, passionfruit (its fruit).
Granadillas, Granadinas, *f.* (*pl.*) Grenadines, an island chain in the West Indies.
granadillo, *m.* 1. (Col.) tamarind (tree). 2. (Guat., Hond.) blackwood; East Indian rosewood (Dalbergia cubilquitzensis). 3. (Ven.) yacca (tree). 4. West Indian red Ebony.
granadina, *f.* 1. (tex.) grenadine (fine silk fabric). 2. (cul.) grenadine (drink made with pomegranate fruit); grenadine syrup. 3. (Sp., mus.) variety of flamenco song believed to have originated in the province of Granada.
granadino, na, *a.* pertaining to pomegranates; pomegranate-colored. —*m.* pomegranate flower.
granadino, na, *a.* of or pertaining to Granada, Spain. —*m., f.* native of Granada. —*m.* flower of the pomegranate tree.
granado, da, *past part. of* **granar.** —*a.* 1. choice, select, illustrious. 2. experienced, mature, expert. 3. (coll.) tall, lanky. —*m.* (bot.) pomegranate tree.
granador, *m.* granulating sieve.
granaje, *m.* granulating powder.
granalla, *f.* granulated metal, metal filings.
granar, *i.v.* (agr.) to seed, form seeds; to granulate; to start forming kernels (corn).
granate, *m.* (min.) garnet (stone); garnet (color); **g. almandino, noble, oriental, sirio,** (jewel.) almandine, almandite.
granazón, *f.* seeding, seeding time.
Gran Bretaña, *f.* Great Britain.
Gran Cañón, *m.* (U.S.) Grand Canyon.
grancé, *a.* red, dyed with madder, Turkey red.
grancero, *m.* madder field.
grancolombiano, na, *a.* (hist.) of or pertaining to the Gran Colombia now divided into Colombia, Venezuela and Ecuador.
granda, *f., var. of* **gándara.**
grande, (see **gran**) *a.* 1. big, large, great. 2. great, notable; eminent. 3. tall. —*m.* grandee, magnate; **en g.,** as a whole; (fig.) in a grand way, on a big scale; **g. de España,** Spanish grandee; **grandes almacenes,** department store.
grandecico, ica; illo, illa; ito, ita, *a.* rather large, fairly big.
grandemente, *adv.* greatly, extremely; grandly.
Grandes Lagos, *m.* (*pl.*) (U.S., Can.) Great Lakes.
grandevo, va, *a.* (poet.) aged, old.
grandeza, *f.* 1. greatness, magnificence, majesty. 2. largeness, bigness, magnitude. 3. grandeeship; Spanish grandees (collectively).
grandillón, na, *a.* (coll.) overgrown, huge, excessively large.
grandilocuencia, *f.* grandiloquence.
grandilocuente, *a.* grandiloquent.
grandílocuo, cua, *a.* grandiloquent.
grandiosamente, *adv.* grandiosely, magnificently.
grandiosidad, *f.* grandeur, greatness, magnificence, splendor.
grandioso, sa, *a.* grandiose, magnificent, grand, splendid.
grandísono, na, *a.* (poet.) high-sounding, resounding.
grandor, *m.* size, extensiveness, bigness; greatness; magnitude.
grandote, ta, *a.* (coll.) huge, hulking, bulky.
grandullón, na, *a.* (coll.) *var. of* **grandillón.**
graneado, da, *past part. of* **granear.** —*a.* 1. granular, powdered. 2. spotted, stippled. 3. grained, granulous. — **fuego g.,** (mil.) drumfire.
graneador, *m.* 1. leather gun powder sieve; sieving or granulating room (in a factory). 2. stipple graver.
granear, *tr.v.* 1. to sow (seeds). 2. to granulate, grain (powder, lithographic stone, paper, leather).
granel, a g., in bulk; in abundance, galore, e.g. *había whisky a g.,* there was whisky galore; **arroz a g.,** rice sold in bulk (not packaged).
granelar, *tr.v.* to grain (leather).
graneo, *m.* 1. sowing. 2. granulating; graining. 3. (art.) stippling.
granero, *m.* 1. granary, barn, grain loft. 2. (fig.) granary, grain-growing country, wheat country.
granete, *m.* center punch; marking awl.
granévano, *m.* (bot.) tragacanth.
granguardia, *f.* (mil.) grand guard, advanced guard of an army.
granífero, ra, *a.* (bot.) graniferous, bearing grains as seeds.
granilla, *f.* (tex.) rough surface on the reverse side of cloth.
granillero, *a.* said of hogs that feed on acorns.
granillo, *m.* 1. *dim. of* **grano,** fine grain; granule, small grain. 2. tiny tumor (on the coccyx of a canary or linnet). 3. profit, gain.
granilloso, sa, *a.* granular, granulous.
granítico, ca, *a.* pertaining to granite, granitic; granite-like.
granitita, *f.* (min.) granitite.
granito, *m.* 1. *dim. of* **grano,** fine grain. 2. pimple, blackhead. 3. (min.) granite. 4. (pharm.) granule. 5. small egg of a silkworm. — **g. de arena,** (fig.) grain of sand (small but effective help).
granívoro, ra, *a.* (zool.) granivorous, grain-eating.
granizada, *f.* 1. hailstorm. 2. (fig.) avalanche, deluge, mass. 3. (Amer., reg.) iced drink.
granizado, *past part. of* **granizar.** —*m.* iced drink, drink consisting of fruit juice or syrup and crushed ice.
granizal, *m.* (Col., Chile) hailstorm.
granizar, (*ref.* 53) *i.v.* to hail. —*tr.v.* (fig.) to hurl, throw.
granizo, *m.* 1. hail, hailstorm. 2. (med.) cataract (on an eye). 3. (fig.) avalanche, mass.
granja, *f.* farm, grange; **g. avícola,** poultry farm; **g. colectiva,** collective farm; **g. lechera,** dairy farm; **g. modelo,** model farm; **ir de g.,** to go on a country excursion or holiday.
granjear, *tr.v., r.v.* 1. to earn; to get, gain, acquire. 2. to win, capture (friendship, sympathy). 3. (Chile) to swindle, rob. 4. (mar.) to approach, get near.
granjeo, *m.* gain, profit; earning, getting; winning; advantage; influence.
granjería, *f.* 1. farming. 2. (fig.) gains, profits.
granjero, ra, *m., f.* 1. farmer, granger, rancher. 2. dealer in commodities.
Gran Lago del Oso, *m.* (Can.) Great Bear Lake.
Gran Lago Salado, *m.* (U.S.) Great Salt Lake.
grano, *m.* 1. grain (of corn); seed. 2. grain, corn (collectively). 3. grain, particle. 4. (med.) pimple, blackhead. 5. (jewel.) grain, fourth of a carat. 6. grain (of leather; of wood). 7. grain (weight). — **apartar el g. de la paja,** to separate the wheat from the chaff; **granos del Paraíso,** (bot.) amomum; **g. malo,** (vet.) carbuncle; **ir al g.,** to come or get to the point.
granodiorita, *f.* (min.) granodiorite.
granofírico, ca, *a.* granophyric.
granófiro, *m.* granophyre, a fine grained granite porphyry.
granolítico, ca, *a.* granolithic.
granolito, *m.* granolith.
granoso, sa, *a.* granular, granulous; grainy.
granuja, *f.* 1. loose grape. 2. seed, pip. —*m.* urchin, ragamuffin, waif, gamin, young rogue.
granujado, da, *a.* grain-shaped, grainlike, granulated; full of stones or seeds.
granujería, *f.* 1. gang of street urchins. 2. deviltry, hooliganism.
granujiento, ta, *a.* pimply, covered with pimples.
granujo, *m.* (coll.) pimple, blackhead.
granujoso, sa, *a.* pimply, full of pimples.
granulación, *f.* granulation, granulating.
granulado, da, *past part. of* **granular.** —*a.* granular.
granulador, ra, *m., f.* granulating machine.
granular, *a.* 1. granular. 2. full of pimples.
granular, *tr.v.* to granulate. —*r.v.* to become covered with pimples.
granulita, ta, *m., f.* (min.) granulite.
gránulo, *m.* 1. *dim. of* **grano,** granule; pellet. 2. (pharm.) small pill.
granulocito, *m.* (physiol.) granulocyte.
granulocitopoyesis, *f.* (physiol.) granulocytopoiesis.
granuloma, *m.* (med.) granuloma.
granulopenía, *f.* (med.) granulopenia.
granulosidad, *f.* granularity.
granuloso, sa, *a.* granular, granulous.
granza, *f.* (bot.) madder; garancine.
granzas, *f.* (*pl.*) 1. chaff; siftings. 2. screenings, refuse. 3. dross of metals.
granzón, *m.* 1. (min.) piece of ore too large to pass through a sieve. 2. (Ven.) coarse sand. 3. (*pl.*) knots of straw left in a sieve.
granzoso, sa, *a.* full of chaff.
grañón, *m.* wheat porridge, cooked grain of wheat, boiled semolina.
grao, *m.* landing, beach, strand, shore.
grapa, *f.* 1. staple, clamp, cramp. 2. (vet.) ulcer (of horses). 3. (Arg.) a brandy of inferior quality. 4. (carp.) holdfast. — **g. de banco,** (mec.) bench clamp.
grapón, *m.* 1. *aug. of* **grapa.** 2. (mec.) **hook,** ram, brace, iron dog.
graptolita, *f.* (min.) dendrite.
grasa, *f.* 1. fat, suet, dripping. 2. grease; filth. 3. grease, lubricant, oil. 4. juniper gum. 5. pounce, powdered sandarac. 6. (*pl.*) dross, slag. 7. (mar.) slush. — **g. de copa,** cup grease; **g. de mantequilla,** butterfat.
grasera, *f.* (cul.) dripping pan or bowl; vessel for grease or fat.
grasería, *f.* tallow candle factory, chandler's shop.
grasero, *m.* (min.) slag heap, slag dumper.
graseza, *f.* fattiness, greasiness.
grasiento, ta, *a.* 1. fatty, greasy, oily. 2. grubby, grimy.
grasilla, *f.* 1. pounce, powdered sandarac. 2. (bot.) juniper resin.
graso, sa, *a.* fatty, unctuous, oily, greasy. —*m.* fattiness, greasiness.
grasones, *m.* (*pl.*) (cul.) wheat porridge with sugar and cinnamon.
grasoso, sa, *a.* fatty, greasy, oily.
graspo, *m.* (bot.) a kind of heath, heather.

grasura, *f., var. of* **grosura.**
grata, grataguja, *f.* metal scrubbing brush, wire brush; rasp; burnisher, smoothing chisel.
gratamente, *adv.* pleasantly, agreeably, graciously; gratefully.
gratar, *tr.v.* to brush, rub, burnish.
gratén, *m.* (cul.) gratin; **al g.,** au gratin, with a cream and cheese sauce.
gratificación, *f.* reward; bonus; recompense, gratuity, tip.
gratificador, ra, *a.* gratifying; rewarding. *—m., f.* rewarder, recompenser; one who tips.
gratificar, *(ref. 50) tr.v.* 1. to recompense, tip, reward. 2. to please, gratify; to delight.
gratifique, gratifiqué, *ref.* **gratificar.**
grátil, gratil, *m.* 1. (mar.) leech (of a sail). 2. (mar.) slings, middle part of a yard.
gratin, *m., var. of* **gratén.**
gratis, *adv.* gratis, free, for nothing.
gratisdato, ta, *a.* given free, gratis, free, gratuitous.
gratitud, *f.* gratitude, gratefulness.
grato, ta, *a.* 1. agreeable, pleasant, pleasing; graceful. 2. free, gratis. 3. (Amer.) grateful.
gratonada, *f.* (cul.) chicken stew, ragout or fricassee.
gratuidad, *f.* gratuitousness, freeness (of tuition, etc.).
gratuitamente, *adv.* 1. gratuitously, free. 2. baselessly, without foundation.
gratuito, ta, *a.* 1. gratuitous, free, gratis. 2. unwarranted, baseless; unfounded, uncalled-for.
gratulación, *f.* congratulation.
gratular, *tr.v.* to congratulate. *—r.v.* to congratulate oneself, rejoice, be pleased.
gratulatorio, ria, *a.* congratulatory.
grauvaca, *f.* (geol.) graywacke, greywacke.
grava, *f.* gravel, coarse sand, broken stone.
gravable, *a.* (law) liable.
gravamen, *m.* 1. tax, obligation, change. 2. burden, load; hardship, inconvenience, encumbrance. 3. (law) mortgage, lien.
gravar, *tr.v.* 1. to tax; to impose (a tax on). 2. to burden, encumber; to oppress.
gravativo, va, *a.* taxing; burdensome, heavy; grievous.
grave, *a.* 1. serious, grave. 2. serious (illness); seriously ill, e.g. *está g.,* he is seriously ill. 3. important (business). 4. solemn, grave. 5. hard, difficult; onerous, burdensome, taxing. 6. deep, low (sound). 7. paroxytone, accented on the penultimate syllable. 8. grave (accent).
gravear, *i.v.* to rest, weigh (on something else); to sink, to gravitate.
gravedad, *f.* 1. gravity, seriousness; importance. 2. circumspection, composure, sobriety of manners. 3. weight, heaviness. 4. (phys.) gravity. — **g. específica,** (chem.) specific gravity; **enfermo de g.,** gravely ill.
gravedoso, sa, *a.* pompous, affectedly serious or solemn; haughty, vain.
gravemente, *adv.* gravely; seriously.
gravidez, *f.* pregnancy.
grávido, da, *a.* 1. (poet.) gravid, heavy, full; abundant. 2. pregnant (woman).
gravimetría, *f.* gravimetry, the measurement of density or weight.
gravimétrico, ca, *a.* (phys.) gravimetric, gravimetrical.
gravímetro, *m.* (phys.) gravimeter.
gravitación, *f.* gravitation.
gravitar, *i.v.* 1. to gravitate. 2. to rest, (on something else). 3. (fig.) to be a burden, weight, e.g. *lo que hice gravita sobre mi conciencia,* what I did weighs on my conscience.
gravoso, sa, *a.* 1. onerous; grievous, offensive, bothersome, troublesome. 2. costly, expensive.
graznador, ra, *a.* cawing, croaking; cackling.
graznar, *i.v.* to caw, croak; to cackle.
graznido, *m.* 1. caw, croak; cackle. 2. (fig.) screeching, unmelodious singing.
greba, *f.* greave (of a leg armor).
greca, *f.* (art., archit.) fret, border, Grecian fret.
Grecia, *f.* Greece.
greciano, na, *a.* Grecian.
grecice, grecicé, *ref.* **grecizar.**
grecisco, ca, *a., var. of* **greguisco.**
grecismo, *m.* Grecism Hellenism.
grecizante, *a.* Grecizing, Hellenizing.
grecizar, *(ref. 53) tr.v., i.v.* to Grecize, Hellenize.
greco, ca, *a., m., f.* Grecian, Greek.
grecolatino, na, *a.* Greco-Latin, Graeco-Latin.
grecorromano, na, *a.* Greco-Roman, Graeco-Roman.
greda, *f.* clay, loam; fuller's earth; chalk, marl.
gredal, *a.* clayey; loamy. *—m.* clayey ground, clay pit; loam pit.
gredoso, sa, *a.* clayey, marly.
grefier, *m.* (hist.) 1. greffier, registrar in the house of Burgundy. 2. official assisting in the investiture of a recipient of the Golden Fleece.
gregal, *m.* north east wind (in the Mediterranean). *—a.* gregarious, fond of company; of or pertaining to a herd or flock.
gregarina, *f.* (zool.) gregarine.
gregario, ria, *a.* 1. gregarious. 2. shared, common, of the herd or flock. 3. servile, slavish, lacking ideas or initiative; dull, stupid.
gregoriano, na, *a.* (hist., mus., lit.) Gregorian.
gregorillo, *m.* short chemise or neckcloth formerly worn by women.
gregorito, *m.* (Mex.) disappointment; practical joke.
greguería, *f.* 1. uproar, din, row, clamor, hullabaloo. 2. image in prose (very personal impression of an aspect of reality); personified metaphor.
gregüescos, *m. (pl.)* pantaloons, loose breeches gathered at the knee; Grecian wide breeches.
greguice, greguicé, *ref.* **greguizar.**
greguisco, ca, *a.* Grecian.
greguizar, *(ref. 53) i.v.* to Grecize, to Hellenize.
greisen, *m.* (geol.) greisen.
gremial, *a.* pertaining to a guild, brotherhood or trade union. *—m.* 1. guild member, gremial; trade union member. 2. (ecc.) gremial, bishop's lap cloth.
gremio, *m.* guild, society, association (of skilled workers); society, brotherhood, fraternity; professors (of a university); union, trade union.
grenchudo, da, *a.* disheveled; with a long mane.
greña, *f.* 1. long, entangled lock of hair. 2. heap of grain not yet thrashed. 3. first leaves on a young vine. — **andar a la g.,** to pull each other's hair; to have a heated argument; **en g.,** (Mex.) raw (said of silk).
greñudo, da, *a.* 1. disheveled, unkempt. 2. shy (said of a horse). *—m.* shy horse.
greñuela, *f.* first shoots of a vine.
gres, *m.* (cer.) siliceous potter's clay; clay and quartzose sand; stoneware, ceramic; *(pl.)* stoneware.
gresca, *f.* quarrel, row, fight; uproar, din, shindy; carousal, brawl.
grevillo, *m.* (C. Rica, bot.) grevillea.
grey, *f.* flock (of sheep; of the faithful); herd (of cattle), people, nation, tribe.
Grial, *m.* Grail; **el Santo G.,** Holy Grail.
griego, ga, *a., m., f.* Greek. *—m.* 1. Greek (language). 2. (coll.) swindler, cheat. 3. (fig.) Greek, unintelligible language, gibberish.
grieta, *f.* 1. crak, crevice, fissure. 2. chink, flaw; cranny, split, vein, rent.
grietado, da, *a,* cracked, split, fissured; flawed.
grietarse, grietearse, *r.v.* to crack, split; to become chapped (the skin); to split in clefts or fissures.
grietoso, sa, *a.* full of cracks or fissures, crannied, flawed.
grifa, *f.* 1. (print.) template, platen. 2. (sl.) marihuana.
grifado, da, *a.* italic (letter, type).
grifalto, *m.* (mil.) small culverin.
grifarse, *r.v., var. of* **engrifarse.**
grifería, *f.* set of taps (for a sink, bath, etc.); tap or faucet shop; **g. sanitaria,** bathroom fixtures.
grifo, fa, *a.* curly, kinky (hair). *—m.* 1. faucet, tap. 2. (myth.) griffin or griffon (a mythical animal). *—m., f.* (Amer.) offspring of a black and an Indian. — **grifo de aparejamiento,** (mec.) priming cock.
grifo, fa, *a.* (print.) italic (letter, type).
grifón, *m.* 1. large faucet or tap. 2. large candlewick. 3. Airedale (dog).
grigallo, *m.* (ornith.) capercaillie (Tetrao urogallus).
gril, *m.* grilse, young salmon returning to fresh water.
grilla, *f.* (ento.) female cricket; **ésa es g.,** (coll.) that is a cock-and-bull story.
grillaje, *m.* (Arg., Col.) grillage.
grillarse, *r.v.* 1. to shoot, sprout. 2. (Cuba) to escape, to run away.
grillera, 1. cricket hole; cricket cage. 2. (coll.) pandemonium, bedlam.
grillero, *m.* jailer, prison warden (who shackles convicts).
grilleta, *f.* grille (in a helmet).
grillete, *m.* shackle, fetter.
grillo, *m.* 1. (bot.) shoot, stalk, sprout. 2. (ento.) cricket. — **g. cebollino** or **real,** mole cricket; **cantar el g.,** (coll.) to clink one's money.
grillos, *m. (pl.)* 1. irons, fetters, shackles. 2. obstacle, encumbrance.
grillotalpa, *m.* (ento.) mole cricket.
grima, *f.* disgust, annoyance, irritation; **dar g.,** to appall, disgust; to annoy, grate on one's nerves.
grimillón, *m.* (Chile) crowd, multitude.
grimoso, sa, *a.* appalling, disgusting; annoying.
grímpola, *f.* (mar.) pennant, streamer.
gringada, *f.* (derog., Amer.) swindle; abuse, indignity; improper action or behavior.
gringo, ga, *a.* (coll., derog.) foreign (said esp. of Americans or British). *—m., f.* foreigner (said esp. of Americans or British); fair-haired person. *—m.* gibberish; **hablar en gringo,** to talk nonsense; **hacerse el gringo,** to play dumb.
griñolera, *f.* (bot.) rose box.
griñon, *m.* 1. (bot.) nectarine (smooth-skinned peach). 2. wimple, medieval headdress; nun's coif.
gripado, da, *a.* (mec.) seized up, stuck (machine parts, due to lack of grease).
gripal, *a.* (med.) pertaining to a cold or influenza, grippy.
griparse, *r.v.* (mec.) to seize up, stick, be stiff (pieces of machinery due to lack of grease).
gripe, *f.* (med.) influenza, cold, grippe.
gripo, *m.* (arch.) cargo boat.
griposo, sa, *a.* said of a person suffering from the grippe or influenza.
gris, *a.* 1. grey, gray. 2. (fig.) dull, dismal, gloomy. *—m.* 1. grey, gray; **g. marengo,** charcoal gray; **g. pizarra,** slate gray. 2. (zool.) Siberian squirrel. 3. (coll.) cold weather, cold wind. 4. (sl., Sp.) political policeman (who wears a gray uniform). — **una tarde g.,** a gray and dismal afternoon.

grisáceo, cea, *a.* greyish, grayish.
grisalla, *f.* (art.) grisaille, chiaroscuro.
gríseo, sea, *a.* griseous, grayish.
griseta, *f.* 1. a kind of patterned silk. 2. (bot.) disease of trees caused by infiltration of water into a tree trunk. 3. (gal.) seamstress, dressmaker.
grisgrís, *m.* grisgris, Moorish amulet or talisman.
grisma, *f.* (Chile, Guat., Hond.) drop, pinch.
grisú, *m.* (min.) firedamp.
grisúmetro, *m.* (min.) firedamp indicator or detector.
grita, *f.* din, uproar; outcry, shouting, clamor; **dar g.,** to hoot, catcall, jeer; **g. foral,** (law) summons, citation.
gritadera, *f.* (Col., Ven.) *var. of* **gritería.**
gritador, ra, *a.* shouting, screaming, crying. *—m., f.* shouter, crier.
gritar, *tr.v.* 1. to shout, scream, call out, e.g. *tuve que gritarle las instrucciones,* I had to shout the instructions to him. 2. to jeer at, catcall. *—i.v.* to shout, scream, call, cry out.
gritería, *f.* **griterío,** *m.* din, uproar; clamor, outcry; shouting, screaming; fight, tumult.
grito, *m.* shout, cry, scream; outcry; **a g. herido** or **pelado, a voz en grito,** with tremendous shouts or screams; **estar en un g.,** to moan in constant pain; **g. de guerra** or **combate,** war cry; **poner el g. en el cielo,** to raise an outcry, raise the roof.
gritón, na, *a.* (coll.) noisy; strident, screeching, clamorous.
gro, *m.* (tex.) grogram, grosgrain, twilled fabric.
groar, *i.v.* to croak (a frog).
groelandés, sa, groenlandés, sa, *a.* Greenlandic. *—m., f.* Greenlander.
Groenlandia, *f.* Greenland.
groera, *f.* (mar.) rope hole.
grog, *m.* rum punch or toddy; any alcoholic drink requiring aromatic ingredients.
gromo, *m.* (bot.) bud, young shoot.
grosella, *f.* red currant (fruit); **g. negra,** black currant; **g. silvestre** or **espinosa,** gooseberry (fruit).
grosellero, *m.* red currant bush; **g. negra,** black currant bush; **g. silvestre** or **espinosa,** goosebery bush.
groseramente, *adv.* rudely, coarsely, vulgarly, grossly.
grosería, *f.* 1. vulgarity, coarseness; vulgar or coarse word or expression. 2. rudeness, discourtesy, ill-breeding; uncouthness.
grosero, ra, *a.* 1. rude, vulgar, coarse. 2. discourteous, rude, ill-bred. 3. rough, coarse (cloth, etc.). *—m., f.* oaf, lout, boor.
grosísimo, ma, *a. super. of* **grueso,** very thick.
groso, *m.* coarse snuff; grain tobacco.
grosor, *m.* thickness, bulk, compactness.
grosso modo, *adv.* more or less, roughly.
grosularia, *f.* (min.) grossularite.
grosularieo, a, *a.* (bot.) grossulariaceous. *—f. (pl.)* (bot.) Grossulariaceae.
grosularita, *m.* (min.) grossularite.
grosulina, *f.* (chem.) grossulin.
grosura, *f.* 1. fat, grease. 2. meat; offal, head and legs (of animals).
grotescamente, *adv.* grotesquely.
grotesco, ca, *a.* grotesque; ridiculous, farcical.
grúa, *f.* (mec.) crane, derrick; **g. alimentadora de agua,** (ry.) water column; **g. corrediza,** traveling crane; **g. de pórtico** or **caballete,** gantry crane; **g. de puente,** traveling crane; **g. de transbordo,** (ry.) transfer crane; **g. gigante,** titan crane.
grúa-remolque, *m.* tow truck.
grúa-torre, *f.* construction crane.
gruero, ra, *a.* (bird) preying on cranes.
gruesa, *f.* 1. gross, twelve dozen. 2. (mar.) bottomry.
gruesamente, *adv.* grossly; in bulk, wholesale.
grueso, sa, *a.* 1. thick; stout; heavy, bulky, big. 2. boring, dull, heavy. 3. coarse, vulgar. *—m.* 1. thickness; (geom.) depth (of a solid figure). 2. bulk, main body or part. 3. thick stroke (of a letter). — **en g.,** in bulk, wholesale.
gruir, (*ref. 48*) *i.v.* to honk like a crane.
grujidor, *m.* glazier's nippers (for trimming glass).
grujir, *tr.v.* to trim (the edge of glass).
grulla, *f.* (ornith.) crane.
grullada, *f.* 1. (coll.) group of idle or insignificant people. 2. (coll.) patrol of constables or police officers. 3. platitude, patently obvious remark.
grullero, ra, *a., var. of* **gruero.**
grullo, lla, *a.* (Amer.) dark grey (horse). *—m.* (Amer.) peso, dollar.
grumete, *m.* (mar.) cabinboy, shipboy.
grumo, *m.* 1. clot (of blood); curd (of milk); lump (in sauce, paste, porridge, etc.). 2. bud (of trees). 3. cluster, bunch. 4. wing tip (of a bird).
grumoso, sa, *a.* lumpy, clotted, full of clots.
gruñido, *past part. of* **gruñir.** *—m.* 1. grunt (of a pig). 2. growl (of a dog). 3. (fig.) grumble, growl, angry grunt (of people).
gruñidor, ra, *a.* 1. grunting. 2. growling. 3. grumbling, grouchy, crotchety, bad-tempered.
gruñimiento, *m.* grunting; growling, muttering, grumbling.
gruñir, (*ref. 66*) *i.v.* 1. to grunt (a pig). 2. to growl (a dog). 3. to creak (a door, etc.). 4. (fig.) to grumble, growl, murmur angrily (people).
gruñón, na, *a.* (coll.) grumbling, grouchy, cranky, irritable, bad-tempered. *—m., f.* (coll.) crosspatch.
grupa, *f.* croup, rump (of a horse); **a la g.,** riding pillion (on the croup, behind the horseman).
grupada, *f.* 1. sudden gust of wind. 2. downpour, rainburst; squall. 3. (Mex., equit.) capriole.
grupal, *a.* group.
grupera, *f.* 1. pillion, cushion behind the saddle for another rider or a satchel; crupper (of the saddle).
grupo, *m.* 1. group, set, cluster, clump. 2. group, assemblage, party. 3. group, type, classification. — **g. de interés** or **presión,** pressure group; **g. de mando,** (mil.) command group; **g. de feligreses,** church congregation; **g. sanguíneo,** blood group or type; **g. de trabajo,** working party; **g. electrogeno,** generator; **g. paritario,** peer group.
gruta, *f.* 1. grotto, cave, grot, cavern. 2. (*pl.*) subterranean galleries, crypts, vaults. — **la g. de Fingal,** (Scotland) Fingal's Cave; **la g. azul,** (Italy) The Blue Grotto.
grutesco, ca, *a., m.* (archit., art.) grotesque, pertaining to or resembling caves and grottos.
gruya, gruye, *ref.* **gruir.**
gua, *interj.* (Amer.) 1. huh! e.g. *¿qué te crees, g.?* who do you think you are, huh? 2. oh!; gracious, heavens (expressing surprise or fear).
gua, *f.* game consisting in knocking or shooting marbles into a hole.
guaba, *f.* (Amer.) *var. of* **guama.**
guabá, (*pl.* **guabaes**), *m.* (C. Amer.) a species of tarantula-like black spider (Phrynus palmatus).
guabairo, *m.* (Cuba) a species of nightjar (Caprimulgus carolinensis).
guabán, *m.* (bot., Cuba) a species of wild tree producing poisonous seeds; its wood is used for making tool handles.
guabico, *m.* (Cuba) annonaceous tree (Xilopia obtusifolia).
guabina, *f.* (Col.) a popular mountain song.
guabirá, (*pl.* **guabiraes**), *m.* (Arg.) a species of myrtle (Campomanesia crenata).
guabiyú, (*pl.* **guabiyúes**), *m* (Arg.) a species of myrtle (Eugenia guabiyu).
guabo, *m., var. of* **guamo.**
guabul, *m.* (Hond.) drink made from bananas.
guaca, *f.* 1. Indian burial mound. 2. (Amer.) buried treasure. 3. (Amer.) hole in the ground where fruit is allowed to ripen. 4. (Ven., coll.) old and unattractive spinster.
guacal, *m.* 1. (Amer.) portable crate (gen. carried on the back). 2. (Amer.) calabash tree. 3. gourd, vessel made from the calabash gourd.
guacalote, *m.* (Cuba) jack bean (climbing plant).
guacamaya, *f.* 1. (C. Amer., Mex., Col.) macaw. 2. (Cuba, Hond.) bladder senna.
guacamayo, *m.* (Amer., ornith.) macaw.
guacamole, *m.* (C. Amer., Mex.) savory spread or salad made of avocado, onions, herbs, and chili peppers.
guacamote, *m.* (Mex.) manioc, bitter cassava.
guachaje, *m.* (Chile) group of calves separated from their mothers.
guachapear, *tr.v.* 1. (coll.) to splash and kick with the feet. 2. (coll.) to do hastily and shoddily, botch. *—i.v.* to rattle, clatter.
guachapelí, *m.* (Ecuad.) a species of mimosa (Pseudosamenea quachapele) whose strong hardwood is used in shipbuilding.
guachar, *tr.v.* (Ecuad.) to furrow for sowing.
guácharo, ra, *a.* 1. sickly, delicate. 2. (Ecuad.) orphaned. *—m.* 1. fledgling, young bird. 3. (ornith.) guacharo. *—f.* (Cuba) lie.
guacharrada, *f.* plop, sudden fall on water or mud.
guacharro, *m.* fledgling, young bird.
guache, *m.* (Amer.) contemptible man, tough, hoodlum.
guachinango, ga, *a.* 1. (Cuba, Mex., P. Rico) said of an artful charmer or flatterer. 2. (Cuba) said of a Mexican. *—m.* (Mex., ichth.) red snapper.
guacho, cha, *a.* 1. (S. Amer.) orphaned, motherless. 2. (Chile) without a mate. 3. (Chile) wild, uncultivated (plant). 4. (Peru) lonely, forlorn, abandoned. *—m., f.* 1. (S. Amer.) orphan, foundling. 2. birdling (of a sparrow). 3. (Ecuad.) furrow.
guacia, *f.* 1. (bot.) acacia. 2. acacia gum, gum arabic.
guácima, *f.* (C. Amer., Cuba, Col.) bastard cedar, a large wild tree producing useful hardwood and cattle fodder.
guácimo, *m.* (Col., Hond., Ven.) *var. of* **guácima.**
guaco, *m.* 1. (bot.) guaco. 2. (ornith.) curassow (Crax globicera). 3. (C. Rica) caracara (Ibycter americanus). 4. (Amer.) ceramic vessel (found in Indian burial mounds).
guadafiones, *m.* (*pl.*) hobbles, hopple, fetterlocks.
guadal, *m.* 1. (Arg.) boggy land; quaking bog. 2. (Arg.) sand dune.
guadalajarense, *a., m., f.* of Guadalajara, Mexico.
guadalajareño, ña. *a., m., f.* of Guadalajara, Spain.
guadamací, guadamacil, *m., var. of* **guadamecí.**
guadamacilería, *f.* leather-embossing; leather embosser's shop.
guadamacilero, *m.* leather embosser.
guadamecí, (*pl.* **guadamecíes**), *m.* embossed leather, tooled leather.
guadameco, *m.* ornament formerly worn by women.
guadaña, *f.* (agr.) scythe; (fig.) death, The Reaper.
guadañador, ra, *a.* mowing. *—f.* mowing machine.
guadañar, *tr.v.* to mow, scythe.
guadañero, *m.* 1. mower, scytheman. 2. (Cuba, Mex., Sp.) owner of a small harbor boat or coastal transport vessel.
guadañil, *m., var. of* **guadañero.**
guadaño, *m.* (Cuba, Mex., Sp.) small harbor boat or coastal transport vessel.

guadapero, *m.* 1. (bot.) wild pear. 2. boy who carries food to rural or field workers.
guadarnés, *m.* 1. harness room; harness keeper. 2. royal armorer; armory.
guadijeño, ña, *a.* of or from Guadix, Spain. —*m., f.* native of Guadix. —*m.* poniard, dagger.
guadramaña, *f.* trick, deceit.
guadua, *f.* (Col., Ecuad., Ven.) guadua (a variety of bamboo).
guáduba, *f.* (Col., Ven.) *var. of* **guadua.**
guagua, *m., f.* (Amer.) baby. —*m.* (Col.) paca (rodent). —*f.* 1. trifle, triviality. 2. (Cuba, P. Rico) bus. 3. (Cuba) orange scale (insect). —**de g.,** (Cuba) free, gratis.
guaguasí, (*pl.* **guaguasíes**), *m.* (Amer.) tree which yields a resin used as a purgative (Loetia apelata).
guagüero, ra, *m., f.* 1. (Cuba, P. Rico) bus driver. 2. (Amer., coll.) sponger.
guaicán, *m.* (ichth.) remora.
guaina, *a.* (Chile) young. —*m.* youth, lad, boy.
guainambi, *m.* (Mex., C. Amer.) humming bird.
guaino *m.* (Peru, Bol.) Indian dance and its plaintive, melancholy tune.
guaipe, *m.* oakum, rag (for wiping machines, etc.).
guaira, *f.* 1. small earthen smelting furnace used by Peruvian Indians. 2. (mar.) leg-of-mutton sail. 3. (C. Amer.) Indian pan pipes.
guairabo, *m.* (Chile, ornith.) night heron.
guairo, *m.* (Amer., mar.) small two-masted vessel with leg-of-mutton sails.
guaita, *f.* (mil.) sentinel, night watch.
guaja, *m., f.* rogue, rascal, scoundrel.
guajacón, *m.* (Cuba) small freshwater fish (Girardinus metallicus).
guajada, *f.* (Mex.) stupid, nonsensical act or talk.
guajamón, na, *a.* (Cuba) bay (colored).
guájaras, *f.* (*pl.*) crags, roughest part of a mountain.
guaje, *a.* (Mex., Hond.) foolish, stupid. —*m.* 1. (Mex., Hond.) bottle gourd. 2. (Mex.) a kind of acacia (Acacia esculenta). 3. (Hond., Mex.) fool. 4. (C. Amer.) useless person, good-for-nothing; **hacer g. a,** to deceive.
guájete, por guájete, (coll.) tit for tat.
guajiro, ra, *m., f.* Cuban peasant. —*f.* (mus., Cuba) a country song set to a famous poem, a legend or the narration of an event.
guajolote, *m.* 1. (Mex.) turkey. 2. (Mex.) fool, simpleton.
guala, *f.* 1. (Ven.) turkey buzzard. 2. (Chile) coot.
gualá, *interj.* certainly!
gualatina, *f.* dish of stewed apples, milk of almonds, rice flour and aromatic spices.
gualda, *f.* (bot.) dyer's rocket, weld, reseda (a European mignonette which produces a golden yellow dye).
gualdado, da, *a.* weld-colored, yellowish.
gualdera, *f.* 1. (carp.) stringboard, bridgeboard (of a stairway). 2. side piece (of a cart, box). 3. (*pl.*) (artil.) trail, bracket. 4. (mar.) whelp, check.
gualdo, da, *a., f.* weld, yellow, golden yellow. —**roja y gualda,** red and gold (poetic description of the Spanish flag).
gualdrapa, *f.* 1. caparison, trappings; long ornamented covering for a horse. 2. (coll.) rag, tatter.
gualdrapazo, *m.* (mar.) flap or flapping sound of a sail; jerk.
gualdrapear, *tr.v.* to place head to tail. —*i.v.* to flap (sails).
gualdrapeo, *m.* flapping of sails.
gualdrapero, *m.* ragamuffin, tatterdemalion; ragged, shabby person.
gualdrín, *m.* weather strip.
guallipén, *m.* (Chile) fool, idiot.
guama, *f.* 1. (Col., Ven.) fruit of the guama. 2. (Col.) guama, tree that provides shade in coffee plantations (Inga laurina).
guamá, *m.* (Cuba) timber tree, the bark of which is used in the making of cordage (Lonchocarpus sericeus).
guamazo, *m.* (C. Amer., Mex.) slap, blow.
guamil, *m.* (Hond.) a kind of weed.
guamo, *m.* 1. (bot., Col., Ven.) guama tree (Inga laurina), gen. used for shading coffee plants. 2. (Cuba) conch shell used as a horn.
guampa, *f.* **guámparo,** *m.* (Arg., Chile) drinking-horn; (Arg., Urug.) horn.
guampo, *m.* (Chile) a kind of pirogue, dugout canoe.
guanabá, *m.* (Cuba, ornith.) a species of heron (Mycoticorax violaceae), wading bird.
guanábana, *f.* (Amer., bot.) soursop, custard apple.
guanabanada, *f.* (Amer.) soursop squash, a refreshing drink made with the fruit, sugar and ice.
guanábano, *m.* (bot.) (Annona muricata) soursop or custard apple tree.
guanabima, *f.* (Cuba) cohune nut.
guanacaste, *m.* (C. Amer.) conacaste, tropical American timber tree.
guanaco, ca, *m., f.* 1. (zool.) guanaco, huanaco (llama guanicoe). 2. (Amer.) churl, rustic; fool, simpleton. 3. (Guat.) any Central American.
guanajo, *m.* (Cuba, P. Rico) 1. turkey. 2. (coll.) fool.
guanaquear, *i.v.* (Chile) to hunt guanacos or huanacos.
guanche, *m., f.* guanche, one of the original inhabitants of the Canary Islands.
guando, *n.* (Col., Chile, Ecuad., Peru) litter, stretcher.
guanera, *f.* guano island or deposit.
guanero, ra, *a.* pertaining to guano. —*m.* ship.
guangoche, *m.* (C. Rica, Mex., Salv.) burlap.
guangocho, cha, *a.* (Mex.) wide, loose, roomy, ample. —*m.* (Hond.) kind of burlap; burlap sack.
guanidina, *f.* (chem.) guanidine.
guanín, *m., var. of* **guañín.**
guanina, *f.* 1. (chem.) guanine. 2. (Amer., bot.) a leguminous plant producing a seed similar to the coffee bean.
guano, *m.* 1. guano, manure derived from sea birds' droppings on Peruvian coasts. 2. manure, fertilizer, derived from the excrement of any animal, e.g. of bats. 3. (Cuba, P. Rico) money. 4. (Cuba) fan palm; the dried palm leaf used for thatching.
guantada, *f.* **guantazo,** *m.* slap.
guante, *m.* 1. glove. 2. (Chile) whip, scourge. 3. (*pl.*) tip, extra money (paid for good measure). —**arrojar el g. (a alguien),** to throw down the gauntlet, challenge; **echar el g. a,** (coll.) to grasp, grab, seize; to arrest, imprison; **echar un g.,** to pass around the hat, collect money for charity; **g. de crin,** massage glove; **guantes de boxeo,** boxing gloves; **guantes de cirujano,** surgical gloves; **guantes de conducir,** driving gloves; **recoger el g.,** to accept a challenge.
guantelete, *m.* gauntlet; (coll.) brass knuckles.
guantería, *f.* glove shop or workshop; glove-making.
guantero, ra, *m., f.* glover, person who makes or sells gloves.
guantón, *m.* (Arg., Col., Peru) slap, blow.
guañín, *a.* base (gold). —*m.* (Amer.) base gold, base gold objects.
guao, *m.* (Cuba, Ecuad., Mex.) guao, tropical American tree which produces seeds as hog feed and whose wood is used for charcoal.
guapamente, *adv.* (coll.) bravely, boldly, courageously.
guapear, *i.v.* 1. (coll.) to act bravely, be brave or bold (in the face of danger). 2. (coll.) to dress handsomely or attractively. 3. (Chile) to boast, brag, bluster.
guapería, *f.* (coll.) bravado, aggressiveness, boastfulness.
guapetón, na, *a.* very handsome or attractive. —*m.* bully, braggart.
guapeza, *f.* 1. (coll.) handsomeness, good looks, attractiveness. 2. (coll.) bravery, courage, daring, boldness. 3. (coll.) bravado, aggressiveness, boastfulness.
guapinal, *m.* (C. Amer.) a resin-yielding tree.
guapo, pa, *a.* 1. (coll.) good-looking, attractive, handsome. 2. (Amer.) bold, brave, daring, courageous. —*m.* 1. bully, braggart, brawler. 2. (Sp.) lady's man, gallant. —*f.* (Sp.) belle; handsomely dressed, provocative young woman.
guapote, ta, *a.* 1. (coll.) good-natured, kindly. 2. (coll.) handsome, good-looking.
guapura, *f.* 1. good looks, handsomeness. 2. aggressiveness, daring.
guaquear, *i.v.* (Amer.) to go in search of buried treasure or ancient Indian pottery.
guaquero, ra, *m., f.* 1. (Amer.) person who digs for ancient Indian pottery or treasure. 2. drinking vessel used by the ancient Peruvians and found buried with the dead.
guara, *f.* 1. (Cuba) guara (tree of the soapberry family). 2. (Hond.) macaw. 3. (Chile) gaudy ornament (on a dress). 4. affected gestures. 5. (Guat.) brandy, spirits.
guará, (*pl.* **guaraes**), *m.* (zool.) agouara, crab-eating raccoon.
guaraca, *f.* 1. (S. Amer.) sling (for hurling missiles). 2. thong, whip.
guaracaro, *m.* (Ven.) hyacinth bean (Dolichos lablab).
guaracha, *f.* 1. (Cuba, P. Rico) guaracha (an old Spanish and now a popular dance, music and song). 2. (Cuba, coll.) noise, joy, fiesta.
guarache, *m.* (Mex.) leather sandal.
guaraguao, *m.* (Cuba, P. Rico, ornith.) red-tailed hawk.
guaraná, *f.* 1. (bot.) supplejack, a Brazilian shrub (Paullinia cupana). 2. (pharm.) guarana, an astringent paste used as a cure for diarrhea.
guarango, ga, *a.* (Amer.) rude, ill-bred, uncivil, impolite. —*m.* 1. (Ecuad., Peru) aroma, huisache (thorny shrub). 2. (Ven.) divi-divi, small tropical American tree (Caesalpina coriaria).
guaraní, (*pl.* **guaraníes**), *a., m., f.* Guarani. —*m.* Guarani (language).
guarapo, *m.* sugar-cane juice; fermented sugar cane juice.
guarapón, *m.* (Chile, Peru) broad-brimmed hat.
guarda, *m., f.* guard, keeper, custodian; **g. forestal,** forest ranger; **g. jurado,** security guard. —*f.* 1. keeping, guarding; custody. 2. guardianship. 3. observance (of a law). 4. outside rib (of a fan). 5. (bkb.) end paper, flyleaf. 6. ward (of a lock or a key). 7. sword guard. 8. (*pl.*) **G.,** (astron.) The Pointers (of the Great Bear).
guardabanderas, *m.* (mar.) yeoman of signals.
guardabarrera, *m., f.* (ry.) grade crossing keeper, gate keeper.
guardabarro, (*pl.* **guardabarros**), *m.* (auto.) mudguard.
guardable, *a.* storable.
guardabosque, *m.* game warden; forest ranger; forest keeper; ranger.
guardabrazo, *m.* brassard (of an armor).
guardabrisa, *m.* 1. glass lampshade (for candles). 2. windscreen, windshield.

guardacabo, *m.* (mar.) thimble (iron ring bound with rope to prevent chafing).
guardacabras, (*pl.* **guardacabras**), *m.* goatherd.
guardacadena, *m.* chain guard.
guardacalada, *f.* attic window.
guardacamisa, *f.* (Ven.) undershirt.
guardacantón, *m.* (bldg., archit.) corner spur stone; spur stone.
guardacartuchos, (*pl.* **guardacartuchos**), *m.* (mar.) cartridge box, cartridge case.
guardacoches, *m., f.* parking lot attendant.
guardacostas, (*pl.* **guardacostas**), *m.* revenue cutter, coastguard cutter; Coast Guard.
guardacuños, (*pl.* **guardacuños**), *m.* die keeper (in the mint).
guardadamente, *adv.* guardedly, warily.
guardado, da, *past part. of* **guardar.** —*a.* guarded, reserved.
guardador, ra, *a.* 1. provident, careful, thrifty. 2. observant (of laws). 3. miserly, stingy. —*m., f.* 1. provident or careful person. 2. observer (of laws). 3. miser. —*m.* 1. (law) guardian. 2. (mil.) keeper of the booty.
guardaespaldas, (*pl.* **guardaespaldas**), *m.* bodyguard.
guardafango, *m.* (auto.) mudguard.
guardafaro, *m.* lighthouse keeper.
guardaflanco, *m.* (mil.) flank guard.
guardafrenos, (*pl.* **guardafrenos**), *m.* (ry.) brakeman.
guardafuego, *m.* (mar.) breaming-boards; fireguard, fender (of a furnace); fire screen (of the hearth or chimney).
guardagujas, (*pl.* **guardagujas**), *m.* (ry.) spurnwater. 2. (carp.) flashing board. 3. (auto.) mudguard, splash leather.
guardagujas, (*pl.* **guardagujas**), *m.* (ry.) switchman, pointsman.
guardahúmo, *m.* (mar.) smoke sail, fire screen.
guardainfante, *m.* 1. farthingale, hoop skirt. 2. (mar.) (capstan) whelps.
guardaja, *f., var. of* **guedeja.**
guardajoyas, (*pl.* **guardajoyas**), *m.* 1. jewel case. 2. keeper of the Crown Jewels.
guardalado, *m.* rail, railing, balustrade, battlement of a bridge.
guardalmacén, *m., f.* warehouse keeper; storeroom keeper.
guardalobo, *m.* (bot.) poet's cassia.
guardalodos, (*pl.* **guardalodos**), *m.* mudguard.
guardamalleta, *f.* lambrequin, valance.
guardamancebo, *m.* (mar.) man-rope.
guardamano, *m.* guard (of a sword).
guardamateriales, (*pl.* **guardamateriales**), *m.* buyer of foundry supplies in the mint.
guardamechones, *m.* locket.
guardameta, *m.* goalkeeper, goalee.
guardamonte, *m.* 1. (mil.) trigger guard. 2. poncho. 3. (Mex.) croup blanket. 4. (Arg.) strips of leather hanging from the saddle to protect the rider's legs from brush, etc.
guardamuebles, (*pl.* **guardamuebles**), *m.* 1. furniture storeroom or repository. 2. palace keeper of the furniture.
guardamujer, *f.* maid of honor (to the queen).
guardapapo, *m.* gorget (in ancient armor).
guardapelo, *m.* locket.
guardapesca, *m.* patrol ship for the protection of national fisheries.
guardapiés, (*pl.* **guardapiés**), *m.* underskirt, petticoat.
guardapolvo, *m.* 1. dust guard, dust sheet or cover. 2. duster, dust-coat. 3. projecting roof (over a balcony). 4. inner lid (of a watch case as additional protection from dust).
guardapuerta, *f.* storm-door.
guardapuntas, (*pl.* **guardapuntas**), *m.* pencil-cap (to protect the point).
guardar, *tr.v.* 1. to guard; to keep, look after; to tend, keep (flocks); to put away; to watch over. 2. to keep, hang on to, (coll.) retain. 3. to keep (the law, one's word, a secret). 4. to have, hold (memories). 5. to save, protect, keep (from harm). 6. to preserve, keep (silence). 7. to save, put by (money). — **guardársela a uno,** to nurse a grudge against someone. —*i.v.* to save (money); **¡guarda!** watch out, look out! —*r.v.* 1. to protect oneself. 2. to keep, hang on to; **guardarse de,** to beware of, avoid, guard against; to take care or be careful not to; **g. silencio,** to keep silent.
guardarraya, *f.* 1. (Cuba) boundary line, path between sugarcane or coffee patches or plantations. 2. (min.) boundary of a drill hole.
guardarriel, *m.* (ry.) safety rail.
guardarrío, *m.* (ornith.) kingfisher.
guardarropa, *m.* 1. cloakroom, checkroom. 2. wardrobe. 3. cloakroom or checkroom attendant. 4. (theat.) wardrobe keeper. 5. (bot.) southernwood. —*f.* 1. cloakroom or checkroom attendant, hatcheck girl (coll.). 2. (theat.) wardrobe mistress.
guardarropía, *f.* (theat.) wardrobe; costumes.
guardarruedas, (*pl.* **guardarruedas**), *m.* spurstone; wheel-guard (protecting the coach entrance or the corners of a building).
guardasellos, *m.* seal keeper.
guardasilla, *f.* chair rail (protecting a wall from the backs of chairs).
guardasol, *m.* (rare) sunshade, parasol.
guardatimón, *m.* (mar.) stern chaser (gun).
guardatrén, *m.* (Arg., ry.) guard.
guardavajilla, *f.* room in which the royal plate or table service is kept.
guardavalla, *m.* (sport.) goalkeeper.
guardavela, *m.* (mar.) rope lashing the main topsail to the masthead.
guardavía, *m.* (ry.) trackwalker.
guardavientos, *m.* (agr.) windbreak.
guardería, *f.* post of guard, keeper or warden; **g. infantil,** nursery, day care center.
guardesa, *f.* female keeper, guard or warden; wife of a guard, keeper or warden.
guardia, *f.* 1. guard (body of soldiers), e.g. *la G. Suiza,* the Swiss Guard. 2. defense, protection. 3. guard (defensive position). 4. police officer, police woman. — **de g.,** (mil.) on guard; **en g.,** on guard (in defensive position; on the alert); **entrar de g.,** (mil.) to go on guard; **estar de g.,** (mil.) to be on guard; **g. cívica,** home guard; **g. civil,** Spanish gendarmery or police force (patrolling the countryside); **g. de cuartillo,** (mar.) dogwatch; **g. de honor,** honor guard; **g. municipal,** local or city police force; **media g.,** (mar.) dogwatch. —*m.* guardsman; police officer, policeman; **g. civil,** gendarme, policeman; **g. de asalto,** riot policeman; shock trooper; **g. marina,** midshipman; **g. municipal,** local or city policeman.
guardián, na, *m., f.* watchman, caretaker, warden. —*m.* 1. (ecc.) guardian. 2. (mar.) boatswain; petty officer (on small craft). 3. (mar.) hawser. 4. (*pl.*) **G.,** (astron.) Pointers.
guardianía, *f.* guardianship (in the Order of St. Francis); territory accorded to each Franciscan convent for the purpose of receiving alms.
guardilla, *f.* 1. attic, garret. 2. (dressm.) seam binding, welting. 3. end tooth of a comb.
guardillón, *m.* loft; small attic.
guardín, *m.* 1. (mar.) rope suspending a ship's gunports. 2. (mar.) tiller cable.
guardoso, sa, *a.* frugal, parsimonious, thrifty; mean, stingy, niggardly, tight-fisted.
guarecer, (*ref. 45*) 1. to shelter, hide, take in, give shelter or protection to. 2. to stow and make secure. 3. to nurse and treat (the sick). —*r.v.* to hide, take refuge or shelter.
guarén, *m.* (zool., Chile) large web-footed rat which feeds on frogs and small fish.
guarentigio, a, *a.* (law) (contract) containing a warranty clause.
guarezca, guarezco, *ref.* **guarecer.**
guaria, *f.* (C. Rica) a tropical American orchid (Cattleya skinnerii).
guaricha, *f.* 1. (Col., Ven., derog.) hussy, female, woman. 2. (Ecuad., derog.) soldier's mistress, camp follower.
guarida, *f.* 1. den, lair (of animals). 2. shelter, refuge. 3. hide-out, den (of criminals). 4. haunt.
guarimán, *m.* (bot.) a tropical American tree of the magnolia family, with aromatic bark, foliage and seeds (Aniba candelilla).
guarín, *m.* suckling pig.
guarisapo, *m.* (Chile) tadpole.
guarismo, *m.* number, cipher, figure, digit; number of two or more figures.
guaritoto, *m.* (bot., Ven.) tree of the suphorbiaceous family (Gnidoscolus quinquelobus).
guarne, *m.* (mar.) each turn (of a cable or tackle).
guarnecedor, ra, *a.* 1. adorning, decorating. 2. trimming, binding, bordering. 3. plastering. 4. garnishing. —*m., f.* trimmer, garnisher, furbisher.
guarnecer, (*ref. 45*) *tr.v.* 1. to decorate, adorn, embellish. 2. to edge, bind, trim, border. 3. (jewel.) to set (a stone). 4. (mil.) to garrison. 5. to fit a guard on (a sword). 6. to provide, equip, supply. 7. (mas.) to plaster. 8. (cul.) to garnish. 9. (mil.) to garrison; to harness.
guarnecido, *past part. of* **guarnecer.** —*m.* (mas.) plastering, stucco, plaster.
guarnés, *m., var. of* **guadarnés.**
guarnezca, guarnezco, *ref.* **guarnecer.**
guarnición, *f.* 1. trimming, edging, border, furbelow; flounce. 2. (jewel.) setting. 3. (mil.) garrison. 4. sword guard. 5. (cul.) garnishing, dressing. 6. (mec.) fitting, fixture (for installing any appliance). 7. (*pl.*) harness. 8. (auto.) lining (of brakes). 9. (mec.) packing. — **estar de g.,** to be on garrison duty.
guarnicionar, *tr.v.* (mil.) to garrison.
guarnicionería, *f.* harness maker's shop; harness shop.
guarnicionero, *m.* harness maker or seller.
guarniel, *m.* 1. pouch, leather bag (used by cattle dealers) strapped over one shoulder. 2. (Mex.) knife or razor case; powder flask.
guarnigón, *m.* (ornith.) young quail.
guarnimiento, *m.* (mar.) rig, rigging.
guarnir, (*ref. 78*) *tr.v.* 1. *var. of* **guarnecer.** 2. (mar.) to rig, to reeve.
guaro, *m.* 1. (ornith.) small parrot. 2. (C. Amer.) rum.
guarrería, *f.* muck, filth; dirty trick.
guarrero, *m.* swineherd.
guarro, rra, *m., f.* hog, swine (*m.*), sow (*f.*).
¡guarte! *interj.* look out! beware!
guaruba, *f.* (ornith.) howling monkey; a red-necked American parrot.
guarura, *f.* (Ven.) shell (used as a horn).
guasa, *f.* 1. (coll.) jest, joke. 2. (Cuba, ichth.) guasa, jewfish. — **de g.,** for fun, in jest.
guasamaco, ca, *a.* (Chile) rough, rude.
guasanga, *f.* (Amer.) noise, din, uproar, hullabaloo.
guasanguero, ra, *a.* (Cuba) jolly, merry, noisy.

guasasa, *f.* (Cuba) a kind of small, annoying fly.
guasca, *f.* 1. (Amer.) thong, cord, strip of rawhide. 2. (Peru, Chile) whip. — **dar g.,** to whip.
guascazo, *m.* (Amer.) lash, whiplash.
guasearse, *r.v.* to jest, joke.
guasería, *f.* (Arg., Chile) rudeness, coarseness, vulgarity.
guásima, *f.* (Cuba, C. Amer.) a large and very useful wild tropical tree producing sturdy wood and cattle fodder.
guaso, sa, *a.* (fig.) rude, coarse, vulgar. —*m., f.* Chilean cowboy, farmhand, ranchhand.
guasón, na, *a.* 1. (coll.) prosaic, dull. 2. (coll.) jocular, gay, comical, humorous, funny. —*m., f.* (coll.) kidder, joker.
guasquear, *tr.v.* to flog, whip. —*r.v.* 1. (Arg.) to jump out of the way. 2. (Urug.) to get annoyed without reason.
guata, *f.* 1. coarse cotton blanket. 2. (Chile) bulging, warping. 3. (Chile) paunch, belly. 4. (Cuba) lie. 5. (Ecuad.) bosom pal or friend. — **echar g.,** (Chile) to become prosperous.
guataca, *f.* 1. (Cuba) spade, short hoe. 2. (Cuba, coll.) big ear. —*m., f.* (Cuba) flatterer, sycophant.
guatacare, *m.* (Ven., bot.) borraginaceous tree (Chytroma idalimon).
guataquear, *tr.v.* 1. (Cuba) to spade. 2. to flatter, play up to (sl.).
guatearse, *r.v.* (Chile) to get fat, develop a belly.
Guatemala, *f.* Guatemala.
guatemalteco, ca, *a., m., f.* Guatemalan.
guatepeor, salir de Guatemala y entrar en g., to jump from the frying pan into the fire.
guateque, *m.* (Cuba) dance, party; spontaneous or improvised festivity.
guatiní, *m.* (Cuba, ornith.) trogon.
guatoco, *m.* (Bol.) chubby, plump, fat person.
guatón, na, *a.* (Chile) fat, with a big paunch or belly.
guatusa, *f.* (C. Rica, Ecuad., Hond., zool.) (a kind of) agouti (Dasyprocta variegata).
guau, *m.* bowwow (dog's bark).
guaucho, *m.* (Chile, bot.) baccharis, American resinous tree (Baccharis concava).
¡guay! *interj.* (poet.) alas! — **g. de mí,** woe is me.
guaya, *f.* lament, sorrow, grief.
guayaba, *f.* 1. (bot.) guava apple; guava jelly. 2. (Amer., coll.) lie, fib, hoax, rumor.
guayabal, *m.* guava tree, plantation or orchard.
guayabera, *f.* (Mex., Car.) loose-fitting men's shirt often worn in lieu of a dinner jacket.
guayabero, ra, *a., m., f.* (Amer.) liar, fiber.
guayabo, *m.* (bot.) guava tree.
guayaca, *f.* 1. (S. Amer.) bag, goatskin bag; (Arg.) purse. 2. (Chile) a dull or silly person.
guayacán, guayaco, *m.* (bot.) guaiacum, lignum vitae.
guayacol, *m.* (pharm.) guaiacol.
Guayana, *f.* Guiana; Guyana (formerly British Guiana).
guayanés, sa, *a., m., f.* Guianese.
guayaquileño, ña, *a.* of or pertaining to Guayaquil, Ecuador. —*m., f.* person born in Guayaquil.
guayuco, *m.* (Col., Ven.) loin cloth.
guayule, *m.* (bot.) guayule.
guayusa, *f.* (Ecuad.) a kind of maté.
guazapa, *f.* (Guat., Hond.) top (spinning toy).
guazubirá, *m.* (Arg., zool.) brocket, small mountain deer (Mazama simplicicornis).
gubán, *m.* (Phil. I.) large canoe.
gubernamental, *a.* governmental.
gubernativamente, *adv.* by an act of government.
gubernativo, va, *a.* governmental, administrative, gubernatorial.
gubernista, *m., f.* (Amer.) person who supports the government.
gubia, *f.* 1. (carp.) gouge. 2. (artil.) vent-cleaner. — **g. acodada or de media caña,** bent gouge.
gubiadura, *f.* notch, channel.
guedeja, *f.* 1. long locks, long hair. 2. lion's mane.
guedejón, na, *a.* long-haired. —*m.* long locks, long hair.
guedejoso, sa, *a., var. of* **guedejón.**
guedejudo, da, *a., var. of* **guedejón.**
güegüecho, *m.* (C. Amer., med.) goiter.
güeldo, *m.* fishing bait (usually shrimp or prawn).
güelfo, fa, *a.* (hist.) Guelphic. —*m., f.* Guelph, Italian partisan of the Pope against the Ghibellines.
güelte, güeltre, *m.* (rare) money.
güemul, *m.* (Arg., Chile, zool.) **guemal,** guemul (Hippocamelus bisuculus).
güepil, *m., var. of* **huipil.**
güérmeces, *m. pl.* (vet.) swelling on the throat of birds of prey.
güero, ra, *a.* (Mex.) blond, light-haired, fair. —*m.* blond. —*f.* blonde.
guerra, *f.* 1. war; warfare; hostility, conflict, strife. 2. kind of billiards. — **armar en g.,** (mar.) to arm for war; **buque de g.,** warship; **dar g.,** to annoy, trouble, cause difficulties; **declarar la g.,** to declare war; **en el amor y la g. todo vale,** all's fair in love and war; **estar en g.,** to be at war; **g. abierta,** open warfare; open hostility; **g. a muerte,** war to the death; **g. bacteriológica,** germ warfare; **g. civil,** civil war; **g. comercial,** trade war; **G. de la Independencia,** War of Independence; **G. de la Sucesión de España,** War of the Spanish Succession; **G. de los Cien Años,** Hundred Years' War; **g. de ondas,** radio jamming, war of the air waves; **G. de los Siete Años,** Seven Years' War; **g. de nervios,** war of nerves; **G. de Peleponeso,** Peloponnesian War; **g. de precios,** price war; **G. de Secesion,** (U.S.) Civil War; **g. de trincheras,** trench warfare; **g. fría,** cold war; **G. Mundial,** World War; **g. nuclear,** nuclear war; **g. psicológica,** psychological warfare; **g. química,** chemical warfare; **g. relámpago,** blitzkrieg; **g. santa,** holy war **Guerras de las Dos Rosas,** War of the Roses; **g. sin cuartel,** all-out war.
guerreador, ra, *a.* warring; warlike. —*m., f.* warrior, fighter.
guerreante, *a.* warring, bellicose.
guerrear, *i.v.* to war, wage war, fight; (fig.) to oppose, quarrel, disagree, resist, argue.
guerrera, *f.* (mil.) high-buttoned tunic, jacket.
guerreramente, *adv.* in a warlike or bellicose manner; martially.
guerrero, ra, *a.* warlike, bellicose, martial; (coll.) mischievous, troublesome. —*m.* warrior, fighter; soldier.
guerrilla, *f.* band of guerrillas; partisans; skirmishers, bushwhackers; independent belligerent.
guerrillear, *i.v.* to wage guerrilla warfare, to skirmish.
guerrillero, *m.* guerrilla; partisan.
guía, *m., f.* 1. guide; adviser. 2. instructor, trainer. —*m.* (mil.) marker, guide (for aligning ranks). —*f.* 1. guide, guidance (guiding light or principle). 2. guide or sign post. 3. guide, handbook, manual; guidebook; (telephone) directory; (railway) timetable. 4. customs permit, clearance certificate. 5. (com.) invoice. 6. fuse. 7. guide shoot (young shoot left on the vine or tree to guide new shoots). 8. (mec.) guide, guide bar. 9. leader (leading horse or mule of team). 10. twisted end (of a moustache). 11. cheating trick (in cards). 12. outside rib (of a fan). 13. (Col.) check rein. 14. (mar.) guy; leader, guide pulley. 15. (min.) leader (small vein leading to a big one). 16. handlebar (of a bicycle). 17. (mus.) leading voice. 18. (*pl.*) reins to control leaders. — **echarse con las guías** or **con guías y todo,** to ride roughshod over (someone); **g. colorimétrica,** color chart; **g. de ondas,** (rad.) wave guide; **g. de entrega,** invoice; **g. telefónica,** telephone directory.
guiabara, *f.* (bot.) sea grape (Coccolaba uvifera).
guiadera, *f.* (mec.) guide, conductor.
guiado, da, *past part. of* **guiar.** —*a.* accompanied by a permit or other document.
guiador, ra, *a.* guiding, leading. —*m., f.* guide, leader, adviser.
guiar, (*ref. 54*) *tr.v.* 1. to guide; to lead, conduct; to show the way. 2. to drive, steer. 3. to train (plants). 4. (fig.) to guide, advise, counsel. —*i.v.* to sprout (plants). —*r.v.* to be guided; **guiarse de** or **por,** to be guided or governed by.
guiguí, *m.* (zool.) flying squirrel (Pteromys petaurista).
guija, *f.* 1. round smooth pebble. 2. (bot.) vetch (Vicia sativa).
guijarral, *m.* pebbly land.
guijarrazo, *m.* blow with a pebble.
guijarreño, ña, *a.* 1. full of pebbles, pebbly. 2. (fig.) hardy, strong (person).
guijarro, *m.* small round pebble.
guijarroso, sa, *a.* pebbly, pebbled, full of pebbles.
güije, *m.* (Cuba) an African term applied to a dangerous spirit such as that of a poisonous snake, a hostile ghost, etc.
guijeño, ña, *a.* 1. pebble-like, pebble-shaped. 2. (fig.) hard, relentless.
guijo, *m.* 1. gravel. 2. (mec.) male pivot, stub shaft.
guijón, *m.* (dent.) caries, tooth decay.
guijoso, sa, *a.* 1. gravelly, full of gravel. 2. hard, stony, relentless.
guilalo, *m.* (Phil. I.) light sailing vessel rigged with sails of matting.
guilda, *f.* guild, medieval organization of artisans, etc.
guildismo, *m.* (econ., polit.) guild socialism.
guileña, *f.* (bot.) columbine (Aquilegia vulgaris).
guilindujes, *m.* (*pl.*) (Hond.) harness with hanging ornaments.
guilla, *f.* good harvest; bounty.
guillado, da, *a.* crazy; equivocal; infatuated.
guilladura, *f.* madness, foolishness; infatuation.
guillame, *m.* (carp.) rabbet plane.
guillarse, *r.v.* 1. to run away, flee. 2. to lose one's head, go crazy.
guillati, *a.* (coll.) crazy, nuts (sl.), mad.
guillatún, *m.* (Chile) Araucan rain-making ceremony.
guillín, *m.* (zool.) otter (Lutra hnidobria).
guillomo, *m.* (bot.) shadberry, serviceberry, juneberry.
guillote, *m.* usufructuary or harvester of a crop. —*a.* 1. lazy, idle. 2. inexperienced, green.
guillotina, *f.* 1. guillotine. 2. paper and cardboard cutter. — **de g.,** sash (window).
guillotinar, *tr.v.* 1. to guillotine (a person). 2. to cut (paper or cardboard) with a single-blade paper cutter.
guimbalete, *m.* pump handle, pump brake.
guimbarda, *f.* (carp.) grooving plane.
güin, *m.* soft thin cane shoot.
guinchar, *tr.v.* to prod, prick, stab.
güinche, *m.* (Amer.) winch, crane.
guincho, *m.* 1. prod, prick, goad. 2. (Cuba, ornith.) osprey (Pandion carolinensis).
guinchón, *m.* tear, rent, rip.
guinda, *f.* 1. (bot.) sour cherry (fruit) (Prunus cerasus); **g. garrafal,** large sweet cherry. 2. (mar.) height of the masts.

guindada, *f.* (Chile) sour cherry drink.
guindado, da, *past part. of* **guindar.** —*a.* 1. made with sour cherries. 2. hanging, suspended; hoisted.
guindajos, *m.* (*pl.*) (Cuba) fringe, hangings, tassels.
guindal, *m.* (bot.) sour cherry tree (Prunus cerasus).
guindalera, *f.* sour cherry tree orchard.
guindaleta, *f.* 1. thick hemp or leather cord. 2. fulcrum (of a balance).
guindaleza, *f.* (mar.) hawser, ship's cable.
guindamaina, *f.* (mar.) salute given by dipping a ship's flag.
guindar, *tr.v.* 1. to hang up, hoist; to hang (execute). 2. (coll.) to win; to beat someone to. —*r.v.* to hang, be suspended; **guindarse a alguien,** (Chile, Peru) to kill, knock off (someone) (sl.). —*i.v.* to hang, be suspended.
guindaste, *m.* (mar.) jib crane, hoisting scaffold.
guindilla, *f.* 1. bird pepper pod; bird pepper (Capsicum baccatum). 2. (derog., Sp.) policeman, cop.
guindillo, *m.* **guindillo de indias,** (bot.) bird pepper (Capsicum baccatum).
guindo, *m.* (bot.) sour cherry (tree) (Prunus cerasus).
guindola, *f.* 1. (mar.) life buoy. 2. (mar.) boatswain's chair. 3. (mar.) log chip.
guinea, *f.* guinea (old English gold coin, equivalent to 21 shillings).
guineo, a, *a.* Guinean, of or pertaining to Guinea; **gallina guinea,** Guinea hen. —*m., f.* Guinean, inhabitant of Guinea. —*m.* 1. negro dance. 2. a variety of banana. —*f.* **G., Guinea; G. Portuguesa,** Portuguese Guinea.
guinga, *f.* gingham (fabric).
guinguear, *i.v.* (Col., Ecuad., Peru) to zigzag.
guingos, *m. p.l.* (Col., Ecuad., Peru) zigzag.
guinja, *f.* jujube berry.
guinjo, *m.* (bot.) jujube tree (Ziziphus sativa).
guinjol, *m, var. of* **guinja.**
guinjolero, *m., var. of* **guinjo.**
guiñada, *f.* 1. wink. 2. (mar.) yaw, lurch.
guiñador, ra, *a.* inclined to wink. —*m., f.* winker.
guiñadura, *f.* wink.
guiñapiento, ta, *a.* ragged, tattered.
guiñapo, *m.* 1. rag, tatter, shred. 2. (fig.) ragamuffin, slovenly person, slattern. 3. (fig.) wretch, reprobate. 4. (Peru, Bol., Chile) ground corn fermented to brew chicha.
guiñaposo, sa, *a.* ragged, tattered.
guiñar, *tr.v.* 1. to wink. 2. (mar.) to yaw. —*r.v.* to wink at one another.
guiño, *m.* wink.
guiñol, *m.* 1. puppet theater. 2. puppet. 3. (fig.) freak, ridiculous-looking person.
guiñote, *m.* a card game similar to tute.
guión, *a.* leading (dog of a pack). —*m.* 1. cross (carried before a prelate). 2. standard, banner. 3. scenario, libretto; screen play, film script. 4. leader (of a dance). 5. leading bird (of a migratory flock). 6. note, instruction. 7. (gram.) hyphen, dash. 8. (mar.) loom (narrowest part of an oar). 9. (mus.) repeat sign. — **g. de escuadrilla,** (aer.) squadron leader.
guionista, *m, f.* script writer, librettist; scenarist, scenario writer.
guipar, *tr.v.* (coll.) to notice, see, perceive.
güipil, *m.* (Mex.) *var. of* **hulpll,** sleeveless blouse or tunic.
guipur, *m.* guipure (type of lace).
güira, *f.* (bot.) calabash tree; calabash (fruit).
guiri, *m.* 1. anti-Carlist, liberal. 2. (coll.) civil guard, policeman.
guirigay, *m.* 1. (coll.) gibberish. 2. hubbub, uproar, confusion.
guirindola, *f.* frill (on the front of a shirt).
güiris, *m.* (Hond.) miner.
guirlache, *m.* candy made with toasted almonds and caramel.
guirnalda, *f.* 1. garland, wreath. 2. (bot.) globe amaranth.
güiro, *m.* 1. gourd, fruit of the calabash. 2. (Amer., mus.) percussion instrument made of the dried gourd. 3. (Bol., Peru) green corn stalk. 4. (Amer.) liana. — **coger el g.,** (Col.) to investigate matters.
guisa, *f.* guise, manner, fashion; **a g. de,** like, in the manner of, e.g. *el niño usa una escoba a guisa de caballo,* the child uses a broomstick as if this were a horse.
Guisa, *m.* (hist.) Guise, French ducal family.
guisado, *past part. of* **guisar.** —*m.* stew; casserole dish, ragout; **estar uno mal g.,** (coll.) to be in a stew (about something), be upset (about something).
guisador, ra, *m., f.* cook (gen. one cooking for a family).
guisandero, ra, *m., f.* (coll.) *var. of* **guisador.**
guisantal, *m.* pea patch or field.
guisante, *m.* (bot.) pea (plant and seed); **g. de olor,** (bot.) sweet pea (Lathyrus odoratus).
guisar, *tr.v.* 1. to cook or prepare food. 2. (fig.) to arrange, put in order, adjust.
guisaso, *m.* (Cuba, bot.) burbark.
guiso, *m.* stew, casserole dish, ragout, fricassee.
guisopillo, *m.* 1. (bot.) winter savory (Batureia montana). 2. mouth swab.
guisote, *m.* poorly made stew or dish.
guita, *f.* 1. twine, string, cord. 2. (coll.) money, dough.
guitar, *tr.v.* to sew or bind with twine or string.
guitarra, *f.* 1. (mus.) guitar; **g. eléctria,** electric guitar; **g. española,** Spanish guitar. 2. pestle (for pounding gypsum).
guitarrazo, *m.* blow dealt with a guitar.
guitarrear, *i.v.* to strum the guitar.
guitarreo, *m.* casual, simple strumming of a guitar.
guitarrería, *f.* guitar workshop or store.
guitarrero, ra, *m., f.* person who designs, makes or sells guitars; (coll.) guitar player.
guitarresco, ca, *a.* of or pertaining to guitars, e.g. *música g.,* music written for the guitar.
guitarrillo, *m.* small four-stringed, high-pitched guitar.
guitarrista, *m., f.* guitarist, guitar player.
guitarro, *m., var. of* **guitarrillo.**
guitarrón, *m.* 1. large guitar, base guitar. 2. (coll.) cunning scoundrel.
guitero, ra, *m., f.* person who makes or sells twine.
güito, *m.* 1. (coll.) hat, bowler hat. 2. stone, pit (of fruit).
guitón, na, *m., f.* tramp, bum; rogue, rascal. —*m.* an ancient coin (formerly used as a gambling chip).
guitonear, *i.v.* to idle, loaf, bum around.
guitonería, *f.* loafing, idling, bumming.
guizacillo, *m.* (bot.) grass (Conchus equinatus).
guizazo, *m.* (Cuba, bot.) crowfoot; the burlike prickly fruit of the crowfoot.
guizgar, (*ref. 51*) *tr.v., var. of* **enguizgar.**
guizque, *m.* long, hooked pole used to extend the arm's reach.
guja, *f.* vouge, type of halberd.
gula, *f.* gluttony, greed for food; gormandizing.
gulden, *m.* guilder, Dutch monetary unit.
gules, *m.* (her.) gules, red.
gullería, *f., var. of* **gollería.**
gulloría, *f.* 1. (ornith.) calandra lark, calander. 2. delicacy, dainty morsel.
gulosidad, *f.* gluttony, greed.
guloso, sa, *a.* gluttonous, greedy. —*m., f.* glutton.
gulusmear, *i.v.* to sniff at the cooking, to hover in the kitchen hoping to get a taste.
gumamela, *f.* (Phil. I., bot.) China rose.
gúmena, *f.* (mar.) thick cable.
gumía, *f.* curved Moorish dagger or poignard.
gumífero, ra, *a.* gummiferous, gum-producing.
gumita, *f.* (min.) gummite.
gura, *f.* (ornith.) crowned pigeon (Goura victoriae).
gurbio, bia, *a.* curved (tool or instrument).
gurbión, *m.* 1. corded silk cloth. 2. silk twist, thread or twine. 3. (pharm.) euphorbium (acrid gum resin).
gurbionado, da, *a.* made of corded silk or silk twist.
gurdo, da, *a.* stupid, simple. —*m.* gourde, monetary unit of Haiti.
guripa, *m.* 1. (coll.) rascal, scamp, imp, rogue. 2. (coll.) soldier.
gurriato, *m.* nestling sparrow.
gurrufero, *m.* (coll.) mean and ugly nag.
gurrumino, na, *a.* weak, sickly. —*m.* 1. doting or hen-pecked husband. 2. (Mex.) young boy. —*f.* 1. (coll.) uxoriousness. 2. (Ecuad., Guat., Mex.) bother, annoyance. 3. (Amer.) trifle, small matter. 4. (Hond.) shrewd person. 5. (Mex.) young girl. 6. (Col.) melancholia, sadness.
gurullada, *f.* (coll.) crowd of nobodies, gang of idlers; (coll.) a squad of policemen.
gurullo, *m.* lump, knot.
gurupa, *f., var. of* **grupa.**
gurupera, *f.* cushion at the back of a saddle.
gurupetín, *m.* small cushion at the back of a saddle.
gurupié, *m.* (Amer.) croupier, gambling table attendant.
gurvio, a, *a.* curved (tools).
gusanear, *i.v.* to teem, swarm, abound.
gusanera, *f.* 1. worm nest. 2. (coll.) blinding passion.
gusanería, *f.* mass of worms.
gusaniento, ta, *a.* wormy, grubby, full of worms or maggots, worm-eaten.
gusanillo, *m.* 1. small worm or grub. 2. delicate embroidery; gold, silver or silk twist. — **matar el g.,** (coll.) to take a nip first thing in the morning.
gusano, *m.* 1. worm; maggot, grub, caterpillar. 2. (fig.) worm, wretch, contemptible person. — **g. de la conciencia,** remorse; **g. de luz,** (ento.) glowworm; **g. de San Antón,** (ento.) ladybird; **g. de sangre roja,** (zool.) amelid; **g. de seda,** silkworm; **g. revoltón,** vine fretter, vine louse; **matar el g.,** (Ecuad., Peru) to satisfy a strong desire or longing; (Mex.) to satisfy partially a whim or caprice; to have a bite to eat.
gusanoso, sa, *a.* wormy, grubby, full of worms, worm-eaten.
gusarapiento, ta, *a.* 1. wormy, full of worms. 2. filthy, dirty, rotten.
gusarapo, pa, *m., f.* waterworm, annelid found in liquids, esp. in vinegar.
gustable, *a.* 1. of taste or flavor. 2. (Chile) tasty, flavorsome.
gustación, *f.* tasting, gustation, sampling.
gustadura, *f.* tasting, sampling.
gustar, *tr.v.* 1. to taste, sample, savor. 2. to try, test. —*i.v.* to please, be pleasing, e.g. *me gusta el vino,* I like wine, *le gusta bailar,* he likes dancing, he likes to dance; **como Ud. guste,** as you like or wish; **g. de,** to like, enjoy, e.g. *él gusta de bromas,* he likes jokes; **g. de** + *inf.,* to like + *inf.* or *ger.,* e.g. *gusto de correr en mi auto,* I like to race in my car.
gustativo, va, *a.* gustative, gustatory.

gustazo, *m.* (coll.) great pleasure; inordinate desire to do something at any cost; **por un g. un trancazo,** a kingdom for a kiss (if the kiss is desired enough).

gustillo, *m.* aftertaste, relish.

gusto, *m.* 1. taste, sense of taste, e.g. *he perdido el g.,* I've lost my sense of taste. 2. taste, flavor. 3. pleasure, delight. 4. whim, caprice, wish. 5. taste (aesthetic discernment; aesthetic quality), e.g. *una casa arreglada con mucho g.,* a house appointed with great taste, *él tiene muy buen g.,* he has very good taste. 6. taste, style, e.g. *según los dictados del g. moderno,* according to the dictates of modern taste. 7. taste, individual liking, e.g. *no hay nada escrito sobre gustos,* there's no accounting for tastes. — **a.g.,** as one wants or wishes; at will; comfortable, e.g. *con las ventanas abiertas me siento muy a g.,* I feel very comfortable with the windows open; (cul.) to taste; **al g.,** (cul.) to individual taste, to order, e.g. *eche sal al g.,* add salt to taste; **a su g.,** as one wants or wishes; at will; **con mucho g.,** gladly, with pleasure; **dar g. a,** to please; **encontrarse** or **estar a g.,** to be or feel comfortable, feel at home; **perder el g. por,** to lose one's taste for; **por g.,** for the sake of it, for a whim or caprice, e.g. *comer por g.,* to eat for the sake of eating; **¡qué g. de +** *inf.,* what a pleasure to + *inf.,* e.g. *¡qué g. de verte!* how nice to see you; **tener el g. de +** *inf.,* to have the pleasure of + *ger.;* **tener g. en +** *inf.,* to be glad to + *inf.;* **tomar el g. a,** to take a liking to, become fond of.

gustosamente, *adv.* 1. gladly, with pleasure. 2. tastefully.

gustoso, sa, *a.* 1. tasty, savory, agreeable to the palate. 2. glad, pleased, willing, ready. 3. agreeable, pleasurable, delightful. — **g. le escribo que,** I am glad to inform you that.

gutagamba, *f.* (bot.) garcinia (Garcinia morella); gambedge (resin).

gutapercha, *f.* 1. gutta-percha. 2. cloth treated with gutta-percha.

gutiámbar, *f.* a yellow resin, gamboge.

gutífero, ra, *a.* (bot.) guttiferous. —*f.* (*pl.*) Guttiferae.

gutural, *a.* (phonet.) guttural.

guturalización, *f.* gutturalization.

guturalizar, (*ref.* 53) *tr.v.* to gutturalize.

guturalmente, *adv.* gutturally.

guzla, *f.* (mus.) gusla, a one-string rebec.

guzmán, *m.* nobleman who served as a cadet or midshipman but with certain privileges.

guzpatarra, *f.* an ancient children's game.

H

H, *f.* h, eighth letter of the Spanish alphabet.
H *sym. of* **hidrógeno,** hydrogen (H).
H., *abbrev. of* **haber,** credit (cr.).
ha, *interj.* ah!
ha, has, han, *ref.* **haber.**
haba, *f.* 1. (bot.) broad bean; bean (of cocoa, coffee, etc.). 2. voting or ballot ball. 3. nodule (in stone); (min.) nugget, globule of ore (surrounded by gangue). 4. swelling, bump (caused by insect bite). 5. (vet.) tumor on horses's palate. — **h. caballar** or **caballuno,** (bot.) horsebean; **h. de Egipto,** (bot.) taro; **h. de las Indias,** (bot.) sweet pea; **h. marina,** (zool.) sea bean (round operculum of various mollusks); **en todas partes se cuecen habas,** it's no different anywhere else; **esas son habas contadas,** it's absolutely certain; it's quite clear.
habado, da, *a.* 1. (vet.) suffering from a tumor on the palate (horse). 2. dappled (animal); mottled (bird).
habanero, ra, *a.* from Havana, Cuba. —*m., f.* native of Havana. 2. (hist.) European emigré who returned home after acquiring wealth in the Americas. —*f.* (mus.) habanera.
habano, na, *a.* 1. from Havana, Cuba. 2. brown (color). —*m.* Havana cigar. —*f.* **La Habana,** Havana, capital of Cuba.
habar, *m.* bean field.
hábeas corpus, *m.* (law) habeas corpus.
háber, *m.* Jewish doctor of law.
haber, (*ref. 9*) *tr.v.* 1. (arch.) to have, possess. 2. to lay one's hands on, get; to catch, capture, e.g. *los contrabandistas no pudieron ser habidos,* the smugglers could not be caught. —*aux.v.* to have, e.g. *he roto el vaso,* I have broken the glass; **¡bien haya(n) . . . !,** blessings on . . . !; **h. de** + *inf.,* to have to, must *inf.* —*imper.v.* (forms used in present: **ha, hay**) 1. **ha,** ago, e.g. *poco tiempo ha,* a short time ago. 2. **hay,** to be (used in phrases there is, there are), e.g. *hay dos niños,* there are two boys. — **hay que** + *inf.,* to be necessary to + *inf.,* e.g. *hay que llegar temprano,* you have to get there early, *hay que ver lo que pasa,* we must wait and see what happens, *para llegar allí, hay que tomar el tren,* to get there, it is necessary to take the train; **hay — que** + *inf.,* there is — to + *inf.,* e.g. *hay mucho que hacer,* there is a lot to do; **¡mal haya(n) . . . !,** curses on . . . !; **no hay de qué,** you're welcome, don't mention it; **no hay nada que hacer,** there is nothing to be done; **¿qué hay?** hi, hello; what's up?; what's the matter?; **¿qué hay de nuevo?** what's new? —*r.v.* to behave; **habérselas con,** to deal with, have it out with; **tener que habérselas con alguien,** to have to face someone; **¡habráse visto!** did you ever! fancy that!
haber, *m.* 1. property, estate; fortune, wealth. 2. salary, wages. 3. (com.) credit (as opposed to debit). — **h. monedado,** hard cash; **tener a su h.,** to have to one's credit.
haberío, *m.* beast of burden; livestock, cattle.
habichuela, *f.* 1. (bot.) kidney bean. 2. (Cuba) string bean. 3. bean.
habiente, *a.* having, possessing.
hábil, *a.* 1. clever, skillful, able, competent. 2. capable, suitable, apt. 3. working (day); court (day). 4. (law) competent (legally able).
habilidad, *f.* 1. ability, capacity; skill. 2. talent, accomplishment. 3. trick, scheme.
habilidoso, sa, *a.* skillful, able, capable.
habilitación, *f.* 1. qualification. 2. equipment. 3. equipping, fitting out, supplying. 4. financing. 5. authorization. 6. (mil.) paymastership. 7. trousseau, hope chest. — **h. de bandera,** permission to foreign ships to trade in national waters.
habilitado, da, *past part. of* **habilitar.** —*a.* 1. qualified; competent, legally authorized; validated (on stamps). 2. outfitted (bride, soldier, etc.). —*m.* 1. paymaster. 2. authorized deputy of judge's secretary. 3. business man financed by someone else.
habilitador, ra, *m., f.* 1. financial backer. 2. outfitter.
habilitar, *tr.v.* 1. to qualify, enable. 2. to furnish, fit out, equip. 3. to supply, provide. 4. to finance. 5. (law) to authorize. — **h. de,** to supply or equip with. —*r.v.* to outfit oneself (bride, soldier, etc.).
habilmente, *adv.* ably, skillfully; cunningly.
habiloso, sa, *a.* (Chile) able, capable, competent, smart.
habitabilidad, *f.* habitability; inhabitability.
habitable, *a.* habitable (house, etc.); inhabitable (region, etc.).
habitación, *f.* room; habitation; residence, dwelling, house; (bot., zool.) habitat.
habitáculo, *m.* habitation, dwelling, house, residence.
habitador, ra, *a., m., f.* inhabitant, dweller.
habitante, *a.* inhabiting. —*m., f.* inhabitant (of a region, country, etc.).
habitar, *tr.v.* to inhabit; to live or reside in. —*i.v.* to live, reside, dwell.
habitat, *m.* (Fr.) habitat; native environment (of a group of persons or of a species of plants, animals, etc.).
hábito, *m.* 1. habit, dress, garb, attire; habit (of monks, etc.); (*pl.*) vestments (of priest). 2. habit, custom. — **colgar los hábitos,** to leave the church; to change one's career; **el h. no hace al monje,** clothes don't make the man; **tener por h.,** to have the habit; **tomar los hábitos,** to become a priest or nun.
habituación, *f.* habituation, accustoming.
habituado, da, *past part. of* **habituar.** —*m.* habitué, habitual customer or client.
habitual, *a.* customary, habitual.
habitualmente, *adv.* habitually, customarily, usually.
habituar, (*ref. 55*) *tr.v.* (with a) to accustom (to), familiarize (with). —*r.v.* to become accustomed or used (to).
habitud, *f.* relation, connection.
habiz, (*pl.* **habices**), *m.* donation or bequest of property to a mosque.
habla, *f.* 1. speech, faculty of speech; speaking. 2. language. 3. speech, address. — **al h.,** in communication, in conversation; within speaking distance; **quedarse sin h.,** to become speechless.
habladas, *f.* (Amer.) boasts, boasting, bragging.
hablado, da, *past part. of* **hablar.** —*a.* **bien** or **mal h.,** polite or rude (speech).
hablador, ra, *a.* talkative; gossipy. —*m., f.* chatterbox; gossip.
habladuría, *f.* nasty talk; piece of idle talk, gossip, rumor; (*pl.*) (coll.) gossip.
hablanchín, na, *a.* (coll.) talkative; gossipy. —*m., f.* chatterbox; gossip.
hablante, *a.* talking, speaking.
hablantín, na, *a., m., f., var. of* **hablanchín.**
hablar, *tr.v.* to speak (a language); to talk, e.g. *h. disparates,* to talk nonsense; **hablarlo todo,** to tell everything. —*i.v.* to speak, talk; **es h. por demás,** it's just wasted breath or talk; **eso es h.,** now you are talking; **estar hablando,** to be almost lifelike; **h. a** or **con,** to court, woo; **h. a tontas y a locas,** to talk without rhyme or reason; **h. consigo mismo,** to talk to oneself; **h. claro,** to talk frankly; **h. gordo,** to brag, boast; **h. hasta por los codos,** to talk a blue streak; **h. por,** to speak or intercede for; **h. por h.,** to talk for the sake of talking; **ni habla ni parla,** as quiet as the grave (a person); **quien mucho habla mucho yerra,** he who talks too much, errs exceedingly. —*r.v.* to talk or speak with one another.
hablilla, *f.* story rumor, piece of gossip.
hablista, *m., f.* good speaker, eloquent talker.
hablistán, *a.* (coll.) talkative; gossipy. —*m., f.* chatterbox; gossip.
habón, *m.* 1. welt, wheal (from insect bite). 2. (bot.) horse bean.
habré, *ref.* **haber.**
Habsburgo, *m.* Hapsburg, Habsburg.
habus, *m., var. of* **habiz.**
haca, *f.* pony, small horse.
hacán, *m.* Jewish scholar or physician.
hacanea, *f.* strong, small horse.
hacecillo, *m.* 1. *dim. of* **haz,** small bundle. 2. fascicle, glomerule.
hacedero, ra, *a.* feasible, practicable, possible.
hacedor, ra, *a.* making. —*m., f.* maker. —*m.* administrator, manager (of an estate). — el **H.,** the Creator.
hacendado, da, *past part. of* **hacendar.** —*a.* landed, owning real estate. —*m., f.* 1. landowner. 2. farmer, planter; (Arg., Chile) rancher, cattle-dealer; (Cuba) plantation owner.
hacendar, (*ref. 29*) *tr.v.* to make over or transfer (property) to. —*r.v.* to acquire property, settle down on the land.
hacendeja, *f. dim. of* **hacienda,** small estate, ranch or farm.
hacendera, *f.* community work, work done by a neighborhood.
hacendero, ra, *a.* industrious, hard-working.
hacendista, *m.* economist, public finance expert.
hacendoso, sa, *a.* industrious, hard-working.
hacenduela, *f. dim. of* **hacienda, small** estate, farm or ranch.
hacer, (*ref. 10*) *tr.v.* 1. to make. 2. to do. 3. to pack (suitcase). 4. to work (miracles). 5. to contain, hold. 6. to assemble, gather. 7. to accustom, e.g. *h. el cuerpo a las fatigas,* to accustom the body

to fatigue. 8. to train (birds of prey). 9. to cut, trim (nails). 10. to bet (a certain amount though not having requisite money). 11. to think to be, e.g. *yo hacía a Elana ya casada,* I thought Elena was already married. 12. to provide, e.g. *h. a uno con libros,* to provide one with books. 13. to act, play (a part; the fool). 14. (math.) to make, equal, be (in addition sums). 15. to make, force, oblige. 16. to evacuate (the bowels or bladder). — **h.** + *inf.,* to get or have + *past part.,* e.g. *haré pintar la casa,* I will get the house painted; to get to + *inf.,* ask to + *inf.,* e.g. *h. pasar, subir* or *bajar,* to ask to come in, up or down, get to come in, up or down; **h. alusión,** to allude; **h. buena una cosa,** to prove or justify something; to perform, carry something out; **h. burla de,** to make fun of; **h. cola,** to queue; **h. conocer,** to make known; **h. daño,** to hurt; **h. el amor,** to make love; **h. estimación,** to estimate; **h. gestos,** to gesture, gesticulate; **h. la barba,** to shave; **h. mofa,** to mock jeer; **h. pedazos,** to break or tear to pieces; **h. que** + *subj.,* to get + *inf.,* e.g. *haré que me planche la camisa,* I will get her to iron my shirt; **h. saber,** to inform, make known; **h. señas,** to signal, make signs. —*i.v.* 1. to do, e.g. *esta máquina hace de todo,* this machine does everything. 2. to be relevant, have to do with, e.g. *eso no hace al caso,* this has nothing to do with the case. 3. to correspond, to fit, e.g. *esta llave hace a dos cerraduras,* this key fits two locks. 4. to try, strive, endeavor, e.g. *h. por llegar a tiempo,* to try to arrive on time. 5. to pretend or feign to be, act, play, e.g. *h. el tonto,* to act dumb. 6. to pretend, act, e.g. *h. como,* to pretend that, act as if. 7. to work, act, e.g. *h. de,* to work as. 8. to evacuate (bowels, bladder), e.g. *h. del cuerpo,* to ease nature; *h. de las suyas,* (coll.) to do what one pleases. 9. to play, e.g. *mi hermana hace de casa,* my sister is playing house. —*r.v.* 1. to make oneself. 2. to become; to grow; to turn (into). 3. to accustom oneself. 4. to cut one's (nails). 5. to evacuate (the bowels). 6. to pretend or feign to be, act, play, e.g. *hacerse el tonto,* to act dumb, pretend not to understand. 7. to go to or towards, e.g. *hacerse a un lado,* to step aside. — **hacerse con,** to provide oneself with, to filch; **hacérsela,** (vulg.) to masturbate, jerk off (vulg.); **hacérsele a uno (una cosa),** to appear, seem. —*impers. v.* 1. to be, e.g. *hace calor, frío* or *buen día,* it is hot, cold or a fine day; **mañana hará calor** or **frío,** it will be hot or cold tomorrow. 2. to be — since, e.g. *hace un mes que se fue,* it's been a month since he left, *hacía tres años que no le había visto,* it had been three years since I had seen him. 3. for, e.g. *hace un mes que no lo veo,* I haven't seen him for a month. 4. ago, e.g. *hace cinco años,* five years ago. — **desde hace,** for, e.g. *él está aquí desde hace siete meses,* he has been here for seven months.

hacera, *f., var. of* **acera.**

hacezuelo, *m. dim. of* **haz,** small bundle.

hacha, *f.* 1. ax. 2. large candle. 3. torch, flambeau. 4. bundle, sheaf (of straw). 5. (Chile) game of marbles. 6. old Spanish dance. — **h. de armas,** battle axe; **ser un h.,** to be outstanding (at something).

hachar, *tr.v., var. of* **hachear.**

hachazo, *m.* 1. ax blow or stroke. 2. (taur.) side blow with the horns. 3. (Col.) sudden shying (of horse).

hache, *f.* aitch (name of the letter "h"). — **por h. o por be,** for whatever reason.

hachear, *tr.v.* to ax or cut with an ax, hew; to trim.

hachero, *m.* 1. woodcutter, woodsman. 2. (mil.) sapper. 3. torch stand; heavy candlestick.

hacheta, *f. dim. of* **hacha,** hatchet, small ax.

hachich, hachís, haschich, *m.* hasheesh, hashish.

hacho, *m.* 1. torch, firebrand, flambeau. 2. (geog.) beacon hill.

hachón, *m.* 1. large heavy candle. 2. cresset, torch holder.

hachote, *m.* 1. (mar.) short heavy sail. 2. a short, thick candle.

hachudo, *m.* (Cuba) anchovy (Engraulis productus).

hachuela, *f. dim. of* **hacha,** hatchet; small ax; (Chile) stonemason's pickax.

hacia, *prep.* 1. towards, toward, in the direction of. 2. about (of time). — **h. abajo,** downwards; **h. acá,** here, hither; **h. adelante,** forwards; **h. arriba,** upwards; **h. atrás,** backwards; **h. donde,** where, whither; **h. un lado,** to one side; **hacia la una,** at about one.

hacienda, *f.* 1. farm, ranch. 2. property, estate, fortune, wealth. 3. (*pl.*) household duties or chores. 4. **H.,** Ministry of Finance. 5. (Arg., Chile) livestock, cattle. — **h. pública,** public finance.

haciende, haciendo, *ref.* **hacendar.**

hacina, *f.* stack, pile, heap.

hacinación, *f., var. of* **hacinamiento.**

hacinador, ra, *m., f.* stacker.

hacinamiento, *m.* stacking; heaping, piling; accumulation.

hacinar, *tr.v.* to stack; to pile or heap up. —*r.v.* to pile or heap up.

hada, *f.* fairy. — **cuento de hadas,** fairytale.

hadado, da, *past part. of* **hadar.** —*a.* magic, enchanted. — **bien h.,** lucky; **mal h.,** unlucky, fateful.

hadar, *tr.v.* 1. to destine, predetermine. 2. to divine, foretell. 3. to enchant, put a spell on.

hades, *m.* (myth.) Hades, the infernal regions governed by Pluto.

hado, *m.* (lit.) fate, destiny.

hafiz, (*pl.* **hafices**), *m.* (Arabic) guardian, keeper, warden.

hafnio, *m.* (chem.) hafnium.

haga, *ref.* **hacer.**

Hagar, *f.* (Bib.) Hagar, a concubine of Abraham.

hagiografía, *f.* (ecc.) hagiography, biography of the saints.

hagiográfico, ca, *a.* hagiographic, hagiographical.

hagiógrafo, *m.* 1. (rel.) hagiographer, an author of the Sacred Scriptures. 2. the biographer of a saint.

hagiológico, ca, *a.* hagiologic.

hagiólogo, *m., var. of* **hagiógrafo.**

hago, *ref.* **hacer.**

Haifa, *f.* Haifa, principal Mediterranean seaport of Israel.

haiga, *m.* 1. improper use of **haya.** 2. (coll.) luxury car or automobile.

Haití, *m.* Haiti.

haitiano, na, *a., m., f.* Haitian.

¡hala! *interj.* come on! hurry up!; hey! come here!

halacabuyas, *m.* (mar.) greenhorn, sailor, cabin boy.

halacuerda, *m.* (mar.) common hand, unskilled sailor.

halagador, ra, *a.* 1. flattering. 2. gratifying, pleasing.

halagar, (*ref. 51*) *tr.v.* 1. to flatter. 2. to treat affectionately, show one's affection for. 3. to please, delight, gratify.

halago, *m.* 1. piece of flattery, flattering word: (*pl.*) flattery, flattering words. 2. gratification.

halague, halagué, *ref.* **halagar.**

halagüeño, ña, *a.* 1. flattering. 2. gratifying, pleasing. 3. pleasant, attractive.

halar, *tr.v.* 1. (coll.) *ref.* **jalar.** 2. to pull, pull on. 3. (mar.) to haul. —*i.v.* (mar.) to pull; to pull ahead. — **h. hacia tierra,** to pull towards the land.

halcón, *m.* (ornith.) falcon, hawk. — **h. lanero,** lanner, African falcon.

halconado, da, *a.* hawk- or falcon-like.

halconear, *i.v.* to vamp, use one's charms to attract another person; to cruise (sl.).

halconera, *f.* mew, place where falcons are kept.

halconería, *f.* falconry, hawking.

halconero, ra, *a.* brazen. —*m.* falconer, hawker.

halda, *f.* 1. skirt. 2. packing burlap. 3. skirtful.

haldada, *f.* skirtful.

haldear, *i.v.* to rush along with skirts billowing.

haldeta, *f.* (dressm.) peplum, short skirt.

¡hale! *interj.* come on! hurry up! pull!

haleche, *m.* (ichth.) a small sardine (Sardinella allecia).

Halicarnaso, *m.* Halicarnassus, ancient Greek city in Asia Minor.

halieto, *m.* (ornith.) sea eagle, osprey, fish hawk.

halita, *f.* (min.) halite.

hálito, *m.* halitus, breath, vapor; (poet.) breath of air, breeze.

halitosis, *f.* (med.) halitosis, bad breath.

hall, *m.* hall, vestibule.

hallada, *f.* discovery, find.

hallado, da, *past part. of* **hallar.** —*a.* **tan** or **bien h.,** easy, at ease; **mal h.,** uneasy, constrained.

hallador, ra, *a.* discovering, finding. —*m., f.* discoverer, finder. —*m.* (mar.) rescue ship.

hallar, *tr.v.* to find; to discover. —*r.v.* to be present; to be, e.g. *hallarse perdido,* to be lost; **no hallarse,** to be uncomfortable, discontented, annoyed.

hallazgo, *m.* 1. finding, discovery; find. 2. reward.

hallullo, lla, *m., f.* bread baked on hot stones; (Chile) special flat bread.

hallus, hallux, *m.* (anat., ornith.) hallux.

halo, *m.* (astron., rel., fig.) halo.

halobionte, *m.* (biol.) halobiont.

halófilo, la, *a.* (bot.) halophilous, halophytic.

halófito, *m.* (bot.) halophyte.

halogenación, *f.* (chem.) halogenation.

halogenar, *tr.v.* (chem.) to halogenate.

halógeno, na, *a.* (chem.) halogenous. —*m.* (chem.) halogen.

halografía, *f.* (chem.) halography.

haloide, *m.* (chem.) haloid, halide.

haloideo, a, *a., m.* (chem.) haloid, halide.

halón, *m., var. of* **halo.**

haloque, *m.* (mar.) felucca, small ancient vessel.

halotecnia, *f.* (chem.) science of extracting industrial salts.

haloza, *f.* clog, wooden overshoe.

haltera, *f.* barbell.

halterofilia, *f.* weightlifting.

halterófilo, la, *m., f.* weightlifter.

haluro, *m.* (chem.) halide.

hamaca, *f.* hammock; hammock litter.

hámago, *m.* 1. beebread. 2. disgust, nausea, loathing.

hamamelidáceo, a, *a.* (bot.) hamamelidaceous. —*f.* (*pl.*) Hamamelidaceae.

hamaquear, *tr.v., r.v.* (Amer.) to rock, swing.

hamaquero, *m.* 1. hammock maker. 2. hammock-litter bearer. 3. peg from which hammock is hung.

hambre, *f.* 1. hunger; starvation. 2. famine. 3. hunger, desire, longing. — **cuando hay h. no hay mal pan,** when one is hungry everything tastes good; **h. canina,** uncontrollable hunger; longing, craving; **morir de h.,** to die of starvation,

starve to death; to be destitute or poverty-stricken; **ser más listo que el h.,** to be very bright, be as sharp as a needle; **tener h.,** to be hungry.
hambrear, *tr.v.* to starve, famish; to be hungry. —*i.v.* to hunger, starve; to be hungry.
hambriento, ta, *a.* hungry, starving; (fig.) hungry, longing; **h. de,** hungry for. —*m., f.* hungry person, (*pl.*) the hungry.
hambrón, na, *a.* (coll.) famished, starving. —*m., f.* hungry person.
hambruna, *f.* (coll., Amer.) great hunger; (Ecuad.) famine.
hamburgués, sa, *a.* pertaining to Hamburg, Germany. —*m.* Hamburger, native of Hamburg. —*f.* (cul.) hamburger.
hamburguesería, *f.* hamburger stand.
hamo, *m.* fishing hook, fishhook.
hampa, *f.* underworld, criminal world; life of vagrancy, delinquency.
hampesco, ca, *a.* vagrant, vagabond; criminal, underworld.
hampo, pa, *a.* vagrant, vagabond; criminal, underworld. —*m.* underworld; life of vagrancy.
hampón, *a.* rowdy, bullying, tough; delinquent. —*m., f.* rowdy, tough, ruffian; gangster, criminal, tough, roughneck.
hanega, *f.* (rare), *var. of* **fanega,** a dry measure.
hanegada, *f.* (rare), *var. of* **fanegada.**
hangar, *m.* (aer.) hangar; shed, shelter.
hannoveriano, na, *a., m., f.* (hist., geog.) Hanoverian.
Hanoi, *n.* Hanoi, capital of North Vietnam.
hansa, *f.* Hanse, Hanseatic League.
hanseático, ca, *a.* Hanseatic.
haploide, *a.* (biol.) haploid.
haplología, *f.* (philol.) haplology.
haplonte, *m.* (biol.) haplont.
haragán, na, *a.* idle, indolent, lazy. —*m., f.* idler, loafer.
haraganamente, *adv.* idly, lazily.
haraganear, *i.v.* to idle, lead an idle life, loaf around.
haraganería, *f.* idleness, laziness, loafing.
haraganoso, sa, *a.* (rare), *var. of* **haragán.**
harakiri, *m.* hara-kiri; **hacerse el h.,** to commit hara-kiri.
harapiento, ta, *a.* ragged; unkempt.
harapo, *m.* 1. rag, tatter. 2. low-grade alcohol. — **andar hecho un h.,** to go around in rags.
haraposo, sa, *a.* ragged, tattered, torn; unkempt.
haraquiri, *m.* hara-kiri.
haras, *m.* (Amer.) stud farm, stud.
harbullar, *tr.v., var. of* **farfullar.**
harca, *f.* harka, Moroccan military expedition; group of Moroccan rebels.
haré, *ref.* **hacer.**
harem, harén, *m.* harem, seraglio.
haría, *ref.* **hacer.**
harija, *f.* mill dust (floating dust caused by grinding wheat).
harina, *f.* 1. flour; meal, e.g. *h. de pescado,* fish meal. 2. dust, powder. — **estar metido en h.,** to be tough and heavy (bread); to be stout and heavy; to be hard at work; **hacer h.,** to pulverize, break into pieces; **h. de avena,** oatmeal; **h. de flor,** extrafine flour; **h. de huesos,** bone meal; **h. de maíz,** cornmeal; **h. de pescada,** fish meal; **h. de trigo,** wheat flour; **h. fósil,** (min.) kieselguhr, diatomaceous or infusorial earth; **h. integral,** wholewheat flour; **h. leudante** or **con levadura** or **con polvos de hornear,** self-rising flour; **ser h. de otro costal,** to be a horse of a different color.
harinado, *m.* flour dissolved in water.
harinero, ra, *a.* floury. —*m.* 1. flour dealer. 2. flour chest.
harinoso, sa, *a.* mealy, floury; farinaceous.
harma, *f., var. of* **alharma.**
harmonía, *f., var. of* **armonía.**
harmónico, ca, *a., var. of* **armónico.**
harmonio, *m., var. of* **armonio.**
harmonioso, sa, *a., var. of* **armonioso.**
harmonizable, *a., var. of* **armonizable.**
harmonización, *f.* (mus.) *var. of* **armonización.**
harmonizar, (*ref. 53*) *tr.v., var. of* **armonizar.**
harnear, *tr.v.* (Col., Chile) to sift, sieve, screen.
harnerero, *m.* sieve maker or seller.
harnero, *m.* sieve.
harneruelo, *m.* (archit.) central part of a wooden ceiling.
harón, na, *a.* lazy, idle, slothful; slow, sluggish.
haronear, *i.v.* to be lazy or idle; to dawdle, walk sluggishly.
haronía, *f.* laziness, idleness, indolence, sloth.
harpa, *f., var. of* **arpa.**
harpado, da, *a., var. of* **arpado.**
harpía, *f., var. of* **arpía.**
harpillera, *f.* burlap, sackcloth.
harqueño, ña, *a.* pertaining to a harka. —*m.* raider, skirmisher, member of a harka.
harrado, *m.* (archit.) angle of cylindrical arch; (archit.) spandrel.
harre, *interj., var. of* **arre.**
harrear, *tr.v., var. of* **arrear.**
harria, *f., var. of* **arria.**
harriero, *m.* 1. muleteer, mule-driver. 2. (Cuba, ornith.) a large cuckoo (Coccysus americanus).
hartada, *f.* fill, bellyful.
hartar, *tr.v.* 1. to fill, stuff. 2. to satisfy, satiate. 3. to annoy, tire, bore. — **h. de palos,** to give, deliver blows; to deluge with. —*r.v.* 1. to stuff or fill oneself, gorge. 2. to get bored or fed up (coll.) tired.
hartazgo, *m.* fill, bellyful, surfeit; **darse uno un h.,** to eat one's fill; **darse uno un h. de,** (coll.) to have one's fill of, have a bellyful of.
hartazón, *m., var. of* **hartazgo.**
harto, *adv.* very, e.g. *él es h. tonto,* he is very stupid.
harto, ta, *irr. past part. of* **hartar.** —*a.* 1. full, satiated, replete. 2. fed up, sick and tired, e.g. *estar h. de su estupidez,* to be sick and tired of his stupidity.
hartura, *f.* 1. satiety, fill. 2. abundance, plenty. 3. (fig.) achievement, gratification, fulfillment.
Hasidismo, *m.* (rel.) Hasidism.
hasta, *prep.* 1. until, till. 2. up to; down to; as far as. 3. up to, around, about. — **h. la vista** or **h. luego,** so long, cheerio; **h. que,** until, till. —*adv.* even; also.
hastado, da, *a.* (bot.) hastate.
hastial, *m.* 1. gable wall. 2. (min.) side wall (of an excavation). 3. (fig.) oaf, uncouth person.
hastiar, (*ref. 54*) *tr.v.* to bore, tire; to sicken, cloy.
hastío, *m.* 1. ennui, boredom, tedium. 2. surfeit, loathing, revulsion (towards food).
hastiosamente, *adv.* with ennui or boredom.
hastioso, sa, *a.* 1. boring, tedious. 2. nauseous, revolting.
hataca, *f.* 1. big wooden ladle. 2. rolling pin.
hatajador, *m.* (Mex.) drover, herdsman.
hatajo, *m.* 1. small herd or flock. 2. (coll.) lot (e.g. of nonsense).
hatear, *i.v.* 1. to pack up, get one's things together. 2. to provide (shepherds) with provisions.
hatería, *f.* provisions, supplies, equipment (of shepherds, herdsmen, miners, etc.).
hatero, ra, *a.* pack (horse). —*m.* carrier of provisions (to shepherds). —*m., f.* (Cuba) rancher.
hatijo, *m.* straw or mat covering (of beehives).
hatillo, *m.* clothes, belongings, things; **echar uno el h. al mar,** to get angry, get annoyed; **coger** or **tomar uno el h.,** to leave, go away.
hato, *m.* 1. flock, herd. 2. shepherd's hut. 3. supplies, provisions, equipment. 4. everyday clothes; belongings, things. 5. (Cuba) ranch, farm. 6. (fig.) gang, band (of criminals); group, circle. 7. lot (e.g. of nonsense). — **andar uno con el h. a cuestas,** to wander, be constantly on the move; **liar uno el h.,** (coll.) to pack one's things; **menear el h. a uno,** (coll.) to thrash, beat; **revolver el h.,** (coll.) to start or provoke a quarrel.
haustorio, *m.* (bot.) haustorium.
haute, *m.* (her.) escutcheon representing coats of arms of different lineages.
Havre, *m.* **El H.,** Le Havre, port in France.
Hawai, *m.* Hawaii.
hawaiano, na, *a., m., f.* Hawaiian.
haxix, *m.* hashish, hasheesh.
haya, *ref.* **haber.**
haya, *f.* 1. (bot.) beech, beech tree; beech wood. 2. (arch.) gift, present.
Haya, *f.* **La H.,** The Hague, city in the Netherlands.
hayaca, *f.* (cul., Ven.) pie with meat or fish, wrapped in banana leaves.
hayal, *m.* beech-tree grove.
hayedo, *m., var. of* **hayal.**
hayo, *m.* 1. (bot.) coca. 2. mixture of coca leaves and lime (chewed by Indians).
hayuco, *m.* (bot.) beechnut.
haz, (*pl.* **haces**), *m.* 1. bundle, bunch, sheaf, fagot. 2. pencil, beam (of rays). 3. (anat.) fascicle (of fibers). 4. (ry.) group (of lines). 5. (*pl.*) fasces (of Roman lictors). 6. battle line, line of troops formed in divisions. — **h. de láser,** laser beam; **h. electrónico,** electron beam.
haz, (*pl.* **haces**), *f.* 1. face, countenance, outward appearance. 2. right side (of cloth). — **a dos haces,** with an ulterior motive; **a sobre h.,** on the surface; **h. de la tierra,** surface of the earth; **ser uno de dos haces,** to be two-faced or hypocritical.
haza, *f.* plot (of arable land).
hazaleja, *f.* face towel.
hazaña, *f.* exploit, deed, heroic feat.
hazañería, *f.* fuss; exaggerated fear, admiration or excitement.
hazañero, ra, *a.* fussy, effusive, shoving exaggerated fear or admiration.
hazañosamente, *adv.* heroically, bravely.
hazañoso, sa, *a.* brave, heroic.
hazmerreír, *m.* (coll.) butt, laughingstock, clown.
hazuela, *f.* small plot (of land).
he, hemos, *ref.* **haber.**
he, *dem. adv.* look, behold; there or here (is or are), e.g. *helo,* look, there he is, *helos aquí,* here they are; it is at this point; **he aquí el hombre,** Ecce Homo, Behold the Man.
He *sym. of* **helio,** helium (He).
hebdómada, *f.* 1. hebdomad, week. 2. seven years.
hebdomadariamente, *adv.* hebdomadally, every week, weekly.
hebdomadario, ria, *a.* hebdomadal, weekly. —*m.* (ecc.) hebdomadary.
Hebe, *f.* (myth.) Hebe, goddess of youth.
hebefrenia, *f.* (med.) hebephrenia.
hebefrénico, ca, *a.* (med.) hebephrenic
hebén, *a.* 1. large and white (grape). 2. (fig.) insignificant, of no account.
hebetar, *tr.v.* (rare) to blunt; to weaken, debilitate, enfeeble, enervate.
hebetud, *f.* (med.) hebetude.
hebijón, *m.* catch (of buckle).
hebilla, *f.* buckle.

hebillaje, *m.* set of buckles.
hebillero, ra, *m., f.* buckle maker or seller.
hebilleta, *f.* small buckle.
hebillón, *m.* large buckle.
hebilluela, *f.* small buckle.
hebra, *f.* 1. thread, strand. 2. fiber (of textile); sinew, nerve (of meat); grain (of wood). 3. thread, gist (of conversation, speech, etc.). 4. (min.) vein, layer. 5. (*pl.*) (poet.) hair. — **cortar a uno la hebra de la vida,** to kill someone; **de una hebra,** all at once, in one breath; **pegar la hebra,** (coll.) to chat; to get into conversation (unexpectedly), prolong a conversation.
hebraico, ca, *a.* Hebraic, Hebraical.
hebraísmo, *m.* Hebraism.
hebraísta, *m.* Hebraist (scholar of Hebrew literature and language).
hebraizante, *a.* Hebraizing. —*m.* Hebraist; Judaist, Judaizer.
hebraizar, (*ref. 53*) *i.v.* to Hebraize, employ Hebraism.
hebreo, a, *a., m., f.* Hebrew. —*m.* 1. Hebrew (language). 2. (coll.) merchant.
hebrero, *m.* esophagus (of a ruminant).
Hébridas, *f.* (*pl.*) (geog.) Hebrides.
Hebrón, *m.* (Bib., geog.) Hebron.
hebroso, sa, *a.* fibrous; sinewy (meat).
Hécate, *f.* (myth.) Hecate, pertaining to several Greek goddesses.
hecatombe, *f.* hecatomb; disaster, catastrophe.
hecha, *f.* (arch.) action, deed. — **de esta h.,** from now on, as of now.
hechice, hechicé, *ref.* **hechizar.**
hechiceresco, ca, *a.* magic, magical; pertaining to witchcraft.
hechicería, *f.* witchcraft, sorcery, black magic; spell, charm.
hechicero, ra, *a.* 1. magic. 2. bewitching, enchanting. —*m.* 1. magician, sorcerer, wizard. 2. enchanter, charmer. —*f.* 1. witch, sorceress. 2. enchantress, charmer.
hechizar, (*ref. 53*) *tr.v.* 1. to bewitch, cast a spell on. 2. to charm, enchant, bewitch.
hechizo, za, *a.* 1. false, fake, imitation; false, removable, detachable. 2. made, manufactured. —*m.* spell, charm.
hecho, cha, *irr. past part. of* **hacer.** —*a.* 1. done, finished, complete. 2. ready-made (clothes). 3. accustomed, inured. 4. mature (man, wine). 5. like, e.g. *h. un león,* like a lion. 6. well over, a good, e.g. *cien kilos bien hechos,* a good hundred kilos. 7. proportioned, e.g. *bien* or *mal h.,* well or badly proportioned. — **a lo h., pecho,** it's no use crying over spilt milk; **¡hecho!** done, agreed; **h. sobre pedido,** made to order; **h. y derecho,** fully mature and capable, complete, perfect. —*m.* 1. act, action; deed, feat. 2. fact. 3. event, occurrence. — **a. h.,** uninterruptedly, continuously; indiscriminately; **de h.,** truly, really, actually; in fact; (law) de facto; **de hecho y derecho,** in fact and by right; **h. consumado,** fait accompli; **h. de armas,** feat of arms; **h. probado,** (law) proved fact; **Hechos de los Apóstoles,** (Bib.) Acts of the Apostles; **pasar a los hechos,** to turn to violence.
hechor, *m.* 1. (Arg., Chile) stallion jackass. 2. (Chile, reg.) malefactor.
hechura, *f.* 1. making. 2. creation, creature. 3. creature, minion, servile dependent. 4. workmanship; price paid for workmanship. 5. form, shape; build (of body). — **no tener h.,** to be impossible, not to be feasible.
hechusgo, *m.* (Hond.) shape, form.
hect. *abbrev. of* **hectárea,** hectare (ha).
hectárea, *f.* hectare.
héctico, ca, *a.* (med.) hectic, consumptive (fever). —*f.* hectic fever. —*m., f.* consumptive, person suffering from tuberculosis.
hectiquez, *f.* (med.) chronic consumption.
hectocótilo, *m.* (zool.) hectocotylus.
hectógrafo, *m.* hectograph, instrument for making copies of manuscripts or drawings.
hectogramo, *m.* hectogram (100 grams).
hectolitro, *m.* hectoliter (100 liters).
hectómetro, *m.* hectometer (100 meters).
hectovatio, *m.* (elec.) hectowatt.
Hécuba, *f.* (myth.) Hecuba, Hecabe, mother of Paris and Hector.
hedentina, *f.* stench, stink.
heder, (*ref. 30*) *i.v.* 1. to stink, smell bad. 2. to annoy, tire, irritate.
hediento, ta, *a.* stinking, fetid, smelly.
hediondamente, *adv.* stinkingly, fetidly.
hediondez, *f.* stench, stink, fetidity.
hediondo, da, *a.* 1. stinking, fetid. 2. (fig.) irritating, insufferable, annoying. 3. filthy, dirty, obscene. —*m.* 1. (bot.) bean trefoil. 2. (zool.) skunk, polecat.
hedónica, *f.* (philos., psyc.) hedonics.
hedonismo, *m.* (philos., psyc.) hedonism.
hedonista, *a.* hedonistic; hedonic. —*m., f.* hedonist.
hedor, *m.* stench, stink.
hegelianismo, *m.* (philos.) Hegelianism.
hegeliano, na, *a., m., f.* Hegelian.
hegemonía, *f.* hegemony, supremacy of a state or people over another.
hégira, *f.* (rel.) hegira, hejira, Muslim era.
heguemonía, *f.* hegemony.
héjira, *f.* (rel.) hegira, hejira.
helable, *a.* freezable.
helada, *f.* freezing; frost; freezing weather, freeze. — **h. blanca,** hoarfrost, frost.
Hélade, *f.* Hellas, ancient name of Greece.
heladera, *f.* refrigerator.
heladería, *f.* ice cream parlor.
heladero, *m.* (Amer.) ice cream vendor.
heladizo, za, *a.* easily frozen.
helado, da, *past part. of* **helar.** —*a.* 1. freezing, icy, very cold. 2. (fig.) dumbfounded, astonished. —*m.* ice cream; sherbet.
helador, ra, *a.* freezing. —*f.* ice cream machine.
heladura, *f.* crack in wood caused by the cold.
helaje, *m.* (Col.) intense cold, frost.
helamiento, *m.* freezing; icing.
helar, (*ref. 29*) *tr.v.* 1. to freeze, ice; to chill. 2. to dumbfound, astonish. 3. to intimidate, discourage. —*i.v.* to freeze. —*r.v.* 1. to freeze, become frozen. 2. to harden, set, solidify. 3. to get blighted (by the frost). 4. to get frostbitten.
helear, *tr.v., var. of* **ahelear.**
helechal, *m.* bog of ferns, land covered with ferns.
helecho, *m.* (bot.) fern; (*pl.*) Ferns, Filicales (family). — **h. hembra,** (bot.) common brake, bracken; **h. macho,** male fern, shield fern.
helena, *f.* St. Elmo's fire.
helenice, *ref.* **helenizar.**
helénico, ca, *a.* Hellenic, Greek.
helenio, *m.* (bot.) elecampane.
helenismo, *m.* (hist.) Hellenism.
helenista, *m.* Hellenist.
helenístico, ca, *a.* Hellenistic, Hellenistical.
helenización, *f.* (hist.) Hellenization.
helenizante, *a.* Hellenizing. —*m.* Hellenizer.
helenizar, (*ref. 53*) *tr.v.* to Helenize. —*r.v.* to become Hellenized.
heleno, na, *a.* Hellenic, Greek. —*m., f.* Hellene, Greek.
helera, *f.* small tumor (on coccyx of canary or linnet).
helero, *m.* snowcap (on mountains); glacier.
helespóntico, ca, *a.* Hellespontine.
helesponto, *m.* Hellespont, ancient name for the Dardanelles.
helgado, da, *a.* jag-toothed, gap-toothed.
helgadura, *f.* gap (between teeth), unevenness (of teeth).
helíaco, ca, *a.* (astron.) Heliacal.
heliantemo, *m.* (bot.) helianthemum.
heliantina, *f.* (chem.) helianthin, methyl orange.
helianto, *m.* (bot.) sunflower, helianthus.
hélice, *f.* 1. helix, spiral; (anat., geom., archit.) helix. 2. propeller (of boat, airplane). 3. (astron.) **H.,** Great Bear, Ursa Major — **h. del avión,** airscrew; **h. tractora,** (aer.) tractor propeller.
helicoidal, *a.* helicoid, helicoidal, spiral.
helicoide, *m.* (geom.) helicoid.
helicómetro, *m.* torsion meter, torque meter (that measures the rotating force of a ship's propeller).
helicón, *m.* 1. **H.,** (myth., fig.) Helicon. 2. (mus.) helicon.
helicónides, *f.* (*pl.*) Muses.
heliconio, nia, *a.* Heliconian.
helicóptero, *m.* (aer.) helicopter.
helio, *m.* (chem.) helium.
heliocéntrico, ca, *a.* (astron.) heliocentric, heliocentrical.
heliogábalo, *m.* 1. (fig.) glutton. 2. **H.,** Heliogabalus.
heliograbado, *m.* (print.) helioengraving, heliogravure.
heliografía, *f.* 1. heliography. 2. blue print.
heliógrafo, *m.* heliograph (apparatus for telegraphing with sun's rays on a mirror).
heliograma, *m.* heliogram.
heliométrico, ca, *a.* (astron.) heliometric.
heliómetro, *m.* heliometer.
helioplastia, *f.* (print.) heliotypy.
Heliópolis, *f.* Heliopolis, ancient Egyptian city.
Helios, *m.* (myth.) Helios, the Sun god.
helioscopio, *m.* (astron.) helioscope, solar telescope.
heliosis, *f.* (med.) heliosis, insolation, sunburn.
helióstato, *m.* (top.) heliostat.
heliotelegrafía, *f.* heliotelegraphy, solar telegraphic communication.
helioterapia, *f.* (med.) heliotherapy.
heliotipia, *f.* (print.) heliotypy.
heliotropina, *f.* (chem.) heliotropin, piperonal.
heliotropio, *m., var. of* **heliotropo.**
heliotropismo, *m.* (bot.) heliotropism.
heliotropo, *m.* 1. (bot., min.) heliotrope. 2. (surv.) heliostat, geodetic heliotrope.
heliozoide, *a.* (zool.) heliozoan.
heliozoo, *m.* (zool.) heliozoan.
helipuerto, *m.* heliport, helicopter airport.
helix, *m.* (anat., zool.) helix.
helmintiasis, *f.* (med.) helminthiasis.
helmíntico, ca, *a.* helminthic, helminthical.
helminto, *m.* (zool.) helminth; (*pl.*) Helminthes.
helmintología, *f.* (biol.) helminthology.
helmintológico, ca, *a.* helminthologic, helminthological.
Helsinki, *m.* Helsinki, capital of Finland.
helvecio, cia, *a., m., f.* Helvetian, Swiss. —*f.* (hist.) **H.,** Helvetia, Switzerland.
helvético, ca, *a.* Helvetic. —*m., f.* Helvetian.
hemacrimo, *a.* (zool.) cold-blooded (as reptiles, etc.).
hemaglutinación, *f.* (biol.) hemagglutination.
hemaglutinina, *f.* (biol.) hemagglutinin.
hemal, *a.* (physiol.) hemal, hematal.
hemateína, *f.* (chem.) hematein, hematin, haematein.
hematemesis, *f.* (med.) hematemesis, vomiting of blood.

hematermo, *a.* warm-blooded (animal).
hemático, ca, *a.* hematic, blood-like.
hematidrosis, *f.* sweating of blood, caused by hemorrhage of the sudoriferous glands.
hematíe, *m.* (med.) red corpuscle.
hematímetro, *m.* (med.) hemocytometer.
hematina, *f.* (med.) hematin.
hematínico, ca, *a., m.* (med.) hematinic, haematinic.
hematita, *f.* (min.) hematite, haematite, iron oxide.
hematites, *f.* (min.) hematite.
hematoblasto, *m.* (biol.) hematoblast.
hematocele, *m.* (med.) hematocele.
hematócrito, *m.* (physiol.) hematocrit.
hematófago, *a.* hematophagous, feeding on blood.
hematógeno, na, *a.* (physiol.) hematogenous.
hematoide, *a.* (physiol.) hematoid.
hematología, *f.* (med.) hematology.
hematólogo, *m.* (med.) hematologist.
hematoma, *m.* (med.) hematoma.
hematómetro, *m.* (med.) hematometer.
hematopoyesis, *f.* (physiol.) hematopoeisis.
hematopoyético, ca, *a.* (physiol.) hematopoietic.
hematosis, *f.* (physiol.) hematosis, hematopoeisis.
hematoso, sa, *a.* (med.) hematose.
hematoxilina, *f.* (chem.) hematoxylin.
hematozoario, *m.* (zool.) hematozoon.
hematozoico, ca, *a.* (zool.) hematozoic.
hematuria, *f.* (med.) hematuria.
hembra, *a.* 1. (bot., mec.) female. 2. fine, delicate, weak. —*f.* 1. female, woman. 2. (zool., bot.) female. 3. (mec.) female coupling or part, socket; strike (of lock); nut (of screw or bolt); eye (of hook and eye). 4. hollow mold. 5. horse tail with little hair. — **h. de cerrojo** or **pestillo,** lock strike or bolt socket; **h. del timón,** (mar.) gudgeon.
hembraje, *m.* (Amer.) female stock (on cattle farm).
hembrear, *i.v.* 1. to be attracted towards the female. 2. to produce females or more females than males.
hembrilla, *f.* (mec.) female coupling or part, nut, socket; (mec.) eyebolt.
hemélitro, *m.* (ento.) hemelytron, hemelytrum.
hemerálope, *a.* (med.) hemeralopic.
hemeralopía, *f.* (med.) hemeralopia.
hemerocala, *f.* (bot.) hemerocallis.
hemeroteca, *f.* periodicals and newspaper library.
hemialgia, *f.* (med.) hemialgia.
hemicelulosa, *f.* (chem.) hemicellulose.
hemiciclo, *m.* hemicycle, semi-circle; hemicycle (semicircular structure, as of an arena).
hémico, ca, *a.* hemic, pertaining to the blood.
hemicordio, dia, *a., m.* (zool.) hemichordate.
hemicránea, *f.* (med.) hemicrania, migraine, splitting headache.
hemiedría, *f.* (min.) hemihedrism, hemihedry.
hemiédrico, ca, *a.* hemihedral.
hemiedro, ra, *a.* hemihedral.
hemiélitro, *m.* (ento.) hemelytron, hemelytrum.
hemihidrato, *m.* (chem.) hemihydrate.
hemimetabolia, *f.* (ento.) hemimetabolism.
hemimetabolismo, *m.* (ento.) hemimetabolism.
hemimorfismo, *m.* (min.) hemimorphism.
hemimorfita, *f.* (min.) hemimorphite.
hemina, *f.* 1. (biochem.) hemin. 2. (hist.) hemina (measure of capacity used in ancient Rome and Greece).
hemíono, *m.* (zool.) hemionus, kiang (type of wild ass).
hemiparásito, *m.* (bot.) hemiparasite, semiparasite.
hemiplejía, *f.* (med.) hemiplegy, hemiplegia.
hemipléjico, ca, *a.* hemiplegic.
hemíptero, ra, *a.* (ento.) hemipterous. —*m.* (ento.) hemipteran; (*pl.*) Hemiptera.
hemipteroide, *a.* (ento.) hemipteroid.
hemisférico, ca, *a.* hemispherical, hemispheric.
hemisferio, *m.* hemisphere. — **h. austral,** southern hemisphere; **h. boreal,** northern hemisphere; **h. cerebral,** (anat.) cerebral hemisphere; **h. occidental,** western hemisphere.
hemisferoide, *m.* hemispheroid.
hemistiquio, *m.* (poet.) hemistich.
hemiterpeno, *m.* (chem.) hemiterpene.
hemítropo, pa, *a.* (min.) hemitropic. —*m.* (min.) hemitrope.
hemoblasto, *m.* (biol.) hemoblast.
hemocianina, *f.* (chem.) hemocyanin.
hemocito, *m.* (biol.) hemocyte.
hemocitómetro, *m.* (med.) hemocytometer.
hemodinamómetro, *m.* blood-pressure gauge.
hemofilia, *f.* (med.) hemophilia, haemophilia.
hemofílico, ca, *a.* hemophilic. —*m., f.* hemophiliac.
hemófilo, la, *a.* (biol.) hemophilic.
hemoflagelado, *m.* (zool.) hemoflagellate.
hemoglobina, *f.* (biochem.) hemoglobin, haemoglobin.
hemoglobinado, da, *a.* (biochem.) hemoglobinous.
hemoglobinuria, *f.* (med.) hemoglobinuria.
hemograma, *m.* blood count.
hemoide, *a.* (physiol.) hemoid.
hemoideo, a, *a.* (physiol.) hemoid.
hemoleucocitario, ria, *a.* (anat.) hemoleucocytic, hemoleukocytic.
hemoleucocítico, ca, *a.* (anat.) hemoleucocytic, hemoleukocytic.
hemoleucocito, *m.* (anat.) hemoleucocyte, hemoleukocyte.
hemolisina, *f.* (biochem.) hemolysin.
hemólisis, *f.* (physiol.) hemolysis.
hemolítico, ca, *a.* hemolytic.
hemopatía, *f.* (med.) hemopathy, haemopathy, disease of the blood.
hemopoyesis, *f.* (physiol.) hematopoiesis.
hemóptico, ca, *a.* (med.) pertaining to hemoptysis.
hemoptisis, *f.* (med.) hemoptysis, haemoptysis.
hemorragia, *f.* (med.) hemorrhage. — **h. nasal,** nosebleed.
hemorrágico, ca, *a.* hemorrhagic.
hemorrea, *f.* (med.) hemorrhea.
hemorroida, *f.* (med.) *var. of* **hemorroide.**
hemorroidal, *a.* (med.) hemorrhoidal.
hemorroide, *f.* (med.) hemorrhoid; (*pl.*) piles, hemorrhoids.
hemorroidectomía, *f.* (med.) hemorrhoidectom, hemorrhoidectomy.
hemorroisa, *f.* woman who suffers from an abnormal discharge of blood.
hemorroo, *m.* (zool.) cerastes, horned viper.
hemosiderina, *f.* (biol.) hemosiderin.
hemostasis, *f.* (med.) hemostasia, haemostasia.
hemostático, ca, *a.* (med.) hemostatic, haemostatic. —*m.* (med.) hemostat, hemostatic.
hemóstato, *m.* (med.) hemostat.
henaje, *m.* tedding, haymaking.
henal, *m.* hayloft, hay barn.
henar, *m.* hayfield.
henchidor, ra *a.* filling, stuffing. —*m.* filler.
henchidura, *f.* filling, stuffing.
henchimiento, *m.* 1. filling, stuffing. 2. floor of trough (in a paper mill). 3. (mar.) strip of wood for covering holes.
henchir, (*ref. 39*) *tr.v.* to fill, stuff. —*r.v.* to stuff oneself, gorge (with food).
hendedor, ra, *a.* splitting, cleaving. —*m.* splitter (wedge for splitting slate).
hendedura, *f., var. of* **hendidura.**
hender, (*ref. 30*) *tr.v.* 1. to split, cleave, crack. 2. to cleave, cut through (air, water, etc.). —*r.v.* to split, crack.
hendible, *a.* splittable, cleavable.
hendidura, *f.* cleft, crack, split, slit.
hendiente, *m.* down stroke (of a sword).
hendija, *f.* slit, crack, split.
hendimiento, *m.* slitting, cleavage, cleaving, cracking.
hendir, (*ref. 31*) *tr.v.* (rare) *var. of* **hender.**
heneador, ra, *m., f.* tedder, haymaker.
henear, *tr.v.* to ted, make hay.
henequén, *m.* (bot.) henequen; sisal (plant, fiber).
hénide, *f.* (poet.) meadow nymph.
henificación, *f.* tedding, haymaking.
henificadora, *f.* (agr.) tedder (machine).
henificar, (*ref. 50*) *tr.v.* to hay, ted, cut and cure grass for hay or forage, to make hay.
henifique, *ref.* **henificar.**
henil, *m.* hayloft, hay barn.
henné, *m.* (bot.) henne.
heno, *m.* hay. — **h. blanco,** (bot.) velvet grass; **fiebre del h.,** hay fever.
henojil, *m.* garter (for stockings).
henojo, *m.* (imp. u.) (Mex., bot.) fennel.
henoteísmo, *m.* (rel.) henotheism.
henoteísta, *m., f.* (rel.) henotheist.
henrio, henry, *m.* (elec.) henry.
heñir, (*ref. 41*) *tr.v.* to knead (as dough).
hépar, *m.* (chem.) hepar.
heparina, *f.* (biochem.) heparin.
hepatalgia, *f.* (med.) hepatalgia, pain of the liver.
hepática, *f.* (bot.) hepatica, liverwort.
hepático, ca, *a.* (bot., anat., med.) hepatic, liver. —*m., f.* patient suffering from liver disorders. —*f.* (*pl.*) (bot.) Hepaticae.
hepatitis, *f.* (med.) hepatitis, inflammation of the liver.
hepatización, *f.* (med.) hepatization.
hepatocele, *f.* (med.) hepatocele, hernia of the liver.
hepatología, *f.* (med.) hepatology.
heptacordio, *m.* (mus.) heptachord.
heptacordo, *m.* (mus.) heptachord (diatonic scale of seven notes, interval of a seventh).
heptaédrico, ca, *a.* heptahedral.
heptaedro, *m.* (geom.) heptahedron.
heptagonal, *a.* heptagonal.
heptágono, na, *a.* heptagonal. —*m.* (geom.) heptagon.
heptámetro, *m.* (poet.) heptameter.
heptano, *m.* (chem.) heptane.
heptarca, *m.* (pol.) heptarch.
heptarquía, *f.* (pol.) heptarchy.
heptasílabo, ba, *a.* heptasyllabic. —*m.* heptasyllable.
heptateuco, *m.* (Bib.) Heptateuch.
heptosa, *f.* (chem.) heptose.
Hera, *f.* (myth.) Hera, Greek goddess of marriage.
Heracles, *m.* (myth.) Heracles, **Herakles,** Greek name of Hercules.
heraclida, *a.* Heraclean. —*m.* (*pl.*) Heraclidae, descendents of Herakles.
Heráclito, *m.* Heraclitus, Greek philosopher.
heráldica, *f.* heraldry.
heráldico, ca, *a.* heraldic. —*m., f.* heraldist.
heraldista, *m.* heraldist (student of heraldry).
heraldo, *m.* herald, harbinger.
herbáceo, a, *a.* (bot.) herbaceous.
herbada, *f.* (bot.) soapwort.
herbajar, *tr.v.* to graze, put out to graze. —*i.v.* to graze, pasture (said of cattle).
herbaje, *m.* 1. herbage. 2. grazing or pasture fee. 3. coarse woolen cloth.

herbajear, *tr.v., i.v., var. of* **herbajar.**
herbajero, *m.* renter of pasture land.
herbar, (*ref. 29*) *tr.v.* to dress (skins) with herbs.
herbario, ria, *a.* herbal. —*m.* 1. herbalist, botanist. 2. herbarium. 3. rumen (first stomach of ruminants).
herbazal, *m.* grassland, pasture-ground.
herbecer, (*ref. 45*) *i.v.* to begin to grow grass.
herbero, *m.* esophagus (of ruminants).
herbezca, *ref.* **herbecer.**
herbicida, *m.* weed killer, herbicide.
herbívoro, ra, *a.* herbivorous, grass-eating. —*m.* herbivore; (*pl.*) Herbivora.
herbolar, *tr.v., var. of* **enherbolar.**
herbolario, ria, *a.* mad, crazy. —*m., f.* madcap, crazy character. *m.* 1. herbalist, herb man. 2. herb or herbalist's shop.
herborice, *ref.* **herborizar.**
herborista, *m., f.* herborist, herbalist.
herborización, *f.* herborization, herb collection.
herborizador, ra, *m., f.* herbalist, herb collector.
herborizar, (*ref. 53*) *i.v.* (bot.) to herborize, gather herbs.
herboso, sa, *a.* grassy, herbaceous, herby.
hercio, *m.* (phys.) hertz.
hercúleo, a, *a.* Herculean.
Hércules, *m.* (myth., astron.) Hercules.
heredable, *a.* inheritable.
heredad, *f.* estate, country estate or property. — **h. residual** or **residuaria,** (law) residual estate.
heredado, da, *a.* landed (gentry), owning real-estate —*m., f.* heir (to property).
heredamiento, *m.* 1. country estate, place. 2. (law) bequest, endowment.
heredar, *tr.v.* to inherit.
heredero, ra, *a.* inheriting. —*m., f.* heir, inheritor. — **h. forzoso,** heir apparent, forced heir; **presunto h.,** heir presumptive; **h. universal,** residuary legatee; **instituir h.** or **por h. a,** to name as heir. —*m.* heir. —*f.* heiress.
heredípeta, *m., f.* legacy-hunter.
hereditario, ria, *a.* hereditary.
hereje, *m., f.* heretic.
herejía, *f.* 1. heresy; misbelief. 2. insult.
herejote, ta, *m., f.* incorrigible heretic.
herén, *m., var. of* **yero.**
herencia, *f.* inheritance; heritage; heredity. — **h. yacente,** (law) undivided estate; estate of which the heir has not taken possession.
heresiarca, *m.* (rel.) heresiarch, leader of an heretic sect.
heretical, *a.* heretical.
herético, ca, *a.* heretical.
herida, *f.* 1. wound, injury. 2. insult, offense. 3. (hunt.) place where game swoops down chased by hawk. — **remover la h.,** to open up an old wound; **resollar** or **respirar por la h.,** to feel (something) very bitterly; **tocarle a uno en la h.,** to put the finger of the sore spot.
herido, da, *past part. of* **herir.** —*a.* wounded, hurt. — **mal herido,** badly wounded, badly hurt.
heridor, ra, *a.* wounding.
herir, (*ref. 42*) *tr.v.* 1. to wound; to injure, hurt. 2. to knock, strike. 3. to shine on, bathe with its rays (sun). 4. to hurt, wound (e.g. sensibilities, etc.); to offend, insult. 5. to pluck (string), play (stringed instrument). 6. to grate on, jar (strident sound on ears), hurt, blind (e.g. bright light).
herma, *m.* herma, column topped by a bust (of Hermes in ancient Greece).
hermafrodita, *a.* hermaphroditic, hermaphrodite. —*m.* hermaphrodite.
hermafroditismo, *m.* hermaphroditism.
hermafrodito, *m.* hermaphrodite; (myth.) **H.,** Hermaphroditus.
hermanable, *a.* fraternal, brotherly; sisterly.
hermanablemente, *adv.* 1. fraternally. 2. uniformly.
hermanado, da, *past part. of* **hermanar.** —*a.* 1. equal, matching, exactly alike or matched. 2. (Chile) similar, alike. 3. (bot.) didymous, twin.
hermanal, *a.* fraternal.
hermanamiento, *m.* mating, matching.
hermanar, *tr.v.* 1. to join, combine; to match; to harmonize. 2. to make brothers (in spirit). —*r.v.* 1. to combine; to match; to harmonize, be similar. 2. to become brothers (in spirit).
hermanastro, tra, *m., f.* stepbrother, stepsister.
hermanazgo, *m., var. of* **hermandad.**
hermandad, *f.* 1. brotherhood, fraternity; sisterhood, sorority. 2. intimate friendship. 3. close relationship or likeness. 4. alliance, league.
hermanear, *i.v.* to call each other brother or sister.
hermanecer, (*ref. 45*) *i.v.* to have a brother born to one.
hermanezca, hermanezco, *ref.* **hermanecer.**
hermano, na, *m.* brother; **h. carnal,** full or blood brother; **h. consanguíneo,** half brother by the same father; **h. de la Doctrina,** Christian brother; **h. de leche,** foster brother; **h. de madre,** half brother by the same mother; **h. de padre,** half brother by the same father; **h. de sangre,** blood brother; **h. gemelo,** twin brother; **h. mayor,** eldest brother; president (of a brotherhood); **h. político,** brother-in-law; **h. uterino,** half brother by same mother; **medio h.,** half brother; **primo h.,** first cousin. —*f.* sister; **h. de la caridad,** Sister of Charity; **h. mayor,** eldest sister; **h. política,** sister-in-law; **media h.,** half sister; **prima h.,** first cousin.
hermanuco, *m.* (derog.) lay brother.
hermeneuta, *m., f.* hermeneut, hermeneutist.
hermenéutico, ca, *a.* hermeneutic, hermeneutical. —*f.* (rel., philos.) hermeneutics.
Hermes, *m.* (myth.) Hermes, messenger of the gods. — **H. Trismegisto,** Hermes Trismegistus.
herméticamente, *adv.* hermetically.
hermeticidad, *f.* 1. airtightness. 2. impenetrability, impenetrableness.
hermético, ca, *a.* 1. hermetic, airtight. 2. impenetrable. 3. reticent, secretive. 4. hermetic, Hermetic, of Hermes (philosopher).
hermetismo, *m.* secrecy, secretiveness, reticence.
hermodátil, *m.* (bot.) meadow saffron, autumn crocus.
hermosamente, *adv.* beautifully; handsomely; (fig.) perfectly, properly.
hermoseador, ra, *a.* beautifying. —*m., f.* beautifier.
hermoseamiento, *m.* beautification; embellishing; grooming.
hermosear, *tr.v.* to beautify, embellish; groom.
hermoseo, *m.* beautification, embellishment; grooming.
hermoso, sa, *a.* beautiful, beauteous, lovely, handsome; (coll.) healthy, robust (said of children and youths).
hermosura, *f.* 1. beauty, handsomeness; fairness; freshness. 2. beauty, belle.
hernia, *f.* (med.) hernia.
herniado, da, *a.* ruptured, suffering from a hernia or rupture. —*m., f.* ruptured person.
herniario, ria, *a.* (med.) hernial.
hernioso, sa, *a.* (med.) ruptured, suffering from a hernia or rupture.
hernista, *m.* (med.) hernia surgeon, herniotomist.
Herodes, *m.* (Bib., hist.) Herod; **andar** or **ir de H. a Pilatos,** to jump from the frying pan into the fire; to go from pillar to post.
herodiano, na, *a.* Herodian, pertaining to Herod.
Herodías, *f.* (Bib., hist.) Herodias, wife of King Herod.
héroe, *m.* hero, champion; (lit., theat.) main character (protagonist).
heroicamente, *adv.* heroically.
heroicidad, *f.* 1. heroism. 2. heroic deed, act of heroism.
heroico, ca, *a.* heroic; **hazaña heroica,** a heroic exploit; **remedio heroico,** a heroic (or desperate) solution.
heroida, *f.* heroic verse, epic poetry.
heroína, *f.* 1. heroine, heroic woman; (lit., theat.) main character (protagonist). 2. (pharm.) heroin.
heroísmo, *m.* heroism; **un acto de h.,** a heroic deed or action.
herpe, *m., f.* (med.) herpes (*gen. pl.*), tetter.
herpético, ca, *a.* (med.) herpetic.
herpetismo, *m.* (med.) herpetism, constitutional predisposition toward herpes.
herpetología, *f.* (zool.) herpetology, the study of reptiles.
herpil, *m.* esparto net sack (for carrying fruits, etc.).
herrada, *f.* 1. water in which red-hot iron has been cooled. 2. wooden pail or bucket.
herradero, *m.* branding (of cattle); branding place; branding season.
herrado, *past part. of* **herrar.** —*m.* shoeing (of horses).
herrador, *m.* blacksmith, horseshoer.
herradora, *f.* (coll.) blacksmith's wife.
herradura, *f.* 1. horseshoe. 2. hoof guard (put on hoof when shoeing). 3. (zool.) horseshoe bat. — **arco de h.,** (archit.) Moorish arch; **h. hechiza,** horseshoe with the nails already fixed; **mostrar las herraduras,** to kick; to run away.
herraj, *m., var. of* **erraj,** coal made from olive pits.
herraje, *m.* iron-work, iron fittings, iron parts, metal fittings, hardware.
herramental, *a.* tool (bag). —*m.* tool bag; tool kit, tools.
herramienta, *f.* 1. tool, instrument, implement; (*pl.*) tools, set of instruments. 2. (coll.) the bull's horns. 3. (coll.) teeth. 4. (coll.) knife, gun, weapon. — **h. cortante** or **de corte,** cutting tool; **h. de cable** or **percusión,** cable tool; **h. neumática,** pneumatic tool.
herranza, *f.* (Col.) horseshoeing.
herrar, (*ref. 29*) *tr.v.* 1. to shoe (a horse). 2. to brand (cattle). 3. to bind with iron.
herrén, *m.* mixed grain, maslin, cattle fodder.
herrenal, *m.* mixed fodder field or patch.
herreñal, *m., var. of* **herrenal.**
herrera, *f.* (coll.) blacksmith's or farrier's wife.
herrería, *f.* 1. blacksmithing. 2. smithy, blacksmith's shop or forge. 3. foundry, ironworks. 4. (fig.) uproar, confusion.
herrerillo, *m.* (ornith.) greater titmouse, blue titmouse.
herrero, *m.* smith, blacksmith; ironworker; horseshoer.
herrerón, *m.* clumsy, incompetent smith.
herreruelo, *m.* 1. (ornith.) coal tit or titmouse. 2. (hist.) German cavalry trooper. 3. plain, short cape without a collar.
herrete, *m.* 1. tag (of shoestring, etc.), tip, ferrule, aiguillete. 2. (Amer.) branding iron.
herretear, *tr.v.* to attach tags or tips to (shoestrings, ribbands, etc.).
herrezuelo, *m.* light, small piece of iron.
herrial, *a.* said of a variety of large black grape and of the vine producing it.
herrín, *m.* rust, iron rust.
herrón, *m.* 1. quoit, iron ring (for games). 2. hob (game played with iron rings and pins). 3. (mec.) washer. 4. iron rod used to plant vines, etc. 5. (Col.) iron point (of a spinning top).

herronada, *f.* 1. violent blow (with an iron rod). 2. hard peck (dealt by a bird).
herrumbrar, *tr.v., r.v., var. of* **aherrumbrar.**
herrumbre, *f.* 1. rust. 2. iron taste (in water, etc.). 3. (bot.) rust (parasitic fungus).
herrumbroso, sa, *a.* rusty, rusted; drossy, scaly.
hertziana, *a.* (phys.) Hertzian (wave).
hertzio, *m.* (phys.) hertz.
hérulo, la, *a.* (hist.) Herulian, pertaining to a Germanic people. *—m., f.* Herulian; (*pl.*) Heruli.
hervenica, *f.* boiling to death (medieval form of execution).
herventar, (*ref. 29*) *tr.v.* to boil, to immerse and seethe (something) in a liquid.
herver, (*ref. 30*) *i.v.* (Mex., reg.) *var. of* **hervir.**
hervidero, *m.* 1. bubbling, ebullition, boiling. 2. bubbling spring. 3. wheezing sound (in the throat or chest); bubbling noise. 4. (fig.) crowd, swarm.
hervido, *past part. of* **hervir.** **—*m.*** (Amer.) stew.
hervidor, *m.* boiler, cooker, saucepan, boiling pan, kettle.
herviente, *a.* boiling, seething.
hervir, (*ref. 42*) *i.v.* 1. to boil, to seethe (in a liquid). 2. to boil (with anger). 3. to surge (the sea). 4. to swarm or teem with.
hervor, *m.* 1. boil, boiling, ebullition. 2. fervor, fire, vigor, restlessness. 3. noise and upsurge of waters. — **alzar** or **levantar el h.,** to come to a boil; **h. de la sangre,** skin rash.
hervoroso, sa, *a.* 1. fiery, ardent, impetuous. 2. boiling, appearing to boil.
hesita, *f.* (min.) hessite.
hesitación, *f.* (rare) hesitation, doubt, perplexity.
hesitar, *i.v.* (rare) to hesitate, vacillate.
hesonita, *f.* (min.) hessonite.
Hesperia, *f.* (hist.) western land; name given by the Greeks to Italy and by the Romans to Spain.
hespérico, ca, *a.* Hesperic, Hesperian, western.
hespérides, *f.* (*pl.*) 1. (myth.) Hesperides, nymphs, daughters of Atlas, who guarded the garden of the golden apples. 2. **H.,** mythical islands once believed to rise to the W. of Europe (probably the Canary Islands).
hesperidina, *f.* (chem.) hesperidin.
hesperidio, *m.* (bot.) hesperidium, fruit of a citrus plant.
hespérido, da, *a.* 1. (poet.) Hesperian (pertaining to the Hesperides). 2. (poet.) Hesperian, western. 3. (astron.) pertaining to the Hesperus, the evening star.
hesperio, ria, *a., m., f.* Hesperian, of or pertaining to Hesperia (ancient name for Europe's westernmost land, Italy to the Greeks, Spain to the Romans).
héspero, ra, *a., var. of* **hesperio.**
hetaira, *f.* hetaera, hetaira, courtesan in ancient Greece; (fig.) a refined prostitute.
heteo, a, *a., m.* (hist.) Hittite, pertaining to an ancient people of Asia Minor.
hetera, *f., var. of* **hetaira.**
heterocerca, *a.* (ichth.) heterocercal.
heterocíclico, ca, *a.* (chem.) heterocyclic.
heterócigo, ga, heterocigótico, ca, *a.* (biol.) heterozygous.
heterocigosis, *f.* (biol.) heterozygosis.
heterocigoto, *m.* (biol.) heterozygote.
heteróclito, ta, *a.* (gram.) heteroclite, irregular; abnormal.
heterocromático, ca, *a.* heterochrome, heterochromatic, many-colored.
heterocromatina, *f.* (biol.) heterochromatin.
heterocromatismo, *m.* (zool.) heterochromatism.
heterocromo, ma, *a.* heterochrome, heterochromatic, heterochromous.
heterocromosoma, *m.* (biol.) heterochromosome.
heterodinar, *tr.v.* (rad.) to heterodyne.
heterodino, na, *a.* (rad.) heterodyne.
heterodoxia, *f.* (philos., rel.) heterodoxy, disbelief.
heterodoxo, xa, *a.* heterodox, disbelieving. *—m., f.* heterodox person, disbeliever.
heteroecio, a, *a.* (biol.) heteroecious. *—f.* (biol.) heteroecism.
heterofilia, *f.* (bot.) heterophylly.
heterófilo, la, *a.* (bot.) heterophyllous.
heterófito, *m.* (bot.) heterophyte.
heterogameto, *m.* (biol.) heterogamete.
heterogamia, *f.* (bot.) heterogamy.
heterógamo, ma, *a.* (biol., bot.) heterogamous.
heterogeneidad, *f.* heterogeneity, heterogeneousness; diversity, variety.
heterogéneo, a, *a.* heterogeneous; dissimilar, different.
heterogénesis, *f.* (biol.) heterogeny, heterogenesis.
heterogenia, *f.* (biol.) heterogenesis, abiogenesis, spontaneous generation.
heterogonía, *f.* (biol., bot.) heterogony.
heterólisis, *f.* (biochem.) heterolysis.
heterología, *f.* (biol.) heterology.
heterólogo, ga, *a.* (biol.) heterologous.
heteromancia, *f.* divination by the flight of birds.
heterómero, ra, *a.* (bot., ento.) heteromerous. *—m.* (*pl.*) (ento.) Heteromera, Heteromeri.
heterometabolia, *f.* (ento.) heterometabolism.
heterometábolo, la, *a.* (ento.) heterometabolic, heterometabolous.
heteromorfia, *f., var. of* **heteromorfismo.**
heteromorfismo, *m.* heteromorphism, diversity of forms.
heteromorfo, fa, *a.* heteromorphous, presenting different forms at various stages of development.
heterónomo, ma, *a.* heteronomous, subject to an alien power.
heteropétalo, la, *a.* (bot.) heteropetalous.
heteroplastia, *f.* (surg.) heteroplasty.
heteroploide, *a.* (med.) heteroploid.
heteropolar, *a.* (chem.) heteropolar.
heteropolaridad, *f.* (chem.) heteropolarity.
heterópsido, da, *a.* lusterless (said of metals which lack characteristic luster).
heteróptero, ra, *a.* (ento.) heteropterous. *—m.* (ento.) heteropter; (*pl.*) Heteroptera.
heteroscio, a, *a., m., f.* (geog.) heteroscian (inhabitant of temperate zones of the earth).
heterosexual, *a.* heterosexual, attracted by the opposite sex.
heterosis, *f.* (biol.) heterosis.
heterotálico, ca, *a.* (bot.) heterothallic.
heterotaxia, *f.* heterotaxis, heterotaxia, heterotaxy, abnormal position or arrangement.
heterotáxico, ca, *a.* heterotaxic, subject to an abnormal position or arrangement.
heterotaxis, *f., var. of* **heterotaxia.**
heterotopia, *f.* (biol.) heterotopia, heterotopy.
heterotópico, ca, *a.* (biol.) heterotopic, heterotopous.
heterótrofo, fa, *a.* (physiol.) heterotrophic.
hético, ca, *a.* hectic, consumptive; thin, emaciated. *—m., f.* consumptive, hectic.
hetiquez, *f.* (med.) consumption, tuberculosis.
heulandita, *f.* (min.) heulandite.
heurística, *f.* heuristics, the art or science of devising or discovering new methods.
heurístico, ca, *a.* heuristic, heuristical, helping to discover; devising a new method.
hévea, *f.* (bot.) hevea, rubber tree.
hexabásico, ca, *a.* (chem.) hexabasic.
hexacordo, *m.* (mus.) hexachord; **h. mayor,** (mus.) a major sixth; **h. menor,** (mus.) minor sixth.
hexaédrico, ca, *a.* (geom.) hexahedral, six-sided (cubes, etc.).
hexaedro, *m.* (geom.) hexahedron; **h. regular,** cube.
hexagonal, *a.* hexagonal, six-sided, with six faces.
hexágono, na, *a.* (geom.) hexagonal. *—m.* hexagon.
hexahidrato, *m.* (chem.) hexahydrate.
hexahídrico, ca, *a.* (chem.) hexahydric.
hexámero, ra, *a.* (bot., zool.) hexamerous.
hexamerón, *m.* hexaemeron.
hexametilentetramina, *f.* (chem.) hexamethylenetetramine.
hexámetro, *a., m.* (poet.) hexameter.
hexángulo, la, *a., var. of* **hexágono.**
hexano, *m.* (chem.) hexane.
hexápeda, *f.* an ancient French linear measurement.
hexapétalo, la, *a.* (bot.) hexapetalous, sixpetaled.
Hexapla, *m.* (Bib.) Hexapla, Origen's edition of the Old Testament.
hexaploide, *a.* (biol.) hexaploid.
hexápodo, da, *a., m.* (zool.) hexapodal.
hexasílabo, ba, *a.* (poet., gram.) six-syllabled, hexasyllabic. *—m.* hexasyllabic verse.
hexástilo, *m.* (archit.) hexastyle, portico with six columns.
hexil, *m.* (chem.) hexyl.
hexilo, *m.* (chem.) hexyl.
hexilresorcinal, *m.* (chem.) hexylresorcinol.
hexosa, *f.* (chem.) hexose.
hez, (*pl.* **heces**), *f.* 1. (fig.) scum, dregs (e.g. of mankind). 2. (*pl.*) dregs, lees (of liquid). 3. (*pl.*) faeces, excrement. 4. sediment.
Hf *sym. of* **hafnio,** hafnium (Hf).
Hg *sym. of* **mercurio,** hydrargyrium-mercury (Hg).
hg. *abbrev. of* **hectogramo,** hectogram (hg., hectog.).
hi, *m., f. contr. of* **hijo, hija,** used in phrases such as: **hi de puta, hi de perra,** (sl.) son of a bitch (vulg.).
Híadas, Híades, *f.* (*pl.*) (myth., astron.) Hyades, Hyads, nymphs, daughters of Atlas; a cluster of stars in the constellation Taurus.
hialino, na, *a.* hyaline, crystalline, transparent, translucent.
hialita, *f.* (min.) hyalite.
hialitis, *f.* (med.) hyalitis.
hialógeno, *m.* (biochem.) hyalogen.
hialografía, *f.* hyalography, art of writing or drawing on glass.
hialógrafo, *m.* hyalograph, instrument for tracing designs on glass.
hialoideo, a, *a.* hyaloid, glassy, transparent, (anat.) hyaloid.
hialoplasma, *m.* (biol.) hyaloplasm.
hialotecnia, *f.* glass making, glassworking.
hialurgia, *f., var. of* **hialotecnia.**
hialuronidasa, *f.* (biochem.) hyaluronidase.
hiante, *a.* (poet.) having hiatus (verse).
hiato, *m.* (gram., poet.) hiatus.
hibernación, *f.* hibernation.
hibernáculo, *m.* (bot., zool.) hibernaculum.
hibernal, *a.* hibernal, wintry.
hibernar, *i.v.* (zool.) to hibernate.
hibernés, sa, *a., m., f.* Hibernian, Irish.
hibérnico, ca, *a.* Hibernian, Irish.
hibernizo, za, *a., var. of* **hibernal.**
hibisco, *m.* (bot.) hibiscus.
hibridación, *f.* hybridization.
hibridez, *f.* hybridism.
hibridismo, *m.* hybridity, hybridism.
híbrido, da, *a., m.* hybrid.
hicaco, *m.* (bot.) coco plum (plant and fruit).
hicadura, *f.* (Cuba) hammock cords (holding up hammock).

hice, hiciera, hiciese, *ref.* **hacer.**

hico, *m.* (Amer.) hammock clew (cord supporting hammock).

hicotea, *f.* (zool.) hicatee, West Indian turtle.

hidalgamente, *adv.* nobly, magnanimously.

hidalgo, ga, *a.* noble, illustrious, of noble blood; generous, magnanimous. —*m.* nobleman; **h. de bragueta,** father who sired seven male heirs in succession within a legitimate marriage and who acquired the right to nobility; **h. de cuatro costados,** noble on four sides (of noble grandparents). —*f.* noblewoman.

hidalgote, ta, *m., f.* pompous old nobleman or noblewoman.

hidalguejo, ja, *m., f.* petty nobleman or noblewoman.

hidalgüelo, la, *m., f.* petty nobleman or noblewoman.

hidalguete, ta, *m., f.* (coll.) down and out nobleman.

hidalguez, *f., var. of* **hidalguía.**

hidalguía, *f.* nobility, nobleness; (fig.) chivalry, generosity, magnanimity.

hidátide, *f.* (med., zool.) hydatid.

hidatídico, ca, *a.* (vet.) hydatid.

hidra, *f.* 1. (zool.) hydra. 2. (zool.) poisonous water snake (Hydrus platyurus). 3. **H.,** (myth., astron.) Hydra.

hidrácido, *m.* (chem.) hydracid.

hidracina, *f.* (chem.) hydrazine.

hidranto, *m.* (zool.) hydranth.

hidrargírico, ca, *a.* hydrargyric.

hidrargirio, *m.* (chem.) hydrargyrum, mercury.

hidrargirismo, *m.* (med.) hydrargyrism, mercurialism, chronic mercury poisoning.

hidrargirita, *f.* (min.) native oxide of mercury.

hidrargiro, *m.* (chem.) hydrargyrum, mercury.

hidrartrosis, *f.* (med.) hydrarthrosis.

hidrastina, *f.* (chem.) hydrastine.

hidratable, *a.* hydratable.

hidratación, *f.* hydration, hydrating.

hidratado, da, *past part. of* **hidratar.** —*a.* hydrate.

hidratar, *tr.v., r.v.* (chem.) to hydrate; **cal hidratada,** hydrated lime.

hidrato, *m.* (chem.) hydrate; **h. de calcio,** calcium hydrate; **h. de carbono,** carbohydrate.

hidráulica, *f.* hydraulics; hydraulic engineering.

hidráulico, ca, *a.* hydraulic. —*m.* hydraulic engineer, hydraulician.

hidrazina, *f.* (chem.) hydrazine.

hidrazoico, ca, *a.* (chem.) hydrazoic.

hidremia, *f., var. of* **hidrohemia.**

hidria, *f.* hydria (water jar).

hídrico, ca, *a.* (chem.) hydric.

hidroaeroplano, *m.* (aer.) hydroplane, seaplane.

hidroavión, *m.* hydroplane.

hidrobarómetro, *m.* hydrobarometer.

hidrobiología, *f.* hydrobiology.

hidrobrómico, ca, *a.* (chem.) hydrobromic.

hidrocarburo, *m.* (chem.) hydrocarbon.

hidrocefalia, *f.* (med.) hydrocephalus, hydrocephaly.

hidrocéfalo, la, *a.* (med.) hydrocephalous.

hidrocele, *f.* (med.) hydrocele.

hidrocinético, ca, *a.* (phys.) hydrokinetic. —*f.* (phys.) hydrokinetics.

hidroclorato, *m.* (chem.) hydrochloride.

hidroclórico, ca, *a.* (chem.) hydrochloric.

hidrocortisona, *f.* (biochem.) hydrocortisone.

hidrodinámica, *f.* (phys.) hydrodynamics.

hidrodinámico, ca, *a.* hydrodynamic, hydrodynamical.

hidroeléctrico, ca, *a.* hydroelectric, hydroelectrical.

hidrófana, *f.* (min.) hydrophane.

hidrofilacio, *m.* hydrophylacium, subterranean store or reservoir of water.

hidrofílidos, *m.* (*pl.*) (ento.) Hydrophilidae.

hidrófilo, la, *a.* water-loving; absorbent; (chem.) hydrophile; (bot.) hydrophilous. —*m.* (ento.) hydrophilid.

hidrófito, ta, *a.* (bot.) hydrophytic. —*f.* (bot.) hydrophyte.

hidrofobia, *f.* (med.) hydrophobia, rabies.

hidrofóbico, ca, *a.* (med.) hydrophobic, rabid.

hidrófobo, ba, *a.* hydrophobic. —*m., f.* hydrophobe, one suffering from hydrophobia.

hidrofoil, *m.* (mar.) hydrofoil (U.S.); hovercraft (G.B.).

hidrófono, *m.* hydrophone, an instrument used for ascertaining the distance traveled by sound transmitted through water.

hidroformación, *f.* (chem.) hydroforming.

hidroftalmía, *f.* (med.) hydrophthalmos.

hidrófugo, ga, *a.* waterproof.

hidrogenación, *f.* (chem.) hydrogenation.

hidrogenado, da, *a.* hydrogenous, containing hydrogen.

hidrogenar, *tr.v.* (chem.) to hydrogenate.

hidrógeno, *m.* hydrogen; **h. sulfurado,** sulfhydric acid.

hidrogeológico, ca, *a.* hydrogeological.

hidrognosia, *f.* (geol.) hydrognosy.

hidrogogía, *f.* channel hydraulics, science of canal-making.

hidrografía, *f.* (geog.) hydrography.

hidrográfico, ca, *a.* hydrographic, hydrographical.

hidrógrafo, *m.* (geog.) hydrographer.

hidrohemia, *f.* (med.) hydraemia, hydremia.

hidroideo, a, *a., m.* (zool.) hydroid.

hidrólisis, *f.* (chem.) hydrolysis.

hidrolítico, ca, *a.* (chem.) hydrolytic.

hidrolizable, *a.* (chem.) hydrolyzable.

hidrolizar, (*ref. 53*) *tr.v., i.v.* (chem.) to hydrolyze.

hidrología, *f.* (geol.) hydrology.

hidrológico, ca, *a.* (geol.) hydrologic, hydrological.

hidrólogo, ga, *a.* (geol.) hydrologic. —*m., f.* hydrologist.

hidromancia, *f.* hydromancy, divination by signs observed in water.

hidromántico, ca, *a.* hydromantic. —*m.* hydromancer.

hidromecánico, ca, *a.* (phys.) hydromechanical. —*f.* hydromechanics.

hidromedusa, *f.* (zool.) hydromedusa.

hidromel, *m.* hydromel, mead.

hidrometalurgia, *f.* hydrometallurgy, a process of recovering metal from ore.

hidrometalúrgico, ca, *a.* hydrometallurgical.

hidrometeoro, *m.* (phys.) hydrometeor.

hidrómetra, *m.* current gauger, expert in current-gauging (person who measures the force, speed or volume of currents).

hidrometría, *f.* measurement of the speed, force or volume of currents or water flow; current-gauging.

hidrométrico, ca, *a.* hydrometric, hydrometrical, pertaining to current-gauging or to the measurement of the speed, force or volume of currents.

hidrómetro, *m.* 1. current gauge, hydrodynamometer, hydrometer (instrument for measuring the speed, force or volume of a current). 2. (Arg., Chile) hydrometer, densimeter.

hidromiel, *m., var. of* **hidromel.**

hidroneumático, ca, *a.* hydropneumatic, made operative by air and water.

hidrópata, *m.* (med.) hydrotherapist, hydropathist.

hidropatía, *f.* (med.) hydropathy.

hidropático, ca, *a.* (med.) hydropathic, hydropathical.

hidropesía, *f.* (med.) dropsy, hydrops, hydropsy.

hidropicarse, (*ref. 50*) *r.v.* (Hond.) to suffer from dropsy.

hidrópico, ca, *a.* 1. dropsical, hydropic. 2. very thirsty. 3. insatiable. —*m., f.* someone suffering from dropsy.

hidroplano, *m.* (aer.) hydroplane.

hidropónico, ca, *a.* hydroponic, grown in water (rather than in earth).

hidroquinona, *f.* (chem.) hydroquinone.

hidroscopía, *f.* exploring for deep or hidden waters.

hidroscopio, *m.* hydroscope, a device for viewing deeply below water surface.

hidrosfera, *f.* hydrosphere, all the waters on the surface of the earth.

hidrosilicato, *m.* (chem.) hydrosilicate, hydrous silicate.

hidrosis, *f.* (physiol., med.) hidrosis.

hidrosol, *m.* (chem.) hydrosol.

hidrostática, *f.* (phys.) hydrostatics.

hidrostáticamente, *adv.* hydrostatically.

hidrostático, ca, *a.* hydrostatic, hydrostatical.

hidrostato, *m.* hydrostat, instrument that measures the pressure of fluids.

hidrosulfito, *m.* (chem.) hydrosulfite.

hidrosulfúrico, *a.* hydrosulfuric.

hidrosulfuro, *m.* (chem.) hydrosulfide.

hidrosulfuroso, sa, *a.* (chem.) hydrosulfurous.

hidrotaxis, *f.* (biol.) hydrotaxis.

hidrotaxismo, *m.* (biol.) hydrotaxis.

hidrotecnia, *f.* hydrotechny, hydraulic engineering.

hidroterapia, *f.* (med.) hydrotherapy.

hidroterápico, ca, *a.* hydrotherapeutic, hydrotherapeutical.

hidrotermal, *a.* hydrothermal, pertaining to hot water springs and minerals thereof.

hidrotérmico, ca, *a.* hydrothermal.

hidrotórax, *m.* (med.) hydrothorax, dropsy of the chest.

hidrotrópico, ca, *a.* (biol.) hydrotropic.

hidrotropismo, *m.* (biol.) hydrotropism.

hidróxido, *m.* (chem.) hydroxide; **h. de potasio,** (chem.) potassium hydroxide; **h. de sodio,** (chem.) sodium hydroxide.

hidroxilamina, *f.* (chem.) hydroxylamine.

hidroxilo, *m.* (chem.) hydroxyl.

hidrozoario, *a., m.* (zool.) hydrozoan.

hidruro, *m.* (chem.) hydride.

hieda, hiedo, *ref.* **heder.**

hiedra, *f.* (bot.) ivy; **h. terrestre,** ground ivy; **h. inglesa,** English ivy.

hiel, *f.* 1. bile, gall. 2. (fig.) bitterness. 3. (*pl.*) (fig.) adversities, troubles, sorrows. — **h. de la tierra,** (bot.) centaury (Centaurium umbellatum); **echar la h.,** to work very hard, sweat and strain; **no tener h.,** to be simple and easygoing.

hiela, hiele, *ref.* **helar.**

hielo, *m.* 1. ice. 2. cold, coldness. 3. freezing. 4. coldness, coolness (e.g. of feelings). 5. astonishment, stupefaction. — **banco de h.,** ice field; **capa de h.,** icecap; **estar hecho un h.,** to be very cold; **hacer h.,** to be freezing, be freezingly cold; **hacerle h. a uno,** to give the cold shoulder, ignore (someone); **h. seco,** dry ice; **manta de h.,** icecap, ice floe; **romper el h.,** (fig.) to break the ice.

hiemación, *f.* (bot.) winter-blooming.

hiemal, *a.* wintry, hibernal.

hiena, *f.* (zool.) hyena; **h. manchada,** spotted hyena; **h. rayada,** striped hyena.

hienda, *f.* dung.
hienda, hiendo, *ref.* **hender.**
hiera, *ref.* **herir.**
hierático, ca, *a.* 1. hieratic, hieratical, sacred. 2. affectedly solemn or pompous.
hierba, *f.* 1. grass. 2. herb. 3. flaw in emerald. 4. (*pl.*) vegetable stew eaten by monks. 5. (*pl.*) pasture, grass (for livestock). 6. (*pl.*) years of age (applied to cattle). 7. (*sl.*) grass, marihuana. — **h. ballestera,** (bot.) hellebore; **h. luisa,** (bot.) lemon verbena; **h. mate,** (bot.) maté; **h. meona,** (bot.) milfoil, yarrow; **h. santa,** (bot.) mint; **ver crecer la h.,** to be very sharp or intelligent; **y otras hierbas,** (hum.) and so forth and so on.
hierbabuena, *f.* (bot.) mint.
hierbatero, ra, *m., f.* 1. maté gatherer; one who prepares the maté. 2. herb doctor.
hierbe, hierbo, *ref.* **herbar.**
hiero, *ref.* **herir.**
hierocracia, *f.* hierocracy, government by priests.
hieródulo, *m.* hierodule, a slave at the service of a god (in ancient Greece).
hierofanta, *m., var. of* **hierofante.**
hierofante, *m.* hierophant (chief priest of the Eleusinian rites performed in ancient Greece).
hieroglífico, ca, *a., m., var. of* **jeroglífico.**
hierología, *f.* hierology, the religious literature of a people.
hieros, *m.* (*pl.*) (bot.) (species of) lentil (Ervum ervilia).
hierosolimitano, na, *a., var. of* **jerosolimitano.**
hierre, *ref.* **herrar.** —*f.* (Amer.) branding.
hierrezuelo, *m. dim. of* **hierro,** a small iron object or tool.
hierro, *m.* 1. iron. 2. brand (mark on cattle). 3. iron tip, point (on spears, arrows, etc.). 4. weapon; instrument. 5. (Cuba) plowing. 6. (*pl.*) irons, fetters, shackles. — **a h. caliente, batir de repente,** strike while the iron is hot; **a h. y sangre** or **fuego,** without mercy; violently; **cargar de h.,** to put in irons; **h. acanalado,** corrugated iron; **h. albo,** white-hot iron; **h. angular,** angle iron; **h. bruto,** pig iron; **h. colado,** cast iron; **h. corrugado,** corrugated iron; **h. de canal** or **en U,** channel iron; **h. dulce,** soft iron; wrought iron; **h. en barras,** bar iron; **h. espático,** (chem.) spathic iron, siderite; **h. forjado,** wrought iron; **h. fundido,** cast iron; **h. laminado,** sheet iron; **h. ondulado,** corrugated iron; **llevar h. a Vizcaya,** to carry coals to Newcastle; **machacar** or **martillar en h. frío,** to knock one's head against a brick wall (in trying to teach someone something); **quien a h. mata a h. muere,** he who lives by the sword shall die by the sword; **ser de h.,** to be as strong as nails.
hierro, *ref.* **herrar.**
hierva, hiervo, *ref.* **hervir.**
hietografía, *f.* (meteorol.) hyetography.
hietográfico, ca, *a.* hyetographic, hyetographical, pertaining to the distribution of rain.
hietógrafo, *m.* (meteorol.) hyetograph.
hifa, *f.* (bot.) hypha.
hifal, *a.* (bot.) hyphal.
hi-fi, *a. invar. & m.* hi-fi.
higa, *f.* 1. talisman, amulet. 2. derisive gesture with the fist. 3. scorn, contempt, disdain; **no dar dos higas por,** not to care a damn about.
higadillo, lla, *m., f.* liver (of small animals). —*m.* (Hond.) stew of kidneys and livers.
hígado, *m.* 1. liver. 2. (*pl.*) (coll.) guts, courage, bravery. — **h. de azufre,** liver of sulfur, hepar; **echar los hígados,** to toil, work hard; **echar los hígados por,** to strive to get; **malos hígados,** (coll.) ill will; **moler los hígados,** to bother, annoy.
higate, *m.* fig stew.
higiene, *f.* hygiene, sanitation.
higiénicamente, *adv.* hygienically.
higienice, higienicé, *ref.* **higienizar.**
higiénico, ca, *a.* hygienic, sanitary.
higienista, *m., f.* hygienist.
higienizar, (*ref. 53*) *tr.v.* to make hygienic or sanitary.
higo, *m.* 1. fig (fruit). 2. (med.) acuminate wart or condyloma. — **de higos a brevas,** (coll.) from time to time; **h. chumbo, de pala** or **de tuna,** prickly pear, cactus fruit; **no dársele a uno un h.,** not to care a fig or give a damn.
higrófito, ta, *a.* (bot.) hygrophytic. —*m.* (bot.) hygrophyte.
higrógrafo, *m.* (phys.) hygrograph, instrument that registers the degree of humidity in the atmosphere.
higrometría, *f.* (phys.) hygrometry.
higrométrico, ca, *a.* hygrometric.
higrómetro, *m.* (phys.) hygrometer.
higroscopía, *f., var. of* **higrometría.**
higroscopicidad, *f.* (phys.) hygroscopicity, capacity for absorption and release of moisture.
higroscópico, ca, *a.* (phys.) hygroscopic.
higroscopio, *m.* (phys.) hygroscope, instrument indicating humidity in the air.
higróstato, *m.* (phys.) humidistat.
higrotermógrafo, *m.* (phys.) hygrothermograph.
higuana, *f., var. of* **iguana.**
higuera, *f.* (bot.) fig tree; **h. chumba, de Indias, de pala** or **de tuna,** (bot.) prickly pear, prickly pear cactus. — **h. de Egipto,** caprifig, wild fig tree; **h. de Bengala,** (bot.) banyan; **h. infernal** or **h. del infierno,** castor-oil plant; **h. loca, moral** or **silvestre,** sycamore, sycamore fig; **estar en la h.,** (coll.) to be in a dream, be in a daze.
higueral, *m.* fig orchard or garden.
higuereta, higuerilla, *f.* (bot.) castor-oil plant.
higuerillo, *m.* (Guat., bot.) castor-oil plant.
higüero, *m.* (bot.) calabash tree.
higuerón, *m.* (bot.) American timber tree (Ficus subtriplinervia).
higuerote, *m., var. of* **higuerón.**
hijadalgo, *f., var. of* **hidalgo.**
hijastro, tra, *m.* stepson. —*f.* stepdaughter.
hijato, *m.* sprout, shoot.
hijear, *i.v.* (Hond.) to sprout.
hijo, ja, *m., f.* 1. child. 2. brainchild, creation, fruit. 3. love, darling, honey (term of affection between intimate friends or parents and children). — **h. adoptivo,** adopted child; **h. bastardo, h. natural,** illegitimate child, natural child; **h. de algo,** nobleman, person of noble birth; **h. de bendición,** legitimate child; **h. de familia,** minor; **h. de la cuna,** foundling; **h. de la piedra,** foundling; **h. de la tierra,** orphan; **h. del diablo,** mischievous child; **h. de leche,** foster child; **h. de su padre** or **su madre,** (coll.) chip off the old block (child resembling his parents); **h. ilegítimo,** illegitimate son; **h. legítimo,** legitimate son; **h. pródigo,** prodigal son; **h. unico,** only child. —*m.* 1. son. 2. native son (of a country, region, etc.). 3. sprout, shoot. 4. spongy interior of antlers. 5. (*pl.*) children; descendants. 6. junior, Jr., e.g. *Juan Gómez, Hijo,* John Gomez, Jr. — **h. de Dios,** Son of God; **h. del hombre,** Son of Man (Jesus Christ); **h. de puta, h. de perra,** (vulg.) bastard, son of a bitch; **h. político,** son-in-law. —*f.* 1. daughter. 2. native daughter (of a country, region, etc.). — **h. política,** daughter-in-law.
hijodalgo, *m., var. of* **hidalgo.**
hijuela, *f.* 1. little daughter, little girl. 2. (dressm.) widening gore, widening strip (to widen dress). 3. accessory. 4. thin narrow mattress (placed under regular one to prevent it from sagging). 5. (ecc.) pall, cloth for covering the chalice. 6. branch irrigation ditch, branch drain; branch road, side path. 7. rural postal service. 8. estate; inventory of inheritance due to each heir. 9. palm seed. 10. (Chile, Peru) small rural estate (formed by the division of a big one).
hijuelación, *f.* (Chile) parceling, division (of land).
hijuelar, *tr.v.* 1. (Chile) to parcel, divide (land). 2. (Chile) to give (the heir) his portion of an inheritance while the ascendant is still alive.
hijuelero, *m.* rural postman.
hijuelo, *m.* (bot.) sucker, shoot (of trees).
hila, *f.* 1. row, line. 2. thin gut. 3. (*pl.*) lint. — **a la h.,** in single file, one after the other; **h. de agua,** small irrigation ditch.
hilachento, ta, *a.* (Chile) fraying, frayed; (Chile) ragged, tattered.
hilacho, cha, *m., f.* thread, strand (unraveling from cloth); (*pl.*) (Mex.) tatters, rags.
hilachoso, sa, *a.* frayed, ragged, in tatters; fibrous (as certain fruits).
hilada, *f.* row, line; (archit.) course, line, row (of bricks or stones).
hiladillo, *m.* 1. silk thread (made from outside part of silk cocoon). 2. strong narrow ribbon, braid, tape.
hiladizo, za, *a.* spinnable.
hilado, *m.* spinning; yarn, thread.
hilador, ra, *m., f.* spinner (usually of silk). —*f.* spinning machine.
hilandera, *f.* spinner.
hilandería, *f.* 1. spinning (art). 2. spinning mill.
hilandero, *m., f.* spinner. —*m.* spinning mill.
hilanza, *f.* 1. spinning. 2. yarn, thread.
hilar, *tr.v.* 1. to spin (silk, wool, cocoon). 2. to infer, conjecture. — **h. delgado or fino,** to talk or discuss very subtly; to act very carefully.
hilaracha, *f., var. of* **hilacha.**
hilarante, *a.* very funny, hilarious; laughing (gas).
hilaridad, *f.* hilarity, mirth, laughter.
hilatura, *f.* the art of spinning.
hilaza, *f.* yarn, thread, fibre; uneven thick thread. — **descubrir uno la h.,** (coll.) to discover someone's faults.
hilera, *f.* 1. row, line, file. 2. thread, fine thread. 3. (mec.) drawplate, wiredrawing maching. 4. (mil.) file, rank. 5. (archit.) ridgepole. 6. (mar.) cable. 7. (*pl.*) (zool.) spinneret. — **hileras abiertas,** open ranks.
hilero, *m.* 1. eddy, whirl (caused by two opposing currents). 2. stream, current.
hililllo, *m.* trickle (of water, blood, etc.).
hilo, *m.* 1. thread, yarn; filament; string (of pearls). 2. linen, linen cloth. 3. wire, fine wire. 4. trickle, thin stream, thin jet. 5. thread (of conversation, etc.; of spider's web). 6. (bot.) hilum. 7. edge. — **a h.,** uninterruptedly, parallel, in line; **al h.,** along the thread (of cloth), with the grain (of wood); **al h. del viento,** with the wind; **colgar de un h.,** to hang by a thread, be in imminent danger; **de h.,** straight, directly; **h. bramante** or **de empalomar,** twine, hempcord; **h. de cajas,** fine thread; **h. de la vida,** course or thread of life; **h. dental,** dental floss; **perder el h.,** to lose the thread (of conversation, thought, etc.); **tener el alma en un h.,** to have one's heart in one's mouth.
hilomorfismo, *m.* (philos.) hylomorphism.
hilozoísmo, *m.* (philos.) hylozoism.
hilozoísta, *m. f.* (philos.) hylozoist.
hilván, *m.* (dressm.) basting, tacking; (Amer.) basting thread.
hilvanar, *tr.v.* 1. to baste, tack; (Amer.) to hem. 2. to do hastily. 3. to plan.

himen, *m.* (anat.) hymen.
himeneo, *m.* 1. wedding. 2. wedding song, nuptial song, epithalamium.
himenio, *m.* (bot.) hymenium.
himenóptero, ra, *a.* (ento.) hymenopterous, hymenopteran. —*m.* (ento.) hymenopteron, hymenopter; (*pl.*) Hymenoptera.
himnario, *m.* hymnal, hymnbook.
himno, *m.* hymn; anthem; **h. nacional,** national anthem.
himnología, *f.* hymnology.
himnólogo, *m.* hymnologist.
himplar, *i.v.* to growl, roar (panther, wildcat, etc.).
hin, *m.* whinny, neigh.
hincadura, *f.* 1. prick; pricking. 2. thrusting, driving (something into something else). 3. sinking (teeth into something).
hincapié, *m.* digging one's feet in; **hacer h.,** to dig one's feet in, stand firm; **hacer h. en,** to insist on, demand; to stress, emphasize.
hincar, (*ref.* 50) *tr.v.* 1. to prick. 2. to thrust, drive or push (something) into (something else); to dig (one's feet) in; to sink (one's teeth) into. —*r.v.* to kneel, kneel down; **hincarse de rodillas,** to kneel, kneel down, genuflect.
hincha, *f.* (coll.) hate, enmity, grudge. —. (coll.) supporter, fan.
hincha, *ref.* **henchir.**
hinchable, *a.* inflatable; bubble (as in bubble gum).
hinchadamente, *adv.* pompously, conceitedly, in an overbearing manner.
hinchado, da, *past part. of* **hinchar.** —*a.* 1. (fig.) vain, conceited. 2. bombastic, turgid (style).
hinchamiento, *m., var. of* **hinchazón.**
hinchar, *tr.v.* 1. to make swell, swell. 2. to inflate, blow up. 3. to exaggerate, inflate. —*r.v.* 1. to swell up, become swollen (a bruise, etc.). 2. to become swollen (a river). 3. to become conceited, swell headed or vain. —*i.v.* to swell, swell up.
hinchazón, *m.* 1. swelling. 2. conceit, vanity, pride. 3. turgidity (of style).
hinchiendo, hinchiera, hinchiese, hinchió, *ref.* **henchir.**
hincho, *ref.* **henchir.**
hinco, *m.* post, stake, pile.
hincón, *m.* mooring post or stake; hitching post.
hindi, *m.* Hindi, one of the languages of India.
hindú, (*pl.* **hindúes**), *a, m., f.* Hindu, Hindustani.
hinduísmo, *m.* Hinduism, Hindooism.
hiniesta, *f.* (bot.) broom, genista.
hinojal, *m.* fennel, patch, field of fennel.
hinojo, *m.* (bot.) fennel; **h. marino,** (bot.) samphire (Crithmum maritimum).
hinojo, *m.* knee; **de hinojos,** kneeling.
hinque, hinqué, *ref.* **hincar.**
hintero, *m.* baker's kneading table.
hiña, hiñendo, hiñera, hiñese, hiño, *ref.* **heñir.**
hiogloso, sa, *a.* hyoglossal. —*m.* (anat.) hyoglossus.
hioideo, a, *a.* (anat.) hyoid.
hioides, *m.* (anat.) hyoid, hyoid bone.
hioscina, *f.* (chem.) hyoscine.
hipálage, *f.* (gram.) hypallage.
hipantio, *m.* (bot.) hypanthium.
hipanto, *m.* (bot.) hypanthium.
hipar, *i.v.* 1. to hiccup, have hiccups. 2. to pant. 3. to wear or tire oneself out. 4. to whine. — **h. por,** to want, yearn for.
hiparca, *m.* (hist.) hipparch, a cavalry commander (in ancient Greece).
hiperacidez, *f.* (med.) hyperacidity.
hiperactivo, va, *a.* (med.) hyperactive.
hiperalgesia, *f.* (med.) hyperalgesia, hyperalgesis.
hiperalgésico, ca, *a.* (med.d) hyperalgesic.
hiperbático, ca, *a.* hyperbatic.
hipérbaton, *m.* (gram.) hyperbaton.
hipérbola, *f.* (geom.) hyperbola.
hipérbole, *f.* (rhet.) hyperbole.
hiperbólicamente, *adv.* hyperbolically.
hiperbolice, *ref.* **hiperbolizar.**
hiperbólico, ca, *a.* hyperbolical, hyperbolic.
hiperbolizar, (*ref.* 53) i. v. to hyperbolize.
hiperboloide, *m.* (geom.) hyperboloid.
hiperbóreo, a, hyperborean, northern; (myth.) Hyperborean.
hipercinesia, *f.* (med.) hyperkinesia, hyperkinesis.
hipercinesis, *f.* (med.) hyperkinesia, hyperkinesis.
hiperclorhidria, *f.* (med.) hyperchlorhydria.
hipercrisis, *f.* (med.) grave crisis.
hipercrítica, *f.* severe criticism, carping criticism.
hipercrítico, ca, *a.* hypercritical. —*m.* hypercritic, carping critic.
hiperdulía, *f.* (theol.) hyperdulia.
hiperemia, *f.* (med.) hyperemia, hyperaemia.
hiperémico, ca, *a.* (med., physiol.) hyperemic, hyperaemic.
hiperestesia, *f.* (med.) hyperesthesia.
hiperestésico, ca, *a.* (med.) hyperesthetic.
hipereutéctico, ca, *a.* (phys., chem., metal.) hypereutectic.
hiperfunción, *f.* (med.) hyperfunction.
hipergeométrico, ca, *a.* (math.) hypergeometric.
hiperglicemia, *f.* (med.) hyperglycemia.
hipericíneo, a, *a.* (bot.) hypericaceous. —*f.* (*pl.*) Hypericaceae.
hipérico, *m.* (bot.) St.-John's-wort (Hypericum perforatum).
hiperinsulinismo, *m.* (med.) hyperinsulinism.
Hiperión, *m.* (astron., myth.) Hyperion.
hiperirritabilidad, *f.* (med.) hyperirritability.
hiperirritable, *a.* (med.) hyperirritable.
hipermetamorfosis, *f.* (zool.) hypermetamorphosis, multiple metamorphosis.
hipermetría, *f.* (poet.) enjambment achieved by finishing a line with part of a word and beginning the next with the rest of it.
hipermétrope, *a.* (ophthal.) hypermetropic, hyperopic.
hipermetropía, *f.* (ophthal.) hypermetropia, hyperopia, far-sightedness.
hipermnesia, *f.* (med.) hypermnesia, abnormal activity or excitement of the memory.
hipermorfo, *m.* (med.) hypermorph.
hiperón, *m.* (phys.) hyperon.
hiperope, *m.* (med.) hyperope.
hiperopía, *f.* (med.) hyperopia, hypermetropia.
hiperostosis, *f.* (anat., med.) hyperostosis.
hiperpiesia, *f.* (med.) hyperpiesia.
hiperpirexia, *f.* (med.) hyperpyrexia.
hiperpituitarismo, *m.* (med.) hyperpituitarism.
hiperplasia, *f.* (med., biol.) hyperplasia.
hiperploide, *a.* (biol.) hyperploid.
hiperpnea, *f.* (physiol.) hyperpnea, hyperpnoea.
hiperqueratosis, *f.* (med.) hyperkeratosis.
hipersensibilidad, *f.* hypersensitiveness, hypersensibility.
hipersensible, *a.* hypersensitive.
hipersónico, ca, *a.* hypersonic.
hiperstena, *f.* (min.) hypersthene.
hiperesténico, ca, *a.* (min.) hypersthenic.
hipersteno, *m.* (min.) hypersthene.
hipertensión, *f.* (med.) hypertension.
hipertensivo, va, *a.* (med.) hypertensive.
hipertenso, sa, *a.* hypertense, very tense.
hipertiroidia, *f.* (med.) hyperthyroidism.
hipertiroidismo, *m.* (med.) hyperthyroidism.
hipertonicidad, *f.* (phys., chem.) hypertonicity.
hipertónico, ca, *a.* (phys., chem.) hypertonic.
hipertrofia, *f.* (med., biol.) hypertrophy.
hipertrofiarse, *r.v.* (med.) to become hypertrophied.
hipertrófico, ca, *a.* (med.) hypertrophic.
hiperventilación, *f.* (med.) hyperventilation.
hipervitaminosis, *f.* (med.) hypervitaminosis.
hipestesia, *f.* (med.) hypesthesia, hypaesthesia.
hipetro, ra, *a.* (archit.) hypaethral, hypethral.
hípico, ca, *a.* equine, pertaining to horses and horseback-riding; **club h.,** riding club.
hipido, *m.* sob, moan.
hipnal, *m.* hypnale, type of adder thought to kill by causing sleep.
hipnoanálisis, *m.* (med.) hypnoanalysis.
hipnoide, *a.* hypnoid, hypnoidal, resembling sleep or hypnosis.
hipnoideo, a, hypnoid, hypnoidal.
hipnología, *f.* hypnology, the study of sleep and hypnotism.
hipnológico, ca, *a.* hypnologic, hypnological; pertaining to sleep or to hypnotism.
Hipnos, *m.* (myth.) Hypnos, the god of sleep.
hipnosis, *f.* hypnosis.
hipnoterapia, *f.* (med.) hypnotherapy.
hipnotice, hipnoticé, *ref.* hipnotizar.
hipnótico, ca, *a., f., m.* hypnotic.
hipnotismo, *m.* (med.) hypnotism.
hipnotizable, *a.* hypnotizable.
hipnotización, *f.* hypnotization.
hipnotizador, ra, *a.* hypnotizing. —*m., f.* hypnotist.
hipnotizar, (*ref.* 53) tr.v. to hypnotize.
hipo, *m.* 1. hiccup, hiccough. 2. yearning, wish, desire. 3. grudge, dislike, aversion. — **quitar el h. a,** (coll.) to amaze, surprise, take by surprise; **tener h.,** to have hiccups; **tener h. contra** or **con,** to have a grudge against, have an aversion for; **tener h. por,** to yearn or long for.
hipo, *m.* (photog.) hypo.
hipoblástico, ca, *a.* (biol.) hypoblastic.
hipoblasto, *m.* (biol.) hypoblast.
hipobosco, *m.* (ento.) horsetick.
hipobranquio, a, *a.* (ichth.) hypobranchial.
hipocampo, *m.* (anat., ichth., myth.) hippocampus, sea-horse.
hipocastáneas, *f.* (*pl.*) (bot.) Hippocastanaceae.
hipocausto, *m.* (archit.) hypocaust, a room heated from below (in ancient Rome).
hipocentauro, *m.* (myth.) centaur.
hipocentro, *m.* (phys.) hypocenter.
hipocicloidal, *a.* (geom.) hypocycloidal.
hipocicloide, *f.* (geom.) hypocycloid.
hipoclorito, *m.* (chem.) hypochlorite.
hipocloroso, sa, *a.* (chem.) hypochlorous.
hipocondría, *f.* (med.) hypochondria.
hipocondríaco, ca, *a., m., f.* hypochondriac.
hipocóndrico, ca, *a.* hypochondriacal.
hipocondrio, *m.* (anat.) hypochondrium.
hipocotíleo, *m.* (bot.) hypocotyl.
hipocótilo, *m.* (bot.) hypocotyl.
hipocrás, *m.* hippocras, a medicinal cordial made with wine and spices.
Hipócrates, *m.* Hippocrates, Greek physician, called the Father of Medicine.
hipocrático, ca, *a.* Hippocratic, pertaining to Hippocrates.
hipocratismo, *m.* Hippocratism, Hippocratic doctrine.
Hipocrene, *f.* (myth.) Hippocrene, sacred fountain of the Muses, created by Pegasus, the winged horse.
hipocresía, *f.* hypocrisy, falseness; dissimulation.
hipócrita, *a.* hypocritical. —*m., f.* hypocrite.
hipócritamente, *adv.* hypocritically.

hipocromatemia, *f.* (med.) hypochromic anemia.
hipocromemia, *f.* (med.) hypochromic anemia.
hipodérmico, ca, *a.* hypodermic, under the skin.
hipodermis, *f.* (bot., zool.) hypodermis.
hipodermo, ma, *a.* (bot.) hypodermal.
hipódromo, *m.* racecourse, race track, hippodrome.
hipoeutéctico, ca, *a.* (phys.) hypoeutectic.
hipofagia, *f.* hippophagy, the habit of eating horse meat.
hipófago, ga, *a.* hippophagous. —*m., f.* hippophagous person, one who prefers horse meat.
hipofaringe, *m.* (ento.) hypopharynx.
hipófisis, *f.* (anat.) hypophysis.
hipofosfato, *m.* (chem.) hypophosphate.
hipofosfito, *m.* (chem.) hypophosphite.
hipofosfórico, *m.* (chem.) hypophosphoric.
hipofosforoso, sa, *a.* (chem.) hypophosphorous.
hipofunción, *f.* (med.) hypofunction.
hipogástrico, ca, *a.* (anat.) hypogastric.
hipogastrio, *m.* (anat.) hypogastrium.
hipogénico, ca, *a.* (geol.) hypogene.
hipogeo, a, *a.* (bot.) hypogeous. —*m.* (archit.) hypogeum.
hipoginia, *f.* (bot.) hypogyny.
hipógino, na, *a.* (bot.) hypogynous.
hipoglicemia, *f.* (med.) hypoglycemia.
hipogloso, sa, *a., m.* (anat.) hypoglossal.
hipognato, ta, *a.* (anat.) hypognathous.
hipogrifo, *m.* (myth.) hippogriff.
Hipólita, *f.* (myth.) Hippolyte, queen of the Amazons, lover of Theseus.
hipología, *m.* hippology, the study of horses.
hipólogo, *m.* hippologist, horse veterinarian.
hipómanes, *m.* (vet.) hippomanes, vaginal discharge from mares in heat.
hipomanía, *f.* (med.) hypomania.
hipomaníaco, ca, *a.* (med.) hypomanic.
hipomoclio, *m.* (phys.) fulcrum.
hipomoclion, *m., var. of* **hipomoclio.**
hiponastia, *f.* (bot.) hyponasty.
hiponástico, ca, *a.* (bot.) hyponastic.
hiponitrato, *m.* (chem.) subnitrate.
hiponitrito, *m.* (chem.) hyponitrite.
hiponitroso, sa, *a.* (chem.) hiponitrous.
hipopión, *m.* (med.) hypopyon.
hipopituitarismo, *m.* (med.) hypopituitarism.
hipoplasia, *f.* (med.) hypoplasia.
hipoplástico, ca, *a.* (med.) hypoplastic.
hipoploide, *a.* (biol.) hypoploid.
hipopótamo, *m.* (zool.) hippopotamus.
hiposcenio, *m.* (archit.) hyposcenium (in Greek theater).
hiposecreción, *f.* (med.) hyposecretion.
hiposensibilización, *f.* (med.) hyposensitization.
hiposo, sa, *a.* having hiccoughs.
hipóstasis, *f.* (theol.) hypostasis.
hipostáticamente, *adv.* (theol.) hypostatically.
hipostático, ca, *a.* (theol.) hypostatic.
hipostatización, *f.* (philos.) hypostatization.
hipostenia, *f.* hyposthenia, weakening, lessening of strength.
hipóstilo, la, *a.* (archit.) hypostyle.
hiposulfato, *m.* (chem.) dithionate.
hiposulfito, *m.* (chem.) hyposulfite, hyposulphite. —**h. de sodio,** sodium hyposulfite.
hiposulfúrico, *a.* (chem.) hyposulphuric, dithionic.
hiposulfuroso, *a.* (chem.) hyposulfurous, hyposulphurous.
hipotálamo, *m.* (anat.) hypothalamus.
hipotaxis, *f.* (gram.) hypotaxis.
hipoteca, *f.* mortgage; **h. conjunta** or **de participación,** participating mortgage; **redimir una h.,** to pay off a mortgage.
hipotecable, *a.* mortgageable.
hipotecar, (*ref. 50*) *tr.v.* to mortgage.
hipotecario, ria, *a.* mortgage.
hipotecnia, *f.* the science of horse-breeding.
hipotenar, *m.* (anat.) hypothenar.
hipotensión, *f.* (med.) hypotension, abnormally low blood pressure.
hipotensivo, va, *a.* (med.) hypotensive.
hipotenusa, *f.* (geom.) hypotenuse.
hipoteque, hipotequé, *ref.* **hipotecar.**
hipotermia, *f.* hypothermia, hypothermy, subnormal body temperature.
hipótesi, *f., var. of* **hipótesis.**
hipótesis, *f.* hypothesis, unproved theory; supposition.
hipotéticamente, *adv.* hypothetically.
hipotético, ca, *a.* hypothetical; conditional.
hipotiposis, *f.* (rhet.) hypotyposis (vivid description).
hipotiroide, *m.* (med.) hypothyroid.
hipotiroideo, *m.* (med.) hypothyroid.
hipotiroidia, *f.* (med.) hypothyroidism.
hipotiroidismo, *m.* (med.) hypothyroidism, insufficient activity of the thyroid gland.
hipotonía, *f.* (physiol.) hypotonicity, abnormally low muscle tension or tone.
hipotónico, ca, *a.* (physiol.) hypotonic.
hipotrofia, *f.* (med.) hypotrophy.
hipoxantina, *f.* (chem.) hypoxanthine.
hipoxia, *f.* (physiol.) hypoxia.
hipsografía, *f.* (geog.) hypsography.
hipsográfico, ca, *a.* (geog.) hypsographic, hypsographical.
hipsometría, *f.* (geog.) hypsometry.
hipsométrico, ca, *a.* (geog.) hypsometric, hypsometrical.
hipsómetro, *m.* (geog.) hypsometer.
hipúrico, ca, *a.* (chem.) hippuric.
hipurita, *f.* (paleon.) hippurite.
hiráceo, *m.* (zool.) hyrax.
Hircania, *f.* (hist.) Hyrcania, province of the ancient Macedonian and Persian empires.
hircino, na, *a.* hircine; pertaining to a goat or its smell.
hirco, *m.* wild goat.
hircocervo, *m.* 1. hircocervus (mythical creature, half goat, half stag). 2. (fig.) chimera, fantasy.
hiriendo, *ref.* **herir.**
hiriente, *a.* 1. wounding, cutting, e.g. *una observación h.,* a cutting remark. 2. (fig.) offensive.
hiriera, hiriese, hirió, *ref.* **herir.**
hirma, *f.* (tex.) selvage, edge.
hirmar, *tr.v.* to make firm, fasten, tighten.
hirsuto, ta, *a.* 1. hirsute, hairy, shaggy, bristly, rough; stiff, coarse (hair). 2. surly, gruff, rough.
hirudina, *f.* hirudin, a substance found in the salivary glands of leeches.
hirudíneos, *f.* (*pl.*) (zool.) Herudinea.
hirundinaria, *f.* (bot.) celandine.
hirviendo, *ref.* **hervir.**
hirviente, *a.* boiling, seething.
hirviera, hirviese, hirvió, *ref.* **hervir.**
hisca, *f.* birdlime.
hiscal, *m.* three-strand esparto rope.
hisopada, *f.* sprinkling of holy water with the aspergill.
hisopadura, *f., var. of* **hisopada.**
hisopar, *tr.v.* to sprinkle holy water with the aspergill.
hisopazo, *m.* 1. sprinkling with holy water. 2. blow inflicted with a sprinkler or the aspergill.
hisopear, *tr.v., var. of* **hisopar.**
hisopillo, *m.* 1. (med.) mouth swab. 2. (bot.) winter savory. 3. small aspergill or sprinkler.
hisopo, *m.* 1. (bot.) hyssop (Hissopus officinalis). 2. (ecc.) aspergill, hyssop. 3. (Amer.) brush, paint brush, shaving brush.
hisopo húmedo, *m.* (pharm.) wool fat, wool grease, lanolin.
hispalense, *a., m., f.* Sevillian, of or pertaining to the Spanish province and city of Seville.
hispalio, lia, *a., var. of* **hispalense.**
Hispania, *f.* Hispania, ancient name for the Iberian Peninsula; (poet.) Spain.
hispanice, *ref.* **hispanizar.**
hispánico, ca, *a.* Hispanic.
hispanidad, *f.* Spanish spirit, Spanishness; Spanish world, cultural community of Spanish-speaking nations.
hispanismo, *m.* 1. Hispanicism. 2. Spanish studies, interest in Spanish literature and culture. 3. a typically Spanish idiom, custom, word.
hispanista, *m, f.* Hispanicist, Spanish scholar.
hispanizado, da, *past part. of* **hispanizar.** —*a.* Spanish-like.
hispanizar, (*ref. 53*) *tr.v.* to hispanicize. —*r.v.* to become hispanicized.
hispano, na, *a.* Hispanic, Spanish, Spanish-American. —*m., f.* Spaniard; Spanish American.
hispanoamericanismo, *m.* Spanish Americanism (doctrine advocating cultural union of Spanish America).
hispanoamericano, na, *a., m., f.* Spanish American, Latin American.
hispanoárabe, *a., m., f.* (hist., archit.) Hispano-Arabic.
hispanófilo, la, *a., m., f.* Hispanophile, liking, admirer of, all things Spanish.
hispanofobia, *f.* Hispanophobia, dislike for all things Spanish.
hispanohablante, *a.* Spanish-speaking. —*m., f.* Spanish speaker.
hispanoparlante, *a.* Spanish-speaking. —*m., f.* Spanish speaker.
híspido, da, *a.* hispid, bristly, hirsute.
hispídulo, la, *a.* (bot.) hispidulous.
hispir, *tr.v.* to make or become spongy. —*i.v.* to swell.
histamina, *f.* (biochem.) histamine.
histaminasa, *f.* (biochem.) histaminase, an enzyme found in the digestive system of animals.
histamínico, ca, *a.* (biochem.) histaminic.
histerectomía, *f.* (med.) hysterectomy, surgical removal of the uterus or part of it.
histéresis, *f.* (phys.) hysteresis.
histeria, *f.* 1. (med.) hysteria. 2. hysterics.
histérico, ca, *a.* 1. hysterical, hysteric. 2. uterine. —*m., f.* (med.) hysteric, hysterical person. —*m.* (med.) hysteria.
histerismo, *m.* 1. (med.) hysteria. 2. hysterics; **h. colectivo** or **en masa,** mass hysteria.
histerocatalepsia, *f.* (med.) hysterocatalepsy.
histerogénico, ca, *a.* (med.) hysterogenic.
histerógeno, na, *a.* (med.) hysterogenic.
histeroide, *a.* (med., psyc.) hysteroid.
histeroneurastenia, *f.* (med., psyc.) hysteroneurasthenia.
histerotomía, *f.* (med.) hysterotomy, incision of the uterus.
histidina, *f.* (biochem.) histidine.
histiocito, *m.* (physiol.) histiocyte.
histofisiología, *f.* (physiol.) histophysiology.
histogénesis, *f.* (biol.) histogenesis (tissue development).
histogenia, *f.* (biol.) histogeny, histogenesis.
histograma, *m.* histogram, chart (gen. used to record statistics).
histoideo, a, *a.* (med.) histoid.
histólisis, *f.* (physiol.) histolysis.
histolítico, ca, *a.* (physiol.) histolytic.
histología, *f.* (biol.) histology, the study of the structure of tissues.

histológico, ca, *a.* (biol.) histological.
histólogo, *m.* histologist.
histona, *m.* (biochem.) histone.
histopatología, *f.* (physiol.) histopathology.
histoplasmosis, *f.* (med.) histoplasmosis.
histoquímica, *f.* (med., biol.) histochemistry, the study of the chemical components of organic tissues.
historia, *f.* 1. history; story, tale; yarn. 2. (*pl.*) (coll.) gossip, tattle. 3. record, analysis. — **dejarse de historias,** (coll.) to come or get to the point, get down to brass tacks; **h. antigua,** ancient history; **h. clínica,** clinical record, medical history; **h. moderna,** modern history; **h. natural,** natural history; **h. sagrada,** Biblical history; **h. universal,** world history.
historiado, da, *past part. of* **historiar.** —*a.* 1. (coll.) ornate, overdecorated, gaudy. 2. elaborate (letter). 3. (p.) storied (representing a story).
historiador, ra, *m., f.* historian.
historial, *a.* historical, historic. —*m.* history, record, dossier; background, e.g. *ella tiene un h. muy interesante,* she has a very interesting background; **h. clínico** or **médico,** medical history; **h. personal,** resumé, curriculum vitae.
historialmente, *adv.* historically.
historiar, *tr.v.* 1. to record or write the history of; to tell the story of. 2. (p.) to depict, represent (historical events).
históricamente, *adv.* historically.
historicidad, *f.* historicity, authenticity.
historicismo, *m.* (philos.) historicism.
histórico, ca, *a.* historic, historical.
historieta, *f.* short story; anecdote; **h. cómica,** comic strip.
historiografía, *f.* historiography.
historiográfico, ca, *a.* historiographical.
historiógrafo, *m.* historiographer, historian.
historión, *m. aug. of* **historia,** tedious, long story.
histrión, *m.* (arch.) actor; juggler, clown.
histriónico, ca, *a.* histrionic.
histrionisa, *f.* (arch.) actress; dancer.
histrionismo, *m.* theatricals, histrionism, acting; histrionics, artificial manners.
hit, *m.* (Amer.) hit, popular success (of a book, play, song, etc.).
hita, *f.* 1. headless nail, brad. 2. milestone, landmark, signpost; boundary stone.
hitación, *f.* marking with milestones or boundary stones.
hitar, *tr.v.* to mark with milestones or sign posts; to mark with boundary stones.
hitita, *a., m, f.* (hist.) Hittite, of an ancient empire of Asia Minor, its languages and people.
hitlerismo, *m.* (pol.) Hitlerism, Nazism.
hitlerista, *a., m., f.* Hitlerite, Nazi.
hito, ta, *a.* 1. adjoining (street or house). 2. fixed, firm. 3. black (horse). —*m.* 1. signpost, milestone; landmark, boundary stone. 2. form of quoits (game). 3. target, point of aim. — **a h.,** permanently, fixedly; **dar en el h.,** to hit the nail on the head, get to the crux of the matter; **mirar de h. en h.,** to look fixedly at, to stare.
hitón, *m.* (min.) large, square, headless nail.
hizo, *ref.* **hacer.**
hl. *abbrev. of* **hectolitro,** hectoliter (hl.).
hm. *abbrev. of* **hectómetro,** hectometer (hectom., hm.).
Hnos. *abbrev. of* **hermanos,** brothers (Bros.).
Ho *sym. of* **holmio,** holmium (Ho).
hoatzín, *m.* (ornith.) hoatzin.
hobachón, na, *a.* fat and lazy person.
hobachonería, *f.* laziness, sluggishness.
hobby, *m.* (Amer.) hobby, pastime.
hobismo, *m.* (philos.) Hobbism, the social theories of Thomas Hobbes, English author and philosopher of the 17th century.
hobo, *m., var. of* **jobo.**
hoce, *ref.* **hozar.**
hocicada, *f.* blow on the nose or snout; blow with the snout or nose.
hocicar, (*ref. 50*) *tr.v.* to root, nuzzle, grub around in, turn up (ground) with its snout. —*i.v.* 1. to fall on one's face, knock one's face against. 2. (coll.) to come up against difficulties. 3. (coll.) to kiss repeatedly. 4. (mar.) to pitch at the bow.
hocico, *m.* 1. snout, muzzle; mouth; (coll.) face. 2. (coll.) sour face, frown, annoyed look. — **caer** or **dar de hocicos,** (coll.) to fall on one's face; **poner h.,** (coll.) to make a face, look sour; **meter el h.,** to stick one's nose into someone's business.
hocicón, na, *a., var. of* **hocicudo.**
hocicudo, da, *a.* big-snouted; thick-lipped, large-mouthed, blubber-lipped.
hocino, *m.* 1. glen, valley. 2. gorge, narrows (of river between mountains). 3. (*pl.*) riverside fields or land. 4. (agr.) sickle, billhook.
hocique, *ref.* **hocicar.**
hociquear, *tr.v.* to root, nuzzle, grub around in, turn up (ground) with the snout.
hociquillo, ito, *m. dim. of* **hocico,** small snout.
hockey, *m.* (sport.) hockey; **h. sobre hielo,** ice hockey.
hodómetro, *m.* odometer, cyclometer.
hogañazo, *adv., var. of* **hogaño.**
hogaño, *adv.* (coll.) this year; nowadays, in our time.
hogar, *m.* 1. hearth, fireplace. 2. home. 3. home life, family life. 4. bonfire; **h. de ancianos,** old people's home.
hogareño, ña, *a.* home-loving; homey, domestic.
hogaza, *f.* large loaf of bread; whole wheat bread, rough, coarse bread.
hoguera, *f.* bonfire.
hoja, *f.* 1. (bot.) leaf; petal. 2. leaf, sheet (of paper); leaf, page (of book); layer, foil, sheet (of metal, etc.); layer (of pastry). 3. blade (of knife, etc.). 4. strip of land cultivated every other year. 5. leaf (of a door); pane (of a window). 6. half of each of the principal parts of a dress. 7. each of the plates composing a suit of armor. 8. (fig.) sword. — **batir h.,** to beat or work metal; **h. abrazadora,** (bot.) amplexicaul leaf; **h. acicular,** (bot.) acicular leaf; **h. aserrada,** (bot.) serrate leaf; **h. batiente,** casement sash; **h. berberisca,** (med.) thin copper plate used to cover certain wounds; **h. compuesta,** (bot.) compound or divided leaf; **h. de afeitar,** razor blade; **h. de aluminio,** aluminum foil; **h. de cálculo,** spreadsheet; **h. de empuje angular,** (bldg.) angledozer; **h. de estaño,** tinfoil; **h. dentada,** (bot.) dentate leaf; **h. de lata,** tinplate, tin; **h. de parra,** (fig.) fig leaf; cover, blind (for some dishonest act); **h. de pedido,** order form; **h. de plata,** silver foil; **h. de reclamación,** complaint form; **h. de ruta,** waybill; **h. de servicios,** service record; **h. de trabajo,** worksheet; **h. de vida,** resumé, curriculum vitae; **h. escurrida,** (bot.) decurrent leaf; **h. intercalar,** interleaf; **h. perfoliada,** (bot) perfoliate leaf; **h. sentada,** (bot.) sessile leaf; **h. suelta,** leaflet, handbill; **h. venosa,** (bot.) veined leaf; **h. volante,** leaflet, pamphlet; **volver la h.,** (fig.) to change the subject.
hojalata, *f.* tin, tinplate.
hojalatería, *f.* tinsmith's shop; tinware, tin articles.
hojalatero, *m.* tinsmith, sheet-metal worker.
hojalde, *m., var. of* **hojaldre.**
hojaldra, *f.* (Amer.) *var. of* **hojaldre.**
hojaldrado, da, *past part. of* **hojaldrar.** —*a.* puff, flaky (pastry).
hojaldrar, *tr.v.* to make into puff pastry.
hojaldre, *m., f.* puff paste or pastry.
hojaldrero, ra, *m., f., var. of* **hojaldrista.**
hojaldrista, *m., f.* puff pastry baker.
hojaranzo, *m.* 1. (bot.) hornbeam, yoke elm. 2. (bot.) oleander.
hojarasca, *f.* 1. fallen leaves, dead leaves. 2. excess foliage. 3. rubbish, trash.
hojear, *tr.v.* to leaf through, skim through, glance through (a book, periodical, etc.) —*i.v.* to flake, scale off; to move or rustle its leaves (a tree).
hojica, illa, ita, *f. dim. of* **hoja,** small leaf.
hojoso, sa, *a.* leafy, abundant in foliage.
hojudo, da, *a., var. of* **hojoso.**
hojuela, *f.* 1. leaflet, small leaf. 2. pancake. 3. pressed olive skins. 4. flat gold or silver thread (used for embroidery). 5. (Cuba) puff pastry, flaky pastry. — **h. de maíz,** corn flake.
hokey, *m.* hockey; **h. sobre hierba,** field hockey; **h. sobre patines,** ice hockey.
¡hola! *interj.* hello! hullo! hi!
holán, *m.* 1. bastite, fine cotton or linen fabric. 2. (Mex.) flounce, furbelow, ruffle.
holancina, *f.* 1. (Cuba) holland cloth, fine Dutch linen.
holanda, *f.* 1. holland, fine Dutch linen. 2. low grade alcohol. 3. **H.,** Holland, the Netherlands.
holandés, sa, *a.* Dutch. —*m.* 1. Dutch (languaje). 2. Dutchman, Hollander. —*f.* Dutchwoman. — **a la holandesa,** (bkb.) half-bound.
holandeta, *f.* (tex.), *var. of* **holandilla.**
holandilla, *f.* (tex.), holland, brown holland, lining material. — **tabaco h.,** poor quality tobacco grown in Holland.
holándrico, ca, *a.* (biol.) holandric.
holding, *m.* holding company.
holgachón, na, *a.* (coll.) lazy and comfort-loving.
holgadamente, *adv.* 1. (to live) comfortably, easily. 2. (to fit) loosely, amply. 3. in a leisurely way, calmly; carelessly.
holgado, da, *past part. of* **holgar.** —*a.* 1. loose, roomy, spacious (clothes). 2. easy, comfortable, leisurely, lax. 3. unemployed, at leisure.
holganza, *f.* 1. rest, repose, leisure. 2. idleness, laziness. 3. fun, pleasure, enjoyment; diversion, recreation.
holgar, (*ref. 72*) *i.v.* 1. to rest. 2. to be idle, not to work. 3. to be glad or happy (at). 4. to be loose, not to fit (clothes). 5. to be useless, unnecessary or needless; **huelga** + *inf.*, it is unnecessary to + *inf.*, e.g. *huelga decir que vino sin invitación,* needless to say, he came uninvited. —*r.v.* to make merry, enjoy oneself, relax.
holgazán, na, *a.* idle, lazy, indolent. —*m., f.* idler, loafer.
holgazanear, *i.v.* to idle, loaf.
holgazanería, *f.* idleness, laziness, loafing.
holgón, na, *a.* lazy and pleasureloving. —*m., f.* pleasureseeker, pleasurelover.
holgorio, *m.* (coll.) gaiety, rejoicing, merriment, merry-making; spree, noisy party.
holgué, *ref.* **holgar.**
holgueta, *f.* (coll.) enjoyment, merriment, party.
holgura, *f.* 1. ease, comfort. 2. looseness (of clothes). 3. enjoyment, mirth, merriment. 4. (mec.) play, give, room.
holladero, ra, *a.* trodden (part of road).
holladura, *f.* 1. treading, trampling. 2. fee paid for passage of cattle through a certain area.
hollar, (*ref. 33*) *tr.v.* to tread on; (fig.) to tread upon, trample on.
hollejo, *m.* skin (of fruits).
hollejudo, da, *a.* (Chile) having a thick, tough skin (a fruit).
hollejuelo, *m. dim. of* **hollejo,** thin skin (of fruits).

hollín, *m.* soot, lampblack.
hollinar, *tr.v.* (Chile) to cover with soot.
holliniento, ta, *a.* sooty.
holmio, *m.* (chem.) holmium.
holoblástico, ca, *a.* (biol.) holoblastic.
holocaína, *f.* (chem.) holocaine.
holocausto, *m.* 1. holocaust, burnt offering, sacrifice. 2. holocaust, complete destruction.
holocéfalo, la, *a.* (ichth.) holocephalan. *—m.* (ichth.) holocephalan; (*pl.*) Holocephali.
holocénico, ca, *a.* (geol.) holocenic.
holocrino, na, *a.* (physiol.) holocrine.
holoédrico, ca, *a.* (cryst.) holohedral.
holofítico, ca, *a.* (biol.) holophytic.
holofrástico, ca, *a.* (philol.) holophrastic.
hologamia, *f.* (biol.) hologamy.
holágrafo, fa, *a.* (law) holograph, holographical. *—m.* (law) holograph.
holómetro, *m.* holometer, pantometer.
holosérico, ca, *a.* made of pure silk.
holostérico, ca, *a.* (phys.) holosteric (barometer).
holotipo, *m.* (biol.) holotype.
holoturia, *f.* (zool.) holothurian, sea cucumber.
holotúrido, da, *a., m., f.* (zool.) holothurian.
holozoico, ca, *a.* (biol.) holozoic.
homarrache, *m.* jester, clown.
hombracho, *m.* tall, husky fellow.
hombrada, *f.* manly action or gesture.
hombradía, *f.* manliness, bravery, courage.
hombre, *m.* 1. man. 2. boy (a male child). 3. omber ombre (card game). 4. player who plays against the rest in card games. 5. (coll.) husband, man. 6. (coll.) fellow, old chap, old boy, man. — **el hombre,** mankind; **el h. propone y Dios dispone,** man proposes and God disposes; **¡hombre!** well! what a surprise! **¡h. al agua!** man overboard!; **h. anuncio,** sandwich-board man; **h. bueno,** (law) arbitrater, referee; **h. de acción,** man of action; **h. de armas,** man-at-arms; **h. de asiento,** solid citizen. **h. de barba,** stern and upright man; **h. de bien,** honorable man, upright man; **h. de bigotes,** (coll.) stern and upright man; **h. de cabeza,** talented man, gifted man; **h. de ciencia,** man of science; **h. de confianza,** right-hand man; **h. de copete,** man of high rank, distinguished man; **h. de corazón,** brave, generous man; **h. de dinero,** man of means; **h. de distinción,** man of distinction; **h. de dos caras,** double-dealer, hypocrite, two-faced man; **h. de estado,** statesman; **h. de fuste,** bigwig, big shot; **h. de guerra,** soldier, man-at-arms; **h. de iglesia,** man of God; **h. de la calle,** man in the street; **h. de las cavernas,** caveman; **h. de letras,** scholar, man of letters; **h. del momento,** man of the hour; **h. del tiempo,** weatherman; **h. de mundo,** man of the world; **h. de mar,** seaman, sailor; **h. de negocios,** businessman; **h. de paja,** puppet, front man, straw man; **h. de palabra,** man of his word; **h. de pelo en pecho,** (coll.) bold and resolute man; **h. de puños,** (coll.) brave, strong man; **h. lobo,** werewolf; **h. orquesta,** one-man band; **h. público,** public figure **h. rana,** frogman; **pobre h.,** poor man, poor wretch; **ser el h. para,** to be suitable for, be the man for (a job); **ser muy h.,** to be very courageous; **ser otro h.,** to be a different man, be greatly changed.
hombrear, *i.v.* 1. to act the man (young boy). 2. (Mex.) to be mannish (a woman). 3. to try to be equal (to). 4. (Col., Mex.) to shoulder, push with the shoulder; to help, protect. *—r.v.* to try to be equal (to).
hombrecillo, ito, *m. dim, of.* **hombre,** little man, youth; **hombrecillo de agua y lana,** weakling, timid man.
hombrecillos, *m.* (*pl.*) (bot.) hops.
hombrera, *f.* (mil.) epaulet; pauldron, shoulder piece on on armor; yoke, shoulder reinforcement (on shirt, jacket, etc.).
hombrezuelo, *m. dim. of* **hombre,** petty little man.
hombría, *f.* manliness, courage. — **h. de bien,** honesty.
hombrillo, *m.* (tail.) yoke, shoulder reinforcement.
hombro, *m.* 1. shoulder. 2. (print.) shoulder; kern. — **a hombros,** on one's shoulders; **arrimar el h.,** to put one's shoulder to the wheel; to lend a hand, help; **echar algo al h.,** to make oneself responsible for something; **encogerse uno de hombros,** to shrug one's shoulders (to show indifference or ignorance); **h. a h.,** shoulder to shoulder; **mirar a uno por encima del h.,** (coll.) to look down on, look down one's nose at, despise.
hombrón, hombronazo, *m. aug. of* **hombre,** hefty or lusty man.
hombruno, na, *a.* manly; mannish (woman).
homenaje, *m.* 1. homage; allegiance, fealty. 2. homage, respect. 3. gift. — **en h. a,** in homage to; **rendir h. a,** to pay homage to; to pay tribute to; to swear allegiance to.
homenajear, *tr.v.* (Amer.) to pay homage to (someone) with a banquet or reception.
homeomorfo, fa, *a.* homeomorphous.
homeópata, *a.* (pharm., med.) homeopathic. *—m., f.* homeopath, homeopathist.
homeopatía, *f.* (med., pharm.) homeopathy.
homeopáticamente, *adv.* in small doses.
homeopático, ca, *a.* homeopathic.
homeotermo, ma, *a.* (zool.) homeothermal, homeothermic, homeothermous.
homeotípico, ca, *a.* (biol.) homeotypic.
homérico, ca, *a.* Homeric, Homerical, pertaining to Homer or his Greek epics. — **risa homérica,** Homeric laughter, unrestrained laughter.
Homero, *m.* Homer, Greek epic poet.
homicida, *a.* homicidal. *—m., f.* homicide, manslayer, murderer.
homicidio, *m.* homicide (act), murder; **h. culposo,** (law) voluntary manslaughter; **h. premeditato,** murder in the first degree.
homilética, *f.* (theol.) homiletics.
homilía, *f.* (rel.) homily.
homiliario, *m.* homiliarium.
homilista, *m., f.* homilist.
hominal, *a.* (zool.) hominid, hominoid; manlike.
hominicaco, *f.* (coll.) weakling, timid man.
homínido, da, *m.* (zool., biol.) hominid.
hominoideo, *a., m.* hominoid.
homocéntrico, ca, *a.* homocentric, concentric.
homocerco, ca, *a.* (ichth.) homocercal.
homocigosidad, *f.* (biol.) homozygosis.
homocigótico, ca, *a.* (biol.) homozygous.
homocigoto, *m.* (biol.) homozygote.
homocromático, ca, *a.* homochromatic, homochromous, consisting of one color.
homodino, *m.* (rad.) homodyne.
homoeroticismo, *m.* homoeroticism.
homoerótico, ca, *a.* homoerotic.
homófilo, la, *m., f.* homophile.
homofobia, *f.* homophobia.
homofóbico, ca, *a,* homophobic.
homófobo, ba, *m., f.* homophobe.
homofonía, *f.* (phonet., mus.) homophony.
homófono, na, *a.* 1. (phonet.) homophonous. 2. (mus.) homophonic. *—m.* homophone.
homogamia, *f.* (bot.) homogamy.
homógamo, ma, *a.* (bot.) homogamous.
homogéneamente, *adv.* homogeneously.
homogeneíce, homogeneicé, *ref.* **homo-**geneizar.
homogeneidad, *f.* homogeneity, similarity.
homogeneizacion, *f.* homogenization.
homogeneizador, *m.* homogenizer.
homogeneizar, (*ref. 53*) *tr.v.* to homogenize.
homogéneo, a, *a.* homogeneous, similar.
homógono, na, *a.* (bot.) homogonous.
homógrafo, fa, *a.* homographic. *—m.* homograph, a word spelled the same as another but having a different meaning.
homoinjerto, *m.* homograft, homotransplant.
homoiusiano, na, *m., f.* (theol.) Homoiusian.
homologación, *f.* (law) homologation; approval; confirmation.
homologar, (*ref. 51*) *tr.v.* (law) to homologate, approve, confirm, ratify.
homología, *f.* (biol., chem.) homology.
homólogo, ga, *a.* 1. (geom., chem.) homologous. 2. (log.) synonymous.
homolográfico, ca, *a.* homolographic, even, level, matched.
homologue, homologué, *ref.* **homologar.**
homomorfía, *f.* (biol., bot.) homomorphy, homomorphism.
homomorfo, fa, *a.* (biol., bot.) homomorphic, homomorphous.
homonimia, *f.* homonymy, similarity of spelling or pronunciation between words of different meanings.
homónimo, ma, *a.* homonymous; with the same name. *—m., f.* namesake. *—m.* homonym.
homopétalo, la, *a.* (bot.) homopetalous.
homoplastia, *f.* homograft, homoplasy.
homoplástico, ca, *a.* (biol.) homoplastic.
homopolar, *a.* (chem., elec.) homopolar.
homóptero, *a.* (ento.) homopterous. *—m., f.* (*pl.*) Homoptera.
homosexual, *a., m., f.* homosexual.
homosexualidad, *f.* homosexuality.
homósporo, ra, *a.* (bot.) homosporous.
homotalia, *f.* (bot.) homothallism.
homotaxia, *f.* (geol.) homotaxis.
homotáxico, ca, *a.* homotaxial.
homotecia, *f.* (geom.) homothety.
homotermo, ma, *a.* (physiol., zool.) homoiothermal, homoiothermic, homoiothermous.
homotético, ca, *a.* (geom.) homothetic.
homotrasplante, *m.* homograft, homotrans. plant.
homozigosis, *f.* (biol.) homozygosis.
homozigótico, ca, *a.* (biol.) homozygotic.
homúnculo, *m.* homunculus; (derog.) little runt, whippersnapper.
honcejo, *m.* (agr.) billhook, scythe.
honda, *f.* sling.
hondable, *a.* (mar.) fit for anchoring, soundable.
hondada, *f., var. of* **hondazo.**
hondamente, *adv.* deeply, profoundly.
hondarras, *f.* (*pl.*) dregs, lees, sediment.
hondazo, *m.* shot from a sling.
hondear, *tr.v.* 1. (mar.) to sound. 2. (mar.) to unload. *—i.v.* to sling, hurl with a sling.
hondero, *m.* slinger, soldier armed with a sling.
hondijo, *m.* sling.
hondillos, *m.* (*pl.*) pieces forming the crotch or seat of the trousers.
hondo, da, *a.* 1. deep; profound; low. 2. (fig.) intense (feeling). *—m.* 1. bottom (of hollow object). 2. depth, e.g. *tiene tres metros de h.,* it is three meters deep.
hondón, *m.* 1. bottom (of hollow object). 2. glen, dale, dell, hollow. 3. eye (of a needle). 4. foot piece (of stirrup).
hondonada, *f.* dell, dale, hollow; ravine, depression.
hondura, *f.* 1. depth, profundity. 2. (fig.) intensity. — **meterse en honduras,** to get into trouble.

Honduras, *f.* Honduras; **H. Británica,** British Honduras.
hondureño, ña, *a., m., f.* Honduran.
honestamente, *adv.* 1. decently, chastely, modestly. 2. decorously.
honestar, *tr.v.* 1. to honor, dignify. 2. to gloss over, excuse.
honestidad, *f.* 1. decency, modesty; chastity, purity. 2. decorum, propriety. 3. honesty, uprightness.
honesto, ta, *a.* 1. chaste, pure, modest. 2. decent, seemly, decorous. 3. honest, upright. 4. reasonable, just.
hongarina, *f.* farmer's sleeveless smock.
hongo, *m.* 1. (bot.) mushroom; toadstool; fungus; (*pl.*) fungi. 2. bowler, derby (hat). 3. (med.) fungus. — **h. atómico,** (Chile) mushroom cloud; — **h. marino,** (zool.) sea anemone; **h. yesquero,** (bot.) touchwood, tinder fungus, punk.
hongoso, sa, *a.* fungous.
honor, *m.* 1. honor, fame, glory, reputation. 2. purity, chastity. 3. (*pl.*) rank, dignity; post, position. 4. (*pl.*) honors (cards and points in bridge.) 5. (*pl.*) honors, marks of respect; honorary privileges, status or position. — **hacer los honores,** to do the honors.
honorabilidad, *f.* honor; good name, honesty.
honorable, *a.* honorable, reliable, honest.
honorablemente, *adv.* honorably.
honorario, ria, *a.* honorary. —*m.* (*pl.*) fees, honorariums.
honoríficamente, *adv.* honorarily; honorably.
honorífico, ca, *a.* honorific.
honra, *f.* 1. honor; fame; respect; purity, chastity. 2. (*pl.*) honors, obsequies, exequies. — **tener a mucha h.,** to be very proud of.
honradamente, *adv.* honestly, uprightly, honorably.
honradero, ra, *a., var. of* **honrador.**
honradez, *f.* honesty, integrity, uprightness, rectitude.
honrado, da, *past part. of* **honrar.** —*a.* honest, upright.
honrador, ra, *a.* honoring. —*m., f.* honorer.
honramiento, *m.* honoring.
honrar, *tr.v.* to honor, respect. —*r.v.* to be honored, feel it an honor (to do something).
honrilla, *f.* concern (for what people might say). — **por la negra h.,** out of concern for what people might say.
honrosamente, *adv.* honorably, with dignity.
honroso, sa, *a.* honorable; decent, decorous, proper.
hontanal, *a.* (pagan feast) in honor of springs and fountains. —*f.* feast in honor of a spring. —*m.* place abounding in springs.
hontanar, *m.* place abounding in springs.
hopa, *f.* tunic, cassock. —*interj.* (S. Amer.) hello!
hopalanda, *f.* smock, pinafore (formerly used by school children).
hopear, *i.v.* 1. to wag the tail. 2. (fig.) to run around, chase around.
hopeo, *m.* 1. wagging of the tail. 2. running around, romping around.
hoplita, *m.* (mil., hist.) hoplite, infantry soldier in ancient Greece.
hoploteca, *f.* collection of weapons on display.
hopo, *m.* tuft of hair; bushy tail; **seguir el h.,** to keep after someone; **sudar el h.,** to work very hard, sweat. —*interj.* get out of here! go away!
hoque, *m.* banquet given at the closing of a business deal.
hoquis, de h., (Mex.) free, gratis.
hora, *f.* 1. hour. 2. time, e.g. *es h. de comer,* it's time to eat. 3. time, hour, end, e.g. *le ha llegado su h.,* his time has come. 4. league (distance traveled in an hour). 5. (*pl.*) book of devotions. 6. (astron.) hour, fifteen degrees. — **a buena h.,** opportunely, in good time; (iron.) late; **a la h.,** on time, punctually; **a todas horas,** at all hours; **dar h.,** to fix or appoint a time; **dar la h.,** to strike (a clock); to hit the spot; to a knockout (a beautiful woman); **en h. buena,** fortunately, luckily; **en h. mala,** unfortunately; **h. astronómica** or **solar,** astronomical or solar time; **h. cero** or **H,** zero hour; **h. de cierre,** news deadline; **h. de comer,** mealtime; **h. del Pacífico,** Pacific standard time; **h. de mayor** or **máxima afluencia, h. punta,** (Sp.) **h. pico,** (Amer.) rush hour; **h. oficial,** standard time; **h. puente** or **sandwich,** free period; **horas canónicas,** (ecc.) the hours, the canonical hours; **horas de ocio,** leisure time; **horas de oficina,** office hours; **horas de trabajo,** working hours; **horas de visita,** visiting hours; **horas de vuelo,** flying time; **horas extras** or **extraordinarias,** overtime; **horas libres,** free time, spare time; **horas menores,** (ecc.) little hours (prime, tierce, sext, nones); **horas muertas,** wasted hours; **por h.,** by the hour; **¿qué h. es?** what time is it?; **tener las horas contadas,** to be about to die, be at death's door. —*adv.* now.
horaciano, na, *a.* Horatian, pertaining to Horace or his odes.
Horacio, *m.* Horace, Latin poet.
horadable, *a.* capable of being drilled, bored or perforated.
horadación, *f.* drilling, boring; perforation, piercing.
horadado, da, *past part. of* **horadar.** —*m.* silkworm's cocoon bored on both sides.
horadador, ra, *a.* boring, drilling, perforating. —*m., f.* borer, driller, burrower.
horadar, *tr.v.* to drill, bore; burrow; to pierce, perforate.
horado, *m.* hole; cave, cavern, grotto.
horambre, *m.* hole (where the counterpoise is fixed in the guide of a mill).
horario, ria, *a.* hourly; horary. —*m.* 1. timetable, schedule; **h. de atención al público,** business hours; **h. de visitas,** visiting hours. 2. hour hand (of clock). 3. clock.
horca, *f.* 1. gallows; gibbet. 2. yoke for hogs or dogs. 3. hayfork, pitchfork. 4. forked prop (for trees or vines); string (of onions, garlic, etc.). — **dejar h. y pendón,** to prune trees leaving two main branches on the trunk; **Horcas Caudinas,** (hist.) Caudine Forks; **pasar uno por las horcas caudinas,** to suffer great humiliation.
horcado, da, *a.* forked, fork-shaped.
horcadura, *f.* fork (of a tree or branch).
horcaja, *f.* (Chile) *var. of* **horcajadura.**
horcajadas, a h., astride, astraddle.
horcajadura, *f.* crotch (formed by two legs).
horcajo, *m.* yoke (for mules); fork (between rivers); junction (between two hills).
horcate, *m.* hames (of the harness).
horchata, *f.* orgeat, a beverage made from barley, almonds, etc.
horchatería, *f.* orgeat shop; milkshake parlor.
horchatero, ra, *m., f.* person who makes or sells orgeat.
horco, *m.* string (of onions or garlic).
horcón, *m.* 1. (agr.) pitchfork. 2. (agr.) forked prop (for trees or vines). 3. (Amer.) wooden column (supporting beams, etc.).
horconada, *f.* 1. blow given with a pitchfork. 2. pitchforkful.
horconadura, *f.* (agr.) pitchforks, collection of pitchforks.
horda, *f.* 1. horde, mob, throng. 2. a nomadic tribe, a wild army, e.g. *las hordas de Atila,* Attila's hordes.
hordeína, *f.* (biochem.) hordein.
hordiate, *m.* pearl barley; barley water.
horero, *m.* (Amer.) hour hand (of the clock).
horizontal, *a., f.* horizontal.
horizontalmente, *adv.* horizontally.
horizonte, *m.* horizon; (fig.) outlook, knowledge. — **ampliar los horizontes,** to broaden one's horizons, to gain experience; **h. artificial,** artificial or false horizon; **h. de la mar,** sensible horizon; **h. racional,** rational, geometrical or true horizon.
horma, *f.* 1. form, mold; last, shoe block, shoe tree; hat block. 2. drywall. 3. (Cuba, Peru) sugar loaf mold. — **hallar uno la h. de su zapato,** to find just what one was looking for; to meet one's match.
hormadoras, *f.* (*pl.*) (Col.) underskirt, petticoat.
hormaza, *f.* (mas.) dry stone wall.
hormazo, *m.* 1. blow given with a mold, block or last. 2. pile of loose stones.
hormero, *m.* shoe-block or last maker.
hormiga, *f.* 1. (ento.) ant. 2. (med.) itch. — **h. blanca,** (ento.) white ant; **h. león,** (ento.) ant lion; **h. obrera,** worker ant; **ser una h.,** to be thrifty or hardworking.
hormigante, *a.* irritating (causing an itch).
hormigo, *m.* 1. (cul.) porridge. 2. (min.) sifted ash for smelting quicksilver. 3. (*pl.*) semola, coarse grain. 4. (cul.) pudding made of bread crumbs, almonds and honey.
hormigón, *m.* 1. (mas.) concrete. 2. disease of plants. 3. disease of cattle. — **h. armado,** reinforced concrete; **h. hidráulico,** hydraulic lime mortar; **h. pretensado,** prestressed concrete.
hormigonera, *f.* (mas.) cement mixer; **h. por cargas,** batch mixer.
hormigoso, sa, *a.* ant-ridden, ant-eaten.
hormigueamiento, *m., var. of* **hormigueo.**
hormigueante, *a.* itching; tingling.
hormiguear, *i.v.* 1. to tingle, itch (as with pins and needles). 2. to swarm (like ants). 3. to abound.
hormigüela, *f. dim. of* **hormiga,** small ant.
hormigueo, *m.* 1. swarming. 2. tingling, crawling sensation, pins and needles. 3. shiver (from fear); sinking feeling (in the stomach).
hormiguero, *m.* 1. anthill. 2. (ornith.) wryneck (Jynx torquilla). 3. (*pl.*) piles of weeds burnt and used as compost. 4. swarm (of people).
hormiguilla, *f.* 1. itching, itch. 2. (coll.) worry, obsession; guilt feeling.
hormiguillar, *tr.v.* (Amer., min.) to mix (silver ore and salt).
hormiguillo, *m.* 1. (vet.) (form of) founder. 2. human chain (passing objects one to another). 3. (cul.) pudding made of bread crumbs, almonds and honey. 4. itch, itching. 5. (Amer.) amalgamation (of silver); reaction between silver ore and a mixture of ferrous oxide and copper sulfate (in silver processing).
hormiguita, *f. dim. of* **hormiga,** small ant.
hormilla, *f.* buttonmold.
hormón, *m.* (physiol.) hormone.
hormona, *f.* (physiol.) hormone; **h. vegetal,** plant hormone.
hormonal, *a.* (med.) pertaining to hormones, hormonal.
hormónico, ca, *a.* (physiol.) hormonal, hormonic.
hormonoterapia, *f.* hormone treatment.
hornabeque, *m.* (fort.) hornwork.
hornablenda, *f.* (min.) hornblende.
hornacero, *m.* furnace keeper or tender, keeper of a silversmith's furnace; crucible operator.
hornacho, *m.* opening, excavation (in a mine).
hornachuela, *f.* hovel, hut.
hornacina, *f.* (archit.) vaulted niche.

hornada, *f.* batch (of bread, bricks, etc. baked at the same time).
hornaguear, *tr.v.* to dig (soil) for coal.
hornagueo, *m.* digging for coal.
hornaguera, *f.* coal, pit coal, hard coal.
hornaguero, ra, *a.* 1. coal-bearing (soil). 2. loose, roomy, spacious.
hornaza, *f.* 1. silversmith's furnace. 2. (cer.) yellow glazing.
hornazo, *m.* 1. Easter cake decorated with eggs. 2. gift given in Easter to priest who has preached during Lent.
hornear, *i.v.* to be a baker. —*tr.v.* (Amer.) to bake.
hornecino, na, *a.* 1. bastard. 2. barren (fruit trees).
hornería, *f.* baking (trade), bakery.
hornero, ra, *m.* 1. baker. 2. (ornith., Amer.) baker bird (Furnarius rufus). —*f.* 1. baker. 2. oven floor.
hornija, *f.* brushwood, small wood for feeding oven fire.
hornilla, *f.* 1. heating hole, stew hole (of a coal stove or range), gas ring (of gas stove), plate (of electric stove). 2. nesting hole (in a dovecot).
hornillo, *m.* 1. portable furnace or stove. 2. (min.) blasthole. 3. (mil.) fougasse. — **h. de atanor,** athanor furnace.
hornito, *m.* (geol.) hornito.
horno, *m.* 1. furnace; kiln; oven. 2. (fig.) oven, very hot place. 3. cavity where bees lodge. — **alto h.,** blast furnace; **en la puerta del h. se quema el pan,** (Amer.) there's many a slip twixt the cup and the lip; **h. castellano,** low lead smelting furnace; **h. crematorio,** crematorium; **h. de cal,** limekiln; **h. de calcinación,** calcining kiln; **h. de carbón,** pile of wood for charring; **h. de copela,** cupeling furnace; **h. de cuba,** blast or shaft furnace; **h. de fundición,** smelting furnace; **h. de ladrillos,** brickkiln; **h. de microondas,** microwave oven; **h. de mufla,** (ceram.) muffle furnace; **h. de pudelar,** puddling furnace; **h. de regeneración,** regenerative furnace; **h. de reverbero,** reverberatory furnace; **no estar el h. para tortas** or **bollos,** to be untimely or inopportune.
horología, *f.* horology, the science of measuring time.
horológico, ca, *a.* horologic, horological.
horometría, *f.* horometry, the measuring of time.
horón, *m.* large round hamper or frail.
horondo, da, *a., var. of* **orondo,** swaggering, boastful; showy.
horópter, *m.* (opt.) horopter.
horoptérico, ca, *a.* (opt.) horopteric.
horóptero, *m.* (opt.) *var. of* **horópter.**
horóscopo, *m.* (astrol.) horoscope.
horqueta, *f.* 1. fork (of a slingshot angle formed by two branches); forked prop or stake. 2. (Arg.) sharp turn (in river); fork of land. 3. (Chile, Ven., Cuba) fork (in road). 4. (Chile) pitchfork.
horquetilla, *f.* 1. (C. Rica, P. Rico) weed. 2. (Cuba) split end (of hair).
horquilla, *f.* 1. fork, forked pole or prop. 2. hairpin. 3. fork (of a bicycle, holding front wheel). 4. hair condition which causes split ends. 5. crutch (forked rod moving pendulum in clock). 6. (archit.) crutch, fork. 7. (anat., surg.) fourchette.
horrar, *tr.v.* (Col., Salv., Mex.) to save. —*r.v.* (Amer.) to remain barren for a year (cattle).
horrendamente, *adv.* horribly, dreadfully, hideously.
horrendo, da, *a.* horrible, dreadful, hideous.
hórreo, *m.* Galician corncrib (raised on pillars for protection from mice and dampness).
horrero, *m.* granary keeper.
horribilidad, *f.* dreadfulness, hideousness, horribleness.
horribilísimo, ma, *a. super. of* **horrible,** very horrible.
horrible, *a.* horrible, hideous, awful.
horriblemente, *adv.* horribly.
horridez, *f.* hideousness, dreadfulness.
hórrido, da, *a.* horrible, hideous, dreadful.
horrífico, ca, *a.* horrible, hideous, dreadful.
horripilación, *f.* 1. fright, dread, horror; aversion, repugnance. 2. bristling of the hair. 3. (med.) horripilation.
horripilante, *a.* hair-raising, terrifying, horrifying.
horripilar, *tr.v.* to make (someone's) hair bristle or stand on end; to terrify, horrify. —*r.v.* to become terrified; to have one's hair stand on end.
horripilativo, va, *a.* causing horripilation, hair-raising, terrifying, frightening.
horrisonante, *a., var. of* **horrísono.**
horrísono, na, *a.* terrifying (said of a sound).
horro, rra, *a.* 1. freed, emancipated, enfranchised. 2. free, unencumbered. 3. temporarily barren or sterile (said of cattle). 4. poor quality (tobacco).
horror, *m.* horror, fear, dread; (fig.) atrocity; **¡qué h.!** how dreadful or ghastly!; **tener h. a,** to be repelled by, hate.
horrorizar, (*ref. 53*) *tr.v.* to horrify, terrify. —*r.v.* to be horrified or terrified.
horrorosamente, *adv.* horribly.
horroroso, sa, *a.* 1. horrible, dreadful, frightful; ugly, hideous, horrid. 2. (coll.) tremendous, terrible, e.g. *hace un calor horroroso,* the heat is terrible.
horrura, *f.* filth, dirt; refuse; (min.) scoria, dross, slag.
hortaliza, *f.* vegetable; (*pl.*) vegetables, garden produce.
hortatorio, ria, *a.* exhortatory, hortatory.
hortecillo, *m.* small garden or orchard.
hortelano, na, *a.* pertaining to orchards. —*m., f.* truck farmer, keeper of an orchard. —*m.* (ornith.) ortolan, European bunting (Emberiza hortulana).
hortense, *a.* pertaining to orchards or truck farms.
hortensia, *f.* (bot.) hydrangea (Hydrangea opuloides).
hortera, *f.* wooden bowl. —*m.* (in Madrid) a person who dresses in bad taste; a store clerk.
hortícola, *a.* horticultural.
horticultor, ra, *m., f.* horticulturist.
horticultura, *f.* horticulture.
horuelo, *m.* (Sp., reg.) meeting place for young people.
hosanna, *m.* (ecc.) hosanna, glory to God.
hosco, ca, *a.* 1. surly, sullen, gruff, bad-tempered, unsociable. 2. dark-skinned.
hoscoso, sa, *a.* bristly, rough.
hospedador, ra, *a.* providing lodging. —*m., f.* host, innkeeper.
hospedaje, *m.* lodging; cost of lodging.
hospedamiento, *m., var. of* **hospedaje.**
hospedante, *a.* providing lodging.
hospedar, *tr.v.* to lodge, put up, harbor, give lodging to. —*r.v.* to lodge (at), stop (at), put up (at).
hospedería, *f.* hospice; inn for travelers, hostel; inn.
hospedero, ra, *m., f.* host; innkeeper.
hospiciano, na, *m., f.* inmate of an orphan asylum or a poorhouse.
hospicio, *m.* hospice, hostel; poorhouse, orphan asylum.
hospital, *m.* hospital; **h. de sangre,** (mil.) field hospital, first aid post; **h. robado,** (coll.) empty bare house (without furniture or decoration).
hospitalariamente, *adv.* hospitably.
hospitalario, ria, *a.* 1. hospitable. 2. of or pertaining to Hospitalers. —*m., f.* (hist.) Hospitaler; hospitable person.
hospitalero, ra, *m., f.* 1. hospital manager, hospitaler. 2. (rare) charitable person.
hospitalice, hospitalicé, *ref.* **hospitalizar.**
hospitalidad, *f.* 1. hospitality. 2. period or stay in a hospital.
hospitalización, *f.* hospitalization.
hospitalizar, (*ref. 53*) *tr.v.* to hospitalize.
hospitalmente, *adv.* hospitably.
hosquedad, *f.* 1. surliness, sullenness, unfriendliness. 2. darkness (of skin).
hostal, *m.,* cheap hotel.
hostelería, *f.* hotel management; hotel industry.
hostelero, ra, *m., f.* landlord.
hostería, *f.* small hotel.
hostia, *f.* 1. sacrifice, sacrificial victim. 2. (ecc.) host, Eucharistic bread or wafer. 3. wafer, biscuit. —*interj.* (Arg.) dislike, bother. — **ser uno la h.,** (P. Rico) to be importunate, to annoy.
hostiario, *m.* (ecc.) wafer box; wafer mold.
hostiero, ra, *m., f.* wafer maker. —*m.* (ecc.) wafer box; wafer mold.
hostigador, ra, *a.* harassing; plaguing, pestering. —*m., f.* harasser; plaguer, pesterer.
hostigamiento, *m.* 1. harassing; pestering, plaguing. 2. whipping, lashing, scourging.
hostigar, (*ref. 51*) *tr.v.* 1. to lash, whip, scourge. 2. to harass, harry; to trouble, plague, pester. 3. (Chile, Guat., Mex.) to cloy.
hostigo, *m.* 1. lash, blow with a whip. 2. weather-beaten wall. 3. beating with wind or rain.
hostigoso, sa, *a.* (Amer.) annoying, irritating.
hostigue, hostigué, *ref.* **hostigar.**
hostil, *a.* hostile.
hostilice, hostilicé, *ref.* **hostilizar.**
hostilidad, *f.* hostility; (*pl.*) hostilities, warfare; **romper las hostilidades,** to start hostilities.
hostilizar, (*ref. 53*) *tr.v.* 1. to antagonize. 2. to harass, harry.
hotel, *m.* hotel; mansion, villa; **h. residencia,** guesthouse, boarding house.
hotelero, ra, *m., f.* hotel manager, hotelier.
hotentote, ta, *a., m., f.* Hottentot, the S. African tribe. —*m.* Hottentot (language).
hoto, *m.* confidence, hope, trust.
hovero, ra, *a.* peach-colored (said of animals, gen. of a horse).
hoy, *adv.* today; now, nowadays; at the present time; **de h. a mañana,** from one day to the next; **de h. en adelante,** from now on, from this day onward; **h. día,** nowadays; today; **h. por h.,** nowadays, today; **por h.,** for the time being.
hoya, *f.* 1. hole, pit; grave. 2. dale, glen. 3. (agr.) seedbed. 4. whirlpool (in a river). 5. (Amer.) river basin. — **plantar a h.,** to plant in holes; **tener un pie en la h.,** to have one foot in the grave.
hoyada, *f.* hollow, depression, dale.
hoyador, *m.* (Col., Cuba, Mex.) grub hoe.
hoyanca, *f.* (coll.) potter's field, common grave.
hoyar, *i.v.* (Amer.) to dig holes with a hoe.
hoyita, *f.* (Hond., Ven., Cuba) *var. of* **hoyuela.**
hoyito, *m.* 1. *dim. of* **hoyo,** small hole or pit. 2. (Amer.) pitching pennies or marbles. 3. (Amer.) dimple (gen. used in *pl.*).
hoyo, *m.* 1. hole, pit; grave, tomb. 2. pockmark.
hoyoso, sa, *a.* full of holes.
hoyuela, *f.* fonticulus, depression at front of the neck.
hoyuelo, *m.* 1. *dim. of* **hoyo,** small pit or hole. 2. dimple. 3. pitching pennies or marbles. 4. fonticulus, depression at front of the neck.
hoz, (*pl.* **hoces**), *f.* 1. sickle, scythe. 2. narrow pass, ravine. — **de h. y de coz,** without thinking, headlong; **h. de cerebelo,** (anat.) falx cerebelli; **h. de cerebro,** (anat.) falx cerebri; **h. y martillo,** hammer and sickle.

hozada, *f.* stroke with a sickle; sheaf of corn or grass cut with one stroke of the sickle.
hozadero, *m.* rooting place (of hogs and wild boar).
hozador, ra, *a.* rooting, nuzzling the ground (said of hogs and wild boar).
hozadura, *f.* rooting hole or mark (left by a rooting hog).
hozar, (*ref. 53*) *tr.v.* to root up, dig up with its snout (said of hogs).
huaca, *f.* (S. Amer.) *var. of* **guaca,** Indian burial grounds.
huacal, *m., var. of* **guacal.**
huacamole, *m.* (Mex.) *var. of* **guacamole.**
huacatay, *m.* (cul., Peru) a kind of mint.
huachache, *m.* (Peru, ento.) variety of white mosquito.
huaco, *m., var. of* **guaco.**
huaico, *m.* 1. (Peru) landslide. 2. (Peru, Chile) gorge, ravine, gulch.
huaino, *m.* (Peru) Indian dance.
huairo, *m.* (bot.) coral tree (Erythrina coralloides).
huairona, *f.* (Peru) limekiln.
huairuro, *m.* coral bean (fruit of coral tree).
hualcal, *m.* (Mex.) crate.
huamanga, *f.* (Peru) kind of alabaster (from Ayacucho).
huanchaco, *m.* (ornith.) Peruvian variety of linnet.
huango, *m.* pigtail, braid (of Ecuadorian Indian women).
huapango, *m.* one of the most popular folkloric dances, music and rhythms of Mexico.
huaquero, *m.* (Peru, archeol.) urn or pitcher found in ancient Indian burial grounds.
huaraca, *f.* (Col., Peru) sling.
huarache, *m., var. of* **guarache,** Mexican style of leather sandal.
huarahua, *f.* (Guat.) lie.
huaro, *m.* (Peru, Ecuad.) cable ferry.
huasca, *f.* (S. Amer.) *var. of* **guasca,** whip; bridle.
huaso, sa, *m., f., var. of* **guaso,** Chilean cowboy, horseman.
hube, hubo, *ref.* **haber.**
hubiera, hubiese, *ref.* **haber.**
hucha, *f.* large chest; money box, piggybank; (fig.) savings.
huchear, *i.v.* to shout, cry; to yelp; to call the dogs (in hunting).
hucho, *interj., var. of* **huchohó.**
huchohó, *interj.,* hunting call to recall birds.
huebra, *f.* 1. day's plowing by a yoke of oxen; pair of mules and plowman hired for day's work. 2. fallow, fallow land.
huebrero, *m.* plowman hired with a pair of mules; owner of a pair of mules leased to farmers by the day.
hueca, *f.* spiral groove in a spindle.
hueco, ca, *a.* 1. hollow (not solid). 2. empty. hollow, pompous (words, language). 3. empty, empty-headed, frivolous (person). 4. deep, resounding (voice). 5. fluffy, soft. —*m.* 1. hole, hollow. 2. lapse, interval, gap. 3. (coll.) vacancy. 4. (archit.) opening. — **h. del ascensor,** lift or elevator shaft.
huecograbado, *m.* photogravure.
huecú, (*pl.* **huecúes**), *m.* (Chile) bog, swamp.
huela, *ref.* oler.
huelán, *a.* (Chile) half-dry, half-ripe (said of timber and plants).
huélfago, *m.* (vet.) heaves.
huelga, *f.* 1. (labor) strike. 2. rest, repose, leisure; diversion, recreation, spree, merriment. 3. (agr.) fallow (season, period). 4. pleasant, attractive place. 5. (mec.) play, give, room (between two parts). — **ir a la h.,** to go on strike; **h. de brazos caídos,** sit-down strike; **h. de celo,** (Sp.) go-slow strike, work-to-rule; **h. de hambre,** hunger strike; **h. general,** general strike; **h. relámpago,** lightning strike; **h. salvaje,** (Sp.) wildcat strike; **h. patronal,** lockout.
huelgo, *m.* 1. breath. 2. room, space; (mec.) play. — **tomar h.,** to catch one's breath.
huelgo, huelgue, *ref.* **holgar.**
huelguista, *m.* striker.
huelguístico, ca, *a.* pertaining to a strike.
huella, *f.* 1. footprint, track; trace, mark, sign; print, imprint, impression. 2. treading. 3. tread (of stairs). — **h. dactilar** or **digital,** fingerprint; **seguir las huellas de,** to follow in the footsteps of, follow the example of.
huelle, huello, *ref.* **hollar.**
huello, *m.* 1. trail, trodden path. 2. tread, bottom of a hoof. 3. step, tread (of a horse).
huelo, *ref.* oler.
huemul, *m.* (zool., Arg., Chile) **guemal,** guemul.
hueñi, *m.* 1. (Chile) male Araucan Indian child; (Chile) houseboy; servant. 2. (Chile) darling (word of endearment among simple folk and peasants).
huequecito, *m. dim. of* **hueco,** small hole or space.
huerco, *m.* 1. disconsolate person, moaner. 2. (arch.) hell.
huérfago, *m., var. of* **huélfago.**
huerfanito, ta, *a., m., f. dim. of* **huerfano,** orphaned child.
huérfano, na, *a.* 1. orphan, orphaned. 2. (poet.) childless. 3. abandoned, unprotected, deserted. — **h. de,** devoid of, without. —*m., f.* orphan.
huero, ra, *a.* 1. addle, rotten, bad. 2. (fig.) addle, empty. 3. (Mex.) blonde, fair. — **salir h.,** to be a failure, flop.
huerta, *f.* garden, vegetable garden; orchard; cultivated land, irrigated land.
huertero, ra, *a.* (Chile) pertaining to gardens or orchards. —*m., f.* (Arg., Chile, Peru) one who tends or owns an orchard.
huertezuela, *f. dim. of* **huerta,** small vegetable garden or orchard.
huertezuelo, *m. dim. of* **huerto,** small fruit or vegetable garden.
huerto, *m.* fruit or vegetable garden, orchard.
huesa, *f.* grave, tomb.
huesarrón, *m. aug. of* **hueso,** large bone.
huesera, *f.* (Chile) ossuary, depository for bones of the dead.
huesezuelo, *m. dim. of* **hueso,** small bone.
huesillo, *m.* 1. *dim. of* **hueso,** small bone. 2. (S. Amer.) dried peach.
hueso, *m.* 1. bone. 2. stone, pit (of fruit). 3. unburnt core of limestone. 4. rotten job, hard job, drudgery. 5. piece of junk or rubbish. 6. (*pl.*) (coll.) hands. — **a otro perro con ese h.,** tell it to the marines; **calarse hasta los huesos,** to get soaked to the skin; **estar uno en los huesos,** (coll.) to be nothing but skin and bones; **h. coronal** or **frontal,** (anat.) frontal bone; **h. cuboides,** (anat.) cuboid bone; **h. cuneiforme,** (anat.) cuneiform bone; **h. de la alegría,** funny bone, crazy bone; **h. de santo,** roll of marzipan with various fillings; **h. de la suerte,** wishbone; **h. escafoides,** (anat.) scaphoid, scaphoid bone; **h. esfenoides,** (anat.) sphenoid bone; **h. etmoides,** (anat.) ethmoid bone; **h. hioides,** (anat.) hyoid bone; **h. innominado,** (anat.) innominate bone; **h. intermaxilar,** (anat.) intermaxillary bone, premaxilla; **h. maxilar,** (anat.) maxillary bone, maxilla; **h. occipital,** (anat.) occipital bone; **h. palomo,** (anat.) coccyx; **h. parietal,** (anat.) parietal bone; **h. sacro,** (anat.) sacrum; **h. temporal,** (anat.) temporal bone; **la sin hueso,** (coll.) tongue; **muy suelto de huesos,** as bold as brass; **no dejar a uno h. sano,** to pick someone to pieces, run someone down; **soltar la sin h.,** to break out into a stream of abuse; **tener los huesos molidos,** to be exhausted or fagged out.
huesoso, sa, *a.* bony, osseous.
huésped, da, *m., f.* 1. guest, lodger. 2. host, hostess; innkeeper. — **h. definitivo** or **primario,** (biol.) definitive host.
hueste, *f.* host, army; followers (gen. used in *pl.*), e.g. *las huestes de los hunos,* the armies of the Huns.
huesudo, da, *a.* bony, raw-boned; full of bones.
hueva, *f.* roe, fish eggs, spawn of fishes.
huevar, *i.v.* (Bol.) to begin to lay (said of fowls).
huevecito, huevecillo, *m. dim. of* **huevo,** small egg.
huevera, *f.* 1. egg seller. 2. (zool.) oviduct (of birds). 3. eggcup. 4. (*pl.*) (Peru) roe, fish roe or spawn.
huevería, *f.* egg shop, egg store.
huevero, ra, *m., f.* 1. egg dealer, egg seller. 2. eggcup.
huevo, *m.* 1. egg. 2. hollow wooden block for molding shoe soles. 3. darning ball or egg. 4. (vulg.) (*pl.*) balls (vulg.), testicles. — **a h.,** very cheaply, for a song; **h. de Colón** or **de Juanelo,** (coll.) something that looks difficult at first but turns out to be easy; **h. de fraile, (Mex.)** St. Ignatius bean; **h. de Pascua,** Easter egg; **h. duro,** hard-boiled egg; **h. escalfado,** poached egg; **h. frito,** fried egg; **h. huero,** addle egg; bad or rotten egg; **h. pasado por agua,** soft-boiled egg; **h. poché,** poached egg; **huevos rancheros,** ranch-style eggs; **huevos revueltos,** scrambled eggs; **h. tibio,** (Amer.) soft-boiled egg.
huevón, na, *a.* (derog., vulg., Amer.) stupid; lazy; sluggish; simple minded; coward.
hueytlatoani, *m.* (Mex.) king of the Aztecs.
hugonote, ta, *a., m., f.* Huguenot, French Protestant of the 16th and 17th centuries.
huida, *f.* 1. flight, escape. 2. widening splay (at the mouth of a hole). 3. hole, outlet. 4. (equit.) shying (of horses).
huidero, ra, *a.* fugitive. —*m.* 1. worker in quicksilver mines who makes holes for pit props. 2. cover, shelter (of game).
huidizo, za, *a.* fugitive; illusive, evasive.
huído, da, *a.* suspicious, fearful, distrustful.
huidor, ra, *a.* fleeing. —*m., f.* fleer.
huiliento, ta, *a.* (Chile) ragged, tattered, shabby.
huillín, *m.* (Chile) a species of otter (Lutra huidobria).
huilte, *m.* (Chile) edible stem of a brown alga (Durvillea utilis).
huincha, *f.* 1. (Bol., Chile, Peru) hair ribbon. 2. (Chile) measuring tape. 3. (Chile, Peru) starting wires (on a racecourse). 4. (Peru) (*pl.*) tape (at end of a race).
huinche, *m.* (Chile) winch, crane.
huinchero, *m.* (Chile) winch operator.
huipil, *m.* (Guat., Mex.) loosely fitting blouse; (Hond., Mex.) sleeveless blouse.
huir, (*ref. 48*) *i.v.* 1. to flee, run away, to escape. 2. to fly by (e.g. time). 3. to slip quickly away (from dock — a ship). —*r.v.* to flee, run away. —*tr.v.* to avoid, shun. — **¡huye!** run! escape!
huira, *f.* (Chile) bark rope or twine.
huiro, *m.* (bot., Peru) brown seaweed.
huisache, *m.* (Guat.) pettifogger, shyster-lawyer.
huistora, *f.* (Hond.) turtle.
huitrín, *m.* (Chile) string of corn cobs.
hulado, *m.* (Hond.) oilcloth.
hule, *m.* 1. oilcloth, oilskin. 2. rubber. 3. (coll.) operating (surgical) table.

hulear, *i.v.* (C. Amer.) to gather rubber (from trees).
hulero, *m.* (C. Amer.) rubber tapper, rubber gatherer.
hulla, *f.* pit-coal; **h. atracitosa,** anthracite; **h. blanca,** hydraulic or water power.
hullero, ra, *a.* pertaining to coal. —*f.* colliery, coal mine.
huma, *f.* (Chile) sweet corn cake.
humada, *f.* smoke signal, fire signal.
humadera, *f.* (Guat.) name given by country folk to smoking gear or accessories.
humanal, *a.* human.
humanamente, *adv.* humanly.
humanar, *tr.v.* to humanize, make human. —*r.v.* to become more human. — **humanarse a,** (Amer.) to condescend to.
humanice, humanice, *ref.* **humanizar.**
humanidad, *f.* 1. humanity, mankind; humaneness. 2. (coll.) corpulence, stoutness. 3. (*pl.*) humanities.
humanismo, *m.* humanism.
humanista, *m., f.* humanist.
humanístico, ca, *a.* humanistic.
humanitario, ria, *a.* humanitarian.
humanitarismo, *m.* humanitarianism.
humanizar, (*ref.* *53*) *tr.v.* to humanize, make human. —*r.v.* to soften.
humano, na, *a.* 1. human. 2. humane, kind, merciful. —*m.* human, human being, man.
humarada, *f., var. of* **humareda.**
humarazo, *m., var. of* **humazo.**
humareda, *f.* dense smoke, cloud of smoke.
humaza, *f., var. of* **humazo.**
humazga, *f.* hearth money, tax formerly paid for the use of chimneys.
humazo, *m.* dense smoke; fumigation (for killing rats or smoking out animals); **dar h. a,** to smoke out.
humeante, *a.* smoking; steaming; fuming.
humear, *i.v.* 1. to smoke; to steam. 2. to smolder (enmity); to remain (traces of love; a quarrel). 3. to become arrogant or proud. —*tr.v.* (Amer.) to fumigate, smoke.
humectación, *f.* dampening, moistening, humidifying.
humectante, *a.* humectant, moistening; (med.) humectant, diluent. —*m.* 1. (chem.) humectant. 2. (med.) humectant, diluent.
humectar, *tr.v.* (med.) to moisten, to wet.
humectativo, va, *a.* moistening, humectant.
humedad, *f.* dampness, moisture, humidity; **h. absoluta,** (meteorol.) absolute humidity; **h. relativa,** (meteorol.) relative humidity.
humedal, *m.* moist or humid soil.
humedecedor, *m.* humidifier.
humedecer, (*ref.* *45*) *tr.v.* to dampen, moisten, humidify.
humedecimiento, *m.* humidification.
humedezco, humedezca, *ref.* **humedecer.**
húmedo, da, *a.* humid; moist, damp, wet.
humera, (with aspirate **h**) *f.* (coll.) drunkenness.
humeral, *a.* (anat.) humeral. —*m.* (ecc.) humeral veil.
húmero, *m.* (zool.) humerus (long bone of upper arm).
humero, *m.* 1. smokestack, chimney. 2. (Col.) dense smoke. 3. room where fish or meat is cured and smoked.
húmico, ca, *a.* (chem.) humic.
húmido, da, *a.* (poet.) humid, damp, moist.
humifuso, sa, *a.* (bot.) humifuse.
humildad, *f.* humility; humbleness, meekness; humbleness, lowliness (of birth); **h. de garabato,** affected humbleness.
humilde, *a.* humble, meek; lowly, e.g. *de humilde origen,* of humble birth or origin.
humildemente, *adv.* humbly.
humillación, *f.* humiliation; humbling.
humilladero, *m.* roadside chapel or shrine.
humillador, ra, *a.* humiliating. —*m., f.* humiliator.
humillante, *a.* humiliating; degrading.
humillar, *tr.v.* 1. to humble; to humiliate. 2. to bow (the head), bend (the knee). —*r.v.* 1. to humble oneself; to grovel. 2. to bend its head (the bull).
humillo, *m.* 1. (vet.) illness in suckling pigs (caused by deficiencies in sow's milk). 2. (*pl.*) pride, airs, vanity.
humina, *f.* (chem.) humin.
humiria, *f.* (bot.) humiria.
humita, *f.* 1. (Amer.) sweet tamale (corn cake). 2. (min.) humite.
humitero, ra, *m., f.* (Arg., Chile, Peru) tamale maker or vendor.
humo, *m.* 1. smoke, steam, vapor. 2. (*pl.*) homes, houses (collectively in a town). 3. (*pl.*) airs, conceit, pride. — **a h. de pajas,** lightly, without reflexion; **bajarle a uno los humos,** to take someone down a peg; **donde fuego se hace h. sale,** where there is smoke there is fire; **hacer h. a,** to receive coldly; **hacer h.,** to smoke (e.g. a fire); **hacerse h.,** to vanish into thin air; **pesar el h.,** to split hairs.
humor, *m.* 1. humor, fluid. 2. humor, wit. 3. mood, temper, humor. — **estar de buen** or **mal h.,** to be in a good or bad mood or temper; **h. ácueo,** (anat.) aqueous humor; **h. vítreo,** (anat.) vitreous humor; **seguirle a uno el h.,** to humor someone.
humorada, *f.* 1. fancy, whim or mood. 2. pleasant joke; witty remark.
humorado, da, *a.* **bien h.,** good-humored or tempered; **mal h.,** bad-humored or tempered.
humoral, *a.* (physiol.) humoral, pertaining to body fluids.
humorismo, *m.* 1. humor, wit (esp. in literary style).
humorista, *a.* 1. humorous. 2. (med.) humoralistic. —*m., f.* 1. humorist (writer). 2. (med.) humoralist.
humorísticamente, *adv.* humorously.
humorístico, ca, *a.* humorous.
humorosidad, *f.* abundance of body fluid.
humoroso, sa, *a.* humorous, full of humor, watery.
humosidad, *f.* smokiness.
humoso, sa, *a.* smoky; smoking, fumy.
humus, *m.* (agr.) humus, organic part of soil.
hunco, *m.* (Bol.) woolen cape.
hundible, *a.* sinkable.
hundido, da, *past part. of* **hundir.** —*a.* deep-set (e.g. the eyes, cheeks, etc.).
hundimiento, *m.* 1. sinking. 2. collapse, downfall; destruction. 3. cave-in, sag.
hundir, *tr.v.* 1. to sink; submerge. 2. to press in (button, bell, etc.); to plunge (sword into). 3. to overcome, overwhelm, defeat. 4. to destroy, ruin. —*r.v.* 1. to sink. 2. to collapse, fall. 3. to vanish, disappear.
húngaro, ra, *a., m., f.* Hungarian. —*m.* Hungarian (language).
Hungría, *f.* Hungary.
huno, na, *a.* (hist.) Hunnish. —*m., f.* Hun.
hupe, *f.* punk, touchwood.
hura, *f.* carbuncle, small tumor on the head. 2. small hole, burrow.
huracán, *m.* hurricane; (Amer.) cyclone; (coll.) a hyper-active person, a whirlwind of energy.
huracanado, da, *a.* hurricane-like (said of the weather).
huracanarse, *r v.* to blow into a hurricane, blow like a hurricane.
huraco, *m.* hole.
hurañamente, *adv.* unsociably; reticently.
hurañia, *f.* unsociability; reticence.
huraño, ña, *a.* unsociable; reticent, taciturn.
hureque, *m.* (Col.) hole.
hurera, *f.* hole; ferret hole or burrow.
hurgador, ra, *a.* poking, rummaging. —*m.* poker, rummager.
hurgamiento, *m.* poking; stirring up, rummaging.
hurgar, (*ref.* *51*) *tr.v.* to poke, rummage; to stir up, agitate, e.g. *h. la lumbre,* to poke or stir the fire.
hurgón, *m.* 1. poker, coal-rake, fire-rake. 2. (coll.) sword.
hurgonada, *f.* 1. poking. 2. (coll.) thrust, jab.
hurgonazo, *m.* blow with a poker; (fig.) thrust.
hurgonear, *tr.v.* 1. to poke (the fire). 2. to make a thrust, jab (with a sword).
hurgonero, *m.* poker (instrument).
hurgue, hurgué, *ref.* **hurgar.**
hurguete, *m.* (Arg., Urug., Chile) prier, snooper.
hurguetear, *tr.v.* (Amer.) to poke.
hurguillas, *m., f.* busybody.
hurí, (*pl.* **huríes**), *f.* houri; beautiful, seductive woman.
hurón, na, *a.* shy, reserved; unsociable. —*m., f.* 1. shy or unsociable person. 2. prier, snooper. —*m.* (zool.) ferret.
huronear, *i.v.* 1. to ferret, go ferreting. 2. to pry, snoop, ferret out.
huronera, *f.* 1. ferret-hole or burrow. 2. hideout, lurking place.
huronero, *m.* keeper of ferrets, ferret-keeper.
¡hurra! *interj.* hurrah!
hurraca, *f.* (ornith.) magpie.
hurtadillas, a h., furtively, on the sly, stealthily.
hurtadineros, *m.* money box, piggy bank.
hurtador, ra, *a.* stealing, thieving. —*m., f.* thief.
hurtagua, *f.* watering pot.
hurtar, *tr.v.* 1. to steal; to cheat (in weights or measures), give short weight or measure; to plagiarize, steal. 2. to withdraw, deflect. 3. to wash away land on the shore or a riverbank. 4. to turn away (the eyes). —*r.v.* to hide, withdraw.
hurto, *m.* theft, robbery; stealing; larceny; stolen object; **h. menor,** (law) petty larceny; **h. sencillo,** (law) simple larceny.
husada, *f.* spindleful (of yarn).
húsar, *m.* (mil.) hussar.
husera, *f.* (bot.) spindle tree.
husero, *m.* straight antler (of a deer).
husillo, *m.* 1. screw, worm (used in presses, etc.). 2. drainage ditch or canal. — **escalera de h.,** (archit.) spiral staircase; **h. transportador,** Archimedean screw.
husita, *m., f.* Hussite, follower of John Huss, religious reformer of the 15th century.
husma, *f.* scenting; prying, snooping; **andar uno a la h.,** to be snooping or investigating.
husmeador, ra, *a.* prying, snooping (coll.). —*m., f.* prier, snooper.
husmear, *tr.v.* to smell out, scent; to spy on, snoop on (coll.); to peek into, pry into. —*i.v.* 1. to nose about, snoop around; to look. 2. to begin to smell bad or high (said of meat).
husmeo, *m.* scenting; prying, snooping.
husmo, *m.* high smell (of meat); **andarse al h.,** (coll.) to go snooping (coll.) or investigating; **estar al h.,** to be on the lookout.
huso, *m.* 1. spindle; bobbin; drum (of a windlass). 2. (her.) large narrow lozenge. — **h. esférico,** surface of a spherical wedge; **h., horario,** time zone.
huta, *f.* hunter's blind, hut.
hutía, *f.* (zool.) hutia
¡huy! *interj.* ouch! (of pain); wow! (of wonder or surprise).
huya, huyendo, huyera, huyese, huyó, *ref.* **huir.**

I

I, *f.* i, ninth letter of the Spanish alphabet; i griega, wye, y.
I *sym. of* **yodo,** iodine (I).
ib, *m.* (Mex.) small kidney bean.
Iberia, *f.* Iberia, ancient and poetic name for Spain (as Portugal's is Lusitania).
ibérico, ca, *a.* Iberian, of or pertaining to Iberia (ancient name for Spain); Spanish; **la península ibérica,** the Iberian Peninsula (comprising Spain and Portugal).
iberio, ria, *a., var. of* **ibérico.**
ibero, ra, *a, m., f., var. of* **ibérico.**
Iberoamérica, *f.* Latin America, Ibero-America.
iberoamericano, na, *a., m., f.* Ibero-American, Latin American.
ibice, *m.* (zool.) ibex, kind of wild goat.
ibicenco, ca, *a.* of or pertaining to Ibiza or Iviza, one of the Islands of the Balearic group (Sp.) —*m., f.* native or inhabitant of Iviza.
ibídem, *adv.* (Lat.) ibidem, in the same place.
ibis, *f.* (ornith.) ibis, a long billed wading bird.
ibiyaú, *m.* an Argentine night bird.
ibón, *m.* lake or basin on the slopes of the Pyrenees.
ibsenismo, *m.* Ibsenism, liking for or adherence to the literary style or social concepts of Henrik Ibsen, the Norwegian playwright.
icaco, *m.* (bot.) icaco, icaco plum, the cocoa plum.
icáreo, a, *a.* 1. Icarian, characteristic of Icarus; daring, foolhardy. 2. Icarian, pertaining to the Greek isle of Icaria.
icario, ria, *a., var. of* **icáreo.**
icaro, *m.* (myth.) Icarus, who attempted to fly but fell and drowned in the Aegean Sea when the sun melted the wax with which his wings had been attached; symbol of man's first flight.
icástico, ca, *a.* natural, plain, unadorned.
ice, icé, *ref.* **izar.**
iceberg, *m.* (geol.) iceberg.
ichal, *m.* field of Andean grass or icho.
icho, *m.* (bot.) icho, a type of Andean grass.
icipo, *m.* (Arg.) a creeping plant used for thatching.
icneumón, *m.* 1. (zool.) mongoose. 2. (ento.) ichneumon fly, ichneumon.
icneumónidos, *m.* (*pl.*) (ento.) Ichneumonidae.
icografía, *f.* (archit.) ichnography; plan, plot, geometric sketch.
icnográfico, ca, *a.* (archit.) ichnographical.
icónico, ca, *a.* iconic, of or pertaining to an icon.
icono, *m.* (art., rel.) icon, a Byzantine style religious representation, usually associated with the Eastern Orthodox Church.
iconoclasta, *a.* iconoclastic, iconoclastical. —*m., f.* iconoclast, one who rejects traditional values.
iconógeno, *m.* (photog.) developer.
iconografía, *f.* iconography, description of ancient or religious works of art; a collection of portraits of a famous person.
iconográfico, ca, *a.* iconographic, iconographical.
iconólatra, *a.* iconolatrous. —*m., f.* iconolater, worshiper of images or icons.
iconolatría, *f.* iconolatry, the worship of images or icons.
iconología, *f.* iconology, science or lore of icons.
iconómaco, ca, *a.* iconoclastic. —*m., f.* iconoclast.
iconoscopio, *m.* (tel.) iconoscope.
iconostasio, *m.* (ecc.) iconostasis, altar screen (in the Eastern Orthodox Church).
icor, *m.* (med.) ichor, thin acrid fluid discharge from an ulcer or wound.
icoroso, sa, *a.* (med.) ichorous, serous.
icosaedro, *m.* (geom.) icosahedron.
icterícia, *f.* (med.) jaundice, icterus.
ictericiado, da, *a.* (med.) jaundiced, icterical. —*m., f.* person with jaundice.
ictérico, ca, *a.* (med.) icteric, suffering from jaundice. —*m., f.* (med.) person suffering from jaundice.
icterodes, *a.* (med.) yellow fever.
íctico, ca, *a.* ichthyic, pertaining to or characteristic of fish.
ictíneo, *m.* 1. submarine vessel. 2. **I.,** name of the submarine designed by Narciso Monturiol, Spanish inventor, in 1859.
Ictino, *m.* (hist.) Ictinus, Greek architect, chief designer of the Parthenon.
ictiofagia, *f.* ichthyophagy, nutrition based on a diet of fish.
ictiófago, ga, *a.* ichthyophagous, fish-eating. —*m., f.* ichthyophagist.
ictioideo, a, *a.* ichthyoid. —*m.* (zool.) ichthyoid.
ictiol, *m.* (pharm.) ichthyol.
ictiología, *f.* ichthyology, the branch of zoology dealing with the study of fishes.
ictiológico, ca, *a.* ichthyologic, ichthyological.
ictiólogo, *m.* ichthyologist.
ictiornis, *m.* (paleon.) ichthyornis.
ictiosauro, *m.* ichthyosaurus, ichthyosaur, a species of prehistoric marine reptiles.
ictiosis, *f.* (med.) ichthyosis.
ictus, *m.* (med.) ictus, stroke, attack.
ida, *f.* 1. going, departure; trip. 2. impetuosity, rash act. 3. (fenc.) sally, initial thrust. 4. track, trail (left by wild game). — **billete de i. y vuelta,** round trip ticket; **idas y venidas,** comings and goings; **en dos idas y venidas,** in a jiffy.
idea, *f.* 1. idea. 2. image, picture. 3. concept, idea, notion, e.g. *la justicia es i. innata del hombre,* justice is an innate concept in man. 4. ideas, imagination, e.g. *es hombre de ideas,* he's a man of ideas; *cambiar de i.,* to change one's mind; **i. fija,** (psyc.) idée fixe, fixed idea; **i. brillante,** (coll.) brain storm, brilliant idea; **ideas afines,** associated ideas; **no puedo hacerme a la i. de que,** I cannot conceive that.
ideación, *f.* (philos.) ideation, the formulation of ideas.
ideal, *a., m.* ideal; **lo i.,** (coll.) the ideal, the ideal thing.
idealice, idealicé, *ref.* **idealizar.**
idealidad, *f.* ideality, ideal.
idealismo, *m.* idealism.
idealista, *a.* idealistic. —*m., f.* idealist.
idealización, *f.* idealization.
idealizador, ra, *a.* idealizing.
idealizar, (*ref. 53*) *tr.v.* to idealize.
idealmente, *adv.* 1. ideally, perfectly. 2. mentally, intellectually, ideally.
idear, *tr.v.* 1. to plan, think up; meditate. 2. to imagine, conceive; to invent, contrive.
ideario, *m.* ideas, thought, philosophy, body of principles, ideology.
ideático, ca, *a.* capricious, subject to sudden fancies, whimsical.
idem, *pron., adv.* idem, the same, ditto.
idénticamente, *adv.* identically.
idéntico, ca, *a.* identical, the same, identic; congenerous.
identidad, *f.* identity; identicalness, sameness; (law) identity; **cédula de i.,** identity card; **documentos de i.;** identity papers; **placa de i.,** identity disc or tag.
identificable, *a.* identifiable.
identificación, *f.* identification.
identificar, (*ref. 50*) *tr.v.* to identify. —*r.v.* to be identified or associated inseparably; **identificarse con,** to identify oneself with.
identifique, identifiqué, *ref.* **identificar.**
ideografía, *f.* ideography, the representation of ideas by graphic symbols.
ideográfico, ca, *a.* ideographic, ideographical.
ideograma, *m.* ideogram, a symbol representing an idea.
ideología, *f.* ideology, body of ideas on which a particular doctrine or system is based.
ideológico, ca, *a.* ideological.
ideólogo, ga, *m., f.* 1. ideologist. 2. dreamer.
idílico, ca, *a.* idyllic.
idilio, *m.* idyl, romance; pastoral poem; (mus.) a simple, pastoral composition.
idioblasto, *m.* (biol., bot.) idioblast.
idioeléctrico, ca, *a.* (phys.) idioelectric, idioelectrical.
idioma, *m.* language, tongue.
idiomático, ca, *a.* idiomatic, characteristic of a particular language; **expresión idiomática,** idiomatic expression, idiom.
idiomorfismo, *m.* (min.) idiomorphism.
idiomorfo, fa, *a.* (min.) idiomorphic.
idiopatía, *f.* (med.) idiopathy.
idiopático, ca, *a.* (med.) idiopathic.
idioplasma, *m.* (biol.) idioplasm.
idioplasmático, ca, *a.* (biol.) idioplasmatic.
idiosincrasia, *f.* idiosyncrasy; peculiarity.
idiosincrásico, ca, *a.* idiosyncratic, idiosyncratical.
idiota, *a.* idiotic, foolish, nonsensical. —*m., f.* idiot, fool.
idiotez, (*pl.* **idioteces**), *f.* idiocy, foolishness; idiotic remark, stupidity.
idiotismo, *m.* 1. idiocy, folly, ignorance. 2. (gram.) idiom, idiomatic expression.
ido, da, *past part. of* **ir.** —*a.* 1. (coll.) absent-minded. 2. (coll.) crazy, screwy, loony, mad.
idocrasa, *f.* (min.) idocrase.
idólatra, *a.* idolatrous, heathen, pagan; idolizing, adoring. —*m., f.* idolizer, idolater, (coll.) admirer, ardent follower.
idolatradamente, *adv.* idolatrously, extremely fond or admiring.
idolatrar, *tr.v.* to idolize, adore, love with passion, e.g. *te idolatro,* I adore you.

idolatría, *f.* idolatry; adoration, idolizing; (coll.) passion, e.g. *tengo i. por la música,* I have a passion for music.
idolátrico, ca, *a.* idolatrous, heathenish, paganish.
ídolo, *m* 1. idol, image; false deity. 2. (coll.) ideal, most admired or loved person; **í. del cine,** movie idol, film star.
idolología, *f.* branch of learning dealing with idols.
idolopeya, *f.* (rhet.) rhetorical device consisting of putting words into the mouth of a dead person.
Idomeneo, *m.* (myth.) Idomeneus, king of Crete who led his subjects against Troy in the Trojan War.
idoneidad, *f.* suitability, aptness, fitness, capability.
idóneo, nea, *a.* suitable, fit, apt, proper.
idos, *m.* (*pl.*) *var. of* **idus.**
idumeo, a, *a., m., f.* (hist.) Idumaean. —*f.* **I.,** Idumaea, Idumea, Edom (ancient kingdom between the Dead Sea and the Gulf of Aqaba).
Idún, *f.* (myth.) Idun, goddess of youth and springtime in the Norse legends.
idus, *m.* (*pl.*) (hist.) ides (special days in the calendar of the ancient Romans); **los i. de marzo,** the ides of March (when Julius Caesar was assassinated).
Ificles, *m.* (myth.) Iphicles, the twin brother of Hercules.
Ifigenia, *f.* (myth.) Iphigenia, the daughter of Clytemnestra and Agamemnon; **I. en Aúlida,** Iphigenia in Aulis; **I. en Táurida,** Iphigenia in Tauris.
Igl. *abbrev. of* **Iglesia,** Church.
iglesia, *f.* church; temple; the ecclesiastical state, the clergy; **acogerse a la i.,** to enter the church (become a priest); **cumplir con la i.,** to take holy communion at Easter; **entrar en la i.,** to enter the church; **i. anglicana,** the Church of England; **i. catedral,** cathedral church; **i. conventual,** convent church; **i. fría,** church granting asylum; **i. militante,** church militant; **i. oriental,** Eastern church; **i. griega ortodoxa,** Greek Orthodox Church; **i. triunfante,** church triumphant; **ir a la i.,** to go to church; **llevar a una mujer a la i.,** to lead a woman to the altar (marry her).
iglú, *m.* igloo, ice hut, Eskimo house.
ignaciano, na, *a.* (rel.) Ignatian, of or pertaining to Ignatius of Loyola.
ignaro, ra, *a.* ignorant, unlearned.
ignavia, *f.* laziness, sloth, idleness; carelessness.
ígneo, a, *a.* igneous, pertaining to or produced by fire; fiery.
ignición, *f.* ignition; the act of setting or catching on fire.
ignícola, *a.* fire-worshiping. —*m.* worshiper of fire.
ignífero, ra, *a.* (poet.) igniferous, firebearing.
ignifugar, (*ref. 51*) *tr.v.* to fireproof.
ignífugo, ga, *a.* fireproof.
ignipotente, *a.* (poet.) ignipotent, having power over fire.
igniscencia, *f.* incandescence.
ignito, ta, *a.* ignited, red-hot; inflamed, afire.
ignitrón, *m.* (elec.) ignitron.
ignívomo, ma, *a.* (poet.) emitting or vomiting fire.
ignografía, *f.* (archit.) ichnography, tracing out, scale drawing of the ground plan of a building.
ignominia, *f.* ignominy, disgrace, infamy.
ignominiosamente, *adv.* ignominiously, disgracefully.
ignominioso, sa, *a.* ignominious, disgraceful, opprobrious.
ignorado, da, *past part. of* **ignorar. —***a.* ignored, unknown, obscure, e.g. *ella vive ignorada,* she lives in obscurity.
ignorancia, *f.* 1. ignorance, lack of education. 2. unawareness. — **i. supina,** ignorance from negligence, crass ignorance.
ignorante, *a.* 1. ignorant, unlearned; stupid. 2. uninformed, unaware. —*m., f.* ignorant person, ignoramus, (fig.) uncouth, ill-bred person.
ignorantemente, *adv.* ignorantly.
ignorantismo, *m.* ignorantism, obscurantism.
ignorantista, *m., f.* obscurantist.
ignorar, *tr.v.* to be ignorant of, unaware of, uninformed about, not to know.
ignoto, ta, *a.* unknown, undiscovered.
igorrote, *m., f.* (Phil. I.) Igorot, member of a savage tribe of the island of Luzon.
igual, *a.* 1. equal; same. 2. similar; alike. 3. level, flat. 4. like it, e.g. *nunca he visto cosa i.,* I have never seen anything like it. 5. even, consistent, equable (temperament). 6. even, constant (temperature). — **i. a,** equal to; **todo le es i.,** it's all the same to him. —*m.* 1. equal. 2. (math.) equal sign, equals sign; **al i. que,** just as, like; **igual de joven,** as young as ever; **i. que,** the same as, e.g. *haremos i. que ayer,* we'll do the same as yesterday; **sin i.,** unparalleled, peerless, matchless.
iguala, *f.* 1. equalization; equating. 2. agreement, contract. 3. fee, payment. 4. (bldg.) level.
igualación, *f.* 1. equalization; leveling. 2. (fig.) agreement; stipulation. 3. (math.) equating. 4. (carp.) counter-gauge.
igualado, da, *past part, of* **igualar. —***a.* 1. with even plumage (birds). 2. (Guat., Mex.) upstart. — **estar i. con,** to receive a fixed sum or set fee from.
igualador, ra, *a.* equalizing, leveling. —*m., f.* equalizer, leveler, evener.
igualamiento, *m.* equalizing, equalization, leveling.
igualar, *tr.v.* 1. to make equal, equalize; to even up; to mate, match; to cut to the same length. 2. to equate, consider the same or equal. 3. to level, smooth off, flatten, make flat. —*i.v.* to equal, be equal; **i. a** or **con,** ito be equal to. —*r.v.* 1. to become equal; to be equal. 2. to come to an agreement; **igualarse a** or **con,** to be equal to.
igualatorio, *m.* private medical care scheme or contract.
igualdad, *f.* 1. equality; sameness, uniformity. 2. evenness, levelness, smoothness (of land). 3. equableness, evenness (of temper). 4. likeness, similarity. — **en i. de condiciones,** on an equal footing; **i. ante la ley,** equality before the law; **i. racial,** racial equality; **i. de ánimo,** stable, even disposition, equanimity.
igualitario, a, *a., m., f.* equalitarian, egalitarian.
igualitarismo, *m.* egalitarianism, equalitarianism.
igualmente, *adv.* 1. equally. 2. likewise, also. 3. (coll.) the same to you, e.g. *"Felices Pascuas", "Igualmente",* "Merry Christmas", "The same to you".
iguana, *f.* (zool.) iguana.
iguánido, *a.* (zool.) iguanid, iguanian. —*m.* (*pl.*) Iguanidae.
iguanodonte, *m.* (zool.) iguanodon.
igüedo, *m.* (zool.) buck, he-goat.
ijada, *f.* 1. flank (of an animal); loin. 2. stitch, pain in the side. — **tener su i.,** to have a weak point or a vulnerable spot.
ijadear, *i.v.* to pant, palpitate.
ijar, *m., var. of* **ijada,** flank of an animal.
ijujú, (*pl.* **ijujúes**), *m.* cry of joy.
ilación, *f.* illation; connection, inference.
ilapso, *m.* ecstatic trance, trance.
ilativo, va, *a.* illative, inferential.
ilécebra, *f.* cajolery, flattery.
ilegal, *a.* illegal, unlawful.
ilegalidad, *f.* illegality, unlawfulness.
ilegalmente, *adv.* illegally, unlawfully.
ilegibilidad, *f.* illegibility.
ilegible, *a.* illegible.
ilegítimamente, *adv.* illegitimately, illegally.
ilegitimar, *tr.v.* to make or prove illegitimate.
ilegitimidad, *f.* illegitimacy.
ilegítimo, ma, *a.* illegitimate; unlawful, illegal.
ileítis, *f.* (med.) ileitis.
íleo, *m.* (med.) ileus, colic.
ileocecal, *a.* (anat.) ileocaecal.
íleon, *m.* (anat.) ileum.
ileso, sa, *a.* unhurt, uninjured.
iletrado, da, *a.* uncultured, illiterate, ignorant. —*m., f.* illiterate, ignorant person.
ilíaco, ca, *a.* (anat.) iliac. —*m.* (anat.) ilium, iliac bone.
ilíaco, ca, *a.* Ilian, pertaining to Ilium, Trojan.
Ilíada, *f.* Iliad' Homer's Greek epic poem.
iliberal, *a.* illiberal.
ilicíneo, a, *a.* (bot.) ilicineous, ilicaceous. *f.* (*pl.*) Ilicaceae.
ilícitamente, *adv.* illicitly, unlawfully.
ilícito, ta, *a.* illicit, unlawful; immoral.
ilicitud, *f.* illicitness, unlawfulness.
ilidiable, *a.* (taur.) unfightable, unsuitable for fighting.
iliense, *a., m., f.* Ilian, Trojan.
ilimitable, *a.* illimitable.
ilimitadamente, *adv.* unlimitedly, limitlessly, boundlessly.
ilimitado, da, *a.* unlimited, boundless, limitless, unrestricted, unconditional.
ilinio, *m.* (chem.) illinium.
ilion, *m.* (anat.) ilium.
Ilión, *m.* (hist.) Ilion, Ilium, Troy.
ilíquido, da, *a.* unliquidated (debts, accounts).
Iliria, *f.* (hist.) Illyria, ancient name of a Balkan region along the coast of the Adriatic Sea.
ilita, *f.* (min.) illite.
iliterato, ta, *a.* illiterate, ignorant, unlearned.
Ilma., Ilmo. *abbrev. of* **Ilustrísima, Ilustrísimo,** Most Illustrious.
ilmenita, *f.* (min.) ilmenite.
ilógico, ca, *a.* illogical.
ilota, *m., f.* 1. (hist.) Helot, serf of the Spartans. 2. (fig.) wretch, object creature. 3. person deprived of civil rights.
ilotismo, *m.* helotism, serfdom.
iluminación, *f.* 1. illumination, lighting. 2. (p.) painting in tempera or distemper. 3. illumination (adornment of letters, books, manuscripts, etc.). 4. intellectual or spiritual enlightenment. 5. (phys.) illumination (surface light density); **i. indirecta,** indirect lighting.
iluminado, da, *past part. of* **iluminar. —***a.* illuminated; enlightened. —*m., f.* 1. visionary. 2. (*pl.*) Illuminati, members of certain sects of heretics who believed themselves especially enlightened.
iluminador, ra, *a.* illuminating. —*m., f.* illuminator, illustrator (of books, etc.).
iluminancia, *f.* (phys.) illuminance.
iluminante, *a.* illuminating, illuminant.
iluminar, *tr.v.* 1. to illuminate, light up. 2. to illuminate, decorate (books, manuscripts, etc.). 3. to illumine, enlighten (spiritually or mentally).
iluminarias, *f.* (*pl.*) festive lights or lighting arrangement.
iluminativo, va, *a.* illuminative.
iluminismo, *m.* (rel.) Illuminism, the doctrines of the Illuminati.
ilusamente, *adv.* 1. deceptively, falsely. 2. ingenuously.

ilusión, *f.* 1. illusion (mistaken impression). 2. (*pl.*) hopes, illusions, wishful thinking, dreams. 3. pleasure, joy, happiness. — **hacerle ilusión a uno,** to dream of having, e.g. *¿le hace ilusión una casa de campo?* do you dream of having a country house?; **hacerse la i.** or **ilusiones de que,** to have hopes that; **i. óptica,** optical illusion; **vivir de ilusiones,** to live on dreams.
ilusionado, da, *a.* hopeful; dreamy.
ilusionar, *tr.v.* to fascinate; to offer hopes to. —*r.v.* to harbor hopes, to have illusions.
ilusionismo, *m.* 1. (philos.) illusionism. 2. the use of illusion in art and performances.
ilusionista, *m., f.* illusionist, conjurer, (theat.) magician.
ilusivo, va, *a.* illusive, illusory, unreal, false, deceptive.
iluso, sa, *a.* deluded; misguided; beguiled. —*m., f.* dreamer, person suffering from delusions.
ilusoriamente, *adv.* illusorily, deceptively.
ilusorio, ria, *a.* 1. illusory, deceptive. 2. (law) null, void.
ilustración, *f.* 1. illustration; picture. 2. exposition, explanation, elucidation. 3. enlightenment; learning. 4. (philos.) Enlightenment.
ilustrado, da, *past part. of* **ilustrar.** —*a.* 1. enlightened, wise, intelligent. 2. learned, well-informed.
ilustrador, ra, *a.* illustrative; enlightening. —*m., f.* illustrator (artist).
ilustrar, *tr v.* 1. to illustrate (a point; a book). 2. to make illustrious or famous. 3. to enlighten; to educate, civilize. 4. to illumine, illuminate (spiritually). —*r.v.* to become enlightened; to become civilized or educated.
ilustrativo, va, *a.* illustrative.
ilustre, *a.* illustrious; distinguished; famous, celebrated, renowned.
ilustremente, *adv.* illustriously.
ilustrísimo, ma, *a. super. of* **ilustre,** very or most illustrious, most distinguished (title applied to bishops).
iluviación, *f.* (geog.) illuviation.
iluvial, *a.* (geog.) illuvial.
imadas, *f.* (mar.) ways, sliding planks.
imagen, *f.* 1. image; picture; effigy, statue. 2. appearance, conception. 3. (opt.) spectrum. — **i. accidental** or **consecutiva,** afterimage; **i. confusa,** blurred image; **i. especular,** mirror image; **i. fantasma,** (tel.) double image; **i. real,** living image; (phys.) real image; **i. virtual,** (phys.) virtual image; **ser la i. viva de,** to be the living or very image of.
imaginable, *a.* imaginable, conceivable.
imaginación, *f.* imagination; vivid mind; inventiveness.
imaginar, *tr.v.* 1. to imagine, figure out; think up. 2. to imagine, suppose, presume. —*r.v.* to imagine, fancy, suspect. — **¡imagínate!** imagine that!; **me lo imagino,** I can just imagine.
imaginariamente, *adv.* imaginarily; in a visionary manner.
imaginario, ria, *a.* 1. imaginary, fancied, fictitious. 2. (math.) imaginary. —*f.* (mil.) reserve guard (corps).
imaginativa, *f.* imagination; vision, inventiveness.
imaginativo, va, *a.* imaginative, fanciful; visionary.
imaginería, *f.* 1. imagery. 2. floral or pictorial embroidery. 3. carving or painting of sacred images.
imaginero, *m.* sculptor or painter of religious images.
imago, *m.* (ento.) imago. —*f.* (psyc.) imago.
imán, *m.* 1. (min., phys.) magnet. 2. (fig.) magnet, charm, attraction. — **i. artificial,** artificial magnet; **i. de herradura,** horseshoe magnet; **i. inductor** or **del campo,** field magnet; **i. laminado,** compound magnet; **i. permanente,** permanent magnet.
imán, *m.* imam, Mohammedan priest; title given to some Moslem rulers.
imanación, *f.* magnetization.
imanar, *tr.v.* to magnetize. —*r.v.* to become magnetized.
imanato, *m.* imamate, territory ruled by an imam; the office of an imam.
imantación, *f.* magnetization.
imantar, *tr.v.* to magnetize. —*r.v.* to become magnetized.
imareto, *m.* imaret (Turkish hostelry).
imbécil, *a.* imbecile; feeble-minded, stupid, silly, foolish, idiotic. —*m., f.* cretin, moron, fool, idiot.
imbecilidad, *f.* imbecility, feeblemindedness; stupidity, foolishness.
imbécilmente, *adv.* idiotically, stupidly, foolishly.
imbele, *a.* incapable of warring, unfit for war.
imberbe, *a.* beardless. —*m.* young and inexperienced man.
imbibición, *f.* imbibing, imbibition; absorption.
imbíbito, ta, *a.* (Mex., Guat.) included, comprised.
imbira, *f.* (bot., Arg.) anonaceous tree whose bark is used for making ropes (Xylopia sericea).
imbornal, *m.* drain hole; (mar.) scupper hole; **ir por los imbornales,** (coll., Ven.) to wander, digress, roam (in a conversation, etc.).
imborrable, *a.* indelible; (fig.) unforgettable.
imbricación, *f.* (archit.) imbrication, overlapping.
imbricado, da, *a.* 1. (bot., zool.) imbricate. 2. overlapped, imbricated.
imbuir, (*ref. 48*) *tr.v.* to imbue, infuse; to impart; to permeate.
imbunchar, *tr.v.* (Chile) 1. to bewitch, cast a spell over. 2. to cheat, swindle.
imbunche, *m.* (Chile) 1. witch who steals small children. 2. fat ugly little boy. 3. magic spell. 4. imbroglio, mess, tangle, complicated situation.
imbuya, imbuyendo, imbuyera, imbuyese, imbuyo, *ref.* **imbuir.**
imida, *f.* (chem.) imide.
imidazol, *m.* (chem.) imidazole, imidazol.
imidógeno, *m.* (chem.) imidogen.
imilla, *f.* (Bol., Peru) Indian maid or servant.
imina, *f.* (chem.) imine.
imitable, *a.* imitable; worthy of imitation, easy to imitate.
imitación, *f.* imitation, copy; impersonation. —*a.* imitation, e.g. *i. cuero,* imitation leather.
imitado, da, *past part. of* **imitar.** —*a.* imitation (as *a.*), simulated, mock, artificial, e.g. *cuero i.,* imitation leather.
imitador, ra, *a.* imitative. —*m., f.* imitator, follower, copyist.
imitar, *tr v.* to imitate, to counterfeit; to ape or mimic.
imitativo, va, *a.* imitative, copying, following (trends, art, fashions, etc.).
imoscapo, *m.* (archit.) apophyge.
impacción, *f.* (dent.) impaction.
impaciencia, *f.* 1. impatience, restlessness; eagerness, hastiness. 2. irritation.
impacientar, *tr.v.* to make impatient, to vex, irritate. —*r.v.* to become impatient, lose one's patience, e.g. *me impacienté,* I became impatient.
impaciente, *a.* impatient, fidgety, restless; anxious.
impacientemente, *adv.* impatiently, anxiously.
impactado, da, *a.* (dent.) impacted.
impacto, *m.* impact; shock; (fig.) influence, repercussion.
impagable, *a.* unpayable.
impago, ga, *a.* (Arg., Chile) unpaid (person). —*m., f.* (Amer.) creditor.
impalpabilidad, *f.* impalpability.
impalpable, *a.* impalpable; (fig.) subtle.
impanación, *f.* (theol.) impanation.
impar, *a.* (math.) odd, uneven; unmatched; (anat.) unpaired, impar, azygous. —*m.* odd or uneven number.
imparcial, *a.* impartial, equitable; unbiased; neutral.
imparcialidad, *f.* impartiality; fairness.
imparcialmente, *adv.* impartially, equitably.
imparidígito, ta, *a.* (zool.) imparidigitate.
imparisílabo, ba, *a.* imparisyllabic.
impartible, *a.* indivisible.
impartir, *tr.v.* to impart, grant; (law) to demand (e.g. assistance).
impasibilidad, *f.* impassibility; (fig.) immobility.
impasible, *a.* impassible, impassive; unfeeling.
impasiblemente, *adv.* impassively, impassibly.
impávidamente, *adv.* intrepidly, fearlessly, undauntedly.
impavidez, *f.* dauntlessness, fearlessness, intrepidity.
impávido, da, *a.* fearless, impavid, intrepid, dauntless.
impecabilidad, *f.* impeccability, faultlessness.
impecable, *a.* impeccable, faultless.
impedancia, *f.* (elec.) impedance; **i. de entrada,** (elec., rad.) input impedance.
impedido, da, *past part. of* **impedir.** —*a.* disabled, invalid, crippled, maimed. —*m., f.* cripple, disabled person, invalid.
impedidor, ra, *a.* obstructive. —*m., f.* obstructor.
impediente, *a.* hindering, obstructive, impeding.
impedimenta, *f.* (mil.) impedimenta, equipment, supplies (all that hinders or delays a march).
impedimento, *m.* impediment, obstacle, hindrance, obstruction, encumbrance; (law) impediment, estoppel; **i. dirimente,** diriment impediment; **i. impediente,** prohibitive impediment.
impedir, (*ref. 39*) *tr.v.* to impede, hinder, obstruct; to prevent, constrain, restrain.
impeditivo, va, *a.* obstructive, preventive, hindering.
impelente, *a.* impelling, propelling; forcing; inciting, spurring.
impeler, *tr.v.* to impel, push, spur, drive; to incite, to urge. — **i. a alguien a** + *inf.,* to impel someone to + *inf.*
impender, *tr.v.* to expend, spend; to invest.
impenetrabilidad, *f.* impenetrability.
impenetrable, *a.* impenetrable, impervious; (fig.) incomprehensible, unfathomable.
impenitencia, *f.* impenitence.
impenitente, *a.* impenitent, unrepentant, obdurate.
impensa, *f.* (law) expense, expenditure.
impensable, *a.* unthinkable.
impensadamente, *adv.* inadvertently, unintentionally.
impensado, da, *a.* unexpected, unforeseen; fortuitous.
impepinable, *a.* (coll.) sure, certain, true.
imperante, *a.* 1. ruling, dominating, commanding. 2. (astrol.) dominant.
imperar, *i.v.* to reign, rule; to prevail; to be in command; to be emperor.
imperativamente, *adv.* imperiously.

imperativo, va, *a.* imperative; imperious, dictatorial; (gram.) imperative. —*m.* (gram.) imperative; **i. categórico,** (philos.) categorical imperative.
imperator, *m.* (hist.) imperator, title given to victorious generals in ancient Rome.
imperatoria, *f.* (bot.) masterwort.
imperatorio, ria, *a.* (hist.) imperatorial, pertaining to the emperor or the empire.
imperceptibilidad, *f.* imperceptibility, imperceptiveness.
imperceptible, *a.* imperceptible; (fig.) invisible.
imperceptiblemente, *adv.* imperceptibly.
imperdible, *a.* that cannot be lost. —*m.* safety pin.
imperdonable, *a.* unpardonable, unforgivable, inexcusable; irremissible.
imperdonablemente, *adv.* unpardonably, unforgivably; inexcusably.
imperecedero, ra, *a.* imperishable, indestructible; undying.
imperfección, *f.* imperfection, fault, flaw, blemish.
imperfectamente, *adv.* imperfectly, inadequately, faultily.
imperfectivo, *a.* (gram.) imperfective.
imperfecto, ta, *a.* imperfect, defective, faulty; unfinished; (gram.) imperfect.
imperforación, *f.* (med.) imperforation.
imperforado, da, *a.* imperforate. —*m.* (*pl.*) (zool.) Imperforata.
imperial, *a.* imperial. —*f.* 1. imperial, coach top seats; roof or top of a coach. 2. imperial (card game). 3. (mar.) poop royal. — **águila i.,** imperial eagle.
imperialismo, *m.* (pol.) imperialism; colonialism.
imperialista, *m., f.* (pol.) imperialist.
impericia, *f.* unskillfulness, lack of skill, inexperience.
imperio, *a.* characteristic of the art and fashions of the time of Napoleon I. —*m.* 1. empire. 2. rule, reign; dominion, sway. 3. reign or status of emperor. 4. pride, arrogance. — **estilo i.,** empire style (in dress, coiffure, décor); **i. celeste,** Celestial Empire; **i. de la ley,** the rule of law; **I. de Occidente,** Western Empire, Western Roman Empire; **I. de Oriente,** Eastern Empire, Eastern Roman Empire.
imperiosamente, *adv.* imperiously, arrogantly; overbearingly.
imperiosidad, *f.* imperiousness.
imperioso, sa, *a.* 1. imperious. arrogant, domineering, overbearing. 2. urgent, imperative.
imperitamente, *adv.* inexpertly, unskillfully.
imperito, ta, *a.* unskilled, inexpert.
impermeabilice, *ref.* **impermeabilizar.**
impermeabilidad, *f.* impermeability, the quality of being waterproof.
impermeabilización, *f.* waterproofing.
impermeabilizar, (*ref. 53*) *tr.v.* to waterproof, make waterproof.
impermeable, *a.* waterproof; impermeable, impervious. —*m.* raincoat, mackintosh.
impermutabilidad, *f.* unexchangeability.
impermutable, *a.* impermutable; unexchangeable.
imperscrutable, *a.* inscrutable.
impersonal, *a.* impersonal; (gram.) impersonal.
impersonalice, *ref.* **impersonalizar.**
impersonalidad, *f.* impersonality, lack of personality.
impersonalizar, (*ref. 53*) *tr.v.* (gram.) to use impersonally, impersonalize.
impersonalmente, *adv.* impersonally.
impersuasible, *a.* not susceptible to persuasion.
impertérrito, ta, *a.* intrepid, dauntless, bold, fearless; serene.
impertinencia, *f.* impertinence, cheek; intrusion.
impertinente, *a.* 1. impertinent, insolent, importunate, cheeky (coll.). 2. impertinent, irrelevant. —*m., f.* impertinent person. —*m.* (*pl.*) lorgnette, eyeglasses or opera glasses with a short handle.
impertinentemente, *adv.* impertinently.
impertir, *tr.v., var. of* **impartir.**
imperturbabililad, *f.* imperturbability.
imperturbable, *a.* imperturbable, immovable, impassive.
imperturbablemente, *adv.* imperturbably, impassively.
impetigo, *m.* (med.) impetigo.
impetra, *f.* 1. permission, license. 2. (ecc.) papal bull granting a dubious benefice.
impetrable, *a.* (law) impetrable, that can be obtained.
impetración, *f.* impetration, begging for, soliciting; obtaining by entreaty.
impetrador, ra, *m., f.* impetrator, one seeking a favor or benefice.
impetrante, *a.* impetrating. —*m.* impetrator, one receiving a favor or benefice.
impetrar, *tr.v.* 1. to beg for, ask for. 2. to impetrate, obtain by entreaty.
impetratorio, ria, *a.* impetratory, impetrative.
ímpetu, *m.* 1. impetus, momentum, impulse. 2. drive, vigor, energy. 3. vehemence, impetuousness. 4. rush, haste, e.g. *salir con í.,* to rush out.
impetuosamente, *adv.* impetuously; vehemently.
impetuosidad, *f.* impetuousness; vehemence.
impetuoso, sa, *a.* impetuous; vehement.
impíamente, *adv.* 1. impiously, irreverently, profanely. 2. cruelly, pitilessly.
impida, impido, *ref.* **impedir.**
impidiendo, impidiera, impidiese, impidió, *ref.* **impedir.**
impiedad, *f.* impiety, ungodliness, irreverence.
impiedoso, sa, *a.* impious, irreverent, ungodly.
impío, a, *a.* impious, irreverent, ungodly; (fig.) irreligious. —*m., f.* infidel.
impla, *f.* wimple; headdress.
implacabilidad, *f.* implacability.
implacable, *a.* implacable, inexorable.
implacablemente, *adv.* implacably.
implacentario, ria, *a.* (zool.) implacental.
implantación, *f.* implantation; introduction (of new ideas, methods, etc.).
implantar, *tr.v.* to implant; to introduce; to establish.
implaticable, *a.* unmentionable; averse to conversation.
implemento, *m.* implement; tool; device.
implicación, *f.* 1. involvement, complicity, implication. 2. contradiction.
implicancia, *f.* (Amer.) legal impediment.
implicante, *a.* compromising, implicating.
implicar, (*ref. 50*) *tr.v.* 1. to involve, implicate. 2. to imply, mean. —*i.v.* 1. to imply contradiction. 2. to stand in someone's way, to impede someone. —*r.v.* to become involved, get involved.
implicatorio, ria, *a.* implicatory, implicative; contradictive.
implícitamente, *adv.* implicitly.
implícito, ta, *a.* implicit.
implique, impliqué, *ref.* **implicar.**
imploración, *f.* imploration, entreaty.
implorante, *a.* entreating, imploring. —*m., f.* implorer, supplicant.
implorar, *tr.v.* to implore, beseech, entreat, beg.
implosión, *f.* (phonet.) implosion.
implosivo, va, *a., f.* (phonet.) implosive.
implume, *a.* featherless, unfledged.
impluvio, *m.* (hist., archit.) impluvium.
impolítica, *f.* discourtesy, rudeness, impoliteness, tactlessness.
impolíticamente, *adv.* impolitely, discourteously, rudely.
impolítico, ca, *a.* impolitic, discourteous, rude.
impoluto, ta, *a.* unpolluted, clean, spotless; stainless; pure, untarnished.
imponderabilidad, *f.* imponderability.
imponderable, *a.* imponderable, beyond praise or measure. —*m.* imponderable.
imponderablemente, *adv.* imponderably.
impondré, impondría, *ref.* **imponer.**
imponedor, *m.* 1. (print.) lockup, stone head. 2. imposer, assessor.
imponente, *a.* 1. imposing, grandiose, majestic; solemn. 2. beyond praise. —*m., f.* depositor; investor.
imponer, (*ref. 15*) *tr.v.* 1. to impose (a sentence; taxes; silence, etc.). 2. to impute falsely. 3. to inform; to teach, instruct. 4. to instil, infuse (fear, respect). 5. to invest, deposit (money). 6. (print.) to impose. —*r.v.* to be impressive, command attention and respect; **imponerse a,** to dominate, get control of; **imponerse de,** to learn, find out about; to inform oneself of.
imponga, impongo, *ref.* **imponer.**
imponible, *a.* taxable, subject to duty.
impopular, *a.* unpopular.
impopularidad, *f.* unpopularity.
importable, *a.* (com.) importable.
importación, *f.* importation; imported goods, imports.
importador, ra, *a.* importing. —*m., f.* importer.
importancia, *f.* importance, significance, import, moment, consequence; urgency. — **darse uno i.,** (coll.) to put on airs; **asunto de i,** a matter of consequence.
importante, *a.* important, momentous, weighty, considerable.
importantemente, *adv.* importantly, momentously; significantly.
importar, *tr.v.* 1. to import, to bring in from abroad. 2. to cost, be valued at, to amount to. 3. to take or bring along. —*i.v.* to be important; to matter, e.g. *no importa lo que digan,* it doesn't matter what they say; to care, e.g. *no me importa,* I don't care, *¿qué importa?* what does it matter? *¿a ti qué te importa?* what business is it of yours?
importe, *m.* amount, price, cost, value.
importunación, *f.* pestering, bothering, importuning.
importunadamente, *adv.* importunately, pesteringly, troublesomely; inconveniently, inopportunely.
importunamente, *adv.* importunately, pesteringly, troublesomely; inopportunely, inconveniently.
importunar, *tr.v.* to importune, pester, bother.
importunidad, *f.* importunity, annoyance, inconvenience, nuisance, bother.
importuno, na, *a.* importune, importunate; inopportune, untimely, inconvenient; troublesome, bothersome.
imposibilidad, *f.* impossibility; (law) disability (excusing one from public duties).
imposibilitado, da, *past part. of* **imposibilitar.** —*a.* invalid, maimed, disabled.
imposibilitar, *tr.v.* 1. to prevent, stop; to make impossible; to make unable. 2. to disable, to render unfit (for service, etc.).
imposible, *a.* 1. impossible. 2. unbearable, impossible, intolerable, unendurable. 3. (Amer.) filthy, dirty, unkempt. — **i. de** + *inf.,* impossible to + *inf.* —*m.* impossibility.
imposiblemente, *adv.* impossibly.

imposición, *f.* 1. imposition, imposing. 2. burden, imposition. 3. tax, levy, imposition. 4. domination, control. 5. (print.) imposition. — **i. de manos,** (ecc.) imposition, laying on of hands.
impositivo, va, *a.* tax; inescapable, unavoidable. —*f.* (S. Amer.) office of the tax collector.
impositor, *m.* (print.) lockup, stoneman.
imposta, *f.* (archit.) impost; fascia; springer.
impostergable, *a.* unpostponable.
impostor, ra, *a.* 1. fraudulent. 2. slanderous. —*m., f.* 1. impostor. 2. slanderer.
impostura, *f.* 1. imposture, fraud. 2. imputation, slander.
impotable, *a.* undrinkable, unpotable.
impotencia, *f.* 1. impotence. 2. powerlessness.
impotente, *a.* 1. impotent. 2. powerless.
impotentemente, *adv.* 1. impotently. 2. powerlessly.
impracticabilidad, *f.* impracticability.
impracticable, *a.* 1. impracticable, unfeasible. 2. impassable.
imprecación, *f.* imprecation, curse.
imprecar, (*ref. 50*) *tr.v.* to imprecate, curse.
imprecatorio, a, *a.* imprecatory.
imprecisión, *f.* lack of precision, inexactness, vagueness.
impreciso, sa, *a.* unprecise, inexact; vague, undefined.
impregnable, *a.* saturable.
impregnación, *f.* 1. impregnation, saturation. 2. (biol.) impregnation, fecundation, fertilization.
impregnado, da, *a.* impregnated.
impregnador, *m.* impregnator.
impregnar, *tr.v.* to impregnate; to saturate, soak; **i. con** or **de,** to saturate with. —*r.v.* to become impregnated or saturated.
impremeditación, *f.* lack of premeditation.
impremeditadamente, *adv.* without premeditation.
impremeditado, da, *a.* unpremeditated.
imprenta, *f.* 1. printing. 2. printer's shop, printshop, printing house. 3. print (size or style of type). 4. press. — **en i.,** in print; **estar en la i.,** to be at the printer's; **libertad de i.,** freedom of the press.
impreque, imprequé, *ref.* **imprecar.**
imprescindible, *a.* indispensable; imperative.
imprescindiblemente, *adv.* absolutely; necessarily, unavoidably.
imprescriptible, *a.* imprescriptible.
impresentable, *a.* unpresentable.
impresión, *f.* 1. printing. 2. print (quality of printed matter), e.g. *la i. es un poco borrosa,* the print is rather blurred. 3. impression, print run, printout. 4. impression, effect, influence; shock. 5. impression, imprint, mark; **i. dactilar,** or **digital,** fingerprint; **i. en cuatricromía,** four-color printing; **i. en policromía,** multicolor printing; **i. fotográfica,** photoprint. 6. pressing (of a record).
impresionabilidad, *f.* impressionability, impressionableness.
impresionable, *a.* impressionable; emotional.
impresionante, *a.* impressing, impressive; amazing.
impresionar, *tr.v.* 1. to impress, make an impression on, to move, to affect or influence. 2. to cause chemical changes on (a photographic plate). 3. to cut a phonograph record. —*r.v.* to be impressed, affected or moved deeply.
impresionismo, *m.* (p., lit., mus.) impressionism, an art form which expresses the mood and the impression rather than the reality of a theme or subject.
impresionista, *a.* impressionistic; impressionist. —*m., f.* (art.) impressionist, e.g. *Monet fue el primer impresionista francés,* Monet was the first French impressionist.
impreso, sa, *irr. past part. of* **imprimir.** —*a.* printed. —*m.* book, article; (*pl.*) printed matter.
impresor, ra, *m., f.* printer; owner of a printing shop or printing house. —*f.* (comput.) printer; **i. de margarita,** daisywheel printer; **i. de matriz,** dot-matrix printer; **i. láser** or **de láser,** laser printer; **i. matricial,** dot-matrix printer.
imprestable, *a.* not lendable, not to be borrowed.
imprevisible, *a.* unforeseeable, unpredictable.
imprevisión, *f.* 1. lack of foresight or forethought, improvidence. 2. oversight, thoughtlessness.
imprevisor, ra, *a.* lacking forethought.
imprevisto, ta, *a.* unforeseen, unexpected. —*m.* (*pl.*) incidental expenses.
imprimación, *f.* (p.) priming (e.g. a canvas); priming material.
imprimadera, *f.* (p.) priming tool, artist's priming knife or spatula.
imprimador, *m.* (p.) primer, one who primes.
imprimar, *tr.v.* to prime (e.g. canvas for painting).
imprimátur, *m.* (ecc.) imprimatur.
imprimir, *tr.v.* 1. to print, stamp, publish (books, designs on cloth; footprints). 2. (fig.) to imprint, stamp, impress, fix (in the mind). 3. to transmit, impart.
improbabilidad, *f.* improbability.
improbable, *a.* improbable, unlikely.
improbablemente, *adv.* improbably.
improbar, (*ref. 33*) *tr.v.* to disapprove of, condemn.
improbidad, *f.* improbity, dishonesty, lack of integrity.
ímprobo, ba, *a.* 1. dishonest, corrupt. 2. arduous, laborious, hard (work).
improcedencia, *f.* 1. inappropriateness, irrelevance. 2. inadmissibility.
improcedente, *a.* 1. inappropriate, unfit, inadequate. 2. inadmissible, contrary to law.
improductivamente, *adv.* unproductively; unprofitably.
improductivo, va, *a.* unproductive; unfruitful, barren; unprofitable.
impromptu, *m.* (mus.) impromptu; improvised composition; short, free-style piece.
impronta, *f.* 1. impression (e.g. of a medal in plaster). 2. (print.) cast, plate, stereotype cast (or plate), casting.
impronunciable, *a.* unpronounceable.
improperar, *tr.v.* to insult, abuse, revile.
improperio, *m.* 1. insult, affront. 2. (ecc.) (*pl.*) versicles sung at the mass on Good Friday, improperia.
impropiamente, *adv.* incorrectly, improperly.
impropiedad, *f.* impropriety, unfitness; incorrect use of words.
impropio, pia, *a.* 1. unsuited, unsuitable, unfitting, inappropriate. 2. out of place. 3. incorrect (use of words). 4. (math.) improper. — **i. de** or **para,** unsuitable.
improporción, *f.* (rare) disproportion.
improporcionado, da, *a.* (rare) disproportionate.
improrrogable, *a.* unpostponable.
impróspero, ra, *a.* (rare) unprosperous, unsuccessful.
impróvidamente, *adv.* improvidently, unpreparedly.
impróvido, da, *a.* unprepared, improvident, thoughtless.
improvisación, *f.* 1. improvisation, extemporization. 2. sudden rise or success (usually undeserved).
improvisadamente, *adv., var. of* **improvisamente.**
improvisado, da, *past part. of* **improvisar.** —*a.* makeshift.
improvisador, ra, *a.* improvising. —*m., f.* improviser, extemporizer.
improvisamente, *adv.* suddenly, unexpectedly, without warning.
improvisar, *tr.v.* to improvise, devise; to make up (poetry, music); to extemporize.
improviso, sa, *a.* unexpected, unforeseen; **al** or de **improviso,** unexpectedly, suddenly.
improvisto, ta, *a., var. of* **improviso.**
imprudencia, *f.* imprudence, indiscretion; (law) criminal negligence.
imprudente, *a.* imprudent, indiscreet.
imprudentemente, *adv.* imprudently.
impúber, *a.* impuberate, immature, below the age of puberty.
impúbero, ra, *a., var. of* **impúber.**
impudencia, *f.* impudence, shamelessness, insolence.
impudente, *a.* impudent, insolent, shameless.
impúdicamente, *adv.* 1. immodestly; indecently, improperly. 2. shamelessly, brazenly.
impudicia, *f.* immodesty, indecency, shamelessness.
impudicicia, *f., var. of* **impudicia.**
impúdico, ca, *a.* immodest; indecent, improper; lewd, prurient, dirty (coll.).
impudor, *m.* immodesty; shamelessness.
impuesto, ta, *past part. of* **imponer.** —*a.* informed, apprised, cognizant; **estar** or **quedar i. de,** to be informed of or about. —*m.* tax, duty; **i. al valor añadido** or **agregado, i. sobre el valor añadido** or **agregado,** value-added tax; **i. de consumo, i. interno,** excise tax; **i. de lujo,** luxury tax; **i. de retención** or **retenido,** (law) withholding tax; **i. sobre la plusvalía,** capital gains tax; **i. sobre la renta** or **los ingresos,** income tax; **i. sobre las utilidades excedentes** or **ganancias excesivas,** excess profits tax; **i. sobre las ventas,** sales tax; **i. sucesorio, i. sobre sucesiones, i. a la herencia,** inheritance tax; **i. único,** flat tax.
impugnable, *a.* impugnable, refutable, contestable.
impugnación, *f.* refutation, challenge, contestation, contradiction, impugnation.
impugnador, ra, *a.* impugning, refuting. —*m., f.* impugner, refuter, challenger; attacker.
impugnar, *tr.v.* to contradict, refute, contest, attack, impugn, confute.
impugnativo, va, *a.* combative, impugning.
impulsar, *tr v.* to impel, drive, force.
impulsión, *f.* 1. impulsion, impulse, impetus, (mec.) drive. 3. motive, influence. — **i. por fricción,** (auto.) friction drive; **i. por engranaje reductor,** (auto.) backgear power.
impulsivamente, *adv.* impulsively, thoughtlessly.
impulsividad, *f.* impulsiveness.
impulsivo, va, *a.* impulsive or impelling, impellent, driving; impulsive, impetuous.
impulso, *m.* 1. impulse, impulsion; impetus, momentum. 2. prompting, e.g. *los impulsos de mi corazón,* the promptings of my heart. — **dar i.,** to set off, to trigger; **i. vital,** (philos.) vital force.
impulsor, ra, *a.* propellent, impelling, driving. —*m., f.* propellant, impeller; driving force.
impune, *a.* unpunished.
impunemente, *adv.* with impunity.
impunidad, *f.* impunity.
impuntual, *a.* unpunctual.
impuramente, *adv.* impurely; unchastely.
impureza, *f.* 1. impurity, unchasteness. 2. pollution, foulness.
impurificación, *f.* defilement, pollution.
impurificar, (*ref. 50*) *tr.v.* to make unclean or impure; to adulterate; to defile, pollute; to sully, stain, blemish, tarnish.

impurifique, *ref.* **impurificar.**
impuro, ra, *a.* 1. impure, unchaste. 2. impure, defiled, adulterated.
impuse, impusiera, impusiese, *ref.* **imponer.**
imputabilidad, *f.* imputability.
imputable, *a.* imputable, chargeable.
imputación, *f.* imputation, attribution, accusation, charge.
imputador, ra, *a.* imputative, charging. —*m., f.* imputer, accuser.
imputar, *tr.v.* 1. to impute; to accuse of, charge with. 2. to assign (money for a definite purpose). 3. to attribute; to ascribe, lay at the door of.
In *sym. of* **indio,** indium (In).
inabarcable, *a.* that cannot be embraced or encompassed.
inabordable, *a.* unapproachable, inaccessible.
inabrogable, *a.* unrepealable, irrevocable, indefeasible.
inacabable, *a.* interminable, unending, endless.
inaccesibilidad, *f.* inaccessibility, unapproachability.
inaccesible, *a.* inaccessible, unapproachable.
inaccesiblemente, *adv.* inaccessibly.
inacción, *f.* inaction, inactivity; idleness, quiescence.
inacentuado, da, *a.* unaccented, unaccentuated, unstressed; atonic.
inaceptable, *a.* unacceptable.
inactivamente, *adv.* inactively, idly.
inactividad, *f.* inactivity, idleness.
inactivo, va, *a.* inactive, idle, quiescent.
inadaptabilidad, *f.* unadaptability.
inadaptable, *a.* unadaptable.
inadaptación, *f.* inadaptation.
inadaptado, da, *a.* unadapted, unadjusted.
inadecuado, da, *a.* inadequate, unsuitable; insufficient; unequal; incapable.
inadmisible, *a.* inadmissible.
inadoptable, *a.* unadoptable.
inadvertencia, *f.* negligence, oversight, inadvertence, carelessness.
inadvertidamente, *adv.* unawares, inadvertently, unwittingly.
inadvertido, da, *a.* 1. unseen, unnoticed, unobserved. 2. careless, thoughtless.
inafectado, da, *a.* unaffected, natural, simple, sincere.
inagotable, *a.* inexhaustible; bottomless.
inaguantable, *a.* insupportable, unbearable, insufferable, intolerable.
inajenable, *a.* inalienable.
inalámbrico, ca, *a.* cordless (telephone); wireless (communications).
in albis, *adv.* (Lat.) 1. blank, in the dark, without understanding what one hears. 2. without attaining what one sought.
inalcanzable, *a.* unreachable, unattainable.
inalienabilidad, *f.* inalienability.
inalienable, *a.* inalienable.
inalterabilidad, *f.* 1. unalterability, immutability. 2. stability, equanimity, calmness (of character).
inalterable, *a.* 1. unalterable, unchangeable, immutable. 2. stable, equable, calm (in character).
inalterablemente, *adv.* unalterably, inalterably.
inalterado, da, *a.* 1. unaltered, unchanged. 2. unmoved, impassive.
inameno, na, *a.* unpleasant, disagreeable; dull.
inamisible, *a.* not likely to be lost.
inamovible, *a.* unremovable; undetachable, immovable.
inamovilidad, *f.* unremovability, undetachability.
inanalizable, *a.* unanalyzable.
inane, *a.* inane, empty, void, senseless, pointless.
inanición, *f.* (med.) inanition, weakness through lack of food.
inanidad, *f.* inanity, emptiness, vacuousness.
inanimación, *f.* inanimation.
inanimado, da, *a.* inanimate, inert; spiritless, lifeless, dead.
inánime, *a.* dead, lifeless, spiritless.
inapagable, *a.* inextinguishable, unquenchable.
inapeable, *a.* 1. obstinate, stubborn. 2. incomprehensible, inconceivable, unfathomable.
inapelable, *a.* 1. unappealable, final. 2. inevitable, unavoidable.
inapercibido, da, *a.* unnoticed, unseen; unfelt; undetected.
inapetencia, *f.* lack of appetite, inappetence.
inapetente, *a.* having no appetite, inappetent.
inaplazable, *a.* undeferable, unpostponable.
inaplicable, *a.* inapplicable.
inaplicación, *f.* laziness, indolence; lack of application.
inaplicado, da, *a.* lazy, indolent; lax, remiss.
inapreciable, *a.* 1. invaluable, inestimable, inappreciable. 2. imperceptible.
inaprensivo, va, *a.* inapprehensive.
inapropiable, *a.* unappropriable, unattachable.
inaprovechado, da, *a.* unused, wasted, not taken advantage of.
inarmónico, ca, *a.* inharmonious, inharmonic.
inarticulable, *a.* that cannot be articulated, unpronounceable.
inarticulado, da, *a.* 1. inarticulate. 2. ineloquent.
in artículo mortis, (Lat., law) at the point of death, about to die.
inartístico, ca, *a.* inartistic.
inasequibilidad, *f.* inaccessibility, unapproachability.
inasequible, *a.* unapproachable, inaccessible; unattainable.
inasible, *a.* ungraspable.
inasimilable, *a.* unassimilable.
inasistencia, *f.* absence.
inasistente, *a.* absent. —*m., f.* absentee.
inastillable, *a.* non-splintering, splinterproof.
inatacable, *a.* unattackable; impregnable, inviolable.
inatención, *f.* inattention.
inatento, ta, *a.* unattentive; careless; rude, incivil.
inaudible, *a.* inaudible.
inaudito, ta, *a.* unheard of, extraordinary; astounding, outrageous.
inauguración, *f.* inauguration, opening; debut, initiation; (art.) unveiling, vernissage.
inaugural, *a.* inaugural.
inaugurar, *tr.v.* to inaugurate, open; to initiate (art.) to open (an exhibition); to unveil (a sculpture, a plaque).
inaveriguable, *a.* unascertainable.
inaveriguado, da, *a.* unascertained, undiscovered.
inca, *m.* (hist., ethnol.) Inca.
incaico, ca, *a.* Inca, Incan; **el imperio i.,** the Inca empire.
incalculable, *a.* incalculable.
incalificable, *a.* unspeakable, indescribable; most reprehensible.
incalmable, *a.* unsubduable, unappeasable.
incambiable, *a.* unexchangeable, unchangeable.
incanato, *m.* (Peru) period of the Inca Empire.
incandescencia, *f.* incandescence.
incandescente, *a.* incandescent.
incansable, *a.* indefatigable, untiring; inexhaustible.
incansablemente, *adv.* untiringly, indefatigably.
incantable, *a.* unsingable.
incapacidad, *f.* 1. incapacity, inability, unfitness, incapability, incompetence. 2. incapacity (lack of intellectual power or legal qualifications). 3. (physical) disability.— **i. absoluta,** total disability; **i. laboral transitoria,** temporary disability.
incapacitado, da, *past part. of* **incapacitar.** —*a.* incapacitated; disabled.
incapacitar, *tr.v.* 1. to incapacitate, disqualify. 2. to disable. 3. (law) to declare incapable.
incapaz, (*pl.* **incapaces**), *a.* incapable, unable; incompetent.
incardinación, *f.* (ecc.) incardination.
incardinar, *tr.v.* (ecc.) to incardinate.
incasable, *a.* unmarriageable, unmarriable; averse to marriage.
incásico, ca, *a.* Inca, Incan, pertaining to the Incas.
incasto, ta, *a.* unchaste; impure.
incausto, *m.* (p.) encaustic.
incautación, *f.* (law) seizure, attachment.
incautamente, *adv.* incautiously, unwarily, heedlessly.
incautarse, *r.v.* (law) to seize, attach (money or property).
incauto, ta, *a.* incautious, unwary, heedless; gullible.
incendaja, *f.* (usually in *pl.*) kindling.
incendiar, *tr.v.* to set on fire, set fire to. —*r.v.* to catch fire; (fig.) to become enraged, e.g. *me incendié al oírlo,* I flared up when I heard it.
incendiario, ria, *a.* 1. incendiary. 2. (fig.) incendiary, inflammatory, trouble-making, seditious, e.g. *artículo incendiario,* inflammatory article. —*m., f.* 1. incendiary, firebug (coll.); arsonist. 2. firebrand.
incendio, *m.* fire; conflagration, combustion.— **i. forestal** or **de bosques,** forest fire; **i. intencionado** or **provocado,** arson.
incensación, *f.* incensing, censing, perfuming with incense.
incensada, *f.* 1. movement or swing of the censer or thurible. 2. (fig.) flattery.
incensario, *m.* censer, thurible.
incensar, *tr.v.* 1. to incense, cense, perfume with incense, make an incense offering to. 2. (fig.) to flatter.
incensurable, *a.* unblamable, uncensurable, not culpable.
incentivo, *m.* incentive; encouragement, spur, inducement.
incertidumbre, *f.* uncertainty, doubt, hesitancy.
incertinidad, *f., var. of* **incertidumbre.**
incertísimo, ma, *a. super. of* **incierto,** very uncertain, extremely doubtful.
incesable, *a.* incessant, unceasing, interminable.
incesablemente, *adv.* incessantly, unceasingly, interminably.
incesante, *a.* incessant, continual, unceasing, uninterrupted.
incesantemente, *adv.* incessantly, unceasingly, continually.
incesto, *m.* incest.
incestuosamente, *adv.* incestuously.
incestuoso, sa, *a.* incestuous.
incidencia, *f.* incidence; (phys., geom.) incidence. — **ángulo de i.,** angle of incidence; **por i.,** accidentally, by chance.
incidental, *a.* 1. incidental; subsidiary, subordinate, side (issue). 2. (gram.) parenthetic. 3. (law) incident.
incidentalmente, *adv.* incidentally.
incidente, *a.* incidental; (phys., law) incident. —*m.* incident, occurrence; (fig.) unpleasantness.
incidentemente, *adv.* 1. incidentally. 2. accidentally, by chance.
incidir, *i v.* to fall (into fault or error); **i. sobre,** to influence, have a bearing on, determine. —*tr.v.* (surg.) to cut, make an incision in.
incienso, *m.* 1. incense; frankincense, olibanum. 2. (fig.) flattery, incense, adulation. 3. (bot.) incense tree; **i. hembra,** incense gum obtained

by tapping; **i. macho,** incense gum obtained from natural exudations.
inciertamente, *adv.* uncertainly, doubtfully, dubiously, vaguely.
incierto, ta, *a.* 1. untrue, false. 2. uncertain, unsure. 3. unstable, inconstant, changeable. 4. unknown.
incinerable, *a.* incinerable (said of bank notes withdrawn from circulation for burning).
incineración, *f.* incineration, cremation.
incinerador, *m.* incinerator, furnace (e.g. for disposal of trash).
incinerar, *tr.v.* to incinerate, cremate, burn.
incipiente, *a.* incipient, beginning, inceptive, initial.
incircunciso, sa, *a.* uncircumcised.
incircunscripto, ta, *a.* uncircumscribed, not confined within certain limits, not hemmed in.
incisión, *f.* 1. incision, cut, gash. 2. (poet.) caesura, break, pause.
incisivo, va, *a.* 1. incisive, sharp, cutting. 2. (fig.) keen, incisive, cutting, trenchant, sharp (criticism). 3. (anat.) incisive. —*m.* (*pl.*) (anat.) incisors.
inciso, sa, *a.* cut, divided. —*m.* (gram.) sentence; clause; (gram.) comma.
incisorio, ria, *a.* (surg.) incisory, cutting.
incisura, *f.* (med.) depression, cavity.
incitación, *f.* incitement, incitation.
incitador, *f.* incitement, incitation.
incitador, ra, *m., f.* inciter, agitator; inducer.
incitamento, incitamiento, *m.* incitement, incentive.
incitante, *a.* inciting, exciting, stimulating, inducing.
incitar, *tr.v.* to incite; to induce, **lead to;** to provoke; **i. a** + *inf.,* to incite to + *inf.*
incitativo, va, *a.* inciting; inducive, provocative. —*m.* incitement. —*f.* (law.) mandatory injunction from a higher to a lower court, ordering justice to be carried out.
incivil, *a.* uncivil, rude, discourteous.
incivilidad, *f.* incivility, rudeness, discourtesy.
incivilizable, *a.* uncivilizable.
incivilmente, *adv.* uncivilly, rudely, dicourteously.
inclasificable, *a.* unclassifiable.
inclaustración, *f.* entrance into a monastic order or a convent.
inclemencia, *f.* 1. inclemency, severity, unmercifulness (said of human character) 2. inclemency, rigors, severity (said of weather).
inclemente, *a.* inclement, severe, harsh.
inclinable, *a.* inclinable.
inclinación, *f.* 1. inclination, incline, slope, slant; tilt, pitch, declivity. 2. inclination, tendency, bent, leaning, propensity; fancy. 3. inclination (of the head), bow, obeisance, nod, reverence. 4. (geom.) inclination. 5. (min.) dip, underlay. — **i. de la aguja,** dip or inclination of a magnetic needle; **de malas inclinaciones,** evilly inclined (said of a person).
inclinado, da, *past part. of* **inclinar.** —*a.* inclined, slanted, slanting, sloping. — **bien i.,** well-disposed; **mal i.,** ill-disposed; **plano i.,** inclined plane.
inclinador, ra, *a.* inclining. —*m., f.* **incliner**
inclinante, *a.* sloping, slanting.
inclinar, *tr.v.* 1. to bow, bend, incline. 2. to incline, induce, dispose, persuade. —*i.v.* to be slightly similar. —*r.v.* 1. to bow; to bend down, stoop; to lean, slant, incline, slope. 2. to be similar. 3. to feel or be inclined. — **inclinarse a** + *inf.,* to be or feel inclined to + *inf.;* **se inclinó a recoger la pelota,** he bent or stooped down to pick up the ball.
inclinómetro, *m.* (phys.) inclinometer.
ínclito, ta, *a.* illustrious, renowned, eminent, distinguished.
incluir, (*ref. 48*) *tr.v.* to include; to enclose; to contain.
inclusa, *f.* foundling home.
inclusero, ra, *a.* of or pertaining to a person who has been reared in a foundling home.
inclusión, *f.* inclusion.
inclusivamente, *adv.* inclusive, inclusively.
inclusive, *adv.* 1. inclusive, e.g. *desde el lunes hasta el viernes i.,* from Monday to Friday inclusive; including, e.g. *todos estaban, Juan i.,* everyone was there, including John. 2. moreover, and what is more, even (coll.), e.g. *te busqué, i. te escribí,* I looked for you, I even wrote to you.
inclusivo, va, *a.* inclusive, including.
incluso, *adv.* 1. (coll.) even; including, e.g. *todos se emborracharon, el cura i.,* everyone got drunk, including the priest.
incluso, sa, *past part. of* **incluir.** —*a.* enclosed, included.
incluya, incluyendo, *ref.* **incluir.**
incluyente, *a.* including, inclosing.
incluyera, incluyese, incluyo, *ref.* **incluir.**
incoación, *f.* initiation, inchoation, commencement.
incoagulable, *a.* uncoagulable, unable to thicken (blood, milk, etc.).
incoar, *tr.v.* initiate, begin, commence.
incoativo, va, *a.* (gram.) inchoative; inchoate, incipient, inceptive.
incobrable, *a.* uncollectable; irrecoverable, irretrievable.
incoercible, *a.* incoercible, unable to be forced.
incógnita, f. (math.) unknown quantity; (fig.) mystery, hidden reason or cause, unknown quantity, e.g. *su visita es una i.,* his visit is a mystery.
incógnito, ta, *a.* incognito, unknown, unrecognized. —*m., f.* incognito. —*f.* (math., fig.) unknown quantity. — **de i.,** incognito, e.g. *él viajó de i.,* he traveled incognito.
incognoscible, *a.* unknowable.
incoherencia, *f.* incoherence.
incoherente, *a.* incoherent, disconnected, disjointed.
incoherentemente, *adv.* incoherently, disconnectedly.
íncola, *m.* inhabitant, resident.
incoloro, ra, *a.* colorless.
incólume, *a.* safe, unharmed, uninjured, whole, sound.
incolumidad, *f.* safety, soundness, wholeness.
incombinable, *a.* uncombinable.
incombustibilidad, *f.* incombustibility.
incombustible, *a.* incombustible, fireproof.
incombusto, ta, *a.* not burned.
incomerciable, *a.* unmarketable, not marketable.
incomestible, *a.* inedible; indigestible.
incomible, *a.* uneatable, inedible.
incomodador, ra, *a.* 1. inconvenient. 2. annoying, vexatious.
incómodamente, *adv.* uncomfortably; inconveniently.
incomodar, *tr.v.* 1. to inconvenience, bother, trouble, disturb. 2. to annoy, vex. —*r.v.* to get or become annoyed, angry or vexed; to trouble oneself.
incomodidad, *f.* 1. discomfort; uncomfortableness. 2. inconvenience. 3. annoyance, nuisance; vexation, anger.
incómodo, da, *a.* 1. uncomfortable; uneasy. 2. troublesome, bothersome. 3. inconvenient. —*m.* discomfort, uncomfortableness. 2. inconvenience.
incomparable, *a.* incomparable, matchless.
incomparablemente, *adv.* incomparably.
incomparado, da, *a.* incomparable, matchless.
incomparencia, *f.* nonappearance.
incompartible, *a.* unsharable; indivisible.
incompasible, *a., var. of* **incompasivo.**
incompasivo, va, *a.* uncompassionate, unsympathetic, pitiless.
incompatibilidad, *f.* incompatibility, uncongeniality; inconsistency; discordance.
incompatible, *a.* incompatible, uncongenial.
incompensable, *a.* incapable of being compensated or repaid; unindemnifiable.
incompetencia, *f.* 1. incompetence, unfitness; lack of skill. 2. lack of jurisdiction.
incompetente, *a.* 1. incompetent, incapable, unfit. 2. (law) unauthorized.
incomplejo, ja, *a., var. of* **incomplexo.**
incompletamente, *adv.* incompletely.
incompleto, ta, *a.* incomplete, unfinished; lacking some part or feature.
incomplexo, xa, *a.* 1. incomplex, simple. 2. disunited, disconnected, disjointed.
incomponible, *a.* unmendable, unrepairable, irreparable.
incomportable, *a.* insupportable, unbearable, intolerable.
incomposibilidad, *f.* incompatibility, irreconcilability.
incomposible, *a.* unmendable, unrepairable, irreparable.
incomposición, *f.* lack of proportion; disrepair.
incomprehensibilidad, *f., var. of* **incomprehensibilidad.**
incomprehensible, *a., var. of* **incomprensible.**
incomprensibilidad, *f.* incomprehensibility.
incomprensible, *a.* incomprehensible, not understandable.
incomprensiblemente, *adv.* incomprehensibly, beyond understanding.
incomprensión, *f.* incomprehension, lack of understanding.
incompresibilidad, *f.* (phys.) incompressibility.
incompresible, *a.* (phys.) incompressible.
incomprimible, *a.* incompressible.
incomunicabilidad, *f.* incommunicability.
incomunicable, *a.* incommunicable.
incomunicación, *f.* 1. isolation. 2. solitary confinement.
incomunicado, da, *past part. of* **incomunicar.** —*a.* incomunicado, in confinement. —*m., f.* an isolated prisoner.
incomunicar, (*ref. 50*) *tr.v.* to isolate, confine; to put in solitary confinement. —*r.v.* to isolate oneself, shut oneself off.
incomunique, incomuniqué, *ref.* **incomunicar.**
inconcebible, *a.* inconceivable, unimaginable.
inconciliable, *a.* irreconcilable; incompatible.
inconcino, na, *a.* disarranged, disordered.
inconcluso, sa, *a.* unfinished, incomplete; **sinfonía inconclusa,** unfinished symphony.
inconcusamente, *adv.* assuredly, certainly, unquestionably, indubitably, undeniably.
inconcuso, sa, *a.* unquestionable, undeniable, incontrovertible, indisputable.
incondicional, *a.* unconditional, absolute, without reservation. —*m.* sworn follower or disciple (of a man or an idea).
incondicionalmente, *adv.* unconditionally, absolutely, categorically.
inconducente, *a.* unconducive, not contributive.
inconexión, *f.* 1. disconnection. 2. irrelevance. 3. incoherence.
inconexo, xa, *a.* unconnected, disconnected; irrelevant, not pertinent.

inconfesable, *a.* unspeakable, shameful.
inconfeso, sa, *a.* unconfessed, without confessing, without admitting his (her) guilt.
inconfidencia, *f.* distrust, mistrust.
inconfidente, *a.* distrustful, mistrustful; unreliable.
inconfundible, *a.* unmistakable.
incongruamente, *adv., var. of* **incongruentemente.**
incongruencia, *f.* incongruousness, incongruity, incongruence.
incongruente, *a.* incongruous, incongruent.
incongruentemente, *adv.* incongruously, incongruently.
incongruidad, *f., var. of* **incongruencia.**
incongruo, rua, *a.* 1. incongruous, incongruent. 2. (ecc.) lacking the necessary income to be ordained a priest. 3. disproportionate. 4. unsuitable.
inconmensurabilidad, *f.* incommensurability.
inconmensurable, *a.* incommensurable, immeasurable.
inconmovible, *a.* firm, unyielding, unbending, inexorable.
inconmutabilidad, *f.* incommutability; immutability, unchangeability, changelessness.
inconmutable, *a.* incommutable; immutable, unchangeable.
inconquistable, *a.* 1. unconquerable, invincible. 2. unbending, inexorable.
inconsciencia, *f.* 1. (physical) unconsciousness. 2. irresponsibility, unconscientiousness. 3. unawareness, unconsciousness.
inconsciente, *a.* 1. unconscious (having lost physical consciousness). 2. unaware, unconscious, uncognizant. 3. irresponsible, unconscientious, unthinking. — **el i., lo i.,** (psyc.) the unconscious. —*m., f.* irresponsible, thoughtless person.
inconscientemente, *adv.* 1. unconsciously. 2. unawares, unwittingly, unknowingly. 3. irresponsibly.
inconsecuencia, *f.* 1. inconsequence; irrelevance. 2. inconsistency.
inconsecuente, *a.* 1. inconsistent; unstable, changeable; **i. en sus opiniones,** inconsistent in one's opinions. 2. fickle, changeable; **i. con los amigos,** fickle with one's friends. 3. irrelevant, inconsequent.
inconsideración, *f.* 1. inconsiderateness, thoughtlessness. 2. rashness, impetuosity.
inconsideradamente, *adv.* 1. inconsiderately, thoughtlessly. 2. rashly, impetuously.
inconsiderado, da, *a.* 1. inconsiderate, thoughtless. 2. rash, impetuous. —*m., f.* madcap, rash person.
inconsiguiente, *a.* inconsequent; irrelevant; illogical.
inconsistencia, *f.* 1. inconsistency, instability. 2. unsubstantiality.
inconsistente, *a.* 1. inconsistent, unstable. 2. unsubstantial.
inconsolable, *a.* unconsolable, inconsolable, disconsolate, broken-hearted.
inconsolablemente, *adv.* unconsolably.
inconstancia, *f.* 1. inconstancy, fickleness, changeableness. 2. levity; volubility.
inconstante, *a.* inconstant, fickle, changeable, variable, voluble.
inconstantemente, *adv.* inconstantly, variably.
inconstitucional, *a.* unconstitutional.
inconstitucionalidad, *f.* unconstitutionality.
inconstruible, *a.* unbuildable.
inconsútil, *a.* seamless.
incontable, *a.* uncountable; innumerable, countless.
incontaminado, da, *a.* uncontaminated, unpolluted, undefiled; pure.
incontenible, *a.* uncontainable, irrepressible; **júbilo i.,** irrepressible joy.
incontestabilidad, *f.* incontestability, incontrovertibility.
incontestable, *a.* incontestable, unquestionable, indisputable, incontrovertible.
incontestablemente, *adv.* incontestably, unquestionably, indisputably.
incontestado, da, *a.* uncontested, unquestioned.
incontinencia, *f.* 1. incontinence, lack of chastity. 2. (med.) incontinence.
incontinente, *a.* 1. incontinent; unbound, unbridled, uncontrollable, unrestrained. 2. incontinent, unchaste. 3. (med.) incontinent.
incontinente, *adv., var. of* **incontinenti.**
incontinentemente, *adv.* incontinently.
incontinenti, *adv.* at once, instantly, immediately.
incontinuo, a, *a.* interrupted, not continuous.
incontrastable, *a.* irresistible, invincible; insurmountable; unshakable.
incontratable, *a.* unmanageable, unruly, intractable; unsociable, surly.
incontrito, ta, *a.* uncontrite, unashamed, unabashed.
incontrolable, *a.* uncontrollable.
incontrovertible, *a.* incontrovertible, unarguable, indisputable.
inconvencible, *a.* unconvincible; invincible.
inconvenible, *a.* 1. intractable, uncompromising, difficult. 2. unreasonable.
inconveniencia, *f.* 1. inconvenience. 2. unsuitability, unsuitableness. 3. senseless or absurd remark.
inconveniente, *a.* inconvenient, unsuitable, inappropriate; not advantageous. —*m.* 1. drawback, obstacle, difficulty. 2. objection. 3. disadvantage. — **no tener i.,** not to mind, to have nothing against; **poner inconvenientes,** to object, to present difficulties.
inconversable, *a.* unsociable; uncommunicative; intractable, surly.
inconvertible, *a.* inconvertible.
incopiable, *a.* inimitable.
incordiar, *tr.v.* to inconvenience, cause inconvenience or difficulties to, annoy, irritate.
incordio, *m.* 1. (med.) bubo. 2. (coll.) nuisance, bore, pest.
incorporación, *f.* 1. incorporation. 2. sitting up. 3. joining a group, a corps, organization, etc. 4. installation (into a new job).
incorporadero, *m.* (metal.) yard in which quicksilver is added to silver ore.
incorporador, ra, *m., f.* incorporator.
incorporal, *a.* incorporeal; intangible, without material body or substance.
incorporalmente, *adv.* incorporeally, intangibly.
incorporar, *tr.v.* 1. to incorporate, unite; to mix (one substance with others); to add (one thing to another). 2. to embody. 3. (mil.) to induct (new recruits). —*r.v.* 1. to sit up (from a reclining position). 2. to incorporate, join together. — **incorporarse a,** to become a part of, to join, e.g. *incorporarse al batallón,* to join the batallion.
incorporeidad, *f.* incorporeity, insubstantiality.
incorpóreo, a, *a.* incorporeal, bodiless.
incorporo, *m.* incorporation.
incorrección, *f.* incorrectness, lack of propriety; improper act or remark.
incorrectamente, *adv.* 1. incorrectly; inaccurately. 2. incorrectly, without propriety.
incorrecto, ta, *a.* 1. incorrect, improper. 2. incorrect, inaccurate.
incorregibilidad, *f.* incorrigibility, incorrigibleness.
incorregible, *a.* incorrigible, froward, unruly.
incorregiblemente, *adv.* incorrigibly.
incorrosible, *a.* noncorrosive.
incorrupción, *f.* incorruptness, purity, integrity; honesty.
incorruptamente, *adv.* incorruptly.
incorruptibilidad, *f.* incorruptibility.
incorruptible, *a.* 1. incorruptible, not receptive to bribes. 2. incorruptible, not vulnerable to seduction.
incorrupto, ta, *a.* incorrupt, uncorrupted; (fig.) chaste, pure.
incrasante, *a.* (med.) thickening, incrassating, inspissating. —*m.* (med.) thickening agent.
incrasar, *tr.v.* (med.) to thicken, incrassate, inspissate.
increado, *a.* uncreated.
incredibilidad, *f.* incredibility.
incrédulamente, *adv.* incredulously.
incredulidad, *f.* incredulity, incredulousness, disbelief; (ecc.) lack of faith or belief.
incrédulo, la, *a.* incredulous; (ecc.) unbelieving. —*m., f.* unbeliever, miscreant.
increíble, *a.* incredible, unbelievable.
increíblemente, *adv.* incredibly, unbelievably.
incrementar, *tr.v.* to increase, augment, intensify.
incremento, *m.* 1. increase, increment. 2. (gram.) suffix (to form augmentatives, diminutives, etc.). 3. (math.) increment.
increpación, *f.* severe rebuke or reprimand, chiding, reproach, upbraiding.
increpador, ra, *a.* rebuking, scolding, reprimanding. —*m., f.* rebuker, scolder.
increpante, *a.* rebuking, scolding, reprimanding.
increpar, *tr.v.* to rebuke or reprimand severely; to chide, scold, reprehend.
incretorio, a, *a.* (physiol.) incretory.
incriminación, *f.* incrimination, charging (someone) with a crime.
incriminar, *tr.v.* 1. to incriminate, accuse. 2. to exaggerate (a crime, fault, etc.).
incristalizable, *a.* uncrystallizable.
incruentamente, *adv.* bloodlessly, without shedding blood.
incruento, ta, *a.* bloodless (said of an offering).
incrustación, *f.* 1. incrustation; scale; mineral residue in a water boiler, etc. 2. (geol.) sinter. 3. (art.) inlay, inlaying.
incrustador, ra, *m., f.* inlayer.
incrustante, *a.* incrusting, incrustive, scale-forming (liquids).
incrustar, *tr.v.* 1. to incrust. 2. (art.) to inlay.
incuartación, *f.* (chem.) quartation.
incubación, *f.* incubation, hatching; (med.) incubation (period).
incubadora, *f.* incubator (device, receptacle).
incubar, *tr.v.* to incubate, hatch.
íncubo, *m.* 1. incubus (evil spirit having intercourse with women). 2. (med.) incubus, nightmare.
incuestionable, *a.* unquestionable, indisputable.
incuestionablemente, *adv.* unquestionably, indubitably.
inculcación, *f.* 1. inculcation, implantation (of ideas, etc.). 2. pressing one thing against another. 3. (print.) binding or wedging in a form.
inculcador, *a.* inculcating. —*m.* inculcator.
inculcar, (*ref. 50*) *tr.v.* 1. to inculcate, implant (ideas, knowledge). 2. to press together. 3. (print.) to crowd, set (type) with too little spacing. —*r.v.* to be obstinate, insistent or persistent.
inculpabilidad, *f.* innocence, guiltlessness, blamelessness. — **veredicto de i.,** (law) acquittal.
inculpable, *a.* inculpable, blameless, guiltless.

inculpablemente, *adv.* inculpably, blamelessly.
inculpación, *f.* inculpation, accusation.
inculpadamente, *adv.* guiltlessly, innocently.
inculpado, da, *past part. of* **inculpar.** —*a.* guiltless, innocent. —*m., f.* (Amer.) **el i.,** the accused.
inculpar, *tr.v.* to inculpate, blame, accuse.
inculque, inculqué, *ref.* **inculcar.**
incultamente, *adv.* uncouthly, coarsely, boorishly, rudely.
incultivable, *a.* uncultivatable, untillable, not arable.
inculto, ta, *a.* 1. uncultured, uncivilized; unrefined; uncouth, coarse, boorish. 2. uncultivated, untilled, unimproved (land).
incultura, *f.* lack of culture or refinement.
incumbencia, *f.* incumbency, obligation, duty, concern.
incumbir, *i.v.* to be incumbent, to be of concern, to pertain, e.g. *eso me incumbe a mí,* that concerns me; **i.a,** to be incumbent on (or upon).
incumplido, da, *past part. of* **incumplir.** —*a.* 1. unfulfilled (promise, etc.). 2. unpunctual. 3. remiss. —*m., f.* person breaking a promise or failing to meet an obligation.
incumplimiento, *m.* unfulfillment, nonfulfillment; breach (of contract, promise, etc.).
incumplir, *tr.v.* to fail to fulfill; to break (a contract, date, promise, etc.).
incunable, *a.* incunabular, said of books printed before the year 1501. —*m.* incunabulum, (*pl.*) incunabula.
incurabilidad, *f.* incurability, incurableness.
incurable, *a.* incurable; hopeless, irremediable.
incuria, *f.* carelessness, negligence, shiftlessness.
incurioso, sa, *a.* 1. careless, negligent; sloppy. 2. inattentive. —*m., f.* negligent or careless person.
incurrimiento, *m.* incurring; committing.
incurrir, *i.v.* to incur, become liable to (a fine, punishment, etc.). — **i. en,** to make, commit (an error); to incur, earn, bring upon oneself (hatred, anger, disdain).
incursión, *f.* incursion, raid, inroad; (mil.) incursion.
incurso, sa, *irr. past part. of* **incurrir.**
incusar, *tr.v.* to accuse, charge, impute.
incuso, sa, *a.* (numis.) incuse, stamped in.
indagación, *f.* 1. investigation, examination, inquiry; (law) inquest. 2. search.
indagador, ra, *a.* investigating, inquiring. —*m., f.* investigator, inquirer, examiner, interrogator.
indagar, (*ref. 51*) *tr.v.* to investigate, examine, inquire into or about.
indagatoria, *f.* (law) unsworn statement (required of a defendant).
indagatorio, ria, *a.* investigatory.
indague, indagué, *ref.* **indagar.**
indamina, *f.* (chem.) indamine, indamin.
indebidamente, *adv.* wrongly, unduly, improperly; unlawfully, illegally.
indebido, da, *a.* improper; illegal, unlawful.
indecencia, *f.* 1. indecency, unseemliness; unseemly remark or act. 2. indecency, obscenity.
indecente, *a.* 1. indecent, unseemly. 2. obscene, lewd. 3. wretched, miserable. 4. filthy.
indecentemente, *adv.* indecently, obscenely, lewdly.
indecible, *a.* unspeakable, inexpressible, unutterable.
indeciblemente, *adv.* unspeakably, inexpressibly, unutterably; (fig.) exceedingly.
indeciduado, da, *a.* indeciduate; (biol.) not shedding (leaves of trees, wings of insects, etc.).
indecisamente, *adv.* irresolutely.
indecisión, *f.* indecision, irresolution.
indeciso, sa, *a.* 1. undecided, hesitant, irresolute. 2. undecisive, inconclusive.
indeclinable, *a.* unavoidable, undeclinable; (gram.) undeclinable; (law) undeclinable, unwaivable.
indecoro, *m.* indecorousness, indecorum, impropriety.
indecorosamente, *adv.* indecorously, immodestly, improperly.
indecoroso, sa, *a.* indecorous, immodest, improper.
indefectibilidad, *f.* indefectibility, imperishability, immortality (said of the Roman Catholic Church).
indefectible, *a.* 1. indefectible, unfailing, unperishable. 2. unextendible (term of payment, etc.); undeferable, unpostponable (date).
indefectiblemente, *adv.* without fail, unfailingly, indefectibly.
indefendible, *a.* indefensible, unjustifiable.
indefensible, *a., var. of* **indefendible.**
indefensión, *f.* defenselessness.
indefenso, sa, *a.* defenseless; helpless.
indeficiente, *a.* unfailing, indefectible; certain.
indefinible, *a.* indefinable, undefinable.
indefinidamente, *adv.* indefinitely.
indefinido, da, *a.* 1. indefinite, vague, general; indefinite, unspecified. 2. (log., gram.) indefinite.
indehiscencia, *f.* (bot.) indehiscence.
indehiscente, *a.* (bot.) indehiscent.
indelebilidad, *f.* indelibility.
indeleble, *a.* indelible; unerasable, ineffaceable.
indeleblemente, *adv.* indelibly.
indelegable, *a.* unable to be delegated.
indeliberación, *f.* undeliberateness, indeliberateness, lack of premeditation.
indeliberadamente, *adv.* undeliberately, indeliberately, unpremeditatedly.
indeliberado, da, *a.* undeliberate, unpremeditated, indeliberate.
indelicadeza, *f.* indelicacy, discourtesy, grossness, coarseness.
indelicado, da, *a.* indelicate, gross, coarse.
indemne, *a.* undamaged, uninjured, unhurt.
indemnice, indemnicé, *ref.* **indemnizar.**
indemnidad, *f.* indemnity (security or protection against injury, damage or loss).
indemnizable, *a.* that can be indemnified.
indemnización, *f.* indemnification; indemnity, compensation.
indemnizar, (*ref. 53*) *tr.v.* to indemnify, compensate.
indemorable, *a.* undelayable.
indemostrable, *a.* undemonstrable, indemonstrable.
independencia, *f.* independence; freedom; autonomy.
independice, independicé, *ref.* **independizar.**
independiente, *a.* 1. independent, free. 2. (polit.) sovereign, autonomous, self-governing. — **i. de,** independent of. —*m., f.* (polit.) independent.
independientemente, *adv.* independently.
independizar, (*ref. 53*) *tr.v.* (neol.) to emancipate, liberate, make independent. —*r.v.* 1. to become independent or emancipated; to win freedom. 2. (polit.) to become self-governing.
indescifrable, *a.* undecipherable; incomprehensible.
indescriptible, *a.* indescribable.
indeseable, *a.* undesirable, unwanted. —*m., f.* an undesirable or despised person.
indesignable, *a.* unnameable; that cannot be designated.
indestructibilidad, *f.* indestructibility.
indestructible, *a.* indestructible.
indeterminable, *a.* 1. indeterminable, undeterminable, unascertainable. 2. indecisive, pusillanimous, hesitating, irresolute.
indeterminación, *f.* 1. indetermination, non-resolution (of a problem). 2. indetermination, irresolution, indecision, hesitancy.
indeterminadamente, *adv.* indeterminately.
indeterminado, da, *a.* 1. indeterminate, indefinite. 2. (gram.) indefinite (article). 3. (math.) indeterminate. 4. indeterminate, indecisive, pusillanimous, irresolute, hesitating, vacillating.
indeterminismo, *m.* (philos.) indeterminism.
indeterminista, *m., f.* (philos.) indeterminist.
indevoción, *f.* impiety; lack of devotion.
indevoto, ta, *a.* irreverent, undevout, irreligious.
index, *m.* index.
indezuelo, la, *m., f. dim. of* **indio,** little Indian.
India, *f.* 1. La I., India. 2. (fig.) great wealth (*gen. in pl.*) 3. (*pl.*) Indies; **Indias Occidentales Británicas,** British West Indies.
indiada, *f.* 1. (Amer.) crowd or mass of Indians. 2. expression or action typical of an Indian.
indiana, *f.* (tex.) printed calico.
indianés, sa, *a.* (arch.) native or inhabitant of India.
indianismo, *m.* (Amer.) interest in or study of the Indians of the Western Hemisphere.
indianista, *m., f.* 1. Indianist, specialist or expert in Hindustani culture. 2. (Amer.) specialist or expert in the Indian cultures of the Western Hemisphere.
indiano, na, *a.* Spanish American; West or East Indian. —*m., f.* Spanish American; West or East Indian; nabob, person returning to Europe from South America with great wealth; **i. de hilo negro,** (coll.) tightwad, skinflint.
indicación, *f.* indication; suggestion, hint, clue; instruction; direction. — **dar indicaciones,** to give (someone) instructions (for the use of a medicine, etc.), give (someone) directions or direct (someone) to a street, etc.; **por i. de,** at the indication or suggestion of.
indicado, da, *past part. of* **indicar.** —*a.* indicated, appropriate, e.g. *ése es el traje i. para esta ocasión,* that's the appropriate dress for this occasion.
indicador, ra, *a.* indicating; indicatory. —*m.* 1. indicator, register, gauge, index, pointer. 2. (mar.) draft and trim indicator. — **i. de deriva,** (aer.) drift indicator; **i. de foco del farol,** (auto.) beam indicator light; **i. de humo,** smoke detector; **i. de rayo,** (auto.) beam indicator light; **i. de régimen ascensional,** (aer.) climb indicator; **i. de sintonía,** (rad.) tuning eye; **i. de techo,** (aer.) ceiling height indicator.
indicano, *m.* (chem.) indican.
indicante, *a.* 1. indicating, indicant. 2. (med.) indicant.
indicar, (*ref. 50*) *tr.v.* 1. to indicate; to show, point out. 2. to hint, suggest.
indicativo, va, *a.* indicative, showing, pointing out; (gram.) indicative. —*m.* 1. (gram.) indicative. 2. (rad.) call sign. 3. code (of a telephone number).
indicción, *f.* 1. indiction. 2. (ecc.) convocation, convening (of a synod or council).
índice, *a.* index (finger). —*m.* 1. index; list, catalogue; library room containing the catalogue. 2. indication, sign, index. 3. ratio, index. 4. (anat.) index finger. 5. index, hand (of a clock), needle (of a measuring gauge), gnomon (of a sundial). 6. (math.) exponent, index, (*pl.*) indices. — **i. alfabético,** alphabetical index; **i. cefálico,** (zool.) cephalic index; **í. de audiencia,** (tel.) audience ratings; **í. de cetano,** cetane rating; **í. de cobre,** (chem.) copper value; **í. de compresión,** (engin.) compression ratio; **í. del costo de vida,** cost of living index; **í. de deflación,**

(econ.) deflator; **i. de mortalidad,** death rate; **i. de natalidad,** birth rate; **í. de precios,** price index; **í. de refracción,** (opt.) refractive index; refraction; **i. de vida,** life expectancy; **í. expurgatorio,** (rel.) Index Expurgatorius (Lat.) (list of books to be amended); **i. temático** or **de materias,** table of contents.
indiciado, da, *past part. of* **indiciar.** —*a.* suspect (of having committed a crime).
indiciador, ra, *a.* indicatory, indicative; suggestive.
indiciar, *tr.v.* 1. to indicate, suggest. 2. to suspect, surmise.
indiciario, ria, *a.* (law) circumstancial; **pruebas indiciarias,** circumstantial evidence.
indicio, *m.* indication, sign, token; trace, clue, track; (law) (*pl.*) evidence, clues; **indicios vehementes,** (law) circumstancial evidence.
indicioso, sa, *a.* suspicious.
índico, ca, *a.* Indian, East Indian; **Océano Indico,** Indian Ocean.
indiferencia, *f.* indifference, apathy, neglect; neutrality.
indiferente, *a.* indifferent, apathetic, unconcerned; inattentive, listless, e.g. *me es i.,* it's all the same to me.
indiferentemente, *adv.* indifferently, apathetically.
indiferentismo, *m.* (philos.) indifferentism.
indígena, *a.* indigenous, native. —*m, f.* native, aboriginal.
indigencia, *f.* indigence, poverty, need, want, penury.
indigenismo, *m.* the study of or predilection for the history, culture, protection and development of the Indians of the Western Hemisphere.
indigenista, *a.* 1. dealing with or writing about Western Hemisphere Indian subjects and themes. 2. defending the interest of the Indian population (of the Western Hemisphere). —*m., f.* 1. supporter of the interests and rights of the Indian population (of the Western Hemisphere). 2. writer on Indian themes and subjects.
indigente, *a.* indigent, destitute, poor, needy, in want.
indigestarse, *r.v.* 1. to cause or give indigestion, e.g. *se le indigestó la comida,* the meal gave him indigestion; to get indigestion, e.g. *se indigestó,* he got indigestion. 2. to dislike, e.g. *este tipo me indigesta,* I dislike that fellow.
indigestible, *a.* indigestible.
indigestión, *f.* indigestion.
indigesto, ta, *a.* 1. indigestible, not easily digested. 2. undigested. 3. (fig.) undigested, jumbled, confused (e.g. facts). 4. rough, uncouth. 5. grouchy, surly, disagreeable.
indignación, *f.* indignation, righteous wrath.
indignado, da, *past part. of* **indignar.** —*a.* indignant, outraged.
indignamente, *adv.* unworthily, unbecomingly, despicably.
indignante, *a.* irritating, causing indignation.
indignar, *tr.v.* to make indignant, irritate, anger. —*r.v.* to become indignant; **indignarse con** or **contra,** to become indignant with (someone); **indignarse de** or **por,** to become indignant at (a base or unjust act).
indignidad, *f.* indignity; unworthiness.
indigno, na, *a.* 1. unworthy; contemptible. 2. despicable, base, low. — **i. de,** unworthy of.
índigo, *m.* indigo (plant, dye, color).
indigotina, *f.* indigotin, indigotine (coloring principle of indigo).
indiligencia, *f.* negligence, carelessness, laziness; lack of diligence.
indinar, *tr.v., r.v.* (coll.) *var. of* **indignar.**
indino, na, *a.* 1. (coll.) despicable, base, contemptible. 2. mischievous, cheeky, saucy.
indio, dia, *a.* 1. Indian. 2. blue. —*m., f.* Indian (of America or Asia). —*m.* (chem.) indium.
indiófilo, la, *m., f.* protector or friend of the Indians.
indique, indiqué, *ref.* **indicar.**
indirecta, *f.* hint, insinuation, innuendo. — **i. del padre Cobos,** (coll.) broad hint.
indirectamente, *adv.* indirectly.
indirecto, ta, *a.* indirect.
indiscernible, *a.* undiscernible, inconspicuous, imperceptible.
indisciplina, *f.* indiscipline, lack of discipline.
indisciplinable, *a.* untrainable, intractable, unmanageable.
indisciplinado, da, *past part. of* **indisciplinarse.** —*a.* undisciplined, untrained.
indisciplinarse, *r.v.* to become undisciplined, unruly, disorderly.
indiscreción, *f.* indiscretion, imprudence.
indiscretamente, *adv.* indiscreetly, imprudently.
indiscreto, ta, *a.* indiscreet; injudicious, unwise, imprudent. —*m., f.* imprudent person.
indisculpable, *a.* inexcusable, unpardonable.
indiscutible, *a.* indisputable, unquestionable.
indiscutiblemente, *adv.* indisputably, unquestionably.
indisolubilidad, *f.* indissolubility.
indisoluble, *a.* indissoluble, undissolvable.
indisolublemente, *adv.* indissolubly.
indispensabilidad, *f.* indispensableness, indispensability.
indispensable, *a.* 1. indispensable, essential. 2. unpardonable.
indispensablemente, *adv.* indispensably, necessarily, unfailingly.
indispondré, indispondría, *ref.* **indisponer.**
indisponer, (*ref. 15*) *tr.v.* 1. to upset, make unwell, indispose. 2. to make unfit, disabled. 3. to prejudice, set (one person) against (another), to estrange. — **i. con,** to put on bad terms with, estrange from. —*r.v.* 1. to fall ill, become indisposed, be upset. 2. to fall out, become estranged; **indisponerse con,** to fall out with.
indisponga, indispongo, *ref.* **indisponer.**
indisposición, *f.* 1. indisposition, slight illness. 2. unpreparedness. 3. dislike, aversion.
indispuesto, *irr. past part. of* **indisponer.** —*a.* 1. indisposed, slightly ill, unwell. 2. at variance, on bad terms.
indispuse, indispusiera, indispusiese, *ref.* **indisponer.**
indisputabilidad, *f.* indisputability.
indisputable, *a.* indisputable, unquestionable.
indisputablemente, *adv.* indisputably, unquestionably.
indistinción, *f.* 1. vagueness (of concepts). 2. lack of distinction (in persons).
indistinguible, *a.* indistinguishable, undistinguishable.
indistintamente, *adv.* indistinctly, not distinctly, not clearly; indifferently, indiscriminately.
indistinto, ta, *a.* indistinct, vague, unclear.
individuación, *f.* individuation.
individual, *a.* individual, personal, characteristic.
individualice, individualicé, *ref.* **individualizar.**
individualidad, *f.* 1. individuality. 2. (fig.) personality.
individualismo, *m.* individualism.
individualista, *a.* individualistic. —*m., f.* individualist.
individualizar, (*ref. 53*) *tr.v.* to particularize, indicate individually, individualize; (Amer.) to know, to identify.
individualmente, *adv.* individually; one by one.
individuamente, *adv.* indivisibly, inseparably.
individuar, (*ref. 55*) *tr.v.* to individuate, treat individually; to particularize.
individuo, a, *a.* individual; indivisible, inseparable. —*m., f.* (coll.) individual, person. —*m.* individual, person; member fellow (of a society, etc.). —*f.* (derog.) woman, broad (sl.).
indivisamente, *adv.* undividedly, indivisibly, not separable.
indivisibilidad, *f.* indivisibility, permanent wholeness or togetherness; integrity.
indivisible, *a.* 1. indivisible. 2. (math.) leaving a remainder when divided.
indivisiblemente, *adv.* indivisibly.
indivisión, *f.* 1. oneness, entirety, indivision. 2. (law) joint ownership.
indiviso, sa, *a.* (law) undivided.
indo, da, *a., m., f.* Indian, Hindu. —*m.* **I.,** Indus.
indochino, na, *a., m., f.* Indo-Chinese. —*f.* **I.,** Indochina.
indócil, *a.* 1. unruly, headstrong, unmanageable. 2. intractable, indocile, inflexible. 3. unteachable.
indocilidad, *f.* unruliness, intractableness, indocility.
indoctamente, *adv.* ignorantly, illiterately.
indocto, ta, *a.* ignorant, illiterate; unschooled, untaught, uneducated.
indoctrinado, da, *a.* indoctrinated.
indocumentado, da, *a.* 1. without identification papers. 2. groundless (statement). 3. (fig.) rootless, unsettled. —*m., f.* (fig.) rootless person.
indoeuropeo, a, *a., m., f.* Indo-European.
indofenol, *m.* (chem.) indophenol.
indogermánico, ca, *a., m., f.* Indo-Germanic.
indol, *m.* (chem.) indole.
indolacético, ca, *a.* (bot.) indoleacetic.
indolbutírico, ca, *a.* (bot.) indolbutyric.
índole, *f.* 1. nature, character, disposition. 2. class, kind, type.
indolencia, *f.* 1. indolence, sloth, laziness, apathy. 2. absence of pain.
indolente, *a.* 1. indolent, lazy, slothful, apathetic. 2. (med.) indolent.
indolentemente, *adv.* indolently, lazily, sluggishly, apathetically.
indoloro, ra, *a.* (med.) painless, indolent.
indomabilidad, *f.* untamableness; dauntlessness, indomitableness.
indomable, *a.* 1. untamable; indomitable, dauntless. 2. unmanageable.
indomado, da, *a.* untamed.
indomesticable, *a.* wild, untamable, not susceptible to domestication.
indomesticado, da, *a.* wild, undomesticated, untamed.
indoméstico, ca, *a.* wild, undomesticated, untamed.
indómito, ta, *a.* untamed; indomitable, unsubduable, unruly.
Indonesia, *f.* Indonesia.
Indonesio, sia, *a., m., f.* Indonesian.
Indostán, *m.* Hindustan.
indostanés, sa, *a.* Hindustani. —*m., f.* native of Hindustan.
indostani, *m.* Hindustani (language).
indostánico, ca, *a.* Hindustani, Hindu.
indotación, *f.* lack of a dowry.
indotado, da, *a.* without a dowry, unendowed.
indoxilo, *m.* (chem.) indoxyl.
indri, *m.* (zool.) indri.
indubitable, *a.* indubitable, doubtless, certain, unquestionable.
indubitablemente, *adv.* indubitably, doubtlessly, undoubtedly, unquestionably.

indubitadamente, *adv.* indubitably, doubtlessly.
indubitado, da, *a.* certain, undoubted, unquestionable.
inducción, *f.* (log., elec.) induction; **bobina** or **carrete de i.,** induction coil.
inducia, *f.* truce, respite; delay.
inducido, *m.* (phys.) armature (of a dynamo).
inducidor, ra, *a.* inducive. *—m., f.* inducer, persuader.
inducimiento, *m.* inducement.
inducir, (*ref. 47*) *tr.v.* 1. to induce, lead, persuade, influence. 2. (log.) to induce, infer. 3. (elec.) to induce. — **i. a** + *inf.*, to induce or lead to + *inf.*
inductancia, *f.* (elec.) inductance.
inductividad, *f.* (elec.) inductivity.
inductivo, va, *a.* inductive.
inductor, ra, *a.* (elec.) inductive. *—m.* (elec.) inductor, magnetic field (of a dynamo). — **i. variable,** (elec.) variable inductor.
indudable, *a.* doubtless, indubitable, certain.
indudablemente, *adv.* undoubtedly, indubitably, certainly.
induje, indujera, indujese, *ref.* **inducir.**
indulgencia, *f.* 1. indulgence, leniency, forbearance. 2. (rel.) indulgence, pardon (in the Catholic church); **i. parcial,** partial indulgence; **i. plenaria,** plenary indulgence.
indulgente, *a.* indulgent, forbearing, lenient.
indulgentemente, *adv.* indulgingly, indulgently.
indulina, *f.* (chem.) induline, indulin.
indultar, *tr.v.* to pardon, exonerate; exempt; (law) to grant amnesty, to pardon.
indulto, *m.* 1. pardon, exoneration; indult. 2. (law) pardon, exoneration, amnesty, commutation.
indumentaria, *f.* 1. clothes, clothing, garments. 2. study of ancient garments.
indumentario, a, *a.* of or pertaining to clothes or clothing.
indumento, *m.* 1. clothing, garments; vestment. 2. (bot.) indumentum.
induración, *f.* hardening, induration; (med.) induration.
indurado, da, *a.* (med.) indurated.
indurar, *tr.v.* (med.) to indurate, harden.
indusio, *m.* (bot.) indusium.
industria, *f.* 1. industry, manufacturing, e.g. *i. algodonera,* cotton industry. 2. skill, ingenuity, cleverness. — **de i.,** on purpose, intentionally, deliberately; **i. artesanal,** cottage industry; **i. automovilística** or **del automóvil,** automobile industry; **i. casera,** cottage industry; **i. ligera,** light industry; **i. militar,** defense industry; **i. pesada,** heavy industry; **i. pesquera,** fishing industry; **industrias básicas,** staple industries; **i. siderúrgica,** iron and steel industry; **i. terciaria,** service industry.
industrial, *a.* industrial. *—m.* industrialist, manufacturer.
industrialice, industrialicé, *ref.* **industrializar.**
industrialismo, *m.* 1. industrialism. 2. mercantilism, commercialism.
industrialista, *a.* pertaining to or in favor of industrialism.
industrialización, *f.* industrialization.
industrializar, 1. *tr.v.* to industrialize. 2. *i.v.* to be or become industrialized.
industriar, *tr.v.* to instruct, train, teach, coach. *—r.v.* to manage, find a way (of doing something).
industriosamente, *adv.* 1. industriously. 2. skillfully.
industrioso, sa, *a.* 1. industrious, assiduous, hard-working, diligent. 2. skillful, clever.
induzca, induzco, *ref.* **inducir.**
inebriar, *tr.v.* to intoxicate, inebriate, make drunk.
inecuación, *f.* (math.) inequality.
inedia, *f.* 1. fasting, abstinence from food. 2. inanition, weakness from malnutrition or starvation.
inédito, ta, *a.* 1. unpublished. 2. unprecedented, new, hitherto unheard of.
ineducable, *a.* ineducable.
ineducación, *f.* 1. unmannerliness, rudeness, impoliteness. 2. lack of education.
ineducado, da, *a.* 1. unmannerly, uncivil, impolite. 2. uneducated.
inefabilidad, *f.* ineffability, unspeakableness.
inefable, *a.* ineffable, inexpressible, unutterable, indescribable.
inefablemente, *adv.* ineffably.
ineficacia, *f.* inefficacy, inefficaciousness.
ineficaz, (*pl.* **ineficaces**), *a.* inefficacious, ineffective, inefficient, ineffectual.
ineficazmente, *adv.* inefficaciously, ineffectively.
inejecución, *f.* nonperformance; nonfulfillment.
inejecutable, *a.* impracticable, not feasible.
inelegancia, *f.* inelegance.
inelegante, *a.* inelegant.
inelegibilidad, *f.* ineligibility.
inelegible, *a.* ineligible.
ineluctable, *a.* ineluctable, irresistible, inevitable.
ineludible, *a.* inevitable, unavoidable, unescapable.
inembargable, *a.* that can not be seized or embargoed.
inenarrable, *a.* inexpressible, undescribable.
inepcia, *f.* foolishness, stupidity; (Hond.) ineptitude, incompetence, inability.
ineptamente, *adv.* ineptly, incompetently.
ineptitud, *f.* ineptitude, ineptness, incompetence.
inepto, ta, *a.* inept, incompetent, incapable, inefficient, unfit. *—m., f.* incompetent, inept or incompetent person.
inequívoco, ca, *a.* unequivocal, unmistakable, certain.
inercia, *f.* inertia, inertness; (mec.) inertia.
inerme, *a.* 1. unarmed; defenseless. 2. (bot., zool.) thornless, without prickles or spines.
inerrable, *a.* inerrable, incapable of erring, infallible.
inerrante, *a.* (astron.) fixed (star).
inerte, *a.* 1. inert, motionless. 2. sluggish, dull, slow. 3. lazy, indolent; inactive.
inervación, *f.* (physiol.) innervation.
inervador, ra, *a.* innerving, innervating.
inescrutabilidad, *f.* inscrutability.
inescrutable, *a.* inscrutable, incomprehensible, unfathomable.
inescudriñable, *a., var. of* **inescrutable.**
inesperadamente, *adv.* suddenly, unexpectedly.
inesperado, da, *a.* unexpected, unforeseen.
inestabilidad, *f.* instability.
inestable, *a.* unstable.
inestabilizar, (*ref. 53*) *tr.v.* to make changeable, make variable (the weather or atmosphere).
inestimabilidad, *f.* inestimability.
inestimable, *a.* inestimable; priceless, invaluable.
inestimablemente, *adv.* invaluably.
inestimado, da, *a.* 1. unestimated, not appraised. 2. underestimated.
inevitable, *a.* inevitable, unavoidable.
inevitablemente, *adv.* inevitably.
inexactamente, *adv.* inaccurately, inexactly.
inexactitud, *f.* inaccuracy, inexactness.
inexacto, ta, *a.* inaccurate, inexact; untrue.
inexcusabilidad, *f.* inexcusability, inexcusableness.
inexcusable, *a.* inexcusable, unpardonable, unforgivable.
inexcusablemente, *adv.* inexcusably.
inexhausto, ta, *a.* unexhausted, inexhaustible, unspent.
inexistencia, *f.* inexistence, non-existence.
inexistente, *a.* inexistent, non-existent.
inexorabilidad, *f.* inexorability, inexorableness.
inexorable, *a.* inexorable, unyielding, relentless.
inexorablemente, *adv.* inexorably.
inexperiencia, *f.* inexperience, lack of experience.
inexperto, ta, *a.* inexperienced; inexpert, unskilled. *—m., f.* greenhorn, novice, inexperienced person.
inexpiable, *a.* inexpiable, unatonable.
inexplicable, *a.* inexplicable, unexplainable.
inexplicablemente, *adv.* inexplicably.
inexplicado, da, *a.* unexplained.
inexplorado, da, *a.* unexplored.
inexplosible, *a.* (phys.) unexplosive, non-explosive.
inexplotable, *a.* unexploitable, unworkable (mine, land, etc.).
inexpresable, *a.* inexpressible; unutterable, unspeakable.
inexpresado, da, *a.* unexpressed.
inexpresivo, va, *a.* inexpressive.
inexpugnable, *a.* impregnable, inexpugnable; unassailable.
inextensibilidad, *f.* inextensibility.
inextensible, *a.* inextensible, unextendible.
inextenso, sa, *a.* short, limited.
in extenso, (Lat.) at full length.
inextinguible, *a.* inextinguishable, unquenchable; (fig.) perpetual, eternal.
inextirpable, *a.* inextirpable, ineradicable.
in extremis, (Lat.) at the point of death.
inextricable, *a.* inextricable.
infacundo, da, *a.* ineloquent, inexpressive.
infalibilidad, *f.* infallibility.
infalible, *a.* infallible, never-failing
infaliblemente, *adv.* infallibly.
infalsificable, *a.* unfalsifiable.
infamación, *f.* 1. defamation, discrediting; calumny. 2. dishonoring, disgracing; dishonor, discredit.
infamadamente, *adv.* slanderously, calumniously.
infamador, ra, *a.* defamatory, slanderous, calumnious. *—m., f.* defamer, detractor.
infamante, *a.* defamatory, slanderous, calumnious; disgraceful, shameful, ignominious.
infamar, *tr.v.* to defame, slander; to dishonor, discredit. *—r.v.* to be dishonored or discredited; to be in disgrace.
infamativo, va, *a.* defamatory, slanderous, libelous.
infamatorio, ria, *a.* defamatory, slanderous, libelous.
infame, *a.* 1. infamous, base, vile. 2. disgusting, dirty. *—m.* scoundrel, blackguard.
infamemente, *adv.* infamously.
infamia, *f.* 1. infamy, baseness, vileness. 2. disgrace, dishonor, discredit.
infancia, *f.* 1. infancy. 2. (fig.) babies, children (collectively). 3. (fig.) infancy, beginning, first stage.
infando, da, *a.* unmentionable, unspeakable, disgusting.
infanta, *f.* 1. female infant. 2. Infanta (any daughter of a king of Spain or Portugal, except the eldest); wife of an Infante.
infantado, *m.* appanage, territory belonging to the younger children of a king of Spain or Portugal.
infante, *m.* 1. male infant. 2. infante (any son of a king of Spain or Portugal, except the eldest). 3. (mil.) infantryman. — **i. de coro,** choirboy; **i. de marina,** marine.
infantería, *f.* infantry; **i. de línea,** infantry of the line; **i. de marina,** marines; Marine Corps; **i. ligera,** light infantry.

infanticida, *a.* infanticidal. *—m., f.* infanticide, person who has killed a child.
infanticidio, *m.* infanticide (murder of a child).
infantil, *a.* infantile, e.g. *parálisis i.,* infantile paralysis; child, e.g. *psicología i.,* child psychology; children's, e.g. *juegos infantiles,* children's games; childlike, simple, innocent; infantile, childish, babyish, silly.
infantilismo, *m.* (med.) infantilism.
infantino, na, *a., var. of* **infantil.**
infanzón, na, *m., f.* nobleman (*m.*) or noblewoman (*f.*) with limited privileges.
infanzonado, da, *a.* of or pertaining to an **infanzón, na.**
infanzonazgo, *m.* property of an **infanzón, na.**
infanzonía, *f.* dignity or position of an **infanzón, na.**
infartar, *tr.v.* (med.) to cause an infarct in. *—r.v.* to suffer an infarct.
infarto, *m.* (med.) heart attack; **i. de miocardio,** myocardial infarction, heart attack; **i. pulmonar,** pulmonary infarction.
infatigable, *a.* indefatigable, inexhaustible, untiring.
infatigablemente, *adv.* indefatigably, untiringly, tirelessly.
infatuación, *f.* conceit, presumption, vanity.
infatuar, (*ref. 55*) *tr.v.* to make vain or conceited. *—r.v.* to become vain or conceited.
infaustamente, *adv.* unluckily, unfortunately.
infausto, ta, *a.* unlucky, unhappy; unfortunate; accursed.
infebril, *a.* without fever, fever-free, (med.) afebrile.
infección, *f.* 1. infection, contamination. 2. (fig.) moral corruption, perversion.
infeccionar, *tr.v.* to infect, contaminate.
infeccioso, sa, *a.* infectious.
infectar, *tr.v.* to infect, corrupt, contaminate. *—r.v.* to become infected, (fig.) to become corrupted or tainted.
infectivo, va, *a.* infective, infectious, contagious.
infecto, ta, *a.* 1. infected, contaminated. 2. tainted, corrupted.
infecundidad, *f.* infecundity, sterility, barrenness.
infecundo, da, *a.* infecund, sterile, barren.
infelice, *a.* (poet.) unhappy, wretched.
infelicemente, *adv.* unhappily, unluckily.
infelicidad, *f.* unhappiness, infelicity, wretchedness.
infeliz, (*pl.* **infelices**), *a.* 1. unhappy; unfortunate, luckless. 2. (coll.) simple, good-hearted. *—m., f.* 1. poor devil, wretch. 2. simple soul.
infelizmente, *adv.* unfortunately, unluckily; unhappily.
inferencia, *f.* inference.
inferior, *a.* inferior; lower; (geog.) lower, nether. *—m.* inferior, subject, subordinate. — **labio inferior,** lower lip.
inferioridad, *f.* inferiority; **complejo de i.,** inferiority complex.
inferir, (*ref. 42*) *tr.v.* 1. to infer, deduce, conclude. 2. to lead to. 3. to cause, inflict (a wound, an insult).
infernáculo, *m.* a kind of hopscotch (a children's game).
infernal, *a.* 1. infernal, hellish. 2. (fig.) wicked, diabolic, fiendish (plan, idea, etc.). 3. (coll.) confounded, infernal, infuriating (din, etc.); **máquina i.,** (mil.) infernal machine (military incendiary contrivance); **nave i.,** fire ship; **piedra i.,** infernal stone, silver nitrate (used for cauterizing).
infernalmente, *adv.* infernally, hellishly.
infernar, (*ref. 29*) *tr.v.* 1. to damn. 2. (coll.) to irritate, disturb, annoy, vex, provoke.
infernillo, *m.* spirit lamp; small portable stove.
inferno, na, *a.* (poet.) infernal, hellish.
infero, ra, *a.* (bot.) inferior, lower.
infestación, *f.* infestation.
infestar, *tr.v.* 1. to infest; proliferate in; overrun. 2. to infest, plague. 3. (fig.) to overrun. *—r.v.* to become infested.
infesto, ta, *a.* (poet.) noxious, harmful, prejudicial, dangerous.
infeudación, *f.* (law) enfeoffment.
infeudar, *tr.v.* (law) to enfeoff.
infibulación, *f.* (vet.) infibulation.
infibular, *tr.v.* (vet.) to infibulate (to attach a ring or clasp to the genital organs to prevent copulation).
inficcionar, *tr.v.* imp. u. *var. of* **inficionar.**
inficionar, *tr.v.* 1. to infect, contaminate. 2. to taint, poison, (fig.) to defile; corrupt, pervert. *—r.v.* 1. to become infected or contaminated. 2. (fig.) to become corrupted.
infidelidad, *f.* 1. infidelity, unfaithfulness. 2. disbelief, unbelief in Christianity.
infidelísimo, ma, *a. super. of* **infiel,** very or most unfaithful.
infidencia, *f.* 1. treason. 2. unfaithfulness, disloyalty, faithlessness.
infidente, *a.* 1. unfaithful, disloyal. 2. treasonous, treasonable. *—m., f.* 1. disloyal person. 2. traitor.
infiel, *a.* 1. unfaithful; disloyal, faithless. 2. inaccurate, inexact, unfaithful. 3. infidel. *—m., f.* infidel, unbeliever, pagan.
infielmente, *adv.* unfaithfully, disloyally.
infiera, infiero, *ref.* **inferir.**
infierne, *ref.* **infernar.**
infiernillo, *m.* spirit lamp, small portable stove.
infierno, *m.* 1. hell; (*pl.*) Hades, nether world (of the pagans). 2. torture, punishment. 3. (fig.) inferno, hell. 4. Limbo, (theol.) Abraham's bosom. 5. underground foundation (for a mill wheel). 6. vat containing the water used in scalding the paste of crushed olives. 7. (coll.) madhouse, bedlam, noisy disorderly place. — **en los quintos infiernos,** in hell and beyond, very far away.
infierno, *ref.* **infernar.**
infigurable, *a.* unportrayable; incorporeal.
infijo, *m.* (gram.) infix.
infiltración, *f.* infiltration; percolation; permeation.
infiltrar, *tr.v., r.v.* 1. to infiltrate, filter, infuse; to permeate. 2. to imbue, seep in. 3. (fig., pol.) to undermine.
ínfimo, ma, *a.* 1. lowest; smallest, least. 2. vilest, most abject, meanest. 3. humblest.
infinidad, *f.* infinity, an infinite number; (coll.) a lot.
infinitamente, *adv.* infinitely, forever.
infinitesimal, *a.* infinitesimal.
infinitésimo, *m.* (math.) infinitesimal.
infinitivo, *a., m.* (gram.) infinitive.
infinito, ta, *a.* infinite, limitless, immense, unbounded. — **a lo infinito,** ad infinitum. *—m.* infinite; (math., opt.) infinity.
infinito, *adv.* infinitely, extremely, exceedingly, immensely.
infinitud, *f.* 1. infinity, the immeasurable; (math.) infinity.
infiriendo, infiriera, infiriese, infirió, *ref.* **inferir.**
infirmar, *tr v.* (law) to invalidate, nullify, render null and void.
inflable, *a.* inflatable.
inflación, *f.* 1. (econ.) inflation. 2. swelling, distension. 3. (fig.) vanity, conceit. — **i. galopante,** (econ.) runaway inflation.
inflacionario, ria, *a.* inflationary.
inflacionismo, *m.* (econ.) inflationism.
inflacionista, *a.* inflationary. *—m., f.* (econ.) inflationist (advocate of inflation).
inflado, da, *past part. of* **inflar.** *—a.* inflated, swollen.
inflamabilidad, *f.* inflammability, combustibility.
inflamable, *a.* inflammable, combustible.
inflamación, *f.* inflammation. — **punto de i.,** (phys.) flash point.
inflamar, *tr.v.* 1. to inflame, stir up (passions, emotions). 2. to set on fire, set fire to. *—r.v.* 1. to become inflamed or stirred up (passions). 2. to become inflamed (wounds). 3. to burst into flame, catch fire.
inflamatorio, ria, *a.* inflammatory.
inflamiento, *m., var. of* **inflación.**
inflar, *tr.v.* 1. to inflate, blow up (balloon, tire, etc.). 2. to inflate or puff up with pride. 3. to exaggerate, inflate. 4. (econ.) to inflate. *—r.v.* 1. to become inflated or blown up. 2. to become puffed up with pride, become proud. 3. (econ.) to become inflated.
inflativo, va, *a.* inflating.
inflectivo, va, *a.* (gram.) inflective, inflectional.
inflexibilidad, *f.* inflexibility; firmness, unbending quality or nature (of character).
inflexible, *a.* 1. inflexible. 2. firm, unbending, unyielding (character).
inflexiblemente, *adv.* inflexibly; unyieldingly, firmly.
inflexión, *f.* inflection; (gram.) inflection, modulation.
inflictivo, va, *a.* inflictive.
infligir, (*ref. 62*) *tr.v.* to inflict; to condemn.
inflija, inflijo, *ref.* **infligir.**
inflorescencia, *f.* (bot.) inflorescence.
influencia, *f.* 1. influence. 2. (theol.) divine grace. 3. (fig.) authority.
influenciar, *tr.v.* (Amer.) to influence.
influente, *a.* influential.
influenza, *f.* (med.) influenza, flu.
influir, (*ref. 48*) *tr.v.* 1. to influence, have influence on. 2. (theol.) to inspire with grace. *—i.v.* 1. to have influence. 2. to have or produce an effect. — **i. en** or **sobre,** to bear upon; to have or produce an effect on; **i. sobre alguien para que** + *subj.,* to bear upon someone to + *inf.*
influjo, *m.* 1. influence. 2. rise (of the tide).
influya, influyendo, *ref.* **influir.**
influyente, *a.* influential.
influyera, influyese, influyo, *ref.* **influir.**
infolio, *m.* (print.) folio, book in folio.
inforciado, *m.* infortiate, second part of Justinian's Pandects.
información, *f.* 1. information, data. 2. report, testimonial. 3. inquiry, investigation, inquest. — **fuente de i.,** source of information.
informado, da, *past part. of* **informar.** *—a.* informed.
informador, ra, *a.* informing. *—m., f.* 1. informant. 2. reporter, journalist. — **i. de policía,** informer; **i. gráfico,** press photographer.
informal, *a.* unreliable; unconventional. *—m., f.* unreliable person. — **traje i.,** casual dress.
informalidad, *f.* unreliability.
informalmente, *adv.* informally; casually.
informante, *a.* informing. *—m.* informant, informer.
informar, *tr.v.* 1. to inform, tell. 2. to write a report on, report on. 3. (philos.) to shape, give form, inform. *—i.v.* 1. to inform. 2. (law) to plead. 3. to pronounce (on), give an opinion (on). *—r.v.* 1. to find out, get information. 2. to inquire, investigate.

informática, *f.* computer science, computing; information storage.
informático, ca, *a,* computer. —*m., f.* computer specialist; programmer.
informativo, va, *a,* informative, information, news; **programa i.,** news program; **un folleto i.,** an information booklet. —*m.* news program, news.
informatización, *f.* computerization.
informatizar, (*ref. 53*) *tr.v.* to computerize. —*r.v.* to become computerized.
informe, *a.* shapeless, formless. —*m.* 1. report; **i. a la prensa,** press release; **i. annual,** annual report; **i. de gestión,** chairman's report; **i. médico,** medical report; **i. policial,** police report. 2. (*pl.*) information, particulars. 3. (*pl.*) references; **pedir informes,** to ask for references. 4. (law) pleading.
informidad, *f.* 1. shapelessness; ugliness. 2. vagueness.
infortificable, *a.* unfortifiable.
infortuna, *f.* (astrol.) adverse influence of the stars.
infortunadamente, *adv.* unfortunately.
infortunado, da, *a.* unlucky, unfortunate. —*m., f.* unlucky or poor wretch.
infortunio, *m.* misfortune, misery.
infosura, *f.* (vet.) (form of) founder.
infracción, *f.* infraction, infringement.
infracto, ta, *a.* steady, firm, stolid.
infractor, ra, *a.* infringing; violating, transgressing. —*m., f.* violator, infringer.
infraestructura, *f.* substructure, infrastructure.
in fraganti, *adv.* in the act, redhanded.
infrahumano, na, *a.* subhuman; infrahuman, unworthy (of human beings).
infralapsarismo, *m.* (rel.) infralapsarianism.
inframaxilar, *a.* (med.) inframaxillary.
infrangible, *a.* infrangible, unbreakable.
infranqueable, *a.* unsurmountable (of obstacles); unenterable (of doors); impassable (road).
infraoctavo, va, *a.* (ecc.) within the octave, pertaining to the six days between the first and last of the octave. —*f.* the six days between the first and last of an octave.
infraorbitario, ria, *a.* (anat.) infraorbital.
infrarrojo, ja, *a.* infrared.
infrascripto, ta, *a.* 1. written hereafter. 2. undersigned. —*m., f.* undersigned, signer.
infrascrito, ta, *a., m., f., var. of* **infrascripto.**
infrasónico, ca, *a.* (phys.) infrasonic.
infrecuencia, *f.* infrequency, infrequence, uncommonness, rarity.
infrecuente, *a.* infrequent.
infrecuentemente, *adv.* infrequently, rarely.
infringir, (*ref. 62*) *tr.v.* to infringe, violate, break.
infrinja, infrinjo, *ref.* **infringir.**
infructífero, ra, *a.* unfruitful; unprofitable.
infructuosamente, *adv.* unfruitfully, fruitlessly.
infructuosidad, *f.* unfruitfulness, fruitlessness.
infructuoso, sa, *a* unfruitful, fruitless, unsuccessful.
infrugífero, ra, *a., var. of* **infructífero.**
infrutescencia, *f.* (bot.) racemose formation of fruits or berries.
ínfula, *f.* 1. infula (fillet symbolizing religious consecration or inviolability; lappet of bishop's miter). 2. (*pl.*) airs, conceit, presumption, vanity. — **darse ínfulas,** to put on airs.
infumable, *a.* 1. unsmokable, very low quality (tobacco). 2. (Mex., Cuba) unbearable.
infundadamente, *adv.* groundlessly.
infundado, da, *a.* groundless.
infundibular, *a.* (anat.) infundibular.
infundibuliforme, *a.* (bot.) infundibuliform, infundibular, funnel-shaped.
infundíbulo, *m.* (anat.) infundibulum.
infundio, *m.* (coll.) lie, fib.
infundioso, sa, *a.* (coll.) lying. —*m., f.* liar, fibber.
infundir, *tr.v.* to infuse, fill, inspire with; to instil, fill.
infurción, *f.* (arch.) tribute paid to the landlord.
infurcioniego, ga, *a.* pertaining to the tribute paid to the landlord.
infurtir, *tr.v.* (tex.) to full (cloth).
infusibilidad, *f.* infusibility.
infusible, *a.* infusible.
infusión, *f.* 1. infusion; brew. 2. (pharm.) infusion. 3. (rel.) pouring on of holy water (in baptism).
infuso, sa, *irr. past part. of* **infundir.** —*a.* (rel.) given or instilled by God's grace.
infusorio, *a.* (zool.) infusorial. —*m.* (zool.) infusorian; (*pl.*) Infusoria.
ing. *abbrev. of* **ingeniero,** engineer (eng., engr.).
inga, *m.* 1. (bot.) inga. 2. (Peru) Indian dance.
ingenerable, *a.* incapable of being engendered, ungenerable.
ingeniar, *tr.v.* to devise, think up, contrive. —*r.v.* to use one's wits. — **ingeniarse a** or **para,** to use one's wits to; **ingeniárselas,** to find a way (to).
ingeniatura, *f.* (coll.) ingeniousness, ingenuity, cleverness.
ingeniería, *f.* engineering; **i. civil,** civil engineering; **i. de sistemas,** systems engineering; **i. genética,** genetic engineering; **i. industrial,** industrial engineering; **i. mecánica,** mechanical engineering; **i. química,** chemical engineering.
ingeniero, ra, *m., f.* engineer. — **i. aeronáutico,** aircraft engineer; **i. agrónomo,** agricultural engineer; **i. civil,** civil engineer; **i. de caminos** or **vial,** highway engineer; **i. de estructuras,** structural engineer; **i. de la armada** or **de marina,** naval engineer; **i. de minas,** mining engineer; **i. de montes,** forestry expert; **i. electricista,** electrical engineer; **i. mecánico,** mechanical engineer; **i. militar,** army engineer; **i. naval,** naval shipbuilder; **i. pecuario,** veterinary surgeon; **i. químico,** chemical engineer.
ingenio, *m.* 1. ingenuity, ingeniousness, inventiveness, creativeness; talent, skill, cleverness. 2. wit, humor, liveliness of mind. 3. genius, talented person. 4. machine, engine, apparatus. 5. (bkb.) paper cutter. 6. sugar mill; sugar plantation. — **afilar** or **aguzar el i.,** to sharpen one's wit; **i. de azúcar,** sugar mill; sugar plantation; **i. espacial,** spacecraft; **i. nuclear,** nuclear device.
ingeniosamente, *adv.* 1. ingeniously, cleverly. 2. wittily, amusingly.
ingeniosidad, *f.* ingenuity, ingeniousness, cleverness.
ingenioso, sa, *a.* 1. ingenious, clever. 2. witty, amusing, humorous.
ingénito, ta, *a.* 1. unbegotten. 2. inborn, innate; natural.
ingente, *a.* huge, enormous.
ingenuamente, *adv.* ingenuously, naively.
ingenuidad, *f.* ingenuousness, naiveté; simplicity, candor.
ingenuo, nua, *a.* 1. ingenuous, naive. 2. (law) freeborn.
ingerencia, *f., var. of* **injerencia.**
ingeridura, *f., var. of* **injeridura.**
ingerir, (*ref. 42*) *tr.v., var. of* **injerir.**
ingestión, *f.* ingestion, swallowing.
Inglaterra, *f.* England.
ingle, *f.* (anat.) groin.
inglés, sa, *a.* English, pertaining to England. —*m.* 1. English language. 2. Englishman. 3. type of cloth. 4. (coll.) creditor. —*f.* Englishwoman. — **a la inglesa,** in the English manner; **inglés primitivo,** (archit.) Early English style.
inglesismo, *m.* Anglicism.
inglete, *m.* 1. (geom.) angle of forty-five degrees. 2. miter, miter joint. — **escuadra de i.,** miter square; **caja de** or **a ingletes,** miter box.
ingletear, *tr.v.* to miter, join by a miter joint.
inglosable, *a.* unglossable.
ingobernable, *a.* ungovernable, unruly, unmanageable.
ingratamente, *adv.* ungratefully.
ingratitud, *f.* ingratitude, ungratefulness.
ingrato, ta, *a.* 1. ungrateful. 2. disagreeable, unpleasant. 3. unrewarding, thankless. —*m., f.* ingrate, ungrateful person.
ingravescente, *a.* (med.) ingravescent.
ingravidez, *f.* lightness.
ingrávido, da, *a.* light, delicate, soft.
ingrediente, *m.* (cul., pharm.) **ingredient.**
ingresar, *tr.v.* 1. to enter, become a member (of). 2. to come in; deposit (money). — **i. en la universidad,** to enter the university (as a student).
ingreso, *m.* 1. entry (into an organization), e.g. *su i. en la organización,* his entry into the organization. 2. deposit. 3. (*pl.*) (personal) income; (*pl.*) takings, receipts, money received (e.g. in a shop); (*pl.*) earnings; revenue (e.g. from government tax) — **i. gravable,** taxable income; **ingresos accesorios,** additional income, fringe benefits; **ingresos brutos,** gross income; **ingresos de operación,** operating income; **ingresos diferidos,** accrued income; **ingresos netos,** net income; **ingresos por trabajo personal,** earned income.
íngrimo, ma, *a.* (Amer.) alone, solitary.
inguinal, *a., var. of* **inguinario.**
inguinario, ria, *a.* (anat.) inguinal, of the groin.
ingurgitación, *f.* (med.) ingurgitation, swallowing.
ingurgitar, *tr.v.* (med.) to ingurgitate, swallow.
ingustable, *a.* unpalatable.
inhábil, *a.* 1. incapable, incompetent, inept; unqualified, unskilled. 2. unfit. — **día i.,** holiday.
inhabilidad, *f.* incapacity, incompetence, ineptitude.
inhabilitación, *f.* 1. disablement, incapacitation. 2. disqualification, debarment.
inhabilitar, *tr.v.* 1. to disqualify, debar. 2. to incapacitate, disable. —*r.v.* 1. to become incapacitated or disabled. 2. to be disqualified or debarred.
inhabitable, *a.* uninhabitable.
inhabitado, da, *a.* uninhabited.
inhabituado, da, *a.* unaccustomed.
inhacedero, ra, *a.* unfeasible.
inhalable, *a.* inspirable, breathable.
inhalación, *f.* inhalation; **hacer inhalaciones,** to inhale; **i. de pegamento,** glue sniffing.
inhalador, *m.* (med.) inhaler (apparatus facilitating inhalation).
inhalar, *tr.v.* to inhale, breathe in.
inhereditable, *a.* uninheritable.
inherencia, *f.* (philos.) inherence.
inherente, *a.* inherent; (Amer.) essential.
inhesión, *f.* (philos.) *var. of* **inherencia.**
inhestar, (*ref. 29*) *tr.v., var. of* **enhestar.**
inhibición, *f.* inhibition.
inhibido, da, *a.* inhibited, restricted.
inhibir, *tr.v.* 1. to inhibit, restrain. 2. (law) to inhibit (a judge) from further proceedings. 3. (physiol.) to inhibit, stop (function of an organ). —*r.v.* 1. to stay out (of), withdraw (from). 2. (law) to disqualify oneself, withdraw (from a case - a judge). 3. (physiol.) to be inhibited.
inhibitorio, ria, *a.* (law) inhibitory. —*f.* (law) writ of prohibition; restraining order (stopping a judge from continuing proceedings).

inhiesto, ta, *a.* straight, upright, erect.
inhomogeneidad, *f.* inhomogeneity.
inhonestamente, *adv.* indecently, improperly, immodestly.
inhonestidad, *f.* indecency, immodesty.
inhonesto, ta, *a.* indecent, immodest.
inhospedable, *a., var. of* **inhospitalario.**
inhospitable, *a., var. of* **inhospitalario.**
inhospital, *a., var. of* **inhospitalario.**
inhospitalario, ria, *a.* 1. inhospitable, unhospitable. 2. barren, desolate (place); exposed, unsheltered (place). 3. dangerous, unsafe (e.g. beach).
inhospitalidad, *f.* inhospitality.
inhóspito, ta, *a.* barren, desolate; exposed, unsheltered.
inhumación, *f.* burial, inhumation.
inhumanamente, *adv.* inhumanly, cruelly.
inhumanidad, *f.* inhumanity, cruelty.
inhumano, na, *a.* 1. inhuman, cruel. 2. (Chile) dirty.
inhumar, *tr v.* to inhume, bury (a body).
iniciación, *f.* initiation.
iniciado, da, *past part. of* **iniciar.** —*a.* initiated. —*m., f.* initiate.
iniciador, ra, *a.* initiatory. —*m., f.* initiator, introducer.
inicial, *a.* initial. —*f.* initial.
iniciar, *tr.v.* 1. to initiate (into a secret society, a sect, etc.). 2. to start, begin. 3. to instruct, introduce (to). —*r.v.* to be initiated, admitted (into society, mystery, secret); (ecc.) to receive minor orders.
iniciativa, *f.* initiative. — **tener mucha i.,** to have a lot of initiative; **tomar la i.,** to take the initiative.
iniciativo, va, *a.* initiative, initiating, beginning.
inicuamente, *adv.* iniquitously.
inicuo, cua, *a.* unjust, unfair.
inigulado, da, *a.* unequaled; peerless.
in illo tempore, *adv.* (Lat.) formerly, in other times.
inimaginable, *a.* unimaginable, inconceivable.
inimicísimo, ma, *a.* very or most hostile.
inimitable, *a.* inimitable.
inimitablemente, *adv.* inimitably.
ininteligible, *a.* unintelligible; difficult to decipher.
ininterrumpido, da, *a.* uninterrupted, continuous.
inio, *m.* (anat.) inion.
iniquidad, *f.* iniquity, wickedness.
iniquísimo, ma, *a. super. of* **inicuo,** very unjust or unfair.
injerencia, *f.* meddling, interference. — **dar i. a uno en,** to introduce someone into.
injeridura, *f.* (agr.) graft (point at which a scion is inserted in the stock).
injerir, (*ref.* 42) *tr.v.* 1. to insert, introduce. 2. (Amer.) to eat, drink, swallow. —*r.v.* to interfere, meddle (in).
injerta, *f.* (agr.) grafting.
injertador, *m.* (agr.) grafter.
injertar, *tr.v.* (agr., surg.) to graft. — **i. en,** to graft onto.
injertera, *f.* (agr.) orchard of transplanted trees.
injerto, ta, *irr. past part. of* **injertar.** —*m.* 1. (agr.) graft, scion. 2. (agr., surg.) grafting, graft (action). 3. (agr.) graft, plant onto which a scion has been inserted. — **i. de acoplamiento,** whip or tongue grafting; **i. de corona** or **coronilla,** crown or bark grafting; **i. de escudete,** side grafting; **i. de hendiduras,** cleft grafting.
injiera, injiero, *ref.* **injerir.**
injiriendo, injiriera, injiriese, injirió, *ref.* **injerir.**
injundia, *f.* (coll.) *var. of* **enjundia.**
injuria, *f.* 1. insult, affront, offense. 2. wrong, injustice; injury, harm.
injuriado, da, *a.* (Cuba) inferior tobacco (leaf).
injuriador, ra, *a.* offensive, abusive, insulting. —*m., f.* insulter, offender.
injuriante, *a.* injuring; insulting.
injuriar, *tr.v.* 1. to abuse, insult, offend. 2. to injure, wrong, harm. —*r.v.* to insult or abuse each other.
injuriosamente, *adv.* insultingly, offensively, abusively.
injurioso, sa, *a.* offensive, abusive, insulting.
injustamente, *adv.* unjustly; unfairly.
injusticia, *f.* injustice; unfairness.
injustificable, *a.* unjustifiable.
injustificadamente, *adv.* unjustifiedly, unwarrantedly.
injustificado, da, *a.* unjustified, unwarranted.
injusto, ta, *a.* unjust; unfair.
inllevable, *a.* unbearable, intolerable.
inmaculadamente, *adv.* immaculately, spotlessly.
inmaculado, da, *a.* immaculate, spotless. —*f.* (ecc.) Virgin Mary.
inmadurez, *f.* immaturity.
inmaduro, ra, *a.* immature, unripened, unmellowed.
inmanejable, *a.* unmanageable.
inmanencia, *f.* immanence.
inmanente, *a.* immanent.
inmarcesible, *a.* unwithering, imperishable; unfading
inmarchitable, *a., var. of* **inmarcesible.**
inmaterial, *a.* immaterial, incorporeal.
inmaterialidad, *f.* immateriality, incorporeity.
inmaterialismo, *m.* (philos.) inmaterialism.
inmaturo, ra, *a.* immature.
inmediación, *f.* 1. immediacy. 2. (*pl.*) environs, outskirts.
inmediatamente, *adv.* immediately.
inmediato, ta, *a.* immediate; next, adjoining; contiguous. — **darle (a uno)** por las inmediatas, to hit (someone) in his sore spot; to leave (someone) unable to reply; de **inmediato,** immediately; **inmediato** a, next to, adjoining; **llegar** or **venir** a las **inmediatas,** to reach the basic point (in an argument) or toughest part (of a fight).
inmedicable, *a.* incurable.
inmejorable, *a.* perfect, excellent, unbetterable, unbeatable.
inmejorablemente, *adv.* perfectly, unbeatably.
inmemorable, *a.* immemorial.
inmemorablemente, *adv.* immemorially, immemoriably.
inmemorial, *a.* immemorial.
inmensamente, *adv.* immensely.
inmensidad, *f.* 1. immensity, immenseness. 2. (fig.) sea, immense crowd.
inmenso, sa, *a.* immense, enormous, countless; deep; extraordinary, endless.
inmensurable, *a.* immensurable, immeasurable.
inmerecidamente, *adv.* undeservedly, unmeritedly.
inmerecido, da, *a.* undeserved, unmerited.
inmergir, (*ref.* 62) *tr.v.* (rare) to inmerse.
inméritamente, *adv.* undeservedly, unmeritedly.
inmérito, ta, *a.* unmerited, undeserved.
inmeritorio, ria, *a.* not meritorious, undeserving.
inmerja, inmerjo, *ref.* **inmergir.**
inmersión, *f.* immersion.
inmerso, sa, *a.* immersed; engrossed.
inmetódico, ca, *a.* unmethodical.
inmigración, *f.* immigration.
inmigrante, *a* immigrant, immigrating. —*m., f.* immigrant.
inmigrar, *i.v.* to immigrate.
inmigratorio, ria, *a.* immigratory, pertaining to immigration.
inminencia, *f.* imminence, imminency.
inminente, *a.* imminent; menacing. — **peligro i.,** imminent danger.
inmiscible, *a.* immiscible, that cannot be mixed.
inmiscuir, (*ref.* 48) *tr.v.* to mix. —*r.v.* 1. to meddle, interfere. 2. to begin to appear.
inmiscuya, inmiscuyendo, inmiscuyera, inmiscuyese, inmiscuyo, *ref.* **inmiscuir.**
inmisericorde, *a.* (Amer.) merciless, ruthless.
inmisión, *f.* inspiration.
inmobiliario, ria, *a.* pertaining to real estate.
inmoble, *a.* 1. immovable, unmovable, fixed. 2. immobile, motionless. 3. firm, unshakable, constant (character).
inmoderación, *f.* immoderation, lack of moderation.
inmoderadamente, *adv.* immoderately.
inmoderado, da, *a.* immoderate.
inmodestamente, *adv.* immodestly.
inmodestia, *f.* immodesty.
inmodesto, ta, *a.* immodest.
inmódico, ca, *a.* excessive, exorbitant.
inmolación, *f.* immolation, sacrifice.
inmolador, ra, *a.* immolating. —*m., f.* immolator, sacrificer.
inmolar, *tr.v.* to immolate, sacrifice. —*r.v.* (fig.) to sacrifice oneself.
inmoral, *a.* immoral.
inmoralidad, *f.* immorality.
inmoralista, *m., f.* immoralist.
inmoralmente, *adv.* immorally.
inmortal, *a.* immortal.
inmortalice, inmortalicé, *ref.* **inmortalizar.**
inmortalidad, *f.* immortality.
inmortalización, *f.* immortalization.
inmortalizar, (*ref.* 53) *tr.v.* to inmortalize. —*r.v.* to become immortal.
inmortalmente, *adv.* immortally.
inmotivadamente, *adv.* for no reason, without cause or reason.
inmotivado, da, *a.* unmotivated, unprovoked; groundless, unjustified.
inmoto, ta, *a.* motionless, immobile, unmoving.
inmovible, *a., var. of* **inmoble.**
inmóvil, *a.* 1. immobile, motionless, unmoving; fixed, set. 2. constant, firm (character).
inmovilice, inmovilicé, *ref.* **inmovilizar.**
inmovilidad, *f.* immobility.
inmovilización, *f.* 1. immobilization. 2. (com.) tying up (of capital).
inmovilizar, (*ref.* 53) *tr.v.* 1. to immobilize. 2. (com.) to tie up (capital). —*r.v.* to become motionless or immobilized.
inmudable, *a.* immutable, unchangeable.
inmueble, *a.* (law) immovable. —*m.* (*pl.*) (law) immovables, real estate.
inmundicia, *f.* 1. filth, dirt. 2. indecency, filth, lewdness, obscenity.
inmundo, da, *a.* 1. filthy, dirty. **2. (fig.)** impure, indecent, obscene. 3. unclean (said of things proscribed by Jewish law).
inmune, *a.* immune; exempt, free.
inmunice, inmunicé, *ref.* **inmunizar.**
inmunidad, *f.* immunity; exemption. — **i. adquirida,** (med.) acquired immunity; **i. parlamentaria** or **diplomática,** diplomatic or parliamentary immunity.
inmunización, *f.* immunization.
inmunizador, ra, *a.* immunizing.
inmunizar, (*ref.* 53) *tr.v.* to inmunize.
inmunología, *f.* immunology.
inmunoquímica, *f.* (med.) inmunochemistry.
inmutabilidad, *f.* immutability.

inmutable, *a.* immutable, unchangeable.
inmutación, *f.* alteration, change.
inmutar, *tr.v.* to alter, change. —*r.v.* (fig.) to become or look agitated or worried.
inmutativo, va, *a.* changeable, alterable.
innatismo, *m.* (philos.) innatism.
innato, ta, *a.* innate.
innatural, *a.* unnatural.
innavegabilidad, *f.* (mar., Chile) unseaworthiness.
innavegable, *a.* (mar.) unnavigable; unseaworthy.
innecesariamente, *adv.* unnecessarily.
innecesario, a, *a.* unnecessary.
innegable, *a.* undeniable.
innegablemente, *adv.* undeniably.
innoble, *a.* 1. ignoble. 2. ignoble, base, mean, ignominious.
innocuidad, *f.* innocuousness, harmlessness.
innocuo, cua, *a.* innocuous, harmless.
innominable, *a.* (rare) unnameable.
innominado, da, *a.* innominate, unnamed; anonymous; (anat.) innominate (bone).
innovación, *f.* innovation.
innovador, ra, *a.* innovative. —*m., f.* innovator.
innovamiento, *m, var. of* **innovación.**
innovar, *tr.v.* to innovate, make changes in.
innumerabilidad, *f.* innumerableness, numberlessness, innumerability.
innumerable, *a.* innumerable, countless, numberless.
innumerablemente, *adv.* innumerably.
innúmero, ra, *a.* numberless, countless.
inobediencia, *f.* disobedience, inobedience.
inobediente, *a.* disobedient, inobedient.
inobservable, *a.* unobservable.
inobservado, da, *a.* unobserved.
inobservancia, *f.* inobservance, nonobservance.
inobservante, *a.* unobservant.
inocencia, *f.* 1. innocence, guiltlessness. 2. innocence; candor, simplicity.
inocentada, *f.* 1. (coll.) ingenuous or naive remark or action; naive blunder or mistake. 2. (coll.) April Fool's joke.
inocente, *a.* 1. innocent; simple, candorous, ingenuous; harmless, innocuous. 2. innocent, guiltless. —*m., f.* innocent. — **la matanza de los inocentes,** the slaughter of the Innocents.
inocentemente, *adv.* innocently.
inocentón, na, *a.* simple, credulous, naive. —*m., f.* booby, simpleton, credulous person.
inocuidad, *f.* innocuousness, harmlessness.
inoculable, *a.* inoculable.
inoculación, *f.* inoculation.
inoculador, ra, *m., f.* inoculator.
inoculante, *a.* inoculating. —*m.* inoculant.
inocular, *tr.v.* 1. to inoculate. 2. to contaminate, pervert, corrupt. —*r.v.* 1. to be inoculated. 2. to become contaminated, corrupted or perverted.
inocultable, *a.* unconcealable, undisguisable.
inocuo, cua, *a.* innocuous, harmless.
inodoro, ra, *a.* odorless, inodorous. —*m.* toilet, privy, lavatory (apparatus).
inofensivo, va, *a.* inoffensive; harmless.
inoficioso, sa, *a.* 1. inofficious. 2. (Amer.) useless, idle, inefficient. — **testamento inoficioso,** (law) inofficious will or testament.
inolvidable, *a.* unforgettable.
inope, *a.* poor, indigent, penurious, destitute.
inoperable, *a.* (surg.) inoperable.
inoperancia, *f.* 1. inapplicability; invalidity. 2. impracticality.
inoperante, *a.* 1. inapplicable, unworkable, unable to be applied; without force, invalid. 2. impractical, ineffective.
inopia, *f.* indigence, poverty, penury, destitution.
inopinable, *a.* indisputable.
inopinadamente, *adv.* unexpectedly.
inopinado, da, *a.* unexpected, unforeseen.
inoportunamente, *adv.* inopportunely, untimely.
inoportunidad, *f.* inopportuneness, untimeliness.
inoportuno, na, *a.* inopportune, untimely.
inordenadamente, *adv.* in a disorderly fashion or way.
inordenado, da, *a.* disordered, in disorder.
inordinado, da, *a., var. of* **inordenado.**
inorgánico, ca, *a.* inorganic.
inoxidable, *a.* stainless, unrustable; inoxidizable, inoxidable.
in pace, *adv.* (Lat.) in peace.
in péctore, *adv.* (Lat., coll.) in secret (said of resolutions).
in perpétuum, *adv.* (Lat.) in perpetuity, forever.
in promptu, *adv.* (Lat.) impromptu, off the cuff.
in púribus, *adv.* (Lat.) naked.
inquebrantable, *a.* unbreakable; indomitable.
inquiera, inquiero, *ref.* **inquirir.**
inquietador, ra, *a.* disquieting, disturbing, worrying, alarming. —*m., f.* disturber.
inquietamente, *adv.* uneasily, anxiously, restlessly, agitatedly, restively.
inquietante, *a.* disquieting, disturbing, perturbing, worrying, alarming.
inquietar, *tr.v.* to disquiet, disturb, perturb, trouble, worry, alarm; to harass. —*r.v.* to be disturbed, perturbed, upset, worried or troubled. — **inquietarse con,** or **por,** to be disturbed, upset or worried by.
inquieto, ta, *a.* restless, restive, fidgety, uneasy, anxious, disturbed, troubled.
inquietud, *f.* disquiet, disquietude, uneasiness, discomposure; restlessness, restiveness.
inquilinaje, *m.* 1. rent, lease. 2. (Chile, Mex.) tenants (collectively).
inquilinato, *m.* 1. lease, leasehold. 2. tenancy, occupancy.
inquilino, na, *m., f.* tenant, lessee.
inquina, *f.* aversion, dislike, ill will, animosity, hatred; **tenerle i. a,** to dislike, have it in for.
inquinamento, *m.* infection, contamination.
inquinar, *tr.v.* to contaminate, infect.
inquiridor, ra, *a.* inquiring, investigating. —*m., f.* inquirer, investigator.
inquirir, (*ref. 43*) *tr.v.* to investigate, inquire into.
inquisición, *f.* inquisition; (hist.) **I.,** Inquisition; Court of the Inquisition.
inquisidor, ra, *a.* inquiring, inquisitive. —*m., f.* inquirer, investigator. —*m.* 1. investigator. 2. **I.,** (ecc.) Inquisitor; **I. General,** Grand Inquisitor.
inquisitivo, va, *a.* inquisitive; inquiring. — **mente inquisitiva,** inquiring mind; **mirada inquisitiva,** inquisitive look.
inquisitorial, *a.* inquisitorial.
inquisitorio, ria, *a.* inquisitive; inquiring.
insabible, *a.* unknowable, unascertainable.
insaciabilidad, *f.* insatiability.
insaciable, *a.* insatiable.
insaciablemente, *adv.* insatiably.
insaculación, *f.* balloting, voting by ballot.
insaculador, *m.* balloter.
insacular, *tr.v.* to ballot, choose by ballot.
insalivación, *f.* insalivation.
insalivar, *tr.v.* to insalivate, mix with saliva.
insalubre, *a.* unhealthy, insanitary, unsanitary, insalubrious.
insalubridad, *f.* unsanitariness, insalubrity, unsanitary condition.
insanable, *a.* incurable.
insania, *f.* insanity, madness.
insanidad, *f.* (neol.) *var. of* **insania.**
insano, na, *a.* 1. insane, mad. 2. unhealthy.
insatisfecho, cha, *a.* unsatisfied.
inscribible, *a.* (law) inscribable.
inscribir, *tr v.* 1. to inscribe, engrave. 2. to register; to enroll; to write down. 3. (law) to record (deeds). 4. (geom.) to inscribe. —*r.v.* to enroll; to register; to write or sign one's name (on a list).
inscripción, *f.* 1. inscription, engraving (esp. on metal, stone etc.). 2. record, entry. 3. enrollment; registration, writing down, recording.
inscripto, ta, *a., var. of* **inscrito.**
inscrito, ta, *irr. past part. of* **inscribir.** —*a.* engraved, inscribed; registered, recorded, enrolled.
insculpido, da, *a.* insculptured, engraved.
insculpir, *tr.v.* to sculpture, insculp, engrave.
insecable, *a.* 1. (coll.) undryable, difficult to dry. 2. uncuttable, indivisible.
insecticida, *a.* insecticide, insecticidal. —*m.* insecticide.
insectil, *a.* insectile, pertaining to insects.
insectívoro, ra, *a.* (zool.) insectivorous. —*m.* (*pl.*) (zool.) Insectivora.
insecto, *m.* insect; (*pl.*) (zool.) Insecta.
insectología, *f.* (neol.) insectology, entomology.
insectólogo, *m.* (neol.) insectologer, entomologist.
inseguramente, *adv.* 1. insecurely. 2. uncertainly.
inseguridad, *f.* 1. insecurity. 2. uncertainty.
inseguro, ra, *a.* 1. insecure; unsafe. 2. uncertain, unsure.
inseminación, *f.* insemination. — **i. artificial,** artificial insemination.
inseminar, *tr.v.* to inseminate.
insenescencia, *f.* agelessness.
insensatamente, *adv.* insensately, stupidly.
insensatez, (*pl.* **insensateces**), *f.* senselessness, stupidity, folly, foolishness; stupidity, foolish or stupid remark.
insensato, ta, *a.* senseless, foolish, stupid. —*m., f.* madcap, madman (coll.), hare-brained person.
insensibilidad, *f.* 1. insensibility, insentience. 2. unconsciousness. 3. insensitivity, impassivity. 4. hardheartedness, callousness.
insensibilizador, ra, *a.* insensibilizing; anesthetizing. —*m.* anesthetic.
insensibilizar, (*ref. 53*) *tr.v.* to make insensible; to anesthetize. —*r.v.* to become insensible.
insensible, *a.* 1. insensitive, impassive, indifferent. 2. insentient, insensible. 3. unconscious, insensible, senseless. 4. imperceptible.
insensiblemente, *adv.* 1. insensitively, impassively. 2. unconsciously. 3. imperceptibly.
inseparabilidad, *f.* inseparability.
inseparable, *a.* inseparable; bosom (friends, couple, etc.).
inseparablemente, *adv.* inseparably.
insepulto, ta, *a.* unburied, uninterred.
inserción, *f.* insertion.
inserir, *tr.v.* 1. to insert. 2. to graft. 3. to swallow, ingest.
insertar, *tr.v.* to insert; to include. —*r.v.* (bot., zool.) to be inserted (*i.e.* attached by natural growth).
inserto, ta, *irr. past part. of* **inserir.** —*a.* inserted.
inservible, *a.* unserviceable, useless.
insidia, *f.* malicious trap, trick, snare or plot; malice.
insidiador, ra, *a.* ensnaring, tricking. —*m., f.* ensnarer, betrayer, plotter.
insidiar, *tr.v.* to plot against, entrap, ensnare, set a trap for.
insidiosamente, *adv.* insidiously.
insidioso, sa, *a.* insidious.
insigne, *a.* celebrated, famous, distinguished, renowned, illustrious.
insignemente, *adv.* notably, illustriously.

insignia, *f.* badge, emblem; standard, flag, banner; (mar.) pennant, flag (denoting captain's rank); (*pl.*) insignia. — **buque i.,** flagship.
insignificancia, *f.* insignificance.
insignificante, *a.* insignificant, unimportant.
insinceridad, *f.* insincerity.
insincero, ra, *a.* insincere.
insinuación, *f.* 1. insinuation, intimation, hint, innuendo, suggestion. 2. (law) insinuation, the presentation of a public document to a judge in order to establish its authenticity. 3. (rhet.) part of introduction in which the orator tries to win the sympathy of his audience.
insinuador, ra, *a.* insinuating, suggestive.
insinuante, *a.* insinuating.
insinuar, (*ref.* 55) *tr.v.* 1. to insinuate, intimate, suggest, hint. 2. (law) to present (a public document) before a judge. —*r.v.* 1. to wheedle or work one's way, insinuate oneself (into someone's confidence). 3. to grow on (habits, vices, etc.).
insinuativo, va, *a.* insinuative, suggestive.
insípidamente, *adv.* insipidly.
insipidez, *f.* insipidity, insipidness.
insípido, da, *a.* 1. insipid, tasteless, flavorless. 2. insipid, vapid, lifeless, dull.
insipiencia, *f.* insipience, stupidity; ignorance.
insipiente, *a.* insipient, foolish, stupid; ignorant.
insistencia, *f.* insistence, persistence.
insistente, *a.* insistent, persistent.
insistentemente, *adv.* insistently.
insistir, *i.v.* to insist; to persist. — **i. en,** to insist on; **i. en que** + *ind.,* to insist. or maintain that, e.g. *insisto en que no se equivocaron,* I insist that they did not make a mistake.
ínsito, ta, *a.* innate, inbred, inborn, inherent.
in situ, *adv.* (Lat.) in situ, on-the-spot.
insociabilidad, *f.* unsociability.
insociable, *a.* unsociable.
insocial, *a., var. of* **insociable.**
insolación, *f.* sunstroke, insolation; (meteorol.) insolation (amount of sunshine received in one day).
insolar, *tr.v.* to insolate, expose to the sun. —*r.v.* to get sunstroke.
insoldable, *a.* unsolderable.
insolencia, *f.* insolence, impertinence.
insolentar, *tr.v.* to make insolent. —*r.v.* to become insolent.
insolente, *a.* 1. insolent, impertinent. 2. haughty, arrogant. —*m., f.* insolent person.
insolentemente, *adv.* 1. insolently, impertinently. 2. haughtily, arrogantly.
in sólidum, *adv.* (law) jointly and severally, in solido, in solidum.
insólito, ta, *a.* unusual, uncommon, strange.
insolubilidad, *f.* insolubility.
insolubilizar, *tr.v.* to insolubilize.
insoluble, *a.* insoluble; unsolvable.
insoluto, ta, *a.* unpaid (debt, account).
insolvencia, *f.* insolvency.
insolvente, *a., m, f.* insolvent.
insomne, *a.* sleepless, insomnious, suffering from insomnia.
insomnio, *m.* insomnia, sleeplessness.
insondable, *a.* unsoundable, unfathomable; (fig.) inscrutable, incomprehensible.
insonorice, insonoricé, *ref.* **insonorizar.**
insonorización, *f.* soundproofing.
insonorizar, (*ref.* 53) *tr.v.* to soundproof.
insonoro, ra, *a.* soundless.
insoportable, *a.* insufferable, intolerable, unbearable.
insospechable, *a.* beyond suspicion.
insospechado, da, *a.* unsuspected.
insostenible, *a.* unsustainable, untenable, indefensible.
inspección, *f.* 1. inspection, examination. 2. inspectorship; inspector's office.
inspeccionar, *tr.v.* to inspect, examine.
inspector, ra, *a.* inspecting. —*m., f.* inspector, examiner, officer. — **i. general,** inspector general; **i. de aduanas,** custom house officer; **i. de Hacienda,** revenue agent; **i. de policiá,** police inspector.
inspectoría, *f.* (Chile) body of police under the command of an inspector; inspectorate.
inspiración, *f.* 1. (physiol.) inspiration, inhalation, breathing in. 2. inspiration, animating influence on the mind or the emotions. 3. inspiration, a sudden solution or idea. 4. (theol.) inspiration.
inspiradamente, *adv.* inspiredly, by inspiration.
inspirador, ra, *a.* inspiring; (zool.) inspiratory (muscles, etc.). —*m., f.* inspirer; instigator.
inspirante, *a.* inspiring.
inspirar, *tr.v.* 1. to inspire, stimulate, animate. 2. to inspire, breathe in, inhale. —*r.v.* to be inspired, become inspired, get inspiration; **inspirarse en,** to be inspired by, get inspiration from.
inspirativo, va, *a.* inspirational.
instabilidad, *f.* instability, unstableness.
instable, *a.* unstable.
instalación, *f.* 1. installation, installing. 2. installation, plant, equipment. 3. appointments, fittings. — **i. sanitaria,** plumbing; **instalaciones deportivas,** sports facilities.
instalador, ra, *a.* installing. —*m., f.* installer, fitter.
instalar, *tr.v.* to install. —*r.v.* to establish oneself, install oneself.
instancia, *f.* 1. insistence, petition, pressing, request. 2. rebuttal, refutation (of an argument in a debate). 3. (law) instance. — **a i. de,** at the request of; **tribunal de primera i.,** court of the first instance; **en última i.,** in the last resort.
instantánea, *f.* (photog.) snap, snapshot.
instantáneamente, *adv.* instantaneously.
instantáneo, a, *a.* instantaneous.
instante, *a.* pressing, urging, insistent. —*m.* instant, moment. — **a cada i.** or **cada i.,** every moment, all the time; **al i.,** immediately, right away; **por instantes,** incessantly, uninterruptedly; from one moment to another.
instantemente, *adv.* 1. insistently, pressingly. 2. (arch.) instantly, immediately.
instar, *tr.v.* 1. to urge, press. 2. to refute, reply (in a debate). —*i.v.* to press, urge; to insist. — **i. para** or **por,** to press for; **i. sobre,** to insist on; **i. a que,** to press or urge to.
instauración, *f.* 1. establishment. 2. restoration, re-establishment.
instaurador, ra, *a.* 1. establishing, institutive. 2. restorative. —*m., f.* 1. restorer. 2. establisher, founder.
instaurar, *tr.v.* 1. to establish, institute, set up. 2. to restore, re-establish.
instaurativo, va, *a.* restorative.
instigación, *f.* instigation, provocation, incitement.
instigador, ra, *a.* instigating, provocative. —*m., f.* instigator.
instigar, (*ref.* 51) *tr.v.* to provoke, incite, induce, instigate.
instigue, instigué, *ref.* **instigar.**
instilación, *f.* 1. instillation (of a doctrine, etc.). 2. (pharm.) instillation, dropping in (of a liquid).
instilar, *tr.v.* 1. to instill (a doctrine, etc.) 2. to pour drop by drop, drop in, instill.
instintivamente, *adv.* instinctively.
instintivo, va, *a.* instinctive; spontaneous.
instinto, *m.* instinct. — **por i.,** by instinct.
institución, *f.* institution; (*pl.*) institutions (established customs, practices, etc.); principles, elements (of the law; an art, a science, etc.); instruction, education. — **i. de heredero,** (law) institution or appointment of an heir.
institucional, *a.* institutional.
institucionalizar, *tr.v.* institutionalize.
instituente, *a.* institutive, founding.
instituidor, ra, *a.* founding. —*m., f.* founder, institutor.
instituir, (*ref.* 48) *tr.v.* 1. to institute, establish, found. 2. to teach, instruct.
Instituta, *f. pl.,* Institutes (of Roman civil laws).
instituto, *m.* 1. institute, society (scientific, literary, etc.). 2. institute, high school, secondary school. 3. precept, rule, institute (e.g. of a religious order). — **i. de segunda enseñanza,** high school, secondary school.
institutor, ra, *a.* founding. —*m., f.* founder, institutor.
institutriz, (*pl.* **institutrices**), *f.* governess, instructress.
instituya, instituyendo, *ref.* **instituir.**
instituyente, *a.* founding, institutive.
instituyera, instituyese, instituyo, *ref.* **instituir.**
instridente, *a.* strident, grating, shrill.
instrucción, *f.* 1. instruction, teaching, tuition, education. 2. knowledge. 3. (law) investigation, hearing (of a case). 4. (*pl.*) instructions, directions, orders. — **i. primaria,** primary education; **i. pública,** public education.
instructivamente, *adv.* instructively, educationally.
instructivo, va, *a.* instructive, educational.
instructor, ra, *a.* instructing. —*m.* instructor. —*f.* instructress.
instruido, da, *a.* well-educated; enlightened.
instruir, (*ref.* 48) *tr.v.* 1. to instruct, train, teach. 2. to inform, tell, advise. 3. (law) to investigate, hear (a case — a judge). —*r.v.* to be informed.
instrumentación, *f.* (mus.) instrumentation, orchestration.
instrumental, *a.* 1. instrumental, pertaining to musical instruments. 2. documentary, supported by documents. —*m.* 1. instruments (of an orchestra; of a surgeon). 2. (gram.) instrumental (case).
instrumentalmente, *adv.* instrumentally.
instrumentar, *tr.v.* (mus.) to instrument, orchestrate.
instrumentista, *m.* 1. instrumentalist. 2. instrument-maker.
instrumento, *m.* instrument; implement, tool; device; document. — **i. de cuerda,** string instrument; **i. de percusión,** percussion instrument; **i. de viento,** wind instrument.
instruya, instruyendo, instruyera, instruyese, instruyo, *ref.* **instruir.**
insuave, *a.* rough; unpleasant, disagreeable.
insuavidad, *f.* roughness; unpleasantness, disagreeableness.
insubordinación, *f.* insubordination, rebelliousness.
insubordinado, da, *past part. of* **insubordinar.** —*a.* insubordinate, rebellious, mutinous. —*m.* mutineer, rebel.
insubordinar, *tr.v.* to incite to insubordination or rebellion. —*r.v.* to mutiny, rebel.
insubsanable, *a.* irreparable, unrepairable, uncorrectable.
insubsistencia, *f.* 1. impermanence, instability. 2. groundlessness, baselessness. 3. nullity (of a law).

insubsistente, *a.* 1. impermanent, unstable. 2. groundless, baseless. 3. null, void (law).
insubstancial, *a.* 1. insubstantial, unsubstantial. 2. incorporeal, immaterial. 3. inane, vapid, empty.
insubstancialidad, *f.* 1. insubstantiality. 2. incorporeity, immateriality. 3. inanity, emptiness.
insubstancialmente, *adv.* insubstantially.
insubstituible, *a.* irreplaceable.
insudar, *i.v.* to strive, toil, labor.
insuficiencia, *f.* 1. insufficiency, scarcity, lack, dearth. 2. incapacity, ineptness, incompetence. 3. inadequacy, deficiency. — **i. cardíaca,** heart failure; **i. renal,** kidney failure.
insuficiente, *a.* insufficient; incompetent.
insuficientemente, *adv.* insufficiently, inadequately.
insuflación, *f.* (med.) insufflation, blowing.
insuflador, *m.* (med.) insufflator (apparatus for blowing air into the lungs).
insuflar, *tr.v.* (med.) to insufflate.
insufrible, *a.* insufferable, intolerable, unbearable, insupportable.
insufriblemente, *adv.* insufferably, intolerably, unbearably, insupportably.
ínsula, *f.* (arch., poet.) island, isle; (fig.) unimportant or insignificant region (of a country).
insulano, na, *a.* (arch.) insular. —*m., f.* (arch.) islander.
insular, *a.* insular. —*m., f.* islander.
insulina, *f.* (med.) insulin.
insulsamente, *adv.* insipidly, vapidly.
insulsez, (*pl.* **insulseces**), *f.* 1. dullness, flatness, insipidity, vapidity. 2. insipidness, vapidness, inanity.
insulso, sa, *a.* dull, colorless, insipid, vapid, inane.
insultada, *f.* (Amer., imp. u.) insult.
insultador, ra, *a.* insulting. —*m., f.* insulter.
insultante, *a.* insulting, abusive, offensive.
insultar, *tr.v.* to insult, affront, abuse. —*r.v.* (rare) to faint, have a fainting fit; to suffer an accident.
insulto, *m.* 1. insult, affront. 2. (coll.) fainting fit; accident; sudden attack. 3. (Mex., Nic.) indigestion.
insumable, *a.* unaddable.
insume, *a.* expensive, costly.
insumergibilidad, *f.* insubmergibility.
insumergible, *a.* insubmergible, unsinkable.
insumisión, *f.* unsubmissiveness; disobedience.
insumiso, sa, *a.* unsubmissive; disobedient.
insuperabilidad, *f.* insuperability.
insuperable, *a.* insuperable, unbeatable; insurmountable.
insupurable, *a.* (rare) that cannot suppurate.
insurgente, *a., m., f.* insurgent, rebel.
insurrección, *f.* insurrection, rebellion, uprising.
insurreccional, *a.* insurrectionary, pertaining to insurrection.
insurreccionar, *tr.v.* to incite to rebellion. —*r.v.* to rebel, rise up in arms.
insurrecto, ta, *a.* insurgent, insurrectionary. —*m., f.,* insurgent, rebel.
insustancial, *a., var. of* **insubstancial.**
insustancialidad, *f., var. of* **insubstancialidad.**
insustancialmente, *adv, var. of* **insubstancialmente.**
insustituible, *a.* irreplaceable.
intacto, ta, *a.* 1. intact, undamaged, unbroken; whole, entire. 2. pure, unadulterated. 3. untouched, unresolved (matter, subject or grievance).
intachable, *a.* irreproachable; **exemplary.**
intangibilidad, *f.* intangibility.
intangible, *a.* intangible; untouchable.
integérrimo, ma, *a super. of* **íntegro.**
integrable, *a.* (math.) integrable.
integración, *f.* 1. (math.) integration. 2. integration, equality. — **i. racial,** racial integration.
integracionista, *m., f.* integrationist.
integral, *a.* integral, whole. —*m.* (math.) integral. — **i. definitivo,** (math.) definitive integral; **alimento i.,** whole meal (bread, flour).
integralmente, *adv.* with integrity, entirely, completely.
íntegramente, *adv.* entirely, completely; (fig.) honestly.
integrante, *a.* integrant, constituent; **parte i.,** constituent part.
integrar, *tr.v.* 1. to integrate; to form, make up. 2. to reimburse. 3. (math.) to integrate.
integridad, *f.* 1. integrity, completeness. 2. honesty, uprightness, probity. 3. maidenhood, virginity.
integrismo, *m.* Spanish political party founded at the end of the 19th century for preserving national traditions and ways of life.
integrista, *a.* pertaining to **integrismo.** —*m., f.* advocate of **integrismo.**
íntegro, gra, *a.* 1. whole, complete, integral. 2. honest, upright, honorable.
integumento, *m.* integument; (fig.) disguise, fiction.
intelección, *f.* intellection, comprehension, understanding (act of).
intelectivo, va, *a.* intellective. —*f.* intellect, understanding.
intelecto, *m.* intellect, understanding.
intelectual, *a., m., f.* intellectual.
intelectualidad, *f.* 1. intellectuality. 2. intellect, understanding. 3. (fig.) intelligentsia, (body of) intellectuals.
intelectualismo, *m.* intellectualism.
intelectualista, *a.* intellectualistic. —*m., f.* intellectualist.
intelectualmente, *adv.* intellectually.
inteligencia, *f.* 1. intelligence, intellect. 2. comprehension, knowledge. 3. ability, talent. 4. (mil., pol.) intelligence. — **i. artificial,** artificial intelligence; **servicios de i.,** intelligence services.
inteligenciado, da, *a.* (coll.) well-informed, instructed.
inteligente, *a.* intelligent, smart, clever. —*m., f.* intelligent person.
inteligentemente, *adv* intelligently, cleverly, smartly.
inteligibilidad, *f.* intelligibility, comprehensibility.
inteligible, *a.* intelligible, comprehensible; (philos.) intelligible, understandable by the intellect only; distinctly audible.
inteligiblemente, *adv.* intelligibly, comprehensibly; audibly.
intelligentsia, *f.* intelligentsia.
intemperado, da, *a.* intemperate, immoderate.
intemperancia, *f.* intemperance, excess.
intemperante, *a* intemperate, immoderate.
intemperie, *f.* inclemency (of weather). — **a la i.,** outdoors, unsheltered, in the open.
intempesta, *a.* **noche intempesta,** (poet.) late at night, dead of the night.
intempestivamente, *adv.* 1. ill-timed, inopportunely. 2. unjustly, without due warning (of dismissals from work).
intempestivo, va, *a.* 1. unseasonable, inopportune, ill-timed. 2. unjust, without due warning.
intemporal, *a.* untemporal, independent of time.
intención, *f.* 1. intention, aim, desire; purpose. 2. viciousness (in certain animals). 3. discretion, caution. — **con i.,** intentionally; **curar de primera i.,** to administer firts aid to; **primera i.,** (coll.) frankness, openness, impetuosity; **segunda i.,** (coll.) underhandedness, deceitfulness.
intencionadamente, *adv.* intentionally.
intencionado, da, *a.* intentioned. — **bien i.,** well-intentioned; **mal i.,** ill-intentioned.
intencional, *a.* intentional, intended, deliberate.
intencionalmente, *adv.* intentionally.
intendencia, *f.* 1. intendance, superintendence; administration. 2. intendancy (post or headquarters of an intendant; district under intendant's jurisdiction). — **depósito de i.,** quartermaster depot or stores; **Servicio de I.,** Quartermaster Corps (U.S.), Royal Army Service Corps (G.B.).
intendenta, *f.* intendant's wife.
intendente, *m.* 1. intendant, superintendent. 2. (mil.) Quartermaster General.
intensamente, *adv.* intensely.
intensar, *tr.v.* to intensify, make intense. —*r.v.* to intensify, become intense.
intensidad, *f.* intensity; vehemence. — **i. de la gravedad,** (phys.) gravitational intensity; **i. de. señal,** (rad.) signal strength; **i. maxima de corriente,** (elec.) peak current.
intensificación, *f.* intensification.
intensificador, *m.* intensifier.
intensificar, (*ref. 50*) *tr.v.* to intensify.
intensifique, intensifiqué, *ref.* **intensificar.**
intensión, *f.* intensity.
intensivamente, *adv.* intensively.
intensivo, va, *a.* intensive; intense. — **cultivo i.,** intensive cultivation.
intenso, sa, *a.* intense, acute; (fig.) intense, vehement, ardent; **dolor i.,** acute pain.
intentar, *tr.v.* 1. to attempt, try, endeavor. 2. (law) to begin (a suit). — **i.** + *inf.,* to try to + *inf.*
intento, *m.* attempt, intention, aim, design. — **de i.,** purposely, on purpose, intentionally; **al i. de,** (Arg.) with the purpose of, with the intention of; **i. de suicidio,** suicide attempt.
intentona, *f.* (coll.) rash attempt, ill-advised attempt.
ínter, *adv.* meanwhile. —*m.* meanwhile, interim. — **en el í.,** in the meantime.
interacción, *f.* interaction.
interamericano, na, *a.* inter-American.
interandino, na, *a.* (Chile) inter-Andean.
interarticular, *a.* interarticular, between two articulations.
interatómico, ca, *a.* interatomic.
intercadencia, *f.* 1. inconsistency; unevenness (of character; of style or language). 2. (med.) intercadence, irregular rhythm (of pulse).
intercadente, *a.* 1. inconsistent, uneven. 2. (med.) intercadent, beating irregularly (the pulse).
intercadentemente, *adv.* inconsistently, unevenly.
intercalación, *f.* intercalation, insertion.
intercaladura, *f., var. of* **intercalación.**
intercalar, *tr.v.* to intercalate, insert.
intercambiable, *a.* interchangeable.
intercambiar, *tr.v.* to interchange; to exchange.
intercambio, *m.* interchange, exchange. — **i. comercial (entre naciones),** international trade.
interceder, *i.v.* to intercede; to mediate.
intercelular, *a.* (anat.) intercellular.
interceptación, *f.* interception. — **avión de i.,** interceptor (plane), pursuit plane.
interceptar, *tr.v.* to intercept; to obstruct.
interceptor, *a.* intercepting. —*m., f.* interceptor, intercepter. —*m.* (elec.) switch, current-breaker, interrupter.
intercesión, *f.* intercession; mediation.
intercesor, ra, *a.* interceding. —*m., f.* intercessor, mediator.

intercesoriamente, *adv.* by intercession.
interciso, *a.* half (holiday).
intercolumnio, *m.* (archit.) intercolumniation, space between two columns.
intercolunio, *m., var. of* **intercolumnio.**
intercomunicación, *f.* intercommunication.
intercomunicador, *m.* intercom, intercommunication system.
intercomunicar, *i.v.* to intercommunicate.
interconexión, *f.* interconnection.
intercontinental, *a.* intercontinental.
intercostal, *a.* (anat.) intercostal.
intercurrente, *a.* (med.) intercurrent (said of an illness intervening in the course of another).
intercutáneo, a, *a.* intercutaneous.
interdecir, (*ref.* 3) *tr.v.* to interdict, prohibit, forbid.
interdental, *a.* interdental.
interdependencia, *f.* interdependence.
interdicción, *f.* interdiction, prohibition; interdict.
interdiciendo, *ref.* **interdecir.**
interdicto, *m.* interdict, prohibition.
interdiga, *ref.* **interdecir.**
interdigital, *a.* (anat.) interdigital.
interdigo, *ref.* **interdecir.**
interdije, interdijera, interdijese, *ref.* interdecir.
interés, *m.* 1. interest; benefit. 2. interest, attraction. 3. (*pl.*) interests, possessions, property. — **i. acumulado** or **devengado,** accrued interest; **i. compuesto,** compound interest; **i. dominante** or **predominante,** controlling interest; **i. simple,** simple interest; **intereses creados,** vested interests; **intereses futuros,** executory interests.
interesable, *a.* mercenary, venal, avaricious.
interesadamente, *adv.* interestedly.
interesado, da, *past part. of* **interesar.** —*a.* 1. interested, concerned. 2. governed by self-interest, mercenary, venal. —*m., f.* interested party or person.
interesal, *a., var. of* **interesable.**
interesante, *a.* interesting.
interesar, *tr.v.* 1. to interest, inspire interest in, e.g. *la interesé en mi proyecto,* I interested her in my project. 2. to affect, attack (e.g. an illness — an organism). 3. to take into, give (someone) an interest in (a business). —*i.v.* to be of interest, concern, or importance, e.g. *el pasado no interesa,* the past is of no importance. —*r.v.* to be interested; to become interested; **interesarse en** or **por,** to be interested in, take an interest in.
interescolar, *a.* interscholastic, inter-school.
interesencia, *f.* personal attendance (at a function).
interesente, *a.* present.
interestatal, *a.* (Amer.) interstate.
interestelar, *a.* interstellar.
interfascicular, *a.* (anat.) interfascicular.
interfecto, ta, *a.* (law) murdered. —*m., f.* murdered person.
interferencia, *f.* 1. (phys., rad.) interference. 2. (*pl.*) atmospherics, interference. 3. (Amer.) intervention, intromission.
interferir, (*ref.* 42) *i.v.* to interfere; (Amer.) to impede; to obstruct.
interferometría, *f.* (phys.) interferometry.
interferómetro, *m.* (phys.) interferometer.
interfiera, interfiere, *ref.* **interferir.**
interfiriendo, interfiriera, interfiriese, *ref.* interferir.
interfoliar, *tr.v.* to interfoliate, interleave.
intergenérico, ca, *a.* (biol.) intergeneric.
interglacial, *a.* (geol.) interglacial.
intergubernamental, *a.* intergovernmental.
ínterin, *m.* 1. temporary employment; interim. 2. (ecc.) Interim, e.g. *í. de Augsburg,* Augsburg Interim. —*adv.* interim, meanwhile. — **en el í.,** in the meantime or interim.
interinamente, *adv.* temporarily, provisionally.
interinar, *tr.v.* to fill or occupy (a post temporarily.
interinato, *m.* (Chile, Hond.) temporary post.
interinidad, *f.* 1. temporariness. 2. temporary employment.
interino, na, *a.* temporary; provisional. —*m. f.* replacement, stand-in.
interior, *a.* 1. interior; inner, inside. 2. inner (feelings, thoughts). 3. domestic, internal (trade, politics, etc.). — **ropa i.,** underclothes, underclothing. —*m.* 1. interior, inside. 2. spirit, soul. 3. (sport.) inside, e.g. *el i. izquierdo,* the inside left. 4. (*pl.*) insides, innards, entrails.
interioridad, *f.* inside; (*pl*) personal or family secrets or affairs; internal affairs.
interiorizarse, (*ref.* 53) *r.v.* (Amer.) (with de) to acquaint oneself (with), find out, learn about.
interiormente, *adv.* inwardly, interiorly; internally.
interjección, *f.* (gram.) interjection.
interjectivo, va, *a.* (gram.) interjectional.
interlínea, *f.* 1. (print.) lead (strip of metal put between the lines). 2. (print.) space line.
interlineación, *f.* 1. interlineation, interlining. 2. (print.) leading (putting leads between lines).
interlineado, da, *a.* (print.) leaded.
interlineal, *a.* interlineal, interlinear.
interlinear, *tr.v.* 1. to interlineate, interline, write or print between the lines. 2. (print.) to lead, lead out, space out.
interlocución, *f.* interlocution, conversation, dialogue; exchange.
interlocutor, ra, *m., f.* interlocutor, talker, speaker.
interlocutoriamente, *adv.* (law) interlocutorily.
interlocutorio, ria, *a.* (law) interlocutory.
intérlope, *a.* 1. interloping, intruding. 2. said of a ship which trades illegally.
interludio, *m.* (mus.) interlude.
interlunio, *m.* (astron.) interlunation, interlunar period.
intermaxilar, *a.* (anat.) intermaxillary.
intermediar, *i.v.* to stand between, be between, to mediate.
intermediario, ria, *a.* intermediary. —*m., f.* intermediary. —*m.* (com.) middleman. — **i. financiero,** broker.
intermedina, *f.* (biochem.) intermedin.
intermedio, dia, *a.* medium, intermediate; interposed. —*m.* 1. interval, interim. 2. (theat.) interval, intermission; interval music, interlude.
interminable, *a.* interminable, endless.
interminación, *f.* (rare) menace, threat.
intermisión, *f.* intermission, interruption, pause.
intermiso, sa, *a.* interrupted, suspended.
intermisor, *m.* intermitter, interruptor.
intermitencia, *f.* intermittence, intermittency; (med.) intermission (temporary cessation of fever. etc.).
intermitente, *a.* intermittent, occurring at intervals; **luz i.,** intermittent light.
intermitir, *tr.v.* to intermit, suspend.
intermolecular, *a.* (phys.) intermolecular.
intermuscular, *a.* (anat.) intermuscular.
internación, *f.* 1. internment, detention (in prison camp, etc.); confinement (in hospital). 2. penetration, going inland.
internacional, *a.* international. —*f.* 1. **I.,** International (the Socialist organization). 2. **La I.,** The Internationale (the Communist anthem).
internacionalice, *ref.* **internacionalizar.**
internacionalidad, *f.* internationality.
internacionalismo, *m.* internationalism, cooperation among nations.
internacionalista, *a., m., f.* internationalist, advocate of world harmony and cooperation.
internacionalizar, (*ref.* 53) *tr.v.* to internationalize, make international.
internado, *past part. of* **internar.** —*m.* boarding school; boarders, body of students of a boarding school.
internamente, *adv.* internally.
internamiento, *m.* (mil.) internment.
internar, *tr v.* 1. to send inland; to import. 2. to intern, detain (in an internment camp, etc.); to confine, put into (a hospital, mental institution). —*i.v.* to penetrate, go into. —*r.v.* 1. to go, press or move inland. 2. to go deeply into (a subject of study). 3. to work one's way into (someone's confidence, etc.). 4. to hide. 5. to enter (a convent, a hospital, etc.).
internista, *m., f.* (med.) internist.
interno, na, *a.* 1. internal, interior, inward. 2. boarding (student). —*m., f.* 1. boarder, boarding-school student. 2. intern (resident doctor).
internodio, *m.* (bot.) internode.
internunciatura, *f.* 1. (rel.) post of internuncio. 2. internuncio's home or office.
internuncio, *m.* 1. (ecc.) internuncio, papal representative. 2. envoy.
interoceánico, ca, *a.* interoceanic.
interoceptor, ra, *a.* (physiol.) interoceptive. —*m.* interoceptor.
interocular, *a.* between the eyes, interocular.
interóseo, a, *a.* (anat.) interosseous, between the bones.
interpaginar, *tr.v.* to interleave, interpage, place between pages or leaves of a book.
interparietal, *a.* (anat.) interparietal.
interparlamentario, ria, *a.* interparliamentary, pertaining to communications between legislative bodies.
interpelación, *f.* 1. interpellation, questioning, summoning. 2. beseeching, appealing, imploring.
interpelante, *a.* 1. interpellating, questioning. 2. imploring, beseeching. —*m., f.* 1. interpellator, questioner. 2. implorer, beseecher.
interpelar, *tr.v.* 1. to interpellate, to summon, to question, ask for explanations. 2. to appeal to, ask for aid.
interpenetración, *f.* interpenetration, mutual penetration.
interpenetrar, *tr.v.* interpenetrate.
interplanetario, ria, *a.* interplanetary, between planets.
Interpol, *f.* Interpol, international police; International Criminal Police Organization.
interpolación, *f.* 1. interpolation, insertion; (math.) interpolation. 2. interruption.
interpoladamente, *adv.* interpolatively, interpolatedly.
interpolador, ra, *a.* interpolative. —*m., f.* interpolator.
interpolar, *tr.v.* 1. to interpolate, insert; (math.) to interpolate. 2. to interrupt, to stop briefly (a speech, conversation, etc.).
interponer, (*ref.* 15) *tr.v.* 1. to interpose; to put or bring between. 2. to appoint (someone) as mediator. 3. (law) to present, file (an appeal); to bring in (an exception). —*r.v.* 1. to intervene, intercede. 2. to put oneself between.
interposición, *f.* interposition, interference; mediation.
interposita persona, (Lat., law) mediator, intermediary.

interprender, *tr.v.* to take by surprise.
interpresa, *f.* taking by surprise, surprise attack or action.
interpretable, *a.* interpretable, understandable, decipherable.
interpretación, *f.* interpretation; (**mus.,** theat.) performance; translation; reading. — **i. auténtica,** (law) authentic interpretation; **i. de lenguas,** translation bureau (in Spanish foreign office); **i. doctrinal,** (law) doctrinal interpretation; **i. por comparación,** (law) comparative interpretation.
interpretador, ra, *a.* interpreting. —*m., f.* interpreter, performer.
interpretar, *tr.v.* 1. to interpret, explain, decipher. 2. to translate orally. 3. (theat.) to act a part. 4. (mus.) to perform.
interpretativamente, *adv.* interpretatively.
interpretativo, va, *a.* interpretative.
intérprete, *m., f.* interpreter; oral translator; (mus.) performer; (theat.) actor, actress.
interpuesto, ta, *irr. past part. of* **interponer.** —*a.* interposed, intervening.
interregno, *m.* (pol.) interregnum, time lapse between monarchs.
interrogación, *f.* 1. interrogation, questioning. 2. question, interrogation, inquiry, query. 3. (gram.) question or interrogation mark; (rhet.) rhetorical question.
interrogador, ra, *a.* interrogating. —*m., f.* interrogator, questioner.
interrogante, *a.* questioning, interrogating; question, interrogation (mark). —*m., f.* questioner, interrogator. —*m.* 1. question or interrogation mark. 2. (fig.) quandary, uncertainty. —*f.* questioning look.
interrogar, (*ref. 51*) *tr.v.* to interrogate, to question.
interrogativamente, *adv.* interrogatively, questioningly.
interrogativo, va, *a.* questioning; (gram.) interrogative.
interrogatorio, *m.* cross-examination, interrogation; series of questions put to a suspect.
interrogue, interrogué, *ref.* **interrogar.**
interrumpidamente, *adv.* interruptedly.
interrumpido, da, *past part. of* **interrumpir.** —*a.* broken, discontinued, interrupted.
interrumpir, *tr.v.* 1. to interrupt, discontinue; to pause; to break into or upon, to stop temporarily. 2. to obstruct or impede.
interrupción, *f.* interruption, break, temporary cessation.
interruptor, ra, *a.* interrupting. —*m.* (elec.) switch; interrupter, circuit breaker; **i. de botón,** (elec.) push button switch; **i. de contacto,** (elec.) contact switch; **i. de corriente,** (elec.) current breaker; **i. de dos polos,** (elec.) double-break switch; **i. de dos vías,** (elec.) double-throw switch; **i. de mando,** (elec.) control switch; **i. de reloj,** (elec.) time switch; **i. de vía única,** (elec.) single-throw switch; **i. de volquete,** (elec.) tumbler switch; **i. horario,** time switch; **i. protector,** circuit breaker.
intersecarse, (*ref. 50*) *r.v.* (geom.) to intersect (two lines).
intersección, *f.* (geom.) intersection.
intersectar, *tr.v.* to intersect; to meet or cross (two streets, highways, etc.).
intersexual, *a.* 1. intersexual, with characteristics of both sexes. 2. between sexes.
intersexualidad, *f.* intersexuality.
intersideral, *a.* (astron.) interstellar.
intersticial, *a.* interstitial.
intersticio, *m.* 1. interstice, gap, space. 2. interval (of time). 3. (ecc.) obligatory lapse of time between the reception of two orders.
intertrigo, *m.* (med.) intertrigo.
intertropical, *a.* (geog.) intertropical, between the tropic of Cancer and the tropic of Capricorn.
interurbano, na, *a.* interurban (bus services, railway, etc.).
interusorio, *m.* (law) interest owed to a woman for delay in repaying her marriage dowry.
intervalo, *m.* interval; stretch of time; space; (mus.) interval. — **i. lúcido** or **claro,** lucid interval, interval of sanity.
intervalómetro, *m.* (photog.) intervalometer.
intervención, *f.* 1. intervention; interference. 2. participation. 3. auditing (of books). 4. (surg.) operation. — **política de no-intervención,** policy of nonintervention.
intervencionismo, *m.* interventionism, the act of interfering in the affairs of others, esp. of one nation in the affairs of another.
intervencionista, *a., m., f.* interventionist, one who advocates interventionism.
intervenga, intervengo, *ref.* **intervenir.**
intervenir, (*ref. 26*) *i.v.* 1. to take part in, participate. 2. to intervene, intercede, mediate. 3. to meddle. 4. to intervene, happen. —*tr.v.* 1. (com.) to audit (accounts). 2. to offer to pay (a draft). 3. to place under government control, take control of, to control, to regulate. 4. (surg.) to operate. 5. (Chile) to take over (*said of the police*).
interventor, ra, *a.* intervening, participating. —*m., f.* intervener; participator. —*m.* 1. supervisor, inspector, controller; election supervisor. 2. (com.) auditor.
intervertebral, *a.* (anat.) intervertebral.
intervine, interviniendo, interviniera, interviniese, *ref.* **intervenir.**
intervocálico, ca, *a.* (phonet.) intervocalic, between vowels.
interyacente, *a.* interjacent, intervening.
intestado, da, *a., m., f.* (law) intestate, without testament. —*m.* (law) estate of an intestate.
intestinal, *a.* intestinal, pertaining to the intestines.
intestino, na, *a.* internal; intestine, civil. —*m.* intestine; **i. ciego,** (anat.) caecum, blind gut; **i. delgado,** (anat.) small intestine; **i. grueso,** (anat.) large intestine.
intima, *f, var. of* **intimación.**
intimacion, *f.* announcement; notification; warning, notice.
íntimamente, *adv.* intimately, closely; personally.
intimar, *tr.v.* to make known, announce; to notify; to convey (an order); to state with authority. —*i.v.* to become intimate or well acquainted (with someone). —*r.v.* 1. to become intimate or well acquainted (with someone). 2. to interpenetrate.
intimatorio, ria, *a.* (law) notificatory, notifying.
intimidación, *f.* intimidation.
intimidad, *f.* intimacy, closeness, privacy, e.g. *en la intimidad del hogar,* in the privacy of the home.
intimidar, *tr.v.* to intimidate, cow, dismay, threaten; to bully, frighten; daunt. —*r.v.* to become intimidated.
íntimo, ma, *a.* 1. intimate. 2. cherished, innermost, fondest (desire, wish). 3. close, e.g. *mis más íntimos amigos,* my closest friends.
intitular, *tr.v.* to entitle, give a title to. —*r.v.* to receive a title; (Guat.) to be called.
intocable, *m.* untouchable; (*pl.*) untouchables (a caste in India).
intolerabilidad, *f.* intolerability, intolerableness.
intolerable, *a.* intolerable, unbearable, insufferable.
intolerancia, *f.* 1. intolerance; (med.) allergy. 2. intransigence. — **i. racial,** racial intolerance.
intolerante, *a.* intolerant, intransigent. —*m., f.* intolerant person.
intomable, *a.* undrinkable; uneatable, inedible.
intonso, sa, *a.* 1. (poet.) unshorn. 2. (fig.) ignorant, uncouth, rustic. 3. (fig.) uncut, with uncut pages (book). —*m., f.* ignorant person.
intorsión, *f.* (bot.) intorsion.
intoxicación, *f.* 1. poisoning, intoxication; **i. saturnina,** (med.) saturnine poisoning. 2. (fig.) drunkenness; ecstasy.
intoxicado, da, *a.* intoxicated, poisoned; (fig.) drunk; ecstatic.
intoxicar, (*ref. 50*) *tr.v.* to poison, intoxicate. —*r.v.* to be poisoned.
intoxique, intoxiqué, *ref.* **intoxicar.**
intraatómico, ca, *a.* intra-atomic, contained within the atom.
intracelular, *a.* (physiol.) intracellular.
intracutáneo, a, *a.* (med.) intracutaneous.
intradérmico, ca, *a.* (anat.) intradermal, intradermic.
intradós, *m.* (archit.) intrados.
intraducibilidad, *f.* untranslatableness, untranslatability.
intraducible, *a.* untranslatable, undecipherable, unanalyzable.
intramolecular, *a.* intramolecular, within molecules.
intramuros, *adv.* within a city or town; (fig.) within a body or an organization.
intramuscular, *a.* (anat.) intramuscular.
intranquilice, intranquilicé, *ref.* **intranquilizar.**
intranquilidad, *f.* uneasiness, restlessness; preoccupation.
intranquilizador, ra, *a.* disquieting, worrying; preoccupying.
intranquilizar, (*ref. 53*) *tr.v.* to make uneasy, restless, worry, disquiet, to preoccupy. —*r.v.* to get restless or uneasy.
intranquilo, la, *a.* restless, uneasy, worried; preoccupied.
intransferible, *a.* untransferable, non-transferable.
intransigencia, *f.* intransigence, stubbornness; intolerance.
intransigente, *a.* intransigent, uncompromising, intolerant.
intransitable, *a.* impassable (road, street, etc.).
intransitivo, va, *a.* (gram.) intransitive.
intransmutabilidad, *f.* intransmutability.
intransmutable, *a.* intransmutable, unconvertible, unchangeable.
intrascendente, *a.* unimportant; that will not harm.
intrasmisible, *a.* untransmissible.
intratabilidad, *f.* 1. unsociability. 2. intractability.
intratable, *a.* 1. unsociable; grouchy; rude. 2. intractable, hard to manage, unruly. 3. difficult to cross or climb (road, hill, etc.).
intrauterino, na, *a.* (med.) intrauterine.
intravenoso, sa, *a.* (med.) intravenous.
intrépidamente, *adv.* intrepidly, fearlessly.
intrepidez, *f.* intrepidity, boldness, fearlessness, bravery, temerity.
intrépido, da, *a.* intrepid, daring, fearless; (fig.) impulsive.
intriga, *f.* 1. intrigue, plot, machination; scheme. 2. entanglement, embroilment.
intrigante, *a.* intriguing. —*m., f.* intriguer, plotter; schemer.
intrigar, (*ref. 51*) *i.v.* to intrigue, plot, scheme. —*tr.v.* to intrigue, puzzle, perplex, fascinate, e.g. *me intriga esa mujer,* that woman fascinates me.

intrigue, intrigué, *ref.* **intrigar.**
intrincable, *a.* capable of being confused or entangled.
intrincación, *f.* intricacy, confusion, complicatedness.
intrincadamente, *adv.* intricately, complicatedly.
intrincado, da, *past part. of* **intrincar.** —*a.* intricate, involved, complicated.
intrincamiento, *m., var. of* **intrincación.**
intrincar, (*ref. 50*) *tr.v.* to tangle, involve, complicate, confuse. —*r.v.* to become tangled, involved or confused.
intríngulis, *m.* (coll.) hidden intention or motive; enigma, puzzle, e.g. *ese asunto tiene su i.,* that's a ticklish problem.
intrinque, intrinqué, *ref.* **intrincar.**
intrínsecamente, *adv.* intrinsically, essentially.
intrínseco, ca, *a.* intrinsic, intrinsical; essential, inherent; **valor i.,** real value.
intrique, intriqué, *ref.* **intrincar.**
introducción, *f.* 1. introduction; insertion. 2. (lit.) foreword, preface. 3. (mus.) introduction. 4. introduction, beginning, initiation.
introducir, (*ref. 47*) *tr.v.* 1. to introduce, bring in (new customs, ideas, words, industries, etc.). 2. to present (at court). 3. to show, bring, usher (into a room). 4. to put (into), insert. 5. to cause, bring about. —*r.v.* 1. to get into, enter, break into. 2. to meddle, interfere, intrude.
introductivo, va, *a.* introductory, introductive.
introductor, ra, *a.* introductory. —*m., f.* introducer; innovator.
introduje, introdujera, introdujese, *ref.* **introducir.**
introduzca, introduzco, *ref.* **introducir.**
introito, *m.* 1. (lit., rhet.) introduction. 2. (ecc.) introit. 3. (theat.) prologue.
intromisión, *f.* 1. insertion. 2. meddling, intruding, interfering.
introspección, *f.* introspection, self-examination.
introspectivo, va, *a.* introspective.
introversión, *f.* introversion, abstraction.
introverso, sa, *a.* introverted, introvert.
introvertido, da, *a.* introverted; (fig.) shy, quiet. —*m., f.* introvert.
introyección, *f.* (psyc.) introjection.
intrusamente, *adv.* intrusively.
intrusarse, *r.v.* to seize unlawfully, to encroach, usurp.
intrusión, *f.* intrusion, interloping; encroachment.
intrusismo, *m.* quackery, practice of a profession without bona fide qualifications.
intruso, sa, *a.* intruding, meddlesome. —*m., f.* intruder, interloper; unauthorized guest or participant.
intubación, *f.* (med.) intubation.
intubar, *tr v.* (med.) to intubate.
intuición, *f.* intuition, perception; (theol.) vision. — **i. femenina,** femenine intuition.
intuicionismo, *m.* (philos.) intuitionism.
intuicionista, *a., m., f.* (philos.) intuitionist.
intuir, (*ref. 48*) *tr.v.* to sense, guess or perceive intuitively, intuit.
intuitivamente, *adv.* intuitively, by intuition.
intuitivo, va, *a.* intuitive.
intuito, *m.* glance, look, view; **por i.,** in view of.
intumescencia, *f.* (med.) intumescence, swelling.
intumescente, *a.* (med.) intumescent, swelling.
intumescer, *i v.* to intumesce, swell.
intususcepción, *f.* (biol.) intussusception; (med.) intussusception, invagination.
intususceptivo, va, *a.* (med., biol.) intussusceptive.
intuya, intuyendo, intuyera, intuyese, intuyo, *ref.* **intuir.**
ínula, *f.* (bot.) inula.
inulina, *f.* (biochem.) inulin.
inulinasa, *f.* (biochem.) inulase, inulinase.
inulto, ta, *a.* (poet.) unavenged, unpunished.
inundación, *f.* 1. inundation, flood, overflow, deluge. 2. (fig.) great abundance.
inundante, *a.* inundating, flooding.
inundar, *tr.v.* to inundate, flood; (fig.) to inundate, flood, fill. —*r.v.* to become inundated or flooded; **inundarse de,** to be flooded with.
inurbanamente, *adv.* discourteously, rudely; uncivilly.
inurbanidad, *f.* discourtesy, rudeness; incivility.
inurbano, na, *a.* discourteous, impolite, rude; uncivil.
inusitadamente, *adv.* unusually, uncommonly; unexpectedly.
inusitado, da, *a.* unusual, uncommon.
inútil, *a.* useless; fruitless, pointless; needless, unnecessary; good-for-nothing, unserviceable. — **i. es decir,** needless to say. —*m., f.* useless person.
inutilice, inutilicé, *ref.* **inutilizar.**
inutilidad, *f.* uselessness; incapacity, incompetence; pointlessness, fruitlessness.
inutilizado, da, *past part. of* **inutilizar.** —*a.* unused; unemployed, without use.
inutilizar, (*ref. 53*) *tr.v.* to make useless; to put out of action or use; to disable, to ruin. —*r.v.* to become useless; to be put out of action or use; to be disabled.
inútilmente, *adv.* uselessly, needlessly, to no avail.
invadeable, *a.* unwadeable, unfordable.
invadir, *tr.v.* to invade; (fig.) to encroach on, meddle in, interfere with; to enter (by force), to trespass.
invaginación, *f.* (med.) invagination.
invaginar, *tr.v.* (med.) to invaginate.
invalidación, *f.* invalidation, nullification, annulment.
inválidamente, *adv.* invalidly.
invalidar, *tr.v.* to invalidate, nullify; to annul; to deprive (of force or effect).
invalidez, *f.* invalidity (disability; nullity); **i. absoluta,** total disability.
inválido, da, *a.* 1. invalid, infirmed, crippled, maimed, disabled. 2. invalid, null and void (law). —*m., f.* invalid; disabled soldier.
invar, *m.* invar (nickel steel).
invariabilidad, *f.* invariability.
invariable, *a.* invariable, unchanging, constant; immutable.
invariablemente, *adv.* invariably.
invariación, *f.* invariableness, invariability.
invariadamente, *adv.* invariably.
invariado, da, *a.* unchanged, constant.
invariante, *f.* (math.) invariant.
invasión, *f.* invasion; entrance by force, prolonged incursion.
invasor, ra, *a.* invading. —*m., f.* invader; intruder.
invectiva, *f.* invective, abuse.
invencibilidad, *f.* invincibility; unconquerability.
invencible, *a.* invincible; unconquerable, undefeatable; **la Armada Invencible,** (hist.) the Spanish Armada or the Invincible Armada (of Philip II, defeated by the British in 1588).
invenciblemente, *adv.* invincibly; unconquerably.
invención, *f.* 1. invention; creation, discovery. 2. invention, fiction, lie, e.g. *esas son invenciones tuyas,* those are figments of your imagination.
invencionero, ra, *m., f.* 1. inventor, discoverer. 2. liar, cheat.
invendible, *a.* unsaleable.
inventar, *tr.v.* 1. to invent, discover. 2. to invent, to imagine, to think up; to concoct, fabricate, make up (falsehood, etc.).
inventariar, *tr.v.* to inventory, make an inventory of; to count.
inventario, *m.* inventory; list; (fig.) instock; **hacer i.,** to take inventory.
inventiva, *f.* inventiveness, inventive faculty; creativity, imagination; resourcefulness.
inventivo, va, *a.* inventive; creative; imaginative; resourceful.
invento, *m.* 1. invention, discovery. 2. (fig.) invention, lie, fiction.
inventor, ra, *a.* inventive; creative. —*m., f.* 1. inventor, creator. 2. storyteller, fibber.
inverecundia, *f.* shamelessness, brazenness, impudence, cheek, impertinence.
inverecundo, da, *a.* shameless, brazen, impudent, cheeky, impertinent.
inverisímil, *a., var. of* **inverosímil.**
inverisimilitud, *f., var. of* **inverosimilitud.**
inverna, *f.* (Peru) winter pastures; wintering period spent in winter pastures.
invernáculo, *m.* greenhouse, conservatory, hothouse.
invernada, *f.* 1. wintertime. 2. (Amer.) winter pastures (for cattle); wintering, period spent in winter pastures.
invernadero, *m.* 1. winter quarters. 2. hothouse, conservatory, greenhouse. 3. winter pastures.
invernal, *a.* wintry, hibernal. —*m.* winter stable, seasonal shed for cattle.
invernar, (*ref. 29*) *i.v.* to hibernate, to winter, spend the winter; to be winter; (Arg.) to pasture in winter pastures.
invernizo, za, *a.* wintry, hibernal.
inverosímil, *a.* unlikely, hard to believe; fantastic, unimaginable.
inverosímilitud, *f.* unlikelihood, improbability; inverosimilitude.
inverosímilmente, *adv.* in an unlikely or improbable manner; improbably.
inversamente, *adv.* inversely; **i. a,** contrary to.
inversión, *f.* 1. inversion; (chem., med., theat., mus., meteorol.) inversion. 2. (com.) investment. — **i. del muerto,** dummy reversal (in bridge).
inversionista, *m., f.* (com.) investor.
inverso, sa, *a.* inverse; opposite, reverse. — **a** or **por la inversa,** on the contrary; **en sentido i.,** in the opposite direction; **figuras inversas,** (math.) inverse figures; **funciones inversas,** (math.) inverse functions.
inversor, sora, *a.* inverting, reversing. —*m., f.* investor. —*m.* (elec.) reversing mechanism.
invertasa, *f.* (biochem.) invertase.
invertebrado, da, *a.* (zool.) invertebrate. —*m.* (zool.) invertebrate; (*pl.*) Invertebrata.
invertido, da, *past part. of* **invertir.** —*a.* 1. inverted. 2. (chem.) invert (sugar). —*m., f.* homosexual.
invertina, *f.* (chem.) invertase.
invertir, (*ref. 42*) *tr.v.* 1. to invert; to reverse. 2. (com.) to invest (capital).
invertosa, *f.* (chem.) invert sugar.
investidura, *f.* investiture.
investigable, *a.* investigable; explorable; researchable.
investigación, *f.* 1. investigation, exploration; research, study. 2. (law) investigation, inquet; **i. de mercados,** market research; **i. operativa,** operations research; **i. y desarrollo,** research and development.
investigador, ra, *a.* investigating, researching. —*m., f.* investigator, researcher.
investigar, (*ref. 51*) *tr.v.* to investigate, examine, inquire into; to do research on; to survey, to study.

investigue, investigué, *ref.* **investigar.**
investir, (*ref.* 39) *tr.v.* (used with **con** or **de**) to invest, endow (with), confer (on).
inveteradamente, *adv.* inveterately.
inveterado, da, *past part. of* **inveterarse.** —*a.* inveterate, confirmed; deep-rooted.
inveterarse, *r.v.* to become inveterate, firmly established; to become old or antiquated.
invictamente, *adv.* victoriously, triumphantly; unconquerably.
invicto, ta, *a.* triumphant, unconquered; unbeaten.
invidencia, *f.* (fig.) 1. blindness; lack of vision. 2. envy.
invido, da, *a.* envious.
invierne, invierno, *ref.* **invernar.**
invierno, *m.* winter; (in equatorial regions) rainy season.
invierta, invierto, *ref.* **invertir.**
invigilar, *i v.* to watch something carefully.
inviolabilidad, *f.* inviolability; **i. parlamentaria,** parliamentary immunity.
inviolable, *a.* inviolable, immune.
inviolablemente, *adv.* inviolably.
inviolado, da, *a.* inviolate, unprofaned; uninjured.
invirtiendo, invirtiera, invirtiese, invirtió, *ref.* **invertir.**
invisibilidad, *f.* invisibility; imperceptibility.
invisible, *a.* invisible — **tinta i.,** invisible ink.
invisiblemente, *adv.* invisibility; imperceptibility.
invista, invisto, *ref.* **investir.**
invistiendo, invistiera, invistiese, invistió, *ref.* **investir.**
invitación, *f.* invitation. — **tarjeta de i.,** invitation card.
invitado, *m.* guest. — **i. de honor,** guest of honor; **i. de piedra,** unwanted guest.
invitador, ra, *m., f.* inviter, one who invites.
invitar, *tr.v.* to invite; to induce.
invitatorio, *m.* (ecc.) invitatory, antiphon to **venite exaltemus.**
invocación, *f.* invocation; (poet.) invocation.
invocador, ra, *a.* invoking. —*m., f.* invoker.
invocar, (*ref.* 50) *tr.v.* to appeal to, call upon (for aid or protection); to cite, invoke (authority, law or custom).
invocatorio, ria, *a.* invocatory.
involucelo, *m.* (bot.) involucel.
involución, *f.* (math., med.) involution.
involucrado, da, *past part. of* **involucrar.** —*a.* (bot.) involucrate.
involucral, *a.* (bot.) involucral.
involucral, *tr.v.* 1. to digress in, introduce irrelevant matter in (speech or writing). 2. to involve, implicate.
involucro, *m.* (bot.) involucre.
involuntariamente, *adv.* 1. involuntarily; unintentionally, without thinking, e.g. *perdóname, lo hice i.,* pardon me, I did it unintentionally.
involuntariedad, *f.* involuntariness.
involuntario, ria, *a.* involuntary; unwilling; unintentional.
involuta, *f.* (geom., bot.) involute.
invoque, invoqué, *ref.* **invocar.**
invulnerabilidad, *f.* invulnerability; unassailability.
invulnerable, *a.* invulnerable, unassailable; impregnable.
inyección, *f.* (med.) injection (action; liquid injected); **i. de refuerzo, (med.)** booster shot; **i. de entusiasmo,** (fig.) a shot in the arm (coll.), a morale boost.
inyectable, *a.* injectable. —*m.* injection (substance injected); ampule.
inyectado, da, *a.* (imp. u.) bloodshot (eyes).
inyectar, *tr.v.* to inject.
inyector, *m.* (mec.) injector.
iñiguista, *a.* Jesuitical. —*m., f.* Jesuit.
iodo, *m.* (pharm., chem.) iodine.
iolita, *f.* (min.) iolite.
ion, *m.* (chem., phys.) ion, electrically charged atom or group of atoms.
iónico, ca, *a.* (chem., phys.) ionic.
iodo, *m.* (pharm., chem.) iodine.
ionizable, *a.* (chem.) ionizable.
ionización, *f.* (chem., phys.) ionization.
ionizador, *m.* (chem., phys.) ionizer.
ionizar, (*ref.* 53) *tr.v., i v., r.v.* to ionize.
ionona, *f.* (chem.) ionone.
ionógeno, *a.* ionogenic. —*m.* (chem.) ionogen.
ionósfera, *f.* (meteorol.) ionosphere.
ionosférico, ca, *a.* ionospheric.
iota, *f.* iota, ninth letter of Greek alphabet.
iotacismo, *m.* (phonet.) iotacism.
ipecacuana, *f.* (bot.) ipecacuanha (Cephaelis ipecuanha); **i. de las Antillas,** bastard ipecac (Asclepsias curassavica); ipecac root.
iperita, *f.* (chem.) yperite.
ipil, *m.* 1. (bot.) ipil tree (Intsia bijuga). 2. (Mex.) sleeveless shirt worn by Indian women.
ípsilon, *f.* upsilon (Greek letter).
ipso facto, (Lat.) ipso facto; at once, immediately.
ir, (*ref.* 11) *i.v.* 1. to go, move, walk. 2. to lead, go. 3. to stretch, extend. 4. to act, proceed. 5. to lead (in cards). 6. to differ, e.g. *¡lo que va del padre al hijo!* what a difference between father and son! 7. to suit, fit, be becoming, e.g. *este color te va muy bien,* this color suits you very well. 8. to be, to fare, be doing, e.g. *Juan va muy bien en sus estudios,* John is doing very well in his studies. 9. (math.) to carry, e.g. *cinco y van dos,* five and carry two. 10. to bet, to wager, e.g. *va un peso a que llego primero,* I bet a peso that I arrive first. — **ir** + *ger.* implies the beginning of the action or its occurrence, e.g. *él va comprendiendo,* he is beginning to understand, e.g. *va anocheciendo,* it is getting dark; **ir** + *past part.,* to be + *past part., e.g. voy rendido,* I am exhausted; **ir a** + *inf.,* to be about, be just going + *inf.,* e.g. *yo iba a salir cuando llegó él,* I was about to leave, when he arrived; **ir a** + *inf.* implies the future tense, e.g. *voy a salir dentro de poco,* I am going to leave very soon; **ir a caballo,** to ride, go on horseback; **ir a pie,** to walk, go on foot; **ir de brazo,** to walk arm in arm; **ir de paseo,** to go for a walk; **ir en,** to concern, affect, have to do with, e.g. *¿qué te va a ti en ese asunto?* how does this matter concern you? what has this matter to do with you?; **ir en auto,** to drive, go by car; **ir para** or **con,** to be directed at or meant for, e.g. *lo que dice no va para nosotros,* what he says is not meant for us; **ir por,** to go for, to go to fetch or get; **ir tirando,** to manage (in life), overcome adversities; **¿quién va?** who goes there; **¿cómo te va?** how are you? how are you doing?; ¡vaya! really! is that so! get out! at last!; **vete a saber** or **vaya Ud. a saber,** who knows? go and find out for yourself (indicating it will be difficult). —*r.v.* 1. to go away, depart, leave; to die. **2.** to ooze or leak away; to evaporate. 3. to exceed, e.g. *se me fue la mano,* I went too far. 4. to give way; to wear out, fray, become thread-bare; grow old. — **irse abajo,** to topple, to crash down; **irse a pique,** (mar.) to sink, to founder; **írsele a uno los ojos,** to gaze longingly or admiringly; **írsele a uno los pies,** to lose one's footing.
Ir *sym. of* **iridio,** iridium (Ir).
ira, *f.* anger, ire, wrath.
iracundia, *f.* anger, ire, wrath; irascibility.
iracundo, da, *a.* irascible, angry, irate, wrathful.
Irán, *m.* Iran (Persia).
iraní, *a., m., f.* Iranian, Persian.
iraniano, na, iranio, nia, *a., m., f.* Iranian, Persian. —*m.* Iranian (language).
Iraq, *m.* Iraq.
iraqués, sa, iraquí, *a., m., f.* Iraqui. —*m.* Iraqui (language).
irascibilidad, *f.* irascibility, bad temper; anger.
irascible, *a.* irascible, irritable, ill-tempered.
irenarca, *m.* (hist.) irenarch, Roman magistrate in charge of order and pacification.
irga, irgo, *ref.* **erguir.**
irguiendo, irguiera, irguiese, irguió, *ref.* **erguir.**
iribú, *m.* (Amer.) aura, turkey, buzzard.
iridáceo, a, *a.* (bot.) iridaceous. —*f.* (*pl.*) (bot.) Iridaceae.
íride, *m.* (bot.) stinking iris, gladdon.
iridectomía, *f.* (surg.) iridectomy.
irídeo, a, *a.* (bot.) irideous, iridaceous. —*f.* (*pl.*) (bot.) Iridaceae.
irídico, ca, *a.* (anat.) iridic.
iridio, *m.* (chem.) iridium.
iridiscencia, *f.* iridescence.
iridiscente, *a.* iridescent.
iridosmina, *f.* (min.) iridosmine.
iridosmio, *m.* (min.) iridosmium.
irire, *m.* (Bol.) oval gourd (for drinking chicha).
irirear, *i.v.* (Bol.) to drink chicha.
iris, *m.* 1. rainbow, iris. 2. (anat.) iris. 3. (min.) noble opal. 4. (myth.) **I.,** Iris, winged female messenger of the gods. — **arco i.,** rainbow, iris.
irisación, *f.* iridescence.
irisar, *tr.v.* to make iridescent. —*i.v.* to iridesce, be iridescent.
iritis, *f.* (med.) iritis.
Irlanda, *f.* 1. Ireland. **2. i.,** Irish linen. — **Estado Libre de I.,** Irish Free State; **I. del Norte,** Northern Ireland.
irlandés, sa, *a.* Irish. —*m.* Irishman; Irish (language); (*pl.*) Irish. —*f.* Irishwoman.
ironía, *f.* irony.
irónicamente, *a.* ironically.
ironice, ironicé, *ref.* **ironizar.**
irónico, ca, *a.* ironic; ironical.
ironista, *m., f.* ironist.
ironizar, (*ref.* 53) *tr.v.* to ridicule, ironize; to make fun of.
iroqués, sa, *a.* (U.S., hist.) Iroquoian. —*m., f.* Iroquoian, Iroquois. —*m.* Iroquoian language.
irracional, *a.* irrational; absurd.
irracionalidad, *f.* irrationality, absurdity.
irracionalmente, *adv.* irrationally, absurdly.
irradiación, *f.* irradiation, radiation.
irradiar, *tr.v., i.v.* to irradiate, radiate; **i. felicidad,** to show great happiness.
irrazonable, *a.* unreasonable.
irreal, *a.* unreal.
irrealidad, *f.* unreality.
irrealizable, *a.* unrealizable; unattainable.
irrebatible, *a.* irrefutable.
irreciprocidad, *f.* lack of reciprocity.
irreconciliable, *a.* unreconcilable.
irreconciliablemente, *adv.* irreconcilably.
irreconocible, *a.* unrecognizable; (fig.) transformed, changed.
irrecordable, *a.* unable to be remembered; (fig.) horrible, painful.
irrecuperable, *a.* irrecoverable; irretrievable; last.
irrecusable, *a.* unchallengeable, unable to be challenged or rejected.
irredentismo, *m.* 1. Irredentism; political movement organized in Italy, 1878, seeking to recover Italian territory under foreign control. 2. any

movement advocating the recovery of territory lost by a nation to foreign control.
irredentista, *a., m., f.* (polit.) Irredentist, pertaining to or one who advocates Irredentism.
irredento, ta, *a.* unredeemed (said especially of a region that has been separated from a nation to which it remains linked by ties of history, race, language, etc.).
irredimible, *a.* unredeemable; unexchangeable.
irreducible, irreductible, *a.* irreducible.
irreemplazable, *a.* unreplaceable, irreplaceable.
irreflexión, *f.* rashness, impetuosity, irreflection.
irreflexivamente, *adv.* unthinkingly, rashly, impetuously.
irreflexivo, va, *a.* unreflecting, rash, impetuous, thoughtless, impulsive.
irreformable, *a.* incorrigible, irreformable.
irrefragable, *a.* irrefragable, unanswerable, irresistible.
irrefragablemente, *adv.* irrefutably.
irrefrenable, *a.* unrestrainable, uncontrollable, unmanageable.
irrefutable, *a.* irrefutable.
irregular, *a.* irregular; abnormal; unmethodical; disorderly.
irregularidad, *f.* irregularity; abnormality; disorder.
irregularmente, *adv.* irregularly.
irreligión, *f.* irreligion, lack of a religion, impiety.
irreligiosidad, *f.* irreligiousness; impiety.
irreligioso, sa, *a.* irreligious; unreligious. —*m., f.* irreligious person; unreligious person.
irremediable, *a.* irremediable; incurable, hopeless.
irremediablemente, *adv.* irremediably; hopelessly.
irremisible, *a.* irremissible, unforgivable, unpardonable.
irremisiblemente, *adv.* irremissibly, unforgivably, unpardonably.
irremunerado, da, *a.* unremunerated, unpaid.
irreparable, *a.* irreparable, unmendable.
irreparablemente, *adv.* irreparably.
irreprensible, *a.* irreproachable; irreprehensible, faultless.
irreprensiblemente, *adv.* irreproachably, blamelessly.
irreprimible, *a.* irrepressible, unrestrainable.
irreprochable, *a.* irreproachable, faultless; impeccable.
irreprochablemente, *adv.* irreproachably, faultlessly.
irresistible, *a.* irresistible; fascinating, compelling.
irresistiblemente, *adv.* irresistibly.
irresoluble, *a.* unsolvable, irresolute.
irresolución, *f.* irresolution, irresoluteness, indecision, hesitation; insecurity.
irresolutamente, *adv.* irresolutely.
irresoluto, ta, *a.* irresolute, wavering, hesitant. —*m., f.* irresolute person.
irrespetuoso, sa, *a.* disrespectful; irreverent.
irrespirable, *a.* unbreathable, suffocating.
irresponsabilidad, *f.* irresponsibility; unreliability.
irresponsable, *a.* irresponsible; unreliable.
irresuelto, ta, *a.* irresolute, wavering, hesitant.
irretroactividad, *f.* (law) non-retroactive principle of law.
irretroactivo, *a.* non-retroactive.
irrevelable, *a.* unrevealable.
irrevelado, da, *a.* unrevealed.
irreverencia, *f.* irreverence, disrespect.
irreverenciar, *tr.v.* to treat irreverently, profane; to disrespect.
irreverente, *a.* irreverent; disrespectful, rude; impolite.
irreverentemente, *adv.* irreverently.
irreversible, *a.* irreversible.
irrevocabilidad, *f.* irrevocability.
irrevocable, *a.* irrevocable.
irrevocablemente, *adv.* irrevocably.
irrigable, *a.* irrigable.
irrigación, *f.* irrigation; (med.) irrigation, douching.
irrigador, *m.* (med.) irrigator, douche.
irrigar, (*ref. 51*) *tr.v.* to irrigate, water; (med.) to irrigate, douche.
irrigue, irrigué, *ref.* **irrigar.**
irrisible, *a.* laughable, ridiculous.
irrisión, *f.* derision, ridicule, mockery; (coll.) laughingstock.
irrisoriamente, *adv.* laughably, ridiculously, derisively.
irrisorio, a, *a.* laughable, ridiculous, derisive.
irritabilidad, *f.* irritability.
irritable, *a.* 1. irritable, annoying. 2. (law) voidable, annulable.
irritación, *f.* 1. irritation, annoyance, exasperation. 2. (med., physiol.) irritation. 3. (law) irritancy, invalidation, annulment.
irritador, ra, *a.* irritating. —*m., f.* irritator.
írritamente, *adv.* (law) invalidly.
irritamiento, *m.* irritation, the state of being irritated.
irritante, *a.* 1. irritating, annoying. 2. (law) annulling, voiding. —*m.* (med.) irritant.
irritar, *tr.v.* to irritate, vex, annoy; to stir up, excite (anger, jealousy); (med.) to irritate. —*r.v.* to become irritated.
irritar, *tr.v.* (law) to irritate, make null and void.
írrito, ta, *a.* (law) null and void, invalid.
irrogación, *f.* causing (of damage).
irrogar, (*ref. 51*) *tr.v.* to cause (damage).
irrogue, irrogué, *ref.* **irrogar.**
irrompible, *a.* unbreakable.
irruir, (*ref. 48*) *tr.v.* to raid, invade, assault.
irrumpir, *i.v.* to burst in; to invade, to break into.
irrupción, *f.* bursting in, irruption; invasion.
irruya, irruyendo, irruyera, irruyese, irruyo, *ref.* **irruir.**
irupé, *m.* (bot) giant or royal water lily.
isabelino, na, *a.* 1. pearl-colored, whitish-yellow (said of a horse). 2. bearing the bust of Isabella II (a coin). 3. Isabelline; Elizabethan. — **arquitectura isabelina,** Elizabethan or Tudor architecture. —*m., f.* 1. Isabelline, partisan of Isabella II (in the Carlist Wars). 2. Elizabethan.
isabelita, *f.* (ichth.) isabelita, angelfish.
isagoge, *f.* isagoge, introduction, exordium.
isagógico, ca, *a.* isagogic, introductory.
Isaías, *m.* (Bib.) Isaiah.
isalobara, *f.* (meteorol.) isallobar.
isangas, *f.* (*pl.*) (Peru) wickerwork prawn trap.
isatina, *f.* (chem.) isatin.
isatis, *m.* (zool.) Arctic fox.
isba, *f.* isbah, Russian log cabin.
iscariote, *m.* (Bib.) Iscariot.
isidoriano, na, *a.* Isidorian, pertaining to Saint Isidore.
isidro, dra, *m., f.* (coll.) name given by the people of Madrid to a rustic, yokel, country bumpkin.
Isis, *f.* (myth.) Isis, Egyptian goddess of medicine and fertility.
isla, *f.* 1. island, isle. 2. block (of houses). 3. grove (in the middle of a plain). 4. (fig.) a solitary person, an isolated event or situation. — **I. del Diablo,** Devil's Island; **I. de Man,** Isle of Man; **I. de Pinos,** Isle of Pines; **i. de seguridad,** safety island or zone; **I. Príncipe Eduardo,** Prince Edward Island; **I. Real,** Isle Royale (on Lake Superior); **Islas Aleutas, Aleutianas** or **Aleutinas,** Aleutian Islands; **Islas Anglonormandas,** Channel Islands; **Islas Baleares,** Balearic Islands; **Islas Británicas,** British Isles; **Islas Canarians,** Canary Islands; **Islas Carolinas,** Caroline Islands; **Islas de Almirantazgo,** Admiralty Islands; **Islas de Barlovento,** Windward Islands; **Islas de Sotavento,** Leeward Islands; **Islas Filipinas,** Philippines, Philippine Islands; **Islas Laquedivas,** Laccadive Islands; **Islas Malvinas,** Falkland Islands; **Islas Salomón,** Solomon Islands; **Islas Vírgenes,** Virgin Islands.
Islam, *m.* Islam (the people, history and civilization of the Moslems and their lands); the Moslems (collectively).
islamice, islamicé, *ref.* **islamizar.**
islámico, ca, *a.* Islamic, pertaining to Islam.
islamismo, *m.* Islamism, the Moslem world; its people, concepts and civilization.
islamita, *a.* Islamitic. —*m., f.* Islamite.
islamizar, (*ref. 53*) *i.v., r.v.* to Islamize, become a Moslem or acquaint with the Moslem civilization.
islán, *m.* lace-edged veil.
islandés, sa, *a.* Icelandic. —*m., f.* Icelander. —*m.* Icelandic (language).
Islandia, *f.* Iceland.
islándico, ca, *a.* Icelandic, of or pertaining to Iceland.
islario, *m.* map or description of islands.
isleño, ña, *a.* of or pertaining to an island. —*m., f.* islander; (Amer.) a native of the Canary Islands.
isleo, *m.* 1. islet, small island. 2. island of land, isolated tract of land.
isleta, *f.* islet, isle, holm.
islilla, *f.* (anat.) armpit; collar bone.
islote, *m.* islet, key; barren isle.
ismael, *m.* (Bib.) Ishmael.
ismaelita, *a.* (Bib., hist.) Ishmaelitic. —*m., f.* Ishmaelite.
isoaglutinación, *f.* (med.) isoagglutination.
isoaglutinina, *f.* (med.) isoagglutinin.
isoaloxazina, *f.* (biochem.) isoalloxazine.
isoanticuerpo, *m.* (biochem.) isoantibody.
isobárico, ca, *a.* (meteorol.) isobaric.
isobaro, ra, *a.* isobaric. —*m.* (chem.) isobar, isobare. —*f.* (meteorol.) isobar.
isobato, ta, *a, f.* (bathymetry) isobath.
isocianato, *m.* (chem.) isocyanate.
isoclinal, *a.* (geol.) isoclinal.
isoclínico, ca, *a.* (geol.) isoclinal.
isoclino, na, *a.* isoclinal, isoclinic. —*f.* (geol.) isoclinal line, isoclinal, isoclinic.
isocromático, ca, *a.* (opt.) isochromatic.
isocronismo, *m.* (phys.) isochronism.
isócrono, na, *a.* (phys.) isochronous.
isodáctilo, la, *a.* (zool.) isodactylous.
isodiáfero, *m.* (phys.) isodiaphere.
isodiamétrico, ca, *a.* isodiametric.
isodimorfismo, *m.* (chem.) isodimorphism.
isodinámico, ca, *a.* (phys.) isodynamic.
isodósico, ca, *a.* (phys.) isodose.
isoeléctrico, ca, *a.* (phys.) isoelectric.
isoelectrónico, ca, *a.* (phys.) isoelectronic.
isogameto, *m.* (biol.) isogamete.
isogamia, *f.* (biol.) isogamy.
isogamo, ma, *a.* (biol.) isogamous.
isogénesis, *f.* (biol.) isogeny.
isogenia, *f.* (biol.) isogeny.
isógeno, na, *a.* (biol.) isogenous.
isogloso, sa, *a.* (linguistics) isoglossal. —*f.* (gram.) isogloss.
isogónico, ca, *a.* (geom.) isogonic, isogonal.

isógono, na, *a.* isogonic. —*f.* (geol.) isogonic, isogonic line.
isograma, *m.* (meteorol.) isogram, isoline.
isohieto, ta, *a.* (meteorol.) isohyetal. —*f.* (meteorol.) isohyet.
isohipsa, *f.* (meteorol.) contour.
Isolda, *f.* (lit., mus.) Isolda, Isolde, lover of Tristan in the Nordic legend.
isoleucina, *f.* (biochem.) isoleucine.
isólogo, ga, *a.* (chem.) isologous.
isomagnético, ca, *a.* (phys.) isomagnetic.
isomagnetismo, *m.* (phys.) isomagnetism.
isomería, *f.* (chem.) isomerism, isomery.
isomérico, ca, *a.* (chem.) isomeric, isomerical.
isomerismo, *m.* (chem., bot.) isomerism.
isómero, ra, *a.* (chem.) isomeric. —*m.* (chem.) isomer.
isométrico, ca, *a.* isometric, isometrical.
isometropía, *f.* (opt.) isometropia.
isomorfismo, *m.* (biol., chem.) isomorphism.
isomorfo, fa, *a.* (biol.) isomorphous.
isoniacida, *f.* (chem.) isoniazid.
isoperímetro, tra, *a.* (geom.) isoperimetrical, isoperimetric.
isopiéstico, ca, *a.* (phys.) isopiestic.
isopleto, *m.* isopleth.
isoploide, *a.* (biol.) isoploid.
isópodo, da, *a.* (zool.) isopodous, isopod, isopodan. —*m.* (zool.) isopod, isopodan, (*pl.*) Isopoda.
isopreno, *m.* (chem.) isoprene.
isoquímeno, na, *a.* (geog.) isocheimal, isocheimenal; **línea isoquímena,** (geog.) isocheim.
isósceles, *a.* (geom.) isosceles.
isoséismico, ca, *a.* (geol.) isoseismal.
isospora, *f.* (biol., bot.) isospore.
isospóreo, a, *a.* (biol., bot.) isosperous.
isostasia, *f.* (geol.) isostasy.
isostático, ca, *a.* (phys., geol.) isostatic.
isotermo, ma, *a.* (meteorol.) isothermal. —*f.* isotherm.
isótero, ra, *a.* (meteorol.) isotheral.
isotonicidad, *f.* (biochem., chem., phys.) isotonicity.
isotónico, ca, *a.* (biochem., chem., phys.) isotonic.
isótono, na, *a.* (biochem., chem., phys.) isotonic.
isotopía, *f.* (chem., phys.) isotopy.
isotópico, ca, *a.* (chem., phys.) isotopic.
isótopo, *m.* (phys.) isotope.
isotropía, *f.* (phys.) isotropy.
isotrópico, ca, *a.* (phys.) isotropic, isotropous.
isotropismo, *m.* (phys.) isotropy.
isótropo, pa, *a.* (phys.) isotropous, isotropic.
isquemia, *f.* (med., biol.) ischemia, ischaemia.
isquémico, ca, *a.* (biol.) ischemic.
isquiático, ca, *a.* (zool.) ischial, ischiatic.
isquión, *m.* (zool.) ischium.
Israel, *m.* Israel.
israelí, *a., m., f.* Israeli.
israelita, *a, m., f.* Israelite, Hebrew.
israelítico, ca, *a.* Israelitic, Israelite.
istmeño, ña, *a.* isthmian, of or pertaining to an isthmus.
ístmico, ca, *a.* isthmian; (hist.) Isthmian, Isthmic; **juegos ísmicos,** Isthmian games (played in Corinth, in honor of Poseidon).
istmo, *m.* (geog., anat., zool.) isthmus. — **i. de Corinto,** Isthmus of Corinth; **i. de las fauces,** (anat.) isthmus of the fauces; **i. del encéfalo,** (anat.) isthmus rhombencephali.
istriar, *tr.v., var. of* **estriar.**
isuate, *m.* (Mex.) palm tree from whose bark mattresses are made.
ita, *m., f., var. of* **acta.**
Ítaca, *f.* Ithaca, one of the Ionic islands, legendary home of Odysseus.
itacate, *m.* (Mex.) traveling provisions.
itacolumita, *f.* (geol.) itacolumite.
itacónico, ca, *a.* (chem.) itaconic.
Italia, *f.* Italy.
italianice, italianicé, *ref.* **italianizar.**
italianismo, *m.* Italianism.
italianizar, (*ref. 53*) *tr.v.* to Italianize. —*r.v.* to become Italianized.
italiano, na, *a., m., f.* Italian. — **a la i.,** in the Italian manner. —*m.* Italian (language).
itálico, ca, *a.* Italic, Italian; Italic (languages); (print.) italic. —*m.* Italic (language).
italiota, *m., f.* (hist.) Italiot, Italiote.
ítalo, la, *a., m., f.* (poet.) Italian.
ítamo, *m.* (bot.) *var. of* **díctamo.**
itea, *f.* (bot.) itea.
item, *adv.* (law) furthermore, moreover, also, likewise. —*m.* 1. (law) item, article. 2. addition.
iterable, *a.* repeatable.
iteración, *f.* iteration, repetition.
iterar, *tr.v.* to iterate, repeat.
iterativo, va, *a.* iterative, repetitive.
iterbina, *f.* (chem.) ytterbia.
iterbio, *m.* (chem.) ytterbium.
itinerario, ria, *a.* itinerary. —*m.* 1. itinerary, route; time-table. 2. (mil.) billet-seeking party going ahead of army.
itria, *f.* (min.) yttria.
ítrico, ca, *a.* (chem.) yttric.
itrio, *m.* (min.) yttrium.
ivierno, *m.* (imp. u.) winter.
ixia, *f.* (bot.) ixia.
ixiolita, *f.* (min.) ixiolite.
izador, ra, *a.* hoisting. —*m., f.* hoister.
izaga, *f.* land full of rushes and reeds.
izar, (*ref. 53*) *tr.v.* (mar.) to hoist, to haul up; to heave.
izote, *m.* (bot.) izote.
izquierda, *f.* left hand; left hand side; (pol.) left; **a la i.,** left, to the left; on the left; **a la i., I,** to the left, left turn.
izquierdear, *i.v.* (fig.) to veer off-course, go astray.
izquierdista, *a., m., f.* (pol.) leftist.
izquierdo, da, *a.* 1. left; left-hand, e.g. *en el lado i.,* on the left-hand side; left-handed. 2. crooked. — **levantarse con el pie i.,** to get up on the wrong side of the bed.

J

J, *f.* j, tenth letter of the Spanish alphabet.
jaba, *f.* 1. (Amer.) light cage-like crate (used for transporting fragile objects). 2. (Cuba) small wicker basket, shopping bag.
jabado, da, *a.* 1. mottled (said of birds). 2. said of someone who wavers between two sides or causes.
jabalcón, *m.* 1. (bldg.) strut, brace, tie-beam. 2. (Col.) ravine.
jabalconar, *tr.v.* (bldg.) to brace, shore or support with struts, to reinforce a roof with tie beams.
jabalí, (*pl.* **jabalíes**), *m.* (zool.) wild boar; **j. verrugoso,** (zool.) warthog.
jabalina, *f.* 1. (hist., sport.) javelin. 2. (zool.) female boar.
jabalón, *m.* (bldg.), *var. of* **jabalcón.**
jabalonar, *tr.v., var. of* **jabalconar.**
jabardear, *i.v.* to produce an afterswarm or second swarm, produce a small prime swarm (said of beehives). —*tr.v.* to swarm.
jabardillo, *m.* swarm (of bees or insects); flock (of birds); (fig.) swarm, crowd (of people), noisy throng.
jabardo, *m.* 1. afterswarm, second swarm, small prime or first swarm (produced by the hive). 2. swarm, crowd, mob.
jabato, *m.* 1. young wild boar. 2. (fig., coll.) boastful young man.
jabear, *tr.v.* (Guat.) to steal.
jabeba, *f., var. of* **jabega,** a type of Moorish flute.
jabeca, *f.* (min.) quicksilver smelting furnace.
jábeca, *f.* sweep net (cast from the shore).
jabega, *f.* a type of Moorish flute.
jábega, *f.* 1. sweep net (cast from the shore). 2. (mar.) fishing smack or sloop.
jabegote, *m.* sweep-net fisherman.
jabeguero, ra, *a.* of or pertaining to a sweep-net. —*m.* sweep-net fisherman.
jabeque, *m.* 1. (mar.) xebec, sailing boat gen. used in the Mediterranean. 2. gash or knife wound on the face.
jabera, *f.* (mus.) old, lively Andalusian folk song.
jabí, (*pl.* **jabíes**), *m.* 1. small wild apple; small wild grape grown mostly in Granada, Spain. 2. (bot.) quebracho.
jabillo, *m.* (bot.) sandbox tree.
jabín, *m.* (Mex.) quebracho.
jabino, *m.* (bot.) dwarf variety of juniper bush.
jabirú, (*pl.* **jabirúes**), *m.* (ornith.) jabiru, Brazilian wading bird, similar to the stork.
jabladera, *f.* (carp.) croze, cooper's plane for cutting grooves in staves.
jable, *m.* croze, groove near end of stave in which the head is inserted in a cask or barrel.
jabón, *m.* soap; cake or bar of soap; **dar j.,** to soft-soap, flatter; **j. de afeitar,** shaving soap; **j. de Castilla,** Castile soap; **j. de sastre,** soapstone, tailor's chalk, French chalk; **j. de tocador,** toilet soap; **j. en escamas,** soapflakes; **j. neutro,** mild soap.
jabonada, *f.* 1. (Chile) soaping, lathering. 2. (Mex.) dressing down, reprimand.
jabonado, *m.* 1. soaping, lathering. 2. laundry, the wash (clothes).
jabonador, ra, *a.* lathering, soaping. —*m., f.* latherer, soaper.
jabonadura, *f.* 1. soaping, lathering. 2. (*pl.*) soapsuds; lather. — **dar a uno una j.,** to give one a dressing down, to upbraid, reprimand.
jabonar, *tr.v.* 1. to soap (clothes), lather (the beard). 2. (coll.) to give someone a dressing down, to upbraid, reprimand.
jaboncillo, *m.* 1. cake of scented soap; (pharm.) medicinal soap. 2. (bot.) soapberry tree; soapberry. 3. (Chile) powdered or liquid shaving soap. — **j. de sastre,** French chalk, soapstone.
jabonera, *f.* 1. woman who makes or sells soap. 2. soap dish. 3. (bot.) soapwort.
jabonería, *f.* soap factory or shop.
jabonero, ra, *a.* (taur.) dull yellowish white (said of the color of a bull). —*m.* soapmaker; soap seller.
jaboneta, *f., var. of* **jabonete.**
jabonete, *m.* cake of scented soap.
jabonoso, sa, *a.* soapy, saponaceous.
jaborandi, *m.* (bot.) jaborandi.
jabuco, *m.* (Cuba) large straw basket.
jaca, *f.* 1. cob, pony, jennet. 2. (Arg.) fighting cock. 3. (Amer., coll.) bidet.
jacal, *m.* (Mex.) hut, shed, wigwam.
jacalón, *m.* (Mex.) large, poorly constructed shed, similar to a hangar, often used for country dances.
jacamar, *m., var. of* **jacamara.**
jacamara, *m.* (ornith.) jacamar.
jacana, *f.* (ornith.) jacana, a wading bird found in tropical America.
jácara, *f.* 1. an old, ribald type ballad of the picaresque genre in which Quevedo excelled. 2. revelers, group of merrymakers who stroll the streets singing and dancing. 3. (coll.) annoyance, nuisance. 4. (coll.) lie, fib. 5. (coll.) yarn, tale, story.
jacarandá, *m.* (bot.) jacaranda.
jacarandana, *f.* 1. band of thieves or rogues. 2. thieves' jargon; vulgar talk.
jacarandoso, sa, *a.* (coll.) merry, gay, carefree, debonair.
jacarear, *i.v.* 1. to sing ribald or picaresque ballads. 2. (coll.) to stroll the streets at nighttime, singing and making merry. 3. (coll.) to taunt, annoy, irritate.
jacarero, ra, *m., f.* 1. ballad singer. 2. (coll.) joker; gay, carefree person.
jacarilla, *f. dim. of* **jácara,** a short risqué poem.
jacarista, *m., var. of* **jacarero.**
jácaro, ra, *a.* boastful, swaggering, bragging. —*m.* boaster, braggart, swaggerer; **a lo jácaro,** boastfully, swaggeringly.
jácena, *f.* (archit.) girder, main beam.
jacerina, *f.* coat of mail.
jacilla, *f.* imprint on the ground (left by any object standing on the same spot a long time).
jacintino, na, *a.* (poet.) hyacinthine, violet.
jacinto, *m.* 1. (bot.) hyacinth. 2. (min.) hyacinth, variety of zircon. — **j. de agua,** (bot.) water hyacinth; **j. occidental,** (min.) topaz; **j. oriental,** (min.) ruby.
Jack el destripador, Jack the Ripper.
jaco, *m.* 1. habergeon, short-sleeved coat of mail; soldier's tunic. 2. hack, nag, jade.
jacobeo, a, *a.* of or pertaining to Saint James.
jacobínico, ca, *a.* Jacobinic, Jacobinical.
jacobinismo, *m.* (hist.) Jacobinism; (pol.) any extreme or radical doctrine or concept.
jacobino, na, *a.* 1. Jacobin, Jacobinical, radical (revolutionist), pertaining to the French Jacobins. 2. Jacobean (pertaining to James I of England). 3. jacobinical, extreme, radical. —*m., f.* 1. Jacobin. 2. Jacobean. 3. Jacobin, extreme radical.
jacobita, *a., m.* (hist., rel.) Jacobite.
jaconta, *f.* (Bol.) meat and vegetable stew.
jactancia, *f.* boasting, bragging, arrogance.
jactanciosamente, *adv.* boastfully.
jactancioso, sa, *a.* boasting, boastful, bragging. —*m., f.* braggart, boaster.
jactarse, *r.v.* to boast, brag, vaunt.
jacú, *m.* (Bol.) bread, banana or yucca used as an accompanying dish.
jaculatoria, *f.* ejaculatory prayer, short, fervent prayer.
jaculatorio, ria, *a.* ejaculatory, brief and fervent.
jachado, da, *a.* (Hond.) scar-faced.
jachalí, (*pl.* **jachalíes**), *m.* (bot.) (variety of) custard apple.
jachi, *m.* (Bol.) bran.
jada, *f.* (agr.) hoe; spade.
jade, *m.* (min.) jade; axestone.
jadeante, *a.* panting, out of breath.
jadear, *i.v.* to pant, heave, to breathe with difficulty.
jadeíta, *f.* (min.) jadeite.
jadeo, *m.* panting, heaving, difficult breathing.
jadiar, *tr.v.* to dig up with a spade, to hoe.
jaece, jaecé, *ref.* **jaezar.**
jaecero, ra, *m., f.* harness maker.
jaén, *a.* large white (grape). —*f.* large white grape.
jaez, (*pl.* **jaeces**), *m.* 1. harness; (*pl.*) trappings. 2. character, type, sort.
jaezar, (*ref. 53*) *tr.v., var. of* **enjaezar.**
jafético, ca, *a.* Japhetic, Indo-Germanic, Indo-European.
jagua, *f.* (bot.) genipap (tree and fruit), inaja palm.
jagual, *m.* genipap plantation.
jaguar, *m.* (zool.) jaguar.
jaguarzo, *m.* (bot.) (variety of) rockrose, helianthemum.
jagüey, *m.* 1. (Cuba, bot.) banyan tree. 2. (S. Amer.) large pool or basin.
jagüilla, *f.* 1. (bot.) genipa (Genipa caruto). 2. (Hond.) (type of) wild pig.
jaharí, (*pl.* **jaharíes**), *a.* said of a type of fig grown in Andalusia.
jaharrar, *tr.v.* to plaster (a wall).
jaharro, *m.* plaster; plastering.
jahuel, *m.* (S. Amer.) large pool or basin; reservoir.
jai alai, *m.* (sport.) jai alai, pelota, a Basque ball game.
jaiba, *f.* (Amer.) (species of) crab, crayfish.
jaique, *m.* haik, Moorish hooded cape.
jaira, *f.* bevel of a plane bit.
jairar, *tr.v.* (shoemaking) to bevel (leather).

jaire, *m.* (shoemaking) bevel cut.
¡ja, ja, ja! *interj.* ha, ha!
jal, *m.* (Mex.) piece of pumice stone.
jala, *f.* (Col.) drunk, drunken bout or spree.
jalapa, *f.* (bot.) jalap.
jalapina, *f.* (chem.) jalapin, jalap resin.
jalar, *tr.v.* 1. (coll.) to pull. 2. (C. Amer.) to make love to. 3. (Peru) to fail, flunk (test, examination). —*r.v.* 1. (Amer.) to get drunk. 2. (P. Rico) to leave, go away.
jalbegador, ra, *a.* whitewashing. —*m., f.* whitewasher.
jalbegar, (*ref. 51*) *tr.v.* 1. to whitewash. 2. to make up (the face). —*r.v.* to make up.
jalbegue, *m.* 1. whitewash. 2. (coll.) cosmetics, make-up.
jalbegue, jalbegué, *ref.* **jalbegar.**
jaldado, da, *a.* deep yellow, gold-colored.
jalde, *a.* deep yellow, gold-colored.
jaldo, da, *a., var. of* **jalde.**
jaldre, *m.* a bright yellow color peculiar to certain birds.
jalea, *f.* (cul., pharm.) jelly, jam, fruit paste; **hacerse una j.,** to become cloyingly affectionate; **j. de membrillo,** quince jelly; **j. real,** royal jelly (obtained from bees); **j. de guayaba,** guava jelly.
jaleador, ra, *m., f.* one who encourages folk dancers.
jalear, *tr.v.* 1. to hoick, urge on (dogs) with shouts; to encourage (dancers) with expressions of acknowledgment and clapping; to encourage, urge on. 2. (Chile) to annoy, bother, tease.
jaleco, *m.* short-sleeved Turkish jacket or vest.
jaleo, *m.* 1. cheering on, urging on. 2. a gay Andalusian dance. 3. noisy party, do (sl.). 4. (C. Amer.) courting, necking (sl.).
jalera, *f.* (Col.) drunk, drunken spree or bout.
jaletina, *f.* gelatine, jelly; calf's-foot jelly.
jalifa, *f.* (hist.) native governor of Spanish Morocco (delegated by the Sultan to work together with the Spanish commissioner).
jalifato, *m.* (hist.) post and territory of native governor of Spanish Morocco.
jalisco, ca, *a.* (Mex.) drunk. —*m.* (Mex.) straw hat made in Jalisco.
jallo, lla, *a.* 1. (Mex.) peevish, touchy. 2. conceited, vain, arrogant.
jallulo, *m.* bread toasted on embers.
jalma, *f.* packsaddle.
jalmería, *f.* harness maker (shop), packsaddler's trade.
jalmero, *m.* harness maker.
jalón, *m.* 1. (surv.) range pole, ranging pole. 2. (Bol.) distance, stretch. 3. (Amer.) jerk, tug, pull. 4. (Mex., Guat.) swig, drink, slug (sl.).
jalonar, *tr.v.* (surv.) to mark with range poles.
jalonero, *m.* (surv.) rodman.
jaloque, *m.* southeast wind.
jalpacar, (*ref. 50*) *tr.v.* (Mex., min.) to sluice (ores in vats).
jalpaque, jalpaqué, *ref.* **jalpacar.**
jama, *f.* (Hond.) small iguana.
jamaica, *f.* 1. (Mex.) charity fete or fair. 2. **J.,** Jamaica.
jamaicano, na, *a, m., f.* Jamaican.
jamaiquino, na, *a., m., f.* Jamaican; pertaining to Jamaica.
jamar, *tr.v.* (coll.) to eat.
jamás, *adv.* never; **nunca j.,** never again.
jamba, *f.* (archit.) jamb (of a door); pier (of an arch); window post.
jambaje, *m.* (archit.) doorway or window frame.
jambar, *tr.v.* (Hond., Mex.) to eat.
jámbico, ca, *a.* (poet.) iambic.
jamelgo, *m.* (coll.) old nag, hack, jade.
jamerdana, *f.* sewer of a slaughterhouse.
jamerdar, *tr.v.* 1. to clean the innards of (slaughtered animals). 2. to wash quickly and badly, give a lick and a promise to.
jamete, *m.* (tex.) samite, rich silk cloth interwoven with gold or silver thread.
jametería, *f., var. of* **zalamería,** flattery.
jámila, *f., var. of* **alpechín,** oozing olive juice.
jamo, *m.* (Cuba) bag, net, fyke.
jamón, *m.* ham — **un j. con chorreras,** you should be so lucky.
jamona, *a.* (coll.) buxom middle-aged (woman). —*f.* buxom middle-aged woman.
jámparo, *m.* (Col.) small boat or canoe.
jamuga, *f., var. of* **jamugas.**
jamugas, *f.* (*pl.*) side-saddle; **ir en j.,** to ride side-saddle.
jamurar, *tr.v.* to bail out, scoop out (water).
jan, *m.* (Cuba) stake (used for fences); dibble (pointed instrument for making holes for seeds).
janano, na, *a.* (Guat., Salv.) harelipped, having a harelip.
jandalesco, ca, *a.* (coll., Sp.) Andalusian.
jándalo, la, *a., m., f.* 1. (coll.) Andalusian. 2. (Sp.) said of a Spaniard with a marked Andalusian or Southern accent.
jane, *a.* (Hond.) harelipped, having a harelip.
janear, *tr.v.* 1. (Cuba) to put stakes in. 2. (Cuba) to leap on to (horse). —*r.v.* 1. (Cuba) to stop dead. 2. (Cuba) to stand up.
jangada, *f.* 1. (coll.) foolish remark. 2. (coll.) dirty trick. 3. (mar.) raft, float.
jangua, *f.* small armed vessel (used in the East).
janiche, *a.* (Hond.) harelipped, having a harelip.
Jano, *m.* (myth.) Janus, ancient Roman god, depicted with two faces looking in opposite directions.
jansenismo, *m.* (rel., philos.) Jansenism.
jansenista, *a.* (rel., philos.) Jansenist, Jansenistic. —*m., f.* Jansenist.
jantato, *m.* (chem.) xanthate.
jántico, ca, *a.* (chem.) xanthic.
jantina, *f.* (chem.) xanthin, xanthine.
jantofilia, *f.* (biochem.) xanthophyll, xanthophyl.
jantoxilo, *m.* (bot.) zanthoxylum, xanthoxylum.
japón, na, *a., m., f.* Japanese. —*m.* **J.,** Japan.
japonés, sa, *a., m., f.* Japanese. —*m.* Japanese (language).
japuta, *f.* (ichth.) pomfret (Brama raii).
jaque, *m.* 1. check (in chess). 2. bully, braggart. 3. a former style of smooth hairdress. — **dar j.,** to check (in chess); **dar j. mate,** to checkmate; **¡j.!** get out! scram! clear off!; **tener a uno en j.,** to hold a sword over someone's head, have someone in one's power.
jaqué, *m.* (Mex.) morning coat.
jaquear, *tr.v.* 1. to check (in chess). 2. to harass (an enemy).
jaqueca, *f.* headache, migraine, splitting headache; **dar a uno una j.,** (coll.) to give one a pain in the neck, to bore to death.
jaquecoso, sa, *a.* irksome, bothersome, tiresome, annoying.
jaquel, *m.* (her.) square. —*a.* (Mex.) bittersweet (orange).
jaquelado, da, *a.* 1. (her.) checkered. 2. square-faceted (jewels).
jaquero, *m.* a small, formerly used fine-toothed comb.
jaqueta, *f.* (arch.) jacket, short loose coat.
jaquetilla, *f.* short jacket.
jaquetón, *m.* 1. (coll.) braggart, bully. 2. (zool.) man-eating shark. 3. long, loose jacket.
jáquima, *f.* 1. rope headstall. 2. (Amer.) drunkenness; drunken bout.
jaquimazo, *m.* 1. blow with a headstall. 2. (coll.) great blow or misfortune, great disappointment.
jaquimero, *m.* headstall maker or seller.
jaquimón, *m.* (Amer.) headstall; (Cuba) headstall with ring (to which halter is attached); (Chile, Peru) large ornamental headstall.
jara, *f.* 1. (bot.) rockrose. 2. sharp, pointed dart or spear; (Mex.) arrow. 3. (Bol.) halt, stop, rest. 4. (Mex.) police. 5. (sl., P. Rico) fuzz, cops, police. — **j. blanca,** white-leaved rockrose.
jarabe, *m.* syrup; **j. de maíz,** corn syrup; **j. de pico,** (coll.) empty talk, idle promises. —*m.* (Mex.) **j. tapatío,** a popular folk dance, often called the Mexican hat dance.
jarabear, *tr.v.* to dose with syrups, prescribe syrups for (a patient). —*r.v.* to take syrups, dose oneself with syrups.
jaracatal, *m.* (Guat.) crowd, abundance.
jaracolito, *m.* (Peru) popular Indian dance.
jaraíz, (*pl.* **jaraíces**), *m.* wine press, oil press.
jaral, *m.* 1. thicket or patch of rockroses. 2. (coll.) maze, puzzle, intricate situation.
jaramago, *m.* (bot.) wall rocket (Diplotaxis virgata).
jarameño, ña, *a.* (Sp.) of or from the Jarama river.
jaramugo, *m.* small or young fish, used as bait.
jarana, *f.* 1. spree, party, binge; revelry; (Amer.) dance. 2. (coll.) rumpus; scuffle, fight, quarrel. 3. (coll.) trick, trickery. 4. (Amer.) joke, jest. 5. (Hond.) debt — **estar de j.,** to be having a party, be drinking and dancing, be on a binge; **andar** or **ir de j.,** to go on a spree or binge.
jaranear, *i.v.* to be on a spree, be dancing and drinking, be making merry.
jaranero, ra, *a.* gay, merry, fond of parties, fond of drinking and dancing. —*m., f.* partygoer, reveler.
jaranista, *a.* (Peru), *var. of* **jaranero.**
jarano, *m.* low-crowned, wide-brimmed hat.
jarapote, *m.* (coll.) the drug habit.
jarapotear, *tr.v.* to stuff with drugs or medicines.
jaratar, *tr.v.* (Ecuad.) to fence.
jarazo, *m.* blow or wound made with a dart or spear.
jarca, *f.* (Bol., bot.) acacia.
jarcia, *f.* 1. (mar.) rigging (*gen. in pl.*); fishing tackle. 2. (coll.) bundle or heap of things, jumble. 3. (Cuba) thick hemp rope, (Mex.) rope, cord. — **j. muerta,** (mar.) standing rigging; **jarcias de labor,** (mar.) running rigging.
jarciar, *tr.v., var. of* **enjarciar.**
jarcio, cia, *a.* (Mex.) drunk.
jardín, *m.* 1. garden. 2. (mar.) latrine, privy, water closet. 3. cloud, flaw, spot (in an emerald). 4. (sport.) outfield (in baseball). — **j. botánico,** botanical gardens; **j. central,** center field (in baseball); **j. de infantes** or **de la infancia,** kindergarten; **j. infantil,** (Chile) kindergarten; **j. izquierdo,** left field (in baseball); **j. zoológico,** zoo, zoological gardens; **jardines colgantes de Babilonia,** Hanging Gardens of Babylon.
jardincito, *m. dim. of* **jardín,** small garden.
jardinera, *f.* 1. (female) gardener. 2. gardener's wife. 3. flower-stand, jardiniere, flower-box. 4. basket carriage, wicker-work, four-seater carriage; open trolley car, open-side tramcar.
jardinería, *f.* gardening, art of gardening.
jardinero, *m.* 1. gardener. 2. (sport.) out-fielder (in baseball). 3. (tex.) overalls, dungarees. — **j. central** or **centro,** center fielder; **j. izquierdo,** left fielder (in baseball).
jarea, *f.* (Mex., coll.) hunger.
jarearse, *r.v.* 1. (Mex.) to starve to death. 2. (Mex.) to flee. 3. (Mex.) to sway, stagger.
jareta, *f.* 1. (dressm.) casing (to hold a tightening cord, as in pajama trousers). 2. (mar.) netting, trelliswork (as defense against boarding parties).

3. (mar.) reinforcement cable (for securing masts, when the rigging has become loose in a storm).
jaretera, *f., var. of* **jarretera.**
jaretón, *m.* broad tuck or fold; wide casing.
jarico, *m.* (Cuba) male hicatee (freshwater tortoise).
jarife, *m., var. of* **jerife.**
jarifiano, na, *a., var. of* **jerifiano.**
jarifo, fa, *a.* magnificent, elegant, resplendent, showy.
jarillo, *m.* (bot.) arum.
jaripeo, *m.* (Bol., Mex.) rodeo, bronco-busting.
jaro, *m.* 1. (bot.) arum. 2. thicket, copse. 3. (reg.) small oak.
jaro, ra, *a.* carroty, red-haired. *—m., f.* red-haired person.
jarocho, cha, *a.* boorish, brusque, rude, uncouth. *—m., f.* 1. boor, rude person. 2. (Mex.) native of Veracruz.
jaropar, *tr.v.* 1. (coll.) to dose with syrups or medicines. 2. (coll.) to stuff with liquor or drinks.
jarope, *m.* syrup; (coll.) unpleasant drink.
jaropear, *tr.v.* (coll.), *var. of* **jaropar.**
jaropeo, *m.* overdosing with syrups or medicines.
jaroso, sa, *a.* full of rockroses or brambles.
jarra, *f.* 1. jug, pitcher, jar. 2. ancient order of chivalry in Aragon. — **con los brazos de jarras, en jarra** or **en jarras,** with arms akimbo.
jarrar, *tr.v.* to plaster (a wall).
jarrazo, *m.* 1. *aug. of* **jarro,** large jug. 2. blow with a jug or pitcher.
jarrear, *i.v.* 1. to draw wine or water with a jug or pitcher. 2. to pour, rain cats and dogs.
jarrero, *m.* one who makes or sells jugs or pitchers.
jarreta, *f. dim. of* **jarra,** small jug or pitcher.
jarretar, *tr.v.* to enervate, weaken, enfeeble.
jarrete, *m.* 1. ham, back of knee (in man). 2. hock, gambrel (in quadrupeds). 3. upper part of calf (of leg).
jarretera, *f.* 1. garter; **La Orden de la J.,** the Order of the Garter.
jarrito, *m. dim. of* **jarro,** small jug or pitcher.
jarro, *m.* jug, pitcher — **a boca de j.,** (Amer.) at point-blank range; **echar un j. de agua (fría) a,** to pour cold water on, discourage.
jarrón, *m.* large vase, urn, flower vase.
Jartum, *m.* Khartoum, capital of Sudan.
jasa, *f.* cut, incision.
jasador, *m.* bloodletter, bleeder.
jasadura, *f.* cut, incision.
jasar, *tr.v.* to cut, make an incision in.
Jasón, *m.* (myth.) Jason, leader of the Argonauts.
jaspe, *m.* (min.) jasper; mottled marble, veined marble.
jaspeado, da, *past part. of* **jaspear.** *—a.* speckled, marbled, veined, spotted, mottled. *—m.* speckling, marbling; speckled, mottled or marbled effect.
jaspeadura, *f.* marbling.
jaspear, *tr.v.* to marble, speckle, vein, mottle; to paint in imitation of marble.
jaspón, *m.* thickly-grained marble.
jata, *f.* (Cuba, bot.) variety of palm tree (Copernicia hospita).
jatata, *f.* (Bol.) variety of royal palm.
jateo, a, *a.* foxhunting. *—m.* foxhound.
játib, *m.* Moslem preacher in charge of Friday prayers and sermon.
jato, ta, *m., f.* calf.
¡jau! *interj.* to incite animals, esp. bulls.
Jauja, *f.* Cockaigne, Utopia; **¿estamos aquí o en J.?** where do you think you are? just be careful what you say! **estamos en J.,** we've got it made (coll.).
jaula, *f.* 1. cage; cell. 2. crate (for transporting goods). — **j. de Faraday,** (elec.) Faraday cage; **j. vagón,** (Amer., ry.) cattle truck.
jauría, *f.* pack (of hounds).
jauto, ta, *a.* insipid, flat, tasteless.
javanés, sa, *a., m., f.* Javanese. *—m.* Javanese (language).
javera, *f., var. of* **jabera.**
jayán, na, *m., f.* big husky person.
jayanazo, za, *m., f., aug. of* **jayán,** huge, burly person.
jayún, *m.* (Cuba) (type of) reed.
jazarán, *m.* coat of mail.
jazmín, *m.* (bot.) jasmine. — **j. amarillo,** yellow jasmine; **j. de España,** Spanish jasmine; **j. de la India,** gardenia.
jazmíneo, a, *a.* jasmine (as *a.*). *—f.* (*pl.*) jasmine family.
J.C. *abbrev. of* **Jesucristo,** Jesus Christ.
jea, *f.* ancient duty on Moorish goods.
jebe, *m.* 1. alum. 2. (Amer.) rubber; (Amer.) elastic band; (Amer., coll.) rubber, condom, contraceptive.
jebuseo, a, *a.* (rel., hist.) Jebusitic, Jebusitical, Jebusitish. *—m., f.* Jebusite.
jedive, *m.* Khedive (title of the former viceroy of Egypt).
jedrea, *f.* (coll.) savory (plant).
Jeep, *m.* (auto.) Jeep (TM).
jefa, *f.* female leader or chief; forelady (in a workshop or factory).
jefactura, *f.* (Mex., imp. u.), *var. of* **jefatura.**
jefatura, *f.* 1. chieftainship; leadership. 2. headquarters, command; police station. — **j. del gobierno,** premiership.
jefe, *m.* 1. chief, leader; boss; superior (in one's employment); head, e.g. *los jefes de departamento,* the heads of the departments; master (e.g. of station, harbor, etc.); chief, chieftain (of a tribe); (mil., mar.) commanding officer, superior officer; (mil.) field officer. 2. (Amer.) sir, boss; governor (G.B.), chief (coll.). 3. (Peru) officer (when addressing a policeman). — **comandante en j.,** commander in chief; **j. de bomberos,** fire chief; **j. de camareros,** head waiter; **j. de cocina,** chef, head chef; **j. de estación,** (ry.) stationmaster; **j. de estado mayor,** (mil.) chief of staff; **j. del estado,** head of state; **j. de estudios,** director of studies; **j. de gobierno,** prime minister; president; **j. de máquinas,** chief engineer; **j. de negociado,** head of department; **j. de personal,** personnel manager; **j. de policía,** chief of police; **j. político,** governor of a province; **j. del puerto,** harbormaster; **j. de redacción,** editor-in-chief; **j. de sección,** floorwalker; **j. de taller,** supervisor, foreman; **j. de ventas,** sales manager; **mandar en j.,** to be commander in chief, be the chief in command.
Jehová, *m.* (Bib.) Jehovah.
jehuite, *m.* (Mex.) weeds, brambles.
jeito, *m.* anchovy or sardine fishing net (used mostly on the Cantabric coast).
je, je, je, *interj.* ha, ha, ha, (laughter).
jeja, *f.* white wheat.
jején, *m.* gnat, mosquito; (Cuba) gallmidge.
jeliz, (*pl.* **jelices**), *m.* (hist.) public silk auctioneer in the kingdom of Granada.
jema, *f.* badly-squared part of a beam.
jeme, *m.* 1. distance between the tip of the thumb and the tip of the forefinger. 2. (coll.) woman's face.
jemiquear, *i.v.* (Chile) to snivel, whine.
jemiqueo, *m.* (Chile) snivelling, whining.
jemoso, sa, *a.* said of a badly-squared beam.
jenabe, *m.* mustard.
jenable, *m.* mustard.
jengibre, *m.* ginger (plant, root, spice).
jeniquén, *m.* (Cuba) henequen; sisal, hemp.
jenízaro, ra, *a.* (fig.) mixed, hybrid; (Mex.) of Chinese and Indian parents. *—m.* Janizary (Turkish infantry soldier).
Jenófanes, *m.* Xenophanes, one of the founders of the Eleatic school of philosophy.
Jenofonte, *m.* (hist.) Xenophon, Greek general and historian.
jeque, *m.* sheik, Moorish chief.
jera, *f.* 1. present, gift. 2. ground that can be plowed in a day with a pair of oxen.
jerapellina, *f.* old ragged garment.
jerarca, *m.* hierarch; dignitary, high official.
jerarquía, *f.* hierarchy, rank.
jerárquicamente, *adv.* hierarchically.
jerarquice, jerarquicé, *ref.* **jerarquizar.**
jerárquico, ca, *a.* hierarchic, hierarchical.
jerarquizar, (*ref.* 53) *tr.v.* to arrange hierarchically.
jerbo, *m.* (zool.) jerboa; mouse.
jeremiada, *f.* (coll.) jeremiad, exaggerated lamentation.
jeremías, *m., f.* 1. jeremiah, constant complainer. 2. **J.,** (Bib.) Jeremy, Jeremiah, Jeremias.
jeremiquear, *i.v.* to moan, complain; to whine, whimper, snivel.
jeremiqueo, *m.* moaning, complaining; whining, sniveling, whimpering.
jerez, (*pl.* **jereces**), *m.* sherry (wine).
jerezano, na, *a.* from or of Jerez de la Frontera, Sp. *—m., f.* native of Jerez. — **manta jerezana,** saddle blanket.
jerga, *f.* slang, lingo; jargon, cant, argot; gibberish, any language difficult to understand.
jerga, *f.* 1. coarse woolen cloth, coarse frieze. 2. straw mattress, paillasse, pallet.
jergal, *a.* pertaining to the slang of a trade, profession or group (word, idiom, etc.).
jergón, *m.* 1. straw mattress, paillasse. 2. sack, ill-fitting clothes. 3. (coll.) lump, slob, (sl.) fat, lazy person. 4. (min.) jargoon, jargon, greenish zircon.
jergueta, *f. dim. of* **jerga,** coarse cloth.
jerguilla, *f.* thin wool or silk cloth.
jeribeque, *m.* grimace; wink.
jericoplear, *tr.v.* (Guat., Hond.) to annoy, irritate.
jerifalte, *m., var. of* **gerifalte.**
jerife, *m.* 1. sherif, shereef; Arab prince. 2. descendant of Mohammed. 3. member of the royal dynasty ruling Morocco.
jerifiano, na, *a.* pertaining to the Moslem sherif; **su majestad jerifiana,** His Majesty the Sultan of Morocco.
jerigonza, *f.* 1. jargon, cant, argot; slang, gibberish, lingo; any lenguage difficult to understand. 2. piece of folly; foolish action. — **andar en jerigonzas,** to twist or misrepresent the facts, to talk in riddles.
jeringa, *f.* 1. syringe; gun (for injecting grease or oil); stuffer (for filling sausages). 2. (coll.) nuisance, bore, annoyance. — **j. de engrase,** grease gun; **j. hipodérmica,** hypodermic syringe; **j. para aceite,** oil gun.
jeringador, ra, *a.* annoying, irritating, pestering. *—m., f.* plague, pest, nuisance.
jeringar, (*ref.* 51) *tr.v.* 1. to inject, squirt, syringe. 2. to syringe, wash by injections, give an enema to. 3. (coll.) to vex, annoy, irritate. *—r.v.* 1. to syringe oneself, give oneself an enema. 2. to get annoyed.
jeringazo, *m.* 1. syringing, injecting, injection. 2. injection, fluid injected.
jeringón, *a.* (coll.) annoying, irritating, pestering.

jeringue, jeringué, *ref.* **jeringar.**
jeringuear, *tr.v.* (Amer.) to annoy, irritate, plague.
jeringuilla, *f.* (bot.) syringa, mock orange.
jeringuilla, *f. dim. of* **jeringa,** small syringe; hypodermic syringe.
jerjén, *m.* (Chile) gnat, mosquito.
jeroglífico, ca, *a.* hieroglyphic, hieroglyphical. —*m.* 1. hieroglyphic. 2. rebus (verbal riddle solved by interpreting a series of pictures which represent syllables or words).
jerónimo, ma, *a., m., f.* (ecc.) Hieronymite.
jerosolimitano, na, *a., m., f.* of or pertaining to Jerusalem.
jerpa, *f.* barren shoot (stemming from the trunk of the vine).
jersey, *m.* jersey, sweater.
Jerusalén, *m.* Jerusalem, capital of Israel.
jeruza, *f.* (Guat., Hond.) prison, jail.
jervilla, *f.* slipper (footwear).
jesnato, ta, *a.* dedicated to Jesus from birth. —*m., f.* person dedicated to Jesus from birth.
Jesucristo, *m.* Jesus Christ.
jesuita, *a., m.* 1. Jesuit. 2. (Amer., coll.) hypocrite.
jesuíticamente, *adv.* 1. Jesuitically. 2. hypocritically.
jesuítico, ca, *a.* 1. Jesuitical, Jesuitic. 2. hypocritical.
jesuitismo, *m.* Jesuitism.
Jesús, *m.* Jesus; **en un decir J.,** in a jiffy, in two shakes of a duck's tail; **estar con el J. en la boca,** (Amer.) to be with one's heart in one's mouth; **hasta verte, J. mío,** to the last drop (when drinking); **J., María y José,** goodness gracious; **morir sin decir J.,** to drop dead suddenly. —*interj.* goodness gracious! what do you know!
jesusear, *i.v.* to repeatedly invoke the name of Jesus.
jet, *m.* jet, jet plane.
jeta, *f.* 1. thick-lipped mouth. 2. (coll.) mug (sl.); dial, face. 3. tap, faucet — **estar con tanta j.,** to pull a long face (in displeasure, bad temper, etc.).
jetar, *tr.v.* to dilute, dissolve.
jet lag, *m.* (aer.) jet lag.
jeto, *m.* empty beehive rubbed with honey to attract bees.
jetón, na, *a., var. of* **jetudo.**
jet set, *f. or m.* (sociol.) jet set.
jetudo, da, *a.* thick-lipped.
jíbaro, ra, *a.* 1. (S. Amer.) Jivaran (Indians). 2. (Amer.) rural, rustic. 3. (Dom. Rep., Cuba) wild, undomesticated (animal). —*m., f.* 1. Jivaro (Indian). 2. (Amer.) peasant. —*m.* 1. (Hond.) tall husky man. 2. (P. Rico) peasant; poor farmer.
jibe, *m.* (Cuba) sieve.
jibia, *f.* (zool.) cuttlefish.
jibión, *m.* (zool.) cuttlebone.
jibraltareño, ña, *a.* of or from Gibraltar. —*m., f.* native of Gibraltar.
jícama, *f.* (C. Amer., Mex.) name given to various medicinal and edible plants.
jícara, *f.* 1. cup, small bowl. 2. (Amer.) gourd cup or bowl (made from a calabash gourd). 3. (Guat.) calabash (fruit).
jicarazo, *m.* 1. blow given with a gourd bowl. 2. poisoning.
jícaro, *m.* (Amer.) calabash tree.
jicarón, *m.* (Amer.) *aug. of* **jícara,** large cup or bowl.
jico, *m.* (Cuba, P. Rico) hammock clew (cord supporting hammock).
jicote, *m.* (Hond.) large wasp; (Hond.) wasp nest.
jicotea, *f.* (zool.) hicotee (freshwater tortoise).
jiennense, *a.* from or of the Spanish province of Jaen. —*m., f.* native of Jaen.
jifa, *f.* offal (of a slaughtered animal).
jiferada, *f.* blow with a slaughterer's knife.
jifería, *f.* slaughtering (cattle).
jifero, ra, *a.* 1. of or pertaining to a slaughterhouse. 2. (coll.) dirty, filthy. —*m.* 1. slaughterer's knife. 2. slaughterer.
jifia, *f.* (ichth.) swordfish.
jifosuro, ra, *a.* (zool.) xiphosuran.
jiga, *f.* jig, ancient dance and music of Italian origin.
jigote, *m.* fricassee; braised meat stew.
jigua, *f.* (bot.) jigua, Cuban hardwood tree.
jiguagua, *f.* (ichth.) (variety of) cavalla (Caranx carangus).
jigüera, *f.* (Cuba) gourd, calabash vessel.
jiguilete, *m., var. of* **jiquilete.**
jijallar, *m.* saltwort thicket; bramble.
jijallo, *m.* (bot.) saltwort, prickly broom.
jijene, *m.* (S. Amer.) sand fly.
ji, ji, ji, *interj.* denoting laughter.
jijón, *m.* (Cuba) hardwood tree similar to the mahogany.
jijona, *f.* 1. long, yellow-grained wheat. 2. **turrón de Jijona,** variety of almond paste confection made in Jijona, Spain.
jileco, *m.* Turkish jacket or vest.
jilguera, *f.* (ornith.) female goldfinch.
jilguero, ra, *m., f.* (ornith.) goldfinch, linnet.
jilibioso, sa, *a.* 1. (Chile) finicky, fastidious, difficult. 2. (Chile) restless, fidgety (horse).
jilmaestre, *m.* (mil.) artillery officer in charge of horses or mules.
jilote, *m.* (C. Amer., Mex.) unripened ear of corn.
jilotear, *i.v.* (Mex.) to begin to ripen (said of corn on the cob).
jimagua, *a., m, f.* (Cuba, Mex.) twin.
jimelga, *f.* (mar.) fish, fish-shaped timber used to reinforce masts.
jimenzar, *tr.v.* to ripple (flax or hemp).
jimerito, *m.* (Hond.) small bee.
jimilille, *m.* (Hond.) thin flexible reed.
jimio, a, *m., f.* ape.
jinestada, *f.* (cul.) milk sauce, thickened with rice flour and seasoned with spices.
jineta, *f.* (zool.) genet.
jineta, *f.* 1. style of riding with stirrups short and legs bent. 2. short lance (carried by cavalry captain). 3. sergeant's silk epaulet.
jinetada, *f.* (rare) boasting, bragging.
jinete, *m.* 1. horseman, rider; cavalryman, trooper. 2. thoroughbred horse.
jinetear, *tr.v.* (Amer.) to break in (a horse). —*i.v.* to ride about on horseback.
jinglar, *i.v.* to swing, vibrate, oscillate.
jingoísmo, *m.* jingoism, chauvinism; aggressive foreign policies.
jingoísta, *a., m., f.* jingoist; jingoistic.
jínjol, *m.* (bot.) jujube berry.
jinjolero, *m.* (bot.) jujube tree.
jiña, *f.* 1. (Chile) trifle, knick-knack. 2. (Cuba) human excrement.
jiote, *m.* (C. Amer., Mex., med.) impetigo.
jiotoso, sa, *a.* suffering from impetigo.
jipa, *f.* (Amer., coll.) jipijapa, Panama hat.
jipar, *i.v.* (coll.) to hiccup, hiccough.
jipato, pa, *a.* 1. (Amer.) pale, wan, anaemic. 2. (Cuba) insipid (fruit).
jipe, *m.* (Mex.) jipijapa, Panama hat.
jipi, *m.* (Cuba) jipijapa, Panama hat.
jipijapa, *f.* straw of the jipijapa palm. —*m.* jipijapa hat, Panama hat (actually made in Ecuador).
jiquilete, *m.* (bot.) indigo plant.
jíquima, *f.* (Cuba, Ecuad.), *var. of* **jícama.**
jira, *f.* 1. strip (of cloth); shred, tatter (of cloth). 2. excursion, picnic, outing; tour, trip; **en j.,** on tour; **j. de inspección,** tour of inspection.
jirafa, *f.* (zool.) giraffe.
jirapliega, *f.* (pharm.) purgative, laxative.
jirasal, *f.* (bot.) soursop (fruit).
jirel, *m.* rich caparison (for a horse).
jíride, *f.* (bot.) stinking iris.
jirimiquear, *i.v.* (Chile, Guat., Mex.) to moan, whine, complain.
jirimiquiento, ta, *a.* (Guat.) snivelling, whining, grizzling (G.B.); complaining, moaning.
jiro, *m.* turn, trend, direction, bias; turn, rotation.
jiroflé, *m.* (bot.) clove tree.
jirón, *m.* 1. shred, tatter (of cloth). 2. facing (of skirt). 3. pennant. 4. portion, bit, small part. 5. (her.) gyron. — **hacer jirones una cosa,** to tear something to shreds.
jironado, da, *a.* 1. torn, tattered, torn to shreds. 2. (her.) divided in gyrons.
jirpear, *tr.v.* to sink holes around (vines for water to accumulate).
jisca, *f.* (bot.) sedge, common reed grass.
jiste, *m.* foam on beer; yeast, barm.
jitar, *tr.v.* to throw up, to vomit.
jitomate, *m.* (Mex.) (variety of) tomato.
jiu-jitsu, *m.* jujitsu.
jo, *m.* Mexican coin of three centavos. —*interj.* whoa!
Job, *m.* (Bib.) Job; (coll.) patient person.
jobo, *m.* (bot.) hog plum, yellow mombin (tree).
jockey, *m.* jockey, professional rider.
jocó, (*pl.* **jocóes**), *m.* jocko, chimpanzee.
jocomico, *m.* (Hond.) paradise tree (Simareuba glauca).
jocoque, *m.* (Mex.) curdled milk; yogurt.
jocosamente, *adv.* 1. amusingly, wittily, jocosely. 2. jocularly, gaily.
jocoserio, ria, *a.* tragicomic, tragicomical.
jocosidad, *f.* 1. humor, wit, waggishness, jocoseness. 2. jocularity, gaiety. 3. joke, witty remark.
jocoso, sa, *a.* 1. amusing, funny, witty, waggish, jocose. 2. jocular, festive, gay.
jocotal, *m.* (bot.) (variety of) hog plum tree (spondias purpurea).
jocote, *m.* (C. Amer.) hog plum (fruit).
jocoyote, *m.* (Mex.) youngest child, baby (of the family), pet.
jocú, (*pl.* **jocúes**), *m.* (ichth.) dog snapper.
jocuma amarilla, *f.* (bot.) (variety of) ironwood (sideroxylon foetidissimum).
jocundidad, *f.* jocundity, gaiety, joviality.
jocundo, da, *a.* jocund, gay, jovial.
joder, *tr.v.* 1. (vulg.) to fuck (vulg.), have sexual intercourse with. 2. (vulg.) to annoy, pester, plague.
jofaina, *f.* basin, washbasin, washbowl.
jojoto, *m.* (Ven.) unripe corn.
jolgorio, *m.* (coll.) boisterous frolic.
jolines, *interj.* (Sp.) expressing surprise or disgust.
jolito, *m.* rest, leisure, pause. — **en jolito,** duped, cheated.
jollín, *m.* (coll.) noisy party, merry or boisterous get-together.
jolote, *m.* (Hond., Guat., Mex.) turkey.
joma, *f.* (Mex.) hump.
jomado, da, *a.* (Mex.) hunchbacked, humpbacked.
jónico, ca, *a.* Ionian, Ionic; (archit.) Ionic. —*m., f.* Ionian, native of Ionia, a colony of ancient Greece. —*m.* 1. (poet.) Ionic, foot of four syllables. 2. Ionic (dialect).
jonio, nia, *a.* Ionian, Ionic, of or pertaining to a colony of ancient Greece. —*m., f.* Ionian.
jonja, *f.* (Chile) mocking raillery, joke or jest; sneer.
jonjabar, *tr.v.* to inveigle, cajole, flatter.
jonjabero, ra, *a.* wheedling, cajoling, flattering.

jonrón, *m.* (Amer.) home run (in baseball).
jonuco, *m.* (Mex.) small dark room.
jopo, *interj.* clear off! be off! get out! —*m.* 1. (reg.) crest, tuft; (reg.) tail (of vixen). 2. (Arg.) quiff, forelock. 3. (Bol.) large hairpin.
jora, *f.* (S. Amer.) the type of corn used for making chicha.
jorcar, *tr.v., var. of* **aechar,** to sift (grain).
jorco, *m.* a loose, vulgar fiesta or party.
Jordán, *m.* 1. Jordan (river). 2. (fig.) anything which beautifies, rejuvenates or purifies; **ir al J.,** to be rejuvenated.
Jordania, *f.* the Hachemite Kingdom of Jordan.
jordanio, nia, *a., m., f.* Jordanian; of or pertaining to Jordan.
jorfe, *m.* 1. buttress, sustaining wall. 2. tor, steep craggy hill, cliff.
jorguín, na, *m.* sorcerer, wizard. —*f.* witch, sorceress.
jorguinería, *f.* witchcraft, sorcery.
jorja, *f.* (Mex.) straw hat.
jornada, *f.* 1. day's journey. 2. journey, trip. 3. military expedition. 4. progress, tour (made by the king). 5. episode in a film or a novel. 6. day's work (number of hours). 7. occasion, circumstance, event. 8. life span, lifetime. 9. passing away (death). 10. (arch.) act (of a play). 11. (print.) day's printing, amount printed in one day. — **a grandes** or **largas jornadas,** quickly; **caminar por sus jornadas,** to proceed or go carefully; **j. continuada** or **intensiva** or **única,** working day with a short break; **j. partida,** working day with a long break.
jornal, *m.* day's wages; day's work; wage daily grind; **a j.,** by the day; **j. mínimo,** minimum wage.
jornalero, ra, *m., f.* day laborer.
joroba, *f.* 1. hump. 2. (coll.) annoyance, nuisance, bother.
jorobado, da, *past part. of* **jorobar.** —*a.* hunchbacked, humpbacked; crooked, lopsided. —*m., f.* hunchback, humpback.
jorobar, *tr.v.* to annoy, bother, irritate, importune, to exasperate.
jorobeta, *m.* (coll.) hunchback, humpback.
jorongo, *m.* (Mex.) poncho; woolen blanket.
jorrar, *tr.v.* to tow, pull (a net); **red de j.,** dragnet.
jorro, *a.* (Cuba) poor quality (tobacco). —*m.* dragnet; **a. j.,** towing, dragging; **red de j.,** dragnet.
josa, *f.* unfenced orchard or garden.
José, *m.* Joseph; **J. de Arimatea,** (Bib.) Joseph of Arimathea.
jostrado, da, *a.* with iron bands and a round head (a dart).
jota, *f.* jot, bit. — **no saber** or **entender ni j.,** to be completely ignorant, not to understand in the least; **sin faltar una j.,** (coll.) without missing a single detail.
jota, *f.* 1. one of Spain's principal folk dances and its music, originating in the region of Aragon. 2. vegetable stew. 3. (Amer.) Indian sandal.
jote, *m.* (Chile) turkey buzzard, vulture.
joto, *a.* (Mex., sl.) effeminate, homosexual.
joule, *m.* (phys.) joule.
jovada, *f.* (reg.) day's plowing (with a pair of mules).
Jove, *m.* (myth.) Jove, the god Jupiter.
joven, *a.* young; youthful, juvenile. —*m., f.* youth, young person; young man, young boy (*m.*); young woman, young girl (*f.*).
jovenado, *m.* (ecc.) juniorate, period of instruction (in some orders); juniorate, seminary (for novices).
jovencillo, illa, *m., f.* youngster, lad, lass.
jovenzuelo, la, *m, f.* youngster, teenager.
jovial, *a.* 1. Jovial, Jove-like. 2. jovial, merry, cheerful.
jovialidad, *f.* joviality, merriment, gaiety.
jovialmente, *adv.* jovially, cheerfully.
joya, *f.* 1. jewel, piece of jewelry; large jeweled brooch. 2. present, gift. 3. jewel (valued person or thing). 4. (artil., archit.) astragal. 5. (*pl.*) trousseau; jewels, jewelry; **j. de fantasía,** piece of costume jewelry.
joyante, *a.* glossy (said of silk).
joyel, *m.* small jewel, valuable trinket.
joyelero, *m.* jewel case or box.
joyería, *f.* 1. jewelry business. 2. jewelry shop or store. 3. jeweler's workshop.
joyero, *m.* 1. jeweler, owner of a jewelry shop; (Amer.) goldsmith. 2. jewel box or case.
joyita, *f.* 1. *dim. of* **joya,** small jewel. 2. (fig.) precious person or object.
joyo, *m.* (bot.) bearded darnel, darnel grass.
joyolina, *f.* (coll., Guat.) prison, jail.
joystick *m.* (aer.) joystick.
joyuela, *f. dim. of* **joya,** dainty little jewel.
juagar, (*ref. 51*) *tr.v.* (Col., Mex.) to rinse.
juagarzo, *m.* (bot.) variety of rockrose.
juagaza, *f.* (Col.) sugary water (left in sugar mill vats).
juague, juagué, *ref.* **juagar.**
Juan, *m.* 1. John. 2. simple, good man. 3. (Mex., Bol.) soldier, private. — **Buen J.,** (coll.) sap, dope, gullible fellow; **J. Bautista,** John the Baptist; **J. de Gante,** John of Gaunt; **J. Lanas,** simpleton, Simple Simon; **J. Palomo,** good-for-nothing; **J. sin tierra,** King John (of England); **J. Soldado,** symbol of the humble Spanish peasant turned soldier by the military draft.
Juana, *f.* Joan, Jane, Jean; **J. de Arco,** Joan of Arc; **J. de Orleáns,** Maid of Orleans.
juanas, *f.* (*pl.*) glove-stretchers.
juancagado, *m.* (Hond.) (species of) owl.
juanete, *m.* 1. high cheek bone. 2. (med.) bunion. 3. (mar.) topgallant; topgallant sail. 4. (vet.) buttress (horny protuberance on horse's hoof). 5. (*pl.*) (Hond.) hips. — **j. mayor,** main-topgallant sail; **j. de proa,** fore-topgallant sail.
juanetero, *m.* (mar.) topman (sailor in charge of top-gallant sails).
juanetudo, da, *a.* bunioned, having bunions.
juanillo, *m.* (Chile, Peru) tip, gratuity.
juarda, *f.* (tex.) grease stain or spot (in silk cloth).
juardoso, sa, *a.* stained, having grease stains (said of silk cloth).
juay, *m.* (Mex.) knife.
juba, *f.* jupon, jubbah (garment used formerly).
jubete, *m.* doublet, covered with chain mail.
jubetería, *f.* formerly said of the trade of mail doublet-making.
jubetero, *m* maker or seller of mail doublets.
jubilación, *f.* retirement; pension (emolument); pensioning-off; **j. anticipada,** early retirement; **j. forzosa,** compulsory retirement; **j. voluntaria,** voluntary retirement.
jubilar, *a.* pertaining to retirement or to a jubilee.
jubilar, *tr.v.* 1. to retire, pension off; to put on the retired list. 2. to excuse or exempt from (duties). 3. (coll.) to discard as useless, pension off. —*i.v.* 1. to rejoice, jubilate. 2. to retire, be pensioned off. —*r.v.* 1. to retire, be pensioned off. 2. to rejoice, jubilate. 3. (Cuba, Mex.) to become expert or skilled (in). 4. (Col.) to come down in the world, go to pieces. 5. (Ven., Guat.) to play truant, play hookie.
jubileo, *m* 1. (hist.) jubilee (Jewish festival celebrated every fiftieth year). 2. (ecc.) jubilee, plenary indulgence. 3. (fig.) bustle, stir, coming and going. — **por j.,** once in a lifetime, once in a blue moon.
júbilo, *m.* joy, jubilation, rejoicing, euphoria.
jubilosamente, *adv.* jubilantly.
jubiloso, sa, *a.* jubilant, joyful, merry.
jubo, *m.* (zool.) small Cuban non-poisonous snake (Coluber cantherigerus).
jubón, *m.* doublet, jerkin, close-fitting jacket; bodice. — **j. de azotes,** (coll.) public whipping; **j. de nudillos,** coat of mail; **j. ojeteado,** doublet covered with chain mail.
jubonero, *m.* one who makes doublets, waists or jackets.
júcaro, *m.* (bot.) (variety of) myrobalan (tree).
juco, ca, *a.* (Hond.) sour.
judaica, *f.* spine of fossil sea-urchin.
judaice, judaicé, *ref.* **judaizar.**
judaico, ca, *a.* Judaic, Jewish.
judaísmo, *m.* Judaism.
judaización, *f.* Judaizing, observance of the teachings of Judaism.
judaizante, *a.* Judaizing. —*m., f.* Judaizer, Judaist.
judaizar, (*ref. 53*) *i.v.* to Judaize, observe the teachings of Judaism.
Judas, *m.* 1. (Bib.) Judas. 2. (fig.) Judas, traitor, treacherous person. 3. silkworm which dies before spinning its cocoon. 4. effigy of Judas burnt in the streets during Holy Week. — **J. Iscariote,** (Bib.) Judas Iscariot.
Judea, *f.* (hist., Bib.) Judea, Judaea.
judeo-español, la, *a.* Judeo-Spanish. —*m., f.* Spanish Jew. —*m.* Judaeo-Spanish (language), Ladino.
judería, *f.* 1. ghetto, Jewry. 2. (arch.) tax paid by Jews.
judía, *f.* 1. (bot.) kidney bean, French bean. 2. (any) face card (in monte). 3. Jewess.
judiada, *f.* 1. crowd of Jews. 2. (coll.) exorbitant profit, usury.
judiar, *m.* kidney bean field or patch.
judicatura, *f.* judicature (post of judge; judge's term of office; body of judges).
judicial, *a.* judicial; juridical.
judicialmente, *adv.* judicially.
judiciario, ria, *a.* 1. (law) judicial, judiciary. 2. (astrol.) judicial. —*m.* astrologer, adherent of judicial astrology.
judiego, *f.* inferior kind of olives.
judío, a, *a.* 1. Jewish, Hebrew. 2. (derog.) miserly, avaricious. —*m.* 1. Jew. 2. (ornith.) ani. —*f.* Jewess.
judión, *m.* a large variety of French bean.
judo, *m.* (sport.) judo.
judoka, *m., f.* judoka, one who practices judo.
juego, *m.* 1. game. 2. play, playing. 3. fun, jest, e.g. *lo dijo en j.,* he said it in fun. 4. gambling; cards, card-playing; hand (cards dealt to each player). 5. (mec.) play, clearance, slack (room in which joints or interlocking parts can move); play (movement of interlocking parts). 6. set (of crockery, cutlery, etc.); suite (of furniture); **j. de baño,** set of towels; **j. de café,** coffee set; **j. de cama,** set of matching sheets and pillowcases; **j. de comedor,** dining room suite; **j. de cubiertos,** set of cutlery; **j. de dormitorio,** bedroom suite; **j. de escritorio,** desk set; **j. de llaves,** set of keys; **j. de té,** tea set. 7. running gear (of four-wheeled carriage). 8. play (of water, lights, etc.). 9. (sport.) court, field. 10. (coll.) game, scheme, plan. 11 (*pl.*) games, e.g. *juegos olímpicos,* Olympic Games. — **casa de j.,** gambling house; **conocerle a alguien el j.,** to be on to someone's game, discover someone's plans or intentions; **dar bien el j.,** to be in luck, have good luck; **dar mal el j.,** to be out of luck, have bad luck; **estar en j.,** to be at work, e.g. *están en j. poderosas influencias,* powerful influences

are at work; to be at stake, e.g. *aquí está en j. el prestigio del colegio,* here the prestige of the school is at stake; **hacer j.,** to match, go together, harmonize; **hacer j. con,** to match, go with; **hacerle a alguien el j.,** to play into someone's hands; to go or play along with someone; **j. a lo largo,** pitch-and-toss (ball game); **j. carteado,** card game not played for money; **j. de azar,** game of chance; **j. de aprieto,** (bridge) squeeze play; **j. de billar,** billiards; **j. de bolas,** (mec.) ball bearing; **j. de comedor,** dining-room suite; **j. de cubiletes,** trickery, deception; dice; **j. de damas,** checkers, draughts (G.B.); **j. de desquite,** return game or match; **j. de dormitorio,** bedroom suite; **j. de envite,** gambling game; **j. de evasión,** (bridge) avoidance play; **j. de ingenio,** guessing game (riddles, charades); **j. de cantillos,** jackstones; **j. de manos,** sleight of hand, conjuring trick, (*pl.*) conjuring; slapping, hitting, pushing; **j. de naipes,** cards, card game; **j. de niños,** child's play (easy thing); **j. de palabras,** pun, play upon words; **j. de pelota,** pelota, jai alai; any ball game; **j. de prendas,** forfeits, game of forfeits; **j. de suerte,** game of chance; **juegos florales,** (hist.) Floral Games, poetry competition for troubadours; **j. limpio,** fair play; **j. longitudinal,** (mec.) end play; **juegos malabares,** juggling; **j. sucio,** foul play; **por j.,** for fun; **verle a alguien el j.,** to tumble to someone's intentions.

juego, juegue, *ref.* **jugar.**

Juegos Olímpicos, *m. pl.* Olympic Games, Olympics.

juera, *f.* sieve made of esparto.

juerga, *f.* (coll.) spree; **correrse una j., ir de j.,** to go on a spree, go on a binge.

juerguearse, *r.v.* 1. (coll.) to go on a spree or binge; to paint the town red; to enjoy oneself. 2. (coll.) to make fun (of), laugh (at).

juerguista, *a.* reveling; boisterous, gay. —*m., f.* reveler, merrymaker; boisterous and gay person.

jueves, *m.* Thursday; **j. de comadres,** penultimate Thursday before Lent; **j. de compadres,** antepenultimate Thursday before Lent; **j. gordo,** Thursday before Lent; **j. santo,** Maundy Thursday; **nada del otro j.,** nothing to write home about, nothing special.

juez, (*pl.* **jueces**), *m.* 1. judge, juryman. 2. critic, connoisseur, expert. 3. (sport.) referee. 4. (arch.) governor of Castile. — **j. arbitrador** or **árbitro,** (law) arbiter, umpire; **j. avenidor,** umpire, arbitrator, referee (not a lawyer); **j. de alzadas** or **apelaciones,** judge of the court of appeals; **j. de línea,** (sport) linesman; **j. de palo,** (coll.) ignorant judge; **j. de partida** or **salida,** (sport) starter; **j. de paz,** justice of the peace; **j. de primera instancia,** judge of the first instance; **j. de raya,** (Amer.) judge (at the finish, on a racecourse); **j. municipal,** judge of a municipal court.

jugada, *f.* 1. play, act of playing, e.g. *¡qué maravillosa j.!* what a marvelous play; move (in chess, checkers, etc.). 2. dirty trick; **hacerle a alguien una mala j.,** to play a dirty trick on someone.

jugadera, *f.* shuttle (used in weaving).

jugador, ra, *m., f.* 1. player. 2. gamester, gambler. — **j. de manos,** conjurer; **j. de ventaja,** cheat, swindler.

jugar, (*ref. 73*) *i.v.* 1. to play; to frolic. 2. to gamble. 3. to move, work, function. 4. (mec.) to be loose (joints or interlocking parts). 5. to come or enter into action (weapons in a battle). 6. to match, go together. 7. to take part, participate. — **j. a,** to play, e.g. *j. al fútbol,* to play football; **j. al alza,** (com.) to bull the market, speculate on a rise in prices; **j. a la baja,** (com.) to bear the market, speculate on a drop in prices; **j. a la bolsa,** (com.) to speculate on the stock exchange; **j. a la mala carta,** to back the wrong horse; **j. con,** to play with, make fun of; to toy with; to match, go with; **j. con dos barajas,** to run with the hare and hunt with the hounds; **j. fuerte,** to gamble heavily. —*tr.v.* 1. to play (a card, a chess piece; a game of chess, etc.). 2. to gamble, stake, wager; to risk; to gamble away. 3. to work, make function, set in motion; to move (limbs). 4. to wield, handle (e.g. a sword).

jugarreta, *f.* 1. (coll.) bad play, bad move. 2. (coll.) dirty trick.

juglándeo, a, *a.* (bot.) juglandaceous, of the walnut family. —*f.* (bot.) juglandaceous plant; (*pl.*) (bot.) Juglandaceae.

juglar, *a.* 1. of minstrels or jongleurs. 2. funny, witty. —*m.* 1. minstrel, jongleur, troubador. 2. jester, juggler, conjurer.

juglaresco, ca, 1. of minstrels or jongleurs. 2. of jesters or jugglers.

juglaría, *f.* minstrelsy; the art of minstrelsy.

juglería, *f.* buffoonery, juggling, mimicry.

jugo, *m.* 1. juice, sap. 2. (cul.) gravy. 3. (fig.) pith, marrow, essence, substance. — **j. gástrico,** (physiol.) gastric juice; **j. pancreático,** (physiol.) pancreatic juice; **j. de fruta,** fruit juice.

jugosidad, *f.* juiciness, succulence.

jugoso, sa, *a.* 1. juicy, succulent. 2. large, big, e.g. *ganancias jugosas,* large profits.

jugué, *ref.* **jugar.**

juguete, *m.* 1. toy, plaything. 2. joke, jest. 3. short light piece of music; short play. 4. (fig.) plaything. — **de j.,** toy (as *a.*); **carro de j.,** toy car.

juguetear, *i.v.* to play, romp, frisk, gambol, frolic.

jugueteo, *m.* playing, frolicking, romping.

juguetería, *f.* toy business; toyshop.

juguetero, *m.* 1. toy dealer; toy maker. 2. place where toys are kept. 3. bric-a-brac cabinet.

juguetón, na, *a.* playful, frisky, frolicsome.

juicio, *m.* 1. sense of judgment, discernment. 2. mind, sound mind, sanity. 3. opinion; decision, judgment; forecast (of astrologers). 4. sense, common sense, sound judgment. 5. (law) trial; lawsuit, action. 6. (theol.) judgment. — **entablar j. a,** to file a suit against; **estar en su j.,** to be of sound mind, be in one's right mind; **estar fuera de su j.,** to be out of one's mind; **j. civil,** civil proceedings; **j. criminal,** criminal proceedings; **j. de Dios,** (hist.) trial by ordeal; **j. final** or **universal,** (theol.) Last Judgment; **meter j. a,** (coll.) to prosecute, file a suit against; **pedir en j.,** to sue for; **perder el j.,** to go out of one's mind; **poner en tela de j.,** to call into question; **quitar el j. a alguien,** to fill whit joy or delight; to go to one's head; to drive (one) mad, infuriate; to turn someone's head, drive someone mad with love.

juiciosamente, *adv.* judiciously, wisely, sensibly.

juicioso, sa, *a.* judicious, wise, mature, sensible.

juico, ca, *a.* (Hond.) deaf.

juil, *m.* a kind of Mexican lake trout.

julepe, *m.* 1. julep, medicinal drink. 2. (coll.) scolding, reprimand, dressing-down. 3. (Amer.) scare, fright. 4. (Amer.) work, strenuous activity, hustle and bustle.

julepear, *tr.v.* 1. (Amer.) to tire, annoy, exhaust. 2. (Amer.) to scare.

juliana, *f.* 1. (bot.) damewort, dame's violet or gillyflower. 2. (cul.) soup made with finely chopped vegetables.

juliano, na, *a.* Julian; **calendario j.,** Julian calendar. —*m.* **J.,** Julian; **J. el Apóstata,** Julian the Apostate.

julio, *m.* 1. July (month). 2. (elec.) joule, watt-second; **Julio César,** Julius Caesar.

julo, *m.* lead cow; horse or mule leading the pack.

juma, *f.* (coll.), *var. of* **jumera.**

jumarse, *r.v.* (coll.) to get drunk.

jumental, *a.* of or pertaining to an ass or donkey.

jumentice, jumenticé, *ref.* **jumentizar.**

jumentil, *a., var. of* **jumental.**

jumento, ta, *m., f.* 1. donkey, ass; jenny; beast of burden. 2. (fig.) stupid person.

jumera, *f.* (coll.) drunk, drunken bout or spree.

juncáceo, a, *a.* (bot.) juncaceous, pertaining to rushes. —*f.* (*pl.*) Juncaceae.

juncada, *f.* 1. kind of fritter. 2. clump of rushes. 3. (vet.) medicine used to cure glanders.

juncal, *a.* 1. slim, willowy; rush-like. 2. generous; handsome. —*m.* clump of rushes.

juncar, *m.* clump of rushes.

júnceo, a, *a.* (bot.) juncaceous, rush-like. —*f.* juncaceous plant; (*pl.*) Juncaceae.

juncia, *f.* (bot.) (variety of) sedge (Cyperus longus). — **vender j.,** to brag, boast.

juncial, *m.* clump of sedge.

junciana, *f.* (coll.) brag, boast.

junciera, *f.* earthenware vessel with perforated lid, allowing the perfume of aromatic herbs to escape.

juncino, na, *a.* made of rushes.

junco, *m.* 1. (bot.) rush, bulrush; stem of bulrush. 2. cane, stick. 3. junk, Chinese sailing vessel. — **j. de Indias,** (bot.) rattan, rattan palm; **j. florido,** (bot.) flowering rush; **j. oloroso,** (bot.) camel grass.

juncoso, sa, *a.* rush-like; rushy.

jungla, *f.* jungle.

junglada, *f.* (cul.) hare fricassee.

junio, *m.* June (month).

júnior, *m.* 1. (ecc.) junior or young priest (still subject to a tutor). 2. junior, the younger of two persons having the same name, e.g. *Rogelio Jackson, J.,* Roger Jackson, Jr.

junípero, *m.* (bot.) juniper.

Juno, *f.* (myth.) Juno, Roman goddess of marriage.

junquera, *f.* (bot.) rush, bulrush.

junqueral, *m.* clump of rushes.

junquillo, *m.* (bot.) jonquil; reed, **rattan;** (archit.) bolted molding.

junta, *f.* 1. council; board; junta; tribunal. 2. meeting, conference, session, assembly. 3. whole, entirety, entity. 4. union, junction; (bldg.) joint; (carp.) joint, scarf; (mar.) seam (in sail, etc.); (mec.) coupling. — j. **cardánica,** universal or cardan joint; **j. de educación,** board of education; **j. de comercio,** board of trade; **j. de culata,** head gasket; **j. de dilatación** or **de expansión,** expansion joint; **j. de sanidad,** board of health; **j. directiva,** board of directors; **j. esférica,** ball, joint; **j. militar,** military junta or government; **j. universal,** universal joint.

juntamente, *adv.* jointly; together.

juntar, *tr.v.* 1. to join; to unite. 2. to assemble, gather, collect. 3. to half-close. —*r.v.* 1. to meet, assemble, gather. 2. to associate closely with one another. 3. to copulate, have sexual intercourse.

juntera, *f.* (carp.) jointing plane.

junterilla, *f.* (carp.) small jointing plane.

junto, ta, *a.* 1. joined, united, connected. 2. (*pl.*) together, e.g. *se fueron juntos,* they left together.

junto, *adv.* together; at the same time; near; **en j.,** or **por j.,** all together, in all, all told; **j. a.,** near, next to; **j. con,** along with, together with.

juntorio, *m.* an ancient tax.

juntura, *f.* 1. joint; coupling; seam. 2. (anat.) joint. 3. (bot.) knuckle. 4. (mar.) scarf.

jupa, *f.* 1. (C. Amer.) round squash or pumpkin. 2. (C. Amer.) head.

Júpiter, *m.* 1. (astron., myth.) Jupiter. 2. (chem.) tin (in alchemy).
juque, *m.* (C. Rica, Salv.) boor, lout, oaf, ill-bred person.
jura, *f.* oath; oath of allegiance; act of swearing or administering an oath of allegiance (to sovereign, flag, country).
jurado, da, *past part. of* **jurar.** *—a.* 1. sworn, declared. 2. under oath, e.g. *intérprete jurado,* an interpreter under oath. *—m.* 1. jury; juror, juryman. 2. examiner; judge, adjudicator; board of examiners; judges, adjudicators, board of judges or adjudicators.
jurador, ra, *m., f.* swearer; one who uses profane language.
juraduría, *f.* office of a juror; office of an examiner or adjudicator.
juramentar, *tr.v.* to swear in. *—r.v.* to pledge oneself on oath, be sworn in.
juramento, *m.* 1. oath. 2. curse, oath, blasphemy. — **bajo j.,** under oath; **j. asertorio,** assertory oath; **j. decisorio** or **j. deferido,** (law) decisory or decisive oath; **j. falso,** perjury; **j. hipocrático,** Hippocratic oath.
jurar, *tr.v.* 1. to swear, declare upon oath. 2. to swear (allegiance, vengeance). 3. to swear, to use profane language. — **jurárselas** or **jurársela a uno,** to threaten with revenge, to swear revenge against; **tenérselas juradas a uno,** to have it in for. *—i.v.* to swear, curse, blaspheme; **j. como un carretero,** to swear like a trooper; **j. en falso,** to commit perjury.
jurásico, *a., m.* (geol.) Jurassic.
juratoria, *f.* (hist.) Gospel tablet for administering the oath (in the ancient courts of Aragon).
juratorio, ria, *a.* (law) juratory. *—m.* (arch.) document on which an oath was registered.
jurdía, *f.* a type of fishing net.
jure, (Lat.) **de j.,** by right, legally.
jurel, *m.* (ichth.) saurel, jurel, yellow jack (Trachurus trachurus).
jurero, *m.* (Chile, Ecuad.) false witness.
jurguina, *f.* witch, sorceress.
jurídicamente, *adv.* juridically, legally.
juridicidad, *f.* lawfulness, legality.
jurídico, ca, *a.* juridical, legal.
jurisconsulto, *m.* jurisconsult, jurist, legal expert.
jurisdicción, *f.* jurisdiction, boundary. — **j. territorial,** (law) territorial jurisdiction; **traslado de j.,** (law) change of venue.
jurisdiccional, *a.* jurisdictional.
jurispericia, *f., var. of* **jurisprudencia.**
jurisperito, *m.* legal expert, jurist.
jurisprudencia, *f.* jurisprudence, law; legislation.
jurisprudente, *m.* jurisprudent, jurist, legal expert.
jurista, *m., f.* 1. jurist, lawyer, legal expert. 2. one who enjoys the right of perpetual ownership. 3. one who has a perpetual annuity or perpetuity, pensioner.
juro, *m.* 1. right of perpetual ownership. 2. perpetual annuity, pension, perpetuity. — **de j.,** inevitably, certainly.
jurón, *m.* (Ecuad., coll.) large basket.
jusbarba, *f.* (bot.) butcher's boom, field myrtle.
jusello, *m.* (cul.) a rich meat stew.
jusi, *m.* a fine dress fabric, similar to voile.
justa, *f.* joust, tournament; (fig.) competition, contest.
justador, *m.* jouster, tilter.
justamente, *adv.* 1. justly, fairly. 2. just, exactly, precisely. 3. tightly. 4. in that very, in that very place, e.g. *Antonio se hallaba j. en aquel pueblo,* Antonio was in that very town.
justar, *i v.* to joust, tilt, tourney.
justicia, *f.* 1. justice; rightness, fairness. 2. punishment, retribution. 3. court (of justice), tribunal. 4. execution (of a criminal). 5. law, police, authorities. — **administrar j.,** to administer justice; **de j.,** justly, duly, deservedly; by rights; **hacer j. a uno,** to do someone justice; **ir por j.,** to go to court or law; **j. distributiva,** distributive justice; **pedir en j.,** to go to court; **tener la j. de su parte,** to have right on one's side.
justiciable, *a.* that can be judged, justiciable; (law) actionable.
justiciar, *tr.v.* to execute (a criminal).
justiciazgo, *m.* judgeship, justiceship, office of judge.
justiciero, ra, *a.* 1. just, fair. 2. severe, strict.
justificable, *a.* justifiable.
justificación, *f.* 1. justification, defense. 2. proof; authentication. 3. (theol., print.) justification.
justificadamente, *adv.* justifiably, justly.
justificado, da, *past part. of* **justificar.** *—a.* 1. justified. 2. just, reasonable, upright.
justificador, *m.* 1. (theol.) sanctifier, justifier. 2. (print.) justification bar; justifier (workman).
justificar, (*ref. 50*) *tr.v.* 1. to justify. 2. (theol.) to free from sin, to absolve. 3. (print.) to justify. 4. to prove, verify. 5. to prove innocent. *—r.v.* 1. to be justified; to justify oneself. 2. to prove one's innocence, prove oneself innocent.
justificativo, va, *a.* justificatory, justifying.
justifique, justifiqué, *ref.* **justificar.**
justillo, *m.* waistcoat, jerkin, bodice.
justinianeo, a, *a.* (hist., law) Justinian.
justipreciación, *f.* valuing, estimate, appraisal.
justipreciador, ra, *m., f.* appraiser.
justipreciar, *tr.v.* to value, estimate, evaluate; to appraise.
justiprecio, *m.* valuing, estimate, appraisal.
justo, ta, *a.* 1. just; fair, reasonable; fitting. 2. exact, precise, right, correct, punctual. 3. tight, tight-fitting. 4. upright, God-fearing. — **con las justas,** (coll.) just in time; **la palabra justa,** mot juste (Fr.), right word. *—m.* (*pl.*) the elect, the just. *—adv.* 1. justly, fairly. 2. in straitened circumstances.
juta, *f.* (Ecuad., Peru) (variety of) goose.
jute, *m.* (Hond., Guat.) small edible freshwater snail.
jutía, *f.* (Cuba) hutia, a rodent.
Jutlandés, sa, *a.* Jutlandish, of the N. European peninsula, Jutland. *—m., f.* Jutlander.
juvenil, *a.* juvenile; youthful, e.g. *ardor j.,* youthful ardor; youth, *club j.,* youth club.
juventud, *f.* 1. youth (age between adolescence and maturity). 2. young people (collectively).
juvia, *f.* (bot.) juvia, Brazil nut; Brazil nut tree.
juyaca, *f.* (Amer.) primitive fire-kindling device.
juzgado, *m.* 1. court, tribunal. 2. territory under court's jurisdiction. 3. judgeship, post of judge. — **j. de circuito,** circuit court; **j. de guardia,** police court; **j. de municipal,** city court.
juzgador, ra, *a.* judging. *—m., f.* judge.
juzgamundos, (*pl.* **juzgamundos**), *m., f.* (coll.) faultfinder.
juzgante, *a.* judging; *m., f.* judge.
juzgar, (*ref. 51*) *tr.v.* 1. to judge, pass judgment on; to form or give an opinion. 2. to judge; to think about, consider.
juzgue, juzgué, *ref.* **juzgar.**

K

K, *f.* k, eleventh letter of the Spanish alphabet.
K *sym. of* **potasio,** potassium (K).
Kabúl, *m.* Kabul, capital of Afghanistan.
kaftén, *m.* (Arg.) pimp, procurer.
kainita, *m.* (min.) kainite.
káiser, *m.* kaiser; emperor.
kaiserismo, *m.* rule and system of government of a Kaiser.
kakapú, *m.* (ornith.) kakapo.
kakemono, *m.* kakemono, Japanese hanging or scroll.
kaki, *m.* khaki, yellowish brown color, gen. associated with military attire.
kaleidoscopio, *m.* kaleidoscope.
kalmia, *f.* (bot., Amer.) kalmia, evergreen shrub of N. America (mountain laurel).
kamala, *f.* (bot.) kamala.
Kampala, *f.* Kampala, capital of Uganda.
kan, *m.* Khan, Tartar prince or chief.
kanato, *m.* Khanate, rule of a Khan; country under such government.
kantiano, na, *a.* (philos.) Kantian, pertaining to the doctrines of Emmanuel Kant, the German philosopher.
kantismo, *m.* Kantianism, the philosophy and doctrines of Emmanuel Kant.
kantista, *m., f.* (philos.) Kantist, Kantian, follower of Kant.
kaolín, *m.* kaolin, fine white clay used in making porcelain and (med.) in the treatment of diarrhea.
kapoc, *m.* kapok, fibre used as a filler for mattresses and pillows.
kappa, *f.* kappa (Greek letter corresponding to the K).
karate, *m.* karate, Japanese system of self-defense.
karma, *f.* (rel.) Karma.
Kartum, Jartum, *m.* Khartoum, capital of Sudan.
kayak, *m.* kayak, Eskimo canoe.
kedive, *m.* Khedive, Turkish prince, ruler, viceroy.
kéfir, *m.* (cul.) kefir, fermented milk.
Kenia, Kenya, *f.* Kenya, African state, member of the British Commonwealth.
kenotrón, *m.* (elec.) kenotron.
Kéops, *m.* Cheops.
kepis, *m.* kepi, military cap, small shako.
keralila, *f.* (Mex.) horny flint.
keratectomía, *f.* (surg.) keratectomy.
keratina, *f.* (biochem.) keratin.
keratitis, *f.* (med.) keratitis.
keratosis, *f.* (med.) keratosis.
kermes, *m., var. of* **quermes.**
kermesse, *f.* fair, fete, festival, carnival.
kernita, *f.* (min.) kernite.
kerógeno, *m.* (min.) kerogen.
kerosén, *m.* kerosene, kerosine.
kerosene, *f.* kerosene, kerosine.
kg. *abbrev. of* **kilogramo,** kilogram (kg).
kibutz, *m.* kibbutz, Israeli collective settlement.
kieselgur, *m.* kieselghur, earthy sediment.
kif, *m.* kef, kief, hashish, intoxicating and narcotic leaves of the Indian hemp.
kiliárea, *f.* kiloare, measure of 1,000 ares or about 24 acres.
kilo, *m.* kilo, kilogram.
kiloamperio, *m.* (elec.) kiloampere.
kilocaloría, *f.* (phys.) kilocalorie.
kilociclo, *m.* (rad., elec.) kilocycle.
kiloergio, *m.* (phys.) kiloerg.
kilográmetro, *m.* (mec.) kilogram-meter.
kilogramo, *m.* kilogram, kilo.
kilohertzio, *m.* kilohertz.
kilojulio, *m.* (phys.) kilojoule.
kilolitro, *m.* kiloliter.
kilometraje, *m.* speed measure by kilometers per hour.
kilométrico, ca, *a.* 1. kilometric. 2. (coll.) very long, extensive. 3. travel ticket applying to a specific number of kilometers in any direction.
kilómetro, *m.* kilometer (about five-eighths of a mile).
kilotón, *m.* (phys.) kiloton, the explosive force of 1,000 tons of TNT.
kilovatio, *m.* (elec.) kilowatt.
kilovatio-hora, *m.* (elec.) kilowatt-hour.
kilovolt, *m.* (elec.) kilovolt.
kilovoltamperio, *m.* (elec.) kilovolt-ampere.
kilovoltio, *m.* (elec.) kilovolt.
kilowat, *m.* (Amer., elec.) kilowatt.
kimógrafo, *m.* (med.) kymograph.
kimona, *f.* (Cuba, Mex.) kimono, robe, dressing gown.
kimono, *m.* kimono, Japanese robe.
kindergarten, *m.* kindergarten, infants' school.
Kingston, *m.* Kingston, capital of Jamaica.
kiosco, *m.* kiosk; newsstand, small shop; candy and refreshments stand.
kirie, *m.* (ecc.) Kyrie; **llorar los kiries,** (coll.) to cry by the bucketful.
kirieleison, *m.* (ecc.) Kyrie eleison. — **cantar el k.,** (coll.) to beg for mercy.
kirsch, *m.* (Amer.) kirsch, dry cherry brandy.
kiwi, *m.* (ornith.) kiwi.
kl. *abbrev. of* **kilolitro,** kiloliter.
klaxon, *m.* horn, hooter (of a car).
klefto, *m.* (hist.) klepht.
klipspringer, *m.* (zool.) klipspringer.
klystron, *m.* (phys.) klystron.
knut, *m.* knout (Russian whip).
KO *abbrev. of* **knock-out,** knock-out (KO).
koljoz, *m.* kolkhoz, collective farm in the Soviet Union.
kopek, *m.* Russian coin equivalent to 1/100 of a ruble.
krausismo, *m.* philosophic system of Karl Christian Krause (which interested Spanish intellectuals in the 19th century).
krausista, *a.* of or pertaining to Krause's philosophic system. —*m., f.* follower of Krause.
Kremlín, *m.* Kremlin, the citadel of Moscow; seat of the government of the Soviet Union.
Krisna, *m.* (myth.) Krishna.
Kuala Lumpur, *f.* Kuala Lumpur, capital of Malaysia.
kulak, *m.* Kulak (well-to-do Russian farmer).
kumis, *m.* kumiss, koomiss, fermented milk used as a drink by the Tartar nomads.
kuncuat, *m.* (bot.) kumquat.
kunzita, *f.* (min.) kunzite.
kurdo, da, *a.* Kurdish, of or pertaining to a nomadic Moslem people, their language or culture. —*m., f.* Kurd.
Kuriles, *f.* (*pl.*) Kurile Islands, chain of islands belonging to the U.S.S.R.
Kuwait, *m.* Kuwait, independent Arab state.
kV *abbrev. of* **kilovoltio,** kilovolt (kV).
kvas, *m.* kvass, a beer made by fermenting cereals.
kW *abbrev. of* **kilovatio,** kilowatt (kW).
kWh *abbrev. of* **kilovatio-hora,** kilowatt-hour (kwh).

K L M

L

L, *f.* l, twelfth letter of the Spanish alphabet.
l, *abbrev. of* **litro,** liter (l., lit.).
la, *f. def. art.* the. —*f. pers. pron.* 1. her, e.g. *la vi a ella en el parque,* I saw her in the park. 2. it (referring to inanimate objects of the feminine gender), e.g. *le di la carta, y él la perdio,* I gave him the letter and he lost it. 3. you (when addressing a woman with the **Ud.** form), e.g. *no la vi* (*a Ud.*) *en el teatro,* I did not see you at the theater.
la, *m.* (mus.) **A,** the sixth tone or note in the C major scale.
La *sym. of* **lantano,** lanthanum (La).
Labán, *m.* (Bib.) Laban.
labanco, *m.* (Amer., ornith.) a South American duck.
lábaro, *m.* (hist.) labarum, an ecclesiastical banner; the banner adopted by Constantine the Great.
labe, *f.* stain, spot.
labelado, da, *a.* (bot.) labellate.
labelo, *m.* (bot.) labellum.
laberíntico, ca, *a.* labyrinthine, labyrinthic.
laberinto, *m.* 1. labyrinth, maze. 2. (poet.) palindrome (poetic composition which is the same read backward or forward). 3. (anat.) labyrinth (inner ear). 4. (fig.) difficulty, intricate problem.
labia, *f.* (coll.) gift of gab, (coll.) loquacity, verbal fluency or facility. — **tener mucha l.,** to have the gift of gab.
labiado, da, *a.* (bot.) labiate (plant). —*f.* labiate.
labial, *a.* labial, of or pertaining to the lips.
labialice, labialicé, *ref.* **labializar.**
labialismo, *m.* (phonet.) labialism.
labializar, (*ref. 53*) *tr.v.* (philol.) to labialize.
labiérnago, *m.* (bot.) mock privet, laburnum.
labihendido, da, *a.* harelipped.
lábil, *a.* 1. (chem., phys.) labile, readily undergoing change. 2. labile, slippery. 3. frail, weak, doddering.
labio, *m.* 1. lip (of the mouth). 2. lip, brim (of a cup, etc.). 3. lip (of a wound). 4. (bot., ento., anat.) labium. 5. lip, mouth, words (also *pl.*). — **cerrar los labios,** to keep one's mouth shut, keep quiet; **l. leporino,** harelip; **leer los labios,** to lip-read; **morderse los labios,** to bite one's lips (in annoyance, to repress laughter, etc.); **no despegar los labios,** not to say a word, to keep absolutely silent.
labiodental, *a.* (phonet.) labiodental.
labionasal, *a.* (phonet.) labionasal.
labioso, sa, *a.* (Hond., Mex.) eloquent, honey-tongued, wily.
labiovelar, *a.* (phonet.) labiovelar.
labor, *f.* 1. labor, work. 2. embroidery, needlework, sewing. 3. sewing or needlework school (for small girls). 4. tilling, plowing; farming, farm work, husbandry (usually in *pl.*) 5. batch of a thousand bricks or tiles. 6. silkworm egg. 7. (min.) working, digging (usually in *pl.*). — **l. blanca,** linen embroidery.
laborable, *a.* workable; tillable, plowable; work (day).
laborador, ra, *m., f.* tiller, farmer, worker.
laboral, *a.* pertaining to work or labor; **conflictos laborales,** labor troubles; **leyes laborales,** labor laws.
laborante, *a.* laboring, toiling, tilling, working. —*m.* political intriguer or schemer.
laborar, *tr.v.* to work, toil, labor. —*i.v.* to intrigue, scheme.
laboratorio, *m.* laboratory; **l. de idiomas,** language laboratory; **l. espacial,** space laboratory.
laborcica, illa, ita, *f. dim. of* **labor,** delicate, intricate needlework.
laborear, *tr.v.* 1. to work, labor. 2. (min.) to work, excavate. —*i.v.* (mar.) to run, pass, reeve (a cable through a block).
laboreo, *m.* 1. (agr.) tilling (of the soil). 2. (min.) working (of a mine). 3. (mar.) reeving (arrangement of cables to enable easy handling of sails yards, etc.). — **l. en avance,** (min.) advancing system.
laborero, ra, *a.* expert or skilled in needlework. —*m.* (Amer.) foreman (in a mine). —*m., f.* clever, skillful worker.
laborío, *m.* labor, work.
laboriosamente, *adv.* laboriously; industriously, conscientiously.
laboriosidad, *f.* laboriousness, industriousness, industry, dedication (to the task at hand).
laborioso, sa, *a.* 1. laborious, arduous; painstaking. 2. industrious, hardworking.
laborismo, *m.* British Labor Party; labor movement, working class.
laborista, *a.* pertaining to labor. — **club l.,** Labor club; **partido l.,** Labor Party. —*m., f.* Labourite (G.B.), Laborite, member of a labor party.
labra, *f.* cutting, carving, working, engraving, bas-relief or intaglio work.
labrada, *f.* land left fallow and tilled, ready for sowing the following year.
labradero, ra, *a.* workable; tillable, arable.
labradío, a, *a.* tillable, arable. —*m.* tillable, arable soil.
labrado, da, *past part. of* **labrar.** —*a.* 1. embroidered, patterned (cloth). 2. carved, wrought, engraved, tooled, worked. 3. tilled, worked (fields). —*m.* 1. cutting, carving, tooling, engraving, bas-relief, intaglio. 2. (*pl.*) plowed fields.
labrador, ra, *m., f.* farmer; farm laborer, farm worker, peasant. —*m.* plowman; (Mex.) driver of a team of oxen or mules. —*a.* industrious.
labradoresco, ca, *a.* peasant's, farmer's, farm worker's; rural, rustic, of the country.
labradoril, *a., var. of* **labradoresco.**
labradorita, *f.* (min.) labradorite.
labrandera, *f.* skilled needlewoman or embroiderer.
labrantín, *m.* poor farmer, small farmer.
labrantío, *a., var. of* **labradío.**
labranza, *f.* 1. plowing, tilling, working. 2. farm; farm land.
labrar, *tr.v.* 1. to farm, cultivate; to till, plow (land). 2. to cut, dress (stone); to carve (wood); to work (silver). 3. to build, erect. 4. to embroider, pattern (material). 5. (fig.) to cause, bring about, e.g. *labrar la propia desgracia,* to bring about or cause one's own misfortune. —*i.v.* to make a lasting impression.
labrero, ra, *a.* pertaining to shark-fishing nets. —*m.* (Chile) mine overseer or foreman.
lábrido, *a.* (ichth.) labroid.
labriego, ga, *m., f.* peasant, farm worker, farm laborer, rustic.
labro, *m.* (zool.) labrum.
labroideo, a, *a.* (ichth.) labroid.
labrusca, *f.* (bot.) wild grapevine.
laburno, *m.* (bot.) laburnum.
laca, *f.* 1. lac (resin). 2. lacquer, japan, shellac (varnish). 3. lacquer, lacquered object. 4. lake, carmine (color prepared from cochineal).
Lacadivas, *f.* (*pl.*) Laccadive Islands in the Arabian Sea, off the Malabar coast.
lacaya, *f.* roofless house or hut.
lacayo, *m.* 1. lackey, footman, groom; squire, knight's attendant. 2. bow knot of ribbons (on a sleeve or cuff). 3. (fig.) lackey, toady, servile person.
lacayuelo, *m. dim. of* **lacayo,** footman, groom.
lacayuno, na, *a.* (coll., derog.) servile, e.g. *conducta lacayana,* servile behavior.
lace, lacé, *ref.* **lazar.**
laceador, *m.* (Amer.) lassoer (of animals).
lacear, *tr.v.* 1. to tie with bows; to adorn with bows. 2. (hunt.) to drive (game) within shot. 3. to snare, trap (small game). 4. (Chile) to lasso; (Arg.) to lash with a lasso.
lacedemón, *a., m., f.* (hist.) Lacedaemonian (pertaining to Sparta).
lacedemonio, nia, *var. of* **lacedemón.**
lacena, *f.* cupboard, chest; pantry cabinet for food or dishes.
laceración, *f.* laceration, tearing.
lacerado, da, *past part. of* **lacerar.** —*a.* 1. unlucky, unhappy, unfortunate. 2. leprous. —*m., f.* leper.
lacerar, *tr.v.* 1. to lacerate, wound. 2. (fig.) to damage (one's honor). —*r.v.* to be lacerated; to lacerate oneself. —*i.v.* to suffer, to undergo hardships.
laceria, *f.* 1. poverty, misery. 2. trouble; toil, drudgery.
lacería, *f.* bows, knots; (archit.) ornamentation imitating bows and sashes.
lacerioso, sa, *a.* poor, wretched, miserable.
lacero, *m.* 1. lassoer, cowboy. 2. poacher; snarer, trapper (of small game).
lacertilio, *a, m.* (zool.) lacertilian.
lacertoso, sa, *a.* muscular, strong, brawny, athletic.
lacha, *f.* (ichth.) small variety of sardine (Sardinella allecia); anchovy. —*f.* 1. (fig., coll.) honor, integrity, e.g. *hombre de poca l.,* a man of questionable honor. 2. (Chile), (coll.) man-chaser; live-in partner.
lacho, *m.* (Chile). (coll.) womanizer; live-in partner; suitor, beau.
lacinia, *f.* (bot.) lacinia.
laciniado, da, *a.* (bot.) laciniate, laciniated, slashed.
lacio, cia, *a.* 1. limp, lifeless, flaccid; languid. 2. dried up, withered. 3. lank, straight (hair).
lacolito, *m.* (geol.) laccolith.
lacón, *m.* shoulder of pork, picnic ham.

lacónicamente, *adv.* laconically, briefly.
lacónico, ca, *a.* laconic, brief, concise.
laconio, nia, *a., m., f.* (hist.) Laconian (of an ancient Grecian region dominated by the city of Sparta).
laconismo, *m.* laconism, brevity, conciseness.
lacra, *f.* 1. scar, mark (left by an illness). 2. fault, flaw, defect. — **l. social,** social disgrace (such as poverty, mendicancy, etc.).
lacrar, *tr.v.* 1. to seal (with sealing wax). 2. to damage or injure someone's health. 3. to damage, harm, injure. —*r.v.* to have one's health impaired; to be stricken.
lacre, *a.* red. —*m.* 1. sealing wax. 2. (Cuba) beeswax, propolis.
lacrimación, *f.* (med.) lacrimation.
lacrimal, *a.* lachrymal, pertaining to tears.
lacrimatorio, ria, *a.* lachrymatory, causing tears. —*m.* small vessels or vials found in old Roman sepulchers.
lacrimógeno, na, *a.* lachrymatory, tear-producing. — **gas lacrimógeno,** tear gas.
lacrimosamente, *adv.* lachrymosely, tearfully.
lacrimoso, sa, *a.* lachrymose, tearful.
lactación, *f.* lactation, suckling.
lactama, *f.* (chem.) lactam.
lactancia, *f.* lactation; suckling period, nursing period. — **l. artificial,** bottlefeeding; **l. materna** or **natural,** breastfeeding.
lactante, *a.* suckling, nursing. —*m., f.* suckling, milkfed baby; unweaned infant.
lactar, *tr.v.* to nurse, suckle, to feed with milk. —*i.v.* to suckle, nurse, be breastfed, to feed on milk.
lactario, ria, *a.* milky, lacteous.
lactasa, *f.* (chem.) lactase.
lactato, *m.* (chem.) lactate.
lácteo, a, *a.* 1. milky; milk (as *a.*) 2. (anat.) lacteal. — **fiebre láctea,** (med.) milk fever; **régimen lácteo,** (med.) milk diet; **venas lácteas,** (anat.) lacteal channels or vessels (conveying chyle in the stomach); **Vía Láctea,** (astron.) Milky Way.
lactescencia, *f.* lactescence, milkiness.
lactescente, *a.* lactescent, milky.
lacticíneo, a, *a.* lacteous, milky, milk (as *a.*).
lacticinio, *m.* milk, any dairy product or food prepared with milk.
láctico, *a.* (chem.) lactic. — **ácido láctico,** lactic acid.
lactífero, ra, *a.* lactiferous.
lactina, *f.* (chem.) lactose, lactin, milk sugar.
lactoflavina, *f.* (chem.) lactoflavin.
lactómetro, *m.* lactometer, an instrument for determining the richness of milk.
lactona, *f.* (chem.) lactone.
lactoproteína, *f.* (chem.) lactoprotein, lactoproteid.
lactosa, *f.* (chem.) lactose.
lactucario, *m.* (pharm.) lactucarium.
lactumen, *m.* (med.) milk crust.
lacunario, *m.* (archit.) *var. of* **lagunar.**
lacustre, *a.* lacustrine, lacustrian, marshy; pertaining to lakes.
ládano, *m.* labdanum, laudanum.
ladeado, da, *past part. of* **ladear.** —*a.* 1. tilted, leaning. 2. (bot.) inclining to one side (said of flowers, leaves, etc.).
ladear, *tr.v.* to tilt, tip; to incline. —*i.v.* 1. to tilt, tip; to lean, incline. 2. to swerve, skirt, turn off; to deviate (a compass needle). —*r.v.* 1. to tip, tilt; to lean, incline. 2. to lean, incline (towards an opinion, etc.). 3. to be equal or even. 4. (Chile) to fall in love. — **ladearse a.,** to lean or incline towards (an opinion).
ladeo, *m.* inclination, tilt, leaning.
ladera, *f.* hillside, slope, side (of a mountain, etc.).
ladería, *f.* small plateau or platform on a mountain side.
ladero, ra, *a.* lateral, side.
ladi, *f.* Lady (English title).
ladierno, *m.* (bot.) buckthorn.
ladilla, *f.* 1. (ento.) crab louse. 2. (bot.) common barley. — **prenderse** or **pegarse como ladilla,** (sl.) to stick like a leech.
ladillo, *m.* 1. side panel of a coach; side (of a wagon). 2. (print.) subhead, sidehead (marginal note explaining contents).
ladinamente, *adv.* artfully, cunningly, craftily.
ladino, na, *a.* 1. astute, crafty, artful, cunning. 2. multilingual. —*m.* 1. Old Castilian (today used commonly only in Israel). 2. (Amer.) half-breed, mestizo.
lado, *m.* 1. side; wickerwork side (of a cart); (geom.) side. 2. room, space. 3. aspect, angle, point of view. 4. direction, road. 5. border, margin, edge. 6. protection, patronage; (*pl.*) patrons, protectors; (*pl.*) advisers. — **al l. de,** at the side of, next to; **a un l.,** out of the way! move to one side!; **dar de l. a uno,** to drop someone, keep away from someone; **del otro l.,** (Amer.) queer (sl.), homosexual; **dejar a un l. una cosa,** to omit something, leave something out; **echar a un l.,** to cast or throw aside; **hacerse a un l.,** to step or move to one side; **l. a l.,** side by side; **l. débil,** weak side; **l. materno,** mother's or maternal side (of a family tree); **l. paterno,** father's or paternal side (of a family tree); **malos lados,** bad friends, bad company; **mirar de l.,** to look disdainfully at; to look sideways at; **por todos lados,** on all sides.
ladón, *m.* (bot.) rockrose, cystus.
ladra, *f.* the act of barking (dogs), baying (of hounds).
ladrador, ra, *a.* barking, baying. —*m., f.* barker.
ladrar, *tr.v.* to bark out (orders, etc.). —*i.v.* 1. to bark, bay. 2. (coll.) to threaten idly, bark at.
ladrería, *f.* 1. lazaretto, leprosy hospital. 2. (vet.) swine cysticercosis.
ladrido, *m.* 1. bark, barking. 2. (coll.) outcry; calumny, slander.
ladrillado, *m.* brick flooring, brick work (on walls, fences, etc.).
ladrillador, *m.* bricklayer.
ladrillal, *m.* brickyard.
ladrillar, *tr.v.* to brick, pave with bricks, to lay bricks.
ladrillazo, *m.* blow with a brick.
ladrillejo, *m.* small brick or tile.
ladrillera, *f.* (Amer.) place where bricks are made.
ladrillería, *f.* (Chile, coll.) brick mold.
ladrillero, ra, *m., f.* brick maker. —*m.* brick dealer.
ladrillo, *m.* 1. brick; tile. 2. bar, cake. — **l. crudo,** unburned brick, adobe; **l. hueco,** perforated brick; **l. refractario,** fireproof brick; **l. vidriado,** glazed brick.
ladrilloso, sa, *a.* brick-like, bricky.
ladrón, na, *a.* thieving, thievish, light-fingered. —*m., f.* thief, burglar, robber. —*m.* 1. sluicegate. 2. fragment of wick falling and sticking to the side of the candle. 3. (print.) bite, blank space. 4. (elec.) adaptor. — **jugar a ladrones y celadores,** to play at cops and robbers; **l. cuatrero,** rustler, cattle thief; **l. de cadáveres,** body snatcher; **l. de corazones,** (coll.) lady killer, heartbreaker.
ladronamente, *adv.* (fig.) furtively, stealthily, thievishly.
ladroncillo, *m. dim. of* **ladrón,** petty thief, filcher.
ladronear, *i.v.* to go about stealing or shoplifting.
ladronera, *f.* 1. thieves' den; (fig.) store or shop that overcharges customers. 2. sluicegate. 3. larceny, theft. 4. money box. 5. (fort.) machicolation.
ladronería, *f.* larceny, theft, robbery.
ladronesca, *f.* (coll.) gang, band of thieves.
ladronesco, ca, *a.* (coll.) thievish.
ladronicio, *m.* larceny, theft, robbery.
ladronzuelo, la, *m., f.* petty thief, filcher, pickpocket.
lagaña, *f., var. of* **legaña,** bleariness.
lagañoso, sa, *a., var. of* **legañoso,** bleary-eyed.
lagar, *m.* wine, olive or apple press; olive farm.
lagarejo, *m.* small wine or olive press. — **hacerse l.,** (fig.) to become bruised or squashed (table grapes); to push or jostle each other about.
lagarero, *m.* wine or olive presser.
lagareta, *f.* 1. small wine or olive press. 2. puddle, pool.
lagarta, *f.* 1. female lizard. 2. (ento.) gypsy moth, tussock moth (Lymantra dispar). 3. (coll.) sly, cunning woman.
lagartado, da, *a., var. of* **alagartado, variegated.**
lagartear, *tr.v.* (Chile) to pinion the arms of, grab or hold by the biceps.
lagarteo, *m.* (Chile) pinioning, holding by the biceps.
lagartero, ra, *a.* lizard-hunter. —*f.* lizard's hole.
lagartija, *f.* 1. wall lizard. 2. (Amer.) rogue, rascal.
lagartijero, ra, *a.* lizard-hunting, lizard-eating. —*m., f.* eft-catcher. —*f.* (taur.) a swift, masterly thrust of the sword.
lagartijo, *m.* 1. small lizard. 2. (Mex.) dandy.
lagarto, *m.* 1. (zool.) lizard; (Amer.) alligator. 2. biceps. 3. (coll.) rogue, rascal, cunning devil. 4. (coll.) red sword (insignia of the Order of Santiago). — **¡lagarto!** get away! (when shooing away bad luck). — **l. cornudo,** (zool.) horned toad; **l. de las Indias,** alligator, cayman.
lago, *m.* lake. — **Gran L. Salado,** Great Salt Lake; **l. de leones,** lions' den; **L. de Tiberíades,** Sea of Tiberias, Sea of Galilee; **la región de los lagos,** the Lake district; **los Grandes Lagos,** the Great Lakes.
lagomorfo, *m.* (zool.) lagomorph.
lagopo, *m.* (bot.) rabbit foot clover.
Lagos, *m.* Lagos, capital of Nigeria.
lagotear, *i.v.* to flatter, soft-soap (coll.); cajole, wheedle.
lagotería, *f.* (coll.) flattery, cajolery; soft-soaping (coll.).
lagotero, ra, *a.* (coll.) flattering. —*m., f.* flatterer, cajoler.
lágrima, *f.* 1. tear. 2. drop, spot. 3. juice, sap; juice exuded by the grape. 4. (*pl.*) sorrows, adversities. 5. (Chile) crystal (of a candelabrum). — **deshacerse en lágrimas,** to dissolve in tears; **l. de Batavia,** Rupert's drop, ball or tear; **lágrimas de cocodrilo,** crocodile tears; **lágrimas de David** or **Job,** (bot.) Job's tears; **llorar a l. viva,** to weep bitterly; **mover a lágrimas,** to move to tears.
lagrimal, *a.* (anat.) lachrymal. —*m.* 1. (anat.) lachrymal caruncle. 2. (bot.) rot formed between the trunk and branch (when the branch breaks slightly away).
lagrimar, *i.v.* to weep, cry, to shed tears.
lagrimear, *i.v.* to become moist (eyes), to begin to show tears.
lagrimeo, *m.* the prelude to weeping.
lagrimón, *m.* large tear.
lagrimoso, sa, *a.* 1. tearful, moving. 2. watery (eyes). 3. (bot.) exuding.
lagua, *f.* (Bol., Peru) type of gruel made with potato flour.
laguna, *f.* 1. lagoon, small lake. 2. (anat., biol.) lacuna. 3. lacuna, hiatus, gap (in a manuscript, knowledge).
lagunajo, *m.* pond, puddle, small pool.

lagunar, *m.* (archit.) lacunar, caisson.
lagunato, *m.* (Cuba, Hond.) puddle, pool.
lagunazo, *m.* puddle, pool.
lagunero, ra, *a.* pertaining to a small lake or a lagoon. —*m.* (Chile) lagoon keeper or warden.
lagunoso, sa, *a.* full of lagoons; swampy, marshy.
La Haya, *f.* The Hague.
laical, *a.* laical, lay.
laicalice, laicalicé, *ref.* **laicalizar.**
laicalización, *f.* (Chile) 1. secularization, laicization. 2. disentailing, disentailment.
laicalizar, (*ref. 53*) *tr.v.* (Chile) 1. to secularize, laicize. 2. to disentail, free from mortmain.
laicice, laicicé, *ref.* **laicizar.**
laicidad, *f.* secularity, the quality of laicism.
laicismo, *m.* laicism.
laicista, *a., m., f.* secularist.
laicización, *f.* secularization, laicization.
laicizar, (*ref. 53*) *tr.v.* to secularize, laicize, transfer to civil or secular control.
laico, ca, *a.* lay, secular, laic; nonreligious, e.g. *escuela laica,* nonreligious or lay school. —*m., f.* layman, lay person.
lairén, *a.* **uva l.,** grape with a tough skin and large seeds.
laja, *f.* 1. stone slab, flagstone. 2. (mar.) shallow bank or shoal of flat rock. 3. (Col.) sisal cord.
lakista, *a., m.* (lit.) said of the English poets who lived in the lake region, e.g. Wordsworth and Coleridge.
lama, *f.* 1. slime, mud silt. 2. (bot.) variety of algae, seaweed. 3. (Bol., Col.) verdigris. 4. (min.) ore dust or mud. 5. fine sand used for mortar.
lama, *f.* 1. lamé, gold or silver fabric. 2. (Amer.) moss. —*m., f.* Lama, Tibetan monk or nun.
lamaico, *a.* Lamaic, of or pertaining to the Lamas.
lamaísmo, *m.* (rel.) Lamaism, the form of Buddhism practiced in Tibet and Mongolia.
lamaísta, *m., f.* (rel.) Lamaist, a follower of Lamaism, Buddhism as practiced in Tibet.
lamantino, *m.* (zool.) manatee, lamantin.
lamarquiano, na, *a.* Lamarckian, of or pertaining to the French naturalist, Jean Baptiste Lamarck.
lamarquismo, *m.* (biol.) Lamarckism.
lamarquista, *a., m., f.* Lamarckian, advocate of the theories of Jean Baptiste Lamarck, French naturalist.
lamasería, *f.* lamasery (lama monastery).
lambarear, *i.v.* (Cuba) to loaf around; to wander aimlessly.
lambdoideo, a, *a.* (anat.) lambdoid, lambdoidal.
lambel, *m.* (her.) label, lambel.
lambeo, *m., var. of* **lambel.**
lambeplatos, *m., var. of* **lameplatos.**
lamber, *tr.v.* (Amer.) to lick.
lambert, *m.* (phys.) lambert.
lambetazo, *m.* lick.
lambido, da, *a.* 1. (C. Amer.) prissy, fastidious; foppish. 2. (Col., Ecuad., Cuba) brazen, barefaced; conceited. —*f.* (coll.) lick, licking.
lambisquear, *tr.v.* to scrounge (for delicacies).
lambón, na, *a.* (Col.) fawning, flattering.
lambrequín, *m.* (her.) lambrequin, mantlet.
lambriche, *a.* (Mex.) flattering, fawning.
lambrija, *f.* 1. earthworm. 2. skeleton, very thin person.
lambrijo, ja, *a.* (Mex.) thin, slender.
lambrusco, ca, *a.* (Chile, Mex.) hungry, ravenous.
lameculos, *m., f.* (vulg.) ass-kisser (vulg.) bootlicker.
lamedal, *m.* mire, muddy place.
lamedero, *m.* (animal husbandry) saltlick.
lamedor, ra, *a.* licking. —*m., f.* licker. —*m.* 1. syrup. 2. flattery. — **dar lamedor,** to feign a losing game in order to make one's opponent lose from over-confidence.
lamedura, *f.* lick; licking.
lamelar, *tr.v.* (metal.) to roll copper into sheets.
lamelibranquio, quia, *a.* (zool.) lamellibranch, lamellibranchiate. —*m.* (zool.) lamellibranch; (*pl.*) Lamellibranchia, Lamellibranchiata.
lamelicornio, nia, *a.* (zool.) lamellicorn. —*m.* (zool.) lamellicorn; (*pl.*) Lamellicornia.
lameliforme, *a.* (bot.) lamelliform.
lamelirrostro, tra, *a.* (zool.) lamellirostral. —*m.* (zool.) (*pl.*) Lamellirostres.
lameloso, sa, *a.* (zool.) lamellose.
lamentable, *a.* 1. lamentable, deplorable. 2. sad, mournful.
lamentablemente, *adv.* lamentably, unfortunately.
lamentación, *f.* lamentation, wail, lament.
lamentador, ra, *a.* lamenting. —*m., f.* lamenter.
lamentar, *tr.v., i.v., r.v.* to lament, bewail, mourn; **lamentarse de** or **por,** to mourn, lament.
lamento, *m.* lament, moan, wail.
lamentoso, sa, *a.* 1. lamentable, deplorable. 2. lamenting, mournful.
lameplatos, *m., f.* 1. (coll.) scavenger, person who lives off scraps. 2. (coll.) glutton, gorger.
lamer, *tr.v.* to lick. —*r.v.* to lick oneself; **lamerse de gusto,** to lick one's chops.
lamerón, na, *a.* (coll.) fond of delicacies, sweet-toothed. —*m., f.* sweet tooth.
lametón, *m.* greedy, lick.
lamia, *f.* 1. (ichth.) lamia, cub shark. 2. (myth.) fabulous monster with the face of a woman and the body of a dragon.
lamiáceo, a, *a.* (bot.) lamiaceous.
lamido, da, *past part. of* **lamer.** —*a.* 1. thin. 2. fastidiously clean, spruce, neat, spick and span; affected, dandified. 3. (rare) worn, wasted. 4. (p.) polished, finely finished (said of a painting).
lamilla, *f.* (Chile) seaweed used for fertilizer.
lámina, *f.* 1. lamina, thin plate or sheet. 2. engraved copper plate (for printing illustrations). 3. illustration, print (of a book). 4. painting on copper. 5. (bot., anat.) lamine. — **l. acuífera,** (geoph.) waterbearing stratum; **l. de ballesta,** (mec.) spring leaf; **l. estañada,** (metal.) tin plate.
laminable, *a.* laminable.
laminación, *f.* lamination.
laminado, da, *a.* laminated. — **l. en frío,** (metal.) cold-rolled. —*m.* 1. lamination. 2. (metal.) rolling (of metal).
laminador, ra, *a.* rolling. —*m.* 1. rolling press, rolling mill (for rolling metal into sheets). 2. rolling mill operator. — **l. de temple,** (metal.) temper mill; **l. de tiras,** (metal.) strip mill.
laminagrafía, *f.* (med.) laminagraphy.
laminar, *a.* laminar, laminate.
laminar, *tr.v.* 1. to laminate, plate. 2. to roll (metal) into sheets, laminate.
laminaria, *f.* (bot.) laminaria.
laminariáceo, a, *a.* (bot.) laminariaceous.
laminero, ra, *m., f.* 1. maker of metal plates. 2. maker of prints or illustrations. 3. engraver of copper plates. —*a.* fond of sweets. —*m., f.* sweet tooth.
laminilla, *f.* scale (rust), flake; **l. metálica,** metal foil.
laminita, *f.* shim, small plate.
laminitis, *f.* (vet.) laminitis.
laminoso, sa, *a.* laminate, laminar, laminose.
lamiscar, (*ref. 50*) *tr.v.* (coll.) to lick greedily, to lap.
lamisque, lamisqué, *ref.* **lamiscar.**
lamoso, sa, *a.* slimy, muddy.
lampa, *f.* (S. Amer.) shovel, spade; miner's pick.
lampacear, *tr.v.* (mar.) to swab, mop.
lampar, *i.v., r.v., var. of* **alampar.**
lámpara, *f.* 1. lamp. 2. light; luminous body. 3. (rad.) valve, tube. 4. oil spot, oil stain. — **l. de aceite,** oil lamp; **l. de acetileno,** acetylene lamp; **l. de bolsillo,** flashlight; **l. de cátodo frío,** (phys.) cold-cathode lamp; **l. de contraste** or **comparación,** comparison lamp; **l. de cuarzo,** quartz lamp; **l. de escritorio,** desk lamp; **l. de lectura,** reading lamp; **l. de mesa,** table lamp; **l. de mineros** or **de seguridad,** safety lamp; Davy lamp; **l. de radio,** valve, tube; **l. de soldar;** blowlamp; blowtorch; **l. de vapor de mercurio,** mercury-vapor lamp; **l. de vapor de sodio,** (elec.) sodium lamp; sodium-vapor lamp; **l. flash** or **de destello,** (photog.) flash bulb; **l. neón,** neon lamp, neon light; **l. proyectante,** searchlight, floodlight; **l. solar,** sun lamp; **l. testigo,** (elec.) pilot lamp or light; **l. votiva,** votive lamp.
lamparazo, *m.* (Col.) drink.
lamparería, *f.* lamp factory or shop.
lamparero, ra, *m., f.* lamp-maker or seller; lamp-lighter.
lamparilla, *f.* 1. small lamp; night light, small oil lamp. 2. (bot.) aspen (Populus tremula). 3. (coll.) a shot of brandy.
lamparín, *m.* lamp holder (in a church).
lamparista, *m., f., var. of* **lamparero.**
lámparo, ra, *a.* (Col.) broke (coll.), penniless.
lamparón, *m.* 1. large lamp. 2. grease spot (on clothes). 3. (med.) scrofula, king's evil. 4. (vet.) (*pl.*) glanders, farcy.
lampatán, *m.* (bot.) chinaroot.
lampazo, *m.* 1. (bot.) burdock. 2. (mar.) swab, mop. 3. (min.) broom made of fresh branches and used to dampen and cool the sides of a furnace.
lampear, *tr.v.* (Chile, Peru) to shovel, remove (earth) with a shovel.
lampeón, *m.* lamp, lantern.
lampero, *m.* (Chile, Peru) shoveler.
lampino, na, *a., var. of* **lampiño.**
lampiño, ña, *a.* beardless; hairless.
lampión, *m.* large lamp, lantern.
lampista, *m, f., var. of* **lamparero.**
lampistería, *f., var. of* **lamparería.**
lampo, *m.* (poet.) flash of light.
lampote, *m.* (Phil. I.) domestic cotton cloth.
lamprea, *f.* (ichth.) lamprey.
lampreada, *f.* (Guat.) whipping, flogging.
lampreado, *m.* (Chile) stew prepared with jerked beef.
lamprear, *tr.v.* to braise food in wine and herbs.
lampreazo, *m.* (coll.) lash, whiplash.
lamprehuela, *f.* (ichth.) small lamprey.
lampreílla, *f.* (ichth.) river lamprey.
lampróf ilo, *m.* (geol.) lamprophyre.
lámpsana, *f.* (bot.) nipplewort.
lampuga, *f.* (ichth.) yellow mackerel.
lampuso, sa, *a.* (Cuba, P. Rico) impudent, shameless.
lana, *f.* 1. wool, fleece. 2. wool, woolen fabric. 3. (coll.) money. —*m.* (C. Amer.) the riffraff, the rabble. — **l. de acero,** steel wool; **l. de caídas,** wool on sheep's legs; **l. de vidrio,** glass wool; **l. mineral,** mineral wool; **l. virgen,** virgin wool; **ir por l. y salir trasquilado,** to expect a bargain and come out the loser instead.
lanada, *f.* (artil.) sponge (cylindrical brush for cleaning gun barrels).
lanado, da, *a.* wooly, fleecy, lanate.
lanar, *a.* wool-bearing; **ganado l.,** sheep.
lanaria, *f.* (bot.) soapwort.
lancán, *m.* (Phil. I.) tugboat.
lancasteriano, na, *a.* Lancastrian, of or pertaining to Lancaster or Lancashire, England.

lance, *m.* 1. throw, cast. 2. casting (of a fishing net). 3. catch, haul (fish caught). 4. difficult moment; difficult situation, jam (coll.), squeeze (coll.). 5. incident, episode, event. 6. fight, quarrel. 7. move (in game). 8. missile-shot from a crossbow). 9. (taur.) pass (with a cape). — **a pocos lances,** in a very short time; **echar buen** or **mal l.,** to achieve or fail to achieve one's aims; **jugar el l.,** to handle a difficult situation; **l. apretado,** (coll.) jam, difficult situation; **l. de fortuna,** chance or unexpected event; **l. de honor,** challenge, duel; **de l.,** at a bargain price, cheap; **tener pocos lances,** to be a dull person.
lance, lancé, *ref.* **lanzar.**
lanceado, da, *a.* (bot.) lanceolate.
lancear, *tr.v., var. of* **alancear;** to wound with a lance.
lancéola, *f.* (bot) ribwort.
lanceolado, da, *a.* (bot.) lanceolate.
lancera, *f.* lance rack (in an armory).
lancería, *f.* lancers, troop of lancers.
lancero, *m.* 1. lancer, pikeman. 2. lance maker. 3. (*pl.*) lancers, lanciers (dance).
lanceta, *f.* 1. (surg.) lancet. 2. (vet.) fleam.
lancetada, *f.* lancing, opening or wounding with a lancet.
lancetazo, *m., var. of* **lancetada.**
lancetero, *m.* lancet case.
lancha, *f.* 1. (mar.) launch, cutter, sloop; long boat; barge, lighter. 2. partridge snare. 3. stone slab, flagstone. 4. (Ecuad.) frost. 5. (Ecuad.) fog, mist. — **l. automóvil,** motor launch; **l. cañonera,** gunboat; **l. de carga,** lighter, barge; **l. de desembarco,** landing craft; **l. neumática,** rubber dinghy; **l. de pesca,** fishing boat; **l. rapida** or **de carreras,** speedboat **l. de rescate,** rescue craft; **l. patrullera,** patrol launch; **l. de salvavidas** or **de socorro** or **de salvamento,** lifeboat; **l. torpedera,** torpedo boat.
lanchada, *f.* lighter load, barge load, boatload.
lanchaje, *m.* lighterage, ferriage, freight charge (on a lighter or barge).
lanchar, *m.* flagstone quarry.
lanchar, *i.v.* (Ecuad.) to freeze, become covered with frost.
lanchazo, *m.* blow with a flagstone.
lanchero, *m.* bargeman, boatman, lighterman; oarsman; captain or owner of a lighter or barge.
lanchón, *m.* launch, lighter, barge, scow.
lanchonero, *m.* lighterman, bargeman.
lanchuela, *f.* small flagstone.
lancinante, *a.* stabbing, piercing (pain).
lancinar, *tr.v.* to stab, pierce, prick, lance.
lanco, *m.* (bot.) bromegrass (Bromus uniclodus).
lancurdia, *f.* small trout.
landa, *f.* barren moorland; wasteland; pasture.
landgrave, *m.* landgrave (title in German nobility).
landgraviato, *m.* landgraviate; pertaining to a landgrave.
landó, (*pl.* **landóes**), *m.* landau, carriage with a folding top.
landre, *f.* 1. (med.) bubo, small tumor (forming on the neck, under the armpits and in the groin). 2. hidden pocket (used to hide money).
landrecilla, *f.* small round piece of flesh (found in various parts of the body).
landrero, ra, *a.* niggardly; said of a person who hoards money in a concealed pocket.
landrilla, *f.* (zool.) tongue worm; swelling raised by a tongue worm bite.
lanería, *f.* shop where wool and woolen fabrics are sold.
lanero, ra, *a.* of or pertaining to wool. —*m.* 1. wool merchant. 2. wool warehouse.
langa, *f.* small dried codfish.
lángara, *a.* (Mex.) astute, cunning.
lángaro, ra, *a.* 1. (Mex.) hungry. 2. (C. Amer.) wandering, vagrant. 3. (C. Rica) lanky, tall.
langarucho, cha, *a.* (Amer.) lanky, tall and thin (person).
langaruto, ta, *a., var. of* **langarucho.**
langbeinita, *f.* (min.) langbeinite.
langor, *m.* (Gal.) languor.
langoroso, sa, *a.* (Gal.) languorous.
langosta, *f.* 1. (ento.) locust. 2. (ichth.) lobster.
langostero, ra, *m., f.* lobster fisherman. —*a.* pertaining to lobster fishing.
langostín, *m., var. of* **langostino.**
langostino, *m.* prawn, crawfish.
langostón, *m.* (ento.) green grasshopper.
languedociano, na, *a.* Languedocian, pertaining to the French region of Languedoc or to the dialects thereof (e.g. the Provencal).
lánguidamente, *adv.* languidly.
languidecer, (*ref. 45*) *i.v.* to languish.
languidez, *f.* languor, languidness, languishment, lassitude; faintness.
languidezca, languidezco, *ref.* **languidecer.**
lánguido, da, *a.* languid, languorous; listless; heartless, faint.
languor, *m., var. of* **languidez.**
languso, sa, *a.* 1. (Mex.) astute, cunning, sly. 2. (Mex., coll.) tall and thin, lanky.
lanicio, cia, *a.* pertaining to wool, woolen.
lanífero, ra, *a.* woolly, fleecy, laniferous.
lanificación, *f., var. of* **lanificio.**
lanificio, *m.* wool manufacturing; woolen goods.
lanilla, *f.* 1. nap (of cloth). 2. fine flannel, swanskin. 3. (arch.) kind of make-up, cosmetic. 4. (mar.) bunting.
lanío, a, *a., var. of* **lanar.**
lanolina, *f.* (chem.) lanolin.
lanosidad, *f.* (bot.) down, pubescence (on leaves, stalks, etc.).
lanoso, sa, *a.* woolly, fleecy.
lansquenete, *m.* (hist.) lansquenet (mercenary German infantryman during the 15th-17th centuries).
lantaca, *f.* (Phil. I.) lantaca, lantaka (a small culverin).
lantana, *f.* (bot.) wayfaring tree (Viburnum lantanan).
lantanido, *m.* (chem.) lanthanide.
lantano, *m.* (chem.) lanthanum.
lantén, *m.* (Mex.), *var. of* **llantén,** medicinal herb, rib grass.
lantia, *f.* (mar.) binnacle lamp; boom guy.
lanudo, da, *a.* 1. woolly, fleecy. 2. (Ven.) coarse, uncouth, rude.
lanuginoso, sa, *a.* lanuginous, downy, covered with down.
lanza, *f.* 1. lance, spear, pike. 2. lance, lancer, pikeman. 3. shaft, thill (of a carriage). 4. nozzle (of a hose). 5. (*pl.*) tax paid by nobility instead of furnishing troops. — **correr lanzas,** to joust; **con la l. en ristre,** ready for action; **no romper lanzas con nadie,** to be a peaceful person; **quebrar lanzas,** to cross swords, quarrel; **romper lanzas por,** to intercede for; **ser una l.,** to be an expert, be a wizard.
lanzabombas, *m.* 1. (mil.) trench mortar. 2. (aer.) bomb release.
lanzacabos, *a.* (mar.) rope-throwing (said of a small cannon that throws a rope to help the shipwrecked).
lanzacohetes, *m.* rocket launcher.
lanzada, *f.* thrust or wound made with a lance or a spear.
lanzadera, *f.* shuttle (of a sewing machine or hand-operated loom). — **parecer una l.,** to bustle about.
lanzado, da, *past part. of* **lanzar.** —*a.* (mar.) raking, inclined.
lanzador, ra, *a.* throwing, thrusting, hurling. —*m., f.* thrower, hurler, pitcher (in baseball). — **l. de electrones,** electron gun; **l. del disco,** discus thrower.
lanzafuego, *m.* (artil.) linstock, matchstaff.
lanzagranadas, *m.* mortar, grenade launcher.
lanzallamas, *m.* (mil.) flamethrower.
lanzamiento, *m.* 1. throwing, hurling, casting. 2. launching (of a rocket, attack, new product). 3. (law) dispossession. 4. (mar.) steeve, steeving. — **l. de abastecimientos,** (mil.) airdrop (of supplies); **l. de bala,** shot put, putting the shot or weight; **l. de jabalina,** javelin throwing; **l. del disco,** throwing the discus.
lanzaminas, *m.* mine thrower, mine-laying boat.
lanzar, (*ref. 53*) *tr.v.* 1. to throw, hurl, fling, cast; to throw (the discus). 2. to fire, shoot (an arrow). 3. to shoot, cast (a glance). 4. to let loose (a curse). 5. to launch (a rocket, attack, new industrial product). 6. (law) to dispossess. —*r.v.* 1. to throw, hurl or fling oneself, jump; to dash, rush. 2. to embark on, to launch into, engage in. 3. (coll.) to take the plunge. — **lanzarse a,** (Amer.) to begin to; to break into, e.g. *se lanzó a correr,* he broke into a run; **lanzarse al agua de cabeza,** to plunge in headfirst.
Lanzarote, *m.* Lancelot.
lanzatorpedos, *a.* (mar.) torpedo-launching. —*m.* (mar.) torpedo tube.
lanzazo, *m., var. of* **lanzada.**
lanzón, *m. aug. of* **lanza,** short, thick spear or pike.
lanzuela, *f. dim. of* **lanza,** small lance or spear.
laña, *f.* 1. clamp, cramp iron. 2. (bot.) green coconut.
lañador, *m.* clamper, one who repairs by fastening with clamps.
lañar, *tr.v.* 1. to clamp, fasten with clamps or cramps. 2. to clean (fish).
Laoconte, *m.* (myth.) Laocoon, Apollo's priest in Troy, crushed with his two sons by two giant snakes.
laodicense, *a., m., f.* Laodicean, (fig.) said of a person who is lukewarm or indifferent to religion.
Laos, *m.* Laos.
laosiano, na, *a., m., f.* Laotian, of or pertaining to Laos.
laotiano, a, *a., m., f.* Laotian, Lao. —*m.* Laotian (language).
lapa, *f.* 1. scum (vegetable film forming on surface of some liquids). 2. (zool.) limpet; barnacle. 3. (bot.) burdock. — **prenderse como una l.,** to stick like a leech.
lapachar, *m.* swampy land, swamp, marsh, morass.
lapacho, *m.* (bot.) lapacho, American timber tree.
lápade, *f.* (zool.) limpet, lepalid, barnacle.
lapalapa, *f.* (Mex.) drizzle, light rain.
laparotomía, *f.* (surg.) laparotomy.
La Paz, *f.* La Paz; capital of Bolivia.
lapice, lapicé, *ref.* **lapizar.**
lapicero, *m.* pencil holder; mechanical penholder.
lápida, *f.* tablet, slab (of stone), gravestone.
lapidación, *f.* 1. stoning to death, lapidation. 2. (Amer.) stonework, stone carving.
lapidar, *tr.v.* 1. to stone to death, to kill by stoning, to lapidate. 2. (Amer.) to work, carve (precious stones).
lapidario, ria, *a.* lapidary. —*m.* 1. lapidary (person who cuts, engraves and polishes precious stones). 2. dealer in precious stones.
lapídeo, dea, *a.* lapidary, pertaining to a stone.
lapidificación, *f.* (chem.) lapidification, petrification, turning into stone.

lapidificar, (*ref. 50*) *tr.v., r.v.* (chem.) to lapidify, petrify, turn into stone.
lapidífico, ca, *a.* (chem.) lapidifying, lapidific.
lapidifique, lapidifiqué, *ref.* **lapidificar.**
lapidoso, sa, *a.* lapidary, pertaining to a stone.
lapilla, *f.* (bot.) hound's tongue.
lapilli, *m.* (*pl.*) (geol.) lapilli.
lapislázuli, *m.* (min.) lapis lazuli.
lapita, *m.* (myth.) Lapith, (*pl.*) Lapithae, a mythical people of Thessaly who fought the centaurs.
lápiz, (*pl* **lápices**), *m.* 1. pencil; crayon. 2. (min.) black lead, graphite. — **l. de cejas** eyebrow pencil; **l. de color,** colored pencil; crayon; **l. de labios,** lipstick; **l. de ojos,** eye pencil; **l. de plomo,** lead pencil; **l. fotosensible** or **óptico,** light pen; **l. negro,** blue pencil (used to censure).
lapizar, (*ref. 53*) *tr.v.* to pencil, draw with a pencil. —*m.* black-lead mine.
lapo, *m.* 1. blow (with a belt or stick), slap (with the hand). 2. (Amer.) drink, swig.
lapón, na, *a.* Laplandian, Lappic, Lappish. —*m., f.* Laplander, Lapp. —*m.* Lapp, Lappish (language).
Laponia, *f.* Lapland.
lapso, *m.* 1. lapse, passing of time. 2. falling into sin or error, slip.
lapsus, *m.* (Lat.) lapsus, slip, error. — **l. cálami,** slip of the pen; **l. linguae,** slip of the tongue.
laqueado, da, *past part. of* **laquear.** —*a.* lacquered. —*m.* lacquering.
laquear, *tr.v.* to lacquer.
Laquedivas, *f.* (*pl.*) Laccadive Islands, islands off the Malabar coast.
laques, *f., var. of* **boleadoras,** lariat.
Láquesis, *f.* (myth.) Lachesis, one of the three Fates.
lar, *m.* Lar, god of the home and households; (fig.) home, homestead.
larario, *m.* altar or shrine for the lares or household gods.
lardáceo, a, *a.* fatty (said of meats).
lardar, *tr.v., var. of* **lardear.**
lardear, *tr.v.* (cul.) to baste, lard.
lardero, *a.* **jueves l.,** Thursday before Lent.
lardo, *m.* lard, fatty part of bacon.
lardón, *m.* 1. (print.) blank space left on a printed page. 2. (print.) insert, addition to be inserted.
lardoso, sa, *a.* greasy, fatty, smearing.
lares, *m.* (*pl.*) 1. home. 2. lares (Roman household gods). 3. (Sp.) home, homestead.
larga, *f.* 1. piece of leather added to a last to make it longer. 2. longest billiard cue. — **dar largas a,** to delay, postpone.
largamente, *adv.* 1. comfortably. 2. liberally. 3. at length, for a long time. — **hablar l.,** to speak frankly and completely; **vivir l.,** to live comfortably.
largar, (*ref. 51*) *tr.v.* 1. to release, let go. 2. to slacken or ease out (e.g. a cable). 3. to utter, let out (a curse). 4. (mar.) to unfurl. 5. (Amer.) to give, let go, strike (a blow). 6. to dismiss, fire (from a job); to throw out (of a house, meeting, etc.); to drive away. —*r.v.* 1. (coll.) to leave, go away; to make off, sneak away, scram (coll.), hop it (G.B.), beat it (coll.). 2. (mar.) to set out to sea. 3. (Amer.) to begin to, break into, e.g. *se largó a correr,* he broke into a run.
largo, ga, *a.* 1. long. 2. generous, liberal. 3. abundant, copious. 4. quick, fast, efficient. 5. (coll.) shrewd, cunning. 6. (*pl.*) many, e.g. *largos años,* many years. 7. (mar.) loose, slack. — **a la larga,** in the long run, in the end; **a lo largo,** lengthwise; at a great distance, far away; **a lo largo de,** along; throughout, throughout the course of; **a lo largo y a lo ancho de,** all over, throughout; **de largo,** in long robes, in long or formal dress; in long skirt and full length stockings (said of a young girl beginning to dress more maturely); **echado de largo a largo,** stretched to its or his full length; **¡largo!** or **¡largo de aquí!** get out of here! beat it! (coll.), scram! (coll.); **largo de uñas,** (coll.) light-fingered, thievish; **largo y tendido,** (coll.) extensively, at length.
largo, *m.* 1. length. 2. (mus.) largo, slow and stately. — **de l.,** in length; **tener . . . de l.,** to be . . . long, be . . . in length. —*adv.* abundantly.
largometraje, *m.* feature, full-length movie.
largomira, *m.* telescope.
largona, *f.* (Chile, Peru) delay, postponement.
largor, *m.* length, longitude.
largucho, cha, *a.* (coll.) longish.
largue, largué, *ref.* **largar.**
largueado, da, *a.* striped.
larguero, *m.* 1. (carp.) stringer, longitudinal beam; jamb-post. 2. bolster, long narrow cushion. 3. (aer.) longeron; nose spar, boom.
largueza, *f.* 1. length; extent. 2. liberality, generosity, munificence, largesse.
larguirucho, cha, *a.* (coll.) lanky, tall and thin.
larguito, ta, *a.* somewhat long, longish.
largura, *f.* length, stretch, extent.
lárice, *m.* (bot.) larch tree.
laricino, na, *a.* pertaining to the larch tree.
larije, *a., var. of* **alarije.**
laringe, *f.* (anat.) larynx.
laríngeo, a, *a.* (anat.) laryngeal.
laringitis, *f.* (med.) laryngitis.
laringófono, *m.* (med.) laryngophone, throat microphone.
laringología, *f.* (med.) laryngology.
laringológico, ca, *a.* (med.) laryngological.
laringólogo, *m.* (med.) laryngologist, specialist in laryngeal illnesses.
laringoscopia, *f.* (med.) laryngoscopy, examination of larynx.
laringoscópico, ca, *a.* laryngoscopic, laryngoscopical.
laringoscopio, *m.* (med.) laryngoscope, instrument for examining the larynx.
laringoscopista, *m.* (med.) laryngoscopist.
laringotomía, *f.* (surg.) laryngotomy.
laringótomo, *m.* (surg.) laryngotome.
larva, *f.* 1. (zool.) larva. 2. (biochem.) (*pl.*) larvae.
larvado, da, *a.* (med.) larvate, larval (said of an illness in which the true nature of the symptoms is hidden).
larval, *a.* larval.
larvicida, *a.* larvicidal. —*m.* (biochem.) larvicide.
las, *pl. f. def. art.* the. —*pl. f. pers. pron.* them.
lasaña, *f.* 1. (cul.) leaf-shaped fritter. 2. (cul.) lasagna (Italian pasta dish).
lasca, *f.* chip of stone; (fig.) chip or thin slice, e.g. *una lasca de jamón,* a thin slice of ham.
lascadura, *f.* (Mex.) graze, bruise.
lascar, (*ref. 50*) *tr.v.* 1. (mar.) to pay out, loosen slowly. 2. (Mex.) to bruise, graze.
lascivamente, *adv.* lasciviously, lustfully.
lascivia, *f.* lasciviousness, lewdness.
lascivo, va, *a.* 1. lascivious, lustful. 2. merry, playful, gay, frisky.
láser *m.* (electron.) laser.
laserpicio, *m.* (bot.) laserwort.
lasitud, *f.* lassitude, weariness, languor, faintness.
laso, sa, *a.* 1. weary, sluggish, tired, lifeless, weak, languid. 2. untwisted (thread).
lasque, lasqué, *ref.* **lascar.**
lastar, *tr.v.* 1. to pay (money) for someone else. 2. (fig.) to suffer, pay (for another's fault).
lástima, *f.* 1. pity, compassion. 2. plaint, lamentation. — **dar l.,** to inspire pity; **¡que l.!** what a shame!; **tener l. de,** to feel sorry for, be moved to compassion by.
lastimador, ra, *a.* hurtful, injurious.
lastimadura, *f.* injury, wound, bruise; graze, sore.
lastimar, *tr.v.* 1. to injure, hurt; to chafe, graze; to bruise. 2. to upset, make sad or sorry. 3. to hurt, offend. —*r.v.* to be injured; to be grazed, chafed or bruised; to hurt or injure oneself. — **lastimarse de,** to feel sorry for or about; to be upset at or by.
lastimeramente, *adv.* pitifully, piteously, sadly, sorrowfully.
lastimero, ra, *a.* pitiful, piteous, sad, doleful.
lastimosamente, *adv.* pitifully, sadly.
lastimoso, sa, *a.* pitiful, piteous, doleful, sad.
lasto, *m.* receipt (given to a person who pays for someone else).
lastón, *m.* (bot.) fescue grass (Festuca granatensis).
lastra, *f.* flagstone, slab.
lastrar, *tr.v.* 1. (mar., aer.) to ballast (a ship). 2. to weight down. 3. to surface with gravel.
lastre, *m.* 1. rubble, broken uneven rocks (not acceptable for masonry and used in rubblework). 2. (mar., aer.) ballast. 3. (fig.) judgment, judiciousness, sense, maturity.
lastrón, *m. aug. of* **lastre,** rubble, broken uneven rocks (used in rubblework).
lasún, *m.* (ichth.), *var. of* **locha.**
lata, *f.* 1. length of timber. 2. (Ven.) cane, stick. 3. tin, tin plate; tin can. 4. roof lath (to which tiles are attached).
lata, *f.* (coll.) bore, annoyance, nuisance, boring person or thing; long boring speech or conversation. — **dar la l.,** to annoy, irritate; to bore; **¡qué l.!** what a bore!
latamente, *adv.* at great length; broadly, amply.
latania, *f.* (bot.) Chinese fan palm (Latania).
latastro, *m.* (archit.) plinth.
lataz, (*pl.* **lataces**), *m.* (zool.) sea otter.
latear, *tr.v.* (S. Amer.) to bore, to talk too much, bend someone's ear (coll.).
latebra, *f.* cave, den, hiding place.
latebroso, sa, *a.* furtive, secretive.
latencia, *f.* (med.) latency.
latente, *a.* 1. latent, hidden, present but unseen. 2. concealed, dormant. — **calor l.,** latent heat.
lateral, *a.* lateral, side (as *a.*). —*m.* throw-in (in soccer).
lateralmente, *adv.* laterally, sideways.
lateranense, *a.* Lateran, pertaining to the Pope's cathedral as bishop of Rome.
latería, *f.* 1. preserves, cans of preserves. 2. (Amer.) tinsmith's shop.
laterita, *f.* (geol.) laterite.
laterización, *f.* (geol.) laterization.
latero, ra, *a.* boring; vexing (said only of a person). —*m.* (Amer.) tinsmith.
latescente, *a.* (bot.) latescent.
látex, *m.* (bot.) latex.
laticífero, *a.* (bot.) laticiferous, containing or secreting latex.
latido, *past part. of* **latir.** —*m.* 1. beat, beating, throb, throbbing. 2. palpitation, pant. 3. short bark, intermittent yelp.
latiente, *a.* beating, throbbing, palpitating.
latifolio, a, *a.* (bot.) latifoliate.
latifundio, *m.* latifundium, large landed estate.
latifundista, *m., f.* owner of a latifundium or large estate.
latigadera, *f.* strap or thong for lashing the yoke.
latigazo, *m.* 1. lash, whiplash. 2. crack (of a whip). 3. lashing, reprimand. 4. (coll.) drink.
látigo, *m.* 1. whip, horsewhip. 2. lashing cord; cord used to tie an object to be weighed; cinch strap. 3. (Chile) finish (in horse races). 4. (Ecuad., Hond.) lash, whiplash. 5. (ichth.) ribbonfish. — **l. de montar,** riding crop.

latigudo, da, *a.* (Chile) flexible, pliable, pliant.
latigueada, *f.* (Hond.) flogging, whipping.
latiguear, *i.v.* to crack the whip. —*tr.v.* (Amer.) to flog, whip.
latigueo, *m.* the act of cracking a whip.
latiguera, *f.* 1. whip, strap, cord. 2. (Peru) flogging, whipping.
latiguero, *m.* person who makes or sells whips.
latiguillo, *m.* 1. *dim. of* **látigo,** small whip. 2. (bot.) stolon, runner, shoot. 3. (theat.) claptrap, hamming (exaggeration of action or emotion to gain applause).
latín, *m.* Latin (language); Latin word or phrase. — **bajo l.,** Low Latin; **decirle** or **echarle a alguien los latines,** to marry, administer the marriage sacrament to someone; **l. clásico,** Classical Latin, **l. rústico** or **vulgar,** Vulgar Latin; **saber l.** or **mucho l.,** to be very astute; **ese toro habla l.,** (taur.) that's a bull to reckon with.
latinajo, *m.* (coll.) dog Latin, bad Latin; (coll.) Latin word or quotation.
latinamente, *adv.* in Latin; in a Latin way.
latinear, *i.v.* (coll.) to use Latin words and phrases in common conversation.
latinice, latinicé, *ref.* **latinizar.**
latinidad, *f.* Latin (language). — **baja l.,** Low Latin.
latiniparla, *f.* Latinized speech.
latinismo, *m.* Latinism, Latin word or syntax; use of Latin words or syntax.
latinista, *m., f.* Latinist, Latin scholar.
latinización, *f.* Latinization.
latinizador, ra, *a.* Latinizing.
latinizante, *a.* Latinizing.
latinizar, (*ref.* 53) *tr.v.* to Latinize. —*i.v.* (coll.) to use Latin words and phrases.
latino, na, *a.* 1. Latin. 2. (mar.) lateen. —*m., f.* Latin.
Latinoamérica, *f.* Latin America.
latinoamericano, na, *a.* Latin American. —*m., f.* Latin American.
latir, *i.v.* to beat, throb, pulsate, palpitate. —*tr.v.* (Ven.) to annoy, bother, irritate.
latita, *f.* (geol.) latite.
latitud, *f.* 1. (astron., geog.) latitude. 2. (fig.) latitude, freedom; scope. 3. latitude, climate. 4. extent, width, size. — **l. geográfica,** geographical latitude, geodetic latitude.
latitudinal, *a.* latitudinal.
latitudinario, ria, *a., m., f.* (theol.) latitudinarian.
latitudinarismo, *m.* (theol.) latitudinarianism.
lato, ta, *a.* 1. extensive, lengthy, long. 2. broad (sense of a word).
latón, *m.* 1. brass. 2. (Bol., Col.) cutlass, sword. — **l. de aluminio,** aluminum brass; **l. cobrizo,** (metal.) red brass; **l. en hojas** or **planchas,** latten brass, sheet brass.
latonado, *a.* brass-plated.
latonería, *f.* brass factory, brass shop.
latonero, *m.* brazier, brassworker, worker in brass.
latoso, sa, *a.* annoying, boring, irritating, vexing, tiresome.
latría, *f.* (theol.) latria, worship due to God only.
latrocinio, *m.* robbery, thievery.
latvio, via, *a., m., f.* Latvian.
lauca, *f.* (Chile) baldness.
laucadura, *f.* (Chile), *var. of* **lauca.**
laucar, (*ref.* 50) *tr.v.* (Chile) to cut the hair of, shear.
laucha, *f.* (Arg., Chile) mouse. —*m.* 1. (Arg., Urug.) clever fellow. 2. (Chile) lanky boy. — **aguaitar uno la l.,** (Chile) to wait for one's chance.
lauco, ca, *a.* (Chile) bald, hairless.
laúd, *m.* 1. (mus.) lute. 2. (mar.) small lateener, small lateen-rigged vessel, cat-boat. 3. (zool.) leatherback, striped turtle.
laudable, *a.* laudable, praiseworthy.
laudablemente, *adv.* laudably.
láudano, *m.* (pharm.) laudanum.
laudar, *tr.v.* to give a decision on.
laudatorio, ria, *a.* laudatory, laudative, full of praise. —*m., f.* eulogy, panegyric.
laude, *f.* tombstone.
laudemio, *m.* dues paid to the lord of the manor on all transfers of his landed property held in emphyteusis.
laudes, *f.* (*pl.*) (ecc.) lauds (religious service).
laudo, *m.* (law) decision, award, finding; arbitration.
launa, *f.* 1. metal sheet. 2. impermeable clay (used to cover roofs).
lauráceo, a, *a.* (bot.) lauraceous. —*f.* (*pl.*) Lauraceae.
láurea, *f.* laurel wreath.
laureado, da, *a.* laureate, laureled. — **poeta laureado,** poet laureate.
laureando, *m.* graduate, person receiving an academic degree.
laurear, *tr.v.* to crown with laurels; (fig.) to honor, reward, decorate; to confer a degree on.
lauredal, *m.* laurel grove or thicket.
laurel, *m.* (bot.) laurel; (fig.) (*pl.*) laurels (honor, reward). — **dormirse en sus laureles,** to rest on one's laurels; **l. alejandrino,** (bot.), ornamental evergreen shrub (Ruscus hypophyllum); **l. cerezo** or **l. real,** (bot.) cherry laurel; **l. rosa,** (bot.) oleander.
laurente, *m.* workman in charge of the paper molds in a paper mill.
laurentino, na, *a., m., f.* (geol.) Laurentian.
láureo, a, *a.* laurel (as *a.*).
lauréola, *f.* 1. laurel crown, laurel wreath. 2. (bot.) spurge laurel (Daphne laureola). 3. halo, aureola; **l. hembra,** (bot.) mezereon; **l. macho,** (bot.) spurge laurel (Daphne laureola).
láurico, ca, *a.* (chem.) lauric.
laurífero, ra, *a.* (poet.) lauriferous, laurel-bearing.
lauríneo, nea, *a.* (bot.) lauraceous. —*f.* (bot.) lauraceous plant.
laurino, na, *a.* laurel (as *a.*).
lauro, *m.* 1. (bot.) laurel. 2. (fig.) laurels, glory, fame, honors.
lauroceraso, *m.* (bot.) cherry laurel.
laus deo, (Lat.) praise be to God.
lautamente, *adv.* splendidly, sumptuously.
lava, *f.* 1. lava, volcanic rock. 2. (min.) washing (of minerals).
lavable, *a.* washable.
lavabo, *m.* 1. washstand, lavabo, washbasin. 2. washroom, lavatory, bathroom.
lavacaras, (*pl.* **lavacaras**), *m., f.* (coll.) fawner, flatterer, bootlicker.
lavación, *f.* (pharm.) lotion, wash.
lavada, *f.* 1. washing; wash. 2. (p.) wash. 3. (Chile) washing (of minerals).
lavadero, *m.* 1. washing place (e.g. alongside a river); laundry; washroom, bathroom; sink, washbasin. 2. (min.) washery (where ore is washed); (min.) buddle (washing trough for ore); (Amer.) placer (place or river bank where gold is obtained by washing gold-bearing deposits).
lavadientes, *m.* (rare) mouth rinse.
lavado, *past part. of* **lavar.** —*m.* 1. washing, wash, cleaning; cleansing. 2. wash, laundry. 3. (p.) wash, watercolor in a single tint. — **l. automático,** carwash; **l. de cerebro,** brain washing; **l. en seco,** dry cleaning.
lavador, ra, *a.* washing. —*m.* 1. (photog.) washer (for washing photographic plates). 2. burnisher (for cleaning fire arms). 3. (Guat.) washstand, washbasin. —*f.* washing machine; **lavadora de platos** or **de vajilla,** dishwasher.
lavadura, *f.* 1. wash, washing. 2. dirty water (left from washing), slops. 3. dressing for glove-leather.
lavafrutas, *m.* fruit-washing bowl.
lavaje, *m.* 1. washing (of wool). 2. (med.) lavage.
lavajo, *m.* 1. rain puddle; morass. 2. watering ditch or pond for cattle.
lavamanos, *m.* washstand, washbasin, lavatory.
lavamiento, *m.* 1. washing, cleaning, wash. 2. (med.) clyster, enema.
lavanco, *m.* a species of wild duck.
lavanda, *f.* 1. (bot.) lavender. 2. lavender (water).
lavandería, *f.* (Amer.) laundry.
lavandero, ra, *m.* launderer, laundryman. —*f.* launderess, laundrywoman, washerwoman.
lavándula, *f.* (bot.) lavender.
lavaojos, *m.* eyecup.
lavaplatos, (*pl.* **lavaplatos**), *m., f.* dishwasher (person). —*m.* sink, kitchen sink; dishwasher (machine).
lavar, *tr.v.* 1. to wash; to cleanse, purify. 2. (bldg., min., p., fig.) to wash. 3. (mas.) to whitewash, calcimine. 4. (p.) to paint in water colors. —*r.v.* to wash; to wash oneself; to wash one's (hands, face, etc.); **lavarse las manos de,** to wash one's hands of; **la ropa sucia se lava en casa,** dirty linen should not be washed in public.
lavarropas, *m.* washing machine; **l. automático,** automatic washing machine.
lavasecadora, *f.* washer dryer.
lavativa, *f.* 1. enema (liquid and syringe), clyster. 2. nuisance, annoyance, bother, bore.
lavatorio, *m.* 1. washing, wash. 2. (rel.) maundy (ceremony of washing the feet of the poor on Maundy Thursday). 3. (ecc.) lavatory (ritual washing of hands by celebrant of the Eucharist). 4. (med.) lotion, wash. 5. washbasin, sink.
lavavajillas, *m.* 1. dishwasher detergent. 2. dishwasher.
lavazas, *f.* (*pl.*) dirty water, washing water, slops. 2. soapsuds.
lave, *m.* (min.) washing (of metals).
lavotear, *tr.v., r.v.* to wash hurriedly and insufficiently.
lavoteo, *m.* hurried wash or washing.
laxación, *f.* laxation, easing, loosening, slackening.
laxamiento, *m.* 1. laxness, slackness. 2. loosening, slackening.
laxante, *a.* loosening, laxative. —*m.* (med.) laxative.
laxar, *tr.v.* to loosen, slacken; to loosen (the bowels). —*r.v.* to loosen, slacken.
laxativo, va, *a.* laxative, loosening. —*m.* laxative.
laxidad, *f., var. of* **laxitud.**
laxismo, *m.* a system based on lax morals.
laxista, *m., f.* one who tolerates lax conduct or morals.
laxitud, *f.* laxity, laxness, slackness.
laxo, xa, *a.* lax, slack; loose in morals.
lay, *m.* (poet.) lay (narrative poem); short song or ballad in Provençal or French.
laya, *f.* 1. spade, spud. 2. kind, nature, type, class, (fig.) breed, e.g. *eso es de otra laya,* that's a horse of a different color.
layador, ra, *m., f.* spader, spademan, one who digs with a spade.
layar, *tr.v.* (agr.) to dig with a spade or spud.
lazada, *f.* 1. bowknot; bow, knot (as a decoration); truelove knot. 2. lasso.
lazador, *m.* lassoer.
lazar, (*ref.* 53) *tr.v.* to lasso, capture with a lasso; to tie with a bow.

lazareto, *m.* lazaretto, leper's hospital; quarantine station (for travellers with contagious diseases); (Chile) smallpox hospital.
lazarillo, *m.* blindman's guide.
lazarino, na, *a.* leprous. —*m., f.* leper.
lazarista, *m.* Lazarist, Lazarite, (member of the hospital order of St. Lazarus).
lázaro, *m.* 1. ragged beggar. 2. **L., Lazarus.** 3. (Ven., Ecuad.) leper. — **estar hecho un l.,** to be covered with sores.
lazaroso, sa, *a.* leprous. —*m., f.* leper.
lazo, *m.* 1. bow; knot; loop. 2. lasso, lariat. 3. cord, rope, lashing rope. 4. tie, bond, connection. 5. snare, trap. 6. figure (in dancing). 7. knot, topiary design (ornamental design made with plants or flowers). 8. truelove knot. 9. (archit.) knot (design on frieze, molding, etc.). 10. beating or driving game within crossbow shot. — **armar l. a,** to set a trap for; **l. corredizo,** slipknot; **l. de matrimonio,** marriage bond.
lazulita, *f.* (min.) lazulite; lapis lazuli.
lb. *abbrev. of* **libra,** pound (lb.).
le, *pers. pron.* 1. (as direct object) him, e.g. *le vi en el parque,* I saw him in the park; you (when addressing a man in the **Ud.** form), e.g. *no le vi a Ud. en el teatro, I did not see you at the theater.* 2. *(as indirect object) him, to him, her, to her, it, to it, you, to you (when addressing a man or woman in the* **Ud.** form), e.g. *le di el libro,* I gave him, her or you the book or I gave the book to him, to her or to you; him, for him, her, for her, it, for it, you, for you, e.g. *le compré un disco,* I bought him, her or you a record or I bought a record for him, her or you; from him, from her, from it, from you, *le quitaron todos sus bienes,* they took all his (her, your) property away from him (her, you).
lea, *f.* (coll., Car.) woman, girl, chick (sl.).
leal, *a.* 1. loyal, faithful. 2. fair, true, e.g. *según mi l. entender,* to the best of my knowledge.
lealmente, *adv.* loyally, faithfully.
lealtad, *f.* loyalty, faithfulness, fidelity.
lebeche, *m.* levanter, southeastern sea wind on the Mediterranean Spanish coast.
lebení, *m.* leban, lebban, Arab drink made with sour milk.
leberquisa, *f.* (min.) magnetic pyrites.
lebrada, *f.* (cul.) fricassee of hare.
lebrancho, *m.* (Cuba, ichth.) striped mullet.
lebrastón, *m., var. of* **lebrato.**
lebratón, *m., var. of* **lebrato.**
lebrato, *m.* leveret, young hare.
lebrel, la, *m., f.* whippet, greyhound.
lebrero, ra, *a.* hare-hunting. —*m.* harrier, hare-hunting dog.
lebrillo, *m.* basin, washbasin; large bowl, deep pan.
lebrón, *m.* 1. *aug. of* **liebre,** large hare. 2. (coll.) coward, mouse. 3. (Mex.) braggart, bully.
lebroncillo, *m.* leveret, young hare.
lebruno, na, *a.* leporine, pertaining to hares, hare-like.
lecanomancia, *f.* lecanomancy, divination or fortune-telling by the sound of stones dropped into a bowl.
lección, *f.* 1. lesson. 2. lesson, chapter (of a school book). 3. lesson, warning, example. 4. reading, lection (interpretation of a text). 5. (ecc.) lection, lesson (extract of scriptures read at the divine service). 6. lecture. 7. reading (action). — **dar a alguien una l.,** to teach someone a lesson; **dar la l.,** to repeat the lesson (pupil to teacher); to give the lesson (teacher to pupil); **dar l.,** to give a lesson, teach; **que te sirva eso de l.,** let this be a lesson or warning to you; **tomar lecciones,** to take lessons.
leccionario, *m.* (ecc.) lectionary, book or list of lections.
leccioncita, *f. dim. of* **lección,** short lecture or lesson; (fig.) brief scolding.
leccionista, *m., f.* private tutor, coach.
lecha, *f.* (zool.) milt (seminal fluid and sac of fish).
lechada, *f.* 1. (bldg.) grout, thin mortar or plaster. 2. whitewash. 3. pulp (of rags for making paper). 4. emulsion. — **l. de cal,** milk of lime.
lechal, *a.* 1. sucking, unweaned (animal). 2. (bot.) lactiferous, milky, having milk. —*m.* milk, milky juice (in plants).
lechar, *a.* 1. sucking, unweaned (animal), nursing. 2. milky (plant). 3. milch (as *a.*), giving milk, e.g. *vaca l.,* milch cow, milk cow.
lechaza, *f., var. of* **lecha.**
lechazo, *m.* suckling lamb, young lamb.
leche, *f.* 1. milk. 2. (Amer., coll.) luck, good luck, e.g. *¡qué tal l.!* what luck! 3. (vulg.) semen. — **diente de l.,** first tooth; **estar con la l. en los labios,** (coll.) to be wet behind the ears, be inexperienced, be fresh out of college; **estar en l.,** to be unripe, be green (fruit); to be calm, be like a lake (the sea); **l. chocolatada,** chocolate milk; **l. condensada,** condensed milk; **l. de gallina,** (bot.) star of Bethlehem; **l. de los viejos,** (coll.) wine; **l. de magnesia,** milk of magnesia; **l. desnatada,** skim milk; **l. en polvo,** powdered milk; **l. entero,** whole milk; **l. evaporada,** evaporated milk; **l. homogeneizada,** homogenized milk; **l. pasteurizada,** pasteurized milk; **oler a l.,** see estar con la **l. en los labios; mamar una cosa en la l.,** (coll.) to know from birth, learn in childhood; **pedir l. a las cabrillas,** (coll.) to ask for the impossible; **vaca de l.,** milch cow.
lechecillas, *f. (pl.)* sweetbreads; innards, livers and lights (G.B.).
lechera, *f.* 1. milkmaid, dairymaid. 2. milk can; milk jug. — **l. amarga,** (bot.) milkwort.
lechería, *f.* dairy store; dairy barn.
lechero, ra, *a.* 1. milky. 2. milk, milch (cow, goat). 3. niggardly, stingy. 4. (Amer.) lucky. —*m.* milkman, dairyman.
lecherón, *m.* milk vessel, milk pail; flannel wrap for newborn infants.
lechetrezna, *f.* (bot.) sun spurge.
lechigada, *f.* 1. litter, brood. 2. gang, crew. 3. group of people living or working together.
lechín, *m.* 1. variety of olive tree and the olive it produces. 2. (vet.) boil, tumor (in horses).
lechino, *m.* 1. dossil, tent, small roll of lint for keeping a wound open. 2. (vet.) boil, tumor (in horses).
lecho, *m.* 1. bed; couch; litter. 2. bed (of river, ocean). 3. bed, base, foundation (of floor, house foundations, etc.). 4. layer; (geol.) stratum. — **abandonar el l.,** to get up; **l. de plumas,** feather bed (comfortable situation); **l. de rosas,** bed of roses.
lechón, *a.* filthy, dirty. —*m.* 1. suckling pig; pig; **l. asado,** roast suckling pig. 2. (coll.) pig, slob, dirty fellow.
lechona, *a.* filthy, dirty. —*f.* 1. female suckling pig; sow. 2. (coll.) pig, dirty woman.
lechoncillo, ito, *m. dim. of* **lechón,** very young pig.
lechosa, *f.* (bot.) papaya (fruit).
lechoso, sa, *a.* milky. —*m.* (bot.) papaya tree; papaya (fruit). —*f.* (S. Amer.) pawpaw tree, pawpaw.
lechuga, *f.* 1. (bot.) lettuce. 2. frill; highly starched ruff or cuff. — **l. repollada,** iceberg lettuce; **l. romana** or **costina,** romaine lettuce, cos lettuce; **l. silvestre,** prickly lettuce; **más fresco que una l., tan fresco como una l.,** (coll.) very fresh; forward or brazen; as bold as brass, as cool as a cucumber.
lechugado, da, *a.* shaped like a lettuce leaf.
lechuguero, ra, *m., f.* lettuce seller.
lechuguilla, *f.* 1. (bot.) prickly or wild lettuce. 2. (hist.) highly starched ruff or cuff. 3. (bot.) lechuguilla (variety of agave).
lechuguino, na, *a.* fashionable, stylish, modish. —*m.* 1. seedling lettuce; lettuce bed or plot. 2. (coll.) young beau or flirt; dandy, fashionable young man or young woman.
lechuzo, za, *a.* owlish, owl-like. —*m.* 1. (coll.) bill collector; summons server. 2. (coll.) owl, owlish-looking man. 3. suckling (mule colt). —*f.* 1. (ornith.) barn owl, screech owl. 2. (coll.) owl, owlish-looking woman. 3. (Mex.) prostitute, whore.
lecitina, *f.* (biochem.) lecithin.
lecitinasa, *f.* (biochem.) lecithinase.
lecito, *m.* yolk (of an egg).
lectisternio, *m.* lectisternium (Roman religious festival).
lectivo, va, *a.* pertaining to a lecture, teaching, e.g. *tiempo lectivo,* lecture or teaching time; pertaining to school, academic (as *a.*), e.g. *año* or *día lectivo,* school year or day.
lector, ra, *a.* reading; **público l.,** reading public. —*m., f.* 1. reader. 2. (educ.) lector, lecturer; assistant lecturer in modern languages (teaching his own language). —*m.* 1. (ecc.) lector. 2. (ecc.) instructor in theology or in the Gospel. 3. (electron.) playback; **l. digital,** digital scanner; **l. óptico,** optical scanner.
lectorado, *m.* (ecc.) lectorate (order of lectors).
lectoral, *m.* theologian or instructor in theology of a cathedral chapter (also used as *a.*, i.e. *canónigo l.*). —*f.* canonry or post of theologian or instructor in theology of a cathedral chapter (also used as *a.*, i.e. *canonjía l.*).
lectoralía, *f.* canonry or post of theologian of a cathedral chapter.
lectoría, *f.* (ecc.) lectorate (post of lector), lectorship.
lectura, *f.* 1. reading, ability to read. 2. reading matter. 3. lecture. 4. reading, culture. 5. reading (interpretation of text). 6. (ecc.) lectorate (post of lector). 7. (print.) pica — **l. estadimétrica,** top. *stadia reading;* **l. por lector óptico láser,** laser optical scanning; **l. rápida** or **veloz,** speed reading, skim reading.
lecturita, *f.* (print.) small pica.
Leda, *f.* (myth.) Leda, Spartan queen whom Zeus visited in the form of a swan.
ledamente, *adv.* (poet.) cheerfully, placidly.
ledo, da, *a.* (poet.) happy, cheerful, placid.
leedor, ra, *a.* reading. —*m., f.* reader.
leer, *(ref. 60) tr.v.* 1. to read; to lecture; to instruct; (fig.) to read (the mind, a hand, etc.). 2. to interpret, read. — **l. pruebas de imprenta,** to proofread. —*i.v.* 1. to read. 2. to lecture. — **l. entre líneas,** (fig.) to read between the lines.
lega, *f.* (ecc.) lay sister.
legacía, *f.* 1. legateship. 2. legate's mission. 3. legation, territory under a legate's jurisdiction.
legación, *f.* legation, embassy.
legado, *past part. of* **legar.** —*m.* 1. legacy, bequest. 2. (hist., ecc.) legate. — **l. a látere,** legatus a latere (Lat.), confidential papal legate.
legador, *m.* man who ties the feet of sheep for shearing.
legadura, *f.* rope, cord, binding cord or strap, tie.
legajar, *tr.v.* (Col., Chile, Hond.) *var. of* enlegajar.
legajo, *m.* bundle of papers; docket, file; **l. personal,** personal file.
legal, *a.* legal, lawful; faithful, loyal, true, legitimate.

legalice, legalicé, *ref.* **legalizar.**

legalidad, *f.* legality; lawfulness, fidelity.

legalista, *a.* legalistic, that sticks to the letter of the law.

legalización, *f.* legalization; authentication, attestation, notary's certificate.

legalizar, (*ref. 53*) *tr.v.* to legalize; to authenticate.

legalmente, *adv.* legally, lawfully.

legamente, *adv.* ignorantly; as a layman.

légamo, *m.* slime, mud, ooze; clayey soil.

legamoso, sa, *a.* slimy, oozy, greasy.

leganal, *m.* pool of mud, mud hole.

légano, *m, var. of* **légamo.**

leganoso, sa, *a., var. of* **legamoso.**

legaña, *f.* gum (on eyelids).

legañoso, sa, *a.* gummy, rheumy, bleary-eyed.

legar, (*ref. 51*) *tr.v.* 1. (law, fig.) to bequeath, leave. 2. to send as a legate; to depute, deputize.

legatario, ria, *m., f.* (law) legatee, devisee.

legenda, *f.* legend, history (of a saint's life).

legendario, ria, *a.* legendary. —*m.* book of legends.

legible, *a.* legible, readable.

legión, *f.* legion, multitude. — **L. de Honor,** Legion of Honor; **l. extranjera,** Foreign Legion.

legionario, ria, *a.* legionary. —*m.* legionary (in the Roman army); legionnaire (e.g. in the Foreign Legion).

legislable, *a.* subject to legislation.

legislación, *f.* legislation (body of laws).

legislador, ra, *a.* legislative, legislating. —*m., f.* legislator, lawmaker.

legislar, *i.v.* to legislate.

legislativo, va, *a.* legislative, law-making, lawgiving; **poder l.,** legislative power.

legislatura, *f.* session or term of the legislature.

legisperito, *m.* legal expert, jurist, professor (of law).

legista, *m.* legist, lawyer, professor of law; law student.

legítima, *f.* (law) legitim, legitime.

legitimación, *f.* legitimation, making legal or legitimate, giving legal standing.

legitimador, ra, *a.* legitimating, giving legal force to a matter.

legítimamente, *adv.* legitimately, lawfully.

legitimar, *tr.v.* 1. to legitimate, legitimize. 2. to prove or establish the legitimacy of. 3. to make competent, capacitate (for a post).

legitimario, ria, *a.* pertaining to a legitim. —*m., f.* (law) one who inherits a legitim.

legitimidad, *f.* legitimacy; legality; genuineness.

legitimismo, *m.* legitimism, support of legitimate authority, esp. of direct descent as claim to a throne.

legitimista, *a., m., f.* legitimist, person supporting direct descent as claim to the throne.

legítimo, ma, *a.* 1. legitimate, lawful. 2. genuine, authentic; true, certain.

lego, ga, *a.* 1. lay, secular. 2. ignorant, uninformed. —*m., f.* layman. —*m.* laybrother.

legón, *m.* a kind of hoe.

legra, *f.* 1. (surg.) bone scraper, periosteotome. 2. gouge for hollowing out clogs.

legración, *f.* (surg.) periosteotomy, bone scraping.

legradura, *f., var. of* **legración.**

legradura, *f., var. of* **alegradura.**

legrar, *tr.v.* (med.) to scrape (a bone), perform a periosteotomy on.

legrón, *m.* (vet.) large bone scraper or periosteotome.

legua, *f.* league (5,572.7 meters or 3 1/2 miles). — **a la l., a l., a leguas, de cien leguas, de mil leguas, de muchas leguas, desde media l.,** far, far away, miles away.

leguario, ria, *a.* of or pertaining to a league. —*m.* milestone, milepost.

legue, legué, *ref.* **legar.**

leguleyo, *m.* shyster lawyer, pettifogger.

legumbre, *f.* vegetable; (bot.) legume.

legúmina, *f.* (biochem.) legumin.

leguminoso, sa, *a.* (bot.) leguminous. —*f.* (*pl.*) (bot.) Leguminosae.

leíble, *a.* legible, readable.

leída, *f.* reading; the act of perusing or giving something a summary reading.

leído, da, *past part. of* **leer.** —*a.* well-read, well-informed. — **leido y escribido,** (coll.) (one) who sets himself up as learned, one who affects erudition.

leila, *f.* nocturnal party or ball among the Moors.

leima, *m.* (mus.) limma (one of the semitones in Greek music).

leishmaniasis, leishmaniosis, *f.* (med.) leishmaniasis.

lejanía, *f.* distance, remoteness; background.

lejano, na, *a.* distant, remote, far-off.

Lejano Oeste, *m.* Far West.

Lejano Oriente, *m.* Far East.

lejas, *a.* distant, faraway. — **de lejas tierras,** from faraway lands.

lejía, *f.* 1. bleach, lye. 2. (coll.) severe reprimand, dressing down.

lejío, *m.* dyers' lye or bleach.

lejísimos, *adv. super.* very far away.

lejitos, *adv. dim. of* **lejos,** quite far, rather far.

lejos, *adv.* far away, in the distance, far off; a long way off. — **a lo l.,** in the distance; **de l., de muy l., desde l.,** from afar, from a distance; **ir** or **llegar l.,** to go far or a long way (i.e. be successful); **l. de,** far from; far away from. —*m.* 1. appearance at a distance. 2. (*pl.*) background, distant objects in a painting. — **tener buen l.,** to look good at a distance.

lejuelos, *adv.* (reg., Sp.) quite far, at some distance.

lelilí, *m.* Moorish war cry or war whoop (used also as a cry of joy in festivals).

lelo, la, *a.* foolish, stupid, simple. —*m., f.* simpleton, stupid person. — **estar lelo por,** to be head over heels in love with.

lema, *m.* 1. motto, slogan. 2. theme, subject. 3. password; countersign; **l. publicitario,** advertising slogan.

lemanita, *f.* (min.) jade.

lembario, *m.* (arch.) marine; sailor.

lemnáceo, a, *a.* (bot.) lemnaceous. —*f.* lemnad; (*pl.*) Lemnaceae (family).

lemnícola, *a.* Lemnian, pertaining to or native of the Aegean island of Lemnos (Greece).

lemnio, nia, *a., m., f., var. of* **lemnícola.**

lemniscata, *f.* (geom.) lemniscate.

lemnisco, *m.* 1. (zool.) lemniscus. 2. fillet, ribbon (awarded together with palms to winning athletes).

lemosín, na, *a.* of or from Limousin, France. —*m., f.* native of Limousin. —*m.* langue d'oc, Provencal (language).

lémur, *m.* (zool.) lemur.

lémures, *m.* (*pl.*) (Roman, myth.) lemures (nocturnal malevolent spirits), apparitions.

lemurias, *f.* (*pl.*) Lemuria (nocturnal feast held to placate the lemures).

lemúridos, *m.* (zool.) (*pl.*) Lemuridae.

len, *a.* soft, flossy (silk); untwisted thread.

lena, *f.* spirit, vigor, inner strength.

lencería, *f.* linen, linen goods or clothes; linen shop; linen district (of town); linen room (for keeping linen); linen trade.

lencero, ra, *m., f.* lingerie or linen maker or dealer.

lenco, ca, *a.* (Hond.) stuttering, stammering. —*m., f.* stutterer.

lendel, *m.* track made by a mill-horse; gin race or ring (track made by horse working any machine).

lendrera, *f.* fine toothed comb (for removing nits).

lendrero, *m.* place full of nits or lice.

lendroso, sa, *a.* full of nits or lice.

lene, *a.* smooth, soft; sweet, kind, pleasant; light, gentle.

leneas, *f.* (*pl.*) (hist.) Bacchanalia, festivals held in Athens in honor of Bacchus.

lengua, *f.* 1. (anat.) tongue. 2. language, tongue. 3. (cul.) tongue. 4. clapper, tongue (of a bell). 5. (bkb.) cutting knife. 6. information. 7. interpreter. — **andar en lenguas,** to be spoken or gossiped about; **atar la l. a,** to silence (someone); **buscar la l. a uno,** (coll.) to pick a quarrel or fight with someone; **con la** l. **de un palmo,** (coll.) very eagerly; **de l. en l.,** by word of mouth; **hacerse lenguas de,** (coll.) to praise highly, rave about; **írsele a uno la l.,** to let slip, blurt out; **largo de l.,** indiscreet; very talkative; l. **aglutinante,** agglutinative language; l. **canina,** (bot.) hound's tongue; **l. de buey,** (bot.) bugloss, oxtongue, alkanet; l. **de ciervo,** (bot.) hart's tongue; **l. de destino,** target language; **l. de escorpión** backbiter, evil tongue, gossip; **l. de estropajo,** (coll.) babbler, mumbler; **l. de flexión,** inflected language; **l. de fuego,** tongue of fire; **l. de hacha,** (coll.) evil tongue, gossip, backbiter; **l. del agua,** bank (of river), shoreline (of sea); **l. de oc,** langue d'oc, Provençal; **l. de oil,** langue d'oil, northern medieval French; **l. de origen,** source language; **l. de sierpe,** evil tongue, gossip, backbiter; (fort.) outwork in front of the salients of a covert way; **l. de tierra,** tongue or spit of land (projecting into the sea)); **l. de trapo,** (coll.) babbler, mumbler; **l. de víbora,** (paleon.) ichthyodont or fossilized tooth of a shark; (coll.) evil tongue, backbiter; **l. franca,** lingua franca; **l. madre,** parent language; **l. materna,** mother tongue, native language; **l. muerta,** dead language; **l. natural or popular,** native language, mother tongue; **l. santa,** Hebrew; **l. serpentina** or **viperina,** evil tongue, gossip, backbiter; **l. viva,** living language; **mala l.,** evil tongue, gossip, backbiter; **media l.,** (coll.) gabble; gabbler; **malas lenguas,** (coll.) evil tongues, gossips; people (in general); **ligero de l.,** indiscreet, blabbermouthed; **morderse la l.,** to hold one's tongue (keep silent); **no tener pelos en la lengua,** to be frank, to speak freely; **poner l.** or **lenguas en,** to run down, speak ill of; **sacar la l. a,** to stick one's tongue out at; **suelto de l.,** see **ligero de l.; tener una cosa en la l.,** (coll.) to have on the tip of one's tongue; **tener mala l.,** to swear, blaspheme, be foul-mouthed; to be a gossip or backbiter, be evil-tongued; **tener mucha l.,** (coll.) to be very talkative; **tirar de la l. a uno,** (coll.) to draw information from someone; **trabársele a uno la l.,** to get tongue-tied.

lenguadeta, *f.* (ichth.) small sole.

lenguado, *m.* (ichth.) sole, flatfish, flounder.

lenguaje, *m.* language, idiom; parlance; speech, tongue. — **l. vulgar,** everyday language; **el l. de las flores,** the language of flowers.

lenguarada, *f., var. of* **lengüetada.**

lenguaraz, (*pl.* **lenguaraces**), *a.* 1. foul-mouthed, insolent; petulant. 2. talkative, garrulous. 3. accomplished in languages.

lenguaz, (*pl.* **lenguaces**), *a.* garrulous, loquacious.

lenguaza, *f.* (bot.) bugloss, oxtongue.

lengüeta, *f.* 1. tongue (of a shoe, football, etc.). 2. tab, flap (for opening boxes, tins, etc.); fastening flap (of a woman's bag). 3. (anat.) epiglottis. 4.

(mus.) reed (of a reed instrument). 5. pointer, tongue (of scales). 6. barb (of a dart, arrow, etc.). 7. (bkb.) cutting knife (for trimming books). 8. fork or catch holding a bird trap open. 9. widening bit. 10. (archit.) buttress; dividing wall (in chimney). 11. (carp.) tongue. 12. (surg.) long thin compress (for fractures). 13. (mech.) wedge, awl, bore, bit. — **l. y ranura,** (carp.) tongue and groove.

lengüetada, *f.* licking, lick.

lengüetazo, *m., var. of* **lengüetada.**

lengüetear, *tr.v.* (Hond.) to prattle, jabber.

lengüetería, *f.* (mus.) reedwork, reed stops (of an organ).

lengüicorto, ta, *a.* quiet, shy, reserved.

lengüilargo, ga, *a.* (coll.) foul-mouthed, garrulous.

lengüita, illa, *f. dim. of* **lengua,** small tongue.

lenice, lenicé, *ref.* **lenizar.**

lenidad, *f.* leniency, mildness.

lenificación, *f.* 1. softening, lessening; soothing. 2. act of mollifying.

lenificar, (*ref. 50*) *tr.v.* to soften, lessen (punishment, etc.); to soothe (pain).

lenifique, lenifiqué, *ref.* **lenificar.**

Leningrado, *m.* Leningrad, city in Russia (formerly the capital, then called Saint Petersburg and Petrograd).

leninismo, *m.* (pol.) Leninism, the theories of Lenin.

leninista, *a, m., f.* Leninist, advocate of the doctrines and theories of Lenin.

lenitivo, va, *a.* lenitive, lenient. *—m.* lenitive; palliative, emollient, mitigator.

lenizar, (*ref. 53*) *tr.v.* (rare) to soften, lessen; to soothe.

lenocinio, *m.* pandering, procuring; **casa de l.,** brothel.

lenón, *m.* (arch.) procurer, pimp.

lentamente, *adv.* slowly, lingeringly, lazily.

lente, *m.* (opt.) 1. lens. 2. (*pl.*) eyeglasses, spectacles. — **l. de aumento,** magnifying glass; **l. de contacto,** contact lens; **l. electrónico,** (phys.) electron lens; **l. ocular,** eyepiece, eyeglass; **lentes bifocales** or **multifocales,** bifocals; **lentes de aumento** or **de fórmula** or **ópticos,** prescription glasses; **lentes de sol** or **negros** or **oscuros,** sunglasses; **l. telefotográfico,** telephoto lens.

lentecer, (*ref. 45*) *i.v, r.v.* to soften, become soft or tender.

lenteja, *f.* 1. (bot.) lentil (plant and pea). 2. pendulum disk or bob. — **l. acuática,** (bot.) lesser duckweed.

lentejar, *m.* lentil field.

lentejuela, *f.* 1. *dim. of* **lenteja.** 2. (dressm.) spangle, sequin.

lentezca, lentezco, *ref.* **lentecer.**

lenticela, *f.* (bot.) lenticel.

léntico, ca, *a.* (biol., geol.) lentic.

lenticular, *a.* lenticular, shaped like a lentil. *—m.* (anat.) lenticular process (of the ear).

lentiginoso, sa, *a.* (bot.) lentiginous.

lentiscal, *m.* grove or thicket of mastic trees.

lentisco, *m.* (bot.) mastic tree.

lentisquina, *f.* (bot.) fruit of the mastic tree.

lentitud, *f.* slowness, sluggishness.

lento, ta, *a.* 1. slow. 2. sluggish; heavy. 3. (pharm., med.) viscid, glutinous. 4. (mus.) slow. *—adv.* **lento,** slowly.

lentor, *m.* (med.) viscid slime (covering teeth and inside of mouth of typhus victim).

lenzuelo, *m.* (agr.) cloth sheet for transporting cut hay; (rare) pocket handkerchief.

leña, *f.* 1. firewood. 2. (coll.) beating, whipping. — **añadir** or **echar l. al fuego,** to fan the flames (of discord); to make things worse; **dar l. a,** to give (someone) a beating; **llevar l. al monte,** to carry coals to Newcastle.

leñador, ra, *m, f.* 1. woodcutter. 2. firewood seller. *—m.* woodman, woodsman.

leñame, *m.* wood; supply of firewood.

leñar, *tr.v.* (coll.) to cut (wood).

leñatero, *m.* woodcutter, woodman.

leñazgo, *m.* woodpile.

leñazo, *m.* (coll.) blow with a club.

leñera, *f.* woodshed, wood box, woodbin, woodpile.

leñero, *m.* 1. wood dealer, wood seller. 2. woodshed, wood box.

leño, *m.* 1. log; wood. 2. (mar.) galley; (poet.) ship, bark, vessel. 3. (coll.) dullard, dimwit. — **l. hediondo,** (bot.) bean trefoil (Anagyris foetida).

leñoso, sa, *a.* woody, ligneous.

Leo, *m.* (astron.) Leo.

león, *m.* 1. lion. 2. (ento.) ant lion. 3. lion (brave or strong person). 4. (astron.) **L.,** Leo. 5. (Amer.) puma. 6. (mar.) lion-shaped figurehead (on ancient Spanish war ships). — **l. marino,** (zool.) sea lion.

leona, *f.* 1. lioness. 2. (fig.) lioness, brave and haughty woman. 3. (Chile) disorder, confusion; riot.

leonado, da, *a.* tawny (color).

leoncico, illo, ito, *m.* whelp of a lion, lion cub.

leonera, *f.* 1. lion's den or cage. 2. (coll.) gambling house. 3. (coll.) rumpus room, junk room. 4. (Mex.) bachelor's den, secret love nest.

leonería, *f.* fierceness, bravery, bravado.

leonero, ra, *m.* 1. lion keeper. 2. (coll.) keeper of a gambling house.

leónica, *a., f.* (zool.) vein under the tongue.

leonina, *f.* (med.) leontiasis.

leonino, na, *a.* 1. leonine, of or pertaining to the lion. 2. (law) leonine, one-sided, unfair, exorbitant (said of a contract in which advantages are all for one side).

leontina, *f.* (jewel.) watch chain.

leopardo, *m.* (zool.) leopard.

leopoldina, *f.* 1. Spanish helmet or shako. 2. ornamental watch chain.

leotardo, *m.* leotard, one-piece tight-fitting knitted garment worn by ballet dancers and acrobats.

Lepe, saber más que L., to be very clever, lively or alert.

leperada, *f.* (Mex.) gross or vulgar remark.

lépero, ra, *a.* 1. (Mex.) low, gross, foul-mouthed. 2. (Cuba) cunning, astute. 3. (Hond.) roguish. *—m., f.* (Mex.) gross or vulgar person.

leperuza, *f.* (Mex.) prostitute.

lepidia, *f.* (Chile, coll.) indigestion.

lepidio, *m.* (bot.) peppergrass, pepper cress.

lepidolita, *f.* (min.) lepidolite.

lepidóptero, *a.* (ento.) lepidopterous. *—m.* (ento.) lepidopteron, butterfly; (*pl.*) Lepidoptera.

lepidosirena, *f.* (zool.) lepidosiren.

lepisma, *f.* (ento.) silverfish, bristletail.

lepóride, *m.* (zool.) leporid.

lepórido, *m.* (zool.) leporid; (*pl.*) Leporidae.)

leporino, na, *a.* harelike, leporine; **labio l.,** harelip.

lepra, *f.* (med.) leprosy.

leprosería, *f.* leprosarium, lazaretto, leprosy hospital.

leproso, sa, *a.* leprous. *—m.* leper.

leptómetro, *m.* (chem.) leptometer viscosity.

leptón, *m.* (phys.) lepton.

leptorrino, na, *a.* (zool.) leptorrhine, leptorrhynian.

leptosomo, ma, *a.* (physiol.) leptosome.

lercha, *f.* (hunt.) reed used for tying and carrying game.

lerda, *f.* (vet.) *var. of* **lerdón.**

lerdamente, *adv.* lumberingly, heavily, awkwardly, slowly.

lerdo, da, *a.* 1. slow, lumbering, heavy (in movements). 2. slow, dull, dim (in understanding).

lerdón, *m.* 1. (vet.) tumor near (horse's) hoof. 2. slow, lumbering person.

lerneido, *m.* (zool.) lernaean.

les, *pers. pron.* (*pl*) 1. (as direct object) them; you (when addressing two or more people in Ud. form). 2. (as indirect object) them, to them, you, to you, e.g. *les di la dirección,* I gave you (*pl.*) or them the address or I gave the address to you or to them; them, for them, you, for you, e.g. *les compré una caja de chocolates,* I bought them or you a box of chocolates or I bought a box of chocolates for them or for you; from them, from you, e.g. *les quitaron todo,* they took everything away from them.

lesbianismo, *m.* lesbianism.

lesbiano, na, lesbio, bia, *a., m., f.* lesbian.

lésbico, ca, *a.* Lesbian.

lesear, *i.v.* (Chile) to fool around.

lesera, *f.* (Chile) foolishness, stupidity.

lesión, *f.* 1. injury, wound, lesion. 2. damage. 3. (law) injury; injury caused by the sale of an article at an unjust price.

lesionador, ra, *a.* damaging, injurious.

lesionar, *tr.v.* to injure, wound; to damage, harm. *—r.v.* to be injured, injure oneself.

lesivo, va, *a.* detrimental, injurious, prejudicial.

lesna, *f.* awl.

lesnordeste, *m.* (mar.) east-northeast; east-northeast wind.

leso, sa, *a.* 1. hurt, injured, wronged, harmed, offended. 2. warped, perverted, perverse (mind, imagination). 3. (Bol., Chile) silly, foolish. — **l. majestad,** lese majesty.

lessueste, *m.* (mar.) east-southeast; east-southeast wind.

leste, *m.* (mar.) east, east wind.

lestrigón, *m.* (myth.) Lestrigon (legendary cannibals who lived in Sicily).

lesura, *f.* (Chile) stupidity, foolishness.

letal, *a.* lethal, deadly, mortal, destructive.

letame, *m.* manure, mulch, compost.

letanía, *f.* 1. (ecc.) litany (form of liturgical prayer). 2. (ecc.) litany, solemn liturgical procession. 3. (fig.) litany, long list.

letárgico, ca, *a.* lethargic, drowsy, sluggish.

letargo, *m.* lethargy, drowsiness, sluggishness.

letargoso, sa, *a.* soporific, inducing lethargy, lethargic.

Lete, *m.* (myth.) Lethe, the river of forgetfulness in Hades.

leteo, a, *a.* (myth.) Lethean. *—m.* (myth.) Lethe, the river of forgetfulness in Hades.

letificante, *a.* gladdening, exhilarating, cheering.

letificar, (*ref. 50*) *tr.v.* to gladden, make happy, animate.

letífico, ca, *a.* gladdening, bringing cheer and comfort.

letifique, letifiqué, *ref.* **letificar.**

letón, na, *a.* Lettish. *—m., f.* Lett, Latvian. *—m.* Lettish (language).

Letonia, *f.* Latvia.

letra, *f.* 1. letter (of the alphabet). 2. handwriting, hand, penmanship. 3. (print.) type; letter. 4. literal meaning, letter. 5. (poet.) kind of rondeau. 6. (mus.) lyrics, words (of a song). 7. motto; slogan, inscription. 8. (com.) draft, bill of exchange. 9. (coll.) astuteness, cunning, cleverness. 10. (*pl.*) arts, letters (branch of learning). 11. (*pl.*) literature, letters, e.g. *letras peruanas,* Peruvian literature. 12. (*pl.*) order, decree, decision. — **al pie de la l., a la l.,** to the letter;

literrally, exactly; **a l. vista,** (com.) at sight; **atarse a la l.,** to stick to the literal meaning; **bellas** or **buenas letras,** belles lettres, literature; **dos** or **cuatro letras,** (coll.) a short note, a line; **l. abierta,** (com.) letter of credit for unlimited sum; **l. a la vista,** (com.) sight bill or draft, demand bill or draft; **l. aldina,** (print.) Aldine type; **l. aspirada,** (phonet.) aspirate letter; **l. bancaria,** (com.) bank draft; **l. bastarda,** (print.) bastard type; **l. bastardilla,** (print.) italics; italic letter; **l. cancilleresca,** copperplate writing; **l. consonante,** consonant; **l. continua,** (phon.) semi-vocal letter, semivowel; **l. corrida,** running or cursive writing; **l. cursiva,** cursive or running writing; (print.) italics; **l. de caja alta,** (print.) capital letter; **l. de caja baja,** (print.) small letter; **l. de cambio,** (com.) draft, bill of exchange; **l. de cambio a plazo,** (com.) time draft or note; **l. de favor** or **cortesía,** accommodation paper; **l. de guarismo,** Arabic numeral; **l. de imprenta,** (print.) type; **l. de mano,** handwriting; handwritten letter; **l. de molde,** block letter, printed letter; **l. dental,** (phonet.) dental; **l. doble,** double letter (one formed by two letters); **l. dominical,** (ecc.) dominical letter; **l. egipcia,** (print.) boldface, boldfaced type; **l. explosiva** (phonet.) explosive letter, plosive; **l. florida** or **historiada,** (print.) decorative letter or initial; **l. gótica,** Old English, black letter (U.S.), Gothic type (G.B.); **l. gutural,** (phonet.) guttural; **l. itálica,** (print.) italics; italic letter; **l. labial,** (phonet.) labial; **l. labiodental,** (phonet.) labiodental; **l. limpia;** (com.) clean bill of exchange, clean draft; **l. lingual,** (phonet.) lingual; **l. magistral,** (print.) large bastard type; **l. mayúscula,** capital letter, capital; **l. menuda,** (coll.) cunning, astuteness; (print.) fine print; **l. metida,** (print.) crowded print; **l. minúscula,** lower case; **l. muda,** (phonet.) silent letter; explosive letter, plosive; **l. muerta,** (fig.) dead letter (law no longer observed); **l. nasal,** (phonet.) nasal; **l. negrilla,** (print.) boldface, boldfaced type; **l. numeral,** Roman numeral; **l. paladial,** (phonet.) palatal; **l. pancilla,** (print.) round type; **l. pelada,** (print.) Gothic or sans serif type (U.S.) grotesque type (G.B.); **l. pequeña,** small print; **l. redonda. redondilla** or **romanilla,** round hand; (print.) Roman, round or standard type; **letras de identificación,** (rad.) call letters; **letras divinas,** the Scriptures; **letras gordas,** (coll.) rudimentary education; **letras humanas,** literature, the humanities; **letras menudas,** (print.) small print; **letras obedenciales,** (ecc.) document issued by superior permitting monk to travel; **letras patentes,** decree, edict; letters patent; **letras remisorias,** (law) judge's orders transferring a case to another court; **letras sagradas,** the Scriptures; **l. semivocal,** (phonet.) semivocal letter, semivowel; **l. sibilante,** (phonet.) sibilant; **l. sobre el interior,** (com.) domestic bill; **l. tenue,** (phonet.) tenuis, surd, mute; **l. tirada,** flowing handwriting; **l. titular,** (print.) head or display letter; **l. versal,** (print.) capital letter; **l. versalita,** (print.) small capital letter; **l. vocal,** vowel; **levantar l.,** (print.) to set type; **primeras letras,** the three R's, elementary education; **protestar una l.,** (com.) to protest a draft of exchange; **tener letras gordas,** (coll.) to have little education; to lack ability or talent.

letrada, *f.* (coll.) lawyer's wife.

letrado, da, *a.* 1. learned, erudite. 2. (coll.) pedantic. —*m.* lawyer, advocate, counsel, attorney.

letrero, *m.* 1. sign, placard, poster. 2. label, legend.

letrilla, *f.* (poet.) rondel, roundel (poem); roundelay.

letrina, *f.* 1. lavatory, latrine. 2. (fig.) pigsty, filthy place.

letrón, *m.* 1. *aug. of* **letra,** large letter. 2. (*pl.*) (ecc.) ban, list of names of those excommunicated, placed at the door of a church.

letuario, *m.* 1. (cul.) kind of jam or marmalade. 2. (pharm.) a thick or viscose preparation.

leucemia, *f.* (med.) leukemia.

leucina, *f.* (biochem.) leucine.

leucita, *f.* (min.) leucite.

leucocitemia, *f.* (med.) leucocythemia, leukemia.

leucocítico, ca, *a.* (physiol.) leukocytic.

leucocito, *m.* (anat.) leukocyte, white corpuscle.

leucocitoblasto, *m.* (physiol.) leukocytoblast.

leucocitoide, *a.* leukocitoid.

leucocitosis, *f.* (med.) leukocytosis.

leucoma, *f.* (med.) leucoma, leukoma.

leucomaína *f.* (biochem.) leucomaine.

leucopenia, *f.* (med.) leukopenia.

leucoplaquia, leucoplasia, *f.* (med.) leukoplasia, leukoplakia.

leucoplástida, *f.* (bot.) leucoplastid.

leucoplasto, *m.* (bot.) leucoplast.

leucopoyesis, *f.* (physiol.) leukopoiesis.

leucopoyético, ca, *a.* (physiol.) leukopoietic.

leucorrea, *f.* (med.) leucorrhea, whitish discharge from the vagina.

leudar, *tr.v.* to leaven, add yeast to (dough). —*r.v.* to rise, ferment (dough).

leude, *m.* hired soldier (in the armies of the Gothic kings), mercenary.

leudo, da, *a.* leavened (bread or dough).

Lev. *abbrev. of* **Levítico,** Leviticus (Lev.).

leva, *f.* 1. (mil.) levy, press; press gang. 2. (mec.) cam, cog. 3. leaving, going, weighing anchor, departure (of ship). 4. lever. 5. (Amer.) frock coat; (Cuba) coat, jacket. 6. (*pl.*) tricks, shrewd devices. — **halar la l.,** (coll.) to cater to, flatter; **irse a la l. y a monte,** (coll.) to flee; **l. de escape,** (mec.) exhaust cam.

levada, *f.* 1. migratory segment of a breed of silkworms, which moves from one place to another. 2. (fenc.) salute or flourish with the foil; bout of fencing.

levadero, *a.* collectable, demandable.

levadizo, za, *a.* 1. (*puerta*) sliding vertically. 2. (*puente*) bridge; **puente levadizo,** drawbridge.

levador, *m.* 1. piler (in paper mills). 2. (mec.) cam, cog, tooth.

levadura, *f.* 1. yeast, leaven. 2. (carp.) sawed-off plank. — **l. de cerveza,** brewer's yeast.

levantacoches, *m.* (auto.) automobile lift.

levantada, *f.* getting-up (from bed), rising.

levantadamente, *adv.* loftily, sublimely.

levantado, da, *past part. of* **levantar.** —*a.* (fig.) lofty, elevated, sublime, noble.

levantador, ra, *a.* raising, lifting, elevating. —*m., f.* **l. de pesas,** weightlifter. —*f.* bathrobe, dressing gown.

levantamiento, *m.* 1. raising, lifting. 2. uprising, insurrection, revolt, rebellion. 3. (mil.) levying, recruitment. 4. removal, lifting (of a ban, prohibition, etc.). 5. (geol.) upheaval. 6. survey, surveying. — **l. altimétrico,** topographical survey; **l. con apoyo,** press (in weight lifting); **l. con arranque,** snatch (in weight lifting); **l. con impulso,** clean and jerk (in weight lifting); **l. del censo,** census-taking; **l. de pesos,** weight lifting; **l. de planos,** survey, surveying; **l. fotográfico,** (chart.) photographic mapping; **l. taquimétrico** or **estadimétrico,** (surv.) stadia survey.

levantar, *tr.v.* 1. to raise, pick up, lift; to lift up, hold up. 2. to straighten up. 3. to raise (prices; a siege; one's voice; one's spirits; a blister or bump). 4. to move to another place; to strike, break (camp). 5. to remove, take off (a tablecloth; bandage); to clear (the table). 6. to bear (false witness); to bring (false charges). 7. to adjourn (a session; court). 8. to weigh (the anchor). 9. to gather (the harvest). 10. to remove, raise (a prohibition, sentence), e.g. *levantar el destierro de,* to remove the order of banishment from. 11. to recruit, raise (troops). 12. to build, raise. 13. (hunt.) to rouse, raise (game). 14. to institute, found. 15. to cut (the cards). 16. to play a higher card than. 17. to induce people to rebel. 18. (coll.) to lift, (coll.) pinch, steal. 19. to make (a survey). 20. to take (a census). — **l. la voz,** to raise one's voice; **l. vuelo,** (avia.) to take off. —*r.v.* 1. to rise; to stand up; to get up; to straighten up. 2. to rise, rebel. 3. to stand out (in relief); **levantarse con,** (coll.) to pinch (sl.), steal, make off with; **levantarse con el pie izquierdo,** to get up on the wrong side of the bed.

levantarrieles, (*pl.* **levantarrieles**), *m.* (ry.) track jack.

levantaválvula, *m.* (engin.) tappet, push rod; valve lift.

levante, *m.* 1. East, Orient. 2. levanter (wind). 3. **L.,** Levant (countries washed by the eastern Mediterranean). 4. the Mediterranean shores of Spain.

levantino, na, *a.* Levantine, Eastern, of the Levant. —*m., f.* inhabitant of the Levant; inhabitant of the Mediterranean coast of Spain.

levantisco, ca, *a.* turbulent, restless. —*var. of* **levantino.**

levar, *tr.v.* (mar.) to weigh (anchor); **levar anclas,** to weigh anchor. —*r.v.* (mar.) to weigh anchor, set sail.

leve, *a.* 1. light 2. (fig.) trivial, unimportant, slight, trifling.

levedad, *f.* 1. lightness. 2. levity, flippancy. 3. inconstancy.

levemente, *adv.* lightly, gently, venially.

leviatán, *m.* (Bib., fig.) Leviathan.

levigación, *f.* levigation.

levigar, (*ref. 51*) *tr.v.* 1. to levigate (to stir into water so as to separate the finer particles); to free from grit. 2. to polish.

levigue, levigué, *ref.* **levigar.**

levirato, *m.* (rel.) levirate.

levita, *m.* 1. (Bib.) Levite. 2. deacon, priest. 3. frock coat, Prince Albert coat.

levitación, *f.* levitation.

levítico, ca, *a.* 1. Levitical; priestly. 2. (fig.) devoted to church; obedient to priests. —*m.* 1. **L.,** (Bib.) Leviticus. 2. (coll.) ceremonial, ceremony (performed at an official function).

levitón, *m.* heavy frock coat.

levógiro, ra, *a.* (chem., phys.) levogyrate, levorotatory.

levoglucosa, *f.* (chem.) levoglucosan.

levorrotación, *f.* (phys., chem.) levorotation.

levorrotatorio, ria, *a.* (phys., chem.) levorotatory.

levosa, *f.* (coll., hum.) elegant frock coat.

levulina, *f.* (chem.) levulin.

levulosa, *f.* (chem.) levulose.

lewisita, *f.* (mil.) lewisite, a blistering poison gas.

léxico, ca, *a.* lexical. —*m.* 1. lexicon, dictionary. 2. the characteristic vocabulary of an author or a speaker.

lexicografía, *f.* lexicography.

lexicográfico, ca, *a.* lexicographic, lexicographical.

lexicógrafo, *m.* lexicographer.

lexicología, *f.* lexicology.

lexicológico, ca, *a.* lexicologic, lexicological.

lexicólogo, *m.* lexicologist.
lexicón, *m.* lexicon, dictionary.
ley, *f.* 1. law, statute, decree; act; rule; regulation. 2. law, body of laws. 3. law, precept, religion. 4. devotion, attachment, loyalty, e.g. *tomarle l. a alguien,* to become attached or devoted to someone. 5. official standard, quality or weight (of goods as set by law). 6. fineness, quantity of gold or silver in bullion, coins, etc. 7. (min.) quantity of metal (in ore). — **a la l. de caballero,** on the word of a gentleman; **a toda l.,** strictly according to the rules or principle, duly, justly; **bajo de l.,** of low silver or gold content; **dar la l.,** to serve as an example; to force, oblige; **de buena l.,** sterling, excellent; **echar la l.** or **toda la l. a,** to throw the book at, judge with extreme severity; **hecha la l. hecha la trampa,** the law was made to be broken; **hombre de l.,** sterling fellow; **l. adjetiva,** (law) adjective law, procedural law; **l. antigua, l. de Moisés, l. vieja,** Law of Moses, Mosaic Law; **l. de bases,** basic precepts, guiding rules; **l. de Coulomb,** Coulomb's law, law of electrostatic attraction; **l. de Faraday,** Faraday's law, law of electromagnetic induction; **l. decreto,** decree law; **l. de gracia,** teachings of Christ in New Testament; **l. de la gravedad,** law of gravity; **l. de la oferta y la demanda,** law of supply and demand; **l. de la trampa,** (coll.) trick; **l. del embudo,** (coll.) one-sided law (favoring privileged minority); **l. del encaje,** (coll.) decision made at judge's discretion; **l. de patentes,** patent law; **l. de prescripción,** (law) statute of limitations; **l. escrita,** written law; (Bib.) Decalogue, Ten Commandments; **l. evangélica,** law of love (teachings of Christ in New Testament); **l. marcial,** (law) martial law; **l. natural,** natural law; **l. no escrita,** unwritten law; **l. nueva,** law of love (teachings of Christ in New Testament); **l. orgánica,** organic law; **l. positiva,** (law) positive law; **l. sálica,** salic law; **l. seca,** dry law; **l. senoidal,** sine law; **l. suntuaria,** sumptuary law (against excessive luxury).
leyenda, *f.* 1. legend, saga, traditional or fabulous story. 2. life of a saint. 3. legend, motto, inscription on a coin or a medal. 4. the act of reading. 5. (Gal.) caption, footing a photo or illustration.
leyendario, ria, *a.* legendary, pertaining to legends.
leyendo, *ref.* **leer.**
leyente, *a.* reading. —*m., f.* reader.
leyera, leyese, leyó, *ref.* **leer.**
lezda, *f.* (arch.) tax on merchandise.
lezdero, *m.* (arch.) tax-collector.
lezna, *f.* awl; **l. de marcar,** scratch awl.
lezne, *a.* crumbly; fragile, frail.
Li *sym. of* **litio,** lithium (Li).
lía, *f.* 1. rope, esparto rope. 2. dregs, lees (usually in *pl.*); **estar uno hecho una l.,** (coll.) to be drunk or tipsy.
Lía, *f.* (Bib.) Leah.
liana, *f.* (Gal., bot.) liana, vine.
liar, (*ref. 54*) *tr.v.* 1. to tie, bind. 2. to tie up, wrap up, do up. 3. to roll (a cigarette). 4. (coll.) to entangle, involve, embroil; **liarlas,** (coll.) to beat it, scram, duck out, escape. (coll.) to die, kick the bucket; **l. tabaco,** to roll cigarettes. —*r.v.* 1. to join together, become associated. 2. to get involved, embroiled or entangled; to enter into concubinage. — **liarse a golpes,** to come to blows.
liara, *f.* drinking vessel made of a horn.
liásico, ca, *a, m.* (geol.) Liassic.
liatón, *m.* esparto rope, strong twine.
liaza, *f.* 1. ropes (for tying wineskins, etc.). 2. wooden hoops (used in making casks).
lib. *abbrev. of* **libra,** pound (lb.).
libación, *f.* 1. drink, sip. 2. libation, pouring of wine or oil on the ground in honor of a deity.
libamen, *m.* sacrificial offering or libation.
libamiento, *m.* libation, sacrificial offering.
libán, *m.* (rare) esparto rope.
libanés, sa, *a., m., f.* Lebanese, of or from Lebanon.
Líbano, *m.* **El L.,** Lebanon, The Lebanon.
libar, *tr.v.* 1. to taste; to drink, sip; to suck. 2. to pour out as a libation. 3. to suck or extract the juice of flowers (apiculture).
libelar, *tr.v.* (law) to petition.
libelático, ca, *a., m., f.* apostate, renegade (said of early Christians who obtained a certificate of apostasy to avoid persecution); retracting, apostatizing.
libelista, *m., f.* lampoonist, libeler, libelist.
libelo, *m.* 1. lampoon, libel. 2. (coll.) act of discarding, abandoning, giving up. 3. (law) petition. — **l. de repudio,** written repudiation of a wife by her husband; **dar l. de repudio a una cosa,** to give up, discard.
libélula, *f.* (ento.) dragonfly.
líber, *m.* (bot.) liber, bast, inner bark.
liberación, *f.* 1. liberation, freeing; deliverance, independence. 2. discharge, release (from prison). 3. exoneration; exemption (from taxes, obligations). 4. redemption (of a mortgage). 5. receipt in full. — **fuerzas de l.,** (mil.) liberation forces; **la l. de la mujer,** Women's Liberation, Women's Lib.
liberado, da, *a.* 1. freed, released; exempted. 2. (com.) paid-up, e.g. *acción liberada;* paid-up share; free, e.g. *liberado de derechos,* tax-free.
liberador, ra, *a.* liberating. —*m , f.* liberator.
liberal, *a.* 1. liberal, generous, munificent. 2. (polit.) liberal, progressive. 3. liberal (arts). —*m., f.* (polit.) liberal, (Amer.) member of the Liberal Party.
liberalice, liberalicé, *ref.* **liberalizar.**
liberalidad, *f.* liberality, generosity, munificence.
liberalismo, *m.* liberalism; (polit.) Liberalism, Liberal Party.
liberalizar, (*ref. 53*) *tr.v.* to liberalize, make liberal. —*r.v.* to become liberal.
liberalmente, *adv.* 1. liberally, generously, freely. 2. (Arg.) quickly, promptly.
liberar, *tr.v.* to free, liberate, exempt.
liberatorio, ria, *a.* releasing, discharging, exempting; **fuerza l.,** legal tender.
Liberia, *f.* Liberia.
Liberiano, na, *a., m., f.* Liberian, of or from Liberia.
libérrimo, ma, *a. super. of* **libre,** completely free.
libertad, *f.* 1. freedom, liberty, deliverance; independence. 2. privilege, right. 3. liberty, e.g. *tomarse la l. de* + inf., to take the liberty of + *ger.* 4. self-confidence, self-assurance, poise. 5. talent, ability, facility, e.g. *l. de pincel,* talent for painting. 6. exemption, freedom. — **estar en l.,** to be at large; **estar en l. de** + *inf.,* to be at liberty to + *inf.,* to be free to + *inf.;* **l. bajo fianza** or **bajo palabra** or **provisional,** bail; **l. condicional,** parole; **l. de cátedra,** academic freedom; **l. de comercio,** free trade; **l. de conciencia,** freedom of thought; **l. de cultos,** religious freedom, freedom of worship; **l. de enseñanza,** academic freedom; **l. de imprenta,** freedom of the press; **l. del espíritu,** spiritual strength; **l. de los mares,** freedom of the seas; **l. de palabra,** or **expressión;** freedom of speech; **l. de prensa,** freedom of the press; **l. de reunión,** freedom of assembly; **poner en l.,** to set free; **poner a uno en l. de,** to exempt or exonerate from; **tomarse libertades,** to take liberties, be over-familiar.
libertadamente, *adv.* boldly, brashly, impudently, insolently, freely.
libertado, da, *past part. of* **libertar.** —*a.* 1. freed, liberated, emancipated. 2. bold, forward, daring. 3. free, unrestrained.
libertador, ra, *a.* liberating. —*m., f.* liberator; **El Libertador,** (Amer.) Simón Bolívar.
libertar, *tr.v.* 1. to liberate, free, set free. 2. to free, exonerate, acquit. 3. to save, preserve (from danger, death, etc.).
libertario, ria, *a.* anarchistic. —*m., f.* anarchist.
liberticida, *a.* liberticidal. —*m., f.* liberticide (destroyer of liberty).
libertinaje, *m.* 1. libertinism, debauchery, licentiousness. 2. lack of respect for or belief in religion.
libertino, na, *a.* dissolute, profligate, libertine. —*m., f.* 1. libertine, profligate. 2. (Roman hist.) libertine (freed slave or freed slave's son).
liberto, ta, *m., f.* (hist.) freedman, freedwoman, libertine.
Libia, *f.* Libya.
líbico, ca, *a.* Libyan, of or from Libya.
libídine, *f.* (psyc.) libido; lust, desire.
libidinosamente, *adv.* libidinously, lustfully, lasciviously.
libidinoso, sa, *a.* libidinous, lustful, lascivious.
libido, *m.* (psyc.) libido.
libio, bia, *a., m., f.* Libyan, of or from Libya.
Liborio, *m.* personification of a Cuban peasant (symbol of the Cuban people).
libra, *f.* 1. pound (weight, coin). 2. weight (in oil mills for pressing olives). 3. (Cuba) best quality tobacco leaf. 4. **L.,** (astron.) Libra. — **l. esterlina,** pound sterling; **entrar pocos** or **pocas en l.,** to be very few of.
libración, *f.* (astron., phys.) libration; (astron.) oscillation.
libraco, *m.* (derog.) cheap book, trashy book; large and useless book.
libracho, *m.* (derog.) *var. of* **libraco.**
librado, da, *past part. of* **librar.** —*a.* **salir bien** or **mal l.,** to come out unscathed or hurt (from an adventure, danger, risk, business venture, etc.). —*m., f.* (com.) drawee.
librador, ra, *a.* delivering. —*m.* 1. storekeeper of royal stables. 2. grocer's scoop. —*m., f.* 1. deliverer. 2. (com.) drawer (of a check or draft).
libramiento, *m.* 1. deliverance, delivery (from danger). 2. warrant or order of payment.
librancista, *m.* (com.) holder of a draft or order of payment.
libranza, *f.* (com.) draft, bill of exchange; warrant, order of payment, money order.
librar, *tr.v.* 1. to save, rescue, deliver, preserve. 2. to free, exempt. 3. to place, put (hope or trust in). 4. to pass (e.g. a sentence). 5. (com.) to issue, write (a draft check; to draw, e.g. *l. a cargo de,* to draw on. 6. to issue (decree, edict). 7. to make (an appointment). 8. to engage or join in (battle), wage (war). —*i.v.* 1. (med.) to give birth; to expel the placenta. 2. to receive guests in the locutory (a nun). — **a bien** or **buen l.,** as well as could or can be expected; **l. bien** or **mal de,** to come out of (a business) successfully or well (unsuccessfully or badly). —*r.v.* to save, deliver or preserve oneself; to escape. — **librarse de,** to avoid, get rid of.
libratorio, *m.* locutory (of a convent); (rel.) place where visitors are received in a convent.
librazo, *m.* 1. *aug. of* **libro,** large book. 2. blow with a book.
libre, *a.* 1. free; independent. 2. free, exempt, excused. 3. bold, frank, free (in what one says). 4. single, unmarried; unencumbered. 5. loose,

wild, dissolute, free (way of living). 6. vacant (premises. — **comercio l.,** free trade; **entrada l.,** free admission; **amor l.,** free love; **l. cambio,** free exchange, free trade; **l. de culpa,** guiltless, innocent; **l. de derechos,** tax-free; **l. de gastos a bordo,** free-on-board; **l. empresa** or **mercado,** free market; **l. pensador,** freethinker; **verso l.,** (poet.) vers libre, free verse.

librea, *f.* 1. livery (uniform). 2. page, servant (wearing a livery coat). 3. (Chile) lackey.

librear, *tr.v.* 1. to dress, deck, adorn. 2. to weigh or sell by the pound.

librecambio, *m.* free trade or exchange.

librecambismo, *m.* the doctrine advocating free trade.

librecambista, *a.* free-trading. —*m., f.* freetrader.

librejo, *m. dim. of* **libro,** little book, booklet; (derog.) trashy book.

libremente, *adv.* freely, without restraint; boldly, without reserve.

librepensador, ra, *a.* freethinking. —*m., f.* freethinker.

librepensamiento, *m.* (philos.) free thought, freethinking.

librería, *f.* 1. bookshop, bookstore. 2. book business. 3. bookshelf. 4. library. — **l. de lance,** second-hand bookshop.

libreril, *a.* pertaining to the book trade.

librero, *m.* 1. bookseller. 2. (Mex.) bookshelf.

libresco, ca, *a.* book, bookish, e.g. *ciencia libresca,* book learning.

libreta, *f.* 1. notebook, copybook, memo book, bankbook. 2. liturgical calendar. — **l. de ahorros,** savings book; **l. de banco** or **depósitos,** pass book, bankbook; **l. de cheques,** checkbook; **l. militar,** military service record; **l. de notas,** notebook, memo book.

librete, *m.* 1. *dim. of* **libro,** little book, booklet. 2. brazier, foot stove.

libretín, *m. dim. of* **librete,** booklet.

libretista, *m., f.* (theat., mus.) librettist.

libreto, *m.* (theat., mus.) libretto.

librillo, *m.* 1. *dim. of* **libro,** little book, booklet; packet (of cigarette papers). 2. (zool) omasum. — **l. de cera,** wax taper; **l. de oro, de plata,** book of gold or silver foil or sheets.

libro, *m.* 1. book. 2. (mus.) libretto, book. 3. (fig.) tax. 4. (zool.) omasum. — **ahorcar los libros,** (coll.) to give up studying; **hacer l. nuevo,** (coll.) to turn over a new leaf, start a new life; (coll.) to modernize; **l. amarillo, azul, blanco** or **rojo,** yellow, blue, white or red book (government publications or reports); **l. antifonal,** antiphonal, antiphonary; **l. blanco,** white paper, consultation document; **l. borrador,** (com.) rough book, notebook; **l. copiador,** (com.) letter book; **l. de asiento,** (com.) account book; **l. de becerro,** church register; **l. de bolsillo,** paperback; **l. de caballerías,** romance of chivalry; **l. de caja,** (com.) cashbook; **l. de coro,** chant or psalm book; **l. de escolaridad,** school record; **l. de estilo,** style guide; **l. de horas,** (ecc.) Book of Hours; **l. de inventarios,** (com.) general account book (showing state of finances); **l. de las cuarenta hojas,** (coll.) pack of cards; **l. de memoria,** memo book; **l. de música,** music book; **l. de oro,** Golden Book, Who's Who; **l. de pedidos,** order book; **l. de texto,** textbook; **l. en blanco,** blank book; **l. diario,** (com.) diary, journal, daybook; **l. en imágenes,** picture book; **l. mayor,** (com.) ledger; **l. talonario,** stub book, check book; **l. verde,** (coll.) notebook for describing the customs and people of a country; person who writes about the customs and people of a country.

librote, *m. aug. of* **libro,** large book.

licantropía, *f.* (med.) lycanthropy; (med.) zoanthropy.

licántropo, *m.* (med.) lycanthrope.

liceísta, *m., f.* member of a lyceum.

licencia, *f.* 1. permission, authority. 2. leave, license, permit. 3. liberty, e.g. *tomarse la l. de,* to take the liberty of; license, e.g. *l. poética,* poetic license. 4. license, wantonness, dissoluteness, excess. 5. (mil.) leave, furlough. 6. (educ.) licentiate (degree), master's degree. 7. (ecc.) (*pl.*) permission to preach and administer communion. — **dar l.,** to authorize, license, permit; **estar de l.,** to be on leave; **l. absoluta,** (mil.) discharge; **l. de armas,** gun permit; **l. de caza,** hunting permit; **l. de conducción** or **de conducir,** driving license; **l. de edificación** or **para construir,** building permit; **l. de pesca,** fishing license; **l. honrosa,** (mil.) honorable discharge; **l. por enfermedad,** sick leave.

licenciado, da, *past part. of* **licenciar.** — 1. discharged, released. 2. licensed, authorized. 3. pedantic. —*m., f.* licentiate, holder of a licentiate or master's degree. —*m., f.* 1. lawyer. 2. (coll.) university student. —*m.* ex-serviceman, discharged soldier, veteran.

licenciamiento, *m.* 1. graduation (with a licentiate). 2. discharge, release (of soldiers). — **l. honroso,** (mil.) honorable discharge.

licenciar, *tr.v.* 1. (mil.) to discharge, release, demobilize. 2. to confer a licentiate or master's degree on. 3. to license, authorize, permit, allow. —*r.v.* 1. to receive a licentiate or master's degree. 2. to become dissolute or debauched.

licenciatura, *f.* 1. licentiate, master's degree. 2. graduation with a licentiate or master's degree. 3. study leading to a licentiate.

licenciosamente, *adv.* licentiously, wantonly, dissolutely.

licencioso, sa, *a.* licentious, dissolute, wanton.

liceo, *m.* 1. Lyceum (gymnasium where Aristotle taught). 2. lyceum, literary or recreational society. 3. lycée, high school, secondary school (in certain countries); (Mex.) primary school.

lichera, *f.* bedcover, bedspread.

licio, cia, *a., m., f.* Lician. —*f.* **L.,** Lycia, ancient region of Asia Minor.

licitación, *f.* 1. bidding; bid, tender (for public contract). 2. auction. — **abrir la l.,** to open the bidding; **sacar a l. pública,** to put up for public auction (public contracts).

licitador, *m.* bidder (at an auction).

lícitamente, *adv.* licitly, lawfully, justly.

licitante, *m., f.* bidder or buyer at an auction.

licitar, *tr.v.* 1. to bid for, bid on (an item) at an auction; to bid on a public works project or for some other contract. 2. (Amer.) to auction, take bids for. —*i.v.* to bid.

lícito, ta, *a.* licit, lawful; just, right.

licitud, *f.* lawfulness; justness, rightness.

licnobio, a, *m., f.* person who lives by night and sleeps by day, (coll.) night owl.

licnis, *f.* (bot.) lychnis.

lico, *m.* (Bol., bot.) barilla, saltwort.

licoperdo, *m.* (bot.) licoperdo,.

licopodio, *m.* (bot.) licopodium.

licopodio, *m.* (bot.) ground pine, lycopod, lycopodium.

licor, *m.* 1. liquor (liquid; spirit). 2. liqueur (e.g. Benedictine). 3. (chem., pharm.) solution, e.g. *l. arsenical de Fowler,* (chem.) Fowler's solution; *l. de Fehling,* (chem.) Fehling solution.

licorera, *f.* 1. cellaret, liquor cabinet. 2. liqueur glass; liqueur decanter.

licorería, *f.* liquor shop.

licorero, ra, *m., f.* (Chile, Cuba) *var. of* **licorista.**

licorista, *m., f.* distiller; liquor seller or dealer.

licoroso, sa, *a.* spirituous, alcoholic; generous, rich, heady (wine).

lictor, *m.* (hist.) lictor, attendant of a Roman magistrate.

licuable, *a.* liquefiable.

licuación, *f.* liquefying, liquefaction; (metal.) liquation.

licuadora, *f.* (cul.) blender.

licuante, *a.* liquefying.

licuar, (*ref.* 55) *tr.v.* 1. to liquefy. 2. (metal.) to liquate, melt. —*r.v.* to become liquefied or liquated; to melt.

licuefacción, *f.* liquefaction, liquefying.

licuefacer, *tr.v.* to liquefy.

licuefactible, *a.* liquefiable.

licuefactivo, va, *a.* liquefiable.

licurgo, ga, *a.* (fig.) intelligent, keen, smart. —*m.* (fig.) legislator, lawmaker; **L.,** (hist.) Lycurgus.

lid, *f.* 1. combat, fight. 2. (fig.) dispute, argument. 3. (law) trial by duel. — **en buena l.,** fairly, by fair means, in a fair fight.

líder, *m.* leader.

liderato, *m.* leadership.

liderazgo, *m.* leadership.

lidia, *f.* 1. fight, contest, battle. 2. bullfight; **toro de l.,** fighting bull; **capote de l.,** bullfighter's working cape.

lidiadero, ra, *a.* (taur.) fit for fighting; **toro l.,** fighting bull.

lidiador, ra, *m., f.* combatant, fighter. —*m.* bullfighter.

lidiante, *a.* fighting.

lidiar, *i.v.* to fight, battle; (fig.) to oppose, face; (fig.) to contend, struggle (with a nuisance or pest). —*tr.v.* (taur.) to fight (a bull).

lidio, dia, *a., m., f.* Lydian.

lidita, *f.* (chem.) lyddite, a type of explosive.

liebrastón, *m.* leveret, young hare.

liebratico, *m.* leveret, young hare.

liebratón, *m.* leveret, young hare.

liebre, *f.* 1. (zool.) hare. 2. (coll.) mouse, coward. 3. (astron.) **L.,** Lepus, Hare. 4. (*pl.*) (mar.) racks, ribs, dead-eyes. — **coger uno una l.,** to fall without hurting oneself; **comer uno l.,** (coll.) to be a coward; **l. marina,** (zool.) sea hare; **l. mímica,** (zool.) varying hare; **meter gato por l.,** to take in, to fool, swindle.

liebrecilla, *f.* (bot.) cornflower, bluebottle.

liebrezuela, *f.* young or small hare.

Liechtenstein, *m.* Liechtenstein.

liego, ga, *a.* virgin (soil).

Lieja, *f.* Liege, city in Belgium.

lienal, *a.* (anat.) lienal.

liencillo, *m.* (Ecuad., tex.) coarse cotton cloth.

liendra, *f.* (Mex.) *var. of* **liendre.**

liendre, *f.* nit, egg of a louse. — **cascarle** or **machacarle a uno las liendres,** (coll.) to reprehend severely.

lientera, *f.* (med.) *var. of* **lientería.**

lientería, *f.* (med.) lientery, diarrhea.

lientérico, ca, *a.* (med.) lienteric. —*m., f.* (med.) lienteric patient.

liento, ta, *a.* damp, dank.

lienza, *f.* 1. strip of cloth. 2. (Chile) cord, twine; (Chile, imp. u.) leveling line or cord; fishline.

lienzo, *m.* 1. canvas; linen, linen cloth. 2. linen handkerchief. 3. (p.) canvas, painting. 4. front, face (of building or wall). 5. (fort.) curtain.

liero, *a., var. of* **lioso.**

liga, *f.* 1. garter; band. 2. league, alliance, confederacy, e.g. *L. anseática,* Hanseatic League, *L. de Augsburgo,* League of Augsburg. — **L. de Naciones,** League of Nations. 3. league, e.g. *l.*

menor, Little League (in baseball). 4. (bot.) mistletoe. 5. birdlime. 6. (metal.) alloy, binding material; bond; flux. 7. mixture, compound; **hacer buena** or **mala l.,** to mix well or badly (people); **l. de goma,** rubber band; **l. mayor,** Major League (in baseball); **l. metálica,** (metal.) alloy.
ligación, *f.* 1. ligation, tying, binding; tie, bond, union. 2. combination, joining. 3. mixture, compound.
ligada, *f.* (mar.) seizing, lashing (of a rope), tying, binding.
ligado, *past part. of* **ligar. —***a.* tied, bound, linked, confederated. —*m.* (mus., print.) tie, ligature; (mus.) legato.
ligadura, *f.* 1. ligature, tie, bond. 2, tie, trammel. 3. (surg.) ligature. 4. (mus., print.) tie, ligature. 5. seizing, lashing (of a rope). 6. subjection. 7. (mus.) suspension.
ligamaza, *f.* viscous substance surrounding the seeds of some plants.
ligamen, *m.* 1. (arch.) spell supposed to cause impotency. 2. impediment (to marriage); tie, trammel.
ligamento, *m.* 1. (anat.) ligament. 2. tying, binding, ligation. 3. mixture, compound. — **l. anular** (anat.) annular ligament.
ligamentoso, sa, *a.* ligamentous.
ligamiento, *m.* 1. unity, union, concord, accord. 2. tying, binding; bond, tie. 3. mixture, compound.
ligar, *(ref. 51) tr.v.* 1. to tie, bind. 2. to alloy, mix. 3. to join, link, combine. 4. to bind, tie, commit (by an obligation). 5. (Cuba) to buy (a harvest) in advance. —*i.v.* to combine cards. —*r.v.* 1. to unite, join together, ally, league together. 2. to become bound or tied (by an obligation).
ligazón, *f.* 1. bond, union, joining, connection. 2. (mar.) futtock.
ligeramente, *adv.* 1. lightly. 2. in passing, lightly. 3. slightly, a little, e.g. *la carne está l. quemada,* the meat is slightly burnt. 4. unthinkingly, without thinking.
ligereza, *f.* 1. lightness. 2. lightness, agility, nimbleness. 3. levity, frivolity, fickleness. 4. tactlessness, indiscretion, indiscreet remark.
ligero, ra, *a.* 1. light, not heavy. 2. light (sleep; meal; wine). 3. agile, swift, nimble, light. 4. light, slight, trifling. 5. superficial, flippant, frivolous, fickle, giddy; unstable, unsteady. 6. flighty, loose (woman). — **a la ligera,** superficially, without much attention, quickly; without ceremony, simply; **de ligero,** without thinking or reflexion, unthinkingly; **l. de cascos,** flirtatious, frivolous person; **l. de lengua,** garrulous, talkative; **l. de manos,** light-fingered, thievish; **l. de piernas,** light-footed, nimble; **l. de pies,** fleet-footed, fleet of foot, fast.
ligero, *adv.* (Amer.) quickly, fast.
ligeruelo, la, *a.* early grapes.
ligio, *a.* liege, bound by feudal allegiance.
lignario, a, *a.* ligneous, woody, of wood.
lignícola, *f.* (ento.) lignicole.
lignífero, ra, *a.* ligniferous, becoming woody.
lignificación, *f.* lignification.
lignificarse, *(ref. 50) r.v.* to lignify, become wood-like.
lignina, *f.* (chem.) lignin.
lignito, *m.* (min.) lignite (non-caking variety of coal, etc.).
lignocelulosa, *f.* (bot., chem.) lignocellulose.
lignosa, *f.* (chem.) lignose, lignin.
ligón, *m.* hoe.
ligroína, *f.* (chem.) ligroin.
ligua, *f.* battle-axe (used in Philippines).
ligue, ligué, *ref.* **ligar.**
liguilla, *f.* narrow band or bandage; ribbon, garter.
lígula, *f.* 1. (bot.) ligule, ligula. 2. (anat.) epiglottis. 3. (anat.) ligula (of the brain).
ligulado, da, *a.* (bot.) ligulate.
liguliflоro, ra, *a.* liguliflorous.
ligur, ligurino, na, *a.* Ligurian, of or pertaining to the Italian region of Liguria. —*m., f.* Ligurian.
ligústico, *m.* (bot.) lovage.
ligustre, *m.* (bot.) privet blossom.
ligustrino, na, *a.* of or pertaining to privets.
ligustro, *m.* (bot.) privet.
lija, *f.* 1. sandpaper. 2. (Cuba, P. Rico) self-flattery, conceit. 3. (ichth.) dogfish. — **papel de l.,** sand paper; **darse l.,** (Cuba, P. Rico) to flatter oneself.
lijado, *m.* sandpapering.
lijadora, *f.* sandpapering machine, sander; **l. de disco,** disk sander.
lijar, *tr.v.* to sandpaper, smooth with sandpaper.
lila, *f.* 1. (bot.) lilac (shrub; flower). 2. lilac (color). —*a.* 1. lilac-colored. 2. (coll.) foolish, stupid, silly. —*m., f.* fool, stupid person.
Lila, *f.* Lille, French city.
lilac, *f.* (bot.) lilac (shrub; flower).
lilaila, *f.* 1. Moorish war cry or whoop; cry of joy or merriment (at Moorish gatherings. 2. (coll.) trick, crafty scheme. 3. thin wool and silk cloth.
lile, *a.* (Chile) timid, spiritless.
lilequear, *i.v.* (Chile) to shiver, tremble (from fright or illness).
liliáceo, a, *a.* (bot.) liliaceaous. —*f.* (*pl.*) Liliaceae.
lilial, *a.* lily-white.
lililí, *m., var. of* **lilaila.**
liliputiense, *a., m., f.* Lilliputian, tiny.
Lima, *f.* Lima, capital of Peru.
lima, *f.* 1. file (tool); **l. de doble talla** or **de picadura cruzada,** double-cut file; **l. para las uñas,** nail file; **l. muza,** smooth file; **l. sorda,** smooth file; **l. triangular,** three-square file. 2. finish, polish, refining. 3. (bot.) lime (tree and fruit). 4. (archit.) **l. hoya,** valley (of a roof); **l. tesa,** hip (of a roof).
limaciforme, *a.* (zool.) limaciform.
limador, *m.* filer, polisher, smoother.
limadura, *f.* filing, (*pl.*) filings.
limalla, *f.* filings.
limar, *tr.v.* 1. to file; to smooth, polish. 2. to cut down, reduce. 3. to polish, perfect (a piece of writing or artwork). —*m.* (Guat.) lime-tree.
limatón, *m.* round coarse file; rasp.
limaza, *f.* 1. (zool.) slug; snail. 2. (Ven.) a large file or rasp.
limazo, *m.* slime, viscosity.
limbado, da, *a.* (bot.) limbate.
límbico, ca, *a.* (bot.) limbic.
limbo, *m.* 1. (theol.) limbo. 2. state of unconsciousness. 3. edge, hem, border. 4. border of the sun or moon. 5. limb (of an instrument for measuring angles). 6. (astron., bot.) limb. — **estar en el l.,** (coll.) to be in a daze or in a dream; **l. azumital,** horizontal limb, lower plate; **l.-índice,** graduated limb.
limen, *m.* (poet.) threshold.
limeño, ña, *a.* from or of Lima, the capital of Peru; Limean. —*m., f.* native or inhabitant of Lima.
limera, *f.* (mar.) rudderhole; helmpool.
limero, ra, *m., f.* lime vendor. —*m.* (bot.) lime tree.
limeta, *f.* short, squat long-necked bottle; vial; flask.
limícola, *a.* (ornith.) limicolous.
limiste, *m.* fine cloth formerly made in Segovia, Spain.
limitable, *a.* limitable; apt to be measured or restricted.
limitación, *f.* 1. limitation; limit. 2. restriction. 3. district, neighborhood.
limitacorriente, *m.* (elec.) current limiter.
limitadamente, *adv.* limitedly, restrictedly.
limitado, da, *past part. of* **limitar. —***a.* 1. limited, restricted; scanty. 2. dull, uncultivated (said of a person).
limitador, *m.* 1. (elec.) limiter, current limiter. 2. (auto.) fuel or speed regulator. 3. (mec.) a stop. 4. (hydr.) spillway. — **l. de corriente,** (elec.) current limiter; **l. de luz,** (photgmt.) aperture stop.
limitáneo, a, *a.* pertaining to frontiers and boundaries.
limitar, *tr.v.* 1. to limit; to reduce, cut down. 2. to restrain, circumscribe. 3. to fix the boundaries or limits of. —*i.v.* to be bounded, e.g. *el Perú limita por el norte con Ecuador y por el sur con Chile y Bolivia,* Peru is bounded in the north by Ecuador and in the south by Chile and Bolivia.
limitativo, va, *a.* limitative, restrictive.
límite, *m.* limit; boundary, frontier; the end. — **l. de elasticidad,** (engin.) elastic limit; **l. de plástico,** plastic limit.
limítrofe, *a.* bordering, conterminous, limiting; **naciones limítrofes,** bordering nations.
limnético, ca, *a.* (biol.) limnetic.
limnita, *f.* (min.) limnite, bog iron ore.
limnología, *f.* (biol.) limnology.
limo, *m.* 1. slime, mud. 2. (Col., Chile) lime tree.
limón, *m.* 1. (bot.) lemon (fruit); lemon tree. 2. shaft, thill (of a carriage).
limonada, *f.* lemonade; **l. de vino,** sangaree, sangria, wine and lemonade.
limonado, da, *a.* lemon, lemon-colored.
limonar, *m.* 1. lemon grove. 2. (Guat.) lemon tree.
limoneno, *m.* (chem.) limonene.
limonera, *f.* shaft, thill (of a carriage).
limonero, ra, *a.* shaft (of a horse cart or carriage). —*m.* lemon tree. —*m., f.* 1. shaft horse. 2. lemon seller.
limonita, *f.* (min.) limonite.
limonitizado, da, *a.* (min.) limonitic.
limosidad, *f.* 1. muddiness, sliminess. 2. tartar (accumulation on the teeth).
limosna, *f.* alms, charity.
limosnear, *i.v.* to beg (for alms).
limosnero, ra, *a.* charitable. —*m.* almsgiver, royal almoner. —*m., f.* (Amer.) beggar. —*f.* alms box.
limoso, sa, *a.* slimy, muddy.
limpia, *f.* 1. cleaning, cleansing. 2. (sl.) a shot of liquor.
limpiabarros, (*pl.* **limpiabarros**), *m.* foot-scraper, bootscraper.
limpiabotas, (*pl.* **limpiabotas**), *m.* shoeshine boy, bootblack.
limpiachimeneas, (*pl.* **limpiachimeneas**), *m.* chimney-sweep.
limpiada, *f.* the act of cleaning; brushing.
limpiadera, *f.* 1. carpenter's brush. 2. plowstaff.
limpiadientes, (*pl.* **limpiadientes**), *m.* toothpick.
limpiador, ra, *a.* cleaning. —*m., f.* cleaner; cleanser, scourer.
limpiadura, *f.* cleaning; (*pl.*) cleanings, waste, refuse; dirt (from something being cleaned).
limpiamanos, (*pl.* **limpiamanos**), *m.* towel, hand towel.
limpiamente, *adv.* 1. cleanly. 2. skillfully, dexterously, ably. 3. sincerely, simply. 4. unselfishly.
limpiamiento, *m.* the act of cleaning or disinfecting.
limpiaoídos, (*pl.* **limpiaoídos**), *m.* earpick.
limpiaparabrisas, (*pl.* **limpiaparabrisas**), *m.* (auto.) windshield or windscreen wiper.
limpiapeines, (*pl.* **limpiapeines**), *m.* comb cleaner.
limpiapipas, (*pl.* **limpiapipas**), *m.* pipe cleaner.

limpiaplumas, (*pl.* **limpiaplumas**), *m.* pen cleaner, penwiper.
limpiar, *tr.v.* 1. to clean; to cleanse; to clean out. 2. to clear (the land of undergrowth or enemies). 3. to clear, exonerate (of guilt). 4. to prune. 5. (coll.) to steal, pinch (coll.), lift. 6. (coll.) to win from; to clean out (win all money from). 7. (Mex.) to punish, to beat. 8. (Chile) to weed. —*r.v.* to clear oneself of blame. — **l. en seco,** to dryclean.
limpiauñas, (*pl.* **limpiauñas**), *m.* nail cleaner.
limpiavia, *m.* (ry.) cowcatcher.
limpidez, *f.* (poet.) limpidity.
límpido, da, *a.* (poet.) limpid, pure, clear.
limpieza, *f.* 1. cleaning. 2. cleanliness; cleanness. 3. purity; chastity. 4. integrity, honesty. 5. skill, ability. 6. clean play, fair play (in games). — **l. de bolsa,** (coll.) poverty, penury; **l. de corazón,** honesty, integrity; **l. de manos,** honesty, integrity; **l. de sangre,** racial purity; **l. en** or **a seco,** drycleaning; **l. étnica,** ethnic cleansing; **l. general,** spring house cleaning.
limpio, pia, *a.* 1. clean. 2. pure. 3. neat, spotless. 4. (fig.) sincere, artless. — **en limpio,** net (profit, income, etc.); **estar** or **quedar l.,** to be cleaned out, be without money; **poner en limpio,** to make a clean copy of; **sacar en limpio,** to get straight, get a clear idea of; to make a clean copy of.
limpio, *adv.* 1. cleanly, neatly; purely. 2. sincerely.
limpión, *m.* 1. superficial or light cleaning. 2. (coll.) cleaner. 3. (Col., Ven.) dish-cloth. — **date un l.,** you'll never make it, you'll never succeed.
límulo, *m.* (zool.) limulus; king crab.
lina, *f.* (Chile) coarse wool.
lináceo, a, *a.* (bot.) linaceous. —*m.* (*pl.*) (bot.) Linaceae.
linaje, *m.* lineage, ancestry, nobility; class, condition.
linajista, *m.* genealogist; writer of pedigrees.
linajudo, da, *a.* highborn, of noble descent (or boasting of it).
lináloe, *m.* (bot.) aloe.
linalol, *m.* (chem.) linalool.
linao, *m.* (Chile) a type of pelota game.
linar, *m.* flax field.
linaria, *f.* (bot.) wild flax.
linaza, *f.* linseed, flax-seed.
lince, *m.* 1. (zool.) lynx. 2. (fig.) very discerning or shrewd person. — **tener ojos de l.,** to be lynx-eyed. —*a.* 1. keen, sharp (eyes, sight). 2. shrewd, discerning (person).
lincear, *tr.v.* (coll.) to spot, discover (something seen with difficulty).
linchamiento, *m.* lynching.
linchar, *tr.v.* to lynch.
linches, *m. pl.* (Mex.) hemp saddlebags.
lincurio, *m.* semi-precious stone (thought by the ancients to consist of petrified lynx urine.
lindamente, *adv.* prettily, neatly, elegantly, beautifully.
lindano, *m.* (chem.) lindane.
lindante, *a.* adjacent, adjoining, contiguous; bordering.
lindar, *i.v.* to adjoin, abut; to be adjacent or adjoining, lie next to one another; to border; **l. con,** to be bounded by (have as its boundaries); to be adjacent to, lie next to; **l. en la locura,** to be bordering on madness.
lindazo, *m.* boundary, boundary line.
linde, *m, f.* boundary, limit; landmark, road sign.
lindel, *m.* (archit.) lintel.
lindera, *f.* boundary, limit.
lindería, *f., var. of* **lindera.**
lindero, ra, *a.* adjacent, adjoining, contiguous. —*m.* boundary, limit; landmark, boundary stone; **con linderos y arrabales,** (coll.) with every detail, the whole kit and caboodle.
lindeza, *f.* 1. prettiness, loveliness; neatness, elegance. 2. witticism, funny remark. 3. (ironic) insult.
lindo, da, *a.* pretty, lovely, beautiful; exquisite, elegant, neat; **de lo lindo,** marvelously, wonderfully, in a grand manner; greatly, very much. —*m.* (coll., derog.) effeminate dandy.
lindón, *m.* (agr.) ridge of earth (in which asparagus is planted).
lindura, *f.* prettiness, loveliness; pretty or lovely thing; **¡qué l.!** how lovely!
línea, *f.* 1. line. 2. (geom., geog.) line. 3. (geog.) Line, Equator. 4. line, limit, boundary. 5. (bus, steamship, etc.) line. 6. line (of words, print, etc.). 7. (ry.) line, track. 8. (sport.) line. 9. line, family, lineage. 10. (mil., mar.) line, e.g. *l. Maginot,* Maginot Line. 11. (fishing) line. 12. (fenc.) line (each of the positions of one's sword to counter the opponent's thrust). — **a la l. tirada,** (print.) all the way across the page; **buque de l.,** (mar.) ship of the line; **caída de potencial de l.,** (elec.) line drop; **correr** la l., (mil.) to inspect the lines; **echar líneas,** to draw lines; to discuss ways and means; to take measures; **en toda la l.,** all along the line, completely; **l. abscisa,** (geom.) abscissa; **l. aclínica,** (geog.) acline line, magnetic equator; **l. aérea,** (avia.) airline; (elec.) aerial line, overhead line; **l. ágata,** (print.) agate line; **l. agónica,** (phys.) agonic line; **l. bisectriz,** halving line; **l. coordenada,** (geom.) coordinate; **l. de abastecimiento,** (mil.) supply line; **l. de agua,** water line; **l. de aguas altas,** highwater line or mark; **l. de aguas mínimas,** low-water mark; **l. de arranque,** spring line; **l. de bajamar,** low-water mark; **l. de banda,** sideline, touchline; **l. de cambio de fecha,** date line; **l. de carga máxima,** (mar.) deep-water line; **l. de circunvalación,** (ry.) belt line; (fort.) line of circumvallation; **l. de contacto** or **golpeo,** line of scrimmage; **l. de contravalación,** (fort.) line of contravalation; **l. de cuadro,** balk line (parallel to one of the sides); **l. de edificación,** building line; **l. de defensa,** line of defense; **l. de flotación,** flotation line, water line; **l. de fondo,** base line (in tennis); **l. de fuego,** (mil.) firing line; **l. de fuerza,** (phys.) line of force; **l. de gol,** (sport.) goal line; **l. de la fecha,** date line; **l. delantera,** (sport.) forward line; **l. de la marea alta,** high-water line or mark; **l. de la tierra,** ground line; **l. de llegada** or **meta,** finishing line; **l. de mira,** (artil.) line of sight; **l. de montaje,** assembly line; **l. de nivel,** (surv.) contour line; **l. de partida,** starting line (of a race); balk line (in billiards); scratch line; **l. de policía,** police line; **l. de puntería,** line of sight; **l. de puntos,** dotted line; **l. de saque,** service line (in tennis); balk line (in billiards); **l. de servicio,** service line (in tennis); **línea de tiro,** line of fire, line of elevation; **l. de viento,** (mar.) direction of the wind; **l. de vuelo,** line of flight; **l. de zagueros,** fullback line; **l. equinoccial,** (geog.) Line, Equator; **l. férrea,** railway line; **l. fundamental,** ground line (perspective); **línea horaria internacional, l. internacional del cambio de fecha,** international date line; **l. isocórica,** (phys.) isochor, isochore; **l. maestra,** screed, floating screed, each of the ridges of a plaster laid on a wall and then leveled out in plastering; **l. media,** (sport.) halfback line; (geom.) center line; **l. meridiana,** meridian; **l. neutra,** (phys.) neutral position or line (of a magnet); **l. ordenada,** (geom.) ordinate; **l. quebrada,** (geom.) broken line; **l. recta,** (geom.) straight line; **l. telefónica,** telephone line; **l. telegráfica,** telegraph line; **l. transversal,** (geom.) transversal, intersecting line; **l. trigonométrica,** (geom.) trigonometric line; **líneas de comunicaciones,** lines of communication; **líneas de Fraunhofer,** (phys.) Fraunhofer lines; **l. visual,** visual line.
lineal, *a.* lineal, linear; composed of lines; (bot.) linear (leaf). — **medida l.,** lineal measurement.
lineamento, *m.* lineament, outline, feature.
lineámetro, *m.* (top.) lineameter.
lineamiento, *m., var. of* **lineamento.**
linear, *tr.v.* 1. to sketch, outline. 2. to line, draw lines on. —*a.* (bot.) linear (leaf).
líneo, a, *a., f.* (bot.) *var. of* **lináceo.**
lineolado, da, *a.* (zool., bot.) lineolate.
lineómetro, *m.* line gauge.
linero, ra, *a.* made of or pertaining to linen or canvas.
linfa, *f.* 1. (anat., physiol.) lymph. 2. (poet.) water. — **l. vacuna,** (med.) vaccine lymph.
linfadenitis, *f.* (med.) lymphadenitis.
linfangitis, *f.* (med.) lymphangitis.
linfático, ca, *a.* lymphatic.
linfatismo, *m.* (med.) lymphatism.
linfoblástico, ca, *a.* (anat.) lymphoblastic.
linfoblasto, *m.* (anat.) lymphoblast.
linfocito, *m.* (anat.) lymphocyte.
linfocitosis, *f.* (med.) lymphocytosis.
linfogranulomatosis, *f.* (med.) lymphogranulomatosis.
linfoide, *a.* (anat.) lymphoid.
linfoideo, a, *a.* (anat.) lymphoid.
linfoma, *m.* (med.) lymphoma.
linfopoyesis, *f.* (physiol.) lymphopoiesis.
lingo, *m.* (Amer.) leapfrog (children's game).
lingote, *m.* 1. ingot, pig, slug. 2. (mar.) iron bar used in securing cargo. 3. (print.) slug.
lingotera, *f.* ingot mold.
lingual, *a.* lingual. —*f.* (phonet.) lingual.
lingue, *m.* (bot.) lingue (Persea lingue).
linguete, *m.* pawl, ratchet; (mar.) pawl of the capstan.
lingüiforme, *a.* linguiform, tongue-shaped.
lingüista, *m.* linguist, expert in the language arts.
lingüística, *f.* linguistics.
lingüístico, ca, *a.* linguistic.
linimento, *m.* (med., pharm.) liniment.
linimiento, *m., var. of* **linimento.**
linina, *f.* (chem.) linin.
linio, *m.* row of plants or trees.
lino, *m.* 1. (bot.) flax. 2. linen; canvas, (poet.) sail. — **l. bayal,** flax sown in Autumn; **l. caliente,** flax sown in Spring.
linoleato, *m.* (chem.) linoleate.
linoleico, ca, *a.* (chem.) linoleic.
linóleo, *m.* linoleum.
linón, *m.* (tex.) buckram.
linotipia, *f.* (print.) linotype.
linotipista, *m., f.* linotypist, linotyper.
lintel, *m.* (archit.) lintel.
linterna, *f.* 1. lantern; lamp, (electric) torch, flashlight. 2. (archit.) lantern. 3. (mar.) lighthouse, lantern. 4. (mec.) lantern wheel or pinion. — **l. avisadora,** signal light; **l. mágica,** magic lantern; **l. sorda** or **flamenca,** dark lantern; **l. trasera,** (auto.) taillight, tail lamp.
linternazo, *m.* blow with a lantern; (fig.) blow, bang.
linternero, *m.* one who makes or sells lanterns.
linternón, *m.* 1. *aug. of* **linterna,** large lantern. 2. (mar.) poop lantern or lamp.
linudo, da, *a.* (Chile) fleecy, wooly.
linuezo, *m.* (coll.) linseed.
liño, *a.* row of plants or trees; ridge between furrows.
liñuelo, *m.* strand (of a rope or cord).
lío, *m.* 1. bundle, package. 2. (coll.) mess, jam, fix (coll.); intrigue, conspiracy. 3. (coll.) row, rumpus, trouble, uproar. 4. (coll.) nuisance,

bother. — **armar un l.,** (coll.) to cause a row, kick up a rumpus; **hacerse uno un l.,** (coll.) to get into a fix or jam.
liofílico, ca, *a.* (chem.) lyophilic, lyophile.
liofilizado, da, *a.* freeze-dried.
liofilizar, (*ref. 53*) *tr.v.* to freeze-dry.
liófilo, la, *a.* (chem.) lyophile, lyophilic.
Lión, *m.* Lyons, city in France.
liona, *f.* (Chile) *var. of* **liorna.**
lionés, sa, *a.* Lyonese, from the French city of Lyon. —*m., f.* Lyonese.
liorna, *f.* (coll.) uproar, confusion, hubbub.
Liorna, *f.* Leghorn, city in Italy.
lioso, sa, *a.* 1. trouble-making (person). 2. confusing, involved (problem).
lipasa, *f.* (biochem.) lipase.
lipegüe, *m.* (C. Amer.) extra (given to the buyer).
lipemania, *f.* (med.) lypethymia, lypemania, manic depression, melancholia.
lipemaníaco, ca, *a., m., f.* manic depressive.
lipemia, *f.* (physiol.) lipemia.
lipes, *f.* (chem.) blue vitriol, copper sulfate.
lipidia, *f.* 1. (Cuba, Mex.) impertinence, annoyance. 2. (C. Amer.) poverty, indigence. 3. (Chile, Peru) indigestion. —*m., f.* (Cuba, Mex.) pest, nuisance, bother.
lipidiar, *tr.v.* (Mex.) to annoy, bother, to make trouble for.
lipidioso, sa, *a.* (Cuba, Mex.) annoying, tiresome, bothersome, troublesome.
lípido, *m.* (biochem.) lipide.
lipiria, *f.* fever and chills, ague.
lipis, *f.* (chem.) blue vitriol, copper sulfate.
lipocaico, *m.* (biochem.) lipocaic.
lipodistrofia, *f.* (med.) lipodystrophy.
lipoideo, a, *a.* lipoid; fatty.
lipólisis, *f.* (chem.) lipolysis.
lipoma, *m.* (med.) lipoma.
lipoproteína, *f.* (biochem.) lipoprotein.
lipotimia, *f.* (med.) lipothymy; swoon, faint.
lipotrópico, ca, *a.* (biochem.) lipotropic.
lipovacuna, *f.* (med.) lipovaccine.
liquefacción, *f.* liquefying, liquefaction.
liquen, *m.* (bot.) lichen.
liquenina, *f.* (chem.) lichenin.
liquenología, *f.* (bot.) lichenology, the study of lichens.
liquidable, *a.* liquefiable; that can be melted.
liquidación, *f.* 1. liquidation, winding-up (of a firm). 2. clearance sale. 3. settlement, liquidation (of debts). 4. liquidation, extermination, killing. 5. liquefying, liquefaction.
liquidador, ra, *a.* liquidating. —*m.* (fin., law) liquidator (G.B.), receiver (U.S.).
liquidámbar, *m.* (pharm.) liquidambar.
líquidamente, *adv.* liquidly, in a melted or liquid manner.
liquidar, *tr.v.* 1. to liquidate, wind up (a firm). 2. to pay off, settle, liquidate (debts). 3. to sell off, sell at bargain prices. 4. to liquidate, kill. 5. to liquefy. —*r.v.* to liquefy, become liquid.
liquidez, *f.* liquidness, liquidity, fluidity.
líquido, da, *a.* 1. liquid. 2. (com.) net, clear. 3. (phonet.) liquid. —*m.* 1. liquid. 2. (com.) net. — **l. anticongelante,** antifreeze; **l. corrector,** correction fluid; **l. de frenos,** brake fluid; **l. imponible,** taxable income. —*f.* (phonet.) liquid.
lira, *f.* 1. (mus.) lyre. 2. (poet.) metrical form of five heptasyllabic verses. 3. (fig.) muse, inspiration. 4. (astron.) **L.,** Lyra. 5. lire, Italian monetary unit.
lirado, da, *a.* (bot.) lyrate, lyre-shaped.
liria, *f.* birdlime.
lírica, *f.* lyric poetry.
lírico, ca, *a.* lyric, lyrical. —*m., f.* lyric poet. —*f.* lyric soprano.
lirio, *m.* (bot.) iris; **l. blanco,** (bot.) Madonna lily; **l. de agua,** (bot.) calla lily; **l. de los valles,** (bot.) lily of the valley; **l. hediondo,** (bot.) stinking iris, gladden, gladwin; **l. tigrado,** tiger lily.
liriodendro, *m.* (bot.) liriodendron.
lirismo, *m.* lyricism.
lirón, *m.* 1. (zool.) dormouse. 2. (fig.) sleepyhead. 3. (mar.) jackscrew. 4. (bot.) water plantain.
lirondo, mondo y lirondo, pure and unsullied, neat, clean.
lis, *f.* (bot.) iris; **flor de l.,** (her.) fleur-delis.
lisa, *f.* (ichth.) striped mullet; (ichth.) a kind of leach (Gobitis taenia).
lisado, *m.* (med., biochem.) lysate.
lisamente, *adv.* smoothly; **lisa y llanamente,** plainly, frankly and openly; (law) taking words at their face value.
Lisboa, *f.* Lisbon, capital of Portugal.
lisbonense, lisbonés, sa, *a.* of or from Lisbon. —*m., f.* native of Lisbon, Portugal.
lisera, *f.* (fort.) berm; ledge or space between the ditch and parapet; narrow terrace.
lisiado, da, *a.* disabled, maimed, crippled. —*m., f.* crippled, disabled person.
lisiar, *tr.v.* to cripple, disable, injure. —*r.v.* to become crippled, disabled or maimed.
lisimaquia, *f.* (bot.) loosestrife.
lisímetro, *m.* (chem., pharm.) lysimeter.
lisina, *f.* (biochem.) lysin, lysine.
lisis, *f.* (med., biochem.) lysis.
liso, sa, *a.* 1. smooth; even. 2. plain, unadorned, unpatterned. 3. (Amer.) saucy, brazen. 4. plaindealing. — **l. y llano,** simple, easy, straightforward. —*m.* smooth face (of a rock).
lisogénesis, *f.* (physiol.) lysogenesis.
lisogénico, ca, *a.* (physiol.) lysogenetic.
lisonja, *f.* piece of flattery; (*pl.*) flattery, adulation, fawning; sweet nothings.
lisonja, *f.* (her.) lozenge.
lisonjado, da, *a.* (her.) rhombic, lozenged.
lisonjeador, ra, *m., f.* flatterer, one who cajoles or fawns. —*a.* 1. flattering. 2. pleasing.
lisonjeante, *a.* flattering, cajoling.
lisonjear, *tr.v.* 1. to flatter, compliment, fawn. 2. to please, delight.
lisonjeramente, *adv.* 1. flatteringly, fawningly. 2. agreeably, pleasantly.
lisonjero, ra, *a.* 1. flattering. 2. (fig.) pleasing, agreeable. —*m., f.* flatterer.
lisozima, *f.* (biochem.) lysozyme.
lista, *f.* 1. list; roll, register, list of names; menu, bill of fare (in a restaurant). 2. strip (of paper, cloth); colored stripe. — **l. civil,** civil list (allowance given to the royal family); **l. de boda,** wedding list; **l. de direcciones,** mailing list; **l. de espera,** waiting list; **l. de éxitos,** best-seller list; **l. de pagos,** payroll; **l. de vinos,** wine list; **l. electoral,** slate of candidates; **l. de correos,** general delivery;**l. grande,** complete list of lottery winners; **l. negra,** black list; **pasar l.,** to call the roll, call the register, call the muster.
listado, da, *past part. of* **listar.** —*a.* striped.
listar, *tr.v.* 1. to list; to enter in a list. 2. to get (something or someone) ready.
listeado, da, *a.* striped.
listel, *m.* (arch.) listel, moulding, fillet, tringle.
listerina, *f.* Listerine, mouthwash (trademark).
listero, *m.* roll keeper, roll taker (one who checks on attendance), timekeeper.
listeza, *f.* smartness, alertness, cleverness.
listín, *m.* 1. telephone directory. 2. (Dom. Rep.) newspaper. 3. small list, short list.
listo, ta, *a.* 1. ready; prepared. 2. smart, clever, bright. 3. quick, prompt. — **estar l.,** to be ready; **pasarse de l.,** to be too clever, be too clever by half; **ser más l. que el hambre,** to be very bright, be very sharp or shrewd.
listón, *m.* 1. ribbon. 2. (archit.) listel. 3. (mar.) battens. 4. (carp.) strip of wood, lath, cleat. —*a.* having a white stripe down its back (bull).
listonado, *m.* (carp.) lathing.
listonar, *tr.v.* (carp.) to make with laths or strips of wood; to batten.
listonería, *f.* 1. bunch of ribbons, ribbons; ribbon factory or store. 2. (carp.) lathing.
listonero, ra, *m., f.* 1. ribbon maker. 2. lath maker.
listura, *f.* smartness, cleverness, shrewdness.
lisura, *f.* 1. smoothness, evenness. 2. (fig.) sincerity, candor, frankness. 3. (Amer.) obscene word, oath. 4. (Amer.) impudence, insolence, sauce, cheek, e.g. *¡qué l.!* what a nerve!
lita, *f.* (vet.) tongue worm (in dogs).
litación, *f.* sacrifice to a deity.
litar, *tr.v.* to sacrifice to a deity.
litagre, *m., var. of* **litargirio.**
litargirio, *m.* (chem.) litharge. — **l. de plata,** silver litharge.
lite, *f.* (law) lawsuit.
litemia, *f.* (med.) lithemia, lithaemia.
litémico, ca, *a.* (med.) lithemic, lithaemic.
litera, *f.* 1. litter, sedan chair. 2. berth (in a train or boat); bunk.
literal, *a.* literal, to the letter; **traducción l.,** literal translation.
literalmente, *adv.* literally, adhering to the letter rather than to the spirit of an issue.
literariamente, *adv.* literarily, in a literary manner.
literario, ria, *a.* literary; **revista l.,** literary review.
literato, ta, *a.* well-read, versed in literature, cultured. —*m., f.* man or woman of letters, writer; (*pl.*) literati, men or women of letters.
literatura, *f.* 1. literature. 2. (fig.) empty words. — **l. comparada,** comparative literature; **l. de cordel,** popular literature, cheap literature; **l. de evasión,** escapist literature; **l. infantil,** juvenile books, children's books; **l. rosa,** romantic fiction.
literero, *m.* 1. one who makes or sells berths or litters. 2. litter bearer.
litiasis, *f.* (med.) lithiasis. — **l. biliar,** gallstones.
lítico, ca, *a.* (chem., biochem., med., physiol.) lithic, pertaining to stones.
litigación, *f.* litigation; quarrel.
litigante, *m., f.* litigant, party in a lawsuit. —*a.* litigant.
litigar, (*ref. 51*) *i.v.* 1. to litigate, to contest something at law with someone. 2. to argue, quarrel, contend, dispute.
litigio, *m.* lawsuit, litigation; dispute, quarrel, argument.
litigioso, sa, *a.* 1. litigious, contentious. 2. quarrelsome, belligerent.
litigue, litigué, *ref.* **litigar.**
litina, *f.* (chem.) lithia, oxide of lithium.
litio, *m.* (metal.) lithium.
litis, *f.* (law) lawsuit.
litisconsorte, *m., f.* (law) associate in lawsuit, joint litigant.
litiscontestación, *f.* (law) litiscontestation, contestation of suit (state of proceedings at which legal action begins).
litisexpensas, *f.* (*pl.*) (law) costs of lawsuit.
litispendencia, *f.* (law) lis pendens, state of lawsuit being judged.
litocálamo, *m.* fossilized or petrified reed.
litoclasa, *f.* (geol.) lithoclase, fissure in a rock.
litocola, *f.* lapidary's cement.
litocromía, *f.* (art., print.) lithochromy.
litófago, ga, *a.* (zool.) lithophagous; rock-eating, rock-boring (molluscs).

litófito, *m.* (bot.) lithophyte.
litofotografía, *f.* lithophotography, photolithography (process); photolithograph (picture produced).
litofotografiar, (*ref.* 54) *tr.v.* to photolithograph.
litogenesia, *f.* (geol.) lithogenesy, lithogenesis.
litoglifia, *f.* engraving on stone.
litografía, *f.* lithography (process); lithograph (picture produced); lithographer's workshop.
litografiar, (*ref.* 54) *tr.v.* to lithograph.
litográfico, ca, *a.* lithographic, lithographical.
litógrafo, *m.* lithographer; printer.
litoideo, a, *a.* (geol.) lithoid, lithoidal.
litología, *f.* (geol.) lithology, the study of rocks, their structure and formations.
litológico, ca, *a.* lithologic, lithological.
litólogo, *m.* (min.) lithologist.
litomarga, *f.* (min.) lithomarge.
litopón, *m.* lithopone, white pigment used in paints, linoleum, etc.
litoral, *a.* littoral. —*m.* littoral, coast, shore.
litosfera, *f.* (geol.) lithosphere.
litosol, *m.* (geog.) lithosol.
litospermo, *m.* (bot.) lithosperm.
lítote, *f.* (rhet.) litotes, attenuation, understatement.
litotomía, *f.* (surg.) lithotomy.
litótomo, *m.* (surg.) lithotome.
litotricia, *f.* (surg.) lithotrity.
litotritor, *m.* (surg.) lithotrite.
litráceo, a, *a.* (bot.) lythraceous. —*f.* (*pl.*) Lythraceae.
litrarieo, a, *a.* (bot.) lythraceous. —*f.* (*pl.*) Lythraceae.
litre, *m.* 1. (bot.) litri, litre (Lithraea caustica). 2. (Chile) rash caused by the leaves of the litri or litre.
litro, *m.* 1. liter, litre, a cubic decimeter. 2. (Chile) coarse wool fabric.
Lituania, *f.* Lithuania.
lituano, na, *a.*, *m.*, *f.* Lithuanian. —*m.* Lithuanian (language).
lituo, *m.* (hist., mus.) lituus (trumpet; augur's staff); ancient Roman trumpet.
liturgia, *f.* (ecc.) liturgy.
litúrgico, ca, *a.* liturgical.
liudar, *i.v.* (Amer., reg.) *var. of* **leudar.**
liúdo, da, *a.* (Amer., reg.) *var. of* **leudo.**
liuto, *m.* (bot.) variety of alstroemeria (Alstroemeria ligtu).
livianamente, *adv.* 1. loosely, licentiously, unchastely. 2. lightly, without foundation. 3. superficially.
liviandad, *f.* 1. looseness. licentiousness, flightiness (of women). 2. lightness. 3. fickleness, frivolity.
liviano, na, *a.* 1. light. 2. loose, flighty, licentious, unchaste (woman). 3. fickle, unconstant, changeable. 4. light, slight, trivial. —*m.* 1. (*pl.*) lungs, lights. 2. leading donkey.
lividecer, (*ref.* 45) *i.v.* to become livid, to turn ashen (from rage or shock).
lividez, *f.* lividness, lividity.
lividezca, lividezco, *ref.* **lividecer.**
lívido, da, *a.* livid, leaden gray, ashen.
livor, *m.* 1. lividness; purple (color). 2. (fig.) envy, hate, spite.
lixiviación, *f.* (chem.) lixiviation, leaching.
lixiviar, *tr.v.* (chem.) to lixiviate, leach.
lixivio, *m.* (chem.) lixivium.
liza, *f.* 1. lists, tournament field. 2. combat, fight. — **entrar en l.,** to enter the lists. 3. (ichth.) skate, striped mullet.
lizo, *m.* 1. warp thread. 2. heddle, heald.
llábana, *f.* smooth, flagstone.
llaca, (Chile, Arg.) mouse opossum (Marmosa elegans).
llaga, *f.* 1. wound; sore, ulcer. 2. (fig.) wound, injury, pain, sorrow. 3. (bldg.) seam, joint (between bricks). — **poner el dedo en la ll.,** to put one's finger on the sore spot.
llagar, (*ref.* 51) *tr.v.* to wound, hurt, injure.
llague, llagué, *ref.* **llagar.**
llama, *f.* 1. (zool.) llama. 2. swamp, marsh.
llama, *f.* 1. flame. 2. fiery passion. — **en llamas,** ablaze, aflame, in flames; **salir de las llamas y caer en las brasas,** to jump from the frying pan into the fire.
llamada, *f.* 1. call. 2. signal, sign, gesture (to attract attention, etc.). 3. reference mark (to footnote). 4. (mil.) call to arms. 5. (mil.) chamade (signal for parley made on drum and bugle). — **batir ll.,** to sound the call to arms; **ll. a filas,** (mil.) call to the colors; **l. al orden,** call to order; **ll. de larga distancia** or **interurbana,** toll call, long-distance call; **ll. de socorro,** distress call; **l. internacional,** international call; **ll. telefónica,** telephone call; **l. urbana,** local call.
llamadera, *f.* goad stick.
llamado, *past part. of* **llamar.** —*m.*, *var. of* **llamamiento.**
llamador, ra, *m.*, *f.* caller; summoner. —*m.* 1. messenger. 2. door knocker. 3. button (of an electric bell).
llamamiento, *m.* 1. call; appeal. 2. calling, summoning, convocation. 3. (med.) attraction (a drawing of fluid from one part of the body to another).
llamar, *tr.v.* 1. to call; to summon; to convoke. 2. to call, name. 3. to attract, call; **ll. la atención,** to attract attention. 4. (law) to summon; **ll. al orden,** to call to order. —*i.v.* 1. to make one thirsty. 2. to knock (at the door), ring the bell; **ll. a la puerta,** to call at the door, ring the bell. —*r.v.* 1. to be called, e.g. *me llamo Thedford,* my name is Thedford. 2. (mar.) to veer, change direction (the wind).
llamarada, *f.* 1. sudden blaze, flare; flash, flame. 2. (fig.) sudden flush (of the face). 3. (fig.) flare-up, outburst.
llamargo, *m.*, *var. of* **llamazar.**
llamarón, *m.* (Col., Chile), *var. of* **llamarada.**
llamativo, va, *a.* 1. (fig.) showy, gaudy, loud, garish, flashy (e.g. clothes). 2. exciting thirst, thirst-provoking.
llamazar, *m.* swamp, marsh.
llambria, *f.* steep incline, steep flat rock face.
llame, *m.* (Chile) bird snare or trap.
llameante, *a.* flaming, blazing.
llamear, *i.v.* to blaze, flame.
llamón, mona, *a.* (Mex.) cowardly.
llampo, *m.* (Chile, min.) ore dust.
llana, *f.* 1. (bldg.) float, trowel (for plastering). 2. each one of the sides of a sheet of paper. 3. level ground, plain.
llanada, *f.* plain, prairie, level ground.
llanamente, *adv.* 1. smoothly, evening. 2. plainly, simply, straightforwardly.
llanca, *f.* 1. (Chile) bluish green copper ore. 2. (Chile) small pebbles used by Araucan Indians for necklaces and dress adornments.
llanero, ra, *m.*, *f.* plainsman, plainswoman.
llaneza, *f.* 1. simplicity (of character, style). 2. familiarity.
llano, na, *a.* 1. level, flat, even, smooth. 2. simple, straightforward, uncomplicated (character, style). 3. simple, plain (dress, etc.). 4. ready, prepared, e.g. *estoy llano a hacer lo que me manden,* I am prepared to do what they command. 5. clear, evident, plain, obvious. 6. clear, free, open (e.g. a road). 7. common, ordinary (man). 8. (gram.) paroxytone. — **a la llana,** simply; (law) open (bidding); **de llano,** openly, clearly. —*m.* 1. plain, prairie, level ground. 2. (*pl.*) straight part (of sock, stocking).
llanote, ta, *a. aug. of* **llano,** very simple and frank, straightforward, uncomplicated.
llanque, *m.* (Peru) coarse Indian sandal.
llanta, *f.* (bot.) kale cabbage.
llanta, *f.* 1. (iron or rubber) tire (U.S.), tyre (G.B.); tread, wheel band (on carriage wheel). 2. rim (of wheel). — **ll. de goma,** rubber tire or tyre; **ll. de repuesto,** spare tire; **ll. neumática,** pneumatic tire; **ll. metálica,** (auto.) tire rim.
llantén, *m.* (bot.) plantain (Plantago majus); **ll. de aguas,** water plantain; **ll. mayor,** plantain; **ll. menor,** ribwort plantain.
llantencillo, *m.* (Chile) ribwort, ribwort plantain.
llantera, *f.* (coll.) continued crying or weeping.
llantería, *f.* (Chile) weeping, wailing (a group of mourners).
llantina, *f.* (coll.) uninterrupted weeping.
llanto, *m.* 1. weeping, crying, sobbing. 2. (Chile) tear, drop (dew on plants); **anegarse uno en ll.,** (coll.) to weep copiously; **el ll. sobre el difunto,** (coll.) there is a time for everything.
llanura, *f.* 1. evenness, levelness, flatness. 2. plain, prairie, steppe.
llapa, *f.*, *var. of* **yapa.**
llapango, ga, *a.* (Ecuad.) barefoot.
llapar, *tr.v.*, *var. of* **yapar.**
llar, *m.* (reg., Sp.) range, hearth. —*f.* (*pl.* **llares**) pothanger, pothook (in a fireplace).
llareta, *f.* (bot., Amer.) llareta yareta (Laretia acaulis).
llatar, *m.* (arch.) log fence, post fence.
llaucana, *f.* (Chile) iron bar or probe used to locate veins of ore.
llaulláu, *m.* (Chile) (variety of edible) mushroom.
llaupangue, *m.* (bot.), (Chile) pink francoa.
llauquear, *r.v.* (Chile) to cave in, slide in (said of the sides of a ditch, well, etc.).
llauto, *m.* (S. Amer.) headband.
llavazo, *m.* blow with a wrench.
llave, *f.* 1. key (of lock). 2. (elec.) switch, key. 3. faucet, cock, tap. 4. wrench. 5. trigger (of gun); lock, striker (of gun). 6. (clock) key. 7. (mus.) clef. 8. (mus.) key (e.g. lever of a clarinet). 9. (carp.) key, tightening wedge (wedge securing union of two pieces of wood or iron); (mas.) key, keystone, bondstone. 10. (dent.) key (extracting instrument). 11. (print.) brace, bracket. 12. (Mex., print.) nick (of a type piece). 13. (fig.) key (to a problem, code; to success). 14. key, key position, key place (controlling an area, country, etc.). 15. (min.) section of rock left cut in form of arch to reinforce walls. — **bajo ll.,** under lock and key; **bajo siete llaves,** very securely under lock and key; **echar ll.,** to lock, to seal; **ll. conmutadora,** (elec.) change-over switch; **ll. de bola,** ball cock; ball valve; **ll. de casquillo estriado,** box wrench; **ll. de cebar,** (mec.) priming cock; **ll. de combinación,** combination wrench; **ll. de contacto** or **de encendido,** ignition key; **ll. de correa,** strap wrench; **ll. de cruceta,** wheel brace; **ll. de cubo,** socket wrench; **ll. de chispa,** striker (of percussion fuse); **ll. de dos bocas,** double-ended wrench; **ll. de flotador,** ball cock; **ll. de iglesia,** (ecc.) power of the keys; **ll. de lucha,** hold (in wrestling); **ll. dentada,** bulldog wrench; **ll. de paso,** socket wrench; **ll. de percusión** or **pistón,** percussion lock; **ll. del pie,** distance from heel to instep; **ll. de reino,** key frontier position, key to frontier (of a country); **ll. de tiempo,** (mus.) time signature; **ll. de tres puntos,** three-way switch; **ll. de trinquete,** ratchet wrench; **ll. de tubo,** box wrench; **ll. de**

vaso, socket wrench; **ll. espacial,** space bar; **ll. falsa,** picklock, skeleton key; **ll. inglesa,** brass knuckles; monkey wrench; **ll. maestra,** master key, pass key; **ll. nelson,** nelson (hold in wrestling); **ll. para tubos,** pipe wrench; **ll. para tuercas y caños,** combination wrench; **ll. tubular,** socket wrench; **ll. universal,** monkey key.

llavero, ra, *m., f.* keeper of the keys; turn-key; jailer. *—m.* key ring.

llavín, *m.* small key, latch key.

lleco, ca, *a.* virgin (soil). *—m.* virgin soil.

llegada, *f.* arrival.

llegar, (*ref. 51*) *i.v.* 1. to reach, arrive, get, come. 2. to amount, come, e.g. *el gasto llegó a dos pesetas,* the expense came or amounted to two pesetas. — **ll. a,** to reach, get to, arrive at, come to; to amount to; **ll. a** + *inf.,* to manage to + *inf.,* get around to + *ger.;* **no llegarle a la suela del zapato a uno,** not to be able to hold a candle to; **ll. a** (e.g. setenta años), to reach the age of (e.g. seventy); **ll. a entender,** to get to understand, manage to understand; **ll. a las manos,** to come to blows; **ll. a oír,** to get to hear, come to hear; **ll. a saber,** to get to know; **ll. a ser,** to become. *—tr.v.* to push (something) up (to) move (something) close (to). *—r.v.* 1. to approach, come near, move close. 2. to stop by.

llegue, llegué, *ref.* **llegar.**

lleivún, *m.* (bot.) (variety of) sedge (Cyperus laetus).

llena, *f.* freshet, flood, overflow.

llenador, ra, *a.* (Chile) filling (food).

llenamente, *adv.* fully, copiously, abundantly.

llenar, *tr.v.* 1. to fill, fill up; to pack, stuff, crowd, make full. 2. to fill, occupy (post, position). 3. to fill in, fill up (G.B.), fill out (U.S.) (a form, etc.). 4. to fill in, while away (time). 5. to have, possess (requisite qualifications), e.g. *él no llena las condiciones para este puesto,* he does not have the qualifications for this post; to comply with (certain requirements). 6. to satisfy, convince, content, e.g. *mi trabajo no me llena por completo,* my job does not satisfy me completely. 7. to overwhelm (with favors, gifts), lavish (gifts, favors) on; to heap, pile (abuse) on, discharge (one's anger) against. 8. to cover, fecundate. — **ll. de** or **con,** to fill with. *—i.v.* 1. to be full (moon). 2. to be filling (food). *—r.v.* 1. to fill up, become or get full or filled up; to get crowded or packed. 2. to get or become covered (with dust, ink, stains, etc.). 3. to gorge oneself, eat one's fill. 4. (coll.) to get annoyed, get fed up. — **llenarse de deudas,** to get deeply into debt; **llenarse de plata,** to make a pile, get rich.

llenazón, *f.* (Amer.) surfeit, fullness.

llenero, ra, *a.* full, complete, entire.

lleno, na, *a.* 1. full. 2. (mar.) bluff. *—m.* 1. (coll.) plenty, abundance, plenitude. 2. fullness (of moon); full moon. 3. full house (at theater). 4. perfection, completeness. 5. (*pl.*) (mar.) middle part of ship (between runs). — **de ll., de ll. en ll.,** entirely, completely, fully; **ll. de bote a bote,** full to the brim, overcrowded.

llenura, *f.* 1. great abundance, plenitude, plenty. 2. overstuffed, filled (with food).

llera, *f.* gravel pit.

llerén, *m., var. of* **lerén.**

lleta, *f.* sprout, shoot.

lleulle, *a.* (Chile) inept, useless.

lleva, *f., var. of* **llevada.**

llevada, *f.* carrying, transporting.

llevadero, ra, *a.* bearable, tolerable.

llevador, ra, *a.* carrying. *—m., f.* carrier.

llevanza, *f.* leasing, renting.

llevar, *tr.v.* 1. to take, carry, transport. 2. to wear, have on (clothes), have with one, be carrying (documents, money, etc.). 3. to take, lead, e.g. *este camino te lleva a la ciudad,* this road takes you to the town. 4. to keep (books, accounts), manage, run (an estate). 5. to lead, live (a certain kind of life). 6. (math.) to carry (in addition, sums). 7. to win, get, e.g. *llevó el primer premio,* he won the first prize. 8. to have been, e.g. *llevo siete años aquí,* I have been here for seven years, *llevan seis años de casados,* they have been married for six years. 9. to tear off, take off, sever (e.g. shell — limb). 10. to charge (a certain price). 11. to win over, convince, persuade. 12. to bear, endure, put up with. 13. to yield, produce (land, plants, etc.). 14. to lease, rent. — **no llevarlas todas consigo,** not to be very sure, have one's doubts; **ll.** + *past part.,* to have + *past part.,* e.g. *llevo leídos muchos de los libros de texto,* I have read many of the text books; **ll. a** + *measurement of time, distance, weight,* etc., to be (so many years) older than, be (so many miles) in front or ahead of, be (so many pounds) heavier than, e.g. *le llevo dos años a mi hermano,* I am two years older than my brother, *el crucero llevaba dos millas al acorazado,* the cruiser was two miles ahead of the battleship, *Juan le lleva dos kilos a Pedro,* John is two kilos heavier than Peter; **ll. a cabo,** to carry out, perform; **ll. adelante,** to go ahead with; **ll. agarrado por las narices** or **por la punta de las narices,** (coll.) to lead by the nose; **ll. el compás,** to beat time; **ll. el paso,** to keep in step; **ll. consigo,** to take with one; **ll. un chasco,** to get a nasty shock, get a surprise; **ll. la delantera,** to be in front, be ahead; **llevarla hecha,** (coll.) to have something planned or well worked out; **ll. hierro a Vizcaya,** (coll.) to carry coals to Newcastle; **ll. la mejor parte,** to get the upper hand; **ll. las de perder,** (coll.) to be in a losing position; **ll. la peor parte,** (coll.) to get the worst of it; **ll. por delante una cosa,** to keep something in mind; **ll. puesto,** to be wearing, have on (clothes); **ll. a alguien la vencida,** (coll.) to have someone beaten, have someone in one's power; **ll. la ventaja a,** to have the advantage over; **ll. una vida de perros,** (coll.) to lead a dog's life. *—i.v.* to lead, go, e.g. *esta senda lleva al pueblo,* this path leads to the village. *—r.v.* 1. to take away, take; to steal; to carry off; to take with one. 2. to win, get. — **llevarse bien,** to get on well together; **llevarse bien con,** to get on well with; **llevarse mal,** not to get on well together; **llevarse mal con,** not to get on well with.

lliclla, *f.* (S. Amer.) blanket carried on the back by Indian women.

lligues, *m.* (*pl.*) (Chile) colored beans employed as dice in some games.

lloica, *f.* (coll., Chile) *var. of* **loica.**

lloradera, *f.* exaggerated wailing or sobbing.

llorador, ra, *a.* weeping, crying. *—m., f.* weeper.

lloraduelos, *m., f.* (coll.) moaner, mourner, weeper.

lloramico, *m.* crying.

llorar, *i.v.* 1. to cry, weep. 2. to water, run, weep (eye with a humor). 3. to bleed, weep (the stem of a plant). — **llorarle a alguien una cosa,** (Amer.) not to fit, suit or become one; (Chile) to fit, suit or become one. *—tr.v.* 1. to weep, shed (tears). 2. to mourn, weep over, lament, bewail. 3. to exude, drip with. — **niño que no llora no mama,** he who does not speak up, will not obtain what he wants; **ll. a lágrima viva,** to cry one's eyes out.

lloredo, *m.* laurel tree grove.

llorera, *f.* weeping, wailing.

lloriquear, *i.v.* to whimper, whine, grizzle (G.B.), snivel.

lloriqueo, *m.* whimpering, whining, sniveling, grizzling.

llora, *f.* (Ven.) funeral wake.

lloro, *m.* weeping, crying; tears.

llorón, na, *a.* 1. crier, constantly crying, who cries a great deal. 2. weeping (willow). *—m., f.* cry baby, child who cries a lot. *—m.* crest or tuft of long drooping feathers. *—f.* 1. weeper, hired mourner. 2. (Amer.) large cowboy's spur.

llorosamente, *adv.* tearfully, mournfully, weepingly.

lloroso, sa, *a.* tearful, weeping.

llovedero, *m.* or **llovedera,** *f.* (Amer.) rainy spell.

llovedizo, za, *a.* leaky. — **agua llovediza,** rain water.

llover, (*ref. 34*) *i.v.* to rain; **a secas y sin ll.,** without warning, without preparation; **como llovido,** unexpectedly; **ll. a cántaros,** to rain cats and dogs; **llovido del cielo,** heaven-sent; **ll. sobre mojado,** it never rains but it pours (adversities, difficulties, work). *—tr.v.* to rain. *—r.v.* to leak (roof).

llovido, *m.* stowaway.

llovioso, sa, *a., var. of* **lluvioso,** rainy.

llovizna, *f.* drizzle, fine rain.

lloviznar, *i.v.* to drizzle.

llubina, *f.* (ichth.) sea bass.

llueca, *a., f., var. of* **clueca,** broody (hen).

llueva, llueve, *ref.* **llover.**

lluvia, *f.* 1. rain, rain water. 2. (fig.) shower (e.g. of stones, bullets, etc.); heap, mass. 3. (Chile, Nic.) shower, shower bath. 4. (phys.) shower (of cosmic rays). — **ll. acida,** acid rain; **ll. de estrellas** meteor shower; **ll. de oro,** great wealth, heaps of money; (bot.) bean trefoil, golden chain, golden rain; **ll. estratosférica,** (meteorol.) trail, wisps of precipitation, virga; **ll. frontal,** (meteorol.) cyclonic rain; **ll. nuclear** or **radiactiva,** nuclear fallout; **lluvias aisladas,** scattered showers; **ll. torrencial,** (meteorol.) cloudburst.

lluvioso, sa, *a.* rainy, wet.

lo, *accusative sing.* of *m.* and *neut. pers. pron.* 1. him; it. 2. **lo** is often used to refer to an idea already mentioned and is either left untranslated or translated by "it" or "so," e.g. *¿eres tú estudiante? sí, lo soy,* are you a student? yes, I am, *¿viene Juan? no lo creo,* is John coming? I don't think so, *está cansado aunque no lo parece,* he is tired, although he doesn't look it. *—def. neut. art.* (followed by the *m.* form of the *a.,* it forms nouns or substantival phrases. 1. the, e.g. *lo increíble,* the incredible, *lo hermoso,* the beautiful. 2. the . . . thing, e.g. *lo sorprendente de eso,* the surprising thing about this, *lo bueno de eso,* the good thing about this. 3. the . . . things, the . . . stuff, e.g. *lo barato siempre se vende rápido,* the cheap things always sell quickly. 4. what is, that which is, e.g. *lo hecho, hecho está,* what is done, is done, *lo mío, mío,* what's mine is mine. *—neut. dem. pron.* the matter or question of, e.g. *no le mencioné lo del robo,* I didn't mention the question of the robbery to him; **eso es lo de menos,** that's the least important thing; **lo que,** which, a thing which (when referring to a whole preceding clause); what (when introducing a noun clause). *—adv.* how, e.g. *me sorprende lo tranquila que está,* what surprises me is how calm she is, *no puedes imaginar lo tacaños que son,* you can't imagine how stingy they are; **lo más . . . posible,** as . . . as possible, e.g. *lo más pronto posible,* as soon as possible.

loa, *f.* 1. praise, eulogy. 2. short dramatic panegyric in verse. 3. prologue (of the early plays).

loable, *a.* laudable, praiseworthy.

loablemente, *adv.* laudably, praiseworthily, commendably.
loador, ra, *a.* eulogistic, praising, eulogizing. —*m., f.* praiser, eulogizer, eulogist.
loán, *m.* (Phil. I.) loan, agrarian measure equivalent to 2.79 ares.
loanda, *f.* (med.) type of scurvy.
loar, *tr.v.* to praise, eulogize; to approve.
loba, *f.* 1. she-wolf. 2. ridge between furrows. 3. soutane, cassock (worn by priests); student's gown; **l. cerrada,** black hooded student's gown.
lobado, da, *a.* (bot., zool.) lobate. —*m.* (vet.) carbuncular tumor on horses.
lobagante, *m.* (zool.) lobster (Homarus gamarrus).
lobanillo, *m.* 1. (med.) wen, cyst. 2. gall (forming on trees).
lobato, *m.* wolf cub.
lobectomía, *f.* (surg.) lobectomy.
lobelia, *f.* (bot.) lobelia.
lobeliáceo, a, *a.* (bot.) lobeliaceous. —*f.* (*pl.*) Lobeliaceae.
lobera, *f.* 1. place where wolves abound. 2. narrow door or passage.
lobero, ra, *a.* of or pertaining to a wolf. —*m., f.* 1. wolf hunter. 2. (coll.) swindler, confidence trickster.
lobezno, *m.* small wolf, wolf cub.
lobina, *f.* (ichth.) a kind of sea bass (Morone labrax).
lobo, *m.* 1. (zool.) wolf. 2. (ichth.) loach (Cobitis barbatula). 3. hook to repel besiegers (in medieval warfare). 4. (tex.) willow, wolf (machine for cleansing and disentangling fibers). 5. (coll.) drunken bout, drunk (coll.). 6. (astron.) **L.,** Lupus, Wolf. 7. (anat., bot.) lobe. — **coger un l.,** (coll.) to get tight; **desollar** or **dormir el l.,** to sleep off a drunken bout or hangover; **l. acuático** or **de río,** otter; **l. cebado,** (her.) wolf holding its prey; **l. cerval,** (zool.) lynx; wildcat; **l. de dos pelos,** (zool.) fur seal; **l. de mar,** (ichth.) wolf fish, sea wolf; (fig.) old salt, old sea dog; **l. escorchado,** (her.) red wolf (on coat of arms); **l. marino** or **del mar,** (zool.) sea lion, seal; **lobos de una camada,** (coll.) birds of a feather; **meterse en la boca del l.,** to go into the lion's den, go knowingly into danger; **muda el l. los dientes y no las mientes,** the leopard never changes his spots.
lobo, ba, *a., m., f.* 1. (Mex., derog.) half-breed (negro with Indian). 2. (Chile) shy, retiring person, lone wolf.
loboso, sa, *a.* abounding in wolves (region).
lobotomía, *f.* (med.) lobotomy.
lóbrego, ga, *a.* 1. dark, gloomy, lugubrious. 2. (fig.) sad, depressing, melancholy.
lobreguecer, (*ref. 45*) *tr.v.* to make something dark or gloomy. —*i.v.* to grow dark.
lobreguez, *f.* darkness, gloom, gloominess; sadness, depression.
lobreguezca, lobreguezco, *ref.* **lobreguecer.**
lobregura, *f., var. of* **lobreguez.**
lobulado, da, *a.* 1. (bot., zool.) lobed, lobate, lobulate (made up of lobes). 2. (bot., zool.) lobular, lobe-shaped. 3. (archit.) foliated.
lobular, *a.* lobular, lobe-shaped.
lóbulo, *m.* lobe, lobule; (archit.) foil.
lobuloso, sa, *a.* lobulose, lobed, lobate, divided into lobes.
lobuno, na, *a.* wolfish, wolf-like.
loca, *f.* (coll.) drag queen; (sl.) queen (effeminate homosexual).
locación, *f.* (law) lease; **l. y conducción,** (law) leasing contract.
locador, ra, *m, f.* (Chile, Peru, Ven.) lessor, landlord.
local, *a.* local; **anestesia l.,** local anesthetic; **color l.,** local color. —*m.* premises, buildings; locale, place, site.
localice, localicé, *ref.* **localizar.**
localidad, *f.* 1. locality; place, locale, site. 2. seat (in theater, etc.); ticket (to theater, etc.).
localismo, *m.* 1. localism, fondness for local character. 2. regional idiom or expression.
localización, *f.* 1. localization. 2. location, finding, tracking down.
localizador, *m.* position finder; localizer (device).
localizar, (*ref. 53*) *tr.v.* 1. to localize, confine to definite limits. 2. to locate, find, track down. —*r.v.* 1. to become localized. 2. to be located or tracked down.
locamente, *adv.* madly, immoderately, foolishly; exceedingly.
locatario, ria, *m., f.* tenant, lessee.
locatis, *a.* (coll.) crazy, screwy, loony, mad. —*m., f.* (coll.) madman, loon.
locativo, va, *a.* 1. pertaining to a lease, leasing. 2. (gram.) locative. —*m.* (gram.) locative.
locería, *f.* (Amer.) crockery, china; (Amer.) china shop, crockery shop.
locero, ra, *m., f.* (coll.) potter; person who makes or sells pottery.
locha, *f.* **loche,** *m.* (ichth.) loach, a species of fresh water fish.
locho, cha, *a.* (Col.) red, reddish.
loción, *f.* lotion (cosmetic, wash); **l. capilar,** hair lotion; **l. para después de afeitarse** or **del afeitado,** after-shave lotion.
loco, ca, *a.* 1. mad, insane, crazy, out of one's mind. 2. mad, crazy, wild, harum-scarum. 3. mad, crazy, insane, rash, risky, imprudent. 4. tremendous, terrific; huge, enormous. 5. overgrown, rambling (branch of tree). 6. (Chile) mad (dog). 7. loose (pulley). 8. not pointing to magnetic north (compass needle). — **estar l. por,** to be mad or crazy about; to be madly in love with; **l. como una regadera,** as mad as a March hare, as nutty as a fruit cake; **l. de contento,** (coll.) mad with joy. —*m., f.* 1. lunatic, madman, insane person. 2. madcap, madman, harum-scarum; **hacerse el loco,** (coll.) to act dumb, pretend not to understand; **l. de atar** or **remate,** (coll.) raving lunatic; **l. perenne,** permanent lunatic or madman; (coll.) perennial wag, constant joker.
locoísmo, *m.* (vet.) locoism.
locomoción, *f.* locomotion.
locomotivo, va, *a.* locomotive.
locomotor, ra, *a.* locomotor; locomotive. —*f.* (ry.) locomotive, engine; **l. de diesel,** diesel locomotive; **l. de empuje,** (ry.) pusher engine; **l. de maniobras,** (ry.) switching engine; **l. de vapor,** (ry.) steam locomotive; **l. eléctrica,** (ry.) electric locomotive; **l. ténder,** (ry.) tank locomotive.
locomotriz, (*pl.* **locomotrices**), *a.* locomotive.
locomovible, locomóvil, *a.* locomobile, portable, movable; self-propelling. —*m.* locomobile; locomotive.
locro, *m.* (Amer.) meat, potato, corn and pepper dish.
locuacidad, *f.* loquacity, talkativeness, garrulity.
locuaz, (*pl.* **locuaces**), *a.* loquacious, talkative.
locucion, *f.* 1. style of speaking, locution. 2. phrase, idiom, expression, locution.
locuela, *f.* characteristic or individual manner of speaking (of a person).
locuelo, la, *a.* crazy, giddy. —*m., f.* crazy or giddy young boy or girl.
loculado, da, *a.* (bot.) loculate, loculated.
locular, *a.* (bot.) locular, having cavities.
loculicida, *a.* (bot.) loculicidal.
lóculo, *m.* (bot.) locule, loculus.
loculoso, sa, *a.* (bot.) loculate, loculated.
locumba, *f.* grape brandy (made in Peru).
locura, *f.* madness, insanity, craziness, lunacy; folly, absurdity.
locutor, ra, *m., f.* (rad.) announcer, commentator, speaker.
locutorio, *m.* 1. locutory (in monasteries or convents). 2. telephone booth.
lodachar, lodazal, lodazar, *m.* quagmire, mudhole, bog.
lodícula, *f.* (bot.) lodicule.
lodo, *m.* mud, mire; sludge; **poner a uno de l.** or **del l.,** to insult, throw mud at someone, slander.
lodoñero, *m.* (bot.) guaiacum.
lodoso, sa, *a.* muddy, boggy, miry.
loess, *m.* (geol.) loess.
lofobranquio, a, *a., m.* (ichth.) lophobranch, lophobranchiate.
logaédico, ca, *a.* (rhet.) logaoedic (verse).
loganiáceo, a, *a.* (bot.) loganiaceous. —*f.* (bot.) (*pl.*) Loganiaceae.
logarismo, *m.* (math.) logarithm.
logarítmico, ca, *a.* (math.) logarithmic.
logaritmo, *m.* (math.) logarithm; **l. común u ordinario,** common logarithm; **l. hiperbólico o natural,** hyperbolic or natural logarithm; **l. vulgar,** common logarithm.
logia, *f.* 1. lodge (of freemasons). 2. (archit.) loggia.
lógica, *f.* 1. logic. 2. dialectics. — **l. natural,** common sense; **l. parda,** (coll.) astuteness, cunning.
lógicamente, *adv.* logically.
lógico, ca, *a.* logical. —*m., f.* logician, professor of logic.
logístico, ca, *a.* logistic. —*f.* (mil.) logistics.
logógrafo, *m.* logographer (historian, chronicler, recorder of speeches in ancient Greece).
logogrífico, ca, *a.* 1. logogriphic, puzzling. 2. obscure, hard to understand.
logogrifo, *m.* 1. logogriph; riddle. 2. (fig.) obscure speech or dissertation.
logomaquia, *f.* logomachy, war of words.
logorrea, *f.* logorrhea; verbosity.
logotipo, *m.* (print.) logotype.
lograr, *tr.v.* to achieve, attain; to obtain, get; to possess, enjoy; l. + *inf.,* to manage to + *inf.,* succeed in + *ger.* —*r.v.* 1. to be successful, succeed, achieve one's desires. 2. (coll.) to get married.
logrear, *i.v.* to be a moneylender.
logrería, *f.* 1. moneylending, usury. 2. speculating, profiteering.
logrerismo, *m.* (Amer.) graft, peculation.
logrero, ra, *m., f.* 1. moneylender, usurer. 2. speculator, profiteer (on fruit). 3. (Chile) sponger, cadger. —**l. de guerra,** war profiteer.
logro, *m.* 1. attainment, achievement; benefit, success. 2. profit, gain. 3. interest, usury. — **dar** or **prestar a l.,** to lend on interest.
loica, *f.* (ornith., Chile) red-breasted singing bird (Pezite militaris).
Loira, *m.* Loire, river and region in France.
Loki, *m.* (myth.) Loki.
loma, *f.* hill; down, rise, hillock, slope.
lomada, *f.* (Arg.) *var. of* **loma.**
lomaje, *m.* (Chile) hilly ground, land with many hillocks and slopes.
lombarda, *f.* 1. (mil.) lombard (ancient type of cannon). 2. (bot.) (variety of) red cabbage.
lombardear, *tr.v.* to bombard with a lombard (cannon).
lombardería, *f.* battery of lombards.
lombardero, *m.* lombard gunman.
Lombardía, *f.* Lombardy, region in Italy.
lombárdico, ca, *a.* Lombardic, pertaining to the Italian region of Lombardy.

lombardo, da, *a., m, f.* Lombard (of or from Lombardy; native of Lombardy, Italy). —*m.* Lombard, bank, credit house.
lombardo, da, *a.* light hazel-colored (bull).
lombricera, *f.* (Mex., bot.) common tansy.
lombriciento, ta, *a.* (Chile, Hond.) wormridden, full of worms.
lombrigón, *m.* large worm.
lombriguera, *f.* 1. (bot.) common tansy. 2. worm hole.
lombriz, (*pl.* **lombrices**), *f.* (zool.) earthworm, worm; (med.) worm. — **l. intestinal,** intestinal worm; **l. solitaria,** tapeworm.
lomear, *i.v.* to buck (horse).
lomento, *m.* (bot) loment, lomentum (a plant used by Roman women for cosmetic purposes).
lomera, *f.* 1. backstrap (holding the harness in place). 2. (bkb.) backband (of book). 3. (archit.) ridgepole (of a roof).
lometa, *f.* hillock, rise.
lomienhiesto, ta, *a.* 1. high-haunched (horse). 2. (coll.) conceited, vain.
lomillería, *f.* (Amer.) harness shop; harness maker's workshop.
lomillo, *m.* 1. cross-stitch. 2. cantle (of packsaddle). 3. (*pl.*) pads (of packsaddle). 4. small loin.
lominhiesto, ta, *a., var. of* **lomienhiesto, ta.**
lomo, *m.* 1. (anat.) loin; (*pl.*) back, loins. 2. back (of an animal). 3. (cul.) loin, chine, saddle (of pork, beef, mutton, etc.); (cul.) steak, cut of loin. 4. ridge (between furrows). 5. back (of a book or knife). 6. crease (in cloth, paper, skins). 7. (*pl.*) ribs. — **doblar el l.,** to toil, to work very hard; **llevar** or **traer a l.,** to bring on one's back, bring by pack animal.
lomudo, da, *a.* broad-backed; humpy.
lona, *f.* (tex.) canvas, sail cloth, cotton duck.
lonco, *m.* 1. (Chile) neck. 2. (Chile) bonnet, reticulum (second stomach of ruminants).
loncha, *f.* 1. flagstone, slab. 2. thin, neat slice (usually of meat).
lonche, *m.* (Amer., Angl.) lunch.
loncho, *m.* (Col.) piece, hunk.
londinense, *a.* of or pertaining to London. —*m., f.* Londoner.
londonense, *a., var. of* **londinense.**
Londres, *m.* London, capital of Great Britain.
londrina, *f.* woolen cloth formerly woven in London.
loneta, *f.* (Amer.) thin canvas, sail cloth, ravens duck.
longa, *f.* (mus.) long note worth two breves (in early music).
longanimidad, *f.* longanimity, long-suffering, constancy, forbearance.
longánimo, ma, *a.* forbearing, long-suffering, constant, magnanimous.
longaniza, *f.* pork sausage.
longazo, za, *a. aug. of* **luengo,** very long.
longevidad, *f.* longevity.
longevo, va, *a.* longevous, long-lived.
longicaule, *a.* long-stemmed.
longicornio, nia, *a.* (zool.) longicorn. —*m.* (zool.) longicorn; (*pl.*) Longicornia.
longincuo, cua, *a.* distant, far away, remote.
longipenne, *a.* (zool.) longipennate.
longirrostro, tra, *a.* (paleon.) longirostrine; (zool.) longirostral.
longísimo, ma, *a., super. of* **luengo,** very long.
longitud, *f.* 1. length. 2. (astron., geog.) longitude. — **l. de onda,** (phys.) wavelength; **tener tantos metros de l.,** to be so many meters long; **l. calibrada,** gage length; **l. total,** overall length; **l. virtual,** time length.
longitudinal, *a.* longitudinal.
longitudinalmente, *adv.* longitudinally; lengthwise.
longo, ga, *m., f.* (Ecuad.) young Indian.
longorón, *m.* (zool.) piddock (Pholas costata).
longuera, *f.* long narrow strip of land.
longuería, *f.* slowness, tardiness, dilatoriness.
longuetas, *f.* (*pl.*) (med.) bandages.
longui, *a.* dumb, stupid. — **hacerse en longui,** to act dumb, pretend not to understand.
longuísimo, ma, *a.* very long.
lonja, *f.* 1. slice of meat. 2. strap, leather thong. 3. (Arg.) hairless hide. 4. (com.) public exchange, market. 5. wool warehouse or storeroom. 6. (archit.) portico, porch.
lonjear, *tr.v.* (Arg.) to remove hair from (hide), strip of hair.
lonjeta, *f.* 1. small thin slice. 2. arbor (in garden), summerhouse.
lonjero, ra, lonjista, *m., f.* grocer.
lontananza, *f.* far horizon; (p.) background; **en l.,** far away, at a distance.
loor, *m.* praise, eulogy.
lopigia, *f.* (med.) baldness, alopecia.
lopista, *m., f.* (lit.) expert on Lope de Vega.
L.Q.Q.D. *abbrev. of* **lo que queríamos demostrar,** quod erat demonstrandum (Q. E. D.).
loquear, *i.v.* 1. to act or talk like a fool, talk nonsense. 2. to kick up a shindy, to frolic, revel.
loquera, *f.* 1. (female) guard or attendant in a lunatic asylum. 2. lunatic asylum. 3. (Amer., coll.) madness.
loquería, *f.* (Chile, Peru) lunatic asylum; madhouse.
loquero, *m.* (male) guard or attendant in a lunatic asylum.
loquesco, ca, *a.* 1. mad, crazy. 2. wisecracking, funny. — **a la loquesca,** madly, crazily.
loquillo, illa, ito, ita, *a. dim. of* **loco,** wild, frisky.
loquios, *m.* (*pl.*) (med.) lochia.
lora, *f.* (Amer.) female parrot, polly (coll.).
loran, *m.* (mar.) loran, long-range navigational system.
lorantáceo, a, *a.* (bot.) loranthaceous. —*f.* (bot.) loranthaceous plant; (*pl.*) (bot.) Loranthaceae.
lorcha, *f.* lorcha (Chinese transport boat), junk-rigged coaster.
lord, (*pl.* **lores**), *m.* lord; Lord (title); **cámara de lores,** House of Lords.
lordosis, *f.* (med.) lordosis, curvature of the spine.
Lorena, *f.* Lorraine, a region and former province of France.
lorenzana, *f.* linen fabric made in Lorraine (France).
loriga, *f.* 1. lorica, cuirass. 2. horse armor. 3. (zool.) lorica. 4. metal reinforcement for wheel hubs.
lorigado, da, *a.* armed with a lorica or cuirass.
lorigón, *m.* large lorica or cuirass with elbow-length sleeves.
loriguillo, *m.* (bot.) mezereon.
loris, *m.* (zool.) loris.
loro, *m.* 1. (ornith.) parrot. 2. (Chile) spy. 3. (Chile) glass bedpan. 4. ugly, unpleasant woman.
loro, ra, *a.* dark brown. —*m.* (bot.) cherry laurel.
lorza, *f.* (dressm.) pleat, tuck.
los, 1. (*pl. m. def. art.*) the. 2. (accusative *pl.* of *m. pers. pron.*) them. — **los niños,** the children; **los vi,** I saw them.
losa, *f.* 1. slab, stone; flagstone, tile. 2. trap, snare (for birds, rats, etc.). 3. (fig.) grave, tomb. — **l. sepulcral,** tombstone (covering tomb).
losado, *m., var. of* **enlosado.**
losange, *m.* diamond, lozenge; (her., geom.) lozenge.
losar, *tr.v., var. of* **enlosar.**
loseta, losilla, *f.* 1. tile. 2. small slab or flagstone. 3. briquette. 4. trap, trick.
lote, *m.* 1. share, portion, part, lot. 2. lottery prize. 3. number of counters (held by each player in card games). 4. (Amer.) lot, plot (of land). 5. (Arg.) fool, imbecile.
lotear, *tr.v.* to divide into lots.
lotería, *f.* 1. lottery, raffle. 2. lotto (game). 3. lottery office. 4. gamble, chance.
lotero, ra, *m., f.* lottery-ticket seller or vendor.
lótico, ca, *a.* (biol.) lotic.
loto, *m.* (bot.) lotus; **flor de l.,** lotus flower.
lotófago, ga, *a.* lotophagous, lotus-eating. —*m., f.* lotus eater; (*pl.*) Lotophagi, lotus eaters.
loxodromia, *f.* (mar.) loxodrome, rhumb line.
loxodrómico, ca, *a.* (mar.) loxodromic, loxodromical.
loyo, *m.* (bot.) boletus (Boletus loyus).
loza, *f.* crockery; earthenware, chinaware; porcelain. — **ande la l.,** (coll.) noisy mirth, gaiety.
lozanamente, *adv.* 1. luxuriantly. 2. exuberantly, vigorously.
lozanear, *i.v.* to be vigorous or exuberant.
lozanía, *f.* 1. luxuriance, frondosity. 2. vigor, exuberance. 3. haughtiness, arrogance.
lozano, na, *a.* 1. luxuriant, frondose. 2. vigorous, exuberant.
LS *abbrev. of* **locus sigilli** (**lugar del sello**), locus sigilli (place of the seal) (l.s.).
LSD, 1. (coll.) acid. 2. *sym. of* **lysergic acid diethylamide.**
ltda., ltdo., *abbrev. of* **limitada, limitado,** Limited (Ld., Ltd.).
Lu *sym. of* **lutecio,** lutetium (Lu).
lúa, *f.* 1. esparto glove for cleaning horses. 2. saffron bag. 3. (mar.) lee.
luán, *a.* (Chile) yellowish, grayish.
lubigante, *m.* (ichth.) *var. of* **bogavante,** lobster.
lubina, *f.* (ichth.) (variety of) sea bass.
lubricación, *f.* lubrication; **l. por barboteo** or **a salpique,** splash lubrication; **l. forzada,** force-feed lubrication.
lubricador, ra, *a.* lubricating. —*m.* lubricator.
lúbricamente, *adv.* lubriciously, lewdly.
lubricán, *m.* (poet.) dawn.
lubricante, *a., m.* lubricant.
lubricar, (*ref. 50*) *tr.v.* to lubricate.
lubricativo, va, *a.* lubricative, lubricating.
lubricidad, *f.* lubricity; (fig.) lewdness.
lúbrico, ca, *a.* lubricious.
lubrificación, *f.* lubrication.
lubrificante, *a., var. of* **lubricante.**
lubrificar, (*ref. 50*) *tr.v., var. of* **lubricar.**
lubrifique, lubrifiqué, *ref.* **lubrificar.**
lubrique, lubriqué, *ref.* **lubricar.**
lucentísimo, ma, *a., super. of* **luciente,** very bright or shining.
lucera, *f.* skylight.
lucerna, *f.* 1. big chandelier. 2. air shaft or hole, ventilation shaft or hole; light shaft, skylight (hole for admitting air or light). 3. (ichth.) (species of) flying fish. 4. (ento.) glowworm, firefly.
lucérnula, *f.* (bot.) corn cockle.
lucero, *m.* 1. **L.,** Venus (the planet). 2. bright star. 3. unshuttered part of window. 4. star, white spot (on animal's head). 5. (fig.) brilliance, splendor, brightness. 6. (*pl.*) (poet.) eyes. — **l. del alba** or **de la mañana,** morning star; 1. de la tarde, evening star.
lucha, *f.* 1. fight; strife, struggle; wrestling; wrestling match. 2. quarrel, dispute. — **l. cuerpo a cuerpo,** hand-to-hand fighting; **l. de clases,** class struggle; **l. libre,** (sport.) freestyle wrestling; **l. por la existencia** or **por la vida,** struggle for survival.
luchador, ra, *m., f.* fighter, struggler, wrestler.
luchar, *i.v.* to fight; to struggle; to wrestle; to quarrel, argue; **l. con** or **contra,** to fight or struggle with or against; **l. por,** to struggle for + *n.,* struggle to + *inf.*

lucharniego, ga, *a.* night-hunting (dog).
luche, *m.* 1. (Chile) kind of hopscotch. 2. (Chile) sea lettuce, laver (Ulva latissima).
luchicán, *m.* (Chile) stew made with sea lettuce.
lúcidamente, *adv.* lucidly, clearly.
lucidamente, *adv.* 1. splendidly, magnificently, sumptuously. 2. brilliantly, outstandingly.
lucidez, *f.* lucidity, clarity, clearness.
lúcido, da, *a.* 1. lucid, clear. 2. (poet.) bright, shining.
lucido, da, *a.* 1. magnificent, splendid, gorgeous, sumptuous. 2. brilliant, outstanding.
lucidor, ra, *a.* 1. shining, bright. 2. dashing, showy (clothes, etc.).
lucidura, *f.* (coll.) whitewashing (of walls).
luciente, *a.* shining, bright.
luciérnaga, *f.* (ento.) glowworm, firefly.
Lucifer, *m.* 1. Lucifer (prince of the rebel angels). 2. morning star. 3. arrogant wicked man.
luciferasa, *f.* (biochem.) luciferase.
luciferina, *f.* (biochem.) luciferin.
luciferino, na, *a.* Luciferian.
lucífero, ra, *a.* (poet.) resplendent, shining. *—m.* Lucifer, morning star.
lucífugo, ga, *a.* (poet., biol.) lucifugous, lucifugal, light-avoiding.
lucilina, *f.* petroleum.
lucilo, *m., var. of* **lucillo.**
lucillo, *m.* tomb; sarcophagus.
lucimiento, *m.* 1. luster, shine. 2. great success, e.g. *salir con l. del examen,* to pass the examination with honors or flying colors. — **tener mucho l.,** to be very successful.
lucio, cia, *a.* bright, shiny. *—m.* 1. salt pool, salt lagoon. 2. (icth.) pike, luce.
lución, *m.* (zool.) glass-snake.
lucir, (*ref. 46*) *tr.v.* 1. to wear; to display, show, exhibit. 2. to illuminate, light up. 3. to plaster. *—i.v.* 1. to shine. 2. to stand out, excel, shine. 3. to benefit, profit. *—r.v.* 1. to stand out, shine, excel. 2. to dress to one's advantage, look one's best. 3. to come out of (a project) successfully.
lucrar, *tr.v.* to earn, obtain. *—r.v.* to profit, fill one's pockets.
lucrativo, va, *a.* lucrative.
lucro, *m.* profit, gain; **l. cesante** (law), loss of profits or earnings; **l. esperado,** (com.) expected profits; **lucros y daños,** (com.) profit and loss.
lucroso, sa, *a.* lucrative, profitable, remunerative.
luctuosa, *f.* feudal death tax.
luctuosamente, *adv.* sadly, mournfully.
luctuoso, sa, *a.* sad, sorrowful, mournful, woeful.
lucubración, *f.* lucubration, laborious work, study.
lucubrar, *tr.v.* to lucubrate, dwell upon (a problem, etc.).
Lúculo, *m.* Lucullus, Roman general famous for his luxurious life.
lúcuma, *f.* (bot.) (variety of) eggfruit (Lucuma valparadisease); (variety of) eggfruit tree.
lúcumo, *m.* (bot.) (variety of) eggfruit tree.
ludada, *f.* hair braid (formerly used by women).
ludibrio, *m.* derision, mockery, scorn.
ludimiento, *m.* rubbing.
ludión, *m.* (phys.) Cartesian devil.
ludir, *tr.v.* to rub, chafe. *—r.v.* to rub together.
ludópata, *m., f.* compulsive gambler.
ludopatía, *f.* compulsive gambling.
lúe, *f., var. of* **lúes.**
luego, *adv.* 1. soon; at once, immediately. 2. then, e.g., *él se fue, l. el otro vino,* he went, then the other came. — **con tres luegos,** (coll.) in great haste; **de l. a l., in a jiffy; desde l.,** of course, naturally; **hasta l.,** so long, goodbye for now; **l. como,** as soon as; **l. de,** after; **l. l.,** at once, immediately; **l. que,** as soon as. *—conj.* therefore, then, e.g. *pienso, l. existo,* I think, therefore I am.
luengo, ga, *a.* long.
lúes, *f.* 1. epidemic, plague, pestilence, infection. 2. (med.) syphilis.
luético, ca, *a.* luetic, syphilitic.
lugano, *m.* (ornith.) (variety of) linnet (Acanthis spinus).
lugar, *m.* 1. place, spot, site. 2. (geom.) locus. 3. room, space. 4. town, village, hamlet. 5. opportunity, occasion, time. 6. post, place, position. 7. motive, reason. 8. (Chile) toilet, lavatory. — **dar l. a,** to make room or space for; to give rise to, cause; **en l. de,** instead of; **en primer l.,** in the first place; **en su l., descanso,** (mil.) stand at ease; **fuera de l.,** out of place, irrelevant; **hacer l.,** to make space or room; **hacerse l.,** to make room for oneself; to make a name for oneself; **l. común,** commonplace, cliché, platitude; toilet, lavatory; **l. geometrico** (geom.), locus; **lugares comunes,** commonplaces, platitudes; general principles; **no ha l.,** (law) the petition is denied; **tener l.,** to take place, happen; to fit, go in; to have time, occasion or opportunity.
lugarejo, *m. dim. of* **lugar,** hamlet, small village.
lugareño, ña, *a.* village (as a.), rural, rustic, country (as a.). *—m., f.* villager.
lugarete, *m. dim. of* **lugar,** little village, hamlet (often used despectively).
lugarote, *m. aug. of* **lugar,** ugly village.
lugartenencia, *f.* lieutenancy.
lugarteniente, *m.* deputy, 2nd. lieutenant, substitute.
lugre, *m.* (mar.) lugger, small vessel.
lúgubre, *a.* dismal, gloomy, doleful, lugubrious.
lúgubremente, *adv.* gloomily, dismally, lugubriously.
luición, *f.* paying off or redeeming of a mortgage.
luir, (*ref. 48*) *tr.v.* 1. to redeem, pay off (a mortgage). 2. (mar.) to rub, chafe. 3. (Chile) to crumple, rumple, crease. 4. (Chile) to burnish (pottery). *—r.v.* (Chile) to rub together, wear away.
luis, *m.* Louis (20 franc gold coin).
luisa, *f.* (bot.) lemon verbena, aloysia.
luismo, *m., var. of* **laudemio.**
lujación, *f.* dislocation, luxation.
lujar, *tr.v.* (Amer., reg.) to shine, polish (shoes).
lujo, *m.* luxury; **de l.,** de luxe, e.g. *modelo de l.,* de luxe model; luxury, e.g. *artículos de l.,* luxury articles; **l. asiático,** excessive luxury; **darse el l. de,** to give oneself the satisfaction or pleasure of.
lujosamente, *adv.* luxuriously, sumptuously.
lujoso, sa, *a.* luxurious, sumptuous.
lujuria, *f.* lechery, lust; excess.
lujuriante, *a.* 1. lecherous, lustful. 2. luxuriant, exuberant.
lujuriar, *i.v.* 1. to lust, be lustful or lecherous. 2. to copulate, mate (animals).
lujuriosamente, *adv.* lustfully, lecherously.
lujurioso, sa, *a.* lustful, lecherous, lascivious, libidinous. *—m., f.* lecher.
luliano, na, *a.* (phil.) Lullian. *—m., f.* Lullianist, Lullist.
lulismo, *m.* (phil.) Lullian philosophy.
lulista, *a.* (phil.) Lullian. *—m., f.* Lullianist, Lullist.
lulo, la, *a.* (Chile) 1. dim, dull. 2. lanky, tall and thin. *—m.* 1. (Chile) small cylindrical bundle. 2. (Chile) curl, spit curl. 3. (Col.) a variety of fruit-yielding plant.
luma, *f.* (bot., Chile) myrtaceous tree (Myrtus luma).
lumaquela, *f.* (min.) lumachel, lumachella, fire marble.
lumbago, *m.* (med.) lumbago.
lumbar, *a.* (anat.) lumbar.
lumbeta, *f.* (Chile, bkb.) paper folding or cutting instrument.
lumbrada, *f.* bonfire, great blaze.
lumbral, *m., var. of* **umbral.**
lumbrarada, *f., var. of* **lumbrada.**
lumbre, *f.* 1. fire. 2. glow, light (of fire). 3. light (for cigarette). 4. brilliance, brightness, splendor. 5. opening, lighthole, unshuttered space in window, door, etc., to admit light. 6. hammer (of flint lock). 7. toe (of horseshoe). 8. (*pl.*) tinder box. — **a l. de pajas,** very quickly, in the twinkling of an eye; **dar l.,** to light; to give (someone) a light; **l. de agua,** surface of the water; **l. mansa,** slow fire; **ni por l.,** by no means; **ser la l. de los ojos de uno,** to be the apple of someone's eye.
lumbrera, *f.* 1. light, body emitting light. 2. skylight; louver (opening to let in light or air); light, air or ventilation shaft or hole. 3. (mec.) opening, port. 4. (carp.) opening, slit (in a plane to let out shavings). 5. luminary, genius, expert, marvel, learned person. 6. (mar.) air duct, porthole. 7. (Mex.) box (in bull ring). 8. (*pl.*) eyes. — **l. de admisión** (mec.), intake port; **l. de escape,** (mec.) escape port.
lumbrerada, *f.* bonfire, great blaze.
lumbrical, *a.* (anat.) lumbrical.
lumbricoide, *a.* (anat.) lumbricoid.
lumbricosis, *f.* (med.) lumbricosis.
lumbroso, sa, *a.* luminous, bright, shining.
lumen, *m.* (phys., anat., zool.) lumen.
lumenmetro, *m.* illuminometer, luminometer.
lumia, *f.* prostitute.
luminal, *m.* (pharm.) luminal (trademark).
luminar, *m.* 1. luminary (heavenly body). 2. (fig.) luminary, genius, expert.
luminaria, *f.* 1. (ecc.) altar lights, sanctuary lights. 2. (*pl.*) lights, illuminations (at festivals).
lumínico, pertaining to light, photic. — **anuncio l.,** neon sign.
luminífero, *a.* luminiferous.
luminiscencia, *f.* luminescence; **l. catódica,** (rad.) cathodoluminescence.
luminiscente, luminescente, *a.* luminescent.
luminista, *a., m., f.* luminist (of a painter especially interested in portraying effects of light).
luminosamente, *adv.* luminously.
luminosidad, *f.* luminosity; **l. remanente o residual,** (rad.) afterglow.
luminoso, sa, *a.* 1. luminous. 2. bright, brilliant (idea).
luminotecnia, *f.* 1. illuminating or lighting engineering. 2. (theat., tel.) lighting.
liminotécnico, ca, *f., m.* (theat., tel.) lighting technician. *—a.* of or pertaining to lighting.
luna, *f.* 1. moon (satellite of the Earth). 2. moonlight, moon. 3. month, moon. 4. window; plate glass; mirror, lens, glass (of spectacles). 5. (ichth.) ocean sunfish, moonfish. 6. (fig.) lunacy, madness; wild idea, caprice, whim. 7. spread eagle (figure in skating). — **dejar en la l. de Paita,** (Peru, Chile) to leave in the dark (i.e., without understanding); to leave stranded; **estar de buena o mala l.,** to be in a good or bad mood; **estar en la l., estar en la l. de Valencia,** to be daydreaming; **ladrar a la l.,** to bark at the moon; **l. creciente,** crescent moon; **l. de miel,** honeymoon; **l. en lleno, l. llena,** full moon; **l. menguante,** waning moon; **l. nueva,** new moon; **luz de la l.,** moonlight; **media l.,** half moon; crescent-shaped gem or jewel; hamstringing knife; Turkish crescent, Islam; (fort.) demilune; (cul.) crescent-shaped roll, croissant; **pedir la l.,** to ask for the moon; **quedarse a la l., a la l.**

de Valencia, to be disappointed; **quedarse en la l.,** to be left stranded; to be left in the dark.
lunación, *f.* (astron.) lunation.
lunado, da, *a.* lunate, crescent-shaped.
lunanco, ca, *a.* having one haunch higher than the other (said of a horse).
lunar, *m.* 1. mole (spot on human body). 2. stain, blot. 3. blemish, defect. —*a.* lunar, of the moon.
lunarejo, ja, *a.* (Amer.) having many moles, covered with moles.
lunario, ria, *a.* of a lunar month. —*m.* calendar. —*f.* honesty.
lunático, ca, *a.* lunatic, mad. —*m., f.*lunatic, mad person.
lunch, *m.* (Amer.) lunch; snack.
lunecilla, *f.* crescent-shaped jewel.
lunel, *m.* (her.) heraldic charge composed of four crescent moons.
lunes, *m.* Monday; **cada l. y. cada martes,** every day, all the time.
luneta, *f.* 1. (theat.) orchestra seat. 2. lens, glass, lunette (of spectacles). 3. lunette, crescent-shaped adornment (used by women in hair and children on shoes). 4. front tile (of each line of roof tiling). 5. (archit.) lunette. 6. (fort.) lunette. 7. (mec.) rest (of lathe). 8. (auto.) window; **l. trasera,** rear window.
luneto, *m.* (archit.) lunette.
lunfa, *m.* (Arg.) thief.
lunfardismo, *m.* slang word or expression used in the region of the River Plate (Argentina and Uruguay).
lunfardo, da, *a.* (S. Amer.) underworld. —*m.* 1. (Arg., Urug.) thief; crook, ruffian. 2. (Arg., Urug.) underworld slang, thieves' jargon.
lunilla, *f.* crescent-shaped jewel.
lúnula, *f.* 1. lunule, moon (of fingernail). 2. (geom.) lune (arc of circle). 3. (astron.) moon (satellite of planets). 4. (zool.) lunule. 5. (ecc.) small monstrance lining a larger one.
lupa, *f.* magnifying glass.
lupanar, *m.* brothel.
lupanario, ria, *a.* of a brothel.
lupercales, *f.* (*pl.*) Lupercalia, festivities in ancient Rome in honor of Pan.
lupia, *f.* 1. cyst, wen. 2. (Col.) small change. —*m., f.* (Hond.) quack, witch doctor.
lupicia, *f.* alopecia, baldness.
lupino, na, *a.* lupine. —*m.* (bot.) lupine.
lupulina, *f.* (bot.) black medic.
lupulino, *m.* (bot.) lupulin (fine yellow powder on strobiles of hops).
lúpulo, *m.* 1. (bot.) hop (vine). 2. hops (ingredient of beer).
lupus, *m.* (med.) lupus.
luquete, *m.* 1. slice of lemon (put into wine). 2. sulfur match. 3. (Chile) untilled patch in fallow land. 4. (Chile) round bald patch. 5. (Chile) round stain or hole (in clothing). 6. (archit.) dome (of vault).
Lurdes, *m.* Lourdes.
lurio, a, *a.* 1. (Mex.) mad, crazy. 2. (Mex.) fatuous, pedantic.
lurte, *m.* landslide, avalanche.
Lusaka, *f.* Lusaka, capital of Zambia.
lusitánico, ca, *a.* Lusitanian, Portuguese.
lusitanismo, *m.* Lusitanism, Portuguese idiom, use of Portuguese words or idioms in other languages.
lusitano, na, *a., m., f.* Lusitanian, Portuguese.
luso, sa, *a.* Lusitanian; Luso, e.g. *lusobrasilero,* Luso-Brazilian. —*m., f.* Lusitanian.
lustrabotas, *m.* 1. (Amer.) bootblack, shoeshine boy. 2. (Amer., derog.) lackey, bootlicker.
lustración, *f.* lustration.
lustrada, *f.* (Amer.) (shoe) shine.
lustral, *a.* lustral.
lustrar, *tr.v.* 1. to polish. 2. to lustrate, purify, cleanse. —*i.v.* to travel, roam, wander.
lustre, *m.* 1. shine, luster, gloss. 2. (fig.) luster, glory, fame, splendor. — **dar l. a,** to polish, shine, shine up; **tener l.,** to be shiny; (fig.) to be famous or noble.
lustrear, *tr.v.* (Chile) to polish, shine.
lústrico, ca, *a.* lustral, lustrical.
lustrín, *m.* (Chile) kiosk where shoes are shined.
lustrina, *f.* 1. (tex.) lustring, lustrine. 2. alpaca-like cloth. 3. (Chile) shoe polish, boot polish.
lustro, *m.* lustrum (five years); (hist.) lustrum (ceremony).
lustrosamente, *adv.* shinily, glossily, lustrously.
lustroso, sa, *a.* lustrous, shiny, glossy.
lútea, *f.* (ornith.) golden oriole.
lutecio, *m.* (chem.) lutetium.
luteína, *f.* (biochem.) lutein.
luteinización, *f.* (biochem.) luteinizing.
lúteo, a, *a.* muddy, luteous, miry.
luteolina, *f.* (chem.) luteolin.
luteranismo, *m.* Lutheranism.
luterano, na, *a.* Lutheran.
Lutero, *m.* (rel., hist.) Luther, German theologian, leader of the Protestant Reformation.
lutita, *f.* (min.) shale.
luto, *m.* 1. mourning; sorrow, bereavement. 2. mourning, mourning clothes; (*pl.*) mourning draperies; **aliviar el l.,** to come out of deep mourning; **estar de l.,** to be in mourning; **medio l.,** half mourning; **l. riguroso,** deep mourning; **ponerse de l.,** to go into mourning.
lutocar, *m.* (Chile) hand-driven cart used to collect garbage.
lutona, *f.* (Ecuad.) ghost, black-clad woman in folk tales.
lutoso, sa, *a., var. of* **luctuoso.**
lutria, *f.* (zool.) otter.
lux, *m.* (phys.) lux (unit of light).
luxación, *f.* (med.) luxation, dislocation.
Luxemburgo, *m.* Luxembourg, Luxemburg.
luxemburgués, sa, *a.* Luxemburgian. —*m., f.* Luxemburger.
luz, (*pl.* **luces**), *f.* 1. light. 2. (fig.) guiding light, beacon light, luminary. 3. (archit.) window, opening, skylight, light-shaft. 4. (coll.) money. 5. day, daylight. 6. piece of information or news. 7. (*pl.*) learning, enlightenment, culture. 8. (archit.) span. 9. (*pl.*) (Mex.) evening party. — **a buena l.,** carefully, after due examination; **a la l. de,** by the light of, in the light of; **a toda l.** or **a todas luces,** from every point of view, manifestly; by all means; **dar a l.,** to give birth, bring forth; **dar a la l.,** (print.) to publish; **dar l.,** to illuminate, light up; **echar l.,** to shed or throw light (on); **entre dos luces,** at twilight, at dawn, at sunset; (coll.) tipsy, half-drunk; **luces de aterrizaje,** landing lights; **luces cortas** or **bajas** or **de cruce,** dipped headlights; **luces de estacionamiento** or **de ciudad** or **de situación** parking lights; **luces de gálibo,** clearance lights; **luces de navegación,** navigation lights; **luces de marcha,** running lights; **luces del tablero,** (auto.) panel lights; **luces largas** or **altas,** full beam, brights; **l. artificial,** artificial lighting; **l. de anclaje,** anchor light; **l. cenicienta** or **cinérea,** earthlight (faintly illuminating dark part of new moon); **l. cenital,** skylight; (auto.) dome lamp or light; **l. de balizaje,** (mil.) boundary light; **l. de Bengala,** flare; sparkler (fireworks); **l. de carretera,** (auto.) full beam, brights; **l. de cortesía** or **estribo,** courtesy light; **l. de estacionamiento,** or **de ciudad** or **de situación,** parking light; **l. de la razón,** light of reason; **l. de frenado,** brake light; **l. de luz,** reflected light, indirect light; **l. de neón,** neon light; **l. de pedestal** or **pie,** (aer.) pedestal light; **l. de situación,** (mar., aer.) position light; **l. de techo,** (auto.) dome lamp or light; **l. del día,** daylight; **l. de tránsito** or **tráfico,** traffic light; **l. de zaga** or **trasera,** (auto.) tail light; **l. eléctrica,** electric light or lighting; **l. y sonido,** son et lumière (spectacle for the public in which is included the lighting of historic buildings); **media l.,** halflight, subdued light; **primera l.,** direct light; **sacar a la l.,** to publish; to disclose, reveal; **salir a la l.,** to come to light, be revealed; to be published or printed; to be produced, come out; **taparle a uno la l.,** to stand in one's light; **traje de luces,** bullfighter's suit; **ver uno la l.,** to be born, see the light of day; (fig.) to understand.
luzbel, *m.* Lucifer (Satan).
luzca, luzco, *ref.* **lucir.**

M

M, *f.,* m, thirteenth letter of the Spanish alphabet.

m., *m. abbrev. of* 1. **metro,** meter (m). 2. **Monsieur,** Monsieur (M.). 3. **masculino,** masculine, male (m.). 4. **Majestad,** Majesty (M.).

mabinga, *f.* 1. (Cuba, Mex.) dung, manure. 2. (Cuba, Mex.) inferior quality tobacco.

mabita, *m., f.* (Ven.) unlucky person. —*f.* evil eye, jinx.

mabolo, *m.* (Phil. I., bot.) camabon tree.

Mac. *abbrev. of* **Macabeos,** (Bib.) Maccabees (Mac.).

maca, *f.* 1. bruise, blemish (on fruit); flaw, defect (spiritual or material); spot, stain (e.g. on cloth). 2. trick; (*pl.*) slyness, cunning, deceit. — **tener muchas macas,** to be very sly or cunning. 3. hammock (by aphaeresis).

Macabeo, *m.* (Bib.) Maccabaeus, Maccabeus, (*pl.*) Maccabees.

macabí, *m.* (Cuba, ichth.) banana fish.

macabro, bra, *a.* macabre, funereal, pertaining to the dead; **danza macabra,** dance of death.

macaca, *f.* 1. (zool.) female macaque. 2. (Chile) binge, (coll.) drunken spree, drunk, jag.

macaco, ca, *a.* (Amer.) ugly, misshapen, deformed; squat. —*m.* 1. (zool.) macaque. 2. (Mex.) bogie, hobgoblin. —*f.* (Hond.) small coin, value of one peso.

macacoa, *f.* (Ven.) bad mood, the dumps, melancholy.

macadam, *m., var. of* **macadán.**

macadamizado, da, *a.* macadamized, macadam.

macadamizar, (*ref. 53*) *tr.v.* to macadamize, to pave with macadam.

macadán, *m.* macadam.

macagua, *f.* 1. (ornith.) laughing falcon. 2. (zool.) Venezuelan poisonous snake. 3. (bot.) (a kind of) breadfruit tree (Pseudolmedia havanensis).

macagüita, *f.* (Ven.) a thorny palm tree.

macal, *m.* (Mex.) taro, eddo, yam (Colocasia antiquorum).

macana, *f.* 1. macana, wooden swordlike weapon (used by American Indians); (Amer.) heavy wooden club. 2. rubbish, dud stock (unsaleable articles). 3. (Amer.) rumor, fib, lie; joke. 4. (fig.) drug on the market. 5. (Amer.) botched job; 6. (Arg.) gadget. 7. (Arg.) tiresome gossip. 8. (C. Amer., Mex.) hoe.

macanazo, *m.* blow with a macana or club.

macanear, *tr.v.* 1. (Arg.) to talk nonsense or rubbish; to fib, to joke. 2. (Arg.) to botch, do poorly. —*r.v.* (Hond.) to work hard, labor, exert oneself.

macano, *m.* (Chile) dark color used to dye wool.

macanudo, da, *a.* (Arg., Urug., Chile) excellent, wonderful, fine, fabulous, grand.

Macao, *m.* Macao, Portuguese-held territory on a Chinese peninsula.

macao, *m.* (zool., Cuba) hermit-crab (Pagurus granulatus).

macaquear, *tr.v.* (C. Amer.) to rob, cheat. —*i.v.* (S.Amer.) to make faces.

macarelo, *m.* bully, troublemaker.

macareno, *m.* (reg., Sp.) braggart, tough guy, swaggerer.

macareo, *m.* tidal bore, tide-rip in a river.

macarro, *m.* bread, bun.

macarrón, *m.* 1. (cul.) macaroon. 2. (*pl.*) macaroni, pasta. 3. (*pl.*) (mar.) stanchions.

macarronea, *f.* macaronic, burlesque poetry or composition written in jumbled Latin.

macarrónicamente, *adv.* macaronically.

macarrónico, ca, *a.* macaronic, pertaining to burlesque parlance imitating Latin.

macarse, (*ref. 50*) *r.v.* to begin to rot, to spoil (fruit).

macatrullo, lla, *a.* stupid, dull, dim.

macaurel, *f.* (zool.) *a.* Venezuelan non-poisonous snake (Xiphosoma canimum).

macaz, (*pl.* **macaces**), *m.* (Peru, zool.) (a kind of) paca.

macazuchil, *m.* piperaceous plant used in Mexico to flavor drinks (Pieper amalago).

mace, macé, *ref.* **mazar.**

maceador, *m.* hammerer, pounder.

macear, *tr.v.* to hammer, pound, to maul, knock. —*i.v.* (fig.) to pester, to insist or harp on an issue.

macedón, na, *a., m., f.* (hist., geog.) Macedonian, of or pertaining to Macedonia.

Macedonia, *f.* 1. Macedonia. 2. (hist.) Macedon, Macedonia, ancient kingdom in N. Greece.

macedónico, ca, *a.* Macedonian.

macedonio, a, *a., m., f.* Macedonian.

macelo, *m.* slaughterhouse, abattoir.

maceo, *m.* hammering, pounding, mauling.

maceración, *f.* 1. (cul.) maceration, marinading; kneading, pounding. 2. mortification of the flesh.

maceramiento, *m., var. of* **maceración.**

macerar, *tr.v.* 1. to macerate, soak, steep, marinate. 2. (fig.) to macerate, mortify (the flesh). —*r.v.* to mortify oneself (in penance).

macerina, *f., var. of* **mancerina.**

macero, *m.* mace-bearer, staff-bearer.

maceta, *f.* 1. handle (of tools). 2. stone-mason's hammer. 3. (Bol.) mallet. 4. flowerpot. 5. (Chile) bunch (of flowers). 6. (Mex.) head. 7. (bot.) corymb. — **m. de hojalatero,** tinner's mallet.

macetero, *m.* flowerpot stand, flowerpot.

macfarlán, macferlán, *m.* macfarlane, sleeveless coat.

macha, *f.* 1. (zool.) razor clam (Ensis macha). 2. (Amer.) mannish woman. 3. (Arg.) drinking spree.

machaca, *f.* crusher, pounder. —*m., f.* (fig.) bore, tiresome person.

machacadera, *f.* pestle, crusher, pounder.

machacador, ra, *a.* crushing, pounding. —*m., f.* pestle, crusher, pounder. —*f.* crusher (machine).

machacante, *m.* 1. (mil.) sergeant's aid. 2. (coll.) five peseta piece.

machacar, (*ref. 50*) *tr.v.* to crush, pound, beat, mash. —*i.v.* (fig.) to pester, bore, bother; to insist on harping on a subject.

machacón, na, *a.* boring, tiresome, bothersome. —*m., f.* bore, pest.

machaconería, *f.* (coll.) insistence, obstinacy; tiresomeness, bother.

machada, *f.* 1. flock of billy goats. 2. (coll.) stupidity, foolish act or remark.

machado, *a.* mashed, crushed, pounded. —*m.* hatchet.

machaje, *m.* (Chile, Arg., Urug.) male animals (collectively); herd of male animals.

machamartillo, *a., m.* firmly, solidly.

machanga, *f.* (Chile) tiresomeness, bother, dullness.

machango, ga, *a.* 1. (Chile) boring, tiresome, bothersome. 2. (Cuba) rude, unrefined, boorish. —*m.* 1. (Cuba, Ven.) capuchin (Cebus apella). 2. (Hond.) poor mount, poor horse.

machaqueo, *m.* crushing, pounding, beating.

machaquería, *f.* tiresomeness, bother, dullness; insistence, importunity.

machar, *tr.v.* to crush, pound, beat; to hammer, maul. —*r.v.* (Arg.) to get drunk.

machear, *i.v.* to beget more males than females (animals).

machetazo, *m.* cut or blow with a machete.

machete, *m.* machete, large heavy knife, cutlass.

machetear, *tr.v.* 1. to wound, cut or strike with a machete. 2. (mar.) to drive in (stakes or piles).

machetero, *m.* 1. cutter, clearer (of wooded or jungle land). 2. cane-cutter (on sugar cane plantation). 3. saber rattler, ignorant military chief. 4. (Amer.) grind (sl., student).

machi, *m., f.* (Chile) medicine man, quack, healer.

machí, (*pl.* **machíes**), *m., f.* (Arg.) *var. of* **machi.**

máchica, *f.* (Peru) roasted cornmeal.

machiega, *a.* **abeja m.,** queen bee.

machigua, *f.* (Hond.) crushed-corn washings.

machihembrado, *a.* (carp.) tongued and grooved, matched.

machihembradora, *f.* (carp.) tonguing and grooving machines; mortiser.

machihembrar, *tr.v.* (carp.) to groove and tongue; to feather, mortise; to dovetail.

machimbre, *m.* a tongued and grooved board.

machín, *m.* (Col., Ven.) (zool.) capuchin monkey (Cebus nigrivittatus).

machina, *f.* 1. crane, derrick. 2. pile driver, drop hammer.

machincuepa, *f.* (Mex.) somersault; (fig.) the act of changing political alliances.

machío, a, *a.* (rare) fruitless, not bearing fruit.

machismo, *m.* machismo, male chauvinism; exaltation of masculinity, he-manship.

machmetro, *m.* (phys., aer.) machmeter (mach number indicator).

macho, *a.* 1. (bot., zool.) male. 2. (mec.) male (part of socket, etc.). 3. manly, virile; strong; robust. 4. stupid, foolish. —*m.* 1. male (animal). 2. he-mule. 3. male flower. 4. hook (of hook and eye); (mec.) male part (of coupling). 5. fool, dolt, idiot. 6. root (of animal's tail). 7. (archit.) abutment, buttress pillar; pier (of arch). 8. (geol.) dike. 9. (min.) unproductive vein. 10. (Cuba) unshelled rice grain. 11. (C. Rica) foreigner, Anglo-Saxon; blond. — **m. cabrío, m. de cabrío,** he-goat, billy goat; **m. de aterraja,** tap, screw tap; **m. de timón,** (mar.) rudder pintle; **m. romo,** hinny, mule; **m. y campana,** bell-and-spigot.

machon, *m.* (archit.) pillar, buttress, large piece of timber.

machorro, rra, *a.* 1. barren, sterile. 2. (derog.) masculine. —*f.* barren female.
machota, *f.* 1. mallet, hammer. 2. (Mex., coll.) tomboy, hoyden, virago, amazon.
machote, *m.* 1. hammer, mallet. 2. (coll.) virile man, he-man. 3. (Mex., min.) boundary stone. 4. (Amer.) rough draft, model, pattern.
machucador, ra, *a.* 1. bruising. 2. pounding, crushing.
machucadura, *f.* 1. bruising, bruise, contusion. 2. crushing, pounding.
machucamiento, *m., var. of* **machucadura.**
machucante, *m.* (coll., Col.) individual, guy, fellow.
machucar, (*ref. 50*) *tr.v.* 1. to bruise, to maul. 2. to crush, pound.
machucón, *m.* (Amer.) *var. of* **machucadura.**
machucho, cha, *a.* 1. calm, level-headed, judicious. 2. mature, elderly.
machuelo, *m.* 1. small he-mule. 2. germ (of any organic body). 3. clove of garlic. 4. (ichth., Chile) shad (Ethmidium maculatum).
machuno, na, *a.* mannish, masculine.
machuque, machuqué, *ref.* **machucar.**
macia, *f., var. of* **macis.**
macice, macicé, *ref.* **macizar.**
macicez, *f.* solidity, solidness, compactness.
macilento, ta, *a.* wan, lean, emaciated, withered.
macillo, *m.* 1. hammer (of a piano). 2. small hammer. 3. (elec.) tapper (of a bell).
macío, *m.* (Cuba, bot.) cattail, reed, bulrush.
macis, *f.* mace (aromatic bark of the nutmeg plant).
macizamente, *adv.* solidly, strongly, compactly.
macizar, (*ref. 53*) *tr.v.* to fill up, stop up, to form into a compact mass.
macizo, za, *a.* 1. solid, strong, firm, compact. 2. solid (not hollow). 3. sound, well-founded (arguments). —*m.* 1. mass, bulk. 2. (geol.) massif. 3. (archit.) solid wall, wall space (wall between two bays). 4. block, group of buildings; flowerbed; clump of flowers. — **M. Central,** Central Massif.
macla, *f.* 1. (min.) macle, chastolitolite. 2. (her.) mascle, macle. 3. (bot.) water caltrops.
maco, ca, *a.* (sl.) artful, cunning.
macoca, *f.* 1. knock on the head with the knuckles. 2. a large variety of fig.
macolla, *f.* bunch, cluster (of flowers, roots).
macollar, *i.v.* to sprout or grow clusters of shoots, flowers, etc.
macollo, *m.* (Hond.) *var. of* **macolla.**
macón, *m.* dark dry honeycomb. —*a.* (Col.) big, huge.
macona, *f.* large basket, hamper.
macono, *m.* Bolivian song bird.
macramé, *m.* macramé, coarse lacework, knotwork and fringe used mostly for upholstery purposes.
macrobio, *a.* (biochem.) macrobian, long-lived.
macrobiótica, *f.* macrobiotics, art of prolonging life.
macrocefalia, *f.* (med.) macrocephaly, macrocephalia.
macrocéfalo, la, *a.* macrocephalous, large-headed.
macrocélula, *f.* (bioichem.) macrocell.
macrocisto, *m.* (bot.) macrocyst.
macrocito, *m.* (med.) macrocyte.
macrocitosis, *f.* (med.) macrocytosis.
macroclima, *m.* (meteorol.) macroclimate.
macrocosmo, *m.* macrocosm, the whole universe in relation to Man.
macrocristalino, *m.* (geol.) macrocrystalline.
macrófago, ga, *a.* (geol.) macrophagic. —*m.* macrophag.
macrofísica, *f.* macrophysics.
macrogameto, *m.* (biol.) macrogamete.
macrografía, *f.* 1. macrography. 2. (med.) macrography, abnormally large handwriting.
macrómero, *m.* (biol.) macromere.
macromolécula, *f.* macromolecule.
macronúcleo, *m.* (biol.) macronucleus.
macroscópico, ca, *a.* macroscopic; large enough to be seen with the naked eye.
macrosección, *f.* macrosection.
macrosísmico, *a.* (geol.) macroseismic.
macrosismo, *m.* (geol.) macroseism, severe earthquake.
macrosismógrafo, *m.* macroseismograph.
macrósporo, *m.* (bot.) macrospore.
macruro, *a.* (zool.) macrural. —*m.* (zool.) macruran; (*pl.*) Macrura.
macsura, *f.* reserved place in a mosque for persons regarded as holy.
macuache, *m.* (Mex.) poor or illiterate Indian.
macuba, *f.* 1. maccaboy, aromatic snuff cultivated in Martinique. 2. (ento.) musk beetle (Aromia moschala).
macuca, *f.* 1. (bot.) umbelliferous plant, with fruit resembling aniseed (Brunium macuca). 2. type of wild pear. 3. (ornith.) macuca.
macuco, ca, *a.* 1. (Chile) sly, cunning, crafty. 2. (Amer.) big, strong, husky. 3. (Amer.) excellent, fine, swell. —*m.* overgrown boy.
macueliro, *m.* (Hond., bot.) hard timber tree (Tabebuia pentaphylla).
macuenco, ca, *a.* (Cuba) thin, skinny (said of an animal).
mácula, *f.* 1. stain, spot, blot, blemish. 2. (coll.) deception, trick. 3. (astron., med., anat.) macula. 4. (print.) mackle, smudge.
macular, *tr.v.* 1. to stain, blemish. 2. (print.) to mackle, smudge. 3. to defame, to defile. —*r.v.* (print.) to mackle, smudge.
maculatura, *f.* (print.) spoiled sheet of print.
maculoso, sa, *a.* stained, blemished, full of spots.
macún, *m.* (Chile) poncho.
macuquero, *m.* clandestine miner (extracting ore from a mine without owner's permission), bootleg miner.
macuquino, na, *a.* said of a gold or silver coin which circulated until middle of 19th century.
macurca, *f.* (Chile, Bol.) aches and pains (after exertion).
macurije, *m.* (bot.) guara (Cupania oppositofolia), medicinal tree.
macuteno, *m.* (Mex.) petty thief.
macuto, *m.* 1. (soldier's) knapsack. 2. alms basket. 3. (Ven.) bag made of palm leaves.
Madagascar, *f.* Madagascar, large island in the Indian Ocean.
madama, *f.* 1. madame. 2. (Cuba, bot.) balsam, balsam apple.
madamisela, *f.* damsel, young girl, miss, young lady.
madapolán, *m.* (tex.) madapollam, a kind of percale.
madefacción, *f.* (pharm.) wetting, moistening.
madeja, *f.* 1. skein, hank. 2. tangle of hair. 3. (coll.) slovenly, lazy person. — **enredar** or **enredarse la m.,** to confuse or become confused (an affair, business, etc.); **hacer m.,** to become ropy (a liqueur or liquor); **m. sin cuenda,** (coll.) hopeless mess, tremendous tangle or confusion; sloppy disorderly person.
madejeta, madejuela, *f.* small skein.
Madera, *f.* Madeira, Portuguese island in the Atlantic.
madera, *f.* 1. wood; piece of wood; timber, lumber. 2. horny part (of a hoof). 3. (coll.) qualities, gift, ability, talent (for a particular activity). 4. (*pl.*) (mus.) woodwinds. — **aguar la m.,** to push timber into river (to float it downstream); **m. aglomerada** or **conglomerada** or **prensada,** chipboard; **m. blanda,** softwood; **m. brava,** hard, snapping wood; **m. de hilo,** wood or timber worked on four sides; **m. del aire,** horn (of animals); **m. de raja,** split timber; **m. de sierra, serradiza,** sawed timber; **m. desecada,** seasoned lumber; **m. dura,** hardwood; **m. laminada,** plywood; **m. en blanco,** unpainted or unvarnished wood; **m. en rollo,** whole, uncut timber; **m. enteriza,** whole log; **m. fósil,** lignite; **m. pasmada,** cracked or split timber; **sangrar la m.,** to tap a tree, draw resin from tree; **tener mala m.,** to be lazy, be a loafer. —*m.* madeira (wine).
maderable, *a.* timber-yielding.
maderación, *f.* (rare) *var. of* **maderamen.**
maderada, *f.* raft, float; lumber floated downstream.
maderaje, *m.* (bldg.) timbers, woodwork, timberwork (of a building).
maderamen, *m.* (bldg.) timbers, woodwork, timberwork.
maderamiento, *m.* woodwork, wainscoting, timbering, planking, boarding.
maderería, *f.* timber-yard, lumber-yard.
maderero, ra, *a.* of or pertaining to timber, lumber. —*m.* 1. timber dealer. 2. carpenter.
madero, *m.* 1. log, piece of timber. 2. beam, scantling. 3. (fig.) ship, bark, vessel. 4. (coll.) insensitive, unfeeling person.
maderuelo, *m. dim. of* **madero,** small log, small beam.
madi, *m.* (Chile) *var. of* **madia.**
madia, *f.* (bot.) melosa, tarweed (Madia sativa), oily plant of Chile.
madianita, *a., m., f.* (Bibl.) Midianite.
madona, *f.* madonna, image of the Virgin (said generally of a work of art).
mador, *m.* moisture, slight sweat.
madoroso, sa, *a.* moist, slightly sweaty.
madrás, *m.* (tex.) madras, striped or checkered cotton fabric.
madrasta, *f.* 1. stepmother. 2. (fig.) nuisance, bother, something unpleasant.
madraza, *f.* (coll.) pampering, doting mother.
madre, *f.* 1. mother. 2. mother, sister (when addressing a nun), e.g. *m. superiora,* mother superior. 3. matron (of hospital). 4. womb, matrix. 5. (fig.) mother, cause, origin, source; cradle. 6. bed (of river); main irrigation ditch; main sewer. 7. mothers, mother liquor (of vinegar); lees, dregs. 8. spindle, axle, shaft, main piece (of capstan, rudder, etc. to which others are fixed). 9. (Cuba) wood prepared for burning into charcoal. — **ésa es la m. del cordero,** this is the real reason; **m. de clavo,** clove of two years' growth; **m. de leche,** wet nurse; **m. de niños,** (med.) kind of epilepsy; **m. patria,** mother country; **m. política,** mother-in-law; stepmother; **salirse de m.,** to go off or change its course (river).
madrearse, *f.* to turn ropy, grow sour (yeast, wine, etc.).
madrecilla, *f.* ovarium of birds.
madreclavo, *m.* spice clove of two years' growth.
madreña, *f.* sabot, clog, wooden shoe.
madreperla, *f.* (zool.) pearl oyster; mother-of-pearl.
madrépora, *f.* (zool.) madrepore, white coral.
madreporarios, *m.* (*pl.*) (zool.) Madreporaria.
madrepórico, ca, *a.* madreporic.
madrero, ra, *a.* (coll.) very attached to one's mother.

madreselva, *f.* (bot.) honeysuckle.
Madrid, *m.* Madrid (capital of Spain).
madrigado, da, *a.* 1. (coll.) experienced, practical. 2. twice-married (said of a woman). 3. that has sired (said of a bull).
madrigal, *m.* (poet., mus.) madrigal.
madrigalesco, ca, *a.* (fig.) elegant; precious.
madriguera, *f.* 1. burrow, hole (of rabbit, etc.). 2. (fig.) den, haunt, hideout, lurking place.
madrileño, ña, *m., f.* Madrilenian, native or inhabitant of Madrid. —*a.* of, from or pertaining to Madrid.
Madriles, los, *m. pl.* (coll.) Madrid.
madrilla, *f.* (ichth.) small river fish.
madrina, *f.* 1. godmother; patroness, protectress, sponsor; matron of honor (at a wedding). 2. prop, upright bar, shore. 3. strap joining halters of leading horses of a team. 4. lead mare. 5. (Hond.) tame animal tied to a wild one. 6. (Ven.) small group of tame animals used to lead wild ones. 7. (mar.) reinforcing timber or prop.
madrinazgo, *m.* godmothership; sponsorship.
madrinero, ra, *a.* (Ven.) lead, tame (cattle).
madrona, *f.* 1. main sewer. 2. (coll.) doting, pampering mother.
madroncillo, *m.* (Sp.) strawberry (fruit).
madroñal, *m.* patch or thicket of madrone trees (arbutus unedo).
madroñera, *f.* 1. patch or thicket of madrone trees. 2. (bot.) madrone tree (Arbutus unedo).
madroño, *m.* 1. (bot.) madrone, arbutus tree and fruit. 2. berry-shaped tassel (used in Spain to trim snoods and mantillas). 3. (Mex.) spring lily.
madroñuelo, *m. dim. of* **madroño,** small madrone tree.
madrugada, *f.* 1. dawn, daybreak. 2. early rising. — **a la m., de m.,** at daybreak, early, at the crack of dawn.
madrugador, ra, *a.* 1. early-rising. 2. smart, astute. —*m., f.* early riser.
madrugar, (*ref.* 51) *tr.v.* (Arg., sl.) to get the better of. —*i.v.* 1. to get up early. 2. to be ahead, get a good start. — **al que madruga Dios le ayuda,** the early bird catches the worm.
madrugón, na, *a.* early-rising. —*m.* (coll.) very early-rising.
madrugue, madrugué, *ref.* **madrugar.**
maduración, *f.* 1. ripeness, ripening; maturing. 2. (med.) maturation, suppuration (of a wound).
maduradero, *m.* place for ripening fruit.
madurador, ra, *a.* ripening; maturing.
maduramente, *adv.* maturely, wisely.
madurante, *a.* ripening; maturing.
madurar, *tr.v.* 1. to ripen, make ripe (fruit). 2. to mature, think out, work out (plans). 3. to maturate, come to a head, begin to suppurate (a wound, a growth). —*i.v., r.v.* 1. to ripen, become ripe. 2. to mature, get experience. 3. to maturate, suppurate (a wound, a growth).
madurativo, va, *a.* maturative. —*m.* 1. maturative. 2. (coll.) inducement; device or argument to make a person accede to a wish or a request.
madurez, *f.* 1. ripeness; maturity. 2. maturity, experience; prudence, wisdom.
madureza, *f., var. of* **madurez.**
madurillo, lla, *a.* beginning to ripen.
maduro, ra, *a.* 1. ripe; mature, full-grown. 2. mature, experienced. 3. aging, aged, mellow.
maesa, *f.* **abeja m.,** queen bee.
maese, *m.* (arch.) master, maestro. — **m. coral,** conjuring trick, legerdemain.
maesil, *m, var. of* **maestril.**
maesilla, *f.* cord for raising and lowering heddles of lacemaking bobbins.
maestoso, sa, *a.* (mus.) majestic, maestoso.)
maestra, *f.* 1. school mistress or teacher; teacher's wife. 2. (fig.) teacher, guide. 3. queen bee. 4. (mas.) screed, floating screed. 5. (mas.) plumb rule (piece of wood hung vertically to guide a bricklayer). 6. (mas.) guide line of bricks (indicating area to be paved).
maestral, *a.* 1. masterly, brilliant, skillful. 2. pertaining to a grand master of a military order. —*m.* 1. queen cell (in a beehive). 2. mistral, north-west wind.
maestralice, maestralicé, *ref.* **maestralizar.**
maestralizar, (*ref.* 53) *i.v.* (mar.) to point towards the northwest (compass needle).
maestramente, *adv.* skillfully, in a masterly fashion.
maestrante, *m.* member of a riding club.
maestranza, *f.* 1. (Sp.) riding club. 2. arsenal, artillery repair works, naval dockyard or shipyard; workshops. 3. arsenal workers, artillery repair men, naval dockyard or shipyard workers. 4. (Chile, ry.) machine shop, repair shop.
maestrazgo, *m.* mastership (of military order); territory under the jurisdiction of a master.
maestre, *m.* master (of military order); (mar., arch.) master (of merchant ship). — **m. coral,** conjuring trick, legerdemain.
maestrear, *tr.v.* 1. to direct, manage. 2. to prune, lop, trim (vines). 3. (mas.) to screed, apply floating screed to (walls). —*i.v.* (coll.) to domineer, be bossy, play the master.
maestreescuela, *m., var. of* **maestrescuela.**
maestresala, *m.* (arch.) chief waiter or butler (of a nobleman).
maestrescuela, *m.* (ecc.) canon; teacher of theology.
maestría, *f.* 1. mastery, skill. 2. teacher's degree; teacher's status.
maestril, *m.* queen cell (in a beehive).
maestro, ra, *a.* 1. master, main, principal, e.g. *obra maestra,* master work, *llave maestra,* master key, main switch, *cloaca maestra,* main sewer, *maestros cantores,* mastersingers. 2. trained, e.g. *perro maestro,* trained dog. —*m.* 1. teacher, master, schoolteacher, schoolmaster. 2. master, expert, specialist, chief exponent, e.g. *los grandes maestros,* the great masters. 3. master, master craftsman, e.g. *m. sastre,* master tailor. 4. (educ.) master (academic degree). 5. maestro, musician, composer. 6. (mar.) mainmast. — **Gran M.,** Grand Master (of masons); **gran m.,** grand master (in chess); **m. aguañón, m. de ribera,** master builder of water works; **m. de armas,** fencing master; **m. de artes,** (educ.) master of arts; **m. de atar escobas,** (coll.) master in dish washing and bottle opening (disparaging name given to a person who boasts of being an expert in some ridiculous or useless thing); **m. de capilla,** choirmaster; **m. de ceremonias,** master of ceremonies; **m. de equitación,** riding master; **m. de escuela** or **de niños,** elementary schoolteacher or schoolmaster; **m. de obra prima,** shoemaker; **m. de obras,** master builder, construction foreman; **m. de postas,** postmaster; chief postmaster; **m. de primera enseñanza** or **primeras letras,** elementary schoolteacher or schoolmaster.
maffia, mafia, *f.* 1. Maffia, crime syndicate. 2. (fig.) gang, exclusive group.
Magallanes, *m.* Magellan, Portuguese navigator; **Estrecho de M.,** Magellan Straits.
magallánico, ca, *a.* Magellanic.
magancear, *i.v.* (Col., Chile) to be lazy, lead an idle life, loaf around, to lounge about.
magancería, *f.* trick, trickery, deception.
magancés, *a.* treacherous, evil.
magancia, *f.* (Chile), *var. of* **magancería.**
maganel, *m.* (mil.) battering ram.
magante, *a.* (Chile), *var. of* **maganto.**
maganto, ta, *a.* sad, wan, languid, spiritless.
maganza, *f.* (Col.) idleness, laziness, indolence.
maganzón, na, *a.* (Col., C. Rica) idle, lazy, indolent. —*m., f.* idler, lounger, bum.
magaña, *f.* 1. trick, ruse. 2. flaw (in the bore of a gun).
magarza, *f.* (bot.) feverfew, downy camomile.
magarzuela, *f.* (bot.) stinking camomile, mayweed.
magdalena, *f.* 1. magdalen, repentant woman. 2. (cul.) madeleine, a kind of biscuit or bun. — **estar hecha una M.,** (coll.) to be disconsolate.
magdaleniense, *a., m.* (geol) Magdalenian.
magdaleón, *m.* (pharm.) cylindrical roll of plaster.
magia, *f.* magic; (fig.) magic, enchantment, charm, spell; **m. blanca, m. natural,** white magic; **m. negra,** black magic.
magiar, *a., m., f.* Magyar, Hungarian. —*m.* Magyar (language).
mágico, ca, *a.* magic, magical. —*m., f.* 1. magician, sorcerer, sorceress, witch, charmer. 2. enchanter, enchantress.
magín, *m.* (coll.) imagination, mind, fancy.
magisterial, *a.* magisterial; pertaining to teaching.
magisterio, *m.* 1. teaching; teaching profession; teachers (collectively); degree in education. 2. affected solemnity. 3. (chem.) precipitate.
magistrado, *m.* 1. magistrate. 2. judge, justice, member of a court of justice.
magistral, *a.* 1. masterly, brilliant, perfect, skillful, excellent. 2. magisterial (august, dignified; authoritative, domineering, lordly). 3. master testing (of control machine used for testing others of the same kind). 4. (ecc.) preaching (prebendary; canonship). 5. (pharm.) magistral (medicine). —*m.* 1. (pharm., metal.) magistral. 2. (ecc.) preaching prebendary or canonship.
magistralmente, *adv.* 1. in a masterly fashion, brilliantly. 2. magisterially, authoritatively.
magistratura, *f.* magistracy, judgeship; **la suprema m.,** the office of the chief executive.
magma, *m.* (geol.) magma.
magnalio, *m.* (metal.) magnalium.
magnánimamente, *adv.* magnanimously, generously.
magnanimidad, *f.* magnanimity; generosity.
magnánimo, ma, *a.* magnanimous; generous.
magnate, *m.* magnate, person of great wealth, V.I.P. (coll.).
magnesia, *f.* (chem.) magnesia. — **leche de m.,** (pharm.) milk of magnesia.
magnesiano, na, *a.* (chem.) magnesian.
magnésico, ca, *a.* (chem.) magnesic.
magnesio, *m.* 1. (chem.) magnesium. 2. (photog.) flashlight.
magnesita, *f.* (min.) magnesite; meerschaum.
magnetice, magneticé, *ref.* **magnetizar.**
magnético, ca, *a.* 1. magnetic. 2. (fig.) attractive, irresistible.
magnetismo, *m.* 1. magnetism. 2. (fig.) attraction. — **m. animal,** animal magnetism; **m. remanente,** remnant or residual magnetism; **m. terrestre,** terrestrial magnetism.
magnetita, *f.* (min.) magnetite.
magnetizable, *a.* magnetizable.
magnetización, *f.* magnetization.
magnetizador, ra, *a.* magnetizing. —*m., f.* 1. magnetizer. 2. mesmerizer.
magnetizar, (*ref.* 53) *tr.v.* 1. to magnetize. 2. to mesmerize.
magneto, *f.* (elec.) magneto.
magnetodínamo, *m.* (elec.) magnetodynamo.

magnetoelectricidad, *f.* magnetoelectricity.
magnetoeléctrico, ca, *a.* magnetoelectric.
magnetofónico, ca, *a.* magnetophonic; **cinta m.,** recording tape.
magnetófono, magnetofón, *m.* (phys.) magnetophone.
magnetógrafo, *m.* (phys.) magnetograph.
magnetoiónico, ca, *a.* magnetoionic.
magnetomecánica, *f.* magnetomechanics.
magnetómetro, *m.* magnetometer.
magnetomotriz, *a.* magnetomotive.
magnetón, *m.* (phys.) magneton.
magnetoóptica, *f.* (phys.) magnetooptics.
magnetoquímica, *f.* magnetochemistry.
magnetoscopio, *m.* (phys.) magnetoscope.
magnetostricción, *f.* (phys.) magnetostriction.
magnetotérmico, ca, *a.* magnetothermal.
magnetrón, *m.* (rad., geoph.) magnetron.
magnicidio, *m.* assassination of a public figure.
magnificable, *a.* magnifiable.
magnificación, *f.* magnification, exaggeration; (opt.) magnification, enlargement.
magnificador, ra, *a.* 1. magnifying, enlarging. 2. praising, extolling, glorifying.
magníficamente, *adv.* magnificently.
magnificar, (*ref. 50*) *tr.v.* 1. to magnify, exaggerate; (opt.) to magnify, enlarge. 2. to extol, exalt, glorify.
magníficat, *m.* (rel.) Magnificat.
magnificencia, *f.* magnificence; splendor, grandeur.
magnificente, *a.* magnificent, splendorous, grand.
magnificentísimo, *a. super. of* **magnificente,** most magnificent.
magnífico, ca, *a.* magnificent; excellent; splendid; great.
magnifique, magnifiqué, *ref.* **magnificar.**
magnitud, *f.* 1. magnitude; size, bulk; greatness; extent. 2. (astron.) magnitude.
magno, na, *a.* great; outstanding, foremost. — **Alejandro M.,** Alexander the Great; **m. acontecimiento,** outstanding event.
magnolia, *f.* (bot.) magnolia.
magnoliáceo, a, *a.* (bot.) magnoliaceous. —*f.* (bot.) magnoliaceous tree; (*pl.*) Magnoliaceae.
magnolio, *m.* (Chile), *var. of* **magnolia.**
mago, ga, *a.* 1. Magian, of the Magi. 2. magical, magic. — **los tres Reyes Magos,** the three Wise Men, the Magi. —*m.* 1. magus, magician, wizard, necromancer. 2. Magus (Persian priest). 3. (Bib.) Magus, Wise Man. 4. (Canar. I.) young peasant, country boy or girl.
magostar, *i.v.* to roast chestnuts outdoors.
magosto, *m.* 1. bonfire for roasting chestnuts outdoors. 2. roast chestnuts.
magra, *f.* slice of ham, rasher.
magrez, *f.* leanness, thinness.
magro, gra, *a.* lean, thin, gaunt. —*m.* lean cut of pork.
magrura, *f., var. of* **magrez.**
magua, *f.* (Cuba) disappointment, surprise; joke, jest.
maguarse, (*ref. 52*) *r.v.* (Cuba) to be disappointed; to get a surprise or shock.
magüeto, ta, *m.* young bull. —*f.* heifer.
maguey, magüey, *m.* (bot.) maguey, American agave.
maguillo, *m.* (bot.) crab apple (tree); wild apple.
magüira, *f.* (Cuba, bot.) calabash tree; calabash (fruit).
magujo, *m.* (mar.) ravehook.
magulladura, *f., var. of* **magullamiento.**
magullamiento, *m.* battering and bruising; bruise, contusion.
magullar, *tr.v.* to batter and bruise. —*r.v. to be battered and bruised.*
magullón, *m.* (Chile) *var. of* **magullamiento.**
Maguncia, *f.* Mainz, city of Germany, birthplace of Gutenberg (inventor of typography).
maguntino, na, *a.* of or from Mainz. —*m., f.* native or inhabitant of Mainz, Germany.
magyar, *a., m., f., var. of* **magiar.**
maharajá, *m.* maharaja, maharajah, prince (in India).
maharani, *f.* maharani, maharanee, princess (in India).
maharrana, *f.* (reg., Sp.) fresh bacon.
Mahoma, *m.* Mohammed, Muhammad.
mahometano, na, *a., m., f.* Mohammedan, Muslim.
mahometice, mahometicé, *ref.* **mahometizar.**
mahomético, ca, *a.* Mohammedan, Islamic.
mahometismo, *m.* Mohammedanism.
mahometista, *a.* Mohammedan. —*m., f.* 1. Mohammedan. 2. Mohammedan converted to Christianity who returns to his original religion.
mahometizar, (*ref. 53*) *tr.v.* to Mohammedanize.
mahón, *m.* (tex.) nankeen, a sturdy cotton fabric.
mahona, *f.* (mar.) mahone, Turkish transport boat.
mahonés, sa, *a.* of or from Mahon, Balearic Islands. —*m., f.* native or inhabitant of Mahon. —*f.* 1. mayonnaise (sauce). 2. (bot.) Mahon Stock, Virginia Stock.
maicena, *f.* cornstarch, corn flour.
maicería, *f.* (Cuba) corn shop or store.
maicero, *m.* 1. (Cuba) corn dealer or seller. 2. (Col., ornith.) ani.
maicillo, *m.* 1. (bot.) gama grass. 2. (Amer.) gravel. 3. (Amer.) millet.
maído, *m.* meow, miau (of a cat).
maílla, *f.* (bot.) crab apple (fruit).
maillechort, *m.* argenton, maillechort, German silver.
maimón, *m.* 1. (zool.) maimon, monkey. 2. (*pl.*) (Sp., reg.) an Andalusian soup made with olive oil.
maimona, *f.* spindle beam of horse-driven flour mill.
maimonetes, *m.* (mar.) belaying pins.
Maimónides, *m.* Maimonides, Spanish-Jewish philosopher and physician.
maimonismo, *m.* philosophic system taught by Maimonides.
mainel, *m.* (archit.) mullion.
maitén, *m.* (bot.) mayten (Maytenus boaria).
maitencito, *m.* (Chile) (kind of) blindman's bluff (children's game).
maitinada, *f.* 1. dawn. 2. (mus.) aubade, sunrise serenade.
maitinante, *m.* (ecc.) priest who attends the matins.
maitines, *m.* (*pl.*) (ecc.) matins.
maíz, (*pl.* **maíces**), *m.* (bot.) corn; **m. dentado** or **hendido,** (bot.) dent corn; **m. morocho, m. de Guinea,** (bot.) Guinea corn, durra.
maizal, *m.* corn field, corn plantation.
majá, (*pl.* **majaes**), *f.* 1. (zool.) Cuban boa (Epicrates angulifer), a non-poisonous snake. 2. (coll.) handle of a mortar. 3. (sl.) flashy dame.
majada, *f.* 1. sheepfold. 2. dung, manure. 3. (Arg., Chile) flock of sheep.
majadal, *m.* 1. grazing ground for sheep. 2. sheepfold. 3. land well manured after having served as a sheepfold.
majadear, *tr.v.* to manure, spread dung on. —*i.v.* to stay the night in a fold or pen (sheep).
majaderear, *tr.v.* (Amer.) to annoy, pester, bother. —*i.v.* (Amer.) to be a nuisance or pest.
majadería, *f.* bother, nuisance, annoyance; insolence; bothersome or irritating act or remark.
majaderico, *m.* 1. old-fashioned dress trimming. 2. lacemaking bobbin.
majaderillo, *m.* lacemaking bobbin.
majadero, ra, *a.* irritating, annoying, bothersome, finicky, difficult. —*m., f.* nuisance, pest, annoying or irritating person. —*m.* 1. pestle (for pounding in a mortar). 2. lacemaking bobbin.
majado, *a.* mashed, puréed. —*m.* (Chile) puréed corn or wheat.
majador, ra, *a.* pounding, crushing, mashing. —*m., f.* pounder, crusher, masher.
majadura, *f.* pounding, mashing, crushing.
majagranzas, *m.* (coll.) oaf, clod, fool.
majagua, *f.* 1. (bot.) majagua, tree of the linden family. 2. (Cuba, coll.) man's linen jacket.
majagual, *m.* tract of land planted with majagua trees.
majagüero, *m.* (Cuba) ropemaker (who makes ropes from majagua fiber).
majagüilla, *f.* (Cuba, bot.) species of majagua.
majal, *m.* shoal, school (of fish).
majamiento, *m.* pounding, crushing, mashing.
majano, *m.* heap of stones used as landmark.
majar, *tr.v.* 1. to crush, pound, mash. 2. (coll.) to bother, annoy, pester. 3. (coll.) to beat, thrash.
majareta, *a.* (coll.) mad, nuts.
majarete, *m.* (cul.) pudding made of milk, sugar and corn.
majencia, *f.* (coll.) *var. of* **majeza.**
majeño, *m.* (Bol.) purple-skinned banana.
majería, *f.* (Sp.) group of flashily-dressed people.
majestad, *f.* 1. majesty, sovereignty, kingship, power. 2. dignity, loftiness, stateliness. — **Su M.,** Your Majesty.
majestoso, sa, *a., var. of* **majestuoso.**
majestuosamente, *adv.* majestically, in a royal manner; grandly.
majestuosidad, *f.* majesty, stateliness.
majestuoso, sa, *a.* majestic, august, stately.
majeza, *f.* (Sp.) a quality of flashy elegance combined with cockiness, attributed to the popular classes in Madrid and Andalusia.
majo, ja, *a.* 1. (Sp.) showy, flashy; (coll.) dressed up. 2. pretty, attractive, simpatico. —*m., f.* provocative young woman or dandy.
majolar, *m.* hawthorn patch or thicket.
majoleta, *f.* haw, hawthorn berry (of English hawthorn).
majoleto, *m.* (bot.) English hawthorn.
majorca, *f., var. of* **mazorca.**
majuela, *f.* 1. haw, hawthorn berry (of Crataegus monogyna). 2. shoelace, leather shoestring.
majuelo, *m.* 1. (bot.) hawthorn (Crataegus monogyna). 2. new vine yielding fruit.
majzén, *m.* government, national assembly (in Morocco).
mal, *a.* apocopated form of **malo,** used only before masculine singular nouns. —*m.* 1. wrong; evil. 2. damage, harm. 3. disease, illness, sickness. 4. misfortune, disaster. — **decir m.,** to curse; to slander; **del m., el menos,** the lesser of two evils; **de m. en peor,** (coll.) from bad to worse; **echar a m.,** to scorn, have a low opinion of; **hacer m.,** to do harm, hurt, damage; **llevar a m.,** to take amiss, take badly; **m. ardiente, m. de los ardientes,** (med.) ergotism, St. Anthony's fire; **m. caduco,** (med.) epilepsy; **m. de Alzheimer,** (med.) Alzheimer's disease; **m. de amores,** (coll.) lovesickness; **m. de Bright,** (med.) Bright's disease; **m. de bubas,** (med.) syphilis; **m. de corazón,** (med.) epilepsy; **m. de la rosa,** (med.) pellagra; **m. de las alturas,** altitude sickness; **m. de la tierra,** homesickness; **m. de Loanda,** (med.) scurvy; **m. de madre,** (med.) hysterics; **m. de mar,** sea-sickness; **m. de montaña,** altitude sickness; **m. de ojo,** evil eye; **m. de Parkinson,** (med.) Parkinson's disease; **m.**

de piedra, (med.) lithiasis, gallstones; **m. de San Antón,** (med.) St. Anthony's fire; **m. de San Lázaro,** (med.) elephantiasis; **m. francés,** (hist.) syphilis; **¡malhaya!** (*interj.*) damn!; **m. que bien,** one way or the other; **no hay m. que por bien no venga,** every cloud has a silver lining; **parar en m.,** to come to a bad end.

mal, *adv.* 1. badly, poorly; wrong, wrongly, incorrectly. 2. hardly, scarcely, e.g. *m. puedo yo ir,* I can hardly go; **estar m.,** to be ill or sick; **estar m. con,** to be on bad terms with; **estar m. de,** to suffer from, be ill with, e.g. *estar m. del hígado,* to suffer from the liver; to be out or short of, e.g. *estar m. de dinero,* to be out or short of money; **m. que bien,** willingly or unwillingly, willy nilly; **ponerse m. con,** (Amer.) to fall out with, quarrel with.

mala, *f.* 1. mail (from France and England); mail-bag. 2. manille, manilla (in cards).

malabar, *a.* Malabar, of or from Malabar, region in S.W. India. —*m., f.* native or inhabitant of Malabar. —*m.* Malabar language. — **juegos malabares,** juggling; (fig.) cunning, deftness.

malabárico, ca, *a.* Malabar, of or from Malabar.

malabarismo, *m.* juggling.

malabarista, *m., f.* 1. juggler. 2. cunning person. 3. (Chile) sly thief.

Malaca, *f.* Malacca (Malay Peninsula).

malaca, *f.* 1. (Mex.) hairdo with braids crossing on the top of the head. 2. walking stick made of Malacca cane.

malacara, *a.* (Arg.) (horse) with a white spot on the forehead.

malacate, *m.* 1. whim, winch. 2. (Amer.) spindle.

malacia, *f.* (med.) malacia, bizarre appetite.

malacitano, na, *a.* of or from Malaga. —*m., f.* native or inhabitant of Malaga, Spain.

malacología, *f.* malacology, the study of mollusks.

malacológico, ca, *a.* malacological.

malaconsejado, da, *a.* ill-advised. —*m., f.* ill-advised person.

malacopterigio, gia, *a.* (zool.) malacopterygian. —*m.* (zool.) malacopterygian, (*pl.*) Malacopterygii.

malacostráceo, a, malacóstraco, ca, *a.* (zool.) malacostracan, malacostracous. —*m.* (zool.) malacostracan.

malacostumbrado, da, *a.* having bad habits; spoiled, pampered.

malacrianza, *f.* (Amer.) impudence; bad behavior or manners.

malacuenda, *f.* 1. burlap, sackcloth. 2. oakum, tow.

malafa, *f.* (tail.) body-length Moorish robe.

málaga, *m.* malaga (sweet wine, originally from the city of Malaga, Spain).

malagana, *f.* (coll.) faintness, dizziness.

malagaña, *f.* pole set up with dry furze to catch swarming bees.

malagradecido, da, *a.* (Amer.) ungrateful, unappreciative.

malagua, *f.* (Peru) jellyfish.

malagueña, *f.* malaguena (song and dance).

malagueño, ña, *a.* of or from Malaga. —*m., f.* native or inhabitant of Malaga, Spain. —*f.* (mus.) malaguena, sweeping, rhythmic song and dance of the province of Malaga.

malagueta, *f.* (cul.) malegueta pepper; grains of Paradise.

malambo, *m.* 1. (Cuba, bot.) dogbane (Rauwolfia tetraphylla). 2. (Arg.) one of the typical dances of the gaucho.

malamente, *adv.* badly, poorly; wrongly.

malamistado, da, *a.* 1. (Chile) fallen out, not on speaking terms. 2. (Chile) living in concubinage.

malandante, *a.* unfortunate, unlucky.

malandanza, *f.* misfortune, calamity.

malandar, *m.* pig not going with the herd; wild hog.

malandrín, na, *a.* perverse, evil, wicked. —*m., f.* scoundrel, rascal.

malanga, *a.* 1. incompetent, unskillful, awkward, useless. 2. timid, cowardly. —*f.* (bot.) malanga, taro, an edible tropical root.

malangar, *m.* malanga-planted patch or field.

malapata, *m., f.* (coll.) unlucky person.

Malaquías, *m.* (Bib.) Malachi.

malaquita, *f.* (min.) malachite.

malar, *a., m.* (anat.) malar, pertaining to the cheek.

malaria, *f.* (med.) malaria.

malariólogo, ga, (med.) malariologist.

malarrabia, *f.* (Cuba, cul.) pudding made with sugar and banana, guava or sweet potato pulp.

Malasia, *f.* Malaysia.

malasombra, *m., f.* dull person, lifeless person.

malatería, *f.* (arch.) leprosarium.

malatía, *f.* (med., obs.) leprosy.

malato, ta, *a.* (obs.) leprous. —*m., f.* (obs.) leper. —*m.* (chem.) malate.

malavenido, da, *a.* incompatible, querulous, quarrelsome.

malaventura, *f.* misfortune, calamity.

malaventurado, *a.* unfortunate, unlucky, ill-fated.

malaventuranza, *f.* misfortune, bad luck.

Malawi, *m.* Malawi.

malaxación, *f.* mixing, blending (of cement, dough, etc.); rubbing, kneading.

malaxador, *m.* mixer, blender; kneader.

malaxar, *tr.v.* to mix, blend; to rub, to knead.

Malayo, ya, *a., m., f.* Malay; **Archipiélago Malayo,** Malay Archipelago; **Estados Malayos,** Malay States; **Federación Malaya,** Federation of Malaya. —*f.* Malaya.

malbaratador, ra, *a.* 1. underselling. 2. squandering. —*m., f.* 1. underseller. 2. spendthrift, squanderer.

malbaratar, *tr.v.* 1. to undersell (an article). 2. to squander, to misspend.

malbaratillo, *m.* second-hand shop or stall, bric-a-brac or knickknack shop or stall.

malbarato, *m.* 1. underselling. 2. squandering.

malcarado, da, *a.* evil-looking, ugly-looking, grim-faced.

malcasado, da, *a.* unfaithful, adulterous (spouse).

malcasar, *tr.v.* to mismate, mismarry. —*r.v.* to be mismated or mismarried.

malcaso, *m.* treachery, perfidy, infamous act.

malcocinado, *m.* 1. (cul.) tripe, liver and lights, offal. 2. shop where these are sold.

malcomer, *i.v., tr.v.* to eat poorly.

malcomido, da, *a.* underfed, undernourished.

malconsiderado, da, *a.* inconsiderate, thoughtless.

malcontado, *m.* (Chile) money given to treasurer or accountant to balance the books.

malcontentadizo, za, *a.* faultfinding, hard to please.

malcontento, ta, *a.* 1. malcontent, displeased. 2. rebellious. —*m., f.* malcontent, troublemaker. —*m.* a card game.

malcoraje, *m.* (bot.) herb mercury.

malcorte, *m.* violation of forest laws by illegally cutting timber.

malcote, *m.* (Hond.) tree similar to the oak.

malcriadez, *f.* (Amer.) bad manners, ill-breeding.

malcriadeza, *f., var. of* **malcriadez.**

malcriado, da, *a.* bad-mannered, ill-bred.

malcriar, (*ref. 54*) *tr v.* to spoil, pamper.

maldad, *f.* wickedness, evil, iniquity; evil act.

maldadoso, sa, *a.* wicked, bad, perverse. —*m., f.* wicked person.

maldecido, da, *a.* wicked, depraved. —*m., f.* wicked person.

maldecidor, ra, *a.* 1. cursing. 2. slanderous, defaming. —*m., f.* 1. curser. 2. defamer.

maldecir, (*ref. 3*) *tr.v.* to curse. —*i.v.* 1. to curse, damn. 2. to speak ill, defame, slander. — **m. de,** to curse; to speak ill of.

maldiciendo, *ref.* **maldecir.**

maldiciente, *a.* slanderous, defaming; cursing. —*m., f.* slanderer, detractor, defamer, curser.

maldición, *f.* curse, imprecation, malediction; damnation.

maldigo, maldiga, *ref.* **maldecir.**

maldije, maldijera, maldijese, *ref.* **maldecir.**

maldispuesto, ta, *a.* 1. indisposed, unwell. 2. ill-disposed, unwilling, reluctant.

maldita, *f.* (coll.) the tongue; **soltar uno la m.,** (coll.) to speak one's mind freely.

malditamente, *adv.* (coll.) damnably, accursedly.

maldito, ta, *irr. past part. of* **maldecir.** —*a.* 1. damned, accursed. 2. bad, wicked, mean, perverse. 3. awful, bloody, confounded. 4. (coll.) nary, little, none, e.g. *m. lo que me importa,* little do I care; *m. lo que sé yo de eso,* I don't know a damned thing about that. —*m.* the devil, the evil one.

maldoso, sa, *a.* (Mex.) *var. of* **maldadoso.**

maleabilidad, *f.* 1. (metal.) malleability. 2. pliability.

maleable, *a.* (metal.) malleable.

maleador, ra, *a., m., f., var. of* **maleante.**

maleamiento, *m.* 1. spoiling, ruining. 2. corruption, perversion.

maleante, *a.* 1. bad, wicked, perverse. 2. corrupting, perverting. 3. scoffing, ridiculing. —*m.* hoodlum, thug, roughneck; ex-convict.

malear, *tr.v.* 1. to spoil, ruin, harm. 2. (fig.) to corrupt, pervert. —*r.v.* 1. to become spoiled or ruined. 2. (fig.) to be corrupted or perverted; to go bad or wrong.

malecón, *m.* sea wall, dike; embankment, breakwater.

maledicencia, *f.* slander, evil talk, verbal abuse.

maleficencia, *f.* wickedness, maleficence.

maleficiar, *tr.v.* 1. to damage, injure, harm, do harm to. 2. to bewitch, cast a spell on.

maleficio, *m.* 1. spell, curse, charm. 2. injury, harm (caused by witchcraft).

maléfico, ca, *a.* harmful, pernicious, malefic. —*m.* sorcerer.

malejo, ja, *a. dim. of* **malo,** rather bad, pretty bad.

malentendido, *m.* (gal.) misunderstanding.

maleolar, *a.* (anat.) malleolar.

maléolo, *m.* (anat.) malleolus.

malestar, *m.* 1. malaise, indisposition. 2. uneasiness, unease, disquietude.

maleta, *f.* 1. suitcase, valise, traveling bag, portmanteau. 2. (Amer.) bundle of clothes. 3. (Arg.) saddlebag, knapsack. — **hacer la m.** or **las maletas,** to pack one's bags, pack one's suitcase; **largar** or **soltar la m.,** (Chile) to die. —*m.* 1. (coll.) bungler, useless character. 2. (taur., derog.) unskilled bullfighter.

maletera, *f.* boot (G.B.), luggage compartment (of a car).

maletero, *m.* 1. suitcase or valise maker or seller. 2. station porter, porter. 3. (Chile) pickpocket, thief. 4. (Ecuad.) saddlebag.

maletín, *m.* small suitcase or valise, grip, attaché case; traveling bag; satchel. — **m. de grupa,** (mil.) saddle bag.

maletón, *m.* 1. large suitcase. 2. (Ecuad.) cover for traveling or camp bed.

malevo, va, *a.* (Arg., Bol.) malevolent, evil.
malevolencia, *f.* malevolence, ill-will.
malévolo, la, *a.* malevolent, evil.
maleza, *f.* 1. undergrowth of weeds; brambly undergrowth, underbrush, brake, coppice. 2. (Chile, Arg.) pus.
malformación, *f.* malformation.
malfuncionamiento, *m.* malfunction.
malgache, *a., m., f.* Madagascan, of or pertaining to Madagascar or the Malagasy Republic.
malgama, *f.* (chem.) amalgam (of mercury with another metal).
malgastador, ra, *a.* extravagant, prodigal. *—m., f.* spendthrift, squanderer.
malgastar, *tr.v.* to squander, waste, misspend.
malgeniado, da, *a.* (Amer.) bad-tempered, irritable, irascible.
malgenioso, sa, *a.* (Amer.) bad-tempered, testy.
malhablado, da, *a.* foulmouthed.
malhadado, da, *a.* unfortunate, unlucky, wretched.
malhecho, cha, *a.* deformed, misshapen, malformed. *—m.* misdeed, evil deed.
malhechor, ra, *a.* bad, wicked. *—m.* malefactor, misdoer, wrong-doer. *—f.* malefactress.
malherido, da, *a.* badly wounded.
malherir, (*ref. 42*) *tr.v.* to wound or injure seriously.
malhiera, malhiero, *ref.* **malherir.**
malhiriendo, *ref.* **malherir.**
malhiriera, malhiriese, malhirió, *ref.* **malherir.**
malhojo, *a.* trimmings, refuse (from plants).
malhumorado, da, *a.* bad-tempered, ill-humored, peeved.
malhumorar, *tr.v.* to irritate, annoy. *—r.v.* to become bad-tempered, irritated or peeved.
Malí, *m.* Mali, African republic.
malicia, *f.* 1. malice, maliciousness. 2. wickedness, badness; perverseness. 3. cunning, trickiness, guile. 4. (coll.) suspicion, apprehension.
maliciar, *tr.v.* 1. to suspect, fear. 2. to spoil, ruin.
maliciosamente, *adv.* maliciously; cunningly.
malicioso, sa, *a.* 1. malicious, nasty, evil. 2. astute, cunning, clever; sly, tricky. 3. suspicious, apprehensive, evil-minded.
málico, ca, *a.* (chem.) malic.
malignamente, *adv.* maliciously.
malignante, *a.* malicious. *—m., f.* maligner.
malignar, *tr.v.* to vitiate, corrupt, deprave. *—r.v.* to become vitiated or corrupted, to grow worse.
malignidad, *f.* malignity, malignancy.
maligno, na, *a.* malignant, evil; (med.) malignant.
malilla, *f.* (cards) manille, manilla (second-best trump).
malingrar, *tr.v., var. of* **malignar.**
malino, na, *a.* (coll.) *var. of* **maligno.**
malintencionado, da, *a.* evilly-disposed, with evil intentions.
malla, *f.* 1. mesh (of a net). 2. netting, meshwork. 3. chainmail, mail. 4. tights (of dancers and acrobats); skin-tight trousers; (Arg., Urug.) swimming trunks. 5. (Chile) variety of potato. — **cota de m.,** coat of mail; **m. de alambre,** wire netting.
mallar, *i.v.* 1. to make meshing. 2. to become enmeshed, get caught in the meshing. 3. to arm or outfit with a coat of mail.
mallero, *m.* mesh or seller; maker of coats of mail.
mallete, *m.* 1. mallet; gavel. 2. (mar.) partner, wooden wedge (to make mast or cannon secure). 3. crossbar of chain link.
malleto, *m.* paper-beating mallet (in paper mills).
mallo, *m.* 1. hammer, mallet. 2. pall-mall; pall-mall alley; game of croquet; game of bowling. 3. (Chile) potato stew.

Mallorca, *f.* Majorca, largest of the Balearic Islands.
mallorquín, na, *a., m., f.* Mallorcan, Majorcan.
malmandado, da, *a.* disobedient; unwilling, grudging, recalcitrant.
malmaridada, *a.* unfaithful, adulterous (said of a wife). *—f.* unfaithful wife.
malmeter, *tr.v.* 1. to waste, squander. 2. (fig.) to lead astray, corrupt. 3. to alienate, cause enmity or estrangement between friends.
malmirado, da, *a.* 1. inconsiderate, discourteous, disobliging. 2. disliked, out of favor.
malo, la, *a.* 1. bad, poor (quality). 2. bad, wicked, evil. 3. harmful, bad, injurious. 4. ill, unwell, bad. 5. unpleasant, nasty, dirty, rude, disagreeable, obnoxious, dissolute. 6. (coll.) mischievous, naughty, roguish. 7. shabby, old; imperfect, defective. — **aceptar lo bueno con lo malo,** to take the good with the bad; **a la mala,** (Amer.) by all means at one's disposal, by force; **a las malas,** (Amer.) by force; **estar de malas,** to be unlucky, be out of luck; **lo malo,** the trouble, the worst thing; **lo malo, cuando viene, viene junto,** it never rains but it pours; **m. con,** mean to; **por la mala, por las malas** or **por malas,** by force; **por malas o por buenas,** willingly or by force; **venir de malas,** to come with bad intentions. *—m.* the Devil.
maloca, *f.* 1. (Amer.) sortie into or attack on Indian lands. 2. (Amer.) sudden attack by Indians. 3. (Col.) Indian village or hideout.
malogrado, da, *past part. of* **malograr.** *—a.* 1. deceased or having died before producing his best work (said of a promising writer, etc.). 2. unfortunate, lamented.
malogramiento, *m., var. of* **malogro,** failure.
malograr, *tr.v.* 1. to waste (time); to miss (opportunity). 2. to ruin, spoil, break. 3. to lead astray, corrupt, pervert. *—r.v.* 1. to come to nothing, fall through, miscarry, fail (one's plans, desires). 2. to become ruined or spoiled (crops, etc.). 3. to break down (a machine). 4. to go bad (food). — **estar malogrado,** (Peru) to be out of order, be broken.
malogro, *m.* failure, miscarriage (of plans), untimely end.
maloja, *f.* (Cuba) corn leaves and stalks used as fodder.
malojal, *m.* (Ven., agr.) land planted with green corn (used as fodder).
malojero, *m.* (Cuba) seller of corn leaves and stalks.
malojo, *m.* (Ven.) *var. of* **maloja.**
maloliente, *a.* smelly, foul-smelling, fetid.
malón, *m.* 1. mean or dirty trick. 2. (Amer.) sudden attack by Indians. 3. (Amer.) surprise visit by a group of friends, surprise party.
malónico, ca, *a.* (chem.) malonic.
maloquear, *i.v.* to raid, attack (said of Indians).
malparado, da, *past part. of* **malparar.** *—a.* damaged, hurt; impaired; **salir m. de,** to come out badly from.
malparar, *tr.v.* to harm, hurt (people); to injure, damage (objects); to impair.
malparida, *f.* woman who has miscarried.
malparir, *i.v.* to abort, miscarry.
malparto, *m.* miscarriage.
malpensado, da, *a.* malicious, evil-minded.
malpigláceo, a, *a.* (bot.) malpighiaceous. *—f.* (bot.) malpighiaceous plant; (*pl.*) Malpighiaceae.
malquerencia, *f.* antipathy, hatred, ill will.
malquerer, (*ref. 17*) *tr.v.* to dislike, bear ill will towards, hate.
malqueriente, *a.* hating, bearing ill will.

malquiera, malquiero, *ref.* **malquerer.**
malquise, malquisiera, malquisiese, *ref.* malquerer.
malquistar, *tr.v.* to alienate, estrange, set against. *—r.v.* to become enemies, alienated or estranged.
malquisto, ta, *a.* disliked, out of favor, unpopular, detested.
malquita, *f.* (geol.) malchite.
malro, *m.* (Chile) root of horse's tail.
malrotador, ra, *a.* wasteful, squandering. *—m., f.* spendthrift, squanderer.
malrotar, *tr.v.* to waste, squander, misspend.
malsano, na, *a.* 1. noxious, harmful, injurious (for health). 2. sickly, unwell.
malsín, *m.* backbiter, evil gossip, mischief-maker, talebearer.
malsonante, *a.* offensive; harsh, ill-sounding.
malsufrido, da, *a.* impatient, unresigned.
malta, *f.* 1. malt. 2. roast barley. 3. (Amer.) black beer.
Malta, *f.* Malta, Mediterranean island.
maltasa, *f.* (biochem.) maltase.
malteado, da, *a.* malted; **leche malteada,** malted milk.
maltés, sa, *a., m., f.* Maltese, from or pertaining to the island of Malta.
maltón, na, *a.* (Bol., Ecuad., Peru) overgrown (boy or girl); youth.
maltosa, *f.* (chem.) maltose.
maltrabaja, *m.* (coll.) idler, lounger.
maltraer, *tr.v., var. of* **maltratar.**
maltraído, da, *a.* (Chile, Peru) untidy, disheveled.
maltrapillo, *m.* street urchin, ragamuffin.
maltratamiento, *m.* ill-treatment, maltreatment.
maltratar, *tr.v.* 1. to maltreat, abuse, ill-treat. 2. to damage, harm, spoil.
maltrato, *m.* ill treatment, maltreatment.
maltrecho, cha, *a.* maltreated, damaged, battered.
maltusianismo, *m.* (sociol.) Malthusianism.
maltusiano, na, *a., m., f.* Malthusian.
malucho, cha, *a.* 1. (coll.) rather unwell, sickly. 2. of poor quality.
maluco, ca, *a.* Moluccan, from or pertaining to the Molucca Islands (a province of Indonesia). *—m., f.* Moluccan.
maluco, ca, *a.* (coll.) *var. of* **malucho.**
malura, *f.* (Chile) indisposition, illness.
malva, *f.* (bot.) mallow. — **m. arbórea, loca, real, rósea** (bot.) hollyhock; **haber nacido uno en las malvas,** (coll.) to be of humble origin; **ser uno como una malva,** (coll.) to be obedient, be meek and mild.
malváceo, a, *a.* (bot.) malvaceous. *—f.* malvaceous plant; (*pl.*) Malvaceae.
malvadamente, *adv.* wickedly, perversely, evilly.
malvado, da, *past part. of* **malvar.** *—a.* wicked, evil, perverse; fiendish. *—m., f.* wicked person, evildoer; knave, villain.
malvar, *m.* land covered with mallows.
malvar, *tr.v.* to corrupt, pervert, deprave, vitiate.
malvarrosa, *f.* (bot.) hollyhock.
malvasía, *f.* 1. (bot.) malvasia grape. 2. malmsey (wine).
malvavisco, *m.* (bot.) marsh mallow.
malvece, malvecé, *ref.* **malvezar.**
malvender, *tr.v.* to sell at a loss, to sacrifice.
malversación, *f.* misappropriation, embezzlement, peculation.
malversador, ra, *a.* embezzling, peculating. *—m., f.* embezzler, peculator.
malversar, *tr.v.* to embezzle, peculate.
malvezar, (*ref. 53*) *tr.v.* to cause or encourage bad habits in. *—r.v.* to fall into bad habits.
Malvinas, las Islas Malvinas, the Falkland Islands.

malvinero, ra, *a.* of or from the Falkland Islands. —*m., f.* native or inhabitant of the Falkland Islands.
malvís, *m.* (ornith.) redwing (Turdus musicus).
malviz, (*pl.* **malvices**), *m., var. of* **malvís.**
malvón, *m.* (Mex.) geranium.
mama, *f.* 1. (coll.) mama, mamma, mother, mommy. 2. (anat.) mamma, mammary gland.
mamá, (*pl.* **mamás**), *f.* (coll.) mamma, mother.
mamacallos, *m.* (coll.) dolt, simpleton, fool.
mamacona, *f.* 1. (hist.) elderly virgin among the ancient Incas. 2. (Bol.) halter.
mamada, *f.* 1. (coll.) sucking, nursing; time taken in sucking. 2. (Chile, Peru) cinch, piece of luck, something obtained without any effort.
mamadera, *f.* 1. breast pump (to remove excess milk). 2. (Amer.) baby's bottle, nursing bottle. 3. (Amer.) rubber nipple (of baby's bottle).
mamado, da, *past part. of* **mamar. —***a.* (vulg.) drunk, intoxicated.
mamador, ra, *a.* sucking. —*m., f.* sucker.
mamalón, na, *a.* (Cuba) lazy, idle, sponger, parasite.
mamamama, *f.* (Peru) granny.
mamancona, *f.* (Chile) fat old woman.
mamandurria, *f.* (Amer.) bargain; sinecure, soft job (coll.).
mamante, *a.* sucking, suckling.
mamantón, na, *a.* suckling (animal).
mamar, *tr.v.* 1. to suck, suckle. 2. to swallow, eat. 3. to learn as a small child. 4. to wangle, obtain, get, land oneself (a job, etc.). —*i.v.* to nurse, suck (child at the breast). —*r.v.* 1. (coll.) to get drunk. 2. to wangle, get, obtain. 3. to swallow, eat; **mamarse a (uno),** to cheat, take (someone) in; to kill, do in, (coll.) knock off (coll.).
mamario, ria, *a.* (zool.) mammary.
mamarrachada, *f.* 1. (coll.) junk, rubbish. 2. piece of folly, ridiculous action. 3. something grotesque or ridiculous. 4. (art.) bunk, worthless daub.
mamarrachista, *m., f.* (coll.) botcher, bungler, one who produces rubbish; bad writer, bad painter, dauber.
mamarracho, *m.* 1. rubbish or nonsense; stupidity. 2. scarecrow, guy, ridiculous figure. 3. (*pl.*) junk, rubbish, useless odds and ends. 4. grotesque, ridiculous masquerade seen at a carnival or Mardi Gras.
mamá-señora, *f.* (Amer.) grandmamma.
mambí, isa, *m., f.* Cuban patriot or rebel during the Spanish domination of the island.
mambla, *f.* small hillock, knoll, mound.
mambo, *m.* (mus.) mambo, a Latin-American dance of Cuban origin.
mamboretá, *f.* (Arg., ento.) praying mantis.
mambrú, *m.* (mar.) kitchen smoke stack or chimney.
mambullita, *f.* (Chile) blind man's buff.
mamella, *f.* mammilla, mamilla (excrescence); protuberance on the neck of goats.
mamellado, da, *a.* mammillated, mammillate, having mammillas.
mamelón, *m.* 1. hillock, knoll, mound. 2. (med.) mammilla, small nipple-shaped protuberance on scars. 3. (anat.) mammilla, nipple.
mamelonado, da, *a.* (med.) mammilated, covered with nipple-shaped excrescences.
mameluco, ca, *m., f.* mameluco (Brazilian half-breed). —*m.* 1. Mameluke (Egyptian soldier). 2. fool, boob, simpleton. 3. (Amer.) union suit, overall (trousers and vest joined together). —*f.* (Chile) prostitute.
mamey, *m.* (bot.) mammee, mamey.
mamífero, *a.* (zool.) mammalian. —*m.* (zool.) mammal.
mamila, *f.* (anat.) mammilla, nipple.
mamilado, da, *a.* mammilate, mammilated.
mamilar, *a.* mammillary.
mamitis, *f.* (med.) inflammation of the nipples.
mamola, *f.* chuck (under the chin), e.g. *hacer a uno la m.,* to chuck under the chin in a scorning or mocking manner; (coll.) to deceive, fool; ¡mamola! what nonsense! hard luck!
mamón, na, *a.* 1. nursing (baby). 2. (baby) who nurses a long time, fond of sucking. —*m., f.* suckling, nursling, child who is still nursing. —*m.* 1. (bot.) sucker, shoot. 2. (bot.) genip (Melicocca bijuga). 3. (Amer.) papaya. 4. (Mex.) cake made of egg and cornstarch. 5. (Amer., coll.) drunkard.
mamona, *f., var. of* **mamola,** (Ecuad.) drunken spree.
mamoncillo, *m.* (Cuba, bot.) genip (Melicocca bijuga), honey berry.
mamoso, sa, *a.* having a good appetite (baby). —*m.* a variety of panic grass.
mamotreto, *m.* 1. notebook, memorandum. 2. (coll.) bulky notebook; bulky bundle of papers. 3. big hulking machine or piece of furniture.
mampara, *f.* screen; lowered door; room divider; glass door.
mamparo, *m.* (mar.) bulkhead, partition (dividing ship in cabins, etc.). — **m. contraincendio,** fire wall.
mampato, ta, *a.* (Chile) short-legged (animal).
mamperlán, *m.* stringboard, wooden guard (on the steps of a staircase).
mamporro, *m.* (coll.) bump, cuff, tap; light blow on the head.
mampostear, *tr.v.* (bldg.) to build with rubble, to cement with mortar.
mampostería, *f.* (bldg.) rubblework; **m. en seco** or **a hueso,** dry masonry.
mampostero, *m.* 1. (mason.) rubbleworker, mason who does rubblework. 2. tithe, rent or alms collector.
mampresar, *tr.v.* to begin to break in (horses).
mampuesta, *f.* (mas.) course or line of rubblework.
mampuesto, ta, *a.* rubble, rough, uncut (stone). —*m.* 1. (bldg.) rubble, rough or uncut stone. 2. parapet, ledge. 3. (Chile) support for firearms (when taking aim). — **de m.,** spare, extra, emergency; from undercover, from a sheltered position.
mamujar, *tr.v.* to nurse or suck intermittently.
mamullar, *tr.v.* 1. to eat as though sucking. 2. (coll.) to mumble, mutter.
mamut, *f.* (paleon.) mammoth.
mana, *f.* (C. Amer., Col.) stream, spring.
maná, *m.* 1. (Bib.) manna. 2. (bot.) manna (sweetish exudate flowing from certain trees). 3. (Bol.) peanut sweet.
manada, *f.* 1. herd, flock, drove, pack. — **a manadas,** in herds or flocks. 2. handful, cluster.
manadero, *m.* herdsman, shepherd.
manadero, ra, *a.* flowing, springing, issuing. —*m.* 1. spring (of water). 2. source, origin.
manadilla, *f. dim. of* **manada,** small flock.
Managua, *f.* Managua, capital of Nicaragua.
managuaco, ca, *a.* 1. (Cuba) rustic, awkward, boorish. 2. (Cuba) having white snout and feet (said of livestock).
manajú, (*pl.* **manajúes**), *f.* (Cuba, bot.) garcinia (Garcinia morella).
Manama, *f.* Manama, capital of the Bahrein Islands.
manante, *a.* flowing, springing, issuing, proceeding.
manantial, *a.* flowing, running, issuing; **agua de m.,** spring water. —*m.* 1. spring (of water). 2. origin, source.
manantío, a, *a.* springing, flowing, issuing, welling, oozing.
manar, *tr.v.* to run or flow with. —*i.v.* 1. to spring, flow forth, issue, run, well forth, rise (a spring); to flow, run (blood, any liquid, etc.). 2. (with **en**) to abound (in), be full (of), flow (with).
manare, *m.* (Ven.) sieve for yucca starch.
manatí, (*pl.* **manatíes**), *m.* 1. (zool.) manatee, sea cow. 2. strip of dried manatee (made into whips, sticks); (Col.) whip.
manato, *m., var. of* **manatí.**
manaza, *f.* large hand, hefty hand.
manazo, *m.* (Amer.) slap.
mancamiento, *m.* 1. maiming, disabling. 2. deficiency, lack; defect.
mancaperro, *m.* 1. (bot.) woody plant growing in Sierra Nevada. 2. (Cuba, ento.) variety of centipede (Spirobulus grandis).
mancar, (*ref. 50*) *tr.v.* to maim (esp. the hand), lame, cripple, disable. —*i.v.* 1. to go lame (a horse), be maimed or crippled. 2. to calm down (sea, wind). — **m. de,** to lack, not have. —*r.v.* to be maimed or crippled.
mancarrón, na, *a.* 1. very crippled, very lame. 2. worn-out (horse). 3. (Chile) disabled (person). —*m.* (Chile, Peru) dike (made to hold back or divert water).
manceba, *f.* concubine, mistress.
mancebete, *m. dim. of* **mancebo,** stripling, youth.
mancebía, *f.* 1. brothel, bawdyhouse. 2. youthful prank or lark, youthful carousing; licentious living.
mancebo, *m.* 1. youth, stripling. 2. bachelor. 3. shop assistant, (office) clerk.
máncer, *m.* prostitute's son.
mancera, *f.* plow handle.
mancerina, *f.* saucer with a holder for a chocolate cup.
mancha, *f.* 1. stain, spot (of oil, dirt, etc.); blot, smudge (of ink); spot (on skin; on sun, etc.). 2. patch (of different-colored cloth; of flowers; of land different from the surroundings). 3. (fig.) stain, blemish (on reputation). 4. (p.) sketch. 5. (Arg.) carbuncle (in cattle). 6. (Hond.) small circle on the ground used in game with tops. 7. (Ecuad.) disease in cocoa plant. **cundir como m. de aceite,** to spread like wild fire, spread rapidly (news, gossip); **m. de hielo,** patch of ice; **m. de petróleo,** oil slick; **m. solar,** sun spot.
manchadizo, za, *a.* easily stained or soiled.
manchado, da, *past part. of* **manchar. —***a.* 1. spotted, speckled. 2. stained, smudged, tarnished.
manchar, *tr.v.* 1. to stain, spot; to blot, smudge (with ink). 2. to blemish, defile, stain (reputation). 3. (p.) to daub, paint in certain parts of (picture) before blending. — **m. su hoja de servicios,** to spoil one's record.
manchego, ga, *a.* of or from La Mancha. —*m., f.* 1. native or inhabitant of La Mancha. 2. (Sp.) rustic, bumpkin.
manchita, *f. dim. of* **mancha,** small stain.
manchón, *m.* 1. large stain; large blot. 2. area of thick growth. 3. patch of land left for pasture.
manchonero, *m.* (Hond.) man who works with indigo dyes.
manchoso, sa, *a.* easily spotted or stained.
manchú, (*pl.* **manchúes**), *a., m., f.* Manchu, Manchurian. —*m.* Manchu (language).
manchuela, *f. dim. of* **mancha,** small spot or stain.
manchuriano, na, *a., m., f., var. of* **Manchú.**
mancilla, *f.* blemish, spot, stain.
mancillado, da, *past part. of* **mancillar. —***a.* spurious, bastard, illegitimate.
mancillar, *tr.v.* to spot, stain, blemish. —*r.v.* to become spotted, blemished or stained.

mancipación, *f.* (Roman law) mancipation, conveyance, transfer (of property).
mancipar, *tr.v.* to enslave. *—r.v.* to become enslaved.
manco, ca, *a.* 1. one-handed; one-armed; maimed. 2. defective, faulty. 3. oarless, without oars (a ship). — **no ser m.,** to be very experienced, be very intelligent; to be talented; (coll.) to be unscrupulous or dishonest. *—m.* (Chile) old hack, poor horse.
mancomún, *adv.* **de m.,** jointly, together; in common, in agreement.
mancomunadamente, *adv.* jointly, together; in common, in agreement.
mancomunar, *tr.v.* 1. to unite, join, combine, associate. 2. (law) to oblige (two or more persons) to pay or perform jointly. *—r.v.* to unite, join together.
mancomunidad, *f.* association, union; community, commonwealth.
mancorna, *f.* 1. (Mex.) snap button. 2. (Amer.) cuff links (also in *pl.*).
mancornar, (*ref. 33*) *tr.v.* 1. to hold (a steer) down by the horns; to tie one horn and one front hoof (of a steer) together (to prevent its escaping); to tie (cattle) together by the horns. 2. (fig.) to tie together, join.
mancornera, *f.* (Chile) raising or lowering strap (on stirrups).
mancuerda, *f.* rack (torture); each turn of the rack (in torture).
mancuerna, *f.* 1. pair (of animals or objects tied together). 2. leather strap used to tie down cattle. 3. (Cuba) part of tobacco plant with a pair of leaves attached. 4. (Phil. I.) pair of prisoners tied together. 5. (Mex.) (*pl.*) cuff links.
mancuerne, mancuerno, *ref.* **mancornar.**
mancuernillas, *f.* (*pl.*) (Hond.) cuff links.
manda, *f.* 1. offer, gift, promise. 2. legacy, bequest. 3. (Chile, imp. u.) religious vow or promise.
mandadero, ra, *a.* obedient. *—m., f.* messenger, porter, errand boy or girl.
mandado, *past part. of* **mandar.** *—m.* 1. order, mandate, command. 2. errand. — **a su m.,** (Arg.) at your service, at your orders. *—a.* **bien m.,** obedient, well-behaved; **mal m.** disobedient, badly behaved.
mandamás, *m.* (coll.) chief, boss, V.I.P.
mandamiento, *m.* 1. command, order. 2. (Bib.) commandment. 3. (law) writ, warrant. 4. (*pl.*) (coll.) five fingers of the hand. — **m. de embargo,** (law) writ of attachment; (*pl.*) **los diez mandamientos de la ley de Dios,** the Ten Commandments.
mandanga, *f.* laziness, indolence, slothfulness.
mandante, *a.* commanding, ordering. *—m., f.* (law) mandator, principal, constituent (one who appoints another to act for him).
mandar, *tr.v.* 1. to order, command, decree, direct. 2. to send. 3. to bequeath, leave (in a will). 4. to offer, promise. 5. to dominate (a horse). 6. (Chile) to start (races, etc.). 7. (Amer.) to give, deliver (a blow); to throw (a stone). 8. (Amer.) to invite to, ask to. 9. (Amer.) to dominate, overlook (e.g. a mountain — a valley); **m.** + *inf.,* to have + *past part.,* e.g. *m. a componer la mesa,* to have the table repaired; **m. a paseo,** to send packing or about one's business; **mande,** (Amer.) what can I do for you? what can I get you? excuse me, what did you say? **m. por,** to send for. *—i.v.* to give the orders, be in charge, be in command, be the boss (coll.). *—r.v.* 1. to move about unassisted (a sick person). 2. to communicate with one another (rooms). 3. to make use (of a doorway, stairway, etc.). 4. (Cuba, Chile) to leave, go away. 5. (Arg., Mex., Urug.) to drink. 6. (Chile) to offer to undertake (an errand, etc.); **bien mandado,** obedient, docile; **mandarse con,** (Cuba) to be rude to; **mal mandado,** disobedient, unmanageable.
mandarín, *m.* 1. mandarin (Chinese civil servant). 2. (coll.) official accorded little respect.
mandarina, *a.* pertaining to Mandarin (language) or mandarin (orange). *—f.* 1. (bot.) mandarin, mandarin orange. 2. Mandarin (language).
mandarinato, *m.* mandarinate (office of mandarin).
mandarria, *f.* (mar.) iron maul, sledge hammer.
mandatario, *m.* (law) agent, attorney, mandatary (one who acts for someone else). 2. (Amer.) leader, president. — **primer m.,** head of the government.
mandato, *m.* 1. command, order, mandate. 2. precept, instruction, ordinance. 3. charge, trust, commission. 4. (ecc.) maundy, ceremony of washing the feet on Maundy Thursday; Maundy Thursday sermon. 5. (law) mandate, power of attorney. 6. (pol.) mandate (power given to elected members by constituents). 7. mandate (power over mandated territory; mandated territory itself).
manderecha, *f.* right hand; **buena m.,** good luck.
mandí, (*pl.* **mandíes**), *m.* (Arg.) (variety of) catfish (Pimelodello gracillis).
mandíbula, *f.* jaw, (anat., zool.) mandible. — **reír a m. batiente,** to laugh uproariously, laugh one's head off.
mandibulado, da, *a.* mandibulate.
mandibular, *a.* mandibular.
mandil, *m.* 1. apron, pinafore; freemason's apron. 2. cloth for rubbing down a horse. 3. fine-meshed fishing net. 4. (Chile) horse blanket.
mandilandinga, *f.* the lower depths, the world of rogues and knaves.
mandilar, *tr.v.* to rub (a horse) down with a cloth or shammy.
mandilejo, *m.* small apron or pinafore.
mandilete, *m.* 1. gauntlet (of coat of arms). 2. (fort.) door of a loophole or embrasure.
mandilón, *m.* (coll.) coward, weakling; mean fellow.
mandinga, *a.* (ethnol.) *a.* Mandingan, negro of the Sudan. *—m., f.* (ethnol.) Mandingo, Mandinga. *—m.* 1. (coll.) devil. 2. (Arg., coll.) young imp, mischievous rogue. 3. (Arg.) black magic, sorcery. 4. (C. Rica) male homosexual. 5. (Arg.) magic, sorcery.
mandioca, *f.* (bot.) bitter cassava, manioc (root and starch).
mando, *m.* 1. command; authority, power, rule. 2. (mec.) drive, control; (*pl.*) controls (of a machine). — **alto m.,** high command; **entregar el m.,** to hand over the command; **estar al m.,** to be in command; **m. a distancia,** remote control; **m. a mano,** hand control; **m. digital,** fingertip control; (auto.), gearshift on the steering column; **m. doble,** (auto.) dual drive; **m. hidráulico,** (auto.) fluid drive; **tener mucho m.,** to have the qualities of leadership, have a commanding presence; **tener el m. y el palo,** to rule the roost; **tomar el m.,** to take command.
mandoble, *m.* 1. two-handed slash or blow with a sword. 2. a large sword. 3. (fig.) severe reprimand.
mandolín, *m.* **mandolina,** *f.* **mandolino,** *m.* mandolin (musical instrument).
mandón, na, *a.* imperious, domineering, bossy. *—m., f.* bossy person, imperious domineering person. *—m.* 1. (Amer.) foreman, boss. 2. (Chile) starter (in horse races).
mandonear, *tr.v.* (Amer.) to boss someone around. *—i.v.* to throw one's weight around.
mandrache, *m.* gambling house.
mandrachero, *m.* owner of a gambling house; croupier, operator of a gambling table.
mandracho, *m, var. of* **mandrache.**
mandrágora, *f.* (bot.) mandrake, mandragora.
mandrágula, *f.* (coll.), *var. of* **mandrágora.**
mandria, *a.* 1. pusillanimous, cowardly, timid. 2. worthless, useless. 3. stupid, foolish. 4. lazy. *—m.* coward, worthless pusillanimous person.
mandril, *m.* 1. (mec.) chuck; mandril, mandrel; reamer, boring tool. 2. (surg.) mandrin. — **m. de quijadas** or **garras,** (mec.) jaw chuck. 3. (zool.) mandrill.
mandrón, *m.* 1. stone or wooden missile. 2. mangonel (catapult for throwing stone missiles).
mandubí, (*pl.* **mandubíes**), *m.* (Arg.) peanut.
manducación, *f.* (coll.) eating.
manducar, (*ref. 50*) *i.v., tr.v.* (coll.) to eat.
manducatoria, *f.* (coll.) food, eats, grub.
manduque, manduqué, *ref.* **manducar.**
manea, *f.* shackles, fetters, hobbling strap (to hobble horses, etc.).
maneador, *m.* (S. Amer.) long strap used for hobbling horses or cattle.
manear, *tr.v.* 1. to hobble (horses, cattle). 2. to manage, handle. 3. to chain, fetter. *—r.v.* (Chile) to become involved or entangled in a difficult situation.
manecilla, *f.* 1. small handle. 2. clasp, catch. 3. (print.) fist (index mark). 4. hand (of watch). 5. (bot.) tendril.
manejable, *a.* manageable, tractable.
manejado, da, *a.* **bien or mal m.,** (p.) well or badly handled.
manejar, *tr.v.* 1. to manage, direct, conduct, govern (a business, a machine). 2. to handle, wield (an instrument, weapon). 3. to manage, handle (a person). 4. (Amer.) to drive (a car). 5. to handle (a horse). *—r.v.* 1. to conduct oneself, behave. 2. to manage to get around (after having some physical defect).
manejo, *m.* 1. handling. 2. management, administration (of a business). 3. (equit.) manege, horsemanship. 4. (Amer.) driving (a car). 5. trick, intrigue, device. — **m. doméstico,** housekeeping.
maneota, *f.* shackles, fetters, hobble, hobbling strap (to hobble horses).
manequí, (*pl.* **manequíes**), *m.* (Chile, Ecuad.) *var. of* **maniquí.**
manera, *f.* 1. way, manner, method, mode. 2. slit (in skirt); fly (on trousers). 3. style (of painting, writing, etc.). 4. manner, kind, sort. 5. (*pl.*) manners, habits. — **a la m. de,** like, in the manner of; **de esa m.,** in this way, thus; **de ninguna m.,** by no means, in no way whatsoever; **de m. que,** so that, in such a way that; **de todas maneras,** whatever happens, by all means; **sobre m.,** extremely, exceedingly.
manerismo, *m.* mannerism.
manerista, *m., f.* mannerist.
manero, ra, *a.* trained, tame (said of falcons, hawks, etc.).
manes, *m.* (*pl.*) manes, ancestral spirits. (among the ancient Romans).
maneto, ta, *a.* 1. (Hond.) one-handed, withered-armed. 2. (Guat., Ven.) knock-kneed.
manezuela, *f.* 1. little hand. 2. clasp, catch. 3. handle, haft.
manfla, *f.* 1. (coll.) mistress, concubine. 2. old sow. 3. (sl.) brothel.
manga, *f.* 1. sleeve; (mec.) sleeve. 2. (water) hose. 3. cloth strainer. 4. band of armed men. 5. (Amer.) crowd, mob, gang. 6. conical fishing

net. 7. (aer.) wind cone. 8. bag or portmanteau open at the sides. 9. (mec.) journal, arm of axle tree turning the wheel. 10. ventilation tube or shaft. 11. (mar.) beam (widest part of ship). 12. waterspout (caused by a tornado). 13. cylindrical cover or framework around the cross. 14. (hunt.) line of beaters. 15. (Arg., Chile, Cuba) narrowing gangway or lane (leading cattle to a corral or loading platform). 16. (Mex.) poncho, manga. 17. (Hond.) coarse cloak. 18. (*pl.*) extras, bonus; profits. — **andar m. por hombro,** to be careless and slovenly around the house; **de m. corta,** shortsleeved, e.g. *camisa de m. corta,* short-sleeved shirt; **de m. larga,** long-sleeved; **en mangas de camisa,** in shirt sleeves; **estar de m.,** (coll.) to be hand in glove, be in league; **hacer mangas y capirotes,** (coll.) to act haphazardly, do hastily and without thought; **m. boba,** wide loose-fitting sleeve; **m. corta,** short sleeve; **m. de agua,** cloudburst, downpour; waterspout; **m. de aire,** (meteorol.) wind cone; **m. de camisa,** shirt sleeve; **m. de incendio,** fire hose; **m. de jamón,** leg-of-mutton sleeve; **m. de riego,** hosepipe; **m. de ventilación,** ventilation shaft; **m. de viento,** whirlwind, tornado; windsock; **m. murciélago,** batwing sleeve; **m. perdida,** angel sleeve, open or hanging sleeve; **ser de** or **tener m. ancha,** to be very lenient, easy-going or generous.

manga, *f.* (bot.) (variety of) mango (tree and fruit).

mangachapuy, *m.* (variety of) gurjun, dipterocarpous tree important in the Philippines for its timber.

mangajarro, *m.* (coll.) long, dirty sleeve; ill-shaped sleeve.

mangajo, *m.* awkward, graceless person.

mangana, *f.* lasso, lariat.

manganato, *m.* (chem.) manganate.

manganear, *tr.v.* 1. to lasso. 2. (Peru) to annoy, vex, bother.

manganeo, *m.* 1. lassoing. 2. a sort of loose, free-for-all rodeo.

manganesa, *f.* (min.) manganese dioxide, pyrolusite.

manganesia, *f., var. of* **manganesa.**

manganesífero, ra, *a.* (chem.) manganiferous, containing manganese.

manganeso, *m.* (chem.) manganese.

manganeta, *f.* (Hond.) trick, scheme, ruse.

mangánico, ca, *a.* (chem.) manganic.

manganilla, *f.* 1. trick, scheme, ruse, stratagem. 2. sleight of hand. 3. battering ram. 4. (reg.) pole for shaking down acorns.

manganina, *f.* (metal.) manganin.

manganita, *m.* (min.) manganite.

manganito, *m.* (chem.) manganite.

manganoso, sa, *a.* (chem.) manganous.

mangante, *a.* shameless, brazen, rascally. —*m.* (coll.) beggar, sponger, cadger; thief.

manganzón, na, *a.* (Amer.) idle, lazy. —*m., f.* idler, loafer, lounger.

mangar, (*ref. 51*) *tr.v.* (coll.) to sponge, cadge, beg, scrounge; to steal, pinch, swipe.

mangaveleta, *f.* (avia.) wind sock.

mangla, *f.* gum from the rockrose.

manglar, *m.* mangrove swamp, thicket of mangrove.

mangle, *m.* (bot.) mangrove tree.

mango, *m.* 1. (bot.) mango (fruit, tree). 2. (sl., Mex.) an attractive woman. 3. handle, haft. — **m. de cuchillo,** (zool.) razor clam; **m. de escoba,** broomstick; **tener la sartén por el m.,** to be in the driver's seat, to be sitting on top of the world.

mangón, na, *m., f.* second-hand dealer, retailer. —*m.* (Arg.) corral.

mangonada, *f.* blow or shove with the arm.

mangoneador, ra, *a.* 1. loafing, loitering. 2. meddling. 3. (Amer.) fiddling, swindling (making a profit from public office).

mangonear, *i.v.* 1. (coll.) to loaf about, loiter about. 2. (coll.) to meddle, pry. 3. (Amer.) to profit illicitly from public office. 4. (Mex.) to steal.

mangoneo, *m.* 1. (coll.) meddling, prying. 2. (Amer.) graft, (coll.) fiddling, swindling.

mangonero, ra, *a.* (coll.) meddlesome, fond of prying.

mangorrero, ra, *a.* 1. (coll.) handled, passing from hand to hand. 2. rough, crude (knife). 3. (coll.) worthless, useless. 4. wandering, roving, rambling.

mangorrillo, *m.* plow handle.

mangosta, *f.* (zool.) mongoose.

mangostán, *m.* (bot.) mangosteen (tree).

mangote, *m.* (coll.) long wide sleeve; sleeve protector, clerk's oversleeve.

mangrullo, *m.* 1. (Arg.) tree lookout; pole lookout (used by scouts to observe Indian raids). 2. (Arg.) (variety of) catfish.

mangual, *m.* war flail, morning star (medieval weapon consisting of spiked heavy balls tied by chains to a wooden handle).

manguardia, *f.* buttress (of a bridge).

mangudo, da, *a.* long-handled.

manguear, *tr.v.* 1. (Arg., Chile) to force (the cattle) to enter the gangway. 2. (coll.) to entice or lure with flattery. —*i.v.* (P. Rico) to loaf, waste time.

manguera, *f.* 1. (water) hose; tube, duct. 2. (mar.) ventilation duct, tube or shaft. 3. waterspout. 4. (Arg.) corral, enclosure.

manguero, *m.* hoseman, fireman.

mangueta, *f.* 1. fountain syringe. 2. door jamb (for glass doors, trellis doors, etc.). 3. tiebeam (in roof). 4. instrument which regulates the speed of wool shears. 5. lever, pole (used by two for carrying great weights). 6. U-tube (of toilet drain pipe).

manguilla, *f.* (Chile) sleeve protector, clerk's oversleeve; (Chile) wristlet, lace half-sleeve (worn by women).

manguindo, *m.* (Cuba) idler, loafer, loiterer.

manguita, *f.* case, cover, sheath.

manguitería, *f.* furrier's shop.

manguitero, *m.* furrier.

manguito, *m.* 1. muff (for the hands). 2. wristlet, lace half-sleeve. 3. (cul.) ring-shaped biscuit. 4. sleeve protector, over-sleeve. 5. (mec.) sleeve, bushing; coupling. — **m. de colector,** (elec.) commutator shell.

manguruyú, *m.* (ichth.) Argentinian river fish (Pseudopimelodus zungaro).

manguzada, *f.* slap, swipe.

maní, (*pl.* **maníes**), *m.* 1. (Cuba, P. Rico, Dom. Rep., bot.) peanut; peanuts. 2. (W. Indies) dough (money).

manía, *f.* 1. mania. 2. craze, whim, fad. 3. hobby; habit. 4. dislike.

maníaco, ca, *a.* maniacal, maniac, mad, frantic. —*m., f.* maniac, madman; **m. sexual,** sex maniac.

maníacodrepresivo, va, *a.* (psyc.) manic depressive.

manialbo, ba, *a.* white-footed (said of horses).

maniatar, *tr.v.* to manacle, handcuff, tie the hands of; (fig.) to frustrate someone, get in the way, prevent someone's action.

maniate, *m.* (Ecuad.) hobble, hobbling strap (for horses, etc.).

maniático, ca, *a.* finicky, fussy; obsessed, neurotic. *m., f.* finicky person; fanatic; **m. de la ecología,** ecology fanatic.

maniblanco, ca, *a., var. of* **manialbo.**

manicato, ta, *a.* (Cuba) strong, brave, courageous.

manicero, *m.* (Cuba) peanut vendor.

manicomio, *m.* insane asylum, lunatic asylum, madhouse.

manicordio, *m., var. of* **monacordio.**

manicorto, ta, *a.* (coll.) stingy, mean, tightfisted, closefisted; parsimonious. —*m., f.* miser, skinflint.

manicurista, *m., f. var. of* **manicuro.**

manicuro, ra, *m., f.* manicurist. —*f.* manicure.

manida, *f.* abode, sheltering place; hangout, haunt; den, lair; nest.

manido, da, *a.* stale; worn-out; high, bad, rotten (meat, fish, etc.).

maniego, ga, *a.* (rare) ambidextrous.

manifacero, ra, *a.* (coll.) meddlesome, troublemaking. —*m., f.* meddler, troublemaker.

manifactura, *f.* 1. manufacture. 2. form, shape.

manifestación, *f.* 1. expression, revelation, manifestation. 2. (pol.) demonstration, public meeting, manifestation. 3. declaration, statement.

manifestador, ra, *a.* manifesting. —*m.* (ecc.) monstrance.

manifestante, *m., f.* demonstrator (participant in a public demonstration or meeting).

manifestar, (*ref. 29*) *tr.v.* to express; to say, declare; to show, reveal; (ecc.) to display, expose (Holy Eucharist). —*r.v.* to show or reveal oneself.

manifiestamente, *adv.* manifestly, clearly, evidently.

manifiesto, ta, *a.* manifest, plain, obvious. —*m.* 1. manifesto, public declaration. 2. (ecc.) exhibition of the Host. 3. manifest, list of ship's cargo. — **poner de m.,** to show, reveal, make evident.

manifiesto, manifieste, *ref.* **manifestar.**

manigordo, *m.* (C. Rica, zool.) ocelot.

manigua, *f.* (Cuba) jungle, thicket (in Cuba).

manigueta, *f.* 1. handle, haft. 2. (mar.) kevels.

manija, *f.* 1. handle, haft; crank. 2. hobble, fetters, hobbling strap. 3. clamp, collar. 4. leather glove (used to prevent chafing when scything, etc.).

manijero, *m.* foreman, manager, contractor of farm laborers.

Manila, *f.* Manila, capital of the Philippines.

manilargo, ga, *a.* 1. long-handed. 2. (fig.) open-handed, generous. 3. rough, ready-fisted.

manilense, *a., m., f., var. of* **manileño.**

manileño, ña, *a.* pertaining to Manila. —*m., f.* native or inhabitant of Manila.

manilla, *f.* 1. bracelet; handcuff, manacle. 2. small handle. 3. (P. Rico) wad of tobacco leaves.

manillar, *m.* handlebar.

maniluvio, *m.* (med.) hand bath (usually used in *pl.*).

maniobra, *f.* 1. handling, operation. 2. maneuver, move. 3. (fig.) maneuver, stratagem. 3. (*pl.*) (mil., mar.) maneuvers. 4. (mar.) gear, rigging, tackle. 5. (mar.) seamanship; art of navigation. 6. (*pl.*) (ry.) shifting, switch work. — **estar de maniobras,** to be on maneuvers.

maniobrabilidad, *f.* maneuverability.

maniobrable, *a.* maneuverable.

maniobrar, *i.v.* to maneuver. —*tr.v.* 1. to maneuver. 2. to operate, work. 3. (mar.) to handle (a ship).

maniobrero, ra, *a.* (mil.) maneuvering (troops); (mil.) skilled in maneuvering.

maniobrista, *a.* (mar.) skilled in maneuvering. —*m.* (mar.) skillful naval tactician.

maniota, *f.* hobble, hobbling strap (for horses, etc.); manacle, fetlock.

manipulación, *f.* 1. manipulation. 2. (fig.) act of controlling someone or something by artful means.

manipulador, ra, *a.* manipulating. —*m., f.* manipulator, handler. —*m.* (elec.) key, telegraph key.
manipulante, *a.* manipulating. —*m., f.* manipulator.
manipular, *tr.v.* to manipulate, manage, handle; (fig.) to manipulate (to one's own purposes).
manipuleo, *m.* (coll.) 1. manipulation (of business to one's own advantage). 2. tactful handling, maneuvering.
manípulo, *m.* 1. (hist.) maniple, standard; subdivision of the Roman legion. 2. (med.) handful. 3. (ecc.) maniple.
maniqueísmo, *m.* (philos., rel.) Manicheanism, the doctrines of Mani or Manichaeus.
maniqueo, a, *a., m, f.* (philos., rel.) Manichean.
maniquete, *m.* 1. black lace mitten. 2. mitten, hand-protector (for mowers).
maniquí, (*pl.* **maniquíes**), *m.* 1. mannekin, jointed model, lay figure (of dressmakers, artists, etc.). 2. puppet, weak-willed person.
manir, *tr.v.* to keep meat until it is high or gamey; to tenderize meat.
manirroto, ta, *a.* lavish, prodigal, spend-thrift, wasteful. —*m., f.* spendthrift, prodigal.
manita, *f.* (chem.) mannite; manna sugar.
manito, *m.* (pharm.) manna.
manito, manita, *f.* small hand, little hand (used in both cases with the fem. article, la). —*m., f.* (Mex., coll.) friend, colleague, brother, sister.
manitol, *m.* (chem.) mannitol.
manitosa, *f.* (chem.) mannitose.
manivacío, a, *a.* (coll.) empty-handed.
manivela, *f.* crank, handle; **m. de arranque,** (auto.) crank handle, starting crank; **m. motriz,** (mec.) driving crank.
manizuela, *f.* (Chile) taphole (in barrel or wine bag).
manjar, *m.* 1. food, dish. 2. (fig.) invigorating pastime or entertainment. — **m. blanco,** (cul.) blancmange.
manjarejo, *m. dim. of* **manjar,** savory dish, tidbit.
manjarete, *m. dim. of* **manjar,** (Cuba, cul.) blancmange made with corn, milk and sugar.
manjarria, *f.* (Cuba) driving beam of a canemill.
manjolar, *tr.v.* (hunt.) to carry (the hawk) in a cage, basket or on the hand.
manjorrada, *f.* (derog.) mass of dull food, abundance of ordinary victuals.
manjúa, *f.* (Cuba, ichth.) (kind of) anchovy (Engraulis cubanus).
manlieva, *f.* tax collected from house to house, or from hand to hand.
manlieve. *m.* confidence game; swindle.
mano, *f.* 1. hand; forefoot (of quadrupeds); leg, trotter (of slaughtered animals); hand (of clock, etc.). 2. coat (of paint). 3. hand, game, round (of cards, domino, etc.). 4. (fig.) time, turn. 5. first player, the lead, e.g. *soy m.,* I lead. 6. pestle, pounder; mano, grinding stone. 7. (elephant's) trunk. 8. quire (of paper). 9. (fig.) reprimand, censure. 10. side, e.g. *a m. izquierda de,* on the left hand side of. 11. (Amer.) bunch (of bananas, etc.); cluster, group (of objects). 12. (fig.) group, band (of people). 13. (tex.) set of teasels. 14. six or eight skeins of thread (in silk-making). 15. thirty four rolls or buns. 16. (hunt.) each of the tours of inspection of the area to be hunted. 17. (fig.) means, way. 18. (fig.) ability, skill, hand. 19. (fig.) power, authority. 20. (fig.) support, favor, patronage. 21. (fig.) hand, help, assistance. 22. (Amer.) mishap, misfortune. 23. grooves cut in a stone to facilitate lifting it. 24. (mus.) scale. 25. (*pl.*) hands, labor. — **abrir la m.,** to give generously; to be lenient; **a dos manos,** (coll.) readily, eagerly, with open arms; **a la m.,** at hand, on hand; within reach; **alzar la m. a,** to raise one's hand to, threaten; **a m.,** (made) by hand; at hand, on hand, nearby; artificially; **a m. abierta,** open-handedly, generously; **a m. airada,** violently, by violence; **a m. armada,** at gunpoint; resolutely; **a m. salva,** without danger, without running any risk; **a manos llenas,** liberally, generously; abundantly; **apretar la m.,** to shake hands; (coll.) to become more strict, clamp down; (coll.) to hurry up, urge on (the carrying out of); **a salva m.,** without danger, without running any risk; **asentar la m. a,** to strike, hit, punish; to reprimand; to be strict with; **atar las manos,** to tie someone's hands, stop from acting; **atarse las manos,** to bind oneself (with a promise, etc.); **a una m.,** in one direction; (fig.) in agreement; **bajar la m.,** to come down in price (goods); **bajo m.,** underhandedly, secretly, clandestinely; **buena m.,** luck, success; **buenas manos,** skill, dexterity; **cargar la m.,** to insist doggedly; to overcharge; to treat severely; **cargar la m. en,** (coll.) to be heavy handed with, use too much of; **con las manos cruzadas,** idly, without doing anything; **(salir) con las manos en la cabeza,** (coll.) (to come out) losing, at a disadvantage, the loser, unsuccessfully; **con las manos en la masa,** (coll.) red-handed, in the very act, on the spot, in the middle of doing something; **con las manos vacías,** empty-handed; unsuccessfully; **correr (una cosa) por m. de uno,** to be in someone's charge, be entrusted to someone; **corto de manos,** slow, inefficient; **cruzar las manos** or **cruzarse de manos,** to sit idly, sit quiet and still; **dar de m.,** to leave, suspend (work); to leave, abandon (a person); (bldg.) to plaster; **dar la m. a,** to give or stretch one's hand to; to lend a hand, help; to shake hands with; **dar la última m. a,** to give the finishing touch to; **darse buena m. en una cosa,** (coll.) to do something well or quickly; **darse la m. una cosa con otra,** to be near to one another; to be closely related, be connected with one another; **darse las manos,** to join hands, unite (in a common enterprise); to become reconciled; to harmonize; **dejar de la m.,** to abandon, forget about, drop, leave, neglect; **dejar en manos de uno,** to leave in someone's hands, entrust to; **de la m. a la boca se cae la sopa,** there's many a slip 'twixt the cup and the lip; **de m. en m.,** from hand to hand, from person to person; (fig.) from father to son; **de manos a boca,** (coll.) suddenly, unexpectedly; **de primera m.,** brand new, new, first-hand; **descargar la m. sobre,** (coll.) to thrash, give a beating to; **de segunda m.,** second-hand; **echar la m., las manos** or **m. a,** to take, catch or get hold of, grasp; **echar m. a la bolsa,** to take money out of one's purse; **echar m. a la espalda,** to make as if to draw one's sword; **echar m. de,** to take, catch or get hold of, grasp; to use, make use; of; **echar una m. a,** to lend a hand, help; **ensuciar** or **ensuciarse las manos,** (coll.) to steal, filch, pinch; to accept bribes; **escribir a la m.,** to take dictation; **estar con una m. atrás y otra adelante,** to be naked; to be destitute, have nothing; **estar dejado de la m. de Dios,** to be forsaken by God; (fig.) to fail in everything, be an utter failure; **estar en buenas manos,** to be in good hands; **estar en m. de uno,** to be up to one, be in one's hands; **estrechar a uno la m.,** to shake someone's hand; **ganar a uno por la m., ganar de m.,** to steal a march on someone, beat someone to it; **hablar por la m.,** to use sign language, communicate by signs; **imponer las manos,** (ecc.) to lay hands on, perform the laying on of hands; **ir a la m. a uno,** (coll.) to check or restrain someone; **irse de la m. (una cosa),** to slip, drop or fall from one's hands; **írsele a uno una cosa de entre las manos,** to let slip through one's fingers, e.g. *se le fue el negocio de entre las manos,* he let the business slip through his fingers; **írsele a uno la m.,** to slip (the hand), put too much, e.g. *se me fue la m. en la sal,* I put too much salt in; to go too far, be excessive (in praises, gifts, punishment, etc.), e.g. *se le fue la m. castigando a Pedro,* he went too far when punishing Peter; **largo de manos,** ready-fisted, aggressive, rough; **lavarse las manos de,** to wash one's hands of; **levantar m.** or **la m. de,** to abandon, forsake; **limpio de manos,** upright, honest, guiltless; **llegar a las manos,** to come to blows; **m. a m.,** together, hand-in-hand; on equal terms; (taur.) match between two star matadors, each handling a bull alternately; **m. apalmada,** (her.) hand appaumé (hand opened out so as to show the palm); **m. de almirez,** pestle; **m. de cazo,** (coll.) left-handed person; **m. de gato,** (coll.) cat's paw; powder puff; skin lotion or treatment; expert hand, correction by an expert; **m. de Judas,** hand-shaped candle extinguisher; **m. de obra,** manual labor; **m. de obra calificada,** skilled labor; **m. derecha** or **diestra,** right hand; right-hand man; **m. de santo,** (coll.) sure cure, unfailing remedy; **m. interior,** undercoat (of paint); **m. izquierda** or **zurda,** left hand; **m. oculta,** hidden power; **mala m.,** lack of skill; bad luck, misfortune, lack of success; **manos a la obra,** let's get to work; **manos largas,** ready-fisted person, rough person; **manos limpias,** (coll.) integrity, honesty, uprightness; (fig.) perquisites, perks, extras (payment in addition to salary); **manos muertas,** (law) mort-main, dead hand; **m. sobre m.,** idly, without doing anything; **manos sucias,** (coll.) graft, ill-gotten gains; **meter la m. en,** to meddle or interfere with; to pinch or steal from; **morderse las manos,** to kick oneself, reproach oneself (for missing an opportunity, etc.); **muchas manos en un plato,** too many cooks spoil the broth; **mudar de manos,** to change hands; **no dejar una cosa de la m.,** not to leave a thing for one minute, do a thing without stopping; **no saber dónde tiene la m. derecha,** (coll.) to be incompetent or stupid; **no saber lo que trae entre manos,** (coll.) to be hopelessly unfit (for a job); **pedir la m.,** to ask for someone's hand in marriage; **poner en manos de,** to put into someone's hands, entrust to; **poner la m. en,** to examine closely, study; to undertake or attempt something; **poner la m.** or **las manos en,** to hit, attack, assault, give a beating; **poner las manos en la masa,** (coll.) to undertake something, get involved in something; **ponerse en manos de,** to place oneself in someone's hands; **por debajo m.,** secretly, clandestinely; **por segunda m.,** with the help of or through someone else; **por su m.,** by oneself, on one own's authority; **primera m.,** undercoat (of paint); **probar la m. en,** to try one's hand in; **sentar la m. a,** (coll.) to beat, punish, thrash, hit; to reprimand; **si a m. viene,** if the case should arise, perhaps; **sin levantar m.,** without stopping work, without stop; **suelto de manos,** ready-fisted, rough, aggressive; **tender a uno la m.** or **una m.,** to hold out or offer one's hand; to offer a hand, offer help; **tener a m.,** to restrain, hold back, check; **tener atadas las manos,** to have one's hands tied, be unable to act; **tener en su m.** or **en sus manos,**

to have (something or someone) in one's hands or power; **tener la m. manca,** (coll.) to be mean or stingy; **tener las manos largas,** (coll.) to be ready-fisted, rough or aggressive; **tener m. con,** to have influence on, have pull with, be in with someone (sl.); **tener m. en,** to have a hand in; **tener m. izquierda,** (coll.) to have one's wits about one, be clever or astute; **tener muchas manos,** to be very skillful; **tener muchos asuntos entre manos,** to have many irons in the fire; **traer entre manos una cosa,** to handle or manage something, be involved in some project; to have some plan in mind; **untar la m.** or **las manos a uno,** to bribe, grease someone's palm; **venir a uno a la mano** or **a las manos,** to drop into one's lap, get (something) without any effort; **venir a las manos,** to come to blows; **venir** or **venirse con sus manos lavadas,** to want to reap where others have sown, want to benefit from others' efforts; **vivir de la m. a la boca,** to live from hand to mouth; **vivir de** or **por sus manos,** (coll.) to earn one's living by one's own efforts.

mano, na, *m., f.* (Mex.) friend, companion, colleague, brother, sister.

manobra, *f.* raw material.

manobrar, *tr.v.* (Chile), *var. of* **maniobrar.**

manobre, *m.* hodman, hod carrier.

manobrero, *m.* cleaner or keeper of irrigation ditches.

manojear, *tr.v.* (Cuba, Chile) to tie (leaves of tobacco) into bundles or bunches.

manojera, *f.* bundle of brushwood.

manojillo, ito, *m. dim. of* **manojo,** small bundle or fagot.

manojo, *m.* handful, bunch, bundle (of twigs, etc.); (Amer.) hand (of tobacco); **a manojos,** abundantly.

manojuelo, *m. dim. of* **manojo,** small bunch or handful.

manolo, la, *m., f.* formerly, popular class Madrilenian, (distinguished by flashy dress and sassy manners).

manométrico, ca, *a.* manometric, manometrical.

manómetro, *m.* manometer, pressure gauge; **m. para neumáticos,** tire gage.

manopla, *f.* 1. gauntlet. 2. coachman's whip. 3. (coll.) big hand. 4. (Amer.) knuckle-duster (a weapon), brass knuckles.

manosa, *f.* (chem.) mannose.

manoseador, ra, *a.* fingering, mussing, rumpling.

manosear, *tr.v.* 1. to finger, handle, touch, paw. 2. to feel. 3. to rumple, muss.

manoseo, *m.* 1. fingering, handling; feeling, pawing. 2. mussing, rumpling.

manota, *f. aug. of* **mano,** large hand.

manotada, *f.* slap, cuff or blow with the hand.

manotazo, *m., var. of* **manotada.**

manoteado, *past part. of* **manotear.** —*m.* slapping; gesticulation.

manoteador, ra, *a.* slapping.

manotear, *tr.v.* to slap. —*i.v.* to gesticulate, wave one's arms about.

manoteo, *m.* 1. slapping. 2. gesticulation with the hands.

manotón, *m.* a resounding blow from the hand.

manque, manqué, *ref.* **mancar.**

manquear, *i.v.* to pretend to be maimed or crippled.

manquedad, *f.* 1. one-handedness, lack of one or both hands. 2. maimed condition, physical defect, fault.

manquera, *f., var. of* **manquedad.**

mansalino, na, *a.* (Chile) enormous; extraordinary.

mansalva, *adv.* **a m.,** without running any risk, without any danger.

mansamente, *adv.* 1. meekly, mildly. 2. slowly, gently. 3. quietly, noiselessly.

mansarda, *f.* (archit.) mansard, garret.

mansedumbre, *f.* tameness, gentleness; meekness, peaceableness.

mansejón, na, *a.* very gentle and tame (an animal).

manseque, *m.* (Chile) children's party or dance.

mansera, *f.* (Cuba) vat for the cane juice.

mansión, *f.* 1. mansion, residence, abode. 2. stay, sojourn. — **hacer m.,** to stop over.

mansito, *a. dim. of* **manso,** very tame; very meek or mild. —*adv.* quietly, softly.

manso, sa, *a.* 1. meek, mild, gentle. 2. tame (animal). 3. gentle, soft (breeze). 4. (Chile) enormous, extraordinary. —*m.* 1. bellwether (leading flock of sheep), leading ox or cow (of herd). 2. farmhouse.

mansurrón, na, *a.* extremely mild, meek or gentle; extremely tame.

manta, *f.* 1. blanket; horse blanket; traveling rug. 2. large shawl; (Arg.) poncho. 3. (mil.) manta, mantelet. 4. thrashing, beating 5. feather on tip of hawk's wing. 6. (Mex.) coarse cotton cloth. 7. (Amer.) burlap bag (used in mines). 8. (Col.) popular dance. 9. (ichth.) manta, devil fish. — **a m.,** (irrigation) by flooding; plentifully, in great quantities, cats and dogs (of rain); **a m. de Dios,** plentifully; in great quantities; cats and dogs (of rain); **liarse la m. a la cabeza,** to ride roughshod over everything; **m. de viaje,** traveling rug, lap robe; **m. eléctrica,** electric blanket; **tirar de la m.,** to reveal a secret.

mantadril, *m.* (Hond., Guat.) drill (cloth).

mantalona, *f.* (Phil. I.) cotton cloth for sails.

mantaterilla, *f.* coarse hemp and wool cloth (used for horse blankets).

manteado, *m.* (Hond.) camp tent.

manteador, ra, *a.* tossing. —*m., f.* tosser, one who tosses another in a blanket.

manteamiento, *m.* tossing in a blanket (formerly a form of diversion or punishment).

mantear, *tr.v.* 1. to toss in the air. 2. (Arg.) to rough up. —*i.v.* (reg.) to gad about (women). —*r.v.* (min., Chile) to extend into a stratum (of a vein).

manteca, *f.* 1. lard, grease, fat. 2. butter. 3. ointment, pomade. 4. (hum.) money. — **como m.,** as smooth as butter; **m. de cacahuete** or **maní,** peanut butter; **m. de cacao,** cocoa butter; **m. de cerdo,** lard; **m. de coco,** coconut butter; **m. de vaca,** butter.

mantecada, *f.* slice of bread and butter sprinkled with sugar; kind of butter cake; buttered toast.

mantecado, *f.* 1. cake made with lard. 2. milk shake, milk sherbet. 3. ice cream; (Cuba) vanilla ice cream.

mantecón, na, *m., f.* pampered person, milksop, person who is fond of ease and leisure.

mantecoso, sa, *a.* buttery, rich in butter.

manteísta, *m.* day student in a seminary.

mantel, *m.* 1. tablecloth. 2. (ecc.) altar cloth. — **levantar los manteles,** to clear the table.

mantelería, *f.* table linen, napery.

manteleta, *f.* wrap, shawl, small mantle, shoulder scarf.

mantelete, *m.* 1. (ecc.) manteletta. 2. (mil.) mantelet. 3. (her.) mantling.

mantelillo, *m.* place mat or napkin.

mantellina, *f.* mantilla, veil.

mantención, *f.* (coll.) maintenance.

mantenedor, *m.* president of a joust, contest or tournament.

mantenencia, *f.* 1. maintenance. 2. aliment, victuals.

mantener, (*ref. 23*) *tr.v.* 1. to maintain, support (a family, etc.). 2. to keep (in a certain condition) e.g. *m. la casa en buen estado,* to keep the house in good condition. 3. to maintain, keep up (an estate, correspondence, relations, a conversation). 4. to hold, maintain, continue to hold (an opinion). 5. to maintain, affirm, e.g. *yo mantengo que,* I maintain that. 6. to hold (a tournament, contest). 7. (law) to uphold, support. — **m. en funcionamiento,** to keep working, keep in operation. —*r.v.* to maintain oneself; to keep oneself; to keep; to stand or remain firm (in opinions, etc.); **mantenerse a distancia,** to keep one's distance; **mantenerse a flote,** to keep afloat; to keep one's head above water; **mantenerse al día con,** to keep up to date with, keep abreast of; **mantenerse aparte,** to keep to oneself, keep oneself apart; **mantenerse en forma,** to keep in shape; **mantenerse en práctica,** to keep in practice, keep one's hand in; **mantenerse firme,** to stand firm (in position, convictions); **mantenerse informado,** to keep informed, keep oneself informed.

mantenga, matengo, *ref.* **mantener.**

mantenido, da, *m., f.* (Arg.) guzzler. —*m.* (Guat., & Mex.) gigolo. —*f.* (Guat., Mex.) kept woman.

manteniente, a m., with all one's might; with both hands.

mantenimiento, *m.* 1. maintenance; sustenance; rations, food; (*pl.*) food; 2. allowance, support.

manteo, *m.* 1. tossing in a blanket. 2. long cloak worn by Roman Catholic priests and formerly by students.

mantequera, *f.* 1. woman who makes or sells butter; milkmaid. 2. butter churn; butter dish.

mantequería, *f.* creamery, butter factory, dairy.

mantequero, *m.* 1. (Amer.) man who makes or sells butter. 2. butter dish. 3. (bot.) cohune palm, corozo palm.

mantequilla, *f.* butter; butter cream (mixture of butter with sugar).

mantequillera, *f.* (Amer.) butter dish.

mantequillero, *m., f.* 1. man who makes or sells butter. 2. butter dish.

mantero, ra, *m., f.* blanket maker or seller.

mantés, sa, *a.* (coll.) roguish, rascally. —*m., f.* (coll.) rogue, rascal, scoundrel.

mantilla, *f.* 1. mantilla, veil. 2. (*pl.*) swaddling clothes, baby's flannel wrap. 3. horsecloth. 4. (print.) blanket. — **estar una cosa en m.,** (coll.) to be in its infancy, be in embryo (said of a project, a book, etc.); **haber salido uno de m.,** (coll.) to be no longer wet behind the ears, have reached the age of judgment. —*m.* 1. (Hond.) coward. 2. (*pl.*) present for the birth of a prince.

mantilleja, *f. dim. of* **mantilla,** small mantilla.

mantillo, *m.* humus; manure.

mantillón, na, *a.* 1. dirty, slovenly. 2. (Mex.) shameless.

mantis, *f.* (zool.) **m. religiosa,** praying mantis.

mantisa, *f.* (math.) mantissa.

manto, *m.* 1. mantle, cloak; robe, gown; (student's) gown; long mantilla; shawl. 2. (zool.) mantle. 3. mantel (of fireplace). 4. (min.) thin almost horizontal stratum. 5. layer of fat (covering newborn baby). 6. (fig.) cloak.

mantón, *m.* 1. shawl. 2. (hunt.) feather on the top of hawk's wing. — **m. de Manila,** (coll.) embroidered shawl.

mantón, na, *a., var. of* **mantudo.**

mantuano, na, *a.* Mantuan, of or from Mantua, Italy. —*m., f.* Mantuan.

mantudo, da, *a.* with drooping wings.

mantuve, mantuviera, mantuviese, *ref.* **mantener.**

manuable, *a.* easy to handle, manageable.
manual, *a.* 1. manual; **trabajo m.,** manual work. 2. easy to handle, manageable, pliant, tractable. 3. easily done. —*m.* 1. manual, handbook; (ecc.) manual. 2. notebook; (com.) roughdraft diary. 3. (*pl.*) perquisites received by priests for attending the choir.
manualmente, *adv.* manually, by hand.
manubrio, *m.* 1. handle; crank. 2. (anat., bot.) manubrium.
manucodiata, *f.* (ornith.) bird of paradise.
manuela, *f.* open hackney carriage (formerly a typical urban conveyance of Madrid).
manuella, *f.* (mar.) capstan bar.
manufactura, *f.* manufacture; manufactory; manufactured article.
manufacturado, da, *a.* manufactured; made in a plant or factory.
manufacturar, *tr.v.* to manufacture, make; to produce by mechanical means.
manufacturero, ra, *a.* manufacturing. —*m., f.* (Gal.) manufacturer, producer.
manumisión, *f.* (law) manumission, freeing.
manumiso, sa, *a.* freed, emancipated (slave).
manumisor, *m.* (law) manumitter, liberator.
manumitir, *tr.v.* (law) to manumit, set free (slaves).
manuscribir, *tr.v.* to write by hand.
manuscrito, ta, *past part. of* **manuscribir.** —*a.* hand-written. —*m.* manuscript; **Manuscritos del Mar Muerto,** Dead Sea Scrolls.
manutención, *f.* 1. maintenance, support. 2. upkeep; conservation.
manutener, (*ref. 23*) *tr.v.* (law) to maintain, support.
manutenga, manutengo, *ref.* **manutener.**
manutigio, *m.* (med.) friction, light rub.
manutisa, *f.* (bot.) sweet william.
manutuve, manutuviera, manutuviese, *ref.* **manutener.**
manvacío, a, *a.* (coll.) empty-handed.
manzana, *f.* 1. apple. 2. block, block of buildings. 3. knob (on furniture). 4. pommel (of sword). 5. (Amer.) Adam's apple. — **m. asperiega,** cider apple; **m. de discordia,** apple of discord, bone of contention; **sano como una m.,** as fit as a fiddle.
manzanal, *m.* 1. apple orchard. 2. apple tree.
manzanar, *m.* apple orchard.
manzanear, *tr.v.* (Guat., Mex.) to divide (a property); (Ven.) to flatter, fawn on. —*i.v.* (Guat.) to steal apples.
manzanera, *f.* (bot.) crab apple, wild apple tree.
manzanero, *m.* (Ecuad.) apple tree.
manzanil, *a.* apple-like, apple-shaped.
manzanilla, *f.* 1. (bot.) camomile. 2. camomile tea. 3. manzanilla (pale dry sherry). 4. tip (of the chin). 5. pad, cushion (of animal's foot). 6. knob (on furniture or balcony). 7. small, round, very tasty olive. — **m. bastarda,** (bot.) mayweed, stinking camomile; **m. hedionda,** (bot.) stinking camomile, mayweed; **m. loca,** (bot.) oxeye; oxeye camomile, yellow camomile; **m. romana,** (bot.) camomile.
manzanillo, *m.* 1. (bot.) manzanilla olive tree. 2. (bot.) manchineel.
manzanita, *f. dim. of* **manzana,** small apple.
manzano, *m.* (bot.) apple tree; (C. Amer., Col., Car.) apple banana; **m. asperiego,** (bot.) cider apple tree.
maña, *f.* 1. skill, knack, ability, dexterity. 2. artfulness, craftiness, astuteness; tact, cunning. 3. custom, habit. 4. bundle, bunch (of flax or hemp). — **darse m.,** to manage, to contrive to or find a way to; **más vale m. que fuerza,** tact or skill will do where mere force won't; **tener malas mañas,** to have bad habits.
mañana, *f.* morning, forenoon; **en or por la m.,** in the morning. —*m.* the future, tomorrow. —*adv.* tomorrow; (fig.) in the future; **de m.,** early in the morning; **hasta m.,** so long, till tomorrow; **m. será otro día,** better luck tomorrow; **muy de m.,** very early in the morning; **no dejes para m. lo que puedes hacer hoy,** don't put off until tomorrow what you can do today; **pasado m.,** the day after tomorrow; **tomar la m.,** to get up at dawn; (coll.) to drink liquor before breakfast.
mañanear, *i.v.* to rise at dawn, get up at dawn habitually.
mañanero, ra, *a.* early-rising.
mañanita, *f.* bed jacket.
mañear, *tr.v.* to manage skillfully. —*i.v.* to behave artfully, to act craftily.
mañería, *f.* 1. barrenness, sterility. 2. feudal right of inheriting without legitimate succession.
mañero, ra, *a.* 1. artful, cunning, shrewd. 2. easy; handy. 3. (Chile) shy (horse).
mañigal, *m.* (Chile) land planted with maniu trees.
mañiu, *m.* (Chile, bot.) maniu.
maño, ña, *m., f.* 1. (Sp., coll.) Aragonese. 2. (reg., Chile) brother, sister. 3. (reg., Chile) darling, dear.
mañoco, *m.* 1. tapioca. 2. (Ven.) Indian corn meal.
mañosamente, *adv.* 1. skillfully, craftily, artfully. 2. maliciously.
mañosear, *i.v.* (Chile) to act craftily or cunningly.
mañoso, sa, *a.* 1. skillful. 2. tricky, artful, cunning, crafty. 3. having bad habits.
mañuela, *f.* 1. craftiness, artfulness. 2. (*pl.*) cunning, crafty person.
mapa, *m.* map, chart. — **m. acotado,** contour map; **m. celeste,** chart of the heavens; **m. de carreteras or rutas,** road map; **m del tiempo,** weather map; **m. de vuelo,** (avia.) flight map; **m. geológico,** geologic map; **m. mudo,** map without geographical names; **m. topográfico,** contour map, topographical plan; **no estar en el m.,** (coll.) to be off the map, be extraordinary. —*f.* (coll.) top, finest of its kind; **llevarse la m.,** (coll.) to take the cake, take the prize.
mapache, *m.* (zool.) raccoon.
mapachín, *m.* (Guat., Hond.) raccoon.
mapamundi, *m.* 1. map of the world. 2. (coll.) the behind, the buttocks.
mapanare, *f.* (zool.) fer-de-lance, bush master (a highly poisonous snake).
mapo, *m.* (ichth.) mapo, a river fish.
mapuche, *a.* (S. Amer.) Araucan, of or pertaining to the Araucan Indians, their culture or customs.
mapuey, *m.* (bot.) edible plant (Discorea tufidae).
mapurite, *m.* (zool.) skunk.
mapurito, *m.* (Col.), *var. of* **mapurite.**
maque, maqué, *ref.* **macarse.**
maque, *m.* 1. lacquer; shellac. 2. (bot.) tree of heaven.
maquear, *tr.v.* to lacquer, to shellac; (Guat., Mex.) to varnish.
maqueño, *m.* (Bol.) large-sized banana.
maqueta, *f.* 1. (art., archit.) model, maquette. 2. (print.) dummy.
maqui, *m.* 1. (bot.) maqui. 2. (zool.) macao.
maquiavélico, ca, *a.* 1. Machiavellian, like or pertaining to the political craftiness of Machiavelli. 2. (fig.) crafty, deceitful.
maquiavelismo, *m.* Machiavellianism.
maquiavelista, *a., m., f.* Machiavellian.
Maquiavelo, *m.* Machiavelli (Niccolo), Florentine politician and writer of the Renaissance.
maquila, *f.* 1. multure, toll of grain or flour paid to the miller or lord of the manor. 2. quarter of a peck, measure used to calculate multure. 3. (Hond.) a unit of weight equivalent to 125 pounds.
maquilar, *tr.v.* to exact the toll (in corn or grain) for grinding at a mill.
maquilear, *tr.v.* (Chile), *var. of* **maquilar.**
maquilero, *m.* collector of multure or miller's toll.
maquillaje, *m.* make-up (on face); cosmetics.
maquillar, *tr.v., r.v.* to make up (the face), to apply cosmetics.
máquina, *f.* 1. machine; engine; apparatus; (ry.) locomotive. 2. (theat., lit.) machine. 3. (fig.) plan, project, scheme. 4. (coll.) enormous quantity. — **m. alternativa,** reciprocating engine; **m. apisonadora,** steam roller; **m. calculadora,** calculating machine; **m. condensadora,** condensing engine; **m. de afeitar,** electric razor; **m. de aire,** air engine; **m. de calcular,** calculator; **m. de coser,** sewing machine; **m. de discos,** jukebox; **m. de escribir,** typewriter; **m. de frutas** or **tragamonedas,** slot machine; **m. de hacer punto** or **tricotar,** knitting machine; **m. de lavar,** washing machine; **m. de ranurar,** slotting machine; **m. de simple expansión,** simple engine; **m. a** or **de vapor,** steam engine; **m. de vapor de triple expansión,** triple expansion engine; **m. eléctrica,** electric machine; **m. expendedora,** vending machine; **m. franqueadora,** postage meter; **m. herramienta,** machine tool; **m. infernal,** infernal machine; **m. neumática,** air pump; **m. perforadora,** (pet.) drill rig; **m. sin escape libre,** condensing engine; **m. sopladora,** blast engine; **m. sumadora,** adding machine; **m. tragaperras,** (Sp.) slot machine; **m. voladora,** flying machine.
maquinabilidad, *f.* machinability, the state or condition of what can be made, shaped or finished by machine.
maquinación, *f.* machination, scheming, plotting.
maquinador, ra, *a.* scheming, plotting. —*m., f.* schemer, plotter, contriver.
máquina-herramienta, *f.* machine tool.
maquinal, *a.* 1. mechanical, pertaining to a machine. 2. mechanical, automatic, unconscious.
maquinalmente, *adv.* mechanically.
maquinar, *tr.v.* to scheme, plot, hatch, contrive.
maquinaria, *f.* 1. machinery. 2. mechanics, art of building machines. 3. applied mechanics.
maquinilla, *f.* 1. winch; clippers. 2. (Amer.) typewriter. — **contestar en m.** (Amer.) to typewrite the answer; **escribir en m.,** (Amer.) to typewrite; **m. cortapelos,** hair clippers; **m. de afeitar** or **de seguridad,** safety razor; **m. de rizar,** curling iron.
maquinismo, *m.* (econ.) mechanization.
maquinista, *m., f.* machinist, mechanic; engine driver, locomotive driver, engineer.
maquís, *m.* partisan, guerrilla, member of the French underground in World War II.
mar, *m., f.* 1. sea, ocean; tide. 2. (fig.) sea, floods, oceans (e.g. of tears). 3. large quantity or number, e.g. *la mar de cosas,* a great many things. — **alta m.,** high seas, open sea; **a mares,** by the bucketful, copiously (after **llorar**), profusely (after **sudar**), cats and dogs (after **llover**); **arrojarse al m.,** to take the plunge, take the risk; **de m. a m.,** from end to end, in great abundance; **en el m.,** at sea; **hacerse a la m.,** to put out to sea; **la m. de,** very, e.g. *es la m. de tonto,* he is very foolish; **Mar Adriático,** Adriatic Sea; **m. agitado** or **bravo,** rough sea; **M. Amarillo,** Yellow Sea; **m. ancha,** open sea, high seas; **M. Báltico,** Baltic Sea; **m. bonanza,** calm sea; **Mar Caribe,** Caribean Sea; **Mar Caspio,** Caspian Sea; **m. cerrada,** closed sea; **M. de Aral,** Lake Aral; **m. de fondo,** ground swell; **M. de Galilea,** Sea of Galilee; **M. de las Antillas,** Caribbean

Sea; **M. de la China Meridional,** South China Sea; **M. del Coral,** Coral Sea; **m. de leva,** ground swell; **M. del Japón,** Sea of Japan; **M. del Norte,** North Sea; **M. de los Sargazos,** Sargasso Sea; **m. en calma, en bonanza** or **en leche,** calm sea; **Mares del Sur,** South Seas; **Mar Egeo,** Aegean Sea; **m. gruesa,** heavy sea; **Mar Jónico,** Ionian Sea; **m. jurisdiccional,** territorial waters; **m. larga,** open sea, high seas; **M. Mediterráneo,** Mediterranean Sea; **M. Muerto,** Dead Sea; **M. Negro,** Black Sea; **M. Rojo,** Red Sea; **m. territorial,** territorial waters or sea; **meter la m. en un pozo,** to attempt the impossible; **picarse el m.** or **la m.,** to begin to get rough (the sea); **quebrar** or **romperse el m.,** to break, lash (the sea); **quien no se aventura no pasa la m.,** nothing ventured, nothing gained; **Mar Tirreno,** Tyrrenian Sea.

mar. *abbrev. of* **marzo,** March (Mar.).

marabú, (*pl.* **marabúes**), *m.* 1. (ornith.) marabou (Leptoptilus ciconidae). 2. (dressm.) marabou, fur stole or trimming. 3. (Cuba, bot.) brush, weeds.

marabuto, *m.* ribat, Mohammedan hermitage.

maraca, *m.* (Amer., mus.) maraca, percussion instrument, made of a dry gourd. —*f.* (Chile) prostitute.

maracaná, (*pl.* **maracanáes**), *m.* (**Arg.,** ornith.) maracan, Brazil macaw.

maracayá, (*pl.* **maracayáes**), *m.* (zool., Amer.) ocelot.

maracure, *m.* (bot.) curare plant.

maragato, ta, *m.* 1. neck trimming formerly worn by women. 2. (Sp.) native of a district called the Maragateria in the province of Leon.

maranta, *f.* (bot.) arrowroot plant.

maraña, 1. thicket, bramble patch, jungle. 2. outer fibers of silk cocoon; coarse silk (made with this silk). 3. tangle (of hair, threads, etc.). 4. (fig.) tangle, mess. 5. lie, trick, scheme (to confuse situation). 6. (bot.) kermes oak.

marañado, da, *a.* entangled, perplexed.

marañal, *m.* kermes oak grove.

marañar, *tr.v.* to tangle; to entangle. —*r.v.* to become tangled or entangled.

marañento, ta, *a.* (Chile), *var. of* **marañero.**

marañero, ra, *a.* tricky, scheming, intriguing, ensnaring. —*m., f.* schemer, intriguer, trickster.

marañón, *m.* (bot.) cashew tree, cashew nut.

marañoso, sa, *a.* 1. tangled. 2. tricky; scheming. —*m., f.* trickster, schemer, intriguer.

marañuela, *f.* (bot.) nasturtium. —*m.* a deep poppy-orange color.

marapa, *f.* (Mex., bot.) hog plum, yellow moubin.

marasmo, *m.* 1. (med.) marasmus. 2. (fig.) apathy, inactivity.

maratón, *m.* 1. (sports) marathon. 2. (fig.) endurance contest.

maravedí, (*pl.* **maravedíes**), *m.* 1. (numis.) maravedi, an ancient Spanish coin. 2. (Sp.) ancient tax on property (in Aragon).

maravedinada, *f.* ancient grain measure.

maravilla, *f.* 1. wonder, marvel. 2. (bot.) four-o'clock, marvel of Peru; morning glory (Convolvulus tricolor); pot marigold, calendula. — **a las mil maravillas,** wonderfully, excellently; — **hacer maravillas,** (coll.) to perform wonders; **por m.,** rarely, seldom, by the merest chance; **ser la octava m.,** to be the eighth wonder of the world.

maravillar, *tr.v.* to amaze, astound, cause to marvel, regard with wonder or admiration. —*r.v.* (with **con** or **de**) to marvel (at), wonder (at), be astonished.

maravillosamente, *adv.* marvelously, wonderfully.

maravilloso, sa, *a.* marvelous, wonderful, wondrous.

maray, *m.* (Chile) millstone in a sugarmill.

marbella, *f.* (ornith.) snakebird.

marbete, *m.* 1. label, tag; luggage label or tag. 2. edge, border, outline, fillet.

marca, *f.* 1. mark; stamp. 2. brand, branding mark, brand (on cattle). 3. make, brand. 4. march, frontier town. 5. height-measuring bar. 6. standard, standard size. 7. (mar.) seamark, landmark. 8. (sport) score; record. — **m. de agua,** watermark; **m. de fábrica,** trademark; **de m.,** (fig.) outstanding; **de m. mayor,** very outstanding; **m. de ley,** hallmark; **m. de marea,** tidemark; **m. líder,** leading brand; **m. registrada,** trademark.

marcación, *f.* 1. (mar.) relative bearing; taking ship's bearing. 2. marking (in football). — **m. brújula,** compass bearing; **m. magnética,** (mar.) magnetic bearing.

marcadamente, *adv.* markedly, notably.

marcado, da, *past part. of* **marcar.** —*a.* marked, pronounced; underlined, stressed.

marcador, ra, *a.* marking; branding. —*m., f.* marker; brander. —*m.* 1. sampler (of embroidery). 2. (print.) feeder (person); (print.) feedboard. 3. public assayer (of the mint); public inspector of weights and measures. 4. (sport) scoreboard. 5. bookmark.

marcar, (*ref. 50*) *tr.v.* 1. to mark; to stamp, stencil; to brand (cattle); to label, embroider initials on. 2. to point out. 3. to mark out, designate, destine. 4. to cover (e.g. someone in soccer). 5. to score (e.g. a goal). 6. to indicate, show. 7. (mar.) to take (a bearing). 8. to dial (a telephone number). 9. (print.) to feed (a press). — **m. el compás,** (mus.) to beat time; **m. el paso,** (mil.) to mark time; **señal para m.,** dial tone. —*r.v.* (mar.) to take its bearings (a ship).

marcasita, *f.* (min.) marcasite.

marceador, ra, *a.* shearing.

marcear, *tr.v.* to shear (animals). —*i.v.* to be typical of March (the weather).

marcelianista, *a., m., f.* (rel.) Marcellian (one of a sect following the heresy of Marcellus, Bishop of Ancyra).

marceño, ña, *a.* of, like or pertaining to the month of March.

marceo, *m.* springtime cleaning or trimming of honeycombs.

marcero, ra, *a.* shearing.

marcescente, *a.* (bot.) marcescent, withering.

marcha, *f.* 1. march; walk; trek. 2. speed, velocity. 3. (mil., mus.) march. 4. (fig.) march, progress, advance, e.g. *la m. del tiempo,* the march of time. 5. motion, operation, function, e.g. *poner en m.,* to put into or set in motion or operation, *ponerse en m.,* to start. — **a largas marchas,** speedily, hastily; **batir la m. or batir m.,** to strike up a march; **dar m. atrás,** (auto.) to go into reverse; **en m.,** in motion, while moving or running; **m. atrás,** (auto.) reverse; **m. de hambre,** hunger march; **m. forzada,** (mil.) forced march; **m. fúnebre,** funeral march; **m. nupcial,** wedding march; **sobre la m.,** on the double, immediately.

marchador, ra, *a.* (Cuba, Chile) ambling, loping, pacing.

marchamar, *tr.v.* to mark, stamp (merchandise and goods in the custom house).

marchamero, *m.* customshouse marker.

marchamo, *m.* 1. customshouse stamp. 2. (Arg.) tax on each head of slaughtered cattle.

marchante, *a.* commercial. —*m.* 1. merchant, salesman, dealer. 2. (Amer.) customer, patron.

marchantería, *f.* (Cuba) clientele.

marchapié, *m.* 1. (mar.) footrope. 2. footboard.

marchar, *i.v.* 1. to go, go away, leave, depart. 2. (mil.) to march. 3. to go, proceed, progress, come along, e.g. *cómo marchan los negocios?* how's business? 4. to go, work, e.g. *mi reloj marcha bien,* my watch works well. 5. to develop (a plot, etc.). —*r.v.* to go, go away, leave, depart, e.g. *me marcho,* I am leaving.

marchitable, *a.* perishable, liable to wilt.

marchitamiento, *m.* wilting, withering, fading.

marchitar, *tr.v.* 1. to wither, wilt; to fade. 2. (fig.) to debilitate, weaken. —*r.v.* 1. to wither, wilt; to fade. 2. to languish, wilt, become thin or debilitated.

marchitez, *f.* 1. withered or faded condition. 2. languor, weakness.

marchito, ta, *a.* 1. withered, wilted, faded. 2. languid, weak, debilitated.

marcial, *a.* 1. martial, war-like; soldierly. 2. (pharm.) martial, containing iron. 3. (fig.) dashing. —*m.* aromatic powder for dusting gloves.

marcialidad, *f.* martialness.

marciano, na, *a.* Martian, of or pertaining to the planet Mars. —*m., f.* Martian, legendary being from Mars.

marcionista, *a.* (rel.) Marcionitic. —*m., f.* Marcionite, Marcionist.

marco, *m.* 1. frame, doorcase, window case. 2. picture frame; (fig.) setting, background. 3. mark (currency). 4. shoemaker's size stick. 5. standard timber measurement. 5. standard weight (for assaying weights). — **m. hidráulico,** small tank with different sized pipes regulating the distribution of water in gardens, etc.; **m. real,** surface measurement equivalent to 4,480 sq. meters.

márcola, *f.* long pruning stick or hook.

marcolador, ra, *m., f.* pruner.

marconigrafía, *f.* wireless telegraphy.

marconigrama, *m.* marconigram, wireless telegram.

marea, *f.* 1. tide. 2. sea shore, beach. 3. soft sea breeze. 4. drizzle, mist. 5. street dirt or garbage. — **m. alta,** high tide; **m. baja,** low tide; **m. diurna,** diurnal tide; **m. creciente** or **entrante,** rising or flood tide; **m. descendiente** or **menguante,** ebb tide; **m. muerta,** neap tide; **m. viva,** spring tide.

mareado, da, *a.* seasick, carsick, airsick; dizzy, nauseated.

mareaje, *m.* 1. (mar.) seamanship, art of navigation. 2. (mar.) route, course.

mareamiento, *m.* 1. sickness, traveling sickness, seasickness. 2. annoyance, bother.

mareante, *a.* 1. causing seasickness, nausea or dizziness. 2. skilled in navigation. —*m.* seaman.

marear, *tr.v.* 1. to navigate, sail. 2. to make sick, cause nausea. 3. (coll.) to confuse, muddle, mix up. 4. (coll.) to annoy, vex, bother. 5. to sell, retail. — **aguja de m.,** ship's compass. —*r.v.* 1. to become dizzy or seasick. 2. to become damaged at sea (merchandise).

marecanita, *f.* (min.) marekanite.

marejada, *f.* 1. (mar.) groundswell, swell. 2. undercurrent, murmur (of discontent).

maremagno, maremágnum, *m.* 1. (coll.) confusion, mess; confused crowd. 2. abundance.

maremoto, *m.* sea earthquake; tidal wave, ground swell.

mareo, *m.* 1. sickness, travel sickness, seasickness, dizziness. 2. (coll.) annoyance, vexation.

mareógrafo, *m.* mareograph, instrument registering the rise and fall of the tide.

mareómetro, *m.* tide gage.

marero, *a.* (mar.) sea (breeze).

mareta, *f.* 1. choppiness (of sea). 2. murmuring, rumbling (of crowd). 3. agitation, disturbance.
maretazo, *m.* huge wave; heavy sea.
márfaga, *f.* coarse woolen cloth.
marfil, *m.* ivory. — **m. vegetal,** (bot.) ivory nut.
marfilense, *a.* of or pertaining to the Ivory Coast. —*m., f.* person from the Ivory Coast.
marfileño, ña, *a.* pertaining to ivory; (poet.) ivory-like.
marfilina, *f.* imitation ivory.
marfuz, za, (*pl.* **marfuces**), *a.* 1. cast aside, rejected, repudiated. 2. false, deceiving, fallacious.
marga, *f.* 1. marl, loam. 2. coarse woolen cloth, burlap.
margajita, *f.* (min.) marcasite, white pyrites.
margal, *m.* marly ground, marlpit.
margallón, *m.* (bot.) dwarf fan palm, hemp palm, palmetto.
margar, (*ref. 51*) *tr.v.* to marl, fertilize (soil) with marl.
margarato, *m.* (chem.) margarate.
margárico, ca, *a.* (chem.) margaric (acid).
margarina, *f.* margarine.
margarita, *f.* 1. (bot.) daisy, marguerite. 2. pearl. 3. (zool.) periwinkle. 4. (min.) margarite. 5. margarita, (Mex.) cocktail made with tequila and lime juice. — **echar margaritas a los puercos,** to cast pearls before swine.
margay, *m.* (Amer., zool.) margay, tiger cat.
margen, *m., f.* 1. margin; border; side, edge. 2. verge; fringe, border. 3. note, marginal note. 4. occasion, cause, reason. 5. (*pl.*) limits. 6. (com.) margin. — **al m. de,** on the border of; at the side or edge of; in the margin of; **andarse por las márgenes,** to beat about the bush; **dar m. para,** to give occasion for; **estar** or **quedarse al m.,** to be or be left on the sidelines, be left out; **m. de beneficio** or **ganancias,** profit margin; **m. de error,** margin of error; **m. de seguridad,** safety margin; **m. de tolerancia,** tolerance.
margenar, *tr.v., var. of* **marginar.**
margesí, (*pl.* **margesíes**), *m.* (Peru) list or inventory of corporation holdings.
marginado, da, *a.* (bot.) marginated, marginate, having an edge.
marginal, *a.* marginal.
marginar, *tr.v.* 1. to write marginal notes on. 2. to leave a margin on. 3. to overlook, disregard.
margoso, sa, *a.* marly, containing marl, loamy.
margrave, *m.* margrave, former title of certain German princes and military governors.
margraviato, *m.* margraviate; territory governed by a margrave.
margravina, *f.* margravine; the wife or widow of a margrave.
marguera, *f.* marl deposit; marlpit, loam pit.
margullar, *tr.v.* (Cuba) to layer (vines or plants).
margullo, *m.* (agr.) (Cuba, Ven.) layer (shoot).
marhojo, *m.* refuse cut from plants, trimmings.
maría, *f.* (coll.) white wax taper. — **baño de m.,** (cul.) double boiler, bain-marie.
mariache, mariachi, *m.* (Mex.) popular music and orchestra; street singer; **los mariachis de Jalisco,** the famous street bands of the state of Jalisco, Mexico.
marial, *a.* in praise of the Virgin Mary (books). —*m.* book in praise of the Virgin Mary.
mariano, na, *a.* (ecc.) Marian.
marica, *f.* 1. (ornith.) magpie. 2. jack of diamonds.—*m.* (derog.) sissy, effeminate man, pansy (sl.).
Maricastaña, en los tiempos de M., (coll.) in the olden days, in the year one.
maricón, *m.* 1. (derog.) queer, pansy, sissy.

maridable, *a.* conjugal, matrimonial.
maridablemente, *adv.* conjugally; uxoriously.
maridaje, *m.* 1. conjugal bond; married life. 2. union, close connection.
maridar, *i.v.* to wed, marry; to lead conjugal life. —*tr.v.* to join, unite.
maridazo, *m.* (coll.) doting husband.
maridillo, *m.* foot-warmer, small brazier.
marido, *m.* husband, spouse.
mariguana, *f.* marijuana, marihuana (Cannabis sativa; Nicotiana glauca).
marihuana, *f., var. of* **mariguana.**
marimacho, *m.* (coll.) mannish, masculine woman. tombov. virago.
marimandona, *f.* domineering and bossy woman, virago.
marimanta, *f.* (coll.) spook, hobgoblin, bugbear.
marimarica, *m.* (coll.) pansy, sissy.
marimba, *f.* 1. (mus.) marimba. 2. (Arg.) beating. 3. a kind of drum used by Africans.
marimoña, *f.* (bot.) Asiatic crowfoot, turban buttercup.
marimorena, *f.* (coll., Sp.) fight, row, quarrel.
marina, *f.* 1. navy. 2. seamanship. 3. (p.) seascape, marine. — **m. de guerra,** navy; **m. mercante,** merchant marine, merchant navy, mercantile marine.
marinaje, *m.* 1. sailoring, seamanship. 2. seamen, sailors, ship's crew.
marinar, *tr.v.* 1. (cul.) to marinate. 2. to man (a ship), put a crew on.
marinear, *i.v.* to be a sailor, work as a seaman.
marinerado, da, *a.* manned, outfitted (said of a ship).
marinerazo, *m. aug. of* **marinero,** experienced seaman, expert seaman.
marinería, *f.* 1. sailoring, seamanship, naval profession. 2. seamen, sailors, ship's crew.
marinero, ra, *a.* easily handled, seaworthy (ship); **a la marinera,** in a nautical or sailor's fashion. —*m.* 1. seaman, sailor, mariner. 2. (zool.) argonaut, paper nautilus. —*f.* 1. middy blouse. 2. (Chile, Ecuad., Peru) popular folk dance.
marinesco, ca, *a.* pertaining to sailors. — a la m., in a seaman-like manner, shipshape.
marinismo, *m.* (lit.) Marinism (of Marini, Italian poet of the Renaissance), euphuism; artificial style.
marinista, *a., m., f.* marine painter, sea-scape painter.
marino, na, *a.* marine, of the sea; (her.) fishtailed. —*m.* seaman, sailor, mariner.
mariol, *m.* (rare) homosexual, sodomite, pansy, queer (sl.).
marión, *m.* (ichth.) sturgeon.
mariona, *f.* old Spanish dance and tune.
marioneta, *f.* marionette, puppet.
maripérez, *f.* 1. primitive type grill, improvised with an iron hoop or triangle. 2. servant girl.
mariposa, *f.* 1. (ento., fig.) butterfly. 2. night light. 3. wing nut. 4. (Cuba) (variety of) finch (Passerina ciris). 5. (Cuba, bot.) butterfly jasmin, the national flower of Cuba. 6. (Chile) each of two bearings which support the pressing cylinder of a cotton gin. — **m. nocturna,** (fig.) prostitute.
mariposeador, ra, *a.* fickle, changeable, capricious.
mariposear, *i.v.* to flit about (from place to place or person to person), be a butterfly, be fickle.
mariposón, *m.* 1. flirt, Don Juan. 2. (Peru) homosexual, pansy, queer (sl.)
mariquita, *f.* 1. (ento.) ladybird (Coccinella septempuctata). 2. (ento.) firebug (Pyrrhocoris apterus). 3. (ornith) parakeet. —*m.* 1. (coll.) sissy; effeminate man. 2. (Cuba) fried chips of plantain (a snack or appetizer).

marisabidilla, *f.* (coll.) bluestocking; pedantic, bookish woman.
marisca, *f.* (Hond., sl.) sexual attraction.
mariscada, *f.* (cul.) shellfish casserole.
mariscador, ra, *a.* shellfish (gatherer). —*m., f.* shellfish gatherer.
mariscal, *m.* 1. (mil.) marshal; (arch.) officer in charge of finding quarters for the cavalry. 2. blacksmith, farrier. — **m. de campo,** field marshal.
mariscala, *f.* marshal's wife.
mariscalato, *m., var. of* **mariscalía.**
mariscalía, *f.* marshalcy, rank of marshal.
mariscar, (*ref. 50*) *tr.v.* to gather (shellfish).
marisco, *m.* shellfish, aquatic crustacean.
marisma, *f.* salt marsh (on sea shore).
marismeño, ña, *a.* swampy, marshy.
marismo, *m.* (bot.) orach (Altriplex halymus).
marisque, marisqué, *ref.* **mariscar.**
marisquería, *f.* seafood bar; fish market.
marista, *a., m., f.* (ecc.) Marist.
marital, *a.* marital, pertaining to marriage.
maritata, *f.* 1. (Chile) trough lined with sheepskins used for retaining metal-bearing dust. 2. (Chile) sieve (used in mines). 3. (*pl.*) (Guat., Hond.) trifles, trinkets.
marítimo, ma, *a.* maritime; sea, marine, nautical. — **derecho marítimo,** maritime law; **por correo marítimo,** by sea mail; **por vía marítima,** by sea.
maritornes, *f.* (coll.) slovenly maidservant.
marizápalos, *f.* disturbance; fight.
marjal, *m.* 1. marsh, fen, moorland. 2. agrarian measure (equivalent to 5 ares, 25 centiares or 5,650 sq. feet).
marjoleta, *f.* hawthorn berry, haw.
marjoleto, *m.* (bot.) white English hawthorn.
marlo, *m.* (Arg., Col., Mex.) grainless stalk of corn.
marlota, *f.* Moorish gown.
marlotar, *tr.v.* (rare) to dissipate, waste; to destroy, undo.
marmaja, *f.* (Col., Mex., min.) marcasite.
marmatita, *f.* (min.) marmatite.
marmella, *f.* mammilla, mamilla (excrescence); protuberance on goat's neck.
marmellado, da, *a.* mammillated, mammillate, having mammillas.
marmita, *f.* marmite, saucepan, pot, boiler.
marmitón, *m.* scullion, kitchen boy.
mármol, *m.* 1. marble (stone; sculpture). 2. marver (iron plate used in shaping glass). 3. (print.) imposing stone. — **m. brecha,** brecciated marble; **m. brocatel,** Spanish white veined marble; **m. estatuario,** marble used for statuary; **m. lumaquela,** shell marble; **m. serpentino,** serpentine marble, verdantique.
marmolejo, *m.* small marble column.
marmoleño, ña, *a.* pertaining to marble, made of or resembling marble.
marmolería, *f.* marble work; marble works or workshop.
marmolillo, *m.* 1. spur stone. 2. (fig.) ignoramus, dolt, unfeeling person.
marmolina, *f.* (Chile) stucco.
marmolista, *m.* marble worker; marble dealer; sculptor.
marmoración, *f.* stucco; plastering.
marmóreo, a, *a.* marble-like, marmoreal, made of or resembling marble.
marmoroso, sa, *a., var. of* **marmóreo.**
marmosa, *f.* (zool.) mouse or murine opossum.
marmosete, *m.* (print.) vignette, small decorative cut.
marmota, *f.* 1. (zool.) marmot. 2. worsted bonnet or cap. 3. sleepyhead.

marmotear, *i.v.* to chatter, jabber.
maro, *m.* 1. (bot.) cat thyme, germander. 2. (bot.) common clary.
marocha, *f.* (Hond.) giddy, empty-headed girl.
marojal, *m.* oak or durmast grove.
marojo, *m.* 1. (bot.) red-berried mistletoe (Viscum cruciatus). 2. (bot.) variety of oak (Quercus pubescens), durmast. 3. leaves used for animal fodder.
marola, *f.* (mar.) groundswell, swell, surge.
maroma, *f.* 1. thick rope. 2. (Amer.) acrobatics, tightrope-walking. — **andar uno en la m.,** (fig.) to have the right backing or support.
maromear, *i.v.* 1. (Amer.) to perform on a tightrope. 2. to swing in a hammock. 3. (Amer.) to take sides according to circumstances.
maromero, ra, *a.* cunning, astute (person); (Cuba, Mex., Peru) opportunist (politician). —*m., f.* (Amer.) tightrope walker, acrobat.
marón, *m.* 1. (ichth.) sturgeon. 2. male sheep; ram.
maronita, *m., f.* Maronite, member of a Christian sect founded in Lebanon in the 5th century.
marota, *f.* (Mex.) mannish woman, virago, amazon.
marque, marqué, *ref.* **marcar.**
marqués, *m.* marquis.
marquesa, *f.* 1. marquise, marchioness. 2. awning, marquee (over a field tent). 3. (Amer.) couch; easy chair. 4. (Chile, Peru, P. Rico, jewel.) marquise.
marquesado, *m.* marquisate (title).
Marquesas, *f.* Marquesas, group of islands in French Polynesia.
marquesina, *f.* marquee, canopy (over an entrance).
marquesita, *f.* 1. (min.) marcasite. 2. small armchair.
marquesota, *f.* high white collar (formerly worn by men).
marquesote, *m.* 1. (derog.) marquis. 2. (Hond.) cake made of corn or rice flour, sugar and eggs.
marqueta, *f.* 1. crude cake of wax. 2. (Chile) bundle of brown crude sugar lumps. 3. (Chile) bundle or bale of raw tobacco.
marquetería, *f.* 1. marqueterie, marquetry, inlaid work. 2. cabinet making, woodwork.
marquilla, *f.* demy, a particular size of paper.
marquista, *m.* (Sp.) wholesale dealer in sherry.
marquito, *m. dim. of* **marco,** small frame.
marra, *f.* 1. gap (in row of vines); lack, want; deficiency. 2. stone hammer.
márraga, *f.* coarse cotton cloth, mattress ticking.
marrajo, ja, *a.* cunning, sly (bull); (fig.) cunning, crafty, wily. —*m.* (ichth.) shark.
marramao, *m.* caterwaul, wail.
marramáu, *m., var. of* **marramao.**
marramice, *ref.* **marramizar.**
marramizar, (*ref. 53*) i.v. to caterwaul.
marrana, *a.* 1. dirty, sluttish. 2. mean, base. —*f.* 1. sow. 2. slut, slattern. 3. (coll.) pig, cat, bitch. 4. axle driving a chain pump.
marranada, *f.* 1. (coll.) filth, filthiness, piggishness. 2. (coll.) dirty or rotten trick.
marranalla, *f.* (coll.) rabble, mob, riffraff.
marrancho, *m.* 1. pig, hog. 2. dirty person.
marranchón, na, *m., f.* pig; small pig, suckling pig.
marranería, *f.* (coll.), *var. of* **marranada.**
marranillo, *m.* suckling pig, piglet, little pig.
marrano, *a.* 1. dirty, slobbish. 2. rotten, mean. —*m.* 1. male hog, boar. 2. (coll.) pig, slob, hog (dirty person). 3. (coll.) swine, pig, rotter (unprincipled person). 4. (derog., hist.) Jew.
marrano, *m.* 1. tooth or cog in water wheel drum. 2. timber (composing framework of a well bottom). 3. timber on pressing board of oil press to equalize pressure.
marraqueta, *f.* (Chile) long loaf of bread.
marrar, *i.v.* 1. to miss (a shot); to fail, miscarry. 2. to go astray, slip. 3. to deviate from truth and justice.
marras, *adv.* long ago, of yore; **de m.,** mentioned before, in question, of whom or which we were talking, e.g. *volvemos al problema de m.,* we're back to the old problem.
marrasquino, *m.* maraschino (cherry cordial).
marrazo, *m.* mattock, double-bitted ax; (Mex.) short machete.
marrear, *tr.v.* to strike with a stone hammer.
márrega, *f.* 1. (tex.) coarse mattress ticking. 2. straw-filled pallet.
marrillo, *m.* short, thick stick.
marro, *m.* 1. game similar to quoits. 2. kind of tag played in teams (game). 3. swerve, dodge, feint (to avoid capture). 4. mistake, error, slip. 5. bat, catstick (for playing tipcat). 6. (Mex.) mallet, hammer.
marrón, *a.* chestnut-colored; dark brown; maroon; dark red. —*m.* 1. candied chestnut. 2. (Col.) paper curler, haircurling paper. 3. stone used in **marro** game.
marronazo, *m.* (taur.) miss, mistake (esp. in the **pica** play).
marroquí, (*pl.* **marroquíes**), *a., m., f.* Moroccan. —*m.* morocco leather.
marroquín, na, *a., m., f.* Moroccan. —*m.* Moroccan leather.
marroquinería, *f.* morocco leatherwork; stamping on fine leather.
marrubial, *m.* (bot.) horehound patch.
marrubio, *m.* (bot.) horehound.
marrueco, ca, *a., m., f.* Moroccan. —*m.* (Chile) fly (on trousers).
Marruecos, *m.* Morocco.
marrulla, *f.* (Col.) flattery, wheedling, cajolery.
marrullería, *f.* flattery, wheedling, cajolery.
marrullero, ra, *a.* cajoling, wheedling, flattering. —*m., f.* flatterer, cajoler, wheedler.
Marsella, *f.* Marseilles.
marsellés, sa, *a.* Marseilles (as *a.*), of or from Marseilles. —*m., f.* inhabitat or native of Marseilles. —*m.* coarse cloth jacket. —*f.* **M.,** Marsellaise (the French national anthem).
marso, sa, *a.* Marsian. —*m.* (*pl.*) Marsi (an ancient people of Italy; an ancient tribe of Westphalia).
marsopa, *f.* (zool.) common porpoise, harbor porpoise.
marsopla, *f., var. of* **marsopa.**
marsupial, *a., m.* (zool.) marsupial.
marta, *f.* (zool.) pine marten; **m. cebellina,** (zool.) sable.
martagón, na, *m., f.* (coll.) shrewd, astute person. —*m.* (bot.) turk's-cap lily, wild lily.
martajar, *tr.v.* (Hond., Mex.) to crush (corn) on a stone.
Marte, *m.* 1. (astron., myth.) Mars (planet; Roman god of war). 2. (alchemy) iron. 3. (fig.) war.
martellina, *f.* marteline, millstone hammer.
martensita, *f.* (metal.) martensite.
martes, *m.* Tuesday; **cada lunes y cada m.,** every day, all the time; **dar a uno con la del m.,** (coll.) to call to task, haul over the coals; **m. de carnaval** o **carnestolendas,** Shrove Tuesday.
martillada, *f.* hammer-blow, blow given with a hammer.
martillador, ra, *a.* hammering. —*m., f.* hammerer.
martillar, *tr.v.* 1. to hammer. 2. to oppress, torment. 3. (artil.) to bombard intensively.
martillazo, *m.* hard blow of the hammer.
martillear, *tr.v., var. of* **martillar.**
martillejo, *m. dim. of* **martillo,** small hammer, smith's hammer.
martilleo, *m.* hammering; (fig.) clatter, banging, hammering.
martillero, *m.* (Amer.) auctioneer.
martillo, *m.* 1. hammer; (mus.) tuning hammer. 2. (fig.) hammer, scourge, persecutor. 3. (anat.) hammer, malleus (bone of the ear). 4. (fig.) auction room. 5. (sport) hammer. 6. (ichth.) hammerhead shark. — **a macha m.,** strongly but crudely (built); definitely, firmly; **a. m.,** by hammering, with a hammer; **de m.,** hammered, wrought (metal); **m. de agua,** (phys.) water hammer; **m. de caída libre** or **de fragua,** drop hammer; **m. de orejas,** claw hammer; **m. macho,** sledge-hammer; **m. neumático,** air hammer; **m. percutor,** percussion hammer; **m. perforador,** jackhammer; **m. pilón,** pile hammer, drop hammer; **m. remachador,** riveting hammer.
Martín, *m.* Martin; **San M.,** hog-killing season; **a cada uno le llega su San M.,** the day of reckoning comes to everyone.
martina, *f.* (ichth.) cusk eel, sand cusk (Ophidium Carbatum).
martín del río, (*pl.* **martines del río**) *m.* (ornith) (species of) heron.
martinete, *m.* 1. (ornith.) (species of) heron. 2. heron plumes.
martinete, *m.* 1. hammer (of piano); drop-hammer; drop-hammer shed (where drop hammer is used); pile hammer, pile driver. 2. Andalusian Gypsy song performed without guitar accompaniment. 3. (ornith.) night heron. — **m. a vapor,** steam hammer; **picar de m.,** to spur (a horse).
martingala, *f.* 1. cunning. 2. system, plan, stratagem (for winning games). 3. stake in the game of **monte.** 4. (*pl.*) cuisse breeches, breeches worn under armor.
Martinica, *f.* **La M.,** Martinique, one of the French Antilles.
martinico, *m.* (coll.) goblin, sprite.
martiniega, *f.* (arch.) tribute paid on St. Martin's Day.
martín pescador, (*pl.* **martín pescadores**) *m.* (ornith.) kingfisher.
mártir, *m., f.* martyr.
martirice, martiricé, *ref.* **martirizar.**
martirio, *m.* martyrdom; torture.
martirizador, ra, *a.* persecuting; tormenting. —*m., f.* persecutor; tormentor.
martirizar, (*ref. 53*) *tr.v.* 1. to martyr, martyrize. 2. (fig.) to torment.
martirologio, *m.* martyrology, historical account of the lives of the religious martyrs.
martirologista, *m.* martyrologist, historian specialized in the lives of the religious martyrs.
marullo, *m.* swell, surge, sea waves.
marxismo, *m.* (pol., econ., philos.) Marxism, the system developed by Karl Marx and his followers.
marxista, *a., m., f.* Marxist, advocate of the theories of Marx.
marzadga, *f.* (Sp., arch.) former tax levied in March.
marzal, *a.* pertaining to the month of March.
marzo, *m.* March (month).
marzoleta, *f.* (bot.) haw, hawthorn berry.
marzoleto, *m.* (bot.) white hawthorn.
mas, *conj.* but, however, although, even if, e.g. *corre, m. no te caigas,* run but don't fall, *no la vi, m. le escribí,* I didn't see her, however I wrote to her; *iré, m. no me quedaré,* I'll go, although I won't stay. —*m.* 1. (Phil. I.) unit for weighing gold and silver. 2. farmhouse, farmstead.
más, *adv.* 1. more (used to form the comparative), e.g. *m. inteligente,* more intelligent, *m. grande,* bigger, *m. rápidamente,* more quickly, *m. + a.*

+ que, more + *a.* + than, e.g. *él es m. inteligente que Juan,* he is more intelligent than John. 2. most (used to form the superlative), e.g. *el m. inteligente,* the most intelligent, *el m. grande,* the biggest. 3. more, longer, e.g. *no te demores m.,* don't delay any longer or more. 4. rather, e.g. *m. quiero perder mi caudal que la honra,* I would rather lose my fortune than my honor. 5. more, a greater number of, e.g. *necesitamos m. sillas,* we need more chairs; **m.** + *n.* + **que, more** + n. than, e.g. *él tiene m. plata que yo,* he has more money than I. 6. (in absolute construction) more, e.g. *no quiero m., I don't want any more, no digas m.,* don't say any more; **m. + de + numerals,** more than, e.g. *necesitamos m. de sesenta sillas,* we need more than sixty chairs; **m. que + n., more than + n.,** e.g. *él tiene m. que yo,* he has more than I. — **a lo m.,** at the most; **a m.,** besides, in addition; **a m. de,** besides, in addition to; **cada vez m.,** more and more, increasingly; **como el que m.,** as much as anyone; **con su m. y su menos,** with an ulterior motive; **cuando m.,** at the most; **de m.,** too much, extra, superfluous, e.g. *astar de m.,* to be superfluous, to be in the way; only too well, e.g. *tú sabes de m.,* you know only too well; **no m.,** no more; no longer; **m. acá,** over this way more, closer; **m. adelante,** later on; further forward; **m. + adverb of place + de,** e.g. *m. allá de,* farther than, beyond; **m. bien,** rather; **m. o menos,** more or less; **m. que,** except, but; though, although; **m. que nunca,** more than ever; **m. tarde** o **m. temprano,** sooner or later; **m. vale tarde que nunca,** better late than never; **ni m. ni menos,** neither more nor less; no more, no less; **por m. que,** however much, no matter how much; **¿qué m. da?** what difference does it make?; **sin m. ni m.,** suddenly, in a rush, without more ado. *—m.* 1. more. 2. (math.) plug sign; **el m. y el menos,** the pros and the cons, the advantages and disadvantages. *—prep.* plus, e.g. *nueve m. diez son diecinueve,* nine plus ten are nineteen.

masa, *f.* 1. mass, lump, volume, quantity. 2. mass, body, group; (*pl.*) the masses, the people. 3. (phys.) mass. 4. dough, mix, paste; mortar mixture. 5. whole, totality, mass, aggregate, bulk, e.g. *la m. de su fortuna,* the bulk of his fortune. 6. nature, disposition. 7. the people. — **con las manos en la m.,** red-handed, in the act; **en m.,** in mass, en masse, in a body; mass (*as an a.*), e.g. *manifestación en m.,* mass meeting; **en la m. de la sangre,** in the blood, innate; **m. crítica,** (phys.) critical mass; **m. de aire,** (meteorol.) air mass; **m. de la sangre,** the total quantity of blood in the body; **m. imponible,** (law) total contributory value (i.e. taxable value); **m. molecular,** (phys.) molecular mass.

masaco, *m.* (Bol.) dish of banana plantains with ground meat.

masacrar, *tr.v.* (Gal.) to massacre.

masacre, *m.* (Gal.) massacre.

masada, *f.* farmhouse, farmstead; country estate.

masadero, *m.* farmer; resident of a country estate or a farmstead.

masaje, *m.* massage, rubdown.

masajista, *m.* masseur. *—f.* masseuse.

masar, *tr.v.* to knead.

masato, *m.* (Bol., Col., Ecuad., Peru) drink made of fermented corn, bananas or cassava; (Col.) sweet meat made of coconut, corn and sugar; (Peru, Ecuad.) soup of boiled or ground banana.

mascabado, da, *a.* muscovado, brown or unrefined (sugar).

mascada, *f.* 1. (Arg., Chile) mouthful (of food). 2. (Arg., Urug.) benefit. 3. (C. Amer.) profit, money. 4. (Mex.) silk pocket handkerchief, silk necktie. 5. (Mex.) punch. 6. (S. Amer.) chew (of tobacco).

mascadijo, *m.* breath deodorant (aromatic vegetable substance).

mascadón, *m.* (Mex.) silk pocket handkerchief.

mascador, ra, *a.* chewing, masticating. *—m., f.* chewer, masticator.

mascadura, *f.* 1. chewing, mastication. 2. (Hond.) bread bun.

mascar, (*ref. 50*) *tr.v.* 1. to chew, masticate. 2. (coll.) to mumble. *—r.v.* (mar.) to rub, chafe; (fig.) fret, gall.

máscara, *f.* 1. mask. 2. masquerade, disguise, fancy dress costume. 3. (fig.) mask, cover, pretense. 4. (*pl.*) masquerade, masque; fancy dress party. — **baile de máscaras,** masked ball, costume ball; **m. antigás,** gas mask; **m. de belleza,** face-pack; **m. de hierro,** man in the iron mask; **m. de oxígeno,** oxygen mask; **m. facial,** face pack; **quitar la m. a,** to unmask, expose; **quitarse la m.,** to come out into the open, speak one's mind, show oneself as one really is. *—m., f.* masker, mask, masquerader.

mascarada, *f.* 1. masquerade, masque. 2. group of maskers. 3. (fig.) farce, put-on (sl.).

mascarero, ra, *m., f.* one who sells or rents masks and costumes.

mascareta, *f. dim. of* **máscara,** little mask.

mascarilla, *f.* 1. half mask, little mask. 2. (art.) death mask.

mascarón, *m.* 1. *aug. of* **máscara,** hideous mask, large mask. 2. (archit.) grotesque face, mask. — **m. de proa,** (mar.) figurehead.

mascón, *m.* (Hond.) mop, swab.

mascota, *f.* mascot; good-luck charm.

mascujada, *f.* 1. bad or hurried chewing. 2. mumbling, muttering.

mascujar, *tr.v.* 1. (coll.) to chew badly or hurriedly. 2. (coll.) to mumble, mutter.

masculinidad, *f.* masculinity.

masculinizar, (*ref. 53*) *tr.v.* (gram.) to make masculine.

masculino, na, *a.* masculine, virile, manly; (bot., biol.) male; (gram.) masculine. *—m.* (gram.) masculine.

mascullar, *tr.v.* (coll.) to mumble, mutter.

masecoral, *m.* sleight of hand, legerdemain.

masejicomar, *m., var. of* **masecoral.**

masera, *f.* kneading trough; kneading trough cloth.

masería, *f., var. of* **masada,** farmhouse, farmstead.

masetérico, ca, *a.* (anat.) masseteric.

masetero, *m.* (anat.) masseter.

masi, *f.* (Bol., zool.) a species of American squirrel.

masica, *f.* (C. Amer.) breadnut tree.

masicoral, *m., var. of* **masecoral.**

masicote, *m.* (chem.) massicot, lead monoxide.

masiliense, *a.* Marseilles (as *a.*), of or from Marseilles. *—m., f.* native or inhabitant of Marseilles.

masilla, *f.* putty, mastic.

masita, *f.* 1. (mil.) clothing money (deducted from military pay to cover the cost of uniforms). 2. (Arg., Bol., Urug.) biscuit, small cake, petit four.

masivo, va, *a.* massive; mass, e.g. *concentración masiva,* mass gathering.

maslo, *m.* 1. (zool.) dock, root (of the tail). 2. (bot.) stem.

masón, *m.* 1. mixture of flour and water used for fattening fowl. 2. Mason (Freemason).

masonería, *f.* Masonry (Freemasonry).

masónico, ca, *a.* Masonic.

masoquismo, *m.* (psyc.) masochism.

masoquista, *a.* masochistic; self-punishing. *—m., f.* masochist; (fig.) one who derives pleasure from pain or suffering.

masora, *f.* (rel.) Masora.

masoreta, *m.* (rel.) Masorete.

masoterapia, *f.* (med.) massotherapy.

masovero, *m.* (Sp., reg.) farmer.

masque, masqué, *ref.* **mascar.**

mastectomía, *f.* (surg.) mastectomy.

mastelerillo, *m.* (mar.) topgallant mast; — **m. de juanete,** topgallant mast; **m. de mayor,** main-topgallant mast; **m. de perico** or **de popa,** mizzen-topgallant mast; **m. de proa,** fore-topgallant mast.

mastelero, *m.* (mar.) topmast; **m. de gavia,** topmast; **m. de mayor,** main-topmast; **m. de popa** or **de sobremesana,** mizzen-topmast; **m. de proa** or **de velacho,** fore-topmast.

masticación, *f.* mastication, chewing.

masticador, *m.* 1. masticator (machine for shredding food). 2. bit causing salivation and provoking hunger.

masticar, (*ref. 50*) *tr.v.* 1. to masticate, chew. 2. (fig.) to ponder, meditate about, ruminate.

masticatorio, a, *a., m.* masticatory.

masticino, na, *a.* mastic, pertaining to mastic.

mastigador, *m.* bit causing salivation and provoking hunger.

mastigóforo, *m.* (zool.) mastigophoran.

mástil, *m.* 1. (mar.) mast; topmast. 2. pole, post. 3. stalk (of plant). 4. shaft (of feather). 5. neck (of guitar, violin). 6. breechcloth, loincloth (used by Indians). — **m. mayor,** (mar.) main mast; **m. totémico,** totem pole.

mastín, na, *m., f.* mastiff. — **m. danés,** Great Dane.

mastingal, *m.* (Mex.) martingale.

mastique, mastiqué, *ref.* **masticar.**

mástique, *m.* mastic (resin; cement).

mastitis, *f.* (med.) mastitis.

masto, *m.* (bot.) stock into which a scion is grafted.

mastodonte, *m.* (zool.) mastodon.

mastoidectomía, *f.* (med.) mastoidectomy.

mastoideo, a, *a.* (anat.) mastoid.

mastoides, *a., m.* (anat.) mastoid.

mastoiditis, *f.* (med.) mastoiditis.

mastranto, *m., var. of* **mastranzo.**

mastranzo, *m.* (bot.) apple mint.

mastuerzo, *m.* 1. (bot.) pepper cress, peppergrass; watercress. 2. (fig.) dolt, simpleton.

masturbación, *f.* masturbation.

masturbarse, *r.v.* to masturbate.

masurio, *m.* (chem.) masurium.

masvale, *m., var. of* **malvasía.**

mata, *f.* 1. bush, shrub. 2. sprig, blade. 3. grove, copse, thicket. 4. (bot.) mastic tree. 5. (Mex.) hill. 6. (min.) matte. — **m. de pelo,** head, shock or crop of hair; **m. parda,** dwarf oak; **m. rubia,** kermes oak; **seguir hasta la m.,** to pursue to the bitter end.

matabuey, *f.* (bot.) buplever (Bupleurum fruticosum).

matacabras, *m.* very cold north wind.

matacán, *m.* 1. dog poison. 2. (fort.) machicolation. 3. (bot.) nux vomica. 4. (bldg.) large piece of rubble. 5. hare hunted previously. 6. two of clubs.

matacandelas, (*pl.* **matacandelas**), *m.* candle-extinguisher, snuffer.

matacandil, *m.* 1. (bot.) London rocket. 2. (reg.) lobster.

matacandiles, (*pl.* **matacandiles**), *m.* (bot.) star of Bethlehem (Ornithogalum umbellatum).

matachín, *m.* 1. buffoon, clown. 2. grotesque, clowning dance. 3. slaughterer, butcher. 4. swashbuckler.

matacía, *f.* slaughter; (fig.) havoc.

mataco, *m.* 1. (Arg., zool.) species of armadillo. 2. Chaco Indian.

matadero, *m.* 1. abattoir, slaughterhouse. 2. (coll.) drudgery, bore. 3. bachelor's den, hideaway, garçonnière. — **ir or venir al m,** to put one's life in grave danger; **llevar a otro al m.,** to put someone else's life in grave danger.
matador, ra, *a.* killing. —*m., f.* killer. —*m.* 1. (cards) matador, one of principal trumps. 2. (taur.) matador.
matadura, *f.* (vet.) sore, gall; **dar a uno en las mataduras,** to hit or criticize someone in a sensitive or sore spot.
matafuego, *m.* fire extinguisher; fireman.
matagallegos, (*pl.* **matagallegos**), *m.* (bot.) centaury.
matagallina, *f.* (bot.) flax-leaved daphne.
matagallos, (*pl.* **matagallos**), *m.* (bot.) Jerusalem sage (Phlomis purpurea).
matagusano, *m.* (Guat., Hond.) preserve of orange peel and brown sugar.
matahambre, *m.* 1. (Arg.) large plate (cut of meat). 2. (Cuba) dessert made of egg, sugar and cassava; marzipan.
matajudío, *m.* (ichth.) striped mullet.
matalahuga, *f., var. of* **matalahuva.**
matalahuva, *f.* (bot.) anise (plant); aniseed, anise (seed).
matalobos, (*pl.* **matalobos**), *m.* (bot.) aconite, wolfsbane, monkshood.
matalón, na, *a.* skinny and full of sores (said of a horse). —*m.* skinny old nag; old worn-out horse.
matalotaje, *m.* 1. (mar.) ship stores. 2. (coll.) mess, jumble, heap.
matalote, *a., m., var. of* **matalón. —***m.* (mar.) next ship (forward or astern, in a convoy).
matambre, *m.* (S. Amer.) plate (cut of meat).
matamoros, (*pl.* **matamoros**), *m.* bully, braggart.
matamoscas, (*pl.* **matamoscas**), *m.* flyswatter, flypaper.
matancero, ra, *a., m., f.* of or pertaining to Matanzas, Cuba. —*m.* (Chile, Mex., Peru) slaughterman, butcher.
matanza, *f.* 1. butchering, slaughtering. 2. slaughter, massacre. 3. pig-slaughtering; pig-slaughtering season; pork products; pigs kept for slaughter. 4. eagerness, concern, obstinacy.
matapalo, *m.* (bot.) tree yielding rubber and sackcloth fiber (Ficus dendrocida).
mataparda, *f.* dwarf or scrub oak.
mataperico, *m.* (Col., Ven.) fillip, flip.
mataperrada, *f.* madcap action, piece of deviltry; street urchin's prank.
mataperrear, *i.v.* (Amer.) to play rough, waste time at mischief, roam the streets (said usually of truants and rowdy youngsters).
mataperros, (*pl.* **mataperros**), *m.* (coll.) madcap, truant, street urchin.
matapiojos, (*pl.* **matapiojos**), *m.* (Col., Chile) dragonfly.
matapolvo, *m.* light rain, shower.
matapulgas, (*pl.* **matapulgas**), *f.* (bot.) apple mint.
matar, *tr.v.* 1. to kill; to butcher, slaughter (animals). 2. to put out (fire, light). 3. to slake (lime). 4. to stave off, keep off (hunger). 5. to pass, kill (time). 6. to beat, top (opponent's card); to mark, spot (cards for cheating). 7. (sport) to kill (e.g. ball in tennis). 8. (p.) to tone down (colors). 9. to mat, dull (metals). 10. to gall, chafe, cause sores on (a horse). 11. to cancel, obliterate (a postage stamp). 12. to round off, smooth off (corners, sharp edges). 13. to plague, pester, bother. 14. to ruin, wreck (a business). — **estar a m. con uno,** to be deadly enemies with, be at drawn daggers with; **m. dos pájaros de un tiro,** to kill two birds with one stone; **m. el polvo,** to lay the dust; **matarlas callando,** (coll.) to feather one's nest on the quiet; **¡que me maten!** I swear it!; **¡que me maten, si miento!** strike me dead if I lie. —*r.v.* 1. to kill oneself, commit suicide. 2. to be killed, meet one's death. 3. to become galled or chafed, get sores (a horse). 4. to kill oneself, wear oneself out (with work, debauchery); **matarse por** + *inf.*, to work like mad to + *inf.;* **matarse por una cosa,** to work like mad to get something.
matarife, *m.* butcher, slaughterer.
matarrata, *f.* a card game.
matarratas, *m.* (coll.) rotgut (drink).
matarrubia, *f.* (bot.) kermes, kermes oak.
matasano, *m.* (Hond., Salv., bot.) white sapota.
matasanos, (*pl.* **matasanos**), *m.* sawbones, (sl.) quack, unskilled doctor.
matasarna, *m.* (bot.) Jamaica dogwood.
matasellos, *m.* (*pl.* **matasellos**), canceller, post office cancelling stamp.
matasiete, *m.* (coll.) braggart, bully.
matasuelo, *m.* (Chile) bump, blow (when falling on one's back).
matate, *m.* (Hond.) bag-shaped net.
matatías, (*pl.* **matatías**), *m.* moneylender, pawnbroker.
matatudo, da, *a.* 1. (Bol.) long-snouted. 2. (Guat.) brave, agile.
matazón, *f.* (Cuba) 1. slaughter, killing, massacre. 2. (fig.) arduous work, hard toil.
match, *m.* (sport) match.
mate, *a.* 1. dull, flat (sound). 2. mat, matte, lusterless; dull (surface). —*m.* 1. checkmate (in chess). 2. matador, any of the three principal trumps (in cards). — **dar m. a,** to checkmate (in chess); to make fun of, laugh at; **m. ahogado,** smothered mate; **m. de las charreteras,** epaulet mate (in chess).
mate, *m.* 1. (bot.) maté (tea, plant). 2. (S. Amer.) maté gourd, maté vessel. 3. (Chile) large bald patch. 4. (Cuba) liana.
matear, *tr.v.* to plant at regular intervals —*i.v.* 1. to spread, send out shoots. 2. to hunt through the bushes (hunting dog). —*r.v.* to spread, send out shoots.
matear, *i.v.* 1. (S. Amer.) to drink maté. 2. (Chile) to mix (a liquid) with another. —*tr.v.* 1. (Chile) to checkmate. 2. to make matte or dull.
matemática, *f.* (usually in *pl.*) mathematics. — **matemáticas aplicadas or mixtas,** applied mathematics; **matemáticas puras,** pure mathematics; **m. superior,** higher mathematics.
matemáticamente, *adv.* mathematically.
matemático, ca, *a.* mathematical; (fig.) mathematical, exact, precise. —*m.* mathematician.
materia, *f.* 1. matter; material, substance, stuff. 2. matter, question. 3. subject, theme, subject matter. 4. (educ.) subject (studied at school, etc.). 5. (med.) pus, matter. — **en m. de,** in questions of, regarding, in the matter of; **entrar en m.,** to get to the point, get to the subject; **m. colorante,** coloring matter; **m. de Estado,** matter of state; **m. orgánica,** organic matter; **m. parva,** small amount of food; **m. prima,** raw material.
material, *a.* 1. material. 2. physical. 3. (fig.) crude, coarse. —*m.* 1. material; ingredient; (*pl.*) materials. 2. equipment, supplies, requisites, matériel. — **m. bélico,** military equipment; **m. de demoliciones** or **derribo,** reclaimed or secondhand building materials; **m. de escritorio,** stationery; **m. de laboratorio,** laboratory apparatus; **m. de oficina,** office stationery; **m. didáctico,** teaching materials; **m. escolar,** school things; **m. fotográfico,** photographic materials; photographic equipment; **m. móvil** or **rodante,** rolling stock.
materialice, *ref.* **materializar.**
materialidad, *f.* 1. materiality; corporeity, physicalness. 2. outward appearance. 3. literal meaning, literalness.
materialismo, *m.* materialism.
materialista, *a.* materialistic. —*m., f.* materialist.
materialización, *f.* 1. materialization (of thoughts, ideas). 2. (phys.) creation, production.
materializar, (*ref. 53*) *tr.v.* to materialize. —*r.v.* to become materialistic.
materialmente, *adv.* 1. materially, physically; corporeally. 2. absolutely.
maternal, *a.* maternal, motherly.
maternalmente, *adv.* maternally.
maternidad, *f.* 1. maternity, motherhood. 2. maternity hospital.
materno, na, *a.* maternal; mother, e.g. *lengua materna,* mother tongue.
matero, ra, *a.* (S. Amer.) maté-drinking. —*m., f.* maté-drinker.
matete, *m.* 1. (Arg., Urug.) mixture, mess. 2. (Arg.) quarrel, dispute.
matice, maticé, *ref.* **matizar.**
matico, *m.* (bot.) matico.
matidez, *f.* flatness, deadness (of a sound); dullness, lack of color.
matihuelo, *m., var. of* **dominguillo,** tumbler (toy).
matinal, *a.* for or pertaining to morning, matinal, matutinal.
matinée, *f.* 1. matinée, afternoon performance. 2. dressing gown, wrapper.
matiz, (*pl.* **matices**), *m.* 1. hue, tint, shade (of colors). 2. shade, nuance (of meaning of words).
matizar, (*ref. 53*) *tr.v.* 1. to color; to tint, shade. 2. to blend, combine, match (colors).
mato, *m., var. of* **matorral;** coppice.
matoco, *m.* (Chile, coll.) devil.
matoide, *m.* (med.) mattoid.
matojo, *m.* 1. shrub, bush. 2. (bot.) sal-solaceous plant (Halexylon articulatum).
matón, *m.* (coll.) bully, troublemaker, browbeater.
matonear, *i.v.* to bully, to boast.
matonismo, *m.* bullying.
matorral, *m.* thicket, underbrush, heath, brake; brambly ground.
matoso, sa, *a.* full of bushes and shrubs, brushy, weedy.
matraca, *f.* 1. wooden rattle. 2. (coll.) pestering, plaguing. — **dar m. a,** to chaff, taunt.
matracalada, *f.* mob, swarm of people.
matraquear, *i.v.* 1. (coll.) to make a noise or racket (with a rattle). 2. (coll.) to jeer, taunt, chaff, rag.
matraqueo, *m.* 1. (coll.) racket, din. 2. (coll.) chaffing, jeering, taunting, ragging.
matraquista, *m., f.* (coll.) jeerer, taunter, ragger.
matraz, (*pl.* **matraces**), *m.* glass flask, matrass, druggist's vessel.
matreramente, *adv.* cunningly, shrewdly.
matrerear, *i.v.* (Arg.) 1. to be a fugitive; to flee. 2. to wander, loiter.
matrería, *f.* shrewdness, astuteness, cunning.
matrero, ra, *a.* 1. shrewd, cunning, sagacious; cautious. 2. (Arg.) fugitive. 3. (Col., Ecuad., Hond.) cautious (said of a bull). —*m., f.* shrewd person.
matriarcado, *m.* matriarchy, matriarchate.
matriarcal, *a.* matriarchal, pertaining to a society in which the mother holds the chief authority.
matricaria, *f.* (bot.) feverfew.
matricida, *m., f.* matricide (person who murders his own mother).
matricidio, *m.* matricide (murder of the mother by her offspring).
matrícula, *f.* 1. register, list, roster, roll. 2. matriculation (e.g. in a university, school, etc.); enrollment, registration. 3. registration number (of a

vehicle), license plate; 4. matriculation, enrollment or registration certificate. 5. cost of matriculation. — **la m. está abierta,** matriculation applications are being received; **m. de buques,** register of ships (list of merchant ships registered at certain marine posts); **m. de mar,** seamen's or mariners' register (list of seamen in service).

matriculado, da, *a.* matriculated; registered.

matriculador, ra, *m., f.* matriculator.

matricular, *tr.v.* 1. to register, enroll; to matriculate. 2. (mar.) to matriculate, register (a merchant ship at a marine post). —*r.v.* to matriculate; to enroll; to enter a contest.

matrimonesco, ca, *a.* (hum.) matrimonial.

matrimonial, *a.* matrimonial, connubial, nuptial.

matrimonialmente, *adv.* matrimonially.

matrimoniar, *i.v.* to get married, to marry.

matrimonio, *m.* 1. marriage, matrimony. 2. (coll.) married couple; e.g. *un matrimonio feliz,* a happily married couple; a happy marriage. — **contraer m.,** to get married; **fuera del. m.,** out of wedlock; **m. civil,** civil marriage; **m. de la mano izquierda,** left-handed marriage; **m. morganático,** morganatic marriage; **m. por poder,** marriage by proxy, proxy marriage; **m. religioso,** church wedding; **palabra de m.,** marriage promise.

matrimoño, *m.* (Ecuad.) *var. of* **matrimonio.**

matritense, *a., m., f.* Madrilenian (of Madrid).

matriz, (*pl.* **matrices**), *a.* 1. main, chief, principal, e.g. *casa m.,* main office (of a firm, etc.). 2. mother, e.g. *lengua m.,* mother tongue. 3. original (draft, manuscript). —*m.* 1. matrix, womb. 2. matrix, mold, die. 3. screw nut. 4. stub (of a check book). 5. (bot., math., min., geol., anat.) matrix. — **m. combinada,** combination die; **m. múltiple,** gang dies.

matrizar, *tr.v.* (mech.) to form with a die, to die-cast.

matriz-patrón, *f* (mech.) master die.

matrona, *f.* 1. matron. 2. midwife. 3. matron (woman supervisor in certain institutions).

matronal, *a.* matronly.

matropa, *f.* (Hond.) hysterics.

matuasto, *m.* (zool.) poisonous Argentinian lizard (Leisaurus belli).

matula, *f.* (rare) wick, lamp wick.

matungo, ga, *a.* (Arg., Cuba) *var. of* **matalón.**

maturrango, ga, *a.* (Arg., Peru) poor (horseman); (Chile) clumsy, awkward. —*m., f.* poor rider, poor horseman or horsewoman. —*f.* trick, cunning, cajolery.

maturranguero, ra, *a.* (Cuba) tricky, coaxing, wheedling.

Matusalén, matuselah, *m.* (Bib.) Methuselah.

matute, *m.* 1. smuggling, contraband; smuggled goods. 2. gambling den.

matutear, *i.v.* to smuggle.

matutero, ra, *m., f.* smuggler.

matutinal, *m.* matutinal, pertaining to the morning.

matutino, na, *a.* matutinal, pertaining to the morning.

maula, *f.* 1. trash, rubbish, junk. 2. remnant. 2. trick, ruse. —*m., f.* (coll.) cheat, swindler, rogue; lazy ne'er-do-well; poor payer.

maular, *i.v.* **sin paular ni m.,** without saying a word.

maulear, *i.v.* (Chile, Urug.) to cheat.

maulería, *f.* 1. remnant shop, shop where cloth remnants are sold. 2. cheating, trickery.

maulero, ra, *m., f.* 1. remnant seller, seller of cloth remnants. 2. swindler, trickster, cheat.

maullador, ra, *a.* meowing, mewing (said of a cat).

maullar, *i.v.* to miaow, mew.

maullido, *m.* miaow; miaowing, mewing.

maúllo, *m., var. of* **maullido.**

mauraca, *f.* roasting chestnuts, fish, etc. over coals outdoors.

maure, *m.* sash, belt, band (around a blouse or tunic).

Mauretania, *f.* Mauritania.

mauritano, na, *a., m., f.* Mauritanian.

mauseolo, *m.* (rare) *var. of* **mausoleo.**

máuser, *m.* Mauser (firearm).

mausoleo, *m.* mausoleum.

mauveína, *f.* (chem.) mauveine (violet dye).

mavorcio, cia, *a.* (poet.) martial, warlike.

mavorte, *m.* (poet.) Mars (god of war).

maxilar, *a., m.* (anat.) maxillary.

máxima, *f.* 1. maxim; principle, axiom. 2. (mus.) maxima (the equivalent of 4 breves).

maximalista, *m., f.* (pol., hist.) maximalist, extremist (during the Russian Revolution).

máximamente, *adv.* particularly, chiefly, principally.

máxime, *adv.* particularly, chiefly, principally.

máximo, ma, *a.* maximum; greatest, top; chief, principal; **máximo común divisor,** (math.) greatest common divisor; **máxima velocidad,** top speed. —*m.* maximum.

máximum, *m.* maximum; extreme limit.

máxwell, maxwelio, *m.* (elec.) maxwell.

maya, *f.* 1. (bot.) daisy. 2. May queen. 3. clown, jester, merry-andrew. 4. (Cuba, bot.) variety of pineapple.

maya, *a.* Maya, Mayan. —*m., f.* Mayan Indian. —*m.* Mayan language.

mayador, ra, *a.* meowing, mewing (said of a cat).

mayal, *m.* 1. horse-powered shaft (driving an oil-mill). 2. threshing flail.

mayar, *i.v.* to mew, meaow.

mayear, *i.v.* to be like May (said of the weather).

mayestático, ca, *a.* majestic.

mayido, *m.* mewing, meaowing; mew, meaow.

mayo, *m.* 1. May (month). 2. Maypole. 3. love wreath placed at sweetheart's door. 4. (*pl.*) serenades sung on the eve of May Day. — **para m.,** (coll., Chile) until doomsday; till the cows come home.

mayólica, *f.* majolica, a type and style of china (dishes, ware) typical of Majorca (Balearic Islands).

mayonesa, *f.* (cul.) mayonnaise.

mayor, *a.* 1. great, e.g. *no tiene m. importancia si vas mañana u hoy,* it is not of great importance whether you go tomorrow or today. 2. greater, larger; greatest, largest; bigger, biggest. 3. older; oldest, eldest. 4. adult, grown-up, of age, e.g. *él tiene varios hijos mayores,* he has several grown-up or adult sons. 5. main, principal, chief, head. 6. high, main (altar); high (mass). 7. (mus.) major, *e.g. tercera or sexta m.,* major third or sixth, *tono m.,* major key. 8. (log.) major. 9. (ecc.) major (orders). 10. (mar.) main (mast). — **calle m.,** main street; **estudios mayores,** university studies; **palo m.,** (mar.) mainmast; **por m.,** (com.) wholesale; (fig.) summarily; **sargento m.,** sergeant major; **ser m. de edad,** to be of age. —*m.* 1. (mil.) major. 2. chief, superior. 3. (*pl.*) elders; ancestors; **m. de edad,** major (person of legal age). —*f.* (log.) major, major premise.

mayoral, *m.* 1. head shepherd. 2. coachman, driver of stagecoach. 3. foreman, boss, overseer. 4. tithe collector, rent collector.

mayorala, *m.* head shepherd's, coachman's or overseer's wife.

mayoralía, *f.* flock, herd; herdsman's wages.

mayorana, *f.* (bot.) *var. of* **mejorana,** marjoram.

mayorazga, *f.* 1. (female) owner of an estate inherited by primogeniture. 2. heiress to an estate inherited by primogeniture. 3. wife of owner of an estate inherited by primogeniture.

mayorazgo, *m.* 1. primogeniture (exclusive right of first-born to inherit). 2. estate inherited by primogeniture. 3. owner of estate inherited by primogeniture. 4. first-born son. 5. (coll.) primogeniture (state of being first-born).

mayorazgüelo, la, *m, f. dim. of* **mayorazgo.**

mayorazguete, *m., f. derog. dim. of* **mayorazgo.**

mayorazguista, *m.* (law) person who writes on primogeniture.

mayorcito, ta, *a.* older. —*m.* boy, young man.

mayordoma, *f.* housekeeper, stewardess; butler's or steward's wife.

mayordomear, *tr.v.* to manage, administer (an estate or household).

mayordomía, *f.* stewardship, butlership (of house); administratorship (of estate); controllership.

mayordomo, *m.* 1. majordomo, steward (of a house); administrator (of an estate). 2. one of several officials of a brotherhood, responsible for organizing its activities. 3. (Chile) foreman, overseer. 4. (Amer.) butler, manservant. — **m. de propios,** treasurer in charge of town funds; **m. de semana,** under-steward; **m. mayor,** chief or head steward.

mayoría, *f.* 1. majority (status of being of legal age); **al alcanzar a la m. de edad,** on coming of age. 2. larger number or part. 3. (pol.) majority, plurality. — **m. absoluta,** absolute majority; **m. relativa,** relative majority; **m. silenciosa,** silent majority; **m. simple,** simple majority.

mayoridad, *f.* 1. majority (status of being of legal age). 2. superiority.

mayorista, *a.* (com.) wholesale. —*m.* 1. (com.) wholesaler. 2. pupil of the upper grades in school.

mayoritario, ria, *a.* pertaining to or depending on the majority.

mayormente, *adv.* principally, chiefly, mainly, particularly.

mayu, *m.* (Chile, bot.) (species of) sophora (Sophora macrocarpa).

mayúsculo, la, *a.* 1. capital (letter). 2. large; important; (coll.) awful, tremendous. —*f.* capital (letter).

maza, *f.* 1. mace (weapon, symbol of authority). 2. hemp brake; mallet. 3. drumstick of a base drum. 4. hammer of drop hammer or pile driver. 5. trunk, post. 6. rag tied to person's clothes as practical joke. 7. thick end of billiard cue. 8. (Chile) hub (of wheel). 9. (Cuba) roller (of sugar mill). 10. (coll.) bore, pest, plague. — **m. de Fraga,** drop hammer, pile driver; (coll.) authoritative person; (coll.) overwhelming truth; **m. sorda,** cattail, reed mace; **la m. y la mona,** (coll.) bosom friends.

mazacote, *m.* 1. barilla, soda ash. 2. mortar, cement, concrete. 3. (coll.) stodge, doughy mess (custard, sauce or food in general). 4. an unsightly piece of artwork. 5. (coll.) pest, plague, bore. 6. (Arg.) hard lumps of sugar residue.

mazacuate, *m.* (Hond.) species of boa.

mazada, *f.* blow with a mace. — **dar m. a,** to harm, injure.

mazagatos, quarrel, row, dispute; difficulty, e.g. *se armó la de m.,* there was a tremendous rumpus.

mazamorra, *f.* 1. (Amer.) sweet made of cornflour, kind of custard or blancmange; soup made of corn or barley. 2. biscuit crumbs; mush made

of broken hardtack. 3. (fig.) mess, stodge, stodgy mixture. 4. crumbs, bits; anything broken into small pieces.
mazaneta, *f.* apple-shaped ornament in jewelry.
mazapán, *m.* marzipan, marchpane, almond paste.
mazar, (*ref.* 53) *tr.v.* to churn (milk).
mazarí, *m.* floor brick or tile.
mazarota, *f.* (metal.) deadhead, sprue.
mazazo, *m.* blow with a mace.
mazdeísmo, *m.* (rel.) Mazdaism, Mazdeism.
mazmorra, *f.* dungeon (underground cell or prison).
maznar, *tr.v.* 1. to knead, squeeze, soften. 2. to beat (iron while it is hot).
mazo, *m.* 1. mallet, heavy wooden hammer. 2. bundle, handful. 3. bore, pest, plague. 4. clapper of a bell.
mazonado, da, *a.* (her.) masoned.
mazonear, *tr.v.* (rare) to ram.
mazonería, *f.* stone masonry; (sculp.) relief work.
mazorca, *f.* 1. spindleful (of thread). 2. ear (of corn, etc.). 3. cocoa bean. 4. certain decoration on banisters. 5. (Chile) tyrannical government; tyrannical ruling clique.
mazorquero, *m.* (Chile) member of a despotic government junta.
mazorral, *a.* 1. rude, uncouth, unmannerly. 2. (print.) solid.
mazorralmente, *adv.* rudely, uncouthly, unmannerly.
mazuelo, *m.* 1. *dim. of* **mazo,** small mallet. 2. pestle.
mazurca, *f.* (mus.) mazurka, a dance of Polish origin.
m./c. *abbrev. of* 1. **mi cargo,** on me. 2. **mi cuenta,** my account. 3. **moneda corriente,** legal tender.
M.C.A. *abbrev. of* **Mercado Común Centroamericano,** Central American Common Market.
M.C.E. *abbrev. of* **Mercado Común Europeo,** European Economic Community (E. E. C.).
me, *pers. pron.* 1. (as direct object pronoun) me, e.g. *me llevó al cine,* he took me to the movies. 2. (as indirect object pronoun) me, to me, e.g. *me dio el libro,* he gave me the book, or the book to me; me, for me, e.g. *cómprame un helado,* buy me an ice-cream, or buy an ice-cream for me; from me, e.g. *cómpremelo, señor,* buy it from me, sir; *me quitaron la pluma,* they took my pen away from me. 3. (as reflexive, pronoun) myself; to myself, e.g. *yo me dije,* I said to myself.
meada, *f.* urine; urine stain; puddle of urine.
meadero, *m.* urinal.
meados, *m.* (*pl.*) urine.
meaja, *f.* 1. ancient coin. 2. dues formerly paid to the judge after a trial. 3. crumb. — **m. de huevo,** embryo of an egg.
meajuela, *f.* 1. small crumb. 2. each of the pieces hanging from horse's bit.
meandro, *m.* 1. meander, curve, bend (e.g. of a river). 2. (archit.) meander (intricate ornamentation).
mear, *tr.v., i.v., r.v.,* (vulg.) to piss, urinate.
meato, *m.* (anat.) meatus, e.g. *m. auditivo,* auditory meatus; (bot.) pore.
meauca, *f.* (ornith.) shearwater.
Meca, *f.* **de la Ceca a la Meca,** from pillar to post, hither and thither.
meca, *f.* 1. (Chile) dung, excrement. 2. (Ecuad., Peru) prostitute.
¡mecachis! *interj., var. of* **caramba.**
mecánica, *f.* 1. (phys.) mechanics. 2. machinery, mechanism. 3. (coll.) contemptible thing. 4. (coll.) dirty trick, meanness. 5. (mil.) fatigues (internal work of a camp). — **m. aplicada,** applied mechanics; **m. cuántica,** (phys.) quantum mechanics; **m. de ondas,** (phys.) wave mechanics.
mecánicamente, *adv.* mechanically.
mecanice, mecanicé, *ref.* **mecanizar.**
mecanicismo, *m.* (biol., philos.) mechanism; mechanistic system or theory.
mecanicista, *m., f.* (biol., philos.) mechanist.
mecánico, ca, *a.* 1. mechanical, machine-made or operated. 2. (coll.) mean, low. —*m.* 1. mechanic, repairman. 2. (auto.) driver, chauffeur. — **m. dental** or **dentista,** dental technician; **m. de vuelo,** flight engineer.
mecanismo, *m.* mechanism; machinery, works; gear. — **m. de avance,** travel mechanism; **m. de cambio europeo** or **de paridades,** Exchange Rate Mechanism; **m. de defensa,** defense mechanism; **m. de dirección,** steering gear; **m. de disparo** or **del disparador,** trigger or firing mechanism; **m. del eyector,** ejector mechanism; **m. de maniobra,** operating mechanism; **m. de retroceso,** recoil mechanism.
mecanización, *f.* mechanization.
mecanizar, (*ref.* 53) *tr.v.* to mechanize; (fig.) to divest of human spirit.
mecanografía, *f.* typewriting, typing.
mecanografiar, *tr.v.* to type, write on a typewriter.
mecanográfico, ca, *a.* of or pertaining to typing or typewriting.
mecanografista, *m., f., var. of* **mecanógrafo.**
mecanógrafo, fa, *m., f.* typist.
mecanorregulable, *a.* power-controlled.
mecanoterapia, *f.* (med.) mechanotherapy.
mecapal, *m.* leather harness used by Mexican carriers and porters.
mecatazo, *m.* (Hond., Mex.) whiplash.
mecate, *m.* (Phil. I., Hond., Mex.) hemp rope or cord.
mecatear, *tr.v.* (Mex.) to whip, thrash.
mecatona, *f.* (Mex.) daily food.
mecedero, *m.* swizzle stick, stirrer (implement for mixing drinks).
mecedor, ra, *a.* rocking, swaying; swinging. —*m.* 1. stirrer, stirring paddle. 2. swing. —*f.* rocking chair.
mecedura, *f.* 1. rocking; swing, swinging. 2. stirring, shaking.
Mecenas, *m.* (hist., lit.) Maecenas, Roman statesman, patron of Virgil and Horace; (fig.) any wealthy or influential patron of the arts.
mecenazgo, *m.* patronage of arts and literature; patronage (of an artist or writer).
mecer, (*ref.* 56) *tr.v.* 1. to rock; to swing, to dangle. 2. to stir. —*r.v.* to swing; to rock, move to and fro.
mecereón, *m.* (bot.) mezereon.
mecha, *f.* 1. wick (of a lamp). 2. fuse, match (to detonate gunpowder, dynamite, etc.). 3. (med.) lint pad, tent. 4. (cul.) strip of larding bacon. 5. lock (of hair). 6. drill bit. 7. (mar.) spindle, main part of mast. 8. (Col., Peru, Ven.) ragging, kidding, joking, fun. — **alargar la m.,** (coll.) to increase one's pay or salary; (coll.) to spin out a business transaction for one's own benefit; **aguantar la m.,** to endure danger, reprimand or adversity with resignation; **encender la m.,** to stir up trouble; **hablar de m.,** (Col.) to speak in fun; **m. de seguridad,** safety fuse; **tener m.,** (Col.) to be witty.
mechar, *tr.v.* (cul.) to lard, stuff, dress (meat). —*r.v.* (Peru sl.) to begin a fight or scrap.
mechazo, *m.* (min.) fizzle (of a blast fuse); **dar m.,** to fizzle.
mechera, *a.* larding (needle). — f. 1. larding needle. 2. shoplifter (female). 3. (tex.) roving frame, fly-frame.
mechero, *m.* 1. burner (of gas lamp or stove); lamp wick tube or holder (of oil lamp). 2. candle socket (of candlestick). 3. cigarette lighter. 4. (coll.) shoplifter. 5. (Ven.) wag, joker, wit, wisecracker. — **m. de Bunsen,** Bunsen burner; **m. de gas,** gas burner; **m. piloto,** pilot, pilot burner.
mechificar, (*ref.* 50) *i.v.* (Ecuad., Peru, Ven.) to tease, rag, kid, taunt.
mechinal, *m.* 1. (mas.) putlog hole. 2. (coll.) cubbyhole, tiny room.
mechoacán, *m.* (bot.) (variety of) jalap (Ipomoea purga); **m. negro,** (bot.) jalap (Exogorium purga).
mechón, *m.* lock, tuft (of hair); bundle (of threads, wool, etc.).
mechoso, sa, *a.* bushy-headed, shockheaded, tufty.
mechudo, da, *a.* (Amer.) *var. of* **mechoso.**
mecida, *f.* rocking; swing, swinging.
mecimiento, *m., var. of* **mecida.**
meco, ca, *a.* (Mex.) brownish black (said of animals). —*m., f.* (Mex.) wild Indian.
meconato, *m.* (chem.) meconate.
mecónico, ca, *a.* (chem.) meconic.
meconio, *m.* 1. (med.) meconium. 2. (pharm.) poppy juice.
medalla, *f.* medal; medallion; (coll.) piece of eight, doubloon (coin).
medallón, *m.* medallion; locket.
medanal, *m.* (Chile, Urug.) marshy, boggy land.
médano, *m.* dune, sand dune; sandbank.
medaño, *m., var. of* **médano.**
media, *f.* 1. sock, stocking. 2. (math.) mean, average. 3. half an hour, e.g. *son las dos y m.,* it is half past two. 4. (Peru) secondary school; secondary school education. — **m. aritmética** or **diferencial,** arithmetic mean; **m. corta** or **m. media,** (Amer.) ankle-length sock; **m. diferencial,** arithmetical mean; **m. geométrica** or **proporcional,** geometric mean, mean proportional; **m. elásticas,** surgical stockings.
mediacaña, *f.* 1. (archit.) cavetto molding, semicircular molding. 2. (carp.) decorative strip of wood. 3. gouge (chisel). 4. curling tongs or irons. 5. (formerly) billiard cue. 6. nose band (of horse's harness). 7. (print.) double rule.
mediación, *f.* mediation; intercession.
mediado, da, *past part. of* **mediar.** —*a.* half-full; **a mediados de,** halfway through, in the middle of (the month, year).
mediador, ra, *a.* mediating, mediative. —*m., f.* mediator; intercessor.
mediagua, *f.* (Col., Chile) sloping roof; building with sloping roof.
medial, *a.* (phonet.) medial; (anat.) median.
medialuna, *f.* 1. hamstringing or hacking knife. 2. (fort.) demilune. 3. (cul.) crescent-shaped roll, croissant. 4. Turkish crescent. 5. (fig.) Islam, Mohammedanism.
mediana, *f.* 1. (in billiards) long cue. 2. strong cord (attaching yoke ring to plow). 3. (geom.) median.
medianamente, *adv.* 1. moderately. 2. middling, so-so, fairly well.
medianejo, ja, *a.* (coll.) rather poor, rather bad, mediocre.
medianería, *f.* party wall, partition wall (separating contiguous houses); dividing hedge (separating two estates).
medianero, ra, *a.* 1. dividing, intermediate. 2. mediating. —*m., f.* mediator. —*m.* 1. owner of a house adjoining another. 2. partner with another in the ownership of land or a farm.
medianía, *f.* 1. halfway stage. 2. (fig.) mediocrity. 3. moderately comfortable (economic) circumstances. 4. (Col.) party or partition wall.
medianidad, *f., var. of* **medianía.**
medianil, *m.* 1. (agr.) middle piece of ground. 2. (print.) crossbar, gutter stick. 3. party or partition wall.

mediano, na, *a.* 1. medium, average, middling. 2. (coll.) mediocre, rather bad. 3. (Chile) small. 4. (anat.) median.
medianoche, *f.* 1. midnight. 2. small meatpie.
mediante, *a.* intervening; interceding; willing, e.g. *Dios m.,* God willing. *—adv.* with the help of, by means of, through.
mediar, *i.v.* 1. to get halfway, be halfway; to be half-finished; to be in the middle. 2. to intervene, intercede, come between. 3. to go by, elapse. 4. to occur in the meantime, intervene.
mediastínico, ca, *a.* (anat.) mediastinal.
mediastino, *m.* (anat.) mediastinum.
mediatamente, *adv.* mediately, indirectly.
mediatice, mediaticé, *ref.* **mediatizar.**
mediatizar, (*ref.* 53) *tr.v.* to mediatize; to annex a small or weak state or ruler to a larger or more powerful one.
mediato, ta, *a.* mediate.
mediator, *m.* omber, ombre (card game).
mediatriz, *f.* median line.
médica, *f.* woman doctor; (coll.) doctor's wife.
medicable, *a.* medicable, curable.
medicación, *f.* medication, medical treatment; medicines prescribed.
medical, *a.* (Gal.) medical.
medicamentar, *tr.v.* to treat medically. *—r.v.* to take medicines.
medicamento, *m.* medicine, medicament.
medicamentoso, sa, *a.* medicinal, curative.
medicastro, *m.* medicaster, quack, charlatan.
medicina, *f.* 1. medicine, art of healing. 2. medicine, remedy. — **m. forense** or **legal,** forensic medicine; **m. interna,** internal medicine; **m. preventiva,** preventive medicine; **m. socializada,** socialized medicine.
medicinal, *a.* medicinal, curative.
medicinalmente, *adv.* medicinally.
medicinante, *m.* 1. charlatan, empiric, quack. 2. medical student, intern (esp. one who practices before receiving his degree).
medicinar, *tr.v.* to medicate, administer medicine to, treat medically. *—r.v.* to take medicine; to dose oneself.
medición, *f.* measurement, measuring.
médico, ca, *a.* medical *—m., f.* doctor, physician. — **m. cirujano,** surgeon; **m. de apelación,** consulting physician; **m. de cabecera,** family doctor, bedside doctor; **m. espiritual,** spiritual counselor; **m. forense,** forensic doctor; **m. general,** general practitioner; **m. interno residente,** intern; **m. podólogo,** chiropodist, podiatrist; **m. rural,** country doctor.
medicucho, *m.* medicaster, quack; unskilled physician.
medida, *f.* 1. measuring unit or standard, measurement, measure. 2. (action of) measuring, measurement. 3. rule, measure, measuring stick or tape (instrument for measuring). 4. (poet.) meter, measure. 5. proportion, e.g. *a m. de,* in proportion to, according to. 6. measure, step, precaution. 7. moderation, prudence. — **a m. que,** as, at the same time as; **colmarse** or **llenarse la m.,** to drain the cup of sorrow, have one's fill of adversities; **hecho a la** or **sobre m.,** made to measure; **m. agraria,** land measure; **m. común,** common divisor, common measure; **m. en radianes,** (geom.) circular measure; **m. lineal,** linear measure; **m. métrica,** metric measure; **m. para áridos,** dry measure; **m. para líquidos,** liquid measure; **m. para sólidos,** solid measure; **medidas prontas de seguridad,** emergency security measures; **tomar sus medidas,** to size up a situation; **tomarle a uno sus medidas,** to size someone up; **tomar medidas,** to take measures, take steps (to correct a situation).
medidamente, *adv.* moderately, with moderation.
medido, da, *a.* measured.
medidor, ra, *a.* measuring, gauging. *—m., f.* measurer. *—m.* measure; (Amer.) meter (for gas, electricity). — **m. de combustible,** fuel gage; **m. de condensadores,** (rad.) condenser meter; **m. de la intensidad de señal,** (rad.) signal meter; **m. de torsión,** torque meter.
mediero, ra, *m., f.* 1. hosier, stocking maker or seller. 2. partner on cattle ranch or farm.
medieval, *a.* medieval.
medievalidad, *f.* medievalism.
mediavalismo, *m.* medievalism.
medievalista, *m., f.* medievalist.
medio, dia, *a.* 1. half, half a, e.g. *media hora,* half an hour, *media naranja,* half an orange. 2. middle, e.g. *medio fondo,* (sport.) middle distance, *corredor de medio fondo,* middle-distance runner, *clase media,* middle class. 3. mid, in the middle of, e.g. *a media tarde,* in mid-afternoon, in the middle of the afternoon. 4. mean, average, e.g. *la velocidad media,* the mean or average speed. 5. (coll.) a bit of a, somewhat of a, e.g. *él es medio idiota,* he is somewhat or a bit of an idiot. — **a media luz,** in a half light; **a media voz,** in a low voice, softly, sotto voce; **a medias,** half, e.g. *dueño a medias,* half owner, *dormido a medias,* half asleep, *pagar a medias,* to pay half; half each, half and half, fifty-fifty, halves, e.g. *lo haremos a medias,* we'll do it half each, or half and half, *pagaremos a medias,* we'll pay half each or fifty-fifty, *ir a medias,* to go halves or fifty-fifty; **media hermana,** half sister; **media luna,** half moon, crescent moon, (cul.) croissant, moon-shaped roll; **medio hermano,** half brother; **medio luto,** half mourning; **medio pasaje,** half fare; **medio tiempo,** (sport.) half time, e.g. *a medio tiempo los equipos descansaron,* at half time the teams rested; **m. voleo,** half volley; **por término medio,** on the average, as an average; **término medio,** average; compromise, middle way; (cul.) medium, not too rare (said of meat). *—m.* 1. middle center. 2. (math.) half. 3. medium (in spiritualism). 4. method, way, (*pl.*) means (to obtain an end), e.g. *los fines no justifican los medios,* the end does not justify the means. 5. medium, vehicle, channel, (*pl.*) media. 6. (*pl.*) means, resources, funds (financial). 7. environment, medium, surroundings, milieu. 8. society, e.g. *es el sentido cívico, lo que falta en nuestro m.,* civic sense is what is lacking in our society. 9. (bot., biol.) medium, habitat. 10. (phys.) medium (through which a force acts). 11. (log.) medium (middle term of a syllogism). 12. (sport) halfback (in football). 13. middle course, mean, medium. 14. ancient Mexican coin; (Peru, Cuba) five cents, e.g. *no tengo ni m.,* I haven't a cent or a penny. — **atrasado de medios,** poor, not well-off, in reduced circumstances; **corto** or **estrecho de medios,** short of or low in funds, short of cash; **de m. a m.,** right on, smack on, plumb in the middle, right on the target, e.g. *la pedrada le acertó de m. a m.,* the stone hit him spot or smack on; entirely, completely, *Ud. se engaña de m. a m.,* you are completely mistaken; **de por m.,** half, e.g. *pagar de por m.,* to pay half; in between, between, e.g. *poner tierra de por m.,* to run away (i.e. to put land in between); **día por** (or **de por**) **m.,** every other day, alternate days; **estar de por m.,** to intervene, participate (in a transaction); to be involved, come into the question, e.g. *está por m. el prestigio de la empresa,* the firm's prestige is involved; **en m.,** in the middle or the center; in between; meanwhile, in the meantime; in spite of, notwithstanding; **los medios informativos** or **de comunicación,** the media; **los medios de comunicación sociales,** the mass media; **medio ambiente,** environment; **m. de cambio** or **trueque,** medium of exchange; **m. de communicación** or **m. informativo,** medium of communication **m. derecho,** (sport.) right half; **m. de transporte,** means of transport; **m. izquierdo,** (sport.) left half; **m. proporcional,** (math.) mean proportional, geometric mean; **medios audiovisuales,** audiovisual aids; **medios de produccion,** means of production; **meterse de por m.** or **en m.,** to intervene, come between; **por todos los medios,** by all means, at all costs; **quitar de en m.,** to get rid of, eliminate; **quitarse uno de en m.,** to get out, quit, withdraw, retire; **por m. de,** by means of; **tomar el m.** or **los medios,** to take measures, take steps.
medio, *adv.* half, partly, e.g. *m. vestido,* half-dressed, *m. borracho,* half-drunk, *m. asado,* half-roasted; **a m.** + *inf.,* half + *past part.,* e.g. *a m. vestir,* half-dressed.
medioambiental, *a,* environmental.
mediocre, *a.* mediocre.
mediocremente, *a.* in a mediocre **manner.**
mediocridad, *f.* mediocrity.
mediodía, *m.* 1. midday, noon; noontide; meridian. 2. south. — **hacer m.,** to stop for lunch; **pleno m.,** high noon.
medioeval, *a.* medieval.
medioevo, va, *a.* medieval. *—m.* Middle Ages.
mediopaño, *m.* light woolen cloth.
mediquillo, *m.* quack, medicaster; unqualified doctor.
medir, (*ref.* 39) *tr.v.* 1. to measure; to gauge; to weigh. 2. (poet.) to scan; **m. con la vista,** to size up. *—i.v.* to measure; **¿cuánto mides?** how tall are you? *—r.v.* 1. to measure oneself. 2. to be moderate, act with restraint.
meditabundo, da, *a.* meditative, pensive, musing, thoughtful.
meditación, *f.* meditation.
meditador, ra, *a.* meditating, meditative, contemplative.
meditar, *tr.v.* 1. to meditate, contemplate, think about, ponder, muse. 2. to plan. *—i.v.* to meditate.
meditativo, va, *a.* meditative, pensive.
mediterráneo, a, *a.* 1. mediterranean, landlocked, inland. 2. **M.,** Mediterranean (pertaining to the Mediterranean Sea). *—m.* Mediterranean (Sea).
médium, *m.* medium (in spiritualism).
medo, da, *a.* Median. *—m., f.* Mede (native or inhabitant of Media, an ancient kingdom in S. W. Asia).
medra, *f.* improvement, progress; growth, increase.
medrana, *f.* (coll.) fear.
medrar, *i.v.* 1. to grow, thrive. 2. to prosper, flourish. — **medrados estamos,** now look what's happened, now we're in a pretty mess.
medregal, *m.* (Cuba, ichth.) medregal.
medriñaque, *m.* 1. buckram (a stiffening cloth for lining and shaping bouffant skirts). 2. short skirt or kirtle.
medro, *m.* growth, increase; improvement, progress; (*pl.*) progress, improvements, growth.
medrosamente, *adv.* timorously, fearfully.
medroso, sa, *a.* 1. timorous, fainthearted, timid, fearful. 2. frightening, terrifying. *—m., f.* coward.
medula, médula, *f.* 1. (anat.) marrow, medulla; (bot.) medulla, pith. 2. (fig.) marrow, essence, pith, substance. — **m. espinal,** (anat.) spinal cord; **m. oblonga** or **oblongada,** (anat.) medulla oblongata.

medular, *a.* medullary, medullar.
meduloso, sa, *a.* full of marrow, marrowy; (bot.) pithy.
medusa, *f.* (zool.) medusa, jellyfish.
meduseo, a, *a.* 1. (myth.) pertaining to Medusa. 2. pertaining to jellyfish.
Mefistófeles, *m.* Mephistopheles.
mefistofélico, ca, *a.* Mephistophelian.
mefítico, *a.* mephitic, noxious; foul-smelling.
megaciclo, *m.* (phys.) megacycle.
megáfono, *m.* megaphone.
megagameto, *m.* (biol.) megagamete.
megalítico, ca, *a.* (archeol.) megalithic.
megalito, *m.* (archeol.) megalith.
megalocéfalo, la, *a.* megalocephalous.
megalomanía, *f.* (psyc.) megalomania.
megalómano, na, *a.* (psyc.) megalomaniacal. —*m., f.* megalomaniac.
megalópodo, da, *a.* (zool.) megapod.
megalópolis, *f.* megalopolis.
megalopolitano, na, *a.* megalopolitan.
megalosaurio, *m.* (paleon.) megalosaur.
megamperio, *m.* (elec.) megampere.
mégano, *m., var. of* **médano,** dune.
megapodo, *m.* (ornith.) megapode.
megarense, *a.* Megarian, of or from the ancient Greek city of Megara. —*m., f.* Megarian.
megascópico, ca, *a.* megascopic, visible to the naked eye.
megáspora, *f.* (bot.) megaspore.
megasporangio, *m.* (bot.) megasporangium.
megasporofilo, *m.* (bot.) megasporophyll.
megaterio, *m.* (paleon.) megathere.
megatón, *m.* (atomic energy) megaton.
megavatio, *m.* (elec.) megawatt.
mego, ga, *a.* meek, gentle, mild, docile, peaceful.
megohmio, *m.* (elec.) megohm.
mehala, *f.* mehalla, mahalla (Moroccan army unit).
meharí, *m.* African dromedary.
mehedí, *m.* Mahdi, Mohammedan Messiah.
meiosis, meyosis, *f.* (biol.) meiosis.
meiótico, ca, *a.* (biol.) meiotic.
mejana, *f.* islet, holm (in a river).
mejicanismo, *m.* Mexican idiom, Mexicanism.
mejicano, na, *a., m., f.* Mexican.
mejido, da, *a.* (cul.) beaten up with sugar and milk (said of an egg).
mejilla, *f.* (anat.) cheek.
mejillón, *m.* (ichth.) mussel.
mejor, *a. comp. of* **bueno,** better; best. —*adv. comp. of* **bien,** better; best; rather; **a lo m.,** maybe, perhaps, as like as not; **en el m. de los casos,** at best. — **m. dicho,** more specifically, rather; **m. que m.,** even better; **tanto m.,** better still, so much the better.
mejora, *f.* 1. improvement, betterment. 2. higher bid (at an auction). 3. (law) special bequest, additional bequest. 4. (law) development, improvement.
mejorable, *a.* improvable, ameliorable.
mejoramiento, *m.* improvement, amelioration, melioration.
mejorana, *f.* (bot.) marjoram (Origanum majorana).
mejorar, *tr.v.* 1. to improve, make better, ameliorate, enhance. 2. to make better (in health). 3. to raise (a bid). 4. (law) to leave an additional bequest to. —*i.v., r.v.* to get better, improve.
mejoría, *f.* 1. improvement, betterment. 2. advantage. 3. superiority. 4. improvement (in health, conditions, etc.).
mejunje, *m.* mixture, potion (medicinal, cosmetic).
melado, da, *a.* honey-colored, roan. —*m.* thick cane syrup; small honey-tart sprinkled with hempseeds. —*f.* toast dipped in honey; dried marmalade.
meladora, *f.* (Cuba) last sugar-boiling pan (in sugar refinery).
meladucha, *f.* sweet, mealy apple.
meladura, *f.* concentrated cane syrup (ready for making sugar).
meláfido, meláfiro, *m.* (geol.) melaphyre.
melamina, *f.* (chem.) melamine.
melampo, *m.* (theat.) prompter's light.
melancolía, *f.* 1. (med.) melancholia. 2. melancholy, gloom, sadness, the blues (coll.).
melancólicamente, *adv.* melancholically, gloomily.
melancolice, melancolicé, *ref.* **melancolizar.**
melancólico, ca, *a.* melancholy, melancholic, sad, gloomy.
melancolizar, (*ref.* 53) *tr.v.* to make sad, gloomy or dejected; to affect with melancholy. —*r.v.* to become melancholy or sad.
melandro, *m.* (zool.) badger.
melanemia, *f.* (med.) melanaemia.
melanesio, a, *a., m., f.* Melanesian. —*m.* Melanesian (language). —*f.* **M., Melanesia,** one of the three major divisions of the Pacific Islands.
melánico, ca, *a.* (med.) melanic.
melanina, *f.* (biochem.) melanin.
melanismo, *m.* (physiol., zool.) melanism.
melanita, *f.* (min.) melanite.
melanoide, *a.* (biol.) melanoid.
melanoideo, a, *a.* (biol.) melanoid.
melanoma, *f.* (med.) melanoma (dark malignant tumor).
melanosis, *f.* (med.) melanosis, black cancer.
melantáceo, a, *a.* (bot.) melanthaceous.
melanuria, *f.* (med.) melanuria.
melafia, *f.* pearmain, semi-sweet apple.
melar, *a.* honey-sweet (said of fruit or sugarcane).
melar, (*ref.* 29) *tr.v.* to fill (the combs) with honey. —*i.v.* 1. to boil (cane juice) for a second time; to boil clear. 2. to fill the combs with honey.
melastomáceas, *f.* (bot.) (*pl.*) Melastomaceae.
melaza, *f.* molasses; dregs of honey.
melca, *f.* (bot.) sorghum.
melcocha, *f.* taffy, molasses candy.
melcochero, ra, *m., f.* taffy maker or seller.
Melchor, *m.* (Bib.) Melchior.
meleagrina, *f.* (zool.) pearl oyster.
melena, *f.* 1. long lock (of hair), loose hair, bob; mane (of lion). 2. yoke pad (of oxen). — **andar a la m.,** (coll.) to quarrel heatedly; **hacer venir** or **traer a la m.,** to force, compel; **venir a la m.,** to yield, give in.
melena, *f.* (med.) melaena, melena, intestinal hemorrhage.
melenera, *f.* forehead of ox (where yoke is placed); yoke pad.
meleno, *a.* (said of a bull) having a tuft of hair on the forehead. —*m.* yokel, rustic.
melenudo, da, *a.* long-haired, bushy-haired.
melera, *f.* 1. honey vendor (female). 2. bruise on melons caused by rain and hail. 3. (bot.) bugloss, oxtongue.
melero, *m.* 1. honey seller or dealer. 2. place where honey is kept.
melga, *f.* (bot.) sorghum.
melga, *f.* (Col., Chile) *var. of* **amelga.**
melgacho, *m.* (ichth.) dogfish.
melgar, *m.* wild alfalfa field or patch.
melgar, *tr.v.* (Chile) *var. of* **amelgar.**
melgo, ga, *a.* twin.
meliáceo, a, *a.* (bot.) meliaceous. —*f.* (*pl.*) (bot.) Meliaceae.
mélico, ca, *a.* melic, lyrical.
melífago, ga, *a.* meliphagous, feeding on honey.
melífero, ra, *a.* (poet.) melliferous, honey-bearing.
melificación, *f.* honey-making, mellification.
melificado, da, *past part. of* **melificar.** —*a.* mellifluous.
melificar, (*ref.* 50) *tr.v.* to make or draw honey from flowers (bees). —*i.v.* to make honey.
melifique, melifiqué, *ref.* **melificar.**
melifluamente, *adv.* mellifluously, mellifluently.
melifluencia, *f.* mellifluousness, mellifluence.
melifluidad, *f.* mellifluousness, mellifluence.
melifluo, flua, *a.* mellifluous, mellifluent, honeyed.
meliloto, ta, *a.* silly, stupid. —*m., f.* simpleton, fool. —*m.* (bot.) melilot, sweet clover.
melindre, *m.* 1. (*pl.*) finickiness, fastidiousness, affectedness, affectation. 2. fritter made with flour and honey. 3. very narrow ribbon. 4. marzipan coated with sugar icing.
melindrear, *i.v.* to speak or act with affectation, be finicky, be fastidious.
melindrería, *f.* finickiness, fastidiousness, affectation, affectedness.
melindrero, ra, *a., var. of* **melindroso.**
melindrice, melindricé, *ref.* **melindrizar.**
melindrillo, *m.* ferret, narrow tape.
melindroso, sa, *a.* finicky, affected, fastidious.
melinita, *f.* melinite; a high explosive.
meliorismo, *m.* (philos.) meliorism.
melisa, *f.* (bot.) lemon balm, garden balm, sweet balm.
melisma, *m.* (mus.) melisma, trill.
melito, *m.* (pharm.) hydromel (honey dissolved in water and mixed with medicinal substances).
mella, *f.* 1. nick, notch (in cutting edge); dent (in metal surface); chip (in plate); gap, hole. 2. harm, injury. — **hacer m. a,** to have an effect on (a person); **hacer m. en,** to harm, injure (reputation, career).
mellado, da, *past part. of* **mellar.** —*a.* gap-toothed; toothless.
melladura, *f., var. of* **mella.**
mellar, *tr.v.* 1. to nick, notch (cutting edge), chip (a plate), dent (metal surface). 2. to harm, injure (someone's honor, credit, etc.). —*r.v.* 1. to become nicked, dented or chipped. 2. to be harmed or injured.
melliza, *f.* a type of sausage prepared with honey.
mellizo, za, *a., m., f.* twin (brother, sister).
mellón, *m.* straw torch.
melocotón, *m.* (bot.) peach tree; peach (fruit).
melocotonar, *m.* peach orchard.
melocotonero, ra, *m.* (bot.) peach tree. —*m., f.* vender of peaches.
melodía, *f.* 1. (mus.) melody. 2. melodiousness.
melódico, ca, *a.* melodic.
melodión, *m.* (mus.) melodeon (instrument).
melodiosamente, *adv.* melodiously, tunefully.
melodioso, sa, *a.* melodious, tuneful, musical.
melodrama, *m.* (theat., lit.) melodrama; (coll.) domestic strife.
melodramáticamente, *adv.* melodramatically.
melodramático, ca, *a.* melodramatic, melodramatical.
melodreña, *a.* whetting (stone).
meloe, *m.* (ento.) meloe, oil beetle.
melófago, *m.* (zool.) parasitic insect in sheep's wool.
melografía, *f.* art of writing music.
meloja, *f.* honey water; mead, metheglin.
melojar, *m.* oak grove.
melojo, *m.* (species of) oak (Quercus pubescens).
melolonta, *m.* (ento.) Melolontha (genus); (ento.) cockchafer.
melolóntido, *m.* (ento.) melolonthid.
melomanía, *f.* melomania, fanatic love of music.
melómano, na, *m., f.* melomaniac, music bug (sl.).

melón, *m.* 1. (bot.) muskmelon, melon. 2. (fig.) dolt, idiot, ignoramus. — **catar el m.,** to sound out (a person or situation), see how the land lies; **decentar el m.,** to run a great risk; **m. de agua,** watermelon; **m. de Castilla,** cantaloupe.
melón, *m.* (zool.) ichneumon (Herpestes ichneumon iddringtoni).
melonada, *f.* foolishness, stupidity.
melonar, *m.* melon field or patch.
meloncillo, *m.* (zool.) ichneumon (Herpestes ichneumon iddringtoni).
melonero, ra, *m., f.* melon grower or seller.
melonhue, *m.* (Chile, zool.) top shell, trochus.
melonzapote, *m.* (Mex., bot.) papaya.
melopea, *f.* 1. monotonous singing. 2. drunken bout, drunk.
melopeya, *f.* (mus., lit.) melopoeia, art of inventing melodies; rhythmical accompaniment to a verse.
melosa, *f.* (Chile, bot.) melosa, tarweed.
melosidad, *f.* 1. smoothness, softness. 2. sweetness, syrupiness.
melosilla, *f.* disease of the oak tree causing the acorns to drop.
meloso, sa, *a.* honey-like, sweet, syrupy; (fig.) soft, smooth, smooth-tongued (said of speech).
melote, *m.* 1. dregs of molasses, residue left after boiling molasses. 2. (Sp., reg.) fruit preserve prepared with honey.
Melpómene, *f.* (myth.) Melpomene, the Muse of tragedy.
melquita, *m.* (rel.) Melchite, Melkite, Arabic-speaking Middle Eastern Christian.
melsa, *f.* 1. spleen. 2. (fig.) dullness, apathy.
meltón, *m.* (Cuba) melton (cloth).
meluza, *f.* cane juice scum sticking to one's hands or garments.
melva, *f.* (ichth.) corvina.
memada, *f.* (coll.) stupidity, foolishness.
membrado, da, *a.* (her.) 1. membered. 2. (arch.) celebrated.
membrana, *f.* (bot., anat.) membrane; **m. alantoides,** (anat.) allantois, allantois membrane; **m. caduca,** (anat.) decidua, caduca; **m. mucosa,** (anat.) mucous membrane; **m. nictitante,** (zool.) nictitating membrane; **m. pituitaria,** (anat.) pituitary membrane; **m. plasmática,** (biol.) plasma membrane; **m. serosa,** (anat.) serous membrane.
membranáceo, a, *a., var. of* **membranoso.**
membranoso, sa, *a.* membranous, membranaceous.
membresía, *f.* (P. Rico) membership.
membrete, *m.* 1. note, memo. 2. invitation (card). 3. heading, letter head (on writing paper); address (on writing paper or envelope).
membrilla, *f.* (bot.) variety of quince.
membrillada, *f.* (Ecuad.) quince jam.
membrillar, *m.* 1. quince tree orchard. 2. quince tree.
membrillate, *m.* quince jam.
membrillero, *m.* quince tree.
membrillo, *m.* quince tree; quince (fruit); quince jam.
membrudamente, *adv.* robustly, strongly.
membrudo, da, *a.* brawny, muscular, husky, corpulent.
memela, *f.* (Mex., C. Amer.) oval-shaped corn tortilla.
memento, *m.* (ecc.) Memento.
memez, *f.* foolishness, stupidity.
memo, ma, *a.* foolish, simple, stupid. —*m., f.* fool, simpleton, dolt.
memorable, *a.* 1. memorable. 2. notable.
memorablemente, *adv.* memorably, unforgettably.
memorando, da, *a., var. of* **memorable.**
memorándum, *m.* 1. memo-book, notebook. 2. (dipl.) memorandum.
memorar, *tr.v.* to remember, to evoke or recall.
memoratísimo, ma, *a.* most memorable, worthy of eternal memory; never to be forgotten.
memorativo, va, *a.* commemorative.
memoria, *f.* 1. memory (faculty); remembrance, recollection. 2. report, study, account (on certain subject). 3. account, financial report. 4. memorial, memorial monument. 5. (*pl.*) regards, greetings (sent to friends by letter or third party). 6. (*pl.*) memoirs (biography). 7. (*pl.*) notebook. — **borrar** or **borrarse de la m.,** to wipe from one's mind, forget completely; **conservar la m. de,** to remember; **de m.,** (to learn) by heart, (to speak) from memory; **en m. de,** in memory of; **flaco** or **olvidadizo de m.,** forgetful, absent-minded; **hacer m. de,** to remember; **m. artificial,** mnemotechny, mnemonics; **m. electrónica,** electronic (memory) storage; **m. de grillo** or **gallo,** scatterbrain; **perder la m.,** to lose one's memory; **saber de m.,** to know by heart.
memorial, *m.* 1. memo-book, notebook. 2. written request. 3. (law) brief. 4. bulletin, publication. — **haber perdido uno los memoriales,** (coll.) to have forgotten.
memorialesco, ca, *a.* memorial (style).
memorialista, *m.* memorialist, amanuensis; secretary.
memorión, riona, *a.* having a prodigious memory. —*m., f.* 1. prodigious memory. 2. person having a prodigious memory.
memorioso, sa, *a.* having a retentive memory, of good memory. —*m., f.* memorist, person with a good or retentive memory.
memorismo, *m.* (system of) learning by heart or by rote.
memorista, *a.* (Hond., Mex., Peru) *var. of* **memorioso.**
mena, *f.* 1. (Phil. I.) size and shape of cigar. 2. (mar.) thickness of cordage. 3. (min.) ore. 4. (ichth.) pickerel.
ménade, *f.* 1. (hist., myth.) maenad, bacchante. 2. (fig.) dissolute woman.
menadiona, *f.* (pharm.) menadione.
menador, ra, *m., f.* winder of silk.
menaje, *m.* 1. household furniture and wares. 2. school supplies or equipment.
menar, *tr.v.* 1. to wind (silk) on a jenny. 2. (fig.) to reflect upon. to ponder.
menchevique, *m.* (polit.) Menshevik, member or advocate of moderate Socialism in Russia, opposed after 1903 by the more radical party of the Bolsheviks.
menchevismo, *m.* (polit.) Menshevism.
menchuca, *f.* (Chile. coll.) lie, fib.
mención, *f.* mention; **hacer m.,** to mention, make mention of; **m. honorífica,** honorable mention.
mencionar, *tr.v.* to mention; to name; **antes mencionado,** above-mentioned.
mendacidad, *f.* mendacity, lying; the habit of lying.
mendaz, (*pl.* **mendaces**), *a.* lying, mendacious. —*m., f.* liar.
mendazmente, *adv.* mendaciously, untruthfully.
mendelevio, *m.* (chem.) mendelevium.
mendeliano, na, *a.* Mendelian, of or pertaining to Gregor Mendel or to his theory of genetics.
mendelismo, *m.* Mendelism, Mendelianism.
mendicación, *f.* begging.
mendicante, *a., m., f.* mendicant.
mendicidad, *f.* begging, mendicity, mendicancy.
mendigante, *a.* begging, mendicant. —*m., f.* beggar, mendicant.
mendigar, (*ref. 51*) *tr.v.* to beg, beg for. —*i.v.* to beg; to live on alms.
mendigo, ga, *m., f.* beggar, mendicant.
mendigue, mendigué, *ref.* **mendigar.**
mendiguez, *f.* begging, beggary; indigence.
mendocino, na, *a.* of or from Mendoza, Argentina. —*m., f.* native or inhabitant of Mendoza.
mendosamente, *adv.* 1. falsely, lyingly. 2. mistakenly, erroneously, wrongly.
mendoso, sa, *a.* 1. false, lying, mendacious. 2. mistaken, wrong.
mendrugo, *m.* 1. crust, crumb. 2. (coll.) fool, idiot.
mendruguillo, *m. dim. of* **mendrugo,** small crumb of bread.
meneador, ra *a.* shaking, moving; wagging (of tail); wiggling, swaying (of the hips). —*m., f.* stirrer, shaker.
menear, *tr.v.* 1. to shake, stir, move; to wag (the tail); to waggle, wiggle (one's behind); to sway (the hips). 2. to manage, run (a business). — **m. el rabo,** to waggle or wiggle one's behind; **peor es menearlo,** let sleeping dogs lie, better let it alone. —*r.v.* 1. to shake, move; to wag (the tail); to wiggle (one's behind); to sway (one's hips). 2. to get a move on, act quickly or efficiently.
menegilda, *f.* (coll.) maidservant.
Menelao, *m.* (myth.) Menelaus, husband of Helen of Troy.
meneo, *m.* 1. shaking, moving; wagging (of the tail); wiggling, waggling (of the behind); swaying (of one's hips). 2. management, running (of a business). 3. whipping, thrashing, flogging.
menequeteo, *m.* (S. Amer.) affected shaking, wiggling or swaying (of the hips).
menester, *m.* 1. necessity, need; want, lack, dearth. 2. occupation, job, post. 3. (*pl.*) bodily needs. 4. (*pl.*) tools, implements. — **haber m.,** to need; **ser m.,** to be necessary.
menesteroso, sa, *a.* needy. —*m., f.* needy person, indigent.
menestra, *f.* 1. vegetable and meat stew. 2. (*pl.*) dried vegetables.
menestral, la, *m., f.* artisan, worker, manual laborer, mechanic.
menestralería, *f.* artisanship.
menestralía, *f.* artisans, manual workers (as a group).
menestrete, *m.* (mar.) nail puller.
Menfis, *f.* (hist.) Memphis, capital of ancient Egypt.
menfita, *a., m., f.* Memphian, Memphite, native of Memphis, capital of ancient Egypt. —*f.* onyx with white and black layers.
menfítico, ca, *a.* Memphian, Memphite.
mengajo, *m.* rag, tatter.
mengala, *f.* (C. Amer.) maidservant.
mengano, na, *m., f.* so and so, what's-his-name; **Fulano, Zutano y M.,** Tom, Dick and Harry.
mengua, *f.* 1. decrease, diminution, lessening, waning; decline, decay. 2. waning (of moon). 3. fall (of tide). 4. discredit, disgrace, shame. 5. poverty, want, need.
menguadamente, *adv.* ignominiously, in a cowardly manner.
menguado, da, *past part. of* **menguar.** —*a.* 1. cowardly, timid. 2. silly, foolish. 3. stingy, miserly. 4. impaired, stunted; **m. de talla,** short, undersize. —*m.* drop stitch (stitch taken in when decreasing in knitting). —*m., f.* 1. coward, weakling. 2. fool, dolt. 3. miser, skinflint.
menguamiento, *m., var. of* **mengua.**
menguante, *a.* 1. diminishing, decreasing; decaying, declining. 2. waning (said of the moon). 3. ebb (tide). —*m.* 1. low tide, ebb tide; low water. 2. decrease, diminution; decline, decay. — **m. de la luna,** waning of the moon.

menguar, (*ref.* 52) *tr.v.* 1. to diminish, lessen, decrease. 2. to discredit, defame. —*r.v.* 1. to diminish, decrease, lessen. 2. to decline; to decay. 3. to decrease (in knitting). 4. to wane (the moon). 5. to fall, go out (the tide).
mengue, *m.* (coll.) devil, the deuce.
menhir, *m.* (archeol.) menhir.
menina, *f.* (hist., Sp.) young lady-in-waiting at the service of the queen or the princesses.
meninge, *f.* (anat.) meninx, (*pl.*) meninges.
meníngeo, a, *a.* (anat., physiol., med.) meningeal.
meningítico, ca, *a.* (med.) meningeal, meningitic.
meningitis, *f.* (med.) meningitis.
meningococo, *m.* (bac.) meningococcus.
menino, *m.* (hist., Sp.) young page of the royal family at the service of the queen or the princes.
menique, *a.* (obs.) *var. of* **meñique.**
menisco, *m.* (anat., opt., phys.) meniscus.
menispermáceo, a, *a.* (bot.) menispermaceous. —*f.* (*pl.*) Menispermaceae.
menjuí, (*pl.* **menjuíes**), *m.* benzoin, benjamin (aromatic balsam extracted from the aromatic styrax benzoin tree).
menjunje, *m., var. of* **mejunje.**
menjurje, *m.* 1. mixture, potion (cosmetic, food or medicine). 2. (coll.) mix-up, mishmash; confusion.
menologio, *m.* (ecc.) menology.
menonita, *a., m., f.* (Rel.) Mennonite, member of an Anabaptist sect founded in the 16th century and still existing in W. Europe and N. America.
menopausia, *f.* (med.) menopause, change of life.
menor, *a.* 1. younger; youngest. 2. smaller; smallest. 3. lesser, least. 4. slightest, least, e.g. *no tengo la m. idea,* I haven't the slightest idea. 5. (ecc.) minor (orders). 6. under age, not of age. 7. (mus., log.) minor. — **al por m.,** (com.) retail; in detail, minutely; **m. de edad,** under age; minor; **m. edad,** minority; **paños menores,** underclothes; **por m.,** (com.) retail; in detail, minutely. —*m.* 1. minor (person under age). 2. (ecc.) Minorite, Franciscan monk; **m. de edad,** minor. —*f.* (log.) minor, minor term.
menorá, *f.* (ecc.) menorah, seven-armed candelabra, symbol of Judaism.
Menorca, *m.* Minorca, Menorca, one of the Balearic Islands.
menorete, al m. or **por m.,** (coll.) at the least.
menoría, *f.* 1. subordination, position of being under another's instructions or command. 2. minority (period of being under age).
menorista, *a.* (Amer.) retail. —*m.* (Amer.) retailer, retail dealer.
menorquín, na, *a.* Minorcan, of or pertaining to the Balearic island of Minorca. —*m., f.* Minorcan.
menorragia, *f.* (med.) menorrhagia.
menos, *adv.* less; least; fewer; fewest; **al, a lo** or **por lo m.,** at least; **a de m. que** + *subj.,* unless + *ind.;* **a m. que** + *subj.,* unless + *ind.;* **de m.,** short, less, e.g. *me has dado una peseta de m.,* you have given me a peseta short; **echar de m.,** to miss (to pine for; not to find); **el que m.,** the most insignificant person; **en m.,** in less; **eso es lo de m.,** that's the least important thing; **lo m.,** the least; **lo m. posible,** the least possible, as little as possible; **más o m.,** more or less; **m. de** + *numeral,* less than + numeral; **m. que,** less than; **no poder m. de** + *inf.,* not to do be able to help + *ger.,* not to be able but + *inf.,* e.g. *no pude m. que reír,* I couldn't help laughing, I couldn't but laugh, e.g. *no pude m. que ayudarle,* I couldn't but help him; **tener a** or **en m.,** to look down on, despise. —*m.* (math.) minus sign. —*prep.* 1. except, but, e.g. *todo m. eso,* everything except that. 2. (math.) minus, take away, less, e.g. *cuatro m. dos,* four minus two. 3. (in time) to, e.g. *son las cinco m. cuarto,* it's a quarter to five. — **todo m. eso,** anything but that; **venir a m.,** to lose rank, fortune or position.
menoscabador, ra, *a.* 1. reducing, decreasing. 2. spoiling, impairing, damaging. 3. discrediting, damaging. —*m., f.* impairer, defamer, detractor.
menoscabar, *tr.v.* 1. to lessen, reduce, diminish. 2. to damage, spoil, impair. 3. to damage, discredit, tarnish (someone's reputation). —*r.v.* to decrease, lessen, diminish.
menoscabo, *m.* 1. reduction, decrease, diminution. 2. damage, impairment, spoiling. 3. discredit, damage (to reputation).
menoscuenta, *f.* payment on account, part payment (of debt).
menospreciable, *a.* contemptible, despicable.
menospreciablemente, *adv.* contemptuously.
menospreciador, ra, *a.* despising, contemptuous. —*m., f.* despiser, scorner.
menospreciar, *tr.v.* 1. to despise, look down on. 2. to underrate, undervalue.
menospreciativo, va, *a.* contemptuous, scornful, disdainful, belittling.
menosprecio, *m.* 1. contempt, scorn. 2. underestimation, underrating, undervaluation.
menostasia, *f.* (med.) menostasia.
mensaje, *m.* message; dispatch; errand; communication; **m. cifrado, m. en clave** or **código,** cipher or code message.
mensajería, *f.* 1. stagecoach. 2. (*pl.*) stage coach company or service; transport company or agency. 3. (*pl.*) steamship line, shipping line; shipping office.
mensajero, ra, *m., f.* messenger, carrier; errand boy or girl; **paloma mensajera,** carrier pigeon.
menso, sa, *a.* (Mex.) foolish, stupid.
menstruación, *f.* menstruation.
menstrual, *a.* menstrual.
menstrualmente, *adv.* menstrually, monthly.
menstruante, *a.* menstruant, menstruating.
menstruar, (*ref.* 55) *i.v.* to menstruate.
menstruo, trua, *a.* menstrual, menstruous. —*m.* 1. menstruation. 2. menses, menstrual blood. 3. (chem.) menstruum, solvent.
menstruoso, sa, *a.* menstruous, menstruating. —*f.* menstruating female.
mensual, *a.* monthly; **revista m.,** monthly, monthly magazine.
mensualidad, *f.* monthly salary or allowance; monthly installment.
mensualmente, *adv.* monthly, every month.
ménsula, *f.* 1. elbow rest. 2. bracket; (archit.) corbel, console.
mensura, *f.* measurement, measuring.
mensurabilidad, *f.* (geom.) mensurability, mensurableness.
mensurable, *a.* mensurable, measurable.
mensuración, *f.* mensuration, measurement.
mensurador, ra, *a.* measuring. —*m., f.* measurer, meter.
mensural, *a.* mensural, measuring.
mensurar, *tr.v.* to measure.
menta, *f.* (bot.) mint; peppermint.
mentado, da, *past part. of* **mentar.** —*a.* famous, renowned, spoken-of, celebrated.
mental, *a.* mental; of the mind or the intellect.
mentalidad, *f.* mentality.
mentalmente, *adv.* mentally; intellectually.
mentar, (*ref.* 29) *tr.v.* to name, mention. — **mentarle la madre a alguien,** (sl.) to insult someone, call someone a bastard.
mentastro, *m.* (bot.) apple mint.
mente, *f.* mind; understanding, intellect, sense; will, disposition. — **tener en la m. una cosa,** to have something in mind.
mentecada, *f., var. of* **mentecatería.**
mentecatería, *f.* 1. foolishness, stupidity, nonsense. 2. foolish or stupid remark or action.
mentecatez, *f., var. of* **mentecatería.**
mentecato, ta, *a.* silly, foolish, stupid, doltish. —*m., f.* simpleton, fool, dolt, fathead (coll.).
menteno, *m.* (chem.) menthene.
mentidero, *m.* (coll.) gossiping place, loafing place.
mentido, da, *past part. of* **mentir.** —*a.* deceiving, false.
mentir, (*ref.* 42) *i.v.* 1. to lie, tell lies, fib (coll.). 2. to deceive, be deceptive. 3. to appear to be. 4. to belie, contradict. 5. to disguise, falsify. —*tr.v.* to fail to keep, break (a promise); to disappoint.
mentira, *f.* 1. lie, untruth, story (coll.), fib (coll.); illusion; deception. 2. error (in manuscript). 3. white spot (on fingernails). 4. (Amer.) cracking of knuckles. — **coger en una m.,** to catch someone lying or in a lie; **parece m.,** it seems incredible or unbelievable; **m. inocente** or **oficiosa,** or **piadosa,** white lie.
mentirijillas, de m., in fun, jokingly.
mentirilla, *f. dim. of* **mentira,** white lie, fib; **de mentirillas,** in fun, jokingly.
mentirón, *m. aug. of* **mentira,** whopper, whopping lie.
mentirosamente, *adv.* lyingly, deceitfully, falsely.
mentirosito, ta, *a. dim. of* **mentiroso,** white liar, little fibber.
mentiroso, sa, *a.* 1. lying, mendacious. 2. full of errors or misprints. 3. false, deceptive. —*m., f.* liar.
mentís, *m.* complete refutation (of a statement), flat denial; **dar un m. a,** to give the lie to.
mentol, *m.* (pharm.) menthol.
mentolado, da, *a.* mentholated.
mentón, *m.* (anat.) chin.
mentor, *m.* mentor, counselor; guide.
menú, (*pl.* **menúes**), *m.* menu, bill of fare.
menudamente, *adv.* 1. minutely. 2. in detail, in particulars.
menudear, *tr.v.* 1. to do frequently or over and over. 2. (Col.) to sell retail, retail. —*i.v.* 1. to occur or happen frequently; to fall rapidly or in abundance (drops, rain); to increase (work). 2. to go into detail, tell in detail. 3. to chatter, talk trivialities.
menudencia, *f.* 1. minuteness, littleness. 2. meticulousness, minuteness. 3. trifle (thing of little value). 4. (*pl.*) pork products. 5. (*pl*) (Amer.) giblets, offal.
menudeo, *m.* 1. frequent repetition; detailed account. 2. retail. — **vender al m.,** to sell retail, retail.
menudero, ra, *m., f.* 1. retailer, retail salesman. 2. person receiving a tithe of fruits and minor products of a farm. 3. dealer in tripes, offal, giblets, etc.
menudillo, *m.* 1. fetlock joint. 2. (*pl.*) giblets, offal, tripes, etc.
menudo, da, *a.* 1. minute, small. 2. trifling, unimportant. 3. minute, meticulous. 4. small (change). 5. common, vulgar. — **a menudo,** often, frequently; **gente menuda,** small fry, children; **por menudo,** in detail; retail. —*m.* 1. (*pl.*) offal (of cattle); giblets (of fowl). 2. (*pl.*) tithe of fruits and minor products. 3. small change, coppers.
menuzo, *m.* bit, fragment, small piece.
meñique, *a.* little (finger); (coll.) tiny, small. —*m.* little finger.
meollar, *m.* (mar.) spun yarn.

meollo, *m.* 1. marrow (of bone). 2. brain, grey matter. 3. brains, grey matter, intelligence. 4. pith, essence, marrow.
meón, na, *a.* urinating frequently. —*m., f.* 1. (vulg.) person who urinates frequently. 2. (coll.) newborn baby.
meple, *m.* (bot.) maple.
meprobamato, *m.* (pharm.) meprobamate.
meque, *m.* (Cuba) slap, hit, blow dealt with the knuckles.
mequetrefe, *m.* coxcomb, jackanapes.
mequiote, *m.* (Mex.) spike of the maguey.
meramente, *adv.* merely, solely, purely, only.
merar, *tr.v.* to mix (two liquids).
merbromina, *f.* (pharm.) merbromin.
merca, *f.* (coll.) purchase.
mercachifle, *m.* pedlar, peddler, hawker; trinket seller.
mercadear, *i.v.* to trade, deal, do business.
mercader, *m.* merchant, dealer; **el M. de Venecia,** the Merchant of Venice; **m. de grueso,** wholesale dealer.
mercadera, *f.* woman shopkeeper; merchant's wife.
mercadería, *f.* 1. piece of merchandise, article, commodity. 2. (both in *sing.* and *pl.*) merchandise, goods, wares.
mercado, *m.* market, mart, market place; **estudio de los mercados,** market research; **m. abierto,** open market, free market; **m. cambiario,** foreign exchange market; **M. Común,** Common Market; **m. de dinero,** money market; **m. de futures,** futures market; **m. de materias primas,** commodities market; **m. laboral,** labor market; **m. monetario,** money market; **m. negro,** black market; **m. de valores,** stock market.
mercadotecnia, *f.* marketing.
mercaduría, *f., var. of* **mercancía.**
mercancía, *f.* 1. (both in *sing.* and *pl.*) merchandise, wares, goods. 2. piece of merchandise, article, commodity. 3. trade, commerce.
mercante, *a.* merchant, mercantile, commercial; **la marina m.,** the merchant marine. —*m.* merchant, trader, dealer.
mercantil, *a.* mercantile, commercial, pertaining to commerce; **agencia m.,** mercantile agency; **derecho m.,** mercantile law; **sistema m.,** mercantile system.
mercantilice, mercantilicé, *ref.* **mercantilizar.**
mercantilismo, *m.* mercantilism, commercialism.
mercantilista, *a.* 1. mercantilist, supporting mercantilism. 2. expert in mercantile law. —*m., f.* 1. mercantilist, advocate of mercantilism. 2. expert in mercantile law.
mercantilizar, (*ref.* 53) *tr.v.* to commercialize; to encourage or promote trade in.
mercantilmente, *adv.* commercially.
mercantivo, va, *a., var. of* **mercantil.**
mercaptán, *m.* (chem.) mercaptan.
mercar, (*ref.* 50) *tr.v.* to buy, purchase.
merced, *f.* 1. mercy, will, pleasure, e.g. *estar a* (*la*) *m. de,* to be at the mercy of. 2. favor, help, grace, good turn. 3. grant, gift, perquisite. 4. worship, grace (courteous appellation), e.g. *Su* or *Vuestra M.,* Your Worship or Grace. 5. (Rel.) Order of Our Lady of Mercy. — **a m. or a mercedes,** without pay, unpaid, voluntarily; **m. de agua,** free distribution of water; **m.** or **muchas mercedes,** thanks, many thanks; **m. a,** thanks to.
mercenario, ria, *a.* 1. mercenary (soldier); hired (worker). 2. mercenary, venal, eager for gain. 3. (Rel.) of the Order of Our Lady of Mercy. —*m.* 1. mercenary (soldier). 2. farm worker; hired laborer. 3. (Rel.) Mercedarian.
mercería, *f.* notions, small wares; notions store, dry-goods store.
mercerice, mercericé, *ref.* **mercerizar.**
mercerizar, (*ref.* 53) *tr.v.* (tex.) to mercerize.
mercero, *m.* haberdasher, mercer, notions dealer or seller.
merchante, *a.* merchant (as *a.*). —*m.* merchant, trader, jobber.
mercurial, *a.* 1. mercurial, pertaining to mercury (the metal). 2. Mercurial, pertaining to Mercury (planet and god). —*m.* 1. (med.) mercurial. 2. (bot.) herb mercury.
mercurialismo, *m.* (med.) mercurialism.
mercúrico, ca, *a.* (chem.) mercuric.
mercurio, *m.* 1. (chem.) mercury. 2. (astron., myth.) **M.,** Mercury. — **m. dulce,** calomel.
mercurioso, sa, *a.* (chem.) mercurous.
mercurocromo, *m.* (chem.) Mercurochrome.
merdellón, na, *m., f.* (coll.) slovenly servant.
merecedor, ra, *a.* deserving, worthy (of reward, punishment, censure).
merecer, (*ref.* 45) *tr.v.* 1. to deserve, merit, warrant. 2. to earn, obtain, get. 3. to be worth. — **m.** + *inf.,* to deserve to + *inf.* —*i.v.* to deserve, be deserving. — **m. bien de uno,** to deserve one's gratitude.
merecidamente, *adv.* deservedly, justly.
merecido, da, *past part. of* **merecer.** —*a.* deserved. —*m.* just deserts or punishment.
merecimiento, *m.* merit, worth; claim to commendation.
merendar, (*ref.* 29) *i.v.* to have a snack, a collation, tea or refreshments. —*tr.v.* to have at tea-time or as a snack, e.g. *vamos a m. jamón,* we are going to have ham at tea or snack-time.
merendero, *m.* 1. lunchroom, snack bar, café, tea garden. 2. (coll.) arbor, pergola. 3. picnic grounds.
merendilla, *f. dim. of* **merienda,** light snack or tea, light lunch.
merendona, *f.* (fig.) high tea, elaborate collation, large snack.
merengar, (*ref.* 51) *tr.v.* to whip (cream, milk).
merengue, *m.* 1. (cul.) meringue. 2. (mus.) merengue, the national popular dance of the Dominican Republic and Haiti. 3. (coll.) slender or delicate person.
meretricio, cia, *a.* meretricious, pertaining to prostitutes.
meretriz, (*pl.* **meretrices**), *f.* prostitute, harlot, whore.
merey, *m.* (bot.) cashew tree.
merezca, merezco, *ref.* **merecer.**
mergánsar, *m., var. of* **mergo.**
mergo, *m.* (ornith.) merganser, cormorant.
meridiana, *f.* 1. couch, chaise longue, divan. 2. afternoon nap.
meridiano, na, *a.* meridian, midday, noon. —*m.* (math., geog., astron.) **meridian; primer m.,** (geog.) prime meridian.
meridional, *a.* southern, meridional; **América M.,** South America; **Europa M.,** Southern Europe; **temperamento m.,** Southern temperament. —*m., f.* southerner.
merienda, *f.* snack, light meal; tea, lunch. — **m. de negros,** (coll.) bedlam, confusion, disorder; **juntar meriendas,** (coll.) to join forces.
meriende, meriendo, *ref.* **merendar.**
merindad, *f.* 1. jurisdiction and post of a district judge. 2. district whose interests were looked after by township within that territory.
merino, na, *a.* merino (sheep). —*m., f.* merino (sheep). —*m.* 1. merino sheep, wool, cloth. 2. shepherd who tends merino sheep. 3. (obs.) a certain district judge in some Spanish towns.
meristema, *f.* (bot.) meristem.
meristemático, ca, *a.* (bot.) meristematic.
merístico, ca, *a.* (bot.) meristic.
méritamente, *adv., var. of* **merecidamente.**
meritísimo, ma, *a.* highly deserving, most worthy.
mérito, *m.* merit; worth, value. — **cuadro de m.,** roll of honor; **de m.,** notable, worthy; **hacer m. de,** to mention, make mention of; **hacer méritos de,** to try to distinguish oneself by exemplary service or conduct; **méritos del proceso,** (law) merits of the case.
meritoriamente, *adv.* meritoriously, deservingly, worthily.
meritorio, ria, *a.* meritorious, worthy, deserving. —*m.* probationer, learner (without pay).
merla, *f.* (ornith.) merle, blackbird.
merláchico, ca, *a.* (Mex.) pale, sick.
merleta, *f.* (her.) martlet, merlette.
merlín, *m.* 1. (mar.) marline. 2. **M., Merlin,** magician. — **saber más que M.,** to be very sharp or keen.
merlo, *m.* (ichth.) black wrasse, **marine fish.**
merlón, *m.* (fort.) merlon.
merluza, *f.* 1. (ichth.) hake. 2. (coll.) drunken bout, drunk.
merma, *f.* decrease, reduction, diminution, shrinkage.
mermador, ra, *a.* decreasing, diminishing, reducing; leaking, wasting, shrinking; consuming.
mermar, *i.v., r.v.* to diminish, reduce, lessen, dwindle. —*tr.v.* to reduce, lessen.
mermelada, *f.* jam; marmalade.
mero, *m.* (ichth.) grouper, hind; sea bass.
mero, ra, *a.* 1. mere, pure, simple, unadorned. 2. (Guat., Col., Mex.) very, right, e.g. *se cayó en la mera esquina,* he fell right on the corner or on the very corner. 3. (Col., Ven.) only, e.g. *sacaron una mera cosa,* they took one thing only. 4. (Mex.) very, exact, e.g. *llegó en el mero momento,* he arrived at that very moment. —*adv.* (Guat., Mex.) soon; almost, nearly.
meroblástico, ca, *a.* (biol.) meroblastic.
merocrino, na, *a.* (physiol.) merocrine.
merodeador, ra, *a.* marauding, plundering. —*m., f.* marauder, plunderer.
merodear, *i.v.* (mil.) to maraud, pillage, sack, loot, plunder.
merodeo, *m.* marauding, plundering.
merodista, *m., f.* marauder, pillager, plunderer.
merovingio, gia, *a., m., f.* (hist.) Merovingian, pertaining to the dynasty of the first kings of France.
merque, merqué, *ref. of* **mercar.**
merquén, *m.* (Chile) condiment of chili and salt.
mes, *m.* 1. month. 2. menses. 3. month's pay. — **mes anomalístico,** (astron.) anomalistic month; **mes lunar periódico,** (astron.) sidereal month; **mes lunar sinódico,** (astron.) nodical month; **mes mayor,** the final month of pregnancy; **meses mayores,** the last few months of pregnancy; (amongst farmers) the months approaching haverst time.
mesa, *f.* 1. table. 2. food, fare, table. 3. board, directing board or body. 4. meseta, tableland, plateau; landing (of a staircase). 5. face, principal facet (of a gem); face, flat side (of a blade). 6. duties entrusted to one officer or official, e.g. *Juan tiene la m. de infantería,* John is in charge of infantry affairs. 7. game (e.g. of billiards); charge for game. 8. (ecc.) host, communion bread and wine. 9. total income (of churches, religious orders, etc.). 10. (bkb.) side frame or board of a bookbinding machine. — **alzar la m.,** to clear the table; **a m. puesta,** without trouble or worries, without cost or expense; **conversación de sobre m.,** after-dinner talk; **estar a m. y**

mantel de otro, to live off someone or at another's expense; **levantar la m.,** to clear the table; **levantarse de la m.,** to leave the table, rise from the table; **m. auxiliar,** side table; **m. de altar,** altar; **m. de batalla,** post office sorting table; **m. de billar,** billiard table; **m. de cambios,** commercial bank; **m. de centro,** coffee table; **m. de dibujo,** drawing board; **m. de guarnición,** (mar.) channel; **m. de juego,** gambling or gaming table; **m. de lavar,** (min.) sluice box; **m. de milanos,** (coll.) scanty fare; **m. de navegación,** (aer.) plotting board; **m. de noche,** bedside table, night table; **m. franca,** open table (for any guest that might arrive); **m. gallega,** (coll.) frugal table; **m. giratoria,** turntable; swivel table; rotary table; **m. nido,** nest of tables; **m. operatoria** or **de operaciones,** operating table; **m. redonda,** round table (i.e. for discussions); table d'hote, ordinary, common table for guests at inn (serving set meal at set time); **m. rodante,** tea trolley; **m. traviesa,** high table (occupied by superiors of a community, convent, etc.); **m. trazadora,** (mil.) plotting board; **poner la m.,** to set or lay the table; **sentarse a la mesa,** to sit at the table; **sobre m.,** after-dinner talk.

mesada, *f.* monthly pay or allowance, stipend.

mesadura, *f.* the act of tearing one's hair (in anguish or despair).

mesalina, *f.* (fig.) dissolute woman.

mesana, *f.* (mar.) mizzen mast or sail.

mesar, *tr.v., r.v.* to tear or pull (one's hair or beard).

mescal, *m.* 1. (bot.) mescal. 2. (Mex.) mescal, liquor made from the maguey plant.

mescalina, *f.* (chem.) mescaline.

mescolanza, *f.* (coll.) mixture, hodgepodge, jumble.

mesdado, da, *a.* mixed, mingled, motley.

meseguería, *f.* harvest watch; amount paid for harvest watch.

meseguero, ra, *a.* pertaining to the harvest. —*m.* harvest watchman.

mesembriantemo, *m.* (bot.) mesembryanthemum.

mesencefálico, ca, *a.* (anat.) mesencephalic.

mesencéfalo, *m.* (anat.) mesencephalon.

mesénquima, *m.* (biol.) mesenchyme.

mesenquimatoso, sa, *a.* (biol.) mesenchymal, mesenchymatous.

mesentérico, ca, *a.* (anat.) mesenteric.

mesenterio, *m.* (anat.) mesentery.

mesenteritis, *f.* (med.) mesenteritis.

mesenterón, *m.* (zool.) mesenteron.

meseraico, ca, *a.* (anat.) mesenteric.

mesero, *m.* 1. worker receiving monthly wages with board. 2. (Mex.) waiter (in a restaurant).

meseta, *f.* staircase landing; meseta, plateau, tableland.

mesiánico, ca, *a.* Messianic, pertaining to the Messiah.

mesianismo, *m.* Messianism, belief in the Messiah.

Mesías, *m.* Messiah; **esperar uno al Mesías,** to wait for a person who has already arrived.

mesidor, *m.* Messidor (tenth month of the French Revolutionary Calendar).

mesilla, *f.* 1. landing (of staircase). 2. window sill, tile on window sill or balustrade. 3. bedside table, night table. 4. mild reproof.

mesillo, *m.* first menses after childbirth.

mesita, *f. dim. of* **mesa,** small table.

mesitileno, *m.* (chem.) mesitylene.

mesmedad, *f.* (coll.) **por su propia m.,** all by itself, without outside help, under its own power; by the very fact.

mesmeriano, na, *a.* mesmeric, mesmerian. —*m., f.* mesmerite, mesmerian.

mesmerismo, *m.* mesmerism, doctrine of animal magnetism.

mesmerista, *a.* mesmeric. —*m., f.* mesmerist, mesmerizer.

mesmo, ma, *a., var. of* **mismo,** same, similar.

mesnada, *f.* 1. company of soldiers, armed retinue (serving under a king or knight). 2. (fig.) gathering, body, group.

mesnadería, *f.* pay of a soldier at arms as member of a king's armed retinue.

mesnadero, *m.* soldier at arms, member of a king's armed retinue.

mesoblástico, ca, *a.* (physiol.) mesoblastic.

mesoblasto, *m.* (zool.) mesoblast.

mesocarpio, *m.* (bot.) mesocarp.

mesocefálico, ca, *a.* (anat., anth.) mesocephalic.

mesocéfalo, la, *a.* (anth.) mesocephalic. —*m.* (anat.) mesencephalon.

mesocracia, *f.* 1. mesocracy, government by the middle class. 2. the bourgeoisie.

mesodérmico, ca, *a.* (biol.) mesodermal.

mesodermo, *m.* (anat.) mesoderm.

mesofilo, *m.* (bot.) mesophyll.

mesófito, *m.* (bot.) mesophyte.

mesogástrico, ca, *a.* (biol.) mesogastric.

mesogastrio, *m.* (anat.) mesogastrium.

mesoglea, *f.* (zool.) mesoglea, mesogloea.

mesognático, ca, *a.* (anth.) mesognathous, mesognathic.

mesolítico, ca, *a.* (geol.) Mesolithic.

mesología, *f.* (biol.) mesology.

mesomería, *f.* (chem.) mesomerism.

mesómero, *m.* (biol.) mesomere.

mesomorfo, fa, *a.* (anth.) mesomorphic. —*m.* (anth.) mesomorph.

mesón, *m.* 1. inn, hostelry, tavern. 2. (Chile) shop counter. 3. (phys.) meson, mesotron. — **estar una casa como m.** or **parecer un m.,** to be crowded to the roof.

mesonaje, *m.* quarter or street having many inns or taverns.

mesonefros, *m.* (*pl.*) (biol.) mesonephros.

mesonero, ra, *a.* inn (as *a.*). —*m., f.* innkeeper; landlord, landlady; host, hostess.

mesónico, ca, *a.* (phys.) mesonic.

mesonista, *a.* pertaining to an inn.

mesopotámico, ca, *a., m., f.* Mesopotamian.

mesosfera, *f.* mesosphere.

mesotélico, ca, *a.* (biol.) mesothelial.

mesotelio, *m.* (biol.) mesothelium.

mesotorácico, ca, *a.* (ento.) mesothoracic.

mesotórax, *m.* 1. (anat.) mid-chest, mid-thorax. 2. (ento.) mesothorax.

mesotorio, *m.* (chem.) mesothorium.

mesotrón, *m.* (phys.) mesotron, meson.

mesozoico, ca, *a., m.* (geol.) Mesozoic.

mesta, *f.* 1. association and meeting of cattle breeders. 2. (*pl.*) confluence (of streams).

mestal, *m.* grove or copse of bastard cork oaks; thicket, growth of shrubs.

mesteño, ña, *a.* 1. stray (animals). 2. wild, untamed, e.g. *caballo m.,* mustang.

mester, *m.* (arch.) trade, craft; **m. de clerecía,** (lit.) clerical verse form (used in Spain in the Middle Ages); **m. de juglaria,** (lit.) verse of troubadours or minstrels.

mestice, mesticé, *ref.* **mestizar.**

mesticia, *f.* (arch.) sadness.

mestizaje, *m.* (Amer.) crossbreeding, crossing to the white and Indian races.

mestizar, (*ref. 53*) *tr.v.* to crossbreed, to mix the races.

mestizo, za, *a.* crossbred, mongrel, hybrid. —*m., f.* 1. half-breed, mestizo; hybrid, mongrel. 2. (Col.) bran bread; whole meal bread.

mesto, *m.* 1. (bot.) bastard cork oak (hybrid between oak and cork oak). 2. (bot.) Turkey oak (Quercus cerris). 3. (bot.) buckthorn.

mestura, *f.* mashlin, mixed wheat and rye.

mesura, *f.* 1. seriousness, sedateness; calm, composure. 2. politeness, civility, respect. 3. moderation, restraint, control.

mesuradamente, *adv.* prudently, sensibly, calmly, with restraint or control.

mesurado, da, *past part. of* **mesurar.** —*a.* moderate, controlled, restrained; circumspect, prudent, sensible.

mesurar, *tr.v.* to moderate, make moderate. —*r.v.* to control oneself, act with restraint or moderation.

meta, *f.* 1. goal, object, aim (of desires). 2. finish (of a race). 3. goal (place where goalkeeper stands in football); (Amer.) goalkeeper. 4. (hist.) meta (in Roman arena).

metabólico, ca, *a.* (biol., physiol.) metabolic.

metabolismo, *m.* metabolism; **m. basal,** (biol.) basal metabolism.

metabolito, *m.* (physiol.) metabolite.

metábolo, la, *a.* (ento.) metabolic.

metacarpiano, *a., m.* (anat.) metacarpal.

metacarpo, *m.* (anat.) metacarpus.

metacéntrico, ca, *a.* (phys.) metacentric.

metacentro, *m.* (phys.) metacenter, metacentre.

metaclasa, *f.* (geol.) metaclase, rock showing cleavage.

metacrilato, *m.* (chem.) methacrylate.

metacrílico, ca, *a.* (chem.) methacrylic.

metacromatismo, *m.* (physiol., chem.) metachromatism.

metacronismo, *m.* metachronism, mistake in dating an event.

metadona, *f.* (pharm.) methadone, methadon.

metafase, *f.* (biol.) metaphase.

metafísica, *f.* 1. metaphysics. 2. abstract theory or talk.

metafísicamente, *adv.* metaphysically.

metafísico, ca, *a.* 1. metaphysical. 2. (fig.) over-subtle, very abstract or obscure. —*m.* metaphysician.

metafisiquear, *i.v.* to discuss in obscure or over-subtle language.

metafonía, *f.* (phonet.) metaphony, umlaut.

metáfora, *f.* (lit., rhet.) metaphor.

metafóricamente, *adv.* metaphorically; figuratively.

metaforice, metaforicé, *ref.* **metaforizar.**

metafórico, ca, *a.* metaphorical; figurative.

metaforista, *m., f.* metaphorist.

metaforizar, (*ref. 53*) *tr.v.* to express in metaphors.

metafosfato, *m.* (chem.) metaphosphate.

metafosfórico, ca, *a.* (chem.) metaphosphoric.

metafrasis, *f.* metaphrase, interpretation of writings.

metafrasta, *m., f.* (rhet.) metaphrast.

metafrástico, ca, *a.* (rhet.) metaphrastic.

metagénesis, *f.* (biol.) metagenesis.

metagenético, ca, *a.* (biol.) metagenetic.

metagoge, *f.* (rhet.) a kind of metaphor.

metahemoglobina, *f.* (biochem.) metahemoglobin.

metal, *m.* 1. metal. 2. brass. 3. timbre, tone (of voice). 4. quality, nature, condition. 5. (her.) metal. 6. (mus.) (*pl*) brass. — **acostarse el m.,** (min.) to change abruptly in level or direction (vein of ore); **m. amarillo,** brass; **m. babbitt** or **antifricción,** Babbitt metal; **m. blanco,** white metal; **m. campanil,** bell metal; **m. de imprenta,** type metal; **m. delta,** delta metal; **m. duro,** hard metal, hard bronze, bell metal; **m. en lámina,** sheet metal; **m. machacado,** native gold

and silver found in layers between rocks; **m. monel,** Monel metal; **m. precioso,** precious metal; **vil m.,** filthy lucre.
metalada, *f.* (Chile, min.) metal contained in a vein.
metalado, da, *a.* (fig.) mixed, impure.
metalario, ria, *m, f.* metal worker; metallist.
metalepsis, *f.* (rhet.) metalepsis.
metalero, ra, *a.* (Chile) pertaining to metal. —*m.* metalworker.
metálica, *f.* metallurgy.
metalice, metalicé, *ref.* **metalizar.**
metálico, ca, *a.* 1. metallic. 2. of medals, e.g. *historia metálica,* history of medals. —*m.* 1. metal worker. 2. coin, currency, bullion, specie, cash; **m. en caja,** (com.) cash on hand; **pagar en m.,** to pay in hard cash.
metalífero, ra, *a.* metal-bearing, metalliferous.
metalina, *f.* (chem.) metaline (alloy).
metalista, *m., f.* metal worker.
metalistería, *f.* metal work, metalworking.
metalización, *f.* (chem.) metalization; converting into metal.
metalizar, (*ref.* 53) *tr.v.* (chem.) to metalize, metallize. —*r.v.* 1. to become metalized. 2. (fig.) to become obsessed with love of money, become mercenary.
metalla, *f.* particles of gold used by gilders to remedy defects.
metalografía, *f.* metallography, the study of metals.
metalográfico, ca, *a.* metallographic.
metalógrafo, *m.* metallographer.
metaloide, *m.* (chem.) metalloid.
metaloideo, a, *a.* (chem.) metalloid, metalloidal, nonmetallic.
metaloterapia, *f.* (med.) metallotherapy.
metalurgia, *f.* metallurgy.
metalúrgico, ca, *a.* metallurgical. —*m., f.* metallurgist.
metalurgista, *m., f.* metallurgist.
metámera, *f.* (zool.) metamere.
metamería, *f.* (chem., zool.) metamerism.
metamérico, ca, *a.* (zool., chem.) metameric.
metamerismo, *m.* (chem., zool.) metamerism.
metamerizado, da, *a.* (zool.) metamerized.
metámero, ra, *a.* (chem., zool.) metameric. —*m.* (zool.) metamere.
metamórfico, ca, *a.* (geol.) metamorphic.
metamorfismo, *m.* (geol.) metamorphism.
metamorfoseado, da, *a.* (geol.) metamorphosed.
metamorfosear, *tr.v., r.v.* to metamorphose, to transform.
metamorfosi, *f., var. of* **metamorfosis.**
metamorfosis, *f.* metamorphosis, transformation.
metanefro, metanefron, *m.* (biol.) metanephros, metanephron.
metano, *m.* (chem.) methane.
metanol, *m.* (chem.) methanol.
metaplasia, *f.* (biol.) metaplasia.
metaplásico, ca, *a.* (biol.) metaplastic.
metaplasma, *f.* (biol.) metaplasm.
metaplasmo, *m.* (gram.) metaplasm.
metaproteína, *f.* (chem.) metaprotein.
metapsicología, *f.* metapsychology.
metapsíquica, *f.* (psyc.) metapsychology.
metasomático, ca, *a.* (geol.) metasomatic.
metasomatismo, *m.* (geol.) metasomatism.
metastable, *a.* (phys., chem.) metastable.
metástasis, *f.* (med.) metastasis.
metastático, ca, *a.* (med.) metastatic.
metasticizar, (*ref.* 53) *i.v.* (med.) to metastasize.
metatarsiano, *a., m.* (anat.) metatarsal.
metatarso, *m.* (anat.) metatarsus.
metate, *m.* metate, stone with a concave upper surface used in Latin America for grinding and pulping seeds, vegetables, etc.
metátesis, *f.* (philol.) metathesis.
metatice, metaticé, *ref.* **metatizar.**
metatizar, (*ref.* 53) *tr.v.* (philol.) to change the letters and sounds of (a word).
metatórax, *m.* (ento.) metathorax.
metaxilema, *m.* (bot.) metaxylem.
metazoario, a, *a.* (zool.) metazoal, metazoan, metazoic. —*m.* (zool.) metazoan.
metazoo, *m.* (zool.) metazoan.
meteco, *a.* foreign. —*m., f.* foreigner (term used in ancient Greece); newcomer, immigrant.
metedor, ra, *m., f.* smuggler. —*m.* 1. small diaper or nappy. 2. (print.) feed board.
meteduría, *f.* the act of smuggling.
metelón, na, *a.* (Mex.) meddling, nosey.
metempsicosis, metempsícosis, *f.* (philos.) metempsychosis.
metemuertos, *m.* 1. stagehand. 2. meddler, busybody.
metencefálico, ca, *a.* (anat.) metencephalic.
metencéfalo, *m.* (anat.) metencephalon.
meteorice, meteoricé, *ref.* **meteorizar.**
meteórico, ca, *a.* meteoric, pertaining to meteors.
meteorismo, *m.* (med.) meteorism.
meteorito, *m.* (astron.) meteorite.
meteorización, *f.* (agr.) effect of the elements on soil.
meteorizar, (*ref.* 53) *tr.v.* (med.) to meteorize, cause meteorism in. —*r.v.* 1. (med.) to become meteorized. 2. to be affected by the weather (soil).
meteoro, metéoro, *m.* (astron.) meteor.
meteorógrafo, *m. meteorograph.*
meteorología, *f.* meteorology, study of the weather and climate.
meteorológico, ca, *a.* meteorological.
meteorologista, *m., f.* meteorologist.
meteorólogo, *m.* meteorologist.
meter, *tr.v.* 1. to put in, put into; to insert, introduce, thrust. 2. to smuggle in, bring in illegally. 3. to start, spread (rumors); to make (noise), cause (trouble, fear, commotion, panic), e.g. *m. chismes,* to start rumors; *m. cizaña,* to sow discord; *m. líos,* to cause trouble; *m. bulla,* to make a noise; *m. alboroto,* to cause a commotion. 4. to get into, e.g. *m. en líos,* to get (someone) into trouble. 5. to play (trumps). 6. to stake (money), place (one's bet). 7. (sew.) to take in (a seam). 8. to put in (an application), to send in (a memorandum); to bring, file (a suit against someone), e.g. *m. pleito* or *juicio a,* to bring a suit against. 9. to squash together, squeeze in, e.g. *m. entre líneas,* to squeeze in between the lines (of a letter). 10. (mar.) to take in (a sail). 11. to hole (a golf ball); to pocket (a billiard ball). — **estar metido con,** to be on intimate terms with; **estar muy metido en (algo),** to be deeply involved in (something); to be dead set on (something); **m. por vereda,** to bring to heel, bring in line; **meterle miedo a,** to make afraid. —*r.v.* 1. to get into, enter (a business, profession, etc.), e.g. *se metió a monja,* she became a nun. 2. to intrude, butt in, interfere, meddle, e.g. *no te metas entre marido y mujer,* don't butt in between husband and wife. 3. to get in with, become associated or get on intimate terms with. 4. to get mixed up or entangled (in trouble, love affairs, etc.), e.g. *me metí en camisa de once varas,* I got into a lot of trouble. 5. to flow, enter, disembogue (river into sea). 6. to throw oneself (upon), attack. 7. to become, e.g. *meterse a soldado,* to become a soldier. 8. to project far (a cape into the sea). — **meterse a,** to set oneself up as, pass oneself off as; to become; **meterse a** + *inf.,* to take it upon oneself to + *inf.;* **meterse de,** (Amer.) to become; **meterse con otro,** to pick a quarrel; **meterse en sí mismo,** to think things out alone, think for oneself; **meterse en todo,** (coll.) to meddle or interfere in everything; **metérsele a uno en la cabeza,** to get it into one's head; **meterse donde no lo llaman,** to stick one's nose in where one is not wanted.
metereología, *f.* (imp. u.) *var. of* **meteorología.**
metesillas y sacamuertos, *m.* 1. (theat.) stagehand. 2. busybody.
metete, *m.* (C. Amer.) meddler, busybody.
metiche, *m.* (Mex.) meddler, busybody.
meticón, na, *a.* nosy, nosey, meddlesome. —*m., f.* nosey parker, meddlesome person.
meticulosamente, *adv.* meticulously.
meticulosidad, *f.* meticulousness, meticulosity; fear, shyness.
meticuloso, sa, *a.* meticulous, finicky. —*m., f.* meticulous person.
metidillo, *m.* infant's diaper, nappy (G.B.).
metido, da, *past part. of* **meter.** —*a.* abundant or abounding (in), rich (in), full (of), e.g. *m. en carnes,* fat, stout, *m. en harina,* full of flour, with lots of flour. 2. (Amer.) meddlesome. — **estar muy m. con,** to be on intimate terms with; **estar muy m. en,** to be deeply involved in. —*m.* 1. punch, blow, blow in the midriff. 2. material allowed in seams. 3. diaper, nappy (G.B.). 4. (coll.) lecture, reprimand.
metijón, na, *a., m., f., var. of* **meticón.**
metilal, *m.* (chem.) methylal.
metilamina, *f.* (chem.) methylamine.
metilato, *m.* (chem.) methylate.
metileno, *m.* (chem.) methylene.
metílico, ca, *a.* (chem.) methylic.
metilo, *m.* (chem.) methyl.
metimiento, *m.* 1. introduction, insertion, putting in. 2. (coll.) favor, influence.
metionina, *f.* (chem.) methionine.
metlapil, *m.* (Mex.) roller used for grinding corn in the metate or stone.
metódicamente, *adv.* methodically.
metodice, metodicé, *ref.* **metodizar.**
metódico, ca, *a.* 1. methodical. 2. subject (index).
metodismo, *m.* 1. (rel.) Methodism. 2. (med.) methodism.
metodista, *a., m., f.* (rel.) Methodist.
metodizar, (*ref.* 53) *tr.v.* to methodize, systematize, organize.
método, *m.* method, technique, manner, form, order, custom.
metodología, *f.* methodology.
metol, *m.* (chem.) metol.
metonimia, *f.* (rhet.) metonymy.
metonímico, ca, *a.* metonymical.
métopa, *f.* (archit.) metope.
metópico, ca, *a.* (anat.) metopic.
metoposcopia, *f.* metoposcopy; reading the future by the lines on the face.
metoxiclor, *m.* (chem.) methoxychlor.
metraje, *m.* length, meterage, footage (of a film); **película de corto m.,** short film (i.e. documentary); **película de largo m.,** feature film.
metralgia, *f.* (med.) metralgia.
metralla, *f.* 1. (artil.) grapeshot, canister shot, case shot; shrapnel. 2. scraps of iron (left out of the mold when making iron ingots).
metrallazo, *m.* discharge of grapeshot or shrapnel.
metralleta, *f.* submachine gun, tommy gun.
metraucán, *m.* 1. (Chile) swill, refuse. 2. (Chile) mixture, jumble, hodgepodge.
metreta, *f.* metretes (Greek and Roman liquid measure).
métrica, *f.* metrics (part of prosody dealing with metrical measurement and composition); metrical art, prosody, poetry.

métricamente, *adv.* (poet.) metrically.
métrico, ca, *a.* metric, metrical.
metrificación, *f.* versification, metrification (rare).
metrificador, ra, *m., f.* versifier, metrifier.
metrificar, (*ref. 50*) *tr.v.* to versify, metrify, turn into verse. —*i.v.* to versify, write verses.
metrifique, metrifiqué, *ref.* **metrificar.**
metritis, *f.* (med.) metritis.
metro, *m., abbrev. of* **metropolitano,** subway (U.S.), tube (G.B.), underground railway.
metro, *m.* 1. meter, metre (measurement). 2. rule, ruler; tape measure. 3. (poet.) meter, measure (e.g. decameter, etc.). — **m. cuadrado,** square meter; **m. cúbico,** cubic meter; **m. plegadizo, m. de trancos** folding rule or ruler.
metrógrafo, *m.* (ry.) metrograph.
metrología, *f.* metrology, the science of weights and measures.
metrón, *m.* (Chile, bot.) evening primrose (Oenothera berteriana).
metrónomo, *m.* (mus.) metronome.
metrópoli, *f.* 1. metropolis, capital. 2. mother country. 3. (ecc.) metropolis.
metropolitano, na, *a.* metropolitan. —*m.* 1. subway, underground or elevated railway. 2. (ecc.) metropolitan.
metrorragia, *f.* (med.) metrorrhagia.
metroscopio, *m.* (med.) metroscope.
metrotomía, *f.* (surg.) hysterotomy.
metrótomo, *m.* (surg.) metrotome, hysterotome.
meucar, (*ref. 50*) *i.v.* (Chile) to doze, snooze, nap.
meucón, *m.* (Chile) doze, snooze, nap.
MEV *abbrev. of* **megaelectronvoltio,** million electron volts (MEV).
mexicano, na, *a., m., f.* Mexican.
México, *m.* 1. Mexico. 2. **M., D. F.,** federal district of Mexico (the capital).
meya, *f.* (zool.) spider crab.
mezala, *m.* oratory, place for prayer.
mezcal, *m.* 1. (bot.) mescal (a variety of cactus). 2. mescal (alcoholic drink made of the maguey (plant). 3. prepared fiber of the maguey for making hemp cord or rope.
mezcla, *f.* 1. mixture, compound. 2. tweed, cloth woven with varicolored threads. 3. (bldg.) mortar. — **m. en frío,** (bldg.) cold mix.
mezclable, *a.* mixable.
mezcladamente, *adv.* in a mixture; higgledy-piggledy, confusedly.
mezclado, da, *a.* mixed; medley; miscellaneous. —*m.* (arch.) tweed, cloth made with different color threads.
mezclador, ra, *a.* mixing, blending. —*m., f.* mixing machine, blender, agitator. —*f.* (bldg.) cement mixer; **m. por lotes,** batch mixer.
mezcladura, *f.* mixture.
mezclamiento, *m.* mixture, mix.
mezclar, *tr.v.* to mix; to blend, unite. —*r.v.* 1. to mix, to mingle. 2. to intermarry. 3. to meddle, become involved (in).
mezclilla, *f.* (tex.) tweed, cloth of varicolored threads.
mezcolanza, *f.* (coll.) mixture, hodgepodge, jumble, mishmash.
mezereón, *m.* (bot.) mezereon.
mezo, meza, *ref.* **mecer.**
mezquinamente, *adv.* meanly, stingily.
mezquinar, *i.v.* (Amer.) to be mean or stingy, skimp.
mezquindad, *f.* 1. meanness, stinginess. 2. poverty, indigence, neediness.
mezquino, na, *a.* 1. mean, stingy, niggardly. 2. poor, needy. 3. small, tiny, puny. 4. wretched, unfortunate. —*m.* (Mex.) wart.
mezquita, *f.* mosque, Moslem temple.
mezquital, *m.* clump of mesquite shrubs.
mezquite, *m.* (bot.) mesquite.
mg. *abbrev. of* **miligramo,** milligram (mg).
Mg *sym. of* **magnesio,** magnesium (Mg).
mho, *m.* (elec.) mho, conductance unit.
mi, *m.* (mus.) mi, E, third note of the scale.
mí, *pers. pron.* (used only as object of prepositions) me. —*reflex. pron.,* myself; **a mí,** to me.
mi, mis, *pos. a.* my, e.g. *mi casa,* my house, *mis hijas,* my daughters, *mis libros,* my books.
mía, *f.* (hist.) Moroccan troops at the service of Spain in Morocco.
miador, ra, *a.* that which miaows a lot.
miaja, *f.* crumb, bit, morsel.
mialgia, *f.* (med.) myalgia.
mialmas, como unas m., (coll.) with the greatest of pleasure.
miar, *i.v.* to miaow, mew.
miasma, *m.* miasma.
miasmático, ca, *a.* miasmatic; unwholesome.
miastenia, *f.* (med.) myasthenia.
miasténico, ca, *a.* (med.) myasthenic.
miau, *m.* miaow (of a cat.).
mica, *f.* 1. (zool.) female long-tailed monkey. 2. (Guat.) coquette, flirtatious woman. 3. (min.) mica. — **m. rubia,** brown mica.
micáceo, a, *a.* (min.) micaceous.
micacita, *f.* (min.) mica schist.
micado, *m.* (hist.) Mikado, emperor of Japan.
micasquisto, *m.* (min.) mica schist.
micción, *f.* (med.) micturition, urination.
micela, *f.* (biol., chem.) micelle.
micelial, *a.* (bot.) mycelial, mycelian.
micélico, ca, *a.* (bot.) mycelial, mycelian.
micelio, *m.* (bot.) mycelium.
micelioide, *a.* (bot.) mycelioid.
Micenas, *f.* (hist.) Mycenae, ancient city in Argolis.
micénico, ca, *a.* (hist.) Mycenaean.
micer, *m.* ancient title of respect (in certain regions of Spain).
micetófago, ga, *a.* (biol.) mycetophagous.
micetoma, *m.* (med.) mycetoma.
michi, *m.* 1. (Peru) bow tie. 2. here, kitty . . . (in calling a cat).
michino, na, *m., f.* kitty, pussycat.
michito, *m. dim. of* **micho,** kitten, pussycat.
micho, cha, *m., f.* (coll.) cat, pussy.
mico, *m.* 1. mico, long-tailed monkey. 2. (coll.) roué, rake, lecher. — **m. capuchino,** (Col.) capuchin monkey; **dar** or **hacer m.,** to miss an appointment or date, not to keep a date or appointment; **dejar a uno hecho un m.,** to make a monkey out of one, make one look ridiculous; **quedarse hecho un m.,** to be made a monkey out of, be made to look ridiculous.
micobacteria, *f.* (bac.) mycobacterium.
micoderma, *f.* (bac.) mycoderma, mycoderm.
micología, *f.* (bot.) mycology, the study of fungi.
micológico, ca, *a.* (bot.) mycologic.
micólogo, ga, *m., f.* mycologist.
micorriza, *f.* (bot.) mycorrhiza.
micosis, *f.* (med.) mycosis.
micótico, ca, *a.* (med.) mycotic.
micra, *f.* micron; one thousandth of a millimeter.
micro, *m.* 1. (tel.) mike, microphone. 2. (Chile) bus.
microanálisis, *f.* (chem.) microanalysis.
microbarógrafo, *m.* microbarograph, an instrument for measuring very small changes in atmospheric pressure.
microbiano, na, *a., var. of* **micróbico.**
microbicida, *a.* microbicidal. —*m.* microbicide, germ-killer.
micróbico, ca, *a.* microbic, microbial.
microbio, *m.* microbe.
microbiología, *f.* microbiology, the study of microscopic organisms.
microbiológico, ca, *a.* microbiological.
microbiólogo, *m.* microbiologist.
microbús, *m.* microbus.
microcefalia, *f.* microcephalia, microcephaly.
microcéfalo, la, *a.* microcephalic, microcephalous; small-headed.
microcito, *m.* (anat.) microcyte.
microclima, *m.* (biol.) microclimate.
microclimatología, *f.* (med.) microclimatology
microclino, *m.* (min.) microcline.
micrococo, *m.* (bac.) micrococcus.
microcopia, *f.* microcopy, microcard, microprint.
microcósmico, ca, *a.* microcosmic, microcosmical.
microcosmo, *m.* (philos.) microcosm.
microcristal, *m.* (geol.) microcrystal, microlite.
microcristalino, na, *a.* (geol.) microcrystalline.
microcristalografía, *f.* microcrystallography.
microcurie, *m.* (phys.) microcurie.
microestructura, *f.* microstructure.
micrófago, *m.* (physiol.) microphage.
microfarad, microfaradio, *m.* (phys.) microfarad.
microfilaria, *f.* (zool.) microfilaria.
microfilm, microfilme, *m.* microfilm.
microfilmar, *tr.v.* to microfilm.
microfísica, *f.* microphysics.
microfítico, ca, *a.* (bot.) microphytic.
micrófito, *m.* (bot.) microphyte.
micrófono, *m.* microphone; **m. electroestático,** condenser microphone.
microfoto, *f.* microphotograph.
microfotografía, *f.* microphotography; microphotograph.
microfotográfico, ca, *a.* microphotographic.
microgameto, *m.* (biol.) microgamete.
micrografía, *f.* micrography, the study or description of microscopic objects.
micrográfico, ca, *a.* micrographic.
micrógrafo, *m.* micrographer, micrographist.
micrógramo, *m.* microgram, one millionth of a gram.
microhmio, *m.* (elec.) microhm.
microinterruptor, *m.* (elec.) microswitch.
microlítico, ca, *a.* (geol.) microlithic.
microlito, *m.* (geol.) microlite.
micromanipulador, *m.* (biol.) micromanipulator.
micrómero, *m.* (biol.) micromere.
micrometría, *f.* micrometry, measuring with a micrometer.
micrométrico, ca, *a.* micrometrical.
micrómetro, *m.* micrometer, an instrument for measuring very small distances (used under a microscope or telescope).
micromicrón, *m.* (med.) micromicron.
micrón, *m.* micron; one thousandth of a millimeter.
Micronesia, *f.* (geog.) **la M.,** Micronesia.
micronesio, a, *a.* Micronesian, of or pertaining to Micronesia. —*m., f.* Micronesian.
micronúcleo, *m.* (zool.) micronucleus.
microonda, *f.* (phys.) microwave.
microorganismo, *m.* (biol.) microorganism.
micropaleontología, *f.* micropaleontology.
microparásito, *m.* (med.) microparasite.
micropelícula, *f.* microfilm.
micropilar, *a.* (bot., zool.) micropylar.
micrópilo, *m.* (bot., zool.) micropyle.
micropirómetro, *m.* (phys.) micropyrometer.
microplaquita, *m.* computer chip.
microquímica, *f.* microchemistry.
microorganismo, *m.* (biol.) microorganism.
microrradiografía, *f.* microradiograph, an X-ray plate showing very small details.

microscopía, *f.* microscopy.
microscópico, ca, *a.* microscopic.
microscopio, *m.* microscope; **m. de comparación,** comparison microscope; **m. electrónico,** electron microscope; **m. estereoscópico,** stereomicroscope.
microscopista, *m.* microscopist.
microsegundo, *m.* microsecond.
microsísmico, ca, *a.* (geol.) microseismic, microseismical.
microsismo, *m.* (geol.) microseism.
microsismógrafo, *m.* microseismograph, microseismometer.
microsoma, *m.* (biol.) microsome.
microspora, *f.* (bot.) microspore.
microsporangio, *m.* (bot.) microsporangium.
microsporofilo, *m.* (bot.) microsporophyll.
micróstomo, ma, *a.* (zool.) microstomatous, microstomous.
microsurco, *m.* 1. microgroove. 2. long play, long-playing record.
microtomía, *f.* microtomy; preparation of thin slices for microscopic studies.
micrótomo, *m.* microtome, instrument for cutting tissue into thin slices, prior to microscopic examination.
microvoltio, *m.* (elec., rad.) microvolt.
micuré. *m.* (zool.) (kind of) opossum.
mida, *f.* (ento.) plant louse; bean fly.
mida, mido, *ref.* **medir.**
Midas, *m.* (myth.) Midas, king of Phrygia who had the power to turn all he touched into gold; (fig.) one who has a golden touch, person who succeeds in every endeavor.
midiera, midiese, midió, *ref.* **medir.**
midríasis, *f.* (med.) mydriasis.
midriático, ca, *a., m.* (med.) mydriatic.
mieditis, *f.* (coll.) fear.
miedo, *m.* fear, dread, apprehension; **dar m., meter m.,** to frighten, make afraid; **m. cerval,** dreadful fear, intense fear; **morirse de m.,** to be quaking with fear; **mucho m. y poca vergüenza,** shame on you, you ought to be ashamed of yourself!; **tener m. (a),** to be afraid (of).
miedoso, sa, *a.* cowardly, timorous. *—m., f.* coward.
miel, *f.* 1. honey. 2. treacle, molasses (G.B.), syrup (U.S.). **— dejar a uno con la m. en los labios,** to stop one's fun; **luna de m.,** honeymoon; **m. de caña,** sugar cane syrup, molasses, treacle; **m. rosada,** (pharm.) honey of rose; **m. silvestre,** wild honey; **m. virgen,** virgin honey; **m. sobre hojuelas,** (coll.) it's a delicious combination, nothing could be better; **no hay m. sin hiel,** life can't be all peaches and cream; **quedarse uno a media m.,** (coll.) to be stopped in the middle of one's enjoyment; to catch only half of what is being said.
miele, mielo, *ref.* **melar.**
mielencéfalo, *m.* (anat.) myelencephalon.
mielga, *f.* 1. (agr.) plot of ground marked for sowing. 2. (agr.) winnowing fork. 3. (bot.) alfalfa, medic, lucerne. 4. (ichth.) spiny dogfish.
mielgo, ga, *a., m., f.* twin.
mielina, *f.* (anat.) myelin.
mielítico, ca, *a.* (med.) myelitic.
mielitis, *f.* (med.) myelitis.
mielógeno, na, *a.* (med.) myelogenous, myelogenic.
mieloide, *a.* (anat.) myeloid.
mieloma, *m.* (med.) myeloma.
miembro, *m.* 1. (anat.) member, limb; penis. 2. member (of a group, society, etc.). 3. part, member. 4. (archit., math.) member. **— m. viril,** (anat.) penis, virile member.
mienta, *f.* (bot.) mint.
miente, *f.* (*gen. pl.*) mind, thought; **caer en m.** or **en las mientes,** to come to mind; **parar** or **poner mientes en (una cosa),** to consider, meditate on, ponder; **pasar por las m.,** to cross one's mind; **traer (una cosa) a las mientes,** to bring to mind, make remember; **venírsele (a uno una cosa) a las mientes,** to occur to one, come to mind.
miento, *ref.* **mentir; mentar.**
mientras, *conj.* while, whilst, when. *—adv.* when, meanwhile. **— m. más mejor,** the more the better; **m. tanto,** in the meanwhile, meanwhile, meantime.
miera, *f.* juniper oil; pine turpentine.
miércoles, *m.* Wednesday; **m. de ceniza, m. corvillo,** (rel.) Ash Wednesday.
mierda, *f.* (vulg.) shit (vulg.); excrement, faeces; filth, dirt; **mandar a la m.,** (vulg.) to send to hell.
mierra, *f.* sled, sledge, drag (vehicle for dragging loads).
mies, *f.* 1. grain, cereal. 2. harvest time; harvest. 3. (fig.) crop, harvest. 4. (*pl.*) grain fields.
miga, *f.* 1. crumb (of soft part of bread). 2. bit, part, fragment. 3. (fig.) meat, pith, marrow, substance. 4. (*pl.*) fried breadcrumbs. **— hacer buenas migas con,** (coll.) to get along well with, to hit it off with; **hacer malas migas con,** to get along badly with; **no ser** or **no estar para dar migas a un gato,** to be completely incompetent or useless.
migaja, *f.* 1. crumb. 2. bit, fragment. 3. nothing, next to nothing. 4. (*pl.*) crumbs, leavings. **— reparar en migajas,** to quibble about trifles.
migajada, *f.* bit, fragment, portion.
migajica, illa, ita, *f. dim. of* **migaja,** little bit.
migajón, *m.* 1. crumb. 2. (fig.) meat, pith, marrow, substance. 3. (Chile) tread or embryo (of egg).
migar, (*ref. 51*) *tr.v.* 1. to crumb, break into crumbs. 2. to put crumbs into.
migración, *f.* migration.
migraña, *f.* migraine, headache.
migratorio, ria, *a.* migratory, migrating.
migue, migué, *ref.* **migar.**
Miguel Angel, (art., lit., hist.) Michelangelo (Buonarroti).
miguelear, *tr.v.* (C. Amer.) to court, woo.
miguelete, *m.* (Sp.) formerly, a mountain fusilier in Catalonia; member of the Basque mountain militia.
miguero, ra, *a.* pertaining to bread crumbs or dough. **— lucero m.,** (coll.) the morning star.
mihrab, *m.* mihrab (niche in a mosque).
miiasis, miasis, *f.* (med.) myasis.
mijar, *m.* millet field.
mijo, *m.* (bot.) millet; **m. ceburro,** white wheat.
mikado, *m.* Mikado; emperor of Japan.
mil, *a., m., f.* thousand, one thousand, a thousandth, a thousandfold. **— m. veces,** a thousand times; one thousand, e.g. *el año mil,* the year one thousand; **las m. y quinientas,** the eleventh hour, the last minute, very late; **las M. y una noches,** the Arabian Nights.
miladi, *f.* milady.
milagrería, *f.* tale of miracles.
milagrero, ra, *a.* superstitious; miracle-faking; (coll.) miraculous, miracle-working.
milagro, *m.* 1. miracle; wonder, marvel. 2. votive offering. **— colgar a uno el m.,** to put the blame on someone; **hacer milagros,** to perform wonders, do miracles; **¡m.!** extraordinary!; **vivir de m.,** to just manage to keep body and soul together, scrape a living; to have escaped from a grave danger.
milagrón, *m.* (coll.) fuss, excitement, e.g. *hacer milagrones,* to make a fuss.
milagrosamente, *adv.* miraculously.
milagroso, sa, *a.* miraculous.
milamores, *f.* (bot.) red valerian.
milanés, sa, *a.* Milanese, of or pertaining to the city of Milan, Italy. *—m., f.* Milanese.
milano, *m.* 1. (ornith.) kite; (ornith.) goshawk. 2. (ichth.) flying fish. 3. burr or down of thistle.
milcao, *m.* (Chile, cul.) dish of seasoned mashed potatoes.
Milcíades, *m.* (hist.) Miltiades, Athenian general who won the battle of Marathon.
mildeu, *m.* (agr.) mildew (said esp. of grape vines).
milenario, ria, *a.* 1. millenary (pertaining to a thousand). 2. millenarian. *—m., f.* (rel.) millenarian. *—m.* millenium (thousand years; thousandth anniversary).
milenarismo, *m.* (rel.) millenarianism.
milenio, *m.* millenium (a thousand years).
mileno, na, *a.* (tex.) containing 1,000 threads in the warp.
milenrama, *f.* (bot.) yarrow, milfoil.
milenta, *m.* (coll.) thousand, one thousand.
milépora, *f.* (zool.) millepore.
milerita, *f.* (min.) millerite.
milésimo, ma, *a.* thousandth. *—f.* mill (thousandth part of a monetary unit).
milesio, sia, *a., m., f.* (hist., lit.) Milesian.
milgranar, *m.* field planted with pomegranate trees.
milhojas, *f.* (bot.) yarrow.
miliamperímetro, *m.* (phys.) milliammeter.
miliamperio, *m.* (phys.) milliampere.
miliar, *a.* 1. millet-sized, or shaped. 2. (med.) miliary. 3. milliary (e.g. a column, post, stone marking one thousand paces on the road). *—f.* (med.) miliaria.
miliario, ria, *a.* milliary, pertaining to the distance of 1,000 paces (the Roman mile).
milibar, *m.* (phys.) millibar.
milicia, *f.* 1. militia, armed forces. 2. soldiering, art of warfare. 3. military service. 4. choirs of angels. **— m. nacional,** national guard.
miliciano, na, *a.* military. *—m.* militiaman.
milico, *m.* (Amer., derog.) soldier.
milicurie, *m.* (phys.) millicurie.
milifaradio, *m.* (elec.) millifarad.
miligal, *m.* (phys.) milligal.
miligramo, *m.* milligram.
milihenrio, milihenry, *m.* (elec.) millihenry.
mililambert, *m.* (phys.) millilambert.
mililitro, *m.* milliliter, millilitre.
milímetro, *m.* millimeter, millimetre.
milimicrón, *m.* millimicron (one-thousandth of a micron or one-millionth of a millimeter).
milipulgada, *f.* mil, unit equal to one one-thousandth of an inch.
miliroentgen, *m.* (phys.) milliroentgen.
milisegundo, *m.* millisecond, one-thousandth of a second.
militante, *a.* militant; (pol.) activist.
militar, *a.* military. *—m.* soldier, army man.
militar, *i.v.* to serve in the army; to fight, struggle; to be a militant member (of a party, group, etc.), militate.
militara, *f.* (coll.) soldier's wife, widow or daughter.
militarice, militaricé, *ref.* **militarizar.**
militarismo, *m.* militarism.
militarista, *a., m., f.* militarist.
militarización, *f.* militarization.
militarizar, (*ref. 53*) *tr.v.* to militarize.
militarmente, *adv.* militarily.
mílite, *m.* soldier.

milivoltio, *m.* (elec.) millivolt.
milla, *f.* mile; **m. cuadrada,** square mile; **m. de estatuto,** statute mile; **m. náutica,** nautical mile.
millaje, *m.* mileage.
millar, *m.* 1. a thousand; (*pl.*) thousands, scores, millions (a great number). 2. about three and a half pounds of cacao. 3. land for grazing a thousand sheep or two herds of cattle. — **a millares,** by the thousand.
millarada, *f.* thousand; **a millaradas,** by the thousands; thousands of times.
millo, *m.* (bot.) millet.
millón, *m.* 1. million. 2. (*pl.*) (arch.) tax on wine, vinegar, oil, meat, soap and candles.
millonada, *f.* million.
millonario, ria, *a.* millionaire; (fig.) very wealthy. —*m., f.* millionaire; (fig.) a wealthy person.
millonésimo, ma, *a., m.* millionth.
milmillonésimo, ma, *a., m.* billionth (U.S.), thousand millionth (G.B.).
milo, *m.* earthworm.
miloca, *f.* (ornith.) species of saw-whet owl (Aegolius funeraria).
milocha, *f.* kite (child's toy).
milodonte, *m.* (paleon.) mylodont.
miloguate, *m.* (Mex.) maize stalk.
milonga, *f.* (Arg.) popular song or dance; (Arg.) family party. — **irse de m.,** (Arg.) to go out on the town, go on a spree.
milonguero, ra, *a.* fond of parties or drinking. —*m., f.* 1. person fond of parties. 2. singer or dancer of **milonga.**
milord, *m.* 1. milord, my lord. 2. low, light barouche, a four-wheeled carriage.
milpa, *f.* (C. Amer., Mex.) corn field, corn patch.
milpear, *i.v.* (Mex.) to begin sprouting (corn).
milpiés, *m.* (ento.) millipede.
milréis, *m.* milreis (Portuguese and Brazilian coin).
mimado, da, *past part. of* **mimar.** —*a.* spoiled, overindulged.
mimador, ra, *a.* pampering, doting.
mimar, *tr.v.* 1. to spoil, pamper, indulge. 2. to pet, fondle.
mimbral, *m., var. of* **mimbreral,** plantation of osiers.
mimbrar, *tr.v.* to overwhelm, humble. —*r.v.* to cower, humble oneself.
mimbre, *m., f.* 1. (bot.) osier, osier willow. 2. wicker, withe, osier, osier rod.
mimbrear, *i.v., r.v.* to bend, sway.
mimbreño, ña, *a.* osier-like, willowy.
mimbrera, *f.* 1. (bot.) osier, osier willow. 2. osiery, tract of land planted with osiers.
mimbreral, *m.* osiery, tract of land planted with osiers.
mimbrón, *m.* (bot.) osier, osier willow.
mimbroso, sa, *a.* 1. wicker; made of wicker. 2. full of osiers.
mimeografiar, (*ref.* 54) *tr.v.* to mimeograph.
mimeógrafo, *m.* mimeograph.
mimesis, *f.* 1. (rhet.) mimesis, mimicry. 2. (med.) mimesis.
mimético, ca, *a.* (biol., zool.) mimetic.
mimetismo, *m.* 1. (biol., zool.) mimicry, mimesis; protective coloration. 2. (min.) mimesis, mimetism (apparent existence of greater symmetry in crystals). 3. (fig.) automatical imitation of speech or gestures.
mímica, *f.* 1. mime (method of acting; theatrical genre). 2. imitation, mimicry.
mímico, ca, *a.* mimic; imitative (language).
mimo, *m.* 1. mimer, mime, mimic. 2. mime (kind of drama). 3. (*pl*) fondling, pampering, indulging. — **hacerle mimos a un niño,** to fondle, pamper or indulge a child.
mimógrafo, *m.* writer of mimes.
mimología, *f.* the study of mime.
mimosa, *f.* (bot.) mimosa; **m. púdica** or **vergonzosa,** mimosa, sensitive plant.
mimosamente, *adv.* fondly, affectionately, tenderly.
mimoso, sa, *a.* 1. finicky, fussy. 2. pampered, spoiled, mollycoddled.
mímulo, *m.* (bot.) mimulus, monkey flower.
mina, *f.* (numis.) mina (ancient coin).
mina, *f.* mine (mineral pit). 2. mine, abundant source, (fig.) sinecure. 3. underground passage. 4. (mil.) mine. 5. (S. Amer.) concubine, mistress. — **denunciar una m.,** to file a claim to a mine; **encontrar una m.,** to find a gold mine (a profitable business); **m. a cielo abierto,** opencut mine; **m. acústica,** acoustic mine, sonic mine; **m. antipersonal** or **contra personal,** antipersonnel mine; **m. antitanque,** antitank mine; **m. de contacto,** contact mine; **m. de fondo,** ground mine; **m. de metralla,** shrapnel mine; **m. de noticias** or **de información,** mine of information; **m. de oro,** a gold mine (a profitable business, etc.); **m. magnética,** magnetic mine; **m. simulada,** dummy mine; **m. submarina,** submarine mine; **m. terrestre,** land mine.
minador, ra, *a.* (mil., mar.) mine-laying. —*m.* mining engineer; (mil., mar.) mine layer; sapper.
minal, *a.* mine, pertaining to a mine or to mining.
minar, *tr.v.* 1. (mil.) to mine, sap, dig mines under. 2. (mar., mil.) to mine, lay mines in. 3. to undermine, destroy (health, confidence, etc.). 4. to wear away (e.g. rock by water).
minarete, *m.* minaret, tower of a mosque.
mineraje, *m.* mining, work and production of a mine.
mineral, *a.* mineral. —*m.* 1. mineral. 2. ore. 3. source, fountainhead (of a spring). 4. (fig.) source, origin. — **m. graso,** rich ore; **m. pobre,** **m. de baja ley,** low-grade ore.
mineralice, mineralicé, *ref.* **mineralizar.**
mineralización, *f.* mineralization, transformation into a mineral.
mineralizador, *m.* (chem.) mineralizer.
mineralizar, (*ref.* 53) *tr.v.* (min.) to mineralize. —*r.v.* to become mineralized.
mineralogía, *f.* mineralogy.
mineralógico, ca, *a.* mineralogical.
mineralogista, *m.* mineralogist.
minería, *f.* 1. mining. 2. miners; mine operators. 3. mines (of a nation or region).
minero, ra, *a.* mining. —*m.* 1. miner; mine operator. 2. mine, seam. 3. (fig.) source, origin.
mineromedicinal, *a.* mineral water, medicinal water.
minerva, *f.* 1. (myth.) **M.,** Minerva, Roman goddess of knowledge. 2. (religious) procession. 3. (print.) platen press. — **de propia M.,** out of one's own head.
minervista, *m., f.* platen press operator.
minestrón, *m.* (Ital. cul.) minestrone, vegetable and bean soup.
minga, *f.* (S. Amer.) communal work.
mingaco, *m.* (Chile) community work (paid with a meal).
mingitorio, ria, *a.* urinary. —*m.* urinal.
mingo, *m.* object ball (in billiards); **poner el m.,** (coll.) to excel, stand out; **coger de m.,** to take or use as a scapegoat.
mingón, na, *a.* (Ven.) spoiled, pampered (child).
minguí, *m.* (Hond.) chicha, Indian beer.
mini-, *prefix* mini-, e.g. *miniooche,* minicar; small, e.g. *minimedios,* small means.
miniado, da, *a.* decorated or illuminated with red or vermilion.
miniar, *tr.v.* to paint in miniature.
miniatura, *f.* miniature.
miniaturista, *m., f.* miniaturist, painter of miniatures.
miniaturización, *f.* (elec.) miniaturization.
minifalda, *f.* miniskirt.
minifundio, *m.* small farmstead.
mínima, *f.* 1. (mus.) minim. 2. slightest thing, little bit.
minimalista, *m., f.* (pol.) minimalist.
minimización, *f.* minimization.
minimizar, (*ref.* 53) *tr.v.* to minimize; (fig.) to make light of.
mínimo, ma, *a.* 1. minimum; very small, minute, minimal. 2. (ecc.) of or belonging to the Order of St. Francis of Paola. —*m.* 1. minimum. 2. **M.,** (ecc.) Minim, member of the Order of St. Francis of Paola.
mínimum, *m.* minimum.
minino, na, *m., f.* (coll.) kitty, puss, cat, pussy cat.
mininoticias, *f. pl.* news briefs.
minio, *m.* (chem.) minium.
ministerial, *a.* (polit.) ministerial, pertaining to a minister or ministry.
ministerialmente, *adv.* ministerially.
ministerio, *m.* 1. (polit.) ministry (office and tenure of a minister). 2. ministry (government department and building housing it). 3. cabinet, government, ministry. 4. post, job, occupation, ministry. — **M. de Agricultura,** Department of Agriculture (U.S.); Ministry of Agriculture (G.B.); **M. de Comunicaciones,** Ministry of Communications; **M. de Estado,** State Department, Department of State (U.S.); Foreign Office (G.B.); **M. de Fomento,** Ministry of Development, Ministry of Works; **M. de Hacienda,** Treasury Department (U.S.); Treasury (G.B.), **M. de Instrucción Pública y Bellas Artes** or **de Educación,** Ministry of Education; **M. de Gobernación,** Department of the Interior (U.S.); Home Office (G.B.); **M. de Trabajo,** Department of Labor (U.S.); Ministry of Labor (G.B.); **M. de Marina,** Department of the Navy, Navy Department (U.S.); Admiralty (G.B.); **M. de Obras Públicas,** Ministry of Public Works; **M. de Relaciones Exteriores,** State Department (U.S.); Foreign Office (G.B.); **M. de Ultramar,** (obs.) Colonial Office.
ministra, *f.* (polit.) woman minister; minister's wife.
ministrable, *a.* capable of being or becoming a minister.
ministrador, ra, *a.* pertaining to one who practices a profession, e.g. a lawyer. —*m., f.* professional.
ministrante, *a.* administering; ministrant. —*m.* hospital nurse.
ministrar, *tr.v.* 1. to administer; to supply, provide, furnish. 2. to hold office or practice a profession. —*i.v.* to minister.
ministril, *m.* 1. constable, tipstaff, petty official. 2. minstrel.
ministro, *m.* 1. minister. 2. judge. 3. (polit., dipl., ecc.) minister. — **M. de Agricultura,** Secretary of Agriculture (U.S.); Minister of Agriculture (G.B.); **M. de Colonias Británico,** (obs.) Colonial Secretary; **M. de Dios** or **del Señor,** priest; **M. de Educación,** Secretary of Education (U.S.); Minister of Education (G.B.); **M. de Estado** or **Relaciones Exteriores,** Secretary of State (U.S.); Foreign Secretary (G.B.); **M. de Fomento,** Minister of Works; **M. de Hacienda,** Secretary of the Treasury (U.S.); Chancellor of the Exchequer (G.B.); **M. de Gobernación,** Secretary of the Interior (U.S.); Home Secretary

(G.B.); **M. de Labor,** Secretary of Labor (U.S.); Minister of Labor (G.B.); **M. de Marina,** Secretary of the Navy (U.S.), First Lord of the Admiralty (G.B.); **M. plenipotenciario,** minister plenipotenciary; **m. sin cartera,** minister without portfolio; **primer ministro,** Prime Minister, premier.
mino, *interj.* pussy, pussy. . . . (said in calling a cat).
minoración, *f.* reduction, lessening, diminution.
minorar, *tr.v., r.v.* to reduce, lessen, diminish.
minorativo, va, *a.* lessening, diminishing; (med.) laxative. —*m., f.* (med.) laxative.
minoría, *f.* 1. minority (smaller number or part). 2. (polit.) minority. 3. minority, state of being a minor or under age.
minoridad, *f., var. of* **minoría.**
minorista, *a.* retail. —*m.* 1. clergyman of a minor order. 2. retailer.
minorita, *m.* Minorite, Franciscan monk.
minoritario, ria, *a.* minority (as *a.*).
Minos, *m.* (myth.) Minos, king of Crete.
Minotauro, *m.* (myth.) Minotaur, monster with the head of a bull, who inhabited the Labyrinth.
Minsk, *m.* Minsk, capital of Byelorussia.
minstral, *m.* mistral (wind).
mintiendo, mintiera, mintiese, mintió, *ref.* **mentir.**
minucia, *f.* 1. trifle. 2. (*pl.*) minor tithes.
minuciosamente, *adv.* minutely, thoroughly, meticulously.
minuciosidad, *f.* meticulousness, thoroughness.
minucioso, sa, *a.* meticulous, thorough, detailed.
minué, *m.* (mus.) minuet.
minuendo, *m.* (math.) minuend.
minuete, *m., var. of* **minué.**
minúsculo, la, *a.* very small, minute, tiny; small (letter). —*f.* small letter, lower case letter.
minusválido, *m.* underprivileged person; **el m. físico y psíquico,** handicapped person.
minuta, *f.* 1. rough draft (of a contract, of instructions, etc.); minute, summary, record. 2. note (to remind one of something). 3. lawyer's bill or account. 4. list; menu, bill of fare. 5. (cul.) breaded cutlet of fish, fowl or meat.
minutar, *tr.v.* to make a rough draft of; to make a summary of, to take the minutes of (a meeting, etc.).
minutario, *m.* notary; ledger.
minutero, *m.* minute hand (of a clock, watch).
minutisa, *f.* (bot.) sweet william, garden flower (Dianthus barbatus).
minuto, *m.* minute (sixtieth part of a degree and hour); **al minuto,** cooked to order (food); instantly, at once.
miñaque, *m.* (Chile, coll.) lace trimming.
miñardí, *m.* (Chile) heavy lace.
miñón, *m.* 1. border guard; forester, forest guard. 2. slag, dross, scoria.
miñona, *f.* (print.) minion, 7-point type.
miñosa, *f.* intestinal worm.
mío, mía, míos, mías, *m.* and *f. pos. a.,* 1. mine, e.g. *esta cosa es mía,* this thing is mine. 2. of mine, e.g. *son íntimos amigos míos,* they are intimate friends of mine. 3. of me, e.g. *estaba sentado delante mío,* he was sitting in front of me. — **es cosa mía, tuya, suya,** or **nuestra,** it is my, your, his, her, their or our affair; **ésta es la mía,** this is my big chance. —*m.* and *f. pos. pron.* (used with *def. art.*) mine, e.g. *tuve que usar su pluma, la mía estaba rota,* I had to use his pen, mine was broken; **de mío,** on my own, by myself, without help.
miocardiaco, ca, *a.* (med.) myocardial.
miocárdico, ca, *a.* (med.) myocardial.
miocardio, *m.* (anat.) myocardium.
miocardiógrafo, *m.* (med.) myocardiograph.
miocardiograma, *m.* (med.) myocardiogram.
miocarditis, *f.* (med.) myocarditis.
mioceno, *a., m.* (geol.) Miocene.
miodinia, *f.* (med.) myalgia, muscular pain.
miogénico, ca, *a.* (med.) myogenic.
miógeno, na, *a.* (med.) myogenic.
mioglobina, *f.* (physiol.) myoglobin.
miografía, *f.* (med.) myography.
miógrafo, *m.* (med.) myograph.
miograma, *m.* (med.) myogram.
miolema, *m.* (anat.) sarcolemma, myolemma.
miología, *f.* (med.) myology.
miológico, ca, *a.* (anat.) myologic.
mioma, *m.* (med.) myoma.
miomatoso, sa, *a.* (med.) myomatous.
mioneural, *a.* (anat.) myoneural.
miope, *a.* myopic, near-sighted, short-sighted. —*m., f.* myopic person, myope.
miopía, *f.* (med.) myopia, near-sightedness.
miosina, *f.* (biochem.) myosin.
miosis, *f.* (med.) miosis.
miosota, *f.* (bot.) German madwort, forget-me-not.
miótico, ca, *a.* (med.) miotic.
miotoma, *m.* (anat.) myotome.
miotonía, *f.* (med.) myotonia.
miotónico, ca, *a.* (med.) myotonic.
miquelete, *m.* 1. miquelet, (mil.) Spanish guerrilla who fought in the Peninsular War; infantryman. 2. Spanish flint lock.
miquilo, *m.* (zool., Arg., Bol.) otter.
mira, *f.* 1. sight (of a firearm, theodolite, etc.). 2. (surv.) leveling rod, staff or pole. 3. aim, object, purpose. 4. care, vigilance. 5. watchtower. 6. upper corner of a shield. — **andar, estar** or **quedar a la m.,** to be on the lookout; **andar, estar** or **quedar a la m. de que** + *subj.,* to be on the lookout to see that; **con miras a,** with an eye to, having in mind, with a view to; **m. taquimétrica,** (surv.) stadia rod; **poner la m. en,** to set one's eyes on, have designs on.
¡mira! *interj.* look! behold! take care!
mirabel, *m.* (bot.) mock cypress; (bot.) sunflower.
mirabolano, *m., var. of* **mirobálano.**
mirada, *f.* look, glance, gaze, view; **echar una m. a,** to take a look at.
miradero, *m.* 1. cynosure, center of attraction. 2. watchtower, lookout, observatory.
mirado, da, *past part. of* **mirar.** —*a.* cautious, prudent, circumspect; **bien** or **mal m.,** well or poorly thought of.
mirador, ra, *a.* looking, overlooking. —*m.* mirador, watchtower; closed porch, bay window, oriel window, balcony.
miradura, *f.* look, act of looking.
miraguano, *m.* (bot.) fan palm, Corypha palm (Corypha miraguano).
miraje, *m.* (Gal.) mirage.
miramamolín, *m.* title of a Caliph.
miramelindos, *m.* (bot.) balsam.
miramiento, *m.* 1. consideration, attention, care. 2. caution, care, circumspection (in planning a project or course of action).
miranda, *f.* eminence; vantage point.
mirante, *a.* looking, gazing. —*m., f.* looker, gazer.
mirar, *tr.v.* 1. to look at, watch, observe; to gaze at; to scan. 2. to contemplate; to consider. — **bien mirado,** taking everything into consideration, all things considered; **mira lo que haces,** be careful, watch out; **mírame y no me toques,** (coll.) very fragile (thing), very sensitive or weak (person); **mira quién habla,** look who's talking; **m. bien a,** to esteem, like, look with favor at; **m. de frente,** to look in the face; **m. mal a,** to dislike, disapprove of, have a bad opinion of; **m. una cosa por encima,** to glance at something, look at superficially; **m. por encima del hombro,** to look down one's nose at; **mire a quién se lo cuenta,** you're telling me (I know perfectly well already); **mire cómo habla, con quién habla** or **lo que habla,** watch your tongue. —*i.v.* to look; to watch; to glance; **mira,** watch out, be careful; **m. a,** to face, look towards, e.g. *la casa mira al norte,* the house faces the north; to look out on, e.g. *el hotel mira a la plaza de armas,* the hotel looks out on the central square of the town; to look out for, look after, e.g. *él mira sólo a su provecho,* he only looks after his own benefit; **m. por,** to look out for, look after. —*r.v.* to look at oneself or at one another; to watch oneself or one another; **mirarse al espejo,** to look at oneself in the mirror; **mirarse en otro,** to be wrapped up in someone, dote on someone, be very fond of someone; **mirarse unos a otros,** to gape at one another, stand dumbfounded looking at one another.
mirasol, *m.* (bot.) sunflower.
miria, *prefix* ten thousand.
miríada, *f.* myriad, large quantity or number.
miriagramo, *m.* myriagram.
mirialitro, *m.* myrialiter.
miriámetro, *m.* myriameter, ten thousand meters.
miriápodo, *a.* (zool.) myriapodous, myriapod. —*m.* (zool.) myriapod; (*pl.*) Myriapoda.
mírica, *f.* (bot.) mirica.
miricáceas, *f.* (bot.) (*pl.*) Myricaceae.
mirificar, (*ref. 50*) *tr.v.* (rare) to exalt, extol.
mirífico, ca, *a.* (poet.) marvelous, wonderful.
mirifique, mirifiqué, *ref.* **mirificar** (rare).
mirilla, *f.* 1. peephole. 2. (surv.) target.
miriñaque, *m.* 1. trinket, bauble, gewgaw. 2. crinoline, hoop skirt. 3. (Arg.) cowcatcher. 4. (Cuba, Mex.) cotton fabric. 5. (Ecuad.) frippery. 6. (Mex.) screen (to keep flies out of the house). 8. (Ven.) crookedness, dishonesty.
miriópodo, *a.* (zool.) myriapod, myriapodous.
mirística, *f.* (bot.) nutmeg (tree).
mirla, *f.* (ornith.) blackbird.
mirlamiento, *m.* self-importance, airs.
mirlarse, *r.v.* to act self-importantly, put on airs.
mirlo, *m.* 1. (ornith.) blackbird. 2. (coll.) self-importance. — **ser una cosa** or **persona un m. blanco,** to be an extraordinary thing or person; to be a rare bird; **soltar el m.,** (coll.) to start chattering or jabbering.
mirmecófago, ga, *a.* (zool.) myrmecophagous.
mirmecófilo, la, *a.* (bot., zool.) myrmecophilous. —*f.* (zool.) myrmecophile.
mirmecología, *f.* (ento.) myrmecology.
mirobálano, *m.* (bot.) myrobalan (tree and fruit), the cherry plum.
mirón, na, *a.* inquisitive, nosy, curious. —*m., f.* onlooker, spectator, bystander.
mirotón, *m.* (Chile) angry glance.
mirra, *f.* myrrh.
mirrado, da, *a.* myrrhed, composed of or mixed with myrrh.
mirranga, *f.* (Col.) scrap; small piece.
mirrauste, *m.* (cul.) pigeon pie; sauce for pigeon fricassee.
mirrino, na, *a.* myrrhic, myrrh-like.
mirruña, *f.* (Hond., Mex.) particle, fragment, bit.
mirsináceas, *f.* (*pl.*) (bot.) Myrsinaceae.
mirtáceo, a, *a.* (bot.) myrtaceous. —*f.* myrtaceous tree; (*pl.*) Myrtaceae.
mirtídano, *m.* (bot.) myrtle sprout.
mirtino, na, *a.* myrtle-like, myrtiform.
mirto, *m.* (bot.) myrtle.
miruello, lla, *m., f.* (Sp., reg.) blackbird.
misa, *f.* 1. (ecc., mus.) mass. 2. priesthood. — **allá te lo dirán de misas,** you'll pay for that; **ayudar a m.,** to serve at mass; **cantar m.,** to say his

first mass (newly ordained priest); **como en m.,** in complete silence; **decir m.,** to say or celebrate mass; **de m. y ollas,** uncouth, ignorant (priest); **¿en qué acabarán estas misas?** how will all this end?; **no saber uno de la m. la media,** not to know what a thing is about; **oír m.,** to hear mass; **m. cantada,** sung mass; **m. de campaña,** mass said in a camp; outdoor mass; **m. de cuerpo presente,** requiem mass with the body present; **m. de difuntos** or **de requiem,** requiem mass; **m. del alba** or **de los cazadores,** early mass; **m. del gallo,** Christmas Eve or midnight mass; **m. de relaciones,** marriage service; **m. en seco,** mass without communion; **m. mayor,** High Mass; **m. nueva,** first mass said by newly ordained priest; **m. privada** or **m. rezada,** Low Mass; **m. solemne,** Solemn Mass; **m. votiva,** votive mass.

misacantano, *m.* fully ordained priest; priest who celebrates mass for the first time.

misal, *a., m.* 1. (ecc.) missal, Mass book. 2. (print.) two-line pica.

misantropía, *f.* misanthropy.

misantrópico, ca, *a.* misanthropic.

misántropo, *m.* misanthrope.

misar, *i.v.* (coll.) 1. to say mass. 2. (coll.) to hear mass.

misario, *m.* (ecc.) acolyte, server.

miscelánea, *f.* miscellany.

misceláneo, a, *a.* miscellaneous.

miscibilidad, *f.* miscibility.

miscible, *a.* miscible, mixable.

miserabilísimo, ma, *a. super. of* **miserable.** 1. very wretched or unfortunate. 2. extremely mean or niggardly.

miserable, *a.* 1. wretched, unfortunate. 2. stingy, niggardly. 3. despicable, vile, mean. —*m., f.* 1. wretch, unfortunate person. 2. miser, skinflint. 3. wretch, cur, cad.

miserablemente, *adv.* wretchedly; despicably.

miseración, *f.* pity, mercy, sympathy.

miseraico, ca, *a.* (anat.) mesenteric.

míseramente, *adv., var. of* **miserablemente.**

miserear, *i.v.* (coll.) to be niggardly or stingy.

miserere, *m.* 1. (ecc., mus.) Miserere. 2. (med.) ileus.

miseria, *f.* 1. misery, wretchedness, distress. 2. poverty, misery. 3. meanness, niggardliness, stinginess. 4. (coll.) pittance, very small amount of money. — **comerse de m.,** to live in great poverty.

misericordia, *f.* 1. mercy, compassion, pity. 2. misericord (dagger). 3. miserere, misericord (projection on hinged choir seat, on which a standing person can rest.

misericordiosamente, *adv.* mercifully, with compassion.

misericordioso, sa, *a.* merciful, compassionate. —*m., f.* merciful person.

mísero, ra, *a.* 1. unfortunate, wretched. 2. miserly, stingy.

misero, ra, *a.* 1. (coll.) mass-loving, church-going. 2. paid only for saying mass (a priest).

misérrimo, ma, *a. super. of* **mísero.** 1. extremely wretched or unfortunate. 2. extremely stingy or niggardly.

misia, misiá, *f.* Mistress, Miss (preceding a woman's given name).

misil, *m.* missile; **m. antiaéreo,** antiaircraft missile; **m. balístico,** ballistic missile; **m. de corto alcance,** short-range missile; **m. de crucereo,** cruise missile; **m. de medio alcance,** medium-range missile; **m. de largo alcance,** long-range missile; **m. superficie-aire,** surface-to-air missile; **m. superficie-superficie,** surface-to-surface missile; **m. tierra-aire,** ground-to-air missile.

misión, *f.* 1. mission, charge, errand, commission; the journey and activities related to a mission or an errand. 2. building housing the staff and offices of a religious or diplomatic mission. 3. moral duties arising from a calling, status or profession, e.g. *la m. del médico es curar al enfermo,* a doctor's duty is to cure the patient. 4. series of sermons preached in one given church. 5. food and pay given to reapers during harvest. — **m. científica,** scientific mission; **m. diplomática,** diplomatic mission; **m. religiosa,** religious mission; **m. secreta,** secret mission.

misional, *a.* missionary, pertaining to a calling, duty or profession, e.g. *fervor m.,* missionary fervor.

misionar, *i.v.* to preach, give a sermon, do missionary work.

misionario, *m.* 1. missionary, envoy, emissary. 2. (ecc.) missionary.

misionera, *f.* missionary, nun working in a mission.

misionero, ra, *a., m., f.* (ecc.) missionary.

Misisipí, *m.* (U.S.) Mississippi (river and state).

misivo, va, *a.* missive, sent. —*f.* missive, letter.

mismamente, *adv.* (coll.) exactly, precisely.

mismísimo, ma, *a. super. of* **mismo,** very, identical, selfsame, e.g. *él es el mismísimo diablo,* he is the very devil.

mismo, ma, *a.* 1. same. 2. myself, yourself, himself, herself, itself, ourselves, yourselves, themselves, e.g. *yo mismo lo haré,* I will do it myself, *ellos mismos lo hicieron,* they did it themselves; *el m. hombre,* the same man. 3. very, e.g. *en el mismo centro de Lima,* in the very center of Lima. — **así mismo,** likewise; in the same way; also; that's right!; **el mismo que viste y calza,** that I am, that's me; **lo mismo,** the same thing; **me da lo mismo,** it's all the same to me; **por lo mismo,** for that very reason.

mismo, *adv.* 1. right (in the very instant, place, etc.), e.g. *ahora m.,* right now, *desde París m.,* right from Paris, all the way from Paris; from Paris, no less. 2. itself, e.g. *en Madrid m.,* in Madrid itself.

miso, *m.* pussy, cat.

misogamia, *f.* misogamy, hatred of marriage.

misógamo, ma, *a.* misogamic. —*m., f.* misogamist; one who hates marriage.

misoginia, *f.* misogyny, hatred of women.

misógino, *a.* misogynic, misogynous. —*m. f.* misogynist, woman hater.

misología, *f.* misology, hatred of reason.

misoneísmo, *m.* misoneism, hatred of change or novelty.

misoneísta, *a.* misoneistic, having an aversion to change, to anything new.

mispíquel, *m.* (min.) mispickel, arsenopyrite.

mistagógico, ca, *a.* mystagogic, pertaining to religious mysteries.

mistagogo, *m.* mystagogue, interpreter or initiator of religious mysteries.

mistar, *tr.v.* to mumble, mutter.

mistela, *f.* flavored brandy; drink made of grape juice and alcohol.

misterio, *m.* 1. mystery; enigma. 2. secret.

misteriosamente, *adv.* mysteriously; enigmatically.

misterioso, sa, *a.* mysterious; enigmatic.

mística, *f.* mystical theology.

místicamente, *adv.* mystically; spiritually.

misticismo, *m.* mysticism.

místico, ca, *a.* mystic, mystical. —*m., f.* mystic. —*m.* (mar.) a small coastal boat used in the Mediterranean.

misticón, na, *a., m., f.* affectedly pious, ascetic or religious (person).

mistificación, *f.* hoax, trick, fraud.

mistificar, (*ref. 50*) *tr.v.* to hoax, trick, deceive.

mistifique, mistifiqué, *ref.* **mistificar.**

mistifori, *m., var. of* **mixtifori.**

mistilíneo, nea, *a.* (geom.) mixtilineal, mixtilinear.

mistión, *f.* mixture.

misto, ta, *a., m., var. of* **mixto.**

mistol, *m.* (Arg., Peru) jujube tree.

mistral, *a., m.* mistral (wind).

mistura, *f., var. of* **mixtura.**

misturar, *tr.v. var. of* **mixturar.**

misturera, *f.* (Amer.) flower girl.

misturero, ra, *a., m., f., var. of* **mixturero.**

Misuri, *m.* (U.S.) Missouri (state and river).

mita, *f.* 1. drafting of selected Indians for public works (during the Incaic period); forced labor (imposed on South American Indians by the Spanish). 2. tax paid by Peruvian Indians. 3. (Bol.) coca harvest. 4. (Arg.) lot of cattle to be transported by train.

mitaca, *f.* (Bol.) harvest.

mitad, *f.* half; middle; center. — **a** or **en la m. (de),** in the middle; **cara m.,** better half (husband or wife); **m. y m.,** half and half; **plantar** or **poner a uno en la m. del arroyo,** to throw someone out of the house; **por la m.,** in half, in the middle, e.g. *partir por la m.,* to cut in half.

mitadenco, *a.* (said of a tax) payable in two kinds of produce. —*m.* mixture of half wheat and half rye.

mitán, *m.* (tex.) holland, brown holland (linen).

mitayo, *m.* 1. South American Indian assigned to paid public or forced labor. 2. Indian collecting his fee for forced or public labor. 3. (Amer., derog.) Indian.

mítico, ca, *a.* mythical, mythic.

mitigación, *f.* mitigation, allaying, alleviation, palliation; calming, mollifying.

mitigadamente, *adv.* less severely or rigorously; less violently or painfully.

mitigador, ra, *a.* mitigating, allaying, alleviating; calming, mollifying. —*m.* mitigator; mollifier.

mitigante, *a.* mitigating, allaying, palliating, alleviating; calming, mollifying.

mitigar, (*ref. 51*) *tr.v.* to allay, mitigate, alleviate, palliate (pain, sorrow, distress); to calm, moderate, mollify (anger, impatience).

mitigativo, va, *a., var. of* **mitigante.**

mitigatorio, ria, *a., var. of* **mitigante.**

mitigue, mitigué, *ref.* **mitigar.**

Mitilene, *m.* Mytilene, Greek island, known in antiquity as Lesbos.

mitin, *m.* meeting, rally.

mito, *m.* myth.

mitocondrio, *m.* (biol.) mitochondrion.

mitografía, *f.* mythography, the descriptions of myths.

mitógrafo, fa, *m., f.* mythographer, writer who specializes in mythography.

mitología, *f.* mythology.

mitológico, ca, *a.* mythological. —*m.* mythologist.

mitologista, mitólogo, *m., f.* mythologist.

mitomanía, *f.* (psyc.) mythomania.

mitómano, na, *a., m., f.* (psyc.) mythomaniac.

mitón, *m.* knitted glove with half fingers only.

mitósico, ca, *a.* (biol.) mitotic.

mitosis, *f.* (biol.) mitosis.

mitote, *m.* 1. (Mex.) Indian dance. 2. house party. 3. (Amer.) finickiness, fussiness. 4. (Mex.) rumpus, uproar, disturbance, shindy.

mitotero, ra, *a.* 1. (Amer.) finicky, fussy. 2. (Mex.) rowdy, noisy, boisterous. 3. (Mex.) gossipy, gossiping, mischief-making. —*m., f.* 1. finicky or fussy person. 2. rowdy, noisy person.

mitótico, ca, *a.* (biol.) mitotic.
mitra, *f.* 1. (ecc.) miter, mitre. 2. miter, bishopric, archbishopric. 3. total revenue of a bishopric or archbishopric. 4. (coll.) parson's nose.
mitrado, da, *a.* (ecc.) mitered, mitred.
mitral, *a.* (anat.) mitral.
mitrar, *i.v.* (ecc.) to become a bishop.
mitridatismo, *m.* (med.) mithridatism.
mitridatizar, (*ref. 53*) *tr.v.* to mithridatize, make immune to poison.
mitridato, *m.* (pharm.) mithridate, antidote.
mitú, (*pl.* **mitúes**), *m.* (ornith.) crax (Crax solateri).
mítulo, *m.* (zool.) mussel.
Miura, *m.* a breed of fighting bull known for its fierceness and bravery; (fig.) an easily infuriated person.
mixedema, *m.* (med.) myxedema.
mixedematoso, sa, *a.* (med.) myxedematous.
mixoma, *m.* (med.) myxoma.
mixomatoso, sa, *a.* (med.) myxomatous.
mixomiceto, *m.* (bot.) myxomycete.
mixtamente, *adv.* mixedly; (law) belonging to both ecclesiastical and civil courts.
mixtela, *f., var. of* **mistela.**
mixtificación, *f., var. of* **mistificación,** hoax, trick, fraud.
mixtificar, (*ref. 50*) *tr.v.* to hoax, trick, deceive.
mixtifique, mixtifiqué, *ref.* **mixtificar.**
mixtifori, *m.* (coll.) hodgepodge, jumble, muddle.
mixtilíneo, a, *a.* (geom.) mixtilineal, mixtilinear.
mixtión, *f.* mixture.
mixto, ta, *a.* mixed, mingled; composite. — **número mixto,** mixed number. —*m.* 1. mixture, compound, blend. 2. match. 3. explosive compound, gunpowder.
mixtura, *f.* 1. mixture. 2. maslin, bread of different types of grain.
mixturar, *tr.v.* to mix.
mixturero, ra, *a.* mixing. —*m., f.* mixer.
miz, *interj.* here, pussy. . . . (to call a cat).
miza, *f.* (coll.) pussy cat, tabby.
Mizar, *f.* (astron.) Mizar.
mizcal, *m.* (Morocco) small coin.
mízcalo, *m.* edible milk mushroom (Lactarius deliciosus).
mizo, za, *m., f.* (coll.) tom cat; tabby cat.
ml. *abbrev. of* **mililitro,** milliliter (ml.).
Mlle. *abbrev. of* **Mademoiselle,** Mademoiselle (Mlle.).
Mlles. *abbrev. of* **Mesdemoiselles,** Mesdemoiselles (Mlles.).
mm. *abbrev. of* **milímetro,** millimeter (mm.).
MM. *abbrev. of* **Messieurs,** Messieurs (MM.).
Mme. *abbrev. of* **Madame,** Madame (Mme.).
Mmes. *abbrev. of* **Mesdames,** Mesdames (Mmes.).
Mn *sym. of* **manganeso,** manganese (Mn).
mnemónica, *f.* mnemonics, a system to improve or develop the memory.
mnemónico, ca, *a.* mnemonic, pertaining to the memory.
Mnemosine, *f.* (myth.) Mnemosyne, the goddess of memory, mother of the Muses.
mnemotecnia, mnemotécnica, *f.* mnemonics, mnemotechny, technique for improving the memory.
mnemotécnico, ca, *a.* mnemonic, mnemotechnical, pertaining to formulas and techniques for improving the memory.
Mo *sym. of* **molibdeno,** molybdenum (Mo).
M. O. *abbrev. of* **moneda oficial,** official currency.
moabita, *a.* Moabite, of or pertaining to Moab. —*m., f.* Moabite, member of an ancient Arab people.
moaré, *m.* (tex.) moire, watered silk.
mobiliario, ria, *a.* movable (property). —*m.* furniture, household appointments.
moblaje, *m.* household furniture and appointments.
moblar, (*ref. 33*) *tr.v.* to furnish, appoint, provide with furniture.
moble, *a.* mobile, movable.
moca, *f.* Mocha coffee.
mocador, ra, *m.* pocket handkerchief.
mocar, (*ref. 50*) *tr.v.* to wipe or blow the nose of. —*r.v.* to wipe one's nose, blow one's nose.
mocárabe, *m.* (archit., carp.) loop-shaped ornament.
mocarra, *m., f.* (coll.) brat, scamp; whippersnapper.
mocarro, *m.* (coll.) nasal mucus, snot (vulg.)
mocasín, *m.,* **mocasina,** *f.* moccasin (shoe).
mocear, *i.v.* to run around, sow one's wild oats, to act like a rowdy youth.
mocedad, *f.* 1. youth, youthfulness. 2. debauchery, dissoluteness, wildness, wild living. 3. (*pl*) youthful adventures or scrapes, wild oats (coll.).
mocejón, *m.* (zool.) mussel.
moceril, *a.* (neol.) youthful, juvenile.
mocerío, *m.* young people, youth, crowd of young people.
mocero, *a.* lewd, woman-chasing. —*m.* young rake, wencher.
mocetón, na, *m.* strapping lad, hefty young man. —*f.* buxom young woman or lass.
mocha, *f.* 1. reverent bow. 2. (Cuba) a type of machete.
mochada, *f.* butt (with the head).
mochales, *a.* (coll.) madly in love; crazy, screwy, mad, loony.
mochar, *tr.v.* 1. to cut, lop off. 2. (Arg.) to steal.
mochazo, *m.* blow dealt with a rifle butt.
moche, *adv.* **a troche y m.,** helter-skelter, pell-mell.
mocheta, *f.* 1. blunt or flat end (of some tools or implements). 2. (bldg.) rabbet, recess, rebate (in a door or window frame). 3. (archit.) reentrant angle. 4. (archit.) reveal, jamb.
mochete, *m.* (ornith.) kestrel, sparrow hawk, small falcon.
mochil, *m.* errand boy for farm laborers.
mochila, *f.* 1. pack, knapsack, haversack; rucksack; game bag; tool bag; (Mex.) small trunk. 2. (mil.) soldiers' provisions to last a specific number of days.
mochilero, *m.* (mil.) pack-carrier; person carrying a pack or knapsack.
mochín, *m.* executioner.
mocho, cha, *a.* 1. blunt, flat, without a point. 2. (coll.) cropped, shorn. 3. (Chile) lay (brother or sister). 4. (Mex.) conservative (in politics). —*m.* butt end, flat or blunt end. —*m., f.* (Chile) lay brother or sister.
mochongada, *f.* (Mex.) clowning, buffoonery.
mochongo, *m.* (Mex.) laughingstock, clown.
mochuelo, *m.* 1. little owl (Athene noctua). 2. (coll.) difficult or distasteful work. — **cada m. a su olivo,** time to be going, time to get to work; **cargar uno con el m.** or **tocarle a uno el m.,** to get stuck with dirty work to do, get the worst part to do.
mocil, *a.* young, youthful, callow.
moción, *f.* 1. motion, movement. 2. inclination, tendency, leaning. 3. divine inspiration. 4. motion (put to a meeting). 5. vowel sign (in semitic languages). — **presentar una m.,** to present or bring forward a motion.
mocionar, *tr.v.* to propose, present a motion to an assembly.
mocito, ta, *a.* young, adolescent. —*m.* lad, youngster. —*f.* young girl, lass.
moco, *m.* 1. mucus (nasal); snot (vulg.). 2. mucilage, soft sticky mass. 3. burning end of candlewick. 4. cinder, scale, red-hot slag (flying off red-hot iron when hammered). 5. candle drippings. 6. (mar.) dolphin striker, martingale. — **a m. de candil,** (coll.) by candle-light; **buscar** or **escoger a m. de candil,** (coll.) to search for or choose with the utmost care; **caérsele a uno el m.,** to be a simpleton, be wet behind the ears; **llorar a m. tendido,** to weep, sob, bawl; **m. de pavo,** crest of a turkey; (bot.) lovelies-bleeding; trifle, mere bagatelle.
mococoa, *f.* (Bol., Col.) sadness, dejection; bad temper.
mocoso, sa, *a.* 1. snotty-nosed. 2. impudent, insolent. 3. inexperienced, callow. 4. unimportant, insignificant. —*m., f.* impudent brat; inexperienced or callow youth.
mocosuelo, la, *m., f.* child, brat; callow youth.
mocosuena, *adv.* (coll.) **traducir m.,** to translate word for word.
moda, *f.* custom, form; fashion, mode, style. — **a la m.,** fashionable, a la mode, in fashion; **a la m. de,** in the fashion, way or style of; **de m.,** in fashion, fashionable; **estar de m., ser m., ser de m.,** to be in fashion, be the fashion; **fuera de m.,** out of fashion; **pasar de m.,** to go out of fashion; **ponerse de m.,** to come into fashion.
modado, da, *a.* (Col.) mannered; **bien or mal m.,** well or ill-mannered.
modal, *a.* modal. —*m.* (*pl.*) manners, ways, behavior.
modalidad, *f.* 1. way, manner. 2. type, kind, sort, variety. 3. peculiarity, characteristic. 4. course of action, method. 5. (log., med.) modality.
modelado, *past part. of* **modelar.** —*m.* modeling; **m. en cera,** wax modeling.
modelador, ra, *a., m., f.* modeler.
modelaje, *m.* shaping, forming; pattern-making.
modelar, *tr.v.* to model; to mold, shape, form. —*r.v.* to model or mold oneself.
modelista, *m.* 1. modelist, model maker. 2. mold-maker.
modelo, *m.* model; pattern; specimen, example; **m. a escala,** scale model; **m. de paciencia,** a model of patience. —*m., f.* model, fashion model, mannequin. —*a.* model, e.g. *un alumno m.,* a model student, *un marido m.,* a model husband.
moderación, *f.* moderation.
moderadamente, *adv.* moderately, with moderation; with restraint or control.
moderado, da, *past part. of* **moderar.** —*a.* moderate; controlled, restrained. — **a fuego moderado,** (cul.) at a moderate heat.
moderador, ra, *a.* moderating, restraining. —*m., f.* moderator (one who moderates or regulates). —*m.* (rel., chem., phys.) moderator.
moderante, *a.* moderating.
moderantismo, *m.* (Sp., hist.) formerly a conservative party.
moderar, *tr.v.* to moderate, regulate, restrain, control. —*r.v.* to control or restrain oneself; to become moderate; to calm down.
moderativo, va, *a.* moderating; restraining, controlling.
moderatorio, ria, *a.* moderating.
modernamente, *adv.* modernly; recently, lately.
modernice, modernicé, *ref.* **modernizar.**
modernidad, *f.* modernity, modernness.
modernismo, *m.* modernism.
modernista, *a.* modernist, modernistic. —*m., f.* modernist.
modernización, *f.* modernization.
modernizador, ra, modernizing. —*m., f.* modernizer.
modernizar, (*ref. 53*) *tr.v.* to modernize.
moderno, na, *a.* 1. modern, late, recent, novel. 2. new (in an employment). — **a la moderna, a lo moderno,** in the modern manner; **edad moderna,** modern age; **historia moderna,** modern

history. —*m.* 1. modern, (*pl.*) moderns (people of modern times; modern artists or writers). 2. freshman (in college); new man, newcomer (in an employment).
modestamente, *adv.* modestly.
modestia, *f.* 1. modesty, lack of pretense. 2. modesty, chastity.
modesto, ta, *a.* 1. modest, unassuming. 2. chaste.
módicamente, *adv.* moderately, sparingly.
modicidad, *f.* moderateness, reasonableness, cheapness.
módico, ca, *a.* moderate; reasonable, economical, cheap (price).
modificable, *a.* modifiable.
modificación, *f.* modification, alteration.
modificador, ra, *a.* modifying. —*m., f.* modifier.
modificante, *a.* modifying.
modificar, (*ref. 50.*) *tr.v.* to modify, to alter; to improve. —*r.v.* to become modified or improved.
modificativo, va, *a.* modifying.
modificatorio, ria, *a.* modifying.
modifique, modifiqué, *ref.* **modificar.**
modillón, *a.* (archit.) modillion, bracket.
modio, *m.* modius (ancient Roman unit of measure).
modiolo, *m.* (anat.) modiolus.
modismo, *m.* (gram.) idiom, idiomatic expression.
modista, *m., f.* dressmaker, modiste.
modistería, *f.* (Amer.) ladies' dress shop.
modistilla, *f.* apprentice dressmaker, seamstress.
modisto, *m., f.* ladies' tailor, fashion designer.
modo, *m.* 1. manner, way, fashion, mode, method. 2. (gram.) mood, mode. 3. (mus.) mode. 4. (philos., log.) mode. 5. (*pl.*) manners, ways (of behavior). — **al m. de,** like, in the manner of, in the same way as; **a mi m.,** in my own way, after my own fashion; **a su m.,** in his way or fashion, as best he can; **de buen m.,** gladly, willingly; **de ese m.,** at this rate; **del mismo m.,** in the same way, similarly; **de mal m.,** unwillingly; **de m. que,** so that; **de ningún m.,** by no means whatsoever; **de todos modos,** by all means, definitely; anyway; **m. adverbial,** (gram.) adverbial phrase; **m. auténtico,** (mus.) authentic mode; **m. conjuntivo,** (gram.) conjunctival phrase; **m. deprecativo,** (gram.) imperative mood (when making a request); **m. de ser,** nature, disposition; **m. discípulo,** (mus.) plagal mode; **m. imperativo,** (gram.) imperative mood; **m. indicativo,** (gram.) indicative mood; **m. infinitivo,** (gram.) infinitive mood; **m. maestro,** (mus.) authentic mode; **m. mayor,** (mus.) major mode; **m. menor,** (mus.) minor mode; **m. optativo,** (gram.) optative mood; **m. plagal,** (mus.) plagal mode; **m. potencial,** (gram.) potential mood; **m. subjuntivo,** (gram.) subjunctive mood; **por m. de,** by way of; **por m. de juego,** by way of a joke, in fun.
modorra, *f.* 1. heaviness, drowsiness. 2. (vet.) gid, staggers.
modorrar, *tr.v.* to make heavy, drowsy or sleepy. —*r.v.* to turn soft (fruit).
modorrilla, *f.* (mil.) third night watch.
modorro, rra, *a.* 1. sleepy, heavy, drowsy. 2. poisoned by mercury (in a mine). 3. soft, flabby (fruit). 4. (fig.) ignorant, dull, stupid. —*m.* 1. miner with mercury poisoning. 2. ignoramus, fool.
modoso, sa, *a.* quiet, decorous, well-behaved.
modrego, *m.* (coll.) awkward, clumsy fellow, dunce.
modulación, *f.* (mus., elec., rad.) modulation; **m. de amplitud,** amplitude modulation; **m. de fase,** phase modulation; **m. de frecuencia,** frequency modulation.
modulador, ra, *a.* modulating. —*m., f.* modulator. —*m.* (rad.) modulator.
modulante, *a.* modulating.
modular, *tr.v, i.v.* to modulate.
modular, *a.* modular. —*m.* shelf unit, modular shelving; modular sofa.
módulo, *m.* (archit., hydr., numis., mec.) module; (math., phys.) modulus; (mus.) modulation. **m. de elasticidad,** (phys.) modulus of elasticity; **m. de maniobra y mando,** command module; **m. lunar,** lunar module; **m. prefabricado,** prefabricated module, prefabricated unit.
moduloso, sa, *a.* modulated, melodious, harmonious.
moer, *m.* (tex.) moire, watered silk.
mofa, *f.* mockery, fun, jeer, gibe, derision; **hacer m. de,** to jeer at, mock, gibe, deride.
mofador, ra, *a.* mocking, jeering, taunting, gibing, deriding. —*m., f.* mocker, taunter, derider.
mofadura, *f.* *var. of* **mofa.**
mofante, *a., m., f., var. of* **mofador.**
mofar, *i.v, r.v.* to mock, jeer, taunt, gibe, deride, sneer; **mofarse de,** to mock, jeer at, taunt, gibe at, deride, sneer.
mofeta, *f.* 1. (geol., min.) mofette, moffette (vent from which poisonous gas escapes). 2. blackdamp, chokedamp (poisonous mine gas); firedamp (explosive mine gas). 3. (zool.) skunk, polecat.
moflete, *m.* fat or chubby cheek.
mofletudo, da, *a.* chubby-cheeked, fat-cheeked.
Mogadiscio, *m.* Mogadishu, capital of Somalia.
mogataz, *m.* Moor serving in the Spanish garrisons in Africa.
mogate, *m.* (cer.) glaze, glazing; **a medio m.,** halfdone, carelessly.
mogato, ta, *a., m., f., var. of* **mojigato.**
mogol, la, *a., m., f.* Mongol, Mongolian; **Gran M.,** Great Mogul. —*m.* Mongolian (language).
mogólico, ca, *a.* Mongolian, Mongolic.
mogollar, *tr.v.* (Bol.) to cheat.
mogollón, *a.* (rare) lazy, sponging, drifting. —*m.* intrusion, butting in. — **comer de m.,** to sponge or cadge a meal; **de m.,** free, without paying.
mogomogo, *m.* (Hond.) dish of green banana and pumpkin; (Mex., Cuba) thick stew.
mogón, na, *a.* one-horned; broken-horned; blunt-horned.
mogote, *m.* 1. hummock, hillock, knoll. 2. pile of faggots. 3. (zool.) budding antler.
mogrollo, *m.* 1. sponger, cadger. 2. boor, rustic.
moharra, *f.* head, point (of a lance).
moharrache, *m., var. of* **moharracho.**
moharracho, *m.* a ridiculous costume or mascarade; clown, buffoon.
mohatra, *f.* fraudulent sale; fraud, trick.
mohatrar, *i.v.* to make fraudulent transactions.
mohatrero, ra, *m., f.* swindler, cheat.
mohatrón, na, *m., f., var. of* **mohatrero.**
mohecer, (*ref. 45*) *tr.v.* to make moldy or mildewy; to rust, make rusty. —*r.v.* to get moldy or mildewy; to rust, get rusty; to become covered with rust.
moheda, *f.* hill overgrown with brambles and undergrowth.
mohedal, *m., var. of* **moheda.**
moheña, *a.* (bot.) variety of nettle.
mohiento, ta, *a.* 1. moldy, mildewy; rusty. 2. mossy.
mohín, *m.* grimace, gesture, face.
mohína, *f.* annoyance, anger, displeasure (with someone).
mohindad, *f., var of* **mohína.**
mohíno, na, *a.* 1. sad, gloomy; displeased, peeved. 2. crossed between a stallion and a she-ass. 3. black, black-nosed (cattle, horses). —*m., f.* 1. hinny. 2. black horse or cow. —*m.* 1. (kind of) magpie (Pica cooki). 2. in certain card games, one who plays against several others.
moho, *m.* 1. moss; mold, mildew. 2. rust; verdigris. 3. (fig.) sluggishness caused by disuse. — **criar m.,** to get moldy or rusty; **no criar m. una cosa,** to keep moving, functioning or working; **m. azul,** tobacco mildew.
mohoso, sa, *a.* 1. moldy, mildewy; rusty. 2. mossy.
moisés, *m.* 1. (Bib.) **M.,** Moses. 2. bassinet, crib.
mojábana, *f.* cheese cake; cruller, fritter.
mojada, *f.* 1. wetting; drenching, dousing, soaking; moistening. 2. (coll.) stab (with a knife). 3. (Sp., reg.) a soup made with bread or tack dipped in any liquid.
mojado, da, *past part. of* **mojar.** —*a.* wet; drenched, sodden, soaked; moistened.
mojador, ra, *a.* wetting; drenching, soaking; moistening. —*m., f.* wetter. —*m.* moistener (for fingers when counting banknotes); (print.) moistening tank.
mojadura, *f.* wetting; drenching, soaking; moistening.
mojama, *f.* dried and salted tuna fish.
mojar, *tr.v.* 1. to wet; to drench, douse, soak; to moisten, dampen. 2. (coll.) to stab. 3. to dip or dunk (bread, toast, cake, into milk, coffee, etc.). —*r.v.* to get wet, drenched, soaked, moistened, damp. —*i.v.* (fig.) to get (into a business), get mixed up (in).
mojarra, *f.* 1. (ichth.) mojarra, moharra. 2. (S. Amer.) short broad knife.
mojarilla, *m., f.* gay, jolly person.
moje, *m.,* the gravy, sauce, broth or liquid of a stew or casserole dish.
mojel, *m.* (mar.) braided rope (for hoisting the anchor).
mojí, (*pl.* **mojíes**), *m., var. of* **mojicón.**
mojicón, *m.* 1. small iced cake; a crisp bun (for dunking into chocolate). 2. (coll.) punch in the face.
mojiganga, *f.* 1. masquerade, costume party. 2. (theat.) farce, short light comedy. 3. joke, prank.
mojigatería, *f.* hypocrisy, sanctimoniousness, prudery, religious fanaticism, bigotry.
mojigatez, *f., var. of* **mojigatería,** hypocrisy, sanctimoniousness, prudery.
mojigato, ta, *a.* hypocritical, dissimulating, dissembling; sanctimonious, unctuous. —*m., f.* hypocrite, prude, prig.
mojinete, *m.* 1. coping; ridge (of a roof). 2. (Amer.) gable. 3. (rare) pat on the face.
mojo, *m.* 1. (Cuba, Sp., cul.) a garnish of chopped parsley and onion with lemon. 2. (Cuba) a rum cocktail made with lime juice and crushed sweet basil.
mojón, *m.* 1. boundary stone; landmark. 2. peg (used in the game of pitching). 3. heap, pile. 4. piece of solid excrement. 5. winetaster.
mojona, *f.* 1. surveying and demarcation of boundaries. 2. excise tax on wine.
mojonación, *f., var. of* **amojonamiento,** setting up of boundary marks.
mojonar, *tr.v, var. of* **amojonar,** to set up boundary marks around.
mojonera, *f.* boundary stones, line of boundary stones; landmark.
mojonero, *m.* appraiser, estimator, assessor, gauger.
moka, *f.* Mocha coffee.
mol, *m.* (chem.) mole, mol.
mola, *f.* 1. barley cake made by the ancient Romans. 2. (med.) mole (in uterus).
molada, *f.* (p.) portion of pigment; the amount of color ground at one time.

molal, *a.* (chem.) molal.
molar, *a., m.* (anat.) molar.
molaridad, *f.* (chem.) molarity.
molcajete, *m.* stone or pottery mortar on a tripod.
moldar, *tr.v.* 1. to mold. 2. (archit.) to put molding on.
moldavo, va, *a., m., f.* Moldavian.
molde, *m.* 1. mold, mould; matrix, cast; pattern, model. 2. (print.) form (type made up for printing). — **de m.,** fitting, exactly for the purpose; **letra de m.,** printed letter; block letter.
moldeado, *m.* molding, moulding, casting.
moldeador, ra, *a.* molding, casting, shaping. —*m., f.* molder, moulder; cast maker.
moldeadora, *f.* molding or sand-packing machine.
moldear, *tr.v.* 1. to mould, mold, cast. 2. to provide or trim with moldings. — **m. como la cera,** to mold like wax.
moldura, *f.* 1. (archit.) molding. 2. (Ecuad.) picture frame.
molduradora, *f.* (mach.) molding plane.
moldurar, *tr.v.* to apply moldings to, e.g. *m. un cielo raso,* to put moldings on a plain ceiling.
mole, *a.* soft, mellow; **huevos m.,** (cul.) an egg yolk cream. —*f.* large mass, bulk, lump. —*m.* (Mex.) casserole dish prepared with meat and chili sauce; **m. verde,** stew prepared with chili and green tomatoes.
molécula, *f.* molecule; **m.-gramo,** (chem.) mole, gram molecule.
molecular, *a.* molecular, pertaining to molecules.
moledera, *f.* 1. grinding stone. 2. (coll.) bother, bore, nuisance.
moledero, ra, *a.* 1. to be ground, for grinding. 2. grindable, millable.
moledor, ra, *a.* 1. grinding. 2. (coll.) bothersome, annoying, tiresome. —*m., f.* 1. grinder. 2. bore, bother, nuisance. —*m.* roller, crushing cylinder (in sugar mill.).
moledura, *f., var. of* **molimiento.**
molejón, *m.* 1. grinding stone. 2. (Cuba) ridge or rock near the surface.
molendero, ra, *m., f.* miller, grinder. —*m.* chocolate grinder or manufacturer.
moleño, ña, *a.* said of a rock suitable for millstones. —*f.* (min.) flint.
moler, (*ref. 34*) *tr.v.* 1. to grind, mill, pulverize. 2. to pester, annoy, bother; to tire out, exhaust. 3. (Cuba) to run (a sugar mill); to press sugar cane. 4. to thrash, beat, hurt. — **m. a golpes** or **palos,** to beat up, do in, (coll.) knock silly.
molero, *m.* millstone maker or seller.
molestador, ra, *a.* tiresome, bothersome, vexing, annoying. —*m., f.* bother, pest, annoying person.
molestamente, *adv.* tiresomely, bothersomely, annoyingly, vexatiously.
molestar, *tr.v.* to annoy, bother, pester, vex; to disturb, molest. —*r.v.* to get annoyed or bothered; to bother; **no te molestes,** don't worry, don't bother; **molestarse con,** to get annoyed with; **molestarse en** + *inf.,* to bother to + *inf.,* take the trouble to + *inf.,* e.g. *molestarse en llamar,* to bother to call; **molestarse por una cosa,** to get annoyed at something.
molestia, *f.* annoyance, nuisance, bother, trouble; discomfort; unpleasantness; **tomarse la m. de** + *inf.,* to take the trouble to + *inf.*
molesto, ta, *a.* 1. annoyed, uncomfortable; bothered. 2. annoying, tiresome, bothersome.
molestoso, sa, *a.* annoying, tiresome, bothersome.
moleta, *f.* 1. muller, grinding stone. 2. glass polisher. 3. knurling tool, knurl; roller (for making patterns on hard-surface materials). 4. (print.) ink grinder. 5. (her.) star with a circle inside.
moletón, *m.* (tex.) a kind of cotton flannel.
molibdato, *m.* (chem.) molybdate.
molibdenita, *f.* (min.) molybdenite.
molibdeno, *m.* (chem.) molybdenum.
molíbdico, ca, *a.* (chem.) molybdic.
molibdoso, sa, *a.* (chem.) molybdous.
molicie, *f.* softness; sybaritism, voluptuousness, love of luxury and sensual pleasures.
molido, da, *past part. of* **moler.** —*a.* 1. exhausted, fagged, beat, dead (with exhaustion). 2. ground, grated. — **oro m.,** ormolu; **pan m.,** grated bread (for breading cutlets, fritters, etc.).
molienda, *f.* 1. grinding. 2. quantity being ground. 3. mill. 4. milling or grinding season. 5. (coll.) annoyance, bother, nuisance, bore. 6. (coll.) tiredness, fatigue, exhaustion. — **la m.,** (Cuba) sugar cane harvest and milling time of the year.
moliente, *a.* grinding; **moliente y corriente,** regular, normal.
molificable, *a.* able to be softened; mollifiable.
molificación, *f.* softening; mollification.
molificante, *a.* softening.
molificar, (*ref. 50*) *tr.v., r.v.* to soften, mollify.
molificativo, va, *a.* softening, mollifying, lenitive.
molifique, molifiqué, *ref.* **molificar.**
molimiento, *m.* 1. grinding, milling. 2. weariness, fatigue, exhaustion.
molinar, *m.* place where there are many mills.
molinejo, *m. dim. of* **molino,** small mill.
molinera, *f.* miller's wife; woman miller.
molinería, *f.* group of mills; milling, milling industry.
molinero, ra, *a.* pertaining to milling or grinding. —*m.* miller, owner or operator of a mill.
molinete, *m.* 1. small mill. 2. ventilating fan or wheel. 3. pinwheel, pin wheel (toy). 4. (fenc., taur., dancing) moulinet, circular swing. 5. winch; drum, moulinet (of winch or capstan). 6. (Mex.) catherine wheel (firework). 7. turnstile. 8. meter (measuring speed of motor); current meter (measuring speed of current). 9. spinwheel (moving clothes in dyeing vat). — **m. acústico,** (hydr.) acoustic current meter.
molinillo, *m.* 1. mill, grinder, hand mill. 2. (chocolate) beater, whisk. — **m. de café,** coffee mill or grinder; **m. de pimienta,** pepper mill.
molinito, *m. dim. of* **molino,** small mill.
molino, *m.* 1. mill. 2. jack-in-the-box, restless person. 3. nuisance, pest, annoying person. 4. (coll.) mouth. — **arremeter contra molinos de viento,** to tilt at windmills; **empatársele a uno el m.,** to run into difficulties or trouble; **está picado el m.,** the time or occasion is ripe; **m. arrocero,** rice mill; **m. de agua,** waterwheel; **m. de arcilla,** clay mill; **m. de cilindros,** roller mill; **m. de papel,** paper mill; **m. de sangre,** animal-driven mill; man-driven mill; **m. de viento,** windmill; **molinos de viento,** imaginary enemies; **m. hidráulico,** water mill.
molitivo, va, *a.* softening, mollifying.
molla, *f.* 1. lean meat. 2. soft bread crumb.
mollar, *a.* 1. soft, tender; soft-shelled. 2. easy, very productive, undemanding work. 3. (coll.) gullible, credulous. 4. boneless meat.
molle, *m.* (Bol., Ecuad., Arg., Chile, Peru, bot.) pepper tree.
mollear, *i.v.* to give, yield; to bend; to become pliable.
molledo, *m.* 1. fleshy part (of arms and legs). 2. crumb (soft part of bread).
molleja, *f.* gizzard, maw. 2. sweetbread, thymus gland (in an animal). 3. (*pl.*) (cul.) sweetbreads. — **criar m.,** (coll.) to grow lazy.
mollejón, *m.* 1. grindstone. 2. (coll.) slob, fat loafer. 3. (coll.) easy-going fellow.
mollejuela, *f. dim. of* **molleja,** sweetbread.
mollera, *f.* 1. crown (of the head). 2. (coll.) brains, ability. 3. (anat.) fontanelle. — **cerrado de m.,** stupid; **duro de m.,** obstinate; dull, slow on the uptake.
mollero, *m.* (coll.) fleshy part (of limb); (Cuba, reg. Sp., coll.) biceps.
molleta, *f.* 1. whole wheat bread; brown bread; bisquit. 2. (*pl.*) candle snuffers.
mollete, *m.* 1. small roll (of bread). 2. fleshy part (of limb). 3. fat or chubby cheek.
molletero, ra, *m., f.* person who bakes or sells rolls.
molletudo, da, *a.* fat-checked, chubby-cheeked.
mollino, na, *a.* drizzling, soft (rain).
mollizna, *f.* drizzle, mist.
molliznar, molliznear, *i.v.* to drizzle, to rain lightly.
molo, *m.* 1. (Chile) mole, breakwater. 2. (Ecuad.) mashed potatoes.
moloc, *m.* (zool.) moloch, lizard.
Moloc, *m.* Moloch, an Ammonite deity.
mololoa, *f.* (Hond.) noisy conversation.
molondro, *m.* (coll.) ne'er-do-well, bum (coll.), good-for-nothing.
molondrón, *m., var. of* **molondro.** — (Ven.) a considerable sum or property.
molote, *m.* 1. (Cuba) uproar, shindy, rumpus, riot, row. 2. (Mex.) bun, chignon (hair). 3. (Mex.) tortilla filled with meat, chile, onions, etc.
molotera, *f.* (Guat., Hond.) uproar, shindy, rumpus, row.
moltura, *f.* grinding.
Molucas, *f.* (*pl.*) Moluccas, archipelago in Indonesia.
molusco, ca, *a.* (zool.) molluscan. —*m.* (zool.) mollusk; (*pl*) Mollusca.
moma, *f.* (Mex.) blindman's buff.
momear, *i.v.* to grimace, clown, act the buffoon.
momentáneamente, *adv.* 1. momentarily. 2. immediately, instantly.
momentáneo, a, *a.* 1. momentary, temporary. 2. prompt.
momento, *m.* 1. moment, instant. 2. importance, consequence, moment. 3. moment, occasion. 4. (phys.) moment. — **a cada m.,** at every moment, continuously; **al m.,** immediately, instantly; **de un m. al otro,** momentarily; from one moment to another, at any time; **m. de fuerza,** (phys.) moment of force; **m. de quiñada,** (aer.) yawing moment; **m. de inercia,** (phys.) moment of inertia; **m. de torsión,** (phys.) torsional moment; **m. de torsión de arranque,** (phys.) starting torque; **m. magnético,** (phys.) magnetic moment, moment of magnet; **por el m.** or **de m.,** for the time being; **por momentos,** continuously.
momería, *f.* buffoonery, clowning.
momero, ra, *a.* buffoonish, clowning. —*m., f.* clown, buffoon.
momia, *f.* 1. mummy (embalmed corpse). 2. (fig.) lean, leathery-skinned person.
momificación, *f.* mummification.
momificar, (*ref. 50*) *tr.v.* to mummify. —*r.v.* to become mummified.
momifique, momifiqué, *ref.* **momificar.**
momio, a, *a.* thin, lean. —*m.* 1. extra; bargain. 2. lean person. 3. (Chile), (sl.) bureaucrat. — **de m.,** gratis, free.
momo, *m.* grimace, funny face (coll.).
momórdiga, *f.* (bot.) balsam apple.
mona, *f.* 1. female monkey; (zool.) Barbary ape, macaque monkey (Macaccus sylvanus). 2. (coll.) copycat, ape. 3. (coll.) drunk, drunken bout; hangover; drunk, drunken person. 4. shin guard (of bullfighter fighting on horseback). 5.

old maid (card game). 6. (Chile) manequin, dressmaker's dummy or figure. 7. (Mex.) coward. — **aunque la m. se vista de seda, m. se queda,** you can't make a duchess out of a fishwife, you can't make a silk purse out of a sow's ear; **dormir la m.,** to sleep off a hangover; **pillar** or **pegarse una m.,** to get drunk; **m. de Pascua,** Easter cake.
monacal, *a.* monastic, monkish, pertaining to monks or monasteries.
monacalmente, *adv.* monastically.
monacato, *m.* monkhood; monasticism; a monastic way of life.
monacillo, *m.* altar boy, acolyte, server.
monacita, *f.* (min.) monazite.
Mónaco, *m.* Monaco, independent principality on the S.E. coast of France.
monacordio, *m.* (mus.) a kind of spinet.
monada, *f.* 1. cute little thing, sweet little thing. 2. monkey face, funny face, grimace. 3. crazy action, madness, stupidity, foolishness. 4. flattery, flattering word.
mónada, *f.* (philos., chem., biol., bot., zool.) monad.
monadelfo, fa, *a.* (bot.) monadelphous.
monadismo, *m.* (philos.) monadism.
monadología, *f.* (philos.) monadology.
monago, *m.* (coll.) *var. of* **monaguillo.**
monaguillo, *m.* acolyte, altar boy, server.
monanto, ta, *a.* (bot.) monanthous.
monaquismo, *m.* monasticism; monkhood.
monarca, *m.* monarch, king, sovereign.
monarquía, *f.* monarchy, kingdom.
monárquicamente, *adv.* monarchically.
monárquico, ca, *a.* monarchical, monarchic. —*m., f.* advocate of a monarchy.
monarquismo, *m.* monarchism.
monarquista, *a., m., f.* monarchist.
monasterial, *a.* monasterial.
monasterio, *m.* monastery; convent; cloister.
monásticamente, *adv.* monastically; austerely.
monástico, ca, *a.* monastic, monastical; austere, disciplined; **vida m.,** monastic life.
monatómico, ca, *a.* (chem.) monatomic.
monazita, *f.* (min.) monazite.
monda, *f.* 1. pruning, trimming; pruning season. 2. cleaning. 3. peeling, paring; shelling. 4. clearing cemetery of bones (to make way for new burials). 5. (Cuba, Col., Mex., P. Rico) beating, thrashing; spanking.
mondadientes, *m.* toothpick.
mondador, ra, *a.* cleaning; pruning, trimming; peeling, shelling. —*m., f.* cleaner; pruner, trimmer; peeler, parer.
mondadura, *f.* pruning, trimming; peeling, shelling; (*pl.*) trimmings, rubbish; peelings.
mondaoídos, *m.* earpick, ear spoon.
mondaorejas, *m., var. of* **mondaoídos.**
mondapozos, *m.* well cleaner.
mondar, *tr.v.* 1. to clean, cleanse. 2. to prune, trim. 3. to peel, pare (fruit); to shell (nuts). 4. to cut (someone's) hair, cut the hair of. 5. (coll.) to clean (someone) out (e.g. of money). —*r.v.* **mondarse de risa,** to split with laughter.
mondarajas, *f.* (*pl.*) (coll.) peelings, parings (from fruit, vegetables).
mondejo, *m.* stuffed pig's or sheep's stomach.
mondo, da, *a.* clean, pure, neat; **mondo y lirondo,** (coll.) unadulterated, pure; without beating about the bush.
mondón, *m.* stripped tree trunk, tree trunk without bark.
mondonga, *f.* kitchen wench; slovenly and rude servant girl.
mondongo, *m.* 1. (cul.) tripe. 2. (coll.) guts, human intestines. 3. (Guat., P. Rico) something ugly or botched up.
mondonguería, *f.* tripe shop.
mondonguero, ra, *m., f.* person who sells or cooks tripe.
mondonguil, *a.* pertaining to tripe.
monear, *i.v.* 1. to clown around, make funny faces. 2. (Amer.) to boast, preen oneself. 3. (Ven.) to climb.
moneda, *f.* coin, currency, money, specie; (coll.) wealth, estate, riches. — **corre la m.,** money is circulating; money is plentiful; **cuñar, batir** or **labrar m.,** to mint money or currency; **m. blanda** or **débil,** soft currency; **m. sonante y contante,** hard money or cash, specie; **m. circulante,** cash; **m. corriente,** currency; **m. cortada,** unmilled coin; **m. de reserva,** reserve currency; **m. divisionaria,** divisional coin (coin representing a fraction of a monetary unit); **m. fiduciaria,** fiat money; **m. fuerte,** strong currency; **m. imaginaria,** money of account; **m. legal** or **de curso legal,** legal tender; **m. metálica,** specie, hard money or cash; **m. sonante,** specie, hard money or cash; **pagar en buena m.,** to pay in good measure, give complete satisfaction; **pagar con la misma m.,** to repay (someone) in his own coin; to give tit for tat; **ser m. corriente,** (coll.) to be common knowledge, be well-known.
monedaje, *m.* seigniorage, brassage, coinage.
monedar, monedear, *tr.v.* to mint, coin (money).
monedería, *f.* minting, mintage.
monedero, *a.* **sobre monedero,** cardboard wrapping for mailing coins. —*m.* 1. change purse. 2. coiner, minter. — **m. falso,** counterfeiter.
monegasco, ca, *a.* Monacan, of or pertaining to Monaco. —*m., f.* Monacan.
monería, *f.* 1. amusing trick or gesture, cuteness. 2. foolishness, childishness, silliness. 3. bauble, trifle, amusing gew-gaw.
monesco, ca, *a.* (coll.) apelike, apish, monkeylike.
monetario, ria, *a.* monetary, financial. —*m.* coin collection; cabinet for a coin collection.
monetice, moneticé, *ref.* **monetizar.**
monetización, *f.* monetization.
monetizar, (*ref. 53*) *tr.v.* 1. to monetize. 2. to mint.
monfí, (*pl.* **monfíes**), *m.* (hist., Sp.) Moorish highwayman.
monga, *f.* (P. Rico, coll.) grippe, influenza; a bad cold.
mongol, *a.* Mongol, Mongolian.
Mongolia, *f.* Mongolia; **M. Exterior,** Outer Mongolia; **M. Interior,** Inner Mongolia.
mongólico, ca, *a.* Mongolian.
mongolismo, *m.* (med.) Mongolism, Down's syndrome.
monguera, *f.* (P. Rico, coll.) lassitude, laziness; weakness.
moniato, *m.* (bot.) sweet potato.
monicaco, *m.* 1. unimportant but self-assertive little man. 2. (Col.) hypocrite, prude; zealot.
monición, *f.* admonition.
monigote, *m.* 1. childishly drawn picture, grotesque puppet. 2. (coll.) boob, sap, dope, ignoramus. 3. (coll.) puppet, rag doll. 4. lay brother.
moniliforme, *a.* (bot., zool.) moniliform.
monillo, *m.* (dressm.) bodice, waist, basque.
monín, na, *a.* cute, pretty, amusing.
monipodio, *m.* illegal agreement or deal, cabal.
monís, *f.* 1. pretty trinket, pretty little thing. 2. a kind of fritter. —*m.* (coll.) money (*gen. pl.*).
monismo, *m.* (philos.) monism.
monista, *a., m.* (philos.) monist.
mónita, *f.* cunning, craftiness, cleverness.
monitor, *m.* 1. monitor, adviser, trainer. 2. (mar.) monitor.
monitorio, ria, *a.* monitory, monitorial. —*m.* (ecc.) monitory, admonition.
monja, *f.* 1. nun. 2. (Mex.) a round sweet bread. 3. (*pl.*) glowing sparks left by burning paper.
monje, *m.* 1. monk. 2. (fig.) recluse, retiring person. 3. (ornith.) great titmouse, brown peacock.
monjía, *f.* monkhood, monk's prebend.
monjil, *a.* nun-like, nunnish, of a nun. —*m.* nun's habit; mourning dress.
manjío, *m.* nunhood; taking the veil.
monjita, *f.* 1. *dim. of* **monja,** dear nun (affectionate term for a nun). 2. (Arg.) small bird of the pampas.
mono, na, *a.* cute, pretty, amusing, dainty. —*m.* 1. (zool.) monkey, ape. 2. mimic, ape (person). 3. nincompoop, dope, sap. 4. childlike drawing or painting, primitively drawn figure. 5. (*pl.*) overalls; (mil.) fatigue clothes. 6. (Chile) pile of fruit or vegetables (in a market). 7. (Ecuad., Peru) chamberpot. — **estar de monos,** (coll.) to be on bad terms, be at odds, have fallen out with one another; **meterle los monos a,** (Col.) to frighten, scare; **quedarse hecho un m.,** to be made a monkey of, be made to look ridiculous; **m. araña,** (zool.) spider monkey; **m. aullador,** (zool.) howling monkey; **m. capuchino,** (zool.) capuchin; **m. sabio,** (taur.) bullring assistant or attendant (who cleans the ring, pulls the dead bull out, etc.).
monoácido, da, *a., m.* (chem.) monoacid.
monoatómico, ca, *a.* (phys.) monatomic.
monoáxico, ca, *a.* (bot.) monaxial.
monobásico, ca, *a.* (chem.) monobasic.
monobloque, *m.* in one piece, in one solid block.
monocarpelar, *a.* (bot.) monocarpellary.
monocárpico, ca, *a.* (bot.) monocarpic.
monocarpo, a, *a.* (bot.) monocarpous.
monocarril, *m.* monorail, one-track railway.
monocasco, *m.* (aer.) monocoque.
monócero, *m.* (astron.) Monoceros.
monoceronte, *m.* unicorn.
monocíclico, ca, *a.* (elec.) monocyclic.
monociclo, a, *a.* monocyclic. —*m.* monocycle.
monocilíndrico, ca, *a.* single-cylinder.
monocito, *m.* (physiol.) monocyte.
monoclamídea, *a.* (bot.) monochlamydeous. —*f.* (*pl.*) Monochlamydeae.
monoclinal, *a.* (geol.) monoclinal.
monoclínico, ca, *a.* (min.) monoclinic.
monoclino, na, *a.* (bot.) monoclinous.
monocontrol, *m.* single-dial control.
monocordio, *m.* (mus.) monochord.
monocotiledón, *a.* (bot.) monocotyledonous. —*m.* (bot.) monocotyledon; (*pl.*) Monocotyledones.
monocotiledóneo, a, *a.* (bot.) monocotyledonous. —*f.* (bot.) monocotyledon; (*pl.*) Monocotyledoneae.
monocromático, ca, *a.* monochromatic, in one color.
monocromo, ma, *a.* monochrome, monochromic, of one color.
monocular, *a.* monocular.
monóculo, la, *a.* monocular, one-eyed. —*m.* 1. monocle. 2. (med.) monoculus, eye patch.
monocultivo, *m.* (agr.) monoculture.
monocultura, *f.* (agr.) monoculture.
monodáctilo, la, *a.* (zool.) monodactylous, having one finger, toe, or claw.
monodia, *f.* (mus.) monody, song for one single voice.
monódico, ca, *a.* monodic.
monoenergético, ca, *a.* (nuclear phys.) monoenergetic.
monofase, *a.* (elec.) single-phase.
monofásico, ca, *a.* (elec.) single-phase, monophase, monophasic.

monofilético, ca, *a.* (biol.) monophyletic.
monofilo, la, *a.* (bot.) monophyllous, having only one leaf.
monofisismo, *m.* (rel.) Monophysitism.
monofisita, *a.* (rel.) Monophysitic. —*m., f.* Monophysite.
monofobia, *f.* (med.) monophobia, fear of being alone.
monofónico, ca, *a.* (elec.) monophonic.
monófono, na, *a.* (mus.) monophonic.
monogamia, *f.* monogamy.
monogámico, ca, *a.* monogamic.
monogamista, *a., m, f.* monogamist.
monógamo, ma, *a.* monogamous. —*m.* monogamist.
monogenésico, ca, *a.* (biol.) monogenetic.
monogénesis, *f.* (biol.) monogenesis.
monogenia, *f.* (biol.) monogeny.
monogénico, ca, *a.* (biol.) monogenic.
monogenismo, *m.* monogenism, monogenesis, theory that mankind has descended from a single pair of ancestors.
monogenista, *m.* monogenist.
monografía, *f.* monograph, writing on a specific subject.
monográfico, ca, *a.* monographic, monographical.
monografista, *m., f.* monographist, monographer.
monograma, *m.* monogram; initials (combined in a design).
monohidratado, da, *a.* (chem.) monohydrated.
monohidrato, *m.* (chem.) monohydrate.
monohídrico, ca, *a.* (chem.) monohydric.
monoico, ca, *a.*(bot.) monoecious.
monolítico, ca, *a.* monolithic.
monolito, *m.* monolith, large block of stone used in architecture or sculpture.
monologar, (*ref. 51*) *i.v.* to soliloquize, make a long speech or monologue.
monólogo, *m.* monologue, soliloquy.
monologue, monologué, *ref.* **monologar.**
monomanía, *f.* monomania, obsession with one idea.
monomaníaco, ca, *a.* monomaniacal. —*m., f.* monomaniac.
monomaníatico, ca, *a.* monomaniac; monomaniacal.
monómero, ra, *a.* (chem.) monomeric. —*m.* (chem.) monomer.
monometálico, *a.* monometallic.
monometalismo, *m.* monometallism, the use of only one metal as a standard of money.
monometalista, *m., f.* monometallist, advocate of monometalism.
monomio, *m.* (math.) monomial.
monomolecular, *a.* (phys., chem.) monomolecular.
monomorfo, fa, *a.* (chem., biol.) monomorphic, monomorphous.
monomotor, *a.* single-motor.
monono, na, *a.* (coll.) cute, pretty, sweet, amusing.
mononuclear, *a.* (bot., chem.) mononuclear.
monopastos, (*pl.* **monopastos**), *m.* pulley, sheave.
monopatín, *m.* scooter.
monopétalo, la, *a.* (bot.) monopetalous.
monoplano, *m.* monoplane.
monoplaza, *m.* single-seater (airplane).
monoplejía, *f.* (med.) monoplegia.
monopléjico, ca, *a.* (med.) monoplegic.
monopodio, *m.* (bot.) monopode.
monopolar, *a.* (elec.) single-pole.
monopolice, monopolicé *ref.* **monopolizar.**
monopolio, *m.* monopoly.
monopolismo, *m.* monopoly.
monopolista, *m., f.* monopolist, monopolizer.
monopolización, *f.* monopolization.
monopolizador, ra, *a.* monopolizing. —*m.* monopolizer.
monopolizar, (*ref. 53*) *tr.v.* to monopolize.
monopsonio, *m.* (com., econ.) monopsony.
monóptero, ra, *a.* (archit.) monopteral (said of a structure formed by a circle of columns, with a ceiling but without walls, e.g. a kiosk, a pergola).
monoquini, *m.* woman's bikini-like topless bathing suit.
monorquidia, *f.* (med.) monorchism, monorchidism.
monorriel, *m.* monorail, railway system with one track.
monorrimo, ma, *a.* (poet.) monorhymed, having only one rhyme.
monorrítmico, ca, *a.* (poet.) monorhythmic.
monosabio, *m.* (taur.) bullring attendant or assistant (who cleans the ring, pulls the dead bull out, etc.).
monosacárido, *m.* (chem.) monosaccharide.
monosépalo, la, *a.* (bot.) monosepalous.
monosilábico, ca, *a.* monosyllabic.
monosílabo, ba, *a.* (gram.) monosyllabic. —*m.* (gram.) monosyllable.
monosimétrico, ca, *a.* monosymmetric, monoclinic.
monosoma, *m.* (biol.) monosome.
monospastos, (*pl.* **monospastos**), *m.* pulley.
monospermo, ma, *a.* (bot.) monospermous.
monostela, *f.* (bot.) monostele.
monostelia, *f.* (bot.) monostely.
monostélico, ca, *a.* (bot.) monostelic.
monostíleo, a, *a.* (bot.) monostylous.
monóstrofe, *f.* (poet.) monostrophe.
monostrófico, ca, *a.* (poet.) monostrophic.
monote, *m.* (coll.) person stricken dumb, dumbfounded person.
monoteísmo, *m.* (theol.) monotheism, belief in one god.
monoteísta, *a.* (theol.) monotheistic. —*m., f.* (theol.) monotheist.
monotelismo, *m.* (rel.) Monothelism, Monotheletism, Monothelitism.
monotelita, *a.* (rel.) Monothelitic, Monotheletic. —*m., f.* (rel.) Monothelite, Monothelete.
monotipia, *f.* (print.) monotype process, monotyping.
monotipo, *m.* (print.) monotype, monotype machine.
monótonamente, *adv.* monotonously; droningly; boringly.
monotonía, *f.* monotony.
monótono, na, *a.* monotonous; unvarying.
monotrema, *a.* (zool.) monotrematous, monotreme. —*m.* (zool.) monotreme; (*pl.*) Monotremata.
monotremado, da, *a.* (zool.) monotrematous.
monotrico, ca, *a.* (biol.) monotrichous, monotrichic.
monovalencia, *f.* (chem.) monovalence, univalence.
monovalente, *a.* (chem.) monovalent, univalent.
monóxido, *m.* (chem.) monoxide. — **m. de carbono,** (chem.) carbon monoxide.
Monrovia, *m.* Monrovia, capital of Liberia.
Mons. *abbrev. of* **Monseñor,** Monsignor.
monseñor, *m.* monseigneur (title).
monserga, *f.* (coll.) gibberish, confused talk; **no me vengas con monsergas,** don't bother me.
monstruo, *m.* monster, monstrosity; something huge and hideous.
monstruosamente, *adv.* monstrously.
monstruosidad, *f.* monstrosity.
monstruoso, sa, *a.* monstrous; huge; extraordinary; hideous; shocking; hateful.
monta, *f.* 1. importance, significance, account, e.g. *de poca m.,* of little importance or significance, of little account. 2. sum, total, price, amount. 3. mounting (action). 4. stud farm. 5. (mil.) mounting call (to the cavalry). 6. (Urug.) jockey, rider.
montacargas, *m.* freight lift or elevator; **m. de cadena,** chain hoist or block.
montada, *f.* (equit.) port, tongue, groove (of horse's bit).
montadero, *m.* mounting block.
montado, da, *past part. of* **montar.** —*a.* mounted. —*m.* trooper, cavalryman, horseman.
montador, *m.* 1. mounting block. 2. (mec.) assembler, installer. — **m. de tuberías,** pipe fitter.
montadura, *f.* 1. mounting. 2. harness, saddle. 3. (jewel.) setting, mounting.
montaje, *m.* 1. assembly, installation (of machine, car, etc.). 2. (artil.) (*pl.*) mount. 3. (rad., cine., photog.) montage. — **m. en Y** or **en estrella,** (elec.) Y grouping; **planta de m,** assembly plant.
montanera, *f.* acorn and mast pasture for hogs; acorn or mast feeding season.
montanero, *m.* forest keeper or ranger, forest warden.
montanismo, *m.* (rel.) Montanism.
montanista, *a.* (rel.) Montanistic. —*m., f.* (rel.) Montanist.
montano, na, *a.* of or pertaining to mountains.
montantada, *f.* 1. boasting, braggadocio. 2. crowd, multitude.
montante, *m.* 1. (carp.) upright post, strut (of a frame, of a supporting stand); stile (of door). 2. (archit.) mullion (slender bar between two lights of a window). 3. (archit) transom window, transom. 4. broadsword. 5. (Hond.) uproar, rumpus, shindy. 6. (Amer.) sum, amount. — **meter el m.,** to separate two fencers; to separate two opponents in a fight or dispute. —*f.* (mar.) flood tide.
montantear, *i.v.* 1. (fenc.) to wield the broadsword. 2. to throw one's weight around, try to boss everyone around.
montantero, *m.* fighter with a broadsword.
montaña, *f.* 1. mountain; mountainous region; highlands. 2. (fig.) large quantity, heap. — **Montañas Rocosas** or **Rocallosas,** Rocky Mountains, Rockies; **m. rusa,** roller coaster, switchback (G.B.).
montañero, ra, *m., f.* mountaineer, mountain climber.
montañes, sa, *a.* 1. highland, mountain (as *a.*). 2. of or from the province of Santander (Spain). —*m., f.* 1. highlander. 2. inhabitant of Santander.
montañeta, *f. dim. of* **montaña,** hill, small mountain.
montañismo, *m.* mountaineering, mountain climbing.
montañoso, sa, *a.* mountainous.
montañuela, *f. dim. of* **montaña,** hill, small mountain.
montar, *tr.v.* 1. to ride (a horse, bicycle, etc.). 2. to mount; to get on, get on top of. 3. to impose a fine for the trespassing of cattle. 4. to cover (a mare). 5. to amount to, add up to. 6. to assemble, mount, set up (a machine); (mil.) to mount (a gun). 7. (mil.) to mount (guard). 8. (jewel.) to mount, set. 9. (mil.) to cock (a gun). 10. (mar.) to command (a ship). 11. (mar.) to mount, have (certain number of guns). 12. (mar.) to round (a cape). 13. (cine.) to edit. — **m. bien la ola,** to ride the wave well; **m. una ofensiva,** to mount an offensive. —*i.v.* 1. to ride. 2. to mount; to get on top. 3. to be important; to be valuable; to be worth. — **m. a,** to amount to, add up to; **m. a caballo,** to ride horseback, ride a horse,

ride; **m. en bicicleta,** to ride a bicycle; **m. en cólera,** to get angry; **tanto monta,** it amounts to the same, it's worth the same.
montaraz, (*pl.* **montaraces**), *a.* 1. pertaining to the backwoods. 2. wild, untamed. —*m.* forest warden or keeper.
montazgar, (*ref. 51*) *tr.v.* to levy or collect cattle toll from.
montazgo, *m.* toll, cattle toll, tax on passage of cattle.
montazgue, montazgué, *ref.* **montazgar.**
monte, *m.* 1. mountain, mount. 2. woodland, wood; brush, underbrush. 3. (cards) monte; bank, kitty; stack (cards or chips left after dealing). 4. unsurmountable difficulty. 5. (coll.) matted mop of hair. 6. (coll.) pawnshop. — **andar a m.,** to take to the woods, be an outlaw; (coll.) to make oneself scarce, keep away from people; **batir** or **correr el m.,** to go hunting; **m. alto;** forest, woodland with tall trees; tall trees; **m. bajo,** land covered with underbrush; underbrush, brushwood; **m. blanco,** land for re-foresting; **M. Blanco,** Mont Blanc; **M. Carmelo,** Mount Carmel; **m. cerrado,** dense woodland; **M. Cervino,** (the) Matterhorn; **M. de los Olivos,** Mount of Olives; **m. de piedad,** pawnshop; **m. de Venus,** (anat.) Mons Veneris, Mountain of Venus; (in palmistry) mount of Venus; **m. hueco,** growth of tall trees with no undergrowth; **m. pardo,** oak grove; **m. pío,** widows' and orphans' fund; public assistance office; **m. público,** common land; **Montes Azules,** Blue Mountains; **Montes de Transilvania,** Transylvanian Alps; **Montes Grampianos,** Grampian Hills.
montea, *f.* 1. beating the wood to rouse game. 2. (archit.) stonecutting. 3. (archit.) rise in arch. 4. (archit.) full-scale drawing (of each part of a work of masonry).
monteador, *m.* 1. beater (who raises game). 2. (archit.) draftsman, one who draws a life-size sketch of each part of a building.
montear, *tr.v.* 1. to hunt, track down. 2. (archit.) to make a full-size drawing of. 3. to arch, vault, form arches in.
montecillo, *m. dim. of* **monte,** small forest; hillock.
montepío, *m.* widows' and orphans' fund; public assistance office.
montera, *f.* 1. cloth cap; (taur.) bullfighter's hat; (Bol.) conical hat used by the Indians. 2. skylight. 3. lid, head (of boiler in a still). 4. (mar.) moonsail.
montera, *f.* 1. wife of hunter or huntsman. 2. huntress. 3. (Hond.) drunken bout, drunk.
monterería, *f.* cloth cap shop.
monterero, ra, *m., f.* cloth cap maker or seller.
montería, *f.* 1. hunt; hunting; chase; big-game hunting. 2. (Cuba) leftover meats. 3. (Sp., reg.) hunting breakfast (brunch).
monterilla, *f.* 1. (mar.) moonsail. 2. (Sp.) small town mayor.
montero, *m.,* hunter, huntsman; beater (at the hunt). — **m. de cámara** or **m. mayor,** royal huntsman.
monterrey, *m.* (cul.) meat pie.
monteruca, *f.* big ugly cap.
montés, sa, *a.* wild, undomesticated, uncultivated; mountain-bred. — **gato m.,** mountain lion.
montesco, *m.* member of the house of Montague, Romeo's family. — **habrá Montescos y Capuletos,** (coll.) there will be fireworks, there will be a tremendous rumpus, row or fight.
montesino, na, *a., var. of* **montés.**
montevideano, na, *a.* of or from Montevideo. —*m., f.* native or inhabitant of Montevideo.
Montevideo, *m.* Montevideo, capital of Uruguay.
montículo, *m.* knoll, hillock, mound.
montilla, *m.* montilla (a type of pale dry sherry).
montmorillonita, *f.* (min.) montmorillonite.
monto, *m.* sum, total, amount.
montón, *m.* heap, pile; crowd; (coll.) lot, a great deal. — **a m.,** wholesale, in bulk; **a, de** or **en m.,** (coll.) all together, taken together; **a montones,** in large quantities, abundantly; **ser del m.,** (coll.) to be mediocre.
montonera, *f.* 1. (Amer.) troop of mounted rebels. 2. large crowd. 3. (Col.) haystack.
montonero, *m.* 1. coward who fights only when surrounded by his cronies. 2. insurgent or rebel soldier; (Amer.) guerrilla soldier. 3. (Mex.) troublemaker.
montoso, sa, *a., var. of* **montuoso.**
montuno, na, *a.* 1. of or pertaining to the mountains. 2. (Amer.) wild, untamed. —*m.* (mus.) the rhythmic, dancing coda of Cuban country songs.
montuosidad, *f.* ruggedness, hilliness, woodiness, wilderness.
montuoso, sa, *a.* wooded; hilly, rugged.
montura, *f.* 1. mount (horse, mule, etc.). 2. harness, saddle. 3. (mec.) assembly, mounting (of a machine). 4. mounting, support (for telescope). 5. (Amer., jewel.) setting.
monuelo, la, *a.* foolish, affected. —*m.* fop, coxcomb.
monumental, *a.* monumental, huge; (coll.) excellent.
monumento, *m.* 1. (art., archit.) monument. 2. mausoleum. 3. (ecc.) side altar to the saints.
monzón, *m.* monsoon.
monzonita, *f.* (min.) monzonite.
moña, *f.* 1. mannequin, lay figure. 2. bow, knot of ribbons; (taur.) rosette (on neck of bull identifying its owner or its breeding ranch); knot of black ribbons (placed on a bull fighter's queue). 3. (coll.) drunk, drunken bout.
moñajo, *m.* big ugly topknot, bun or chignon.
moño, *m.* 1. bun, chignon, topknot (of hair). 2. rosette of ribbons, topknot. 3. crest (of feathers on some birds). 4. (*pl.*) fripperies, baubles (adornments in poor taste). 5. (Chile) forelock (of horse). 6. (Mex.) bow, bowknot. 7. (Col.) whim, caprice. — **hacerse el m.,** (coll.) to do one's hair, comb one's hair; **ponérsele a uno una cosa en el m.,** (coll.) to get a bee in one's bonnet; **ponerse uno moños, to put on airs.**
moñón, na, moñudo, da, *a.* 1. crested (birds). 2. (Col.) pouting, sulky.
moque, moqué, *ref.* **mocar.**
moquear, *i.v.* to snivel, have a runny nose.
moqueo, *m.* sniveling, running at the nose.
moquero, *m.* handkerchief.
moqueta, *f.* (tex.) strong pile cloth used for carpeting.
moquete, *m.* punch in the face.
moquetear, *i.v.* (coll.) to snivel, run at the nose constantly. —*tr.v.* to punch someone in the nose.
moquillo, *m.* 1. (vet.) distemper (of dogs, cats). 2. (vet.) pip (of birds, fowls). 3. (Ecuad., equit.) twitch (stick drawn lightly over upper lip to keep horse quiet).
moquita, *f.* watery mucus.
mora, *f.* 1. (law) mora, negligent delay. 2. Moorish woman. 3. (bot.) mulberry, blackberry, brambleberry. 4. (Bol.) rifle bullet.
morabito, *m.* Mohammedan hermit or hermitage.
morabuto, *m., var. of* **morabito.**
moráceo, a, *a.* (bot.) moraceous. —*f.* moraceous plant; (*pl.*) Moraceae.
moracho, cha, *a., m.* light purple.
morada, *f.* 1. dwelling, abode, home. 2. stay, sojourn.
morado, da, *a.* 1. royal purple, murrey. 2. (Arg.) cowardly. —*m.* royal purple color.
morador, ra, *a.* dwelling, residing; sojourning. —*m., f.* dweller, resident; sojourner.
moraga, *f.* 1. sheaf, bundle (of gleaned corn). 2. outdoor barbecue (of fish, fruit).
moragada, *f.* toasting of pine cones (to extract seeds).
morago, *m., var. of* **moraga.**
moral, *a.* moral. —*f.* 1. morals, ethics; morality. 2. morale (of soldiers, etc.). —*m.* (bot.) black mulberry tree (Morus nigra).
moraleja, *f.* moral, maxim, lesson (of a fable, story, etc.).
moralice, moralicé, *ref.* **moralizar.**
moralidad, *f.* morality; ethics, morals.
moralista, *m.* moralist.
moralización, *f.* moralization.
moralizador, ra, *a.* moralizing. —*m., f.* moralizer.
moralizar, (*ref. 53*) *tr.v.* to moralize, make moral. —*i.v.* to moralize, indulge in moral reflexion. —*r.v.* to become moral.
moralmente, *adv.* morally.
moranza, *f.* dwelling, abode, residence.
morapio, *m.* (coll.) red table wine.
morar, *i.v.* to dwell, live, stay, sojourn.
moratiniano, na, *a.* (lit.) characteristic of the style of Moratín (18th century playwright, called the Spanish Moliére).
moratoria, *f.* (law) moratorium.
moravo, va, *a., m., f.* Moravian.
morbidez, *f.* softness, smoothness (of contours, skin, etc.).
morbididad, *f.* (med.) morbidity, sick rate, amount of disease (in a given region or country).
mórbido, da, *a.* 1. soft, smooth, fine-grained; subtle (colors, contours). 2. (med.) morbid, sick, diseased.
morbífico, ca, *a.* (med.) morbific, unhealthy, causing disease.
morbilidad, *f., var. of* **morbididad.**
morbo, *m.* (med.) illness, disease; **m. comicial,** (med.) epilepsy; **m. gálico,** (med.) syphilis; **m. regio,** (med.) jaundice.
morbosidad, *f.* 1. (med.) morbidity, sickness, disease. 2. (med.) morbidity, sick rate, amount of disease.
morboso, sa, *a.* sick, diseased, morbid; unhealthy.
morcajo, *m.* maslin, mixture of wheat and rye.
morceguila, *f.* bat's excrement.
morcella, *f.* spark from candle or lamp.
morciguillo, *m.* (ornith.) bat.
morcilla, *f.* 1. (cul.) blood pudding, blood sausage. 2. poisoned meat to kill dogs. 3. (theat.) ad-lib, improvisation, gag. 4. (Cuba) lie, fib, boast.
morcillero, ra, *m., f.* 1. sausage maker or seller. 2. ad-libber, improvising actor.
morcillo, *m.* fleshy part (of upper arm).
morcillo, lla, *a.* reddish black (said of a horse).
morcillón, *m.* (cul.) (type of) haggis.
morcón, *m.* 1. large blood pudding; sausage. 2. (coll.) short fat fellow. 3. (coll.) slob; dirty, slovenly person.
morcuero, *m.* loose pile of stone.
mordacidad, *f.* sarcasm; mordacity, mordancy.
mordaga, *f.* drunk, drunken bout.
mordante, *m.* (print.) guide, typesetter's double rule.
mordaz, (*pl.* **mordaces**), *a.* mordant, biting, caustic (e.g. style, criticism, etc.); sarcastic; corrosive, burning; stinging, biting (to the palate).
mordaza, *f.* 1. gag; (fig.) gag. 2. (mec.) clamp, grip, holder; (mec.) jaw (of pincers, tongs). 3. (artil.) recoil mechanism (on some guns). 4.

(mar.) hawschole clamp (stopping or impeding exit of anchor chain). 5. (vet.) clamp (securing upper part of scrotum and avoiding hemorrhages during castration).
mordazmente, *adv.* bitingly, caustically, mordantly.
mordedor, ra, *a.* 1. biting. 2. biting; satirical, mordant. —*m., f.* biter, backbiter.
mordedura, *f.* bite; **m. de serpiente,** snakebite.
mordente, *m.* 1. mordant. 2. (mus.) mordent.
morder, (*ref. 34*) *tr.v.* 1. to bite; to nip; to gnaw. 2. to grasp, clutch. 3. to wear away, wear down (a file-metal); to eat into (an acid-metal). 4. to criticize, run down, gossip about, find fault with. — **m. el polvo,** to bite the dust.
mordicacíon, *f.* nipping, biting; stinging, smarting.
mordicante, *a.* burning, biting, corrosive; sarcastic, caustic, mordant.
mordicar, (*ref. 50*) *tr.v.* to nip, bite; to sting.
mordicativo, va, *a.* biting, burning, corrosive.
mordido, da, *past part. of* **morder.** —*a.* (fig.) diminished, lessened, wasted away.
mordiente, *a.* mordant, biting. —*m.* caustic acid used in etching and engraving; color fixative used in dyeing.
mordihuí, (*pl.* **mordihuíes**), *m.* (ento.) weevil.
mordimiento, *m.* bite, biting.
mordique, mordiqué, *ref.* **mordicar.**
mordiscar, (*ref. 50*) *tr.v.* to nibble; to bite.
mordisco, *m.* nibble, bite; fragment bitten off.
mordiscón, *m. aug. of* **mordisco,** big bite.
mordisque, mordisqué, *ref.* **mordiscar.**
mordisquear, *tr.v., var. of* **mordiscar.**
morduyo, *m.* (Mex.) *var. of* **mordihuí.**
moreda, *f.* (bot.) black mulberry tree; group of black mulberry bushes.
morel de sal, *m.* crimson (used in painting frescoes).
morena, *f.* 1. stack of newly cut corn. 2. (geol.) moraine. 3. loaf of brown bread. 4. (ichth.) moray (Muraena helena).
morenillo, *m.* paste of ground charcoal and vinegar used by shearers for dressing cuts.
moreno, na, *a.* 1. brown, tawny (color). 2. brown-skinned, dark, dark-skinned, swarthy. 3. mulatto, colored. —*m., f.* 1. (Cuba) black person; Negro, Negress. 2. (Sp.) brunet, brunette; (coll.) darling; beautiful; lover.
morenote, ta, *a.* very dark, brown-skinned or swarthy.
móreo, a, *a.* (bot.) moraceous. —*f.* (*pl.*) (bot.) Moraceae.
morera, *f.* (bot.) white mulberry tree; **m. negra,** (bot.) black mulberry tree.
moreral, *m.* group of mulberry trees.
morería, *f.* (Sp., hist.) Moorish quarter; Moorish territory.
morete, *m.* (Hond., Mex.) bruise.
moreteado, da, *a.* 1. bruised, covered with bruises. 2. purplish.
moretón, *m.* (coll.) bruise; discoloration left on the skin by a bruise.
morfa, *f.* (bot.) citrus scab, fungus disease (on citrus trees).
morfema, *m.* (gram.) morpheme.
Morfeo, *m.* (myth.) Morpheus, god of sleep and dreams.
mórfico, ca, *a.* morphine (salt).
morfina, *f.* (pharm.) morphine.
morfínico, ca, *a.* morphinic.
morfinismo, *m.* (med.) morphinism.
morfinomanía, *f.* morphinomania, drug habit.
morfinómano, na, *a.* morphinomaniacal. —*m., f.* morphinomaniac, drug addict.
morfogénesis, *f.* (biol.) morphogenesis.
morfogénico, ca, *a.* (biol.) morphogenic.
morfología, *f.* (biol., philol.) morphology.
morfológico, ca, *a.* morphological.
morfosis, *f.* (biol.) morphosis.
morga, *f.* 1. foul-smelling juice from crushed olives. 2. (bot.) Indian berry tree.
morganático, ca, *a.* morganatic.
moriángano, *m.* (Can. I.) strawberry.
moribundo, da, *a.* moribund, dying. —*m., f.* dying person.
morichal, *m.* tract of land planted with mirity palms.
moriche, *m.* (bot.) mirity palm.
moriego, ga, *a.* Moorish.
morigeración, *f.* moderation, restraint, temperance.
morigerado, da, *a.* moderate, restrained, abstemious, temperate.
morigerar, *tr.v.* to moderate, temper, restrain.
morilla, *f.* (bot.) morel.
morillo, *m. dim. of* **moro,** little Moor. 2. firedog, andiron (*gen. pl.*).
moringa, *f.* (Cuba) bogeyman, ghost.
morir, (*ref. 38*) *i.v.* 1. to die, expire, decease, pass away. 2. to go out, die (fire). 3. to end, expire (the day). 4. to die away (e.g. a voice in the distance). 5. to be considered unplayed (a hand in cards). — **¡muera!** death to! down with!; **m. de aburrimiento,** to be bored stiff, die of boredom; **m. ahogado,** to drown, die by drowning; **m. asesinado,** to be assassinated, die by assassination: **m. como chinches,** to die like flies; **m. con las botas puestas,** to die with one's boots on; **m. de frío,** to freeze to death; (coll.) to be freezing, be very cold; **m. de hambre,** to starve to death, die of hunger; (coll.) to be ravenous, be very hungry; **m. de risa,** to die laughing; **m. de sed,** to be parched, die or be dying of thirst; **m. en gracia,** to die in a state of grace; **m. en la cama,** to die in one's bed; **m. por** + *n.*, to die for + *n.;* **m. por** + *inf.*, to die trying to + *inf.;* to die because of trying to + *inf.;* **m. quemado,** to burn to death, be burnt to death; **m. vestido,** to die a violent death; to die with one's boots on. —*r.v.* 1. to die, expire; to end. 2. to go out, die (fire). 3. to expire, end (the day). 4. to die away (e.g. voice in the distance). 5. to go to sleep, become numb (limbs). — **morirse por** + *n.*, to be mad or crazy about + *n.;* **morirse por** + *inf.*, to be dying or yearning to + *inf.*
morisco, ca, *a.* 1. Moorish, Morisco, Moresque. 2. (Chile) thin, lean. 3. (Mex.) quadroon. —*m., f.* 1. (Sp.) Moor converted to Christianity. 2. Morisco, child of a Spaniard and a mulatto.
morisma, *f.* 1. Moors, crowd of Moors. 2. Moorish sect. — **a la m.,** in the Moorish way.
morisqueta, *f.* 1. Moorish trick; (coll.) mean trick. 2. (Phil. I.) rice boiled in unsalted water. 3. (Amer.) face, grimace.
morito, *m.* (ornith.) eastern glossy ibis.
morlaco, ca, *a.* pretending to be stupid or ignorant. —*m., f.* 1. one who pretends to be stupid or ignorant. 2. (taur.) bull. 3. (Arg., coll.) buck, peso (any national coin). 4. (Col.) nag, tired old horse.
morlés, *m.* (a kind of) linen fabric similar to lawn.
morlón, na, *a.* pretending to be stupid or ignorant. —*m., f.* one who pretends to be ignorant or stupid.
mormón, na, *m., f.* (rel.) Mormon.
mormónico, ca, *a.* (rel.) Mormon.
mormonismo, *m.* (rel.) Mormonism.
mormullar, *i.v., var. of* **murmullar.**
mormullo, *m., var. of* **murmullo.**
mormurar, *i.v., var. of* **murmurar.**
moro, ra, *a.* 1. Moorish. 2. Moslem. 3. Moro (pertaining to members of any of the Mohammedan tribes of the southern Philippine Islands). 4. (coll.) strong, undiluted (wine). 5. (coll.) unbaptized. 6. black with white star on forehead (horse). 7. (Hond.) dapple grey (horse). —*m., f.* 1. Moor. 2. Moslem. 3. Moro (member of any Mohammedan tribe of the southern Philippine Islands). — **como moros sin señor,** like bedlam, chaotically; **m. de paz,** peaceful person; **moros y cristianos,** (in public festivals) mock fight between Moors and Christians; (Cuba) casserole of white rice and black beans; **no hay moros en la costa,** (coll.) the coast is clear; **hubo moros y cristianos,** (coll.) there was a colossal fight.
morocada, *f.* butt of a ram.
morocho, cha, *a.* 1. (bot.) Guinea (corn). 2. (Amer., coll.) strong, robust. 3. (Amer.) brunet, brunette; dark, swarthy. 4. (Ven.) twin. 5. (Ecuad.) dry, hard (wood, coal). 6. (Chile) shorn to the scalp (a man, a boy).
morolo, la, *a.* (Hond.) simple, dim, unintelligent.
morón, *m.* hillock, mound, hummock.
morona, *f.* (Col.) breadcrumb.
moroncho, cha, *a.* hairless; leafless; bare, stripped (of leaves, hair).
morondanga, *f.* (coll.) load of junk, jumble of rubbish.
morondo, da, *a.* hairless; leafless; bare, stripped (of hair or leaves).
moronga, *f.* (Hond., Mex.) blood sausage or pudding.
moronía, *f.* casserole dish made of eggplant, tomatoes, squash and pepper.
morosamente, *adv.* slowly, tardily.
morisidad, *f.* slowness, tardiness, delay; (law) delay in payment, delinquency.
moroso, sa, *a.* tardy, slow, sluggish; (law) delinquent, in default (in payment of a debt).
morquera, *f.* (bot.) winter savory; Spanish thyme.
morra, *f.* 1. mora, morra (game); clenched fist (signifying zero in this game). 2. crown, top (of the head). — **andar la m.,** (coll.) to be always fighting. —*interj.* pussy! (in calling a cat).
morrada, *f.* bump, butt (of two heads together); blow, slap.
morral, *m.* 1. feed bag; knapsack; game bag. 2. (coll.) oaf, rustic, boor. 3. (mar.) boomsail, spinnaker.
morralla, *f.* 1. small fish, small fry. 2. crowd, rabble; (fig.) junk, rubbish. 3. (Mex.) small change.
morrena, *f.* (geol.) moraine.
morrilla, *f.* (bot.) wild artichoke.
morrillo, *m.* 1. fat on the back of the neck (of cattle and sheep); (fig.) thick neck. 2. pebble.
morriña, *f.* 1. (vet.) murrain, generalized dropsy. 2. (coll.) sadness, melancholy, dumps (coll.), the blues (coll.). — **m. negra,** (vet.) blackleg, symptomatic anthrax.
morriñoso, sa, *a.* 1. weak, rachitic. 2. dropsical. 3. sad, melancholy, blue.
morrión, *m.* 1. morion; helmet. 2. (kind of) vertigo (suffered by hawks).
morrisqueta, *f.* (Col.) face, grimace.
morro, *m.* 1. knob; butt (of pistol). 2. knoll, hillock, mound; (mar.) headland, promontory. 3. pebble. 4. thick lips. — **andar al m.,** (coll.) to be always fighting; **estar de morros,** (coll.) to be at odds, be on bad terms; **jugar al m. con,** (coll.) to deceive, pull the wool over (someone's) eyes.
morrocotudo, da, *a.* 1. very important or difficult. 2. (Amer.) excellent, terrific (coll.), fabulous. 3. (Col.) wealthy, well-off. 4. (Mex.) big, enormous; strong, stout.

morrocoy, *m., var. of* **morrocoyo.**
morrocoyo, *m.* giant tortoise (Testudo imbricata).
morrón, *a.* large, red, sweet (pepper). —*m.* 1. (mar.) knotted flag. 2. (coll.) blow, punch.
morroncho, cha, *a.* (Sp.) mild, tame, peaceful.
morrongo, ga, *m.,* 1. (coll.) kitty, pussy, cat. 2. (Mex.) servant.
morronguear, *i.v.* 1. (S. Amer.) to drink. 2. (Chile) to doze.
morroño, ña, *m., f., var. of* **morrongo.**
morroñoso, sa, *a.* 1. (Guat., Hond.) rough, wrinkled. 2. (Peru) rachitic, undernourished, weak, sickly (people); small (fruit).
morrudo, da, *a.* snouted; thick-lipped, blubber-lipped.
morsa, *f.* (zool.) walrus.
morsana, *f.* (bot.) bean caper.
mortadela, *f.* mortadella, bologna (sausage).
mortaja, *f.* 1. shroud, winding sheet. 2. (Amer.) cigarette paper. 3. mortise, mortice. — **m. ciega,** stub mortise.
mortal, *a.* 1. mortal, subject to death. 2. mortal, fatal (wound); mortal (sin). 3. mortal, deadly, implacable (hatred, enemies, etc.). 4. dying, moribund, mortally ill. 5. exhausting, hard. 6. conclusive, definitive; terminal. — **los mortales,** mankind; **restos mortales,** mortal remains.
mortalidad, *f.* 1. mortality (condition of being mortal). 2. death rate, mortality.
mortalmente, *adv.* 1. mortally, fatally, deadly. 2. implacably.
mortandad, *f.* 1. death toll, mortality. 2. slaughter, butchery.
mortecino, na, *a.* 1. pale, grey, deathly, wan. 2. dying, waning; dying a natural death. — **hacer la mortecina,** (coll.) to pretend to be dead, play possum.
mortera, *f.* wooden bowl (used for both carrying lunch and drinking.
morterada, *f.* 1. contents of a mortar bowl; food or condiments prepared therein. 2. (artil.) shot from a mortar.
morterete, *m.* 1. small mortar (used in artillery and in firework displays). 2. thick candle. 3. cone-shaped groove (in gun carriages). 4. (Sp.) mortar used for tapping out the rhythm for certain country dances.
mortero, *m.* 1. mortar (bowl for pounding solids). 2. (artil.) mortar. 3. (bldg.) mortar. 4. lower stone (of olive mill.). 5. (her.) cap, bonnet (used on coat of arms by certain ministers of justice instead of a crown). — **m. de trinchera,** trench mortar; **m. de brújula,** inner compass box.
morteruelo, *m.* 1. (type of) rattle. 2. dish made of pig's liver, spices and breadcrumbs.
mortífero, ra, *a.* lethal, deadly, mortiferous, fatal.
mortificación, *f.* mortification; bother, annoyance, vexation.
mortificador, ra, *a.* mortifying; annoying, bothering, vexing.
mortificante, *a.* mortifying; annoying, bothering, vexing.
mortificar, (*ref. 50*) *tr.v.* 1. to annoy, vex, irritate, bother. 2. to mortify, chastise, subdue (passions, the flesh). 3. (med.) to mortify, deprive of vitality. —*r.v.* 1. to get or become annoyed, vexed or irritated. 2. to mortify oneself, subdue the flesh. 3. (med.) to lose vitality.
mortifique, mortifiqué, *ref.* **mortificar.**
mortual, *f.* (Mex., C. Amer.) inheritance.
mortuorio, ria, *a.* funereal; mortuary, pertaining to a burial or the dead. —*m.* funeral.
morucho, cha, *a.* (coll.) darling, beloved.—*m.* (taur.) young bull whose horn tips have been covered with wooden balls.
morueco, *m.* ram, tup, male sheep.
morula, *f.* (biol.) morula.
morulla, *f.* (Mex.) blood pudding.
móruno, na, *a.* Moorish. —*m.* (Cuba) sturdy peasant shoe.
moruro, *m.* (species of) acacia (Acacia arborea).
morusa, *f.* 1. (coll.) money, cash, dough. 2. (P. Rico, Ven.) a lock of matted hair.
mosaico, ca, *a.* Mosaic, pertaining to Moses; **ley mosaica,** Mosaic law.
mosaico, ca, *a., m.* 1. (art., archit., bldg.) mosaic. 2. (fig., lit., mus.) any work or piece composed of variegated fragments; **m. musical,** medley.
mosaísmo, *m.* Mosaism, Judaism, Mosaic law.
mosca, *f.* 1. (ento.) fly. 2. Vandyke beard (between underlip and chin). 3. (coll.) money, dough (coll.), cash. 4. (coll.) bore, nuisance, pest. 5. (coll.) annoyance, irritation, e.g. *estar con m.,* to be annoyed or irritated. 6. (astron.) **M.,** Musca. — **aflojar** or **soltar la m.,** (coll.) to fork out, give money grudgingly; **cazar moscas,** (coll.) to waste one's time; **m. azul,** (ento.) bluefly, blowfly; **m. de burro,** (ento.) horsefly; **m. de España,** (ento.) Spanish fly; **m. de Milán,** blister plaster; **m. de mula,** horsefly; **m. muerta,** (coll.) hypocrite (feigning meekness but never failing to take advantage of an opportunity); **moscas volantes,** (med.) spots before the eyes, muscae volitantes; **papar moscas,** to gape open-mouthed; **picarle a uno la m.,** (coll.) to have an unpleasant memory, have a twinge of conscience; **por si las moscas,** just in case.
moscabado, da, *a.* raw, unrefined, brown (sugar).
moscada, *a.* **nuez m.,** (bot.) nutmeg.
moscarda, *f.* 1. (ento.) flesh fly, meat fly; (ento.) bluebottle, blowfly. 2. eggs of queen bee.
moscardear, *i.v.* to lay eggs (queen bee).
moscardón, *m.* 1 (ento.) botfly; (ento.) flesh fly, bluebottle, blowfly; (ento.) hornet, drone. 2. (coll.) importunate person; pest, nuisance.
moscareta, *f.* (ornith.) spotted flycatcher.
moscarrón, *m.* (coll.) botfly.
moscatel, *a., m.* muscatel (grape, wine, vineyard).
moscella, *f.* spark from a wick or lamp.
mosco, ca, *a.* (Chile) black with a few white hairs (said of a horse). —*m.* mosquito, gnat.
moscón, *m.* 1. large fly; (ento.) meat or flesh fly, bluebottle, bumblebee, blowfly. 2. (bot.) maple tree. 3. pest, bore, nuisance, importunate person.
moscona, *f.* hussy, shameless woman.
mosconear, *tr.v.* to pester, annoy, vex. —*i.v.* to be a nuisance, make a nuisance of oneself.
mosconeo, *m.* pestering, annoying.
moscorrofio, *m.* (Col., Hond.) fright, ugly person.
moscovia, *f.* (Cuba) very soft tanned steer skin.
moscovita, *a.* Muscovite, of or pertaining to Moscow. —*m., f.* Muscovite. —*f.* (min.) muscovite.
Moscú, *m.* Moscow, capital of the U.S.S.R.
Mosela, *f.* Moselle, river originating in northeastern France.
mosqueado, da, *a.* spotted, mottled, dotted, brindled.
mosqueador, *m.,* 1. fly swatter, flytrap. 2. (coll.) tail (of a horse or a cow).
mosquear, *tr.v.* 1. to swat or shoo away (flies). 2. to bite back at, retort angrily. 3. to whip, thrash, flog. —*r.v.* 1. to take offense. 2. to rid oneself violently of difficulties or obstacles.
mosqueo, *m.* 1. fly-swatting. 2. resentment, annoyance.
mosquero, *m.* 1. flytrap. 2. (Amer.) swarm of flies.
mosquerola, mosqueruela, *f.* small, very sweet pear.
mosqueta, *f.* (bot.) Japan globeflower; — **m. silvestre,** (bot.) dog rose.
mosquetazo, *m.* musket shot; musket shot wound.
mosquete, *m.* (artil.) musket.
mosquetería, *f.* 1. musketry, musketeers, body of musketeers. 2. (theat.) groundlings, group of groundlings (spectators standing in the pit of a theater in the time of Lope de Vega or Shakespeare).
mosqueteril, *a.* (coll.) pertaining to the crowd in the pit, groundling, of the groundlings (in the theater of Lope de Vega or Shakespeare).
mosquetero, *m.* 1. musketeer. 2. (theat.) groundling (spectator in the pit of the theater in the time of Lope de Vega or Shakespeare). 3. (Arg., Bol.) party-crasher.
mosquetón, *m.* (artil.) short musket.
mosquil, *a.* of or pertaining to flies.
mosquino, na, *a., var. of* **mosquil.**
mosquita, *f.* 1. *dim. of* **mosca,** small fly. 2. (ornith.) bird similar to the white-throat; **m. muerta,** (coll.) hypocrite; **hacerse la m. muerta,** to look as if butter wouldn't melt in one's mouth.
mosquitero, *m.* mosquito net or its frame.
mosquito, *m.* 1. (ento.) mosquito; gnat. 2. (coll.) tippler.
mostacero, ra, *m., f.* mustard pot, mustard server.
mostacho, *m.* 1. moustache. 2. (coll.) blemish, mark (on the face). 3. (mar.) bowsprit shroud.
mostachón, *m.* 1. small sugar bun made with almonds, sugar and spice. 2. a diamond-shaped ornament.
mostachoso, sa, *a.* mustachioed.
mostacilla, *f.* 1. bird shot, mustard-seed shot. 2. small bead; embroidery beads.
mostagán, *m.* (coll.) wine.
mostajo, *m.* (bot.) white beam tree.
mostaza, *f.* 1. (bot.) mustard plant; mustard seed. 2. (cul.) mustard. 3. mustard-seed shot, bird shot. — **hacerle la m. a uno,** to give someone a bloody nose, make someone's nose bleed; **subirse a uno la m. a las narices,** (coll.) to get annoyed.
mostazal, *m* mustard field.
mostazo, *m.* 1. strong syrupy must, heavy new wine. 2. mustard plant.
mostear, *i.v.* 1. to yield must. 2. to put must into vats. 3. to mix must with old wine.
mostela, *f.* (agr.) sheaf, gavel, bundle.
mostelera, *f.* (agr.) stacking place, place where sheaves are stacked.
mostellar, *m.* (bot.) white beam tree.
mostense, *a., m.* (coll., rel.) Premonstratensian, belonging to an order of canons.
mostillo, *m.* 1. paste made of must cooked with aniseed, cloves and cinnamon. 2. must cake (made with must, flour and spices). 3. sauce made of must and mustard.
mosto, *m.* must (unfermented grape juice); **desliar el m.,** to separate the dregs from the must; **m. agustín,** must cake (made with must, flour and spices).
mostrable, *a.* showable; demonstrable.
mostrado, da, *past part. of* **mostrar.** —*a.* habituated, accustomed, inured.
mostrador, ra, *a.* showing, pointing. —*m., f.* 1. counter (in a shop). 2. dial (of a watch, a clock).
mostrar, (*ref. 33*) *tr.v.* 1. to show; to exhibit, display. 2. to show, demonstrate, expound, explain, point out, prove. —*r.v.* to show oneself to be, e.g. *mostrarse amigo,* to show oneself to be a friend.
mostrenco, ca, *a.* 1. ownerless; masterless. 2. (coll.) homeless, wandering, vagabond, vagrant. 3. (coll.) stray, masterless (animal). 4. (coll.) dim, dull, unintelligent. 5. (coll.) fat, stout. —*m., f.* 1. (coll.) dolt, dullard. 2. (coll.) fat person.
mota, *f.* 1. burl, mote (in cloth). 2. mote, speck (of mud), piece of thread or fluff (sticking to clothing). 3. small fault or defect. 4. hillock,

mound, rise, hummock. 5. (Chile) small tuft of wool. 6. (Ven.) fluff enclosing cotton seed. 7. kinky hair; (Arg.) blacks' hair. 8. (Mex., Cuba, coll.) marihuana, pot (sl.).
motacila, *f.* (ornith.) white wagtail.
mote, *m.* 1. nickname, ej., *le pusieron como m. 'Sweet Knot'.* 2. device, emblem. 3. riddle, enigmatic phrase. 4. (Chile) error, mistake. 5. (Amer.) stewed corn.
moteado, da, *a.* speckled, spotted, mottled.
motear, *tr.v.* to speckle, mottle, fleck. —*i.v.* (Peru) to eat stewed corn.
motejador, ra, *a.* name-calling. —*m., f.* name-caller.
motejar, *tr.v.* to call names; to chaff; to censure, ridicule; **m. de,** to brand as, accuse of being.
motejo, *m.* name-calling.
motero, ra, *m., f.* (Chile) person who prepares or sells stewed corn; one who is fond of this dish. —*f.* (Cuba) vanity case; powder puff; face-powder box.
motete, *m.* 1. (mus.) motet. 2. nickname. 3. (C. Amer., P. Rico) bundle, parcel.
motil, *m., var. of* **mochil,** farmer's boy.
motilar, *tr.v.* to shear, shave (the head).
motilidad, *f.* (biol.) motility.
motilón, na, *a.* hairless. —*m., f.* 1. hairless person, one with little or cropped hair. 2. member of a tribe of Indians of Colombia and Venezuela. —*m.* (coll.) lay brother.
motín, *m.* mutiny, insurrection; uprising, riot.
motita, *f. dim. of* **mota,** mote, speck, mite.
motivación, *f.* motivation.
motivar, *tr.v.* 1. to motivate, cause. 2. to explain, give reason for.
motivo, va, *a.* moving, motive. —*m.* 1. motive, reason. 2. (mus., p.) motif, motive. 3. (*pl.*) (Chile) finickiness. — **con m. de,** on the occasion of; because of; **dar m.,** to give cause; **por ningún m.,** under no circumstances.
moto, ta, *a.* (Hond.) orphan. —*m.* landmark, guidepost; boundary stone. —*f.* (coll.) motorcycle.
motobomba, *f.* pump and engine, pumping engine.
motocicleta, *f.* motorcycle.
motociclismo, *m.* motorcycling.
motociclista, *m., f.* motorcyclist.
motocine, *m.* (cine.) drive-in (movie theater).
motocompresor, *m.* motor-driven compressor.
motocultivo, *m.* **motocultura,** *f.* mechanized farming.
motolita, *f.* (ornith.) white wagtail.
motolito, ta, *a.* silly, foolish. —*m., f.* fool, ninny, dolt. — **vivir uno de m.,** to live at another's expense.
motón, *m.* pulley, block; **m. de amantillar,** (mar.) topping block; **m. violín** (mec.) fiddle block.
motonave, *f.* motor ship, motorboat.
motonería, *f.* (mar.) tackle, set of pulleys or block.
motoneurona, *f.* (physiol.) motoneuron.
motonieve, *f.* snowmobile.
motopropulsor, *m.* moto-propeller, electric drive.
motor, ra, *a.* motor, motive. —*m.* motor, engine; **m. acelerador,** booster motor; **m. a inyección,** fuel-injected engine; **m. a reacción,** jet engine; **m. cohético,** aerojet, rocket engine; **m. de arranque,** starter motor; **m. de combustión,** combustion engine; **m. de combustión interna** or de explosión, internal combustion engine; **m. de dos tiempos,** two-stroke engine; **m. de propulsión a chorro,** jet engine; **m. Diesel,** Diesel engine; **m. eléctrico,** electric motor; **m. en estrella,** radial engine; **m. fuera de borda,** outboard motor; **m. invertible,** reversible motor; **m. hidráulico,** hydraulic engine; **m. pulsorreactor,** (aer.) pulse-jet engine; **m. radial,** (mec.) radial engine; **m. sincrónico,** synchronous motor; **primer m.,** (philos.) prime mover. —*f.* small motorboat.
motorice, motoricé, *ref.* **motorizar.**
motorismo, *m.* motoring (as a sport).
motorista, *m., f.* motorist, driver, motorman, motorwoman, motorcyclist.
motorización, *f.* motorization.
motorizar, (*ref. 53*) *tr.v.* to motorize.
motricidad, *f.* (physiol.) motor function, motor faculty.
motril, *m.* shop boy, errand boy; errand boy for laborers.
motriz, (*pl.* **motrices**), *a.* motive, motor, moving.
motu propio, (Lat.) by his own will.
movedizo, za, *a.* moving, shifting; unsteady, shaky, unfirm; fickle, variable, changeable; **arenas movedizas,** quicksand.
movedor, ra, *a.* moving. —*m., f.* mover.
movedura, *f.* 1. movement. 2. (med.) miscarriage.
mover, (*ref. 34*) tr.v. 1. to move; to shift; to nod (the head); to wag (the tail). 2. to induce (to), bring (to), e.g. *m. a alguien a + inf.,* to induce someone to + *inf.* 3. to cause, provoke, e.g. *m. guerra,* to cause war. 4. to move, affect, e.g. *m. a lágrimas,* to move to tears, *m. a compasión,* to move to pity; *m. a cólera,* to move to anger. — **mover cielo y tierra,** to move heaven and earth. —*i.v.* 1. to have a miscarriage. 2. to begin to sprout. 3. (archit.) to spring, begin (an arch, vault). —*r.v.* to move.
movible, *a.* 1. movable. 2. variable, changeable, fickle. 3. (astron.) movable.
movición, *f.* 1. (coll.) movement. 2. (vulg.) abortion.
movido, da, *past part. of* **mover.** —*a.* 1. (Amer.) fidgety; active. 2. (Amer.) rough, choppy (sea). 3. (C. Amer., Mex.) irresolute, variable, inconstant. 4. (Guat., Hond.) weak, feeble, rachitic. 5. moved, blurred (said of a photo). 6. (Amer.) laid without a shell (eggs). —*f.* move (in chess).
moviente, *a.* 1. moving, motive. 2. (her.) starting at the border (of coat of arms) and moving towards the center.
móvil, *a.* 1. mobile. 2. unstable, changeable, fickle. —*m.* motive, reason, incentive, inducement.
movilice, movilicé, *ref.* **movilizar.**
movilidad, *f.* mobility; changeableness; fickleness, inconstancy; unsteadiness; **m. ascendente,** upward mobility; **m. social,** social mobility.
movilización, *f.* mobilization.
movilizar, (*ref. 53*) *tr.v.* to mobilize; (mil.) to mobilize.
movimiento, *m.* 1. movement; motion; moving. 2. (p., lit.) movement (flow of verse, action in writing or painting). 3. movement, trend (literary, religious, political, etc.). 4. (med.) motion, movement (of bowels). 5. (mus.) movement. 6. (com.) movement, activity; uprising, rebellion. 7. feeling (of pity), fit (of anger, etc.). 8. (astron.) clock error (loss or gain of clock in fixed interval). — **en m.,** in motion; **m. acelerado,** (mec.) accelerated motion; **m. compuesto,** (mec.) compound motion; **m. continuo** or **perpetuo,** perpetual motion; **m. de flanqueo,** flanking movement; **m. de reducción,** (fenc.) inward thrust (of sword); **m. de rotación,** (mec.) rotary motion; **m. de traslación,** orbital movement; **m. diurno** or **primario,** (astron.) diurnal motion; **m. extraño,** (fenc.) feint, removal of the sword; **m. giratorio,** gyratory motion, rotary motion; **m. ondulatorio,** wave movement; **m. oratorio,** oratorical gesture; **m. perdido,** (mec.) lost motion; **m. propio,** (astron.) proper movement; **m. remiso,** (fenc.) outward thrust (of sword); **m. retardado,** (mec.) retarded motion; **m. simple,** (mec.) simple motion; **m. sismico,** earth tremor; **m. uniforme,** (mec.) uniform motion or velocity; **m. variado,** (mec.) varying or variable motion; **m. vibratorio,** wave movement; **m. paraláctico,** (astron.) parallactic motion; **m. rectilíneo,** (mec.) straight-line motion; **poner en m.,** to put into motion; **primer m.,** sudden fit or feeling (of passion, etc.).
moxa, *f.* (med.) moxa, cautery; cauterization (of the skin).
moxte, *interj.* get away! keep off! — **sin decir oxte ni m.,** without saying a word.
moya, *m.* (Cuba) daisy, marguerite.
moyana, *f.* 1. (artil.) cannon with larger caliber than that of a culverin. 2. (coll.) lie, fib, falsehood. 3. bran biscuit (given to sheep dogs).
moyo, *m.* liquid measure (258 liters).
moyote, *m.* (Mex.) mosquito; gnat.
moyuelo, *m.* very fine bran.
moza, *f.* 1. girl, lass, maid. 2. maid servant. 3. mistress, concubine. 4. washing paddle or bat (for pounding clothes). 5. bracket on trivet to hold frying pan handle secure. 6. last hand (in cards). — **buena m.,** good-looking; good-looking girl or woman, good-looker; **m. de cámara,** chambermaid; **m. de fortuna** or **partido,** prostitute; **real m.,** (coll.) swell or real chick or doll.
mozalbete, *m.* youth, lad, young fellow, stripling.
mozalbillo, *m., var. of* **mozalbete.**
mozallón, na, *m., f.* husky young person.
mozancón, na, *m.* husky young fellow. —*f.* husky young lass or wench.
mozárabe, *a.* (hist.) Mozarabic. —*m., f.* Mozarab.
mozarabía, *f.* Mozarabic population.
mozcorra, *f.* (coll.) prostitute.
mozo, za, *a.* 1. young, youthful. 2. single, unmarried. —*m.* 1. youth, lad, young man; bachelor. 2. servant; boy, hand; waiter. 3. cloak or clothes' rack. 4. prop, shore. — **buen m.,** handsome, good-looking; good-looking or handsome man; **m. de caballerías** or **caballos,** groom, stable boy; **m. de cocina,** kitchen boy or hand; **m. de cordel, cuerda** or **esquina,** public porter or errand boy; **m. de espuela,** footman; **m. de estación,** station porter; **m. de estoques,** sword boy (bullfighter's assistant in charge of swords); **m. de hotel,** bellboy, bellhop; **m. de paja y cebada,** hostler; **m. de restaurante,** waiter.
mozón, na, *a.* (Peru) joking, wisecracking.
mozonada, *f.* (Peru) joke, wisecrack.
mozonear, *i.v.* (Peru) to joke, wisecrack.
mozuelo, la, *m.* lad, youth, youngster. —*f.* young girl.
m.p.g. *abbrev. of* **millas por galón,** miles per gallon (mpg).
m.p.h. *abbrev. of* **millas por hora,** miles per hour (mph).
M.S. *abbrev. of* **manuscrito,** manuscript (MS.).
M.SS. *abbrev. of* **manuscritos,** manuscripts (MSS.).
mu, *m.* moo, lowing of cattle. —*f.* bed, sleep, beddy-bye (children's word). — **vamos a la m.,** lets go beddy-bye, go to sleep.
muaré, *m.* (tex.) moiré, watered silk.
mucamo, ma, *m., f.* (Amer.) servant.
múcara, *f.* (mar.) shoal, shallow.
mucepo, *m.* (Hond.) sadness, gloom, depression.
muceta, *f.* (ecc.) mozzetta; hood (worn by certain academics).
muchachada, *f.* 1. boyish prank or joke; girlish joke or prank. 2. group of boys or girls; assemblage of young people.
muchachear, *i.v.* to play or fool around, act like a youngster.

muchachería, *f., var. of* **muchachada.**
muchachez, *f.* boyhood; girlhood; childhood.
muchachil, *a.* 1. boyish; girlish. 2. pertaining to youth or young people.
muchacho, cha, *m., f.* 1. youngster, youth, young person. *—m.* 1. boy, lad, youth. 2. servant, manservant, houseboy. *—f.* 1. girl, young girl. 2. maid, maidservant.
muchedumbre, *f.* crowd, multitude, flock; populace, rabble.
muchísimo, ma, *a. super. of* **mucho,** very much. *—adv.* a great deal.
muchitanga, *f.* (Peru, P. Rico) mob, rabble.
mucho, cha, *a.* 1. much, a great deal of, a lot of; abundant, plentiful. 2. (*pl.*) many. — **muchas gracias,** many thanks, thanks a lot; **mucho ruido y pocas nueces,** much ado about nothing.
mucho, *adv.* 1. a lot, much, very much. 2. a long time, e.g. *m. antes,* a long time before, *tardará m. en llegar,* it will be a long time before he arrives. 3. yes indeed. — **con** or **por m.,** by far, by a long shot; **la quiere m.,** he loves her dearly; **m. que sí,** yes indeed; **ni m. menos,** not by any means; **por m. que,** however much, no matter how much; **ser m. que** + *subj.,* to be unlikely that, e.g. *será m. que nos paguen hoy,* it's very unlikely that we'll get paid today. *—m.* much, a lot; **tener en m.,** to think very highly of, esteem greatly.
muchos, chas, *pron.* many, e.g. *m. asistieron,* many attended.
múcico, ca, *a.* (chem.) mucic.
mucífero, ra, *a.* muciferous, producing mucus.
mucilaginoso, sa, *a.* mucilaginous, slimy.
mucílago, *m., var. of* **mucilago.**
mucilago, *m.* mucilage.
mucina, *f.* (biochem.) mucin.
mucinógeno, *m.* (biochem.) mucinogen.
mucinoso, sa, *a.* mucinous.
mucle, *m.* (Hond.) illness in infants caused by inability to digest milk.
muco, *m.* (Bol.) chewed corn (used in the preparation of chicha).
mucocutáneo, a, *a.* (anat.) mucocutaneous.
mucoide, *m.* (biochem.) mucoid.
mucoideo, a, *a.* mucoid.
mucoproteína, *f.* (biochem.) mucoprotein.
múcor, *m.* (bot.) mucor.
mucoseroso, sa, *a.* (physiol.) mucoserous.
mucosidad, *f.* mucosity.
mucoso, sa, *a.* mucous. *—f.* (anat.) mucosa, mucous membrane.
mucre, *a.* (Chile) acrid, sharp, astringent.
mucronato, ta, *a.* mucronate, ending in a point.
múcura, *m., f.* (Amer.) 1. pitcher, ewer (used for carrying and keeping fresh water). 2. (Col.) blockhead.
mucus, *m.* (physiol.) mucus.
mucuy, *m.* (Mex.) turtledove.
muda, *f.* 1. change; alteration. 2. change of clothing. 3. change or breaking of voice (in boys). 4. molting, molt; molting season. 5. mew (cage for hawks when molting); nest (of birds of prey). — **está de m.,** his voice is changing; **estar en m.,** to be completely silent.
mudable, *a.* changeable; fickle, inconstant.
mudada, *f.* (Amer.) 1. change of clothes. 2. (Cuba) moving, change of domicile.
mudadizo, za, *a.* changeable, fickle, variable.
mudamente, *adv.* silently, mutely.
mudamiento, *m., var. of* **mudanza.**
mudanza, *f.* 1. change. 2. moving (change of domicile). 3. figure (in a dance). 4. (mus.) mutation. 5. fickleness, changeableness, inconstancy. **camión** or **carro de mudanzas,** moving van; **estar de m.,** to be moving to new quarters; **hacer m.** or **mudanzas,** to be fickle, changeable or inconstant.
mudar, *m.* (bot.) mudar.
mudar, *tr.v.* 1. to change, alter, vary; to convert. 2. to move, move to another place. 3. to shed, molt (feathers; skin). 4. to change his voice (said of a boy). *—i.v.* to change; **m. de,** to change (opinions); to move, move to another house, location; to shed, molt (skin; feathers). *—r.v.* 1. to change, alter (way of living, etc.). 2. to move, move away, move to another house, location. 3. to change one's clothes. — **mudarse de,** to change (one's clothes); to move (to another house, location); **se le está mudando la voz,** his voice is changing.
muday, *m.* (Chile) corn or barley beer or **chicha.**
mudéjar, *a.* (hist., art.) Mudejar. *—m.* Mudejar (Mohammedan living under a Christian King in Spain).
mudenco, ca, *a.* (Hond.) stuttering, stammering.
mudez, *f.* dumbness, muteness; stubborn silence; inability or unwillingness to speak.
mudo, da, *a.* dumb, mute, silent; speechless; (gram.) mute, silent (letter). *—m., f.* mute person. — **a la muda,** silently; **cine mudo,** silent films; **hacer hablar a los mudos,** to be capable of doing anything. *—m., f.* mute (person).
mué, *m.* (tex.) moiré.
mueblaje, *m., var. of* **moblaje,** household furniture.
mueblar, *tr.v., var. of* **amueblar,** to furnish, supply with furniture.
mueble, *a.* movable. *—m.* 1. piece of furniture; (*pl.*) furniture. 2. (her.) armorial bearings.
mueble, mueblo, *ref.* **moblar.**
mueblería, *f.* furniture factory; furniture shop.
mueblista, *m, f.* furniture maker or dealer.
mueca, *f.* grimace, face, grin; **hacerle muecas a,** to make faces at.
muecín, *m.* muezzin, crier who calls faithful Moslems to prayer from the minaret of a mosque.
muela, *f.* 1. upper millstone. 2. sharpening stone, whetstone, grindstone. 3. (anat.) molar tooth, grinder. 4. steep flat-topped hill; mound, hillock. 5. water enough to keep a mill in motion; measure of water (used to gauge the water carried by an irrigation ditch). 6. (bot.) purple vetch. 7. (fig.) circle, ring. — **costarle a uno muelas,** to give one a lot of work; **m. cordal** or **del juicio,** wisdom tooth; **m. de esmeril,** emery wheel; **haberle salido a uno la m. de juicio,** to have reached the age of reason or wisdom, be sensible and prudent; **m. pulidora,** polishing wheel.
muela, muelo, *ref.* **moler.**
muelar, *m.* purple vetch field, field sown with purple vetch.
muellaje, *m.* wharfage, fee for using a wharf, dockage.
muelle, *a.* 1. soft, tender. 2. voluptuous, luxurious; easy. *—m.* 1. pier, wharf, dock. 2. (mach.) spring. 3. (ry.) freight platform, unloading platform. 4. chatelaine, decorative clasp worn at the waist. — **m. antagonista,** (mec.) recoil, antagonist, or reactive spring; **flojo de muelles,** (coll.) having a weak bladder or bowels; **m. de retroceso,** recoil spring; **m. de válvula,** valve spring; **m. real,** mainspring (of a watch), spring (in firearms); **m. tensor,** tension spring.
muellemente, *adv.* softly, luxuriously, easily, tenderly, gently.
muelo, *m.* heap of thrashed grain.
muenda, *f.* (Col.) flogging, beating, thrashing.
muengo, ga, *a.* (Cuba) one-eared.
muequear, *iv.* to make faces, grimace.
muera, muero, *ref.* **morir.**
muerda, muerdo, *ref.* **morder.**
muérdago, *m.* (bot.) mistletoe.
muerdo, *m.* (coll.) bite; bite, morsel, mouthful.
muérgano, *m.* 1. (zool.) razor clam. 2. (obs.) organ (instrument). 3. (Col., Ven.) useless object, worthless thing. 4. (Col., Ven., Ecuad.) shabbily dressed, unkempt person.
muergo, *m.* (zool.) razor clam.
muermera, *f.* (bot.) tabernaemontana (Tabernaemontana amygdalifolia).
muermo, *m.* 1. (vet.) glanders. 2. (bot.) muermo, Chilean timber tree.
muermoso, sa, *a.* (vet.) glanderous.
muero, muera, *ref.* **morir.**
muerte, *f.* 1. death, demise, decease. 2. death, ruin, end, destruction, extinction, havoc. 3. homicide, murder, bloodshed. 4. personification of death (in the figure of a black-clad skeleton carrying a scythe; The Reaper). — **a las puertas de la m.,** at death's door; **a m.,** to death, to the death, e.g. *condenar a m.,* to condemn to death, *duelo a m.,* duel to the death; **dar la m. a,** to put to death; **de mala m.,** (coll.) crummy (coll.), insignificant, unimportant; **de m.,** mortal, fatal, e.g. *golpe de m.,* death blow; hopelessly, seriously e.g. *estar enfermo de m.,* to be hopelessly ill; **estar a la m.,** to be at death's door; **hasta la m.,** to the bitter end, to the death; **m. a mano airada** or **violenta,** violent death; **m. cerebral,** brain death; **m. civil,** (law) civil death; **m. súbita,** (sport.) sudden death, tiebreaker; **m. piadosa,** mercy killing; **m. clínica,** clinical death, state of being clinically dead; **m. de cuna,** sudden infant death syndrome, cot death; **sentir de m.,** to feel (something) very deeply; **ser la m.,** to be ghastly, terrible or dreadful.
muerto, ta, *irr. past part. of* **morir,** killed, e.g. *he muerto un conejo,* I have killed a rabbit. *—a.* 1. dead; deceased; defunct. 2. lifeless, dead; dull, vapid. 3. (fig.) exhausted. 4. slaked (lime). 5. flat (drink). — **estar m. por,** (coll.) to be mad or crazy about; **más m. que vivo,** more dead than alive; **m. de,** (coll.) dying of (e.g. hunger); **m. y bien m.,** dead as a doornail; **naturaleza muerta** (p.), still life. *—m., f.* dead person, deceased person, corpse, dead body. — **contar a uno con los muertos,** to take no notice of someone; to despise someone utterly; **desenterrar los muertos,** (coll.) to speak ill of the dead; **echarle a uno el muerto, hacerle cargar con el muerto,** to put the blame on someone; **hacer el muerto,** to float (in the sea); **hacerse el muerto,** to play possum, keep quiet; **los muertos no hablan,** dead men tell no tales. *—m.* 1. dummy hand (in bridge). 2. deadman, anchorage, buoy; **inversión del m.,** dummy reversal; **m. de amarre,** anchor buoy.
muesca, *f.* 1. mortise, mortice, notch, groove. 2. identification nick (on ear of cattle). 3. dovetail scarf.
mueso, *m.* (coll.) puerperal pains, post-childbirth pains.
mueso, sa, *a.* small-eared (said of a lamb).
muestra, *f.* 1. sample, specimen; proof, demonstration. 2. model, pattern (to be followed). 3. sign (on a shop, etc.). 4. sign, indication. 5. card turned up to show which suit is trumps. 6. (mil.) **review,** inspection. 7. (hunt.) set (of a dog when spotting game). 8. edge or fag end of cloth bearing manufacturer's name. 9. dial, face (of a clock, watch). — **dar muestras de,** to show signs of; **para m., basta un botón,** one example will suffice to prove it; **pasar m.,** to examine carefully; (mil.) to review, inspect; **por la m. se**

conoce el paño, you know a person by the way he acts.
muestrario, *m.* sample book, collection of samples, sample case.
muestre, muestro, *ref.* **mostrar.**
mueva, muevo, *ref.* **mover.**
muévedo, *m.* stillborn, aborted fetus.
muezín, *m., var. of* **muecín,** muezzin.
mufla, *f.* muffle (oven inside a furnace).
muftí, (*pl.* **muftíes**), *m.* mufti (official expounder of Moslem law).
muga, *f.* 1. boundary mark, landmark. 2. spawning; spawning season; fecundation of spawn or roe.
mugar, (*ref.* *51*) *i.v.* to spawn; to fecundate the spawn.
mugido, *past part. of* **mugir.** —*m.* moo, low; bellow (of cattle).
mugidor, ra, *a.* mooing, lowing; bellowing.
mugiente, *a.* mooing, lowing; bellowing.
múgil, *m.* (ichth.) mullet, striped mullet.
mugílidos, *m.* (*pl.*) (zool.) Mugilidae.
mugir, (*ref.* *62*) *i.v.* to moo, low; to bellow; (fig.) to roar, bellow.
mugre, *f.* filth, grime, dirt.
mugriento, ta, *a.* filthy, dirty; greasy.
mugrón, *m.* layer (of vine); shoot, runner, tiller, sprig, sucker.
mugroso, sa, *a., var. of* **mugriento.**
muguete, *m.* (bot.) lily-of-the-valley.
muharra, *f., var. of* **moharra,** head of a spear.
muisca, *a., m., f.* (Amer.) Muysca, Chibcha.
mujalata, *f.* farming partnership between a Moslem and a Jew or a Christian.
mujer, *f.* woman, wife, mate. — **m. de gobierno,** housekeeper; **m. de la limpieza,** cleaning lady; **m. del arte, de la vida airada, del partido, de mala vida, de mal vivir,** prostitute; **m. de negocios,** businesswoman; **m. fatal,** femme fatale, vamp; **m. de su casa,** housewife; **m. golpeada** or **maltratada,** battered wife, battered woman; **m. mundana, perdida** or **pública,** prostitute; **m. policía,** policewoman; **m. taxista,** woman taxidriver. **tomar m.,** to take a wife, to marry.
mujercilla, *f.* little woman; insignificant woman.
mujercita, *f.* little woman, young lady; little wife (term of endearment).
mujerengo, *a.* (C. Amer.) effeminate.
mujerero, *a.* (Chile, Hond., Mex.) *var. of* **mujeriego.**
mujeriego, ga, *a.* 1. philandering, donjuanish, fond of women, woman-chasing. 2. womanly, womanish, woman's. — **a la mujeriega, a mujeriegas,** (to ride) side-saddle. —*m.* 1. philanderer, ladies' man, roué, rake, woman-chaser. 2. women, skirts (sl.), e.g. *en este pueblo hay buen m.,* there are good-looking women in this town.
mujeril, *a.* 1. womanly, womanish, feminine; woman's, e.g. *trabajos mujeriles,* woman's work. 2. effeminate.
mujerilmente, *adv.* effeminately; in a womanish manner.
mujerío, *m.* women, skirts (sl.), gathering of women.
mujerona, *f. aug. of* **mujer,** strapping, stout woman; matron.
mujerzuela, *f.* 1. uncouth, loudmouthed woman; fishwife. 2. prostitute; worthless female.
mujo, ja, *ref.* **mugir.**
mújol, *m.* (ichth.) mullet, striped mullet.
mula, *f.* 1. mule, she-mule. 2. (Mex.) (porter's) shoulder pad. 3. (Mex.) trash, junk, unsaleable goods. 4. (Guat., Hond.) shame; anger. — **hacer la m.,** (coll.) to be difficult, like to be coaxed (into doing something); **en la m. de San Francisco,** shank's mare, on foot; **írsele a uno la m.,** (coll.) to slip out, be indiscreet, let something out; **m. cabañil,** grain-carrying mule; **m. de paso,** riding mule; **ser una m.,** to be very stupid or obstinate.
mula, *f.* mule, kind of slipper (worn by the Romans); shoe worn by the Pope.
mulada, *f.* 1. (Amer.) drove of mules, herd of mules. 2. a stupid act or gesture.
muladar, *m.* 1. dung heap, dunghill, rubbish heap. 2. (fig.) source of corruption.
muladí, (*pl.* **muladíes**), *m., f.* (hist.) Christian Spaniard who embraced the Moslem faith; (fig.) renegade Christian.
mulante, *m.* muleteer; mule boy.
mular, *a.* pertaining to mules; **ganado m.,** mules.
mulatada, *f.* (Chile) fit of temper.
mulatero, *m.* 1. mule-hirer. 2. mule boy, muleteer, mule driver.
mulato, ta, *a., m., f.* mulatto. —*m.* (Amer.) dark colored silver ore, greenish-colored silver ore.
múleo, *m.* mule, kind of slipper with up-turned point (worn by the Romans).
muléolo, *m., var. of* **múleo.**
muleque, *m.* (Cuba, hist.) little slave; black boy.
mulero, *a.* (horse) fond of mules. —*m.* mule boy, muleteer.
muleta, *f.* 1. crutch (for a cripple). 2. (taur.) muleta, cane bearing bullfighter's small killing cape. 3. (fig.) prop, support. 4. (fig.) bite, snack, light meal. — **pasar de m. al toro,** to deceive the bull; **tener muletas una cosa,** (coll.) to be as old as Methuselah, be old news.
muletada, *f.* drove of mules.
muletero, *m., var. of* **mulatero.**
muletilla, *f.* 1. cross-handle cane. 2. cross-piece (on crutch, on end of stick). 3. (dressm.) frog, toggle button. 4. pet word, pet phrase. 5. (taur.) muleta, cane bearing bullfighter's small killing cape. 6. (min.) nail with cross-like head.
muletillero, ra, *m., f.* person who always uses pet words or phrases in conversation.
muleto, ta, *m., f.* young mule, unbroken mule.
muletón, *m.* (tex.) canton flannel, swanskin.
muliebridad, *f.* muliebrity, femininity.
mulilla, *f., var. of* **múleo.**
mulita, *f.* (min.) mullite.
mulita, *f.* 1. (Arg., Urug.) armadillo. 2. (Chile, ento.) water bug, water strider (Gerris chilensis).
mulito, *m.* (Mex.) turkey.
mullendo, mullera, mullese, mulló, *ref.* **mullir.**
mullida, *f.* pile of straw (serving as bed for cattle); litter, bedding (for animals).
mullido, *past part. of* **mullir.** —*m.* soft filling, soft stuffing (for cushions, etc.).
mullidor, ra, *m., f.* fluffer, softener.
mullir, (*ref.* *65*) *tr.v.* 1. to fluff up, soften up, shake up, punch to make soft (e.g. wool in cushion). 2. to get ready, prepare. 3. (agr.) to loosen, dig up (earth around a vinestock). — **mullírselas a uno,** (coll.) to punish someone.
mullo, *m.* 1. (ichth.) red mullet. 2. (Ecuad.) colored head.
mulo, *m.* (zool.) mule or hinny; **m. castellano,** mule.
mulón, na, *a.* (Chile, Peru) slow in learning to speak; (Chile, Peru) stammering, mumbling.
mulquía, *f.* (in Morocco) title deed (attesting ownership of land).
mulso, a, *a.* sweetened with honey or sugar.
multa, *f.* fine, mulet, forfeit; traffic ticket.
multar, *tr.v.* to fine, mulet, penalize.
multibanda, *f.* (rad.) multiband.
multicapsular, *a.* (bot.) multicapsular.
multicaule, *a.* (bot.) having many shoots.
multicelular, *a.* multicellular.
multicolor, *a.* multicolored, of many colors, many-colored.
multicopista, *m.* duplicating machine, copying machine.
multidentado, da, *a.* multidentate, having many teeth.
multidimensional, *a.* multidimensional.
multidireccional, *a.* multidirectional.
multietapa, *a.* (phys.) multistage.
multifacético, ca, *a.* many-sided.
multifásico, *a.* (elec.) polyphase.
multífido, da, *a.* (bot.) multifid.
multiflor, *f.* (Chile, bot.) multiflora, multiflora rose.
multifloro, ra, *a.* multiflorous, many-flowered.
multiforme, *a. multiform, having many forms.*
multifrecuencia, *a.* (elec.) multifrequency.
multigrafiar, *tr.v.* to multigraph.
multilátero, a, *a.* multilateral, many-sided.
multilobulado, da, *a.* (med.) multilobulate.
multilocular, *a.* (med.) multilocular.
multímetro, *m.* (elec.) multimeter, multiple-purpose tester.
multimillonario, a, *a., m., f.* multimillionaire.
multimotor, *a.* multi-engined, polymotor.
multinacional, *a.* multinational.
multinomio, *m.* (math.) multinomial.
multinucleado, da, *a.* multinucleated.
multinuclear, *a.* multinuclear.
multípara, *a.* multiparous. —*f.* multipara, female who has had more than one offspring.
multiparidad, *f.* multiparity, the state of having had more than one offspring.
multípedo, da, *a.* (zool.) multiped, many-footed.
múltiple, *a.* multiple, manifold; complex; gang, e.g. *condensador m.,* gang condenser. —*m.* manifold; **m. de admisión,** (auto.) intake manifold; **m. de escape,** (auto.) exhaust manifold.
multiplete, *m.* (phys.) multiplet.
multiplex, *a.* (rad., tel.) multiplex, sending or receiving more than one message at a time.
multiplicable, *a.* multipliable, multiplicable.
multiplicación, *f.* multiplication.
multiplicado, da, *a.* multiplicate.
multiplicador, ra, *a.* multiplying. —*m., f.* multiplier; **multiplicadora electrónica** or **fotoeléctrica,** (phys.) electron multiplier. —*m.* (math.) multiplier.
multiplicando, *m.* (math.) multiplicand.
multiplicar, (*ref.* *50*) *tr.v., i.v., r.v.* 1. (math.) to multiply. 2. to increase in number. — **tablas de m.,** multiplication tables.
multiplicativo, va, *a.* multiplicative.
multíplice, *a.* multiple, manifold; complex.
multiplicidad, *f.* multiplicity; great number, multitude.
multiplique, multipliqué, *ref.* **multiplicar.**
múltiplo, pla, *a.* (math.) multiple. —*m.* (math.) multiple. — **mínimo común m.,** (math.) lowest common multiple.
multipolar, *a.* multipolar.
multisimétrico, ca, *a.* (geom.) multisymmetrical.
multitud, *f.* crowd, multitude; populace, people.
multitudinario, a, *a.* multitudinous, mass.
multivalente, *a.* (chem., biol.) multivalent, polyvalent.
multivoltage, *a.* (elec.) variable voltage, multivoltage.
mumuga, *f.* (Hond.) tobacco chaff.
mundanal, *a., var. of* **mundano,** wordly, mundane.
mundanalidad, *f.* worldliness, mundanity.
mundanamente, *adv.* mundanely.
mundanear, *i.v.* to be wordly-minded; to indulge in wordly things.

mundanería, *f.* worldliness, sophistication; worldly behavior.
mundano, na, *a.* worldly, mundane.
mundial, *a.* pertaining to the world; worldwide, universal; **guerra m.,** World War.
mundicia, *f.* cleanness, cleanliness.
mundificación, *f.* cleansing.
mundificante, *a.* cleansing, purifying.
mundificar, (*ref.* *50*) *tr.v.* to clean, cleanse, purify.
mundificativo, va, *a.* (med.) cleansing.
mundifique, mundifiqué, *ref.* **mundificar.**
mundillo, *m.* 1. arched clotheshorse. 2. warming pan. 3. lace-making cushion. 3. (bot.) guelder-rose, snowball. 4. inner circle (of artists, actors, politicians, etc.).
mundinovi, *m., var. of* **tutilimundi.**
mundo, *m.* 1. world, earth; sphere, globe. 2. experience, sophistication. 3. (coll.) crowd, flock (of people), multitude. 4. Saratoga trunk. 5. (bot.) guelder rose, snowball. — **conocer m.,** to see the world, travel; **desde que el m. es m.,** (coll.) ever since the world began; **echar al m.,** to bring forth, create, bring into the world; **echarse al m.,** to give oneself up to dissipation and debauchery; **el m. anda** or **está al revés,** the world is topsyturvy; **entrar en el m.,** to go into society; **este m. y el otro,** (coll.) all this and heaven too; **gran m.,** high society; **m. antiguo,** ancient world, antiquity; **m. elegante,** high society; **m. mayor,** macrocosm, great world, universe; **m. menor,** microcosm, little world; **(El) Nuevo M.,** (the) New World; **(el) otro m.,** the other world; **medio m.,** (coll.) crowds or thousands of people; **nada del otro m.,** nothing to write home about, nothing special; **ponerse el m. por montera,** (coll.) to pay no attention to public opinion; **salir de este m.,** to die; **tener m.** or **mucho m.,** (coll.) to be experienced or sophisticated; **todo el m.,** everybody, everyone; **venir al m.,** to be born; **ver m.,** to see the world, travel.
mundología, *f.* worldly experience, worldly wisdom.
mundonuevo, *m., var. of* **tutilimundi.**
munición, *f.* 1. ammunition, munitions. 2. buckshot, small shot. 3. charge (of firearms). 4. (Hond.) soldier's uniform. — **de m.,** government issue; (coll.) hurriedly done or made. — **depósito de municiones,** ammunition dump; **municiones de boca,** (mil.) food, provisions; **m. de fogueo,** dummy ammunition; **m. de guerra,** (mil.) ammunition, war supplies; **m. perforante,** (arm.) armor-piercing ammunition; **m. trazadora,** tracing ammunition.
municionamiento, *m.* munitioning, supplying with munition.
municionar, *tr.v.* to munition, supply with ammunition, provide with supplies.
municionera, *f.* (Col., Chile) cartridge pouch.
municionero, ra, *m., f.* supplier of ammunition. —*f.* (Ven.) ball bearing.
municipal, *a.* municipal. —*m.* 1. city policeman. 2. (Chile) councilor.
municipalice, municipalicé, *ref.* **municipalizar.**
municipalidad, *f.* town council; municipality; town hall.
municipalización, *f.* municipalization.
municipalizar, (*ref.* *53*) *tr.v.* to municipalize.
munícipe, *m.* citizen, community member, town councilor; denizen of a town or city.
municipio, *m.* 1. (Roman hist.) municipium, municipality. 2. municipality (community under municipal corporation). 3. town council, municipal corporation. 4. town hall. 5. municipal boundary. 6. town, city.
munido, da, *a.* (Chile) defended, fortified; armed.
munificencia, *f.* munificence, liberality.
munificente, *a.* munificent, generous, liberal.
munificentísimo, ma, *a. super. of* **munífice,** exceedingly munificent.
munífico, ca, *a.* munificent, liberal, generous.
munitoria, *f.* art of fortification.
muntyac, *m.* (zool.) muntjac, muntjak.
muñeca, *f.* 1. (anat.) wrist. 2. doll (toy). 3. mannequin, dressmaker's dummy or lay figure. 4. muslin bag; tea bag; pounce bag; polishing bag. 5. coquette; pretty girl. — **menear las muñecas,** to work hard; **m. de estarcir,** pounce bag; **m. de trapo,** rag doll.
muñeco, *m.* 1. doll, puppet (toy figure representing male child). 2. effeminate young man, fop. — **tener muñecos en la cabeza,** (coll.) to have exaggerated ideas of one's abilities; to build castles in the air.
muñeira, *f.* (Sp.) popular Galician dance and its music (usually played on bagpipes).
muñendo, muñera, muñese, muño, *ref.* **muñir.**
muñequear, *i.v.* 1. (fenc.) to use wrist-play. 2. (Chile) to bud, sprout.
muñequera, *f.* watch strap, wrist strap.
muñequería, *f.* 1. (coll.) overdressing, effeminate fripperies. 2. doll shop.
muñequilla, *f.* 1. small doll. 2. pounce bag. 3. (Chile) young ear of corn.
muñequitos, *m.* (*pl.*) comics, comic book; cartoons.
muñidor, *m.* 1. beadle (of a brotherhood or fraternity). 2. messenger, go-between. 3. intriguer, plotter.
muñir, (*ref.* *66*) *tr.v.* to summon, convoke, call (to meetings); to arrange; to handle, manage.
muñón, *m.* 1. stump (of an amputated limb). 2. (anat.) deltoid, shoulder muscle. 3. (artil.) trunnion. 4. (mec.) trunnion, pivot, journal, gudgcon pin, wrist-pin.
muñonera, *f.* 1. (artil.) trunnion plate. 2. (mec.) gudgeon socket, journal box bearing.
muón, *m.* (phys.) muon.
mura, *f., var. of* **amura.**
muradal, *m., var. of* **muladar.**
murajes, *m.* (*pl.*) (bot.) pimpernel.
mural, *a.* mural; pertaining to walls; wall; **mapa m.,** wall map; **pintura m.,** (p.) mural, mural painting.
muralla, *f.* city wall; (fort.) rampart; (Chile, Ecuad., Guat., P. Rico) wall (of a building); **la Gran M.** or **la M. China,** the Great Wall of China.
murallón, *m.* thick strong wall.
murar, *tr.v.* to wall, fortify with a wall, surround with a rampart.
murceguillo, *m.* (zool.) bat.
murciélago, *m.* (zool.) bat.
murena, *f.* (ichth.) moray.
murete, *m.* low wall, small wall.
murexida, *f.* (chem.) murexide.
murga, *f.* 1. lees of olives. 2. (coll.) band of street musicians. — **dar m.,** to bother, pester, annoy.
murgón, *m.* (ichth.) parr, smelt, samlet.
murguista, *m.* member of a band of street musicians.
muriacita, *f.* (min.) anhydrite.
muriático, ca, *a.* (chem.) muriatic.
muriato, *m.* (chem.) muriate.
muricado, da, *a.* (bot.) muricate, muricated.
múrice, 1. (zool.) murex. 2. (poet.) purple.
múridos, *m.* (*pl.*) (zool.) Muridae.
muriendo, muriera, muriese, murió, *ref.* **morir.**
murmujear, *tr.v., i.v.* (coll.) to murmur, to whisper.
murmullar, *i.v.* to murmur, to whisper.
murmullo, *m.* 1. murmur, murmuring (of people); ripple, rippling (of water); babbling (of brook); whisper, whispering, sighing (of wind); rustle, rustling (of leaves). 2. murmur, complaint, grumble. 3. (med.) murmur.
murmuración, *f.* malicious gossip, backbiting, slander.
murmurador, ra, *a.* 1. murmuring; whispering; sighing; rippling, babbling; rustling. 2. moaning; grumbling. 3. gossiping. —*m., f.* 1. murmurer. 2. moaner, grumbler. 3. gossip, gossiper, slanderer.
murmurante, *a., var. of* **murmurador,** murmuring, purling, whispering.
murmurar, *i.v.* 1. to murmur (people), whisper, sigh (wind), rustle (leaves), ripple (water), babble (brook). 2. to mutter, grumble, moan. 3. to gossip (about). —*tr.v.* 1. to mutter, grumble or moan about. 2. to gossip about, slander.
murmureo, *m.* constant murmuring, whispering, rippling, babbling or rustling.
murmurio, *m., f.* murmur, whisper, ripple, babbling, rustle.
muro, *m.* (outside) wall; rampart; **m. cortafuegos,** fire wall; **m. de alma** or **pantalla,** (hydr.) core wall; **M. de Berlín,** Berlin Wall; **m. de carga,** load-bearing wall; **m. de cerramiento,** curtain wall; **M. de las Lamentaciones** or **los Lamentos,** Wailing Wall; **m. del calor** or **térmico,** (aer.) heat barrier; **m. de retención** or **sostenimiento,** or **contención,** retaining wall.
murria, *f.* 1. (coll.) melancholy, dejection, sadness, the blues. 2. (obs.) a home-concocted lotion, formerly used as a mild antiseptic.
múrrino, na, *a.* murrhine, of an ancient Roman semi-precious stone, used for making vessels, goblets, etc.
murriña, *f., var. of* **morriña,** 1. murrain, cattle disease. 2. melancholy, dejection, sadness.
murrio, rria, *a.* sad, dejected, blue (coll.), melancholy.
murro, *m.* (Chile) frown, angry or stern look.
murruz, *a.* (Hond.) curly, kinky (hair).
murta, *f.* (bot.) myrtle; myrtle berry.
murtal, murtela, *m.* myrtle grove.
murtilla, murtina, *f.* (Chile) (species of) myrtle (Myrtus ugni); liquor made from the berry of this tree.
murtón, *m.* (bot.) myrtle berry.
murucuyá, *f.* (bot.) passionflower.
murueco, *m., var. of* **morueco,** ram, male sheep.
mus, *m.* card game. — **no hay m.,** cannot be granted; **sin decir tus ni m.,** without saying a word.
musa, *f.* 1. (myth.) Muse. 2. muse, inspiration. 3. (*pl.*) Muses, the liberal arts. — **soplarle a uno la m.,** (coll.) to be inspired, get inspiration; to be lucky at gambling.
musáceo, cea, *a.* (bot.) musaceous. —*f.* (*pl.*) Musaceae.
musaraña, *f.* 1. (zool.) shrew. 2. small animal, insect, bug, worm. 3. (coll.) caricature, ridiculous figure (of someone). 4. (coll.) floating speck in the eye. — **mirar a las musarañas, pensar en las musarañas,** (coll.) to let one's mind wander.
muscardina, *f.* muscardine (fungus disease of some insects).
muscaria, *f.* (ornith.) spotted flycatcher.
muscarina, *f.* (chem.) muscarine.
muscícapa, *f.* (ornith.) spotted flycatcher.
múscido, da, *a.* (ento.) muscid.
musco, *m.* (bot.) moss.
musco, ca, *a.* dark brown. —*m.* (bot.) *var. of* **musgo,** moss.
muscovita, *f.* (min.) muscovite (mica).

musculación, *f.* (Col., Guat., Mex.) *var. of* **musculatura.**
muscular, *a.* muscular, pertaining to the muscles.
muscularidad, *f.* muscularity.
musculatura, *f.* musculature.
músculo, *m.* 1. muscle. 2. (zool.) rorqual, finback, razorback whale. — **m. abductor,** (anat.) abductor muscle; **m. aductor** (anat.) adductor muscle; **m. agonista,** (anat.) agonist muscle; **m. glúteo,** (anat.) gluteal muscle; **m. lumbrical,** (anat.) lumbrical muscle; **m. sartorio,** (anat.) sartorius, sartorial muscle; **m. subscapular,** (anat.) subscapular muscle; **m. voluntario,** (anat.) voluntary muscle.
musculoso, sa, *a.* muscular, brawny.
muselina, *f.* (tex.) muslin.
museo, *m.* museum.
museología, *f.* the study of museums, their organization, functioning, etc.
muserola, *f.* noseband (of a horse's bridle fittings).
musgaño, *m.* (zool.) shrew.
musgo, *m.* (bot.) moss. — **m. marino** (bot.) coralline (calcareous alga); **m.** or **liquen de Islandia,** (bot.) Iceland moss.
musgo, ga, *a.* dark brown.
musgoso, sa, *a.* mossy, moss-covered.
música, *f.* 1. music. 2. band; choir. 3. (coll.) row, racket, noise. 4. musical composition. 5. sheet music. — **ir la m. por dentro,** to keep one's feelings hidden or under control; **irse con la m. a otra parte,** (coll,) to up and go; **mandar con la m. a otra parte,** (coll.) to send packing; **m. armónica,** vocal music; **m. bailable,** dance music; **m. celestial,** (coll.) idle promises; **m. clásica,** or **culta,** classical music; **m. coral,** choral music; **m. de acompañamiento** or **incidental,** incidental music; **m. de baile,** dance music; **m. de cámara,** chamber music; **m. de fondo,** background music; **m. folk,** folk music; **m. instrumental,** instrumental music; **m. ligera,** light music; **m. llana,** plain song; **m. sacra,** sacred music; **m. vocal,** vocal music; **m. y acompañamiento,** (coll.) small fry; **no entender la m.,** to act dumb; **váyase con la m. a otra parte,** (coll.) clear off, don't bother me.
musical, *a.* musical.
musicalidad, *f.* musicality, melodiousness.
musicalmente, *adv.* musically.
musicastro, *m.* (derog.) musician.
músico, ca, *a.* musical. —*m., f.* 1. musician. 2. (Col.) tippler, one who likes drinking. 3. (C. Amer.) poor horseman or horsewoman. 4. (Mex.) hypocrite.
musicógrafo, *m.* one who writes about music and composers.
musicología, *f.* musicology, the study of the theory and history of music.
musicólogo, ga, *m., f.* musicologist.
musicomanía, *f.* fanaticism for music.
musicómano, na, *m., f.* music fan, music buff (coll.).
musiquero, *m.* music cabinet or shelf.
musitar, *i.v.* to mumble, whisper, mutter.
musivo, *a.* mosaic (gold).
muslera, *f.* armor for the thigh, cuisse.
muslime, *a., m., f.* Moslem, Muslem, Muslim, Islamic, Mohammedan.
muslímico, ca, *a.* Moslem, Muslim, Mohammedan.
muslo, *m.* (anat.) thigh.
musmón, *m.* (zool.) moufflon, mountain sheep or goat.
musquerola, *f.* small very sweet pear, muscadine pear.
mustaco, *m.* must cake, cake made with must and butter.
mustang, mustango, *m.* mustang, wild horse.
mustela, *f.* 1. (ichth.) dogfish (Mustelus vulgaris). 2. (zool.) weasel.
mustélidos, *m.* (*pl.*) (zool.) Mustelidae.
mustiamente, *adv.* sadly, languidly, glumly.
mustiarse, *r.v.* to wither, become withered.
mustio, tia, *a.* 1. sad, gloomy, dejected. 2. withered, faded. 3. (Mex.) (fig.) hypocritical, false.
musuco, ca, *a.* (Hond.) curly, kinky (hair).
musulmán, na, *a.* Mussulmanic, Moslem, Muslin, Mohammedan. —*m., f.* Mussulman, Moslem, Muslim, Mohammedan.
muta, *f.* pack of dogs or hounds.
mutabilidad, *f.* mutability, changeableness.
mutación, *f.* 1. mutation, change. 2. (theat.) scene change, change of scenery. 3. change of weather. 4. (biol.) mutation.
mutacionismo, *m.* (biol.) mutationism.
mutagénico, ca, *a.* (biol.) mutagenic, capable of inducing a mutation.
mutágeno, na, *a.* (biol.) mutagenic.
mutante, *m.* (biol.) mutant.
mutatis mutandis, (Lat.) with the necessary changes (in words, etc.).
mute, *m.* (Col.) stew made of corn and potatoes.
mútico, ca, *a.* (bot.) muticate, muticous.
mutilación, *f.* 1. mutilation; disablement, crippling. 2. defacement, disfigurement.
mutilado, da, *past part. of* **mutilar.** —*a.* 1. mutilated; disabled, crippled, maimed. 2. defaced, disfigured. —*m., f.* crippled or disabled person. — **m. de guerra,** disabled serviceman.
mutilador, ra, *a.* 1. mutilating; crippling, disabling, maiming. 2. defacing, disfiguring. —*m., f.* mutilator.
mutilar, *tr.v.* 1. to mutilate; to cripple, disable, maim. 2. to deface, disfigure; cut short.
mútilo, la, *a.* 1. mutilated; crippled, maimed. 2. defaced, disfigured.
mutis, *m.* (theat.) exit; **hacer m.,** to keep quiet, say nothing.
mutismo, *m.* mutism, dumbness; silence, muteness.
mutual, *a.* mutual, reciprocal.
mutualidad, *f.* 1. mutuality, interdependence, reciprocity. 2. benefit society, mutual benefit society. 3. mutual benefit or aid.
mutualismo, *m.* mutualism, system of organized mutual aid.
mutualista, *a.* mutualist, mutualistic; mutual benefit society (*as a.*). —*m., f.* member of a mutual benefit society.
mutuamente, *adv.* mutually, reciprocally.
mutuante, *m., f.* lender, loaner.
mutuario, ria, *m., f., var. of* **mutuatario.**
mutuatario, ria, *m., f.* (law) mutuary, borrower.
mútulo, *m.* (archit.) mutule, part of the corona of the Doric cornice.
mutún, *m.* (ornith., Bol.) curassow.
mutuo, tua, *a.* mutual, reciprocal. —*m.* (law) mutuum, loan.
muy, *adv.* 1. very, much, greatly. 2. too, e.g. *está m. enfermo para venir a la oficina,* he is too ill to come to the office. 3. quite a, very much a, e.g. *él es m. hombre,* he's quite a man. — **m. de madrugada,** very early in the morning; **m. de noche,** very late at night; **m. de prisa,** very quickly; **m. de su casa,** very homeloving; **m. señor mío,** my dear sir (a form of address in a formal or business letter).
muz, (*pl.* **muces**), *m.* (mar.) upper extremity of outwater.
muzárabe, *a.* (hist.) Mozarabic, Mozarab.
muzo, za, *a.* dead-smooth (file). —*f.* dead-smooth file.
Mv *sym. of* **mendelevio,** mendelevium (Md).
mV. *abbrev. of* **milivoltio,** millivolt (mv).
mw. *abbrev. of* **milivatio,** milliwatt (mw).

N

N, *f.* 1. n, fourteenth letter of the Spanish alphabet. 2. (math.) n (indefinite number).
N *sym. of* **nitrógeno,** nitrogen (N).
N. *abbrev. of* **norte,** north (N.).
Na *sym. of* **sodio,** natrium, sodium (Na).
N.A. *abbrev. of* **Norte América,** North America.
naba, *f.* (bot.) rape, Swedish turnip, rutabaga.
nabab, *m.* 1. nabob, governor of a province in India. 2. (fig.) a very rich or important man.
nababo, *m., var. of* **nabab.**
nabal, *a., m., var. of* **nabar.**
nabar, *a.* pertaining to turnips. —*m.* turnip field.
nabateo, tea, *a.* Nabataean, Nabatean, pertaining to an ancient Arab kingdom in S.W. Asia.
nabería, *f.* heap or pile of turnips; turnip soup or stew.
nabí, (*pl.* **nabíes**), *m.* Moorish prophet.
nabicol, *m.* (bot.) kohlrabi.
nabina, *f.* rape or turnip seed.
nabiza, *f.* rape rootlets; (*pl.*) turnip greens or leaves.
nabla, *f.* (mus.) ancient harp.
nabo, *m.* (bot.) turnip; (any) thick root. 2. stock, root (of a horse's tail). 3. (archit.) newel (of stairs); kingpost (of a roof). 4. (mar.) mast. 5. heart (of split wood). — **n. de. Suecia,** Swedish turnip; **n. gallego,** (bot.) rape.
naborí, (*pl.* **naboríes**), *m., f.* (Amer.) free Indian servant.
naboría, *f.* (Amer.) allocation of Indians as domestic servants (at the beginning of the Spanish Conquest).
Nabucodonosor, *m.* (Bib.) Nebuchadnezzar, Nabuchodonosor.
nácar, *m.* mother-of-pearl, nacre.
nácara, *f.* ancient cavalry drum.
nacarado, da, *a.* set or decorated with mother-of-pearl; nacreous, made of mother-of-pearl, nacrine.
nacáreo, rea, *a., var. of* **nacarino.**
nacarigüe, *m.* (Hond.) dish of meat and spice.
nacarino, na, *a.* pertaining to, made of, or resembling mother-of-pearl; nacarine, nacreous.
nacarón, *m.* inferior quality mother-of-pearl.
nacascolo, *m.* (C. Amer., bot.) divi-divi.
nacatamal, *m.* (C. Amer.) pork tamale.
nacatamalera, *f.* (C. Amer.) tamale vendor.
nacatete, *m.* (Mex.) unfledged chick.
nacela, *f.* 1. (archit.) scotia. 2. (aer.) nacelle.
nacencia, *f.* (fig.) growth, tumor.
nacer, (*ref. 45*) *i.v.* 1. to be born, come into the world; to be hatched. 2. to sprout; to begin to grow; to bud, blossom. 3. to appear, to rise, come out (the sun, a star). 4. to spring, issue, start to flow (a spring). 5. to spring, derive, originate (from). — **n. para** + *inf.*, to be born to + *inf.*, e.g. *n. para ser maestro,* to be born to be a teacher; **n. para** + *n.*, to be born for + *n.*, e.g. *n. para la iglesia,* to be born for the church. —*r.v.* 1. to sprout, shoot, bud. 2. to split, come apart (clothes at the seams).
nacho, cha, *a.* pug-nosed, flat-nosed.
nacido, da, *past part. of* **nacer.** —*a.* 1. born. 2. innate, inborn, natural. — **bien n.,** wellborn, highborn, well-bred; **n. para,** born for; **mal n.,** lowborn, ill-bred. —*m.* 1. human being. 2. inflamed boil; growth, tumor.
naciente, *a.* 1. nascent; incipient; very recent, growing. 2. rising (sun). 3. (her.) naissant. —*m.* East, Orient. — **el sol n.,** the rising sun.
nacimiento, *m.* 1. birth; hatching. 2. source, spring (of a stream); stream. 3. beginning; origin; birth. 4. birth, descent, origin. 5. crib, crèche (Nativity scene). — **de n.,** from birth, e.g. *ciego de n.,* blind from birth; **de noble** or **humilde n.,** of noble or humble birth or origin; **n. de nuevo,** rebirth; **por n.,** by birth.
nación, *f.* 1. nation, country, state. 2. race, tribe, people (of the same ethnic origin and language). — **de n.,** by birth; from birth; **naciones del Eje,** Axis nations; **Naciones Unidas,** United Nations.
nacional, *a., m., f.* national, native, domestic. —*m.* militiaman; **guardia n.,** National Guard.
nacionalice, nacionalicé, *ref.* **nacionalizar.**
nacionalidad, *f.* nationality, citizenship; **doble n.,** dual citizenship.
nacionalismo, *m.* nationalism.
nacionalista, *a.* nationalistic, nationalist. —*m., f.* nationalist.
nacionalización, *f.* 1. nationalization. 2. naturalization. 3. (pol., econ.) expropriation, nationalization.
nacionalizar, (*ref. 53*) *tr.v.* 1. to nationalize. 2. to naturalize. —*r.v.* 1. to be nationalized. 2. to become naturalized.
nacionalmente, *adv.* nationally.
nacionalsocialismo, *m.* (pol.) National Socialism; Nazism, Fascism.
nacionalsocialista, *a., m., f.* National Socialist; Nazi, fascist.
nacismo, *m.* Nazism.
nacista, *m., f.* Nazi.
naco, *m.* 1. (Arg., Bol., Urug.) rolled tobacco leaf. 2. (Col.) cream of corn; mashed potatoes. 3. (Arg.) fear, scare. 4. (C. Amer.) coward, sissy. 5. black chewing tobacco.
nacrita, *f.* (min.) variety of talc.
nada, *f.* nothing, naught, nothingness. —*indef pron.* nothing; **n. del otro mundo, n. del otro jueves,** nothing to write home about, nothing special; **n. de eso,** not at all, none of that, not so; **n. nuevo,** nothing new; **de n.,** (after thank you) you are welcome; **n. del otro jueves,** nothing else; **n. más,** nothing else, nothing more, no more; **n. menos,** no less, nothing less; **no es n.,** it's nothing at all; **por n.,** for nothing; for nothing in the world or at all; **por nada del mundo,** not for all the world, for nothing in the world. —*adv.* not at all, e.g. *no me parece n. gracioso,* it does not seem at all funny to me, *no es n. extraño que no venga,* it's not at all surprising that he doesn't come.
nadaderas, *f.* (*pl.*) water wings, water bladders (used to keep afloat in learning how to swim).
nadadero, *m.* swimming place.
nadador, ra, *a.* swimming. —*m., f.* swimmer.
nadante, *a.* swimming, natan (poet.).
nadar, *i.v.* 1. to swim; to float. 2. (fig.) to be lost in, to swim in (oversize clothing), e.g. *yo nado en estas botas,* I am swimming in these boots. — **n. contra la corriente,** to swim against the tide; **n. de espaldas,** to swim on one's back; **n. en riquezas** or **la opulencia,** to be rolling in dough, be filthy rich; **n. entre dos aguas,** to be on the fence, undecided.
nadería, *f.* trifle, nothing, insignificant thing.
nadie, *indef. pron.* nobody, not anybody, no one, none. —*m.* nobody (person of no importance).
nádir, *m.* nazir, one who administers a public assistance fund (in Morocco).
nadir, *m.* (astron., fig.) nadir, opposite to the zenith. — **n. fotográfico,** (photgmt.) plate nadir point, photographic nadir.
nado, a n., *adv.* swimming; **pasar a n.,** to swim across.
nafta, *f.* (chem.) naphtha.
NAFTA, *m.* NAFTA.
naftalina, *f.* (chem.) naphthalene.
nafteno, *m.* (chem.) naphthene.
naftílico, ca, *a.* (chem.) naphthalic.
naftilo, *m.* (chem.) naphthyl.
naftol, *m.* (chem.) naphthol, naphtol.
nagana, *f.* (vet.) nagana; an infectious disease affecting horses and cattle in tropical Africa.
nagual, *m.* 1. (Mex.) wizard, sorcerer. 2. (Hond.) inseparable pet (animal).
naguas, *f.* (coll.) (*pl.*) petticoat.
naguatlato, ta, *m., f.* (Mex., hist.) Indian interpreter (between Spaniards and Nahuatl Indians).
naguatle, *a., var. of* **nahuatle.**
nahuatl, nahuatle, *a.* Nahuatl. —*m.* Uto-Aztecan language.
naide, *indef. pron.* (imp. u.) nobody **(nadie).**
naife, *m.* (jewel.) diamond of the first water, fine quality diamond.
naipe, *m.* (playing) card; pack or deck of cards. — **cortar el n.,** to cut the cards; **dar bien el n.,** to be in luck, have good luck; **dar el n. (a uno) para (una cosa),** to have a knack for (something); **dar mal el n.,** to have bad luck, be out of luck; **florear el n.,** to stack or mark the cards (for cheating); **peinar los naipes,** to shuffle the cards thoroughly; **truco de naipes,** card trick.
naire, *m.* mahout, elephant keeper, trainer.
Nairobi, *m.* Nairobi (capital of Kenya).
naja, *f.* (zool.) cobra.
nalca, *f.* (Chile) edible stalk.
nalga, *f.* (anat.) buttock, rump.
nalgada, *f.* 1. spanking, spank; slap given on the buttocks. 2. pork cut; ham.
nalgar, *a.* pertaining to the buttocks, gluteal.
nalgatorio, *m.* (coll.) bottom, buttocks, posterior, behind, fanny (coll.).
nalgón, na, *a.* (Amer.) big-buttocked.
nalgudo, da, *a.* broad in the beam, having a large posterior or behind.
nalguear, *i.v.* to waggle or wiggle one's behind (when walking).
nambí, *m.* (Arg., Urug.) said of a horse with drooping ears.
nambimba, *f.* (Mex.) frothy stew made with corn, honey, cacao and chili.
nambira, *f.* (Hond.) gourd, gourd bowl or vessel.
nana, *f.* 1. (coll.) grannie, grandmother. 2. lullaby. 3. (Amer.) nanny, nurse. 4. (Hond.) mummy, mother. 5. (S. Amer.) injury, harm, pain (in baby language). — **el año de la n.,** the year one.

nanacate, *m.* (Mex.) mushroom.
nance, *m.* (C. Amer., bot.) nance, golden spoon (Byrsonima crassifolia).
nancear, *i.v.* (Hond.) to catch; to reach.
nancer, *m.* (Cuba) *var. of* **nance.**
nanear, *i.v.* to waddle.
nango, ga, *a.* (Mex.) 1. strange, foreign. 2. silly, foolish.
nanismo, *m.* dwarfishness.
nanita, *f. dim. of* **nana.**
nanjea, *f.* (bot.) jack, breadfruit (Artocarpus maxima).
nanquín, *m.* (tex.) nankeen, nankin, a fine cotton fabric made in China.
nansa, *f.* 1. fyke, bag net (bag-shaped net for catching fish). 2. fish pond.
nansú, *m.* (tex.) nainsook, fine lawn.
nao, *f.* (poet., hist.) ship, vessel.
naonato, ta, *a.* born on board ship.
napa, *f.* undeground sheet of water; **n. freática,** (geoph.) ground water, water table.
napalm, *m.* (chem., mil.) napalm, jellied gasoline (bomb).
napea, *f.* (myth.) wood nymph; (*pl.*) Napaese.
napelo, *m.* (bot.) aconite, monkshood, wolfsbane.
napeo, a, *a.* (myth.) pertaining to wood nymphs.
napias, *f.* (*pl.*) (coll.) noses.
napiforme, *a.* (bot.) napiform, turnipshaped.
napoleón, *m.* 1. (numis.) napoleon, French coin. 2. **N.,** Napoleon (Bonaparte).
napoleónico, ca, *a.* Napoleonic.
Nápoles, *m.* Naples, city in Italy.
napolitana, *f.* (in certain card games) combination of cards.
napolitano, na, *a., m., f.* Neapolitan.
naque, *m.* formerly, a pair of strolling comedians.
narango, *m.* (C. Amer.) banshee, goblin, bogey man.
naranja, *f.* 1. orange; (Mex.) grapefruit. 2. cannon ball. — **media n.,** better half (spouse); bosom friend; (archit.) dome; **n. agria,** Seville orange; **n. mandarina,** mandarin orange; **n. navel,** navel orange; **¡naranjas!,** (coll.) phooey!, nuts!; **n. sanguínea,** blood orange.
naranjada, *f.* 1. orangeade, orange cordial, orange juice. 2. (coll.) coarse or vulgar remark.
naranjado, da, *a., var. of* **anaranjado,** orange-colored.
naranjal, *m.* orange grove.
naranjazo, *m.* blow with an orange.
naranjera, *f.* large blunderbuss.
naranjero, ra, *a.* of three and a half-inch caliber (pipe, cannon). —*m., f.* orange-seller. —*m.* (reg.) orange tree.
naranjilla, *f.* green orange for making preserves.
naranjillada, *f.* (Ecuad.) orangeade, orange cordial (made with the **naranjilla**).
naranjo, *m.* 1. (bot.) orange tree; orange-wood. 2. (coll.) rustic, bumpkin.
narbonense, *a., var of* **narbonés.**
narbonés, sa, *a.* Narbonne, of or from Narbonne, France. —*m., f.* inhabitant or native of Narbonne.
narceína, *f.* (chem.) narceine.
narcisismo, *m.* narcissism.
narciso, *m.* (bot.) narcissus, daffodil.
narciso, *m.* 1. (bot.) narcissus. 2. (fig.) narcissus (fop, dandy). 3. (myth.) **N.,** Narcissus, a beautiful youth who fell in love with his own reflection.
narcoanálisis, *m.* (med.) narcoanalysis.
narcolepsia, *f.* (med.) narcolepsy, a condition of frequent and uncontrollable desire for sleep.
narcosíntesis, *f.* (med.) narcosynthesis.
narcosis, *f.* (med.) narcosis.
narcotice, narcoticé, *ref.* **narcotizar.**
narcótico, ca, *a., m.* narcotic.
narcotina, *f.* (chem.) narcotine.
narcotismo, *m.* (med.) narcotism.
narcotización, *f.* narcotization.
narcotizador, ra, *a.* narcotizing.
narcotizar, (*ref. 53*) *tr.v.* to narcotize, drug, dope.
nardino, na, *a.* nardine; nard-like, made of or resembling spikenard.
nardo, *m.* (bot.) nard; (pharm., bot.) spikenard; (bot.) tuberose; **n. índico,** tuberose.
narguile, *m.* narghile (Turkish pipe).
narguilé, *m., var. of* **narguile.**
narigada, *f.* (Amer.) pinch (e.g. of snuff).
narigón, na, *a.* large-nosed. —*m.,* large-nosed person. —*m.* 1. big nose. 2. hole in the nose (for wearing a ring). 3. (Cuba) nose ring. 4. (Cuba) hole in a tree trunk (to facilitate dragging).
narigudo, da, *a.* large-nosed. —*m., f.* large-nosed person.
nariguera, *f.* nose ring or pendant.
nariqueta, ita, *f. dim. of* **nariz,** small nose.
nariz, (*pl.* **narices**), *f.* 1. (anat.) nose; nostril. 2. nose, sense of smell. 3. bouquet (of wine). 4. socket of a bolt or latch. 5. cutwater (of a boat, bridge). 6. nozzle, spout (of a retort). — **darle a uno en la n. una cosa,** to smell (food, trouble); to suspect (someone's intentions); **darse con la puerta en las narices,** to come up against a stone wall; **en sus propias narices,** under one's nose; **hinchársele a uno las narices,** (coll.) to get angry; **meter las narices en todo,** (coll.) to stick one's nose into everything; **n. aguileña,** aquiline nose; **n. perfilada,** Grecian nose; **n. respingona,** turned-up nose; **n. chata,** snub nose; **no ver más allá de sus narices,** (coll.) to see no farther than one's nose, be short-sighted; **sonarse la n.,** to blow one's nose; **tener a uno montado en las narices,** (coll.) to be constantly plagued by someone; **tenerle a alguien agarrado por las narices,** (coll.) to lead by the nose, have someone under one's thumb; **torcer las narices,** (coll.) to turn one's nose up at, reject.
narizón, na, *a.* large-nosed.
narizota, *f. aug. of* **nariz,** large ugly nose.
narizudo, da, *a.* (Mex., coll.) large-nosed.
narra, *m.* (bot.) red sandalwood (Pterocarpus santalinus).
narrable, *a.* that can be narrated, apt for narration.
narración, *f.* narration, chronicle, account; recounting, telling; **n. retrospectiva,** flashback (in a novel).
narrador, ra, *a.* narrating. —*m., f.* narrator, chronicler.
narrar, *tr.v.* to narrate, relate, tell.
narrativa, *f.* 1. narrative, tale, story. 2. narrative art or talent, skill in telling stories.
narrativo, va, *a.* narrative.
narratorio, ria, *a., var. of* **narrativo.**
narria, *f.* 1. sled, sledge; drag, dray (low cart for hauling very heavy loads). 2. (fig.) heavy, bulky woman.
nártex, *m.* (archit.) narthex.
narval, *m.* (zool.) narwhal.
narvaso, *m.* cornstalks (used as fodder).
nasa, *f.* 1. fish trap; lobster pot. 2. fishing basket; bread basket, breadbox; flour bin.
NASA f. — **la N.,** NASA.
nasal, *a., f.* nasal, pertaining to the nose.
nasalidad, *f.* (phonet.) nasality.
nasalización, *f.* (phonet.) nasalization.
nasalizar, (*ref. 53*) *tr.v.* (phonet.) to nasalize.
nasardo, *m.* (mus.) nasard, organ stop.
nasico, *m.* (zool.) proboscis monkey.
nasio, nasión, *f.* (anat.) nasion.
naso, *m.* (coll.) large nose.
nasofaringe, *m.* (anat.) nasopharynx.
nasofaríngeo, a, *a.* (med.) nasopharyngeal.
nasón, *m. augm. of* **nasa,** large fyke or bag net.
nástico, ca, *a.* (bot.) nastic.
nastuerzo, *m.* (bot.), *var. of* **mastuerzo.**
nata, *f.* 1. cream (of milk). 2. skim (on boiled milk); skim (on wine). 3. (fig.) (the) elite, (the) cream. 4. (Amer.) scum (of metals). 5. (*pl.*) (cul.) whipped cream; custard.
natación, *f.* swimming.
natal, *a.* 1. natal (pertaining to birth). 2. native (country); **día n.,** birthday; **país n.,** native country. —*m.* birthday; birth.
natalicio, cia, *a.* natal. —*m.* birthday.
natalidad, *f.* natality, birthrate.
natátil, *a.* natant; able to swim or float.
natatorio, ria, *a.* 1. natatory, natatorial. 2. (ichth.) **vejiga n.,** air bladder, swim bladder. —*m.* swimming pool or place, natatorium.
naterón, *m.* (cul.) cottage cheese.
natillas, *f.* (*pl.*) (cul.) cream custard.
natío, a, *a.* native; **oro n.,** native gold. —*m.* nature, birth; **de su n.,** by nature, naturally.
natividad, *f.* 1. nativity, birth. 2. (rel.) Nativity; crèche, Nativity scene. 3. Christmas time, yuletide.
nativo, va, *a.* 1. native, indigenous, native born, autochthonous, aboriginal, e.g. *lengua nativa,* native language, *país nativo,* native country. 2. (min.) native. 3. natural, inborn, innate, native.
nato, ta, *a.* born, implied by or inherent in an office or position, e.g. *es un actor nato,* he is a born actor.
natrio, *m.* (chem.) natrium.
natrolita, *f.* (min.) natrolite.
natrón, *m.* 1. (chem.) natron. 2. soda ash, barilla.
natura, *f.* 1. nature. 2. (anat.) genitals. 3. (mus.) major scale. — **a or de n.,** naturally.
natural, *a.* 1. natural; native (of a country or region). 2. spontaneous; unstudied, ingenuous. 3 innate. 4. (mus.) natural. — **ciencias naturales,** natural sciences; **historia n.,** natural history; **ley n.,** natural law. —*m., f.* native. —*m.* 1. nature, disposition, temperament. 2. instinct. — **al n.,** naked, in the nude; without art or affectation; (cul.) without dressing, uncooked, au naturel; **del n.,** (p.) from life, from a live figure.
naturaleza, *f.* 1. nature. 2. genitals, female genitals. 3. nationality. 4. type, kind. 5. temperament, disposition, character, nature. — **n. humana,** human nature; **n. muerta,** (p.) still life.
naturalice, naturalicé, *ref.* **naturalizar.**
naturalidad, *f.* 1. naturalness. 2. nationality; birthright.
naturalismo, *m.* (lit., philos.) naturalism; (art.) realism.
naturalista, *a.* naturalist; naturalistic. —*m., f.* naturalist.
naturalización, *f.* naturalization.
naturalizar, (*ref. 53*) *tr.v.* to naturalize, to nationalize. —*r.v.* to become naturalized, become nationalized.
naturalmente, *adv.* naturally; of course; obviously.
naturismo, *m.* 1. belief in natural healing practices. 2. nudism.
naturopatía, *f.* (med.) naturopathy.
naufragante, *a.* shipwrecked; sinking; perishing.
naufragar, (*ref. 51*) *i.v.* 1. to be shipwrecked or wrecked. 2. to go on the rocks, come to grief, fail, fall through (a project, etc.).
naufragio, *m.* 1. shipwreck. 2. (fig.) ruin, disaster, failure, calamity.

náufrago, ga, *a.* wrecked, shipwrecked. *—m., f.* shipwrecked person. *—m.* shark.
naufrague, naufragué, *ref.* **naufragar.**
naumaquia, *f.* naumachia; naumachy; in ancient Rome, a mock sea battle and its stage.
nauplio, *m.* (zool.) nauplius.
náusea, *f.* (*gen. in pl.*) 1. nausea, sickness, retching. 2. repugnance, disgust. — **dar náuseas,** to disgust; **sentir** or **tener náuseas,** to feel sick.
nauseabundo, da, *a.* nauseating, sickening, nauseous, loathsome.
nauseado, da, *past part. of* **nausear.** *—a.* nauseated; disgusted.
nauseante, *a., var. of* **nauseabundo.**
nausear, *i.v.* to feel nauseated or sick.
nauseativo, va, *a., var. of* **nauseabundo.**
nauseoso, sa, *a., var. of* **nauseabundo.**
nauta, *m.* seaman, sailor, mariner, seafarer.
náutica, *f.* art of navigation, seamanship, nautics.
náutico, ca, *a.* nautical, e.g. *deportes náuticos,* water sports.
nautilo, *m.* (zool.) nautilus.
nautilóideo, a, *a., m.* (zool.) nautiloid.
nava, *f.* dale, dell, vale, hollow plain, gen. swampy and surrounded by mountains.
navacero, ra, *m., f.* (Sp., reg.) gardener in sandy marshland.
navaja, *f.* 1. razor, shaver; clasp knife, jack knife. 2. sting (of an insect). 3. (zool.) razor clam. 4. (wild boar's) tusk, razor. 5. (coll.) malicious or evil tongue. — **n. automática** or **de boton** or **de resorte,** switchblade; **n. cabritera,** skinning knife; **n. de afeitar,** razor, shaver; **n. de muelle, n. de resorte,** switchblade, switchblade knife, flickknife (G.B.); **navajas de ga-** gallos, cockspurs; **n. suiza,** Swiss army knife; **n. eléctrica,** electric razor.
navajada, *f.* gash, slash (administered with a razor or switchblade knife).
navajazo, *m., var. of* **navajada.**
navajero, *m.* razor case; jug for cleaning a razor; razor cleaning cloth.
navajita, *f. dim. of* **navaja,** small knife or razor; razor blade.
navajo, *m.* 1. hollow, dale, dell. 2. puddle or pool of rain water (watering place for cattle). 3. **N.,** (U.S.) Navaho, Navajo (Indian).
navajón, *m.* large clasp knife.
navajonazo, *m.* deep gash made with a large clasp knife or a razor.
navajudo, da, *a.* (Mex.) sly, cunning.
navajuela, *f. dim. of* **navaja,** small clasp knife.
naval, *a.* naval; **batalla n.,** sea battle; **escuela n.,** naval academy.
navarca, *m.* commander of a Greek fleet; captain of a Roman ship.
navarro, rra, *a., m., f.* Navarrese. *—f.* **N.** Navarre, region of N.E. Spain and S.W. France.
navazo, *m.* (Sp., reg.) orchard or vegetable garden (in coastal marshlands).
nave, *f.* 1. ship. 2. (archit.) nave, aisle. — **n. aérea,** airship; **n. capitana,** flagship; **n. de San Pedro,** Roman Catholic Church; **quemar las naves,** (fig.) to burn one's bridges; **n. espacial,** spaceship.
navecilla, *f.* 1. small ship. 2. (ecc.) navicula, censer, thurible.
navegable, *a.* navigable (river, lake, etc.).
navegación, *f.* 1. navigation; sailing. 2. sea voyage. 3. navigation, art of navigation, nautics. — **acta de n.,** Navigation Act; **n. aérea,** air navigation; aerial navigation; **n. a estima,** (mar.) dead reckoning; **n. astronómica** or **de altura,** celestial navigation; **n. a vela,** sailing; **n. costera** or **de altura,** coastal shipping; coasting; **n. en círculo máximo,** great-circle sailing; **n. espacial,** space travel; **n. fluvial,** river navigation, inland navigation; **n. ortodrómica,** circular sailing; **n. por un paralelo,** parallel sailing.
navegador, ra, *a.* navigating, sailing. *—m., f.* navigator, sailor, seaman.
navegante, *a., m., f., var. of* **navegador.**
navegar, (*ref. 51*) *tr.v.* to sail, navigate. *—i.v.* 1. to sail, navigate, steer, travel. 2. to bustle about; to move about.
navegue, navegué, *ref.* **navegar.**
naveta, *f.* 1. small ship. 2. (ecc.) navicula, censer, thurible. 3. drawer (of a desk).
navichuelo, la, *m., f.* small ship, cockleshell.
navícula, *f.* 1. small ship. 2. (bot.) navicula, boat-shaped alga.
navicular, *a.* navicular, boat-shaped.
naviculario, *m.* owner or captain of a Roman merchant ship.
Navidad, *f.* 1. Christmas, Christmas time, yuletide; Christmas Day. 2. (ecc.) Nativity. — **tener muchas Navidades,** to be pretty old; **feliz N.,** Merry Christmas.
navideño, ña, *a.* pertaining to Christmas or yuletide.
naviero, ra, *a.* pertaining to shipping; **empresa naviera,** shipping company. *—m.* ship owner, shipping owner.
navío, *m.* ship, vessel; **montar un n.,** to command a ship; **N. Argo,** (astron.) Argo, Argo Navis; **n. de guerra,** warship; **n. de transporte,** transport ship; **n. mercante,** merchant ship.
náyade, *f.* (myth.) naiad, water nymph.
nayuribe, *f.* (bot.) an amarantaceous herb.
nazareno, na, *a.* 1. Nazarene (of or from Nazareth). 2. Nazarene, Christian. *—m., f.* 1. Nazarene, native of Nazareth. 2. Nazarite (among the Jews, person consecrated to God). *—m.* penitent dressed in a purple robe in Holy Week processions. — **El Divino N., El N.,** The Nazarene (Christ); **estar hecho un n.,** to be in a terrible state, to look a sight.
nazareo, rea, *a., m., f.* Nazarene, Nazarite.
Nazaret, *m.* Nazareth, city in Israel.
nazca, nazco, *ref.* **nacer.**
nazi, *a., f.* (hist., pol.) Nazi, pertaining to or of the German fascist political party. *—m., f.* Nazi.
nazificar, (*ref. 50*) *tr.v.* to nazify.
nazismo, *m.* (hist., pol.) Nazism.
nazista, *a., m., f.* (hist., pol.) Nazi.
názula, *f.* cottage cheese.
Nb *sym. of* **niobio,** niobium (Nb).
N.B. *abbrev. of* **nota bene,** nota bene (NB).
nc., NC. *abbrev. of* 1. **nuestra cuenta,** our account. 2. **nuestro cargo,** on us.
Nd *sym. of* **neodimio,** neodymium (Nd).
Ne *sym. of* **néon,** neon (Ne).
NE *abbrev. of* **nordeste,** northeast (NE).
nea, *f.* (bot.) cattail, reed mace, bulrush.
neandertal, (paleon.) *a.* Neanderthal.
neandertaloide, (paleon.) *a.* Neanderthaloid.
nearca, *m.* commander of a Greek fleet; captain of a Roman ship.
nébada, *f.* (bot.) catnip, catmint.
nebí, (*pl.* **nebíes**), *m., var. of* **neblí.**
nebladura, *f.* 1. damage to crops from mist. 2. (vet.) gid, staggers (in sheep).
neblí, (*pl.* **neblíes**), *m.* (ornith.) (species of) falcon.
neblina, *f.* fog, mist.
neblinoso, sa, *a.* misty, foggy.
nebral, *m.* juniper grove.
nebreda, *f.* juniper grove.
nebrina, *f.* juniper berry.
nebro, *m.* juniper tree or shrub.
nebulice, nebulicé, *ref.* **nebulizar.**
nebulizar, (*ref. 53*) *tr.v.* to nebulize, to reduce (a liquid) to a fine spray.
nebulón, *m.* hypocrite; sly, cunning man.
nebulosa, *f.* (astron.) nebula.
nebulosamente, *adv.* nebulously, mistily.
nebulosidad, *f.* 1. cloudiness, mistiness, fogginess, haziness. 2. nebulousness, vagueness, haziness, obscurity, abstruseness. 3. gloom, somberness, gloominess. 4. shadow, cloud.
nebuloso, sa, *a.* 1. misty, foggy, cloudy, hazy. 2. nebulous, vague, hazy; obscure, difficult, abstruse. 3. gloomy, somber.
necear, *i.v.* to talk nonsense; to act foolishly; to persist stupidly.
necedad, *f.* stupidity, foolishness; folly; foolish remark or act, (*pl.*) nonsense, rubbish, e.g. *él habla necedades,* he talks nonsense.
necesaria, *f.* (rare) water closet, toilet, privy.
necesariamente, *adv.* necessarily; unavoidably, inevitably.
necesario, ria, *a.* necessary; essential, required; inevitable.
neceser, *m.* dressing case, toilet case; **n. de costura,** work basket, sewing case.
necesidad, *f.* necessity, need, want; **de primera n.,** basic (commodity); **de n.,** by necessity, necessarily, unavoidably, inevitably; **en n. de,** in need of; **n. extrema,** extreme need, dire straits; **la n. es madre de la invención,** necessity is the mother of invention; **n. mayor,** defecation; **n. menor,** urination; **necesidades de la vida,** necessities of life; **pasar n.,** to undergo or experience need, hardship or want; **por n.,** of, through or out of necessity.
necesitado, da, *past part. of* **necesitar.** *—a.* needy, poor. *—m., f.* needy or indigent person, (*pl.*) the needy.
necesitar, *tr.v.* 1. to need, necessitate, require; want. 2. to have to, need to. *—i.v.* to be in need; **n. de,** to be in need of.
neciamente, *adv.* stupidly, foolishly, injudiciously.
necio, cia, *a.* 1. foolish, stupid; injudicious. 2. stubborn, pigheaded. *—m., f.* fool, idiot; **a necias,** stupidly, foolishly.
necrófago, ga, *a.* necrophagous, carrion-eating.
necrología, *f.* 1. necrology, list of the dead. 2. obituary.
necrológico, ca, *a.* necrological.
necromancia, *f.* necromancy, divination by alleged communication with the dead; black magic.
necrópolis, *f.* necropolis, burying ground.
necropsia, *f., var. of* **necroscopia.**
necroscopia, *f.* necroscopy, necropsy, autopsy, post-mortem examination.
necroscópico, ca, *a.* necroscopic, necroscopical, pertaining to autopsy.
necrosis, *f.* (med., biol.) necrosis.
necrótico, ca, *a.* (med., bot.) necrotic.
necrotomía, *f.* (med.) necrotomy, the dissection of corpses.
necrotómico, ca, *a.* (med.) necrotomic.
néctar, *m.* (myth., fig., bot.) nectar; any delicious drink.
nectáreo, rea, *a.* nectarean, nectareous, nectareal, nectarous.
nectarino, na, *a., var. of* **nectáreo.**
nectario, *m.* (bot.) nectary, part of the flower that secretes the nectar.
neerlandés, sa, *a.* of the Netherlands, Dutch. *—m., f.* Netherlander; (*pl.*) Dutch. *—m.* Dutchman. *—f.* Dutchwoman.
nefandamente, *adv.* abominably, infamously, execrably.

nefandario, ria, *a.* infamous, abominable, vile.
nefando, da, *a.* infamous, abominable, execrable, vile.
nefariamente, *adv.* nefariously, heinously, abominably.
nefario, ria, *a.* nefarious, abominable, vile.
nefas, *adv.* **por fas o por n.,** justly or unjustly, rightly or wrongly; for one thing or for another.
nefasto, ta, *a.* ominous, fateful, unlucky.
nefelina, *f.* (min.) nepheline, nephelite.
nefelinita, *f.* (min.) nephelinite.
nefelio, *m.* (ophthal.) cloud (on the cornea).
nefelismo, *m.* (meteorol.) characteristics of cloud formations.
nefelita, *f.* (min.) nepheline, nephelite.
nefelometría, *m.* (chem.) nephelometry.
nefelómetro, *m.* (phys.) nephelometer.
nefoscopio, *m.* (meteorol.) nephoscope; instrument for determining the direction and velocity of clouds.
nefralgia, *f.* (med.) nephralgia.
nefrectomía, *f.* (med.) nephrectomy.
néfrico, ca, *a.* (med.) nephritic, pertaining to the kidneys.
nefridio, *m.* (zool.) nephridium.
nefrismo, *m.* (med.) nephrism.
nefrita, *f.* (min.) nephrite (jade).
nefrítico, ca, *a.* (med.) nephritic. —*m.* 1. nephritic wood, rosilla wood. 2. nephritic stone, nephrite, jade.
nefritis, *f.* (med.) nephritis, disease or inflammation of the kidneys.
nefrocele, *f.* (med.) nephrocele, hernia of the kidney.
nefrógeno, na, *a.* (med.) nephrogenic.
nefrolito, *m.* (med.) nephrolith.
nefrosis, *f.* (med.) nephrosis, a disease of the kidneys.
nefrotomía, *f.* (surg.) nephrotomy.
Neftalí, *m.* (Bib.) Nephtali.
negable, *a.* 1. deniable, refutable, controvertible. 2. refusable.
negación, *f.* 1. denial, negation. 2. refusal. 3. (gram.) negative, negative particle, negation. 4. (philos.) negation. 5. lack, want, dearth.
negado, da, *past part. of* **negar.** —*a.* 1. incapable, incompetent, inept, unfit. 2. apostate (Christian). —*m.* 1. dullard, useless person, dimwit. 2. renegade, apostate (Christian).
negador, ra, *m., f.* 1. denier, disclaimer, recanter. 2. refuser.
negamiento, *a., var. of* **negación.**
negar, (*ref. 67*) *tr.v.* 1. to deny, declare untrue, e.g. *él negó haberlo hecho,* he denied having done it. 2. to deny, refuse, withhold, e.g. *nos negaron ayuda,* they refused to help us. 3. to disavow, disclaim, disown, e.g. *n. a su hijo,* to disown one's child. 4. to forbid, prohibit, e.g. *n. la entrada al país,* to deny entry (into a country). —*i.v.* (Amer.) to misfire (gun, rifle, etc.). —*r.v.* to deny oneself (gratification, pleasure), to practice self-denial; to decline to do, e.g. *me negué a comer,* I declined dinner, *me negué a parcipar,* I abstained from participating.
negativa, *f.* 1. negative; denial, negation. 2. refusal.
negativamente, *adv.* negatively.
negativismo, *m.* (philos.) negativism.
negativo, va, *a.* negative; (gram., elec., photog.) negative; (math.) negative, minus; **cantidad negativa,** minus quantity; **electricidad negativa,** negative electricity; **número negativo,** negative or minus number; **signo negativo,** minus sign. —*m.* (photog.) negative.
negatrón, *m.* (phys., chem.) negatron (electron).
neglígé, *m.* negligee, peignoir, housedress.
negligencia, *f.* negligence; neglect; carelessness, slackness; **n. comparativa,** (law) comparative negligence; **n. criminal,** criminal negligence; **n. temeraria,** gross negligence.
negligente, *a.* negligent, neglectful, careless, slack. —*m., f.* neglecter, neglector.
negligentemente, *adv.* negligently, neglectfully; carelessly.
negociable, *a.* negotiable.
negociación, *f.* 1. negotiation. 2. deal, transaction. — **negociaciones colectivas,** collective bargaining.
negociado, *m.* 1. department, section, office, bureau; **N. Federal de Investigaciones,** Federal Bureau of Investigation (FBI). 2. transaction, deal. 3. (S. Amer.) shady deal, illicit transaction. 4. (Chile) shop, store.
negociador, ra, *a.* negotiating. —*m., f.* negotiator, business agent, businessman.
negociante, *a.* negotiating. —*m., f.* dealer, trader, merchant.
negociar, *tr.v.* 1. to negotiate (a treaty, political deal, loan). 2. (com.) to negotiate (a draft, bill of exchange); to buy or sell (goods, stock, etc.). —*i.v.* 1. to negotiate, discuss, talk. 2. to trade, deal, do business. — **n. en,** to trade in; **n. sobre,** to negotiate, discuss, talk about.
negocio, *m.* 1. business, business concern, commercial establishment. 2. job, work, occupation. 3. affair, business. 4. deal, transaction; piece of business. 5. (Arg., Chile, Urug.) shop, store. — **cerrar un n.,** (coll.) to conclude a deal; **hombre de negocios,** businessman; **n. redondo,** very good or lucrative business or deal; **n. sucio,** dirty or illegal business; (coll.) monkey business.
negocioso, sa, *a.* businesslike, active, diligent.
negozuelo, *m. dim. of* **negocio,** petty business, unimportant deal.
negra, *f.* 1. (mus.) quarter note. 2. black woman, Negress. 3. fencing sword.
negrada, *f.* 1. (Cuba) body of workers in a plantation. 2. (hist.) body of slaves belonging to a plantation. 3. (coll.) the plebe, the rabble.
negral, *a.* blackish.
negrear, *i.v.* to turn black; to be blackish.
negrecer, (*ref. 45*) *i.v., r.v.* to turn black, to blacken.
negreguear, *i.v., var. of* **negrear.**
negregura, *f.* blackness.
negrería, *f.* Negroes, body or crowd of blacks.
negrero, ra, *a.* slave-trading; (fig.) slave-driving. —*m., f.* 1. slave trader. 2. (fig.) slave-driver, harsh taskmaster or employer.
negrestino, na, *a.* blackish.
negreta, *f.* (ornith.) coot (Oidemia nigra).
negrezca, *ref.* **negrecer.**
negrilla, *f.* 1. (ichth.) black conger eel. 2. fumagine (plant fungus). 3. (print.) boldface.
negrillera, *f.* elm grove, poplar grove.
negrillo, *m.* 1. elm. 2. (reg.) blight (on grain crops). 3. (Arg.) (variety of) finch (Pyrrhula nigra). 4. (S. Amer.) black cupriferous silver ore.
negrito, ta, *m., f.* 1. (ethnol.) member of a Central African people. 2. little Negro or Negress. 3. (coll.) darling, dearest. —*m.* (Cuba) variety of finch (Pyrrhula nigra).
negrizco, ca, *a.* blackish.
negro, gra, *a.* 1. black. 2. negro, black, colored. 3. brown (bread). 4. bad (temper); unlucky, unfortunate. — **pasarlas negras,** to have a lot of trouble, have a bad time of it. —*m., f.* (coll.) dear, darling, honey. —*m.* 1. black (color). 2. black; Negro (obs.) — **en blanco y n.,** in black and white; **n. animal,** bone black, animal black, animal charcoal; **n. de humo,** lampblack; **n. de marfil,** ivory black. —*f.* 1. black woman; Negress (derog.); 2. bad luck, bad time; **tener la n.,** to have a run of bad luck.
negrófilo, la, *m., f.* 1. Negrophile, Negrophil, a person who admires, likes or champions blacks, their culture, etc. 2. enemy of slavery.
negrofobia, *f.* Negrophobia, hatred or fear of blacks.
negrófobo, ba, *m., f.* Negrophobe, one who hates or fears the blacks.
negroide, *a.* negroid.
negror, *m., var. of* **negrura.**
negrura, *f.* blackness, darkness.
negruzco, ca, *a.* blackish, darkish.
negué, *ref.* **negar.**
neguijón, *m.* tooth decay, caries.
neguilla, *f.* 1. (bot.) corn cockle; corn cockle seed. 2. (bot.) love-in-a-mist. 3. age-mark (on a horse's teeth).
neguillón, *m.* (bot.) corn cockle.
negundo, *m.* (bot.) box elder, ash-leaved maple (Acer negundo).
negus, *m.* Negus (title of the ruler of Ethiopia).
neis, *m.* (geol.) gneiss.
neísico, *a.* (geol.) gneissic.
neja, *f.* 1. (Chile) gore (in a dress). 2. (Mex.) corn cake.
nejayote, *m.* (Mex.) water in which corn has been boiled.
neldo, *m., var of* **eneldo.**
nelumbio, *m.* (bot.) nelumbo, Indian lotus, sacred bean.
nema, *f.* seal (of a letter); sealing.
nematelminto, *m.* (zool.) nemathelminth; (*pl.*) Nemathelminthes.
nematocida, *a.* (zool.) nematocidal. —*m.* nematocide.
nematocisto, *m.* (zool.) nematocyst.
nemátodo, *a., m.* (zool.) nematode, (*pl.*) Nematoda.
nematodes, *m.* (*pl.*) (zool.) Nematoda.
nematología, *f.* (med.) nematology.
neme, *m.* (Col.) asphalt.
nemeo, mea, *a.* Nemean, of the ancient Greek city of Nemea; **Juegos nemeos,** Nemean games (in honor of Hercules).
Némesis, *f.* (myth.) Nemesis, the goddess of retributive justice or vengeance.
némine discrepante, (Lat.) unanimously.
nemoroso, sa, *a.* (poet.) sylvan, nemoral; (poet.) wooded, woody.
nemotecnia, *f., var. of* **mnemotecnia,** mnemonics, a technique or system of improving the memory.
nene, na, *m., f.* 1. (coll.) baby, infant. 2. dear, darling, honey. 3. (iron.) scoundrel, villain.
neneque, *m.* (Hond.) weakling.
nenia, *f.* funeral song; eulogy (for a deceased person).
nenúfar, *m.* (bot.) nenuphar, white water lily; **n. amarillo,** (bot.) yellow water lily, spatterdock.
neo, *pref.* neo-(new, recent). —*m.* (chem.) neon.
neoarsfenamina, *f.* (pharm.) neoarsphenamine.
neocatolicismo, *m.* Neo-Catholicism.
neocatólico, ca, *a., m., f.* Neo-Catholic.
neocelandés, sa, *a.* New Zealand. —*m., f.* New Zealander.
neoclasicismo, *m.* (art, lit., archit.) neo-classicism.
neoclásico, ca, *a.* neoclassic. —*m., f.* neo-classicist.
neocristianismo, *m.* Neo-Christianity.
neodarwinismo, *m.* Neo-Darwinism.
neodarwinista, *m.* Neo-Darwinist.
neodimio, *m.* (chem.) neodymium.
neoescocés, cesa, *a.* Nova Scotian. —*m., f.* (coll.) bluenose; Nova Scotian.

neoescolasticismo, *m.* (philos.) Neo-Scholasticism.
neoescolástico, ca, *a.* Neo-Scholastic.
neófito, ta, *m., f.* neophyte, novice, beginner.
neofobia, *f.* aversion to innovations, hostility to change.
neogénesis, *f.* (biol.) neogenesis.
neogenético, ca, *a.* (biol.) neogenetic.
neogótico, ca, *a.* (art., archit.) Neo-Gothic.
neogranadino, na, *a.* (hist.) of or from New Granada (colonial name for Colombia). —*m., f.* native or inhabitant of New Granada.
neogriego, ga, *a.* pertaining to modern Greece.
neohegelianismo, *m.* (philos.) Neo-Hegelianism.
neoimpresionismo, *m.* (art) neo-impressionism.
neoimpresionista, *a., m., f.* (art) neo-impressionist.
neolatino, na, *a.* Neo-Latin. —*m., f.* Neo-Latin (person). —*m.* Neo-Latin, Romance (language).
neolítico, ca, *a.* neolithic, designating or of a period in the latter part of the Stone Age.
neología, *f.* neology, the study and introduction of new words in a language.
neológico, ca, *a.* neologistic, neologistical.
neologismo, *m.* neologism, a new word or a new meaning of an established word.
neólogo, ga, *m., f.* neologist, coiner of words.
neomenia, *f.* 1. (hist.) festival of the new moon. 2. (astron.) new moon; first day of the new moon.
neomicina, *f.* (med.) neomycin.
neón, *m.* (chem.) neon.
neo-nazi, *a., m., f.* (pol.) Neo-Nazi, pertaining to a revival of German fascism.
neoplasia, *f.* (med.) neoplasia.
neoplásico, ca, *a.* (med.) neoplastic.
neoplasma, *m.* (med.) neoplasm.
neoplasticismo, *m.* (art) neoplasticism, principles and methods of the Stijl movement in painting, of which the works of Mondrian are exemplary.
neoplasticista, *m., f.* (art.) neoplasticist.
neoplástico, ca, *a.* (med.) neoplastic.
neoplatonicismo, *m.* (philos.) Neoplatonism.
neoplatónico, ca, *a.* (philos.) Neoplatonic. —*m., f.* Neoplatonist.
neopreno, *m.* neoprene, synthetic rubber.
neorama, *m.* cyclorama.
neosalvasán, *m.* (pharm.) Neosalvarsan.
neotenia, *f.* (zool.) neoteny, neoteinia, neotenia.
neotérico, ca, *a.* neoteric; newly invented. —*m., f.* person who is receptive to new ideas (esp. physicians and philosophers).
neotomismo, *m.* (rel., philos.) Neo-Thomism, modern philosophical doctrines based on the religious concepts of Saint Thomas Aquinas.
neoyorquino, na, *a.* of or pertaining to New York. —*m., f.* New Yorker.
neozelandés, sa, *m., f.* New Zealander. —*a.* of or from New Zealand.
neozoico, ca, *a.* (geol.) Neozoic, former name for Cenozoic.
Nepal, *m.* Nepal.
nepalense, *a.* Nepalese, of or pertaining to Nepal. —*m., f.* Nepalese.
nepalés, sa, *a., m., f. var. of* **nepalense.**
nepente, *m.* 1. (bot.) nepenthe, pitcher plant, monkey cup. 2. nepenthe (ancient potion or drug used for relieving pain or sorrow).
néper, (math.) neper.
neperiano, na, *a.* Napierian, pertaining to John Napier, Scottish mathematician.
nepote, *m.* privileged relative and favorite of the Pope.
nepotismo, *m.* nepotism, favoritism shown to relatives.
neptúneo, nea, *a.* (poet.) Neptunian.
neptuniano, na, *a.* (geol.) *var. of* **neptúnico.**
neptúnico, ca, *a.* (geol.) neptunian.
neptunio, *m.* (chem.) neptunium.
neptunismo, *m.* (geol.) neptunism.
neptunista, *a., m., f.* (geol.) neptunist.
Neptuno, *m.* 1. (myth., astron.) Neptune (Roman god of the sea). 2. (poet.) the sea.
nequáquam, *adv.* (Lat., coll.) by no means, certainly not.
nequicia, *f.* perversity, malevolence.
nereida, *f.* (myth.) Nereid (sea nymph).
nereido, *m.* (zool.) nereis.
Néreo, *m.* 1. (myth.) Nereus, a sea god, father of the Nereids. 2. (astron.) Nereid.
nerita, *f.* (zool.) nerita, a mollusk.
nerítico, ca, *a.* (geol.) neritic.
nerol, *m.* (chem.) nerol.
Nerón, *m.* 1. (hist.) Nero. 2. (fig.) cruel, ruthless person.
neroniano, na, *a.* Neronian, pertaining to Nero or his reign.
nervado, da, *a.* (bot.) nervate, having nerves or veins.
nervadura, *f.* 1. (archit.) rib, nervure. 2. (bot.) nervation (system of veins in a leaf); (ento.) nervure (rib of insect's wing).
nérveo, vea, *a.* nerval, pertaining to nerves.
nerviación, *f.* (ento.) nervure (rib of insect's wing).
nervino, na, *a.* (med.) nervine.
nervio, *m.* 1. (anat.) nerve, sinew. 2. (cul.) sinew (in meat). 3. string (of musical instrument). 4. (bot.) vein, nerve. 5. (bkb.) rib (in the back of a book). 6. stocks (instruments of punishment). 7. nerve (physical and mental strength and endurance). 8. (archit.) rib (of a vault) 9. (mar.) jackstay. — **n. auditivo,** auditory nerve; **n. ciatico,** (anat.) sciatic nerve; **n. de buey,** pizzle; **n. óptico,** (anat.) optic nerve; **n. vago,** (anat.) vagus, vagus nerve; **guerra de nervios,** war of nerves.
nerviosamente, *adv.* nervously.
nerviosidad, *f.* nervousness, nervous excitement.
nervioso, sa, *a.* 1. nervous (pertaining to the nerves). 2. nerve (containing nerves). 3. nervous, excitable. 4. energetic, vigorous. — **célula nerviosa,** nerve cell; **crisis nerviosa,** nervous breakdown; **enfermedad nerviosa,** nervous disease; **sistema nervioso,** nervous system; **tejido nervioso,** nerve tissue; **poner n.,** to get on one's nerves.
nervosamente, *adv.* vigorously, energetically.
nervosidad, *f.* 1. nervousness. 2. ductibility, flexibility (of metals). 3. cogency, potency (of arguments and reasons).
nervoso, sa, *a. var. of* **nervioso.**
nervudo, da, *a.* 1. having strong nerves; vigorous. 2. (cul.) sinewy (meat).
nervura, *f.* (bkb.) ribbing, ribs, backbone (forming the back of a book).
nesciencia, *f.* nescience, ignorance.
nesciente, *a.* nescient, ignorant.
nescientemente, *adv.* ignorantly.
nesga, *f.* (dressm.) gore, gusset, triangular piece.
nesgado, da, *past part. of* **nesgar.** —*a.* (dressm.) having gores, gored, gusseted, on the bias.
nesgar, (*ref. 51*) *tr.v.* (dressm.) to gore, gusset; to cut (cloth) on the bias.
nesgue, nesgué, *ref.* **nesgar.**
néspera, *f.* (bot.) medlar tree.
nestorianismo, *m.* (ecc.) Nestorianism, the doctrines of Nestorius.
nestoriano, na, *a., m., f.* (ecc.) Nestorian.
netamente, *adv.* clearly, distinctly, exactly.
netezuelo, la, *m., f. dim. of* **nieto,** small grandchild.
neto, ta, *a.* 1. pure, genuine. 2. (com.) net; **peso neto,** net weight. —*m.* (archit.) dado.
neuma, *m.* 1. (mus.) neume, set of signs used in medieval church music. 2. (rhet.) expression by gestures, signs or interjections.
neumático, ca, *a.* pneumatic. —*m.* tire (of a car); **n. acordonado** or **de cuerdas,** (auto.) cord tire; **n. balón,** balloon tire. —*f.* (phys.) pneumatics.
neumatóforo, *m.* (bot.) pneumatophore.
neumatógrafo, *m.* (med.) pneumograph.
neumatólisis, *f.* (min.) pneumatolysis.
neumatolítico, ca, *a.* (geol.) pneumatolytic.
neumatología, *f.* (theol.) pneumatology, the study of spirits or spiritual phenomena.
neumatómetro, *m.* (physiol.) pneumatometer, an instrument for measuring the capacity and functioning of the lungs.
neumectomía, *f.* (surg.) pneumonectomy.
neumobacilo, *m.* (bac.) pneumobacillus.
neumocócico, ca, *a.* (bac.) pneumococcic, pneumococcous.
neumococo, *m.* (bac.) pneumococcus.
neumoconiosis, *f.* (med.) pneumoconiosis.
neumogástrico, ca, *a., m.* (anat.) pneumogastric.
neumógrafo, *m.* (physiol.) pneumograph.
neumonectomía, *f.* (med.) pneumonectomy.
neumonía, *f.* (med.) pneumonia; **n. atípica primaria,** (med.) primary atypical pneumonia.
neumónico, ca, *a.* (med.) pneumonic.
neumotórax, *m.* (med.) pneumothorax.
neumotrópico, ca, *a.* (med.) pneumotropic.
neuralgia, *f.* (med.) neuralgia.
neurálgico, ca, *a.* (med.) neuralgic.
neurastenia, *f.* (med.) neurasthenia, nervous prostration.
neurasténico, ca, *a., m., f.* (med.) neurasthenic.
neurilema, *m.* (anat.) neurilemma.
neurilemático, ca, *a.* (anat.) neurilemmatic.
neurisma, *f., var. of* **aneurisma.**
neurita, *f.* (anat., physiol.) neurite.
neurítico, ca, *a.* (anat.) neuritic.
neuritis, *f.* (med.) neuritis.
neurocirugía, *f.* neurosurgery.
neurocirujano, *m.* neurosurgeon.
neurocrinia, *f.* (physiol.) neurocrinism.
neuroesqueleto, *m.* (anat.) neuroskeleton.
neurofibrila, *a.* (physiol.) neurofibril.
neurofibrilar, *a.* (physiol.) neurofibrillary.
neurofibrilla *f.* (physiol.) neurofibril.
neurógeno, na, *a.* (physiol.) neurogenic, originating in nervous tissue.
neuroglia, *f.* (anat.) neuroglia.
neurografía, *f.* (anat.) neurography.
neurología, *f.* (anat.) neurology.
neurólogo, ga, *m., f.* neurologist.
neuroma, *m.* (med.) neuroma.
neuromuscular, *a.* (physiol.) neuromuscular, of or involving both nerves and muscles.
neurona, *f.* (anat.) neuron, neurone.
neurónico, ca, *a.* (anat.) neuronic.
neurópata, *m., f.* neuropath.
neuropatía, *f.* (med.) neuropathy.
neuropático, ca, *a.* neuropathic.
neuropatología, *f.* (med.) neuropathology.
neuropsiquiatra, *m.* (med.) neuropsychiatrist.
neuróptero, ra, *a.* (zool.) neuropterous, neuropteran. —*m.* neuropteran; (*pl.*) Neuroptera.
neurosis, *f.* (med.) neurosis; **n. de angustia** or **de ansiedad,** (med.) anxiety neurosis; **n. de guerra,** shell shock; battle fatigue.
neurótico, ca, *a., m., f.* neurotic.
neurotomía, *f.* (med.) neurotomy (dissection of a nerve).
neurótomo, *m.* (med.) instrument for dissecting nerves.

neurotoxicidad, *f.* (med.) neurotoxicity.
neurotóxico, ca, *a.* (med.) neurotoxic.
neurótropo, a, *a.* (med.) neurotropic.
neurovegetativo, va, *a.* (med.) neurovegetative.
neutral, *a., m., f.* neutral, not taking any part or side, not causing a reaction.
neutralice, neutralicé, *ref.* **neutralizar.**
neutralidad, *f.* neutrality; impartiality.
neutralismo, *m.* (pol.) neutralism.
neutralista, *m., f.* (pol.) neutralist.
neutralización, *f.* neutralization.
neutralizar, (*ref.* 53) *tr.v.* to neutralize. —*r.v.* to be neutralized.
neutrino, *m.* (phys.) neutrino.
neutro, ra, *a.* 1. neutral (color). 2. (gram.) neuter (pronoun, noun); (gram.) intransitive. 3. (bot., biol.) neutral. 4. (elec., chem.) neutral.
neutrófilo, *m.* (physiol.) neutrophil, neutrophile.
neutrón, *m.* (phys.) neutron; **n. hiperenergético,** hyperenergetic neutron, high energy neutron; **n. hipoenergético,** hypoenergetic neutron, low energy neutron.
nevadilla, *f.* (bot.) whitlow-wort (Paronychia argentea).
nevado, da, *a.* snow-covered, snowy; snow-white, as white as snow. —*f.* snowfall.
nevar, (*ref.* 29) *i.v.* to snow. —*tr.v.* to make snow-white.
nevasca, *f.* 1. snowfall. 2. blizzard, snowstorm.
nevatilla, *f.* (ornith.) white wagtail.
nevazo, *m.* snowfall.
nevazón, *f.* (Arg. Chile, Ecuad.) snowstorm, blizzard.
nevera, *f.* 1. refrigerator; icebox. 2. woman who sells ice. 3. (fig.) icebox, very cold room. 4. (P. Rico) cooler (sl.), prison.
nevereta, *f.* (ornith.) white wagtail.
nevería, *f.* ice shop, ice cream parlor.
nevero, *m.* 1. ice cream vendor, ice vendor. 2. snowcap; site where perpetual snow lies; perpetual snow.
nevisca, *f.* light snowfall, sleet.
neviscar, *i.v.* to snow lightly.
nevisque, *ref.* **neviscar.**
nevo, *m.* (med.) naevus, nevus, birth mark.
nevoso, sa, *a.* snowy (place, weather).
newtoniano, na, *a.* Newtonian, pertaining to Isaac Newton or his theories and discoveries.
nexo, *m.* nexus, link, tie, union.
ni, *conj.* 1. neither, nor. 2. not even, e.g. *no recibe a nadie, ni a sus amigos íntimos,* he is not receiving anyone, not even his intimate friends, *ni me preguntes,* don't even bother to ask; **ni — ni,** neither — nor, either — or, *no descansa ni de día ni de noche,* neither by day nor by night does he rest; **ni chicha ni limonada,** neither fish nor fowl; **no — ni,** neither — nor, e.g. *no como ni duermo,* I neither eat nor sleep; **ni bien,** not quite, not altogether; **ni que,** as if, e.g. *¡ni que fuera yo tan tonto!* as if I were fool enough (to do, think, believe etc. something); **ni — siquiera,** not even.
Ni *sym. of* **níquel,** nickel (Ni).
niacina, *f.* (chem.) niacin, nicotinic acid.
Niágara, *f.* Niagara; **(las) cataratas del N.,** Niagara Falls.
niara, *f.* haystack, hayrick, rick or stack of straw.
nibelungos, *m.* (*pl.*) (myth.) Nibelungs (Germanic legend).
nícalo, *m.* (bot.) edible milk mushroom (Lactarius deliciosus).
nicaragua, *f.* 1. **N.,** Nicaragua. 2. (bot.) balsam apple.
nicaragüense, *a., m., f.* Nicaraguan.
niccolita, *f.* (min.) niccolite.
niceno, na, *a., m., f.* (rel.) Nicene.
nicho, *m.* niche, recess.
nicle, *m.* (min.) agate.
nicociana, *f.* (bot.) tobacco plant.
Nicodemo, *m.* (Bib.) Nicodemus.
nicol, *m.* (phys.) Nicol, Nicol or Nicol's prism.
Nicosia, *f.* Nicosia, capital of Cyprus.
nicotiana, *f.* (bot.) nicotiana, tobacco.
nicótico, ca, *a.* pertaining to nicotinism.
nicotina, *f.* (chem.) nicotine.
nicotinamida, *f.* (chem.) nicotinamide, a white crystalline powder, the amide of nicotinic acid.
nicotínico, ca, *a.* nicotinic.
nicotinismo, *m.* (med.) nicotinism, nicotine poisoning.
nicotismo, *m.* (med.) nicotinism.
nictagináceo, cea, *a.* (bot.) nyctaginaceous. —*f.* (*pl.*) Nyctaginaceae.
nictálope, *a.* 1. (med.) hemeralopic, nyctalopic. 2. nyctalopic, hemeralopic. —*m., f.* hemeralope; nyctalope.
nictalopia, *f.* 1. (med.) hemeralopia, nyctalopia, day blindness. 2. nyctalopia, hemeralopia, night blindness.
nictitante, *a.* (zool., ornith.) nictitating (membrane).
nidada, *f.* nest, nestful (of eggs); brood, nest (of newly hatched birds).
nidal, *m.* 1. nest, nest box, nesting place (where hen lays eggs). 2. nest egg (egg left in nest to induce hen to lay in certain place). 3. haunt, hangout.
nidícola, *a.* (ornith.) nidicolous.
nidificar, (*ref.* 50) *i.v.* to nest, build a nest.
nidifique, *ref.* **nidificar.**
nidífugo, ga, *a.* (ornith.) nidifugous, leaving the nest almost immediately after hatching.
nido, *m.* 1. nest. 2. (fig.) home, nest. 3. den, nest. — **haberse caído de un n.,** to be very credulous, be rather simple or credulous; **n. de ametralladoras,** (mil.) machine gun nest; **n. de amor,** love nest; **n. de avispas,** hornets' nest; **n. de cuervo,** (mar.) crow's nest; **n. de ladrones,** thieves' den.
niebla, *f.* 1. fog, mist. 2. film, cloud (on the cornea). 3. mildew (on plants). 4. fogginess, confusion. 5. dust shot, mustard seed shot. 6. clotting of urine (in certain illnesses). — **n. meona,** dripping fog.
niego, *a.* newborn (falcon).
niego, niegue, *ref.* **negar.**
niel, *m.* (min., chem.) niello.
nielado, *m.* niello work, nielloing; decorated with niello.
nielar, *tr.v.* to niello, decorate with niello.
niéspera, *f.* (bot.) medlar (fruit).
nietastro, tra, *m., f.* step grandchild. —*m.* step grandson. —*f.* step granddaughter.
nieto, ta, *m., f.* grandchild. —*m.* grandson. —*f.* granddaughter.
nietzscheano, na, *a.* (philos.) Nietzschean.
nietzscheismo, *m.* (philos.) Nietzscheanism, Nietzscheism.
nieva, nieve, *ref.* **nevar.**
nieve, *f.* 1. snow. 2. snowy whiteness. 3. water ice, ice-cream.
Níger, *m.* Niger (river and country).
Nigeria, *f.* Nigeria.
nigeriano, na, *a., m., f.* Nigerian.
nigola, *f.* (mar.) ratline.
nigrescente, *a.* nigrescent, becoming or tending to become black.
nigromancía, *f.* necromancy, black magic, the practice of claiming to foretell the future by alleged communication with the dead.
nigromante, *m.* necromancer, practitioner of necromancy (black magic).
nigromántico, ca, *a.* necromantic. —*m., f.* necromantic, necromancer.
nigua, *f.* (ento.) chigoe, chigger (Dermatophilus penetrans), jigger flea.
niguatero, ra, *a.* (Amer.) contaminated with jigger fleas.
nihilismo, *m.* 1. nihilism, the belief that there is no meaning or purpose in existence. 2. the denial of the existence of any basis for knowledge or truth.
nihilista, *a.* nihilist, nihilistic. —*m., f.* nihilist.
Nika, Niké, *f.* (myth.) Nike, the winged goddess of victory.
Nilo, *m.* Nile. — **N. Alto,** Upper Nile; **N. Azul,** Blue Nile; **N. Blanco,** White Nile.
nilómetro, *m.* (hist.) Nilometer, marked columns in ancient Egypt to measure the floods of the river Nile.
nilón, *m.* nylon, synthetic material.
nilótico, ca, *a.* Nilotic, of the Nile or the Nile Valley (people, languages, etc.).
nimbar, *tr.v.* to halo, encircle with a halo or nimbus.
nimbo, *m.* nimbus, halo, aureole; (meteorol.) nimbus; (numis.) nimbus, aureole (surrounding ruler's head on some coins).
nimiamente, *adv.* excessively, extremely.
nimiedad, *f.* 1. excess, prolixity; great or excessive detail; great or excessive care. 2. trifle, small, trivial or insignificant thing. 3. (coll.) timidity.
nimio, mia, *a.* 1. excessive, extreme. 2. minute, extremely detailed. 3. very careful. 4. small, trivial, insignificant. 5. stingy.
ninfa, *f.* 1. (myth.) nymph; (fig.) nymph, beautiful young woman. 2. (zool.) nymph, pupa. 3. (anat.) small lips (of the vulva). — **ninfa Egeria,** Egeria adviser.
ninfálido, da, *a., m.,* (zool.) nymphalid.
ninfea, *m.* (bot.) white water lily.
ninfeáceo, a, *a.* (bot.) nympheaceous. —*f.* (*pl.*) Nympheaceae.
ninfo, *m.* (coll.) effeminate fop, dandy, narcissus.
ninfómana, *f.* nymphomaniac.
ninfomanía, *f.* (med.) nymphomania.
ninfomaníaco, ca, *a.* nymphomaniac.
ningún, *a., var. of* **ninguno** (shortened form of **ninguno,** used only before singular masculine nouns and adjectives), e.g. *de ningún modo,* by no means, under no circumstances.
ninguno, na, *a.* no, not any, none, not one, neither. —*m., f. pron.* not one, not any, e.g. *ninguno de los estudiantes fue arrestado,* not one of the students was arrested; neither, e.g. *ninguno de los dos vino,* neither of the two came.
ninivita, *a.* (hist.) Ninevitical, Ninevitish. —*m., f.* Ninevite, pertaining to Assyria.
niña, *f.* 1. child, young girl. 2. (anat.) pupil; **n. de los ojos,** apple of one's eyes; **n. bien,** well-bred girl.
niñada, *f.* childishness, childish remark or act, puerility.
niñato, *m.* unborn calf (in slaughtered cow).
niñear, *i.v.* to behave in a childish manner, act childishly.
niñería, *f.* 1. childish act, (*pl.*) childish behavior, childishness. 2. childish remark. 3. trifle.
niñero, ra, *a.* fond of children. —*f.* nursemaid, baby sitter.
niñeta, *f.* pupil (of the eye).
niñez, *f.* 1. childhood. 2. (fig.) childishness. 3. (fig.) infancy, cradle; **segunda n.,** second childhood.
niño, ña, *a.* 1. young, inexperienced. 2. childish, childlike. —*m., f.* child. — **niña bonita,** number fifteen; **n. bien,** (coll.) rich kid; **n. de brazos,** babe-in-arms; **n. de la doctrina,** orphan raised in a public orphanage; **n. de los azotes,** whipping

boy, scapegoat; **n. de pecho,** young baby **n. de teta,** babe in arms, suckling babe; **n. mimado,** favorite, pet. (fig.) novice, learner, apprentice. —*m.* boy, little boy. — **¡ni qué n. muerto!** nonsense! rubbish! (said when denying something); **n. de coro,** choirboy, chorister; **n. de la bola,** image of the infant Christ; (coll.) lucky fellow; **n. gótico,** fop, dandy; **n. Jesús,** Baby Jesus; **n. prodigio,** child prodigy; **niños envueltos,** beef olives; stuffed cabbage leaves; **n. zangolotino,** (coll.) youth who wants to pass as a child.
niόbico, ca, *a.* (chem.) niobic.
niobio, *m.* (chem.) niobium.
nioto, *m.* (ichth.) smooth dogfish (Mustelus canis).
nipa, *f.* (bot.) nipa palm, sugar palm.
nipe, *m.* (Cuba, Mex.) *var. of* **nipis.**
nipis, *m.* fine Manila hemp cloth.
nipόn, na, *a., m., f.* Nipponese, Japanese. —*m.* **N., (poet., hist.) Nippon, Japanese name for Japan.**
níquel, *m.* 1. (chem.) nickel. 2. (Urug.) money; (Mex.) (*pl.*) money. — **n. arsenical,** niccolite, arsenical nickel.
niquelado, *past part. of* **niquelar.** —*m.* nickel-plated.
niquelador, *m.* nickel-plater.
niqueladura, *f.* nickel-plating.
niquelar, *tr.v.* to nickel-plate.
niquélico, ca, *a.* (chem.) nickelic.
niquelífero, ra, *a.* (min.) nickeliferous, containing nickel.
niquelina, *f.* (min.) niccolite.
niquelita, *f.* (min.) niccolite.
niquelocre, *m.* (min.) nickel ocher, annabergite.
niquiscocio, *m.* (coll.) trifle, unimportant thing.
nirvana, *m.* (rel., Hinduism, Buddhism.) nirvana, any place or condition of great peace or bliss.
níscalo, *m.* (bot.) edible milk mushroom (Lactarius deliciosus).
niscome, niscόmel, *m.* (Mex.) cornmeal pot, saucepan in which the maize is cooked for tortillas.
níspero, *m.* (bot.) medlar tree; medlar (fruit); **n. del Japón,** (bot.) loquat; **n. espinoso silvestre,** (bot.) hawthorn; **no mondar nísperos,** to be or keep oneself informed; to keep on one's toes, not to let the grass grow under one's feet.
níspola, *f.* (bot.) fruit of the medlar tree.
nistágmico, ca, *a.* (med.) nystagmic.
nistagmo, *m.* (med.) nystagmus.
nitidez, *f.* 1. clarity, clearness, brightness. 2. sharpness (of photograph).
nítido, da, *a.* 1. clear, bright. 2. sharp (photograph).
nito, *m.* (bot.) nito, climbing fern (Lygodium semihastatum).
nitόn, *m.* (chem.) niton, former name of radon.
nitraciόn, *f.* (chem.) nitration.
nitral, *m.* niter bed, saltpeter bed.
nitrar, *tr.v.* to nitrate.
nitratina, *f.* nitratine, caliche, native sodium nitrate.
nitrato, *m.* (chem.) nitrate; **n. de potasio,** (chem.) potassium nitrate; **n. de sodio,** (chem.) sodium nitrate.
nitrería, *f.* niter works, saltpeter works.
nítrico, ca, *a.* (chem.) nitric.
nitrificaciόn, *f.* nitrification.
nitrificar, (*ref. 50*) *tr.v.* to nitrify.
nitrifique nitrifiqué, *ref.* **nitrificar.**
nitrilo, *m.* (chem.) nitrile.
nitrito, *m.* (chem.) nitrite.
nitro, *m.* niter, saltpeter, potassium nitrate. — **n. cúbico,** (chem.) sodium nitrate, Chilean saltpeter, cubic or soda niter.
nitroalgodόn, *m.* (pyro.) nitrocotton, guncotton.
nitroalmidόn, *m.* (pyro.) nitrostarch.
nitrobacteria, *f.* (bac.) nitric bacteria.
nitrobenceno, *m.* (chem.) nitrobenzene.
nitrobencina, *f.* (chem.) nitrobenzene.
nitrocelulosa, *f.* (chem.) nitrocellulose, cellulose nitrate.
nitrogelatina, *f.* nitrogelatin.
nitrogenado, da, *a.* nitrogenous, containing nitrogen.
nitrogenar, *tr.v.* to nitrogenize.
nitrόgeno, *m.* (chem.) nitrogen; **fijaciόn del n.,** (chem.) nitrogen fixation.
nitroglicerina, *f.* (chem.) nitroglycerine.
nitrόlico, ca, *a.* (chem.) nitrolic.
nitrόmetro, *m.* nitrometer.
nitroparafina, *f.* (chem.) nitroparaffin.
nitroprusiato, *m.* (chem.) nitroprussiate.
nitrosaciόn, *f.* nitrification.
nitrosamina, *f.* (chem.) nitrosamine, nitrosamin.
nitrosidad, *f.* nitrous condition.
nitrosilo, *m.* nitrosyl.
nitroso, sa, *a.* (chem.) nitrous.
nitrotolueno, *m.* nitrotoluene.
nitruraciόn, *f.* (metal.) nitriding.
nitruro, *m.* (chem.) nitride.
nivel, *m.* level (in all senses). — **a n.,** perfectly level; **a n. del mar,** at sea level; **n. de agua,** water level; **n. de aire,** spirit level; **n. de albañil,** mason's level, plumb rule; **n. de base,** base level (of river); **n. del mar,** sea level; **n. de vida,** standard of living; **n. en Y or de horquetas,** Y level; **n. freático,** water table; **n. geodésico,** (geophys.) geodetic level.
nivelaciόn, *f.* leveling; leveling up; grading. — **n. barométrica,** (meteorol.) barometric leveling; **n. taquimétrica,** (top.) stadia leveling.
nivelador, ra, *a.* leveling. —*m., f.* leveler; grader.
nivelar, *tr.v.* to level; to level up; to make even or level; to grade; (surv.) to level, survey. —*r.v.* to become level; to put oneself on a level (with someone).
niveleta, *f.* (top.) T-shaped rod for sighting in points on a grade.
níveo, a, *a.* (poet.) snowy, niveous.
nivόmetro, *m.* snow gage.
nivoso, sa, *a.* snowy. —*m.* Nivose (fourth month of the French Revolutionary calendar).
nixtamal, *m.* (Mex.) corn especially processed for making tortillas.
Niza, *f.* Nice, city of France.
nizardo, da, *a.* Nice (as *a.*), of or from Nice, France. —*m., f.* native or inhabitant of Nice.
NNE *abbrev. of* **nornordeste,** north-northeast (N N E).
NNO *abbrev. of* **nornoroeste,** north-northwest (N N W).
no, *adv.* 1. not, e.g. *no bebo,* I do not drink, *no conozco a nadie,* I don't know anyone. 2. no, e.g. *¿quieres más? no, gracias,* do you want any more? no, thank you. 3. haven't you? weren't you? didn't he? didn't they? isn't it? wasn't it? etc. (used after an affirmative question and expecting a reply in the affirmative), e.g. *¿tú has estado en la China, no?* you've been in China, haven't you? *¿está roto, no?* it's broken, isn't it? — **a que no,** I bet you don't; **¿cόmo no?** with the greatest of pleasure, gladly, of course (I'll do it); **creer que no,** not to think so, e.g. *creo que no,* I don't think so; **no bien,** as soon as, no sooner; **no más,** only, no more; (Amer.) go right ahead (used to invite someone to do or carry on doing something), e.g. *hágalo no más,* go right ahead and do it, *pase no más,* come right in please, *siga no más,* carry right on, carry on, don't worry about me; **no menos,** no less; **no sea que,** lest; **no sin,** not without; **no tal,** certainly not; **ya no,** no longer, e.g. *ya no trabaja aquí,* he doesn't work here any longer; not any more, not now, e.g. *¿quieres ir al cine? ya no, es demasiado tarde,* do you want to go to the cinema? not now, it's too late.
No *sym. of* **nobelio,** nobelium (No).
No. *abbrev. of* **número,** number, e.g. *Quinta Avenida No. 4,* 4 Fifth Avenue.
NO *abbrev. of* **noroeste,** northwest (N W).
nobelio, *m.* (chem.) nobelium.
nobiliario, ria, *a.* nobiliary, pert. to nobility; of peer, of a peer. —*m.* peerage list.
nobilísimamente, *adv. super. of* **noblemente,** most nobly.
nobilísimo, ma, *a., super. of* **noble,** most or very noble.
noble, *a.* noble. —*m.* 1. noble, nobleman. 2. (numis.) noble.
noblemente, *adv.* nobly.
nobleza, *f.* 1. nobility, nobleness. 2. nobility (nobles collectively). 3. plain silk damask.
noblote, ta, *a.* (coll.) very kind, very noble.
noca, *f.* (zool.) (variety of) spider crab.
noceda, *f.* walnut grove.
nocedal, *m.* walnut tree.
nocente, *a.* 1. harmful, noxious. 2. guilty.
nocharniego, ga, *a., var. of* **nocherniego.**
noche, *f.* night; darkness; **a prima** or **primera n.,** just after dark; **ayer n.,** last night; **buenas noches,** good evening; good night; **cerrar la n.,** to fall (the night); **de la n. a la mañana,** overnight, suddenly; **de n.,** at night (*as adv.*); night (as *a.*); **esta n.,** tonight; **hacerse de n.,** to grow dark; **hacerse n.,** to disappear; **Nochebuena,** Christmas Eve; **n. de bodas,** wedding night; **n. de estreno,** (theat.) opening night; **n. de Reyes,** Twelfth Night; **n. de verbena,** party, festive evening; **n. de vigilia,** watchful night; **n. toledana,** restless or sleepless night; **N. Vieja,** New Year's Eve; **media n.,** midnight; **n. y día,** night and day, continuously; **pasar de claro en claro la n.,** to have a sleepless night; **por la n.,** at night.
Nochebuena, *f.* Christmas Eve.
nochebueno, *m.* 1. Christmas cake. 2. Yule log.
nochecita, *f.* (Amer.) twilight, dusk, nightfall; **a la n.,** at nightfall.
nocherniego, ga, *a.* noctambulous, night-walking, night-wandering.
nochero, ra, *m., f.* 1. (Amer.) night watchman. 2. (Guat.) night worker. —*m.* (Col.) bedside table.
nochizo, *m.* (bot.) wild hazel (tree).
nocible, *a.* harmful, noxious.
nociceptivo, va, *a.* (physiol.) nociceptive, causing or reacting to pain.
nociceptor, a, *a.* (physiol.) nociceptive.
nociόn, *f.* notion, idea; (*pl.*) rudiments, rudimentary knowledge.
nocional, *a.* notional.
nocividad, *f.* harmfulness, noxiousness.
nocivo, va, *a.* harmful, noxious, injurious.
nocla, *f.* (zool.) *var. of* **noca.**
noctambular, *i.v.* to wander about at night.
noctambulismo, *m.* noctambulism, wandering about at night; going out at night, sleepwalking.
noctámbulo, la, *a.* noctambulous, night-walking. —*m., f.* 1. night bird, night owl (one who stays up or goes out late at night). 2. nightwalker.
noctífloro, ra, *a.* (bot.) noctiflorous, night-blooming.
noctiluco, ca, *a.* noctilucent. 1. (zool.) noctiluca. 2. (ento.) glowworm.
noctívago, ga, *a.* (poet.) noctambulous, nightwalking, sleepwalking.

nocturnal, *a.* nocturnal, pertaining to the night.
nocturnidad, *f.* (law) aggravation of an offense because it was committed at night.
nocturnino, na, *a.* night, nocturnal.
nocturno, na, *a.* 1. pertaining to night, nocturnal. 2. (fig.) sad, lonely, melancholy. *—m.* (mus.) nocturne.
nodación, *f.* (med.) impediment caused by a node.
nodal, *a.* (astron., med.) nodal.
nodátil, *a.* (anat.) nodal.
nodo, *m.* (astron., phys., med.) node; **n. ascendente** or **boreal,** (astron.) ascending node; **n. austral** or **descendente,** (astron.) descending node.
nodriza, *f.* 1. wetnurse. 2. (auto.) vacuum tank.
nódulo, *m.* nodule, lump; (anat., med., min., geol.) nodule.
Noé, *m.* (Bib.) Noah.
noético, ca, *a.* noetic, of or existing or originating in the intellect.
nogada, *f.* nut and spice sauce for dressing fish.
nogal, *m.* (bot.) walnut tree; walnut (wood).
nogalina, *f.* walnut brown (color).
noguera, *f. var. of* **nogal.**
noguerado, da, *a.* walnut-colored.
nogueral, *m.* walnut grove.
nogueruela, *f.* (bot.) (variety of) spurge (Euphorbia chamaesyce).
noli, *m.* (Col.) kindling (obtained from a lichen).
nolición, *f.* (philos.) nolition, unwillingness.
noluntad, *f., var. of* **nolición.**
noma, *f.* (med.) noma.
nómada, *a.* nomadic. *—m., f* nomad.
nómade, *a.* nomadic.
nomadismo, *m.* nomadism, nomadic state.
nomarca, *m.* nomarch, the governor of a nome or nomarchy.
nomarquía, *f.* nomarchy, province.
nombradamente, *adv.* expressly.
nombradía, *f.* fame, renown, reputation.
nombrado, da, *past part. of* **nombrar.** *—a.* famous, renowned, well-known.
nombramiento, *m.* appointment; election; nomination; commission.
nombrar, *tr.v.* 1. to name, mention by name; to mention. 2. to appoint, elect.
nombre, *m.* 1. name; Christian name. 2. name, fame, renown. 3. name, authority, e.g. *en n. de,* in the name of. 4. name, nickname. 5. (gram.) noun. *—hacerse n.,* to make a name for oneself; **n. adjectivo,** (gram.) adjective; **n. apelativo,** apellation, cognomen; (gram.) common noun; **n. artístico,** stage name; **n. colectivo,** (gram.) collective noun; **n. comercial,** firm name, registered name of a commercial enterprise; **n. compuesto,** compound; **n. común,** (gram.) common noun; **n. contable,** countable noun; **n. de guerra,** nom de guerre, pseudonym; **n. de lugar,** place name; **n. de pila,** Christian or first name; **n. de pluma,** pen name, nom de plume; **n. de soltera,** maiden name; **n. en clave,** code name; **n. genérico,** (gram.) common noun; **n. masivo** or **no contable,** countable noun; **n. postizo,** alias, assumed name; **n. propio,** (gram.) proper noun; **n. substantivo,** (gram.) noun, substantive; **n. trivial,** (chem.) trivial name; **no tener n.,** to be unspeakable or unmentionable; **poner n. a,** to name, put a name to; to set a price on; **por el n. de,** by the name of.
nomenclador, *m.* list, nomenclator; technical glossary.
nomenclátor, *m., var. of* **nomenclador.**
nomenclatura, *f.* nomenclature, terminology; list, catalogue.
nomeolvides, *f.* (bot.) forget-me-not (flower).
nómina, *f.* list, roll; payroll. — **n. de pagos,** payroll.
nominación, *f.* nomination, appointment.
nominador, ra, *m., f.* nominator, appointer.
nominal, *a.* 1. nominal, titular. 2. (gram.) nominal, substantival. 3. (com.) nominal. 4. (philos.) nominalist. *—m., f.* (philos.) nominalist.
nominalismo, *m.* (philos.) nominalism.
nominaslista, *a.* nominalist, nominalistic. *—m., f.* (philos.) nominalist.
nominalmente, *adv.* nominally.
nominar, *tr.v.* to nominate, name.
nominativo, va, *a.* 1. (com.) nominative (bearing a person's name), registered (as bonds). 2. (gram.) nominative. *—m.* (gram.) nominative.
nominilla, *f.* voucher, pay warrant.
nómino, *m.* nominee (person named for office, duty or position).
nomo, *m.* 1. nome, province. 2. gnome.
nomografía, *f.* 1. nomography, the art of drafting laws. 2. nomography, the science of drawing nomographs.
nomograma, *m.* (math., engin.) nomogram, nomograph, alignment chart.
nomología, *f.* nomology.
nomoteta, *a.* nomothetic, giving or enacting laws.
nomparell, *m.* (print.) nonpareil, six-point.
non, *a.* odd, uneven. *—m.* 1. odd number. 2. (*pl.*) repeated negation or denial; refusal. — **andar** or **estar de nones,** (coll.) to be idle, be unemployed; (coll.) to be unique or unequaled; **decir nones,** to say no, refuse; **de n.,** alone; odd, unmatched; unique, unmatched; **estar de n.,** (coll.) to be unique or unmatched; to be useless; **jugar a pares o nones,** to play odds and evens; **quedar de n.,** (coll.) to be odd man out, be without a companion.
nona, *f.* 1. (ecc.) nones. 2. (*pl.*) nones (in Roman calendar).
nonada, *f.* trifle, nothing.
nonagenario, ria, *a., m., f.* nonagenarian, between the ages of ninety and one hundred.
nonagésimo, ma, *a., m.* ninetieth. — **n. de la Eclíptica,** (astron.) nonagesimal.
nonagonal, *a.* nine-sided.
nonágono, na, *a.* (geom.) nine-sided. *—m.* (geom.) nonagon.
nonato, ta, *a.* 1. nonexistant, unborn. 2. not born naturally, born by a Caesarean operation.
noningentésimo, ma, *a., m.* nine-hundredth.
nonio, *m.* vernier, a measuring instrument.
nono, na, *a., m.* ninth.
non plus ultra, *m.* (Lat.) ne plus ultra, unsurpassable.
non sancta, (coll.) loose, dissipated, immoral; **casa n. s.,** bawdy house.
nopal, *m.* (bot.) prickly pear; **n. de la cochinilla,** cochineal fig tree, cochineal cactus.
nopaleda, *f., var. of* **nopalera.**
nopalera, *f.* prickly pear growth or thicket.
nopalito, *m.* (Mex.) boiled tender prickly pear leaf.
noque, *m.* 1. tanning vat. 2. heap of squashed olives.
noquear, *tr.v.* (coll.) to knock out.
noquero, *m.* tanner, currier, leather dresser.
norabuena, *f., adv., var. of* **enhorabuena, congratulations.**
noramala, *adv., var. of* **enhoramala,** unfortunately.
nora tal, nora en tal, *adv., var. of* **enhoramala.**
noray, *m.* (mar.) bollard, mooring stone or post; (mar.) mooring line or cable.
nordestal, *a.* northeast; northeastern.
nordeste, *m.* 1. northeast. 2. northeast wind, northeaster. — **n. cuarta al norte,** northeast by north; **n. cuarta al este,** northeast by east.
nordestear, *i.v.* (mar.) to turn from north towards northeast (a compass needle.)
nórdico, ca, *a.* Nordic (peoples); Norse, Scandinavian, Nordic (languages). *—m.* Norse, Nordic (language).
noria, *f.* 1. chain pump, Persian wheel; chain pump well. 2. (coll.) treadmill (drudgery).
norial, *a.* pertaining to a chain pump.
norma, *f.* 1. norm, standard. 2. rule, regulation. 3. pattern, template, model. 4. (mason's, carpenter's, etc.) rule, square, template.
normal, *a.* normal, usual, standard; (chem., mus., math., geom., phys.) normal. *—f.* normal school, teachers' training college.
normalice, normalicé, *ref.* **normalizar.**
normalidad, *f.* normality, normalcy; (chem.) normality; **volver a la n.,** to get back to normality.
normalista, *a.* of or from a normal school or teachers' training college. *—m., f.* normal school student, student of a teachers' training college.
normalización, *f.* normalization; standardization.
normalizar, (*ref. 53*) *tr.v.* 1. to normalize, make normal. 2. to standardize, make standard. *—r.v.* to return or get back to normal.
normalmente, *adv.* normally.
Normandía, *f.* Normandy, region of France.
normando, da, *a., m., f.* Norman.
normano, na, *a., m., f., var. of* **normando.**
normativo, va, *a., m., f.* standard.
nornordeste, *m.* 1. north-northeast. 2. north-northeast wind.
nornoroeste, *m., var. of* **nornorueste.**
nornorueste, *m.* 1. north-northweast. 2. north-northwest wind.
noroeste, *m.* 1. northwest. 2. northwester, north-west wind. — **n. cuarta al oeste,** northwest by west; **n. cuarta al norte,** northwest by north.
noroestear, *i.v.* (mar.) to turn from north to north-west (compass needle, wind).
nororiental, *a.* northeast, northeastern.
nortada, *f.* continuous north wind.
norte, *m.* 1. north; North Pole. 2. north wind, norther. 3. **N.,** polestar, North Star. 4. (fig.) polestar, guide, guiding principle. — **n. magnético,** magnetic north; **n. cuarta al noreste,** north by northeast; **n. cuarta al noroeste,** north by north-west; **n. verdadero,** true north.
Norteamérica, *f.* North America.
norteamericano, na, *a., m., f.* North American (of the U.S.A.).
nortear, *tr.v.* to steer to the north. *—i.v.* to veer towards the north (wind).
norteño, ña, *a.* northern. *—m., f.* northerner.
nórtico, ca, *a.* northern, northerly.
nortino, na, *a.* (Amer.) northern. *—m., f.* (Amer.) northerner.
Noruega, *f.* Norway
noruego, ga, *a., m., f.* Norwegian. *—m.* Norwegian (language). *—f.* **N.,** Norway.
norueste, *n.* northwest.
noruestear, *i.v.* (mar.), *var. of* **noroestear.**
nos, *pers. pron.* 1. (as direct object) us. 2. (as indirect object) to us, us, e.g. *nos dieron el libro,* the gave us the book, or they gave the book to us; for us, us, e.g. *nos compraron estas flores,* they bought us these flowers, or they bought these flowers for us; from us, e.g. *nos sacaron un montón de plata,* they got an enormous amount of money from us. 3. (as *reflex. pron.*) ourselves; (as *rec. pron.*) one another, each other, e.g. *nos ayudamos el uno al otro,* we help one another.
nosogenia, *f.* (med.) nosogeny.
nosografía, *f.* (med.) nosography.
nosología, *f.* (med.) nosology, classification of diseases.
nosológico, ca, *a.* (med.) nosological.

nosologista, *m., f.* (med.) nosologist.
nosomántica, *f.* cure by enchantment or spell.
nosotros, tras, *pers. pron.* 1. we (when subject of verb). 2. us (when governed by a preposition).
nostalgia, *f.* nostaliga; homesickness.
nostálgico, ca, *a.* nostalgic; homesick.
nosticismo, *m.* (Rel., philos.) Gnosticism.
nóstico, ca, *a.* (Rel., philos.) Gnostic.
nostología, *f.* nostology, the scientific study of the process of aging and of the problems of the aged.
nostológico, ca, *a.* nostologic.
nostramo, ma, *m.* 1. (mar. boatswain (word used when addressing a boatswain). 2. master. —*f.* mistress.
nostras, *a.* (med.) local (disease).
nota, *f.* 1. note (short letter; diplomatic communication). 2. note, marginal note, comment, observation, e.g. *tomar* or *hacer notas,* to take or make notes. 3. note, heed, notice, e.g. *tomar n. de,* to take note of, fix one's attention on. 4. note, fame, renown, repute. 5. (mus.) note. 6. mark, grade (in examination). 7. (*pl.*) records (of public notary). — **caer en n.,** to cause a scandal; **forzar la n.,** to carry things too far; **dar la n.,** to draw attention; **n. de adorno,** grace note; **n. a pie de página,** footnote; **n. de crédito,** (com.) credit memorandum or note; **n. de débito or cargo,** (acc.) debit note; **n. de prensa,** press release; **n. de sobresaliente,** first-class mark or grade; **n. diplomática,** diplomatic note; **n. falsa,** (mus.) wrong note; **n. marginal,** marginal note; **n. verbal,** verbal note; **n. musical,** note; **n. necrológica,** death announcement; **tomar n. de,** to take note of.
notabilidad, *f.* notability; a notable (person).
notabilísimo, ma, *a. super. of* **notable,** most or very notable.
notable, *a.* notable, noteworthy; outstanding. —*m.* worthy, notable.
notablemente, *adv.* notably, noticeably, remarkably.
notación, *f.* (math., mus.) notation; note, annotation.
notar, *tr.v.* 1. to note, notice, observe. 2. to point out, indicate. 3. to jot down, take down, make note of. 4. to annotate, write notes in (a text). 5. to criticize, find fault with, censure; to discredit. 6. to dictate.
notaría, *f.* 1. notary's office. 2. profession of notary.
notariado, da, *a.* notarized. —*m.* profession of a notary; body of notaries.
notarial, *a.* notarial.
notariato, *m.* 1. notary's degree or certificate. 2. practice of a notary.
notario, *m.* 1. notary, notary public. 2. clerk, actuary amanuensis.
noticia, *f.* 1. piece of news, news, news item; (*pl.*) news. 2. notion, idea, rudimentary knowledge, (*pl.*) basic or rudimentary knowledge. — **atrasado de noticias,** out of date (uninformed of latest events); **n. bomba,** (coll., fig.) bombshell; **n. remota,** vague idea, recollection or notion; **noticias de última hora,** stoppress news; **primera n.,** that's the first thing I've heard about it.
noticiar, *tr.v.* to inform, notify.
noticiario, *m.* news; (cine.) news, newsreel; (rad.) newscast, news. — **n. deportivo,** sports news; **n. teatral,** theater news.
noticiero, ra, *a.* news (as *a.*). —*m.* 1. newsman, reporter. 2. (Amer.) newscast, news, news bulletin.
notición, *m.* 1. great news; scoop, headline news. 2. (coll.) wild or extravagant piece of news.
noticioso, sa, *a.* 1. informed, full of news. 2. learned, erudite. 3. news (as *a.*), **agencia noticiosa,** news agency.

notificación, *f.* notification, notice.
notificado, da, *past part. of* **notificar.** —*a.* notified.
notificar, (*ref. 50*) *tr.v.* to notify, inform.
notificativo, va, *a.* notifying.
notifique, notifiqué, *ref.* **notificar.**
notita, *f. dim of* **nota,** short note, memorandum.
noto, ta, *a.* 1. well-known, widely known. 2. illegitimate, bastard.
noto, *m.* Notus, south wind.
notocordio, *m.* (zool.) notochord.
notoriamente, *adv.* manifestly, conspicuously, glaringly.
notoriedad, *f.* reputation, fame, renown, notoriety.
notorio, ria, *a.* well-known, widely known; evident, manifest.
notungulado, da, *a., m.* (paleon.) notungulate.
noumeno, *m.* (philos.) neumenon, an object reached by intellectual intuition.
nov. *abbrev. of* **noviembre,** November (Nov.).
nova, *f.* (astron.) nova (star).
novación, *f.* (law) novation.
novador, ra, *m., f.* innovator.
noval, *a.* newly broken up (land).
novallo, lla, *a.* (arch.) *var. of* **noval.**
novar, *tr.v.* (law) to novate, to renew by novation.
novatada, *f.* 1. ragging, hazing (of new students). 2. beginner's blunder.
novato, ta, *a.* beginning. —*m., f.* novice, beginner, freshman.
novator, ra, *m., f.* innovator, novator.
novecientos, tas, *a., m.* nine hundred.
novedad, *f.* 1. novelty, newness. 2. novelty, new thing, innovation. 3. recent event, piece of news; (*pl.*) news. 4. change, alteration, new development. 5. surprise. — **hacer n.,** to surprise; to make innovations; **sin n.,** as usual, no news.
novedoso, sa, *a.* novel, new, recent; (Amer.) fictional.
novel, *a.* new, inexperienced, beginning.
novela, *f.* 1. (lit.) novel. 2. lie, story, fiction, falsehood. 3. (Roman law) novel. — **n. de amores,** love story, romance; **n. científica** or **de cienca ficción,** science fiction story; **n. policíaca,** detective novel; **n. por entregas,** serialized novel; **n. radiofónica,** radio serial; **n. rosa,** romantic novel.
novelador, ra, *m., f.* novelist.
novelar, *i.v.* 1. to write novels. 2. to tell lies or fabulous stories.
novelería, *f.* 1. fondness for novelties, curiosity, inquisitiveness. 2. fondness for fiction. 3. poor fiction. 4. collection of novels.
novelero, ra, *a.* 1. fond of novelty or novelties; curious, inquisitive. 2. gossipy, newsmongering. 3. inconstant, fickle. —*m., f.* novelty or curiosity seeker; newsmongerer.
novelesco, ca, *a.* 1. novelesque, like a novel, fantastic. 2. novelistic, fictional.
novelice, novelicé, *ref.* **novelizar.**
novelista, *m., f.* novelist.
novelística, *f.* 1. fiction, novels (collectively). 2. treatise on the novel, study of the novel. 3. novel writing.
novelístico, ca, *a.* novelistic; novel (as *a.*).
novelizar, (*ref. 53*) *tr.v.* to novelize, put into the form of a novel, fictionalize.
novelón, *m.* long poorly written novel.
novena, *f.* 1. novena, novene, the recitation of prayers on nine days, usually to seek some special favor. 2. book containing prayers for novenas.
novenario, *m.* novenary period of nine days of prayers or mourning.
novendial, *a.* novendial. —*m.* (Roman hist.) novendial, nine days of sacrifices and celebrations in honor of the gods.

noveno, na, *a.* ninth. —*m.* 1. ninth. 2. tithe consisting of ninth part of produce or income. —*f.* (rel.) novena.
noventa, *a., m.* ninety, ninetieth.
noventavo, va, *a., m., f.* ninetieth.
noventayochista, *a.* of the Generation of 98.
noventón, na, *a., m., f.* nonagenarian.
novia, *f.* fiancée, girlfriend (coll.), girl (coll.); bride; sweetheart; **pedir la n.,** to ask for the hand of one's fiancée.
noviazgo, *m.* engagement, courtship, betrothal.
noviciado, *m.* 1. (ecc.) novitiate, noviciate, apprenticeship of novice; seminary; novices (collectively). 2. apprenticeship, novitiate.
novicio, cia, *a.* new, inexperienced. —*m., f.* novice, beginner, apprentice; (ecc.) novice; freshman.
noviembre, *m.* November.
novilla, *f.* heifer, young cow.
novillada, *f.* 1. drove of young cattle. 2. (taur.) fight with young bulls by aspiring fighters.
novillejo, eja, *m., f. dim. of* **novillo, lla,** bullock (heifer).
novillero, *m.* 1. herdsman who looks after young cattle. 2. (taur.) bullfighter who fights young bulls (one stage prior to becoming a matador). 3. stable for young cattle. 4. pasture ground for young cattle. 5. (coll.) truant, idler.
novillo, *m.* 1. young bull. 2. (coll.) cuckold. 3. (*pl.*) bullfight of young bull. — **hacer novillos,** to play truant or hooky.
novilunio, *m.* new moon.
novio, *m.* fiancé, boyfriend; bridegroom, (*pl.*) bride and groom, newlyweds.
novísimo, ma, *a. super. of* **nuevo,** newest, latest, most recent. —*m.* each of the last stages of man, i.e. death, judgment, hell, heaven. —*f.* **N.,** *abbrev. of* **Novísima Recopilación,** revised Spanish legal code (1805).
novocaína, *f.* (med., pharm.) novocaine.
noyó, *m.* a bitter liquour made of brandy, sugar and almonds.
Np *sym. of* **neptunio,** neptunium (Np).
N.S.J. *abbrev. of* **Nuestro Señor Jesucristo,** Our Lord Jesus Christ.
N.U. *abbrev. of* **Naciones Unidas,** United Nations.
nubada, *f.* 1. cloudburst, sudden shower or downpour. 2. (fig.) abundance, plenty.
nubado, da, *a.* clouded, shaped like clouds.
nubarrada, *f., var. of* **nubada.**
nubarrado, da, *a.* decorated with cloud designs.
nubarrón, *m.* large black storm cloud.
nube, *f.* 1. cloud (in the sky). 2. cloud, haze, smokescreen (obscuring something). 3. cloud, flock, multitude, host (of locusts, birds, etc.). 4. cloud, shade (in a diamond). 5. lace head scarf. 6. (med.) film, white spot on cornea. — **andar** or **estar por las nubes,** to be very high, be skyhigh (prices); **bajarse de las nubes,** to come down to earth; **banco de nubes,** cloud bank; **capa de nubes,** cloud layer; **como caído de las nubes,** out of the blue, unexpectedly; **coronado de nubes,** cloud-capped; **levantarse a las nubes,** to become proud or haughty; **n. de lluvia,** rain cloud; **n. de verano,** sudden shower, summer shower; passing annoyance; **poner por las nubes,** to praise to the skies; **remontarse a las nubes,** to become very highflown (e.g. in style); **subir a las nubes,** to go skyhigh (prices); **n. atómica,** atomic cloud; **n. cósmica,** (astr.) cosmic cloud.
nubecita, *f.* small cloud.
nube-hongo, *f.* mushroom cloud.
nubiense, *a., m., f.* Nubian; of Nubia, its people or their language.

nubífero, ra, *a.* (poet.) cloud-bringing.
núbil, *a.* nubile, young but of marriageable age.
nubilidad, *f.* nubility, marriageability, marriageable age.
nubiloso, sa, *a.* (poet.) *var. of* **nubloso.**
nublado, da, *past part. of* **nublar.** —*a.* cloudy. —*m.* 1. storm cloud. 2. (fig.) storm cloud, impending danger. 3. cloud, flock; crowd, host, multitude. — **descargar el n.,** to pour with rain, snow or hail hard; to vent one's anger in a stream of expletives.
nublar, *tr.v.* to cloud. —*r.v.* to become overcast or cloudy.
nublo, bla, *a.* cloudy. —*m.* 1. storm cloud. 2. fungus (of plants).
nubloso, sa, *a.* cloudy, dark, overcast.
nubosidad, *f.* cloudiness.
nuboso, sa, *a.* cloudy.
nuca, *f.* nape (of neck).
nucela, *f.* (bot.) nucellus.
nucelar, *a.* (bot.) nucellar.
nuche, *m.* (ento., Col.) (variety of) botfly.
nucleado, da, *a.* (biol., bot.) nucleate.
nuclear, *a.* (biol., phys.) nuclear.
nuclearío, ria, *a.* (biol.) nuclear, nucleal.
nucleasa, *f.* (biochem.) nuclease.
nucleico, ca, *a.* (biochem.) nucleic.
nucleínas, *f.* (chem.) nuclein.
núcleo, *m.* 1. nucleus, core; focal point. 2. nucleus, kernel (of nut). 3. (astron., biol., anat., chem., phys., gram.) nucleus. — **n. celular,** cellular core; **n. magnético,** magnetic core; **n. testigo,** boring or sample core.
nucleolado, da, *a.* (biol.) nucleolated, nucleolate.
nucleolar, *a.* (biol.) nucleolar.
nucléolo, *m.* (biol.) nucleolus, nucleola.
nucleón, *m.* (phys.) nucleon.
nucleónico, ca, *a.* (phys.) nucleonic. —*f.* (phys.) nucleonics.
nucleoplasma, *m.* (biol.) nucleoplasm.
nucleoplásmico, ca, *a.* (biol.) nucleoplasmic.
nucleoproteína, *f.* (biochem.) nucleoprotein.
nucleósido, *m.* (chem.) nucleoside.
nucleótido, *m.* (chem.) nucleotide.
núclido, *m.* (phys.) nuclide.
nuco, *m.* (Chile., ornith.) barn owl.
nudamente, *adv.* nakedly, plainly.
nudibranquio, *a., m.* (zool.) nudibranchiate.
nudicaule, *a.* (bot.) nudicaul, nudicaulus, having stems without leaves.
nudicaulo, la, *a.* (bot.) nudicaul, nudicaulus.
nudillo, *m.* 1. knuckle (of finger). 2. knot (forming seam of stocking). 3. plug, plug in a wall.
nudismo, *m.* nudism.
nudo, *m.* 1. knot (in rope). 2. (bot.) knot (part of trunk where branches emerge); node, knot (in grass, sugar-cane, etc.). 3. knot (in texture of plank of wood). 4. bond, tie, knot. 5. lump, node, knot, protuberance (in tendon, bone, etc.). 6. joint (in animal's bones). 7. impediment (to marriage); spell supposed to cause impotency. 8. climax (of novel, drama, etc.). 9. problem, difficulty, knot. 10. (geog.) knot. 11. (mar.) knot. — **dar or echar otro n. a la bolsa,** to tighten one's purse-strings; **n. corredizo,** slip knot; **n. de guerra,** tug-of-war; **n. de vuelta redonda y cote,** round turn and half hitch; **n. en la garganta,** lump in one's throat, e.g. *hacérsele a uno un n. en la garganta,* to get a lump in one's throat; e.g. *cortar el n. gordiano,* to cut the Gordian knot.
nudo, da, *a.* naked, nude.
nudosidad, *f.* (med.) node, knotty swelling, knot.
nudoso, sa, *a.* knotty, knotted.
nuecero, ra, *m., f.* nut vendor, walnut vendor.
nuégado, *m.* 1. nougat. 2. concrete.
nuera, *f.* daughter-in-law.
nuestramo, ma, *m.* master. —*f.* mistress.
nuestro, tra, *pos. a.* our; of ours, e.g. *un amigo nuestro,* a friend of ours. —*pos. pron.* ours; **los nuestros,** our side, our friends, our allies.
nueva, *f.* news; (*pl.*) news.
nuevamente, *adv.* 1. again, anew. 2. newly, recently.
nueve, *a.* nine. —*m.* nine; ninth (in dates).
nuevo, va, *a.* new. — **de nuevo,** again, anew; **Nueva Escocia,** Nova Scotia; **Nuevo Gales del Sur,** New South Wales; **Nueva Inglaterra,** New England; **Nueva Orleans,** New Orleans; **n. ola,** new wave; n. rico, nouveau riche; **N. Testamento,** New Testament; **Nueva York,** New York; **Nueva Zelandia,** New Zealand; **Nuevo Méjico** or **México,** New Mexico; **¿qué hay de nuevo?** what's new?
nuez, (*pl.* **nueces**), *f.* 1. walnut; nut (of any tree). 2. Adam's apple. 3. nut (to tighten hairs on violin bow or strings on arbalest). — **apretarle a uno la n.,** to throttle someone, choke someone to death; **cascarle a uno las nueces,** to give someone a beating; **n. de betel,** betel nut; **n. de ciprés,** cypress cone; **n. de especia, n. moscada,** nutmeg; **n. de la garganta,** Adam's apple; **n. de tagua,** ivory nut; **n. vómica,** (bot.) nux vomica; **volver las nueces al cántaro,** to renew old quarrels or disputes; to restore friendly relations.
nueza, *f.* (bot.) briony.
nugatorio, ria, *a.* nugatory, deceiving, futile.
nulamente, *adv.* invalidly, without value or effect.
nulidad, *f.* 1. nullity, invalidity, invalidness. 2. worthlessness. 3. incapacity, incompetence, uselessness. 4. incompetent, useless incompetent person.
nulificar, (*ref.* 50) *tr.v.* to nullify.
nulifique, nulifiqué, *ref.* **nulificar.**
nulípara, *a.* nulliparous, a woman who has never given birth to a child.
nulípora, *f.* (bot.) nullipore.
nulo, la, *a.* 1. null, void, invalid. 2. worthless, useless. 3. nil, non-existent, e.g. *la interferencia es casi nula en esta radio,* the interference is almost null or non-existent on this radio set.
núm, *abbrev. of* **número,** number.
Numancia, *f.* (hist., lit.) Numantia.
numantino, na, *a., m., f.* Numantian, of the ancient Celtic city of Numantia (Spain).
numen, *m.* 1. numen, deity. 2. muse, inspiration.
numerable, *a.* numerable.
numeración, *f.* numbering, numeration; (math.) numeration.
numerador, *m.* 1. numbering stamp. 2. (math.) numerator.
numeradora, *f.* (print.) numbering machine.
numeral, *a., m., f.* numeral.
numerar, *tr.v.* 1. to number. 2. to express numerically.
numerario, ria, *a.* numerary. —*m.* coin, cash, currency.
numéricamente, *adv.* numerically.
numérico, ca, *a.* numerical.
número, *m.* 1. number; numeral. 2. number, group. 3. number, issue (e.g. of a magazine). 4. (mus., poet.) number (regular count of syllables or beats); (*pl.*) numbers (metrical verses). 5. (gram.) number. 6. (Bib.) Numbers, Book of Numbers. — **áureo n.,** golden number (in chronology); **de n.,** regular (member of an association, e.g. a national academy); **hacer n.** or **llenar el n.,** to make up the number; **n. arábigo,** Arabic numeral; **n. atómico,** atomic number; **n. atrasado,** back number (of a publication); **n. cardinal,** cardinal number; **n. complejo,** complex number; compound number; **n. compuesto,** composite number (not prime); **n. cuántico,** (phys.) quantum number; **n. deficiente,** deficient or defective number; **n. de fax,** fax number; **n. de guarismo,** see **n. arábigo; n. de Mach,** (aer.) Mach; **n. de masa,** mass number; **n. de matrícula,** license number; **n. de serie,** serial number; **n. de teléfono** telephone number; **n. denominado,** see **n. complejo; n. de octano,** octane number or rating; **n. dígito,** digit; **n. dual,** dual number; **n. entero,** whole number; **n. fraccionario** or **quebrado,** fraction; **n. impar,** odd number; **n. índice,** index number; **n. natural,** (math.) natural number; **n. ordinal,** ordinal number; **n. par,** even number; **n. plano,** product of two whole numbers multiplied together; **n. plural,** (gram.) plural number; **n. primo,** prime number; **n. redondo,** round number, round figure; **n. romano,** Roman numeral; **n. simple,** prime number; digit; **n. superante,** abundant number; **n. uno,** (coll.) number one, oneself; number one, best, e.g. *el n. uno,* the best; **sin número,** countless.
numerología, *f.* numerology, a system of occultism built around numbers; divination by numbers.
numerosamente, *adv.* 1. in great numbers, numerously. 2. rhythmically.
numerosidad, *f.* numerousness, numerosity.
numeroso, sa, *a.* 1. numerous. 2. harmonious, rhythmical.
numisma, *m.* (numis.) coin, money.
numismática, *f.* numismatics, the study or collection of coins, medals, paper money, etc.
numismático, ca, *a.* numismatic, numismatical. —*m.* numismatist, numismatician.
numismatología, *f.* numismatology.
numo, *m.* coin, money.
núms, *abbrev. of* **números,** numbers.
numular, *a.* nummular; coin-shaped, circular or oval.
numulario, *m.* money broker.
numulita, *f.* (zool.) nummulite.
numulítico, ca, *a.* nummulitic, coin-shaped.
nutante, *a.* (bot.) nutant; with the top bent downward, drooping.
nunca, *adv.* never, at no time. — **nunca jamás,** nevermore.
nunciatura, *f.* 1. nunciature (office and dignity of a nuncio). 2. nuncio's residence.
nuncio, *m.* messenger; papal ambassador; harbinger; (ecc.) nuncio; **n. apostólico,** papal nuncio.
nuncupativo, va, *a.* nuncupative, oral (said of wills).
nuncupatorio, ria, *a.* designative, nuncupative, named before witnesses as one's heir.
nuño, *m.* (Chile, bot.) blue-eyed grass.
nupcial, *a.* nuptial, hymeneal.
nupcialidad, *f.* nuptiality, marriage rate.
nupcias, *f.* (*pl.*) nuptials, marriage, wedding. — **casarse en segundas nupcias,** to marry for the second time.
nutación, *f.* (astr., bot.) nutation.
nutra, *f., var. of* **nutria.**
nutria, *f.* (zool.) otter.
nutricio, cia, *a.* nutritious, nutritive, nourishing.
nutrición, *f.* nutrition, nourishing; (biol.) nutrition.
nutrido, da, *past part. of* **nutrir.** —*a.* 1. full, abundant, abounding, e.g. *n. de,* full of, abounding in. 2. very big, heavily attended, e.g. *una*

nutrida manifestación, a very big or heavily attended demonstration or meeting. 3. incessant, heavy (gunfire).

nutrimental, *a.* nutrimental, nutritious, nourishing.

nutrimento, *m.* nutriment, nourishment, food.

nutrimiento, *m., var. of.* **nutrimento.**

nutrir, *tr.v.* 1. to nourish, to feed. 2. (fig.) to nourish, encourage, promote, support. 3. to fill.

nutritivo, va, *a.* nutritive, nourishing, nutritious. — **valor n.,** food value.

nutriz, (*pl.* **nutrices**), *f.* wetnurse.

nutual, *a.* (ecc.) removable (said of chaplainship or civil offices, which can be taken away at the patron's will).

nylon, *m.* nylon.

Ñ

Ñ, *f.* fifteenth letter of the Spanish alphabet.
ña, *f.* (Amer., coll.) *dim. of* **Doña,** lady (a title used only before the Christian name, e.g. *Ña María.*)
ñacanina, *f.* (Arg.) black-spotted viper (Cyclagras gigas).
ñaco, *m.* (S. Amer.) porridge, gruel made of corn.
ñacurutú, (*pl.* **ñacurutúes**), *m.* (Arg., Par., Urug.) great horned owl (Buho virginianus nacurutu).
ñagaza, *f. var. of* **añagaza,** bird call, decoy.
ñame, *m.* edible tuberose root of the yam family, a popular table fare in the tropics.
ñandú, (*pl.* **ñandúes**), *m.* (ornith.) nandu, American ostrich.
ñandubay, *m.* (S. Amer., bot.) nandubay; a kind of hard wood.
ñandutí, *m.* nanduty (fine lace made in Paraguay).
ñangado, da, *a.* (Cuba) malformed, crooked legged.
ñango, ga, *a.* (Amer.) awkward, clumsy, ungainly.
ñangué, *m.* (Cuba) thorn apple.
ñañigo, ga, *a.* (Cuba) pertaining to a secret society of Negroes, nowadays a folkloric culture chiefly expressed in music, songs and dances of African origin.
ñaño, ña, *a.* 1. (Amer.) intimate, very close. 2. (Amer.) spoiled, pampered. —*m., f.* (Amer.) intimate or bosom friend; brother, sister. —*f.* 1. children's nurse, nanny. 2. (C. Amer.) human excrement.
ñapa, *f.* (Amer.) gratuity, bonus, tip, something extra. — **de ñapa,** to boot, into the bargain.
ñapango, ga, *a.* (Col.) mestizo, half-breed.
ñapindá, (*pl.* **ñapindaes**) *m.* (bot., Arg.) variety of acacia (Acacia bonariensis).
ñapo, *m.* (Chile) fiber used in basketry.
ñaque, *m.* junk, rubbish, odds and ends.
ñaruso, sa, *a.* (Ecuad.) pockmarked.
ñato, ta, (coll., Amer.) pug-nosed, flat-nosed.
ñeque, *a.* 1. (Amer.) strong, full of vim, vigorous. 2. (Amer.) brave; bullying, swaggering. —*m.* (Amer.) strength, vigor, pep; courage. — **hombre de ñ.,** a real man, a he-man.
ñiquiñaque, *m.* (coll.) piece of trash or rubbish; good for nothing person.
ñire, ñirre, *m.* (Chile) antarctic beech.
ñire, *m.* a semihard Argentine lumber.
ñisca, ñizca, *f.* (Amer.) bit, pinch, fragment.
ñisñil, *m.* (Chile) cattail, reed mace.
ño, *m.* (Amer., coll.) *apocopated form of* **Señor,** sir (a title used only before the Christian name, e.g. *Ño Antonio*).
ñocha, *f.* (Chile) variety of sedge (Cyperus lechleri).
ñoclo, *m.* aniseed-flavored cake, a kind of macaroon.
ñoñería, *f.* timid, babyish or infantile behavior; shyness; dotage.
ñoñez, (*pl.* **ñoñeces**), *f.* 1. timidity, shyness, babyishness. 2. senility, dotage.
ñoño, ña, *a.* 1. timid, shy, babyish, infantile. 2. insipid, tasteless. 3. senile, whiny. 4. (Amer.) outmoded, old-fashioned.
ñoque, ñoqui, *m.* (cul.) gnoccho, (*pl.*) gnocchi.
ñorbo, *m.* (Ecuad., Peru, bot.) passion flower.
ñu, (*pl.* **ñúes**), *m.* (zool.) gnu. — **ñ. azul,** brindled gnu, blue wildebeest; **ñ. negro,** white-tailed gnu, black wildebeest.
ñudillo, *m., var. of* **nudillo.**
ñudo, *m.* knot.
ñudoso, sa, *a., var. of* **nudoso,** knotty, knotted.
ñusta, *f.* ancient Inca princess.
ñuto, ta, *a.* (Ecuad.) ground, powdered. — **carne ñuta,** tender, boneless cut of beef.

O

O, *f.* o, sixteenth letter of the Spanish alphabet.

o, *conj.* or; either; **o sea,** that is.

ó, *conj.* or (conjunction used between Arabic numerals to avoid confusion with zero).

O *abbrev. of* **oeste,** west (W).

OACI *abbrev. of* **Organización de Aviación Civil Internacional,** International Civil Aviation Organization (ICAO).

oasis, (*pl.* **oasis**), *m.* oasis.

obcecación, *f.* blindness, stubbornness, obsession.

obcecadamente, *adv.* blindly, stubbornly, obsessedly.

obcecar, (*ref. 50*) *tr.v.* to blind, obfuscate; to obsess.

obceque, obcequé, *ref.* **obcecar.**

obcónico, ca, *a.* (bot.) obconic.

obcordiforme, *a.* (bot.) obcordate.

obduración, *f.* obstinacy, obduracy.

obedecedor, ra, *a.* obedient. —*m., f.* obeyer.

obedecer, (*ref. 45*) *tr.v.* to obey; to respond (to). — **o. a,** to obey; to respond to; to be due to, arise from, spring from; to follow.

obedecible, *a.* obeyable.

obedecimiento, *m.* obedience (to), compliance (with).

obedezca, obedezco, *ref.* **obedecer.**

obediencia, *f.* obedience; **a la o.,** your obedient servant; **o. ciega,** blind obedience.

obediencial, *a.* pertaining to obedience.

obediente, *a.* obedient, docile.

obedientemente, *adv.* obediently.

obelisco, *m.* 1. obelisk. 2. (print.) dagger. — **o. doble,** (print) double dagger.

obelo, *m.* 1. obelisk. 2. (print.) obelus, dagger.

obencadura, *f.* (mar.) shrouds.

obenque, *m.* (mar.) shroud, guy, shifters.

obertura, *f.* (mus.) overture.

obesidad, *f.* obesity, fatness.

obeso, sa, *a.* fat, obese.

óbice, *m.* obstacle, impediment, hindrance.

obispado, *m.* bishopric, episcopate.

obispal, *a.* episcopal, pertaining to a bishop.

obispalía, *f.* 1. bishop's palace. 2. bishopric, diocese.

obispar, *i.v.* to become a bishop, be appointed bishop.

obispillo, *m.* 1. mock bishop, boy bishop (boy or new student dressed as a bishop for a mock or initiation ceremony). 2. large pork sausage. 3. rump (of a fowl).

obispo, *m.* 1. (ecc.) bishop. 2. (ichth.) bishop ray, spotted sting ray. 3. large pork sausage.

óbito, *m.* death, decease, demise.

obituario, *m.* obituary.

obiubi, *m.* (zool., Ven.) night ape.

objeción, *f.* objection. — **o. denegada,** objection overruled.

objetable, *a.* objectionable, apt to be objected to.

objetante, *a.* objecting. —*m., f.* objector.

objetar, *tr.v.* 1. to raise, bring up, put forward (difficulties). 2. to object to, raise objections to. 3. to ask questions on (a university thesis). — **no tener nada que o.,** to have no objections. —*i.v.* to object.

objetivación, *f.* objectivization.

objetivamente, *adv.* objectively.

objetivar, *tr.v.* to objectivize, objectify.

objetividad, *f.* objectivity.

objetivismo, *m.* objectivism.

objetivo, va, *a.* objective; (gram., philos., opt., med.) objective. —*m.* 1. objective, aim, goal. 2. (opt.) objective. — **o. zoom, o. de distancia focal variable,** (photog.) zoom lens.

objeto, *m.* 1. object, thing. 2. object, purpose, aim. 3. subject, subject matter; **o. de arte,** objet d'art; **objetos perdidos,** (señal) lost and found; **o. volador** (or **volante**) **no identificado (OVNI),** unidentified flying object, UFO.

objetor, tora, *m., f.* objector: **o. de conciencia,** conscientious objector.

oblación, *f.* oblation, offering, gift.

oblada, *f.* (ecc.) offering of bread given for the dead at a requiem mass.

oblata, *f.* (ecc.) 1. gift or oblation for church expenses. 2. wine and bread of the Eucharist before being consecrated. 3. lay sister oblate, belonging to the Order of the Redeemer.

oblativo, va, *a.* (ecc.) oblatery.

oblato, ta, *a., m., f.* (ecc.) oblate.

oblea, *f.* 1. sealing wafer, lozenge of gum (for sealing letters). 2. (coll.) bag of bones, extremely thin person. — **salir de algo hecho una o.,** to come out of something as thin as a rake or like a bag of bones.

obleera, *f.* sealing wafer case or box.

oblicuamente, *adv.* obliquely.

oblicuángulo, *a.* (geom.) oblique-angled.

oblicuar, *tr.v.* to cant, slant. —*i.v.* (mil.) to oblique; to change the direction of the march to a 45 degree angle.

oblicuidad, *f.* obliquity. — **o. de la eclíptica,** (astron.) obliquity of the ecliptic.

oblicuo, cua. *a.* oblique, slanting.

obligación, *f.* 1. obligation; responsibility, duty; (*pl.*) obligations; family responsibilities. 2. (com.) obligation, liability; bond. 3. (law) obligation. — **constituirse en o. de** + *inf.,* to bind oneself to + *inf.;* **o. mancomunada,** concurrent obligation; **o. natural,** natural or moral obligation; **o. solidaria,** joint and several or solidary debt; **obligaciones de capital,** capital liabilities.

obligacionista, *m., f.* (com.) bondholder.

obligado, da, *past part. of* **obligar.** —*a.* 1. obliged, compelled. 2. obliged, indebted. —*m.* 1. city or town purveyor or supplier. 2. (law) obligor; debtor. 3. (mus.) obbligato.

obligante, *a.* obliging, obligating.

obligar, (*ref. 51*) *tr.v.* 1. to oblige, force, make, compel, obligate. 2. (law) to oblige, pledge as security. 3. to force, push (into). 4. to oblige, make indebted. — **o. a** + *inf.,* to oblige to + *inf.* —*r.v.* to bind oneself (to do something).

obligativo, va, *a.* obligatory.

obligatorio, ria, *a.* obligatory, compulsory.

obligue, obligué, *ref.* **obligar.**

obliteración, *f.* 1. obstruction; cancellation. 2. (med.) obliteration.

obliterado, da, *past part. of* **obliterar.** —*a.* 1. (med.) obliterated. 2. canceled (a postage stamp).

obliterador, ra, *a.* obliterating.

obliterar, *tr.v.* 1. (med.) to obliterate. 2. to erase, efface, obliterate. 3. to obliterate, cancel (a stamp).

oblongada, *a.* oblongated, e.g. *médula o.,* oblongated marrow.

oblongo, ga, *a.* oblong, longer than broad, elongated.

obnoxio, xia, *a.* obnoxious.

obnubilación, *f.* 1. cloudiness, obfuscation. 2. (med.) cloudiness of vision. — **o. mental** or **intelectual,** mental confusion or disorientation.

oboe, *m.* (mus.) oboe; oboist.

óbolo, *m.* 1. small gift or donation. 2. obolus (weight measure and coin in ancient Greece).

obovado, da, *a.* (bot.) obovate.

obovoide, *a.* (bot.) obovoid.

obra, *f.* 1. work; product. 2. work (book, painting); (mus.) work, opus; (*pl.*) works (books, paintings or music collectively of one man or school). 3. building, construction. 4. repairs, repair work. 5. work, action, act. 6. work, labor, workmanship, e.g. *esta pieza tiene mucha o.,* a lot of work went into this piece. 7. (metal.) hearth (of blast furnace). — **buena o.,** good work, act or deed; **es o.** or **ya es o.,** this is really tough work; **hacer mala o.,** to do a bad turn, do harm; **meter en o.,** to begin, set in motion, set to work; **o. accesoria** or **accidental,** (fort.) earthwork, bulkwark; **o. de arte,** work of art; **o. de caridad,** work of charity; **o. de consulta,** reference work; **o. de Dios,** act of God; **o. del diablo,** work of the devil; **o. de fábrica,** construction work; **o. de manos,** manual labor; **o. de misericordia,** act of mercy or charity; **o. de romanos,** titanic piece of work, titanic task; **o. exterior,** (fort.) outwork; **o. maestra,** masterpiece; **o. muerta,** (mar.) upperworks, freeboard; **o. pía,** charitable institution; good work, act of charity; **obras públicas,** public works; (mar.) quickwork (part of ship under waterline); **sentarse la o.,** to set and dry (concrete, cement); **tomar una o.,** to undertake a job.

obrada, *f.* 1. day's plowing or digging. 2. agricultural measurement (varying between 54 and 39 ares).

obrador, ra, *a.* working. —*m., f.* worker. —*m.* 1. workman. 2. workshop. —*f.* working woman.

obradura, *f.* quantity of olives pressed at each pressing.

obraje, *m.* 1. manufacturing. 2. workshop; wool mill.

obrajero, *m.* foreman, overseer, superintendent.

obrar, *tr.v.* 1. to work (e.g. wood, metal, etc.). 2. to construct, build. 3. to have an effect on. —*i.v.* 1. to act, proceed. 2. to be. 3. to evacuate the bowels.

obrepción, *f.* (law) obreption.

obrepticio, cia, *a.* (law) obreptitious.

obrería, *f.* 1. (ecc.) funds for church repairs; upkeep of church; churchwarden's office. 2. task of a workman.

obrerismo, *m.* 1. laborism, labor movement. 2. labor, workers.

obrerista, *a.* pertaining to or partial to labor.
obrero, ra, *a.* 1. working, laboring, e.g. *clase obrera,* working class. 2. (ento.) worker, e.g. *hormiga obrera,* worker ant. —*m., f.* (manual) worker; laborer. —*m.* 1. workman. 2. churchwarden. — **o. autónomo,** self-employed worker; **o. de villa,** mason; **o. especializado,** skilled worker. —*f.* 1. working woman. 2. (*pl.*) (ento.) workers.
obrita, *f. dim. of* **obra,** small or little work; booklet.
obrizo, *a.* pure, refined (gold).
obscenamente, *adv.* obscenely.
obscenidad, *f.* obscenity.
obsceno, na, *a.* obscene.
obscuración, *f.* darkness, obscurity.
obscuramente, *adv.* obscurely.
obscurantismo, *m.* obscurantism; opposition to the spreading of knowledge among the people.
obscurantista, *a., m., f.* obscurantist, opposed to progress.
obscurecer, (*ref. 45*) *tr.v.* 1. to darken; to cloud. 2. to obscure, cover up. 3. to tarnish. 4. to confuse, muddle. 5. to obscure, make obscure or difficult. 6. (p.) to shade, shadow. —*i.v.* to get dark, grow dark. —*r.v.* 1. to cloud over, get cloudy. 2. (coll.) to disappear (a person).
obscurecimiento, *m.* 1. darkening, clouding; obscuring. 2. (p.) shading.
obscurezca, *ref.* **obscurecer.**
obscuridad, *f.* 1. darkness; gloom; cloudiness. 2. obscurity (of origin, of social position). 3. obscurity (of a written passage, of language). 4. uncertainty, lack of clarity or information.
obscuro, ra, *a.* 1. dark; cloudy; gloomy. 2. dark (color). 3. obscure (origin, social position). 4. obscure, difficult (language, passage). 5. uncertain, dangerous. — **a obscuras,** in the dark. —*m.* (p.) shading, dark part (of picture); **estar o.,** to be dark, overcast or cloudy.
obsecración, *f.* obsecration, supplication.
obsecrar, *tr.v.* to implore, beseech, entreat.
obsecuente, *a.* submissive, obedient.
obseder, *tr.v.* to obsess.
obsequiador, ra, *a.* generous, hospitable. —*m., f.* entertainer; giver.
obsequiante, *a., m., f., var. of* **obsequiador.**
obsequiar, *tr.v.* 1. to entertain, regale, compliment. 2. to court, woo. 3. to give, present with.
obsequio, *m.* 1. obsequiousness. 2. gift, present. 3. courtesy, deference.
obsequiosamente, *adv.* obsequiously, courteously, obligingly.
obsequiosidad, *f.* courteousness, deference.
obsequioso, sa, *a.* obsequious, courteous, obliging, polite.
observable, *a.* observable, noticeable.
observación, *f.* observation. — **bajo o.,** under observation.
observador, ra, *a.* observant. —*m., f.* obserserver. — **o. de pájaros,** bird watcher; **o. meteorológico,** meteorologist, weather forecaster.
observancia, *f.* 1. observance; (ecc.) observance. 2. courtesy, deference, respectfulness. — **poner en o.,** to put into action, to enforce.
observante, *a.* observant. —*m., f.* (ecc.) observant, observantist.
observar, *tr.v.* 1. to observe, obey, heed. 2. to observe, watch. 3. to observe, notice, see. 4. to remark, observe, say.
observatorio, *m.* observatory.
obsesión, *f.* obsession.
obsesionar, *tr.v.* to obsess.
obsesivo, va, *a.* obsessive.
obseso, sa, *a.* obsessed.
obsidiana, *f.* (min.) obsidian.
obsidional, *a.* (mil.) pertaining to a citadel under siege.
obsolescencia, *f.* obsolescence.
obsolescente, *a.* obsolescent.
obsoleto, ta, *a.* obsolete; no longer in use, discarded.
obstaculice, obstaculicé, *ref.* **obstaculizar.**
obstaculizar, (*ref. 53*) *tr.v.* to hinder, hold up, obstruct, put obstacles in the way of.
obstáculo, *m.* obstacle, impediment, hindrance.
obstante, *a.* obstructing, hindering. — **no o.,** notwithstanding, nevertheless.
obstar, *i.v.* to stand in the way; to obstruct, hinder, impede.
obstetricia, *f.* (med.) obstetrics.
obstinación, *f.* obstinacy, stubbornness.
obstinadamente, *adv.* obstinately, stubbornly.
obstinado, da, *past part. of* **obstinarse.** —*a.* obstinate, stubborn, obdurate, headstrong.
obstinarse, *r.v.* to persist; to be obstinate or stubborn.
obstrucción, *f.* obstruction, stoppage.
obstruccionismo, *m.* obstructionism, filibustering.
obstruccionista, *a.* obstructionist. —*m., f.* obstructionist, filibusterer.
obstructivo, va, *a.* obstructive.
obstructor, ra, *a.* obstructive, obstructing. —*m., f.* obstructor.
obstruir, (*ref. 48*) *tr.v.* to obstruct; to block, stop; to block or stop up. —*r.v.* to get blocked or stopped up.
obstruya, obstruyendo, obstruyera, obstruyese, obstruyo, *ref.* **obstruir.**
obtemperar, *tr.v.* to obey.
obtención, *f.* obtaining, obtainment, obtention.
obtener, (*ref. 23*) *tr.v.* 1. to obtain, get. 2. to have, keep.
obtenga, obtengo, *ref.* **obtener.**
obtenible, *a.* obtainable.
obtento, *m.* (ecc.) benefice, prebend.
obtentor, *m.* (ecc.) person who obtains a prebend.
obtestación, *f.* (rhet.) obtestation, supplication (to God or audience), protestation.
obturación, *f.* obturation, plugging, stopping up.
obturador, triz, *a.* plugging, stopping, obturating; (anat.) obturator. —*m.* 1. plug, stopper, obturator. 2. (auto.) choke, throttle. 3. (photog.) shutter, obturator. 4. (artil.) obturator. 5. (anat., bot.) obturator. 6. (surg.) obturator. — **o. de guillotina,** (photog.) drop shutter; **o. de plano focal,** (photog.) focal plane shutter.
obturar, *tr.v.* to obturate, close; to plug, stop up; (dent.) to stop (a tooth); (auto.) to throttle.
obtusángulo, *a.* (geom.) obtuse-angled.
obtuso, sa, *a.* obtuse, blunt; (geom.) obtuse; (fig.) obtuse, dull, dim witted.
obtuve, obtuviera, obtuviese, *ref.* **obtener.**
obué, *m.* (mus.) oboe.
obús, *m.* (mil.) howitzer, mortar.
obusera, *a.* ship carrying a howitzer.
obvención, *f.* perquisite, privilege or benefit obtained from a position or status.
obviar, *tr.v.* to clear away, remove, obviate.
obvio, via, *a.* obvious, evident.
obvoluto, ta, *a.* (bot.) obvolute.
obyecto, *m.* objection, reply.
oc, lengua de o., langue d'oc, ancient French dialect.
oca, *f.* 1. (ornith.) goose. 2. goose (game). 3. (bot.) oca.
ocal, *a.* 1. delicious, tasty (fruit). 2. delicately colored (roses). 3. double (cocoon). —*m.* dupion, double cocoon. —*f.* doupion, dupion (silk made from double cocoons).
ocalmar, *i.v.* to make dupions or double cocoons (silk worms).
ocarina, *f.* (mus.) ocarina.
ocasión, *f.* 1. occasion, opportunity, chance. 2. occasion, time. 3. occasion, reason, cause. 4. chance, accident. 5. danger, risk. 6. bargain. — **asir, coger** or **tomar la o. por los cabellos,** to seize an opportunity in both hands; **compra de o.,** bargain; **de o.,** second hand; reduced, at a bargain price; **en la primera o.,** at the first opportunity; **por o.,** by chance.
ocasionado, da, *past part. of* **ocasionar.** —*a.* 1. dangerous, hazardous. 2. annoying, provoking, irritating.
ocasionador, ra, *a.* causal, causative. —*m., f.* causer.
ocasional, *a.* occasional, incidental, by chance.
ocasionalismo, *m.* (philos.) occasionalism.
ocasionalista, *a.* (philos.) pertaining to the philosophy of occasionalism.
ocasionalmente, *adv.* occasionally, from time to time, by chance.
ocasionar, *tr.v.* 1. to occasion, cause. 2. to stir up, provoke. 3. to endanger, jeopardize.
ocaso, *m.* 1. sunset; setting (of star). 2. west. 3. (fig.) decline, fall, end.
occidental, *a.* 1. western, occidental. 2. (astron.) occidental.
occidentalizar, (*ref. 53*) *tr.v.* to occidentalize, westernize.
occidente, *m.* 1. west, occident (cardinal point). 2. O., West. — **la Decadencia de O.,** the Decline of the West.
occiduo, dua, *a.* occidental, western; pertaining to the setting of the sun, etc.
occipital, *a.* occipital. —*m.* (anat.) occipital, occipital bone.
occipucio, *m.* (anat.) occiput.
occisión, *f.* violent death, murder.
occiso, sa, *a.* dead, killed. —*m., f.* the deceased.
Oceanía, *f.* Oceania, Australian continent.
oceánico, ca, *a.* oceanic.
Oceánidas, *f.* (myth.) Oceanid, (*pl.*) Oceanides.
océano, *m.* ocean; (myth.) **O.,** Oceanus; **O. Atlántico,** Atlantic Ocean; **O. glacial Antártico,** Antartic Ocean; **O. glacial Ártico,** Arctic Ocean; **O. Índico,** Indian Ocean; **O. Pacífico,** Pacific Ocean.
oceanografía, *f.* oceanography.
oceanográfico, ca, *a.* oceanographic.
oceanógrafo, fa, *m., f.* oceanographer.
oceanología, *f.* oceanology.
oceanólogo, ga, *m., f.* oceanologist.
ocelado, da, *a.* (ento.) ocellated, ocellate.
ocelar, *a.* (zool.) ocellar.
ocelo, *m.* (ento.) ocellus, (*pl.*) ocelli.
ocelote, *m.* (zool.) ocelot.
ocena, *f.* (med.) ozena.
ochava, *f.* 1. eighth. 2. (ecc.) octave.
ochavado, da, *past part. of* **ochavar.** —*a.* octagonal, eight-sided.
ochavar, *tr.v.* to make octagonal, make eight-sided.
ochavario, *m., var. of* **octavario.**
ochavo, *m.* 1. (numis.) ochavo, brass coin. 2. octagon, octagonal building.
ochavón, na, *a.* (Cuba) octoroon; mestizo.
ochenta, *a., m.* eighty.
ochentavo, va, *a., m. f.* eightieth.
ochenteno, na, *a.* eightieth.
ochentón, na, *a., m., f.* (coll.) octogenarian.
ocho, *a.* eight. —*m.* eight; eighth (in dates). — **te veo a las o.,** I'll see you at eight.
ochocientos, tas, *a., m. f.* eight hundred.
ociar, *i.v., r.v.* to idle, loaf around.
ocio, *m.* 1. idleness, inactivity, inaction. 2. leisure, spare time. 3. pastime, diversion; (*pl.*) pastime pursuit; hobby. — **ratos de o.,** spare time, leisure time.

ociosamente, *adv.* 1. idly. 2. pointlessly, uselessly; needlessly.
ociosidad, *f.* idleness, laziness; dolce far niente (Ital.).
ocioso, sa, *a.* 1. idle, lazy. 2. idle, pointless, useless (question). —*m., f.* idler, loafer.
oclocracia, *f.* (polit.) ochlocracy, mob rule.
oclocrático, ca, *a.* (polit.) ochlocratic, ochlocratical.
oclofobia, *f.* (med.) oclophobia.
ocluir, (*ref.* 48) *tr.v.* to occlude. —*r.v.* to be or become occluded.
oclusal, *a.* (anat., dent.) occlusal.
oclusión, *f.* occlusion; stop; **o. glótica,** (phonet.) glottal stop.
oclusivo, va, *a.* occlusive. —*f.* (phonet.) occlusive.
ocluya, ocluyendo, ocluyera, ocluyese, *ref.* **ocluir.**
ocosial, *m.* (Peru) boggy lowland, morass.
ocotal, *m.* (Mex.) ocote grove or plantation.
ocote, *m.* (Mex.) ocote, torch pine.
ocotillo, *m.* (bot.) ocotillo.
ocozoal, *m.* (Mex.) rattlesnake.
ocozol, *m.* (bot.) sweet gum, laquidambar tree.
ocre, *m.* (min.) ocher; **o. calcinado, quemado** or **tostado,** burnt ocher; **o. rojo,** red ocher.
ocrea, *f.* (bot.) ocrea.
ocreado, da, *a.* (bot.) ocreate.
oct. *abbrev. of* **octubre,** October (Oct.).
octacordio, *m.* (mus.) octachord.
octaédrico, ca, *a.* (geom.) octahedral.
octaedrita, *f.* (min.) octahedrite.
octaedro, *m.* (geom.) octahedron.
octagonal, *a.* octagonal.
octágono, na, *a.* octagonal. —*m.* octagon.
octanaje, *m.* (chem.) octane number or rating. — **de alto o.,** high-octane.
octandro, a, *a.* (bot.) octandrious.
octano, *m.* (chem.) octane. — **gasolina de** noventa **octanos,** ninety octane gasoline; **índice** or **número de o.,** octane rating or number.
octanol, *m.* (chem.) octanol.
octante, *m.* 1. (astron., geom.) octant. 2. (astron.) **O.,** Octans, Octant.
octario, *m.* (med.) octarius.
octava, *f.* 1. (ecc.) octave (eight days following a church festival, eighth day of this period). 2. (mus.) octave; (poet.) eight-line stanza.
octavar, *i.v.* 1. to deduct the eighth part. 2. (mus.) to play in octaves.
octavario, *m.* 1. period of eight days. 2. (ecc.) festival celebrated in an octave.
octaviano, na, *a.* (hist.) Octavian, Augustan. —*m.* **O.,** Octavian.
octavilla, *f.* 1. leaflet. 2. (poet.) octet.
octavín, *m.* (mus.) piccolo (flute).
octavo, va, *a., m.* eighth; **en octavo,** (print.) octavo.
octeto, *m.* (mus.) octet.
octingentésimo, ma, *a., m., f.* eight hundredth.
octogenario, ria, *a., m., f.* octogenarian.
octogésimo, ma, *a., m., f.* eightieth.
octogonal, *a.* octagonal.
octógono, na, *a.* (geom.) octagonal. —*m.* octagon.
octonario, *m.* octonary, a group of eight, a stanza of eight lines.
octopétalo, la, *a.* (bot.) octopetalous.
octoploide, *a.* (physiol.) octoploid.
octópodo, da, *a.* (zool.) octopod, octopodan. —*m.* (zool.) octopod, octopodan; (*pl.*) Octopoda.
octosilábico, ca, *a.* octosyllabic.
octosílabo, ba, *a.* octosyllabic. —*m.* octosyllable (octosyllabic line).
octóstilo, la, *a.* (archit.) octastyle, octostyle.
octubre, *m.* October.

óctuple, *a.* octuple, eightfold.
óctuplo, pla, *a., var. of* **óctuple.**
ocuje, *m.* (Cuba, bot.) Santa Maria tree.
ocular, *a.* ocular, pertaining to the eye. — **testigo o.,** eyewitness. —*m.* eyepiece, ocular.
ocularmente, *adv.* ocularly, visually.
oculista, *m., f.* oculist, eye doctor.
oculomotor, ra, *a., m.* (physiol.) oculomotor.
ocultación, *f.* (astron.) occultation.
ocultador, ra, *a.* hiding. —*m., f.* hider, concealer.
ocultamente, *adv.* hidden from view, stealthily, secretly, surreptitiously, e.g. *avanzó o. hacia la fortaleza,* he advanced hidden from view towards the fortress.
ocultar, *tr.v.* to hide, conceal; **o. alguna** cosa a or **de alguien,** to hide something from someone. —*r.v.* to hide; to be hidden.
ocultismo, *m.* occultism.
ocultista, *a., m., f.* occultist.
oculto, ta, *a.* hidden, concealed; occult. — **de oculto,** incognito; stealthily, hidden from view; **en oculto,** secretly.
ocumo, *m.* (Ven., bot.) taro.
ocupación, *f.* 1. occupation; possession, occupancy. 2. occupation, employment, job. 3. (rhet.) prolepsis.
ocupado, da, *past part. of* **ocupar.** —*a.* 1. busy, occupied, engaged. 2. (coll.) pregnant. 3. (tel.) busy (Am.); engaged (G.B.).
ocupador, ra, *a.* occupying. —*m., f.* occupier, occupant.
ocupante, *a.* occupying. —*m., f.* occupant.
ocupar, *tr.v.* 1. to occupy; to take possession of. 2. to occupy (post, position). 3. to occupy, fill (space). 4. to occupy, live in, inhabit. 5. to occupy, keep busy; to give work or employment to. 6. to bother, annoy. —*r.v.* to occupy, busy or employ oneself; to be busy, occupied or engaged. — **ocuparse de,** to attend to, be in charge of; to concern oneself, bother or worry about; **ocuparse de, en or con,** to occupy, busy or employ oneself in or with; to be busy, occupied or engaged in.
ocurrencia, *f.* 1. occurrence, incident. 2. witticism, witty remark. — **¡qué ocurrencia!** what a crazy idea!
ocurrente, *a.* 1. occurring. 2. witty, bright, amusing; full of ideas, imaginative, humorous.
ocurrir, *i.v.* 1. to occur, happen. 2. to coincide (festivals). —*r.v.* to occur, come (to mind).
ocurso, *m.* (Mex.) petition, claim, appeal.
oda, *f.* (poet.) ode.
odalisca, *f.* odalisque, slave or concubine (in a harem).
ODECA *abbrev. of* **Organización de los Estados Centroamericanos,** Organization of Central American States (OCAS).
odeón, *m.* odeum, concert hall.
odiar, *tr.v.* to hate, to loath.
odio, *m.* hate, hatred, odium.
odiosamente, *adv.* odiously, hatefully.
odiosidad, *f.* hatefulness, odiousness; hatred, hate.
odioso, sa, *a.* hateful, odious.
odisea, *f.* 1. **O.,** (myth.) Odyssey. 2. (fig.) odyssey, adventure.
odógrafo, fa, *m., f.* odograph, a device for measuring the distance traveled on a road.
odómetro, *m.* odometer, taximeter; cyclometer.
odonato, *m.* (ento.) odonate.
odontalgia, *f.* (dent.) odontalgia, toothache.
odontálgico, ca, *a.* (dent.) odontalgical.
odontoblasto, *m.* (anat.) odontoblast.
odontogloso, *m.* (bot.) odontoglossum.
odontógrafo, *m.* (med.) odontograph.
odontoideo, a, *a.* (anat., zool.) odontoid.

odontología, *f.* (med.) odontology, dentistry.
odontológico, ca, *a.* (med.) odontological.
odontólogo, *m.* (med.) odontologist.
odorante, *a.* odorous, fragant.
odorífero, *a.* odoriferous, fragant.
odorífico, ca, *a., var. of* **odorífero.**
odre, *m.* 1. wineskin. 2. (coll.) drunkard.
odrería, *f.* wineskin shop.
odrezuelo, *m. dim. of* **odre,** small wineskin.
odrina, *f.* oxskin wine boot.
OEA *abbrev. of* **Organización de Estados Americanos,** Organization of American States (OAS).
OECA *abbrev. of* **Organización de los Estados Centroamericanos,** Organization of Central American States (OCAS).
OECE *abbrev. of* **Organización Europea de Cooperación Económica,** European Economic Cooperation Organization (EECO).
oersted, *m.* (elec.) oersted.
oerstedio, *m.* (elec.) oersted.
oesnoroeste, *m.* west-northwest; west-northwest wind.
oessudoeste, *m.* west-southwest; west-southwest wind.
oeste, *m.* west; west wind. — **o. cuarta al noroeste,** west by northwest; **o. cuarta al suroeste,** west by southwest.
ofendedor, ra, *a.* offending. —*m., f.* offender.
ofender, *tr.v.* 1. to **offend, give offense to. 2.** to insult, hurt. —*i.v.* to be unpleasant or disagreeable. —*r.v.* to take offense.
ofendido, da, *past part. of* **ofender.**
ofensa, *f.* 1. offense, affront, insult. 2. offense, crime.
ofensión, *f.* 1. insult, hurt. 2. annoyance, bother, grievance.
ofensiva, *f.* offensive. **montar una o.,** to mount an offensive; **tomar la o.,** to take the offensive.
ofensivamente, *adv.* offensively.
ofensivo, va, *a.* offensive.
ofensor, ra, *a.* offending. —*m., f.* offender.
oferente, *a.* offering. —*m., f.* offerer.
oferta, *f.* offer. — **o. firme,** positive **offer; o pública hostil,** hostile takeover bid; **ofertas de trabajo,** (señal) job vacancies, help wanted; **o. y demanda,** supply and demand.
ofertar, *tr.v.* (Arg., Mex., imp. u.) to offer.
ofertorio, *m.* (ecc.) offertory.
off, *adv.* (Amer., theat., rad., t.v., cine.) **hablar en o.,** to speak offstage or off mike in order to convey the idea of distance.
offset, *m.* (print.) offset.
oficial, *a.* official. —*m.* 1. official, officer, functionary. 2. (mil., mar.) officer. 3. clerk, office worker. 4. skilled workman, artisan. 5. butcher. 6. executioner. - **o. de aduanas,** customs officer; - **o. de artillería,** (mar.) gunnery officer; **o. de guardia,** officer of the watch; **o. de la reserva,** (mil.) reserve officer; **o. del día** or **de servicio,** (mil.) **officer** of the day; **o. de transmisiones,** (mil.) signals officer; **o. general,** general officer; **o. subalterno,** junior officer; **o. superior,** senior officer; **segundo o.,** (mar.) first mate; **ser buen o.,** to be clever and able.
oficiala, *f.* 1. skilled **working woman or** craftswoman. 2. female clerk or office worker.
oficialía, *f.* 1. clerkship in a public office, status of clerk. 2. status of craftsman.
oficialidad, *f.* officers, body of officers.
oficialismo, *m.* (Amer.) the party in power in the government.
oficialista, *m.* (Arg.) an ardent follower of the government's policies.
oficialmente, *adv.* **officially.**
oficiante, *a.* officiating. —*m.* (ecc.) officiating priest.

oficiar, *tr.v.* 1. to communicate officially or in writing. 2. (ecc.) to officiate, celebrate (mass, etc.). —*i.v.* (ecc.) to officiate. — **o. de,** to act as.
oficina, *f.* 1. office; workshop; laboratory. 2. (*pl.*) offices (parts of a house devoted to household work). — **o. de cambio,** currency exchange; **o. de empleo,** employment office; **o. de objetos perdidos,** lost and found office; **o. pública,** government office; **o. de turísmo,** tourist office.
oficinal, *a.* (pharm., med.) officinal.
oficinesco, ca, *a.* departmental, clerical, pertaining to an office.
oficinismo, *m.* office routine, bureaucracy, red tape.
oficinista, *m.* clerk, office worker.
oficio, *m.* 1. occupation, job, work. 2. craft, trade. 3. office, post, position. 4. function, work, job. 5. written communication. 6. king's room (in a palace). 7. office (where people work). 8. (ecc.) office, service. — **buenos oficios,** good offices (mediation); **no tener o. ni beneficio,** to be an idler, be a layabout; **haber aprendido buen o.,** to have a cushy, well-paying job; **tomar por o. una cosa,** to take something up, dedicate oneself to something; **o. público,** public office; **o. servil,** mechanical or manual labor or craft; **Santo O.,** Holy Office, Inquisition; **zapatero de o.,** shoemaker by trade.
oficionario, *m.* (ecc.) book containing canonical offices.
oficiosamente, *adv.* 1. officiously. 2. diligently, assiduously. 3. obligingly, helpfully.
oficiosidad, *f.* 1. diligence, assiduousness. 2. officiousness, meddlesomeness.
oficioso, sa, *a.* 1. diligent, assiduous, hardworking. 2. meddlesome, interfering, officious. 3. semi-official (newspaper).
oficleide, *m.* (mus.) ophicleide.
oficleido, *m.* (mus.) ophicleide.
ofidio, dia, *a., m., f.* (zool.) ophidian; (*pl.*) Ophidia.
ofiolatría, *f.* ophiolatry, worship of snakes.
ofiolátrico, ca, *a.* ophiolatrous.
ofiología, *f.* ophiology, branch of zoology dealing with snakes.
ofiológico, ca, *a.* ophiological, dealing with snakes.
ofita, *f.* (min.) ophite.
ofítico, ca, *a.* (min.) ophitic.
Ofiuco, *m.* (astron.) Ophiuchus, Serpentarius.
ofrecedor, ra, *a.* offering. —*m., f.* offerer.
ofrecer, (*ref. 45*) *tr.v.* to offer. — **o.** + *inf.*, to offer to + *inf.* — *r.v.* 1. to offer oneself, volunteer. 2. to offer itself, present itself (e.g. an opportunity). — **ofrecerse a** + *inf.*, to offer or volunteer to + *inf.*
ofreciente, *a.* offering. —*m., f.* offerer.
ofrecimiento, *m.* offer, offering.
ofrenda, *f.* offering; gift; **o. floral,** wreath.
ofrendar, *tr.v.* to make an offering of; to make a gift of.
ofrezca, ofrezco, *ref.* **ofrecer.**
oftalmía, *f.* (med.) ophthalmia.
oftálmico, ca, *a.* (med.) ophthalmic.
oftalmitis, *f.* (med.) ophthalmitis.
oftalmología, *f.* ophthalmology, branch of medicine dealing with the structure, functions, and diseases of the eye.
oftalmológico, ca, *a.* ophthalmological.
oftalmólogo, *m.* ophthalmologist, oculist.
oftalmoscopia, *f.* ophthalmoscopy.
oftalmoscópico, ca, *a.* ophthalmoscopic, ophthalmoscopical.
oftalmoscopio, *m.* ophthalmoscope, instrument used to examine the eye.
ofuscación, *f., var. of* **ofuscamiento.**
ofuscador, ra, *a.* 1. dazzling, blinding. 2. confusing, bewildering. —*m., f.* confuser, bewilderer.
ofuscamiento, *m.* 1. blinding, dazzling, obfuscation. 2. confusion, bewilderment.
ofuscar, (*ref. 50*) *tr.v.* 1. to dazzle, blind, obfuscate. 2. to confuse, bewilder. 3. to obscure. —*r.v.* 1. to be dazzled or blinded. 2. to be confused; to lose control of oneself.
ofusque, ofusqué, *ref.* **ofuscar.**
ogaño, *adv., var. of* **hogaño,** in these days, currently.
ogro, *m.* 1. ogre, monster. 2. (fig.) a tyrant.
¡oh! *interj.* oh! (expression of wonder).
ohm, *m.* (phys.) ohm.
óhmico, ca, *a.* (phys.) ohmic.
ohmímetro, ohmiómetro, óhmetro, *m.* ohmmeter.
ohmio, *m.* (phys.) ohm.
ohmiómetro, *m.* (elec.) ohmmeter.
oíble, *a.* audible, able to be heard.
oída, *f.* hearing; **de** or **por oídas,** by hearsay.
oídio, *m.* (bot.) oidium, powdery mildew.
oído, *m.* 1. (anat.) ear; inner ear. 2. hearing, sense of hearing, e.g. *los perros tienen el o. muy fino,* dogs have a very acute sense of hearing. 3. (mus.) ear, ear for music, musical sense, e.g. *Juan tiene buen o.,* John has a good ear for music. 4. priming hole, vent (of a gun). — **abrir los oídos,** to listen attentively; **aguzar los oídos,** to prick up one's ears; **al alcance del o.,** within earshot; **al o.,** by listening; into one's ear, e.g. *me dijo al o.,* he whispered into my ear; confidentially; **aplicar el o. a,** to put one's ear to; to pay attention to; **caer en oídos sordos,** to fall on deaf ears; **cerrarle a uno los oídos,** to bamboozle someone, pull the wool over one's eyes (stop him from hearing the truth); **cerrar los oídos a,** to turn a deaf ear to; **dar oídos a,** to listen favorably to, believe; **de o.,** by ear; **entrar por un o. y salir por el otro,** to go in one ear and out the other; **falto de o. musical,** tone-deaf; **llegar a oídos de uno,** to come to one's ears, **negar los oídos,** to refuse to listen; **o. absoluto,** (mus.) absolute pitch; **o. externo,** (anat.) outer ear; **o. interno,** (anat.) inner ear; **prestar oídos,** to lend an ear; **regalar a uno el o.,** (coll.) to flatter someone; **ser todo oídos,** to be all ears; **silbido** or **zumbido de los oídos,** ringing or buzzing in the ears; **taparse los oídos,** to stop up one's ears.
oidor, ra, *a.* hearing, listening. —*m., f.* hearer. —*m.* (arch.) judge.
oidoría, *f.* (arch.) judgeship.
oiga, oigo, *ref.* **oír.**
oír, (*ref. 12*) *tr.v.* 1. to hear. 2. to listen, pay attention to. 3. to understand. 4. to attend (lectures). — **¡ahora lo oigo!** that's the first I've heard about it; **como quien oye llover,** (coll.) without the least interest; **!oiga! ¡oigan!** listen! look here!; **o.** + *inf.*, to hear + *inf.* or *ger.*, e.g. *le oí decir que iba al cine,* I heard him say that he was going to the cinema; **o. bien,** to hear with pleasure; **o. misa,** to attend mass; **o., ver y callar,** mind your own business; **oye,** see; **oiga; oiga bien,** listen closely.
OIT *abbrev. of* **Organización Internacional del Trabajo,** International Labor Organization (I L O).
ojal, *m.* 1. buttonhole; hole. 2. eyelet. 3. loop (in a rope or halyard).
ojalá, *interj.* I hope so; let's hope so; God willing (affirmative or negative according to context). — **o. que** + *subj.*, I hope that, let's hope that, God grant that.
ojaladera, *f.* buttonhole-maker.
ojalado, da, *a.* (vet.) having dark colored hair around the eyes.
ojalador, ra, *m., f.* buttonhole-maker. —*m.* buttonhole machine.
ojaladura, *f.* set of buttonholes.
ojalar, *tr.v.* to put buttonholes in.
ojalatero, *m.* armchair partisan or supporter; stay-at-home military strategist.
ojalete, *m.* (sew.) eyelet.
ojaranzo, *m.* (bot.) witch hazel.
ojeada, *f.* glance, glimpse, quick look.
ojeador, *m.* beater (in game-hunting).
ojear, *tr.v.* 1. to stare at, eye, ogle. 2. to put the evil eye on. 3. (hunt.) to beat bushes (in order to startle the game). 4. (hunt.) to frighten or startle (game).
ojén, *m.* beverage made with anisette, ice and sugar.
ojeo, *m.* 1. perusal, look-over. 2. (hunt.) beating for game. — **echar un o.,** (hunt.) to go beating for game.
ojera, *f.* 1. dark circle under the eye, (*pl.*) circles under the eyes. 2. eyeglass, eyecup.
ojeriza, *f.* animosity, grudge, ill-will. — **tener o. a,** to have a grudge against.
ojeroso, sa, *a.* with dark circles under the eyes; (fig.) dissipated.
ojerudo, da, *a.* with dark circles under the eyes.
ojete, *m.* 1. eyelet, eyehole, drawstring hole. 2. (coll.) hole (vulg.), anus.
ojetear, *tr.v.* to make eyelets in, make drawstring openings in.
ojetera, *f.* line of eyelets (in a corset, garment, etc.).
ojialegre, *a.* (coll.) bright-eyed; having sparkling or twinkling eyes.
ojienjuto, ta, *a.* dry-eyed, tearless.
ojigarzo, za, *a.* (coll.) blue-eyed.
ojimel, *m.* (pharm.) oxymel.
ojimiel, *m.* (pharm.) oxymel.
ojimoreno, na, *a.* (coll.) brown-eyed.
ojinegro, gra, *a.* (coll.) dark-eyed.
ojiprieto, ta, *a., var. of* **ojinegro.**
ojituerto, ta, *a.* cross-eyed.
ojiva, *f.* 1. (archit.) ogive, pointed arch. 2. (astronaut.) nose cone (of a space vehicle or capsule).
ojival, *a.* (archit.) ogival.
ojizaino, na, *a.* squint-eyed, cross-eyed.
ojizarco, ca, *a.* (coll.) blue-eyed.
ojo, *m.* 1. (anat.) eye. 2. eye of needle; hole in hammer, hoe or ax to receive shaft. 3. hole, opening. 4. bow (of key); (*pl.*) bows (of scissors). 5. keyhole. 6. spring, eye (of water). 7. spot of fat (floating on liquid). 8. eye in peacock's tail. 9. span, arch (of bridge). 10. lathering, scrubbing. 11. N.B. (nota bene). 12. care, attention. 13. eye, hole (in bread, cheese or other spongy material). 14. eye, loop (in net). 15. (print.) width (of type). 16. (print.) face (of type). 17. (bot.) eye (center of flower). 18. well (of stair). — **abrir el o.,** to keep one's eyes open, keep alert; **abrir los ojos a uno,** to open someone else's eyes (to truth); **a cierra ojos,** blindly, rashly, recklessly, precipitately; **alegrársele a uno los ojos,** to sparkle with joy (one's eyes); **al o.,** roughly, by a rough estimate; nearby, closeby, at a short distance; **andar con cien ojos,** to be on the alert or watch-out; **a o. de cubero,** roughly, by a rough estimate or guess; **a ojos cerrados, a ojos vistas,** clearly, patently, obviously; **bailarle a uno los ojos,** to have dancing eyes, be merry; **cerrar el o.,** to die, kick the bucket (sl.); **cerrar los ojos,** to rest, sleep, doze; to die; to obey blindly; **clavar los ojos en,** to fix one's eyes on, stare at; **comerse con los ojos a una persona,** to devour someone with one's gaze; **costar un o. de la cara,** to cost a fortune;

con mucho o., very carefully; **cuatro ojos,** glasses, person wearing glasses; **dar en los ojos (una cosa),** to be self evident, be obvious at first sight; **delante de los ojos de uno,** before one's very eyes; **desencapotar los ojos,** to stop frowning and look pleased; **dichosos los ojos que te ven,** what a pleasure to see you after so long; **dormir con los ojos abiertos,** to sleep with one's eyes open, keep on the alert; **echar el o. a una cosa,** to set one's eye on something (longingly); **entrar a ojos cerrados,** to plunge blindly into; **en un abrir y cerrar de ojos,** in the twinkling of an eye, in a wink; **hablar con los ojos,** to speak with the eyes; **hacerle ojos a uno,** to make eyes at; **hasta los ojos,** (to be in something) up to the eyes; **írsele a uno los ojos por,** to long or yearn for; **más ven cuatro ojos que dos,** two heads are better than one; **mirar con buenos** or **malos ojos a,** to look on with approval or disapproval, approve or disapprove of; **mirar a uno con otros ojos,** to see someone in a different light, see someone with different eyes; **¡mucho ojo!** take care! beware! careful!; **no decir a uno "buenos ojos tienes",** to ignore someone, take no notice of; **no pegar el o.** or **los ojos,** not to sleep a wink all night; **no quitar los ojos de,** not to take one's eyes off, keep one's eyes on; **no tener donde volver los ojos,** to be completely destitute; **¡o.!** watch out!; **o. avizor,** eagle eye, sharp eye; on the lookout, alert; **o. clínico** or **médico,** clinical eye, practiced diagnostician's eye; **o. compuesto,** (zool.) compound eye; **o. de buey,** (bot.) oxeye; (archit.) bull's eye; (mar.) porthole; **o. de gato,** (min.) cat's eye; **o. de la escalera,** stairwell; **o. de la tempestad,** eye of the storm; **o. eléctrico,** electric eye; **o. de pez,** fish-eye lens; **o. de pollo** or **gallo,** corn (on the toe); **o. mágico,** peephole; **o. morado,** black eye; **o. por o. y diente por diente,** an eye for an eye and a tooth for a tooth; **ojos que no ven, corazón que no siente,** out of sight, out of mind; **ojos que te vieron ir,** that's the last I'll see of you; **ojos rasgados,** slant eyes; **ojos reventones** or **saltones,** bulging or pop eyes; **ojos vivos,** sparkling eyes; **pasar los ojos por,** to glance over; **permanecer o. avizor,** to keep one's eyes open; **poner los ojos en blanco,** to roll one's eyes; **por sus lindos ojos,** for nothing, gratis; **arrasársele a uno los ojos de** or **en lágrimas,** to be filled with tears (one's eyes); **saltar a los ojos,** to catch the eye, attract attention; **tener entre ojos** or **sobre o. a uno,** to loathe someone; **vendarse los ojos,** to close one's eyes to reason; **vidriarse los ojos,** to become glazed or glassy (one's eyes); **volver los ojos,** to squint; **eres la niña de mis ojos,** you're the apple of my eye.

ojoche, *m.* (bot., C. Rica) breadnut tree (Brosimum alicastrum).

ojón, na, *a.* (Amer.) big-eyed.

ojoso, sa, *a.* full of holes or eyes, holey (e.g. bread or cheese).

ojota, *f.* (Amer.) Indian sandal.

ojuelos, *m.* (*pl.*) 1. sparkling or laughing eyes. 2. glasses, spectacles.

okapí, *m.* (zool.) okapi.

ola, *f.* 1. wave. 2. crowd, wave (of people). — **o. de asalto,** (mil.) assault wave; **o. de calor,** heat wave; **o. de crímenes,** crime wave; **o. de frío,** cold spell. —*interj.,* hello, greetings (gen. spelled **hola**).

olaje, *m., var. of* **oleaje.**

¡olé! *interj.* bravo! —*m.* **el o.,** an old Andalusian dance.

oleáceo, cea, *a.* (bot.) oleaceous. —*f.* (*pl.*) Oleaceae.

oleada, *f.* 1. big wave. 2. beating of waves. 3. wave, surge (of people). —*f.* large crop of olive oil.

oleaginosidad, *f.* oiliness, oleaginousness.

oleaginoso, sa, *a.* oily, oleaginous.

oleaje, *m.* surf, breaking waves. motion of the waves.

oleandro, *m.* (bot.) oleander.

olear, *tr.v.* to administer extreme unction to.

olear, *i.v.* to surge, swell (the sea).

oleario, ria, *a.* oily, oleaginous.

oleastro, *m.* (bot.) wild olive tree.

oleato, *m.* (chem.) oleato.

olécranon, *m.* (anat.) olecranon.

oledero, ra, *a.* odorous, fragrant.

oledor, ra, *a.* smelling. —*m., f.* smeller.

olefina, *f.* (chem.) olefin.

oleico, ca, *a.* (chem.) oleic.

oleícola, *a.* pertaining to olive-growing.

oleicultura, *f.* olive growing.

oleífero, ra, *a.* oleiferous, oil-producing (plants).

oleína, *f.* (chem.) olein.

óleo, *m.* oil; holy oil; oil painting. — **al ó.,** in oils (portrait, etc.); **andar** or **estar al ó.,** (coll.) to be well adorned or groomed; **cuadro** or **pintura al ó.,** oil painting; **santos óleos,** (ecc.) extreme unction, holy oils.

oleoducto, *m.* oil pipeline.

oleografía, *f.* (p.) oleograph; oleography.

oleomargarina, *f.* oleomargarine.

oleómetro, *m.* oleometer, instrument for testing the density of oil.

oleorresina, *m.* oleoresin.

oleosidad, *f.* oiliness.

oleoso, sa, *a.* oily.

oler, (*ref. 37*) *tr.v.* 1. to smell. 2. to scent, guess, perceive. 3. to smell out, inquire into. —*i.v.* 1. to smell. 2. to smack (of), look (like), appear, have the look or appearance of. — **no o. bien,** to be fishy, look suspicious; **o. a,** to smell of or like; to smack of, look like, appear to be; **o. donde guisan,** to keep on the lookout for good opportunities; **o. a rosa,** to smell like a rose; **o. a gloria,** to smell delicious (food).

olfacción, *f.* olfaction, act of smelling.

olfatear, *tr.v.* to smell, sniff, scent; (coll.) to get wind of (a good deal, etc.).

olfateo, *m.* sniffing, smelling; (coll.) snooping.

olfativo, va, *a.* olfactory.

olfato, *m.* 1. smell, sense of smell, e.g. *el sentido del o.,* the sense of smell. 2. (coll.) nose, intuition, e.g. *él tiene muy buen o. para los negocios,* he has a very good nose for business.

olfatorio, ria, *a.* olfactory.

olíbano, *m.* olibanum, frankincense.

oliente, *a.* smelling; odorous.

oliera, *f.* (ecc.) chrismal (vessel holding holy oil).

oligarca, *m.* oligarch.

oligarquía, *f.* oligarchy, a form of government in which the ruling power belongs to a privileged few.

oligárquico, ca, *a.* oligarchical.

oligisto, *m.* (min.) oligist. — **o. rojo,** hematite.

oligoceno, *a., m.* (geol.) Oligocene.

oligocitemia, *f.* (med.) oligocythemia.

oligoclasa, *f.* (min.) oligoclase.

oligofrenia, *f.* (med.) oligophrenia.

oligopolio, *m.* oligopoly, control of a commodity or service in a given market by a small number of companies or suppliers.

oliguria, *f.* (med.) oliguresis.

olimpíada, *f.* Olympiad, Olympic games.

olímpico, ca, *a.* 1. Olympic; Olympian. 2. arrogant, haughty.

Olimpo, *m.* (myth., geog.) Mount Olympus, highest peak in Greece; home of the gods.

olio, *m.* oil.

oliscar, (*ref. 50*) *tr.v.* 1. to sniff, smell. 2. to investigate, sniff around, make inquiries about. —*i.v.* to smell strong, smell high (meat).

olisque, olisqué, *ref.* **oliscar.**

olisquear, *tr.v.* 1. to sniff, smell. 2. to investigate, sniff around, make inquiries.

olisqueo, *m.* sniffing.

oliva, *f.* 1. olive (fruit). 2. (ornith.) owl. 3. (fig.) olive branch, peace. 4. (anat.) olive. 5. (archit.) olive molding. — **color o.,** olive-colored.

oliváceo, a, *a.* olive, olive-colored, olivaceous.

olivar, *m.* olive grove. —*tr.v.* to prune or trim off lower branches.

olivarda, *f.* 1. (ornith.) green peregrine falcon. 2. (bot.) elecampane.

olivavero, ra, *a.* olive-growing. —*m., f.* olive-grower.

olivarse, *r.v.* to form bubbles when baking (bread).

olivastro de rodas, *m.* (bot.) **aloe.**

olivenita, *f.* (min.) olivenite.

olivera, *f.* (bot.) olive tree.

olivero, *m.* place where olives are stored before being pressed.

olivícola, *a.* pertaining to olive-growing.

olivicultor, ra, *m., f.* olive-grower.

olivicultura, *f.* olive cultivation or growing.

olivífero, ra, *a.* (poet.) rich in olives.

olivillo, *m.* (bot.) (variety of) terebinth shrub.

olivina, *f.* (min.) olivine.

olivino, *m.* (min.) olivine, peridot.

olivo, *m.* (bot.) olive tree. — **o. acebucheno,** wild olive tree; **o. arbequín,** manzanilla olive tree; **o. manzanillo,** manzanilla olive tree; **o. silvestre,** wild olive tree; **tomar el o.,** (taur.) to take shelter or cover (behind a barrier).

olivoso, sa, *a.* (poet.) rich in olives.

olla, *f.* 1. saucepan, pot; kettle. 2. stew. 3. eddy (in river). — **estar a la o. de otro,** to sponge off someone; **o. ciega,** piggy bank, money box; **o. de campaña,** field kitchen pot or saucepan; **o. commun** or **popular,** soup kitchen; **o. de fuego,** primitive clay grenade; **o. de grillos,** (coll.) bedlam, pandemonium; nest of intrigues; **o. de presión,** (cul.) pressure cooker; **o. freidora,** deep fryer; **o. podrida,** meat and vegetable stew; **las ollas de Egipto,** the good old times.

ollado, *m., var. of* **ollao.**

ollao, *m.* (mar.) eyelet hole (in sail).

ollar, *m.* nostril (of horse). —*a.* **piedra o.,** rock formed by serpentine, talc or chlorite.

ollaza, *f. aug. of* **olla,** very large pot. — **a cada o. su coberteraza,** to each his own.

ollera, *f.* (ornith.) greater titmouse, blue titmouse.

ollería, *f.* pottery; earthenware shop or store; pots, earthenware set.

ollero, ra, *m., f.* potter; dealer in earthenware.

olleta, *f.* 1. (Ven.) stew of Indian corn. 2. (Col., Peru) pot for cooking chocolate.

ollita, *f. dim. of* **olla,** small saucepan or pot.

olluco, *m.* (Peru, bot.) ullucu, olluco, an Andean plant with tuberous roots like a small new potato (Ullucus tuberosa).

olluela, *f. dim. of* **olla,** small pot or saucepan.

olma, *f.* thick, luxuriously branched elm.

olmeda, *f.* elm grove.

olmedo, *m., var. of* **olmeda,** elm grove.

olmo, *m.* (bot.) elm.

ológrafo, fa, *a.* (law) holographic, holograph. —*m.* holograph.

olomórfico, ca, *a.* (cryst.) holomorphic.

olopopo, *m.* (C. Rica) (variety of) screech owl (Ciccaba virgata).

olor, *m.* 1. smell, odor, fragrance. 2. hope, promise. — **estar al o.,** (coll.) to be on the lookout for; **o. a,** smell of; **tener o. a,** to smell of; **o. de santidad,** the odor of sanctity.

olorizar, (*ref. 53*) *tr.v.* to perfume, scent.
oloroso, sa, *a.* fragrant, odorous.
olvidadizo, za, *a.* 1. forgetful. 2. ungrateful.
olvidado, da, *past part. of* **olvidar.** —*a.* 1. forgetful. 2. ungrateful.
olvidar, *tr.v.* 1. to forget. 2. to leave, leave behind. 3. to leave off, omit. — **o.** + *inf.,* to forget to. —*r.v.* 1. to forget. 2. to leave. 3. to leave off, omit. — **olvidarse de** + *inf.,* to forget to; **no se te olvide hacerlo,** don't forget to do it; **se le olvidaron los guantes en casa,** he left his gloves at home.
olvido, *m.* 1. forgetfulness. 2. oblivion. — **enterrar en el o.,** to forget completely.
omaso, *m.* (zool.) omasum.
omátida, *f.* (zool.) ommatidium.
omatidia, *f.* **omatidio,** *m.* (zool.) ommatidium.
ombligada, *f.* (tanning) navel area of a hide.
ombligo, *m.* 1. (anat.) navel. 2. (anat.) umbilical cord. 3. center, middle point. — **o. de Venus,** (bot.) Venus' navelwort; (zool.) small elliptical shell (which serves as the operculum of gastropod mollusks); **haberle cortado el o. a uno,** (coll.) to win someone over, win a person's good will.
ombliguero, *m.* navel bandage (for newborn child)
ombría, *f.* shade, shady place.
ombrómetro, *m.* (meteorol.) ombrometer, rain gage.
ombú, (*pl.* **ombúes**), *m.* (bot.) umbra tree, ombu.
omega, *f.* omega, final letter of the Greek alphabet. — **de alfa a o.,** from A to Z.
omental, *a.* (anat.) omental.
omento, *m.* (anat.) omentum.
ómicron, *f.* omicron, fifteenth letter of the Greek alphabet.
ominar, *tr.v.* to predict, foretell, forecast, prophesy, prognosticate.
ominoso, sa, *a.* foreboding, ominous, menacing.
omisión, *f.* omission; neglect.
omiso, sa, *a.* neglectful, careless, **remiss,** negligent. — **hacer caso o. de,** to ignore, pay no attention to.
omitir, *tr.v.* to omit, leave out. — **no o. esfuerzos,** to do all one can, spare no efforts. —*r.v.* to be omitted, left out or neglected.
ómnibus, *m.* omnibus. — **o. escolar,** school bus; **ó. de dos pisos,** double-decker bus.
omnidireccional, *a.* (rad.) omnidirectional.
omnímodo, da, *a.* all-embracing.
omnipotencia, *f.* omnipotence.
omnipotente, *a.* omnipotent, all-powerful.
omnipotentemente, *adv.* omnipotently.
omnipresencia, *f.* omnipresence.
omnipresente, *a.* omnipresent.
omnisapiente, *a.* omniscient, all-knowing.
omnisciencia, *f.* omniscience.
omnisciente, *a.* omniscient.
omniscio, cia, *a.* omniscient.
omnívoro, ra, *a.* (zool.) omnivorous. —*m.* omnivore.
omóplato, *m.* (anat.) shoulder blade, scapula.
OMS *abbrev. of* **Organización Mundial de la Salud,** World Health Organization (WHO).
onagra, *f.* (bot.) evening primrose.
onagrarieo, a, *a.* (bot.) onagraceous. —*f.* (*pl.*) Onagraceae.
onagro, *m.* 1. (zool.) onager. 2. (mil.) onager (military catapult).
onanismo, *m.* 1. onanism. 2. male masturbation.
once, *a.* eleven. —*m.* eleven; eleventh (in dates); (soccer) eleven. — **hacer or tomar las o.,** (coll.) to have a coffee break; **las o.,** eleven o'clock.
oncear, *tr.v.* to weigh out in ounces.
oncejera, *f.* snare (for small birds).
oncejo, *m.* (ornith.) black martin, European swift.
onceno, na, *a., m.* eleventh. — **el o., no molestar,** the "Eleventh Commandment" thou shall not disturb.
oncijera, *f., var. of* **oncejera.**
oncología, *f.* (med.) oncology.
onda, *f.* 1. wave (on sea, water). 2. flicker (of flame). 3. wave, curl (in hair). 4. undulation (in cloth, paper). 5. (phys.) wave. 6. (archit.) wave molding. — **de toda o.,** (rad.) all-wave; **o. amortiguada,** (phys.) damped wave; **o. continua** or **entretenida,** continuous wave; **o. corta,** (rad.) short wave; **o. de choque,** (phys.) shock or blast wave; **o. eléctrica,** (phys.) electric wave; **o. electromagnética,** (phys.) electromagnetic wave; **o. de empuje** or **de compresión,** (phys.) push wave; **o. de presión y depresión,** (mil.) shock wave (of a bomb); **o. de reposo,** (rad.) spacing wave; **o. estacionaria,** (phys.) stationary vibration or wave; **o. expansiva,** blast, shock wave; **o. herciana** or **herziana,** (phys.) Hertizian wave; **o. larga,** (rad.) long wave; **o. longitudinal,** (phys.) longitudinal wave; **o. luminosa,** (phys.) light wave; **o. portadora,** (elec., rad.) carrier wave; **o. sinusoidal,** (math.) sine wave; **o. sonora,** (phys.) sound wave; **o. transversal,** (phys.) transverse wave.
ondámetro, *m.* wave meter.
ondeado, da, *past part. of* **ondear.** —*a.* wavy.
ondeante, *a.* waving, undulating.
ondear, *i.v.* to wave; to ripple; to undulate. —*r.v.* to sway, swing.
ondeo, *m.* waving; rippling; undulating; swaying.
ondímetro, *m.* wave meter.
ondina, *f.* undine, water nymph.
ondisonante, *a.* (poet.) ripply, billowy (water).
ondógrafo, *m.* (elec.) ondograph.
ondómetro, *m.* wave meter.
ondoso, sa, *a.* wavy, undulating.
ondulación, *f.* undulation; winding (of river, road); (phys.) undulation, wave. — **o. permanente,** permanent wave.
ondulado, da, *past part. of* **ondular.** —*a.* wavy, curly (hair); rolling, undulating (country); corrugated (surface). —*m.* wave. — **o permanente,** permanent wave.
ondulante, *a.* undulating; (med.) undulant (fever, temperature).
ondular, *i.v.* to undulate; to wind (river, road). —*tr.v.* to wave (hair).
ondulatorio, ria, *a.* undulatory.
onerario, ria, *a.* (arch.) onerary, **cargo,** transport (ship).
oneroso, sa, *a.* onerous, burdensome, heavy; (law) onerous.
onfacino, *a.* omphacine (oil made from unripe olives).
onfaloflebitis, *f.* (med.) omphalophlebitis.
ónice, *m.* (min.) onyx.
ónique, *f.* (min.) onyx.
oniquina, *f.* (arch.) onyx.
oníríco, ca, *a.* oneiric, pertaining to dreams.
onirocrítico, ca, *a.* oneirocritical, concerning the interpretation of dreams. —*m.* oneirocritic.
oniromancia, *f.* oneiromancy (divination by dreams).
ónix, *f.* (min.) onyx.
ONO *abbrev. of* **oesnoroeste,** west-northwest (WNW).
onocrótalo, *m.* (ornith.) solan gannet.
onomancía, *f.* onomancy, divination from names.
onomástico, ca, *a.* onomastic. — **día o.,** name or saint's day, birthday. —*m.* birthday, saint's day. —*f.* study of proper names.
onomatopeya, *f.* onomatopoeia, the formation of a word by imitating the natural sound associated with the object or action involved.
onomatopéyico, ca, *a.* onomatopoeic.
onoquiles, *f.* (bot.) alkanet, dyer's alkanet.
onoto, *m.* (Ven., bot.) annatto tree.
óntico, ca, *a.* (philos.) ontic.
ontina, *f.* (bot.) white sage (Artemisia herba-alba).
ontogénesis, *f.* (biol.) ontogenesis.
ontogenia, *f.* ontogeny, the life cycle of a single organism.
ontogénico, ca, *a.* ontogenetic, ontogenic.
ontogenista, *m., f.* (biol.) ontogenist.
ontología, *f.* ontology, the branch of metaphysics dealing with the nature of being, reality or ultimate substance.
ontológico, ca, *a.* ontological.
ontologismo, *m.* ontologism.
ontólogo, *m.* ontologist.
ONU *abbrev. of* **Organización de las Naciones Unidas,** United Nations Organization (UNO).
ONUDI *abbrev. of* **Organización de las Naciones Unidas para el Desarrollo Industrial,** United Nations Industrial Development Organization (UNIDO).
onz. *abbrev. of* **onza,** ounce (oz).
onza, *f.* ounce (measure). — **por onzas,** niggardly; by the ounce, in small portions; **o. de oro,** Spanish doubloon.
onza, *f.* (zool.) ounce, snow leopard.
onzavo, va, *a., m.* eleventh.
oocito, *m.* (biol.) oocyte.
oofítico, ca, *a.* (bot.) oophytic.
oofito, *m.* oophyte, in plants undergoing alternations of generations, that generation in which the reproductive organs are developed.
ooforectomía, *f.* (med.) oophorectomy.
oógamo, ma, *a.* (biol.) oogamous.
oogénesis, *f.* (biol.) oogenesis, gonogenesis.
oogenia, *f.* (biol.) gonogenesis.
oogonio, *m.* (biol.) oogonium.
oolítico, ca, *a.* (geol.) oolitic.
oolito, *m.* (geol.) oolite.
oología, *f.* (ornith.) oology, the study of birds' eggs.
oológico, ca, *a.* (ornith.) oological.
oosfera, *f.* (biol.) oosphere.
oospermo, *m.* (zool.) oosperm.
oospora, *f.* (bot.) oospore.
oosporo, *m.* (bot.) oospore.
ooteca, *f.* (zool.) ootheca.
oótide, *m.* ootid, a large haploid cell that quickly becomes an egg cell.
opa, *a.* (Amer.) stupid, idiotic. —*m., f.* (Amer.) idiot, fool.
opacamente, *adv.* obscurely, darkly.
opacar, (*ref. 50*) *tr.v.* (Amer.) to cloud, darken; (fig.) to eclipse. —*r.v.* (Amer.) to become cloudy or dark.
opacidad, *f.* opaqueness, opacity.
opaco, ca, *a.* 1. opaque. 2. gloomy, dull; uninteresting. 3. (fig.) murky, unclear.
opado, da, *a.* 1. swollen, puffed. 2. (Bol., Ven.) pale, drawn (countenance).
opalescencia, *f.* opalescence, iridescence.
opalescente, *a.* opalescent, iridescent.
opalino, na, *a.* opaline, iridescent.
ópalo, *m.* (min.) opal; **ó. de fuego,** fire opal; **ó. girasol,** girasol; **ó. noble,** precious opal.
opción, *f.* option, right, choice; (com., law) option; **o. de compra,** call option; **o. de enajenación** or **venta,** put option; **o. de futuro,** futures option.
opcional, *a.* optional.
ópera, *f.* 1. opera, musical drama; **ó. bufa,** opéra bouffe; **ó. ligera,** light opera. 2. theatre where, by design or tradition, operas are performed.
operable, *a.* operable; practicable, feasible; (surg.) operable.
operación, *f.* 1. operation, action, working. 2. (med., surg.) operation, surgery; **o. de corazón expuesto,** open heart surgery. 2. (com.) operation, transaction; **o. bancaria,** banking transaction. 3. (chem.) process. 4. (math.) operation,

calculation. 5. (*pl.*) (mil., mar.) operations, maneuvers.
operador, ra, *a.* (surg.) operating. —*m., f.* 1. (mach., tech.) operator. 2. (surg.) operating surgeon, operator. 3. (math.) operator. 4. (tel.) cameraman, camerawoman. 5. (fin.) trader. — **o. cambiaro,** foreign exchange operator; **o. de consola,** keyboarder; **o. turistico,** tour operator.
operante, *a.* operating, working, operative. —*m., f.* operator.
operar, *tr.v.* to operate on. —*i.v.* to operate, work, act, take effect; (com., mil., surg.) to operate. —*r.v.* to be operated on, e.g. *me operé de apendicitis,* I was operated on for appendicitis.
operario, ria, *m., f.* 1. operator, laborer, worker. 2. friar who ministers to the sick or the dying.
operativo, va, *a.* operative, operating, effective.
operatorio, ria, *a.* operative; (med.) operative.
operculado, da, *a.* (zool., bot.) operculate.
opercular, *a.* (zool.) opercular.
opérculo, *m.* (bot., zool.) operculum.
opereta, *f.* operetta, light opera.
operista, *m., f.* opera singer.
operístico, ca, *a.* operatic, pertaining to operas.
operoso, sa, *a.* 1. industrious, hard-working, energetic. 2. tiring, arduous, fatiguing.
opiáceo, cea, *a.* 1. opiate (containing opium). 2. (pharm.) soothing, quieting, assuaging.
opiado, da, *a.* opiate, containing opium.
opiata, *f.* opiate.
opiato, ta, *a.* opiate, containing opium. —*m.* opiate.
opilación, *f.* (med.) obstruction, oppilation; (med.) amenorrhoea; (med.) dropsy.
opilarse, *r.v.* to contract amenorrhoea.
opilativo, va, *a.* oppilative, obstructive, constipative.
opimo, ma, *a.* rich, fertile, abundant, fruitful.
opinable, *a.* debatable, arguable, disputable, moot.
opinante, *a.* arguing. —*m., f.* arguer.
opinar, *i.v.* 1. to think, opine, judge. 2. to form, express or have an opinion, e.g. *opino que haces mal,* in my opinion you are doing wrong. 3. to give one's opinion, opine. — **o. de,** to think of, have an opinion of, e.g., *¿qué opinas tú de este tipo?* what is your opinion of this fellow?; **o. en** or **sobre,** to give one's opinion on.
opinión, *f.* opinion; reputation, public image; **cambiar** or **mudar de o.,** to change one's mind; **casarse uno con su o.,** to stick to one's opinion or belief; **o. pública,** public opinion; **tener mala o. de,** to have a poor opinion of.
opio, *m.* 1. (pharm.) opium. 2. (fig.) opiate, distraction.
opiomanía, *f.* (med.) opiumism, addiction to opium.
opíparamente, *adv.* sumptuously, splendidly, magnificently, abundantly.
opíparo, ra, *a.* sumptuous, splendid, magnificent, plentiful (meal, banquet).
opistognacia, *f.* (zool.) opisthognathism.
opistognatismo, *m.* opisthognathism.
opistognato, ta, *a.* opisthognathous.
oploteca, *f.* museum of ancient, precious or rare weapons.
opobálsamo, *m.* balm of Gilead, opobalsam.
opodeldoch, *m.* (pharm.) opodeldoc.
opondré, opondría, *ref.* **oponer.**
oponente, *a.* opponent; rival.
oponer, (*ref. 15*) *tr.v.* to put up, offer (resistance, arguments); **o. una cosa a otra,** to set or put one thing against another. —*r.v.* 1. to object, oppose e.g, *yo me opongo,* I object. 2. to oppose each other. 3. to face or be opposite one another. — **oponerse a,** to oppose, be opposed to, resist; to run or compete for; to stand in competition with.
oponga, opongo, *ref.* **oponer.**
oponible, *a.* opposable.
opopánax, *m., var. of* **opopónaco.**
opopónace, *f.* (bot.) Hercules' allheal.
opopónaco, *m.* (pharm.) opopanax, a gum resin.
oporto, *m.* port (wine).
oportunamente, *adv.* 1. opportunely, conveniently, at the right time. 2. in due time.
oportunidad, *f.* 1. opportunity, chance. 2. opportuneness.
oportunismo, *m.* (pol.) opportunism.
oportunista, *a.* opportunistic. —*m., f.* opportunist.
oportuno, na, *a.* 1. opportune, timely, convenient; well-timed; seasonable, suitable; proper, necessary. 2. witty, amusing (in conversation)
oposición, *f.* 1. opposition, resistance, antagonism. 2. contrast, juxtaposition. 3. competitive examination (for employment). 4. (pol.) opposition (minority). 5. (law, log., astron.) opposition. — **leer de o.,** to give a lecture or read a thesis in a competitive examination; **poder leer de o.,** (fig.) to be an authority on science or art.
oposicionista, *a.* oppositionist, oppositional. —*m.* oppositionist; (pol.) member of the opposition.
opositar, *i.v.* to take part or be a candidate in an examination for a public post; **o. a,** to compete for.
opositor, ra, *m., f.* 1. opponent. 2. competitor, candidate (for a competitive post or in sports).
oposum, *m.* (zool.) opossum.
opoterapia, *f.* (med.) organotherapy, opotherapy.
opoterápico, ca, *a.* organotherapeutic.
opresión, *f.* 1. oppression; tyranny. 2. congestion, oppression, pressure, e.g. *o. del pecho,* congestion or oppression of the chest, pressure on the chest. 3. distress, affliction, oppression (of the spirit).
opresivamente, *adv.* oppressively.
opresivo, va, *a.* oppressive.
opreso, sa, *a.* oppressed.
opresor, ra, *a.* oppressive, tyrannical. —*m., f.* oppressor, tyrant.
oprimir, *tr.v.* 1. to oppress, tyrannize. 2. to lie heavily upon. 3. to press, squeeze, e.g. *oprima el botón,* press the button.
oprobiar, *tr.v.* to vilify, revile, defame, calumniate, slander.
oprobio, *m.* opprobrium, ignominy, shame, disgrace, dishonor.
oprobiosamente, *adv.* opprobriously, ignominiously, shamefully, disgracefully.
oprobioso, sa, *a.* opprobrious, ignominious, shameful, disgraceful.
opsónico, ca, *a.* (bac.) opsonic.
opsonificación, *f.* (bac.) opsonification.
opsonina, *f.* (bac.) opsonin.
optación, *f.* (rhet.) optation.
optante, *m., f.* chooser, one who opts.
optar, *tr.v.* to choose, select. —*i.v.* to choose, opt; **o. a,** to be a candidate for (an office or position); **o. entre,** to choose between; **o. por** + *inf.,* to choose + *inf.;* decide in favor of + *ger.;* **o. por** + *n.,* to choose + *n.,* decide in favor of + *n.,* opt for + *n.*
optativo, va, *a.* optative, optional; (gram.) optative. —*m.* (gram.) optative.
óptica, *f.* 1. (phys.) optics. 2. stereoscope.
óptico, ca, *a.* optical, optic. —*m.* 1. optician. 2. stereoscope.
óptimamente, *adv.* perfectly, excellently, in the best manner.
optimate, *m.* 1. hero, great leader. 2. (Roman hist.) optimate. 3. (*pl*) grandees, worthies.
optimismo, *m.* optimism.
optimista, *a.* optimistic, sanguine. —*m., f.* optimist.
óptimo, ma, *a.* excellent, best, most favorable, optimum, optimal.
optómetra, *m., f.* optometrist.
optometría, *f.* optometry.
optometrista, *m., f.* optometrist.
optómetro, *m.* optometer.
opuestamente, *adv.* oppositely, contrarily, contradictorily, on the contrary.
opuesto, ta, *past part. of* **oponer.** —*a.* 1. opposing, adverse, contrary, antagonistic, e.g., *intereses opuestos,* opposing interests. 2. opposite, opposing, e.g. *las orillas opuestas del río,* the opposite banks of the river. 3. (geom., bot.) opposite.
opugnación, *f.* 1. attack, assault. 2. refutation, contradiction.
opugnador, *m.* oppugner, attacker, assaulter.
opugnante, *a.* attacking, opposing. —*m., f.* oppugner, attacker.
opugnar, *tr.v.* 1. to oppugn, attack, assault. 2. to resist, oppose, refute.
opulencia, *f.* opulence, wealth, riches, affluence; superabundance.
opulentamente, *adv.* opulently, affluently.
opulento, ta, *a.* opulent, wealthy, rich, affluent.
opúsculo, *m.* opuscule, short work, tract, booklet.
opuse, opusiera, opusiese, *ref.* **oponer.**
oque, (coll.) **de o.,** free, gratis, for nothing.
oquedad, *f.* 1. hollow, cavity. 2. hollowness, insincerity.
oquedal, *m.* woodland of tall and lofty trees, bare of undergrowth.
oquerucla, *f.* kink (in thread), tangled, knotted thread.
ora, *conj.* (*apheresis of* **ahora**) now, whether, either then; **tomando o. la espada, o. la pluma,** taking now the sword, now the pen.
oración, *f.* 1. oration; speech. 2. prayer, orison. 3. (gram.) sentence, clause. 4. (*pl.*) first part of the catechism, prayers. 5. (*pl.*) prayers, prayer time. 6. (*pl.*) sunset, dusk, the Angelus hour. — **casa de o.,** house of prayer, church; **o compuesta,** (gram.) compound sentence; complex sentence; **o. coordinada** (gram.) compound sentence; **o. fúnebre,** funeral oration; **o. inaugural,** inaugural speech; **o. jaculatoria,** brief fervent prayer; **o. principal,** main clause; **o. relativa,** (gram.) relative clause; **o. relativa determinativa,** (gram.) restrictive clause; **o. relativa incidental,** (gram.) non-restrictive clause; **o. simple,** (gram.) simple sentence; **o. subordinada,** (gram.) subordinate clause; **parte de la o.,** (gram.) part of speech.
oracional, *a.* (gram.) sentence, sentential. —*m.* prayer book.
oracular, *a.* oracular.
oráculo, *m.* oracle; (fig.) prophesy, prediction.
orador, *m., f.* 1. orator, speaker. 2. petitioner, supplicant.
oraje, *m.* severe, wintry weather.
oral, *a.* 1. oral, verbal, vocal, e.g., *examen o.,* oral examination. 2. (Col.) place abounding in gold ore; a quantity of ore.
oralmente, *adv.* orally, verbally.
Orán, *m.* Oran, city and port in Algeria.
orangután, *m.* (zool.) orangutan.
orante, *a.* orant, in a praying position; said of an artistic representation of a person praying.
orar, *i.v.* 1. to pray; **o. por,** to pray for. 2. to speak, make a speech.
orario, *m.* (ecc.) orarium, orarion.
orate, *m., f.* lunatic, maniac, madman, madwoman.
oratoria, *f.* oratory, art of public speaking, eloquence; rhetoric.

oratoriamente, *adv.* oratorically.
oratorio, *m.* 1. oratory, small private chapel. 2. (ecc.) **O.,** Oratory (Oratory of St. Philip Neri). 3. (mus.) oratorio.
orbe, *m.* 1. orb; globe; world. 2. (ichth.) globefish. 3. (astron.) orb.
orbicular, *a.* orbicular, globular, spherical, circular.
orbicularmente, *adv.* orbicularly, spherically, circularly.
órbita, *f.* (astron., anat., zool., fig.) orbit; field (of action); sphere; eye socket. — **entrar en ó.,** to go into orbit.
orbital, *a.* orbital.
orbitario, ria, *a.* (astron.) orbital.
orca, *f.* (zool.) killer whale, orca, grampus.
orcadas, *f.* (*pl.*) Orkneys, Orkney Islands (N. of Scotland).
orcaneta, *f.* (bot.) alkanet, dyer's alkanet. — **o. amarilla,** (bot.) false gromwell.
orce, *ref.* **orzar.**
orcella, *f.* (bot.) Angela wood, archil.
orchilla, *f.* (bot., chem.) archil.
orcina, *f.* (bot., chem.) orcinol, orcin.
Orco, *m.* 1. Orcus, Hades, the underworld. 2. (myth.) Orcus, Pluto.
órdago, de ó., excellent, first-class; tremendous, grand, e.g. *dio un discurso de ó.,* he gave a first-class speech, *armó un escándalo de ó.,* he created a tremendous scandal.
ordalías, *f.* (*pl.*) ordeal, trials by ordeal.
orden, *m.* 1. order; methodical, regular or harmonious arrangement; system, method; orderly series or succession of things, e.g. *el o. cronológico,* the chronological order, *poner en o.,* to put in order; sequence, succession. 2. order, peace, harmony. 3. (biol., archit., math.) order. 4. (ecc.) order (sixth sacrament). 5. (mil.) order, formation — **del o. de,** in the neighborhood of (an amount of money); **de primer o.,** first-rate, first-class; **en o.,** in order; **en o. de aparición,** in order of appearance; **llamar al o.,** to call to order; **o. abierto,** (mil.) open order; **o. atlántico,** (archit.) order in which atlantes support the entablature; **o. cerrado,** (mil.) close order; **o. compuesto,** (archit.) Composite order; **o. corintio,** (archit.) Corinthian order; **o. de batalla,** (mil., **mar.**) order of battle, battle array; **o. de encendido,** (auto., mec.) firing order; **o. de marcha,** (mil.) march order; (mar.) cruising formation (of line of battleships); **o. dórico,** (archit.) Doric order; **o. jónico,** (archit.) Ionic order; **o. paranínfico,** (archit.) order in which figures of nymphs support the entablature; **o. permanente de pago,** standing order; **o. público,** public order; (law) public policy; **o. sacerdotal,** holy order; **o. toscano,** (archit.) Tuscan order; **por su o.,** in its or their order or turn. —*f.* 1. order, command. 2. (civil, knightly, etc.) order. 3. (ecc.) order (monastic brotherhood or society; rank in Christian ministry), e.g. *la O. de Malta,* the Order of Malta, *las órdenes mayores* or *sagradas,* the major, holy or sacred orders, *las órdenes menores,* the minor orders. 4. (theol.) choir (of angels). 5. (law) order, warrant. — **a la o.** or **las órdenes de,** at the orders or service of; **a la o. de,** (com.) to the order of; **a sus órdenes,** at your orders or service; **consignar las órdenes,** (mil.) to give instructions or orders; **dar** or **hacer órdenes,** (ecc.) to ordain; **orden de allanamiento** or **registro,** search warrant; **o. de arresto, captura** or **detención,** warrant of arrest; **o. de caballería,** order of knighthood or chivalry; knighthood (title); **o. de desalojo,** notice to quit; **o. de la Jarretera,** (G.B.) Order of the Garter; **o. del Cister,** Cistercian Order; **o. del día,** agenda, order of the day; (mil.) order of the day; **O. del Templo,** Order of Knights Templars; **órdenes de marcha,** marching orders; **o. judicial,** court order; **o. militar,** military order; **por o. de,** by order of, at the order of.
ordenación, *f.* 1. (ecc.) ordination. 2. arrangement, array, disposition, order, putting in order. 3. rule, regulation; order. 4. auditor's or paymaster's office. 5. (archit., p.) ordinance (planned arrangement of parts or objects in a building or picture).
ordenada, *f.* (geom.) ordinate.
ordenadamente, *adv.* tidily, in an orderly fashion.
ordenado, da, *past part. of* **ordenar.** —*a.* tidy, methodical, orderly.
ordenador, ra, *a.* 1. arranging, ordering. 2. ordaining. —*m., f.* 1. arranger. 2. controller, chief auditor. 3. ordainer. 4. (electron.) computer; **o. central,** central computer, mainframe; **o. de a bordo,** onboard computer; **o. de sobremesa** or **de mesa,** desktop computer; **o. doméstico,** home computer; **o. patrón,** server; **o. personal,** personal computer; **o. portátil,** portable computer, laptop computer.
ordenamiento, *m.* 1. arranging, ordering. 2. order, edict, regulation, ordinance. 3. code or set of laws.
ordenancista, *a.* strict, rigid. —*m., f.* martinet, disciplinarian.
ordenando, ordenante, *m.* (ecc.) ordinand.
ordenanza, *f.* 1. ordinance, statute, law; (*pl.*) set or code of regulations or laws. 2. order, system, method. 3. command, order. 4. (archit., p.) ordinance (planned arrangement of parts or objects of a building or picture). —*m.* 1. (mil.) orderly, batman. 2. clerk, office worker.
ordenar, *tr.v.* 1. to arrange, put in order; to classify. 2. to order, command, ordain. 3. to regulate, direct. 4. to establish, enjoin, prescribe, decree. 5. (ecc.) to ordain. 6. (math.) to arrange (a polynomial). —*r.v.* to become ordained, take holy orders.
ordeñadero, *m.* milk pail; milking place.
ordeñador, ra, *a.* milking. —*m., f.* milker.
ordeñar, *tr.v.* 1. to milk. 2. to strip (olives) from a branch.
ordeño, *m.* 1. milking. 2. stripping olives from a branch.
ordinal, *a.* (gram.) ordinal (number); (biol.) ordinal (relating to a biological order).
ordinariamente, *adv.* 1. ordinarily, usually, generally, customarily. 2. rudely, uncouthly, coarsely.
ordinariez, *f.* uncouthness, vulgarity, bad manners, coarseness, grossness.
ordinario, ria, *a.* 1. ordinary, common; usual, customary. 2. vulgar, uncouth, coarse. 3. regular, daily (meals, expenses). —*m.* 1. ordinary (judge or bishop). 2. daily household expenses. 3. carrier; delivery man. 4. regular mail or post. — **de o.,** ordinarily, usually, customarily.
ordinativo, va, *a.* ordering, regulating, arranging, ordinative.
ordo, *m.* (ecc.) ordo, ordinal.
ordovícico, ca, *a., m.* (geol.) Ordovician.
orea, *f., var. of* **oréade.**
oréada, *f., var. of* **oréade.**
oréade, *f.* (myth.) oread, mountain nymph.
oreante, *a.* airing, drying; refreshing, cooling.
orear, *tr.v.* to air, dry in the air; to aerate; to refresh. —*r.v.* 1. to become aired, dry in the air. 2. to take an airing, take the air.
orégano, *m.* (bot.) oregano, wild marjoram.
oreja, *f.* 1. (anat.) ear; outer ear. 2. (each) side of the uppers of a shoe (with eyelets and shoelaces). 3. (mec.) ear, lug, flange. 4. (fig.) gossip. — **aguzar las orejas,** to prick up one's ears; **apearse por las orejas,** (coll) to fall from one's horse; to make a stupid remark; **bajar las orejas,** (coll.) to yield, assent or agree humbly; **calentar a uno las orejas,** (coll.) to give someone a dressing-down or ticking off; **cerrar la o.,** to close one's ears to, turn a deaf ear to; **con las orejas caídas or gachas,** (coll.) crestfallen; **con las orejas tan largas,** all ears; **de cuatro orejas,** (coll.) with horns, horned (animal); **descubrir** or **enseñar la o.,** (coll.) to show the cloven hoof, reveal one's true self; **hacer orejas de mercader,** to turn a deaf ear to; **mojar la o.,** to insult, look for a fight; **o. de abad** or **monje,** leaf-shaped fritter; (bot.) navelwort; **o. de fraile,** (bot.) hazelwort, asarabacca; **o. del ancla,** anchor fluke or palm; **o. de oso,** (bot.) auricula, bear's ear; **o. de ratón,** (bot.) mouse-ear (Hieracium pilosella); **o. marina,** (zool.) abalone (Haliotis cracherodi); **pabellón de la o.,** pinna, auricle; **poner a uno las orejas coloradas,** (coll.) to give someone a dressing-down or ticking off, to make someone blush; **tener a uno de la o.,** to have someone under one's thumb, lead by the nose; **tener la mosca en la o.,** to be very suspicious or wary; **tirar a uno de la o.,** to pull someone's ear; **ver uno las orejas del lobo,** to find oneself in great danger.
orejano, na, *a.* unbranded (said of cattle).
orejeado, da, *a.* warned, instructed, advised, ready to answer, ready with an answer.
orejear, *i.v.* 1. to shake or wiggle the ears (said of animals). 2. to do something reluctantly.
orejera, *f.* 1. earflap, earmuff, earcap; earguard (on helmet). 2. moldboard, earthboard (of plow). 3. type of earring worn by Peruvian Indians.
orejeta, *f. dim. of* **oreja,** ear, lug, an earlike handle on a vessel or machine.
orejisano, na, *a.* unbranded (said of cattle).
orejón, na, *a.* 1. (Amer.) big-eared. 2. (Amer.) coarse, uncouth (person). —*m., f.* (Hond.) simpleton, fool.
orejón, *m.* 1. peeled dried peach or apricot half. 2. a pull at the ear. 3. (hist.) name given by Spaniards to any Inca nobleman. 4. (S. Amer.) rancher, dweller of the plains. 5. (Col.) cuckold, deceived husband. 6. (fort.) orillion (projection of a bastion).
orejudo, da, *a.* flap-eared; big-eared. —*m.* (zool.) long-eared bat (Plecotus auritus).
orejuela, *f.* 1. *dim. of* **oreja,** small ear. 2. handle (as of a pitcher or a tray).
orenga, *f.* (mar.) floor timber; (mar.) frame.
oreo, *m.* 1. airing, freshening. 2. gentle breeze.
oreoselino, *m.* (bot.) mountain parsley.
Orestes, *m.* (myth.) Orestes, brother of Electra.
Orestíada, *f.* (lit.) Oresteia, Aeschylus' dramatic trilogy.
orfanato, *m.* orphanage.
orfandad, *f.* 1. orphanhood. 2. orphan's pension. 3. neglect, abandonment.
orfebre, *m.* goldsmith, silversmith; jeweler.
orfebrería, *f.* gold or silver work.
orfelinato, *m.* orphanage.
Orfeo, *m.* (myth.) Orpheus, the musician, who descended to Hades in search of his wife, Eurydice.
orfeón, *m.* (mus.) choral ensemble; choral society.
orfeonista, *m.* (mus.) member of a choral ensemble or society.
órfico, ca, *a.* Orphean, Orphic; (fig.) mystic, occult.

orfismo, *m.* (myth., rel.) orphism.
orfo, *m.* (ichth.) (variety of) sea bream.
organdí, *m.* (tex.) organdy.
organero, *m.* organ maker, organ builder.
orgánicamente, *adv.* organically.
organice, organicé, *ref.* **organizar.**
organicismo, *m.* (med., biol., philos.) organicism.
organicista, *a.* organicistic. —*m., f.* organicist.
orgánico, ca, *a.* organic.
organillero, ra, *m., f.* organ grinder.
organillo, *m.* barrel organ, hand organ, hurdy-gurdy.
organismo, *m.* 1. organism. 2. body, organization, institution.
organista, *m., f.* (mus.) organist, organ player.
organizable, *a.* organizable.
organización, *f.* 1. organization, club, union, society, body of organized members, e.g. *o. obrera,* labor union. 2. organization, order, arrangement.
organizado, da, *a.* 1. organized. 2. (biol.) organized, organic.
organizador, ra, *a.* organizing; **comité o.,** organizing committee. —*m., f.* organizer.
organizar, (*ref. 53*) *tr.v.* 1. to organize; to arrange, set up, start. 2. to tune (an organ). —*r.v.* to be organized, become or get organized.
órgano, *m.* 1. (mus., anat.) organ. 2. tube refrigerator. 3. organ, instrument, medium, agency. — **ó. de lengüetas,** reed organ; **ó. de la voz,** vocal organ; **ó. de manubrio,** barrel organ, hurdy-gurdy; **ó. eléctrico,** electric organ; **ó. electrónico,** electronic organ; **ó. expresivo,** harmonium; **órganos genitales,** genital organs; **órganos sensorios** or **de los sentidos,** sense organs; **ó. táctil,** tactile organ, organ of touch.
organogénesis, organogenia, *f.* (biol.) organogenesis, organogeny.
organografía, *f.* (biol.) organography.
organográfico, ca, *a.* (biol.) organographic.
organoléptico, ca, *a.* (physiol.) organoleptic.
organología, *f.* (biol.) organology.
órganon, *m.* (philos.) organon, organum.
organoterapia, *f.* (med.) organotherapy.
organotropía, *f.* (med.) organotropy.
organotrópico, ca, *a.* (med.) organotropic.
organotropismo, *m.* (med.) organotropism.
organum, *m.* (mus.) organum.
organza, *f.* (tex.) organza, silk organdy.
organzín, *f.* (tex.) organzine.
orgasmo, *m.* (physiol.) orgasm.
orgástico, ca, *a.* orgasmic, orgastic.
orgia, *f., var. of* **orgía.**
orgía, *f.* orgy, excess, revel.
orgiástico, ca, *a.* orgiastic.
orgullo, *m.* 1. pride. 2. arrogance, haughtiness.
orgullosamente, *adv.* proudly; haughtily, arrogantly.
orgulloso, sa, *a.* 1. proud. 2. haughty, arrogant. 3. conceited, overbearing.
orientación, *f.* 1. orientation, direction, guidance. 2. (archit.) orientation, exposure, position (of a building). 3. (mar.) trimming (of sails). 4. bearings, position. 5. (psyc.) orientation. — **o. profesional** or **vocacional,** vocational guidance.
orientador, ra, *a.* orientating, guiding. —*m.* counselor.
oriental, *a.* oriental; eastern; **Alemania O.,** East Germany. —*m., f.* Oriental.
orientalismo, *m.* orientalism.
orientalista, *m., f.* orientalist.
orientalizar, (*ref. 53*) *tr.v.* orientalize.
orientar, *tr.v.* 1. to orientate, orient; to place in a certain position; to determine position of something in relation with cardinal points. 2. to orientate, guide, direct; to give (someone) his bearings. 3. (chem.) to orient (molecules). 4. (mar.) to trim (sails). —*r.v.* to orientate oneself, get or find one's bearings; **o. hacia,** to turn toward.
oriente, *m.* 1. east (cardinal point). 2. **O.,** the Orient, the East. 3. source, origin, birth. 4. east wind. 5. orient (luster of a pearl). — **Extremo O.,** Far East; **Gran O.,** Grand Lodge (of Masons); **Cercano O.,** Near East; **O. Medio,** Middle East; **O. Próximo,** Near East.
orificación, *f.* (dent.) gold filling.
orificador, *m.* (dent.) plugger.
orificar, (*ref. 50*) *tr.v.* (dent.) to fill (a tooth) with gold.
orífice, *m.* goldsmith.
orificio, *m.* orifice, hole; opening, vent.
orifique, orifiqué, *ref.* **orificar.**
oriflama, *f.* 1. oriflamme, the ancient royal French standard. 2. any banner or battle standard.
orifrés, *m.* gold or silver braid.
origen, *m.* 1. origin, beginning, source, e.g. *el o. del problema,* the source of the problem. 2. origin, ancestry, e.g. *un hombre de o. humilde,* a man of humble origin. 3. origin, native country, e.g. *soy de o. español,* I am of Spanish origin.
originador, ra, *m., f.* originator.
original, *a.* 1. original, initial, first, earliest, e.g. *el pecado o.,* the original sin. 2. original, new, fresh, novel, e.g. *¡qué idea más o.!* what a novel idea! 3. original, authentic, not copied, e.g. *este es un dibujo o. de Picasso,* this is an original drawing by Picasso. 4. quaint, queer, strange, peculiar, e.g. *ahí tienes un tipo o.,* there's an odd character for you. —*m.* (print.) original (copy to be typeset), manuscript. — **de buen o.,** on good authority; **o. de imprenta,** original manuscript.
originalidad, *f.* 1. originality, spontaneity, novelty. 2. strangeness, oddness, quaintness.
originalmente, *adv.* 1. originally, at the beginning. 2. with originality.
originar, *tr.v.* to originate, create, invent, give an origin to. —*r.v.* to originate, arise, spring, derive.
originariamente, *adv.* originally, primarily.
originario, ria, *a.* 1. originating (giving origin, causing). 2. originating, native, descendant, derived, coming, e.g. *o. de,* originating or coming from, native of.
orilla, *f.* 1. bank (of a river), shore (of the sea). 2. edge, border, margin. 3. sidewalk, pavement, edge of a road. 4. (Amer.) (*pl.*) outskirts. 5. (tex.) selvage, border, edge. — **a la o.,** near, on the brink; **a la orilla del camino,** at the wayside; **a orillas de,** on the banks or shores of; **salir a la o.,** to come through, surmount one's difficulties.
orillar, *tr.v.* 1. to settle, arrange, conclude, wind up. 2. to skirt, go around the edge of. 3. to put a border on. 4. to trim or decorate the border of. 5. to surmount (a difficulty). —*i.v., r.v.* to approach the shore.
orillo, *m.* selvage, edge (of cloth).
orín, *m.* 1. urine (usually used in *pl.*). 2. rust (caused by dampness).
orina, *f.* urine; **o. negra,** blackwater.
orinal, *m.* urinal, chamber pot; potty (coll.).
orinar, *tr.v., i.v., r.v.* to urinate.
oriniento, ta, *a.* rusty, moldy.
orinque, *m.* (mar.) buoy rope.
oriol, *m.* (ornith.) oriole, gold thrush.
Orión, *m.* (myth., astron.) Orion, the hunter, loved by Diana.
Oriónida, *f.* (astron.) Orionid.
oriundez, *f.* origin (place, nationality).
oriundo, da, *a.* native, originating, derived, coming. — **o. de,** native of, coming from; **ser o. de,** to come or hail from, be a native of.
orix, *m.* (zool.) oryx.
orla, *f.* 1. border, edge, selvage; fringe, trimming. 2. (print.) ornamental border or edge. 3. (her.) orle.
orlador, ra, *m., f.* borderer, edger.
orladura, *f.* 1. trimming, edging, ornamental border. 2. border, edge.
orlar, *tr.v.* 1. to border, edge, trim. 2. (her.) to put an orle on, provide with an orle.
orleanista, *a., m., f.* Orleanist.
orlo, *m.* 1. Alpine horn. 2. (mus.) horn stop (of an organ). 3. (archit.) plinth.
orlón, *m.* (tex.) orlon (trademark).
ormesí, *m.* (tex.) shimmering shot silk.
ormino, *m.* (bot.) vervain sage, wild sage, wild clary (Salvia verbenaca).
ornadamente, *adv.* ornately.
ornado, da, *past part. of* **ornar.** —*a.* ornate, ornamented.
ornamentación, *f.* ornamentation.
ornamental, *a.* ornamental.
ornamentar, *tr.v.* to adorn, decorate, ornament, embellish.
ornamento, *m.* 1. ornament, adornment, embellishment. 2. (*pl.*) vestments (of priests); sacred ornaments (of altar). 3. (fig.) accomplishment, gift. 4. (archit.) ornament.
ornar, *tr.v.* to adorn, bedeck, decorate. —*r.v.* to adorn or bedeck oneself.
ornato, *m.* ornament, finery; show.
ornitodelfo, fa, *a.* (zool.) monotreme, monotrematous. —*m.* monotreme; (*pl.*) Monotremata.
ornitología, *f.* ornithology, the branch of zoology that deals with birds.
ornitológico, ca, *a.* ornithological.
ornitólogo, *m.* ornithologist.
ornitomancia, *f.* ornithomancy, divination by the flight or the song of birds.
ornitópodo, da, *a., m.* (zool.) ornithopod.
ornitóptero, *m.* (aer.) ornithopter.
ornitorrinco, *m.* (zool.) duckbill, ornithorhynchus, platypus.
ornitosis, *f.* (med.) ornithosis.
oro, *m.* 1. gold (metal, color). 2. gold, jewels; wealth, riches. 3. playing card representing a gold coin; (*pl.*) suit of cards equivalent to diamonds (in Spanish packs). 4. (her.) or. — **como mil oros, como un o.,** as neat as a pin; **(guardar) como o. en paño,** (to look after) as if it were pure gold; **de o.,** golden, of gold, e.g. *edad de o.,* Golden Age, *corazón de o.,* heart of gold; **de o. y azul,** very smart and elegant, all dressed up; **el o. del Rin,** (myth., mus.) Rhinegold; **el o. y el moro,** (coll.) all this and heaven too (a fabulous offer); **no es o. todo lo que reluce,** all that glitters is not gold; **o. batido,** gold foil, gold leaf; **o. blanco,** white gold; **o. coronario,** fine gold, high-carat gold; **o. de ley,** standard gold; **o. en barras,** bullion, bar gold; **o. en polvo,** gold dust; **o. fulminante,** fulminating gold; **o. mate, unburnished or mat gold; o. molido,** ormolu (ground gold for gilding); (fig.) pure gold, excellent or outstanding thing; **o. musivo,** mosaic gold; **o. nativo,** native gold; **o. verde,** green gold; **oros son triunfos,** always look after number one (oneself); **patrón o.,** gold standard; **pesar a uno en o.,** to pay someone very handsomely; **valer su peso en o.,** to be worth one's weight in gold.
orobanca, *f.* (bot.) broom rape.
orobancáceo, a, *a.* (bot.) orobanchaceous. —*f.* (bot.) Orobanchaceae.
orobías, *m.* grain incense.
orogenia, *f.* (geol.) orogeny.
orogénico, ca, *a.* (geol.) orogenic.
orografía, *f.* (geog.) orography, the branch of geography that deals with mountains.

orográfico, ca, *a.* (geog.) orographic.
orología, *f.* (geol.) orology, the study of mountains.
orológico, ca, *a.* orological.
oronasal, *a.* (phonet.) orinasal.
orondo, da, *a.* 1. pompous, vain, conceited, self-satisfied. 2. hollow, swollen, puffed up. 3. big-bellied, pot-bellied (bottle, vessel).
oropel, *m.* 1. tinsel, tinfoil. 2. (fig.) tinsel, glitter, cheap gaudy ornament; hollow show.
oropelero, *m.* foil or tinsel maker or seller.
oropéndola, *f.* (ornith.) golden oriole.
oropimente, *m.* (min.) orpiment.
oroya, *f.* hanging basket, carrier (of a cableway or ropeway).
orozuz, *m.* (bot.) licorice.
orquesta, *f.* orchestra; band; orchestra pit. — **o. bailable** or **de baile,** dance band; **o. de cámara,** chamber orchestra; **o. de cuerda,** string orchestra; **o. de jazz,** jazz band; **o. sinfónica,** symphony orchestra.
orquestación, *f.* (mus.) orchestration.
orquestal, *a.* orchestral.
orquestar, *tr.v.* to orchestrate.
orquestina, *f.* band, dance band.
orquidáceas, *f.* (*pl.*) (bot.) Orchidaceae.
orquídeo, a, *a.* (bot.) orchidaceous. —*f.* orchid.
orquitis, *f.* (med.) orchitis.
orre, *adv.* **en o.,** loose, in bulk; in large quantities.
ortega, *f.* (ornith.) sand grouse (Pterocles orientalis).
orticón, *m.* (photog.) orthicon.
ortiga, *f.* (bot.) nettle. — **o. de mar,** (zool.) sea nettle; **o. muerta,** (bot.) hedge nettle (Stachys palustris); **ser como unas ortigas,** (coll.) to be surly, be irritable or crabby.
ortigal, *m.* bed or field of nettles.
ortivo, va, *a.* (astron.) ortive, pertaining to the rising of the sun or a star; **amplitud ortiva,** (astron.) ortive amplitude.
orto, *m.* (astron.) rise (of the sun or a star).
ortocefalia, *f.* (anth.) orthocephaly.
ortocéfalo, la, *a.* (anth.) orthocephalic, orthocephalous.
ortoclasa, *f.* (min.) orthoclase.
ortocromático, ca, *a.* (photog.) orthochromatic, ortho.
ortodoncia, *f.* (dent.) orthodontics, orthodontia.
ortodóntico, ca, *a.* (dent.) orthodontic.
ortodontista, *m., f.* (dent.) orthodontist.
ortodoxia, *f.* 1. (rel.) orthodoxy. 2. adherence to established beliefs.
ortodoxo, xa, *a.* 1. orthodox; **O.,** Orthodox (church). 2. conforming to established doctrines; conventional. —*m., f.* 1. **O.,** Orthodox, member of the Orthodox Church. 2. a conventional person.
ortodromía, *f.* (mar.) great circle.
ortodrómico, ca, *a.* (mar.) orthodromic, great-circle. — **navegación ortodrómica,** great-circle sailing.
ortoepía, *f.* (phonet.) orthoepy.
ortofonía, *f.* orthophony.
ortofosfato, *m.* (chem.) orthophosphate.
ortofosfórico, ca, *a.* (chem.) orthophosphoric (acid).
ortogénesis, *f.* (biol.) orthogenesis.
ortogenético, ca, *a.* orthogenetic, orthogenic.
ortognatismo, *m.* (anth.) orthognathism, orthognathy.
ortognato, ta, *a.* (anat.) orthognathous.
ortogonal, *a.* (geom.) orthogonal.
ortogonio, *m.* (geom.) right-angled, orthogonal (triangle).
ortografía, *f.* 1. (gram.) orthography; spelling. 2. orthography, elevation. — **o. degradada** o **en perspectiva,** (geom.) linear perspective; **o. geométrica** (geom.) orthogonal projection, orthographic projection; **tener mala o.,** to be a poor speller.
ortográficamente, *adv.* orthographically.
ortográfico, ca, *a.* orthographical; spelling; **error ortográfico,** spelling mistake.
ortógrafo, fa, *m., f.* orthographer.
ortología, *f.* orthoepy, the study of the pronunciation of words.
ortológico, ca, *a.* orthoepic.
ortólogo, *m., f.* orthoepist.
ortopedia, *f.* (med.) orthopedics.
ortopédico, ca, *a.* (med.) orthopedic. —*m., f.* orthopedist.
ortopedista, *m., f.* (med.) orthopedist.
ortopsiquiatría, *f.* (med.) orthopsychiatry.
ortóptero, *a.* (ento.) orthopterous. —*m.* (ento.) orthopteran; (*pl.*) Orthoptera.
ortóptico, ca, *a.* (med.) orthoptic.
ortorrómbico, ca, *a.* (opt.) orthorhombic.
ortosa, *f.* (min.) orthoclase.
ortoscópico, ca, *a.* (opt.) orthoscopic.
ortóstico, *m.* (bot.) orthostichy.
ortotropía, *f.* (bot.) orthotropy.
ortotropismo, *m.* (bot.) orthotropism.
ortótropo, pa, *a.* (bot.) orthotropous.
ortoza, *f.* (min.) orthoclase, orthose.
oruga, *f.* 1. (bot.) rocket (Eruca longirostris). 2. (ento.) caterpillar. 3. caterpillar tractor.
orujo, *m.* 1. crushed grape skin (after wine is extracted). 2. residue of the olives after pressing (yielding inferior oil).
orvallar, *i.v.* to drizzle, rain lightly.
orvalle, *m.* (bot.) wild sage.
orvallo, *m.* drizzle; dew.
orza, *f.* crock, earthenware jar, gallipot.
orza, *f.* 1. (mar.) luff; luffing. 2. (mar.) centerboard, sliding or drop keel. — **a o.,** (mar.) (to sail) into the wind; (fig.) to go awry, askew (plans, etc.).
orzaga, *f.* (bot.) orach.
orzar, (*ref. 53*) *i.v.* (mar.) to luff, turn into the wind.
orzaya, *f.* nanny, children's nurse.
orzoyo, *m.* (tex.) silk yarn (ready for making velvet pile).
orzuela, *f.* (Mex.) split ends (a poor condition of human hair).
orzuelo, *m.* 1. snare (for birds); trap (for wild animals). 2. (med.) sty.
os, *pers. pron.* (direct and indirect object form and reflexive form of *vos* and *vosotros*). 1. (as direct object) you, e.g. *os perdono,* I forgive you. 2. (as indirect object) you, to you, e.g. *os di el libro,* I gave you the book; you, for you, e.g. *os compré lo que me pedisteis,* I bought (for) you what you asked; from you, e.g. *os quitará todo lo que poseéis,* he will take away from you all that you possess.
Os *sym. of* **osmio,** osmium (Os).
osa, *f.* (zool.) she-bear. — **O. Mayor,** (astron.) Great Bear, Ursa Major, the Dipper; **O. Menor,** (astron.) Little Bear, Ursa Minor.
osadamente, *adv.* boldly, daringly, audaciously.
osadía, *f.* audacity, boldness, daring.
osado, da, *past part. of* **osar.** —*a.* daring, audacious, bold; **a osadas,** boldly.
osambre, *m., var. of* **osamenta.**
osamenta, *f.* skeleton, bones.
osar, *m., var. of* **osario.**
osar, *i.v.* to venture; dare; **o. +** *inf.,* to dare + *inf.*
osario, *m.* ossuary, charnel house.
oscar, *m.* (coll., cinem.) Oscar, popular name for the statuette awarded yearly in the U.S. to film notables.
oscilación, *f.* oscillation; **o. de la frecuencia,** (rad.) frequency swing; **o. parásita,** (rad.) parasitic oscillation.
oscilador, *m.* (phys.) oscillator; **o. de pulsación,** (rad.) beat oscillator; **o. de toda onda,** (rad.) signal generator.
oscilante, *f.* oscillating; swinging; oscillatory; **circuito o.,** oscillatory circuit.
oscilar, *i.v.* 1. to oscillate; to swing. 2. to fluctuate, change. 3. to hesitate, waver.
oscilatorio, ria, *a.* oscillatory.
oscilógrafo, *m.* (phys.) oscillograph.
oscilograma, *f.* (phys.) oscillogram.
osciloscopio, *m.* (phys.) oscilloscope.
oscina, *f.* (ornith.) oscine.
oscitancia, *f.* negligence, carelessness.
ósculo, *m.* kiss.
oscuramente, *adv., var. of* **obscuramente.**
oscurantismo, *m., var. of* **obscurantismo.**
oscurantista, *a., m., f., var. of* **obscurantista.**
oscurecer, (*ref. 45*) *tr.v., r.v., var. of* **obscurecer.**
oscurecimiento, *m., var. of* **obscurecimiento.**
oscurezca, *ref.* **obscurecer.**
oscuridad, *f., var. of* **obscuridad.**
oscuro, ra, *a., var. of* **obscuro.**
osecico, osecillo, osecito, *m. dim. of* **hueso,** little bone, bonelet.
oseína, *f.* (biochem.) ossein.
óseo, a, *a.* bony; pertaining to bone, osseous; **tumor óseo,** bone tumor.
osera, *f.* bear's lair or den.
osero, *m.* ossuary, charnel house.
osezno, *m.* bear cub.
osezuelo, *m.* little bone.
osículo, *m.* (anat., zool.) ossicle.
osificación, *f.* ossification.
osificarse, (*ref. 50*) *r.v.* to ossify, become ossified, become bone.
osifique, *ref.* **osificarse.**
osífraga, *f.* (ornith.) *var. of* **osífrago.**
osífrago, *m.* (ornith.) ossifrage, lammergeier.
Osiris, *m.* (myth.) Osiris, ancient Egyptian god of the lower world.
Oslo, *m.* Oslo, capital of Norway.
osmanlí, (*pl.* **osmanlíes**), *m., f.* Osmanli, Ottoman Turk.
osmático, ca, *a.* osmatic, osmic, having a sense of smell.
osmazomo, *m.* (chem.) osmazome.
ósmico, ca, *a.* (chem.) osmatic, osmic.
osmio, *m.* (metal.) osmium.
osmiridio, *m.* (min.) osmiridium.
ósmosis, *f.* (phys.) osmosis.
osmótico, ca, *a.* osmotic.
oso, *m.* bear; **hacer el o.,** (coll.) to play the fool; (coll.) to court or woo quite openly; **o. blanco, marítimo** or **polar,** polar or white bear; **o. colmenero,** little anteater; **o. de felpa** or **peluche,** teddy bear; **o. gris,** grizzly bear; **o. hormiguero,** ant bear, great anteater; **o. marino,** fur seal; **o. marsupial,** koala, Australian bear; wombat; **Osa Mayor,** *f.* Great Bear; **Osa Menor,** *f.* Little Bear; **o. negro,** black bear; **o. panda,** panda; **o. pardo,** brown bear; **o. perezoso,** sloth.
OSO *abbrev. of* **oessudoeste,** west-southwest (WSW).
ososo, sa, *a.* osseous, bony.
OSP *abbrev. of* **Organización Sanitaria Panamericana,** Pan-American Health Organization.
osta, *f.* (mar.) vang; brace, guy rope.
ostaga, *f.* (mar.) tye, tie, runner.
ostalgia, *f.* (med.) ostalgia, ostealgia, pain in the bones.
¡oste! *interj.* off! go away! (to persons); **sin decir o. ni moxte,** without saying a word.
ostealgia, *f.* (med.) ostalgia, pain in the bones.
osteálgico, ca, *a.* ostalgic, ostealgic.
osteico, ca, *a.* osteal, osseous, bony.
osteína, *f.* (biochem.) ostein, ossein.
osteítis, *f.* (med.) osteitis.
ostensible, *a.* ostensible, obvious, clear, patent, manifest.

ostensiblemente, *adv.* ostensibly, obviously, clearly, patently.
ostensivo, va, *a.* ostensive, showing.
ostensorio, *m.* (ecc.) monstrance, ostensory.
ostentación, *f.* ostentation, show or boast; obvious pomp or luxury, e.g. *hacer o. de sus riquezas,* to boast of one's wealth.
ostentador, ra, *a.* ostentatious, boastful. —*m., f.* 1. ostentatious person. 2. holder (of title, championship, etc.).
ostentar, *tr.v.* to make a show of, brag about, boast of; to display or flaunt (luxury or wealth).
ostentativo, va, *a.* ostentatious, exhibiting, displaying.
ostento, *m.* portent, miraculous or monstrous thing.
ostentosamente, *adv.* ostentatiously, boastfully.
ostentoso, sa, *a.* ostentatious, magnificent, sumptuous.
osteoartritis, *f.* (med.) osteoarthritis.
osteoblasto, *m.* (anat.) osteoblast.
osteoclasia, *f.* (med.) osteoclasis.
osteoclasis, *f.* (med., surg.) osteoclasis.
osteoclasto, *m.* (surg.) osteoclast.
osteocráneo, *m.* (anat.) osteocranium.
osteocranium, *m.* (anat.) osteocranium.
osteófito, *m.* (med.) osteophyte.
osteogénesis, *f.* (physiol.) osteogenesis, formation of bone.
osteoide, *a.* (anat.) osteoid.
osteolita, *f.* (min.) osteolite.
osteolito, *m.* (paleon.) bone fossile.
osteología, *f.* osteology.
osteológico, ca, *a.* (anat.) osteological.
osteólogo, *m.* osteologist.
osteoma, *m.* (med.) osteoma.
osteomalacia, *f.* (med.) osteomalacia.
osteomielitis, *f.* (med.) osteomyelitis.
osteópata, *m., f.* (med.) osteopath.
osteopatía, *f.* (med.) osteopathy.
osteopático, ca, *a.* (med.) osteopathic.
osteoplastia, *f.* (med.) osteoplasty.
osteoplástico, ca, *a.* (med.) osteoplastic.
osteotomía, *f.* (surg.) osteotomy.
osteótomo, *m.* (surg.) osteotome.
ostia, *f.* (zool.) oyster.
ostiario, *m.* (ecc.) ostiary, doorkeeper.
ostíolo, *m.* (bot.) ostiole.
ostión, *m.* (zool.) large oyster.
ostra, *f.* (zool.) oyster; **o. perlera,** pearl oyster.
ostracismo, *m.* ostracism.
ostrácodo, *m.* (zool.) ostracod.
ostral, *m.* oyster bed; oyster farm.
ostrera, *f.* (reg.) oyster bed.
ostrería, *f.* oyster shop; restaurant specializing in oysters.
ostrero, ra, *a.* oysterlike. —*m.* 1. oysterman, oyster seller. 2. oyster bed, oyster farm. 3. (ornith.) oyster catcher, oyster bird. —*f.* oysterwoman.
ostrícola, *a.* pertaining to oyster-breeding and marketing.
ostricultura, *f.* the art, occupation or business of oyster-breeding.
ostrífero, ra, *a.* abounding in or producing oysters.
ostro, *m.* 1. large oyster. 2. purple dye from mollusks. 3. Auster, south wind.
ostrogodo, da, *m., f.* (hist.) Ostrogoth, East Goth, member of an ancient European tribe.
ostrón, *m.* large, ordinary oyster.
ostugo, *m.* 1. nook, corner. 2. bit, pinch.
osudo, da, *a.* bony.
osuno, na, *a.* bearlike, pertaining to bears.
otacústico, ca, *a.* otacoustic.
otalgia, *f.* (med.) otalgia, earache.
otálgico, ca, *a.* (med.) otalgic.
OTAN *abbrev. of* **Organización del Tratado del Atlántico del Norte,** North Atlantic Treaty Organization (NATO).
otáñez, *m.* (coll.) elderly squire who escorted a lady as chaperon.
otario, ria, *a.* (Arg.) foolish, gullible, easily deceived.
oteador, ra, *a.* vigilant, watchful. —*m., f.* watcher, observer, spy.
otear, *tr.v.* 1. to survey, scan, to observe from a height. 2. to watch, keep an eye on. 3. to examine, inspect, spy, search.
Otelo, *m.* (lit.) Othello.
otero, *m.* hill, butte, height, knoll.
oteruelo, *m. dim. of* **otero,** knoll, hillock.
otitis, *f.* (med.) otitis.
oto, *m.* (ornith.) tawny owl.
otocisto, *m.* (zool.) otocyst.
otolaringología, *f.* (med.) otolaryngology.
otolaringólogo, *m.* (med.) otolaryngologist.
otolito, *m.* (anat., zool.) otolith.
otología, *f.* (med.) otology.
otólogo, *m.* (med.) otologist, aurist.
otomán, *m.* (tex.) ottoman, corded silk or rayon fabric.
otomano, na, *a., m., f.* Ottoman, Turkish. —*f.* ottoman, low cushioned seat or divan.
otoñada, *f.* autumn time; autumn pastures.
otoñal, *a.* autumnal, pertaining to fall; in the autumn of life, ripe in years. —*m., f.* oldster.
otoñar, *i.v.* 1. to spend the autumn. 2. to sprout or grow in autumn. —*r.v.* to become seasoned or softened by the autumn rains (said of earth or dirt).
otoño, *m.* autumn, fall.
otorgadero, ra, *a.* grantable, that can be granted.
otorgador, ra, *a.* granting; issuing. —*m., f.* grantor; issuer.
otorgamiento, *m.* 1. granting, giving, awarding. 2. execution, issuing (of a deed, document, etc.). 3. approval, consent; authorization, permission, license, permit. 4. contract; will.
otorgante, *a.* granting; issuing. —*m., f.* granter; issuer, authorizer.
otorgar, (*ref. 51*) *tr.v.* 1. to grant, give, award, concede. 2. (law) to grant, award; to execute (a deed, will). — **quien calla otorga,** silence grants consent.
otorgue, otorgué, *ref.* **otorgar.**
otorrea, *f.* (med.) otorrhea.
otorrinolaringología, *f.* (med.) otorhinolaryngology.
otorrinolaringólogo, *m.* (med.) otorhinolaryngologist.
otosclerosis, *f.* (med.) otosclerosis.
otoscopia, *f.* (med.) otoscopy.
otoscopio, *m.* (med.) otoscope.
otro, tra, *a.* other; another; a different one. — **al o. día,** the next day, the day after; **el o. día,** the other day; **o. cosa,** something else; **o. tantos,** as many; **o. vez,** again, once more; **por o. parte,** on the other hand; **¡otra!** encore!; **unos a otros,** one another, each other.
otrora, *adv.* formerly, in other times, of yore.
otrosí, *adv.* furthermore, besides, moreover. —*m.* (law) each additional petition after the principal one.
Ottawa, *m.* Ottawa, capital of Canada.
ova, *f.* 1. (bot.) green algae. 2. (*pl.*) (zool.) roe. 3. (archit.) egg (in an egg and dart ornament).
ovación, *f.* ovation.
ovacionar, *tr.v.* to give an ovation to, acclaim, applaud.
ovado, da, *past part. of* **ovar.** —*a.* 1. ovate, oval, egg-shaped. 2. impregnated, fecundated (fowl).
oval, *a., var. of* **ovalado.**
ovalado, da, *a.* oval, egg-shaped.
ovalar, *tr.v.* to make oval.
óvalo, *m.* 1. oval. 2. (archit.) egg, ovum, egg-shaped ornament.
ovante, *a.* victorious, triumphant.
ovar, *i.v.* to lay eggs.
ovárico, ca, *a.* ovarian.
ovariectomía, *f.* (surg.) ovariectomy.
ovario, *m.* 1. (biol.) ovary. 2. (archit.) molding with egg-shaped ornaments.
ovariotomía, *f.* (med.) ovariotomy.
ovaritis, *f.* (med.) ovaritis.
ovas, *f. pl.* (reg., Sp.) roe, fish roe.
oveja, *f.* ewe, female sheep; **cada o. con su pareja,** let every man keep his place; birds of a feather flock together; **o. negra,** black sheep (e.g. of the family); **o. perdida** or **descarriada,** lost sheep; **o. renil,** spayed or castrated ewe.
ovejero, ra, *a.* sheep. —*m.* shepherd. —*f.* shepherdess. — **perro ovejero,** (Arg.) sheep dog.
ovejuela, *f.* small or young ewe, lamb.
ovejuno, na, *a.* pertaining to sheep, e.g. *leche ovejuna,* ewe's milk.
overa, *f.* ovary (of birds).
overo, ra, *a.* 1. golden, golden-colored (animal). 2. (*pl.*) (coll.) said of bulging eyes.
overol, *m.* (Amer.) overalls.
ovetense, *a.* Oviedo, of or from Oviedo, Spain. —*m., f.* native of Oviedo.
ovezuelo, *m. dim. of* **ovo,** small egg.
Ovidio, *m.* (lit.) Ovid, Roman poet.
óvidos, *m. (pl.)* (zool.) Ovidae, Capridae.
oviducto, *m.* (anat., zool.) oviduct.
oviforme, *a.* oviform, egg-shaped.
ovil, *m.* sheepfold, sheepcote.
ovillar, *tr.v.* to roll or wind (yarn, thread) into a ball. —*r.v.* to roll or curl into a ball.
ovillejo, *m.* 1. (poet.) metric combination composed of three octosyllabic lines, a kind of rondel or rondeau. 2. small ball (of yarn or thread).
ovillo, *m.* 1. ball (of wool, silk, etc.) 2. tangled ball; heap, jumbled mess. — **hacerse un o.,** to hunch oneself up, crouch; to get all mixed or tangled up (when talking).
ovino, na, *a.* ovine. —*m.* ovine; (*pl.*) (zool.) Ovinae.
ovíparo, ra, *a.* oviparous. —*m.* oviparous animal; (*pl.*) (zool.) Ovipara (oviparous animals).
oviscapto, *m.* (zool.) ovipositor.
OVNI *abbrev. of* **objeto volador no identificado,** unidentified flying object (UFO).
ovo, *m.* (archit.) egg, ovum, egg-shaped ornament.
ovoide, ovoideo, *a.* ovoid.
óvolo, *m.* 1. (archit.) ovolo. 2. (archit.) egg, ovum (in egg-and-dart ornaments).
ovoso, sa, *a.* containing roe, full of roe.
ovotestis, *f.* (biol.) ovotestis.
ovovivíparo, *a.* (zool.) ovoviviparous. —*m.* ovoviviparous animal; (*pl.*) Ovovivipara.
ovulación, *f.* (biol.) ovulation.
óvulo, *m.* (biol.) ovule.
¡ox! *interj.* shoo! (said to chase away fowl or to scare birds).
oxácido, *m.* (chem.) oxyacid.
oxalato, *m.* (chem.) oxalate; **o. potásico,** (chem.), potassium oxalate.
oxálico, ca, *a.* (chem.) oxalic.
oxalidáceo, a, *a.* (bot.) oxalidaceous. —*f.* (*pl.*) Oxalidaceae.
oxalídeo, a, *a., var. of* **oxalidáceo.**
oxalme, *m.* brine and vinegar.
oxazina, *f.* (chem.) oxazine, oxazin.
¡oxe! *interj.* shoo!
oxear, *tr.v.* to shoo away (fowl, birds).

oxhídrico, ca, *a.* (chem.) oxyhydrogen.
oxhidrilo, oxidrilo, *m.* (chem.) hydroxyl.
oxiacanta, *f.* (bot.) hawthorn, whitethorn.
oxiácido, *m.* (chem.) oxyacid.
oxibromuro, *m.* (chem.) oxybromide.
oxicloruro, *m.* (chem.) oxychloride.
oxidable, *a.* oxidizable.
oxidación, *f.* oxidation.
oxidante, *a.* oxidizing. —*m.* (chem.) oxidizer, oxidizing agent, oxidant.
oxidar, *tr.v.* (chem.) to oxidize; to rust. —*r.v.* to become oxidized.
oxidasa, *f.* (biochem.) oxidase.
óxido, *m.* (chem.) oxide; **ó. de zinc,** zinc oxide; (min.) iron oxide.
oxidorreducción, *f.* (chem.) oxidation-reduction.
oxídrico, ca, *a.* (chem.) oxyhydrogen.
oxífilo, la, *a.* oxyphile, oxyphil, oxyphilic. oxyphilous.
oxigenable, *a.* (chem.) oxygenizable.
oxigenación, *f.* (chem.) oxygenation.
oxigenado, da, *past part. of* **oxigenar.** —*a.* oxygenated.
oxigenar, *tr.v.* (chem.) to oxygenate; —*r.v.* 1. to become oxygenated. 2. to take some fresh air.
oxígeno, *m.* (chem.) oxygen.
oxigonio, *a.* (geom.) acute-angled.
oxihemoglobina, *f.* (biochem.) oxyhemoglobin.
oxima, *f.* (chem.) oxime, oxim.
oximel, oxymiel, *m.* (pharm.) oxymel.
oxímoron, *m.* (rhet.) oxymoron.
oxipétalo, *m.* (bot.) a Brazilian vine.
oxisal, *f.* (chem.) oxysalt.
oxisulfuro, *m.* (chem.) oxysulfide, oxysulphyde, oxysulfid, oxysulphid.
oxitetraciclina, *f.* (pharm.) oxytetracycline.
oxitócico, ca, *a.* (med.) oxytocic.
oxitocina, *f.* (physiol.) oxytocin.
oxítono, na, *a.* oxytone, stressed on the last syllable.
oxiuriasis, *f.* oxyuriasis.
oxiuriosis, *f.* oxyuriasis.
oxiuro, *m.* (zool.) pinworm; (*pl.*) Oxyuridae.
oxoniense, *a., m., f.* Oxonian, of or pertaining to Oxford University.
¡oxte! *interj.* shoo, go away! get out!; **sin decir oxte ni moxte,** (coll.) without so much as a by-your-leave; without a word.
oyendo, *ref.* **oír.**
oyente, *a.* listening. —*m., f.* listener. —*m.* auditor (one who listens to classes or lectures without being an enrolled student). — **los oyentes,** the audience.
oyera, oyese, oyó, *ref.* **oír.**
ozocerita, ozokerita, *f.* (min.) ozocerite.
ozona, *f., var. of* **ozono.**
ozonar, ozonizar, (*ref.* 53) *tr.v.* to ozonize.
ozónico, ca, *a.* ozonic.
ozonización, *f.* ozonization.
ozonizado, da, *a.* ozonic.
ozonizador, *m.* ozonizer.
ozonizar, (*ref.* 53) *tr.v.* to ozonize.
ozono, *m.* (chem.) ozone.
ozonólisis, *f.* (chem.) ozonolysis.
ozonómetro, *m.* (chem.) ozonometer.
ozoquerita, *f.* (min.) ozocerite.
ozostomía, *f.* (med.) ozostomia.

P

P, *f.* p, seventeenth letter of the Spanish alphabet.
P. *abbrev. of* **padre,** priest.
Pa *sym. of* **protactinio,** protactinium (Pa).
pabellón, *m.* 1. pavillion, bell tent. 2. pavilion, canopy. 3. (archit.) pavilion building in an exposition. 4. flag, banner; (mar.) national flag, colors. 5. (jewel.) pavilion (faceted part of a precious stone). 6. bell (flaring mouth of wind instruments). 7. (mil.) stack (of rifles). 8. (fig.) protection. 9. (anat.) pavilion. — **p. auricular** or **de la oreja,** outer ear; **p. de caza,** hunting lodge.
pabilo, pábilo, *m.* 1. candle wick. 2. snuff (charred end of candle wick).
pabilón, *m.* tuft or bunch of flax or silk hanging from the distaff.
pablar, *i.v.* (hum.) to speak.
Pablo, *m.* **¡guarda, P.!** (coll.) be careful!; take care! watch out!
pábulo, *m.* 1. food, pabulum, aliment. 2. (fig.) support, encouragement, food, fuel, pabulum. — **dar p. a,** to add fuel to the fire, feed the flames of, e.g. *dar p. a la murmuración,* to encourage gossip.
paca, *f.* 1. (zool.) paca, spotted cavy. 2. bale, bundle.
pacana, *f.* (bot.) pecan tree, pecan nut.
pacato, ta, *a.* gentle, mild, peaceful quiet; timid.
pacay, (*pl.* **pacayes** or **pacaes**), *m.* (bot.) pacay (tree and fruit).
pacaya, *m.* (C. Rica, Hond., bot.) pacaya, shrub with palm leaves.
pacayar, *m.* (Peru) plantation or grove of pacay trees.
pacedero, ra, *a.* good for grazing, pasture, pasturable (land).
pacedura, *f.* pasture-ground.
pacense, *a.* of or from Badajoz, Spain. —*m., f.* native or inhabitant of Badajoz.
paceño, ña, *a.* of or from La Paz, Bolivia. —*m., f.* native or inhabitant of La Paz.
pacer, (*ref. 45*) *i.v.* to graze, pasture. —*tr.v.* 1. to graze, pasture, put out to pasture. 2. to eat away, nibble, gnaw.
pachá, *m.* pasha, title of rank or honor in certain Eastern countries.
pachacho, cha, *a.* 1. (Chile) short-legged. 2. (Chile) chubby, tubby.
pachamanca, *f.* (Peru) barbecue.
pacho, cha, *a.* 1. (C. Amer., Chile) short, chubby, stumpy. 2. (C. Amer.) flat.
pachocha, *f.* (Chile, Peru) sluggishness, laziness; slowness.
pachochudo, da, *a.* (Peru) *var. of* **pachorrudo.**
pachón, na, *a.* 1. (Amer.) shaggy, hairy, wooly. 2. (Peru) dim, dull, unintelligent. —*m.* 1. pointer (dog). 2. calm quiet fellow.
pachorra, *f.* (Cuba, P. Rico) sluggishness, laziness, slowness.
pachorrudo, da, *a.* (coll.) slow, phlegmatic, sluggish, lazy.
pachucho, cha, *a.* 1. overripe. 2. (fig.) floppy, droopy, languid.
pachulí, *m.* (bot.) patchouli (plant and scent).
paciencia, *f.* 1. patience, forbearance. 2. small almond cake. — **acabársele a uno la p.,** to get to the end of one's patience, lose patience; **perder la p.,** to lose one's patience.
paciente, *a.* patient, long-suffering, forbearing. —*m., f.* (med.) patient. —*m.* patient, recipient of an action.
pacientemente, *adv.* patiently.
pacienzudo, da, *a.* very patient or long-suffering.
pacificación, *f.* pacification; peace, quiet.
pacificador, ra, *a.* pacifying. —*m., f.* pacifier, peacemaker.
pacíficamente, *adv.* pacifically, peaceably.
pacificar, (*ref. 50*) *tr.v.* to pacify. —*i.v. to negotiate a peace.* —*r.v.* (fig.) to calm down, become calm.
pacífico, ca, *a.* 1. pacific, peaceful, peaceable. 2. **P.,** Pacific (Ocean). —*m.* **P.,** the Pacific (Ocean).
pacifique, pacifiqué, *ref.* pacificar.
pacifismo, *m.* pacifism.
pacifista, *a., m., f.* pacifist.
paco, *m.* 1. (zool.) paco, alpaca. 2. (min.) paco. 3. (Sp.) Moroccan sniper. 4. (Chile) policeman.
paco, ca, *a.* (Arg., Urug.) reddish-brown.
pacón, *m.* (Hond., bot.) soapberry tree.
pacotilla, *f.* 1. venture, goods carried by sailors and officers free of freight charges. 2. inferior quality or shoddily made goods, trash, junk. 3. (Guat., Ecuad., Chile) mob, rabble. — **hacer su p.,** to make one's pile, make a bundle, feather one's nest; **ser de p.,** to be of inferior quality; to be poorly or shoddily made.
pacotillero, *m.* (Amer.) peddler, street hawker.
pactar, *tr.v.* to contract, stipulate; to agree upon, agree to. —*i.v.* to agree, come to an agreement; to make a pact or agreement.
pacto, *m.* pact, agreement, covenant, contract. — **p. de caballeros,** gentlemen's agreement; **p. de no agresión,** non-aggression pact; **p. social,** social contract.
pacú, *m.* (ichth., Arg.) a large river fish.
pácul, *m.* (bot., Phil. I.) wild plantain.
padecer, (*ref. 45*) *tr.v.* 1. to suffer from. 2. to put up with, endure, tolerate, suffer. 3. to be the victim of (an illusion, mistake). —*i.v.* to suffer; to be injured or damaged, e.g. *p. del estómago* or *de los nervios,* to suffer from the stomach or from nerves; *las cosechas han padecido con el frío reciente,* the crops have suffered from or been damaged by the recent cold.
padecimiento, *m.* 1. suffering. 2. ailment.
padezca, padezco, *ref.* **padecer.**
padilla; *f.* small frying pan; small oven.
padrastro, *m.* 1. stepfather; (fig.) severe father. 2. (fig.) obstacle, difficulty, impediment. 3. (fig.) hangnail.
padrazo, *m.* (coll.) overindulgent father.
padre, *m.* 1. father. 2. **P.,** (theol.) Father (first person of the Trinity). 3. father (reverential form of addressing a priest). 4. sire, stallion. 5. (fig.) father, originator, e.g. *Herodoto es el p. de la historia,* Herodotus is the father of history. 6. (*pl.*) parents; ancestors. 7. (*pl.*) (theol.) Fathers (of the Church). — **hallar p. y madre,** to find oneself a home; **P. Apostólico,** Apostolic Father; **p. conscripto,** (Roman hist.) conscript father; **p. de almas,** spiritual adviser; **p. de familia,** head of the family, pater-familias; **p. de la patria,** founding father (of a nation); **p. de pila,** godfather; **p. espiritual,** confessor; **P. Eterno,** Eternal Father, God Almighty; **P. Nuestro,** Our Father, Our Maker; **p. político,** father-in-law; **P. Santo,** Holy Father, the Pope; **Santo P.,** Father of the Church; **sin p. ni madre,** totally independent; all alone in the world; **tener el p. alcalde,** to have influential friends.
padrear, *i.v.* 1. to resemble one's father. 2. to breed (animals). 3. (coll.) to sow one's wild oats.
padrenuestro, *m.* Lord's prayer; **P.,** Our Father.
padrillo, *m.* (Amer.) sire, stallion.
padrinazgo, *m.* 1. godfathership, sponsorship, status of godfather or sponsor. 2. patronage, favor, protection.
padrino, *m.* 1. godfather; sponsor. 2. best man or person who presents a bride for marriage. 3. second (in a duel). 4. (*pl.*) godparents.
padrón, *m.* 1. census list or register (of people living in a certain place area). 2. model, pattern. 3. inscribed column or pillar. 4. blemish, stain or mark of infamy (on a reputation). 5. (coll.) overindulgent father. 6. (Amer.) sire, stallion. — **p. electoral,** electoral roll.
paella, *f.* Valencian rice dish with meat, fish or seafood and vegetables.
¡paf! *interj.* bang!
paflón, *m.* (archit.) soffit.
pág. *abbrev. of* **página,** page.
paga, *f.* 1. pay, fee, wages, earnings. 2. payment. 3. amends, satisfaction; fine. 4. requiting (of love), repayment (of favor). — **buena p.,** good pay; one who pays promptly; **mala p.,** poor pay; one who pays slowly.
pagable, *a.* payable.
pagadero, ra, *a.* payable; **p. a la demanda,** payable on sight. —*m.* time and place of payment.
pagado, da, *past part. of* **pagar.** —*a.* 1. paid; compensated. 2. vain, conceited, e.g. *p. de su suerte* or *de sí mismo,* vain, conceited, self-satisfied.
pagador, ra, *a.* paying. —*m., f.* 1. payer. 2. teller (in a bank); paymaster.
pagaduría, *f.* paymaster's office; disbursement office.
pagamento, pagamiento, *m.* payment.
paganice, paganicé, *ref.* **paganizar.**
paganismo, *m.* paganism; heathenism.
paganizar, (*ref. 53*) *i.v.* to paganize. —*r.v.* to become pagan.
pagano, na, *a., m., f.* pagan, heathen. —*m.* (coll.) one who pays for others; easy mark, sucker (sl.).
pagar, (*ref.51*) *tr.v.* 1. to pay; to pay for; to return (visit, favor). 2. to requite, atone, make amends for; to return (love, friendship, etc.). — **pagarla** or pagarlas, to pay for it. —*i.v.* to pay. — **a luego p.,** cash, for cash; **p. con la misma moneda,** to pay in the same coin; **p. los platos rotos,** to pay the piper; to pay the fiddler. —*r.v.* 1. to become fond (of). 2. to boast, brag (about).
pagaré, *m.* (com.) promissory note, i.o.u.; **p de favor or cortesia,** accommodation paper.
pagaya, *f.* large-bladed scull (used in Phil. I. to propel and steer the boat).
pagel, *m.* (ichth.) red sea bream.

página, *f.* 1. page (of a book); folio. 2. (fig.) page (in life, history).
paginacion, *f.* pagination, paging, page numbering.
paginar, *tr.v.* to page, paginate, number the pages of (a book, etc.).
pago, *m.* 1. payment; repayment, requital, recompense. 2. district, region, estate; village. — **balance de pagos,** (econ.) balance of payments; **en p. (de),** in payment (of); as recompense (for); **p. a plazos,** payment in installments; **p. contra entrega,** cash on delivery (C.O.D.). —*a.* (coll.) paid.
pagoda, *f.* pagoda.
pagote, *m.* (coll.) 1. one who pays. 2. scapegoat.
pagro, *m.* (ichth.) porgy.
pague, pagué, *ref.* **pagar.**
paguro, *m.* (zool.) hermit crab.
paico, *m.* (Arg., Col., Chile, Ecuad., bot.) wormseed, Mexican tea.
paila, *f.* 1. large shallow pan; cauldron. 2. (Cuba) sugar pan, evaporator.
pailebot, pailebote, *m.* (mar.) small schooner; pilot's boat.
pailero, *m.* (Col.) pan-mender; (Cuba) workman in charge of sugar pans (in sugar mill).
pailón, *m.* 1. *aug. of* **paila,** very large pan. 2. (Hond.) round-bottomed ravine or gully.
paipai, *m.* (Phil. I.) palm fan.
painel, *m.* (archit.) panel.
pairar, *i.v.* (mar.) to lie to (a vessel).
pairo, *m.* (mar.) lying to; **al p.,** lying to with all sails set.
país, *m.* 1. country, land, nation; region, territory. 2. (p.) landscape. 3. paper or cloth backing of a fan.
paisaje, *m.* landscape.
paisajista, *a.* landscape (painter). —*m., f.* landscape artist or painter.
paisanaje, *m.* 1. civilians, civilian population. 2. state of being compatriots. 3. peasantry, peasants, country people.
paisano, na, *a.* of the same country or region. —*m.* 1. fellow countryman, compatriot. 2. peasant, countryman. 3. civilian, e.g. *vestido de p.,* (mil.) in civilian clothes, in mufti. —*f.* 1. fellow countrywoman. 2. peasant woman, countrywoman. 3. country dance.
Países Bajos, *m.* Low Countries, Netherlands, Belgium and Luxembourg.
paisista, *a., var. of* **paisajista.**
paja, *f.* 1. straw. 2. rubbish, trash, chaff, deadwood. 3. (fig.) straw, light, unimportant thing. — **apartar el grano de la p.,** to separate the wheat from the chaff; **buscar la p. en el oído,** (coll.) to look for a quarrel or trouble, look for an opportunity to annoy someone; **echar pajas,** to draw lots; **quítame allá esas pajas,** in a jiffy, in two shakes of a donkey's tail; **hacerse la p.,** (vulg.) to masturbate; **no dormirse en las pajas,** (coll.) to be alert and wide awake, be on the lookout for opportunities; **no importar** or **montar una p.,** to be utterly unimportant or useless; **p. cebadaza,** barley straw; **p. centenaza,** rye straw; **p. colorada,** paspalum (Paspalum cuadrifarium); **p. de agua.** (arch.) two cubic centimeters of water per second; (Col., Guat., Nic.) water tap, faucet; **p. de camello, de esquenanto** or **de Meca,** camel grass; **p. larga,** unthreshed barley straw; **por quítame allá esas pajas,** on account of a very unimportant thing; **quitar** or **sacar la p.,** to start a bottle (of wine); **ver la p. en el ojo ajeno, y no la viga en el propio,** to see the mote in another's eye and not the beam in one's own.
pajado, da, *a.* straw-colored, pale. —*f.* mix of bran and straw (a kind of fodder for horses).
pajar, *m.* barn, straw loft; haystack, hayrick.
pájara, *f.* 1. small bird. 2. kite (child's toy). 3. paper bird. 4. (fig.) crafty woman. — **p. pinta,** game of forfeits.
pajarear, *i.v.* 1. to hunt birds. 2. (fig.) to loiter about, loaf around. 3. (Amer.) to shy (a horse).
pajarel, *m.* (ornith.) linnet (Acanthis cannabina).
pajarera, *f.* aviary; large bird cage.
pajarería, *f.* 1. flock of birds. 2. bird shop.
pajarero, ra, *a.* 1. pertaining to birds, e.g. *redes pajareras,* bird nets. 2. perky, bright, cheerful, merry, gay. 3. flashy, gaudy, loud, bright-colored. — **caballo pajarero,** (Amer.) shyer (horse). —*m.* bird catcher; bird fancier.
pajarete, *m.* fine sherry wine.
pajaril, hacer p., (mar.) to passaree, pull the sails tight.
pajarilla, *f.* 1. (bot.) columbine (Aquilegia vulgaris). 2. milt, spleen (of a hog). 3. kite (child's toy). — **alegrársele a uno las pajarillas,** (coll.) to be greatly pleased, be delighted; **hacer temblar la p. a uno,** (coll.) to make one shake in his boots; **traerle a uno las pajarillas volando,** (coll.) to gratify a person's every wish, wait hand and foot on someone.
pajarita, *f.* 1. paper kite. 2. paper bird. 3. wing collar. — **p. de las nieves,** white wagtail.
pájaro, *m.* 1. bird. 2. (fig.) important man. 3. sly, crafty fellow. 4. (vulg.) penis. — **p. bebe,** (ornith.) penguin; **p. bitango,** kite (toy); **p. bobo,** (ornith.) penguin; **p. burro** (ornith.) frigate bird (Fregata aguila); **p. carpintero,** (ornith.) woodpecker; **p. de cuenta,** (coll.) big shot; **p. del sol,** (ornith.) bird of paradise; **p. diablo,** (ornith.) European coot, bald coot; **p. gordo,** (coll.) big noise, important wealthy person; **p. mosca,** (ornith.) humming bird; **p. moscón,** (ornith.) (species of) titmouse; **p. niño,** (ornith.) penguin; **p. polilla,** (ornith.) kingfisher; **p. resucitado,** (ornith.) tailorbird; **p. solitario,** (ornith.) solitaire; **p. tonto,** (ornith.) yellowhammer; **más vale p. en mano que ciento volando,** a bird in the hand is worth two in the bush; **matar dos pájaros de un tiro,** to kill two birds with one stone.
pajarota, pajarotada, *f.* (coll.) hoax, canard.
pajarote, *m.* large ugly bird.
pajarraco, *m.* 1. ugly bird. 2. (coll.) sly, crafty fellow, sharp customer.
pajaruco, *m., var. of* **pajarraco.**
pajaza, *f.* refuse or waste fodder.
pajazo, *m.* scar on the cornea of a horse's eye.
paje, *m.* 1. page (of a king, knight, etc.); valet. 2. (mar.) cabin boy. 3. familiar, servant (in bishop's residence). 4. dressing table. — **p. de armas** or **de lanza,** squire, armorbearer; **p. de cámara,** valet; **p. de escoba,** (mar.) cabin boy; **p. de hacha,** link boy.
pajea, *f.* (bot.) mugwort.
pajear, *i.v.* 1. to feed well, eat a lot of straw (said of a horse). 2. to behave, conduct oneself properly.
pajecillo, *m.* 1. *dim. of* **paje,** little page. 2. washstand.
pajel, *m.* (ichth.) sea bream.
pajera, *f.* straw loft (in a stable).
pajero, *m.* 1. straw dealer. 2. masturbator, one who masturbates frequently.
pajil, *a.* of or pertaining to a page.
pajilla, *f.* cigarette rolled in a corn leaf.
pajizo, za, *a.* 1. made or covered with straw. 2. thatched with straw. 3. straw-colored, pale yellow.
pajolero, ra, *a.* (Sp., coll.) disagreeable, unpleasant; ornery (dial.).
pajón, *m.* coarse straw.
pajonal, *m.* (Amer.) place abounding in straw or gleanings.
pajoso, sa, *a.* 1. full of straw. 2. straw-like, strawy.
pajote, *m.* straw mat used for protecting plants.
pajucero, *m.* place where straw is kept to rot for fertilizer.
pajuela, *f.* 1. short straw. 2. straw taper or spill. 3. (Bol.) sulphur match. 4. (Bol., Col.) earpick; toothpick. 5. (Ven.) mandolin plectrum.
pajuno, na, *a., var. of* **pajil.**
pajuz, *m.* refuse of straw used for manure.
Pakistán, *m.* Pakistan.
pal, *m.* (her.) pale.
pala, *f.* 1. shovel; spade; (baker's) peel. 2. blade (of ax, hoe, spade); flat part (of various instruments). 3. pelota bat; (badminton) racket. 4. wash beetle, battledore. 5. (tanner's) scraping knife. 6. vamp, upper (of shoes). 7. wide flat surface (of teeth). 8. (vet.) milk molar (of colt). 9. section of a prickly pear. 10. leaf (of a hinge). 11. top (of the epaulet, from which the fringe hangs). 12. (coll.) ruse, trick (to obtain information). 13. (coll.) skill, ability (in pelota). 14. (mar.) small sail. 15. (mus.) flat part of key (of flute, etc., pressed by the finger). — **meter la p.,** (coll.) to trick, deceive, pull the wool over someone's eyes; **meter su media p.,** (coll.) to share in, take part; **p. de cuchara,** bowl of a spoon; **p. de timón,** rudder blade; **p. a vapor,** steam shovel; **p. empujadora,** dozer shovel; **p. excavadora,** power shovel; **p. mecánica,** power shovel.
palabra, *f.* 1. word, term. 2. faculty of speech. 3. word, promise, assurance. 4. right to speak, turn to speak. 5. (theol.) P., the Word. 6. (*pl.*) witch's formula (when weaving spells). 7. (ecc.) formula (for sacraments). — **a media p.,** at the least word or hint; **a palabras necias oídos sordos,** to turn a deaf ear to nonsense; **cruzar una p. con,** to talk with, engage in conversation; **bajo su p.,** on one's word of honor; **beber las palabras a uno,** to wait upon attentively; **coger la p.,** to keep one to one's word; **comerse las palabras,** (coll.) to swallow one's words, speak indistinctly; to skip a word (in writing); **cuatro** or **dos palabras,** a word, a few words; **dar la p.,** to give (someone) the floor or the right to speak; **dar su p.,** to give one's word, promise; **dejar a uno con la p. en la boca,** to turn one's back on (not listen to what someone is saying); **de p.,** orally, by word of mouth; **dirigir la p. a,** to address, speak to; **empeñar la p.,** to pledge one's word; **en dos palabras, en una p., en pocas palabras,** in short, briefly, in a word; **estar colgado** or **pendiente de las palabras de uno,** to hang on one's words; **faltar a su p.,** to fail to keep one's promise; **gastar palabras,** to waste one's breath; **llevar la p.,** to be the spokesman; **mantener su p.,** to keep one's word; **medir las palabras,** to weigh one's words, speak carefully; **no tener más que palabras,** to be a braggart or boaster; **no tener p.,** to be unreliable; **medias palabras,** garbled speech; veiled insinuations, veiled remarks; **¡palabra!** really, truly, upon my word of honor; **p. de clave,** code word; **p. compuesta,** compound word; **p. de Dios,** Word of God; **p. de honor,** word of honor; **p. de matrimonio,** promise of marriage; **p. divina,** Word of God; **p. funcional** or **vacía,** function word; **p. por p.,** word for word; **palabras cruzadas,** crossword puzzle; **palabras gruesas,** (coll.) strong words, strong language; **palabras mayores,** offensive or insulting words or language; **pedir la p.,** to ask to be allowed to speak, ask for the floor; **quitarle a uno la p.**

de la boca, to take the words out of one's mouth; **¡santa p.!** thank God!; **sobre su p.,** on one's word of honor; **tener la p.,** to have the floor, have the right to speak; **tener palabras,** to have words, have an argument; **tomar la p.,** to begin to speak, take the floor; **torcer las palabras,** to twist one's words; **trabarse de palabras,** to have words with one another, have an argument; **usar de la p.,** to speak, make a speech; **venir contra su p.,** to go against one's word.

palabrada, *f.* swearword, obscenity.

palabrear, *tr.v.* (Amer.) to chat, prattle.

palabreja, *f.* unimportant or odd word.

palabreo, *m.* chatter, prattle.

palabrería, *f.* talk, chatter, prattle; empty talk, wordiness.

palabrero, ra, *a.* 1. talkative, loquacious. 2. unreliable (who does not keep promises). —*m., f.* 1. chatterbox, prattler, chatterer. 2. vain talker, windbag.

palabrimujer, *a.* with a feminine voice. —*m.* man with a feminine voice.

palabrista, *a., m., f., var. of* **palabrero.**

palabrita, *f.* 1. *dim. of* **palabra,** small or short word. 2. word full of meaning.

palabrón, na, *a., var. of* **palabrero.**

palabrota, *f.* swearword, coarse word, obscenity.

palacete, *m.* elegant country house.

palaciego, ga, *a.* of or pertaining to a palace or court; palatial, splendid. —*m.* courtier.

palacio, *m.* 1. palace; mansion; royal residence. 2. official building of a court of justice. — **P. Real,** Royal Palace.

palacra, palacrana, *f.* gold nugget.

palada, *f.* 1. shovelful. 2. (mar.) stroke of an oar.

paladar, *m.* 1. (anat.) palate, roof of the mouth. 2. (fig.) palate, taste, sensibility. — **p. blando,** (anat.) soft palate; **p. duro,** hard palate.

paladear, *tr.v.* 1. to savor, taste, relish. 2. to clean or wash the palate of an animal (to induce him to eat). 3. to rub a baby's palate with something sweet to induce him to suckle. —*i.v.* to show its desire for suckling (a baby). —*r.v.* to savor, taste, relish.

paladeo, *m.* the act of savoring, tasting, relishing.

paladial, *a., f.* (phonet.) palatal.

paladín, *m.* paladin, champion, knight.

paladinamente, *adv.* publicly, openly, clearly.

paladino, na, *a.* public, open, manifest, clear. —*m.* paladin.

paladio, *m.* (chem.) palladium.

paladión, *m.* palladium, safeguard.

palado, da, *a.* (her.) paly.

palafito, *m.* palafitte, a lake dwelling.

palafrén, *m.* palfrey, woman's or groom's horse.

palafrenero, *m.* groom, hostler. — **p. mayor,** royal groom; first equerry.

palahierro, *m.* shaft socket (in a millstone).

palamallo, *m.* pall-mall (game).

palamenta, *f.* oarage, oars, set of oars.

palanca, *f.* 1. lever; crowbar; pole (for carrying weights). 2. (fig.) pull, influence. 3. (fort.) outworks made of stakes and earth. 4. (mar.) clew garnet. — **p. de cambio,** gear lever, switch lever; (auto.) gearshift lever; quick-change or change-gear lever; **p. de disparo,** trip lever; **p. de mando,** control stick or lever; **p. de pie** or **cabra,** (mec.) pinch bar; **p. oscilante,** (mec.) rocker lever; **p. ruptora,** (auto.) breaker arm.

palancada, *f.* blow given with a lever.

palancana, *f., var. of* **palangana.**

palangana, *f.* 1. washbowl, washbasin. 2. (C. Amer., Col.) platter, dish. —*m.* (Amer.) boaster, braggart.

palanganero, *m.* portable washstand.

palangre, *m.* boulter, setline, trotline, trawl line (fishing line with several hooks attached).

palangrero, *m.* 1. fishing vessel using a boulter. 2. boulterer, fisherman using a boulter.

palanquear, *tr.v.* to pry.

palanquera, *f.* wooden stockade, wooden fence.

palanquero, *m.* 1. leverman, leverer. 2. bellows blower (in a forge). 3. (Chile, Bol., ry.) brakeman.

palanqueta, *f.* 1. crowbar, jimmy. 2. (mar.) bar shot. 3. (Cuba) sweetmeat made with cane syrup. 4. (Mex.) dumbbell.

palanquín, *m.* 1. errand boy, porter. 2. palanquin, palankeen, covered litter. 3. (mar.) clew garnet. 4. (mar.) gun tackle.

palas, *m.* (astron.) Pallas (asteroid). —*f.* (myth.) Pallas; **P. Atena** or **Atenea,** Pallas Athene or Athena.

palasan, *m.* (bot.) rattan, rotang.

palastro, *m.* 1. sheet iron, steel plate. 2. plate of the bolt (in a lock).

palatal, *a., f.* (phonet.) palatal.

palatalice, *ref.* **palatalizar.**

palatalización, *f.* (phonet.) palatalization.

palatalizar, (*ref. 53*) *tr.v., r.v.* to palatalize.

palatice, *ref.* palaticar.

palatina, *f.* scarf, tippet, palatine.

palatinado, *m.* 1. palatinate. 2. **P.,** Palatinate (part of Germany). — **el Alto P.,** the Upper Palatinate; **el Bajo P.,** the Lower Palatinate.

palatino, na, *a.* (anat.) palatine. —*m.* (anat.) palatine, palatine bone.

palatino, na, *a.* palatine; **conde palatino,** count palatine. —*m.* palatine; **P.,** Palatine (one of the seven hills of Rome).

palatizar, (*ref. 53*) *tr.v.* (phonet.) to palatalize.

palay, *m.* (Phil. I.) palay, rice in the husk.

palazo, *m.* blow given with a spade or shovel.

palazón, *f.* woodwork, timbering (of house, hut); masting (of vessels).

palca, *f.* 1. (Bol.) juncture (of two roads or rivers). 2. (Bol.) fork (formed by a branch).

palco, *m.* (theat.) box; raised stand for spectators. — **p. de platea,** parterre box; **p. escénico,** stage.

paleador, *m.* shoveler, stoker.

palear, *tr.v.* 1. to winnow (grain). 2. to shovel; to beat or pound.

paleártico, ca, *a.* (geol., zool.) Paleartic.

palenque, *m.* 1. paling, fence, palisade. 2. enclosure; arena. 3. (Arg., Bol., Urug.) hitching post (for horses). 4. (Amer.) noisy place.

palentino, na, *a.* of or from Palencia, Spain. —*m., f.* native or inhabitant of Palencia.

paleoarqueología, *f.* paleoarchaeology.

paleobotánica, *f.* paleobotany.

paleoceno, na, *a., m.* (geol.) Paleocene.

paleoetnología, *f.* paleethnology.

paleoetnológico, ca, *a.* paleethnologic, paleethnological.

paleoetnólogo, *m.* paleethnologist.

paleografía, *f.* paleography.

paleográfico, ca, *a.* paleographic, paleographical.

paleógrafo, *m.* paleographer.

paleolítico, ca, *a.* (geol.) paleolithic, paleolithical.

paleología, *f.* paleology.

paleontografía, *f.* paleontography.

paleontográfico, ca, *a.* paleontographic, paleontographical.

paleontología, *f.* paleontology.

paleontológico, ca, *a.* paleontologic, paleontological.

paleontólogo, *m.* paleontologist.

paleoterio, *m.* (paleon.) paleothere.

paleozoico, ca, *a., m.* Paleozoic.

paleozoología, *f.* paleozoology.

paleozoólogo, *m.* paleozoologist.

palería, *f.* (agr.) drainage, draining.

palermitano, na, *a.* of or from Palermo, Italy; Palermitan. —*m., f.* native or inhabitant of Palermo, Palermitan.

palero, *m.* 1. shovel maker or seller. 2. drainer, ditcher, shoveler. 3. (mil.) sapper, pioneer.

palestino, na, *a., m., f.* Palestinian. —*f.* 1. (print.) two-line pica. 2. P., Palestine.

palestra, *f.* 1. palaestra, gymnasium, wrestling court; arena. 2. wrestling. 3. contest, competition, tournament.

paléstrico, ca, *a.* palaestric, palaestral, palaestrian.

palestrita, *m.* wrestler.

paleta, *f.* 1. small shovel, fire shovel. 2. (p.) palette. 3. (cul.) serving ladle; spatula. 4. poker (for fire). 5. (mas.) trowel. 6. (anat.) shoulder blade. 7. paddle, blade (of water wheel); vane, blade (of ventilator, windmill, etc.); blade (of propeller). 8. (Amer.) (washing) paddle (for beating clothes). 9. (Amer.) racket, bat. — **de p.,** at hand, handy; **en dos paletas,** in a twinkling, in a jiffy; **p. directriz,** (hydr.) guide vane, wicket gate.

paletada, *f.* 1. trowelful. 2. blow given with a trowel, shovel or bat. — **en dos paletadas,** in a jiffy.

paletazo, *m.* glancing blow with the bull's horns.

paletear, *i.v.* to thrash about with the oars or beat the water without advancing.

paleteo, *m.* ineffective thrashing or flapping with paddles or oars.

paletero, *m.* (hunt.) two-year-old fallow deer.

paletilla, *f.* 1. (anat.) shoulder blade. 2. (anat.) sternum cartilage. 3. short candlestick. — **levantarle a uno la p.,** (coll.) to give someone very bad news; **ponerle a uno la p. en su lugar,** (coll.) to give someone a dressing-down, to reprimand severely.

paletizar, (*ref. 53*) *tr.v.* to palletize.

paleto, *m.* 1. fallow deer. 2. (fig.) yokel, rustic, rube (U.S.).

paletó, *m.* paletot, overcoat, greatcoat.

paletón, *m.* bit web (of a key).

paletoque, *m.* mantlet, short cape, scapular.

pali, *a., m.* Pali (religious language of Buddhism).

palia, *f.* (ecc.) altar cloth or frontal; curtain or pall covering tabernacle; pall, chalice cover.

paliación, *f.* palliation, extenuation; alleviation, mitigation.

paliadamente, *adv.* secretly, on the sly, stealthily.

paliar, *tr.v.* to palliate, extenuate; to alleviate, lessen.

paliativo, va, *a., m.* palliative.

paliatorio, ria, *a.* palliative.

palidecer, (*ref. 45*) *i.v.* to turn pale, grow pale, to pale.

palidez, *f.* pallor, paleness.

palidezca, palidezco, *ref.* **palidecer.**

pálido, da, *a.* 1. pale, pallid, wan. 2. (fig.) colorless (novel or play).

paliducho, cha, *a.* palish, pale, sickly, wan.

palillero, ra, *m., f.* toothpick maker or seller. —*m.* toothpick holder.

palillo, *m.* 1. knitting needle holder. 2. toothpick; cocktail stirrer. 3. bobbin (for lace-making). 4. drumstick. 5. vein or stem of a thick tobacco leaf. 6. (fig.) chitchat, small talk. 7. (*pl.*) pins (in billiards). 8. (*pl.*) castanets. 9. (*pl.*) modeling sticks (used by sculptors). 10. (*pl.*) (coll.) rudiments, first principles. 11. (*pl.*) (coll.) trifles. — **como p. de barquillero,** coming and going; **palillos,** chopsticks; **tocar todos los palillos,** (coll.) to try all methods (to obtain something).

palimpsesto, *m.* palimpsest (ancient document imperfectly erased and reused).

palíndromo, ma, *a.* palindromic. —*m.* palindrome, word that has the same sound and meaning when read backwards, e.g. Anna.
palingenesia, *f.* palingenesis, rebirth, regeneration.
palingenésico, ca, *a.* palingenetic.
palingénesis, *f.* (min., biol.) palingenesis.
palinodia, *f.* palinode, retraction, recanting. — **cantar la p.,** to retract.
palinología, *f.* (bot.) palynology.
Palinuros, *m.* (myth.) Palinurus, Aeneas' pilot (in the Oddysey).
palio, *m.* 1. pallium, himation (Greek cloak); cloak, mantle. 2. (ecc.) pallium (insignia of archbishops and some bishops). 3. baldachin, canopy. 4. (anat.) pallium. 5. winner's prize for racing. 6. (her.) pairle, pall, shakefork. — **recibir con** or **bajo p.,** to receive with great pomp.
palique, *m.* (coll.) chitchat, small talk.
paliquear, *i.v.* to chatter, prattle.
palisandro, *m.* (bot.) palisander, Brazilian rosewood.
palito, *m.* 1. (P. Rico, coll.) drink, cocktail. 2. cocktail stirrer.
palitoque, *m., var. of* **palitroque.**
palitroque, palitoque, *m.* 1. small roughly carved stick. 2. breadstick.
paliza, *f.* beating, thrashing, caning, bastinado.
palizada, *f.* 1. (mil.) palisade, stockade. 2. embankment. 3. fenced-in enclosure. 4. (her.) barry-pily field.
palla, *f.* 1. (Chile) improvised popular vocal duet. 2. (Bol., Chile) extraction of metal from ore.
pallaco, *m.* (Chile) pay dirt (left in abandoned mine).
pallador, *m.* (Amer.) minstrel, roving singer, wandering poet.
pallaquear, *tr.v.* (Peru) to extract (metal) from ore.
pallar, *tr.v., var. of* **pallaquear.** —*m.* (Peru) sieva bean, civet bean, butter bean.
pallas, *f.* indigenous Peruvian dance.
pallón, *m.* assay button (globule of gold remaining in crucible after assaying gold or silver ore); assaying of gold by cupellation.
palma, *f.* 1. (bot.) palm tree, palm; (*pl.*) Palmae (palm family); (bot.) palmetto, dwarf fan palm; (bot.) date palm. 2. palm leaf. 3. palm (of hand). 4. (vet.) palm, sole (of horse's hoof). 5. glory, triumph; victory. 6. (*pl.*) applause. — **andar en palmas,** to be universally applauded and esteemed; **batir palmas,** to clap one's hands, applaud; **ganar** or **llevarse la p.,** to carry the day, triumph, win; **llevar** or **traer en palmas,** (coll.) to pamper or spoil someone, gratify someone's every whim; **p. enana,** dwarf fan palm, palmetto.
palmacristi, *f.* palma Christi; castor oil plant.
palmada, *f.* slap; handclap, clap, (*pl.*) clapping, applause; **dar palmadas,** to clap, applaud; **dar una p.,** to clap one's hand (to attract attention); **dar unas cuantas palmadas a,** to spank, give a spanking to; **un par de palmadas,** a spank or spanking.
palmado, da, *past part. of* **palmar.**
palmar, *a.* 1. of or pertaining to palms. 2. (anat.) palmar. 3. clear, obvious, patent. —*m.* 1. palm grove. 2. fuller's teasel or thistle. — **ser más viejo que un p.,** to be as old as Methuselah.
palmar, *i.v.* to die, expire.
palmariamente, *adv.* obviously, clearly, evidently.
palmario, ria, *a.* clear, obvious, evident.
palmatífido, *m.* (bot.) palmatifid.
palmatoria, *f.* 1. teacher's rod, palmer, ferule. 2. small candlestick. — **ganar la p.,** to be first to school; to get somewhere first; to beat or anticipate someone.
palmeado, da, *past part. of* **palmear.** —*a.* palmate; (bot., zool.) palmate.
palmear, *i.v.* to clap, clap one's hands. —*tr.v.* 1. (print.) to plane down, level off (form with type plane or mallet). 2. to propel (a boat) by pulling on objects close at hand. —*r.v.* (mar.) to pull oneself along or up by means of a rope or cable.
palmejar, *m.* (mar.) keelson, thick stuff.
palmeo, *m.* measurement or measuring by spans.
pálmer, *f.* micrometer caliper.
palmera, *f.* palm tree, date palm; **p. datilera** or **de dátiles,** date palm.
palmeral, *m.* palm grove, date palm grove or plantation.
palmero, *m.* 1. palmer, pilgrim visiting the Holy Land. 2. palm tree keeper.
palmeta, *f.* 1. teacher's rod or ferule. 2. blow with a rod or ferule. — **ganar la p.,** to be the first to arrive at school; to get somewhere first; to beat or anticipate someone.
palmetazo, *m.* 1. blow with a rod or ferule. 2. discourteous or rough rebuke.
palmiche, *m.* 1. royal palm; royal palm nut. 2. (Cuba, tex.) palm beach (a fine suiting fabric).
palmífero, ra, *a.* (poet.) palmiferous, palm-bearing; abounding in palms.
palmilla, *f.* 1. inner sole (of shoe). 2. blue woolen cloth.
palmípedo, da, *a.* (zool.) webfooted. —*f.* (zool.) web-footed animal.
Palmira, *f.* Palmyra (ancient city of Syria).
palmista, *f.* (Amer.) palmist, hand reader, fortuneteller.
palmitato, *m.* (chem.) palmitate.
palmítico, ca, *a.* (chem.) palmitic.
palmitieso, sa, *a.* (vet.) flat-hoofed.
palmitina, *f.* (chem.) palmitin.
palmito, *m.* (bot.) 1. palmetto, dwarf fan palm. 2. heart of palmetto trunk used as a vegetable. 3. (coll.) woman's face, e.g. *buen p.,* beautiful face.
palmo, *m.* span, palm, measure of length (8 inches). — **crecer a palmos,** to grow by leaps and bounds; **dejar con un p. de narices,** (coll.) to disappoint, thwart, frustrate; **p. a p.,** little by little; **p. de tierra,** small stretch of land; **tener medido** or **conocer a palmos,** to know like the back of one's hand, know every inch of.
palmotear, *i.v.* to clap, clap hands, applaud.
palmoteo, *m.* 1. hand-clapping. 2. striking with a rod or ferule.
palo, *m.* 1. stick; staff; pole; club, cudgel. 2. wood, timber. 3. (mar.) mast, spar. 4. blow with a stick, whack. 5. hanging, garroting. 6. suit (in pack of cards). 7. stalk (by which fruit hangs from the tree). 8. stroke (of some letters). 9. (P. Rico, coll.) drink, cocktail. 10. (her.) pale. 11. (falcon's perch.) 12. (*pl.*) pins (in billiards); knocking down the pins in billiards. 13. (arch.) quinine. — **a p. seco,** (mar.) with sails hauled in; (fig.) without ceremony; **dar de palos,** to thrash, beat; **dar palos de ciego,** to swing out wildly; **de tal p., tal astilla,** like father, like son; **estar del mismo p.,** to be in the same position or condition; **meter el p. en la candela,** (coll.) to stir up trouble, pour oil on the flames; **no se dan palos de balde,** (coll.) you don't do anything for nothing; **p. áloe,** (bot.) aloeswood, agalloch, eaglewood; **p. bañon,** (bot.) alaternus, buckthorn; **p. corto,** short suit (in cards); **p. de campeche,** (bot.) logwood, campeachy or campeche wood; **p. de ciego,** unintentional blow, unintentional injury; **p. de escoba,** broomstick; **p. de esteva,** reach (of a carriage); **p. de favor,** trump suit (in cards); **p. de Pernambuco,** (bot.) Pernambuco wood; **p. de hule,** (bot.) rubber tree; **p. de jabón,** (bot.) soapbark, quillai; **p. de águila,** (bot.) eaglewood; **p. de la rosa,** (bot.) barberry, aspalathus; rosewood; **p. de las Indias,** (bot.) lignum vitae, holy wood; **p. del Brasil,** (bot.) brazilwood; Pernambuco wood; **p. de mesana,** (mar.) mizzenmast; **p. de rosa,** (bot.) rosewood; **p. de trinquete,** (mar.) foremast; **p. dulce,** (bot.) licorice root; **p. ensebado,** (Amer.) greasy pole; **p. fuerte,** long suit (in cards); **p. macho,** (mar.) mast; spar; **p. mayor,** (mar.) mainmast; **p. nefrítico,** (bot.) nephritic wood; **p. piche,** (Arg., bot.) pichi; **p. santo,** (bot.) lignum vitae, holy wood; **poner a uno en un p.,** to garrot, hang, put in the pillory; **portador de palos,** caddie, caddy; **terciar el p.,** to raise a stick as if to strike.
paloduz, *m.* (bot.) licorice root.
paloma, *f.* 1. pigeon, dove. 2. (fig.) dove, lamb, quiet meek person. 3. (astron.) **P.,** Dove, Columba. 4. (mar.) sling (middle part of a yard). 5. (coll.) high collar. 6. (coll.) brandy and soda. 7. (*pl.*) whitecaps, white horses (waves breaking into white foam). — **p. brava,** (ornith.) stock dove (Columba oenas); **p. buchona,** (ornith.) pouter pigeon; **p. capuchina,** (ornith.) capuchin (pigeon); **p. colipava,** (ornith.) fantail pigeon; **p. de la paz,** dove of peace; **p. de moño,** (ornith.) ruff pigeon; **p. de toca,** (ornith.) nun (pigeon); **p. duenda,** (ornith.) domestic pigeon; **p. mensajera,** (ornith.) homing or carrier pigeon; **p. monjil,** (ornith.) nun (pigeon); **p. moñuda,** (ornith.) ruff (pigeon); **p. silvestre,** (ornith.) wild pigeon, stock dove; **p. torcaz,** (ornith.) ringdove, wood pigeon (Columbia palumbus).
palomadura, *f.* (mar.) boltrope tie.
palomar, *a.* hard-twisted (said of twine). —*m.* pigeon house, dovecot. — **alborotar el p.,** (coll.) to put the cat among the pigeons, cause a commotion.
palomariego, palomariega, *a.* domestic (pigeon).
palomear, *i.v.* 1. to go pigeon shooting. 2. to spend a great deal of time looking after or breeding pigeons.
palomera, *f.* 1. small dovecot. 2. small moor or heath, bleak spot.
palomería, *f.* pigeon shooting.
palomero, ra, *m., f.* pigeon dealer; pigeon breeder, pigeon fancier.
palometa, *f.* 1. (ichth.) caribe, piranha. 2. (ichth.) (kind of) saurel or yellow jack.
palomilla, *f.* 1. small dove or pigeon. 2. (ento.) grain moth; small butterfly. 3. (bot.) fumitory. 4. (bot.) alkanet, dyer's alkanet. 5. back, forerump (of horse). 6. white horse. 7. peak (of packsaddle). 8. wall bracket. 9. journal or axle, bearing. 10. piece of iron connecting the carriage body with the back springs. 11. (ento.) nymph, pupa. 12. (Chile, Peru) street urchin, scamp; rabble, mob. 13. (*pl.*) whitecaps, white horses (white tops of waves). — **p. de tintes,** (bot.) alkanet, dyer's alkanet.
palomina, *f.* 1. pigeon droppings. 2. (bot.) fumitory.
palomino, *m.* 1. young stock dove. 2. (coll.) dirty mark on a shirttail.
palomita, *f.* 1. small dove. 2. (*pl.*) popcorn. 3. (Amer.) darling.
palomo, *m.* cock pigeon; (ornith.) ringdrove.
palón, *m.* (her.) guidon.
palor, *m.* pallor, paleness.
palotada, *f.* blow given with drumstick; **no dar p. uno,** (coll.) to do or say nothing right; not to do a stroke of work.
palote, *m.* 1. drumstick. 2. downstroke (in learning to write).

paloteado, *m.* 1. stick dance. 2. (coll.) noisy quarrel, argument or fight, scuffle.
palotear, *i.v.* 1. to beat sticks together. 2. to wrangle, argue.
paloteo, *m.* noisy quarrel, argument or fight.
palpabilidad, *f.* palpability.
palpable, *a.* 1. palpable; touchable. 2. (fig.) palpable, patent, clear, obvious.
palpablemente, *adv.* palpably, patently, clearly.
palpación, *f.* 1. touching, feeling, palpation. 2. (med.) palpation.
palpadura, *f.* touching, feeling; groping.
palpalén, palpallén, *m.* (bot., Chile) groundsel (Senecio dentidulata).
palpamiento, *m., var. of* palpadura.
palpar, *tr.v.* 1. to feel, touch, grope. 2. (med.) to palpate. 3. to see as self-evident. —*i.v.* to grope or feel one's way.
pálpebra, *f.* (anat.) eyelid, palpebra.
pálpebral, *a.* (anat.) palpebral.
palpitación, *f.* 1. palpitation, beating, throbbing. 2. (med.) palpitation.
palpitante, *a.* 1. palpitating, beating, throbbing. 2. burning (question, issue).
palpitar, *i.v.* to palpitate; to beat, throb, quiver.
pálpito, *m.* (Amer.) hunch, idea, presentiment; **por puro p.,** (Peru) just on a hunch.
palpo, *m.* (ento.) palpus, feeler.
palta, *f.* (Arg., Urug., bot.) avocado pear.
palto, *m.* (bot.) avocado pear tree.
paludamento, *m.* (Roman hist.) paludamentum (military cloak).
palúdico, ca, *a.* malarial, paludal, marshy, swampy. — **fiebre palúdica, malarial,** swamp or marsh fever, malaria. —*m., f.* malaria patient.
paludismo, *m.* (med.) malaria.
paludoso, sa, *a.* swampy, marshy, boggy.
paludrina, *f.* (pharm.) paludrine, paludrin.
palumbario, *a.* dove hunting; **halcón p.,** goshawk.
palurdo, da, *a.* uncouth, boorish. —*m., f.* rustic, yokel.
palustre, *m.* (mas.) trowel.
palustre, *a.* marshy, boggy.
pamandabuán, *m.* (Phil. I.) large dugout canoe, snake boat.
pambil, *m.* (Ecuad.) stilt palm.
pamela, *f.* pamela, picture hat, broadbrimmed straw hat, cartwheel hat.
pamena, *f.* 1. (coll.) unimportant trifle. 2. (coll.) cajolery, flattery.
pampa, *f.* pampas, pampa, extensive plain. — **La P.,** (geog.) the Pampas.
pámpana, *f.* vine leaf; **tocar** or **zurrarle la p. a uno,** (coll.) to thrash, beat.
pampanada, *f.* juice of vine shoots.
pampanaje, *m.* 1. abundant growth of vine shoots. 2. (fig.) empty words or promises.
pampanilla, *f.* loincloth.
pámpano, *m.* 1. vine shoot or tendril; vine leaf. 2. (ichth.) gilthead (Boops salpa). 3. (Amer., ichth.) pompano.
pampanoso, sa, *a.* full of shoots or tendrils (a grapevine).
pampeano, na, *a.* of or from the pampas, pampean. —*m., f.* pampean, native of the pampas.
pampear, *i.v.* (S. Amer.) to travel over or rove the pampas.
pampero, ra, *a.* of or from the pampas, pampean. —*m., f.* pampean, native of the pampas. —*m.* pampero (violent wind from the pampas).
pampirolada, *f.* 1. (cul.) bread sauce seasoned with garlic. 2. (coll.) piece of nonsense, silly thing.
pamplina, *f.* 1. (bot.) chickweed; largeflowered yellow poppy, pimpernel. 2. (coll.) nonsense, foolish thing, trifle. — **p. de agua,** (bot.) brookweed; **p. de canarios,** (bot.) chickweed; **¡pamplinas!** fiddlesticks! nonsense! rubbish!
pamplinada, *f.* nonsense, trifle, frivolity.
pamplinero, ra, pamplinoso, sa, *a.* foolish, silly, nonsensical.
pamplonés, sa, *a.* of or from Pamplona, Spain. —*m., f.* native or inhabitant of Pamplona.
pampón, *m.* (Peru) large yard or corral.
pamporcino, *m.* (bot.) sowbread, cyclamen.
pamposado, da, *a.* lazy, idle, indolent.
pamprigada, *f.* 1. slice of bread dipped in gravy. 2. (coll.) stupidity; ridiculous thing or act.
pampsiquismo, *m.* (philos.) panpsychism.
pan, *m.* 1. bread; loaf, loaf of bread. 2. dough. 3. cake (of soap), loaf (of sugar, etc.). 4. (fig.) bread, food, sustenance. 5. (fig.) wheat, corn; (*pl.*) grain crops. 6. (fig.) anything good or wholesome. 7. (gold or silver) leaf or foil. — **a falta de p., buenas son tortas,** for want of something better, faute de mieux (Fr.); **a p. y agua,** on bread and water; **comer p. y corteza,** (coll.) to stand on one's own two feet; (coll.) to be fully recovered (from an illness); **con su p. se lo coma,** he's welcome to it (for all I care); **contigo p. y cebolla,** for better or for worse, through thick and thin; **¡el p. de cada día!** always whining! the same old thing!; **(llamar) al p., p. y al vino, vino,** (to call) a spade a spade; **ganarse el p.,** to earn one's living; **hacer un p. como unas hostias,** (coll.) to botch a job; **no cocérsele a uno el p.,** (coll.) to be restless to do, say or know something; **p. aflorado,** bread made with superfine flour; **p. ázimo,** unleavened bread; **p. bazo,** brown bread; **p. bendito,** communion bread; (coll.) hot cakes, e.g. *se vende como p. bendito,* it sells like hot cakes; **p. candeal,** soft white bread; **p. cenceno,** unleavened bread; **p. de azúcar,** sugar loaf; **p. de carne,** meatloaf; **p. de centeno,** rye bread; **p. de flor,** bread made with superfine flour; **p. del día,** fresh bread; **p. de los angeles,** communion wafer; **pan de maíz,** corn bread, corn pone; **p. de munición,** army bread; prison bread; **p. de oro,** gold leaf; **p. de proposición,** (Bib.) shewbread, showbread; **(buscar) p. de trasrigo,** (coll.) (to look for) trouble; **p. duro,** stale bread; **p. eucarístico,** (ecc.) consecrated bread, host; **p. fermentado,** leavened bread; **p. floreado,** bread made with superfine flour; **p. francés,** French bread; baguette; **p. integral,** whole-wheat bread; **p. mollete,** bun, soft roll; **p. negro,** black bread; **p. perdido,** tramp, vagabond; **p. porcino,** (bot.) sowbread; **p. por mitad,** rental of land paid for in grain; **p. rallado,** breadcrumbs; **p. seco,** bread alone (without butter); **p. sentado,** doughy bread; **p. tierno,** fresh bread; **p. y agua,** bread and water; **p. y quesillo,** (bot.) shepherd's purse; **ser el p. de cada día,** (coll.) to happen every day, be completely normal.
pana, *f.* 1. (Arg., Chile) animal's liver. 2. (Chile) courage. — **helársele a uno la p.,** to become frightened, turn chicken. 2. corduroy, panne, velveteen, plush. 3. (mar.) deck timber, flooring board.
pánace, *f.* (bot.) Hercules' allheal, opopanax.
panacea, *f.* panacea. — **p. universal,** universal panacea or remedy.
panadear, *i.v.* to make bread, be a baker.
panadeo, *m.* making bread, bread-making.
panadería, *f.* 1. bakery, baker's shop. 2. bread making, job of a baker.
panadero, ra, *m., f.* baker. —*m.* (*pl.*) Spanish heel-tapping dance.
panadizo, *m.* 1. (med.) whitlow. 2. (coll.) pale and sickly person.
panado, da, *a.* toast soaked in milk, broth or hot water.
panal, *m.* 1. honeycomb. 2. (cul.) sponge sugar bar. — **p. longar,** honeycomb attached to the length of the hive; **p. saetero,** honeycomb attached crosswise to the cover of a hive.
panamá, *m.* panama hat. —*f.* **P., Panama.**
panameño, ña, *a., m., f.* Panamanian.
panamericanismo, *m.* Pan-Americanism.
panamericanista, *m., f.* Pan-Americanist, supporter of Pan-Americanism.
panamericano, na, *a.* Pan-American.
panarabismo, *m.* Pan-Arabism.
panarizo, *m., var. of* **panadizo.**
panarra, *m.* (coll.) simpleton, lazy person.
panatela, *f.* long thin spongecake.
panateneas, *f.* (*pl.*) (hist.) Panathenaea, festival celebrated in honor of the goddess Athene.
panática, *f.* (mar.) bread supplies.
panatier, *m., var. of* **panetero.**
panca, *f.* 1. (Phil. I.) Philippine fishing boat. 2. (Arg., Bol., Peru) cornhusk.
pancada, *f.* 1. lump sale, job lot. 2. sudden kick.
pancarpia, *f.* garland made of various different flowers.
pancarta, *f.* 1. poster, placard. 2. panchart, parchment containing records, documents.
pancellar, *m., var. of* **pancera.**
pancera, *f.* (mil.) belly plate (of armor).
pancho, *m.* 1. (ichth.) spawn of sea bream. 2. (coll.) belly, paunch.
pancilla, *f.* (print.) type used in manual or choir book.
pancista, *a.* (coll.) one who is on the fence, opportunistic. —*m., f.* political fence-sitter, opportunist.
panco, *m.* (Phil. I.) coasting cargo vessel similar to a pontin.
pancraciasta, *m.* (hist.) pancratist, pancratiast.
pancracio, *m.* (hist.) pancratium, in ancient Greece, an athletic show or contest combining boxing and wrestling.
pancrático, ca, *a.* (anat.) *var. of* **pancreático.**
páncreas, *m.* (anat.) pancreas.
pancreático, ca, *a.* (anat.) pancreatic.
pancreatina, *f.* (biochem.) pancreatin.
pancromático, ca, *a.* panchromatic, sensitive to all visible colors (e.g. a photographic film).
panda, *f.* gallery of a cloister. —*m.* (zool.) panda. — **p. gigante,** giant panda.
pandán, *m.* **hacer p.,** to go together; to form a pair.
pandanáceo, a, *a.* (bot.) pandanaceous. —*f.* (bot.) pandan, pandanus; (*pl.*) Pandanaceae.
pandáneo, a, *a.* (bot.) pandanaceous. —*f.* (bot.) pandan, pandanus; (*pl.*) Pandanaceae.
pandantif, *m.* (Gal., jewel.) pendant.
pandear, *i.v., r.v.* to warp, bend (wood); to sag, buckle, bulge (a wall).
Pandectas, *f.* (*pl.*) Pandects, body or code of laws (Roman Law).
pandemia, *f.* (med.) pandemia, pandemic, pandemic disease.
pandémico, ca, *a.* (med.) pandemic.
pandemonio, pandemonium, *m.* pandemonium.
pandeo, *m.* warping, bending (of wood); sagging, buckling, bulging (of walls or beams).
pandera, *f.* (mus.) large tambourine.
panderada, *f.* 1. (mus.) ensemble or collection of tambourines. 2. (coll.) stupid or foolish remark, (*pl.*) nonsense, poppycock.
panderazo, *m.* blow given with a tambourine.
pandereta, *f.* (mus.) *dim. of* **pandera,** small tambourine.
panderetazo, *m.* blow given with a tambourine.

panderete, *m.* 1. *dim. of* **pandero,** tambourine (musical instrument). 2. (bldg.) wall of bricks laid on edge.
panderetear, *i.v.* to play the tambourine; to sing and dance to the tambourine.
pandereteo, *m.* 1. tambourine-playing, noise of tambourines. 2. merrymaking; dancing and singing.
panderetero, ra, *m., f.* 1. tambourine-player. 2. tambourine maker or seller.
pandero, *m.* 1. (mus.) large tambourine. 2. kite (toy). 3. (coll.) silly jabberer or prattler.
pandiculación, *f.* stretching (of the arms), pandiculation.
pandilla, *f.* 1. gang, band; clique, party, group of people, e.g. *una p. de muchachos,* (coll.) a gang of kids. 2. picnic or excursion party.
pandillaje, *m.* intriguing, racketeering; action or influence of a gang.
pandillero, pandillista, *m.* leader or member of a gang, band or mob; gangster.
Pandit, *m.* pundit, pandit; a wise, erudite, scholarly man (in India).
pando, da, *a.* 1. bulging, sagging, buckling; warped. 2. slow-moving (e.g. a river). 3. slow, deliberate, ponderous. *—m.* plain between two mountains.
Pandora, *f.* (myth.) Pandora, the first mortal woman, who let all the evils of mankind escape out of a box.
pandorga, *f.* 1. (coll.) fat lazy woman. 2. kite (toy).
pandurado, da, *a.* (bot.) pandurate.
panduriforme, *a.* panduriform, pandurate.
panecillo, *m.* bread roll, bun.
panegirice, panegiricé, *ref.* **panegirizar.**
panegírico, ca, *a. panegyrical. —m.* panegyric; eulogy.
panegirista, *m.* panegyrist; eulogizer, eulogist.
panegirizar, (*ref. 53*) *tr.v.* to panegyrize; to eulogize.
panel, *m.* 1. (archit., p.) panel. 2. (mar.) floor board (of deck). 3. panel (e.g. advisory, research, etc.).
panela, *f.* 1. (cul.) diamond-shaped sponge-cake. 2. (Amer.) brown sugar loaf. 3. (her.) poplar leaf (on shield).
pane lucrando, de p. l., done for profit only (said of artistic and literary works).
panera, *f.* 1. barn, granary. 2. breadbasket; pannier.
panero, *m.* 1. baker's basket. 2. small round rush mat.
paneslavismo, *m.* Pan-Slavism.
paneslavista, *a.* Pan-Slavistic. *—m., f.* Pan-Slavist.
panetela, *f.* 1. panatela, thin cigar. 2. (cul.) dish of broth or milk with broken toast. 3. (Amer.) spongecake.
panetería, *f.* pantry of a royal palace.
panetero ra, *m., f.* steward in charge of a royal pantry.
panfilismo, *m.* extreme kindness, excessive benignity.
pánfilo, la, *a.* sluggish, slow. *—m., f.* sluggard, slow and sluggish person.
panfletista, *m.* pamphleteer.
panfleto, *m.* pamphlet.
pangelín, *m.* (bot.) angelin.
pangenésico, ca, *a.* (biol.) pangenetic.
pangénesis, *f.* (biol.) pangenesis.
pangermanismo, *m.* Pan-Germanism.
pangermanista, *a.* Pan-Germanic. *—m., f.* Pan-Germanist.
pangolín, *m.* (zool.) pangolin.
panhelénico, ca. *a.* Panhellenic.
panhelenismo, *m.* Panhellenism.
panhelenista, *m., f.* Panhellenist.
paniaguado, *m.* 1. servant, minion. 2. favorite, protégé.
pánico, ca, *a.* panic, panicky. *—m.* panic.
panícula, *f.* (bot.) panicle.
paniculado, da, *a.* (bot.) paniculate, panicle-shaped.
panicular, *a.* pannicular (having a panniculus).
panículo, *m.* (anat.) panniculus.
paniego, ga, *a.* 1. fond of bread. 2. corn or wheat-producing (land). 3. burlap bag.
panificación, *f.* making or converting into bread, panification.
panificar, (*ref. 50*) *tr.v.* 1. to make (flour) into bread. 2. to convert (pasture land) into corn or wheat fields.
panifique, panifiqué, *ref.* **panificar.**
panilla, *f.* oil measure (equivalent to — lb.).
panique, *m.* (zool.) flying fox (Pteropus vampyrus).
panislamismo, *m.* Pan-Islamism.
panislamista, *a.* Pan-Islamic. *—m., f.* Pan-Islamist.
panizo, *m.* 1. Italian millet. 2. (Chile) seam, vein, mineral deposit or bed. 3. (Chile) abundance. 4. one of the names given to corn.
panjí, (*pl.* **panjíes**), *m.* (bot.) China tree.
panocha, *f.* 1. corn cob; ear (of corn, millet, etc.); (bot.) panicle. 2. (Col., C. Rica, Chile) large cornmeal and cheese pancake. 3. (Mex.) panocha, coarse brown sugar.
panoja, *f.* 1. corn cob; (bot.) panicle. 2. bunch (of fruit hung for keeping). 3. batch of fish fried with tails fastened together.
panol, *m.* (mar.) storeroom.
panoli, *a.* simple, foolish. *—m., f.* simpleton, fool.
panoplia, *f.* 1. panoply, suit of armor. 2. study of ancient weapons. 3. collection of arms exhibited on a board.
panóptico, ca, *a.* panoptical. *—m.* panopticon (building or prison built radially so that someone at a central position can observe all parts of it).
panorama, *m.* panorama.
panorámico, ca, *a.* panoramic.
panormitano, na, *a.* Palermitan, of or from Palermo, Italy. *—m., f.* Palermitan, native or inhabitant of Palermo.
panoso, sa, *a.* mealy, doughy.
panqué, panqueque, *m.* (Amer.) plain pound cake.
panslavismo, *m.* Pan-Slavism.
panslavista, *a.* Pan-Slavistic. *—m., f.* Pan-Slavist.
pansofía, *f.* (philos.) pansophy, universal wisdom or knowledge.
pansofismo, *m.* (philos.) pansophism, pretension to universal knowledge or wisdom.
panspermia, *f.* (biol.) panspermia, panspermy.
pantagruélico, ca, *a.* Pantagruelic, Pantagruelian, sumptuous (banquet, dinner).
pantalán, *m.* (Phil. I.) wooden or cane quay or pier.
pantaletas, *f. pl.* (Amer.) pantalettes, panties.
pantalla, *f.* 1. shade, lampshade. 2. screen (television or cinema screen). 3. fire screen or guard. 4. (fig.) screen (person or thing hiding someone or something). 5. (phys.) screen, shield. 6. (photog.) screen, filter. 7. (tech.) shield, screen, guard (guarding the body from sparks, winds, dazzling light, radioactive rays, etc.). 8. (*pl.*) (P. Rico), earrings. — **p. acustica,** (rad.) baffle; **p. antideslumbrante,** (auto.) antiglare shield or screen; **p. antidifusora,** (photgmt.) spill shield; **p. chica,** television screen; **p. de chimenea,** fire screen; **p. de radar,** radar screen; **p. eléctrica,** electric screen; **p. Faraday,** (elec.) Faraday cage, electrostatic screen; **p. interior,** (hydr.) core wall; **p. magnética,** magnetic screen; **servir de p. a,** to act as a blind for, cover up for.
pantalón, *m.* (*gen. pl.*) trousers, pants (U.S.); breeches (G.B.). — **llevar, ponerse** or **tener los pantalones,** to wear the pants (or trousers), be the boss (in the family); **p. abotinado,** breeches; **p. bombacho,** knickers; balloon trousers, gaucho's wide trousers; **p. cortos,** shorts; **p. de peto,** overalls; **p. tejanos** or **vaqueros** or **de mezclilla,** jeans; **pantalones de montar,** riding breeches; **p. sastre,** pants suit.
pantalonera, *f.* 1. trouser maker (woman). 2. (Mex.) charro (cowboy) pants (buttoned down the leg).
pantana, *f.* (bot., Can. I.) small green calabash.
pantanal, *m.* swampy or marshy land, swampland.
pantano, *m.* 1. swamp, marsh, bog, morass. 2. reservoir, dam. 3. (fig.) obstacle, hindrance, difficulty. — **gas de los pantanos,** marsh gas.
pantanoso, sa, *a.* 1. swampy, marshy, boggy; miry. 2. difficult, fraught with difficulties and obstacles.
pantasana, *f.* fishing seine surrounded by horizontal nets.
panteísmo, *m.* (philos.) pantheism.
panteísta, *a.* (philos.) pantheistic. *—m., f.* pantheist.
panteístico, ca, *a.* (philos.) pantheistic.
panteón, *m.* pantheon; mausoleum; (Amer.) graveyard.
pantera, *f.* (zool.) panther.
pantógrafo, *m.* pantograph (copying instrument).
pantómetra, *f.* pantometer (making and measuring instrument).
pantomima, *f.* pantomime.
pantomímico, ca, *a.* pantomimic, pantomimical.
pantomimista, *m.* pantomimist (writer of pantomimes).
pantomimo, *m.* pantomimic, pantomime actor, pantomimist.
pantoque, *m.* (mar.) bilge.
pantorra, *f.* (coll.) *var. of* **pantorrilla.**
pantorrilla, *f.* calf (of the leg).
pantorrillera, *f.* padded stocking.
pantorrilludo, da, *a.* thick-calved.
pantoscopio, *m.* (photog.) pantoscope.
pantotenato, *m.* (chem.) pantothenate.
pantoténico, ca, *a.* (chem.) pantothenic.
pantufla, *f.* babouche, slipper, house slipper.
pantuflazo, *m.* blow given with a slipper.
pantuflo, *m.* slipper, house slipper.
panuco, *m.* (Chile) handful of toasted flour.
panucho, *m.* (Mex.) cornmeal cake filled with beans and meat.
panudo, *a.* (Cuba) firm (avocado pear).
panul, *m.* (Chile, bot.) celery.
panza, *f.* 1. belly; paunch, pot-belly; (zool.) rumen (of ruminants). 2. belly (e.g. of a bowl). 3. (coll.) sponger. — **p. de burra,** (coll.) grey, overcast sky; **aterrizar de p.,** to belly-land.
panzada, *f.* 1. push given with belly or paunch. 2. (coll.) bellyful, e.g. *darse una p. de,* to have one's fill of (some favorite food).
panzón, na, *a.* pot-bellied, paunchy. *—m.* paunch, large stomach.
panzudo, da, *a.* pot-bellied, paunchy.
pañal, *m.* 1. diaper (U.S.), nappy (G.B.). 2. shirttail. 3. (*pl.*) swaddling clothes. 4. (*pl.*) (fig.) swaddling clothes, infancy, early stages. — **estar en pañales,** to be in its infancy or early stages; to be wet behind the ears, be inexperienced; **haber salido de pañales,** to be experienced, have reached the age of reason.
pañería, *f.* 1. draper's shop, dry goods store (U.S.). 2. materials, textiles, drapery, dry goods (U.S.).
pañero, ra, *a.* dry goods, textile. *—m., f.* draper, dry goods dealer.

pañete, *m.* 1. poor quality cloth; thin cloth. 2. (*pl.*) trunks (worn by workers who can't wear trousers while they work, e.g. fishermen, tanners). 3. peplum or drape clothing a crucifix below the waist.
pañizuelo, *m.* handkerchief, kerchief.
paño, *m.* 1. cloth, material, fabric. 2. flannel, woolen cloth. 3. (dressm.) panel, width of the fabric. 4. tapestry, hanging. 5. cloth, rag (for cleaning). 6. (med.) compress, lint pad. 7. spot (on the face or body). 8. growth over the eye. 9. blur, blemish, spot (on a shiny surface). 10. coat of plaster or whitewash. 11. face (of a wall). 12. (mar.) unfurled sails. 13. (*pl.*) drape (in sculpture or picture). — **al p.,** offstage, backstage; **conocer el p. de,** to know the real character of; **hay p. de que cortar,** (coll.) there is lots of material available, there is lots to talk about; **p. buriel,** grey flannel; **p. de altar,** altar cloth; **p. de Arrás,** arras; **p. de cáliz,** pall, chalice cover; **p. de cocina,** kitchen towel, teatowel; dishcloth; **p. de hombros,** (ecc.) humeral veil; **p. de lágrimas,** sympathetic friend; **p. de manos,** hand towel; **p. de mesa,** tablecloth; **p. de púlpito,** pulpit drape or hanging; **p. de ras,** arras; **p. de tumba,** crape over a funeral bier; **p. pardillo,** coarse woolen cloth; **paños calientes or tibios,** (coll.) half measures; mitigating or softening measures; encouragement; **p. higiénico,** sanitary napkin; **paños menores,** underclothes, underwear; **poner** or **tender el p. al púlpito,** (coll.) to talk tediously and at great length.
pañol, *m.* (mar.) storeroom.
pañolería, *f.* handkerchief shop; handkerchief trade.
pañolero, ra, *m., f.* handkerchief seller or maker.
pañolero, *m.* (mar.) storeroom keeper.
pañoleta, *f.* 1. neckerchief, woman's triangular shawl. 2. (taur.) bullfighter's necktie.
pañolito, *m. dim. of* **pañuelo,** small handkerchief.
pañolón, *m.* large square shawl.
pañoso, sa, *a.* ragged, tattered. —*m.* (coll.) large woolen cape.
pañuelo, *m.* handkerchief; kerchief; **p. de bolsillo** or **de mano,** pocket handkerchief; **p. de cuello,** neckerchief.
papa, *m.* **1. P.,** (ecc.) pope. 2. (coll.) papa, daddy. — **ser uno más papista que el p.,** to be exceedingly radical in one's beliefs.
papa, *f.* (bot.) potato; **p. de caña,** Jerusalem artichoke; **p. dulce,** sweet potato; **papas chip** or **fritas,** potato chips.
papa, *f.* **1.** (coll.) false rumor, hoax. 2. (coll.) food, grub; din-din (when addressing children). 3. (*pl.*) pap, mush; porridge, gruel.
papá, (*pl.* **papás**), *m.* (coll.) papa, daddy, father.
papable, *a.* papable, eligible for the papacy (said of a cardinal).
papachar, *tr.v.* (Mex.) to caress, fondle.
papacho, *m.* (Mex.) caress.
papada, *f.* double chin; dewlap.
papadilla, *f.* flesh under the chin.
papado, *m.* papacy.
papafigo, *m.* 1. (ornith.) beccafico, figpecker (Sylvia hortensis). 2. (ornith.) golden oriole. 3. (mar.) course.
papagaya, *f.* female parrot.
papagayo, *m.* 1. (ornith.) parrot. 2. (bot.) Joseph's coat (Amaranthus tricolor). 3. (bot.) caladium (Caladium bicolor). 4. (zool.) very poisonous green snake. 5. (ichth.) (species of) wrasse (Labrus bimaculatus).
papahigo, *m.* 1. Balaclava helmet (winter cap covering head and neck). 2. (ornith.) beccafico, figpecker (Sylvia hortensis). 3. (mar.) course.
papahuevos, *m.* (coll.) dolt, simpleton, fool.
papaína, *f.* (chem.) papain.
papal, *a.* papal.
papalina, *f.* 1. cap with ear flaps. 2. woman's coif. 3. (coll.) drunk, drunken bout.
papalino, na, *a.* papal.
papalmente, *adv.* in a papal manner, as a pope.
papalote, *m.* (Mex., Cuba) paper kite.
papamoscas, (*pl.* **papamoscas**), *m.* 1. (ornith.) flycatcher. 2. (coll.) dolt, simpleton.
papanatas, (*pl.* **papanatas**), *m.* (coll.) dolt, simpleton, fool.
papandujo, ja, *a.* (coll.) too soft, overripe.
papar, *tr.v.* 1. to swallow (soft food) without chewing; (coll.) to eat. 2. (coll.) to pay little attention to.
páparo, *m.* yokel, rustic; simpleton.
paparote, ta, *m., f.* simpleton, dolt, fool, dimwit.
paparrabias, (*pl.* **paparrabias**), *m., f.* (coll.) crab, crosspatch, bad-tempered person.
paparrasolla, *f.* bogeyman.
paparrucha, *f.* 1. (coll.) false rumor, hoax. 2. (coll.) silliness, nonsense.
papasal, *m.* 1. trifle, bagatelle. 2. children's game.
papatoste, *m.* dolt, simpleton, fool.
papaveráceo, a, *a.* (bot.) papaveraceous. —*f.* (*pl.*) (bot.) Papaveraceae.
papaverina, *f.* (chem.) papaverine.
papaya, *f.* 1. (bot.) papaya (fruit). 2. (C. Amer., Cuba, P. Rico, vulg.) vulva.
papayáceo, a, *a.* (bot.) caricaceous. —*f.* (*pl.*) (bot.) Papayaceae, Caricaceae.
papayo, *m.* (bot.) papaya tree.
pápaz, (*pl.* **pápaces**), *m.* Christian priest (in N. Africa).
papazgo, *m.* papacy, pontificate.
papel, *m.* 1. paper; piece of paper. 2. paper, document; (*pl.*) papers, documents, credentials (of identity, etc.). 3. (theat., cinem.) role, part. 4. (fig.) role, function. 5. (com.) paper money, bank notes, credit; security, bond. — **desempeñar** or **hacer un p.,** to play a role or part; **embadurnar, embarrar, emborronar** or **manchar p.,** to write trash; **hacer buen** or **mal p.,** to cut a good or bad figure; to come out or act well or badly; **hacer el p.,** to act, pretend; (theat.) to play a role, a part; **hacer su p.,** to do one's job; **p. ahuesado,** bone-colored paper; **p. alquitranado,** tar paper; **p. atlántico,** atlas folio, atlas; **p. avitelado,** vellum paper; **p. bancario,** bank paper; **p. Biblia,** Bible paper; **p. blanco,** blank paper; **p. bond,** bond paper; **p. carbón** or **carbónico,** carbon paper; **p. cebolla,** onionskin paper; **p. comercial,** commercial paper; **p. continuo,** paper in reels; **p. costero,** wrapping paper, spoiled paper used for wrapping reams; **p. crepé,** crepe paper; **p. cuadriculado,** graph paper, squared paper; **p. cuché,** glossy or coated paper, art paper; **p. de aluminio,** aluminum foil; **p. de añafea,** brown wrapping paper; **p. de arroz,** rice paper; **p. de barbas,** untrimmed paper; **p. de calcar,** tracing paper; **p. de cartas,** writing paper; **p. de cúrcuma,** (chem.) curcuma paper, turmeric paper; **p. de China,** Chinese paper; **p. de dibujo,** drawing paper; **p. de empapelar,** wallpaper; **p. de envolver,** wrapping paper; **p. de escribir,** writing paper; **p. de esmeril,** emery paper; **p. de estaño,** tin foil; **p. de estracilla,** brown paper; **p. de estraza,** brown wrapping paper; **p. de filtro,** filter paper; **p. de fumar,** cigarette paper; **p. de granate,** garnet paper; **p. de hilo,** rag paper; **p. del estado,** government bond; **p. de lija,** sandpaper; **p. de Japón,** Japanese paper; **p. de luto,** black-edged stationery; **p. de mano,** vat paper; handmade paper; **p. de marca,** vat paper; **p. de marca mayor,** double-sized vat paper; **p. de música,** music paper; **p. de pagos,** stamped paper; **p. de periódico,** newsprint; **p. de seda,** tissue paper; **p. de tina,** vat paper, handmade paper; **p. de tornasol,** litmus paper; **p. en blanco,** blank paper; **p. en derecho,** (law) printed pleading; **p. escarchado,** ice paper; **p. esténcil,** stencil paper; **p. florete,** first quality paper, superfine paper; **p. fotográfico,** photographic paper; **p. higiénico,** toilet paper; **p. indicador,** test paper; **p. japonés,** Japanese paper; **p. matamoscas,** flypaper; **p. mojado,** worthless document; (coll.) trifle, unimportant thing; **p. moneda,** paper currency, paper money; **p. ondulado,** corrugated paper; **p. pautado,** lined paper for teaching people to write; **p. pergamino,** parchment paper; **p. periódico,** newsprint; **p. pintado,** wallpaper; **p. plateado,** silver paper; **p. pluma,** featherweight paper; **p. quebrado,** wrapping paper, spoiled paper used for wrapping reams; **p. rayado,** lined paper; **p. reactivo,** test paper; **p. secante,** blotting paper; **p. sellado,** official stamped paper; **p. semilogarítmico,** selogarithmic paper; **p. sensible,** photographic paper; **p. sulfito,** sulfite paper; **p. tela,** tracing cloth or linen; **p. vergé** or **vergueteado,** marbled paper; **p. volante,** pamphlet.
papelear, *i.v.* 1. to rummage or look through papers. 2. (coll.) to cut a figure; to play a part, pretend.
papeleo, *m.* looking or rummaging through papers; paper work, red tape.
papelera, *f.* 1. writing desk, paper case. 2. mass or lot of papers. 3. wastepaper basket.
papelería, *f.* 1. pile or mass of papers. 2. stationery shop. 3. litter.
papelero, ra, *a.* 1. pertaining to paper, papermaking. 2. boastful, bragging. —*m., f.* 1. paper manufacturer or dealer. 2. showoff, boaster.
papeleta, *f.* 1. card, ticket, slip, form. 2. (coll.) difficult matter, a hard nut to crack. 3. (Peru) ticket, fine (for traffic offense). — **p. de empeño** or **del monte,** pawn ticket.
papelillo, *m.* 1. *dim. of* **papel,** slip of paper. 2. cigarette. 3. paper containing a dose of medicine.
papelina, *f.* 1. tall wide-mouthed drinking glass. 2. (tex.) poplin.
papelista, *m.* 1. paper manufacturer. 2. paper dealer. 3. paper hanger. 4. archivist (one in charge of documents).
papelón, na, *a.* showy, ostentatious. —*m.* 1. showoff. 2. useless document. 3. thin cardboard. 4. (Amer.) raw sugar loaf. — **hacer un p.,** (Amer.) to make a fool of oneself.
papelonado, *a.* (her.) papélonné.
papelonear, *i.v.* (coll.) to boast, brag, make a show of influence or power.
papelorio, *m.* mass or pile or papers.
papelote, papelucho, *m.* 1. useless document, worthless piece of paper. 2. scurrilous piece of writing.
papera, *f.* 1. (med.) goiter. 2. (*pl.*) (med.) mumps. 3. (*pl.*) (med.) scrofula. 4. (vet.) glanders, farcy.
papero, *m.* pap pot, saucepan in which children's pap is prepared.
papi, *m.* (coll.) daddy.
papialbillo, *m.* (zool.) genet.
papila, *f.* (bot., anat.) papilla.
papilar, *a.* (bot., anat.) papillary, papillar.
papilionáceo, a, *a.* (bot.) papilionaceous. —*f.* (*pl.*) Papilionaceae.
papilla, *f.* 1. pap, soft food. 2. (fig.) deceit, guile. — **dar p. a,** (coll.) to deceive, delude; **echar hasta la p.,** (coll.) to be as sick as a dog.
papillote, *m.* hair in curlpaper; **a la p.,** wrapped in paper (food to be broiled).

papiloma, *m.* (med.) papilloma.
papilomatoso, sa, *a.* (med.) papillomatous.
papiloso, sa, *a.* papillose.
papín, *m.* homemade candy.
papión, *m.* (zool.) papion.
papiráceo, a, *a.* papyraceous.
papiro, *m.* papyrus (paper; scroll); (bot.) papyrus.
papirolada, *f.* 1. (cul.) bread sauce seasoned with garlic. 2. (coll.) piece of nonsense, silly thing.
papirotada, *f.* fillip, flip.
papirotazo, *m.* fillip, flip.
papirote, *m.* 1. fillip, flip. 2. (coll.) fool, dolt, nincompoop.
papismo, *m.* papism, papistry, popery, papalism.
papista, *a.* papist, pertaining to popes, adherent of the pope. —*m., f.* papist.
papo, *m.* 1. dewlap. 2. maw, craw, crop. 3. (coll.) goiter. 4. puffed-up cloth seen through ornamental slashes in dresses. 5. portion of food given to hawking birds. 6. (*pl.*) woman's coif with ear flaps. — **estar una cosa en p. de buitre,** (coll.) to be in the hands of vultures; **hablar de p.,** (coll.) to boast, brag; **hablar p. a p.,** to speak one's mind, speak frankly; **p. de viento,** (mar.) pocket of wind (in a sail).
papo, *m.* (bot.) pappus, thistledown.
papón, *m.* bogeyman, hobgoblin.
paporrear, *tr.v.* to whip, flog.
papú, papúa, (*pl.* **papúes, papúas**) *a.* Papuan, of or pertaining to a people of New Guinea. —*m., f.* Papuan.
Papuasia, *f.* Papua, a territory in New Guinea.
papudo, da, *a.* 1. double-chinned. 2. with a large maw or crop.
papujado, da, *a.* 1. full-gorged (fowl). 2. (fig.) swollen, puffed-up.
pápula, *f.* (med.) papule, pimple.
papuloso, sa, *a.* papulous, pimply.
paquear, *tr.v.* to snipe at.
paquebot, paquebote, *m.* packet boat, mail boat.
paqueo, *m.* sniping.
paquete, *a.* (coll.) spruce, elegant; self-important, pompous. —*m.* 1. package, parcel, bundle. 2. packet, packet boat. 3. (coll.) dandy, natty dresser. 4. (print.) stick, stickful, piece of composition. 5. (Amer.) washout, dead loss, waste of time (incompetent person). 6. (coll.) lie, rumor. 7. (Cuba, coll.) frame-up.
paquetería, *f.* small goods; small goods business, retail trade shop.
paquetero, ra, *m., f.* parcel maker, wrapper, packager. —*m.* 1. general deliveryman, distributor of bundles of newspapers to street sellers. 2. (print.) typesetter, compositor.
paquidermo, *a.* (zool.) pachydermous. —*m.* pachyderm.
Paquistán, *m.* Pakistan.
paquistaní, *a., m., f.* Pakistani, of or pertaining to Pakistan.
paquistano, na, *a., m., f.* Pakistani.
par, *a.* 1. equal, absolutely alike. 2. (math.) even. 3. (zool.) paired (organs in corresponding places of the body). —*m.* 1. pair, couple; brace (of pheasants, etc.); pair of oxen. 2. peer (nobleman). 3. (archit.) principal rafter. 4. (math.) even number. 5. (elec., mec.) couple. 6. pair (in poker). — **al p.,** at the same time; together, jointly; even, equal; on an equal footing; **a pares,** in pairs, in twos; **de p. en p.,** wide open, open wide; clearly, patently, obviously; **jugar a pares y nones,** to play at odds and evens; **p. doble,** two pairs (in poker); **p. eléctrico,** electric moment, electric cell; **p. estereoscópico,** (photgmt.) stereo pair; **p. magnético,** magnetic couple; **p. motor,** torque; **p. voltaico,** (elec.) voltaic couple; **sentir a p. de muerte,** to feel (something) very deeply; **sin p.,** peerless, without equal. —*f.* 1. par. 2. (*pl.*) placenta. — **a la p.,** at the same time; together, jointly; even, equal; on an equal footing; (com.) at par; **ir a la p.,** to work together or jointly; to go halves or fifty-fifty.
para, *prep.* 1. for, e.g. *él es muy apropiado p. el puesto,* he is very suitable for the position; good for, e.g. *Antonio no es p. nada,* Anthony is no good for anything. 2. for, on behalf of, e.g. *una colecta p. los pobres,* a collection for the poor, *lo compré p. él,* I bought it for him. 3. in order to, to, for, e.g. *p.* + *inf.,* in order to or to + *inf.,* for + *ger.,* e.g. *hay que trabajar p. vivir,* one must work (in order) to live, *lo han comprado p. regar el jardín,* they have bought it for watering the garden. 4. towards, for, to, e.g. *voy p. el campo,* I'm going to the country. 5. to (time), e.g. *son un cuarto p. las nueve,* it is a quarter to nine. 6. for, by, at, e.g. *lo tendrá listo p. mañana,* he will have it ready for or by tomorrow, *pagará p. Pascua,* he will pay at Christmas. 7. considering, e.g. *¡con buena calma te vienes p. la prisa que tengo!* you take your time, considering the hurry I'm in! 8. for, as far as one is concerned, e.g. *p. mí no es una cuestión muy importante,* as far as I am concerned, it is not a very important question. — **dar p.,** to give money for or to buy, e.g. *le dí p. fruta,* I gave her money for or to buy fruit; **estar p.,** to be about to, be on the point of; to be up to, be in condition for; to be in the mood for; **leer p. sí,** to read to oneself (i.e. silently); **p. con,** towards, e.g. *no me gusta su actitud p. con nosotros,* I do not like his attitude towards us; compared with, e.g. *¿quién es Ud. p. conmigo?* who are you compared with me?; **p. eso,** just or only for this; **p. mí, tí** or **sí,** for me or myself, for you or yourself, for him or himself, for her or herself, for oneself, for themselves; **p. que** + *subj.,* in order that + *subj,* in order to + *inf.,* to + *inf.* **¿p. qué?** why? what for? for what use or object?; **p. siempre,** forever.
paraba, *f.* (ornith., Bol.) macaw.
parabién, *m.* congratulation, greeting, compliment; **dar el p.,** to congratulate.
parabiosis, *f.* (biol.) parabiosis.
parablasto, *m.* (biol.) parablast.
parábola, *f.* 1. (rhet.) parable. 2. (geom.) parabola.
parabolano, *m.* 1. (rel.) parabolanus (in the early Eastern Church). 2. one who speaks in parables. 3. (coll.) rumor-monger. 4. liar; trickster.
parabólico, ca, *a.* 1. parabolical, allegoric. 2. (geom.) parabolic.
parabolizar, (*ref. 53*) *i.v.* to speak in parables, allegorize.
paraboloide, *m.* (geom.) paraboloid.
parabrisas, *m.* (auto.) windscreen, windshield.
paraca, *f.* (Chile, Peru) strong offshore breeze (blowing in from the Pacific).
paracaídas, (*pl.* **paracaídas**), *m.* parachute.
paracaidismo, *m.* parachute jumping.
paracaidista, *m., f.* parachutist; (mil.) paratrooper.
paracaseína, *f.* (biochem.) paracasein.
Paracelso, *m.* Paracelsus, Swiss alchemist and physician.
paracentesis, *f.* (surg.) paracentesis.
parachispas, (*pl.* parachispas), *m.* spark arrester; fireguard.
parachoques, (*pl.* parachoques), *m.* (auto.) bumper, fender.
parachutar, *i.v.* to parachute.
paracimeno, *m.* (chem.) paracymene.
paracleto, paráclito, *m.* Paraclete, Comforter, Helper (applied to the Holy Spirit).
paracomando, *m.* paratrooper, airborne commando.
paracronismo, *m.* parachronism, an error in chronology.
parada, *f.* 1. stop, halt; stopping, halting. 2. halt, stop, stopping-place. 3. finish, end. 4. break, pause (esp. in music). 5. stall, corral (for cattle). 6. stud farm. 7. relay (team of horses or mules at a post station). 8. post station. 9. dam (holding water). 10. bet, stake. 11. (fenc.) parry. 12. (mil.) parade, review; parade ground. 13. (Amer.) call down, rebuff. 14. (Peru) market. — **doblar la p.,** to double one's stake or bid; **p. de taxi** or **coches,** taxi stand, hack stand; **p. en firme,** dead stop or halt; **salirle a la p.,** to go out to meet someone.
paradera, *f.* 1. sluice-gate. 2. seine net.
paradero, *m.* 1. whereabouts. 2. stopping place. 3. finish, end. 4. (Arg., Cuba, Chile, Guat., Peru) railway halt; bus-stop.
paradetas, *f.* (*pl.*) old Spanish dance.
paradiástole, *f.* (rhet.) paradiastole.
paradigma, *m.* paradigm, example.
paradigmático, ca, *a.* exemplary, paradigmatic.
paradilla, *f. dim. of* **parada,** a short pause or stop.
paradina, *f.* pastureland used for penning sheep.
paradisíaco, ca, *a.* paradisiac, paradisiacal, paradisaical.
paradislero, *m.* 1. hunter lying in wait. 2. newshound, newsmonger.
parado, da, *past part. of* **parar.** —*a.* 1. lazy, idle; unemployed. 2. slow, listless, sluggish. 3. stopped, arrested, motionless. 4. (Amer.) erect, straight, standing. 5. shut down (factory). —*m.* unemployed worker. — **caer p.,** (Amer.) to land on one's feet; **estar p.,** to be standing; **estarse p.,** to be immobile; **lo mejor parado,** the best; **quedar** or **salir bien** or **mal p. de,** to come out of well or badly.
paradoja, *f.* paradox.
paradójico, ca, *a.* paradoxical.
paradojo, ja, *a.* paradoxical.
parador, ra, *a.* 1. stopping, halting. 2. heavy-betting. 3. which stops and stands smartly (a horse). —*m., f.* heavy bettor. —*m.* inn, hostelry, roadhouse.
paraestatal, *a.* semi-state (said of institutions or organisms which are set up by the state to give public services without actually forming part of the public administration).
parafasia, *f.* (med.) paraphasia.
parafernales, *a. pl.* (law) **bienes p.,** paraphernalia (wife's property not remaining under control of husband).
parafina, *f.* paraffin.
parafinado, da, *a.* paraffin-dipped, treated with paraffin.
parafinar, *tr.v.* to paraffin, saturate with paraffin.
parafínico, ca, *a.* paraffinic.
parafinoso, sa, *a.* containing paraffin.
paráfisis, *f.* (bot.) paraphysis.
parafraseador, ra, *a.* paraphrasing. —*m., f.* paraphraser.
parafrasear, *tr.v.* to paraphrase.
paráfrasis, *f.* paraphrase.
parafraste, *m.* paraphrast, paraphraser, expounder.
parafrásticamente, *adv.* paraphrastically.
parafrástico, ca, *a.* paraphrastic.
parafuego, *m.* fire wall.
paragénesis, *f.* (geol.) paragenesis, paragenesia.
paragoge, *f.* (gram.) paragoge.
paragógico, ca, *a.* paragogic.

paragolpes, *m.* (auto., ry.) bumper; fender; buffer; bumping post; door stop.
paragonar, *tr.v., var. of* **parangonar,** to compare.
paragonita, *f.* (min.) paragonite.
parágrafo, *m., var. of* **párrafo.**
paragranizo, *m.* (agr.) hail cover, covering for fruit trees as a protection from hail.
paraguas, *m.* umbrella.
paraguatán, *m.* (C. Amer., bot.) arariba (Sickingia tinctoria).
Paraguay, *m.* Paraguay.
paraguay, *m.* 1. Paraguayan parrot. 2. **té del P.,** Paraguay tea, maté.
paraguayano, na, *a., m., f.* Paraguayan.
paraguayo, ya, *a., m., f.* Paraguayan. —*f.* variety of peach.
paragüería, *f.* 1. umbrella shop. 2. (Cuba) inept motorcar driving, driver's blunder.
paragüero, ra, *m., f.* umbrella maker or seller. —*m.* 1. umbrella stand. 2. inept motorcar driver.
parahusar, *tr.v.* to drill with a pump drill.
parahúso, *m.* pump drill; jeweler's bow drill.
paraíso, *m.* 1. paradise. 2. (theat.) top gallery, paradise. 3. (fig.) paradise, bliss. 4. (Amer.) chinaberry, azederach. — **p. de los bobos,** fool's paradise; **p. terrenal,** earthly paradise.
paraje, *m.* 1. place, spot. 2. condition, state.
paral, *m.* 1. (bldg.) putlog; scaffold prop. 2. (mar.) launching ways.
paraláctico, ca, *a.* (astron.) parallactic.
paralaje, *f.* (astron.) parallax. — **p. angular** (opt.) angular parallax; **p. anual,** annual, heliocentric or stellar parallax; **p. de altura,** diurnal or geocentric parallax; **p. horizontal,** horizontal parallax.
paralasis, *f., var. of* **paralaje.**
paralaxi, *f., var. of* **paralaje.**
paraldehido, *m.* (chem.) paraldehyde.
paralela, *f.* 1. (fort.) parallel (trench). 2. (*pl.*) parallel lines. 3. (*pl.*) parallel bars (gymnastics).
paralelamente, *adv.* parallel. — **p. a,** parallel to.
paralelar, *tr.v.* to parallel, compare.
paralelepípedo, *m.* (geom.) parallelepiped, parallelepipedon.
paralelismo, *m.* parallelism. — **p. psicofísico,** (psyc.) psychophysical parallelism.
paralelo, la, *a.* parallel. —*m.* 1. parallel, comparison. 2. (fig.) similar. 3. (geog.) parallel. — **p. de latitud,** (geog.) parallel of latitude.
paralelogramo, *m.* (geom.) parallelogram.
paralice, paralicé, *ref.* paralizar.
paralipómenos, *m.* (*pl.*) (Bibl.) Paralipomen, Paralipomena.
paralipsis, *f.* (rhet.) paraleipsis, paralepsis.
parálisis, *f.* 1. paralysis, stoppage, absence of action. 2. (med.) paralysis. — **p. agitante,** or **temblorosa,** Parkinson's disease; **p. infantil,** infantile paralysis, poliomyelitis; **p. motora,** motor paralysis; **p. progresiva,** creeping paralysis.
paraliticado, da, *past part. of* **paraliticarse.** —*a.* (med.) paralyzed, palsied.
paraliticarse, (*ref. 50*) *r.v.* to become paralyzed, to become palsied.
paralítico, ca, *a.* (med.) paralytic, palsied. —*m., f.* paralytic.
paralización, *f.* 1. paralyzation; immobilization. 2. (com.) stagnation.
paralizador, ra, *a.* paralyzing; (fig.) stunning.
paralizar, (*ref. 53*) *tr.v.* to paralyze, immobilize, stop. —*r.v.* to become paralyzed, stunned, immobilized.
paralogice, paralogicé, *ref.* **paralogizar.**
paralogismo, *m.* paralogism, false reasoning.
paralogizar, (*ref. 53*) *tr.v.* to try to convince with specious arguments. —*r.v.* to paralogize.
parallamas, *m.* flame arrester or check; fire stop or wall.
paramagnético, ca, *a.* (phys.) paramagnetic.
paramagnetismo, *m.* (phys.) paramagnetism.
paramecio, *m.* (zool.) paramecium.
paramentar, *tr.v.* to adorn, decorate, embellish, beautify, bedeck.
paramento, *m.* 1. adornment, decoration, ornament; hanging. 2. caparison. 3. (archit.) face, surface (of walls, masonry, etc.). — **paramentos sacerdotales,** clerical vestments; altar hangings.
paramera, *f.* moorland, heathland, barren country.
paramétrico, *a.* (math.) parametric.
parámetro, *m.* (geom.) parameter.
paramilitar, *a.* paramilitary, pertaining to an organization operating in substitution of a regular military force.
paramilo, *m.* (biol.) paramylum.
paramnesia, *f.* (med.) paramnesia.
páramo, *m.* 1. moor, heath; (Amer.) high barren plateau. 2. (fig.) wilderness, bleak cold spot. 3. (Bol., Col., Ecuad.) drizzle.
paramorfismo, *m.* (min.) paramorphism.
parancero, *m.* snarer, bird or rabbit catcher.
paranéfrico, ca, *a.* paranephric.
parangón, *m.* comparison, parallel.
parangona, *f.* (print.) paragon type.
parangonar, *tr.v.* 1. to compare, parallel. 2. (print.) to align, line up (type).
paranínfico, *a.* (archit.) **orden p.,** order in which figures of nymphs support the entablature in lieu of plain columns.
paraninfo, *m.* 1. paranymph, best man (at a wedding). 2. announcer of good news, harbinger of happiness. 3. salutatorian (one who makes the inaugural speech for the new scholastic year). 4. assembly hall (of a school, university).
paranoia, *f.* (psyc.) paranoia.
paranoico, ca, *a., m., f.* (psyc.) paranoiac.
paranoide, *a.* (med.) paranoid.
paranomasia, *f., var. of* **paronomasia.**
paranza, *f.* 1. hunter's hut or blind. 2. wickerwork fishing trap.
parao, *m.* large Philippine passenger vessel.
parapara, *f.* (Ven., bot.) soapberry.
paraparo, *m.* (Ven., bot.) soapberry tree.
parapetar, *tr.v.* to fortify with parapets. —*r.v.* to protect oneself with parapets; to protect oneself, hide behind a parapet.
parapeto, *m.* 1. (fort.) rampart, parapet, breastwork. 2. (archit.) railing, parapet, balustrade. 3. (Ecuad.) screen, screen door.
paraplejía, *f.* (med.) paraplegia.
parapléjico, ca, *a., m., f.* (med.) paraplegic.
parapoco, *m., f.* (coll.) 1. numbskull. 2. timid person.
parapsicología, *f.* parapsychology.
parar, *m.* lansquenet, faro (card game).
parar, *tr.v.* 1. to stop, halt, arrest, detain, check. 2. to bet, stake, put up. 3. to prepare, make ready. 4. to point game (a hunting dog). 5. to fix, put (e.g. attention on). 6. to change, alter. 7. to parry (blow, sword thrust, etc.). 8. (print.) to set (type). 9. (Amer.) to prick up (one's ears). —*i.v.* 1. to stop, halt; to finish, end. 2. to end up, land up (in someone's hands), e.g. *la nota vino a p. a sus manos,* the note landed or ended up in his hands. 3. to lodge, put up (at), stay (at). — **no p.,** without stopping, unceasingly, ceaselessly; **p. en seco,** to stop dead; **pararle los pies a uno,** (coll) to put someone in his place; **p. mal,** to end up badly; **sin p.,** unceasingly, ceaselessly; right away, immediately. —*r.v.* 1. to stop; to halt; to stop working. 2. to stand up; to stand on end (hair). 3. to turn, become. 4. (Cuba, Ecuad., Guat.) to prosper, become rich. — **pararse a** *+inf.,* to stop or pause + *inf.;* **pararse en,** to occupy oneself with, pay attention to; **pararse en pelillos,** to split hairs, argue over trifles.
pararrayo, pararrayos, *m.* lightning rod, lightning conductor; lightning arrester. — **p. electrostático,** electrostatic arrester.
pararrosanilina, *f.* (chem.) pararosaniline.
parasanga, *f.* parasang (ancient Persian measure of length).
parasceve, *f.* parasceve, Good Friday.
paraselene, *f.* (meteorol.) paraselene, mock moon.
parasemo, *f.* figurehead (on ancient Greek and Roman ships).
parasimpático, ca, *a.* (anat., physiol.) parasympathetic.
parasinapsis, *f.* (biol.) parasynapsis.
parasíntesis, *f.* (gram.) parasynthesis.
parasintético, ca, *a.* (gram.) parasynthetic.
parasismo, *m.* paroxysm, fit.
parasitario, ria, *a.* parasitic, parasitary, parasitical.
parasiticida, *a.* parasiticide.
parasítico, ca, *a.* parasitic, parasitical.
parasitismo, *m.* parasitism; (fig.) the habit of sponging or taking advantage of others.
parásito, ta, *a.* 1. parasitic, parasitical. 2. (rad.) atmospheric (noises). —*m.* 1. (biol., fig.) parasite. 2. (*pl.*) (rad.) atmospherics, strays. — **p. atmosféricos,** (rad.) atmospherics, static.
parasitología, *f.* parasitology.
parasitólogo, *m.* parasitologist.
parasol, *m.* 1. parasol, sunshade. 2. (bot.) umbel.
parástade, *m.* (archit.) parastas, anta, pilaster.
parata, *f.* (agr.) cultivation terrace, artificial land terrace.
parataxia, *f* (gram) parataxis
paratífico, ca, *a.* (med.) paratyphoid.
paratifoidea, *f.* (med.) paratyphoid fever.
paratión, *m.* (chem.) parathion.
paratiroideo, a, *a.* (anat.) parathyroid.
paratiroides, *a., f.* (anat.) parathyroid.
paratopes, *m.* (ry.) buffer, bumper.
paraulata, *f.* (Ven.) (variety of) thrush.
parca, *f.* 1. (poet.) death. 2. **P.,** (*pl.*) the Parcae, the Fates.
parcamente, *adv.* frugally, sparingly, parsimoniously, economically.
parce, *m.* prize card (given to absolve a pupil from some future offense).
parcela, *f.* 1. plot, lot, parcel (of ground). 2. particle.
parcelación, *f.* (law) parceling, division into lots.
parcelar, *tr.v.* (law) to parcel, divide (land) into lots.
parcelario, ria, *a.* parceling, parcelling; pertaining to parceled lands.
parcha, *f.* (bot., Amer.) passion flower.
parchar, *tr.v.* (Arg., Chile, Mex.) to mend, patch.
parchazo, *m.* 1. big plaster. 2. (mar.) bang of sail against mast or yard. 3. (coll.) deception, trick. — **pegar un p.,** to swindle, gyp or trick out of money, etc.
parche, *m.* 1. plaster (on a wound, etc.). 2. patch (on clothing, tire, etc.). 3. (taur.) ornamental rosette stuck by a daring bullfighter on the bull's forehead. 4. drumhead; drum. 5. camouflaging patch. 6. poorly retouched part (of a picture, etc.). — **pegar un p.,** (fig.) to swindle, gyp or trick out of money.
parchista, *m.* (coll.) sponger, moocher, cadger.
parcial, *a.* 1. partial, incomplete, e.g. *eclipse p.,* partial eclipse. 2. part (pertaining to part of a whole), e.g. *pago p.,* part payment. 3. biased, partial. 4. partisan. 5. participating, participant.

— **a tiempo p.,** part-time. —*m., f.* 1. partisan, follower, adherent, supporter. 2. participant, sharer.
parcialidad, *f.* 1. partiality, bias, partisanship. 2. party, faction, clique. 3. friendship, affableness.
parcialmente, *adv.* 1. partially, partly, incompletely. 2. one-sidedly, partially, prejudicially.
parcidad, *f., var. of* **parquedad.**
parcionero, ra, *a.* participating, sharing. —*m., f.* participant, sharer, partner.
parcísimo, ma, *a. super. of* **parco,** very scanty or frugal; very sparing or economical; very moderate.
parco, ca, *a.* 1. scanty, frugal. 2. sparing, economical, parsimonious. 3. temperate, moderate.
pardal, *a.* rural, rustic. —*m.* 1. (zool.) leopard. 2. (zool.) giraffe, camelopard. 3. (ornith.) sparrow. 4. (ornith.) linnet. 5. (bot.) aconite, monkshood, wolfsbane. 6. (coll.) crafty fellow, rogue, scoundrel.
pardear, *i.v.* to look brownish or grayish, to look grey or drab.
pardela, *f.* (ornith.) variety of tern.
¡pardiez! *interj.* by Jove! Good God!
pardillo, lla, *a.* 1. rural, rustic. 2. pertaining to a type of grape and its wine. —*m., f.* yokel, rustic. —*m.* (ornith.) linnet.
pardisco, ca, *a., var. of* **pardusco.**
pardo, da, *a.* 1. gray; brown, drab; dark. 2. flat, dull, toneless (voice). —*m., f.* (Cuba, P. Rico) mulatto. —*m.* (zool.) leopard; pard (poet.).
pardusco, ca, *a.* grayish; brownish; drab.
pareado, *m.* (poet.) couplet.
parear, *tr.v.* 1. to pair, match. 2. to put in pairs or couples, pair off. 3. (taur.) to impale the banderillas in.
parecencia, *f.* resemblance, likeness, similarity.
parecer, *m.* 1. opinion, way of thinking, view, mind. 2. appearance, looks. — **a mi p.,** in my opinion, to my way of thinking, to my mind; **arrimarse al p. de uno,** to agree with someone's way of thinking or view; **cambiar** or **mudar de p.,** to change one's mind or opinion; **casarse con su p.,** to stick to one's own opinion or way of thinking; **tomar p. de uno,** to ask for someone's opinion, confer with someone.
parecer, (*ref. 45*) *i.v.* 1. to appear, seem, look; to look like, seem or appear to be. 2. to appear, turn up, show up. — **a lo que parece, al p.,** apparently; **aunque parezca mentira,** although it seems incredible; **me parece que sí,** it seems so, I think so; **p.** + *inf.,* to appear to + *inf.,* seem to + *inf.;* **parece mentira,** it seems unbelievable or incredible; **p. que,** to look as if, seem that, appear that; **p. bien** or **mal,** to seem a good or bad idea, seem a plausible or impractical plan; **por el bien p.,** for appearances' sake; **¿qué le parece?** what do you think?; **según parece,** apparently, as it seems. —*r.v.* to look alike, resemble one another, e.g. *estos hermanos se parecen mucho,* these brothers look very much alike. — **parecerse a,** to look like, be like, resemble.
parecido, da, *a.* alike, similar. — **bien p.,** good-looking; **mal p.,** ill-favored, ugly; **p. a,** like, similar to; **ser bien p.,** to be seemly; **ser mal p.,** to be unseemly. —*m.* similarity, resemblance, likeness; analogy.
pareciente, *a.* similar, alike, resembling.
pared, *f.* wall. — **andar a tienta paredes,** to feel one's way, to grope one's way; **darse uno contra la p.,** to knock one's head against the wall (trying and failing to do something); **descargar las paredes,** (archit.) to lighten walls with arches or abutments; **entre cuatro paredes,** between four walls, shut in, withdrawn, retired; **estar entre la espada y la p.,** to have one's back against the wall; **hasta la p. de enfrente,** (coll.) resolutely, unwaveringly, with all one's might; **las paredes oyen,** walls have ears; **p. maestra,** main or bearing wall; **p. común** or **medianera,** party wall, partition wall; **p. cortafuego,** fire wall; **p. en** or **por medio,** next door, very close or near; **pegado a la p.,** nonplussed, confused; squashed; embarrassed.
paredaño, ña, *a.* adjoining, nearby, contiguous, having only a wall between.
paredón, *m. aug. of* **pared,** large thick wall. — **mandar al p.,** to condemn to be shot, send before the firing squad.
paregór—co, ca, *a., m.* (pharm.) paregor—c.
pareja, *f.* 1. pair, couple, team, brace, yoke. 2. partners, dancing partners. 3. pair of soldiers, guards, policemen. 4. (sport.) doubles, e.g. *parejas mixtas,* mixed doubles. 5. pair (of cards, dice). — **correr parejas** or **a las parejas,** to be on a par, to go together.
parejero, ra, *a.* 1. (S. Amer.) fast, race (horse). 2. (Bol., Cuba, P. Rico, Ven.) vain, presumptuous. 3. (Ven.) sycophantic, fawning. —*m.* (S. Amer.) race horse.
parejo, ja, *a.* 1. equal, alike. 2. level, even, smooth. — **por p.** or **por un p.** evenly; in the same way, on a par; **ir parejos,** to go neck and neck (said of racing horses); to be equal. —*adv.* evenly.
parejura, *f.* equality, similarity; evenness.
paremia, *f.* paroemia, proverb, adage, saying.
paremiología, *f.* paroemiology, study of proverbs.
paremiológico, ca, *a.* paroemiologic.
paremiólogo, *m.* paroemiologist, student of proverbs.
parénesis, *f.* admonition, exhortation; warning; precept.
parenético, ca, *a.* admonitory, exhortative.
parénquima, *m.* (anat., bot.) parenchyma.
parenquimatoso, sa, *a.* parenchymatous.
parentales, *f.* (*pl.*) Parentalia (Roman festival in honor of the dead).
parentela, *f.* relations, kinfolk, relatives.
parentesco, *m.* kinship, relationship; tie, bond.
paréntesis, (*pl,* **paréntesis**), *m.* 1. parenthesis, parenthetical statement. 2. (gram.) bracket, parenthesis. 3. (fig.) break, pause, interval. — **abrir** or **cerrar el p.,** to open or close brackets or parentheses; **entre p.,** in brackets or parentheses; incidentally, by the way.
pareo, *m.* pairing, coupling; matching.
pares, *f.* (*pl.*) placenta, afterbirth.
paresa, *f.* peeress.
paresia, *f.* (med.) paresis.
parestesia, *f.* (med., physiol.) paresthesia, paraesthesia.
parético, ca, *a., m., f.* paretic.
parezca, parezco, *ref.* **parecer.**
pargo, *m.* (icth.) porgy; (Cuba) red snapper.
parhelia, parhelio, *f., m.* (meteor.) parhelion.
parhélico, ca, *a.* parhelic, parhelical.
parhilera, *f.* (archit.) ridgepole, ridgepiece.
paria, *m., f.* outcast, pariah.
paría, *f.* peerage.
parias, *f.* (*pl.*) 1. (anat.) placenta. 2. tribute, submission, homage.
parición, *f.* parturition time of cattle; calving time.
parida, *a.* having recently given birth (said of a woman or an animal).
paridad, *f.* 1. parity, equality. 2. comparison, parallel; similarity.
paridera, *a.* prolific (female). —*f.* parturition place (of cattle); parturition (of cattle).
pariente, ta, *m., f.* relation, relative, kinsman, kinswoman. — **p. consanguíneo,** blood relation.
parietal, *a.* parietal; (bot., anat.) parietal. —*m.* (anat.) parietal (bone).
parietaria, *f.* (bot.) pellitory, wall pellitory.
parificación, *f.* exemplification, illustration.
parificar, (*ref. 50*) *tr.v.* to exemplify, illustrate, show by comparison.
parigual, *a.* very similar, very much alike.
parihuela, *f.* 1. handbarrow. 2. stretcher, litter (also used in *pl.*).
parima, *f.* (Arg., bot.) large heron.
pario, ria, *a., m., f.* Parian, pertaining to the Greek isle of Paros, famous for its marble; thus, pertaining to marble.
paripé, hacer el p., (coll.) to put on airs; to feign, deceive.
paripinado, da, *a.* (bot.) paripinnate.
parir, *tr.v.* 1. to give birth to, bear, bring forth. 2. to cause, originate. —*i.v.* 1. to give birth; to lay eggs. 2. to become known, come to light.
Paris, *m.* (myth.) Paris, prince of Troy, abductor of Helen.
París, *m.* Paris, capital of France.
parisién, parisiense, *a., m., f.* Parisian.
parisilábico, ca, *a.* parisyllabic.
parisílabo, ba, *a.* parisyllabic.
parisino, na, *a.* Parisian.
paritario, ria, *a.* pertaining to organizations in which management and workers meet on equal terms.
parkinsonismo, *m.* (med.) parkinsonism.
parla, *f.* 1. talk, chatter. 2. garrulity, verbal fluency or facility, loquacity, eloquence.
parlador, ra, *a.* talkative, gossipy. —*m., f.* chatterbox; gossip.
parladuría, *f.* talk, gossip, chatter.
parlaembalde, *m., f.* (coll.) chatterbox.
parlamentar, *i.v.* to talk, converse; to parley, confer, discuss.
parlamentariamente, *adv.* according to parliamentary rules and procedures.
parlamentario, ria, *a.* parliamentary. —*m.* 1. member of parliament. 2. parleyer, negotiator. 3. (mil.) flag of truce.
parlamentarismo, *m.* parliamentarianism.
parlamento, *m.* 1. parliament. 2. parleying, parley. 3. speech, address; (theat.) speech.
parlanchín, na, *a.* (coll.) chattering, jabbering, talkative. —*m., f.* chatterbox, jabberer.
parlante, *a.* speaking, talking; **cine p.,** talking pictures.
parlar, *tr.v.* to talk, speak. —*i.v.* to talk, speak; to chatter, gossip, jabber.
parlatorio, *m.* 1. talk, chat. 2. parlor; place teeming with chatter. 3. parlatory, locutory (in monasteries).
parlería, *f.* 1. garrulity, verbal fluency or facility, loquacity. 2. tale, piece of gossip.
parlero, ra, *a.* 1. talkative, garrulous; gossipy. 2. singing (bird); expressive (eyes). 3. babbling (brook, etc.).
parleta, *f.* (coll.) chat, idle talk.
parlón, na, *a.* (coll.) talkative, garrulous, chattering. —*m., f.* chatterbox.
parlotear, *i.v.* (coll.) to chatter, jabber, prattle.
parloteo, *m.* prattle, chatter.
parmesano, na, *a.* Parmesan, of or pertaining to Parma, Italy. —*m., f.* Parmesan. — **queso p.,** Parmesan cheese.
parmetro, *m.* (mec.) torquemeter.
parnaso, *m.* 1. (fig.) poets (collectively); (fig.) Parnassus, collection of poems. 2. **P.,** (myth.) Mount Parnassus.
parné, *m.* (coll.) cash, money.
paro, *m.* (coll.) 1. stop, stoppage (of work); lockout (by employers); **p. forzoso,** lay-off, shutdown, unemployment (not caused by strike or lockout).

2. (ornith.) titmouse; **p. carbonero,** great titmouse.
parodia, *f.* parody.
parodiar, *tr.v.* to parody.
paródico, ca, *a.* parodical, parodistic.
parodista, *m., f.* parodist, writer of parodies.
parola, *f.* 1. (coll.) volubility, loquacity, eloquence, verbal fluency. 2. (coll.) long chat, idle chatter or talk.
parolero, ra, *a.* (coll.) garrulous, talkative.
pároli, *m.* paroli, placing of staked money and its winnings as a further stake.
parolina, *f.* (coll.) *var. of* **parola.**
paronimia, *f.* paronymy (of words).
parónimo, ma, *a.* paronymous (of words).
paroniquieas, *f.* (bot.) (*pl.*) Paronychia.
paronomasia, *f.* 1. paronymy, resemblance between two or more words. 2. (rhet.) paronomasia, play upon words, pun.
paronomásticamente, *adv.* 1. paronymously. 2. paronomastically.
paronomástico, ca, *a.* 1. paronymous. 2. paronomastic.
parótida, *f.* 1. (anat.) parotid, parotid gland. 2. (med.) tumor on a parotid gland.
parotiditis, *f.* (med.) parotitis, mumps.
paroxismal, *a.* paroxysmal.
paroxismo, *m.* paroxysm; extreme feeling of pain, pleasure, passion, etc.
paroxítono, na *a.* (phonet., gram.) paroxytone.
parpadear, *i.v.* to blink; to wink.
parpadeo, *m.* blinking; winking.
párpado, *m.* eyelid.
parpalla, parpallota, *f.* (arch.) copper coin, pataca, milled copper piece.
parpar, *i.v.* to quack (said of ducks).
parque, *m.* 1. park, garden, preserve. 2. park (storage depot). 3. supplies, equipment (military, fire, etc.). 4. parking area. — **p. botánico,** botanical gardens; **p. de artillería,** gun park; **p. de atracciones** or **diversiones** (Arg., Col.) or **entretenciones** (Chile), amusement park; **p. empresarial,** business park, industrial park; **p. eólico,** windfarm; **p. nacional,** national park; **p. temático,** theme park; **p. zoológico,** zoo, zoological gardens.
parqué, *m., var. of* **parquet.**
parqueadero, *m.* (Amer.) parking space.
parquear, *tr.v.* (Amer.) to park (a car).
parquedad, *f.* 1. frugality, economy, sparingness, paucity. 2. moderation, temperance, parsimony.
parquet, *m.* parquet, parquetry, parquet flooring.
parquímetro, *m.* (auto.) parking meter.
parra, *f.* 1. grapevine; **hoja de p.,** grape of fig leaf. 2. earthenware jar with wide handles.
parrado, da, *a.* vinelike, spreading.
parrafada, *f.* (coll.) confidential talk, intimate talk.
parrafear, *i.v.* to chat confidentially.
parrafeo, *m.* confidential chat.
párrafo, *m.* 1. paragraph. 2. (coll.) chat. — **echar un p.,** to have a chat; **p. aparte,** to change the subject (of a conversation).
parragón, *m.* assayer's standard silver bar.
parral, *m.* 1. vine arbor, bower; untrimmed vineyard. 2. large earthenware jar.
parranda, *f.* 1. (coll.) spree, party, revel. 2. group of musicians or singers (performing on the streets at night). — **andar de p.,** to go out on a spree, paint the town red.
parrandear, *i.v.* to go out on a spree.
parrandeo, *m.* spree, celebrating, reveling.
parrandero, ra, *a.* reveling, carousing. —*m., f.* reveler, carouser.
parrandista, *m., var. of* **parrandero.**
parrar, *i.v.* to spread out (in branches).
parresia, *f.* (rhet.) parrhesia.
parricida, *a.* parricidal. —*m., f.* parricide (person), slayer of his father or mother.
parricidio, *m.* parricide (act).
parrilla, *f.* earthenware jug with a broad bottom and narrow neck.
parrilla, *f.* 1. gridiron, grill broiler. 2. grate (of furnace). 3. wide earthenware jug.
parriza, *f.* (bot.) wild grapevine.
parro, *m.* (ornith.) duck.
párroco, *a.* parish. —*m.* parson, parish priest.
parrocha, *f.* (ichth.) small pickled sardine.
parrón, *m.* (bot.) wild grapevine.
parroquia, *f.* 1. parish (ecclesiastical territory). 2. parish, parishioners, congregation of a parish. 3. parish church. 4. priests of a parish. 5. customers, clientele.
parroquial, *a.* parochial, pertaining to a parish.
parroquialidad, *f.* membership of a parish, parochial right.
parroquiano, na, *a.* parochial, parish. —*m., f.* 1. parishioner. 2. customer, client.
parsec, *m.* (astron.) parsec, unit of astronomical length equal to 3.26 light years.
parsi, *a.* Parsic. —*m., f.* Parsi, Parsee. —*m.* Parsi, Zoroastrian; Parsee (language).
parsimonia, *f.* 1. sobriety, circumspection, temperance, moderation, discretion. 2. parsimony, economy, frugality.
parsimonioso, sa, *a.* 1. sober, circumspect, solemn. 2. parsimonious, frugal, thrifty.
parsismo, *m.* (hist., rel.) Parsiism, Parseeism.
parte, *f.* 1. part, fragment, fraction. 2. part, share, portion. 3. part, place, spot. 4. part, volume, book. 5. (law) party (in a lawsuit). 6. party (in a contract). 7. (theat.) part, role. 8. member (of a theatrical company). 9. direction, way. 10. side, faction, party. 11. each word in a line. 12. (*pl.*) private parts. 13. (*pl.*) parts, gifts, talents. 14. (*pl.*) faction, party. 15. (mus.) part. — **a partes,** in parts; **a esta p.,** ago, e.g. *de un año a esta p.,* a year ago; **de mi (su) p.,** as far as I (he, she, etc.) am (is) concerned, for my (his, her, etc.) part; **de p. a p.,** from one side to another; through and through; **de p. de,** on the side of; on behalf of; in the name of; at the command of; **¿de parte de quién?** who is calling?; **echar a mala p.,** to misinterpret, take it ill or badly, be offended; **echar por otra p.,** to go in another direction; **en cualquier p.,** anywhere, everywhere; **en ninguna p.,** nowhere; **en todas partes,** everywhere; **en todas partes cuecen habas,** this happens everywhere, that's not exclusive to this part of the world; **estar de p. de,** to be on the side of, to side with; **hacer de su p.,** to do one's bit or share; **la mayor p.,** the majority; **llevar la mejor p.,** to have the upper hand, be in the winning position; **llevar la peor p.,** to get the worst of it, be in the losing position; **mandarse la p.,** (Peru) to act big, act the big shot, e.g. *mandarse la p. de gerente,* to act the big managing director; **no ser p. de la oración,** to have no say in, be of no account in; **p. actora,** (law) plaintiff; **p. alicuanta,** (math.) aliquant part; **p. alícuota,** (math.) aliquot part; **p. de la oración,** (gram.) part of speech; **p. del león,** lion's share (i.e. the biggest part); **p. de por medio,** (theat.) bit actor, small part actor; **p. esencial,** essential part; **p. inferior,** body (as opposed to the soul); **p. integral** or **integrante,** integral part; **p. meteorológico,** meteorological report, weather report; **p. por p.,** bit by bit; **p. superior,** soul (as opposed to the body); **partes contratantes,** contracting parties; **partes litigantes** or **contendientes,** contending parties; **partes naturales, pudendas** or **vergonzosas,** private parts, genitals; **poner de su p.,** to do one's bit or share; **ponerse de p. de uno,** to side with someone, take someone's side; **por la mayor p.,** in the main, in the most part; **por mi (su) p.,** as far as I (he, she, etc.) am (is, etc.) concerned; **por otra p.,** on the other hand; in another direction; **por p. de madre** or **padre,** on one's mother's or father's side; **por partes,** step by step, e.g. *vayamos por partes,* let's take it step by step; **por todas partes,** everywhere; **saber de buena p.,** to know on good authority; **salva sea la p.,** (coll.) the unmentionable part (of the body); e.g. *me dió un tremendo puntapié en salva sea la p.,* he gave me a tremendous kick in the backside; **ser p.** or **tener p. en una cosa,** to take part in, participate in; **tener de su parte,** to have on one's side; **tomar p. en una cosa,** to participate in, take part in something. —*m.* 1. note, message, dispatch, communiqué; report. 2. notification of marriage (sent to relatives or friends). 3. (arch.) royal post service; schedule, timetable of or for royal post riders; **dar, p.** to report; **dar p. a,** to notify, inform; to let participate, admit into a business or concern; **dar p. de,** to report; **dar p. sin novedad,** to report that all is well; **p. de guerra,** war dispatch; **p. de luto,** (Chile) obituary card.
partear, *tr.v.* to assist (a woman) in childbirth.
parteluz, *m.* (archit.) mullion, slender column dividing a window.
partencia, *f.* departure, leaving.
partenocarpia, *f.* (bot.) parthenocarpy.
partenogenesia, *f.* (bot.) parthenogenesis, parthenogeny.
partenogénesis, *f.* (bot.) parthenogenesis.
partenogenético, ca, *a.* parthenogenetic.
Partenón, *m.* (hist., archit.) Parthenon.
partera, *f.* midwife.
partería, *f.* midwifery.
partero, *m.* accoucheur, obstetrician, male midwife.
parterre, *m.* 1. parterre, flower garden. 2. the orchestra or ground floor of a theatre.
partesana, *f.* (archit.) halberd.
partesanero, *m.* halberdier.
partible, *a.* divisible, separable.
partición, *f.* 1. division, partition, separation. 2. (math.) division.
particionero, ra, *a., var. of* **partícipe.**
participación, *f.* 1. participation, share; joint action. 2. notification; communication. — **p. en las utilidades,** profit-sharing.
participante, *a.* participating, sharing. —*m., f.* 1. participant, participator, sharer. 2. notifier.
participar, *tr.v.* to communicate; to inform, notify of. —*i.v.* 1. to participate, partake, take part. 2. to share, have a share. — **p. de,** to have a share of or in; **p. en,** to take part in, participate in.
partícipe, *a.* 1. participating, participant. 2. sharing. —*m., f.* 1. participator, participant. 2. sharer.
participial, *a.* (gram.) participial.
participio, *m.* (gram.) participle.
partícula, *f.* particle, minute fraction; (gram., phys.) particle. — **p. alpha,** (phys.) alpha particle; **p. beta,** (phys.) beta particle; **p. subatómica,** (phys.) subatom; **p. V,** (phys.) V particle.
particular, *a.* 1. particular; special, peculiar; extraordinary, e.g. *es algo muy p.,* it's something very special; *nada tiene de p.,* there's nothing unusual (about that). 2. private, personal, e.g. *residencia p,* private residence. —*m.* 1. private person, individual, e.g. *vino a verte un p.,* an individual came to see you. 2. subject, item, matter, e.g. *hablemos de ese p.,* let's talk about that subject. —*adv.* specially; **en p.,** specially, particularly.

particularidad, *f.* 1. particular property or feature, particularity, peculiarity, individuality. 2. detail, individual feature. 3. friendship.
particularismo, *m.* 1. particularism; individualism. 2. (philos., theol.) particularism.
particularista, *a., m., f.* (philos.) particularist, adherent of the doctrine of particularism.
particularizar, (*ref. 53*) *tr.v.* 1. to particularize, specify, itemize, detail. 2. to show special attention to. —*r.v.* to distinguish oneself, stand out.
particularmente, *adv.* 1. particularly, specially. 2. privately, individually.
partida, *f.* 1. departure, leave; starting, start (of a race). 2. record; certificate. 3. (com.) entry, item (in ledger, balance sheet, etc.); item, financial allotment (in a budget). 4. lot, shipment (of merchandise, goods, etc.). 5. band, gang, crew; guerrilla group; hunting party; search detail. 6. hand, round (of cards). 7. stake (bet in a round of cards). 8. (coll.) turn, deed. 9. (fig.) departure, death, decease, passing away. — **echar una p.,** to play a round or hand of cards; **p. de bautismo,** baptismal certificate; **p. de campo,** picnic, excursion; **p. de caza,** hunting party; **p. doble,** (com.) double entry; **p. de defunción,** death certificate; **p. de matrimonio,** marriage or wedding certificate; **p. de nacimiento,** birth certificate; **p. serrana,** (coll.) dirty trick, mean turn.
partidamente, *adv.* separately.
partidario, ria, *m., f.* supporter, follower, adherent, partisan; advocate. —*m.* guerilla fighter.
partidismo, *m.* partisanship.
partidista, *a.* (Amer.) of a party or faction, partisan.
partido, da, *past part. of* **partir.** —*a.* 1. divided; cleft; broken. 2. (her.) party, parted. 3. (bot., ento.) partite, divided. 4. frank; generous, liberal. —*m.* 1. (political) party, group, faction. 2. match, game (of football, tennis, etc.) 3. team (of players). 4. profit, advantage, e.g. *sacar p. de,* to profit from. 5. backing, protection, aid, favor. 6. handicap (advantage given to one player over another). 7. treaty, agreement, pact. 8. measure, step. 9. county, district; area or district under the care of a state paid doctor. 10. match (marriage partner). — **formar p.,** to seek aid, enlist aid; **p. de desquite,** return game or match; **p. de exhibición.** exhibition game or match; **p. de homenaje,** benefit game or match; **p. judicial,** district under jurisdiction of circuit judge; **p. robado,** uneven game, uneven match; **ser buen** or **mal p.,** to be a good or bad match (in marriage); **tomar p.,** to decide, make up one's mind; to take sides; to enlist.
partidor, *m.* 1. divider; distributor. 2. breaker; splitter; cracker; cutter, cleaver, splitter. 3. device for distributing water equally to various sluice gates. 4. (arch.) parting comb (for parting the hair). 5. (math.) divisor. — **p. de leña,** woodcutter; **p. de nueces,** nutcracker; **p. de tensión,** (elec.) voltage divider.
partidura, *f.* part (in hair).
partija, *f.* 1. *dim. of* **parte,** small part. 2. division, partition.
partimento, partimiento, *m.* division, partition.
partiquino, na, *m., f.* singer of small parts (in opera).
partir, *tr.v.* 1. to split, divide, cut in two, cleave; to break, crack. 2. to divide, split up; to distribute, share. 3. (coll.) to ruin (someone's) plans, put out, disconcert. 4. (math.) to divide. — **p. la diferencia,** to split the difference. —*i.v.* 1. to depart, leave, set out. 2. to decide, make up one's mind; **a p. de,** as of, from (this moment, that date, etc.); **estar a p. de confite con,** to be bosom friends with, be on intimate terms with; **p. de,** to depart from; to reckon from; to start from. —*r.v.* 1. to split, crack, break. 2. to become divided, split up (into factions, etc.). 3. to depart, leave, set out.
partitivo, va, *a.* (gram.) partitive.
partitura, *f.* (mus.) score.
parto, *m.* 1. delivery, childbirth, parturition. 2. baby, newborn child. 3. (fig.) product, creation, brain child. 4. (fig.) important event. — **estar de p.,** to be in labor; **p. de los montes,** anticlimax; **p. prematuro,** premature birth; **p. revesado,** difficult delivery; **p. sin dolor,** pain-free labor; **supresión de p.,** abortion; **venir el p. derecho,** to occur as hoped.
parto, ta, *a.* Parthian, of or pertaining to ancient country in W. Asia (now a part of Iran). —*m., f.* Parthian.
parturición, *f.* (med.) parturition, delivery.
parturienta, parturiente, *a.* parturient. —*f.* woman in labor.
párulis, *m.* (med.) parulis, gumboil.
parva, *f.* 1. heap of unthreshed or unwinnowed grain. 2. heap, pile, large amount. 3. light breakfast (on fast days).
parvada, *f.* 1. (agr.) heap of unthreshed corn. 2. batch of newly hatched chicks.
parvedad, *f.* 1. smallness, minuteness, littleness. 2. light breakfast (on fast days).
parvero, *m.* large heap of grain to be winnowed.
parvidad, *f., var. of* **parvedad.**
parvo, va, *a.* small, little.
parvulario, ria, *m., f.* (Chile) nursery school teacher. —*m.* nursery school, kindergarten.
parvulez, *f.* 1. smallness, littleness. 2. innocence, candor, simplicity.
párvulo, la, *a.* 1. small, little. 2. innocent, simple. —*m., f.* small child, tot.
parvulez, *f.* 1. smallness, littleness. 2. innocence, candor, simplicity.
párvulo, la, *a.* 1. small, little. 2. innocent, simple. —*m., f.* small child, tot.
pasa, *f.* 1. raisin; currant; sultana. 2. cosmetic made with raisins. 3. (Cuba, Car.) tight curl or kink (in hair). 4. (mar.) channel (between shallows). — **estar hecho** or **quedarse como una p.,** to become all dried up and wrinkled; **p. de Corinto,** currant; **p. garrona,** large raisin.
pasable, *a.* passable, fair.
pasablemente, *adv.* passably.
pasacalle, *m.* (mus.) lively march; two-step; passacaglia.
pasacólica, *f.* (med.) colic.
pasada, *f.* 1. passing, passage; traverse, traversing. 2. geometrical or great pace. 3. (ecc.) maintenance, stipend. 4. hand, round, game (of cards). 5. (coll.) mean trick, bad turn. 6. big stitch. 7. (C. Amer.) reprimand. — **dar p. a,** to tolerate, let pass; **de p.,** in passing; **mala p.,** (coll.) mean trick, bad turn; **p. de lanzadera,** shuttle traverse.
pasadera, *f.* 1. stepping stone. 2. (mar.) spun yarn.
pasaderamente, *adv.* passably.
pasadero, ra, *a.* 1. bearable, tolerable. 2. passable, fair, fairly good. 3. fairly well (in health). —*m., f.* stepping stone. —*f.* (mar.) spun yarn, furling line.
pasadillo, *m.* embroidery on both sides of the cloth.
pasadizo, *m.* passage, corridor; alley.
pasado, da, *past part. of* **pasar.** —*a.* 1. past, gone by, elapsed. 2. outmoded, antiquated, old-fashioned, passé. 3. boiled (egg). 4. rotten, overripe (fruit); spoiled, sour, curdled (meat, milk); stale (bread, cheese); rancid (butter); rotten (eggs). 5. overcooked, overdone (food). 6. last (week, year). 7. (gram.). past (tense). — **p. de moda,** old-fashioned. —*m.* 1. past. (gram.) past. 2. (gram.) past (tense). 3. turncoat, deserter. 4. (*pl.*) ancestors, forebears. —*adv.* **pasado mañana,** the day after tomorrow; **pasado meridiano,** post meridian (p.m.).
pasador, ra, *a.* smuggling. —*m., f.* smuggler. —*m.* 1. pin, cotter. 2. door or window bolt. 3. (arch.) thin arrow. 4. large hair pin, hat pin. 5. skirt pin or brooch; safety pin (for holding a medal). 6. strainer, colander. 7. (mar.) marline spike. 8. (Peru) lace, shoestring. — **p. ahusado,** (mec.) taper pin, driftpin; **p. hendido,** (mec.) cotter pin; **p. horquilla** (mec.) clevis pin; **p. de enganche,** coupling pin; **p. de seguridad,** safety bolt.
pasadura, *f.* 1. passage, transit. 2. (child's) convulsive fit of sobbing.
pasagonzalo, *m.* (coll.) light slap.
pasaje, *m.* 1. passage, pass, way, road (e.g. through mountains, etc.); passage, alley (between two streets); (mar.) channel, strait, narrow. 2. fare (amount paid for train or bus journey); passage (amount paid for boat or airplane journey). 3. passage (in a text). 4. (total number of) passengers (on a ship). 5. passage, journey, voyage. 6. reception, treatment. 7. (mus.) passage, run, flourish; (mus.) transition, modulation (of voice). — **medio p.,** half fare.
pasajero, ra, *a.* 1. passing; transient; fleeting. 2. frequented (street, place). —*m., f.* passenger; traveler.
pasajeros-kilómetro, *m. pl.* passenger miles.
pasajuego, *m.* return (of the ball in pelota).
pasamanar, *tr.v.* to passement, trim with passementerie.
pasamanería, *f.* passementerie (gimp, lace, bead and ribbon embroidery).
pasamanero, *m.* passementerie maker or seller.
pasamano, *m.* 1. handrail (of banister, railling, etc.). 2. passementerie. 3. (mar.) gangway.
pasamiento, *m.* passage, transit.
pasante, *a.* 1. passing. 2. (her.) passant. —*m.* 1. assistant (of lawyer, teacher, doctor). 2. tutor, coach. — **p. de pluma,** lawyer's clerk.
pasantía, *f.* 1. tutorship. 2. assistantship, apprenticeship.
pasapalo, (*pl.* **pasapalos**), *m.* (Ven.) cocktail canapé, appetizer, tidbit.
pasapán, *m.* (coll.) gullet, windpipe.
pasapasa, *m.* sleight of hand, conjuring trick, legerdemain.
pasaperro, coser a p., to fasten thin books with a thong.
pasaporte, *m.* 1. passport, safe conduct. 2. (mil.) furlough. 3. (fig.) carte blanche, full discretionary powers.
pasapuré, *m.* potato masher.
pasar, *tr.v.* 1. to pass, transfer, hand, e.g. *pásame la sal, por favor,* pass or hand me the salt please; to pass on, communicate (a message, disease). 2. to take or carry across, e.g. *pasaron el carro en un barco,* they took the car across in a boat; to transfer, move, take, e.g. *pasa sus maletas a otro cuarto,* take or move his bags to another room. 3. to pass, while away (the time); to spend (a holiday). 4. to pass (an examination). 5. to cross, go over, pass. 6. to go or pass through, penetrate, pierce. 7. to pass, go beyond (limit, etc.). 8. to smuggle in. 9. to pass, circulate (counterfeit money). 10. to go through, undergo, suffer, e.g. *p. muchas privaciones,* to undergo many privations, *p. hambre,* to go hungry. 11. to run, pass, wipe, brush, sweep, e.g. *p. la mano por la cara,* to run one's hand over one's face, *p un peine por el pelo,* to run a comb through one's hair; *p. un trapo por la mesa,* to wipe the table

with a rag, go over the table with a rag, *p. la escoba por el piso,* to sweep the floor, give the floor a quick brush. 12. to pass, put, e.g. *p. por,* to put or pass through, *p. por el colador,* to strain, put through a strainer. 13. to percolate (coffee). 14. to swallow. 15. to show or run (a film). 16. to tolerate, stand for, allow, pass over. 17. to let pass, let through. 18. to omit, leave out. 19. to study as an assistant with (a lawyer, doctor, etc.). 20. to review, revise (a lesson). 21. to study superficially; to say (a prayer) inattentively. — **p. a (alguien) la voz** or **el dato,** to inform, let know, tip (someone) off; **p. a cuchillo,** to put to the sword, kill; **p. de largo,** to pass by; to skim through, read or glance at superficially; **p. en blanco** or **claro,** to omit, leave out, skip; **p. en limpio,** to make a fair copy of (manuscript, document, etc.); **p. la noche en blanco** or **claro,** not to sleep a wink all night; **p. por agua,** to boil (an egg); **p. por alto,** to disregard; to leave out, omit, overlook; **p. por las armas,** to shoot, execute; **p. lista,** to call the roll or register, pass muster; **pasarlo,** to live, fare, do, get along, manage; **pasarlo bien** or **mal,** to have a good or bad time, fare well or badly. —*i.v.* 1. to pass, go; to go by. 2. to spread (disease, news, etc.). 3. to pass, go by, elapse (time). 4. to pass or go (through), pierce, penetrate. 5. to go in, come in. 6. to pass (in a game of cards). 7. to manage, get by, have enough to live on, e.g. *vamos pasando,* we get by. 8. to let pass, let through (as of being of no importance). 9. to last, do, e.g. *este vestido puede p. el verano,* this dress will last the summer. 10. to pass, calm down, die down, to get over, e.g. *le pasará el mal humor,* he'll get over his bad mood. 11. to pass (through one's mind). 12. to happen, occur, e.g. *¿qué pasó?* what happened? what's the matter? — **hacerse p. por,** to pass oneself off as; **¿qué te pasa?** what's the matter with you?; **lo pasado, pasado,** let bygones be bygones; **pase, por favor,** come in, please; **p. a** + *inf.*, to go or come in + *inf.;* to go on + *inf.;* **p. a ser,** to become; **p. de,** to be more than, exceed (a certain number or amount), be more than (a certain number of years) old; **p. por,** to pass by, stop or call at (somewhere on an errand); to be considered or held to be; to go through, undergo (an experience); to pass or go through, be handled by; **p. por encima de,** to go over (someone's) head (not go through the normal channels); **p. sin,** to do or go without. —*r.v.* 1. to pass, go. 2. to overdo it, go too far, go beyond oneself, e.g. *te pasaste con la sal,* you put too much salt. 3. to pass, calm down, die down, get over, e.g. *se le pasó el susto,* his shock has passed, he has got over his fright. 4. to go over to, e.g. *se pasó al enemigo,* he went over to the enemy. 5. to cease, finish. 6. to forget, e.g. *se me pasó de la memoria lo que dijo,* I have forgotten what he said. 7. to become overripe (fruit); to go off, become tainted, go bad (meat, milk, eggs); to go stale (bread, cheese); to go rancid (butter); to get overcooked. 8. to burn out (fire). 9. to burn well (coal). 10. to leak, be porous. 11. to take an examination. 12. to get too many points in certain card games. 13. to be loose (fittings, locks). — **pasarse de,** to exceed, be too, be excessively, e.g. *él se pasa de listo,* he's a smart alec, he's too smart; **pasarse de rosca,** to go too far, go beyond the limits; **pasarse de la raya,** to go too far (in one's behavior); **pasarse la gran vida,** to live it up, have a high old time, live well; **pasarse la mano,** to go too far, to overdo it; **pasarse sin,** to do or go without.

pasarela, *f.* 1. footbridge; catwalk. 2. (mar.) gangplank; bridge.

pasatiempo, *m.* pastime, amusement; hobby.

pasatoro, *m.* (taur.) thrust with the sword as the bull is passing.

pasavante, *m.* (mar.) sea letter or brief, safe conduct.

pasavolante, *m.* 1. hasty act, thoughtless act. 2. small caliber culverin.

pasavoleo, *m.* hitting ball back over the service line (in pelota).

pascana, *f.* 1. (S. Amer.) stage, stop (during journey). 2. (S. Amer.) inn, tavern, hostelry.

pascasio, *m.* (coll.) university student who spends Easter or Christmas holidays in his home town.

pascua, *f.* 1. (rel.) church festival commemorating Easter, Christmas, Pentecost, Epiphany; (*pl.*) Christmas time, Christmastide. 2. (rel.) Passover. — **dar las Pascuas,** to wish (someone) a Merry Christmas or Happy New Year; **de Pascuas a Ramos,** from time to time, occasionally, once in a blue moon; **estar como una p.,** (coll.) to be as happy as a lark; **¡Felices Pascuas!** Merry Christmas!; **P. Florida** or **de Resurrección,** Easter; **P. del Espíritu Santo,** Pentecost; **santas pascuas,** there's no way out, we'll have to conform.

pascual, *a.* paschal. — **el cordero p.,** paschal lamb.

pascuilla, *f.* first Sunday after Easter.

pase, *m.* 1. pass, permit. 2. pass, free ticket. 3. pass (in cards). 4. pass (movement of hands by mesmerist). 5. exequatur. 6. (fenc.) feint. 7. (taur.) pass. 8. pass (in football, etc.) — **p. de cortesía,** complimentary ticket.

paseadero, *m.* walk, promenade, avenue.

paseador, ra, *a.* fond of walking or strolling. —*m., f.* stroller, promenader.

paseante, *a.* strolling. —*m., f.* stroller, promenader; **p. en corte,** (coll.) idler, loafer.

pasear, *tr.v.* 1. to take for a walk or stroll. 2. to show off, exhibit. —*i.v., r.v.* 1. to walk, stroll, take a stroll or walk; to take a ride, go riding (on a horse, in a coach); to go for a ride (in a car). — **p. a caballo,** to go riding; **p. en barco,** to go sailing, go for a boat trip; **p. en bicicleta,** to go bicycling; **p. en canoa,** to go canoing; **p. en carro, coche** or **automóvil,** to take a ride in a car, go for a drive. —*i.v.* to pace (a horse); **mandar a pasear,** to send (someone) about (his) business. —*r.v.* to take it easy, laze around, loaf about.

paseata, *f.* walk, stroll, promenade; ride; drive.

paseo, *m.* 1. walk, stroll; ride; drive; trip, excursion. 2. walk, promenade, avenue. — **anda** or **vete a p.,** (coll.) go take a walk, go jump in the lake; **dar un p.,** to take a walk, stroll or ride; **echar, mandar a p.,** (coll.) to send packing, send (someone) about (his) business; **ir de p.,** to go on a trip or excursion, go for a walk; **p. marítimo,** esplanade, seafront.

pasera, *f.* 1. drying place, drying table, drying room (for fruit). 2. drying of fruit.

pasero, ra, *a.* (equit.) pacing (horse). —*m., f.* raisin seller.

pasibilidad, *f.* sensibility.

pasible, *a.* sensible, capable of suffering. — **p. de,** deserving; subject to.

pasicorto, ta, *a.* short-paced.

pasiega, *f.* (coll.) wet nurse.

Pasifae, *f.* (myth.) Pasiphae, wife of Minos and mother, by a white bull, of the Minotaur.

pasiflora, *f.* (bot.) passionflower.

pasifloráceo, a, pasiflóreo, a, *a.* (bot.) passifloraceous. —*f.* (*pl.*) Passifloraceae.

pasilargo, ga, *a.* long-paced.

pasillo, *m.* 1. short step. 2. passage, corridor. 3. basting stitch. 4. short play, sketch, skit. 4. (S. Amer.) a typical folkloric dance and composition. 5. (aer.) aisle. — **p. rodante,** moving walkway or sidewalk.

pasión, *f.* 1. passion; strong emotion. 2. enthusiasm, vehemence. 3. (rel.) **P.,** Passion. — **tener p. por,** to have a passion for.

pasional, *a.* passional, emotional; passionate. — **crimen p.,** crime passionel (Fr.), crime of passion.

pasionaria, pasionario, *f.* (bot.) passion flower (plant and flower). —*m.* (ecc.) Passion songbook.

pasioncilla, *f.* 1. passing fancy. 2. grudge, aversion (towards someone).

pasionero, pasionista, *m.* 1. chorister who sings the Passion during Holy Week. 2. priest assigned to hospital as spiritual adviser.

pasitamente, *adv.* (coll.) gently, softly, lightly.

pasito, *m.* short pace or step. —*adv.* gently, softly, lightly, leisurely.

pasitrote, *m.* (equit.) short trot.

pasivamente, *adv.* passively.

pasividad, *f.* passivity, passiveness; (chem.) passivity.

pasivo, va, *a.* 1. passive; unresisting; unresponsive. 2. (com., law, gram., chem.) passive. 3. retirement (pension). — **clases pasivas,** pensioners; **resistencia pasiva,** passive resistance. —*m.* (com.) liabilities; **p. corriente** or **exigible,** current liabilities; **p. eventual** or **contingent,** contingent liability; **p. fijo,** capital liabilities.

pasmado, da, *a.* 1. (coll.) astounded, stunned. 2. (her.) open-mouthed (fish).

pasmar, *tr.v.* 1. to stun, astound, leave dumbfounded. 2. to chill, freeze, benumb. 3. to wither, freeze, blight (plants). —*r.v.* 1. to be stunned, astounded or dumbfounded. 2. to become chilled, frozen or numbed. 3. to get tetanus or lockjaw. 4. to become blighted, get blight (plants). 5. to become dull or blurred (colors).

pasmarota, pasmarotada, *f.* exaggerated gesture of astonishment.

pasmarote, *m.* gawk, fool, vacant-looking person.

pasmo, *m.* 1. astonishment, amazement. 2. wonder, object of wonder or amazement. 3. (med.) tetanus, lockjaw. 4. muscular spasm, convulsion or ache, rheumatic pain.

pasmosamente, *adv.* astonishingly, amazingly.

pasmoso, sa, *a.* astonishing, amazing.

paso, *m.* 1. step, pace (movement of feet). 2. pace (length of step). 3. (fig.) step, movement, e.g. *un p. hacia el entendimiento internacional,* a step towards international understanding. 4. step (in dance); (mil.) step. 5. stair, step (of stairs). 6. (equit.) gait, walk, step. 7. passing, passage; crossing. 8. pass (e.g. between mountains); (geog.) strait (narrow passage of water). 9. (*pl.*) steps, measures; negotiations. 10. footprint, step. 11. permit, pass, safe conduct. 12. permission, authority; exequatur. 13. promotion (of student to higher grade). 14. examination, review, revision (of lesson). 15. progress, improvement (in employment, health, etc.). 16. (each) stage (in Christ's Passion); effigy representing stage in Christ's Passion. 17. passage (in text). 18. basting stitch. 19. (theat.) sketch, skit. 20. (hunt.) part of terrain where game is accustomed to pass. 21. migration (of birds). 22. (mec.) pitch (of screw, nut, etc.). — **abrir p. (para),** to make way (for); **abrirse p.,** to force one's way; **a buen p.,** quickly, rapidly; **a cada p.,** at every turn; at each step, frequently, repeatedly; **a dos pasos de,** a short distance from, a stone's throw from;

a ese p., at this rate, in this way; **alargar el p.,** (coll.) to quicken one's pace, speed up; **al p.,** in passing, on the way; without stopping; **al p. que,** while, at the same time as; **anchura de p.,** (mec.) clearance width; **a p. de buey** or **tortuga,** at a snail's pace, very slowly; **a p. de carga,** rashly, precipitately; **a p. largo,** rapidly, quickly; **a p. llano,** smoothly, without difficulty; **a p. tirado,** quickly, rapidly; **a pocos pasos,** at a short distance, a stone's throw (from); easily, without difficulties; **apretar** or **avivar el p.,** to quicken or hasten one's step; **asentar el p.,** to live quietly and sensibly; **ave de p.,** migratory bird; fickle friend; **buen p,** (coll.) easy life; **cada p. es un gazapo** or **tropiezo,** (coll.) he makes a mistake at every turn; **cambiar el p.,** (mil.) to change step; **ceder p. (a),** to make way (for), step aside; **cerrar el p.,** to block the way, put oneself in the way, hinder, obstruct; **coger al p.,** to take (a pawn) en passant (in chess); **coger los pasos,** to guard the paths and routes (along which an enemy is expected); **contar los pasos a uno,** to watch someone's every step; **cortar el p.,** to intercept, cut off, hinder, obstruct; **dar p. atrás,** to step backwards; to withdraw; to back down; **dar pasos,** to take steps or measures; **dar un p.,** to take a step; **de cuatro pasos,** four-way, e.g. *válvula de cuatro pasos,* four-way valve; **de p.,** in passing, en passant, incidentally, lightly; (Amer.) ambling, e.g. *caballo de p.,* ambler; **de p. en p.,** step by step, gradually; **estar de p.,** to be just passing through or by; **hacer el p.,** to make a fool of oneself; **llevar el p.,** to keep in step; keep pace; **marcar el p.,** (mil.) to mark time; **no dar p.,** to make no effort, take no steps; **no poder dar un p.,** to be unable to walk; to be unable to make any progress; **¡paso!** gangway! open up!; **p. a desnivel** or **p. elevado,** overpass (Am.), flyover (G.B.); **p. a nivel,** (ry.) level crossing (G.B.), grade crossing (Am.); **p. a. p.,** step by step, little by little; **p. aparente,** (engin.) apparent pitch; **p. atrás,** (mil.) back step; step backwards; **p. castellano,** long easy pace; **p. circunferencial,** (mec.) circumferential pitch, circular pitch, arc-pitch (gearing); **p. corto,** (mil.) half step, short step; **p. de ambladura** or **andadura,** ambling pace; **p. de ataque** or **carga,** (mil.) *var. of* **p. ligero; p. de cebra,** zebra crossing; **p. de comedia,** incident, passage (in drama or real life); **p. de gallina,** (coll.) ineffective step, half measure; **p. de ganso,** (mil.) goose step; **P. de Khaiber,** Khyber Pass; **p. del collector,** (elec.) commutator pitch; **P. del Noroeste,** Northwest Passage; **p. de peatones,** crosswalk, pedestrian crossing; **p. diametral,** (mec.) diametral pitch; **p. doble,** (mus.) pasodoble; **p. fronterizo,** border crossing; **p. geométrico,** geometrical or great pace; **p. lateral,** (mil.) side step; **p. lento,** (mil.) slow step; **p. libre,** free or unobstructed passage, e.g. *dejar el p. libre,* to leave the way clear or open; **p. ligero,** (mil.) double time; **p. ordinario,** (mil.) quick step, quick march; **p. polar,** (elec.) pole pitch; **p. por p.,** step by step; **p. portante,** ambling pace; **p. redoblado,** (mil.) quick step, quick march; **p. regulable,** (hydr., avia.) variable pitch; **p. subterraneo,** underpass; **salir del p.,** to get out of a fix, jam or difficult situation; **salirle a uno al p.,** to go out to meet; to waylay; to interrupt, contradict, oppose, thwart; **seguir los pasos a uno,** to keep an eye on, check, watch (someone) closely; **seguir los pasos de uno,** to follow in someone's footsteps; **volver sobre los pasos,** to retrace one's steps. —*adv.* softly, gently.

paso, sa, *a.* sun-dried (raisins, figs, etc.); **ciruelas p.,** prunes.

pasote, *m.* (bot.) wormseed, Mexican tea.

paspa, *f.* (Amer.) crack (in the lips or the skin).

pasparse, *r.v.* (Amer.) to crack, become cracked (the skin, the lips).

paspartú, *m.* passe-partout, decorative mat for framing a picture.

paspié, *m.* (mus.) passepied, a lively French dance of the 18th century.

pasquín, *m.* 1. poster, street advertisement. 2. rag, scandal sheet, low-grade newspaper.

pasquinada, *f.* pasquinade, lampoon, squib.

passim, *adv.* (Lat.) passim, in various places (in a book, such as quotations, etc.).

pasta, *f.* 1. paste, e.g. *p. de almendras,* almond paste, *p. dentífrica,* toothpaste. 2. (cul.) pastry, pie crust. 3. (cul.) pasta (spaghetti, macaroni, etc.); (*pl.*) spaghetti, macaroni, ravioli (in general); biscuit, cookie. 4. (metal.) bullion. 5. makings, qualities, e.g. *tiene p. de campeón,* he has the makings of a champion. 6. pasteboard, cardboard. 7. pulp (for making paper). 8. (bkb.) stiff marbled leather binding. 9. (p.) perfect blending (of colors). — **buena p.,** placid and pleasant temperament; **p. de chocolate,** chocolate in tablets; **p. de hojaldre,** puff pastry; **p. de madera,** wood pulp; **p. de papel,** wood pulp; **p. dental** or **dentífrica** or **de dientes,** toothpaste; **p. española,** (bkb.) stiff marbled binding; **p. italiana,** (bkb.) parchment binding; **p. para soldar,** soldering paste; **media p.,** (bkb.) half binding; cloth binding.

pastadero, *m.* pastureland, grazing field.

pastaflora, *f.* (cul.) fine puff pastry.

pastar, *tr.v.* to take (cattle) to graze. —*i.v.* to graze, pasture.

paste, *m.* (C. Rica, Hond.) luffa, dishcloth gourd, sponge gourd.

pastear, *tr.v.* (Peru) to spy.

pasteca, *f.* (mar.) snatch block.

pastel, *m.* 1. (cul.) pastry; pie, cake. 2. pastel (crayon, color, drawing). 3. (bot.) dyer's weed. 4. tablet of dye. 5. cheating (when shuffling cards), card sharping. 6. (coll.) underhand or shady deal. 7. (print.) pie, pi. — **cuadro al p.,** pastel drawing; **descubrirse el p.,** (coll.) to come to light, be revealed; **p. de boda,** wedding cake; **p. de carne,** meat pie; **p. de cumpleaños,** birthday cake; **pastelito de carne,** meat turnover, piroshki.

pastelear, *i.v.* (coll.) to temporize, compromise (in politics).

pastelejo, *m., var. of* **pastelito.**

pasteleo, *m.* deal, compromise (in politics).

pastelería, *f.* cake shop, patisserie; the art of pastry-making.

pastelero, ra, *m., f.* 1. pastry cook. 2. (coll.) temporizer, one who compromises or makes deals (in politics).

pastelillo, *m.* (cul.) sweet made of almond paste and candied fruit.

pastelista, *m., f.* pastel painter, pastelist.

pastelito, *m. dim. of* **pastel,** patty, small pie or pastry, tart, tartelette.

pastelón, *m.* 1. (Chile) large cement tile. 2. (cul.) large meat pie.

pastenco, ca, *a.* newly-weaned (calf.) —*m.* newly-weaned calf.

pasterización, *f., var. of* **pasteurización.**

pasterizar, (*ref. 53*) *tr.v., var. of* **pasteurizar.**

pastero, *m.* workman who puts the crushed olives into pressing bags.

pasteurice, pasteuricé, *ref.* **pasteurizar.**

pasteurización, *f.* pasteurization.

pasteurizar, (*ref. 53*) *tr.v.* to pasteurize.

pastilla, *f.* 1. pastille, tablet; lozenge; drop. 2. cake (of soap); bar (of chocolate). — **p. de freno,** brake shoe; **p. de silicio,** silicon chip; **p. magnética,** (elec.) magnetic cartridge.

pastillero, *m.* pill box.

pastinaca, *f.* 1. (bot.) parsnip. 2. (ichth.) stingray.

pastizal, *m.* pastureland, pasture.

pasto, *m.* 1. pasture, grass, hay; fodder, food, nourishment. 2. pastureland, pasture. 3. grazing, pasturing. 4. (fig.) fuel, e.g. *el edificio fue p. de las llamas,* the building was fuel for the flames; food, e.g. *él fue p. para los cocodrilos,* he was food for the crocodiles. — **a p.,** to excess; **a todo p.,** freely, without restriction; **de p.,** ordinary, everyday; **p. espiritual,** spiritual nourishment (religious teaching); **p. seco,** dried fodder; **p. verde,** green grass.

pastor, ra, *m.* 1. shepherd, herdsman. 2. pastor, parish priest. — **el Buen P.,** (Bib.) the Good Shepherd; **p. alemán,** German shepherd; **perro p.,** sheep dog. —*f.* shepherdess.

pastoral, *a.* 1. pastoral, pertaining to shepherds. 2. pastoral, rustic; bucolic, idyllic, Arcadian. —*f.* 1. (ecc.) pastoral. 2. (mus., lit.) pastoral, pastorale.

pastoralmente, *adv.* pastorally.

pastorcico, illo, ito, *m. dim. of* **pastor,** little shepherd.

pastorear, *tr.v.* to shepherd, pasture (cattle); (fig.) to minister to, lead (the faithful).

pastorela, *f.* shepherd's song; (lit.) pastourelle.

pastoreo, *m.* shepherding, tending flocks.

pastoría, *f.* shepherding; shepherds; pastoral life.

pastoricio, cia, *a., var. of* **pastoril.**

pastoril, *a.* pastoral, bucolic, of shepherds.

pastorilmente, *adv.* pastorally, in the manner of shepherds.

pastosidad, *f.* 1. doughiness, pastiness. 2. mellowness (of the voice, the sound of a cello, etc.). 3. (p.) pastosity (as in impasto painting).

pastoso, sa, *a.* 1. doughy, pasty. 2. soft, mellow (voice). 3. (p.) pastose.

pastueño *a.* (taur.) impetuous (bull) which charges straight on.

pastura, *f.* 1. pasture, fodder. 2. pastureland, pasture, grazing field.

pasturaje, *m.* 1. common pasture, pasturage. 2. grazing fee.

pasudo, da, *a.* (Amer.) kinky (hair).

pata, *f.* 1. paw, foot, leg (of animal). 2. leg (of a stand, a piece of furniture). 3. (coll.) leg, foot (of human being). 4. pocket flap. 5. tie, draw. 6. (ornith.) duck. — **a cuatro patas,** (coll.) on all fours, crawling; **a la p. coja,** game of hopping on one foot; **a la p. llana or a p. llana,** plainly, unaffectedly, simply; **ancorar a p. de ganso,** (mar.) to moor with three anchors; **andar a p. coja, renca** or **renga,** to limp, hobble; **a p.,** on foot; **a p. pelada,** (Amer.) barefoot; **bailar en una p.,** (Amer.) to be merry as a cricket; **echar las patas por alto,** (coll.) to rant, rave, talk unrestrainedly; **enseñar la p.** or **su p.,** (coll.) to show the cloven hoof, give oneself away, show one's real self; **estirar la p.,** (coll.) to kick the bucket, die; **meter la p.,** (coll.) to put one's foot in it, make a faux pas; **p. de banco,** (coll.) foolish remark; **p. de cabra,** (in shoemaking) heel burnisher; crowbar; **p. de gallina,** radial crack (in trees); **p. de gallo,** (bot.) crowfoot (Ranunculus muricatus); (coll.) crow's-foot, wrinkle around the eye; **p. de león,** (bot.) lion's foot; **p. de palo,** wooden leg, peg leg; **p. galana,** (coll.) game or lame foot; (coll.) clubfooted or lame person; **patas arriba,** (coll.) upside-down; topsy-turvy; **patas de rana,** flippers; **poner de patas en la calle,** (coll.) to throw someone out on his ear; **quedar patas,** (coll.) to tie, draw, come out even; **¡qué mala p.!** what bad luck; **tener la mala p. de + *inf.*,** (coll.) to have the bad luck + *inf.;* **tener mala p.,** (coll.) to be unlucky.

patabán, *m.* (Cuba) white mangrove.
pataca, *f.* 1. (numis.) pataca, silver coin. 2. (bot.) Jerusalem artichoke (plant and tuber).
patache, *m.* (mar.) tender.
pataco, ca, *a., m., f., var. of* **patán.**
patacón, *m.* (numis.) patacoon, silver dollar; (coll.) duro, five pesetas.
patada, *f.* 1. kick; stamp (with the foot). 2. (coll.) step (movement of foot). 3. (coll.) footstep, footprint. — **a patadas,** (coll.) in abundance, plenty; **darle a uno una p.,** to kick someone; **p. corta,** onside kick; **p. de inicio,** kickoff; **p. fija,** placekick; **p. voladora,** dropkick.
patadión, *m.* sarong (used in some Philippine islands).
patagio, *m.* (zool.) patagium.
patagón, na, *a., m., f.* Patagonian.
patagónico, ca, *a.* Patagonian.
patagorillo, lla, *m., f.* (cul.) hash of liver and lights.
patagua, *f.* (Chile) linden, whitewood.
pataje, *m. var. of* **patache,** (mar.) tender.
patalear, *i.v.* to kick; to stamp one's feet.
pataleo, *m.* kicking; stamping.
pataleta, *f.* (coll.) feigned fit; fit of kicking or stamping.
pataletilla, *f.* an old dance; a kind of pirouette.
patán, *a.* (coll.) uncouth, vulgar, boorish, churlish. —*m.* 1. (coll.) boor, churlish person. 2. (coll.) peasant, rustic.
patanada, *f.* rudeness, incivility.
patanco, *m.* (Cuba) tropical cactus (Harrisia criophora).
patanería, *f.* uncouthness, vulgarity, boorishness, incivility.
patarata, *f.* 1. foolish trifle, idle talk. 2. affectedness; overpoliteness, effusive politeness.
pataratero, ra, *a.* affected, effusively polite.
patarráez, *m.* (mar.) reinforcing or preventer shroud, Bentinck shroud (to strengthen the rigging), guy, back rope.
patas, *m.* (coll.) the devil.
patasca, *f.* 1. (Arg.) pork and corn stew. 2. (Peru) row, dispute.
patata, *f.* potato; **p. de caña,** Jerusalem artichoke; **p. dulce,** sweet potato, yam; **patatas fritas,** fried potatoes, chips, potato chips, crisps.
patatal, patatar, *m.* potato field.
patatero, ra, *a.* potato-eating. 2. (mil.) up from the ranks. —*m.* 1. potato seller. 2. (coll.) ranker (G.B.), officer who has come up from the ranks.
patatín, patatán, (que) subterfuges; this and that; and so on.
patatús, *m.* (coll.) fainting fit; swoon.
patavino, na, *a., m., f.* Paduan, of or pertaining to Padua, Italy.
patay, *m.* (S. Amer.) dried carob paste or bread.
paté, *a.* (her.) patté (said of a cross).
pateador, ra, *a.* kicker (said of a horse, a mule).
pateadura, *f.* 1. kicking; stamping. 2. beating up. 3. (coll.) severe scolding, harsh reprimand.
pateamiento, *m., var. of* **pateadura.**
patear, *tr.v.* 1. (coll.) to kick. 2. (coll.) to be rude to, treat rudely. 3. to stamp the feet in disapproval (an audience). —*i.v.* 1. (coll.) to stamp (with rage). 2. (coll.) to be boiling with rage. 3. (coll.) to rush about a lot (trying to obtain something). 4. (Amer.) to kick (a gun, horse).
patena, *f.* 1. medallion worn by peasant women. 2. (ecc.) paten. — **limpio como una p.,** as neat as a pin, clean as a whistle.
patentar, *tr.v.* to patent.
patente, *a.* patent, clear, evident, manifest, obvious. —*f.* 1. patent, letters patent. 2. license, warrant, patent. 3. patent (for an invention). 4. membership card (of certain societies guaranteeing privileges to members). 5. (ecc.) travel warrant (given to monks). — **p. de contramarca** o **de corso,** (mar.) letters of marque; **p. de invención,** (registered) patent; **p. de navegación,** ship's registration papers; **p. de sanidad,** (mar.) bill of health.
patentemente, *adv.* patently, clearly, evidently, obviously.
patentice, patenticé, *ref.* **patentizar.**
patentizar, (*ref.* 53) *tr.v.* to make patent, evident or obvious.
pateo, *m.* (coll.) stamping, kicking.
pátera, *f.* patera, shallow earthenware dish or saucer.
paternal, *a.* paternal, fatherly.
paternalmente, *adv.* paternally, in a fatherly manner.
paternidad, *f.* 1. paternity; fatherhood. 2. authorship.
paterno, na, *a.* paternal; from the male line.
paternóster, *m.* 1. (rel.) paternoster, Our Father, Lord's Prayer. 2. (coll.) thick tight knot.
pateta, *m.* 1. (coll.) Old Nick, the Devil. 2. (coll.) cripple, lame person.
patéticamente, *adv.* pathetically, movingly.
patético, ca, *a.* 1. pathetic, moving, touching. 2. plaintive.
patetismo, *m.* pathos; suffering.
patiabierto, ta, *a.* bowlegged; straddling.
patialbillo, *m.* (zool.) genet, a kind of weasel.
patialbo, ba, *a., var. of* **patiblanco.**
patiblanco, ca, *a.* white-legged, white-footed.
patibulario, ria, *a.* 1. pertaining to scaffolds. 2. horrifying, harrowing; hair-raising.
patíbulo, *m.* scaffold, gallows, gibbet.
patico, *m. dim. of* **pato,** young duck, duckling.
paticojo, ja, *a.* lame, limping; crippled. —*m., f.* lame person, cripple.
patidifuso, sa, *a.* (coll.) dumbfounded, stunned, amazed, astounded.
patiecillo, *m. dim. of* **patio,** small courtyard.
patiestevado, da, *a.* bowlegged, bandy-legged. —*m., f.* bowlegged person.
patihendido, da, *a.* cloven-footed; clovenhoofed.
patilla, *f.* 1. sideburn, sidewhiskers, mutton chops. 2. chape (of a buckle). 3. trigger (of certain firearms). 4. (rare) certain position of fingers on guitar fret. 5. pocket flap. 6. (carp.) tongue, tenon. 7. (mar.) compass; spike of rudder. 8. (*pl.*) Old Nick, the Devil. 9. (Col., Ven.) watermelon. 10. (Arg., Bol.) seat (running along the side of a wall). 11. (Arg., Bol.) balcony railing. — **levantar a uno de p.,** (coll.) to exasperate, get one's goat.
patilludo, da, *a.* bewhiskered; heavily sidewhiskered.
patimuleño, ña, *a.* with hooves like a mule (said of a horse).
patín, *m.* 1. *dim. of* **patio,** small courtyard. 2. (ornith.) petrel.
patín, *m.* 1. skate, ice skate, roller skate; (aer.) skid; **p. de freno,** brake shoe; **p. de hielo,** ice skate; **p. de ruedas,** roller skate. 2. (ornith.) petrel; goosander, a species of duck. 3. (rare) *dim. of* **patio,** small courtyard.
pátina, *f.* patina; (metal., art.) patina; film.
patinada, *f.* skid.
patinadero, *m.* skating rink, skating place.
patinador, ra, *a.* skating. —*m. f.* skater.
patinaje, *m.* 1. skating; **p. artístico,** figure skating; **p. de velocidad,** speed skating. 2. skidding (of a vehicle).
patinar, *i.v.* 1. to skate. 2. to skid; to slide, slip. 3. (fig.) to make a blunder. —*tr.v.* to patinate.
patinazo, *m.* 1. skid, sudden skid. 2. (fig.) slip, boner, blunder.
patinejo, *m.* 1. *dim. of* **patín,** small courtyard. 2. small skate.
patineta, *f.* scooter (child's toy vehicle).
patinillo, *m. dim. of* **patín,** small courtyard.
patio, *m.* 1. yard, courtyard, court; quadrangle; (ry.) yard. 2. (theat.) pit, stalls, orchestra (parterre). — **p. de armas,** parade ground; **p. de butacas,** (theat.) orchestra, parterre; **p. de carga,** (ry.) freight yard; **p. de maniobras,** (ry.) switching yard, switchyard; **p. de operaciones,** floor (of an exchange); **p. de recreo,** playground.
patiquebrar, (*ref.* 29) *tr.v.* to break an animal's leg. —*r.v.* to break its leg (an animal).
patiquiebre, patiquiebro, *ref.* **patiquebrar.**
patita, *f.* 1. *dim. of* **pata,** young duck (female of the drake). 2. small paw, leg or foot. — **poner de patitas en la calle,** to bounce (sl.), throw out, discharge.
patitieso, sa, *a.* 1. (coll.) stiff-legged. 2. (coll.) stunned, dumbfounded, amazed. 3. (coll.) stiff, starchy, haughty.
patito, *m. dim. of* **pato,** young drake or male duck, duckling.
patituerto, ta, *a.* 1. crooked-legged, knock-kneed. 2. crooked, misshapen; lopsided. 3. (fig., coll.) ill-disposed.
patizambo, ba, *a.* bowlegged.
pato, *m.* (ornith.) 1. duck; drake. 2. (derog., vulg.) queer, faggot, sissy. — **estar hecho un p.** or **un p. de agua,** (coll.) to be soaked to the skin; **p. de reclamo,** decoy duck; **pagar el p.,** (coll.) to be the scapegoat, pay, pay for it, take the rap; **p. flojel,** eider, eider duck; **p. negro,** black sooter; **salga p. o gallareta,** (coll.) whatever happens, come what may.
patochada, *f.* blunder; stupidity; coarse remark.
patogénesis, *f.* (med.) pathogenesis.
patogenia, *f.* (med.) pathogeny, pathogenesis.
patogénico, ca, *a.* (med.) pathogenic (pertaining to pathogeny).
patógeno, na, *a.* (med.) pathogenic. —*m. pathogen, pathogene.*
patognomónico, ca, *a.* (med.) pathognomonic.
patojear, *i.v.* (Cuba) to waddle in walking.
patojera, *f.* 1. crooked-leggedness. 2. waddling gait.
patojo, ja, *a.* crooked-legged, with a waddling gait. —*m., f.* 1. (C. Amer.) street urchin. 2. (C. Amer.) affectionate term for a young person, kid.
patología, *f.* pathology; **p. vegetal,** plant pathology.
patológico, ca, *a.* pathological, pathologic.
patólogo, *m.* (med.) pathologist.
patón, na, *a.* (coll.) big-footed, big-pawed; clumsy-footed.
patoso, sa, *a.* (coll.) boring, dull. —*m., f.* presumptuous bore.
patota, *f.* (Arg., Urug.) street gang, gang of young braggarts.
patotero, ra, *m., f.* (Arg., Urug.) member of a street gang, young braggart.
patraña, *f.* lie, humbug, falsehood.
patrañero, ra, *a.* lying, false. —*m., f.* liar, hoaxer.
patria, *f.* country, native land, fatherland, motherland. — **madre p.,** motherland; **p. chica,** home town; **p. potestad,** custody, guardianship.
patriarca, *m.* patriarch.
patriarcado, *m.* patriarchate; patriarchy.
patriarcal, *a.* patriarchal. —*f.* 1. patriarchal church. 2. patriarchate (territory).
patriciado, *m.* patriciate (patrician rank).
patricio, cia, *a.* patrician; aristocratic. —*m., f.* patrician; aristocrat.

patrilineal, *a.* patrilineal, derived from the paternal side.
patrimonial, *a.* patrimonial.
patrimonio, *m.* patrimony; heritage; inheritance.
patrio, tria, *a.* 1. native, of one's country. 2. paternal, of the father. — **amor patrio, love of one's country; suelo patrio,** native land or soil. 2. paternal; **patria potestad,** (law) patria potestas (parental authority over minor children).
patriota, *m.* patriot.
patriotería, *f.* exaggerated patriotism, jingoism.
patriotero, ra, *a.* (derog.) exaggeratedly patriotic; jingoist, jingo. —*m., f.* jingoist.
patrióticamente, *adv.* patriotically.
patriótico, ca, *a.* patriotic.
patriotismo, *m.* patriotism.
patrística, *f.* (ecc.) patristics.
patrístico, ca, *a.* (ecc.) patristic.
patrocinador, ra, *a.* sponsoring. —*m., f.* sponsor; patron; backer.
patrocinar, *tr.v.* to sponsor; to patronize; to support, favor. — **p. las artes,** to sponsor the arts; **p. un programa de televisión,** to sponsor a television program.
patrocinio, *m.* sponsorship, patronage, support, auspices, e.g. *bajo el p. de,* under the auspices of.
patrología, *f.* (ecc.) patrology, patristics.
patrón, na, *m.* 1. patron, patron saint. 2. defender, patron, protector. 3. master, owner; employer, boss, chief; landlord, proprietor; (mar.) skipper, captain. 4. pattern, model. 5. standard (of measure, money). — **p. oro,** gold standard. —*f.* 1. patroness, patron saint. 2. defender, patroness, protectress. 3. owner, mistress; landlady, proprietress. 4. (mar.) ship ranking next to the flagship.
patronado, da, *a.* (ecc.) having a patron saint.
patronal, *a.* pertaining to employers, e.g. *relaciones obrero-patronales,* worker-employer relations, *asociación p,* employers' association. 2. patronal, pertaining to a patron saint, e.g. *fiesta p.,* patronal feast or festival.
patronato, *m.* 1. trust, foundation, institution. 2. employer's association. 3. trusteeship; board of trustees. 4. sponsorship. — **p. de las Artes,** Arts Council (organization to encourage artistic activity); **p. de turismo,** travel association (organization promoting travel); **p. del libro universitario,** trust to encourage the printing of university books.
patronazgo, *m., var. of* **patronato.**
patronear, *tr.v.* (mar.) to steer or command a ship.
patronímico, ca, *a., m.* patronymic; surname.
patronita, *f.* (geol.) patronite (vanadium ore).
patrono, na, *m., f.* 1. employer, boss, master, mistress. 2. patron, patroness, patron saint. 3. protector, patron, defender. 4. lord or lady (of the manor).
patrulla, *f.* 1. (mil.) squad, patrol. 2. gang, band, group.
patrullar, *tr.v., i.v.* to patrol.
patrullero, *a.* patrol, patrolling. —*m.* patrol car (of police); patrol ship or plane.
patuá, *m.* (gal.) patois; jargon.
patudo, da, *a.* (coll.) big-footed, big-pawed.
patulea, *f.* (coll.) disorderly soldiers; (coll.) mob, gang of toughs; bevy of unruly children.
patuleco, ca, *a.* 1. crippled, lame. 2. (Amer.) crooked-legged.
patullar, *i.v.* 1. to trample, stamp, tramp. 2. (coll.) to hurry about, tramp or hustle around. 3. (coll.) to chat, babble noisily.
paturro, rra, *a.* (Col.) chubby; short, stocky person.
paují, paujil, *m.* (ornith., Peru) guan, cashew bird. — **p. de copete,** curassow.
paúl, paular, *m.* bog, marsh, fen, moor.
paular, *i.v.* to talk, chat (used only in the expression **sin p. ni maular,** without saying a word).
paulatinamente, *adv.* little by little, gradually, slowly, by degrees.
paulatino, na, *a.* slow, gradual.
paulilla, *f.* (ento.) grain moth.
paulina, *f.* 1. letter or decree of excommunication. 2. (coll.) reproof, reprimand. 3. (coll.) poison-pen letter, offensive anonymous letter.
paulinia, *f.* (bot.) paullinia, supplejack (Paullinia cupana).
paulino, na, *a.* (ecc.) Pauline, pertaining to the order of St. Paul.
paulonia, *f.* (bot.) pawlonia.
pauperismo, *m.* pauperism, poverty.
pauperización, *f.* pauperization.
paupérrimo, ma, *a. super. of* **pobre,** very poor, poverty-stricken.
pausa, *f.* 1. pause, break, interval. 2. calm, slowness. 3. (mus.) rest. — **a pausas,** at intervals; **con p.,** slowly, calmly.
pausadamente, *adv.* slowly, unhurriedly, deliberately.
pausado, da, *past part. of* **pausar.** —*a.* slow, unhurried, calm, deliberate. —*adv.* slowly, deliberately.
pausar, *tr.v.* to make pauses in, interrupt. —*i.v.* to pause; to rest; to slow down; to hesitate.
pauta, *f.* 1. ruler, rule. 2. guideline (for handwriting). 3. (fig.) guide, rule, pattern, model. 4. (fig.) guiding principle, guideline.
pautado, da, *past part. of* **pautar.** —*a.* lined, ruled (paper). —*f.* (mus.) musical stave or staff.
pautar, *tr.v.* 1. to rule, rule lines on; (mus.) to draw a musical stave or staff on. 2. (fig.) to give directions or guiding principles for.
pava, *f.* 1. (ornith.) turkey hen. 2. (coll.) ungainly, awkward woman. 3. furnace bellows. 4. (Arg., Bol., Par.) kettle, teakettle. 5. (Amer.) wide-brimmed hat; (P. Rico) typical peasant hat. — **pelar la p.,** to court at the window; **hacerle a uno la p.,** (Bol., Peru) to make fun of.
pavada, *f.* 1. flock of turkeys. 2. (coll.) inanity, foolishness. 3. child's game.
pavana, *f.* 1. (mus.) pavan, pavane, ancient, stately dance of Spanish origin. 2. (arch.) woman's cloak or cape.
pavero, ra, *m., f.* turkey breeder, dealer. —*m.* (Sp.) wide-brimmed hat.
pavés, *m.* pavis, large shield. — **alzar** or **levantar sobre el p.,** to exalt, praise.
pavesa, *f.* ember, spark; hot cinders; burnt candle-wick. — **estar uno hecno una p.,** (coll.) to be exhausted or weak; **ser uno una p.,** (coll.) to be very docile or placid.
pavesada, *f., var. of* **empavesada.**
pavesina, *f.* small pavis, small shield.
pavezno, *m. dim. of* **pavo,** young turkey.
pavía, *f.* (bot.) pavy, clingstone peach (tree and fruit).
pávido, da, *a.* fearful; timid.
pavimentación, *f.* paving, flooring.
pavimentar, *tr.v.* to pave, to floor.
pavimento, *m.* pavement, paving.
paviota, *f.* (ornith.) sea-gull, mew.
pavipollo, *m.* young turkey.
pavisoso, sa, *a.* dull, graceless, colorless.
pavitonto, ta, *a.* stupid, foolish.
pavo, *m.* 1. (ornith.) turkey. 2. (coll.) dull, colorless person. 3. (Chile, Pan., Peru) stowaway. 4. (ichth.) peacock fish. — **comer p.,** (coll.) to be a wallflower (at a dance); **ponerse hecho un p., subírsele a uno el p.,** (coll.) to blush; **p. de matorral,** (ornith.) brush turkey; **p. real** or **ruán,** (ornith.) peacock; **p. ruante,** (her.) strutting peacock; **p. silvestre,** wood grouse.
pavón, *m.* 1. (ornith.) peacock. 2. (ento.) peacock butterfly. 3. bluing, browning (on steel or iron to prevent rust). 4. (astron.) **P.,** Peacock, Pavo.
pavonada, *f.* 1. (coll.) short period of relaxation or amusement, short walk, stroll. 2. (fig.) show, ostentation, display. — **darse uno una p.,** (coll.) to go for a spin, stroll or walk.
pavonado, da, *a.* dark blue. —*m.* bluing, browning (on steel or iron to prevent rust).
pavonar, *tr.v.* to blue, brown (iron or steel to prevent rusting).
pavonazo, *m.* (p.) dark red pigment (used in fresco painting).
pavonear, *i.v., r.v.* to show off, strut about, swagger, swank.
pavoneo, *m.* showing off, swaggering.
pavor, *m.* terror, fear, fright.
pavorde, *m.* (ecc.) provost; professor of divinity.
pavordear, *i.v.* to swarm (said of bees).
pavordía, *f.* (ecc.) provostship.
pavorido, da, *a.* terrified, fearful.
pavorosamente, *adv.* fearfully, terrifiedly.
pavoroso, sa, *a.* frightful, terrible, frightening, terrifying.
pavura, *f.* terror, fright, fear, dread.
paya, *f.* (S. Amer.) improvised song, poetic composition improvised by strolling singers.
payacate, *m.* (Mex.) handkerchief.
payada, *f.* (Arg., Chile, Urug.) improvised composition sung by strolling or traveling singers. — **p. de contrapunto,** (S. Amer.) contest between traveling singers.
payador, *m.* (S. Amer.) traveling country singer who accompanies himself on the guitar.
payar, *i.v.* (Arg., Chile, Urug.) to improvise songs.
payasada, *f.* clownish jest or act. — **hacer payasadas,** to clown about.
payasear, *i.v.* (Chile, Cuba) to clown, clown about.
payaso, *m.* 1. clown. 2. (coll.) show-off.
payés, sa, *m., f.* (Sp.) Catalonian peasant.
payo, ya, *a.* 1. rustic, churlish. 2. (coll.) stupid, foolish. —*m., f.* peasant, country man, country woman.
payuelas, *f. pl.* (med.) chicken pox.
paz, (*pl.* **paces**), *f.* 1. peace; peacefulness; tranquility. 2. peace, freedom from war. 3. (ecc.) pax (ceremony and tablet kissed by officiating priest). — **a la p. de Dios,** (coll.) God be with you; **anda la p. por el coro,** (iron.) there is trouble or unrest (in a community or family); **dejar en p.,** to leave in peace; **descansar en p.,** to rest in peace; **estar en p.,** to be at peace; to be even, be quits; **ir en p.,** or **con la p. de Dios,** to go in peace; **hacer las paces,** to make up (after quarrel); **meter** or **poner p. entre,** to bring peace between, reconcile; ¡paz! peace! quiet!; **p. de la conciencia,** peace of mind; **p. sea en esta casa,** God bless this house; **poner en p.,** to reconcile; **tratado de p.,** peace treaty; **venir uno en son de p.,** to come as friend, come in peace.
pazca, *ref.* **pacer.**
pazguatería, *f.* simpleness, foolishness.
pazguato, ta, *a.* simple, foolish. —*m., f.* simpleton, fool, dolt.
pazote, *m.* (bot.) wormseed, Mexican tea.
pazpuerca, *a.* (coll.) sluttish, slovenly (woman). —*f.* slut, slattern.
Pb *sym. of* **plomo,** plumbum, lead (Pb).
¡pche! ¡pchs! *interj.* pshaw!
Pd *sym. of* **paladio,** palladium (Pd).
P.D. *abbrev. of* **postdata,** postscript (P.S.).
pe, *f.* name of letter "p". — **de pe a pa,** (coll.) from A to Z, from beginning to end.

pea, *f.* (sl.) drunk, drunken spree or bout.
peaje, *m.* toll, ferriage.
peajero, *m.* toll collector.
peal, *m.* 1. foot (of a stocking). 2. legging. 3. (coll.) good-for-nothing, ne'er-do-well.
peán, *m.* paean, pean; song of war, victory or rejoicing.
peana, peaña, *f.* 1. base, pedestal, stand. 2. altar platform, altar step.
peatón, *m.* 1. pedestrian, walker. 2. rural postman.
pebete, ta, *m.* 1. joss stick. 2. fuse. 3. (coll.) incense taper. 4. smelly object. —*m., f.* (Arg., Urug.) boy, girl, kid.
pebetero, *m.* perfume censer, incense burner.
pebrada, *f.* (cul.) sauce made of garlic, green pepper, parsley and vinegar.
pebre, *m.* 1. *var. of* **pebrada.** 2. pepper, black pepper.
peca, *f.* freckle; speck, spot (on the human skin).
pecable, *a.* peccable, prone to sin.
pecadillo, ito, *m.* 1. *dim. of* **pecado,** slight sin. 2. peccadillo.
pecado, *m.* 1. sin; transgression; guilt. 2. defect, fault. — **estar en p.,** not to be in a state of grace; **p. actual,** actual sin; **p. capital,** mortal sin; **p. contra natura,** or **naturaleza,** unnatural sin, bestialism, sodomy; **p. mortal,** mortal, deadly sin; **p. nefando,** sodomy; **p. original,** original sin; **p. venial,** venial sin; **¡qué p.!** what a shame!
pecador, ra, *a.* sinning, sinful. —*m., f.* sinner. —*f.* (fig.) prostitute.
pecaminosamente, *adv.* sinfully, wickedly.
pecaminoso, sa, *a.* sinful, wicked.
pecante, *a.* sinning; excessive. —*m., f.* sinner.
pecar, (*ref. 50*) *i.v.* to sin, to transgress. — **p. de,** to be extremely, excessively, e.g. *p. de confiado,* to be excessively or over-confident, *p. de goloso,* to be extremely fond of food, esp. of sweets; to be, e.g. *p. de grosero,* to be rude or gross; **esto peca de largo (corto, sucio,** etc.), this is too long (short, soiled, etc.).
pécari, *m.* (S. Amer., zool.) peccary.
pecblenda, *f.* (min.) pitchblende (ore of radium and uranium).
peccata minuta, (Lat., coll.) slight fault or mistake; peccadillo.
pece, *f.* mud or mortar for building. —*m.* ridge between furrows.
pececillo, ito, *m. dim. of* **pez,** little fish.
peceño, ña, *a.* 1. pitchy, pitch-colored. 2. tasting of pitch.
pecera, *f.* fish bowl, aquarium.
pecezuela, *f. dim. of* **pieza,** little piece, small piece.
pecezuelo, *m.* 1. *dim. of* **pie,** small foot. 2. *dim. of* **pez,** small fish.
pechada, *f.* 1. (S. Amer.) blow on the chest. 2. (Arg.) touch for a loan.
pechador, *m.* (S. Amer.) cadger, sponger.
pechar, *tr.v.* 1. to pay as a tax. 2. to shoulder, assume (e.g. a responsibility). 3. (S. Amer.) to push, shove or bump with the chest; to collide with, ride one's horse against. 4. (S. Amer.) to touch for a loan. —*i.v.* to put up with, accept (disagreeable work, duty, etc.).
pechblenda, *f.* (min.) pitchblende.
peche, *m., var. of* **pechina.**
peche, *a.* (C. Amer.) 1. thin, frail. 2. orphaned (child).
pechera, *f.* 1. shirt front; jabot, shirt frill. 2. chest protector. 3. breast strap (of a harness). 4. (coll.) bosom, chest, woman's bosom.
pechería, *f.* taxes; tax roll or register; revenue.
pechero, ra, *a.* 1. taxable. 2. common, plebeian. —*m., f.* 1. taxpayer. 2. commoner, plebeian. —*m.* bib (child's small apron).
pechiblanco, ca, *a.* white-breasted (animal).
pechicatería, *f.* (Mex.) meanness, stinginess.
pechicolorado, *m.* (ornith.) linnet.
pechigonga, *f.* a card game.
pechina, *f.* 1. pilgrim's shell or scallop. 2. (archit.) pendentive.
pechirrojo, *m.* (ornith.) linnet.
pechisacado, da, *a.* (coll.) vain, arrogant.
pechito, *m. dim. of* **pecho,** small breast or teat.
pecho, *m.* 1. (anat.) chest; breast, bosom. 2. (anat.) bosom, teat (mammary gland). 3. short steep slope or incline. 4. (fig.) courage, spirit, heart. 5. (fig.) strength of voice. — **abrir** or **descubrir su p. a otro,** to unbosom oneself to, take into one's confidence; **a lo hecho, p.,** on with it and don't look back; **a p. abierto,** frankly; **a p. descubierto,** defenseless, undefended; sincerely, frankly; **dar el p. a un niño,** to breast-feed a child; **de p.,** breast-fed, still suckling; **de pechos,** face down, on one's chest; **echarse a pechos (una cosa, una bebida),** to undertake (something) resolutely, go into (something) boldly; to drink thirstily; **entre p. y espalda,** (coll.) in the stomach; **no caber una cosa en el p.,** to be burning to reveal something; **¡p. al agua!** courage! take heart!; **p. arriba,** uphill; **p. de pichón,** (med.) pigeon chest or breast; **p. por el suelo** or **tierra,** humbly, submissively, meekly; (hunt.) flying near the ground (hawking birds); **poner una pistola en el p.,** to leave one no alternative, to put one against the wall; **poner el p. a,** to face, confront; **quedarse con una cosa en el p.,** to leave a thing unsaid or untold; **sacar el p.,** to throw out one's chest; **tomar a p. (una cosa),** to take (something) to heart, take seriously.
pechón, *a.* (Mex.) sponging, cadging, brazen.
pechoño, ña, *a.* (Arg., Chile) sanctimonious, hypocritical, overly pious. —*m., f.* sanctimonious person.
pechuelo, *m. dim. of* **pecho,** small chest or breast.
pechuga, *f.* 1. breast (of a fowl); (coll.) chest, breast (of a person). 2. (coll.) slope, incline. 3. (Amer.) nerve, audacity, impudence.
pechugón, na, *a.* 1. (coll.) big-chested or breasted. 2. (Amer.) brazen, nervy, impudent. —*m.* 1. blow on the chest; fall on the chest. 2. great effort, hard push.
pechuguera, *f.* hoarse cough, deep cough.
peciento, ta, *a.* pitchy, pitch-colored.
pecilotermo, ma, *a.* (ichth.) poikilothermic, poikilothermal.
peciluengo, ga, *a.* long-stalked (fruit).
pecina, *f.* 1. slime, viscous mud. 2. fishpool.
pecinal, *m.* slimy hole, swamp.
pecinoso, sa, *a.* slimy, muddy.
pecio, *m.* (mar.) flotsam, jetsam, wreckage.
peciolado, da, *a.* (bot.) petiolate. —*m.* (*pl.*) (zool.) Petiolata.
peciolo, *m.* (bot.) petiole.
peciólulo, *m.* (bot.) petiolule.
pécora, *f.* 1. sheep, head of sheep. 2. shrewd, wicked person, e.g. *¡mala p.!* wicked one!
pecorea, *f.* 1. (mil.) marauding, looting, pillage. 2. gadding about, roaming around.
pecorear, *tr.v.* to steal (cattle). —*i.v.* (mil.) to loot, pillage, maraud.
pecoso, sa, *a.* freckled, freckly, freckle-faced.
pectato, *m.* (chem.) pectate.
pectén, *m.* (zool.) pecten.
péctico, ca, *a.* (chem.) pectic.
pectina, *f.* (chem.) pectin.
pectíneo, *m.* (anat.) pectineus (muscle).
pectiniforme, *a.* pectiniform, pectinate, comb-like.
pectoral, *a.* pectoral. —*m.* 1. pectoral, breastplate. 2. (ecc.) pectoral, pectoral cross. 3. (rel.) pectoral, breastplate worn by Jewish priest. 4. (anat.) pectoral, pectoral muscle. 5. (pharm.) pectoral.
pectosa, *f.* (chem.) protopectin, pectose.
pecuario, ria, *a.* pertaining to cattle.
peculado, *m.* (law) peculation, embezzlement.
peculiar, *a.* peculiar; characteristic, innate.
peculiaridad, *f.* peculiarity.
peculiarmente, *adv.* peculiarly.
peculio, *m.* (law) peculium; (fig.) private money, private property.
pecunia, *f.* (coll.) money, cash.
pecuniariamente, *adv.* pecuniarily, in money or cash; from the financial point of view, financially.
pecuniario, ria, *a.* pecuniary, monetary, financial.
pedagogía, *f.* pedagogy, teaching.
pedagógicamente, *adv.* pedagogically.
pedagógico, ca, *a.* pedagogic, pedagogical, pertaining to teaching; **métodos pedagógicos,** teaching methods.
pedagogo, *m.* pedagogue, educator, teacher.
pedaje, *m.* toll, bridge toll.
pedal, *m.* 1. pedal. 2. (mec.) treadle. — **p. de sordina,** (mus.) soft pedal; **p. acelerador,** (auto.) accelerator pedal; **p. de embrague,** (auto.) clutch pedal; **p. de frenos,** (auto.) brake pedal.
pedalear, *i.v.* to pedal.
pedáneo, *a.* junior, petty; puisne (G.B., law) (judge).
pedante, *a.* pedantic. —*m., f.* pedant.
pedantear, *i.v.* to be pedantic, to boast of being scholarly.
pedantería, *f.* pedantry; flaunted erudition.
pedantescamente, *adv.* pedantically.
pedantesco, ca, *a.* pedantic.
pedantismo, *m.* pedantry.
pedantón, *m. aug. of* **pedante,** great pedant.
pedazo, *m.* piece, bit, fragment, part, portion. — **a pedazos,** in bits, in pieces; **caerse a pedazos,** (fig.) to fall to pieces, (coll.) to be exhausted or fagged out; **en pedazos,** in bits, in pieces; **estar hecho pedazos,** (coll.) to be worn out, be exhausted; **hacer (una cosa) pedazos,** to break to pieces, tear to pieces; **hacerse pedazos,** to break into smithereens, break to pieces; to wear oneself out, exhaust oneself; **morirse por sus pedazos,** (coll.) to be head over heels in love with someone; **p. de alcornoque,** dolt, nitwit, blockhead, imbecile, cretin; **p. del alma, de las entrañas** or **del corazón,** (coll.) darling, apple of one's eye; **ser un p. de pan,** (coll.) to be very kind or easy-going.
pedazuelo, *m. dim. of* **pedazo,** small fragment, particle.
pederasta, *m.* pederast.
pederastia, *f.* pederasty.
pedernal, *m.* 1. flint. 2. (fig.) flintiness, hardness.
pedernalino, na, *a.* flinty; (fig.) flinty, hard.
pedestal, *m.* pedestal, stand; base, support. — **p. de chumacera,** (mec.) bearing pedestal.
pedestre, *a.* 1. walking, on foot; 2. (fig.) pedestrian, dull, prosaic, uninspired.
pedestrismo, *m.* 1. (sport) walking, marathon racing, foot racing.
pediatra, pediatra, *m.* (med.) pediatrician, pediatrist.
pediatría, *f.* (med.) pediatrics.
pediátrico, ca, *a.* pediatric.
pedicelado, da, *a.* (bot., zool.) pedicellate.
pedicelo, *m.* (bot., zool.) pedicel.
pedicoj, *m.* jump, hop (performed on one foot).
pediculado, da, *a.* (ichth.) pediculate.
pedicular, *a.* pedicular, pediculous.

pedículo, *m.* (bot.) peduncle, pedicle.
pediculosis, *f.* (med.) pediculosis.
pedicuro, *m.* podiatrist; chiropodist.
pedido, *past part. of* **pedir.** —*m.* 1. request, petition. 2. (com.) order, purchase. — **a p. de,** at the request of; **a p. del público,** by public request; **hecho sobre p.,** made to order; **p. de ensayo,** trial order; **p. en firme,** positive order; **p. por correo,** mail order.
pedidor, ra, *a.* said of a person who frequently borrows money or possessions. —*m., f.* petitioner.
pedidura, *f.* asking, requesting, petitioning.
pediforme, *a.* pediform, foot-shaped.
pedigón, na, *a., m., f., var. of* **pedigüeño.**
pedigree, *m.* pedigree.
pedigüeño, ña, *a.* persistent in asking; importunate, pestering. —*m., f.* importunate beggar; persistent asker or petitioner.
pediluvio, *m.* (med.) foot-bath, pediluvium.
pedimento, *m.* petition, request; (law) claim, bill; **a p.,** on request.
pedipalpo, *m.* (zool.) pedipalpus.
pedir, (*ref. 39*) *tr.v.* 1. to ask, request, bid (someone to do something). 2. to ask for, request (something). 3. to demand, require, call for. 4. to order (food in a restaurant; goods in a store). 5. to ask (a price). 6. to ask the hand of (a woman in marriage). — **a p. de boca,** as desired; just as one wants or wanted; **dejarse p.,** (coll.) to ask without batting an eyelid (an obviously exorbitant price); **p. alguna cosa a alguien,** to ask someone for something; **p. en justicia** or **contra,** to bring a suit or action against; **p. que alguien** + *subj.,* to ask someone + *inf.,* e.g. *pedí que trajera el auto inmediatamente,* I asked him to bring the car immediately; **p. la palabra,** to ask for the floor, ask to speak; **p. peras al olmo,** to ask for the impossible; **p. prestado,** to borrow.
pedo, *m.* fart (vulg.), wind from the anus, flatulence.
pedogénesis, *f.* (geol.) pedogenesis, paedogenesis.
pedología, *f.* 1. pedology, the scientific study of soils. 2. pedology, the study of the behavior and development of children.
pedómetro, *m.* pedometer, a device that registers the steps taken by a walker.
pedorrera, *f.* 1. wind or gas expelled by the anus. 2. (*pl.*) tights, skintight breeches.
pedorrero, ra, *a.* that breaks wind frequently.
pedorreta, *f.* raspberry, Bronx cheer (sl.), noise of derision or disapproval (made with the mouth).
pedorro, rra, *a., m., f., var. of* **pedorrero.**
pedrada, *f.* 1. blow with a stone; bruise, wound, mark or dent made with a stone. 2. cockade, rosette (securing brim to the crown of a hat); bow (on the hair). 3. (coll.) sneer, taunt, pointed remark intended to offend. — **como p. en ojo de boticario,** (coll.) very opportunely, just at the right time; **matar a pedradas,** to stone to death.
pedral, *m.* (mar.) stone sinker (for holding fishing net or cable in place).
pedrea, *f.* 1. stoning; stonefight. 2. hailstorm, hailing. 3. (coll.) smaller prizes (of a lottery).
pedregal, *m.* stony ground.
pedregoso, sa, *a.* 1. stony, rocky. 2. (med.) suffering from gallstones. —*m., f.* sufferer from gallstones.
pedrejón, *m.* boulder.
pedreñal, *m.* flintlock, firelock.
pedrera, *f.* stone quarry, stone pit.
pedreral, *m.* packsaddle for carrying stones.
pedrería, *f.* precious stones, jewelry (collectively).
pedrero, *m.* 1. stonecutter, quarryman. 2. petrary, stone-throwing mortar. 3. slinger.
pedrés, *a.* rock (salt), e.g. *sal p.,* rock salt.
pedreta, pedrezuela, *f. dim. of* **piedra,** small stone, pebble.
pedrisca, *f., var. of* **pedrisco.**
pedriscal, *m.* stony ground.
pedrisco, *m.* 1. hailstorm. 2. shower or hail of stones. 3. pile of small stones.
pedrisquero, *m.* hailstorm.
pedrizo, za, *a.* stony. —*f.* 1. stony ground. 2. stone fence.
Pedro, *m.* **P. Botero,** (coll.) the Devil, Old Nick; **P. el Ermitaño,** Peter the Hermit; **P. el Grande,** Peter the Great; **viejo es P. para cabrero,** you can't teach an old dog new tricks.
pedroche, *m.* stony ground.
pedrojiménez, *m.* variety of Andalusian grape and wine.
pedrusco, *m.* (coll.) rough, uncut stone.
pedunculado, da, *a.* (bot.) pedunculate.
peduncular, *a.* (bot.) peduncular.
pedúnculo, *m.* (bot.) peduncle.
peer, *i.v., r.v.* to break wind, to fart (vulg.).
pega, *f.* 1. gluing, cementing; sticking or joining together. 2. pitch varnish applied to earthenware vessels. 3. (min.) detonation (of an explosive), firing (of a blast). 4. (coll.) practical joke, trick, jest. 5. beating, spanking, drubbing. 6. poser, difficult or catch question. 7. (ichth.) remora. 8. (ornith.) magpie. — **p. reborda,** (ornith.) shrike; **saber a la p.,** to have bad manners; **sabio de p.,** false prophet, sham philosopher.
pegadillo, *m. dim. of* **pegado,** small patch, sticking plaster; **p. de mal de madre,** pest, bore, nuisance.
pegadizo, za, *a.* 1. sticky, adhesive. 2. catching, contagious; infectious, catchy (a tune, habit, etc.). 3. parasitic, cadging, sponging. 4. false, imitation, artificial.
pegado, da, *past part. of* **pegar.** —*a.* close together, tied (to). —*m.* sticking plaster, patch.
pegador, *m.* 1. (min.) blaster. 2. gluer, sticker, affixer; paper hanger. — **p. de carteles,** billposter.
pegadura, *f.* sticking, gluing.
pegajosidad, *f.* stickiness, clamminess.
pegajoso, sa, *a.* 1. sticky, adhesive, clammy. 2. catching, contagious (tune, bad habit). 3. alluring, tempting, attractive. 4. cloyingly friendly or familiar.
pegamiento, *m.* sticking, joining, gluing, cementing.
pegamoide, *m.* waterproofing cellulose (used in making oilcloth).
pegamoscas, (*pl.* **pegamoscas**), *f.* (bot.) catchfly.
peganita, *f.* (min.) peganite.
pegante, *a.* sticking, sticky, gluing, adhesive; glutinous.
pegar, (*ref. 51*) *tr.v.* 1. to stick, paste, glue, cement. 2. to fasten, attach, unite. 3. to sew or stitch on. 4. to move or push close together. 5. to pass on (a disease, bad habit, opinion, etc.). 6. to hit, beat, knock, strike. 7. to give (a kick, slap, beating, shout, jump), fire (a shot). — **no p. los ojos en toda la noche,** not to sleep a wink all night long; **p. fuego a,** to set fire to, set alight; **p. saltos,** to jump; **p. un bofetón,** to slap, give a slap; **p. una paliza,** to beat, give a beating; **p. un grito,** to let out a shout, shout; **p. un puntapié,** to kick, give a kick; **p. un susto,** to frighten, give a shock; **p. un tiro,** to shoot; **p. voces,** to shout. —*i.v.* 1. to match, go together, go with one another (e.g. colors); to go, e.g. *p. con,* to go with, match. 2. to take root (e.g. a plant). 3. to make an impression. 4. to be near or close to. 5. to knock, beat, bang. 6. to catch (fire). — **p.** or **pegarla con,** to attack; to have words with; **p. con uno,** to hurt someone's feelings. —*r.v.* 1. to stick; to stick together. 2. (cul.) to stick (to the pan, e.g. burnt food). 3. to stick (to), hang on (to) (someone who is not wanted). 4. to become obsessed (with), fond (of) or addicted (to) e.g. *pegársele a uno una canción,* to become obsessed with a song, not to be able to get a song out of one's head. 5. to be catching (a disease, bad habit). 6. to move close (to), keep close (to); to move or keep close together. — **pegársela a uno,** to fool, make a fool of, cheat; **pegarse una borrachera,** to get drunk; **pegarse un susto,** to get a shock; **pegarse un tiro,** to shoot oneself.
pegaseo, a, *a.* Pegasean, pertaining to Pegasus or to the Muses.
pegásides, *f.* (*pl.*) the Muses.
Pegaso, *m.* (astron., myth.) Pegasus, the winged horse.
pegata, *f.* (coll.) trick, deception, fraud.
pegatoste, *m.* plaster, sticking plaster.
pegmatita, *f.* (min.) pegmatite.
pego, *m.* cheating by sticking two cards together; **dar** o **tirar el p.,** to win by cheating; to deceive, trick.
pegollo, *m.* pillar, post (in a barn, hayloft or stable).
pegote, *m.* 1. sticking plaster. 2. crude, rough patch. 3. (coll.) sponger, hanger-on. 4. (coll.) crude addition (to literary or artistic work). 5. sticky mess; lumpy stew or dish.
pegotear, *i.v.* to sponge, be a sponger or parasite.
pegotería, *f.* (coll.) sponging.
pegual, *m.* (S. Amer.) saddle cinch or girth (with rings).
pegue, pegué, *ref.* **pegar.**
peguera, *f.* pit where pinewood is burned to obtain pitch; place where pitch is heated for branding cattle or marking sheep.
peguero, *m.* pitch manufacturer or dealer.
pegujal, *m.* 1. (law) peculium. 2. (coll.) small holding; small estate; small fund or amount of money.
pegujalero, *m.* small farmer; small cattle farmer.
pegujar, *m., var. of* **pegujal.**
pegujarero, *m., var. of* **pegujalero.**
pegujón, *m.* lump of wool or hair.
pegullón, *m., var. of* **pegujón.**
pegunta, *f.* pitch mark (on sheep or cattle).
peguntar, *tr.v.* to mark (sheep or cattle) with pitch.
peguntoso, sa, *a.* sticky, glutinous.
pehuén, *m.* (Chile) araucaria (tree).
peina, *f.* ornamental comb, Spanish comb.
peinada, *f.* (coll.) combing, dressing of the hair.
peinado, da, *past part. of* **peinar.** —*a.* 1. combed, groomed. 2. highly polished (style). 3. effeminately elegant. —*m.* hairdo, coiffure, hair style.
peinador, ra, *m., f.* hairdresser. —*m.* housecoat, peignoir, wrapper, dressing gown.
peinadura, *f.* 1. combing, dressing the hair. 2. combings, hairs coming out when combed.
peinar, *tr.v.* 1. to comb (hair, wool). 2. to dress, do, fix (the hair). 3. to touch, rub slightly. 4. to comb, search thoroughly. —*r.v.* to comb one's hair; to do, fix or dress one's hair.
peinazo, *m.* (carp.) rail (e.g. of door).
peine, *m.* 1. comb (for the hair). 2. comb, card (for wool or cotton). 3. (tex.) reed (of a loom). 4. (anat.) hypogastrium (lower middle part of the abdomen). 4. sly fellow. — **p. de balas,** cartridge clip; **sobre p.,** lightly, superficially.
peinecillo, ito, *m. dim. of* **peine,** small comb.
peinería, *f.* comb factory; comb shop.
peinero, *m.* comb maker; comb seller.
peineta, *f.* ornamental comb, side comb, back comb. — **p. de teja,** tile-shaped large Spanish comb.

peinetero, *m., var. of* **peinero.**
peinilla, *f.* (P. Rico) comb, dressing comb.
p. ej. *abbrev. of* **por ejemplo,** for example (e.g.).
peje, *m.* 1. fish. 2. (fig.) sly, crafty fellow. — **p. araña,** (ichth.) greater weaver, stingbull; **p. buey,** (Amer., zool.) manatee; **p. diablo,** (ichth.) scorpene, hogfish, grouper.
pejebuey, *m.* (zool.) manatee.
pejegallo, *m.* (ichth.) (species of) chimaera (Callorhynchus callorhynchus).
pejemuller, *m.* (zool.) manatee.
pejepalo, *m.* unsplit smoked codfish; stockfish.
pejerrey, *m.* (ichth.) atherine, variety of mackerel.
pejesapo, *m.* (ichth.) angler, goosefish.
pejiguera, *f.* (coll.) nuisance, annoyance, bother.
Pekín, *m.* Peking, capital of China.
pela, *f., var. of* **peladura.**
pelada, *f.* pelt, sheepskin (stripped of wool).
peladera, *f.* (med.) alopecia, baldness.
peladero, *m.* 1. place where hogs and fowls are stripped or scalded. 2. (coll.) sharper's den. 3. (Col., Chile) wasteland.
peladilla, *f.* 1. candied almond. 2. small pebble.
peladillo, *m.* 1. (bot.) clingstone peach (tree and fruit). 2. (*pl.*) wool stripped from sheepskin pelts.
pelado, da, *past part. of* **pelar.** —*a.* 1. bare, barren, treeless (country, field, mountain). 2. hairless, bald. 3. meatless (bone). 4. unadorned, bald (piece of writing, talk). 5. smooth (stone). 6. round (number). 7. (coll.) penniless, poor, broke (coll.). 8. (Mex.) brazen, shameless; ragged. 9. worn down (brush). — **bailar el pelado,** (coll.) to be broke or penniless.
pelador, *m.* peeler, plucker, stripper.
peladura, *f.* 1. peeling; plucking; barking, stripping. 2. parings, peelings.
pelafustán, na, *m., f.* (coll.) good-for-nothing, ne'er-do-well, vagabond, idler.
pelagallos, *m., f.* (coll.) bum, tramp.
pelagatos, *m.* (coll.) poor, penniless person, ragamuffin.
pelagianismo, *m.* (rel.) Pelagianism.
pelagiano, na, *a., m., f.* (rel.) Pelagian.
pelágico, ca, *a.* pelagic, oceanic, of the open sea.
Pelagio, *m.* (rel.) Pelagius.
pelagoscopio, *m.* instrument for studying the bottom of the sea.
pelagra, *f.* (med.) pellagra.
pelagroso, sa, *a.* (med.) pellagrous, pellagrose. —*m., f.* pellagrin, person suffering from pellagra.
pelaire, *m.* wool carder or teaseler.
pelairía, *f.* carding, teaseling; wool comber's trade.
pelaje, *m.* 1. hair, fur coat (of an animal). 2. (coll.) appearance; clothes, apparel.
pelambrar, *tr.v.* (tanning) to strip off (hides).
pelambre, *m.* 1. batch of hides (to be steeped in lime solution). 2. hair, coat, pelt. 3. lime, lime solution (for soaking hides). 4. baldness (in certain parts of body).
pelambrera, *f.* 1. liming room (where skins are steeped in lime). 2. thick body hair. 3. baldness, alopecia.
pelambrero, *m.* limer (workman who limes hides), steeper.
pelamen, *m.* (coll.) *var. of* **pelambre.**
pelamesa, *f.* 1. hair-pulling scuffle. 2. tuft of hair.
pelana, *m.* (coll.) nobody, person of no importance.
pelanas (*pl.* **pelanas**), *m.* poor wretch.
pelandusca, *f.* harlot, strumpet.
pelantrín, *m.* small farmer.
pelar, *tr.v.* 1. to peel, pare (e.g. fruit); to pluck (a fowl); to bark, strip (a tree); to crop (hair), shave (someone's head); to remove hair from (the skin). 2. to skin, fleece, trick or cheat out of possessions; (coll.) to clean out (in gambling). 3. (a hawk) to eat (a bird) with its feathers. 4. (Amer.) to slander, run down. — **duro de p.,** (coll.) difficult to do. —*r.v.* 1. (coll.) to get a haircut. 2. to go bald. 3. to peel (as after a sun tan). — **pelarse de fino,** (coll.) to be too smart or astute; **pelarse de frío,** to be frozen stiff; **pelárselas,** (coll.) to yearn, long, crave.
pelarela, *f.* baldness, alopecia.
pelargonio, *m.* (bot.) pelargonium.
pelarruecas, *f.* (coll.) spinner, woman who makes a living by spinning.
pelásgico, ca, *a.* (hist.) Pelasgian, Pelasgic.
pelasgo, ga, *a., m., f.* (hist.) Pelasgian.
pelaza, *a.* **paja p.,** beaten barley straw (used for fodder). —*f.* quarrel, row.
pelazga, *f.* quarrel, row, scuffle.
peldaño, *m.* step (of a staircase).
pelde, *f.* flight, escape.
peldefebre, *m.* (tex.) mohair, mockado; camlet, camel hair.
pelea, *f.* fight; struggle; quarrel, dispute. — **ni en p. de perros,** (Chile, Peru) never in one's life; absolutely never; **p. a tiros,** gunfight; **p. de gallos,** cockfight.
peleado, da, *past part. of* **pelear.** —*a.* **estar p. con,** not to be on speaking terms, be at loggerheads with.
peleador, ra, *a.* fighting; quarrelsome; game, e.g. *gallo p.,* game or fighting cock. —*m., f.* fighter.
pelear, *i.v.* 1. to fight; to struggle; to contend. 2. to quarrel. —*r.v.* 1. to fight, fight with one another. 2. to quarrel, have a disagreement.
pelechar, *i.v.* 1. to grow a new coat (of feathers or hair). 2. (coll.) to start to prosper or thrive; to start to recover or get better (in health).
pelel, *m.* light beer, pale ale.
pelele, *m.* 1. stuffed figure. 2. baby's knitted pajamas. 3. (coll.) simpleton, nincompoop.
pelendengue, *m., var. of* **perendengue.**
Peleo, *m.* (myth.) Peleus, father of Achilles.
peleón, na, *a.* 1. quarrelsome; pugnacious, aggressive. 2. cheap (wine or liquor). —*m.* cheap wine, cheap liquor.
peleona, *f.* (coll.) quarrel, dispute, row.
pelerina, *f.* pelerine, cape.
pelete, *m.* 1. punter (in gambling). 2. (coll.) poor man. — **en p.,** naked, nakedly.
peletería, *f.* 1. furriery, fur business or trade; fur shop. 2. (Cuba) leather goods, store; shoe store.
peletero, *m.* 1. furrier. 2. (Cuba) shoe or leather goods dealer or salesman.
pelgar, *m.* (coll.) bum, tramp.
peliagudo, da, *a.* 1. furry, long-haired. 2. (coll.) tough, difficult (to solve). 3. (coll.) astute, crafty, clever.
peliblanco, ca, *a.* white-haired.
peliblando, da, *a.* soft-haired.
pelícano, *m.* 1. (ornith.) pelican. 2. (dent.) pelican, dentist's forceps. 3. (*pl.*) (bot.) colombine.
pelicano, na, *a.* grey-haired, gray-haired.
pelicorto, ta, *a.* short-haired.
película, *f.* 1. film, pellicle; skin. 2. (photog.) film. 3. (cine.) film, picture, movie. — **p. biológica,** biological film; **p. de corto metraje,** (cine.) short film; **p. de dibujos animados,** cartoon; **p. de estreno,** first-run movie; **p. de largo metraje,** (cine.) full-length film; **p. del Oeste,** or **de vaqueros,** Western; **p. de seguridad,** (photog.) safety film; **p. en carrete,** roll film; **p. en colores,** (photog.) color film; (cine.) technicolor film; **p. hablada,** (cine.) talkie, talking picture; **p. muda,** (cine.) silent picture or film; **p. sonora,** (cine.) sound film; **p. X,** X-rated movie; **rodar una p.,** to shoot a film.
pelicular, *a.* pellicular, skin-like; filmy.
peliculero, ra, *a.* of a film or movie, film, movie, cinema. —*m., f.* (derog.) person who works in the motion picture industry.
peliforra, *f.* (coll.) prostitute.
peligrar, *i.v.* to be in danger, peril.
peligro, *m.* danger, peril, risk, hazard. — **correr p.** or **estar en p.,** to be in danger, run a risk; **fuera de p.,** out of danger; **señal de p.,** danger signal.
peligrosamente, *adv.* dangerously, perilously, hazardously.
peligroso, sa, *a.* dangerous, perilous, hazardous.
pelilargo, ga, *a.* long-haired.
pelillo, *m.* 1. short hair or fibre. 2. (coll.) trifle. — **echar pelillos al mar,** (coll.) to bury the hatchet, make up, make friends; **no tener uno pelillos en la lengua,** (coll.) to be forthright and outspoken, say what one thinks; **pararse** or **reparar en pelillos,** (coll.) to bother about trifles.
pelilloso, sa, *a.* (coll.) touchy, finicky, difficult, peevish, querulous.
pelinegro, gra, *a.* black-haired.
pelirrojo, ja, *a.* red-haired, redheaded, ginger, ginger-haired. —*m., f.* redhead, carrot-top.
pelirrubio, bia, *a.* blond, fair-haired.
pelitieso, sa, *a.* stiff-haired.
pelito, *m. dim. of* **pelo,** small hair or fibre.
pelitre, *m.* (bot.) pyrethrum, chrysanthemum (Pyrethrum cinerariaefolium).
pelitrique, *m.* trifle, bauble, trinket.
pella, *f.* 1. pellet, ball, lump. 2. tender head or shoot (of cauliflower, etc.). 3. incendiary cannon ball. 4. raw lard. 5. blob, drop (of meringue, cream, etc. decorating a desert). 6. (coll.) amount, sum (of money). 7. (min.) lump (of metal).
pellada, *f.* 1. trowelful or handful of mortar. 2. pellet, lump. — **no dar p. en,** not to do a lick of work in (a construction project).
pelleja, *f.* 1. hide, skin; lambskin, sheepskin. 2. (coll.) prostitute. — **dar la p.,** (coll.) to give one's life, die; **dejar, perder** or **soltar la p.,** (coll.) to lose one's life, die; **salvar la p.,** (coll.) to save one's life.
pellejería, *f.* 1. leather dressing or tanning shop. 2. leather dressing, tanning, occupation of leather dresser. 3. skins, hides. 4. (Amer.) jam, fix, trouble, difficulty.
pellejero, ra, *m., f.* 1. leather dresser, tanner. 2. leather dealer.
pellejina, *f.* small skin or pelt.
pellejo, *m.* 1. skin, hide, rawhide. 2. skin, rind. 3. wineskin. 4. (coll.) sot, drunkard. — **dar el p.,** (coll.) to give one's life; **dejar** or **perder el p.,** (coll.) to lose one's life, die; **estar** or **hallarse en el p. de otro,** (coll.) to be in someone else's shoes; **mudar el p.,** (coll.) to change one's ways; **no caber uno en el p.,** (coll.) to be bursting at the seams, be very fat; to be very happy; to be too big for one's boots, be very vain or bigheaded; **no tener uno más que el p.,** (coll.) to be all skin and bones, be very thin; **pagar con el p.,** (coll.) to pay with one's life; **quitar a uno el p.,** (coll.) to speak ill of, run down; to clean out, fleece, skin alive, leave penniless; **salvar el p.,** (coll.) to save one's skin or life; **soltar uno el p.,** (coll.) to lose one's life, get killed.
pellejudo, da, *a.* flabby-skinned.
pellejuela, *f. dim. of* **pelleja,** small pelt, skin or hide.
pellejuelo, *m. dim. of* **pellejo,** small skin, pelt or hide.
pelleta, *f.* pelt, hide, skin.
pelletería, *f., var. of* **pellejería.**
pelletero, *m., var. of* **pellejero.**
pellica, *f.* 1. coverlet (made of fine furs). 2. shepherd's jacket (made of fur). 3. small dressed skin or pelt.

pellico, *m.* shepherd's skin jacket; pelisse, fur-lined jacket.
pellijero, *m., var. of* **pellejero.**
pellín, *m.* 1. (Chile) (variety of) oak. 2. (Chile) hard inner core of oak. 3. (Chile, fig.) tough, sturdy person or object.
pelliquero, *m.* maker or seller of fur coverlets.
pelliza, *f.* pelisse, fur-lined or quilted jacket; (mil.) dolman.
pellizcador, ra, *a.* pinching. —*m., f.* pincher.
pellizcar, (*ref. 50*) *tr.v.* 1. to pinch; to nip; to prune. 2. to take a pinch of. 3. (coll.) to nibble at everything and eat little.
pellizco, *m.* 1. pinch, nip. 2. pinch, small portion. — **p. de monja,** small cookie.
pellizque, pellizqué, *ref.* **pellizcar.**
pello, *m.* fine fur jacket; pelisse.
pellón, pellote, *m.* 1. long fur robe. 2. (Amer.) fur saddle pad.
pellote, *m.* long fur robe.
pelluzgón, *m.* tuft, bunch (of wool, threads, hair, etc.).
pelma, *m., var. of* **pelmazo.**
pelmacería, *f.* (coll.) slowness, sluggishness.
pelmazo, *m.* 1. squashed mass. 2. heavy, undigested food. 3. (coll.) sluggard, slow dull person; bore.
pelo, *m.* 1. (one) hair. 2. hair; fur (collectively); down (on fruit; soft fluffy feathers on birds). 3. thread, fiber, filament. 4. thread, piece of fluff. 5. hair trigger, hair (secondary spring device in lock mechanism of firearms). 6. nap, fluff (on cloth). 7. color (of animal's coat). 8. raw silk. 9. flaw, cloud (in precious stone). 10. crack, split (in glass, metal, etc.). 11. (med.) breast abscess, inflamed galactocele. 12. grain (in wood). 13. kiss (in billiards). 15. (fig.) trifle, nothing; hair's breadth, inch, short distance. 16. (vet.) split hoof. 17. pile (of a carpet). — **agarrarse o asirse de un p.,** (coll.) to grab at a straw, use any argument available; **al p.,** with the hair or nap; just right, just as one wants, e.g. *este puesto me cae al p.,* this post suits me just fine; just on time, opportunely, conveniently; **a medios pelos,** (coll.) tipsy, merry; **a p.,** with the hair or nap; without saddle, bareback; **buscar el p. al huevo,** (coll.) to look for a quarrel or fight; **contra p.,** the wrong way, against the hair or nap, against the normal direction (of fur, hair or nap); inopportunely; **cortar un p. en el aire,** to be very clear-sighted, shrewd or clever; **de medio p.,** (coll.) unimportant, of little or no account; (Amer.) lower class: (Amer.) social climber; **de p. en pecho,** (coll.) robust, vigorous, strong, e.g. *hombre de p. en pecho,* grown man; brave man, real man, strong man, he-man; **de poco p.,** (coll.) unimportant, of little account; **echar buen p.,** (coll.) to make good, prosper, thrive; **echar pelos a la mar,** to bury the hatchet, make up; **en p.,** without a saddle, bareback; (coll.) naked, unadorned; **estar hasta los pelos,** (coll.) to be fed up to the teeth, be sick and tired; **hacer el p. a,** to do or fix (someone's) hair; **hacerse el p.,** to do one's hair; **no tener p. de tonto,** to be nobody's fool; e.g. *no tiene p de tonto,* nothing stupid about him; **no tener pelos en la lengua,** (coll.) to be outspoken, speak one's mind; **no tocarle a uno un p.,** not to touch a hair of someone's head, not to touch someone at all; **p. arriba,** the wrong way, against the normal direction of the hair, fur or nap; **p. de camello,** camel hair (cloth); **pelos de estadia,** (surv.) stadia hairs; **pelos y señales,** (coll.) pertinent details; exact details; **ponérsele a uno los pelos de punta,** (the hair) to stand on end (with fear); **por un p.,** by a hair's breadth, e.g. *salvarse por un p.,* to be saved by a hair's breadth; **relucirle a uno el p.,** to glow with health; **tener pelos,** (coll.) to be difficult (a problem); **tomar el p. a,** (coll.) to pull (someone's) leg; to tease; **venirle a uno al p.,** to suit one just fine.
pelón, na, *a.* 1. bald, hairless; balding, going bald. 2. (coll.) poor, penniless. 3. (coll.) stupid, foolish. —*m., f.* 1. bald person. 2. (coll.) poor person. 3. (coll.) nitwit.
pelona, *f.* 1. alopecia, baldness. 2. (coll.) death.
pelonería, *f.* (coll.) poverty, neediness, want.
pelonía, *f., var. of* **pelona.**
peloponense, *a., m., f.* (hist., geog.) Peloponnesian.
peloponesíaco, ca, *a.* (hist., geog.) Peloponnesian.
Peloponeso, *m.* Peloponnesus, peninsula forming the S. part of Greece.
Pélops, *m.* (myth.) Pelops, son of Tantalus.
peloria, *f.* (bot.) peloria.
pelórico, ca, *a.* (bot.) peloric.
pelosilla, *f.* (bot.) mouse-ear, mouse-ear hawkweed (Hieracium pilosella).
peloso, sa, *a.* hairy.
pelota, *f.* 1. ball. 2. pelota (Spanish game similar to squash), jai alai; catch, ball, ball game, e.g. *jugar a la p.,* to play catch, play ball. 3. cannon ball, musket ball. 4. (Amer.) cowhide ferry barge or boat. 5. (fig.) pile (of debts), series, succession (of misfortunes). 6. (cul.) lump (i.e. in a sauce). 7. (*pl.*) (vulg.) balls, testicles. 8. (Cuba, Mex.) passion, crush, e.g. *tener p. por,* to be passionately in love with, have a crush on. — **estar la p. en el tejado,** (coll.) to be still undecided, be doubtful (outcome of something); **hacerse una p.,** (coll.) to curl or roll up into a ball; **hinchar las pelotas,** (vulg.) to annoy; **jugar a la p. con alguien,** to have someone on a string, play around with someone (making him come and go for no apparent reason); **no tocar p.,** not to get to the root of a problem; **p. medicinal,** medicine ball; **p. vasca,** pelota (game), jai alai; **rechazar** or **volver la p.,** to reply with the same arguments; **sacar pelotas de una alcuza,** (coll.) to be able to get blood out of a stone; **tirarse la p.,** to pass the buck.
pelota, *adv.* **en p.,** naked, stripped; **dejar en p.,** to strip, undress; to clean out, leave penniless.
pelotari, *m., f.* pelota player; professional jai alai player.
pelotazo, *m.* blow or hit with a ball.
pelote, *m.* goat's hair (used in upholstery); tuft of wool.
pelotear, *tr.v.* to go over, check (an account). —*i.v.* 1. to knock about, knock a ball about. 2. to throw back and forth. 3. to argue, wrangle; to have a discussion, discuss. 4. (S, Amer.) to cross a river (in a cowhide boat).
pelotera, *f.* (coll.) brawl, quarrel, squabble.
pelotería, *f.* 1. heap of balls. 2. heap of goat's hair.
pelotero, *m.* 1. ball maker. 2. baseball player, ballplayer. 3. (coll.) brawl, quarrel.
pelotilla, *f.* 1. *dim. of* **pelota,** small ball, pellet, small lump. 2. small wax ball with pieces of glass used as a scourge. — **hacer la p. a,** to butter up, soft-soap, flatter.
pelotillero, ra, *a.* flattering, adulating. —*m., f.* flatterer, soft-soaper.
peloto, *m.* beardless wheat.
pelotón, *m.* 1. large ball, lump. 2. tuft of matted hair. 3. (fig.) crowd. 4. (mil.) squad, platoon. — **p. de ejecución** or **fusilamiento,** firing squad.
pelta, *f.* pelta, leather shield (used by Greeks and Romans).
peltre, *m.* pewter, spelter.
peltrero, *m.* pewterer.
pelú, (*pl.* **pelúes**), *m.* (bot.) pelu.
peluca, *f.* 1. wig, toupee. 2. severe reprimand, dressing down.
pelúcido, da, *a.* (bot.) pellucid.
pelucón, na, *a.* 1. long-haired, bushy-haired. 2. (Chile) conservative. —*m., f.* 1. (Ecuad.) big wig (person of high position). 2. (Chile) conservative. —*m.* large wig.
pelucona, *f.* gold doubloon.
peluche, *m.* (tex.) plush.
peludo, da, *a.* 1. hairy, furry, shaggy. 2. difficult, tricky. —*m.* 1. thick mat. 2. (Arg., zool.) armadillo.
peluqueada, *f.* (Col., Ven.) haircut.
peluquear, *tr.v.* (Col, Ven.) to cut the hair of. —*i.v.* (Col., Ven.) to get a haircut.
peluquera, *f.* barber's wife; lady hairdresser or wigmaker.
peluquería, *f.* barber shop; hairdresser shop.
peluquero, *m* barber, hairdresser; wigmaker.
peluquilla, ita, *f. dim. of* **peluca,** small wig.
peluquín, *m.* 1. toupee, small wig. 2. periwig, peruke.
pelusa, *f.* 1. down (on fruit); fuzz, fluff (on clothes). 2. (tex.) nap, pile. 3. (coll.) envy, jealousy (in child).
pelusilla, *f.* (bot.) mouse-ear, mouse-ear hawkweed (Hieracium pilosella).
pelvi, *a., m.* Parsee, Parsi, Pahlavi (ancient Persian language).
pelviano, na, *a.* (anat.) pelvic.
pélvico, ca, *a.* (anat.) pelvic.
pelvímetro, *m.* (med.) pelvimeter.
pelvis, (*pl.* **pelvis**), *f.* (anat.) pelvis.
pena, *f.* 1. penalty, punishment. 2. sorrow, grief. 3. pain, suffering. 4. trouble, difficulty. 5. mourning drape or fall (worn around the hat). 6. embarrassment; chagrin. — **a duras, malas** or **graves penas,** with great difficulty; **a penas,** hardly, barely; **bajo p. de,** under penalty of; **es una p.,** it's a pity; **merecer** or **valer la p.,** to be worthwhile, be worth the trouble or effort, be worth it; **valer la p.** + *inf.,* to be worth + *ger.,* be worthwhile + *ger.,* be worth the effort or trouble to + *inf.,* e.g. *no vale la p. salir en esta lluvia,* it's not worth going out in this rain; **pasar la p. negra,** (coll.) to go through hell, suffer terribly; **p. accesoria,** (law) cumulative penalty; **p. capital,** (law) capital punishment, death penalty; **p. corporal,** (law) corporal punishment; **p. correccional,** (law) corrective punishment; **p. de galera,** the galleys, e.g. *condenar a la p. de galera,* to sentence to the galleys; **p. de muerte,** (law) death penalty; **p. del talión,** (law) law of an eye for an eye, lex tallionis; **p. pecuniaria,** (law) fine; **p. privativa de libertad,** custodial sentence; **¡qué p.!** what a pity; **so p. de,** (arch.) under pain or penalty of.
pena, *f.* 1. penna, quill feather. 2. (mar.) peak (of lateen yard).
penable, *a.* punishable.
penachera, *f., var. of* **penacho.**
penacho, *m.* 1. plume, crest, panache, tuft of feathers. 2. (fig.) pride, arrogance, haughtiness.
penachudo, da, *a.* plumed, crested, tufted.
penachuelo, *m. dim. of* **penacho,** small plume or crest.
penadamente, *adv., var. of* **penosamente.**
penadilla, *f.* narrow-mouthed drinking vessel.
penado, da, *past part. of* **penar.** —*a.* 1. sorrowful, sad, grieved. 2. arduous, difficult, laborious. 3. narrow-mouthed (vessel). —*m., f.* convict. —*m.* narrow-mouthed drinking vessel.

penal, *a.* penal, e.g. *código p.,* penal code; penalty. —*m.* prison, penitentiary.
penalice, penalicé, *ref.* **penalizar.**
penalidad, *f.* 1. suffering, hardship. 2. (law) penalty.
penalista, *a.* versed in penal law. —*m., f.* penologist.
penalización, *f.* (sport.) penalization, handicap.
penalizar, (*ref. 53*) *tr.v.* to penalize, punish.
penalty, *m.* (sport.) penalty.
penante, *a.* 1. suffering, afflicted. 2. narrow-mouthed (drinking vessel).
penar, *tr.v.* to punish, chastise, penalize. —*i.v.* 1. to suffer (pain or sorrow). 2. (rel.) to suffer in purgatory. — **p. por,** to crave or yearn for. —*r.v.* to grieve, to mourn.
penates, *m.* (*pl.*) penates, household gods.
penca, *f.* 1. cowhide whip. 2. fleshy leaf (e.g. of cactus); fleshy part (of a leaf). 3. (Amer.) bunch (of bananas). 4. (Ven.) stock (of a tail). 5. (C. Rica, Urug.) drunk, drunken bout, e.g. *coger una p.,* to get drunk. — **a la pura p.,** (Amer.) nude, naked; **dar** or **echar p.,** (Arg., Chile) to whip; **hacerse de pencas,** (coll.) to let oneself be coaxed, play hard to get.
pencazo, *m.* whiplash.
penco, *m.* 1. (coll.) nag, hack. 2. (Hond., coll.) rustic, bumpkin.
pencón, cona, *a.* (Guat.) fine, excellent; (Guat.) bold, daring; (Guat.) good, skillful.
pencudo, da, *a.* having fleshy leaves.
pendanga, *f.* 1. jack of diamonds. 2. (coll.) prostitute, whore.
pendejear, *i.v.* (Amer., vulg.) to fool around, loaf, waste time.
pendejo, ja, *a.* (vulg.) 1. (Car.) foolish, stupid. 2. (Car.) cowardly. 3. (Peru) smart, clever, crafty. —*m.* 1. pubic hair. 2. (coll.) coward. 3. (Amer.) fool.
pendencia, *f.* 1. quarrel, fight, fray, dispute. 2. (law) pending suit, lis pendens.
pendenciar, *i.v.* to quarrel, wrangle, dispute, fight.
pendenciero, ra, *a.* quarrelsome, belligerent, pugnacious. —*m., f.* troublemaker.
pendenzuela, *f. dim. of* **pendencia,** disagreement, squabble, petty quarrel.
pender, *i.v.* 1. to hang, dangle. 2. to depend. 3. to be pending, be undecided.
pendiente, *a.* 1. pendent, hanging. 2. pending, unresolved. — **asuntos** or **negocios pendientes,** pending business; **cuenta p.,** outstanding or unpaid account or bill; **estar p. de,** to hang on (someone's words); to depend on; to be in the process of; to be aware of the presence of; **p. de pago,** unpaid. —*m.* (jewel.) drop earring; pendant. —*f.* 1. slope, gradient; dip, pitch; (math.) slope. 2. (her.) lower part (of flag). — **p. abajo,** (top.) downgrade; **p. arriba,** (top.) upgrade; **p. barométrica,** (meteorol.) barometric gradient; **p. magnética,** (geoph.) magnetic slope; **p. piezométrica,** hydraulic slope or gradient; **p. de temperatura,** temperature gradient.
pendil, *m.* woman's cloak; **tomar el p.,** to go away, leave.
pendingue, tomar el p., (coll.) to go away, leave.
pendol, *m.* (mar.) boot-topping.
péndola, *f.* 1. pendulum; pendulum clock. 2. (archit.) queen post (in roof); suspension cable (of suspension bridge). 3. feather; quill, pen.
pendolaje, *m.* right to seize deck cargo of a captured vessel.
pendolario, *m., var. of* **pendolista.**
pendolista, *m., f.* penman, calligrapher.
pendolón, *m.* (archit.) kingpost, crown post.
pendón, *m.* 1. standard, pennon, banner. 2. (bot.) shoot (of trees). 3. (coll.) whore; slut, slattern. 4. (coll.) despicable person. 5. (*pl.*) reins of leading mules. — **a p. herido,** with all speed; **alzar** or **levantar p.** or **pendones,** to raise troops or men; **seguir el p. de,** to serve or enlist under (someone's) command.
pendonear, *i.v.* to be much about town, to go out often.
pendoneta, *f.* small standard or pennon.
pendonista, *a.* standard-bearing. —*m., f.* standard bearer.
pendular, *a.* pendulous.
péndulo, la, *a.* hanging, pendent. —*m.* pendulum; **p. compuesto,** (phys.) compound or physical pendulum; **p. de compensación,** (phys.) compensation pendulum; **p. de torsión,** (phys.) torsion pendulum; **p. simple,** (phys.) simple or mathematical pendulum.
pendura, a la p., (mar.) hanging, hanging at the cathead.
pene, *m.* (anat.) penis.
peneca, *f.* (Chile) primary school. —*m., f.* (Chile) first grader, primary school student.
Penélope, *f.* (myth.) Penelope, wife of Ulysses.
peneque, *a.* (coll.) drunk, tipsy.
penesísmico, *a.* (geoph.) peneseismic.
penetrabilidad, *f.* penetrability.
penetrable, *a.* 1. penetrable. 2. (fig.) comprehensible, intelligible, understandable.
penetración, *f.* 1. penetration; piercing. 2. (fig.) penetration, insight, sagacity.
penetrador, ra, *a.* penetrating, discerning; acute, keen (mind).
penetrales, *m.* (*pl.*) penetralia, innermost recesses or parts.
penetrante, *a.* 1. penetrating, piercing. 2. (fig.) penetrating, acute, keen, clear-sighted.
penetrar, *tr.v.* 1. to penetrate, pierce; to enter, go into. 2. to permeate, pervade. 3. (fig.) to pierce, penetrate (the wind; a shout; grief). 4. (fig.) to penetrate, fathom, understand, get to the bottom of. — **estar penetrado de,** to be overwhelmed (e.g. by grief); to be convinced of (e.g. one's importance); to be imbued with, be steeped in. —*i.v.* to penetrate; **p. en,** to penetrate; to go into; **p. por** or **p. entre,** to enter, penetrate; **p. hasta,** to penetrate up to, go in up to. —*r.v.* to fathom, comprehend; **penetrarse de,** to get to the bottom of (reason for something); to steep oneself in (a subject).
penetrativo, va, *a.* penetrating; piercing.
penetrómetro, *m.* (phys.) penetrometer, penetrameter.
pénfigo, *m.* (med.) pemphigus.
peni, *f.* (Amer.) jail.
penicilado, da, *a.* (bot., zool.) penicillate.
peniciliforme, *a.* (bot., zool.) penicilliform, penicillate.
penicilina, *f.* (pharm.) penicillin.
penígero, ra, *a.* (poet.) feathered, winged.
penillanura, *f.* (geol.) peneplain, peneplane.
Peninos, *a.* **Alpes P.,** Pennine Alps.
península, *f.* peninsula.
peninsular, *a.* peninsular. —*m., f.* 1. peninsular, native or inhabitant of a peninsula. 2. (Amer., coll.) Spaniard.
peniplanicie, *f.* (geol.) peneplain, peneplane.
penique, *m.* (G. B.) penny.
penitenciado, da, *past part. of* **penitenciar.** —*a.* 1. condemned. 2. (hist.) punished by the Inquisition. —*m., f.* convict.
penitencial, *a.* penitential.
penitenciar, *tr.v.* to impose penance on; to punish.
penitenciaría, *f.* 1. penitentiary, prison, jail. 2. (ecc.) penitentiary (tribunal of Roman Curia). 3. (ecc.) post of Grand Penitentiary.
penitenciario, ria, *a.* penitentiary, pertaining to prison. —*m.* (ecc.) penitentiary, confessor (priest); (ecc.) Grand Penitentiary.
penitente, *a.* penitent; repentant, contrite. —*m., f.* penitent; repenter.
Penjab, *m.* Punjab, region and state in India.
penjabi, *m.* Punjabi, Panjabi (language).
penjabo, *a., m., f.* Punjabi (inhabitant of Punjab).
Pennina, *a.* **Cordillera P.,** Pennine Chain (in England).
peno, na, *a., m., f.* (hist.) Carthaginian.
penol, *m.* (mar.) yardarm, peak; **a toca penoles,** (mar.) grazingly, very close.
penología, *f.* penology.
penológico, ca, *a.* penological.
penólogo, ga, *m., f.* penologist.
penosamente, *adv.* 1. painfully, grievously, sorrowfully. 2. laboriously, arduously, with difficulty.
penoso, sa, *a.* 1. distressing, sad. 2. difficult, laborious, arduous. 3. embarrassing, unpleasant.
pensado, da, *past part. of* **pensar.** —*a.* thought-out, devised; premeditated. — **bien p.,** well thought-out or devised; **mal p.,** poorly thought-out or devised; evilminded; **tener pensado,** to have in mind, in view; to be planning to.
pensador, ra, *a.* thinking. —*m.* 1. thinker. 2. (coll.) philosopher.
pensamiento, *m.* 1. thought; idea. 2. thought, thinking, faculty of thought. 3. (p.) rough sketch or draft. 4. (bot.) pansy. — **beberle a uno sus pensamientos,** (coll.) to anticipate a person's wishes; **como el p.,** in a jiffy, in a wink; **el p.,** thought, e.g. *el p. médico contemporáneo,* contemporary medical thought; **en un p.,** in a twinkling, in a jiffy, in a trice; **leer el p. a,** to thought-read; **ni por** or **con p.,** not even in thought; **no pasarle a uno por el p.,** not to occur to, not to pass through one's mind.
pensante, *a.* thinking.
pensar, (*ref. 29*) *tr.v.* 1. to think. 2. to think over, consider, study, e.g. *voy a pensarlo,* I'm going to think it over. 3. to think of, intend to, e.g. *estaba pensando ir al teatro,* I was thinking of going to the theater. — **¡ni pensarlo!** I wouldn't dream or think of it!; **pensándolo mejor,** on second thought. —*i.v.* to think; **p. de,** to think about or of (i.e. have an opinion of); **p. en,** to think about (i.e. focus one's thoughts on); **p. en** + *inf.,* to think about or of + *ger.;* **p. mal,** to be evil-minded; **p. mal de,** to think ill of; **sin p.,** without thinking, thoughtlessly.
pensar, (*ref. 29*) *tr.v.* to feed (animals).
pensativo, va, *a.* pensive, thoughtful; (fig.) absorbed.
pensel, *m.* (bot.) turnsole.
penseque, *m.* (coll.) oversight, thoughtlessness.
pensil, *a.* pensile, hanging, pendent. —*m.* (fig.) idyllic garden.
Pensilvania, Pennsylvania, *f.* (U.S.) Pennsylvania.
pensilvano, na, *a., m., f.* (U.S.) Pennsylvanian.
pensión, *f.* 1. pension, allowance; annuity. 2. board, cost of lodgings; boarding house. 3. grant, allowance, fellowship (for study). 4. pension, tax (paid on an estate). — **p. alimenticia,** maintenance; **p. de invalidez,** disability allowance; **p. de jubilación,** retirement pension; **p. de viudedad** or **viudez,** widow's pension; **p. vitalicia,** annuity, retirement allowance, life pension.
pensionado, da, *past part. of* **pensionar.** —*a.* pensioned, having a pension. —*m., f.* pensioner. —*m.* boarding school.
pensionar, *tr.v.* 1. to pension, grant a pension. 2. to impose a tax or pension on.
pensionario, *m.* 1. pensionary; magistrate. 2. one who pays a tax or pension.
pensionista, *m., f.* 1. pensioner, retiree. 2. boarder (in boarding house).

pent-, penta-, *prefix,* five, e.g. *pentágono,* pentagon.
pentaclorofenol, *a.* (chem.) pentachlorophenol.
pentacordio, *m.* (mus.) pentachord (instrument).
pentadáctilo, la, *a.* pentadactyl, pentadactylate.
pentadecágono, *a., var. of* **pentedecágono.**
pentaédrico, ca, *a.* pentahedral.
pentaedro, *m.* (geom.) pentahedron.
pentafásico, ca, *a.* (elec.) five-phase.
pentagonal, *a.* (geom.) pentagonal.
pentágono, na, *a.* (geom.) pentagonal. —*m.* (geom.) pentagon; **P.,** the Pentagon (U.S. Dept. of Defense building).
pentagrama, *m.* (mus.) staff, stave.
pentámero, ra, *a.* (bot., zool.) pentamerous. —*m.* (zool.) pentameron; (*pl.*) Pentamera.
pentámetro, *a., m.* (poet.) pentameter.
pentano, *m.* (chem.) pentane.
pentapolar, *a.* (elec.) five-pole.
pentápolis, *f.* pentapolis (group of five cities).
pentaquina, *f.* (pharm.) pentaquine, pentaquin.
pentarquía, *f.* (pol., hist.) pentarchy, government consisting of five persons.
pentasílabo, ba, *a., m.* pentasyllabic.
pentateuco, *m.* (Bib.) Pentateuch.
pentatlón, pentatlo, *m.* (sport.) pentathlon.
peñasco, *m.* 1. crag, steep rugged rock. 2. (tex.) strong silk material. 3. (zool.) murex. 4. (anat.) petrous portion (of the temporal bone).
peñascoso, sa, *a.* rocky, craggy.
peño, *m.* (Sp., reg.) foundling.
peñol, *m., var. of* **peñón.**
peñola, *f.* pen, quill, quill pen.
peñolada, *f.* the act of writing a short note.
peñón, *m. aug. of* **peña,** crag, steep rugged hill of rock. — **p. de Gibraltar,** Rock of Gibraltar.
peón, *m.* 1. pedestrian. 2. laborer, worker. 3. foot soldier, infantryman. 4. top, spinning top (toy). 5. pawn (in chess); man (in checkers). 6. (mec.) axle, spindle. 7. beehive. 8. (poet.) paeon (foot). — **a p.,** (coll.) on foot; **a torna p.,** (coll.) mutually; **p. caminero,** road worker, road laborer; **p. de mano,** (mas.) hodman, mason's help.
peonada, *f.* 1. day's work (of a laborer). 2. team or gang of laborers. — **pagar uno la p.,** (coll.) to repay a favor.
peonaje, *m.* 1. gang of laborers. 2. squad of infantrymen; foot soldiers (collectively).
peonería, *f.* day's plowing per man.
peonía, *f.* 1. (bot.) peony. 2. (hist.) land apportioned to a foot soldier (after the conquest of a territory). 3. (Amer.) day's plowing.
peonza, *f.* 1. whip top (toy). 2. (coll.) noisy little squirt. — **a p.,** (coll.) on foot.
peor, *adv., a. comp. of* **malo,** worse; worst; **en el p. de los casos,** at worst; **p. es meneallo,** let sleeping dogs lie; **p. que p., tanto p.,** worse still; **si pasa lo p.,** if the worst comes to the worst.
peoría, *f.* 1. worseness. 2. worsening, deterioration.
pepa, *f.* 1. (Amer.) seed, stone, pip. 2. (Col.) lie, hoax. 3. (Arg.) marble (toy).
pepe, *m.* (coll.) 1. bad, tasteless melon. 2. (Bol., Ven.) dandy, dude. 3. (Amer.) bib; **Pepe,** Joe. —*m., f.* (Amer.) foundling.
pepena, *f.* (C. Amer., Mex.) collecting, gathering, scavenging.
pepenado, *m.* (Mex.) adopted child, foundling.
pentatómico, ca, *a.* (chem.) pentatomic.
pentatónico, ca, *a.* (mus.) pentatonic.
pentavalente, *a.* (chem.) pentavalent.
pentecostés, *m.* Pentecost, Whitsunday.
pentedecágono, *a.* pentadecagonal. —*m.* pentadecagon.
Pentesilea, *f.* (myth.) Penthesilea, queen of the Amazons, slain by Achilles.
pentilo, *m.* (chem.) pentyl.
pentlandita, *f.* (min.) pentlandite.
pentobarbital, *m.* (chem.) pentobarbital.
pentodo, péntodo, *m.* (rad.) pentode.
pentosa, *f.* (chem.) pentose.
pentosano, *m.* (chem.) pentosan.
pentósido, *m.* (chem.) pentoside.
pentotal, pentothal, *m.* (chem.) pentothal.
penúltimo, ma, *a.* penultimate. —*m., f.* penultimate.
penumbra, *f.* 1. semi-darkness; border area. 2. (astron.) penumbra. 3. (p.) chiaroscuro.
penumbroso, sa, *a.* penumbral, penumbrous.
penuria, *f.* penury, want, need, poverty.
peña, *f.* 1. rock, boulder. 2. crag, craggy or rugged mountain. 3. group, circle, coterie; club. — **durar por peñas,** to last for ages, last an eternity; **ser p. or una p.,** to be as hard as stone, be insensible.
peñaranda, *f.* (coll.) pawnshop; debt; **estar en p.,** to be in debt.
peñascal, *m.* rocky terrain, craggy country or terrain.
pepenador, ra, *m., f.* (Mex.) scavenger.
pepenar, *tr.v.* 1. (C. Amer., Mex., Col.) to pick up, gather, collect, scavenge. 2. (Mex.) to sift (ore). 3. (Mex.) to grab, seize.
pepián, *m., var. of* **pipián,** an. American Indian stew or fricassee.
pepinar, *m.* cucumber bed, cucumber patch or field.
pepinillo, *m.* cucumber; gherkin.
pepino, *m.* (bot.) cucumber; **no importarle a uno un p.,** (coll.) not to care a fig about; **p. del diablo, p. purgante, p. silvestre,** (bot.) squirting cucumber; **p. de mar,** (zool.) sea cucumber.
pepión, *m.* formerly used Spanish gold coin.
pepita, *f.* 1. pip, seed (in fruit). 2. (vet.) pip (disease of fowls). 3. (min.) nugget (of gold), lump (of native metal). — **no tener pepitas en la lengua,** to be outspoken, to speak one's mind.
pepitoria, *f.* 1. (cul.) giblet stew; chicken fricassee with egg sauce. 2. jumble, hodgepodge.
pepitoso, sa, *a.* 1. pippy, full of pips or seeds. 2. (vet.) suffering from pip.
peplo, *m.* peplum (short, sleeveless Grecian or Roman tunic).
pepón, *m.* (bot.) watermelon.
pepona, *f.* large paper doll.
pepónide, *f.* (bot.) pepol (generic name for pumpkin, melon, squash, and other gourd-like fruit).
pepsina, *f.* (biochem.) pepsin, pepsine.
pepsinógeno, *m.* (biochem.) pepsinogen.
péptico, ca, *a.* peptic.
péptido, *m.* (biochem.) peptide, peptid.
peptizar, (*ref. 53*) *tr.v.* to peptize.
peptona, *f.* (biochem.) peptone.
peptonificación, *f.* peptonization.
peptonificar, (*ref. 50*) *tr.v.* to peptonize.
pepú, (*pl.* **pepúes**), *m.* (Cuba, bot.) alpinia (Alpinia nutans).
peque, pequé, *ref.* **pecar.**
pequén, *m.* (Chile, ornith.) (variety of) burrowing owl.
pequeñamente, *adv.* in a small degree or way.
pequeñez, (*pl.* **pequeñeces**), *f.* 1. smallness. 2. infancy, childhood. 3. trifle, unimportant thing. 4. (fig.) smallness, pettiness, meanness.
pequeñín, na, *a.* tiny, very small. —*m.* tiny tot; tiny person.
pequeño, ña, *a.* 1. small, little. 2. small, young; of tender age. 3. (fig.) small, humble, modest. —*m., f.* child.
pequeñuelo, la, *a. dim. of* **pequeño,** tiny, small; very young. —*m., f.* small child, baby, tot.
Pequín, *m.* Peking, capital of China.
pequín, *m.* (tex.) pekin (a silk fabric).
pequinés, *m.* Pekingese (dog).
pera, *f.* 1. (bot.) pear. 2. goatee, imperial (beard). 3. (fig.) sinecure, cushy job, cinch. 4. (vet.) inflammation on feet of sheep. — **dar para peras a uno,** (coll.) to threaten, promise a thrashing; **escoger como entre peras,** (coll.) to choose very carefully; **partir peras con,** (coll.) to be on intimate terms with, be very friendly with; **pedir peras al olmo,** (coll.) to ask for the moon, ask for the impossible; **p. bergamota,** bergamot; **poner a uno las peras a cuarto,** (coll.) to put the squeeze on someone, force or coerce someone.
perácido, *m.* (chem.) peracid.
perada, *f.* 1. pear jam. 2. pear brandy.
peral, *m.* (bot.) pear tree; pear wood.
peraleda, *f.* pear orchard.
peralejo, *m.* (bot.) nance, golden spoon (Byrsonima crassifolia).
peraltar, *tr.v.* 1. (archit.) to stilt, elevate (an arch). 2. (ry.) to raise, elevate, bank (outer rail).
peralte, *m.* 1. (archit.) stilt; rise, height (of arch). 2. (ry.) superelevation, bank (of outer rail).
peralto, *m.* (geom.) height.
perantón, *m.* 1. (bot.) mock cypress. 2. large fan. 3. (coll.) very tall person.
perborato, *m.* (chem.) perborate.
perbórico, ca, *a.* (chem.) perboric.
perca, *f.* (ichth.) perch.
percal, *m.* (tex.) percale.
percalina, *f.* (tex.) percaline.
percance, *m.* 1. mishap, mischance, misfortune; accident. 2. (*pl.*) perquisites. — **percances del oficio,** part and parcel of the job (unpleasant features of a job).
percatarse, *r.v.* **p. de,** to notice, realize, to become aware of.
percebe, *m.* 1. (zool.) goose barnacle. 2. (coll.) fool, idiot.
percebimiento, *m.* preparation; awareness.
percepción, *f.* 1. perception; sensing. 2. the act of collecting or receiving rents, monies, taxes, etc.
perceptibilidad, *f.* perceptibility.
perceptible, *a.* 1. perceptible. 2. collectable, receivable.
perceptiblemente, *adv.* perceptibly.
perceptividad, *f.* perceptivity.
perceptivo, va, *a.* perceptive.
perceptor, ra, *a.* percipient, perceiving. —*m., f.* 1. percipient, perceiver. 2. collector, receiver.
percha, *f.* 1. pole, prop, staff, perch. 2. clothes rack, hat rack. 3. (tex.) napping (action); teaseling. 4. (hunt.) snare. 5. hunter's belt to which game is attached. 6. (bird's) perch. 7. barber's pole. 8. (mar.) spar. 9. (mar.) headrail. 10. (ichth.) perch. — **estar en p.,** to be in the bag; **p. de barbero,** barber's pole.
perchado, da, *a.* (her.) on a perch.
perchador, ra, *m., f.* (tex.) carder, teaseler.
perchar, *tr.v.* to teasel, nap, raise the nap on (cloth).
perchel, *m.* (Sp.) fishing device consisting of a net hung on various poles; place where this device is used.
perchero, *m.* 1. clothes hanger; coat and hat rack. 2. cloakroom.
percherón, na, *a., m., f.* Percheron (horse).
perchón, *m.* poorly pruned shoot, shoot with too many buds left on.
perchonar, *i.v.* 1. to leave poorly pruned shoots on the vine. 2. (hunt.) to set traps.
percibir, *tr.v.* 1. to perceive, sense. 2. to collect; to receive.
percibo, *m.* receiving, collecting.

perclorato, *m.* (chem.) perchlorate.
perclórico, ca, *a.* (chem.) perchloric.
percloruro, *m.* (chem.) perchloride, perchlorid.
percocería, *f.* delicate hammered silver work.
percolación, *f.* (pharm.) percolation; leakage, seepage.
percolador, *m.* percolator, filter.
percromato, *m.* (chem.) perchromate.
percrómico, ca, *a.* (chem.) perchromic.
percuciente, *a.* percussive, percutient; striking, knocking.
percudir, *tr.v.* to tarnish, dull; to dirty, stain, soil. —*r.v.* to become permanently stained or soiled (laundry, linen, clothing).
percusión, *f.* 1. percussion; impact. 2. (med.) percussion.
percusor, *m.* 1. firing pin. 2. (med.) percussor, percussion hammer. 3. percussor, striker.
percutáneo, a, *a.* (med.) percutaneous.
percutir, *tr.v.* 1. to percuss, knock, strike. 2. (med.) to percuss.
percutor, *m.* (arm.) firing pin, striker, firing needle, cock. — **p. eléctrico,** (arm.) electric firing mechanism.
perdedero, *m.* 1. cause or reason for losing. 2. hiding place (of hunted hare).
perdedor, ra, *a.* losing. —*m., f.* loser.
perder, (*ref. 30*) *tr.v.* 1. to lose; to mislay. 2. to waste (time). 3. to miss (bus, train; opportunity, vocation). 4. to lose (be separated by death), e.g. *p. a un hijo en la guerra,* to lose a son in the war. 5. to lose, be beaten in (a championship, game, contest, battle). 6. to lose (esteem, respect); forget (one's good manners). 7. to spoil, harm, damage. 8. to ruin, cause the ruin of. — **no tener nada que p.,** to have nothing to lose; **p. de vista,** to lose sight of; **p. el habla,** to become speechless; **p. la razón** or **el juicio,** to lose one's reason, go out of one's mind; **p. la vista,** to lose one's eyesight; **p. sustentación,** (avia.) to stall; **p. terreno,** to lose ground. —*i.v.* 1. to lose (in a game, contest, etc.). 2. to fade, discolor. —*r.v.* 1. to get lost, lose oneself, lose one's way. 2. to lose, mislay, e.g. *se me ha perdido el paraguas,* I have mislaid my umbrella. 3. to lose control of oneself (through shock, etc.), get carried away (by passion). 4. to abandon oneself (to), wallow (in) (vice). 5. to fade, disappear, get lost (sound, object - in darkness, distance, etc.). 6. to be lost (at sea), sink, go to the bottom. 7. to be passionately in love (with), be mad (about), e.g. *se perdía por ella,* he was passionately in love with her. 8. to lose one's honor. 9. to disappear (horizon), go underground (a stream). 10. to be wasted, e.g. *esta carne se va a perder si no se come hoy,* this meat will be wasted if it's not eaten today. — **estar perdido,** to be lost, to be damned; **perderse de vista,** to go out of sight, fade from view, to disappear.
perdición, *f.* 1. perdition, eternal damnation. 2. loss, ruin, ruination. 3. unbridled passion. 4. outrage, disgrace.
pérdida, *f.* 1. loss, waste; damage. 2. (com.) shrinkage; shortage; leakage. — **estar** or **ir a pérdidas y ganancias,** to share profit and loss; **es una p. de tiempo,** it's a waste of time; **no tener p. una cosa,** (coll.) to be easy to find or to achieve; **p. de transmisión,** (elec.) line loss; **pérdidas y ganancias,** (com.) profit and loss.
perdidamente, *adv.* 1. madly, wildly, desperately. 2. uselessly.
perdidizo, za, *a.* supposed to be lost; lost by design or on purpose; **hacer perdidizo,** (coll.) to hide; **hacerse el p.** (coll.) to sneak away, make oneself scarce; **hacerse p.,** (coll.) to lose on purpose (at cards, etc.).
perdido, da, *past part. of* **perder.** —*a.* 1. lost; mislaid. 2. wasted. 3. damned; misguided; dissolute, profligate. 4. stray (bullet). 5. (coll.) filthy, very dirty. 6. (coll.) inveterate, confirmed (e.g. drunkard). 7. leisure, spare, e.g. *ratos perdidos, horas perdidas,* spare time, leisure time. — **p. por,** madly in love with (a person), mad about, very fond of (something). — **ser un perdido,** to be a wastrel, rake or dissolute person. —*m.* rake, scoundrel; black sheep. —*f.* loose woman; harlot.
perdidoso, sa, *a.* 1. losing, sustaining loss. 2. easily lost.
perdigana, *f.* young partridge.
perdigar, (*ref. 51*) *tr.v.* 1. (cul.) to brown, broil slightly. 2. (cul.) to braise. 3. (coll.) to prepare, make ready.
perdigón, *m.* 1. young partridge; decoy partridge. 2. pellet, bird shot, (*pl.*) shot, pellets. — **p. zorrero,** buckshot.
perdigón, *m.* 1. (coll.) heavy loser (in gambling). 2. (coll.) wastrel, squanderer, prodigal.
perdigonada, *f.* shot with bird shot; wound caused by bird shot.
perdigonera, *f.* shot pouch or bag.
perdigue, perdigué, *ref.* **perdigar.**
perdiguero, ra, *a.* partridge hunting. —*m.* 1. game dealer. 2. pointer, setter (dog).
perdimiento, *m., var. of* **of perdición, pérdida.**
perdis, *m.* (coll.) rake, good-for-nothing, wastrel, gay blade.
perdiz, (*pl.* **perdices**), *f.* (ornith.) partridge. — **p. blanca,** rock ptarmigan; **p. pardilla,** gray partridge; **p. real** or **roja,** red-legged partridge; **perdices en campo raso,** something very difficult to obtain.
perdón, *m.* pardon, forgiveness, grace, reprieve. 2. burning drop of oil or fat. — **con p.,** by your leave; **¡p.!** excuse me! pardon me; **no tener p. de Dios,** to be inexcusable, unforgivable.
perdonable, *a.* pardonable, forgivable.
perdonador, ra, *a.* pardoning, forgiving. —*m., f.* pardoner, forgiver.
perdonante, *a.* pardoning, forgiving.
perdonar, *tr.v.* 1. to pardon, forgive, excuse. 2. to forego (a privilege). 3. to exempt, to spare. — **no p.,** not to spare; **no p. detalle,** not to miss or omit a detail; **no p. ocasión de,** not to miss a chance to, not to miss an opportunity to.
perdonavidas, *m.* (coll.) bully, braggart.
perdulario, ria, *a.* 1. careless, sloppy, slovenly. 2. dissolute, debauched. —*m., f.* bohemian. 2. good-for-nothing, wastrel, rake.
perdurable, *a.* lasting, long-lasting; everlasting.
perdurablemente, *adv.* everlastingly, lastingly.
perdurar, *i.v.* to last, last a long time.
perecear, *tr.v.* (coll.) to protract, delay, to put off, postpone (out of laziness or negligence). —*i.v.* to idle, to loaf.
perecedero, ra, *a.* perishable; mortal. —*m.* (coll.) poverty, need, want.
perecer, (*ref. 45*) *i.v.* to perish; to end; to die. —*r.v.* **perecerse de pasión** or **amor,** to be consumed with passion or love; **perecerse por,** to long for, yearn for, be mad about.
pereciente, *a.* perishing, ending, dying.
perecimiento, *m.* 1. perishing, end, demise, death. 2. decline.
pereda, *f.* pear orchard.
peregrinación, *f.* 1. peregrination, journey; pilgrimage. 2. (fig.) life (as a journey).
peregrinaje, *m., var. of* **peregrinación.**
peregrinamente, *adv.* 1. strangely, singularly, curiously. 2. beautifully, exquisitely.
peregrinante, *a.* on pilgrimage, traveling. —*m.* pilgrim, traveler.
peregrinar, *i.v.* 1. to peregrinate, journey, wander; to go on a pilgrimage. 2. (fig.) to journey through life.
peregrinidad, *f.* strangeness, rareness, rarity.
peregrino, na, *a.* 1. traveling, journeying, wandering. 2. pilgriming, on a pilgrimage. 3. migratory (bird). 4. strange, singular, rare, odd; foreign. 5. fine, perfect, beautiful. —*m., f.* pilgrim, palmer, traveler.
pereirina, *f.* (chem.) pereirine, pereirin.
perejil, *m.* 1. (bot.) parsley. 2. (coll.) furbelows, frippery, showy ornaments. 3. (*pl.*) (coll.) titles, decorations. — **huyendo del p. le nació en la frente,** be careful not to jump from the frying pan into the fire; **p. de mar,** (bot.) samphire; **p. de monte,** (bot.) mountain parsley; **p. de perro,** (bot.) poison parsley; **p. macedonio,** (bot.) smallage, wild celery; **p. mal sembrado,** (coll.) thin beard; **p. marino,** (bot.) samphire.
perejila, *f.* card game in which the seven of hearts is used as a joker; the seven of hearts in this game.
perenal, *a., var. of* **perennal.**
perencejo, *m.* so-and-so, what's-his-name.
perención, *f.* (law) lapsing, expiration (of a legal action).
perendeca, *f.* (coll.) prostitute, tart.
perendengue, *m.* earring; trinket, bauble, cheap jewelry.
perene, *a., var. of* **perenne.**
perengano, na, *m., f., var. of* **perencejo.**
perennal, *a.* perennial.
perennalmente, *adv., var. of* **perennemente.**
perenne, *a.* perennial, perpetual; (bot.) perennial.
perennemente, *adv.* 1. perennially, perpetually. 2. continually.
perennidad, *f.* perpetuity.
perentoriamente, *adv.* peremptorily; urgently, pressingly.
perentoriedad, *f.* peremptoriness, urgency.
perentorio, ria, *a.* 1. peremptory, decisive. 2. urgent, pressing, peremptory. 3. (law) peremptory.
perero, *m.* fruit parer (instrument).
pereza, *f.* 1. laziness; sloth. 2. slowness.
perezca, perezco, *ref.* **perecer.**
perezosamente, *adv.* lazily; slowly, sluggishly.
perezoso, sa, *a.* 1. lazy, indolent, idle, slothful. 2. slow, sluggish. —*m., f.* loafer, slacker, lay-about. —*m.* 1. (zool.) sloth. 2. (Urug.) folding chair. 3. (Mex.) safety pin. —*f.* (Arg.) chair with a leg rest; (Chile) bolster.
perfección, *f.* 1. perfection, perfectness. 2. (fig.) beauty, grace. 3. (law) fulfillment of requisites for legal validity. — **a la p.,** perfectly, to perfection.
perfeccionador, ra, *a.* perfecting, improving; finishing.
perfeccionamiento, *m.* perfecting, improvement; finish.
perfeccionar, *tr.v.* 1. to perfect, make perfect; to improve; to finish. 2. (law) to fulfill (requisites for legal validity). —*r.v.* 1. to be perfected. 2. to become fully qualified (in).
perfeccionismo, *m.* perfectionism.
perfeccionista, *a., m., f.* perfectionist.
perfectamente, *adv.* perfectly.
perfectibilidad, *f.* perfectibility.
perfectible, *a.* perfectible, that can be perfected or improved.
perfectivo, va, *a.* perfective.
perfecto, ta, *a.* perfect; (gram.) perfect (tense).
perficiente, *a.* perfecting.
pérfidamente, *adv.* perfidiously.
perfidia, *f.* perfidy.

pérfido, da, *a.* perfidious, treacherous. —*m., f.* perfidious person.
perfil, *m.* 1. profile; side view; cross section. 2. (p.) outline, sketch. 3. decorations, traceries, side ornament or adornment. 4. thin stroke (in writing). 5. (*pl.*) finishing strokes. 6. (*pl.*) refinement, good manners. — **de p.,** sideways, profile, e.g. *foto de p.,* profile photograph; **medio p.,** half profile; **p. aerodinámico,** streamlining; **p. atar,** (aer.) wing profile, wing section, wing contour; **p. edafológico,** soil profile; **p. estratigráfico,** (geol.) stratigraphic logging; **p. magnético,** (geoph.) magnetic profile; **p. supersónico,** (aer.) supersonic profile, supersonic airfoil; **p. T.,** (bldg.) T bar; **tomar perfiles,** to trace.
perfilado, da, *a.* 1. in profile; outlined. 2. streamlined. 3. finished, complete. 4. well-formed (nose). 5. long and thin (face); elongated.
perfiladora, *f.* (mach.) profiling machine.
perfiladura, *f.* 1. profiling; profile. 2. outlining.
perfilar, *tr.v.* 1. to profile, outline. 2. to finish, give finishing touches to, polish. —*r.v.* 1. to show one's profile, stand sideways. 2. (coll.) to dress up, smarten oneself up.
perfilógrafo, *m.* (geoph.) profilograph.
perfoliada, *f.* (bot.) hare's ear (Bupleurum rotundifolium).
perfoliado, da, *a.* (bot.) perfoliate.
perfoliata, *f.* (bot.) hare's ear.
perfolla, *f.* shucks; corn husk.
perforación, *f.* 1. perforation, piercing. 2. drilling, boring. 3. hole, puncture. 4. (comp.) keypunching.
perforador, ra, *a.* 1. perforating, piercing, puncturing. 2. drilling, boring. —*m., f.* perforator; driller, borer. —*f.* 1. perforator (machine). 2. (min.) drill, drilling machine; hammer drill; piston drill; rock drill. — **p. de percusión,** percussion drill; **p. giratoria,** rotary drill.
perforante, *a.* piercing.
perforar, *tr.v.* 1. to perforate, puncture, pierce. 2. to drill, bore, punch.
perforista, *m., f.* (comp.) keypuncher.
performancia, *f.* (mech.) performance.
perfumadero, *m.* cassolette, perfume pan.
perfumado, da, *past part. of* **perfumar.** —*a.* perfumed, sweet-smelling.
perfumador, ra, *a.* perfuming. —*m., f.* perfumer, perfume maker. —*m.* cassolette, perfume pan; perfumer, perfume atomizer.
perfumar, *tr.v.* to perfume. —*r.v.* to become perfumed. —*i.v.* to exhale perfume.
perfume, *m.* 1. perfume; fragrance, sweet smell; aroma. 2. (fig.) something that evokes a pleasant memory.
perfumear, *tr.v., var. of* **perfumar.**
perfumería, *f.* perfumery; perfumer's shop or trade; perfume and toiletries collectively.
perfumero, ra, *m., f., var. of* **perfumista.**
perfumista, *m., f.* perfumer, perfume maker or seller.
perfunctoriamente, *adv.* (rare) perfunctorily.
perfusión, *f.* perfusion, bath.
pergal, *m.* leather paring for sandal tongs or shoe laces.
pergaminero, *m.* parchment maker or seller.
pergamino, *m.* 1. parchment (paper), vellum. 2. parchment, manuscript, document. 3. (*pl.*) (fig.) titles of nobility. — **en p.,** (print.) parchment bound.
Pérgamo, *m.* (hist.) Pergamum, ancient Greek kingdom in Asia Minor.
pergenio, *m.,* (Chile, Urug.) boy, kid, brat.
pergeñar, *tr.v.* (coll.) to arrange, prepare, to get ready for; to perform competently.
pergeño, *m.* (coll.) appearance, looks, mien.
pérgola, *f.* 1. pergola, arbor, bower. 2. roof garden.
peri, *f.* peri, fairy, elf.
periantio, *m.* (bot.) perianth.
periarteritis, *f.* (med.) periarteritis.
periartritis, *f.* (med.) periarthritis.
pericárdico, ca, *a.* (anat., zool.) pericardial, pericardic.
pericardio, *m.* (anat.) pericardium.
pericarditis, *f.* (med.) pericarditis.
pericarpio, *m.* (bot.) pericarp.
pericia, *f.* skill, expertness, proficiency, know-how (coll.).
pericial, *a.* expert, of experts.
pericialmente, *adv.* expertly.
periciclo, *m.* (bot.) pericycle.
Pericles, *m.* (hist.) Pericles, Athenian statesman, orator and strategist.
periclinal, *a.* (geol.) periclinal.
periclitar, *i.v.* 1. to be in danger. 2. to decline, decay.
perico, *m.* 1. periwig. 2. (ornith.) conure, parakeet. 3. (mar.) mizzen top gallant; (mar.) mizzen top gallant sail. 4. queen of clubs in the Spanish card game of **truque.** 5. large fan. 6. large asparagus. 7. (coll.) chamber pot. — **p. de los palotes,** so-and-so; John Doe; **p. entre ellas,** (coll.) ladies' man; **p. ligero,** (zool.) sloth.
pericón, na, *a.* fit for all uses (esp. a horse, a mule). —*m.* 1. large fan. 2. queen of clubs in the game of reversi. 3. (Arg.) popular dance to music of guitars with intervals of reciting or improvising couplets.
pericondrio, *m.* (anat.) perichondrium.
pericote, *m.* (Amer.) large rat; **mientras los gatos duermen, los pericotes se pasean,** (Amer.) while the cat's away, the mice will play.
pericráneo, *m.* (anat.) pericranium.
peridental, *a.* (anat.) periodontal, peridental.
peridérmico, ca, *a.* (bot.) peridermal, peridermic.
peridermis, *f.* (bot.) periderm.
peridotita, *f.* (min.) peridotite.
peridoto, *m.* (min.) peridot, olivine.
perieco, ca, *a.* (geog.) perioecic. —*m.* (*pl.*) (geog.) Perioeci.
periferia, *f.* periphery.
periférico, ca, *a.* peripheral.
perifollo, *m.* 1. (bot.) chervil. 2. (*pl.*) (coll.) frippery, gaudy ornaments in woman's dress or hair — **p. oloroso,** (bot.) sweet cicely.
perifonear, *tr.v.* (rad.) to broadcast, transmit.
perifonía, *f.* (rad.) broadcasting; broadcast.
perífono, *m.* (rad.) transmitter, broadcasting equipment.
periforme, *a.* pear-shaped.
perifrasear, *i.v.* to periphrase, use periphrase or circumlocution.
perífrasi, perífrasis, (*pl.* **perífrasis**), *f.* (rhet.) periphrasis, periphrase, circumlocution.
perifrástico, ca, *a.* periphrastic, circumlocutory.
perigallo, *m.* 1. loose skin under the chin, dewlap. 2. brightly colored hair ribbon. 3. sling (made of twine). 4. tall, skinny person. 5. (mar.) topping lift.
perigeo, *m.* (astron.) perigee.
perigonio, *m.* (bot.) perigonium, perigone.
perihelio, *m.* (astron.) perihelion.
perilla, *f.* 1. knob, handle (on a drawer); pear-shaped ornament. 2. goatee, imperial (beard). 3. mouth end of a cigar. 4. pommel (of saddle). 5. (anat.) lobe (of ear). — **de p.** or **perillas,** (coll.) just right; just at the right time; **venir de p.,** to be just the thing needed.
perillán, na, *a.* (coll.) roguish, crafty. —*m., f.* (coll.) rogue, sly or crafty person.
perillo, *m.* sweet, scalloped bun.
perilustre, *a.* very illustrious, famous.
perimetría, *m.* (opt.) perimetry.
perimétrico, ca, *a.* perimetric, perimetrical.
perímetro, *m.* perimeter.
perimisio, *m.* (anat.) perimysium.
perínclito, ta, *a.* illustrious, renowned.
perineal, *a.* (anat.) perineal.
perinefrio, *m.* (anat.) perinephrium.
perineo, *m.* (anat.) perineum.
perineumonía, *f.* (med.) pneumonia.
perineumónico, ca, *a.* (med.) pneumonic.
perineurio, *m.* (anat.) perineurium.
perineuritis, *f.* (anat.) perineuritis.
perinola, *f.* 1. teetotum (top used in gambling). 2. pear-shaped ornament. 3. (coll.) lively little woman.
perinquina, *f.* (rare) hatred, animosity, hostility.
perinquinoso, sa, *a.* (rare) hostile, unfriendly.
perioca, *f.* summary; synopsis.
periódicamente, *adv.* periodically.
periodicidad, *f.* periodicity.
periódico, ca, *a.* periodic, periodical; (math., astron., chem., elec.) periodic. —*m.* newspaper, journal; periodical; **p. dominical** or **del domingo,** Sunday paper; **p. matutino** or **de la mañana,** morning newspaper; **p. vespertino** or **de la tarde,** evening newspaper.
periodicucho, *m.* (derog.) rag, poor newspaper, scandal sheet.
periodismo, *m.* journalism; **p. gráfico,** photojournalism.
periodista, *m., f.* journalist, newspaperman, reporter, newspaperwoman. — **p. gráfico,** press photographer; **p. policíaco,** police reporter.
periodístico, ca, *a.* journalistic.
período, *m.* 1. period, space of time, age, era, epoch. 2. (math., astron., chron., gram., rhet., med., geol., hist., phys., elec.) period. 3. (physiol.) period, menstruation. 4. (educ.) term. — **p. de incubación,** (med.) incubation period; **p. de semidesintegración,** half-life; **p. de una substancia radioactiva, p. de vida media,** (phys.) period, half-life, half-life period; **p. glacial,** ice age; **p. geocrático,** (geoph.) geocratic period; **p. latente,** (med.) latent period; **p. mesolítico,** (geoph.) mesolithic period.
periodoncia, *f.* (med.) periodontics.
periodontal, *a.* (anat.) periodontal, peridental.
perióstico, ca, *a.* (anat.) periosteal.
periostio, *m.* (anat.) periosteum.
periostitis, *f.* (med.) periostitis.
periostosis, *f.* (med.) periostosis.
periótico, ca, *a.* (zool.) periotic.
peripatético, ca, *a.* 1. (philos.) Peripatetic, Aristotelian. 2. (coll.) ridiculous (opinions, concepts), wild.
peripatetismo, *m.* (philos.) Peripateticism, the philosophy of Aristotle.
peripato, *m.* (philos.) Peripateticism (doctrine of Peripatetics); Peripatetics (members of Peripatetic school).
peripecia, *f.* 1. (theat.) peripeteia, sudden change of fortune in a drama. 2. vicissitude, peripeteia, change of fortune.
periplo, *m.* periplus, voyage.
períptero, ra, *a.* (archit.) peripteral, surrounded by columns. —*m.* (archit.) peripteros, peripteral building.
peripuesto, ta, *a.* (coll.) all dressed up, all spruced up.
periquear, *i.v.* 1. to take too many liberties (said of women). 2. (C. Amer.) to flirt and court.
periquete, *m.* jiffy, instant; **en un p.,** in a jiffy.
periquillo, *m.* a very light sweet tidbit.

periquito, *m.* (ornith.) parakeet, love bird; small parrot.
perisarco, *m.* (zool.) perisarc.
periscio, cia, *a.* (geog.) periscian. —*m.* (*pl.*) periscii.
periscópico, ca, *a.* (opt.) periscopic.
periscopio, *m.* (opt., mar.) periscope.
perisodáctilo, *a.* (zool.) perissodactyl. —*m.* (zool.) perissodactyl, (*pl.*) Perissodactyla.
perisología, *f.* (rhet.) pleonasm, verbiage.
peristalsis, *f.* (physiol.) peristalsis.
peristáltico, ca, *a.* (physiol.) peristaltic.
peristaltismo, *m.* (physiol.) peristalsis.
perístasis, *f.* (rhet.) subject matter, theme.
peristilo, *m.* (archit.) peristyle, colonnade.
perístole, *f.* (physiol.) peristole, peristalsis.
peristoma, *m.* (bot., zool.) peristome.
peritación, *f.*, *var. of* **peritaje.**
peritaje, *m.* work of an expert, expert's investigations or studies.
peritecio, *m.* (bot.) perithecium.
perito, ta, *a.* expert, experienced, skilled. —*m.* expert; appraiser; connoisseur; **p. de montes,** forestry technician; **p. industrial,** engineer; **p. mercantil,** qualified accountant.
peritoneal, *a.* (anat.) peritoneal.
peritoneo, *m.* (anat.) peritoneum.
peritonitis, *f.* (med.) peritonitis.
perjudicado, da, *past part. of* **perjudicar.** —*a.* harmed, damaged. —*m.* injured party.
perjudicador, ra, *a.* harmful, damaging. —*m., f.* harmer, damager.
perjudicante, *a.* harmful, damaging.
perjudicar, (*ref.* 50) *tr.v.* to harm, injure, do harm to; to be or go against (someone's) interests; to impair, damage. —*r.v.* to do oneself harm.
perjudicial, *a.* harmful, damaging; prejudicial, detrimental.
perjudicialmente, *adv.* harmfully, damagingly, detrimentally.
perjudique, perjudiqué, *ref.* **perjudicar.**
perjuicio, *m.* harm, injury, damage, detriment.
perjurador, ra, *a.* perjurious, perjured. —*m., f.* perjurer, forswearer.
perjurar, *i.v.* to commit perjury, to forswear. —*r.v.* to commit perjury; to perjure oneself.
perjurio, *m.* perjury.
perjuro, ra, *a.* perjured, forsworn. —*m., f.* perjurer, forswearer.
perla, *f.* 1. (jewel.) pearl. 2. (fig.) pearl, jewel (invaluable or exquisite person or thing). 3. (pharm.) pearl, capsule. 4. (her.) pairle, pall, shakefork. 5. (print.) pearl. — **de perlas,** just right, perfect, to a tee (coll.); **p. barroca,** baroque pearl; **p. de cultivo,** cultured pearl.
perlado, da, *a.* 1. pearly, pearl-colored. 2. pearl (barley).
perlático, ca, *a.* (med.) paralyzed, palsied. —*m., f.* (med.) paralytic, palsy patient.
perlería, *f.* large quantity of pearls.
perlero, ra, *a.* pertaining to pearls, e.g. *industria perlera,* the pearl industry.
perlesía, *f.* (med.) paralysis, palsy.
perlino, na, *a.* pearl-colored, pearly.
perlita, *f.* (min.) perlite, pearlite; (metal.) pearlite.
perlítico, ca, *a.* (min.) perlitic.
perlongar, (*ref.* 51) *i.v.* 1. (mar.) to sail along the coast. 2. (mar.) to pay out a cable.
perlongue, *ref.* **perlongar.**
permalloy, *m.* (metal.) permalloy.
permanecer, (*ref.* 45) *i.v.* to stay, remain.
permaneciente, *a.* remaining, staying; permanent.
permanencia, *f.* 1. permanence, permanency. 2. stay, residence, sojourn.
permanente, *a.* permanent. —*m.* permanent wave.
permanentemente, *adv.* permanently.
permanezca, permanezco, *ref.* **permanecer.**
permanganato, *m.* (chem.) permanganate.
permangánico, ca, *a.* (chem.) permanganic.
permansión, *f.*, *var. of* **permanencia.**
permeabilidad, *f.* permeability. — **p. hidráulica,** hydraulic permeability.
permeable, *a.* permeable; non-waterproof.
permeancia, *f.* (elec.) permeance.
pérmico, ca, *a.* (geol.) Permian. —*m.* Permian period.
permisible, *a.* permissible.
permisión, *f.* 1. permission, leave; authorization. 2. the act of permitting another to do what one has censured.
permisivamente, *adv.* permissively.
permisivo, va, *a.* permissive.
permiso, *m.* 1. permission; permit; license; (mil.) leave of absence, furlough. 2. (numis.) tolerance (amount which coins are allowed to weigh above or under the standard weight). — **con su p.** or **p.,** excuse me; **p. de conducir,** driver's license.
permisor, ra, *a., m., f., var. of* **permitidor.**
permistión, *f.* mixture, concoction.
permitente, *a.* permissive; permitting, allowing.
permitidero, ra, *a.* permissible, allowable.
permitidor, ra, *a.* permitting, granting. —*m., f.* permitter, granter.
permitir, *tr.v.* 1. to permit, allow. 2. to grant, admit. 3. to permit, tolerate, consent. — **p.** + *inf.*, to permit or allow + *inf.;* **p. que** + *sub.*, to permit or allow + *inf.* —*r.v.* to be permitted or allowed; to permit or allow oneself, to take the liberty (to).
permitividad, *f.* (elec.) permittivity, specific inductive capacity.
permuta, *f.* exchange; permutation, interchange, barter.
permutable, *a.* permutable, interchangeable; exchangeable.
permutación, *f.* exchange; permutation, interchange, barter; (math.) permutation.
permutador térmico, *m.* (elec.) heat exchanger.
permutar, *tr.v.* to exchange; to interchange; to change, permute, barter.
permutatriz, *m.* (elec.) commutator, rectifier, transverter.
perna, *f.* black tropical shell fish.
pernada, *f.* 1. kick. 2. (mar.) leg, branch (of some object).
pernambuco, palo de P., (bot.) Pernambuco wood.
pernaza, *f. aug. of* **pierna,** large, fat leg.
perneador, ra, *a.* strong-legged, brawny-legged.
pernear, *i.v.* 1. to kick about, kick one's legs. 2. (coll.) to traipse, bustle or hurry about (trying to get something). 3. (coll.) to get impatient, to fuss, worry, fret.
pernera, *f.* leg (of trousers or pants).
pernería, *f.* (mar.) stock or provision of bolts.
perneta, *f. dim. of* **pierna,** small leg; **en pernetas,** barelegged.
pernete, *m. dim. of* **perno,** small bolt, pin or peg.
perniabierto, ta, *a.* bowlegged.
perniciosamente, *adv.* perniciously.
pernicioso, sa, *a.* pernicious, harmful, injurious.
pernigón, *m.* preserved plum formerly imported from Genoa.
pernil, *m.* 1. thigh (of animal); hock, ham. 2. leg (of trousers or pants).
pernio, *m.* door or window hinge.
perniquebrar, (*ref.* 29) *tr.v.* to break the leg or legs of. —*r.v.* to break one's leg or legs.
pernítrico, *a.* (chem.) pernitric.
pernituerto, ta, *a.* crooked-legged.
perno, *m.* 1. bolt, pin, spike. 2. knuckle, hook (of a door hinge). 3. (mec.) crank pin, joint pin. — **p. común,** machine bolt; **p. de cabeza en T,** T bolt; **p. de expansión,** expansion bolt; **p. de gancho,** (ry) clutch bolt; **p. maestro,** kingbolt; **p. pasante,** through bolt; **p. prisionero,** stud bolt; **p. torneado,** machined bolt; **p. U,** U bolt; **p. zurdo,** left-hand thread bolt.
pernoctar, *i.v.* to pass or spend the night, to stop for the night.
pernotar, *tr.v.* to note, observe.
pero, *m.* (variety of) apple.
pero, *conj.* 1. but, yet, and yet, e.g. *éste es chico p. me gusta más,* this one is smaller but (and yet) I like it better. 2. but, except, e.g. *hice buen viaje, p. empezó a llover,* I had a good trip, but (except that) it started to rain. 3. (coll.) but, so (a superfluous element used for emphasis at the beginning of some sentences), e.g. *p. ¿ya regresaste?* so, back already?; *p. ¡qué bien bailas!* but . . . how well you dance! —*m* objection, fault, defect, e.g. *siempre pones p. a todo,* you're always finding fault with everything; **¡no hay peros que valgan!** no ifs and buts!
perogrullada, *f.* (coll.) platitude, trite remark, obvious truth, truism.
perogrullesco, ca, *a.* platitudinous, trite, inane.
perojimén, *m., var. of* **pirojiménez.**
perojiménez, *m.* variety of grape grown in Andalusia; sherry made with this grape.
perol, *m.* pot, cauldron, kettle.
perola, *f.* small pot, cauldron or kettle.
perón, *m.* (Mex.) pear-shaped apple.
peroné, *m.* (anat.) fibula.
peroneo, a, *a.* (anat.) peroneal, fibular. —*m.* (anat.) peroneus; **p. lateral corto,** (anat.) peroneus brevis; **p. lateral largo,** (anat.) peroneus longus.
peroración, *f.* peroration, speech; (rhet.) peroration (conclusion of speech).
perorar, *i.v.* 1. to perorate, make a speech, orate. 2. to beseech.
perorata, *f.* long tiresome speech.
peroxidasa, *f.* (chem.) peroxidase.
peróxido, *m.* (chem.) peroxide.
perpejana, *f.* copper coin, pataca.
perpendicular, *a., f.* (geom.) perpendicular. — **p. media,** (geom.) mid-perpendicular.
perpendicularidad, *f.* perpendicularity.
perpendicularmente, *adv.* perpendicularly.
perpendículo, *m.* 1. plumb bob, plummet. 2. (geom.) altitude of triangle. 3. (mec.) pendulum.
perpetración, *f.* perpetration.
perpetrador, ra, *a.* perpetrating. —*m., f.* perpetrator, aggressor.
perpetrar, *tr.v.* to perpetrate, commit.
perpetua, *f.* (bot.) globe amaranth; **p. amarilla,** (bot.) everlasting flower; **p. encarnada,** (bot.) globe amaranth.
perpetuación, *f.* perpetuation.
perpetuamente, *adv.* perpetually, everlastingly.
perpetuán, *m.* (tex.) durance, coarse woolen fabric.
perpetuar, (*ref.* 55) *tr.v.* to perpetuate, make perpetual. —*r.v.* to be perpetuated.
perpetuidad, *f.* perpetuity.
perpetuo, tua, *a.* 1. perpetual, everlasting, endless, unending. 2. life, e.g. *cadena perpetua,* life imprisonment.
perpiaño, *a.* (archit.) with a projecting rib (an arch). —*m.* (archit.) bondstone, perpend.
perplejamente, *adv.* perplexedly.
perplejidad, *f.* perplexity, confusion, bewilderment.
perplejo, ja, *a.* perplexed, confused, bewildered.

perpunte, *m.* pourpoint, quilted doublet.
perqué, *m.* 1. old form of satirical composition. 2. lampoon, pasquinade.
perquiera, perquiero, *ref.* **perquirir.**
perquirir, (*ref. 43*) *tr.v.* to investigate, inquire into.
perra, *f.* 1. bitch, she-dog. 2. (vulg.) bitch, vixen (unpleasant woman). 3. (coll.) drunk, drunken bout. 4. (coll.) (child's) tantrum, fit. — **p. gorda,** (Sp., coll.) tencentime piece; **soltar la p.,** (coll.) to boast prematurely of having something.
perrada, *f.* 1. pack of dogs. 2. (vulg.) dirty or mean trick.
perramente, *adv.* (vulg.) very badly, despicably.
perrengue, *m.* 1. (coll.) peevish person, irritable, snappy person. 2. (derog.) Negro, black.
perrera, *f.* 1. kennel, doghouse; dog compartment (in train). 2. (coll.) arduous and poorly-paid job. 3. (coll.) poor payer, financial risk (person). 4. (coll.) (child's) tantrum, fit of temper.
perrería, *f.* 1. pack of dogs; gang of toughs or hoodlums. 2. angry remark or word. 3. dirty or mean trick.
perrero, *m.* 1. dog-catcher. 2. kennelman, keeper or master of hounds (for hunting). 3. dog-lover, dog-fancier.
perrezno, *m.* whelp, pup, puppy.
perrillo, *m.* 1. little dog. 2. trigger (of a gun). 3. curb (chain or strap attached to bit). — **p. de falda or faldero,** lap dog, pug; **p. de todas bodas,** (coll.) party-goer, party-lover.
perrito, *m.* little dog, doggie.
perro, rra, *a.* 1. (coll.) rotten, mean, miserable, hard, e.g. *este perro mundo,* this rotten world, *esta perra vida,* this bitch of a life. 2. (coll.) stubborn, tenacious. —*m.* 1. (zool.) dog. 2. dog, rotter (G.B.), cad, louse (sl.). 3. obstinate, tenacious person. — **a otro p. con ese hueso,** (coll.) tell it to the marines; **andar como perro y gato,** (coll.) to be like cat and dog, be at daggers drawn; **atar los perros con longaniza,** to live off the fat of the land; **darse a perros,** (coll.) to get furious; **de perros,** very bad, filthy, e.g. *tiempo de perros,* filthy weather, *humor de perros,* filthy temper; **echar a perros,** (coll.) to misuse (something), use badly; **hinchar el p.,** to exaggerate; **el p. del hortelano,** dog in the manger; **p. alano,** alan; **p. braco,** pointer, setter; **p. cobrador,** retriever; **p. de aguas,** spaniel; **p. de ajeo,** pointer, partridge-hunting dog; **p. de busca,** retriever; **p. de casta,** pedigreed dog; **p. de lanas,** poodle; lap dog; **p. de muestra,** pointer, setter; **p. de presa,** bulldog; **p. de San Bernardo,** St. Bernard; **p. de terranova,** Newfoundland dog, Labrador; **p. dogo,** bulldog; **p. faldero,** lapdog; **p. galgo,** greyhound; **p. gosque,** small yapping dog; **p. jateo,** foxhound; **p. ladrador, poco mordedor,** his bark is worse than his bite; **p. lebrel,** whippet; **p. lebrero,** harehound, harrier, rabbiter; **p. lobo,** wolfhound; **p. marino,** (ichth.) dogfish; **p. mastín,** mastiff; **p. mudo,** raccoon; **p. ovejero** or **pastor,** sheep dog; **p. pachón,** pointer; **p. pelado mexicano,** chihuahua; **p. perdiguero,** pointer, setter; **p. podenco,** hound; **p. policía,** police dog; **p. raposero,** foxhound; **p. rastrero,** sleuthhound; **p. sabueso,** bloodhound; **p. viejo,** (coll.) old dog, experienced person; **p. zorrero,** foxhound; **todo junto, como al p. los palos,** (coll.) it never rains but it pours; **tratar como a un p.,** (coll.) to treat like a dog.
perroquete, *m.* (mar.) topgallant mast.
perruna, *f.* dog bread (coarse bread given to dogs).
perruno, na, *a.* of or pertaining to dogs, canine.
persa, *a., m., f.* Persian. —*m.* Persian (language).
per se, (Lat.) by, of, for or in itself.
persecución, *f.* 1. persecution, harassment. 2. pursuit, chase. 3. (fig.) annoyance, harassing, pestering.
persecutorio, ria, *a.* 1. pursuing. 2. persecuting.
Perséfone, *f.* (myth.) Persephone, Proserpine, queen of Hades.
perseguidor, ra, *a.* 1. pursuing. 2. perse-cuting. —*m.,f.* 1. pursuer. 2. persecutor. —*f.* 1. (Peru) hangover (after drinking). 2. (Cuba) police car, patrol car.
perseguimiento, *m., var. of* **persecución.**
perseguir, (*ref. 77*) *tr.v.* 1. to pursue, chase, run after. 2. to persecute. 3. to chase around, pester, harass, pursue.
perseidas, *f.* (astron.) Perseids.
perseo, *m.* 1. (astron.) Perseus. 2. (myth.) Perseus, rescuer of Andromeda.
Persépolis, *m.* Persepolis, ancient capital of Persia.
persevante, *m.* pursuivant, pursuivant of arms.
perseverancia, *f.* perseverance.
perseverante, *a.* persevering.
perseverantemente, *adv.* perseveringly.
perseverar, *i.v.* to persevere, persist.
persiano, na, *a.* Persian. —*f.* 1. Venetian blind. 2. (tex.) flowered silk fabric.
persicaria, *f.* (bot.) persicary, lady's thumb.
pérsico, ca, *a.* Persian. —*m.* (bot.) peach (tree and fruit).
persignar, *tr.v.* to make the sign of the cross on. —*r.v.* 1. to cross oneself, make the sign of the cross. 2. (coll.) to make the first sale of the day. 3. (coll.) to cross oneself as sign of surprise or wonder.
pérsigo, *m.* (bot.) peach (tree and fruit).
Persio Flacco, *m.* (lit., hist.) Persius Flaccus, Roman satirist.
persistencia, *f.* persistence; obstinacy.
persistente, *a.* persistent, persisting.
persistir, *i.v.* 1. to persist. 2. to continue; **p. en,** to persist in.
persona, *f.* 1. person, individual; (*pl.*) people. 2. personage, personality. 3. (gram.) person. 4. (theat., lit.) character. 5. (theol.) person. — **de p. a p.,** person to person, man to man; **en p.,** in person; **hacer de su p.,** (coll.) to ease nature, evacuate the bladder, to have a bowel movement; **hacerse p.,** (coll.) to pretend to be someone; **p. agente,** (gram.) agent; **p. desplazada,** displaced person; **p. expatriada,** displaced person; **p. grata,** persona grata; **p. jurídica,** legal entity; **p. natural,** (law) natural person; **p. no grata,** persona non grata; **p. paciente,** (gram.) patient, recipient of action; **por su p.,** in person; **primera p.,** (gram.) first person.
personada, *a.* (bot.) personate.
personado, *m.* (ecc.) benefice (without jurisdiction).
personaje, *m.* 1. personage, personality. 2. (theat., lit.) character.
personal, *a.* 1. personal, private. 2. (gram.) personal. —*m.* personnel, staff. — **gastos de personal,** personnel expenses; **p. de cabina,** cabin staff; **p. de tierra,** (aer.) ground crew, ground staff; **p. de vuelo,** flight crew.
personalice, personalicé, *ref.* personalizar.
personalidad, *f.* 1. personality, distinctive character or nature. 2. personality, personal remark. 3. personality, (public) figure, personage. 4. (law) personality, legal status or capacity. 5. (psyc., philos.) personality. — **p. alternante** or **dual,** (psyc.) alternating, dual or double personality; **tener mucha p.,** to have a lot of personality.
personalismo, *m.* 1. personal remark, personality. 2. egotism. 3. antagonism, enmity, hostility. 4. (philos.) personalism.
personalista, *m., f.* (philos.) personalist.
personalizar, (*ref. 53*) *tr.v.* 1. to personalize. 2. (gram.) to make personal (an impersonal verb).
personalmente, *adv.* personally, in person.
personarse, *r.v.* 1. to have an interview, meet. 2. to appear in person. 3. (law) to appear (in court).
personería, *f.* 1. representation, duty or post of representative or agent. 2. (law) personality, legal capacity.
personero, *m.* representative, deputy, agent; solicitor.
personificación, *f.* personification.
personificar, (*ref. 50*) *tr.v.* to personify.
personifique, pesonifiqué, *ref.* **personificar.**
personilla, *f.* (derog.) shabby little person.
personudo, da, *a.* well-built, husky.
perspectiva, *f.* 1. perspective. 2. scene, vista, panorama, view. 3. outlook, prospect. 4. appearance. — **p. aérea,** aerial perspective; **p. cónica,** conical perspective; **p. isométrica,** isometric perspective; **p. lineal,** linear perspective.
perspectivo, *m.* expert in perspective.
perspectógrafo, *m.* perspectograph.
perspicacia, *f.* 1. perspicacity, shrewdness, sagacity. 2. keen sight.
perspicacidad, *f., var. of* **perspicacia.**
perspicaz, (*pl.* **perspicaces**), *a.* perspicacious, shrewd; keen-sighted.
perspicuidad, *f.* perspicuity, clearness, lucidity.
perspicuo, cua, *a.* perspicuous, clear.
persuadidor, ra, *m., f.* persuader. —*a.* persuasive.
persuadir, *tr.v.* to persuade. —*r.v.* to become persuaded or convinced.
persuasible, *a.* credible, plausible.
persuasión, *f.* persuasion, conviction.
persuasiva, *f.* persuasiveness.
persuasivamente, *adv.* urgently.
persuasivo, va, *a.* persuasive.
persuasor, ra, *a.* persuasive. —*m., f.* persuader.
persulfato, *m.* (chem.) persulfate.
pertenecer, (*ref. 45*) *i.v.* to belong; to pertain, appertain, concern, refer.
pertenecido, *m., var. of* **pertenencia.**
perteneciente, *a.* pertaining, referring; belonging.
pertenencia, *f.* 1. belonging. 2. ownership. 3. property, possession, holding. 4. appurtenance, accessory. 5. mining concession; claim.
pertenezca, pertenezco, *ref.* **pertenecer.**
pértiga, *f.* 1. perch (linear measurement). 2. pole, staff, rod; **p. del trole,** trolley pole.
pertigal, *m., var. of* **pértiga.**
pértigo, *m.* shaft, thill (of a wagon or carriage).
pertiguería, *f.* (ecc.) vergership, office of verger.
pertiguero, *m.* (ecc.) verger.
pertinacia, *f.* insistence, obstinacy, stubbornness, pertinacity, doggedness.
pertinaz, (*pl.* **pertinaces**), *a.* 1. pertinacious, tenacious, obstinate. 2. persistent.
pertinazmente, *adv.* pertinaciously, tenaciously.
pertinencia, *f.* pertinence, pertinency, relevancy, fitness.
pertinente, *a.* 1. pertinent, relevant; apt, fitting, appropriate. 2. (law) concerning, pertaining.
pertinentemente, *adv.* pertinently, appropriately, fittingly, opportunely.
pertrechar, *tr.v.* to equip, supply; to prepare; to store. —*r.v.* to equip, provide or supply oneself.
pertrechos, *m.* 1. (mil.) (*pl.*) supplies, stores; equipment. 2. tools, implements.
perturbable, *a.* perturbable, easily perturbed.
perturbación, *f.* disturbance; perturbation, agitation, excitement. — **p. atmosférica,** (meteorol.) atmospheric disturbance; **p. de la aguja,** (mar.) deviation of compass needle; **p. geomagnética,** (geoph.) geomagnetic disturbance.

perturbadamente, *adv.* in confusion, agitatedly, confusedly.
perturbador, ra, *a.* disturbing, upsetting; perturbing. —*m., f.* disturber; perturber.
perturbar, *tr.v.* to disturb, upset; to perturb; to interrupt. —*r.v.* to get disturbed, to become upset or perturbed.
Perú, *m.* Peru. — **valer un P.,** (coll.) to be worth a fortune.
peruanismo, *m.* Peruvianism.
peruano, na, *a., m., f.* Peruvian.
peruétano, *m.* 1. (bot.) wild pear (tree and fruit). 2. pointed tip or projection.
perulero, *m.* wide-bellied narrow-necked pitcher.
perulero, ra, *a., m., f.* Peruvian. —*m., f.* one who returns from Peru with a fortune.
perversamente, *adv.* perversely, wickedly.
perversidad, *f.* perversity, wickedness.
perversión, *f.* 1. perversion, perverting, corrupting. 2. perversion, depravity, depravation, corruption; wickedness.
perverso, sa, *a.* perverse, evil, depraved, wicked.
pervertido, da, *past part. of* **pervertir.** —*m., f.* pervert.
pervertidor, ra, *a.* perverting, corrupting. —*m., f.* perverter, corrupter.
pervertimiento, *m.* perversion, corruption.
pervertir, (*ref. 42*) *tr.v.* to pervert, corrupt, deprave. —*r.v.* to become perverted or corrupted.
pervibración, *f.* internal vibration.
pervierta, pervierto, *ref.* **pervertir.**
pervigilio, *m.* insomnia, sleeplessness, wakefulness.
pervirtiendo, pervirtiera, pervirtiese, pervirtió, *ref.* **pervertir.**
pervulgar, (*ref. 51*) *tr.v.* to divulge, publish, make known, proclaim.
peryodato, *m.* (chem.) periodate.
peryódico, ca, *a.* (chem.) periodic (acid).
peryoduro, *m.* (chem.) periodide.
pesa, *f.* 1. weight (for weighing). 2. dumbbell, weight (for weight lifting). 3. counterweight, weight. — **como caigan las pesas,** depending on the circumstances.
pesaácido, *m.* acidimeter.
pesacartas, *m.* letter-scales.
pesada, *f.* quantity weighed at one time.
pesadamente, *adv.* 1. heavily. 2. annoyingly, irritatingly, tiresomely. 3. slowly, sluggishly; clumsily.
pesadez, *f.* 1. heaviness; weightiness. 2. oppressiveness, heaviness (of the weather). 3. heaviness (of the head); drowsiness. 4. obesity, fatness. 5. tiresomeness, dullness; annoyance, nuisance. 6. slowness, sluggishness; clumsiness. 7. (phys.) gravity.
pesadilla, *f.* nightmare.
pesado, da, *past part. of* **pesar.** —*a.* 1. heavy, massive, weighty. 2. obese, corpulent. 3. deep, heavy (sleep). 4. heavy (head). 5. oppressive, heavy, sultry (weather). 6. slow, sluggish; clumsy. 7. dull, tiresome; annoying, irritating. 8. hard, onerous, arduous.
pesador, ra, *a.* weighing. —*m., f.* weigher.
pesadumbre, *f.* 1. grief, pain, sorrow; regret. 2. trouble, unpleasantness, harm. 3. heaviness, weight.
pesalicores, *m.* hydrometer.
pésame, *m.* condolences; **dar el p. por,** to send or express one's condolences for.
pesante, *a.* 1. weighty, weighing. 2. sad, contrite, regretful. —*m.* weight of half a drachm.
pesantez, *f.* (phys.) gravity.
pesar, *m.* sorrow, grief; regret, repentance; **a p. de,** in spite of, notwithstanding, withal; **a p. de todo,** for all that, nevertheless; **a. p. mío,** in spite of me, against my will.
pesar, *tr.v.* 1. to weigh. 2. (fig.) to weigh, examine, consider, ponder, e.g. *p. sus palabras,* to weigh one's words. 2. (Col.) to sell (meat). —*i.v.* 1. to weigh; to have weight. 2. to be heavy, e.g. *¡cómo pesa ésta caja!* how heavy this box is! 3. to grieve, cause sorrow or regret, make sad, e.g. *me pesa,* I'm sorry, I regret it. 4. to be important, have influence, carry weight, e.g. *su opinión pesa acá,* his opinion carries weight here; **mal que me, te, le, nos, os** or **les pese,** against my, your, her, his, our, or their wishes; **pese a,** in spite of; **pese a quien pese,** regardless of what anybody says, whatever happens.
pesario, *m.* (med.) pessary.
pesaroso, sa, *a.* 1. sorry, repentant, regretful. 2. sad, sorrowful.
pesca, *f.* 1. fishing, angling. 2. catch, haul. 3. fishing industry. — **¡brava, buena** or **linda p.!** (coll.) smart or clever customer; scoundrel, rogue; **p. costera** or **litoral,** coastal fishing; **p. de alta mar or altura,** deep-sea fishing; **p. de arrastre,** trawler fishing, trawling.
pescada, *f.* (ichth.) hake.
pescadería, *f.* fish market, fish shop.
pescadero, ra, *m.* fishmonger. —*f.* fishwife.
pescadilla, *f.* (ichth.) (variety of) weakfish (Cynoscion striatus), whiting.
pescado, *m.* fish (when caught); salted codfish. — **ahumársele a uno el p.,** (coll.) to get annoyed or huffy.
pescador, ra, *a.* fishing. —*m.* 1. fisherman; angler. 2. (ichth.) angler, goosefish. —*f.* fisherwoman.
pescante, *m.* 1. jib, boom (of crane or derrick). 2. (mar.) davit. 3. coach box; driver's seat or cab, coachman's seat. 4. (theat.) hoist. — **p. de la ancla,** (mar.) cathead.
pescar, (*ref. 50*) *tr.v.* 1. to fish, fish for. 2. to catch (fish; someone doing something). 3. (coll.) to get, catch, obtain; to manage to get. 4. (coll.) to hook, i.e. to marry (someone). —*i.v.* to fish; to angle.
pescozada, pescozón, *m.* blow on the neck or head.
pescozudo, da, *a.* thick-necked, bull-necked.
pescuezo, *m.* 1. neck, throat. 2. (fig.) haughtiness. — **andar al p.,** (coll.) to be on very bad terms, be at daggers drawn; **apretar** or **estirar el p. a,** (coll.) to throttle (someone); **torcer (uno) el p.,** (coll.) to die; **torcer el p. a,** (coll.) to wring someone's neck; to throttle (someone), wring (someone's) neck.
pescuño, *m.* wedge holding moldboard, coulter wedge (in plowhandle).
pesebre, *m.* manger; crib; **conocer el p.,** (coll.) to know where one can freeload.
pesebrejo, *m.* 1. *dim. of* **pesebre,** small manger. 2. alveolus, alveole (in horse's jaw).
pesebrera, *f.* rows or racks in a stable; mangers.
pesebrón, *m.* compartment under coach floor, boot (of a coach).
pesero, *m.* (Mex.) jitney, passanger vehicle, car pool.
peseta, *f.* peseta, monetary unit of Spain. — **cambiar la p.,** (coll.) to vomit, be sick.
pésete, *m.* curse, imprecation.
pesetero, ra, *a.* 1. cheap, costing a peseta. 2. (Guat., Ven., Peru) sponging, cadging. 3. (Cuba) tight-fisted, mean.
pesgua, *f.* (Ven., bot.) wintergreen (Gaultheria odorata).
¡pesia! *interj.* blast it! darn! confound it!
pesiar, *i.v.* to curse, swear.
pesillo, *m.* small scales (for weighing coins).
pésimamente, *adv.* very badly, wretchedly.
pesimismo, *m.* pessimism.
pesimista, *a.* pessimistic. —*m., f.* pessimist.
pésimo, ma, *a.* very bad, appalling, terrible.
peso, *m.* 1. weight; heaviness. 2. scales, balance. 3. importance, weight, influence; good sense, judgment. 4. burden, load, weight. 5. (numis.) piece of eight; (Amer.) peso (monetary unit, Argentina, Colombia, Cuba, the Dominican Republic, Mexico, Philippines, Uruguay). 6. food shop. — **a p. de dinero, oro** or **plata,** at an exorbitant price; **caerse de su p.,** (coll.) to be self evident, be patently obvious; **dar buen p.,** to give good weight; **de p.,** of the correct weight; sensible, serious; important, weighty; **de su p.,** naturally, by its own momentum; **en p.,** in the air; all, whole, entire, e.g. *el día y la noche en p.,* the whole night and day; doubtful, uncertain, undecided; **llevar en p. una cosa,** to have sole charge of something; **no valer a p. de oveja,** (coll.) to be contemptible; **p. absoluto,** (phys.) absolute weight; **p. atómico,** (phys.) atomic weight; **p. bruto,** gross weight; **p. de cruz,** beam and scales, balance; **p. de la prueba,** burden of proof; **p. dinámico,** live or moving load; **p. duro,** (numis.) piece of eight; **p. específico,** (phys.) specific gravity; **p. estático,** dead weight, dead load; **p. fuerte,** (numis.) piece of eight; **p. gallo,** (sport.) bantamweight; **p. liviano,** (sport) lightweight; **p. mediano,** (sport.) middleweight; **p. medio mediano,** (sport.) welterweight; **p. medio pesado,** (sport.) middleheavyweight; **p. molecular,** (phys.) molecular weight; **p. mosca,** (sport.) flyweight; **p. muerto,** dead weight; **p. neto,** net weight; **p. pesado,** (sport.) heavyweight; **p. pluma,** (sport.) featherweight; **p. semipesado.** (sport.) light heavyweight; **p. unitario,** unit weight; **p. welter,** welterweight, **tomar a p.,** to take the weight of, estimate the weight of (by lifting something); to examine, inspect.
pésol, *m.* pea.
pespuntador, ra, *a.* (sew.) backstitching, overcasting. —*m., f.* backstitcher, overcaster.
pespuntar, *tr.v.* (sew.) to backstitch, overcast.
pespunte, *m.* (sew.) backstitching; backstitch, overcasting.
pespuntear, *tr.v.* (sew.) to backstitch, overcast.
pesque, pesqué, *ref.* **pescar.**
pesquera, *f.* fishing ground, fishery.
pesquería, *f.* 1. fishing; fishing trade. 2. fishing ground, fishery.
pesquero, ra, *a.* fishing (boat, industry, etc.).
pesquis, *m.* (coll.) acumen, shrewdness, perspicacity.
pesquisa, *f.* inquiry, investigation, search.
pesquisante, *a.* inquiring, investigating.
pesquisar, *tr.v.* to inquire into, investigate, make inquiries into.
pesquisidor, ra, *a.* inquiring, investigating. —*m., f.* investigator, inquirer.
pestalociano, na, *a.* Pestalozzian, pertaining to the theories of the Swiss educator, J. H. Pestalozzi.
pestaña, *f.* 1. eyelash. 2. fringe, edging (on lace, cloth); edge of linen (left so that edge threads do not get entangled with stitches); edge, border (of paper, sheet or metal); rim (of wheel). 3. (*pl.*) (bot.) cilia, hairs. 4. (mec.) flange. — **no mover p.,** not to bat an eyelid, remain completely calm; **no pegar p.,** (coll.) not to sleep a wink; **pestañas vibrátiles,** (bot.) cilia; **quemarse las pestañas,** to burn the midnight oil.
pestañear, *i.v.* 1. to blink, wink. 2. (fig.) to be alive. — **no p.,** not to bat an eyelid; **sin p.,** without batting an eyelid.
pestañeo, *m.* blinking, winking.

pestañoso, sa, *a.* 1. having long eyelashes, having thick eyelashes. 2. (bot.) ciliate, hairy.
peste, *f.* 1. plague, pest; epidemic disease. 2. stench, stink, foul smell. 3. pestilence, evil, evil influence. 4. corruption, depravity. 5. (coll.) abundance. 6. (*pl.*) threats; curses, abuse. — **decir** or **hablar pestes de,** (coll.) to speak very badly of, run down; **p. blanca,** (med.) white plague (tuberculosis); **p. bubónica,** (med.) bubonic plague; **p. negra,** (med.) Black Death.
pesticida, *m.* (chem.) pesticide.
pestíferamente, *adv.* pestiferously.
pestífero, ra, *a.* stinking, foul; pestiferous, pestilential, noxious.
pestilencia, *f.* 1. pestilence, plague, pest. 2. stench, stink.
pestilencial, *a.* foul, stinking, pestilential, pestiferous, noxious.
pestilencioso, sa, *a.* pestilential.
pestilente, *a.* stinking, foul; pestilent, pestiferous, noxious.
pestillo, *m.* bolt (of lock); bolt, latch (on door). — **echar p.,** to bolt; **estar con p.,** to be bolted; **p. de golpe,** spring bolt.
pestiño, *m.* (cul.) honeyed fritters, honeyed doughnuts.
pestorejazo, *m.* blow on the back of the neck.
pestorejo, *m.* back of the neck.
pestorejón, *m.* blow on the back of the neck.
pesuña, *f.* 1. hoof (of cloven-hoofed animal). 2. (Arg., Chile) dirt or grime on the feet. 3. (Ecuad., Peru) smell of dirty feet.
pesuño, *m.* each half of a cloven hoof.
petaca, *a.* 1. (Amer.) heavy, awkward, slow. 2. (Amer.) lazy, idle. —*f.* 1. leather trunk; suitcase. 2. cigarette case, tobacco pouch. 3. (C. Amer.) hump (on back). 4. (Arg., Chile) tub, short fat person. 5. (Col., Hond.) belly, stomach. 6. (*pl.*) (Mex.) buttocks. 7. (P. Rico, Dom. Rep.) washing trough. 8. (Col.) laziness, sluggishness.
petacón, na, *a.* 1. (C. Amer.) humpbacked. 2. (Arg., Peru) tubby, fat, chubby. 3. (Ecuad., Mex.) big-buttocked.
petalismo, *m.* (hist.) petalism (form of ostracism practiced in ancient Syracuse).
pétalo, *m.* (bot.) petal.
petaloide, *a.* (bot.) petaloid.
petanque, *m.* (min.) silver ore.
petaquilla, *f.* small trunk or suitcase.
petar, *tr.v.* (coll.) to please, to gratify.
petardear, *tr.v.* 1. (mil., arch.) to batter with petards. 2. to cheat, swindle. —*i.v.* (auto.) to backfire.
petardeo, *m.* (auto.) backfire.
petardero, *m.* 1. (mil., arch.) petardier, soldier who sets a petard. 2. cheat, swindler.
petardista, *m., f.* cheat, swindler.
petardo, *m.* 1. (mil.) petard, bomb. 2. swindle, cheat, trick, fraud. — **pegar un p. a,** (coll.) to swindle or cheat (someone) out of money, to touch (someone) for money.
petaso, *m.* petasos, petasus (wide-brimmed hat used by Romans).
petate, *m.* 1. straw sleeping mat. 2. bed roll, bedding (of soldier, sailor or prisoner). 3. (coll.) baggage, belongings. 4. (coll.) swindler, cheat. 5. (coll.) good-for-nothing, scoundrel. — **liar el p.,** (coll.) to pack one's bags, leave, go away, move; to be dismissed or fired; to die, kick the bucket, turn up one's toes.
petenera, *f.* popular Andalusian song; **salir por peteneras,** (coll.) to speak out of turn, put one's foot in it.
petequia, *f.* (med.) petechia.
petequial, *a.* (med.) petechial.
petera, *f.* 1. (coll.) brawl, row. 2. (coll.) tantrum, fit of temper.
peteretes, *m.* (*pl.*) sweets, appetizing morsels, tidbits.
peticano, peticanon, *m.* (print.) petitcanon, two-line pica (26 point type).
petición, *f.* 1. petition, request; (law) claim, demand. 2. prayer, petition. — **p. de divorcio,** petition for divorce; **p. de extradición,** extradition request; **p. de mano,** formal asking for the hand of a woman; **p. de principio,** (log.) petitio principii (Lat.).
peticionario, ria, *a.* petitionary. —*m., f.* petitioner.
petifoque, *m.* (mar.) flying jib.
petigrís, *m.* common grey squirrel (name used in the fur trade).
petillo, *m.* stomacher, breast ornament formerly worn by women.
petimetra, *f.* overdressed woman; fashion plate (U.S., coll.)
petimetre, *m.* dandy, dude, fop.
petirrojo, *m.* (ornith.) robin, robin redbreast.
petiso, sa, *a.* (S. Amer.) short, stubby; chubby.
petitorio, ria, *a.* petitionary. —*m.* 1. (coll.) tiresome and constantly repeated request. 2. (pharm.) medicine catalogue. —*f.* (coll.) request, petition.
peto, *m.* 1. breastplate (of armor). 2. stommacher (ornamental covering for the chest). 3. (fenc.) plastron. 4. (zool.) plastron. — **p. volante,** second breastplate.
peto, *m.* (ichth.) peto, wahoo; (ichth.) pipefish, needlefish.
petra, *f.* (bot., Chile) (variety of) myrtle (Myrceugenia pitra).
petral, *m.* breastband, breast strap (of a horse's harness).
Petrarca, *m.* Petrarch, Italian lyric poet.
petraria, *f.* (hist., mil.) petrary, ballista.
petrarquesco, ca, *a.* Petrarchan, Petrarchian, pertaining to Petrarch.
petrarquista, *a.* Petrarchistic. —*m.* Petrarchist, admirer of Petrarch or his poetry.
petrel, *m.* (ornith.) petrel.
pétreo, a, *a.* stony, rocky, full of rocks; hard, rock-like; rock, of rock.
petrificación, *f.* petrification.
petrificante, *a.* petrifying.
petrificar, (*ref. 50*) *tr.v.* to petrify. —*r.v.* to become petrified.
petrífico, ca, *a.* petrifying.
petrifique, petrifiqué, *ref.* **petrificar.**
petrofísica, *f.* (pet.) petrophysics.
petroglifo, *m.* petroglyph, ancient stone or rock carving.
petrografía, *f.* petrography.
petrográfico, ca, *a.* (geoph.) petrographic.
petrógrafo, fa, *m., f.* (geoph.) petrographer.
petrolato, *m.* (pharm.) petrolatum, petroleum jelly.
petróleo, *m.* petroleum. — **p. bruto,** crude oil; oil in bulk; **p. combustible,** fuel oil.
petrolero, ra, *a.* 1. petroleum, e.g. *industria petrolera,* petroleum industry; oil, petrol, e.g. *buque petrolero,* oil or petrol tanker. 2. incendiary. —*m.* 1. petrol dealer (G. B.), gas or gasoline dealer. 2. petroleur (Fr.), incendiary. 3. petrol or oil tanker.
petrolífero, ra, *a.* oil-bearing, petroliferous, oil, e.g. *yacimientos petrolíferos,* oil deposits.
petrolífico, ca, *a.* petrolific.
petrolítico, ca, *a.* petrolithic.
petrología, *f.* petrology.
petrólogo, ga, *m., f.* petrologist.
Petronio, *m.* Petronius, Roman satirist.
petroquímica, *f.* petrochemistry.
petroquímico, ca, *a.* petrochemical.
petroso, sa, *a.* 1. petrous, stony, rocky. 2. (anat.) petrous. —*f.* (anat.) petrosal bone.
petulancia, *f.* 1. presumptuousness, arrogance, haughtiness. 2. sauciness; flippancy, impertinence.
petulante, *a.* 1. presumptuous, arrogant, haughty. 2. saucy; impertinent.
petulantemente, *adv.* 1. presumptuously, arrogantly. 2. saucily.
petunia, *f.* (bot.) petunia.
peucédano, *m.* (bot.) brimstonewort, hog's fennel.
peuco, *m.* (ornith.) rough-legged hawk (Buteo uncinatis).
peyorativo, va, *a.* derogatory, pejorative, disparaging, depreciatory; (gram.) pejorative.
peyote, *m.* peyote, mescal (plant and drink).
pez, (*pl.* **peces**), *m.* 1. fish (alive). 2. (coll.) a desirable thing or circumstance, e.g. *al fin cayó el p.,* at last (it happened, I got it, it came, etc.). 3. (*pl.*) (astron.) **P.,** the Fishes, Pisces. — **estar como el p. en el agua,** (coll.) to feel completely at home, be in one's element; **p. aguja,** (ichth.) needlefish, garfish; **P. Austral,** (astron.) Southern Fish, Piscis Australis; **p. ballesta,** (ichth.) triggerfish; **p. cofre,** (ichth.) boxfish, trunkfish; **p. de colores,** goldfish; **p. de San Pedro,** (ichth.) dory; **p. elefante** or **gallo,** (ichth.) elephant fish; **p. espada,** (ichth.) swordfish; **p. gordo,** (coll.) big noise; ringleader, key man, important person; **p. luna,** (ichth.) sunfish, moonfish; **p. martillo,** (ichth.) hammerhead; **p. mujer,** (zool.) manatee; **p. piloto,** (ichth.) pilot fish; **p. reverso,** (ichth.) remora, sucking fish; **p. sierra,** (ichth.) sawfish; **p. vela,** (ichth.) sailfish; **p. volador** or **volante,** (ichth.) flying fish; **picar el p.,** (coll.) to be taken in, fall for the bait or trap; (coll.) to win at cards; **salga p. o salga rana,** (coll.) whatever happens, regardless.
pez, (*pl.* **peces**), *f.* 1. pitch, tar. 2. meconium. — **dar la p.,** to get to the end or bottom of something; **estar p.,** (coll.) to be in the dark, know absolutely nothing; **p. blanca** or **de Borgoña,** white or Burgundy pitch; **p. elástica,** elastic bitumen, elaterite; **p. con p.,** completely empty or bare; **p. griega,** rosin, colophony.
pezolada, *f.* fag end (of cloth).
pezón, *m.* 1. stalk, stem. 2. nipple, teat. 3. end (of spindle or axle). 4. peg (in ox harness shaft to which the yoke is secured). 5. point, projection, cape (of land). 6. nipple, umbo (on lemon, etc.). 7. point, end (of various objects).
pezonera, *f.* 1. (mec.) linchpin. 2. nipple shield.
pezpalo, *m.* unsplit smoked codfish, stockfish.
pezpita, *f.* (ornith.) wagtail.
pezpítalo, *m., var. of* **pezpita.**
pezuelo, *m.* selvage (of cloth).
pezuña, *f.* hoof (esp. of cloven-hoofed animals).
Phnom Penh, *m.* Pnom Penh, capital of Cambodia.
pi, *f.* pi (sixteenth letter of Greek alphabet).
pi, *f.* (math.) pi.
piache, tarde p., (coll.) too late.
piada, *f.* 1. cheeping, chirping, peeping. 2. (coll.) borrowed phrase or expression.
piador, ra, *a.* cheeping, peeping, chirping.
piadosamente, *adv.* 1. piously, devoutly. 2. compassionately.
piadoso, sa, *a.* 1. merciful, compassionate. 2. pious, devout.
piafar, *i.v.* to paw, stamp (said of a horse).
pial, *m.* (Amer.) 1. lasso, lariat. 2. (Amer). snare, trap.
pialar, *tr.v.* (Amer.) to hobble (a horse).

piale, *m.* (Amer.) throw of the lasso.
piamadre, piamáter, *f.* (anat.) pia mater.
píamente, *adv.* 1. piously. 2. compassionately.
piamontés, sa, *a.* Piedmontese, of or pertaining to Piedmont, region of Italy. *—m., f.* Piedmontese.
pianista, *m., f.* 1. pianist, piano player. 2. piano manufacturer or dealer.
pianístico, ca, *a.* (mus.) of or pertaining to the piano.
piano, *m.* (mus.) piano; **p. de cola,** grand piano; **p. de manubrio,** piano organ, street piano; **p. de media cola,** baby grand; **p. mecánico,** player piano; **p. vertical,** upright piano; **tocar p.,** to play the piano. *—adv.* (mus.) piano, softly.
pianoforte, *m.* pianoforte, piano.
pianola, *f.* pianola.
pian, piano, *adv.* (coll.) little by little, slowly.
piante, chirping, peeping, cheeping. — **ni p. ni mamante,** not a living soul, e.g. *no quedó ni p. ni mamante,* not a living soul remained.
piar, (*ref. 54*) *i.v.* to cheep, chirp, peep; **p. por,** (coll.) to ask for, whine for.
piara, *f.* herd (of swine); drove (of mules, horses, etc.).
piariego, ga, *a.* said of one who owns a herd or drove of animals.
piastra, *f.* (numis.) piaster, piastre.
pibe, ba, *m., f.* (Arg., Urug.) kid, child.
pica, *f.* 1. (mil.) pike; pikeman. 2. (taur.) lance (of the picador). 3. stonecutter's hammer. 4. measurement of 14 feet for measuring depths. 5. (Amer.) annoyance, pique. 6. (Col., Ecuad., Guat., Ven.) narrow path. 7. (med.) pica, abnormal craving for unnatural foods. — **a p. seca,** by very hard and profitless work; **pasar por las picas,** to go through a lot of troubles; **poner una p. en Flandes,** (coll.) to achieve a triumph, perform a great feat; **sacarle p. a alguien,** (Amer.) to annoy, peeve or pique someone.
picacero, ra, *a.* magpie-hunting (said of a hawk).
picacho, *m.* sharp peak or summit (of a mountain).
picada, *f.* 1. bite, peck, pricking. 2. (Amer.) path, trail. 3. (Arg.) narrow ford. 4. (aer.) dive, nose-dive. 4. (Cuba, coll.) a hinted request for a loan.
picadero, *m.* 1. riding school; school where picadors train their horses. 2. (carp.) planing board. 3. hole dug by a buck (when sharpening its horns against a tree during the rutting season). 4. (mar.) boat skid, boat block. 5. (coll.) bachelor apartment.
picadillo, *m.* (cul.) hash; minced meat; filling (for sausages, meat turnovers, piroshky, etc.).
picado, da, *past part. of* **picar.** *—a.* 1. pinked, perforated; pitted. 2. pricked; pecked, bitten. 3. minced, chopped, shredded, cut. 4. choppy (sea). 5. decayed (tooth). 6. (Amer.) merry, tipsy, lit up. 7. (mus.) staccato. — **p. de viruelas,** pock-marked. *—m.* 1. (cul.) hash. 2. (aer.) dive, nose-dive.
picador, *m.* 1. horsebreaker; (taur.) picador. 2. (kitchen) chopping block. 3. (min.) cutter (miner who extracts ore). — **p. de limas,** (mec.) file cutter.
picadura, *f.* 1. bite, sting; peck; prick. 2. perforation. 3. pit, hole, mark (caused by smallpox, woodworm, corrosion); pitting (caused by corrosion). 4. cut, nick (in a dress). 5. shag, shredded tobacco, pipe tobacco. 6. cavity, decayed spot (in tooth). — **p. bastarda,** bastard cut (file); **p. cruzada,** double cut (file).
picafigo, *m.* (ornith.) beccafico, figpecker.
picaflor, *m.* 1. (ornith.) hummingbird. 2. (Amer.) Casanova, girl chaser.
picagallina, *f.* (bot.) chickweed.
picagrega, *f.* (ornith.) shrike.
picajón, picajoso, sa, *a.* touchy, querulous, easily offended.
pical, *m.* crossroads.
picamaderos, *m.* (ornith.) woodpecker.
picana, *f.* (S. Amer.) goad; **p. eléctrica,** electric shock torture.
picanear, *tr.v.* (S. Amer.) to goad, goad on.
picante, *a.* 1. pricking; biting, stinging. 2. very hot, highly seasoned (sauce, stew). 3. stinging, biting, mordant (remarks). 4. risqué, blue (joke). *—m.* 1. piquancy. 2. mordacity, acrimoniousness. 3. (Amer.) very hot sauce, highly seasoned sauce.
picantemente, *adv.* sharply; piquantly.
picantería, *f.* (Peru) restaurant, food stall, tavern (where highly spiced foods are sold).
picaño, ña, *a.* lazy, shameless, ragged. *—m.* patch (on a shoe).
picapedrero, ra, *m.* stonecutter, quarry worker.
picapica, *f.* 1. itch-producing plant. 2. (coll.) itch, itching.
picapleitos, *m.* 1. troublemaker, quarrelsome person. 2. pettifogging lawyer.
picaporte, *m.* latch; latchkey; door knocker; **p. de resbalón,** spring latch.
picaposte, *m.* (ornith.) woodpecker.
picapuerco, *m.* (ornith.) spotted woodpecker (Dryobates medius).
picar, (*ref. 50*) *tr.v.* 1. to prick, puncture, pierce (with needle, etc.). 2. to punch (a bus ticket). 3. (taur.) to prick (the bull) with a lance. 4. to pit, mark (the skin). 5. to peck (bird); to sting, bite (insect, snake). 6. to chop, mince, shred. 7. to peck at (food), bite, nibble (baitfish). 8. (fig.) to fall for (a trick). 9. to cause itching; to make sting or burn. 10. to burn, sting (the mouth or tongue, e.g. pepper). 11. to nibble, pick at. 12. to spur (a horse). 13. to train (a horse). 14. to hit (a billiard ball) vertically at the side. 15. to perforate, pink (paper or cloth with ornamental patterns). 16. to cut (stones); to chip (walls for re-plastering). 17. to roughen, make rough (a grindstone). 18. to arouse, provoke, incite. 19. to annoy, vex, pique. 20. (mar.) to cut, chop. 21. (mar.) to speed up (rate of rowing). 22. (mar.) to operate (a pump). 23. (mil.) to pursue, harass. 24. (mus.) to play staccato. 25. (p.) to stipple, to surface (with a tool). *—i.v.* 1. to itch; to burn, smart. 2. to be hot, burn (highly spiced food). 3. to nibble, peck, eat little amounts (of food). 4. to burn, be very hot (the sun). 5. to pick up, become brisk (business). 6. to begin, start; to break out (an epidemic). 7. to have a slight knowledge (of), have a smattering (of). 8. to dive. — **p. en,** to be something of, have pretensions to being; **p. muy alto,** to fly too high, aim too high. *—r.v.* 1. to become moth-eaten; to become worm-eaten. 2. to begin to rot or go rotten; to decay (a tooth); to go vinegary or sour (wine). 3. to be in heat (animal). 4. to become choppy (sea). 5. to get annoyed, take offense, become piqued. 6. to think a lot of oneself. — **picarse de,** to boast of being, have pretensions to being.
pícaramente, *adv.* 1. roguishly, mischievously, impishly. 2. crookedly, schemingly; basely. 3. cunningly, craftily.
picaraza, *f.* (ornith.) magpie.
picarazado, da, *a.* (Cuba) pock-marked.
picardear, *i.v.* to be a rogue or scoundrel; to be lewd, mischievous or roguish. *—r.v.* to acquire bad habits.
picardía, *f.* 1. mischievousness, roguishness, impishness. 2. roguish remark, impish remark. 3. cunning, craftiness, astuteness. 4. crookedness, knavery; baseness, vileness. 5. trick, ruse, game. 6. gang of rogues.
picardihuela, *f. dim. of* **picardía,** prank, mischief, trick.
picaresca, *f.* gang of rogues; life of a rogue or vagabond.
picarescamente, *adv.* roguishly; impishly, mischievously.
picaresco, ca, *a.* 1. roguish; mischievous, impish, gay, saucy. 2. (lit.) picaresque, ribald. 3. (fig.) picaresque, colorful (e.g. life).
picaril, *a., var. of* **picaresco.**
pícaro, ra, *a.* 1. roguish; mischievous. 2. swindling, scheming, crooked; vile, low, base. 3. cunning, crafty, astute. *—m., f.* 1. rogue; rascal, scamp, imp, little devil. 2. scoundrel, swindler, cheat. *—m.* (lit.) rogue, vagabond (hero of the picaresque novel). — **p. de cocina,** scullion, kitchen boy.
picarón, na, *a. aug. of* **pícaro,** roguish, mischievous, impish. *—m., f.* rogue, scamp, rascal. *—m.* (Chile) ring-shaped cruller or fritter.
picaronazo, za, picarote, *a. aug. of* **picarón,** notorious rogue.
picarrelincho, *m.* (ornith.) woodpecker.
picarro, *m.* (ornith.) woodpecker.
picatoste, *m.* (Sp., cul.) fried bread; buttered toast.
picaza, *f.* (ornith.) magpie; **p. chillona** or **manchada,** (ornith.) shrike; **p. marina,** (ornith.) flamingo.
picazo, *m.* 1. jab, jab with a pike or spear; pike or spear wound. 2. peck, bite. 3. young magpie.
picazo, za, *a.* piebald, black and white. *—m.* piebald horse.
picazón, *f.* 1. itch, itching, smarting. 2. annoyance, displeasure, peevishness.
picazuroba, *f.* (ornith.) purple-breasted bird similar to the turtledove.
pícea, *f.* (bot.) spruce.
píceo, a, *a.* piceous, pitchy, of or pertinent to pitch.
pichagua, *f.* (Ven., bot.) calabash.
pichagüero, *m.* (Ven., bot.) calabash tree.
pichana, *f.* (Arg., Chile, Peru) bass broom.
pichanga, *f.* (Col.) broom.
piche, *a.* 1. white (wheat). 2. (Col., Ven.) rotten, bad, sour. 3. (C. Amer.) mean, stingy, niggardly. *—m.* 1. white wheat. 2. (Amer., coll.) fear. 3. (Col.) push, shove. 4. (Arg.) (variety of) armadillo. 5. (Col.) curd (of sour milk).
pichel, *m.* pewter tankard or beer mug.
pichelería, *f.* tankard or pitcher factory or shop.
pichelero, *m.* one who makes pitchers or tankards.
pichelingue, *m., var. of* **pechelingue,** pirate.
pichi, *m.* (bot.) pichi.
pichicato, ta, *a.* (Amer.) mean, stingy.
pichicho, *m.* (Arg.) doggie, little dog.
pichihuén, *m.* (ichth.) umbra (Umbrina ophicephala).
pichincha, *f.* (Arg.) bargain; lucky break.
pichinchero, ra, *a.* (Arg.) bargain-hunting. *—m., f.* bargain hunter.
pichiñique, *a.* (Chile, coll.) stingy, niggardly. *—m.* (Chile) effeminate little man.
pichirre, *a.* (Ven., coll.) stingy, niggardly.
picho, *m.* (Chile) doggie, little dog.
pichoa, *f.* (Chile, bot.) (variety of) spurge (Euphorbia portulacoides).
pichocal, *m.* (Mex.) pigsty.
picholear, *i.v.* 1. (Hond., Mex.) to play for low stakes. 2. (Guat.) to cheat. 3. (Chile, Hond.) to go out on a spree, have a party. 4. (Arg.) to pilfer, be a petty thief. 5. (Arg., Bol.) to make a living by doing odd jobs.
picholeo, *m.* 1. (Chile) spree, merry-making. 2. (Arg.) small business deal.

pichón, *m.* 1. young pigeon, squab. 2. (coll.) dear, darling, pigeon.
pichona, *f.* (coll.) dear, darling.
pichopisque, *m.* (Mex.) swineherd.
pichoso, sa, *a.* (Col.) watery-eyed.
pichulear, *i.v.* (Arg.) to do odd jobs for a living. —*t.v.* (Chile, vulg.) deceive, trick.
Picio, más feo que P., as ugly as sin.
pickup, (Angl.) *m.* pickup (of record player).
picles, *m.* pickles, gherkins.
picnic, *m.* (gal.) picnic.
pícnico, ca, *a.*, pyknic, of or designating a fleshy, squatty body.
picnidio, *m.* (bot.) pycnidium.
picnogónido, *m.* (zool.) pycnogonid.
picnómetro, *m.* (phys.) pycnometer.
pico, *m.* 1. beak, bill (of bird). 2. sharp point; corner, tip. 3. spout (of teapot); spout, mouth, lip (of jug). 4. (Chile, vulg.) penis. 5. pick, pickax. 6. peak, summit (of mountain); peak (mountain with a sharp peak). 7. bit, small amount, fraction, e.g. *son las tres y p.,* it's a little after three o'clock, *cuesta mu y p.,* it costs a bit more than a thousand. 8. (coll.) mouth, trap, (coll.) e.g. *ciérrate el p.,* close your trap. 9. loquacity, gift of gab; garrulity. 10. small herd of cows. 11. (Chile) edible acorn barnacle. 12. (mar.) gaff. — **andar de picos pardos,** (coll.) to loaf around, to go out looking for an escapade; **a p. de jarro,** (to drink) like a fish, to excess; **callar el p.,** (coll.) to keep quiet, shut up, keep one's mouth shut; **hacer el p. a uno,** to feed someone, provide someone with food; **hincar el p.,** (coll.) to die; **perder** or **perderse por el p.,** (coll.) to talk too much for one's own good; **p. cangrejo,** (mar.) gaff; **p. de cigüeña,** (bot.) heron's bill; **p. del ancla,** anchor bill; **p. de oro,** silver tongue, good speaker; **tener mucho p.,** (coll.) to talk a lot, be garrulous.
pico, *m.* (ornith.) woodpecker; **p. barreno** or **carpintero,** woodpecker; **p. de frasco,** (Ven.) toucan; **p. verde,** (ornith.) green woodpecker.
picofaradio, *m.* (elec.) micromicrofarad.
picofeo, *m.* (Col., ornith.) toucan.
picola, *f.* (stonecutter's) small pick.
picolete, *m.* bolt staple.
picolina, *f.* (chem.) picoline, picolin.
picón, na, *a.* 1. having protruding upper teeth (said of animals). 2. touchy, sensitive, easily offended. —*m.* 1. lampoon, jest. 2. charcoal for braziers. 3. broken rice. 4. small fresh-water fish.
piconero, *m.* 1. charcoal maker or dealer. 2. (taur.) picador.
picor, *m.* burning (of the mouth); itch, itching.
picoso, sa, *a.* pock-marked.
picota, *f.* 1. gibbet, pillory. 2. spire, top, peak, point. 3. (mar.) cheek (of pump). 4. children's game.
picotada, picotazo, *m.* peck; bite, sting; blow with the beak.
picote, *m.* (tex.) 1. goat's hair cloth. 2. work jacket.
picoteado, da, *a.* 1. having many points or corners. 2. nibbled, pecked. 3. pinked, shredded, cut (paper, cloth.).
picotear, *tr.v.* 1. to peck, to bite (with the beak). 2. to nibble food. —*i.v.* 1. to toss the head (said of horse). 2. (coll.) to chatter, prattle, jabber. —*r.v.* (coll.) to wrangle, quarrel.
picotería, *f.* (coll.) garrulity, talkativeness, gossip.
picotero, ra, *a.* (coll.) garrulous, talkative. —*m., f.* (coll.) chatterbox, garrulous person, jabberer.
picotillo, *m.* low quality goat's hair cloth.
picrato, *m.* (chem.) picrate.
pícrico, *a.* (chem.) picric.
picrita, *f.* (min.) picrite.
picrotoxina, *f.* (chem.) picrotoxin.
picto, picta, *a.* Pictish. —*m., f.* Pict (member of an ancient tribe of N. Britain).
pictografía, *f.* pictography, picture writing.
pictográfico, ca, *a.* pictographic.
pictórico, ca, *a.* pictorial.
picuda, *f.* (Cuba, ichth.) great barracuda, picuda.
picudilla, *f.* 1. (ornith.) (variety of) rail. 2. (Cuba, ichth.) picudilla, small barracuda.
picudo, da, *a.* 1. beaked; pointed; spouted, having a spout. 2. long-snouted. 3. (coll.) jabbering, garrulous, talkative. 4. (Mex.) smart, clever. 5. (Dom. Rep.) cowardly, weak. —*m.* 1. long spit or skewer. 2. (ento.) weevil, grub. 3. (Cuba) ridiculous person.
pida, *ref.* **pedir.**
pidén, *m.* (Chile, ornith.) bird similar to a coot.
pidiendo, *ref.* **pedir.**
pidientero, *m.* beggar.
pidiera, pidieron, pidiese, *ref.* **pedir.**
pido, *ref.* **pedir.**
pídola, *f.* leapfrog (children's game).
pidón, na, *a.* (coll.) *var. of* **pedigüeño.**
pie, *m.* 1. (anat.) foot. 2. foot (of sock, stocking). 3. base (e.g. of column). 4. basis, foundation. 5. foot, bottom, end. 6. foot (linear measurement); (poet.) foot (group of syllables comprising a metrical unit). 7. occasion, opportunity, reason, cause. 8. trunk (of tree), stem (of plant). 9. small plant, tree, young tree. 10. sediment, lees. 11. mass of trodden grapes ready for pressing. 12. caption, legend (under a photo or an illustration). 13. (theat.) cue. 14. (print.) foot (lower part of a letter). 15. (Chile) down payment. — **a cuatro pies,** on all fours; **a los pies de Ud.,** at your service (said only to women); **al p. de,** at the foot of, at the bottom of; near, close to; nearly, almost; **al p. de la letra,** literally, to the letter, exactly according to instructions; **al p. de la fábrica** or **la obra,** (com.) at the factory or delivered to the site; **andar de p. quebrado,** (coll.) to be crestfallen or low (in spirits); to be low (in health); to be down and out (in fortune); **a p.,** on foot; **a p. enjuto,** dry-shod, without wetting one's feet; without risk; without effort; **a p. firme,** without moving, standing fast; **a p. juntillas,** firmly, steadfastly, stubbornly; **a p. llano,** flat, smooth; easily, without obstacles; **arrastrar los pies,** to be old and weak; **buscar cinco** or **tres pies al gato,** (coll.) to go looking for trouble; **caer de pie,** to land on one's feet; **cerrado como p. de muleto,** (coll.) stubborn, obstinate; **comer por los pies a,** to cause (someone) great expense; **con buen p.,** well, successfully; **con mal p.,** on the wrong foot, unfortunately, badly; **con p. derecho,** well, successfully; **con pies de plomo,** very slowly, very carefully; **cortar por el p.,** to cut down; **dar p.,** to give reason or cause; **de a p.,** foot, e.g. *soldado de a p.,* foot soldier; **dejar a uno a p.,** to dismiss or fire someone to leave someone out on the street; **del p. a la mano,** from one moment to another, at any moment; **de p.,** standing (as opposed to sitting), e.g. *estar de p.,* to be standing, be standing up; **de pies a cabeza,** from head to foot; **echar p. a tierra,** to alight, get down, dismount; **en buen p.,** in good order; well, successfully; **en p.,** standing (as opposed to being knocked down), e.g. *no quedó ni un edificio en p.,* not one building was left standing; up, working, e.g. *estuve en p. hasta las once,* I was up till eleven o'clock; up and about (after illness), e.g. *ya anda* or *está en p.,* he's already up and about again; **en p. de guerra,** on a war footing, ready for war; **entrar con buen p.** or **con el p. derecho,** to make a good start; **estar con el p. en el estribo,** to be about to leave; **estar con un p. en la sepultura,** to have one foot in the grave; **faltarle a uno los pies,** to lose one's balance; **hacer con los pies,** to do (something) very badly; **hacer p.,** to be in one's depth, be able to stand, have a firm footing (i.e. to reach the bottom of river with one's feet); to make a pile (of grapes for pressing); to be confident, be sure of oneself; **ir a p.,** to walk, go on foot; **írsele los pies a uno,** to slip, slide; to make a slip or an error; **irse por pies,** to run away, escape; **levantarse con el p. izquierdo,** to get up on the wrong side of the bed; **mirarse los pies,** to look down at one's feet (in humility, etc.); **buenos pies,** agility, swiftness; **nacer de p.,** to be born with a silver spoon in one's mouth, be born lucky; **no dar p. con bola,** to make one mistake after another, do nothing right; **no dar p. ni patada,** to do nothing at all; **no dejar a uno sentar el p. en el suelo,** to keep a person constantly on the run; **no tener pies ni cabeza,** to make no sense whatsoever, have neither head nor tail, be without rhyme or reason; **no poner los pies en el suelo,** to fly, go like the wind; **pararle los pies a uno,** to put someone in his place; **perder p.,** to lose one's footing; to go out of one's depth (in the water or in a conversation); **p. ante p.,** step by step; **p. con p.,** very closely; **¡p. a tierra!** dismount! (order given to cavalry); **piebujía,** (phys.) candle-foot; **p. columbino,** (bot.) alkanet, dyer's alkanet; **p. cuadrado,** square foot; **p. cúbico,** cubic foot; **p. de altar,** perquisites received by clergy apart from their salary; **p. de amigo,** bracket, support, prop; **p. de atleta,** (med.) athlete's foot; **p. de burro,** (zool.) acorn barnacle; **p. de cabalgar,** left foot of mounted rider; **p. de cabra,** crowbar; **p. de fotografía,** caption; **p. de guerra,** war footing, combat readiness; **p. de imprenta,** (print.) imprint, printer's mark; **p. de león,** (bot.) lion's foot; **p. de liebre,** (bot.) hare's-foot or rabbit-foot clover; **p. de paloma,** (bot.) alkanet, dyer's alkanet; **p. derecho,** (archit.) upright, upright or vertical prop; **p. de rey,** caliper square, slide caliper; **p. de tierra,** small plot of land; **p. de trinchera,** (med.) trench foot; **p. equino,** clubfoot; **p. forzado,** (poet.) rhyme established beforehand for certain poetic compositions; **p. por segundo, (engin.) foot-second; p. quebrado,** (poet.) short line; **pies planos,** flat feet; **p. tonelada,** (mec.) foot-ton; **poner a uno a los pies de los caballos,** (coll.) to treat someone like dirt; to talk very badly about someone; **poner pies en la pared,** (coll.) to stand firm, dig one's heels in, insist (on one's opinion, point of view); **poner pies en polvorosa,** (coll.) to run away, flee, take it on the lam; **ponerse de p.,** to stand up, rise; **ponerse de pie en un negocio,** (coll.) to understand a business completely; to take charge of a business; **quedarse a p.,** to miss (a plane, train); **recalcarse el p.,** to twist one's foot; **sacar a uno el p. del lodo,** (coll.) to help someone out of a spot or fix; **sacar los pies del plato,** (coll.) to become independent, begin to take certain liberties; **salir por pies,** (coll.) to beat it, take a powder; **ser pies y manos de alguien,** to be someone's right hand man, be someone's constant helper; **tener el p. en dos zapatos,** to have several irons in the fire; **tomar p.,** to gain strength; to take root; **tomar p. de,** to make use of (something as a pretext); **un p. tras otro,** time to go, off you go now; **vestirse por los pies,** (coll.) to be a man; **volver p. atrás,** to go back, retrace one's footsteps; (fig.) to back out, withdraw.

pie-acre, *m.* acre-foot.
pie-bujía, *m.* foot-candle.
piececillo, piececito, *m. dim. of* **pie,** little foot.
piecezuela, *f. dim. of* **pieza,** little piece.
piecezuelo, *m. dim. of* **pie,** little foot.
piedad, *f.* 1. piety, piousness. 2. pity, mercy. 3. (art.) Pietà (representation of the Virgin Mary holding body of Jesus Christ on her lap). — **tener p. de,** to have pity for, have mercy on.
piedra, *f.* 1. rock, stone. 2. (med.) stone (in bladder). 3. hail. 4. foundling home. 5. flint (in musket). 6. grindstone, millstone. 7. trick, point (in cards). — **a p. y lodo,** shut tight; **echar a p.** or **en la p.,** to place (one's child) in a foundling home; **hallar la p. filosofal,** to find the keystone to power or riches; **no dejar p. por mover,** to leave no stone unturned; **no dejar p. sobre p.,** to raze to the ground, destroy completely. **no quedar p. sobre p.,** to be razed to the ground; **picar la p.,** to work or cut stone; to roughen the surface of a millstone; **p. abrasiva,** abrasive stone, honing stone; **p. afiladera** or **aguzadera,** whetstone, grindstone; **p. alumbre,** (min.) alum rock salumite; (chem.) alum; **p. amarga,** (min.) picrolite; **p. amoladera,** whetstone, grindstone; **p. angular,** (bldg., fig.) corner stone, keystone; **p. arcillosa,** clay stone; **p. arenisca,** sandstone; **p. aromática,** (min.) amber; **p. azufre,** (min.) brimstone, sulphur; **p. bendita** or **de cubierta,** (mar.) holystone; **p. berenguela,** (min.) alabaster; **p. berroqueña,** (min.) granite; **p. bezar** or **bezoar,** bezoar, bezoar rock; **p. biliar,** (med.) gallstone; **p. ciega,** opaque precious stone; **p. de aceite,** oilstone; **p. de afilar** or **amolar,** whetstone, grindstone; **p. de albardilla,** (archit.) coping stone; **p. de cal,** (min.) limestone; **p. de campana,** (Col.) clinkstone, phonolite; **p. de chispa,** flint, flintstone; **p. de escandalo,** source of gossip; **p. de escopeta** or **de fusil,** flint, flintstone; **p. del águila,** (min.) eaglestone; **p. de eslabón,** (min.) flint; **p. de granizo,** hail, hailstone; **p. de Huamanga,** (Peru) alabaster; **p. de jabón,** (min.) saponite; **p. de la luna,** (min.) moonstone; **p. de las Amazonas,** (min.) amazonite; **p. del Labrador,** (min.) Labrador stone, Labradorite; **p. del sol,** (min.) sunstone; **p. de lumbre,** flint, flintstone; **p. de Moca,** (min.) Mocha stone, moss agate; **p. movediza nunca moho la cobija,** a rolling stone gathers no moss; **p. de pipa,** (min.) meerschaum; **p. de rayo,** thunderbolt, thunderstone; **p. de remate,** (archit.) coping stone; **p. de Rosetta** or **Roseta,** (archaeol.) Rosetta stone; **p. de sapo,** (Arg.) mica; **p. de toque,** (min.) touchstone; (fig.) touchstone; **p. falsa,** imitation precious stone; **p. filosofal,** philosopher's stone; **p. fina,** precious stone; **p. fundamental,** (bldg., fig.) foundation stone; **p. imán,** lodestone; **p. infernal,** lunar caustic, silver nitrate; **p. jaspe,** jasper; **p. lipis,** (chem.) copper sulfate, blue vitriol; **p. mármol,** marble; **p. meteórica,** meteoric stone, meteorite; **p. nefrítica,** (min.) nephrite, nephritic stone; **p. pómez,** pumice stone; **p. preciosa,** precious stone; **p. rodada,** smooth pebble; **p. sanguínea,** (min.) bloodstone; **p. seca,** (bldg.) dry stone, loose gravel; **p. sonora,** (min.) clinkstone, phonolite; **p. voladora,** millstone for grinding olives; **poner la primera p.,** to lay the foundation stone (of a building or enterprise); **señalar con p. blanca,** to put out the flags on (a certain day in celebration); **señalar con p. negra,** to remember (a day) with sadness; **tener uno su p. en el rollo,** to be an important person or a prominent citizen; **tirar uno piedras,** (coll.) to be furious, be boiling with anger.
piedrezuela, *f. dim. of* **piedra,** small stone.
piel, *f.* skin; fur; hide, pelt; leather; peel (of fruit). — **abrigo de pieles,** fur coat; **dar** or **soltar uno la p.,** (coll.) to kick the bucket, die; **p. brillante** or **luciente,** (med.) glossy skin; **p. de cabra,** goatskin; **p. de cabritilla,** kidskin; **p. de foca,** sealskin; **p. de gallina,** goose flesh; **p. de león,** lion skin; **p. de naranja,** orange peeling; **p. de Rusia,** Russian leather; **p. de serpiente,** snakeskin; **p. de zorro,** fox fur; **p. roja** (*m., f.*) redskin (derog.); **p. sintetica,** synthetic leather; **ser la p. del diablo,** (coll.) to be a handful, be a little devil, be unruly; **vender la p. del oso antes de cazarlo,** to count one's chickens before they are hatched.
piélago, *m.* 1. (poet.) sea, ocean, high, open sea. 2. (fig.) sea, mass, countless number; abundance.
pielecita, *f. dim. of* **piel,** smooth skin; small hide or skin.
pielgo, *m., var. of* **piezgo.**
pie-libra, *m.* (engin.) foot-pound.
pielitis, *f.* (med.) pyelitis.
pielografía, *f.* (med.) pyelography.
pielograma, *m.* (med.) pyelogram, pyelograph.
pielonefritis, *f.* (med.) pyelonephritis.
piemia, *f.* (med.) pyemia, pyaemia.
piémico, ca, *a.* pyemic, pyaemic.
piense, pienso, *ref.* **pensar.**
pienso, *m.* fodder, dry hay, feed.
pienso, *m.* idea, thought; **ni por p.,** absolutely not, not even in dreams.
pierdo, pierda, *ref.* **perder.**
piérides, *f.* (*pl.*) (myth.) Pierides, the Muses.
pierio, ria, *a.* (poet.) Pierian, pertaining to the Muses.
pierna, *f.* three of a kind (in poker).
pierna, *f.* 1. leg. 2. branch, leg (of a compass). 3. unevenness of sides of cloth. 4. jar or small pitcher. 5. down stroke (in writing). 6. quarter (of a nut kernel). — **dormir a p. suelta** or **tendida,** to sleep like a log; **echar a uno la p. encima,** (coll.) to beat or do better than someone; **en piernas,** (coll.) barelegged; **estirar la p.,** (coll.) to kick the bucket, die; **estirar** or **extender las piernas,** (coll.) to stretch one's legs, go for a walk; **hacer piernas,** to be firm on its legs (a horse); to stand one's ground, be steadfast; **meter** or **poner la p. al caballo,** to spur a horse on; **ser una buena p.,** (Arg., Urug.) to be a good sport.
piernitendido, da, *a.* with legs extended.
pietismo, *m.* (rel.) pietism.
pietista, *a.* pietist, pietistic. —*m., f.* pietist.
pieza, *f.* 1. piece (of music; of ordnance; of jewelry; of furniture; of game, quarry; work of art). 2. piece, bit (coin). 3. piece, length, roll (of cloth, paper). 4. part (of machine, apparatus). 5. room (in house). 6. period (of time); plot (of land). 7. (theat.) play, piece. 8. (her.) ordinary heraldic charge. 9. piece, man (in chess, checkers). 10. component (of a whole). — **buena, gentil** or **linda p.,** (coll.) rogue, sly fox, scoundrel (man); minx, hussy (woman); little devil, rogue, scamp (child); **de una p.,** honest, upright; **jugar una p. a,** to play a dirty trick on; **p. de autos,** (law) item entered in evidence; documentary evidence; **p. de batir,** siege gun; **p. de convicción,** piece of evidence; **p. de examen,** examination piece (examinations); (fig.) excellent piece of work; **p. de leva,** (mar.) farewell salute (fired by ship when setting sail); **p. dentaria,** tooth; **p. de oro,** gold piece; **p. de recibo,** reception room; **p. de repuesto,** spare part; **p. honorable,** (her.) honorable ordinary; **p. por p.,** bit by bit; very carefully; **quedarse de una p.** or **hecho una p.,** (coll.) to be dumbfounded, be greatly surprised.
piezgo, *m.* 1. hole (of the animal's leg or paw) in a hide or a skin. 2. wineskin.
piezodieléctrico, *a.* (elec.) piezodielectric.
piezoelectricidad, *f.* piezoelectricity.
piezoeléctrico, ca, *a.* piezoelectric.
piezógrafo, *m.* (phys.) piezograph.
piezometría, *f.* (phys.) piezometry.
piezométrico, ca, *a.* (phys.) piezometric.
piezómetro, *m.* (phys.) piezometer.
piezorresonador, *m.* (acous.) piezo resonator.
pífano, *m.* (mus.) fife; fife player.
pifia, *f.* 1. miscue (in billiards). 2. (coll.) slip, blunder, fumble.
pifiar, *tr.v.* 1. to make a miscue of (a stroke in billiards). 2. (Amer.) to boo, whistle at, to make fun of, jeer. —*i.v.* to make the blowing too audible, to wheeze (in playing a flute). — **pifiarse de,** (Amer.) to make fun of.
pigargo, *m.* (ornith.) sea eagle, osprey, fish hawk.
pigidio, *m.* (zool.) pygidium.
Pigmalión, *m.* (myth.) Pygmalion, sculptor and lover of Galatea.
pigmentación, *f.* pigmentation.
pigmentar, *tr.v.* to pigment, to color with pigment.
pigmentario, ria, *a.* pigmentary, pertaining to pigment.
pigmento, *m.* pigment.
pigmeo, a, *a.* very small, dwarfish. —*m., f.* 1. (myth., ethnol.) Pygmy. 2. pygmy, dwarf, very small person. 3. (fig.) insignificant, unimportant person.
pigmoide, *a.* pygmoid; (fig.) very small, Pygmy-like.
pignoración, *f.* pledging, pawning.
pignorar, *tr.v.* to pledge, pawn, hypothecate.
pignoraticio, cia, *a.* pignorative, pledging; pertaining to a pledge or security.
pigre, *a.* sluggish, lazy, slothful; negligent.
pigricia, *f.* sloth, sluggishness, laziness, negligence.
pigro, gra, *a., var. of* **pigre.**
píhua, *f.* sandal.
pihuela, *f.* 1. jess (on hawk's legs). 2. obstacle, hindrance. 3. (*pl.*) shackles, fetters.
píico, ca, *a.* (med.) pyic.
piina, *f.* (biochem.) pyin.
pijama, piyama, payama, (gen. *pl.*) *m.* pajamas. —*f.* (Car.) pajamas.
pijibay, *m.* (C. Rica, Hond.) (variety of) cohune palm (Bactris utilis).
pijije, *m.* (C. Rica, El Salv., Guat.) tree duck (Dendrocygna arborea).
pijojo, *m.* (Cuba) wild tree yielding yellow hardwood.
pijota, *f.* (ichth.) (variety of) weakfish (Cynoscion striatus). — **hacer pijotas,** to play at ducks and drakes.
pijote, *m.* (artil.) small caliber gun; swivel gun for grapeshot.
pijotería, *f.* annoying trifle, annoying remark.
pijotero, ra, *a.* 1. annoying, tiresome, bothersome. 2. (Cuba, Mex.) stingy, niggardly.
pila, *f.* 1. sink, basin; trough, tank; (baptismal) font. 2. pile, heap. 3. parish, parishioners. 4. (engin.) pier, pillar, buttress (of bridge). 5. (her.) pile. 6. (phys., elec.) pile. 7. (elec.) battery, cell. 8. amount of wool cut each year by one sheep farmer. 9. (Arg.) hairless dog. 10. (Amer.) fountain. 11. (Cuba) tap, faucet. — **nombre de p.,** Christian name; **p. atómica,** (phys.) atomic pile; **p. atómica de reacción en cadena,** (phys.) chain reactor, chain-reacting pile; **p. de bicromato,** (elec.) bichromate cell; **p. de circuito**

cerrado, (elec.) closed-circuit battery; **p. de gravedad,** (elec.) gravity cell; **p. de selenio,** (elec.) selenium cell; **p. húmeda,** (elec.) wet cell; **p. patrón,** (elec.) standard cell; **p. primera,** (elec.) primary cell; **p. seca,** (elec.) dry cell, dry battery; **p. voltaica** or **de Volta,** (chem.) voltaic pile, electric column; **sacar de p.** or **tener en p. a,** to stand as godfather for.

pilada, *f.* 1. pile, heap. 2. batch of mortar or cement. 3. quantity of cloth fulled at one time.

pilapila, *f.* (Chile) malvaceous plant used medicinally (Modiola caroliniana).

pilar, *m.* 1. basin, tank, trough (of fountain). 2. pillar, column. 3. (fig.) pillar, column, prop (person). 4. milestone. 5. bedpost.

pilar, *tr.v.* to hull or husk (grain) by pounding.

pilarejo, *m. dim. of* **pilar,** small pillar.

pilastra, *f.* (archit.) pilaster, square column.

pilastrón, *m. aug. of* **pilastra,** large pilaster.

pilatero, *m.* (tex.) fuller (of cloth).

Pilatos, *m.* (Bib., hist.) **Poncio P.,** Pontius Pilate.

pilca, *f.* (S. Amer.) stone wall.

pilcha, *f.* (Amer.) piece of clothing; (*pl.*) clothes, belongings.

pilche, *m.* (Peru) wooden bowl or cup.

píldora, *f.* 1. (pharm.) pill, pellet. 2. (coll.). unpleasant chore or news. — **dorar la p.,** (coll.) to sugarcoat the pill; **p. soporífera** or **para dormir,** sleeping pill; **tragarse la p.,** (coll.) to fall for the story, swallow a tall story.

pildorero, *m.* (pharm.) pill roller (device).

píleo, *m.* pileus, skullcap; (ecc.) pileus, Cardinal's biretta.

pilero, *m.* workman who mixes clay for bricks or pottery.

pileta, *f.* 1. *dim. of* **pila,** small basin, tank or trough. 2. holy water font. 3. (Arg.) swimming pool; water tank.

pilífero, ra, *a.* piliferous, hairy.

pilla, *f.* plunder, pillage.

pillada, *f.* (coll.) prank, trick, knavery.

pillador, ra, *a.* pillaging, plundering. —*m., f.* pillager, plunderer.

pillaje, *m.* 1. theft, larceny. 2. pillaging, plundering, looting.

pillar, *tr.v.* 1. to plunder, pillage, loot. 2. to catch. 3. (coll.) to catch (someone doing something).

pillastre, pillastrón, *m.* (coll.) rogue, rascal.

pillear, *i.v.* to be a rogue or rascal.

pillería, *f.* 1. (coll.) gang of rogues or rascals. 2. (coll.) prank, knavery.

pillete, pillín, *m.* (coll.) street urchin; little scamp, young rascal.

pillo, lla, *a.* 1. roguish, mischievous, rascally. 2. (coll.) crafty, sly, astute. —*m.* 1. rogue, rascal, scamp, scalawag, little devil. 2. crafty fellow, rogue. 3. thief, housebreaker. 4. (ornith.) ibis (Pseudocolopteryx acutipennis).

pilluelo, *m.* (coll.) 1. little rogue, rascal, scamp; little devil. 2. street urchin.

pilme, *m.* (Chile, ento.) blister beetle (Cantharis femoralis).

pilo, *m.* pilum, javelin (used in ancient Rome).

pilo, *m.* (Chile, bot.) pelu.

pilocarpina, *f.* (chem.) pilocarpine.

pilón, *m.* 1. basin, trough (of a fountain). 2. pounding mortar. 3. conical sugar loaf. 4. movable weight (of a steelyard). 5. counterpoise, counterweight (of an olive press). 6. heap of plaster. 7. pounder, drop hammer (for pounding earth or asphalt). 8. (archit.) pylon. — **beber del p.,** (coll.) to pass on gossip; **haber bebido del p.,** to become less severe (a judge); **llevar (a uno) al p.,** (coll.) to lead one by the nose.

piloncillo, *m.* (Mex.) brown sugar, unrefined sugar.

pilonero, ra, *a.* gossiping, gossipmongering. —*m., f.* newsmonger.

pilongo, ga, *a.* 1. thin, emaciated. 2. (benefice) granted to those baptized in certain fonts or parishes. — **castaña pilonga,** peeled and dried chestnut.

pilórico, ca, *a.* (anat.) pyloric.

píloro, *m.* (anat.) pylorus.

pilosidad, *f.* hairiness, pilosity.

piloso, sa, *a.* pilose, pilous, hairy.

pilotaje, *m.* 1. (mar.) piloting, art of piloting. 2. (mar.) pilotage (fee paid to pilot). 3. (bldg.) piles, piling, pilework.

pilotar, *tr.v.* to pilot (boat, plane); to drive (car.)

pilotáxico, ca, *a.* (geol.) pilotaxitic.

pilote, *m.* (bldg.) pile; **p. de arena,** (bldg.) sand pile; **p. de pedestal** or **pie abultado,** pedestal pile; **p. de rosca,** screw pile.

pilotear, *tr.v., var. of* **pilotar.**

pilotín, *m. dim. of* **piloto,** pilot's mate, second pilot.

piloto, —*a.* pilot. *m.* 1. pilot, navigator; driver (of car). 2. (mar.) mate, first mate. 3. (fig.) pilot, leader, director. 4. (auto.) taillight, parking light. — **co-p.,** co-pilot; **p. automático,** (avia.) automatic pilot, pilot aid; gyropilot, mechanical pilot; **p. de altura,** helmsman, steersman (on high seas); **p. de carreras,** racing driver; **p. de pruebas,** (aer.) test pilot; **p. de puerto,** harbor pilot; **primer p.,** (mar.) first officer.

pilpilén, *m.* (Chile, ornith.) oyster catcher (Hoematopus palliatus).

piltrafa, *f.* 1. sinewy meat. 2. (*pl.*) scraps (of food). — **estar hecho una p.,** to be a complete wreck.

pilucho, cha, *a.* (Chile, coll.) naked.

pilvén, *m.* (Chile) fresh-water fish.

pimental, *m.* pepper field or plot.

pimentero, *m.* 1. (bot.) pepper plant, black pepper. 2. pepper pot, pepperbox. — **p. falso,** pepper tree.

pimentón, *m.* (cul.) paprika (powdered red pepper fruit used as a condiment).

pimienta, *f.* 1. pepper (spice). 2. (fig., coll.) piquancy, vivacity. — **comer uno p.,** (coll.) to get angry; **p. blanca,** white pepper; **p. de Chiapa** or **de Tabasco,** grains of Paradise, melegueta pepper, allspice (seeds of allspice tree); **p. falsa,** pepper tree seed; **p. inglesa,** (cul.) allspice; **p. loca** or **silvestre,** (bot.) chaste tree, agnus castus; **p. malagueta,** allspice tree; **p. negra,** black pepper; **ser como una p.,** (coll.) to be very sharp, smart or quick; **tener mucha p.,** (coll.) to be very lively or provocative.

pimiento, *m.* 1. (bot.) capsicum, pepper (plant and fruit), sweet or bell pepper, green pepper, red (ripe) pepper, chili (sweet and hot varieties). 2. (cul.) paprika. 3. rust (parasitic fungus). — **p. de bonete,** (bot.) bonnet pepper; **p. de cerecilla,** (bot.) bird pepper; **p. de cornetilla,** (bot.) hot pepper, chili; **p. de hocico de buey,** (bot.) bonnet pepper; **p. de las Indias,** (bot.) bird pepper; **p. loco, montano or silvestre,** (bot.) chaste tree, agnus castus; **p. morrón,** (bot.) bonnet pepper.

pimpante, *a.* 1. elegantly dressed, elegant. 2. graceful, poised, self-assured.

pimpido, *m.* (ichth.) dogfish.

pimpín, *m.* children's pinching game.

pimpina, *f.* (Ven.) earthenware water-cooling jug.

pimpinela, *f.* (bot.) salad burnet, pimpernel.

pimplar, *tr.v., r.v.* (coll.) to drink (wine).

pimpleo, a, *a.* of the Muses.

pimpollada, *f.* **pimpollar,** *m.* tree nursery; plantation of young trees.

pimpollecer, (*ref. 45*) *i.v.* to sprout, bud.

pimpollejo, *m. dim. of* **pimpollo,** young sprout, sucker or shoot; tender bud.

pimpollezca, *ref.* **pimpollecer.**

pimpollo, *m.* 1. sprout, shoot (of plants or trees). 2. flower bud, bloom. 3. young tree. 4. (coll.) handsome child, handsome young man or girl.

pimpolludo, da, *a.* full of sprouts, shoots or buds.

pina, *f.* 1. conical boundary stone or landmark. 2. felloe, felly, rim (of wheel).

pinabete, *m.* (bot.) fir tree.

pinacate, *m.* (Mex., ento.) black stinkbug.

pinacoteca, *f.* art gallery, pinacotheca.

pináculo, *m.* 1. (archit.) pinnacle, top. 2. (fig.) pinnacle, acme, summit.

pinado, da, *a.* (bot.) pinnate (leaf).

pinar, *m.* pine grove.

pinarejo, *m. dim. of* **pinar,** small pine grove.

pinariego, ga, *a.* pertaining to a pine.

pinastro, *m.* (bot.) pinaster, cluster pine.

pinatero, *m.* (Cuba, ornith.) crow.

pinatífido, da, *a.* (bot.) pinnatifid.

pinatipartido, da, *a.* (bot.) pinnatisect.

pinatisecto, ta, *a.* (bot.) pinnatisect.

pinaza, *f.* (mar.) pinnace.

pincarrasca, *f., var. of* **pincarrasco.**

pincarrascal, *m.* (bot.) Aleppo pine grove.

pincarrasco, *m.* (bot.) Aleppo pine.

pincel, *m.* 1. (artist's) paint brush, pencil. 2. brush (artist's style, technique), artist, painter. 3. (mar.) tar brush. 4. filoplume, second feather in a martin's wing.

pincelación, *f.* (med.) pencilling, painting a wound by means of a brush.

pincelada, *f.* brush stroke; **dar la última p. a,** to give the last touches to.

pincelar, *tr.v.* (art.) to paint; to paint a portrait of.

pincelero, ra, *m., f.* paintbrush maker or seller. —*m.* artist's brush case or box.

pincelote, *m. aug. of* **pincel,** big brush.

pincerna, *m., f.* cupbearer, one who serves drinks.

pinchadura, *f.* prick, jab, puncture, piercing.

pinchar, *tr.v.* 1. to prick, jab; to puncture, pierce. 2. (fig.) to stir up, provoke. 3. to anger, annoy. — **no p. ni cortar,** to have little influence, voice or say (in an affair).

pinchaúvas, (*pl.* **pinchaúvas**), *m.* 1. (coll.) grape pilferer, grape sampler (in a store or market). 2. (coll.) good-for-nothing, ne'er-do-well.

pinchazo, *m.* 1. prick, stab, jab; puncture. 2. prod, push (someone to do something). — **a prueba de pinchazos,** (auto.) puncture-proof, punctureless (tire); (fig.) immune to barbs and darts.

pinche, *m.* scullion, kitchen boy.

pincho, *m.* 1. thorn, spine (on plants). 2. prod, goad; skewer; sharp point; (Amer.) hatpin. 3. exciseman's sampling stick. 3. (cul.) tidbits broiled and served on skewers.

pinchón, *m.* (ornith.) chaffinch.

pinchudo, da, *a.* (coll.) prickly.

pindárico, ca, *a.* (lit.) Pindaric, characteristic of the Greek poet Pindar.

Píndaro, *m.* Pindar, lyric poet of ancient Greece.

Pindo, *m.* Pindus, mountain range in Greece.

pindonga, *f.* (coll.) gadabout (woman).

pindonguear, *i.v.* (coll.) to gad about, gallivant about, be always out of the house (a woman).

pineal, *a.* (anat.) pineal.

pineda, *f.* 1. pine grove or forest. 2. (Sp., arch.) embroidered cotton ribbon formerly used for making garters.

pinedo, *m.* (S. Amer.) pine grove.

pineno, *m.* (chem.) pinene.

pinga, *f.* 1. (Phil. I.) shoulder yoke (for carrying loads). 2. (Cuba, vulg.) penis, prick (vulg.).

pingajo, *m.* (coll.) rag, tatter.

pingajoso, sa, *a.* ragged, tattered.

pinganello, pinganillo, *m.* icicle.

pinganitos, en p. (coll.) in good fortune, in a high position.
pingar, (*ref. 51*) *i.v.* 1. to drip. 2. to jump. 3. to hang, droop.
pingo, *m.* 1. (coll.) rag, tatter. 2. (coll.) horse; (Arg., Bol., Urug.) fast horse; (Peru, Chile) nag, hack. 3. good-for-nothing, ne'er-do-well. 4. (Mex.) devil. 5. (*pl.*) (coll.) cheap clothes. — **andar, estar or ir de p.,** (coll.) to gad about (women).
pingopingo, *m.* (Chile) joint fir (Ephedra andina).
pingorote, *m.* (coll.) pointed tip or object; projection.
pingorotudo, da, *a.* (coll.) lofty, high.
pingotear, *i.v.* to jump, buck (horse).
pingue, *m.* turreted steamer, cargo boat with built-up sides (in order to carry more cargo).
pingue, pingué, *ref.* **pingar.**
pingüe, *a.* 1. greasy, oily, fatty. 2. plentiful, abundant. 3. substantial (profits).
pingüedinoso, sa, *a.* fatty, greasy, oily.
pingüino, *m.* (ornith.) penguin.
pinguosidad, *f.* fattiness, oiliness, greasiness.
pinífero, ra, *a.* (poet.) piniferous, full of pines.
pinillo, *m.* (bot.) ground pine, herb ivy, yellow bugle (Ajuga chamaepytis); (bot.) mock cypress.
pinita, *f.* (chem.) pinite, pinitol.
pinito, *m.* first step; **hacer pinitos,** to begin to walk, take its first steps (a child).
pinjante, *a.* pendent, hanging. —*m.* 1. pendant (jewel). 2. (archit.) pendant, boss.
pinnípedo, da, *a.* (zool.) pinnipedian, pinniped. —*m.* (zool.) pinniped; (*pl.*) Pinnipedia.
pino, *m.* 1. (bot.) pine, pine tree. 2. (poet.) bark, vessel, ship. 3. (Chile) meat-pie filling. — **p. albar** (bot.) Scotch pine; nut pine, piñón; **p. alerce,** (bot.) larch; **p. aparrado,** (bot.) Scotch pine; **p. araucano,** (bot.) Chilean pine, monkey puzzle; **p. blanco americano,** (bot.) white pine; **p. carrasco or carrasqueño,** (bot.) Aleppo pine; **p. cascalbo,** (bot.) Austrian pine; **p. de Brasil,** (bot.) Brazilian pine, Paraná pine; **p. de Valsaín,** (bot.) Scotch pine; **p. doncel** o **manso,** (bot.) nut pine, piñón; **p. gigantesco,** redwood; **p. marítimo,** (bot.) seaside pine, cluster pine, pinaster; **p. melis,** (bot.) variety of Austrian pine; **p. negral,** (bot.) Austrian pine; **p. negro,** (bot.) mountain pine; Swiss mountain pine; **p. Oregón,** (bot.) Oregon Pine, Paraná pine; **p. piñonero,** (bot.) piñón, nut pine; **p. pudio,** (bot.) Austrian pine; **p. rodeno,** (bot.) cluster pine, seaside pine, pinaster; **p. rojo,** redwood; red or Norway pine; red fir; red spruce; **p. salgareño,** (bot.) Austrian pine; **p. tea,** (bot.) pitch pine; **ser uno como un p. de oro,** (coll.) to be handsome, have good bearing and appearance.
pino, na, *a.* steep. —*m.* (coll.) first step (of a child or convalescent); **a pino,** turning them completely around (bells); **en pino,** standing, straight, upright; **hacer pinos,** to start to walk, take one's first steps.
pinocha, *f.* pine needle, pine leaf.
pinol, *m.* 1. (C. Rica, Ecuad., Guat.) pinole (aromatic powder formerly used in chocolate). 2. (C. Amer., Mex.) drink made from ground toasted corn, sugar, water and ice. 3. (Ecuad.) pinole (flour made from any of various cereals).
pinolate, *m.* (Guat.) beverage made of pinole flour, water and sugar.
pinole, *m.* 1. pinole (aromatic powder formerly used for flavoring chocolate). 2. (Mex., C. Amer.) pinole (flour made from any of various cereals). 3. (C. Amer.) refreshing drink made with ground toasted corn, honey and water.
pinolillo, *m.* 1. (Mex.) small red tick. 2. (Hond.) drink made from pinole mixed with sugar, cocoa and cinnamon.
pinoso, sa, *a.* piny.
pinsapar, *m.* grove of Spanish firs.
pinsapo, *m.* (bot.) Spanish fir.
pinta, *f.* 1. spot, mark; dot. 2. drop (of liquid). 3. edge mark on Spanish cards denoting suit. 4. look, appearance, mien, aspect; characteristic trait or feature. 5. cue ball (in billiards). 6. (*pl.*) lansquenet, faro (card game). 7. (*pl.*) (med.) kind of psoriasis. 8. (Arg., Col., Ecuad., P. Rico) lineage, caste. 9. (Arg., Peru, P. Rico) color (of animals). 10. (Bol., Chile, Peru) dice game. 11. pint (liquid measure). — **descubrir a uno por la p.,** (coll.) to recognize someone by some characteristic feature or trait; **hacer la p.,** (Mex.) **irse de p.,** (C. Amer.) to play hooky or truant; **no dejarse ver la p.,** (Col., Peru., P. Rico) to keep one's intentions secret; **no tener p. de,** not to look like, not to have the appearance of; **ser pura p.,** to be all show, be all window dressing.
pintacilgo, *m.* (ornith.) goldfinch.
pintada, *f.* (ornith.) guinea fowl.
pintadera, *f.* baker's tool for decorating cakes, bread, etc.
pintadillo, *m.* (ornith.) goldfinch.
pintado, da, *past part. of* pintar. —*a.* spotted, dotted, mottled, speckled. **el más pintado,** the cleverest, the most prudent, sensible or experienced; the best one; **pintado** or **como pintado,** just right, exactly, perfectly, e.g. *eso me cae como pintado,* this suits me just fine; **estar** or **venir pintado** or **como pintado,** to be just right, be just the thing.
pintamonas, *m., f.* (coll.) dauber, poor painter.
pintar, *tr.v.* 1. to paint (a picture, a wall). 2. to decorate (pastry, etc.). 3. to write (an accent mark, letter). 4. to paint, describe, depict. 5. to exaggerate. — **p. de,** to paint, e.g. *p. el cuarto de azul,* to paint the room blue; **pintarla,** to put on airs. —*i.v.* 1. to paint. 2. to begin to ripen or turn red. 3. (coll.) to show up to be, turn out to be. 4. to be one's business, e.g. *¿qué pintas tú aquí?* what are you doing here? — **p. como querer,** to indulge in wishful thinking. —*r.v.* 1. to make up, paint one's face. 2. to begin to ripen or turn red. — **pintarse solo para,** (coll.) to have a special ability or aptitude for, be right up one's alley, e.g. *me pinto solo para este trabajo,* this work is just up my alley.
pintarrajar, pintarrajear, *tr.v.* 1. to daub, paint. 2. to make up in a gaudy fashion, put heavy make-up on.
pintarrajo, *m.* (coll.) daub, daubing (poorly painted picture).
pintarroja, *f.* (ichth.) dogfish.
pintear, *i.v.* to drizzle.
pintica, illa, *f. dim. of* **pinta,** small spot or dot.
pintiparado, da, *past part. of* **pintiparar.** —*a.* 1. exactly like. 2. just right, ideal. **p. a** or **para,** ideal or just right for.
pintiparar, *tr.v.* 1. to liken, make alike. 2. to compare.
Pinto, estar uno entre Pinto y Valdemoro, (coll.) to be half-drunk.
pintojo, ja, *a.* spotted, mottled, speckled.
pintón, na, *a.* 1. ripening, half-ripe (fruit) 2. half-baked (brick). 3. (Peru) very handsome or well-dressed. —*m.* 1. (ento.) corn borer. 2. disease caused to grain crops by corn borer.
pintor, ra, *m., f.* 1. painter, artist. 2. house painter. — **p. abstractor,** abstract painter; **p. de brocha gorda,** house painter; **p. de paisajes,** landscape painter; **p. de retratos,** portrait painter.
pintoresco, ca, *a.* picturesque.
pintorrear, *tr.v.* (coll.) to daub.
pintura, *f.* 1. painting, art of painting. 2. painting, picture. 3. paint, pigment. 4. picture, portrayal, description. — **hacer pinturas,** (coll.) to caper (a horse); **no poder ver a nuno ni en p.,** (coll.) not to be able to stand the sight of somebody; **p. a la aguada,** water color; **p. al encausto,** (p.) encaustic painting; **p. al fresco,** (p.) fresco, wall painting; **p. al óleo,** (p.) oil painting; **p. al pastel,** (p.) pastel (drawing); **p. al temple,** (p.) tempera painting; **p. alumínea** or **aluminica,** aluminum painting; **p. anticorrosiva,** anticorrosive paint; **p. de aguazo,** (p.) gouache; **p. grafitada,** graphite paint; **p. ignífuga,** fireproof paint; **p. rupestre,** cave painting or drawing; p. termorreflectora, heat-reflecting paint; **p. vidriada,** enamel paint.
pinturero, ra, *a.* vain, conceited, conscious of his or her good looks. —*m., f.* vain person; one who flaunts his or her good looks.
pinuca, *f.* (Chile) edible shellfish.
pínula, *f.* 1. pinnule, sight (of an optical instrument). 2. (zool.) pinnule.
pinza, *f.* 1. (sew.) tuck (in a dress). 2. (*pl.*) tweezers; pliers, nippers; clamp (also in sing.). 3. (*pl.*) (dent., surg.) forceps, clamp. 4. (*pl.*) (zool.) pincers, nippers (claws of crab, scorpion, etc.).
pinzón, *m.* 1. (mar.) pumphandle (of suction pump). 2. (ornith.) chaffinch. — **p. real,** (ornith.) bullfinch.
pinzote, *m.* (mar.) tiller; (mar.) pintle.
piña, *f.* 1. (bot.) pine cone, pine nut. 2. (bot.) pineapple. 3. (Phil. I.) piña cloth. 4. knot, crush, cluster (of people); cluster (of things). 5. (mar.) wall knot. 6. (metal.) pina, conical mass of spongy silver left after retorting. 7. (Amer., reg.) blow, punch. — **darse de piñas,** (Amer.) to come to blows; **p. de América,** pineapple; **p. de ciprés,** cypress cone.
piñal, *m.* (Amer.) pineapple plantation.
piñata, *f.* piñata, hanging pot filled with candies and small gifts which is broken with a stick at a masquerade or children's party; party featuring this entertainment.
piñatería, *f.* (Ven.) armed holdup.
piñon, *m.* 1. pine nut, piñon. 2. (bot.) pignole (nut). 3. (ornith.) pinion (last bone on a bird's wing); pinion, flight feather. 4. last mule (in drove). 5. catch (in trigger of some firearms). — **comer los piñones en alguna parte,** to spend Christmas Eve somewhere; **estar a partir un p. con,** to be intimate friends with.
piñón, *m.* 1. (ornith.) pinion, flight feather. 2. (mec.) pinion. — **p. diferencial,** (aut.) gear differential; **p. motor,** (mec.) driving pinion.
piñonata, *f.* conserve of almonds.
piñonate, *m.* 1. pine nut candy. 2. fritters bathed in honey.
piñoncillo, *m.* (ornith.) pinion, flight feather.
piñonear, *i.v.* 1. to click (as a gun when being cocked). 2. to cry (said of partridges in rut). 3. (coll.) to show signs of growing up (said of children). 4. (coll.) to behave like a young buck (said of mature men).
piñoneo, *m.* 1. click, clicking (the trigger of a gun). 2. squawk, cry of partridges in rut.
piñonero, ra, *a.* **pino piñonero,** (bot.) nut pine, piñon. —*m.* (ornith.) bullfinch.
piñuela, *f.* 1. silk cloth. 2. (bot.) cypress nut.
pío, *m.* 1. cheeping, peeping (of chickens). 2. longing, yearning. — **no decir ni p.,** (coll.) not to say a word.
pío, a, *a.* 1. pious, devout. 2. merciful, compassionate. 3. pinto, piebald (said of horses).
piocha, *f.* 1. jeweled hair ornament. 2. handmade feather flower. 3. (Mex.) pointed beard, Vandyke beard. 4. bricklayer's hammer.
pioderma, *f.* (med.) pyoderma.
piodermatosis, *f.* (med.) pyodermatosis.

piodermia, *f.* (med.) pyoderma.
piogenia, *f.* (med.) pyogenesis, formation of pus.
piogénico, ca, piógeno, na, *a.* (med.) pyogenic.
piojento, ta, *a.* lousy, louse-ridden.
piojería, *f.* 1. lousiness, abundance of lice. 2. (fig.) poverty.
piojillo, *m.* (ento.) bird louse.
piojo, *m.* 1. (ento.) louse. 2. (min.) splinter shooting off the head of drill when struck by a hammer. — **como p.** or **piojos en costura,** (coll.) like sardines in a can (cramped); **p. de mar,** whale louse; **p. pegadizo,** (coll.) pest, leech (someone difficult to get rid of); **p. resucitado,** (coll.) upstart, parvenu.
piojoso, sa, *a.* 1. lousy, louse-ridden. 2. mean, stingy.
piojuelo, *m. dim. of* **piojo,** small louse; plant louse, green fly.
piola, *f.* 1. (mar.) cord (string); housing line. 2. (Amer.) packthread.
piolar, *i.v.* to cheep, chirp (chickens, birds).
piolín, *m.* (Amer.) packthread.
pión, na, *a.* cheeping or peeping a great deal. —*m.* (phys.) pion.
pionero, ra, *a., m., f.* pioneer.
pionía, *f.* seed of coral bean tree; (Ven.) bucare seeds used as beads.
piornal, piorneda, *f.* patch or growth of Spanish broom.
piorno, *m.* (bot.) Spanish broom; (bot.) variety of cytisus.
piorrea, *f.* (med., dent.) pyorrhea.
piosis, *f.* (med.) pyosis.
pipa, *f.* 1. pipe (for smoking tobacco). 2. cask, keg (for wine). 3. reed (of a flute). 4. flute made out of a green barley stem. 5. fuse (of bomb, etc.). 6. (Amer., coll.) belly, stomach. 7. pip, seed. — **p. de espuma de mar,** meerschaum pipe; **p. de la paz,** peace pipe, pipe of peace; **tomar p.,** to leave, go, take a powder (coll.).
pipar, *i.v.* to smoke a pipe.
piperáceo, a, *a.* (bot.) piperaceous. —*f.* (*pl.*) Piperaceae.
piperazina, *f.* (chem.) piperazine, piperazin.
pipería, *f.* casks, kegs; (mar.) water tanks.
piperidina, *f.* (chem.) piperidine.
piperina, *f.* (chem.) piperine.
pipero, *m.* copper pipe maker.
piperonal, *m.* (chem.) piperonal.
pipeta, *f.* pipette; **p. medidora,** measuring pipette.
pipí, *m.* 1. (ornith.) pitpit, guitguit, honey creeper (Dacius cavana). 2. wee-wee, urine; **hacer p.,** to wee-wee, urinate (in baby talk).
pipián, *m.* an American Indian dish made with meat, bacon and almonds.
pipiar, *i.v.* to cheep, peep (chicks).
pipiola, *f.* (Mex.) small bee.
pipiolo, *m.* (coll.) novice, rookie, greenhorn.
pipirigallo, *m.* (bot.) sainfoin.
pipirijaina, *f.* (coll.) band of strolling comedians.
pipiripao, *m.* (coll.) banquet, feast, sumptuous party. — **de p.,** (Amer.) unimportant.
pipiritaña, pipitaña, *f.* flute made out of a green cane.
pipo, *m.* (ornith.) woodpecker (Dryobates minor).
pipón, na, *a.* 1. (Amer.) paunchy, potbellied. 2. (Amer.) full, replete.
piporro, *m.* (mus., coll.) bassoon (instrument).
pipote, *m.* keg, barrel, cask.
pipudo, da, *a.* (coll.) terrific, marvelous, cool (sl.).
pique, *a.* steep (coastline). —*m.* 1. pique, annoyance, irritation. 2. eagerness, zeal, anxiousness (to do something). 3. (ento.) chigger, chigoe. 4. spade (in cards). 5. (mar.) crutch, crotch. — **a p. de,** in danger of, in peril of, on the point of; **echar a p.,** (mar.) to sink; to ruin; **estar a p. de,** to be on the verge of; **irse a p.,** (mar.) to sink; to be ruined.
piqué, *m.* (tex.) piqué.
pique, piqué, *ref.* **picar.**
piquera, *f.* 1. opening (in beehive); bunghole (in cask); taphole (in furnace). 2. wick tube or hole (in oil lamp). 3. (Cuba) hackstand.
piquería, *f.* body of pikemen.
piquero, *m.* pikeman; (Peru, Chile, ornith.) booby (Sula variegata).
piqueta, *f.* pickax, pick; mason's pick or hammer.
piquete, *m.* 1. prick, jab. 2. small hole, small cut. 3. pole, stake, picket. 4. (mil.) picket (small squad of soldiers). 5. (Arg.) small pen or corral. 6. (Col.) picnic. 7. (Col.) edge (of scissors). 8. (Cuba) small band. 9. (Ven.) cattle mark (cut in the animal's ear).
piquetero, *m.* (min.) tool boy (boy who carries miners' pickaxes).
piquetilla, *f.* mason's small pick or hammer.
piquillín, *m.* (Arg., bot.) (variety of) buckthorn (Condalia lineata).
piquituerto, *m.* (ornith.) crossbill.
pira, *f.* 1. pyre, funeral pyre. 2. (her.) point.
piracanta, *f.* (bot.) pyracantha.
piragón, *m.* 1. (myth.) fabulous firefly which lived in fire. 2. (ento.) pyralidid moth.
piragua, *f.* 1. piragua, pirogue; light canoe. 2. (bot.) anthurium (Anthurium violaceum).
piragüero, *m.* steersman of a piragua; canoeist.
piral, *m., var. of* **piragón.**
pirálido, *a.* (zool.) pyralidan, pyralidid. —*m.* (zool.) pyralidan, pyralidid, (*pl.*) Pyralididae.
piramidal, *a.* pyramidal.
piramidalmente, *adv.* in the shape of a pyramid.
pirámide, *f.* pyramid.
pirandeliano, na, *a.* (theat., lit.) Pirandellian, characteristic of the plays of Luigi Pirandello.
pirano, *m.* (chem.) pyran.
piranómetro, *m.* (astrol.) pyranometer.
piraña, *f.* (ichth.) piranha, caribe.
pirargirita, *f.* (min.) pyrargyrite.
pirarse, *r.v.* (coll.) to flee, run away; **pirárselas,** (coll.) to cut class; (coll.) to beat it.
pirata, *a.* piratical, piratic. —*m.* 1. pirate. 2. (fig.) cruel person, brute.
piratear, *i.v.* to practice piracy, be a pirate. —*tr.v.* (fig.) to copy, publish illegally; to steal an idea, a design.
piratería, *f.* piracy; theft, robbery.
pirático, ca, *a.* piratic, piratical.
pirausta, *f.* (myth.) mythical firefly believed to live in fire.
pirca, *f.* (S. Amer.) dry-stone wall.
pircar, (*ref. 50*) *tr.v.* (S. Amer.) to enclose with a dry-stone wall.
pirco, *m.* (Chile) succotash; dish of beans, corn and pumpkin.
pireliómetro, *m.* (phys.) pyrheliometer.
pirenaico, ca, *a.* Pyrenean, or pertaining to the Pyrenees.
Pireo, *m.* Piraeus (the port of Athens).
pirético, ca, *a.* (med.) pyretic.
piretogénico, ca, *a.* (med.) pyrogenic. —*m.* (med.) pyrogen.
piretógeno, na, *a.* (med.) pyrogenic. —*m.* (med.) pyrogen.
piretología, *f.* (med.) pyretology.
piretoterapia, *f.* (med.) pyretotherapy.
piretro, *m.* (bot.) pyrethrum.
pirexia, *f.* (med.) pyrexia.
pirgüín, *m.* (Chile, zool.) liver fluke; illness caused by liver fluke.
pirheliómetro, *m.* (phys.) pyrheliometer.
pirhuín, *m., var. of* **pirgüín.**
pírico, ca, *a.* pertaining to fire or fireworks.
pirídico, ca, *a.* (chem.) pyridic.
piridina, *f.* (chem.) piridine.
piridoxina, *f.* (chem., pharm.) pyridoxine, pyridoxin.
piriforme, *a.* pear-shaped, pyriform.
pirimetamina, *f.* (pharm.) pyrimethamine.
pirimidina, *f.* (chem.) pyrimidine.
pirineo, a, *a.* Pyrenean. —*m.* (*pl.*) Pyrenees (mountain range).
pirita, *f.* (min.) pyrites; pyrite, iron pyrites; **p. arsenical,** arsenopyrite, arsenical pyrites; **p. blanca,** (geol.) marcasite, white iron pyrites; **p. cobriza** or **de cobre,** copper pyrites; **p. de hierro** or **marcial,** iron pyrites; firestone; **p. magnética,** magnetic pyrites, pyrrhotite.
piritoso, sa, *a.* (min.) pyritic, pyritical, pyritous.
pirlitero, *m.* (bot.) hawthorn (Crataegus monogyna).
pirobolista, *m.* (mil.) mine builder.
pirocatequina, *f.* (chem.) pyrocatechin, pyrocatechol.
piroclástico, ca, *a.* (geol.) pyroclastic.
pirocloro, *m.* (chem.) pyrochlore.
pirocondensación, *f.* (phys.) pyrocondensation.
piroconductibilidad, *f.* (phys.) pyroconductivity.
piroelectricidad, *f.* (phys.) pyroelectricity.
piroeléctrico, ca, *a.* pyroelectric.
pirofilacio, *m.* cave filled with flames formerly thought to exist in the center of the earth.
pirofilita, *f.* (min.) pyrophyllite.
pirofobia, *f.* (med.) pyrophobia.
pirofórico, *a.* (phys., metal.) pyrophoric.
piróforo, *m.* (chem.) pyrophorus.
pirofosfato, *m.* (chem.) pyrophosphate.
pirofosfórico, ca, *a.* (chem.) pyrophosphoric.
pirofotómetro, *m.* (phys.) pyrophotometer.
pirogalato, *m.* (chem.) pyrogallate.
pirogálico, ca, *a.* (chem.) pyrogallic.
pirogalol, *m.* (chem.) pyrogallol.
pirogénico, *a.* (geol.) pyrogenic.
pirógeno, na, *a.* pyrogenic, pyrogenous.
pirograbado, *m.* pyrography, pyrogravure.
pirograbar, *tr.v.* to decorate by pyrography.
pirolatría, *f.* pyrolatry, fire worship.
piroleñoso, sa, *a.* (chem.) pyroligneous, pyrolignic.
pirólisis, *f.* (chem.) pyrolisis.
pirolusita, *f.* (min.) pyrolusite.
piromagnético, ca, *a.* (phys.) pyromagnetic.
piromancia, *f.* pyromancy, divination by fire.
piromanía, *f.* pyromania.
piromaníaco, ca, *a.* pyromaniacal. —*m., f.* pyromaniac.
pirómano, na, *a.* pyromaniacal. —*m., f.* pyromaniac.
piromántico, ca, *a.* pyromantic. —*m.* pyromancer.
pirometalurgia, *f.* pyrometallurgy.
pirometría, *f.* (phys., metal.) pyrometry.
pirométrico, ca, *a.* (phys., metal.) pyrometric.
pirómetro, *m.* pyrometer; **p. fotoeléctrico,** photoelectric pyrometer.
piromorfita, *f.* (min.) pyromorphite.
pirón, *m.* (Arg.) cassava flour bread (eaten with soup or stew).
pirona, *f.* (chem.) pyrone.
pironina, *f.* (chem.) pyronine.
piropear, *tr.v.* (coll.) to pay flattering compliments to (a woman), make flirtatious remarks to.
piroplasma, *m.* (zool.) piroplasm, piroplasma.
piropo, *m.* 1. (coll.) flattering compliment, flirtatious remark. 2. (min.) pyrope, garnet. 3. carbuncle.

piroquímico, ca, *a.* pyrochemical.
piróscafo, *m.* early name for steamship.
piroscopio, *m.* (phys.) pyroscope.
pirosfera, *f.* (geol.) pyrosphere.
pirosis, *f.* (med.) pyrosis.
piróstato, *m.* (phys.) pyrostat.
pirosulfato, *m.* (chem.) pyrosulfate.
pirosulfúrico, ca, *a.* (chem.) pyrosulfuric.
pirotecnia, *f.* pyrotechnics, pyrotechny.
pirotécnico, ca, *a.* pyrotechnic, pyrotechnical. —*m.* pyrotechnist, firework maker.
pirotoxina, *f.* (biochem.) pyrotoxin.
piroxena, *f.* (min.) pyroxene.
piroxenita, *f.* (min.) pyroxenite.
piroxeno, *m.* (min.) piroxene.
piroxilina, *f.* (chem.) pyroxylin.
piroxilo, *m.* (chem.) cellulose nitrate, nitrocellulose.
pirque, pirqué, *ref.* **pircar.**
pirrarse, *r.v.* (coll.) to long, yearn; **pirrarse por,** to yearn for, long for.
pírrico, ca, *a.* pyrrhic, e.g. *una victoria pírrica,* a Pyrrhic victory. —*f.* pyrrhic (ancient Greek war dance).
pirriquio, *m.* (poet.) pyrrhic (foot).
Pirro, *m.* (hist.) Pyrrhus; **victoria a lo Pirro,** Pyrrhic victory.
pirrol, *m.* (chem.) pyrrole, pyrrol.
pirroniano, na, *a.* Pyrrhonic.
pirrónico, ca, *a.* (philos.) Pyrrhonistic. —*m., f.* Pyrrhonist.
pirronismo, *m.* (philos.) Pyrrhonism.
pirrotina, *f.* (min.) pyrrhotite, pyrrhotine.
pirrotita, *f.* (min.) pyrrhotite, pyrrhotine, magnetic pyrites.
pirueta, *f.* pirouette (of a dancer); caper (of a horse); somersault (of a plane); **hacer piruetas,** to pirouette, caper, turn somersaults.
piruétano, *m.* (bot.) wild pear tree.
piruetear, *i.v.* to pirouette (dancer); to caper (a horse); to turn somersaults (a plane).
piruja, *f.* uninhibited young woman, sassy girl.
pirúvico, ca, *a.* (chem.) pyruvic.
pisa, *f.* 1. treading, step. 2. batch of grapes or olives for pressing. 3. (coll.) kicking, hiding, beating.
pisada, *f.* 1. step, tread. 2. footprint, footstep. 3. kick. — **seguir las pisadas de,** to follow in the footsteps of.
pisador, ra, *a.* prancer, high stepping (horse). —*m.* grape treader.
pisadura, *f., var. of* **pisada.**
pisano, na, *a., m., f.* Pisan, of or pertaining to Pisa, Italy.
pisapapeles, *m.* paperweight.
pisar, *tr.v.* 1. to tread on, step on. 2. to tread, press (grapes) with the feet; to tamp, pack down, tread down (earth); to beat (cloth). 3. to cover part of. 4. to tread, copulate with, cover (said of birds). 5. to strike (the keys of a piano), pluck (the strings of an instrument). 6. to trample on, squash, abuse, tread on. 7. to be on top of (one room above another). — **no p. el césped,** keep off the lawn or grass; **p. el arrancador,** to step on the starter; **pisarle algo a alguien,** (coll.) to beat someone to something; (coll.) to snitch something from someone; **pisarle los talones a,** to keep on someone's heels, follow someone closely.
pisasfalto, *m.* pitch, asphalt; mixture of bitumen and pitch.
pisaúvas, (*pl.* **pisaúvas**), *m.* grape treader.
pisaverde, *m.* (coll.) dandy, fop.
piscator, *m.* meteorological almanac (listing forecasts).
piscatorio, ria, *a.* piscatorial, piscatory, pertaining to fish, fishing, or fishermen.
piscicultor, ra, *m., f.* pisciculturist, fish breeder.
piscicultura, *f.* pisciculture, fish-breeding.
piscifactoría, *f.* fish hatchery.
pisciforme, *a.* pisciform, fish-shaped.
piscina, *f.* 1. swimming pool; fishbowl. 2. (ecc.) piscina. — **p. probática,** (Bib.) tank in which sacrificial animals were washed (in the temple of Solomon).
Piscis, *m.* (astron.) Pisces.
piscívoro, ra, *a.* (zool.) piscivorous, fish-eating.
pisco, *m.* 1. (Chile, Peru) pisco, grape brandy. 2. (Col.) turkey. 3. (Ven.) drunk, inebriated person.
piscolabis, *m.* 1. (coll.) snack, bite. 2. overtrumping (at cards).
pisiforme, *a.* pisiform, pea-shaped; (anat.) pisiform.
piso, *m.* 1. floor; flooring; ground, pavement, surface. 2. floor, story, storey. 3. flat, apartment. 4. layman's room (in monastery or convent). 5. (min.) level (all the workings on the same level of a mine). 6. (geol.) stage. 7. (Chile, Peru) table runner; place mat, table mat. 8. (Chile) stool, footstool. 9. (Cuba) pasturing fee. — **de pisos a desnivel,** (archit.) split-level; **p. alto,** top floor, upper floor; **p. bajo,** ground floor; **p. mojado,** (señal) wet floor.
pisolita, *f.* (geol.) pisolite.
pisolítico, ca, *a.* pisolitic.
pisón, *m.* rammer, tamper, beetle; **a p.,** by ramming or tamping.
pisonear, *tr.v.* to ram down, tamp, pound down, make compact.
pisotear, *tr.v.* 1. to trample down, tread down, stamp on. 2. (fig.) to trample on, squash (treat abusively or contemptuously).
pisoteo, *m.* trampling.
pisotón, *m.* stamp, heavy tread or step on someone's foot.
pispa, *f.* 1. (Can. I.) canary. 2. gay, bright young girl.
pista, *f.* 1. track, trail (footprints of an animal, provisional road). 2. racetrack. 3. road; road surface. 4. (aer.) runway. 5. (fig.) track, scent (leading to the solving of a crime, discovery of a criminal, etc.). — **en medio de la p.,** in the middle of the road; **estar sobre la p. (de),** to be on the track (of), have picked up the scent (of); **p. cubierta,** indoor track; **p. de aterrizaje,** landing strip, air strip; **p. de baile,** dance floor; **p. de despegue,** air strip; **p. de esquí,** ski slope, ski run; **p. de hielo,** ice rink; **p. de patinaje,** skating rink; **p. de rodaje** or **maniobras,** (aer.) taxiway; **p. de carretera,** (Amer.) highway lane; **seguir la p. a,** to trail, be on the trail of.
pistache, *m.* sweet or ice made from the pistachio nut.
pistachero, *m.* (bot.) pistachio tree (Pistacia vera).
pistacho, *m.* pistachio nut.
pistadero, *m.* pestle, crusher, squeezer.
pistar, *tr.v.* to pound, crush with a pestle.
pistero, *m.* feeding cup with nozzle or spout.
pistilado, da, *a.* (bot.) pistillate.
pistilo, *m.* (bot.) pistil.
pisto, *m.* 1. chicken broth (for the sick). 2. fried hash of chopped peppers, tomato, onions, etc. 3. hodgepodge or jumble of ideas (in a speech). — **a pistos,** in little amounts, sparingly; **darse p.,** to put on airs.
pistola, *f.* 1. pistol, gun. 2. spray gun, paint sprayer; (grease) gun. — **p. de aire,** air gun; **p. de arzón,** horse pistol; **p. de bolsillo,** pocket pistol; **p. de cinto,** holster pistol; **p. de fogueo,** dummy pistol, pistol shooting dummy bullets; **p. de grasa, p. lubricadora,** grease or oil gun; **p. de laser,** láser gun; **p. de pintura,** paint sprayer; **p. de pulverización, p. pulverizadora,** spray gun, paint sprayer, airbrush; **p. remachadora,** riveting hammer.
pistolera, *f.* holster.
pistolero, *m.* gunman, gangster.
pistoletazo, *m.* pistol shot.
pistolete, *m.* 1. small pocket pistol. 2. spray gun, paint sprayer.
pistón, *m.* 1. (mec., mus.) piston. 2. percussion cap (on bullet).
pistonada, *f.* piston stroke (of an engine).
pistonudo, da, *a.* (coll.) super, terrific, excellent.
pistoresa, *f.* short dagger.
pistraje, *m.* (coll.) unpleasant drink or dish.
pistraque, *m.* (coll.) *var. of* **pistraje.**
pistura, *f.* pounding, crushing.
pita, *f.* 1. (bot.) century plant. 2. string, cord, pita fiber, pita thread. 3. hen. 4. glass marble; (*pl.*) marbles (game). 5. whistling, hissing (as sign of disapproval).
pita, *f.* chicken.
pitaco, *m.* (bot.) stem of the century plant.
pitada, *f.* 1. whistle; whistling. 2. improper remark, inopportune remark. 3. (S. Amer.) puff (of cigarette smoke).
Pitágoras, *m.* Pythagoras, Greek philosopher and mathematician.
pitagórico, ca, *a., m., f.* Pythagorean.
pitahaya, *f.* (bot.) pitahaya.
pitancería, *f.* 1. place where food, dole or alms are distributed. 2. distribution of food, dole and alms.
pitancero, *m.* 1. distributor of food, dole or alms. 2. roll caller of choir. 3. steward, purveyor (in military orders).
pitanga, *f.* (Arg., bot.) Surinam cherry.
pitanza, *f.* 1. pittance, food, alms, dole. 2. daily ration of food (distributed among the poor). 3. daily food, daily bread; wage, remuneration. 4. (Arg., Urug., Guat.) bargain, gift. 5. (Chile) hoax.
pitaña, *f., var. of* **legaña,** gum (on eyelids).
pitañoso, sa, *a., var. of* **legañoso.**
pitar, *tr.v.* 1. to pay (a debt). 2. to apportion alms to. —*i.v.* 1. to whistle, blow a whistle. 2. (S. Amer.) to smoke (tobacco). 3. (Mex.) to whistle, hiss (in disapprobation). 4. (Cuba) to run away, flee. — **salir pitando,** to leave in a hurry.
pitarra, *f., var. of* **legaña,** 1. gum (in the eyelids). 2. second-run cider.
pitarroso, sa, *a., var. of* **legañoso.** gummy (eyelids).
pitazo, *m.* sound or blast of a whistle.
pitear, *i.v.* (Amer.) to whistle, hiss; to protest.
pitecántropo, *m.* (anth.) pithecanthropus.
pitezna, *f.* catch (releasing spring of a trap).
pitias, *m.* (hist.) Pythias, Greek philosopher.
pítico, ca, *a.* (hist.) Pythian.
pitido, *m.* whistling, whistle.
pitillera, *f.* 1. cigarette maker. 2. cigarette case.
pitillo, *m.* cigarette.
pítima, *f.* 1. (pharm.) plaster containing saffron. 2. (coll.) drunkenness.
pitiminí, *m.* 1. (bot.) variety of small rose. 2. (Amer.) fastidious, finicky person.
pitio, tia, *a.* (hist.) Pythian.
pitío, *m.* (coll.) whistle, whistling; whistling sound of certain small birds.
pitipié, *m.* graduated scale (applied to drawings, maps, etc.).
pitiriasis, *f.* (med.) pityriasis.
pitirre, *m.* (Cuba, ornith.) kingbird (Tyrrannus melancholius).
pito, *m.* 1. whistle (instrument); catcall; earthenware vessel which produces a whistling sound when blown into. 2. (ento.) bed tick. 3. knucklebone (used in game of knucklebones). 4. cigarette. 5. (vulg.) penis. 6. (Arg., Bol., Chile,

Urug.) pipe (for smoking). 7. (C. Amer.) ripe coffee bean. 8. fife; fifer. — **no dársele** or **importarle a uno un p.,** not to care a fig (G.B.), not to give a damn about; **no tocar pitos en,** (coll.) to have nothing to do with, have no hand in; **no valer un p.,** (coll.) not to be worth a straw, to be utterly useless; **pitos flautos,** (coll.) foolish, frivolous entertainment or pastime; **por pitos o por flautas,** (coll.) for one reason or another; **¿qué p. tocas tú aquí?** what are you doing here, what's your business here?

pito, *m.* (ornith.) woodpecker; **p. real,** green woodpecker.

pitoflero, ra, *m., f.* 1. (coll.) mediocre musician. 2. gossip, busybody.

pitón, *m.* (zool.) python.

pitón, *m.* 1. budding horn (of bull, deer, goat, etc.). 2. spout (of a jug, etc.). 3. protuberance, lump. 4. shoot (of a tree). 5. stem of the century plant. 6. (Amer.) nozzle (of a hose pipe). 7. (Chile) dibble, dibber (digging tool). 8. (Mex.) weaned colt or mare. 9. spike (mountain-climbing aid).

Pitón, *m.* (myth.) Python, gigantic serpent slain by Apollo.

pitónico, ca, *a.* pythonic, oracular, prophetic.

pitonisa, *f.* pythoness; soothsayer.

pitorra, *f.* (ornith.) woodcock.

pitorrearse, *r.v.* to make fun (of), jeer (at).

pitorreo, *m.* mockery, ridicule, jeering.

pitorro, *m.* spout (of an earthen jar or vessel).

pitpit, *m.* (ornith.) honey creeper, pitpit, guitguit.

pitreo, *m.* (bot.) stem of century plant.

pituco, ca, *m., f.* (Arg., Chile) dashing young man or woman; young member of the fashionable set.

pituita, *f.* pituite, mucus, phlegm.

pituitario, ria, *a., m., f.* (med., physiol.) pituitary.

pituitoso, sa, *a.* pituitous.

pituso, sa, *a.* cute, small. —*m., f.* cute child.

piular, *i.v.* to peep, cheep, chirp.

piulido, *m.* peeping, cheeping, chirping.

piuquén, *m.* (ornith.) (variety of) bustard.

piure, *m.* (Chile) edible shellfish.

piuria, *f.* (med.) pyuria.

pivotar, *i.v.* to pivot.

pivote, *m.* pivot, king pin.

píxide, *f.* (ecc.) pyx, ciborium.

pixidio, *m.* (bot.) pyxidium, pyxis.

piyama, *m.* pajama.

pizarra, *f.* 1. (min.) slate, shale. 2. slate; blackboard.

pizarral, *m.* slate deposit or quarry, shale bed.

pizarreño, ña, *a.* slaty, slate-like, slate-colored.

pizarrería, *f.* slate quarry.

pizarrero, *m.* slate cutter.

pizarrín, *m.* slate pencil.

pizarrón, *m.* (Amer.) blackboard.

pizarroso, sa, *a.* full of slate; slaty, slate-like.

pizate, *m.* (bot.) wormseed, Mexican tea.

pizca, *f.* pinch, bit, small amount, crumb, whit.

pizcar, (*ref. 50*) *tr.v.* (coll.) 1. to pinch, pick at (food). 2. (Mex.) to glean (corn).

pizco, *m.* (coll.) pinch (act of pinching).

pizmiento, ta, *a.* pitch-colored.

pizote, *m.* (C. Amer., Mex., zool.) red coati.

pizpereta, pizpireta, *a.* (coll.) lively, vivacious (woman).

pizpirigaña, *f.* children's pinching game.

pizpita, *f.* (ornith.) wagtail.

pizpitillo, *m., var. of* **pizpita.**

pizque, pizqué, *ref.* **pizcar.**

pizzicato, *a., m.* (mus.) pizzicato.

placa, *f.* 1. plaque, tablet. 2. badge (of sheriff, policeman, etc.); plaque, insignia (of an honorary order). 3. plate, sheet. 4. (carp.) veneer, layer of wood. 5. plack, small coin used in the Low Countries. 6. (auto.) license plate. 7. microscope slide or plate. 8. (photog.) plate. 9. (elec.) plate, flat electrode. 10. (rad.) plate. 11. (Amer.) spot (caused by a throat or mouth infection). — **corriente de p.,** (elec.) plate current; **p. de asiento,** (ry.) railway chair, tie plate; **p. base,** circuit board; **p. de cabeza,** crown sheet (of a furnace); **p. de circuitos impresos,** printed circuit board; **p. de energía solar,** solar cell; **p. deflectora,** baffle plate; **p. de hielo,** black ice; **p. de horno,** baking tray, baking sheet; **p. de matrícula,** license plate; **p. de silicio,** silicon chip; **p. difusora,** diffuser plate; **p. eléctrica de cuarzo,** (elec.) quartz plate; **p. ecuatorial,** (biol.) equatorial plate; **p. fotomecánica,** process plate; **p. giratoria,** (ry.) turntable; **p. madre,** main board, mother board; **p. seca,** (photog.) dry plate; **p. terminal,** (anat.) end plate; **p. volada,** cantilever slab.

placabilidad, *f.* placability.

placable, *a.* placable, able to be placated.

placa-marca, *f.* (mec.) name plate.

placativo, va, *a.* placatory.

placear, *tr.v.* 1. to sell retail. 2. to publish, make known.

placel, *m.* (mar.) sandbank, reef.

pláceme, *m.* congratulations; **dar el p. a,** to congratulate; **estar de plácemes,** to be lucky or happy enough to be congratulated.

placenta, *f.* (zool., anat., bot.) placenta.

placentario, ria, *a.* placental. —*m.* (zool.) placental; (*pl.*) Placentalia.

placenteramente, *adv.* gladly, joyfully, with pleasure.

placentero, ra, *a.* pleasant, agreeable.

placer, *m.* 1. pleasure, joy. 2. desire, will. 3. sandbank, sand bar; reef. 4. (min.) placer. 5. pearl fishery. 6. (Cuba) lot, plot of vacant land.

placer, (*ref. 13*) *tr.v.* to please, content.

placero, ra, *a.* pertaining to the market place. —*m., f.* 1. stallkeeper, market woman or man. 2. loafer, layabout, town gossip.

placeta, placetuela, *f. dim. of* **plaza,** small town square.

placibilidad, *f.* agreeableness, pleasantness.

placible, *a.* agreeable, pleasant.

plácidamente, *adv.* placidly.

placidez, *f.* 1. placidness, tranquility, serenity. 2. pleasantness, agreeableness.

plácido, da, *a.* 1. placid, quiet, serene. 2. pleasant, agreeable.

placiente, *a.* pleasing, pleasant, agreeable.

plácito, *m.* opinion, judgment.

placoideo, a, *a.* (ichth.) placoid.

plafón, *m.* (archit.) soffit of an architrave.

plaga, *f.* 1. plague, calamity, scourge. 2. plague, pestilence, disease. 3. sore, ulcer. 4. plague, pest, nuisance. 5. superabundance, glut. 6. plague (e.g. of locusts, etc.).

plaga, *f.* 1. climatic zone. 2. (mar.) bearing, course.

plagado, da, *past part. of* **plagar.** —*a.* infested, full, crawling, smitten. — **p. de,** infested with, full of, crawling with, smitten with.

plagal, *a.* (mus.) plagal.

plagar, (*ref. 51*) *tr.v.* to infest, to plague. —*r.v.* to become infested or overrun (with) or full (of).

plagiar, *tr.v.* 1. to plagiarize, copy. 2. (Amer.) to kidnap.

plagiario, ria, *a.* plagiaristic, plagiarizing. —*m., f.* plagiarist.

plagio, *m.* plagiarism, copying.

plagioclasa, *f.* (min.) plagioclase.

plagioclásico, ca, *a.* (min.) plagioclastic.

plagiófido, *m.* (geol.) plagiophyre.

plagióstomos, *m.* (*pl.*) (zool.) Plagiostomi.

plagiótropismo, *m.* (bot.) plagiotropism.

plagiotropo, pa, *a.* (bot.) plagiotropous, plagiotropic.

plague, plagué, *ref.* **plagar.**

plan, *m.* 1. plan, project, scheme; outline, draft. 2. level, height. 3. plan, diagram, graphic representation. 4. (mar.) floor timber. 5. (min.) mine floor. 6. (Arg., Chile, Guat., Mex., Ven.) plain, plateau. — **p. de campaña,** plan of action; **p. de estudios,** curriculum, syllabus; **p. de jubilación,** retirement plan; **p. quinquenal,** five-year plan.; **p. maestro,** master plan.

plana, *f.* 1. side (of a page of paper). 2. (print.) page; type page. 2. level ground, plain. 3. (mas.) trowel. 4. roster, list, roll. — **a p. y renglón,** line for line (exactly the same as the original in content and lay-out); (fig.) just right; **cerrar la p.,** to finish, conclude; **corregir** or **enmendar la p.,** to correct, find fault with; to do better than, surpass, excel; **de primera p.,** front-page; **p. mayor,** (mil., mar.) staff.

planada, *f.* plain, level ground.

planador, *m.* (metal.) planisher.

planario, *m.* (zool.) planarian.

plancha, *f.* 1. sheet, plate (of metal). 2. iron, flatiron. 3. ironing; ironed linen. 4. press-up, press-up on horizontal bar (in gymnastics). 5. (coll.) blunder, error, faux pas. 6. (print.) plate. 7. (mar.) gangplank, plank. — **hacer una p.,** to make a blunder or faux pas, put one's foot in it; **p. a vapor,** steam iron; **p. cizallada,** (metal.) sheared plate, plate with sheared edges; **p. de blindaje,** armor plate; **p. de vela** or **de windsurf,** sailboard, windsurfer; **p. de viento,** (mar.) hanging platform (used for painting or calking a ship); **p. estriada,** checkered plate; **p. litográfica,** (print.) lithographic printing plate; **p. seca,** (photog.) dry plate.

planchada, *f.* (mar.) gangplank, plank.

planchado, da, *past part. of* **planchar.** —*a.* (Amer., coll.) without a cent, broke (sl.). —*m.* ironing; clothes ironed or to be ironed; **día de p.,** ironing day.

planchador, ra, *m., f.* ironer, presser (person). —*f.* ironing machine.

planchar, *tr.v.* to iron, press (clothes).

planchazo, *m.* mistake, faux pas.

planchear, *tr.v.* to plate, cover with metal plates.

plancheta, *f.* (surv.) plane table.

planchón, *m. aug. of* **plancha,** large plate or sheet (of metal).

planchón, *m.* 1. (Chile, Bol.) glacier, plateau, meseta. 2. (Col.) barge (boat).

planchuela, *f.* 1. *dim. of* **plancha,** small sheet or plate (of metal). 2. strip iron.

planco, *m.* (ornith.) gannet.

plancton, *m.* (biol.) plankton.

planctónico, ca, *a.* (biol.) planktonic.

planeador, *m.* (aer.) glider.

planear, *tr.v.* to plan, design. —*i.v.* (aer.) to glide.

planeo, *m.* (aer.) gliding.

planeta, *m.* (astron.) planet. —*f.* (ecc.) planeta, short chasuble.

planetario, ria, *a.* planetary. —*m.* 1. planetarium, orrery. 2. (mec.) planet differential, planetary gearing.

planetícola, *m., f.* inhabitant of another planet.

planetoide, *m.* (astron.) planetoid.

planga, *f.* (ornith.) gannet.

planialtimetría, *f.* contour map; topographical survey.

planicie, *f.* plain, level ground.

planificación, *f.* planning; **p. familiar,** family planning; **p. urbana,** urban planning.

planificado, da, *past part. of* **planificar.** —*a.* planned.

planificador, dora, *a,* planning. *—m., f.* planner.
planificar, (*ref. 50*) *tr.v.* to plan, to draw up a plan for.
planifique, planifiqué, *ref.* **planificar.**
planígrafo, *m.* planigraph.
planilla, *f.* 1. (Amer.) list, roll, table. 2. (Amer.) payroll. 3. (Mex.) voting ballot.
planimetrar, *tr.v.* to measure with a planimeter.
planimetría, *f.* (top.) planimetry.
planimétrico, ca, *a.* (top.) planimetric.
planímetro, *m.* planimeter; **p. polar,** (chart.) polar planimeter.
planisferio, *m.* planisphere.
plano, na, *a.* flat, level, even, smooth; (math.) plane. *—m.* 1. plane, surface, face; (math.) plane. 2. plan, diagram, map, chart, plot. 3. (cine., p., photog.) ground, distance, e.g. *primer plano,* foreground, *medio plano,* middle ground, middle distance. 4. (aer.) fin, wing, surface. 5. part of a film script. 6. base (of bellows). — **dar de plano,** to hit with the flat of a knife or hand; **de plano,** clearly, plainly, flatly, flat; **levantar un p.,** (surv.) to make a survey; **p. acotado,** (chart.) topographical plan, dimensioned drawing; **p. aerodinámico,** (aer.) airfoil; **p. altimétrico,** topographical plan; **p. azul,** blueprint; **p. catastral,** real estate map; **p. conjugado,** (phys., math.) conjugate plane; **p. corto,** close-up; **p. de cola,** (aer.) tail plane; **p. de comparación, de nivel** or **de referencia,** (surv.) datum plane, datum level; **p. de desenfilada,** (mil.) plane of desfilade; **p. de exfoliación,** (min.) cleavage plane; **p. de incidencia,** (opt.) plane of incidence; **p. de objetivos,** (mil.) target map; **p. de proyección,** plane of projection; **p. de prueba,** (phys.) proof plane; **p. de simetría,** (phys.) plane of symmetry; **p. de taller, ejecución** or **construcción,** (archit., mec.) working drawing; **p. de tiro,** (mil.) plane of sight; **p. diagonal,** diagonal plane; **p. estabilizador,** (aer.) stabilizer; **p. fijo horizontal,** (aer.) horizontal stabilizer; **p. focal,** (opt.) focal plane; **p. geométrico,** ground plane, geometric plane (in perspective); **p. horizontal,** horizontal plane (in perspective); **p. inclinado,** (mec.) inclined plane; **p. intermedio,** (theat., p.) the near distance; **p. osculador,** (math.) plane of osculation, osculating plane; **p. perspectivo,** perspective plane; **p. picado,** aerial view; **p. rectificante,** (math.) plane of rectification, rectifying plane; **p. topográfico,** contour map, topographical plan; **p. vertical,** vertical plane (in perspective); **segundo p.,** middle distance (in painting).
planocóncavo, va, *a.* plano-concave.
planoconvexo, a, *a.* plano-convex.
planta, *f.* 1. (bot.) plant. 2. sole (of the foot). 3. recently planted patch; nursery of young plants. 4. plan, drawing, sketch. 5. plan, scheme, project. 6. list or roster of staff. 7. (archit.) ground plan, floor plan. 8. stance, position (in dancing or fencing). 9. (Amer.) plant, factory. — **buena p.,** good appearance; **de nueva p.,** right from the start or from the beginning; **de p.,** from the foundations, from the beginning; **echar plantas,** (coll.) to swagger, bully; **fijar las plantas,** to dig one's heels in (keeping to one's opinion); **p. alta,** upper floor or story; **p. baja,** ground floor (G.B) first floor (Am.); **p. de goma,** (bot.) gum plant; **p. eléctrica, p. de energía,** electric power plant; **p. generadora,** generating station, electric power plant; **p. de interior,** houseplant; **p. motriz,** power plant.
plantación, *f.* plantation, planting.
plantado, da, *a.* standing; upright; erect.
plantador, ra, *a.* planting. *—m., f.* planter. *—m.* dibble, dibber.

plantagináceo, a, *a.* (bot.) plantaginaceous *—f.* (*pl.*) Plantaginaceae.
plantaina, *f.* (bot.) plantain, ribwort.
plantaje, *m.* plants, shrubs (collectively).
plantar, *a.* (anat.) plantar (pertaining to the sole of the foot).
plantar, *tr.v.* 1. to plant, sow (plants); to plant, sow with plants. 2. to plant, erect, set up, fix upright. 3. to put, place; to throw (into the street or prison). 4. to establish, found. 5. to give, deliver (blows). 6. to stand (someone) up, leave in the lurch, jilt, disappoint (usually **dejar plantado**). *—r.v.* 1. (coll.) to stand, plant or put oneself upright. 2. to land (in), arrive (in), get to (quickly). 3. (coll.) to balk (said of an animal). 4. (coll.) to stand pat (in card games). 5. to stand firm, make a stand.
plantario, *m.* (agr.) seedbed; nursery.
plante, *m.* ganging together, concerted action of a group for or against something.
planteamiento, *m.* 1. statement, exposition, outlining. 2. raising, posing (of problem, doubt, question, etc.); proposal (of a solution, etc.). 3. establishment, setting up.
plantear, *tr.v.* 1. to outline, set forth, state, expound. 2. to raise, pose (problem, doubt, question); to propose, put forward (solution, etc.). 3. to establish, set up, put into operation.
plantel, *m.* 1. nursery (of plants). 2. establishment, institution; school, educational institution.
planteo, *m.* 1. *var. of* **planteamiento.** 2. layout, arrangement.
plantificación, *f.* establishment, setting-up.
plantificar, (*ref. 50*) *tr.v.* 1. to establish, set up. 2. to deal, give, plant (a blow). 3. to put, place, plant; to throw (into the street).
plantifique, plantifiqué, *ref.* **plantificar.**
plantígrado, da, *a.* (zool.) plantigrade. *—m.* (zool.) plantigrade; (*pl.*) Plantigrada.
plantilla, *f.* 1. insole, inner sole (of a shoe). 2. patch used for covering holes in socks. 3. lockplate (of gun, etc.). 4. template, jig, pattern, mold. 5. reduced plan; part of plan. 6. list or roll of staff. 7. list of duties (in public departments). 8. (astrol.) celestial configuration. 9. (carp.) full-scale drawing (of part or whole of structure). — **p. curva,** irregular curve, French curve; **p. de radio,** radius gauge; **p. mecánica,** mechanical template.
plantillar, *tr.v.* to sole (shoes).
plantillero, ra, *a.* swaggering, bullying. *—m., f.* bully, swaggerer.
plantío, a, *a.* 1. planted. 2. ready to be planted. *—m.* 1. planting. 2. bed, patch, plantation; plants (in a bed or patch).
plantista, *m.* 1. landscape gardener. 2. (coll.) bully, braggart.
plantón, *m.* 1. shoot (to be transplanted); cutting, scion (section of plant used for propagation). 2. sentry on long punishment guard. 3. watchman, guard. 4. tax officer, tax-enforcement officer. — **dar un p.,** to keep (someone) waiting; **estar de** or **en p.,** (coll.) to be standing around a long time (in one place); **llevarse** or **pegarse un p.,** to be kept waiting; to be stood up.
plántula, *f.* 1. (bot.) plantule, plantlet. 2. (zool.) plantula, pulvillus.
planudo, da, *a.* (mar.) flat-bottomed.
plánula, *f.* (zool.) planula.
plañidero, ra, *a.* plaintive, mournful, weeping, moaning. *—f.* weeper, hired mourner.
plañido, *m.* wail, cry, moan, lament.
plañimiento, *m.* lamentation, wailing, weeping, moaning.
plañir, (*ref. 66*) *i.v.* to wail, lament, cry, weep, moan. *—tr.v.* to bemoan, grieve over.

plaqué, *m.* plate, plating; plated metal, cladding, filled gold.
plaquear, *tr.v.* to veneer.
plaqueta, *f.* (biol.) blood platelet.
plaquín, *m.* hauberk, long coat of mail.
plasma, *f.* (biol.) plasma. 2. (min.) plasma, dark green agate. — **p. iónico,** (phys.) ionic plasma.
plasmador, ra, *m., f.* maker, molder. *—m.* **P.,** the Creator.
plasmagén, *m.* (biol.) plasmagene.
plasmalema, *f.* (zool.) plasmalemma.
plasmante, *a.* forming, shaping, molding.
plasmar, *tr.v.* to form, shape, mold, create.
plasmasol, *m.* (zool.) plasmasol.
plasmático, ca, *a.* (biol.) plasmatic.
plasmodio, *m.* (biol.) plasmodium.
plasmólisis, *f.* (physiol.) plasmolysis.
plasmología, *f.* (phys.) plasmology.
plasta, *f.* 1. paste, soft mass, soft mixture. 2. flattened object. 3. (coll.) poor job, mess.
plaste, *m.* size, filler (for filling holes prior to painting).
plastecer, (*ref. 45*) *tr.v.* to fill, size (prior to painting).
plastecido, *m.* sizing, filling.
plastezca, plastezco, *ref.* **plastecer.**
plástica, *f.* art of modeling in clay.
plasticidad, *f.* plasticity.
plástico, ca, *a.* 1. plastic, soft, pliable. 2. aesthetic, well-formed; harmoniously conceived and executed (said of works of art); **artes plásticas,** fine arts. *—m.* 1. (chem.) plastic (material). 2. (chem.) certain explosive. *—f.* art of modeling in clay and other pliable media. — **plástico alveolar,** plastic foam; **plástico celular,** foam rubber.
plástida, *f* (biol.) plastid.
plastilina, *f.* modeling clay.
plastrón, *m.* 1. leather apron. 2. large cravat. 3. (fencing) plastron.
plata, *f.* 1. (min.) silver. 2. silver, silver coins; (coll.) small change. 3. money; wealth, riches. 4. (her.) argent. — **en p.,** (coll.) briefly, without beating about the bush; in a word, in a nutshell; **p. agria,** (min.), black silver, stephanite; **p. alemana,** (min.) German silver; **p. córnea,** (min.) horn silver, cerargyrite; **p. de ley,** hallmarked silver; **p. de piña,** (min.) piña, conical mass of spongy silver left after retorting; **p. gris,** (min.) silver glance, argentite; **p. labrada,** silverware, silver plate; **p. mexicana,** silver not coined in the mint but of sterling quality; **p. nativa,** native silver; **p. roja clara,** (min.) proustite; **p. roja oscura,** (min.) dark red silver ore; ruby silver ore, pyrargyrite; **p. vítrea,** argentite, vitreous silver, silver glance.
platabanda, *f.* 1. narrow flower bed. 2. (archit.) flat molding.
plataforma, *f.* 1. platform; stage. 2. (bus or train) platform. 3. (ry.) platform car, flatcar. 4. (fort.) platform (for guns). 5. (geog.) platform, shelf. 6. (mec.) index plate. 7. platform, program (of a political party). — **p. continental,** (geog.) continental shelf; **p. de lanzamiento,** launching pad; **p. de perforación,** drilling rig; **p. electoral,** electoral platform, party platform; **p. espacial,** space station; **p. giratoria,** turntable; revolving stage; **p. petrolífera** or **petrolera,** oil rig.
platal, *m.* (Amer.) fortune, pile of money, mint (U.S., sl.).
platalea, *f.* (ornith.) pelican.
platanáceo, a, platáneo, a, *a.* (bot.) platanaceous. *—f.* (*pl.*) Platanaceae.
platanal, platanar, *m.* banana or plantain grove or plantation.

platanero, ra, *a.* (Cuba) strong (wind). *—m.* banana tree, plantain tree.
plátano, *m.* (bot.) banana (tree and fruit); (bot.) plantain (Musa paradisiaca - tree and fruit); (bot.) plane tree. — **p. falso** (bot.) sycamore, maple.
platea, *f.* (theat.) orchestra floor, stalls (G.B.), parquet; **p. alta,** dress circle.
plateado, da, *past part. of* **platear.** *—a.* 1. silver-plated. 2. silvery, silver. — **p. galvanoplástico,** (chem.) electrosilvered. *—m.* silver plating.
plateador, *m.* plater, silverer.
plateadura, *m.* silver plating; silver (used in plating).
platear, *tr.v.* to plate or coat with silver, to silver-plate.
platel, *m.* platter, tray.
platelminto, *a.* (zool.) platyhelminthic. *—m.* platyhelminth; (*pl.*) Platyhelminthes.
plateresco, ca, *a.* (archit., art) plateresque, pertaining to an ornate Spanish style of the 16th century.
platería, *f.* silversmith's trade or workshop; silverware shop.
platero, *a.* silver-grey (color). *—m.* silversmith; dealer in silverware; **p. de oro,** goldsmith.
plática, *f.* conversation, chat, talk; address, talk; **libre p.,** (mar.) pratique.
platicar, (*ref. 50*) *tr.v.* to talk over, discuss. *—i.v.* to converse, talk, chat, discuss.
platicéfalo, la, *a.* (anat.) platycephalous.
platija, *f.* (ichth.) plaice, European flounder.
platilla, *f.* (tex.) Silesian linen (a sheer but coarse fabric).
platillo, *m.* 1. small dish, small plate, saucer. 2. plate, disk. 3. pan (of scales). 4. (cul.) ragout of meat and vegetables. 5. extra dish (served in monasteries on feast days). 6. subject of gossip. 7. (mus.) cymbal. — **platillo volador** or **volante,** flying saucer.
platina, *f.* (chem.) platinum.
platina, *f.* 1. platen, flat metal plate. 2. (min.) ore of platinum. 3. stage (small platform in microscope on which specimen to be studied is placed). 4. (print.) imposing table or stone. 5. (print.) bed (part of the press on which the form is laid); **p. a cassette,** tape deck.
platinado, *m.* platinum plating.
platinar, *tr.v.* to platinize, coat or plate with platinum.
platínico, ca, *a.* (chem.) platinic.
platinífero, ra, *a.* platinum-bearing.
platinista, *m.* platinum worker.
platinita, *f.* (metal.) platinite; (geol.) platynite, platinite.
platino, *m.* (chem.) platinum.
platinociánico, ca, *a.* (chem.) platinocyamic.
platinocianuro, *m.* (chem.) platinocyanide, platinocyanid.
platinoide, *m.* (metal.) platinoid.
platinos, *m.* (auto.) contact points.
platinoso, sa, *a.* (chem.) platinous.
platinotipia, *f.* (photog.) platinotype.
platique, platiqué, *ref.* **platicar.**
platirrinia, *f.* platyrrhinism.
platirrino, na, *a.* (zool.) platyrrhinian, platyrrhine. *—m.* (zool.) platyrrhine; (*pl.*) Platyrrhina.
plató, *m.* (cinem.) film studio set.
plato, *m.* 1. plate, dish (tableware). 2. pan (of scales). 3. (cul.) dish, culinary specialty. 4. course (part of a meal), e.g. *primer p.,* first course, *p. de fondo,* main course. 5. daily food. 6. (coll.) subject of gossip. 7. (archit.) gutta (ornament on metope of Doric frieze). 8. (mec.) plate, disk. — **comer en un mismo p.,** (coll.) to be close friends, be intimate friends; **entre dos platos,** with much bowing and scraping, with a great deal of ceremony; **hacer el p. a uno,** (coll.) to maintain, feed, keep someone (provide with food); **no haber quebrado un p.,** to be completely innocent; **pagar los platos rotos,** to pay the piper, to be the goat; **p. combinado,** (mec.) combination chuck; **p. de postre,** dessert plate; **p. hondo,** soup dish; **p. llano** or **liso,** dinner plate, plate; **p. sopero,** soup plate; **p. trinchero,** carving plate, trencher; dinner plate; **p. universal,** (mec.) universal chuck; **ser p. del gusto de uno,** (coll.) to be one's cup of tea, be just what one likes; **ser p. de segunda mesa,** (coll.) to play second fiddle.
platón, *m.* (Amer.) big plate or dish; wash bowl, wash basin.
Platón, *m.* Plato, Greek philosopher.
platónicamente, *adv.* platonically.
platónico, ca, *a.* Platonic. *—m., f.* Platonist.
platonismo, *m.* (philos.) Platonism.
platudo, da, *a.* (Amer., coll.) wealthy, rich.
platuja, *f.* (ichth.) plaice.
plausibilidad, *f.* 1. plausibility. 2. praiseworthiness, commendability.
plausible, *a.* 1. commendable, laudable; worthy of applause. 2. admissible, plausible.
plausiblemente, *adv.* 1. plausibily. 2. commendably, laudably.
plausivo, va, *a.* 1. plausive. 2. laudatory.
plauso, *m.* applause.
plaustro, *m.* (poet.) cart, wagon, carriage.
plautino, na, *a.* Plautine, pertaining to Plautus, Roman playwright.
playa, *f.* 1. beach, shore. 2. (mar.) open space (on ship). 3. (Amer.) piece of clear land, open space. 4. (geol.) playa. — **cabeza de p.,** (mil.), beachhead; **p. de carga,** (ry.) freight yard; **p. de distribución,** (ry.) switching yard, switchyard; **p. de estacionamiento,** (Amer.) car park, parking lot; **p. ferroviaria,** (Amer.) railway yard.
playado, da, *a.* having a beach.
playazo, *m.* large beach; extended shore.
playeras, *f.* (mus.) a style of Andalusian song.
playero, ra, *a.* of or pertaining to the beach, e.g. *bata playera,* beach robe. *—m., f.* one who sells fish or seafood at the seaside.
playón, *m.* large beach.
playuela, playita, *f. dim. of* **playa,** small beach.
plaza, *f.* 1. plaza, square, town square. 2. market place, market. 3. (mil.) fortified town, fortress, stronghold. 4. place, space, room. 5. job, work; post, employment, position. 6. entry of enlistment (in enlistment register). 7. emporium, financial and commercial center. 8. (mil.) parade ground. 9. furnace floor. — **sentar p.,** to enlist, join up (in the armed forces); **atacar bien la p.,** (coll.) to eat well; **de una p.** or **dos plazas,** single or double (bed, sheet, etc.); **echar en la p.,** (coll.) to publish, make public; **hacer p.,** to sell retail; to make room, clear the way; **hacer la p.,** to do the marketing, go shopping at the market; **¡plaza!** clear the way, out of the way; **p. de aparcamiento,** parking space; **p. de armas,** stronghold, fortress; parade ground; (Amer.) central or main square (of a town); **p. de garaje,** parking space; **p. de toros,** bullring; **p. fuerte,** fortified town, stronghold, fortress; **p. mayor,** main square; **p. montada,** (mil.) trooper, cavalry soldier; **sacar a la p.,** (coll.) to publish, make public; **sentar p.,** to enlist, join up (in the armed forces); **socorrer la p.,** to help the needy.
plazca, plazco, *ref.* **placer.**
plazo, *m.* 1. period, term, space (of time); time limit. 2. installment. — **comprar a plazos,** to buy on credit, buy in installments, buy on time, buy on the never-never (G.B.). — **en breve p.,** in a short time; **vender a plazos,** to sell on credit.
plazoleta, *f. dim. of* **plazuela,** small square; small square or space in a garden or walk.
plazuela, *f. dim. of* **plaza,** small square.
ple, *m.* handball game.
pleamar, *m.* (mar.) high water, high tide; high tide mark; **p. media,** mean high water.
plébano, *m.* parish priest.
plebe, *f.* common people, populace; crowd, rabble.
plebeyez, *f.* plebeianism.
plebeyo, ya, *a.* plebeian. *—m., f.* plebeian; commoner.
plebiscitario, ria, *a.* pertaining to a plebiscite.
plebiscito, *m.* plebiscite.
pleca, *f.* (print.) thin-lined rule.
plectognato, *a.* (ichth.) plectognathous, plectognath. *—m.* plectognath; (*pl.*) Plectognathi.
plectro, *m.* 1. (mus.) plectrum. 2. (fig.) inspiration, style (in poetry).
plegable, *a.* folding, collapsible.
plegadamente, *adv.* 1. confusedly. 2. wholesale.
plegadera, *f.* paper knife, paper folder.
plegadizo, za, *a.* pliable, pliant; folding; foldable, easy to fold; **silla plegadiza,** folding chair.
plegado, *m., var. of* **plegadura.**
plegador, ra, *a.* folding. *—m., f.* folder; plaiter. *—m.* warp beam (of a silk loom).
plegadura, *f.* folding; fold; pleat, crease.
plegamiento, *m.* (geol.) fold.
plegar, (*ref. 67*) *tr.v.* 1. to fold, double. 2. to pleat, e.g. *una falda plegada,* a pleated skirt. 3. to wind (warp) on to a warp beam. *—r.v.* 1. to fold. 2. to yield, submit. 3. to join, adhere, e.g. *plegarse a una huelga, un movimiento, etc.,* to join a strike, a movement, etc.
plegaria, *f.* 1. prayer, supplication. 2. midday call to prayer. — **hacer plegarias,** to implore, beseech.
plegué, *ref.* **plegar.**
pleguería, *f.* pleats, folds (esp. in robes and drapery).
pleguete, *m.* vine tendril.
pleistoceno, *a.* (geol.) Pleistocene.
pleita, *f.* plaited strand of esparto grass.
pleiteador, ra, *a.* litigating, litigious; troublemaking. *—m., f.* litigious person; troublemaker.
pleiteante, *a.* litigating.
pleitear, *i.v.* to litigate, go to court; to engage in legal action, bring legal action.
pleitesía, *f.* homage, reverence; **rendir p.,** to do homage.
pleitista, *a.* troublemaking, trouble-picking, litigious. *—m., f.* troublemaker, litigious person.
pleito, *m.* 1. lawsuit, suit; court or judicial action or proceedings. 2. quarrel, dispute, argument. 3. fight, battle. — **arrastrar el p.,** to remove a case to a superior court; **contestar el p.,** to oppose the claim, defend the suit; **dar el p. por concluso,** to close a case; **p. civil,** (law) civil suit; **p. criminal,** (law) criminal prosecution; **p. de acreedores,** bankruptcy proceedings; **poner p. a,** to bring a suit against; **salir con el p.,** to win a suit; **ver el p. mal parado,** to recognize the risk of something.
plenamar, *f., var. of* **pleamar.**
plenamente, *adv.* fully, completely.
plenariamente, *adv.* 1. completely, fully. 2. (law) plenarily.
plenario, ria, *a.* 1. plenary, full, complete, entire. 2. (law) plenary.
plenilunio, *m.* full moon.
plenipotencia, *f.* full powers.
plenipotenciario, ria, *a., m., f.* plenipotentiary.
plenitud, *f.* plenitude, fullness; abundance, plenty. — **en la p. de la vida,** in the prime of life.

pleno, na, *a.* full, complete; **en p.** + *n.*, in the middle of + *n.*, at the height of + *n.*; **en plena calle,** right in the middle of the street; **en plena carrera,** right in the middle of the race; **en pleno día,** in broad daylight; **en plena guerra,** in the middle of the war; **en pleno invierno,** in the depth of winter; **en plena juventud,** in the flower of youth; **a pleno sol,** at high noon; **en pleno verano,** at the height of summer. —*m.* plenum, general assembly, joint session.
pleonasmo, *m.* (rhet.) pleonasm, redundancy.
pleonásticamente, *adv.* pleonastically.
pleonástico, ca, *a.* pleonastic.
pleópodo, *m.* (zool.) pleopod.
plepa, *f.* person, animal or object full of defects or faults.
plerocercoide, *m.* (med.) plerocercoid.
plesímetro, *m.* (med.) pleximeter.
plesiosauro, *m.* (paleon.) plesiosaur.
pletina, *f.* sheet metal, sheet iron; small iron plate.
plétora, *f.* 1. (med.) plethora. 2. (fig.) plethora, superabundance.
pletórico, ca, *a.* plethoric.
pleura, *f.* (anat.) pleura.
pleural, *a.* (anat.) pleural.
pleurectomía, *f.* (med.) pleurectomy.
pleuresía, *f.* (med.) pleurisy; **p. seca,** (med.) dry pleurisy.
pleurítico, ca, *a.* (med.) pleuritic; (anat.) pleural.
pleuritis, *f.* (med.) pleuritis.
pleurodinia, *f.* (med.) pleurodynia, pain in the side of the chest.
pleurodonte, *a.* (zool.) pleurodont.
pleuronecto, *m.* (ichth.) pleuronectid; (*pl.*) Pleuronectes.
pleuroneumonía, *f.* (med.) pleuropneumonia.
pleuroperitoneo, *m.* (anat.) pleuroperitoneum.
pleuston, *m.* (bot.) pleuston.
plexiglás, *m.* plexiglass, plexiglas.
plexo, *m.* (anat.) plexus; **p. sacro,** (anat.) sacral plexus; **p. solar,** (anat.) solar plexus.
Pléyadas, *f.* (*pl.*) (astron.) Pleiades.
pléyade, *f.* pleiad, group (esp. of poets or writers).
Pléyades, *f.* (*pl.*) (astron., myth.) Pleiades.
plica, *f.* 1. sealed document or letter to be opened on a certain date; (law) escrow. 2. (med.) plica.
pliego, *m.* 1. sheet (of paper). 2. section (of book or newspaper of two or more sheets). 3. sealed letter, envelope or document. 4. list (of claims, conditions, etc.). — **p. de cargos,** list of charges; **p. de condiciones,** specifications, list of conditions; **pliegos de cordel,** popular ballads, romances, etc. (published in loose sheets); **p. de costas,** (law) bill of costs; **p. de prensa,** (print.) proof sheet (taken from press to check errors); **p. perdido,** (print.) spoil, spoiled sheet.
pliego, pliegue, *ref.* **plegar.**
pliegue, *m.* fold; pleat, crease, gather. — **p. anticlinical,** (geol.) upwarp, anticlinal fold; **p. de arrastre,** (geol.) drag fold; **p. isoclínico,** (geol.) isoclinal or closed fold; **p. sinclinal,** (geol.) downwarp, synclinal fold.
plieguecillo, *m.* half sheet, small pleat.
Plinio, *m.* Pliny; **P. el Joven,** Pliny the Younger, Roman writer and statesman; **P. el Viejo,** Pliny the Elder, Roman naturalist and writer.
plinto, *m.* (archit.) plinth.
plioceno, *a., m.* (geol.) Pliocene.
pliodinatrón, *m.* (rad.) pliodynatron.
pliotrón, *m.* (rad.) pliotron.
plisado, da, *past part. of* **plisar.** —*a.* pleated. —*m.* pleat, pleating.
plisamiento, *m.* (geol.) fold.
plisar, *tr.v.* to pleat, to accordion-pleat (fabric, garment).
plomada, *f.* 1. lead pencil (used by some craftsmen). 2. plumb, plummet, plumb bob. 3. (mar.) sounding line, plumb line. 4. sinker, lead weight (on fishing line or net). 5. cat-o-nine-tails (with lead balls attached). 6. lead touch-hole cover (on cannon).
plomar, *tr.v.* to put a lead seal on.
plomazo, *m.* bullet wound, shot wound.
plomazón, *f.* gilder's cushion (on which goldsmith cuts gold leaf).
plombagina, *f.* plumbago, graphite.
plomería, *f.* 1. lead roofing. 2. plumber's workshop. 3. lead warehouse. 4. plumbing, plumber's trade. 5. plumbing, lead-work (of house).
plomero, *m.* lead worker; plumber.
plomífero, ra, *a.* plumbiferous, lead-bearing. —*m., f.* (coll.) bore, nuisance, bother.
plomizo, za, *a.* 1. leaden, gray, lead-colored. 2. leaden, lead-like.
plomo, *m.* 1. (chem.) lead. 2. lead, lead weight; lead, sinker (of net); plumb bob, plummet (of plumb line). 3. bullet. 4. (coll.) bore, nuisance, pest. 5. (elec.) fuse. — **andar con pies de p.,** to proceed with great caution; **a p.,** vertically, plumb; flat; **caer a p.,** to fall flat; **p. amarillo,** (min.) yellow lead ore, wulfenite; **p. blanco,** (chem.) white lead; **p. corto,** buckshot lead; **p. de obra,** silver-bearing lead ore; **p. dulce,** pure lead, refined lead; **p. fundido,** (elec.) blown fuse; **p. pobre,** lead ore poor in silver; **p. rico,** lead ore rich in silver; **p. rojo,** crocoite; red lead; **p. verde,** green lead ore, pyromorphite.
plomoso, sa, *a., var.* of **plomizo.**
pluguiera, pluguieron, pluguiese, plugo, *ref.* **placer.**
pluma, *f.* 1. feather. 2. quill, quill pen. 3. pen nib; pen. 4. shaving (produced when shaping something on a lathe). 5. penmanship, handwriting, calligraphy. 6. writer, pen, author. 7. style, pen. 8. writing profession. 9. (coll.) flatulence. 10. derrick, boom. 11. (C. Amer.) hoax, rumor, story. 12. (Col., Cuba, P. Rico) tap, faucet. — **al correr de la p., a vuela p.,** (to write) without stopping to think, carried away by the mood or inspiration; **hacer a p. y a pelo,** (coll.) to be very versatile, be a jack-of-all-trades; **p. atómico,** (Mex.) ballpoint pen; **p. de contorno,** contour feather; **p. estilográfica,** stylographic pen; **p. fuente,** fountain pen; **poner la p. bien** or **mal,** to write well or badly, express oneself well or badly; **vivir de su p.,** to live by writing.
plumada, *f.* 1. pen stroke, flourish. 2. feathers swallowed by a hawk. 3. plumage (feathers given to hawks as casting).
plumado, da, *a.* feathered, feathery, plumed.
plumaje, *m.* plumage; plume, crest.
plumajería, *f.* plumes, plumage, crests.
plumajero, *m.* feather-dresser.
plumaria, *a.* art of embroidering with feathers (as was done in pre-Columbian Mexico).
plumario, *m.* featherworker, feather embroiderer.
plumazo, *m.* 1. feather bed or mattress, feather pillow. 2. pen stroke, dash, stroke crossing out what has been written. — **de un p.,** with one stroke of the pen.
plumazón, *f.* plumage; plumes.
plumbado, da, *a.* sealed with lead, with a lead seal.
plumbagina, *f., var. of* **plombagina.**
plumbagináceo, a, plumbagíneo, a, *a.* (bot.) plumbaginaceous. —*f.* (*pl.*) Plumbaginaceae.
plúmbeo, a, *a.* 1. leaden, lead-like. 2. leaden, heavy, weighty.
plúmbico, ca, *a.* (chem.) plumbic.
plumbífero, *a.* containing lead.
plumbismo, *m.* (med.) plumbism.
plumeado, *m.* (p.) hatching (feather brush strokes employed in miniature painting).
plumear, *tr.v.* (p.) 1. to hatch. 2. to write with a quill.
plúmeo, a, *a.* feathered.
plumería, *f.* feathers, plumes (collectively); plumosity.
plumerilla, *f.* (Arg., Urug.) red-flowered mimosa.
plumerío, *m., var. of* **plumería.**
plumero, *m.* 1. feather duster. 2. pen box; (Amer.) penholder. 3. plumes, crest, panache.
plumier, *m.* pencil and pen case.
plumífero, a, *a.* (poet.) plumed, feathered. —*m., f.* (derog.) hack, hack journalist or writer.
plumilla, *f.* 1. *dim. of* **pluma,** small feather. 2. (bot.) plumule. 3. (Peru, coll.) windshield wiper.
plumión, *m., var. of* **plumón.**
plumista, *m.* 1. clerk, scrivener. 2. plumassier, person who makes objects with feathers.
plumita, *f. dim. of* **pluma,** small pen or feather.
plumón, *m.* 1. (ornith.) down, plumule. 2. feather bed. 3. (Sp.) pillow.
plumoso, sa, *a.* feathery, downy, plumy.
plúmula, *f.* (bot.) plumule.
plural, *a., m.* (gram.) plural.
pluralice, pluralicé, *ref.* **pluralizar.**
pluralidad, *f.* plurality, majority, large number; **a p. de votos,** by a majority of votes.
pluralismo, *m.* pluralism.
pluralizar, (*ref. 53*), *tr.v.* to pluralize.
pluriaxial, *a.* (bot.) pluriaxial.
pluriáxico, ca, *a.* (bot.) pluriaxial.
pluriglandular, *a.* (physiol.) polyglandular.
plurilingüe, *a.* plurilingual.
plurivalencia, *f.* multivalence, multivalency.
plus, *m.* (mil.) extra pay, extra, bonus.
pluscafé, *m.* (Amer.) liqueur (taken after a meal).
pluscuamperfecto, *a., m.* (gram.) pluperfect, past perfect.
plus minusve, (Lat.) about, more or less.
plusvalía, *f.* capital gain, increased value; (*in Marxian economics*) surplus value; **impuesto sobre la p.,** capital gains tax.
Plutarco, *m.* Plutarch, Greek historian and biographer.
plúteo, *m.* shelf, bookshelf.
plutocracia, *f.* plutocracy.
plutócrata, *m., f.* plutocrat.
plutocrático, ca, *a.* plutocratic.
Plutón, *m.* (astron., myth.) Pluto.
plutoniano, na, *a.* (geol.) plutonian, plutonic. —*m., f.* (geol.) plutonist.
plutónico, ca, *a.* (geol.) plutonic.
plutonio, *m.* (chem.) plutonium.
plutonismo, *m.* (geol.) plutonism, theory that rocks of the earth solidified from igneous fusion.
plutonista, *a., m., f.* (geol.) plutonist.
pluvia, *f.* (rare, poet.) rain.
pluvial, *a.* pluvial, rain; **agua p.,** rain water; **capa p.,** (ecc.) pluvial.
pluvímetro, *m., var. of* **pluviómetro.**
pluviografía, *f.* pluviography.
pluviógrafo, *m.* rain gauge, pluviograph; **p. registrador,** (meteorol.) udomograph, hyetograph, self-registering rain gage.
pluviometría, *f.* pluviometry.
pluviométrico, ca, *a.* pluviometric, pluviometrical.
pluviómetro, *m.* pluviometer, rain gage.
pluvionivómetro, *m.* (meteorol.) pluvionivometer, rain-snow gage.
pluvioso, sa, *a.* rainy, pluvious. —*m.* Pluviose (fifth month in the calendar of the French Revolution).

Pm *sym. of* **promecio,** promethium (Pm).
PNUD *abbrev. of* **Programa de las Naciones Unidas para el Desarrollo,** United Nations Development Program (UNDP).
Po *sym. of* **polonio,** polonium (Po).
P.O. *abbrev. of* **por orden,** by order.
poa, *f.* (mar.) bowline bridle.
poáceo, a, *a.* (bot.) poaceous. —*f.* (*pl.*) (bot.) Poaceae.
pobeda, *f.* white poplar grove.
poblacho, *m.* (derog.) poor shabby village, shabby broken-down village.
población, *f.* 1. population, citizenry. 2. city, town, village; **p. activa,** working population; **p. fija,** permanent population.
poblado, *m.* town, village; settlement, inhabited place.
poblador, ra, *a.* founding, settling, establishing. —*m., f.* inhabitant, settler; founder.
poblano, na, *a.* (Amer.) rustic, rural. —*m., f.* villager, peasant; townsman.
poblar, (*ref. 33*) *tr.v.* 1. to people, populate; to settle, colonize; to found. 2. to stock (a fishpond, beehive); to plant (with trees). —*i.v.* 1. to settle. 2. to multiply or procreate prolifically. —*r.v.* 1. to become peopled or populated. 2. to become covered with leaves. — **poblarse de,** to become full of, become covered with.
poblazo, *m., var. of* **poblacho.**
poblezuelo, *m. dim. of* **pueblo,** small village.
pobo, *m.* (bot.) white poplar.
pobre, *a.* 1. poor, needy, indigent. 2. poor, lacking, inadequate, paltry; barren. 3. poor, unfortunate. 4. poor, modest, humble, meek. — **más p. que una rata,** (coll.) as poor as a church mouse; **p. de espíritu,** poor in spirit; **p. de mí,** poor old me. —*m., f.* 1. poor person, poor man, poor woman; (*pl.*) the poor, poor people. 2. beggar, pauper. 3. poor devil, poor wretch; **p. de solemnidad,** pauper, very poor person.
pobrecillo, ito, *m. dim. of* **pobre,** poor little thing.
pobremente, *adv.* 1. poorly, indigently. 2. poorly, inadequately, scantily; sorrily.
pobrería, *f., var. of* **pobretería.**
pobrero, *m.* distributor of alms.
pobrete, ta, *a.* poor, unfortunate, wretched. —*m., f.* poor devil, unfortunate person, wretch.
pobretear, *i.v.* (coll.) to act the poor man, play the pauper.
pobretería, *f.* 1. poor people, beggars. 2. poverty, penury; niggardliness.
pobretón, na, *a.* very poor, needy. —*m., f.* very poor man or woman.
pobreza, *f.* 1. poverty, indigence, want, penury, destitution. 2. deficiency, scantiness. 3. barrenness, sterility. 4. (fig.) lack of magnanimity, meanness of spirit. 5. (ecc.) vow of poverty.
pobrezuelo, la, *m., f. dim. of* **pobre,** poor devil, poor wretch; poor little boy or girl, poor little child.
pobrísimo, ma, *a. super. of* **pobre,** extremely poor.
pobrismo, *m., var. of* **pobretería.**
pocero, *m.* 1. well digger, well driller; cesspool cleaner; sewerman. 2. (min.) pitman.
pochismo, *m.* (Mex.) Americanized Mexicanism.
pocho, cha, *a.* 1. faded, discolored. 2. overripe; rotten, bad (fruit). 3. (Chile) fat, chubby. —*m., f.* (Mex., derog.) Americanized Mexican.
pochote, *m.* (C. Rica, Hond., bot.) bombax (Bombax ellipticum).
pocilga, *f.* 1. pigpen, pigsty. 2. (fig.) hovel, filthy place.
pocillo, *m.* 1. sump, catch basin; vessel sunk in the ground in oil mills and wine presses. 2. chocolate cup. 3. (P. Rico) demitasse.
pócima, *f.* potion, concoction, draught; medicinal drink.
poción, *f.* drink; concoction; (pharm.) potion, medicinal preparation.
poco, ca, *a.* 1. little, scanty, not much, e.g. *hay poca comida,* there is little food. 2. (with collective nouns and in the pl.) few, not many, e.g. *ha venido poca gente,* few people have come, *pocos hombres han visto tal cosa,* few men have seen such a thing.
poco, *m.* little, small amount, little bit; **otro p.,** a little more; **un p. de,** a little; e.g. *un p. de agua, por favor,* a little water, please. —*adv.* 1. little, e.g. *habló p. pero bien,* he spoke little but well. 2. not very, e.g. *es un hombre p inteligente,* he is not a very intelligent man; **a p.,** shortly afterwards; **a p. de** + *inf.,* shortly after + *ger.;* **p. a p.,** little by little; take it easy, steady; **p. más o menos,** more or less; **por p.,** almost, nearly, e.g. *por p. se cae,* he nearly fell; **tener en p. a,** not to think much of, think little of.
póculo, *m.* goblet, drinking glass or cup.
poda, *f.* pruning; pruning season.
podadera, *f.* pruning hook or knife; hedging bill.
podador, ra, *a.* pruning. —*m., f.* pruner.
podadura, *f.* (rare), *var. of* **poda.**
podagra, *f.* (med.) gout, podagra.
podar, *tr.v.* to prune, lop, trim.
podazón, *f.* pruning season.
podenco, *m.* hound (dog).
podenquero, *m.* (hunt.) keeper of the hounds.
poder, *m.* 1. power, authority, command, sway, e.g. *no está en mi p. hacer tal cosa,* it is not within my power to do such a thing; (*pl.*) powers, e.g. *plenos poderes,* full powers. 2. power, strength, might. 3. power, possession, hands, tenure. 4. power of attorney, proxy. 5. (armed) forces. 6. government. — **en su p.,** in one's hands or possession; within one's power; **p. absorbente,** (chem.) absorbent power, absorptive power, absorptivity; **p. adquisitivo,** purchasing power; **p. calórico,** caloricity, calorific value, heating capacity, heat value; **p. dióptrico,** (opt.) dioptric power; **p. ejecutivo,** the executive; **p. judicial,** the judiciary; **p. legislativo,** the legislature; **p. resolvente,** (opt., photog.) resolving power; **poderes notariales,** power of attorney; **poderes públicos,** authorities.
poder, (*ref. 14*) *tr.v.* to be able, e.g. *no puedo venir mañana,* I cannot or am not able to come tomorrow, *no pudo ir al colegio,* he could not or was not able to go to school; **no p. ver a uno ni pintado,** not to be able to stand the sight of someone. —*i.v.* to be able, to have the power or strength; **a más no p.,** to the limits of one's power or endurance; as much as possible, e.g. *corrió a más no p.,* he ran as fast as he could; *comió a más no p.,* he ate as much as he could; **hasta más no p.,** as much as possible, with all one's might or strength; **no p. con,** not to be able to cope with, not to be able to manage or handle, not to be able to deal with; not to be able to stand (someone); **no p. más,** to be worn-out, exhausted, all-in; **no p. menos de** + *inf.,* cannot but + *inf.,* not to be able to help + *ger.* —*impers. v.* to be possible; **puede que** + *subj.* it's possible that + *subj.,* it may + *inf.* —*r.v.* to be able; **no poderse valer,** to be helpless.
poderdante, *m., f.* (law) constituent, principal.
poderhabiente, *m., f.* (law) attorney, proxy.
poderío, *m.* 1. power, strength, might. 2. power, authority, jurisdiction, dominion. 3. riches, wealth.
poderosamente, *adv.* powerfully, mightily.
poderoso, sa, *a.* 1. powerful, mighty. 2. rich, wealthy.
podestá, *m.* (hist.) podesta.
podíatra, *m.* (med.) podiatrist.
podiatría, *f.* (med.) podiatry.
podio, *m.* 1. podium, dais. 2. (archit.) podium.
podofilina, *f.* (chem.) podophyllin, podophyllum resin.
podofilotoxina, *f.* (chem.) podophyllotoxin.
podómetro, *m.* pedometer.
podón, *m.* large pruning hook, large billhook, mattock.
podre, *f.* putrid matter; (med.) pus, matter.
podrecer, (*ref. 45*) *tr.v., i.v., r.v.* to rot.
podrecimiento, *m., var. of* **podredura.**
podredumbre, *f.* 1. rottenness, putrefaction; rot, decay. 2. (fig.) corruption, moral breakdown. 3. (med.) pus, matter. 4. hidden sorrow, grief.
podredura, *f.* putrefaction, corruption.
podrición, *f., var. of* **podredura.**
podridero, *m.* 1. compost heap. 2. temporary vault (for corpses).
podrido, da, *past part. of* **podrir.** —*a.* rotten, putrid, putrescent. — **estar p. en plata,** to be rolling in money.
podrigorio, *m.* (coll.) person full of aches and pains, valetudinarian.
podrimiento, *m.* rotting, rottenness, putrefaction.
podrir, *tr.v., r.v.* to rot, putrefy, decay (used only in *inf.* and *past part.*); **podrirse en plata,** to be rolling in money.
podsol, *m.* podsol, podzol (barren, poor soil in cold damp regions).
poema, *m.* poem; **p. sinfónico,** (mus.) symphonic poem, tone poem.
poemario, *m.* collection of poetry.
poemático, ca, *a.* poetical.
poesía, *f.* 1. poetry, (*pl.*) poetical works, poems. 2. poem, poetical composition.
poeta, *m.* poet; **p. laureado,** poet laureate.
poetastro, *m.* poetaster.
poética, *f.* poetics, art of poetry.
poéticamente, *adv.* poetically.
poetice, poeticé, *ref.* **poetizar.**
poético, ca, *a.* poetic, poetical.
poetisa, *f.* poetess, woman poet.
poetizar, (*ref. 53*) *tr.v.* to poeticize, make poetic. —*i.v.* to write poetry, poeticize, poetize.
pogo, *m.* **pogo saltarín,** pogo stick (children's toy).
pogromo, *m.* (hist.) pogrom.
poíno, *m.* gantry, stilling, barrelstand.
poiquilotermo, ma, *a.* (ichth.) poikilothermic, poikilothermal.
poker, *m.* poker (card game).
polaca, *f.* (mil.) tunic.
polaco, ca, *a.* Polish. —*m., f.* Pole; (*pl.*) Poles, Polish. —*m.* Polish (language).
polacra, *f.* (mar.) polacre.
polaina, *f.* legging; gaiter, spat.
polar, *a.* polar; pole. —*f.* 1. (math.) polar. 2. (astron.) pole star.
polarice, polaricé, *ref.* **polarizar.**
polaridad, *f.* (phys., fig.) polarity; **p. invertida,** (elec.) reversed polarity.
polarimetría, *f.* (opt.) polarimetry.
polarimétrico, ca, *a.* polarimetric.
polarímetro, *m.* (phys.) polarimeter.
polariscopio, *m.* (phys.) polariscope.
polarización, *f.* polarization; **p. de rejilla,** (rad.) grid bias; **p. atómica,** (phys.) atomic polarization.
polarizador, ra, *a.* polarizing. —*m.* (opt., photog.) polarizer.
polarizar, (*ref. 53*) *tr.v.* to polarize. —*r.v.* to become polarized.
polarografía, *f.* (chem.) polarography.
polarógrafo, *m.* (phys., elec., chem.) polarograph.

polca, *f.* (mus.) polka.
polcar, (*ref. 50*) *i.v.* to dance the polka, to polka.
pólder, *m.* polder.
polea, *f.* (mec.) pulley, sheave; (mar.) tackle, purchase block; wheel of a conveyor belt; **p. de cadena,** (mec.) chain pulley; **p. de cono,** cone pulley; **p. muerta,** (mec.) idler pulley; **p. tensora,** (mec.) tension pulley, tightening pulley.
poleadas, *f.* (*pl.*) porridge, pap.
poleame, *m.* (mar.) act of pulleys, tackle.
polemarca, *m.* (hist.) polemarch (Greek military commander).
polémica, *f.* 1. polemics (art of disputation; polemic theology). 2. polemic (controversy). 3. (mil.) science of fortification.
polemice, polemicé, *ref.* **polemizar.**
polémico, ca, *a.* polemic, polemical.
polemista, *m., f.* polemicist, polemist.
polemizar, (*ref. 53*) *i.v.* to engage in controversy.
polemoniáceo, a, *a.* (bot.) polemoniaceous. —*f.* (bot.) polemonium, polemoniaceous plant; (*pl.*) Polemoniaceae.
polemonio, *m.* (bot.) polemonium, Greek valerian, Jacob's ladder.
polen, *m.* (bot.) pollen.
polenta, *f.* (cul.) polenta.
poleo, *m.* 1. (bot.) pennyroyal (Mentha polegium). 2. (coll.) cold wind. 3. (coll.) swagger, strutting gait.
polevi, *m.* (obs.) shoe with high wooden heel.
poli, *m.* (Sp., sl.) policeman.
poliadelfo, a, *a.* (bot.) polyadelphous.
poliamida, *f.* (chem.) polyamide.
poliandria, *f.* 1. polyandry, the state of having more than one husband at the same time. 2. (bot.) polyandry.
poliandro, ra, *a.* (bot.) polyandrous.
poliantea, *f.* miscellany of news items.
poliarquía, *f.* polyarchy, government by many.
poliárquico, ca, *a.* polyarchic.
poliatómico, *a.* (phys.) polyatomic.
polibásico, ca, *a.* (chem.) polybasic.
polibasita, *f.* (min.) polybasite.
policarpelar, *a.* (bot.) polycarpellary.
policarpelario, a, *a.* (bot.) polycarpellary.
policárpico, ca, *a.* (bot.) polycarpic, polycarpous.
policasio, *m.* (bot.) polychasium.
pólice, *m.* thumb (finger).
policelular, *a.* (engin.) polycellular, multicellular.
policía, *f.* 1. police. 2. (rare) politeness, courtesy, propriety. 3. (rare) cleanliness, neatness. 4. policewoman, police officer. — **p. antidisturbios,** riot police; **p. de tráfico** or **de tránsito,** traffic police; traffic policewoman; **p. judicial,** court officials or officers; **p. secreta,** secret police; **p. militar,** military police. —*m.* policeman, police officer.
policíaco, ca, *a.* 1. pertaining to police, e.g. *procedimientos policíacos,* police methods or procedure. 2. detective, e.g. *novela policíaca,* detective novel.
policial, *a.* 1. pertaining to police. 2. detective (novel). —*m.* (Amer.) policeman.
policíclico, ca, *a.* (elec., chem.) polycyclic.
policitación, *f.* (law) pollicitation, offer not yet accepted.
policitemia, *f.* (med.) polycythemia.
Policleto, *m.* Polyclitus, Polycleitus, Policletus, Greek sculptor of the 5th century B.C.
policlínica, *f.* (med.) polyclinic.
policondensación, *f.* (phys., chem.) polycondensation.
policónico, ca, *a.* polyconic.
policopia, *f.* multigraph, polygraph, copying machine.
policotiledóneo, a, *a.* (bot.) polycotyledonous. —*m.* polycotyledon.
policótomo, a, *a.* (bot.) polychotomous.
policroísmo, *m.* (min.) pleochroism, polychroism.
policromía, *f.* polychromy, polychrome effect.
policromo, ma, *a.* polychrome, many-colored.
policultura, *f.* diversified farming.
polichinela, *m.* punchinello, buffoon, clown.
polidáctilo, la, *a.* (zool.) polydactyl, polydactyle, polydactylous.
polidipsia, *f.* (med.) polydipsia, excessive thirst.
poliédrico, ca, *a.* (geom.) polyhedral, polyhedric.
poliedro, *m.* (geom.) polyhedron.
poliembrional, *a.* (biol.) polyembryonic.
poliembrionía, *f.* (biol.) polyembryony.
poliéster, *m.* (chem.) polyester.
poliestireno, *m.* (chem.) polystryrene.
polietileno, *m.* (chem.) polythene, polyethylene.
polifacético, ca, *a.* versatile, many-sided, diverse.
polifagia, *f.* 1. (med.) polyphagia, polyphagy, excessive hunger. 2. (zool.) polyphagism, feeding on many foods.
polífago, ga, *a.* 1. (med.) polyphagian, excessively hungry. 2. (zool.) polyphagous, feeding on many foods.
polifarmacia, *f.* dosing with a great number of medicines.
polifásico, ca, *a.* (elec.) polyphase, multiphase.
Polifemo, *m.* (myth.) Polyphemus, a Cyclops blinded by Odysseus.
polifilar, *a.* multiple-wire, multiwire.
polifilético, ca, *a.* polyphyletic.
polifonía, *f.* (mus.) polyphony.
polifónico, ca, *a.* polyphonic.
polífono, na, *a., var. of* **polifónico.**
polígala, *f.* (bot.) milkwort.
poligaláceo, a, poligáleo, a, *a.* (bot.) polygalaceous. —*f.* (*pl.*) Polygalaceae.
poligalia, *f.* (med.) polygalactia, excessive milk secretion in post-partum women.
poligamia, *f.* polygamy.
polígamo, ma, *a.* polygamous. —*m., f.* polygamist.
poligénico, ca, *a.* (biol.) polygenetic.
poligenismo, *m.* polygenism, polygeny.
poligenista, *m.* polygenist.
poliginia, *f.* 1. polygyny, practice or state of having several wives. 2. (bot.) state of having several pistils.
polígino, na, *a.* (bot.) polygynous.
poligloto, ta, *a.* polyglot. —*f.* polyglot Bible. —*m., f.* polyglot.
poligonáceo, a, *a.* (bot.) polygonaceous. —*f.* (*pl.*) Polygonaceae.
poligonación, *f.* (top.) survey by means of a series of polygons.
poligonal, *a.* (geom.) polygonal.
polígono, na, *a.* polygonal. —*m.* (geom., fort.) polygon; **p. de descongestión,** apartment development.
poligonometría, *f.* (top.) determination of areas.
poligrafía, *f.* polygraphy, art of writing in or interpreting ciphers.
poligráfico, ca, *a.* polygraphic.
polígrafo, *m.* 1. writer on widely differing subjects. 2. polygraph, copying machine. 3. (med.) polygraph.
polilla, *f.* 1. (ento.) moth, clothes moth, carpet moth. 2. (fig.) destroyer, consumer, waster. — **no tener p. en la lengua,** (coll.) to be outspoken or frank; **p. de biblioteca,** (fig.) bookworm; **p. de la harina,** (ento.) flour moth; **p. de las colmenas,** (ento.) bee or honey moth; **p. de las manzanas,** (ento.) codling moth, apple moth; **p. de trigo,** (agr.) corn weevil.
polimastigoto, ta, *a.* (zool.) polymastigote.
polimatía, *f.* polymathy, wide knowledge.
polimería, *f.* (biol., chem.) polymery.
polimerismo, *m.* (chem., biol.) polymerism.
polimerización, *f.* (chem., biol.) polymerization.
polimerizar, (*ref. 53*) *tr.v.* (chem.) to polymerize.
polímero, ra, *a.* 1. (bot.) polymerous. 2. (chem.) polymeric. —*m.* (chem.) polymer.
polimetría, *f.* (rhet.) polymetry.
polimétrico, ca, *a.* (rhet.) polymetric.
polímita, *a.* (tex.) varicolored (cloth).
polimixina, *f.* (chem.) polymyxin.
Polimnia, *f.* (myth.) Polyhymnia, Polymnia, one of the Muses.
polimórfico, ca, *a.* polymorphic.
polimorfismo, *m.* polymorphism.
polimorfo, fa, *a.* polymorphous.
polimorfonuclear, *a.* (physiol.) polymorphonuclear.
polín, *m.* wooden roller, skid.
polinación, *f.* (bot.) pollination.
polinesio, sia, *a., m., f.* Polynesian. —*f.* **P.,** Polynesia.
polineuritis, *f.* (med.) polyneuritis.
polinice, polinicé, *ref.* **polinizar.**
polínico, ca, *a.* (bot.) pollinic, pollinical, pollen.
polinio, *m.* (bot.) pollinium.
polinización, *f.* (bot.) pollination, pollinization.
polinizar, (*ref. 53*) *tr.v.* to pollinate, pollinize.
polinomio, *m.* (math.) polynomial.
polinosis, *f.* (med.) pollinosis, hay fever.
polio, *m.* (bot.) poly.
poliomielitis, *f.* (med.) poliomyelitis.
poliorcética, *f.* (mil.) poliorcetics, science of conducting sieges.
polipasto, *m.* tackle, pulleys; **p. diferencial,** differential hoist.
polipéptido, *m.* (biochem.) polypeptide, polypeptid.
polipero, *m.* (zool.) polypary.
polipétalo, la, *a.* (bot.) polypetalous.
polípido, *m.* (zool.) polypide.
poliploide, *a., m.* (biol.) polyploid.
poliploidia, *f.* (bot.) polyploidy.
polipnea, *f.* (med.) polypnea.
pólipo, *m.* 1. (zool.) polyp. 2. (zool.) octopus, polypus. 3. (med.) polypus, polyp.
polipodiáceas, *f.* (*pl.*) (bot.) Polypodiaceae.
polipodio, *m.* (bot.) polypody, sweet fern.
polipoide, *a.* (zool., med.) polypoid.
poliposo, sa, *a.* (med., zool.) polypous.
políptico, *m.* (p.) polyptych, set of painted panels.
poliptoton, *f.* (rhet.) polyptoton.
poliqueto, ta, *a., m.* (zool.) polychaete, polychaetous.
polisacárido, *m.* (chem.) polysaccharide, polysaccharid.
polisarcia, *f.* (med.) polysarcia, obesity.
poliscopio, *m.* (med.) polyscope.
polisemia, *f.* (gram.) polysemia, polysemy.
polisépalo, la, *a.* (bot.) having many sepals.
polisílabo, ba, *a.* polysyllabic. —*m.* polysyllable.
polisíndetum, *m.* (rhet.) polysyndeton.
polisintético, ca, *a.* (gram.) polysynthetic.
polisón, *m.* bustle (of woman's dress).
polispasto, *m.* pulleys, burton, hoisting tackle.
polista, *m.* (Phil. I.) native serving on communal works.
polista, *a.* polo playing. —*m., f.* polo player.
polistilo, la, *a.* 1. (archit.) polystyle, having many pillars. 2. (bot.) polystylous.
polisulfuro, *m.* (chem.) polysulfide, polysulphide, polysulfid, polysulphid.
politécnico, ca, *a.* polytechnic.
politeísmo, *m.* (rel.) polytheism.

politeísta, *a.* (rel.) polytheistic. —*m., f.* polytheist.
política, *f.* 1. politics. 2. policy. 3. politeness, tact, good manners, courtesy. — **p. de apaciguamiento,** policy of appeasement; **p. del Buen Vecino,** Good Neighbor Policy; **p. exterior,** foreign policy; **p. fiscal,** fiscal policy.
políticamente, *adv.* politically; politely.
politicastro, *m.* politicaster, petty politician.
político, ca, *a.* 1. political. 2. polite, courteous, tactful. 3. in-law, e.g. *padre político,* father-in-law. 4. cold, reserved. —*m., f.* politician.
politicón, na, *a.* 1. excessively polite, ceremonious. 2. extremely interesed in politics.
politípico, ca, *a.* (biol.) polytypical, polytypic.
politiquear, *i.v.* 1. (coll.) to make political maneuvers, to scheme politically. 2. (coll.) to talk politics, dabble in politics.
politiqueo, *m.* (coll.) political maneuvering, political scheming.
politiquería, *f., var. of* **politiqueo.**
politiquero, ra, *m., f.* political maneuverer, political schemer.
politiquero, *m.* politicaster.
politonalidad, *f.* (mus.) polytonality.
politono, na, *a.* (mus.) polytonal.
politrófico, ca, *a.* (bac.) polytrophic.
poliuretano, *m.* (chem.) polyurethane, polyurethan.
poliuria, *f.* (med.) polyuria.
poliúrico, ca, *a.* (med.) polyuric.
polivalencia, *f.* (bac., chem.) polyvalence.
polivalente, *a.* (bac., chem.) polyvalent, multivalent; manifold.
polivalvo, va, *a.* (zool.) multivalve (shellfish).
poliviníllico, ca, *a.* (chem.) polyvinyl.
polivinilo, *m.* (chem.) polyvinyl.
póliza, *f.* 1. (insurance) policy; (freight, stock exchange, etc.) contract. 2. draft, check, money order. 3. customs clearance certificate. 4. tax stamp. 5. entrance ticket. 6. anonymous note. — **p. flotante,** floating policy (in insurance).
polizoario, *m.* (zool.) polizoan.
polizón, *m.* 1. stowaway. 2. tramp, hobo, bum.
polizonte, *m.* (coll.) cop, copper, dick, policeman, fuzz (U.S., sl.).
polizoo, a, *a., m.* (zool.) polyzoan.
polla, *f.* 1. pullet, young hen. 2. (ornith.) coot. 3. bet, stake. 4. (coll.) young girl, lassie. 5. (Arg., Chile, Guat., Peru) gambling pool. 6. (Sp., sl.) penis. — **p. de agua,** water hen, gallinule, moor hen; water rail.
pollada, *f.* 1. hatch, brood, covey. 2. (artil.) volley (with howitzers).
pollancón, na, *m., f.* 1. large chicken. 2. strapping lad or lass, hefty youngster.
pollastre, *m.* 1. crafty fellow. 2. (coll.) young braggart.
pollastro, tra, *m., f.* large chicken. —*m.* (coll.) 1. crafty fellow. 2. young braggart.
pollazón, *f.* hatch, brood.
pollera, *f.* 1. woman poulterer, woman chicken breeder or dealer. 2. chicken coop; chicken yard; chicken basket. 3. hooped underskirt; (S. Amer.) skirt. 4. (type of) go-cart, child's wickerwork stroller.
pollería, *f.* 1. poultry shop, poultry market. 2. (coll.) gathering of young people.
pollero, *m.* 1. poulterer, chicken breeder or dealer. 2. chicken or poultry yard; chicken coop.
pollerón, *m.* (Arg.) riding skirt.
pollinarmente, *adv.* riding on a donkey.
pollinejo, ja, *m., f. dim. of* **pollino,** small donkey or ass.
pollino, na, *m., f.* 1. donkey, ass. 2. (fig.) ass, fool, dolt.
pollito, ta, *m., f.* 1. chick, baby chicken. 2. (coll.) chick, youngster.
pollo, *m.* 1. chicken. 2. young bee. 3. (coll.) chicken, young person, fledgling. 4. (coll.) wise guy, crafty fellow. — **estar hecho un p.,** (coll.) to look young and handsome; **mojado como un p.,** wet to the skin; **sacar pollos,** to hatch eggs.
polluelo, la, *m., f. dim. of* **pollo,** chick.
polo, *m.* 1. (geog., astron., biol., anat., bot., math., elec., fig.) pole. 2. (fig.) foundation, base. — **de p. a p.,** from pole to pole, from end to end; **p. antártico, austral** or **sur,** South Pole; **p. ártico, boreal** or **norte,** North Pole; **p. de frío,** (meteorol.) cold pole; **p. de un círculo en la esfera,** (math.) pole or axis of a circle of a sphere; **p. geográfico,** geographical pole; **p. magnético,** magnetic pole; **p. negativo,** (elec.) negative pole; (chem.) zinc pole; **p. positivo,** (elec.) positive pole; **polos opuestos se atraen,** opposite poles attract; **p. norte,** (geog.) North Pole; **p. sur,** (geog.) South Pole.
polo, *m.* 1. (sport.) polo; **p. acuático,** water polo. 2. (mus.) Andalusian popular dance and song. 3. (Phil. I.) yearly service rendered by the inhabitants during the Spanish domination.
pololear, *i.v.* (Chile) to flirt. —*tr.v.* (Amer.) to bother, annoy; (Chile) to flirt with.
pololo, la, *m., f.* (Chile, Ecuad.) youngster. —*m.* (Chile) flirt; (Chile) side job.
polonés, sa, *a.* Polish. —*m., f.* Pole. —*f.* 1. (mus.) polonaise. 2. polonaise, 18th century dress with an elaborate skirt.
Polonia, *f.* Poland.
polonio, *m.* (metal.) polonium.
poltrón, na, *a.* lazy, idle. —*m., f.* lazy person, lazybones (coll.). —*m.* poltroon.
poltronería, *f.* laziness, idleness, indolence.
poltronizarse, (*ref. 53*) *r.v.* to become lazy or idle.
polución, *f.* 1. (neol.) pollution (of the environment). 2. (med.) pollution, emission of semen.
poluto, ta, *a.* polluted, unclean.
Pólux, *m.* 1. (myth.) Pollux, twin of Castor. 2. (astron.) Pollux.
polvareda, *f.* 1. cloud of dust. 2. (fig.) disturbance, rumpus, hullaballoo.
polvera, *f.* powder-box; compact, powder case.
polvificar, (*ref. 50*) *tr.v.* (coll.) to pulverize.
polvillo, *m.* 1. fine dust. 2. (Amer., agr.) fungus, rot (on grains).
polvo, *m,* 1. dust (minute particle of earth; dirt settling on objects). 2. powder (result of solids being pulverized). 3. powder (cosmetic). — **en p.,** powdered, e.g. *leche en p.,* powdered milk; **estar hecho p.** (coll.), to be worn out, be a wreck; to be overcome or weighed down (by worries, etc.); **hacer p. a,** (coll.) to knock to pieces, knock the stuffing out of; **hacer morder el p.,** to beat, conquer, overcome, make someone bite the dust; **levantar** or **sacar del p.,** to raise from nothing; **limpio de p. y paja,** (coll.) with no strings attached; net, pure (profit); **matar el p.,** to settle the dust (before sweeping); **morder el p.,** (coll.) to bite the dust, be conquered or beaten; **p. de ángel,** (sl.) angel dust (drug); **p. de arroz,** rice powder; **p. de blanquear,** bleaching powder; **p. de azúcar,** powdery mildew; **p. de capuchino,** powdered sabadilla seed; **p. de cartas** or **de salvadera,** sand (to dry ink); **p. de hornear,** (cul.) baking powder; **p. de la madre Celestina,** (coll.) magic formula (for doing something), hocus-pocus; **p. dentífrico,** tooth powder; **p. limpiador** or **de limpieza,** scouring powder; **polvos compactos,** face powder; **polvos de talco,** talcum powder; **polvos para dormir** or **soporíferos,** sleeping powder; **p. radiactivo,** atomic dust; **sacar p. debajo del agua,** (coll.) to be very smart or clever; **sacudir el p. a,** (coll.) to give a beating, beat up; (coll.) to refute.
pólvora, *f.* 1. gunpowder, powder. 2. fireworks. 3. bad temper. 4. liveliness, briskness. — **Conspiración de la P.,** (hist.) Gunpowder Plot; **gastar p. en salvas,** to waste one's energy to no effect, waste one's time; **mojar la p. a,** to calm (someone) down; **no haber inventado la p.,** (coll.) not to be overbright, be rather dim; **p. de algodón,** guncotton; **p. de combustión lenta,** slow-burning powder; **p. detonante** or **fulminante,** fulminating powder; **p. lenta** or **progresiva,** slow burning powder, progressive powder; **p. negra,** blasting or black powder; **p. prismática,** prismatic powder; **p. sin humo,** smokeless powder; **p. sorda,** (fig.) snake in the grass, underhanded person; **ser la p.,** to be very quick, lively or efficient; **tirar con p. ajena,** (coll.) to spend someone else's money at gambling.
polvoraduque, *f.* (cul., rare) sauce made with cloves, ginger, cinnamon and sugar.
polvoreamiento, *m.* sprinkling, dusting, powdering.
polvorear, *tr.v.* to sprinkle, dust, powder.
polvoriento, ta, *a.* dusty; pulverulent; floury (soil).
polvorín, *m.* 1. powder magazine. 2. powder flask, powder horn. 3. fine gunpowder. 4. (fig.) powder keg, explosive trouble spot. 5. (Arg., Chile, Mex.) spitfire, quick-tempered person. 6. (Arg.) small tick (insect).
polvorista, *m.* pyrotechnist, maker of fireworks.
polvorón, *m.* (cul.) crumb cake; shortcake; sugar cookie.
polvoroso, sa, *a.* dusty; **poner pies en polvorosa,** to beat it, run away, take it on the lam (U.S., sl.).
polvoscopio, *m.* dust-counter (device).
poma, *f.* 1. apple. 2. cassolette (pan for burning perfume; perfume box). 3. pomander, pomander box.
pomáceo, a, *a.* (bot.) pomaceous. —*f.* (*pl.*) Pomaceae.
pomada, *f.* ointment, pomade; salve; **divina p.,** (Peru) cat's whiskers, hot stuff, e.g. *se cree la divina p.,* he thinks he's the cat's whiskers.
pomar, *m.* orchard, apple orchard.
pomarada, *f.* apple orchard.
pomarrosa, *f.* (bot.) rose apple.
pomelo, *m.* (S. Amer., bot.) grapefruit.
pomerano, na, *a., m., f.* Pomeranian.
pomez, *f.* pumice, pumice stone.
pomicultura, *f.* (bot.) pomiculture.
pomífero, ra, *a.* (poet.) pomiferous, apple-bearing.
pomo, *m.* 1. (small) bottle, vial, flagon (for perfume, etc.). 2. pommel (of sword hilt). 3. pomander, pomander box. 4. (bot.) pome.
pomol, *m.* (Mex.) corn tortilla.
pomología, *f.* (bot.) pomology.
pomólogo, *m.* (bot.) pomologist.
pompa, *f.* 1. pomp, ostentation, pageantry, splendor. 2. procession, pageant. 3. bubble. 4. billow, bulge, swell. 5. spread of a peacock's tail. 6. (mar.) pump. — **hacer p.,** to show off; **p. de jabón,** soap bubble; **pompas fúnebres,** funeral.
pompear, *i.v.* to show off, swagger, strut. —*r.v.* to show off, strut about.
Pompeya, *f.* (hist.) Pompeii.
pompeyano, na, *a., m., f.* (hist.) Pompeian.
pompo, pa, *a.* (Col.) blunt (knife, scissors, etc.).
pompón, *m.* 1. pompon (ornamental ball). 2. (Cuba, ichth.) pompon, pompoon.
pomponearse, *r.v.* to show off, strut about.

pomposamente, *adv.* 1. magnificently, sumptuously, pompously. 2. grandiloquently, pompously. 3. pompously, self-importantly.
pomposidad, *f.* 1. magnificence, sumptuousness, pompousness. 2. grandiloquence, pompousness. 3. pomposity, pompousness.
pomposo, sa, *a.* 1. magnificent, sumptuous, pompous, imposing, ostentatious. 2. grandiloquent, ornate, pompous (speech).
pómulo, *m.* (anat.) cheekbone.
pon, *m.* (P. Rico) lift, ride: **ofrecer p.,** to offer a ride; **pedir p.,** to thumb a ride.
ponasí, *m.* (Cuba, bot.) hamelia (Hamelia patens).
ponchada, *f.* 1. bowlful of punch. 2. (Amer.) ponchoful, contents of a poncho. 3. (Arg., Chile, Urug.) large quantity (of anything).
ponche, *m.* punch (drink); **p. de huevo,** eggnog.
ponchera, *f.* punch bowl.
poncho, *m.* (Amer.) poncho, cape, cloak; (mil.) military cape; **estar a p. en,** (Peru) to be in the dark about, know nothing about.
poncho, cha, *a.* 1. idle, lazy; soft, careless. 2. (Col.) tubby, chubby, chunky.
poncí, poncidre, poncil, *a., m.* pertaining to a variety of bitter lemon or citron.
ponderable, *a.* 1. ponderable, weighable. 2. worthy of attention.
ponderación, *f.* 1. consideration, deliberation, thought, care. 2. weighing. 3. excessive praise; exaggeration. 4. balance, equilibrium.
ponderadamente, *adv.* judiciously, soberly.
ponderado, da, *a.* prudent, cautious, careful.
ponderador, ra, *a.* 1. pondering, examining. 2. exaggerating. 3. balancing. —*m., f.* 1. exaggerator. 2. ponderer, examiner.
ponderal, *a.* ponderal; gravimetric.
ponderar, *tr.v.* 1. to ponder, ponder over, examine, consider. 2. to weigh. 3. to overpraise, overvalue; to exaggerate. 4. to balance, counterpoise.
ponderativo, va, *a.* exaggerating.
ponderosamente, *adv.* 1. carefully, circumspectly. 2. heavily, ponderously.
ponderosidad, *f.* carefulness, deliberation, care, thought, circumspection.
ponderoso, sa, *a.* 1. careful, circumspect, grave. 2. heavy, ponderous.
pondo, *m.* (Ecuad.) large earthenware jug.
ponedero, ra, *a.* egg-laying (hen). —*m.* hen's nest.
ponedor, ra, *a.* 1. egg-laying (hen). 2. trained to rear on its hind legs (a horse). —*m.* bidder, bettor, wagerer.
ponencia, *f.* 1. paper; report. 2. post or office of person in charge of submitting a report.
ponente, *m.* 1. person who submits a paper or report; reporter. 2. referee, arbitrator, chairman.
ponentino, na, ponentisco, ca, *a.* occidental, western. —*m., f.* westerner, occidental.
poner, (*ref. 15*) *tr.v.* 1. to put, place, set, lay. 2. to put, levy (a tax), e.g. *p. un impuesto en, a* or *sobre,* to put a tax on. 3. to set, lay (the table). 4. to suppose, assume. 5. to put, bet, wager, e.g. *p. dos pesetas al as,* to put two pesetas on the ace. 6. to price, tag, e.g. *p. precious a la mercancía,* to price or tag the goods. 7. to write, set down, put (on paper). 8. to lay (eggs). 9. to apply, put, pay, e.g. *p. grasa a las ruedas,* to apply grease to the wheels, *p. empeño en,* to take pains with; put effort into, *p. atención en,* to pay attention to, *p. los ojos en,* to look at, set eyes upon. 10. to call, give (a name, nickname). 11. to put on (a play), e.g. *p. en escena,* put on the stage. 12. to expose (to dangers, insults, etc.). 13. to contribute, pay. 14. to add (to a story). 15. to abuse, insult, e.g. *lo puso verde,* he called him all the names under the sun. 16. to pass, establish, institute (a law, a tax, etc.). 17. to make, cause, put, e.g. *p. enfermo,* to make ill, *p. furioso,* to make furious, *p. de mal humor,* to make ill-tempered, put in a bad mood. — **p. + a +** *inf.,* to put + *inf.,* e.g. *p. la ropa a secar,* to hang the clothes out to dry; **p. algunos renglones,** to write a few lines; **p. bien a uno,** to speak well of someone, give someone a good name or reputation; to set someone up comfortably, provide someone with comfortable means of support; **p. casa,** to set up house; **p. colorado a,** (coll.) to embarrass, make blush; **p. como nuevo,** to renovate completely; (coll.) to insult, embarrass; **p. como un trapo,** to give a severe dressing down, wipe the floor with; **p. el grito en el cielo,** to complain bitterly, cry out to heaven; **p. en +** *n.,* to make + *a.,* put in + *n.,* e.g. *p. en duda,* to make doubtful, put in doubt; **p. en apuros,** to put in a fix or jam; **p. en claro,** to explain; **p. en disputa** or **discusión,** to lay open to discussion; **p. en libertad,** to set free; **p. en limpio,** to make a clean copy of; **p. en movimiento,** to put into motion, set in motion; **p. en ridículo,** to ridicule; **p. mal a,** to run down, give a bad name, speak ill of; **p. por,** to use as, e.g. *p. por intercesor,* to use as intercessor; **p. por delante a uno,** to put (an obstacle) in someone's way; **p. por encima,** to prefer; **p. por escrito,** to put in writing; **p. por las nubes,** to praise to the skies; **p. una carta,** to post a letter; **p. un colegio,** to open a school; **p. un negocio,** to set up a business, open a business. —*r.v.* 1. to put, place or set oneself. 2. to begin, set oneself, set about, e.g. *se puso a trabajar,* he began or set himself to work, *se puso a limpiar el cuarto,* he set about cleaning the room. 3. to expose oneself (to danger, ridicule, etc.). 4. to become, get, turn, grow, e.g. *se puso furioso,* he got furious, *se puso pálido,* he turned pale, *se puso de mal humor,* he got into a bad mood or temper. 5. to put on (clothes); to dress up. 6. to get, e.g. *ponerse de lodo,* to get muddy, *ponerse de hollín,* to get sooty. 7. to set (sun, planets). 8. to arrive (in), get (to), e.g. *me pondré en Barcelona en cuatro horas,* I'll get to Barcelona in four hours. — **no ponérsele a uno nada por delante,** to stop at nothing, ride roughshod over everything; **ponerse al corriente** or **al tanto,** to bring oneself or get up to date, become acquainted with what is going on; **ponerse al corriente** or **al tanto de,** to find out about, inform oneself about; **ponerse al día,** to bring oneself or get up to date; **ponerse bien,** to get better, recover; to set oneself up well, look after one's interests, feather one's nest; **ponerse de acuerdo,** to come to an agreement; **ponerse de pie,** to stand up, rise; **ponerse de punta,** to stand on end (hair); **ponerse en atención,** to come to attention.
ponga, pongo, *ref.* **poner.**
póngido, *m.* (zool.) pongid.
pongo, *m.* 1. (zool.) orangutan. 2. (Bol., Peru) Indian servant. 3. (Peru, Ecuad.) gully, ravine.
ponientada, *f.* steady west wind.
poniente, *m.* 1. west. 2. west wind.
ponimiento, *m.* placing, putting, laying; setting.
ponleví, (*pl.* **ponlevíes**), *m.* French-heeled shoe, shoe with high curved heel.
pontaje, *m., var. of* **pontazgo.**
pontana, *f.* flagstone or slab on the bed of a brook or river.
pontazgo, *m.* pontage, bridge toll.
pontazguero, ra, *m., f.* toll-bridge keeper.
pontear, *tr.v.* to bridge, build a bridge over.
pontederiáceo, a, *a.* (bot.) pontederiaceous. —*f.* (*pl.*) Pontederiaceae.
pontezuelo, *m. dim. of* **puente,** small bridge.
póntico, ca, *a.* (hist.) Pontic.
pontificado, *m.* 1. pontificate (office or position of pontiff). 2. papacy, popedom (Pope's term of office).
pontifical, *a.* pontifical. — **estar de** or **ponerse de p.,** to be in full dress. —*m.* 1. (*pl.*) pontificals (episcopal attire). 2. pontifical (book). 3. parochial tithes corresponding to each church.
pontificalmente, *adv.* pontifically.
pontificar, (*ref. 50*) *i.v.* 1. to pontificate, to act as a pontiff. 2. to pontificate, talk with authority; **p. sobre,** to pontificate on.
pontífice, *m.* 1. pontifex (in ancient Rome). 2. (ecc.) pontiff; Pope. — **p. máximo,** Pontifex Maximus; **Sumo P.** or **P. Romano,** Pope, Sovereign or Supreme Pontiff.
pontificio, cia, *a.* pontifical, papal.
pontifique, pontifiqué, *ref.* **pontificar.**
pontil, *m.* punty or pontil (glassmaking).
pontín, *m.* (Phil. I.) pontin, coasting vessel.
ponto, *m.* 1. (poet.) sea. 2. (hist.) **P.,** Pontus (country). — **P. Euxino,** Euxine or Black Sea.
pontocón, *m.* kick (with the foot).
pontón, *m.* 1. pontoon (flat-bottomed lighter used for building bridges); pontoon bridge. 2. (mar.) pontoon, pontoon dock (low flat-bottomed ship used for certain harbor work). 3. old ship, hulk tied to the dock used as a warehouse, hospital or prison. — **p. flotante,** floating bridge, pontoon bridge.
pontonero, *m.* (mil.) pontonier, pontoneer.
ponzoña, *f.* poison, venom.
ponzoñosamente, *adv.* poisonously, venomously.
ponzoñoso, sa, *a.* poisonous; venomous; (fig.) poisonous, noxious, harmful.
popa, *f.* (mar.) poop, stern; **amollar en p.,** to bring the stern around to windward; **a p.,** astern; **de p. a proa,** totally, entirely.
popamiento, *m.* 1. scorn, despising. 2. fondling, caressing. 3. indulging, spoiling, pampering.
popar, *tr.v.* 1. to despise, scorn, make fun of. 2. to caress, fondle. 3. to indulge, spoil, pamper.
pope, *m.* pope (priest of the Greek Orthodox Church).
popel, *a.* sternmost, aftermost.
popelina, *f.* (tex.) poplin.
poplíteo, a, *a.* (anat.) popliteal.
popo, *m.* (Col.) tube, small pipe.
popocho, cha, *a.* (Col.) full, sated.
poporo, *m.* 1. (Ven.) wooden club. 2. (Ven.) bump (on the head).
popotal, *m.* (Mex.) straw field, brush field.
popote, *m.* 1. (Mex.) straw for brooms. 2. (Mex.) drinking straw. — **hecho un p.,** as thin as a rake; **no levantar un p.,** not to do a lick of work.
popotillo, *m.* (bot.), (Mex.) ephedra; (Mex.) braid, corded ribbon.
populachería, *f.* cheap popularity, mass appeal.
populachero, ra, *a.* 1. of the masses, popular. 2. cheap, vulgar, common.
populacho, *m.* rabble, mob, plebs.
población, *f.* population (the act of populating).
popular, *a.* 1. popular, of the people, people's. 2. popular, well-liked. — **música p.,** popular music; **República P.,** People's Republic; **voto p.,** popular vote, people's choice.
popularice, popularicé, *ref.* **popularizar.**
popularidad, *f.* popularity.
popularización, *f.* popularization.
popularizar, (*ref. 53*) *tr.v.* to make popular, popularize. —*r.v.* to become popular, generally liked or known.
popularmente, *adv.* popularly.
populazo, *m.* rabble, mob, plebs.

populeón, *m.* ointment containing extract of black poplar buds.
populismo, *m.* (hist.) Populism.
populista, *a.* populist, populistic. —*m.* (hist.) Populist.
populoso, sa, *a.* populous; crowded; thickly-populated.
popurrí, *m.* 1. potpourri, miscellany. 2. (mus.) potpourri, medley.
popusa, *f.* (Bol., El Salv., Guat.) tortilla filled with cheese or meat.
poquedad, *f.* 1. timidity, pusillanimity. 2. paucity, scantiness, scarcity. 3. trifle, thing of little value.
póquer, *m.* poker (card game); four of a kind.
poquitico, ica, ito, ita, *a. dim. of* **poco,** very little bit, almost nothing.
poquito, ta, *a. dim. of* **poco,** very little; (*pl.*) very few.
poquito, *m.* little bit, wee bit; **a p.,** little by little; **a poquitos,** in small portions, bit by bit; **de p.,** fainthearted, timid; inept. —*adv.* very little.
por, *prep.* by; for; through; along; over; by way of, via; around; about; in; at; by means of, with, in exchange for, in return for; times, multiplied by; to, in order to; as, for, as being. *A,* in phrases indicating place: 1. by, e.g. *pasar p. la iglesia,* to pass by the church. 2. along, e.g. *ir p. la acera,* to go along the curb. 3. over, e.g. *pasar la mano p. la cara,* to pass one's hand over one's face. 4. through, via, by way of. 5. around, e.g. *p allí,* around there, over there; in that place. 6. in, e.g. *p. este barrio,* in this neighborhood. 7. through, e.g. *mirar p. la ventana,* to look through the window, *pasar p. la guerra,* to go through the war, *p. todo el mundo,* throughout the world. *B,* in phrases indicating time: 1. around, about, e.g. *p. agosto,* around August, *p. el año 1900,* about the year 1900. 2. for, e.g. *estudió p un año,* she studied for a year, *p. ahora, p. lo pronto,* for the time being, for the moment. 3. in, e.g. *p. la mañana,* in the morning. 4. at, e.g. *p. la noche,* at night. *C,* in phrases indicating an agent: by, e.g. *fue pintado p. Picasso,* it was painted by Picasso. *D,* in phrases indicating manner or means: 1. by, through, by means of, with, e.g. *llamó la atención p. señas,* he attracted attention by means of or with signs, *p. sus actos los conoceréis,* by their acts thou shalt know them. 2. in, e.g. *p. adelantado,* in advance, *p. duplicado,* in duplicate, *p. escrito,* in writing, *p. separado,* separately. *E,* in concessive phrases: however, e.g. *p. rico que sea no lo puedo comer,* however delicious it may be, I can't eat it, *p. mucho que haya hecho,* however much he may have done. *F,* in phrases indicating price, exchange measurement or rate: 1. for, in exchange for, in return for, e.g. *lo compré p. dos pesetas,* I bought it for two pesetas, *golpe p. golpe,* blow for blow, *le di dos gatitos p. su perro,* I gave him two kittens for his dog. 2. per, a, for each, e.g. *son tres dólares p. pareja,* it's three dollars per couple. 3. by, e.g. *vender p. libras,* to sell by the pound, *p. miles,* by the thousands. 4. times, multiplied by, by, e.g. *cuatro p. tres,* four by three, three times four. 5. per, e.g. *p. ciento,* per cent. *G,* in phrases indicating purpose or motive: in order, e.g. *p. no causar un escándalo,* in order not to cause a scandal. *H,* in phrases indicating cause or reason: through, because of, on account of, for, e.g. *no bailé mucho p. estar cansada,* I didn't dance much because I was tired. *I,* in phrases indicating sequence: by, after, e.g. *me los comí uno p. uno,* I ate them one by one, *día p. día,* day by day, day after day. *J,* in miscellaneous uses: 1. as, for, as being, e.g. *tomar p. esposa,* to take as one's wife, *yo tuve a mi padre p. maestro,* I had my father as or for my teacher, *lo tomé p. cura,* I took him for a priest, I thought he was a priest. 2. for, in the stead of, on behalf of, e.g. *lo haré p. ti,* I will do it for you or in your stead; for, on behalf of, e.g. *daría mi vida p él,* I would give my life for him. 3. for, in favor of, e.g. *estar p.,* to be in favor of, be for, *es p tu bien,* it's for your own good. 4. for, to get, to fetch, e.g. *ir p,* to go for, go to fetch or get, *preguntar p.,* to ask for (when one comes to see someone). 5. to be, still or yet to be, not yet, e.g. *hay muchas cosas p. hacer,* there are many things still or yet to be done, there many things not yet done, *p. pagar,* to be paid, *p. cobrar,* to be collected; to be, still to be, *la carta está p. escribir,* the letter is still to be or remains to be written. 6. about to, on the point of, e.g. *estar p. ir,* to be about to go, on the point of going. 7. (used in oaths) by, e.g. *p. Dios,* by God. — **dar p.,** to consider, think, e.g. *lo dí p. perdido,* I gave it up for lost; **p. alquilar,** to let, to rent; **p. ahí,** around there, about that (when stating approximate price or distance); **p. aquí y p. allá,** here and there; **p. tierra, mar y aire,** by land, sea and air; **p. bondad,** out of kindness; **p. completo,** completely; **p. correo aéreo** or **marítimo,** by airmail, by seamail; **p. consiguiente,** therefore, consequently; **p. cuanto,** inasmuch as, whereas; **p. dentro,** on the inside; **p. donde,** because of this; **p. entre,** in between, between; **p. fuera,** on the outside; **p. eso,** for that reason; **p. lo tanto,** therefore; **p. mí** or **ti solo,** by myself, by yourself, on my own, on your own; **p. otra parte,** on the other hand; **porque,** because; in order that, so that; **¿p. qué?** why?; **p. si,** in case; **p. si acaso,** just in case; **p. sí solo, sola, solos** or **solas,** by himself, herself or themselves, on his, her or their own; **p. todas partes, p. todos lados,** everywhere, on all sides; **p. valor de,** at the value of, to the tune of; **tener p.,** to think, consider.
porcachón, na, *a., m., f., var. of* **porcallón.**
porcal, *a.* **ciruela p.,** large fleshy plum.
porcallón, na, *a.* filthy, piggish. —*m., f.* 1. large hog. 2. dirty person.
porcelana, *f.* 1. porcelain, chinaware. 2. vitreous enamel, porcelain enamel. 3. porcelain blue.
porcelanita, *f.* (geol.) porcelanite, porcellanite.
porcentaje, *m.* percentage.
porcino, na, *a.* pertaining to pigs or hogs; **ganado porcino,** pigs, hogs. —*m.* 1. pig, hog; small pig. 2. bump, bruise; **cría de porcinos,** hog breeding.
porción, *f.* 1. portion, part, lot. 2. portion, share. 3. daily ration of food. 4. (coll.) large number, crowd; group. 5. (ecc.) stipend, prebend.
porcionero, ra, *a.* participating. —*m., f.* participant.
porcionista, *m., f.* 1. shareholder. 2. boarding school pupil.
porcipelo, *m.* (coll.) bristle (of hog).
porcuno, na, *a.* porcine, swinish, hoggish.
porche, *m.* porch, portico.
pordiosear, *i.v.* to beg, go begging.
pordiosería, *f.* beggary; begging.
pordiosero, ra, *m., f.* beggar.
porfía, *f.* 1. persistence; stubbornness, insistence, importunity. 2. dispute; competition; **a p.,** vying or competing with, insistently.
porfiadamente, *adv.* persistently; stubbornly, obstinately.
porfiado, da, *past part. of* **porfiar.** —*a.* persistent, insistent; obstinate, stubborn. —*m., f.* stubborn or obstinate person. —*m.* (Peru) tumbler (toy).
porfiador, ra, *a.* persistent, insistent; obstinate, stubborn.
porfiar, (*ref. 54*) *i.v.* 1. to insist, persist. 2. to argue obstinately.
porfídico, ca, *a.* (min.) porphyritic.
pórfido, *m.* (min.) porphyry.
porfioso, sa, *a., var. of* **porfiado.**
porfiria, *f.* (med.) porphyria.
porfirina, *f.* (biochem.) porphyrin.
porfirita, *f.* (min.) porphyrite.
porfirizar, (*ref. 53*) *tr.v.* to pulverize.
pórfiro, *m.* (min.) porphyry.
porfirogéneto, *m.* (hist.) porphyrogenite, porphyrogenitus.
porfolio, *m.* portfolio, album.
porisma, *m.* (math.) porism.
pormenor, *m.* detail, particular; **entrar en pormenores,** to go into details.
pormenorizar, (*ref. 53*) *tr.v.* to describe in detail, itemize, enter into details about.
pornografía, *f.* pornography.
pornográfico, ca, *a.* pornographic.
pornógrafo, *m.* pornographer.
poro, *m.* 1. (biol.) pore. 2. interstice.
porongo, *m.* (Peru) milk can or churn; (Amer.) pot, container (for liquids).
pororó, *m.* (S. Amer.) popcorn.
pororoca, *f.* (Arg.) tidal bore.
porosidad, *f.* porousness, porosity; **p. subcutánea,** (metal.) subcutaneous porosity.
poroso, sa, *a.* porous.
poroto, *m.* 1. (S. Amer.) dry bean; pigeon pea. 2. (cul.) bean stew.
porque, *conj.* because; as, in order that.
¿por qué? *interrog.* why? wherefore?
porqué, *m.* 1. reason, cause, motive. 2. (coll.) amount, quantity; allowance.
porquecilla, *f. dim. of* **puerca,** small sow.
porquera, *f.* 1. wild boar's lair. 2. short lance.
porquería, *f.* 1. dirt, filth. 2. (coll.) junk, rubbish, botch, worthless thing. 3. (coll.) dirty trick. 4. trifle.
porqueriza, *f.* pigsty.
porquerizo, za, *m., f.* swineherd.
porquero, ra, *m., f.* swineherd.
porquerón, *m.* (coll.) constable, catchpole, petty officer.
porqueta, *f.* (ento.) wood louse.
porquezuelo, la, *m., f. dim. of* **puerco,** piglet, small pig.
porra, *f.* 1. club, bludgeon. 2. maul, sledgehammer. 3. last one to play in a game. 4. (coll.) braggadocio, boasting. — **gastar p.,** to swagger, boast. 5. (coll.) bore, pest, nuisance. 6. *euphem. for* **mierda,** shit (vulg.). — **vete a la p.,** go to the devil; **¡p.!** damn! blast! **mandar a la p.,** to send to hell, send packing.
porráceo, a, *a.* 1. (bot.) pertaining to leeks. 2. leek-green.
porrada, *f.* 1. blow; slap, bang. 2. stupidity, folly. 3. pile, heap, e.g. *una p. de dinero,* a pile of money.
porral, *m.* leek patch, leek field.
porrazo, *m.* clubbing, bludgeoning; blow, bump, knock.
porrear, *i.v.* (coll.) to be a pest, make a nuisance of oneself; to insist, persist.
porrería, *f.* 1. (coll.) folly, stupidity. 2. (coll.) tiresomeness, slowness.
porreta, *f.* green leaves of leek, onion or garlic; **en p.,** (coll.) naked.
porretada, *f.* pile, heap.
porrilla, *f.* 1. forge hammer. 2. (vet.) osseous tumor in the joints.
porrillo, *adv.* **a p.,** (coll.) in abundance, abundantly, galore.
porrina, *f.* 1. young green crop. 2. green leaves of leek.

porrino, *m.* (bot.) leek seed; leek ready for transplanting.
porro, rra, *a.* (coll.) dull, stupid. —*m., f.* dolt, oaf, fool. —*m.* 1. (Col.) drum in a conical shape. 2. (bot.) leek.
porrón, *m.* earthenware jug; large bottle (for beer); wine carafe with long side spout (used for communal drinking).
porrón, na, *a.* (coll.) heavy, sluggish, slow.
porrudo, da, *a.* obstinate, hard-headed. —*m.* shepherd's crook.
porta, *f.* 1. (artil.) cover of a loophole. 2. (mar.) port, gun port, porthole.
porta-, *prefix* denoting "holder", "bearer", "carrier", "socket" or "support", e.g. *portaplumas,* penholder.
portaaviones, (*pl.* **portaaviones**), *m.* aircraft carrier.
portabandera, *f.* flagpole socket.
portabombas, (*pl.* **portabombas**), bomb carrier, bomb rack.
portabrocas, (*pl.* **portabrocas**), *m.* drill chuck or holder.
portacaja, *f.* (mil.) drum strap, drumsash.
portacarabina, *f.* (mil.) carbine holster.
portacartas, (*pl.* **portacartas**), *m.* pouch, mailbag.
portacilindros, (*pl.* **portacilindros**), *m.* cylinder support (of weaving loom).
portacruz, (*pl.* **portacruces**), *m.* crucifer, cross bearer (in a religious procession).
portachuelo, *m.* gorge, mountain pass.
portada, *f.* 1. title page, frontispiece (of a book). 2. cover, jacket (of a book or magazine). 3. (archit.) frontispiece, portal, facade. 4. (tex.) division of the warp.
portadera, *f.* saddle coffer.
portadilla, *f.* (print.) half title, bastard title.
portadiscos, *m.* (mus.) record case.
portado, da, *past part. of* **portar.** —*a.* **bien p.,** well-dressed; well-behaved; **mal p.,** badly dressed; ill-behaved.
portador, ra, *a.* bearing, carrying. —*m., f.* bearer, carrier. —*m.* 1. (com.) bearer (e.g. holder of a check). 2. (med.) carrier (of a disease). 3. (chem.) catalyst. 4. waiter's tray. — **p. de palos,** (golf) caddy; **cheque al p.,** cashier's check.
portaelectrodo, *m.* electrode holder.
portaequipajes, (*pl.* **portaequipajes**), *m.* luggage rack; boot (compartment for luggage).
portaestandarte, *m.* standard bearer.
portaféretro, *m.* pallbearer.
portafolio, *m.* portfolio, attaché case, briefcase.
portafusil, *m.* sling (of a rifle).
portaguión, *m.* (mil.) guidon, guidon bearer.
portahachón, *m.* torchbearer.
portaherramienta, *f.* (mec.) tool rest, toolstock, toolpost.
portaherramientas, (*pl.* **portaherramientas**), *m.* toolholder, chuck.
portaje, *m., var. of* **portazgo.**
portal, *m.* 1. arcade, portico, porch. 2. vestibule, entrance hall. 3. town or city gate. 4. (Amer.) crib, crèche.
portalada, *f.* portal, large gate.
portalámparas, (*pl.* **portalámparas**), *m.* (elec.) socket, bulb socket, lamp holder. — **p. de bayoneta,** bayonet socket; **p. de cadena,** chain-pull lamp holder.
portalápiz, (*pl.* **portalápices**), *m.* pencil holder.
portaleña, *f.* (mar.) port, gun port.
portalero, *m.* tax collector, octroi guard.
portalibros, (*pl.* **portalibros**), *m.* straps for carrying schoolbooks.
portaligas, (*pl.* **portaligas**), *m.* garter belt.
portallaves, *m.* (*pl.* **portallaves**) (Mex., Ven.) key ring.
portalón, *m.* 1. gateway, portal. 2. (mar.) gangway (opening in side of ship).
portamanteo, *m.* portmanteau, valise.
portamira, *m.* (surv.) rodman.
portamonedas, (*pl.* **portamonedas**), *m.* change purse; pocketbook.
portanario, *m.* (anat.) pylorus.
portaneumáticos, (*pl.* **portaneumáticos**), *m.* (auto.) tire rack.
portante, *m.* ambling gait (of a horse). — **tomar el p.,** (coll.) to go, leave; **tomar un p.,** to take a step.
portantillo, *m.* quick trotting step or pace.
portanuevas, (*pl.* **portanuevas**), *m., f.* newsmonger.
portañola, *f.* (mar.) gun port.
portañuela, *f.* fly (of trousers).
portaobjeto, *m.* slide (of microscope); stage (of microscope).
portapapeles, (*pl.* **portapapeles**), *m.* briefcase.
portaparaguas, *m.* umbrella stand.
portapaz, (*pl.* **portapaces**), *m., f.* (ecc.) pax, pyx.
portapliegos, (*pl.* **portapliegos**), *m.* briefcase.
portaplumas, (*pl.* **portaplumas**), *m.* penholder.
portaprobeta, *f.* test tube stand or rack.
portar, *tr.v.* 1. to carry, bear. 2. (hunt.) to retrieve. —*i.v.* to fill (the sails with wind). —*r.v.* to behave, conduct oneself, e.g. *portarse bien,* to behave properly.
portarremo, *m.* rowlock, oarlock.
portarretrato, *m.* picture frame.
portátil, *a.* portable.
portatostadas, (*pl.* **portatostadas**), *m.* toast rack or caddy.
portavasos, (*pl.* **portavasos**), *m.* rack or stand for glasses.
portaventanero, *m.* door and window maker.
portaviandas, (*pl.* **portaviandas**), *m.* dinner pail.
portavoz, (*pl.* **portavoces**), *m.* 1. spokesman, mouthpiece. 2. megaphone.
portazgo, *m.* toll, tollhouse.
portazguero, *m.* toll gatherer, toll collector.
portazo, *m.* slam, bang (of a door); slamming a door in one's face.
porte, *m.* 1. transporting, carrying. 2. carrying charge, transport charge, portage, freightage; postage, mail or postage charge. 3. behavior, conduct. 4. bearing, presence. 5. size, capacity. 6. (mar.) burden. — **p. bruto,** (mar.) deadweight tonnage; **p. pagado,** freight prepaid; **portes,** freight.
porteador, ra, *a.* carrying. —*m., f.* carrier, porter.
portear, *tr.v.* to carry, convey, transport. —*r.v.* to migrate, to pass (said especially of birds). —*i.v.* to slam (door, window).
portento, *m.* wonder, prodigy, portent, marvel.
portentosamente, *adv.* amazingly, extraordinarily, prodigiously.
portentoso, sa, *a.* amazing, portentous, marvelous, prodigious.
porteño, ña, *a., m., f.* of or from Buenos Aires, Valparaiso, Buenaventura (Col.), or Santa María (port of Cadiz, Sp.).
porteo, *m.* carrying, portage, cartage.
portería, *f.* 1. porter's lodge or office; job of porter or concierge. 2. (sport.) goal (in football, hockey, etc.). 3. (mar.) portholes (collectively).
porteril, *a.* pertaining to the porter or the main door.
portero, ra, *m., f.* 1. porter, janitor, gatekeeper, doorkeeper; concierge. 2. goalkeeper. — **p. de estrados,** usher (in a court room).
portezuela, *f.* 1. *dim. of* **puerta,** small door. 2. door of an automobile, taxi, truck, lorry. 3. pocket flap.
pórtico, *m.* 1. (archit.) portico, porch, arcade, colonnade. 2. (philos.) Porch, Stoic school.
portier, *m.* portiere, door curtain, drape over a doorway.
portilla, *f.* 1. private cart or cattle road; opening, gate (in a fence). 2. (mar.) porthole.
portillera, *f.* private road (on a farm or ranch).
portillo, *m.* 1. gap, opening, breach. 2. wicket (small gate within larger one); postern gate, side gate. 3. narrow pass, narrow path (through mountains). 4. nick, chip, dent, notch. 5. small sluicegate.
Port-Luís, *m.* Port Louis, capital of Mauritius.
Port of Spain, *m.* Port of Spain, capital of Trinidad and Tobago.
portón, *m. aug. of* **puerta,** large door, vestibule door, main door of house.
Porto Novo, *m. Porto Novo, capital of Dahomey.*
portorriqueño, ña, *a., m., f.* Puerto Rican.
portuario, ria, *a.* pertaining to a port; **autoridades portuarias,** port authorities.
Portugal, *m.* Portugal.
portugués, sa, *a., m., f.* Portuguese. —*m.* 1. Portuguese (language). 2. (arch.) portuguese (coin).
portuguesada, *f.* (coll.) exaggeration.
portulacáceo, a, *a.* (bot.) portulacaceous. —*f.* (*pl.*) (bot.) Portulacaceae.
portulano, *m.* collection of harbor charts.
porvenir, *m.* future; (fig.) promise, expectations.
¡porvida! *interj.* by the living saints!
pos, en p. de, after; in pursuit of.
posa, *f.* 1. knell, toll. 2. pause in funeral procession to sing the responses. 3. (*pl.*) buttocks, seat, behind.
posada, *f.* 1. inn, hostelry. 2. lodging, boarding house. 3. (Cuba) hideaway, trysting place. 4. traveling set of knife, fork and spoon. 5. (Mex., Hond.) Christmas party, (*pl.*) Christmas festivities.
posaderas, *f.* (*pl.*) buttocks, seat, behind.
posadero, ra, *m., f.* innkeeper. —*m.* rush or canework seat.
posante, *a.* (mar.) smooth-sailing (said of a ship).
posar, *i.v.* 1. to pose (for a painting, photograph). 2. to perch, alight, sit (birds). 3. to lodge, put up, board. 4. to rest, repose. —*r.v.* 1. to perch, alight, sit (birds). 2. to settle (dust, sediment). —*tr.v.* to put or lay down (a load in order to rest).
posaverga, *f.* (mar.) yard prop.
posbélico, ca, *a.* postwar.
posca, *f.* drink of vinegar and water.
poscafé, *m.* liqueur, pousse-café (served after dinner).
poscombustión, *m.* afterburning.
poscomunión, *f.* (ecc.) Post-Communion.
posdata, *f.* postscript.
pose, *f.* 1. pose, posture. 2. pose, affectation. 3. (photog.) exposure.
poseedor, ra, *a.* owning, possessing. —*m., f.* owner, possessor; holder; **p. de acciones,** stockholder; **p. de buena fe,** (law) bona fide possessor; **p. del título mundial,** holder of the world title; **p. de mala fe,** (law) mala fide possessor.
poseer, (*ref. 60*) *tr.v.* 1. to possess; to own; to hold. 2. to know perfectly, master (e.g. a language). —*r.v.* to control oneself.
poseído, da, *past part. of* **poseer.** —*a.* possessed; owned, held. —*m., f.* possessed person (controlled by an emotion, evil spirit, etc.).
Poseidón, *m.* (myth.) Poseidon, Greek god of the sea.
posesión, *f.* possession (in all senses); (*pl.*) possessions, property, estate; **aprehender la p.** or **tomar p. de,** to take possession of; **dar p. de,**

to give possession of; **p. civil,** (law) civilis possessio; **p. natural,** (law) detention, naturalis possessio; **p. pretoria,** (law) possession by court order; **recobrar** or **retener p. de,** to recover or retain possession of.
posesional, *a.* possessory, possessional.
posesionar, *tr.v.* to give possession of, to install, induct. —*r.v.* to take possession of, be installed (in an office, post, etc.).
posesionero, *m.* pasture-owning cattle breeder.
posesivo, va, *a.* possessive; (gram.) possessive; (law) possessory. —*m.* (gram.) possessive.
poseso, sa, *irr. past part. of* **poseer.** —*a.* possessed (person). —*m., f.* possessed person (controlled by an emotion, evil spirit, etc.).
posesor, ra, *m., f.* owner, possessor, holder.
posesorio, ria, *a.* possessory.
poseyendo, *ref.* **poseer.**
poseyente, *a.* owning, possessing.
poseyera, poseyese, poseyó, *ref.* **poseer.**
posfecha, *f.* postdate.
posguerra, *f.* postwar period.
posibilidad, *f.* 1. possibility; power, capacity, ability. 2. (*pl.*) means, property.
posibilitar, *tr.v.* to facilitate, make possible.
posible, *a.* possible; **hacer lo p.** or **todo lo p.,** to do everything possible; **ser p. que** + *subj.,* to be possible that + *subj.,* e.g. *es p. que venga,* it's possible that he will or might come. —*m.* (*pl.*) means, income, wealth.
posiblemente, *adv.* possibly.
posición, *f.* 1. position; place, situation; posture, attitude; standing, status. 2. (mil.) position. 3. (law) (*pl.*) questions and answers. 4. supposition; postulate. — **absolver posiciones,** (law) to answer questions; **p. de apresto** or **espera,** (mil.) position in readiness; **p. simulada,** (mil.) dummy position.
positivamente, *adv.* positively, absolutely.
positivismo, *m.* 1. positivism. 2. materialism. 3. matter-of-factness.
positivista, *m., f.* positivist. —*a.* positivist, positivistic; realistic, practical; matter-of-fact. —*m., f.* positivist.
positivo, va, *a.* positive; certain, indisputable; absolute; affirmative. —*m.* (gram., photog.) positive.
pósito, *m.* 1. public granary. 2. cooperative.
positón, positrón, *m.* (phys., chem.) positron; positive electron.
positronio, *m.* (phys., chem.) positronium.
positura, *f.* position; condition, state, disposition.
posliminio, *m.* (law) postliminy, postliminium.
posma, *a.* dull, slow, sluggish. —*f.* sluggishness, slowness, dullness. —*m., f.* (coll.) slow, sluggish person.
poso, *m.* 1. sediment, dregs, less; residue. 2. repose, rest, quiet. 3. (Phil. I.) bun or knot of hair secured by gold or silver pins.
posología, *f.* (med.) posology.
posón, *m.* cane or rattan seat.
pospelo, *adv.* **a p.,** 1. against the natural direction (of fur, hair, pile), against the grain. 2. (fig.) the wrong way; contrary to the normal practice; against one's will, reluctantly.
pospierna, *f.* thigh (of animal).
posponer, (*ref. 15*) *tr.v.* 1. to postpone, put off, defer, delay. 2. to think less of. 3. (gram.) to postpone, place after. 4. to place after (in order of preference, precedence, importance, etc.).
posponga, pospongo, *ref.* **posponer.**
posposición, *f.* 1. postponement, putting after, subordination. 2. (gram.) postposition.
pospositivo, va, *a.* (gram.) postpositive.
pospuesto, ta, *irr. past part. of* **posponer.**
pospuse, pospusiera, pospusiese, *ref.* **posponer.**
posta, *f.* 1. relay team, post horse. 2. post station, posthouse, post, stage. 3. post, stage, (distance between two post stations). 4. slice (of meat, fish, etc.). 5. small bullet. 6. stake, bet. 7. commemorative plaque or tablet. 8. (archit.) scroll pattern (used in friezes). —*m., f.* postrider. — **caballo de p.,** post horse; **correr la p.,** to ride post; **por la p.,** posthaste, speedily, rapidly.
postal, *a.* postal; **giro p.,** postal money order. —*f.* postcard, postal card.
postdata, *f.* postscript.
postdiluviano, na, *a.* (Bib.) postdiluvian.
poste, *m.* 1. post, pole; pillar. 2. punishment consisting in making children stand in a certain place. — **asistir al p.** or **quedarse al p.,** to answer questions (lecturer after speaking); **dar p.,** (coll.) to keep someone waiting; **llevar p.,** (coll.) to be kept waiting; **oler el p.,** (coll.) to smell trouble; **p. de amarre,** (mar.) mooring post; **p. de conexión sujetahilo,** (elec.) binding post; **p. de flagelación,** whipping post; **p. de llegada,** (sport.) finishing post; **p. de partida,** (sport.) starting post; **p. indicador,** signpost; **p. telegráfico,** telegraph pole; **ser un p.,** (coll.) to be very stupid, dumb or dull; (coll.) to be as deaf as a post.
postelero, *m.* (mar.) skid, skeed.
postema, *f.* 1. (med.) abscess, sore. 2. bore, pest, nuisance. — **no criarle** or **no hacérsele a uno p. una cosa** (coll.) to be outspoken.
postemero, *m.* (surg.) large lancet.
postergación, *f.* 1. delay, postponement. 2. passing over, holding back.
postergar, (*ref. 51*) *tr.v.* 1. to postpone. 2. to pass over, hold back (an employee expecting promotion).
postergue, postergué, *ref.* **postergar.**
posteridad, *f.* posterity.
posterior, ra, *a.* 1. posterior, back, rear. 2. later, subsequent; **p. a,** subsequent to, after, later than.
posterioridad, *f.* posteriority; **con p.,** afterwards, subsequently; **con p. a,** after, subsequent to.
posteriormente, *adv.* afterwards, subsequently, later on.
posteta, *f.* (bkb.) number of printed sheets stitched together at a time.
postfijo, ja, *a.* (gram.) suffixal. —*m.* (gram.) suffix.
postglacial, *a.* (geol.) postglacial.
postgraduado, da, *a., m., f.* postgraduate.
postguerra, *f.* postwar period.
post-hipnótico, ca, *a.* posthypnotic.
póstico, ca, *a.* (bot.) posticous.
postigo, *m.* 1. window shutter. 2. postern, postern gate, side gate. 3. wicket, small gate in larger one.
postila, *f.* marginal note, footnote, comment.
postilación, *f.* annotation, adding footnotes or comments.
postilador, *m.* annotator.
postilar, *tr.v.* to annotate, make marginal notes in.
postilla, *f.* 1. scab (on healing wound). 2. note, comment, footnote.
postillón, *m.* postilion, postboy.
postilloso, sa, *a.* scabby.
postimpresionismo, *m.* (art) postimpressionism.
postimpresionista, *a., m., f.* (art) postimpressionist.
postín, *m.* (coll.) conceit, presumption, airs; **darse p.,** to put on airs; **fiesta de mucho p.,** posh party (G.B.), swanky party.
postinero, ra, *a.* swanky, posh; vain, conceited.
postizo, za, *a.* false, artificial; detachable. — **dentadura postiza,** false teeth; **pelo postizo,** false hair, wig; **senos postizos,** falsies. —*m.* switch, false hair. —*f.* 1. (mar.) outrigger increasing beam of galleys. 2. (arch., obs.) castanet.
postliminio, *m.* (law) postliminium, postliminy.
postludio, *m.* (mus.) postlude.
postmeridiano, na, *a.* postmeridian, p.m. —*m.* any point on the trajectory of a celestial body after passing an observer's meridian.
postnatal, *a.* postnatal.
postnupcial, *a.* postnuptial.
postónica, *a.* (phonet.) posttonic (syllable).
postoperatorio, ria, *a.* (med.) postoperative.
postor, *m.* bidder; **mejor p., p. mayor,** highest bidder.
postorbitario, a, *a.* (anat., zool.) postorbital.
postpalatal, *a., f.* (phonet.) postpalatal.
postparto, ta, *a.* postpartum, postpartal. —*m.* postpartum period.
postprandial, *a.* postprandial, after dinner.
postración, *f.* prostration, exhaustion; dejection.
postrador, ra, *a.* prostrating. —*m.* footstool, kneeling stool, priedieu.
postrar, *tr.v.* 1. to prostrate, humble, humiliate. 2. to overthrow. 3. to weaken, exhaust, debilitate. —*r.v.* 1. to be prostrated, exhausted or debilitated. 2. to prostrate oneself, kneel down.
postre, *a.* final, last; **a la p., al p.,** in the end, finally. —*m.* dessert, sweet. — **llegar a los postres,** to arrive late or too late.
postrer, *a.* last, final (apocopated form of **postrero,** used only before masculine singular nouns).
postreramente, *adv.* lastly, finally.
postrero, ra, *a.* last, final. —*m., f.* last one, last, hindermost.
postrimer, *a.* last, final (apocopated form of **postrimero,** used only before masculine singular nouns).
postrimeramente, *adv.* finally, at last.
postrimería, *f.* 1. twilight, last years, end, latter part, e.g. *en las postrimerías del imperio romano,* in the last years or the twilight of the Roman Empire. 2. (theol.) each of the last stages of man, i.e. death, judgment, hell, and heaven.
postrimero, ra, *a.* last, final; hindmost.
post scriptum, *m.* postscript.
póstula, postulación, *f.* 1. application; request, demand. 2. (ecc.) postulation.
postulado, *past part. of* **postular.** —*m.* postulate; axiom; basic principle. — **p. de las paralelas,** (math.) parallel postulate.
postulador, *m.* (ecc.) postulator.
postulanta, *f.* (ecc.) female postulant (candidate for admission to a religious order).
postulante, *a.* applying. —*m., f.* applicant; petitioner. —*m.* (ecc.) postulant (candidate for admission to a religious order).
postular, *tr.v.* 1. to apply for (e.g. a job); to stand for, stand as candidate for; to seek; to ask for, claim, demand. 2. (ecc.) to postulate. —*i.v.* to apply; to stand, take part (as a candidate in an election, as a candidate for a professorship). — **p. a una senaduría,** to stand as candidate for a senatorship; **p. a** or **para la universidad,** to apply for admission to a university.
póstumo, ma, *a.* posthumous.
postura, *f.* 1. posture, position, attitude. 2. price (officially set on food). 3. bid, offer. 4. agreement, arrangement. 5. stake, wager, bet. 6. (bird's) egg. 7. laying (of an egg). 8. transplanting. 9. seedling, young plant (for transplanting). — **hacer p.,** to bid, make a bid (at an auction); **p. del sol,** sunset; **plantar de p.,** to plant as seedlings, transplant.
potabilidad, *f.* potability.
potabilizar, (*ref. 53*) *tr.v.* to make drinkable.
potable, *a.* drinkable, potable, drinking, e.g. *agua p.,* drinking water.

potación, *f.* potation, drinking, beverage, drink.
potador, ra, *a.* drinking. —*m., f.* drinker.
potaje, *m.* 1. pottage; stewed vegetables. 2. dried vegetables. 3. brew, drink with several ingredients. 4. hodgepodge, jumble, mixture.
potajería, *f.* pulse, dried vegetables; storeroom for pulse or dried vegetables.
potajier, *m.* (Gal.) keeper of vegetable storeroom (in royal household).
potala, *f.* 1. (mar.) anchor weight or stone. 2. (mar.) tub, unseaworthy vessel.
potámlde, *f.* (myth.) naiad.
potar, *tr.v.* 1. to correct and mark (weights and measures). 2. to drink.
potasa, *f.* (chem.) potash; **p. cáustica,** caustic potash.
potásico, ca, *a.* (chem.) potassium, potassic.
potasio, *m.* (chem.) potassium.
pote, *m.* 1. pot, jug, jar; flowerpot; saucepan, cooking pot. 2. standard measure or weight. 3. stew, boiled dinner, hotpot. 4. (coll.) pout, puckering of lips (in children about to cry). — **a p.,** in abundance, galore.
potencia, *f.* 1. power, strength, force. 2. power, faculty. 3. potency, power of procreation. 4. power, nation. 5. (philos.) potency (capacity for acting or being acted upon). 6. (phys., math., elec., mec., opt.) power. 7. (geol.) thickness (of stratum or vein). 8. power, reach (of guns). — **factor de p.,** (elec.) power factor; **las grandes potencias,** the Great Powers; **p. aérea,** (mil.) air power; **p. al freno,** (engin.) brake horsepower, actual power; **p. ascensional,** (avia.) climbing power; **p. combatiente,** (mil.) fighting power; **p. de entrada,** (elec.) input power; **p. de fuego,** (mil.) fire power; **p. de salida,** (elec.) output power; **p. de salida de cresta,** (elec., rad.) peak power output; **p. hidráulica,** water power; **p. mundial,** world power; **p. nuclear,** nuclear power; **Potencias Centrales,** Central Powers (in First World War).
potencial, *a., m., f.* potential. — **caída de p. de línea,** (elec.) line drop; **barrera de p.,** (phys.) potential barrier; **p. de óxido-reducción,** (chem.) oxidation-reduction potential; **p. vectorial,** vector potential; **pozo de p.,** (phys.) potential well or hole.
potencialidad, *f.* potentiality, potential.
potencialmente, *adv.* potentially.
potenciómetro, *m.* (elec.) potentiometer.
potentado, *m.* 1. potentate, sovereign. 2. (fig.) potentate, tycoon.
potente, *a.* 1. potent, strong, powerful, mighty, vigorous. 2. potent (sexually). 3. (coll.) huge, bulky.
potentemente, *adv.* powerfully.
potentilla, *f.* (bot.) potentilla, cinquefoil.
potenza, *f.* (her.) potent, horizontal bar, tace.
poterna, *f.* (fort.) postern, sally port.
potero, *m.* drinker.
potestad, *f.* 1. power, authority, jurisdiction. 2. podesta (Italian official). 3. potentate, prince. 4. angelic power, (*pl.*) Powers (order of angels). — **patria p.,** (law) patria potestas, parental authority.
potestativo, va, *a.* facultative, optional.
potingue, *m.* (coll.) potion, concoction.
potísimo, ma, *a.* very strong; very special.
potista, *m., f.* (coll.) drinker, tippler, boozer (sl.).
poto, *m.* 1. (Arg., Chile, Peru, Ecuad.) backside, bottom, ass (vulg.); bottom (of an object). 2. (Chile, Ecuad., Peru) bowl (made from a gourd or clay).
potoco, ca, *a.* (Chile) tubby, short. —*m., f.* tubby, short person.
potosí, *m.* extraordinary wealth, fortune, e.g. *vale un P.,* it's worth a fortune.
potra, *f.* 1. filly. 2. (coll.) hernia, rupture; scrotal rupture. — **cantarle a uno la p.,** (coll.) to cause pain, throb (hernia).
potrada, *f.* herd of foals.
potranca, *f.* filly, young mare.
potrear, *tr.v.* 1. to annoy, tease, vex. 2. (Guat., Hond., Peru) to thrash, beat. 3. (Amer.) to break (a horse). —*i.v.* to frisk, frolic (like a colt).
potrera, *a.* **cabezada p.,** hempen halter for colts.
potrero, *m.* 1. herdsman for colts, cowboy looking after colts. 2. pasture ground. 3. (Amer.) cattle ranch. 4. (coll.) hernia specialist.
potrico, illo, *m. dim. of* **potro,** small colt.
potril, *m.* pasture ground for colts.
potrilla, *m.* (coll.) merry old man; older man who affects young manners.
potro, *m.* 1. colt, foal. 2. shoeing frame (for horses). 3. obstetrical chair. 4. horse (in gymnasium). 5. pit dug in ground for dividing a beehive. 6. nuisance, bore. 7. (arch.) rack (instrument of torture).
potroso, sa, *a.* 1. ruptured. 2. (coll.) fortunate, lucky.
poundal, (phys.) poundal (unit of force).
poya, *f.* 1. tax paid in bread at the public oven. 2. hemp bagasse.
poyal, *m.* 1. striped cloth bench cover. 2. stone seat or bench.
poyar, *i.v.* to pay the baking fee in bread.
poyata, *f.* shelf, cupboard.
poyo, *m.* 1. stone bench built against a wall. 2. fee formerly paid to judges.
poza, *f.* 1. puddle, pool. 2. tank for retting and breaking hemp. — **lamerle la p. a uno,** (coll.) to milk someone of his money.
pozal, *m.* 1. pail, bucket (of a well). 2. curbstone (of a well). 3. sump, catch basin.
pozanco, *m.* pool or puddle in a river bank.
pozo, *m.* 1. well. 2. pit, hole, ditch. 3. deep pool (in river). 4. kitty, pool (in gambling games). 5. (fig.) fountain, mine, e.g. *un p. de sabiduría,* a mine of knowledge. 6. (mar.) well, hold. 7. (min.) shaft. 8. (Ecuad.) spring, stream. 9. (Chile, Col.) puddle, pool. — **caer en un p.,** to fall into oblivion; **p. airón,** bottomless pit; **p. artesiano,** artesian well; **p. ciego,** septic tank, cesspool; **p. de la hélice,** propeller shaft or well; **p. de petróleo,** oil well; **p. de potencial,** (phys.) potential well or hole; **p. de registro,** manhole; **p. de ventilación** or **aire,** (min.) air shaft or well; **p. negro,** cesspool, cesspit; **p. séptico,** septic tank; **p. surgente,** flowing well.
pozol, *m.* (C. Rica, Hond.) *var. of* **pozole.**
pozole, *m.* 1. (Mex.) stew of young corn, meat and chili. 2. (Mex.) drink made from red corn and sugar.
pozuelo, la, *m., f.* 1. *dim. of* **pozo,** small well. 2. sump, catch basin. —*f. dim. of* **poza,** small puddle.
pp. *abbrev. of* **páginas,** pages (pp.).
P.P. *abbrev. of* **porte pagado,** postage paid.
Pr *sym. of* **praseodimio,** praseodymium (Pr.).
pracrito, prácrito, *m.* Prakrit, old Indic language.
práctica, *f.* 1. practice; experience, skill; method, manner. 2. (usually in *pl.*) training, apprenticeship. — **en la p.,** in practice; **poner en p.,** to put into practice; **práticas de tiro,** target practice; **tener mucha** or **poca p.,** to have a lot of or little practice; to be experienced or inexperienced.
practicable, *a.* practicable, feasible.
practicador, ra, *m., f.* practitioner, practicer.
practicaje, *m.* (mar.) pilotage.
prácticamente, *adv.* practically.
practicanta, *f.* 1. hospital nurse. 2. prescription clerk, druggist's assistant.
practicante, *m., f.* 1. trainee, apprentice. 2. hospital nurse. 3. prescription clerk, druggist's assistant. —*m.* (med.) hospital intern.
practicar, (*ref. 50*) *tr.v.* to practice; to perform, carry out; to do, e.g. *p. una buena acción,* to do a good deed, *p. una intervención quirúrgica,* to perform a surgical operation on.
práctico, ca, *a.* practical; experienced, skillful, expert. —*m.* (mar.) pilot.
practicón, na, *m., f.* expert (through practical rather than theoretical knowledge).
practique, practiqué, *ref.* **practicar.**
pradal, *m.* meadow, field.
pradejón, *m.* small meadow.
pradeño, ña, *a.* pertaining to meadows.
pradera, *f.* meadowland; large prairie.
pradería, *f.* meadowland, prairie.
praderoso, sa, *a.* abounding in or pertaining to prairies.
pradial, *m.* Prairial (ninth month of the French Revolutionary Calendar).
prado, *m.* meadow, field; walk, promenade; **a p.,** out to pasture, grazing in the meadow; **p. de guadaña,** meadow mowed yearly.
Praga, *f.* Prague, capital of Czechoslovakia.
pragmático, ca, *a.* pragmatic, pragmatical. —*m.* writer or interpreter of national laws.
pragmatismo, *m.* (philos.) pragmatism.
pragmatista, *a.* (philos.) pragmatist, pragmatistic. —*m., f.* pragmatist.
prao, *m.* proa (double-bowed Malayan sailing vessel).
praseodimio, *m.* (chem.) praseodymium.
prasio, *m.* (min.) prase, translucent chalcedony.
prasma, *m.* (min.) plasma, dark green agate.
pratense, *a.* growing or living in a meadow.
praticultura, *f.* meadow cultivation.
pratíncola, *f.* (ornith.) pratincole.
pravedad, *f.* depravity, perversity, iniquity, wickedness.
praviana, *f.* (Sp.) Asturian popular song.
pravo, va, *a.* depraved, wicked, perverse.
praxiología, *f.* (philos.) praxeology.
Praxíteles, *m.* Praxiteles, one of the great sculptors of ancient Greece.
pre, *m.* soldier's daily pay.
pre-, prefix meaning before, prior to, in advance of, beforehand, early, in front of.
preadamita, *m.* preadamite (supposed ancestor of Adam).
preadamítico, ca, *a.* preadamic, preadamite (before Adam).
preámbulo, *m.* preamble; digression.
preamplificador, *m.* (elec.) preamplifier.
preatómico, ca, *a.* preatomic.
prebenda, *f.* 1. (ecc.) prebend, benefice, canonry. 2. dowry, dower (given to a woman about to marry or enter a convent). 3. (coll.) sinecure, cushy job, feather bed (coll., U.S.).
prebendado, *m.* (ecc.) prebendary.
prebostal, *a.* provostal, provost.
prebostazgo, *m.* provostship.
precalentador, *m.* preheater.
precalentar, (*ref. 29*) *tr.v.* to preheat.
precanceroso, sa, *a.* (med.) precancerous.
precariamente, *adv.* precariously.
precario, ria, *a.* precarious; (law) precarious, held as a loan.
precaución, *f.* precaution.
precaucionarse, *r.v.* to take precautions.
precautelar, *tr.v.* to take precautions against, to ward off.

precautorio, ria, *a.* precautionary, preventive.
precaver, *tr.v.* to prevent, provide against, take measures or precautions against. —*r.v.* **precaverse de** or **contra,** to guard against, provide against.
precavidamente, *adv.* cautiously, warily.
precavido, da, *past part. of* **precaver.** —*a.* cautious, wary, careful, guarded.
precedencia, *f.* 1. precedence, priority. 2. precedence, superiority, primacy.
precedente, *a.* preceding, foregoing. —*m.* precedent.
preceder, *tr.v., i.v.* to precede, go before.
precelente, *a.* (rare) most excellent.
preceptista, *a.* preceptive. —*m., f.* one who teaches or sets rules or precepts.
preceptivamente, *adv.* preceptively.
preceptivo, va, *a.* preceptive.
precepto, *m.* precept; injunction, order, rule. —**día de p.,** holy day of obligation; **los preceptos del Decálogo,** the Ten Commandments.
preceptor, ra, *m., f.* preceptor, master, teacher; private tutor.
preceptoril, *a.* (derog.) preceptorial, pertaining to a teacher or tutor.
preceptuar, (*ref. 55*) *tr.v.* to command, issue as a precept.
preces, *f.* (*pl.*) prayers, supplications.
precesión, *f.* (rhet.) incomplete phrase, half-sentence. — **p. de los equinoccios,** (astron.) precession of the equinoxes.
preciado, da, *past part. of* **preciar.** —*a.* 1. valued, esteemed; valuable, precious. 2. conceited, vain, proud, boastful.
preciador, ra, *a.* appraising. —*m., f.* appraiser.
preciar, *tr.v.* to value, price, appraise. —*r.v.* to brag, boast; **preciarse de** + *n.* or *a.*, to think one is, boast of being, e.g. *él se precia de gran deportista,* he thinks he is or boasts of being a great sportsman; **preciarse de** + *inf.*, to boast of + *ger.*
precinta, *f.* 1. strap, band (for reinforcing corners of boxes). 2. revenue seal or stamp (affixed by customs). 3. (mar.) parceling.
precintar, *tr.v.* 1. to reinforce or bind with straps. 2. to seal. 3. (mar.) to parcel.
precinto, *m.* binding, strapping; sealed strap.
precio, *m.* 1. price; cost. 2. worth, merit, esteem, value, credit. 3. prize, reward (in jousts). — **abrir p., romper p.,** to put an opening price to; **al p. de,** at the cost of; **alzar el p.,** to raise the price; **no tener p.,** to be priceless; **poner a p. su cabeza,** to put a price on his head; **poner p. a,** to price, put a price on; **p. al contado,** cash price; **p. al por mayor,** wholesale price; **p. al por menor,** retail price; **p. callejero,** (com.) street price; **p. cerrado,** fixed price; **p. corriente,** current or market price; **p. de abertura,** opening price; **p. de cierre,** closing price; **p. de compra,** purchase price; **p. de costo** or **de fábrica,** cost price; **p. de factura,** invoice price, invoiced price; **p. de venta,** selling price; **p. de venta al público,** recommended retail price, published price; **p. fuera de la bolsa,** (com.) street price; **p. máximo, techo** or **tope,** ceiling price; **p. unitario** or **por unidad,** unit price; **tener en p.,** to esteem, regard highly.
preciosa, *f.* (ecc.) allowance to prebendaries.
preciosamente, *adv.* exquisitely, beautifully.
preciosidad, *f.* 1. preciousness, value. 2. exquisiteness, excellence. 3. (fig.) jewel, delight, beautiful thing. 4. beauty (beautiful woman or child).
preciosismo, *m.* (lit.) preciosity, euphuism.
preciosista, *a.* (lit.) euphuistic. —*m., f.* (lit.) euphuist.
precioso, sa, *a.* 1. precious (metals, stones, etc.). 2. precious, valuable, costly. 3. (coll.) beautiful, lovely.
preciosura, *f.* (Amer.) beauty, delight; beautiful or delightful person, object, act.
precipicio, *m.* 1. precipice, cliff, chasm. 2. headlong or violent fall. 3. (fig.) ruin, downfall, destruction.
precipitable, *a.* (chem.) precipitable.
precipitación, *f.* 1. precipitation, haste, rush, impetuosity. 2. (meteorol.) precipitation, rainfall. — **p. radioactiva,** fallout.
precipitadamente, *adv.* precipitately, impetuously, hastily.
precipitadero, *m., var. of* **precipicio.**
precipitado, da, *past part. of* **precipitar.** —*a.* hasty, rash, hurried; impetuous, precipitate, reckless. —*m.* (chem.) precipitate, deposit.
precipitante, *a.* precipitating. —*m.* (chem.) precipitating agent, precipitant.
precipitar, *tr.v.* 1. to precipitate, throw, cast, hurl, fling. 2. to hurry, hasten. 3. (chem.) to precipitate. —*r.v.* to rush headlong, to move or act recklessly or hastily.
precípite, *a.* in danger of falling, about to fall.
precipitina, *f.* (med.) precipitin.
precipitinógeno, *m.* (med.) precipitinogen.
precipitosamente, *adv.* precipitately, impetuously.
precipitoso, sa, *a.* 1. precipitous; reckless; impetuous.
precipuamente, *adv.* principally, mainly, chiefly.
precipuo, pua, *a.* principal, main, chief.
precisamente, *adv.* precisely, exactly; necessarily, unavoidably.
precisar, *tr.v.* 1. to specify, state precisely, determine. 2. to force, oblige, compel. 3. (Amer.) to need. — **p. a alguien a** + *inf.*, to oblige someone + *inf.*; **p. que alguien** + *subj.*, to force or oblige someone + *inf.* —*i.v.* to be necessary, e.g. *precisa que lo escribas cuanto antes,* it is necessary that you write it as soon as possible.
precisión, *f.* 1. precision, exactness, accuracy; conciseness. 2. necessity, obligation.
preciso, sa, *a.* 1. necessary, indispensable, compulsory. 2. definite, exact. 3. precise, concise. 4. distinct, clear.
precitado, da, *a.* aforementioned, aforesaid, above-mentioned.
precito, ta, *a.* damned, condemned to hell. —*m., f.* reprobate.
preclaramente, *adv.* illustriously.
preclaro, ra, *a.* illustrious, distinguished, eminent, prominent, famous.
preclásico, ca, *a.* preclassical, preclassic.
preclínico, ca, *a.* (med.) preclinical.
precocidad, *f.* precocity, precociousness.
precognición, *f.* precognition, foreknowledge.
precolombino, na, *a.* pre-Columbian.
precombustión, *f.* (mec.) precombustion.
preconcebir, (*ref. 39*) *tr.v.* to preconceive.
preconciba, preconcibiera, preconcibiese, *ref.* **preconcebir.**
preconice, preconicé, *ref.* **preconizar.**
preconización, *f.* 1. praising, eulogy, commendation, preconization. 2. (ecc.) preconization.
preconizador, ra, *a.* laudatory, commendatory. —*m., f.* praiser, lauder, commender.
preconizar, (*ref. 53*) *tr.v.* 1. to praise, commend, preconize. 2. (ecc.) to preconize. 3. to recommend, suggest, propose.
preconocer, (*ref. 45*) *tr.v.* to foresee, know beforehand.
preconozca, preconozco, *ref.* **preconocer.**
precoz, (*pl.* **precoces**), *a.* precocious, advanced.
precrítico, ca, *a.* (med.) precritical.
precursor, ra, *a.* preceding, precursory. —*m., f.* precursor, forerunner, harbinger.
predecesor, ra, *m., f.* 1. predecessor. 2. ancestor, forefather.
predecir, (*ref. 7*) *tr.v.* to predict, forecast, foretell.
predefinición, *f.* (theol.) predefinition, predetermination.
predefinir, *tr.v.* (theol.) to predefine, predetermine.
predestinación, *f.* predestination.
predestinacionismo, *m.* (rel.) predestinarianism.
predestinado, da, *past part. of* **predestinar.** —*a.* predestined, predestinated. —*m., f.* (theol.) predestinate.
predestinante, *a.* predestinating.
predestinar, *tr.v.* to predestine, predestinate, foreordain.
predeterminación, *f.* predetermination.
predeterminar, *tr.v.* to predetermine, foreordain; foredoom.
predial, *a.* praedial, predial, land, e.g. *impuesto p.,* land tax.
prédica, *f.* 1. sermon. 2. (coll.) harangue.
predicable, *a.* preachable, predicable. —*m.* (log.) predicable.
predicación, *f.* preaching; sermon.
predicaderas, *f.* (*pl.*) preaching abilities.
predicado, *m.* predicate; **p. nominativo,** (gram.) predicate nominative.
predicador, ra, *a.* preaching. —*m.* 1. preacher. 2. (ento.) praying mantis.
predicamental, *a.* (log.) predicamental.
predicamento, *m.* 1. esteem, reputation, regard. 2. (log.) predicament, category.
predicante, *a.* preaching, predicant. —*m.* preacher, predicant.
predicar, (*ref. 50*) *tr.v.* 1. to preach (a sermon, theory, doctrine). 2. to praise excessively. 3. to scold, sermon, lecture, reprove. —*i.v.* to preach.
predicativo, va, *a.* (gram.) predicative, pertaining to the predicate.
predicción, *f.* prediction, forecast.
predicho, cha, *irr. past part. of* **predecir.**
prediciendo, *ref.* **predecir.**
predictor, *m.* (mil.) predictor.
prediga, *ref.* **predecir.**
predigestión, *f.* predigestion.
predigo, *ref.* **predecir.**
predije, predijera, predijese, *ref.* **predecir.**
predilección, *f.* predilection, market preference.
predilecto, ta, *a.* favorite, preferred.
predio, *m.* property, estate, piece of land; **impuesto a los predios,** land tax; **p. dominante,** (law) dominant tenement; **p. rústico,** farm, rural property; **p. sirviente,** (law) servient tenement; **p. urbano,** city property.
predique, prediqué, *ref.* **predicar.**
predisponer, (*ref. 15*) *tr.v.* 1. to predispose; to make susceptible. 2. to prejudice. 3. to prearrange.
predisponga, predispongo, *ref.* **predisponer.**
predisposición, *f.* predisposition; prejudice.
predispuesto, ta, *a.* inclined, predisposed; biased, prejudiced.
predispuse, predispusiera, predispusiese, *ref.* **predisponer.**
predominación, predominancia, *f.* predominance, predomination.
predominante, *a.* predominant, prevailing.
predominar, *tr.v.* to predominate, prevail; to tower over, rise above, overlook. —*i.v.* to predominate, command.
predominio, *m.* predominance, superiority.
predorsal, *a.* (anat., phonet.) pre-dorsal. —*f.* (phonet.) pre-dorsal consonant.

preelegir, (*ref. 62*) *tr.v.* to elect beforehand; to predestine.
preelige, preeligiera, preeligiese, preeligió, *ref.* **preelegir.**
preelija, preelijo, *ref.* **preelegir.**
preeminencia, *f.* 1. preeminence, superiority, mastery. 2. privilege (due to rank, merit, etc.).
preeminente, *a.* preeminent, superior.
preencendido, *m.* (auto.) preignition.
pre-encogido, da, *a.* (tex.) preshrunk.
preescolar, *a.* preschool.
preestablecido, da, *a.* preestablished.
preexcelso, sa, *a.* most illustrious.
preexistencia, *f.* preexistence.
preexistente, *a.* preexistent.
preexistir, *i.v.* to preexist.
prefabricación, *f.* prefabrication (processes).
prefabricado, da, *a.* prefabricated.
prefabricar, (*ref. 50*) *tr.v.* to prefabricate.
prefacio, *m.* 1. preface, introduction. 2. (ecc.) preface (to the mass).
prefación, *f.* preface, introduction.
prefecto, *m.* 1. prefect, chief administrative officer of a department or region. 2. prefect, chief officer, president, superintendent. 3. prefect (high Roman official). 4. (ecc.) prefect (head of a congregation of ecclesiastics).
prefectura, *f.* prefecture.
preferencia, *f.* preference; **con** or **de p.,** preferably.
preferencial, *a.* preferential.
preferente, *a.* preferential; (law) preferent, preferential, having priority (claim); (com.) preferred, preferential, preference (stock bond).
preferentemente, *adv.* preferably; preferentially.
preferible, *a.* preferable.
preferiblemente, *adv.* preferably.
preferido, da, *past part. of* **preferir.** —*a.* favorite; **acción preferida,** (com.) preferred share.
preferir, (*ref. 42*) *tr.v.* to prefer.
prefiera, prefiero, *ref.* **preferir.**
prefiguración, *f.* prefiguration, foreshadowing.
prefigurar, *tr.v.* to prefigure, foreshadow, foretell.
prefijación, *f.* (gram.) prefixion.
prefijar, *tr.v.* 1. to arrange or fix beforehand, prearrange, predetermine. 2. (gram.) to prefix.
prefijo, ja, *irr. past part. of* **prefijar.** —*a.* prefixed. —*m.* (gram.) prefix.
prefinición, *f.* setting of a time limit.
prefinir, *tr.v.* to set a time limit for.
prefiriendo, prefiriera, prefiriese, prefirió, *ref.* **preferir.**
prefloración, *f.* (bot.) praefloration, estivation.
prefoliación, *f.* (bot.) praefoliation, vernation.
preformación, *f.* preformation.
prefrontal, *a.* (anat.) prefrontal.
prefulgente, *a.* resplendent, bright, brilliant.
preganglionar, *a.* (med.) preganglionic.
pregón, *m.* 1. public proclamation or announcement. 2. street vendor's cry.
pregonar, *tr.v.* 1. to proclaim, announce publicly. 2. to hawk, peddle (merchandise). 3. to make public (secret, news). 4. to praise openly. 5. to outlaw, proscribe.
pregoneo, *m.* crying or announcing wares on the street.
pregonería, *f.* office of common crier.
pregonero, ra, *a.* proclaiming, announcing. —*m., f.* 1. discloser, gossip. 2. street vendor. —*m.* town crier.
preguerra, *f.* prewar period.
pregunta, *f.* question, query, inquiry. — **absolver las preguntas,** (law) to answer under oath; **estar a la cuarta p.,** (coll.) to be hard up or penniless; **hacer una p.,** to ask a question.
preguntador, ra, *a.* inquisitive, nosey, (coll.) questioning. —*m., f.* 1. inquisitive person, nosey parker (coll., G.B.). 2. questioner, inquirer.
preguntante, *a.* questioning, inquiring. —*m., f.* questioner, inquirer.
preguntar, *tr.v.* to ask (a question), to inquire after or about; to question, interrogate. —*i.v.* to ask, inquire; **quien pregunta, no yerra,** it's always best to ask beforehand. —*r.v.* to wonder; to ask oneself.
pregunteo, *m.* (coll.) snooping.
preguntón, na, *a.* inquisitive, nosey (coll.). —*m., f.* inquisitive person, snooper (coll.).
pregustación, *f.* the act of tasting food and drink before it is served to the king.
pregustar, *tr.v.* to taste (food and drink) before it is served to the king.
prehelénico, ca, *a.* (hist., art) pre-Hellenic.
prehistoria, *f.* prehistory, prehistoric times.
prehistórico, ca, *a.* prehistoric.
preignición, *f.* (auto.) preignition.
preincaico, ca, *a.* pre-Incan.
preinserto, ta, *a.* previously inserted.
prejudicial, *a.* (law) pre-judicial, requiring judicial decision before final sentence.
prejudicio, *m., var. of* **prejuicio.**
prejuicio, *m.* 1. prejudice, bias. 2. prejudgment.
prejuzgar, (*ref. 51*) *tr.v.* to prejudge.
prejuzgue, prejuzgué, *ref.* **prejuzgar.**
prelacía, *f.* prelacy.
prelación, *f.* priority, preference.
prelada, *f.* prelatess, abbess, mother superior.
prelado, *m.* prelate.
prelaticio, cia, *a.* prelatic, prelatical; **traje p.,** prelatic gown.
prelatura, *f., var. of* **prelacía.**
preliminar, *a.* preliminary; introductory. —*m.* 1. preliminary; preparation. 2. (*pl.*) basic principles.
preliminarmente, *adv.* preliminarily, in advance.
prelucir, (*ref. 46*) *i.v.* to shine forth, shine ahead.
preludiar, *i.v.* (mus.) to prelude, to run over the scales (before beginning to play or sing). —*tr.v.* to pave the way for, clear the ground for.
preludio, *m.* 1. introduction. 2. (mus.) prelude; warming-up practice; overture.
prelusión, *f.* introduction, preface.
preluzca, preluzco, *ref.* **prelucir.**
prematuramente, *adv.* prematurely.
prematuro, ra, *a.* premature; untimely, inopportune. —*f.* (law) impubertal.
premédico, ca, *a.* premed, premedical.
premeditación, *f.* premeditation; (law) malice aforethought, premeditation.
premeditadamente, *adv.* 1. premeditatedly. 2. (law) with malice aforethought.
premeditado, da, *past part. of* **premeditar.** —*a.* premeditated.
premeditar, *tr.v.* to premeditate.
premenstrual, *a.* (physiol.) premenstrual.
premezclar, *tr.v.* to premix.
premiador, ra, *a.* rewarding. —*m., f.* rewarder.
premiar, *tr.v.* 1. to reward, recompense, repay, requite. 2. to award a prize to.
premidera, *f.* (tex.) treadle, loom lever moved by foot.
premier, *m.* (pol.) premier, prime minister.
premio, *m.* 1. prize, award; recompense, reward. 2. (econ.) premium (greater value of one form of money over another). 3. (com.) premium (of insurance contract). 4. premium, bonus, additional sum. — **a p.,** at a premium, with interest; **p. de consuelo,** or **de consolación,** consolation prize; **p. en efectivo,** cash prize; **p. gordo,** (coll.) jackpot, first prize (in the lottery); **p. Nóbel,** Nobel prize.
premiosamente, *adv.* 1. tightly. 2. onerously, bothersomely. 3. by force, by pressure. 4. rigidly, strictly. 5. slowly, haltingly (said of speech); awkwardly, heavily (said of movement).
premioso, sa, *a.* 1. tight, narrow. 2. burdensome, onerous. 3. pressing, urgent. 4. rigid, strict. 5. awkward, slow, heavy (movement); slow (speech or writing); heavy, plodding, pedestrian (literary style).
premisa, *f.* 1. (log.) premise. 2. indication, sign, clue. — **p. mayor** or **menor,** (log.) major or minor premise.
premiso, sa, *a.* 1. anticipated, presupposed; sent in advance. 2. (law) preceding, precedent.
premoción, *f.* (theol.) premotion, (divine) predetermination (of a human act).
premolar, *a.* (anat., zool.) premolar.
premonitorio, ria, *a.* (med.) premonitory, giving previous warning.
premonstratense, *a., m.* Premonstratensian, member of a regular order of canons founded at Premontre in 1119.
premoriencia, *f.* (law) predecease, prior death.
premoriente, *a., m., f.* (law) predeceasing.
premorir, (*ref. 38*) *i.v.* (law) to predecease, die first.
premorso, sa, *a.* (bot., ento.) premorse.
premostrar, (*ref. 33*) *tr.v.* to preview, to show prior to a formal demonstration.
premostratense, *a., var. of* **premonstratense.**
premuera, premuero, *ref.* **premorir.**
premuerto, ta, *a., m., f.* predeceased.
premuestre, premuestro, *ref.* **premostrar.**
premura, *f.* urgency, pressure, haste.
premuriendo, premuriera, premuriese, premurió, *ref.* **premorir.**
prenatal, *a.* (biol.) prenatal.
prenda, *f.* 1. security, pledge, guaranty. 2. jewel; household article (especially when offered for sale). 3. garment, article of clothing. 4. token, sign (of love, etc.). 5. loved one, darling. 6. (*pl.*) natural gifts, talents; moral qualities. 7. (*pl.*) forfeits (game). — **en p., en prendas,** in pawn; as a pledge; as a guaranty; **es por más la p.,** this is more than I can thank you for; **hacer p.,** to hold a valuable as security; to hold something against someone; **juego de prendas,** (game of) forfeits; **meter prendas,** to get oneself into business; **no dolerle prendas a uno,** to keep one's promise; to spare no effort or expense; **no soltar prenda,** to keep one's mouth shut, give nothing away; **p. perdida,** forfeit; **prendas intimas,** or **interiores,** underclothes; **soltar p.,** (coll.) to commit oneself, promise.
prendado, da, *past part. of* **prendar.** —*a.* **estar p. de,** to be taken with, to be very admiring of.
prendador, ra, *a.* pawning, pledging. —*m., f.* pawner, pledger.
prendamiento, *m.* 1. pawning, pledging. 2. falling in love; crush (coll., U.S.).
prendar, *tr.v.* 1. to pawn, pledge, give as security. 2. to charm, captivate, please. —*r.v.* **prendarse de,** to become fond of, take a great liking to; to fall in love with.
prendedera, *f.* (Col) waitress.
prendedero, *m.* 1. clasp, catch, hook. 2. brooch, ornamental clasp. 3. hair ribbon, hair band, bandeau; barrette.
prendedor, *m.* 1. apprehender, catcher. 2. clasp, catch, hook. 3. ornamental clasp, brooch. 4. hair ribbon, hair band, fillet, bandeau.
prendedura, *f.* tread, cicatricle (of an egg).
prender, *tr.v.* 1. to grasp, seize; to arrest, catch, apprehend. 2. to secure, fasten, fix, e.g. *p. con alfileres,* to pin, secure with pins. 3. to cover

the female, mate with. 4. to dress up, doll up, adorn. 5. (Amer.) to switch on (light, radio). — **p. fuego a,** to set afire, set fire to. —*i.v.* 1. to take root; to take (e.g. an inoculation). 2. to catch, light, catch fire. —*r.v.* to dress up, doll oneself up; **prenderse de,** (coll.) to hang or hold on to.

prendería, *f.* second-hand shop; pawn shop.

prendero, ra, *m., f.* second-hand dealer; pawnbroker.

prendido, da, *past part. of* **prender.** —*a.* on, e.g. *dejé la luz prendida,* I left the light on. —*m.* 1. ornamental hair clasp, fillet. 2. pattern for bobbin lace.

prendimiento, *m.* capture, arrest, seizure, apprehension.

prenoción, *f.* (philos.) prenotion, first knowledge.

prenombre, *m.* praenomen, first name, Christian name, given name.

prenotar, *tr.v.* to note in advance, note beforehand.

prensa, *f.* 1. press; clamp, vise. 2. printing press; the press, newspapers. — **dar a la p.,** to print, publish; **entrar** or **meter en p.,** to go to press; **meter en p. a uno,** to force or put the squeeze on someone; **p. a cadena,** (mec.) chain vise; **p. amarillo,** tabloids, "yellow press"; **p. de aceite,** oil press; **p. de cilindro,** cylinder press; **p. de encuadernador,** book clamp; **p. de filtrar, filtro-p.,** filter press; **p. de imprenta,** printing press; **p. de rebordear,** (mec.) flanging press; **p. de uva,** wine press; **p. hidráulica,** hydraulic press; **p. plana,** (print.) flatbed; **p. rotativa,** rotary press; **sudar la p.,** to print continuously; **tener buena** or **mala p.,** to have good or bad press reviews (an artist, etc.).

prensado, *m.* (tex.) luster, gloss.

prensador, ra, *m., f.* presser, press operator.

prensadura, *f.* pressing, pressure; compressing.

prensaestopas, *m.* (mec.) stuffing box.

prensar, *tr.v.* to press; to compress.

prensero, *m.* (Col.) sugar mill feeder or operator.

prensil, *a.* prehensile.

prensión, *f.* seizing, grasping, prehension.

prensista, *m.* (print.) pressman.

prensor, ra, *a.* (ornith.) psittacine. —*f.* psittacine, (*pl.*) Psittaciformes, Psittasi.

prenunciar, *tr.v.* to announce in advance, presage, foretell, prognosticate, predict.

prenuncio, *m.* presage, prognostication, prediction.

preñado, da, *a.* 1. pregnant. 2. (fig.) bulging, sagging (said of a wall). 3. (fig.) pregnant, full, charged, e.g. *una palabra preñada de significado,* a word pregnant or charged with meaning. —*m.* 1. pregnancy. 2. foetus.

preñar, *tr.v.* 1. to make pregnant, to impregnate. 2. (fig.) to fill, stuff.

preñez, *f.* 1. pregnancy. 2. impending trouble or danger. 3. confusion, obscurity.

preocupación, *f.* 1. preoccupation, concern, worry, anxiety. 2. preconception, preconceived notion, prejudice.

preocupadamente, *adv.* worriedly, with concern.

preocupado, da, *past part. of* **preocupar.** —*a.* preoccupied, worried, concerned.

preocupar, *tr.v.* 1. to preoccupy, worry, concern. 2. to prejudice, predispose. 3. to preoccupy, prepossess, take previous possession of. —*r.v.* 1. to worry; to be preoccupied, worried or concerned. 2. to be prejudiced. — **preocuparse con, de** or **por,** to worry about; to be preoccupied or worried with or about.

preoperatorio, a, *a.* (med.) preoperative.

preopinante, *a.* speaking previously. —*m., f.* previous speaker, predecessor (in a debate).

preoral, *a.* (zool.) preoral.

preordinación, *f.* (theol.) preordination.

preordinadamente, *adv.* in a preordained or foreordained manner.

preordinar, *tr.v.* (theol.) to preordain, foreordain.

prepalatal, *a., f.* (phonet.) prepalatal.

preparación, *f.* 1. preparation, getting ready. 2. preparation, compound, concoction; medicine.

preparado, *m.* pharmaceutical preparation.

preparador, ra, *m., f.* preparer; **p. de caballos,** horse trainer.

preparamento, preparamiento, *m.* preparation, prearrangements.

preparar, *tr.v.* to prepare; to make ready, get ready. —*r.v.* to prepare, get ready; **prepararse** a or **para** + *inf.,* to prepare or get ready to + *inf.*

preparativo, va, *a.* preparatory, preparative. —*m.* (*pl.*) preparations, e.g. *hacer p.,* to make preparations, to get ready.

preparatoriamente, *adv.* preparatorily.

preparatorio, ria, *a.* preparatory.

preponderancia, *f.* preponderance, superiority.

preponderante, *a.* preponderant, prevailing.

preponderar, *i.v.* to preponderate; to prevail, predominate.

preponer, (*ref. 15*) *tr.v.* to put before, prefer.

preponga, prepongo, *ref.* **preponer.**

preposición, *f.* (gram.) preposition; **p. inseparable.** (gram.) prefix.

preposicional, *a.* (gram.) prepositional.

prepositivo, va, *a.* (gram.) prepositive, prepositional.

prepósito, *m.* chairman, president; (ecc.) provost, prepositus.

prepositura, *f.* chairmanship, presidency; (ecc.) prepositure, provostship.

preposteración, *f.* reversal, reversion of order.

prepósteramente, *adv.* out of place or order, untimely.

preposterar, *tr.v.* to reverse, change the order of, disarrange, upset.

prepóstero, ra, *a.* reversed, upset, out of order, disarranged.

prepotencia, *f.* 1. arrogance, hauteur, haughtiness. 2. prepotency, great power or influence.

prepotente, *a.* 1. overbearing, haughty, arrogant. 2. prepotent, very powerful or influential.

prepucio, *m.* (anat.) prepuce, foreskin.

prepuesto, ta, *irr. past part. of* **preponer.**

prepuse, prepusiera, prepusiese, *ref.* **preponer.**

prerrafaelismo, *m.* (art) Pre-Raphaelitism.

prerrafaelista, *a., m.* (art) Pre-Raphaelite.

prerrogativa, *f.* prerogative, privilege.

prerromanticismo, *m.* (art, lit.) preromanticism.

prerromántico, ca, *a.* (art, lit.) pre-romantic.

presa, *f.* 1. seizure, capture. 2. (mil.) booty, spoils; (mar.) prize (captured enemy vessel); (hunt.) prey, catch. 3. irrigation channel or ditch. 4. dam, weir. 5. channel (conducting water in watermill). 6. piece, slice (of food). 7. fang, tusk. 8. (hunt.) claw (of bird of prey). — **ave de p.,** bird of prey; **buena** or **mala p.,** lawful or unlawful prize (vessel lawfully or unlawfully seized); **hacer p.,** to capture; to seize, grasp; (fig.) to seize, take advantage (of a chance or opportunity); **parte de p.,** (mar.) prize money; **ser p. de,** to be seized with.

presada, *f.* reservoir, reserve water (in watermill).

presado, da, *a.* pale green.

presagiar, *tr.v.* to presage, forebode, predict, foretell.

presagio, *m.* presage, omen, token.

presagioso, sa, *a.* presaging, foreboding, betokening.

presago, présago, ga, *a.* presaging, foreboding, betokening.

presbicia, *f.* (med.) presbytia, far-sightedness.

presbiope, *m., f.* (med.) presbyope.

presbiopía, *f.* (med.) presbyopia, far-sightedness.

presbiópico, ca, *a.* (med.) presbyopic, far-sighted.

présbita, *a.* (med.) presbytic, far-sighted. —*m., f.* presbyte.

présbite, *a., m., f., var. of* **présbita.**

presbiterado, *m.* priesthood.

presbiteral, *a.* priestly, sacerdotal.

presbiterato, *m., var. of* **presbiterado.**

presbiterianismo, *m.* (rel.) Presbyterianism.

presbiteriano, na, *a., m., f.* (rel.) Presbyterian.

presbiterio, *m.* presbytery; chancel.

presbítero, *m.* presbyter, priest.

presciencia, *f.* prescience, foreknowledge.

presciente, *a.* prescient.

prescindencia, *f.* (Amer.) leaving aside; omission; **con p. de,** without.

prescindible, *a.* dispensable, that can be dispensed with.

prescindir, *i.v.* **p. de,** to do without, dispense with; to leave out, omit.

prescito, ta, *a., m., f., var. of* **precito.**

prescribir, *irr. past part.* **prescrito.** —*tr.v.* 1. to lay down, order, prescribe, dispose, specify. 2. to prescribe (medicine). 3. (law) to prescribe, invalidate (through default over lapse of time). 4. (law) to acquire by uninterrupted possession. —*i.v.* 1. (law) to prescribe, become invalid (rights, possession, etc. through default over lapse of time). 2. (law) to prescribe, become valid (rights, property, etc. through uninterrupted possession). 3. to finish, end, come to an end; to lapse, become invalid (debt, prison sentence, etc. through lapse of time).

prescripción, *f.* prescription; (law, med.) prescription; **ley de p.,** (law) statute of limitations; **p. adquisitiva,** (law) acquisitive prescription; **p. extintiva,** (law) extinctive prescription.

prescriptible, *a.* prescriptible.

prescripto, ta, prescrito, ta, *irr. past part. of* **prescribir.**

presea, *f.* gem, jewel; priceless object.

preselección, *f.* 1. preselection, previous selection. 2. (sport) trial team.

preselector, *m.* (rad.) preselector.

presencia, *f.* 1. presence (being present). 2. presence, bearing, mien. 3. show, display, ostentation. — **en p. de,** in the presence of; **p. de ánimo,** presence of mind; **p. real,** (theol.) real presence.

presencial, *a.* presential, pertaining to presence; **testigo p.,** eyewitness.

presencialmente, *adv.* in person.

presenciar, *tr.v.* to witness, be present at, see, attend.

presentable, *a.* presentable.

presentación, *f.* 1. presentation; introduction. 2. display, exhibition. 3. external appearance (of a book, etc.). 4. (med.) presentation (position of fetus in labor). 5. (theat.) staging. 6. (theol.) Presentation.

presentado, *m.* (ecc.) presentee.

presentador, ra, *a.* presenting. —*m., f.* presenter.

presentalla, *f.* (ecc.) votive offering.

presentáneamente, *adv.* immediately, on the spot, at once.

presentáneo, a, *a.* quick-acting.

presentante, *a.* introducing, presenting.

presentar, *tr.v.* 1. to present, submit (e.g. application). 2. to present, give, offer. 3. to introduce (one person to another). 4. to display, show; (theat.) to put on stage. 5. (ecc.) to present, put

forward (for benefice, office, etc.). — **p. batalla,** to offer battle; **p. las armas,** to present arms. —*r.v.* 1. to appear; to show up, present oneself, report; to turn up. 2. to introduce oneself (to a new acquaintance). 3. to occur, present itself, e.g. *si se presenta la oportunidad,* if the opportunity occurs or presents itself. 4. to offer oneself, offer one's services.
presente, *a.* 1. present, current. 2. (gram.) present. 3. delivered by hand. — **al p., de p.,** at present, at the present time, now; **mejorando lo p.,** present company excepted; **la p.,** this letter, the present writing; **tener p.,** to keep in mind. —*m.* 1. present, gift. 2. (gram.) present. —*interj.* present, here.
presentemente, *adv.* at present, now.
presentero, *m.* (ecc.) sponsor.
presentimiento, *m.* presentiment, premonition; foreboding, misgiving.
presentir, (*ref. 42*) *tr.v.* to have a presentiment of; to predict, forebode, to sense.
presepio, *m.* manger; stable; crib, rack.
presera, *f.* (bot.) bedstraw, cleavers.
presero, *m.* keeper of an irrigation ditch or dam.
preservación, *f.* preservation, conservation.
preservador, ra, *a.* preserver, preserving. —*m., f.* preserver.
preservar, *tr.v.* to preserve, keep; to protect, defend.
preservativamente, *adv.* preservatively.
preservativo, va, *a.* preservative. —*m.* 1. prophylactic, preventive. 2. contraceptive, condom.
presidario, *m., var. of* **presidiario.**
presidencia, *f.* 1. presidency. 2. presidential term. 3. president's office or residence. 4. chairmanship.
presidencial, *a.* presidential.
presidenta, *f.* 1. (woman) president; president's wife. 2. woman chairman, chairwoman.
presidente, *m.* 1. president. 2. presiding judge or officer. 3. chairman. 4. speaker (of a parliamentary body). — **dirigirse al p.,** to address the chair.
presidiar, *tr.v.* to garrison, furnish with soldiers.
presidiario, *m.* convict.
presidio, *m.* 1. garrison; fortress, citadel. 2. prison, penitentiary; prisoners, convicts (collectively); imprisonment, hard labor.
presidir, *tr.v.* to preside over; to govern. —*i.v.* to preside.
presienta, presiento, *ref.* **presentir.**
presilla, *f.* 1. paper clip; hair clip. 2. loop, fastener. 3. kind of linen cloth. 4. buttonhole stitching. — **p. aislante,** cleat insulator.
presintiendo, presintiera, presintiese, presintió, *ref.* **presentir.**
presión, *f.* pressure; **a p.,** under pressure; pressurized, e.g. *cabina a p.,* pressurized cabin; **olla de p.,** pressure cooker; **p. acústica,** sound pressure; **p. arterial** or **sanguínea,** blood pressure; **p. atmosférica,** atmospheric pressure; **p. de apoyo,** (bldg.) bearing pressure; **p. del aire, p. neumática,** air pressure; **p. osmótica,** osmotic pressure; **p. sobre la chumacera,** (mec.) bearing pressure.
presionar, *tr.v.* (Amer.) to urge, press.
preso, sa, *irr. past part. of* **prender.** —*a.* imprisoned, arrested, under arrest. — **p. por mil, p. por mil y quinientos,** (coll.) in for a penny, in for a pound. —*m., f.* prisoner, convict; **p. político** or **política,** political prisoner; **p. preventivo** or **preventiva,** prisoner held in preventive detention.
presocrático, ca, *a.* (philos.) pre-Socratic.
prest, *m.* (arch.) soldier's wages.
prestación, *f.* 1. lending, loaning; loan. 2. rendering (of services). 3. service; payment. — **p. personal,** obligatory communal work.
prestadizo, za, *a.* lendable.
prestado, da, *past part. of* **prestar.** —*a.* lent, loaned; borrowed. — **dar prestado,** to lend; **de prestado,** as a loan; **pedir** or **tomar prestado,** to borrow.
prestador, ra, *a.* lending. —*m., f.* lender.
prestamente, *adv.* speedily, quickly.
prestamera, *f.* 1. (ecc.) benefice, living, allowance. 2. sinecure.
prestamería, *f.* 1. (ecc.) dignity of beneficiary. 2. benefice, church living.
prestamero, *m.* (ecc.) beneficiary, priest receiving a benefice.
prestamista, *m., f.* moneylender, pawnbroker.
préstamo, *m.* 1. loan, loaning, lending. 2. (engin.) borrow pit. — **casa de préstamos,** pawnshop; **p. a plazo fijo,** time loan or money; **p. a vista** or **a la demanda,** call loan, demand loan.
prestancia, *f.* excellence.
prestante, *a.* excellent.
prestar, *tr.v.* to lend, loan; to give, render (information, statement; help, assistance, services); to pay (attention); to keep (silence); to show (patience). —*i.v.* 1. to stretch, give (cloth). 2. to be good, be useful, e.g. *p. para,* to be good for. —*r.v.* 1. to lend itself, be suitable, e.g. *este salón se presta para un baile,* this salon is suitable for a ball. 2. to submit, e.g. *prestarse para,* to submit to. 3. to offer, e.g. *prestarse a ayudar,* to offer to help.
prestatario, ria, *a.* borrowing. —*m., f.* borrower.
preste, *m.* prester, priest; **P. Juan,** Prester John.
presteza, *f.* quickness, promptness, celerity.
prestidigitación, *f.* prestidigitation, sleight of hand, legerdemain.
prestidigitador, ra, *m., f.* prestidigitator, magician.
prestigiador, ra, *a.* causing prestige. —*m., f.* deceiver, trickster.
prestigiar, *tr.v.* (Amer.) to do credit to; to lend prestige or authority to.
prestigio, *m.* 1. prestige, good standing or reputation. 2. illusion, deception. 3. spell, fascination.
prestigioso, sa, *a.* 1. prestigious, famous, renowned. 2. deceiving, illusory.
prestimonio, *m.* 1. loan. 2. (ecc.) prestimony.
prestiño, *m., var. of* **pestiño.**
presto, ta, *a.* 1. quick, swift, prompt. 2. ready, prepared. —*adv.* 1. immediately, promptly. 2. (mus.) presto.
presumible, *a.* presumable.
presumido, da, *past part. of* **presumir.** —*a.* presumptuous, conceited, vain. —*m., f.* vain or conceited person.
presumir, *tr.v.* to presume, surmise, conjecture. —*i.v.* to be vain or conceited; to boast. — **p. de,** to think one is, boast of being, e.g. *él presume de ser un experto,* he boasts of being an expert.
presunción, *f.* 1. presumption, assumption. 2. presumptuousness, vanity, conceit. 3. (law) presumption.
presuntamente, *adv.* presumably, supposedly.
presuntivamente, *adv.* conjecturally.
presuntivo, va, *a.* presumptive, supposed.
presunto, ta, *irr. past part. of* **presumir.** —*a.* supposed, presumed; **presunto heredero,** heir presumptive.
presuntuosamente, *adv.* presumptuously, conceitedly.
presuntuosidad, *f.* presumptuousness, conceit, vainglory.
presuntuoso, sa, *a.* presumptuous, conceited. —*m., f.* presumptuous or conceited person.
presupe, presupiera, presupiese, *ref.* **presuponer.**
presuponer, (*ref. 15*) *tr.v.* 1. to presuppose. 2. to budget, estimate.
presuponga, presupongo, *ref.* **presuponer.**
presuposición, *f.* presupposition.
presupuestar, *tr.v.* to budget; to estimate.
presupuestario, ria, *a.* budgetary.
presupuesto, ta, *irr. past part. of* **presuponer.** —*a.* presupposed, estimated. —*m.* 1. budget; estimate. 2. motive, cause. 3. assumption, supposition.
presura, *f.* 1. anxiety, worry. 2. quickness, speed, promptness. 3. earnestness, zeal, persistence.
presurice, presuricé, *ref.* **presurizar.**
presurizar, (*ref. 53*) *tr.v.* to pressurize.
presurosamente, *adv.* hastily, hurriedly; promptly.
presuroso, sa, *a.* quick, speedy, hasty, hurried.
pretal, *m.* 1. breast band or strap (of horse's harness); strap. 2. (Hond.) trouser belt.
pretencioso, sa, *a.* 1. conceited, vain, presumptuous. 2. pretentious, showy.
pretendencia, *f., var. of* **pretensión.**
pretender, *tr.v.* 1. to try to get, seek, endeavor, be after, e.g. *no sé qué pretende,* I don't know what he's after. 2. to claim, pretend to (e.g. a throne). 3. to be a suitor for (a woman's hand). 4. to claim, pretend, e.g. *no pretendo saber tanto,* I don't claim to know that much.
pretendido, da, *past part. of* **pretender.** —*a.* supposed, presumed.
pretendienta, *f.* (woman) claimant; pretender (to a throne).
pretendiente, *m.* 1. claimant, seeker; pretender (to a throne); candidate (for office). 2. suitor (for a woman's hand).
pretensión, *f.* 1. claim, pretension. 2. aspiration, intention, desire, plan. 3. pretentiousness, pretention, showiness. 4. conceit, presumption; **pretensiones de sueldo,** salary expected.
pretensioso, sa, *a., var. of* **pretencioso.**
pretenso, sa, *irr. past part. of* **pretender.** —*a.* supposed, presumed.
pretensor, ra, *m., f.* pretender, claimant; seeker.
preterición, *f.* preterition; (law, rhet.) preterition.
preterir, *tr.v.* to pass over, omit, disregard, overlook; (law) to omit (lawful heirs) in a will.
pretérito, ta, *a.* preterit, past, bygone; (gram.) preterit. —*m.* (gram.) past; preterit, past absolute or historic. — **p. anterior,** (gram.) past anterior; **p. imperfecto,** (gram.) imperfect; **p. indefinido,** (gram.) preterit, past absolute; **p. perfecto,** (gram.) present perfect; **p. pluscuamperfecto,** (gram.) past perfect, pluperfect.
pretermision, *f.* omission, pretermission; (rhet.) pretermission, paraleipsis.
pretermitir, *tr.v.* to omit, pretermit.
preternatural, *a.* preternatural, abnormal.
preternaturalice, preternaturalicé, *ref.* **preternaturalizar.**
preternaturalizar, (*ref. 53*) *tr.v.* to render preternatural or abnormal.
preternaturalmente, *adv.* preternaturally.
pretexta, *f.* praetexta (Roman toga).
pretextar, *tr.v.* to give as a pretext.
pretexto, *m.* pretext, excuse.
pretil, *m.* 1. stone or brick railing; battlement, parapet. 2. sidewalk, pavement. 3. (Ven.) stone bench. 4. (Amer.) portico (of church).
pretina, *f.* belt, waistband; girdle. — **meter** or **poner a uno en p.,** to restrain, control someone.
pretinazo, *m.* blow with a belt.
pretinero, *m.* one who makes girdles or belts.
pretinilla, *f. dim. of* **pretina,** ladies' belt or girdle.

pretor, *m.* 1. (hist.) praetor. 2. blackness of water where tuna abound.
pretoría, *f.* praetorship.
Pretoria, *f.* Pretoria (capital of South Africa).
pretorial, *a.* praetorian, praetorial.
pretorianismo, *m.* praetorianism, military intervention in politics, political militarism.
pretoriano, na, *a., m.* praetorian.
pretoriense, *a.* of a praetorium (Roman governor's residence).
pretorio, ria, *a.* praetorian. —*m.* praetorium (Roman governor's residence).
pretura, *f.* praetorship.
prevalecer, (*ref. 45*) *i.v.* 1. to prevail, triumph, overcome. 2. to take root, thrive; (fig.) to thrive, prosper, flourish. — **p. sobre,** to prevail over.
prevaleciente, *a.* prevailing, prevalent.
prevaler, (*ref. 25*) *i.v.* to prevail. —*r.v.* **prevalerse de,** to avail oneself of, take advantage of.
prevalezca, *ref.* **prevalecer.**
prevaricación, *f.* 1. breach of duty, dishonesty, collusion; breach of trust. 2. (law) prevarication.
prevaricador, ra, *a.* failing in one's duty, dishonest; corrupt, corrupting. —*m., f.* one who fails in his duty; corrupter.
prevaricar, (*ref. 50*) *i.v.* 1. to act dishonestly in the discharge of a public trust; to fail in one's duty. 2. (law) to prevaricate. 3. (coll.) to rave, talk deliriously.
prevaricato, *m.* corrupt practice; (law) prevarication.
prevarique, prevariqué, *ref.* **prevaricar.**
prevención, *f.* 1. prevention; warning; foresight; precaution, precautionary measure. 2. stock, supply (provisions). 3. prejudice, bias. 4. police station or post, jail. 5. (mil.) military police; guardhouse. 6. (law) preliminary hearing, anticipated hearing of a case. — **a** or **de p.,** spare, reserve, emergency.
prevenga, prevengo, *ref.* **prevenir.**
prevenidamente, *adv.* beforehand, previously; with preparation.
prevenido, da, *past part. of* **prevenir.** —*a.* 1. prepared, ready. 2. careful, foresighted, forewarned. 3. stocked, supplied.
preveniente, *a.* preparing, disposing; prudent, foresighted.
prevenir, (*ref.26*) *tr.v.* 1. to warn, caution. 2. to foresee. 3. to prevent, forestall, anticipate. 4. to make ready. 5. to prejudice, bias, predispose. 6. (law) to conduct a preliminary hearing of (a case). —*r.v.* to take precautions; to prepare oneself, get ready.
preventivamente, *adv.* preventively.
preventivo, va, *a.* preventive; warning.
preventorio, *m.* preventorium, clinic or hospital for contagious diseases.
prever, (*ref. 27*) *tr.v.* to foresee, anticipate.
previamente, *adv.* previously, beforehand.
previne, previniendo, previniera, previniese, *ref.* **prevenir.**
previo, via, *a.* 1. previous, former. 2. upon, after, e.g. *previo pago de los derechos correspondientes,* upon or after payment of the corresponding fees.
previsible, *a.* foreseeable.
previsión, *f.* 1. foresight, prevision, foresightedness; forecast. 2. (acc.) provision (sum put aside for contingencies or incidentals). — **p. meteorológica,** weather forecast; **p. obrera,** workers' pension plan; **p. social,** social security.
previsor, ra, *a.* foresighted, cautious, wise, careful, prudent.
previsto, ta, *irr. past part. of* **prever.** —*a.* foreseen.
prez, *m., f.* honor, glory, renown.
priado, *adv.* quickly, rapidly, promptly.
Príamo, *m.* (myth.) Priam, last king of Troy.
priapismo, *m.* (med.) Priapism.
Príapo, *m.* (myth.) Priapus, son of Aphrodite who personifies sexual power.
priesa, *f., var. of* **prisa.**
prieto, ta, *a.* 1. dark, swarthy; 2. tight, compact. 3. stingy, niggardly.
prima, *f.* 1. (insurance) premium. 2. bonus, premium; bounty. 3. female cousin. 4. early morning. 5. (ecc.) first tonsure. 6. (mus.) treble (in stringed instruments). 7. (mil.) first quarter of the night.
primacía, *f.* 1. primacy, supremacy. 2. (ecc.) primacy, primateship.
primacial, *a.* primatial.
primada, *f.* 1. (coll.) act or remark typical of a naive or gullible person. 2. trick, fraud, deception.
primado, da, *a.* primatial, of a primate. —*m., f.* (ecc.) primate. —*m.* primacy, supremacy.
primal, la, *a.* yearling (sheep or goat). —*m.* 1. yearling. 2. silk cord or braid.
primariamente, *adv.* primarily, principally, chiefly.
primario, ria, *a.* 1. primary. 2. first, e.g. *delincuente primario,* (law) first offender. 3. (educ., geol., biol., elec.) primary.
primate, *m.* 1. illustrious citizen, distinguished person. 2. (zool.) (*pl.*) Primates.
primavera, *f.* 1. spring, springtime. 2. (bot.) cowslip, primrose. 3. flowered silk. 4. (fig.) bright colorful object. 5. (fig.) prime of life, spring.
primaveral, *a.* pertaining to spring, vernal.
primazgo, *m.* 1. cousinship. 2. primateship, primacy.
primearse, *r.v.* to call each other cousins (royalty).
primer, *a.* first (apocopated form of **primero** used only before singular masculine nouns and adjectives), e.g. *p. actor,* (theat.) leading man; *p. ministro,* prime minister; *p piso,* ground floor, main floor; *p. plano,* foreground; *p. teniente,* first lieutenant; *en p. lugar,* in the first place, first of all.
primera, *f.* 1. (auto.) low (gear, speed). 2. (ry., avia.) first (class). 3. primero (card game). 4. (fenc.) prime. 5. (ballet) first (position).
primeramente, *adv.* first, previously, before; in the first place.
primerizo, za, *a.* 1. beginning. 2. primiparous, giving birth for the first time. —*m., f.* beginner, novice. —*f.* primipara, woman bearing her first child.
primero, ra, [see **primer**] *a.* 1. first. 2. foremost, best, top (sl.). 3. chief, leading, principal. 4. early, former, original. 5. prime, primary. 6. (math.) prime (number). 7. front, e.g. *primera página,* front page. — **a las primeras de cambio,** the first thing, right off; **a p. vista,** at first sight; **primero de año,** New Year's Day; **primeros auxilios,** first aid; **p. actor** or **actriz,** leading man; leading lady; **p. bailarin** or **bailarina,** leading dancer; prima ballerina; **p. base,** (baseball) first base; **p. clase,** first class; **la primera dama,** the first lady (of the nation); **de buenas a primeras,** suddenly, all at once; **de primera,** (com.) highest quality, prime; **de p. instancia,** in the first place, on first impulse; **p. edición,** first edition; **p. enseñanza,** primary education; **p. fila,** front rank, first row; **primeras horas,** the small hours; **p. mano,** priming coat (of paint); **p. ministro,** Prime Minister; **p. persona,** (gram.) first person; **p. piedra,** cornerstone; **p. plana,** front page; **p. plano,** close-up shot; **p. plato,** (cul.) first course; p. violin, concertmaster.
primero, *adv.* 1. firstly, in the first place. 2. rather, first, sooner.
primevo, va, *a.* primeval; oldest; original.
primicerio, ria, *a.* principal, top, foremost, first (in rank). —*m.* (ecc.) precentor, cantor.
primicia, *f.* 1. first fruits. 2. (ecc.) primitiae, first fruits (gift made to the church). 3. (fig.) (*pl.*) early results, first products of an endeavor.
primicial, *a.* pertaining to the first fruits; (fig.) pertaining to the first results of an endeavor.
primichón, *m.* skein of embroidery silk.
primigenio, nia, *a.* original, pristine, primitive.
primilla, *f.* pardon for first offense.
primina, *f.* (bot.) primine.
primípara, *f.* primipara, woman giving birth for the first time.
primitivamente, *adv.* 1. originally. 2. primitively, in a primitive manner.
primitivismo, *m.* primitivism.
primitivo, va, *a.* 1. primitive, primeval; original. 2. primitive, rudimentary, crude. 3. (geol.) primitive, primary. 4. primitive (language). —*m.* primitive (artist, sculptor).
primo, ma, *a.* 1. prime (number). 2. raw (material). 3. first. 4. prime, excellent. —*m., f.* 1. cousin. 2. cousin (form of address used by king to grandees). 3. (coll.) booby, simpleton, ninny. — **materia p.,** raw material; **primo hermano** or **carnal,** first cousin; **primo segundo,** second cousin.
primogénito, ta, *a., m., f.* first-born.
primogenitura, *f.* primogeniture.
primor, *m.* 1. beauty, exquisiteness. 2. skill, excellence, fineness of workmanship or execution. 3. (coll.) exquisite or beautiful thing.
primordial, *a.* primordial, fundamental.
primordio, *m.* (biol.) primordium.
primorear, *i.v.* to work with skill, to perform excellently.
primorosamente, *adv.* 1. beautifully, exquisitely, delicately. 2. skillfully, finely.
primoroso, sa, *a.* 1. beautiful, exquisite, delicate, fine. 2. skillful.
prímula, *f.* (bot.) cowslip, primrose.
primuláceo, a, *a.* (bot.) primulaceous. —*f.* (*pl.*) Primulaceae.
princesa, *f.* princess; **p. real,** princess royal.
principada, *f.* (coll.) abuse of authority.
principado, *m.* 1. princedom, princehood (rank or title of prince). 2. princedom, principality, principate. 3. preeminence, primacy. 4. (*pl.*) (rel.) principalities (celestial choir).
principal, *a.* 1. main, principal; head, chief; essential, fundamental. 2. (print.) princeps, first (edition). 3. (gram.) main (clause). 4. illustrious, foremost, renowned. — **lo p.,** the principal thing, the main thing; **piso p.,** second floor (U.S.), first floor (G.B.). —*m.* 1. chief, head, director. 2. (com.) principal (capital). 3. (law) principal, constituent. 4. (mil.) main guard.
principalía, *f.* (Phil. I.) board of town officials, town council.
principalidad, *f.* pre-eminence, superiority, supremacy.
principalmente, *adv.* principally, mainly.
príncipe, *m.* 1. prince; sovereign, ruler. 2. male offspring of the queen bee. — **p. azul,** (hum.) Prince Charming; **p. consorte,** prince consort; **p. de Asturias,** crown prince of Spain; **p. de la Iglesia,** Prince of the Church; **p. de las tinieblas,** Prince of Darkness, Satan; **p. heredero,** crown prince; **p. regente,** prince regent.
principela, *f.* (tex., obs.) thin rough wool cloth.
principesco, ca, *a.* princely, regal, noble.
principiador, ra, *a.* beginning. —*m., f.* beginner.

principiante, ta, *m., f.* beginner, learner, novice, apprentice, tyro.
principiar, *tr.v.* to begin, start, commence.
principio, *m.* 1. beginning, start, commencement. 2. principle, fundamental; axiom, tenet. 3. principle, idea, theoretical basis. 4. principle, moral scruple, e.g. *este hombre no tiene principios,* this man has no principles. 5. principle, source, basis. 6. principle, component, ingredient. 7. (*pl.*) introductory matter (of a book). 8. (cul.) entrée. — **al p., a los principios,** in or at the beginning; **a principios de,** at the beginning of (month, year, etc.); **del p. al fin,** from beginning to end, from start to finish; **cuestión de principios,** matter of principles; **de principios elevados,** high-principled; **en p.,** in principle; **por p.,** on principle; **p. de contradicción,** (log.) principle of contradiction; **p. de exclusión,** (phys.) exclusion principle; **p. de identidad,** (log.) principle of identity; **p. de incertidumbre,** (phys.) uncertainty principle; **p. del tercer excluido,** (log.) principle of the excluded middle; **p. inmediato,** (chem.) element, principle; **tener** or **tomar p. de,** to spring from, come from.
principote, *m.* (coll.) upstart, social climber.
pringada, *f.* bread soaked in drippings.
pringamoza, *f.* 1. (Amer.) liana covered with hairs which cause itching (Platygna urens). 2. (Col., Hond.) nettle.
pringar, (*ref.* 51) *tr.v.* 1. to dip or soak in fat or drippings. 2. to scald with boiling fat. 3. to spatter, spot or stain with fat. 4. (coll.) to stab, to wound. 5. (coll.) to run down, slander. —*i.v.* to take part (in a business, etc.). — **p. en todo,** (coll.) to have many irons in the fire. —*r.v.* 1. to get spattered, spotted or stained with fat or grease. 2. (coll.) to embezzle, make illegal profits from.
pringón, na, *a.* (coll.) filthy, dirty, greasy. —*m.* (coll.) the act of getting greasy or dirty; (coll.) grease stain.
pringoso, sa, *a.* greasy, dirty, grease-stained.
pringote, *m.* mixture of foods; mass made of the mashed components of a stew.
pringue, *m., f.* 1. fat, drippings, grease. 2. grease, dirt.
pringue, pringué, *ref.* **pringar.**
prionodonte, *m.* (zool.) giant armadillo.
prior, *a.* prior, preceding. —*m.* 1. (ecc.) prior; curate, parish priest. 2. commercial attaché (in a consulate).
priora, *f.* prioress, abbess.
prioral, *a.* pertaining to a prior or prioress.
priorato, *m.* 1. priorate; priory. 2. (Sp.) a type of red wine.
priorazgo, *m.* priorship.
prioridad, *f.* priority; precedence.
prioste, *m.* steward of a brotherhood.
prisa, *f.* 1. haste, hurry, dispatch, speed, promptness, urgency, rush. 2. bitter fight or skirmish. — **a gran p., más vagar,** haste makes waste; **andar de p.,** to be in a hurry; **a p.,** quickly, hurriedly; **a toda p.,** as quickly as possible, with all possible haste; **correr p.,** to be urgent; **dar p.,** to rush, hurry; **darse p.,** to hasten, hurry, look alive; **de p.,** quickly, rapidly; **de p. y corriendo,** with great speed, with utmost dispatch, without delay; **estar de p., tener p.,** to be in a hurry; **vísteme despacio que estoy de p.,** (coll.) haste makes waste; **vivir de p.,** to burn the candle at both ends.
priscal, *m.* night enclosure or shelter for cattle in the fields.
priscilianismo, *m.* (rel.) Priscillianism.
prisciliano, na, *a., m., f.* (rel.) Priscillianist.
prisco, *m.* (variety of) peach.
prisión, *f.* 1. prison, gaol. 2. imprisonment. 3. seizure, capture. 4. bond, tie (for falcons); (fig.) fetter; (*pl.*) fetters, shackles. — **p. de alta seguridad,** high-security prison; **p. de máxima seguridad,** maximum-security prison; **p. mayor,** long-term prison sentence; **p. preventiva,** (law) protective custody; preventive detention.
prisionero, ra, *m., f.* 1. prisoner. 2. (fig.) captive (of love). — **p. de guerra,** prisoner of war.
prisma, *m.* (geom., opt.) prism.
prismático, ca, *a.* prismatic. —*m.* (*pl.*) binoculars.
prismoide, *m.* (geom.) prismoid.
priste, *m.* (ichth.) sawfish.
pristino, na, *a.* pristine, first, original.
prisuelo, *m.* muzzle put on ferrets for rabbit hunting.
privación, *f.* 1. privation, lack, want. 2. deprivation, loss.
privada, *f.* 1. toilet, privy, water closet. 2. piece of dung or filth.
privadamente, *adv.* privately, in private.
privadero, *m.* cesspool cleaner.
privado, da, *a.* 1. private, separate, personal. 2. confidential. 3. stunned, unconscious. —*m.* favorite (person in someone's favor).
privanza, *f.* favor, preference (at court).
privar, *tr.v.* 1. to deprive, deny. 2. to stun, daze, knock unconscious. 3. to forbid, prohibit; to impede. —*i.v.* to be in favor; to be current or in vogue. —*r.v.* 1. to faint, lose consciousness. 2. to deprive oneself (of), abstain (from). — **privarse de,** to give up, abstain from.
privativamente, *adv.* privately, solely, personally.
privativo, va, *a.* 1. privative, depriving. 2. private, personal, exclusive.
privilegiadamente, *adv.* in a privileged manner.
privilegiado, da, *past part. of* **privilegiar.** —*a.* privileged, gifted; uncommon.
privilegiar, *tr.v.* to privilege, favor, grant a privilege to.
privilegiativo, va, *a.* containing a privilege.
privilegio, *m.* privilege, grant, concession, exemption; franchise, patent. — **p. de invención,** patent; patent rights.
pro, *m., f.* profit, advantage, benefit. — **el p. y el contra,** the pros and cons; **en p. de,** for, pro, on behalf of; **hombre de p.,** upright or useful citizen.
proa, *f.* (mar.) prow; bow; (aer.) nose; **poner la p. a uno,** to oppose someone.
proal, *a.* (mar.) pertaining to the prow or bow.
probabilidad, *f.* probability, likelihood, prospect.
probabilísimo, ma, *a. super. of* **probable,** most probable.
probabilismo, *m.* (theol., philos.) probabilism.
probabilista, *a.* (theol., philos.) probabilistic. —*m., f.* probabilist.
probable, *a.* 1. probable, likely. 2. provable, that may be proved.
probablemente, *adv.* probably, likely.
probación, *f.* 1. probation. 2. trial, test.
probado, da, *past part. of* **probar.** —*a.* tested, tried; proved, demonstrated.
probador, ra, *m., f.* 1. tester; taster; sampler. 2. (dressm.) fitter. —*m.* fitting room (in dress shop for trying on clothes).
probadura, *f.* testing; tasting; sampling.
probanza, *f.* (law) proof, proving; (law) proof, evidence.
probar, (*ref.* 33) *tr.v.* 1. to prove, show, demonstrate. 2. to test; to try; to try out; to try on (clothes); to taste, sample (food). —*i.v.* **p. a** + *inf.,* to try + *inf.,* attempt + *inf.;* **p. de,** to taste, try, sample; **p. bien** or **mal,** to suit or not to suit, be suitable or not be suitable, agree with or not agree with. —*r.v.* to try on (clothes).
probatoria, *f.* (law) probatory term (time allowed for producing evidence).
probatorio, ria, *a.* probatory, probative. —*f.* probatory term (time allowed for producing evidence).
probatura, *f.* (coll.) trial, test, attempt.
probeta, *f.* 1. manometer, pressure gauge. 2. test tube, laboratory flask or beaker. 3. (phot.) developing tray. 4. powder tester (measuring explosive power of gunpowder). — **p. de presión,** (chem.) pressure tube.
probidad, *f.* probity, honesty, integrity; rectitude, uprightness.
problema, *m.* problem.
problemáticamente, *adv.* problematically.
problemático, ca, *a.* problematical, problematic.
probo, ba, *a.* upright, honest.
proboscidio, dia, *a.* (zool.) proboscidian. —*m.* (zool.) proboscidian; (*pl.*) Proboscidea.
procacidad, *f.* impudence, insolence.
procaína, *f.* (chem.) procaine.
procambial, *a.* procambial.
procaz, (*pl.* **procaces**), *a.* impudent, insolent; bold, daring.
procedencia, *f.* 1. origin, source. 2. point of departure. 3. (law) justification, legal basis.
procedente, *a.* 1. coming, originating, proceeding (from). 2. justified; according to rules or practice.
proceder, *m.* conduct, behavior; action.
proceder, *i.v.* 1. to proceed, go on or ahead, continue. 2. to proceed, come, issue, originate. 3. to proceed, act, behave. 4. to go on, proceed (to do something). 5. to be right, proper or fit; to be wise or convenient, e.g. *procede ir con cuidado,* it is wise to go carefully. — **p. a** + *inf.,* to proceed or go on + *inf.;* **p. contra,** (law) to proceed against, bring proceedings or legal actions against; **p. de,** to proceed, originate or come from.
procedimiento, *m.* 1. procedure; process, method. 2. (law) proceedings. — **p. al carbón,** carbon process; **p. básico,** (chem., metal.) basic process.
procefálico, ca, *a.* (zool.) procephalic.
procela, *f.* (poet.) storm, tempest.
proceleusmático, *m.* (poet.) proceleusmatic (foot of four short syllables).
proceloso, sa, *a.* (poet.) stormy, tempestuous.
prócer, *a.* 1. tall, high, lofty. 2. eminent, exalted. —*m.* 1. illustrious citizen, national hero or leader. 2. (Amer.) founding father (of the nation). 3. (*pl.*) the grandees and titled nobility of Spain.
procerato, *m.* position of national hero or leader; exalted station.
procercoide, *m.* (zool.) procercoid.
proceridad, *f.* 1. tallness, height; vigor, growth. 2. eminence.
prócero, ra, procero, ra, *a., var. of* **prócer.**
proceroso, sa, *a.* big-built and serious-looking (said of a portly and impressive-looking person).
procesado, da, *past part. of* **procesar.** —*a.* (law) accused, prosecuted, indicted. —*m., f.* (law) accused, defendant. —*m.* processing.
procesador, *m.* processor; **p. de textos** or **de palabras,** word processor.
procesal, *a.* (law) legal, of a trial, e.g. *costas procesales,* legal costs.
procesamiento, *m.* 1. (law) trial, trying; prosecution, indictment. 2. processing; **p. de datos,** data processing; **p. de textos** or **palabras,** word processing.

procesar, *tr.v.* (law) to try; to prosecute, indict; to sue.
procesión, *f.* 1. act of proceeding or originating. 2. procession; parade, pageant.
procesional, *a.* processional.
procesionalmente, *adv.* in procession.
procesionaria, *f.* (ento.) processionary moth.
procesionario, *a., m.* processional (hymn-book).
proceso, *m.* 1. process (set of changes, phenomena, etc.), e.g. *p. evolutivo,* evolutionary process, *p. revolucionario,* revolutionary process. 2. (law) trial; lawsuit, action. 3. process, passing, lapse (of time). 4. (anat., bot.) process, outgrowth, e.g. *p. ciliar,* (anat.) ciliary process. 5. (neol.) process, method, procedure, e.g. *un p. químico,* a chemical process. 6. (med.) process (set of symptoms, developments, etc.). — **fulminar el p.,** (law) to carry through a legal action; **p. criminal,** criminal proceedings; **p. de datos,** data processing; **p. de textos,** word processing; **p. verbal,** (Amer.) minutes (of a meeting); written report.
Proción, *m.* (astron.) Procyon.
proclama, *f.* 1. proclamation, announcement, declaration. 2. (*pl.*) marriage banns. — **correr las proclamas,** to publish the banns.
proclamación, *f.* 1. proclamation, declaration. 2. public acclamation or applause.
proclamar, *tr.v.* 1. to proclaim, declare. 2. to acclaim. —*r.v.* to proclaim oneself. — **proclamarse rey,** to proclaim oneself king.
proclítico, ca, *a.* (gram.) proclitic.
proclive, *a.* inclined, disposed; **p. a,** inclined towards, disposed to.
proclividad, *f.* proclivity, propensity, inclination.
procomún, procomunal, *m.* public good, public welfare.
procónsul, *m.* proconsul.
proconsulado, *m.* proconsulate.
proconsular, *a.* proconsular.
procreación, *f.* procreation.
procreador, ra, *a.* procreative, procreating, procreant, producing. —*m., f.* procreator, begetter, producer.
procreante, *a.* procreating.
procrear, *tr.v.* to procreate, beget; to produce.
proctodeo, *m.* (zool.) proctodaeum.
proctología, *f.* (med.) proctology.
proctólogo, *m.* (med.) proctologist.
proctoscopia, *f.* (med.) proctoscopy.
proctoscopio, *m.* (med.) proctoscope.
procura, *f.* power of attorney, proxy.
procuración, *f.* 1. power of attorney, proxy. 2. attorney's, lawyer's or solicitor's office, law office. 3. post of attorney, solicitor or lawyer. 4. careful or diligent management.
procurador, *m.* 1. attorney, solicitor; public prosecutor. 2. proxy, agent, attorney. 3. procurator (Roman agent or administrator). 4. town clerk or treasurer; village or town representative. — **p. a, de or en Cortes,** member of parliament, representative in the Spanish Parliament; **p. general,** attorney general; **p. síndico general,** village representative on a town or borough council.
procuradora, *f.* manageress (of a nunnery).
procuraduría, *f.* law office, lawyer's or attorney's office; post of attorney or public prosecutor.
procurante, *m., f.* intendant, solicitor.
procurar, *tr.v.* 1. to try, endeavor, seek, strive for. 2. to give, produce. 3. to transact or manage for another. —*i.v.* to act as an attorney or agent; **p. por,** to act as an attorney for.
procurrente, *m.* (geog.) peninsula.
prodición, *f.* treason; treachery, perfidy.
prodigalidad, *f.* 1. prodigality. 2. lavishness, abundance.
pródigamente, *adv.* 1. prodigally. 2. lavishly.
prodigar, (*ref. 51*) *tr.v.* 1. to squander, waste, spend lavishly. 2. to lavish, e.g. *p. elogios a,* to lavish praises on. —*r.v.* to devote oneself to too many activities.
prodigio, *m.* prodigy, wonder, marvel; **niño p.,** child prodigy.
prodigiosamente, *adv.* prodigiously; wonderfully, marvelously; extremely.
prodigiosidad, *f.* prodigiousness.
prodigioso, sa, *a.* prodigious; wondrous; marvelous, excellent.
pródigo, ga, *a.* 1. prodigal, wasteful, extravagant. 2. lavish, generous. — **hijo pródigo,** prodigal son. —*m., f.* prodigal, wastrel.
prodigue, prodigué, *ref.* **prodigar.**
prodrómico, ca, *a.* (med.) prodromal.
pródromo, *m.* (med.) prodrome, premonitory symptom.
producción, *f.* production; produce, products; crops, yield. — **p. automática,** automation; **p. en masa** or **serie,** mass production; **p. piloto,** pilot production.
producente, *a.* producing, causing.
producibilidad, *f.* producibility.
producible, *a.* producible, that can be produced.
producidor, ra, *a.* producing. —*m., f.* producer.
producir, (*ref. 47*) *tr.v.* 1. to produce; to yield; to bear; to manufacture. 2. to cause, bring about. 3. (law) to produce (evidence). —*r.v.* 1. to express or explain oneself. 2. to happen, take place.
productividad, *f.* productivity.
productivo, va, *a.* productive; profitable; fruitful.
producto, *irr. past part. of* **producir.** —*m.* product; (com.) yield, profit; (chem., math.) product; **p. alimenticio,** foodstuff; **p. de belleza,** cosmetic; **p. de marca,** brand name product; **p. final,** end product; **p. lácteo,** dairy product; **p. nacional bruto,** gross national product, GNP; **p. neto,** (com.) net produce; **p. secundario,** by-product; **p. vectorial,** (math.) vector product.
productor, ra, *a.* producing. —*m., f.* producer; (cinem., theat.) producer.
produje, produjera, produjese, *ref.* **producir.**
produzca, produzco, *ref.* **producir.**
proejar, *i.v.* to row against the wind or current.
proel, *a.* (mar.) fore. —*m.* bow hand, bowman.
proemial, *a.* proemial, introductory, prefatory.
proemio, *m.* proem, introduction, preface.
proenzima, *f.* (biochem.) proenzyme.
proeza, *f.* prowess, exploit, feat.
profanación, *f.* profanation, desecration.
profanador, ra, *a.* profaning, profanatory. —*m., f.* profaner, defiler.
profanamente, *adv.* profanely.
profanamiento, *m.* profanation, desecration.
profanar, *tr.v.* 1. to profane, desecrate, defile. 2. to profane, debase, abuse.
profanidad, *f.* 1. profanity. 2. excess.
profano, na, *a.* 1. profane, secular, worldly. 2. profane, irreverent, blasphemous. 3. indecent, immodest. 4. uninitiated, lay, profane. —*m., f.* 1. wordly person. 2. (*pl.*) (the) profane, (the) uninitiated.
profase, *f.* (biol.) prophase.
profazar, (*ref. 53*) *tr.v.* to abominate, curse.
profe, *m.* (Amer., sl.) prof (coll.), professor.
profecía, *f.* prophecy.
profecticio, cia, *a.* (law) profectitious.
proferir, (*ref. 42*) *tr.v.* to say, utter, express, speak.
profesar, *tr.v.* 1. to profess (a faith, doctrine, principle, loyalty, etc.). 2. to profess, practice the profession of. —*i.v.* to profess, join a religious order by professing faith and taking vows.
profesión, *f.* 1. profession, occupation. 2. profession, avowal, declaration.
profesional, *a., m., f.* professional, e.g. *artista p.,* professional artist; *un p. del ajedrez,* a professional chess player.
profesionalismo, *m.* professionalism, professional status in a field of endeavor; solidarity with the tenets of one's field.
profeso, sa, *a., m., f.* (rel.) professed (monk, priest, nun).
profesor, ra, *m., f.* teacher, schoolmaster, schoolmistress; professor; **p. asociado,** associate professor; **p. auxiliar,** assistant professor; **p. honorario,** professor emeritus; **p. mercantil,** certified public accountant; **p. suplente,** supply or substitute professor.
profesorado, *m.* post of teacher or professor, professorship; teachers, teaching staff, professorate, professors, the faculty (U.S.).
profesoral, *a.* professorial; pertaining to professors.
profeta, *m.* prophet.
profetal, *a.* prophetic.
profetante, *a.* prophesying.
proféticamente, *adv.* prophetically.
profetice, profeticé, *ref.* **profetizar.**
profético, ca, *a.* prophetic.
profetisa, *f.* prophetess.
profetizador, ra, *a.* prophesying. —*m., f.* prophesier.
profetizante, *a.* prophesying.
profetizar, (*ref. 53*) *tr.v.* to prophesy.
proficiente, *a.* proficient, advanced.
proficuo, cua, *a.* advantageous, fruitful.
profiera, profiero, *ref.* **proferir.**
profiláctica, *f.* (med.) hygiene, prophylaxis.
profiláctico, ca, *a.* (med.) prophylactic; preventive. —*m.* prophylactic.
profilaxis, *f.* (med.) prophylaxis.
profiriendo, profiriera, profiriese, profirió, *ref.* **proferir.**
prófugo, ga, *a., m., f.* fugitive. —*m.* 1. fugitive, escapee. 2. (mil.) draft dodger.
profundamente, *adv.* profoundly, deeply.
profundar, *tr.v., var. of* **profundizar.**
profundice, profundicé, *ref.* **profundizar.**
profundidad, *f.* 1. depth; deepness. 2. profundity, profoundness; intensity. — **carga de p.,** depth charge; **de p.,** deep, e.g. *cinco pies de p.,* five feet deep; **p. de campo,** (opt., photog.) depth of field; **p. efectiva,** (mec.) working depth; **p. de foco,** (opt.) depth of focus or definition.
profundizar, (*ref. 53*) *tr.v.* 1. to deepen, make deeper. 2. (fig.) to delve deeply into (a subject). 3. to fathom, explore. —*i.v.* to go deep into a subject.
profundo, da, *a.* 1. deep (hole; jungle; root; wound; sleep). 2. pitch (darkness). 3. profound, intense, deep (grief; reverence). 4. profound, deep (thinker, idea). 5. difficult, obscure, recondite. —*m.* (poet.) (the) deep, sea; (poet.) hell. — **lo p.,** the bottom, depths, e.g. *en lo p. de mi corazón,* in the bottom of my heart, in my heart of hearts.
profusamente, *adv.* profusely; lavishly, extravagantly.
profusión, *f.* profusion; lavishness.
profuso, sa, *a.* profuse, plentiful; lavish.
progenie, *f.* progeny, offspring, issue.
progenitor, *m.* progenitor, direct ancestor.
progenitura, *f., var. of* **progenie.**
progesterona, *f.* (biochem.) progesterone.
progestina, *f.* (biochem.) progestin.
progimnasma, *m.* (rhet.) preparatory exercise.
proglotis, *m.* (zool.) proglottid, proglottis.

prognatismo, *m.* (physiol.) prognathism.
prognato, ta, *a., m., f.* (physiol.) prognathous.
progne, *f.* (poet.) swallow.
prognosis, *f.* prognosis, forecast.
programa, *m.* 1. (theat., mus., cinem., rad., tel.) program, programme. 2. plans; schedule. 3. (pol.) platform, projection of policies; proclamation. 4. public notice. — **p. doble,** double feature; **p. de estudios,** curriculum; **p. espacial,** space program; **p. de urgencia,** crash program.
programador, *m.* 1. (tel., rad.) program director. 2. (computers) programmer.
programar, *tr.v.* to make a program or a plan; to include in a program or a plan.
programático, ca, *a.* programmatic.
progresar, *i.v.* to progress; to advance or improve.
progresión, *f.* progression; (math., mus.) progression. — **p. aritmética,** arithmetical progression; **p. ascendente,** (math.) increasing progression; **p. descendente,** (math.) decreasing progression; **p. geométrica,** geometrical progression.
progresismo, *m.* 1. (pol.) progressivism, advocation of progress. 2. progressive party.
progresista, *a.* progressive (devoted to progress). —*m., f.* member of a progressive party.
progresivamente, *adv.* progressively.
progresivo, va, *a.* progressive, advancing.
progreso, *m.* 1. progress, advancement, development; improvement. 2. progress, civilization. 3. (*pl.*) progress (e.g. in studies). — **hacer progresos,** to advance, make progress, move forward.
prohibición, *f.* prohibition; denial.
prohibicionismo, *m.* prohibitionism.
prohibicionista, *a., m., f.* prohibitionist.
prohibir, *tr.v.* to forbid, prohibit; to ban. **prohibida la entrada,** keep out, no admittance; **p.** + *inf.,* to prohibit from + *ger.,* forbid to + *inf.,* **prohibido estacionarse,** no parking; **se prohíbe fumar,** no smoking; **se prohíbe el paso,** no thoroughfare; **se prohíbe la entrada,** keep out, no admittance.
prohibitivo, va, *a.* prohibitive, forbidding.
prohibitorio, ria, *a.* prohibitory.
prohijación, *f., var. of* **prohijamiento.**
prohijador, ra, *a.* adopting. —*m., f.* adopter.
prohijamiento, *m.* adoption.
prohijar, *tr.v.* to adopt (a child, ideas, customs, etc.).
prohombre, *m.* master (of a guild); leading man, top man (of a group).
proindivisión, *f.* (law) state of being undivided or proindiviso (an estate).
proindiviso, sa, *a.* undivided, in joint tenancy.
proís, proíz, *m.* (mar.) mooring stone; (mar.) mooring cable.
prójima, *f.* (coll.) slut, jade.
prójimo, *m.* 1. fellow man, neighbor. 2. mankind. — **al p., contra una esquina,** (coll.) every man for himself; **no tener p. uno,** to be hard-hearted, be as hard as nails.
prolactina, *f.* (biochem.) prolactin.
prolamina, *f.* (biochem.) prolamin, prolamine.
prolán, *m.* (biochem.) prolan.
prolapso, *m.* (med.) prolapse.
prole, *f.* progeny, offspring, issue.
prolegómeno, *m.* (lit.) prolegomenon, (*pl.*) prolegomena.
prolepsis, *f.* (rhet.) prolepsis.
proletariado, *m.* proletariat.
proletarice, proletaricé, *ref.* **proletarizar.**
proletario, ria, *a., m., f.* 1. proletarian. 2. (fig.) plebeian.
proletarización, *f.* proletarianization.
proletarizar, (*ref. 53*) *tr.v.* to proletarianize.
proliferante, *a.* multiplying, proliferating.
proliferar, *i.v.* to proliferate, multiply.
prolífico, ca, *a.* prolific, fertile; productive.
prolijamente, *adv.* 1. prolixly, tediously, tiresomely; long-windedly. 2. extensively, lengthily; meticulously.
prolijidad, *f.* 1. prolixity, tediousness, tiresomeness; long-windedness. 2. extensiveness; lengthiness; meticulousness.
prolijo, ja, *a.* 1. prolix, tedious, tiresome, wearisome; long-winded. 2. extensive, lengthy; meticulous, detailed.
prolina, *f.* (biochem.) proline, prolin.
prologal, *a.* introductory, prefatory.
prologar, (*ref. 51*) *tr.v.* to prologue, to preface; to write a prologue to.
prólogo, *m.* prologue, preface.
prologue, prologué, *ref.* **prologar.**
prologuista, *m., f.* writer of prologues.
prolonga, *f.* (artil.) prolonge.
prolongable, *a.* prolongable; extendible.
prolongación, *f.* prolongation; extension; lengthening; protraction.
prolongadamente, *adv.* at great length.
prolongado, da, *past part. of* **prolongar. —***a.* 1. prolonged, lengthy. 2. oblong.
prolongamiento, *m., var. of* **prolongación.**
prolongar, (*ref. 51*) *tr.v.* to prolong, extend, continue; to protract. —*r.v.* to be prolonged or extended; to linger.
prolongue, prolongué, *ref.* **prolongar.**
proloquio, *m.* maxim, aphorism, apothegm.
prolusión, *f.* introduction, preface; prelude.
promanar, *i.v.* to spring, originate, arise.
promediar, *tr.v.* to average. —*i.v.* 1. to divide in two equal parts. 2. to be half-way through, be half over, e.g. *al p. el mes,* half-way through the month.
promedio, *m.* average, mean. — **por p.,** on the average; **p. aritmético,** arithmetical mean; **p. geométrico,** geometric mean.
promesa, *f.* 1. promise; offer. 2. vow, pledge.
prometedor, ra, *a.* promising, hopeful. —*m., f.* promiser.
Prometeo, *m.* (myth.) Prometheus, who stole fire from heaven and offered it to mankind; **P. encadenado,** (lit.) Prometheus Bound.
prometer, *tr.v.* to promise; to offer; vow or pledge; **p.** + *inf.,* to promise to + *inf.* — *i.v.* to promise, show promise, e.g. *este muchacho promete,* this boy shows promise. —*r.v.* 1. to become engaged. 2. to offer oneself to God.
prometida, *f.* fiancée.
prometido, da, *past part. of* **prometer. —***a.* 1. promised, offered. 2. engaged, betrothed. —*m., f.* fiancé, fiancée.
prometiente, *a.* promising.
prometimiento, *m.* promise, offer.
prometio, *m.* (chem.) promethium.
prominencia, *f.* prominence; rise; protuberance; elevation.
prominente, *a.* 1. prominent; elevated; rising; projecting. 2. prominent, notable, distinguished.
promiscuación, *f.* (ecc.) eating meat with fish in the same meal on days of fasting.
promiscuamente, *adv.* promiscuously.
promiscuar, (*ref. 55*) *i.v.* 1. (ecc.) to eat meat with fish on days of fasting. 2. (fig.) to participate in diverse activities.
promiscuidad, *f.* promiscuity, promiscuousness; **p. sexual,** sexual promiscuity.
promiscuo, cua, *a.* 1. promiscuous. 2. ambiguous.
promisión, *f.* promise; **la tierra de p.,** the promised land.
promisorio, ria, *a.* promissory.
promoción, *f.* 1. promotion, advancement. 2. class, year, group (of students, cadets, employees, who have graduated or joined an organization on the same year). 3. (Amer.) promotion, publicity; **p. de ventas,** (com.) sales promotion.
promontorio, *m.* 1. promontory, headland. 2. (fig.) encumbrance, hindrance.
promotor, ra, *m., f.* 1. promoter. 2. causer, provoker, instigator. — **p. comercial,** sales representative; **p. de la fe,** (ecc.) devil's advocate; **p. de ventas,** sales representative; **p. fiscal,** (law) government attorney, public prosecutor; **p. inmobiliario,** developer (of property).
promovedor, ra, *m., f.* 1. promoter. 2. causer, provoker, instigator.
promover, (*ref. 34*) *tr.v.* 1. to promote (an industrial product, etc.); to foster, further, encourage (friendship, the arts, etc.). 2. to promote, upgrade (in rank). 3. to cause, provoke, give rise to (a scandal, debate, etc.).
promueva, promuevo, *ref.* **promover.**
promulgación, *f.* promulgation.
promulgador, ra, *a.* promulgating. —*m., f.* promulgator.
promulgar, (*ref. 51*) *tr.v.* 1. to proclaim, announce, promulgate. 2. (law) to promulgate, put (law) into force.
promulgue, promulgué, *ref.* **promulgar.**
pronación, *f.* (physiol.) pronation.
pronador, ra, *a.* pronating. —*m.* (anat.) pronator.
pronaos, *m.* (archit.) pronaos, portico of a temple.
pronéfrico, ca, *a.* (anat.) pronephric.
pronefros, *m.* (anat.) pronephros.
prono, na, *a.* prone, inclined, bent over.
pronombre, *m.* (gram.) pronoun; **p. demostrativo,** (gram.) demonstrative pronoun; **p. indeterminado,** (gram.) indefinite pronoun; **p. personal,** (gram.) personal pronoun; **p. posesivo,** (gram.) possessive pronoun; **p. relativo,** (gram.) relative pronoun.
pronominado, *a.* (gram.) reflexive (verb).
pronominal, *a.* (gram.) pronominal.
pronosticable, *a.* foreseeable, predictable, prognosticable.
pronosticación, *f.* prognostication, prediction, forecast.
pronosticador, ra, *a.* prognosticating. —*m., f.* prognosticator, forecaster.
pronosticar, (*ref. 50*) *tr.v.* to prognosticate, foretell, augur.
pronóstico, *m.* 1. prognostic, omen, sign, portent. 2. prognostication, prediction, forecast, prognostic. 3. almanac. 4. (med.) prognosis. — **p. del tiempo,** or **p. meteorológico,** weather forecast.
pronostique, pronostiqué, *ref.* **pronosticar.**
prontamente, *adv.* promptly, diligently.
prontitud, *f.* promptness, dispatch; briskness, speed; keenness, quickness, sharpness (of mind).
pronto, ta, *a.* 1. prompt, quick, rapid, speedy. 2. ready, prepared.
pronto, *adv.* soon; quickly, swiftly; promptly; **lo más p. posible,** as soon as possible; **de p.,** hastily, hurriedly; suddenly; **por lo p.,** for the present, for the moment; **tan p. como,** as soon as. —*m.* sudden impulse, fit or idea; **al p.,** at first.
prontuario, *m.* 1. handbook, manual. 2. notebook. 3. resumé, summary, compendium. 4. (Amer., police) dossier, blotter (U.S.).
prónuba, *f.* (poet.) pronuba, woman attending the bride at a wedding.
pronúcleo, *m.* (biol.) pronucleus.
pronunciable, *a.* pronounceable, utterable.
pronunciación, *f.* pronunciation, articulation.
pronunciado, da, *past part. of* **pronunciar. —***a.* pronounced, marked; steep, sharp (curve).

pronunciador, ra, *a.* pronouncing. —*m., f.* pronouncer.
pronunciamiento, *m.* 1. rising, rebellion, insurrection. 2. (law) pronouncement (of a sentence or judgment).
pronunciar, *tr.v.* 1. to pronounce, articulate, enunciate (a word); to deliver (a speech). 2. to pronounce, pass (judgment). —*r.v.* 1. to go on record with one's opinion. 2. to rise, rebel. — **pronunciarse por,** to declare oneself to be in favor of.
pronuncio, *m.* (ecc.) internuncio, temporary nuncio.
propagabilidad, *f.* (acoust.) propagability.
propagación, *f.* propagation; spreading; dissemination. — **p. ultrasónica,** (acous.) hypersonic propagation.
propagador, ra, *a.* propagating; promoting. —*m., f.* propagator; disseminator; promotor.
propaganda, *f.* 1. publicity, advertising, propaganda. 2. (rel.) Propaganda. — **hacer p.,** to advertise.
propagandismo, *m.* propagandism.
propagandista, *m., f.* propagandist, publicist, promoter.
propagandístico, ca, *a.* pertaining to advertising, propaganda.
propagar, (*ref. 51*) *tr.v., r.v.* 1. to propagate, increase by reproduction. 2. to propagate, spread, disseminate (belief, ideas, doctrines, etc.). 3. to multiply.
propagativo, va, *a.* propagative.
propague, propagué, *ref.* **propagar.**
propalador, ra, *m., f.* divulger.
propalar, *tr.v.* to reveal, divulge (a secret).
propano, *m.* (chem.) propane.
propao, *m.* (mar.) breastwork.
proparoxítono, na, *a.* (gram.) proparoxytone.
propartida, *f.* time preceding a departure.
propasar, *tr.v.* to go beyond (the limits). —*r.v.* to go too far, take undue liberties, to exceed one's authority; to forget oneself.
propedéutico, ca, *a.* propaedeutic. —*f.* propaedeutics, preparatory studies or instruction.
propender, *i.v.* to incline, be inclined, lean, have a tendency. — **p. a,** to tend, be inclined towards.
propensamente, *adv.* with an inclination or tendency.
propensión, *f.* propensity, inclination, tendency, bent. — **tener p. a,** to have a propensity for or inclination to.
propenso, sa, *a.* prone, inclined, predisposed; **ser p. a,** to be prone or inclined to.
propiamente, *adv.* properly, correctly, fittingly.
propiciación, *f.* propitiation, sacrifice, atonement.
propiciador, ra, *a.* propitiating. —*m., f.* propitiator.
propiciamente, *adv.* propitiously, favorably.
propiciar, *tr.v.* 1. to propitiate, conciliate. 2. (Amer.) to propose. 3. (Amer.) to sponsor.
propiciatorio, ria, *a.* propiciatory. —*m.* 1. propitiatory, mercy seat. 2. footstool, prie-dieu.
propicio, cia, *a.* propitious, favorable; auspicious.
propiedad, *f.* 1. property; holding, estate. 2. ownership, proprietorship. 3. property, attribute, quality. 4. perfect likeness or resemblance. 5. complete exactness or correctness, exact meaning of a word, e.g. *hablar con p.,* to speak exactly or correctly. — **de mi, tu, su** or **nuestra p.,** belonging to me, you, him, her or us; **p. horizontal,** condominium; **p. industrial,** patent rights; **p. inmobiliaria,** real estate; **p. intelectual,** copyright; **p. literaria,** literary property, copyright.
propienda, *f.* strip of cloth on cheeks of embroidery frame to which piece to be worked is attached.
propietariamente, *adv.* with the right of possession or property.
propietario, ria, *a.* proprietary. —*m.* owner; proprietor, landlord. —*f.* owner; proprietress, landlady.
propileno, *m.* (chem.) propylene.
propileo, *m.* (archit.) propylaeum, vestibule of a temple or a palace; (*pl.*) propylaea.
propílico, ca, *a.* (chem.) propylic.
propilita, *f.* (min.) propylite.
propilo, *m.* (chem.) propyl.
propina, *f.* 1. tip, gratuity, perquisite, perk (G.B., sl.). 2. pocket money, spending money, allowance. — **de p.,** as a tip; (coll.) in addition, into the bargain.
propinar, *tr.v.* 1. to give (a blow). 2. to invite or treat to (a drink). 3. to prescribe (a medicine).
propincuidad, *f.* propinquity, proximity, nearness.
propincuo, cua, *a.* near, contiguous.
propio, pia, *a.* 1. one's own, e.g. *mi propia madre,* my own mother. 2. typical, characteristic, inherent, e.g. *eso es muy propio de ella,* that's very typical of her. 3. own, natural, genuine, e.g. *es su propio pelo,* it's her own hair. 4. very, exact, precise, e.g. *esas fueron sus propias palabras,* those were his very words. 5. self, e.g. *amor propio,* amour propre, self-esteem; *defensa propia,* self-defense. 6. same, e.g. *lo propio,* the same to you (returning a wish, a compliment). 7. himself, herself, themselves, e.g. *el propio embajador,* the ambassador himself; *los propios dueños,* the owners themselves. 8. proper, fitting, suitable, e.g. *eso es lo propio en ese caso,* that's the proper thing in that case. 9. (gram.) proper (noun). 10. (math.) proper (fraction). 11. (astron.) proper (motion). —*m.* 1. messenger, courier. 2. (*pl.*) public lands or property.
propioceptor, ra, *a.* (physiol.) propioceptive. —*m.* (physiol.) propioceptor.
propionato, *m.* (chem.) propionate.
propiónico, ca, *a.* (chem.) propionic (acid).
propóleos, *m.* propolis, bee glue.
proponedor, ra, *a.* proposing. —*m., f.* proposer; propounder, proponent.
proponente, *a.* proposing; propounding. —*m., f.* proposer, proponent.
proponer, (*ref. 15*) *tr.v.* to propose; to propound; to suggest, bring or put forward, move; to name, present. —*r.v.* to propose, plan, intend, mean; **proponerse a** + *inf,* to propose to + *inf.*
proponga, propongo, *ref.* **proponer.**
proporción, *f.* 1. proportion; symmetry. 2. occasion, opportunity. 3. (*pl.*) proportions, dimensions, size. 4. (math.) proportion. — **en p. a,** in proportion to; **fuera de p.,** out of proportion; **guardar p. con,** to be in proportion with; **p. dimensional,** (tel.) aspect ratio.
proporcionable, *a.* proportionable.
proporcionablemente,
proporcionadamente, *adv.* proportionately, proportionally, in proportion.
proporcionado, da, *past part. of* **proporcionar.** —*a.* 1. proportioned, commensurate, proportionate, e.g. *un edificio bien proporcionado,* a well proportioned building. 2. fit, suitable.
proporcionador, *m.* (chem.) proportioner.
proporcional, *a.* proportional; (gram., math.) proportional. — **representación p.,** (pol.) proportional representation.
proporcionalidad, *f.* proportion, proportionality.
proporcionalmente, *adv.* proportionally.
proporcionar, *tr.v.* 1. to furnish, supply, provide; to apportion. 2. to proportion, put in proportion, make proportionate; to adapt, adjust. —*r.v.* **proporcionarse** + *n.,* to get, obtain, to furnish or provide oneself with.
proposición, *f.* 1. proposition, proposal, e.g. *p. de matrimonio,* marriage proposal. 2. motion, resolution (in a meeting, a legislative body, etc.). 3. (log., math., rhet.) proposition. 4. (gram.) clause.
propósito, *m.* 1. aim, object, purpose, design. 2. intention, resolve. 3. subject matter. — **a p.,** by the way; suitable, fitting, e.g. *no venir a p.,* not to be suitable or fitting; on purpose, deliberately; **a p. de,** apropos of, with respect or regard to; **de p.,** on purpose, deliberately; **fuera de p.,** irrelevant, beside the point; unsuitable, out of place, inopportune.
propretor, *m.* (hist.) propraetor (Roman Magistrate).
propretura, *f.* (hist.) propraetorship (office or dignity of a propraetor).
proptosis, *f.* (med.) proptosis.
propuesta, *f.* 1. proposal, proposition. 2. offer, tender. 3. nomination (for office or membership). — **p. de ley,** bill (introduced in a legislative body).
propuesto, ta, *irr. past part. of* **proponer.** —*a.* proposed.
propugnáculo, *m.* fortress; (fig.) bulwark, defense.
propugnar, *tr.v.* to defend, protect, advocate.
propulsa, *f.* 1. repulse, rejection, rebuff. 2. propelling.
propulsar, *tr.v.* 1. to reject, repulse, rebuff. 2. to propel, drive.
propulsión, *f.* 1. propulsion, propelling, drive. 2. repulse, reject. — **p. a chorro,** jet propulsion; **p. delantera,** (auto.) front-wheel drive; **p. por correa,** belt drive.
propulsor, ra, *a.* driving, propelling, propellent, pushing, e.g. *fuerza propulsora,* driving force. —*m.* propellent, pusher.
propuse, propusiera, propusiese, *ref.* **proponer.**
prora, *f.* (poet.) bow, prow (of a ship).
prorrata, *f.* share, quota, prorate; **a p.,** in proportion, proportionately, pro rata.
prorratear, *tr.v.* to prorate, apportion, distribute proportionally.
prorrateo, *m.* proration, prorating, apportionment, pro rata division.
prórroga, *f.* prorogation, extension (of time).
prorrogable, *a.* prorogable, that can be deferred or postponed.
prorrogación, *f.* prorogation, extension, postponement.
prorrogar, (*ref. 51*) *tr.v.* to prorogue, extend; to postpone, put off, defer, prolong.
prorrogativo, va, *a.* prorogative, extending, prolonging (in time).
prorrogue, prorrogué, *ref.* **prorrogar.**
prorrumpir, *i.v.* 1. to burst (into a room). 2. to break out, burst out (in oaths, curses, etc.).
prosa, *f.* 1. prose (as opposed to poetry). 2. prose (hymn used on some occasions in the mass). 3. (coll.) tedious boring talk, verbiage. 4. (fig.) prose, ordinariness, matter-of-factness.
prosado, da, *a.* written in prose.
prosador, ra, *m., f.* 1. prose writer. 2. (coll.) tedious talker, windbag (sl.).
prosaico, ca, *a.* 1. prosaic; prosy. 2. (coll.) pedestrian, uninspired.
prosaísmo, *m.* 1. prosaism, prosiness. 2. commonplaceness.
prosapia, *f.* ancestry, lineage.
proscenio, *m.* 1. forestage; apron (of the stage). 2. (hist.) proscenium.
proscribir, *past part.* **proscrito.** —*tr.v.* to prescribe; to banish; to outlaw.

proscripción, *f.* proscription, exile, banishment. — **escrito de p. y confiscación,** (law) bill of attainder.
proscripto, ta, *irr. past part. of* **proscribir.** —*a.* proscribed, exiled, banished. —*m.* proscript, exile.
proscriptor, ra, *a.* proscribing. —*m., f.* proscriber.
proscrito, ta, *irr. past part. of* **proscribir.** —*m., f.* proscript, exile, outlaw.
prosecución, *f.* 1. continuation. 2. pursuit, pursuance (e.g. of an aim).
proseguible, *a.* pursuable.
proseguimiento, *m., var. of* **prosecución.**
proseguir, (*ref. 77*) *tr.v.* to continue, proceed, go on with. —*i.v.* **p. con,** to continue, proceed, go on with.
proselitismo, *m.* proselytism.
proselitista, *a.* converting, proselytizing. —*m., f.* converter, proselytizer.
prosélito, *m.* proselyte, convert.
prosencéfalo, *m.* (anat.) prosencephalon.
prosénquima, *m.* (bot.) prosenchyma.
prosenquimatoso, sa, *a.* (bot.) prosenchymatous.
Proserpina, *f.* (myth.) Proserpina, Proserpine, queen of Hades.
prosificación, *f.* prosification, turning into prose.
prosificador, ra, *m., f.* one who turns poetry into prose.
prosificar, (*ref. 50*) *tr.v.* to convert into prose, put into prose.
prosifique, prosifiqué, *ref.* **prosificar.**
prosiga, prosigo, *ref.* **proseguir.**
prosimio, mia, *a.* (zool.) prosimian. —*m.* (zool.) prosimian; (*pl.*) Prosimias.
prosista, *m., f.* prose writer.
prosístico, ca, *a.* pertaining to prose.
prosita, *f.* short piece of prose.
prosodia, *f.* orthoepy, prosody, study and art of pronunciation and accentuation.
prosódico, ca, *a.* orthoepic, orthoepical.
prosoma, *f.* (zool.) prosoma.
prosopografía, *f.* (rhet.) physical description of a person or an animal.
prosopopeya, *f.* 1. (rhet.) prosopopoeia. 2. (coll.) pomposity, exaggerated solemnity or seriousness.
prospección, *f.* prospecting, exploration, survey.
prospecto, *m.* prospectus, booklet, brochure.
prosperado, da, *a.* prosperous, rich, flourishing.
prósperamente, *adv.* prosperously, successfully.
prosperar, *tr.v.* to render successful, prosper, make prosperous. —*i.v.* to prosper, thrive, flourish.
prosperidad, *f.* prosperity.
próspero, ra, *a.* prosperous, thriving, successful.
prostaféresis, *f.* (astron.) prosthaphaeresis, difference between the mean and true anomaly of a celestial body.
próstata, *f.* (anat.) prostate, prostate gland.
prostatectomía, *f.* (surg.) prostatectomy, removal of the prostate gland.
prostático, ca, *a.* (anat.) prostatic.
prostatismo, *m.* (med.) prostatism.
prostatitis, *f.* (med.) prostatitis.
prosternarse, *r.v.* to prostrate oneself, throw oneself on one's knees.
próstesis, *f.* (gram.) prosthesis, prefixing of a sound or syllable to a word.
prostético, ca, *a.* (gram.) prosthetic.
prostibulario, ria, *a.* pertaining to a brothel.
prostíbulo, *m.* brothel.
próstilo, *a., m.* (archit.) prostyle.
prostitución, *f.* prostitution.
prostituido, da, *past part. of* **prostituir.** —*a.* corrupted, debased, prostitute.

prostituir, (*ref. 48*) *tr.v.* to prostitute, corrupt. —*r.v.* to prostitute oneself; to become a prostitute; (fig.) to debase or sell oneself or one's integrity.
prostituta, *f.* prostitute, harlot.
prostituyendo, prostituyera, prostituyese, prostituyo, *ref.* **prostituir.**
prostodontia, *f.* (dent.) prosthodontia, prosthodontics.
prostomio, *m.* (zool.) prostomium.
prosudo, da, *a.* (Chile, Ecuad., Peru) pompous, affectedly formal.
protactinio, *m.* (chem.) protactinium, protroactinium.
protagonista, *m., f.* (theat., lit., fig.) protagonist, hero, heroine.
protagonizar, (*ref. 53*) *tr.v.* to be the protagonist of, take a leading part in, take a main role in.
protaliano, na, *a.* (bot.) prothallial, prothalline.
protálico, ca, *a.* (bot.) prothallial, prothalline.
prótalo, *m.* (bot.) prothallium.
protamina, *f.* (biochem.) protamine, protamin.
protargol, *m.* (pharm.) protargol.
prótasis, (*pl.* **prótasis**), *f.* (poet., rhet.) protasis.
protático, ca, *a.* (poet., rhet.) protatic.
proteáceo, a, *a.* (bot.) proteaceous. —*f.* proteaceous plant; (*pl.*) Proteaceae.
proteasa, *f.* (biochem.) protease.
protección, *f.* protection.
proteccionismo, *m.* (pol., econ.) protectionism.
proteccionista, *a., m., f.* (pol., econ.) protectionist.
protector, ra, *a.* protective, protecting, defensive. —*m.* protector, defender, patron. —*f.* protectress, patroness. — **p. de las artes,** patron of the arts.
protectorado, *m.* protectorate.
protectoría, *f.* protectorate, protectorship.
protectorio, ria, *a.* protectory, protective.
protectriz, (*pl.* **protectrices**), *a.* protective. —*f.* protectress.
proteger, (*ref. 57*) *tr.v.* to protect, defend.
protegido, da, *past part. of* **proteger.** —*a.* protected; secluded. —*m.* protégé. —*f.* protégée.
proteico, ca, *a.* 1. protean, changeable, varied. 2. (biochem.) protein, proteid, proteinaceous.
proteína, *f.* (chem.) protein, proteid; **p. conjugada,** (physiol., biochem.) conjugated protein.
proteinasa, *f.* (biochem.) proteinase.
proteinato, *m.* (chem.) proteinate.
proteínico, ca, *a.* with protein, proteid.
proteinuria, *f.* (med.) proteinuria.
proteja, protejo, *ref.* **proteger.**
proteo, *m.* 1. (fig.) protean, changeable person. 2. (myth.) **P.,** Proteus, sea god who could change his appearence at will.
proteoclástico, ca, *a.* (chem.) proteoclastic.
proteólisis, *f.* (biochem.) proteolysis.
proteosa, *f.* (biochem.) proteose.
proteranto, ta, *a.* (bot.) proteranthous.
proterozoico, ca, *a, m.* (geol.) Proterozoic.
protervamente, *adv.* perversely.
protervia, *f.* perversity, wickedness, evil.
protervidad, *f.* perversity, wickedness, malignity.
protervo, va, *a.* perverse, wicked, evil, malignant.
protésico, ca, *a.* (med.) prosthetic.
prótesis, *f.* (surg.) prosthesis.
protesta, *f.* protest; protestation, declaration, affirmation; (law) protest. — **manifestación de p.,** protest demonstration. — **p. de mar,** ship's or captain's protest.
protestación, *f.* protestation; **p. de la fe,** declaration of faith.
protestante, *a.* 1. protestant, protesting. 2. Protestant (Church). —*m., f.* 1. protestant, protester. 2. Protestant (member of a Protestant Church).

protestantismo, *m.* (rel.) Protestantism.
protestar, *tr.v.* 1. to protest, declare, affirm; to profess (faith). 2. (com.) to protest (e.g., a note). —*i.v.* to protest, object; **p. contra,** to protest against, object to; **p. de,** to affirm, declare; to profess.
protestativo, va, *a.* declaratory, affirmatory; which declares or testifies something.
protesto, *m.* protest; (com.) protest (of a bill).
protético, ca, *a.* (med.) prosthetic. —*f.* prosthetics.
prótido, *m.* (chem.) protide.
protilo, *m.* (chem.) protyle, protyl.
protio, *m.* (chem.) protium.
protista, *f.* (biol.) protist.
protisto, *m.* (biol.) protist.
proto, *pre.* first; foremost; earliest form of.
protoactinio, *m.* (chem.) protoactinium, protactinium.
protoalbéitar, *m.* chief veterinary surgeon.
protoalbeiterato, *m.* examining board for veterinary surgeons.
protocloruro, *m.* (chem.) protochloride.
protocolar, *a.* 1. protocolar; formal, official. 2. ceremonial.
protocolar, *tr.v.* to protocol, protocolize, record in a protocol.
protocolario, ria, *a.* (coll.) protocolar.
protocolice, protocolicé, *ref.* **protocolizar.**
protocolización, *f.* protocolization, recording in a protocol.
protocolizar, (*ref. 53*) *tr.v.* to protocol, protocolize, record in a protocol.
protocolo, *m.* 1. protocol. 2. diplomatic ceremonial forms. 3. registry, record.
protofloema, *m.* (bot.) protophloem.
protohistoria, *f.* protohistory.
protohistórico, ca, *a.* protohistoric.
protomártir, *m.* protomartyr.
protomedicato, *m.* examining board of physicians; position of royal physicians.
protomédico, *m.* royal physician.
protón, *m.* (phys., chem.) proton; **p.-sincrotón** (phys.), proton-synchroton.
protonema, *m.* (bot.) protonema.
protonotario, *m.* protonotary, prothonotary.
protoplasma, *m.* (biol.) protoplasm.
protoplasmático, ca, protoplásmico, ca, *a.* (biol.) protoplasmic.
protoplástico, ca, *a.* (biol.) protoplastic.
protoplasto, *m.* (biol.) protoplast.
protórax, *m.* (zool.) prothorax.
protostela, *f.* (bot.) protostele.
protostélico, ca, *a.* (bot.) protostelic.
prototipo, *m.* prototype, model, original; archetype.
prototrófico, ca, *a.* (physiol.) prototrophic.
protóxido, *m.* (chem.) protoxide; **p. de hierro** (chem.), ferrous oxide.
protoxilema, *m.* (bot.) protoxylem.
protozoario, ria, *a.* (zool.) protozoan, protozoic. —*m.* protozoan, protozoon; (*pl.*) Protozoa.
protozoico, ca, *a.* (zool.) protozoic.
protozoo, *m.* (zool.) protozoan, protozoon.
protozoología, *f.* (zool.) protozoology.
protrombina, *f.* (physiol.) prothrombin.
protrusión, *f.* (med.) protrusion.
protuberancia, *f.* protuberance; projection, bulge.
protuberante, *a.* protuberant, bulging, projecting.
protutor, *m.* (law) protutor.
provascular, *a.* (bot.) provascular.
provecho, *m.* 1. benefit, advantage; profit, gain. 2. progress, advancement, improvement. — **buen p.,** enjoy your meal, bon appetit; **de p.,**

useful, hardworking; **sacar p. de,** to benefit from, get benefit from, turn to account.
provechosamente, *adv.* profitably, beneficially; advantageously.
provechoso, sa, *a.* profitable, beneficial; advantageous.
provecto, ta, *a.* old, advanced, mature.
proveedor, ra, *m., f.* supplier, purveyor, provider.
proveeduría, *f.* 1. storehouse, warehouse. 2. post or office of supplier or purveyor.
proveer, (*ref. 60*) *tr.v.* 1. to provide, supply, equip, furnish; to stock. 2. to decide, resolve, settle. 3. to bestow, give, grant. 4. (law) to decide. 5. to fill (a vacancy); to appoint (a person to a post or office). —*i.v.* (law) to give a decision, decide. —*r.v.* 1. to supply oneself. 2. to empty the bowels.
proveído, *m.* (law) judgment, decision, resolution.
proveimiento, *m.* providing, provisioning, supplying.
provena, *f.* layer, offshoot (of vine).
provenga, provengo, *ref.* **provenir.**
proveniente, *a.* proceeding, originating, issuing, resulting.
provenir, (*ref. 26*) *i.v.* to come, proceed, originate, issue, arise from.
provento, *m.* rent, revenue, net product.
proventrículo, *m.* (zool.) proventriculus.
provenzal, *a., m., f.* Provençal (language).
provenzalismo, *m.* Provençalism, Provençal word or phrase.
proverbiador, *m.* book of proverbs or sayings.
proverbial, *a.* proverbial; well-known.
proverbialmente, *adv.* proverbially.
proverbiar, *i.v.* (coll.) to use proverbs frequently.
proverbio, *m.* 1. proverb; saying, adage, maxim. 2. prediction, omen. 3. **P.,** (Bib.) (*pl.*) Proverbs, Book of Proverbs.
proverbista, *m., f.* (coll.) person who collects or uses proverbs.
proveyendo, proveyera, proveyese, proveyo, *ref.* **proveer.**
provicero, *m.* prophet, forecaster.
próvidamente, *adv.* providently, carefully, prudently, diligently.
providencia, *f.* 1. **P.,** Providence, divine power or guidance; God. 2. prevention, disposition, measure, step. 3. foresight, forethought. 4. plan, scheme. 5. (law) judgment, decision, ruling, sentence. — **tomar providencias,** to take measures, make a decision.
providencial, *a.* providential; fortunate.
providencialismo, *m.* providentialism, belief that everything is determined by Divine Providence.
providencialmente, *adv.* providentially; fortunately.
providenciar, *tr.v.* 1. to decide, rule, make a decision on. 2. to take steps or measures for.
providente, *a.* provident, prudent, wise; careful.
próvido, da, *a.* 1. provident, cautious, careful. 2. propitious, favorable; benevolent.
provincia, *f.* province; **en provincias,** in the provinces, outside the capital, e.g. *vivir en provincias,* to live outside the capital or in the provinces.
provincial, *a.* provincial. —*m.* (ecc.) provincial.
provinciala, *f.* (ecc.) provincial, abbess in charge of religious houses in the provinces.
provincialato, *m.* (ecc.) position of provincial, provincialship.
provincialismo, *m.* provincialism; (fig.) parochialism.
provinciano, na, *a.* provincial, from the provinces; countrified. —*m., f.* provincial.
provine, proviniendo, proviniera, proviniese, *ref.* **provenir.**
provisión, *f.* 1. supply, stock, provision; (*pl.*) provisions, supplies, stocks, provender. 2. provision, supplying. 3. measure, step. 4. decree, mandamus. — **p. de fondos,** (com.) provision of funds; **provisiones de boca,** snacks.
provisional, *a.* provisional, temporary, interim.
provisionalmente, *adv.* provisionally, temporarily.
proviso, al p., instantly, immediately.
provisor, *m.* 1. provider, supplier, purveyor. 2. (ecc.) vicar general, ecclesiastical judge authorized by bishop. —*f.* purveyor, nun in charge of stores.
provisorato, *m.* purveyorship, post of supplier.
provisoría, *f.* 1. purveyorship, post of supplier. 2. storeroom (in convents).
provisorio, ria, *a.* (Amer.) provisional, provisory, temporary.
provisto, ta, *irr. past part. of* **proveer.** —*a.* provided, stocked, supplied.
provitamina, *f.* (biochem.) provitamin.
provocación, *f.* provocation, incitement, instigation; challenge.
provocador, ra, *a.* provocative; provoking. —*m., f.* provoker, inciter, challenger.
provocante, *a.* provocative, provoking.
provocar, (*ref. 50*) *tr.v.* 1. to provoke, incite, dare. 2. to annoy, incense, anger. 3. to tempt, e.g. *no me provoca nadar hoy,* I'm not tempted to swim today; to make one feel like, e.g. *no me provoca ir al cine,* I don't feel like going to the cinema. 4. to make, cause, move, e.g. *p. a risa,* to make one laugh, *p. a lástima,* to cause sorrow, make sad. 5. (coll.) to make one feel sick, make one want to vomit.
provocativo, va, *a.* provocative, provoking, tempting, inciting.
provoque, provoqué, *ref.* **provocar.**
proxeneta, *m.* procurer, pimp. —*f.* procuress.
proxenético, ca, *a.* pertaining to a procurer or procuress.
proxenetismo, *m.* procuring, pimping.
próximamente, *adv.* 1. soon, in the near future, before long. 2. approximately.
proximidad, *f.* proximity, nearness, closeness.
próximo, ma, *a.* 1. near, nearby, close. 2. next, e.g. *el p. mes,* next month. — **de p.,** soon, in the near future; **el año** or **mes p. pasado,** last year or month; **p. a,** near to, close to; about to.
proyección, *f.* 1. projection. 2. (cinem.) screening. — **p. axonométrica,** axonometric projection; **p. central,** gnomonic projection; **p. policónica,** polyconic projection.
proyectante, *a.* projecting, designing.
proyectar, *tr.v.* 1. to project, shoot, cast or throw forward. 2. to plan, map out, project, design. 3. to project (an image, film, etc.), to cast a shadow. 4. (geom.) to project. — **p. +** *inf.,* to plan to + *inf.* —*r v.* 1. to project, stick out. 2. to be cast, to fall (a shadow).
proyectil, *m.* projectile; missile; **p. atómico,** atomic missile; **p. dirigido,** guided missile; **p. de iluminación, p. luminoso,** (mil.) illuminating projectile.
proyectista, *m., f.* (com.) designer, planner, maker of projects.
proyecto, ta, *a.* (geom.) projected, in perspective. —*m.* project, plan, draft, design, (archit.) project; **en p.,** being planned, projected; **p. de ley,** bill, proposed law.
proyector, *m.* 1. projector. 2. searchlight; spotlight. — **p. amplificador,** (photog.) enlarging projector; **p. de orientacion,** (aer.) bearing projector.
proyectoscopio, *m.* (opt.) projectoscope.
proyectura, *f.* (archit.) projection.
prudencia, *f.* prudence, discretion; wisdom.
prudencial, *a.* 1. prudential, sensible, judicious. 2. approximate, rough, e.g. *un cálculo p.,* an approximate estimate.
prudencialmente, *adv.* prudentially.
prudente, *a.* prudent, wise, judicious, discreet.
prudentemente, *adv.* prudently, wisely; cautiously.
prueba, *f.* 1. proof, trial, test. 2. proof, evidence, demonstration; token, e.g. *dar una p. de,* to give proof of, *es una p de,* it's proof of. 3. sample, piece to be tested. 4. (math., print., photog.) proof. 5. (tail., dressm.) fitting. 6. (Amer.) (*pl.*) acrobatics; sleight of hand. 7. trial (moral), temptation; ordeal. 8. (sport.) match, competition, race. — **a p.,** on trial or approval; perfect; **a p. de,** proof against, - proof, e.g. *a p. de ácidos,* acid-fast; *a p. de agua,* waterproof, watertight, *a p. de bomba,* bombproof, *a p. de aire,* airtight, *a p. de bala,* bulletproof; **corregir pruebas,** (print.) to proofread; **de p.,** proved, tested; **poner a p.,** to put to the test; **p. antes de la letra,** proof impression (engraving); **p. cinematográfica,** screen test; **p. de aptitud,** aptitude test; **p. de Babcock,** Babcock test; **p. de fluidez,** (mec.) pour test; **p. de fuego,** acid test; **p. de galera,** (print.) slip or galley proof; **p. de impresión,** (print.) proof sheet; **p. de indicios** or **indiciaria,** circumstantial evidence; **p. de inteligencia,** intelligence test; **p. del laboratorio,** laboratory trial test; **p. del absurdo,** reductio ad absurdum; **p. del alcohol** or **de la alcoholemia,** sobriety test; **p. del embarazo,** pregnancy test; **p. de nivel,** placement test; **p. de ruta,** road race; **p. de Schick,** (med.) Schick test; **p. negativa,** (photog.) negative; **p. nuclear,** nuclear test; **p. patrón** or **de referencia,** benchmark; **p. positiva,** (photog.) positive print; **p. primaria,** (law) primary evidence; **p. semiplena,** (law) imperfect evidence; **pruebas materiales,** material evidence; **p. supletoria,** (law) supplementary evidence; **tomar a p.,** to take on trial.
pruebe, *ref.* **probar.**
pruebista, *m.* (Amer.) acrobat.
pruebo, *ref.* probar.
pruna, *f.* plum, prune.
prunela, *a.* (chem.) prunella (salt).
pruno, *m.* plum tree.
pruriginoso, sa, *a.* (med.) pruriginous.
prurigo, *m.* (med.) prurigo.
prurito, *m.* 1. (med.) pruritus, itch. 2. (fig.) urge, desire, itch (to do or have something).
Prusia, *f.* Prussia; **P. Oriental,** East Prussia.
prusiano, na, *a, m., f.* Prussian.
prusiato, *m.* (chem.) prussiate.
prúsico, *a.* (chem.) prussic.
P.S. *abbrev. of* **post scriptum,** postscript (PS).
psefita, *f.* (geol.) psephite.
pseudo, *a.* pseudo, false.
psicastenia, *f.* (med.) psychasthenia.
psicasténico, ca, *a.* (med.) psychasthenic.
psicoanalice, psicoanalicé, *ref.* **psicoanalizar.**
psicoanálisis, *m., f.* psychoanalysis.
psicoanalista, *m., f.* psychoanalyst.
psicoanalítico, ca, *a.* psychoanalytic, psychoanalytical.
psicoanalizar, (*ref. 53*) *tr.v.* to psychoanalyze.
psicobiología, *f.* psychobiology.
psicocirugía, *f.* psychosurgery.
psicodinámico, ca, *a.* psychodynamic.
psicodrama, *m.* (psych.) psychodrama.
psicofísica, *f.* psychophysics.
psicogénesis, *f.* psychogenesis.

psicogenia, *f.* psychogenesis.
psicógeno, na, *a.* psychogenic.
psicognosia, psicognosis, *f.* psychognosis.
psicógrafo, *m.* (psych.) psychograph.
psicología, *f.* psychology.
psicológico, ca, *a.* psychological.
psicologismo, *m.* psychologism.
psicólogo, *m.* psychologist.
psicometría, *f.* psychometry.
psicométrico, ca, *a.* psychometric.
psicomotor, ra, *a.* psychomotor.
psiconeurosis, (*pl.* **psiconeurosis**) *f.* psychoneurosis.
psiconeurótico, ca, *a., m., f.* psychoneurotic.
psicópata, *m., f.* psychopath.
psicopatía, *f.* psychopathy.
psicopático, ca, *a.* psychopathic.
psicopatología, *f.* psychopathology.
psicosis, *f.* (med.) psychosis.
psicosomático, ca, *a.* psychosomatic.
psicotecnia, *f.* psychotechnology.
psicoterapéutico, ca, *a.* psychotherapeutic. —*f.* psychotherapeutics.
psicoterapia, *f.* (med.) psychotherapy.
psicrófilo, la, *a.* (biol.) psychrophilic.
psicrómetro, *m.* psychrometer; **p. giratorio,** sling psychrometer.
psílido, *m.* (ento.) psyllid, psylla.
psilomelana, *f.* (min.) psilomelane.
psilomelano, *m.* (min.) psilomelane.
psilosis, *f.* (med.) psilosis.
psique, *m.* psyche (soul; mind; spirit).
psiquíatra, *m.* (med.) psychiatrist.
psiquiatría, *f.* psychiatry.
psíquico, ca, *a.* psychic, psychical.
Psiquis, *f.* (myth.) Psyche, maiden abducted by Eros.
psitácidos, *m.* (*pl.*) (zool.) Psittacidae.
psitacismo, *m.* learning or teaching by rote, psittacism.
psitacosis, *f.* (med.) psittacosis.
psoas, *m.* (anat.) psoas.
psócido, *m.* (ento.) psocid.
psofómetro, *m.* (tel.) psophometer.
psoriasis, *f.* (med.) psoriasis.
Pt *sym. of* **platino,** platinum (Pt).
ptas. *abbrev. of* **pesetas,** pesetas.
pteridoesperma, *f.* (paleon.) pteridosperm.
pteridófito, ta, *a.* (bot.) pteridophytic, pteridophytous. —*f.* (bot.) pteridophyte.
pteridoide, *a.* (bot.) pteridoid.
pteridología, *f.* (bot.) pteridology.
pterigoideo, *a., m.* (anat.) pterygoid.
pterodáctilo, *m.* (paleon.) pterodactyl.
pterópodo, *a., m.* (zool.) pteropod.
pterosaurio, *m.* (paleon.) pterosaur.
ptialina, *f.* (biochem.) ptyalin.
ptialismo, *m.* (med.) ptyalism.
pto. *abbrev. of* **puerto,** port.
Ptolomeos, *m.* (hist.) Ptolemies, dynasty of Egyptian rulers.
ptomaína, *f.* (biochem.) ptomaine.
ptosis, *f.* (med.) ptosis.
Pu *sym. of* **plutonio,** plutonium (Pu).
púa, *f.* 1. barb, spike, prong, tine, point. 2. spine (on hedgehog, porcupine, etc.). 3. thorn (of thistle, holly leaf, etc.). 4. tooth (of comb). 5. (bot.) graft, scion. 6. (mus.) plectrum (for playing guitar). 7. metal point (of spinning top). 8. sting (of remorse or sorrow). 9. crafty person. — **alambre de púas,** barbed wire; **saber uno cuantas púas tiene un peine,** to know the score; **sacar la p. al trompo,** to get to the bottom of something.
puado, *m.* set of teeth, prongs or tines.
puar, *tr.v.* to put teeth on (e.g. **a comb**), put prongs on.
puazo, *m.* (S. Amer.) slash (made by the spur of a cock).
púber, púbera, púbero, *a.* pubescent, having reached puberty. —*m., f.* person who has reached puberty.
pubertad, *f.* puberty, pubescence.
pubes, (*pl.* **pubes**), *m.,* (anat.) *var. of* **pubis.**
pubescencia, *f.* pubescence.
pubescente, *a.* pubescent, reaching **puberty.**
pubescer, *i.v.* to reach the age of puberty.
pubiano, na, *a.* (anat.) pubic.
púbico, ca, *a.* (anat.) pubic.
pubis, (*pl.* **pubis**), *m.* (anat.) pubes (lower part of abdomen; hair covering it); (anat.) pubis (part of innominate bone).
pública, *f.* public defense of a thesis in the final examination at university.
publicación, *f.* 1. publication. 2. proclamation; **p. periódica,** periodical.
publicador, ra, *a.* publishing. —*m., f.* publisher, divulger.
públicamente, *adv.* publicly, openly.
publicano, *m.* (hist.) publican, Roman tax collector.
publicar, (*ref. 50*) *tr.v.* 1. to publish, issue (book, periodical, etc.). 2. to announce, broadcast, proclaim; to divulge, publicize. 3. to publish (banns).
publicata, *f.* (ecc.) certificate of publication.
publicidad, *f.* publicity; promotion, advertising; **agencia de p.,** advertising agency, publicity bureau; **en p.,** publicly; **p. estática,** billboard advertising.
publicista, *m., f.* 1. publicist, writer on public law or on topics of public interest. 2. (Amer.) publicity agent.
publicitario, ria, *a.* advertising, publicity, e.g. *agencia publicitaria,* advertising agency.
público, ca, *a.* public, general; known, open. —*m.* public; audience, spectators. — **dar** or **sacar al p.,** to publish; **en p.,** publicly, in public; **la opinión del p.,** public opinion.
publique, publiqué, *ref.* **publicar.**
pucelana, *f.* (geol.) pozzuolana, pozzolana.
pucha, *f.* (Cuba) nosegay or bouquet.
puchada, *f.* 1. flour poultice. 2. hogwash, hog feed.
puchera, *f.* (cul., coll.) stew, boiled dinner.
pucherazo, *m.* blow with a pot. — **dar p.,** (coll.) to count votes that were not cast.
pucherear, *i.v.* (Chile) to pout, screw up one's face (prior to crying).
pucherito, ico, *m. dim. of* **puchero,** pouting of a child before crying.
puchero, *m.* 1. cooking pot. 2. stew, boiled dinner, olla. 3. (coll.) daily bread or food. 4. pout, pouting. — **empinar el p.,** (coll.) to manage to live decently; **hacer pucheros,** (coll.) to pout, screw up one's face (in weeping); **p. de enfermo,** invalid's broth; **salírsele a uno el p.,** to have one's plans miscarry; **volcar p.,** (coll.) to count votes that were not cast.
puches, *m., f.* (*pl.*) porridge, gruel, pap, mush.
puchiganga, *f.* (Col.) distaff.
pucho, *m.* 1. (S. Amer.) cigar or cigarette end or stump. 2. (S. Amer.) trifle, bit, small amount; leftover, residue. 3. (Chile, Ecuad.) baby, youngest child (of family). 4. (Chile, Ecuad.) candle-stump.
pucia, *f.* closed pharmaceutical vessel.
puco, *m.* (Ecuad., Arg., Col.) wide wooden bowl.
pude, *ref.* **poder.**
pudelación, *f.* (metal.) puddling.
pudelador, *m.* (metal.) puddler.
pudelar, *tr.v.* (metal.) to puddle.
pudendo, da, *a.* shameful, obscene; private (parts); **partes pudendas,** genitals.
pudibundez, *f.* prudishness, affected modesty, overmodesty.
pudibundo, da, *a.* modest, shy, bashful.
pudicia, *f.* pudency, modesty, chastity.
púdico, ca, *a.* modesty, shy, chaste.
pudiendo, *ref.* **poder.**
pudiente, *a.* rich, affluent, well-to-do. —*m., f.* person of means.
pudiera, pudiese, *ref.* **poder.**
pudín, *m.* (cul.) pudding.
pudinga, *f.* (geol.) pudding stone conglomerate.
pudio, *a.* **pino p.,** Austrian pine.
pudor, *m.* modesty, shyness; chastity; **atentado contra el p.,** indecent assault; **ultraje al p.,** indecent exposure.
pudoroso, sa, *a.* modest, shy, bashful.
pudrición, *f.* rot, putrefaction, rotting; **p. roja,** plant rot.
pudridero, *m.* 1. rotting place, place of decomposition; compost heap. 2. temporary vault (for a body).
pudridor, *m.* fermenting vat (used in paper making).
pudrigorio, *m.* (coll.) sickly person, wreck (sl.).
pudrimiento, *m.* rot, rotting, putrefaction.
pudrir, *past part.* **podrido.** —*tr.v.* 1. to rot, putrefy, decay. 2. (fig.) to worry, vex, harass. —*r.v.* 1. to rot, putrefy. 2. to be irritated, vexed or harassed. —*i.v.* to be dead and buried.
pudú, *m.* Chilean mountain goat.
puebla, *f.* (agr.) planting or vegetable seeds.
pueblada, *f.* (Amer.) riot, mutiny, popular uprising.
pueble, *m.* (min.) gang of workmen.
pueble, *ref.* **poblar.**
pueblecito, ico, *m. dim. of* **pueblo,** small village or town.
puebleño, ña, *m., f.* (Col.) an inhabitant of small town, villager.
pueblerino, na, *a.* village, rural. —*m., f.* villager.
pueblo, *m.* 1. town, village. 2. common people, people, working classes. 3. people, nation, population; **p. de mala muerte,** one-horse town; **p. fantasma,** ghost town; **p. llano,** ordinary people, everyday people.
pueblo, *ref.* **poblar.**
pueda, puedo, *ref.* **poder.**
puelche, *m.* (Chile) 1. native living on the eastern side of the Andes. 2. (Chile) east wind.
puente, *m.* (originally *f.*) 1. bridge. 2. (mus.) bridge (on stringed instruments); capo. 3. (mus.) tailpiece (on stringed instruments). 4. crossbeam, crosspiece, transom. 5. (mar.) bridge. 6. (mar.) gun-carrying deck. 7. (dent.) bridge. — **cabeza de p.,** bridgehead; **calar el p.,** to lower the drawbridge; **ponerle p. de plata a uno,** (coll.) to smooth the way for, make things easy for; **hacer p.,** to take the intervening day off; **p. aéreo,** airlift, air bridge; **p. basculante,** bascule bridge; **p. cantilever,** cantilever bridge; **p. cerril,** narrow cattle bridge; **p. colgante,** suspension bridge; **p. de barcas,** pontoon bridge; **p. de caballetes,** trestle bridge; **p. de los asnos,** (coll.) stumbling block, discouraging difficulty; **p. de los suspiros,** Bridge of Sighs; **p. de peatones,** footbridge; **p. de pontones,** (mil.) pontoon bridge; **p. de tablero inferior,** through bridge; **p. giratorio,** swing bridge; **p. levadizo,** drawbridge; **p. suspendido,** suspension bridge, chain bridge; **p. transbordador,** transporter bridge.
puentecilla, *f.* (mus.) bridge (of a stringed instrument); (mus.) tailpiece (of a stringed instrument).

puentezuela, *f.* small bridge.
puerca, *f.* 1. (zool.) sow. 2. (ento.) wood louse, sow bug. 3. (med.) scrofula. 4. eye (of a hinge). 5. (fig.) slut, slattern; slovenly woman. — **p. montés, p. salvaje,** sow of wild boar.
puercamente, *adv.* 1. (coll.) dirtily, filthily. 2. (coll.) despicably, contemptibly, basely.
puerco, *m.* 1. (zool.) hog, swine, pig; wild boar. 2. pig, hog, filthy ill-mannered person; swine; base, mean man. — **p. de mar,** (zool.) common porpoise, harbor porpoise, sea hog; **p. de simiente,** boar, stud boar; **p. espín, p. espino,** (zool.) porcupine; (fort.) spiked timber; **p. marino,** (zool.) dolphin; **p. montés, p. salvaje,** wild boar.
puerco, ca, *a.* 1. dirty, filthy, foul, piggish, hoggish. 2. despicable, base, contemptible, mean.
puericia, *f.* childhood (state between infancy and adolescence).
puericultor, ra, *m., f.* one who studies puericulture, child educator.
puericultura, *f.* puericulture.
pueril, *a.* puerile, childish.
puerilidad, *f.* puerility, childishness; puerile remark or act.
puerilmente, *adv.* puerilely, childishly.
puérpera, *f.* puerpera, woman who has just given birth.
puerperal, *a.* puerperal, pertaining to childbirth.
puerperio, *m.* (med.) puerperium, time directly after childbirth.
puerro, *m.* (bot.) leek, scallion; **p. silvestre,** wild leek.
puerta, *f.* 1. door; gate; doorway; gateway. 2. entrance, exit, access. 3. (fig.) door, path, way (e.g. to success). — **abrir la p. a** or **para,** to open the door for, prepare the way for; **a las puertas de la muerte,** at death's door; **a p. cerrada,** secretly, behind closed doors; **cerrar a uno la p.,** to close the door on, refuse help to; **cerrársele a uno todas las puertas,** to have no way out, to find all avenues closed; **coger la p., tomar la p.,** to leave; **dar a uno con la p. en las narices,** (coll.) to slam the door in one's face, close the door on, refuse help to; **de p. en p.,** from door to door; **echar las puertas abajo,** (coll.) to knock violently, knock the door down; **enseñarle a uno la p. de la calle,** (coll.) to show someone the door, ask someone to leave; **estar a la p., llamar a la p.,** to be imminent, be near at hand; **poner a uno en la p. de la calle,** to throw into the street, put one out of the house; to sack, fire, dismiss; **p. abierta,** (dipl.) open door, free trade; **p. accesoria,** side door; **p. cochera,** portecochere, carriage gateway; **p. corredera,** sliding door; **p. de embarque,** gate; **p. de servicio,** service entrance; **p. de vaivén,** swing door; **p. excusada, p. falsa,** back door, side door; **p. franca,** open door, free entrance, free entry; exemption from import duty; **p. giratoria,** revolving door; **p. plegadiza,** folding door; **p. secreta,** concealed door; **Puerta de Hierro,** Iron Gate (Madrid); **p. trasera,** back door; (hum.) anus, back passage; **p. ventana,** French doors; **p. vidriera,** glass door; **Sublime P.,** Sublime Porte (Turkey).
puertaventana, *f.* window shutter.
puertezuela, *f. dim. of* **puerta,** small door.
puertezuelo, *m. dim. of* **puerto,** small harbor.
puerto, *m.* 1. port, harbor; haven. 2. mountain pass; mountain range with passes. 3. (fig.) shelter, haven, refuge, asylum. 4. (sl.) roadside inn, lodging house. — **agarrar un barco el p.,** (mar.) to reach port after rough seas; **naufragar en el p.,** to be wrecked in the last stages; **p. abierto,** open port (open to foreign trade); **p. aduanero** or **de entrada,** port of entry; **p. de arribada** or **de escala,** (mar.) port of call; **p. de estadía** or **de refugio,** port or harbor of refuge; **p. deportivo,** marina; **p. fluvial,** river port; **p. franco, p. libre,** free port; **p. marítimo,** seaport; **p. pesquero,** fishing port; **p. seco,** frontier customs house; **tomar p.,** to reach port; (fig.) to take refuge or asylum.
Puerto Príncipe, *m.* Port-au-Prince, capital of Haiti.
Puerto Rico, *m.* Puerto Rico, Porto Rico.
puertorriqueño, ña, *a., m., f.* Puerto Rican.
pues, *conj.* since, because, for, as, inasmuch as; **p. que,** since, because. —*adv.* 1. then; well, all right, e.g. *repito, p., que no debes hacerlo,* I repeat, then, that you should not do it, *¿no quieres seguir mis consejos? p., te arrepentirás,* you don't want to follow my advice? well or all right, you'll regret it, *así es p.,* that's how it is, then, *p. bien,* well then, *¿p. qué? ¿y p.?* well, what about it? well and so what? 2. certainly, of course, e.g. *claro p.,* of course, *p. no,* certainly or of course not, *sí p., p. sí,* yes, of course, yes, certainly. 3. really, well, e.g. *p. no faltaba más,* really (well), that's the last straw.
puesta, *f.* 1. setting (e.g. of the sun). 2. putting, e.g. *p. en servicio* or *operación,* putting into service or operation. 3. laying (of eggs). 4. (in games) stake, bet. 5. (astron.) set, setting. — **puesta(s) del sol,** sunset, sundown; **primera p.,** (mil.) new outfit (issued to a recruit); **p. a** or **en punto,** adjusting, regulating; **p. de mano,** touch, e.g. *ganar por p. de mano,* to win by a touch (in swimming); **p. en escena,** (theat.) staging; **p. en marcha,** starting; starting-up; launching.
puestero, *m.* (Arg., Urug.) tender of livestock (on a ranch), administrator of a cattle station.
puesto, ta, *irr. past part. of* **poner.** —*a.* put; placed; set. — **bien** or **mal p.,** well or badly dressed; **tener** or **llevar puesto** or **puesta,** to be wearing, have on, e.g. *¿qué ropa tenía puesta?* what clothes did he have on? —*m.* 1. post, position, place, e.g. *p. de primeros auxilios,* first-aid post, *p. de centinela* (mil.) sentry post; stall, stand, booth (e.g. in a market, exhibition, etc.). 2. post, position, job. 3. blind (for hunters). 4. stud farm, stud; (Arg.) cattle station. 5. condition, situation, state. 6. post. — **p. de mando,** (mil.) command post; **puestos de combate,** action stations; **p. de observación,** observation post; **p. de periódicos,** newsstand; **p. de policía,** police station; **p. de socorro,** first-aid station; **p. fronterizo,** border post. —*conj.* **puesto que,** because, inasmuch as, since, e.g. *déjalo aquí, p. que pesa tanto,* leave it here, since it weighs so much, *me voy, p. que no me necesitas,* I'm leaving, inasmuch as you don't need me, *te ayudo p. que te quiero,* I help you because I care for you.
¡puf! *interj.* (denoting revulsion, rejection) ugh! pugh!
puf, *m.* pouf (ottoman, upholstered taboret).
pufo, *m.* (coll.) petard, bomb.
púgil, *m.* boxer, pugilist, prizefighter.
pugilar, *m.* Hebrew manual of the scriptures as used in synagogues.
pugilato, *m.* 1. boxing, pugilism (sport.). 2. fight, scrap; heated controversy.
pugilismo, *m.* pugilism.
pugilista, *m.* boxer, pugilist, prizefighter.
pugna, *f.* fight, battle; struggle, conflict; **estar en p.,** to be in conflict, disagree, oppose each other.
pugnacidad, *f.* pugnacity, pugnaciousness.
pugnante, *a.* 1. fighting, struggling. 2. hostile, opposing.
pugnar, *i.v.* to fight; to struggle, strive; to be opposed (to); to conflict (with); to persist; **p. por** + *inf.,* to struggle to + *inf.*
pugnaz, (*pl.* **pugnaces**), *a.* pugnacious, bellicose.
puja, *f.* 1. struggle, effort; **sacar de la p. a uno,** (coll.) to beat, outwit; to outstrip; to be stronger than; (coll.) to get someone out of a jam. 2. bid; higher bid; raising a bid, outbidding (in a game, at an auction).
pujador, ra, *m., f.* bidder, outbidder.
pujame, pujamen, *m.* (mar.) foot of a sail, bottom part of the sails.
pujamiento, *m.* abundant flow of the blood or body fluids.
pujante, *a.* vigorous, strong, powerful.
pujantemente, *adv.* vigorously, forcefully, powerfully.
pujanza, *f.* vigor, energy, power, might, strength, force.
pujar, *i.v.* 1. to struggle, strain, strive. 2. to struggle, grope (for words), e.g. *p. por hablar,* to struggle to speak, grope for words. 3. to hesitate, falter (in action). 4. (coll.) to pout, make a face as if to cry. — **p. con** or **contra,** to struggle with or against; **p. para adentro,** (Amer.) to repress one's feelings, keep one's feelings to oneself. —*tr.v.* to raise, bid up, outbid.
pujavante, *m.* hoof parer (tool used by horseshoer).
pujo, *m.* 1. strong desire or urge, irresistible impulse or desire (e.g. to laugh or cry). 2. (coll.) attempt, effort. 3. (med.) straining, tenesmus (strong desire to evacuate the bowels or bladder with great difficulty in doing so). — **a pujos,** (coll.) little by little, with great difficulty.
pulchinela, *m.* punchinello, Punch.
pulcritud, *f.* 1. neatness, tidiness; beauty, pulchritude. 2. honesty; ethical conduct.
pulcro, cra, *a.* 1. neat, tidy; beautiful. 2. ethical, clean, decent (legitimate), e.g. *es un negocio p.,* it's a clean, legitimate business.
pulga, *f.* 1. (ento.) flea. 2. small top (toy). — **buscarle las pulgas a alguien,** to look for a fight with someone; **cada uno tiene su modo de matar pulgas,** everyone has his own way of doing things; **tener la p. tras la oreja,** (coll.) to be restless, upset; **hacer de una p. un camello** or **un elefante,** (coll.) to make a mountain out of a molehill; **p. de agua,** water flea; **sacudirse las pulgas,** (coll.) to take no notice of irritations; **tener malas pulgas,** (coll.) to take offense easily; to be touchy or easily annoyed; **tener pulgas,** (coll.) to be restless or too lively, be a jack-in-the-box, to have ants in the pants (U.S., coll.); **p. acuática,** (ento.) water flea.
pulgada, *f.* inch; **no ceder una p.,** (coll.) not to give an inch.
pulgar, *a.* **dedo p.,** thumb. —*m.* 1. thumb. 2. shoot (left on a vine). — **menear uno los pulgares,** to uncover one's cards gradually; (coll.) to work quickly (with the fingers); **por sus pulgares,** (coll.) with one's own hands, by oneself.
pulgarada, *f.* 1. flip, fillip (with thumb). 2. pinch (e.g. of salt). 3. inch.
Pulgarcito, *m.* Tom Thumb.
pulgón, *m.* (ento.) plant louse.
pulgoso, sa, *a.* flea-ridden, full of fleas.
pulguera, *f.* 1. fleapit, place full of fleas. 2. (bot.) fleawort. 3. notch, nock (of crossbow).
pulguillas, *m.* (coll.) touchy, irritable person.
pulicán, *m.* dentist's forceps.
pulidamente, *adv.* carefully, neatly, exquisitely.
pulidero, *m.* polisher, glosser (wad of cloth or leather).
pulidez, *f.* polish, shine; neatness.

pulido, da, *past part. of* **pulir.** —*a.* 1. polished, shiny; neat, beautiful, trim. 2. polished (as a style or type of finish). 3. (fig.) refined, well-bred.
pulidor, ra, *a.* polishing. —*m., f.* polisher. —*m.* 1. polishing machine. 2. leather protector for the fingers (when winding thread onto spool).
pulimentadora, *f.* lapping or buffing machine.
pulimentar, *tr.v.* to polish, finish, burnish.
pulimento, *m.* polish, shine, gloss; finish.
pulir, *tr.v.* 1. to polish, burnish. 2. to apply a finish to. 3. to make refined or well-bred. 4. (coll.) to steal, lift, swipe, pinch (a thing); to rob (a person). —*r.v.* 1. to become polished or refined. 2. to dress up; to get neatly attired.
pulla, *f.* 1. obscenity. 2. caustic or cutting remark. 3. witty remark, quip. 4. (ornith.) gannet.
pullista, *m., f.* scoffer, giber; wit, joker.
pulmón, *m.* (anat.) lung; **p. artificial, p. de acero,** iron lung; **p. marino,** (zool.) jellyfish.
pulmonado, da, *a.* (zool.) pulmonate.
pulmonar, *a.* pulmonary, pertaining to the lungs.
pulmonaria, *f.* (bot.) lungwort (Pulmonaria officinalis); (bot.) brown lichen (Sticta pulmonacea).
pulmonía, *f.* (med.) pneumonia; **coger una p.,** to catch pneumonia.
pulmoníaco, ca, *a.* (med.) pneumonic. —*m., f.* (med.) person with pneumonia.
pulmotor, *m.* Pulmotor (trademark).
pulpa, *f.* 1. pulp, flesh (e.g. of fruit). 2. pulp, mass (e.g., of wood).
pulpejo, *m.* soft flesh (of the ear, finger, etc.); bulb (of a horse's hoof).
pulpería, *f.* (Amer.) grocery store, general store.
pulpero, *m.* 1. (Amer.) grocer, storekeeper. 2. one who catches or fishes squids or cuttlefish.
pulpeta, *f.* slice of meat.
pulpetón, *m. aug. of* **pulpeta,** large slice of meat.
pulpitis, *f.* (med.) pulpitis.
púlpito, *m.* 1. pulpit. 2. office or occupation of a preacher.
pulpo, *m.* (zool.) octopus, cuttlefish.
pulposo, sa, *a.* pulpy, fleshy.
pulque, *m.* (Amer.) pulque (the fermented juice of the agave or maguey plant).
pulquería, *f.* pulque shop; (Mex., coll.) a low-class, rowdy bar.
pulquero, *m.* (Mex.) pulque seller.
pulquérrimo, ma, *a. super. of* **pulcro,** extremely neat, tidy, beautiful or wellbred.
pulsación, *f.* pulsation, throb, beat, pulse; (phys., physiol.) pulsation.
pulsada, *f.* pulsation, beat (of the pulse).
pulsador, ra, *a.* pulsating. —*m.* 1. pulsator. 2. buzzer, push-button bell.
pulsante, *a.* pulsating.
pulsar, *tr.v.* 1. to play, strum (e.g. a guitar). 2. to take the pulse of. 3. to sound out, explore, examine. —*i.v.* to pulse, throb, beat.
pulsátil, *a.* beating, pulsating, pulsatile.
pulsatila, *f.* (bot.) pasqueflower.
pulsativo, va, *a.* beating, pulsating, pulsative.
pulsear, *i.v.* to hand-wrestle.
pulsera, *f.* 1. bracelet; watchband. 2. (med.) wrist bandage. 3. lock of hair over the temple. — **p. de pedida,** engagement bracelet; **reloj de p.,** wristwatch.
pulsímetro, *m.* (med.) pulsimeter.
pulso, *m.* 1. pulse. 2. steadiness, steady hand. 3. place where the pulse is felt (gen. the wrist). 4. (Cuba) bracelet. 5. (fig.) care, caution. — **a p.,** with hand and wrist, with the strength of the hand; freehand (drawing); **de p.,** sensible, prudent, cautious; **p. formicante,** (med.) low or weak pulse; **p. sentado,** (med.) steady pulse; **quedarse uno sin p.,** to be left speechless; **sacar a p.,** (coll.) to achieve against great difficulties; **tomar el p.,** to feel or take the pulse of, feel or take someone's pulse; to examine, sound out, explore, investigate.
pulsómetro, *m.* (hydr.) pulsometer.
pulsorreactor, ra, *a.* (aer.) pulse-jet; **motor p.,** pulse-jet engine.
pultáceo, a, *a.* 1. pulpy, soft. 2. (med.) putrescent, approaching gangrene.
pululante, *a.* pullulating, germinating.
pulular, *i.v.* 1. to teem, abound, swarm, pullulate. 2. to bud, sprout, germinate, grow new shoots. 3. to teem, multiply prolifically.
pulverice, pulverice, *ref.* **pulverizar.**
pulverizable, *a.* pulverizable.
pulverización, *f.* pulverization; atomization.
pulverizador, *m.* atomizer; sprayer, spray, pulverizer. — **p. de pintura,** paint sprayer.
pulverizar, (*ref. 53*) *tr.v.* 1. to pulverize, reduce to powder. 2. to atomize, spray. —*r.v.* to become pulverized.
pulverulento, ta, *a.* dusty, reduced to dust.
pulvillo, *m.* (zool.) pulvillus.
¡pum! *interj.* bang!
puma, *m.* (sometimes *f.*) (zool.) puma, American panther.
pumarada, *f.* apple orchard.
pumita, *f.* pumice stone.
puna, *f.* 1. (S. Amer.) bleak, desolate plateau (in the higher Andes), puna. 2. (S. Amer.) mountain sickness, puna, soroche.
puncha, *f.* prickle, thorn, sharp point.
punchar, *tr.v.* to prick, puncture, pierce.
punches, *m.* (*pl.*) (Hond.) popcorn.
punción, *f.* 1. (surg.) puncture. 2. stab, sudden pain.
puncionar, *tr.v.* (surg.) to puncture.
pundonor, *f.* honor, integrity.
pundonorosamente, *adv.* honorably, honestly, with integrity.
pundonoroso, sa, *a.* honorable, honest, upstanding.
pungente, *a.* pricking; stinging.
pungimiento, *m.* prick; sting.
pungir, (*ref. 62*) *tr.v.* 1. to prick. 2. (fig.) to sting.
pungitivo, va, *a.* pricking; stinging.
punguista, *m.* (Arg.) petty thief, pickpocket.
punibilidad, *f.* punishability.
punible, *a.* punishable.
punición, *f.* punishment.
púnico, ca, *a.* (hist.) Punic, Carthaginian; guerras **púnicas,** Punic Wars.
punitivo, va, *a.* (law) punitive.
punta, *f.* 1. point, sharp end. 2. tip; apex, top, end; (cigarette) end, butt or stub. 3. small part of a herd. 4. point, tine, snag (of antlers). 5. (bull's) horn. 6. point, cape, promontory, headland. 7. sourish taste (e.g. of wine turning to vinegar). 8. (hunt.) point, the position assumed by a pointer when it finds the game. 9. touch, trace, tinge (often in *pl*), e.g. *tiene una p. de loco,* he has a touch of the madman in him. 10. (Cuba) small leaf of first quality tobacco. 11. unusable end of a tree trunk. 12. (her.) point. 13. (print.) bodkin (sharp instrument for pushing out letters from body of set type). 14. (*pl.*) point lace, needle-point lace. 15. (*pl.*) headstreams, headwaters, sources (of a river). 16. point, graver, style, burin. 17. (Amer.) crowd, lot, big number. — **andar en puntas,** (coll.) to be on bad terms with one another; **a p. de,** by dint of; by means of; **a torna p.,** (coll.) mutually, reciprocally; **de p.,** on tiptoe; **de p. a cabo,** from end to end, from tip to toe; **de p. en blanco,** in full armor; (coll.) in full regalia; **en puntas de pies,** (Amer.) on tiptoe; **estar de p. con,** (coll.) to be at odds or be on bad terms with; **estar hasta la p. de los pelos,** (coll.) to be fed up, be tired; **hacer p. uno,** (fig.) to lead, go first; (fig.) to oppose; (fig.) to stand out, lead, excel; **poner los nervios de p.,** to put one's nerves on edge; **poner los pelos de p.,** to make one's hair stand on end; **ponerse de p. con,** to get annoyed with, fall out with; **p. de diamante,** diamond pencil, diamond point (for cutting); small pyramid (cut into stones, etc. as decoration); **p. de espárrago,** asparagus tips; **p. de lanza,** spearhead; **p. de París,** wire nail; **p. detectora,** (rad.) cat's whisker; **p. seca,** graver, burin, engraving needle; **sacar p. a,** (coll.) to sharpen; to interpret maliciously, give a malicious interpretation to; **tener en la p. de la lengua,** to have on the tip of one's tongue; **tener los nervios de p.,** to have one's nerves on edge; **tocar a uno en la p. de un cabello,** to offend slightly.
puntación, *f.* pointing (of letters in Semitic languages).
puntada, *f.* 1. stitch; stitch hole. 2. hint. 3. (Amer.) stitch, stabbing pain (in the side). — **no dar una p. en,** (coll.) to leave untouched, take no action in; (coll.) not to have the slightest knowledge or idea of.
puntador, *m., var. of* **apuntador.**
puntal, *m.* 1. prop, support, shore; stanchion. 2. elevation, rise (in the ground). 3. (fig.) prop, backing, support. 4. (mar.) depth of hold. 5. (Amer.) snack, bite.
puntapié, *m.* kick (with the foot of the boot); **dar un p.,** to kick; **echar a puntapiés,** to kick out; **mandar a uno a puntapiés,** (coll.) to boss about, order about dictatorially.
puntar, *tr.v.* to dot, mark with points and dots; to point (letters in Semitic languages).
puntazo, *m.* (Amer.) stab, jab.
punteado, *m.* 1. dotted line. 2. (mus.) plucking (as against strumming a guitar, lute, etc.).
puntear, *tr.v.* 1. to dot, mark with dots or points. 2. to stipple, engrave or paint by means of dots. 3. to stitch, sew. 4. (mus.) to pluck (a string instrument). 5. to check off (a bill). —*i.v.* (mar.) to tack.
puntel, *m.* pontil, punty, pointed rod used for fashioning hot glass.
punteo, *m.* 1. (mus.) plucking (as against strumming stringed instruments). 2. checking off (a bill).
puntera, *f.* 1. toecap (of a shoe); toe patch, new toe (on stocking). 2. (coll.) kick.
puntería, *f.* 1. aim, aiming. 2. marksmanship. 3. (fig.) skill. — **afinar la p.,** to aim carefully; **dirigir** or **poner la p. (en),** to aim (at), direct one's aim (towards); to fire or shoot (at); **hacer p. (en),** to fire or shoot (at); to aim (at); **hacer un poco de p.,** to do a bit of shooting; **p. directa,** direct aiming; **tener buena** or **mala p.,** to be a good or bad shot or marksman.
puntero, ra, *a.* sharpshooting. —*m.* 1. pointer, thin rod. 2. rod to anoint confirmands with oil. 3. punch (for making holes in metal). 4. stone-cutter's chisel. 5. (Amer.) leader, leading, animal in flock or drove. 6. (Amer.) hand (of the clock).
punterola, *f.* (min.) miner's pick, poll pick.
puntiagudo, da, *a.* sharp, sharp-pointed; tapering (to a sharp point).
puntico, ito, *m. dim. of* **punto,** small point, fine point.
puntido, *m.* (Arg.) landing (of stairs).
puntilla, *f.* 1. narrow lace, lace edging. 2. tack, brad, short nail. 3. carpenter's tracing point. 4. dagger, short poniard. — **dar la p.,** to stab, stick

a dagger into; (coll.) to finish off, bring about the final ruin of; (taur.) give the coup de grâce; **de** or **en puntillas,** on tiptoe.

puntillado, da, *a.* (her.) pointillé, decorated with gold dots.

puntillazo, *m.* (coll.) kick, booting.

puntillero, *m.* (taur.) puntillero, bullfighter (who gives the coup de grâce to the bull with a dagger).

puntillismo, *m.* (p.) pointillism (method of painting practiced by certain French impressionists).

puntillo, *m.* 1. *dim. of* **punto,** small point. 2. punctilio. 3. (mus.) dot, point of augmentation.

puntillón, *m.* (coll.) kick.

puntilloso, sa, *a.* punctilious.

puntiseco, ca, *a.* dry at the tips (said of plants).

puntizón, *m.* (print.) frisket mark or hole.

punto, *m.* 1. point, dot; (geom., math.) point. 2. (gram.) dot (over i or j); period (U.S.), full stop (G.B.). 3. point (unit for counting scores in games, contests, examinations, etc.), e.g. *ganar por puntos,* to win on points. 4. point, spot, place; (mil.) point, e.g. *p de aprovisionamiento,* supply point. 5. point, verge, e.g. *estar a p de,* to be on the verge of. 6. point (occasion, opportunity), e.g. *llegó a p. de lograr su deseo,* he reached the point of achieving his wish. 7. point (stage, condition), e.g. *llegaron a tal p. que no podían entenderse,* they got to such a stage that they couldn't understand one another, *p. de ebullición,* boiling point. 8. point, degree, e.g. *hasta cierto p.,* to a certain point. 9. point, item, e.g. *entiendo todo menos el primer p.,* I understand everything except the first item. 10. questions, point, subject, e.g. *p. filosófico,* philosophical question or point. 11. point, main idea, aim, object, e.g. *vamos al p.,* let's get to the point. 12. stitch (in sewing), point (in embroidery). 13. (surg.) stick. 14. (print.) point, 1/72 of an inch, e.g. *carácter de cinco puntos,* five-point type. 15. 1/6 of a millimeter. 1/12 of a line. 16. 2/3 centimeter division on shoemaker's measuring stick. 17. hole (in knitted or woven fabrics). 18. adjusting hole (in belts, straps, etc.). 19. nib, each of two divisions of the point of a pen. 20. gun sight. 21. catch (on the trigger of some firearms). 22. taxi stand, hack stand. 23. ace (in some card games). 24. (cul.) point at which certain foods are cooked or reach the desired consistency. 25. stabbing pain, stitch. 26. (mus.) pitch. 27. (mar.) estimated position (of a ship). 28. break, rest, holiday. 29. each of the errors made when committing a lesson to memory. 30. (Amer.) man who works with someone else's union card or work permit (usually on the docks). 31. honor, integrity, honesty. 32. gambler who stakes against the banker. — **a buen p.,** on time, opportunely; **al p.,** immediately, at once; **a p. de,** on the point of, about to; **a p. fijo,** precisely, with certainty, exactly; **a p. largo,** (coll.) roughly, carelessly; **a p. que,** just as, just when; **aquí finca el p.,** that's where the problem lies; **bajar de p.,** to decline, decay; **bajar el p.,** (mus.) to lower the pitch; **bajar el p. a,** to moderate, lower; **ya sé cuantos puntos calza,** I know his good and bad points; **dar en el p.,** to locate the difficulty, hit the nail on the head; **darse un p. en la boca,** (coll.) to keep quiet, not to speak; **de p.,** knitted, e.g. *medias de p.,* knitted socks; **de todo p.,** entirely, completely; **dos puntos,** (gram.) colon; **echar el p.,** (mar.) to mark the estimated position of a ship on the map; **en buen** or **mal p.,** fortunately, luckily or unfortunately, unluckily; **en p.,** on the dot, sharp, exactly (of time); **en su p.,** just right, ready, just perfect; **estar a** or **en p. de,** to be on the point of, be about to; **hacer p.,** to stop; **hasta cierto p.,** up to a point; **medio p.,** (archit.) arch formed by an exact semicircle; **meter en p.,** (sculp.) to point, scabble, roughdress (wood, stone, etc. in preparation for sculpturing); **no perder p.,** to procede carefully, act with care; **no poder pasar por otro p.,** to be forced to, have to; **poner en su p.,** (coll.) to perfect, make perfect; (coll.) to appreciate; **poner los puntos en,** to direct one's attention towards; **poner los puntos muy altos,** to aim too high, fix one's sights too high; **poner los puntos sobre las íes,** (coll.) to dot one's i's and cross one's t's, do with precision and care; **poner p. final a,** to put a stop to; **por p. general,** as a general rule; **por puntos,** from one moment to another; (to win) on points; **p. accidental,** accidental point (in perspective); **p. aparte,** full stop or period at the end of a paragraph; **p. atrás,** (sew.) backstitch; **p. cardinal,** cardinal point; **P. Cuarto,** (econ.) Point Four; **p. céntrico, center, central point; (fig.) central point or aim; p. ciego,** (anat.) blind spot; **p. crítico,** (phys.) critical point; **p. crudo,** (coll.) the very moment; **p. cruzado** or **de cruz,** cross-stitch; **p. de absorción,** absorption point; **p. de admiración,** (gram.) exclamation mark or point; **p. de aguja,** needle point (in embroidery); **p. de apoyo,** (mec.) fulcrum, support; (mil.) strong point; **p. débil,** weak point; **p. de cadeneta,** (sew.) chain stitch; **p. de caída,** (artil.) point of fall; **p. de caramelo,** (cul.) hard ball syrup stage; **p. decisivo,** turning point; **p. de congelación,** freezing point; **p. de cordoncillo,** (sew.) cord stitch, twist stitch; **p. de costado,** (med.) sharp stabbing pain, stitch; **p. de distancia,** point of distance (in perspective); **p. de ebullición,** boiling point; **p. de encaje,** (sew.) lace stitch; **p. de encendido,** ignition point, flash point; **p. de explosión,** (mil.) bursting point; **p. de fuga,** vanishing point (in perspective); **p. de fusión,** melting point; **p. de galibo** or **de cartabón,** (ry.) clearance point; **p. de honor,** point of honor; (her.) honor point; **p. de honra,** honor, integrity; **p. de inflamabilidad,** flash point; **p. de inflexión,** (math.) point of inflection; **p. de interrogación,** (gram.) question mark; **p. de observación,** observation point; **p. de ojal,** (sew.) buttonhole stitch; **p. de partida,** starting point, point of departure; **p. de resistencia,** (mil.) strongpoint; **p. de rocío,** (meteorol.) dew point; **p. de saturación,** saturation point; **p. de tafetán,** (tex.) taffeta or plain weave; **p. de tangencia,** (math.) point of inflection; **p. de vista,** (fig.) viewpoint, point of view; **p. en boca,** silence, mum's the word, don't say a word; **p. equinoccial,** (astron., geog.) equinoctial point, equinox; **p. final,** final full stop or period (at the end of a piece of writing); **p. interrogante,** (gram.) question or interrogation mark or point; **p. muerto,** dead point or center; **p. muerto superior,** top dead center; **p. de candelilla,** carpet stitch, overhand stitch; over-and-over stitch; **p. principal,** principal point, center of vision (in perspective); **p. radiante,** (astron.) radiant, radiant point (point from which a star radiates); **p. redondo,** final full stop or period (at the end or a piece of writing); **p. y seguido,** full stop or period within a paragraph; **p. vocálico,** vowel point; **puntos suspensivos,** (gram.) suspension points, dots and dashes, dotted line; **p. torcido,** (sew.) cord stitch, twist stitch; **p. y coma,** (gram.) semicolon; **p. por p.,** point by point, in detail; **sacar de p.,** (sculp.) to copy exactly; **sin faltar p. ni coma,** (coll.) in the minutest detail, exactly; **subir de p.,** to grow, increase; to get worse.

puntoso, sa, *a.* 1. full of points, spiky. 2. punctilious, scrupulous, honorable, honest.

puntuación, *f.* punctuation.

puntual, *a.* 1. punctual, prompt. 2. sure, certain. 3. adequate, convenient.

puntualice, puntualicé, *ref.* **puntualizar.**

puntualidad, *f.* punctuality.

puntualizar, (*ref. 53*) *tr.v.* 1. to fix, stamp, imprint (in the mind or memory). 2. to detail, report or describe in detail, give a detailed account of. 3. to perfect, finish, give the finishing touch to.

puntualmente, *adv.* punctually, exactly, accurately.

puntuar, (*ref. 55*) *tr.v.* 1. to punctuate. 2. to score.

puntuoso, sa, *a.* punctilious, scrupulous, honorable, honest.

puntura, *f.* 1. puncture, prick. 2. (print.) register point, point. 3. (vet.) bloodletting of a horse's hoof.

punzada, *f.* 1. prick; stab. 2. stabbing or shooting pain, stitch. 3. pang (of grief, etc.).

punzador, ra, *m.* puncher (person). —*f.* punch, punching machine.

punzadura, *f.* prick, puncture.

punzante, *a.* sharp, stabbing, shooting (pain).

punzar, (*ref. 53*) *tr.v.* 1. to prick, puncture; to punch, pierce, perforate. 2. to grieve, sting (remorse, regret). —*i.v.* to cause a sharp pain, throb.

punzó, *m.* bright red (color).

punzón, *m.* 1. punch, awl, bodkin, boring tool; burin, graver. 2. punch, puncheon, figured stamp. 3. budding horn (of an animal). 4. (mach.) mandril, drift punch. — **p. ahusado,** taper punch; **p. de centrar,** center punch; **p. múltiple,** gang punch.

punzonería, *f.* (print.) set of puncheons (of a font of type).

puñada, *f.* punch, cuff, blow.

puñado, *m.* handful, fistful; (fig.) handful, a few, e.g. *un puñado de soldados,* a few soldiers. — **a puñados,** in handfuls (when it should be in driblets), in driblets (when it should be in handfuls).

puñal, *m.* dagger, poniard.

puñalada, *f.* 1. stab (with a dagger or a knife). 2. (fig.) sudden stab of pain or shock of grief. — **p. de misericordia,** coup de grace, finishing stroke; **coser a puñaladas a uno,** (coll.) to cut one up, cut to pieces.

puñalejo, *m. dim. of* **puñal,** small dagger.

puñalero, *m.* maker or seller of daggers or poniards.

puñera, *f.* 1. contents of both cupped hands, double handful. 2. flour measure (about a third of a peck).

puñeta, *f.* (vulg.) masturbation; **hacer la p.,** to masturbate.

puñetazo, *m.* punch, blow, cuff, fisticuff.

puñete, *m.* 1. fisticuff, punch, blow. 2. bracelet, wristband.

puño, *m.* 1. fist. 2. handful, fistful. 3. wristband, cuff (of a sleeve). 4. hilt (of a sword); handle (of an umbrella, cane, etc.); head (of a walking stick); handlebar (of a bicycle). 5. handful, little bit, e.g. *un p. de casa,* a tiny house. 6. (mar.) corner (of a sail). 7. (*pl.*) courage, pluck, strength, e.g. *hombre de puños,* strong or brave man. — **apretar los puños,** (coll.) to buckle to, do one's utmost (to accomplish or finish something); **a p. cerrado,** with the fists (blows); **creer a p. cerrado,** (coll.) to believe firmly; **de propio p.,** by one's own hand, in one's own hand;

jugarla de p., or **pegarla de p. a uno,** (coll.) to bamboozle, take in or deceive; **meter en un p. a uno** (coll.) to intimidate, squash (coll.); **partir al p.,** (mar.) to luff; **por sus puños,** (coll.) through one's own efforts, with great personal effort, sweating blood; **p. en rostro,** (coll.) miser, tight-fisted person, tightwad, skinflint.
pupa, *f.* 1. pustule, pimple; scab. 2. injury, harm, pain (in baby language). 3. (ento.) pupa. — **hacer p. a,** (coll.) to hurt, do harm to, injure.
pupila, *f. ref.* **pupilo.**
pupilaje, *m.* 1. pupilage, wardship, tutelage. 2. boarding house; board, boarding-house rate.
pupilar, *a.* 1. pupillary (pertaining to a ward). 2. (anat.) pupillary, pupilary.
pupilero, ra, *m., f.* boarding-house keeper.
pupilo, la, *m., f.* 1. boarder (person living in a boarding house; student at boarding school). 2. pupil, ward (under guardian). — **a pupilo,** as a boarder, on bed and board; **medio pupilo,** boarder who eats only midday meal in a boarding house; student who stays at school for lunch. —*f.* 1. (anat.) pupil (of the eye). 2. (iron.) prostitute. — **tener p.,** to be very smart.
pupitre, *m.* school desk, writing desk. — **p. de distribución,** (elec.) control desk, control panel.
pupo, *m.* (S. Amer.) navel.
puposo, sa, *a.* pustulous, pimply, scabby.
pupusa, *f.* (Hond., cul.) corn and cheese turnover.
pupuso, sa, *a.* 1. (Guat.) chubby, stout. 2. swollen. 3. conceited, vain.
puquio, *m.* (S. Amer.) spring (of water).
puramente, *adv.* 1. purely, chastely. 2. purely, strictly. 3. (law) without qualification, restriction or time limit.
purana, *m.* purana (Hindu epic or legend).
puré, *m.* (cul.) purée; thick soup; **p. de guisantes,** pea soup; **p. de papas,** mashed potatoes.
purear, *i.v.* (coll.) to smoke cigars.
purera, *f.* cigar box or case, humidor.
pureza, *f.* purity, pureness; limpidity; genuineness.
purga, *f.* 1. purgative, laxative, purge, cathartic. 2. (pol.) purge. 3. residues, dregs (of some industrial processes).
purgable, *a.* that can or should be purged.
purgación, *f.* 1. purging, purgation, purge. 2. serving (of a prison sentence). 3. expiation (of), atonement (for sins). 4. cleansing, purification. 5. menstrual blood. 6. gonorrhea, clap (sl.).
purgamiento, *m.* 1. purging, purgation. 2. atonement, expiation. 3. cleansing, purification.
purgante, *a.* purgative. —*m.* purgative, laxative, physic, cathartic.
purgar, (*ref. 51*) *tr.v.* 1. to purge, cleanse; to purify; to drain. 2. to atone for, expiate (one's sins). 3. to purge, give a purge or laxative to. 4. (law) to clear (of guilt, suspicions, etc.) —*r v.* 1. to take a purge or laxative. 2. to free, clear or rid oneself (of a moral guilt, a nuisance).
purgativo, va, *a.* purgative, cathartic.
purgatorio, ria, *a., var. of* **purgativo** —*m.* (rel., fig.) purgatory.
purgue, purgué, *ref.* **purgar.**
puridad, *f.* 1. purity, pureness. 2. secret; secrecy, stealth. — **en p.,** clearly, plainly, frankly; in secret, secretly, stealthily.
purificación, *f.* 1. purification, purifying; cleansing. 2. (ecc.) purification (of the chalice).
purificadero, ra, *a.* purifying, cleansing.
purificador, ra, *a.* purifying, cleansing. —*m., f.* purifier, cleanser. —*m.* (ecc.) purificator.
purificante, *a.* purifying.
purificar, (*ref. 50*) *tr.v.* to purify, depurate; to cleanse. —*r.v.* to become purified or cleansed.
purificatorio, ria, *a.* purifying.
purifique, purifiqué, *ref.* **purificar.**
purina, *f.* (chem.) purine, purin.
purísima, *f. abbrev. of* **la Purísima Concepción,** the Immaculate Conception; **la P.,** the Virgin Mary.
purismo, *m.* (art, lit., philos.) purism.
purista, *a.* (art, lit., philos.) purist, puristic. —*m., f.* purist.
puritanismo, *m.* 1. (rel.) Puritanism. 2. (fig.) puritanism, strictness, austerity.
puritano, na, *a.* 1. (rel.) Puritan. 2. (fig.) puritanical, puritanic, austere, strict. —*m., f.* 1. Puritan (member of the religious sect). 2. (fig.) puritan, austere person.
puro, ra, *a.* 1. pure (unadulterated, unalloyed; disinterested; uncorrupted, innocent; chaste; unsullied, spotless). 2. solid, pure (gold, silver). 3. clear (sky). 4. utter, absolute, e.g. *es la pura verdad,* that's the absolute truth. 5. sheer, pure, mere, e.g. *de pura chiripa,* by a sheer fluke, by mere chance. 6. black (coffee), neat, straight (alcoholic drinks). — **a puro,** by dint of, e.g. *a puros golpes,* by dint of blows; **de puro,** completely, extremely, totally. —*m.* cigar.
púrpura, *f.* 1. purple (color; purple cloth; imperial, regal or cardinal's rank or power). 2. (zool.) purple, murex. 3. purple dye. 4. (poet.) blood. 5. (her.) purple, purpura. 6. (med.) purpura, purples. — **p. de Casio,** purple of Cassius.
purpurado, *m.* (ecc.) cardinal.
purpurante, *a.* purpling, giving a purple color.
purpurar, *tr.v.* 1. to dye or color purple. 2. to dress in purple.
purpúrea, *f.* (bot.) burdock.
purpurear, *i.v.* to have or show a purplish tinge.
purpúreo, rea, *a.* purple, purple-colored, purplish.
purpurina, *f.* 1. (chem.) purpurin. 2. (art) bronze or white metal powder (to impart a gold or silver finish).
purpurino, na, *a., var. of* **purpúreo.**
purrela, *f.* poor wine.
purriela, *f.* (coll.) piece of junk or trash.
purulencia, *f.* (med.) purulence, purulency.
purulento, ta, *a.* (med.) purulent.
pus, *m.* (med.) pus.
puse, pusiera, pusiese, *ref.* **poner.**
pusilánime, *a.* pusillanimous, weak, faint-hearted, chicken-hearted.
pusilanimidad, *f.* pusillanimity, faint-heartedness, weakness.
pusinesco, ca, *a.* (Fr.) one-third its natural size (said of a painting).
pústula, *f.* (med., bot.) pustule. — **p. maligna,** (med.) malignant postule, anthrax.
pustuloso, sa, *a.* (med.) pustular.
pusuquear, *i.v.* (Arg.) to sponge, be a sponger or parasite.
puta, *f.* whore, prostitute; **hijo de p.,** (vulg.) son of a bitch.
putaísmo, putanismo, *m.* 1. whoredom, prostitution. 2. brothel. 3. group of prostitutes.
putañear, *i.v.* (coll.) to whore around, go whoring, visit prostitutes or brothels.
putañero, *a.* whoring, libertine, debauched.
putativo, va, *a.* putative, supposed.
putear, *i.v.* 1. (coll.) to whore around, go whoring, visit prostitutes or brothels. 2. to solicit, accost; to propose an illicit assignation; to cruise (U.S., sl.).
putería, *f.* 1. whoredom, prostitution. 2. brothel. 3. (coll.) coquetry, feminine wiles; sexual provocation.
putero, *m.* (coll.) *var. of* **putañero.**
putesco, ca, *a.* (coll.) whorish, pertaining to prostitutes or whoredom.
puto, ta, *a.* loose, promiscuous. —*m.* 1. (derog., vulg.) male prostitute; fag (homosexual). 2. (vulg.) son of a bitch, bastard. 3. (vulg.) pimp.
putrefacción, *f.* putrefaction, rotting, decay.
putrefactivo, va, *a.* putrefactive, putrescent, putrefying.
putrefacto, ta, *a.* rotten, decayed, putrid.
putrescente, *a.* putrescent, rotting, decaying.
putrescible, *a.* putrescible, liable to decay.
putrescina, *f.* (biochem.) putrescine.
putridez, *f.* rottenness, putridness, decay.
pútrido, da, *a.* putrid, rotten, decayed.
puya, *f.* 1. goad, steel point. 2. (Pan.) machete.
puyada, *f.* (Hond.) bullfight.
puyador, *m.* (Hond., Guat., taur.) picador (in a bullfight).
puyar, *tr.v.* 1. (Amer.) to jab or wound with a goad or sharp point. 2. (C. Amer.) to annoy, irritate. —*i.v.* (Chile) to work hard.
puyazo, *m.* wound or jab with a goad.
puyo, *m.* (Arg.) short woolen poncho.
puzol, *m., var. of* **puzolana.**
puzolana, *f.* (min.) pozzolana.
Pyong Yang, *m.* Pyong Yang (capital of North Korea).

Q

Q, *f.* q, eighteenth letter of the Spanish alphabet.
Q.B.S.M., q.b.s.m. *abbrev. of* **que besa su mano,** your humble servant.
Q.E.P.D., q.e.p.d. *abbrev. of* **que en paz descanse,** rest in peace (R.I.P.).
ql. *abbrev. of* **quintal,** hundredweight (cwt).
quántico, ca, *a.* (math.) quantic.
quantum, (*pl.* **quanta**), *m.* quantum; **q. de luz** (phys.) light quantum; **teoría de los quanta,** quantum theory.
que, *rel. pron.* who; whom; that; which; **el q.,** he who; the one who; the one which; **la q.,** she who, the one who; the one which; **los** or **las q.,** those who; the ones who; those which; the one which; **lo q.,** which, a thing which (when referring to a whole preceding clause), e.g. *es bonita, lo que no quita que sea inteligente,* she's pretty, which doesn't preclude her being smart; what (when introducing a noun clause), e.g. *no sé lo q. quieres decir con esas palabras,* I don't know what you mean with those words; **el q. más y el q. menos,** everybody, more or less, everyone. —*conj.* 1. that, e.g. *dijeron q. la habían despachado,* they said that they had posted it. 2. than, e.g. *sabe mucho más q. Juan,* he knows much more than John. 3. because, since, for, e.g. *lo hará, q. ha prometido hacerlo,* he will do it, since he has promised to. 4. that, with the result that, e.g. *habló tan rápido, q. no entendí una palabra,* he spoke so quickly that I didn't understand one word. 5. and, e.g. *suyo es el error, q. no el mío,* it is his error (and) not mine. 6. following a command, wish, etc., and followed by the subjunctive, it can be translated by "that" + *subj.,* by an infinitive or by the indicative alone, e.g. *quiero q. venga,* I want him to come, *espero q. venga,* I hope he comes, *le dije q. lo hiciera,* I told him that he should do it. 7. let, e.g. *q. venga, si quiere,* let him come if he wants to. 8. let's hope, e.g. *q. no llueva,* let's hope it doesn't rain. 9. as if, as though, e.g: *corre q. vuela,* he runs as if he were flying. 10. and (used for emphasis), e.g. *uno trabaja q. trabaja y no consigue nada,* one works and works and doesn't get anything. 11. definitely (when used with "sí" and "no"), e.g. *sí, q. lo haré,* yes, I'll definitely do it; **a q.,** I bet, e.g. *a q. no lo hace,* I bet he doesn't do it.
qué, *a.* 1. which, e.g. *¿q. libro sacaste de la biblioteca?* which book did you take out of the library? 2. what, e.g. *¡q placer verte otra vez!* what a pleasure to see you again! —*adv.* how, e.g. *¡q. bonito!* how pretty! —*pron.* what, e.g. *no sé q. decir,* I don't know what to say. — **¡a mí q.!** so what, what does it matter to me; **no hay de q.,** you're welcome, don't mention it; **¿para q.?** what for? why?; **¿por q.?** why?; **q. de,** what a crowd of, how many, e.g. *q. de gente en la plaza,* what a crowd of people in the square; **¡q. sé yo!** how should I know! **¿q. tal?** how are you? **sin q. ni para q.,** for no reason at all; **¿y q.?** so what?
quebracho, *m.* (bot.) quebracho, quebracho bark.
quebrada, *f.* 1. ravine, gorge; crack, break, fissure (in the ground). 2. (Amer.) stream, rivulet.
quebradero, *m.* (obs.) breaker, splitter. — **q. de cabeza,** (coll.) worry, bother.
quebradillo, *m.* 1. French heel, high curved heel. 2. bending of the body (in dancing).
quebradizo, za, *a.* 1. fragile, weak, easily broken, brittle, friable. 2. frail, delicate, weak, sickly. 3. trilling (voice).
quebrado, da, *past part. of* **quebrar.** —*a.* 1. broken. 2. weak, weakened. 3. bankrupt. 4. (med.) ruptured. 5. broken, rough, uneven (terrain). —*m., f.* 1. bankrupt person. 2. (med.) person afflicted with a hernia. —*m.* 1. (math.) fraction. 2. (Cuba) tobacco leaf full of holes. — **q. compuesto,** (math.) compound fraction; **q. decimal,** (math.) decimal fraction; **q. impropio,** (math.) improper fraction; **q. propio,** (math.) proper fraction.
quebrador, ra, *a.* breaking. —*m., f.* breaker; violator (of law).
quebradura, *f.* 1. break, split, crack; fissure, gap. 2. (med.) fracture; rupture, hernia.
quebraja, *f.* crack, split, fissure; flaw.
quebrajar, *tr.v., i.v., r.v.* to crack, split.
quebrajoso, sa, *a.* 1. fragile, weak, easily broken. 2. full of cracks.
quebrantable, *a.* delicate, fragile, frangible.
quebrantado, da, *a.* split, broken, fractured.
quebrantador, ra, *a.* breaking; crushing; weakening. —*m., f.* breaker; violator, transgressor. —*f.* crusher, breaker (machine).
quebrantadura, *f., var. of* **quebrantamiento.**
quebrantahuesos, (*pl.* **quebrantahuesos**), *m.* 1. (ornith.) osprey, sea eagle; lammergeier (Gypaetus barbatus). 2. children's game. 3. (coll.) bore, tiresome person.
quebrantamiento, *m.* 1. breaking; crushing; grinding. 2. violation, breaking (of law, promise, etc.). 3. fatigue, exhaustion; ill-being.
quebrantaolas, (*pl.* **quebrantaolas**), *m.* 1. (mar.) breakwater, old ship used as a breakwater. 2. (mar.) small auxiliary buoy (tied to a larger buoy).
quebrantapiedras, (*pl.* **quebrantapiedras**), *f.* (bot.) burstwort.
quebrantar, *tr.v.* 1. to break; to crush, grind. 2. to break (law, contract, promise, etc.). 3. to break out of (prison). 4. to weaken, break (health, strength); to crush (one's spirit). 5. to desecrate, defile. 6. to moderate, diminish (heat, cold); to tone down (a color). 7. to annoy, vex. 8. (law) to revoke, annul (a will). 9. (Amer.) to break in (a horse). —*r.v.* 1. to break, crack, split, become cracked or split. 2. to break down (one's health); to be crushed (one's spirit); to be weakened, go to pieces (in health).
quebranto, *m.* 1. weakness (of health); ruin, undermining (of health). 2. sorrow, affliction, grief. 3. ruin, loss, damage or injury. 4. breaking; crushing.
quebrar, (*ref. 29*) tr.v. 1. to break; to grind, crush. 2. to break (promise, contract, law, etc.). 3. to bend, twist. 4. to interrupt, break off (inspiration, concentration, etc.). 5. to temper, soften, moderate. 6. to discolor, wrinkle (complexion). —*i.v.* 1. to break (with someone). 2. (com.) to go bankrupt. —*r.v.* 1. to break, be broken 2. to be broken or crushed (in spirit). 3. to become discolored or faded, lose its color, become wrinkled (the complexion). 4. to get a rupture or hernia. 5. to be broken (a range of hills).
quebrazas, *f.* (*pl.*) flaws in a sword blade.
quebrazón, *m.* (Amer.) crashing, breakage (of glass, china, etc.).
queche, *m.* (mar.) ketch, smack.
quechemarín, *m.* (mar.) two-masted lugger.
quechol, *m.* (Mex., ornith.) flamingo.
quechua, *a., m., f.* Quechuan. —*m.* Quechua (language).
queda, *f.* 1. curfew. 2. (mil.) taps. 3. (arch.) curfew bell.
quedada, *f.* stay, sojourn.
quedamente, *adv.* softly, in a low voice.
quedar, *i.v.* 1. to remain, stay, stay behind. 2. to be left, be left over, e.g. *me quedan dos pesetas,* I have two pesetas left. 3. to finish, stop, e.g. *allí quedó la discusión,* the argument stopped there, there the argument remained. 4. to be, be situated, e.g. *¿dónde queda el museo?* where is the museum? 5. to be, get, e.g. *él quedó herido del choque,* he was or got wounded in the crash, *quedamos conformes,* we are in agreement, we agree. — **¿en qué quedamos?** where do we stand? **q. atrás,** to be left behind, get left behind, be surpassed; to fail to understand completely; **q. (uno) bien or mal,** to make a good or bad impression; to come out well or badly (from a business transaction, etc.); **q. en que,** to agree that; **q. (uno) limpio,** (coll.) to be cleaned out, be left flat, broke or penniless; **q. por** + *inf.,* to remain to be + *past part.,* be still to be + *past part.,* e.g. *mucho queda por hacer,* much remains to be done; **q. por,** to come out as, come to be regarded as, be left as, e.g. *él quedó por inteligente,* he came to be regarded as intelligent. —*r.v.* 1. to remain, stay. 2. to be left, e.g. *se quedó todo sin vender,* all was left unsold. — **quedarse a oscuras,** (coll.) to be left in the dark, fail to understand; **quedarse atrás,** to get left behind; to lose heart, become discouraged, back out; **quedarse con,** to keep, take, e.g. *él se quedó con el libro,* he kept the book; **q. dormido,** to fall asleep; **quedarse frío,** to be dumbfounded, flabbergasted or frozen with surprise; **quedarse muerto,** (coll.) to be frozen or petrified (with surprise, horror), be overcome (with grief); **quedarse riendo,** (coll.) to thumb one's nose, snap one's fingers; **quedarse yerto,** to be petrified (with shock).
quede, (print.) let stand; stet.
quedito, *adv.* quietly, noiselessly, softly; gently.
quedo, da, *a.* 1. quiet, soft, low (voice). 2. quiet, tranquil.
quedo, *adv.* 1. softly, in a whisper, quietly. 2. carefully. — **de q.,** little by little, slowly; **¡quedo!** quiet! gently! easy!
quehacer, *m.* work, task, chore; occupation, business. — (*pl.*) **quehaceres de casa,** household chores.

queja, *f.* 1. complaint; plaint, lament; moan, groan. 2. grudge, resentment.
quejar, *r.v.* to complain; to groan, moan; **quejarse de una cosa,** to complain of or about something; **quejarse de** + *inf.,* to complain of + *ger.*
quejicoso, sa, *a.* whiny, querulous, grumbling, complaining, plaintive.
quejido, *m.* moan, lament.
quejigal, quejigar, *m.* grove of gall oaks.
quejigo, *m.* (bot.) gall oak; young oak tree.
quejilloso, sa, *a., var. of* **quejicoso.**
quejosamente, *adv.* complainingly, plaintively; querulously, grumblingly.
quejoso, sa, *a.* plaintive, complaining; querulous.
quejumbre, *f.* whining, grumbling.
quejumbroso, sa, *a.* plaintive, complaining, whining, grumbling.
quela, *f.* (zool.) chela.
quelato, *m.* (chem.) chelate.
quelícero, *m.* (zool.) chelicera.
quelonio, nia, *a., m.* (zool.) chelonian; (*pl.*) (zool.) Chelonia (turtle family).
quema, *f.* burning; fire; **a q. ropa,** pointblank; **hacer q.** (Arg., Bol.), to hit the target; **huir de la q.,** to run away from danger; to sidestep or dodge an obligation.
quemada, *f.* 1. burnt forest or brush. 2. (Mex.) fire (disaster). 3. (Cuba) disappointment.
quemadero, ra, *a.* to be burned. —*m.* stake (for the burning of those sentenced to death by fire); incinerator (of dead animals and garbage).
quemado, da, *past part. of* **quemar.** —*a.* 1. burnt, scorched. 2. angry, irritated. —*m.* burnt forest or brush; (coll.) something burning; **q. por el sol,** sunburned.
quemador, ra, *a.* burning; incendiary (guilty of arson). —*m., f.* burner; incendiary, firebug (U.S., coll.). —*m.* burner (gas, oil, etc.); **q. de gas,** gas ring or burner; **q. auxiliar,** (aer.) afterburner of jet engine.
quemadura, *f.* 1. burn; scald. 2. smut (plant disease). 3. plant blight. — **q. de segundo grado,** (med.) second-degree burn; **q. de tercer grado,** (med.) third-degree burn.
quemajoso, sa, *a.* burning, smarting.
quemante, *a.* burning.
quemar, *tr.v.* 1. to burn; to burn down; to parch, scorch. 2. to burn, to sting, smart. 3. to sell cheaply. 4. to blight, blast, wither (the sun or frost - plants). 5. (coll.) to annoy, irritate, make impatient. 6. to distill (wine). — **q. balas** or **cartuchos,** to fire shots; **q. sus barcos,** to burn one's ships. —*i.v.* to be very hot. —*r.v.* 1. to burn; to get burnt. 2. to burn (with passion). 3. (coll.) to get annoyed, irritated or steamed up. 4. (coll.) to be hot, be warm, be near the solution of. 5. to become scorched or frostbitten (plants). 6. to blow, burn out (fuses); **quemarse las pestañas or cejas,** to burn the midnight oil.
quemarropa, a q., pointblank.
quemazón, *f.* 1. burning, burn; intense heat. 2. (coll.) itch, itching. 3. (coll.) cutting remark. 4. (coll.) pique, annoyance. 5. bargain sale. 6. (Arg., Bol., Chile) mirage on the pampas.
quena, *f.* (Amer.) Indian reed flute.
quenopodiáceo, cea, *a.* (bot.) chenopodiaceous. —*f.* (*pl.*) Chenopodiaceae.
quenopodio, *m.* (bot.) chenopod, goosefoot.
quepis, *m.* (mil.) kepi.
quepo, quepa, *ref.* **caber.**
queque, *m.* (Amer.) cake.
querando, *m.* an ancient tribe of South American Indians.
queratina, *f.* (biochem.) keratin.
queratitis, *f.* (med.) keratitis, inflammation of the cornea.
queratófiro, *m.* (geol.) keratophyre.
queratosis, *f.* (med.) keratosis.
quercético, ca, *a.* (chem.) quercetic.
quercetina, *f.* (chem.) quercetin.
quercitol, *m.* (chem.) quercitol, acorn sugar.
quercitrón, *m.* (bot., chem.) quercitron.
querella, *f.* 1. quarrel, controversy, dispute. 2. moan, wail. 3. (law) complaint, accusation; action, suit; petition, appeal.
querellador, ra, querellante, *m., f.* (law) complainant, plaintiff.
querellarse, *r.v.* 1. (law) to file a complaint, bring suit (against). 2. to lament, moan, bewail.
querellosamente, *adv.* plaintively, querulously.
querelloso, sa, *a.* querulous, whining, grumbling; complaining. —*m., f.* complainant, plaintiff.
querencia, *f.* 1. haunt, lair (favorite place frequented by animals); (coll.) home, lair, favorite spot; (taur.) favorite spot (of the bull in the bull ring). 2. fondness, liking, affection, attraction, inclination; attachment to one's home or early environment.
querencioso, sa, *a.* home-loving; haunt-loving; fond of its lair (said of animals).
querendón, na, *a.* (Chile) very affectionate, loving.
querer, *m.* love, affection, fondness.
querer, (*ref. 17*) *t.v.* 1. to want; to wish, will, desire. 2. to love, be fond of, like. 3. to require, need. 4. to accept a bet. — **como quiera que,** however, in whatever way; inasmuch as, since; **cuando quiera,** any time; **cuando quiera que,** whenever; **cuanto quiera que,** however, in whatever way; inasmuch as, since; **donde quiera,** anywhere, everywhere; **do quiera,** anywhere, everywhere; **¿qué más quieres?** what more do you want?; **que quiera, que no quiera,** whether he wants it or not; **¿qué quiere decir eso?** what do you mean by that?; **¡qué quieres!** or **¡qué quieres que le haga!,** what can one do! there's nothing to be done about it!; **q.** + *inf.,* to want, wish or desire to + *inf.;* **q. a alguien,** to like, love or be fond of someone; **q. bien a,** to love very much; **q. es poder,** where there's a will there's a way; **sin q.,** unintentionally, without meaning to; by chance, fortuitously. —*impers. v.* to look like, look as if it were about or going to, be trying to (rain, shine), e.g. *quiere llover,* it looks as if it's going to rain.
queresa, *f., var. of* **cresa.**
querido, da, *past part. of* **querer.** —*a.* dear, e.g. *Querido Juan,* Dear John (beginning of a letter). —*m., f.* 1. paramour. 2. (coll.) honey, darling. —*m.* lover. —*f.* mistress.
queriente, *a.* 1. loving. 2. willing.
quermes, *m.* 1. (ento.) kermes insect. 2. (chem.) kermes (dye). — **q. mineral,** (chem.) kermes mineral.
quermese, *f.* charity bazaar or fair.
querocha, *f., var. of* **cresa.**
querochar, *i.v.* to lay eggs (said of bees and other insects).
querosén, querosene, queroseno, querosín, *m.* kerosene.
quersoneso, *m.* chersonese, peninsula.
querub, querube, *m.* (poet.) cherub, cherubim.
querúbico, ca, *a.* cherubic.
querubín, *m.* cherubim, cherub.
querva, *f.* (bot.) castor-oil plant.
quesadilla, *f.* cheesecake; pastry filled with syrup and conserves; (Hond., Mex.) corn meal pie filled with cheese.
quesear, *i.v.* to make cheese.
quesera, *f.* 1. (woman) cheese maker or seller, dairymaid. 2. cheese dish; cheese mold; cheese board. 3. dairy.
quesería, *f.* 1. cheese factory, dairy. 2. cheese shop or store. 3. cheese-making season.
quesero, ra, *a.* caseous, cheesy. —*m.* cheese maker or seller.
queso, *m.* cheese; **medio q.,** tailor's ironing board; **q. de bola,** Edam cheese; **q. de cerdo,** headcheese; **q. de Emmenthal,** Swiss cheese; **q. de nata,** cream cheese; **q. fresco,** cottage cheese; **q. helado,** ice cream brick; **q. para untar,** cheese spread; **q. suizo,** Swiss cheese.
quetona, *f.* (chem.) ketone.
quetro, *m.* (ornith.) Chilean duck with featherless wings.
quetzal, *m.* 1. monetary unit of Guatemala. 2. (ornith.) quetzal.
quevedos, *m.* (*pl.*) pince-nez.
¡quía! *interj.* (coll.) not really! come, now!
quiasma, *m.* (anat., biol.) chiasma.
quiché, *a., m., f.* Quiche (member of a Mayan tribe in southern Guatemala). —*m.* Quiche (language).
quichua, *a.* Quechuan. —*m., f.* Quechua. —*m.* Quechua, Quechuan (language).
quicial, era, *m., f.* hanging stile; hinge pole.
quicio, *m.* 1. pivot hole. 2. frame jamb (of door or window). — **estar fuera de q.,** to be beside oneself (with fury, joy); **fuera de q.,** out of joint; **sacar de q.,** to put out of joint or kilter; **sacar de q. a uno,** to exasperate, infuriate.
quid, *m.* quiddity, essence, gist.
quídam, *m.* (coll.) so-and-so; (coll.) nobody.
quid pro quo, (Lat.) *m.* 1. an equivalent, a substitute. 2. mistake; mistaken identity.
quiebra, *f.* 1. break, breach; crack, fissure; fracture. 2. loss, injury, damage. 3. bankruptcy, failure.
quiebrahacha, *m.* (bot.) breakax, quebracho.
quiebre, quiebro, *ref.* **quebrar.**
quiebro, *m.* 1. bending at the waist. 2. (mus.) trill. — **dar el q. a,** to avoid, keep away from.
quien, (*pl.* **quienes**), *rel. and interrog. pron.* who, whom; he or she who, the person who, they who, those who; whoever, whomever.
quién, (*pl.* **quiénes**), *interrog., exclam. pron.,* who, whose, e.g. *¿quién me llamó?* who called me? *¿de quién es este libro?* whose book is this? *¡quién lo hubiera creído!* who would have believed it!
quienquiera, (*pl.* **quienesquiera**), *indef. pron.* anyone, anybody; whoever; whomever.
quiera, quiero, *ref.* **querer.**
quietación, *f.* quieting, calming; appeasing.
quietador, ra, *a.* calming, quieting; appeasing. —*m, f.* quieter, calmer; appeaser.
quietamente, *adv.* quietly, calmly.
quietar, *tr.v.* to quiet, calm. —*r.v.* to calm down, become quiet.
quiete, *f.* hour of repose or recreation (after meals).
quietismo, *m.* quietism, a form of religious mysticism.
quietista, *m., f.* quietist.
quieto, ta, *a.* 1. quiet, still, motionless; quiet, peaceful, calm. 2. quiet, silent. 3. orderly, moderate, virtuous.
quietud, *f.* quiet, stillness, tranquility; repose, calm, rest.
quijada, *f.* (anat.) jawbone, jaw.
quijal, quijar, *m.* 1. (anat.) jaw. 2. (anat.) back tooth, molar, grinder.
quijarudo, da, *a.* large-jawed.
quijera, *f.* 1. cheek of crossbow. 2. cheek strap, cheekpiece (of harness). 3. (carp.) tenon.
quijero, *m.* sloping side (of irrigation ditch).
quijo, *m.* quartz (generally acting as matrix for gold or silver).

quijones, *m.* (bot.) (variety of) chervil (Scandix australis).
quijongo, *m.* (C. Rica) stringed instrument used by the Mayan Indians.
quijotada, *f.* quixotism, quixotic act or deed.
quijote, *m.* 1. cuisse (piece of armor). 2. croup, rump (of horse, mule or ass). 3. **Q.,** Quixote, quixotic person.
quijotería, *f.* quixotism, quixotic behavior.
quijotescamente, *adv.* quixotically.
quijotesco, ca, *a.* quixotic, quixotical.
quijotismo, *m.* quixotism, quixotic behavior.
quil. *abrev. of* **quilate,** carat.
quila, *f.* (S. Amer.) quila (type of bamboo).
quilatador, *m.* assayer (of precious metals).
quilatar, *tr.v.* to assay (gems or precious metals).
quilate, *m.* 1. carat. 2. worth, value, carat. — **por quilates,** (coll.) in minute portions, in small amounts.
quilatera, *f.* pearl or diamond sieve (for gauging the size of gems).
quilco, *m.* (Chile) large basket.
quiliárea, *f.* land measure equivalent to 1,000 ares.
quilífero, ra, *a.* (physiol.) chyliferous.
quilificación, *f.* (physiol.) chylification.
quilificar, (*ref. 50*) *tr.v.* (physiol.) to chylify. —*r.v.* to chylify, become chylified.
quilla, *f.* (mar., zool., bot.) keel; **dar de q.,** to keel, keel over, turn keel up; **q. de balance,** (mar.) bilge keel; **q. falsa,** false keel; **q. lateral,** (mar.) bilge keel.
quillango, *m.* (Arg.) fur blanket.
quillay, *m.* (Chile, Arg.) quillai, soapbark tree.
quillotrar, *tr.v.* 1. (coll.) to incite, stir up, excite; to make love to, woo, court; to charm, captivate. 2. to think over, ponder, study. 3. to adorn, dress up. —*r.v.* 1. to fall in love. 2. to dress oneself up, adorn oneself. 3. to complain.
quillotro, *m.* 1. (coll.) incitement, stimulus. 2. (coll.) sign, symptom, indication. 3. (coll.) love affair, love. 4. (coll.) ornament, trimming. 5. (coll.) friend, favorite.
quilma, *f.* large, rough sack.
quilo, *m.* (physiol.) chyle; **sudar el q.,** (coll.) to sweat blood, work oneself to the bone, slave away.
quilo, quilogramo, *m.* kilo, kilogram.
quilográmetro, *m.* kilogrammeter.
quilolitro, *m.* kiloliter.
quilombo, *m.* 1. (Ven.) hut, cabin, shanty. 2. (Chile, Arg.) brothel.
quilométrico, ca, *a.* kilometric.
quilómetro, *m.* kilometer.
quiloso, sa, *a.* (physiol.) chylous.
quilquil, *m.* (Chile) tropical fern.
quiltro, *m.* (Chile) yapper, little yapper (dog).
quimba, *f.* (Col., Ecuad., Ven.) rustic shoe.
quimera, *f.* 1. chimera, chimaera, fantastic idea, fancy. 2. quarrel, dispute. 3. (zool.) chimaera. 4. **Q.,** (myth.) fabulous monster.
quimérico, ca, *a.* chimerical, unreal, unrealistic, illusory.
quimerista, *a.* 1. imaginative, fanciful, fond of fantastic ideas. 2. troublemaking, quarrelsome. —*m., f.* 1. fanciful or imaginative person. 2. troublemaker, wrangler.
quimerizar, (*ref. 53*) *i.v.* to indulge in fanciful ideas.
química, *f.* chemistry. — **q. analítica,** analytical chemistry; **q. geológica,** geo-chemistry; **q. inorgánica,** inorganic chemistry; **q. magnética,** magnetochemistry; **q. nuclear,** nuclear chemistry; **q. orgánica,** organic chemistry.
químicamente, *adv.* chemically.
químico, ca, *a.* chemical. —*m.* chemist.
quimicultura, *f.* hydroponics.
quimífero, ra, *a.* (phys.) chymiferous.
quimificación, *f.* (physiol.) chymification.
quimificar, (*ref. 50*) *tr.v.* (physiol.) to chymify, convert into chyme. —*r.v.* to turn into chyme.
quimiosíntesis, *f.* (physiol.) chemosynthesis.
quimiotaxis, *f.* (biol.) chemotaxis.
quimioterapéutica, *f.* chemotherapy.
quimioterapia, *f.* chemotherapy.
quimista, *m.* alchemist.
quimo, *m.* (physiol.) chyme.
quimógrafo, *m.* (med.) kymograph.
quimón, *m.* (tex.) fine printed cotton.
quimono, *m.* kimono, Japanese robe.
quimoso, sa, *a.* chymous.
quimotaxia, *f.* (bac.) chemotaxis.
quimotripsina, *f.* (biol.) chymotrypsin.
quimurgia, *f.* (chem.) chemurgy.
quina, *f.* 1. horizontal line of five numbers in lotto. 2. (*pl.*) Portuguese coat-of-arms. 3. (*pl.*) double fives (in game of backgammon). 4. (pharm.) cinchona bark, Peruvian bark.
quinado, da, *a.* mixed with quinine.
quinal, *m.* (mar.) preventer (auxiliary cable or rope).
quinaquina, *f.* cinchona bark, Peruvian bark.
quinario, ria, *a.* quinary, consisting of five. —*m.* 1. quinarius (Roman coin). 2. five-day period of devotion.
quincalla, *f.* miscellany of small hardware.
quincallería, *f.* hardware shop; small hardware store or business.
quincallero, ra, *m., f.* maker or seller of small hardware.
quince, *a.* fifteen. —*m.* 1. fifteen; fifteenth (in dates). 2. game of cards.
quincena, *f.* 1. fifteen days, two weeks, fortnight. 2. half-month's pay. 3. (mus.) fifteenth.
quincenal, *a.* fortnightly, semi-monthly.
quincenalmente, *adv.* twice a month, fortnightly.
quinceno, na, *a.* fifteenth. —*m., f.* fifteen-month-old mule. —*f.* (mus.) organ stop; two-octave interval.
quincha, *f.* 1. (S. Amer.) latticework or wicker-work. 2. (Chile, Peru) wall of reeds and adobe.
quinchamalí, *m.* (Chile, bot.) santalaceous medicinal plant (Quinchamalium chilensis).
quinchar, *tr.v.* (S. Amer.) to cover or fence with reed and adobe; to roof or wall with reeds and rush.
quinchihue, *m.* (S. Amer., bot.) (variety of) marigold (Tagetes minuta).
quinchoncho, *m.* (bot.) (variety of) pigeon pea (Cajanus indicus).
quincuagena, *f.* fifty, group of fifty.
quincuagenario, ria, *a., m., f.* quinquagenarian, person over fifty years old.
quincuagésimo, ma, *a.* fiftieth. —*f.* Quinquagesima Sunday.
quincunce, *m.* (hort.) quincunx (arrangement of trees in square with one in the center).
quindécimo, ma, *a., m.,* fifteenth.
quindenial, *a.* fifteen year (lasting fifteen years); fifteen yearly (occuring every fifteen years).
quindenio, *m.* 1. period of fifteen years. 2. portion of ecclesiastical incomes paid to Rome.
quinfa, *f.* (Col.) sandal.
quingentésimo, ma, *a., m.* five-hundredth.
quingombó, *m.* (bot.) okra, gumbo.
quingos, *m.* (*pl.*) (Col., Ecuad., Peru) zigzags.
quinguear, *i.v.* to zigzag.
quinidina, *f.* (chem.) quinidine, quinidin.
quiniela, *f.* punt, a game in which someone bets against the banker.
quinielista, *m., f.* (coll.) 1. punter. 2. wager.
quinientos, tas, *a., m.* five hundred.
quinina, *f.* (chem.) quinine.
quinismo, *m.* (med.) cinchonism, effects of the use of quinine.
quino, *m.* 1. (bot.) cinchona tree. 2. (pharm.) cinchona bark.
quinoa, *f.* (S. Amer.) quinoa, pigweed; quinoa seed (used ground as cereal).
quinoidina, *f.* (chem.) quinoidine, quinoidin.
quínola, *f.* 1. sequence of four cards of same suit. 2. (coll.) strange thing, rarity. — **estar de quínolas,** (coll.) to have various types of things or colors mixed together; to be dressed in various colors.
quinolear, *tr.v.* to arrange cards (for game of quínola).
quinoleína, *f.* (chem.) quinoline, quinolin.
quinona, *f.* (chem.) quinone.
quino-quino, *m.* (Bol., Peru) myroxylon (tree and tolu balsam).
quinoxalina, *f.* (chem.) quinoxaline, quinoxalin.
quinqué, *m.* hurricane lamp; oil or kerosene lamp.
quinquefolio, *m.* (bot.) cinquefoil.
quinquelingüe, *a.* speaking or knowing five languages; written in five languages.
quinquenal, *a.* five-year, quinquennial; **plan q.,** five-year plan.
quinquenervia, *f.* (bot.) ribwort.
quinquenio, *m.* quinquennium, five-year period.
quinquevalente, *a.* (chem.) quinquevalent.
quinta, *f.* 1. country house, manor, villa; (Peru) group of town houses with a common entrance. 2. sequence of five of the same suit, quint (in cards). 3. (Sp.) annual draft, induction of recruits for the army. 4. (mus.) fifth, quint. 5. (fenc.) quinte. — **estar en quintas,** to become liable for military service.
quintacolumnista, *m., f.* (pol.) fifth columnist.
quintador, *m.* official who drafts men for military service.
quintaesencia, *f.* quintessence.
quintaesenciar, *tr.v.* to refine, distill.
quintal, *m.* quintal (46 kilograms, 100 pounds); **q. métrico,** hundred kilograms.
quintalada, *f.* (mar.) primage, hat money.
quintaleño, ña, *a.* capable of containing a quintal.
quintalero, ra, *a.* weighing a quintal.
quintana, *f.* 1. country house, villa. 2. food stall, market stall (in Roman camp).
quintante, *m.* (astron.) quintant.
quintañón, na, *a., m., f.* (coll.) centenarian.
quintar, *tr.v.* 1. to draw one out of every five. 2. to choose by lot (for military service). 3. to plow for the fifth time. 4. to pay the king the fifth part of the booty. —*i.v.* 1. to raise the bid by one fifth (at an auction). 2. to reach the fifth day (the moon).
quintería, *f.* grange, farm house.
quinterno, *m.* 1. section of five sheets of paper, quinternion. 2. horizontal line of five numbers (in lotto).
quintero, *m.* farmer; farm hand.
quinteto, *m.* 1. (mus.) quintet. 2. five line stanza.
Quintiliano, *m.* Quintilian, Roman rhetorician born in Spain.
quintilla, *f.* (poet.) stanza of five octosyllabic lines; any five-lined stanza with two rhymes.
quintillo, *m.* game of ombre played by five.
quintillón, *m.* quintillion.
quintín, *m.* (tex.) quintin (fine linen).
Quintín, Se armó la de San Q., there was a tremendous rumpus.
quinto, ta, *a.* fifth. —*m.* 1. fifth, fifth part. 2. (Sp.) draftee, conscript (chosen by lot). 3. tax of 20%. 4. (Mex., Chile) five centavo piece. 5. (mar.)

fifth part of an hour. — **por los quintos infiernos,** in hell and beyond, in the middle of nowhere, out in the sticks.
quintral, *m.* (bot.) 1. red variety of mistletoe. 2. blight (on watermelons and beans).
quintuplicación, *f.* quintuplication.
quintuplicar, (*ref. 50*) *tr.v., r.v.* to quintuple, quintuplicate.
quíntuplo, pla, *a.* quintuple, fivefold. —*m.* quintuple.
quinua, *f.* (S. Amer., bot.) quinoa, pigweed; (cul.) quinoa seed (used ground as cereal).
quinzavo, va, *a., m.* fifteenth.
quiñado, da, *past part. of* **quiñar.** —*a.* dented, chipped; pockmarked.
quiñar, *tr.v.* 1. (Peru) to dent, chip, nick. 2. (Peru) to hit, knock, bang (two spinning tops). —*r.v.* (Peru) to get dented, chipped or nicked.
quiñazo, *m.* (Amer.) collision, crash.
quiñón, *m.* 1. share, portion. 2. plot of land. 3. (Phil. I.) square measurement of 2.79 hectares.
quío, a, *a., m., f.* Chian, of the Greek isle of Chios. —*m.* **Q.,** Chios.
quiolita, *f.* (min.) chiolite.
quiosco, *m.* kiosk; stand, newsstand, bandstand; pavilion. — **q. de necesidad,** public lavatory.
quipe, *m.* 1. (Peru, Ecuad.) bundle. 2. (Bol., Chile) knapsack.
quipo, quipú, *m.* quipu (ancient Peruvian device used for recording facts and events).
quiquiriquí, (*pl.* **quiquiriquíes**), *m.* 1. cocka-doodle-do (sound of cock). 2. (coll.) cock of the walk.
quiragra, *f.* (med.) chiragra.
quirie, *m.* (ecc.) kirie.
quirinal, *a.* Quirinal. —*m.* **Q.,** Quirinal, palace and hill of Rome.
quirite, *m.* (hist.) quirite, civilian citizen in ancient Rome.
quirófano, *m.* operating theater, operating room.
quirografía, *f.* chirography, handwriting, penmanship.
quirógrafo, *m.* chirograph (document).
quiromancia, *f.* chiromancy, palmistry.
quiromántico, ca, *a.* chiromantic. —*m., f.* chiromancer.
quiropodia, *f.* chiropody.
quiropodista, *m., f.* chiropodist.
quiropráctica, *f.* (med.) chiropractic (system of treatment).
quiropráctico, ca, *m., f.* chiropractor.
quiropraxia, *f.* (med.) chiropraxis, chiropractice (system of treatment).
quiróptero, ra, *a.* (zool.) chiropterous, chiropteran. —*m.* (zool.) chiropteran; (*pl.*) Chiroptera.
quiroteca, *f.* (coll.) glove.
quirquincho, *m.* (Amer.) armadillo.
quirúrgico, ca, *a.* surgical.
quirurgo, *m.* surgeon.
quisca, *f.* 1. (Chile) night blooming cereus (Cereus chilensis); thorn of the night blooming cereus. 2. (Arg., Chile) thick stiff hair.
quiscudo, da, *a.* (Arg., Chile) having thick stiff hair.
quise, *ref.* **querer.**
quiselgur, *m.* (geol.) kieselguhr.
quisicosa, *f.* (coll.) puzzle, riddle, enigma.
quisiera, quisiese, *ref.* **querer.**
quisque, cada q., (coll.) each one.
quisquido, da, *a.* (Arg.) constipated.
quisquilla, *f.* 1. trifle, triviality, quibble. 2. (zool.) shrimp, prawn. — **dejarse de quisquillas,** to stop fussing or quibbling; **pararse en quisquillas,** to fuss or quibble.
quisquilloso, sa, *a.* 1. fussy, fastidious. 2. touchy, irritable. —*m., f.* 1. fusser, quibbler. 2. touchy or irritable person.
quiste, *m.* (med., bot., zool.) cyst.
quisto, ta, *a.* (arch.) liked; **bien q.,** well-received; **mal q.,** disliked.
quita, *f.* (law) acquittance, release, discharge. — **de q. y pon,** removable, detachable. —*interj.* get out; nonsense; God forbid; **¡q. de ahí!** away with you!
quitación, *f.* 1. income, salary. 2. (law) release, acquittance.
quitador, ra, *a.* removing. —*m., f.* remover.
quitaipón, *m., var. of* **quitapón.**
quitamanchas, (*pl.* **quitamanchas**), *m., f.* spot-remover (person). —*m.* spot remover (product).
quitameriendas, (*pl.* **quitameriendas**), *f.* (bot.) meadow saffron, autumn crocus (Colchicum autumnalis).
quitamiento, *m., var. of* **quita.**
quitamotas, (*pl.* **quitamotas**), *m., f.* (coll.) bootlicker, flatterer, obsequious person.
quitanieves, (*pl.* **quitanieves**), *m.* snowplow.
quitanza, *f.* quittance (document indicating payment in full).
quitapelillos, (*pl.* **quitapelillos**), *m., f.* (coll.) bootlicker, flatterer, fawner.
quitapesares, (*pl.* **quitapesares**), *m.* (coll.) solace, comfort.
quitapón, *m.* headstall for mules; **de q.,** detachable, removable.
quitar, *tr.v.* 1. to remove, subtract, take away, e.g. *le quitaron el puesto a Juan,* they took the job away from John; to take off, e.g. *le quité la chaqueta,* I took his jacket off. 2. to eliminate, erase, delete, e.g. *q. una coma,* to delete a comma. 3. to steal, take; to deprive of. 4. to release or redeem (a pledge). 5. (law) to repeal, annul, abrogate. 6. to free or exonerate (from an obligation, guilt, etc.). 7. (fenc.) to parry. — **al q.,** impermanent; (law) redeemable; **de quita y pon,** removable, detachable; **¡quita!** or **¡quite!,** (coll.) nonsense! I don't believe a word of it!; **q. la mesa,** to clear the table; **quitarle a uno las palabras de la boca,** to take the words out of one's mouth; **sin q. ni poner,** faithfully, accurately, exactly, without additions or omissions; **vender al q.,** (law) to sell with the option to buy back. —*r.v.* 1. to remove, take off (one's clothing). 2. to take (i.e., one's life). 3. to withdraw, leave, quit. 4. to come out (a stain). — **quitarse de encima,** to get rid of, free oneself of.
quitasol, *m.* sunshade, parasol.
quitasueño, *m.* (coll.) worry, preoccupation.
quite, *m.* 1. dodge, dodging. 2. (fenc.) parry. 3. hindrance, obstacle. 4. (taur.) attracting the bull to save another man from danger. — **estar al q.,** to be ready to defend someone; **ir al q.,** to go to someone's help; **no tener q.,** to be unavoidable.
quiteño, ña, *a.* of or from Quito. —*m., f.* inhabitant or native of Quito, Ecuador.
quitina, *f.* (biochem.) chitin.
quitinoso, sa, *a.* chitinous.
quito, ta, *a.* free, released, clear, exempt.
Quito, *m.* Quito, capital of Ecuador.
quitón, *m.* 1. (zool.) chiton. 2. (hist.) chiton (Greek garment).
quitrín, *m.* (Cuba) gig, light, open horse-drawn carriage.
quizá, quizás, *adv.* maybe, perhaps.
quorum, *m.* quorum.

R

R, *f. r.* nineteenth letter of the Spanish alphabet.
Ra, *m.* (myth.) Ra, the principal deity of the ancient Egyptians.
Ra, *sym. of* **radio,** radium (Ra).
raba, *f.* fishing bait made of codfish roe.
rabada, *f.* hind quarter, rump (of slaughtered animal).
rabadán, *m.* head shepherd.
rabadilla, *f.* (anat.) coccyx; uropygium (in birds); (coll.) Pope's nose, parson's nose.
rabanal, *m.* radish field, plot or patch.
rabanero, ra, *a.* 1. (coll.) short (skirt). 2. (coll.) vulgar, coarse (language, manners). —*m., f.* radish seller. —*f.* fishwife, vulgar, sluttish woman.
rabanillo, *m.* 1. *dim. of* **rábano,** small radish. 2. (bot.) jointed charlock. 3. sour taste (of turning wine). 4. (coll.) coolness, disdain. 5. (fig., coll.) eagerness, longing.
rabaniza, *f.* 1. radish seed. 2. (bot.) jointed charlock.
rábano, *m.* 1. (bot.) radish. 2. sour taste (of wine). — **r. silvestre,** (bot.) jointed charlock; **tomar el r. por las hojas,** (coll.) to be entirely mistaken, to be off the track.
Rabat, *m.* Rabat (capital of Morocco).
rabazuz, *m.* licorice extract.
rabdomancia, *f.* rhabdomancy, divination by a rod or wand.
rabear, *i.v.* to wag the tail.
rabel, *m.* 1. (mus.) rebec, ancient stringed instrument. 2. (hum.) backside, behind.
rabelejo, *m. dim. of* **rabel,** small rebec.
rabeo, *m.* wagging of the tail.
rabera, *f.* 1. tail end. 2. chaff (of corn). 3. handle (of a crossbow, of a tool).
raberón, *m.* top part of felled tree.
rabí, (*pl.* **rabíes**), *m.* rabbi, rabbin.
rabia, *f.* 1. anger, fury, rage. 2. (med., vet.) rabies, hydrophobia. 3. (Guat.) game of tag. —**con r.,** (Car.) hard, e.g. *llueve con r.,* it is raining hard; **tener r. a (una persona),** (coll.) to have a grudge against someone; **tomar r.,** to contract the rabies; to get very angry, get furious.
rabiacana, *f.* (bot.) wake robin.
rabiada, *f.* (Hond.) fit of fury or anger.
rabiar, *i.v.* 1. to get furious or mad, be furious, rave; to get or be impatient. 2. to be in great pain, scream or moan with pain. 3. to have rabies. — **a r.,** tremendously, enormously, exceedingly; **estar a r. con,** (coll.) to be furious with; **que rabia,** (coll.) like mad, e.g. *pica que rabia,* it stings like mad; **r. de** + *a.,* to be exceedingly + *a.,* e.g. *rabia de tonto,* he is extremely stupid; **r. por algo,** to yearn or be dying for something; **r. por** + *inf.,* to yearn or be dying.
rabiatar, *tr.v.* to tie by the tail.
rabiazorras, *m.* (coll.) east wind.
rabicán, rabicano, na, *a.* white-tailed.
rábico, ca, *a.* (med., vet.) rabid.
rabicorto, ta, *a.* short-tailed, bob-tailed, docked.
rábida, *f.* convent, monastery (in Morocco).
rábido, da, *a., var. of* **rabioso.**
rabieta, *f.* (coll.) tantrum, fit of temper.
rabihorcado, *m.* (ornith.) frigate bird.
rabilargo, ga, *a.* long-tailed. —*m.* (ornith.) blue magpie.
rabillo, *m.* 1. *dim. of* **rabo,** small tail. 2. (bot.) leafstalk; flower stalk. 3. (bot.) bearded darnel. 4. (agr.) mildew spots (on cereals). 5. back straps of trousers. — **mirar con el r. del ojo,** to look out of the corner of one's eye.
rabínico, ca, *a.* rabbinical, rabbinic.
rabinismo, *m.* rabbinism.
rabinista, *m., f.* rabbinist.
rabino, *m.* rabbi, rabbin.
rabión, *m.* (*pl.*) rapids (in a river).
rabiosamente, *adv.* angrily, furiously.
rabioso, sa, *a.* 1. furious, angry. 2. violent, rabid, vehement, raving. 3. (med.) rabid, affected with rabies.
rabisalsera, *a.* (coll.) pert, forward (woman).
rabiza, *f.* 1. tip, end (esp. of fishing rod). 2. (mar.) short rope or cable.
rabo, *m.* 1. tail (of a quadruped). 2. (bot.) flower stalk. 3. (coll., fig.) tail, train. 4. rag pinned to a person's dress as a joke. — **con el r. entre las piernas,** with one's tail between one's legs, crestfallen; **ir al r. de otro,** (coll.) to follow fawningly or servilely at someone's heels; **ir** or **salir con el r. entre las piernas,** (coll.) to go or come out with one's tail between one's legs, be completely squashed or abashed; **mirar uno con el r. del ojo,** (coll.) to look out of the corner of one's eye; **quien tiene r. de paja no debe acercarse al fuego,** people who live in glass houses should not throw stones; **r. de junco,** (ornith.) a tropical bird; **r. del ojo,** corner of (one's) eye; **r. de zorra,** (bot.) foxtail, plume grass; **rabos de gallo,** cirrus (cloud).
rabón, na, *a.* short-tailed, bobtailed; (Guat., Mex.) short; (Guat., Mex.) wearing a short dress.
rabona, *f.* (Amer.) soldier's wife, camp follower. — **hacer r.,** (coll.) to play hooky, play truant.
rabopelado, *m.* (zool.) oppossum.
raboseada, raboseadura, *f.* mussing, ruffling, crumpling; fraying.
rabosear, *tr.v.* to muss, crumple, ruffle; to fray.
raboso, sa, *a.* frayed, ragged, tattered.
rabotada, *f.* coarse remark, insolent reply.
rabotear, *tr.v.* to cut off, crop or dock the tail of.
raboteo, *m.* tail cropping.
rabudo, da, *a.* long-tailed, thick-tailed.
rábula, *m.* pettifogger, shyster lawyer.
raca, *f.* (mar.) traveler.
racamento, ta, *m., f.* (mar.) parral, parrel.
racel, *m.* (mar.) dead-rising (each of the vertical frames in the run of a ship).
racemato, *m.* (chem.) racemate.
racha, *f.* 1. squall, gust of wind. 2. (coll.) streak, run (of luck), series (of robberies, etc.). 3. large chip of wood. 4. split, crack (in wood).
racial, *a.* racial, pertaining to races.
racima, *f.* bunches of small grapes left on vines (after vintage).
racimado, da, *a.* in a cluster, in a bunch.
racimal, *a.* pertaining to clusters or racemes.
racimar, *tr.v.* to pick the remaining grapes from (the vines after vintage). —*r.v.* to form clusters or bunches.
racimo, *m.* cluster, bunch; (bot.) raceme.
racimoso, sa, *a.* full of clusters or bunches; (bot.) racemose.
racimudo, da, *a.* bearing large clusters (fruit).
raciocinación, *f.* reasoning, ratiocination.
raciocinar, *i.v.* to reason, ratiocinate.
raciocinio, *m.* 1. reason, reasoning power. 2. reasoning, ratiocination. 3. reasoning, argument.
ración, *f.* 1. ration; portion; allowance. 2. cup (as capacity measure). 3. (ecc.) cathedral prebend. — **media r.,** (ecc.) small prebend; **r. de hambre,** starvation wages, pittance; **r. de reserva, r. seca,** (mil.) emergency rations.
racionabilidad, *f.* reason, judgment, discernment.
racional, *a.* 1. rational, endowed with reason; reasonable. 2. (math.) rational. —*m.* rational, pectoral (breast plate of the Jewish high priest).
racionalidad, *f.* rationality, reasonableness.
racionalismo, *m.* (philos.) rationalism.
racionalista, *a.* rationalist, rationalistic. —*m., f.* rationalist.
racionalización, *f.* (com., ind.) rationalization.
racionalizar, (*ref. 53*) *tr.v.* to rationalize.
racionalmente, *adv.* rationally.
racionamiento, *m.* rationing.
racionar, *tr.v.* to ration.
racioncita, illa, *f. dim. of* **ración,** small allowance.
racionero, *m.* 1. distributor of rations. 2. (ecc.) prebendary.
racionista, *m., f.* 1. person who lives on an allowance. 2. (theat.) poor actor, small-part actor.
racismo, *m.* racism, racialism.
racista, *m., f.* racist, racialist.
rada, *f.* (mar.) bay, inlet.
radar, *m.* radar. — **r. acústico,** sound radar.
radiación, *f.* 1. radiation. 2. radio broadcast. — **r. dirigida,** beamed radiation; **r. espuria,** (rad.) spurious radiation; **r, cósmica,** cosmic radiation; **r. ionizante,** ionizing radiation; **r. nuclear,** nuclear radiation, atomic radiation; **r. solar,** solar radiation.
radiactividad, *f.* (phys.) radioactivity.
radiactivo, va, *a.* (phys.) radioactive.
radiado, da, *a.* 1. radiated; irradiated. 2. broadcast, transmitted. 3. (bot., zool.) radiate. —*m.* (zool.) radiate; (*pl.*) Radiata, Radiates.
radiador, *m.* 1. radiator (heating device). 2. (auto.) radiator. — **r. de bocina,** (auto.) horn radiator; **r. de panal, r. celular,** (auto.) honeycomb radiator.
radial, *a.* 1. radial. 2. radio, e.g. *programa r.,* radio program.
radián, *m.* (geom.) radian.
radiancia, *f.* (engin.) radiance, specific radiant intensity.
radiante, *a.* 1. radiant; beaming, e.g. *sonrisa r.,* beaming smile. 2. (phys., astron.) radiant.
radiar, *tr.v.* to radio, broadcast. —*i.v.* 1. (phys.) to radiate. 2. to beam, shine.
radicación, *f.* 1. taking root; settling down. 2. (math.) evolution, finding of roots. 3. (bot.) arrangement of roots on stalk.
radical, *a.* radical; (bot., philol., chem., math., pol.) radical. —*m., f.* (pol.) radical. —*m., f.* (pol.) radical. —*m.* (philol., chem., math.) radical. —

r. compuesto, (chem.) compound radical; **r. simple,** (chem.) simple radical.
radicalismo, *m.* radicalism.
radicalmente, *adv.* radically.
radicando, *m.* (math.) radicand.
radicar, (*ref. 50*) *i.v.* 1. to take root. 2. to be, be situated, be located. 3. to live, settle settle down. —*r.v.* 1. to settle, settle down, establish oneself. 2. to take root.
radicícola, *a.* (zool.) radicolous, radicicolous.
radicoso, sa, *a.* pertaining to roots.
radícula, *f.* (bot.) radicle.
radio, *m.* 1. radius, zone, sector. 2. (metal.) radium. 3. radio (instrument, set). 4. radio (wireless message). 5. rung, spoke (of ladder, wheel, etc.). 6. (geom., anat.) radius. — **r. de acción,** operating range; **r. vector,** radius vector.
radio, *f.* radio, wireless; broadcasting (as a medium).
radío, a, *a.* wandering.
radioactividad, *f.* (phys.) radioactivity.
radioactivo, va, *a.* (phys.) radioactive.
radioaficionado, da, *m., f.* radio ham, radio amateur.
radioastronomía, *f.* (astron.) radio astronomy.
radiobaliza, *f.* (nav.) radio range beacon.
radiobiología, *f.* radiobiology.
radiobrújula, *f.* radio compass.
radiocarbono, *m.* (chem.) radiocarbon.
radiocomunicación, *f.* radio communication.
radioconductor, *m.* (elec.) radio conductor.
radiodetector, *m.* radiodetector.
radiodifundir, *tr.v., i.v.* (rad.) to broadcast.
radiodifusión, *f.* broadcasting, radiobroadcasting.
radiodifusor, ra, *a.* broadcasting. —*f.* broadcasting or radio station.
radioelemento, *m.* radioelement, radioactive element.
radioemisión, *f.* broadcasting.
radioemisora, *f.* broadcasting station.
radioescucha, *m., f.* radio listener.
radioespectro, *m.* (rad.) radio spectrum.
radiofaro, *m.* radio beacon. — **r. marcador,** radio marker beacon.
radiofonía, *f.* (phys., rad.) radiophony.
radiofónico, ca, *a.* radiophonic.
radiófono, *m.* (phys., rad.) radiophone.
radiofoto, *f.* radiophotograph.
radiofotografía, *f.* radiophotography.
radiofrecuencia, *f.* (rad.) radio frequency.
radiogénico, ca, *a.* radiogenic.
radiógeno, na, *a.* radiogenic, produced by radioactivity.
radiogoniometría, *f.* (rad.) radiogoniometry.
radiogoniómetro, *m.* (rad.) radiogoniometer.
radiografía, *f.* 1. X-ray, radiograph. 2. radiography.
radiografiar, (*ref. 54*) *tr.v.* to X-ray, radiograph.
radiográfico, ca, *a.* radiographic, X-ray.
radiograma, *m.* radiogram, radio message.
radioisótopo, *m.* (phys., chem.) radioisotope.
radiolario, ria, *a.* (zool.) radiolarian. —*m.* (zool.) radiolarian; (*pl.*) Radiolaria.
radiolisis, *f.* (phys., chem.) radiolysis.
radiología, *f.* (med.) radiology.
radiólogo, *m.* (med.) radiologist.
radiolúcido, da, *a.* (med.) radiolucent.
radiometría, *f.* radiometry.
radiómetro, *m.* (phys.) radiometer.
radionúclido, *m.* (phys.) radionuclide.
radiopatrulla, *f.* (Amer.) prowl car, squad car.
radioquímica, *f.* radiochemistry.
radiorientador, *m.* radio direction finder.
radiorreceptor, *m.* (rad.) receiver, radio receiver, receiving set.
radioscopia, *f.* radioscopy.
radioscopio, *m.* radioscope.
radiosensibilidad, *f.* (med.) radiosensitivity.
radioso, sa, *a.* radiant.
radiosonda, *f.* (meteorol.) radiosonde.
radiotécnica, *f.* radiotechnology; radio engineering.
radiotelefonía, *f.* radiotelephony.
radiotelefónico, ca, *a.* radiotelephonic.
radioteléfono, *m.* radiotelephone.
radiotelegrafía, *f.* radiotelegraphy, wireless.
radiotelegrafiar, (*ref. 54*) *tr.v.* to radiotelegraph, to wireless.
radiotelegráfico, ca, *a.* radiotelegraphic, wireless.
radiotelegrafista, *m., f.* wireless operator.
radiotelégrafo, *m.* radiotelegraph, wireless telegraph.
radiotelegrama, *m.* radiotelegram, radiogram.
radioteletipo, *m.* radioteletypewriter.
radioterapia, *f.* (med.) radiotherapy.
radiotermia, *f.* (med.) radiothermy.
radiotorio, *m.* (chem.) radiothorium.
radiotransmisión, *f.* radio transmission.
radiotransmisor, *m.* radio transmitter.
radiotrón, *m.* (phys.) radiotron.
radioyente, *m., f.* radio listener.
radique, radiqué, *ref.* **radicar.**
raditerapia, radiumterapia, *f.* (med.) radiotherapy.
radón, *m.* (chem.) radon.
raedera, *f.* scraper (instrument).
raedizo, za, *a.* easily scraped or scratched.
raedor, ra, *a.* scraping. —*m., f.* scraper. —*m.* strickle, strike (instrument for leveling grain measurements).
raedura, *f.* scraping; (*pl.*) scrapings, filings.
raer, (*ref. 18*) *tr.v.* 1. to scrape. 2. to strike, level with a strickle or strike. 3. to uproot, extirpate. —*r.v.* to become threadbare or worn.
rafa, *f.* 1. (vet.) crack in hoof. 2. irrigation side ditch. 3. (archit.) buttress. 4. (min.) skewback.
Rafael, *m.* Raphael, Italian painter and architect of the Renaissance.
rafaelesco, ca, *a.* Raphaelesque.
ráfaga, *f.* 1. gust of wind. 2. small cloud. 3. flash of light. 4. burst (of machine-gun fire).
rafania, *f.* (med.) raphania.
rafe, *m.* (archit.) eaves. —*m., f.* (bot., anat.) raphe.
rafear, *tr.v.* to reinforce with buttresses, to buttress.
rafia, *f.* (bot.) raffia palm; raffia (fiber).
raglán, *m.* raglan.
ragú, *m.* (cul.) ragout.
ragua, *f.* top of sugar cane.
rahez, (*pl.* **raheces**), *a.* vile, base, low, contemptible.
raíble, *a.* that can be scraped or frayed.
raicear, *i.v.* (C. Amer., Ven.) to take roots.
raiceja, *f. dim. of* **raíz,** rootlet.
raicilla, ita, *f. dim. of* **raíz,** (bot.) rootlet; (bot.) radicle (lower portion of axis of embryo plant).
raid, *m.* (Angl.) 1. raid, attack. 2. long tour, trip or journey.
raído, da, *past part. of* **raer.** —*a.* 1. frayed, threadbare, worn out (clothes). 2. barefaced, shameless.
raigal, *a.* radical (of the root). —*m.* foot of tree trunk.
raigambre, *f.* 1. matted roots. 2. (fig.) deeprootedness.
raigo, raiga, *ref.* **raer.**
raigón, *m. aug. of* **raíz,** large root; root (of a tooth); **r. del Canadá,** (bot.) Kentucky coffee tree.
rail, *m.* (ry.) rail.
raimiento, *m.* 1. scraping. 2. impudence, barefacedness.
raíz, (*pl.* **raíces**), *f.* (fig., bot., anat., math., gram.) root. — **a r. de,** as a result of, because of; right after; **bienes raíces,** real estate; **cortar de r.** or **la r.,** to nip in the bud, cut out at the root; **de r.,** by the root or roots; completely; **echar raíces,** to take root; to settle down; **r. cuadrada,** (math.) square root; **r. cúbica,** (math.) cube root; **r. del moro,** (bot.) elecampane; **r. entera,** (math.) integral root; **r. irracional** or **sorda,** (math.) irrational root; **sacar de r.,** to pull up by the roots.
raja, *f.* 1. splinter, chip. 2. split, crack. 3. slice. 4. coarse cloth.
rajá, (*pl.* **rajaes**), rajah (Indian prince).
rajable, *a.* easily split.
rajabroqueles, (*pl.* **rajabroqueles**), *m.* (coll.) bully, boaster, braggart.
rajadillo, *m.* (cul.) sliced sugared almonds.
rajadizo, za, *a.* easily split, cleavable, fissile.
rajado, da, *a.* cracked, split.
rajador, *m.* wood splitter.
rajadura, *f.* split, crack, fissure.
rajamacana, *m.* (Ven.) expert; (Ven.) tough work, hard chore.
rajante, *a.* splitting.
rajar, *tr.v.* 1. to split, rend, cleave; to crack. 2. to slice. —*i.v.* 1. (coll.) to boast, brag. 2. (coll.) to jabber, chatter. —*r.v.* 1. to split, cleave; to crack. 2. (coll.) to back down, go back on one's word. 3. (Peru) to put oneself out, take a lot of trouble. 4. (Amer.) to escape. 5. (Amer.) to squander. 6. (Col.) to be mistaken. 7. (P. Rico) to get drunk.
rajatabla, a r., at any cost, regardless.
rajeta, *f.* thin varicolored cloth.
rajuela, *f.* 1. *dim. of* **raja,** small crack. 2. thin flagstone.
ralea, *f.* 1. (derog.) type, kind, sort, ilk, breed. 2. (hunt.) prey.
ralear, *i.v.* 1. to become sparse or thin. 2. to yield thin bunches (grapevine). 3. to show his or her true nature.
ralentí, *m.* (cine.) slow motion.
raleón, na, *a.* predatory (bird of prey).
raleza, *f.* sparseness, thinness, lack of density.
rallador, *m.* (cul.) kitchen grater.
ralladura, *f.* 1. (cul.) gratings. 2. mark left by a grater.
rallar, *tr.v.* 1. to grate (food). 2. to annoy, bother, vex.
rallo, *m.* 1. grater; rasp. 2. earthenware water-cooling jug.
rallón, *m.* arrow with crosshead.
ralo, la, *a.* sparse, thin.
rama, *f.* 1. bough, branch. 2. (fig.) branch (of family, learning, industry). 3. (print.) chase. — **andarse por las ramas,** (coll.) to wander off the point, digress; **asirse a las ramas,** (coll.) to clutch at straws, make excuses; **de r. en r.,** constantly changing; **en r.,** raw, crude; (bkb.) in sheets, not yet bound.
ramada, *f., var. of* **ramaje.**
Ramadán, *m.* Ramadan, ninth month of the Moslem year.
ramaje, *m.* branches, mass or network of branches; arbor.
ramal, *m.* 1. strand (of rope, braid, etc.). 2. halter (for leading a horse). 3. branch line (of a railway), branch (of a cordillera), branch road, branch tunnel (of a mine), branch ditch (from main irrigation ditch).
ramalazo, *m.* 1. lash (stroke with a rope and mark left by it). 2. spot, mark. 3. sharp pain; sudden grief. 4. spot on the face left by a blow or a disease.
ramalear, *i.v.* to allow itself to be led easily by the halter (a horse).

ramazón, *f.* cut-off branches (collectively).
rambla, *f.* 1. sandy or dry ravine, gully. 2. walk, avenue, boulevard. 3. tenter (frame for stretching and drying cloth).
ramblar, *m.* confluence of gullies, junction of several ravines.
ramblazo, ramblizo, *m.* bed of a torrent.
rameado, da, *a.* ramiform, with a design of branches.
rameal, rámeo, a, *a.* (bot.) pertaining to branches or boughs.
ramera, *f.* prostitute, whore, streetwalker.
ramería, *f.* 1. brothel. 2. prostitution, streetwalking.
ramial, *m.* ramie patch, ramie field.
ramificación, *f.* ramification; branching.
ramificarse, (*ref. 50*) *r.v.* to ramify; to divide into branches, to branch off.
ramifique, ramifiqué, *ref.* **ramificarse.**
ramilla, *f.* 1. sprig, twig. 2. (fig.) small help.
ramillete, *m.* 1. bouquet, nosegay. 2. attractively arranged plate of sweets. 3. centerpiece, epergne. 4. collection. 5. (bot.) cluster, umbel. — **r. de Constantinopla,** (bot.) sweet william.
ramilletero, ra, *m., f.* florist, maker and seller of bouquets. —*m.* flower vase.
ramina, *f.* ramie fiber.
ramio, *m.* (bot.) ramie.
ramito, *m. dim. of* **ramo,** small bunch of flowers; spray, sprig.
ramiza, *f.* cut branches; work made from branches.
ramnáceo, a, rámneo, a, *a.* (bot.) rhamnaceous. —*f.* (*pl.*) Rhamnaceae.
ramo, *m.* 1. bouquet, bunch (of flowers); cluster; bough. 2. branch, field (of science, business, learning, etc.). 3. (fig.) touch, trace, e.g. *r. de locura,* touch of madness. — **r. de Navidad,** Christmas wreath.
ramojo, *m.* cut branches, brushwood.
ramón, *m.* browse, foliage cut for cattle fodder; trimmed twigs or branches.
ramonear, *i.v.* 1. to trim twigs, cut the tips of branches or twigs. 2. to browse, eat browse; to graze.
ramoneo, *m.* 1. twig trimming; trimming time. 2. browsing, eating browse, grazing.
ramoso, sa, *a.* ramose, full of branches or boughs.
rampa, *f.* 1. cramp (painful involuntary contraction of a muscle), charley horse. 2. ramp, slope; **r. de lanzamiento,** (astronaut.) launching ramp.
rampante, *a.* (her.) rampant.
rampiñete, *m.* vent drill or gimlet.
ramplón, na, *a.* 1. heavy thick-soled (shoe). 2. (fig.) common, vulgar. —*m.* calk (of horseshoe).
ramplonería, *f.* commonness, vulgarity.
rampojo, *m.* fruitless stems of the grapevine.
rampollo, *m.* (agr.) cutting (for replanting).
Ramsés, *m.* Rameses, Egyptian kings.
rana, *f.* 1. (zool.) frog. 2. (*pl.*) (med.) ranula, tumor under the tongue. — **hombre r.,** frogman; **no ser r.,** (coll.) to be an expert; **r. leopardo,** (zool.) leopard frog; **r. marina** or **pescadora,** (ichth.) angler; **r. voladora,** (zool.) flying frog.
ranacuajo, *m.* (zool.) tadpole, polliwog.
rancajada, *f.* uprooting (of plants).
rancajado, da, *a.* pricked or cut by a splinter.
rancajo, *m.* splinter (in the skin).
rancheadero, *m.* settlement of huts or shanties.
ranchear, *tr.v.* (Amer.) to sack, pillage. —*i.v.* to build huts, form a settlement. —*r.v.* to build or dwell in a hut.
rancheo, *m.* (Amer.) sacking, pillaging.
ranchería, *f.* 1. collection of huts, settlement; hamlet; camp. 2. (Peru) farmworker's hut.
rancherío, *m.* 1. (Amer.) collection of huts, settlement. 2. (Arg., Urug.) one-horse town.
ranchero, ra, *m., f.* 1. (Amer.) rancher. 2. (Mex.) rustic, country person. 3. camp cook.
rancho, *m.* 1. ranch, farm. 2. food, meal, mess (food prepared for gangworkmen, prisoners, soldiers). 3. mess, group of people who eat together. 4. (coll.) gathering, meeting. 5. hut, thatched hut. 6. (mar.) squad of ship's crew. 7. (mar.) provisions. — **alborotar el r.,** (coll.) to cause trouble; **asentar el r.,** (coll.) to stop for a meal and rest; to settle down; **hacer r.,** (coll.) to make room; **hacer r. aparte,** (coll.) to go one's own way; **r. de Santa Bárbara,**(mar.) rudder trunk.
rancidez, ranciedad, *f.* rankness, rancidness, staleness.
rancio, cia, *a.* 1. rank, rancid, stale, sour. 2. old, ancient (nobility, lineage). 3. old-fashioned, antiquated. —*m.* 1. rankness, rancidness. 2. rancid bacon. 3. greasiness on cloth (before milling).
rancioso, sa, *a., var. of* **rancio.**
randa, *f.* lace border, lace trimming. —*m.* (coll.) petty thief, pickpocket.
randado, da, *a.* lace-trimmed.
randera, *f.* lacemaker (woman).
ranero, *m.* frog pond, frogmarsh.
rangífero, *m.* (zool.) reindeer.
rango, *m.* 1. rank; class, order; social position. 2. (Amer.) high social standing. 3. (Amer.) pomp, splendor.
rangoso, sa, *a.* (Chile) generous, liberal spender.
rangua, *f.* (mec.) shaft socket, pivot bearing, pivot box.
Rangún, *m.* Rangoon (capital of Burma).
ránido, *m.* (zool.) ranid.
ranilla, *f.* 1. frog, soft part of horse's hoof. 2. (vet.) disease in the bowels of cattle.
ranina, *a.* (anat.) ranine.
ránula, *f.* (med., vet.) ranula, tongue tumor.
ranunculáceo, a, *a.* (bot.) ranunculaceous. —*f.* (bot.) ranunculus; (*pl.*) Ranunculaceae.
ranúnculo, *m.* (bot.) buttercup; crowfoot.
ranura, *f.* groove, slot.
ranuradora, *f.* grooving machine.
raña, *f.* 1. hook for catching cuttlefish. 2. thicket, copse.
raño, *m.* 1. (ichth.) scorpion fish. 2. oyster rake.
rapa, *f.* blossom of the olive tree.
rapabarbas, (*pl.* **rapabarbas**), *m.* (coll.) barber.
rapacejo, ja, *m., f.* child, urchin. —*m.* border, fringe, edging.
rapacería, *f.* childish prank.
rapacidad, *f.* rapacity.
rapador, ra, *a.* scraping, shaving. —*m., f.* scraper. —*m.* (coll.) barber.
rapadura, *f.* close haircut; shave.
rapagón, *m.* beardless young man, stripling.
rapamiento, *m., var. of* **rapadura.**
rapante, *a.* 1. robbing, thieving, snatching. 2. shaving. 3. (her.) rampant.
rapapiés, (*pl.* **rapapiés**), *m.* (fireworks) squib, cracker.
rapapolvo, *m.* (coll.) dressing down, sharp reprimand.
rapar, *tr.v.* 1. to shave; to shave close; to crop (the hair). 2. (coll.) to snatch, filch, steal.
rapavelas, *m.* (coll.) sexton; altar boy, acolyte.
rapaz, (*pl.* **rapaces**), *a.* 1. thievish; rapacious. 2. of prey, predatory, e.g. *ave r.,* bird of prey. —*m.* (*pl.*) (zool.) Raptores.
rapaz, za, *m.* youngster, young boy. —*f.* young girl.
rapazada, *f.* childish prank or action.
rapazuelo, la, *m., f.* street urchin.
rape, *m.* (coll.) quick shave; **al r.,** cropped or cut very close (to the scalp).
rape, *m.* (ichth.) angler.
rapé, *m.* (tobacco) snuff, rappee.
rápidamente, *adv.* rapidly, quickly, fast.
rapidez, *f.* rapidity, celerity, swiftness, speed.
rápido, da, *a.* rapid, quick, fast, speedy, swift; express, fast (train). —*m.* (*pl.*) 1. rapids (in river). 2. (ry.) express, fast train.
rapiego, ga, *a.* rapacious, predacious, predatory (said of birds).
rapingacho, *m.* (Peru) cheese omelet.
rapiña, *f.* rapine, pillage, plundering; robbery. — **ave de r.,** bird of prey.
rapiñador, ra, *a.* plundering, pillaging; robbing, thieving. —*m., f.* plunderer, pillager; robber, thief.
rapiñar, *tr.v.* (coll.) to plunder, pillage; to steal.
rapista, *m.* (coll.) barber.
rapo, *m.* (bot.) turnip (root).
rapónchigo, *m.* (bot.) rampion.
rapóntico, *m., var. of* **ruipóntico.**
raposa, *f.* 1. (zool.) fox; vixen, she-fox. 2. (coll.) fox, cunning person.
raposear, *i.v.* to be cunning, be foxy, be sly as a fox.
raposeo, *m.* foxiness, cunning, crafty ways.
raposera, *f.* fox hole, fox burrow or den.
raposería, *f.* foxiness, cunning, crafty ways.
raposero, ra, *a.* used for fox-hunting; **perro raposero,** foxhound.
raposía, *f.* foxiness, cunning.
raposino, na, *a.* foxy, vulpine.
raposo, *m.* 1. (zool.) male fox. 2. (coll.) fox, foxy, cunning fellow. — **r. ferrero,** (zool.) blue fox.
raposuno, na, *a.* foxy, vulpine.
rapsoda, *m.* rhapsodist, rhapsode, professional reciter of epic poems (in ancient Greece).
rapsodia, *f.* rhapsody.
raptar, *tr.v.* to abduct; to ravish; to kidnap.
rapto, *m.* 1. abduction; kidnapping. 2. rapture, ecstasy. 3. (med.) raptus, seizure, fit. — **R. de las Sabinas,** the Abduction of the Sabines.
raptor, ra, *m., f.* abductor, ravisher; kidnapper.
rapuzar, (*ref. 53*) *tr.v.* (Sp.) to trim, prune, crop (plants).
raque, *m.* beachcombing; **andar** or **ir al r.,** to go beachcombing.
raquear, *i.v.* to go beachcombing, beachcomb.
raquero, ra, *a.* piratical. —*m.* 1. pirate. 2. beachcomber. 3. dock rat, dock thief.
raqueta, *f.* 1. racket; battledore. 2. battledore and shuttlecock, badminton. 3. racket snowshoe. 4. counter rake (used by croupiers for collecting and moving counters in gambling tables). 5. (bot.) wall rocket (Diplotaxis virgata).
raquetazo, *m.* blow with a racket.
raquetero, ra, *m., f.* racket maker or seller.
raquialgia, *f.* (med.) rachialgia.
raquídeo, a, *a.* (anat.) rachidian.
raquis, *m.* (bot., anat.) rachis.
raquítico, ca, *a.* 1. (med.) rachitic, rickety. 2. (fig.) weak, rickety, feeble. 3. scant, skimpy, niggardly. —*m., f.* person suffering from rickets.
raquitis, raquitismo, *m.* (med.) rickets, rachitis.
raquítomo, *m.* (surg.) rachitome.
raramente, *adv.* 1. rarely, seldom. 2. oddly, strangely.
rarefacción, *f.* rarefaction.
rarefacer, (*ref. 10*) *tr.v.* to rarefy. —*r.v.* to become rarefied.
rarefacto, ta, *irr. past part. of* **rarefacer.** —*a.* rarefied (not dense).
rareza, *f.* 1. rarity, rareness, uncommonness; rarity, rare thing. 2. strangeness, oddness, oddity; curio, freak. 3. eccentricity, peculiarity.
raridad, *f., var. of* **rareza.**
rarificar, (*ref. 50*) *tr.v., r.v.* to rarefy.

rarificativo, va, *a.* rarefying, rarefactive, thinning.
rarifique, rarifiqué, *ref.* **rarificar.**
rarísimo, ma, *a. super. of* **raro,** 1. very rare or uncommon. 2. very odd or strange.
raro, ra, *a.* 1. rare, uncommon. 2. rare, scarce. 3. odd, strange, peculiar, queer. 4. rare, thin (gas). 5. outstanding, excellent, notable. — **r. vez,** seldom, infrequently.
ras, *m.* evenness, levelness. — **a r. or al r.,** level, e.g. *una cucharita de . . . llena a r.,* a level teaspoon of; **a r. de,** close to, level with, flush to; **r. con r., r. a r.,** on the same level, on one level; grazing, touching lightly.
rasa, *f.* 1. thinness (in cloth). 2. tableland, plateau.
rasadura, *f.* leveling with a strickle.
rasamente, *adv.* openly, clearly, frankly, publicly.
rasante, *a.* grazing; touching. — **fuego** or tiro r., (artil.) flat trajectory fire, low-angle fire; **vuelo r.,** flying close to the level of the ground. —*f.* (ry.) grade, grade line.
rasar, *tr.v.* 1. to level with a strickle. 2. to graze, touch lightly, skim.
rasarse, *r.v.* to clear up, become clear (the sky).
rascacielo, *m.* skyscraper.
rascacio, *m.* (ichth.) scorpene.
rascadera, *f.* 1. scraper. 2. (coll.) currycomb.
rascadillar, *tr.v.* (Ecuad.) to weed.
rascado, da, *a.* 1. (Hond.) quick-tempered, irascible. 2. (Ven.) drunk, tipsy.
rascador, *m.* 1. scraper, scaler; rasp. 2. ornamental hairpin. 3. huller, husker, sheller (instrument).
rascadura, *f.* scraping; scratching, scratch.
rascalino, *m.* (bot.) dodder.
rascamiento, *m.* scraping; scratching.
rascamoño, *m.* ornamental hairpin.
rascar, (*ref. 50*) *tr.v.* 1. to scratch. 2. to scrape. —*i.v.* (Amer.) to itch. —*r.v.* 1. to scratch, scratch oneself. 2. (Amer.) to get drunk.
rascarrabias, (*pl.* **rascarrabias**), *m., f.* irritable person, crab.
rascatripas, (*pl.* **rascatripas**), *m., f.* scraper, poor fiddler.
rascazón, *f.* itching, itch.
rascle, *m.* coral-fishing gear.
rascón, na, *a.* rough, harsh, sharp (to palate). —*m.* (ornith.) rail, marsh hen.
rascuñar, *tr.v., var. of* **rasguñar.**
rascuño, *m., var. of* **rasguño.**
rasel, *m.* (mar.) dead-rising (each of the vertical frames in the run of a ship).
rasera, *f.* 1. strike, strickle. 2. (cul.) spatula, egg or pancake turner.
rasero, *m.* strike, strickle. — **medir por un r.,** to treat with strict impartiality.
rasete, *m.* (tex.) satinet, cotton sateen.
rasgado, da, *past part. of* **rasgar.** —*a.* 1. torn, ripped. 2. slit, slant, almond-shaped (eyes). 3. large, wide. —*m.* tear, rip, rent.
rasgador, ra, *a.* tearing, ripping, rending.
rasgadura, *f.* tear, rip, rent; tearing, ripping.
rasgar, (*ref. 51*) *tr.v.* 1. to tear, rip, rent. 2. to strum (a guitar, lute, etc.). —*r.v.* to become torn; to tear.
rasgo, *m.* 1. flourish, stroke (of pen). 2. trait, feature, characteristic. 3. act, deed, feat, e.g. *un r. heroico,* an act or feat of heroism. 4. (bright) remark; flash (of wit). 5. (*pl.*) features (of the face). — **a grandes rasgos,** in broad outlines, broadly, (i.e. without going into details).
rasgón, *m.* tear, rent, rip.
rasgue, rasgué, *ref.* **rasgar.**
rasgueado, *past part. of* **rasguear.** —*m. var. of* **rasgueo.**
rasguear, *tr.v.* to strum, thrum (the guitar, lute, etc.). —*i.v.* to make flourishes (with a pen).
rasgueo, *m.* 1. forming of fine strokes with a pen; flourish, stroke (of a pen). 2. strumming, thrumming (on a guitar).
rasguñar, *tr.v.* 1. to scratch. 2. to sketch, outline.
rasguño, *m.* 1. scratch. 2. sketch, outline.
rasguñuelo, *m.* 1. *dim. of* **rasguño,** slight scratch. 2. rough sketch.
rasilla, *f.* 1. serge, light woolen fabric. 2. thin hollow brick.
rasmilar, *tr.v.* (Chile, Ecuad.) to scratch, graze.
raso, sa, *a.* 1. flat, level, even, unobstructed. 2. cloudless, clear. 3. common, without rank (soldier, private). 4. backless (chair). — **cielo raso,** ceiling. —*m.* (tex.) satin. — **al r.,** in the open air, in the open country.
rasoliso, *m.* (tex.) glossy silk satin.
raspa, *f.* 1. (bot.) beard (of an ear of corn, of wheat). 2. hair, thread (caught on the tip of a writing pen). 3. fishbone (esp. the spine). 4. bunch of grapes; corncob. 5. stalk, stem. 6. shell (of nuts). 7. (coll., Amer.) lecture, sermon, dressing-down. 8. (Cuba) remainder stuck or burnt in the pot. 9. (Arg.) petty thief; **ir a la r.,** (coll.) to go pilfering.
raspada, *f.* (Mex.) reprimand.
raspadilla, *f.* (Peru) ice chips flavored with fruit syrup.
raspador, *m.* scraper, eraser, rasp.
raspadura, *f.* 1. scraping, erasure, rasping; scrapings. 2. (Cuba) dark pan sugar.
raspajo, *m.* grape stem or stalk.
raspamiento, *m.* scraping, erasure, rasping.
raspante, *a.* 1. harsh, rough to the taste (wine). 2. abrasive, scraping.
raspar, *tr.v.* 1. to scrape; to graze. 2. to bite, sting, have a harsh taste. 3. to steal, take away, pinch (coll.). 4. (Amer.) to reprimand.
raspear, *i.v.* to scratch (said of a pen).
raspetón, de r., (coll.) in passing.
raspilla, *f.* (bot.) myosotis, forget-me-not.
raspón, *m.* 1. (Amer.) severe reprimand or dressing-down. 2. (Amer.) graze, scratch. 3. (Col.) large straw hat. — **de r.,** in passing.
rasponazo, *m.* scratch, graze, chafe, abrasion.
rasque, rasqué, *ref.* **rascar.**
rasqueta, *f.* 1. scraper. 2. (S. Amer.) currycomb.
rasquetear, *tr.v.* to curry (a horse).
rasquiña, *f.* itch, skin rash.
rastacuero, *m.* parvenu, social climber.
rastel, *m.* railing, balustrade.
rastillador, ra, *a., m., f., var. of* **rastrillador.**
rastillo, *m., var. of* **rastrillo.**
rastra, *f.* 1. rake; harrow. 2. sled, drag, dray (low cart for hauling heavy loads). 3. vestige, trace, sign, track, trail. 4. string (of dried fruit). 5. something that drags or trails. 6. consequences, outcome. 7. (mar.) drag, grapnel. — **a la r., a r., a rastras,** dragging, trailing; unwillingly; **llevar a rastras,** to drag, drag along.
rastrallar, *i.v.* to crack (a whip).
rastreador, ra, *a.* 1. dredging, dragging; minesweeping. 2. tracking, tracing, trailing. —*m.* 1. tracker. 2. dredger, dredge. — **r. de minas,** mine sweeper.
rastrear, *tr.v.* 1. to track, trail, trace. 2. to drag, dredge, sweep. 3. to investigate, check into, snoop (coll.). 4. to sell (meat) wholesale. —*i.v.* 1. to rake; to hoe. 2. to skim the ground, fly very low.
rastrel, *m.* (archit.) rail, crosspiece, lath, crossbeam.
rastreo, *m.* 1. racking, trailing, tracing. 2. dragging, dredging. — **r. de minas,** mine sweeping.
rastrera, *f.* (mar.) lower studding sail.
rastreramente, *adv.* despicably, basely, shamefully, vilely.
rastrero, ra, *a.* 1. dragging; trailing. 2. skimming over the ground. 3. low, base, despicable, vile. 4. (bot.) creeping, trailing (plant). —*m.* slaughterhouse employee. —*f.* (mar.) lower studding sail.
rastrillada, *f.* 1. rakings, rakeful. 2. (Amer.) track, footstep.
rastrillador, ra, *m., f.* 1. hatcheler, comber (of hemp). 2. raker.
rastrillaje, *m.* 1. raking. 2. hatcheling.
rastrillar, *tr.v.* 1. to rake, to harrow. 2. to hatchel, comb, dress (flax, hemp). 3. (Col.) to fire (a gun); to light (a match). 4. (Arg.) to cock (a gun).
rastrillo, *m.* 1. rake. 2. hatchel, hackel, flax comb. 3. (fort.) portcullis; iron grating or gate. 4. hammer (of gunlock). 5. ward (of lock or key).
rastro, *m.* 1. vestige, trace, sign; track, trail. 2. rake; harrow. 3. wholesale meat market. 4. slaughterhouse. 5. store or market of second-hand goods and antiques.
rastrojal, *m.* 1. stubble ground. 2. (Ecuad.) undergrowth, brush, underbrush.
rastrojar, *tr.v.* to clear (a field) of stubble.
rastrojera, *f.* 1. stubble field. 2. stubblegrazing season.
rastrojo, *m.* stubble, haulm. — **sacar a uno de los rastrojos,** (coll.) to raise (someone) from the mud.
rasura, *f.* 1. shaving. 2. (*pl.*) (chem.) tartar, argol.
rasuración, *f.* 1. shaving. 2. scraping.
rasurar, *tr.v., r.v.* to shave (the beard).
rata, *f.* 1. (zool.) rat; female rat. 2. thin scraggy pigtail. — **r. amizclada,** (zool.) muskrat; **r. blanca,** (zool.) white rat; **r. canguro,** (zool.) kangaroo rat; **r. de agua,** (zool.) water rat; **r. de alcantarilla,** (zool.) brown rat, sewer rat. —*m.* pickpocket, sneak thief.
ratafía, *f.* ratafia, ratafee (liqueur).
ratania, *f.* (bot.) rhatany, Peruvian or knotty rhatany; rhatany (root).
rataplán, *m.* rataplan, rub-a-dub (sound of a drum).
ratear, *tr.v.* 1. to reduce pro rata, to distribute proportionately. 2. to steal, pilfer, filch, pinch (coll.). —*i.v.* to creep, crawl.
ratel, *m.* (zool.) ratel.
rateo, *m.* proration, prorating, apportionment.
rateramente, *adv.* basely, vilely, meanly.
ratería, *f.* 1. pilfering, filching, petty thieving; petty theft. 2. mean or dishonest action, dishonesty.
ratero, ra, *a.* 1. thieving, thievish. 2. dragging, creeping. —*m.* pickpocket, sneak thief, petty thief.
rateruelo, la, *m., f.* petty thief, little pickpocket.
raticida, *m.* raticide.
ratico, ito, *m. dim. of* **rato,** little while, short while.
ratificación, *f.* ratification, confirmation.
ratificar, (*ref. 50*) *tr.v.* to ratify, confirm.
ratificatorio, ria, *a.* ratifying, confirming.
ratifique, ratifiqué, *ref.* **ratificar.**
ratigar, (*ref. 51*) *tr.v.* to secure or fasten a load with a rope.
rátigo, *m.* truckload, cartload.
ratihabición, *f.* (law) ratification, approval, confirmation.
ratina, *f.* (tex.) ratteen, ratiné.
ratito, *m.* short while, little while.
rato, *m.* while, short time or while, little while; **a ratos,** at times, sometimes; from time to time; **a ratos perdidos,** in one's spare time; **buen r.,** good while, quite a long time; a lot, large amount; pleasant experience; **de r. en r.,** from time to time; **hace ya r.,** some time ago; **hasta otro r.,** cheerio, goodbye; **mal r.,** nasty or

unpleasant experience; **pasar el r.,** to while away, kill or spend the time; **ratos perdidos,** free or spare time.
rato, *a.* (law) valid, legalized (marriage).
ratón, *m.* 1. (zool.) (male) mouse. 2. (mar.) jagged rock (that damages underwater cables). — **r. almizclero,** (zool.) desman, muskrat; **r. de biblioteca,** (coll.) bookworm (person); **r. de campo,** (zool.) field mouse.
ratona, *f.* female rat or mouse.
ratonar, *tr.v.* to nibble, gnaw. —*r.v.* to become sick from eating mice (cats).
ratoncito, *m. dim.* little mouse.
ratonera, *f.* mouse trap; mouse hole; nest of mice. — **caer en la r.,** (coll.) to fall into the trap.
ratonero, ra, ratonesco, ca, ratonil, *a.* mousy, mouselike.
RAU *abbrev. of* **República Arabe Unida,** United Arab Republic (UAR).
rauco, ca, *a.* (poet.) raucous, hoarse, husky.
rauda, *f.* Arab cemetery.
raudal, *m.* 1. torrent, rapid stream. 2. (fig.) abundance, plenty. — **a raudales,** in torrents; (fig.) galore.
raudamente, *adv.* rapidly, swiftly.
raudo, da, *a.* rapid, swift, impetuous.
raulí, (*pl.* **raulíes**), *m.* (Chile, bot.) evergreen beech (Nothofagus nervosa).
rauta, *f.* (coll.) route, road, way.
ravenala, *f.* (bot.) traveler's tree.
ravioles, *m.* (*pl.*) (cul.) ravioli.
Rawalpindi, *m.* Rawalpindi (interim capital of Pakistan).
raya, *f.* 1. stripe; line. 2. bound, limit, line; border, frontier. 3. parting (in hair). 4. dash, stroke (in writing, etc.). 5. (phys.) line (of spectrum). 6. spiral groove (in rifling of gun). 7. point (in a score). 8. crease (in trousers). — **a rayas,** striped; **dar quince y r. a,** (coll.) to surpass completely, beat hands down; **echar r.,** to compete; **hacer r.,** to excel, be outstanding; **mantener a r.,** to keep at bay; **pasar de la r.,** to go too far, go beyond the line; **poner** or **tener a r.,** to keep or place within bound or limits; **r. del espectro,** (phys.) spectral line; **r. de mulo,** dark line down horse's back; **r. diplomática,** pin stripe; **tres en r.,** noughts and crosses (G.B.), tick tack toe.
raya, *m.* (ichth.) ray, skate.
rayadillo, *m.* (tex.) striped cotton duck.
rayado, da, *past part. of* **rayar.** —*a.* striped, streaked; ruled, lined. —*m.* 1. stripes, striping; lines. 2. rifling (of rifle barrel); grooving, scoring.
rayador, *m.* 1. (C. Amer., ornith.) black skimmer. 2. grooving tool.
rayano, na, *a.* bordering, contiguous; **rayano en,** bordering on, verging on.
rayar, *tr.v.* 1. to line, draw lines on, rule; to stripe. 2. to underline. 3. to cross out, put a line through. 4. to groove, score, scratch; to rifle (cannon or rifle barrel). 5. (C. Amer., Col., Chile) to spur on (a horse). 6. (Arg., Mex.) to halt (a horse) suddenly. 7. (Mex.) to pay (workers). 8. (Mex.) to collect (wages). —*i.v.* 1. to dawn, break, begin (the day), rise, come forth (sun, light). 2. to stand out, excel, be outstanding. — **r. con,** to be equal to, match; to resemble; **r. en,** to border on.
rayendo, rayera, rayese, rayo, rayó, *ref. raer.*
rayo, *m.* 1. ray, beam. 2. flash of lightning; thunderbolt. 3. spoke (of wheel). 4. whirlwind, live wire (person who works very quickly). 5. wit (person). 6. (fig.) sudden flash of pain; sudden misfortune. — **r. alfa,** (phys.) alpha ray; **r. beta,** (phys.) beta ray; **r. de calor,** heat ray; **r. catódico,** (elec.) cathode ray; **r. del radio,** radio beam; **r. delta,** (phys.) delta ray; **r. de luz,** ray of light; (fig.) ray of light (casting light on an obscure point); **r. electrónico,** (phys.) electron beam; **r. gamma,** gamma ray; **r. infrarrojo,** infrared ray; **r. laser,** (phys.) laser beam; **r. refracto** or **refractado,** (opt.) refracted ray; **r. Roentgen,** Roentgen ray; **r. textorio,** (weaver's) shuttle; **r. ultravioleta,** (phys.) ultraviolet ray; **rayos alfa,** (phys.) alpha rays; **rayos beta,** (phys.) beta rays; **rayos canales** or **positivos,** (chem.) canal or positive rays; **rayos catódicos,** (phys.) cathode rays; **rayos cósmicos,** (phys.) cosmic rays; **rayos gamma,** (phys.) gamma rays; **rayos X,** X rays; **echar rayos,** to be furious, be fuming; **¡que te parta un r.!** drop dead!
rayón, *m.* (tex.) rayon.
rayoso, sa, *a.* striped, streaked; lined.
rayuela, *f.* 1. *dim. of* **raya,** small stripe or line. 2. (type of) chuck or pitch farthing game; hopscotch.
rayuelo, *m.* (ornith.) snipe.
raza, *f.* race (of human beings); breed, strain, lineage; **de pura r.,** thoroughbred; **¡qué tal r.!** (Peru, coll.) what nerve! (coll.); **r. amarilla, (derog.)** yellow race; **r. blanca,** white race; **r. humana,** human race; **r. negra,** (derog.) black race; **tener mucha r.,** (Peru, coll.) to be very courageous.
raza, *f.* 1. cleft, fissure, crack. 2. beam or ray of light (through a crack). 3. crack (in horse's hoof). 4. light stripe (in cloth).
razado, da, *a.* (tex.) having light woven stripes.
rázago, *m.* burlap, sackcloth.
razón, *f.* 1. reason, intellect, faculty of reasoning. 2. reason, sanity. 3. reason, argument, explanation. 4. reason, cause, motive. 5. reasonableness; fairness. 6. rate. 7. (math.) ratio. — **alcanzar de razones,** (coll.) to overwhelm with reasons, beat someone in an argument; **a r. de,** at the rate of; **con r.,** (coll.) that explains it, understandably so, with good reason; **con r. o sin ella,** right or wrong; **dar la r. a,** to agree with, side with; **dar r.,** to inform, tell, give information; **dar r. de sí,** to do exactly as instructed; **entrar en r.,** to come to reason; **envolver a uno en razones,** to confuse, tie someone up (so that he does not know how to reply); **meter a uno en r.,** to bring someone to reason, talk sense into someone; **meterse en r.,** to listen to reason, see reason; **no dar r. de sí,** to disappear or be absent, disappear from the map; **no tener r.,** to be wrong; **perder la r.,** to lose one's mind or reason, go mad; **poner en r.,** to pacify, reconcile; to punish, reprimand; **ponerse a razones con,** to argue with; **ponerse en r.,** to come to an agreement; **privarse de r.,** to go out of one's senses, lose one's senses; to drink oneself senseless; **r. de estado,** reason of state; **r. de ser,** raison d'etre; **r. geométrica** or **por cociente,** (math.) geometric ratio, quotient; **r. inversa,** inverse ratio; **r. natural,** natural reasoning power; **r. social,** (coll.) firm, trade or business name; **reducirse a la r.,** to yield, give in; **tener r.,** to be right; **tomar r.,** to register, enter (in a register).
razonable, *a.* 1. reasonable, sensible; fair, just. 2. reasonable, moderately-sized, fair-sized. — **dentro de lo r.,** within reason.
razonablemente, *adv.* reasonably.
razonadamente, *adv.* in a reasoned manner.
razonado, da, *a.* reasoned, reasoned out.
razonador, ra, *reasoning, explaining.* — *m., f.* reasoner, explainer.
razonamiento, *m.* reasoning, ratiocination.
razonante, *a.* reasoning. —*m., f.* reasoner.
razonar, *i.v.* to reason, ratiocinate. —*tr.v.* to explain, reason out.
razzia, *f.* 1. razzia, raid, foraging expedition. 2. police raid.
Rb *symb. of* **rubidio,** rubidium (Rb).
re, *m.* (mus.) re, D., second note of scale.
Re *symb. of* **renio, rhenium (Re).**
rea, *f.* female offender, defendant.
reabrir, *tr.v., i.v.* to reopen.
reabsorber, *tr.v.* to reabsorb.
reabsorción, *f.* reabsorption.
reacción, *f.* reaction (in all senses); **r. de fisión,** fission reaction; **r. de fusión,** fusion reaction; **r. en cadena,** chain reaction; **r. cutánea,** (med.) skin test; **r. nuclear,** nuclear reaction.
reaccionar, *i.v.* to react.
reaccionario, ria, *a., m., f.* reactionary.
reaccionarismo, *m.* (polit.) reactionism.
reacio, cia, *a.* reluctant, unwilling; stubborn, obstinate; **r. a,** loath to, disinclined.
reacondicionamiento, *m.* reconditioning.
reacondicionar, *tr.v.* to recondition.
reactancia, *f.* (elec.) reactance.
reactivar, *tr.v.* to reactivate.
reactividad, *f.* reactivity.
reactivo, va, *a.* reactive. —*m.* (chem.) reagent.
reactor, *m.* (elec., phys.) reactor; **r. atómico,** atomic reactor; **r. avanzado de gas,** advanced gas-cooled reactor; **r. de agua a presión,** pressurized-water reactor; **r. de agua en ebullición,** boiling-water reactor; **r. de gas,** gas-cooled reactor; **r. engendrador,** breeder reactor; **r. nuclear,** nuclear reactor; **r. refrigerado por gas,** gas-cooled reactor.
reacuñar, *tr.v.* to recoin, mint anew.
readaptación, *f.* readaptation, readjustment.
readaptar, *tr.v.* to readapt; to readjust.
readmisión, *f.* readmission, readmittance.
readmitir, *tr.v.* to readmit.
reafirmación, *f.* reaffirmation.
reafirmar, *tr.v.* reaffirm, reassert.
reagravación, *f.* renewed worsening.
reagravar, *tr.v.* to make worse again. —*r.v.* to get worse again.
reagrupar, *tr.v. & reflex. v.* to regroup.
reajustar, *tr.v.* to readjust.
reajuste, *m.* adjustment; **r. ministerial,** cabinet reshuffle; **r. salarial,** wage settlement.
reagudo, da, *a.* very sharp or acute.
real, *a.* real, actual; true, genuine; **r. moza,** handsome woman, real chick or doll (sl.).
real, *a.* 1. royal. 2. royalist. 3. fine, splendid, magnificent, excellent, very good; beautiful, handsome. —*m.* 1. king's tent or camp; army camp. 2. king's galleon. 3. fairground. 4. real (Spanish coin); (Amer.) ten cents, small coin. — **alzar** or **levantar los reales,** to strike or break camp; **asentar los reales,** to encamp, set up camp; **la R. Academia Española de la Lengua,** the Royal Academy of the Spanish Language; **la r. casa,** the royal house (lineage); **sentar el r. or los reales,** to settle down, set up house; **un r. sobre otro,** (coll.) (to pay) in cash and down to the last cent.
reala, *f., var. of* **rehala.**
realce, *m.* 1. raised work, relief, embossment. 2. luster, splendor. 3. (p.) highlight. — **bordar de r.,** to embroider with raised work; **dar r. a,** to give splendor or luster to.
realce, realcé, *ref.* **realzar.**
realdad, *f.* royal power, sovereignty.
realegrarse, *r.v.* to be overcome with joy, be overjoyed.
realejo, *m.* small hand organ.
realengo, ga, *a.* state, royal (lands). —*m.* royal patrimony.
realera, *f.* queen cell (of beehive).

realeza, *f.* royalty, regal dignity.
realice, realicé, *ref.* **realizar.**
realidad, *f.* reality; truth, fact. — **en r.,** really, truly; **en r. de verdad,** truly, in truth; **ajustarse a la r.,** to face facts.
realimentación, *f.* (elec.) feedback; **r. acústica,** (rad.) acoustic feedback.
realineación, *f.* realignment.
realismo, *m.* 1. realism. 2. royalism.
realista, *a.* 1. realistic. 2. royalist. —*m., f.* 1. realist. 2. royalist.
realizable, *a.* 1. realizable, feasible, practicable. 2. (com.) salable.
realización, *f.* 1. realization, execution, performing, carrying out, putting into effect, fulfillment. 2. (com.) sale, bargain sale.
realizar, (*ref.* *53*) *tr.v.* 1. to carry out, perform, put into effect; to fulfill, realize, accomplish. 2. (com.) to sell out, turn into cash.
realmente, *adv.* really, truly; in reality, actually.
realzar, (*ref.* *53*) *tr.v.* 1. to enhance, heighten, impart luster or splendor to. 2. to make prominent, elevate, exalt. 3. to emboss, decorate with raised work. 4. (p.) to highlight.
reanimar, *tr.v.* 1. to revive, reanimate. 2. to encourage, cheer up, comfort. —*r.v.* to revive, recover.
reanudación, *f.* renewal, resumption.
reanudar, *tr.v.* to renew, resume, take up again. —*r.v.* to be renewed, begin again.
reaparecer, (*ref.* *45*) *i.v.* to reappear.
reaparezca, reaparezco, *ref.* **reaprecer.**
reaparición, *f.* 1. reappearance. 2. (theat.) comeback, return engagement.
reapertura, *f.* reopening.
reapretar, (*ref.* *29*) *tr.v.* to press again; to squeeze tightly.
reapriete, reaprieto, *ref.* **reapretar.**
rearar, *tr.v.* to plow again, replow.
rearmar, *tr.v., r.v.* (mil.) to rearm.
rearme, *m.* (mil.) rearmament.
reasegurar, *tr.v.* (com.) to reinsure.
reaseguro, *m.* reinsurance.
reasumir, *tr.v.* to reassume; to resume, take up again (duties, powers, etc.).
reasunción, *f.* reassumption, resumption.
reata, *f.* 1. riata; rope used to tie horses or mules in single file. 2. single file of horses. 3. additional mule used for pulling wagon or cart. 4. (mar.) woolding. — **de r.,** in single file; (coll.) following the leader submissively.
reatadura, *f.* tying in single file, retying; tying tight.
reatar, *tr.v.* 1. to retie, tie again; to tie tightly; to tie in single file (horses). 2. (mar.) to woold.
reato, *m.* obligation of atonement for sins committed.
reaventar, (*ref.* *29*) *tr.v.* to winnow again.
reavivar, *tr.v.* 1. to revive, revivify, reanimate. 2. to rekindle, reawake, renew.
rebaba, *f.* fin, burr, rough seam; rough edge; rough flange.
rebaja, *f.* reduction, rebate, discount; deduction, diminution.
rebajado, da, *past part. of* **rebajar.** —*a.* 1. relieved from service (soldier). 2. (com.) reduced (in price).
rebajador, *m.* (photog.) weakener, bath for toning down dark images.
rebajamiento, *m.* 1. lowering; reduction. 2. debasement, humiliation.
rebajar, *tr.v.* 1. to lower, bring down; to reduce, lessen. 2. to deflate, lower, humiliate. 3. (p.) to lower, tone down (intensity of colors). 4. (archit.) to drop, depress (an arch.). 5. (photog.) to weaken, tone down (dark images). 6. (carp.) to cut down, scarf, shave off. —*r.v.* 1. to humble or lower oneself. 2. to be relieved of service (a soldier). — **rebajarse a** + *inf.,* to stoop to + *inf.*
rebajo, *m.* (carp.) rabbet, groove.
rebalaje, *m.* current (of water).
rebalsa, *f.* 1. pond, pool. 2. (med.) clotted humor.
rebalsar, *tr.v.* to dam, dam up. —*i.v., r.v.* to get dammed up; to form pools; to overflow.
rebanada, *f.* slice (esp. of bread).
rebanar, *tr.v.* to slice; to divide, cut through.
rebanco, *m.* (archit.) upper socle.
rebañadera, *f.* grapnel, drag hook.
rebañadura, *f.* 1. gathering up; eating up completely, finishing off. 2. (*pl.*) leavings, residues.
rebañar, *tr.v.* 1. to gather up completely. 2. to eat up, finish up the last morsel.
rebañego, ga, *a.* pertaining to the herd or flock; gregarious.
rebaño, *m.* flock; (fig.) flock.
rebañuelo, *m. dim. of* **rebaño,** small herd or flock.
rebasadero, *m.* (mar.) safe place for passing.
rebasar, *tr.v.* 1. to exceed; overflow; to go over, go beyond. 2. (mar.) to sail beyond or past. —*i.v.* to overflow.
rebate, *m.* fight, encounter; dispute, contention.
rebatible, *a.* refutable, disputable.
rebatimiento, *m.* refutation, rebuttal.
rebatiña, *f.* grabbing, scramble; **andar a la r.,** to grab and snatch (from one another); to scramble.
rebatir, *tr.v.* 1. to refute, rebut. 2. to repel, ward off, drive back (physical force); to resist (temptation). 3. to strengthen, reinforce, redouble. 4. to beat again; to beat hard. 5. (com.) to deduct. 6. (fenc.) to parry.
rebato, *m.* 1. call to arms, e.g. *llamar a r.,* to call to arms. 2. alarm, commotion. 3. (mil.) surprise attack. — **de r.,** (coll.) suddenly.
rebautice, rebauticé, *ref.* **rebautizar.**
rebautizar, (*ref.* *53*) *tr.v.* to rebaptize.
rebeco, *m.* (zool.) chamois.
rebelarse, *r.v.* to revolt, rebel; to resist.
rebelde, a. 1. rebellious; unruly, disobedient. 2. unruly (hair). 3. stubborn, unruly, unyielding. 4. (law) defaulting, in default. —*m., f.* 1. rebel, insurgent. 2. (law) defaulter.
rebeldía, *f.* 1. rebelliousness; contumacy, stubbornness. 2. (law) default, contempt of court; **en r.,** (law) by default.
rebelión, *f.* rebellion, revolt, uprising, insurrection.
rebelón, na, *a.* balky, restive (horse).
rebencazo, *m.* lash, whiplash.
rebenque, *m.* 1. whip. 2. (mar.) ratline.
rebenquear, *tr.v.* (Amer.) to whip.
rebién, *adv.* (coll.) very well.
rebina, *f.* (agr.) third earthing-up of vines; third plowing.
rebinar, *tr.v.* (agr.) to earth up (vines) for the third time.
rebisabuelo, la, *m.* great-great-grandfather; (*pl.*) great-great-grandparents. —*f.* great-great-grandmother.
rebisnieto, ta, *m.* great-great-grandson; (*pl.*) great-great-grandchildren. —*f.* great-great-granddaughter.
reblandecer, (*ref.* *45*) *tr.v.* to soften. —*r.v.* to become soft.
reblandecimiento, *m.* softening; (med.) softening.
reblandezca, reblandezco, *ref.* **reblandecer.**
reboce, rebocé, *ref.* **rebozar.**
rebocillo, rebociño, *m.* mantilla, shawl.
rebollar, rebolledo, *m.* tract of land planted with Turkey oaks; thicket of oak saplings.
rebollidura, *f.* (mil.) flaw in the bore of gun.
rebollo, *m.* (bot.) Turkey oak; oak trunk.
rebolludo, da, *a.* 1. stocky, thickset. 2. rough (diamond).
rebombar, *i.v.* to reverberate, resound, to make a loud report.
reborde, *m.* flange, rim, border.
rebordeador, *m.* flanging instrument.
rebordear, *tr.v.* to flange.
rebosadero, *m.* overflow (pipe); spillway.
rebosadura, rebosamiento, *f.* overflow, overflowing.
rebosante, *a.* full, brimming; **r. de,** full of, brimming with, e.g. *r. de salud,* brimming with health.
rebosar, *i.v.* 1. to run over, overflow. 2. to abound, be abundant. — **r. de** or **en,** to be brimming with; to overflow with; to have an abundance of. —*r.v.* to overflow, run over.
rebotación, *f.* 1. rebounding. 2. annoyance.
rebotadera, *f.* nap-raising comb.
rebotador, ra, *a.* 1. rebounding. 2. nap-raising. 3. clinching. 4. upsetting, vexatious. —*m.* 1. rebounder. 2. clincher (of nails).
rebotadura, *f.* 1. bouncing; rebounding. 2. clinching (bending the point of a nail, etc.). 3. raising the nap of cloth. 4. vexation, upsetting.
rebotar, *tr.v.* 1. to bend (a nail) over. 2. to repel, beat back. 3. to change in color or quality. 4. (coll.) to perturb, upset; to annoy, exasperate, infuriate. —*i.v.* to bounce; to rebound. —*r.v.* 1. to change in color or quality. 2. (coll.) to get upset or perturbed; to get annoyed.
rebote, *m.* rebound; bounce (of a ball, etc.); **de r.,** indirectly.
rebotica, *f.* back room of a drugstore (U.S.) or chemist's shop (G.B.).
rebotín, *m.* second growth of mulberry leaves.
rebozar, (*ref.* *53*) *tr.v.* 1. to muffle, wrap, cover (the face). 2. (cul.) to dip in batter or in egg (before frying). —*r.v.* to wrap up or muffle one's face.
rebozo, *m.* 1. (Amer.) long narrow stole or shawl. 2. muffling the face. 3. pretext, pretense. — **de r.,** secretly; **sin r.,** openly, frankly.
rebramar, *i.v.* to bellow repeatedly; to bellow back (an animal).
rebramo, *m.* answering bellow of a deer.
rebrillar, *i.v.* to sparkle, gleam.
rebrotar, *tr.v.* to sprout, shoot.
rebrote, *m.* sprout, shoot.
rebudiar, *i.v.* (hunt.) to sniff and grunt (a boar).
rebudio, *m.* (hunt.) grunt (of wild boar).
rebufar, *i.v.* to snort again; to snort loudly.
rebufe, *m.* snort, snorting (of a bull).
rebufo, *m.* expansion of air around muzzle of a gun, muzzle blast, recoil.
rebujado, da, *a.* 1. tangled-up, entangled. 2. wrapped up, muffled.
rebujal, *m.* 1. cattle herd in excess of fifty or multiple of fifty. 2. small plot of arable land.
rebujar, *tr.v.* to jumble or bundle together. —*r.v.* to tuck oneself in (i.e. in bed), wrap oneself up (in a cloak, etc.).
rebujina, rebujiña, *f.* (coll.) uproar, rumpus, racket, scuffle.
rebujo, *m.* 1. woman's face veil. 2. clumsy bundle or package.
rebullicio, *m.* bustle, hubbub.
rebullir, (*ref.* *65*) *i.v., r.v.* to stir, begin to move.
rebultado, da. *a.* bulky; puffed.
rebumbar, *i.v.* to whiz, whistle (a cannon ball).
rebumbio, *m.* (coll.) noise, uproar, rumpus, confusion.
reburujar, *tr.v.* (coll.) to wrap up in a clumsy bundle.
reburujón, *m.* clumsy bundle.

rebusca, *f.* 1. careful or meticulous search. 2. gleanings; crops left to be gleaned after harvesting. 3. refuse, leavings.
rebuscado, da, *past part. of* **rebuscar.** *—a.* affected, unnatural, pedantic (speech, manners, literary style).
rebuscador, ra, *m., f.* 1. searcher. 2. gleaner.
rebuscamiento, *m.* 1. meticulous search. 2. affectation (in language or manners).
rebuscar, (*ref. 50*) *tr.v.* 1. to search meticulously. 2. to glean.
rebusco, *m., var. of* **rebusca.**
rebutir, *tr.v.* to stuff, pack, fill.
rebuznador, ra, *a.* braying. *—m., f.* brayer.
rebuznar, *i.v.* to bray.
rebuzno, *m.* braying (of a donkey).
recabar, *tr.v.* 1. to succeed in getting; to obtain by entreaty. 2. to request.
recadero, ra, *m., f.* messenger, errand boy or girl.
recado, *m.* 1. message. 2. errand. 3. equipment, gear, outfit, materials; (Amer.) riding gear, saddle and trappings. 4. present, gift. 5. daily marketing or shopping. 6. safety, security. 7. (print.) standing matter, set-up matter used for various sheets. 8. (*pl.*) (Mex., P. Rico) regards, compliments, greetings. — **a buen r., a mucho r.** or **a r.,** in safety; **dar r. para,** to provide the necessities for; **enviar a un r.,** to send on an errand; **r. de escribir,** writing materials.
recaer, (*ref. 5.*) *i.v.* to fall again; to relapse, fall back (into error, heresy or illness). — **r. en,** to fall to, come to (said of an inheritance); **r. sobre,** to fall to, fall on (said of responsibility).
recaída, *f.* relapse.
recaiga, recaigo, *ref.* **recaer.**
recalada, *f.* (mar.) landfall.
recalar, *tr.v.* to saturate. *—i.v.* (mar.) to sight land; to reach a ship (the wind or tide). *—r.v.* to become saturated.
recalcada, *f.* (mar.) listing, heel.
recalcadamente, *adv.* 1. closely, tightly. 2. emphatically, distinctly.
recalcadura, *f.* packing, cramming, pressing.
recalcar, (*ref. 50*) *tr.v.* 1. to emphasize, stress (words). 2. to cram, pack, press. *—i.v.* (mar.) to list, heel. *—r.v.* 1. (coll.) to say repeatedly, harp on a subject. 2. (coll.) to sprawl, make oneself comfortable, stretch out.
recalce, *m.* 1. (agr.) hilling. 2. (carp.) extra felloe used instead of iron tire. 3. (bldg.) reinforcement of a foundation.
recalce, recalcé, *ref.* **recalzar.**
recalcitrante, *a.* recalcitrant, stubborn, obstinate.
recalcitrar, *i.v.* 1. to move back, recede. 2. to resist stubbornly, balk.
recalentador, *m.* superheater.
recalentamiento, *m.* 1. reheating, overheating; superheating. 2. spoiling of stored fruit or tobacco by excessive heat.
recalentar, (*ref. 29*) *tr.v.* 1. to reheat; to overheat; to superheat. 2. to excite sexually. *—r.v.* 1. to be excited sexually. 2. (agr.) to be spoiled by heat (tobacco, wheat, olives, etc.). 3. to overheat, get too hot.
recalescencia, *f.* (metal.) recalescence.
recaliente, recaliento, *ref.* **recalentar.**
recalmón, *m.* (mar.) lull (in wind or sea).
recalque, recalqué, *ref.* **recalcar.**
recalvastro, tra, *a.* (derog.) bald, baldpated.
recalzar, (*ref. 53*) *tr.v.* 1. (agr.) to hill (plants). 2. (bldg.) to reinforce (foundations). 3. (p.) to color, paint (a drawing).
recalzo, *m.* 1. (carp.) extra felloe used instead of iron tire. 2. (bldg.) reinforcement of foundations.
recalzón, *m.* (carp.) extra felloe used instead of an iron tire.
recamado, da, *a.* overlaid, enhanced by raised embroidery. *—m., f.* raised embroidery.
recamador, ra, *m., f.* one who does raised embroidery.
recamar, *tr.v.* to overlay, enhance with raised embroidery.
recámara, *f.* 1. dressing room; wardrobe. 2. reserve furniture, etc. (in houses of the rich). 3. (coll.) caution, reserve, prudence. 4. chamber, breech (of a gun). 5. (mil.) blasthole. 6. (Mex.) bedroom.
recamarera, *f.* (Mex.) chambermaid.
recambiar, *tr.v.* 1. to exchange again, rechange. 2. (com.) to redraw.
recambio, *m.* 1. changing again, rechanging. 2. spare part; **de r.,** spare (part).
recamo, *m.* 1. raised embroidery. 2. gold braid frog (ornamental loop and buttonhole on uniforms).
recancamusa, *f.* (coll.) trick, ruse, artifice.
recancanillla, *f.* 1. hippety-hop, feigned limp. 2. (coll.) emphasis, stress.
recantación, *f.* recantation; retraction.
recantón, *m.* corner spur stone.
recapacitar, *tr.v.* to turn over in one's mind, to reflect upon; to reconsider.
recapitulación, *f.* 1. recapitulation, summing up, summary. 2. (com.) consolidated statement.
recapitular, *tr.v.* to recapitulate, summarize.
recarga, *f.* (mil.) overcharge.
recargado, da, *past part. of* **recargar.** *—a.* overloaded; heavy (schedule, etc.); overdressed, overdecorated.
recargar, (*ref. 51*) *tr.v.* 1. to overload; to reload. 2. to charge extra, surcharge; to overcharge; to recharge, charge again. 3. to decorate excessively, to overdress. 4. to increase (a tax or duty). 5. (elec.) to recharge, reload. 6. to increase (prisoner's sentence). 7. to load (insurance premium). *—r.v.* (med.) to run a higher temperature, become more feverish.
recargable, *a.* rechargeable.
recargo, *m.* 1. extra charge, surcharge. 2. extra or additional load. 3. extra tax. 4. increase (in a prisoner's sentence). 5. (med.) rise in temperature.
recargue, recargué, *ref.* **recargar.**
recata, *f.* retasting, resampling (of food); (med.) taking a fresh specimen (of urine).
recatadamente, *adv.* 1. cautiously, circumspectly, reservedly. 2. modestly, chastely.
recatado, da, *a.* 1. cautious, circumspect, reserved. 2. modest, chaste; shy.
recatar, *tr.v.* 1. to hide, conceal, cover up. 2. to taste again. *—r.v.* 1. to act prudently. 2. to be modest, chaste; to cover oneself up. 3. to be afraid to take a decision.
recatear, *tr.v.* to haggle over (price); to sell retail.
recatería, *f.* 1. retail business. 2. haggle (over price, quantity, etc.).
recato, *m.* 1. caution, prudence, discretion, reserve. 2. modesty, chastity.
recatón, na, *a.* retail, retailing. *—m., f.* retailer, retail seller. *—m.* tip, ferrule, metal cap.
recatonazo, *m.* blow with the tip of a lance.
recatonear, *tr.v.* to retail, sell at retail.
recatonería, *f.* retail business; retailing.
recauchutaje, *m.* (Arg., Urug.) retreading, recapping (of a tire).
recauchutar, *tr.v.* (Amer.) to retread, recap (tires).
recaudación, *f.* 1. collection, collecting. 2. amount collected; receipts (in box-office or ticket office). 3. collector's office.
recaudador, *m.* collector; taxgatherer.
recaudamiento, *m.* 1. collection, collecting; receipts. 2. post of collector; collector's district.
recaudar, *tr.v.* 1. to collect (e.g. taxes); to take (as profits). 2. to look after, keep safe.
recaudatorio, ria, *a.* pertaining to collections or receipts.
recaudo, *m.* 1. collection, collecting. 2. care, precaution. 3. (law) bail, bond, surety. — **a buen r., a r.,** in safety.
recavar, *tr.v.* to dig again, redig.
recayendo, recayera, recayese, recayó, *ref.* **recaer.**
recazo, *m.* guard (of a sword); dull edge, back (of a knife).
rece, recé, *ref.* **rezar.**
recebar, *tr.v.* 1. to level (road) with gravel. 2. to refill (a cask).
recebo, *m.* 1. gravel, gravel on road surface. 2. liquid added to fill up a barrel.
rechar, *tr.v.* (hunt.) *var. of* **acechar.**
rececho, *m.* (hunt.) *var. of* **acecho.**
recelador, *m.* said of a horse used for making a mare receptive to a stud jackass.
recelamiento, *m., var. of* **recelo.**
recelar, *tr.v.* 1. to suspect, fear; to mistrust, distrust. 2. to get a mare in heat. *—i.v., r.v.* **r. de,** to suspect, fear; to mistrust, distrust.
recelo, *m.* fear; mistrust, distrust; misgiving, suspicion.
receloso, sa, *a.* distrustful, mistrustful, suspicious.
recensión, *f.* review, write-up, critique.
recentadura, *f.* leaven, leavening (for raising dough).
recental, *a.* suckling (lamb or calf). *—m.* suckling lamb or calf.
recentar, (*ref. 29*) *tr.v.* (cul.) to leaven (dough, bread). *—r.v.* to become renewed.
recentín, *a., var. of* **recental.**
recentísimo, ma, *a. super. of* **reciente, very recent.**
receñir, (*ref. 41*) *tr.v.* to regird; to re-encircle.
recepción, *f.* 1. reception; receiving; receipt. 2. welcoming, greeting, meeting. 3. admission; (law) examination of witnesses. — **r. heterodina,** (rad.) heterodyne reception; **r. homodina,** (rad.) homodine or zero-beat reception.
recepcionista, *m., f.* (Amer.) receptionist.
recepta, *f.* register of fines (imposed by the Council of Indies in charge of Spain's overseas possessions).
receptáculo, *m.* 1. receptacle, container; vessel. 2. (bot., zool., elec.) receptacle. 3. refuge, shelter. — **r. embutido,** (elec.) flush receptacle.
receptador, ra, *m., f.* (law) receptor (of fugitives from justice); receiver, receptor (of stolen goods); abettor.
receptar, *tr.v.* (law) to hide, conceal (a fugitive from justice); to receive, conceal (stolen goods).
receptividad, *f.* receptivity.
receptivo, va, *a.* receptive.
recepto, *m.* shelter, refuge.
receptor, ra, *a.* receiving. *—m.* receiver; (tel., rad., elec., mec.) receiver; (biochem., physiol.) receptor; (law) receiver. — **r. telefónico,** telephone receiver.
receptoría, *f.* receiver's office; (law) receivership.
recercar, (*ref. 50*) *tr.v.* to refence, fence in again; to fence in.
recésit, *m., var. of* **recle.**
receso, *m.* 1. separation, withdrawal. 2. (Amer.) recess, adjournment. 3. (astron.) deviation.
receta, *f.* 1. recipe, formula; (med.) prescription; (cul.) recipe. 2. (coll.) order memo, memorandum of orders. 3. (com.) amount brought forward.
recetador, *m.* prescriber (of medicines).
recetante, *a.* prescribing (doctor).

recetar, *tr.v.* 1. to prescribe (medicines). 2. (coll.) to request, beg.
recetario, *m.* 1. (med.) prescription book or record; physician's instructions. 2. (pharm.) pharmacopoeia, prescription or formula book, apothecary's file.
recetor, *m.* public treasurer; (law) receiver.
recetoría, *f.* public treasury; receiver's office.
rechace, rechacé, *ref.* **rechazar.**
rechazador, ra, *a.* 1. repelling, repulsing. 2. rejecting. 3. denying. —*m., f.* 1. repeller. 2. rejector.
rechazamiento, *m.* 1. repulsion, repelling. 2. rejection. 3. denial (of an accusation).
rechazar, (*ref. 53*) *tr.v.* 1. to repel, repulse, drive back. 2. to reject, turn down. 3. to deny (an accusation).
rechazo, *m.* 1. recoil, rebound. 2. rejection. 3. denial (of an accusation). — **de r.,** indirectly.
rechifla, *f.* hissing, hooting; hiss, hoot, catcall; derision, mockery, jeering.
rechiflar, *tr.v.* to whistle, hiss, hoot at; to mock, ridicule, to jeer at.
rechinador, ra, *a.* creaking, squeaking, grating.
rechinamiento, *m.* creak, squeak; squeaking, creaking, grating (of teeth).
rechinante, *a.* creaking, squeaking, grating.
rechinar, *i.v.* 1. to creak, squeak, grate. 2. to gnash, grind (one's teeth). 3. to gripe against, do something unwillingly. —*r.v.* (C. Amer., Col.) to burn (food).
rechinido, rechino, *m., var. of* **rechinamiento.**
rechistar, *i.v., var. of* **chistar.**
rechoncho, cha, *a.* (coll.) chubby, tubby, thickset (person).
rechupado, da, *a.* thin, lean.
rechupete, de r., delicious; terrific, fine, splendid.
recial, *m.* rapids, torrent, rapid current (in rivers).
reciamente, *adv.* strongly; vigorously; stoutly.
reciario, *m.* (hist.) retiarius (gladiator armed with net and trident).
recibidero, ra, *a.* receivable.
recibidor, ra, *a.* receiving. —*m., f.* recipient, receiver; receiving teller (in a bank). —*m.* anteroom, reception room.
recibiente, *a.* receiving.
recibimiento, *m.* 1. reception, receiving; greeting, welcome. 2. at-home, reception for guests at home. 3. anteroom, reception room; hall, vestibule.
recibir, *tr.v.* 1. to receive; to get, earn; to accept. 2. to meet, go to meet, welcome. —*i.v.* 1. to receive (visitors), be at home. 2. (rad.) to receive. —*r.v.* to graduate; **recibirse de,** to graduate as, be admitted to practice as.
recibo, *m.* 1. receipt (document acknowledging payment). 2. receipt, receiving. 3. reception room, anteroom. — **acusar r. de,** to acknowledge receipt of; **estar de r.,** to be at home (to visitors); **pieza de r.,** reception room; **ser de r.,** to be acceptable.
recidiva, *f.* (med.) relapse.
reciedumbre, *f.* strength, vigor, stamina.
recién, *adv.* 1. recently, newly; **r. casados,** newlyweds; **r. llegado,** newcomer; **r. nacido,** newborn. 2. (Amer.) just, just now, e.g. *recién lo vi,* I just saw him.
reciente, *a.* recent, late; fresh, new; modern; **noticias recientes,** fresh news.
reciente, reciento, *ref.* **recentar.**
recientemente, *adv.* recently, lately, newly.
recinchar, *tr.v.* to cinch, gird; to bind with a strap or a girdle; to tie together, bind together.
recinto, *m.* enclosure, space, area; ambit, precinct.
reciña, reciñendo, reciñera, reciñese, reciño, *ref.* **receñir.**
recio, cia, *a.* 1. strong, robust. 2. harsh, severe (weather, character). 3. heavy, hard, strong (attack, rain, etc.). 4. heavy, clayey (soil). 5. swift, impetuous. — **en lo más recio del combate,** in the thick of the fighting; **en lo más recio del invierno,** in the dead of winter.
recio, *adv.* strongly; vigorously, stoutly; loudly.
récipe, *m.* 1. (coll.) recipe, prescription. 2. (coll.) scolding, reprimand.
recipiendario, *m.* newly inducted member.
recipiente, *a.* recipient, receiving. —*m.* 1. receptacle, vessel, container. 2. bell glass (of a pump).
reciprocación, *f.* reciprocity, mutuality.
recíprocamente, *adv.* reciprocally, mutually.
reciprocar, (*ref. 50*) to reciprocate; to match a deed or an act; to make mutual.
reciprocidad, *f.* reciprocity.
recíproco, ca, *a.* 1. reciprocal, mutual. 2. (math.) reciprocal.
reciproque, reciproqué, *ref.* **reciprocar.**
recircular, *tr.v.* (phys.) to recycle.
recisión, *f.* (law) rescission, abrogation.
recitación, *f.* recitation, recital.
recitado, *m.* (mus.) recitative.
recitador, ra, *a.* reciting. —*m., f.* reciter, poetry reader, rhapsodist.
recital, *m.* (mus., poet.) recital.
recitar, *tr.v.* to recite (a poem), read out (a list), read (a speech).
recitativo, va, *a.* recitative.
reciura, *f.* 1. strength, robustness. 2. harshness, severeness (of weather).
reclamación, *f.* 1. claim, demand. 2. objection, protest, complaint. 3. (law) remonstration.
reclamante, *a.* claiming. —*m., f.* claimant, claimer; complainer.
reclamar, *tr.v.* 1. to re-claim, recover possession of. 2. to claim, ask for, demand; to clamor for. 3. (hunt.) to decoy, lure, call with a decoy whistle. 4. to look for, seek (a criminal), summon (a defaulting witness). —*i.v.* 1. to protest, object, complain, cry out, clamor, reclaim. 2. (poet.) to resound. —*r.v.* to call each other (birds).
reclamar, *i.v.* to hoist taut, hoist atrip; **a r.,** (mar.) hoisted taut, atrip.
reclame, *m.* (mar.) topmast hole and sheave. —*f.* (neol.) advertisement.
reclamo, *m.* 1. decoy bird; decoy whistle. 2. call; bird call; call with a decoy whistle. 3. attraction, allure. 4. advertisement, publicity. 5. reference mark (of a footnote). 6. (law) protest, claim, complaint, reclamation. 7. (print.) catchword. — **entablar un r.,** to file a claim.
recle, *m.* (ecc.) prebendaries' period of rest from choir duty.
reclinación, *f.* reclining; leaning.
reclinar, *tr.v., r.v.* to recline; to lean; **reclinarse en** or **sobre,** to lean on or upon.
reclinatorio, *m.* 1. couch, chaise lounge. 2. prie-dieu, kneeling stool.
recluir, (*ref. 48*) *tr.v.* to shut in, imprison, confine, seclude. —*r.v.* to go into seclusion; to shut oneself in.
reclusión, *f.* confinement, seclusion; internment, imprisonment; **r. aislada,** solitary confinement.
recluso, sa, *past part. of* **recluir.** —*a.* imprisoned; shut in, confined. —*m., f.* prisoner; inmate.
reclusorio, *m.* place of seclusion or confinement.
recluta, *f.* 1. recruitment. 2. (Arg.) round-up of cattle. —*m.* recruit, rookie, inductee, conscript.
reclutador, *m.* recruiter, recruiting officer.
reclutamiento, *m.* 1. recruitment, recruiting, conscription. 2. year's draft, year's recruits.
reclutar, *tr.v.* 1. to recruit, conscript. 2. (Arg.) to round up (cattle).
recluya, recluyendo, recluyera, recluyese, recluyo, *ref.* **recluir.**
recobrable, *a.* recoverable.
recobrante, *a.* recovering.
recobrar, *tr.v.* to recover, recuperate, regain; to retrieve. — **r. el aliento,** to get one's breath back. —*r.v.* to recover, recuperate.
recobro, *m.* recovery, recuperation.
recocción, *f.* (metal.) annealing.
recocer, (*ref. 75*) *tr.v.* 1. to cook again, recook, boil or bake again; to overcook, cook too much. 2. to anneal (metal). —*r.v.* 1. to overcook, get overcooked. 2. to be burning (with anger, passion, etc.).
recocho, cha, *a.* overcooked, overdone.
recocido, da, *a.* 1. overcooked. 2. annealed. 3. experienced. —*m., f.* 1. recooking; overcooking. 2. (metal.) annealing.
recocina, *f.* back kitchen, pantry.
recodadero, *m.* elbow board, elbow support.
recodar, *i.v., r.v.* to lean or rest one's elbows (on); to rest or lean on one's elbows.
recodar, *i.v.* to wind, bend, turn, twist (a river, road, etc.).
recodo, *m.* bend, angle; twist, turn (of a river, etc.).
recogedero, *m.* 1. gathering or collecting place. 2. collector, collecting pan; dustpan.
recogedor, ra, *m., f.* collector, gatherer; **r. de pelotas,** ball boy (in tennis). —*m.* 1. (agr.) gleaner, rake, scraper. 2. collector, collecting pan; dustpan. 3. workman who takes molten glass from a crucible.
recogegotas, (*pl.* **recogegotas**), *m.* (auto.) drip pan.
recoger, (*ref. 57*) *tr.v.* 1. to pick up, retrieve, take back. 2. to pick up, collect, go for, go to collect. 3. to gather, gather together, collect; to harvest, gather, pick (crops, berries, etc.). 4. (dressm.) to gather, draw together, bunch up (fabric when making pleats), to shorten. 5. to put away, put in a safe place. 6. to save, put away. 7. to take in, shelter, give shelter or protection to. 8. to lock up, put away (in an institution). 9. to suspend, discontinue, withdraw from circulation. —*r.v.* 1. to take shelter or refuge. 2. to withdraw, retire; to seclude oneself, go into seclusion; to abstract oneself. 3. to cut down on one's expenses. 4. to retire (to sleep or rest). 5. to go home.
recogida, *f.* 1. withdrawal, retirement. 2. gathering, collecting, harvesting.
recogidamente, *adv.* introspectively; devoutly.
recogido, da, *past part. of* **recoger.** —*a.* 1. retiring, reserved, withdrawn, abstracted. 2. cloistered (nun, woman). 3. short-trunked (animal). 4. quiet, secluded. —*m., f.* inmate of a hermitage or house of correction; waif.
recogimiento, *m.* 1. spiritual absorption, self-communion, withdrawal into oneself. 2. sheltering; shelter, protection. 3. hermitage, house of seclusion or retreat.
recoja, recojo, *ref.* **recoger.**
recolar, (*ref. 33*) *tr.v.* to strain or sift again.
recolección, *f.* 1. collection, gathering (of money or taxes). 2. harvest, crop. 3. summary, compendium. 4. spiritual absorption or withdrawal. 5. house of retirement or seclusion.
recolectar, *tr.v.* to gather, collect.
recolector, *m.* collector, taxgatherer.
recolegir, (*ref. 76*) *tr.v.* 1. to gather, collect. 2. to surmise, conjecture, deduce.
recoleto, ta, *a.* in retreat or meditation (monk, nun or monastery). —*m.* (ecc.) recollet.
recomendable, *a.* commendable; recommendable, advisable.
recomendablemente, *adv.* commendably.

recomendación, *f.* 1. recommendation, endorsement, praise. 2. request, rejoinder. — **r. del alma,** (ecc.) prayers for the dying.
recomendante, *a.* recommending. —*m., f.* recommender, endorser.
recomendar, (*ref. 29*) *tr.v.* 1. to recommend; to advise. 2. to request, rejoin, ask.
recomendatorio, ria, *a.* recommendatory.
recomenzar, (*ref. 68*) *tr.v.* to recommence, begin again.
recomerse, *r.v., var. of* **concomerse.**
recomience, recomienzo, *ref.* **recomenzar.**
recomiende, recomiendo, *ref.* **recomendar.**
recompensa, *f.* recompense, compensation, reward; **en r.,** in return, as a reward.
recompensable, *a.* recompensable, rewardable.
recompensación, *f., var. of* **recompensa.**
recompensar, *tr.v.* to recompense, compensate; to reward; to remunerate, pay.
recomponer, (*ref. 15*) *tr.v.* 1. to repair again. 2. to recompose.
recomponga, recompongo, *ref.* **recomponer.**
recomposición, *f.* 1. alteration, mending. 2. recomposition.
recompuesto, ta, *past part. of* **recomponer. —***a.* repaired, repaired again; composed again.
recompuse, recompusiera, recompusiese, *ref.* **recomponer.**
reconcentración, reconcentramiento, *m.* 1. concentration, gathering together. 2. mental absorption or abstraction, deep thought. 3. (mil., hist.) concentration (of a vanquished people).
reconcentrar, *tr.v.* 1. to concentrate, gather together. 2. to conceal and intensify (feelings). —*r.v.* 1. to become absorbed in thought, become abstracted, withdraw within oneself. 2. to become concentrated, gather together.
reconciliación, *f.* reconciliation.
reconciliador, ra, *a.* reconciling. —*m., f.* reconciler.
reconciliar, *tr.v.* 1. to reconcile, bring together. 2. to bring back into the Church. 3. to hear a short or summary confession from. 4. to bless (a sacred place which has been desecrated). —*r.v.* 1. to be reconciled, come together. 2. to be brought back into the Church. 3. to make a short confession.
reconcomerse, *r.v., var. of* **concomerse.**
reconcomio, *m.* 1. (coll.) fear, suspicion, misgiving. 2. itch, desire, craving, yen.
reconditez, *f.* (coll.) reconditeness.
recóndito, ta, *a.* recondite, hidden. 2. deep, cherished, e.g. *deseo recóndito,* deep wish.
reconducción, *f.* (law) extension (of a lease).
reconducir, (*ref. 47*) *tr.v.* (law) to extend or renew (a lease).
reconduje, recondujera, recondujese, reconduzca, reconduzco, *ref.* **reconducir.**
reconfortar, *tr.v.* to comfort, cheer up, console, strengthen.
reconocedor, ra, *a.* 1. recognizing. 2. examining, inspecting. —*m., f.* 1. recognizer. 2. examiner, inspector.
reconocer, (*ref. 45*) *tr.v.* 1. to recognize; to acknowledge. 2. to admit, confess. 3. (dipl.) to recognize (a government, a nation). 4. to examine, inspect; (mil.) to reconnoiter. —*r.v.* 1. to be obvious, be clear, apparent. 2. to know oneself.
reconocible, *a.* recognizable.
reconocidamente, *adv.* 1. gratefully. 2. acknowledgedly. 3. confessedly, avowedly.
reconocido, da, *past part. of* **reconocer. —***a.* 1. grateful, appreciative. 2. confessed, acknowledged.
reconociente, *a.* recognizing.
reconocimiento, *m.* 1. recognition; admission, acknowledgment. 2. (dipl.) recognition. 3. gratitude, appreciation. 4. inspection, examination; (mil.) reconnaissance — **r. fotográfico,** (mil.) photo-reconnaissance.
reconozca, reconozco, *ref.* **reconocer.**
reconquista, *f.* 1. reconquest, reconquering. 2. (hist.) **R.,** the struggle to end Moorish rule in Spain.
reconquistar, *tr.v.* to reconquer; to regain, win back, recover.
reconsiderar, *tr.v.* to reconsider.
reconstitución, *f.* reconstitution.
reconstituir, (*ref. 48*) *tr.v.* to reconstitute.
reconstituya, reconstituyendo, *ref.* **reconstituir.**
reconstituyente, *a.* reconstituent. —*m.* (med.) reconstituent, tonic, restorative.
reconstituyera, reconstituyese, reconstituyo, *ref.* **reconstituir.**
reconstrucción, *f.* reconstruction; rebuilding.
reconstructivo, va, *a.* reconstructive.
reconstruir, (*ref. 48*) *tr.v.* to reconstruct; to rebuild.
reconstruya, reconstruyendo, reconstruyera, reconstruyese, reconstruyo, *ref* **reconstruir.**
recontamiento, *m.* recounting, narration.
recontar, (*ref. 33*) *tr.v.* 1. to re-count, count again. 2. to recount, relate, tell, narrate.
recontento, ta, *a.* very happy, greatly pleased. —*m.* great happiness or satisfaction.
reconvalecer, (*ref. 45*) *i.v.* to reconvalesce, convalesce anew.
reconvalezca, reconvalezco, *ref.* **reconvalecer.**
reconvención, *f.* 1. remonstrance, reprimand, reprehension, rebuke. 2. (law) reconvention, cross action (by a defendant).
reconvenga, reconvengo, *ref.* **reconvenir.**
reconvenir, (*ref. 26*) *tr.v.* 1. to remonstrate, reprimand, rebuke, reproach. 2. (law) to countercharge.
reconvine, reconviniendo, reconviniera, reconviniese, *ref.* **reconvenir.**
recopilación, *f.* 1. compendium, collection, compilation. 2. resumé, summary, abridgment. 3. (law) digest.
recopilador, *m.* 1. compiler. 2. abridger.
recopilar, *tr.v.* 1. to compile. 2. to abridge.
recoquín, *m.* (coll.) short, chubby man.
récord, *m.* (sport) record; **batir un r.,** to break a record.
recordable, *a.* memorable; that can be remembered.
recordación, *f.* 1. commemoration. 2. recollection, remembrance.
recordador, ra, *a.* remembering; reminding.
recordar, (*ref. 33*) *tr.v.* 1. to remember; to recollect. 2. to remind; to remind of, bring back, bring to mind. — **r. algo a alguien,** to remind someone of something. —*i.v.* 1. to remember, recollect. 2. to wake up; to come to, revive. —*r.v.* 1. to be commemorated, be remembered. 2. to wake up.
recordativo, va, *a.* reminding, reminiscent. —*m.* reminder, memento.
recordatorio, *m.* reminder, memento.
recorrer, *tr.v.* 1. to travel; to traverse, cross, go over or through. 2. to run over, look over; to peruse (a document, etc.). 3. to repair, overhaul. 4. (print.) to justify.
recorrido, *past part. of* **recorrer. —***m.* 1. space or distance traveled. 2. trip, run, journey. 3. stroke (of a piston). 4. repairing, overhauling. 5. reprimand. — **un auto con muy poco r.,** a car with very little mileage; **r. de aterrizaje,** (avia.) landing run; **r. del émbolo,** (mec.) piston travel; **r. de prueba,** trial run.
recortado, da, *a.* (bot.) notched, indented (leaves). —*m.* cutout (figure).
recortadura, *f.* cutting, trimming, clipping; (*pl.*) cuttings, trimmings.
recortar, *tr.v.* 1. to cut, cut off, cut away, clip, trim off. 2. to cut down, reduce, decrease. 3. (p.) to outline.
recorte, *m.* 1. cutting, trimming, clipping; (*pl.*) cuttings, trimmings; newspaper clipping. 2. (taur.) dodge (to avoid the bull). — **r. de periódico,** press clipping.
recorvar, *tr.v., r.v.* to bend, curve.
recorvo, va, *a.* bent, curved, arched.
recoser, *tr.v.* to sew again; to mend, patch, darn; to overcast (stitch).
recosido, *m.* resewing; mending, darning, patching.
recostadero, *m.* low stool; resting or reclining place.
recostar, (*ref. 33*) *tr.v.* to lean; recline. —*r.v.* to lean, recline; to lie back; to lie down (for a short rest).
recova, *f.* 1. poultry business; poultry market, poultry stand. 2. (hunt.) pack of hunting dogs. 3. (Amer.) market.
recoveco, *m.* 1. turn, twist, bend; nook. 2. trick, ruse, artifice.
recovero, ra, *m., f.* poultry dealer.
recre, *m., var. of* **recle.**
recreación, *f.* recreation; entertainment, amusement.
recrear, *tr.v.* to entertain, amuse, recreate. —*r.v.* to amuse or entertain oneself; to take delight in.
recreativo, va, *a.* entertaining, recreative.
recrecer, (*ref. 45*) *tr.v.* to increase, augment. —*i.v.* 1. to increase, grow. 2. to recur. —*r.v.* to recover one's spirits.
recrecimiento, *m.* increase, growth.
recreído, da, *a.* (hunt.) wild, gone wild (said of falcons).
recrementicio, cia, *a.* (physiol.) recrementitious.
recremento, *m.* (physiol.) recrement.
recreo, *m.* 1. recreation; entertainment, amusement. 2. recess, recreation time (at school).
recrezca, recrezco, *ref.* **recrecer.**
recría, *f.* 1. fattening on new pastures (animals); breeding of colts, etc. 2. regeneration, reanimation. 3. (theol.) redemption.
recriador, *m.* one in charge of fattening or improving breeds; breeder.
recriar, (*ref. 54*) *tr.v.* 1. to fatten new pastures (colts and other animals). 2. to regenerate, give new strength. 3. (theol.) to redeem, re-create.
recriminación, *f.* recrimination.
recriminador, ra, *a.* recriminating. —*m., f.* recriminator.
recriminar, *tr.v.* to recriminate, reproach. —*i.v.* to recriminate, bring a counter accusation against. —*r.v.* to recriminate one another, exchange recriminations.
recriminatorio, ria, *a.* recriminatory, recriminative.
recrudecer, (*ref. 45*) *i.v., r.v.* to get worse; to flare up, break out again, recrudesce.
recrudecimiento, *m.,* **recrudescencia,** *f.* worsening; flaring up; recrudescence.
recrudescente, *a.* recrudescent.
recrudezca, *ref.* **recrudecer.**
recrujir, *i.v.* to creak, crackle or rustle loudly.
recruzar, (*ref. 53*) *tr.v., r.v.* to recross, cross again.
rectal, *a.* (anat.) rectal.
rectamente, *adv.* honestly, in an upright manner, righteously, rightly.

rectangular, *a.* rectangular.
rectángulo, la, *a.* rectangular, right-angled. —*m.* rectangle.
rectificable, *a.* rectifiable.
rectificación, *f.* rectification, correction; (chem., elec., math.) rectification.
rectificador, ra, *a.* rectifying; (elec.) rectifier. —*m.* (elec.) rectifier. —*f.* grinder, dresser (instrument); **r. cilíndrica,** (mec.) cylindrical grinder.
rectificar, (*ref. 50*) *tr.v.* to rectify, correct; to adjust; (chem., elec., math.) to rectify.
rectificativo, va, *a.* rectifying.
rectifique, rectifiqué, *ref.* **rectificar.**
rectilíneo, a, *a.* 1. rectilinear, rectilineal. 2. (fig.) upright, honest, straight; straight-laced, righteous.
rectitud, *f.* 1. rectitude, honesty, uprightness. 2. rightness, correctness, accuracy. 3. straightness.
recto, ta, *a.* 1. straight. 2. honest, honorable, upright, righteous, just, fair; severe. 3. literal (meaning). 4. (geom.) right (angle). 5. (anat.) rectal. —*m.* (anat.) rectum; (anat.) rectus. —*f.* straight line. — **r. final,** home or final stretch (of a racecourse).
rector, ra, *a.* governing, ruling, directing. —*m., f.* principal, superior, superintendent, director; rector, president (of a university). —*m.* rector, parish priest.
rectorado, *m.* rectorate; rectorship; directorship.
rectoral, *a.* rectorial. —*f.* rectory.
rectorar, *i.v.* to become a rector; to become a parish priest.
rectoría, *f.* rectorate; rectorship; office of a rector, principal or superintendent.
recua, *f.* pack, drove (of pack animals); (coll.) pack, crowd.
recuadrar, *tr.v.* (art.) to divide into squares, to reticulate.
recuadro, *m.* (archit.) panel, compartment, square division.
recuaje, *m.* toll for the passage of pack animals.
recuarta, *f.* one of the strings of the ancient guitar.
recubierto, ta, *irr. past part. of* **recubrir.**
recubrimiento, *m.* 1. covering, coating, lining, facing. 2. retiling (roof).
recubrir, *irr. past part.:* **recubierto.** —*tr.v.* to recover, cover again; to retile (roofs); to cover; to coat; to line, face, overlay.
recudimento, recudimiento, *m.* (law) power to collect rents.
recudir, *tr.v.* to pay (what is due). —*i.v.* to return, rebound, spring or come back.
recuele, recuelo, *ref.* **recolar.**
recuelo, *m.* 1. strong lye (used in laundering). 2. warmed up or re-percolated coffee.
recuente, recuento, *ref.* **recontar.**
recuento, *m.* 1. count; re-count, tally. 2. inventory. — **r. de pólenes,** pollen count; **r. de sangre,** (med.) blood count.
recuentro, *m., var. of* **reencuentro.**
recuerde, recuerdo, *ref.* **recordar.**
recuerdo, *m.* 1. memory, recollection. 2. remembrance, keepsake, memento, souvenir. 3. (*pl.*) regards, greetings; compliments.
recuero, *m.* muleteer, pack driver.
recuesta, *f.* request, warning, demand.
recuestar, *tr.v.* to demand, request; to warn.
recueste, recuesto, *ref.* **recostar.**
recuesto, *m.* slope, declivity.
recueza, recuezo, *ref.* **recocer.**
reculada, *f.* backing, backing up, going backwards; (coll.) backing down.
recular, *i.v.* 1. to go back, go backwards, back up; to recoil; (coll.) to back down (in one's opinions). 2. (coll.) to yield, give up. 3. (mar.) to fall astern.
reculo, la, *a.* tailless (poultry).
reculones, a r., (coll.) backwards, backing up.
recuñar, *tr.v.* (min.) to cut (rock or ore in a quarry or mine) by wedging.
recuperable, *a.* recoverable.
recuperación, *f.* recovery, recuperation.
recuperador, ra, *a.* recovering. —*m., f.* recoverer. —*m.* recuperator.
recuperar, *tr.v., r.v.* to recover, recuperate, regain, retrieve. —*r.v.* to recover one's health, losses, etc.
recuperativo, va, *a.* recuperative.
recura, *f.* toothing knife (for forming and cutting the teeth of a comb), comb saw.
recurar, *tr.v.* to tooth (a comb).
recurrente, *a.* recurrent. —*m., f.* (law) appellant; petitioner.
recurrible, *a.* (law) appealable.
recurrido, da, *a.* (law) appealed against. —*m., f.* (law) appellee.
recurrir, *i.v.* 1. to appeal (to), have recourse (to), resort (to). 2. to revert, return (to). 3. (law) to petition, apply; to appeal.
recurso, *m.* 1. way, means, recourse, resort. 2. (*pl.*) means, funds; resources, wealth. 3. (law) appeal; application, petition. 4. return, reversion. — **r. de habeas corpus,** (law) appeal for habeas corpus; **r. de nulidad,** (law) appeal for annulment; **r. de queja,** (law) complaint appeal; **recursos naturales,** natural resources; **sin r.,** irremediably, without appeal; without help.
recusable, *a.* rejectable; objectionable; refusable; (law) recusable, able to be challenged or objected to.
recusación, *f.* rejection; refusal; (law) recusation, objection, challenge, exception.
recusante, *a.* rejecting; objecting, challenging. —*m., f.* objector, challenger; rejector.
recusar, *tr.v.* to object to; to reject, refuse; (law) to object to, challenge the competence or impartiality of, recuse.
red, *f.* net; netting, mesh. 2. (coll.) net, snare, trick. 3. network, system (of communications, supplies, roads, nerves, railways, etc.). 4. (opt.) grating. 5. railing, fence, paling, grating. — **a r. barredera,** sweepingly, overwhelmingly; **caer uno en la r.,** to fall into a trap, be tricked; **echar** or **tender las redes,** to cast fishing nets; (coll.) to take measures, make plans (to obtain something); **r. barredera,** dragnet, seine; **r. de aire,** hanging net used as a bird snare; **r. de difracción,** (opt.) diffraction grating; **r. de discriminación,** (rad.) dividing network; (elec.) crossover network; **r. de emisoras,** radio network; **r. de jorrar** or **de jorro,** dragnet, seine; **r. de torpedos,** torpedo net or netting.
redacción, *f.* writing, editing; editing office, editorial room; editors, editorial staff.
redactar, *tr.v.* 1. to write, redact; draw up. 2. to edit, be the editor of (book, newspaper, etc.).
redactor, ra, *m., f.* writer; editor, member of an editorial staff; **r. deportivo,** sports editor; **r. jefe** or **responsable,** editor-in-chief.
redada, *f.* 1. casting of a net. 2. netful, catch, haul. 3. roundup, dragnet (of suspects, criminals); (pol.) razzia (of conspirators).
redaño, *m.* 1. (anat.) caul, omentum. 2. (*pl.*) (coll.) strength, spirit, pluck, courage, guts (sl.).
redar, *tr.v.* to cast a net, catch in a net, haul in.
redargución, *f.* counter-argument, refutation; (law) impugnation.
redargüir, (*ref. 49*) *tr.v.* to argue in reply, retort; (law) to impugn, object to.
redaya, *f.* river fishing net.
redecilla, *f.* 1. *dim. of* **red,** small net or network; netting, mesh; hair net. 2. (zool.) reticulum (of a ruminant).
redecir, (*ref. 7*) *tr.v.* to say or repeat over and over again.
rededor, *m.* neighborhood, surroundings, environs; **alrededor de,** around, surrounding, circa.
redejón, *m.* large hairnet.
redel, *m.* (mar.) loof frame.
redención, *f.* 1. redemption, salvation, deliverance. 2. (com.) redemption (of a pledge, mortgage, etc.).
redentor, ra, *a.* redeeming. —*m., f.* redeemer. —*m.* (rel.) the Redeemer (Jesus Christ).
redentorista, *a., m.* (ecc.) Redemptorist.
redero, ra, *a.* pertaining to mesh or net, reticular. —*m., f.* netmaker; birdcatcher or fisherman who uses a net.
redescubrir, *irr. past part.:* **redescubierto.** —*tr.v.* to rediscover.
redescuento, *m.* (com.) rediscount.
redhibición, *f.* (law) redhibition.
redhibir, *tr.v.* (law) to return (a purchased article); to annul a sale by right of redhibition.
redhibitorio, ria, *a.* redhibitory.
redicho, cha, *irr. past part. of* **redecir.** —*a.* (coll.) affected (in speech), with affected precision.
redición, *f.* repetition, reiteration.
rediente, *m.* (fort.) redan.
rediezmar, *tr.v.* to tithe a second time.
rediezmo, *m.* second or extra tithe.
redifundir, *tr.v., i.v.* (rad., tel.) to rebroadcast.
rediga, redigo, redije, redijera, redijese, *ref.* **redecir.**
redil, *m.* sheepcote, sheepfold.
redimible, *a.* redeemable.
redimir, *tr.v.* 1. to redeem. 2. to ransom, liberate (a slave); to win back, reconquer (territory). 3. to redeem (something in pawn); to buy back. 4. to free, exempt (from an obligation). 5. to save, free, deliver (from penury, misfortune, etc.).
redingote, *m.* redingote, greatcoat.
redistribución, *f.* 1. redistribution. 2. resettlement (of displaced persons, etc.).
redistribuir, (*ref. 48*) *tr.v.* to redistribute.
rédito, *m.* revenue, income, profit, interest, yield.
redituable, reditual, *a.* revenue-yielding, income-producing.
redituar, (*ref. 55*) *tr.v.* to yield, produce; to draw (a revenue, income, interest, etc.).
redivivo, va, *a.* redivivus, resuscitated, revived.
redoblado, da, *a.* 1. stocky, thick-set (person); strong, resistant, tough (object). 2. (mil.) double-quick (step), double-time.
redobladura, redoblamiento, *m.* 1. redoubling, doubling. 2. repetition. 3. clinching (of a nail, etc.).
redoblante, *m.* (mus.) side or snare drum or drummer.
redoblar, *tr.v.* 1. to redouble, double. 2. to repeat, do again. 3. to clinch, bend back (a nail). —*i.v.* to roll, beat repeatedly (a drum). —*r.v.* to grow louder; to become more intense.
redoble, *m.* 1. (mil., mus.) roll, rolling (of a drum). 2. doubling, redoubling.
redoblegar, (*ref. 51*) *tr.v.* to double, bend, clinch.
redoblegue, redoblegué, *ref.* **redoblegar.**
redoblón, *m.* clinch nail, rivet.
redolente, *a.* slightly painful.
redoma, *f.* (chem.) balloon; vial, flask, phial.
redomado, da, *a.* artful, sly, crafty.
redomón, na, *a.* (S. Amer.) not fully broken (horse, mare).
redonda, *f.* 1. region, district, area. 2. pasture, pasture land. 3. (mus.) semibreve. 4. (mar.) square sail. — **a la r.,** around.
redondamente, *adv.* 1. plainly, categorically, flatly. 2. around, in a circle.

redondeado, da, *a.* round, rounded; spherical.
redondear, *tr.v.* 1. to round, make round. 2. to round off, perfect, complete; to make into a round sum. —*r.v.* 1. to become round. 2. to clear oneself of debts. 3. to become competent or expert.
redondel, *m.* 1. (coll.) circle. 2. round cloak. 3. circular mat. 4. (bull) ring, arena.
redondete, ta, *a. dim. of* **redondo,** roundish.
redondez, *f.* roundness; rotundity. — **r. de la tierra,** the face of the earth, curvature of the earth.
redondilla, *f.* 1. (poet.) octosyllabic quatrain rhyming abba. 2. librarian's round script.
redondo, da, *a.* 1. round, circular. 2. private pasture (land). 3. clear, straight, flat, categorical (denial, rejection, etc.). — **cifra redonda,** round figure; **letra redonda,** (print.) roman round or standard type; **viaje r.,** round trip. —*m.* 1. circle, round, ring. 2. (coll.) cash, ready money; **en r.,** around, roundabout; clearly, categorically, plainly.
redondón, *m.* large circle or sphere.
redopelo, *m.* 1. rubbing the wrong way. 2. (coll.) squabble, scuffle, fight. — **al or a r.,** the wrong way, against the grain; forcibly; against one's will; **traer al redopelo,** (coll.) to treat roughly and with contempt.
redor, *m.* 1. round mat. 2. (poet.) neighborhood, vicinity.
redova, *f.* (mus.) redowa (Polish dance).
redro, *adv.* behind, backward. —*m.* annual ring (on the horns of sheep or goats).
redrojo, *m.* 1. small bunch of grapes remaining after the vintage. 2. second fruit or blossom. 3. (coll.) puny child, runt.
redropelo, *m., var. of* **redopelo.**
redruejo, *m., var. of* **redrojo.**
reducción, *f.* 1. reduction, decrease. 2. (mec.) reducing coupling, reducer (coupling for joining a pipe to another of smaller diameter). 3. (Amer., hist.) settlement of converted Indians. — **r. al absurdo,** reductio ad absurdum (Lat.).
reducible, *a.* reducible.
reducido, da, *past part. of* **reducir.** —*a.* 1. reduced, diminished; small, compact. 2. narrow, limited.
reducimiento, *m.* reduction.
reducir, (*ref. 47*) *tr.v.* 1. to reduce, convert; to change (currency). 2. to reduce; to diminish, decrease, shorten, lessen. 3. to condense, boil down, reduce. 4. to subject, subjugate. 5. to convince. 6. (surg.) to reduce (dislocated bone, displaced organ). 7. (log., math., chem.) to reduce. 8. (p.) to reduce to scale. 9. (Amer.) to receive, buy and dispose of (stolen goods). —*r.v.* 1. to boil down, condense, e.g. *todos los problemas se reducen a uno básico,* all the problems boil down to a basic one. 2. to cut down on one's living expenses. 3. to be compelled to make a decision.
reductible, *a.* reducible.
reducto, *m.* (fort.) redoubt.
reductor, ra, *a.* reducing. —*m.* reducer; **r. de voltaje** or **tensión,** (elec.) voltage divider.
reduje, redujera, redujese, *ref.* **reducir.**
redundancia, *f.* redundancy, redundance, excess.
redundante, *a.* redundant; superfluous.
redundantemente, *adv.* redundantly.
redundar, *tr.v.* 1. to overflow. 2. to redound, result in, lead to.
reduplicación, *f.* 1. reduplication. 2. (rhet.) repetition, anadiplosis.
reduplicado, da, *past part. of* **reduplicar.** —*a.* reduplicated, redoubled.
reduplicar, (*ref. 50*) *tr.v.* to reduplicate, repeat, reiterate.
reduplique, redupliqué, *ref.* **reduplicar.**
reduvio, *m.* (ento.) assassin bug.
reduzca, reduzco, *ref.* **reducir.**
reedición, *f.* reissue, reprint.
reedificación, *f.* rebuilding, reconstruction.
reedificador, ra, *a.* rebuilding, reconstructive. —*m., f.* rebuilder.
reedificar, (*ref. 50*) *tr.v.* to rebuild, reconstruct.
reedifique reedifiqué, *ref.* **reedificar.**
reeditar, *tr.v.* to reprint, publish again.
reeducación, *f.* reeducation.
reeducar, (*ref. 50*) *tr.v.* to re-educate.
reeduque, reeduqué, *ref.* **reeducar.**
reelección, *f.* reelection.
reelecto, ta, *irr. past part. of* **reelegir.**
reelegible, *a.* re-elegible.
reelegir, (*ref. 76*) *tr.v.* to reelect, elect again.
reeligiendo, reeligiera, reeligiese, reeligió, reelija, reelijo, *ref.* **reelegir.**
reembarcar, (*ref. 50*) *tr.v., r.v.* to reship, reembark.
reembargo, *m.* (law) reattachment.
reembarque, *m.* reembarkation, reshipment.
reembarque, reembarqué, *ref.* **reembarcar.**
reembolsable, *a.* reimbursable, repayable.
reembolsar, *tr.v.* to reimburse; to repay, pay back, refund. —*r.v.* to recover (disbursed or expended sum of money).
reembolso, *m.* reimbursement; refund, repayment. — **entrega contra r.,** cash on delivery.
reempacar, *tr.v.* to reeducate.
reemplace, reemplacé, *ref.* **reemplazar.**
reemplazable, *a.* replaceable.
reemplazante, *m.* replacement (person).
reemplazar, (*ref. 53*) *tr.v.* to replace, substitute; to supersede.
reemplazo, *m.* 1. replacement, substitute. 2. (mil.) replacement, reinforcement.
reempleo, *m.* reemployment.
reemplear, *tr.v.* to hire again, to employ a second time.
reencarcelamiento, *m.* (law) remand.
reencarcelar, *tr.v.* to remand.
reencarnación, *f.* reincarnation.
reencarnar, *i.v.* to reincarnate. —*r.v.* to become reincarnated.
reencauchar, *tr.v.* to retread (tires).
reencauche, *m.* retreading (of tires).
reencuardenación, *f.* rebinding, new binding (for a book).
reencuadernar, *tr.v.* to rebind (a book).
reencuentro, *m.* 1. collision; (mil.) clash, skirmish. 2. (coll.) chance meeting (of long-parted friends, enemies, etc.).
reenganchamiento, *m.* (mil.) reenlistment; reenlistment bonus.
reenganchar, *tr.v.* (mil.) to reenlist. —*r.v.* to reenlist (to enroll oneself again).
reenganche, *m.* (mil.) reenlistment; reenlistment bonus.
reengastar, *tr.v.* (jewel.) to reset.
reengendrador, ra, *a.* regenerating. —*m., f.* regenerator, reviver.
reengendrar, *tr.v.* to regenerate, reproduce; to revive, renew.
reensayar, *tr.v.* 1. (theat.) to rehearse anew. 2. to test again, try out again. 3. (metal.) to reassay.
reensaye, *m.* second assay (of metal).
reensayo, *m.* 1. (theat.) second rehearsal. 2. second tryout (of a machine), second test or trial.
reentrada, *f.* reentry.
reenvasar, *tr.v.* to refill, repack.
reenviar, (*ref. 54*) *tr.v.* 1. to send back, return. 2. to forward, send on.
reenvidar, *tr.v.* to raise (the bid, the stake).
reenvío, *m.* return, sending back; forwarding.
reenvite, *m.* extra bid (in gambling).
reestreno, *m.* revival (of a film or play).
reexaminación, *f.* reexamination.
reexaminar, *tr.v.* to reexamine.
reexpedición, *f.* forwarding, reshipment.
reexpedir, (*ref. 39*) *tr.v.* to forward, reship.
reexportación, *f.* reexportation; reexport.
reexportar, *tr.v.* (com.) to reexport.
refacción, *f.* 1. refreshment, snack, collation. 2. renovation, redoing, repair, overhaul. 3. (coll.) extra, bonus. 4. (Mex., Cuba, Peru, P. Rico) running or upkeep expenses. 5. (Mex.) financial aid or assistance.
refaccionar, *tr.v.* 1. (Amer.) to repair, renovate, overhaul. 2. (Cuba, Mex., Peru, P. Rico) to finance, aid.
refajo, *m.* underskirt, slip, petticoat.
refalsado, da, *a.* false, deceiving.
refección, *f.* 1. refreshment, snack, collation. 2. renovation, repair, overhauling.
refectolero, *m., var. of* **refitolero.**
refectorio, *m.* refectory, dining hall (in schools, convents, monasteries).
referencia, *f.* 1. reference, allusion. 2. reference, relationship, relation. 3. narration, account, report. 4. (*pl.*) references (information about someone's character, etc.).
referendario, *m., var. of* **refrendario.**
referéndum, *m.* referendum.
referente, *a.* referring, relating.
referible, *a.* 1. referable. 2. narratable.
referido, da, *a.* related, expressed, said.
referir, (*ref. 42*) *tr.v.* 1. to relate, tell, report, narrate. 2. to refer (to), direct (to). —*r.v.* to refer oneself (to).
refertero, ra, *a.* quarrelsome.
refiera, refiero, *ref.* **referir.**
refigurar, *tr.v.* to conjure up, imagine anew.
refilón, *adv.* obliquely, askance; sideways; **de r.,** in passing; out of the corner of one's eye.
refinación, *f.* refining; refinement.
refinadera, *f.* roller (for making chocolate paste).
refinado, da, *past part. of* **refinar.** —*a.* refined, polished; subtle, artful. — **azúcar refinada,** refined sugar; **crueldad refinada,** refined cruelty; **modales refinados,** refined manners.
refinador, ra, *m., f.* refiner; finisher.
refinadura, *f.* refining, refinement.
refinamiento, *m.* refinement; refining, e.g. *r. de azúcar,* sugar-refining.
refinanciación, *f.* (com.) refinancing.
refinanciar, *tr.v.* (com.) to refinance.
refinar, *tr.v.* to refine; to polish, perfect (literary style, manners, taste, etc.).
refinería, *f.* 1. refinery. 2. distillery.
refino, na, *a.* very fine, extra fine. —*m.* 1. refining. 2. coffee, cocoa and sugar market or commodities' exchange. 3. (Mex.) brandy.
refiriendo, refiriera, refiriese, refirió, *ref.* **referir.**
refirmar, *tr.v.* 1. to support, uphold. 2. to confirm, ratify.
refistolería, *f.* (Cuba) conceit, vanity.
refistolero, ra, *a.* (Cuba) vain, conceited. —*m., f.* (Cuba) conceited person.
refitolero, ra, *a.* 1. (coll.) meddlesome, meddling. 2. (Cuba) flattering, fawning. —*m., f.* 1. refectorian, person in charge of a refectory. 2. (coll.) busybody, meddler. 3. (Cuba) flatterer, fawner.
reflectancia, *f.* (phys.) reflectance.
reflectante, *a.* (phys.) reflecting.
reflectar, *i.v.* (phys.) to reflect.
reflector, ra, *a.* reflecting. —*m.* 1. reflector, reflecting surface. 2. (astron.) reflector, reflecting telescope. 3. searchlight. — **r. buscacampo,** (aer.) bearing projector.

refleja, *f.* reflection, meditation.
reflejado, da, *a.* mirrored, reflected.
reflejar, *tr.v.* to reflect; to show, reveal. *—i.v.* to reflect, ponder, think, consider. *—r.v.* to be reflected.
reflejo, ja, *a.* 1. reflected. 2. (physiol.) reflex. 3. (gram.) reflexive. *—m.* 1. reflection, glare; image; vestige. 2. (physiol.) reflex. — **r. condicionado,** conditioned reflex.
reflexión, *f.* 1. reflection (light, image). 2. reflection (mental).
reflexionar, *tr.v.* to reflect or meditate on. *—i.v.* to reflect, meditate. — **r. en or sobre,** to reflect on.
reflexivamente, *adv.* 1. reflectively. 2. (gram.) reflexively.
reflexivo, va, *a.* reflective, reflexive; (gram.) reflexive.
reflorecer, (*ref. 45*) *i.v.* to blossom or bloom again; to flourish again.
reflorecimiento, *m.* reflorescence; blossoming or blooming afresh.
reflorezca, reflorezco, *ref.* **reflorecer.**
refluente, *a.* refluent, flowing back.
refluir, (*ref. 48*) *i.v.* 1. to flow back, reflow. 2. to redound, result.
reflujo, *m.* reflux, ebb, ebb tide.
refluya, refluyendo, refluyera, refluyese, refluyo, refluyó, *ref.* **refluir.**
refocilación, *f.* joy, pleasure, cheer, exhilaration; recreation, amusement.
refocilar, *tr.v.* to cheer, exhilarate, delight. *—r.v.* to be cheered, enjoy oneself, be exhilarated.
refocilo, *m., var. of* **refocilación.**
reforcé, *ref.* **reforzar.**
reforestación, *f.* reforestation.
reforestar, *tr.v.* to reforest.
reforma, *f.* 1. reform; reformation. 2. alteration, improvement. 3. (rel.) **R.,** Reformation. — **r. agraria,** land reform.
reformable, *a.* reformable.
reformación, *f.* reform; reformation.
reformado, da, *past part. of* **reformar.** *—a.* 1. reformed; corrected; altered, improved. 2. (rel.) Reformed. *—m., f.* (rel.) Protestant.
reformador, ra, *a.* reforming. *—m., f.* reformer.
reformar, *tr.v.* 1. to reform; to correct, improve. 2. to re-form, reshape; to reorganize, alter, revise. 3. to repair, restore, renovate. *—r.v.* 1. to reform; to mend one's ways. 2. to control or restrain oneself.
reformativo, va, *a.* reformative.
reformatorio, ria, *a.* reformative, reforming, correcting. *—m.* reformatory, reform school.
reformista, *a., m., f.* reformist, reformer.
reforzado, da, *past part. of* **reforzar.** *—a.* reinforced. *—m.* tape, ribbon, braid.
reforzador, *m.* (photog.) intensifier, intensifying solution.
reforzar, (*ref. 70*) *tr.v.* 1. to reinforce, strengthen. 2. to cheer, encourage. 3. to intensify. *—r.v.* to cheer up, be encouraged or strengthened.
refracción, *f.* (phys.) refraction. — **r. atmosférica,** (meteorol.) atmospheric refraction.
refractar, *tr.v.* (opt.) to refract. *—r.v.* to be refracted.
refractario, ria, *a.* 1. refractory; unwiling; unruly, obstinate. 2. (phys.) refractory, heat-resistant.
refractividad, *f.* refringence, refractivity.
refractivo, va, *a.* refractive.
refracto, ta, *a.* (opt.) refracted.
refractómetro, *m.* (opt.) refractometer.
refractor, *m.* (opt.) refractor.
refrán, *m.* proverb, saying, adage, aphorism, maxim. — **como dice** or **reza el r.,** as the saying goes; **tener muchos refranes,** or **tener refranes para todo,** (coll.) to know all the answers, be able to explain one's way out of anything.
refranero, *m.* collection of proverbs or maxims.
refranesco, ca, *a.* pertaining to maxims or adages; pat (coll.).
refrangibilidad, *f.* refrangibility.
refrangible, *a.* refrangible.
refranista, *m., f.* person who frequently quotes proverbs.
refregadura, *f.* rubbing, friction, scrubbing; rub, abrasion (mark).
refregamiento, *m.* rubbing, scrubbing.
refregar, (*ref. 67*) *tr.v.* 1. to rub, scrub. 2. to harp on, insist on recalling (something unpleasant). — **refregárselo a uno,** to rub it in.
refregón, *m.* 1. (coll.) rubbing, scrubbing; rub, abrasion. 2. (mar.) gust of wind, squall.
refregue, *ref.* **refregar.**
refreír, (*ref. 40*) *irr. past part.:* **refrito.** *—tr.v.* to fry again; to fry very well; to overfry, fry too much.
refrenable, *a.* curbable, checkable, controllable.
refrenada, *f., var. of* **sofrenada.**
refrenamiento, *m.* curbing, check, restraint.
refrenar, *tr.v.* 1. to curb, rein in, check (a horse). 2. to curb, restrain, control, check. *—r.v.* to restrain oneself, control oneself.
refrendación, *f.* 1. countersignature; legalization, authentication. 2. visé, stamping (of a passport).
refrendar, *tr.v.* to countersign; to legalize, authenticate; to visa, stamp (a passport).
refrendario, *m.* countersigner.
refrendata, *f.* countersignature.
refrendo, *m.* legalization, authentication; countersignature; visa, stamp (in a passport).
refrentado, *m.* (mec.) facing.
refrescador, ra, *a.* refreshing; cooling.
refrescadura, *f.* refreshing; cooling.
refrescamiento, *m., var. of* **refresco.**
refrescante, *a.* refreshing; cooling.
refrescar, (*ref. 50*) *tr.v.* 1. to refresh, freshen, cool. 2. to renew (the fight), revive (a custom), refresh (one's memory). *—i.v.* 1. to become fresh or refreshed (a person); to become cool or fresh (the weather). 2. (mar.) to freshen, increase (the wind). *—r.v.* 1. to become cool. 2. to refresh oneself, take some fresh air. 3. to take some refreshment.
refresco, *m.* 1. refreshment, snack. 2. soft or cold drink. 3. light buffet, refreshments (served at informal gatherings). — **de r.,** anew, again.
refresque, refresqué, *ref.* **refrescar.**
refresquería, *f.* (C. Amer.) refreshment stall or stand.
refriante, *m.* refrigerant, cooling solution.
refriega, *f.* skirmish, affray, fray.
refriego, refriegue, *ref.* **refregar.**
refrigeración, *f.* 1. refrigeration. 2. air conditioning; **r. por agua,** water-cooling; **r. por aire,** air-cooling.
refrigerado, da, *past part. of* **refrigerar.** *—a.* cooled; air-conditioned; **r. por agua,** water-cooled; **r. por aire,** air-cooled.
refrigerador, ra, *a.* refrigerating, cooling. *—m.* 1. refrigerator. 2. cooling unit (of an air conditioner).
refrigerante, *a.* refrigerating, cooling. *—m.* 1. refrigerant, coolant. 2. (chem.) condenser, cooling chamber. 3. cooler, cooling bath (for coil of a still).
refrigerar, *tr.v.* to cool, refrigerate; to refresh; to air-condition. *—r.v.* to become cool, be refreshed; to become air-conditioned.
refrigerativo, va, *a.* refrigerative, refrigeratory, cooling.
refrigerio, *m.* 1. refreshment, snack. 2. comfort, consolation.
refringencia, *f.* refringency, refractivity, power to refract.
refringente, *a.* refracting, refringent, refractive.
refringir, (*ref. 62*) *tr.v.* to refract. *—r.v.* to be refracted.
refrinja, refrinjo, *ref.* **refringir.**
refrito, ta, *irr. past part. of* **refreír.** *—a.* fried again; too fried. *—m.* (fig.) rehash (of a literary work, news, play, etc.).
refuerza, refuerzo, *ref.* **reforzar.**
refuerzo, *m.* 1. reinforcement, strengthening, help, aid; backing, bracing. 2. welt. 3. (*pl.*) (mil.) reinforcements.
refugiado, da, *past part. of* **refugiar.** *—m., f.* refugee.
refugiar, *tr.v.* to shelter, give refuge. *—r.v.* to take refuge.
refugio, *m.* refuge, shelter; retreat, asylum, home, sanctuary; **r. antiaéreo,** air-raid shelter.
refulgencia, *f.* refulgence, radiance, brilliance.
refulgente, *a.* refulgent, radiant, brilliant, shining.
refulgir, (*ref. 62*) *i.v.* to shine, be refulgent.
refundición, *f.* 1. remelting, recasting (of metal). 2. (theat., lit.) adaptation, revision.
refundidor, ra, *m., f.* adapter, rearranger, revisor (of a play, book, etc.).
refundir, *tr.v.* 1. to recast, cast again, remelt (metal). 2. to adapt, rearrange, revise, rehash. 3. to contain, include, embrace. *—i.v.* to redound, result.
refunfuñador, ra, *a.* grumbling, growling; muttering. *—m., f.* grumbler, growler, mutterer.
refunfuñadura, *f.* grumbling, growl; angry muttering.
refunfuñar, *i.v.* to grumble, growl; to mutter angrily.
refunfuño, *m., var. of* **refunfuñadura.**
refutable, *a.* refutable.
refutación, *f.* refutation.
refutar, *tr.v.* to refute.
refutatorio, ria, *a.* refuting.
regadera, *f.* 1. watering-can, water-sprinkler. 2. irrigation ditch. — **loco como una r.,** mad as a March hare, mad as a hatter.
regadero, *m.* irrigation ditch.
regadío, a, *a.* irrigable, irrigated (land). *—m.* irrigated land.
regadizo, za, *a.* irrigable; pertaining to irrigation.
regador, *m.* comb maker's gauge.
regador, ra, *a.* irrigating, watering. *—m., f.* waterer, irrigator. *—f.* water sprinkler, sparger.
regadura, *f.* irrigation, watering, sprinkling.
regaifa, *f.* 1. egg cake (pastry). 2. grooved stone of an oil mill.
regajal, regajo, *m.* puddle, pool; stream, brooklet, rivulet, rill.
regala, *f.* (mar.) gunwale, gunnel.
regalada, *f.* royal stables; king's horses.
regaladamente, *adv.* 1. delicately, daintily. 2. pleasantly, comfortably.
regalado, da, *past part. of* **regalar.** *—a.* 1. delicate, dainty. 2. soft, easy, pleasant. 3. dirt-cheap, very inexpensive.
regalador, ra, *a.* giving; regaling; entertaining. *—m., f.* giver, regaler; entertainer. *—m.* wine skin scraper.
regalamiento, *m.* giving, regaling; entertaining.
regalar, *tr.v.* 1. to give, present, treat. 2. to please, entertain, regale; to flatter. *—r.v.* 1. to indulge oneself, live, dine or feast sumptuously.
regalejo, *m. dim. of* **regalo,** small gift.
regalero, *m.* purveyor of fruit or flowers to the royal family.
regalía, *f.* 1. right; privilege; exemption; royal right, prerogative or privilege, (*pl.*) regalia. 2. perquisite, bonus, gratuity; gift, present. —

tabaco de r., superrior quality tobacco *—m.* superior quality cigar.
regalicia, *f., var. of* **regaliz.**
regalillo, *m.* 1. *dim. of* **regalo,** small gift. 2. muff (for keeping hands warm).
regalismo, *m.* regality; rights and privileges belonging to a king.
regalista, *a., m., f.* regalist.
regalito, *m. dim. of* **regalo,** small gift.
regaliz, regaliza, *m.* (bot.) licorice.
regalo, *m.* 1. gift, present. 2. comfort, luxury. 3. indulgence; pleasure. 4. delicacy, treat (food); **r. de Navidad** or **r. Navideño,** Christmas gift.
regalón, na, *a.* 1. (coll.) spoiled, pampered, fond of ease and luxury. 2. soft, easy (life).
regante, *a.* irrigating, watering. *—m.* 1. irrigator, waterer. 2. person who has irrigation rights.
regañadientes, a r., reluctantly, grudgingly, grumblingly.
regañamiento, *m.* 1. (coll.) scolding, reprimand. 2. growling, snarling, grumbling.
regañar, *tr.v.* (coll.) to scold, grumble at, reprimand, chide. *—i.v.* 1. (coll.) to grumble, mutter. 2. (coll.) to quarrel. 3. to growl, snarl (a dog). 4. to crack, split, open (skin of ripe fruit).
regañir, (*ref. 66*) *i.v.* to yelp repeatedly.
regaño, *m.* 1. (coll) scolding, reprimand. 2. gesture of annoyance or anger. 3. crack in crust of loaf of bread.
regañón, na, *a.* 1. (coll.) snappy, bad-tempered, grumbling. 2. northeast (wind). *—m., f.* grumbler, crab, snappy, bad-tempered person. *—m.* northeast wind.
regar, (*ref. 67*) *tr.v* 1. to water, irrigate, sprinkle, shower. 2. to water, wash a certain region (river). 3. to scatter, strew, sprinkle.
regata, *f.* 1. irrigation ditch or trench. 2. regatta, boat race.
regate, *m.* 1. dodge, duck (the body). 2. (coll.) way out (of a difficulty).
regateador, ra, *m., f.* haggler; person who beats down the price of something.
regatear, *tr.v.* 1. to haggle over, bargain, chaffer. 2. to resell at retail. 3. (coll.) to avoid, evade, shun, dodge (doing something). *—i.v.* to bargain, haggle. 2. to dodge, duck. 3. to race (boats).
regateo, *m.* bargaining, haggling, chaffer.
regatería, *f.* retail, retailing; hucksterism.
regatero, ra, *a.* 1. retailing. 2. hagging, chaffering. *—m., f.* 1. retailer. 2. haggler, chafferer.
regato, *m., var. of* **regajo.**
regatón, na, *a.* 1. retailing. 2. haggling, bargaining. *—m., f.* 1. retailer; hawker, huckster. 2. haggler. *—m.* ferrule, tip, point.
regatonear, *tr.v.* to sell at retail.
regatonería, *f.* retail business, retail sale.
regazar, (*ref. 53*) *tr.v.* to tuck up (the skirt).
regazo, *m.* lap (of a seated person).
regencia, *f.* 1. regency. 2. management.
regeneración, *f.* 1. regeneration. 2. (elec.) feedback. — **r. acústica** (rad.) acoustic feedback.
regenerador, ra, *a.* regenerative. *—m., f.* regenerator. *—m.* 1. (mec.) regenerator. 2. (phys.) breeder reactor.
regenerar, *tr.v., r.v.* to regenerate.
regenta, *f.* 1. wife of a regent. 2. woman teacher or professor.
regentar, *tr.v.* 1. to direct, manage, administrate. 2. to rule, govern. 3. to fill, hold (a post, professorship, etc.).
regente, *a.* governing, ruling. *—m., f.* regent. *—m.* 1. foreman, manager. 2. magistrate in charge of regional court. 3. superintendent of studies (in some religious orders). 4. regent, university professor. 5. (print.) foreman.
regentear, *tr.v., var. of* **regentar.**
regiamente, *adv.* royally, regally, in a kingly manner; (fig.) sumptuously, magnificently.
regicida, *a.* regicidal. *—m., f.* regicide (person).
regicidio, *m.* regicide, murder of a king or queen.
regidor, ra, *a.* ruling, governing. *—m.* councilman, councillor, alderman. *—f.* alderman's or councilman's wife; councilwoman.
régimen, (*pl.* **regímenes**), *m.* 1. regime, regimen; system, regulations, rules. 2. (gram.) government, regimen. 3. (med.) diet, regimen. 4. (elec., mec.) rate, ratio; state. 5. regime, regimen (of a river); flow (of air or water). — **estar** or **poner a r.,** to be or put on a diet; **r. ascensional,** (aer.) rate of climb; **r. de carga,** (elec.) charging rate; **r. de descarga,** (elec.) rate of discharge; **r. de repetición,** repetition rate (of electronic computers); **r. de saturación,** saturation state (of electronics); **r. de selección,** selection ratio (of electronic computers); **r. del aire,** (aer.) airflow, airstream; **r. permanente,** (tel.) permanent state.
regimentación, *f.* regimentation.
regimentar, (*ref. 29*) *tr.v.* to regiment.
regimiento, *m.* 1. (mil.) regiment. 2. government. 3. body of councilmen or aldermen; officer of councilman or alderman. 4. (mar.) pilot's book of rules or sailing instructions.
regio, gia, *a.* 1. royal, regal. 2. (fig.) sumptuous, gorgeous, magnificent. 3. (coll.) super, marvelous, smashing.
región, *f.* region.
regional, *a.* regional.
regionalismo, *m.* regionalism.
regionalista, *a.* regionalistic. *—m., f.* regionalist.
regionario, ria, *a.* (ecc.) regionary. *—m.* (ecc.) regionary bishop.
regir, (*ref. 76*) *tr.v.* 1. to govern, rule; to guide, steer, conduct, manage. 2. to keep (the bowels) in good order. 3. (gram.) to govern. *—i.v.* 1. to be in force. 2. to function, work. 3. (mar.) to steer, obey the helm.
registrado, da, *a.* registered. — **una carta r.,** a registered letter; **marca r.,** trademark.
registrador, ra, *a.* registering; recording. *—m.* 1. registrar, recorder. 2. inspector. 3. register. — **r. de tiempo,** time clock; **r. de títulos de propiedad,** recorder of deeds. *—f.* cash register.
registrar, *tr.v.* 1. to examine, inspect, search. 2. to register, record. 3. to mark with a bookmark. 4. (print.) to register. — **¡a mí que me registren!** (fam.) search me! *—r.v.* to register; to be registered, be recorded.
registro, *m.* 1. register, record, record book. 2. registration, registry, registering, recording. 3. examination, inspection, search. 4. entry, record, register. 5. registry, registration office. 6. (mus.) register, organ stop. 7. (print.) register. 8. receipt of registration. 9. bookmark, bookmarker. 10. regulator (of a clock). 11. (furnace) register, damper. — **echar todos los registros,** to do one's utmost, pull out all the stops; **r. civil,** registry, registrar's office; **r. de actos de última voluntad,** registry office for wills; **r. de la propiedad;** real estate registry; **r. de la propiedad industrial,** trademark registry office; **r. de la propiedad intelectual,** copyright registry office; **r. de patentes y marcas,** patent office; **r. electoral,** electoral roll; **r. parroquial,** parish register. **tocar todos** or **muchos registros,** (coll.) to use all possible means.
regla, *f.* 1. ruler, rule (for ruling lines, etc.). 2. rule, law; principle, precept. 3. rule (of a religious order). 4. moderation, temperance. 5. natural harmony or order. 6. menstruation. 7. (math.) rule. — **en r.,** in order; **la excepción confirma la r.,** the exception proves the rule; **por r. general,** as a rule, generally; **r. áurea,** golden rule; **r. de aligación,** (math.) rule of alligation; **r. de cálculo,** (math.) slide rule; **r. de campo** or **terreno** or **r. local,** ground rule; **r. de falsa posición,** (math.) rule of false position; **r. de oro,** golden rule; **r. de oro, de proporción,** or **de tres,** (math.) rule of three; **r. lesbia,** flexible rule (for ruling curved surfaces); **reglas paralelas,** (engin.) parallel rulers.
reglado, da, *past part. of* **reglar.** *—a.* 1. moderate, temperate. 2. (geom.) ruled (surface).
reglaje, *m.* adjustment; **r. en alcance,** (mil.) range adjustment. — **r. sincronizado,** (engin.) synchronized timing.
reglamentación, *f.* regulation; rules.
reglamentar, *tr.v.* 1. to regulate by rule, decree or law. 2. to establish rules or regulations for.
reglamentario, ria, *a.* 1. pertaining to or prescribed by regulations, rules or by laws. 2. required by social conventions.
reglamento, *m.* regulation; regulations, bylaws.
reglar, *a.* (ecc.) regular (belonging to a religious order).
reglar, *tr.v.* 1. to rule, draw lines on. 2. to regulate. *—r.v.* to be moderate; to restrain oneself.
regleta, *f.* (print.) reglet, lead.
regletear, *tr.v.* (print.) to lead, space (lines).
reglón, *m.* 1. *aug. of* **regla,** large rule or measuring rod. 2. (mas.) level.
regnícola, *m., f.* 1. native of a kingdom. 2. writer on subjects relating to his or her own country.
regocijademente, *adv.* joyfully, merrily.
regocijado, da, *a.* joyful, rejoicing, glad.
regocijador, ra, *a.* gladdening, cheering, rejoicing. *—m., f.* rejoicer.
regocijar, *tr.v.* to delight, rejoice, gladden. *—r.v.* to rejoice, be glad; (fig.) to gloat, feel smug.
regocijo, *m.* joy, gladness, cheer, rejoicing.
regodearse, *r.v.* 1. (coll.) to take delight. 2. (coll.) to joke, jest, banter.
regodeo, *m.* 1. delight. 2. (coll.) merry-making, amusement, diversion.
regojo, *m.* 1. crust, crumb, piece of bread left after a meal. 2. puny boy.
regolaje, *m.* good humor.
regoldano, na, *a.* wild (chestnut).
regoldar, (*ref. 35*) *i.v.* to belch, eruct.
regoldo, *m.* (bot.) wild chestnut tree.
regolfar, *i.v.* 1. to flow back, eddy. 2. to turn, to be deflected (wind). *—r.v.* to flow back, eddy.
regolfo, *m.* 1. eddy, whirlpool. 2. gulf, bay, inlet.
regolita, *f.* (geol.) regolith, mantle.
regona, *f.* large irrigation ditch.
regordete, ta, *a.* chubby, plump, pudgy.
regostarse, *r.v.* to acquire a liking or taste for.
regosto, *m.* liking, taste, craving (for more).
regraciar, *tr.v.* to show gratitude for, to thank.
regresar, *tr.v.* (coll.) to return, give back. *—i.v.* to return, come or go back.
regresión, *f.* regression, retrogression.
regresivo, va, *a.* regressive.
regreso, *m.* return, coming back; **de r.,** return, e.g. *viaje de r.,* return journey; **estar de r.,** to be back (from a trip); (coll.) to be an expert, be a past master.
regruñir, (*ref. 66*) *i.v.* to growl, snarl.
reguardarse, *i.v.* to take care of oneself; to take shelter.
regué, *ref.* **regar.**
regüelde, regüeldo, *ref.* **regoldar.**
regüeldo, *m.* belching, belch, eructation.
reguera, *f.* irrigation ditch.
reguero, *m.* 1. trickle, stream. 2. track, furrow (left by running water). 3. irrigation ditch. — **ser un r. de pólvora,** to spread like wildfire.

reguilete, *m., var. of* **rehilete.**
regulación, *f.* regulation; control; adjustment.
regulado, da, *a.* regular, according to rule.
regulador, ra, *a.* regulating. —*m.* 1. regulator (person). 2. (mec.) governor, regulator; (elec.) regulator; (chem.) buffer, regulator. 3. (mus.) crescendo or decrescendo sign. — **r. de bolas,** (mec.) ball governor; **r. de luz,** dimmer; **r. de voltaje or tension,** (elec.) voltage regulator; **r. de volumen,** (rad.) volume control; **r. dinamométrico,** (engin.) dynamometric governor.
regular, *a.* 1. regular; steady; even. 2. fair, fairly good, average; common, ordinary, middling, so so. 3. (gram., geom., mil., ecc., bot.)regular. — **por lo r.,** usually, as a rule.
regular, *tr.v.* to regulate; to control; to adjust; to put in order.
regularice, regularicé, *ref.* **regularizar.**
regularidad, *f.* 1. regularity. 2. (ecc.) strict observance of the rule.
regularización, *f.* regularization.
regularizador, ra, *a.* regularizing, regulating. —*m., f.* regularizer.
regularizar, (*ref. 53*) *tr.v.* to regularize; to regulate, adjust.
regularmente, *adv.* regularly; ordinarily, as a rule, usually.
regulativo, va, *a.* regulative.
régulo, *m.* 1. regulus, king or ruler of a petty state. 2. regulus, basilisk (mythical reptile). 3. (ornith.) kinglet. 4. **R.,** (astron.) Regulus. 5. (chem., metal.) regulus.
regurgitación, *f.* regurgitation.
regurgitar, *i.v.* to regurgitate.
regustado, da, *a.* (Cuba) delighted; satisfied.
regusto, *m.* aftertaste; new flavor, new appeal.
rehabilitación, *f.* rehabilitation.
rehabilitar, *tr.v.* to rehabilitate; reinstate, restore.
rehacer, (*ref. 10*) *tr.v.* 1. to do over; to make again, remake. 2. to redo, repair, renovate, rebuild, remodel. 3. to give back strength, invigorate. —*r.v.* to recover, rally, regain one's strength; to pull oneself together. 3. (mil.) to rally, reorganize.
rehacimiento, *m.* 1. renovation, renewal, rebuilding. 2. recovery, recuperation.
rehaga, rehago, *ref.* **rehacer.**
rehala, *f.* flock of sheep of different owners under one shepherd.
rehalero, *m.* shepherd of a flock of sheep of different owners.
rehecho, cha, *irr. past part. of* **rehacer.** —*a.* stocky, thickset, sturdy.
rehelear, *i.v.* to taste of gall, taste bitter.
reheleo, *m.* bitterness.
rehén, *m.* hostage; **quedar en rehenes,** to be held hostage; **tener como r.,** to hold hostage.
rehenchido, *m.* filling, stuffing.
rehenchimiento, *m.* refilling; stuffing, filling.
rehenchir, (*ref. 39*) *tr.v.* to refill, fill again; to stuff, fill.
rehendija, *f., var. of* **rendija.**
reherimiento, *m.* repulse, driving back.
reherir, (*ref. 42*) *tr.v.* to repulse, repel.
reherrar, (*ref. 29*) *tr.v.* to reshoe (a horse).
rehervir, (*ref. 42*) *tr.v.* to boil again, reboil. —*i.v.* 1. to boil again, reboil. 2. (fig.) to be blinded by passion. —*r.v.* to turn sour, ferment (preserves).
rehice, rehiciera, rehiciese, *ref.* **rehacer.**
rehiera, rehiero, *ref.* **reherir.**
rehiladillo, *m.* cotton twill ribbon.
rehilandera, *f.* pinwheel, pin wheel (toy).
rehilar, *tr.v.* to twist too hard (in spinning). —*i.v.* 1. to quiver, tremble. 2. to whiz, whir (darts, arrows).
rehilero, rehilete, *m.* 1. dart, small arrow; (taur.) banderilla. 2. shuttlecock. 3. (fig.) dig, cutting remark.
rehilo, *m.* quiver, quivering.
rehincha, rehincho, *ref.* **rehenchir.**
rehiriera, rehiriese, rehirió, *ref.* **reherir.**
rehogar, (*ref. 51*) *tr.v.* to cook in butter or oil over a slow fire.
rehogue, rehogué, *ref.* **rehogar.**
rehollar, (*ref. 33*) *tr.v.* 1. to tread again. 2. to trample under foot.
rehoya, *f., var. of* **rehoyo.**
rehoyar, *i.v.* to dig holes anew.
rehoyo, *m.* deep hole, pit; ravine.
rehuelle, rehuello, *ref.* **rehollar.**
rehuída, *f.* 1. flight, fleeing; avoidance, shunning. 2. (hunt.) backtracking (of game).
rehuir, (*ref. 48*) *tr.v.* 1. to avoid; to shun; to shrink from, flee from. 2. to decline, refuse. 3. to withdraw, retire. —*i.v.* 1. to avoid; to shun; to shrink from, flee from. 2. (hunt.) to flee along the same track. —*r.v.* to avoid; to shun; to shrink from, flee from.
rehumedecer, (*ref. 45*) *tr.v.* to wet through, dampen well.
rehundido, *past part. of* **rehundir.** —*m.* (archit.) hollow (in the base of a pedestal).
rehundir, *tr.v.* 1. to sink deeply. 2. to deepen (hole, excavation). 2. to remelt, recast (metals). 3. to waste, squander. —*r.v.* to sink deeply.
rehuntarse, *r.v.* to flee in an unexpected direction (game).
rehusar, *tr.v.* to refuse, turn down, decline; to reject; **r.** + *inf.*, to refuse + *inf.*
rehuya, rehuyo, rehuyó, *ref.* **rehuir.**
reidero, ra, *a.* (coll.) laughable.
reidor, ra, *a.* laughing, jolly, full of laughter. —*m., f.* one who laughs.
Reikiavik, *m.* Reykjavik, capital of Iceland.
reimpresión, *f.* reprinting, reprint.
reimpreso, sa, *irr. past part. of* **reimprimir.** —*a.* reprinted.
reimprimir, *tr.v.* to reprint.
reina, *f.* 1. queen (female sovereign, king's wife). 2. (chess) queen. 3. (ento.) queen bee. — **r. de belleza,** beauty queen; **r. de la fiestas,** carnival queen; **r. de los bosques,** (bot.) woodruff; **r. luisa,** (bot.) lemon verbena; **r. madre,** queen mother; **r. mora,** hopscotch; **r. viuda,** dowager queen.
reinado, *m.* reign (tenure).
reinador, ra, *m., f.* ruler; monarch.
reinal, *m.* twisted hemp cord.
reinante, *a.* reigning; prevailing, ruling.
reinar, *i.v.* to reign; to prevail, predominate.
reincidencia, *f.* relapse; repetition of an offense, backsliding; (law) recidivism.
reincidente, *a.* backsliding, relapsing. —*m., f.* backslider; (law) second offender.
reincidir, *i.v.* to repeat an offense; to backslide, relapse.
reincorporación, *f.* 1. reincorporation. 2. rejoining.
reincorporar, *tr.v.* to reincorporate. —*r.v.* to become reincorporated; to join again.
reingresar, *i.v.* to re-enter.
reingreso, *m.* re-entry.
reino, *m.* 1. kingdom, realm. 2. (animal, vegetable, mineral) kingdom. — **r. de los cielos,** kingdom of heaven.
Reino Unido, *m.* United Kingdom.
reinstalación, *f.* reinstallation; reinstatement.
reinstalar, *tr.v.* to reinstall; to reinstate.
reintegrable, *a.* restorable, returnable; (com.) reimbursable, repayable.
reintegración, *f.* 1. restoration, return, restitution, reimbursement. 2. return, reintegration.
reintegrar, *tr.v.* to restore, return, reintegrate; to repay, refund. —*r.v.* to recover; to return; **reintegrarse a (sus funciones),** to return to or take up (one's post) again.
reintegro, *m.* restoration, return; reimbursement, refund, repayment.
reintroducir, (*ref. 47*) *tr.v.* to reintroduce.
reinversión, *f.* reinvestment.
reír, (*ref. 40*) *tr.v.* to laugh at; to laugh over. —*i.v.* 1. to laugh. 2. to bubble with laughter, laugh (a brook, etc.). — **r. a. carcajadas,** to laugh one's head off, to laugh loudly; **r. de,** to laugh at. —*r.v.* 1. to laugh. 2. to bubble with laughter, laugh (brook, etc.). 3. (coll.) to begin to split (worn out or flimsy cloth). — **reírse de,** to laugh at, to deride, make fun of; to make little of, dismiss lightly; **reírse en las barbas de alguien,** to laugh in someone's face.
reis, *m.* (*pl.*) reis (Brazilian and Portuguese money of account).
reiteración, *f.* reiteration; (law) habitual criminality, recidivism.
reiteradamente, *adv.* repeatedly.
reiterar, *tr.v.* to reiterate, repeat.
reiterativo, va, *a.* reiterative.
reivindicable, *a.* recoverable; (law) repleviable.
reivindicación, *f.* recovery; (law) replevy, replevin.
reivindicar, (*ref. 50*) *tr.v.* to recover; (law) replevy.
reivindicatorio, ria, *a.* (law) replevying.
reja, *f.* 1. grille, grating, railing; (*pl.*) bars (of prison). 2. plowshare; plowing. — **estar entre rejas,** to be behind bars.
rejacar, (*ref. 50*) *tr.v.* to harrow.
rejada, *f.* plowstaff.
rejado, *m.* railing, grating.
rejal, *m.* pile of bricks laid on edge and crisscross.
rejalgar, *m.* (min.) realgar.
rejera, *f.* (mar.) mooring line, painter, buoy, anchor.
rejería, *f.* 1. ornamental ironwork. 2. set of wrought iron grilles.
rejero, *m.* maker of railings, grilles or grates.
rejilla, *f.* 1. grating, lattice, grille; (rad., elec.) grid. 2. latticed window. 3. wickerwork, canework. 4. foot stove, foot brasier. 5. fire grate. 6. luggage rack. — **r. de difracción,** (opt.) diffraction grating; **r. del radiador,** (auto.) radiator grid; **r. libre, (rad., elec.) floating grid; r. de pantalla,** (rad., elec.) screengrid.
rejitar, *tr.v.* to vomit.
rejo, *m.* 1. sharp point; goad. 2. sting. 3. hob, iron pin (used in the game of quoits). 4. iron frame (of door). 5. strength, vigor. 6. (bot.) radicle.
rejón, *m.* 1. spear; (taur.) short spear; dagger. 2. point (of spinning top).
rejonazo, *m.* blow or wound with a spear.
rejoncillo, *m.* (taur.) short spear.
rejoneador, *m.* (taur.) rejoneador, bullfighter on horseback who uses a short lance.
rejonear, *tr.v.* (taur.) to jab with a short lance.
rejuela, *f.* 1. *dim. of* **reja,** small grille or grating. 2. foot brasier, foot heater.
rejuntar, *tr.v.* to rejoin. —*i.v.* (coll.) to live together (a man and a woman).
rejuvenecer, (*ref. 45*) *tr.v.* to rejuvenate; (fig.) to renew, modernize. —*i.v., r.v.* to become rejuvenated.
rejuvenecimiento, *m.* rejuvenation.
rejuvenezca, rejuvenezco, *ref.* **rejuvenecer.**
relabrar, *tr.v.* to recarve, recut, carve again (stone or wood).
relación, *f.* 1. relation, relationship; ratio; connection. 2. account, report; recounting, telling, narration, reporting. 3. long speech (in a play). 4.

(law) report. — **r. jurada,** sworn statement, sworn report; **relaciones diplomáticas,** diplomatic relations; **r. modular,** (rad.) modular ratio; **relaciones comerciales** or **sociales,** business or social connections; **relaciones públicas,** public relations.
relacionar, *tr.v.* 1. to relate, connect; associate. 2. to relate, report, narrate. —*r.v.* 1. to be or become connected or related. 2. to make connections, get acquainted.
relai, relais, *m.* (elec.) relay.
relajación, *f.* 1. relaxation; slackening; loosening, laxity. 2. (ecc.) delivery (to secular court). 3. (med.) hernia, rupture. 4. (law) mitigation (of a penalty).
relajado, da, *a.* 1. (coll.) dissipated. 2. relaxed.
relajador, ra, *a.* relaxing. —*m., f.* relaxer.
relajamiento, *m., var. of* **relajación.**
relajante, *a.* relaxing. —*m.* (med.) relaxant.
relajar, *tr.v.* 1. to relax, loosen (e.g. muscles), slacken (e.g. a rope). 2. to relax, rest. 3. to relax, slacken, make less severe (e.g. discipline). 4. (law) to release (from an obligation). 5. (ecc.) to deliver (to a secular court). 6. (law) to lessen, make less severe (sentence). —*r.v.* 1. to become relaxed, loosen up (muscles), become slack (rope). 2. to relax (discipline). 3. to rest, relax. 4. to sprain, strain; to get a hernia. 5. to become dissipated or debauched.
relajo, ja, *a., m.* 1. (Amer.) disorder, commotion, rumpus. 2. (Cuba, Dom. Rep., Mex., P. Rico) dissoluteness, depravity; jeer, scorn.
relamer, *tr.v.* to lick again. —*r.v.* 1. to lick one's lips or one's chops (coll.). 2. to slick oneself up; to paint, make up heavily. 3. (fig.) to gloat, relish; to brag.
relamido, da, *a.* affected, prim.
relámpago, *m.* 1. lightning; flash of lightning; flash. 2. (fig.) anything swift in passing. 3. (vet.) blemish (in the eyes of horses). — **como un r.,** like lightning.
relampagueante, *a.* flashing, sparkling.
relampaguear, *i.v.* to lighten, flash with lightning; to flash, sparkle (eyes, etc.).
relampagueo, *m.* lightning, flashing; sparkling.
relance, *m.* 1. second chance or attempt; another round (in gambling). 2. recasting (of net, of votes or lottery tickets). 3. chance happening, fortuitous event. — **de r.,** by chance, unexpectedly.
relanzar, (*ref. 53*) *tr.v.* 1. to repel, repulse, throw back. 2. to cast (ballots, tickets or lots) again.
relapso, sa, *a.* relapsed (into error), backsliding. —*m., f.* backslider, one who relapses into sin.
relatador, ra, *a.* relating, narrating, reporting. —*m., f.* narrator, relater, teller, reporter.
relatante, *a.* reporting, narrating.
relatar, *tr.v.* to relate, narrate, report, tell; (law) to report (a case, a lawsuit).
relativamente, *adv.* relatively.
relatividad, *f.* relativity.
relativismo, *m.* (philos.) relativism.
relativista, *a.* (philos.) relativistic. —*m., f.* relativist.
relativo, va, *a.* relative; (gram.) relative.
relato, *m.* report, account; story, narrative.
relator, ra, *m., f.* relator, reporter; secretary (who reads the minutes). —*m.* court reporter.
relatoría, *f.* (law) post and office of a court reporter.
relauchar, *i.v.* (Chile) to knock off work, sneak away from work.
relavar, *tr.v.* to wash again.
relave, *m.* second washing (of ore); (*pl.*) (metal.) washings, sweepings (of ore).
relazar, (*ref. 53*) *tr.v.* to tie up, tie securely with many bindings.
relé, *m.* (Fr., elec.) relay.
releer, (*ref. 60*) *tr.v.* to read over again, reread; to revise.
relegación, *f.* (law) relegation, banishment, exile.
relegar, (*ref. 51*) *tr.v.* 1. to relegate, banish, exile. 2. to put aside, forget about. — **r. al olvido,** to cast into oblivion.
relegue, relegué, *ref.* **relegar.**
relej, *m., var. of* **releje.**
relejar, *i.v.* (archit.) to taper, slope, batter (said of a wall).
releje, *m.* 1. rut, wheel track. 2. (artil.) ridge (in chamber of cannon to make it narrower). 3. (archit.) slope, talus. 4. (med.) sordes, fur (in the mouth).
relente, *m.* 1. dampness, night dew, light drizzle. 2. (coll.) sarcasm, irony, cheek.
relevación, *f.* 1. exemption, releasing (from obligation, etc.); remission, forgiveness (of sins). 2. removal (from office).
relevador, *m.* (elec.) relay.
relevante, *a.* outstanding, excellent, eminent.
relevar, *tr.v.* 1. (mil.) to relieve. 2. to remove (from office). 3. (sport.) to relay. 4. to exempt, release (from taxes, obligations). 5. to forgive, excuse, pardon. 6. to emboss, make stand out in relief; (p.) to paint in relief. 7. to praise, exalt, aggrandize. —*i.v.* (art) to stand out in relief.
relevo, *m.* 1. (mil.) relief, change of the guard; relief (new guard). 2. (sport.) relay; **carrera de relevos,** relay race.
relicario, *m.* 1. reliquary, shrine. 2. locket; memento.
relicto, *a.* (law) left at one's death (said of an estate). —*m.* (*pl.*) (law) estate.
relieve, *m.* 1. (art) relief, relievo; raised work; embossment. 2. leftovers, leavings. — **alto r., todo r.,** (sculp.) high relief; **bajo r.,** bas-relief; **de mayor r.,** of considerable importance; **en r.,** in relief; **medio r.,** half relief; **poner en r.,** to bring out, emphasize.
religa, *f.* metal added to an alloy (to change its proportions); second alloy.
religación, *f.* 1. binding, tying securely. 2. alloying again.
religar, (*ref. 51*) *tr.v.* 1. to tie again; to bind tightly. 2. to alloy again.
religión, *f.* religion; **entrar en r.,** to go into the church.
religionario, *m.* Protestant.
religiosamente, *adv.* religiously; punctiliously.
religiosidad, *f.* 1. religiousness, religiosity. 2. punctiliousness, scrupulousness.
religioso, sa, *a.* 1. religious. 2. conscientious, punctilious, scrupulous. —*m.* monk; priest. —*f.* nun.
relimpio, pia, *a.* (coll.) very clean, neat, spick-and-span.
relinchador, ra, *a.* neighing, said of a horse who neighs habitually.
relinchante, *a.* neighing, whinnying.
relinchar, *i.v.* to neigh, whinny.
relincho, relinchido, *m.* 1. neigh, neighing. 2. shout of joy, of merriment.
relindo, da, *a.* very pretty, very neat and fine.
relinga, *f.* (mar.) boltrope; rope (of fishing net).
relingar, (*ref. 51*) *tr.v.* (mar.) to rope (a sail); to fasten rope to (a net); to hoist (a sail) till boltrope is tight. —*i.v.* to rustle (sails in the wind).
reliquia, *f.* 1. relic. 2. trace, vestige (of the past). 3. ailment, habitual complaint. — **r. de familia.** heirloom.
rellanar, *tr.v.* to level, smooth or flatten again. —*r.v.* to sprawl in one's seat, to settle comfortably in a seat.
rellano, *m* 1. landing (of staircase). 2. terrace, level stretch (in sloping terrain).
rellenar, *tr.v.* 1. (cul.) to fill, put filling in (a cake), stuff (e.g. poultry). 2. to fill up, fill completely. 3. to fill, pad, wad. 4. to refill, fill again. 5. (coll.) to stuff, cram (with food). —*r.v.* to stuff oneself (with food).
relleno, na, *a.* stuffed, crammed; padded. —*m.* 1. (cul.) filling, stuffing, forcemeat. 2. filling, filler, packing, wadding (for various technical or mechanical operations). 3. stuffing, filling (action). 4. (fig., lit.) padding (superfluous additions). — **darle a uno relleno,** (coll.) to fill someone in, give someone the details; **de relleno,** (coll.) as padding (in a speech, etc.).
reloj, (with silent j in the singular) *m.* 1. clock, watch, timepiece; (coll.) meter, clock meter. 2. (*pl.*) (bot.) stork's bill. — **contra r.,** against the clock (of races in which participants start at different times); **estar como un r.,** to be in fine shape; be in the pink of health; **por r.,** (to work) by the clock, by the hour; **r. de agua,** water clock, clepsydra; **r. de arena,** hourglass, sandglass; **r. de bolsillo,** pocket watch; **r. de caja,** grandfather's clock; **r. de campana,** chiming clock; **r. de carillón,** chiming clock; **r. cuarzo,** quartz clock or watch; **r. de cuco, r. de cuclillo,** cuckoo clock; **r. de cuerda automática,** self-winding watch; **r. de la muerte,** (ento.) deathwatch; **r. de música,** musical clock; **r. de péndola,** pendulum clock; **r. de pie,** tallcase clock; **r. de pulsera,** wristwatch; **r. de repetición,** repeating watch; **r. desconcertado,** scatterbrain, inconsistent and disorderly person; **r. de sol, r. solar,** sundial; **r. de sobremesa,** desk clock; **r. despertador,** alarm clock; **r. digital,** digital clock or watch; **r. magistral,** master clock, standard clock; **r. marino,** marine chronometer; **r. registrador,** time clock.
relojera, *f.* watchcase; watch stand.
relojería, *f.* watchmaker's shop; watchmaking, clockmaking.
relojero, *m.* watchmaker, clockmaker.
reluciente, *a.* shining, gleaming, glittering, bright.
relucir, (*ref. 46*) *i.v.* 1. to shine, glisten, glitter. 2. to excel, shine. — **sacar a r.,** to bring out, bring into play; **salir a r.,** to come to light, appear.
reluctancia, *f.* (phys., elec.) reluctance.
reluctante, *a.* unmanageable, unruly.
reluchar, *i.v.* to struggle, wrestle, strive.
relumbrante, *a.* dazzling, resplendent.
relumbrar, *i.v.* to dazzle, sparkle, shine, glitter.
relumbre, *m.* light, shine, brightness.
relumbrón, *m.* 1. flash of bright light, dazzling brightness, glare. 2. tinsel. — **de relumbrón,** showy, flashy.
relumbroso, sa, *a.* dazzling.
reluzca, reluzco, *ref.* **relucir.**
remachado, *m.* riveting, clinching; **r. en frío,** cold riveting.
remachador, ra, *a.* riveting. —*m.* riveter. —*f.* riveter, riveting machine.
remachar, *tr.v.* 1. to clinch, hammer flat; to rivet, peen. 2. to hammer home, stress (words, etc.). — **r. el clavo,** to drive the point home.
remache, *m.* 1. riveting; clinching. 2. rivet, clinch nail.
remador, ra, *m., f.* rower.
remadura, *f.* rowing.
remallar, *tr.v.* to mend the netting or meshing of.
remamiento, *m.* rowing.
remandar, *tr.v.* to send several times, send over and over again.
remanecer, (*ref. 45*) *i.v.* to reappear unexpectedly.
remaneciente, *a.* reappearing unexpectedly.

remanencia, *f.* (elec.) remanence, residual magnetism.
remanente, *m.* remainder, residue, remnant.
remangar, (*ref.* 51) *tr.v., r.v., var. of* **arremangar.**
remango, *m., var. of* **arremango.**
remansar, *tr.v.* to dam up, form into a pool. *—r.v.* to form into a pool, to eddy.
remanso, *m.* 1. pool; backwater. 2. (fig.) placid retreat, oasis. 3. calm, pause.
remante, *a.* rowing.
remar, *i.v.* 1. to row, paddle. 2. to labor, toil, struggle.
remarcar, (*ref.* 50) *tr.v.* to mark again.
rematadamente, *adv.* completely, absolutely, utterly.
rematado, da, *past part. of* **rematar.** *—a.* 1. complete, hopeless, e.g. *es un loco rematado,* he's completely mad, *es un alcohólico rematado,* he's a hopeless alcoholic. 2. (com.) sold at auction.
rematador, *m.* (Arg.) auctioneer.
rematamiento, *m., var. of* **remate.**
rematante, *m.* highest bidder (at an auction).
rematar, *tr.v.* 1. to terminate, finish off; to complete, put the finishing touch to (something). 2. to auction off. 3. to finish off, kill off. 4. to put the last stitch to. 5. to auction. *—i.v.* to come to an end, terminate, finish. *—r.v.* to come to an end; to be ruined or destroyed.
remate, *m.* 1. end, finish, conclusion. 2. closing (of an account). 3. (archit.) pinnacle, crest, pediment. 4. highest bid. 5. sale (at auction); (Amer.) auction, sale. 6. (archit.) finial, pinnacle. 7. (print.) vignette. — **de r.,** completely, hopelessly, e.g. *está loco de r.,* he is hopelessly mad; **por r.,** finally, in the end.
rematista, *m., f.* (Amer.) auctioneer.
remecedor, *m.* worker who shakes olives down from the trees.
remecer, (*ref.* 56) *tr.v., r.v.* to move, rock, swing.
remedable, *a.* imitable.
remedador, ra, *a.* imitative, imitating, copying. *—m.* imitator, mimic.
remedar, *tr.v.* to imitate, copy; to mimic, mock; ape.
remediable, *a.* remediable.
remediador, ra, *a.* remedial, curing; helping, relieving. *—m., f.* curer; comforter; helper, reliever.
remediar, *tr.v.* 1. to remedy. 2. to help, assist. 3. to save, protect. 4. to prevent, avoid. — **no lo puedo r.,** I can't help it.
remedición, *f.* remeasurement, remeasuring.
remedio, *m.* 1. remedy, cure, solution; way out. 2. medicine, remedy. 3. help, relief. 4. (law) appeal. — **no tener más r.,** to be unavoidable, be unable to be helped; **no tener para un r.,** to be utterly destitute; **no hay r.** or **no tiene más r.,** there's no other way, it can't be helped, there's no help for it; **no tener más r. que,** to have no alternative but + *inf.;* **r. casero,** household remedy; **r. heroico,** last resort, desperate remedy; **sin r.,** unavoidably, inevitably.
remedión, *m.* (theat.) substitute show.
remedir, (*ref.* 39) *tr.v.* to remeasure.
remedo, *m.* imitation, copy; mimicking; mockery.
remellado da, *a.* split, jagged; dented.
remellar, *tr.v.* to scrape, dehair (hides).
remellón, na, *a.* (coll.) jagged; split; dented.
remembranza, *f.* memory, recollection, remembrance.
remembrar, *tr.v.* to remember, recall.
rememoración, *f.* remembrance, recollection, memory.
rememorar, *tr.v.* to remember, recall.
rememorativo, va, *a.* reminding, recalling.
remendado, da, *a.* 1. mended, darned, patched. 2. scuffed, spotted, streaked.
remendar, (*ref.* 29) *tr.v.* to mend, repair; to patch; to darn.
remendón, na, *a.* mending, repairing. *—m., f.* 1. mender, repairer. 2. cobbler.
remeneo, *m.* swaying, wiggling, jogging (in dancing).
remera, *f.* (ornith.) flight feather.
remero, ra, *m., f.* rower, paddler.
remesa, *f.* 1. remittance. 2. (com.) shipment.
remesar, *tr.v., r.v.* to pluck, pull out (one's hair). *—tr.v.* (com.) to remit, send, ship.
remesón, *m.* 1. (equit.) short gallop and halt. 2. (fenc.) deflection ruse. 3. pulling or plucking of hair; tuft of hair.
remeter, *tr.v.* to put back, insert again.
remezón, *m.* (S. Amer.) slight earthquake.
remiche, *m.* space between benches in a galley.
remiel, *m.* syrup obtained from sugar cane at second boiling.
remiende, remiendo, *ref.* **remendar.**
remiendo, *m.* 1. patch; darn; mend, repair. 2. emendation, correction. 3. spot (on animal's skin). 4. (coll.) patch, badge. 5. (print.) small printing job. — **a remiendos,** in bits and pieces, piecemeal; **echar un r. a la vida,** (coll.) to have a snack.
rémige, *f.* (ornith.) flight feather.
remilgadamente, *adv.* affectedly, fastidiously.
remilgado, da, *past part. of* **remilgarse.** *—a.* affected, fastidious, finicky, prudish.
remilgarse, (*ref.* 51) *r.v.* to behave in an affected manner.
remilgo, *m.* affectedness, fastidiousness, finickiness.
rémington, *m.* Remington gun.
reminiscencia, *f.* reminiscence.
remirado, da, *past part. of* **remirar.** *—a.* meticulous, cautious, prudent.
remirar, *tr.v.* to look at over again; to examine carefully. *—r.v.* 1. to contemplate with pleasure or enjoyment. 2. to be painstaking and cautious.
remisamente, *adv.* slackly, lazily, remissly.
remisible, *a.* remissible.
remisión, *f.* 1. remission, forgiveness, pardon. 2. reference (in a book). 3. remittance, shipment. 4. remission, cancellation. 5. (med.) remission, subsidence, abatement (of fever, pain). — **r. de los pecados,** remission of sins.
remisivo, va, *a.* reference, e.g. *nota remisiva,* reference note.
remiso, sa, *a.* remiss, slack, indolent, lazy.
remisor, ra, *a.* remittent, sending. *—m., f.* (Amer.) sender; shipper.
remisorio, ria, *a.* remissory, forgiving. *—f.* (law) remand.
remitente, *a.* 1. remittent, remitting; sending. 2. (med.) remittent. *—m., f.* sender; shipper.
remitir, *tr.v.* 1. to remit, send, transmit, dispatch. 2. to remit, forgive, pardon. 3. to put off, postpone. 4. to remit, slacken. 5. to remit, leave (to someone's judgment). 6. to refer. *—i.v.* to remit, slacken, relax. *—r.v.* 1. to remit, slacken, relax. 2. to refer. 3. to yield (to), defer (to), submit (to), abide (by).
remo, *m.* 1. oar, paddle. 2. arm, leg, wing. 3. long stretch of hard work. 4. (sport.) rowing. — **al r.,** rowing; (coll.) with a great deal of trouble; **a r. y sin sueldo,** (coll.) working hard for nothing; **a r. y vela,** (coll.) quickly, efficiently.
Remo, *m.* (myth.) Remus, twin brother of Romulus.
remoción, *f.* 1. removal, removing. 2. dismissal.
remojadero, *m.* soaking or steeping tank or tub.
remojar, *tr.v.* 1. to soak, steep. 2. (coll.) to celebrate with a drink. — **r. el gaznate,** (coll.) to wet one's whistle, have a drink.
remojo, *m.* soaking, steeping; **echar en r.,** (coll.) to put off or postpone till a more convenient time; **poner en r.,** to soak; **poner las barbas en r.,** to prepare oneself, take precautions.
remojón, *m.* soaking, drenching.
remolacha, *f.* (bot.) beet (plant and root); **r. forrajera,** mangel-wurzel.
remolar, *m.* oar maker; oar maker's shop.
remolcador, ra, *a.* hauling, towing, tugging. *—m.* tug, tugboat.
remolcar, (*ref.* 50) *tr.v.* to tow, haul, drag.
remoler, (*ref.* 34) *tr.v.* 1. to grind up, grind very fine. 2. (Peru) to exasperate, wear out (patience). *—i.v.* (Chile, Peru) to live it up, go out on the town.
remolida, remolimiento, *m.* grinding up, fine grinding.
remolinante, *a.* whirling, swirling.
remolinar, *i.v., r.v.* 1. to whirl around, swirl; to eddy. 2. to mill around (people).
remolinear, *tr.v., i.v., r.v.* to whirl, gyrate.
remolino, *m.* 1. whirlpool, eddy, vortex (in water); whirl, whirling (in air), swirling, flurry (of smoke, dust, snow). 2. cowlick. 3. throng, crowd. 4. commotion, disturbance.
remolón, *m.* upper tusk (of wild boar); point (of horse's tooth).
remolón, na, *a.* shirking, lazy, indolent. *—m., f.* shirker, loafer. *—m.* upper tusk of wild boar; point of horse's tooth.
remolonear, *i.v.* to loaf about, lag, loiter, shun work.
remolque, *m.* 1. tow, towing. 2. towline, towrope, tow. 3. tow, thing being towed. — **a r.,** towing, in tow; at another's instigation; **dar r.,** to tow; **r. volcador,** dump trailer.
remolque, remolqué, *ref.* **remolcar.**
remondar, *tr.v.* to prune a second time.
remonta, *f.* 1. shoe repair, resoling, revamping. 2. stuffing, padding (of a saddle). 3. leather patch (on riding breeches). 4. (mil.) remount, supply of horses; remount establishment (where horses are bought, bred and trained for cavalry).
remontamiento, *m.* remounting, cavalry horses.
remontar, *tr.v.* 1. to frighten away (game). 2. to restuff (a saddle). 3. to remount, furnish with new horses (cavalry). 4. to repair, revamp, resole (shoes). 5. to elevate, raise. 6. to put a patch on (trousers). *—r.v.* 1. to rise; to soar. 2. (hist.) to flee to the hills (slaves). 3. to go back (to some date in the past).
remonte, *m.* 1. repairing, repair. 2. rising; soaring. 3. remounting, furnishing with fresh horses.
remontista, *m.* (mil.) remount commissioner.
remoque, *m.* (coll.) gibe, biting word.
remoquete, *m.* 1. punch, fisticuff. 2. nickname. 3. witticism, sarcastic or clever remark. 4. (coll.) gallantry, flirting. — **dar r.,** to annoy.
rémora, *f.* 1. (ichth.) remora. 2. hindrance, obstacle, drag (coll.).
remordedor, ra, *a.* worrying, disturbing, causing remorse.
remorder, (*ref.* 34) *tr.v.* 1. to bite again. 2. to sting, disturb (one's conscience). *—r.v.* to fret, show one's concern, anguish or remorse.
remordimiento, *m.* remorse.
remosquearse, *r.v.* 1. (coll.) to become suspicious. 2. (print.) to mackle, blur.
remostar, *tr.v.* to put must into old wine. *—r.v.* 1. to rot, spoil (fruit). 2. to taste sweet and musty (wine).
remostecerse, (*ref.* 45) *r.v.* to spoil (fruit).
remosto, *m.* 1. adding must to old wine. 2. sweetness (of wine).
remotamente, *adv.* remotely; vaguely.

remoto, ta, *a.* 1. remote, distant. 2. remote, vague; unlikely.
remover, (*ref. 34*) *tr.v.* 1. to remove, take away, move. 2. to remove, dismiss. 3. to stir (e.g. a liquid). 4. to upset, disturb, stir up. *—r.v.* to stir, move.
removimiento, *m.* removal.
remozamiento, *m.* rejuvenation.
remozar, (*ref. 53*) *tr.v.* 1. to make young, rejuvenate. 2. (fig.) to enrich and update a literary work. *—r.v.* to become rejuvenated, become young again.
rempujar, *tr.v.* to push, shove (improper use of **empujar**).
rempujo, *m.* 1. (coll.) push (improper use of **empuje**). **2. (mar.) sailmaker's palm.**
rempujón, *m.* (coll.) push, shove (improper use of **empujón**).
remuda, remudamiento, *f.* 1. change, replacement. 2. change of clothes.
remudar, *tr.v.* to change, replace. *—r.v.* to change one's underclothes.
remuerda, remuerdo, *ref.* **remorder.**
remueva, remuevo, *ref.* **remover.**
remugar, (*ref. 51*) *tr.v., var. of* **rumiar.**
remullir, (*ref. 65*) *tr.v.* to fluff up (e.g. a pillow).
remuneración, *f.* remuneration.
remunerador, ra, *a.* remunerating. *—m.* remunerator.
remunerar, *tr.v.* to remunerate, recompense.
remunerativo, va, *a.* remunerative.
remuneratorio, ria, *a.* remunerative.
remusgar, (*ref. 51*) *i.v.* to guess, suspect, conjecture.
remusgo, *m.* 1. surmise, conjecture, suspicion. 2. cold breeze.
renacentista, *a.* pertaining to the Renaissance. *—m., f.* expert in the Renaissance.
renacer, (*ref. 45*) *i.v.* to be born again, be reborn; to spring up, bloom again.
renaciente, *a.* renascent, growing again.
renacimiento, *m.* rebirth, renascence; (hist.) **R.,** Renaissance.
renacuajo, *m.* 1. (zool.) tadpole. 2. (coll.) shrimp, little runt (person).
renadío, *m.* aftermath, new crop.
renal, *a.* (anat., med.) renal.
Renania, *f.* Rhineland.
renazca, renazco, *ref.* **renacer.**
rencilla, *f.* grudge, quarrel.
rencilloso, sa, *a.* quarrelsome, peevish, touchy.
renco, ca, *a.* lame, hipshot. *—m., f.* lame person.
rencor, *m.* rancor, ill will, animosity, grudge.
rencorosamente, *adv.* rancorously.
rencoroso, sa, *a.* rancorous, spiteful.
renda, *f.* second hoeing (of vines).
rendaje, *m.* set of reins or bridles.
rendajo, *m.* (ornith.) jay.
rendar, *tr.v.* to hoe (vines) a second time.
rendibú, *m.* (coll.) obsequiousness, lavish attention.
rendición, *f.* 1. surrender, submission, submissiveness. 2. rendering (of accounts). 3. product, yield.
rendidamente, *adv.* submissively, humbly.
rendido, da, *past part. of* **rendir.** *—a.* 1. exhausted, worn out. 2. humble, submissive, devoted, e.g. *rendido admirador,* humble admirer.
rendija, *f.* split, crack, crevice, slit.
rendimiento, *m.* 1. yield, output, product. 2. performance (of a student, athlete, sportsman, etc.); performance, efficiency (of worker, machine, etc.). 3. exhaustion, fatigue. 4. submissiveness, servility, subordination; obsequiousness. — **r. aerodinámico,** (aer.) aerodynamic efficiency; **r. específico,** specific yield or capacity.
rendir, (*ref. 39*) *tr.v.* 1. to yield, produce. 2. to render (thanks, homage, accounts, etc.). 3. to surrender, yield, give up; to hand over. 4. to give, give back, return. 5. to conquer, make surrender, overcome. 6. to exhaust, tire out, wear out. 7. to vomit, throw up. — **r. cuentas de,** to give an explanation or account of; **r. las armas,** to surrender, to lay down arms. *—i.v.* 1. to produce, yield. 2. (mar.) to finish (a journey). *—r.v.* 1. to surrender. 2. to become exhausted or worn out. 3. (mar.) to crack, split (mast, yard, etc.).
renegado, da, *a.* 1. renegade, apostate. 2. gruff, hostile. *—m., f.* renegade, apostate. *—m.* ombre (card game).
renegador, ra, *a.* swearing, blasphemous. *—m., f.* swearer, blasphemer.
renegar, (*ref. 67*) *tr.v.* 1. to renege, deny. 2. to detest, abhor. *—i.v.* 1. to apostatize, renounce one's faith. 2. to blaspheme, swear. — **r. de,** to renounce, give up.
renegón, na, *a.* swearing. *—m., f.* habitual swearer.
renegrear, *i.v.* to turn very black.
renegrido, da, *a.* livid, blackish (bruise).
renegué, *ref.* **renegar.**
rengífero, *m.* (zool.) reindeer.
renglón, *m.* 1. line (of letters or words). 2. item, staple. 3. line (of business, goods, merchandise, etc.). — **a r. seguido,** (coll.) right after, immediately after; **dejar** or **quedarse entre renglones,** to forget, be forgotten; **leer entre renglones,** to read between the lines.
renglonadura, *f.* ruling, ruled lines (on sheet of paper).
rengo, ga, *a.* lame. *—m., f.* lame person; **dar a uno con la de rengo,** (coll.) to disappoint, dash someone's hopes; **hacer la de rengo,** (coll.) to swing the lead, goldbrick.
renguear, *i.v.* (Amer.) to limp, hobble.
renguera, *f.* (Amer.) lameness.
reniego, *m.* curse, blasphemy, oath.
reniego, reniegue, *ref.* **renegar.**
reniforme, *a.* reniform, kidney-shaped.
renil, *a.* barren (ewe).
renina, *f.* (biochem.) renin.
renio, *m.* (chem.) rhenium.
renitencia, *f.* renitency, resistance, opposition.
renitente, *a.* renitent, resistant.
reno, *m.* (zool.) reindeer.
renombrado, da, *a.* renowned, famous.
renombre, *m.* 1. renown, fame. 2. surname.
renovable, *a.* renewable; replaceable.
renovación, *f.* renovation; restoration; renewal; replacement.
renovador, ra, *a.* renewing, restoring. *—m., f.* renovator, restorer, renewer.
renoval, *m.* area or patch planted with new shoots.
renovante, *a.* renewing, restoring.
renovar, (*ref. 33*) *tr.v.* 1. to renovate, restore. 2. to renew; to reestablish. 3. to replace. 4. to repeat, renew. *—r.v.* 1. to be renewed or reestablished. 2. to change, renew oneself, become new.
renovero, ra, *m., f.* usurer, money lender.
renquear, *i.v.* to limp, hobble.
renta, *f.* 1. revenue, income. 2. rent. 3. annuity. 4. government bonds; public debt. — **distribución de la r.,** distribution of wealth; **meterse en la r. del excusado,** (coll.) to meddle in other people's business; **r. bruta,** gross income; **r. de aduanas,** customs duties; **r. decreciente,** (econ.) diminishing returns; **r. estancada,** government monopoly revenue; **r. gravable, r. imponible,** taxable income; **r. líquida,** net income; **r. nacional,** national income or revenue, gross national product; **r. vitalicia,** life annuity; **vivir de sus rentas,** to live on one's investments, live on income from one's capital.
rentabilidad, *f.* (econ.) income-yield capacity.
rentable, *a.* (econ.) income-producing.
rentado, da, *past part. of* **rentar.** *—a.* enjoying a private income, living on one's capital.
rentar, *tr.v.* 1. (Mex.) to hire, rent. 2. to produce, yield (profit).
rentero, ra, *a.* tributary, tax-paying. *—m., f.* rural tenant, farm lessee.
rentilla, *f.* 1. *dim. of* **renta,** small income. 2. a card game. 3. a game played with dice.
rentista, *m., f.* 1. financier. 2. bondholder. 3. person with independent means.
rentístico, ca, *a.* financial.
rento, *m.* annual rent, rental.
rentoso, sa, *a.* income-producing, profit-yielding.
rentoy, *m.* a card game.
renuencia, *f.* reluctance, unwillingness.
renuente, *a.* reluctant, unwilling.
renueve, renuevo, *ref.* **renovar.**
renuevo, *m.* 1. sprout, shoot. 2. renewal.
renuncia, *f.* 1. renunciation. 2. resignation. 3. (law) waiver, disclaimer.
renunciable, *a.* renounceable, that can be waived.
renunciación, *f.,* **renunciamiento,** *m., var. of* **renuncia.**
renunciante, *a.* renouncing, resigning, waiving. *—m., f.* renouncer; resigner.
renunciar, *tr.v.* 1. to renounce, waive, give up (right, claim, etc.). 2. to resign from, resign (post, position). — **r. algo a favor de alguien,** to renounce something in favor of someone. *—i.v.* 1. to resign. 2. to revoke, renege (in cards). — **r. a,** to abandon, give up (plan), renounce (world). *—r.v.* **renunciarse a sí mismo,** to deny oneself.
renunciatorio, *m.* one in whose favor an inheritance is renounced.
renuncio, *m.* 1. revoke, renege. 2. (coll.) untruth, contradiction.
renvalsar, *tr.v.* (carp.) to rabbet, shave off, plane down (edge of door or window).
renvalso, *m.* (carp.) shaving off, rabbet.
renzina, *f.* (geol.) rendzina.
reñidamente, *adv.* bitterly; tenaciously, stubbornly.
reñidero, *m.* pit (for cockfights); **r. de gallos,** cockpit.
reñido, da, *past part. of* **reñir.** *—a.* 1. on bad terms, e.g. *están reñidos,* they're on bad terms with one another, they've fallen out with one another. 2. hard-fought (contest, game, etc.). — **r. con,** at variance with, contrary to, e.g. *actos reñidos con la moral* or *decencia pública,* acts at variance with or contrary to public morality or decency.
reñidor, ra, *a.* 1. scolding. 2. quarrelsome. *—m., f.* quarreler, scolder.
reñir, (*ref. 41*) *i.v.* to fight; to quarrel, fall out. — **r. en buena lid,** to have a fair fight. *—tr.v.* to scold, tell or tick off, reprimand.
reo, a, *a.* guilty. *—m., f.* criminal, offender; (law) accused, defendant. *—m.* (ichth.) trout.
reocupar, *tr.v.* reoccupy.
reóforo, *m.* (elec.) rheophore.
reojo, mirar de r., to look out of the corner of one's eye, look over one's shoulder; to look askance, hostilely or distrustfully.
reología, *f.* (phys.) rheology.
reómetro, *m.* (phys., hydr.) rheometer.
reordenar, *tr.v.* to rearrange; to order again.
reorganice, reorganicé, *ref.* **reorganizar.**

reorganización, *f.* reorganization.
reorganizador, ra, *a.* reorganizing. —*m., f.* reorganizer.
reorganizar, (*ref. 53*) *tr.v.* to reorganize.
reoscopio, *m.* (phys.) rheoscope.
reóstato, *m.* (elec.) rheostat.
reotropismo, *m.* (biol.) rheotropism.
reótropo, *m.* (elec.) rheotrope.
repacer, (*ref. 45*) *tr.v.* to eat up all the grass of.
repagar, (*ref. 51*) *tr.v.* to pay an exorbitant price for.
repajo, *m.* field enclosed by a hedge.
repanchigarse, repantigarse, (*ref. 51*) *r.v.* to stretch or sprawl out.
repapilarse, *r.v.* to glut, stuff oneself (with food).
reparable, *a.* 1. reparable, remediable. 2. noteworthy.
reparación, *f.* 1. reparation, repair. 2. reparation, indemnity. — **en r.,** under repair.
reparada, *f.* (equit.) sudden start or shying away (of a horse).
reparado, da, *past part. of* **reparar.** —*a.* 1. strengthened, reinforced, restored. 2. squint-eyed.
reparador, ra, *a.* 1. repairing, repair. 2. strengthening, restorative, invigorating. 3. fault-finding. —*m., f.* 1. repairer. 2. fault-finder. carper.
reparamiento, *m., var. of* **reparo; reparación.**
reparar, *tr.v.* 1. to repair, mend, fix; to correct. 2. to restore, refresh, invigorate. 3. to notice, heed, perceive, remark. 4. to make amends for. 5. to parry (a blow); to prevent, ward off. —*i.v.* 1. to stop. 2. (Mex., Guat.) to rear (a horse). — **r. en,** to notice, fix on, pay attention to. —*r.v.* 1. to stop. 2. to control, check or restrain oneself.
reparativo, va, *a.* reparative; restorative.
reparo, *m.* 1. objection; misgiving, doubt. 2. observation, remark. 3. repair; repairing. 4. restorative (medicine, poultice). 5. defense, guard. 6. spot (on eye or eyelid). 7. (fenc.) parry. 8. (Guat., Mex., El Salv.) sudden shying away (of horse). — **poner r.** or **reparos a,** to object to; **tener ciertos reparos sobre,** to have certain misgivings about.
reparón, na, *a.* (coll.) fault-finding. —*m., f.* (coll.) fault-finder.
repartible, *a.* distributable.
repartición, *f.* 1. distribution, division. 2. deal, dealing (of cards).
repartidamente, *adv.* distributively.
repartidero, ra, *a.* to be distributed, for distribution.
repartidor, ra, *a.* distributing. —*m., f.* 1. distributor. 2. dealer (of cards).
repartimiento, *m.* 1. distribution; apportionment. 2. deal, dealing (of cards).
repartir, *tr.v.* 1. to distribute; to apportion; to give out, hand out; to parcel out; to allot. 2. to deal (cards).
reparto, *m.* 1. distribution. 2. delivery. 3. deal, dealing (of cards). 4. (theat., cinem.) cast. — **r. de acciones gratis,** stock split; **r. de beneficios** (Sp.) or **utilidades,** (Am.) profit-sharing.
repasadera, *f.* (carp.) finishing plane.
repasador, ra, *m.* (Amer.) dish cloth, dry cloth, dish towel. —*f.* (tex.) wool comber.
repasar, *tr.v.* 1. to repass, pass again. 2. to go through, revise, review (a lesson); to go over, explain again (a lesson); to go over, examine (any object). 3. to scan, peruse, skim through (a book). 4. to comb (dyed wool). 5. to mend (clothing). 6. (min.) to amalgamate (silver ore).
repasata, *f.* (coll.) chiding, ticking off, reprimand.
repaso, *m.* 1. revision, review (of a lesson, etc.); examination, inspection, going over (objects for defects). 2. (coll.) ticking off, chiding, reprimand.
repastar, *tr.v.* 1. to add flour and water to (dough in order to knead it again). 2. (agr.) to put (cattle) to graze again, feed again.
repasto, *m.* extra forage or pasture.
repatriación, *f.* repatriation.
repatriado, da, *past part. of* **repatriar.** —*a.* repatriated. —*m., f.* repatriate.
repatriar, (*ref. 54*) *tr.v.* to repatriate. —*i v., r.v.* to be repatriated; to return to one's country.
repechar, *i.v.* to climb up a hill or a steep incline.
repecho, *m.* short steep incline; **a r.,** uphill.
repeinado, da, *past part. of* **repeinar.** —*a.* all slicked up, sleek, well groomed.
repeinar, *tr.v.* to comb again.
repeladura, *f.* repeeling; restripping; second peeling or cropping.
repelar, *tr.v.* 1. to pull out the hair of, pull the hair of. 2. to make (a horse) take a short gallop. 3. to clip, crop, lop off, cut the top of. 4. to reduce, lessen, cut down. 5. (Mex.) to exasperate, irritate. 6. (Ecuad.) reprimand. —*r.v.* (Chile) to get upset.
repelente, *a.* repellent, repulsive.
repeler, *tr.v.* 1. to repel, repulse. 2. to refute, contradict.
repellar, *tr.v.* (mas.) to plaster a wall.
repelo, *m.* 1. part going against grain, fur or nap; lump. 2. cross fiber, cross grain fibers (in wood). 3. (coll.) scuffle, fight. 4. (coll.) aversion, repugnance. 5. (Ecuad., Mex.) rag, old dress.
repelón, *m.* 1. pull of the hair. 2. snag, pulled thread (in stocking). 3. snatch, fragment, portion. 4. spurt, short gallop. 5. (*pl.*) flames escaping from furnace. **a repelones,** (coll.) little by little, with effort; **de r.,** (coll.) swiftly, in passing; **más viejo que el r.,** (coll.) as old as the hills.
repeloso, sa, *a.* 1. crooked-grained (of wood). 2. (coll.) touchy, peevish.
repeluzno, *m.* shiver, shudder.
repensar, (*ref. 29*) *tr.v.* to think over again, reconsider.
repente, *m.* (coll.) start, sudden movement; **de r.,** suddenly; **hablar de r.,** to say the first thing that enters one's head.
repentinamente, *adv.* suddenly.
repentino, na, *a.* sudden.
repentista, *m., f.* 1. improviser; extemporizer. 2. (mus.) sight reader.
repentizar, (*ref. 53*) *i.v.* (mus.) to sight read.
repentón, *m.* (coll.) *aug. of* **repente,** sudden start or movement.
repeor, *a., adv.* (coll.) much worse.
repercudir, *i.v., var. of* **repercutir.**
repercusión, *f.* repercussion.
repercutir, *tr.v.* (med.) to repel. —*i.v.* 1. to rebound. 2. to reverberate; to echo. — **r. en,** to have a repercussion or repercussions on. —*r.v.* to reverberate, echo.
repertorio, *m.* repertoire, repertory.
repesar, *tr.v.* to reweigh, weigh again.
repeso, *m.* reweighing; reweighing room or office; order for reweighing.
repetición, *f.* 1. repetition. 2. repeating mechanism (of watch, firearm, etc.). 3. (mus., theat.) encore. — **rifle de r.,** repeating rifle.
repetidamente, *adv.* repeatedly.
repetidor, ra, *a.* repeating. —*m.* 1. repeater, person who goes over a student's lessons with him. 2. (tel., mar.) repeater.
repetir, (*ref. 39*) *tr.v.* 1. to repeat. 2. (law) to demand, claim restitution. 3. (theat., mus.) to repeat, rehearse; to recite. 4. to have another helping of (food). —*i.v.* to repeat; to repeat (taste of food). —*r.v.* to repeat oneself or itself. — **¡que se repita!** encore!
repicar, (*ref. 50*) *tr.v.* 1. to ring (bells); to click (castanets). 2. to mince finely, chop well. 3. (cards) to repique (in game of piquet or of ombre). —*i.v.* to ring, peal, chime; **r. gordo,** (coll.) to celebrate with great pomp and ceremony. —*r.v.* to boast.
repicotear, *tr.v.* to decorate with a wavy edge, to scallop.
repinaldo, *m.* large delicious apple.
repinarse, *r.v.* to soar, rise.
repintar, *tr.v.* to repaint, retouch, restore (painting). —*r.v.* 1. to make up one's face with great care. 2. (print.) to mackle, blur.
repinte, *m.* (p.) restoration; retouching.
repique, *m.* 1. peal, chime, ringing (of bells); roll (of castanets). 2. squabble, tiff (coll.) 3. mincing, chopping. 4. repique (in cards).
repique, repiqué, *ref.* **repicar.**
repiquete, *m.* 1. lively pealing or chime. 2. clash, skirmish. 3. (mar.) short tack.
repiquetear, *tr.v.* to peal, ring gaily, toll, click and roll (castanets). —*r.v.* (coll.) to squabble, quarrel, wrangle.
repiqueteo, *m.* 1. lively ringing or pealing of bells; lively playing of castanets. 2. bickering, squabbling.
repisa, *f.* 1. shelf, ledge. 2. bracket, console; mantelpiece.
repisar, *tr.v.* 1. to tread on again; to tamp, pack down. 2. to knock into one's head (knowledge).
repiso, *m.* inferior wine made from retrod grapes.
repita, repitiendo, repitiera, repitiese, repitió, repito, *ref.* **repetir.**
repizcar, (*ref. 50*) *tr.v.* to pinch.
repizco, *m.* pinch.
replantar, *tr.v.* to replant; to transplant.
replantear, *tr.v.* 1. to mark out the ground plan of (a house). 2. to restate (a problem, question, proposal).
replanteo, *m.* marking out the **ground plan** (of a structure).
repleción, *f.* repletion, fullness.
replegable, *a.* folding.
replegar, (*ref. 67*) *tr.v.* to fold over and over. —*r.v.* (mil.) to fall back.
repletar, *tr.v.* to stuff, cram, fill up. —*r.v.* to stuff oneself.
repleto, ta, *a.* replete, full.
réplica, *f.* 1. reply, retort. 2. (art) replica, copy. 3. (law) replication.
replicador, ra, *a.* argumentative. —*m., f.* argumentative person; replier, retorter.
replicante, *a.* answering. —*m., f.* replier, retorter.
replicar, (*ref. 50*) *i.v.* 1. to retort, answer, reply. 2. to argue, contradict. 3. (law) to answer (defendant's plea or answer).
replicato, *m.* 1. objection. 2. (law) replication.
replicón, na, *a., m., f., var. of* **replicador.**
repliego, repliegue, *ref.* **replegar.**
repliegue, *m.* 1. fold, crease; convolution. 2. (mil.) falling back, retreat.
replique, repliqué, *ref.* **replicar.**
repoblación, *f.* repopulation; reforestation.
repoblar, (*ref. 33*) *tr.v.* to repopulate; to restock (fishpond, beehive); to reforest. —*r.v.* to become repopulated.
repodrir, *tr.v.* to rot. —*r.v.* 1. to go completely rotten. 2. to eat one's heart out, pine away.
repollar, *i.v., r.v.* to head, form a head (cabbage).
repollito de Bruselas, *m.* (S. Amer.) Brussels sprouts.
repollo, *m.* (bot.) cabbage; head (of lettuce, cabbage, etc.). — **r. colorado** (Arg.) or **morado** (Arg.), red cabbage.
repolludo, da, *a.* 1. cabbage-headed. 2. short, chubby.

repolluelo, *m. dim. of* **repollo,** small head of cabbage.
reponer, (*ref. 15*) *tr.v.* 1. to replace, put back; to reinstate (dismissed employee). 2. to reply, retort. 3. (theat.) to revive (a play). 4. (law) to restore (a case). —*r.v.* 1. to recover, recuperate (one's losses). 2. to calm down.
reponga, repongo, *ref.* **reponer.**
reportación, *f.* calm, moderation.
reportaje, *m.* (jour.) article, report, write-up, special feature.
reportamiento, *m.* restraint, moderation, forbearance.
reportar, *tr.v.* 1. to check, curb, control. 2. to achieve, obtain, get. 3. to produce. 4. to bring, take. 5. to transfer (drawing to lithographic plate). —*r.v.* 1. to control oneself, curb oneself. 2. (Amer.) to present oneself, show up, report, appear.
reporte, *m.* 1. news, information, report. 2. mischievous rumor or gossip. 3. transfer (drawing in lithographic crayon).
reporteril, *a.* pertaining to a report or a reporter.
reporterismo, *m.* (jour.) reporting, news reporting.
reportero, ra, *m., f.* (jour.) reporter; **r. gráfico,** press photographer; **r. policíaco,** police reporter.
reportorio, *m.* almanac, calendar.
reposadamente, *adv.* restfully, calmly.
reposadero, *m.* (metal.) runner (trough for receiving molten metal).
reposado, da, *a.* calm, peaceful, restful.
reposar, *tr.v.* to let settle (food, liquid, boiling or bubbling mixture). —*i.v.* 1. to rest, take a nap. 2. to rest (in peace), to lie buried. —*r.v.* to settle (food, liquid, etc.).
reposición, *f.* 1. replacement, reinstatement. 2. replacement, repaying. 3. recovery (of health, self-control, etc.). 4. (theat.) revival. — **r. instantánea,** (elec.) instantaneous reset.
repositorio, *m.* repository.
reposo, *m.* rest, repose; calm, quiet; tranquility.
repostarse, *r.v.* to lay in stock.
repostería, *f.* 1. pastry, confectionery (as a culinary field). 2. pastry or confectionery shop. 3. pantry, larder (in a large household).
repostero, *m.* 1. confectioner; pastry cook. 2. drape or hangings ornamented with coat of arms.
repregunta, *f.* (law) cross-examination.
repreguntar, *tr.v.* (law) to cross-examine.
reprehender, *tr.v., var. of* **reprender.**
reprehensible, *a., var. of* **reprensible.**
reprehensión, *f., var. of* **reprensión.**
reprender, *tr.v.* to reprehend, reprimand, reprove, scold.
reprendiente, *a.* reprehending.
reprensible, *a.* reprehensible.
reprensión, *f.* reprehension, reprimand; admonition.
reprensor, ra, *a.* reprehending, rebuking, reproving. —*m., f.* reprehender, reprover.
represa, *f.* 1. dam, dike, sluice. 2. (mar.) recapture, recovery, recuperation (of a captured ship).
represalia, *f.* reprisal; retaliation; **tomar represalias,** to take reprisals.
represar, *tr.v.* 1. to dam up. 2. to recapture (a ship). 3. to repress, hold back, check.
representable, *a.* 1. representable. 2. (theat.) performable.
representación, *f.* 1. representation, delegation. 2. (theat.) production, performance; impersonation. 3. representation, image, figure, likeness. 4. rank, dignity, capacity. 5. petition. 6. (law) right of succession.
representador, ra, *a.* representing. —*m.* actor. —*f.* actress.
representanta, *f.* (rare) actress.
representante, *a.* representing, representative. —*m., f.* 1. representative; agent. 2. (theat.) actor, actress. — **cámara de representantes,** chamber or house of representatives.
representar, *tr.v.* 1. to represent. 2. (theat.) to act, play, impersonate, perform. 3. to state, declare. 4. to show, express. 5. to look, appear to be (a certain age).
representativo, va, *a.* representative.
represión, *f.* repression; check; curb.
represivo, va, *a.* repressive.
represor, ra, *a.* repressive, repressing. —*m., f.* represser.
reprimenda, *f.* reprimand.
reprimir, *tr.v.* to repress, check, curb. —*r.v.* to repress or check oneself.
reprise, *f.* (theat.) repeat performance.
reprobable, *a.* reprehensible, censurable.
reprobación, *f.* reproof, censure, reproval.
reprobadamente, *adv.* reprehensively.
reprobado, da, *a., m., f., var. of* **réprobo.**
reprobador, ra, *a.* reproving, reprobative. —*m., f.* reprover.
reprobar, (*ref. 33*) *tr.v.* 1. to reprove, censure, disapprove. 2. to fail, flunk (coll.) (in an examination).
reprobatorio, ria, *a.* reprobative, reprobationary.
réprobo, ba, *a., m., f.* reprobate.
reprochable, *a.* reproachable, reprovable.
reprochador, ra, *a.* reproachful. —*m., f.* reproacher.
reprochar, *tr.v.* to reproach; **r. algo a alguien,** to reproach someone for something.
reproche, *m.* reproach, rebuke, reproof.
reproducción, *f.* reproduction; copy; (biol.) multiplication.
reproducir, (*ref. 47*) *tr.v., r.v.* to reproduce.
reproductividad, *f.* reproductiveness.
reproductivo, va, *a.* reproductive.
reproductor, ra, *a.* reproducing. —*m., f.* 1. reproducer. 2. breeder (animal used for breeding).
reproduje, reprodujera, reprodujese, reproduzca, reproduzco, *ref.* **reproducir.**
repromisión, *f.* renewed promise.
repropiarse, *r.v.* to get balky (a horse).
repropio, pia, *a.* balky, unruly (horse, mule).
reprueba, *f.* new proof.
repruebe, repruebo, *ref.* **reprobar.**
reps, *m.* (tex.) rep, ribbed fabric.
reptar, *i.v.* to slither, creep, crawl.
reptil, *a., m.* (zool.) reptile.
república, *f.* republic; **La R.,** (Plato's) The Republic; **r. de las letras** or **literaria,** republic of letters.
República Centroafricana, *f.* Central African Republic.
República Dominicana, *f.* Dominican Republic.
republicanismo, *m.* republicanism.
republicano, na, *a., m., f.* republican.
repúblico, *m.* prominent or leading citizen; statesman; patriot.
repudiación, *f.* repudiation.
repudiar, *tr.v.* to repudiate.
repudio, *m.* repudiation (of one's wife).
repudrir, *tr.v.* to rot completely. —*r.v.* 1. to go completely rotten. 2. (coll.) to eat one's heart out, pine away.
repuesto, ta, *irr. past part. of* **reponer.** —*a.* 1. replaced, reinstated; restored. 2. recovered (from illness, shock, etc.). —*m.* 1. stock, supply. 2. spare, spare part. 3. sideboard, cupboard. — **de r.,** spare, extra part.
repugnancia, *f.* 1. repugnance, aversion, loathing, disgust. 2. (philos.) incompatibility, inconsistency, contradiction.
repugnante, *a.* repugnant; loathsome, disgusting, repulsive.
repugnantemente, *adv.* repugnantly, repulsively, disgustingly.
repugnar, *tr.v.* 1. to contradict. 2. to conflict with, be opposite to. 3. to do or admit reluctantly. —*i.v.* to disgust, nauseate, cause repugnance.
repujado, da, *past part. of* **repujar.** —*a.* repoussé. —*m.* repoussage; repoussé work.
repujar, *tr.v.* to do repoussé work on (metals); to emboss (leather).
repulgado, da, *a.* (coll.) affected.
repulgar, (*ref. 51*) *tr.v.* (sew.) to hem; to overcast.
repulgo, *m.* 1. (sew.) hem, overcasting. 2. (cul.) fancy edging (on pies). — **r. de empanada,** (coll.) trifle, ridiculous scruple.
repulgue, repulgué, *ref.* **repulgar.**
repulido, da, *past part. of* **repulir.** —*a.* very smart, neat, spruce.
repulir, *tr.v.* to repolish. —*tr.v., r.v.* to doll up, dress smartly or affectedly.
repullo, *m.* 1. small dart. 2. start, jump.
repulsa, *f.* repulse, rejection; refusal; rebuke.
repulsar, *tr.v.* to repulse, reject; to refuse.
repulsión, *f.* 1. repulsion, repelling, driving back. 2. rejection. 3. repulsion, repugnance; aversion. 4. (phys.) repulsion.
repulsivo, va, *a.* 1. (phys.) repulsive. 2. repulsive, repugnant.
repunta, *f.* 1. cape, point, headland. 2. first sign, indication. 3. quarrel, disagreement, dispute.
repuntar, *tr.v.* (Arg., Chile, Urug.) to round up (scattered cattle). —*i.v.* 1. to begin to turn, begin to ebb (tide). 2. (Amer.) to begin to appear or be visible. 3. (S. Amer.) to begin to rise (river); to begin to improve, gain ground (e.g. in elections). —*r.v.* 1. to begin to turn sour (wine). 2. to fall out, to be displeased with one another.
repunte, *m.* 1. turn (of tide). 2. (Arg., Chile, Urug.) round up (of cattle). 3. (Arg., Chile, Urug., Peru) rise (in river). 4. (com.) rise in prices, rebound.
repurgar, (*ref. 51*) *tr.v.* to cleanse or purify again, repurge.
repuse, repusiera, repusiese, *ref.* **reponer.**
reputación, *f.* reputation, repute.
reputante, *m.* appraiser, estimator.
reputar, *tr.v.* 1. to repute, consider. 2. to esteem, appreciate.
requebrador, ra, *m., f.* wooer, flirt.
requebrar, (*ref. 29*) *tr.v.* 1. to flirt with, make flirtatious or flattering remarks to (a woman). 2. to flatter, compliment. 3. to break again.
requemado, da, *past part. of* **requemar.** —*a.* burnt, brown; tanned, sunburned. —*m.* thin black cloth formerly used for making shawls.
requemamiento, *m., var. of* **resquemo.**
requemar, *tr.v.* 1. to burn again. 2. to overcook, burn, roast too much; to burn (the skin). 3. to parch (plants). 4. to burn, sting, bite (the mouth). 5. to inflame (passions). —*r.v.* 1. to get burnt, burn (food); to get sunburned. 2. to get parched, shrivel up (plants). 3. to get inflamed (passions). 4. to suffer in silence.
requemazón, *f., var. of* **resquemo.**
requeridor, ra, *m., f.* 1. summons server. 2. suitor, wooer.
requeriente, *m.* 1. (law) summons server. 2. inquirer, requester.
requerimiento, *m.* 1. request, requisition; demand; summons; notification. 2. (law) injunction. 3. requirement.
requerir, (*ref. 42*) *tr.v.* 1. to require, need. 2. to notify; to request, summon, order. 3. to court, woo. 4. to induce, persuade. 5. to examine, investigate.

requesón, *m.* cottage cheese; pot cheese; curd.
requeté, *m.* (Sp., hist.) Carlist.
requetebién, *adv.* (coll.) very well, extremely well.
requiebro, *m.* 1. compliment, flattering remark; flirting, flattering, wooing. 2. recrushing; (min.) recrushed mineral.
réquiem, *m.* requiem (mass, music).
requiescat in pace, (Lat.) a religious wish or prayer for the repose of the dead: may the soul rest in peace.
requiera, requiero, *ref.* **requerir.**
requilorios, *m. pl.* (coll.) superfluous formalities, circumlocution, beating about the bush.
requintador, ra, *m., f.* outbidder (at an auction).
requintar, *tr.v.* 1. to outbid by one fifth. 2. to surpass, beat, excel. 3. (mus.) to raise or lower (pitch) by one fifth. 4. (Peru) to swear at, curse, tell or tick off. 5. (Amer.) to squeeze very tight; to make taut. —*i.v.* **r. a,** (P. Rico) to resemble, be like. —*r.v.* **requintarse a** + *inf.,* (Hond.) to begin + *inf.*
requinto, *m.* 1. second fifth removed. 2. raise of a fifth (in an auction). 3. extra services imposed on Indians in Peru during the reign of Philip II. 4. (mus.) fife; fife player. 5. small guitar.
requirente, *m., f.* 1. (law) summons server. 2. suitor, wooer.
requiriendo, requiriera, requiriese, requirió, *ref.* **requerir.**
requisa, *f.* 1. tour or round of inspection. 2. requisition, requisitioning.
requisar, *tr.v.* to requisition.
requisición, *f.* requisition, requisitioning.
requisito, *m.* requirement, requisite.
requisitorio, ria, *a.* (law) requisitory. —*f.* (law) requisition (formal demand for performance of obligation).
requive, *m., var. of* **arrequive.**
res, *f.* head of cattle; animal, beast. — **carne de r.,** beef; **r. de vientre,** (female) breeding animal, breeder.
resaber, (*ref. 20*) *tr.v.* to know very well.
resabiar, *tr.v.* to instill bad habits in. —*r.v.* 1. to acquire bad habits. 2. to get annoyed.
resabido, da, *a.* pedantic, affecting erudition.
resabio, *m.* 1. unpleasant aftertaste. 2. vice, bad habit.
resabioso, sa, *a.* vicious; cross, querulous; ill-tempered.
resaca, *f.* 1. undertow. 2. (com.) redraft. 3. (coll.) hangover.
resacar, (*ref. 50*) *tr.v.* 1. (mar.) to underrun, haul. 2. (com.) to redraw.
resalado, da, *a.* (coll.) witty, charming; attractive.
resalga, *f.* brine.
resalga, resalgo, resaldré, resaldría, *ref.* **resalir.**
resalir, (*ref. 21*) *i.v.* to jut out, project.
resallar, *tr.v.* to reweed, weed again.
resallo, *m.* reweeding.
resaltar, *i.v.* 1. to bounce, rebound. 2. to jut out, project. 3. to stand out, be prominent or conspicuous.
resalte, *m.* projection, ledge, ridge.
resalto, *m.* 1. bounce, rebound. 2. projection, ledge, ridge. 3. (hunt.) method of hunting boar.
resaludar, *tr.v.* to return (someone's) greeting or salute, greet or salute back.
resalutación, *f.* return of a greeting or salute.
resalvo. *m.* sapling, tiller, sprout.
resanar, *tr.v.* 1. to regild, retouch with gilt. 2. (Amer.) to repair, replaster (chipped walls).
resarcible, *a.* compensable, indemnifiable.
resarcimiento, *m.* compensation, reparation, indemnification.
resarcir, (*ref. 61*) *tr.v.* to indemnify, make amends for, redress, compensate. —*r.v.* **resarcirse de,** to recover oneself, recoup one's losses.
resbaladero, ra, *a.* slippery. —*m.* 1. slippery place. 2. chute, slide.
resbaladizo, za, *a.* 1. slippery. 2. (fig.) tempting; elusive.
resbalador, ra, *a.* sliding, slipping. —*m., f.* slider, backslider.
resbaladura, *f.* skid mark, slip mark.
resbalamiento, *m.* slide, slip; skid.
resbalante, *a.* slipping, sliding; skidding.
resbalar, *i.v., r.v.* 1. to slip, slide; to skid. 2. (fig.) to slip, err, go astray.
resbalón, *m.* 1. slip, slide; skid. 2. (fig.) slip, error, blunder.
resbaloso, sa, *a.* slippery. —*m.* (S. Amer.) heel-tapping dance.
rescacio, *m.* (ichth.) dragonet (Gallyonimus lira).
rescaldar, *tr.v.* to scald.
rescaño, *m.* residue.
rescatador, ra, *a.* rescuing, ransoming. —*m., f.* rescuer, ransomer.
rescatar, *tr.v.* 1. to ransom; to rescue. 2. to free, release, save. 3. to make up for, recover (lost time or opportunity). 4. to exchange or trade gold or valuables for (ordinary goods). 5. (Mex.) to resell.
rescate, *m.* 1. rescue; ransom. 2. ransom money.
rescaza, *f.* (ichth.) (species of) scorpene, hogfish.
rescindir, *tr.v.* to rescind.
rescisión, *f.* rescission.
rescisorio, ria, *a.* rescissory, rescinding.
rescoldera, *f.* (med.) pyrosis, heartburn.
rescoldo, *m.* 1. embers, hot ashes. 2. scruple, doubt, apprehension.
rescontrar, (*ref. 33*) *tr.v.* (com.) to offset, set off, balance.
rescripto, *m.* rescript, order, decree (issued by the Pope or a Roman emperor).
rescriptorio, ria, *a.* rescriptive.
rescuentro, *m.* (com.) compensation, offset.
resecación, *f.* thorough drying.
resecar, (*ref. 50*) *tr.v.* to dry thoroughly or excessively. —*r.v.* to become too dry, become bone-dry.
resección, *f.* (surg.) resection.
reseco, ca, *a.* 1. thoroughly dry, too dry. 2. very lean or thin. —*m.* dried part (of tree, bush), honeyless part (of honeycomb).
reseda, *f.* (bot.) mignonette, reseda.
resedáceo, a, *a.* (bot.) resedaceous. —*f.* (bot.) (*pl.*) Resedaceae.
resegar, (*ref. 51*) *tr.v.* to mow again; to mow or cut very short.
reseguir, (*ref. 77*) *tr.v.* to edge (swords).
resellante, *a.* restamping, recoining.
resellar, *tr.v.* 1. to restamp; to reseal. 2. to recoin. —*r.v.* to change camp or party.
resello, *m.* 1. restamping; resealing. 2. recoinage.
resembrar, (*ref. 29*) *tr.v.* to resow.
resentido, da, *past part. of* **resentir.** —*a.* resentful; annoyed; hurt.
resentimiento, *m.* resentment, grudge, umbrage.
resentirse, (*ref. 42*) *r.v.* 1. to become resentful, feel resentment; to feel hurt or offended; to get annoyed. 2. to begin to weaken, begin to give away. — **resentirse de** or **por,** to take offense.
reseña, *f.* 1. outline, sketch, brief description. 2. review, write-up. 3. (mil.) inspection, review. 4. narration, account, report.
reseñar, *tr.v.* 1. to outline, sketch, describe briefly. 2. to review, write a review of. 3. (mil.) to review, inspect.
reseque, resequé, *ref.* **resecar.**
resequido, da, *a.* parched, dried-up.
resero, *m.* a person in charge or who deals with cattle or a flock of sheep; herdsman.
reserpina, *f.* (med., pharm.) reserpine.
reserva, *f.* 1. reserve, stock. 2. reservation, exception. 3. reserve, reticence, self-effacement; discretion, prudence, caution. 4. (ecc.) reservation (retention of part of Holy Sacrament; Holy Sacrament thus reserved). 5. (mil., com., econ., biochem.) reserve. — **a r. de,** subject to, with the purpose of; **con la mayor r.,** in the strictest confidence; **r. alcalina,** (biochem.) alkali reserve; **r. de indios,** Indian reservation (U.S.); **r. mental,** mental reservation; **reservas de excedente,** (com., acc.) surplus reserves; **reservas de oro,** (econ.) gold reserves; **sin r.,** openly, frankly.
reservación, *f.* reservation.
reservadamente, *adv.* reservedly; confidentially.
reservado, da, *past part. of* **reservar.** —*a.* 1. reserved, reticent, self-effacing, retiring. 2. reserved, circumspect, discreet, cautious, careful. —*m.* 1. reserved place; (ry.) reserved compartment. 2. (ecc.) reservation (the Host kept in the ciborium).
reservar, *tr.v.* 1. to reserve, keep, save; to put aside, destine for. 2. to put off, postpone. 3. to exempt, exonerate. 4. to conceal, keep secret. 5. (ecc.) to reserve (put the Host back in the ciborium). —*r.v.* 1. to save oneself. 2. to be wary, be cautious. 3. to bide one's time.
reservativo, va, *a.* reservative.
reservista, *m.* (mil.) reservist.
reservón, na, *a.* 1. (coll.) very reserved or reticent. 2. (taur.) unwilling to attack.
resfriado, *m.* 1. cold chill, catarrh. 2. watering (before plowing). — **coger un r.,** to catch a cold.
resfriador, ra, *a.* cooling.
resfriadura, *f.* (vet.) cold.
resfriamiento, *m.* 1. cooling, chilling. 2. (med.) common cold.
resfriante, *a.* cooling. —*m.* cooler, cooling bath (for coil of a still).
resfriar, (*ref. 54*) *tr.v.* to cool, chill. —*i.v.* to grow or turn cold. —*r.v.* 1. to catch a cold. 2. to cool off, grow cool or cold. 3. to grow cold (as love).
resfrío, *m.* cold (in the head).
resguardar, *tr.v.* to defend, protect, shelter. —*r.v.* to protect oneself, take shelter; **resguardarse de,** to guard against.
resguardo, *m.* 1. protection, shelter, safety. 2. security, certificate, voucher. 3. frontier customs guard. 4. (mar.) wide berth, sea room.
residencia, *f.* 1. residence, domicile, abode, home. 2. residence, mansion, manor. 3. residence, stay, sojourn. 4. (dipl.) function of a resident minister. 5. (law) impeachment.
residencial, *a.* residential; residentiary.
residenciamiento, *m.* (law) impeachment.
residenciar, *tr.v.* (law) to impeach; to call to account.
residente, *a.* resident, residing, residential. —*m., f.* 1. resident, dweller, tenant. 2. (dipl.) resident minister.
residir, *i.v.* 1. to reside; to be in residence. 2. to reside, dwell, live. 3. to inhere, consist, lie, be.
residual, *a.* residual.
residuo, *m.* 1. residue; remainder, rest, remnant. 2. (math.) remainder. — **r. eléctrico,** electric residue, residual charge; **residuos nucleares,** nuclear waste; **residuos radiactivos,** radioactive waste; **residuos sólidos,** refuse, solid waste; **residuos tóxicos,** toxic waste.
resiego, resiegue, *ref.* **resegar.**
resiembra, *f.* (agr.) resowing.
resiembre, resiembro, *ref.* **resembrar.**

resienta, resiento, *ref.* **resentir.**
resigna, *f.* (ecc.) renunciation (of benefice).
resignación, *f.* 1. resignation, patience, submission. 2. relinquishing or handing over power or authority.
resignadamente, *adv.* resignedly.
resignado, da, *a.* resigned; submissive.
resignante, *a.* resigning. —*m., f.* resigner.
resignar, *tr.v.* to resign, hand over, give up (command or post). —*r.v.* to resign oneself.
resignatario, *m.* resignee.
resiguiendo, resiguiera, resiguiese, resiguió, *ref.* **reseguir.**
resina, *f.* resin, rosin; **r. acaroide,** acaroid resin; **r. epoxia,** epoxy resin.
resinación, *f.* extraction of resin.
resinar, *tr.v.* to extract or draw resin from, tap for resin.
resinato, *m.* (chem.) resinate.
resinero, ra, *a.* pertaining to resin. —*m.* resin tapper or extractor.
resinífero, ra, *a.* resiniferous.
resinoso, sa, *a.* resinous.
resintiendo, resintiera, resintiese, resintió, *ref.* **resentir.**
resisar, *tr.v.* to draw one eighth from (each liter of wine, vinegar or oil) as tax.
resistencia, *f.* 1. resistance, opposition. 2. resistance, strength, stamina, endurance. 3. (elec.) resistance, resistor. — **oponer r.,** to put up or offer resistance; **r. a la torsión,** (phys.) torsional strength; **r. al corte** or **al cizallamiento,** (mec.) shearing strength; **r. autorreguladora,** (rad.) ballast resistor; **r. de compensación,** (rad.) bleeder resistance, ballast resistor; **r. de drenaje,** (rad.) bleeder resistor; **r. de placas de carbón,** (elec.) carbon-pile regulator; **r. de polarización negativa,** (rad.) bias resistor; **r. de tensión,** (phys.) tensile strength; **r. derivadora,** (rad.) bleeder resistance; **r. dieléctrica,** (elec.) disruptive strength; **r. pasiva,** passive resistance.
resistente, *a.* 1. resistant, strong, tough. 2. resisting, opposing.
resistero, *m.* 1. hottest part of the day. 2. heat from reflected rays of the sun. 3. very hot place or spot.
resistible, *a.* resistible, endurable.
resistidero, *m., var. of* **resistero.**
resistidor, ra, *a.* resistant.
resistir, *tr.v.* 1. to be able to endure, bear or withstand. 2. to resist, oppose, fight against. —*i.v.* to resist; **r. a,** to resist; to fight against. —*r.v.* to resist, fight; to struggle; **resistirse a** + *inf.,* to refuse + *inf.*
resistividad, *f.* (elec.) resistivity.
resistivo, va, *a.* resistive.
resistor, *m.* (elec.) resistor.
resma, *f.* ream (of paper).
resmilla, *f.* four quires of letter paper.
resnatrón, *m.* (rad., electron.) resnatron.
resobado, da, *a.* trite, hackneyed, commonplace.
resobrar, *tr.v.* to be well over and above, be in excess of.
resobrino, na, *m., f.* grandnephew; grandniece.
resol, *m.* sun glare.
resolano, na, *a.* sunny and windless. —*f.* 1. sunny and windless spot. 2. (Amer.) sun glare.
resolladero, *m.* air hole, vent.
resollar, (*ref. 33*) *i.v.* 1. to breathe; to breathe hard, pant. 2. to take a breather, rest. 3. (coll.) to show up, break one's long silence.
resoluble, *a.* 1. resoluble. 2. solvable, resolvable.
resolución, *f.* 1. resolution, resoluteness, determination, courage. 2. resolution, decision, decree. 3. solution (of a problem). 4. (law) nullification, termination. 5. (med., mus., phys.) resolution. — **en r.,** in short, in a word.
resolutivamente, *adv.* resolutely, with resolution.
resolutivo, va, *a.* analytical. —*m.* (med.) resolvent.
resoluto, ta, *a.* 1. resolute, determined. 2. succinct, compendious, brief. 3. expert, skillful.
resolutorio, ria, *a.* (law) resolutory.
resolvente, *a., m.* (med., math.) resolvent.
resolver, *irr. past part.* **resuelto** (*ref. 34*) *tr.v.* 1. to resolve, decide, determine. 2. to solve, find a solution or answer to. 3. to analyze, break up into component parts. 4. to summarize, sum up. 5. (phys., med.) to resolve. 6. (law) to annul, rescind. —*r.v.* 1. to resolve, decide, make up one's mind. 2. (med.) to resolve, clear up, be over (an infection). — **resolverse a** + *inf.,* to decide + *inf.;* **resolverse en,** to turn into (e.g. steam into water); **resolverse por,** to decide in favor of, decide on.
resonación, *f.* resounding, resonance.
resonador, ra, *a.* resounding, resonating. —*m.* resonator.
resonancia, *f.* 1. resonance. 2. (fig.) importance, renown, e.g. *un artista de r. mundial,* a world-famous artist. — **r. en paralelo,** (rad.) parallel resonance; **tener r.,** to be known, be a V.I.P. (U.S.).
resonante, *a.* resonant, resounding.
resonar, (*ref. 33*) *i.v.* to resound; to resonate.
resondrar, *tr.v.* (Peru) to tell off, tick off, grumble at, scold.
resoplar, *i.v.* to snort, puff, breathe hard.
resoplido, resoplo, *m.* heavy breathing, puffing, snort.
resorber, *tr.v.* to resorb, reabsorb; to sip again.
resorcina, *f.,* **resorcinol,** *m.* (chem.) resorcinol, resorcin.
resorción, *f.* resorption, reabsorption.
resorte, *m.* 1. (mec.) spring. 2. spring, elasticity, resilience. 3. means, way, resources, pull (coll.). — **r. antagonista,** resisting or release spring; **r. espiral,** coil spring; **r. graduable,** coiled spring; **r. tensor,** tension spring.
respailar, *i.v.* to hurry, scurry.
respaldar, *m.* back of a seat.
respaldar, *tr.v.* 1. to indorse, endorse, write on the back of. 2. to back, back up, support, indorse. —*r.v.* 1. to lean back. 2. to dislocate the backbone (a horse).
respaldo, *m.* 1. back (of seat; of sheet of paper). 2. trellis, espalier (supporting plants). 3. endorsement, backing.
respectar, *i.v.* to concern, regard, pertain; **en cuanto** or **por lo que respecta a,** as far as (someone, something) is concerned; as for . . .
respectivamente, *adv.* respectively.
respective, *adv., var. of* **respectivamente.**
respectivo, va, *a.* respective.
respecto, *m.* respect, relation; **al r.,** about the matter, in regard to the matter; **en ese r.,** in that respect; **con r. a, r. a** or **de,** with respect to, with regard to.
résped, *m.* 1. (snake's) tongue; (bee's) sting (organ). 2. spitefulness; mean or malicious remark.
respeluzar, (*ref. 53*) *tr.v., r.v., var. of* **despeluzar.**
respetabilidad, *f.* respectability.
respetable, *a.* 1. respectable, venerable. 2. honorable. 3. considerable; **el r.,** (taur.) the honorable public.
respetador, ra, *a.* respectful, respecting.
respetar, *tr.v.* 1. to respect, honor, revere. 2. to respect, to spare.
respetivo, va, *a.* respectful.
respeto, *m.* 1. respect, deference, reverence. 2. awe, fear. — **campear por sus respetos,** to act independently, do as one pleases; **de r.,** respectable, venerable; extra, spare; **faltar al r.,** to be disrespectful; **ofrecer sus respetos,** to pay one's respects; **r. de sí mismo,** self-respect.
respetuosamente, *adv.* respectfully.
respetuosidad, *f.* respectfulness.
respetuoso, sa, *a.* 1. respectful; considerate. 2. respectable, honorable.
réspice, *m.* 1. (coll.) short dry reply. 2. (coll.) tongue lashing, sharp reproof.
respigador, ra, *a.* gleaner.
respigar, (*ref. 51*) *tr.v.* to glean.
respigón, *m.* 1. hangnail. 2. (vet.) sore on heel (of horse).
respigue, respigué, *ref.* **respigar.**
respingado, da, *past part. of* **respingar.** —*a.* turned-up, snub, retroussé (e.g. nose).
respingar, (*ref. 51*) *i.v.* 1. to give a jerk; to start, balk. 2. (coll.) to curl up (said of a poorly made garment). 3. (coll.) to do reluctantly, be balky; to mutter, grumble.
respingo, *m.* 1. shake, jump, jerk; violent start. 2. (coll.) gesture of disdain or annoyance (on receiving an order); muttering, grumbling. 3. (Chile, Mex.) crease (in clothing).
respingona, *a.* (coll.) **nariz r.,** turned-up nose.
respingue, respingué, *ref.* **respingar.**
respirable, *a.* breathable.
respiración, *f.* 1. respiration, breathing. 2. ventilation. — **r. artificial,** artificial respiration; **r. boca a boca,** mouth-to-mouth resuscitation.
respiradero, *m.* 1. air hole, air vent, air inlet; ventilation shaft. 2. breather, rest. 3. (coll.) respiratory organ.
respirador, ra, *a.* breathing; (anat.) repiratory. —*m.* respirator.
respirante, *a.* breathing, respiring.
respirar, *tr.v.* 1. to breathe. 2. to breathe forth, exude (odor, perfume; ill-will, hatred, etc.). —*i.v.* 1. to breathe, respire. 2. to recover one's spirits, take courage. 3. to rest, take a breather. 4. to smell. — **no r.,** not to breathe a word; **r. por la herida,** to vent one's resentments; **sin r.,** without a rest.
respiratorio, ria, *a.* respiratory.
respiro, *m.* 1. respiration, breathing. 2. rest, breather, respite. 3. extension of time (for payment).
resplandecer, (*ref. 45*) *i.v.* 1. to shine, gleam, glisten, glitter. 2. to shine, excel, stand out.
resplandeciente, *a.* resplendent; shining, bright, glittering, radiant.
resplandecimiento, *m., var. of* **resplandor.**
resplandina, *f.* (coll.) severe reprimand, sharp reprove.
resplandor, *m.* 1. brilliance, radiance; splendor, magnificence. 2. glare, light.
responder, *tr.v.* to answer, reply, respond to. —*i.v.* 1. to answer, reply, respond. 2. to respond, react, perform, e.g. *el paciente no responde al tratamiento,* the patient does not respond to the treatment. 3. to echo back, re-echo. 4. to yield, produce. 5. to correspond, harmonize. 6. to answer back, be pert or impudent. 7. to look towards, face. — **r. a,** to answer, reply to; to answer to, react; **r. de,** to answer or hold oneself responsible for (something); **r. por,** to answer or hold oneself responsible for (a person).
respondiente, *a.* responding, answering. —*m., f.* answerer.
respondón, na, *a.* (coll.) pert, saucy, impudent.
responsabilidad, *f.* 1. responsibility; reliability. 2. liability. — **r. civil** or **pública,** (law) public liability.

responsabilizarse, (*ref. 53*) *r.v.* to make oneself responsible, take the responsibility.
responsable, *a.* responsible; **r. de,** responsible for.
responsar, responsear, *i.v.* to say prayers for the dead.
responso, *m.* 1. prayer for the dead. 2. (coll.) reprimand, reproof.
responsorio, *m.* (ecc.) responsory.
respuesta, *f.* answer, reply, response.
resquebradura, *f.* crack, split, cleft, flaw, fissure.
resquebrajadizo, za, *a.* easily cracked or split.
resquebrajadura, *f., var. of* **resquebradura.**
resquebrajar, *tr.v., r.v.* to crack, split.
resquebrajo, *m., var. of* **resquebradura.**
resquebrajoso, sa, *a.* easily cracked or split.
resquebrar, (*ref. 32*) *i.v.* to crack or split.
resquemar, *tr.v.* to bite, burn, sting (the tongue); to burn (food). —*i.v.* to sting, burn. —*r.v.* to get burned (food).
resquemazón, *f.* **resquemo, resquemor,** *m.* 1. bite, sting (produced by spicy food). 2. burnt taste. 3. misgiving, uneasy feeling. 4. resentment.
resquicio, *m.* 1. chink, crack. 2. chance, opportunity, occasion.
resquiebre, resquiebro, *ref.* **resquebrar.**
resta, *f.* (math.) subtraction; (math.) remainder.
restablecer, (*ref. 45*) *tr.v.* to reestablish, restore, reinstate. —*r.v.* to recover, recuperate.
restablecimiento, *m.* reestablishment, restoration; recovery.
restablezca, restablezco, *ref.* **restablecer.**
restallar, *i.v.* to crack (a whip); to crackle.
restante, *a.* remaining. —*m.* remainder, rest.
restañadero, *m.* estuary; inlet.
restañadura, *f.* retinning.
restañar, *tr.v.* 1. to tin again, retin. 2. to stanch, stop the flow of. —*i.v.* 1. to stanch, cease flowing. 2. to crack (a whip); to crackle.
restañasangre, *f.* (min.) bloodstone.
restaño, *m.* 1. stanching, stopping. 2. pool (of dammed-up water). 3. a formerly used cloth of gold or silver threads.
restar, *tr.v.* 1. to take away, reduce; (math.) to subtract. 2. to return (service in ball games). —*i.v.* 1. to remain, be left. 2. (math.) to substract.
restauración, *f.* 1. restoration, refurbishing, renewal. 2. reinstatement, reestablishing; (pol.) restoration.
restaurador, ra, *a.* restoring. —*m., f.* restorer.
restaurante, *a.* restoring. —*m., f.* restorer. —*m.* restaurant.
restaurar, *tr.v.* 1. to restore, renew, refurbish. 2. to restore, reinstate; (pol.) to restore (a dynasty, a government, etc.).
restaurativo, va, *a., m.* restorative.
restinga, *f.* (mar.) shoal, bar, ledge of rocks.
restingar, *m.* shoaly spot, place full of shoals.
restitución, *f.* restitution, return.
restituible, *a.* returnable, restorable.
restituidor, ra, *a.* returning, restoring. —*m., f.* restorer, returner.
restituir, (*ref. 48*) *tr.v.* 1. to return, refund, give back. 2. to restore, bring back. —*r.v.* to come back, return to the place of departure.
restitutorio, ria, *a.* restitutive.
restituya, restituyendo, restituyera, restituyese, restituyo, *ref.* **restituir.**
resto, *m.* 1. rest, remainder; rest, residue; (math.) remainder. 2. stakes (at cards). 3. player who returns the service; the act of returning the ball. — **r. abierto,** (coll.) without limit; **echar el r.,** to stake all; (coll.) to do one's utmost; **restos mortales,** mortal remains.
restorán, *m.* (Amer.) restaurant.
restregadura, *f.,* **restregamiento,** *m.* hard rubbing or scrubbing.
restregar, (*ref. 67*) *tr.v.* to rub hard, scrub.
restregón, *m.* hard rub or scrub; **a restregones,** by rubbing hard.
restregué, *ref.* **restregar.**
restribar, *i.v.* to rest heavily, lean heavily.
restricción, *f.* restriction; restraint; limitation; **r. de comercio,** (com.) restraint of trade; **r. mental,** mental reservation.
restrictivamente, *adv.* restrictively.
restrictivo, va, *a.* restrictive, restricting.
restricto, ta, *a.* restricted, limited.
restriego, restriegue, *ref.* **restregar.**
restringa, *f., var. of* **restinga.**
restringente, *a.* 1. restricting. 2. binding; astringent.
restringible, *a.* restrainable; limitable.
restringir, (*ref. 62*) *tr.v.* 1. to restrict, limit. 2. to contract, astringe, constrict.
restrinja, restrinjo, *ref* **restringir.**
restriñidor, ra, *a.* constricting, astringent, contracting.
restriñimiento, *m.* contraction, astriction.
restriñir, (*ref. 66*) *tr.v.* to astringe, contract, constrict.
restrojo, *m.* (rare) *var. of* **rastrojo.**
resucitador, ra, *a.* resuscitating, reviving. —*m., f.* resuscitator, reviver.
resucitar, *tr.v.* to bring back to life, resurrect, resuscitate; (coll.) to revive. —*i.v.* to come back to life, rise from the dead, be resurrected; **Él resucitó de entre los muertos,** He rose from the dead.
resudación, *f.* 1. light sweat, light perspiration. 2. oozing.
resudar, *i.v.* 1. to perspire slightly. 2. to ooze.
resudor, *m.* slight perspiration or sweat.
resuelle, resuello, *ref.* **resollar.**
resuello, *m.* breathing, hard breathing; **meterle a uno el r. en el cuerpo,** (coll.) to silence or intimidate someone; **sin r.,** breathless, panting.
resueltamente, *adv.* resolutely.
resuelto, ta, *irr. past part. of* **resolver.** —*a.* 1. resolute, determined. 2. prompt, diligent.
resuelva, resuelvo, *ref.* **resolver.**
resuene, resueno, *ref.* **resonar.**
resulta, *f.* 1. result, effect, consequence. 2. final decision, outcome. 3. vacancy of a post or office. — **de resultas de,** as a result of, as a consequence of.
resultado, *m.* result, effect, outcome, consequence; **como r.,** in consequence.
resultancia, *f.* (rare) result.
resultando, *m.* (law) whereas clause, paragraph, clause.
resultante, *a.* resultant, resulting. —*f.* (math., mec.) resultant.
resultar, *i.v.* 1. to result, come about, arise. 2. to prove to be, turn out to be. 3. to work out, be successful, e.g. *el negocio no resultó,* the business did not work out. 4. to be advantageous. — **r. de,** to result or arise from; **r. ser,** to prove or turn out to be.
resumbruno, na, *a.* (hunt.) brown (said of hawk's coloring).
resumen, *m.* summary, abstract, résumé; **en r.,** in a word, in short, to sum up.
resumidamente, *adv.* briefly, in a word, summarily.
resumidero, *m.* (Amer.) drain.
resumir, *tr.v.* to sum up, summarize, abstract, recapitulate. —*r.v.* to be reduced or transformed.
resunta, *f.* summary, résumé.
resurgente, *a.* resurgent.
resurgimiento, *m.* reappearance, resurgence, revival.
resurgir, (*ref. 62*) *i.v.* to resurge, come to life, appear again, spring up again.
resurrección, *f.* resurrection; (theol.) **R.,** Resurrection; **r. de la carne,** (theol.) resurrection of the body.
resurtida, *f.* rebound, repercussion.
resurtir, *i.v.* to rebound, bounce back.
retablo, *m.* series of paintings or carvings representing a story or event; altar-piece, retable.
retacar, (*ref. 50*) *tr.v.* to hit (the ball) twice (in billiards). —*r.v.* 1. (Chile) to spread one's legs out. 2. (Chile) to refuse to move. 3. (Chile) to back out, back down.
retacear, *tr.v.* 1. to divide into pieces; to trim; to make out of scraps or remnants. 2. (S. Amer.) to scrimp, be stringy with.
retacería, *f.* odds and ends (of fabrics), collection of remnants (e.g. for a crazy quilt).
retaco, *m.* 1. short gun. 2. (billiards) short cue. 3. fellow.
retador, ra, *a.* challenging. —*m.* challenger.
retaguardia, *f.* (mil.) rear, rear guard; **a r.,** in the rear; straggling, lagging; **picar la r.,** to pursue the rear guard closely.
retahíla, *f.* string, line, series.
retajar, *tr.v.* 1. to cut round. 2. to trim (the nib of a quill pen). 3. to circumcise.
retal, *m.* 1. remnant, piece, clipping, scrap. 2. waste leather (used for making glue).
retallar, *tr.v.* 1. to retouch, re-engrave. 2. (archit.) to leave or form ledges or projections.
retallecer, (*ref. 45*) *i.v.* to sprout again.
retallo, *m.* 1. (archit.) ledge, projection. 2. new sprout, bud.
retama, *f.* (bot.) broom, genista; **mascar r.,** (coll.) to be cross, bitter or sour; **r. de escobas, r. negra,** (bot.) broom; **r. de olor, r. macho,** (bot.) Spanish broom; **r. de tintes** or **de tintoreros,** (bot.) woodwaxen.
retamal, retamar, *m.* broom thicket; land covered with furze or Spanish broom.
retamero, ra, *a.* pertaining to broom.
retamilla, *f.* (Mex., bot.) barberry.
retamo, *m.* (S. Amer.) broom (plant).
retar, *tr.v.* 1. to challenge, dare. 2. (coll.) to reprove. 3. (Chile) to reprimand.
retardación, *f.* retardation, delay; slowing down.
retardado, da, *past part. of* **retardar.** —*a.* retarded (mentally).
retardador, ra, *a.* retarding, delaying; decelerating. —*m.* (mec.) retarder.
retardar, *tr.v.* to retard, slow down; to make late, delay, detain. —*r.v.* to slow down; to be or arrive late.
retardatario, ria, *a.* retardant.
retardativo, va, *a.* retardative, retardatory.
retardatriz, (*pl.* **retardatrices**), *a.* (mec.) decelerating, retardative (force).
retardo, *m.* delay, retardation.
retartalillas, *f.* (*pl.*) flow of words.
retasa, retasación, *f.* reappraisement.
retasar, *tr.v.* to reappraise; to reduce the price of (an object left unsold at auction).
retazar, (*ref. 53*) *tr.v. to tear to pieces.*
retazo, *m.* 1. remnant, piece, scrap (of cloth). 2. fragment (of speech, essay, etc.).
retejador, *m.* retiler, tile repairer.
retejar, *tr.v.* 1. to retile (roof). 2. (coll.) to provide with clothing.
retejer, *tr.v.* to weave or knit closely.
retejo, *m.* retiling, roof repairing.
retemblar, (*ref. 29*) *i.v.* to shake, quiver, tremble.
retén, *m.* 1. store, stock, reserve; (mil.) reserve, reserve corps. 2. (mec.) catch, detent, pawl.

retención, *f.* 1. retention. 2. amount withheld. 3. (med.) retention.
retener, (*ref.* 23) *tr.v.* 1. to retain; to keep, withhold; to preserve. 2. to detain, arrest.
retenga, retengo, *ref.* **retener.**
retenida, *f.* (mar.) guy, guy rope.
retenidamente, *adv.* retentively.
retenimiento, *m.* retention.
reteno, *m.* (chem.) retene.
retentado, da, *a.* (Hond.) rash, impetuous, violent.
retentar, (*ref.* 29) *tr.v.* to threaten to return (a disease).
retentiva, *f.* memory, retentive faculty, retentiveness.
retentividad, *f.* (phys.) retentivity.
retentivo, va, *a.* retentive. —*m., f.* retentiveness, memory.
reteñir, (*ref.* 41) *tr.v.* to redye.
reteñir, (*ref.* 41) *i.v., var. of* **retiñir.**
retesamiento, *m.* tightening.
retesar, *tr.v.* to stretch or draw tight.
reteso, *m.* 1. tightening. 2. knoll, slight rise.
reticencia, *f.* (rhet.) implication by omission; deliberate hesitation in speech.
reticente, *a.* knowingly hesitant or vague in speech.
rético, ca, *a.* Rhaetian; Rhaeto-Romanic (language spoken in parts of Switzerland and Italy). —*m.* Rhaeto-Romanic (language).
retícula, *f., var. of* **retículo.**
reticulación, *f.* (top.) reticulation.
reticulado, da, *a.* reticulate.
reticular, *a.* reticular.
retículo, *m.* 1. reticulum, network. 2. (opt.) reticle, cross hairs. 3. (zool., anat., biol., bot.) reticulum.
reticulocito, *m.* (physiol.) reticulocyte.
retín, *m., var. of* **retintín.**
retina, *f.* (anat.) retina.
retináculo, *m.* (med.) retinaculum.
retinar, *tr.v.* to work (wool).
retineno, *m.* (chem.) retinene.
retiniano, na, *a.* retinal.
retinita, *f.* (min.) retinite.
retinitis, *f.* (med.) retinitis.
retinte, *m.* 1. *var. of* **retintín.** 2. second dyeing.
retintín, *m.* 1. ding-dong, jingle, ringing. 2. (coll.) sarcastic tone of voice.
retinto, ta, *a.* 1. dark chestnut. 2. strong, black (coffee).
retiña, retiñendo, retiñera, retiñese, *ref.* **reteñir.**
retiñir, (*ref.* 66) *i.v.* to ding-dong, jingle, ring.
retiración, *f.* (print.) backing, backing up, second impression, printing on the other side of the sheet.
retirada, *f.* 1. withdrawal. 2. (mil.) retreat (act of falling back; signal thereof; taps). 3. place of refuge or shelter. 4. dry river bed (caused by river changing course). — **batirse en r.,** to beat a retreat; **tocar la r.,** to sound the retreat; to sound taps, lights out.
retiradamente, *adv.* secretly.
retirado, da, *past part. of* **retirar.** —*a.* 1. remote, distant, far. 2. retired, inactive; pensioned. —*m.* (mil.) retired officer.
retiramiento, *m., var. of* **retiro.**
retirar, *tr.v.* 1. to retire; withdraw, take away, remove. 2. (print.) to print on the back, back up. —*r.v.* 1. to withdraw, retire. 2. (mil.) to retreat, withdraw. 3. to go into retirement.
retiro, *m.* 1. withdrawal; retirement. 2. retreat, secluded place. 3. (ecc.) retreat. 4. (mil.) retirement, pension. — **pasar al r.,** to go into retirement (army officers).

reto, *m.* 1. challenge, dare. 2. threat. 3. (Chile) reprimand.
retobado, da, *a.* 1. (Amer.) given to grumbling or answering back. 2. (C. Amer.) wild, unruly; stubborn. 3. (Amer.) sly, crafty.
retobar, *tr.v.* 1. (Arg.) to cover with leather. 2. (Chile) to wrap in leather, sackcloth or oilcloth. —*r.v.* (Arg.) to turn ill-humored and surly.
retobo, *m.* 1. (Col., Hond.) junk, refuse, useless thing. 2. (Arg., Chile) sackcloth, oilcloth.
retocador, ra, *m., f.* retoucher.
retocamiento, *m.* retouching.
retocar, (*ref.* 50) *tr.v.* 1. to touch up, retouch; to put the finishing touches to. 2. to touch again, touch repeatedly.
retoce, retocé, *ref.* **retozar.**
retoñar, retoñecer, *i.v.* 1. to sprout. 2. (fig.) to reappear.
retoño, *m.* 1. sprout, shoot. 2. (coll.) child, offspring.
retoque, *m.* 1. retouching, finishing touch. 2. touch (of illness). 3. repeated and frequent touching.
retoque, retoqué, *ref.* **retocar.**
retor, *m.* (tex.) twilled cotton fabric.
retorcedura, *f., var. of* **retorcimiento.**
retorcer, (*ref.* 74) *tr.v.* 1. to twist, wring. 2. to misinterpret, twist, distort, misconstrue. —*r.v.* to twist; to writhe, contort oneself.
retorcido, da, *a.* evil-minded. —*m.* sweetmeat.
retorcijón, *m.* (Amer.), *var. of* **retortijón.**
retorcimiento, *m.* twisting; wringing; writhing.
retórica, *f.* 1. rhetoric. 2. (*pl.*) (coll.) sophistries, subtleties.
retóricamente, *adv.* rhetorically.
retórico, ca, *a.* rhetorical. —*m., f.* rhetorician.
retornamiento, *m.* return.
retornante, *a.* returning.
retornar, *tr.v.* 1. to return, give back. 2. to make go back, back up. 2. to twist again. —*i.v., r.v.* to return, go back.
retornelo, *m.* (mus.) ritornello, ritornel.
retorno, *m.* 1. return, going back; homecoming. 2. return trip. 3. reward, recompense. 4. exchange, barter. 5. return horse, donkey, carriage or transport. 6. (mar.) leading block.
retorromano, na, *a., m.* Rhaeto-Romanic (language).
retorsión, *f.* 1 retortion, twisting. 2. retaliation; (law) retortion.
retorsivo, va, *a.* bending back.
retorta, *f.* 1. (chem.) retort. 2. (tex.) strong linen fabric.
retortero, *m.* twist, turn, twirl; **andar al r.,** (coll.) to scurry around, rush hither and thither; **traer al r.,** (coll.) to drag from pillar to post, harass; (coll.) to lead on, string along; to deceive with false promises.
retortijar, *tr.v.* to twist up, curl up.
retortijón, *m.* curling up, twisting up; **r. de tripas,** stomach cramp.
retostado, da, *a.* dark brown.
retostar, (*ref.* 33) *tr.v.* to toast again; to toast brown.
retozador, ra, *a.* gamboling, romping, frolicking, frisky.
retozadura, *f., var. of* **retozo.**
retozar, (*ref.* 53) *i.v.* 1. to romp, frolic, gambol, frisk about, skip about. 2. to become aroused or inflamed. —*r.v.* to revel, rejoice.
retozo, *m.* romp, gambol, frolic; prank.
retozón, na, *a.* frolicsome, playful, frisky.
retracción, *f.* retraction.
retractable, *a.* retractable (statement, etc.).
retractación, *f.* retraction, recantation.
retractar, *tr.v.* 1. to retract, recant; withdraw, take back. 2. (law) to redeem. —*r.v.* to retract oneself.

retráctil, *a.* retractile.
retractilidad, *f.* retractility.
retracto, *m.* (law) prior right of purchase.
retractor, *a.* (anat.) retractive (muscle). —*m.* (surg., anat.) retractor.
retraer, (*ref.* 24) *tr.v.* 1. to bring again, bring back. 2. to dissuade. —*r.v.* 1. to withdraw, retire; to shun, keep aloof from. 2. to take refuge.
retraído, da, *past part. of* **retraer.**
retraiga, retraigo, *ref.* **retraer.**
retraimiento, *m.* 1. reserve, uncommunicativeness, withdrawn nature. 2. withdrawal, retirement. 3. solitude. 4. asylum, refuge, sanctuary, retreat.
retraje, retrajera, retrajese, *ref.* **retraer.**
retranca, *f.* 1. breeching (of harness). 2. (Col., Cuba) hub brake.
retranquear, *tr.v.* (archit.) to hoist and put (building stones or blocks) in place.
retranqueo, *m.* (archit.) setting stones or blocks in position.
retranquero, *m.* (Cuba, P. Rico, ry.) brakeman.
retransmisión, *f.* (rad., tel.) rebroadcast, relay broadcast.
retransmitir, *tr.v.* to rebroadcast, relay.
retrasado, da, *past part. of* **retrasar.** —*a.* retarded (mentally).
retrasar, *tr.v.* to delay, retard; to defer, put off. —*i.v.* to get or lag behind. —*r.v.* to delay, be late, be delayed, be behind; to get or lag behind; to be slow (watch, clock).
retraso, *m.* delay, slowness; lag; **con r., de r.,** late, e.g. *él siempre llega con media hora de r.,* he always arrives half an hour late.
retratación, *f.* retraction, recantation.
retratador, ra, *m., f., var. of* **retratista.**
retratar, *tr.v.* 1. to paint a portrait of, paint, draw; to photograph. 2. to portray, describe, depict. 3. to imitate, copy. 4. to retract, take back, withdraw. —*r.v.* 1. to be reflected, depicted; to show (e.g. on one's face). 2. to sit for a portrait or photograph.
retratista, *m., f.* portrayer; portrait painter; photographer.
retrato, *m.* 1. portrait, portrait picture or painting; portrait photograph. 2. portrait, description. 3. image, exact likeness. 4. (law) prior right of purchase. — **r. de cuerpo entero,** full-length portrait; **r. de medio cuerpo,** head-and-shoulders portrait; **ser el vivo r. de,** to be the living image of.
retrayendo, *ref.* **retraer.**
retrayente, *m., f.* (law) purchaser by prior right.
retrechar, *i.v.* to back, move backward (horse).
retrechería, *f.* (coll.) evasiveness, cunning.
retrechero, ra, *a.* 1. (coll.) cunning, crafty. 2. (coll.) attractive, fascinating.
retrepado, da, *a.* leaning or slanting backward.
retreparse, *r.v.* to lean back, to sprawl and lean back in a chair.
retreta, *f.* 1. (mil.) retreat (call sounding retreat); (mil.) retreat, tattoo, taps, lights out. 2. tattoo, evening parade. 3. (Amer.) open-air band concert. 4. (Amer.) series, string.
retrete, *m.* (Sp.) water closet, toilet, lavatory.
retribución, *f.* repayment, reward, recompense.
retribuir, (*ref.* 48) *tr.v.* to repay, reward, recompense.
retributivo, va, *a.* retributory; repaying, rewarding.
retribuya, retribuyendo, *ref.* **retribuir.**
retribuyente, *a.* repaying, rewarding.
retribuyera, retribuyese, retribuyo, retribuyó, *ref.* **retribuir.**
retrillar, *tr.v.* (agr.) to thrash again.

retroacción, *f.* retroaction; (mec.) backward action; (elec.) feedback.
retroactividad, *f.* retroactivity.
retroactivo, va, *a.* retroactive.
retroalimentación, *f.* (elec., rad.) feedback. — **r. negativa,** (elec., rad.) negative feedback.
retrocarga, de r., breech-loading.
retroceder, *i.v.* 1. to go back, go backwards; to step back, draw back, back away; to recede, retrocede. 2. to become worse (illness, patient, etc.).
retrocesión, *f.* 1. retrocession. 2. (law) retrocession, ceding back.
retroceso, *m.* 1. retrocession, retrogression; backward motion. 2. recoil, kick (of a gun). 3. reverse, reverse gear (e.g. of car). — **ir en r.,** to back up, go in reverse. 4. (med.) aggravation, worsening.
retrocohete, *m.* retro-rocket.
retrodisparo, *m.* (astronaut.) retro-firing.
retroexcavadora, *f.* backhoe.
retrogradación, *f.* (astron.) retrogradation, retrogression.
retrogradar, *i.v.* (astron.) to retrograde.
retrógrado, da, *a.* 1. retrogressive. 2. (astron.) retrograde. 3. (pol.) retrograde; reactionary. —*m., f.* reactionary.
retrogresión, *f.* retrogression.
retrolingual, *a.* retrolingual.
retronar, (*ref.* 33) *i.v.* to thunder, rumble.
retropilastra, *f.* (archit.) pilaster behind a column.
retropropulsión, *f.* (aer.) jet propulsion.
retropulsión, *f.* (med.) retropulsion.
retroscopio, *m.* retroscope.
retrospección, *f.* retrospection.
retrospectivo, va, *a.* retrospective.
retrotracción, *f.* (law) antedating.
retrotraer, (*ref.* 24) *tr.v.* (law) to antedate, date back.
retrotraiga, retrotraigo, *ref.* **retrotraer.**
retrotraje, retrotrajera, retrotrajese, retrotrayendo, *ref.* **retrotraer.**
retrovender, *tr.v.* (law) to sell back to the vendor.
retrovendición, retroventa, *f.* (law) selling back to the vendor.
retroversión, *f.* (med.) retroversion.
retrovisor, *a.* **espejo r.,** (auto.) rear view mirror.
retrovisual, *f.* backsight.
retrucar, (*ref.* 50) *i.v.* 1. to kiss (billiards). 2. (Arg.) to talk back, retort.
retruco, *m.* kiss (in billiards).
retruécano, *m.* 1. pun, play on words. 2. (rhet.) antithesis.
retruena, retruene, *ref.* **retronar.**
retruque, *m., var. of* **retruco.**
retruque, retruqué, *ref.* **retrucar.**
retuerza, retuerzo, *ref.* **retorcer.**
retueste, retuesto, *ref.* **retostar.**
retumbante, *a.* 1. resonant, resounding, booming, rumbling. 2. (fig.) pompous, bombastic, turgid.
retumbar, *i.v.* to resound, boom, rumble.
retumbo, *m.* boom, rumble, resonance, reverberation.
retundir, *tr.v.* 1. (mas.) to even, smooth (the surface of a wall, etc.); to point (joints). 2. (med.) to repel.
retuve, retuviera, retuviese, *ref.* **retener.**
reucliniano, na, *a., m., f.* Reuchlinian, of or pertaining to Johann Reuchlin, German scholar and humanist.
reuma, *m.* (med.) rheumatism; (med.) rheum, watery discharge.
reumático, ca, *a., m., f.* rheumatic.
reumátide, *f.* (med.) rheumatic dermatosis.
reumatismo, *m.* (med.) rheumatism.
reunión, *f.* 1. reunion, meeting, assembly, gathering. 2. rejoining, consolidation. — **derecho de r.,** right of assembly.
reunir, *tr.v., r.v.* to join, unite; to assemble, gather, collect, get together; to reunite; to collect, accumulate.
reuntar, *tr.v.* to grease again, oil again.
revacunación, *f.* (med.) revaccination.
revacunar, *tr.v.* to revaccinate.
reválida, *f.* final examination for a degree.
revalidación, *f.* revalidation, confirmation; renewal.
revalidar, *tr.v.* to revalidate, confirm, renew. —*r.v.* to take an examination for a degree.
revalorar, *tr.v.* to revalue.
revalorización, *f.* revaluation.
revalorizar, (*ref.* 53) *tr.v.* to revalue.
revaluación, *f.* revaluation, reappraisal.
revancha, *f.* 1. revenge, retaliation. 2. (sport) return match.
revecero, ra, *a.* changing, shifting. —*m., f.* farmhand in charge of oxen relays.
reveedor, *m.* revisor, inspector, overseer.
revejecer, (*ref.* 45) *i.v., r.v.* to grow old prematurely.
revejezca, revejezco, *ref.* **revejecer.**
revejido, da, *a.* prematurely old or aged.
revelable, *a.* revealable.
revelación, *f.* revelation.
revelado, *a.* revealed. —*m.* (photog.) developing, development.
revelador, ra, *a.* revealing. —*m., f.* revealer. —*m.* (photog.) developer (solution).
revelamiento, *m.* revelation, revealing.
revelandero, ra, *m., f.* bogus visionary, one who pretends to have had a divine revelation.
revelante, *a.* revealing.
revelar, *tr.v.* 1. to reveal. 2. (photog.) to develop.
reveler, *tr.v.* (med.) to cause revulsion to.
revellín, *m.* (fort.) ravelin.
revenar, *i.v.* to sprout (trees after pruning).
revendedera, *f., var. of* **revendedora.**
revendedor, ra, *m., f.* 1. reseller; retailer. 2. ticket speculator, scalper (coll.).
revender, *tr.v.* to resell; to retail.
revenga, revengo, *ref.* **revenir.**
revenimiento, *m.* 1. return (to original condition). 2. shrinkage; lessening. 3. souring, turning sour. 4. sweating (of wall, etc.). 5. (min.) cave-in.
revenir, (*ref.* 26) *i.v.* to return (to its original condition). —*r.v.* 1. to shrink; to grow less. 2. to go sour. 3. to exude dampness, sweat. 4. to become soft or runny (from heat or dampness). 5. (coll.) to yield, give in, back down.
reveno, *m.* sprout, shoot (of pruned or grafted trees).
reventa, *f.* resale; retail.
reventadero, *m.* 1. rough or steep ground. 2. (coll.) drudgery, rough job. 3. (Chile) place where ocean waves break.
reventar, (*ref.* 29) *tr.v.* 1. to burst, explode; to squash, smash. 2. to override (a horse); to work to death, exhaust. 3. (coll.) to annoy, bother, irritate; (coll.) to ruin, wreck. —*i.v.* 1. to burst, explode, blow up; to blow (a tire); to break (waves); (coll.) to be bursting (with desire); (coll.) to burst, explode, blow up (with anger). 2. (coll.) to die violently. — **r. de risa,** to burst out laughing; **r. por** + *inf.,* (coll.) to be raring + *inf.,* be dying + *inf.* —*r.v.* 1. to burst, explode, blow up; to blow up (tire). 2. to wind (a horse). 3. (coll.) to be wrecked, exhausted.
reventazón, *f.* 1. bursting, explosion; surf, breaking (of waves); blowout (of a tire). 2. (Arg.) counterfort (of a mountain range).
reventón, *a.* bursting. —*m.* 1. bursting, explosion; blowout (of tire); breaking (of waves). 2. rough steep path. 3. (coll.) difficulty, mess, fix (coll.). 4. (coll.) spurt, all-out effort. 5. (Chile) fit, outburst (of anger, etc.). 6. (Arg., Chile, min.) outcrop.
reveo, revea, *ref.* **rever.**
rever, (*ref.* 27) *tr.v.* 1. to revise, look over, review. 2. (law) to retry (a case).
reverberación, *f.* 1. reflection, reverberation. 2. (chem.) reverberation, calcination in a reverberatory furnace.
reverberante, *a.* reverberating.
reverberar, *i.v.* to reverberate.
reverbero, *m.* 1. reflection, reverberation. 2. reflector. 3. (Amer.) alcohol stove. — **horno de r.,** reverberatory furnace.
reverdecer, (*ref.* 45) *tr.v.* 1. to make green or verdant again. 2. to give new vigor. —*r.v.* 1. to grow green or verdant. 2. to get new vigor or life.
reverdeciente, *a.* 1. verdant, greening (fields). 2. renewed, refreshed, invigorated.
reverdezca, reverdezco, *ref.* **reverdecer.**
reverencia, *f.* 1. reverence, veneration. 2. bow, curtsy, reverence. 3. (ecc.) **R.,** Reverence (title).
reverenciable, *a.* reverend, worthy of reverence, venerable.
reverenciador, ra, *a.* revering, venerating. —*m., f.* one who reveres or venerates.
reverencial, *a.* reverential.
reverenciar, *tr.v.* to revere, reverence, venerate.
reverendas, *f.* (*pl.*) (ecc.) prelate's dimissory letters. 2. virtues, merits, qualities.
reverendísimo, ma, *a. sup. of* **reverendo,** (ecc.) Most Reverend, Right Reverend.
reverendo, da, *a.* 1. (ecc.) Reverend. 2. (coll.) formal, prim, circumspect.
reverente, *a.* reverent.
reverentemente, *adv.* reverently.
reversibilidad, *f.* reversibility.
reversible, *a.* reversible.
reversión, *f.* reversion.
reverso, *m.* reverse, back; reverse (of a coin); **el r. de la medalla,** the very antithesis, the absolute opposite.
reverter, (*ref.* 30) *i.v.* to overflow.
revertir, (*ref.* 42) *i.v.* (law) to revert.
revés, *m.* 1. reverse, back; opposite side; wrong side. 2. backhand, slap with the back of the hand; backhand, backhand stroke (in ball games). 3. (fenc.) reverse stroke. 4. (coll.) setback, reverse. 5. change (of disposition, manner, etc.). 6. (Cuba) tobacco weevil. — **al r.,** upside down, inside out, wrong side out; in the opposite way, backwards; **al r. me las calcé,** I did or understood quite the opposite; **r. alto,** high backhand stroke.
revesa, *f.* (mar.) back water, eddy, counter-current.
revesado, da, *a.* 1. intricate, complicated, obscure. 2. mischievous, skittish, wayward.
revesar, *tr.v.* to throw up, vomit.
revesino, *m.* reversi (game of cards).
revestido, revestimiento, *m.* coating, coat, layer, lining, facing; finish, dressing. — **r. calorífugo,** heat insulation; **r. del embrague,** clutch facing.
revestir, (*ref.* 39) *tr.v.* 1. to coat, line, face, surface, dress, cover with. 2. to adorn, deck. 3. (mas.) to revet. 4. to invest (with dignity, etc.). —*r.v.* 1. to imbue oneself, become imbued, be carried away. 2. to become conceited. 3. to gird or arm oneself (with patience, resignation, etc.). 4. to put on garments or vestments.
revezar, (*ref.* 53) *tr.v.* to replace, relieve. —*i.v.* to alternate, take shifts or turns.

revezo, *m.* replacement, relief; relay, turn.
reviejo, ja, *a.* very old. —*m.* withered branch (of a tree).
revientabuey, *m.* (ento.) buprestid, buprestid beetle.
reviente, reviento, *ref.* **reventar.**
reviernes, *m.* each of the seven Fridays following Easter.
revierta, revierto, *ref.* **reverter; revertir.**
revindicar, (*ref. 50*) *tr.v.* to recover, regain possession of, replevy.
revindique, revindiqué, *ref.* **revindicar.**
revine, reviniendo, reviniera, reviniese, *ref.* **revenir.**
revirado, da, *a.* twisted (tree fibers). —*m., f.* (Cuba) rebel; turncoat.
revirar, *tr.v.* 1. to twist; to turn around. 2. to roll (one's eyes). —*r.v.* (Cuba, coll.) to rebel, revolt. —*i.v.* (mar.) to veer again, retack.
revirtiendo, revirtiera, revirtiese, revirtió, *ref.* **revertir.**
revisada, *f.* (Amer.), *var. of* **revisión.**
revisador, ra, *a., var. of* **revisor.**
revisar, *tr.v.* 1. to revise, examine, inspect, check. 2. to audit. — **r. las cuentas,** to audit accounts.
revisión, *f.* 1. revision, examination, inspection. 2. check; auditing. 3. (law) review, rehearing, new trial. — **r. médica,** checkup, medical examination.
revisita, *f.* reinspection.
revisor, ra, *a.* revising, revisory; examining, inspecting; auditing, checking. —*m., f.* 1. revisor, examiner, inspector, checker; auditor. 2. (ry.) conductor.
revisoría, *f.* office of an inspector, examiner or auditor.
revista, *f.* 1. inspection, review. 2. review, survey; reexamination, reinspection. 3. magazine, journal, review. 4. review, critique, criticism (of book, play, etc.). 5. (theat.) revue, vaudeville or variety show. 6. (mil.) review, muster, parade. 7. (law) retrial, new trial. — **pasar r.,** to inspect, review; to examine very carefully; **r. de modas,** fashion magazine.
revista, *ref.* **revestir.**
revistar, *tr.v.* to review, inspect.
revisteril, *a.* pertaining to a revue or vaudeville show.
revistero, ra, *m., f.* critic, reviewer.
revistiendo, revistiera, revistiese, revistió, revisto, *ref.* **revestir.**
revisto, ta, *irr. past part. of* **rever.**
revitalizar, (*ref. 53*) *tr.v.* to revitalize.
revivídero, *m.* silkworm breeding farm.
revivificación, *f.* revivification, revival.
revivificar, (*ref. 50*) *tr.v.* to revivify, revive.
revivifique, revivifiqué, *ref.* **revivificar.**
revivir, *i.v.* to revive, come back to life.
revocabilidad, *f.* revocability.
revocable, *a.* revocable, annullable, repealable.
revocablemente, *adv.* revocably.
revocación, *f.* revocation, abrogation, repeal, annulment; **r. de una sentencia,** (law) reversal.
revocador, ra, *a.* revoking, repealing, annulling. —*m.* 1. revoker, annuller. 2. plasterer.
revocadura, *f.* 1. plastering, whitewashing. 2. (p.) edge of a canvas turned over the stretcher.
revocante, *a.* revoking, repealing, cancelling, annulling.
revocar, (*ref. 50*) *tr.v.* 1. to revoke, repeal, cancel, annul. 2. to dissuade. 3. to drive back, push back. 4. (mas.) to plaster or whitewash. —*i.v.* to recede, be driven or pushed back.
revocatorio, ria, *a.* revocatory, repealing.
revoco, *m.* 1. driving back; regression, going back. 2. plastering, whitewashing. 3. cover of furze on charcoal baskets.

revolante, *a.* fluttering, hovering.
revolar, (*ref. 33*) *i.v.* to fly again; to fly around, flutter around.
revolcadero, *m.* wallowing place (of animals).
revolcadura, *f.* wallowing, rolling about; weltering.
revolcado, *m.* (Guat.) dish made with toasted bread, chili, tomatoes and spice.
revolcar, (*ref. 69*) *tr.v.* 1. to knock down, trample upon. 2. (coll.) to floor, get the better of, defeat. 3. (coll.) to fail, flunk (coll., U.S.), plough (coll., G.B.). —*r.v.* 1. to wallow, roll about. 2. to be stubborn.
revolcón, *m.* 1. (coll.) wallow, wallowing, rolling about. 2. knocking down.
revolear, *i.v.* to fly or flutter around. —*tr.v.* (Arg.) to swing a lasso around.
revoletear, *i.v.* (S. Amer.) to fly or flutter around.
revolico, *m.* (Cuba) confusion, uproar, disorder.
revolotear, *tr.v.* to whirl up into the air, send spinning up. —*i.v.* to fly or flutter around; to flutter, spin or whirl down.
revoloteo, *m.* fluttering, whirling, hovering.
revolqué, *ref.* **revolcar.**
revoltijo, revoltillo, *m.* 1. jumble, mix-up, mess; confusion. 2. twisted innards or guts. — **revoltillo de huevos,** scrambled eggs.
revoltón, *m.* 1. (ento.) vine fretter, vine grub. 2. small vault (in a ceiling). 3. (archit.) turn, corner, angle (of a molding).
revoltoso, sa, *a.* troublemaking, rioting, agitating, rebellious; unruly, mischievous. —*m., f.* rioter, troublemaker, agitator.
revoltura, *f.* (Amer.) mixture; confusion.
revolución, *f.* 1. revolution, revolt. 2. revolution, complete change. 3. (mec., astron.) revolution, turn.
revolucionar, *tr.v.* 1. to revolutionize, change completely. 2. to incite to rebellion.
revolucionario, ria, *a., m., f.* revolutionary.
revolvedero, *m., var. of* **revolcadero.**
revolvedor, ra, *a.* agitating, turbulent; disturbing, troublemaking, seditious. —*m., f.* agitator, troublemaker. —*m.* (Cuba) mixing vat (in sugar mills).
revólver, *m.* revolver, pistol, gun.
revolver, (*ref. 34*) *irr. past part.* **revuelto.** —*tr.v.* 1. to stir, mix; to jumble up, disarrange. 2. to turn over, poke about, rummage around in (to examine something). 3. to turn over, consider, ponder. 4. to disturb, stir up, upset. 5. to swing (a horse) around swiftly. 6. to retrace (one's steps). 7. to wrap, wrap up. 8. to turn completely round, revolve. — **r. a uno con otro,** to set one person against another. —*r.v.* 1. to turn around and around; to toss and turn (in bed). 2. to retrace one's steps. 3. to swing around swiftly (a horse). 4. to turn stormy (weather), get rough (sea). 5. (astron.) to revolve, make a complete revolution (planet).
revolvimiento, *m.* 1. revolution, rotation. 2. stirring (e.g. liquid). 3. commotion, disturbance. 4. swinging, turning around.
revoque, *m.* plastering, whitewashing; whitewash, plaster.
revoque, revoqué, *ref.* **revocar.**
revotarse, *r.v.* to reverse or reconsider one's vote or ballot.
revuelco, *m.* 1. wallowing, wallow, rolling over. 2. knocking down.
revuelco, *ref.* **revolcar.**
revuelo, *m.* 1. commotion, agitation, stir. 2. second flight. 3. turn, gyration (in flying). 4. (Amer.) spur thrust (of fighting cock). — **de r.,** swiftly, lightly.

revuelque, *ref.* **revolcar.**
revuelta, *f.* 1. revolt, revolution; quarrel, fight; commotion, disturbance. 2. turn; change.
revueltamente, *adv.* confusedly, pell-mell.
revuelto, ta, *irr. past part. of* **revolver.** —*a.* 1. swiftly-turning (horse). 2. mischievous, troublemaking, unruly. 3. intricate, complicated, obscure. 4. scrambled (eggs).
revuelva, revuelvo, *ref.* **revolver.**
revuelvepiedras, *m.* (ornith.) turnstone.
revulsión, *f.* (med.) revulsion.
revulsivo, va, revulsorio, ria, *a., m.* (med.) revulsive.
rey, *a.* king. —*m.* 1. king, sovereign. 2. king (in cards or chess). 3. ancient Spanish dance step. 4. queen bee. 5. (coll.) hog-keeper, swineherd. — **a r. muerto, r. puesto,** the king is dead; long live the king! (a vacant position is soon filled); **el r. que rabió,** or **el r. Perico,** Methuselah, proverbial personage representing antiquity, e.g. *ser de los tiempos del rey que rabió,* to be as old as the hills or Methuselah, *en los tiempos del r. Perico,* in the times of Methuselah; **no temer ni r. ni roque,** (coll.) to be afraid of no one or nothing; **noche de Reyes,** Twelfth night; **r. de armas,** king-of-arms; **r. de bando** or **banda,** leader of a covey of partridges; **R. de reyes,** (Bib.) Jesus Christ; **r. de Romanos,** Holy Roman Emperor; **Reyes Magos,** Three Magi, Three Wise Men; **servir al r.,** to serve king and country, to be a soldier.
reyerta, *f.* quarrel, fight, row, wrangle.
reyezuelo, *m.* 1. *dim. of* **rey,** little king, petty king, kinglet. 2. (ornith.) kinglet.
Reykiavik, *m.* **Reykjavik,** capital of Iceland.
rezado, *m.* (ecc.) prayer, divine service.
rezador, ra, *a.* prayerful, devout. —*m., f.* prayer; devout or prayerful person.
rezaga, *f.* rear guard.
rezagado, da, *past part. of* **rezagar.** —*a.* deferred for examination at a later date. —*m., f.* 1. straggler, lagger. 2. examinee deferred for examination at a later date.
rezagante, *a.* straggling, lagging, left behind.
rezagar, (*ref. 51*) *tr.v.* to leave behind; to put off, defer, postpone. —*r.v.* to remain behind, lag, straggle, fall behind.
rezago, *m.* 1. remainder, left-over. 2. weak cattle put aside for special care.
rezandero, ra, *a.* (Col., Hond., Mex., Ven.) prayerful, devout —*m., f.* prayerful person.
rezar, (*ref. 53*) *tr.v.* 1. pray. 2. to say (the divine office, the Mass, a prayer). 3. (coll.) to say, read. —*i.v.* 1. to pray. 2. (coll.) to grumble, moan. 3. (coll.) to read, e.g. *el titular del periódico rezaba así,* the newspaper headline read as follows. — **r. con,** to concern, have to do with, be the business of.
rezno, *m.* 1. (ento.) bot. 2. (bot.) castor oil plant.
rezo, *m.* prayer; daily prayers.
rezón, *m.* (mar.) grapnel.
rezongador, ra, *a.* grumbling, griping, grouching. —*m., f.* grumbler, griper, grouch.
rezongar, (*ref. 51*) *i.v.* to grumble, gripe, grouch.
rezonglón, na, *a., m., f.* (coll.), *var. of* **rezongón.**
rezongo, *m.* grumbling, griping, grouching.
rezongón, na, *a., m., f.* (coll.), *var. of* **rezongador.**
rezongue, rezongué, *ref.* **rezongar.**
rezonguero, ra, *a.* grumbling, grouching, griping.
rezumadero, *m.* place where something leaks or oozes; leakage, seepage.
rezumar, *tr.v.* to exude, ooze. —*i.v.* to ooze, exude, seep; to leak. —*r.v.* 1. to ooze, exude, seep. 2. (coll.) to leak out (news, etc.).
rezumbador, *m.* (Cuba) whirring spinning top.

Rh *sym. of* **rodio,** rhodium (Rh).
rhesus, *m.* (zool.) rhesus; **factor r.,** (med.) rhesus factor.
ría, *f.* estuary (of a river).
¡ria! cry used by cart drivers to guide horses towards the left.
ría, *ref.* **reír.**
riacho, riachuelo, *m.* rivulet, stream.
riada, *f.* freshet, flood.
riba, *f.* mound, hillock, bank, slope, brae.
ribadoquín, *m.* (artil.) small bronze cannon.
ribaldería, *f.* knavery, rascality.
ribaldo, da, *a.* knavish, rascally. —*m., f.* knave, rascal, rogue.
ribazo, *m., var. of* **riba.**
ribera, *f.* 1. bank, shore, beach; riverside. 2. vicinity of a river.
riberano, na, ribereño, ña, *a.* riparian, riverside. —*m., f.* riverside dweller, owner of a riverside property.
riberiego, ga, *a.* 1. stationary, sedentary, non-roaming (cattle). 2. riparian, riverside. —*m., f.* owner of non-roaming cattle.
ribero, *m.* dike, levee.
ribesiáceo, a, *a.* (bot.) grossulariaceous. —*f.* (*pl.*) (bot.) Grossulariaceae.
ribete, *m.* 1. (sew.) edge, binding, border, trimming. 2. addition, embellishment (to a story). 3. (*pl.*) signs, touches, streaks, e.g. *tener ribetes de loco,* to have a mad streak in oneself.
ribeteado, da, *a.* edged, bound, bordered, trimmed.
ribeteador, ra, *a.* edging, binding, trimming. —*m., f.* edger, binder, trimmer.
ribetear, *tr.v.* to edge, border, bind, trim.
riboflavina, *f.* (biochem.) riboflavin.
ricacho, cha, ricachón, na, *m., f.* (coll.) vulgar rich person.
ricadueña, ricahembra, *f.* (arch.) noblewoman.
ricahombría, *f.* (arch.) grandeeship; the high nobility of Castile.
ricamente, *adv.* 1. richly, opulently; abundantly; magnificently. 2. tastily, deliciously.
rice, ricé, *ref.* **rizar.**
ricial, *a.* growing or sprouting again (stubble field); green (pasture land).
ricina, *f.* (chem.) ricin.
ricino, *m.* (bot.) castor oil plant, Palma Christi.
ricinólico, ca, *a.* (chem.) ricinoleic.
rico, ca, *a.* 1. rich, wealthy. 2. tasty, delicious (food); magnificent, sumptuous (e.g. decorations); abundant, big (crops). 3. dear, darling. —*m., f.* rich person; **nuevo rico,** nouveau riche.
ricohombre, *m.* (arch.) grandee, nobleman; peer of the high nobility of Castile.
rictus, *m.* convulsive contraction of the lips, convulsive grin.
ricura, *f.* (coll.) tastiness, deliciousness.
ridículamente, *adv.* ridiculously.
ridiculez, (*pl.* **ridiculeces**), *f.* 1. ridiculousness, absurdity. 2. oddity, eccentricity. 3. trifle, bagatelle, negligible amount. 4. touchiness, sensitivity.
ridiculice, ridiculicé, *ref.* **ridiculizar.**
ridiculizar, (*ref.* 53) *tr.v.* to ridicule.
ridículo, la, *a.* 1. ridiculous, absurd. 2. touchy. —*m.* 1. ridiculous situation. 2. reticule (lady's handbag). — **hacer el r., ponerse en r.,** to make a fool of oneself; **poner en r.,** to make a fool of; **quedar en r.,** to be made a fool of; **un papel ridículo,** a ridiculous situation.
riego, *m.* irrigation, watering; irrigation water.— **r. continuo,** continuous-flow irrigation; **r. por aspersión,** spray irrigation; **r. por goteo,** drip irrigation; **r. sanguíneo,** blood flow, circulation of the blood.
riego, riegue, *ref.* **regar.**
riel, *m.* 1. ingot, bar. 2. (ry.) rail. — **andar sobre rieles,** to go like clockwork; **r. conductor,** (ry.) third rail; **r. de hongo** or **patín,** (ry.) T rail; **r. de recorrido,** running rail; **r. Vignoles,** (ry.) T rail.
rielar, *i.v.* (poet.) to flicker, glow, glimmer.
rielera, *f.* ingot mold.
rielero, *m.* (ry.) platelayer.
rienda, *f.* rein; (fig.) (*pl.*) reins, control, government; **aflojar las riendas,** (coll.) to ease up, loosen the reins; **a r. suelta,** (coll.) at full speed; freely, unrestrainedly; **dar r. suelta a,** (fig.) to give free rein to; to give (a horse) its head; **falsa r.,** (equit.) checkrein; **tener las riendas,** (fig.) to be in control, control, direct; **tomar las riendas,** (fig.) to take the reins, take control.
riendo, *ref.* **reír.**
riente, *a.* laughing, smiling.
riera, riese, *ref.* **reír.**
riesgo, *m.* risk, danger, hazard, peril; **correr r.,** to take or run a risk; **riesgos contra tercera persona,** third party risks.
riesgoso, sa, *a.* (Amer.) risky, dangerous.
Rif, *m.* **El R.,** Er Rif (a mountain region of Morocco).
rifa, *f.* 1. raffle. 2. quarrel, fight, scuffle.
rifador, *m.* raffler.
rifadura, *f.* (mar.) splitting (of a sail).
rifar, *tr.v.* to raffle. —*i.v.* to quarrel. —*r.v.* to split (of a sail).
rifeño, ña, *a., m., f.* Riff, Riffian (from the Rif, Morocco).
rifirrafe, *m.* (coll.) squabble, row, fight
rifle, *m.* rifle; **r. de repetición,** repeating rifle.
riflero, *m.* (Arg., Chile) rifleman (soldier).
rigente, *a.* (poet.) rigid.
rígidamente, *adv.* rigidly.
rigidez, *f.* rigidity, stiffness; **r. cadavérica,** rigor mortis.
rígido, *a.* 1. rigid, stiff. 2. rigorous, stern, inflexible.
rigiendo, rigiera, rigiese, rigió, *ref.* **regir.**
rigodón, *m.* rigadoon (dance).
rigor, *m.* 1. rigor; severity; harshness. 2. exactness, precision, strictness. 3. (med.) rigor. — **de r.,** prescribed by rules, de rigueur; essential, obligatory; **en r.,** strictly, exactly.
rigorismo, *m.* rigorism, strictness, severeness.
rigorista, *a.* rigoristic. —*m., f.* rigorist.
rigorosamente, *adv., var. of* **rigurosamente.**
rigoroso, *a., var. of* **riguroso.**
rigüe, *m.* (Hond.) tortilla of green corn.
rigurosamente, *adv.* 1. rigorously. 2. scrupulously.
rigurosidad, *f.* rigorousness, severity.
riguroso, sa, *a.* 1. rigorous; severe; harsh; strict, rigid. 2. exact; absolute.
rija, *f.* 1. (med.) lachrymal fistula. 2. fight, quarrel; dispute.
rijador, ra, *a., var. of* **rijoso.**
rija, rijo, *ref.* **regir.**
rijo, *m.* lust, concupiscence, sensuality.
rijoso, sa, *a.* 1. lustful, sexually excited. 2. restless at the sight of the mare (stallion). 3. quarrelsome, belligerent.
rilar, *i.v., r.v.* to shiver, shudder, shake.
rima, *f.* rhyme; consonance; (*pl.*) poems, poetry; **r. imperfecta, media r.,** assonance; **octava r.,** ottava rima; **sexta r.,** sestina; **tercia r.,** terza rima.
rima, *f.* heap, pile.
rimador, ra, *m., f.* poetaster, rhymester, maker of poor verse.
rimar, *i.v.* 1. to rhyme. 2. to compose verse, write poetry. —*tr.v.* to rhyme.
rimbombancia, *f.* 1. resonance, boom. 2. bombast, ostentation.
rimbombante, *a.* 1. resonant, booming, resounding. 2. bombastic, ostentatious.
rimbombar, *i.v.* to resound, boom.
rimbombe, rimbombo, *m.* resonance, boom.
rímel, *m.* mascara.
rimero, *m.* heap, pile, stack.
rimú, (*pl.* **rimúes**), *m.* (Chile, bot.) wood sorrel (Oxalis lobata).
Rin, *m.* Rhine (the river).
rinal, *a.* (anat.) rhinal.
rinalgia, *f.* (med.) rhinalgia.
rinanto, *m.* (bot.) wild sage, vervain sage.
rinche, cha, *a.* (Chile) brimful.
rincocéfalo, *m.* (zool.) rhynchocephalian; (*pl.*) Rhynchocephalia.
rincón, *m.* 1. (inside) corner; angle. 2. nook, cosy corner; haven, retreat, remote place. 3. patch, small piece (of land). 4. bit, end.
rinconada, *f.* corner, angle (formed by houses, streets, etc.).
rinconcillo, *m. dim. of* **rincón,** small corner.
rinconera, *f.* 1. corner piece (of furniture), corner table, cupboard, stand, bracket. 2. (archit.) wall between corner and window.
rinde, *m.* (Arg.) yield.
rindiendo, rindiera, rindiese, rindió, rindo, *ref.* **rendir.**
ringente, *a.* (bot.) ringent.
ringla, *f.,* **ringle,** *m.,* **ringlera,** *f.* (coll.) line, row, tier, file.
ringlero, *m.* ruled line (for writing exercises).
ringorrango, *m.* 1. (coll.) flourish (with a pen). 2. (coll.) frill, frippery.
rinitis, *f.* (med.) rhinitis.
rinoceronte, *m.* (zool.) rhinoceros.
rinofaringitis, *f.* (med.) rhinopharyngitis.
rinolaringología, *f.* (med.) rhinolaryngology.
rinología, *f.* (med.) rhinology.
rinólogo, *m.* (med.) rhinologist.
rinoplastia, *f.* (surg.) rhinoplasty, plastic surgery of the nose.
rinoscopia, *f.* (med.) rhinoscopy.
riña, *f.* quarrel, fight, dispute; **r. de gallos,** cockfight.
riña, riñendo, riñera, riñese, riño, riñó, *ref.* **reñir.**
riñon, *m.* 1. kidney; (*pl.*) loins, back. 2. center, heart (of country, of a matter, etc.). 3. (min.) nodule. 4. (min.) kidney ore. — **ceñirse los riñones,** to gird up one's loins; **riñones de conejo,** (coll.) bean stew; **r. flotante,** floating kidney; **tener bien cubierto los riñones,** to be well off, be wealthy; **tener riñones,** (coll.) to have intestinal fortitude, be brave.
riñonada, *f.* 1. (anat.) cortical tissue of kidney; loins. 2. kidney stew.
río, *m.* river, stream; (fig.) river, great amount; flood, stream (of people); **cuando el r. suena, piedras lleva,** where there is smoke there is fire; **pescar en r. revuelto,** to fish in troubled waters; **r. abajo,** downstream; **R. Amarillo,** Yellow River; **r. arriba,** upstream; **r. de lágrimas,** flood of tears; **R. de la Plata,** (geog.) River Plate; **r. flotable,** river navigable for rafts only.
río, rió, *ref.* **reír.**
riodacita, *f.* (min.) rhyodacite.
riolada, *f.* (coll.) torrent, stream (of people or things).
riolita, *f.* (min.) rhyolite.
rioplatense, *a.* of or from the River Plate Basin, Platine. —*m., f.* native or inhabitant of the River Plate Basin, Argentinian, Uruguayan.

riostra, *f.* (archit.) (diagonal) brace, stay, strut, spur.
riostrar, *tr.v.* to brace, stay by means of oblique struts.
ripia, *f.* slab (outside cut of log); shingle, strip of wood (for roofing).
ripiar, *tr.v.* 1. (mas.) to fill with rubble, riprap. 2. (Cuba) to tear to pieces.
ripio, *m.* 1. refuse, debris, riprap. 2. padding (in writing, speech); verbiage. — **no perder r.,** (coll.) not to miss a word or trick.
ripioso, sa, *a.* 1. rubbly, stony, full of stones or rubble. 2. padded (verse, speech, etc.).
riqueza, *f.* 1. wealth, riches. 2. richness, opulence. 3. abundance. 4. (*pl.*) wealth, riches. — **r. imponible,** taxable wealth or income; **riquezas naturales,** natural resources.
risa, *f.* laugh; laughter; **caerse de r.,** to split one's sides with laughter; **contener la r.,** to keep a straight face; **cosa de r.,** laughing matter; **desternillarse de r.,** to split one's sides with laughter; **mearse de r.,** (vulg.) to wet one's pants from laughter; **morirse de r.,** to die laughing; **reventar de r.,** to burst with laughter; **r. ahogada,** stifled laugh, giggle; **r. de escarnio,** smirk, sneer; **r. del conejo,** false laugh or grin (disguising anger); **r. falsa,** artificial laugh; **tomar a r.,** to take with a laugh.
risada, *f.* guffaw, horselaugh, immoderate laughter.
riscal, *m.* craggy place.
risco, *m.* 1. cliff, crag. 2. honey fritter.
riscoso, sa, *a.* craggy, rocky.
risibilidad, *f.* risibility.
risible, *a.* laughable, risible, ludicrous.
risiblemente, *adv.* laughably, ludicrously, risibly.
risica, risilla, risita, *f. dim. of* **risa,** giggle, titter; feigned laugh.
risotada, *f.* guffaw, horselaugh, boisterous laughter.
rispar, *i.v.* (Hond.) to take to one's heels, take it on the lam (sl., U.S.).
ríspido, da, *a.* surly, gruff, unfriendly (person); (lit.) craggy, rocky, harsh (terrain).
rispo, pa, *a.* harsh, gruff, surly.
risquería, *f.* (Chile) craggy place.
ristra, *f.* string (of onions or garlic); (coll.) string, row, line, bunch.
ristre, *m.* rest or socket (for lance).
ristrel, *m.* (archit.) rail, lath, crosspiece, crossbeam.
risueño, ña, *a.* smiling, laughing; cheerful; pleasant, pretty, e.g. *un prado risueño,* a pleasant meadow, *porvenir risueño,* bright prospects.
¡rita! shepherd's call to sheep.
ritidoma, *m.* (bot.) rhytidome.
rítmico, ca, *a.* rhythmic, rhythmical.
ritmo, *m.* 1. rhythm, cadence. 2. rhythm, rate. — **r. salteado,** (poet.) sprung rhythm.
rito, *m.* rite; ceremony.
ritón, *m.* rhyton (ancient Greek cup).
ritornelo, ritornello, *m.* (mus.) ritornel, ritornelle.
ritual, *a., m.* ritual, ceremonial; **ser de r.** to be prescribed by custom.
ritualidad, *f.* ritualism, observance of formalities.
ritualismo, *m.* ritualism.
ritualista, *a.* ritualistic. —*m., f.* ritualist.
rival, *m., f.* rival; **sin r.,** unrivaled.
rivalice, rivalicé, *ref.* **rivalizar.**
rivalidad, *f.* rivalry.
rivalizar, (*ref. 53*) *i.v.* to rival, vie, compete.
rivera, *f.* brook, stream, creek.
rixdal, *m.* (numis.) rix-dollar.
Riyad, *f.* Riyadh, capital of Saudi Arabia.
riza, *f.* 1. barley stubble; stubbly hay (left by horses). 2. ravage, destruction.
rizado, da, *past part. of* **rizar.** —*a.* curly; ripply; corrugated, wrinkled (face with smile). —*m.* 1. curling; curliness; curls. 2. (sew.) shirring.
rizador, *m.* 1. hair curler; curling iron. 2. shirrer (of sewing machine).
rizal, *a., var. of* **ricial.**
rizar, (*ref. 53*) *tr.v.* to curl, crimp (hair); to ripple (sea); to crinkle, fold (paper); to shirr (cloth). —*r.v.* to curl naturally; to ripple.
rizo, za, *a.* curled; curly; ribbed (velvet). —*m.* 1. curl, ringlet, curled lock of hair. 2. ribbed velvet. 3. (aer.) loop. 4. (mar.) reef point. — **hacer el r.,** (aer.) to loop the loop; **medio r.,** (aer.) wing over; **tomar rizos,** (mar.) to take in the reefs.
rizocárpeo, ca, *a.* (bot.) rhizocarpous.
rizocéfalo, la, *a.* (zool.) rhizocephalous. —*m.* (zool.) rhizocephalan, rhizocephalid.
rizófago, ga, *a.* (zool.) rhizophagous, root-eating.
rizoforáceo, a, rizofóreo, a, *a.* (bot.) rhizophoraceous. —*f.* (*pl.*) (bot.) Rhizophoraceae.
rizoide, *a.* (bot.) rhizoidal. —*m.* (bot.) rhizoid.
rizoma, *m.* (bot.) rhizome.
rizomorfo, fa, *a.* (bot.) rhizomorphous.
rizópodo, *m.* (zool.) rhizopod.
rizoso, sa, *a.* naturally curly.
rizotomía, *f.* (med.) rhizotomy.
Rn *sym. of* **radón,** radon (Rn).
ro, *interj.* bye-bye (word used in repetition to lull children to sleep).
roa, *f.* (mar.) stem, hawse (part of ship's bow).
roa, *ref.* **roer.**
roano, na, *a.* roan, sorrel (horse).
rob, *m.* (pharm.) fruit syrup.
robadera, *f.* (agr.) leveling harrow.
robadizo, *m.* 1. land easily washed away. 2. gully.
robador, ra, *a., m., f.* robber, thief.
robaliza, *f.* (ichth.) female bass or snook.
robalo, róbalo, *m.* (ichth.) (variety of) sea bass (Morone labrax).
robar, *tr.v.* 1. to steal, rob, pilfer, thieve. 2. to abduct; to kidnap. 3. to wash away, eat away (a river—its banks); to round off, smooth. 4. to pick up (cards) from the stack. 5. to steal, captivate (e.g. one's heart). — **estar robado,** to have lost its thread (a screw); **r. algo a alguien,** to steal something from someone, rob someone of something. —*i.v.* to make a false start (in a race). —*r.v.* to lose its thread (a screw).
robda, *f.* (arch.) pasturing fee.
robellón, *m.* (bot.) edible milk mushroom (Lactarius deliciosus).
robezo, *m.* (zool.) chamois.
robín, *m.* rust.
robinete, *m.* valve, cock; bibb, faucet.
robinetería, *f.* taps, set of taps.
robinia, *f.* (bot.) locust, false acacia.
robla, *f.* (arch.) pasturing fee.
robladero, ra, *a.* made to be riveted or clinched.
robladura, *f.* riveting, clinching.
roblar, *tr.v.* to rivet, clinch.
roble, *m.* 1. (bot.) oak. 2. (fig.) bulwark, pillar of strength, very strong person or thing. — **r. albar,** (bot.) British oak; **r. carrasqueño,** (bot.) gall oak; **r. borne, negral, villano,** (bot.) variety of oak (Querous pubescens).
robleda, *f.* **robledal, robledo,** *m.* oak grove or forest.
roblizo, za, *a.* 1. oaken. 2. strong, robust, hard.
roblón, *m.* 1. rivet. 2. ridge of tiles. 3. ridge tile. — **r. embutido,** counter sunk rivet.
roblonar, *tr.v.* to rivet.
robo, *m.* 1. theft, robbery, burglary. 2. drawing of cards or dominoes.
roboración, *f.* 1. strengthening, reinforcing. 2. corroboration.
roborante, *a.* 1. strengthening, reinforcing. 2. corroborating. —*m.* roborant, tonic.
roborar, *tr.v.* 1. to strengthen, reinforce. 2. (fig.) to corroborate, confirm.
roborativo, va, *a.* corroborative.
robot, *m.* robot.
robra, *f., var. of* **alboroque.**
robustecedor, ra, *a.* strengthening.
robre, *var. of* **roble.**
robustamente, *adv.* robustly.
robustecer, (*ref. 45*) *tr.v.* to strengthen, make strong. —*r.v.* to become strong.
robustecimiento, *m.* strengthening.
robustez, robusteza, *f.* robustness, strength, hardiness.
robustezco, robustezca, *ref.* **robustecer.**
robusto, ta, *a.* robust, strong, vigorous, healthy.
roca, *f.* rock, cliff; (fig.) rock (anything hard, hardy, firm). — **r. calcárea,** limestone; **rocas de cubierta,** (min.) cap rock; **r. filoniana,** dike rock.
rocada, *f.* rock, bundle of fibers on a distaff.
rocadero, *m.* 1. cone shaped hat worn by penitents or convicts. 2. knob, rock of a distaff.
rocador, *m.* head of a distaff.
rocalia, *f.* 1. pebbles, stones, talus. 2. large glass beads. 3. (art) rocaille.
rocalloso, sa, *a.* stony, pebbly, rocky; **Montañas Rocallosas,** (U.S.) Rocky Mountains.
rocambola, *f.* (bot.) rocambole.
rocambor, *m.* (S. Amer.) variety of ombre (card game).
roce, *m.* 1. friction, rubbing. 2. frequent contact, intercourse, communication. — **r. resbaladizo,** sliding friction.
roce, rocé, *ref.* **rozar.**
rocera, *a.* **leña r.,** brushwood.
rocha, *f.* clearing, ground cleared of brush or undergrowth.
rochar, *tr.v.* (Chile) to catch (someone) red-handed.
rochela, *f.* (Amer.) hullabaloo, uproar, shindy, racket.
rocho, *m.* (myth.) roc (huge fabulous bird).
rociada, *f.* 1. sprinkling, spraying; spray, shower. 2. dew; dew-drenched grass fed to horses as medicine. 3. sharp reprimand. 4. (mar.) spray, splash.
rociadera, *f.* watering can, sprinkler.
rociado, da, *past part. of* **rociar.** —*a.* 1. dewy, bedewed. 2. sprinkled, splashed.
rociador, *m.* sprinkler, sprayer. — **r. automático,** automatic sprinkler.
rociadura, *f.* **rociamiento,** *m.* sprinkling, spraying; spray.
rociar, (*ref. 54*) *i.v.* to fall (dew) e.g. *está rociando,* dew is falling. —*tr.v.* to sprinkle, spray; to scatter, strew.
rocín, *m.* 1. nag, hack, work horse. 2. (coll.) coarse ignorant man. — **r. matalón,** wornout hack.
rocinal, *a.* pertaining to hack or nag.
rocinante, *m.* 1. worn-out hack or nag. 2. **R.,** (lit.) Don Quixote's sorry mount.
rocino, *m., var. of* **rocín.**
rocío, *m.* 1. dew, dewdrops; short shower. 2. (fig.) sprinkling, spray, light shower. 3. (mar.) spoondrift. — **punto de r.,** (phys.) dew point; **r. de mar or de las olas,** sea spray; **r. de sol,** (bot.) sundew.
rococó, *a., m.* (art.) rococo.
rocola, (Amer.) jukebox.
rocoso, sa, *a.* rocky stony; **Montañas Rocosas,** Rocky Mountains.
rocote, rocoto, *m.* (S. Amer., bot.) variety of large green or bell pepper.
roda, *f.* (mar.) cutwater, stem.
rodaballo, *m.* 1. (ichth.) brill; turbot. 2. (coll.) crafty fellow.

rodada, *f.* rut, wheel track, car track.
rodadero, ra, *a.* 1. rolling easily. 2. shaped to roll, rollable.
rodadizo, za, *a.* easy-rolling.
rodado, da, *past part. of* **rodar.** —*a.* 1. dappled (horse). 2. flowing, rounded (phrase). 3. rounded, smooth (pebble, stone). 4. (min.) scattered (ore). —*m.* 1. (min.) scattered ore. 2. boulder, stone. 3. (Arg., Chile) vehicle, carriage. — **canto r.,** rolling stone.
rodador, ra, *a.* rolling. —*m.* 1. (ichth.) sunfish. 2. (ento.) gnat.
rodadura, *f.* 1. rolling, wheeling. 2. tread (of a wheel).
rodaja, *f.* 1. slice. 2. disk, wheel; caster. 3. rowel (of spur). 4. cutting pastry wheel.
rodaje, *m.* 1. wheels, set of wheels. 2. vehicle tax; (Peru) annual payment for car license. 3. (cinem.) shooting, filming.
rodajuela, *f. dim. of* **rodaja,** small wheel or caster; small slice.
rodal, *m.* 1. patch of land; spot. 2. cart.
rodalán, *m.* (Chile, bot.) evening primrose (Oenothera mutica).
rodamiento, *m.* bearing; **r. de bolas,** ball bearing; **r. de rodillos,** roller bearing.
rodamina, *f.* (chem.) rhodamine, rhodamin.
Ródano, *m.* Rhone (river).
rodante, *a.* 1. rolling. 2. (Chile) ambling, meandering. — **material r.,** (ry.) rolling stock.
rodapelo, *m., var. of* **redopelo.**
rodapié, *m.* 1. foot board (of bed and other pieces of furniture). 2. (archit.) skirting, baseboard, socle; footrail (of balcony). 3. dust ruffle (drapery around bottom of bed).
rodaplancha, *f.* main ward of a key.
rodar, (*ref. 33*) *tr.v.* 1. to roll. 2. (cinem.) to shoot, roll (film). 3. (Hond.) to knock down. —*i.v.* 1. to roll; to move, run (on wheels). 2. to revolve, rotate. 3. to abound. 4. to tumble, fall. 5. to roam, wander. 6. to go or happen in succession. — **echarlo todo a r.,** to upset everything; **r. por,** to fall down, tumble down; to roll down, roll along; **r. por el mundo,** to roam the world; **r. una película,** (cinem.) to shoot a film, a motion picture.
Rodas, *m.* Rhodes (Greek island).
rodeabrazo, a r., swinging the arm for a throw.
rodeado, da, *a.* surrounded, encircled.
rodeador, ra, *a.* surrounding, encircling. —*m., f.* one who surrounds.
rodear, *tr.v.* 1. to surround; to encircle, encompass. 2. (mil.) to invest. 3. (S. Amer.) to round up (cattle). —*i.v.* 1. to go by a roundabout way. 2. to beat about the bush. —*r.v.* 1. to move about, toss and turn. — **rodearse de,** to surround oneself (with good or bad company, luxury, comforts, etc.).
rodela, *f.* 1. target, buckler. 2. (Chile) slice.
rodelero, *m.* 1. targetman, soldier bearing a buckler. 2. swashbuckler.
rodenal, *m.* clump or grove of cluster pines.
rodeno, na, *a.* red (soil, rock, etc.), reddish.
rodeo, *m.* 1. rodeo; cattle roundup; corral. 2. encircling, surrounding. 3. roundabout way. 4. twist, turn (to shake off a pursuer). 5. evasion, subterfuge, circumlocution. — **andar con rodeos,** to beat about the bush; **dejarse de rodeos,** to stop beating about the bush; **sin ambages ni rodeos,** franky, bluntly.
rodeón, *m.* 1. full turn. 2. long detour.
rodera, *f.* track, rut; cart track, wheel track.
rodero, ra, *a.* pertaining to wheels. —*m.* 1. boy in charge of turning wheels of printing machine. 2. collector of pasturing fees.
Rodesia, *f.* Rhodesia.
rodete, *m.* 1. bun, knot, chignon (of hair). 2. cloth pad (worn on head under heavy loads). 3. ward (of lock). 4. fifth wheel (on coach). 5. belt wheel (driving belt in various machines). 6. horizontal water wheel. 7. (her.) circlet (over escutcheon). — **r. impulsor,** pump runner, impeller.
rodezno, *m.* 1. water wheel, tympanum, drum wheel. 2. cogwheel moving millstone.
rodezuela, *f.* small wheel.
rodilla, *f.* 1. (anat.) knee. 2. cloth pad (worn on head under heavy loads). 3. rag, cloth. — **de rodillas,** kneeling, on one's knees; **hacer rodillas,** to bag at the knees; **hincar la r., hincarse de rodillas, ponerse de rodillas,** to kneel down, kneel; **r. de fregona,** (med.) housemaid's knee.
rodillada, *f.* 1. blow given with the knee. 2. blow on the knee. 3. kneeling position.
rodillazo, *m.* blow or push given with the knee.
rodillera, *f.* 1. knee guard, kneepad; knee patch; knee bulge (in old trousers). 2. knee wound or scar (on horse's knee). 3. (mus.) knee swell, swell pedal (of harmonium, clavichord, organ, etc.).
rodillero, ra, *a.* pertaining to the knees.
rodillo, *m.* 1. roller. 2. (cul.) rolling pin. 3. (print.) inking roller. 4. platen (of typewriter). 5. road roller, clod crusher.
rodilludo, da, *a.* having large or bony knees.
rodio, *m.* (chem.) rhodium.
rodio, a, *a., m., f.* Rhodian, of or pertaining to the Greek island of Rhodes.
rodo, *m.* roller; **a r.,** in abundance.
rodocrosita, *f.* (min.) rhodochrosite; manganese spar.
rododafne, *m.* (bot.) oleander, rosebay.
rododendro, *m.* (bot.) rhododendron.
rodofíceas, *f.* (*pl.*) (bot.) Rhodophyceae.
rodolita, *f.* (min.) rhodolite.
rodomiel, *m.* (pharm.) honey of rose.
rodón, *m.* 1. (Chile, archit.) bead molding; plane for carving bead moldings. 2. (print.) proof press.
rodonita, *f.* (min.) rhodonite.
rodoplasto, *m.* (bot.) rhodoplast.
rodopsina, *f.* (physiol.) rhodopsin.
rodrigar, (*ref. 51*) *tr.v.* to prop up (plants).
rodrigazón, *f.* season when plants are propped.
rodrigón, *m.* 1. prop (for plants). 2. (coll.) elderly retainer who accompanied ladies.
rodrigue, rodrigué, *ref.* **rodrigar.**
roedor, ra, *a.* gnawing, biting; (fig.) worrying, tormenting, harassing. —*m.* (zool.) rodent.
roedura, *f.* 1. gnawing; part gnawed or nibbled; nibble. 2. corrosion, eating away.
roel, *m.* (her.) bezant, roundel.
roela, *f.* disk of crude gold or silver.
roentgen, *m.* (phys.) roentgen.
roer, (*ref. 19*) *tr.v.* 1. to gnaw; to pick (a bone). 2. to eat away, corrode; to fret, wear away. 3. (fig.) to worry, torment.
roete, *m.* (pharm.) pomegranate wine.
rogación, *f.* 1. request, petition. 2. (ecc.) (*pl.*) rogations.
rogado, da, *past part. of* **rogar.** —*a.* difficult; fond of being coaxed.
rogador, ra, *m., f.* beseecher, suppliant; requester.
rogante, *a.* praying, entreating.
rogar, (*ref. 72*) *tr.v.* to beg, entreat, implore, pray; to ask, request; **hacerse de r.,** to be difficult, want to be coaxed.
rogativo, va, *a.* supplicatory. —*f.* (ecc.) rogation, public prayer.
rogatorio, ria, *a.* rogatory.
rogo, *m.* (poet.) pyre, fire.
rogué, *ref.* **rogar.**
roído, da, *past part. of* **roer.** —*a.* (coll.) miserly, poor, penurious.
roiga, roigo, *ref.* **roer.**
rojal, *a.* reddish. —*m.* reddish plot of land.
rojeante, *a.* reddish.
rojear, *i.v.* 1. to blush, redden. 2. to have a tinge of red.
rojete, *m.* rouge, red cosmetic.
rojez, *f.* redness, ruddiness.
rojizo, za, *a.* reddish, ruddy; rubicund.
rojo, ja, *a.* 1. red; ruddy (cheeks). 2. (polit.) Red (communist). —*m., f.* (polit.) Red. —*m.* red. — **al r.,** red-hot, e.g. *estar al r., calentar al r.,* to be or make red-hot; **al r. blanco,** white-hot; **el r. y gualda (de la nación),** the flag of Spain; **r. alambrado,** bright red; **r. cereza,** cherry red; **r. Congo,** (chem.) Congo red; **r. de metilo,** methyl red; **r. escarlata,** scarlet red.
rojura, *f.* redness; ruddiness.
rol, *m.* 1. roll, list. 2. (mar.) muster roll. 3. (theat.) role, part.
rolar, *i.v.* 1. (mar.) to veer around. 2. (Chile) to associate, keep company (with), go around (with).
roldana, *f.* 1. pulley, sheave. 2. washer; spool insulator.
rolde, *m.* circle, group (of people).
roleo, *m.* (archit.) volute.
rolla, *f.* padding on collar of draft horse, yoke pad.
rollar, *tr.v.* to roll up.
rollete, *m.* small roll; small roller.
rollizo, za, *a.* 1. plump, stocky, sturdy. 2. round, cylindrical. —*m.* round log.
rollo, *m.* 1. roll, e.g. *r. de papel,* paper roll. 2. roller, rolling pin. 3. unworked roll log. 4. column, pillar. 5. padding on yoke of draft horse. 6. (coll.) long boring speech or conversation, bore, boring thing or person. 7. (Cuba) trouble, mess, confusion. — **soltar el r.,** to burble on, talk a lot.
rollón, *m.* wholemeal flour, graham flour.
rollona, *f.* (coll.) nanny, nurse.
rolo, *m.* (Col., print.) inking roller.
Roma, *f.* Rome, capital of Italy.
romadizarse, (*ref. 53*) *r.v.* to catch cold.
romadizo, *m.* cold, cold in the head.
romaico, ca, *a., m.* Romaic.
romana, *f.* steelyard, Roman balance.
romanador, *m.* weighing inspector, weighmaster.
romanar, *tr.v.* to weigh with a steelyard.
romance, *a.* Romance (language). —*m.* 1. romance, love affair. 2. Romance (language). 3. romance, ballad, tale of chivalry. 4. lyric or narrative poem in octosyllabic meter with alternate lines in assonance. — **en buen r.,** in plain language, plainly, simply; **hablar en r.,** to express oneself plainly or clearly; **r. de gesta,** chanson de geste, epic poem; **r. heroico** or **real,** hendecasyllabic verse with alternate lines in assonance.
romanceador, ra, *m., f.* one who translates into Romance or Spanish language.
romancear, *tr.v.* to translate into Spanish, translate into the vernacular; to paraphrase (to facilitate translation into Latin). —*i.v.* (Chile) to waste time in idle chatter.
romancerista, *m., f.* romancer, writer of romances or ballads.
romancero, ra, *m., f.* 1. romancer, writer of romances or ballads. 2. balladeer, singer of romances or ballads. 3. collection of romances or ballads.
romancesco, ca, *a., var. of* **novelesco.**
romancista, *a.* (one) who wrote in the vernacular or Spanish. —*m., f.* writer in the vernacular, writer in Spanish. —*m.* romancist, writer of ballads or romances.

romanear, *tr.v.* to weigh on the steelyard. —*i.v.* to outweigh.
romaneo, *m.* 1. weighing on a steelyard. 2. balancing up (of cargo or ballast).
romanero, *m.* weighing inspector, weighmaster.
romanesco, ca, *a.* 1. Roman. 2. novelesque, novelistic.
romanía, andar de r. 1. down at the heels. 2. crestfallen.
románico, ca, *a.* (archit.) Romanesque; (philol.) Romanic (language).
romanillo, lla, *a.* **letra romanilla,** (print.) man, roman type. 2. (Ven.) dining room screen, room divider.
romanismo, *m.* Romanism (Roman institutions, culture and political tendencies).
romanista, *a., m., f.* Romanist (expert on Roman law or in Romance languages).
romanización, *f.* Romanization.
romanizar, (*ref.* 53) *tr.v.* to Romanize. —*r.v.* to become Romanized or Latinized.
romano, na, *a., m., f.* Roman; **números romanos,** Roman numerals; **romana de Elzevir,** (print.) Elzevir, Elzevier.
romanticismo, *m.* romanticism; **R.,** Romanticism, Romantic Movement.
romántico, ca, *a., m., f.* romantic, romanticist.
romanza, *f.* (mus.) romance, romanza.
romanzar, (*ref.* 53) *tr.v.* to translate into Spanish, translate into the vernacular.
romaza, *f.* (bot.) sorrel.
rombal, *a.* rhombic.
rombencéfalo, *m.* (anat.) rhombencephalon.
rombo, *m.* 1. (geom.) rhombus, rhomb; diamond, lozenge. 2. (ichth.) brill; turbot.
romboedro, *m.* (geom.) rhombohedron.
romboidal, *a.* rhomboidal.
romboide, *m.* (geom.) rhomboid.
romeo, a, *a.* Romaean (Byzantine Greek).
romeraje, *m.* pilgrimage.
romeral, *m.* rosemary field or patch.
romería, *f.* 1. pilgrimage. 2. picnic, excursion. 3. festival or celebration held near a shrine. 4. crowd, gathering.
romeriego, ga, *a.* fond of pilgrimages or picnic.
romero, ra, *m., f.* pilgrim. —*m.* 1. (bot.) rosemary. 2. (ichth.) whiting; (ichth.) pilot fish.
romí, (*pl.* **romíes**), *a.* **azafrán r.,** (bot.) bastard saffron.
romo, ma, *a.* 1. blunt (without a point). 2. flat-nosed, snub-nosed.
rompeátomos, (*pl.* **rompeátomos**), *m.* atom smasher.
rompecabezas, (*pl.* **rompecabezas**), *m.* 1. jigsaw puzzle; (coll.) puzzle, riddle. 2. slingshot.
rompedera, *f.* 1. iron punch, blacksmith's punch. 2. gunpowder screen or sieve.
rompedero, ra, *a.* breakable; brittle.
rompedor, ra, *a.* breaking. —*m., f.* 1. breaker. 2. one who wears out or tears his clothes.
rompedura, *f.* breakage.
rompegalas, (*pl.* **rompegalas**), *m., f.* (coll.) shabby-looking, slovenly person.
rompehielos, (*pl.* **rompehielos**), *m.* (mar.) icebreaker, iceboat.
rompehuelgas, (*pl.* **rompehuelgas**), *m.* strikebreaker, blackleg (coll.), scab (coll.).
rompenueces, (*pl.* **rompenueces**), *m.* nutcracker.
rompeolas, (*pl.* **rompeolas**), *m.* breakwater, groyne, jetty, mole.
romper, *irr. past part.* **roto.** —*tr.v.* to break, tear, tear up; to pierce, break through, penetrate; to cleave; to break up, plow. — **¡rompan!** (mil.) fall out, dismissed; **r. el hielo,** to break the ice; **r. el paso,** (mil.) to break step; **r. filas,** (mil.) to break ranks, fall out. —*i.v.* 1. to break (the day, waves); to burst open (flowers). 2. (hunt.) to veer, change direction (game). — **de rompe y rasga,** (coll.) resolute undaunted; **r. a** + *inf.*, to begin suddenly + *inf.*, burst out + *ger.*; **r. con,** to break with, dissociate oneself with; **r. en,** to burst into (tears). —*r.v.* to break; to tear; **romperse el alma** or **la crisma,** to break one's neck; **romperse la cabeza,** to rack one's brains.
rompesacos, (*pl.* **rompesacos**), *m.* (bot.) goat grass.
rompesquinas, (*pl.* **rompesquinas**), *m.* (coll.) loafer; neighborhood bully; lay-about.
rompezaragüelles, (*pl.* **rompezaragüelles**), *m.* (bot.) ironweed (Vernonia remotiflora).
rompible, *a.* breakable.
rompido, *m.* earth broken up for cultivation.
rompiente, *m.* reef, rock, shoal.
rompimiento, *m.* 1. breaking; breakage; breaking off (e.g. of diplomatic relations; of an engagement to be married); crack, break. 2. (theat.) short fore curtain. 3. disagreement, quarrel. 4. (min.) breakthrough, driftway. 5. (p.) opening in background showing distant view or object.
rompope, *m.* (Amer.) punch made with rum, milk, eggs, sugar and spice.
Rómulo, *m.* (myth.) Romulus, twin brother of Remus.
ron, *m.* rum.
ronca, *f.* 1. call of the buck in rut; rut, rutting season. 2. bullying, braggadocio. 3. (arm.) halberd. 4. ticking off, reprimand. — **echar roncas,** to bully, threaten.
roncador, ra, *a.* snoring. —*m., f.* snorer. —*m.* (ichth.) grunt, roncador, croaker. —*f.* (Ecuad., Bol.) large-roweled spur.
roncal, *m.* nightingale.
roncamente, *adv.* 1. hoarsely. 2. roughly, rudely.
roncar, (*ref.* 50) *i.v.* 1. to snore. 2. to call the doe (a buck in rut). 3. to roar (sea, wind). 4. (coll.) to threaten, bully. 5. (S. Amer. sl.) to give the orders, e.g. *yo soy el que ronca acá,* I'm the one who gives the orders around here.
ronce, *m.* (coll.) flattery, cajolery.
roncear, *i.v.* 1. to dawdle, go slow, work slowly. 2. to flatter, cajole. 3. (mar.) to sail slowly. —*tr.v.* (Arg., Chile) to lever along, move by levering.
roncería, *f.* 1. dawdling, dilatoriness, slowness. 2. flattery, cajolery. 3. (mar.) slow, sluggish sailing.
roncero, ra, *a.* 1. dilatory, slow. 2. grouchy, grumbling. 3. flattering, cajoling, coaxing. 4. (mar.) slow-sailing.
roncha, *f.* 1. bump or rash; welt, wale, weal. 2. round slice (e.g. of meat). 3. trickery, cheating.
ronchar, *tr.v.* to crunch, chew. —*i.v., r.v.* to raise welts or bumps, become swollen.
ronchón, *m. aug. of* **roncha,** large slice; large welt or bump on the skin.
ronco, ca, *a.* hoarse; raucous. —*m.* (Cuba, ichth.) grunt.
roncón, *a.* (Col.) bullying, bragging. —*m.* drone (one of the largest pipes of a bagpipe).
ronda, *f.* 1. night watch or patrol; round, beat (of a guard, a watchman or policeman). 2. street serenade; group of strolling musicians. 3. round (of drinks, cigars, etc.). 4. (fort.) space outside the walls surrounding a town.
rondador, ra, *m., f.* prowler, night wanderer. —*m.* 1. night watchman. 2. serenader, wooer. 3. (Ecuad.) reed flute.
rondalla, *f.* 1. (Sp.) band of strolling musicians. 2. tale, malicious gossip.
rondar, *tr.v.* 1. to patrol, make the rounds. 2. to haunt, hover, prowl (around). 3. to court, woo, serenade. 4. to threaten to return (disease, sleeplessness, etc.). —*i.v.* to do guard duty.
rondel, *m.* (poet.) rondel, rondeau.
rondeño, ña, *a.* of or pertaining to Ronda, Spain. —*f.* (mus.) Andalusian song and rhythm typical of Ronda.
rondín, *m.* 1. (mil.) corporal's round (to check sentries). 2. (mar.) dock watchman.
rondís, rondiz, *m.* (jewel.) face or table of a gem.
rondó, *m.* (mus.) rondo.
rondón, de r., abruptly, impetuously; **entrar de r.,** (coll.) to burst in unannounced.
rongigata, *f.* pinwheel (toy).
ronque, ronqué, *ref.* **roncar.**
ronquear, *i.v.* to be hoarse, to speak in a husky voice.
ronquedad, ronquera, ronquez, *f.* hoarseness; raucousness.
ronquido, *m.* 1. snore. 2. harsh, raucous sound.
ronrón, *m.* 1. purring sound. 2. (C. Amer.) species of scarab. 3. (C. Amer.) bullroarer (toy).
ronronear, *i.v.* to purr (cat, motor, etc.).
ronroneo, *m.* purring (of a cat).
ronza, ir a la r., (mar.) to fall leeward.
ronzal, *m.* 1. halter (for horses). 2. (mar.) purchase rope, clew garnet.
ronzar, (*ref.* 53) *tr.v.* 1. to crunch, chew. 2. (mar.) to move with a lever.
roña, *f.* 1. rust (in metals). 2. dirt, filth. 3. meanness, stinginess. 4. (Cuba, Dom. Rep., P. Rico) grudge, animosity. 5. mange, scab (in sheep). 6. moral decay. 7. bark of pine trees. 8. blight of the grape vine.
roñería, *f.* stinginess, meanness; avarice.
roñica, *m., f.* miserly person, skinflint, tightwad.
roñoso, sa, *a.* 1. rusty; grimy, filthy. 2. niggardly, stingy, miserly. 3. mangy, scabby. 4. (C. Amer.) spiteful, resentful.
ropa, *f.* 1. clothes, clothing; garments, wearing apparel; wardrobe. 2. dry goods, stuff. 3. costume, dress; robe or gown (of rank, profession, office). — **a quema r.,** point blank, suddenly, unexpectedly; **hay r. tendida,** the walls have ears, don't say too much; **la r. sucia se lava en casa,** don't wash your dirty linen in public; **nadar y guardar la r.,** to be cautious in an undertaking; **r. blanca,** house linens; **r. de baño,** swimsuit; bathing trunks; **r. de cama,** bed clothes; **r. de mesa,** table linen; **r. dominguera,** Sunday clothes, Sunday best; **r. hecha,** ready-made clothes; **r. interior,** underwear, lingerie; **r. sucia,** soiled clothes, laundry, wash; **r. usada,** second-hand clothes; **r. vieja,** old clothes; (cul.) braised shredded beef.
ropaje, *m.* 1. wearing apparel, clothes, vestments; robe, gown. 2. (art) drapery. 3. (fig.) form of expression, style, language.
ropálico, ca, *a.* rhopalic (verse).
ropavejería, *f.* second-hand clothes store.
ropavejero, ra, *m., f.* second-hand clothes dealer.
ropería, *f.* 1. clothier's trade. 2. clothing store or business. 3. wardrobe, clothes room, check room, cloakroom. 4. job of cloakroom attendant.
ropero, ra, *a.* clothes, e.g. *armario r.,* clothes closet. —*m., f.* 1. clothier, clothes dealer. 2. cloakroom and attendant thereof. 3. clothes closet or cupboard, armoire, locker. 4. charity institution distributing clothes to the poor.
ropeta, ropilla, *f.* formerly worn doublet with sleeves. — **dar a uno una ropilla,** to reprove gently.
ropita, *f. dim of* **ropa,** child's clothing.
ropón, *m.* 1. *aug. of* **ropa,** large loose gown; night gown, nightie. 2. (Chile, Col.) riding skirt.
roque, *m.* rook, castle (in chess).
roqueda, *f.*, **roquedal,** *m.* rocky place.
roquedo, *m.* rock, crag.

roqueño, ña, *a.* rocky, hard as a rock, flinty.
roquería, *f.* rookery (of seals).
roquero, ra, *a.* rocky; built on rock.
roqueta, *f.* (fort.) turret.
roquete, *m.* 1. (ecc.) rochet. 2. barbed spearhead. 3. (artil.) rammer, ramrod.
rorcual, *m.* (zool.) rorqual, finback.
rorro, *m.* (coll.) baby, infant.
ros, *m.* (mil.) Spanish shako.
rosa, *f.* 1. (bot.) rose. 2. pink spot (on the body). 3. rose, rosette, rose-shaped decoration. 4. (archit.) rosette; rose window. 5. (jewel.) rose cut diamond. 6. rose (color). 7. (*pl.*) popcorn. — **como las propias rosas,** fine, excellent, great (coll.); **r. de rejalgar,** or **montés,** (bot.) peony; **r. de Jericó,** (bot.) rose of Jericho; **r. del azafrán,** (bot.) saffron flower; **r. de los vientos** or **náutica,** (mar.) compass rose, mariner's compass; **r. de té,** (bot.) tea rose; **r. de tiro,** (mil.) shot pattern; **verlo todo de color de r.,** to see everything through rose-colored glasses.
rosáceo, a, *a.* rosaceous, rose-colored, rosy. —*f.* (*pl.*) (bot.) Rosaceae.
rosacruz, (*pl.* **rosacruces**) *a., m., f.* (rel.) Rosicrucian.
rosada, *f.* frost, hoarfrost, rime.
rosadelfa, *f.* (bot.) azalea.
rosado, da, *a.* 1. pink, rose-colored, rosy. 2. (cul.) rose-flavored. 3. (Amer.) roan (livestock). — **Casa Rosada,** residence of the president of Argentina in Buenos Aires.
rosal, *m.* rosebush or plant; rose garden; **r. de pitiminí,** (bot.) multiflora rose; **r. perruno** or **silvestre,** (bot.) dog rose.
rosaleda, rosalera, *f.* rose garden, rosary.
rosanilina, *f.* (chem.) rosalinine.
rosariero, ra, *m., f.* one who makes or sells rosaries. —*f.* (bot.) chinaberry, bead tree.
rosario, *m.* 1. rosary (prayer, beads). 2. assemblage of people reciting the rosary. 3. string or series of misfortunes. 4. (hydr.) chain pump; water wheel. 5. (coll.) backbone. — **acabar como el r. de la aurora,** to break up in confusion or disorder.
rosarse, *r.v.* to blush.
rosbif, *m.* (cul.) roast beef.
rosca, *f.* 1. (cul.) ring-shaped roll of pastry. 2. thread (of a screw). 3. ring, disk, circle. 4. spiral, coil (turn of a spiral). 5. cockade worn by Spanish students. 6. (Amer.) cloth pad (worn on the head under heavy loads). 7. roll of fat (on body), spare tire (coll.). — **hacer la r.,** to flatter, fawn; **hacerse r. de galgo,** to curl up and go to sleep anywhere; **pasarse de r.,** not to fit (said of a screw); to go too far, take too many liberties; **r. de Arquímedes,** Archimedes screw; **r. autotrabadora,** (mec.) self-locking thread; **r. cónica,** (mec.) taper thread; **r. hembra,** female thread.
roscado, da, *a.* 1. (mec.) threaded. 2. ring-shaped; spiral-shaped.
roscar, (*ref. 50*) *tr.v.* to thread (a screw), make or cut a screw thread on.
roscón, *m.* large ring-shaped roll or pastry.
rosear, *i.v.* to turn pink or rose color.
Rosellón, *m.* (hist., geog.) Roussillon.
róseo, a, *a.* roseate, rosy.
roséola, *f.* (med.) roseola, rose rash.
rosero, ra, *m., f.* one who picks and gathers saffron flowers.
roseta, *f.* 1. small rose. 2. rosy cheek. 3. rosehead, sprinkling nozzle (of watering can). 4. metal tip of steelyard. 5. rosette, cockade, decoration. 6. (*pl.*) popcorn.
rosetón, *m.* (archit.) rose window; rosette.
rosicler, *m.* rose, russet or pink color of the dawn. — **r. claro,** (min.) proustite; **r. oscuro,** (min.) pyrargyrite, ruby silver ore.
rosillo, lla, *a.* 1. light red. 2. roan.
rosita, *f.* 1. *dim. of* **rosa,** small rose. 2. (Chile) earring. — **de r.,** free, for nothing; **r. de maiz,** (Cuba) popcorn.
rosmarino, na, *a.* light red. —*m.* (bot.) rosemary.
rosmaro, *m.* (zool.) manatee, sea cow.
roso, sa, *a.* 1. red. 2. threadbare; hairless. — **a roso y velloso,** without exception.
rosoli, *m.* rosolio (cordial made with rose petals and cinnamon).
rosón, *m.* (ento.) bot (larva).
rosqueado, da, *a.* coiled, twisted; ring-shaped.
rosquete, *m.* (cul.) ring-shaped pastry.
rosquilla, *f.* (cul.) ring-shaped pastry. 2. (ento.) grub. — **saber a rosquillas,** (coll.) to suit one perfectly, be satisfying.
rostelo, *m.* (bot., zool.) rostellum.
rostrado, *a.* rostrate, having a beak.
rostral, *a.* rostral; **columna r.,** (archit.) rostral column.
rostrillo, *m.* 1. headdress on saints' images. 2. small seed pearl.
rostritorcido, da, rostrituerto, ta, *a.* (coll.) angry-looking, sullen, morose.
rostro, *m.* 1. face, countenance. 2. rostrum, bill, beak (of a bird). 3. rostrum, beak (of an ancient war ship). — **a r. firme,** boldly, resolutely; **hacer r. a,** to face, face up to; **torcer el r.,** to make a wry face, show displeasure.
rota, *f.* 1. (mil.) rout, defeat. 2. (bot.) rattan, rattan palm. 3. Rota, ecclesiastical tribunal (Sacra Romana Rota).
rotación, *f.* rotation; **r. de cultivos,** rotation of crops; **r. de existencias** or **stocks,** (fin.) stock turnover; **r. dextrorsa,** clockwise rotation; **r. sinistrórsum,** counterclockwise rotation.
rotacismo, *m.* (phonet.) rhotacism.
rotal, *a.* (ecc.) Rotal, pertaining to the Rota.
rotamente, *adv.* barefacedly, brazenly, impudently.
rotante, *a.* rotating, revolving.
rotar, *i.v.* to rotate.
rotario, ria, *a., m., f.* Rotarian.
rotarismo, *m.* Rotarianism.
rotativo, va, *a.* rotary; revolving. —*f.* (print.) rotary printing press.
rotatorio, ria, *a.* rotary, rotating; **movimiento r.,** rotary motion.
roten, *m.* 1. (bot.) rattan, rattan palm. 2. rattan cane or walking stick.
rotería, *f.* (Chile) populace, rabble.
rotífero, ra, *a.* (zool.) rotiferous. —*m.* (zool.) rotifer; (*pl.*) Rotifera.
roto, ta, *irr. past part. of* **romper.** —*a.* 1. broken, shattered, chipped, cracked; destroyed. 2. torn, worn out, ragged. 3. debauched, licentious. —*m.* 1. (Chile) member of the poorest class. 2. (Arg., Peru, derog.) Chilean. 3. (Mex.) village dandy.
rotograbado, *m.* rotogravure.
rotonda, *f.* rotunda, round building. 2. (ry.) roundhouse. 3. rotonde, round compartment of a stagecoach.
rotor, *m.* (mec., elec., hydr.) rotor.
rotula, *f.* 1. (anat.) rotula, patella kneecap, kneepan. 2. (pharm.) lozenge, troche, rotula. 3. (mec.) ball and socket joint, universal joint.
rotulación, *f.* labeling, lettering.
rotulador, ra, *a.* labeling, lettering. —*m., f.* labeler, sign maker.
rotular, *tr.v.* 1. to label. 2. to design or make a sign, an inscription, etc.
rotulata, *f.* collection of labels, signs, inscriptions, posters.
rotuliano, na, *a.* (anat.) pertaining to the rotula or the kneecap.
rótulo, *m.* 1. label, title; sign, poster. 2. (ecc.) document or certificate for beatification.
rotunda, *f.* (archit.) rotunda, round building.
rotundamente, *adv.* categorically, flatly, peremptorily.
rotundidad, *f.* roundness, rotundity.
rotundo, da, *a.* 1. categorical, peremptory, flat (denial, statement, etc.). 2. round, rotund, circular. 3. rotund, sonorous, full.
rotura, *f.* 1. breakage, breaking; fracture, rupture; tear, rent; crack. 2. (vet.) poultice; plaster applied to a broken bone.
roturacíon, *f.* (agr.) breaking up new ground; newly broken up ground.
roturador, ra, *a.* breaking up. —*m.* plow or harrow.
roturar, *tr.v.* to break up (new ground).
round, *m.* (sport., Angl.) round (in boxing match).
roya, *f.* (bot.) rust, mildew, plant rot.
roya, royendo, royera, royese, royo, royó, *ref.* **roer.**
roza, *f.* 1. grubbing, clearing, stubbing. 2. clearing, stubbed land.
rozadera, *f., var. of* **rozón.**
rozadero, *m.* 1. ground being cleared. 2. (mec.) friction plate.
rozador, ra, *m., f.* grubber, stubber, weeder, clearer (of ground).
rozadura, *f.* 1. rubbing, chafing, friction. 2. chafed, rubbed or sore spot. 3. (bot.) punk knot.
rozagante, *a.* 1. splendid-looking and conscious of it. 2. (arch.) flowing, sweeping (formerly said of robes, gowns, etc.).
rozamiento, *m.* 1. rubbing, friction, chafing. 2. (fig.) friction, disagreement.
rozar, (*ref. 53*) *tr.v.* 1. to grub, stub, clear (land). 2. to nibble grass (livestock). 3. to scrape, scratch; graze. —*i.v.* to touch lightly in passing. —*r.v.* 1. to knock or rub together; to interfere (hooves, legs, etc.). 2. to be on close terms. 3. to stammer, stumble over words. 4. to circulate, associate oneself, be well-connected.
roznar, *tr.v.* to crunch, chew. —*i.v.* to bray.
roznido, *m.* 1. braying of a donkey. 2. crunch, crunching noise.
rozno, *m.* small donkey.
rozo, *m.* stubbing, grubbing, clearing; brushwood. — **ser de buen r.,** (coll.) to have a good appetite.
rozón, *m.* short, broad scythe.
R.P.M., r.p.m. *abbrev. of* **revoluciones por minuto,** revolutions per minute (rpm).
Ru, *sym. of* **rutenio,** ruthenium (Ru).
rúa, *f.* village street; high road.
rúan, *m.* (tex.) cotton fabric manufactured in the French city of Rouen.
ruana, *f.* 1. (Col., Ven.) square poncho. 2. (tex.) woolen fabric.
Ruanda, *f.* Rwanda, republic in central Africa.
ruano, na, *a.* roan (horse, cow).
ruante, *a.* 1. walking or riding through the streets. 2. (her.) with fantail spread (peacock).
ruar, (*ref. 55*) *i.v.* to walk or ride through the streets; to flirt with passersby.
rubefaccíon, *f.* (med.) rubefaction, redness of the skin.
rubefaciente, *a., m.* (med.) rubefacient.
rúbeo, a, *a.* reddish.
rubéola, *f.* (med.) German measles, rubella.
rubescencia, *f.* rubescence, rosiness.
rubescente, *a.* 1. rubescent, reddish, blushing.
rubeta, *f.* (zool.) species of toadlike animals.
rubí, (*pl.* **rubíes**), *m.* (min.) ruby; **r. balaje,** balas, balas ruby; **r. de Bohemia,** rose quartz; **r. espinela,** ruby spinel; **r. oriental,** Oriental or true ruby.

rubia, *f.* 1. blonde (girl, woman). 2. (bot.) madder, madder root. 3. (ichth.) red river fish. 4. station wagon (U.S.), shooting brake (G.B.).
rubiáceo, a, *a.* (bot.) rubiaceous. —*f.* (*pl.*) Rubiaceae.
rubial, *m.* madder thicket, madder field. —*a.* reddish (said of soil and plants).
rubicán, na, *a.* roan flecked with white (horse).
rubicela, *f.* (min.) rubicel.
Rubicón, *m.* (geog.) Rubicon; **pasar el R.,** to pass or cross the Rubicon, take a decisive, irrevocable step.
rubicundez, *f.* rubicundity; reddishness.
rubicundo, da, *a.* 1. rubicund; reddish. 2. rosy with health.
rubidio, *m.* (chem.) rubidium.
rubiera, *f.* 1. (Ven.) prank, mischief, reckless action. 2. (C. Amer., P. Rico) spree; carousal.
rubificar, (*ref. 50*) *tr.v.* to redden, make red.
rubiginoso, sa, *a.* (bot., zool.) rubiginous, rubiginose, rust-colored.
rubilla, *f.* (bot.) woodruff.
rubín, *m.* 1. ruby. 2. rust (on metals).
rubinejo, *m.* small ruby.
rubio, bia, *a.* blond, fair, golden. —*m., f.* blond, blonde (person). —*m.* 1. (ichth.) red gurnard (Trigla Lyra). 2. (*pl.*) middle of the withers (in bulls). 3. blond (color); **r. ceniza,** ash blond; **r. platino,** platinum blond. — **rubia oxigenada,** peroxide blonde; **rubia platinada,** platinum blonde.
rublo, *m.* ruble, rouble (Russian monetary unit).
rubor, *m.* 1. blush, flush; bashfulness, shyness. 2. redness.
ruborizado, da, *a.* flushed, blushing; bashful.
ruborizar, (*ref. 53*) *tr.v.* to make blush. —*r.v.* to blush.
ruborosamente, *adv.* blushingly, bashfully.
ruboroso, sa, *a.* bashful, blushing.
rúbrica, *f.* 1. flourish (of signature). 2. rubric, title, heading. 3. (ecc.) rubric, rule, instruction (for conducting of a service). 4. red mark. — **r. fabril,** red ocher (used by carpenters); **r. lemnia,** Armenian bole; **r. sinópica,** minium; **ser de r. una cosa,** to be in accordance with ritual or custom.
rubricante, *a.* signing, initialing.
rubricar, (*ref. 50*) *tr.v.* 1. to sign, initial, indorse with a flourish, initials, or one's own mark. 2. to sign and seal. 3. to bear witness to, attest.
rubrique, rubriqué, *ref.* **rubricar.**
rubriquista, *m.* expert on church rubrics, rubrician.
rubro, ra, *a.* red. —*m.* (Amer.) title, label, heading.
ruc, *m.* (myth.) roc, a fabulous bird.
ruca, *f.* (Arg., Chile) hut, cabin.
rucio, cia, *a.* silver-grey; (coll.) graying, grey-haired. —*m.* donkey.
ruco, ca, *a.* (C. Amer.) old, worthless.
ruche, *m.* 1. donkey. 2. ruche (trimming).
ruchique, *m.* (Hond.) wooden plate or saucer.
rucho, *m.* donkey.
ruda, *f.* (bot.) rue; **r. cabruna,** (bot.) goat's rue.
rudamente, *adv.* rudely, roughly, harshly.
rudeza, *f.* 1. roughness, coarseness, rudeness. 2. harshness, severity (of climate).
rudimental, *a.* rudimentary.
rudimentario, ria, *a.* rudimentary.
rudimento, *m.* 1. rudiment. 2. (*pl.*) rudiments, elements.
rudo, da, *a.* 1. coarse, rough, gross, unpolished. 2. rough, crude, primitive, rudimentary. 3. dull, dim, unintelligent. 4. severe, harsh (climate, weather); hard, difficult (life).
rueca, *f.* 1. distaff. 2. twist, turn.
rueda, *f.* 1. wheel; caster, roller. 2. ring, circle (of people). 3. (ichth.) sunfish, moonfish. 4. spread (of peacock's tail). 5. round slice. 6. turn, time, successive order. 7. circle printed or painted at the foot of a document stating a royal privilege. 8. threesome at billiards. 9. wheel, rack (form of torture). — **comulgar con ruedas de molino,** (coll.) to swallow anything, believe the most improbable things; **hacer la r. a,** (coll.) to flatter, fawn, cajole; **hacer r.,** to make a circle; **ir con r. libre,** to freewheel; **r. de Santa Catalina,** Catherine wheel; **r. de andar,** treadwheel; **r. de cadena,** (mec.) sprocket wheel, chain gear; **r. de carro,** cart wheel; **r. de ceja** or **de pestaña,** (ry.) flange wheel; **r. de engranaje,** (mec.) gearwheel; **r. de estrella** or **de gatillo,** (mec.) ratchet wheel; **r. de fricción,** (mec.) friction wheel; **r. de la fortuna,** wheel of fortune; **r. de molino,** mill wheel; **r. dentada,** (mec.) cogwheel; **r. de paletas,** (mec.) paddle wheel; **r. paletas,** (mec.) paddle wheel; **r. de periodistas** or **prensa,** press conference; **r. de plato,** disk wheel; **r. de presos,** line-up (of suspects or criminals); **r. de trinquete,** (mec.) ratchet wheel; **r. de timón,** (mec.) steering wheel; **r. hidráulica,** (mec.) water wheel; **r. libre,** (mec.) freewheel; **r. llena,** disk wheel.
ruede, *ref.* **rodar.**
ruedecilla, ica, ita, *f. dim. of* **wheel,** small wheel or ring; caster, roller.
ruedo, *m.* 1. turn, rotation, revolution. 2. (taur.) arena, bullring. 3. skirt hem. 4. round mat; rug. 5. edge, border, fringe.
ruedo, ruede, *ref.* **rodar.**
ruego, *m.* request, petition, plea, entreaty.
ruego, ruegue, *ref.* **rogar.**
ruezno, *m.* walnut burr, outer walnut shell.
rufa, *f.* (Peru) leveling harrow.
rufián, *m.* 1. scoundrel, ruffian. 2. pimp, panderer.
rufianear, *i.v.* to be a ruffian; to procure, pander.
rufianería, *f.* ruffianism.
rufianesca, *f.* gang of ruffians.
rufianesco, ca, *a.* base, scoundrelly.
rufo, fa, *a.* 1. golden-haired; red-haired. 2. curly, curly-haired. 3. stiff, tough.
ruga, *f.,* (rare) *var. of* **arruga.**
rugar, (*ref. 51*) *tr.v., r.v.,* (rare) *var. of* **arrugar.**
rugido, *m.* 1. roar; bellow. 2. (fig.) rumbling (in the stomach).
rugiente, *a.* roaring, bellowing.
ruginoso, sa, *a.* rusty.
rugir, (*ref. 62*) *i.v.* 1. to roar, bellow; to rumble. 2. to come out, be revealed.
rugosidad, *f.* rugosity; wrinkled condition.
rugoso, sa, *a.* rugose, wrinkled, wrinkly; corrugated.
ruibarbo, *m.* (bot.) rhubarb (Rheum palmatum); rhubarb root; **r. blanco,** (bot.) mechoacan.
ruido, *m.* 1. noise. 2. discussion, shindy, rumpus, row. — **hacer** or **meter r.,** to make a noise; to create a stir or sensation; **mucho r. y pocas nueces,** much ado about nothing; **querer r.,** to be looking for a quarrel or row; **r. blanco,** white noise; **r. de fondo,** background noise, **r. de sables,** saber rattling.
ruidosamente, *adv.* noisily, loudly.
ruidoso, sa, *a.* 1. noisy, loud. 2. sensational, much talked about.
ruin, *a.* 1. base, despicable, mean; bad, vicious, wicked. 2. mean, niggardly, paltry; inferior, poor. 3. small, puny, petty. 4. vicious (animals). 5. (Cuba) in rut, in heat. —*m.* tip of cat's tail.
ruina, *f.* 1. ruin, decay, wreck; decline, downfall. 2. (*pl.*) (archeol.) ruins. — **amenazar r.,** to be on the point of collapsing (a building); **estar hecho una r.,** to be a wreck (person).
ruinar, *tr.v., r.v., var. of* **arruinar.**
ruindad, *f.* 1. baseness, meanness; wickedness. 2. meanness, niggardliness.
ruinmente, *adv.* basely, meanly, despicably; wickedly.
ruinoso, sa, *a.* 1. ruinous, broken-down, ruined, dilapidated. 2. ruinous, causing ruin.
ruiponce, *m.* (bot.) rampion.
ruipóntico, *m.* (bot.) rhubarb (Rheum rhaponticum).
ruiseñor, *m.* (ornith.) nightingale.
ruja, rujo, *ref.* **rugir.**
rular, *tr.v., i.v.* to roll.
rulé, *m.* (coll.) behind, backside, posterior.
rulenco, ca, *a.* (Chile) weak, feeble.
ruleta, *f.* roulette (game).
ruletero, *m.* (Mex.) collective taxi driver, jitney chauffeur.
rulo, *m.* 1. lock of hair, curl, ringlet. 2. thick ball. 3. conical millstone. 4. roller (for flattening earth). 5. (Chile) unwatered or dry land.
ruma, *f.* (Amer.) heap, stack, pile.
Rumania, *f.* Rumania, Romania.
rumano, na, *a., m., f.* Rumanian. —*m.* Rumanian (language).
rumazón, *m.* (mar.) bank of clouds (on the horizon).
rumba, *f.* 1. rumba (Cuban dance). 2. (Cuba, P. Rico) spree, party, night out.
rumbada, *f., var. of* **arrumbada.**
rumbantela, *f.* (Cuba, Mex.) fast party, spree, night out.
rumbar, *i.v.* 1. (Col.) to buzz, hum. 2. (Chile) to follow a course, take a direction. —*tr.v.* (Hond.) to throw, hurl.
rumbático, ca, *a.* sumptuous; ostentatious, showy.
rumbeador, *m.* (Arg.) guide, pathfinder.
rumbear, *i.v.* 1. (Arg.) to take a course or direction. 2. (Cuba) to go on a spree.
rumbo, *m.* 1. course, direction; (mar.) rhumb, rhumb line. 2. (coll.) ostentation, show. 3. (coll.) generosity, liberality. 4. (Guat.) spree, night out. 5. (Col.) humming bird. 6. (her.) rustre. 7. (mar.) opening in hull (caused by collision). — **abatir el r.,** (mar.) to fall to leeward; **con r. a,** bound for, in the direction of; bound, e.g. *con r. al norte, sur, etc.,* northbound, southbound, etc.; **corregir el r.,** (mar.) to find the true course; **hacer r. a,** (mar.) to head for; to sail for; **r. a,** bound for; **r. aguja** or **brújula,** (mar.) compass course; **r. computado,** calculated bearing; **r. magnético,** (mar., aer.) magnetic bearing; **r. proa brújula,** (mar.) compass heading.
rumbón, na, *a., var. of* **rumboso.**
rumbosamente, *adv.* 1. grandly, sumptuously. 2. liberally, generously.
rumboso, sa, *a.* 1. (coll.) sumptuous, ostentatious. 2. (coll.) liberal, generous.
rumen, *m.* (zool.) rumen.
rumí, *m.* Christian (among the Moors).
rumia, *f.* rumination.
rumiación, *f.* (med.) rumination, merycism.
rumiador, ra, *a.* ruminating. —*m., f.* ruminator.
rumiadura, *f.* rumination.
rumiante, *a.* ruminant, ruminating; (zool.) ruminant. —*m.* (zool.) ruminant; (*pl.*) Ruminantia.
rumiar, *tr.v.* 1. to ruminate, chew over again. 2. (coll.) to ruminate, reflect on, meditate on. 3. (coll.) to grumble, growl.
rumión, na, *a.* (coll.) ruminative, brooding.
rumo, *m.* (cooperage) first hoop of a cask.
rumor, *m.* 1. rumor; report; gossip. 2. murmur; buzz (of voices). 3. rustle (of trees).
rumorcito, illo, *m. dim. of* **rumor,** petty gossip.

rumorear, *tr.v.* to rumor, spread a rumor. —*r.v.* to be rumored.
rumoroso, sa, *a.* murmurous; murmuring; buzzing.
runa, *f.* rune, runic character (of old Scandinavian alphabet).
runcho, *m.* (Col., zool.) kind of opossum.
rundún, *m.* 1. (Arg.) humming bird. 2. (Arg.) bull-roarer (toy).
runfla, runflada, *f.* (coll.) row, series, sequence.
rungo, ga, *a.* (Hond.) short, small (person).
rungue, *m.* (Chile) bundle of sticks (for turning toasted corn); (*pl.*) (Chile) leafless sticks and stalks.
rúnico, ca, runo, na, *a.* runic (pertaining to ancient Scandinavian language or culture).
runrún, *m.* 1. (coll.) murmur, buzz; drone, droning. 2. purr, purring. 3. (Arg.) bull-roarer (toy).
runrunear, *i.v.* to buzz, drone; to purr. —*r.v.* to be rumored.
ruñar, *tr.v.* to croze (a stave).
rupestre, *a.* 1. (biol.) rupicolous. 2. (archeol., art) rupestrian.
rupia, *f.* 1. rupee (coin). 2. (med.) rupia.
rupicabra, rupicapra, *f.* (zool.) chamois.
rupícola, *a.* (biol.) rupicolous.
ruptor, *m.* (auto.) breaker.
ruptura, *f.* 1. rupture, break, breach. 2. breaking, fracture.
ruqueta, *f.* (bot.) rocket.
rural, *a.* rural, rustic, country.
ruralmente, *adv.* rurally.
rus, *m.* (bot.) sumach; **¡voto a r.!** (coll.) damn it!
rusalca, *f.* water nymph (in Slavic mythology).
rusco, *m.* (bot.) butcher's broom.
rusel, *m.* (tex.) woolen serge.
rusentar, *tr.v.* to make red hot.
Rusia, *f.* Russia; **R. Soviética,** Soviet Russia.
rusiente, *a.* red hot, candent.
rusificar, (*ref.* *50*) tr.v. to Russianize, Russify. —*r.v.* to become Russianized or Russified.
ruso, sa, *a., m., f.* Russian. —*m.* 1. Russian (language). 2. ulster, thick overcoat.
rusófilo, la, *a., m., f.* Russophile.
rustificación, *f.* rustication, living in the country.
rustical, *a.* rustic, rural.
rústicamente, *adv.* rustically, rudely.
rusticano, na, *a.* wild (plants).
rusticar, (*ref.* *50*) *i.v.* to rusticate.
rusticidad, *f.* rusticity; clumsiness, rudeness.
rústico, ca, *a.* 1. rustic, rural, country. 2. rustic, rough, clumsy, unmannerly. — **en rústica,** (bkb.) paper-bound. —*m.* rustic, peasant.
rustique, rustiqué, *ref.* **rusticar.**
rustiquez, rustiqueza, *f.* rusticity.
rustro, *m.* (her.) rustre.
ruta, *f.* route; course, way. — **r. aérea,** air lane.
rutáceo, a, *a.* (bot.) rutaceous. —*f.* (*pl.*) Rutaceae.
rutenio, *m.* (metal.) ruthenium.
rutenioso, sa, *a.* (chem.) ruthenious.
ruteno, na, *a., m., f.* Ruthenian. —*m.* Ruthenian (language).
rutilante, *a.* sparkling, shining, scintillating.
rutilar, *i.v.* (poet.) to sparkle, twinkle, scintillate.
rútilo, la, *a.* sparkling, shining, bright.
rutina, *f.* routine, habit, custom.
rutinario, ria, *a.* routine. —*m., f.* routinist, adherer to routine.
rutinero, ra, *m., f.* routinist, adherer to routine.
rútulos, *m.* (*pl.*) Rutuli.
ruzafa, *f.* garden, park.
Rwanda, *f.* Rwanda.

S

S, *f. s,* twentieth letter of the Spanish alphabet.
S *sym. of* **azufre,** sulfur (S).
S. *abbrev. of* **sur,** south (S.).
S.A. *abbrev. of* 1. **Su Alteza,** Her or His Highness (H.H.). 2. **Sociedad Anónima,** stock company; Incorporated. 3. **Sud América,** South America (S. A.).
Saba, *f.* (hist., geog.) Sheba; **la reina de S.,** the Queen of Sheba.
sábado, *m.* Saturday; Sabbath; **hacer s.,** to do the weekly cleaning; **S. de gloria,** Easter Saturday.
sabalar, *m.* shad net.
sabalera, *f.* 1. grate in reverberatory furnace. 2. shad net.
sabalero, *m.* shad fisherman.
sábalo, *m.* (ichth.) shad (Alosa vulgaris).
sábana, *f.* 1. bed sheet. 2. altar cloth. — **pegársele a uno las sábanas,** (coll.) to oversleep; **s. ajustable** or **de cuatro picos,** fitted sheet; **s. de arriba** or **s. encimera,** top sheet; **S. Santa,** Holy Shroud.
sabana, *f.* savanna, savannah, wide treeless plain; **estar en la s.,** (Ven., coll.), to be sitting pretty, be prosperous.
sabanazo, *m.* (Cuba) small plain or field.
sabandija, *f.* 1. bug, insect. 2. (fig.) vermin, despicable person.
sabanear, *i.v.* (Col., Ven.) to ride the plains rounding up or counting cattle.
sabanero, ra, *a.* pertaining to the savanna or the plain. —*m., f.* savanna or plain dweller. —*m.* 1. cowboy, cattle drover. 2. (Amer., ornith.) starling (Sturnus ludovicianus).
sabanilla, *f.* 1. small sheet; kerchief; hand towel. 2. altar cloth. 3. (Chile) light bedspread.
sabañón, *m.* chilblain; **comer uno como un s.,** (coll.) to eat greedily.
sabara, *f.* (Ven.) haze, very light fog.
sabatario, ria, *a., m., f.* Sabbatarian, of the Sabbath.
sabático, ca, *a.* Sabbatical, sabbatical.
sabatina, *f.* 1. Saturday mass. 2. Saturday review of studies.
sabatino, na, *a.* pertaining to Saturday.
sabatizar, (*ref. 53*) *i.v.* to keep the Sabbath, rest on the Sabbath.
sabedor, ra, *a.* informed, knowing.
sabeísmo, *m.* (rel.) Sabaeanism, Sabaism.
sabela, *f.* (zool.) sabella.
sabelección, *m., f.* (Cuba, bot.) peppercress, peppergrass.
sabelianismo, *m.* (theol.) Sabellianism.
sabeliano, na, *a., m., f.* Sabellian.
sabélico, ca, *a.* (hist.) Sabellian, pertaining to the Samnites and Sabines.
sabelotodo, *m., f.* (coll.) know-all, know-it-all.
sabeo, a, *a., m., f.* (hist., geog.) Sabaean.
saber, *m.* learning, knowledge; **según mi leal s. y entender,** to the best of my knowledge.
saber, (*ref. 20*) *tr.v.* 1. to know, have cognizance of. 2. to know how, be able, e.g. *él no sabe leer,* he can't or doesn't know how to read. 3. to learn, find out, e.g. *fue entonces que supe lo que había pasado,* it was then that I found out what had happened. — **hacer s.,** to inform; **no s. cuántos son dos y dos,** to know nothing at all, not to have a clue; **no s. dónde meterse,** not to know which way to turn; **no sé cuántos,** what's-his-name; **¿qué sé yo?** how should I know?; **que yo sepa,** as far as I know; **¿quién sabe?** perhaps; who knows?; **s. cuántos son cinco,** to know what's what; **s. de,** to hear from or of; to know about; **s. de buena tinta,** to have it on good authority; **un no sé qué,** un je ne sais quoi, a certain something. —*i.v.* to know; **a s.,** that is, namely, to wit; **s. a,** to taste of or like; to smack of.
sabiamente, *adv.* 1. wisely, prudently. 2. learnedly, knowingly.
sabicú, (*pl.* **sabicúes**), *m.* (Cuba, bot.) sabicu.
sabidillo, lla, *a.* (derog.) know-it-all, pedantic. —*m., f.* know-it-all, pedant.
sabido, da, *past part. of* **saber.** —*a.* 1. known. 2. clever, well-informed; learned. — **dar por sabido,** to take for granted; **de sabido,** certainly.
sabiduría, *f.* wisdom; knowledge, learning, erudition.
sabiendas, a s., knowingly, consciously.
sabiente, *a.* knowing.
sabihondez, *f.* (coll.) affectation of knowledge.
sabihondo, da, *a.* (coll.) know-it-all, affecting knowledge. —*m., f.* know-it-all.
sábila, *f.* (Cuba, bot.) aloe.
sabina, *f.* (bot.) savin.
sabinar, *m.* clump of savin.
sabino, na, *a., m., f.* (hist.) Sabine.
sabino, na, *a.* roan (horse).
sabio, bia, *a.* wise; learned. —*m., f.* wise man, sage, scholar, savant; scientist.
sablazo, *m.* 1. saber blow or wound. 2. (coll.) sponging, cadging. — **dar un s. a,** to touch someone for a loan; **vivir de sablazos,** to live by sponging.
sable, *m.* 1. saber; cutlass. 2. (Cuba, ichth.) cutlass fish. 3. (her.) sable, black.
sableador, ra, *m., f.* (coll.) sponger, cadger. —*m.* saber expert, expert with a saber.
sablear, *i.v.* (coll.) to sponge, cadge, live by sponging.
sablista, *m., f.* sponger, cadger; one who borrows from friends.
sablón, *m.* coarse sand.
saboga, *f.* (ichth.) shad.
sabogal, *a.* shad fishing (net). —*m.* shad fishing net.
saboneta, *f.* hunting case watch.
sabor, *m.* 1. taste; flavor; (fig.) flavor, color. 2. (*pl.*) beads on bit. — **a s.,** to one's taste, to one's liking; **tener s. a,** to taste of.
saborcico, saborcillo, saborcito, *dim. of* **sabor,** slight taste or flavor.
saboreamiento, *m.* 1. flavoring, seasoning. 2. savoring, tasting, relishing.
saborear, *tr.v.* 1. to flavor, season, give flavor to. 2. to savor, relish, taste. 3. to allure, attract, entice. —*r.v.* to savor, relish, taste; to be delighted with.
saboreo, *m.* 1. flavoring, seasoning. 2. relishing, savoring, enjoyment.
saborete, *m.* slight taste.
sabotaje, *m.* sabotage.
saboteador, ra, *m., f.* saboteur.
sabotear, *tr.v.* to sabotage.
Saboya, *f.* (geog., hist.) Savoy.
saboyana, *f.* 1. open overskirt. 2. (cul.) baba au rhum (pastry).
saboyano, na, *a., m., f.* Savoyard.
sabré, sabría, *ref.* **saber.**
sabrosamente, *adv.* tastily, deliciously.
sabroso, sa, *a.* 1. delicious, tasty. 2. (coll.) delightful, pleasant.
sabrosura, *f.* (coll., Cuba, Dom. Rep., P. Rico) tastiness; delight; leisure.
sabucal, *m.* grove or clump of elders.
sabuco, *m.* (bot.) elder.
sabueso, sa, *m.* bloodhound; (fig.) bloodhound, sleuth.
sabugal, sabugo, *m. vars. of* **sabucal, sabuco.**
sábulo, *m.* coarse heavy sand.
sabuloso, sa, *a.* sandy, gritty, sabulous.
saburra, *f.* (med.) saburra.
saburral, *a.* (med.) saburral.
saburroso, sa, *a.* (med.) showing symptoms of saburra, furry (tongue).
saca, *f.* 1. removal, extraction, taking out. 2. exportation. 3. certified or notarized copy (of document). 4. withdrawal of goods from state monopoly offices for subsequent sale. 5. large sack. — **estar de s.,** to be for sale; to be marriageable.
sacabala, *f.* bullet-removing pincers or forceps.
sacabalas, (*pl.* **sacabalas**), *m.* (artil.) bullet extractor, bullet screw.
sacabocado, sacabocados, (*pl.* **sacabocados**), *m.* 1. punch (for making holes). 2. sure way or means (of getting what one is after).
sacabotas, (*pl.* **sacabotas**), *m.* bootjack.
sacabrocas, (*pl.* **sacabrocas**), *m.* tack puller, nail puller, tack claw, tack drawer.
sacabuche, *m.* 1. (mus.) sackbut; sackbut player. 2. (mar.) hand pump. 3. (coll.) shrimp, squirt (person).
sacaclavos, (*pl.* **sacaclavos**), *m.* (carp.) nail puller.
sacacorchos, (*pl.* **sacacorchos**), *m.* corkscrew.
sacacuartos, (*pl.* **sacacuartos**), *m.* 1. (coll.) cheap, gaudy show. 2. (coll.) swindler, bamboozler.
sacada, *f.* 1. territory separated from a country or province. 2. removal, drawing out, extraction. 3. (bridge) takeout.
sacadinero, sacadineros, (*pl.* **sacadineros**), *m.* 1. (coll.) cheap, gaudy show. 2. (coll.) small-time swindler, bamboozler.
sacador, ra, *m., f.* remover; extractor. —*m.* (print.) delivery board.
sacadura, *f.* 1. notch cut, sloping cut (made in a garment to make it fit). 2. (Chile) removal, extraction, taking out.
sacafilásticas, (*pl.* **sacafilásticas**), *f.* (artil.) priming wire.
sacalagua, *m.* (Amer.) light-skinned mestizo.
sacaliña, *f.* 1. goad stick. 2. (fig.) trick, cunning.
sacamanchas, (*pl.* **sacamanchas**), *m., f.* spot remover.

sacamantas, (*pl.* **sacamantas**), *m.* (coll.) tax collector.
sacamantecas, (*pl.* **sacamantecas**), *m., f.* (coll.) ripper, criminal who rips open his victims.
sacamiento, *m.* removal, taking out.
sacamolero, (rare), **sacamuelas,** (*pl.* **sacamuelas**), *m., f.* (derog.) 1. dentist. 2. charlatan, swindler.
sacamuestra, *m.* sampler; (pet.) core barrel.
sacanabo, *m.* (artil.) bomb or shell extractor (for extracting bomb from mortar).
sacanete, *m.* lansquenet (card game).
sacapelotas, (*pl.* **sacapelotas**), *m.* 1. bullet screw or extractor (for a harquebus). 2. (fig.) rotter, cur, cad.
sacapotras, (*pl.* **sacapotras**), *m.* (coll.) butcher, quack surgeon.
sacapuntas, (*pl.* **sacapuntas**), *m.* pencil sharpener.
sacar, (*ref. 50*) *tr.v.* 1. to take out; to extract; to remove; to pull out; to get out; to extract (teeth); to pull up (plants); to extract (e.g. oil from olives); to remove (e.g. stain from cloth); to draw (money from bank; sword from sheath); to subtract; to work out, e.g. *s. la cuenta,* to work out the bill. 2. to solve, interpret, deduce. 3. to win (prize, lottery, etc.). 4. to obtain, get. 5. to take (photographs). 6. to quote, cite. 7. to bring out, introduce (a new machine, fashion, etc.); to publish (book). 8. to serve (e.g. ball in tennis). 9. to elect, choose. 10. to show, brandish, stick out. — **s. adelante,** to carry forward, carry out, execute; to rear, nurture; **s. a alguien de un apuro,** to get someone out of a jam; **s. a bailar,** to invite to dance; to drag in, force in (to participate); **s. a luz,** to bring to light; **s. a pasear,** to take out for a walk; **s. a relucir,** to pull out, flash (gun, sword); **s. de,** to free from, deliver from, e.g. *s. de pobre,* to deliver from poverty; to get out of, e.g. *yo voy a sacarle la verdad,* I'm going to get the truth out of him; **s. de sí,** to infuriate, drive mad or crazy; **s. el cuerpo,** to give the slip to (somebody); **s. el jugo,** to make (one) work hard; **s. el pecho,** to put or throw out one's chest; **s. en cara,** to throw in one's face (as a reproach); **s. en claro** or **en limpio,** to get straight, deduce, make out of, e.g. *no puedo s. nada en claro de eso,* I can make nothing out of this; to recopy clearly; **s. la cara por,** to stand for; **s. la cuenta,** to figure out; **s. la lengua,** to stick out one's tongue; **s. la mano,** to put out one's hand; **s. la mugre a,** to knock the living daylights out of; **s. provecho de,** to benefit from, draw benefit from; **s. una copia,** to make a copy (of a document); **s. ventaja sobre,** to gain an advantage over. —*i.v.* to serve (in tennis, etc.), kick off (in soccer), throw in (in soccer).
sacarasa, *f.* (chem.) saccharase.
sacarato, *m.* (chem.) saccharate.
sacárico, ca, *a.* (chem.) saccharic.
sacárido, *m.* (chem.) saccharide.
sacarífero, ra, *a.* sacchariferous.
sacarificación, *f.* saccharification.
sacarificar, (*ref. 50*) *tr.v.* to saccharify.
sacarifique, sacarifiqué, *ref.* **sacarificar.**
sacarígeno, na, *a.* sacchariferous.
sacarimetría, *f.* saccharimetry.
sacarímetro, *m.* saccharimeter.
sacarina, *f.* (chem.) saccharin.
sacarino, na, *a.* saccharine.
sacaroideo, a, *a.* saccharoid, saccharoidal.
sacarómetro, *m.* saccharimeter.
sacaromicético, ca, *a.* (bot.) saccharomycetic.
sacarosa, *f.* (chem.) saccharose.
sacaroso, sa, *a.* similar to saccharine.
sacarrueda, *m.* (auto.) wheel puller.
sacasillas, (*pl.* **sacasillas**), *m.* 1. stagehand. 2. (coll.) busybody.
sacatachuelas, (*pl.* **sacatachuelas**), *f.* tack claw.
sacatapón, *m.* corkscrew.
sacate, *m.* (Mex.) hay; grass, herb.
sacatinta, *f.* (C. Amer.) jacobinia (Jacobinia spicigera - shrub producing blue dye).
sacatrapos, (*pl.* **sacatrapos**), *m.* (artil.) wad hook, wormer.
sacayán, *m.* (Phil. I.) small boat.
sacerdocio, *m.* priesthood.
sacerdotal, *a.* priestly, sacerdotal.
sacerdote, *m.* priest, clergyman; **sumo s.,** high priest.
sacerdotisa, *f.* priestess.
sácere, *m.* (bot.) maple tree.
sachadura, *f.* (agr.) weeding, hoeing.
sachaguasca, *f.* (Arg., bot.) cat's claw.
sachar, *tr.v.* (agr.) to weed.
sachet, *m.* (Fr.) sachet.
sacho, *m.* 1. weeder, weeding tool. 2. (Chile, mar.) sinker, anchor.
saciable, *a.* satiable.
saciar, *tr.v.* to satiate, sate, glut, surfeit. —*r.v.* to be satiated, sated or glutted.
saciedad, *f.* satiety, satiation, surfeit; **hasta la s.,** ad nauseam.
saciña, *f.* (bot.) (variety of) willow (Salix incana).
sacio, cia, *a.* (rare) satiated, sated.
saco, *m.* 1. sack; bag; (bot., zool., anat.) sac. 2. (Amer.) jacket, sports coat. 3. rough coat or dress; loose overcoat; (Roman) sagum. 4. sack (measure of capacity). 5. sacking, pillaging. 6. service, serve (in pelota, tennis, etc.). 7. (mar.) creek, inlet. — **echar en s. roto,** to forget; **entrar** or **meter a s.,** to sack, pillage; **no echar en s. roto,** (coll.) to keep in mind, not to forget; **s. aéreo,** air sac or cell (of birds); **s. de arena,** (sport.) punchbag; **s. de dormir,** sleeping bag; **s. de huesos,** (Amer.) bag of bones (very thin person); **s. de noche,** overnight bag, valise; **s. terrero,** (mil.) sandbag; **s. vitelino,** (biol.) yolk sac.
sácope, *m.* (Phil. I.) subject, citizen.
sacra, *f.* (ecc.) sacring tablet.
sacramentación, *f.* administration of the sacraments.
sacramentado, da, *a.* (ecc.) 1. transubstantiated. 2. having received the last sacraments.
sacramental, *a.* sacramental. —*m.* 1. (ecc.) sacramental. 2. member of brotherhood dedicated to the worship of the Holy Sacrament. —*f.* brotherhood dedicated to the worship of the sacrament.
sacramentalmente, *adv.* sacramentally; in confession.
sacramentar, *tr.v.* 1. (ecc.) to transubstantiate. 2. to administer the sacraments to. 3. to hide, conceal. —*r.v.* (ecc.) to be transubstantiated.
sacramentario, ria, *a., m., f.* sacramentarian.
sacramente, *adv.* sacredly.
sacramento, *m.* sacrament (e.g. baptism, marriage, etc.); Sacrament, Eucharist; **s. del altar,** Sacrament, Eucharist; **Santísimo S.,** Blessed Sacrament; **últimos sacramentos,** extreme unction.
sacratísimo, ma, *a.* most sacred.
sacre, *m.* 1. (ornith., artil.) saker. 2. thief.
sacrificable, *a.* able to be sacrificed, expendable.
sacrificadero, *m.* place of sacrifice, sacrificial altar.
sacrificador, ra, *a.* sacrificing. —*m., f.* sacrificer.
sacrificante, *a.* sacrificing, sacrificial.
sacrificar, (*ref. 50*) *tr.v.* 1. to sacrifice. 2. to slaughter (for the market). —*r.v.* to sacrifice oneself.
sacrificio, *m.* sacrifice; **s. del altar,** (ecc.) Sacrifice of the Mass.
sacrifique, sacrifiqué, *ref.* **sacrificar.**
sacrílegamente, *adv.* sacrilegiously.
sacrilegio, *m.* sacrilege.
sacrílego, ga, *a.* sacrilegious. —*m., f.* sacrilegious person, profaner, desecrator.
sacrismoche, sacrismocho, *m.* (coll.) one who goes about in black.
sacrista, *m.* sacristan, sexton.
sacristán, na, *m.* 1. sacristan, sexton. 2. farthingale, hoop, petticoat. 3. (ornith.) stonechat. —*f.* 1. sacristan's or sexton's wife. 2. nun in charge of the sacristy.
sacristanía, *f.* office of a sacristan or sexton, sacristanship.
sacristía, *f.* 1. sacristy, vestry. 2. office of a sacristan or sexton.
sacro, cra, *a.* 1. sacred, holy. 2. (anat.) sacral. —*m.* (anat.) sacrum.
sacroilíaco, ca, *a.* (anat.) sacroiliac.
sacrosanto, ta, *a.* sacred, sacrosanct.
sacuara, *f.* (Peru) cane shoot.
sacudida, *f.* shake, shaking, jerk, jolt; **s. eléctrica,** electric shock.
sacudido, da, *past part. of* **sacudir.** —*a.* 1. intractable, surly. 2. determined, resolute.
sacudidor, ra, *a.* shaking. —*m., f.* shaker, beater, duster. —*m.* carpet beater (instrument).
sacudidura, *f.* 1. shaking, dusting. 2. jolt, jar, jerk.
sacudimiento, *m.* 1. shaking, shake. 2. jolt, jar; shock.
sacudión, *m.* 1. violent jolt or jar. 2. energetic shaking.
sacudir, *tr.v.* 1. to shake; to jolt, jar. 2. to dust. — **s. de,** to shake from, **e.g.** *s. el polvo de la alfombra,* to shake the dust from the carpet. —*r.v.* to shake; to shake oneself; to shake off, e.g. *sacudirse el polvo,* to shake off the dust.
sacudón, *m.* (Amer.), *var. of* **sacudión.**
saculiforme, *a.* (bot., zool.) saccate.
sáculo, *m.* (anat.) saccule.
sádico, ca, *a.* sadistic. —*m., f.* sadist.
sadismo, *m.* sadism.
sadista, *m., f.* sadist.
sadomasoquismo, *m.* (psyc.) sadomasochism.
saduceísmo, *m.* (hist., rel.) Sadduceeism.
saduceo, a, *a.* (hist., rel.) Sadducean. —*m., f.* Sadducee.
saeta, *f.* 1. arrow, dart. 2. (watch) hand; cock of a sundial. 3. needle. 4. stump of a vine shoot (after pruning). 5. (astron.) **S.,** Sagitta, the Arrow. 6. (Sp.) Andalusian song generally performed in religious ceremonies and Holy Week processions.
saetada, saetazo, *f.* arrow shot or wound.
saetear, *tr.v.* to attack or wound with darts or arrows.
saetero, ra, *a.* arrow, arrow-shooting. —*m.* archer, bowman. —*f.* embrasure, loophole (for shooting arrows); narrow window.
saetí, (*pl.* **saetíes**), *m.* (tex.) satin.
saetía, *f.* 1. (mar.) settee. 2. embrasure, loophole.
saetilla, *f.* 1. *dim. of* **saeta,** dart, small arrow. 2. hand (of a watch, clock, etc.). 3. small magnetic needle. 4. (bot.) arrowhead.
saetín, *m.* 1. brad (nail). 2. millrace, mill run, flume. 3. (tex., Gal.) satin.
saetón, *m. aug. of* **saeta,** large arrow; dart for shooting rabbits.
safacoca, *f.* (Amer.) hullaballoo, **racket,** din, row.
safena, *a.* (anat.) saphenous (vein).
sáfico, ca, *a., m.* (poet.) Sapphic (verse).
safismo, *m.* sapphism, lesbianism.
Safo, *f.* Sappho, Greek poetess of Lesbos.

safrol, *m.* (chem.) safrole, safrol.
saga, *f.* 1. saga, legend. 2. witch, sorceress.
sagacidad, *f.* sagacity, sagaciousness.
sagapeno, *m.* sagapenum (gum).
sagarrera, *f.* (Col.) scuffle, fight, free-for-all.
sagatí, *m.* rough, woven fabric.
sagaz, (*pl.* **sagaces**), *a.* 1. sagacious, astute; far-sighted. 2. keen-scented (hunting dog).
sagazmente, *adv.* sagaciously, astutely.
sagita, *f.* (geom.) vertical height (of an arc); (archit.) rise, height (of arch).
sagitado, da, *a.* (bot.) sagittate.
sagital, *a.* sagittal, arrow-shaped; (anat., zool.) sagittal.
sagitaria, *f.* (bot.) arrowhead.
sagitario, *m.* 1. archer, bowman. 2. (astron.) **S.,** Sagittarius.
ságoma, *f.* (archit.) pattern, templet.
sagradamente, *adv.* sacredly; reverently.
sagrado, da, *a.* sacred. —*m.* sanctuary, asylum, haven, refuge; **acogerse a sagrado,** to take sanctuary; **Sagradas Escrituras** or **S. Escritura,** Holy Scriptures.
sagrario, *m.* sacrarium (where sacred utensils and relics are kept); tabernacle (niche where consecrated elements of the Eucharist are kept); chapel (serving as parish church of a cathedral).
sagú, *m.* 1. (bot.) sago palm; (C. Amer., Cuba, bot.) arrowroot. 2. sago (starch).
saguaipe, *m.* (vet., Arg., Bol., Urug.) liver fluke.
ságula, *f.* short sleeveless robe.
sahárico, ca, *a.* Saharan, Saharian.
sahina, *f.* (bot.) sorghum.
sahinar, *m.* sorghum field.
sahornarse, *r.v.* to become chafed, red or inflamed.
sahorno, *m.* chafing, rawness, redness (of the skin).
sahumado, da, *past part. of* **sahumar.** —*a.* 1. better, better still; improved. 2. (Amer., coll.) lit up, tipsy.
sahumador, *m.* 1. perfume burning pot, incense burner. 2. clothes drier, clothes rack (for drying clothes over heat).
sahumadura, *f., var. of* **sahumerio.**
sahumar, *tr.v.* to perfume by burning aromatic herbs or incense. —*r.v.* to become perfumed, fragrant or aromatic.
sahumerio, sahumo, *m.* perfuming, making fragrant or aromatic; aromatic smoke, aroma, fragrance; aromatic herbs, incense.
Saigón, *m.* Saigon, capital of South Vietnam.
saín, *m.* 1. animal fat; fish oil (used for oil lamps). 2. grease, greasiness.
sainar, *tr.v.* to fatten (animals).
sainete, *m.* 1. (theat.) one-act farce. 2. sauce, seasoning, relish; tidbit, appetizer; tastiness, flavor. 3. style, flare.
sainetear, *i.v.* (theat.) to play one-act farces.
sainetero, *m.* farceur, writer or player of farces.
sainetesco, ca, *a.* farcical, burlesque.
sainetista, *m., var. of* **sainetero.**
saíno, *m.* (zool.) peccary.
saja, *f.* 1. incision, cut. 2. (bot.) leaf stalk of Manila hemp.
sajador, *m.* bleeder, bloodletter; (med.) scarifier.
sajadura, *f.* incision, cut.
sajar, *tr.v.* to cut, make an incision on (the flesh).
sajelar, *tr.v.* to sift and clean (clay).
sajón, na, *a., m., f.* (hist., geog.) Saxon.
Sajonia, *f.* Saxony; **S. Coburgo,** Saxe Coburg.
sajumaya, *f.* (Cuba) swine disease ending in asphyxiation.
sajuriana, *f.* (Chile, Peru) old foot-tapping and shuffling dance.

sakí, *m.* 1. sake, saki (liquor). 2. (zool.) saki.
sal, *f.* 1. (cul., chem.) salt. 2. wit, wittiness. 3. charm, grace. 4. (Cuba, C. Amer.) misfortune, bad luck. — **con su s. y pimienta,** (coll.) piquantly, wittily; **echar en s.,** to hold back, withhold; **s. amoníaca** or **amoníaco,** sal ammoniac; **s. ática,** Attic salt, Attic wit; **s. de acederas,** salt of sorrel; **s. de ajo,** garlic salt; **s. de compás,** rock salt; **s. de Epsom,** Epsom salts; **s. de gema,** rock salt; **s. de la Higuera,** liver salts, Epsom salts; **s. de nitro,** saltpeter; **s. de plomo** or **de Saturno,** lead acetate, salt of Saturn, sugar of lead; **s. de Sedlitz,** Seidlitz powder; **sales aromáticas,** smelling salts; **sales de baño,** bath salts; **s. fumante,** hydrochloric acid; **s. yodada,** iodized salt.
sala, *f.* 1. drawing room, living room, parlor; hall, lounge, salon. 2. court, tribunal. — **s. de apelaciones,** court of appeal; **s. de batalla,** sorting room (in post office); **s. de embarque** or **preembarque,** departure lounge, gate; **s. de equipajes,** luggage or baggage office; **s. de espectáculos,** auditorium, theater, cinema; **s. de espera,** waiting room; **s. de exposiciones,** gallery, exhibition hall; **s. de fiestas,** night club; **s. de juntas,** board room; **s. de justicia,** court of justice; **s. de lectura,** reading room; **s. de mando,** control room; **s. de máquinas,** engine room; **s. de operaciones,** operating theater; **s. de partos,** delivery room (in maternity hospital); **s. de sesiones,** (com.) boardroom (of firm, company, etc.); **s. de subastas,** auction room; salesroom; **s. de urgencias,** (med.) emergency room.
salabardo, *m.* dip net, scoop net.
salacidad, *f.* salaciousness, lasciviousness, lechery.
salacot, *m.* pith helmet, topi, sun helmet.
saladamente, *adv.* wittily, piquantly.
saladar, *m.* salt marsh; saline ground.
saladería, *f.* (Arg.) meat-salting industry.
saladero, *m.* salting room, salting house.
saladillo, lla, *a.* slightly salted. —*m.* slightly salted bacon. —*f.* (bot.) saltbush (Atriplex glauca).
Saladino, *m.* (hist.) Saladin, hero of the Third Crusade.
salado, da, *past part. of* **salar.** —*a.* 1. salty, briny; brackish. 2. witty, peppy, amusing. 3. graceful, winsome, charming. 4. (Cuba, C. Amer.) unlucky, jinxed. 5. (Arg., Chile) expensive, costly. — **agua s.,** salt water. —*m.* (bot.) saltwort.
salador, ra, *a.* salting. —*m., f.* salter. —*m.* salting house, salting room.
saladura, *f.* salting; curing.
salamanca, *f.* 1. (Chile) natural cave in the hills. 2. (Arg., zool.) flat-headed salamander.
salamandra, *f.* 1. (zool.) salamander. 2. salamander, fire sprite. 3. salamander, salamander stove. 4. (chem.) crystallized alum. — **s. acuática,** (zool.) newt.
salamandria, *f., var. of* **salamanquesa.**
salamanqueja, *f.* (Col., Ecuad., Peru), *var. of* **salamanquesa.**
salamanquero, ra, *m., f.* (Phil. I.) juggler; prestidigitator.
salamanquesa, *f.* (zool.) gecko, tarente; s. de agua, (zool.) newt.
salamanquino, na, *a., m., f.* Salamancan.
Salamina, *f.* (hist., geog.) Salamis.
salangana, *f.* (ornith.) swift.
salar, *tr.v.* 1. to salt, cure, corn, brine. 2. to season with salt, salt, put salt on or in. 3. (C. Amer.) to stain, dishonor. 4. (Cuba, C. Amer.) to bring (one) bad luck, jinx. —*m.* (Arg., Chile) salt deposit.

salariar, *tr.v.* to pay wages or a salary to; to assign a wage or salary.
salario, *m.* wages; salary; **s. vital,** living wage.
salaz, (*pl.* **salaces**), *a.* salacious, lascivious, lecherous.
salazón, *f.* 1. salting, brining. 2. great amount of salt meat or fish. 3. salt meat or fish trade. 4. (coll., Cuba) bad luck.
salbadera, *f.* sandbox, pounce box.
salbanda, *f.* (min.) selvage, gouge.
salce, *m.* (bot.) willow.
salceda, *f.,* **salcedo.** *m.* willow grove.
salchicha, *f.* 1. sausage. 2. (fort.) saucisson (long fascine). 3. (mil.) saucisson (fuse).
salchichería, *f.* sausage shop.
salchichero, ra, *m., f.* sausage maker or seller.
salchichón, *m.* 1. *aug. of* **salchicha,** large sausage; salami. 2. (fort.) saucisson, large fascine.
salcochar, *tr.v.* (cul.) to boil.
salcocho, *m.* (cul., Amer.) stew, boiled dinner.
saldado, da, *past part. of* **saldar.** —*a.* even, paid, settled (debt, account).
saldar, *tr.v.* (com.) to settle, pay up (a debt); to sell at bargain prices.
saldista, *m., f.* remnant seller or dealer.
saldo, *m.* 1. payment, settlement. 2. (com.) balance. 3. remnant, remainder. — **s. acreedor,** credit balance; **s. deudor,** debit balance, balance due; **s. disponible,** balance in hand.
saldrá, saldré, *ref.* **salir.**
saledizo, za, *a.* projecting, jutting out. —*m.* (archit.) ledge, projection.
salega, salegar, *m.* lick, salt lick (for cattle).
salema, *f.* (ichth.) gilthead.
salep, *m.* salep (starch).
salera, *f.* receptacle for salt fed to cattle.
salero, *m.* 1. saltcellar, saltshaker, salt dish. 2. salt warehouse, salthouse. 3. salt lick (for cattle). 4. (artil.) base of shrapnel cartridge bags. 5. (coll.) grace, charm, wit. 6. (coll.) wit, witty, lively person.
saleroso, sa, *a.* (coll.) witty, charming, lively, winsome.
salesa, *a., f.* Salesian (pertaining to the Order of the Visitation founded by St. Francis de Sales).
salesiano, na, *a.,* m. Salesian (pertaining to the Order founded by Dom Bosco).
saleta, *f.* 1. *dim. of* **sala,** small living room or sitting room, parlor. 2. royal antechamber.
salga, salgo, *ref.* **salir.**
salgada, salgadera, *f.* (bot.) crach, mountain spinach.
salgar, (*ref. 51*) *tr.v.* to feed salt to cattle.
salgareño, *a.* (bot.) Austrian (pine).
salguera, *f.,* **salguero,** *m.* (bot.) willow.
salicáceo, a, *a.* (bot.) salicaceous. —*f.* (bot.) salicaceous plant; (*pl.*) Salicaceae.
salicaria, *f.* (bot.) purple loosestrife (Lithrum salicaria).
salicilato, *m.* (chem.) salicylate.
salicílico, *a.* (chem.) salicylic.
salicina, *f.* (chem.) salicin.
salicíneo, a, *a.* (bot.) salicaceous. —*f.* (bot.) salicaceous plant; (*pl.*) (bot.) Salicaceae.
sálico, ca, *a.* (hist.) Salic.
salicor, *m.* (bot.) saltwort, barilla.
salida, *f.* 1. leaving; departure, emergence; going out; coming out; exit, way out; outlet; (sport.) start; issue; debut; publication. 2. environs, fields near town. 3. projection, ledge, part jutting out. 4. market, outlet, salableness, marketing potential, e.g. *este artículo tiene mucha s.,* this article is in great demand or sells very well. 5. expenditure, outlay. 6. way out (of a difficult situation). 7. end, conclusion, settlement. 8.

sally, witty remark, witticism. 9. ship's speed, headway. 10. (mil.) attack, sortie. 11. (elec.) outlet. — **s. de baño,** bathing wrap; **s. del sol,** sunrise; **s. de teatro,** evening wrap; **s. de tono,** faux pas, impertinent remark, improper remark; **s. especificada,** (rad.) rated output.
salidero, ra, *a.* gadabout. —*m.* exit, way out.
salidizo, *m.* (archit.) projection, ledge.
salido, da, *past part. of* **salir.** —*a.* 1. projecting; protuberant. 2. in heat, in season (female animal).
saliente, *a.* projecting; salient; prominent. —*m.* 1. east. 2. projection, ledge. 3. (mil.) salient.
salífero, ra, *a.* saliferous.
salificable, *a.* (chem.) salifiable.
salificación, *f.* (chem.) salification.
salificar, (*ref. 50*) *tr.v.* (chem.) to salify.
salifique, salifiqué, *ref.* **salificar.**
salín, *m.* salthouse.
salina, *f.* salt mine, salt pit; salt marsh; salt works.
salinero, *a.* spotted red and white (bull). —*m.* salter, salt maker, salt dealer.
salinidad, *f.* salinity, saltiness.
salino, na, *a.* saline.
salinómetro, *m.* salinometer.
salio, lia, *a.* (hist.) Salian. —*m., f.* Salian, Salian Frank.
salir, (*ref. 21*) *i.v.* 1. to leave, go out; to come out. 2. to get out (of place, out of a difficulty, etc.). 3. to come out, rise (the sun). 4. to come up, begin to appear (plants). 5. to come out (stains). 6. to jut out, stick out, project. 7. to turn out, turn out to be, prove to be. 8. to originate, come, stem. 9. to lead (in card games), make the first move. 10. to get rid (of), dispose (of). 11. to come out, appear (a publication, new fashion, inventions, etc.). 12. to happen, occur, crop up. 13. to work out (to), cost, come (to). 14. to come out right, work out correctly (e.g. a calculation). 15. to emerge, come out (e.g. the winner). 16. to end (season of year). 17. to come out, come off, e.g. *Juan salió ileso,* John came out unhurt. 18. to be drawn (e.g. lottery ticket). 19. (mar.) to get ahead, lead. 20. (theat.) to enter, appear. 21. (coll.) to sell well, have a market. — **salga lo que salga,** (coll.) come what may, whatever happens; **s. a,** to work out to, cost, come to; to come out like, look like, resemble; to lead into (a street); **s. a** + *inf.,* to go or come out + *inf.;* **salirle a cuenta,** to be worth one's while, come out winning; **s. al encuentro de,** to go or come out to meet; **s. adelante,** to get ahead; to lead; **s. con,** to come out with (a remark); to get, e.g. *s. con la suya,* to get one's own way; **s. de,** to get rid of, dispose of; to get out of (place, difficulty, etc.); **s. de compras,** to go shopping; **s. de dudas,** to make sure, overcome one's doubts; **s. pitando,** (coll.) to run off pell-mell; to get mad, blow up. —*r.v.* 1. to leave, go. 2. to come out, e.g. *el tornillo se ha salido,* the screw has come out. 3. to leak, ooze, trickle or seep out. 4. to leak (a cracked vessel). 5. to boil over. — **salirse con la suya,** to get one's own way, get what one wants.
Salisbury, *f.* Salisbury, capital of Rhodesia.
salitrado, da, *a.* saltpetrous.
salitral, *a.* saltpetrous. —*m.* saltpeter bed, saltpeter deposit.
salitre, *m.* saltpeter, niter.
salitrería, *f.* saltpeter works.
salitrero, ra, *a.* saltpeter. —*m.* saltpeter refiner or dealer. —*f.* saltpeter bed or deposit.
salitroso, sa, *a.* saltpetrous, nitrous.
saliva, *f.* saliva, spittle; **gastar s. en balde,** (coll.) to talk in vain; **tragar s.,** (coll.) to suffer an affront; to be speechless, be dumbfounded.
salivación, *f.* 1. salivation. 2. excessive salivation, ptyalism.
salivajo, *m., var. of* **salivazo.**
salival, *a.* salivary.
salivar, *i.v.* to salivate.
salivazo, *m.* spit, spittle.
saliveo, *m.* spitting.
saliveras, *f.* (*pl.*) knobs on horse's bit.
salivoso, sa, *a.* salivating or spitting excessively.
salladura, *f.* (agr.) weeding.
sallar, *tr.v.* 1. to weed. 2. to store (wood) on blocks.
sallete, *m.* weeder, weeding tool.
salma, *f.* ton, ton-weight.
salmanticense, salmantino, na, *a., m., f.* Salamancan (referring to the Spanish province of Salamanca).
salmear, *i.v.* to sing psalms.
salmer, *m.* (archit.) impost (of an arch).
salmista, *m.* psalmist, chanter of psalms.
salmo, *m.* psalm.
salmodia, *f.* (ecc.) psalmody; (fig.) monotonous song.
salmodiar, *i.v.* to sing psalms. —*tr.v.* to sing monotonously.
salmón, *m.* (ichth.) salmon; **s. zancado,** kelt.
salmonado, da, *a.* 1. salmon-like. 2. salmon, salmon-colored, salmon pink.
salmonera, *f.* salmon net.
salmonete, *m.* (ichth.) red mullet, surmullet.
salmónidos, *m.* (*pl.*) (ichth.) Salmonidae.
salmorejo, *m.* sauce made of vinegar, oil, salt and pepper, used for braising rabbit.
salmuera, *f.* brine, pickle.
salmuerarse, *r.v.* to become ill from eating too much salt (cattle).
salobral, *a.* saline (ground). —*m.* saline ground.
salobre, *a.* brackish, briny, saltish; **agua s.,** brackish water.
salobreño, ña, *a.* saline.
salobridad, *f.* brackishness, saltiness.
salol, *m.* (med.) salol.
saloma, *f.* (mar.) chantey, chanty.
salomar, *i.v.* to sing chanteys.
Salomé, *f.* (hist., Bib.) Salome.
Salomón, *m.* 1. (hist., Bib.) Solomon. 2. (fig.) Solomon, very wise man.
salomónico, ca, *a.* Solomonic.
salón, *m.* 1. salon, saloon, drawing room, reception room. 2. salon, fashion assemblage at which celebrities gather. — **s. comedor,** living room-dining room; **s. de baile,** ballroom, dancehall; **s. de belleza,** beauty parlor; **s. de exposiciónes,** exhibition room; **s. de juegos** or **s. recreativo,** amusement arcade; **s. de sesiones,** assembly hall; board room (of board of directors); **s. de té,** tea-room; **s. de ventas,** salesroom.
salón, *m.* salted meat or fish.
saloncillo, cito, *m. dim. of* **salón,** small hall or reception room; special small room (lounge, rest room, etc.).
salpa, *f.* 1. (zool.) salpa, salp. 2. (ichth.) gilthead.
salpicadero, *m.* (auto.) splash guard.
salpicado, da, *a.* splashy, splotchy.
salpicadura, *f.* splash, spatter, splashing, spattering.
salpicar, (*ref. 50*) *tr.v.* 1. to splash, spatter; to splash or spatter with; to sprinkle. 2. to touch on without order.
salpicón, *m.* 1. (cul.) salmagundi, cold hash. 2. splash, spatter. 3. (Amer.) cold fruit juice; **s. de frutas,** (Col., Ecuad.) cold fruit juice; **s. de mariscos,** sea-food cocktail.
salpimentar, (*ref. 29*) *tr.v.* 1. to season with salt and pepper. 2. to make more pleasant or agreeable.
salpimienta, *f.* mixture of salt and pepper.
salpique, salpiqué, *ref.* **salpicar.**
salpresar, *tr.v.* to salt, preserve with salt.
salpreso, sa, *irr. past part. of* **salpresar.** —*a.* preserved with salt.
salpullido, *m.* 1. rash, skin eruption. 2. flea bites.
salpullir, (*ref. 65*) *tr.v.* to cause a rash on. —*r.v.* to get a rash.
salsa, *f.* 1. (cul.) sauce, dressing, gravy. 2. (fig.) seasoning. 3. (Chile) beating, whipping, flogging. — **cocer(se) en su propia s.,** to stew in one's own juice; **s. blanca,** (cul.) white sauce; **s. de San Bernardo,** (coll.) good appetite, hunger; **s. de tomate,** tomato catsup, ketchup; **s. inglesa,** Worcestershire sauce; **s. mahonesa** or **mayonesa,** (cul.) mayonnaise; **s. mayordoma,** (cul.) parsley butter; **s. rubia,** (cul.) brown roux; **s. rusa,** Russian dressing; **s. tártara,** tartar sauce.
salsedumbre, *f.* saltiness.
salsera, *f.* sauce boat, gravy boat.
salsereta, salserilla, salseruela, *f.* small dish (for mixing paints).
salsifí, (*pl.* **salsifíes**), *m.* (bot.) salsify, goat's beard; **s. de España** or **negro,** (bot.) black salsify, viper's grass.
salso, *m.* (geol.) salse, mud volcano.
salsoláceo, a, *a.* (bot.) salsolaceous. —*f.* (*pl.*) (bot.) Salsolaceae.
saltabanco, saltabancos, *m.* 1. mountebank, charlatan, quack. 2. juggler; tumbler. 3. (coll.) show-off, fraud.
saltabardales, (*pl.* **saltabardales**), *m., f.* (coll.) wild youth, madcap.
saltabarrancos, (*pl.* **saltabarrancos**), *m., f., var. of* **saltabardales.**
saltacharquillos, (*pl.* **saltacharquillos**), *m., f.* affected person who goes mincing about.
saltación, *f.* 1. jumping, leaping. 2. dancing, dance.
saltadero, *m.* 1. jumping place. 2. jet, spring.
saltadizo, za, *a.* brittle, breaking easily.
saltador, ra, *a.* jumping, leaping. —*m., f.* jumper, leaper; **s. con garrocha,** pole jumper or vaulter. —*m.* skipping rope.
saltadura, *f.* chip, flaw (in surface of a hewn stone).
saltaembanco, saltaembancos, (*pl.* **saltaembancos**), *m., var. of* **saltabanco.**
saltagatos, (*pl.* **saltagatos**), *m.* (Col.) grasshopper.
saltamimbres, (*pl.* **saltamimbres**), *m.* (ornith.) marsh warbler.
saltamontes, (*pl.* **saltamontes**), *m.* grasshopper.
saltanejoso, sa, *a.* (Cuba) undulating (ground).
saltante, *a.* 1. jumping, leaping; salient. 2. (Chile) outstanding, noteworthy.
saltaojos, (*pl.* **saltaojos**), *m.* (bot.) peony.
saltaparedes, (*pl.* **saltaparedes**), *m., f.* (coll.) madcap, wild youth.
saltaperico, *m.* (Cuba, bot.) manyroot.
saltar, *tr.v.* 1. to jump, jump over, leap; to hop, skip. 2. to cover (a female). 3. to skip, miss out. 4. to jump (as in checkers or chess). 5. to place (a bet on a card). 6. (mar.) to loosen, slacken (a cable). —*i.v.* 1. to jump, spring, leap; to hop, skip; to fly (sparks, chips); to bounce (ball); to gush, shoot up (liquid). 2. to break, crack, burst. 3. to come or fly off. 4. to jump (to the eye). — **hacer s. la banca,** to break the bank; **s. a la vista or a los ojos,** to spring to the eye, be self-evident; **s. con,** to come out with (a remark); **s. de,** to jump with, e.g. *s. de gozo,* to jump with joy. —*r.v.* to skip, miss out.
saltarel, saltarelo, *m.* old Spanish dance based on the Italian saltarello.
saltarén, *m.* 1. dance played on the guitar. 2. (ento.) grasshopper.

saltarilla, *f.* (ento.) grasshopper.
saltarín, na, *a.* dancing, jumping. —*m., f.* 1. dancer, jumper. 2. madcap, unruly youth.
saltarregla, *f.* bevel square.
saltatrás, (*pl.* **saltatrás**), *m., f., var. of* tornatrás.
saltatumbas, (*pl.* **saltatumbas**), *m.* (coll.) priest who makes most of his living from funeral services.
salteador, ra, *m.* highwayman, highway robber. —*f.* highway robber's wench or woman; female robber.
salteamiento, *m.* highway robbery, assault.
saltear, *tr.v.* 1. to hold up, rob, waylay, assault. 2. to do in fits and starts. 3. to beat (someone) to something. 4. to surprise, take by surprise. 5. to sauté, fry lightly.
salteo, *m., var. of* **salteamiento.**
salterio, *m.* 1. Psalter, Book of Psalms. 2. (ecc.) book of services for the canonical hours, horary. 3. rosary. 4. (mus.) psaltery. 5. (zool.) psalterium (third stomach of ruminants).
saltero, ra, *a.* of the highlands.
saltico, to, *m. dim. of* **salto,** little jump, short hop.
saltígrado, da, *a., m., f.* (zool.) saltigrade.
saltimbanco, saltimbanqui, *m.* (coll.) mountebank, juggler, tumbler.
salto, *m.* 1. jump, leap, bound, vault; skip, hop. 2. leapfrog (game). 3. deep ravine. 4. waterfall, falls. 5. sudden palpitation or heart throb. 6. assault, attack. 7. omission (in reading or copying). 8. jump (in promotion). — **a gran s., gran quebranto,** the higher one flies, the harder the fall; **a s. de mata,** fleeing and hiding; **a saltos,** by leaps; **de un s.,** in a leap or jump; **el s. de Niágara,** Niagara Falls; **en un s.,** right away, in a jiffy; **s. a ciegas,** leap in the dark; **s. alto,** (sport.) high jump; **s. atrás,** throwback, reversion; **s. con garrocha** or **pértiga,** (sport.) pole vault; **s. de agua,** waterfall, falls; **s. de altura,** (sport.) high jump; **s. de carnero,** bucking (of a horse); **s. de carpa,** jackknife (dive); **s. de cisne,** swan dive (in swimming); **s. de esquí,** ski jump; **s. del ángel,** swan dive; **s. de lobo,** ditch marking boundary of property; **s. de longitud,** (sport.) long jump; **s. de tijera,** scissors (in gymnastics); **s. largo,** (sport.) broad jump; **s. mortal,** somersault.
saltómetro, *m.* horizontal bar (of high jump).
saltón, na, *a.* 1. jumping, leaping. 2. bulging, protruding. 3. (Peru) jumpy, nervous, worried. 4. (Chile, Col.) half-cooked. —*m.* (ento.) grasshopper.
salubérrimo, ma, *a. super. of* **salubre,** very healthy, salubrious.
salubre, *a.* healthy, healthful, salubrious.
salubridad, *f.* health, healthiness; salubrity.
salud, *f.* 1. health; welfare, well-being. 2. salvation (of the soul). — **beber a la s. de alguien,** to drink to someone's health; **estar bien** or **mal de s.,** to be in good or bad health; **¡salud!** your health, down the hatch, bottoms up (when having a drink); bless you (to someone who sneezes).
saludable, *a.* healthy, wholesome.
saludablemente, *adv.* healthfully, wholesomely.
saludación, *f., var. of* **salutación.**
saludador, ra, *a.* greeting. —*m., f.* greeter. —*m.* quack doctor.
saludar, *tr.v.* 1. to greet, salute, hail. 2. (mil.) to salute, to fire a salute. 3. (mar.) to dip the flag.
saludo, *m.* 1. greeting, salute; compliments, regards. 2. (mil.) salute. — **saludos a,** greetings to, my best wishes to.
salumbre, *f.* flower of salt.
salutación, *f.* salutation, greeting; **s. angélica,** Angelic Salutation.
salute, *m.* (numis.) salute, coin struck by the House of Anjou.
salutífero, ra, *a., var. of* **saludable.**
salva, *f.* 1. salvo, volley. 2. greeting. 3. ordeal (to prove one's innocence). 4. oath, solemn promise. — **hacer la s.,** to request the floor (for speaking); **s. de aplausos,** round of applause.
salvabarros, (*pl.* **salvabarros**), *m.* mudguard.
salvable, *a.* savable.
salvación, *f.* salvation; deliverance. — **Ejército de S.,** Salvation Army.
salvachia, *f.* (mar.) grommet, becket, strap, sling.
salvadera, *f.* sandbox (for sprinkling sand on wet ink).
salvado, *m.* bran (grain).
salvador, ra, *a.* saving. —*m., f.* savior, saver. —*m.* **S.,** Savior, Jesus Christ.
salvadoreño, ña, *a., m., f.* Salvadoran (from El Salvador).
salvaguarda, *f., var. of* **salvaguardia.**
salvaguardar, *tr.v.* to safeguard, protect, shield.
salvaguardia, *f.* 1. safe-conduct, pass, safeguard. 2. safeguard, protection. —*m.* 1. guard, escort. 2. mark or sign of protection (in war).
salvajada, *f.* savage action, brutality, savagery.
salvaje, *a.* 1. wild; uncultivated; untamed. 2. savage, ferocious. 3. (coll.) stupid, ignorant, uncouth. —*m., f.* 1. savage. 2. uncouth, ignorant or stupid person.
salvajemente, *adv.* savagely.
salvajería, *f., var. of* **salvajada.**
salvajez, *f.* savageness, savagery.
salvajina, *f.* 1. wild animals. 2. game, meat of wild animals. 3. wild beast.
salvajino, na, *a.* 1. wild. 2. savage, ferocious. 3. gamy, having the taste of game (meat).
salvajismo, *m.* savagery.
salvamano, a s., safely, without running any risks; cowardly.
salvamanteles, (*pl.* **salvamanteles**), *m.* table mat.
salvamente, *adv.* safely, securely.
salvamento, salvamiento, *m.* 1. saving, rescue; life-saving; salvage, salvaging. 2. place of safety, harbor.
salvante, *a.* saving, rescuing. —*adv.* saving, except.
salvar, *tr.v.* 1. to save (from danger; the soul); to rescue; to salvage; to safeguard, protect, shield. 2. to overcome, get round, avoid (difficulties, obstacles). 3. to clear, jump, jump over, jump across; to cross, go over; to cover (a distance). 4. to rise above, be or stand taller than. 5. to certify (corrections to a document). 6. to except, make an exception of. 7. (law) to save, prove the innocence of. — **s. las apariencias,** to keep up appearances. —*i.v.* to taste food beforehand (to see that it is not poisoned). —*r.v.* to save oneself; to be saved; **sálvese el que pueda,** every man for himself.
salvarsán, *m.* (pharm.) salvarsan.
salvataje, *m.* salvage, salvaging; life saving. — **operaciones de s.,** salvage operations.
salvavidas, (*pl.* **salvavidas**), *a.* life-saving. — **bote s.,** life boat; **chaleco s.,** life jacket; **cinturón s.,** life belt. —*m.* life belt, life preserver; lifeboat; lifesaver, lifeguard.
salve, *interj.* salve, hail.
salvedad, *f.* reservation, proviso; exception.
salvia, *f.* (bot.) sage, salvia.
salvilla, *f.* glass rack or tray; salver.
salvo, va, *a.* 1. safe; saved. 2. excepted, omitted. — **a salvo,** in safety, out of danger; **a salvo de,** safe from; **dejar a salvo,** to set or put aside; **en salvo,** in liberty; in safety, out of danger; **poner a salvo,** to rescue, make safe; **sano y salvo,** safe and sound.
salvo, *adv.* except, excepting, saving, save, barring.
salvoconducto, *m.* safe-conduct, pass.
salvohonor, *m.* (coll.) buttocks, behind, backside.
Salzburgo, *m.* Salzburg, city in Austria.
sámago, *m.* alburnum, sapwood, splintwood.
samán, *m.* (bot.) rain tree, saman.
sámara, *f.* (bot.) samara, key fruit, key.
samarilla, *f.* (bot.) ironwort (Sideritis glacialis).
samario, *m.* (chem.) samarium.
samaritano, na, *a., m., f.* Samaritan. —*m.* Samaritan (language).
samarsquita, *f.* (min.) samarskite.
samaruguera, *f.* small mesh fishing-net.
sambenitar, *tr.v.* to put the Indian sign on (sl.), to stigmatize, hex; to dishonor, discredit.
sambenito, *m.* 1. sanbenito, cap and garment stigmatizing the penitent accused by the Inquisition. 2. church notice listing punishment for penitents. 3. disgrace, stigma, mark of infamy.
sambeque, *m.* (Cuba) noise, shindy, rumpus.
samblaje, *m.* joining, coupling; joint, union.
sambuca, *f.* 1. (mus.) sambuke, sackbut. 2. ancient war machine.
sambumbia, *f.* 1. (Cuba) drink made of cane syrup, water and peppers. 2. (Mex.) cordial made of pineapple, water and sugar. 3. (Col.) pap.
sambumbiería, *f.* (Cuba, Mex.) shop where **sambumbia** is made and sold.
samio, mia, *a., m., f.* (hist., geog.) Samian.
samisén, *m.* (mus.) samisen.
samita, *f.* (geol.) psammite.
samnita, samnite, *a., m., f.* (hist., geog.) Samnite.
samnítico, ca, *a.* (hist., geog.) Samnite.
samotana, *f.* (C. Rica, Hond.) noise, rumpus, shindy.
Samotracia, *f.* (hist., geog.) Samothrace.
samovar, *m.* samovar.
samoyedo, da, *a., m., f.* (geog.) Samoyed, Samoyede.
sampaguita, *f.* (bot.) Arabian jasmine.
sampán, *m.* sampan, Chinese skiff.
sampsuco, *m.* (bot.) marjoram.
samuga, *f., var. of* **jamuga.**
samuro, *m.* (Col., Ven.) turkey buzzard.
san, *a.* apocopated form of **santo,** used before all masculine names of saints except Tomás, Tomé, Toribio and Domingo.
Sana, *f.* Sana, capital of Yemen.
sanable, *a.* curable, healable.
sanaco, ca, *a.* (Cuba) foolish, stupid.
sanador, ra, *a.* healing, curing. —*m., f.* healer, curer.
sanalotodo, *m.* 1. black plaster. 2. (fig.) cure-all, catholicon, panacea.
sanamente, *adv.* 1. healthily, wholesomely. 2. sincerely.
sanar, *tr.v.* to cure, heal, restore to health. —*i.v.* to heal; to get well.
sanativo, va, *a.* healing, curative.
sanatorio, *m.* sanatorium, sanitarium, hospital.
sanchete, *m.* ancient silver coin.
sanchopancesco, ca, *a.* resembling Sancho Panza; practical, down-to-earth, shrewd.
sanción, *f.* 1. sanction; punishment. 2. sanction, approval, authorization. 3. statute, law, decree, sanction.
sancionable, *a.* sanctionable.
sancionador, ra, *a.* sanctioning. —*m., f.* sanctioner.
sancionar, *tr.v.* 1. to sanction, authorize, approve. 2. to sanction, punish.
sancirole, *m.* fool, simpleton, dimwit, dolt, clod.
sanco, *m.* 1. (Chile) toasted corn porridge. 2. (Arg.) stew made of bull's blood. 3. (Chile, fig.) thick mud.

sancochado, *m.* 1. boiling; parboiling. 2. (Peru) boiled dinner.
sancochar, *tr.v.* to boil; to parboil.
sancocho, *m.* 1. (Amer.) boiled dinner. 2. (Cuba) unappetizing dish. 3. (fig.) trouble, disturbance.
sancta, *m.* fore part of the tabernacle.
sanctasanctórum, *m.* 1. sanctum sanctorum, holy of holies. 2. great mystery or secret.
sanctus, *m.* (ecc.) Sanctus.
sandalia, *f.* sandal.
sandalino, na, *a.* pertaining to sandalwood.
sándalo, *m.* 1. (bot.) sandalwood. 2. (bot.) bergamot mint. — **s. blanco,** (bot.) white sandalwood; **s. rojo,** (bot.) red sandalwood.
sandáraca, *f.* sandarac (realgar; resin).
sandez, (*pl.* **sandeces**), *f.* foolishness, stupidity; foolish remark; (*pl.*) nonsense.
sandía, *f.* (bot.) watermelon.
sandiar, *m.* watermelon field or patch.
sandio, dia, *a.* simple, foolish. —*m., f.* simpleton, fool.
sandunga, *f.* 1. wit; charm, winsomeness. 2. (Chile) spree, party, night-out.
sandunguero, ra, *a.* witty; charming, graceful, winsome.
sándwich, *m.* **sándwiche,** *m.* sandwich.
saneado, da, *a.* unencumbered by taxes or mortgages.
saneamiento, *m.* 1. righting, putting on a sound basis or footing. 2. freeing of debts or encumbrances. 3. draining (of land); sanitation. 4. (law) warranty, guarantee, surety. 5. (law) indemnification, reparation, redress.
sanear, *tr.v.* 1. to put right, correct. 2. to make healthy, put on a sound basis or footing (e.g. an economy); to clear of debt, mortgages or encumbrances. 3. to drain (land); to make hygienic or sanitary. 4. (law) to warrant, guarantee, give security to. 5. (law) to indemnify.
sanedrín, *m.* (hist.) Sanhedrin.
sanfasón, *m.* brazenness, cheek, nerve.
sanforizado, da, *a.* Sanforized (TM).
sanfrancia, *f.* (coll.) row, dispute, quarrel.
sangley, *m.* (Phil. I.) sangley, Chinese trader.
sango, *m.* (Peru) kind of porridge.
sangradera, *f.* 1. lancet. 2. basin for bloodletting. 3. side irrigation ditch. 4. overflow sluicegate. 5. (Amer.) bleeding, bloodletting.
sangrador, *m.* 1. bloodletter. 2. outlet, hole, drain.
sangradura, *f.* 1. inner part of the crook of the arm. 2. bloodletting; draining; tapping (of a tree). 3. cut or incision in a vein. 4. outlet, drainage; ditch.
sangrar, *tr.v.* 1. to bleed, let (someone's) blood. 2. to drain. 3. to tap (a tree; a furnace). 4. (coll.) to steal or pilfer from. 5. (print.) to indent. —*i.v.* to bleed. —*r.v.* to be bled.
sangraza, *f.* contaminated blood.
sangre, *f.* 1. blood. 2. blood, lineage. — **a s. fría,** in cold blood; **a s. y fuego,** by fire and sword, ruthlessly; violently; **írsele la s. a los talones,** to go numb or freeze with fear; **hervirle a uno la s.,** (coll.) to be in one's prime, be in the flower of youth; **de s. caliente,** warm-blooded; **encenderse a uno la s.,** to get furious; **lavar con s.,** to avenge with blood; **llevar en la s.,** to have in one's blood; **mala s.,** (coll.) bad blood, enmity; vindictiveness; **no llegará la s. al río,** (coll.) nothing very serious will happen, it won't have serious consequences; **s. azul,** blue blood, noble blood; **(tener) s. de horchata,** (to be) apathetic, indifferent; **s. fría,** sang froid, self-control; **(tener) s. ligera,** (Amer.) (to be) pleasant, agreeable; **s. negra,** venous blood; **(tener) s. pesada,** (Amer.) (to be) disagreeable, unpleasant; **s. roja,** red blood, arterial blood; **s. y leche,** red marble streaked with white; **subírsele a uno la s. a la cabeza,** to get furious; **sudar s.,** to sweat blood.
sangregorda, *m.* (coll.) bore, boring person.
sangría, *f.* 1. bleeding, bloodletting; draining, drainage; tapping (of tree; of furnace). 2. inner part of the crook of the arm. 3. outlet, drain, drainage ditch; (fig.) drain (on resources). 4. cut, incision (made in tree). 5. pilfering. 6. sangaree, wine and fruit drink. 7. (print.) indentation. 8. (metal.) tap (amount of metal run out of furnace at any one time).
sangrientamente, *adv.* bloodily, cruelly.
sangriento, ta, *a.* 1. bloody, bleeding, full of or stained with blood. 2. sanguinary, bloodthirsty, bloody. 3. bloody, bitterly or savagely fought (battle). 4. (poet.) blood-red.
sangriligero, ra, *a.* (Col., Cuba, coll.) witty, genial; pleasant, agreeable, friendly.
sangripesado, da, sangrón, ona, *a.* (Col., Cuba, coll.) disagreeable, unpleasant.
sanguaraña, *f.* 1. (Peru) popular dance. 2. (Peru, Ecuad.) circumlocution, e.g. *dejarse de sanguarañas,* to stop beating about the bush.
sanguaza, *f.* contaminated blood; (fig.) red juice (from certain fruits or vegetables).
sangüeño, *m.* (bot.) dogwood tree.
sangüeso, sa, *m.* (bot.) raspberry bush. —*f.* (bot.) raspberry.
sanguífero, ra, *a.* blood-bearing (vein).
sanguificación, *f.* (med.) hematosis.
sanguificar, (*ref. 50*) *tr.v.* to produce blood from.
sanguijuela, *f.* 1. (zool.) leech. 2. (fig., coll.) leech, pest; sponger.
sanguina, *f.* 1. sanguine (red crayon). 2. blood orange.
sanguinaria, *f.* 1. (min.) bloodstone. 2. **s. mayor,** (bot.) knotgrass; **s. menor,** (bot.) whitlowwort.
sanguinariamente, *adv.* sanguinarily, bloodily.
sanguinario, ria, *a.* sanguinary, cruel, bloodthirsty.
sanguíneo, a, *a.* 1. pertaining to blood, e.g. *corriente sanguínea,* blood stream, *grupo sanguíneo,* blood group, *presión sanguínea,* blood pressure, *vaso sanguíneo,* blood vessel. 2. blood-red, blood-colored.
sanguino, na, *a.* blood-red. —*m.* 1. (bot.) alaternus, buckthorn. 2. (bot.) dogwood tree.
sanguinolencia, *f.* sanguinolency.
sanguinolento, ta, *a.* sanguinolent, bloody, stained with blood.
sanguinoso, sa, *a.* 1. sanguineous, bloody. 2. sanguinary, bloodthirsty.
sanguiñuelo, *m.* (bot.) dogwood tree.
sanguis, *m.* (ecc.) blood of Christ; consecrated wine.
sanguisorba, *f.* (bot.) salad burnet, pimpernel.
sanícula, *f.* (bot.) sanicle.
sanidad, *f.* health, healthiness, soundness; **en s.,** in perfect health; **carnet de s.,** health certificate; **inspección de s.,** health inspection; **s. pública,** health department, Board of Health.
sanidina, *f.* (min.) sanidine.
sanidinita, *f.* (geol.) sanidinite.
sanie, sanies, *f.* (med.) sanies.
sanioso, sa, *a.* (med.) sanious.
sanitario, ria, *a.* sanitary; hygienic; **estación sanitaria,** medical or health station; **instalaciones sanitarias,** sanitary installations; **medidas sanitarias,** health measures; **toalla sanitaria,** sanitary napkin. —*m.* military health officer.
San José, *m.* San José, capital of Costa Rica.
San Juan, *m.* San Juan, capital of Puerto Rico.
sanjuanada, *f.* celebration on St. John's Day.
sanjuanero, ra, *a.* ripe by St. John's Day (said of fruit).
sanjuanista, *a.* of the Order of Saint John of Jerusalem. —*m.* Knight of the Order of Saint John of Jerusalem.
sanmiguelada, *f.* Michaelmastide.
sanmigueleño, ña, *a.* ripe by St. Michael's Day (said of fruit).
sano, na, *a.* 1. healthy; wholesome; sound. 2. unbroken, undamaged, whole. 3. honest, discreet; wise; safe. — **cortar por lo sano,** to use drastic measures or remedies; **s. y salvo,** safe and sound.
San Salvador, *m.* San Salvador, capital of El Salvador.
sanscritista, *m., f.* Sanskritist.
sánscrito, ta, *a., m.* Sanskrit.
sanseacabó, (coll.) that's the end of it, e.g. *he dicho que no voy a ir y s.,* I've said that I'm not going and that's the end of it.
sansimoniano, na, *a., m., f.* Saint-Simonian.
sansimonismo, *m.* Saint-Simonianism.
sansirolé, *m., f.* (coll.) nincompoop, simpleton, nitwit, fool.
Sansón, *m.* 1. (Bib.) Samson. 2. Samson, man of extraordinary physical strength.
santa, *f.* 1. female saint. 2. (fig.) saint (self-sacrificing or godly woman).
santabárbara, *f.* (mar.) powder magazine.
santafesino, na, *a.* of or from Santa Fe (Argentina). —*m., f.* native or inhabitant of Santa Fe.
santaláceo, a, *a.* (bot.) santalaceous. —*f.* (*pl.*) (bot.) Santalaceae.
santalina, *f.* (chem.) santalin.
santamente, *adv.* in a saintly manner; virtuously.
santanderiense, santanderino, na, *a.* of or from Santander. —*m., f.* inhabitant or native of Santander.
Santelmo, *m.* **fuego de S.,** (mar.) St. Elmo's fire.
santero, ra, *a.* image-worshipping. —*m., f.* 1. sanctuary keeper. 2. seller of religious images and objects. 3. (Cuba) witch doctor; medicine man or woman.
Santiago, *m.* Santiago, capital of Chile.
santiago, *interj.* charge! (battle cry of medieval Spaniards fighting the Saracens). —*m.* **S. el Mayor,** Saint James the Greater; **S. el Menor,** Saint James the Less.
santiagueño, ña, *a.* 1. ripe by St. James' Day (said of fruit).
santiaguero, ra, *a.* of or from Santiago de Cuba. —*m., f.* native or inhabitant of Santiago de Cuba.
santiagués, sa, *a.* of or from Santiago de Compostela, Spain. —*m., f.* native or inhabitant of Santiago de Compostela.
santiaguino, na, *a.* of or from Santiago de Chile. —*m., f.* native or inhabitant of Santiago de Chile.
santiaguista, *a.* pertaining to the Order of St. James. —*m.* Knight of the Order of St. James.
santiamén, en un s., (coll.) in a jiffy.
santico, ca, ito, ita, *m., f.* (coll.) good little boy or girl; small sculpture or image of a saint.
santidad, *f.* sanctity, holiness, saintliness; **Su S.,** His Holiness (the Pope).
santificable. *a.* sanctifiable.
santificación, *f.* sanctification; hallowing; keeping holy.
santificador, ra, *a.* sanctifying; hallowing. —*m., f.* sanctifier; hallower.
santificante, *a.* sanctifying; hallowing.
santificar, (*ref. 50*) *tr.v.* to sanctify; to hallow; to make holy; **santificado sea tu nombre,** hallowed be thy name; **s. las fiestas,** (to) keep the Sabbath and holy days. —*r.v.* (coll.) to justify or exculpate oneself.
santifique, santifiqué, *ref.* **santificar.**
santiguada, *f.* 1. making the sign of the cross, crossing oneself; sign of the cross. 2. maltreatment, rough treatment. — **para** or **por mi s.,** upon my faith, upon my soul.

santiguadera, *f.* attempt to heal by meaningless incantation accompanying signs of the cross.
santiguador, ra, *m., f.* quack, fake healer.
santiguamiento, *m.* crossing oneself.
santiguar, (*ref. 52*) *tr.v* 1. to make the sign of the cross upon. 2. to attempt to heal by blessing. 3. (coll.) to beat, maltreat. —*r.v.* 1. to make the sign of the cross, cross oneself. 2. (coll.) to marvel, wonder.
santimonia, *f.* 1. holiness, saintliness. 2. (bot.) chrysanthemum.
santiscario, *m.* **de mi s.,** of my own invention.
santísimo, ma, *a. super. of* **santo,** very or most holy; **Santísima Virgen,** Blessed Virgin. —*m.* Holy Sacrament.
santo, ta, *a.* 1. holy, saintly, hallowed, sacred, blessed, e.g. *Santa Iglesia Católica,* Holy Catholic Church, *Semana Santa,* Holy Week, *Tierra Santa,* Holy Land; saint (used in front of four *m.* names — Tomás, Tomé, Toribio and Domingo, e.g. *Santo Tomás,* Saint Thomas). 2. (coll.) blessed, e.g. *todo el santo día,* the whole blessed day. the whole livelong day; **santo y bueno,** well and good. —*m., f.* saint. —*m.* 1. image or picture of a saint. 2. (coll.) picture, illustration. 3. saint's day, name day. 4. (mil.) password, watchword. — **alzarse** or **cargar con el s. y la limosna,** to make off with everything, take everything but the kitchen sink; **a s. de,** because of, under the pretext of; **¿a s. de qué?** for what reason or motive?; **desnudar a un s. para vestir a otro,** to rob Peter to pay Paul; **írsele a uno el s. al cielo,** (coll.) to forget what one was about to say; **Santa Sede,** Holy See; **S. Grial,** Holy Grail; **s. patrón** or **titular,** patron saint; **s. titular, s. y seña,** (mil.) password, watchword; **tener el s. de espaldas,** (coll.) to do nothing right.
Santo Domingo, *m.* Santo Domingo, capital of the Dominican Republic.
santol, *m.* (bot.) santol, sandal tree.
santón, *m.* 1. Mohammedan hermit or ascetic. 2. (coll.) hypocrite. 3. (coll.) influential man.
santónico, *m.* (bot.) santonica, wormwood.
santonina, *f.* (chem.) santonin.
santoral, *m.* 1. calendar of saints' days. 2. choir book. 3. book of the lives of the saints.
santuario, *m.* 1. sanctuary. 2. (Col.) treasure.
santucho, cha, *a., m., f., var. of* **santurrón.**
santulón, na, *a., m., f., var. of* **santurrón.**
santurrón, na, *a.* sanctimonious, affectedly devout or pious. —*m., f.* sanctimonious person; hypocrite.
santurronería, *f.* sanctimoniousness, sanctimony; hypocrisy.
saña, *f.* 1. rage, fury. 2. brutality, cruelty.
sañosamente, sañudamente, *adv.* 1. furiously. 2. brutally, cruelly.
sañudo, da, *a.* furious; brutal, cruel.
sao, *m.* 1. (bot.) phillyrea, mook privet. 2. (Cuba) small savannah with clusters of trees or bushes.
sapa, *f.* residue of chewing paste made of betel leaf, nut and lime.
sapán, *m.* (bot.) sapanwood, brazilwood.
sapaneco, ca, *a.* (Hond.) chubby, stocky, tubby.
sapidez, *f.* sapidity, taste, flavorsomeness, savoriness.
sápido, da *a.* sapid, flavorsome, savory.
sapiencia, *f.* 1. sapience, wisdom. 2. (Bib.) **S.,** Book of Wisdom, Wisdom of Solomon.
sapiencial, *a.* sapiential.
sapiente, *a.* sapient, wise. —*m., f.* **sage,** wise person.
sapientísimamente, *adv.* learnedly, most wisely.
sapillo, *m.* 1. little toad. 2. (med.) ranula (tumor); (Cuba) mouth sore (in nursing infants).
sapina, *f.* (bot.) saltwort.
sapindáceo, a, (bot.) *a.* sapindaceous. —*f. (pl.)* Sapindaceae.
sapino, *m.* (bot.) fir, fir tree.
sapo, *m.* 1. (zool.) toad. 2. (coll.) (any) animal, beast. 3. (C. Amer.) toadfish. 4. (Chile) fluke, stroke of luck. 5. (Chile, Mex.) scoundrel. — **echar sapos y culebras,** (coll.) to talk nonsense; to be abusive, talk abusively; **s. marino,** (ichth.) angler; **s. partero,** (zool.) obstetrical toad.
saponáceo, a, *a.* saponaceous, soapy.
saponaria, *f.* (bot.) soapwort.
saponificable, *a.* saponifiable, able to be made into soap.
saponificación, *f.* saponification, conversion into soap.
saponificar, (*ref. 50*) *tr.v.* to saponify, make into soap. —*r.v.* to turn into soap.
saponifique, saponifiqué, *ref.* **saponificar.**
saponina, *f.* (chem.) saponin.
saponita, *f.* (min.) saponite.
saporífero, ra, *a.* saporific, able to cause taste.
saporro, rra *a.* (Amer.) tubby, chubby.
sapotáceo, a, *a.* (bot.) sapotaceous. —*f. (pl.)* Sapotaceae.
sapote, *m.* (bot.) *var. of* **zapote.**
saprófito, *m.* (biol.) saprophyte.
saprolita, *f.* (geol.) saprolite.
saprozoico, ca, *a.* (biol.) saprozoic.
saque, *m.* serve, service (in tennis, etc.); service line; server; **s. de meta,** goal kick (in soccer); **s. inicial,** kickoff; **tener buen s.,** (coll.) to be a heavy eater or drinker.
saque, saqué, *ref.* **sacar.**
saqueador, ra, *a.* sacking, plundering, looting. —*m., f.* plunderer, looter.
saqueamiento, *m.* sacking, plundering, pillaging.
saquear, *tr.v.* to sack, plunder, loot, pillage.
saqueo, *m.* sack, sacking, plundering, pillaging.
saquera, *a.* packing (needle).
saquería, *f.* manufacture of sacks; sacks, group of sacks.
saquerío, *m.* sacks (collectively).
saquero, ra, *m., f.* sack maker or seller.
saquete, *m. dim. of* **saco,** small sack; (mil.) cartridge bag.
saquilada, *f.* contents of a bag which is not full.
S.A.R. *abbrev. of* **Su Alteza Real,** Her or His Royal Highness (HRH).
Sara, *f.* (Bib.) Sarah, Abraham's wife.
saraguate, *m.* (C. Amer.) howler monkey.
saragüete, *m.* (coll.) family party, small party, informal get-together.
sarampión, *m.* (med.) measles.
sarao, *m.* soirée, evening party.
sarape, *m.* (Mex.) serape, Mexican heavy shawl or small blanket.
sarapia, *f.* (Amer.) tonka bean (fruit and tree).
sarapico, *m.* (ornith.) curlew.
sarasa, *m.* (coll.) pansy, effeminate man.
saraviado, da, *a.* (Col., Ven.) speckled, spotted.
sarazo, *a.* (Col., Cuba, Mex., Ven.) ripening (corn).
sarcasmo, *m.* sarcasm.
sarcásticamente, *adv.* sarcastically.
sarcástico, ca, *a.* sarcastic.
sarcia, *f.* load, burden.
sarcillo, *m.* weeding hoe.
sarcocarpio, *m.* (bot.) sarcocarp.
sarcocele, *m.* (med.) sarcocele.
sarcocola, *f.* sarcocolla, sarcocolla gum.
sarcófago, *m.* sarcophagous, stone casket or coffin.
sarcoideo, a, *a,* (biol.) sarcoid.
sarcolema, *m.* (anat.) sarcolemma.
sarcoma, *f.* (med.) sarcoma.
sarcomatoso, sa, *a.* sarcomatous.
sarcótico, ca, *a., m.* (med.) sarcotic.
sarda, *f.* (ichth.) horse mackerel.
sardana, *f.* sardana (folk dance of Catalonia).
sardesco, ca, *a.* 1. small (horse or pony). 2. (coll.) gruff, surly; brazen. —*m.* small ass or horse, pony.
sardiano, na, *a., m., f.* (hist.) Sardian.
sardina, *f.* (ichth.) sardine; **como sardinas** en lata, packed like sardines.
sardinal, *m.* sardine net.
sardinel, *m.* (mas.) rowlock.
sardinero, ra, *a.* pertaining to sardines. —*m., f.* sardine dealer.
sardineta, *f.* 1. *dim. of* **sardina,** small sardine. 2. cheese overtopping the vat. 3. (mil.) pointed two-stripe chevron.
sardio, *m.* (min.) sardonyx.
sardo, da, *a., m., f.* Sardinian. —*m.* Sardinian (language).
sardo, da *a.* spotted red, white and black (cattle).
sardonia, *a.* **risa s.,** sardonic (grin or laugh). —*f.* (bot.) Sardinian herb.
sardónica, sardónice, *f.* (min.) sardonyx.
sardónico, ca, *a.* 1. sardonic (laugh or grin). 2. sardonic, ironic, sarcastic.
sardonio, *m.,* **sardónique,** *f.* (min.) sardonyx.
sarga, *f.* 1. (tex.) serge. 2. painted wall frabric. 3. (bot.) willow.
sargadilla, *f.* (bot.) sea blite (Suaeda splendens).
sargado, da, *a.* (tex.) serge-like.
sargal, *m.* willow grove, clump of willows.
sargatillo, *m.* (bot.) variety of willow.
sargazo, *m.* (bot.) sargasso, gulfweed.
sargenta, *f.* 1. sargeant's wife. 2. (coll.) hefty, coarse woman. 3. sargeant's halberd.
sargentear, *tr.v.* 1. to command as a sargeant. 2. (coll.) to boss, bark orders at. 3. to direct, manage, lead, command.
sargentería, *f.* (mil.) sergeant's drill.
sargentía, *f.* rank of sergeant.
sargento, *m.* sergeant.
sargentona, *f.* (coll.) hefty, coarse woman.
sargo, *m.* (ichth.) sargo.
sarguero, ra, *a.* willowy. —*m.* painter of wall fabrics.
sargueta, *f.* (tex.) light serge.
sariama, *f.* (S. Amer., ornith.) crested seriema.
sarilla, *f.* (bot.) marjoram.
sármata, *a., m., f.* (hist.) Sarmatian.
sarmático, ca, *a.* (hist.) Sarmatic, Sarmatian.
sarmentador, ra, *m., f.* gatherer of vine shoots.
sarmentar, (*ref. 29*) *i.v.* to gather pruned vine shoots.
sarmentazo, *m.* 1. *aug. of* **sarmiento, large** vine shoot. 2. lash with vine shoot.
sarmentera, *f.* gathering of vine shoots; place where vine shoots are stored.
sarmenticio, cia, *a.* Christian (applied to early Christians burned at the stake by slow fire).
sarmentillo, *m.* slender vine shoot.
sarmentoso, sa, *a.* 1. vine-like, twining. 2. (bot.) sarmentose, sarmentous.
sarmiente, sarmiento, *ref.* **sarmentar.**
sarmiento, *m.* vine shoot.
sarna, *f.* (itch.) mange, scabies; **más viejo que la s.,** as old as the hills, as old as Methuselah; **s. de los barberos,** barber's itch.
sarnazo, *m. aug. of* **sarna,** persistent itch.
sarnoso, sa, *a.* itchy, mangy.
sarpullido, *m.* (med.) rash, skin eruption.
sarpullir, (*ref. 65*) *tr.v.* to cause a rash to.
sarraceniáceo, a, *a.* (bot.) sarraceniaceous. —*f. (pl.)* Sarraceniaceae.
sarracénico, ca, *a.* (hist.) Saracenic, Saracen.

sarraceno, na, sarracín, na, *a., m., f.* (hist.) Saracen.
sarracina, *f.* scuffle, free-for-all.
Sarre, *m.* Saar; **Territorio del Sarre,** Saarland.
sarria, *f.* 1. coarse net for carrying straw. 2. (Sp., reg.) large basket.
sarrillo, *m.* 1. death rattle. 2. (bot.) arum.
sarro, *m.* 1. deposit, crust (left on vessels); fur (on tongue); tartar (on teeth). 2. (bot.) rust, mildew.
sarroso, sa, *a.* covered with a deposit or crust; furry (tongue); covered with tartar (teeth).
sarta, *f.* string (of beads, pearls, etc.); line, series; **una s. de mentiras,** a string of lies.
sartal, *m.* string (of beads, pearls, etc.).
sartalejo, *m. dim. of* **sartal,** small string (of beads).
sartén, *f.* frying pan, skillet; frying panful; saltar **del s. y caer en las brasas,** to jump from the frying pan into the fire; **tener la s. por el mango,** to have the upper hand, be in control.
sartenada, *f.* contents of a frying pan, as much as can be fried at one time in a skillet.
sartenazo, *m.* blow with a frying pan; (coll.) hard blow.
sarteneja, *f.* 1. *dim. of* **sartén,** small frying pan. 2. (S. Amer.) crack, split, fissure (in ground, caused by drought).
sartorio, a, *a.* (anat.) sartorial, sartorius. *—m.* (anat.) sartorius, sartorius muscle.
sasafrás, *m.* (bot.) sassafras.
sasánida, *a., m.* (hist.) Sassanian, Sasanian, Sassanid.
sastra, *f.* tailor's wife; female tailor.
sastre, *m.* tailor; **traje s.,** (woman's) tailored suit.
sastrería, *f.* tailor's shop; tailor's trade.
Satán, Satanás, *m.* Satan.
satánicamente, *adv.* satanically.
satánico, ca, *a.* Satanic.
satélite, *m.* 1. (astron.) satellite. 2. satellite, minion, follower, sycophant. 3. (pol.) satellite (country dependant on another). — **s. de communicaciones,** communications satellite; **s. espía,** spy satellite; **s. metereológico,** metereological satellite, weather satellite.
satén, *m.* (tex) satin.
satín, *m.* satinwood.
satinado, da, *past part. of* **satinar.** *—a.* satiny, like satin. *—m.* satin finish. — **papel satinado,** (print.) coated paper.
satinador, ra, *a.* glazing, calending. *—m., f.* glazer, calender. *—m.* (photog.) burnisher.
satinar, *tr.v.* 1. to glaze, calender. 2. (photog.) to burnish.
sátira, *f.* 1. satire. 2. mordant remark. 3. (coll.) vixen.
satiriasis, *f.* (med.) satyriasis.
satíricamente, *adv.* satirically; sarcastically.
satirice, satiricé, *ref.* **satirizar.**
satírico, ca, *a.* satirical; sarcastic. *—m.* satirist.
satirio, *m.* (zool.) water rat.
satirión, *m.* (bot.) salep-yielding orchid.
satirizante, *a.* satirizing.
satirizar, (*ref. 53*) *tr.v.* to satirize, to lampoon. *—i.v.* to write satires.
sátiro, *m.* (myth.) satyr; (fig.) satyr (lascivious man).
satisdación, *f.* (law) surety, security, bail.
satisfacción, *f.* 1. satisfaction, content, pleasure, gratification. 2. satisfaction, apology, excuse; amends. 3. self-satisfaction, conceit. — **a s.,** fully; according to one's wishes; **a s. de,** to the satisfaction of; **s. propia,** conceit.
satisfacer, (*ref. 10*) *tr.v.* 1. to satisfy, gratify, please. 2. to expiate, atone for, make amends for. 3. to indemnify, repay; to reward. 4. to answer, reply. 5. to explain; to convince. *—r.v.* 1. to be satisfied, to satisfy oneself. 2. to convince oneself. 3. to get satisfaction, get one's revenge.
satisfaciente, *a.* satisfying, satisfactory.
satisfactoriamente, *adv.* satisfactorily.
satisfactorio, ria *a.* satisfactory.
satisfaga, satisfago, *ref.* **satisfacer.**
satisfecho, cha, *past part. of* **satisfacer.** *—a.* 1. satisfied, content. 2. vain, conceited.
satisfice, satisficiera, satisfizo, *ref.* **satisfacer.**
sato, *m.* (Cuba) mongrel dog.
sátrapa, *m.* 1. satrap, governor in ancient Persia. 2. (coll.) crafty fellow. *—a.* (coll.) sly, crafty.
satrapía, *f.* (hist.) satrapy.
saturable, *a.* capable of being saturated.
saturación, *f.* 1. saturation. 2. (fig.) glutting.
saturador, ra, *a.* saturating. *—m.* saturator.
saturante, *a.* (chem.) saturant.
saturar, *tr.v.* 1. to saturate. 2. (fig.) to fill, glut, sate, satiate. *—r.v.* 1. to become saturated. 2. (fig.) to become sated.
saturnal, *a.* Saturnian; Saturnalisn. *—f.* 1. orgy, saturnalia. 2. (*pl.*) Saturnalia, festival of Saturn.
saturnino, na, *a.* 1. saturnine, melancholy, gloomy, sullen. 2. (chem.) saturnine (pertaining to lead). 3. (med.) lead, saturnine (e.g. poisoning).
saturnio, nia, *a.* Saturnian.
saturnismo, *m.* (med.) saturnism, lead poisoning.
Saturno, *m.* 1. (myth., astron.) Saturn. 2. (chem.) lead.
sauce, *m.* (bot.) willow; **s. blanco,** white willow; **s. cabruno,** goat willow; **s. de Bailonia, s. llorón,** weeping willow.
sauceda, *f.,* **saucedal,** *m.,* **saucera,** *f.* willow grove.
saucillo, *m.* (bot.) knotgrass.
saúco, *m.* 1. (bot.) elder tree, elderberry. 2. second layer of horse's hoof.
saudade, *f.* homesickness, nostalgia.
sauquillo, *m.* (bot.) dwarf elder, snowball, guelder rose.
saurio, ria, *a.* (zool.) saurian. *—m.* (zool. saurian; (*pl.*) Sauria.
sausería, *f.* palace larder or pantry.
sausier, *m.* palace pantry steward or seneschal.
sautor, *m.* (her.) saltier.
sauz, (*pl.* **sauces**), *m.* (bot.) willow.
sauzal, *m.* willow grove.
sauzgatillo, *m.* (bot.) agnus castus, chaste tree.
savia, *f.* sap (of a plant); (fig.) sap, energy, vitality.
saxafrax, *f., var. of* **saxífraga.**
saxátil, *a.* saxatile, saxicolous, growing among rocks.
saxífraga, *f.* 1. (bot.) saxifrage. 2. (bot.) sassafras.
saxifragáceo, a, *a.* (bot.) saxifragaceous. *—f.* (*pl.*) Saxifragaceae.
saxifragia, *f., var. of* **saxífraga.**
saxofón, saxófono, *m.* (mus.) saxophone; **s. tenor,** tenor sax; **s. barítono,** baritone sax.
saxofonista, *m., f.* saxophone player, saxophonist.
saya, *f.* 1. skirt; lower part of a dress; petticoat. 2. (hist.) tunic worn by men in ancient Greece and Rome.
sayal, *m.* coarse woolen cloth.
sayalería, *f.* weaving of coarse woolen cloth.
sayalero, ra, *m., f.* weaver of coarse woolen cloth.
sayalesco, ca, *a.* made of coarse woolen cloth.
sayalete, *m.* light woolen cloth (for undergarments).
sayo, *m.* smock, frock; cassock, loose coat; (coll.) dress, garment, tunic. — **s. baquero,** smock buttoned at the back; **s. bobo,** buttoned-down tights formerly worn by clowns; **cortar un s.,** (coll.) to talk behind (someone's) back; **decir para su s.,** to say to oneself.
sayón, *m.* 1. (in Middle Ages) bailiff, constable. 2. executioner. 3. member of a brotherhood wearing a long tunic in processions. 4. (coll.) fierce-looking fellow.
sayuela, *f.* woolen shirt (worn by some religious orders); (Cuba) petticoat, underskirt.
sazón, *f.* 1. seasoning, flavoring. 2. time, occasion, opportunity. 3. season, time of maturity, ripeness or greatest quality (of fruit, etc.). — **a la s.,** at that time, then; **en s.,** in season, ripe; opportunely; **estar en s.,** to be in season; **tener buena s.,** (Amer.) to be a good cook; to be well-seasoned, to taste good.
sazonadamente, *adv.* seasonably, maturely.
sazonado, da, *a.* 1. tasty, flavorsome, seasoned. 2. ripe, mellow. 3. witty, expressive.
sazonador, ra, *a.* 1. seasoning. 2. ripening.
sazonar, *tr.v.* 1. to season, flavor. 2. to ripen, mature. *—r.v.* to become ripe or mature.
Sb *sym. of* **antimonio,** stibium-antimony (Sb).
Sc. *sym. of* **escandio,** scandium (Sc).
se, *third person form of reflexive pronoun.* 1. equivalent to: "himself, herself, itself, oneself, yourself, themselves, yourselves"; "to himself, to herself, etc.", e.g. *la cocinera se ha quemado,* the cook has burned herself; *el perro se rasca,* the dog scratches itself; *él se dijo,* he said to himself; *los estudiantes se comportan,* the students behave themselves. 2. equivalent to: "each other, one another," e.g. *mis primos se detestan,* my cousins detest each other. 3. to impart possessive value to the *def.* or *indef. article,* e.g. *ella se pinta el pelo,* she dyes her hair; *se cambiaron la ropa,* they changed their clothes. 4 as an expletive forming verbs reflexive only in form, not in meaning, e.g. *el plato se rompió,* the plate broke; *ellos se fueron,* they left, they went away. 5. to form expressions of impersonal or passive sense, e.g. *se espera,* it is expected, it is awaited; *se entiende,* it is understood; *aquí se habla inglés,* English (is) spoken here. — the imperative form of *se* in impersonal expressions is generally rendered by the simple imperative: *sírvase bien frío,* serve very cold; *consúltese un médico,* consult a physician. *—pers. pronoun* equivalent to "to him, to her, to it, to you, to them," used instead of *le* or *les* in the presence of another pers. pronoun, e.g. *se lo di a ella,* I gave it to her.
sé, *ref.* **saber.**
Se *sym. of* **selenio,** selenium (Se).
SE *abbrev. of* **sudeste,** southeast (SE).
S. E. *abbrev. of* **1. salvo errores, errors** excepted (EE). **2. Su Excelencia,** His Her, Your Excellency.
sea, *ref.* **ser.**
sabáceo, a, *a.* sebaceous.
sebastiano, *m., var. of* **sebestén.**
sebe, *f.* high wattle fence.
sebestén, *m.* (bot.) sebesten tree; sebesten plum.
sebillo, *m.* 1. soft light tallow. 2. soft creamy hand soap.
sebista, *m.* (Arg.) loafer, layabout, bum.
sebo, *m.* 1. tallow; fat, grease. 2. (Peru) gift requested from godfather or godmother by children.
seboro, *m.* (Bol., zool.) river crab.
seborrea, *f.* (med.) seborrhea.
seboruco, *m.* 1. (Cuba) porous limestone rock; large stone, rock. 2. (Cuba, coll.) dolt; stupid person. 3. (Mex.) rocky place. 4. (P. Rico) open country.
seboso, sa, *a.* tallowy; greasy, fatty; unctuous.
sebucán, *m.* (Cuba, Ven.) manioc strainer.
seca, *f.* 1. drought; dry season. 2. (med.) infarct, infarction (of a gland). 3. drying up of pustules of certain skin diseases. 4. dry sand bank.
secácul, *m.* (bot.) parsnip (Pastinaca sekakul).
secadal, *m.* 1. dry barren land. 2. dry sand bank.

secadero, ra, *a.* dry, easily kept dry; fit for drying (fruit, tobacco, etc.). —*m.* drying place, drying room or shed.
secadillo, *m.* almond meringue.
secador, ra, *a.* drying. —*m.* dryer; dish towel. —*f.* dryer; hair dryer.
secamente, *adv.* dryly, curtly, coldly, sharply.
secamiento, *m.* drying; withering; desiccation.
secano, *m.* dry barren land; dry sand bank; anything very dry.
secansa, *f.* sequence (in cards).
secante, *a.* drying, blotting, e.g. *papel secante,* blotting paper. —*m.* 1. blotting paper; siccative. 2. drying oil. —*f.* (geom. secant.
secar, (*ref. 50*) *tr.v.* 1. to dry; to wipe dry, dry up; to wither. 2. to annoy, vex, bore. —*r.v.* 1. to get dry; to dry oneself; to dry up; to wither. 2. to become thin or shrunken. 3. to be thirsty.
secaral, *m.* dry barren soil.
secatón, na, *a.* dull, insipid.
secatura, *f.* dullness, inanity, insipidity.
sección, *f.* 1. section; department, division. 2. portion, slice. 3. (geom., mil., surg.) section. — **s. de anuncios,** advertising section (in a newspaper); **s. transversal,** cross section.
seccionado, da, *a.* separated, sectional.
seccionador, *m.* (elec.) section or isolating switch.
seccionar, *tr.v.* to section; to cut or divide into sections; to cut off.
seccionario, ria, *a.* sectional.
secesión, *f.* secession.
secesionista, *a., m., f.* secessionist.
seceso, *m.* stool, bowel movement.
seco, ca, *a.* 1. dry, dried up. 2. dried (fruit). 3. dry (season; wine; cough). 4. dry, laconic, curt; indifferent, cold. 5. dull, dead (sound, knock). 6. withered, dead (plant, tree). 7. plain, unadorned. 8. lean, thin, dried up. 9. strict (justice, truth). 10. sterile, arid (mind, imagination). — **a secas,** plainly, simply, just, e.g. *llámame Roberto a secas,* just call me Robert; **en seco,** (to stop) dead; (mas.) dry, without mortar; high and dry; without cause or reason; without resources; **estar seco,** to be sound asleep; **ley seca,** (U.S.) Prohibition; **limpiar en seco,** to dry-clean; **¡seco y volteado!** bottoms up! down the hatch! your health! —*m.* 1. (Chile) sharp blow, punch. 2. (Chile) knock given by one spinning top to another.
secoya, *f.* (bot.) sequoia.
secreción, *f.* secretion.
secreta, *f.* 1. licenciate's examination (in some universities). 2. secret investigation. 3. (ecc.) secret (prayer). 4. (coll.) secret police. 5. (rare) privy, water closet.
secretamente, *adv.* secretly.
secretar, *tr.v.* (physiol.) to secrete.
secretaria, *f.* woman secretary; wife of a secretary.
secretaría, *f.* secretariat; secretaryship; secretary's office; government office, department or ministry (in some countries).
secretariado, *m., var. of* **secretaría.**
secretario, ria, *m.* 1. secretary. 2. (ornith.) secretary bird.
secretear, *i.v.* (coll.) to whisper, talk in secret, talk confidentially.
secreteo, *m.* (coll.) whispering, confidential talk.
secreter, *m.* writing desk, secretary.
secretico, illo, ito, *m. dim. of* **secreto,** little secret.
secretina, *f.* (biochem.) secretin.
secretista, *m., f.* 1. naturalist. 2. whisperer, secretmonger.
secreto, ta, *a.* 1. secret; confidential, private. 2. secret, hidden, covert. —*m.* 1. secret; secrecy. 2. key (combination for opening a lock). 3. (mus.) soundboard. — **con s.,** with secrecy, secretively; **en s.,** in secret, secretly; **s. a voces,** (coll.) open secret; **s. de alcoba,** intimate secret; **s. de confesión,** secret of the confessional; **s. de Estado,** state secret; **s. commercial** or **industrial, s. de fábrica,** trade secret.
secretor, ra, secretorio, ria, *a.* (physiol.) secretory, secreting.
secta, *f.* sect.
sectador, ra, sectario, ria, *a., m., f.* sectarian, sectary.
sectarismo, *m.* sectarianism.
sectilidad, *f.* (geol.) sectility.
sector, *m.* 1. sector, section, quarter. 2. (geom., astron., mil.) sector.
secua, *f.* (Cuba, bot.) rattan (Fevillea cordifolia).
secuaz, (*pl.* **secuaces**), *a.* partisan. —*m., f.* follower, partisan.
secuela, *f.* 1. sequel, result, upshot; aftermath.
secuencia, *f.* (ecc., mus., geol.) sequence.
secuestrable, *a.* (law) sequestrable.
secuestración, *f.* 1. (law) sequestration. 2. kidnapping.
secuestrador, ra, *m., f.* 1. hijacker. 2. kidnapper, abductor. 3. (law) sequestrator.
secuestrar, *tr.v.* 1. to hijack (esp. an airplane). 2. to kidnap, to abduct. 3. (law) to sequester, sequestrate.
secuestro, *m.* 1. hijacking. 2. kidnapping, abduction. 3. (law) sequestration; sequestered property. 4. (med.) sequestrum (dead portion of a bone). 5. arbiter, umpire.
secular, *a.* 1. secular, lay, temporal. 2. secular, centenary, centennial.
secularice, secularicé, *ref.* **secularizar.**
secularización, *f.* secularization.
secularizar, (*ref. 53*) *tr.v.* to secularize. —*r.v.* to become secularized.
secundar, *tr.v.* to second, to support, to aid.
secundariamente, *adv.* secondarily.
secundario, ria, *a.* secondary; high (school). —*m.* (elec.) secondary (coil or circuit).
secundinas, *f.* (*pl.*) secundines, afterbirth.
secundípara, *a.* secundiparous. —*f.* secundipara.
secura, *f.* dryness, condition of drought.
sed, *f.* thirst; (fig.) thirst, longing, eager desire; **apagar** or **matar la s.,** to quench one's thirst; **tener s.,** to be thirsty; **tener s. de,** to be thirsty for, have a thirst for.
seda, *f.* 1. silk (fabric, yarn, fibre). 2. wild boar's bristles. — **como una s.,** (coll.) smooth as silk; easy as pie, with no difficulty whatsoever; **papel de s.,** tissue paper; **s. de azache,** low quality silk; **s. conchal,** choice silk; **s. cruda,** raw silk; **s. de candongo** or **de candongos,** raw silk; **s. dental,** dental floss; **s. en bruto** or **en rama,** raw silk; **s. floja,** floss silk, untwisted silk; **s. negra,** raw silk; **s. torcida,** twisted silk; **s. verde,** silk from cocoon with the silkworm still alive; **ser una s.,** to be sweet and easy (to get along with).
sedación, *f.* soothing, calming.
sedadera, *f.* hackle (for dressing flax).
sedal, *m.* 1. fishing line. 2. (vet.) rowel; (surg.) seton.
sedalina, *f.* (tex.) silkaline, silkalene.
sedán, *m.* (auto.) sedan.
sedante, *a., m.* sedative.
sedar, *tr.v.* to soothe, quiet, allay.
sedativo, va, *a.* (med.) sedative.
sede, *f.* seat; headquarters; (ecc.) see; **s. provisional,** temporary headquarters; **Santa S.,** Holy See; **s. apostólica,** Apostolic See.
sedear, *tr.v.* to brush (jewels), clean with a brush.
sedentario, ria, *a.* sedentary; (zool.) sedentary. —*m.* (*pl.*) Sedentaria.
sedeña, *f.* fine tow of flax; tow cloth.
sedeño, ña, *a.* silky, silken.
sedera, *f.* bristle brush.
sedería, *f.* 1. silks; silk goods. 2. silk trade or business. 3. fine yard goods store.
sedero, ra, *a.* silk. —*m., f.* silk weaver; silk mercer; silk dealer.
sediciente, *a.* self-styled, e.g. *un escritor s.,* a self-styled writer.
sedición, *f.* sedition, insurrection, rebellion, uprising.
sediciosamente, *adv.* seditiously.
sedicioso, sa, *a.* seditious. —*m., f.* seditionary.
sediento, ta, *a.* 1. thirsty. 2. dry, parched. 3. (fig.) thirsty, eager, longing, e.g. *s. de,* thirsty or eager for.
sedimentación, *f.* sedimentation.
sedimentar, *tr.v.* to deposit as sediment. —*r.v.* to settle, deposit sediment.
sedimentario, ria, *a.* sedimental, sedimentary; (geol.) sedimentary.
sedimento, *m.* sediment, lees, dregs.
sedoso, sa, *a.* silky, silken.
seducción, *f.* 1. seduction; temptation, enticement, corruption. 2. charm, attraction.
seducir, (*ref. 47*) *tr.v.* 1. to seduce; to entice, tempt; to corrupt; to bribe. 2. to charm, captivate.
seductivo, va, *a.* seductive; enticing.
seductor, ra, *a.* seductive, captivating, charming; tempting, enticing. —*m., f.* seducer; charmer.
seduje, sedujera, sedujese, sedujo, seduzca, seduzco, *ref.* **seducir.**
sefardí, (*pl.* **sefardíes**), *a.* Sephardic. —*m., f.* Sephardi, Sephardic Jew, (*pl.*) Sephardim.
sefardita, *a., m., f. var. of* **sefardí.**
sefita, *f.* (geol.) psephite.
segada, *f., var. of* **siega.**
segadera, *f.* sickle.
segadero, ra, *a.* ready for harvesting or reaping.
segador, ra, *m., f.* 1. reaper, harvester, mower. 2. (ento.) harvestman, daddy longlegs.
segar, (*ref. 67*) *tr.v.* 1. to reap, mow, cut. 2. to cut off; to mow down. 3. to cut short (someone's life, the development of something, etc.). —*i.v.* to reap, mow.
segazón, *f.* harvest, reaping; harvest season.
seglar, *a.* secular; lay. —*m.* layman. —*f.* laywoman.
seglarmente, *adv.* secularly.
segmentación, *f.* segmentation; cleavage; **s. del óvulo,** (biol.) egg cleavage; **s. determinada,** (biol.) determinate cleavage.
segmentar, *tr.v.* to segment.
segmento, *m.* segment, part; (geom.) segment; **s. colector,** (elec.) commutator bar; commutator segment.
segoviano, na, segoviense, *a., m., f.* Segovian.
segregación, *f.* 1. segregation; separation. 2. (med.) secretion. — **s. racial,** racial segregation.
segregacionista, *m., f.* segregationalist.
segregado, da, *a.* separate, segregate.
segregar, (*ref. 51*) *tr.v.* 1. to segregate. 2. (med.) to secrete.
segregativo, va, *a.* segregative.
segregue, segregué, *ref.* **segregar.**
segrí, *m.* (tex.) heavy silk fabric.
segué, *ref.* **segar.**
segueta, *f.* marquetry saw, buhl saw; **s. mecánica,** power saw.
seguetear, *i.v.* to cut with a buhl saw.
seguida, *f.* succession, continuation; row, series. — **de s.,** continuously, without interruption; immediately; **en s.,** at once, immediately.
seguidamente, *adv.* 1. consecutively, successively. 2. immediately, forthwith. 3. below.
seguidero, *m.* guide line for writing.

seguidilla, *f.* 1. (poet.) seguidilla (Spanish stanza of four or seven verses). 2. (*pl.*) seguidillas, flamenco song and dance. 3. (coll.) (*pl.*) diarrhea.
seguido, da, *past part. of* **seguir.** —*a.* continued, successive; straight, direct; in a row, running, e.g. *dos semanas seguidas,* two weeks running. —*m.* diminishing stitch in stocking foot.
seguido, *adv.* continuously; consecutively; uninterruptedly.
seguidor, ra, *m., f.* follower. —*m.* guide line for writing.
seguimiento, *m.* 1. following; pursuit, chase, hunt. 2. continuation.
seguir, (*ref. 77*) *tr.v.* 1. to follow; to pursue, chase; to dog, hound. 2. to follow (course of studies). 3. to follow, obey (leader). 4. to follow, go by (instructions). 5. to follow, copy, imitate. —*i.v* 1. to follow, come or go after. 2. to continue; to keep on; continue to be, e.g. *sigue enfermo,* he is still ill, *sigue difícil,* he continues to be difficult; **s.** + *ger.,* to keep + *ger.,* continue + *ger.,* keep on + *ger.,* continue + *inf.* —*r.v.* to follow; to ensue; to issue, spring, originate.
según, *prep.* according to, e.g. *s. el maestro,* according to the teacher. —*conj.* as; according to how, depending on how; according to, depending on; **s. y como, s. y conforme,** just as, exactly as. —*adv.* depending on circumstances; **s. y como** or **conforme,** depending on circumstances.
segunda, *f.* 1. double turn (of a lock). 2. double meaning. 3. (mus.) second. 4. (auto.) second (gear), e.g. *sube el cerro en s.,* it takes the hill in second.
segundar, *tr.v.* 1. to repeat. 2. to second, assist, help. —*i.v.* to be second, follow after the first.
segundariamente, *adv., var. of* **secundariamente.**
segundario, ria, *a., var. of* **secundario.**
segundero, ra, *a.* second (crop, fruit in same year). —*m.* second hand (of a clock or watch).
segundilla, *f.* call bell (in convents).
segundillo, *m.* second serving of bread; second helping.
segundo, da, *a.* second; secondary; **de segunda intención,** on second thought; with hidden meaning; **de segunda mano,** second-hand; **segunda dama,** (theat.) second lead (female); **segunda enseñanza,** secondary education, high school; **segunda niñez,** second childhood; **segundo galán,** (theat.) second lead (male); **segunda mano,** second coat (of paint, etc.). —*m.* 1. second (sixtieth of a minute). 2. second in authority, assistant; **s. de a bordo,** (mar.) matc; **s. en mando,** (mil.) second-in-command. — **sin segundo,** peerles, matchless, without par.
segundogénito, ta, *a., m., f.* second-born.
segundogenitura, *f.* the right and condition of a second-born.
segundón, *m.* second son.
segur, *f.* 1. axe; sickle. 2. axe in fasces carried by lictors.
segurador, *m.* security; bondsman.
seguramente, *adv.* 1. surely; of course. 2. (coll.) probably, likely. 3. securely, safely.
seguridad, *f.* 1. safety; security; safety measures. 2. certainty, assurance. 3. surety bond. 1. police. — **agente de s.,** security police; **alfiler de s.,** safety pin; **cinturón de s.,** safety belt; **con toda s.,** with absolute certainty; very probably; **s. ciudadana,** public safety; **s. del estado,** national security; **s. social,** social security; **s. vial,** road safety; **tener la s. de que,** to be sure that.
seguro, ra, *a.* 1. safe; secure, steady, stable; reliable, dependable, firm, constant, staunch. 2. sure, certain, definite. —*m.* 1. insurance; insurance policy. 2. safety catch, safety latch. 3. security; certainty, assurance. 4. permit, warrant, license. — **a buen s., al s., de s.,** certainly, undoubtedly, truly; **en s.,** in safety; **s. contra accidentes,** accident insurance; **s. contra daños materiales,** property damage insurance; **s. de enfermedad,** medical insurance; **s. de incendios,** fire insurance; **s. sobre la vida,** life insurance; **s. social,** social security; **sobre s.,** without any risk.
segurón, *m. aug. of* **segur,** large axe.
seis, *a.* six; sixth (of the month). —*m.* 1. six. 2. sixth (in dates). 3. (P. Rico) folk dance and its music. — **las s.,** six o'clock.
seisavado, da, *a.* hexagonal.
seisavar, *tr.v.* to make hexagonal.
seisavo, va, *a.* sixth. —*m.* 1. sixth. 2. hexagon.
seiscientos, tas, *a.* six hundredth (in order). —*m.* six hundred.
seise, *m.* singing and dancing choir boy in certain cathedrals in Spain.
seiseno, na, *a.* sixth.
seisillo, *m.* (mus.) sextuplet, sextolet.
seísmo, *m., var. of* **sismo.**
selacio, cia, *a.* (ichth.) selachian. —*m.* selachian, (*pl.*) Selachii.
selección, *f.* selection, choice. — **s. natural,** (biol.) natural selection.
seleccionador, ra, *a.* selecting, choosing. —*m., f.* selector, picker.
seleccionar, *tr.v.* to select, choose.
selectas, *f. (pl.)* analects, selections from an author.
selectividad, *f.* (rad.) selectivity.
selectivo, va, *a.* selective; (rad.) selective.
selecto, ta, *a.* select, choice; **un público selecto,** a distinguished audience.
selector, ra, *a.* selective; selecting. —*m.* (auto., mec., rad., tel.) selector; **s. de ondas,** (rad.) wave trap.
selénico, ca, *a.* (chem.) selenic.
selenio, *m.* (chem.) selenium.
selenita, *m., f.* selenite, supposed inhabitant of the moon. —*f.* (min.) selenite.
seleniuro, *m.* (chem.) selenide.
selenografía, *f.* (astron.) selenography.
selenógrafo, *m.* selenographist, selenographer.
selenosis, (*pl.* **selenosis**), *f.* 1. white spots on nails. 2. (vet.) selenosis.
self, *f.* (Angl., elec.) self-induction coil.
selfactina, *f.* mule jenny (in spinning).
sellador, ra, *a.* sealing, stamping. —*m., f.* sealer, stamper.
selladura, *f.* sealing, stamping.
sellar, *tr.v.* 1. to seal, stamp, put a stamp or seal on. 2. to mark, stamp (give a definite character). 3. to conclude, finish. 4. to cover, close, e.g. *s. los labios,* to silence; to keep silent. — **firmado y sellado por,** under the hand and seal of.
sello, *m.* 1. stamp, seal. 2. stamp (for letters, etc.). 3. stamping or stamp office. 4. stamp, definite character. 5. (pharm.) (pleasant-tasting) cachet, wafer capsule (for taking unpleasant-tasting medicine). — **echar** or **poner el s. a,** to put the finishing touch to, to perfect; **s. corporativo, s. de la corporación,** (com.) corporate seal; **s. de caucho,** rubber stamp; **s. de correos,** postage stamp; **s. de Salomón,** Solomon's seal; (bot.) Solomon's seal; **s. fiscal,** revenue stamp; **s. postal,** postage stamp.
selva, *f.* forest, woods; jungle; **S. Negra,** Black Forest; **s. tropical,** tropical rainforest.
selvático, ca, *a.* 1. of the jungle, of the woods. 2. sylvan. 3. rustic, wild.
selvatiquez, *f.* (rare) wildness.
selvicultor, *m.* forester, forestry engineer.
selvicultura, *f.* forestry.
selvoso, sa, *a.* forestal; wooded, woody; jungly; sylvan.
semafórico, ca, *a.* semaphoric.
semáforo, *m.* semaphore.
semana, *f.* 1. week. 2. (fig.) week's pay. 3. (variety of) hopscotch. — **entre s.,** during the week, any day of the week (but not the first and the last); **s. santa,** Holy Week; **s. inglesa,** working week ending Saturday noon; five-day work week.
semanal, *a.* weekly.
semanalmente, *adv.* weekly, every week.
semanario, ria, *a.* weekly. —*m.* 1. weekly (publication). 2. set of seven razor blades.
semanería, *f.* work by the week.
semanero, ra, *a.* engaged by the week. —*m., f.* worker on a weekly basis.
semántica, *f.* semantics.
semántico, ca, *a.* semantic.
semasiología, *f.* (philos.) semasiology.
semblante, *m.* face, countenance; look, appearance, mien, aspect; **estar de mal s.,** to look ill or pale; **componer el s.,** to put on a calm expression; to look serious; **mudar de s.,** to change color; to take on a different aspect.
semblanza, *f.* biographical sketch or profile.
sembrada, *f.* sown land.
sembradera, *f.* (agr.) seeding or sowing machine, seeder.
sembradío, día, *a.* sowable, arable, suitable for sowing.
sembrado, *m.* sown land, cultivated field.
sembrador, ra, *a.* sowing, seeding. —*m., f.* sower; seeder.
sembradura, *f.* sowing, seeding.
sembrar, (*ref. 29*) *tr.v.* 1. to sow, seed, plant. 2. (fig.) to sow, e.g. *s. las semillas de la discordia,* to sow the seeds of discord. 3. to scatter, sprinkle, spread. 4. to spread (rumor, terror); to spread, disseminate, propagate (doctrine, etc.).
semeja, *f.* 1. resemblance, likeness. 2. sign, mark, indication (*gen. pl.*).
semejable, *a.* capable of resembling.
semejado, da, *past part. of* **semejar.** —*a.* like, resembling, similar.
semejante, *a.* 1. similar, alike. 2. such, of that kind. 3. (geom.) similar. — **s. a,** like, similar to. —*m.* 1. likeness, resemblance. 2. fellow man, fellow creature.
semejantemente, *adv.* similarly; likewise.
semejanza, *f.* 1. similarity, likeness, resemblance. 2. (rhet.) simile. — **a s. de,** like, as.
semejar, *i.v.* to resemble, look like. —*r.v.* to look alike, resemble one another. — **semejarse a,** to look like, resemble.
semen, *m.* 1. (physiol.) semen, **sperm.** 2. (bot.) seed.
semencera, *f., var. of* **sementera.**
semencontra, *m.* (pharm.) santonica.
semental, *a.* sowing; breeding (male animal). —*m.* breeding animal (horse, bull), stud, studhorse.
sementar, *tr.v.* to sow, seed.
sementera, *f.* 1. sown land. 2. sowing, seeding. 3. seeding or sowing time or season.
sementero, *m.* 1. seed bag (carrying seeds for sowing). 2. seed bed, seed plot. 3. sowing, seeding. 4. sown land. 5. seeding or sowing time.
sementino, na, *a.* pertaining to seed.
semestral, *a.* six-month, semestral, semi-annual.
semestralmente, *adv.* every six months, every semester, semiannually.
semestre, *a.* six-month, semestral. —*m.* 1. semester, six-month period. 2. six-month's pay or payment.
semi, *pre.* 1. partly, a portion of, half, semi. 2. almost.
semiacero, *m.* (metal.) semisteel, ferrosteel, high strength gray iron.

semiárido, da, *a.* semiarid.
semiautomático, ca, *a.* semiautomatic.
semibreve, *f.* (mus.) semibreve, whole note.
semicabrón, *m., var. of* **semicapro.**
semicadencia, *f.* (mus.) semicadence.
semicapro, *m.* (myth.) satyr.
semicilindro, *m.* half cylinder.
semicircular, *a.* semicircular.
semicírculo, *m.* (geom.) semicircle.
semicircunferencia, *f.* (geom.) semicircumference.
semicivilizado, da, *a.* half civilized, semicivilized.
semiconductor, ra, *a.* (elec.) semiconductive, semiconducting. —*m.* (elec.) semiconductor.
semiconsciente, *a.* half conscious, semiconscious.
semiconsonante, *a.* (gram.) semiconsonant.
semicopado, da, *a.* (mus.) *var. of* **sincopado.**
semicorchea, *f.* (mus.) semiquaver, sixteenth note.
semicromático, ca, *a.* (mus.) semichromatic.
semicupio, *m.* sitz bath.
semidea, *f.* (poet.) demigoddess.
semideo, *m.* (poet.) demigod.
semidiáfano, na, *a.* semidiaphanous.
semidiámetro, *m.* (geom.) semidiameter.
semidiapasón, *m.* (mus.) semidiapason.
semidifunto, ta, *a.* half-dead, almost dead.
semidiós, *m.* demigod.
semidiosa, *f.* demigoddess.
semidítono, *m.* (mus.) semiditone.
semidiurno, na, *a.* semidiurnal.
semidoble, *a.* (ecc.) semi-solemn (rite, feast-day).
semidormido, da, *a.* half-asleep.
semidragón, *m.* mythological monster half-man half-dragon.
semieje, *m.* 1. axle (on each side of the differential). 2. (geom.) semiaxis.
semiesfera, *f.* hemisphere.
semiesférico, ca, *a.* hemispheric, hemispherical.
semifinal, *a., f.* (sport) semifinal.
semifinalista, *m., f.* (sport.) semifinalist.
semiflósculo, *m.* (bot.) semifloret, semifloscule.
semifluido, da, *a.* semifluid.
semiforme, *a.* half-formed, undeveloped.
semifusa, *f.* (mus.) hemidemisemiquaver, sixty-fourth note.
semigola, *f.* (fort.) demigorge.
semihombre, *m.* (arch.) pygmy, half-man.
semilogarítmico, ca, *a.* (math.) semilogarithmic.
semilunar, *a.* semilunar.
semilunio, *m.* (astron.) half moon, half a lunation.
semilla, *f.* seed.
semillero, *m.* 1. seed bed, seed plot; seed nursery. 2. (fig.) breeding ground, hot-bed (of vice, discord, etc.).
seminación, *f.* (biol.) semination.
seminal, *a.* seminal.
seminario, *m.* 1. seminary, school. 2. seminar (group of students or class engaged on special line of study). — **s. conciliar,** theological seminary.
seminarista, *m.* 1. seminarian, seminarist. 2. student of theology.
seminífero, ra, *a.* (zool.) seminiferous.
semínima, *f.* (mus.) crotchet.
semioficial, *a.* semiofficial.
semiología, *f.* semeiology.
semiótica, *f.* (med.) semeiotics, semeiology, symptomatology.
semipedal, *a.* half-foot long, semipedal.
semiplena, *a.* (law) imperfect, incomplete (evidence).
semiplenamente, *adv.* (law) insufficiently proved, half proved.
semiprecioso, sa, *a.* semiprecious (stone, etc.).
Semíramis, *f.* (hist.) Semiramis.
semirrecto, *a.* (geom.) of 45 degrees (angle).
semirrígido, da, *a.* (aer.) semirigid.
semis, *m.* semis (Roman coin).
semisalvaje, *a.* half-savage. —*m., f.* half savage.
semisólido, da, *m., f.* semisolid.
semita, *a.* Semitic. —*m., f.* Semite. —*f.* (Bol., Ecuad.) kind of bun or biscuit.
semítico, ca, *a.* Semitic.
semitismo, *m.* Semitism.
semitista, *m.* Semitist, specialist in Semitic languages, literature, etc.
semitono, *m.* (mus.) semitone; **s. cromático** or **menor,** chromatic semitone; **s. diatónico** or **mayor,** diatonic semitone.
semitransparente, *a.* semitransparent.
semitropical, *a.* semitropical.
semivivo, va, *a.* half-alive.
semivocal, *a.* (phonet.) semivocal, semivocalic. —*f.* semivowel.
sémola, *f.* semola, semolina, groats, grits.
semoviente, *a.* (law) livestock (property). —*m. (pl.)* livestock property.
sempiternamente, *adv.* everlastingly, eternally, perpetually.
sempiterno, na, *a.* sempiternal, everlasting, eternal, perpetual. —*f.* 1. (tex.) durance. 2. (bot.) globe amaranth.
sen, *m.* 1. (bot., **pharm.**) senna. 2. sen, Japanese coin.
sena, *f.* 1. six (on a dice); (*pl.*) double sixes (in some games). 2. (bot., pharm.) senna.
Sena, *m.* Seine (river).
senado, *m.* senate.
senadoconsulto, *m.* senatus consultum (decree of ancient Roman senate).
senador, *m.* senator.
senaduría, *f.* senatorship.
senara, *f.* 1. land granted to servants for tillage as part of their wages; product of such land. 2. sown land. 3. commons, common land.
senario, ria, *a.* senary, sextuple. —*m.* senarius.
senarmontita, *f.* (metal.) senarmontite (antimony ore).
senatorial, senatorio, ria, *a.* senatorial.
sencillamente, *adv.* 1. simply. 2. easily. 3. plainly, unpretentiously; naturally. 4. ingenuously.
sencillez, *f.* 1. simplicity (plainness; naturalness). 2. easiness. 3. naiveté, artlessness, candor.
sencillo, lla, *a.* 1. simple (plain, unadorned; uncomplicated, easy; natural, unaffected; naive, artless, guileless, innocent, candid). 2. thin, light (fabric). —*m.* change, small change (money).
senda, *f.* 1. path, footpath, trail. 2. (fig.) means, way.
senderar, senderear, *tr.v.* to guide or lead along a path or trail; to open or cut a path through. —*i.v.* (fig.) to employ unusual means, ways or arguments.
sendero, *m.* 1. path, footpath, trail. 2. (fig.) means, way.
senderuelo, *m. dim. of* **sendero,** small or narrow path or trail.
sendos, das, *a.* (*pl.*) each, one each, one to each, e.g. *les repartieron s. libros,* they gave them a book each.
séneca, *m.* 1. (fig.) wise man, man of wisdom, sage. 2. **S.,** Seneca, Spanish-born Roman philosopher.
senectud, *f.* old age, senility.
Senegal, *m.* Senegal.
senegalés, sa, *a., m., f.* Senegalese.
senequista, *a.* Senecan (relating to or following the philosophy of Seneca). —*m., f.* Senecan, Stoic (follower of the philosophy of Seneca).
senescal, *m.* seneschal, household officer.
senescalado, *m.,* **senescalía,** *f.* seneschalship (office of a seneschal).
senescencia, *f.* senescence.
senil, *a.* senile.
seno, *m.* 1. bosom, breast. 2. womb. 3. bosom (part of dress worn on breast). 4. cavity, hollow, hole, recess, indentation. 5. (anat., bot., zool., med.) sinus, cavity. 6. gulf, bay, cove, inlet, indentation in coastline. 7. (mar.) bosom, belly (of a sail). 8. (fig.) bosom, sanctuary, haven, asylum, refuge. 9. (fig.) bosom, heart, inner recess. 10. (math.) sine. 11. (archit.) spandrel. — **s. de Abrahán,** Abraham's bosom; **s. hiperbólico,** (math.) hyperbolic sine; **s. segundo,** (math.) cosine; **s. verso,** (math.) versed sine.
sensación, *f.* sensation; **hacer s.,** to cause a sensation.
sensacional, *a.* sensational.
sensacionalismo, *m.* sensationalism.
sensacionalista, *a.* sensationalistic.
sensatamente, *adv.* sensibly, prudently.
sensatez, *f.* good sense, prudence; good judgment.
sensato, ta, *a.* sensible, prudent, judicious.
sensibilice, sensibilicé, *ref.* **sensibilizar.**
sensibilidad, *f.* sensibility; sensitivity, sensitiveness.
sensibilizador, *m.* sensitizer.
sensibilizar, (*ref. 53*) *tr.v.* to sensitize, make sensitive.
sensible, *a.* 1. sensitive, impressionable (person). 2. sensitive, delicate. 3. (photog.) sensitive, sensitized. 4. regrettable, lamentable, unfortunate. 5. perceptible, noticeable, appreciable. 6. sensible, sentient (able to feel; capable of being perceived by the senses). 7. (mus.) sensible. —*f.* (mus.) sensible note.
sensiblemente, *adv.* 1. perceptibly, noticeably, appreciably. 2. regrettably, grievously.
sensiblería, *f.* mawkishness, oversentimentality.
sensiblero, ra, *a.* mawkish, oversentimental.
sensitiva, *f.* (bot.) sensitive plant.
sensitivo, va, *a.* sensitive; sentient.
sensitómetro, *m.* (photog.) sensitometer.
sensor, *m.* sensor.
sensorio, ria, *a.* sensory, sensorial; sense, e.g. *órganos sensorios,* sense organs. —*m.* (physiol.) sensorium, sense center.
sensual, *a.* sensual; sensuous.
sensualidad, *f.* sensuality; sensuousness.
sensualismo, *m.* 1. sensuality; sensuousness. 2. (philos.) sensualism, sensationalism. 3. (psyc.) sensationism.
sensualista, *a.* 1. sensualistic. 2. (philos.) sensualistic, sensualist, sensationalistic. —*m., f.* 1. sensualist. 2. (philos.) sensualist, sensationalist.
sensualmente, *adv.* sensually, sensuously.
sentada, *f.* sitting; **de una s.,** at one sitting.
sentadero, *m.* sitting place, seat (log, stone, etc.).
sentadillas, *adv.* **a sentadillas,** sidesaddle.
sentado, da, *past part. of* **sentar.** —*a.* 1. seated, sitting. 2. settled, established. 3. judicious, sensible; stable, steady. 4. (bot.) sessile. — **dar por s.,** to take for granted; **esperar s.,** to wait for ages.
sentador, ra, *a.* (Amer.) becoming, well-fitting (of clothes).
sentamiento, *m.* (archit.) settling (of material under pressure).
sentar, *tr.v.* 1. to seat. 2. to set, establish. 3. to assert. 4. (dressm.) to press (the seams). — **s. una denuncia,** to report, e.g. *senté la denuncia sobre el robo,* I reported the theft; **s. los cascos,** to settle down, become more sensible and prudent; **s. plaza,** to enlist, join up. —*i.v.* 1. to

affect, e.g. *la comida me ha sentado bien,* the meal has agreed with me. 2. to do (good), make feel (ill), e.g. *le sentó bien la ducha,* the shower did him good, *el pescado le sentó mal,* the fish made him feel ill. 3. to suit, become, fit, e.g. *este saco no le sienta,* this jacket does not suit or fit him. 4. (coll.) to please or not, e.g. *le sentó bien tu consejo,* he liked your advice, your advice pleased him. —*r.v.* 1. to sit, sit down. 2. to leave a mark on (the skin).

sentazón, *m.* Chile, min.) cave-in.

sentencia, *f.* 1. (law) judgment, verdict, sentence. 2. saying, aphorism, maxim.

sentenciador, *a.* sentencing. —*m.* one who passes judgment or sentence.

sentenciar, *tr.v.* 1. to pass judgment on. 2. (law) to condemn, sentence.

sentenciosamente, *adv.* sententiously.

sentencioso, sa, *a.* sententious.

senticar, *m.* brambly land or patch.

sentidamente, *adv.* 1. with feeling. 2. sadly, regretfully.

sentido, da, *past part. of* **sentir.** —*a.* 1. deeply felt. 2. experienced. 3. sensitive; offended; **darse por sentido,** to take offense. —*m.* 1. sense, faculty of sensation, e.g. *los cinco sentidos,* the five senses, *el s. del oído, de la vista, del olfato, del gusto y del tacto,* the sense of hearing, sight, smell, taste and touch. 2. sense, judgment, common sense, reason. 3. sense, point, meaning, e.g. *este vocablo tiene muchos sentidos,* this word has many meanings. 4. interpretation, e.g. *la Sagrada Escritura tiene varios sentidos,* the Scriptures have several interpretations. 5. way, direction, e.g. *tráfico de doble s.* or *dos sentidos,* two-way traffic; (geom., mec.) sense, direction. 6. (Amer.) temple (of head). — **aguzar el s.,** (coll.) to prick up one's ears; **doble s.,** double meaning; **en el s. de que,** to the effect that; **no tener s.,** to make no sense; **perder el s.,** to lose consciousness, faint; **poner** or **tener puestos sus cinco sentidos en,** (coll.) to devote all one's attention to; to hold dearly or in great esteem; **recobrar el s.,** to recover consciousness; **s. común,** common sense; **s. del humor,** sense of humor; **s. de orientación,** sense of direction; **S. y Sensibilidad,** Sense and Sensibility (Jane Austen's novel); **sin s.,** senseless, foolish; meaningless, pointless, unconscious; **tener s.,** to make sense.

sentimental, *a.* sentimental; emotional.

sentimentalismo, *m.* sentimentalism; sentimentality.

sentimentalmente, *adv.* sentimentally.

sentimiento, *m.* 1. feeling, sentiment; sensation. 2. grief, sorrow, regret.

sentina, *f.* 1. (mar.) bilge. 2. (fig.) pigsty, hovel, filthy place. 3. den of vice, bed of corruption.

sentir, *m.* feeling; opinion, view, judgment.

sentir, (*ref. 42*) *tr.v.* 1. to feel; to experience, e.g. *s. miedo,* to feel afraid, *s. alegría,* to feel happy or joyful, *s. frío,* to feel cold. 2. to feel, think, opine, e.g. *digo lo que siento,* I say what I feel. 3. to regret; feel or be sorry about, be grieved at, e.g. *lo siento,* I'm sorry, *s. la muerte de un amigo,* to be grieved at the death of a friend. 4. to feel, sense, foresee. 5. to hear, e.g. *siento golpes,* I hear knocking. — **dar or tener que s.,** to give or have cause for regret; **s. +** *inf.,* to regret + *inf.,* be sorry + *inf.* —*i.v.* 1. to feel; to notice. 2. to be sorry. — **sin s.,** without noticing. —*r.v.* 1. to feel, be, e.g. ¿ ¿ cómo te sientes? me siento enfermo, how do you feel? I feel ill, *sentirse obligado,* to feel obliged. 2. to begin to crack or split. 3. to begin to decay or rot. 4. to complain, be resentful. 5. (Amer.) to take offense. — **sentirse a sus anchas,** to feel at ease.

sentón, *m.* (Ecuad.) sudden check or stop (of a horse).

seña, *f.* 1. sign, signal, gesture. 2. sign, indication. 3. (mil.) password, watchword. 4. (*pl.*) address, direction. 5. (Chile) ringing or tolling of a church bell. — **dar señas de,** to show signs of; **hablar por señas,** to speak with sign language; **hacer señas,** to make signs, signal, gesture; **por señas** or **por más señas,** more specifically, more exactly; **santo y s.,** password; **señas personales,** (personal) particulars, personal description.

señal, *f.* 1. signal; sign. 2. sign, mark; token, indication. 3. sign, trace, vestige. 4. landmark. 5. scar. 6. brand, earmark (on cattle). 7. earnest money. 8. (med.) sign, symptom. 9. (rad.) signal, e.g. *intensidad de s.,* signal strength. — **en s. de,** as a sign of, as a token of; **hacer señales,** to signal, make signals or signs; **ni s.,** not a sign, not a trace; **s. de cambio,** (ry.) switch signal; **s. de desastre,** distress signal; **s. de la cruz,** sign of the cross; **s. de línea,** (tel.) dial tone; **s. de niebla,** fog signal; **s. de ocupado,** busy signal (in telephoning); **s. de peligro,** danger signal; **s. de tráfico,** traffic signal or sign; **s. horaria,** time signal; **señales entrelazadas,** (ry.) interlocking signals; **s. parásita,** (rad.) interfering signal; **sistema de señales por tramos de vía,** (ry.) block system.

señaladamente, *adv.* particularly, notably.

señalado, da, *past part. of* **señalar.** —*a.* notable, distinguished.

señalamiento, *m.* designation, appointment, indication (of place, time).

señalar, *tr.v.* 1. to point out, point at; to indicate, show. 2. to designate, determine, set, fix (date, place, etc.). 3. to mark, put a mark or sign on. 4. (Arg., Chile) to brand, earmark (cattle). — **s. con el dedo,** to point (a finger) at. —*r.v.* to stand out, distinguish oneself, excel.

señaleja, *f. dim. of* **señal,** small or slight sign or mark.

señalización, *f.* 1. marking with signals, providing with signals. 2. signals, system of signals.

señalizar, (*ref. 53*) *tr.v.* instal signals on or along (a road).

señero, ra, *a.* 1. solitary, only, single. 2. unique, unequalled.

señolear, *i.v.* to hunt with a decoy, snare.

señor, ra, *a.* 1. (coll.) very big, quite a, a whale of a, e.g. *me dio un señor susto,* it gave me a whale of a fright, *me hice una señora herida,* I got quite a wound. 2. (coll.) gentlemanly, noble, e.g. *él es muy señor,* he is very much a gentleman. —*m.* 1. mister, sir, gentleman, man, e.g. *Señor Pérez,* Mr. Pérez, *¿puedo ayudarle, Señor?* can I help you, sir? *Señoras y Señores,* Ladies and Gentlemen. 2. master, owner, lord, e.g. *el s. de la casa,* the master of the house. — **el S.,** the Lord (God); **muy s. mío,** Dear Sir; **s. de campanillas,** bigwig, bigshot; **s. de horca y cuchillo,** absolute lord and master; **s. del argamandijo,** (coll.) chief, boss; **s. de sí,** master of oneself; **s. mayor,** elderly gentleman.

señora, *f.* 1. lady (as correlative of gentleman). 2. mistress, lady, owner, e.g. *la s. de la casa,* the mistress or lady of the house. 3. madam, e.g. *¿puedo ayudarle, S.?* can I help you, madam? 4. wife. 5. mistress, Mrs., e.g. *la S. de Pérez,* Mrs. Pérez. — **muy s. mía,** Dear Madam; **Nuestra S.,** Our Lady, the Virgin Mary; **s. de compañia,** lady companion; chaperon; **s. mayor,** elderly lady, matron.

señorada, *f.* gentlemanly act.

señoreador, ra, *a.* ruling; overbearing, domineering. —*m., f.* ruler, master; overbearing person.

señoreaje, *m.* seigniorage, something claimed by a superior as a prerogative.

señoreante, *a.* ruling; overbearing, domineering.

señorear, *tr.v.* 1. to rule, control, dominate. 2. to take over, take control of, seize. 3. to master, control, dominate, restrain. 4. (coll.) to "sir" (someone) continually. —*r.v.* to have in a dignified manner; (coll.) to put on airs; **señorearse de,** to seize, take over, take control of.

señoría, *f.* 1. lordship, ladyship (title and person). 2. dominion, sway. 3. seigniory, signory (chief executive body of medieval Italian city); (Italian) city state, republic, e.g. *Señoria de Venecia,* Seigniory of Venice.

señorial, *a.* 1. seigniorial, lordly; noble, majestic. 2. feudal (tax).

señoril, *a.* lordly, majestic; dignified.

señorilmente, *adv.* in a lordly manner, nobly, grandly.

señorío, *m.* 1. dominion, sway, rule 2. seigniory, seignioralty, domain of lord of manor. 3. dignity, majesty, gravity. 4. control, mastery, restraint (of passions). 5. gentry, nobility.

señorita, *f.* young lady, little lady, e.g. *ya es una s.,* she's already quite a little lady. 2. Miss, e.g. *Srta. Rodriguez,* Miss. Rodríguez. 3. (coll.) mistress of the house.

señoritingo, ga, *m., f.* (derog.) young pipsqueak, no-account youth.

señorito, *m.* master, young gentleman; (coll.) master of the house; (coll.) playboy, young blade.

señoron, na, *a.* lordly, majestic. —*m., f.* great gentleman or lady.

senuelo, *m.* decoy, lure; live decoy. 2. (fig.) bait; enticement. 3. (Arg.) leader, leading cow or cows (in diving cattle).

seo, *f.* cathedral church.

seó, seor, *m.,* **seora,** *f.* (sl.) *contr. of* **señor, ra,** used before given names, e.g. *seora María,* Miss Mary.

sepa, *ref.* **saber.**

sépalo, *m.* (bot.) **sepal.**

sepaloideo, a, *a.* (bot.) sepaloid.

sepancuantos, *m.* (coll.) beating, spanking; punishment; scolding, reprimand.

separable, *a.* separable, detachable, removable.

separación, *f.* separation; **s. estratigráfica,** (geol.) stratigraphic separation.

separadamente, *adv.* separately.

separado, da, *past part. of* **separar.** —*a.* separated, isolated, apart; por **separado,** separately.

separador, ra, *a.* separating. —*m., f.* separator. —*m.* 1. separator (machine, instrument). 2. (surg.) retractor. — **s. centrífugo,** (mec.) centrifugal separator; **s. ciclónico,** (mec.) cyclone separator.

separante, *a.* separating.

separar, *tr.v.* 1. to separate. 2. to dismiss, discharge (from post, employment). 3. (coll.) to reserve (e.g. seats in theater); to order, put aside (goods in shop). 4. to detach, remove. —*r.v.* 1. to separate, part company. 2. to separate, come apart, come off. 3. to retire, resign. 4. (law) to waive (a right, claim).

separata, *f.* offprint.

separatismo, *m.* separatism; (pol.) secessionism.

separatista, *a., m., f.* separatist; secessionist.

separativo, va, *a.* separating, separative.

sepe, *m.* (Bol.) termite.

sepedón, *m.* (zool.) seps (serpent).

sepelio, *m.* burial, interment.

sepia, *f.* 1. (zool.) sepia, cuttlefish. 2. sepia (pigment, color).

sepiolita, *f.* (min.) sepiolite.
sepsis, *f.* (med.) sepsis.
sept. *abbrev.* **of septiembre,** September (Sept., Sep.).
septal, *a.* (anat.) septal.
septaria, *m.* (min.) septarium.
septectomía, *f.* (med.) septectomy.
septena, *f.* septenary, heptade, group of seven.
septenario, ria, *a.* septenary. —*m.* seven days.
septenio, *m.* septennium, period of seven years.
septeno, na, *a.* seventh.
Septentrión, *m.* 1. (astron.) Septentrion, Great Bear. 2. North (cardinal point).
septentrional, *a.* septentrional, northern.
septeto, *m.* (mus.) septet.
septicemia, *f.* (med.) septicemia, septicaemia.
septicémico, ca, *a.* septicemic, septicaemic.
septicida, *a.* (bot.) septicidal.
septicidad, *f.* septicity.
séptico, ca, *a.* (med.) septic.
septiembre, *m.* September.
septífrago, ga, *a.* (bot.) septifragal.
septillo, *m.* (mus.) septimole, septuplet.
séptimo, ma, *a.* seventh. —*m., f.* seventh. —*f.* (mus.) seventh. — **s. aumentada,** (mus.) augmented seventh; **s. disminuida,** (mus.) diminished seventh; **s. mayor,** (mus.) major seventh; **s. menor,** (mus.) minor seventh.
septingentésimo, ma, *a., m.* seven hundredth.
septisílabo, ba, *a.* heptasyllabic, seven-syllable.
septo, *m.* (anat., zool., bot.) septum.
septuagenario, ria, *a., m., f.* septuagenarian, septuagenary.
septuagésima, *f.* (ecc.) Septuagesima.
septuagésimo, ma, *a., m.* seventieth.
séptum, *m.* (anat.) septum.
septuplicacíon, *f.* septuplication.
septuplicar, (*ref. 50*) *tr.v.* to septuple, septuplicate, multiply by seven. —*r.v.* to increase sevenfold .
séptuplo, pla, *a.* septuple, sevenfold. —*m.* septuple.
sepulcral, *a.* sepulchral; pertaining to tomb, e.g. *inscripción s.,* tomb inscription.
sepulcro, *m.* 1. sepulcher, tomb, grave. 2. (archit.) sepulcher (repository for relics). — **Santo S.,** Holy Sepulcher; **ser un s.,** (coll.) to be as silent as a tomb (in guarding a secret).
sepultador, ra, *a.* burying. —*m., f.* burier, gravedigger.
sepultar, *tr.v.* to bury, inter, entomb; (fig.) to bury, hide, conceal. —*r.v.* (fig.) to be wrapped or buried (in one's thoughts).
sepulto, ta, *irr. past part. of* **sepultar.** —*a.* buried.
sepultura, *f.* 1. interment, burial. 2. tomb, grave. 3. burial place, sepulture. — **dar s. a,** to bury; **estar con un pie en la s.,** to have one foot in the grave.
sepulturero, *m.* gravedigger; sexton.
seque, sequé, *ref.* **secar.**
sequedad, *f.* 1. dryness; aridness, aridity. 2. (fig.) curtness, gruffness.
sequedal, sequeral, *m.* very dry ground or soil.
sequero, *m.* 1. unirrigated land. 2. drying place.
sequeroso, sa, *a.* very dry, lacking in moisture; juiceless.
sequete, *m.* 1. dry crust. 2. blow. 3. (coll.) gruffness, surliness.
sequía, *f.* drought, dry season; (Amer.) thirst.
sequillo, *m.* sweet bun or roll.
sequío, *m.* unirrigated land.
séquito, *m.* 1. retinue, suite, train, entourage, cortege. 2. popularity, following.
sequizo, za, *a.* dryish, apt to dry up.
ser, *m.* being; life, existence; essence, nature, substance; **s. humano,** human being; **S. Supremo,** Supreme Being; **seres queridos,** loved ones.
ser, (*ref. 22*) *aux. v.* to be (used to form the passive voice), e.g. *él fue herido por una bala,* he was wounded by a bullet. —*i.v.* to be; **a no s. por,** but for, if it had not been for; **a no s. que** + *subj.,* unless; **¡cómo es eso!** how is that; what do you mean by that?; **¿ cómo ha sido eso?** how did that happen?; **de s. posible,** if possible; **érase que se era,** (coll.) once upon a time; **es a saber, esto es,** that is, that is to say, namely, to wit; **es de** + *inf.,* it is to be + *past part.,* e.g. *es de esperar,* it is to be hoped; **lo que será, será,** what will be, will be; **no es para menos,** (coll.) justifiably so, with good reason; **no sea que,** lest; **o sea,** that is to say; **pienso luego soy,** I think, therefore I am; **sea lo que sea, sea lo que fuere,** be it as it may, whatever happens; **s. de,** to belong, e.g. *estas tierras son del rey,* these lands belong to the king; to be made of, be of, e.g. *es de oro,* it's made of gold; to be from, come from, e.g. *él es de Buenos Aires,* he's from Buenos Aires; to become of, happen to, e.g. *¿qué ha sido de tu proyecto?* what became of your project; **s. de lo que no hay,** (coll.) to be unique, be without equal; **s. de** or **para ver,** (coll.) to be worth seeing; **s. o no s.,** to be or not to be; **s. otro,** (coll.) to be a changed or different person; **s. para,** to be for, be suited to, e.g. *él no es para este tipo de empleo,* he is not suited to this type of work; **s. para poco,** (coll.) to be timid, have little go or vitality, be useless, have little talent; **soy contigo** o **con Ud.,** I'll be with you in a moment; **soy yo,** it's me, it is I.
sera, *f.* large basket, usually without handles.
serado, *m.* baskets.
seráficamente, *adv.* seraphically.
seráfico, ca, *a.* seraphic.
serafín, *m.* 1. (Rel.) seraph. 2. (fig.) angel, cherub, extremely beautiful person.
serafina, *f.* fine baize.
seraje, *m.* frails, baskets.
serapino, *m.* sagapenum, a kind of gum.
serba, *f.* (bot.) sorb apple, serviceberry.
serbal, serbo, *m.* (bot.) service tree, sorb tree.
serena, *f.* 1. serena, evening love song, serenade. 2. (coll.) evening dew, evening dampness. — **a la s.,** (coll.) in the night air.
serenamente, *adv.* coolly, calmly; serenely.
serenar, *tr.v.* 1. to calm; to calm down, pacify, make calm. 2. to cool (a liquid). 3. to settle, make settle (liquids). —*i.v.* to become or grow calm. —*r.v.* 1. to become or grow calm (e.g. a person, the weather); to calm down. 2. to cool, grow cold. 3. to settle (liquids). 4. (coll.) to become unclouded (a day, a person's face).
serenata, *f.* (mus.) serenade.
serenero, *m.* head scarf (used as protection against cold night air); night wrap.
serení, (*pl.* **sereníes**), *m.* 1. (mar.) small boat, dinghy. 2. (Cuba, bot.) aleluya, wood sorrel.
serenidad, *f.* 1. serenity, calm; self-possession, presence of mind. 2. **S.,** Serenity (title).
serenísimo, ma, *a. super. of* **sereno,** very or most serene or calm; most serene (Highness).
sereno, na, *a.* 1. clear, cloudless. 2. serene, calm, unruffled. —*m.* 1. evening dew, night dew. 2. night watchman. — **al s.,** in the night air, exposed to the night dew.
serete, *m., var. of* **serijo.**
sergas, *f. pl.* exploits, deeds.
sergenta, *f.* lay sister of the order of Santiago.
seriamente, *adv.* 1. seriously, gravely. 2. in earnest.
seriar, *tr.v.* to place in series, put in order.
sericícola, *a.* sericicultural, sericultural.
sericicultor, *m.* sericiculturist, sericulturist.
sericicultura, *f.* sericiculture, sericulture.
sérico, ca, *a.* sericeous, silken.
sericultor, ra, *m., f.* sericulturist, sericiculturist.
sericultura, *f.* sericulture, sericiculture.
serie, *f.* series or group of related numbers or things; **de s.,** stock; e.g. *auto de s.,* (auto.) stock car; **en s.,** mass (production); (elec.) in series; **fuera de s.,** (coll.) excellently made, perfectly made; outstanding, excellent, perfect; **producir en s.,** to mass produce; **s. mundial,** world series (in baseball); **s. parafínica.** (chem.) paraffin series.
seriedad, *f.* 1. seriousness; gravity. 2. reliability, responsibility, dependability. 3. sternness, severity.
serigrafía, *f.* (tex., art.) serigraphy.
serija, *f. dim. of* **sera,** small basket or pannier.
serijo, *m.* small frail, basket or pannier.
serina, *f.* (chem.) serine.
seringa, *f.* (Amer.) rubber.
serio, ria, *a.* 1. serious; thoughtful; sober, solemn; grave. 2. stern, severe. 3. reliable, responsible, dependable. 4. important. — **en serio,** seriously; really, truly; **es una cosa seria,** (coll.) it's a real problem, it's a serious matter; it's a pain in the neck; **tomar en serio,** to take seriously.
sermón, *m.* 1. sermon. 2. (rare) **tongue,** language. 3. (fig.) sermon, admonishment, reprimand. — **S. de la Montaña,** (Bib.) Sermon on the Mount.
sermonar, *i.v.* to preach, sermonize.
sermonario, ria, *a.* sermonic, sermonical. —*m.* collection of sermons.
sermoncillo, ito, *m. dim. of* **sermón,** short sermon, address; brief advice.
sermoneador, ra, *a.* sermonizing.
sermonear, *i.v.* to preach, sermonize. —*tr.v.* to address; to preach to; (coll.) to lecture, reprimand, admonish, sermonize.
sermoneo, *m.* (coll.) sermonizing, preaching; repeated admonition.
serna, *f.* cultivated or sown field.
seroalbúmina, *f.* (med.) serum albumin.
seroglobulina, *f.* (med.) serum globulin.
seroja, *f.,* **serojo,** *m.* brushwood; dry, fallen leaves.
serología, *f.* (med.) serology.
serón, *m.* long narrow pannier or frail.
serondo, da, *a.* (bot.) serotinous, late.
seronero, *m.* pannier or frail maker or seller.
serosidad, *f.* (med.) serosity, serous fluid.
seroso, sa, *a.* serous.
seroterapia, *f.* (med.) serum therapy.
serotino, na, *a.* (bot.) serotinous.
serpa, *f.* (bot.) sterile shoot (of a vine).
serpear, *i.v., var. of* **serpentear.**
serpentaria, *f.* (bot.) green dragon; **s. virginiana,** Virginia snakeroot.
serpentario, *m.* 1. (ornith.) secretary bird. 2. (astron.) **S.,** Serpent bearer, Ophiuchus.
serpenteado, da, *a.* winding, sinuous, serpentine.
serpentear, *i.v.* to wind; to meander; to snake, slither.
serpenteo, *m.* winding; meandering; slithering, snaking.
serpentígero, ra, *a.* (poet.) bearing or containing serpents.
serpentín, *m.* 1. coil (of a still, heater, etc.). 2. serpentine (attachment on harquebus to hold match; ancient piece of artillery); cock on gunlock. 3. (min.) serpentine. — **s. calentador,** (mec.) heating coil; **s. refrigerante,** cooling coil.
serpentina, *f.* 1. (min.) serpentine. 2. paper streamer (thrown in carnivals). 3. snakelike spear. 4. serpentine (attachment on harquebus to hold the match).
serpentinamente, *adv.* windingly, sinuously.

serpentón, *m.* 1. *aug. of* **serpiente,** large serpent or snake. 2. (mus.) serpent (wind instrument).
serpezuela, *f. dim. of* **sierpe,** small snake or serpent.
serpiente, *f.* 1. snake, serpent. 2. (fig.) devil, Satan. 3. (astron.) **S.,** Serpens, Serpent. — **s. boa,** boa constrictor; **s. de cascabel,** rattlesnake; **s. pitón,** python.
serpiginoso, sa, *a.* (med.) serpiginous.
serpigo, *m.* (med.) serpigo, ringworm.
serpol, *m.* (bot.) wild thyme.
serpollar, *i.v.* (bot.) to sprout, grow shoots.
serpollo, *m.* (bot.) shoot, sprout, sapling.
serradizo, za, *a., var. of* **aserradizo.**
serrado, da, *past part. of* **serrar.** —*a.* serrate.
serrador, ra, *a.* sawing. —*m., f.* **sawer,** sawyer.
serraduras, *f.* (*pl.*) sawdust.
serrallo, *m.* 1. seraglio, harem. 2. (fig.) brothel.
serranía, *f.* mountainous country.
serraniego, ga, *a., var. of* **serrano.**
serranil, *m.* dagger, knife.
serranilla, *f.* popular bucolic poem written in short verses.
serrano, na, *a.* mountain, highland. —*m., f.* highlander, mountain dweller. —*f.* bucolic poem.
serrar, (*ref. 29*) *tr.v.* to saw.
serrátil, *a.* (med.) irregular (pulse).
serrato, *a.* (anat.) serratus. —*m.* (anat.) serratus (muscle).
serrería, *f.* sawmill.
serreta, *f.* 1. *dim. of* **sierra,** small saw. 2. cavesson, iron toothed noseband (for horses). 3. gold or silver scallop-edged braid.
serretazo, *m.* 1. jerk or pull on the cavesson. 2. (fig.) reprimand, severe dressing down.
serrezuela, *f. dim. of* **sierra,** small handsaw.
serrijón, *m.* short range of mountains.
serrín, *m.* sawdust.
serrino, na, *a.* 1. saw-like. 2. (med.) irregular (pulse).
serrón, *m. aug. of* **sierra,** large saw; two-handed saw.
serruchar, *tr.v.* (Amer.) to saw.
serrucho, *m.* 1. handsaw. 2. (ichth., Cuba) sawfish. 3. (Chile) tramcar inspector. — **al s.,** (Cuba, coll.) halves, fifty-fifty; **s. de calar** or **de punta,** compass saw; **s. de corte doble,** double-cut saw.
servato, *m.* (bot.) hog's fennel, brimstonewort.
serventesio, *m.* sirvente (Provençal song); quatrain.
serventía, *f.* (Cuba) road for public use cutting across private property.
servible, *a.* usable, useful, serviceable.
serviciador, *m.* tax or fees collector, cattle toll collector.
servicial, *a.* obliging, willing, keen to help or serve, diligent, accommodating. —*m.* (coll.) enema, clyster.
servicialmente, *adv.* obligingly, willingly; diligently.
serviciar, *tr.v.* to pay or collect (tax, fees, cattle toll, etc.).
servicio, *m.* 1. service, serving, e.g. *el s. en este restaurante es excelente,* the service in this restaurant is excellent, *veinte años de servicios,* twenty years' service, *este vestido ha prestado buen s.,* this dress has given good service. 2. service, condition of a servant, e.g. *estar en el s. doméstico,* to be a domestic servant. 3. service, favor, help, e.g. *hacerle un s. a uno,* to do someone a service. 4. toilet, lavatory. 5. enema, clyster. 6. service, set (of plates, etc.). 7. service (organization devoted to some special end), e.g. *s. de correos,* postal service, *s. diplomático,* diplomatic service, *s. de reparaciones,* repair service, *s. de grúa,* (auto.) towing or break-down service. 8. (rel.) service. 9. service, serve (as in tennis), e.g. *línea de s.,* service line. 10. (hist.) voluntary donations given to king or state; (*pl.*) emergency direct tax. — **entrada de servicio,** service entrance; **estar al s. de,** to be in someone's employment or service; **estar de s.,** to be on duty; **hacer un flaco s. a uno,** (coll.) to do someone a disservice; **prestar servicios,** to give one's services; **s. activo,** active service; **s. de combate,** (mil.) combat duty; **s. de fajina,** (mil.) fatigue duty; **s. de limpieza,** street-cleaning department, **s. de mesa,** table service (i.e. china, cutlery, etc.); **s. de transmisiones,** (mil.) signal corps; **s. militar,** military service; **s. permanente** or **de 24 horas,** (seal) 24-hour service, open 24 hours; **s. pesado,** (mec.) heavy duty; **s. secreto,** secret service; **servicios profesionales,** professional services; **servicios públicos,** public services.
servidero, ra, *a.* 1. serviceable, useful. 2. demanding or needing personal attention.
servido, da, *past part. of* **servir.** —*a.* pleased, served.
servidor, ra, *m., f.* servant; employee, worker; server, waiter or waitress. — **su s., su seguro s.,** your humble servant. —*m.* 1. suitor, wooer. 2. chamber pot.
servidumbre, *f.* 1. servitude, slavery, bondage. 2. (hist.) serfdom. 3. servants, maids. 4. inevitable obligation. 5. (law) easement, servitude. 6. (fig.) restraint of emotions. — **s. aparente,** (law) apparent easement or servitude; **s. de acceso,** (law) easement of access; **s. continua,** (law) continuing or continuous easement; **s. de aguas,** (law) water rights; **s. de paso** or **de tránsito,** (law) right of way.
servil, *a.* 1. servile, subservient. 2. abject; lowly, humble.
servilismo, *m.* servility, subservience; abjectedness.
servilla, *f.* 1. slipper. 2. (Cuba) tray (gen. of sweets).
servilleta, *f.* napkin, serviette. — **doblar la s.,** (coll.) to die; **estar de s. en el ojal,** (coll.) to be invited out to dinner.
servilletero, *m.* napkin ring, serviette ring.
servilmente, *adv.* servilely.
servio, via, *a., m., f.* Serbian, Serb. —*f.* **S.,** Serbia.
serviola, *f.* (mar.) cathead, anchor beam. —*m.* (mar.) cathead guard or lookout.
servir, (*ref. 39*) *tr.v.* 1. to serve, wait on. 2. to serve (God; country); to serve, work for (a firm; a person). 3. to serve (food, wine, etc.). 4. to do a service, help; to favor. 5. to court, woo. — **para servirle a Ud.,** at your service. —*i.v.* 1. to serve (at table; in the army; in a post or employment); to work. 2. to be suitable, be useful, be good, e.g. *esta máquina no sirve para este trabajo,* this machine is no good for this work, *él no sirve para nada,* he's completely useless, he's good for nothing. 3. to be useful, be for use, e.g. *eso nos puede s.,* this can be of use to us. 4. to follow suit (in cards). 5. to serve (in tennis). — **s. de,** to serve as, act as. —*r.v.* to serve oneself, help oneself; **servirse** + *inf.,* to be kind enough + *inf.,* e.g. *él se ha servido acompañarnos a la casa,* he has been kind enough to accompany us to the house or home; **sírvase,** please, **e.g.** *sírvase pasar,* please come in; to have the pleasure of + *ger., quiero servirme acompañarte a la casa,* I want to have the pleasure of accompanying you to the house.
servita, *a., m.* (ecc.) Servite.
servocroata, *a., m., f.* Serbo-Croatian.
servomecanismo, *m.* servomechanism.
servomotor, *m.* (mach.) servomotor.
sesada, *f.* 1. (cul.) fried brains. 2. brains (of an animal).
sesámeo, a, *a.* (bot.) pertaining to sesame. —*f.* (*pl.*) sesamum (family).
sésamo, *m.* 1. (bot.) sesame. 2. sesame (magic word used by Ali Baba); **¡Abrete, sésamo!** Open, sesame!
sesamoideo, a, *a.* (anat.) sesamoid, sesamoidal.
sesear, *i.v.* to pronounce the Spanish c, before e and i, or the z as an s (esp. in Spanish-America and Southern Spain).
sesenta, *a., m.* sixty, sixtieth.
sesentavo, va, *a., m.* sixtieth.
sesentón, na, *a., m., f.* (coll.) sexagenarian.
seseo, *m.* pronouncing the Spanish c, before e and i, or z as an s (esp. in Spanish-America and the South of Spain).
sesera, *f.* 1. brainpan. 2. brains, brain.
sesga, *f.* (dressm.) gore, gusset.
sesgadamente, *adv.* 1. slantwise, askew, obliquely. 2. on the bias.
sesgado, da, *past part. of* **sesgar.** —*a.* 1. oblique, slanting. 2. cut on the bias.
sesgadura, *f.* 1. obliqueness, bias, slant. 2. (dressm.) goring; gusset.
sesgamente, *adv., var. of* **sesgadamente.**
sesgar, (*ref. 51*) *tr.v.* 1. to slant; to give an oblique direction to. 2. (dressm.) to cut on the bias.
sesgo, ga, *a.* 1. oblique, slanting, sloping. 2. on the bias. —*m.* 1. slant, slope; bias. 2. middle course, compromise. 3. direction, course. 4. (sew.) bias, bias binding or tape. — **al s.,** on the bias; slanting, slantwise, obliquely.
sesgue, sesgué, *ref.* **sesgar.**
sesí, (*pl.* **sesíes**), *m.* (Cuba, P. Rico, ichth.) sesi, black fin snapper.
sésil, *a.* (bot.) sessile.
sesión, *f.* session; sitting; meeting; conference; **abrir la s.,** to open the meeting or session; **estar en s.,** to be in session; **levantar la s.,** to adjourn the meeting or session; **s. espiritista,** séance.
sesma, *f., var. of* **sexma.**
sesmero, *m., var. of* **sexmero.**
sesmo, *m., var. of* **sexmo.**
seso, *m.* 1. brain. 2. intelligence, brains, sense, common sense. 3. (cul.) (*pl.*) brains. 4. stone to keep a pot steady on the fire. — **calentarse** or **devanarse los sesos,** to rack one's brains (in thought); **perder el s.,** to go mad, go out of one's mind; **tener sorbido el s. a uno,** to dominate, have completely under one's influence; to have someone under one's spell, have someone crazy about one; **tener sorbido el s. por,** to be mad or crazy about, be madly in love with; **levantarse la tapa de los sesos,** to blow one's brains out.
sesquiáltero, ra, *a.* sesquicentennial.
sesquimodio, *m.* one and a half modius or buckets.
sesquióxido, *m.* (chem.) sesquioxide.
sesquipedal, *a.* sesquipedalian, one and a half feet long.
sesteadero, *m.* shaded resting place for cattle.
sestear, *i.v.* 1. to take a rest, take a nap. 2. to rest in the shade (cattle).
sestercio, *m.* sesterce, ancient Roman coin.
sestero, sestil, *m., var. of* **sesteadero.**
sesudamente, *adv.* sensibly, wisely, prudently.
sesudez, *f.* wisdom, common sense, prudence.
sesudo, da, *a.* wise, sensible, prudent.
set, *m.* set (in tennis; in film studio).
seta, *f.* 1. (bot.) mushroom. 2. snuff (of a candle). 3. bristle.
setáceo, a, *a.* setaceous, having bristles.
setal, *m.* mushroom patch.
setecientos, tas, *a., m.* seven hundred.

setena, *f.* 1. seven, group of seven, septenary. 2. (*pl.*) fine amounting to the payment of seven times the sum involved. — **pagar con las setenas,** to pay or suffer excessively.
setenado, da, *a.* punished very severely. —*m.* period of seven years.
setenario, *m., var. of* **septenario.**
setenta, *a., m.* seventy; seventieth.
setentavo, va, *a., m.* seventieth.
setentón, na, *a., m., f.* (coll.) septuagenarian.
setiembre, *m.* September.
séptimo, ma, *a., m., f.* seventh.
seto, *m.* hedge, fence, enclosure; **s. vivo,** hedge, quickset, quickset hedge.
seudo, *a.* pseudo, pretended, false.
seudocarpio, seudocarpo, *m.* (bot.) pseudocarp.
seudomembrana, *f.* (anat.) pseudomembrane.
seudónimo, ma, *a.* pseudonymous. —*m.* pseudonym, nom de plume, pen name.
seudópodo, *m.* (biol.) pseudopod, pseudopodium.
S.E. u O. *abbrev. of* **salvo error u omisión,** errors and omissions excepted (E and O E).
Seúl, *m.* Seoul, capital of South Korea.
severamente, *adv.* severely; sternly.
severidad, *f.* severity; sternness, strictness, harshness; austerity.
severo, ra, *a.* 1. severe, harsh; strict, stern. 2. severe, grim, austere, grave.
seviche, *m.* (cul., Ecuad., Peru) spiced dish of raw fish marinated in lemon juice.
sevicia, *f.* extreme cruelty; maltreatment.
Sevilla, *f.* Seville, city and province in Spain.
sevillanas, *f.* (*pl.*) sevillanas, seguidillas of Seville, lively dance, music and song style typical of Seville.
sevillano, na, *a., m., f.* Sevillian.
sexagenario, ria, *a., m., f.* sexagenarian.
sexagésima, *f.* (ecc.) Sexagesima, second Sunday before Lent.
sexagesimal, *a.* sexagesimal.
sexagésimo, ma, *a.* sexagesimal, sixtieth.
sexagonal, *a.* hexagonal.
sexángulo, la, *a.* (geom.) hexagonal. —*m.* hexagon.
sexapil, *m.* sex appeal.
sexcentésimo, ma, *a., m.* six hundredth.
sexenal, *a.* occurring every six years.
sexenio, *m.* period of six years.
sexismo, *m.* sexism, discrimination or prejudice based on sex (esp. against women).
sexma, *f.* 1. sixth. 2. township, borough.
sexmero, *m.* representative of a township or borough.
sexmo, *m.* township, borough.
sexo, *m.* 1. sex. 2. penis, vulva. — **bello s.,** the fair sex; **s. débil,** the weaker sex; **s. feo, s. fuerte,** the stronger sex.
sexología, *f.* sexology.
sexólogo, ga, *m., f.* sexologist.
sexta, *f.* 1. (ecc.) sext. 2. (mus.) sixth. 3. (in ancient Rome) the third of the four parts of the day, afternoon. — **s. aumentada,** (mus.) augmented sixth; **s. disminuida,** (mus.) diminished sixth; **s. mayor or menor,** (mus.) major or minor sixth.
sextantario, ria, *a.* having the weight of a sextans (ancient Roman coin).
sextante, *m.* 1. sextant (instrument). 2. sextans (Roman coin). 3. (astron.) **S.,** Sextant. — **s. de burbuja,** bubble sextant.
sextario, *m.* sextarius (Roman measure).
sextavado, da, *a.* hexagonal.
sextavar, *tr.v.* to make hexagonal.
sexteto, *m.* (mus.) sextet, sextette.
sextil, *a.* (astron., astrol.) sextile.
sextilla, *f.* (poet.) sestet, sextain.
sextillo, *m.* (mus.) sextolet, sextuplet.
sextina, *f.* sestina (verse form of six hendecasyllabic sestets and one tercet).
sextina, *f.* (ecc.) letter of excommunication issued in order to detect delinquents.
sexto, ta, *a.* sixth. —*m.* 1. sixth. 2. (ecc.) book of canonical decrees. 3. (coll.) the Sixth Commandment.
séxtula, *f.* Roman copper coin.
sextuplicación, *f.* sextuplication, multiplication by six.
sextuplicar, (*ref. 50*) *tr.v., r.v.* to sextuple.
séxtuplo, pla, *a., m.* sextuple, sixfold.
sexuado, da, *a.* sexed.
sexual, *a.* sexual.
sexualidad, *f.* sexuality.
shakesperiano, na, *a.* Shakespearian.
shock, *m.* (med.) shock; **s. insulínico** or **hipoglicénico,** (med.) insulin shock.
short, *m.* shorts (trousers).
si, *m.* (mus.) ti, si, B, seventh note of the scale.
sí, *reflex. pron.* (used as object of prepositions) oneself, himself, itself, themselves, yourself, yourselves, each other; **dar de sí,** to give of oneself; to stretch; **de por sí,** by itself, in itself, alone; **entre sí,** among themselves, to each other; **en sí,** in itself, by itself; **fuera de sí,** beside oneself, etc. (with anger, joy); **para sí,** to oneself, etc., for oneself, etc.; **por sí y ante sí,** of one's own accord; **sobre sí,** carefully, cautiously, haughtily; **volver en sí,** to regain consciousness, come to.
sí, *adv.* 1. yes, yea, aye. 2. certainly, indeed, e.g. *esto sí que es bueno,* this is certainly good, *iré, sí, aunque pierda la vida,* I will certainly go, though I may lose my life. 3. often used for emphasis as an auxiliary verb, e.g. *él no habla francés pero yo sí,* he does not speak French, but I do. — **por sí o por no,** in any case; **sí tal,** indeed, certainly; **un día sí y un día no,** every other day, on alternate days. —*m.* yes; consent, permission. — **dar el sí,** to accept a marriage proposal.
si, *conj.* 1. if. 2. whether, if. 3. even though, although. — **como si,** as if; **por si acaso,** just in case; **si no,** if not; otherwise; **si tú supieras . . . ,** if you only knew . . . ; **¿y, si fuera verdad?** suppose it were true?
sialagogo, ga, *a.* (med.) sialogio, stimulating the secretion of saliva. —*m.* sialagogue.
siálido, da, *a., m.* (ento.) sialid, sialidan.
sialismo, *m.* (med.) salivation, secretion of saliva.
siamés, sa, *a., m., f.* Siamese.
siampán, *m.* (bot.) sapan tree and its wood.
sibarita, *a.* 1. Sybaritic (of or from Sybaris). 2. sybaritic, sensuous, given to pleasure. —*m., f.* 1. Sybarite, native of Sybaris. 2. sybarite, voluptuary.
sibarítico, ca, *a.* 1. Sybaritic (of or from Sybaris). 2. sybaritic, sensuous.
sibaritismo, *m.* sybaritism, love of luxury.
siberiano, na, *a., m., f.* Siberian.
sibil, *m.* cave; cellar, vault (for storing food).
sibila, *f.* sibyl, prophetess.
sibilante, *a.* sibilant, hissing. —*f.* (phonet.) sibilant.
sibilino, na, sibilítico, ca, *a.* 1. sibylline, sibyllic, pertaining to a sibyl. 2. mysterious, awe-inspiring.
sibucao, *m.* (Phil. I., bot.) sapanwood tree.
sicalipsis, *f.* pornography.
sicalíptico, ca, *a.* pornographic.
sicamor, *m.* (bot.) European Judas tree.
sicario, *m.* hired assassin.
sicigia, *f.* (astron.) syzygy, opposition or conjunction of sun and moon.
siciliano, na, *a.* Sicilian. —*m., f.* **Sicilian, native of Sicily, Italy.** —*m.* Sicilian (dialect).
siclo, *m.* shekel, an ancient Jewish silver coin.
sicoanálisis, *m.* (med.) psychoanalysis.
sicofanta, sicofante, *m.* informer, false accuser.
sicología, *f., var. of* **psicología.**
sicómoro, *m.* (bot.) sycamore; plane tree, button wood, sycamore maple.
sicón, *m.* (zool.) sycon.
sicono, *m.* (bot.) syconium, syconus.
sicosis, *f.* (med.) psychosis.
sicote, *m.* (Amer.) sweat and dirt in the toes.
sículo, la, *a., m., f.* Sicilian; (hist.) Siculian.
SIDA, *m.* (síndrome de inmunodeficiencia adquirida) AIDS (Acquired Immune Deficiency Syndrome).
sideral, sidéreo, a, *a.* sidereal, astral; pertaining to space.
siderita, *f.* 1. (min.) siderite. 2. (bot.) ironwort.
siderografía, *f.* siderography.
siderolito, *m.* (geol.) siderolite.
siderosa, *f.* (min.) siderite.
siderosis, *f.* (med.) siderosis.
siderotecnia, *f.* siderurgy.
siderurgia, *f.* siderurgy, iron and steel industry.
siderúrgico, ca, *a.* siderurgical iron and steel; **industria s.,** iron and steel industry.
sidonio, nia, *a., m., f.* (hist.) Sidonian.
sidra, *f.* cider; **s. seca,** hard cider.
sidrería, *f.* cider shop.
siega, *f.* harvesting, reaping; harvest time; harvest, crop gathered.
siego, siegue, *ref.* **segar.**
siembra, *f.* sowing, seed-planting; seedtime, sowing time; sown land.
siembre, siembro, *ref.* **sembrar.**
siempre, *adv.* always, ever, evermore; at all times; **de s.,** usual; **para s., por s.,** forever; **s. jamás,** forever and ever; **s. lo mismo,** always the same; **s. que, s. y cuando,** as long as, on condition that, provided that.
siempretieso, *m.* tumbler (toy **figure**).
siempreviva, *f.* (bot.) everlasting **flower,** immortelle; **s. mayor,** houseleek; **s. menor,** (bot.) white stonecrop.
sien, *f.* (anat.) temple.
siena, *f.* sienna (color).
siendo, *ref.* **ser.**
sienita, *f.* (min.) syenite, sienite.
sienítico, ca, *a.* (min.) syenitic.
sienta, siento, *ref.* **sentir.**
siente, siento, *ref.* **sentar.**
sierpe, *f.* 1. serpent, snake. 2. (fig.) ugly-looking person; angry or dangerous person. 3. (fig.) wriggler, anything that wriggles. 4. (bot.) sprout, shoot, sucker.
sierra, *f.* 1. saw. 2. jagged mountain range, sierra. 3. (ichth.) sawfish, sierra. — **s. abrazadera,** lumberman's saw; **s. caladora,** keyhole or coping saw; **s. cilíndrica,** crown saw; **s. circular,** circular or buzz saw; **s. colgante,** swing saw; **s. con armazón,** bucksaw; **s. continua,** band saw; **s. de arco,** bow saw, box saw; **s. de ballesta,** bucksaw; **s. de bastidor,** bucksaw; **s. de cadena,** chain saw; **s. de calar,** fretsaw; keyhole saw; **s. de cinta,** band saw; **s. de columpio,** swing saw; **s. de contornear,** compass saw, box saw; **s. de cordón,** band saw; **s. de cortar metales,** hacksaw; **s. de mano,** handsaw; **s. de marquetería,** fretsaw; **s. de péndulo,** swing saw; **s. de punta,** compass saw; **s. de recortar,** cutoff saw; **s. de tiro,** dragsaw; **s. de trasdós,** backsaw; **s. de través,** crosscut saw; **s. de trozar,** dragsaw; **s. de tumba,** crosscut saw; **s. en frío,** (metal.) cold saw; **s. huincha,** band saw; **s. mecánica,** power

saw; **s. neumática,** (mach.) pneumatic saw; **s. ranuradora,** grooving saw; **s. sin fin,** band saw; **s. tronzadera,** crosscut saw.
Sierra Leona, *f.* (geog.) Sierra Leone.
sierre, sierro, *ref.* **serrar.**
siervo, va, *m., f.* slave; serf; **s. de Dios,** servant of God; (coll.) poor devil; **s. de la gleba,** serf; **s. de los siervos de Dios,** name adopted by the Pope out of humility.
sieso, *m.* (anat.) anus.
siesta, *f.* 1. siesta, afternoon nap or rest. 2. hottest time of the day. 3. afternoon music in church. — **dormir la s., echar la s.,** to take a nap after lunch; **s. del carnero,** nap before lunch.
siete, *a.* seven. —*m.* 1. seven; seventh (of the month). 2. (carp.) clamp, dog. 3. (coll.) V-shaped tear in a garment. — **hablar más que s.,** to talk a blue streak; **s. y media,** seven-up, card game; **más que s.,** (coll.) very much; **son las s.,** it's seven o'clock.
sietecolores, (*pl.* **sietecolores**), *m.* (ornith.) (Amer.) (species of) tanager.
sietecueros, (*pl.* **sietecueros**), *m.* (Amer.) hard skin, callosity (on the heel); (Amer.) felon, whitlow (on the finger).
sieteenrama, *m.* (bot.) tormentil.
sietemesino, na, *a.* born in seven months (baby). —*m., f.* seven-month baby. —*m.* (coll.) runt, weakling.
sieteñal, *a.* seven-year-old.
sifílide, *f.* (med.) syphilide.
sífilis, *f.* (med.) syphilis.
sifilítico, ca, *a., m., f.* syphilitic.
sifilografía, *f.* (med.) syphilology, branch of medicine dealing with syphilis.
sifilógrafo, *m.* (med.) syphilologist, expert in syphilis.
sifiloma, *m.* (med.) syphiloma, syphilitic tumor.
sifón, *m.* 1. syphon; syphon bottle. 2. trap (in a drainpipe).
sifonóforo, *m.* (zool.) siphonophore.
sifosis, *f.* kyphosis, hump (on the back).
sifué, *m.* surcingle, strap securing the saddle.
siga, *ref.* **seguir.**
sigilación, *f.* sealing, stamping; seal, stamp, impression.
sigilar, *tr.v.* 1. to seal, stamp. 2. to conceal, keep secret.
sigilo, *m.* 1. seal, sigil. 2. secrecy; concealment; prudence, discretion. — **s. profesional,** professional secrecy kept by a lawyer or physician; **s. sacramental,** inviolable secrecy of the confessional.
sigilografía, *f.* sigillography, study of ancient seals.
sigilosamente, *adv.* secretly, silently, stealthily.
sigiloso, sa, *a.* silent, secretive; reserved.
sigla, *f.* abbreviation by initials, e.g. UNESCO.
siglo, *m.* 1. century; age, era, epoch. 2. the world, secular life. — **hace siglos que no lo veo,** it's years since I've seen him, I haven't seen him for years; **por los siglos de los siglos,** forever and ever, until the end of time; **s. de Acuario,** Age of Aquarius; **s. de oro,** Golden Age; **siglos medios,** the Middle Ages.
sigma, *f.* sigma, Greek letter corresponding to s.
sigmoideo, a, *a.* sigmoid, s-shaped.
signáculo, *m.* seal, signet (on documents).
signar, *tr.v.* to sign; to put a mark on, mark with a signet; to make the sign of the cross over. —*r.v.* to cross oneself.
signatario, ria, *a., m., f.* signatory.
signatura, *f.* 1. filing mark (to facilitate filing of documents), library number; (print.) signature. 2. (ecc.) Roman-Catholic court of justice and pardons.
signífero, ra, *a.* (poet.) carrying a mark or sign.
significación, *f.* meaning; significance, implication; importance.
significado, da, *a.* well-known, important, prominent. —*m.* sense, meaning (of a word).
significante, *a.* significant, meaningful.
significar, (*ref. 50*) *tr.v.* 1. to mean; to signify. 2. to indicate, point out, make known. —*i.v.* to be important. —*r.v.* to distinguish oneself; to call attention to oneself.
significativamente, *adv.* significantly.
significativo, va, *a.* significant, meaningful.
signifique, signifiqué, *ref.* **significar.**
signo, *m.* 1. sign, signal; mark; symbol. 2. flourish (in signature). 3. fate, destiny. 4. (astron., math., mus., print.) sign. 5. (gram.) mark (of punctuation). — **s. de admiración,** (gram.) exclamation mark; **s. de igual,** equal sign; **s. de interrogacion,** (gram.) question mark; **s. del Zodíaco,** sign of the Zodiac; **signos de puntuación,** punctuation marks; **s. de radicación,** (math.) radical sign; **s. diacrítico,** (gram.) diacritical mark; **s. fonético,** phonetic symbol; **s. más,** (math.) plus sign; **s. negativo,** (math.) minus sign; **s. positivo,** (math.) plus sign.
sigo, sigue, *ref.* **seguir.**
siguemepollo, *m.* ribbon formerly worn around the neck, with long streamers down the back.
siguiente, *a.* following, next.
siguiera, siguiese, siguió, *ref.* **seguir.**
sijú, (*pl.* **sijúes**), *m.* (ornith.) gnome owl.
sil, *m.* yellow ochre.
sílaba, *f.* syllable; **s. átona,** unaccented syllable; **s. postónica,** syllable following an accented one; **s. protónica,** syllable preceding an accented one; **s. tónica,** accented syllable.
silabar, *i.v.* to pronounce by syllables, to syllable.
silabario, *m.* spelling-book; primer (book to teach reading).
silabear, *i.v., tr.v.* to pronounce by syllables, syllable, syllabicate.
silabeo, *m.* syllabication, pronouncing by syllables.
silábico, ca, *a.* syllable.
sílabo, *m.* index, summary, syllabus.
silanga, *f.* (Phil. I.) channel, strait, inlet.
silba, *f.* whistling, hissing (in disapproval).
silbador, ra, *a.* whistling. —*m., f.* whistler.
silbante, *a.* whistling, hissing; sibilant.
silbar, *i.v.* to whistle; to whiz (as a passing bullet). —*tr.v.* (fig.) to whistle or hiss at (in disapproval).
silbatina, *f.* (Amer.) whistling, hissing (in disapproval).
silbato, *m.* 1. whistle (instrument). 2. crack (letting out air or a liquid with a whistling sound).
silbido, *m.* whistle, whistling; hiss, hissing; **s. de oídos,** ringing in the ears.
silbo, *m.* 1. whistle, whistling. 2. hiss, hissing (of snake). 3. whiz (e.g. of a bullet).
silbón, *m.* (ornith.) (a kind of) whistling widgeon.
silboso, sa, *a.* whistling, hissing.
silenciador, *m.* silencer (on gun, car, etc.); **s. de escape,** (mec.) exhaust silencer, muffler.
silenciar, *tr.v.* 1. to be silent about, pass over without mentioning. 2. to silence, impose silence on.
silenciario, ria, *a.* observing silence. —*m.* officer in charge of enforcing silence.
silenciero, ra, *a.* in charge of enforcing silence.
silencio, *m.* 1. silence. 2. (mus.) **rest. — en s.,** in silence; **guardar s.,** to keep quiet; **imponer s.,** to silence (someone).
silenciosamente, *adv.* silently, noiselessly.
silencioso, sa, *a.* quiet (person, neighborhood); noiseless (machine); taciturn.
Sileno, *m.* (myth.) Silenus, leader of the satyrs.
silente, *a.* quiet, silent, still.
silepsis, *f.* (rhet.) syllepsis.
silería, *f.* group of silos.
silero, *m.* (agr.) silo.
silesiano, na, silesio, sia, *a., m., f.* Silesian (of a region in Central Europe).
sílex, *m.* (chem.) silex.
sílfide, *f.* (myth.) sylph, nymph of the air; (fig.) sylph, slender graceful woman.
silfo, *m.* (myth.) sylph, imaginary beings supposed to inhabit the air.
silgar, (*ref. 51*) *tr.v.* 1. (mar.) to tow. 2. (mar.) to pole, propel (a boat) by the action of an oar at the stern of the boat.
silguero, *m.* (ornith.) linnet.
silicato, *m.* (chem.) silicate.
sílice, *f.* (chem.) silica.
silíceo, a, *a.* siliceous.
silícico, ca, *a.* (chem.) silicic.
silicio, *m.* (chem.) silicon.
siliciuro, *m.* (chem.)silicide.
silicón, *m.* **silicona,** *f.* **silicono,** *m.* (chem.) silicone.
silicosis, *f.* (med.) silicosis.
silicua, *f.* 1. siliqua (ancient weight). 2. (bot.) silique, siliqua.
silícula, *f.* (bot.) silicle, silique broader than it is long.
silicuoso, sa, *a.* (bot.) siliquose, siliquous.
silimanita, *f.* (min.) sillimanite.
silla, *f.* 1. chair, seat; saddle. 2. (ecc.) see. 3. (coll.) behind, seat, anus. — **s. alta,** high chair; **s. curul,** (hist.) curule; (Mex.) seat (in Parliament); **s. de cordero,** saddle of lamb; **s. de cubierta, de extensión,** deck chair; **s. de la reina,** or **de manos,** queen's chair, chair made by two persons crossing hands and grasping wrists; **s. de junco,** rush-bottomed chair; **s. de lona,** canvas chair; **s. de montar,** saddle; **s. de posta,** post chaise; **s. de ruedas,** wheel chair; **s. de tijera,** camp stool, folding chair; **s. eléctrica,** electric chair; **s. gestatoria,** gestatorial chair (used by Pope); **s. giratoria,** swivel chair; **s. mecedora,** rocking chair; **s. poltrona,** easy chair; **sillas apilables,** chairs that can be stacked or nested; **s. turca,** (anat.) Turkish saddle.
sillada, *f.* flat land (on mountain slope).
sillar, *m.* 1. (mas.) ashlar, ashlar stone. 2. horse's back (where saddle rests). — **s. de concreto,** cast stone; **s. de hoja,** (mas.) facing ashlar; **s. lleno,** (mas.) solid ashlar.
sillarejo, *m. dim. of* **sillar,** small ashlar stone, facing ashlar.
sillera, *f.* 1. place for storing sedan chairs. 2. woman who takes care of seats in church.
sillería, *f.* 1. chairs, set of chairs; stalls (of a choir, etc.). 2. chair store or factory. 3. chairmaking, chair business. 4. ashlar stone masonry.
sillero, ra, *m., f.* 1. chairmaker, chairdealer. 2. saddler.
silleta, *f.* 1. *dim. of* **silla,** small chair, stool. 2. bedpan. 3. chocolate grinding stone. 4. (*pl.*) (reg.) sidesaddle.
silletazo, *m.* blow with a chair.
silletero, *m.* 1. sedan chair carrier. 2. (Amer.) chairmaker, chairdealer.
sillico, *m.* chamber pot.
sillín, *m.* 1. fancy sidesaddle; light riding saddle; harness saddle. 2. saddle, seat (of bicycle, etc.).
sillón, *m.* 1. armchair, easy chair; (Cuba) rocking chair. 2. sidesaddle. — **s. de ruedas,** wheel chair.
sillonero, ra, *a.* (Amer.) docile, mountable, ridable (horses, mules).
silo, *m.* 1. silo, dry underground storage place. 2. (fig.) cave, cavern, dark place. 3. (Chile) silage, stored fodder.
silogismo, *m.* (log.) syllogism; **s. cornuto,** (log.) dilemma.

silogístico, ca, *a.* (log.) syllogistic.
silogizar, (*ref. 53*) *i.v.* to syllogize, **argue.**
silueta, *f.* silhouette; outline; profile.
siluriano, na, silúrico, ca, *a., m.* **(geol.)** Silurian.
silúrido, *m.* (ichth.) silurid, (*pl.*) Siluridae.
siluro, *m.* 1. (ichth.) catfish, sheatfish. 2. (fig., mar.) self-propelling torpedo.
silva, *f.* 1. miscellany. 2. (poet.) medieval verse form (revived by Rubén Darío).
silvanita, *f.* (min.) sylvanite, graphic tellurium.
Silvano, *m.* (myth.) Silvanus, Silvan, god of woods and forests.
silvático, ca, *a., var. of* **selvático.**
silvestre, *a.* wild; uncultivated; rustic.
silvicultor, *m.* forester, silviculturist.
silvicultura, *f.* forestry, silviculture.
SIM *abbrev. of* **Servicio de Inteligencia Militar,** Military Intelligence Service.
sima, *f.* chasm, abyss.
simaruba, *f.* (bot., Amer.) mountain damson, paradise tree.
simbiosis, *f.* (biol.) symbiosis.
simbiótico, ca, *a.* symbiotic, symbiotical.
simbólicamente, *adv.* symbolically.
simbolice, simbolicé, *ref.* **simbolizar.**
simbólico, ca, *a.* symbolic, symbolical.
simbolismo, *m.* symbolism.
simbolista, *a.* symbolistic. —*m., f.* symbolist.
simbolización, *f.* symbolization.
simbolizar, (*ref. 53*) *tr.v.* to symbolize; to typify, represent.
símbolo, *m.* symbol; sign, emblem; adage, saying. — **s. de la fe,** or **de los apóstoles,** Apostles' Creed; **s. químico,** chemistry symbol.
simetría, *f.* symmetry.
simétricamente, *adv.* symmetrically.
simétrico, ca, *a.* symmetric, symmetrical.
símico, ca, *a.* simian.
simiente, *f.* 1. seed; germ. 2. semen, sperm. — **s. de papagayos,** (bot.) bastard safflower.
simiesco, ca, *a.* simian, apelike, apish.
símil, *a.* similar, like, alike. —*m.* 1. resemblance, similarity. 2. (rhet.) simile.
similar, *a.* similar, like, resembling.
similicuero, *m.* imitation leather, leatherette.
similitud, *f.* similitude, similarity, resemblance.
similitudinario, ria, *a.* similar.
similor, *m.* similor (alloy of copper and zinc resembling gold); **de s.,** false, fake, sham.
simio, mia, *m., f.* (zool.) simian, monkey, ape.
simón, *m.* hack, cab; hackman, cab driver.
simonía, *f.* simony.
simoníacamente, *adv.* simoniacally.
simoníaco, ca, simoniático, ca, *a.* simoniac, simoniacal. —*m., f.* simonist.
simpa, *f.* (Arg., Peru) plait, braid.
simpatectomía, *f.* (surg.) sympathectomy.
simpatía, *f.* 1. liking, affection, fondness. 2. congeniality; pleasantness, likableness; winsomeness. 3. interest, sympathy, e.g. *recibió la idea con s.,* he received the idea with interest, he was sympathetic to the idea. 4. affinity, relationship, sympathy; (med.) sympathy. — **inspirar s.,** to inspire affection; **tener s. a** or **por,** to be fond of, have affection for.
simpáticamente, *adv.* pleasantly, nicely, congenially, likably.
simpatice, simpaticé, *ref.* **simpatizar.**
simpático, ca, *a.* 1. pleasant, nice, likable; appealing; congenial. 2. (mus., anat., med., phys., physiol.) sympathetic. — **gran simpático,** (anat., physiol.) sympathetic nervous system.
simpatina, *f.* (biochem.) sympathin.
simpatizador, ra, simpatizante, *a.* sympathizing, sympathetic, supporting. —*m., f.* sympathizer, supporter.
simpatizar, (*ref. 53*) *i.v.* to get along well together, be congenial; **s. con,** to get along well with; to sympathize with (e.g. a political party).
simpétalo, la, *a.* (bot.) sympetalous.
simpiezómetro, *m.* (hydr.) sympiesometer.
simple, *a.* 1. simple, uncompounded, uncombined; (bot., log., gram., chem.) simple. 2. single, e.g. *cama* or *cuarto s.,* single bed or room,, *juego de simples,* singles (in tennis), *flor s.,* single flower. 3. simple, uncomplicated, easy. 4. simple, mere. 5. simple, foolish. 6. insipid, tasteless. —*m., f.* simpleton, fool. —*m.* (pharm.) simple.
simplemente, *adv.* simply, plainly; absolutely.
simpleza, *f.* 1. simpleness, stupidity, stupidness; rusticity. 2. stupid remark, (*pl.*) nonsense.
simplicidad, *f.* simplicity.
simplísimo, ma, *a. super. of* **simple,** extremely simple.
simplificable, *a.* able to be simplified, simplifiable.
simplificación, *f.* simplification.
simplificador, ra, *a.* simplifying.
simplificar, (*ref. 50*) *tr.v.* to simplify.
simplifique, simplifiqué, *ref.* **simplificar.**
simplicísimo, ma, *a. super. of* **simple,** extremely simple.
simplismo, *m., var. of* **simplicidad,** simplicity.
simplista, *a.* simplistic, tending to oversimplify. —*m., f.* 1. simplist, advocate of simplification. 2. (med.) simplist, herbalist.
simplón, na, *a.* (coll.) simple, foolish; simplehearted, naive. —*m., f.* simpleton.
simpódico, ca, *a.* (bot.) sympodial.
simpodio, *m.* (bot.) sympodium.
simposio, *m.* symposium; **S.,** Symposium (of Plato).
simulación, *f.* simulation, pretense, feigning.
simulacro, *m.* 1. simulacrum, image, vision. 2. pretense, show, semblance, mock appearance, sham, simulacrum. 3. mockup, mock representation; (mil.) sham battle, war games.
simuladamente, *adv.* feigningly, deceivingly.
simulado, da, *a.* simulated, sham, imitated; pretended.
simulador, ra, *a.* simulative, pretending, feigning. —*m., f.* simulator, pretender, feigner.
simular, *tr.v.* to simulate, feign, sham; to pretend.
simultáneamente, *adv.* simultaneously.
simultanear, *tr.v.* to do or carry out simultaneously; to study (two courses) at the same time. —*r.v.* to happen at the same time.
simultaneidad, *f.* simultaneousness, simultaneity.
simultáneo, a, *a.* simultaneous. —*f.* (Col.) simultaneous showing (of a film in a town or several towns).
simún, *m.* simoom, simoon; sirocco (hot, dry, violent wind).
sin, *prep.* 1. without. 2. besides, apart from, not including; **s.** + *inf.,* without + *ger.,* e.g. *salió s. comer,* he went out without eating; un- + *past part.,* e.g. *dejaron la cuenta s. pagar,* they left the bill unpaid. — **s. embargo,** however, notwithstanding, nevertheless.
sinagoga, *f.* synagogue.
sinalagmático, ca, *a.* (law) mutually obligatory.
sinalefa, *f.* (gram.) synalepha.
sinamay, *m.* (Phil. I.) sinamay, thin cloth of abaca fiber.
sinamayera, *f.* (Phil. I.) woman cloth seller.
sinapismo, *m.* 1. (med.) mustard plaster, sinapism. 2. (coll.) bore, nuisance.
sinapsis, *f.* (physiol.) synapse; (biol.) synapsis.
sináptico, ca, *a.* (physiol., biol.) synaptic.
sinario, *m.* (rare) fate, destiny.
sinartrosis, *f.* (anat.) synarthrosis.
sincario, *m.* (biol.) synkaryon.
sincarion, *m.* (biol.) synkaryon.
sincárpico, ca, *a.* (bot.) syncarpous.
sincarpo, *m.* (bot.) syncarp.
sincerador, ra, *a.* exculpating, exonerating. *m., f.* exonerator, exculpator, defender.
sinceramente, *adv.* sincerely.
sincerar, *tr.v.* to exculpate, justify, exonerate. —*r.v.* to exonerate or vindicate oneself; **sincerarse de,** to exonerate oneself of.
sinceridad, *f.* sincerity, good faith.
sincero, ra, *a.* sincere.
sincipital, *a.* (anat.) sincipital.
sincipucio, *m.* (anat.) sinciput.
sinclástico, ca, *a.* (math., phys.) synclastic.
sinclinal, *a.* (geol.) synclinal. —*m.* (geol.) syncline.
síncopa, *f.* (mus., phonet.) syncope, syncopation.
sincopadamente, *adv.* syncopatedly.
sincopado, da, *past part. of* **sincopar.** —*a.* (mus.) syncopated.
sincopal, *a.* (med.) syncopal.
sincopar, *tr.v.* 1. (phonet., mus.) to syncopate. 2. (fig.) to abridge, abbreviate.
síncope, *m.* 1. (phonet.) syncope. 2. (med.) syncope, fainting spell; **s. cardíaco,** heart attack.
sincopice, sincopicé, *ref.* **sincopizar.**
sincopizar. (*ref. 53*) *tr.v.* to make (someone) faint or swoon. —*r.v.* to faint, swoon.
sincrético, ca, *a.* (philos., rel., gram.) syncretic.
sincretismo, *m.* 1. (philos., rel., gram.) syncretism.
sincrisis, *f.* (rhet.) syncrisis, the comparison of opposites.
sincrociclotrón, *m.* (phys.) synchrocyclotron.
sincronía, *f.* synchrony.
sincronice, sincronicé, *ref.* **sincronizar.**
sincrónico, ca, *a.* synchronous, synchronical, synchronic, simultaneous, contemporary.
sincronismo, *m.* synchronism, simultaneousness, contemporaneousness.
sincronización, *f.* synchronization.
sincronizado, da, *past part. of* **sincronizar.** —*a.* synchromesh.
sincronizador, ra, *m., f.* synchronizer. —*a.* synchronizing.
sincronizar, (ref. 53) tr.v. to synchronize. —*i.v.* to tune in.
sincronoscopio, *m.* (elec.) synchroscope, synchronoscope.
sincrotón, *m.* (phys.) synchrotron.
sindáctilo, la, *a.* (zool., med.) syndactyl, syndactyle.
sindéresis, *f.* good judgment, discretion.
síndesis, *f.* (biol.) syndesis, synapsis.
sindicación, *f.* 1. accusation. 2. syndication.
sindicado, *m.* syndicate (body of syndics).
sindicador, ra, *a.* accusing. —*m., f.* accuser, informer; prosecutor.
sindical, *a.* sindical; of the trade or labor union, e.g. **movimiento s.,** trade union movement.
sindicalice, *ref.* **sindicalizar.**
sindicalismo, *m.* trade unionism, unionism; syndicalism.
sindicalización, *f.* syndicalization, organization into a trade union.
sindicalista, *a.* syndicalistic. —*m., f.* trade unionist, unionist; syndicalist.
sindicalizar, (*ref. 53*) *tr.v.* to syndicate; organize into a trade union. —*r.v.* to organize into a trade union; to join a trade union.
sindicar, (*ref. 50*) *tr.v.* 1. to accuse, denounce, point to (as guilty). 2. to organize into a trade or labor union; to syndicate, organize into a syndicate. 3. to put into trust. —*r.v.* to organize into a trade or labor union; to join a trade or labor union.

sindicato, *m.* 1. labor union, trade union. 2. syndicate.
sindicatura, *f.* 1. (law) trusteeship; receivership (in bankruptcy proceedings). 2. post of syndic or representative (of a business corporation or township).
síndico, *m.* 1. (law) syndic, trustee, receiver (in bankruptcy proceedings). 2. syndic, representative (of a business corporation, a township, etc.).
sindique, sindiqué, *ref.* **sindicar.**
síndrome, *m.* (med.) syndrome; **s. de abstinencia,** withdrawal symptoms; **s. de inmunodeficiencia adquirida,** Acquired Immune Deficiency Syndrome (AIDS).
sinécdoque, *f.* (rhet.) synecdoche.
sinecología, *f.* (med.) synecology.
sinecura, *f.* sinecure, soft job (coll.).
sinedrio, *m., var. of* **sanedrín,** Sanhedrim, Sanhedrin.
sine qua non, (Lat.) absolutely necessary, essential.
sinéresis, *f.* 1. (gram.) synaeresis, syneresis, union of two vowels. 2. (chem.) syneresis.
sinergia, *f.* (physiol., med.) synergy.
sinergismo, *m.* 1. (physiol., med.) synergism, synergy. 2. (theol.) synergism.
sinergista, *m.* (theol.) synergist.
sinestesia, *f.* (physiol., psyc.) synesthesia.
sinfín, *m.* endless number, endless amount, great number.
sínfisis, *f.* (anat., med., biol.) symphysis.
sínfito, *m.* (bot.) comfrey.
sinfonía, *f.* symphony.
sinfónico, ca, *a.* 1. symphonic, e.g. *variaciones sinfónicas,* symphonic variations. 2. symphony, e.g. *orquesta sinfónica,* symphony orchestra.
sinfonista, *m., f.* symphonist.
singa, *f.* (mar.) poling, propelling with an oar or a pole at the stern.
singamia, *f.* (biol.) syngamy, sexual reproduction.
singámico, ca, *a.* (biol.) syngamic, syngamous.
Singapur, *m.* Singapore.
singar, *i.v.* (mar.) 1. to pole, scull, propel with an oar or pole at the stern. 2. (Cuba, vulg.) to have sexual intercourse, to fuck (vulg.).
singenésico, ca, *a.* (biol.) syngenetic.
singénesis, *f.* (biol.) syngenesis, sexual reproduction.
singierita, *f.* (min.) radioactive mineral containing uranium.
singladura, *f.* (mar.) day's run, day (from noon to noon).
singlar, *i.v.* (mar.) to sail, steer, travel over a course.
single, *a.* (mar.) single. —*m.* 1. singles match (in tennis), (*pl.*) singles. 2. (Angl.) single sleeping compartment (on a train).
singlón, *m.* (mar.) futtock.
singular, *a.* 1. singular, single. 2. exceptional, unique, extraordinary. 3. (gram.) singular. —*m.* (gram.) singular.
singularice, singularicé, *ref.* **singularizar.**
singularidad, *f.* 1. singularity. 2. uniqueness. 3. peculiarity.
singularizar, (*ref. 53*) *tr.v.* 1. to make stand out, singularize, distinguish. 2. (gram.) to use in the singular, make singular. —*r.v.* to distinguish oneself, stand out, make oneself conspicuous.
singularmente, *adv.* singularly, individually.
singulto, *m.* 1. sob. 2. (med.) hiccup, singultus.
sinhueso, *f.* (coll.) tongue.
sinícesis, *f.* (biol., gram.) synizesis, synaeresis.
sínico, ca, *a.* Sinic, Chinese, Sinitic.
siniestra, *f.* left hand; left-hand side.
siniestrado, da, *a.* ill-fated; injured, damaged. —*m., f.* victim.
siniestramente, *adv.* sinisterly, perversely.
siniestro, tra, *a.* 1. sinister, evil, wicked. 2. (her.) left, sinister. 3. unlucky, ill-fated, sinister. —*m.* 1. fire, disaster, calamity, accident. 2. perversity, evil disposition or habit.
sinistrorso, sa, *a.* 1. (bot.) sinistrorse, twining upward to the left. 2. counter-clockwise.
sinjusticia, *f.* (reg., P. Rico) injustice.
sinnúmero, *m.* great number, endless number.
sino, *m.* fate, destiny, lot.
sino, *conj.* 1. but (used in contraposition to a preceding negative clause), e.g. *no es verde s. azul,* it's not green but blue. 2. except, apart from, e.g. *no lo sabe nadie s. yo,* no one knows except me. 3. only, solely, e.g. *no te pido s. que me oigas,* I only ask that you hear me, all I ask is that you hear me, *no tengo s. un lápiz,* I have only one pencil; **no sólo . . . s.,** not only . . . but also.
sinoble, *a., m.* 1. (her.) sinople. 2. (obs.) vert, green.
sinocal, sínoco, ca, *a.* (med.) synochal (said of fever). —*f.* (med.) synochus.
sinodal, *a.* synodal (of a council). —*m.* synodal examiner. —*f.* decision made by a synod.
sinodático, *m.* (ecc.) annual donation made to the bishop by priests attending the synod.
sinódico, ca, *a.* 1. (astron.) synodic, synodical. 2. (ecc.) synodal.
sínodo, *m.* (ecc., astron.) synod; **Santo S.,** Holy Synod (of the Eastern Church).
sinojaponés, sa, *a.* Sino-Japanese.
sinología, *f.* Sinology, the study of the language, literature, customs, history, etc. of China.
sinológico, ca, *a.* Sinological.
sinólogo, *m.* Sinologist, person who specializes in Sinology.
sinonimia, *f.* synonymy, synonymity; (rhet.) synonymy.
sinónimo, ma, *a.* synonymous. —*m.* synonym.
sinople, *a.* (her.) synople, vert.
sinopsis, (*pl.* **sinopsis**), *f.* synopsis.
sinóptico, ca, *a.* synoptic, synoptical.
sinovia, *f.* (anat.) synovia.
sinovial, *a.* (anat.) synovial.
sinovitis, *f.* (med.) synovitis.
sinrazón, *f.* 1. unreasonableness; illogical remark or statement. 2. wrong, injustice.
sinsabor, *m.* 1. trouble, sorrow. 2. insipidness.
sinsonte, *m.* (ornith.) mockingbird.
sinsubstancia, *m., f.* (coll.) frivolous, superficial person.
sintáctico, ca, *a.* (gram.) syntactic.
sintaxis, (*pl.* **sintaxis**), *f.* (gram.) syntax.
sinterización, *f.* (metal.) sintering.
sinterizar, *tr.v.* (metal.) to sinter.
síntesis, (*pl.* **síntesis**), *f.* synthesis.
sintéticamente, *adv.* synthetically.
sintetice, sinteticé, *ref.* **sintetizar.**
sintético, ca, *a.* synthetic, synthetical.
sintetizar, (*ref. 53*) *tr.v.* to synthesize.
sintiendo, sintiera, sintiese, sintió, *ref.* **sentir.**
sintoísmo, *m.* Shinto, Shintoism, a principal religion of Japan; the state religion prior to 1945.
sintoísta, *a., m., f.* Shintoist, person who practices the Shinto religion.
síntoma, *m.* symptom; **s. de abstinencia,** withdrawal symptom.
sintomático, ca, *a.* symptomatic.
sintomatología, *f.* (med.) symptomatology.
sintonía, *f.* (rad., psyc.) syntony.
sintonice, sintonicé, *ref.* **sintonizar.**
sintónico, ca, *a.* syntonic, syntonical.
sintonina, *f.* (biochem.) syntonin.
sintonismo, *m.* 1. (rad.) syntony, tuning. 2. (elec.) syntony, oscillation, adjustment.
sintonización, *f.* syntonization, tuning; **s. aguda,** sharp tuning; **s. selectiva,** selective tuning.
sintonizador, *m.* (elec.) syntonizer, tuner.
sintonizar, (*ref. 53*) *tr.v.* to syntonize, make (two or more radio systems) vibrate in unison, tune. —*i.v.* to syntonize. — **s. con,** to tune in.
sinuosidad, *f.* 1. sinuosity. 2. hollow, concavity.
sinuoso, sa, *a.* 1. sinuous, winding, wavy. 2. (fig.) evasive, secretive.
sinusitis, *f.* (med.) sinusitis.
sinusoidal, *a.* (geom.) sinusoidal, sine.
sinusoide, *f.* (geom.) sinusoid.
sinvergonzón, ona, *a.* (coll.) shameless, brazen. —*m., f.* (coll.) scoundrel, rogue, brazen person.
sinvergüencería, *f.* (coll.) shamelessness, brazenness.
sinvergüenza, *a.* shameless, brazen. —*m., f.* scoundrel, rascal, rogue, brazen person.
sinvergüenzada, *f.* (Col.) base action, dirty trick.
Sión, *m.* (Bib., hist.) Zion, Sion.
sionismo, *m.* (hist., pol.) Zionism.
sionista, *a.* Zionist, of or pertaining to Zionism. —*m., f.* supporter of the Zionist cause.
SIP *abbrev. of* **Sociedad Interamericana de Prensa,** Interamerican Press Association.
siquier, siquiera, *adv.* 1. at least, e.g. *déme una peseta siquiera,* give me one peseta at least. 2. even, e.g. *ni una carta siquiera,* not even a letter. —*conj.* although, even though, e.g. *hazme un favor, siquiera el último,* do me a favor, even though it may be the last.
siracusano, na, *a., m., f.* (geog.) Syracusan.
sirena, *f.* 1. (myth.) siren; mermaid. 2. siren, foghorn, signal. 3. (phys.) siren (device for producing musical sounds, especially for acoustical study) — **s. de playa** (hum.) bathing beauty.
sirenio, nia, *a.* (zool.) sirenian. —*m.* sirenian, (*pl.*) Sirenia.
sirga, *f.* (mar.) towrope, towline; **rope for** hauling in nets; **a la s.,** tracking from the bank.
sirgar, (*ref. 51*) *tr.v.* (mar.) to tow, to track.
sirgo, *m.* twisted silk; silk fabric.
sirguero, *m.* (ornith.) linnet.
Siria, *f.* (geog., hist.) Syria.
siríaco, ca, *a.* Syrian; Syriac. —*m., f.* Syrian.
siringa, *f.* 1. (mus.) syrinx. 2. (Bol., Peru, bot.) seringa, rubber yielding tree.
siringe, *f.* (ornith.) syrinx (vocal organs of birds).
siringomielia, *f.* (med.) syringomyelia.
Sirio, *m.* (astron.) Sirius.
Sirio, ria, *a., m., f.* Syrian. —*m.* **S.,** (astron.) Sirius.
sirle, *m.* sheep or goat dung, manure.
siroco, *m.* sirocco, Mediterranean wind that blows from the Southeast.
sirope, *m.* (Amer.) syrup.
sirria, *f., var. of* **sirle.**
sirte, *f.* 1. submerged sand bank. 2. quick-sand, syrtes.
sirviendo, *ref.* **servir.**
sirvienta, *f.* maid, servant.
sirviente, *a.* serving; (law) servient. —*m.* manservant, servant.
sirviera, sirviese, sirvió, *ref.* **servir.**
sisa, *f.* 1. petty theft, snitching, pinching, filching. 2. (dressm.) dart, tapering seam; armhole. 3. (arch.) excise tax on foodstuffs. 4. size (used by gilders.)
sisador, ra, *a.* snitching, thieving, filching. —*m., f.* petty thief, filcher.
sisallo, *m.* (bot.) saltwort.
sisar, *tr.v.* 1. to snitch, filch. 2. (dressm.) to take in. 3. (arch.) to excise, place an excise tax on. 4. (Ecuad.) to glue broken chinaware. 5. to size (for gilding).
sisarcosis, *f.* (anat.) syssarcosis.

sisear, *tr.v.* to hiss, hiss at. —*i.v.* to hiss.
siseo, *m.* hiss. hissing.
sisero, *m.* excise collector (official placing an excise tax on foodstuffs).
Sísifo, *m.* (myth.) Sisyphus, who was doomed to roll a stone uphill forever.
sisimbrio, *m.* (bot.) sisymbrium, hedge mustard.
sísmico, ca, *a.* seismic.
sismo, *m.* earthquake.
sismocronógrafo, *m.* seismochronograph.
sismografía, *f.* seismography.
sismográfico, ca, *a.* seismographic.
sismógrafo, *m.* seismograph.
sismograma, *m.* seismogram.
sismología, *f.* seismology.
sismológico, *a.* seismologic, seismological.
sismólogo, *m.* seismologist, seismographer.
sismómetro, *m.* seismometer.
sisón, na, *a.* (coll.) pilfering, filching, thieving. —*m., f.* (coll.) petty thief, pilferer, filcher. —*m.* (ornith.) little bustard.
sistáltico, ca, *a.* (physiol.) systaltic.
sistema, *m.* system; **s. al tacto,** touch system; **s. astático,** astatic system; **s. automático,** automatic system; **s. cegesimal,** C.G.S. system, centimeter-gram-second system; **s. métrico** or **métrico-decimal,** metric system; **s. montañoso,** mountain range; **s. nervioso central,** central nervous system; **s. operativo de disco,** disk operating system; **s. periódico,** (chem.) periodic system; **s. planetario,** (astrol.) planetary system; **s. solar,** solar system.
sistemáticamente, *adv.* systematically.
sistematice, sistematicé, *ref.* **sistematizar.**
sistemático, ca, *a.* systematic, systematical.
sistematización, *f.* systematization.
sistematizar, (*ref. 53*) *tr.v.* to systematize.
sístilo, *m.* (archit.) systyle.
sístole, *f.* (biol., physiol., poet.) systole.
sistólico, ca, *a.* systolic.
sistro, *m.* (mus.) sistrum, ancient Egyptian instrument.
sitacosis, *f.* (med.) psittacosis, parrot fever.
sitiado, da, *past part. of* **sitiar.** —*a.* **surrounded, besieged.**
sitiador, ra, *a.* besieging. —*m., f.* besieger.
sitial, *m.* seat of honor, high position.
sitiar, *tr.v.* 1. to beleaguer, besiege; (mil.) to lay siege to. 2. to surround, hem in.
sitibundo, da, *a.* (poet.) thirsty.
sitiero, ra, *m., f.* (Cuba) small farmer or rural landowner.
sitio, *m.* 1. place, spot; location, site. 2. space, room. 3. country house, country estate; (Cuba) farm, rural property. 4. taxi stand or station. — **dejar en el s.,** to kill outright; **quedarse uno en el s.,** to die on the spot, die suddenly.
sitio, *m* (mil.) siege; **estado de s., martial** law; **levantar el s.,** to raise the siege; **poner s. a,** to lay siege to.
sito, ta, *a.* situated, located, lying.
situación, *f.* 1. situation, location, site; position. 2. situation, circumstances, position. 3. state, condition. — **buena s.,** good economic conditions, prosperous circumstances; good location; **s. activa,** active service, office or position; **s. ridícula,** ridiculous position.
situado, da, *past part. of* **situar.** —*a.* situated, located, placed. —*m.* fixed income.
situar, (*ref. 55*) *tr.v.* 1. to put, situate, place, locate. 2. to assign (money for payment, investment). —*r.v.* 1. to situate or locate oneself. 2. to take one's stand.
siútico, ca, *a.* (Chile) showy, in poor taste, flashy, vulgar.
siutiquez, *f.* (Chile) showiness, flashiness, lack of taste.
siux, *a., m., f.* (ethnol., U. S.) Sioux.
Sixtina, *a.* Sistine (chapel, etc.).
S. L. *abbrev. of* **sociedad de responsabilidad limitada,** limited company.
slogan, *m.* (Angl.) slogan.
Sm *sym. of* **samario,** samarium (Sm).
S. M. *abbrev. of* **Su Majestad,** Her or His Majesty (H. M.).
smoking, *m.* dinner jacket, tuxedo.
Sn *sym. of* **estaño,** stannum-tin (Sn).
s/n *abbrev. of* **sin número,** without number.
snob, *m., f.* (Angl.) snob.
snobismo, *m.* snobbishness.
!so! *interj.* whoa! (command to a horse).
so, *prep.* under, e.g. *so pena de,* under penalty of, on pain of. — emphatic word used with derogatory adjectives, e.g. *so tonto,* you blithering idiot.
S.O. *abbrev. of* **sudoeste,** southwest (SW).
soasar, *tr.v.* to roast lightly.
soata, *f.* (Ven., bot.) a kind of squash.
soba, *f.* 1. kneading; rubbing; massage. 2. beating, thrashing. 3. (fig., coll.) annoyance.
sobacal, *a.* (anat.) axillary.
sobaco, *m.* 1. (anat.) armpit, axilla. 2. (bot.) axil. 3. (archit.) spandrel.
sobadero, ra, *a.* kneadable; rubbable. —*m.* place where skins are rubbed (in tanning factories).
sobado, da, *past part. of* **sobar.** —*a.* 1. greased with shortening or oil (dough). 2. rumpled, worn, much handled. —*m.* 1. kneading; rubbing; massaging. 2. (C. Rica) kind of taffy (candy).
sobadura, *f.* kneading, rubbing; massaging.
sobajadura, *f.* rumpling, crushing.
sobajamiento, *m., var. of* **sobajadura.**
sobajanero, *m.* (coll., Sp.) messenger.
sobajar, *tr.v.* 1. to rumple, crumple; to paw. 2. (Arg., Ecuad., Mex.) to humiliate.
sobanda, *f.* either end of a barrel or cask.
sobaquera, *f.* armhole (of a garment); armhole reinforcement; shield, underarm shield (for protecting clothes against sweat from armpits).
sobaquina, *f.* perspiration odor from armpits.
sobar, *tr.v.* 1. to knead; to rub; to massage. 2. to paw, pet, feel. 3. to beat, slap, thrash, pummel. 4. to vex, pester, annoy. 5. (Amer.) to soft-soap (coll.), flatter.
sobarba, *f.* 1. noseband (of a horse). 2. double chin.
sobarbada, *f.* 1. sudden checking (of a horse). 2. rebuke, reprimand, scolding.
sobarbo, *m.* bucket, blade (of a water wheel); cam (in a fulling mill).
sobarcar, (*ref. 50*) *tr.v.* to place or carry under the arm; to raise a garment up to the underarm.
sobeo, *m.* thong (to tie the yoke to the pole of a carriage or to a plow handle).
soberado, *m.* (Amer.) attic.
soberanamente, *adv.* 1. with sovereignty or authority. 2. extremely, exceedingly, highly.
soberanear, *i.v.* to lord it (over someone); to domineer, boss.
soberanía, *f.* 1. sovereignty; supremacy. 2. rule, sway.
soberano, na, *a.* 1. sovereign. 2. supreme, unsurpassed. 3. superior. 4. (coll.) tops, great. —*m., f.* sovereign. —*m.* sovereign (coin).
soberbia, *f.* 1. pride, arrogance, haughtiness; conceit, vanity, presumption. 2. sumptuousness, pomp. 3. rage, fury.
soberbiamente, *adv.* 1. arrogantly, haughtily. 2. superbly, sumptuously.
soberbio, bia, *a.* 1. arrogant, haughty, proud. 2. superb, magnificent. 3. enormous, tremendous. 4. spirited, fiery (steed).
sobermejo, ja, *a.* dark vermillion, dark red.
sobina, *f.* peg, wooden pin.
sobón, na, *a.* 1. (coll.) mushy, pawing (given to excessive fondling). 2. (coll.) loafing, slacking, gold-bricking (sl.). 3. (Amer.) fawning, soft-soaping, apple-polishing. —*m., f.* 1. (coll.) mushy person. 2. (coll.) loafer, slacker. 3. (Amer.) soft-soaper, apple-polisher, boot-licker.
sobordo, *m.* (mar.) 1. checking of a ship's cargo against the freight list. 2. freight list, manifest. 3. bonus (paid to a freighter's crew in wartime).
sobornación, *f.* bribing, bribery.
sobornado, da, *a.* misshapen (loaf of bread).
sobornador, ra, *a.* bribing, suborning. —*m., f.* briber.
sobornal, *m.* extra load, overload.
sobornar, *tr.v.* to bribe, suborn.
soborno, *m.* 1. bribing, suborning; bribery; bribe; (coll.) bribe, enticement. 2. (Arg., Bol., Chile) extra load, overload. — **de s.,** (Arg., Bol., Chile) in addition.
sobra, *f.* 1. surplus, excess, extra. 2. (*pl.*) left-overs, leavings; rubbish, trash. — **de s.,** superfluous; more than enough; only too well, e.g. *sabes de s.,* you know only too well; **de s.,** (coll.) to be one too many.
sobradamente, *adv.* only too well, more than enough, in excess.
sobradar, *tr.v.* to build an attic or garret onto.
sobradillo, *m.* (archit.) penthouse, sloping roof over a window or balcony.
sobrado, da, *a.* 1. abundant, more than enough, excessive. 2. bold, licentious, brazen. 3. rich, wealthy. 4. (Peru, coll.) conceited. 5. (Chile) tremendous, terrific. —*m.* 1. attic, garret. 2. (Arg.) china hutch.
sobrado, *adv., var. of* **sobradamente.**
sobrancero, *a.* 1. unemployed, jobless, out of work. 2. (Cuba) excessive, surplus. —*m.* unemployed person.
sobrante, *a.* leftover, remaining; surplus, excess. —*m.* leftover, surplus, remainder.
sobrar, *tr.v.* to exceed, surpass. —*i.v.* 1. to be more than enough, be too much, be in excess; to be left over, be surplus. 2. to be in the way, be unwanted, be intrusive.
sobrasada, *f.* highly-seasoned pork sausage from the island of Majorca.
sobrasar, *tr.v.* to increase the heat (under a pot).
sobre, *prep.* 1. above, over, e.g. *el avión voló s. la ciudad,* the plane flew over the city. 2. on, on top of, upon, e.g. *puso el libro s. la mesa,* he put the book on the table. 3. about, concerning, on, e.g. *hablar s. el costo de la vida,* to talk about the cost of living. 4. about, approximately, around, e.g. *volveré s. las diez,* I'll return around ten. 5. in addition to. 6. on, with surety of, e.g. *préstame veinte pesetas s. esta alhaja,* lend me twenty pesetas on this piece of jewelry. 7. against, on, e.g. *en los últimos años ha girado mucho s. su cuenta corriente,* in the last years he has drawn a great deal on or against his checking account. 8. on or near. 9. on, e.g. *poner un impuesto s.,* to put a tax on. —(com.) **s. la par,** above par; **s. manera,** beyond measure, exceedingly; **s. sí,** on guard. —*m.* 1. envelope. 2. address (on a letter).
sobreabundancia, *f.* superabundance.
sobreabundante, *a.* superabundant.
sobreabundantemente, *adv.* superabundantly.
sobreabundar, *i.v.* to superabound.
sobreaguar, (*ref. 52*) *i.v., r.v.* to float on the water.
sobreagudo, da, *a.* (mus.) treble; high-pitched. —*m.* high-pitched note.
sobrealiento, *m.* hard or labored breathing.

sobrealimentación, *f.* 1. overfeeding. 2. (mec.) supercharging.

sobrealimentar, *tr.v.* to overfeed.

sobrealzar, (*ref. 53*) *tr.v.* to raise, raise higher.

sobreañal, *a.* over a year old (animal).

sobrearco, *m.* (archit.) relieving arch, discharging arch.

sobreasada, *f., var. of* **sobrasada.**

sobrebarato, ta, *a.* very cheap.

sobrebarrer, *tr.v.* to sweep lightly.

sobrebota, *f.* (C. Amer.) leather legging.

sobrecaja, *f.* outer case.

sobrecalentador, *m.* superheater.

sobrecalza, *f.* legging.

sobrecama, *f.* bedspread, coverlet.

sobrecaña, *f.* (vet.) bony tumor (on a horse's leg).

sobrecarga, *f.* 1. overload; extra load. 2. packing strap. 3. supercharge. 4. additional burden or trouble.

sobrecargado, da, *past part. of* **sobrecargar.** —*a.* 1. overloaded. 2. surcharged (stamp).

sobrecargo, *m.* (mar.) supercargo, purser.

sobrecargue, sobrecargué, *ref.* **sobrecargar.**

sobrecarta, *f.* envelope (of a letter).

sobrecédula, *f.* second or confirmatory royal decree.

sobreceja, *f.* brow (part of the forehead above the eyebrows).

sobrecejo, *m.* frown; menacing look.

sobrecenar, *i.v.* to have a second dinner or supper. —*tr.v.* to eat as a second supper.

sobreceño, *m.* frown, scowl.

sobrecerco, *m.* (sew.) reinforcing border or edge.

sobrecerrado, da, *a.* well closed.

sobrecielo, *m.* awning, canopy.

sobrecincha, *f.* **sobrecincho,** *m* surcingle.

sobreclaustra, *f.* **sobreclaustro,** *m.* room or apartment over a cloister.

sobrecogedor, dora, *a.* surprising, startling.

sobrecoger, (*ref. 57*) *tr.v.* to surprise, catch unawares. —*r.v.* to be surprised; to be frightened or scared; **sobrecogerse de,** to be seized with (horror, fear, etc.).

sobrecogimiento, *m.* surprise, awe, fear, apprehension.

sobrecojo, sobrecoja, *ref.* **sobrecoger.**

sobrecopa, *f.* cover or lid (of a glass or cup).

sobrecoser, *tr.v.* (sew.) to whipstitch; to fell (a seam).

sobrecrecer, (*ref. 45*) *i.v.* to grow too much, overgrow.

sobrecreciente, *a.* growing too much, overgrowing.

sobrecruz, (*pl.* **sobrecruses**), *f.* spoke of a water wheel.

sobrecubierta, *f.* 1. extra cover, outside wrapper. 2. (mar.) upper deck. 3. dust jacket (of a book).

sobrecuello, *m.* over-collar (worn over another collar).

sobredicho, cha, *a.* above-mentioned, aforesaid, aforementioned.

sobrediente, *m.* snaggletooth.

sobredorar, *tr.v.* 1. to gold-plate (esp. silver). 2. (fig.) to gloss over, make excuses for.

sobreedificar, (*ref. 50*) *tr.v.* to build on top of (another construction).

sobreempeine, *m.* instep of a legging.

sobreenfriar, (*ref. 54*) *tr.v.* (phys., chem.) to undercool, supercool.

sobreentender, (*ref. 30*) *tr.v., var. of* **sobrentender.**

sobreentendido, da, *past part. of* **sobreentender.** —*a.* implicit.

sobreentienda, sobreentiendo, *ref.* sobreentender.

sobreesdrújulo, la, *a., m., var. of* **sobresdrújulo.**

sobreestadía, *f.* (mar.) days of delay (in port), demurrage; (mar.) demurrage, amount paid for extra lay days.

sobreexcitación, *f.* overexcitement.

sobreexcitar, *tr.v.* to overexcite. —*r.v.* to be or become overexcited.

sobrefalda, *f.* overskirt.

sobrefaz, (*pl.* **sobrefaces**), *f.* surface, outside.

sobreflor, *f.* flower growing within another.

sobrefrenada, *f.* saccade; sudden checking of a horse.

sobrefusión, *f.* (chem., phys.) superfusion, supercooling.

sobregirar, *tr.v.* (com.) to overdraw.

sobregiro, *m.* (com.) overdraft; **s. aparente** or técnico, (com.) technical overdraft.

sobreguarda, *m.* head guard; auxiliary guard.

sobrehaz, (*pl.* **sobrehaces**), *f.* 1. surface, outside. 2. cover, covering. 3. superficial appearance.

sobreherido, da, *a.* slightly wounded.

sobrehilado, *m.* overcast stitch (to prevent raveling).

sobrehilar, *tr.v.* (sew.) to overcast.

sobrehueso, *m.* 1. (vet.) exostosis, bony outgrowth. 2. burden, annoyance; trouble, difficulty.

sobrehumano, na, *a.* superhuman.

sobreimpuesto, *m.* overtax, surtax.

sobrejalma, *f.* blanket placed over a packsaddle.

sobrejuanete, *m.* (mar.) royal mast; royal sail.

sobrelecho, *m.* (archit.) underside of a stone.

sobrellave, *f.* 1. double lock. 2. person authorized to possess the key to the second lock.

sobrellenar, *tr.v.* to fill, to overflow.

sobrelleno, na, *a.* full to the brim, overflowing, running over.

sobrellevar, *tr.v.* 1. to carry, bear. 2. to ease (another's burden). 3. to overlook, be lenient about (another's faults or misdeeds). 4. to put up with, endure, bear.

sobreltado, *m.* (her.) small escutcheon (superimposed on a larger one).

sobremanera, *adv.* excessively, exceedingly, beyond measure.

sobremano, *f.* (vet.) exostosis of bony outgrowth on the forehoof of a horse.

sobremarcha, *f.* (auto.) overdrive.

sobremesa, *f.* 1. tablecloth, table cover. 2. sitting at the table after eating. — **de s.,** at the table after eating; after-dinner, e.g. *charla de s.*, after-dinner conversation.

sobremesana, *f.* (mar.) mizzen topsail.

sobremodo, *adv.* exceedingly, excessively.

sobremuñonera, *f.* (artil.) clamp, capsquare.

sobrenadar, *i.v.* to float.

sobrenatural, *a.* supernatural.

sobrenaturalismo, *m.* supernaturalism.

sobrenaturalmente, *adv.* supernaturally.

sobrenjalma, *f., var. of* **sobrejalma.**

sobrenombre, *m.* surname; agnomen; nickname.

sobrentender, (*ref. 30*) *tr.v.* to understand (something implied) —*r.v.* to be understood go without saying.

sobrentienda, sobrentiendo, *ref.* **sobrentender.**

sobrepaga, *f.* increased pay; extra pay.

sobrepaño, *m.* top cloth.

sobreparto, *m.* confinement, lying-in after childbirth; delicate health after childbirth.

sobrepasar, *tr.v.* to exceed, surpass.

sobrepaso, *m.* (Amer.) amble, gait (of a walking horse).

sobrepeine, *adv.* (coll.) lightly, superficially.

sobrepelo, *m.* (Arg.) horse blanket, saddle blanket.

sobrepelliz, (*pl.* **sobrepellices**), *f.* (ecc.) surplice.

sobrepeso, *m.* overweight; excess weight, excess baggage (fig.).

sobrepié, *m.* (vet.) splint in rear hoof.

sobreplán, *f.* (mar.) rider.

sobreponer, (*ref. 15*) *tr.v.* to put on top; to superimpose. —*r.v.* to control oneself; to pull oneself together; **sobreponerse a,** to overcome, master; to rise above (fig.).

sobreponga, sobrepongo, *ref.* **sobreponer.**

sobreposición, *f.* superposition.

sobreprecio, *m.* extra charge, surcharge.

sobreproducción, *f.* overproduction.

sobrepuerta, *f.* 1. valance, frame for curtains over a door; cornice over a door. 2. door curtain. 3. overdoor (painting, carving or ornamental cloth over a doorway).

sobrepuesto, ta, *irr. past part. of* **sobreponer.** —*a.* appliqué (work). —*m.* 1. appliqué work. 2. honeycomb formed by bees after the hive is full. 3. (Amer.) patch, mend.

sobrepujamiento, *m.* surpassing, excelling.

sobrepujante, *a.* surpassing, excelling.

sobrepujanza, *f.* power, might, vim, vigor.

sobrepujar, *tr.v.* to surpass, outdo, excel.

sobrepuse, sobrepusiera, sobrepusiese, *ref.* sobreponer.

sobrequilla, *f.* (mar.) keelson.

sobrero, *a.* (taur.) standby, substitute (bull).

sobrerrienda, *f.* (Amer.) checkrien.

sobrerronda, *f.* (mil.) sentinel's extra round.

sobrerropa, *f.* overalls; smock.

sobresalga, sobresalgo, *ref.* **sobresalir.**

sobresaliente, *a.* 1. projecting. 2. outstanding, excellent. 3. notable, remarkable, conspicuous. —*m.* 1. the highest grade on an examination 2. (taur.) substitute bullfighter. —*m., f.* substitute, understudy.

sobresalir, (*ref. 21*) *i.v.* 1. to project, jut out. 2. to stand out, excel; to be prominent or distinguish oneself. 3. to stand out, be conspicuous.

sobresaltar, *tr.v.* 1. to fall upon; to attack, assail. 2. to startle, alarm, frighten, scare. —*i.v.* to stand out, be striking. —*r.v.* to be startled, be frightened; to start, jump. — **sobresaltarse con or por,** to be startled or frightened by; to start or jump at.

sobresalto, *m.* sudden fright, scare, alarm; start, shock; **de s.,** suddenly, unexpectedly.

sobresanar, *i.v.* 1. to heal superficially (a wound). 2. (fig.) to cover up a fault.

sobresano, *adv.* 1. healing superficially. 2. feigningly, pretendingly, deceivingly. —*m.* (mar.) tabling, leachlining.

sobresaturación, *f.* (chem.) supersaturation.

sobresaturado, da, *a.* (chem.) supersaturated.

sobrescribir, *irr. past part.:* **sobrescrito, sobrescripto.** —*tr.v.* to superscribe, write over; to address (a letter).

sobrescrito, ta, *irr. past part. of* **sobrescribir.**

sobrescrito, ta, *irr. past part. of* **sobrescribir.** —*m.* address (on a letter).

sobresdrújulo, la, *a.* accented on the syllable preceding the antepenult. —*m.* word accented on the syllable preceding the antepenult.

sobreseer, (*ref. 60*) *i.v.* 1. (law) to supercede; to stay (a judgment); to discontinue; to dismiss. 2. to desist (from a plan); to abandon one's obligations. 3. (law) to yield.

sobreseimiento, *m.* (law) stay of proceedings; dismissal; discontinuance; nonsuit; **s. definitivo,** dismissal; **s. provisional** or **temporal,** temporary stay.

sobresello, *m.* second seal, double seal.

sobresembrar, (*ref. 29*) *tr.v.* to sow over again, sow a second time.

sobresiembre, sobresiembro, *ref.* **sobresembrar.**
sobresolar, (*ref. 33*) *tr.v.* to resole (a shoe); to repave (the floor).
sobrestadía, *f., var. of* **sobreestadía.**
sobrestante, *m.* foreman, overseer, supervisor.
sobrestantía, *f.* foremanship, post of foreman; foreman's office.
sobresuela, *f.* new sole.
sobresueldo, *m.* extra wages, extra pay.
sobresuele, sobresuelo, *ref.* **sobresolar.**
sobresuelo, *m.* floor or pavement laid over another.
sobretarde, *f.* late afternoon.
sobretendón, *m.* (vet.) tumor on a tendon of a horse's leg.
sobretensión, *f.* (elec.) supervoltage.
sobretiro, *m.* (Amer.) offprint.
sobretodo, *m.* overcoat, great coat.
sobreveedor, *m.* chief overseer.
sobrevenga, sobrevengo, *ref.* **sobrevenir.**
sobrevenida, *f.* sudden or unexpected occurrence, supervention.
sobrevenir, (*ref. 26*) *i.v.* 1. to happen or occur suddenly. 2. to supervene, happen later, follow.
sobreverterse, (*ref. 30*) *r.v.* to run over, overflow.
sobrevesta, sobreveste, *f.* surcoat (worn over the armor).
sobrevestir, (*ref. 39*) *tr.v.* to put a garment on over other clothes.
sobrevidriera, *f.* window screen; storm window; window guard.
sobrevienta, *f.* 1. sudden gust of wind. 2. fury, rage. 3. start, surprise. — **a s.,** suddenly, unexpectedly.
sobreviento, *m.* gust of wind.
sobrevierta, sobrevierto, *ref.* **sobreverterse.**
sobreviniendo, sobreviniera, sobreviniese, sobrevino, *ref.* **sobrevenir.**
sobrevista, *f.* beaver (of a helmet).
sobrevista, sobrevisto, *ref.* **sobrevestir.**
sobrevistiendo, sobrevistiera, sobrevistiese, sobrevistió, *ref.* **sobrevestir.**
sobreviviente, *a.* surviving. —*m., f.* surviver.
sobrevivir, *i.v.* to survive, to outlive.
sobrevolar, (*ref. 33*) *tr.v.* to overfly.
sobrexcedente, *a.* exceeding, surpassing.
sobrexceder, *tr.v.* to exceed, to surpass.
sobrexcitación, *f.* overexcitement.
sobrexcitar, *tr.v.* to overexcite. —*r.v.* to become overexcited.
sobriamente, *adv.* soberly, moderately.
sobriedad, *f.* sobriety, moderation.
sobrinazgo, *m.* 1. relationship of nephew or niece. 2. nepotism.
sobrino, na, *m.* nephew; **s. nieto,** great nephew; **s. segundo,** first cousin once removed (child of one's cousin). —*f.* niece. **s. nieta,** great niece; **s. segunda,** first cousin once removed (child of one's cousin).
sobrio, bria, *a.* 1. moderate, temperate; sober. 2. sober, not drunk.
soca, *f.* 1. (Bol., Cuba, Peru, Ven.) ratoon (of sugar cane). 2. (Bol.) sprouting (of rice plants).
socaire, *m.* 1. (mar.) lee. 2. (mar.) slatch. — **al s. de,** under the protection of; **estar al s.,** (coll.) to shirk, to be a slacker.
socairero, *m.* (mar.) slacker, skulker (G.B.).
socaliña, *f.* trick, ruse, cunning.
socaliñar, *tr.v.* to obtain by trickery or cunning.
socaliñero, ra, *m., f.* trickster, cunning person.
socalzar, (*ref. 53*) *tr.v.* (bldg.) to shore up, underpin.
socapa, *f.* pretext, pretense; **a s.,** clandestinely, on the sly.
socapar, *tr.v.* (Bol., Ecuad., Mex.) to cover up for (other people's faults).
socapiscol, *m., var. of* **sochantre.**
socarra, *f.* 1. singeing, scorching. 2. cunning, slyness, craftiness.
socarrar, *tr.v.* to sear, scorch. —*r.v.* to get seared or scorched.
socarrén, *m.* (bldg.) eaves.
socarrena, *f.* 1. cavity, hollow. 2. (bldg.) space between two rafters.
socarrina, *f.* (coll.) singeing, scorching.
socarrón, na, *a.* cunning, crafty. —*m., f.* cunning, sly or crafty person.
socarronamente, *adv.* craftily, cunningly, slyly.
socarronería, *f.* cunning, craftiness; slyness.
socava, *f.* 1. undermining, digging under. 2. (agr.) trench dug around a tree to hold irrigation water.
socavación, *f.* undermining, digging under.
socavar, *tr.v.* 1. to dig under, excavate. 2. (fig.) to undermine.
socavón, *m.* 1. (min.) gallery, adit, shaft, tunnel. 2. cavern, cave.
socavonero, *m.* (Chile) miner.
socaz, (*pl.* **socaces**), *m.* tailrace (of a watermill).
sociabilidad, *f.* sociability, sociableness.
sociable, *a.* sociable, friendly, companionable.
social, *a.* 1. social, pertaining to society, e.g. *la estructura s.,* the social structure, *leyes sociales,* social welfare laws. 2. (com.) company, firm, business, e.g. *razón s.,* firm or business name. 3. social, sociable.
socialice, socialicé, *ref.* **socializar.**
socialismo, *m.* (polit.) socialism; **s. de estado,** state socialism.
socialista, *a., m., f.* (polit.) socialist.
socialización, *f.* socialization; nationalization (of public utilities, industries, etc.).
socializar, (*ref. 53*) *tr.v.* to socialize; to nationalize (public utilities, industries, etc.); to establish state control over.
socianismo, *m.* (rel., philos.) Socianism.
sociedad, *f.* 1. society, social order, community. 2. (coll.) society (fashionable people). 3. (com.) society, company, firm, corporation. — **s. anonima,** (com.) stock company, public corporation (Amer.), public limited company (G.B.); **s. comanditaria por acciones,** (com.) joint stock company; **s. conyugal,** (law) joint ownership of property by husband and wife; **s. cooperativa,** cooperative society; **s. de crédito hipotecario,** savings and loan institution; **S. de las Naciones,** League of Nations; **S. de los Amigos,** (rel.) Society of Friends; **s. en comandita,** (com.) commandite; **S. Fabiana,** Fabian Society; **s. gremial,** trade union; **s. secreta,** secret society.
sociniano, na, *a., m., f.* (rel., philos.) Socinian.
socio, cia, *m., f.* 1. member, fellow (of a club, etc.). 2. partner, business associate. 3. (coll.) pal, friend. — **s. capitalista,** financial partner; **s. comanditario,** silent partner; **s. industrial,** working partner.
socio-económico, ca, *a.* socioeconomic.
sociología, *f.* sociology.
sociológicamente, *adv.* sociologically.
sociológico, ca, *a.* sociological, of or concerning human society.
sociólogo, ga, *m., f.* sociologist, specialist in sociology.
socio-político, ca, *a.* sociopolitical.
socolar, *tr.v.* (C. Amer.) to clear (land) of brush and small trees.
socolor, *m.* pretense, pretext; **s. de,** under the pretext of.
socollada, *f.* (mar.) flapping (of sails); (mar.) pitching.
socollón, *m.* (C. Amer.) shake, jolt, jerk.
soconusco, *m.* **polvos de S.,** chocolate with pinole.
socoro, *m.* (ecc.) space under the choir.
socorredor, ra, *a.* helping, aiding. —*m., f.* helper, aide.
socorrer, *tr.v.* 1. to succor, help, aid. 2. to pay on account.
socorrido, da, *past part. of* **socorrer.** —*a.* 1. ready to help, helpful. 2. handy, convenient. 3. profitable. 4. trite, hackneyed, worn. 5. well stocked, well supplied.
socorro, *m.* 1. succor, help, aid, assistance. 2. (mil.) reinforcements; relief supplies. — **puesto de s.,** first-aid station; **¡s.!** help!
Sócrates, *m.* Socrates, Greek philosopher.
socrático, ca, *a., m., f.* Socratic.
socrocio, *m.* (pharm.) saffron poultice.
socucho, *m.* (Amer.) tiny room, garret, hovel.
sochantre, *m.* (ecc.) subchanter, succentor, subcantor.
soda, *f.* (chem.) soda.
sodalita, *f.* (min.) sodalite.
sódico, ca, *a.* (chem.) sodium.
sodio, *m.* (chem.) sodium.
Sodoma, *f.* (Bib.) Sodom.
sodomía, *f.* sodomy.
sodomita, *m., f.* 1. (Bib.) Sodomite, native of Sodom. 2. sodomite (one who practices sodomy).
sodomítico, ca, *a.* pertaining to sodomy.
soez, (*pl.* **soeces**), *a.* crude, coarse, vulgar, base, indecent, vile.
soezmente, *adv.* coarsely, basely, vilely.
sofá, (*pl.* **sofás),** *m.* sofa.
sofaldar, *tr.v.* to truss up, tuck up (skirts); (fig.) to uncover.
sofaldo, *m.* trussing or tucking up (skirts).
sofí, (*pl.* **sofíes**), *m.* (hist., rel.) Sufi.
Sofía, *f.* Sophia, capital of Bulgaria.
sofión, *m.* 1. snort (of anger); hoot; harsh refusal. 2. blunderbuss.
sofisma, *m.* sophism, specious reasoning; fallacy.
sofismo, *m.* (rel.) Sufism, mysticism of certain Muslim ascetics.
sofista, *m.* 1. (hist.) Sophist. 2. sophist.
sofistería, *f.* 1. sophistry. 2. deceit, falsification; guile.
sofisticación, *f.* 1. sophistication. 2. falsification, doctoring, adulteration (of the truth).
sofisticado, da, *past part. of* **sofisticar.** —*a.* sophisticated.
sofísticamente, *adv.* sophistically, deceptively.
sofisticar, (*ref. 50*) *tr.v.* to sophisticate; to doctor, adulterate.
sofístico, ca, *a.* sophistic, sophistical, fallacious.
sofistique, sofistiqué, *ref.* **sofisticar.**
sofito, *m.* (archit.) soffit.
soflama, *f.* 1. glow, flicker. 2. blush, flush. 3. cheating, trick, bamboozle, deceiving remark. 4. flattery, cajolery. 5. (derog.) speech, harangue.
soflamar, *tr.v.* 1. to trick, bamboozle. 2. to make (someone) blush. —*r.v.* to scorch, get scorched.
soflamero, ra, *a.* conning (sl.), deceiving, bamboozling, cheating. —*m., f.* bamboozler, hypocrite.
sofocación, *f.* suffocation, choking, smothering, stifling.
sofocador, ra, *a.* suffocating, stifling.
sofocante, *a.* suffocating, stifling, close, oppresive (atmosphere, heat, etc.).
sofocar, (*ref. 50*) *tr.v.* 1. to suffocate, stifle, choke, smother. 2. to put down, suppress, smother (an uprising, a revolution, opposition, etc.). 3. to extinguish, put out (fire). 4. to harass, bother, annoy. 5. to make (someone) blush. —*r.v.* 1. to choke, suffocate. 2. to blush, get red, get embarrassed. — **sofocarse por,** to get worked up or excited about.

sofocleo, a, *a.* Sophoclean.
Sófocles, *m.* (hist., theat.) Sophocles, Greek playwright.
sofoco, *m.* 1. blush, embarrassment. 2. (fig.) annoyance, vexation.
sofocón, *m.* (coll.) vexation, chagrin, mortification; embarrassment.
sofoque, sofoqué, *ref.* **sofocar.**
sofoquina, *f.* (coll.) vexation, chagrin, mortification.
sófora, *f.* (bot.) Japanese pagoda tree.
sofreír, (*ref. 40*) *tr.v.* (cul.) to sauté, fry lightly.
sofrenada, *f.* 1. saccade, sudden checking of a horse. 2. harsh reprimand.
sofrenar, *tr.v.* 1. to rein in suddenly, to check a horse. 2. to give a severe dressing-down or reprimand. 3. to control (feelings, passions).
sofreyendo, sofreyera, sofreyese, sofreyó, *ref.* **sofreír.**
sofría, sofrío, *ref.* **sofreír.**
sofrito, ta, *irr. past part, of* **sofreír.**
soga, *f.* 1. rope, cord. 2. variable land measure. 3. (archit.) face (of a brick or stone). 4. (bldg.) stretcher. 5. (Arg.) halter, leather thong (for hitching horses). — **a s.,** (archit.) facewise (bricks); **con la s. al cuello,** with a sword at one's throat, in great risk or danger; **dar s. a,** (coll.) to give (someone) rope or freedom to act; to make fun of; **echar la s. tras el caldero,** (coll.) to let everything go; to throw the helve after the hatchet; **quien no trae s. de sed se ahoga,** always be prepared. —*m.* 1. (coll.) sly fellow. 2. (Amer.) lariat.
soguear, *tr.v.* 1. to measure with a rope. 2. (Amer.) to tie (an animal) with a long rope so it can roam and pasture. 3. (Col.) to make fun of.
soguería, *f.* 1. ropemaking. 2. rope factory or shop. 3. collection of ropes. 4. ropewalk.
soguero, *m.* 1. ropemarker; rope dealer. 2. street porter.
soguilla, *f.* small cord; thin braid of hair. —*m.* porter who carries only light-weight luggage.
soja, *f.* (bot.) soya, soyabean, soybean.
sojuzgador, ra, *a.* subduing, subjugating. —*m., f.* subduer, subjugator, conqueror.
sojuzgamiento, *m.* subjugation, subjugating.
sojuzgar, (*ref. 51*) *tr.v.* to subdue, subjugate, conquer.
sojuzgue, sojuzgué, *ref.* **sojuzgar.**
sol, *m.* 1. sun (planet). 2. sun, sunshine, sunlight, e.g. *sentarse al s.,* to sit in the sun. 3. (mus.) sol, g, fifth note of the scale. 4. sol (Peruvian coin). — **al ponerse el s.,** at sunset; **al salir el s.,** at sunrise; **de s. a s.,** from dawn to dusk; **hacer s.,** to be sunny; **no dejar ni a s. ni a sombra a,** (coll.) to harass, hound; **quemadura de s.,** sunburn; **rayo de s.,** sunbeam, sun's ray; **s. de medianoche,** midnight sun; **s. de las Indias,** (bot.) sunflower; **s. naciente,** rising sun; **s. poniente,** setting sun; **tomar el s.,** to sun oneself, to bask in the sun, sunbathe; (mar.) to take the sun's altitude.
solace, solacé, *ref.* **solazar.**
solacear, *tr.v., var. of* **solazar.**
solada, *f.* dregs, sediment, lees.
solado, *m.* paving, tiling; pavement.
solador, *m.* paver, tiler.
soladura, *f.* paving, tiling; tiles, paving material.
solamente, *adv.* only, solely; **s. que,** provided that.
solana, *f.* 1. strong sunlight. 2. sunny spot; solarium, sun porch, sun gallery.
solanáceo, *a.* (bot.) solanaceous. —*f. (pl.)* Solanaceae.
solanera, *f.* 1. sunburn. 2. hot sunny spot.
solanina, *f.* (chem.) solanine.
solano, *m.* 1. easterly wind. 2. hot wind. 3. (bot.) nightshade, morel.
solapa, *f.* 1. lapel (of a coat). 2. pretext, pretense, dissembling. 3. (vet.) cavity (in sores). — **de s.,** sneakily, secretly, stealthily; **junta de s.,** lap joint.
solapadamente, *adv.* deceitfully, underhandedly, slyly, sneakingly.
solapado, da, *past part. of* **solapar.** —*a.* sneaky, underhanded, sly.
solapamiento, *m.* (vet.) cavity (in a sore).
solapar, *tr.v.* 1. (tailoring) to put lapels on. 2. to overlap. 3. to cover up, conceal. —*i.v.* to overlap (garment).
solape, *m., var. of* **solapa.**
solapo, *m.* 1. lapel. 2. part of a garment overlapped by another. 3. (coll.) chuck under the chin. — **a s.,** sneakily, secretly.
solar, *a.* ancestral (home). —*m.* 1. ancestral home or mansion. 2. house, family, noble lineage. 3. plot, ground, lot. 4. (Cuba) tenement.
solar, *a.* solar, sun, e.g. *sistema s.,* (astron.) solar system.
solar, (*ref. 33*) *tr.v.* 1. to pave, tile, floor. 2. to sole (a shoe).
solariego, ga, *a.* 1. manorial; ancestral, e.g. *casa solariega,* ancestral home. 2. noble, ancient, old.
solas, *adv.* **a s.** alone, in private.
solaz, (*pl.* **solaces**), *m.* 1. recreation, pleasure, relaxation. 2. solace, comfort, relief. — **a. s.,** with pleasure, agrreeably.
solazar, (*ref. 53*) *tr.v.* 1. to solace, cheer, comfort. 2. to rest, relax, entertain, divert. —*r.v.* to relax, rest, entertain oneself.
solazo, *m.* (coll.) scorching or blazing sun or sunshine.
solazoso, sa, *a.* resting, relaxing; comforting; pleasing.
soldada, *f.* 1. salary, wages. 2. soldier's pay.
soldadesca, *f.* 1. soldiering. 2. troops, soldiers. 3. undisciplined troops.
soldadesco, ca, *a.* pertaining to soldiers and barracks, barrack-room, e.g. *lenguaje soldadesco,* barrack-room language.
soldado, *m.* 1. soldier. 2. (ento.) soldier. — **s. de caballería,** cavalryman, trooper; **s. de cuota,** soldier who serves part of his time in the army, paying exemption for the rest; **s. de haber,** soldier who serves his full time in the army; **s. de infantería,** infantryman; **s. de Pavía,** (cul.) slice of haddock dipped in the batter and fried; **s. de sanidad,** medical corpsman; **s. primero,** private first class; **s. raso,** private.
soldador, *m.* 1. solderer, welder. 2. soldering iron. 3. blow torch. — **s. de arco,** arc welder.
soldadora, *f.* soldering gun, welder (machine); **s. de arco,** arc welder (machine).
soldadura, *f.* 1. soldering, welding. 2. soldered or welded joint or part. 3. solder, soldering material. 4. (coll.) repair, mend, e.g. *el daño no tiene s.,* the damage is beyond repair. — **s. al tope,** butt welding; **s. blanda,** soft solder; **s. con arco de hidrógeno atómico,** atomic hydrogen welding; **s. de arco sin protección,** bare-electrode welding; **s. de cantos,** edge weld; **s. de filetes en cadena,** chain fillet weld; **s. de forja a mano,** blacksmith welding; **s. de impacto,** percussive welding; **s. en barras,** bar solder; **s. en la forja,** forge, hammer or blacksmith welding; **s. fuerte,** hard solder; **s. oxídrica,** oxygen-hydrogen welding; **s. por aluminiotermia,** aluminiothermic welding; **s. por arco,** arc welding; **s. por electrodos de carbón,** carbon arc welding; **s. por fusión,** fusion welding; **s. por gas,** gas welding; **s. por percusión,** percussive welding; **s. por presión,** pressure welding; **s. por puntos,** spot-welding; **s. por resistencia,** resistance welding; **s. reforzada** or **con cubrejunta,** strap weld.
soldán, *m.* (arch.) sultan.
soldar, (*ref. 53*) *tr.v.* 1. solder, weld. 2. to repair, patch up (quarrel, disagreement, unfortunate incident). — **s. a tope,** to butt weld; **s por puntos,** to spot-weld. —*r.v.* to knit (bones).
soleamiento, *m.* sunning, sunbathing.
solear, *tr.v.* to sun. —*r.v.* to bask in the sun, sun oneself, sunbathe.
solecismo, *m.* (rhet., gram.) solecism.
soledad, *f.* 1. solitude, solitariness, loneliness. 2. grieving, bereavement, sadness. 3. solitary or lonely spot. 4. melancholy Andalusian song and dance.
soledoso, sa, *a.* solitary; lonely, lonesome.
solejar, *m.* sunny place.
solemne, *a.* 1. solemn, imposing, majestic, stately, impressive. 2. solemn, grave, serious; formal. 3. (derog.) utter and complete, downright (nonsense, lie, etc.), e.g. *es un s. disparate,* it's a downright idiocy.
solemnemente, *adv.* solemnly.
solemnice, solemnicé, *ref.* **solemnizar.**
solemnidad, *f.* 1. solemnity; formality. 2. ceremony, festivity.
solemnización, *f.* solemnization.
solemnizador, ra, *a.* solemnizing. —*m., f.* solemnizer.
solemnizar, (*ref. 53*) *tr.v.* to solemnize.
solenoide, *m.* (elec.) solenoid.
sóleo, *m.* (anat.) soleus.
soler, *m.* (mar.) underflooring.
soler, (*ref. 34*) *i.v.* to be in the habit of, be accustomed to, e.g. *suelo lavar la ropa los lunes,* I usually or generally wash the clothes on Mondays, I am in the habit of washing the clothes on Monday, *suele llover por este tiempo,* it usually rains at this time.
solera, *f.* 1. crossbeam, stringpiece, breastsummer. 2. plinth. 3. nether millstone. 4. floor (of an oven); bed (of a river). 5. lees, mother (remaining in wine barrel). 6. (Chile) curb, stone edging pavement. — **vino de s.,** aged wine used to strengthen new vintage.
solercia, *f.* shrewdness, astuteness.
solería, *f.* 1. paving, tiling; tiling or paving material. 2. leather for making soles.
solerte, *a.* shrewd, cunning, sagacious.
soleta, *f.* 1. patch for the sole of a stocking. 2. (coll.) brazen woman, hussy. 3. (Mex.) a kind of sweet pastry. — **apretar** or **picar de s., tomar s.,** (coll.) to flee, run away.
soletar, soletear, *tr.v.* to put patches on the sole of a stocking.
soletero, ra, *m., f.* one who puts patches on soles of stockings, stockings-mender.
solevación, *f.,* **solevamiento,** *m.* 1. insurrection, uprising, revolt, rebellion 2. upheaval.
solevantado, da, *past part. of* **solevantar.** —*a.* 1. unsettled, perturbed, agitated. 2. rebellious, insurgent, in revolt.
solevantamiento, *m., var. of* **solevamiento.**
solevantar, solevar, *tr.v.* 1. to push up, raise, lift. 2. to stir up, agitate, incite to rebellion. —*r.v.* 1. to rise up, rise. 2. to rebel, rise in rebellion, revolt.
solfa, *f.* 1. sol-fa, tonic sol-fa, solmization. 2. musical notation. 3. music, harmony. 4. (coll.) beating, drubbing. — **poner en s.,** to make (someone) look ridiculous, put in a ridiculous light; to put right, to arrange properly.
solfatara, *f.* (geol.) solfatara.
solfeador, ra, *m., f.* sol-faer, sol-faist.

solfear, *tr.v.* 1. to sol-fa, to solmizate. 2. (coll.) to beat, flog. 3. (coll.) to censure, criticize; to reprehend, tell off, upbraid.
solfeo, *m.* 1. solfeggio, solmization. 2. (coll.) beating, drubbing.
solferino, na, *a.* reddish mauve, magenta.
solfista, *m., f.* sol-faist.
solicitación, *f.* request; application.
solicitado, da, *past part. of* **solicitar.** *—a.* in demand, popular, sought after.
solicitador, ra, *m., f.* requester; applicant; petitioner.
solícitamente, *adv.* solicitously.
solicitante, *m., f.* requester; applicant; petitioner.
solicitar, *tr.v.* 1. to ask for, request; to petition; to apply for. 2. to woo, court. 3. (phys.) to attract.
solícito, ta, *a.* solicitous.
solicitud, *f.* 1. solicitude, solicitousness. 2. application; request, petition. — **a. s.,** on request; **a s. de,** at the request of.
sólidamente, *adv.* solidly; firmly, securely.
solidar, *tr.v.* 1. to make solid or firm. 2. to back up, prove, establish. 3. to consolidate.
solidariamente, *adv.* 1. with solidarity. 2. (law) in solidum.
solidarice, solidaricé, *ref.* **solidarizar.**
solidaridad, *f.* 1. solidarity. 2. common cause.
solidario, ria, *a.* 1. solidary; in common cause. 2. jointly responsible or liable; jointly involved.
solidarismo, *m.* (econ.) solidarism.
solidarizar, (*ref.* 53) *tr.v.* to make jointly responsible or liable. *—r.v.* to become jointly responsible or liable; to make common cause, join together; **solidarizarse con,** to support, back up, make common cause with, join.
solideo, *m.* (ecc.) calotte, skullcap, zuchetto.
solidez, *f.* 1. solidity; strength, firmness; stability. 2. (geom.) volume.
solidificación, *f.* solidification.
solidificar, (*ref.* 50) *tr.v., r.v.* to solidify.
solidifique, solidifiqué, *ref.* **solidificar.**
sólido, da, *a.* 1. solid, compact, consistent. 2. sound, reliable. 3. strong, stable, firm. *—m.* 1. (phys.) solid. 2. (numis.) solidus (Roman coin).
soliloquiar, *i.v.* to soliloquize.
soliloquio, *m.* soliloquy, monologue.
solimán, *m.* (chem.) mercury chloride, corrosive sublimate.
solio, *m.* canopied throne.
solípedo, da, *a,* (zool.) solipede, solidungulate. *—m.* soliped, solidungulate, (*pl.*) Solidungula.
solipsismo, *m.* (philos.) solipsism.
solista, *m.* soloist.
solitaria, *f.* 1. tapeworm. 2. post chaise for single person.
solitariamente, *adv.* solitarily, in solitude.
solitario, ria, *a.* 1. solitary, lone; lonely, secluded, isolated. 2. retiring. *—m., f.* recluse, hermit. *—m.* 1. solitaire (diamond). 2. solitaire, patience (game). 3. (zool.) hermit crab.
sólito, ta, *a.* accustomed, usual.
soliviadura, *f.* raising, lifting; rising partly, getting up partly.
soliviantar, *tr.v.* to stir up, incite, cause to rise or rebel, rouse. *—r.v.* to become aroused, rise, rebel.
soliviar, *tr.v.* 1. to raise, lift. 2. (Arg.) to lift (sl.), steal. *—r.v.* to raise oneself partly, rise partly.
solivio, *m.* raising, lifting, rising partly, getting up partly.
solivión, *m.* powerful heave, jerk or push.
sollado, *m.* (mar.) orlop deck.
sollamar, *tr.v.* to scorch, singe. *—r.v.* to become scorched or singed.
sollastre, *m.* 1. kitchen boy, scullion. 2. (fig.) scoundrel, rogue.
sollastría, *f.* scullery work, kitchen work.
sollo, *m.* (ichth.) sturgeon.
sollozante, *a.* sobbing.
sollozar, (*ref.* 53) *i.v.* to sob.
sollozo, *m.* sob.
solo, la, *a.* 1. alone, by oneself or itself. 2. only, single, sole. 3. lone, lonely, lonesome. — **a solas,** alone, by oneself; **café solo,** black coffee; **una sola vez,** once only, just once. *—m.* 1. (mus.) solo, solo performance. 2. solo (card game). 3. (Arg.) boring conversation; **dar un s. a,** (coll.) to bore with tedious conversation.
sólo, *adv.* only, solely.
solomillo, solomo, *m.* 1. sirloin. 2. loin of pork.
Solón, *m.* (hist.) Solon, Greek statesman and legislator.
solsticial, *a.* solstitial.
solsticio, *m.* (astron.) solstice; **s. de invierno** or **hiemal,** winter solstice; **s. de verano** or **vernal,** summer solstice.
soltadizo, za, *a.* easily removed or untied; easily loosened.
soltador, ra, *a.* unfastening, freeing, untying. *—m., f.* loosener, unfastener, releaser.
soltar, (*ref.* 33) *tr.v.* 1. to untie, loosen, unfasten. 2. to let go, free, set free, let or turn loose. 3. to let go of; to drop. 4. to let out (e.g. water from dam). 5. to let out (a cry, shout, laugh, etc.); to come out with, let slip (a curse, laughter, remark, etc.); to drop (a hint); to give, deliver (a blow). 6. to decipher, solve. 7. to loosen, move (the bowels). — **s. la lengua,** to speak freely; **s. una bofetada,** to slap, give a slap; **s. una indirecta,** to drop a hint. *—r.v.* 1. to get free, get loose. 2. to come loose; to come undone. 3. to become proficient or skilled. 4. to loosen up, let oneself go, become more at ease, more confident or self-assured. — **soltarse a** + *inf.*, to begin + *inf.*
soltería, *f.* bachelorhood, celibacy.
soltero, ra, *a.* single, unmarried. *—m.* bachelor. *—f.* unmarried woman.
solterón, na, *m.* (coll.) old bachelor. *—f.* (coll.) old maid, spinster.
soltura, *f.* 1. ease, confidence, assurance (of manner, behavior); ease, nimbleness, agility (of movement); fluency (of speech). 2. brazenness; laxity. — **con s.,** confidently, with assurance; fluently.
solubilidad, *f.* solubility.
soluble, *a.* 1. soluble. 2. solvable.
solución, *f.* 1. solution (to a problem, question, puzzle, doubt, difficulty). 2. (chem.) solution. 3. issue, termination. 4. (theat., lit.) denouement (in a play, a novel).
solucionar, *tr.v.* to solve.
solutivo, va, *a., m.* (med.) laxative.
soluto, *m.* (chem.) solute.
solutrense, *a.* (geol.) solutrean, solutrian.
solvatación, *f.* (chem.) solvate.
solvato, *m.* (chem.) solvate.
solvencia, *f.* 1. solvency (freedom or ability to pay debts; ability to dissolve); (fig.) solvency, e.g. *s. moral,* moral solvency. 2. reliability, dependability.
solventar, *tr.v.* 1. to settle, pay (debts). 2. to solve (difficulty).
solvente, *a.* 1. solvent (free from or able to pay debts; able to dissolve); (fig.) morally responsible (for one's acts or debts). 2. reliable, dependable. *—m.* solvent, dissolvent, dissolving agent.
soma, *f.* coarse flour.
Somalia, *f.* Somalia, Somali Republic.
somanta, *f.* (coll.) beating, thrashing.
somatar, *tr.v.* (C. Amer.) to beat, thrash.
somatén, *m.* 1. civilian militia, home guard (in Catalonia). 2. (coll.) uproar, commotion. — **¡S.!** ancient war cry of the Catalans.
somatenista, *m.* civilian militiaman (in Catalonia).
somático, ca, *a.* (anat., biol., zool.) somatic; corporeal, physical.
somatología, *f.* somatology.
somatoplasma, *m.* (biol.) somatoplasm.
sombra, *f.* 1. shadow; shade; darkness, gloom. 2. shade, shadow, ghost, phantom. 3. (fig.) ignorance. 4. shelter, protection. 5. shadow, vestige, trace, e.g. *sin s. de sospecha,* without a shadow of doubt, *eso no tiene ni s. de verdad,* this hasn't a vestige of truth. 6. stain, spot. 7. (coll.) shadow, constant companion. 8. (coll.) luck, good fortune. 9. (coll.) charm, wit, pleasantness of manner. 10. sunshade. 11. (p.) shade, shading. — **a la s.,** in the shade; (coll.) in jail; **a la s. de,** in the shadow of; **hacer s.,** to cast a shadow; to stand in the light; to shadow-box; **hacer s. a,** to overshadow, stand in one's light; **luz y s.,** light and shade; **ni por s.,** by no means whatsoever; **no ser ni s. de lo que era,** not to be the shadow of what one was or one's former self; **poner a la s.,** (coll.) to put in jail; **sombras chinescas,** shadow play; **tener buena s.,** (coll.) to be likeable and pleasant; to bring good luck; **tener mala s.,** (coll.) to exert an evil influence; to bring bad luck; to be unpleasant and disagreeable.
sombraje, *m.* sunshade or sun screen made with branches and twigs.
sombrajo, *m.* 1. sunshade or sun screen made with twigs and branches. 2. (coll.) shadow (caused by getting in someone's light), e.g. *no me hagas sombrajos,* don't get in my light.
sombrar, *tr.v.* to shade; to get in the light of.
sombreado, da, *a.* shady, shaded. *—m.* (p.) shading.
sombreador, ra, *a.* shading.
sombrear, *tr.v.* 1. to shade; to cast or throw a shadow upon. 2. (p.) to shade.
sombrerada, *f.* hatful.
sombrerazo, *m.* 1. blow given with hat. 2. (coll.) quick raising or doffing of the hat.
sombrerera, *f.* 1. woman milliner. 2. hatbox, hat stand. 3. hatter's wife.
sombrerería, *f.* 1. millinery shop, hattery; hat making. 2. hat factory. 3. hat shop.
sombrerero, *m.* hatter; male milliner.
sombrerete, *m.* 1. small hat. 2. cowl, hood (of a chimney). 3. cap (of mushroom). 4. spark catcher (of a locomotive).
sombrerillo, *m.* 1. *dim. of* **sombrero,** small hat. 2. (bot.) navelwort.
sombrero, *m.* 1. hat; bonnet. 2. canopy (of pulpit). 3. Spanish Grandee's privilege of keeping his hat on before king. 4. cap (of mushroom). 5. (mar.) head (of capstan). — **s. apuntado,** cocked hat; **s. calañes,** low-crowned black velvet hat with a rolled-up brim, worn by Andalusians; **s. de castor,** beaver hat; felt hat; **s. cordobés,** the wide-brimmed typical Andalusian hat with a tall crown; **s. chambergo,** jaunty fedora; **s. de canal** or **de teja,** shovel hat; **s. de copa,** top hat; **s. de jipijapa or Panamá,** Panama hat; **s. de paja,** straw hat; **s. de tres picos,** three-cornered hat, tricorne; **s. gacho,** slouch hat; **s. hongo,** bowler hat; **s. jarano,** Mexican sombrero; **s. nuclear,** nuclear umbrella.
sombría, *f.* **shady spot.**
sombrilla, *f.* sunshade, parasol; **s. protectora** (mil.), (fig.) umbrella.
sombrillazo, *m.* blow given with a sunshade or parasol.

sombrío, a, *a.* 1. somber, dark, murky, dismal, overcast. 2. gloomy, sullen, taciturn; melancholy. 3. (p.) shaded, dark.

sombrógrafo, *m.* shadowgraph.

sombroso, sa, *a.* dark, shady, shaded, shadowy.

somera, *f.* (print.) sleeper of the press.

someramente, *adv.* superficially; briefly, quickly.

somero, ra, *a.* brief, quick; superficial, shallow.

someter, *tr.v.* 1. to subdue, put down, quell, force to yield. 2. to subject, expose, cause to undergo, e.g. *lo sometieron a un examen médico,* they subjected him to a medical examination. 3. to subordinate, subject, put under the control of. 4. to put forward, submit (an opinion, suggestion). —*r.v.* to submit, yield; to surrender; to undergo, subject oneself.

sometimiento, *m.* 1. submission, subjection, subjugation, subduing. 2. submission, surrender, yielding. 3. submission (for consideration).

somito, *m.* (zool.) somite.

somnambulismo, *m.* sleepwalking, somnambulism.

somnámbulo, la, *a.* sleepwalking, somnambulistic. —*m., f.* sleepwalker, somnambulist.

somnífero, ra, *a.* somniferous.

somnilocuencia, *f.* somniloquence, somniloquy.

somnílocuo, cua, *a.* somniloquous. —*m., f.* somniloquist.

somnolencia, *f.* somnolence, drowsiness, sleepiness; (fig.) laziness.

somonte, *a.* **de s.,** rough, coarse, unpolished.

somorgujador, *m.* diver.

somorgujar, *tr.v.* to submerge, duck, plunge. —*r.v.* to duck or submerge oneself; to dive.

somorgujo, *m.* (ornith.) grebe, dabchick. — **a** or **a lo s.,** under the water; (coll.) secretly, stealthily.

somorgujón, *m., var. of* **somorgujo.**

somormujar, *tr.v., var of* **somorgujar.**

somormujo, *m., var. of* **somorgujo.**

sompesar, *tr.v.* to weigh in one's hand.

son, *m.* 1. sound; tune, melody. 2. news, rumor. 3. reason, motive. 4. manner, way. 5. (mus.) Cuban popular dance. — **al s. de,** to the sound of; **¿a s. de qué?** why? for what reason?; **bailar al s. que le tocan,** (coll.) to adapt oneself to circumstances; **en s. de,** as, by way of, in the way of; **sin s.,** without rhyme or reason.

sonable, *a.* 1. sonorous, noisy, loud. 2.. famous, well-known.

sonada, *f.* (mus.) tune; sonata.

sonadera, *f.* blowing of the nose.

sonadero, *m.* handkerchief.

sonado, da, *past part. of* **sonar.** —*a.* famous, well-known, noted, much talked-of. — **hacer una que sea sonada,** (coll.) to cause a scandal or sensation.

sonador, ra, *a.* noisemaking. —*m., f.* noisemaker . —*m.* handkerchief.

sonaja, *f.* 1. metal disk (in tambourine). 2. child's rattle. 3. (*pl.*) jingle stick. 4. (mus.) timbrel.

sonajero, *m.* baby's rattle.

sonambulismo, *m.* sleepwalking, somnambulism.

sonámbulo, la, *a.* sleepwalking, somnambulistic. —*m., f.* sleepwalker, somnambulist.

sonante, *a.* 1. sounding; jingling, tinkling. 2. (phonet.) sonant. —*m.* (phonet.) sonant.

sonar, (*ref. 33*) *tr.v.* 1. to sound; to ring (a bell); to play (a musical instrument). 2. to blow (the nose). —*i.v.* 1. to sound; to ring, chime; to strike (a clock). 2. to be pronounced or sounded (vowel, letter, consonant). 3. to seem or sound correct, e.g. *esta frase no me suena,* this phrase doesn't sound right to me. 4. (coll.) to ring a bell, mean something, sound familiar, e.g. *¿te suena el nombre de Juan Pérez?* does the name Juan Pérez ring a bell or mean anything to you? 5. to be mentioned. 6. to be said, reported or rumored. —*r.v.* 1. to blow one's nose. 2. to be reported, rumored or said. —*m.* (mar.) sonar.

sonata, *f.* (mus.) sonata.

sonatina, *f.* (mus.) sonatina.

sonda, *f.* 1. sounding, probing, fathoming. 2. (mar.) sounding line or lead, plummet, sound. 3. auger, large drill (for boring soil). 4. (med.) sound, catheter, probe. 5. (mar.) sound, passage of water. — **s. ecoica,** echo sounder.

sondable, *a.* soundable, fathomable.

sondaleza, *f.* (mar.) lead line, sounding line.

sondar, sondear, *tr.v.* 1. to sound, fathom. 2. to sound, explore (nature of subsoil), make borings in. 3. to sound, sound out (a person's intentions). 4. (med.) to sound, probe (with a sound, catheter, etc.).

sondeadora, *f.* sounding line, sounding machine.

sondeo, *m.* sounding, fathoming; probing; exploring.

sonecillo, *m.* 1. slight or barely perceptible sound. 2. gay lively tune.

sonetear, *i.v.* to compose sonnets.

sonetico, *m.* 1. slight sound or noise. 2. drumming of fingers, tapping of fingers (on table. etc.). 3. little sonnet.

sonetillo, *m.* sonnet composed of lines of not more than eight syllables.

sonetista, *m., f.* sonneteer, writer of sonnets.

sonetizar, (*ref. 53*) *i.v.* to write sonnets.

soneto, *m.* sonnet; **s. caudato,** sonnet with additional couplet or triplet.

songo, ga, *a.* (Col., Mex.) cunning, sly; **a la songa** (C. Amer.) craftily, cunningly. —*f.* (Cuba, P. Rico) irony, mockery.

sónico, ca, *a.* sound, e.g. *barrera sónica,* sound barrier.

sonido, *m.* 1. sound; noise. 2. literal meaning. 3. news, rumor. — **barrera del s.,** sound barrier; **s. absoluto,** (mus.) absolute pitch.

soniquete, *m.* 1. slight, unpleasant sound. 2. rhythmical tapping or drumming. 3. catchy tune.

sonochada, *f.* 1. evening, early part of night. 2. night watch.

sonochar, *i.v.* 1. to do the evening watch. 2. to be awake during the early hours of the night.

sonógrafo, *m.* (acous.) sonograph.

sonómetro, *m.* sonometer.

sonoramente, *adv.* 1. sonorously. 2. harmoniously.

sonoridad, *f.* sonority.

sonorización, *f.* 1. dubbing. 2. (phonet.) voicing.

sonorizar, (*ref. 53*) *tr.v.* 1. to dub (a film or tape). 2 (phonet.) to voice. —*r.v.* (phonet.) to be voiced.

sonoro, ra, *a.* 1. sound, e.g. *banda sonora,* sound track (of a film), *onda sonora,* sound wave. 2. talking, e.g. *película sonora,* talking picture or film. 3. sonorous, resonant; loud, clear. 4. (phonet.) voiced.

sonoroso, sa, *a.* sonorous.

sonreír, (*ref. 40*) *i.v., r.v.* to smile.

sonría, sonriendo, sonrío, *ref.* **sonreír.**

sonriente, *a.* smiling.

sonrisa, *f.* smile.

sonrisueño, ña, *a.* pleased, smiling. —*m., f.* smiling person.

sonrodarse, (*ref. 33*) *r.v.* to stick or get stuck in the mud (wheels).

sonrojear, sonrojar, *tr.v.* to make (one) blush. —*r.v.* to blush.

sonrojo, *m.* 1. blush; blushing. 2. embarrassing remark or word.

sonrosar, sonrosear, *tr.v.* to make pink or rose-colored. —*r.v.* to turn pink or rose-colored; to blush.

sonroseo, *m.* blush, flush.

sonsaca, *f.* 1. wheedling, drawing out (e.g. a secret from a person). 2. enticing, coaxing.

sonsacador, ra, *m., f.* enticer, wheedler; one who draws out information, secrets, etc.

sonsacamiento, *m., var. of* **sonsaca.**

sonsacar, (*ref. 50*) *tr.v.* 1. to entice away. 2. to get out of, wheedle or elicit (information from), e.g. *s. un secreto a alguien,* to get a secret out of someone.

sonsaque, *m., var. of* **sonsaca.**

sonsaque, sonsaqué, *ref.* **sonsacar.**

sonsonete, *m.* 1. singsong; repetitious ditty; monotonous voice. 2. rhythmical tapping or drumming.

sonto, ta, *a.* (Guat., Hond.) one-eared.

soñación, *f.* **ni por s.,** (coll.) by no means whatsoever.

soñador, ra, *a.* dreamy, dreaming. —*m., f.* dreamer.

soñante, *a.* dreaming, dreamy.

soñar, (*ref. 33*) *tr.v.* to dream; **ni soñarlo,** it's out of the question. —*i.v.* to dream; to daydream; **s. con,** to dream of; **s. despierto,** to daydream.

soñarrera, *f.* (coll.) excessive dreaming; (coll.) deep or sound sleep; (coll.) sleepiness.

soñera, *f.* sleepiness.

soñolencia, *f.* somnolence, sleepiness.

soñolientamente, *adv.* sleepily, drowsily.

soñoliento, ta, *a.* sleepy, drowsy, somnolent; lazy.

sopa, *f.* 1. (cul.) soup. 2. soup, bread soaked in any liquid. 3. (*pl.*) slices of bread dipped into soup. — **andar a la s.,** to beg from door to door; **comer la s. boba, andar a la s. boba,** to sponge on, live at someone else's expense; **hecho una s.,** soaked to the skin; **s. boba,** soup distributed to the poor in convents; **s. de ajo,** garlic soup; **s. juliana,** julienne, julienne soup; **s. de verduras,** vegetable soup.

sopaipa, *f.* fritter dipped in honey.

sopalancar, (*ref. 50*) *tr.v.* to lift with a lever.

sopanda, *f.* 1. (carp.) joist. 2. brace (of a carriage). 3. (Chile) spring mattress.

sopapear, *tr.v.* 1. to slap, box. 2. to maltreat.

sopapina, *f.* (coll.) slapping, beating.

sopapo, *m.* 1. (coll.) slap, box. 2. chuck under the chin. 3. valve, stop valve.

sopar, sopear, *tr.v.* to dip, dunk, steep.

sopeña, *f.* cavity formed under a rock.

sopero, ra, *a.* soup (plate, bowl). —*f.* tureen, soup tureen.

sopesar, *tr.v.* to heft, to test the weight (of) by lifting.

sopetear, *tr.v.* 1. to dunk or dip (bread) in soup, coffee, etc. 2. to maltreat.

sopeteo, *m.* dunking, sopping, dipping (bread, etc.).

sopetón, *m.* 1. slap, box. 2. toast dipped in olive oil.— **de s.,** (coll.) suddenly, unexpectedly.

sopicaldo, *m.* thin soup.

sopista, *m., f.* formerly, a student living on charity.

sopita, *f. dim. of* **sopa,** light soup; small amount of soup.

sopitipando, *m.* (coll.) fainting fit, swoon.

sopladero, *m.* vent, air hole or passage (of a subterranean cavity).

soplado, da, *a.* 1. (coll.) over-neat, spruce. 2. (coll.) stuck-up, conceited. —*m.* (min.) deep fissure.

soplador, ra, *a.* blowing. —*m.* 1. blower; ventilator. 2. (Ecuad., theat.) prompter. 3. inciter, stirrer.

sopladura, *f.* blowing; blowhole, airhole.

soplamocos, (*pl.* **soplamocos**), *m.* punch on the nose.

soplar, *i.v.* 1. to blow. 2. (coll.) to squeal, sing, blow the gaff, inform the police; to tip off, e.g. *¿ quién sopló a la policía?* who tipped off the police?; to tattle, tell tales. —*tr.v.* 1. to blow up, inflate. 2. to blow away. 3. to prompt, whisper the answer to. 4. to pinch, snitch, swipe, steal. 5. to huff (in checkers). 6. to report (a criminal to the police). —*r.v.* 1. to drink, eat; to wolf down, gobble up. 2. (coll.) to endure, take; (coll.) to spend, e.g. *me soplé las dos horas del viaje parado,* I spent the two hours of the journey standing. 3. (coll.) to become conceited, put on airs. 4. (Guat., Mex.) to kill. 5. (Guat., Mex.) to do, e.g. *mientras Vd. limpie este carro, yo me soplo el otro,* while you clean this car, I will do the other one. 6. (Guat., Mex.) to have sex with.
soplete, *m.* 1. blowpipe, blowtorch, torch. 2. air tube (taking air into bagpipes). — **s. atomizador,** paint sprayer; **s. de arena,** sandblast; **s. oxiacetilénico, oxyacetilene torch; s. oxídrico,** oxyhydrogen blowpipe or torch; **s. soldador,** welding torch.
soplido, *m.* breath, puff, blowing; blast.
soplillo, *m.* 1. breath, puff. 2. blowing fan (for fire). 3. very thin silk, silk gauze. 4. light sponge cake.
soplo, *m.* 1. breath, blowing, puff, gust, e.g. *us s. de viento,* a breath of wind. 2. moment, instant. 3. (coll.) secret information. 4. (coll.) informer, stool pigeon. 5. (coll.) squealing, tipping off, reporting.
soplón, *a.* tale bearing, informing, squealing. —*m., f.* (coll.) stool pigeon, informer, talebearer.
soplonear, *tr.v.* to inform on, give away, squeal on.
soplonería, *f.* informing, squealing, talebearing.
sopón, *m.* 1. *var. of* **sopista.** 2. nourishing, rich soup.
soponcio, *m.* 1. (coll.) swoon, fainting fit. 2. (coll.) nourishing, rich soup.
sopor, *m.* sopor, stupor; lethargy, drowsiness.
soporífero, ra, *a., m.* soporific.
soporífico, ca, *a.* soporific.
soporoso, sa, *a.* soporose, of stupor; sleepy, lethargic.
soportable, *a.* bearable, endurable, supportable.
soportador, ra, *a.* supporting, sustaining. —*m., f.* supporter, sustainer.
soportal, *m.* porch; portico; arcade.
soportar, *tr.v.* 1. to support, hold up. 2. to bear, endure, put up with, suffer.
soporte, *m.* 1. support, prop; base, stand; bearing (in which journal, etc., turns). 2. (fig.) support, provider, e.g. *él es único s. de su familia,* he is his family's sole provider. — **s. de cojinete,** (mec.) bearing pedestal; **s. de cuña,** (mec.) knife-edge bearing.
soprano, *m., f.* (mus.) soprano (singer). —*m.* soprano (voice, register).
sopuntar, *tr.v.* to underscore with dots.
sor, *f.* sister (used before the name of a nun), e.g. *S. Juana,* Sister Joanna.
sora, *f.* (Peru) fermented corn mash.
sorbedor, ra, *a.* absorbing, sipping; sucking. —*m., f.* absorber, sipper; sucker.
sorber, *tr.v.* 1. to sip; to suck. 2. to absorb, suck in, soak up. 3. (fig.) to swallow.
sorbete, *m.* 1. sherbet, water ice. 2. (Mex.) drinking straw.
sorbetera, *f.* ice cream freezer, ice cream maker (machine).
sorbetón, *m.* (coll.) large sip, gulp or draught.
sorbible, *a.* sippable, able to be sipped; absorbable.
sorbita, *f.* (meteorol.) sorbite.
sorbito, *m. dim. of* **sorbo,** small sip.
sorbo, *m.* 1. sip, draught; sipping. 2. sip, drop, small amount.
Sorbona, *f.* Sorbonne, seat of the faculties of arts and letters of the University of Paris.
sorche, *m.* (coll.) recruit, rookie (sl.).
sorda, *f.* 1. (mar.) hawser used in launching. 2. (ornith.) snipe.
sordamente, *adv.* secretly, silently, stealthily.
sordera, sordez, *f.* deafness.
sórdidamente, *adv.* sordidly.
sordidez, *f.* 1. sordidness. 2. squalor.
sórdido, da, *a.* 1. sordid. 2. squalid; dirty. 3. miserly. 4. miserable, abject.
sordina, *f.* 1. (mus.) mute, damper, sordino, sourdine. 2. silencer (in timepieces). — **a la s.,** silently, on the quiet.
sordino, *m.* (mus.) fiddle, small violin.
sordo, da, *a.* 1. deaf. 2. silent, still. 3. muffled, dull. 4. (fig.) deaf, indifferent, insensitive. 5. (phonet.) voiceless, unvoiced, surd. 6. (math.) surd. — **a la sorda, a lo sordo, a sordas,** silently, noiselessly; **s. como una tapia,** stoned-eaf, deaf as a post. —*m., f.* deaf person.
sordomudez, *f.* deaf-muteness.
sordomudo, da, *a.* deaf-and-dumb. —*m., f.* deaf-mute. deaf-and-dumb person.
sordón, *m.* (mus.) ancient type of bassoon.
sorgo, *m.* (bot.) sorghum.
soríasis, *f.* (med.) psoriasis.
sorites, *m.* (log.) sorites.
sorna, *f.* sarcasm, irony, sarcastic or ironic tone.
soro, *a.* young (hawk), (hawk) which has not yet molted. —*m.* (bot.) sorus.
sorocharse, *r.v.* to get mountain sickness or soroche.
soroche, *m.* 1. (Amer.) soroche, mountain sickness. 2. (Bol., Chile) galena, native lead. 3. (Chile) blush, flush.
soroco, ca, *a.* (Amer.) crazy, wild, silly.
sorprendente, *a.* surprising; unusual, extraordinary.
sorprender, *tr.v.* 1. to surprise, astonish. 2. to surprise or catch (someone in the act). —*r.v.* to be surprised, astonished.
sorpresa, *f.* surprise; **tomar por s.,** to take by surprise.
sorpresivo, va, *a.* unexpected, surprising.
sorra, *f.* 1. (mar.) coarse gravel ballast. 2. side of tuna fish.
sorregar, (*ref. 67*) *tr.v.* to irrigate or water accidentally (by overflow from another plot or furrow).
sorregué, *ref.* **sorregar.**
sorriego, *m.* irrigation by overflow; overflow water.
sorriego, sorriegue, *ref.* **sorregar.**
sorrostrada, *f.* insolence, impudence; taunt.
sorteador, ra, *m., f.* 1. one who draws lots. 2. one who evades or eludes. 3. (taur.) skillful, cautious bullfighter.
sorteamiento, *m., var. of* **sorteo.**
sortear, *tr.v.* 1. to raffle, cast or draw lots for. 2. (taur.) to fight cleverly. 3. to dodge, avoid, evade, elude.
sorteo, *m.* 1. raffle, casting of lots, drawing (of lottery). 2. dodging, evasion. 3. (taur.) swift cape passes.
sortero, ra, *m., f.* soothsayer, fortuneteller.
sortiaria, *f.* fortunetelling by cards.
sortija, *f.* 1. ring (jewel). 2. ringlet, curl, lock of hair.
sortijero, *m.* ring box, small jewel case.
sortijilla, *f. dim. of* **sortija,** small ringlet.
sortijuela, *f. dim. of* **sortija,** small ringlet.
sortijón, *m., aug. of* **sortija,** large, showy ring (jewel).
sortilegio, *m.* 1. sortilege, sorcery. 2. **magic** spell.
sortílego, ga, *m., f.* fortune teller, conjurer.
sosa, *f.* 1. (bot.) saltwort, barilla; soda ash. 2. (chem.) soda; **s. cáustica,** caustic soda.
sosaina, *a.* (coll.) dull, colorless (**person**). —*m., f.* (coll.) dull person, drip (sl.).
sosal, *m.* barilla or saltwort field.
sosamente, *adv.* 1. insipidly, **tastelessly.** 2. inanely.
sosar, *m., var. of* **sosal.**
sosegadamente, *adv.* calmly, quietly.
sosegado, da, *past part, of* **sosegar.** —*a.* calm, quiet, peaceful.
sosegador, ra, *a.* calming, quieting. —*m., f.* calmer, quieter, appeaser.
sosegar, (*ref. 67*) *tr.v.* to calm, quiet. —*i.v.* 1. to calm down. 2. to repose, rest. —*r.v.* to calm down, become calm; to regain serenity.
sosegué, *ref.* **sosegar.**
sosera, sosería, *f.* 1. insipidity, dullness, inanity; inane remark, nonsense. 2. tastelessness, insipidity.
sosero, ra, *a.* soda-yielding.
sosiega, *f.* 1. rest from work, break. 2. drink during rest; nightcap.
sosiego, *m.* quiet, calm, tranquility.
sosiego, sosiegue, *ref.* **sosegar.**
soslayar, *tr.v.* 1. to put or place slanting or obliquely. 2. to pass over, ignore, evade, dodge.
soslayo, *a.* oblique, slanting; **al soslayo, de soslayo,** obliquely, slantingly, askance; out of the corner of one's eye; sideways; hastily, in passing.
soso, sa, *a.* 1. insipid, tasteless. 2. (fig.) dull, inane, colorless (person, remark, etc.).
sospecha, *f.* suspicion.
sospechable, *a.* apt to be suspected or surmised.
sospechar, *tr.v.* to suspect. —*i.v.* to be suspicious.
sospechosamente, *adv.* suspiciously.
sospechoso, sa, *a.* suspicious. —*m.* suspect.
sospesar, *tr.v., var. of* **sopesar.**
sosquín, *m.* sneak blow, side blow.
sostén, *m.* 1. support. 2. sustenance. 3. brassiere, bra (coll.). 4. (mar.) steadiness (of a ship).
sostenedor, ra, *a.* supporting. —*m., f.* supporter.
sostener, (*ref. 23*) *tr.v.* 1. to support, hold up, prop, sustain (a weight, etc.). 2. to maintain, hold (an opinion). 3. to support, keep, maintain. 4. to endure, bear (difficulties, misfortunes). 5. to hold (a conference, a conversation). 6. to maintain, keep up (prices, credit, etc.). —*r.v.* to support or maintain oneself.
sostenga, sostengo, *ref.* **sostener.**
sostenido, da, *past part. of* **sostener.** —*a.* 1. supported, sustained; kept up. 2. (mus.) sharp; **doble s.,** double sharp.
sosteniente, *a.* supporting, sustaining.
sostenimiento, *m.* support, maintenance. — **muro** or **pared de s.,** retaining wall.
sostuve, sostuviera, sostuviese, *ref.* **sostener.**
sota, *f.* 1. jack, knave (in cards). 2. hussy, brazen woman. — **s., caballo y rey,** (coll.) meat, vegetables and broth (ingredients of a typical Spanish boiled dinner). —*m.* (Chile) foreman, overseer.
sotabanco, *m.* 1. attic, garret. 2. (**archit.**) impost, springer.
sotabarba, *f.* Lincoln-style beard (under and around the chin).
sotacola, *f.* crupper strap (of horse's harness).
sotacoro, *m., var. of* **socoro.**
sotacura, *m.* (Arg., Col., Chile) assistant priest.
sotalugo, *m.* second hoop (of a cask or barrel).
sotamontero, *m.* assistant to chief huntsman.
sotana, *f.* 1. soutane, cassock. 2. (coll.) beating, drubbing.
sotanear, *tr.v.* (coll.) 1. to beat, drub. 2. reprimand.
sotañi, (*pl.* **sotaníes**), *m.* narrow, short, unpleated skirt.

sótano, *m.* basement, cellar.
sotaventarse, sotaventearse, *r.v.* (mar.) to fall to leeward.
sotavento, *m.* (mar.) leeward, lee; **a s.,** under the lee.
sotechado, *m.* shed.
soteño, ña, *a.* growing in groves.
soteriología, *f.* (rel., philos.) soteriology.
soterramiento, *m.* burial; burying under ground.
soterraño, ña, *a.* underground, subterranean. —*m.* subterranean, place underground.
soterrar, (*ref. 29*) *tr.v.* to bury; (fig.) to bury, hide.
sotierre, sotierro, *ref.* **soterrar.**
sotileza, *f.* leader (fine fiber at the end of a fishing line).
sotillo, *m. dim. of* **soto,** small grove or thicket.
soto, *m.* grove, thicket.
sotole, *m.* (Mex.) thick strong palm (used in the construction of huts).
sotoministro, *m.* chief kitchen or pantry steward or assistant (in some monasteries).
sotreta, *f.* (Arg. nag, useless horse.
sotrozo, *m.* 1. (artil.) linchpin, axle pin. 2. (mar.) futtock staff.
sotuer, *m.* (her.) saltier, saltire.
soturno, na, *a.* saturnine, melancholy, gloomy.
sotuto, *m.* (Bol., ento.) chigoe, chigger.
soviet, *m.* soviet.
soviético, ca, *a.* of the Soviet Union.
sovietización, *f.* sovietization.
sovietizar, (*ref. 53*) *tr.v.* to sovietize.
sovoz, *adv.* **a s.,** sotto voce, in a low voice.
soy, *ref.* **ser.**
soya, *f., var. of* **soja.**
sozina, *f.* (biochem.) sozin.
sport, *m.* (Angl., sport; **chaqueta de sport,** sports jacket.
sprintar, *i.v.* (Angl., sport.) to sprint.
Sr *sym. of* **estroncio,** strontium (Sr).
Sr. *abbrev. of* **Señor,** Mister (Mr.).
Sra. *abbrev. of* **Señora** (Mrs.).
Sres., Srs. *abbrev. of* **Señores,** Messrs.
S.R.L. *abbrev. of* **sociedad de responsabilidad limitada,** limited liability company.
S.R.M. *abbrev. of* **Su Real Majestad,** Her or His Royal Majesty (H R M).
Srta. *abbrev. of* **señorita,** Miss.
SSMO. P. *abbrev. of* **Santísimo Padre,** Most Holy Father.
SSO *abbrev. of* **sur-sudoeste,** south-southwest (S S W).
S.S.S. *abbrev. of* **su seguro servidor,** your faithful servant.
S.S. *abbrev. of* **Su Santidad,** His Holiness (H H).
SSE *abbrev. of* **sur-sudeste,** south-southeast (S S E).
SSMO. *abbrev. of* **Santísimo,** Most Holy.
Sta. *abbrev. of* **Santa,** Saint.
Stábat, Stabat Mater, *m.* Stabat Mater.
staccato, *m., a.* (mus.) staccato, chopped, with distinct stops between successive tones.
stalinismo, *m.* (pol.) Stalinism.
stándard, *a., m.* standard.
standardización, *f.* standardization.
sténcil, *m.* stencil.
Sto. *abbrev. of* **Santo,** Saint (St).
stock, *m.* (Angl.) stock; **en s.,** in stock.
striptease, *m.* striptease.
stripteasero, ra, *m., f.* striptease artist, stripper. —*m.* male stripper.
su, sus, *pos. a.* your, his, her, its,its, their.
suabo, ba, *a., m., f.* Swabian (of a region in Germany).
suarda, *f.* grease stain or spot (in silk cloth due to faulty degumming).
suasorio, ria, *a.* suasive, persuasive.
suave, *a.* 1. smooth, soft; delicate. 2. gentle, mild. 3. sweet, mellow. 4. suave, docile, tractable.
suavemente, *adv.* 1. smoothly, softly; delicately. 2. gently, mildly. 3. suavely.
suavice, suavicé, *ref.* **suavizar.**
suavidad, *f.* 1. smoothness, softness; delicateness. 2. gentleness, mildness. 3. sweetness, mellowness. 4. suavity, tractability.
suavizador, ra, *a.* smoothing; softening; mollifying. —*m.* razor strop.
suavizar, (*ref. 53*) *tr.v.* 1. to smooth, soften. 2. to mollify, mitigate. 3. to ease; to temper. —*r.v.* 1. to become smooth, soft, pliable. 2. to become smoothed, to lessen (pain, etc.); to become lenient, tractable, approachable.
suba, *f.* (Arg.) rise (in prices).
subacetato, *m.* (chem.) subacetate.
subácido, a, *a.* (chem.) subacid.
subacuático, ca, *a.* subaqueous, underwater.
subafluente, *m.* tributary (river, stream).
subagente, *a.* subagent.
subalcaide, *m.* deputy warden.
subalpino, a, *a.* subalpine.
subalternar, *tr.v.* to hold in subordination.
subalterno, na, *a., m., f.* subordinate, subaltern, subalternate.
subálveo, a, *a.* located under a river bed. —*m.* layer under a river bed.
subarrendador, ra, *m., f.* subleaser, subletter.
subarrendamiento, *m., var. of* **subarriendo.**
subarrendar, (*ref. 29*) *tr.v.* 1. to sublet, sublease (grant under a sublease). 2. to sublease (hold under a sublease).
subarrendatario, ria, *m., f.* subtenant, sublessee.
subarriende, subarriendo, *ref.* **subarrendar.**
subarriendo, *m.* sublease, underlease (action, contract); sublease rent.
subártico, ca, *a.* subarctic.
subasta, *f.* auction, auction sale; **en s.,** for auction; **sacar a pública s.,** to sell at auction.
subastador, ra, *m.* auctioneer.
subastar, *tr.v.* to auction, sell at an auction, auction off.
subatómico, ca, *a.* (chem., phys.) subatomic.
subátomo, *m.* (phys.) subatom.
subcalibrado, da, *a.* subcaliber.
subcartilaginoso, sa, *a.* (anat.) subcartilaginous.
subcinericio, *a.* baked under ashes (bread).
subclase, *f.* (biol.) subclass.
subclavero, *m.* assistant keeper of the keys (in some military orders).
subclavio, via, *a.* (anat.) subclavian.
subcolector, *m.* subcollector, assistant collector.
subcomendador, *m.* deputy commander (in military orders).
subcomisión, subcomité, *m., f.* subcommission, subcommittee.
subconsciencia, *f.* (the) subconscious; subconsciousness.
subconsciente, *a.* subconscious.
subcontratar, *tr.v.* to subcontract.
subcontratista, *m., f.* subcontractor.
subcontrato, *m.* subcontract.
subcostal, *a.* (anat., zool.) subcostal.
subcrítico, ca, *a.* (phys., chem.) subcritical.
subcultivo, *m.* (bac.) subculture.
subcutáneo, a, *a.* subcutaneous.
subdelegación, *f.* subdelegation.
subdelegado, da, *m., f.* subdelegate.
subdelegante, *m., f.* one who subdelegates.
subdelegar, (*ref. 51*) *tr.v.* to subdelegate.
subdelegue, subdelegué, *ref.* **subdelegar.**
subdelirio, *m.* (med.) subdelirium.
subdesarrollado, a, *a.* underdeveloped.
subdesarrollo, *m.* underdevelopment.
subdiaconado, subdiaconato, *m.* subdeaconry, subdiaconate.
subdiácono, *m.* subdeacon.
subdirección, *f.* post and office of an assistant director.
subdirector, ra, *m., f.* assistant director.
subdistinción, *f.* subdistinction.
subdistinga, subdistingo, *ref.* **subdistinguir.**
subdistinguir, (*ref.63*) *tr.v.* to make a subdistinction, subdistinguish.
súbdito, ta, *a.,* subject (to authority). —*m., f.* citizen, e.g. *s. francés,* French citizen.
subdividir, *tr.v.* to subdivide.
subdivisión, *f.* subdivision.
subdominante, *f.* (mus.) subdominant.
subduplo, pla, *a.* (math.) subdouble.
subejecutor, *m.* subagent, assistant executor.
subentender, (*ref. 30*) *tr.v.* to understand; to understand what is tacitly implied. —*r.v.* to be understood; to be implied.
subentienda, subentiendo, *ref.* **subentender.**
subeo, *m.* thong (to tie yoke to pole).
subérico, ca, *a.* (chem.) suberic.
suberina, *f.* (biochem.) suberin.
suberización, *f.* (bot.) suberization.
suberoso, sa, *a.* suberose, subereous, corklike.
subespecie, *f.* (biol.) subspecies.
subestación, *f.* (elec.) substation.
subestructura, *f.* substructure.
subfamilia, *f.* (biol.) subfamily.
subfebril, *a.* (med.) subfebrile, slightly above normal (temperature).
subforo, *m.* (law) sublease.
subgénero, *m.* (biol.) subgenus.
subgobernador, *m.* deputy governor, lieutenant governor.
subibaja, *f.* 1. seesaw. 2. (Cuba, coll.) cafe au lait and buttered bread.
subida, *f.* 1. rise; ascent; going up, climb, climbing. 2. ascension (to the throne). 3. rise (of prices, tide, etc.). 4. slope, acclivity.
subidero, ra, *a.* used for mounting, rising, climbing. —*m.* way up, path up.
subido, da, *past part. of* **subir.** —*a.* 1. strong (smell); loud, bright (color). 2. high (price); tall (plant). 3. fine, superior, excellent. — **s. de precio,** highly-priced, expensive; **s. de tono,** suggestive, risqué, off-color (joke, remark).
subidor, *m.* 1. porter. 2. raiser, hoister.
subiente, *a.* rising, ascending. —*m.* (archit.) spiral ornamentation on pillars.
subilla, *f.* awl.
subimiento, *m.* rise; ascent; going up; hoisting, carrying up.
subíndice, *m.* (math.) subindex.
subinquilino, *m.* subtenant.
subinspección, *f.* subinspectorship; subinspector's office.
subinspector, *m.* subinspector, assistant inspector.
subintendencia, *f.* office and post of subintendant or assistant superintendent.
subintendente, *m.* subintendant, assistant superintendent.
subintración, *f.* (surg.) underlapping (of bone); (med.) overlapping (of fevers).
subintrante, *a.* (surg.) underlapping (bone); (med.) overlapping (fevers).
subintrar, *i.v.* to enter after or later; (surg.) to underlap (bone); (med.) to overlap (fevers).
subir, *tr.v.* 1. to go up, climb, mount, ascend. 2. to take up, bring up, carry up. 3. to lift, raise; to make higher. 4. to raise the price of, charge more for; to raise (price). —*i.v.* 1. to rise, go up, come up; to mount; to climb; to get on (a bus, train,

horse, etc.); to get bigger or taller. 2. to enter leaves (silkworm, to spin cocoon). 3. to rise in the world, rise in position. 4. to get worse, spread (epidemic). — **s. a,** to climb, climb up to, go up to; to climb into; to get into, get on; to mount; to add up to, amount to (bill). —*r.v.* to go up, rise; to climb; **s. de tono,** to raise one's voice; to become haughty; **subírsele a uno a la cabeza,** to go to one's head (wine, popularity, etc.); **subirse sobre,** to climb on top of.

súbitamente, subitáneamente, *adv.* suddenly, all of a sudden.

subitáneo, a, *a.* sudden, unexpected.

súbito, ta, *a.* sudden, unexpected; hasty, impetuous. —*m.* (rare) impulse, fit.

súbito, *adv.* suddenly. — **de s.,** suddenly, unexpectedly.

subjefe, *m.* assistant chief, second in command.

subjetivamente, *adv.* subjectively.

subjetividad, *f.* subjectivity.

subjetivismo, *m.* subjectivism.

subjetivo, va, *a.* subjective.

subjuntivo, *a., m.* (gram.) subjunctive.

sublevación, *f.,* **sublevamiento,** *m.* rising, revolt, insurrection.

sublevar, *tr.v.* to incite to rebellion; (fig.) to stir up, arouse. —*r.v.* to revolt, rise in rebellion, rebel.

sublimación, *f.* sublimation.

sublimado, da, *past part. of* **sublimar. —***a.* sublimated; exalted. —*m.* (chem.) sublimate; **s. corrosivo,** (chem.) corrosive sublimate.

sublimar, *tr.v.* 1. to sublime, sublimate, idealize, exalt. 2. (chem.) to sublimate, sublime. 3. (psyc.) to sublimate. —*r.v.* 1. to be sublimed, exalted or idealized. 2. (phys.) to sublime; (chem.) to be sublimated or sublimed. 3. (psyc.) to be sublimated.

sublimatorio, ria, *a.* (chem.) sublimatory.

sublime, *a.* sublime; **S. Puerta,** Sublime Porte (the former Ottoman Empire).

sublimemente, *adv.* sublimely.

sublimidad, *f.* sublimity, sublimeness.

subliminar, *a.* subliminal.

sublingual, *a.* (anat.) sublingual.

sublunar, *a.* 1. sublunar, sublunary. 2. earthly, terrestrial.

submarinismo, *m.* skin diving.

submarino, na, *a.* submarine, underwater. —*m.* (mar., mil.) submarine.

submaxilar, *a.* (anat.) submaxillary.

submicroscópico, ca, *a.* submicroscopic.

submúltiplo, pla, *a., m., f.* (math.) submultiple.

subnivel, *m.* sublevel.

subnormal, *a.* subnormal. —*f.* (geom.) subnormal.

subnota, *f.* (print.) footnote to a footnote.

suboficial, *m.* (mil.) sergeant major.

suborden, *m.* (biol.) suborder.

subordinación, *f.* subordination.

subordinadamente, *adv.* subserviently.

subordinado, da, *a.* 1. subordinate; subservient. 2. (gram.) subordinate. —*m., f.* subordinate (person).

subordinar, *tr.v.* to subordinate. —*r.v.* to become subordinated.

subóxido, *m.* (chem.) suboxide, suboxid.

subpolar, *a.* subpolar.

subprefecto, *m.* subprefect.

subprefectura, *f.* subprefecture.

subproducto, *m.* by-product.

subranquial, *a.* (zool.) sub-branquial.

subrayable, *a.* worth underlining or emphasizing.

subrayado, *a.* underlined, underscored; emphasized.

subrayar, *tr.v.* to underline, underscore; to emphasize.

subreino, *m.* (biol.) subkingdom.

subrepción, *f.* 1. subreption, underhandedness. 2. (law) subreption, concealment of truth.

subrepticiamente, *adv.* surreptitiously.

subrepticio, cia, *a.* surreptitious.

subrigadier, *m.* (mil.) subbrigadier.

subrogación, *f.* subrogation, substitution.

subrogar, (*ref. 51*) *tr.v.* (law) to substitute, subrogate.

subrogue, subrogué, *ref.* **subrogar.**

subsanable, *a.* 1. reparable, remediable. 2. excusable.

subsanación, *f.* 1. reparation, remedying. 2. excusing, exculpation.

subsanar, *tr.v.* 1. to correct, mend, repair. 2. to excuse, exculpate.

subscapular, *a.* (anat.) subscapular. —*m.* subscapular muscle, subscapularis.

subscribir, *irr. past part.* **subscripto,** subscrito. —*tr.v.* 1. to subscribe to, endorse, be in favor of, agree with. 2. (com.) to subscribe, underwrite (shares, bonds). 3. to sign, subscribe. 4. to subscribe to (a periodical). —*r.v.* to subscribe; **subscribirse a,** to subscribe to (a periodical).

subscripción, *f.* subscription.

subscripto, ta, *a., var. of* **subscrito.**

subscriptor, ra, *m., f.* subscriber.

subscrito, ta, *irr. past part. of* **subscribir. —***m., f.* **el subscrito, la subscrita,** the undersigned.

subscritor, ra, *m., f., var. of* **subscriptor.**

subscretaría, *f.* undersecretaryship; undersecretary's office; assistant secretary, assistant secretary's office.

subsecretario, ria, *m., f.* assistant secretary. —*m.* undersecretary (of a government ministry).

subsecuente, *a.* subsequent.

subseguir, (*ref. 77*) *i.v., r.v.* to follow next.

subsidiariamente, *adv.* subsidiarily.

subsidiario, ria, *a.* subsidiary; (law) ancillary.

subsidio, *m.* subsidy; aid, help, assistance; **s. familiar,** family allowance.

subsiga, subsigo, *ref.* **subseguir.**

subsiguiente, *a.* subsequent, succeeding.

subsistencia, *f.* 1. subsistence. 2. livelihood, means of support. 3. (*pl.*) food, provisions, supplies.

subsistente, *a.* subsistent.

subsistir, *i.v.* 1. to subsist, live. 2. to remain, continue to exist, still be.

subsolano, *m.* east wind.

subsónico, ca, *a.* subsonic; **velocidad s.,** subsonic speed.

subsótano, *m.* subbasement, subcellar.

substancia, *f.* 1. substance, matter, material, stuff. 2. substance, essence, marrow. 3. concentrated broth, e.g. *s. de pollo,* concentrated chicken broth; extract, essence (of foods). 4. substance, wealth, fortune. 5. importance. 6. (coll.) personality, maturity, judgment, sense, e.g. *hombre sin s.,* nonetity, man without personality. 7. (philos., theol.) substance. — **en s.,** in brief, in a word, in substance, in brief, in a nutshell; **s. blanca,** (anat.) white matter; **s. gris,** (anat.) gray matter.

substanciación, *f.* 1. abridgment. 2. (law) proceedings (of a case).

substancial, *a.* 1. substantial, material, pertaining to substance or matter. 2. substantial, considerable, e.g. *faltaba una suma s. de dinero,* a substantial sum of money was missing. 3. nourishing, nutritious, substantial. 4. essential, basic, important, substantial, e.g. *lo s.,* the essence or substance.

substancialmente, *adv.* substantially; basically, essentially.

substanciar, *tr.v.* 1. to abridge, abstract. 2. (law) to try (a case).

substancioso, sa, *a.* 1. juicy, substantial, nourishing, nutritious. 2. substantial, important.

substantivamente, *adv.* as a noun, in the function of a noun.

substantivar, *tr.v.* (gram.) to convert into a noun, substantivize, use as a noun.

substantividad, *f.* substantiveness; substantiality.

substantivo, va, *a.* substantive; (gram.) substantive. —*m.* (gram.) substantive, noun.

substitución, *f.* substitution.

substituible, *a.* replaceable.

substituidor, ra, *a.* substitute, substituting. —*m., f.* substitute.

substituir, (*ref. 48*) *tr.v.* to substitute, replace.

substitutivo, va, *a.* substitutive. —*m.* substitute.

substituto, ta, *m., f.* substitute.

substituyente, *a.* substituting.

substracción, *f.* 1. substraction, removal; withdrawal. 2. misappropriation; stealing, theft. 3. (math.) subtraction.

substraendo, *m.* (math.) subtrahend.

substraer, (*ref. 24*) *tr.v.* 1. to take away, remove. 2. to misappropriate; to steal. 3. (math.) to subtract. —*r.v.* to withdraw oneself; to elude; **substraerse de,** to withdraw from, get out of (an obligation, etc.).

substraje, substrajera, substrajese, *ref.* substraer.

substrato, *m.* 1. substratum. 2. (philos.) substance, essence.

substrayendo, *ref.* **substraer.**

subsuelo, *m.* subsoil.

subte, *m.* (Amer.) subterranean railway, subway (U.S.), underground (G.B.).

subtender, (*ref. 30*) *tr.v.* (geom.) to subtend.

subtenencia, *f.* (mil.) second lieutenancy.

subteniente, *m.* mil.) second lieutenant.

subtensa, *f.* (geom.) subtense (chord).

subtenso, sa, *irr. past part. of* **subtender.**

subterfugio, *m. subterfuge, pretext.*

subterráneamente, *adv,* subterraneously.

subterráneo, a, *a.* subterranean, underground. —*m.* 1. cellar, subterranean, underground place, cave. 2. subway, underground, underground railway.

subtienda, subtiendo, *ref.* **subtender.**

subtitular, *tr.v.* to subtitle.

subtítulo, *m.* subtitle.

subtropical, *a.* subtropical.

suburbano, na, *a.* suburban. —*m., f.* suburbanite.

suburbicario, ria, *a.* (ecc.) suburbicarian.

suburbio, *m.* suburb, outskirts; shantytown.

subvención, *f.* subsidy, subvention; aid, financial help.

subvencionar, *tr.v.* to subsidize.

subvenga, subvengo, *ref.* **subvenir.**

subvenir, (*ref. 26*) *i.v* 1. to provide for (needs). 2. to help pay, defray (expenses).

subversión, *f.* subversion.

subversivo, va, *a.* subversive.

subversor, ra, *a.* subversive. —*m., f. subverter.*

subvertir, (*ref. 42*) *tr.v.* to subvert; to upset, disturb.

subvierta, subvierto, *ref.* **subvertir.**

subvine, subviniendo, subviniera, subviniese, *ref.* **subvenir.**

subvirtiendo, subvirtiera, subvirtiese, subvirtió, *ref.* **subvertir.**

subyacente, *a,* subjacent, underlying.

subyugable, *a.* able to subjugated.

subyugación, *f.* subjugation, subjection.

subyugador, ra, *a. s*ubjugating, subjecting. —*m., f.* subjugator, subjecter.

subjugar, (*ref. 51*) *tr.v.* to subjugate; to subdue.

subyugue, subyugué, *ref.* **subyugar.**

Suc. *abbrev. of* **sucursal,** branch.
succinato, *m.* (chem.) succinate.
succínico, ca, *a.* (chem.) succinic.
succino, *m.* succin, amber.
succión, *f.* suction; sucking.
succionar, *tr.v.* to suck, suck in.
sucedáneo, a, *a.* succedaneous, substitute. *—m. substitute.*
suceder, *i.v.* 1. to succeed, follow, be the successor of. 2. to happen, befall, occur; to come to pass. e.g. ¿qué sucede? what's the matter?; **suceda lo que suceda, come what may. —***r.v.* to follow one another, happen one after another.
sucedido, *m.* (coll.) event, happening; **lo s.,** what has happened.
sucediente, *a.* succeeding, following.
sucesible, *a.* capable of succession.
sucesión, *f.* 1. succession, succeeding (e.g. to the throne). 2. succession, estate, fortune (left by deceased). 3. issue, offspring, descendants. — **s. forzosa,** (law) hereditary succession (in some civil law countries); **s, intestada, (law) succession ab intestato, intestate succession.**
sucesivamente, *adv.* successively; **y así s.,** and so on.
sucesivo, va, *a.* successive, succeeding; consecutive; **en la s.,** in the future, hereafter.
suceso, *m.* 1. event happening. 2. course, lapse (of time). 3. outcome, result. 4. success.
sucesor, ra, *a.* succeeding. *—m., f.* successor.
suche, *a.* (Ven.) unripe, sour, green. *—m.* 1. (Ecuad., Peru, bot.) white frangipani. 2. (Arg.) pimple, boil. 3. (Chile, derog.) minor clerk, office boy.
súchel, *m.* (Cuba, bot.) white frangipani.
súchil, *m* Mex., bot.) white frangipani.
suciamente, *adv,* dirtily; nastily; basely.
suciedad, *f.* 1. dirtiness, filthiness; filth, dirt. 2. (fig.) vile, base act or remark.
sucintamente, *adv.* succinctly, briefly.
sucintarse, *r.v.* **to be succinct, brief or concise.**
sucinto, ta, *a.* succinct, brief, concise.
sucio, cia, *a.* 1. dirty, soiled. 2. dishonest; tainted with sin or guilt. 3. (mar.) foul. 4. foul (play, trick); obscene; low, base.
sucio, *adv.* dirtily; **jugar s.,** to play foully.
suco, ca, *a.* 1. (Bol., Ven.) muddy, slimy. 2. (Ecuad.) blond. 3. (Peru) orange. *—m.* 1. juice, sap. 2. (Bol., Chile, Ven.) slimy or muddy ground.
sucoso, sa, *a.* juicy.
sucre, *m.* sucre, Ecuadorian monetary unit and silver coin.
Sucre, *m.* Sucre (nominal capital of Bolivia).
sucrosa, *f.* (chem.) sucrose.
súcubo, *a.* succubine. *—m. succubus, demon.*
sucucho, *m.* 1. corner, nook; (Amer.) room, attic, den, small cubbyhole or corner. 2. (mar.) cranny between frames of the ship.
súcula, *f.* winch.
suculencia, f. succulence, juiciness.
suculentamente, *adv.* succulently.
suculento, ta, *a.* 1. succulent, juicy. 2. (bot.) succulent.
sucumbiente, *a.* succumbing.
sucumbir, *i.v.* 1. to succumb; to yield. 2. to perish. 3. (law) to lose a suit.
sucursal, *a.* ancillary, subsidiary; branch (office, store). *—m.* branch office or store. *—f.* (C. Amer.) mistress.
sucusión, *f.* (med.) succussion.
sud-, *pref.* south, e.g. *Sudamérica,* South America. *—m.* south.
sudadero, *m.* 1. saddle blanket, saddlecloth; sweat cloth. 2. sweating room or booth, sudatorium. 3. damp place, place where water filters through. 4. sweating place for sheep.
sudado, da, *past part. of* **sudar.** *—a.* sweated, sweaty.
Sudáfrica, *f.* South Africa.
sudafricano, na, a., m., f. South African.
Sudamérica, *f.* South America.
sudamericano, na, *a., m., f.* South American.
Sudán, *m.* Sudan.
sudanés, sa, *a., m., f.* Sudanese.
sudante, *a.* sweating, perspiring. *—m., f.* sweater, perspirer.
sudar, *tr.v.* 1. to sweat. 2. (coll.) to cough up, give reluctantly, shell out. *—i.v.* 1. to sweat, perspire; to exude moisture. 2. (coll.) to sweat, work hard. — **s. la gota gorda,** to sweat blood, to overexert oneself.
sudario, *m.* shroud, winding sheet; el Santo S., the Holy Shroud.
sudatorio, ria, *a.* sudorific, sweat-inducing.
sudestada, *f.* (Arg.) rainy southeast wind.
sudeste, *m.* 1. southeast. 2. southeaster, southeast wind. — **s. cuarta al este,** (mar.) southeast by east.
sudoeste, *m.* 1. southwest. 2. southwest wind. — **s. cuarta al sur,** southwest by south.
sudor, *m.* 1. sweat, perspiration; moisture. 2. (coll.) sweat, toil, hard work. 3. (*pl.*) (med.) sweat treatment. — **s. frío,** cold sweat.
sudoriento, ta, *a.* sweaty, sweat-soaked, sweating.
sudorífero, ra, *a.* sudoriferous.
sudorífico, ca, *a., m.* sudorific.
sudoríparo, ra, *a.* (anat.) sudoriferous, sweat (glands).
sudoroso, sa, *a.* sweating, perspiring; sweaty.
sudoso, sa *a.* sweaty.
sudsudeste, *m.* 1. south-southeast. 2. south-southeast wind.
sudsudoeste, *m.* 1. south-southwest. 2. south-southwest wind.
sudueste, *m. var. of* **sudoeste.**
Suecia, *f.* Sweden.
sueco, ca, *a.* Swedish. *—m., f.* Swede; **hacerse el sueco,** (coll.) to play dumb, pretend not to understand. *—m.* Swedish (language).
suegra, *f.* 1. mother-in-law. 2. hard crust (of bread).
suegro, *m.* father-in-law.
suela, *f.* 1. sole (of shoe). 2. tanned leather. 3. leather tip (on billiard cue). 4. (ichth.) sole. 5. (archit.) socle, base (of building). 6. (archit.) rafter or beam placed under a partition. 7. (*pl.*) sandals. — **de siete suelas,** (coll.) out and out, downright; **media s., sole** (underpart of shoe excluding heel); **no llegarle a uno a la s. del zapato,** not to be able to hold a candle to (fig.).
suela, *ref.* **soler.**
suelazo, *m.* (Amer., coll.) bang, bump (on floor).
suelda, *f.* (bot.) comfrey.
sueldacostilla, *f.* (bot.) grape hyacintyh.
suelde, sueldo, *ref,* **soldar.**
sueldo, *m.* 1. salary, pay. 2. (numis.) solidus. — **a s.,** on a salary; **s. regulador,** highest average pay (for calculating pensions, etc.); **tipo de s.,** rate of pay.
suele, suelo, *ref.* **solar.**
suelo, *m.* 1. soil, earth. 2. ground, floor, pavement. 3. soil, land, territory. 4. bottom, base. 5. sediment, dregs. 6. hoof (of horse). 7. earth, world. 8. end, finish. 9 land used for tilling and cultivation. 10. (*pl.*) grain left on threshing floor. — **dar consigo en el s.,** to fall down; **por el s., por los suelos,** very low, in very bad shape, e.g. *estaba con la moral por los suelos,* his morale was very low; **venir** or **venirse al s.,** to fall down, topple down, collapse; **s. de tarima,** floorboards; **s. natal** *or* **patrio,** homeland, native soil. native land, homeland.
suelo, *ref.* **soler.**
suelta, *f.* 1. release, freeing, loosing. 2. hobble, fetters (on horse). 3. relay of oxen, extra oxen (used as replacements). 4. stopping place where oxen rest and graze. 5. offprint, separate. 6. single copy. — **dar s. a,** to free, let loose; to grant a break or a period of recess (at school, etc.).
sueltamente, *adv.* 1. loosely; freely; lightly. 2. easily, nimbly. 3. fluently; flowingly. 4. spontaneously.
suelte, suelto, *ref.* **soltar.**
sueltista, *m., f.* spot news reporter.
suelto, ta, *irr. past part of* **soltar. — a. 1.** loose, free; at large. 2. loose, baggy, slack. 3. loose, unattached, e.g. *hago mis notas en hojas sueltas,* I make my notes on loose sheets of paper, *no vende los cigarrillos sueltos sino en paquetes,* he does not sell cigarettes loose, but in packets; disconnected, isolated, e.g. *es difícil traducir palabras sueltas,* it is difficult to translate isolated words; single, e.g. *muebles sueltos,* single pieces of furniture; by itself, singly, separately, e.g. *los libros de esta colección no se venden sueltos,* the books in this collection are not sold separately (singly). 4. fluent, easy-flowing (style, language). 5. loose, thin, watery. 6. loose (change). 7. free, easy (movements); nimble, agile; quick, swift, fast. 8. blank (verse). — **andar s.,** to be loose; to be at large (a criminal); **dar rienda suelta a,** to give a free rein to, let loose (a horse, an idea, passions, etc.); **s. de lengua,** outspoken; sharp-tongued; **s. de huesos or modos,** brazen, bold; brazenly, boldly. *—m.* 1. loose change (money). 2. short article (in newspaper).
suene, sueno, *ref.***sonar.**
suelvo, suelva, *ref.***solver.**
sueñe, sueño, *ref.***soñar.**
sueño, *m.* 1. sleep. 2. sleepiness, drowsiness. 3. dream. — **caerse de s.,** to be very sleepy, be dog-tired; **conciliar el s.,** to sink into sleep; **descabezar un s.,** to have a nap or doze; **echar un s.,** to have or take a nap; **en sueños,** in one's dreams; **entre sueños,** dozing, while half asleep; in one's dreams; **primer sueño,** beauty sleep; **s. dorado,** cherished dream or wish; **s. eterno,** everlasting sleep; death; **s. hecho realidad,** dream come true; **s. húmedo,** wet dream; **s. paradójico,** rapid-eye-movement sleep, REM sleep; **s. pesado,** sound or heavy sleep; **tener s.,** to be sleepy, be tired.
suero, *m.* 1. (med., biol.) serum.**2. whey.**
sueroso, sa, *a.* serous; watery.
sueroterapia, *f.* (med.) serotherapy, **serum** therapy, serum therapeutics.
suerte, *f.* 1. fate, luck, chance. 2. (good or bad) luck, good luck; piece of luck. 3. fate, lot, destiny, e.g. *ignora cuál será su s.,* he doesn't know what his fate will be. 4. lot, drawing lots, e.g. *elegir por s.,* to choose by lot. 5. lot, condition, state, e.g. *quería mejorar la s. del pueblo,* he wanted to better the lot of the people. 6. fortune, e.g. *leerle la s. a alguien,* to tell someone's fortune. 7. kind, sort, type. 8. manner, way. 9. (taur.) each of the progressive formal stages of the game; a skillful maneuver (with the cape, lance, or banderillas). 10. demarcated area of land for cultivation. 11. quality, grade. 12. (Peru) lottery ticket. 13. (print.) sort. — **buena** or **mala s., good** or bad luck; **caerle** or **tocarle a uno en s. una cosa,** to fall to one by chance or luck; **de s. que,** so that, in such a way that; **echar suertes,** to cast or draw lots; **¡mucha s.!,** best of luck!; **por s.,** by lot; by chance; fortunately, luckily; **s.!** or **¡ buena s.!,** good luck!; **tener (buena)**

s., to be lucky, be in luck; **tener mala s.,** to be unlucky.
suertero, ra, *a.* (Ecuad., Hond.) lucky, fortunate. —*m.* (Peru) seller of lottery tickets.
sueste, *m.* 1. southeast. 2. (mar.) southwester, sou'wester (hat).
suéter, *m.* (Angl.) sweater.
suévico, ca, *a. (hist.) Swabian.*
suevo, va, *a., m., f.* hist.) Swabian.
sufete, *m.* (hist.) Suffete (a Carthaginian magistrate).
sufí, (*pl.* **sufíes**) *a., m.* (hist., rel.) Sufi.
suficiencia, *f.* 1. sufficiency. 2. fitness, suitability, competence, ability. 3. (coll.) cocksureness.
suficiente, *a.* 1. sufficient. 2. fit, suitable, competent, able. 3. (coll.) cocksure. 4. pedantic.
suficientemente, *adv.* sufficiently.
sufijo, ja, *a.* (gram.) suffixed. —*m.* (gram.) suffix.
sufismo, *m.* (hist. rel.) Sufism.
sufista, *a.* (hist., rel.) Sufistic. —*m.* Sufi.
sufra. *f.* ridgeband (of a harness).
sufragáneo, a, *a., m.* suffragan.
sufragar, (*ref. 51*) *tr.v.* 1. to pay, defray. 2. to aid, help. —*i.v.* (Arg., Chile, Ecuad., Peru, Ven.) to vote.
sufragio, *m.* 1. suffrage (vote; franchise). 2. help, assistance, aid. 3. (ecc.) suffrage. — **s. restringido,** restricted suffrage; **s. universal,** universal suffrage.
sufragismo, *m.* female suffrage.
sufragista, *m.* suffragist (advocate of woman suffrage). —*f.* suffragette.
sufrague, sufragué, *ref.* **sufragar.**
sufrible, *a.* sufferable, bearable, endurable.
sufridera, *f.* smith's iron block (placed under piece to be punched).
sufridero, ra, *a., var. of* **sufrible.**
sufrido, da, *past part. of* **sufrir.** —*a.* 1. long-suffering, patient, enduring. 2. practical, that does not show the dirt (color).
sufridor, ra, *a.* suffering. —*m., f.* sufferer.
sufriente, *a.* suffering, enduring.
sufrimiento, *m.* 1. suffering; grief. 2. patience, tolerance.
sufrir, *tr.v.* 1. to suffer; to undergo, experience. 2. to bear, endure, put up with. 3. to permit, allow, suffer. —*i.v.* to suffer.
sufruticoso, sa, *a.* (bot.) suffruticose.
sufumigación, *f.* (med.) suffumigation.
sufusión, *f.* 1. (med.) suffusion (spreading of fluid into surrounding tissues). 2. (ophthal.) cataracts.
sugerencia, *f.* suggestion.
sugerente, sugeridor, ra, *a.* suggestive.
sugerir, (*ref. 42*) *tr.v.* to suggest; to hint, insinuate.
sugestión, *f.* 1. suggestion. 2. (psyc.) suggestion. — **s. hipnótica,** hypnotic suggestion.
sugestionable, *a.* easily influenced.
sugestionar, *tr.v.* 1. to influence (by the power of suggestion). 2. (psyc.) to induce by suggestion.
sugestivo, va, *a.* 1. suggestive; expressive; conspicuous. 2. interesting; alluring, striking, stimulating.
sugiera, sugiero, *ref.* **sugerir.**
sugiriendo, sugiriera, sugiriese, sugirió, *ref.* **sugerir.**
suicida, *a.* suicidal. —*m., f.* suicide (person).
suicidarse, *r.v.* to commit suicide, kill oneself.
suicidio, *m.* suicide (act); self-destruction.
suidos, *m.* (*pl.*) (zool.) Suidae, swine family.
sui géneris, *a.* (Lat.) sui generis, unique, peculiar, characteristic.
suindá, *m.* (Arg., ornith.) white owl.
suita, *f.* (Hond.) kind of grass used for forage and thatching.
Suiza, *f.* Switzerland.
suiza, *f.* 1. ancient military pastime simulating battle maneuvers. 2. (coll.) dispute, fight; contest, competition.
suizo, za, *a., m., f.* Swiss. —*m.* 1. yes-man. 2. (cul.) sweet butter roll.
sujeción, *f.* 1. subjection, domination; control. 2. submission, subordination. 3. (rhet.) prolepsis; rhetorical question. — **con s. a,** according to, in accordance with, subject to.
sujeta-, prefix meaning "holder", "clip", "fastener", "clamp".
sujetador, ra, *m., f.* clip, holder, fastener, clamp.
sujetahilos, (*pl.* **sujetahilos**) *m.* cleat insulator.
sujetalibros, (*pl.* sujetalibros), *m.* book end.
sujetapapeles, (*pl.* **sujetapapeles**), *m.* paper clip or clamp.
sujetar, *tr.v.* 1. to secure, fasten, tie; to hold, hold in place, catch, grasp. 2. to subject, subdue; to bring or put under the control or domination of. —*r.v.* 1. to subject oneself, submit. 2. to abide by, conform to.
sujeto, ta, *past part. irr. of* **sujetar.** —*a.* 1. subject, liable to; contingent upon. 2. held, grasped, tied, fastened. — **s. a,** subject to. —*m.* 1. individual, person. 2. (philos., gram., log., med.) subject. 3. subject, topic, theme. — **buen s.,** nice chap.
sujo, ja, *m., f.* (Chile, derog.) individual, person, character (coll.).
sulfa, *f.* (pharm.) sulfa, sulpha.
sulfadiazina, *f.* (pharm.) sulfadiazine.
sulfamida, *f.* (pharm.) sulfamide.
sulfanilamida, *f.* (pharm.) sulfanilamide.
sulfanílico, ca, *a.* (chem.) sulfanilic.
sulfapiridina, *f.* (pharm.) sulfapyridine.
sulfatación, *f., var. of* **sulfatado.**
sulfatado, *m.* sulfating.
sulfatador, ra, *a.* sulfating. —*m., f.* sulfater; sulfating machine.
sulfatar, *tr.v.* to sulfate, sulphate.
sulfatiazol, *m.* (pharm.) sulfathiazole.
sulfatillo, *m.* (Hond., bot.) plant with panicled purple flowers and heart-shaped leaves.
sulfato, *m.* (chem.) sulfate; **s. de cinc,** (chem.) zinc sulfate; **s. de cobre,** copper sulfate; **s. de magnesio,** magnesium sulfate; **s. de potasio,** (chem.) potassium sulfate; **s. de sodio,** (chem.) sodium sulfate; **s. ferroso,** (chem.) ferrous sulfate.
sulfhidrato, *m.* (chem.) sulfhydrate, hydrosulfide.
sulfhídrico, ca, *a.* (chem.) sulfhydric.
sulfito, *m.* (chem.) sulfite.
sulfonal, *m.* (chem.) sulfonal.
sulfonamida, *f.* (chem.) sulfonamide.
sulfónico, ca, *a.* (chem.) sulfonic.
sulfurar, *tr.v.* 1. to sulfurize, sulfurate. 2. to anger, enrage. —*r.v.* to get angry or furious; to become enraged.
sulfúreo, a, *a.* sulfurous, sulfureous, sulfury.
sulfúrico, ca, *a.* (chem.) sulfuric.
sulfurilo, *m.* (chem.) sulfuryl.
sulfuro, *m.* (chem.) sulfide, sulfuret; **s. de cinc,** (chem.) zinc sulfide.
sulfuroso. sa, *a.* sulfurous.
sulla, *f.* (bot.) sulla clover, French honey-suckle.
sultán, ana, *m., f.* sultan, sultana.
sultanato, *m.* sultanate (rule and rank of a sultan).
sultanía, *f.* sultanate (territory ruled by sultan).
suma, *f.* 1. sum, amount. 2. sum, sum total; aggregate. 3. addition, adding. 4. essence, essential point. 5. summa, summary, sum, substance. 6. (math.) sum. — **en s.,** to sum up, in short, briefly; **s. vectorial,** (math.) vector sum.
sumaca, *f.* (Amer.) two-masted coasting schooner.
sumador, ra, *a.* adding. —*m., f.* adder. —*f.* adding machine.
sumamente, *adv.* extremely, exceedingly, highly.
sumando, *m.* (math.) addend.
sumar, *tr.v.* 1. to add, add up. 2. to amount to, add up to. 3. to summarize, make a summary of. — **suma y sigue,** carry forward (addition); (coll.) to be continued. —*r.v.* **sumarse a,** to join.
sumaria, *f.* 1. (law) written proceedings. 2. (law) preliminary hearing or proceedings, indictment (in military case).
sumariamente, *adv.* summarily, briefly.
sumariar, *tr.v.* (law) to conduct a preliminary hearing of a case.
sumario, ria, *a.* 1. summary, brief, concise, succinct. 2. (law) summary (of civil law proceedings. —*m.* 1. summary, resumé. 2. (law) indictment.
sumarísimo, ma, *a. super. of* **sumario,** (law) swift, expeditious (type of proceedings).
sumergible, *a.* submergible, submersible. —*m.* submergible, submersible, submarine.
sumergimiento, *m.* submersion, sinking.
sumergir, (*ref. 62*) *tr.v.* to submerge, submerse, immerse; to sink, plunge. —*r.v.* to be submerged, submersed, immersed; to plunge, dive.
sumerja, sumerjo, *ref.* **sumergir.**
sumersión, *f.* submersion, immersion.
sumidad, *f.* top, apex, summit.
sumidero, *m.* 1. drain, sewer; sump. 2. (Amer.) cesspit, cesspool.
sumido, da, *past part. of* **sumir.** —*a.* sunken, submerged.
sumiller, *m.* steward, chamberlain (in various royal dependencies). — **s. de cortina,** royal chaplain.
sumillería, *f.* stewardship; chamberlain's office.
suministrable, *a.* that can be supplied.
suministración, *f., var. of* **suministro.**
suministrador, ra, *a.* supplying, providing. —*m., f.* supplier, provider, purveyor.
suministrar, *tr.v.* to supply, provide, furnish, purvey, e.g. *s. tanques al ejército,* to supply tanks to the army, to supply, provide or furnish the army with tanks.
suministro, *m.* supply, providing; (*pl.*) provisions, supplies; **s. por medio de paracaídas,** airdrop.
sumir, *tr.v.* 1. to sink, submerge. 2. to plunge (into despair, etc.). 3. (ecc.) to take (the host and wine in the mass). —*r.v.* 1. to sink, submerge. 2. to become sunken (cheeks). 3. to plunge, sink (into despair); to lose oneself, become wrapped (in thought, study).
sumisamente, *adv.* submissively; obediently.
sumisión, *f.* submission; obedience.
sumiso, sa, *a.* submissive; obedient, docile; humble, meek.
sumista, *m., f.* quick adder or calculator. —*m.* summarizer, summarist.
súmmum, *m.* the acme, the highest degree.
sumo, ma, *a.* supreme, highest, greatest; **a lo sumo,** at the most; **de sumo,** completely, entirely; **en sumo grado,** exceedingly, extremely; **Sumo Pontífice,** Sovereign Pontiff (the Pope).
sumoscapo, *m.* (archit.) projection on the upper part of the shaft of a column, highest part of a scape.
sumpancazo, *m.* (Guat.) punch; fall.
súmulas, *f.* (*pl.*) compendium of the essential elements of logic.
sumulista, *m.* teacher or student of the essentials of logic.
suncho, *m.* 1. hoop, ring, band. 2. Bol., bot.) vellow aster.
sunción, *f.* (ecc.) taking of the host and wine (by a priest).
sunsún, *m.* (Cuba, ornith.) hummingbird.

suntuario, ria, *a.* luxury, e.g. *artículo suntuario,* luxury article.
suntuosamente, *adv.* sumptuously, magnificently, richly.
suntuosidad, *f.* sumptuousness, magnificence, richness.
suntuoso, sa, *a.* sumptuous, magnificent, splendid, gorgeous, rich.
supe, *ref.* **saber.**
supedáneo, *m.* pedestal, base, support (of a crucifix).
supeditación, *f.* subjection; oppression.
supeditar, *tr.v.* 1. to subject, subordinate. 2. to hold down, oppress, subject. —*r.v.* 1. to be subject (to), be subordinated (to). 2. to be oppressed or held down.
superable, *a.* surmountable, superable, able to be overcome.
superabundancia, *f.* superabundance.
superabundante, *a.* superabundant.
superabundar, *i.v.* to superabound.
superación, *f.* 1. surmounting, overcoming. 2. self-improvement, self-betterment.
superádito, ta, *a.* (rare) added, additional.
superante, *a.* surpassing; excelling; overcoming; exceeding.
superar, *tr.v.* 1. to surpass, exceed; excel. 2. to surmount, overcome. —*r.v.* to better oneself, do better, improve oneself.
superávit, *m.* (com.) superavit, surplus; **s. apartado pagado,** (com.) paid-in surplus; **s. de capital,** (com.) capital surplus; **s. reservado,** (com.) surplus reserves.
supercarretera, *f.* (Amer.) superhighway.
superchería, *f.* fraud, hoax, trick, trickery, deceit.
superchero, ra, *a.* fraudulent, deceitful, tricky. *m., f.* trickster, cheat, deceiver.
superciliar, *a.* (anat.) superciliary.
superconductividad, *f.* (elec.) superconductivity.
superconductor, ra, *a.* (elec.) superconductive.
supercrítico, ca, *a.* (phys.) supercritical.
superdominante, *f.* (mus.) superdominant.
superego, *m.* (psyc.) superego.
supereminencia, *f.* supereminence.
supereminente, *a.* supereminent.
superentender, *ref. 30) tr.v.* to superintend, supervise, inspect.
superentienda, superentiendo, *ref.* superentender.
supererogación, *f.* supererogation.
supererogatorio, ria, *a.* supererogatory.
superestructura, *f.* superstructure.
superfecundación, *f.* (physiol.) superfecundation.
superferolítico, ca, *a.* (coll.) extremely fine or delicate, exquisite.
superfetación, *f.* (biol.) superfetation.
superficial, a. superficial; shallow.
superficialidad, *f.* superficiality, shallowness.
superficialmente, *adv.* superficially.
superficiario, ria, *a.* (law) superficiary.
superficie, *f.* surface; area; **s. cónica,** (geom.) conical surface; **s. curva,** (geom.) curved surface; **s. desarrollable,** (geom.) developable surface; **s. esférica,** (geom.) spherical surface; **s. impresora,** (print.) printing surface; **s. plana,** (geom. plane surface; **s. de sustentación,** (aer.) airfoil.
superfino, na, *a.* superfine, extra fine.
superfluamente, *adv.* superfluously.
superfluidad, *f.* superfluity, superfluousness, superfluous thing.
superfluidez, *f.* (phys.) superfluidity.
superfosfato, *m.* (chem.) superphosphate.
superheterodino, na, *a., m.* (rad.) superheterodyne.
superhombre, *m.* superman.
superhumeral, *m.* (ecc.) superhumeral, ephod, stole.
superintendencia, *f.* superintendency, susperintendence; superintendent's office.
superintendente, *m., f.* superintendent; overseer; supervisor.
superior, *a.* 1. top, upper, e.g. *el labio s.,* the upper lip; higher, e.g. *él tiene una posición s. a la mia en la empresa,* he has a higher position than mine in the firm; above, e.g. *viven en el piso s.,* they live on the floor above. 2. superior, better, e.g. *este vino es s. al otro,* this wine is superior to or better than the other. 3. greater, higher, larger, e.g. *una suma s. a mil dólares,* an amount greater or higher than a thousand dollars. 4. superior, excellent. 5. advanced, higher (learning, studies). —*m.* superior.
superiora, *f.* mother superior.
superiorato, *m.* office of a superior or mother superior; term of office of superior or mother superior.
superioridad, *f.* superiority.
superiormente, *adv.* superiorly, masterfully.
superlación, *f.* superlativeness.
superlativamente, *adv.* superlatively.
superlativo, va. *a.* superlative; (gram.) superlative (adjective). —*m.* (gram.) superlative.
supermercado, *m.* supermarket.
superno, na, *a.* (rare) supreme, supernal.
supernova, *f.* (astron.) supernova.
supernumerario, ria, *a., m., f.* supernumerary.
superpoblado, da, *a.* overpopulated.
superponer, (*ref. 15*) *tr.v. to* superpose.
superponga, superpongo, *ref.* superponer.
superposición, *f.* superposition.
superpotencia, *f.* (pol., elec.) superpower.
superproducción, *f.* 1. (cine.) mammoth production. 2. (econ.) overproduction.
superpuse, superpusiera, superpusiese, *ref.* superponer.
supersaturar, *tr.v.* to supersaturate.
supersensible, *a.* supersensitive.
supersónico, ca, *a.* supersonic.
superstición, *f.* superstition.
supersticiosamente, *adv.* superstitiously.
supersticioso, sa, *a.* superstitious.
supérstite, *a.* (law) surviving. —*m., f.* (law) survivor.
supersubstancial, *a.* (ecc.) **pan s.,** the Host.
supertensión, *f.* (elec.) supervoltage.
supervacáneo, a, *a.* (rare) superfluous.
supervención, *f.* (law) supervention.
superveniencia, *f.* (law) supervention.
supervenga, supervengo, *ref.* **supervenir.**
superveniente, *a.* (law) supervening, supervenient.
supervenir, (*ref. 26*) *tr.v.* 1. to happen, take place, come about. 2. to supervene, happen after.
supervine, superviniendo, superviniera, superviniese, *ref.* **supervenir.**
supervisar, *tr.v.* to supervise.
supervisión, *f.* supervision.
supervisor, ra, *a.* supervising. —*m., f.* supervisor.
supervivencia, *f.* survival.
superviviente, *a.* surviving. —*m. f.* survivor.
supiera, supiese, *ref.* **saber.**
supinación, *f.* supination.
supinador, *m.* (anat.) supinator.
supino, na, *a.* supine. —*m.* (gram.) supine.
súpito, ta, *a.* 1. (coll.) impatient. 2. (Chile, Col., Mex.) stunned; stupid, dull.
suplantable, *a* 1. supplantable. 2. forgeable, falsifiable.
suplantación, *f.* 1. supplantation, supplanting. 2. falsification, fraudulent alteration; forging.
suplantador, ra, *a.* 1. supplanting. 2. falsifying, forging. —*m., f.* 1. supplanter. 2. falsifier; forger.
suplantar, *tr.v.* 1. to supplant, **displace,** take the place of. 2. to alter (document) fraudulently, forge (signature). 3. to pass oneself off as.
suple, *m.* (Chile) advance (on wages, saary, account).
suplefaltas, (*pl.* **suplefaltas**), *m., f.* (coll.) fill-in, substitute, replacement (for an absentee).
suplemental, *a.* (rare), *var. of* **suplementario.**
suplementar, *tr.v.* to supplement.
suplementario, ria, *a.* supplementary.
suplementero, *m., f.* (Chile) newspaper vendor.
suplemento, *m.* 1. supplement; complement. 2. (jour., math., geom.) supplement.
suplencia, *f.* substitution, replacement.
suplente, *a.* substituting, replacing. —*m., f.* substitute, replacement, deputy, fill-in (person).
supletorio, ria, *a.* supplementary, suppletory.
súplica, *f.* supplication, entreaty, plea; request, petition; **a s.,** by request.
suplicación, *f.* 1. supplication, entreaty, plea; request, petition. 2. (cul.) rolled wafer. 3. (law) petition for a reversal of a court's decision.
suplicante, *a.* entreating, pleading, suppliant, supplicant, petitioning, requesting. —*m., f.* suppliant, supplicant, entreater, pleader; petitioner, requester.
suplicar, (*ref. 50*) *tr.v.* 1. to entreat, implore, pray, beg, supplicate. 2. (law) to appeal to (a high court) for a reversal of its sentence.
suplicatorio, ria, *a.* supplicatory. —*m.* (law) request made by a judge or court to Parliament, Senate or Congress, for permission to initiate judicial proceedings against one of its members. —*m., f.* (law) communication from a lower court to a higher one.
suplicio, *m.* 1. torture; execution, punishment; place of torture or execution. 2. (fig.) torment, anguish, suffering, agony.
suplidor, ra, *a., m., f., var. of* **suplente.**
suplique, supliqué, *ref.* **suplicar.**
suplir, *tr.v.* 1. to make up for, supplement. 2. to substitute, take the place of, replace. 3. to overlook, excuse (someone's shortcomings).
supo, *ref.* **saber.**
suponedor, ra, *a.* supposing. —*m., f.* supposer.
suponer, (*ref. 15*) *tr.v.* 1. to suppose, assume, presume, imagine. 2. to pretend. 3. to entail, imply. —*i.v.* to have authority.
suponga, supongo, *ref.* **suponer.**
suposición, *f.* 1. supposition, assumption. 2. authority, distinction, high position. 3. imposture, falsehood. 4. (log.) supposition.
supositicio, cia, *a.* (rare) suppositious, supposed, assumed, pretended.
supositivo, va, *a.* suppositive, suppositional, hypothetical.
supositorio, *m.* (med.) suppository.
supradicho, cha, *a.* aforesaid, above-mentioned.
supraorbital, *a.* (anat.) supraorbital.
suprarrenal, *a.* (anat.) suprarenal; cápsula s., (med.) suprarenal capsule, gland or body.
suprasensible, *a.* hypersensitive.
supraspina, *f.* (anat.) supraspinous **fossa.**
suprema, *f.* (hist.) Supreme Council of the Inquisition.
supremacía, *f.* supremacy.
supremamente, *adv.* supremely.
supremo, ma, *a.* 1. supreme; highest, paramount. 2. last, final, definitive.
supresión, *f.* suppression, elimination, omission.
supresivo, va, *a.* suppressive.
supresor, *a.* eliminating, suppressing. —*m.* (mec.) suppressor; **s. de chispas,** (elec.) spark condenser.

suprimible, *a.* suppressible, that can be eliminated.
suprimir, *tr.v.* 1. to suppress, eliminate, do away with. 2. to cut out, leave out, strike out, omit.
suprior, *m.* subprior, deputy or substitute prior.
supriora, *f.* subprioress.
supriorato, *m.* office of subprior or subprioress.
supuesto, ta, *irr. past part. of* **suponer.** **—***a.* 1. supposed, assumed; believed. 2. assumed, pretended, e.g. *nombre supuesto,* assumed name. — **supuesto que,** since as, inasmuch as. **—***m.* supposition, assumption, hypothesis; **por s.,** of course.
supuración, *f.* suppuration.
supurante, *a.* suppurating.
supurar, *i.v.* to suppurate.
supurativo, va, *a., m.* suppurative, suppurant.
supuratorio, ria, *a.* suppurating.
supuse, supusiera, supusiese, *ref.* **suponer.**
suputación, *f.* (rare) calculation, **computation.**
suputar, *tr.v.* (rare) to compute, calculate, reckon.
sur, *m.* south; south wind.
sura, *m.* sura, section or chapter of the Koran.
surá, *m.* (tex.) surah, a soft, twilled silk fabric.
sural, *a.* (anat.) sural.
suramericano, na, *a., m., f.* South American.
surcaño, *m.* boundary, limit.
surcado, da, *a.* furrowed, sulcate, sulcated.
surcar, (*ref. 50*) *tr.v.* 1. to plow, furrow. 2. to cut through (e.g. the sea — a ship).
surco, *m.* 1. furrow; rut. 2. wrinkle (in brow). 3. groove (in gramophone record). 4. ridge between furrows. — **a s.,** adjoining, separated by a furrow; **echarse uno en el s.,** (coll.) to lie down on the job, give up working.
surcoreano, na, *a., m., f.* South Korean.
surculado, da, *a.* (bot.) single-stemmed.
súrculo, *m.* (bot.) single stem.
surculoso, sa, *a.* (bot.) *var. of* **surculado.**
sureño, ña, *a.* southern, southerly. **—***m., f.* southerner. **—***m.* (Chile) south wind.
sureste, *m.* southeast.
surgente, *a.* arising, springing up.
surgidero, *m.* (mar.) roads, anchoring place, anchorage.
surgidor, ra, *m., f.* one who anchors.
surgir, (*ref. 62*) *i.v.* 1. to spring up, arise, present itself, appear. 2. to spring, flow, spout. 3. (mar.) to anchor. 4. (coll.) to get on, be successful, rise in the world.
suri, *m.* (Arg., ornith.) ostrich.
suricate, *m.* (zool.) suricate.
suripanta, *f.* 1. (theat.) formerly a chorine, chorus girl. 2. (derog.) harlot, slut, jade.
surja, surjo, *ref.* **surgir.**
surmenaje, *m.* (gal.) mental fatigue.
suroeste, *m.* southwest.
surplus, *m.* surplus.
surque, surqué, *ref.* **surcar.**
surrealismo, *m.* (art., lit.) surrealism.
surrealista, *a., m., f.* (art., lit.) surrealist.
sursudoeste, *m.* south-southwest; south-southwest wind.
surtida, *f.* 1. (mil.) sally, sortie; (fort.) sally port. 2. (fig.) back door. 3. (mar.) slipway; (mar.) repair dock.
surtidero, *m.* 1. conduit, outlet. 2. fountain, jet, spout, spurt.
surtido, da, *a.* 1. assorted. 2. supplied; stocked. **—***m.* 1. assortment. 2. stock, supply.
surtidor, ra, *a.* supplying, providing. **—***m., f.* purveyor, supplier, stocker. **—***m.* fountain; jet, spout, spurt; **s. de gasolina,** gasoline or petrol pump, filling station.
surtimiento, *m.* 1. supplying, stocking; supply, stock. 2. assortment.
surtir, *tr.v.* 1. to stock, supply, provide, furnish. 2. **s. efecto,** to work, to have the desired effect. — **s. de,** to stock with. **—***i.v.* to gush, spout, spurt, shoot up.
surto, ta, *a.* 1. quiet, still, at rest. 2. anchored; **s. en el muelle,** docked, tied up at the wharf.
súrtuba, (C. Rica) gigantic fern.
surubí, (*pl.* **surubíes**), *m.* (Arg., Bol., ichth.) large fresh-water catfish.
surumpe, *m.* (Peru, med.) inflammation of the eyes (caused by the reflection of the snow).
surúpi, *m.* (Bol.), *var. of* **surumpe.**
sus, *pos. a. pl. of* **su,** his, hers, theirs, your, yours.
¡sus! *interj.* cheer up! up! forward! keep going!
susceptancia, *f.* (elec.) susceptance.
susceptibilidad, *f.* 1. susceptibility. 2. touchiness.
susceptible, susceptivo, va, *a.* 1. susceptible. 2. touchy, sensitive. — **s. de,** susceptible to, susceptible of, capable of.
suscitación, *f.* provocation; excitation.
suscitar, *tr.v.* to cause, provoke; to raise, start, originate. **—***r.v.* to come up, originate (argument, conversation, subject, etc.).
suscribir, *tr.v., var. of* **subscribir.**
suscripción, *f., var. of* **subscripción.**
suscriptor, *m., f., var. of* **subscriptor.**
suscritor, ra, *m., f., var. of* **subscriptor.**
susidio, *m.* restlessness, uneasiness, anxiety.
susodicho, cha, *a.* above-mentioned, aforesaid, said.
suspendedor, ra, *a.* suspending, holding, dangling. **—***m., f.* suspender, holder.
suspender, *tr.v.* 1. to suspend, to hang, hang up. 2. to interrupt, stop temporarily; to adjourn (meeting, session, etc.). 3. to remove temporarily (from a position, office, etc.). 4. to amaze, astound; to enrapture, enthrall. 5. to fail, flunk (coll.), plow (coll.) (in an examination). **—***r.v.* 1. to be suspended, adjourned or stopped. 2. to rear (a horse).
suspensión, *f.* 1. suspension, the act and effect of hanging, dangling or suspending. 2. suspension, interruption, discontinuance, cessation; (auto., chem., ecc., mus., phys., rhet.) suspension. 3. suspense, uncertainty; anxiety. — **s. de armas,** (mil.) truce, temporary cease fire; **s. de garantías,** suspension of constitutional guarantees; **s. de pagos,** (com.) deferral of payments.
suspensivo, va, *a.* suspensive; **puntos suspensivos,** dots or dashes, suspension point.
suspenso, sa, *past part. irr. of* **suspender.** *a.* 1. suspended, hanging. 2. amazed, astonished, baffled, perplexed. **—***m.* 1. suspense, expectancy, anticipation. 2. failing mark (in an examination). — **en s.,** in suspense, in a quandary.
suspensoide, *m.* (chem., phys.) suspensoid.
suspensores, *m.* (*pl.*) (Amer.) suspenders (U.S.), braces (G.B.).
suspensorio, ria, *a.* suspensory. **—***m.* jockstrap, suspensory, supporter.
suspicacia, *f.* suspiciousness, suspicion; distrust.
suspicaz, (*pl.* **suspicaces**), *a.* suspicious, distrustful.
suspicazmente, *adv.* suspiciously, distrustfully.
suspirado, da, *a.* desired, longed for, yearned after.
suspirar, *tr.v.* to sigh; **s. por,** to sigh for, long for; to crave, covet.
suspiro, *m.* 1. sigh, breath. 2. (cul.) ladyfinger. 3. glass whistle. 4. (Chile, bot.) pansy; (Arg., Chile, bot.) morning-glory. 5. (mus.) short pause. **exhalar el último s.,** to breathe one's last.
sustancia, *f., var. of* **substancia.**
sustanciación, *f., var. of* **substanciación.**
sustancial, *a., var. of* **substancial.**
sustancialmente, *adv., var. of* **substancialmente.**
sustanciar, *tr.v., var. of* **substanciar.**
sustantivar, *tr.v., var. of* **substantivar.**
sustantividad, *f., var. of* **substantividad.**
sustantivo, va, *a., m., var. of* **substantivo.**
sustentable, *a.* defensible, arguable, maintainable.
sustentación, *f.* 1. sustenance, nourishment; maintenance, support. 2. supporting, holding up (e.g. of a building). 3. asserting, holding (e.g. of opinion, thesis). 4. (rhet.) suspension. 5. (aer.) lift, buoyancy.
sustentáculo, *m.* prop, stay, support.
sustentador, ra, *a.* 1. sustaining, nourishing. 2. supporting. **—***m., f.* sustainer.
sustentamiento, *m.* 1. sustenance, nourishment; maintenance, support. 2. supporting, holding up (e.g. of building). 3. asserting, holding (e.g. of opinion, thesis).
sustentante, *a.* 1. sustaining, nourishing. 2. supporting. **—***m.* 1. support (of a building). 2. propounder, defender (of a thesis in a university faculty). 3. (mar.) gooseneck.
sustentar, *tr.v.* 1. to sustain, give nourishment to; to maintain, support, feed. 2. to support, hold up, sustain (e.g. a building). 3. to maintain, hold, propound, assert, put forward, defend (e.g. a thesis, opinion). **—***r.v.* 1. to nourish, feed oneself; to maintain or support oneself. 2. to be supported or held up. — **sustentarse con** or **de,** to nourish oneself on; to feed on; to draw strength from; to live off.
sustento, *m.* 1. sustenance, maintenance, food. 2. support.
sustitución, *f., var. of* **substitución.**
sustituíble, *a.* replaceable.
sustituidor, ra, *a., m., f., var. of* **substituidor.**
sustituir, (*ref. 48*) *tr.v., var. of* **substituir.**
sustitutivo, va, *a., var. of* **substitutivo.**
sustituto, ta, *m., f. var. of* **substituto.**
sustituya, sustituyendo, sustituyera, sustituyese, sustituyo, *ref.* **sustituir.**
susto, *m.* scare, fright, shock, startle; **dar un s.,** to give a fright, scare, frighten; **pasar** or **darse un s.,** to get a scare or fright.
sustracción, *f., var. of* **substracción.**
sustractivo, va, *a.* (photog.) subtractive.
sustraendo, *m., var. of* **substraendo.**
sustraer, (*ref. 24*) *tr.v., var. of* **substraer.**
sustraiga, sustraigo, *ref.* **sustraer.**
sustraje, sustrajera, sustrajese, *ref.* **sustraer.**
sustrato, *m.* (biochem.) substrate, substratum.
sustrayendo, *ref.* **sustraer.**
susurración, *f.* whispering.
susurrador, ra, *a.* whispering, murmuring, rustling. **—***m., f.* whisperer.
susurrante, *a.* whispering, murmuring, rustling.
susurrar, *i.v.* 1. to murmur, whisper. 2. to gossip. 3. (fig.) to murmur, whisper (trees, wind), rustle (leaves), purl (stream). **—***r.v.* to be rumored (gossip, etc.).
susurro, *m.* 1. whisper, murmur. 2. (fig.) whisper, murmur, rustle, purling.
susurrón, na, *a.* (coll.) whispering, murmuring, grumbling. **—***m., f.* whisperer, grumbler.
sutás, *m.* soutache (gimp, ribbon, trimming), braid, Russian braid.
sute, *a.* (Col., Ven.) sickly, puny, thin. **—***m.* 1. (Col.) suckling pig. 2. (Hond., bot.) kind of avocado.
sutil, *a.* 1. subtle, delicate, tenuous. 2. keen, cunning.
sutileza, *f.* 1. subtlety; delicateness, tenuousness. 2. cunning, artifice; perspicacity. 3. animal instinct. — **s. de manos,** dexterity, manual skill; (fig.) lightfingeredness (of a thief).

sutilice, sutilicé, *ref.* **sutilizar.**
sutilidad, *f., var. of* **sutileza.**
sutilización, *f.* subtilization.
sutilizador, ra, *a.* 1. polishing, refining. 2. (fig.) subtilizing, discerning. *—m., f.* 1. polisher, refiner. 2. one who subtilizes; one who argues with subtle distinctions.
sutilizar, (*ref. 53*) *tr.v.* 1. to file, taper; to polish, refine. 2. (fig.) to subtilize; to sharpen, make keen or discerning. 3. to argue subtly about. *—i.v.* to make subtle distinctions.
sutilmente, *adv.* 1. subtly. 2. finely, delicately; nicely.
sutorio, ria, *a.* pertaining to the shoemaking art, trade, and industry.
sutura, *f.* seam; (anat., med., bot., zool.) suture.
suyo, suya, suyos, suyas, *pos. pron. (never used before a noun)* his, hers, yours, theirs, its, one's; his own, her own, your own, their own, its own, one's own. — **de suyo,** naturally, by his, her, your or their very nature, e.g. *ella es de suyo tranquila,* she is by her very nature or naturally quiet; **hacer de las suyas,** to be up to one's old tricks; **los suyos,** his, her, your, one's or their relations or family; **salirse con la suya,** to get or have one's way. *—pos. a.* of his, of hers, of yours, of theirs, his, her, your, their, one's, its, e.g. *son amigos suyos,* they are friends of his (etc.) or they are his (etc.) friends.
suzón, *m.* (bot.) groundsel.
svástica, *f.* swastika, swastica.
Swaziland, *f.* Swaziland.
swing, *m.* (mus.) swing.
Sydney, *f.* Sydney, capital of Australia.

T

T, *f.* t, twenty-first letter of the Spanish alphabet.
¡ta! *interj.* easy does it! that's it!; rat-a-tat-tat (rapping sounds).
taba, *f.* 1. anklebone, astragalus. 2. knucklebones (game). 3. (Col.) vent in a water pipe. 4. (Mex.) conversation, talk. — **menear las tabas,** (coll.) to shake a leg, get a move on; to hurry.
tabacal, *m.* tobacco field, tobacco plantation.
tabacalero, ra, *a.* pertaining to tobacco, e.g. *industria tabacalera,* tobacco industry. —*m., f.* tobacco grower or dealer; tobacconist. —*f.* (Sp.) state tobacco monopoly.
tabaco, *a.* (Mex.) bold, determined. —*m.* 1. tobacco; snuff; cigar. 2. black rot (plant disease). — **acabársele el t.,** (Arg., Chile) to run out of or be out of dough or money; **ponerse de mal t.,** (C. Amer.) to get into a bad mood, get bad-tempered or moody; **t. capero,** cigar tobacco; **t. de hoja,** leaf tobacco; **t. de mascar,** chewing tobacco, plug; **t. de montaña,** (bot.) arnica; **t. de pipa,** pipe tobacco; **t. en polvo,** snuff; **t. en rama,** leaf tobacco; **t. rapé,** rappee; **t. turco,** Turkish tobacco; **tomar t.,** to take snuff.
tabacoso, sa, *a.* 1. (coll.) fond of taking snuff. 2. tobacco-stained. 3. attacked by black rot.
tabal, *m.* (reg., Cuba) barrel or cask of sardines or herring.
tabalada, *f.* 1. (coll.) heavy fall on the behind. 2. (coll.) slap; spanking.
tabalario, *m.* (coll.) behind, posterior, rump, backside, buttocks.
tabalear, *tr.v.* to rock to and fro; to shake. —*i.v.* to drum with the fingers. —*r.v.* to rock to and fro; to shake.
tabaleo, *m.* 1. rocking; shaking. 2. drumming with the fingers.
tabanazo, *m.* (coll.) slap, blow.
tabanco, *m.* 1. food stall or stand. 2. (Amer.) attic, loft, garret.
tabanera, *f.* place full of gadflies or horseflies.
tábano, *m.* (ento.) gadfly, horsefly.
tabanque, *m.* potter's wheel; **levantar el t.,** (coll.) to adjourn a meeting; to leave, go away
tabaola, *f.* hubbub, uproar, clamor.
tabaque, *m.* 1. large tack (nail). 2. small wicker basket, hand basket.
tabaquera, *f.* 1. snuffbox. 2. bowl (of a tobacco pipe). 3. (Arg., Chile) tobacco pouch.
tabaquería, *f.* tobacconist's shop, tobacco store; (Cuba) cigar factory.
tabaquero, ra, *a.* tobacco. —*m., f.* cigar or cigarette maker; tobacco dealer; tobacconist.
tabaquismo, *m.* (med.) nicotinism.
tabaquista, *m., f.* 1. tobacco expert. 2. heavy smoker.
tabardete, tabardillo, *m.* 1. form of typhus. 2. (coll.) sunstroke. 3. (coll.) madcap, wild person; annoying person, bore.
tabardo, *m.* (hist.) tabard (loose heavy jacket; long warm blazoned tunic).
tabarra, *f.* 1. bore, nuisance. 2. tiring speech, boring conversation.
tabarrera, *f.* 1. (coll.) *aug. of* **tabarra,** boring conversation. 2. (Sp., reg.) hornet's nest.
tabarro, *m., var. of* **tábano.**
tabear, *i.v.* (Arg.) to chat, prattle.
tabellar, *tr.v.* 1. to fold (cloth) leaving the selvage visible. 2. to mark with a trademark.
taberna, *f.* tavern, saloon, barroom, pub (coll., G.B.).
tabernáculo, *m.* tabernacle; (Bib.) **T.,** Tabernacle.
tabernario, ria, *a.* 1. tavern, saloon. 2. vulgar, low, coarse.
tabernera, *f.* woman who owns or keeps a tavern or a saloon; wife of a saloonkeeper or tavernkeeper; barmaid.
tabernero, *m.* tavern keeper, saloonkeeper, publican (G.B.); bartender.
tabes, *f.* (med.) consumption, tabes; **t. dorsal,** (med.) progressive locomotor ataxia.
tabí, *m.* (tex.) tabby, watered silk, moiré.
tabica, *f.* (archit.) covering board; riser (of a staircase).
tabicar, (*ref. 50*) *tr.v.* to wall up; (fig.) to close up, shut up, block up.
tabicón, *m. aug. of* **tabique,** thick partition wall.
tábido, da, *a.* (med.) putrid, rotting; (med.) tabid, tabetic, wasted by consumption.
tabífico, ca, *a.* (med.) tabific, wasting.
tabinete, *m.* (tex.) tabinet, tabbinet.
tabique, *m.* thin wall; partition wall; partition; **t. de carga,** (bldg.) load-bearing partition; **t. de panderete,** (bldg.) brickon-edge partition; **t. impermeabilizador,** (hydr.) core wall; **t. sordo,** (bldg.) hollow partition, double partition wall, wall with air space.
tabiquería, *f.* partition walls; partitions, series of partitions.
tabiquero, *m.* builder of partitions or partition walls.
tabla, *f.* 1. board, plank; slab, tablet (of marble, stone, etc.); plate, sheet (of metal). 2. width of a plank; widest face of a piece of lumber. 3. bulletin board. 4. table, tablet, e.g. *las tablas eugubinas,* (*pl.*) (Bib.) the Tables (on which the Ten Commandments were written). 5. index, table of contents; table, list (of figures, statistics, etc.); (multiplication, logarithm, cosine, etc.) table. 6. wide part (of a limb or body). 7. (anat.) table. 8. (jewel.) square-cut, flat-faced diamond. 9. (dressm.) panel, straight gore or insert in a skirt. 10. strip of land, land between two rows of trees; garden bed, patch or plot. 11. border customs post. 12. meat block or counter; butcher's stand or stall. 13. (p.) table, panel, painting on a board. 14. cushion between two pockets on a billiard table. 15. (*pl.*) draw, tie, e.g. *llegaron tablas,* they tied for first place, *quedaron tablas,* they tied, drew, finished up equal. 16. (*pl.*) boards, stage, e.g. *pisar las tablas,* to tread the boards; *pisar bien las tablas,* to act well. 17. (*pl.*) barrier (of a bullring). 18. (*pl.*) backgammon. — **a raja t.,** (coll.) by all means, at any cost, come what may; **escapar** or **salvarse en una t.,** to escape by a hair's breadth, have a narrow escape; **hacer t. rasa de,** to ignore entirely, to clear away (all obstacles); **quedar tablas,** to tie, draw, end up equal; **ser de t.,** (coll.) to be common, usual or customary; **t. de juego,** gaming house; **t. de lavar,** washboard; **t. de logaritmos,** logarithm table; **t. de mareas,** tide table; **t. de materias,** table of contents; **t. de multiplicar,** multiplication table; **t. de planchar,** ironing board; **t. de río,** calm wide stretches of a river; **t. de salvación,** last resource, lifesaver; **t. de servicios,** (aer.) service pattern; **t. hawaiana,** surfboard; surf riding; **t. pitagórica,** Pythagorean or multiplication table; **t. periódica,** (chem.) periodic table; **t. rasa,** (philos.) tabula rasa; **tablas reales,** backgammon; **T. Redonda,** (lit.) Round Table; **tener tablas,** (theat.) to have stage presence.
tablachina, *f.* wooden shield or buckler.
tablacho, *m.* sluicegate, floodgate.
tablada, *f.* (Arg., Bol., Urug.) stockyard, cattle yard.
tablado, *m.* 1. flooring; planking, boards. 2. wooden platform, stand or stage. 3. (theat.) boards, stage. 4. scaffold (for executions). 5. wooden target (for lancethrowing).
tablaje, *m.* 1. planking, boards. 2. gambling den, gaming house.
tablajería, *f.* 1. vice or habit of gambling; winnings at gambling. 2. butcher's shop.
tablajero, *m.* 1. builder of platforms or stands. 2. platform or stand attendant (collecting fees for use of a platform or stand). 3. tax collector (formerly collecting royal taxes). 4. gambler. 5. butcher.
tablar, *m.* 1. field of garden plots or beds. 2. wide calm stretch of a river. 3. sideboard, side boards (of a cart).
tablazo, *m.* 1. blow given with a board or plank. 2. shoal, wide shallow part of a river or sea.
tablazón, *f.* planking, boarding, planks, boards. — **t. de la cubierta,** (mar.) deck planks.
tableado, *m.* (dressm.) box pleating.
tablear, *tr.v.* 1. to cut (lumber) into boards or planks. 2. to divide (land) into plots or beds. 3. to level, grade (earth). 4. to convert (iron bars) into strips or plates. 5. (dressm.) to make box pleats in (skirt, etc.).
tableo, *m.* 1. cutting wood into planks. 2. dividing (land, garden) into plots. 3. leveling or grading of earth. 4. converting of iron into strips or bars. 5. box pleating.
tablero, *a.* suitable for planking (wood). —*m.* 1. board (of wood), sheet (of metal, cardboard, etc.), slab (of stone); table top. 2. panel, board, switchboard. 3. chessboard, checkerboard, backgammon board. 4. (tail.) cutting board. 5. blackboard. 6. counter (in a shop). 7. gambling house. 8. hard firm bed (of a dam or canal). 9. (ornith.) variety of petrel. 10. (archit.) abacus; projecting panel; (carp.) panel (of a door). 11. (mar.) bulkhead, partition (dividing a ship into cabins, etc.). 12. stock (of a crossbow). 13. (*pl.*) barrier (of a bull ring). — **poner** or **traer al t.,** to risk; to take a gamble; **t. contador,** abacus, counting frame; **t. de ajedrez,** chessboard; **t. de chaquete,** backgammon board; **t. de damas,** checkerboard; **t. de dibujo,** drawing board; **t. de**

distribución de electricidad, distribution switchboard; **t. de instrumentos,** (aut.) dashboard; (aer.) instrument panel; **t. de mando, control** or **gobierno,** control board or panel.

tablestaca, *f.* sheet pile; (min.) poling board.

tablestacado, *m.* sheetpiling.

tableta, *f.* 1. small plank or board. 2. slab, tablet (of chocolate). 3. lozenge, tablet (e.g. of aspirin). 4. wooden clappers. — **estar en tabletas,** to be dubious or uncertain; **quedarse tocando tabletas,** (coll.) to lose everything.

tableteado, *m.* rattle, rattling (of wooden clappers).

tabletear, *i.v.* 1. to rattle wooden clappers. 2. to fire continuous bursts (machine gun).

tableteo, *m.* 1. rattle, rattling (of wooden clappers). 2. rattling of machine gun fire.

tablilla, *f.* 1. small board or plank; small notice or bulletin board; (surg.) splint. 2. cushion between two pockets on the side of a billiard table. — **tablillas neperianas,** (math.) logarithmic tables.

tabloide, *m.* (Angl.) tabloid (newspaper format).

tablón, *m.* 1. large board or plank, thick board or plank. 2. (mar.) plank, strake. 3. (coll.) drunken bout or spree. — **t. de aparadura,** (mar.) garboard strake.

tablonaje, *m.* planking, boarding.

tabloncillo, *m.* 1. small board or plank; planking. 2. (taur.) last row of seats in bull ring.

tabloza, *f.* painter's palette.

tabo, *m.* (Phil. I.) dish or cup made from hollow coconut shell.

tabón, *m.* (ornith.) mound bird.

tabor, *m.* (hist.) unit of regular Moroccan troops in the Spanish army.

tabú, (*pl.* **tabúes**), *m.* taboo, tabu.

tabuco, *m.* small hut, hovel; narrow room.

tabulación, *f.* tabulation.

tabulador, *m.* tabulator (of typewriter).

tabuladora, *f.* tabulator, tabulating machine.

tabular, *tr.v.* to tabulate. —*a.* tabular.

taburete, *m.* 1. stool, taboret; small armless chair. 2. (*pl.*) semicircular rows of seats in the pit of the theater.

tac, *m.* tick (of clock, heart).

taca, *f.* 1. small cupboard or closet. 2. spot, stain. 3. (min.) crucible plate (each of the plates forming a crucible). 4. (Chile) an edible shellfish.

tacaco, *m.* (C. Rica) cucurbitaceous creeper (Cyclonthera piltieri).

tacada, *f.* 1. stroke (in billiards). 2. run of cannons or caroms (in billiards). 3. (mar.) wedges.

tacamaca, tacamacha, tacamahaca, *f.* (bot.) tacamahac (tree and resin).

tacana, *f.* (min.) rich silver ore.

tacañamente, *adv.* in a miserly or stingy manner, stingily, meanly.

tacañear, *i.v.* to be stingy, mean or niggardly, act stingily or meanly.

tacañería, *f.* stinginess, miserliness, meanness.

tacaño, ña, *a.* stingy, mean, niggardly, miserly. —*m., f.* miser.

tacar, (*ref. 50*) *tr.v.* 1. to mark, put a mark on (e.g. someone's face); to stain. 2. to shoot (in billiards).

tacataca, *f.* go-cart.

tacazo, *m.* blow with a billiard cue or heel; stroke with a billiard cue.

taceta, *f.* copper ladle for transferring olive oil from one container to another.

tacha, *f.* 1. defect, flaw, blemish. 2. large tack. 3. (law) disqualification. — **poner t. a,** to find fault with; **poner tachas,** to make objections; **sin t.,** flawless; honorable.

tacha, *f.* 1. (Amer.) large metal bowl. 2. crystallizing pan or vat (used in sugar refining).

tachable, *a.* 1. censurable, deserving criticism, exceptionable. 2. deserving to be crossed out.

tachador, ra, *a.* censuring, fault-finding. —*m., f.* censurer.

tachadura, *f.* erasure, deletion, crossing out (of a word, a line).

tachar, *tr.v.* 1. to cross out, cross off, strike out; to eliminate. 2. to object to (a witness). 3. to censure, find fault with.

tachero, *m.* worker in charge of sugar pans in a refinery.

tachigual, *m.* (Mex.) a type of cotton cloth.

tacho, *m.* 1. (Amer.) sugar vat or pan, evaporator. 2. (Amer.) deep metal bowl; casserole. — **irse al t.,** (Amer.) to fail, be unsuccessful; **t. de basura,** garbage or refuse can.

tachón, *m.* 1. deleting line (in written material). 2. decorative ribbon, braid trimming. 3. ornamental tack or nail (used in upholstery).

tachonar, *tr.v.* to trim with braid or ribbon; to decorate with ornamental nails or tacks.

tachonería, *f.* ornamentation work with braids and ribbons or with nails and tacks.

tachoso, sa, *a.* faulty, defective.

tachuela, *f.* 1. tack (nail). 2. (Chile, coll.) short stocky person. 3. (Col., Cuba) metal bowl or pot. 4. (Ven.) metal drinking cup.

tacita, *f. dim. of* **taza,** small cup.

tácitamente, *adv.* tacitly, by implication.

tácito, ta, *a.* tacit, implied and understood.

Tácito, *m.* (hist.) Tacitus, Roman historian.

taciturnidad, *f.* taciturnity.

taciturno, na, *a.* 1. taciturn, reserved. 2. melancholy.

taclobo, *m.* (Phil. I.) giant clam.

taco, ca, *a.* 1. (Chile) short, tubby, chubby. 2. (Cuba, P. Rico) very elegant, spruce or dapper.

taco, *m.* 1. plug; wedge; rawl plug. 2. billiard cue. 3. wad, wadding (for pressing down powder of blasting charge); (artil.) ramrod, rammer. 4. blowpipe, blowgun (used by children). 5. calendar pad. 6. (coll.) snack, bite, light meal. 7. (coll.) drink of wine. 8. (coll.) trouble, difficulty; muddle, confusion. 9. (coll.) oath, curse. 10. (Chile) hindrance, impediment, obstruction. 11. (Amer.) heel (of shoe). 12. (Chile) short stocky person. 13. (Mex.) fried tortilla stuffed with cheese, chicken, roast pork, etc. 14. (print.) shooting stick (for loosening and tightening quoins). — **darse t.,** (Amer.) to put on airs; **echar** or **soltar tacos,** (coll.) to curse, swear; **hacerse un taco,** to get muddled; **t. de aguja,** (Amer.) spike heel.

tacógrafo, *m.* tachograph.

tacómetro, *m.* tachometer.

tacón, *m.* heel (of shoe); **t. de aguja,** spike heel; **t. de goma,** rubber heel.

taconazo, *m.* blow with the heel.

taconear, *i.v.* 1. to tap one's heels. 2. to strut, walk in an arrogant manner. —*tr.v.* (Chile) to wad, stuff, fill up.

taconeo, *m.* heel tapping (as in Flamenco dancing).

tacotal, *m.* 1. (C. Rica) dense thicket. 2. (Hond.) marsh, quagmire, swamp.

táctica, *f.* tactics; **gran t.,** (mil.) grand tactics.

táctico, ca, *a.* tactical. —*m.* tactician. —*f.* tactics; **t. militar,** military tactics.

táctil, *a.* tactile, of or pertaining to touch.

tacto, *m.* 1. touch, sense of touch. 2. tact. — **al t.,** by touch; to the touch; **mecanografía al t.,** touch typing.

tacuacha, *f.* (Cuba) artful deceit.

tacuache, *m.* (Cuba, Mex., ento.) almique, solenodon.

tacuacín, *m.* (C. Amer., Mex.) tacuacine, crab-eating oppossum.

tacuaco, *m.* (Chile) short stocky man.

tacuará, *f.* (Arg., Chile, bot.) guadua (variety of bamboo).

tacuaral, *m.* (Arg., Chile) grove of guadua bamboo.

tacurú, (*pl.* **tacurúes**), *m.* 1. (Arg., Par.) variety of small black ant. 2. (S. Amer.) small clay mound found in frequently flooded fields of the Chaco.

tael, *m.* tael (coin and weight).

tafanario, *m.* (coll.) buttocks, seat, behind, backside.

tafetán, *m.* 1. (tex.) taffeta. 2. (*pl.*) **flags.** 3. women's finery, fancy clothing. — **t. de heridas, t. inglés,** court plaster.

tafia, *f.* (Arg., Bol., Ven.) tafia, taffia (a low-grade rum).

tafilete, *m.* morocco leather.

tafiletear, *tr.v.* to decorate with morocco leather.

tafiletería, *f.* 1. art of dressing morocco leather. 2. morocco leather shop.

tafón, *m.* (zool.) gastropod (Taphon striatus).

tafurea, *f.* flat-bottomed barge used to transport horses.

tagalo, la, *a., m., f.* (Phil. I.) **Tagalog,** Tagal. —*m.* Tagalog (language).

tagarino, na, *m., f.* Moor who lived among Christians.

tagarnina, *f.* 1. (bot.) golden thistle. 2. (coll.) poor quality cigar.

tagarote, *m.* 1. (ornith.) hawk. 2. notary's clerk. 3. down-and-out gentleman who lives by sponging, has-been (sl.). 4. (coll.) tall gawky person.

tagarotear, *i.v.* to write rapidly in bold, sweeping hand.

tagua, *f.* 1. (Chile, ornith.) coot. 2. (bot.) tagua, ivory nut palm; ivory nut.

taguán, *m.* (zool.) taguan, flying squirrel.

taha, *f.* district, region.

tahalí, (*pl.* **tahalíes**), *m.* 1. baldric. 2. (rel.) small leather box for carrying relics.

taharal, *m., var. of* **tarayal.**

taheño, ña, *a.* red (hair); red-bearded.

tahitiano, na, *a., m., f.* Tahitian. —*m.* Tahitian, Polynesian language of Tahiti.

tahona, *f.* 1. bakery. 2. horse-driven flour mill.

tahonera, *f.* 1. miller's wife. 2. baker's wife.

tahonero, *m.* 1. baker. 2. miller.

tahulla, *f.* unit of measure of arable land.

tahur, ra, *a.* 1. gambling. 2. cardsharping, cheating. —*m., f.* 1. gambler, gamester. 2. cardsharp.

tahurería, *f.* 1. gambling house. 2. gambling. 3. cheating, cardsharping.

tahuresco, ca, *a.* pertaining to a gambler or cardsharp.

taicún, *m.* tycoon (title of a Japanese shogun).

taifa, *f.* 1. faction, party, band. 2. (coll.) bad lot, disreputable group.

taiga, *f.* (geog.) taiga.

tailandés, sa, *a.* of or from Thailand. —*m., f.* Thailander, Thai.

Tailandia, *f.* Thailand.

taima, *f.* 1. cunning, craftiness. 2. (Chile) sullenness; obstinacy.

taimado, da, *a.* 1. crafty, slick, cunning. 2. (Chile) sullen, obstinate.

taimarse, *r.v.* (Chile) to become obstinate or sullen.

taimería, *f.* cunning, craftiness, slyness; rascality.

Taipei, *m.* Taipei, capital of Taiwan.

taino, na, *a.* Tainan. —*m., f.* Taino, member of an extinct Indian people of the West Indies. —*m.* Taino (language).

taita, *m.* (coll.) 1. child's term of endearment for a loved one (father, mother, nurse). 2. (Car.) title of respect given to a venerable old Negro. 3.

(Chile, Ecuad., Ven., Arg.) father; head of the family.
taja, *f.* 1. tree for a packsaddle, packsaddle frame. 2. share, distribution, apportionment. 3. cut, incision.
tajá, (*pl.* **tajaes**), *f.* (C. Amer.) variety of woodpecker.
tajada, *f.* 1. slice. 2. (coll.) hoarseness; cough. 3. (coll.) drunken bout, spree. 4. (Chile) slash, gash, cut. — **hacer tajadas a,** to slash, cut to pieces; **sacar t.,** to benefit, profit.
tajadera, *f.* 1. semicircular slicing or chopping knife. 2. chopping board. 3. cold chisel.
tajadero, *m.* (cul.) chopping block or board.
tajadilla, *f.* 1. small slice. 2. (cul.) dish of lights.
tajado, da, *past part. of* **tajar.** —*a.* 1. steep, sheer, sharp (cliff, etc.). 2. (her.) divided.
tajador, ra, *a.* cutting, slicing. —*m., f.* cutter, slicer. —*m.* chopping block.
tajadura, *f.* slicing, chopping, cutting.
tajamar, *m.* 1. cutwater (of a ship or bridge). 2. (Chile) embankment, dyke. 3. (Arg.) dam, pond.
tajamiento, *m.* slicing, chopping, cutting.
tajante, *a.* 1. cutting, slicing. 2. categorical, definitive (answer, remark).
tajaplumas, (*pl.* **tajaplumas**), *m.* penknife.
tajar, *tr.v.* to slice, chop, carve; to cut, trim (a quill).
tajea, *f.* watercourse, channel, culvert; drainpipe.
tajo, *m.* 1. cut, slash, gash; incision. 2. gap, mountain pass, cleft, ravine; steep cliff. 3. three-legged stool. 4. chopping block; (hist.) beheading block. 5. work, work load; assignment. 6. (Col., Ven.) horse trail. 7. cut-off point for a work gang.
Tajo, *m.* Tagus (river).
tajón, *m.* chopping blocktcher's block.
tajú, *m.* (Phil. I.) beverage made with tea, ginger and sugar.
tajuelo, la, *m., f.* rustic three-legged stool. —*m.* (mec.) pillow block.
tal, *a.* 1. such, such a, e.g. *nunca he visto t. cosa,* I have never seen such a thing. 2. such, so great, so great a, e.g. *t. es su fuerza,* such or so great is his strength. 3. certain, fellow called, e.g. *un t. Gómez vino a verte,* a fellow called Gómez came to see you. 4. this, that, e.g. *t. es mi parecer,* that is my opinion. — **como si t. cosa,** as if nothing had happened; **el t.,** that fellow, e.g. *el t. Gómez regresó,* that fellow Gómez came back; **¿qué t.?** how are you? how are things?; how, e.g. *¿qué t. estuvo la película?* how was the picture?; **¡qué t.** + *n.* what a + *n.,* e.g. *¡qué t. frescura!* what a nerve!; **t. como,** just as, exactly the same as; **t. cual,** such as; just as, the same as; an or the occasional, e.g. *nadie viene a verlo sino t. cual estudiante,* no one comes to see it except an occasional student; so-so, middling, mediocre; **t. vez,** perhaps. —*pron.* 1. such a thing; this, that. 2. someone, e.g. *siempre t. habrá, que diga calumnias del hombre honrado,* there will always be someone who will slander the honest man. 3. so-and-so. — **con t. que,** provided that, so long as; **fulano de t.,** so-and-so; **t. para cual,** (coll.) made for each other, birds of a feather; **t. por cual,** (coll.) so-and-so. —*adv.* 1. thus, so, in such a way or manner. 2. so, eg. *t. estaba de quisquilloso, que se enojaba de cualquier cosa,* he was so touchy that the slightest thing annoyed him. — **sí** or **no t.,** yes or no indeed.
tala, *f.* 1. felling of trees. 2. destruction, ruin, havoc, devastation. 3. tipcat (game); cat, stick (used in tipcat). 4. (fort.) abatis. 5. (Chile) grazing on stubble. 6. (bot.) hackberry tree (Celtis spinosa).
talabarte, *m.* sword belt.
talabartería, *f.* leather work, saddle or harness-making; leather worker's shop, saddle or harness maker's shop, saddlery.
talabartero, *m.* leather worker, saddler, harness maker.
talacho, *m.* (Mex.) pickaxe.
talador, ra, *a.* 1. felling, cutting. 2. devastating. 3. perforating, drilling. —*m., f.* 1. feller, cutter. 2. devastator, destroyer.
taladrador, ra, *a.* boring, drilling; piercing. —*m., f.* borer, driller. —*f.* drill, borer, drilling or perforating machine; **t. radial,** (mec.) turret drill; **t. torneadora,** (mec.) boring and turning machine.
taladrante, *a.* drilling, boring; piercing.
taladrar, *tr.v.* 1. to drill, bore. 2. (fig.) to pierce the ears (a sound). 3. (fig.) to fathom, get to the bottom of; to elucidate.
taladrilla, *f.* (ento.) borer, boring insect.
taladro, *m.* 1. drill, auger, borer, gimlet. 2. drill hole; mine tunnel. 3. (zool.) shipworm. — **t. de empuje,** push drill; **t. de trinquete,** ratchet drill; **t. múltiple,** gang drill; **t. neumático** or **de aire comprimido,** air drill.
talaje, *m.* (Chile) grazing; grazing fee.
talamera, *f.* (hunt.) tree in which a decoy is placed.
talamete, *m.* (mar.) foredeck.
talámico, ca, *a.* (anat.) thalamic.
talamifloro, ra, *a.* (bot.) thalamifloral, thalamiflorous. —*f.* (*pl.*) Thalamiflorae.
tálamo, *m.* 1. nuptial bed or chamber. 2. (anat., bot.) thalamus. — **t. óptico,** (anat.) optic thalamus.
talán, *m.* clanging (of a bell); ding-dong.
talanquera, *f.* 1. parapet, fortification, breastwork, barricade; place of shelter or cover. 2. (fig.) safety, defense, protection. 3. (Amer.) picket fence.
talante, *m.* 1. manner of doing something. 2. appearance, mien, aspect, countenance. 3. temper, mood, humor, disposition. 4. will, desire. — **de buen t.,** in a good mood; **de mal t.,** in a bad mood.
talar, *a.* long, full-length, ankle-length (gown). —*m.* (*pl.*) (myth.) talaria, winged sandals (of Mercury, Hermes).
talar, *tr.v.* 1. to fell, cut down. 2. to devastate, lay waste, ruin, destroy. 3. (Amer.) to prune (trees). —*m.* (Arg.) grove of hackberry trees.
talasoterapia, *f.* (med.) thalassotherapy, beneficial effects of ocean-bathing or seaside air.
talayote, *m.* (archeol.) talayot (tower-shaped stone structure found on the Balearic Islands).
talco, *m.* 1. (min.) talc. 2. (pharm.) talcum powder. 3. tinsel (material).
talcoso, sa, *a.* talcose, talcous.
talcualillo, lla, *a.* 1. (coll.) fairly good, so-so, fair, middling. 2. (coll.) slightly better (in health).
tálea, *f.* (hist., mil.) stockade in Roman camps.
taled, *m.* tallith (Jewish prayer shawl).
talega, *f.* 1. bag, sack; bagful, sackful. 2. (arch.) bag for keeping hair. 3. diaper, nappy. 4. (*pl.*) (coll.) fortune, wealth, money.
talegada, *f.* bagful, sackful.
talegallo, *m.* (ornith.) brush turkey.
talegazo, *m.* blow dealt with a bag.
talego, *m.* 1. large sack or bag. 2. (coll.) barrel, tub, fat person. — **hacer t.,** to have money tucked away.
taleguilla, *f.* 1. small bag. 2. bullfighter's breeches. — **t. de la sal,** (coll.) daily household expenses.
talento, *m.* 1. talent, cleverness; aptitude. 2. (hist.) talent (ancient coin and weight).
talentoso, sa, talentudo, da, *a.* talented, smart, clever; gifted.
tálero, *m.* (numis.) taler, thaler.
Talía, *f.* (myth.) Thalia, the Muse of dramatic art and idyllic poetry.
tálico, ca, *a.* (chem.) thallic.
talio, *m.* (chem.) thallium.
talión, *m.* talion, the principle of an eye for an eye, a tooth for a tooth; retaliation.
talionar, *tr.v.* to punish by talion, retaliate against.
talipédico, ca, *a.* (med., zool.) taliped.
talipes, *m.* (med.) talipes.
talismán, *m.* talisman, amulet, charm.
talla, *f.* 1. carving, engraving. 2. height, stature; size (of clothing); height-measuring apparatus. 3. hand (in game of cards). 4. reward (offered for the capture of a criminal). 5. amount of coins to be minted from a given quantity of metal. 6. (surg.) lithotomy, removal of gallstones. 7. (C. Amer.) swindle, trick, fraud. 8. (Arg., Chile) chat, jabbering. 9. (mar.) tackle, purchase block. — **en toda su t.,** to one's full height, e.g. **erguirse en toda su t.,** to draw oneself up to one's full height; **poner t. contra,** to put a price on a criminal's head, offer a reward for his capture.
tallado, da, *past part. of* **tallar.** —*a.* cut, carved. — **bien t.,** attractively shaped. —*m.* carving; engraving; cutting.
tallador, *m.* 1. engraver; carver; cutter. 2. cutter, cutting machine. 3. (Arg.) banker, dealer (in cards).
talladura, *f.* carving; engraving; cutting.
tallar, *a.* fit to be cut, ready for cutting (a tree, forest). —*m.* 1. young growth of trees; woodland ready for first cutting. 2. small comb.
tallar, *tr.v.* 1. to carve, engrave; to cut (precious stones). 2. to deal (cards). 3. to value, appraise. 4. to measure the height of. 5. (surg.) to remove gallstones from. 6. (Col.) to beat, thrash; to bother, annoy; to tame, break in. —*i.v.* 1. to lead a conversation. 2. (Chile) to court, flirt. 3. (Arg.) to chat, chit-chat.
tallarín, *m.* (cul.) noodle, spaghetti.
tallarola, *f.* knife for cutting velvet pile.
talle, *m.* 1. waist, bodice. 2. shape, form, figure. 3. (dressm.) fit, adjustment. — **t. corto,** high waist; empire line; **t. largo,** long waist.
tallecer, (*ref. 45*) *i.v.* to sprout, shoot.
taller, *m.* 1. shop, workshop; laboratory; plant, factory. 2. artist's studio, atelier. 3. cruet stand (for oil and vinegar servers). — **t. de fundición,** casting shop; **talleres gráficos,** printing plant; **t. mecánico,** garage, vehicle repair shop.
tallista, *m., f.* wood carver; engraver; sculptor.
tallo, *m.* 1. stem, stalk; sprout, shoot. 2. (Col.) cabbage. 3. (Chile, bot.) holy thistle, blessed thistle.
tallón, *m.* reward (offered for the capture of a criminal or an escapee).
talludo, da, *a.* 1. long-stalked; tall, lanky. 2. inveterate. 3. middle-aged, no longer young.
talluelo, *m. dim. of* **tallo,** small stem, stalk or sprout.
talma, *f.* shoulder cape.
talmente, *adv.* thus, in this manner.
Talmud, *m.* (rel.) Talmud.
talmúdico, ca, *a.* (rel.) Talmudic.
talmudista, *m.* (rel.) Talmudist.
talo, *m.* (bot.) thallus.
talofita, *f.* (bot.) thallophyte.
talón, *m.* 1. heel (part of a foot, shoe, stocking, or horse's hoof). 2. (archit.) talon (molding); heel (lower end of a timber in a frame). 3. check, ticket, receipt, voucher, coupon (detached from stub in a check book, book of tickets, receipts, etc.). 4. (mus.) heel (nut end of a violin bow). 5. (mar.) heel (after end of ship's keel). 6. (auto.) flange, lug (of a tire). — **a t.,** (coll.) on foot;

apretar los talones, (coll.) to take to one's heels; **pisarle a uno los talones,** (coll.) to be at or on someone's heels; **t. de Aquiles,** (anat.) Achilles' heel; **t. de venta,** sales slip.
talón, *m.* monetary standard.
talonada, *f.* kick or dig with the heels (given to horses).
talonario, *m.* stub book.
talonazo, *m.* kick with the heel.
talonear, *i.v.* 1. (coll.) to walk very quickly, dash along. 2. (Arg.) to spur on one's horse.
talonera, *f.* (Chile) leather heel-piece put on a boot to which spurs are attached.
talonesco, *a.* (coll.) pertaining to the heels.
talpa, talparia, *f.* (med.) talpa, mole, wen.
talque, *m.* tasco (refractory clay used in making crucibles).
talqueza, *f.* (C. Rica) paspalum, grass used for thatching (Paspalum virgatum).
talquina, *f.* (Chile) dirty trick; deceit.
talquita, *f.* (min.) talc schist.
taltuza, *f.* (C. Rica, zool.) gopher.
talud, *m.* slope, incline, talus.
taludín, *m.* (Guat.) species of crocodile.
talvina, *f.* porridge made of almonds and milk.
tamagás, *m.* (C. Amer.) highly poisonous snake.
tamal, *m.* 1. (Amer.) tamale, dish made of corn meal, chicken or meat and chili wrapped in banana leaves or corn husk. 2. (Amer.) imbroglio, domestic intrigue. 3. (Amer.) clumsy bundle or package.
tamalero, ra, *m., f.* person who makes or sells tamales.
tamanaco, ca, *a., m., f.* Tamanaco, Tamanac, of or pertaining to an Indian tribe of South America. *—m.* Tamanac language.
tamandúa, (*pl.* **tamanduáes**), *m.* (zool.) tamandus, anteater.
tamango, *m.* (Arg., Chile) sheepskin sandal; (Arg.) gaucho's coarse work boot.
tamañamente, *adv.* as large (as), as great (as).
tamañito, ta, *a.* abashed, embarrassed, small, squelched, squashed; **dejar t.,** to squash, abash, make (someone) feel small; **quedarse t.,** to be squashed or abashed, be made to feel small.
tamaño, ña, *a.* 1. so large, great or big as, such a large, great or big. 2. very big or large; **abrir tamaños ojos,** to open one's eyes wide. *—m.* size, dimension. — **t. bolsillo,** pocket-size; **t. carné,** passport-size; **t. familiar,** family-size; **tamaño natural,** full size, normal size; **tamaño oficio, legal size (stationery).**
támara, *f.* 1. (bot.) date palm. 2. palm grove. 3. cluster of dates. 4. brushwood.
tamarao, *m.* (Phil. I., zool.) tamarau, variety of water buffalo.
tamaricáceo, a, *a.* (bot.) tamaricaceous. *—f.* tamaricaceous plant, (*pl.*) Tamaricaceae.
tamarindo, *m.* (bot.) tamarind (tree and fruit); **t. montero,** (bot.) velvet tamarind.
tamariscíneo, a, *a.* (bot.) tamaricaceous. *—f.* tamaricaceous plant, (*pl.*) Tamaricaceae.
tamarisco, tamariz, (*pl.* **tamarices**), *m.* (bot.) tamarisk.
tamarrizquito, ta, tamarrusquito, ta, *a.* (coll.) tiny, very small.
tamarugal, *m.* (Chile) mesquite grove.
tamarugo, *m.* (Chile, bot.) mesquite (Prosopis tamarugo).
tamba, *f.* (Ecuad.) sarong or wrap-around skirt.
tambaleante, *a.* staggering, tottering, reeling.
tambalear, *i.v., r.v.* to stagger, totter, reel.
tambaleo, *m.* staggering, tottering, reeling.
tambalisa, *f.* (Cuba, bot.) sophora (Sophora tomentosa).
tambanillo, *m.* (archit.) tympanum.
tambarillo, *m.* chest or coffer with an arched lid.
tambarria, *f.* (Col., Ecuad., Hond., Peru) spree, party, night out.
tambero, ra, *a.* 1. (Arg.) dairy (cattle). 2. (Arg.) tame, gentle (said of livestock). 3. (S. Amer.) pertaining to an inn. *—m., f.* (S. Amer.) innkeeper, hostel keeper.
también, *adv.* also, too, as well, likewise.
tambo, *m.* 1. (Quech., S. Amer.) roadside hostelry, inn. 2. (Arg.) dairy farm.
tambobón, *m.* (Phil. I.) stone crock for keeping rice.
tambocha, *f.* (Col.) poisonous red-headed ant.
tambor, *m.* 1. (mus.) drum; drummer. 2. drum, cylinder. 3. (anat.) eardrum. 4. roasting cylinder (for coffee, chestnuts, etc.). 5. (archit.) drum, tambour (cylindrical block composing a column; wall supporting a cupola); (archit.) bell, tambour (part of the capital of a column between abacus and neck). 6. sugar sieve or screen used by confectioners. 7. tambour, embroidery frame. 8. (fort.) tambour. 9. (Cuba, Mex.) burlaps. 10. drum, metal barrel. 11. (Cuba, ichth.) puffer. 12. (Mex.) spring mattress. — **a t. batiente,** with flying colors, triumphantly; **t. de freno,** (auto.) brake drum; **t. mayor,** drum major.
tambora, *f.* 1. (mus.) bass drum. 2. (Cuba) (coll.) lie, hoax, tall tale.
tamborear, *i.v.* to drum with the fingers.
tamboreo, *m.* drumming with the fingers.
tamborete, *m.* 1. (mus.) small timbrel; small drum. 2. (mar.) cap (for joining spars).
tamboril, *m.* (mus.) tabor, timbrel, small drum.
tamborilada, *f.*, **tamborilazo,** *m.* 1. (coll.) bump, fall on one's bottom. 2. (coll.) slap on the head or shoulders.
tamborilear, *i.v.* to drum. *—tr.v.* 1. to praise, extol. 2. (print.) to level, plane down (set type with the planer).
tamborileo, *m.* (mus.) drumming.
tamborilero, *m.* drummer, taborer.
tamborilete, *m.* 1. (mus.) small drum or tabor. 2. (print.) planer.
tamborín, *m.* (mus.) tabor, timbrel.
tamborino, *m.* 1. tabor, timbrel. 2. drummer, taborer.
tamboritear, *i.v.* to drum.
tamboritero, *m.* drummer, taborer.
tamborón, *m. aug. of* **tambora,** large bass drum.
tambre, *m.* (Col.) river dam.
Tamerlán, *m.* (hist.) Tamerlane, Tamburlaine.
Támesis, *m.* Thames (river).
tamice, tamicé, *ref.* **tamizar.**
tamidina, *f.* (elec.) tamidine.
tamínea, taminia, *a.* **uva t.,** (bot.) stavesacre.
tamiz, (*pl.* **tamices**), *m.* sieve, sifter, bolter.
tamizador, *m.* screen, strainer, sifter.
tamizar, (*ref. 53*) *tr.v.* to sift, put through a sieve.
tamo, *m.* 1. fuzz, fluff; dust. 2. chaff, grain dust. 3. household lint and dust (under beds, etc.).
tamojal, *m.* saltwort patch or field.
tamojo, *m.* (bot.) saltwort, glasswort.
tampoco, *adv.* neither, not either, either, e.g. *t. me gusta éste,* I don't like this one either; *si tú no bailas yo tampoco,* if you don't dance neither will I.
tampón, *m.* ink pad, tampon (for inking seals).
tamtam, *m.* tom-tom (African drum).
tamuja, *f.* pine straw, pine tags, dried pine needles.
tamujo, *m.* (bot.) brush.
tan, *m.* (*pl.*) tom-tom (sound of the drum or drumming).
tan, (*apocope of* **tanto**) *adv.* 1. so, as, e.g. *no seas t. curiosa,* don't be so curious; *él es t. alto como tú,* he is as tall as you. 2. at least, only, e.g. *t. siquiera dame la mano,* at least shake hands with me; *si t. sólo me escribiese,* if only he wrote to me. 3. what, how, e.g. *¡qué chica t. linda!* what a pretty girl!; *¿t. poco te quiere?* that's how little he loves you?
tanaceto, *m.* (bot.) tansy.
tanagra, *f.* Tanagra (figurine).
Tananarive, *m.* Tananarive, capital of the Malagasy Republic.
tanate, *m.* (C. Rica, Hond., Mex.) bag, knapsack, haversack; (C. Amer.) bundle, parcel. — **cargar con los tanates,** to move away.
tanatero, ra, *m., f.* (C. Amer., Mex.) porter, carrier.
tanato, *m.* (chem.) tannate.
tanda, *f.* 1. turn, go; shift (of work). 2. relay team, gang or group of workmen or animals (employed on a given assignment). 3. (Amer., theat.) single showing in a series of continuous performances. 4. layer, coat. 5. task, work. 6. number, series, batch, pack, lot. 7. (Arg.) bad habit.
tándem, *m.* tandem (bicycle for two).
tandeo, *m.* distribution of irrigating waters by turns.
tandero, ra, *m., f.* (Chile) joker, wisecracker, jester.
tanela, *f.* (C. Rica, cul.) honey biscuit.
tángana, *f.* (Cuba, coll.) rumpus; brawl.
Tanganica, Tangañica, *f.* Tanganyika (lake and region in E. Africa).
tanganillas, *adv.* **en t.,** unsteady, shaky; waveringly.
tanganillo, *m.* temporary prop, stay.
tángano, na, *a.* (Mex.) short (person). *—m.* 1. dry branch of a tree. 2. hob (boys' game).
tangará, *f.* (Arg., ornith.) tanager.
tangencia, *f.* tangency.
tangencial, *a.* tangential.
tangente, *a., f.* (geom.) tangent. — **escapar, escaparse, irse, salir por la t.,** (coll.) to go off at a tangent, digress; to resort to subterfuge, evade the issue.
Tánger, *m.* Tangier.
tangerino, na, *a., m., f.* Tangerine, of or pertaining to Tangier. *—f.* tangerine, mandarine (orange).
tangible, *a.* tangible, palpable.
tangidera, *f.* (mar.) thick mooring cable.
tango, *m.* 1. tango (music and dance). 2. hob (boys' game). 3. (Amer.) party, dance. 4. (Hond.) drum.
tangón, *m.* (mar.) outrigger.
tanguear, *i.v.* to dance the tango; (Ecuad.) to stagger. *—r.v.* (Amer.) to change parties.
tanguista, *m.* chorus man. *—f.* chorus girl; hostess, B-girl (in a dance hall).
tánico, ca, *a.* tannic.
tanino, *m.* (chem.) tannin.
tano, na, *a., m., f.* (Arg., coll.) *apheretic form of* **napolitano,** Neapolitan, i.e. Italian immigrant.
tanor, ra, *m., f.* (Phil. I., hist.) Malay servant (during the Spanish domination).
tanoría, *f.* (Phil. I., hist.) obligatory domestic service performed by the natives during the Spanish domination.
tanque, *m.* 1. tank, vat (large container for liquids). 2. (mil.) tank (armored car). 3. (Amer.) reservoir. 4. bee glue. — **t. aforador,** (hydr.) gaging tank; **t. de gasolina,** (auto.) gas tank.
tanta, *f.* (Peru) cornbread.
tantalato, *m.* (chem.) tantalate.
tantalio, *m.* (chem.) tantalum.
tantalita, *f.* (min.) tantalite.
tántalo, *m.* 1. (ornith.) wood ibis. 2. **T.,** (myth.) Tantalus.
tantán, *m.* 1. gong. 2. sound of a drum; clanging (of a hammer, etc.).

tantarán, tantarantán, *m.* 1. rub-a-dub, beat of a drum. 2. (coll.) hard smack.
tanteador, ra, *m., f.* scorer; scorekeeper. *—m.* score board.
tantear, *tr.v.* 1. to compare. 2. to scrutinize, consider or think about carefully; to examine, study; to size up, gauge, weigh up; to test, probe, try out; to sound, feel out. 3. to keep the score of. 4. (p.) to outline, sketch. 5. (Col., Chile) to estimate or calculate roughly. *—i.v.* 1. to score, keep the score. 2. to grope, feel one's way.
tanteo, *m.* 1. comparison. 2. sounding, feeling out; probe; trial, test; sizing up, gauging; careful examination or study. 3. (Chile) rough estimate or calculation. 4. scoring; score.
tantico, illo, *m. dim. of* **tanto,** little, a little bit. *—adv.* somewhat, a little.
tanto, ta, *a.* as much; so much; such a; (*pl.*) so many, as many, e.g. *tanto dinero como* or *cuanto necesites,* as much money as you need; *tantos libros como* or *cuantos quepan,* as many books as will fit; *comí tanto pan que me enfermé,* I ate so much bread that I got sick. *—pron.* so much; (*pl.*) so many, e.g. *eran tantos en Madrid como en Nueva York,* there were as many in Madrid as in New York. — **en tanto, entre tanto,** (coll.) meanwhile, meantime; **no ser para tanto,** not to be that or so bad, e.g. *no es para tanto,* it's not that bad; **otro tanto,** the same thing; **por tanto, por lo tanto,** therefore; **t. como** or **cuanto,** as much as; **tantos como** or **cuantos,** as many as; **t. que,** so much that; **tantos que,** so many that; **y tantos,** odd, and a bit, e.g. *¿cuántos alumnos hay? hay mil y tantos,* how many students are there? there are a thousand odd.
tanto, *adv.* 1. so much, so long, so far, so often; to such degree or extent, e.g. *te quiero t.,* I love you so much; *esperaste t.,* you waited so long; *ella viene t. por aquí,* she comes around so often. 2. just as much as, e.g. *t. el occidente como el oriente quieren la paz,* both the West and the East want peace, the West wants peace just as much as the East. — **t. como, t. cuanto,** as much as, as long as, as far as, as often as, e.g. *ganarás t. como merezcas,* you will earn as much as you deserve, *te voy a visitar t. como sea necesario,* I'm going to visit you as often as is necessary; **t. más,** all the more, so much the more, **t. menos,** all the less, so much the less; **t. mejor,** all the better, so much the better; **t. peor,** so much the worse, all the worse; **t. monta,** it's all the same, it comes out to the same thing; **t. que,** so much (long, far, often) that. *—m.* 1. little, bit; certain amount, certain quantity. 2. copy (of document, piece of writing, etc.). 3. chip, counter (used in certain games). 4. point (in a score). — **algún t.,** a little, a little bit; **apuntar los tantos,** to keep the score; **a tantos de,** on a certain day of, on such and such a day of (a month); **estar al t.,** to be informed on, be posted about, be up to date on; **poner al t. de,** to bring up to date; **señalar un t.,** to score a goal (in soccer), score a point; **t. por ciento,** percentage, certain percentage; **y t.,** and a bit, odd, e.g. *me costó mil y t.,* it cost me a thousand odd, it cost me a thousand and a bit; **un t.,** somewhat, a bit.
tanza, *f.* fishing line.
Tanzania, *f.* Tanzania.
tañedor, ra, *m., f.* 1. player of a musical instrument. 2. toller, one who tolls a bell.
tañente, *a.* playing on a musical instrument.
tañer, (*ref. 59*) *tr.v.* to play (a musical instrument); to toll (bells). *—i.v.* to drum with the fingers.
tañido, *m.* 1. sound of a musical instrument. 2. tolling of a bell.
tañimiento, *m.* the act of playing a musical instrument.
taño, *m.* tanbark, tan.
tao, *m.* tau cross, badge or insignia of some religious orders.
taoísmo, *m.* (rel.) Taoism.
tapa, *f.* 1. lid, top, cap, cover; horny cover (of a hoof); hard cover (of a book). 2. lift (on the heel of a shoe). 3. gate (of a sluice). 4. round, round of beef (cut of beef). 5. collar (of a coat). 6. (*pl.*) (Sp.) assortment of tidbits and appetizers served with wine or cocktails. 7. (Hond., bot.) stramonium, Jimson weed. 8. (Chile) shirt front. — **hablar por la t. de la barriga,** (Ven.) to talk through one's hat, talk nonsense; **levantar** or **saltar a alguien la t. de los sesos,** to blow someone's brains out; **levantarse** or **saltarse** la t. **de los sesos,** to blow one's brains out; **ni por las tapas,** (Arg.) not at all; **t. de los sesos,** (coll.) top of the skull.
tapaaguejros, (*pl.* **tapaagujeros**), *m. var. of* tapagujeros.
tapabalazo, *m.* 1. (Col., Mex., vulg.) fly (of trousers). 2. (mar.) shot plug.
tapabarro, *m.* (Chile, Peru) mudguard.
tapaboca, *m.* 1. slap on the mouth. 2. scarf, muffler. 3. (coll.) squelch, squelcher, crushing remark.
tapabocas, (*pl.* **tapabocas**), *m.* 1. muffler. 2. (artil.) tampion.
tapacamino, *m.* (Arg., ornith.) goatsucker.
tapacete, *m.* (mar.) sliding awning.
tapachiche, *m.* (C. Rica) green grasshopper.
tapacubo, *m.* (auto.) hubcap.
tapaculo, *m.* 1. hip (fruit of the dog rose). 2. (Chile) small brownish white-breasted bird (Scelorchilus albicollis). 3. (Cuba) fish resembling sole.
tapada, *f.* woman who covers her face with a veil, mantle or cloak.
tapadera, *f.* 1. lid, cover, cap. 2. blind, front (person who shields another).
tapadero, *m.* stopper, cap, plug.
tapadillo, *m.* 1. the act of concealing the face with a scarf or mantle. 2. (mus.) flute-stop of an organ. — **de t.,** secretly, stealthily.
tapadizo, *m.* shed.
tapado, da, *past part. of* **tapar.** *—a.* 1. covered-up, wrapped-up. 2. hidden, concealed. 3. unspotted, without marks (said of a horse's coat). *—m.* 1. (Arg., Chile) woman's coat, cloak, wrap. 2. (Col.) barbecue, outdoor cooking. 3. (S. Amer.) buried treasure. 4. (coll., Cuba, P. Rico) covert homosexual.
tapador, ra, *a.* 1. covering, concealing. 2. stopping. *—m., f.* coverer. *—m.* lid, cover, top; plug, stopper.
tapadura, *f.* 1. covering; plugging, stopping up. 2. concealing, hiding. 3. obstruction, blocking.
tapafunda, *f.* 1. flap of a holster. 2. (Col.) saddle cover.
tapagoteras, (*pl.* **tapagoteras**), *m.* (Amer.) waterproofing material, roofing cement.
tapagujeros, (*pl.* **tapagujeros**), *m.* 1. (coll.) botcher, poor mason or plasterer. 2. (coll.) substitute worker, makeshift helper.
tapajuntas, (*pl.* **tapajuntas**), *m.* (carp.) window or door sash.
tápalo, *m.* (Mex.) shawl, mantle.
tapamiento, *m., var. of* **tapadura.**
tapanca, *f.* (Chile, Col., Ecuad.) caparison, horse trappings.
tapanco, *m.* (Phil. I.) bamboo awning.
tapaojo, *m.* 1. (Col., Ven.) ornamental headstall (on a harness). 2. blinders (on horses).
tapapiés, *m.* (arch.) 1. rich silken gown or dress. 2. short kirtle formerly worn by soldiers.
tapar, *tr.v.* 1. to cover; to stop up, plug, close up. 2. to wrap up; to cover up, hide; to conceal. 3. to block, obstruct (the view). 4. (Chile) to fill (a tooth). — **t. la boca,** to shut someone up, to bribe; **taparle a uno la luz,** to stand in one's light. *—r.v.* 1. to cover oneself up, wrap up. 2. to partially cover the track of the front hoof with that of the hind one.
tápara, *f.* (bot.) caper.
tapara, *f.* gourd; **vaciarse uno como una t.,** (coll.) to spill everything, tell everything.
taparo, *m.* (bot.) gourd tree.
taparrabo, *m.* 1. loincloth. 2. bikini, short bathing trunks.
tapate, *m.* (C. Rica, bot.) stramonium, Jimson weed.
tapatío, tía, *a.* typical of the state of Jalisco, Mexico; **jarabe tapatío,** Mexican hat dance.
tapayagua, *f.* (Hond., Mex.) mist, drizzle, light rain.
tapera, *f.* (S. Amer.) 1. ruins of a village. 2. ruined house, ruin, shack.
taperujarse, *r.v.* (coll.) to wrap oneself up; to bundle up.
taperujo, *m.* 1. (coll.) badly fitting plug. 2. awkward or careless way of covering the face.
tapesco, *m.* (C. Amer., Mex.) kind of wattle used as a bed.
tapetado, da, *a.* dark, dark-brown.
tapete, *m.* 1. rug, small carpet. 2. table cover, runner. — **t. verde,** (coll.) card table, gambling table; **estar sobre el t.,** to be under discussion; **poner sobre el t.,** to bring under discussion.
tapia, *f.* 1. mud wall, adobe wall. 2. (mas.) square measure of 50 square feet. — **sordo como una t.,** deaf as a post; **t. real,** (mas.) wall made with mixture of adobe and lime.
tapiador, *m.* builder of mud or adobe walls.
tapial, *m.* form or mold for making adobe walls; mud wall.
tapialar, *tr.v.* (Ecuad.), *var. of* **tapiar.**
tapiar, *tr.v.* 1. to wall up, wall in, enclose within walls. 2. to close up, wall up (a door, etc.).
tapice, tapicé, *ref.* **tapizar.**
tapicería, *f.* 1. tapestries, set of tapestries; tapestry shop; tapestry-making. 2. upholstering, upholstery; upholsterer's shop.
tapicero, *m.* 1. tapestry-maker; upholsterer. 2. carpet layer.
tapido, da, *a.* (rare) closely woven (cloth).
tapiería, *f.* mud walls.
tapiero, *m.* (Col.) builder of mud walls.
tapín, *m.* 1. cap (of powder horn). 2. (mar.) small wooden plug covering the head of a nail or bolt.
tapioca, *f.* (cul.) tapioca.
tapir, *m.* (zool.) tapir.
tapirujarse, *r.v., var. of* **taperujarse.**
tapirujo, *m.* (coll.), *var. of* **taperujo.**
tapis, *m.* (Phil. I.) broad sash worn by women.
tapisca, *f.* (C. Rica, Hond.) corn harvest.
tapiscar, (*ref. 50*) *tr.v.* (C. Rica, Hond.) to harvest corn.
tapiz, (*pl.* **tapices**), *m.* tapestry.
tapizar, (*ref. 53*) *tr.v.* to hang with tapestries; to cover (furniture), upholster; to carpet.
tapón, *m.* 1. stopper, cork, cap; bung, plug. 2. (med.) tampon. 3. (fig.) traffic jam. — **t. de cuba,** (coll.) short fat person; **t. de cubo,** (auto.) hubcap; **t. de desagüe, evacuación** or **purga,** drain plug; **t. de radiador,** (auto.) radiator cap; **t. hembra,** pipe cap; **t. macho,** pipe plug.
taponamiento, *m.* (surg.) tamponage, tamponment, tamponade; **t. cardíaco,** (surg.) cardiac tamponade.
taponar, *tr.v.* 1. to plug, stop up. 2. (surg.) to tampon.

taponazo, *m.* pop (of a cork).
taponería, *f.* 1. corks, stoppers, caps, plugs, bungs. 2. cork or stopper industry or factory.
taponero, ra, *a.* cork, stopper, cap, plug, bung (factory, business, etc.). —*m., f.* person who makes or sells corks, stoppers, caps, plugs or bungs.
tapsia, *f.* (bot.) deadly carrot.
tapucho, cha, *a.* (Chile) tailless, short-tailed.
tapujarse, *r.v.* (coll.) to muffle up one's face, cover one's face.
tapujo, *m.* 1. mantle, veil (to hide the face). 2. (coll.) concealment, secrecy.
taque, *m.* click (of a door as it locks); knock, rap (at a door).
taque, taqué, *ref.* **tacar.**
taquear, *tr.v.* (Amer.) to stuff, pack, fill; to ram, tamp (a firearm). —*i.v.* 1. (Arg., Chile) to tap (with one's heels). 2. (Arg., Peru, Mex.) to play billiards.
taquera, *f.* rack (for billiard cues).
taquería, *f.* 1. (Cuba) brazenness, impudence. 2. (Mex.) snack stand, taco stand.
taquero, *m.* (Chile) drain or sewer cleaner.
taquicardia, *f.* (med.) tachycardia.
taquichuela, *f.* (Par.) jackstones, jacks, dibs (game played with pebbles).
taquigrafía, *f.* shorthand, stenography, tachygraphy.
taquigrafiar, (*ref.* *54*) *tr.v.* to write in shorthand, stenograph.
taquigráficamente, *adv.* in shorthand, stenographically, tachygraphically.
taquigráfico, ca, *a.* shorthand, stenographic, tachygraphic, tachygraphical.
taquígrafo, fa, *m., f.* stenographer, tachygraphist.
taquilita, *f.* (min.) tachylyte, tachylite.
taquilla, *f.* 1. ticket office, box office, ticket window. 2. takings, gate (money taken in ticket office). 3. pigeonhole, key rack, rack. 4. (Amer.) small nail. 5. (C. Rica) inn, saloon, bar. — **atracción de t.,** box-office draw; **éxito de t.,** box-office success.
taquillero, ra, *a.* box-office, e.g. *éxito taquillero,* box-office success; good box office, e.g. *este actor es muy taquillero,* this actor is very good box office. —*m., f.* ticket seller, ticket agent.
taquimeca, *f.* (coll.) shorthand typist.
taquimetría, *f.* (surv.) tachymetry.
taquimétrico, ca, *a.* tachymetric.
taquímetro, *m.* 1. (surv.) tachymeter. 2. speedometer.
taquín, *m.* anklebone; knucklebones (game); jackstones.
taquisterol, *m.* (biochem.) tachysterol.
taquistoscopio, *m.* (psyc.) tachistoscope.
tara, *f.* 1. (com.) tare (allowance for the weight of the container, etc.). 2. defect; vice. 3. (biol.) hereditary defect, throw-back. 4. tally stick. 5. (Ven., ento.) green grasshopper. 6. (Col.) a poisonous snake. 7. (S. Amer., bot.) divi-divi (Caesalpinia tintoria).
tarabilla, *f.* 1. millclapper. 2. catch, latch (to fasten doors or windows). 3. (coll.) chatterbox (person). 4. (coll.) jabber, nonsense. 5. (Arg.) bullroarer (toy). — **soltar la t.,** (coll.) to talk a blue streak, jabber.
tarabita, *f.* 1. tongue (of a belt buckle). 2. (S. Amer.) rope, cable (of cableway or ropeway).
taracea, *f.* inlaid work, marquetry, boulle, buhlwork.
taracear, *tr.v.* to decorate with inlaid work, to inlay.
tarado, da, *a.* 1. defective; **damaged,** spoiled. 2. cretinous. —*m., f.* cretin.
taragallo, *m., var. of* **trangallo.**
taraje, *m.* (bot.) salt cedar.
taramba, *f.* (Hond.) one-stringed instrument played with a stick.
tarambana, *a., m., f.* (coll.) scatterbrain; madcap.
tarando, *m.* (zool.) reindeer.
tarangallo, *m., var. of* **trangallo.**
tarángana, *f.* (cul.) blood sausage.
taranta, *f.* 1. (Sp.) Andalusian folk song, music and dance. 2. (Hond.) dizziness, faintness. 3. (Arg., C. Rica, Ecuad.) whim; fit, sudden impulse.
tarantela, *f.* tarantella (dance and music); **darle a uno la t.,** (coll.) to decide suddenly to do something.
tarantín, *m.* 1. (C. Amer., Cuba) kitchen utensil; simple gadget. 2. (Ven.) humble little shop.
tarantismo, *m.* (med.) tarantism.
tarántula, *f.* (ento.) tarantula.
tarantulado, da, *a.* 1. bitten by a tarantula. 2. bewildered, confused; restless.
tarar, *tr.v.* to tare, to calculate the tare of.
tarara, tarará, *f.* imitation of the sound of trumpets.
tararear, *tr.v.* to hum (a tune).
tarareo, *m.* humming (a tune).
tararira, *f.* 1. (coll.) noisy merrymaking or laughter. 2. (Arg.) fresh-water fish (Hoplias malabaricus). —*m., f.* (coll.) noisy madcap.
tarasa, *f.* (Peru, Chile, bot.) sida (malvaceous plant).
tarasca, *f.* 1. dragon (in Corpus Christi procession). 2. (coll.) glutton, gormandizer. 3. (coll.) waster, devourer, drain, consumer. 4. (coll.) hag, coarse ugly woman. 5. (C. Rica, Chile) large mouth.
tarascada, *f.* 1. bite, wound made by a tooth. 2. (coll.) sharp reply, rude rebuff.
tarascar, (*ref.* *50*) *tr.v.* to bite (said of a dog).
tarascón, *m.* (S. Amer.) bite.
taratántara, *f., var. of* **tarara.**
taray, *m.* (bot.) salt cedar; salt cedar gall.
tarayal, *m.* salt cedar patch.
taraza, *f.* (zool.) shipworm.
tarazana, *f.* **tarazanal,** *m., var. of* **atarazana.**
tarazar, (*ref.* *53*) *tr.v.* 1. to bite, tear. 2. to annoy, irritate, bother, harass.
tarazón, *m.* chunk; slice.
tarbea, *f.* large room or hall.
tarco, *m.* (Arg.) rosewood (Weinmannia paullinifolia).
tardador, ra, *a.* delaying, tarrying, dallying. —*m., f.* delayer.
tardanaos, *m.* (ichth.) remora.
tardanza, *f.* 1. delay, tardiness, slowness. 2. dalliance, lingering.
tardar, *i.v.* to be long; to be or take a long time; **t. . . . en** + *inf.,* to be or take (so much time) to + *inf.* or in + *ger.,* be or take (so much) time + *ger.,* e.g. *tardó mucho en llegar aquí,* he took a long time to get here, he took a long time in getting here, he took a long time getting here; **a más t.,** at the latest. —*r.v.* to be long; to be or take a long time.
tarde, *adv.* late; **de t. en t.,** now and then; **más vale t. que nunca,** better late than never; **para luego es t.,** the sooner the better; right now; shake a leg (sl., U.S.); it's later than you think; **t. o temprano,** sooner or later. —*f.* afternoon; evening; **buenas tardes,** good afternoon, good evening; **t. de asueto,** half-holiday.
tardecer, (*ref.* *45*) *i.v.* to get dark, grow late.
tardecica, tardecita, *f.* dusk, twilight, nightfall.
tardecillo, *adv. dim. of* **tarde,** a little or rather late.
tardezca, *ref.* **tardecer.**
tardíamente, *adv.* belatedly, too late.
tardígrado, *a.* (zool.) tardigrade. —*m.* tardigrade, (*pl.*) Tardigrada.
tardío, a, *a.* 1. late; belated, tardy; slow, delayed. 2. slow, dilatory. —*m.* (*pl.*) late crops.
tardo, da, *a.* 1. slow, sluggish, dilatory, lagging behind. 2. late, belated, tardy. 3. slow, dull, dense, dull-witted.
tardón, na, *a.* 1. (coll.) slow, sluggish, dilatory. 2. (coll.) dull, dense, slow. —*m., f.* slowpoke.
tarea, *f.* task, chore, job, work, assignment. — **a t.,** in-class assignment; **t. escolar,** homework; **t. fácil,** easy job, a song (coll., U.S.).
tareche, *m.* (Bol.) caracara, carrion hawk (Polyborus plancus).
tareco, *m.* 1. (Ecuad., Ven.) utensil, gadget, implement, tool. 2. (Cuba) old piece of furniture; (*pl.*) households.
tárgum, *m.* (rel.) Targum (parts of the Hebrew Scriptures).
tarida, *f.* (arch.) military transport vessel (formerly used in the Mediterranean).
tarifa, *f.* 1. tariff, rate; price list. 2. **toll;** fare.
tarifar, *tr.v.* to fix a tariff for. —*i.v.* to quarrel, fall out.
tarima, *f.* wooden stand or platform, dais.
tarimón, *m. aug. of* **tarima,** large wooden platform or stand, dais.
tarín, *m.* 1. (numis.) coin worth twenty five centimes (of a peseta). 2. (ornith.) tarin.
tarín, barín, (coll.) only, just, **barely,** scarcely.
tarja, *f.* 1. shield, buckler. 2. tally, tally stick. 3. (coll.) blow; lash. 4. tally, check, tab. 5. (numis.) old Spanish copper coin. 6. (Amer.) card, visiting card. — **beber sobre t.,** to drink on credit.
tarjador, ra, *m., f.* tally-keeper.
tarjar, *tr.v.* 1. to tally, add to the bill. 2. to cut, slice, chop. 3. (Chile, Peru) to cross out.
tarjero, ra, *m., f.* tally-keeper.
tarjeta, *f.* 1. card (visiting, personal or invitation card). 2. index card, etc. 3. heading, title (on a map). 4. (archit.) ornate or inscribed tablet. — **t. de cobro automático,** debit card; **t. de crédito,** credit card; **t. de embarque,** boarding pass; **t. de identidad,** I.D., identification card; **t. de Navidad,** Christmas card; **t. de negocios,** business card; **t. de visita,** visiting card, calling card; business card; **t. postal,** postcard; **t. telefónica,** (tel.) calling card (used to make telephone calls).
tarjetazo, *m.* (Peru) use of influential personal card in order to get certain favors.
tarjeteo, *m.* (coll.) social exchange of personal cards.
tarjetera, *f., var. of* **tarjetero.**
tarjetero, *m.* 1. card file, index. 2. card tray, visiting card case.
tarjetón, *m. aug. of* **tarjeta,** large card.
tarlatana, *f.* tarlatan (fabric).
taro, *m.* (bot.) taro.
taropé, *m.* (Arg., Par., bot.) Amazon, giant or royal water lily.
tarpón, *m.* (ichth.) tarpon.
tarquín, *m.* mire, slime.
tarquinada, *f.* (coll.) rape, sexual assault.
tarquino, na, *a.* (Arg., Sp.) said of a pedigreed bull or cow.
tarraconense, *a.* of or from Tarragona. —*f.* **T.,** (hist.) Tarraconensis.
tárraga, *f.* 17th century Spanish dance.
tarrago, *m.* (bot.) meadow sage.
tarraja, *f.* 1. (mec.) diestock; threading machine. 2. template, modeling board; (metal.) strickle, sweep board. 3. (Ven.) tally kept by cattlebreeders on a strip of leather.
tarrajadora, *f.* threading machine.
tarralí, *f.* (Col.) climbing plant (Posadea spherocarpa).

tarraya, *f.* (P. Rico, Ven.) casting net.
tarreña, *f.* a crude type of castanet made of clay or tile.
tarrico, *m.* (bot.) saltwort.
tarro, *m.* 1. jar; tin can, pot. 2. (S. Amer.) top hat. 3. (Cuba, Urug., P. Rico) horn (of some quadrupeds). 4. (Arg.) stroke of luck. — **t. de unto,** (Amer.) top hat.
tarsana, *f.* (C. Rica, Ecuad., Peru) soapbark, quillai bark.
tarsiano, na, *a.* (anat.) tarsal.
tarso, *m.* (anat.) tarsus.
tarta, *f.* 1. tart, pastry. 2. baking pan; tart mold.
tártago, *m.* 1. (bot.) caper spurge. 2. (coll.) misfortune. 3. (coll.) practical joke; mean trick. — **t. de Venezuela,** (bot.) castor oil plant.
tartajear, *i.v.* to stutter, stammer.
tartajeo, *m.* stuttering, stammering.
tartajoso, sa, *a.* stuttering, stammering. —*m., f.* stutterer.
tartalear, *i.v.* 1. (coll.) to reel, sway, stagger. 2. (coll.) to splutter, stutter, be dumbfounded or speechless.
tartamudear, *i.v.* to stammer, stutter.
tartamudeo, *m.* (act of) stammering, stuttering.
tartamudez, *f.* (defect of) stammering, stuttering.
tartamudo, da, *a.* stammering, stuttering. *m., f.* stutterer.
tartán, *m.* tartan, Scotch plaid.
tartana, *f.* 1. two-wheeled carriage with a domed top. 2. (mar.) tartan, tartana, a small Mediterranean vessel.
tartanero, *m.* driver of a **tartana** (a two-wheeled carriage with a domed top).
tartáreo, a, *a.* (poet.) Tartarean, infernal.
Tartaria, *f.* (geog., hist.) Tartary, Tatary.
tartárico, ca, *a.* (chem.) tartaric.
tartarín, *m.* (zool.) tartarin.
tartarizar, (*ref. 53*) *tr.v.* (chem.) to tartarize.
tártaro, *m.* 1. (chem.) tartar. 2. tartar (deposit on teeth). 3. T., (myth.) Tartarus, (poet.) hell. —*a., m., f.* Tartar.
tartaruga, *f.* (Bol., zool.) river tortoise or turtle.
tartera, *f.* 1. pan, baking pan. 2. (mil.) billy, billycan; lunch or dinner pail.
tartrato, *m.* (chem.) tartrate.
tártrico, ca, *a.* (chem.) tartaric.
tartufo, *m.* hypocrite.
taruca, taruga, *f.* (zool.) guemal, guemul (Hippocamelus antisensis).
tarugo, *m.* 1. wooden peg; wooden block; chunk of wood. 2. (Cuba) fright, start. 3. (Cuba, Dom. Rep.) stagehand; roust-about. 4. (Guat., Mex.) fool, dolt. 5. (Mex.) rogue, scoundrel, cheat.
tarumá, *m.* (Arg., bot.) vitex (Vitex cymosa).
tarumba, volverle a uno t., to rattle, to confuse (someone); **volverse t.,** to become rattled or confused.
tas, *m.* stake, small anvil used by silver-smiths.
T.A.S. *abbrev. of* **velocidad relativa verdadera,** true airspeed (T A S).
tasa, *f.* 1. rate; **t. de descuento,** (com.) discount rate; **t. de interés,** rate of interest; **t. de interés bancario,** bank rate; **t. de mortalidad,** death rate; **t. de natalidad,** birth rate; **t. impositiva** or **tributaria,** tax rate. 2. measure, moderation, e.g. *sin t. ni medida,* without any moderation whatsoever. 3. measure, rule, standard. 4. appraisal, assessment, valuation; **a t. de,** at the rate of.
tasación, *f.* 1. appraisal, appraisement, valuation. 2. price regulation or control.
tasadamente, *adv.* 1. moderately, with moderation. 2. scarcely, scantily.
tasador, ra, *a.* appraising, assessing, valuing. —*m., f.* appraiser, assessor.

tasajear, *tr.v.* (Amer., cul.) to jerk (beef).
tasajo, *m.* 1. jerked beef, hung beef. 2. (Col.) tall, thin man.
tasajudo, da, *a.* (Amer.) tall and thin.
tasar, *tr.v.* 1. to appraise, assess the value of. 2. to rate; to tax. 3. to regulate. 4. to restrict, limit; to keep within bounds. — **t. en,** to value or estimate at.
tasca, *f.* 1. (coll.) bar, saloon, tavern. 2. low gambling dive or joint. 3. (coll.) fight, quarrel. 4. (Chile, Col.) drunk, drunken spree. 5. (Peru) turbulent and dangerous coastal region (on which to land or unload).
tascador, *m.* swingle, scutcher.
tascar, (*ref. 50*) *tr.v.* 1. to scutch, swingle (flax). 2. champ, champ at, e.g. *t. el freno,* to champ at the bit (a horse); (fig.) to resist curtailment. 3. to gnaw, nibble; to graze on.
tasco, *m.* stalk of hemp or flax (after scutching).
tasconio, *m.* tasco, refractory clay.
tasi, *m.* (Arg., bot.) wild liana (Morrenia odorata).
tasímetro, *m.* (phys.) tasimeter.
tasín, *m.* 1. (Quech., Ecuad.) nest. 2. (Ecuad.) padded ring (for carrying heavy objects on the head).
tasmanio, nia, *a., m., f.* Tasmanian. —*f.* Tasmania, island south of Australia.
tasque, tasqué, *ref.* **tascar.**
tasquera, *f.* (coll.) row, quarrel, wrangle.
tasquero, *m.* (Peru) stevedore who unloads cargo in dangerous coastal regions.
tasquil, *m.* chip (of a stone).
tastana, *f.* 1. hard crust (of dry earth). 2. (bot.) membrane (e.g. dividing sections of an orange).
tástara, *f.* (Arg.) coarse bran.
tastaz, *m.* metal-polishing powder.
tasto, *m.* bad taste (of spoiled or tainted food).
tasugo, *m.* (zool.) badger.
tata, *f.* nanny, nurse. —*m.* 1. (Amer., reg.) daddy, father. 2. (S. Amer.) sir, title of respect (among country folk).
tatabro, *m.* (Col., zool.) capybara; peccary.
tatagua, *f.* (Cuba, ento.) giant owlet moth (Erebus odorata).
tataibá, *m.* (Par., Arg., bot.) mulberry (Morus tataiba).
tatarabuelo, la, *m., f.* great-great-grandparent, great-great-grandfather, great-great-grandmother.
tataradeudo, da, *m., f.* ancestor, distant relative.
tataranieto, ta, *m., f.* great-great-grandchild, great-great-grandson, great-great-granddaughter.
tataré, *m.* (Arg., Par., bot.) wild tamarind (Pithecolobium tortum).
tatarrete, *m.* (derog.) old can, old jar.
tatas, andar a t., to toddle; to crawl on all fours (a baby).
¡tate! *interj.* 1. look out! careful! 2. so that's it!
tatetí, *m.* (Arg.) form of noughts and crosses (G.B.), tick tack toe (game).
tatito, *m.* (Bol., Peru) papa, daddy, father.
tato, ta, *a.* lisping; stammering. —*m.* (coll., Arg., Chile) baby brother, kid brother; baby.
tatú, (*pl.* **tatúes**), *m.* (zool., Arg.) tatouay, giant armadillo.
tatuaje, *m.* tatoo; tattooing (marks or designs on the skin).
tatuar, (*ref. 55*) *tr.v.* to tattoo (mark the skin). —*r.v.* to have tattooed.
tatusia, *f.* (Par., zool.) kind of armadillo.
tatusa, *f.* (S. Amer.) insignificant woman.
tau, *m.* (rel.) tau, tau cross. —*f.* tau, nineteenth letter (of the Greek alphabet).
tauca, *f.* (Chile) large purse.

taujel, *m.* (carp.) narrow strip of wood.
taujía, *f., var. of* **ataujía,** damascene work, damascene, damaskeening.
taumaturgia, *f.* thaumaturgy, the working of miracles or wonders.
taumatúrgico, ca, *a.* thaumaturgical.
taumaturgo, *m.* thaumaturge, thaumaturgist.
taurino, na, *a.* 1. taurine, of or about bulls. 2. bullfighting, e.g. *revista taurina,* bullfighting magazine, *mundo taurino,* bullfighting world. —*f.* (chem.) taurine, taurin.
taurios, *a. pl.* (hist.) taurian, e.g. *Juegos Taurios,* Taurian Games (bullfighting games).
Tauro, *m.* (astron., astrol.) Taurus.
tauróbolo, *m.* (myth.) taurobolium, sacrifice of a bull.
taurocólico, la, *a.* (chem.) taurocholic.
taurófilo, ca, *a.* fond of bullfighting. —*m., f.* bullfighting fan, aficionado (da).
tauromaco, ca, *a.* tauromachian, pertaining to bullfighting. —*m., f.* expert in tauromachy.
tauromaquia, *f.* tauromachy, the art and technique of bullfighting.
tauromáquico, ca, *a.* tauromachian, pertaining to bullfighting.
tautología, *f.* (rhet.) tautology, redundancy; pleonasm.
tautológico, ca, *a.* (rhet.) tautologic, tautological.
tautomería, *f.* (chem.) tautomerism.
tautómero, ra, *a.* (chem.) tautomeric. —*m.* (chem.) tautomer.
taxáceo, a, *a.* (bot.) taxaceous.
taxativamente, *adv.* (law) limitatively; restrictively.
taxativo, va, *a.* (law) limitative, restrictive.
taxi, *m.* (coll.) taxi, taxicab.
taxia, *f.* (biol.) taxis.
taxidermia, *f.* taxidermy.
taxidérmico, ca, *a.* taxidermic, taxidermal.
taxidermista, *m., f.* taxidermist.
taxímetro, *m.* 1. taximeter. 2. taxi, taxicab, taximeter.
taxis, *f.* (biol., surg., archit.) taxis.
taxista, *m., f.* taxi driver, cab driver, cabby.
taxonomía, *f.* (biol.) taxonomy.
taxonómico, ca, *a.* taxonomic, taxonomical.
taylorismo, *m.* (econ.) Taylorism, Taylor System (of scientific management).
tayuyá, *f.* (Arg.) creeper, creeping plant (Cayaponia ficifolia).
tayuyo, *m.* (Guat.) tamale.
taz, t. a t., tit for tat, on an even basis; **t. con t.,** even, equal, tied.
taza, *f.* 1. cup; cupful. 2. basin (in a water fountain). 3. bowl (of a toilet). 4. cup guard (of a sword). — **t. de café,** coffee cup, cup of coffee.
tazaña, *f.* dragon (in Corpus Christi processions).
tazar, (*ref. 53*) *tr.v.* to fray (clothes). —*r.v.* to fray, become frayed.
tazmía, *f.* 1. grain tithe (contributed by a farmer); tithe register. 2. estimate of a growing crop (esp. of sugar cane).
tazón, *m.* 1. *aug. of* **taza,** large cup, bowl. 2. washbowl, basin.
Tb *sym. of* **terbio,** terbium (Tb).
Tc *sym. of* **tecnecio,** technetium (Tc).
te, *pers. pron. 2nd person sing. fam.* 1. you, thee (object. case) e.g. *te amo,* I love you (thee). 2. to you, for you, from you (dative case), e.g. *te lo di,* I gave it to you, *te lo leeré,* I will read it for you, *él te lo quitó,* he took it away from you. 3. yourself, to yourself, for yourself (ref. case), e.g. *serénate,* pull yourself together, *guárdatelo,* keep it to yourself.
té, *m.* (bot.) 1. tea, tea plant; tea (leaf, beverage). 2. tea (reception). 3. T square. — **dar el t.,** to bore, talk to at great length; **t. aguado** or **ralo,**

weak tea; **t. bailable,** tea dance, thé dansant; **t. borde, t. de España, t. de Europa, t. de Méjico,** (bot.) Mexican tea, wormseed; **t. cargado,** strong tea; **t. de los Jesuitas, t. del Paraguay,** (bot.) Paraguay tea, maté.
Te *sym. of* **telurio,** tellurium (Te).
tea, *f.* 1. torch, firebrand. 2. (mar.) cable for raising the anchor. 3. (bot.) candlewood.
teáceo, a, *a.* (bot.) theaceous. —*f.* (bot.) theaceous plant, (*pl*) Theaceae.
teame, teamide, *f.* stone formerly believed to repel iron.
teantropía, *f.* (theol.) theanthropism.
teatina, *f.* (Chile, bot.) wild oat (Avena Hirsuta).
teatino, *a., m.* (rel.) Theatin, Theatine (religious order).
teatral, *a.* 1. theatrical, pertaining to the theater. 2. (fig.) theatrical, spectacular; exaggerated.
teatralidad, *f.* theatricality.
teatralmente, *adv.* theatrically; histrionically.
teatrero, ra, *m., f.* theatergoer.
teatro, *m.* 1. theater. 2. theater (dramatic arts); stage. 3. dramatic works or literature. — **dedicarse al t.,** to go on the stage; **hacer venirse el t. abajo,** to bring the house down; **t. de guiñol** or **marionetas** or **títeres,** puppet theater; **t. de la ópera,** opera house; **t. de variedades,** vaudeville (Amer.), music hall (G.B.).
tebaico, ca, *a.* (hist.) Thebaic, Theban. — **extracto t.,** (pharm.) opium extract.
Tebaida, *f.* 1. (hist.) Thebaid. 2. **t.,** desert, solitary place; solitude.
tebaína, *f.* (chem.) thebaine.
tebano, na, *a., m., f.* (hist.) Theban (pertaining to Thebes).
Tebas, *f.* (hist.) 1. Thebes, city in ancient Egypt. 2. Thebes, capital of Boeotia, a district of ancient Greece.
tebeo, a, *a., m., f.* (hist.) Theban (pertaining to Thebes).
teca, *f.* 1. reliquary. 2. (bot., zool., anat.) theca. 3. teak (wood and tree).
tecali, *m.* (Mex., min.) tecali, Mexican onyx.
techado, *m.* 1. roof, ceiling. 2. shed. — **bajo t.,** indoors, under cover.
techador, *m.* roofer, roof-builder; thatcher.
techar, *tr.v.* to roof, put a roof on or over; to thatch.
techo, *m.* 1. roof; ceiling. 2. (fig.) roof (house, home). 3. (aer.) ceiling. — **t. absoluto** or **teórico,** (aer.) absolute ceiling; **t. a cuatro aguas** or **vertientes,** hip roof; **t. máximo,** (aer.) operating ceiling; **t. práctico,** (aer.) service ceiling.
techumbre, *f.* 1. roofing, roof; ceiling. 2. shed, cover. 3. top (of a vehicle).
tecla, *f.* 1. key (of subject, piano, organ, typewriter, etc.). 2. touchy matter, delicate matter. — **dar en la t.,** (coll.) to get the knack (of); to get into the habit (of); **t. de las mayúsculas,** shift key; **t. de espacios,** space bar; **t. de retroceso,** back spacer; **t. de sujeción,** shift lock; **t. del tabulador,** tabulator key; **tocar una t.,** (coll.) to pull wires, resort to influential help.
teclado, *m.* keyboard (of a piano, typewriter, etc.).
tecle, *m.* (mar.) single block purchase or tackle, single whip.
tecleado, *m.* drumming with the fingers.
teclear, *tr.v.* to try various ways or expedients; to feel one's way (in a situation, etc.). —*i.v.* 1. to run one's fingers over the keys, play the piano, type; (coll.) to drum with the fingers. 2. (S. Amer.) to be ill, be on one's last legs; to be in the throes of death.
tecleo, *m.* drumming with the fingers.
teclo, cla, *a.* (Peru, sl.) old, feeble, ill.
tecnecio, *m.* (chem.) technetium.
técnica, *f.* 1. technique; technic, technics. 2. ability. — **t. electrónica,** electronics; **t. frigorífica,** refrigeration engineering; **t. hidráulica,** hydraulics, hydraulic engineering.
técnicamente, *adv.* technically.
tecnicismo, *m.* 1. technicality. 2. technical term or terminology.
técnico, ca, *a.* technical. —*m.* technician; expert; **t. agrícola,** agronomist, agricultural engineer; **t. electricista,** electrical engineer; **t. forestal,** forestry engineer.
tecnicolor, *m.* (photog., cinem.) technicolor.
tecnocracia, *f.* (polit.) technocracy.
tecnócrata, *m., f.* technocrat.
tecnología, *f.* technology.
tecnológico, ca, *a.* technological.
tecnólogo, ga, *m., f.* technologist.
tecol, *m.* (zool.) maguey worm, agaveworm (Bombix agavis).
tecolines, *m.* (*pl.*) (Mex.) money, cash, dough (sl.), bread (sl.).
tecolote, *a.* 1. (C. Rica) reddish brown. 2. (Guat., El Salv.) drunk, tipsy. —*m.* 1. (Hond., Mex., ornith.) owl. 2. (Mex., Guat.) drunk, drunken spree. 3. (Mex.) policeman, cop (sl.)
tecomate, *m.* 1. (C. Amer.) calabash or gourd cup, bowl or other vessel. 2. (Mex.) earthenware bowl.
tecorral, *m.* (Mex.) stone wall.
tectónico, ca, *a.* tectonic. —*f.* tectonics, tectonic science.
tectriz. (*pl.* **tectrices**), *f.* (zool.) tectrix.
tedero, *m.* cresset, torch holder.
tedéum, *m.* (ecc.) Te Deum.
tediar, *tr.v.* to loathe, abhor; (coll.) to be tired or sick of.
tedio, *m.* 1. tedium, tediousness, boredom. 2. disgust, loathing.
tedioso, sa, *a.* 1. tedious, tiresome, boring. 2. disgusting, irksome.
tefe, *m.* 1. (Col., Ecuad.) strip (of leather or cloth). 2. (Ecuad.) scar (on the face).
tefrita, *f.* (min.) tephrite.
tegmen, *m.* (bot., zool.) tegmen.
Tegucigalpa, *f.* Tegucigalpa, capital of Honduras.
tegue, *m.* (Ven., bot.) caladium (Caladium arboreum).
teguillo, *m.* thin board, batten, strip of wood.
tegumentario, ria, *a.* (bot., zool.) tegumentary.
tegumento, *m.* (bot., zool.) tegument.
Teherán, *m.* Teheran, capital of Iran.
teína, *f.* (chem.) theine, thein.
teinada, *f.* cattle shed.
teísmo, *m.* (theol.) theism.
teísta, *a.* (theol.) theistic. —*m., f.* theist.
teja, *f.* 1. curved roof tile. 2. large Spanish comb (in the shape of a roof tile). 3. priest's shovel hat. 4. steel facing (of a sword blade). 5. (mar.) hollow cut for scarfing. 6. (bot.) linden tree, basswood. — **a t. vana,** under a bare roof, in impecunious circumstances; **a toca t.,** for cash; **de tejas abajo,** without help from above; **de tejas arriba,** with help from heaven; **t. cóncava,** gutter, pantile; **t. de la silla,** (Mex.) cantle of a saddle; **t. de madera,** shingle; **t. lomada** or **de cumbrera,** ridge tile.
tejadillo, *m.* 1. *dim. of* **tejado,** small roof; shed; eave. 2. top, cover; roof or top (of a coach or carriage). 3. cardsharp's manner of holding cards.
tejado, *m.* 1. roof, shed; tile roof. 2. (min.) outcrop, top of a mineral vein. — **empezar la casa por el t.,** to put the cart before the horse; **t. a cuatro aguas** or **vertientes,** hip roof; **t. de vidrio,** (fig.) glass house.
tejamaní, (*pl.* **tajamaníes**), **tejamanil,** *m.* (Cuba, P. Rico, Mex.) shingle, batten (used for covering a roof).
tejano, na, *a., m., f.* Texan.
tejar, *m.* 1. tile works, tile kiln. 2. brickyard, brick works. —*tr.v.* to tile, cover a roof with tiles.
tejaroz, *m.* eaves; tiled shed.
tejavana, *f.* shed, tiled shed.
tejazo, *m.* blow dealt with a tile.
tejedera, *f.* 1. (woman) weaver. 2. (ento.) whirligig beetle.
tejedor, ra, *a.* 1. weaving. 2. (Peru, Chile) scheming. —*m., f.* 1. weaver. 2. (Peru, Chile) schemer. —*m.* 1. (ento.) water strider. 2. (ornith.) weaverbird.
tejedura, *f.* 1. weaving. 2. texture (of a fabric).
tejeduría, *f.* 1. art of weaving. 2. mill, weaving mill, textile factory.
tejemaneje, *m.* 1. (coll.) knack, skill. 2. (coll.) scheming, underhand maneuvering.
tejer, *tr.v.* 1. to weave; to knit; to spin (a spider its web, a silkworm its cocoon). 2. to weave (a story, a pattern). —*i.v.* to weave; to knit; to spin. — **t. y destejer,** to blow hot and cold, take and lose interest.
tejera, *f.* 1. woman who makes tiles. 2. tile works or kiln. 3. brickyard, brick works.
tejería, *f.* 1. tile works, tile kiln. 2. brick works, brickyard.
tejero, *m.* man who makes tiles.
tejido, *m.* 1. weave, texture. 2. fabric, textile, cloth. 3. (anat., biol.) tissue. — **t. adiposo,** adipose tissue; **t. conectivo,** connective tissue; **t. conjuntivo,** conjunctive tissue; **t. de acero,** wire cloth; **t. de alambre,** wire mesh; **t. fibroso,** fibrous tissue; **t. laminoso,** conjunctive tissue; **t. de punto,** knitted fabric.
tejillo, *m.* plaited girdle formerly worn by women.
tejo, *m.* 1. disk, quoit (used in various games); metal disk. 2. (mec.) pillow block, step bearing, pivot bearing. 3. blank coin (before minting). 4. disk of gold, portion of gold paste. 5. game similar to quoits or hob.
tejo, *m.* (bot.) yew.
tejocote, *m.* (Mex., bot.) variety of hawthorn (Crataegus mexicana); haw (fruit).
tejoleta, *f.* 1. piece of tile or brick, brickbat. 2. (*pl.*) crude castanets made of clay.
tejón, *m.* 1. (zool.) badger. 2. gold ingot or disk.
tejonera, *f.* burrow (of a badger).
tejuela, *f.* 1. small roofing tile; piece of tile or brick; brickbat. 2. saddletree.
tejuelo, *m.* 1. *dim. of* **tejo,** small disk. 2. (bkb.) backbone title label. 3. (mec.) pillow block, pivot bearing. 4. (vet.) sole (of a hoof).
tela, *f.* 1. cloth fabric, material, stuff. 2. (anat.) membrane. 3. film, skin (forming on the surface of a liquid). 4. skin (e.g. of an onion). 5. film, cloud (forming on the eye). 6. (p.) canvas, painting. 7. arena; jousting or tilting field. 8. web (e.g. of a spider). 9. (fig.) lie, trick, scheme (to confuse a situation). 10. material, subject matter (for discussion). — **estar** or **quedar en t. de juicio,** to be or remain in doubt or dispute; **hay t. que cortar,** (coll.) it will be a long business; **poner en t. de juicio,** to put in doubt, to question; **t. adhesiva,** adhesive tape; **t. aislante,** insulating tape; **t. de araña,** cobweb, spider's web; **t. de cebolla,** onion skin; (coll.) thin unsubstantial cloth; **t. de esmeril,** emery cloth; **t. de vidrio,** glass wool; **t. metálica,** wire netting; **t. mosquitera,** mosquito netting.
telabrejo, *m.* 1. (Mex.) trinket, piece of junk. 2. (Mex.) schemer, whippersnapper.
telamón, *m.* (archit.) telamon, atlante.

telangiectasia, *f.* (med.) telangiectasis.
telar, *m.* 1. (weaving) loom. 2. (theat.) gridiron. 3. (bkb.) sewing press. 4. (archit.) frame (of a door). — **en el t.,** in the making; **t. de cajas ascendentes,** (tex.) drop-box loom.
telaraña, *f.* 1. spider's web, cobweb. 2. (fig.) trivial matter. — **mirar a las telarañas,** to star-gaze, be absent-minded; **t. mundial,** World Wide Web; **tener telarañas en los ojos,** (coll.) to be blind to what is going on.
telarañoso, sa, *a.* cobwebbed, cobwebby.
telarejo, *m.* small loom.
tele, *f.* (coll.) TV, television, telly (G.B.).
teleadicto, ta, *m., f.* TV addict.
teleautógrafo, *m.* (rad., photog.) teleautograph.
telebanco, *m.* automated-teller machine, ATM.
telecabina, *f.* cable car.
telecine, *m.* television movie.
telecomando, *m.* remote control.
telecomedia, *f.* TV comedy show.
telecomunicación, *f.* telecommunication, long distance communication.
teleconferencia, *f.* (tel.) conference call.
telecontrol, *m.* remote control.
teleculebra, *f.* (coll.) television soap opera.
telediario, *m.* television news.
teledifusión, *f.* (tel.) television broadcasting.
teledinámico, ca, *a.* telodynamic.
teledirección, *f.* remote control.
teledirigido, da, *past part. of* **teledirigir.** —*a.* remote-controlled, guided.
teledirigir, (*ref. 62*) *tr.v.* to steer or guide by remote control.
telefax, *m.* fax, telefax.
teleferaje, *m.* telpherage, telferage, transportation system using cable cars.
teleférico, *m.* cable railway, funicular railway.
telefilm, *m.* made-for-TV movie.
telefio, *m.* (bot.) orpine stonecrop.
telefonazo, *m.* or **telefoneado,** *f.* (coll.) buzz, call, ring, e.g. *le voy a dar un t.,* I'm going to give him a buzz.
telefonear, *tr.v., i.v.* to telephone, to phone.
telefonema, *m.* telephone call, telephone message.
telefonía, *f.* telephony; **t. sin hilos,** wireless telephony, radiotelephony.
telefónicamente, *adv.* telephonically, by telephone.
telefónico, ca, *a.* telephone, phone, telephonic; **cabina telefónica,** telephone box or booth; **guía telefónica,** telephone directory; **llamada telefónica,** telephone call.
telefonista, *m., f.* telephone operator, switchboard operator, telephonist (G.B.).
teléfono, *m.* telephone, phone; **t. automático,** dial telephone; **t. inalámbrico,** cordless telephone; **t. interno,** extension; **t. portátil** or **móvil,** mobile phone; **t. público** or **monedero,** payphone, coin telephone, pubic telephone; **t. rojo,** hot line.
telefoto, telefotografía, *m., f.* phototelegraphy, telephotography; phototelegraph, telephotograph.
telefotográfico, ca, *a.* telephoto, telephotographic.
telefotómetro, *m.* (photog.) telephotometer.
telega, *f.* telega, four-wheeled cart.
telegénico, ca, *a.* (tel.) telegenic, videogenic.
telegonía, *f.* (biol.) telegony.
telegrafía, *f.* telegraphy; **t. sin hilos,** wireless telegraphy.
telegrafiar, (*ref. 54*) *tr.v., i.v.* to telegraph.
telegráficamente, *adv.* telegraphically.
telegráfico, ca, *a.* telegraphic, telegraphical.
telegrafista, *m., f.* telegrapher, telegraphist, telegraph operator.
telégrafo, *m.* telegraph; **hacer telégrafos,** (coll.) to talk by signs; **t. marino,** nautical signals; **t. óptico,** signal telegraph, semaphore; **t. sin hilos,** wireless telegraph.
telegrama, *m.* telegram, wire (coll.); **t. nocturno,** night letter, deferred telegram.
teleguiado, da, *past part. of* **teleguiar.** —*a.* guided or steered by remote control.
teleguiar, (*ref. 54*) *tr.v.* to guide or steer by remote control.
teleimpresor, *m.* teleprinter, teletype.
teleindicador, *m.* (mec.) telegage, remote gage; indicator screen.
telele, *m.* (C. Amer., Mex.) swoon, fainting spell.
Telémaco, *m.* (myth.) Telemachus, the son of Ulysses and Penelope.
telemando, *m.* remote control.
telemárketing, *m.* telemarketing.
telemática, *f.* telematics, data transmission.
telemecánico, ca, *a.* telemechanic. —*f.* telemechanics.
telemetría, *f.* (photgmt.) telemetry.
telemétrico, ca, *a.* telemetric, telemetrical.
telémetro, *m.* telemeter, range finder; **t. lasérico,** laser rangefinder.
telencéfalo, *m.* (anat.) telencephalon.
telendo, da, *a.* lively, spirited, spritely, jaunty.
telenovela, *f.* soap opera.
telenque, *a.* 1. (Arg.) stupid, foolish. 2. (Chile) weak, feeble, sickly.
teleobjetivo, *m.* telephoto lens, telelens.
teleología, *f.* (philos.) teleology.
teleológico, ca, *a.* (philos.) teleologic, teleological.
teleósteo, a, *a.* (ichth.) teleost, teleostean. —*m.* teleost, (*pl.*) Teleostei.
telepatía, *f.* telepathy.
telepático, ca, *a.* telepathic.
telequinesis, *f.* (psyc.) telekinesis.
telera, *f.* 1. plow pin. 2. transom, crosspiece (of a cart frame); (artil.) transom (of a gun carriage). 3. (carp.) jaw (of a vise). 4. sheep pen, sheepfold (enclosed by a board fence). 5. (mar.) rack, rack block. 6. large loaf of brown bread. 7. (Cuba) thin oblong cracker.
telerán, *m.* (electron., aer.) teleran.
telero, *m.* stake (of a cart).
telerón, *m.* (artil.) transom (of a gun carriage).
telerreceptor, *m.* television set.
telescópico, ca, *a.* telescopic.
telescopio, *m.* telescope; **T.,** (astron.) Telescopium, Telescope; **t. de refracción,** refracting telescope; **t. espacial,** space telescope.
Telesforo, *m.* (myth.) Telesphorus, Greek god of health.
telesilla, *m.* chair lift (to transport skiers).
telespectador, ra, *m., f.* viewer, television viewer.
telespectroscopio, *m.* telespectroscope.
telesquí, *m.* ski lift.
telestereoscopio, *m.* telestereoscope.
telestesia, *f.* telesthesia (extrasensory perception).
teleta, *f.* 1. blotting paper. 2. sieve in a paper mill.
teletermómetro, *m.* (phys.) telethermometer.
teletipo, *m.* (tel.) teletypewriter, Teletype (TM), teleprinter (G.B.).
teleutóspora, *f.* (bot.) teleutospore.
televidente, *m., f.* viewer, televiewer.
televisar, *tr.v.* to televise.
televisión, *f.* television; television set; **t. a color** or **en color** or **en colores,** color television; **t. en blanco y negro,** black-and-white television; **t. en circuito cerrado,** closed-circuit television; **t. por abonados,** pay-per-view television; subscription television; **t. por cable,** cable television.
televisivo, va, *a.* television.
televisor, ra, *m.* television set; **t. en blanco y negro,** black-and-white television set; **t. en colores,** color television set.
televisual, *a.* television.
télex, *m.* telex.
telilla, *f.* 1. cloth; thin camlet, thin woolen cloth. 2. film, skin, pellicle.
telina, *f.* 1. (zool.) mussel, sunset shell or clam. 2. (biochem.) theelin.
telio, *m.* (bot.) telium.
telita, *f. dim. of* **tela,** small piece of cloth or fabric.
tellina, *f.* mussel, clam.
telliz, (*pl.* **tellices**), *m.* caparison, horse trappings; horse blanket.
telliza, *f.* bedspread, coverlet.
telofase, *f.* (biol.) telophase.
telón, *m.* (theat.) drop curtain; **t. de acero,** (pol.) iron curtain; **t. de boca,** (theat.) front curtain; **t. de fondo** or **foro,** (theat.) backdrop; **t. de seguridad, t. metálico,** (theat.) safety curtain.
telúrico, ca, *a.* 1. telluric; terrestrial. 2. (chem.) telluric.
telurio, *m.* (chem.) tellurium.
teluroso, sa, *a.* (chem.) tellurous.
telururo, *m.* (chem.) telluride, tellurid.
tema, *m.* 1. subject, theme; essence. 2. (mus.) theme, motif. 3. (educ.) composition, translation exercise; thesis. 4. (gram.) stem, root (of a word). —*f.* 1. obstinacy, persistence. 2. mania, obsession, idée fixe. 3. grudge, ill-will. — **atenerse al t.,** to stick to the point; **tener a t.,** to have a grudge against; **tomar a t.,** to become obstinate.
temar, *i.v.* (Arg.) to persist, insist.
temario, *m.* program, agenda.
temascal, *m.* (Guat., Mex., hist.) bath house.
temático, ca, *a.* 1. thematic, thematical. 2. persistent, obstinate, insistent, stubborn. 3. (gram.) pertaining to the stem or root of a word.
tembetá, *f.* (Guar.) ornamental dowel worn by some Indians in the lower lip.
tembladal, *m.* quaking bog, quagmire.
tembladera, *f.* 1. double-handled bowl or cup made of thin metal or glass. 2. jewel mounted on a spiral spring. 3. (ichth.) torpedo. 4. (bot.) quaking grass. 5. (Amer.) trembling, fit of shaking. 6. (Amer.) quaking bog. 7. (Arg.) horse and cattle disease.
tembladeral, *m.* (Arg.) quaking bog.
tembladerilla, *f.* (Chile, bot.) locoweed; (bot.) minute water fern (Azolla filiculoides).
tembladero, ra, *a.* trembling, shaking. —*m.* quaking bog. —*m., f.* person who trembles severely. —*m.* swamp.
temblador, ra, *a.* trembling, quaking, quivering, shaking. —*m., f.* 1. trembler. 2. (rel.) Shaker. —*m.* (elec.) trembler, make-and-break.
temblante, *a.* trembling, shaking. —*m.* bangle, bracelet.
temblar, (*ref. 29*) *i.v.* 1. to tremble, shake, shudder, quake, quiver, shiver. 2. (fig.) to be afraid. — **t. de frío,** to shiver from cold; **t. de miedo,** to shake with fear; **t. por su vida,** to tremble for one's life.
tembleque, *a.* shaky, unstable, doddering; trembling, shaking. —*m.* 1. jewel mounted on a spiral spring. 2. person who trembles. 3. (P. Rico, cul.) pudding.
temblequear, tembletear, *i.v.* to tremble, shake, shudder, quiver, quake or shiver often; (coll.) to pretend to tremble or shake.
temblequeteo, *m.* (coll.) frequent trembling, shaking or shivering.
temblón, na, *a.* trembling, shaking. —*m.* (bot.) trembling poplar, aspen.

temblor, *m.* 1. tremor, trembling, shaking, quivering, shivering. 2. (med.) tremor. — **t. de tierra,** (Amer.) earthquake.
temblorcillo, *m. dim. of* **temblor,** slight tremor.
tembloroso, sa, tembloso, sa, *a.* trembling, tremulous, shaking.
temedero, ra, *a.* fearful, dreadful, terrifying.
temedor, ra, *a.* frightened, afraid; **t. de,** afraid of, fearing.
temer, *tr.v.* 1. to fear, dread, be afraid of. 2. to fear, suspect, e.g. *temo que habrá más dificultades,* I fear there will be more difficulties. — **t.** + *inf.*, to be afraid of + *ger.* —*i.v.* to be afraid, fear. — **t. por,** to fear for, be worried about.
temerariamente, *adv.* 1. temerariously, recklessly, boldly, daringly. 2. rashly, hastily, foolhardily.
temerario, ria, *a.* 1. temerarious, reckless, bold, daring. 2. rash, hasty, foolhardy; imprudent.
temeridad, *f.* 1. temerity, recklessness, boldness, daring. 2. rashness, foolhardiness.
temerón, na, *a.* 1. blustering, swaggering. 2. cowardly. —*m., f.* blusterer.
temerosamente, *adv.* timorously, timidly.
temeroso, sa, *a.* 1. dreadful, dread, frightening. 2. timid, timorous. 3. fearful, afraid. — **t. de,** fearful or afraid of, e.g. *t. de Dios,* God-fearing.
temible, *a.* to be feared, frightening.
Temis, *f.* (myth.) Themis, Greek goddess of Law and Justice.
Temístocles, *m.* (hist.) Themistocles, Athenian statesman.
temor, *m.* 1. fear, dread; apprehension, foreboding.
temoso, sa, *a.* persistent, insistent; stubborn, obstinate.
tempanador, *m.* knife or cutter used to open the beehives.
tempanar, *tr.v.* to put a cork dome on (a beehive); to put the head on (a barrel).
témpano, *m.* 1. (mus.) small drum. 2. drum-head, drumskin. 3. flitch (of bacon). 4. head top (of a barrel). 5. cork dome (of a beehive), floe. 6. (archit.) tympanum, tympan. — **t. de hielo,** iceberg.
tempera, *f.* (p.) tempera.
temperación, *f.* 1. calming, soothing. 2. moderating, tempering.
temperadamente, *adv.* temperately; moderately.
temperamental, *a.* temperamental, related to temperament.
temperamento, *m.* 1. temperament; nature. 2. weather, climate. 3. compromise, conciliation. 4. (mus.) temperament.
temperancia, *f., var. of* **templanza.**
temperante, *a.* 1. calming, soothing; (med.) sedative. 2. (Amer.) abstemious. —*m., f.* (Amer.) teetotaler.
temperar, *tr.v.* 1. to soothe, calm, mitigate, assuage. 2. to moderate, temper. 3. to bring to a bearable or convenient temperature. 4. (med.) to calm. —*i.v.* (Amer.) to have a change of climate, change climates. —*r.v.* 1. to calm down, become calm. 2. to become moderate or temperate.
temperatura, *f.* 1. temperature. 2. weather, weather conditions. 3. temperature, fever. — **t. absoluta,** absolute temperature; **t. ambiente,** room temperature; **t. crítica,** critical temperature; **t. de saturación,** (meteorol.) saturation temperature, dew point; **t. límite,** breaking or limiting temperature; **tener t.,** to have a temperature or fever.
temperie, *f.* weather, weather or atmospheric conditions.
tempero, *m.* readiness for sowing or cultivation (of soil).
tempestad, *f.* storm, tempest; **levantar una t.,** to cause or raise a storm (of protests, etc.); **ojo de la t.,** eye of the storm; **t. de arena,** sandstorm; **t. de nieve,** snowstorm; **t. en un vaso de agua,** storm in a teacup; **t. magnética,** magnetic storm.
tempestear, *i.v.* 1. to storm, be stormy. 2. (fig.) to become violent, get out of hand.
tempestivamente, *adv.* opportunely, seasonably.
tempestividad, *a.* timeliness, opportuneness
tempestivo, va, *a.* opportune, timely.
tempestuosamente, *adv.* tempestuously, stormily, turbulently.
tempestuoso, sa, *a.* tempestuous, stormy, turbulent.
tempisque, *m.* (C. Rica, Hond., bot.) iron-wood (Sideroxylon capiri).
templa, *f.* 1. (p.) tempera, distemper. 2. (Cuba) amount of fermented sugar cane juice in a vat.
templadamente, *adv.* temperately; moderately.
templadero, *m.* tempering or annealing shop (in a glass or steel factory).
templado, da, *past part. of* **templar.** —*a.* 1. temperate, moderate, self-restrained. 2. warm, lukewarm (liquids, bath, etc.); mild, temperate (zone, climate). 3. (mus.) tuned; tempered. 4. tempered (glass, steel, etc.). 5. brave, courageous; firm. 6. (S. Amer.) in love. 7. (Amer.) drunk, tipsy. 8. (Col., Ven.) severe, strict, hard. 9. (C. Amer., Mex.) clever, able.
templador, ra, *a.* tempering; calming; soothing. —*m.* 1. (mus.) tuning hammer or key. 2. (Peru) shelter for bullfighters (in the center of large bullrings). 3. (Col.) worker in charge of sugar cane vats.
templadura, *f.* tempering; moderation; (mus.) tuning.
templanza, *f.* 1. temperance; moderation, sobriety. 2. mildness, temperateness (of climate). 3. (p.) harmony, blending (of colors).
templar, *tr.v.* 1. to moderate, temper, mitigate. 2. to make temperate, bring to a convenient or bearable temperature, cool down (hot water), warm up (cold water). 3. to temper (steel, glass). 4. to tighten (e.g. a nut) moderately. 5. to appease (anger, etc.). 6. (mar.) to trim (sails) to the wind. 7. (mus.) to tune, temper. 8. (p.) to blend, harmonize (colors); to dilute. 9. (Ecuad., Peru) to kill. 10. (C. Rica) to beat, thrash. 11. (Col., Ecuad.) to knock down. —*i.v.* 1. to become warmer, warm up (weather). 2. (Cuba) to flee, run away. —*r.v.* 1. to be moderate, restrain oneself. 2. (Chile, Peru) to fall in love. 3. (Ecuad.) to face danger. 4. (Col., Ecuad., Guat., Hond.) to die. 5. (Col., Peru, P. Rico) to get drunk.
Templario, *m.* (rel., hist.) Templar, Knight-Templar.
temple, *m.* 1. courage, dash, valor. 2. disposition, temper, mood. 3. weather, weather conditions. 4. temperature. 5. temper (of steel, glass, etc.). 6. average, mean. 7. (mus.) tuning, tempering. — **estar de buen** or **mal t.,** to be in a good or bad mood; **pintura al t.,** tempera painting. — **t. dulce,** (metal.) mild temper; **t. extraduro,** (metal.) very high temper.
temple, *m.* (rel., hist.) Order of Knights Templar or of Knights of the Temple.
templén, *m.* (tex.) temple (on a loom).
templete, *m.* 1. *dim. of* **templo,** small church or temple, chapel. 2. shrine, niche, tabernacle (in which a religious image or icon is kept). 3. pavilion; kiosk.
templista, *m., f.* (p.) artist who paints in tempera or distemper.
templo, *m.* temple; church; shrine.
témpora, *f.* (ecc.) Ember days (usually in the *pl.*).
temporada, *f.* season; period, spell; **estar de t. en,** to spend the season in; **ir por una t. a,** to go for or to spend a period or spell in; **t. de caza y pesca,** open season; **t. de deportes de invierno,** winter sports season; **t. de ópera,** opera season; **t. de veda,** closed season; **t. de verano,** summer season; **t. seca,** dry season.
temporal, *a.* 1. temporal, worldly, secular. 2. temporary, provisional; temporal, passing, transitory. 3. (gram.) temporal. —*m.* 1. storm, tempest. 2. period of rainy or stormy weather. 3. weather conditions. 4. (anat.) temporal bone. 5. (reg., Cuba) swindler, cheat. — **correr un t.,** to go through a storm.
temporalice, temporalicé, *ref.* **temporalizar.**
temporalidad, *f.* 1. temporality, secular or worldly nature. 2. (philos.) transitoriness. 3. (ecc.) (*pl.*) temporalities (revenues from dues, tithes, collections, etc.).
temporalizar, (*ref. 53*) *tr.v.* to make temporal; to secularize.
temporalmente, *adv.* 1. temporarily. 2. temporally, secularly.
temporáneo, a, temporario, ria, *a.* temporary, provisional; transitory, passing, momentary.
temporejar, *i.v.* (mar.) to lie to.
temporero, ra, *a.* seasonal, temporary. —*m., f.* seasonal or temporary worker.
temporice, temporicé, *ref.* **temporizar.**
temporizar, (*ref. 53*) *i.v.* 1. to temporize. 2. to while away the time, kill time.
tempranal, *a.* producing an early yield (land or crops). —*m.* early-cropping land, early crop.
tempranamente, *adv.* early; too early, prematurely.
tempranero, ra, *a.* early, ahead of time.
tempranilla, *a.* early (grape). —*f.* early grape.
tempranito, *adv.* (coll.) very early, good and early.
temprano, na, *a.* early. —*m.* early crop. —*adv.* early; too early, ahead of time. — **tarde o t.,** sooner or later.
temu, *m.* (Chile, bot.) eugenia (Eugenia temu).
temulento, ta, *a.* (rare) drunk, inebriated.
ten, t. con t., tact, adroitness, diplomacy; caution, moderation; **ir con mucho t. con t.,** to proceed with great caution.
tena, *f.* cattle shed.
tenacear, *tr.v., var. of* **atenacear.** —*i.v.* to insist or persist stubbornly.
tenacero, *m.* maker, user or seller of pliers, pincers or tongs.
tenacidad, *f.* 1. tenacity, firmness, perseverance, persistence. 2. (phys.) tenacity (of a metal).
tenacillas, *f.* (*pl.*) 1. *dim. of* **tenaza,** small tongs; tweezers; curling irons or tongs; sugar tongs; small pair of pliers or pincers. 2. snuffers.
tenáculo, *m.* (surg., ento.) tenaculum.
tenada, *f.* cattle shed.
tenallón, *m.* (fort.) tenaille.
tenante, *m.* (her.) supporter (of a shield).
tenar, *m.* (anat.) thenar.
tenaz, (*pl.* **tenaces**), *a.* 1. tenacious, unyielding, firm, strong. 2. tenacious, persevering, stubborn. 3. adhesive, strongly cohesive.
tenaza, *f.* 1. (*pl.*) pliers, pincers, nippers; tongs; (dent.) forceps; (zool.) pincers, nippers, claws (e.g. of a lobster). 2. (fort.) tenaille. 3. tenace, fourchette (in bridge). — **movimiento de tenazas,** (mil.) pincer movement; **tenazas de rizar,** curling tongs or iron.
tenazada, *f.* 1. grasp or grip with pincers, pliers or tongs; click of pincers or pliers, clink of tongs. 2. hard bite.
tenazmente, *adv.* tenaciously, firmly.
tenazón, a or **de t.,** 1. blindly, without taking aim. 2. suddenly.

tenazuelas, *f.* (*pl.*) *dim. of* **tenaza,** small tongs or pincers; tweezers.
tenca, *f.* 1. (ichth.) tench. 2. (Chile, Arg., ornith.) mockingbird (Mimus triurus). 3. (Chile, coll.) lie, hoax, false rumor.
tención, *f.* having, holding, possessing.
tencolote, *m.* (Mex.) cage (in which live poultry is taken to market).
tencua, *a.* (Mex.) with a harelip, harelipped. *—m., f.* person with a harelip.
tendajo, *m., var. of* **tendejón.**
tendal, *m.* 1. awning, covering. 2. canvas used to catch olives. 3. place where clothes are spread out or hung up for drying; clothes hung up or spread out to dry. 4. (Arg.) shearing shed. 5. (Arg., Chile, Peru) jumble of things in disorder. 6. (Chile) vending stand or stall. 7. (Cuba, Ecuad.) drying floor (for drying coffee beans, cocoa beans, etc.).
tendalera, *f.* (coll.) (S. Amer.) litter.
tendalero, *m.* drying place, place where things are hung up to dry.
tendedera, *f.* (Cuba, Guat., Mex.) clothesline.
tendedero, *m., var. of* **tendalero.**
tendedor, ra, *m., f.* person who spreads (clothes, etc.) out to dry.
tendedura, *f.* stretching; spreading; extending, lying.
tendejón, *m.* 1. small shop or vendor's stall. 2. shack, shed.
tendel, *m.* (mas.) leveling line; layer of mortar.
tendencia, *f.* tendency; trend, drift.
tendencioso, sa, *a.* tendentious, slanted (book, report, etc.).
tendente, *a.* 1. tending (to). 2. apt (to), inclined (to).
ténder, *m.* (ry.) tender.
tender, (*ref. 30*) *tr.* 1. to spread, spread out, stretch out. 2. to lay (a cable, a railway track). 3. to make (a bed). 4. to hang (clothes) up or out to dry. 5. to throw, build (a bridge across a river, ravine, etc.). 6. to stretch out, extend (one's hand). 7. to floor, stretch out, e.g. *lo tendió de un golpe,* he floored him with one blow. 8. to cast (a net). 9. to set, lay (a trap). 10. (mas.) to coat (with plaster). *—i.v.* to tend, have a tendency; **t. a** + *inf.,* to tend to + *inf.,* e.g. *él tiende a exagerar,* he tends to exaggerate. *—r.v.* 1. to stretch out, lie down. 2. to place one's cards on the table. 3. to go all out, run at full gallop (a horse). 4. (coll.) to become negligent (e.g. in business). 5. to droop, get beaten down (corn, etc.).
tenderete, *m.* 1. stall, stand, booth. 2. jumble of things, things scattered in disorder on the ground. 3. a card game resembling casino.
tendero, ra, *m., f.* 1. shopkeeper. 2. (Chile) shoplifter. *—m.* 1. tent-maker; person who takes care of the tents in a camp.
tendezuela, *f. dim. of* **tienda,** small shop.
tendidamente, *adv.* diffusely; extensively.
tendido, da, *past part. of* **tender.** *—a.* 1. spread out, extended, stretched out. 2. lying down. 3. full (gallop). *—m.* 1. laying (of cable); spreading. 2. tier or row of seats (in a bullring). 3. portion of lace made at one time. 4. batch of washing (hung up at one time); batch of bread (baked at one time). 5. slope or side of a roof. 6. coat of plaster, plastering. 7. (Arg.) clear sky. 8. (Col., Ecuad., Mex.) bedclothes. — **t. eléctrico,** electric wiring.
tendiente, *a.* tending (to), having a tendency (to).
tendinoso, sa, *a.* tendinous, tendon-like; full of tendons (meat).
tendón, *m.* (anat.) tendon; **t. de Aquiles,** Achilles' tendon.
tenducha, *f.,* **tenducho,** *m.* (derog.) shabby little shop, vending stand or stall.
tenebrario, *m.* (ecc.) tenebrae hearse or candelabrum.
tenebrosamente, *adv.* gloomily, darkly.
tenebrosidad, *f.* 1. darkness, gloominess. 2. obscurity.
tenebroso, sa, *a.* 1. dark, gloomy, tenebrous. 2. shady (business, deal, etc.). 3. obscure, difficult.
tenedero, *m.* (mar.) anchoring ground.
tenedor, *m.* 1. holder; bearer; owner, possessor. 2. fork (eating utensil). 3. (sport.) ball boy. — **t. de acciones,** stockholder; **t. de la póliza,** policyholder; **t. de libros,** bookkeeper.
teneduría, *f.* position of bookkeeper; **t. de libros,** bookkeeping.
tenencia, *f.* 1. tenure, holding, tenancy; occupation; possession. 2. (mil.) lieutenancy. 3. position of mayor's deputy or alderman; alderman's office.
tener, (*ref. 23*) *tr.v.* 1. to have; to possess, own. 2. to have, contain. 3. to have (i.e. to do something), e.g. *tengo una reunión esta tarde,* I have a meeting this afternoon. 4. to have, spend, e.g. *he tenido un día delicioso,* I've had a delightful day. 5. to have in a certain condition, e.g. *me tiene preocupada tu silencio,* your silence worries me, *me tiene loco este muchacho,* this boy is driving me mad, *tenía los ojos cerrados,* he had his eyes closed, *ya tengo la carta escrita,* I already have the letter written. 6. to take hold of, take, hold, e.g. *tenlo,* take it. 7. to have, receive, e.g. *me daría gusto tenerlo en mi casa,* I would be pleased to have him in my house. 8. to be (so many months, days, years, etc.) old, e.g. *tiene veinte años,* he is twenty, he is twenty years old. 9. to be, e.g. *t. calor,* to be hot, *t. celos,* to be jealous, *t. cuidado,* to be careful, *t. éxito,* to be successful, *t. frío,* to be cold, *t. hambre,* to be hungry, *t. miedo,* to be afraid, be scared, *t. razón,* to be right. — **no tenerlas todas consigo,** (coll.) to be worried or concerned, be afraid or scared; **no t. donde caerse muerto,** (coll.) not to have a cent to one's name; **¿qué tiene?** what is the matter with him, her or it; **¿qué tienes?** what's the matter with you?; **t. . . . de alto,** to be (so many feet, etc.) tall; **t. . . . de ancho,** to be (so many feet, etc.) wide; **t. . . . de largo,** to be (so many feet, etc.) long; **t. a menos,** to consider (something) below one's dignity; **t. de** + *a.,* to be + *a.* about or in (used in the interrogative and negative), e.g. *¿qué tiene eso de raro?* what is so unusual about that? *nada tiene de difícil este trabajo,* there is nothing difficult about this work; **t. en contra,** to have (something, nothing, etc.) against; **t. en cuenta,** to keep in mind; **t. en mucho,** to esteem greatly; **t. en poco,** to think little of; **tenga la bondad de** + *inf.,* be so kind as to + *inf.,* please + *imper.;* **t. la culpa,** to be to blame; **t. lugar,** to take place; **t. para sí,** to think, be of the opinion; **t. parte en,** to have to do with, have a say in; **t. por,** to consider (someone) to be; **t. presente,** to remember, keep or bear in mind; **t. prisa,** to be in a hurry; **t. que** + *inf.,* to have to + *inf.,* must + *inf.;* **t. . . . que hacer,** to have (little, nothing, a lot, etc.) to do; **t. . . . que decir,** to have . . . to say; **t. . . . que perder,** to have . . . to lose; **t. que ver con,** to concern, to have to do with. *—i.v.* to be rich, have money. *—aux.v.* 1. to have; **tener que** + *inf.,* to have to + *inf.,* must + *inf.,* e.g. *tienes que comer,* you have to eat, *tengo que salir,* I must go out. 2. to have + *past part.* (agreeing with object), e.g. *tengo leídos tres capítulos,* I have (already) read three chapters, *tengo escritos dos libros,* I have written two books. — **tener entendido que,** to understand that; **tener pensado,** to intend to; **tener planeado** or **proyectado,** to plan to. *—r.v.* 1. to consider oneself, e.g. *él se tiene por inteligente,* he considers himself intelligent. 2. to hold, grasp, steady oneself, e.g. *tenerse de la baranda,* to hold on to the railing. 3. to stop, halt. 4. to stand firm. — **tenerse a,** to stick to, stand by, keep to; **tenerse en pie,** to keep on one's feet; **tenérselas tiesas a** or **con,** (coll.) to stand firm against.
tenería, *f.* tannery, leather works.
tenesmo, *m.* (med.) tenesmus.
tenga, tengo, *ref.* **tener.**
tenguerengue, en t., unstable, wobbly, teetering.
tenia, *f.* 1. (zool.) taenia, tapeworm. 2. (archit.) taenia, fillet. 3. (anat.) taenia.
teniasis, *f.* (med.) taeniasis.
tenicida, *a.* taenicidal. *—m.* taenicide.
tenida, *f.* 1. (Amer.) meeting (of a Masonic lodge). 2. (Chile) uniform, suit.
tenienta, *f.* lieutenant; (hist.) lieutenant's wife.
tenientazgo, *m.* lieutenancy.
teniente, *a.* 1. having, holding, owning. 2. unripe (fruit). 3. (coll.) hard of hearing. 4. miserly, tight-fisted. *—m., f.* lieutenant, deputy, substitute, (mil.) lieutenant. — **t. coronel,** lieutenant colonel; **t. de alcalde,** deputy mayor; **t. general,** lieutenant general; **segundo t.,** second lieutenant.
tenífugo, ga, *a.* (med.) taenifuge, teniafuge.
tenis, *m.* tennis; tennis court.
tenista, *m., f.* tennis player.
Tenochtitlán, capital of the Aztec empire; location of Mexico City.
tenonitis, *f.* (med.) tenonitis.
tenor, *m.* 1. (mus.) tenor. 2. tenor, tone, drift (e.g. of a letter, document). — **a t. de,** according to.
tenorio, *m.* Don Juan, Casanova, lady-killer.
tenotomía, *f.* (surg.) tenotomy.
tensar, *tr.v* to draw, make taut.
tensiómetro, *m.* (mec.) tensiometer.
tensión, *f.* 1. tension; stress, strain. 2. tautness, tightness. 3. (elec.) tension, voltage. — **t. alta,** (elec.) high tension; **t. aplicada,** (elec.) impressed voltage; **t. capilar,** capillary potential; **t. baja,** (elec.) low tension; **t. de desenganche,** (elec.) drop-out voltage; **t. disruptiva,** (elec.) disruptive voltage; **t. final,** (elec.) cutoff voltage; **t. superficial,** (phys.) surface tension.
tenso, sa, *a.* 1. tense, tight, taut. 2. tense, on edge, strained.
tensón, *f.* (poet.) tenson.
tensor, ra, *a.* tensile. *—m.* 1. tension (device to produce desired tension in a loom or sewing machine). 2. (mec.) turnbuckle. 3. (math.) tensor. 4. (anat.) tensor (muscle).
tentación, *f.* temptation; **caer en la t.,** to fall into temptation.
tentaculado, da, *a.* (zool., bot.) tentacled.
tentacular, *a.* tentacular.
tentáculo, *m.* (zool.) tentacle; feeler.
tentadero, *m.* corral where young fighting bulls are tested.
tentador, ra, *a.* tempting, enticing, alluring. *—m.* tempter. *—f.* temptress.
tentadura, *f.* 1. mercury test of silver ore; sample used for such a test. 2. beating, thrashing, drubbing.
tentalear, *tr.v.* to feel, examine by touch; to touch repeatedly.
tentar, (*ref. 29*) *tr.v.* 1. to feel, touch. 2. to grope for, feel (one's way). 3. to examine. 4. to try, attempt. 5. (surg.) to probe. 6. to tempt, entice,

lead (someone) on, to incite. 7. to try, test (someone's endurance, loyalty, etc.). — **t. al diablo,** to look for trouble.
tentativa, *f.* attempt, trial, experiment; endeavor. — **t. de delito,** (law) attempted crime.
tentemozo, *m.* 1. prop, support; whipple-tree prop. 2. tumbler, roly-poly (toy). 3. cheek strap, cheek piece (of bridle).
tentempié, *m.* 1. (coll.) snack, bite. 2. tumbler, roly-poly (toy).
tentenelaire, *m., f.* offspring of a quadroon and a mulatto. —*m.* (ornith.) humming-bird.
tentetieso, *m.* tumbler, roly-poly (toy).
tentón, *m.* 1. (coll.) brusk touch, rough handling. 2. (Guat.) serious wound.
tenue, *a.* 1. faint, dim, subdued, thin (light). 2. delicate, soft (color, shade). 3. thin, delicate, tenuous. 4. simple (style). 5. trifling, insignificant.
tenuemente, *adv.* tenuously, dimly, faintly, thinly.
tenuidad, *f.* 1. tenuousness, faintness, dimness (of light). 2. subtlety, softness (of colors, shades). 3. thinness, tenuousness. 4. trifle (unimportant thing).
tenuirrostro, tra, *a.* (zool.) tenuirostral. —*m.* tenuiroster, (*pl.*) Tenuirostres.
tenuta, *f.* (law) provisional tenure.
tenutario, ria, *a.* (law) pertaining to provisional tenure.
tenzón, *m.* (poet.) tenson.
teñible, *a.* dyeable; stainable.
teñido, da, *past part. of* **teñir.** —*a.* dyed, tinted, stained. —*m.* dyeing, tinting, staining.
teñidura, *f.* dyeing, staining.
teñir, (*ref. 41*) *tr.v.* 1. to dye, tint; to stain. 2. (p.) to darken (colors). 3. (fig.) to imbue.
teobroma, *m.* (bot.) **cacao.**
teobromina, *f.* (chem.) theobromine.
teocali, *m.* (archeol.) teocali, ancient Aztec temple.
teocéntrico, ca, *a.* (theol.) theocentric.
teocinte, *m.* (bot.) teosinte.
teocracia, *f.* theocracy.
teocráta, *m., f.* theocrat.
teocrático, ca, *a.* theocratic.
Teócrito, *m.* (hist.) Theocritus, Greek poet of the 3rd century B.C.
teodicea, *f.* (theol.) theodicy.
teodolito, *m.* theodolite; **t. de tránsito,** transit theodolite.
Teodora, *f.* (hist.) Theodora, Byzantine empress, consort of Justinian.
teodosiano, na, *a.* (hist.) Theodosian, of or pertaining to Theodosius I or Theodosius II.
Teodosio, *m.* 1. (hist.) Theodosius I, Theodosius the Great, Roman emperor of the 4th century A.D. 2. (hist.) Theodosius II, Roman emperor of the 5th century A.D.
teofanía, *f.* (theol.) theophany.
teofilina, *f.* (chem.) theophylline.
teogonía, *f.* theogony, origin of the gods; genealogy of the gods.
teogónico, ca, *a.* theogonic.
teologal, *a.* theological, theologic.
teología, *f.* theology; **no meterse en teologías,** (coll.) to keep to simple subjects or topics.
teológicamente, *adv.* theologically.
teologice, teologicé, *ref.* **teologizar.**
teológico, ca, *a.* theological, theologic.
teologizar, (*ref. 53*) *i.v.* to theologize.
teólogo, ga, *a.* theological. —*m., f.* 1. theologian. 2. theology student, divinity student.
teomanía, *f.* (psyc.) theomania.
teorema, *m.* (math., log.) theorem.
teoría, *f.* 1. theory; **t. cuántica,** quantum theory; **t. de la evolución,** theory of evolution; **t. de la relatividad,** theory of relativity; **t. del dominó,** domino theory; **t. electrónica,** electron theory; **t. germinal,** (biol.) germ theory; **t. unitaria, t. del campo unificado,** (phys.) unitary theory. 2. theoretics.
teórica, *f.* theory, theoretics.
teóricamente, *adv.* theoretically.
teorice, teoricé, *ref.* **teorizar.**
teórico, ca, *a.* theoretical, theoretic. —*m., f.* theoretician; theorist. —*f.* theory, theoretics.
teorizante, *a.* theorizing. —*m., f.* person who theorizes.
teorizar, (*ref. 53*) *tr.v.* to theorize on. —*i.v.* to theorize.
teoso, sa, *a.* resinous, full of resin.
teosofía, *f.* (philos., rel.) theosophy.
teosófico, ca, *a.* theosophical, theosophic.
teosofismo, *m.* theosophism.
teósofo, *m.* theosophist.
tepache, *m.* (Mex.) tepache, beverage made of pulque, water, pineapple and cloves.
tepe, *m.* turf, sod (used for making walls).
tepeizcuinte, *m.* (C. Rica, Mex., zool.) paca, spotted cavy.
tepemechín, *m.* (C. Rica, Hond., ichth.) fresh water fish found near waterfalls.
tepetate, *m.* 1. (Mex.) white rock (used for building). 2. (Mex., Hond., min.) refuse, barren rock (rock containing no ore). 3. (Mex.) rocky terrain or country.
tepexilote, *m.* palm nut used as an ornamental bead.
tepidario, *m.* (hist.) tepidarium, steam room (in Roman baths).
tepozán, *m.* (Mex., bot.) buddleia (Buddleia americana).
tepú, (*pl.* **tepúes**), *m.* (Chile, bot.) small myrtaceous tree (Tepulia stiplularis).
tequiche, *m.* (Ven.) dish made of roasted cornmeal, coconut milk and butter.
tequila, *f.* (Mex.) tequila (liquor distilled from maguey).
tequio, *m.* 1. (C. Rica, Mex.) trouble, nuisance, bother, inconvenience. 2. (Amer.) amount of ore dug by one man. 3. (Mex., hist.) forced labor of Indians.
terapeuta, *m., f.* 1. therapeutist, therapist. 2. (rel.) one of the Therapeutae, (*pl.*) Therapeutae.
terapéutica, *f.* therapeutics.
terapéutico, ca, *a.* therapeutic, therapeutical.
terapia, *f.* therapy; **t. de grupo,** group therapy; **t. de pareja,** marriage counseling; **t.-electroshoc,** electroshock therapy; **t. intensiva,** intensive care; **t. ocupacional,** occupational therapy.
teratología, *f.* (biol.) teratology.
teratológico, ca, *a.* teratological, teratologic.
teratoma, *m.* (med.) teratoma.
terbio, *m.* (chem.) terbium.
tercamente, *adv.* obstinately, stubbornly.
tercelete, *m.* (archit.) tierceron.
tercena, *f.* 1. state monopoly wholesale store (esp. for tobacco). 2. (Ecuad.) butcher's shop.
tercenista, *m., f.* 1. person running a government monopoly store. 2. (Ecuad.) butcher.
tercer, *a.* apocopated form of **tercero,** used only before masculine singular nouns and adjectives, e.g. *al t. día resucitó,* He rose on the third day; **el t. estado.** the third estate; **el T. Mundo,** the Third World.
tercera, *f.* 1. tierce (in cards). 2. go-between; procuress, bawd. 3. (mus.) third. 4. third class. 5. (fenc.) tierce. 6. (auto.) third gear. — **t. edad,** retirement years; **t. mayor,** tierce major (in cards); (mus.) major third; **t. menor,** (mus.) minor third.
terceramente, *adv.* thirdly, in the third place.
tercería, *f.* 1. mediation, arbitration. 2. pimping, procuring. 3. temporary occupation (of a fortress or castle). 4. (law) right of third party.
tercerilla, *f.* (poet.) triplet or tercet.
tercerista, *m., f.* (law) intervener, intervenant.
tercero, ra, *a.* third. —*m., f.* third, third one or person. —*m.* 1. procurer, pimp, pander. 2. (ecc.) tertiary. 3. third party. 4. mediator, arbitrator, referee. 5. (geom.) sixtieth of a second. 6. third floor (of a building). — **t. en discordia,** mediator, arbitrator, referee.
tercerol, *m.* (mar.) third (in order).
tercerola, *f.* 1. short carbine. 2. (com.) tierce; medium-sized barrel. 3. small flute. 4. (ry.) third-class car.
tercerón, na, *m., f.* (Amer.) offspring of white and mulatto parents.
terceto, *m.* (mus.) trio; (poet.) tercet.
tercia, *f.* 1. third, third part. 2. (ecc.) tierce (canonical hour). 3. tierce (in cards). 4. 11 inches, third of a vara (measure). 5. (hist.) forenoon (in ancient Rome). 6. storehouse for tithes (of grain). 7. third digging.
terciado, da, *past part. of* **terciar.** —*a.* 1. tilted, slanting, crosswise. 2. medium sized (bull). —*m.* 1. cutlass, broadsword. 2. wide ribbon.
terciador, ra, *a.* mediating, arbitrating. —*m., f.* mediator, arbitrator.
terciana, *f.* (med.) tertian, tertian fever (sometimes in *pl.*); **t. de cabeza,** intermittent headache.
tercianario, ria, *a.* 1. suffering from or infested with tertian fever. 2. (med.) tertian (fever). —*m., f.* person suffering from tertian fever.
tercianela, *f.* (tex.) heavy silk cloth.
terciar, *tr.v.* 1. to place diagonally across; to place (a rifle) diagonally across the back. 2. to divide into three. 3. to balance (the load on a mule). 4. to plow for the third time. 5. to cut (plants) to one third their size. 6. (Col., Cuba, Chile, Ecuad.) to water down. —*i.v.* 1. to intervene, mediate. 2. to take part; to make up the number. 3. to be in its third day (the moon). — **t. en,** to take part in, to chime in (a conversation). —*r.v.* **si se tercia,** if the opportunity arises or presents itself.
terciario, ria, *a.* tertiary; (geol.) Tertiary. —*m.* 1. (geol.) Tertiary. 2. (ecc.) tertiary. —*f.* (zool.) tertiary, tertial feather.
terciazón, *m.* (agr.) third plowing.
tercio, cia, *a.* third. —*m.* 1. third, third part. 2. pack (each of two carried by beasts of burden). 3. (Sp.) infantry regiment (in 16th and 17th centuries); division of the Spanish Civil Guard; the Spanish army corps of volunteers. 4. (mar.) fishermen's guild or harbor union. 5. calf (of a stocking). 6. (*pl.*) strong limbs. 7. (taur.) each of the three stages of a bullfight; **t. de muerte,** the kill. 8. third of a horse's height. 9. stage, each stage of horse race (start, run, stop). 10. each of the three parts of a rosary. 11. each of three parts into which a sword is divided. 12. (Cuba) hundredweight bale of tobacco. 13. (Ven.) fellow, guy, character (sl.). — **hacer buen** (or mal) t. a, to do (someone) a good (or bad) turn, help (or hinder); **hacer t.,** to participate, join in, make up the number; **mejorado en t. y quinto,** at a great advantage, greatly favored.
terciodécuplo, pla, *a.* containing thirteen an exact number of times. —*m.* multiple of thirteen.
terciopelado, da, *a.* velvety. —*m.* velvetlike cloth or material.
terciopelero, ra, *m., f.* person who weaves or works with velvet.
terciopelo, *m.* velvet.
terco, ca, *a.* 1. obstinate, stubborn. 2. hard, intractable, difficult (to work or fashion). 3. (Ecuad.) cold, aloof, unresponsive.

terebeno, *m.* (chem.) terebene.
terebintáceo, a, *a.* (bot.) terebinthine. —*f.* (*pl.*) Terebinthaceae.
terebinto, *m.* (bot.) terebinth tree.
terebrante, *a.* piercing (pain).
terebrátula, *f.* (zool.) terebratula.
terenciano, na, *a.* (lit.) Terentian, characteristic of the Roman playwright Terence.
tereniabín, *m.* sticky sweet substance obtained from a Persian shrub and used for purgatives.
tereque, *m.* (Amer.) utensil, implement; (*pl.*) belongings, odds and ends, bits and pieces.
terere, *m.* (Par.) cold maté tea.
teresiana, *a.* (ecc.) Teresian, of or pertaining to Saint Theresa. —*f.* T., Teresian, member of a Spanish order of reformed Carmelites. 2. military cap.
teresiano, na, *a.* 1. pertaining to Saint Teresa of Avila. 2. Teresian (religious order).
tergal, *m.* (tex.) a synthetic fabric made in France.
tergiversable, *a.* that can be twisted or distorted.
tergiversación, *f.* twisting, distortion, misrepresentation (e.g. of facts).
tergiversador, ra, *a.* distorting. —*m., f.* distorter.
tergiversar, *tr.v.* to twist, distort (e.g. facts, a statement).
teriaca, *f.* (pharm.) theriaca, antidote.
teriacal, *a.* (pharm.) theriacal.
teristro, *m.* light summer shawl or veil (used by Palestinian women).
terliz, *m.* (tex.) strong cotton cloth.
termal, *a.* thermal; **aguas termales,** hot springs.
termas, *f.* (*pl.*) thermal baths, thermae, hot baths, hot springs.
termes, *m.* (ento.) termite.
termia, *f.* (phys.) therm.
térmico, ca, *a.* thermic, thermal; steam-generated (power); heated (windshield).
termidor, *m.* (hist.) Thermidor, eleventh month in the calendar of the French Revolution.
terminabilidad, *f.* terminability.
terminable, *a.* terminable.
terminacho, *m.* (coll.) rude or vulgar word; barbarism; incorrectly used word or term.
terminación, *f.* 1. termination, ending, completion. 2. finish (given to a product). 3. (gram.) ending.
terminador, ra, *a.* finishing, completing. —*m., f.* finisher.
terminajo, *m., var. of* **terminacho.**
terminal, *a.* terminal, final, last. —*m.* terminal, terminus; (elec.) terminal. — **t. aérea,** (avia.) air terminal; **t. de carga,** freight terminal; **t. de pasajeros,** passenger terminal; **t. nerviosa,** nerve ending.
terminante, *a.* definite, final, conclusive, categorical; peremptory.
terminantemente, *adv.* 1. conclusively, definitely. 2. categorically, peremptorily.
terminar, *tr.v.* to finish, end, terminate, close, conclude. —*i.v.* to finish, end, terminate; to end up, conclude; **nunca terminan de verse los museos de Madrid,** you never can see all the museums of Madrid; **t. de** + *inf.,* to finish + *ger.,* e.g. *cuando termines de lavar los vasos,* when you finish washing the glasses. — **t. en,** to finish in, end up as or in, develop into, come to or end in, e.g. *terminaré en diez minutos,* I'll finish in ten minutes, *vas a t. en cura,* you're going to end up as a priest, *terminó en la cárcel,* he ended up in jail, *eso terminará en pelea,* that's going to develop into a fight, *el lápiz termina en punta,* the pencil comes to (ends in) a point; t. + *ger.* or **por** + *inf.,* to finish or end up by + *ger.,* e.g. *terminé riendo, terminé por reír,* I ended up by laughing. —*r.v.* to finish, end, come to an end, be over, e.g. *se terminó la función,* the show is finished, is over.
terminativo, va, *a.* (philos.) terminative.
terminista, *m., f.* pedant, phrasemonger.
término, *m.* 1. term, word, expression. 2. end, finish, conclusion. 3. limit; boundary, landmark. 4. time limit; term, period, space of time. 5. (log., math.) term. 6. (archit.) term, terminal figure or statue. 7. (p., theat.) ground, e.g. *en primer t. se ven pastores con sus ovejas,* shepherds with their sheep are seen in the foreground. 8. (*pl.*) terms, relations, e.g. *estar en buenos términos con,* to be on good terms with. 9. object, end, goal. 10. state, situation, condition. 11. district (under jurisdiction of a town council). 12. piece of land assigned for specific use. — **en buenos términos,** on good terms (with); **en primer, segundo** or **tercer t.,** in the first, second or third place; **en t.,** on time, e.g. *pague en t.,* pay on time; **llevar a buen t.,** to carry out successfully; **llevar a t.,** to carry out, to complete; **medios términos,** evasions, vague half answers; **poner t. a,** to put an end to; **por t. medio,** on the average; **t. de la distancia,** (law, Peru) space of time necessary to travel a certain distance (in order to appear in court); **t. de prueba,** (law) time allowed for producing evidence; **t. extraordinario,** (law) extended period of time for producing evidence; **t. fatal,** (law) unextendable term; **t. medio,** (math.) average; (fig.) compromise, middle way; (cul.) medium, not too rare; **t. perentorio,** (law) unextendable term.
terminología, *f.* terminology.
terminológico, ca, *a.* terminological.
terminote, *m.* (coll.) big word, pedantic expression.
termión, *m.* (phys.) thermion.
termiónico, ca, *a.* (phys.) thermionic. —*f.* thermionics.
termita, *f.* (chem.) thermite.
termite, *m.* (ento.) termite.
termitero, *m.* nest of termites.
termo, *m.* thermos, vacuum flask.
termoanestesia, *f.* (med.) thermoanesthesia, thermoanaesthesia.
termobarógrafo, *m.* (phys.) thermobarograph.
termobarómetro, *m.* (meteorol.) thermobarometer.
termocauterio, *m.* (surg.) thermocautery.
termodinámica, *f.* (phys.) thermodynamics.
termodinámico, ca, *a.* (phys.) thermodynamic.
termodúrico, ca, *a.* (med.) thermoduric.
termoelectricidad, *f.* (phys.) thermoelectricity.
termoeléctrico, ca, *a.* (phys.) thermoelectrical, thermoelectric.
termoelectromotriz, *a.* (phys.) thermoelectromotive.
termoelectrón, *m.* (phys.) thermoelectron.
termoelemento, *m.* (elec.) thermoelement.
termoendurecible, *a.* thermosetting (plastic).
termófilo, la, *a.* (biol.) thermophile.
termofísica, *f.* thermophysics.
termofraguado, da, *a.* thermosetting (plastic).
termogénesis, *f.* (physiol., biol.) thermogenesis.
termogénico, ca, *a.* (physiol., biol.) thermogenetic.
termógeno, na, *a.* (physiol., biol.) thermogenic, thermogenous.
termografía, *f.* (phys.) thermography.
termógrafo, *m.* thermograph, automatically registering thermometer.
termograma, *m.* (phys.) thermogram.
termointerruptor, *m.* (elec.) thermostat-controlled switch.
termoión, *m.* (phys.) thermion.
termoiónico, ca, *a.* (phys.) thermionic.
termolábil, *a.* (biochem.) thermolabile.
termólisis, *f.* (chem., physiol.) thermolysis.
termología, *f.* (phys.) thermology.
termometría, *f.* (phys., med.) thermometry.
termométrico, ca, *a.* (phys.) thermometrical, thermometric.
termómetro, *m.* thermometer; **t. clínico,** clinical thermometer; **t. de bola seca,** dry-bulb thermometer; **t. de resistencia,** resistance thermometer; **t. diferencial,** differential thermometer; **t. registrador,** recording thermometer; **t. seco,** dry-bulb thermometer; **t. termoeléctrico,** thermoelectric thermometer.
termomultiplicador, *m.* (phys.) thermomultiplier, thermopile.
termonuclear, *a.* thermonuclear.
termopar, *m.* (elec.) thermocouple.
termopila, *f.* (phys.) thermopile.
Termópilas, *f.* (*pl.*) (hist.) Thermopylae.
termoplástico, ca, *a.* thermoplastic.
termoquímico, ca, *a.* thermochemical. —*f.* thermochemistry.
termorregulación, *f.* (phys.) thermoregulation.
termoscopio, *m.* (phys.) thermoscope.
termosifón, *m.* 1. boiler, water heater. 2. (phys.) thermosiphon.
termostático, ca, *a.* thermostatic. —*f.* (phys.) thermostatics.
termostato, *m.* thermostat.
termotaxia, *f.* (biol., physiol.) thermotaxis.
termoterapia, *f.* (med.) thermotherapy.
termotropismo, *m.* (biol.) thermotropism.
termounión, *f.* (elec.) thermojunction.
terna, *f.* 1. list of three candidates for a job or position; (ecc.) terna. 2. pair of threes (in dice). 3. set of dice.
ternario, ria, *a.* 1. ternary, consisting of three parts or elements. 2. (mus.) three-part (time, measure). —*m.* (rel.) three days' devotion.
terne, *a.* 1. bragging, bullying. 2. tenacious, persistent, stubborn. 3. (coll.) husky, robust. —*m.* 1. braggart, bully. 2. (Arg.) gaucho knife or cutlass.
ternecico, ca, to, ta, *a. dim. of* **tierno,** young and tender.
ternejal, *a.* (coll.) bragging, bullying. —*m.* braggart, bully.
ternejo, ja, *a.* (Ecuad., Peru, coll.) energetic, lively.
ternejón, na, *a.* (coll.) sentimental. —*m., f.* sentimental person.
terneraje, *m.* (Chile, Mex.) group of calves.
ternerico, ca, ito, ita, *m., f. dim. of* **ternero, ra,** small or young calf.
ternero, ra, *m., f.* calf; **t. recental,** unweaned calf. —*f.* (cul.) veal; **chuleta de t.,** veal chop.
ternerón, na, *a.* sentimental. —*m., f.* sentimental person.
terneza, *f.* 1. tenderness. 2. (*pl.*) endearments, sweet nothings.
ternilla, *f.* 1. cartilage (of animals); nose or nostril (of an ox, etc.). 2. (Cuba) spare ribs. — **llevar de la t.,** to lead by the nose.
ternilloso, sa, *a.* gristly, cartilaginous.
ternísimo, ma, *a. super. of* **tierno,** very tender.
terno, *m.* 1. suit (of clothes). 2. set of three, triad, triplet. 3. tern (in a lottery). 4. oath, curse. 5. (ecc.) three priests officiating at high mass. 6. (print.) three sheets folded within one another. 7. (Cuba, Col., P. Rico) three-piece set of jewelry. — **t. seco,** (coll.) lucky break.
ternura, *f.* 1. tenderness; love, affection. 2. endearment, sweet nothing.
terpénico, ca, *a.* (chem.) terpenic.

terpeno, *m.* (chem.) terpene.
terpina, *f.* (chem.) terpin hydrate, terpinol hydrate.
terpineol, terpinol, *m.* (chem.) terpineol, terpinol.
terpino, *m.* (chem.) terpinol.
Terpsícore, *f.* (myth.) Terpsichore, the Muse of Dance.
terquear, *i.v.* to be obstinate or stubborn.
terquedad, *f.* 1. obstinacy, stubbornness. 2. (Ecuad.) aloofness, disaffection.
terracota, *f.* terra cotta.
terrado, *m.* flat roof or high terrace (of a house).
terraja, *f.* 1. (mec.) diestock; threading machine. 2. template, modeling board; (metal.) strickle, sweep board.
terraje, *m.* land rent, rent paid for farmland.
terrajero, *m.* tenant farmer.
terral, *a.* land (wind). —*m.* land wind or breeze.
terramicina, *f.* (pharm.) terramycin.
Terranova, *f.* (geog.) Newfoundland; **perro de T.,** Newfoundland dog.
terraplén, *m.* embankment, terreplein; (fort.) terreplein.
terraplenar, *tr.v.* to fill up with earth; to embank, bank up with earth, terrace.
terráqueo, a, *a.* terrestrial, terraqueous; **globo t.,** the earth.
terrateniente, *m., f.* land owner, landholder.
terraza, *f.* 1. terrace, veranda. 2. terrace (for farming). 3. (geol.) terrace. 4. border, edge (containing plants and flowers in a garden). 5. glazed two-handled jug. 6. sidewalk café.
terrazgo, *m.* 1. plot of arable land. 2. land rent, rent paid for farmland.
terrazguero, *m.* tenant farmer.
terrazo, *m.* (p.) ground, earth (as a composition element in a painting).
terrear, *i.v.* to let the soil show through (said of poor crops).
terrecer, (*ref. 45*) *tr.v.* to terrify.
terregoso, sa, *a.* full of clods or lumps (of earth).
terremoto, *m.* earthquake.
terrenal, *a.* earthly, e.g. *paraíso t.,* earthly paradise; worldly, of the world, e.g. *bienes terrenales,* worldly goods.
terrenidad, *f.* earthliness.
terreno, na, *a.* 1. earthly. 2. worldly, mundane. —*m.* 1. land, ground, terrain. 2. piece or plot of land. 3. ground, soil, earth, e.g. *t. arcilloso,* clayey ground. 4. (geol.) terrane, terrain. 5. (fig.) field, sphere. — **ceder t.,** to give ground; **ganar uno t.,** to gain ground; **perder uno t.,** to lose ground; **preparar el t.,** to pave the way; **sobre el t.,** on the spot, face-to-face with the actual facts or situation; **t. abierto** or **descubierto,** (mil.) open ground; **t. de honor,** field of honor, duelling ground or field; **t. franco,** (min.) state land which can be granted freely for mining concessions.
térreo, a, *a.* earthy, earth-like.
terrero, ra, *a.* 1. earthly, worldly. 2. low-flying (said of birds); low-stepping (said of horses). 3. for carrying earth (basket). 4. humble, lowly. 5. (Canar. I., P. Rico) one-floor (house). —*m.* 1. terrace (of a house). 2. pile, heap (of earth or brush). 3. alluvium, sediment, deposit. 4. target, mark. 5. public square. —*f.* 1. steep ground, slope. 2. (ornith.) lark. 3. basket for carrying earth.
terrestre, *a.* terrestrial, earthly.
terrezca, terrezco, *ref.* **terrecer.**
terrezuela, *f. dim. of* **tierra,** small or worthless piece of land.
terribilidad, *f.* terribleness.
terrible, *a.* terrible. 2. gruff, bad-tempered.
terriblemente, *adv.* terribly.
terriblez, terribleza, *f.* (rare) *var. of* terribilidad.
terrícola, *m., f.* earth dweller, inhabitant of the earth.
terrífico, ca, *a.* terrifying, terrific.
terrígeno, na, *a.* earthborn, terrigenous.
terrino, na, *a.* earthly, terrene.
territorial, *a.* territorial.
territorialidad, *f.* territoriality.
territorio, *m.* 1. territory; region. 2. district; zone.
terrizo, za, *a.* earthen, made of earth. —*m., f.* earthen tub or pan.
terromontero, *m.* hill, hillock.
terrón, *m.* 1. clod (of earth). 2. lump (of sugar, salt, etc.). 2. olive residue (in olive oil mills). 3. (coll.) farmland, farm property.
terronazo, *m.* blow with a clod of earth.
terroncillo, *m. dim. of* **terrón,** small lump (of sugar, etc.).
terror, *m.* terror; **T.,** Reign of Terror (French Revolution).
terrorífico, ca, *a.* terrifying, terrific.
terrorismo, *m.* terrorism.
terrorista, *a., m.* terrorist; **t. de alquiler,** goon, hired thug.
terrosidad, *f.* 1. earthiness, cloddiness; dirtiness.
terroso, sa, *a.* earthy, cloddy; dirty, gritty.
terruño, *m.* 1. native land, native soil. 2. piece or plot of land. 3. clod, lump (of earth).
tersar, *tr.v.* to make smooth, glossy or shiny.
tersidad, *f., var. of* **tersura.**
terso, sa, *a.* 1. smooth, glossy, shining, polished. 2. smooth, flowing, fluid (style).
tersura, *f.* 1. smoothness, glossiness, shininess. 2. smoothness, fluidity (of style).
tertel, *a.* (Chile) hard layer of soil (under subsoil).
tertil, *m.* (Sp., arch.) tax formerly paid on every pound of silk.
tertulia, *f.* 1. social gathering, at-home, get-together. 2. (theat.) upper gallery. 3. gambling room (in a café). 4. (Arg.) theater seat. — **estar de t.,** to talk, chat.
tertuliano, na, tertuliante, *m., f.* guest at an informal gathering or get-together.
tertuliar, *i.v.* (Amer.) to gather for conversation.
tertulio, lia, *a., m., f., var. of* **tertuliano.**
teruncio, *m.* (numis.) teruncius, quadrans, ancient Roman coin.
teruteru, *m.* (ornith.) teruteru, American lapwing.
terzón, na, *a., m., f.* a three-year-old heifer.
terzuela, *f.* (ecc.) allotment received by some chapter members for attending choir at the hour of tierce.
terzuelo, *m.* 1. third, third part. 2. (hunt.) tercel, male falcon.
Tesalia, *f.* (hist., geog.) Thessaly.
tesálico, ca, tesaliense, tesalio, lia, tésalo, la, *a., m., f.* Thessalian.
Tesalónica, *f.* (hist., geog.) Thessalonike, Thessalonica.
tesalonicense, tesalónico, ca, *a., m., f.* Thessalonian.
tesar, *tr.v.* (mar.) to make taut (cables, sails, etc.). —*i.v.* to back, back up (yoked oxen).
tesaurizar, (*ref. 53*) *tr.v., var. of* **atesorar.**
tesauro, *m.* thesaurus, lexicon.
tesela, *f.* tessera, mosaic tile.
teselado, da, *a.* tesselated. —*m.* tesselated pavement.
Teseo, *m.* (myth.) Theseus, king of Athens who slayed the Minotaur.
tésera, *f.* tessera (ticket voucher, etc. in ancient Rome).
tesis, (*pl.* **tesis**), *f.* thesis; theory, idea; proposition; dissertation; **t. doctoral,** doctoral thesis.
tesitura, *f.* 1. (mus.) tessitura. 2. attitude, frame of mind, mood.
teso, sa, *irr. past part. of* **tesar.** —*a.* taut, tight. —*m.* 1. hilltop. 2. bulge (on a smooth surface).
tesón, *m.* tenacity, perseverance, doggedness, firmness; fury.
tesonería, *f.* obstinacy, persistence, stubbornness.
tesonero, ra, *a.* tenacious, persevering, persistent, dogged.
tesorería, *f.* treasury, exchequer; treasurer's office; treasurership, post of treasurer.
tesorero, ra, *m., f.* treasurer. —*m.* (ecc.) canon who keeps the jewels and relics of a cathedral.
tesoro, *m.* 1. treasure; (fig.) treasure. 2. national or public funds; treasury, exchequer. 3. thesaurus.
tespíades, *f.* (*pl.*) (poet.) the Muses.
Tespis, *m.* (hist., lit.) Thespis, Greek poet, originator of Greek tragedy.
testa, *f.* 1. head (of man or animal). 2. face, front. 3. (coll.) brains, wisdom. 4. (bot., zool.) testa. — **t. coronada,** sovereign, crowned head; **t. de ferro, testaferro,** figurehead, straw man, front.
testáceo, a, *a., m.* (zool.) testacean, (*pl.*) Testacea.
testación, *f.* erasion, cancellation; obliteration.
testada, *f.* blow with the head.
testado, da, *a.* (law) testate.
testador, ra, *m.* (law) testator. —*f.* (law) testatrix.
testadura, *f.* erasion, cancellation; obliteration.
testaferro, *m.* figurehead, straw man, front.
testamentaría, *f.* (law) 1. testamentary execution, testate proceedings. 2. estate (of deceased). 3. meeting of executors (of a will). 4. testamentary documents. 5. legal proceedings for the partition of an inheritance.
testamentario, ria, *a.* (law) testamentary. —*m.* executor. —*f.* executrix.
testamento, *m.* will, testament; **Antiguo,** or Viejo T., (Bib.) Old Testament; **Nuevo T.,** (Bib.) New Testament; **t. abierto,** (law) nuncupative will; **t. cerrado,** (law) sealed will; **t. ológrafo,** (law) holographic will.
testar, *i.v.* to make a will or testament. —*tr.v.* to erase, cancel, obliterate.
testarada, *f.* 1. blow with the head. 2. obstinacy, stubborness.
testarazo, *m.* blow with the head, butt.
testarrón, na, *a.* (coll.) stubborn, pigheaded, bullheaded. —*m., f.* stubborn or pigheaded person.
testarronería, *f.* (coll.) pigheadedness, stubbornness.
testarudez, *f.* obstinacy, stubbornness.
testarudo, da, *a.* obstinate, stubborn. —*m., f.* stubborn or hardheaded person.
teste, *m.* 1. (anat.) testis, testicle. 2. **(Arg.)** corn or wart (on the fingers).
testera, *f.* 1. face, front, fore part. 2. front-facing seat (in a carriage). 3. forehead (of an animal). 4. crownpiece (of harness). 5. (metal.) wall (of a smelting furnace).
testerada, *f.* blow with the head.
testerillo, lla, *a.* (Arg.) starred, starmarked, having a blaze on the forehead (said of a horse).
testero, *m.* 1. front, face, forepart. 2. fireback, back plate (of a fireplace). 3. (min.) ore rock showing two faces.
testicular, *a.* testicular.
testículo, *m.* (anat.) testicle.
testificación, *f.* testification, attestation.
testifical, *a.* witness (as *a.*).
testificante, *a.* testifying, attesting.
testificar, (*ref. 50*) *tr.v.,* to testify; to witness. —*i.v.* to testify.
testificata, *f.* (law) affidavit.
testificativo, va, *a.* attesting.
testifique, testifiqué, *ref.* **testificar.**

testigo, *m., f.* witness; attestor; **t. abonado,** (law) competent witness; **t. de cargo,** (law) witness for the prosecution; **t. de conocimiento,** (law) attestor of identity (before a notary); **t. de descargo,** (law) witness for the defense; **t. de Jehová,** (rel.) Jehovah's Witness; **t. ocular,** (law) eyewitness; **t. de oídas,** hearsay witness; **t. idoneo,** (law) competent witness; **t. instrumental,** (law) attesting witness; **t. mayor de toda excepción,** (law) fully competent witness. —*m.* 1. witness, testimony, evidence, proof. 2. mound of earth (left along excavations to show amount of earth extracted). 3. testicle. 4. (*pl.*) boundary stones.

testimonial, *a.* testimonial. —*f.* 1. (*pl.*) (ecc.) testimonial. 2. (*pl.*) documentary proof.

testimoniar, *tr.v.* to testify, attest, bear witness to.

testimoniero, ra, *a.* 1. bearing false witness. 2. hypocritical, false. —*m., f.* 1. perjurer, false witness. 2. hypocrite.

testimonio, *m.* testimony; proof, evidence; affidavit; **falso t.,** (law) perjury.

testimoñero, ra *a., m., f., var of* **testimoniero.**

testón, *m.* (numis.) teston, testoon (ancient coin with the image of a head on one side).

testosterona, *f.* (biochem.) testosterone.

testudíneo, a, *a.* testudinal, pertaining to or like a tortoise.

testudo, *m.* (hist., mil.) testudo (**Roman** protective covering and battle tactic).

testuz, (*pl.* **testuces**), **testuzo,** *m.* forehead (of certain animals); nape (of other animals).

tesura, *f., var. of* **tiesura.**

teta, *f.* 1. nipple, teat, tit; breast; **udder.** 2. mound, hummock, knoll. — **dar la t. a,** to nurse, to suckle; **niño de t.,** babe-in-arms; **quitar la t.,** (coll.) to wean; **t. de vaca,** (cul.) conical meringue; (bot.) cut-leaved viper's grass.

tetania, *f.* (med.) tetany.

tetanice *ref.* **tetanizar.**

tetánico, ca, *a.* (med.) titanic.

tetanismo, *m.* (med.) tetanism.

tetanizar, (*ref. 53*) *tr.v.* to tetanize.

tétano, tétanos, *m.* (med.) tetanus, lockjaw.

tetar, *tr.v.* to suckle, give the breast to.

tetartoédrico, ca, *a.* (cryst.) tetartohedral.

tetartoedro, *m.* (cryst.) tetartohedron.

tetera, *f.* 1. teapot, teakettle, kettle. 2. (Cuba, Mex., P. Rico) nipple (of a baby's bottle).

tetero, *m.* (Col.) baby's bottle, nursing bottle.

tetigonia, *f.* (ento.) grouse locust.

tetilla, *f. dim. of* **teta,** nipple (in males); nipple (of a nursing bottle).

Tetis, *f.* (myth.) Thetis, mother of Achilles.

tetón, *m.* stub of a pruned branch (remaining on trunk).

tetona, *a.* (coll.) big-breasted, big-nippled.

tetrabásico, ca, *a.* (chem.) tetrabasic.

tetraborato, *m.* (chem.) tetraborate.

tetrabromuro, *m.* (chem.) tetrabromide.

tetraciclina, *f.* (pharm.) tetracycline.

tetrácido, a, *a.* (chem.) tetracid.

tetracloruro, *m.* (chem.) tetrachloride; **t. de carbono,** carbon tetrachloride.

tetracordio, *m.* (mus.) tetrachord, perfect fourth; the four scale-tones of a perfect fourth.

tetradimita, *f.* (min.) tetradymite.

tetradínamo, ma, *a.* (bot.) tetradynamous.

tetraédrico, ca, *a.* (geom.) tetrahedral.

tetraedrita, *f.* (min.) tetrahedrite.

tetraedro, *m.* (geom.) tetrahedron.

tetraetilato, *m.* (chem.) tetraethyl; **t. de plomo,** tetraethyl lead.

tetragonal, *a.* (geom.) tetragonal.

tetrágono, *m.* (geom.) tetragon.

tetragrama, *m.* (mus.) four-line staff (used in Gregorian chant).

tetragrámaton, *m.* tetragram, word of four letters.

tetralogía, *f.* (theat., mus.) tetralogy.

tetrámero, ra, *a.* (bot., zool.) tetramerous. —*m.* (*pl.*) (zool.) Tetramera.

tetramotor, *a.* four-engined. —*m.* four-engined plane.

tetrandro, a, *a.* (bot.) tetrandrous.

tetrapétalo, la, *a.* (bot.) tetrapetalous.

tetraploide, *a.* (biol.) tetraploid.

tetráptero, a, *a.* (biol.) tetrapterous.

tetrarca, *m.* (hist.) tetrarch.

tetrarquía, *f.* (hist.) tetrarchy.

tetrasílabo, ba, *a.* tetrasyllabic. —*m.* tetrasyllable.

tetraspora, *f.* (bot.) tetraspore.

tetrástico, ca, *a* .1 (poet.) terastich, tetrastichic. 2. (bot.) tetrastichous.

tetratómico, ca, *a.* (chem.) tetratomic.

tetravalencia, *f.* (chem.) tetravalence, tetravalency.

tetravalente, *a.* (chem.) tetravalent.

tétrico, ca, *a.* somber, gloomy, sullen, grave.

tetrilo, *m.* (chem.) tetryl.

tetrodo, *m.* (elec.) tetrode.

tetuda, *a.* large-breasted, big-nippled.

teucrio, *a.* (bot.) germander.

teucro, cra, *a., m., f.* Teucrian, Trojan.

teurgia, *f.* theurgy, an ancient system of magic practices.

teúrgico, ca, *a.* theurgical.

teúrgo, *m.* theurgist.

teutón, na, *a., m., f.* Teuton.

teutónico, ca, *a.* Teutonic. —*m.* Teutonic (language).

textil, *a., m.* textile.

texto, *m.* 1. text. 2. (print.) large primer type. — **libro de t.,** textbook.

textorio, ria, *a.* textile, weaving.

textual, *a.* textual.

textualista, *m.* textualist.

textualmente, *adv.* textually.

textura, *f.* 1. (tex.) texture, nap. 2. weaving. 3. (fig.) texture, structure.

teyolote, *m.* (Mex.) rubble (used in building).

teyú, (*pl.* **teyúes**), *m.* (S. Amer., zool.) iguana.

tez, *f.* complexion (of the face).

tezado, da, *a.* swarthy, dark.

tezontle, *m.* (Mex.) volcanic rock.

Th *sym. of* **torio,** thorium (Th).

Thor, *m.* (myth.) Thor, god of war (in Scandinavian myth.).

ti, *pers. pron.* (used only as object of a preposition), thee, thyself, you, yourself, e.g. *lo traje para ti,* I brought it for you, *lo hiciste por ti, no por mí,* you did it for yourself, not for me.

tía, *f.* 1. aunt. 2. lady (title of respect for a married or elderly woman). 3. (coll.) rustic, coarse woman. 4. (coll.) prostitute. — **cuéntaselo a tu t.,** (coll.) tell it to the marines; **no hay tu t.,** (coll.) it's no use, nothing doing; **quedar para t.,** (coll.) to be left an old maid; **t. abuela,** grandaunt, great-aunt; **t. segunda,** first cousin once removed (cousin to one's parents).

Ti *sym. of* **titanio,** titanium (Ti).

tiaca, *f.* (Chile, bot.) cunoniaceous tree of the genus Weinmannia (Weinmannia paniculata).

tialina, *f.* (biochem.) ptyalin.

tialismo, *m.* (physiol.) ptyalism.

tiamina, *f.* (biochem.) thiamine.

tiánguez, tianguis, *m.* (Mex.) market place.

tiara, *f.* tiara (the Pope's triple crown; ancient Persian headdress).

tiatina, *f.* (Chile, bot.) wild oat (Avena hirsuta).

tiazol, *m.* (chem.) thiazole.

tíbar, *m.* **oro de t.,** pure gold.

tibe, *m.* (Col., min.) corundum; (Cuba) slate used for sharpening instruments.

Tíber, *m.* Tiber (river).

tiberino, na, *a.* Tiberine (of or pertaining to the river Tiber).

tiberio, *m.* (coll.) hullaballoo, racket, uproar, turmoil.

Tiberio, *m.* (hist.) Tiberius, Roman emperor.

Tibet, (geog.) **El T.,** Tibet.

tibetano, na, *a., m., f.* Tibetan. —*m.* Tibetan (language).

tibia, *f.* (anat.) tibia (shinbone).

tibial, *a.* tibial.

tibiamente, *adv.* 1. lukewarmly. 2. indifferently.

tibiera, *f.* (Ven., coll.) nuisance, bother.

tibieza, *f.* 1. lukewarmness, tepidity. 2. indifference, coolness.

tibio, bia, *a.* 1. lukewarm, tepid. 2. (fig.) cool, indifferent (e.g. reception, greeting). 3. (Col., Ven., Peru) annoyed, angry.

tibiotarsiano, na, *a.* (anat.) tibiotarsal.

tibisí, *m.* (Cuba, bot.) wild reed grass.

tibor, *m.* 1. ornamented china or earthenware vase. 2. (Cuba) chamber pot. 3. (Mex.) cup, small bowl (made from a calabash gourd).

tiborna, *f.* (Sp., reg.) piece of bread soaked in oil.

Tibulo, *m.* (lit.) Tibullus, Latin poet.

tiburón, *m.* (ichth.) shark; **t. tigre,** (ichth.) tiger shark.

tic, (*pl.* **tics**), *m.* tic, nervous twitch.

tichela, *f.* (Bol.) tapping cup (to collect latex flowing from rubber tree).

ticholo, *m.* (Arg.) guava paste; small tile or brick.

tictac, *m.* tick, tick-tock; ticking (of a watch or clock).

tiemannita, *f.* (min.) tiemannite.

tiemble, tiemblo, *ref.* **temblar.**

tiemblo, *m.* (bot.) aspen, trembling poplar.

tiempo, *m.* 1. time (period during which something lasts; certain period of time), e.g. *él vivió por mucho t. en la selva,* he lived for a long time in the jungle, *después de un t. se fue,* after a time he left. 2. time, age, era. 3. time, moment, occasion. 4. time, season, e.g. *t. de lluvia,* rainy season. 5. an age, ages, a long time, e.g. *hace t. que no te veo,* it's ages or an age since I saw you. 6. weather, weather conditions. 7. (gram.) tense. 8. (mar.) storm, bad weather. 9. (mus.) time, e.g. *t. de vals,* waltz time. 10. (mec.) stroke, cycle, e.g. *motor de dos tiempos,* two-stroke engine. 11. (sport.) half, e.g. *primer t.,* first half; *segundo t.,* second half; **medio t.,** half. — **abrir, alzar,** or **levantar el t.,** to clear, clear up (weather); **al mal t. buena cara,** face adversity with courage, keep a stiff upper lip; **andando el t.,** in the course of time, as time goes by, in time; **a su t.,** in due time, at the proper time, at the right time, opportunely; **a t.,** in time, opportunely; **a tiempos,** at times, sometimes; once in a while, from time to time; **a un t.,** simultaneously, at the same time; **cada cosa en su t.,** there's a time and place for everything; **cargarse el t.,** to become overcast; **con t.,** in advance; in time, opportunely; **darse buen t.,** to have a good time; **dar t. al t.,** to take things easy, do things in a leisurely manner; **dejar al t.,** to leave it to time (to solve, heal, etc.); **de t. en t.,** from time to time, occasionally; **de un t. a esta parte,** for some time now; **engañar el t.,** to while away the time, kill time; **el t. es oro,** time is money; **en otros tiempos,** in other times, formerly; **en los buenos tiempos,** in the good old times; **en**

los tiempos que corren, these days; **en t. de Maricastaña,** or **del Rey Perico,** (coll.) in the times of Methuselah, in bygone days; **ganar t.,** to save time; **gastar el t.,** to waste time; **hacer buen** or **mal t.,** to be fair or foul weather; **hacer t.,** to mark time, pass the time away, kill time (while waiting); **medio t.,** half (in football); interval; time between seasons; **pasar el t.,** to pass the time; **perder t.** or **el t.,** to waste time; **t. atrás,** some time ago; **t. compartido,** time-sharing; **t. complementario** or **suplementario,** (sport.) overtime; **t. compuesto,** (gram.) compound tense; **t. de compresión,** (engin.) compression stroke; **t. de fortuna,** bad weather, stormy weather; **t. de pasión,** (ecc.) Passion Week; **t. de subida,** (aer.) time of climb; **t. futuro,** (gram.) future tense; **t. grueso,** hazy weather; **t. ha,** a long time ago; **t. inmemorial,** time immemorial; **t. medio,** (astron.) mean time; **t. muerto,** (sport.) time out; **t. pascual,** (ecc.) Eastertide, Eastertime (from Easter to Trinity Sunday); **t. presente,** (gram.) present tense; **t. pretérito,** (gram.) past tense; **t. simple,** (gram.) simple tense; **t. verdadero,** (astron.) true time, solar or apparent time; **tiempos heroicos,** heroic age, heroic times; **tomar t.,** to take time; **tomarse t.,** to take one's time; **y si no, al t.,** time will show that I am right.

tienda, *f.* 1. shop, store. 2. tent. 3. awning; tilt, canvas covering (over a cart.). 4. (med.) tentormin. — **abrir t.,** to set up shop; **alzar** or **levantar t.,** to close up shop; **armar** or **levantar una t.,** to pitch a tent; **batir tiendas,** to strike camp; **desarmar una t.,** to strike a tent, take down a tent; **ir de tiendas,** to go shopping; **t. de abarrotes,** general store; **t. de antigüedades,** antique shop; **t. de campaña,** army tent; **t. de departamentos,** (Mex.) department store; **t. de deportes,** sporting goods store; **t. de modas,** ladies' dress shop, boutique; **t. de muebles,** furniture store; **t. de oxígeno,** (med.) oxygen tent; **t. de regalos,** gift shop; **t. de ultramarinos,** grocery store.

tienta, *f.* 1. (taur.) testing spirit of young bulls. 2. shrewdness, sagacity, cleverness. 3. (bldg.) sounding rod. 4. (surg.) probe. — **andar a tientas,** to grope in the dark; **a tientas,** feeling one's way, gropingly; uncertainly.

tientaguja, *f.* (bldg.) sounding rod (for testing the land prior to building on it).

tientaparedes, (*pl.* **tientaparedes**), *m., f.* (fig.) groper, one who gropes in the dark.

tiente, tiento, *ref.* **tentar.**

tiento, *m.* 1. caution, care. 2. touch, touching, feeling. 3. blindman's walking stick. 4. (ropewalker's) balancing pole. 5. steady hand. 6. blow, hit. 7. (coll.) swig, drink. 8. (mus.) warm-up, preliminary flourish (to test an instrument). 9. (p.) maulstick. 10. (zool.) tentacle. 11. (Arg., Chile) thin strip of leather. 12. (Arg.) snack, bite. 13. (*pl.*) (mus.) one of the flamenco rhythms. — **a t.,** gropingly; by tact; uncertainly; **con t.,** cautiously; **dar un t. a,** (coll.) to take a swig or drink from; (coll.) to try, test; **perder el t.,** to lose the touch or knack; **por el t.,** by touch, by feeling; **tomar el t. a,** (coll.) to feel, examine.

tiernamente, *adv.* tenderly, affectionately.

tiernecito, ta, ico, ca, illo, lla, *a. dim. of* **tierno,** young, tender, soft.

tierno, na, *a.* 1. affectionate, tender. 2. soft, delicate; sensitive. 3. tender, young. 4. tender, e.g. *carne tierna,* tender meat. 5. tearful. 6. (Chile, Ecuad.) green, unripe (vegetables).

tierra, *f.* 1. earth (planet). 2. land (as opposed to sea); ground, earth (as opposed to air). 3. earth, soil, e.g. *un puñado de t.,* a fistful of earth or soil; dirt, dust. 4. native land, country or soil. 5. land (farm land; real estate). 6. land, territory, region. 7. (elec.) earth, ground. — **besar la t.,** to fall flat on the ground; **caer a t.,** to crash (a plane); to fall to earth; **dar en t. con,** to ruin, wreck; to knock down; to bring down; **de la t.,** of the country or region, native, local (produce); **echar por t.,** to wreck, ruin, destroy; **echar t. a,** to hush up, bury (a matter); **en t.,** on land; **mover cielo y t.,** to move heaven and earth; **por estas tierras,** around here, in these parts; **quedarse en t.,** to be left or get left behind (by a vehicle); **t. abrasada,** (mil.) scorched earth; **t. adentro,** inland; **t. amarilla,** (min.) yellow earth, ocher; **t. blanca,** (min.) white earth; **t. de almáciga,** foster earth; **t. de batán,** fuller's earth; **t. de brezo,** heath humus mixed with sand; **t. de Cassel** or **Colonia,** (min.) Cologne or Cassel earth; **t. de cultivo** or **labor,** farm land, cultivated land; **T. del Fuego,** Tierra del Fuego; **t. del sol de medianoche,** Land of the Midnight Sun, Norway; **t. del sol naciente,** Land of the Rising Sun, Japan; **t. de miga,** clayey soil; **t. de nadie,** no man's land; **t. de pan llevar,** cereal-growing land, wheat land; **T. de Promisión,** (Bib.) Promised Land; **t. de promisión,** (fig.) promised land; **t. de Segovia,** white earth; **t. de Siena,** (min.) sienna; **t. de sombra,** umber; **t. de Venecia,** yellow ocher; **t. firme,** terra firma; firm or solid ground (for building); **t. natal,** native land; **t. negra,** humus; **t. perfecta,** (elec., rad.) dead ground; **t. rara,** (chem.) rare earth; **T. Santa,** Holy Land (Palestine); **tierras baldías,** public domain, public land; **t. vegetal,** vegetable mold, humus; **t. verde,** (min.) green earth; glauconite; **tomar t.** (mar.) to make port, arrive (a vessel); to land (airplane); to disembark; to acquire practice, become proficient; to get to know, get on a friendly footing (with a person); **venir** or **venirse a t.,** to crash (a plane); to fail (a project, etc.).

tiesamente, *adv.* stiffly; strongly, firmly.

tieso, sa, *a.* 1. stiff, rigid. 2. tight, taut. 3. strong, hardy, robust. 4. (fig.) courageous, plucky. 5. (fig.) stiff, starchy, aloof. 6. (fig.) stubborn, obstinate.

tieso, *adv.* hard, firmly, strongly.

tiesta, *f.* edge of headings (of barrels).

tiesto, *m.* 1. broken piece of earthenware, potsherd. 2. flowerpot. 3. (Chile) bowl, basin.

tiesura, *f.* 1. stiffness, rigidity. 2. (fig.) stiffness, starchiness.

tifáceo, a, *a.* (bot.) typhaceous. —*f.* typhaceous plant, (*pl.*) Typhaceae.

tífico, ca, *a.* (med.) typhous. —*m., f.* person suffering from typhus.

tiflitis, *f.* (med.) typhlitis.

tiflología, *f.* (med.) typhlology.

tiflosis, *f.* (med.) typhlosis.

tifo, *m.* (med.) typhus; **t. asiático,** Asiatic cholera, cholera morbus; **t. de América,** yellow fever; **t. de Oriente,** bubonic plague.

tifo, fa, *a.* (coll.) full, satiate.

tifogénico, ca, *a.* (med.) typhogenic.

tifógeno, na, *a.* (med.) typhogenic.

tifoideo, a, *a.* (med.) typhoid, typhoidal. —*f.* typhoid fever, typhoid.

tifón, *m.* typhoon, tropical cyclone; waterspout.

tifus, *m.* 1. (med.) typhus. 2. (coll.) spectators who hold passes or free tickets to a performance. — **t. abdominal,** (med.) typhoid fever; **t. exantemático,** (med.) typhus, jail, famine or spotted fever; **t. icteroides,** (med.) yellow fever.

tigmotaxis, *f.* (biol.) thigmotaxis.

tigmotropismo, *m.* (biol.) thigmotropism.

tigra, *f.* (zool.) tigress; (Amer.) female jaguar.

tigre, *m.* 1. (zool.) tiger. 2. (coll.) tiger (cruel, bloodthirsty person). 3. (Amer., zool.) jaguar. 4. (ornith.) tiger bittern.

tigresa, *f.* (gal.) tigress.

tigrillo, *m.* (zool.) wild cat.

tija, *f.* stem (of a key).

tijera, *f.* 1. scissors; shears (used also in *pl.*). 2. sawhorse, sawbuck. 3. sheepshearer. 4. drainage channel or ditch. 5. brace, strap (under body of coach). 6. (coll.) gossip, backbiter. 7. (sport.) scissors (hold in wrestling; jump in high jumping). 8. (ornith.) man-of-war bird, frigate bird. 9. (*pl.*) stringers, crossbeams (forming sides of cart). — **buena t.,** (dressm.) good cutter; (coll.) heavy eater; (coll.) backbiter, gossip; **cama de t.,** cot, folding bed; **silla de t.,** folding chair; **tijeras t. dentadas,** thinning scissors; **tijeras de podar,** pruning shears.

tijerada, *f., var. of* **tijeretada.**

tijeral, *m.* (Chile) roof frame, roof truss.

tijereta, *f.* 1. *dim. of* **tijera,** (*pl.*) small scissors or shears. 2. tendril (of vine). 3. (ento.) earwig. 4. (ornith.) scissor-tail; man-of-war bird, frigate bird.

tijeretada, *f.,* **tijeretazo,** *m.* cut, snip, nip (with a scissors).

tijeretear, *tr.v.* 1. to cut, clip, snip. 2. (coll.) to deal arbitrarily with (someone else's affairs).

tijereteo, *m.* clipping, snipping, cutting; clicking of scissors.

tijerilla, tijeruela, *f.* 1. *dim. of* **tijera,** small scissors. 2. tendril (of vine).

tijuil, *m.* (Hond., ornith.) cowbird (Molothrus pecoris).

tila, *f.* 1. (bot.) linden, basswood. 2. linden flower or blossom. 3. linden flower or blossom tea, tilleul.

tílburi, *m.* tilbury, cart, gig.

tildar, *tr.v.* 1. to put a tilde on. 2. to erase, cross out, strike out. 3. (fig.) to brand, criticize, stigmatize. — **t. de,** to brand as.

tilde, *m., f.* 1. tilde; accent mark. 2. criticism, censure. — **poner t.,** to criticize, censure. —*f.* trifle, jot, bit.

tildón, *m.* crossing-out line, stroke.

tilia, *f.* (bot.) linden, basswood.

tiliáceo, a, *a.* (bot.) tiliaceous. —*f.* (*pl.*) (bot.) Tiliaceae.

tilichero, *m.* (C. Amer.) peddler, hawker.

tiliches, *m.* (C. Amer., Mex.) odds and ends, bits and pieces, trinkets.

tilico, ca, *a.* (coll.) 1. (Bol., Mex.) weak, feeble, thin. 2. (Bol., Mex.) stupid, timid, cowardly.

tilín, *m.* tinkle, ringing (of small bell); **en un t.,** in a jiffy, in a twinkling; (Col., Chile, Ven., coll.) in imminent danger; **hacer t.,** (coll.) to appeal, be appealing; **tener t.,** (coll.)to be pleasant or attractive, have appeal.

tilinches, *m. pl.* (Mex.) rags, tatters.

tilingo, ga, *a.* (S. Amer.) empty-headed, foolish, silly.

tilita, *f.* (geol.) tillite.

tilma, *f.* (Mex.) blanket used as a cloak.

tilo, *m.* 1. (bot.) linden, basswood. 2. (Col.) maize blossom.

tilla, *f.* (mar.) part deck (of a small ship).

tillado, *m.* boarding, planking, floor boarding.

tillar, *tr.v.* to plank, board.

timador, ra, *m., f.* swindler, cheater.

tímalo, *m.* (ichth.) grayling.

timar, *tr.v.* to swindle, cheat, gyp. —*r.v.* to wink at each other, make eyes at one another; **timarse con,** to make eyes at, flirt with.

timba, *f.* 1. (coll.) gambling; gambling house, gambling den. 2. (Phil. I.) well bucket. 3. (Guat., Hond., Mex.) belly, stomach. 4. (Cuba, coll.) guava paste.

timbal, *m.* 1. kettledrum; timbrel, tabor. 2. (cul.) timbale.
timbalero, *m.* kettledrummer.
timbiriche, *m.* 1. (Cuba) small, makeshift store or saloon. 2. (Mex., bot.) pinguin.
timbirimba, *f.* (coll.) gambling game; gambling house or den.
timbó, *m.* (Arg., Par., bot.) timbo (Enterolobium timbouva).
timbrado, da, *past part. of* **timbrar.** *—a.* 1. stamped, bearing stamps. 2. (mus.) having a good timbre (voice).
timbrador, *m.* 1. stamper, person who puts a stamp on. 2. stamp, stamping machine.
timbrar, *tr.v.* 1. to timbre, put the timbre or crest on (a coat of arms). 2. to stamp, put a seal or stamp on.
timbrazo, *m.* loud ring (of a doorbell, telephone, etc.).
timbre, *m.* 1. stamp seal; tax stamp. 2. tax stamp revenue. 3. doorbell; buzzer. 4. timbre (quality of tone of voice, instrument, etc.). 5. (her.) timbre, crest. 6. glorious deed; **t. de agua,** watermark.
timeleáceo, a, *a.* (bot.) thymelacaceous. *—f.* (bot.) (*pl.*) Thymelaeaceae.
timiama, *f.* aromatic incense (used in Jewish religious services).
tímico, ca, *a.* (chem.) thymic.
tímidamente, *adv.* timidly; shyly.
timidez, *f.* timidness, timidity; shyness, bashfulness.
tímido, da, *a.* timid; shy, bashful.
timo, *m.* 1. (coll.) swindle, gypping. 2. (coll.) practical joke. — **dar un t.,** to swindle, gyp; to deceive.
timo, *m.* 1. (anat.) thymus. 2. (ichth.) grayling.
timocracia, *f.* (pol.) timocracy, government influenced by the wealthy classes.
timocrático, ca, *a.* (pol.) timocratic.
timol, *m.* (chem.) thymol.
timón, *m.* 1. rudder, control stick, joy stick (of airplane); (Amer.) steering wheel (of car); rudder, helm (of boat); plow beam. 2. whippletree (of carriage). 3. rocket stick. 4. (fig.) helm, rudder. — **manejar el t.,** to be at the wheel or helm, be in command; **t. de dirreción,** (aer.) rudder; **t. de profundidad,** (aer.) elevator; **t. mecánico,** (mar.) gyropilot, mechanical steering device.
timonear, *tr.v., i.v.* (mar.) to steer.
timonel, *m.* (mar.) helmsman, steersman; **t. automático,** pilot aid.
timonera, *a.* tail (feather). *—f.* 1. rectrix, tail feather. 2. (mar.) wheelhouse, pilothouse.
timonero, *a.* beam (plow). *—m.* helmsman, pilot steersman.
timonucleico, ca, *a.* (chem.) thymonucleic.
timorato, ta, *a.* 1. God-fearing. 2. timid, chickenhearted, cowardly.
timpa, *f.* (metal.) tymp.
timpanice, *ref.* **timpanizarse.**
timpánico, ca, *a.* (anat., med.) tympanic.
timpanillo, *m.* (print.) inner tympan.
timpanítico, ca, *a.* (med.) tympanitic. *—m., f.* (med.) person suffering from tympanites.
timpanitis, *f.* (med.) tympanitis (inflammation of middle ear); (med.) tympanites (distention of abdomen caused by gases).
timpanizarse, (*ref. 53*) *r.v.* (med.) to become distended with gases.
tímpano, *m.* 1. (mus.) kettledrum, (*pl.*) timpani, kettledrums. 2. (mus.) harmonica (glockenspiel with glass strips). 3. (archit.) tympanum, tympan. 4. (print.) tympan. 5. (anat.) tympanum, eardrum. 6. head, top (of barrel).
tina, *f.* bath, bathtub; large earthenware jar; tub, vat.
tinaco, *m.* 1. small wooden tub; (Amer.) earthenware jar. 2. juice oozing from pile of olives.
tinada, *f.* 1. pile of firewood. 2. cattle shed.
tinado, tinador, *m.* cattle shed.
tinaja, *f.* 1. large earthen jar. 2. (Phil. I.) liquid measure of approximately 12 2/3 gallon.
tinajero, *m.* maker or seller of earthenware jars; stand for earthenware jars.
tinajón, *m. aug. of* **tinaja,** large earthenware jar.
tinajuela, *f. dim. of* **tinaja,** small earthenware jar.
tinamú, *m.* (ornith.) tinamou.
tinapá, *m.* (Phil. I.) dry smoked fish.
tinca, *f.* 1. (Bol.) surprise Dutch party. 2. (Chile, Peru) hunch, intuitive idea.
tíncal, *m.* tincal, crude borax.
tincar, (*ref. 50*) *tr.v.* (Chile, Arg.) to fillip, flip, flick (with the nails or fingertip). *—i.v.* (Chile, Peru) **tincarle a uno que,** to have a hunch that, e.g. *me tinca que,* I have a hunch that.
tincazo, *m.* (Arg., Ecuad.) fillip, flip (with the nails or fingertips).
tinción, *f.* dyeing, tinting; dye, tint.
tindalización, *f.* (phys.) Tyndall effect.
Tíndaro, *m.* (myth.) Tyndareus, king of Sparta.
tindío, *m.* (Peru, ornith.) tern.
tineido, *m.* (zool.) tineid.
tinelero, ra, *m., f.* (arch.) keeper of the servants' dining room.
tinelo, *m.* (arch.) servants' dining room.
tineta, *f. dim. of* **tina,** small tub or vat.
tingazo, *m.* (Ecuad.) fillip, flick, flip (with the nails or fingertips).
tinge, *m.* (ornith.) eagle owl.
tingladillo, *m.* (mar.) clinker work.
tinglado, *m.* 1. shed. 2. temporary platform or floor. 3. trick, ruse, device. 4. (Cuba) tilted board for draining sugarcane juice.
tingle, *f.* glazier's tool for leading windows.
tinicla, *f.* hauberk, a type of armor.
tinieblas, *f.* (*pl.*) darkness. 2. (fig.) darkness, ignorance. 3. (ecc.) Tenebrae.
tinillo, *m.* reservoir (of a wine press for collecting grape juice).
tino, *m.* 1. common sense; good judgment. 2. knack, ability. 3. good aim. — **a buen t.,** roughly, by a rough estimate; **a t.,** gropingly; **sin t.,** immoderately, without moderation; **sacar de t.,** to exasperate, drive mad.
tino, *m.* 1. dyeing vat; tank. 2. wine press. 3. (bot.) laurustine.
tinola, *f.* (Phil. I.) chicken and vegetable soup.
tinta, *f.* 1. (writing) ink; (zool.) ink (of squid). 2. tint, dye; tinting, dyeing. 3. (p.) (*pl.*) hues, colors (mixed for painting). — **a medias tintas,** vague, indefinite, e.g. *no me gustan las respuestas a medias tintas,* I don't like vague replies; **media t.,** (p.) halftone; **saber de buena t.,** to have on good authority; **sudar t.,** to sweat blood; **t. china,** India ink; **t. comunicativa,** hectographic ink; **t. de imprenta, printer's ink; t. indeleble,** indelible ink; **t. simpática,** sympathetic or invisible ink.
tintar, *tr.v.* to dye, tint, e.g. *t. de azul,* to dye blue.
tinte, *m.* 1. dyeing, tinting. 2. hue, tint, color. 3. dyer's shop. 4. (fig.) false appearance (given to things) 5. (Sp.) dry cleaner's.
tinterazo, *m.* blow given with an inkwell or inkpot.
tinterillada, *f.* (Amer.) chicanery, trickery; pettifogging.
tinterillo, *m.* 1. (derog.) petty clerk, scrivener. 2. (Amer.) shyster, pettifogger.
tintero, *m.* 1. inkpot, inkwell. 2. (print.) ink fountain. 3. age mark (on horse's teeth). — **quedársele a uno en el t.,** (coll.) to forget, omit.
tintilla, *f.* sweet red wine (made in Rota, Spain).
tintillo, *a.* **vino tintillo,** light red wine, rosé.
tintín, *m.* clink, chink (of glasses); jingling, ting-a-ling (of bell).
tintinar, tintinear, *i.v.* to jingle, ting-a-ling (a bell); clink, chink (glasses); to patter (said of rain).
tintineo, *m.* chinking, clinking (of glasses); jingling, ting-a-ling (of bell); patter (of rain).
tintirintín, *m.* shrill sound of a trumpet, clarion, bugle, etc.
tinto, ta, *a.* 1. dyed, colored, tinted. 2. red (wine); (C. Rica, Hond.) dark-red; (Col.) black (coffee). *—m.* red wine.
tintóreo, a, *a.* tinctorial, dyeing.
tintorera, *f.* 1. female dyer; dyer's wife. 2. (Amer., ichth.) female shark.
tintorería, *f.* 1. dyeing, dyeing trade. 2. dyeing and dry cleaning establishment.
tintorero, *m.* dyer, clothes cleaner.
tintorro, *m.* (coll.) red wine.
tintura, *f.* 1. tincture. 2. tint, dye. 3. rouge, cosmetic. 4. smattering, superficial knowledge. — **t. de yodo,** (pharm.) tincture of iodine.
tinturar, *tr.v.* 1. to tincture, tinge, tint, dye. 2. to teach superficially.
tiña, *f.* 1. bee, beetle. 2. (med.) tinea, scald head, scalp ringworm. 3. (coll.) niggardliness, stinginess. — **t. mucosa,** eczema.
tiña, tiñendo, tiñera, tiñere, *ref.* **teñir.**
tiñería, *f.* (coll.) stinginess, niggardliness, meanness.
tiñese, tiño, *ref.* **teñir.**
tiñoso, sa, *a.* 1. scabby. 2. niggardly, mean, stingy.
tiñuela, *f.* 1. (bot.) dodder. 2. (zool.) shipworm.
tío, *m.* 1. uncle, (*pl.*) uncle and aunt. 2. sir (title of respect for an elderly man). 3. (coll.) guy, fellow. — **el t. Sam,** Uncle Sam; **t. abuelo,** grand uncle, great uncle; **t. segundo,** first cousin once removed (cousin to one's parents).
tioacético, ca, *a.* (chem.) thioacetic.
tioácido, *m.* (chem.) thioacid.
tioarseniato, *m.* (chem.) thioarsenate, thioarseniate.
tioarsenito, *m.* (chem.) thioarsenite.
tiocarbamida, *f.* (chem.) thiocarbamide, thiocarbamid.
tiocianato, *m.* (chem.) thiocyanate.
tiociánico, ca, *a.* (chem.) thiocyanic.
tiofeno, *m.* (chem.) thiophene.
tiofosfórico, ca, *a.* (chem.) thiophosphoric.
tionato, *m.* (chem.) thionate.
tiónico, ca, *a.* (chem.) thionic.
tionilo, *m.* (chem.) thionyl.
tionina, *f.* (chem.) thionine.
tiorba, *f.* (mus.) theorbo, large lute.
Tío Sam, *m.* Uncle Sam.
tiosinamina, *f.* (chem.) thiosinamine.
tiosulfato, *m.* (chem.) thiosulfate; **t. de sodio,** (chem.) sodium hyposulfite, sodium thiosulfate.
tiosulfúrico, ca, *a.* (chem.) thiosulfuric.
tiouracilo, *m.* (chem.) thiouracil.
tiourea, *f.* (chem.) thiourea.
tiovivo, *m.* merry-go-round, carrousel.
tipa, *f.* 1. (bot.) yellow-flowered hard wood tree (Tipuana tipu). 2. (Arg.) wicker basket. 3. (coll.) character, contemptible woman.
tiparraco, ca, *m., f.* (derog.) sap, simpleton.
tipejo, *m.* (derog.) ridiculous little fellow, twerp (sl.), squirt (coll.).
tipiadora, *f.* 1. typewriter. 2. stenographer, typist.
típico, ca, *a.* typical; characteristic.
tipismo, *m.* typical quality or condition.
tiple, *m., f.* 1. soprano, treble (voice), soprano singer. 2. tiple or treble guitar player. *—m.* 1. soprano, treble (voice). 2. treble guitar. 3. (mar.) single-piece mast.

tiplisonante, *a.* (coll.) treble-toned, soprano.
tipo, *m.* 1. type, kind, class, model, pattern, standard. 2. (coll.) guy, fellow, type, chap, character, customer, person. 3. (print.) type. 4. appearance, build. 5. (bot., zool.) phylum. — **jugarse el t.,** to risk one's neck; **t. de cambio,** exchange rate; **t. de descuento,** (com.) discount rate; **t. de interés,** (com.) rate of interest; **tener buen t.,** to be handsome, to cut a good figure.
tipografía, *f.* 1. typography. 2. typesetting plant or shop.
tipográfico, ca, *a.* typographic, typographical.
tipógrafo, *m.* typesetter, typographer.
tipolitografía, *f.* typolithography.
tipología, *f.* typology.
tipológico, ca, *a.* typological.
tipómetro, *m.* (print.) type gauge, type measure.
tipoy, *m.* (Arg., Par.) sleeveless tunic worn by Guaraní Indians.
típula, *f.* (ento.) crane fly.
tíquet, tiquete, *m.* ticket (theater, railway, etc.).
tiquín, *m.* (Phil. I.) punting pole.
tiquis miquis, tiquismiquis, *m.* (*pl.*) finickiness; exaggerated courtesies, affected words or manners.
tiquistiquis, *m.* (Phil. I., bot.) bitterwood.
tiquizque, *m.* (C. Rica, bot.) malanga, spoonflower, arrowleaved spoonflower.
tira, *f.* 1. narrow strip (of cloth, paper, etc.). 2. (mar.) fall. 3. (*pl.*) (Chile, derog.) rags, clothes. 4. (Amer.) (coll.) undercover cop, police plant; **la t.,** (Mex.) (sl., derog.) the fuzz. — **t. cómica,** comic strip (in newspaper); **t. fusible,** (elec.) strip fuse; **t. mosaica,** (chart.) strip mosaic.
tirabala, *m.* popgun (toy).
tirabeque, *m.* 1. (bot.) tender pea. 2. slingshot.
tirabotas, (*pl.* **tirabotas**), *m.* boot hook (to pull on boots).
tirabuzón, *m.* 1. corkscrew. 2. long curl, hanging curl. — **t. plano,** (aer.) flat spin.
tiracol, tiracuello, *m.* baldric, sword belt.
tiracuero, *m.* (derog.) shoemaker, cobbler.
tirada, *f.* 1. throw, cast. 2. distance, stretch. 3. length of time, period. 4. series, group (of things said or written at one time); cloth woven at one time. 5. (print.) printing; number of copies printed, edition; day's printing. — **de** or **en una t.,** at one stretch, at one time; **t. aparte,** (print.) offprint, reprint.
tiradera, *f.* 1. horn-tipped Indian arrow. 2. (Cuba) ridgeband (of a harness).
tiradero, *m.* hunter's post, shooting post.
tirado, da, *past part. of* **tirar.** —*a.* 1. given away, dirt-cheap, very cheap. 2. (mar.) long and low (said of a ship). —*m.* 1. wire drawing. 2. printing, presswork.
tirador, ra, *m., f.* 1. marksman, shot, e.g. *buen t.,* good marksman, *t. certero,* sure shot, sharpshooter. 2. thrower. 3. (sport.) fencer. 4. wire drawer (person). —*m.* 1. handle, knob (of door, drawer, etc.). 2. wire drawer (instrument). 3. bell-pull. 4. iron ruler (used by stonemason). 5. ruling pen (pen for drawing lines). 6. slingshot. 7. (Arg.) gaucho's wide belt. — **t. de oro,** gold-wire drawer; **t. de tiro al vuelo, al platillo** or **al pichón,** trapshooter.
tirafondo, *m.* 1. wood screw. 2. (surg.) bullet extractor; extracting forceps (for brobing the depth of a wound).
tiragomas, (*pl.* **tiragomas**), *m.* slingshot.
tiraje, *m.* print order; number of copies printed (of book, paper, etc.), edition.
tirajo, *m.* (coll.) strip, shred, tatter.
tiralíneas, (*pl.* **tiralíneas**), *m.* ruling pen.
tiramiento, *m.* 1. throwing. 2. shooting; firing. 3. drawing, stretching (of wire).
tiramina, *f.* (chem.) tyramine.
tiramira, *f.* 1. long, narrow range of mountains. 2. series, string (of things). 3. distance, stretch.
tiramollar, *i.v.* (mar.) to pull (a cable) slack, ease, slacken.
tirana, *f.* old Spanish folk song.
Tirana, *f.* Tirana, capital of Albania.
tiranamente, *adv.* tyrannically.
tiranía, *f.* tyranny.
tiránicamente, *adv.* tyrannically.
tiranice, tiranicé, *ref.* **tiranizar.**
tiranicida, *a.* tyrannicidal. —*m., f.* tyrannicide (person).
tiranicidio, *m.* tyrannicide (act of killing a tyrant).
tiránico, ca, *a.* tyrannic, tyrannical.
tiranización, *f.* tyrannizing.
tiranizadamente, *adv.* tyrannically.
tiranizar, (*ref. 53*) *tr.v.* to tyrannize.
tirano, na, *a.* tyrannical, tyrannous. —*m., f.* tyrant.
tirante, *a.* 1. tense, taut, tight; stretched, drawn, pulled. 2. (fig.) tense, strained (relations). —*m.* 1. trace (of harness). 2. (*pl.*) suspenders (U.S.), braces (G.B.). 3. (archit.) tie beam. 4. (mec.) tie rod, tension member.
tirantez, *f.* 1. tenseness, tightness, tautness. 2. strain, tenseness, tension (in relations). 3. distance in a straight line between the ends of something.
tiranuelo, la, *m., f. dim. of* **tirano,** no-account tyrant.
tirapié, *m.* shoemaker's stirrup.
tirar, *tr.v.* 1. to throw, fling, pitch, hurl, cast; to slam (the door). 2. to throw or cast away (e.g. clothes). 3. to squander, waste (money). 4. to fire (a shot, a round). 5. to draw (a line). 6. to give (pinch, bite, kick, etc.). 7. to knock down, tear down, demolish (building). 8. to draw (metal), make (metal) into wire strips. 9. (print.) to print; to reproduce. 10. (Cuba, Chile) to carry, transport. — **tirarla de,** to act the, boast of being, set oneself up as; **tirar la esponja,** to throw in the towel. —*i.v.* 1. to pull, draw, e.g. *tres caballos tiraban del coche,* three horses were pulling the coach. 2. to shoot, fire (at a target, etc.). 3. to draw, e.g. *esta chimenea tira bien,* this chimney draws well. 4. to incline, tend, e.g. *este periódico tira a la izquierda,* this newspaper leans to the left. 5. to approximate (hues), to border on, have a tinge of, e.g. *es un marrón que tira a rojo,* it is a reddish brown. 6. to attract, appeal, have appeal, e.g. *la vida académica le tira,* the academic life appeals to him. 7. to handle, e.g. *tira bien a la espada,* he handles a sword well. 8. to turn, veer (in a certain direction). 9. (coll.) to function, run, e.g. *este coche tira bien,* this car runs well. 10. to last, e.g. *este abrigo no tirará otro año,* this overcoat won't last another year. 11. to aspire (to), aim (at), e.g. *este profesor tira a ser director,* this teacher aims at being principal. — **a todo t.,** at the most; **ir tirando,** to get along, manage, cope, get by; **t. de,** to pull, draw; to pull at, pull on (e.g. one's sleeve, clothes); to pull out, draw (e.g. sword); to take out; **t. de** or **por largo,** (coll.) to spend lavishly; to exaggerate, estimate exaggeratedly; **tira y afloja,** (coll.) from one extreme to another, hot and cold. —*r.v.* 1. to throw, hurl, cast or fling oneself. 2. (Cuba) to go too far. 3. (Amer., vulg.) to have sexual intercourse with, lay (vulg.). — **tirarse un planchazo,** (coll.) to put one's foot in it.
tiratacos, (*pl.* **tiratacos**), *m.* popgun (toy).
tiratrón, *m.* (elec.) thyratron.
tira y afloja, *m.* hard bargaining, horse trading (fig.).
tirela, *f.* striped cloth.
tiricia, *f.* (coll.) jaundice.
tirilla, *f. dim. of* **tira,** neckband (of shirt).
tirio, ria, *a., m., f.* (hist.) Tyrian. — **tirios y troyanos,** opposing factions, Montagues and Capulets.
tirita, *f.* band-aid.
tiritaña, *f.* 1. thin silk cloth. 2. (coll.) trifle.
tiritar, *i.v.* to shiver; **t. de frío,** to shiver from cold.
tiritón, *m.* shiver, chill, shivering.
tiritona, *f.* (coll.) affected shivers.
tiro, *m.* 1. throw, cast. 2. shot, report; shooting, e.g. *el t. es un deporte muy popular,* shooting is a very popular sport; (mil.) gunnery; (mil.) fire, e.g. *t. rasante,* flat-trajectory or low-angle fire, *t. oblicuo,* oblique fire; (artil.) gun, piece of ordnance. 3. (sport.) kick, shot, hit, stroke, drive, throw. 4. (mil.) round, load, charge (of gun). 5. range (of gun). 6. range, shooting range. 7. team (of draft animals). 8. trace (of harness). 9. hoisting rope. 10. draft (of chimney). 11. length (of cloth); width (of dress, of trouser leg). 12. flight (of stairs). 13. injury, damage, hurt. 14. joke, prank, trick. 15. theft, robbery. 16. (coll.) dig, backbiting remark. 17. (min.) shaft; depth of shaft. 18. (*pl.*) sword belts. 19. (Peru, sl.) sexual intercourse. — **al t.,** (Amer.) immediately, right away; **a t.,** within reach or range; **a t. de bala,** within gun shot; **a t. de piedra de,** a stone's throw from, within a stone's throw of; **a t. hecho,** with absolute certainty; deliberately; **a t. de ballesta,** (coll.) at a distance, at a glance; **caballo de t.,** draft horse; **campo de t.,** shooting range or ground; **de a t.,** (Mex., Guat.) completely, absolutely; (Cuba) consequently, as a result; **de t. a t.,** single-shot (rifle); **de t. rápido,** rapidfire; **de tiros largos,** (coll.) in full dress or regalia, dressed to the nines, dressed to kill; **errar el t.,** to miss the mark; to fail, be unsuccessful; **ni a tiros,** (coll.) by no means, not for love or money; **poner el t. muy alto,** to aim high; **salir el t. por la culata,** (coll.) to misfire, backfire (plans, schemes); **t. al arco** or **con arco,** archery; **t. al blanco,** target shooting; **t. al plato,** trapshooting; **t. de contención,** (mil.) holding fire; **t. de defensa,** (mil.) defensive fire; **t. de flanco** or **flanqueante,** (mil.) flanking fire; **t. de gracia,** coup de grâce, last straw, finishing stroke; **t. rasante,** horizontal fire; **t. de rastrilleo,** (mil.) raking fire; **t. de rebote,** (mil.) ricochet fire; **t. directo,** (mil.) direct fire; **t. fijante,** (mil.) plunging fire; **t. indirecto,** (mil.) indirect fire; **t. par,** team of four horses; **t. ventilador,** (min.) air shaft.
tirocidina, *f.* (biochem.) tyrocidine.
tirocinio, *m.* apprenticeship.
tiroidectomía, *f.* (surg.) thyroidectomy.
tiroideo, a, *a.* (anat.) thyroid.
tiroides, *a.* (anat.) thyroid. —*m.* (anat.) thyroid (gland).
tiroidina, *f.* (med.) thyroid extract.
tiroiditis, *f.* (med.) thyroiditis.
Tirol, *m.* (geog.) Tyrol.
tirolés, sa, *a., m., f.* Tyrolese. —*m. peddler, hawker.*
tirón, *m.* tyro, novice.
tirón, *m.* 1. jerk, tug, pull. 2. tyro, tiro, novice. 3. mugger, purse snatcher. — **de un t.,** at a stretch, with one stroke, in one session.
tirona, *f.* fishing net, seine.
tironear, *i.v.* (Arg., Chile, Urug., Mex.) to pull, jerk, tug.
tiroriro, *m.* (coll.) sound of reed instruments; (*pl.*) (coll.) reed instruments.
tirosina, *f.* (biochem.) tyrosine, tyrosin.

tirosinasa, *f.* (biol.) tyrosinase.
tirotear, *tr.v.* to snipe or fire at. —*r.v.* 1. to fire at one another, fire at each other. 2. (coll.) to bicker, quarrel.
tiroteo, *m.* firing, shooting; skirmish.
tirotóxico, ca, *a.* (med.) thyrotoxic.
tirotoxicosis, *f.* (med.) thyrotoxicosis.
tirotricina, *f.* (biochem.) tyrothricin.
tirotropina, *f.* (physiol.) thyrotrophin, thyrotropin.
tiroxina, *f.* (biochem.) thyroxine.
tirreno, na, *a., m., f.* 1. Thyrrhenian. 2. Etruscan.
tirria, *f.* (coll.) dislike, grudge, aversion; **tener t. a,** to have a grudge against.
tirso, *m.* (myth., bot.) thyrsus.
tirsoideo, a, *a.* (bot.) thyrsoid.
tirulato, ta, *a.* (coll.) *var. of* **turulato.**
tisana, *f.* tisane, ptisan, infusion, tea.
tisanóptero, ra, *a., m.* (ento.) thysanopteran.
tisanuro, ra, *a., m.* (ento.) thysanuran, (*pl.*) Thysanura.
tísico, ca, *a.* (med.) tubercular, consumptive, phthisical, suffering from tuberculosis. —*m., f.* (med.) consumptive, person suffering from consumption or tuberculosis, tubercular patient.
tisis, *f.* (med.) tuberculosis, consumption, phthisis.
tiste, *m.* (C. Amer., Mex.) beverage made with toasted corn flour, cocoa and sugar.
tisú, (*pl.* **tisúes**), *m.* lamé (silk interwoven with gold or silver thread).
tisuria, *f.* (med.) weakness caused by excessive urination.
titán, *m.* 1. (myth.) **T.,** Titan. 2. (fig.) titan (person of great size, power, talent or strength).
titanato, *m.* (chem.) titanate.
titánico, ca, *a.* 1. titanic, gigantic, immense. 2. (myth.) Titanic. 3. (chem.) titanic.
titanífero, ra, *a.* (geol.) titaniferous.
titanio, nia, *a.* titanic. —*m.* (chem.) titanium.
titanita, *f.* (min.) titanite.
titanosaurus, *m.* (paleon.) titanosaur.
titanoso, sa, *a.* (chem.) titanous.
titear, *tr.v.* (Arg., Bol., Urug.) to make fun of; to tease, pull (someone's) leg.
titeo, *m.* (Arg.) teasing, legpulling.
títere, *m.* 1. puppet, marionette; (*pl.*) puppet show, marionettes. 2. (fig.) puppet, tool. 3. (coll.) bumptious squirt, whippersnapper. 4. (coll.) nincompoop, fool. — **echar los títeres a rodar,** (coll.) to give someone a piece of one's mind, tell someone where to get off; **no dejar t. con cabeza,** (coll.) to destroy; to upset or disarrange; **no quedar t. con cabeza,** (coll.) to be destroyed; to be upset or disarranged.
titerero, ra, *m., f., var. of* **titiritero.**
titeretada, *f.* (coll.) folly, foolishness; stupid act, stupidity.
titerista, *m., f., var. of* **titiritero.**
tití, (*pl.* **titíes**), *m.* (zool.) titi (small South American monkey).
titiaro, *a.* (bot.) **cambur t.,** banana tree yielding small, delicately-flavored fruit.
titilación, *f.* 1. tremor, quiver, quivering. 2. twinkle, twinkling.
titilador, ra, *a.* 1. quivering. 2. twinkling.
titilante, *a.* 1. quivering. 2. twinkling.
titilar, *i.v.* 1. to quiver. 2. to twinkle.
titileo, *m.* 1. quiver, quivering. 2. twinkle, twinkling.
titímalo, *m.* (bot.) sun spurge.
titimico, ca, *a.* (Guat., coll.) tipsy, drunk.
titirimundi, *m.* cosmorama.
titiritaina, *f.* 1. noise, racket, din; confused noise of instruments. 2. happy bustle, merry noises.
titiritar, *i.v.* to shake, tremble, shiver; **t. de,** to shake, tremble or shiver with.
titiritero, ra, *m., f.* puppeteer; acrobat, juggler, tumbler.
tito, *m.* 1. (bot.) purple vetch. 2. (coll.) chamber pot.
Tito, *m.* Titus, Roman emperor.
titración, *f.* (chem.) titration.
titubeante, *a.* 1. hesitant, hesitating. 2. wavering, indecisive. 3. staggering, tottering.
titubear, *i.v.* 1. to waver, hesitate. 2. to stammer, stutter. 3. to stagger, totter.
titubeo, *m.* 1. wavering, hesitation. 2. stammering. 3. staggering, tottering.
titulación, *f.* (chem.) titration.
titulado, da, *a.* supposed, so-called. —*m., f.* 1. holder of an academic degree. 2. titled person.
titular, *a.* 1. titular, nominal. 2. regular, (as opposed to substitute or part-time), e.g. *profesor t.,* regular teacher. —*m., f.* regular (player, teacher, etc.). —*m.* 1. headline (in newspaper). 2. holder (of a permit, document, etc.). —*f.* (print.) capital letter.
titular, *tr.v.* 1. to title, entitle, call, name (a book, etc.). 2. (chem.) to titrate. —*i.v.* to receive a title of nobility. —*r.v.* to be called, call or style oneself.
titulillo, *m.* (print.) running head, running title.
título, *m.* 1. title, name; sobriquet. 2. headline, caption, heading. 3. section (into which laws and regulations are divided). 3. certificate, (law) title. 4. diploma, (academic) degree; (*pl.*) qualifications. 5. (noble) title; titled person. 6. reason, cause, e.g. *¿a t. de qué vienes a preguntarme eso?* for what reason do you come and ask me this? 7. (com.) bond, security. 8. (chem.) titer (concentration of a solution). — **a t. de,** as a, by way of, e.g. *a t. de prueba,* by way of proof, as proof; **t. al portador,** bearer bond or security; **t. corrido,** (print.) running head or headline; **t. de dominio** or **propiedad,** (law) title deed; **t. lucrativo,** (law) lucrative title; **t. nominativo,** registered bond; **t. universitario,** university degree.
tiufado, *m.* (hist., mil.) Visigothic commander of a thousand men.
tiuque, *m.* 1. (Arg., Chile, ornith.) chimango. 2. (Chile, coll.) crafty fellow.
tiza, *f.* 1. chalk. 2. calcined stag's horn. 3. whiting (for polishing metals).
tizar, (*ref. 53*) *tr.v.* (Chile) to mark with chalk.
Tiziano, *m.* (p.) Titian, Venetian master.
tizna, *f.* blackening, smudging substance.
tiznado, da, *a.* (C. Amer., Arg.) drunk.
tiznadura, *f.* smudge, stain, spot.
tiznajo, *m.* (coll.) *var. of* **tiznón.**
tiznar, *tr.v.* 1. to soil with soot; to soil, stain. 2. (fig.) to tarnish, stain (reputation). —*r.v.* 1. to become soiled or stained. 2. (fig.) to become tarnished (reputation, etc.). 3. (C. Amer., Arg.) to get drunk.
tizne, *m., f.* soot. —*m.* half-burned log.
tiznón, *m.* smudge, spot of soot.
tizo, *m.* half-burned charcoal.
tizón, *m.* 1. firebrand, half-burned log. 2. bunt, wheat smut. 3. (fig.) stain, blemish, brand, stigma (on reputation). 4. (bldg.) header.
tizona, *f.* (coll.) 1. sword. 2. **T.,** (hist.) El Cid's legendary sword.
tizonada, *f.* 1. blow with a firebrand. 2. (coll.) hellfire.
tizoncillo, *m.* bunt, wheat smut.
tizonear, *i.v.* to poke or stir the fire.
tizonera, *f.* heap of half-burned wood prepared for charring.
Tl *sym. of* **talio,** thallium (Tl).
tlaco, *m.* (Mex.) tlaco, ancient Spanish coin.
tlacote, *m.* (Mex., coll.) boil, **furuncle.**
tlacoyo, *m.* (Mex.) large tortilla roll filled with beans.
tlacuache, *m.* (Mex., zool.) opossum.
tlapalería, *f.* (Mex.) paint shop.
tlazol, *m.* (Mex.) corn or sugar cane tops used as fodder.
Tm *sym. of* **tulio,** tulium (Tm).
tmesis, *f.* (gram.) tmesis.
T.N.T. *abbrev. of* **trinitrotolueno,** trinitrotoluene (T.N.T.).
tnte. *abbrev. of* **teniente,** Lieutenant (Lieut., Lt.).
toa, *f.* (mar.) cable, rope, hawser.
toalla, *f.* towel; **t. continua** or **sin fin,** roller towel; **t. de baño,** bath towel; **t. sanitaria,** sanitary napkin.
toallero, *m.* towel rack.
toalleta, *f. dim. of* **toalla,** small towel; napkin.
toar, *tr.v.* (Angl., mar.) to tow.
toba, *f.* 1. (geol.) tufa, tuff. 2. (dent.) tartar. 3. (bot.) cotton thistle. 4. (fig.) crust, cover.
tobar, *m.* tufa quarry.
tobera, *f.* 1. tuyera, tewel (of a blast furnace). 2. nozzle. — **t. de aspiración,** suction nozzle; **t. de presión,** (aer.) pressure nozzle.
tobiano, na, *a.* (Arg., Chile) piebald, pied (horse).
tobillera, *f.* 1. (coll.) bobbysoxer, adolescent girl. 2. bobby sock, short sock. 3. (sport.) ankle support.
tobillo, *m.* ankle.
tobo, *m.* (Ven.) bucket, pail.
toboba, *f.* (C. Amer., zool.) poisonous snake.
tobogán, *m.* 1. toboggan, sledge, sled. 2. slide, chute.
toboso, sa, *a.* (geol.) tufaceous.
toca, *f.* 1. toque, cornet, wimple; headdress, coif. 2. material for making toques. 3. (*pl.*) compensation or aid given to widow of a deceased employee.
tocable, *a.* 1. touchable. 2. (mus.) playable.
tocadiscos, (*pl.* **tocadiscos**), *m.* record player.
tocado, da, *past part. of* **tocar.** —*a.* touched, loony (sl., U.S.), balmy, e.g. *t. de cabeza,* touched in the head. —*m.* 1. hairdo, coiffure. 2. headdress, headgear.
tocador, *m.* 1. dressing table; **boudoir;** dressing room; toilet case. 2. head scarf, head kerchief. — **productos de t.,** toiletries.
tocador, ra, *m., f.* player, performer; **t. de guitarra,** guitar player.
tocadura, *f.* 1. hairdo, coiffure. 2. headdress.
tocamiento, *m.* 1. feeling, touching. 2. (fig.) inspiration.
tocante, *a.* touching; **t. a,** concerning, with reference to.
tocar, (*ref. 50*) *tr.v.* 1. to touch; to feel. 2. to touch, graze, come into contact with. 3. to touch upon, make reference to. 4. to play (musical instrument; record player; piece of music); to sound (alarm, attack, retreat, etc.), strike (a gong), ring, toll (bell), blow (trumpet), beat (drum), knock at (door), blow, sound (car horn). 5. to touch, test (gold or silver) with a touchstone. 6. to tap, knock, strike (e.g. glass, ceramics, etc. - to test their quality). 7. to put into contact with, put next to. 8. to inspire, move, influence. 9. (p.) to touch up. — **t. fondo,** to touch bottom (of the sea); **t. la diana,** (mil.) to sound reveille. —*i.v.* 1. to touch, be touching, e.g. *esto me toca en lo más hondo,* this touches me deeply. 2. to knock, e.g. *t. o la puerta,* to knock at the door. 3. to be up to, be one's job, e.g. *me toca a mí decidir quién va,* it's up to me or it's my job to decide who goes; to be one's turn, e.g. *hoy te toca a ti hacer el té,* today it's your turn to make tea; to be one's responsibility or obligation, behoove,

fall to, be incumbent upon, e.g. *te toca a ti como gerente decírselo,* it's your responsibility as manager to tell him. 4. to get, win, fall to, be one's share or part, e.g. *le tocó una quinta parte de la herencia,* he got a fifth of the estate, a fifth was his share of the estate, *le tocó la lotería,* he won the lottery. 5. to concern, interest, e.g. *esto me toca a mí,* this concerns me. 6. to stop, call, e.g. *este barco no toca en Valparaíso,* this boat does not stop or call at Valparaíso. — **por lo que a mí me toca,** as far as I am concerned; **t. a muerto,** to toll a death knell; **t. a rancho,** (mil.) to sound the mess call; **t. a rebato,** to sound the alarm; **t. de cerca,** to affect, concern deeply; **tocarle a uno en suerte** + *inf.,* to fall to one to + *inf.* —*r.v.* 1. to touch; to touch each other, touch one another. 2. to become touched (in the head), go balmy.

tocar, (*ref. 50*) *tr.v.* to comb, do (the hair). —*r.v.* 1. to comb or do one's hair. 2. to cover one's head.

tocasalva, *f.* glass rack.

tocata, *f.* 1. (mus.) toccata. 2. (coll.) beating, thrashing.

tocatoca, *f.* (Chile) catch ball (game).

tocayo, ya, *m., f.* namesake.

toche, *m.* (Col., Ven., ornith.) American oriole.

tochedad, *f.* boorishness, roughness, coarseness; foolishness, stupidity; boorish remark or act; stupid remark or act.

tochimbo, *m.* (Peru) smelting furnace.

tocho, cha, *a.* 1. boorish, rough, coarse; stupid, foolish. 2. (Chile) spurless (fighting cock), thumbless (person). —*m.* iron ingot.

tochura, *f.* (reg.), *var. of* **tochedad.**

tocía, *f.* tutty, zinc oxide.

tocinería, *f.* bacon and pork shop or stand.

tocinero, ra, *m., f.* bacon and pork dealer. —*f.* pork-salting board.

tocino, *m.* 1. bacon; salt pork. 2. lard, fat. 3. flitch or side of bacon. 4. small quick skip (in rope-skipping). 5. (Cuba) variety of acacia (Acacia paniculata). — **t. del cielo,** (cul.) egg and syrup custard; **t. entreverado,** streaky bacon; **t. saladillo,** half-salted bacon.

tocio, cia, *a.* dwarf (oak).

toco, *m.* (Peru) rectangular niche (in Incan architecture).

tocoferol, *m.* (biochem.) tocopherol.

tocología, *f.* (med.) tocology, obstetrics.

tocólogo, *m.* (med.) tocologist, obstetrician.

tocolotear, *tr.v.* (Cuba) to shuffle (cards).

tocón, na, *a.* (Col.) bobtailed. —*m.* stump (of tree, arm or leg).

toconal, *m.* 1. ground full of tree stumps. 2. olive orchard formed by sprouts of olive tree stumps.

tocororo, *m.* (ornith.) tocororo.

tocotín, *m.* old Mexican folk dance.

tocotoco, *m.* (Ven., ornith.) pelican.

tocte, *m.* (Ecuad., Peru, bot.) black walnut.

tocuyo, *m.* (S. Amer.) coarse cotton cloth.

todabuena, todasana, *f.* (bot.) tutsan.

todavía, *adv.* 1. still, e.g. *está trabajando t.,* he's still working. 2. nevertheless, still, yet, e.g. *es un mentiroso pero t. le tengo afecto,* he's a liar but nevertheless or still I'm fond of him. 3. even, e.g. *este libro es t. más atrevido que el primero,* this book is even more daring than the first. 4. (C. Amer., Car.) not yet, e.g. *¿ha llegado Juan? t.,* has John arrived? not yet.

todito, ta, *a.* (coll.) whole, whole blessed, whole; long, e.g. *todita la familia vino,* the whole blessed family came, *estuve allí todito el día,* I was there the whole day long.

todo, da, *a.* 1. all, whole, e.g. *toda la familia,* all the family, the whole family; all, every, e.g. *todas las flores son bonitas,* all flowers are beautiful, every flower is beautiful. 2. every, each, e.g. *viene todos los meses,* he comes every or each month. 3. full, e.g. *a todo trapo* or *correr,* at full speed. — **todo el que,** everybody who. —*m.* 1. whole; all, everything. 2. (*pl.*) everybody, all, all of them. — **ante t.,** first of all; **así y todo,** notwithstanding, in spite of this; **a t. esto, a todas estas,** meanwhile; **con t., con t. eso, con t. esto,** nevertheless, still, however; **del t.,** wholly, entirely, completely; **jugarse el t. por el t.,** to stake or risk everything; **sobre t.,** above all.

todo, *adv.* wholly, entirely, completely.

todopoderoso, sa, *a.* all-powerful, almighty. —*m.* **T.,** Almighty (God).

todoterreno, *m.* 1. four-wheel-drive vehicle, off-road vehicle. 2. Jack-of-all-trades.

toesa, *f.* toise, old French measurement of length.

tofana, *f.* aqua tofana (poison).

tofo, *m.* 1. (med., vet.) tophus. 2. (Chile) white refractory clay.

toga, *f.* toga (Roman garment); (academic) gown, toga.

togado, da, *a.* togaed, wearing a toga, gown or robe.

Togo, *m.* Togo, country in W. Africa.

Toisón, de Oro, *m.* Golden Fleece (order).

tojal, *m.* furze field, clump of furze.

tojino, *m.* (mar.) bitt, cleat; (mar.) chock.

tojo, *m.* 1. (bot.) furze, ulex (Ulex boethicus). 2. (Bol., ornith.) lark.

tojosa, tojosita, *f.* (Cuba, ornith.) wild pigeon (Columba passerina).

Tokio, *m.* Tokyo, capital of Japan.

tola, *f.* (bot.) tola (Baccharis tola).

tolano, *m.* (usually in *pl.*) 1. short hairs on neck. 2. (vet.) gingivitis.

toldadura, *f.* awning; canopy.

toldar, *tr.v.* to cover with an awning or a canopy.

toldería, *f.* (Arg., Chile) Indian camp.

toldilla, *f.* (mar.) poop, poop deck.

toldillo, *m.* 1. *dim. of* **toldo,** small awning. 2. covered sedan chair. 3. (Col.) mosquito net.

toldo, *m.* 1. awning, canopy; tarpaulin. 2. tilt or awning (covering cart, cab, etc.). 3. (fig.) pride, haughtiness, conceit. 4. (Arg., Chile) Indian tent or hut.

tole, *m.* 1. hubbub, noise, din, **racket.** 2. uproar, clamor, outcry (against something). — **tomar el t.,** (coll.) to beat it, run away, leave in a hurry.

toledano, na, *a., m., f.* Toledan, from Toledo; **noche toledana,** sleepless night.

tolemaico, ca, *a.* (hist.) Ptolemaic.

tolerable, *a.* tolerable, bearable; permissible; sufferable.

tolerablemente, *adv.* tolerably.

tolerancia, *f.* 1. tolerance; toleration; indulgence. 2. (med.) tolerance. 3. (mec.) tolerance, allowance (in minting coins).

tolerante, *a.* tolerant.

tolerantismo, *m.* tolerationism, doctrine of the freedom of worship.

tolerar, *tr.v.* 1. to tolerate, suffer, endure, put up with, stand. 2. to tolerate, allow, permit. 3. to overlook, be indulgent. 4. to hold, keep down, e.g. *mi estómago no tolera el alcohol,* my stomach cannot hold or keep down alcohol.

tolete, *m.* 1. (mar.) rowlock, oarlock, thole, thole-pin. 2. (Amer.) club, cudgel. 3. (Amer.) fool, clod, dolt, nit.

toletole, *m.* 1. noise, hubbub, din. 2. (Amer.) uproar, clamor, outcry, e.g. *se armó un t.,* an uproar broke out.

tolidina, *f.* (chem.) tolidine, tolidin.

tolilo, *m.* (chem.) tolyl.

tolla, *f.* 1. quagmire, soggy marsh. 2. (Cuba) canoe-shaped drinking trough.

tolladar, *m.* quagmire.

tollina, *f.* (coll.) beating, drubbing, thrashing.

tollo, *m.* 1. (ichth.) dogfish. 2. loin (of stag). 3. (hunt.) blind. 4. quagmire, bog.

tollón, *m.* narrow pass, narrow road, gorge.

tolmera, *f.* place full of pillarlike rocks, tors.

tolmo, *m.* pillarlike rock or boulder, tor.

tolobojo, *m.* (Guat., ornith.) penguin.

Tolomeo, *m.* Ptolemy, Greek astronomer and geographer.

tolondro, dra, *a.* scatterbrained, reckless, rash. —*m., f.* scatterbrain. —*m.* bump, lump, swelling (caused by a blow).

tolondrón, na, *a.* scatterbrained, reckless, rash. —*m.* lump, bump, swelling (caused by a blow). — **a tolondrones,** by fits and starts, precipitately.

tolosano, na, *a.* of or from Toulouse, France. —*m., f.* native or inhabitant of Toulouse.

tolteca, *a., m., f.* (hist., anth.) Toltec. —*m.* Toltec language.

toluato, *m.* (chem.) toluate.

tolueno, *m.* (chem.) toluene.

toluico, ca, *a.* (chem.) toluic.

toluidina, *f.* (chem.) toluidine.

toluol, *m.* (chem.) toluol.

tolva, *f.* hopper, chute.

tolvanera, *f.* dust storm, dust whirl.

toma, *f.* 1. taking, take; receiving. 2. hold, grip (in wrestling). 3. (cine.) take. 4. taking, capture, seizure. 5. dose (of medicine). 6. tap, outlet. 7. intake, inlet. 8. (S. Amer.) irrigation ditch. 9. (Chile) dam. — **t. de aire,** air inlet, air intake; **t. de corriente,** (elec.) plug, current tap, power outlet; **t. fuerza,** (auto.) power take-off; **t. de mando,** taking or assumption of office (as by a president); **t. de posesión,** inauguration (presidential, etc.); occupation; **t. de tierra,** (elec.) earth, ground, ground connection; landing (of airplane); **t. de tijera,** scissors (in wrestling); **t. panorámica,** (cine., tel.) panning; **t. y daca,** give-and-takc; **más vale un "t." que dos "te daré",** a bird in the hand is worth two in the bush.

tomacorriente, *f.* 1. (Amer.) socket, plug. 2. (Chile) trolley (of an electric train).

tomada, *f.* taking, capture, seizure.

tomadero, *m.* 1. handle. 2. tap, outlet.

tomado, da, *past part. of* **tomar.** —*a.* muffled (voice). 2. (coll.) drunk, tipsy.

tomador, ra, *m., f.* 1. taker. 2. (Amer.) drinker. —*m.* 1. (com.) drawee. 2. (mar.) gasket. 3. retriever (dog).

tomadura, *f.* taking; **t. de pelo,** (coll.) amusing hoax, practical joke.

tomafuerza, *f.* (mcc.) power take-off.

tomaína, *f.* (biochem.) ptomaine.

tomajón, na, *m., f.* one who takes or borrows indiscriminately.

tomar, *tr.v.* 1. to take; to take hold of, seize, grip. 2. to take, catch (e.g. train, bus, etc.). 3. to take, take up, occupy (time). 4. to take, seize, occupy (fortress, town, etc.). 5. to have (eat, drink, etc.); to take, have (lessons, bath, shower). 6. to take, adopt (measures, precautions; liberties, etc.). 7. to acquire (habits, vices, customs, ways). 8. to take on, employ. 9. to take, interpret, e.g. *t. en* or *a broma,* to take as a joke, *t. en serio,* to take seriously. 10. to take, hire, rent (taxi, house, apartment). 11. to use, borrow, take (quote), e.g. *t. un verso de Lorca,* to borrow a verse from Lorca. 12. to take, steal. 13. to take, buy. 14. to take, accept, e.g. *no quería t. el dinero,* he did not want to take the money. 15. to take, choose, e.g. *t. por ejemplo,* to take as an example, take for example. 16. to copulate with. 17. to take, win (trick at cards); to capture (a piece at chess or checkers). 18. to take (in one's company). 19. to take, gather, gain, e.g. *t. fuerza,* to gather or gain strength, *t. ánimo* or *aliento,* to take courage. — **t. a mal,** to resent, take offense at; **t. a pecho,** to take to heart; **t. asiento,** to take a seat; **t. el aire,** to take the air; **t. el sol,** to take the sun or a sun-bath; **t. en cuenta,** to take into account; **t. la delantera,** to take the lead; **t. las de Villadiego,** to beat it, take to one's heels; to take it on the lam (sl., U.S.); **tomarla con,** to get at or criticize constantly; to have a grudge against; **tomarle el pelo a,** to pull someone's leg; **t. nota de,** to take note of; **t. parte,** to take part; **t. partido,** to take sides; **t. por,** to take for, mistake for; **t. por asalto,** to take by assault; **t. por sorpresa,** to take by surprise; **t. prestado,** to borrow; **t. sobre sí,** to take upon oneself; **t. tiempo,** to take time; **t. tierra,** to land (airplane); to make port, arrive (a ship); to disembark; **t. una fotografía,** to take a photograph. —*i.v.* 1. to go, turn, e.g. *t. a* or *por la izquierda,* to go to the left. 2. (Amer., coll.) to drink, e.g. *él toma mucho,* he drinks a lot. —*r.v.* 1. to take. 2. to go rusty. — **tomarse la libertad de,** to take the liberty of; **tomarse la molestia** or **el trabajo de** + *inf.,* to take the trouble to + *inf.;* **tomarse libertades con,** to take liberties with.

Tomás, *m.* Thomas; **T. Becket,** Thomas à Becket; **T. de Aquino,** Thomas Aquinas; **T. de Kempis,** Thomas à Kempis.

tomatada, *f.* (cul.) batch of fried tomatoes.

tomatal, *m.* tomato patch or field; (Guat.) tomato plant.

tomatazo, *m.* 1. *aug. of* **tomate,** large tomato. 2. blow with a tomato.

tomate, *m.* 1. (bot.) tomato (fruit; plant). 2. (coll.) hole, run, tear (in stocking, glove, etc.).

tomatera, *f.* (bot.) tomato plant.

tomatero, ra, *a.* young, tender (chicken). —*m., f.* tomato grower or seller.

tomaticán, *m.* (Chile) tomato sauce or stew.

tomavistas, *m.* television or motion-picture camera.

tómbola, *f.* tombola, charity raffle, fair.

tome, *m.* (bot.) totora, bulrush, club rush.

tomento, *m.* 1. tow (of flax). 2. (bot.) tomentum.

tomentoso, sa, *a.* (bot.) tomentose, tomentous.

tomillar, *m.* field or patch of thyme.

tomillo, *m.* (bot.) thyme; **t. blanco,** (bot.) white sage; **t. salsero,** thyme (used for seasoning) (Thymus zygis).

tomín, *m.* former Spanish weight unit and small coin.

tomineja, *f.* **tominejo,** *m.* (ornith.) hummingbird.

tomismo, *m.* Thomism, the doctrines of the doctrines of Thomas Aquinas.

tomista, *a., m., f.* Thomist (pertaining to the doctrines of Thomas Aquinas).

tomiza, *f.* base rope, esparto rope.

tomo, *m.* 1. volume, tome. 2. bulk. 3. **(fig.)** importance, value. — **de t. y lomo,** (coll.) bulky, heavy; (coll.) important.

tomografía, *f.* (med.) tomography.

tomón, na, *a., m., f., var. of* tomajón.

ton, *m.* **sin t. ni son,** without rhyme or reason.

ton. *abbrev. of* **tonelada,** ton.

tonada, *f.* 1. tune, air, song, melody. 2. (Arg., Chile) accent (of a particular person or region).

tonadilla, *f. dim. of* **tonada,** light, popular song; ditty.

tonadillero, ra, *m., f.* composer or singer of light, popular songs.

tonal, *a.* (mus.) tonal.

tonalidad, *f.* (mus., p.) tonality.

tonante, *a.* (poet.) thundering.

tonar, *i.v.* (poet.) to thunder.

tonario, *m.* (mus.) antiphonary, antiphonal (book).

tonca, *a.* (bot.) tonka; **haba t.,** tonka bean.

tondero, *m.* (Peru) Peruvian folk dance.

tondino, *m.* (archit.) astragal.

tondiz, *f., var. of* **tundizno.**

tondo, *m.* (archit.) circular ornament or molding (in the face of a wall).

tonel, *m.* 1. cask, barrel. 2. (aer.) roll. — **t. abierto,** (aer.) barrel roll; **t. lento,** (aer.) slow roll.

tonelada, *f.* 1. ton. 2. tax formerly paid by vessels for galley-building. 3. casks, barrels. — **t. bruta,** gross ton; **t. corta,** short ton; **t. de arqueo** or **registro,** register ton; **t. larga,** long ton; **t. métrica,** metric ton.

tonelaje, *m.* 1. tonnage. 2. (com.) tonnage dues. — **t. bruto,** gross tonnage; **t. de carga,** dead tonnage.

tonelería, *f.* cooperage, cooper's shop, casks, barrels.

tonelero, ra, *a.* pertaining to cask, barrel (industry). —*m.* cooper, cask or barrel maker.

tonelete, *m.* 1. *dim. of* **tonel,** keg, small cask or barrel. 2. short skirt.

tonético, ca, *a.* (philol.) tonetic. —*f.* tonetics.

tonga, *f.* 1. layer; coat, covering. 2. (Cuba) pile, mound. 3. (Col.) task, job.

tongada, *f.* 1. layer; coat, covering. 2. pile, mound (of bricks, sticks, gravel, etc.).

tongo, *m.* 1. put-up job, fix (fixed sporting event). 2. (Chile) bowler hat.

tongonearse, *r.v.* (C. Amer., Col., Mex.) to walk affectedly swaying one's hips.

tongoneo, *m.* (C. Amer., Col., Mex.) swaying, suggestive gait or walk.

tonicidad, *f.* (physiol.) tonicity, tonus.

tónico, ca, *a.* tonic, invigorating. —*m.* (med.) tonic. —*f.* (mus., phonet.) tonic.

tonificación, *f.* strengthening, invigorating.

tonificador, ra, *a.* invigorating, strengthening.

tonificante, *a.* invigorating, strengthening.

tonificar, (*ref. 50*) *tr.v.* to invigorate, strengthen, tone up.

tonifique, tonifiqué, *ref.* **tonificar.**

tonillo, *m.* 1. singsong, monotonous tone. 2. intonation (typical of a person or region). 3. emphatic tone (of voice).

tonina, *f.* 1. (ichth.) tuna. 2. (zool.) dolphin.

Tonkín, *m.* (geog.) Tonkin, region in North Vietnam.

tono, *m.* 1. tone (inflection or modulation of voice; manner of writing or expressing oneself). 2. tone, resiliency, energy. 3. tone, color, hue. 4. (p.) tone, shade. 5. (med., physiol.) tone. 6. (mus.) tone (interval); mode, tone; key; slide (of certain instruments). 7. tune, melody, air. — **a este t.,** in this way; **a t. con,** in tune, harmony or agreement with; **bajar el t.,** to curb one's arrogance, become more amenable; **darse t.,** (coll.) to put on airs; **de buen t.,** elegant, stylish; **de mal t.,** vulgar, tasteless, brash; **mudar el t.,** to change one's tone; **salida de t.,** vulgar remark, improper or coarse remark; **subir** or **subirse de t.,** to become arrogant and haughty; to begin living in style; **t. de discar** or **marcar.** dial tone (U.S.), dialling tone (G.G.); **t. de ocupado,** busy signal (U.S.), engaged tone (G.B.); **t. mayor,** (mus.) major key; **t. menor,** (mus.) minor key.

tonómetro, *m.* (mus., med.) tonometer.

Tonquín, *m.* (geog.) Tonkin, region in North Vietnam.

tonsila, *f.* (anat.) tonsil.

tonsilar, *a.* (anat.) tonsillar.

tonsilectomía, *f.* (surg.) tonsillectomy.

tonsilitis, *f.* (med.) tonsillitis.

tonsura, *f.* 1. hair cutting; shearing, clipping. 2. (ecc.) tonsure.

tonsurado, *m.* tonsured man (priest, cleric, monk).

tonsurando, *m.* one about to receive the clerical tonsure.

tonsurar, *tr.v.* 1. to cut the hair of, to shear, clip. 2. (ecc.) to tonsure.

tontada, *f.* foolishness, silliness; nonsense.

tontaina, *m., f.* (coll.) silly thing, fool, nincompoop. —*a.* (coll.) silly, foolish, stupid.

tontamente, *adv.* foolishly, stupidly.

tontear, *i.v.* 1. to talk nonsense, act foolishly. 2. to flirt.

tontedad, tontera, *f., var. of* **tontería.**

tontería, *f.* foolishness, silliness; foolish or silly act or remark; (*pl.*) nonsense, rubbish, e.g. *hablar tonterías,* to talk nonsense.

tontillo, *m.* short hooped petticoat, farthingale.

tontiloco, ca, *a.* foolish, hairbrained.

tontina, *f.* (com.) tontine, annuity, fund.

tontito, *m.* (Chile, ornith.) goatsucker, nighthawk.

tontivano, na, *a.* conceited (fool), fatuous.

tonto, ta, *a.* silly, foolish, stupid; **a tontas y a locas,** haphazardly, any old way, helter-skelter. —*m., f.* fool, dolt, nincompoop; **hacerse el t.,** (coll.) to act dumb, pretend not to know or understand; **no tener pelo de tonto,** (coll.) to be no fool, to be no slouch; **t. de capirote,** (coll.) prize fool, blockhead, dumbbell. —*m.* 1. (Col., C. Rica, Chile) old maid (card game). 2. (Chile) bola, bolas (thong with a ball on the end used in roundup to entangle cattle).

tontucio, cia, *a.* rather silly or foolish, dumb.

tontuelo, la, *a.* silly, foolish. —*m., f.* fool, nit, ninny.

tontuna, tontura, *f.* foolishness, silliness, simple-mindedness.

toña, *f.* tipcat (game).

¡top! *interj.* (mar.) hold! stop!

topacio, *m.* (min.) topaz.

topada, *f.* butt (given with the head).

topadizo, za, *a.* bobbing up or turning up often; encountered by chance.

topador, ra, *a.* 1. butting. 2. hasty in raising stakes (in gambling games). —*m., f.* 1. hasty stake raiser (in gambling games). 2. bulldozer. — **t. hidráulica,** hydraulically operated bulldozer.

topar, *tr.v.* 1. to bump, bump against, knock against. 2. to bump into, run into, encounter; to find, run across. 3. (Amer.) to try (two cocks in a fight). 4. (mar.) to join, butt. —*i.v.* 1. to butt. 2. to accept a bet. 3. (coll.) to work out well, come out well. — **t. con,** to bump into, knock into; to meet, run into; to find, run across; **t. contra,** to bump against, knock into; **t. en,** to bump into, knock into; to consist in, lie in, e.g. *la dificultad topa en eso,* the difficulty lies in this.

toparca, *m.* petty ruler.

toparquía, *f.* petty state.

tope, *m.* 1. butt, end; top, limit. 2. stop, catch, check. 3. (ry.) buffer, bumper. 4. snag, difficulty, difficult point. 5. collision, bump. 6. hard reinforcement (in toecap of shoe). 7. quarrel, fight, scuffle. 8. (mar.) masthead; topmast head; topman (watch, lookout). — **a t.** or **al t.,** end to end; **estar hasta el t.** or **los topes,** to be filled to the brim or limit; to be fed up, be sick and tired (of something); **hasta el t.** or **los topes,** up to the brim; **t. amortiguador,** (mec.) shock-absorbing bumper; **t. de banco,** (mec.) bench hook; **precio t.,** maximum price.

topear, *tr.v.* (Chile) to unhorse, knock from the saddle.

topera, *f.* molehill, molehole.
topetada, *f.* 1. butt (given by horned animal). 2. (coll., fig.) butt, bump (with the head). — **darse de topetadas,** to butt one another.
topetar, *tr.v.* to butt; to bump against. —*i.v.* to butt (with horns or head).
topetazo, *m., var. of* **topetada.**
topetón, *m.* 1. bump, collision, **head-on** encounter. 2. butt.
topetudo, da, *a.* butting (animal).
tópico, ca, *a.* topical, local. —*m.* 1. (neol.) topic, subject. 2. topic, general principle, commonplace. 3. (rhet.) commonplace, hackneyed or trite expression. 4. (med.) external, local medical application.
topinada, *f.* (coll.) blunder, error; clumsiness, awkwardness.
topinambur, *m.* (Arg., Bol., bot.) Jerusalem artichoke.
topinaria, *f.* (med.) talpa, mole, wen.
topinera, *f.* molehill, molehole.
topo, *m.* 1. (zool.) mole. 2. (coll.) stumbler, awkward person; blunderer. 3.(coll.) dunce, dolt. — **más ciego que un t.,** as blind as a bat. —*a.* 1. (coll.) stumbling, blundering; awkward. 2. (coll.) dumb, foolish, stupid.
topo, *m.* 1. (S. Amer.) Indian measure of one and a half leagues. 2. (S. Amer.) large pin (used by Indian women to fasten their shawls).
topocho, cha, *a.* (Ven.) plump, pudgy.
topografía, *f.* 1. topography. 2. surveying.
topográficamente, *adv.* topographically.
topográfico, ca, *a.* topographic, topographical.
topógrafo, *m.* 1. topographer. 2. surveyor.
topón, *m.* (Col., Chile) butt (with the head).
toponimia, *f.* toponymy; toponymics.
toposo, sa, *a.* (Ven.) interfering, meddlesome.
toque, *m.* 1. touch, touching. 2. sounding (of reveille, retreat, etc.); ringing, tolling (of bells); beating (of drum); (mil.) call. 3. essence, quiddity, heart (of a matter). 4. examination, test, check. 5. (coll.) blow, hit. 6. (p.) touch, light brush stroke. 7. (metal.) assaying of gold or silver with a touchstone; touchstone. 8. warning, admonition. — **dar los últimos toques a,** to give the last touches to; **dar t. de atención,** to call (someone's) attention, warn; **dar un t. a,** to put to the test; to sound (someone) out (about something); **t. a muerto,** death knell, passing bell; **t. de asamblea,** (mil.) assembly call; **t. de corneta,** bugle call; **t. del alba,** ringing of church bells at daybreak; **t. de diana,** or **alborada,** reveille; **t. de difuntos,** taps; **t. de incendio,** fire call; **t. de queda,** curfew; **t. de rancho,** mess call; **t. de rebato,** alarm; **t. de retreta,** call to quarters; **t. de silencio,** taps; **último t.,** finishing touch.
toque, toqué, *ref.* **tocar.**
toqueado, *m.* rapping, thumping; stumping, stamping; clapping.
toquería, *f.* toques, headdresses, coifs; toque or coif making, toque or coif maker's trade.
toquero, ra, *m., f.* maker or seller of coifs, toques, headdresses.
toquetear, *tr.v.* to touch repeatedly; to handle.
toqui, *m.* (Chile, anth.) Araucan Indian chief.
toquilla, *f.* 1. *dim. of* **toca,** small toque. 2. triangular scarf, kerchief or bandana. 3. knitted shawl. 4. (Bol., Ecuad.) palmetto fiber (used in straw hat making).
Tor, *m.* (myth.) Thor, Scandinavian god of war.
tora, *a.* **yerba t.,** (bot.) broomrape. —*f.* 1. firework frame in the shape of a bull. 2. Jewish family tax. 3. Torah.
torácico, ca, *a.* (anat.) thoracic.
toracostomía, *f.* (med.) thoracotomy.
torada, *f.* drove of bulls.
toral, *a.* 1. main, principal, chief. 2. unbleached yellow (wax). —*m.* (metal.) mold for copper bars; copper bar.
torax, (*pl.* **torax**), *m.* (anat.) thorax.
torbellino, *m.* whirlwind; vortex; (fig.) whirlwind, avalanche, rush (of things, events); (coll.) whirlwind, lively, restless person.
torca, *f.* cavern, cave, depression; (geol.) corrie.
torcal, *m.* cavernous place abounding in rocks and caves.
torcaz, (*pl.* **torcaces**), *a.* **paloma t.,** (ornith.) ring-dove, woodpigeon.
torcazo, za, *a.* **1. paloma torcaza,** ringdove, woodpigeon. 2. (Col., coll.) stupid, foolish. —*f.* (ornith.) ringdove, woodpigeon.
torcecuello, *m.* (ornith.) wryneck.
torcedero, ra, *a.* twisted, crooked. —*m.* twisting instrument, twister.
torcedor, ra, *a.* twisting. —*m., f.* twister. —*m.* 1. twisting spindle (twisting thread). 2. (fig.) thorn in the side (causing constant annoyance, grief, etc.). 3. (Cuba) cigar maker (worker).
torcedura, *f.* 1. twisting; twist; (med.) sprain; dislocation. 2. watered-down sour wine.
torcer, (*ref. 74*) *tr.v.* 1. to twist, turn, wind twine. 2. to twist, bend, make crooked. 3. to turn (in a certain direction). 4. to break one's eyes away. 5. to twist, wrench, sprain (e.g. ankle, arm, etc.). 6. to twist, contort, screw up (face in pain, displeasure, anger, etc.). 7. to twist, misinterpret, distort (e.g. someone's words, etc.). 8. to corrupt, bribe. — **andar** or **estar torcido con,** (coll.) to be on bad terms with; **t. el rostro,** to make a wry face; **no dar el brazo a torcer,** to be obstinate. —*i.v.* to turn (in a certain direction), e.g. *la senda tuerce a la izquierda,* the path turns to the left. —*r.v.* 1. to twist, wind. 2. to bend, get bent or twisted, become crooked. 3. to turn (in a certain direction). 4. to twist, contort (one's face with pain, etc.); to become twisted or contorted. 5. to twist, wrench, sprain (e.g. one's ankle, etc.). 6. to turn sour (wine); to curdle (milk). 7. to run into difficulties, go on the rocks (a business). 8. to go astray, go crooked, go bad.
torcida, *f.* wick (of lamp or candle).
torcidamente, *adv.* crookedly; twistedly, pervertedly.
torcidillo, *m.* thick silk thread.
torcido, da, *past part. of* **torcer.** —*a.* 1. crooked; twisted; bent; winding, twisting, tortuous. 2. (fig.) dishonest, crooked. 3. (Guat.) unfortunate, unlucky. —*m.* 1. (cul.) candied fruit roll. 2. watered-down sour wine. 3. thick twisted silk thread.
torcijón, *m.* 1. twisting; writhing. 2. stomach pain, gripe, cramp. 3. (vet.) severe enteritis.
torcimiento, *m.* 1. twisting; twist; bending; twining, winding. 2. circumlocution, periphrasis.
torculado, *a.* screw-shaped.
tórculo, *m.* screw press, rolling press.
torda, *f.* (ornith.) female thrush.
tordella, *f.* (ornith.) fieldfare.
tórdiga, *f.* leather thong, strip of leather.
tordillejo, ja, *a.* dapple-gray (horse). —*m., f.* young dapple-gray horse.
tordillo, lla, *a.* dapple-gray (horse). —*m., f.* dapple-gray horse.
tordo, da, *a.* dapple-gray (horse). —*m., f.* dapple-gray horse. —*m.* (ornith.) thrush; (C. Amer., Arg., Chile, ornith.) starling; **t. alirrojo,** (ornith.) redwing; **t. de agua,** (ornith.) water ouzel, water thrush; **t. de campanario,** (ornith.) starling; **t. de mar,** (ichth.) blenny; **t. loco,** (ornith.) solitaire; **t. mayor,** (ornith.) missel thrush; **t. serrano,** (ornith.) black solitaire.
toreador, *m.* toreador, bullfighter.
torear, *i.v.* to fight bulls in the ring. —*tr.v.* 1. to fight (bulls). 2. to string one along, give (someone) false hope. 3. to sidestep (an issue). 4. to tease, quip, pull one's leg. 5. to annoy, pester, harrass.
toreo, *m.* bullfighting.
torera, *f.* tight waist-length jacket; bolero. — **saltarse (una cosa) a la t.,** to fail to keep (date, engagement, etc.).
torería, *f.* 1. bullfighters; bullfighters' guild. 2. (Cuba, Ecuad., Guat.) prank, mischief, antics, caper.
torero, ra, *a.* (coll.) pertaining to bullfighting. —*m., f.* bullfighter.
torés, *m.* (archit.) torus.
torete, *m.* 1. *dim. of* **toro,** young bull. 2. (coll.) serious difficulty, difficult matter. 3. (coll.) common topic of conversation (e.g. the weather, fashions, gossip).
toréutico, ca, *a.* (art.) toreutic. —*f.* toreutics, the art of chasing or embossing (esp. in metal).
torga, *f.* yoke used on hogs and dogs.
toria, *f.* (chem.) thoria.
torianita, *f.* (min.) thorianite.
tórico, ca, *a.* (chem.) toric.
toril, *m.* (taur.) bull pen (adjoining the ring).
torillo, *m.* 1. *dim. of* **toro,** small or young bull. 2. (archit.) torus. 3. (mech.) dowel, dowel pin. 4. (coll.) common topic of conversation. 5. (anat.) raphe. 6. (ichth.) blenny.
torina, *f.* (chem.) thoria.
torio, *m.* (chem.) thorium.
toriondez, *f.* rut (of cattle).
toriondo, da, *a.* in rut, rutting (said of cattle).
torita, *f.* (min.) thorite.
torito, *m.* 1. *dim. of* **toro,** small bull, little bull. 2. (Cuba, ichth.) horned boxfish or trunkfish. 3. (Chile) conical awning-like shelter (of twigs, branches). 4. (Arg., Peru, ento.) rhinoceros beetle, horn bug. 5. (Ecuad., bot.) variety of orchid. 6. (Chile, ornith.) tyrant flycatcher (Elaenia parvirostris).
torloroto, *m.* shepherd's horn.
tormagal, *m.* ground abounding in pillar-like rocks, tors.
tormellera, *f., var. of* **tormagal.**
tormenta, *f.* 1. storm, tempest. 2. (fig.) adversity, misfortune, trouble. 3. (fig.) storm, turmoil; heated discussion; **t. de arena,** sandstorm; **t. de nieve,** snowstorm; blizzard; **t. eléctrica,** electrical storm.
tormentario, ria, *a.* pertaining to ancient war machines.
tormentila, *f.* (bot.) tormentil.
tormentín, *m.* (mar.) jib boom.
tormento, *m.* 1. torture; torment, anguish. 2. tormentum, torment (ancient artillery weapon). — **t. de cuerda,** rack.
tormentoso, sa, *a.* 1. stormy; turbulent. 2. (mar.) storm-ridden, storm-tossed (ship).
tormera, *f., var. of* **tolmera.**
tormo, *m.* 1. *var. of* **tolmo.** 2. clod or clump (of earth).
torna, *f.* 1. return; devolution, restitution. 2. dam (in an irrigation ditch to change course of water). 3. (*pl.*) return, recompense, restitution. — **volver las tornas,** to give tit for tat, give like for like; to turn the tables.
tornaboda, *f.* day after the wedding; celebration of this day.
tornachile, *m.* (Mex.) thick pepper.

tornada, *f.* 1. return (from a journey), return visit. 2. (poet.) envoy (last stanza in a Provençal poem). 3. (vet.) gid.

tornadera, *f.* two-pronged winnowing fork.

tornadizo, za, *a.* changeable, fickle. —*m., f.* changeable or fickle person; turncoat.

tornado, *m.* tornado, hurricane.

tornadura, *f.* 1. return, devolution; recompense. 2. agrarian measure of 2.70 meters.

tornaguía, *f.* (com.) arrival acknowledgment.

tornamiento, *m.* turn, change, alteration.

tornapunta, *f.* brace, strut; prop, shore, stay.

tornar, *tr.v.* 1. to return, give back, restore. 2. to turn, e.g. *t. la espalda,* to turn one's back. 3. to make, turn, cause to be. —*i.v.* 1. to return, come back, go back. 2. to come to, revive, recover consciousness. — **t. a** + *inf., inf.* + again, e.g. *no torné a hablar con él,* I didn't speak to him again. —*r.v.* to become, turn, go, grow. — **tornarse en,** to change into, become, e.g. *se tornó en un ogro,* he became an ogre.

tornasol, *m.* 1. (bot.) sunflower. 2. iridescence, shot effects. 3. (chem.) litmus.

tornasolado, da, *a.* shot, changeable, iridescent (fabrics, colors).

tornasolar, *tr.v.* to make iridescent, give a shot effect to. —*r.v.* to become iridescent, get a shot effect.

tornátil, *a.* 1. turned (on a lathe). 2. changeable, fickle. 3. (poet.) easily gyrating or whirling.

tornatrás, (*pl.* **tornatrás**), *m., f.* (biol.) throwback, atavism.

tornavía, *f.* (ry.) turntable.

tornaviaje, *m.* return trip; baggage or souvenirs brought back from a trip.

tornavirón, *m.* slap.

tornavoz, (*pl.* **tornavoces**), *m.* sounding board.

torneador, *m.* 1. turner, lathe operator. 2. jouster, participant in a joust or tournament.

torneadura, *f.* lathe shavings.

torneante, *a.* tourneying, tilting (in a tournament).

tornear, *tr.v.* to turn (on a lathe). —*i.v.* 1. to turn, go round. 2. to tourney, joust, tilt. 3. to meditate, ponder, muse.

torneo, *m.* 1. tournament, tilt, tourney. 2. contest, competition, championship, tournament. 3. dance in imitation of ancient tournaments. 4. (vet.) gid, staggers, sturdy.

tornera, *f.* 1. doorkeeper of a nunnery. 2. wife of a turner or lathe operator.

tornería, *f.* turnery (turner's shop or trade).

tornero, *m.* 1. turner, lathe operator; operator of potter's wheel; lathe maker. 2. errand man, chore boy in a nunnery.

tornés, sa, *a.* (numis.) tournois. —*m.* (numis.) gros tournois.

tornillazo, *m.* 1. half turn (by horse). 2. (coll.) desertion (by soldier).

tornillero, *m.* (coll.) deserter (soldier).

tornillo, *m.* 1. screw, male screw. 2. small lathe. 3. vise, clamp. 4. (coll.) desertion (of a soldier). 5. (C. Amer., Ven., bot.) screw tree. — **apretarle a uno los tornillos,** (coll.) to put the screws on someone, put pressure on; **faltarle a uno un t.** or **tener flojos los tornillos,** (coll.) to have a screw loose; **t. compuesto** or **doble,** compound screw; **t. de Arquímides,** Archimedes screw; **t. de banco,** bench clamp; **t. de cabeza** or **casquete,** cap screw; **t. de cabeza ranurada,** slotted screw; **t. de cadena,** chain vise; **t. de mariposa** or **de orejas,** thumbscrew; **t. de mordazas,** jaw vise; **t. de paso diferencial,** differential screw; **t. de rosca doble,** double-thread screw; **t. de seguridad** or de **traba,** lockscrew; **t. de tope,** stop or shoulder screw; **t. graduador,** tamper screw; **t. limitador,** stop or shoulder screw; **t. micrométrico,** micrometer screw; **t. opresor,** stud bolt; **t. para metales,** machine screw; **t. pasante,** through bolt; **t. seguro,** lockscrew; **t. sin fin,** worm screw; **t. tensor,** turnbuckle.

torniquete, *m.* 1. bell crank. 2. turnstile. 3. (surg.) tourniquet. 4. (Arg.) turnbuckle (tightening wires of fence).

torniscón, *m.* (coll.) 1. slap, cuff; pinch. 2. (Amer.) hard pinch.

torno, *m.* 1. (mec., carp.) lathe. 2. wheel, drum; potter's wheel. 3. hoisting wheel, winch, windlass, whim. 4. (carp.) vise, clamp. 5. carriage hand brake. 6. turn, revolution. 7. turn, bend (in river). 8. revolving dumbwaiter (passing things through wall); revolving window at entrance to nunneries (to pass things through without the receiver being seen). 9. (law) granting of auctioned land to second bidder when first bidder has failed to effect the stipulated payment. — **a t.,** on a lathe, on the (potter's) wheel; around; **en t.,** in exchange, in return; **en t. a** or **de,** about, in connection with, regarding; **t. de alfarero,** potter's wheel; **t. de bancada,** bed lathe; **t. de conformar,** spinning lathe; **t. de cordelero,** ropemaker's wheel (used in weaving strands of rope); **t. de chapista,** spinning lathe; **t. de extensión,** extension lathe; **t. desbastador,** roughing lathe; **t. de filetear,** chasing lathe; **t. de hilar,** spinning wheel; **t. de roscar,** screw-cutting lathe; **t. de torrecilla,** turret lathe; **t. doble,** duplex lathe; **t. revólver,** turret lathe.

toro, *m.* 1. bull. 2. (fig.) bull, horse, strong man. 3. (astron.) **T.,** Taurus. 4. (*pl.*) bullfight. 5. (Cuba, ichth.) trunkfish. — **ciertos son los toros,** (coll.) it's quite true; **echarle** or **soltarle a uno el t.,** (coll.) to talk straight from the hip, talk frankly; **otro t.,** (coll.) change the record, change the subject; **t. corrido,** (coll.) smart guy, smart cookie; **t. de cola,** (Mex.) bull for throwing by tail twisting (for not fighting); **t. de fuego,** firework frame in the shape of a bull; **t. furioso,** (her.) bull rampant; **t. de lidia,** (taur.) fighting bull, bull used in bullfighting; **t. mexicano,** (zool.) bison.

toro, *m.* 1. (archit.) torus (molding). 2. (geom.) torus, tore.

toroidal, *a.* (elec., math.) toroid, toroidal.

toroide, *a.* toroid, toroidal. —*m.* **(geom.) toroid.**

torón, *m.* (chem.) thoron.

toronja, *f.* (bot.) grapefruit.

toronjil, *m.,* **toronjina,** *f.* (bot.) balm, lemon balm.

toronjo, *m.* (bot.) grapefruit tree.

toroso, sa, *a.* strong, sturdy, husky.

torozón, *m.* 1. (vet.) gripe pains (of animals suffering from enteritis); (vet.) severe enteritis. 2. anxiety, worry, concern.

torpe, *a.* 1. clumsy, awkward. 2. dull, slow, dimwitted. 3. indecent, obscene. 4. ugly, crude.

torpedeamiento, *m.* torpedoing.

torpedear, *tr.v.* 1. to torpedo. 2. to besiege (with questions, chatter, etc.).

torpedeo, *m.* 1. torpedoing. 2. (fig.) barrage (of questions, etc.).

torpedero, *a.* (mar.) torpedo. —*m.* torpedo boat.

torpedista, *m.* torpedoist, torpedoman.

torpedo, *m.* 1. (ichth.) torpedo fish, electric ray. 2. (mar.) torpedo. — **t. aéreo** or **de aviación,** aerial torpedo; **t. de fondo,** ground torpedo; **t. flotante,** submarine mine.

torpemente, *adv.* 1. clumsily, awkwardly. 2. slowly, dimly, stupidly. 3. crudely, uglily.

torpeza, *f.* 1. clumsiness, awkwardness. 2. slowness, dullness, dimness, stupidity. 3. crudeness, ugliness.

tórpido, da, *a.* (med.) torpid, sluggish, reacting slowly to treatment.

torpor, *m.* (med.) torpor, sluggishness.

torques, (*pl.* **torques**), *f.* torque (ancient collar or necklace worn by Romans).

torrado, da, *m.* toasted chickpea.

torrar, *tr.v.* to roast or toast lightly.

torre, *f.* 1. tower; (church) steeple; (mar., mil.) turret. 2. castle, rook (in chess). 3. (reg., Sp.) country house, farm. 4. (Cuba, P. Rico) chimney of a sugar mill. — **t. albarrana,** turret; **t. dama,** queen's rook (in chess); **t. de aguas,** water tower; **T. de Babel,** Tower of Babel; **t. de control,** control tower; **t. del homenaje,** keep, donjon; **t. de costa,** watch tower. **T. de Londres,** Tower of London; **t. de mando,** (mar.) conning tower; (aer.) control tower; **t. de maniobra de cambios,** (ry.) switch tower; **t. de marfil,** ivory tower; **t. de perforación,** drilling rig; **t. de señales,** (ry.) signal tower (U.S.), signal box (G.B.); **t. de vigía** or **de observación,** observation tower; (mar.) crow's nest; **T. Eiffel,** Eiffel Tower; **t. inclinada de Pisa,** leaning tower of Pisa.

torrear, *tr.v.* to fortify with towers or turrets.

torrecilla, *f.* 1. *dim. of* **torre,** turret, tower. 2. (mar.) conning tower (of submarine).

torrefacción, *f.* roasting, torrefaction (drying by heat).

torrefacto, ta, *a.* torrefied, dried by heat.

torreja, *f.* 1. (Amer.) *var. of* **torrija.** 2. (Chile) slice of fruit.

torrejón, *m.* small crooked tower or turret.

torrencial, *a.* torrential; (fig.) overwhelming.

torrente, *m.* torrent; avalanche, rush; (fig.) plenty, abundance. — **t. de voz,** powerful voice.

torrentera, *f.* ravine made by a torrent; gully.

torrentoso, sa, *a.* torrential.

torreón, *m. aug. of* **torre,** large fortified tower.

torrero, *m.* 1. lighthouse keeper, watchtower keeper. 2. overseer of a small farm.

torreta, *f.* (mil.) turret (of tank).

torreznada, *f.* large dish of fried bacon.

torreznero, ra, *a.* (coll.) lazy, indolent, self-indulgent. —*m., f.* lazy person, idler.

torrezno, *m.* rasher of bacon.

tórrido, da, *a.* torrid; ardent; **zona tórrida,** torrid zone.

torrija, *f.* bread soaked in milk or wine, fried and sweetened with syrup or sugar, French toast.

torrontés, *a.* designating a kind of white grape which produces an aromatic wine.

torsión, *f.* torsion; twisting. — **momento de t. de arranque,** starting torque.

torso, *m.* (anat., art.) torso; **el t. desnudo,** stripped to the waist.

torta, *f.* 1. (cul.) cake, torte. 2. (coll.) slap. 3. (print.) font; (print.) solid set matter for distribution. 4. (Amer.) adobe roughcast (used for covering roofs, etc.). — **t. de reyes,** (cul.) Twelfth-Night cake; **costar la t. un pan,** (coll.) to cost a fortune, cost more than expected; **ser una cosa tortas y pan pintado,** (coll.) not to be so bad; to be an easy matter, a cinch or child's play.

tortada, *f.* 1. (cul.) large meat or fruit pie. 2. (mas.) coat or layer of mortar.

tortazo, *m.* (coll.) slap, blow.

tortedad, *f.* the condition of having only one eye.

tortera, *f.* 1. baking pan, pie dish. 2. whorl of a spindle.

tortero, ra, *m., f.* cake maker; cake seller. —*m.* 1. cake box or basket. 2. whorl of a spindle.

torticeramente, *adv.* wrongly, unjustly.

torticero, ra, *a.* wrong, unjust.

tortícolis, *m.* (med.) torticollis, wryneck.

tortilla, *f.* omelet; (Mex.) tortilla (thin unleavened cornmeal pancake). — **hacer t. a,** to flatten, smash or break to pieces; **volverse la t.,** (coll.) to turn out contrary to expectations; e.g. *se me ha vuelto la t.,* my luck has changed.
tortillero, ra, *m., f.* (Amer.) tortilla maker or seller. —*f.* (vulg.) Lesbian.
tortillo, *m.* (her.) roundel, bezant.
tortita, *f.* 1. *dim. of* **torta,** small loaf or cake. 2. (*pl.*) pat-a-cake (child's game).
tórtola, *f.* (ornith.) turtledove; (ornith.) ringdove.
tortolito, ta, *a.* inexperienced, ingenuous. —*f.* (ornith.) small young turtledove.
tórtolo, *m.* 1. (ornith.) male turtledove. 2. (coll.) turtledove, sweetheart.
tortor, *m.* (mar.) tightening bar or stick.
tortozón, *m.* variety of large grape.
tortuga, *f.* 1. (zool.) turtle; tortoise. 2. (mil.) testudo. — **t. amizclada,** (zool.) musk turtle; **t. elefante** or **gigante,** (zool.) giant turtle; **t. emis,** (zool.) diamondback terrapin; **t. laúd,** (zool.) leatherback; **t. mordedora,** (zool.) snapping turtle; **t. verde,** (zool.) green turtle.
tortuguismo, *m.* (Pam.) slowdown.
tortuosamente, *adv.* tortuously.
tortuosidad, *f.* tortuousness, tortuosity.
tortuoso, sa, *a.* winding, tortuous, sinuous; (fig.) tortuous, devious.
tortura, *f.* 1. torture, torment. 2. twisted condition or state, twistedness.
torturador, ra, *a.* torturing, torturous. —*m., f.* torturer, tormentor.
torturar, *tr.v.* to torture, torment. —*r.v.* to torture oneself, to worry.
torunda, *f.* (med.) swab.
toruno, *m.* (Chile) ox castrated after three years of age.
torva, *f.* rain or snow squall.
torvisca, *f., var. of* **torvisco.**
torviscal, *m.* patch or field of spurge flax.
torvisco, *m.* (bot.) spurge flax.
torvo, va, *a.* frowning; fierce, grim, irritable.
torzadillo, *m.* thin silk twist.
torzal, *m.* silk twist; cord, twine; (Arg., Chile) plaited leather lasso.
torzón, *m.* (vet.), *var. of* **torozón.**
torzonado, da, *a.* (vet.) suffering from gripes.
torzuelo, *m.* (hunt.) tiercel, male falcon.
tos, *f.* cough, coughing; **t. convulsiva** or **ferina,** (med.) whooping cough; **t. perruna,** barking cough.
tosa, *f.* (bot.) beardless wheat.
tosca, *f.* 1. (geol.) tufa, tuff. 2. (dent.) tartar.
toscamente, *adv.* rudely, coarsely.
toscano, na, *a., m., f.* Tuscan. —*m.* **Tuscan (dialect).** —*f.* **La T.,** Tuscany, region in Italy.
tosco, ca, *a.* coarse, crude, unpolished; uncouth, unrefined.
tosecilla, *f. dim. of* **tos,** slight cough.
tosedera, *f.* (Col.) frequent coughing.
tosegoso, sa, *a.* having a chronic cough.
toser, *i.v.* to cough. — **t. una persona a otra** (coll.) to be able to rival or compete with; **a mi nadie me tose,** no one can compete with me; **t. fuerte,** (coll.) to brag, boast, swagger.
tosidura, *f.* coughing; cough.
tosigar, (*ref. 51*) *tr.v.* 1. to poison. 2. (fig.) to harrass, pester.
tósigo, *m.* 1. poison. 2. (fig.) grief, pain, anguish, sorrow.
tosigoso, sa, *a.* 1. poisonous, venomous. 2. having a chronic cough.
tosquedad, *f.* coarseness, crudeness; uncouthness, roughness.
tostada, *f.* 1. slice of toast, (*pl.*) toast. 2. (Arg., coll.) bore, nuisance. — **dar** or **pegar a uno la t.,** (coll.) to cheat, swindle; **no ver la t.,** (coll.) to fail to see the point, fail to understand.
tostadero, *m.* roasting room or place.
tostado, da, *past part. of* **tostar.** —*a.* tanned, sunburned, brown. —*m.* toasting; roasting (e.g. of coffee beans).
tostador, ra, *a.* 1. toasting; roasting. 2. (fig.) burning, scorching, roasting. —*m., f.* toaster; roaster (person). —*m.* toaster; roaster (utensil).
tostadura, *f.* toasting; roasting.
tostar, (*ref. 33*) *tr.v.* 1. to roast; to toast. 2. to burn, scorch, roast. 3. to tan the skin (the sun). 4. (coll.) to tan, thrash, beat. —*r.v.* to become scorched; to become tanned or sunburned. — **tostarle algo a alguien,** (Chile) to please someone, take someone's fancy; **tostárselas,** (Mex.) to smoke marihuana.
tostón, *m.* 1. toasted chickpea. 2. piece of toast dipped in olive oil. 3. roast pig. 4. over-roasted or over-toasted piece of food. 5. (P. Rico, cul.) fried plantain patty. 6. (coll.) long boring speech or conversation, bore, boring thing or person.
tostón, *m.* (numis.) Mexican 50-centavo piece; tostao, former Portuguese coin.
tota, a t., (Chile) on one's shoulders or back.
total, *a.* total, complete absolute, whole. —*m.* total (number, amount), sum total, whole, totality. — **en t.,** in a word, in short; **t. que,** the result or upshot is that.
totalice totalicé, *ref.* **totalizar.**
totalidad, *f.* totality, aggregate, whole; **la casi t. de,** almost all of.
totalitario, ria, *a., m., f.* (polit.) totalitarian.
totalitarismo, *m.* (pol.) totalitarianism.
totalizador, ra, *m., f.* totalizer; (sport.) totalizator, pari-mutuel.
totalizar, (*ref. 53*) *tr.v.* to totalize, add up, sum up.
totalmente, *adv.* totally, wholly, entirely, fully.
totanera, *a.* **calabaza t.,** (bot.) pumpkin.
totazo, *m.* (Cuba) knock on the head.
totem, (*pl.* **totems** or **tótemes**), *m.* totem.
totémico, ca, *a.* totemic, totem, e.g. *poste totémico,* totem pole.
totemismo, *m.* totemism.
totilimundi, *m., var. of* **tutilimundi.**
totipalmado, da, *a.* (zool.) totipalmate.
totolate, *m.* (C. Rica, ento.) chicken louse.
totoloque, *m.* Mexican game similar to quoits.
totomoxtle, *m.* (Mex.) cornhusk.
totoposte, *m.* (C. Amer., Mex.) corn pancake, tortilla.
totora, *f.* (S. Amer.) totora (a cattail used as food and for making a fiber; *Typha domingensis).*
totoral, *m.* (Amer.) patch of cattails or bulrushes.
totoreco, ca, *a.* (C. Amer.) stunned, confused, bewildered.
totorero, *m.* (Chile, ornith.) heron (Izobrychus exilis).
totovía, *f.* (ornith.) crested lark.
totuma, *f.* 1. (Cuba, P. Rico) calabash (fruit). 2. calabash (vessel).
totumo, *m.* (Amer.) calabash tree.
tova, *f.* (ornith.) created lark.
toxemia, *f.* (med.) toxemia.
toxémico, ca, *a.* toxemic.
toxialbúmina, *f.* (med.) toxalbumin.
toxicar, (*ref. 50*) *tr.v.* to poison.
toxicidad, *f.* toxicity.
tóxico, ca, *a., m.* (med.) toxic.
toxicología, *f.* toxicology.
toxicológico, ca, *a.* toxicological.
toxicólogo, *m.* toxicologist.
toxicomanía, *f.* drug addiction; (med.) toxicomania.
toxicómano, na, *a.* addicted to drugs. —*m., f.* drug addict.
toxina, *f.* (med.) toxin.
toza, *f.* 1. piece of bark. 2. tree stump.
tozal, *m.* top of a hill or mound.
tozar, *i.v.* to butt (ram, goat).
tozo, za, *a.* short, small, dwarfish, stumpy.
tozolada, *f.* blow on the neck (of an animal).
tozolón, *m., var. of* **tozolada.**
tozudez, *f.* stubbornness, obstinacy, pigheadedness.
tozudo, da, *a.* stubborn, obstinate, pigheaded.
tozuelo, *m.* back of the neck of an animal.
traba, *f.* 1. hobble, trammel (keeping an animal immobile or restricting its freedom of movement); chock, wedge, block (put under coach wheel); (Chile) pole tied to horns of cattle to impede movement. 2. (fig.) obstacle, hindrance, trammel, fetter, shackle. 3. tie, bond; lock; (mas.) bond. 4. (law) attachment, distraint. 5. (Guat., Dom. Rep.) perch for fighting cocks. — **poner trabas a,** to hinder, impede, put things in the way of; **sin trabas,** without restraint; without conditions.
trabacuenta, *f.* 1. error in an account or bill. 2. (fig.) dispute, controversy, argument.
trabadero, *m.* pastern (of a horse).
trabado, da, *past part. of* **trabar.** —*a.* 1. with white forefeet; with a white right forefoot and a white left hind foot. 2. robust, strong, husky.
trabador, *m.* 1. (mec., Chile) saw set. 2. locking device.
trabadura, *f.* union, joining; bond, tie.
trabajadamente, *adv.* laboriously, painfully.
trabajado, da, *past part. of* **trabajar.** —*a.* 1. worked, wrought. 2. worn-out, exhausted. 3. busy, full or work. 4. elaborate, ornate (literary style).
trabajador, ra, *a.* 1. hard-working, industrious. 2. working, e.g. *la clase t.,* the working class. —*m., f.* worker, laborer. —*m.* workman, workingman. —*f.* workingwoman. —*m.* (Chile, ornith.) heron (Izobrychus exilis). — **t. autonomo** or **independiente** or **por cuenta propia,** self-employed worker; **t. calificado,** skilled worker; **t. por cuenta ajena,** employee; **t. social,** (Mex.) social worker
trabajante, *a.* working, toiling, laboring.
trabajar, *tr.v.* 1. to work, shape, form. 2. to work, till (soil). 3. to exercise, work out, train (a horse, etc.). 4. to bother, disturb, harass, worry, trouble. 5. to work, drive, make work hard. —*i.v.* 1. to work; to be employed. 2. to work, toil, labor. 3. to work, function. 4. (coll.) to act (in theater, cinema, etc.). 5. to bend, warp. — **poner a t.,** to put to work; **t. a destajo,** to do piecework; **t. a jornal,** to do timework, work for a fixed wage; **t. para** + *inf.,* to work to + *inf.,* e.g. *t. para subsistir,* to work (in order) to subsist.
trabajera, *f.* (coll.) bothersome chore.
trabajillo, *m. dim. of* **trabajo,** slight work; slight trouble.
trabajo, *m.* 1. work, labor, toil. 2. job, chore, task. 3. employment, position, post. 4. (phys.) work. 5. study, thesis, report. 6. trouble, bother; (*pl.*) hardships. — **bolsa de t.,** labor exchange; **costar t.,** to be hard, take a lot of effort; **costar t.** + *inf.,* to be hard to + *inf.,* take a lot to + *inf.;* **tomarse el t. de** + *inf.,* to take the trouble to + *inf.;* **t. a destajo,** piecework; **t. a jornal,** timework; **t. calificado,** skilled work; **t. de campo,** fieldwork; **t. de manos,** hand or manual work; **t. de taller,** shopwork; **t. de mucho aliento,** long job or undertaking; **t. de zapa,** underhand work; **t. especializado** or **experto,** skilled work; **t. infantil,** child labor; **trabajos de Hércules,** (myth.) labors of Hercules; **trabajos forzados,** hard labor; **t. manuales,** handicrafts; **pasar trabajos,** to have difficulties.

trabajosamente, *adv.* laboriously, painfully.
trabajoso, sa, *a.* 1. hard, difficult, laborious, arduous. 2. labored, unspontaneous. 3. sickly, weak. 4. needy, suffering.
trabal, *a.* **clavo t.,** large finishing nail (for joining beams or joists together).
trabalenguas, (*pl.* **trabalenguas**), *m.* tongue twister, jawbreaker.
trabamiento, *m.* joining, uniting; bond, union.
trabanca, *f.* paperhanger's table, trestle table.
trabanco, *m.* stick attached to a dog's collar to prevent it from nosing the ground.
trabar, *tr.v.* 1. to join, unite; to lock; to bind, fasten; (mas.) to bond. 2. to grasp, grab, seize. 3. to hobble, fetter, shackle. 4. to thicken, inspissate. 5. to set (the teeth of a saw). 6. to begin; to join in (battle); to strike up (a conversation, acquaintance, friendship, etc.). 7. to harmonize, make agree. 8. (law) to seize, attach, distrain. — **t. amistad,** to become friends; **t. batalla,** to join battle. —*i.v.* to take hold. —*r.v.* 1. to get entangled; to jam (machinery), foul (cables). 2. to come together, become locked (e.g. in a fight). — **trabarse de palabras,** to come to words, cross words, insult each other; **trabársele la lengua a uno,** to get tongue-tied.
trabazón, *f.* 1. union; bond; connection. 2. thickness, consistency.
trabe, *f.* beam, joist.
trábea, *f.* (hist.) trabea (dress toga worn by Romans).
trabécula, *f.* (biol.) trabecula.
trabilla, *f.* 1. gaiter or trouser strap (passing under shoe). 2. half belt (on back of coat). 3. dropped stitch (in knitting).
trabón, *m.* 1. hobbling ring, fetter, shackle. 2. cross plank in oil mills.
trabuca, *f.* firecracker.
trabucación, *f.* 1. confusion, disorder, mix-up, jumble. 2. mistake, blunder.
trabucador, ra, *a.* confusing, disarranging, upsetting. —*m., f.* 1. confuser, disarranger. 2. blunderer.
trabucaire, *m.* (hist.) Catalonian guerrilla (armed with a blunderbuss). —*a.* bold, blustering, swaggering.
trabucante, *a.* 1. confusing, disarranging, jumbling. 2. overweight (coin).
trabucar, (*ref.* *50*) *tr.v.* 1. to upset, overturn, disarrange, jumble. 2. to befuddle, mix up, confuse (the mind). 3. to mix up (words, letters or syllables). 4. to interrupt (a conversation). —*r.v.* to become confused or mixed up; to become jumbled up, upset or disarranged.
trabucazo, *m.* 1. blunderbuss shot. 2. (coll.) blow, shock, sudden misfortune, sudden piece of bad news.
trabuco, *a.* (Mex.) small, tight, narrow. —*m.* 1. blunderbuss. 2. (hist., mil.) catapult. 3. (child's) blowpipe (for firing pellets). 4. (Mex., Cuba) large, poor quality cigar. — **t. naranjero,** wide-mouthed blunderbuss.
trabuquete, *m* 1. catapult. 2. small seine.
traca, *f.* 1. string of firecrackers. 2. (mar.) strake.
tracal, *m.* (Chile) large wineskin.
trácala, *f.* (Mex., P. Rico) trick, deception, fraud.
tracalada, *f.* (Amer.) crowd, flock, multitude.
tracalero, ra, *a.* (Mex.) cheating, tricky. —*m., f.* trickster, cheat.
tracamundana, *f.* 1. (coll.) barter, exchange. 2. (coll.) uproar, hubbub, confusion.
tracción, *f.* 1. traction; pulling. 2. (mec.) tension. — **t. a las cuatro ruedas** or **total** or **integral,** four-wheel drive; **t. delantera,** front-wheel drive; **t. específica,** (engin.) unit tension; **t. magnética,** magnetic traction; **t. trasera,** (auto.) rear-wheel drive.
trace, *a., m., f.* (geog., hist.) Thracian.
trace, tracé, *ref.* **trazar.**
tracería, *f.* (archit.) tracery.
Tracia, *f.* (geog., hist.) Thrace.
traciano, na, *a., m., f.* (geog., hist.) Thracian.
tracio, cia, *a., m., f.* (geog., hist.) Thracian.
tracista, *m., f.* 1. designer. 2. schemer, trickster.
tracoma, *m.* (med.) trachoma.
tracomatoso, sa, *a.* (med.) trachomatous.
tracto, *m.* 1. space, stretch. 2. interval, lapse. 3. (ecc.) tractus.
tractor, *m.* tractor, traction engine; **t. agrícola,** farm tractor; **t. de oruga** or **carriles,** caterpillar tractor.
tradición, *f.* 1. tradition. 2. (law) tradition, delivery, transfer. 3. (lit.) story relating a local tradition or custom.
tradicional, *a.* traditional.
tradicionalismo, *m.* traditionalism.
tradicionalista, *a.* traditionalistic. —*m., f.* 1. traditionalist. 2. (Sp., hist.) Carlist.
tradicionalmente, *adv.* traditionally.
tradicionista, *m., f.* writer of stories relating local traditions or customs.
traducción, *f.* 1. translation. 2. interpretation (of a text); **t. directa,** translation into one's native language; **t. inversa,** translation into a foreign language; **t. mecánica,** machine translation; **t. simultánea,** simultaneous translation.
traducianismo, *m.* (theol.) traducianism.
traducible, *a.* translatable.
traducir, (*ref.* *47*) *tr.v.* 1. to translate. 2. to change, convert, transform. 3. to express.
traductor, ra, *a.* translating. —*m., f.* translator.
traduje, tradujera, tradujese, *ref.* **traducir.**
traduzca, traduzco, *ref.* **traducir.**
traedizo, za, *a.* carried, brought, transported.
traedor, ra, *m., f.* carrier, porter, bearer, bringer.
traedura, *f., var. of* **traída.**
traer, (*ref.* *24*) *tr.v.* 1. to bring. 2. to attract, draw, pull. 3. to bring about, cause, occasion. 4. to make, keep, cause to be, have in certain condition, e.g. *t. a uno intranquilo,* to make one restless, to keep one restless. 5. to wear, e.g. *traes un bonito vestido,* you are wearing a pretty dress. 6. to bring forward, advance, adduce (authorities, arguments). 7. to make, oblige, compel. 8. to persuade. 9. to have, carry (a publication), e.g. *lo trae el periódico,* it's in the newspaper. — **t. abajo el teatro,** to bring the house down; **t. (un niño) al mundo,** to bring (a child) into the world; **t. a mal t.,** to treat badly, maltreat, push about; **t. de acá para allá** or **de aquí para allí,** to push from pillar to post, harass; **t. cola,** to have consequences; **t. consigo,** to have or carry with oneself; **t. de cabeza,** to cause worries or headaches; **t. entre manos,** to have in mind; to have on the fire (plan, scheme, etc.); **t. y llevar,** to gossip, to spread rumors. —*r.v.* to be dressed (well or poorly). — **traérselas,** to be or have more than meets the eye, e.g. *este hombre se las trae,* there's more to this fellow than meets the eye.
traeres, *m.* (*pl.*) finery, dress ornaments.
trafagador, *m.* trafficker, dealer, trader.
trafagante, *a.* trafficker, dealing, trading. —*m., f.* dealer, trader, trafficker.
trafagar, (*ref.* *51*) *tr.v.* to travel over or through. —*i.v.* 1. to trade, deal. 2. to travel, journey, go about.
tráfago, *m.* 1. traffic, trade, business. 2. work, chores, drudgery. 3. hustle, bustle.
trafagón, na, *a.* (coll.) hustling, pushing (salesman). —*m., f.* hustler.
trafague, trafagué, *ref.* **trafagar.**
trafalgar, *m.* (tex.) common cotton buckram.
trafalmeja, jo, trafalmejas, (*pl.* **trafalmejas**), *a.* rattlebrain, empty-headed. —*m., f.* rattlebrain, empty-headed person.
traficación, *f., var. of* **tráfico.**
traficante, *a.* dealing, trading. —*m., f.* dealer, trader, trafficker.
traficar, (*ref.* *50*) *i.v.* 1. to traffic, deal, trade. 2. to travel, journey, go about.
tráfico, *m.* 1. traffic, trade, commerce. 2. traffic (movement of people and vehicles). — **t. aéreo,** air traffic; **t. de influencias,** influence peddling; **t. marítimo,** shipping; **t. rodado,** road traffic.
trafique, trafiqué, *ref.* **traficar.**
tragacanta, *f.* **tragacanto,** *m.* (bot.) tragacanth (tree and gum).
tragacete, *m.* javelin, dart, spear.
tragaderas, *f.* (*pl.*) gullet, throat; **tener buenas t.,** to be very gullible.
tragadero, *m.* 1. throat, gullet. 2. pit, gulf, abyss, vortex (swallowing something up).
tragador, ra, *a.* 1. swallowing. 2. gluttonous. —*m., f.* 1. swallower. 2. glutton, gobler.
tragahombres, (*pl.* **tragahombres**), *m.* (coll.) bully.
trágala, *m.* (Sp.) political song of the liberals scorning the absolutists favoring Ferdinand VII. — **cantarle a uno el t.,** to force one to accept what he detests.
tragaldabas, (*pl.* **tragaldabas**), *m., f.* (coll.) glutton.
tragaleguas, (*pl.* **tragaleguas**), *m., f.* indefatigable walker.
tragallón, na, *a.* (Amer.) gluttonous. —*m., f.* glutton, gobbler.
tragaluz, (*pl.* **tragaluces**), *m.* skylight; transom.
tragamallas, (*pl.* **tragamallas**), *m., f.* (coll.) glutton, gobbler.
tragamonedas, (*pl.* **tragamonedas**), *m.* slot machine.
traganíquel, *m.* (Cuba) juke box.
tragantada, *f.* big swig.
tragante, *a.* swallowing. —*m.* 1. (metal.) hopper (of blast furnace); flue (of a reverberatory furnace). 2. (reg.) flume, main channel (carrying water to mill).
tragantón, na, *a.* (coll.) gluttonous. —*m., f.* (coll.) glutton. —*f.* 1. (coll.) large meal, blow-out, big spread. 2. (coll.) gulp, violent swallow. 3. (coll.) hard pill to swallow.
tragaperras, (*pl.* **tragaperras**), *m.* (coll.) slot machine.
tragar, (*ref.* *51*) *tr.v.* 1. to swallow; to devour, gobble, gulp down; to swallow up, engulf. 2. (fig.) to swallow, believe. 3. to put up with, stomach, swallow, tolerate. 4. to consume, use, swallow up. — **no t. a una persona,** not to be able to stand or stomach a person. —*i.v.* to swallow; (coll.) to gorge oneself, eat a lot. —*r.v.* 1. to swallow up, engulf. 2. to swallow, believe. 3. to put up with, stomach, swallow. 4. to use, consume, take up. — **t. el anzuelo,** to believe a lie, to be deceived.
tragasantos, (*pl.* **tragasantos**), *m., f.* (derog.) overdevout person, church mouse.
tragavenado, *f.* (zool.) anaconda.
tragavirotes, (*pl.* **tragavirotes**), *m.* (coll.) stuffed shirt.
tragazón, *f.* (coll.) gluttony, voracity.
tragedia, *f.* tragedy.
trágicamente, *adv.* tragically.
trágico, ca, *a.* tragic. —*m.* tragedian. —*f.* tragedienne.
tragicomedia, *f.* tragicomedy.
tragicómico, ca, *a.* tragicomic, tragicomical.

trago, *m.* 1. drink, e.g. *¿ quieres un t.?* would you like a drink?; draught, swig; (coll.) drink, drinking, e.g. *le gusta el t.,* he likes drinking. 2. (Ecuad.) liquor. 3. (coll.) misfortune, adversity. — **a tragos,** little by little, slowly; **echar un t.,** to have a drink, take a swig; **t. largo,** long drink.
trago, *m* (anat.) tragus.
tragón, na, *a.* gluttonous. —*m., f.* (coll.) glutton, gobbler.
tragonear, *tr.v.* (coll.) to eat frequently.
tragonería, tragonía, *f.* (coll.) gluttony, voracity.
tragontina, *f.* (bot.) cuckoopint, arum.
trague, tragué, *ref.* **tragar.**
traición, *f.* 1. treachery. 2. treason; act of treason. — **alta t.,** high treason; **a t.,** treacherously; (to shoot) in the back, from behind; **hacer t.,** to betray.
traicionar, *tr.v.* to betray.
traicionero, ra, *a.* treacherous; traitorous. —*m., f.* traitor.
traída, *f.* bringing, carrying, conduction; **t. de aguas,** water supply or system.
traído, da, *past part. of* **traer.** —*a.* worn out, old, threadbare (garment).
traidor, ra, *a.* 1. treasonous, traitorous. 2. treacherous; perfidious, false. —*m.* traitor. —*f.* traitress.
traidoramente, *adv.* treacherously, traitorously, perfidiously, falsely.
traiga, traigo, *ref.* **traer.**
traílla, *f.* 1. dog leash; dog leashes joined together. 2. leveling harrow. 3. (hunt.) pack or pair of dogs leashed together. 4. whip; cord, whipcord; snapper at end of whip.
traillar, *tr.v.* to level (ground) with a leveling harrow.
traína, *f.* sardine fishing net, deep-sea fishing net.
trainera, *a.* sardine-fishing (boat or smack). —*f.* sardine-fishing boat.
traiña, *f.* large sardine-fishing net.
traite, *m.* napping (of cloth).
Trajano, *m.* (hist.) Trajan.
traje, *m.* dress, costume; suit; gown. — **en t. de Adán,** in one's birthday suit, naked; **t. a la medida,** tailor-made suit; made-to-order suit or dress; **t. de baño,** bathing suit; **t. de buzo,** diving suit; **t. de calle,** business suit; **t. de campaña,** battle dress; **t. de etiqueta,** full dress, dress uniform; formal dress; **t. de faena,** (mil.) fatigue clothes; **t. de gala** or **noche** or **t. largo,** evening dress; **t. de luces,** embroidered costume worn by bullfighters; **t. de montar,** riding habit or clothes; **t. de novia,** wedding dress; **t. espacial,** space suit; **t. largo,** evening gown; **t. de paisano,** civilian clothes, mufti; **t. sastre** or **chaqueta,** (woman's) tailored suit.
traje, *ref.* **traer.**
trajear, *tr.v.* to dress, clothe, costume.
trajera, trajese, *ref.* **traer.**
trajín, *m.* 1. chore, work; hectic activity; bustle, hustle, going to and fro, rush. 2. carrying, transporting.
trajinante, *a.* carrying, transporting. —*m., f.* carrier, transporter.
trajinar, *i.v.* to bustle about, rush about; to work; to go back and forth, move about. —*tr.v.* 1. to carry to and fro, carry back and forth. 2. (Chile) to examine, inspect. 3. (Chile) to deceive. 4. (Pan.) to annoy, vex. —*r.v.* (Arg.) to be fooled or deceived.
trajinería, *f.* carrying, transporting; carrier's trade.
trajinero, *m.* carrier, transporter.
tralla, *f.* 1. cord, whipcord. 2. snapper or cracker of whip. 3. whip.
trallazo, *m.* 1. lash (with a whip). 2. crack (of a whip). 3. tongue-lashing, scolding.
trama, *f.* 1. weft, woof. 2. tram (silk twist). 3. plot, scheme, stratagem. 4. plot (of play or novel). 5. blossom (esp. of olive trees). 6. screen, line screen (used in photoengraving).
tramador, ra, *a.* 1. weaving. 2. plotting, scheming. —*m., f.* 1. weaver. 2. plotter, schemer.
tramar, *tr.v.* 1. to weave (cloth). 2. to hatch, weave (a scheme, plot); to plan a difficult enterprise. —*i.v.* to blossom (esp. olive trees).
tramilla, *f.* twine.
tramitación, *f.* transaction, negotiation; procedure.
tramitador, *m.* negotiator, transactor.
tramitar, *tr.v.* to transact, negotiate; to carry through.
trámite, *m.* step (in a negotiation, application for license, etc.); (*pl.*) negotiations, form-filling, transactions, procedure, formalities.
tramo, *m.* 1. section, span, stretch (of land, of road, etc.); flight (of stairs). 2. (fig.) passage (of writing). 3. (archit.) panel.
tramojo, *m.* 1. band, tie (for binding sheaves); place where sheaf is tied. 2. (*pl.*) troubles, hardships.
tramontana, *f.* 1. north; north wind; tramontane. 2. vanity, conceit, pride.
tramontano, na, *a.* tramontane, on the other side of the mountains.
tramontar, *i.v.* 1. to cross the mountains. 2. to sink behind the mountains (the sun). —*tr.v.* to help escape or get away.
tramoya, *f.* 1. (theat.) stage machinery. 2. trick, scheme.
tramoyista, *m.* 1. stagehand, scene shifter. 2. swindler, trickster, schemer, impostor, humbug.
trampa, *f.* 1. trap, snare, pitfall; (fig.) trap, trick. 2. cheating, e.g. *eso es t.,* that's cheating. 3. trap door. 4. hinged section of shop counter. 5. bad debt. 6. fly (of trousers). — **armar una t. a,** to lay a trap for; **caer en la t.,** to fall into the trap; **hacer t.** or **trampas,** to cheat; **llevarse la t.,** (coll.) to fail, be unsuccessful; fall through; **t. antitanque,** (mil.) tank trap; **t. de iones,** (tel.) ion trap; **t. de luz,** light trap; **t. estratigráfica,** (pet.) stratigraphic trap; **t. mortal,** death trap.
trampal, *m.* bog, quagmire.
trampantojo, *m.* (coll.) trick; optical illusion.
trampeador, ra, *a.* cheating, swindling. —*m., f.* swindler, cheater, humbug.
trampear, *tr.v.* 1. trick, deceive, cheat, swindle. —*i.v.* 1. to sponge, cadge. 2. to manage to get along. 3. to cheat.
trampería, *f.* cheating, chicanery, trickery, swindling.
trampero, ra, *m., f.* trapper.
trampilla, *f.* 1. peephole, peep window. 2. door of coal bin. 3. fly (on trousers).
trampista, *m., f.* cheat, swindler, trickster.
trampolín, *m.* 1. springboard; diving board; trampoline. 2. (fig.) springboard, stepping stone.
tramposo, sa, *a.* dishonest, cheating, swindling. —*m., f.* cheat, swindler, trickster, card sharp.
tranca, *f.* 1. cudgel, club, truncheon. 2. pole, beam; bar, crossbar. 3. (Amer.) gate (in a fence). 4. (Amer.) drunk, drunken spree, jag, e.g. *estar en t.,* to be drunk, have a jag on. — **pegarse una t.,** to get drunk.
trancada, *f.* stride, long step; **en dos trancadas,** in a jiffy.
trancahilo, *m.* stop knot (in thread or rope).
trancanil, *m.* (mar.) waterway.
trancar, (*ref. 50*) *tr.v.* to put a bar across; to obstruct, stand in the way of, bar (doors, windows). —*i.v.* (coll.) to stride along.
trancazo, *m.* 1. blow with a club or pole. 2. (coll.) grippe, flu, influenza.
trance, *m.* 1. critical moment. 2. (hypnotic) trance. 3. (law) legal seizure. — **a todo t.,** at all cost, in all events; **en t. de,** in the act of; **entrar en t.,** to go into a trance; **estar en t.,** to be in a trance; **estar en t. de,** to be in danger of, be on the verge of; **t. de armas,** battle, fight, duel; **t. último, postrero** or **mortal,** last hours (of life).
trance, trancé, *ref.* **tranzar.**
trancelín, *m.* braid, ribbon, trimming.
trancha, *f.* tinsmith's stake, small anvil (for forming flanges on tinplate).
tranchete, *m.* shoemaker's knife.
trancho, *m.* (ichth.) (small variety of) sardine (Sardinella allecia).
tranco, *m.* 1. stride, long step. 2. threshold. 3. (coll.) basting stitches. — **al t.,** (Arg., Chile) with long paces; **a trancos,** (coll.) hurriedly and carelessly; **en dos trancos,** (coll.) in two ticks, in a jiffy.
trangallo, *m.* stick hung from hunting dog's collar, to prevent it from nosing the ground.
tranque, tranqué, *ref.* **trancar.**
tranquear, *i.v.* 1. (coll.) to stride along. 2. to lever along, push along with a pole or bar.
tranquera, *f.* 1. fence, palisade. 2. (Amer.) rustic gate or fence; roadblock. — **t. de cruce,** (ry.) crossing gate.
tranquero, *m.* angular stone (of a jamb or lintel); stone (used for door frame).
tranquil, *m.* (archit.) plumb line.
tranquilamente, *adv.* quietly, peacefully, calmly, serenely.
tranquilar, *tr.v.* (com.) to check off (entries in an account).
tranquilice, tranquilicé, *ref.* **tranquilizar.**
tranquilidad, *f.* tranquillity, quiet, peace, calm; serenity, ease of mind.
tranquilizador, ra, *a.* tranquilizing, soothing, calming; reassuring.
tranquilizante, *a.* tranquilizing, reassuring. —*m.* (pharm.) tranquilizer.
tranquilizar, (*ref. 53*) *tr.v.* to tranquilize, calm, quiet down. —*r.v.* to become quiet or calm.
tranquilla, *f.* 1. *dim. of* **tranca,** small bar, pole or beam. 2. bolt, pin. 3. (fig.) surreptitious feeler (cleverly introduced into conversation to elicit secrets); red herring.
tranquillo, *m.* knack, trick; **encontrar or coger el t.,** to get the knack.
tranquillón, *m.* maslin, mixture of wheat and rye.
tranquilo, la, *a.* tranquil, calm, quiet, peaceful; reassured.
tranquiza, *f.* (Mex.) beating, thrashing.
transacción, *f.* 1. transaction, negotiation. 2. settlement, agreement, compromise.
transalpino, na, *a.* transalpine.
transandino, na, *a.* transandean.
transar, *i.v.* (Amer.) to compromise, settle, adjust.
transatlántico, ca, *a.* transatlantic. —*m.* transatlantic liner.
transbordador, ra, *a.* transporter, transporting; transshipping. —*m.* ferry boat, ferry; transporter bridge; **t. funicular,** funicular transporter; transporter bridge.
transbordar, *tr.v.* to transship; to transfer (from one vehicle to another).
transbordo, *m.* transshipment; transfer.
transcaspio, pia, *a.* transcaspian.
transcendencia, *f., var. of* **trascendencia.**
transcendental, *a., var. of* **trascendental.**
transcendentalismo, *m.* (philos.) transcendentalism.
transcendente, *a., var. of* **trascendente.**

transcender, (*ref. 30*) *i.v., var. of* **trascender.**
transcienda, transciendo, *ref.* **transcender.**
transcontinental, *a.* transcontinental.
transcribir, *tr.v.* to transcribe.
transcripción, *f.* transcription.
transcripto, ta, *irr. past part. of* **transcribir.**
transcriptor, *m.* transcriber.
transcrito, ta, *irr. past part. of* **transcribir.**
transcurrir, *i.v.* to pass, go by, elapse.
transcurso, *m.* course, passage (of time).
transductor, *m.* (elec.) transducer.
transepto, *m.* (archit.) transept.
transeúnte, *a.* transient, transitory, temporary. —*m., f.* 1. passer-by, pedestrian. 2. transient, temporary resident.
transexual, *a., m., f.* transsexual.
transexualidad, *f.* **transexualismo,** *m.* transsexualism.
transferencia, *f.* transference; transfer.
transferible, *a.* transferable.
transferidor, ra, *a.* transferring. —*m., f.* transferrer.
transferir, (*ref. 42*) *tr.v.* 1. to transfer. 2. to defer, put off, postpone. 3. (law) to transfer, make over to, convey, cede.
transfiera, tranfiero, *ref.* **transferir.**
transfigurable, *a.* transfigurable.
transfiguración, *f.* transfiguration; (Bib., ecc.) **T.,** Transfiguration.
transfigurar, *tr.v.* to transfigure. —*r.v.* to become transfigured.
transfijo, *a.* transfixed, pierced.
transfinito, ta, *a.* (math.) transfinite.
transfiriendo, transfiriera, transfiriese, transfirió, *ref.* **transferir.**
transfixión, *f.* transfixion.
transflor, *m.* (p.) painting on metal.
transflorar, *tr.v.* 1. to paint, paint designs on (metal). 2. to trace, make tracing of. —*i.v.* to show through.
transformable, *a.* transformable, convertible.
transformación, *f.* transformation.
transformador, ra, *a.* transforming. —*m., f.* transformer. —*m.* (elec.) transformer; **t. acorazado,** shell transformer; **t. de corriente,** current transformer; **t. de desenganche,** tripping transformer; **t. de fase,** phasing transformer; **t. de medida,** instrument transformer; **t. de núcleo de hierro,** iron-core transformer; **t. de núcleo de aire,** air-core transformer; **t. de núcleo y bobina,** core-and-coil transformer; **t. de potencial, voltaje** or **tensión,** potential or voltage transformer; **t. elevador,** step-up or booster transformer; **t. en aceite,** oil-insulated transformer; **t. enfriado por aceite,** oil-cooled transformer; **t. enfriado por agua,** water-cooled transformer; **t. enfriado por aire,** air-cooled transformer; **t. erizo,** hedgehog transformer; **t. estático,** stationary or static transformer; **t. reductor,** step-down transformer; **t. rotativo** or **rotatorio,** rotary transformer; synchronous converter.
transformamiento, *m.* transformation.
transformante, *a.* transforming.
transformar, *tr.v.* to transform. —*r.v.* to be or become transformed.
transformativo, va, *a.* transformative.
transformismo, *m.* (biol.) transformism.
transformista, *a.* (biol.) transformist, transformistic. —*m., f.* (biol.) transformist. —*m.* (theat.) quick-change artist.
transfregar, (*ref. 67*) *tr.v.* to rub together.
transfregué, *ref.* **transfregar.**
transfretano, na, *a.* across the strait, on the other side of a strait or point.
transfretar, *tr.v.* to cross (the sea). —*i.v.* to extend, spread.
transfriego, transfriegue, *ref.* **transfregar.**
tránsfuga, tránsfugo, *m., f.* 1. fugitive. 2. deserter, turncoat.
transfundición, *f.* transfusion.
transfundir, *tr.v.* 1. to transfuse, pour from one vessel to another. 2. to transmit, spread (news from one person to another). —*r.v.* to become transmitted, spread (news).
transfusible, *a.* transfusable.
transfusión, *f.* transfusion; **t. de sangre,** (med.) blood transfusion.
transfusor, ra, *a.* transfusing. —*m., f.* transfuser.
transgredir, *tr.v.* to transgress, violate, break (a law).
transgresión, *f.* transgression, violation.
transgresivo, va, *a.* transgressive.
transgresor, ra, *a.* transgressing. —*m., f.* transgressor, violator.
transiberiano, na, *a.* trans-Siberian.
transición, *f.* transition.
transido, da, *a.* 1. racked, torn (with pain), weak, worn out (with hunger), overcome (with emotion, sorrow). 2. miserable, wretched.
transigencia, *f.* tolerance; compromise.
transigente, *a.* compromising, accommodating; tolerant, broad-minded.
transigir, (*ref. 62*) *i.v.* to compromise; to give in; **t. con,** to agree to; to tolerate.
transija, transijo, *ref.* **transigir.**
Transilvania, *f.* Transylvania, region in Rumania.
transilvano, na, *a., m., f.* Transylvanian.
transistor, *m.* (elec.) transistor; **radio a transistores,** transistor radio.
transistorizar, (*ref. 53*) *tr.v.* (elec.) to transistorize.
transitable, *a.* passable, fit for traffic, transitable.
transitar, *i.v.* to travel, journey, pass.
transitivamente, *adv.* transitively.
transitivo, va, *a.* transitive.
tránsito, *m.* 1. transit, movement, passage, journey. 2. traffic (movement of vehicles). 3. road, way, passageway. 4. stopping place. 5. change, transition, transit. 6. death (of a saint). — **en t.,** on one's way, en route; **estar de t.,** to be in transit, be passing through; **policía de t.,** traffic police; **se prohibe el t.,** no thoroughfare; **t. aéreo,** air traffic.
transitoriamente, *adv.* transitorily, temporarily.
transitoriedad, *f.* transitoriness, temporariness.
transitorio, ria, *a.* transitory, temporary.
translación, *f., var. of* **traslación.**
translaticiamente, *adv., var. of* **traslaticiamente.**
translaticio, cia, *a., var. of* **traslaticio.**
translativo, va, *a., var. of* **traslativo.**
translimitación, *f.* 1. trespassing, overstepping, going beyond limits. 2. armed intervention in a bordering state.
translimitar, *tr.v.* 1. to overstep, go beyond the limits or bounds of. 2. to trespass (boundaries). 3. to cross unintentionally or with previous permission (the frontier of a state).
translinear, *i.v.* (law) to pass an entail from one line of heirs to another.
translucidez, *f.* translucence.
translúcido, da, *a.* translucent.
transluciente, *a.* translucent.
translucir, (*ref. 46*) *tr.v., r.v., var. of* **traslucir.**
transmarino, *a.* transmarine.
transmigración, *f.* transmigration.
transmigrar, *i.v.* to transmigrate.
transmisible, *a.* transmissible, transmittable.
transmisión, *f.* transmission; (*pl.*) (mil.) signals; communication, signal corps, e.g. *servicio de transmisiones,* signal corps. — **t. a cardán,** (auto.) drive shaft; **t. de cadena,** (mec.) chain drive; **t. de contramarcha,** reverse drive; **t. delantera,** (auto.) front-wheel drive; **t. de pensamiento,** thought transference, telepathy; **t. en las cuatro ruedas,** (auto.) four-wheel drive; **t. por correa,** belt drive; **t. por onda portadora,** (elec.) carrier transmission.
transmisor, ra, *a.* transmitting. —*m., f.* transmitter. —*m.* (rad., tel.) transmitter; **t. de chispas,** (rad.) spark transmitter.
transmitir, *tr.v.* 1. to transmit. 2. (rad.) to broadcast. 3. (law) to cede.
transmontano, na, *a., var. of* **tramontano.**
transmontar, *tr.v., i.v., r.v., var. of* **tramontar.**
transmudación, *f., var. of* **transmutación.**
transmudamiento, *m., var. of* **transmutación.**
transmudar, *tr.v.* 1. to transfer, move. 2. to transmute, convert, change. 3. to persuade, convince.
transmundano, *a.* transmundane, beyond the world.
transmutable, *a.* transmutable.
transmutación, *f.* transmutation; **t. química,** chemical change.
transmutar, *tr.v.* to transmute, convert, change. —*r.v.* to become transmuted or converted.
transmutativo, va, transmutatorio, ria, *a.* transmutative, transmutational.
transoceánico, ca, *a.* transoceanic.
transpacífico, ca, *a.* transpacific.
transpadano, na, *a., m.* transpadane, on the other side of the river Po.
transparencia, *f.* 1. transparency, transparence. 2. (photog.) transparency, slide.
transparentarse, *r.v.* 1. to show through; to be transparent. 2. (fig.) to become clear or obvious.
transparente, *a.* 1. transparent; translucid. 2. (fig.) clear, obvious. —*m.* 1. window shade, blind. 2. stained glass window (behind an altar).
transpirable, *a.* transpirable.
transpiración, *f.* 1. perspiration, sweating. 2. transpiration, exudation.
transpirar, *i.v.* 1. to perspire, sweat. 2. to transpire, exude.
transpirenaico, ca, *a.* trans-Pyrenean, beyond the Pyrenees.
transplacentario, a, *a.* (med.) transplacental.
transplantar, *tr.v., var. of* **trasplantar.**
transpondré, transpondría, *ref.* **transponer.**
transponedor, ra, *a.* transplanting; moving. —*m., f.* transplanter; mover.
transponer, (*ref. 15*) *tr.v.* 1. to transfer, move; to transplant. 2. to cross (a line, threshold); to go behind (a hill), go round (a corner). —*r.v.* 1. to go out of sight, be lost from sight. 2. to doze, fall half asleep. 3. to set below the horizon (the sun).
transponga, transpongo, *ref.* **transponer.**
transportación, *f.* transportation, transport, transporting.
transportador, ra, *a.* transporting, carrying. —*m., f.* transporter, carrier. —*m.* 1. transporter, carrier. 2. protractor (measuring instrument). — **t. a cadena,** chain conveyor; **t. de banda** or **de cinta sin fin,** belt conveyor; **t. de paletas,** drag conveyor; **t. de rodillos,** roller conveyor; **t. de tornillo sin fin,** screw conveyor.
transportamiento, *m.* 1. transportation, transporting. 2. ecstasy, rapture.
transportar, *tr.v.* to transport, convey, carry; (mus.) to transpose. —*r.v.* to be transported, be carried away.
transporte, *m.* 1. transport, cartage; transportation; conveyance; ferriage. 2. transmission (of electricity). 3. transport, transport ship. 4. (fig.) transport, rapture, ecstasy. — **t. de abastecimientos por aire,** airlift; **t. de tropas,** troop

carrier; **t. fluvial,** river transportation; **t. marítimo,** ocean transportation; **t. público,** public transportation.
transportista, *m., f.* mover, carrier, porter.
transposición, *f.* transposition.
transpositivo, va, *a.* transpositive.
transpuesta, *f., var. of* traspuesta.
transpuesto, ta, *irr. past part. of* **transponer.**
transpuse, transpusiera, transpusiese, *ref.* transponer.
transterminar, *tr.v.* to transfer or send to another jurisdiction.
transtiberino, na, *a., m., f.* trans-Tiber, trans-Tiberian, across the Tiber (river).
transubstanciación, *f.* transubstantiation.
transubstancial, *a.* transubstantial.
transubstanciar, *tr.v.* to transubstantiate. —*r.v.* to be transubstantiated, undergo transubstantiation, transubstantiate.
transuránico, ca, *a.* (phys.) transuranic.
transvasar, *tr.v.* to decant, pour from one vessel to another.
transverberación, *f.* (rel.) transfixion, transverberation.
transversal, *a.* transversal, transverse; cross (street); collateral (relative). —*m., f.* collateral relative. —*f.* cross street.
transversalmente, *adv.* transversally, transversely.
transverso, sa, *a.* transverse. —*m.* (anat.) transverse, transverse muscle.
transvertidor, *m.* (elec.) transverter.
transvestido, da, *a.* transvestite.
tranvía, *m.* trolley car, tram, tramcar, streetcar; tramway, tramline.
tranviario, ria, *a.* trolley, tramway, streetcar. —*m.* tramway employee or worker; streetcar conductor or driver.
tranviero, *m., var. of* **tranviario.**
tranzadera, *f.* plaited cord.
tranzar, (*ref. 53*) *tr.v.* 1. to break, break off, cut off. 2. to braid, plait.
tranzón, *m.* piece, lot (of land); small farm.
trapa, *f.* 1. (mar.) spilling line; (*pl.*) (mar.) tackle for securing lifeboat to deck. 2. stamping or tramping of feet; hullabaloo, racket, uproar. 3. (ecc.) the Trappist order.
trapace, *ref.* **trapazar.**
trapacear, *i.v.* to cheat, swindle.
trapacería, *f.* trick, deception, swindle.
trapacero, ra, *a., m., f., var. of* **trapacista.**
trapacete, *m.* (com.) daybook, entry book.
trapacista, *a.* swindling, cheating, deceiving, tricking. —*m., f.* swindler, cheat, trickster.
trapajería, *f.* rags, tatters.
trapajo, *m.* rag, tatter.
trapajoso, sa, *a.* raggedy, ragged, torn, tattered.
trápala, *f.* 1. (coll.) hubbub, uproar, hullabaloo; confusion. 2. clatter, galloping or trotting noise (of a horse). 3. (coll.) trick, hoax, deception. —*m.* (coll.) chattering, jabbering, prattling, loquacity. —*m., f.* 1. (coll.) chatterbox, chatterer, prattler. 2. (coll.) trickster, swindler, fraud, cheat, liar.
trapalear, *i.v.* 1. (coll.) to chatter, prattle, jabber. 2. (coll.) to lie, cheat, swindle, deceive. 3. to tramp or clatter about.
trapalón, na, *m., f.* cheat, liar, trickster.
trapatiesta, *f.* (coll.) row, brawl, uproar.
trapaza, *f.* trick, fraud, swindle.
trapazar, (*ref. 53*) *i.v., var. of* **trapacear.**
trape, *m.* 1. interlining (formerly used for skirt and jacket pleats). 2. (Chile) woolen cord.
trapeador, *m.* (Amer.) floor mop or rag.
trapear, *tr.v.* (Chile, Ecuad., Mex., Peru) to mop (the floor).
trapecial, *a.* (geom.) trapezoidal.
trapecio, *m.* 1. trapeze (acrobat's swing). 2. (geom.) trapezoid (U.S.), trapezium (G.B.). 3. (anat.) trapezium (bone). 4. (anat.) trapezius (triangular muscle).
trapecista, *m., f.* trapeze artist.
trapense, *a., m., f.* (ecc.) Trappist.
trapería, *f.* rags; old clothes and second-hand shop.
trapero, ra, *m., f.* ragpicker, rag dealer.
trapezoedro, *m.* (cryst.) trapezohedron.
trapezoidal, *a.* (geom.) trapezoidal, trapezoid.
trapezoide, *m.* 1. (geom.) trapezium (G.B.), trapezoid (U.S.). 2. (anat.) trapezoid (bone).
trapiche, *m.* 1. sugar mill. 2. olive press. 3. (Arg., Chile) ore grinding mill.
trapichear, *i.v.* 1. (coll.) to contrive, devise, scheme. 2. to be a retailer; to deal at retail.
trapicheo, *m.* 1. (coll.) scheming, contriving. 2. retail business, retailing.
trapichero, *m.* sugar mill worker.
trapiento, ta, *a.* ragged, tattered.
trapillo, *m.* 1. (coll.) poor suitor, suitor of little means. 2. (coll.) savings, nest egg. — **de t.,** (coll.) in house clothes, in shirt sleeves, untidy.
trapío, *m.* 1. (coll.) graceful, easy style or bearing. 2. (taur., coll.) spirit, daring (said of a bull).
trapisonda, *f.* 1. (coll.) hubbub, racket; brawl, squabble. 2. (coll.) intrigue, scheming, plot. 3. (mar.) choppy sea.
trapisondear, *i.v.* (coll.) to stir up trouble; to scheme, intrigue.
trapisondista, *m., f.* intriguer, schemer.
trapista, *m.* (Arg.) ragpicker, rag dealer.
trapito, *m. dim. of* **trapo,** small rag, small piece of cloth. — **los trapitos de cristianar,** (coll.) Sunday best (clothes), glad rags.
trapo, *m.* 1. rag; tatter. 2. sails (of a ship). 3. (coll.) muleta, smaller cape (used in last phase of bullfight). 4. (*pl.*) (coll.) women's clothes, rags. — **a todo t.,** (mar.) full sail; (coll.) at full speed, at top speed; **poner a uno como un t.,** (coll.) to give a severe reprimand, give a dressing down; **sacar los trapos a la colada, a relucir** or **al sol,** (coll.) to wash one's dirty linen in public; **soltar el t.,** (coll.) to burst out laughing or crying; **t. de cocina,** dishtowel; **t. del polvo** or **de sacudir,** dust cloth.
traque, *m.* 1. bang, crack (report of a rocket, firecracker). 2. gunpowder fuse. — **a t. barraque,** at all times, continuously; for any reason.
tráquea, traquearteria, *f.* (anat., bot., zool.) trachea, windpipe.
traqueado, da, *a.* (Arg.) often-used, trampled (road, etc.); hackneyed.
traqueal, *a.* (anat., bot., zool.) tracheal.
traquear, *tr.v., i.v., var. of* **traquetear.**
traqueida, *f.* (bot.) tracheid.
traqueitis, *f.* (med.) tracheitis.
traqueo, *m., var. of* **traqueteo.**
traqueotomía, *f.* (med.) tracheotomy.
traquetear, *tr.v.* 1. to shake, jolt, jerk. 2. (coll.) to handle a lot, paw about. —*i.v.* to clatter, rattle (e.g. machinery, moving train or vehicle, etc.); to crack, bang (wood or firecrackers).
traqueteo, *m.* 1. clattering, rattling; banging. 2. shaking, jolting, jerking.
traquido, *m.* 1. crack, report (of a firearm). 2. crack, snap (of a piece of wood or something that breaks).
traquinias, *f.* (lit.) (*pl.*) **Las T.,** The Trachiniae, a tragedy by Sophocles.
traquita, *f.* (min.) trachyte.
traquítico, ca, *a.* (min.) trachytic.
trarigüe, *m.* (Chile) ornamental sash or belt used by the Indians.
trarilongo, *m.* (Chile) Indian headband.
traro, *m.* (Chile, ornith.) caracara, carrion hawk.
tras, *prep.* after; behind; in search of, in pursuit of; **t. de,** behind; in addition to. —*m.* 1. (coll.) behind, backside, bottom. 2. sound of loud tapping, banging.
tras, (onomatopoeic word) rat, tap; **¡tras, tras!** rat-a-tat! tap, tap!
trasalcoba, *f.* small room adjoining a bedroom.
trasalpino, na, *a.* transalpine.
trasaltar, *m.* space behind an altar.
trasandino, *a.* trans-Andean.
trasandosco, ca, *a.* slightly over two years old (said of cattle).
trasanteanoche, *adv.* three nights ago.
trasanteayer, trasantier, *adv.* three days ago.
trasañejo, ja, *a.* three years old.
trasatlántico, ca, *a.* transatlantic. —*m.* transatlantic liner.
trasbarrás, *m.* thud, thump (of something falling).
trasbocar, (*ref. 50*) *tr.v.* (Arg., Col.) to throw up, vomit.
trasbodar, *tr.v., var. of* **transbordar.**
trasbordo, *m., var. of* **transbordo.**
trasbotica, *f.* back room (behind shop or store).
trasca, *f.* leather strap or thong.
trascabo, *m.* trip, slip.
trascantón, *m.* 1. spur stone. 2. errand boy or porter. — **darle a uno t.,** (coll.) to give someone the slip, shake someone off.
trascantonada, *f.* spur stone.
trascartarse, *r.v.* to appear after it was needed or expected (a winning card).
trascartón, *m.* drawing of a winning card after the game is lost.
trascendencia, *f.* 1. importance, consequence. 2. (philos., theol.) transcendence. 3. penetration, perspicacity.
trascendental, *a.* 1. transcendent, far-reaching, very important or serious, great, enormous, e.g. *va a tener efectos trascendentales,* it will have far-reaching effects. 2. (philos.) transcendental.
trascendente, *a.* 1. transcendent, of great importance. 2. (math.) transcendental. 3. (philos., theol.) transcendent.
trascender, (*ref. 30*) *i.v.* 1. to become known, to come out. 2. to smell strong, have a strong smell. 3. to spread, extend; to go beyond. 4. (philos.) to transcend. —*tr.v.* to inquire into, find out about.
trascendido, da, *a.* perspicacious, keen.
trascienda, trasciendo, *ref.* **trascender.**
trascocina, *f.* scullery, back kitchen.
trascolar, (*ref. 33*) *tr.v.* 1. to strain. 2. to pass over (road, etc.) —*r.v.* to percolate, seep through.
trasconejarse, *r.v.* 1. to remain behind the hunting dogs (hunted animals); to get trapped in the rabbit hole (ferret). 2. (coll.) to get lost, get mislaid.
trascordarse, (*ref. 33*) *r.v.* to forget.
trascoro, *m.* back choir, retrochoir, place behind the choir.
trascorral, *m.* 1. back yard, back court. 2. (coll.) behind, backside, bottom.
trascorvo, va, *a.* crook-kneed (horse).
trascribir, *tr.v., var. of* **transcribir.**
trascripción, *f., var. of* **transcripción.**
trascripto, ta, trascrito, ta, *irr. past part. of* **transcribir.**
trascuarto, *m.* 1. back room. 2. rear apartment.
trascuenta, *f.* error (in an account).
trascuerde, trascuerdo, *ref.* **trascordarse.**
trascurrir, *i.v., var. of* **transcurrir.**
trascurso, *m., var. of* **transcurso.**
trasdobladura, *f.* 1. trebling, tripling. 2. folding three times.
trasdoblar, *tr.v.* 1. to treble, triple. 2. to fold three times.

trasdoblo, *m.* treble number.
trasdós, *m.* (archit.) extrados; (archit.) pilaster behind a column.
trasdosear, *tr.v.* (archit.) to strengthen the back of.
trasechador, ra, *a., m., f., var. of* **acechador.**
trasechar, *tr.v., var. of* **acechar.**
trasegador, ra, *m., f.* one who racks or decants wine.
trasegadura, *f., var. of* **trasiego.**
trasegar, (*ref. 67*) *tr.v.* 1. to decant, transfer (liquid) from one container to another. 2. to transfer, move. 3. to disarrange, jumble up, turn upside down or topsy-turvy, upset. 4. to tipple, drink (liquor).
trasegué, *ref.* **trasegar.**
traseñalar, *tr.v.* to put a different mark on, change the mark on.
trasero, ra, *a.* 1. back, rear. 2. overloaded in back (a carriage). —*m.* 1. rump, buttocks, behind. 2. (*pl.*) (coll.) ancestors. —*f.* back, rear, back part (of house, carriage, door, etc.).
trasferencia, *f., var. of* **transferencia.**
trasferible, *a., var. of* **transferible.**
trasferidor, ra, *a., m., f.* **transferidor.**
trasferir, (*ref. 42*) *tr.v., var. of* **transferir.**
trasfiera, trasfiero, *ref.* **transferir.**
trasfigurable, *a., var. of* **transfigurable.**
trasfiguración, *f., var. of* **transfiguración.**
trasfigurar, *tr.v., var. of* **transfigurar.**
trasfijo, ja, *a., var. of* **transfijo.**
trasfiriendo, trasfiriera, trasfiriese, *ref.* **trasferir.**
trasfixión, *f., var. of* **transfixión.**
trasflor, *m., var. of* **transflor.**
trasflorar, *tr.v., var. of* **transflorar.**
trasflorear, *tr.v., var. of* **transflorear.**
trasfollado, da, *a.* (vet.) suffering from swollen gambrels or hocks.
trasfollo, *m.* (vet.) swelling on the hock or gambrel.
trasfondo, *m.* background.
trasformación, *f., var. of* **transformación.**
trasformador, ra, *a., m., f., var. of* **transformador.**
trasformamiento, *m., var. of* **transformamiento.**
trasformar, *tr.v., r.v., var. of* **transformar.**
trasformativo, va, *a., var. of* **transformativo.**
trasfregue, trasfregué, *ref.* **trasfregar.**
trásfuga, *m., f., var. of* **tránsfuga.**
trásfugo, *m., var. of* **tránsfugo.**
trasfundición, *f., var. of* **transfundición.**
trasfundir, *tr.v., var. of* **transfundir.**
trasfusión, *f., var. of* **transfusión.**
trasfusor, ra, *a., m., f., var. of* **transfusor.**
trasgo, *m.* sprite, imp, goblin, hobgoblin; (coll.) imp, mischievous child.
trasgredir, *tr.v., var. of* **transgredir.**
trasgresión, *f., var. of* **transgresión.**
trasgresor, ra, *a., m., f., var. of* **transgresor.**
trasguear, *i.v.* to play the spook; to imitate a bogyman.
trasguero, ra, *m., f.* prankster who likes acting the spook.
trashoguero, ra, *a.* lazy, stay-at-home. —*m.* fireback, back plate (of a fireplace); large log (in a fireplace).
trashojar, *tr.v.* to scan, leaf through (a book, etc.).
trashumación, *f.* nomadism, seasonal migration of flocks in search of pastures.
trashumante, *a.* nomad, migrating; grazing in alien pastures (flocks).
trashumar, *i.v.* to migrate seasonally in search of pasture (flocks).
trasiego, *m.* 1. decanting, racking (of wine). 2. transferring, moving. 3. disarranging, disorder, upset.
trasiego, trasiegue, *ref.* **trasegar.**
trasijado, da, *a.* 1. thin-flanked (horse). 2. skinny, lean (person).
traslación, *f.* 1. transfer; transference; moving. 2. translation (into another language). 3. copy, transcription. 4. (rhet.) metaphor. 5. (mec., phys.) translation.
trasladable, *a.* transferable; movable.
trasladación, *f., var. of* **traslación.**
trasladador, ra, *a.* transferring; moving. —*m., f.* transferrer; mover, carrier.
trasladante, *a.* transferring; moving.
trasladar, *tr.v.* 1. to transfer, move. 2. to translate (into another language). 3. to copy, transcribe. —*r.v.* to move, change residence.
traslado, *m.* 1. transfer; move; removal. 2. moving, change (of residence, etc.); transportation. 3. copy, transcript. 4. (law) notification, communication.
traslapar, *tr.v.* to overlap.
traslapo, *m.* overlapping, overlapped object or piece.
traslaticiamente, *adv.* figuratively, metaphorically.
traslaticio, cia, *a.* figurative, metaphorical.
traslativo, va, *a.* translative, transferring, conveying.
traslato, ta, *a., var. of* **traslaticio.**
traslimitar, *tr.v., var. of* **translimitar.**
traslúcido, da, *a., var. of* **translúcido.**
trasluciente, *a., var. of* **translúcido.**
traslucimiento, *m.* showing through, translucency.
traslucir, (*ref. 46*) *tr.v.* to conjecture, guess, deduce. —*r.v.* 1. to be translucid or translucent. 2. to become evident, clear or obvious.
traslumbramiento, *m.* dazzlement, dazzling.
traslumbrar, *tr.v.* to dazzle (light). —*r.v.* to vanish, disappear swiftly.
trasluz, *m.* light seen through a transparent body; reflected light; **al t.,** against the light.
trasluzca, *ref.* **traslucir.**
trasmallo, *m.* 1. trammel net. 2. iron ring reinforcing the head of a pall-mall mallet.
trasmano, *m., f.* second hand (at cards); **a t.,** out of reach; out of the way, remote; out of touch.
trasmañana, *adv.* (rare) day after tomorrow.
trasmañanar, *tr.v.* (rare) to procrastinate; to put off to another day, postpone.
trasmarino, na, *a., var. of* **transmarino.**
trasmatar, *tr.v.* (coll.) to assume that one will outlive, live longer than (another person).
trasmigración, *f., var. of* **transmigración.**
trasmigrar, *i.v., var. of* **transmigrar.**
trasminante, *a.* (Chile) penetrating, piercing cold).
trasminar, *tr.v.* 1. to dig under, undermine. 2. to permeate (an odor), seep through (a liquid).
trasmisible, *a., var of* **transmisible.**
trasmisión, *f., var. of* **transmisión.**
trasmitir, *tr.v., var. of* **transmitir.**
trasmochar, *tr.v.* to trim or prune very closely.
trasmontano, na, *a., var. of* **transmontano.**
trasmontar, *tr.v., i.v., var. of* **transmontar.**
trasmudación, *f., var. of* **transmutación.**
trasmudamiento, *m., var. of* **transmutación.**
trasmudar, *tr.v., var. of* **transmudar.**
trasmutable, *a., var. of* **transmutable.**
trasmutación, *f., var. of* **transmutación.**
trasmutar, *tr.v., r.v., var. of* **transmutar.**
trasmutativo, va, *a., var. of* **transmutativo.**
trasmutatorio, ria, *a., var. of* **transmutatorio.**
trasnochada, *f.* 1. last night. 2. wakeful night. 3. (mil.) night attack.
trasnochado, da, *past part. of* **trasnochar.** —*a.* 1. stale, spoiled, e.g. *ensalada t.,* wilted salad. 2. haggard, gaunt, drawn. 3. stale, hackneyed, old (news, etc.).
trasnochador, ra, *m., f.* one who keeps late hours, night bird, night owl.
trasnochar, *tr.v.* to sleep on, spend the night thinking about (a certain subject). —*i.v.* 1. to stay up late, keep late hours. 2. to spend the night.
trasnoche, trasnocho, *m.* (coll.) staying up late, keeping late hours.
trasnombrar, *tr.v.* to change or confuse the names of.
trasnominación, *f.* (rhet.) metonymy.
trasoiga, trasoigo, *ref.* **trasoir.**
trasoír, (*ref. 12*) *tr.v.* to mishear, hear wrong.
trasojado, da, *a.* gaunt, haggard, drawn; having sunken eyes.
trasoñar, (*ref. 33*) *tr.v.* 1. to imagine wrongly. 2. to see as in a dream.
trasovado, da, *a.* (bot.) obovate.
trasoyendo, trasoyera, trasoyese, *ref.* trasoir.
traspadano, na, *a., m., f., var. of* **transpadano.**
traspalar, traspalear, *tr.v.* 1. to move or remove with a shovel. 2. to transfer, move.
traspaleo, *m.* 1. shoveling. 2. moving.
traspapelar, *tr.v.* to mislay amongst other papers. —*r.v.* to get lost or mislaid amongst other papers.
trasparencia, *f., var. of* **transparencia.**
trasparentarse, *r.v., var. of* **transparentarse.**
trasparente, *a., var. of* **transparente.**
traspasable, *a.* transferable.
traspasación, *f.* transfer, conveyance, cession (of rights or possessions); sale.
traspasador, ra, *a.* transgressing. —*m., f.* transgressor; trespasser.
traspasamiento, *m., var. of* **traspaso.**
traspasar, *tr.v.* 1. to pierce, transfix, run through; (fig.) to pierce (with pain, grief). 2. to transfer, make over (possession, etc.), sell. 3. to cross, go across, go over. 4. to take, move, transfer. 5. to break, violate (law). 6. to exceed, go beyond (limits). 7. to pass again. —*r.v.* to go too far, exceed the limits.
traspaso, *m.* 1. transfer, conveyance, cession (of rights or property); sale. 2. property or goods transferred or sold. 3. cost of things transferred or sold. 4. crossing, going across. 5. transgression, violation. 6. trick, ruse. 7. anguish, grief, pain.
traspatio, *m.* backyard, back court.
traspecho, *m.* bone ornament on crossbow stock.
traspeinar, *tr.v.* to comb over again, to touch up the hair with a comb.
traspellar, *tr.v.* (rare) to close, shut (a door, a book, etc.).
traspié, *m.* stumble; slip, trip; **dar traspiés,** to stumble, trip; to slip, make a mistake.
traspilastra, *f.* (archit.) counterpillar, counterpilaster.
traspillar, *tr.v.* to close, shut. —*r.v.* to get worn out, become weak and emaciated.
traspintar, *tr.v.* to show (one card) and play another. —*r.v.* 1. to show (one card) and play another. 2. to come out wrong, turn out contrary to one's expectations. 3. to show through (writing, fabric).
traspirable, *a., var. of* **transpirable.**
traspiración, *f., var. of* **transpiración.**
traspirenaico, ca, *a., var. of* **transpirenaico.**
trasplantable, *a.* transplantable.
trasplantar, *tr.v.* to transplant. —*r.v.* to settle in another country; to migrate.
trasplante *m.* transplantation, transplanting.
trasponedor, ra, *a., m., f., var. of* **transponedor.**
trasponer, (*ref. 15*) *tr.v., i.v., r.v., var. of* transponer.
traspontín, *m.* 1. bed mat or pad 2. (coll.) behind, bottom, backside.
trasportación, *f., var. of* **transportación.**

trasportador, ra, *a., m., f., var. of* **transportador.**
trasportamiento, *m., var. of* **transportamiento.**
trasportar, *tr.v., var. of* **transportar.**
trasporte, *m.* 1. transportation; transport. 2. (P. Rico) large five-stringed guitar.
trasportín, *m., var. of* **traspuntín.**
trasposición, *f., var. of* **transposición.**
traspositivo, va, *a., var. of* **transpositivo.**
traspuesta, *f.* 1. transposition, transposing. 2. elevation, rise (in terrain impeding view). 3. flight, hiding (of a person). 4. rear buildings, outhouses, outbuilding.
traspunte, *m.* (theat.) call, callboy; prompter in the wings.
traspuntín, *m.* 1. small undermattress. 2. folding seat (in a car).
trasquila, *f., var. of* **trasquiladura.**
trasquilador, *m.* shearer, clipper.
trasquiladura, *f.* 1. clipping, shearing (of sheep, dogs, etc.). 2. clumsy haircut. 3. curtailment.
trasquilar, *tr.v.* 1. to shear (sheep); to clip (dogs); to crop (hair). 2. (coll.) to cut down, lessen, curtail.
trasquilimocho, cha, *m.* (coll.) closecropped, shorn.
trasquilón, *m.* 1. (coll.) cropping; shearing. 2. (coll.) money obtained by a swindle. — **a trasquilones,** irregularly, clumsily.
trasroscarse, *(ref. 50) r.v.* not to fit in, not to screw in properly (a screw).
trasrosque, trasrosqué, *ref.* **trasroscarse.**
trastabillar, *i.v., var. of* **trastrabillar.**
trastabillón, *m.* (Arg., C. Rica, Chile) stumble, trip, slip.
trastada, *f.* (coll.) dirty trick.
trastajo, *m.* piece of junk, old furniture, worthless object.
trastazo, *m.* (coll.) whack, bump, knock, blow.
traste, *m.* 1. (mus.) fret (on guitars, etc.). 2. object, thing, whatnot; (*pl.*) (coll.) housewares; old furniture, knickknacks. 3. (Sp.) wine taster's glass. 4. (Amer., coll.) behind, bottom, backside. — **dar al t. con,** to spoil, wreck, break; to discard, scrap.
trasteado, *m.* set of frets (on some stringed instruments).
trasteador, ra, *a.* noisy, bustling about. —*m., f.* person who makes noise or moves about.
trastear, *tr.v.* 1. to put fets on (a guitar, etc.). 2. to play, strum on (a guitar, etc.). 3. (taur.) to challenge (a bull) with the muleta cape. 4. (coll.) to manage cleverly (a person or business).
trastejador, ra, *a.* 1. tiling. 2. overhauling. —*m., f.* 1. roof tiler. 2. overhauler.
trastejadura, *f.* tiling, re-tiling.
trastejar, *tr.v.* 1. to tile, re-tile (a roof). 2. to overhaul, repair.
trastejo, *m.* 1. tiling, re-tiling. 2. overhauling. 3. aimless bustling about or running around.
trasteo, *m.* 1. (taur.) challenging the bull (with the muleta cape). 2. managing (a person, an affair). 3. bustle, agitation.
trastería, *f.* 1. junk, old furniture or wares. 2. (coll.) dirty trick.
trasterminar, *tr.v.* (law) to transfer to another jurisdiction.
trastero, ra, *a.* storage, attic (room). —*f.* attic.
trastesado, da, *a.* hard, stiff (esp. udders with milk).
trastesón, *m.* abundance of milk (in a cow's udder).
trastiberino, na, *a., m., f., var. of* **transtiberino.**
trastienda, *f.* 1. back room (of a shop). 2. (coll.) tact; cunning; caution.
trasto, *m.* 1. piece of furniture, household utensil. 2. old or useless object or piece of furniture, junk. 3. (theat.) flat, piece of scenery. 4. (coll.) nuisance, good-for-nothing. 5. (*pl.*) weapons; tools, implements, equipment, tackle. — **tirarse los trastos a la cabeza,** (coll.) to quarrel, fight, have a row; **trastos de cocina,** kitchenware; **trastos viejos,** old junk or knickknacks.
trastocar, *(ref. 69) tr.v.* (rare) to upset, disturb, disarrange. —*r.v.* (rare) to go out of one's mind, go mad.
trastoqué, *ref.* **trastocar.**
trastornable, *a.* easily upset.
trastornado, da, *past part. of* **trastornar.** —*a.* upset, perturbed; (coll.) mad.
trastornador, ra, *a.* upsetting, disturbing. —*m., f.* upsetter, disturber; agitator.
trastornadura, *f., var. of* **trastorno.**
trastornamiento, *m., var. of* **trastorno.**
trastornar, *tr.v.* 1. to turn upside down, turn topsy-turvy, disorganize, disarrange. 2. to upset, disturb; to worry, perturb; to derange, turn mad (a person), turn (someone's mind); to change completely. 3. to make dizzy.
trastorno, *m.* 1. upset; upheaval; disturbance, confusion. 2. (med.) disorder; complication.
trastrabado, da, *a.* with a white forefoot and a white, opposite hind foot (horse).
trastrabarse, trastabársele a uno la lengua, to stammer, stutter, become tongue-tied.
trastrabillar, *i.v.* 1. to stumble, trip. 2. to stagger, reel, wobble. 3. to stutter, stammer.
trastrás, *m.* (coll.) next to the last (in children's games).
trastrocamiento, *m.* change, alteration, reversal; permutation.
trastrocar, *(ref. 69) tr.v.* to change, alter, permute. —*r.v.* to become changed or altered.
trastoqué, *ref.* **trastrocar.**
trastrueco, trastrueque, *m., var. of* **trastrocamiento.**
trastuelo, *m. dim. of* **trasto,** small household article; knickknack.
trastulo, *m.* pastime, plaything.
trastumbar, *tr.v.* 1. to drop, let fall; to knock down. 2. to upset, overturn.
trasudación, *f.* perspiration, light sweat.
trasudar, *i.v.* to perspire, sweat lightly.
trasudor, *m.* perspiration, light sweat.
trasuntar, *tr.v.* 1. to copy, transcribe. 2. to summarize; to abridge.
trasuntivamente, *adv.* 1. in a copy. 2. concisely, briefly.
trasunto, *m.* 1. copy, transcription, transcript. 2. copy, imitation.
trasvasar, *tr.v., var. of* **transvasar.**
trasvasijar, *tr.v.* (Chile) to pour (liquid) from one vessel to another, decant.
trasvasijo, *m.* (Chile) transfer (of a liquid) from one container to another, decanting.
trasvenarse, *r.v.* 1. to exude through the veins. 2. to spill, spill over.
trasver, *(ref. 27) tr.v.* 1. to see through (something). 2. to see wrongly.
trasverberación, *f., var. of* **transverberación.**
trasversal, *a., var. of* **transversal.**
trasverso, sa, *a., var. of* **transverso.**
trasverter, *(ref. 30) i.v.* to overflow, run over, spill over.
trasvierta, trasvierto, *ref.* **trasverter.**
trasvinarse, *r.v.* 1. to leak or ooze out (wine from casks). 2. (coll.) to become apparent, obvious or clear.
trasvolar, *(ref. 33) tr.v.* to fly over or across.
trasvuele, trasvuelo, *ref.* **trasvolar.**
trata, *f.* trade, slave trade; **t. de blancas,** white slave traffic; **t. de esclavos,** slave trade.
tratable, *a.* sociable, friendly, courteous; tractable.
tratadista, *m.* writer of a treatise.
tratado, *m.* 1. treaty. 2. treatise.
tratador, ra, *a.* mediating, arbitrating. —*m., f.* mediator, arbitrator.
tratamiento, *m.* 1. treatment. 2. (med., chem., ind.) treatment, process. 3. style, title; form of address. — **apear el t.,** to leave off the title (when addressing a titled person); to leave off one's title (a titled person); **dar t. de,** to address (someone) as; **tragarse el t.,** to leave off one's title (a titled person); **t. de datos** or **de la información,** data processing; **t. del agregado por lavado,** (bldg.) aggregate processing; **t. de textos,** word processing; **t. térmico,** (metal.) heat treatment.
tratante, *m.* dealer, trader; **t. de blancas,** white slaver; **t. de caballos,** horse dealer; **t. de esclavos,** slave dealer.
tratar, *tr.v.* 1. to treat, use, act or behave towards, e.g. *él trata muy bien a sus empleados,* he treats his employees very well. 2. (med.) to treat (a patient for a specific ailment), e.g. *me están tratando de un catarro,* I'm being treated for a cold. 3. (chem., ind.) to treat (with a substance), subject (to a process), e.g. *t. con cloruro,* to treat with chloride. 4. to address as, give the title of, e.g. *al embajador se le trata de Su Excelencia,* the ambassador is addressed as Your Excellency. 5. to call, treat as, charge with being, e.g. *lo tratan de revoltoso,* they charge him with being a troublemaker, *la tratan como una reina,* they treat her as a queen. 6. to deal with (a subject), discuss, e.g. *tratemos ese asunto,* let us discuss or deal with that matter. —*i.v.* 1. **t. de** —*inf.,* to try or endeavor to + inf., e.g. *yo trato de escribir aprisa,* I try to write fast. 2. **t. de, sobre, acerca de,** to deal with, speak about, e.g. *la conferencia trata acerca de ecología,* the conference deals with ecology. 3. (com.) **t. en,** to deal or trade in, e.g. *t. en pieles,* to deal in furs. 4. **t. con.** to deal with, be in touch or speak with, e.g. *t. con el administrador,* to deal with the manager. —*r.v.* 1. to look after oneself, to live (well or badly). 2. to deal or be in contact with, be on speaking or friendly terms with, e.g. *yo me trato bien con el vecino,* I'm on friendly terms with my neighbor. 3. **tratarse de,** to be a question of, be the matter or the subject discussed, e.g. *¿de qué se trata?* what is the matter? what is it about?
trato, *m.* 1. treatment, e.g. *t. preferencial,* preferential treatment. 2. (*pl.*) dealings, negotiations. 3. manner, way of behaving or acting, e.g. *él es muy simpático de t.,* he has a very pleasant manner, he is very pleasant to talk to. 4. style, title, form of address. 5. agreement, deal, contract. 6. business, trade. — **cerrar un t.,** to make a deal; **entrar en tratos con,** to open negotiations or dealings with; **t. de gentes,** social charm, winning ways, savoir faire; **t. colectivo,** collective bargaining; **t. doble,** double-dealing; **¡t. hecho!** (coll.) it's a deal!
trauma, *m.* trauma.
traumático, ca, *a.* traumatic.
traumatismo, *m.* traumatism.
traumatosis, *f.* (med.) traumatosis, traumatism.
travelín, *m.* (cine.) traveling, dollying; dolly (wheeled platform on which camera moves to take a travel or dolly shot).
traversa, *f.* 1. bolster (transverse bar supporting frame of a cart or carriage). 3. (mar.) stay.
travertino, na, *a., m.* (min.) travertine, travertin.
través, *m.* 1. slant, inclination, bias; bend. 2. misfortune, adversity. 3. (archit.) traverse, crosspiece, crossbeam. 4. (fort.) traverse. 5. (mar.) beam (direction at right angles to the keel). —

al t., crosswise; **al t. de, a t. de,** through, across; **dar al t.**, (mar.) to hit sideways or broadsides on; to come a cropper, get into trouble or danger; **dar al t. con,** to ruin, wreck, spoil; **mirar de t.**, to look out of the corner of one's eye, squint.
travesaño, *m.* 1. crosspiece, crossbar. 2. bolster (pillow). 3. (Cuba, ry.) sleeper, tie, crosstie (of railroad).
travesar, (*ref. 29*) *tr.v., r.v.* (rare) *var. of* **atravesar.**
travesear, *i.v.* 1. to be mischievous; to romp, frolic, caper. 2. to be a witty and lively conversationalist. 3. to lead a wild debauched life.
travesero, ra, *a.* crosswise, cross. —*m.* bolster (pillow).
travesía, *f.* 1. voyage, crossing. 2. crossroad, cross street. 3. part of a highway within a town. 4. distance from one place to another. 5. transverse position. 6. amount of money lost or won (at gambling). 7. (Arg.) waterless stretch of land. 8. (fort.) traverses (of a fortification). 9. (mar.) side wind, crosswind. 10 (mar.) sailor's pay for each voyage.
travesío, sía, *a.* 1. wandering (cattle). 2. side (wind). —*m.* crossing place, crossing.
travestido, da, *a.* disguised (dressed in the clothing of the opposite sex).
travestir, (*ref. 39*) *i.v.* to be a transvestite, to dress in the clothing of the opposite sex.
travesura, *f.* 1. prank, mischief, antic, caper. 2. wit, sparkle.
traviesa, *f.* 1. distance across, distance from one place to another. 2. raise on a bet or wager; bet laid on a player by a spectator. 3. (ry.) sleeper, crosstie; crosspiece (joining stringers of floor of railway wagon). 4. (archit.) rafter, crossbeam. 5. (archit.) interior main or bearing wall. 6. (min.) cross or transverse gallery. — **t. de cambio,** (ry.) switch tie.
traviese, travieso, *ref.* **travesar.**
travieso, sa, *a.* 1. mischievous, prankish, roguish. 2. cross, transverse. 3. shrewd, sagacious. 4. debauched, dissolute. 5. (fig.) lively, merry, e.g. *un arroyuelo travieso,* a lively little stream. — **a campo traviesa** or **travieso,** across country, e.g. *una carrera a campo traviesa,* a cross-country race.
trayecto, *m.* way, road, journey; distance, stretch (traveled).
trayectoria, *f.* trajectory, path, course.
trayendo, *ref.* **traer.**
traza, *f.* 1. looks, appearance, mien. 2. sign, trace. 3. plan, design. 4. plan, idea, scheme. 5. (geom.) trace. 6. (Ven.) clothes moth, carpet moth. 7. (chem.) (*pl.*) traces, small amounts (of substance hardly detectable by analysis). — **darse trazas para,** (coll.) to find a way to, manage to; **tener trazas de,** to show signs of, look like.
trazado, da, *past part. of* **trazar.** —*a.* traced, outlined; **bien t.**, well-built, attractive; **mal t.**, poorly-built, ungainly, unattractive. —*m.* 1. sketch, outline; sketching, outlining; tracing, plotting; design, plan. 2. setting out, laying out. 3. course, route, direction (of road, etc.). 4. marking (of stone or wood before cutting). — **t. taquimétrico,** (top.) stadia traverse.
trazador, ra, *a.* 1. planning, designing; plotting. 2. tracer (bullet). —*m., f.* planner, designer; plotter. —*m.* (chem., biol., phys.) tracer.
trazar, (*ref. 53*) *tr.v.* 1. to draw (plans, designs, etc.; lines, curves, angles); to plot, trace (a course, route); to lay or set out, locate (roads, railways). 2. to plan, design. 3. to describe, outline, sketch.
trazo, *m.* 1. line, stroke. 2. outline. 3. (p.) fold in drapery. — **al t.**, drawn in outline; **dar el t.**, to outline; **t. magistral,** thick stroke (of a letter).
trazumarse, *r.v.* to ooze, seep, filter, exude.
treballa, *f.* (cul.) white sauce mixed with garlic bread, eggs, nuts, sugar, condiments, etc.
trébede, *f.* 1. (*pl.*) trivet, cook's tripod. 2. part of a room warmed by an underground fire.
trebejar, *i.v.* to romp, frolic, play, gambol.
trebejo, *m.* 1. implement, tool, utensil (*gen. pl.*). 2. toy, plaything. 3. chess piece.
trébol, *m.* 1. (bot.) clover, trefoil. 2. (archit.) trefoil. 3. club (playing card), (*pl.*) clubs (suit of playing cards). — **t. de Alejandría,** (bot.) Egyptian clover; **t. de Bokhara,** (bot.) Bokhara clover; **t. de olor,** (bot.) sweet clover, melilot.
trebolar, *m.* (S. Amer.) clover field.
trece, *a.* thirteen; thirteenth. —*m.* thirteen; thirteenth (in dates). — **estarse, mantenerse,** or **seguir en sus t.**, to stand firm, stick to one's guns.
trecemecino, na, *a.* of thirteen months; thirteen-month old.
trecén, *m.* (Sp., arch.) thirteenth part of the money earned from a sale, formerly paid to a feudal lord.
trecenario, *a.* period of thirteen days.
treceno, na, *a.* thirteenth.
trecentista, *a.* pertaining to the trecento, the fourteenth century.
trecésimo, ma, *a., m.* thirtieth.
trecha, *f.* trick, ruse, artifice.
trecheador, *m.* (min.) mine worker who passes along baskets of ore, ore transporter.
trechear, *tr.v.* (min.) to pass loads of ore from one man to the next in baskets.
trechel, *a.* (bot.) spring (wheat). —*m.* spring wheat, wheat planted in the spring.
trecheo, *m.* (min.) passing or transporting of baskets of ore from one man to another.
trecho, *m.* stretch, distance, period; **a trechos,** at intervals; **de t. a** or **en t.**, from time to time; from place to place.
trechor, *m.* (her.) tressure, narrow orle.
trecientos, tas, *a., m.* three hundred.
tredécimo, ma, *a.* thirteenth.
trefe, *a.* 1. flimsy, weak, shaky. 2. false, fake (e.g. coin).
trefilado, *m.* wiredrawing.
trefilador, ra, *a.* wiredrawing. —*m., f.* wiredrawer (operator). —*f.* wiredrawer, wiredrawing machine.
trefilar, *tr.v.* to draw (metal), make (metal) into wire.
trefilería, *f.* 1. wiredrawing factory. 2. wiredrawing.
trefina, *f.* (surg.) trephine.
trefinación, *f.* (surg.) trephination.
tregua, *f.* 1. (mil.) truce, temporary cessation of hostilities. 2. rest, respite. — **dar treguas,** to let up, ease up, give one a rest; not to be urgent.
treílla, *f., var. of* **traílla.**
treinta, *a.* thirty. —*m.* 1. thirty; thirtieth (in dates). 2. card game. —*f.* (*pl.*) **treinta y cuarenta,** rouge et noir, trente et quarante.
treintadosavo, va, *a.* thirty-second.
treintaidoseno, na, *a.* thirty-second.
treintanario, *m.* period of thirty days.
treintañal, *a.* of thirty years duration or age.
treintavo, va, *a., m.* thirtieth.
treintena, *f.* thirty, group of thirty; thirtieth.
treinteno, na, *a.* thirtieth.
treja, *f.* cushion shot (in game of pool).
tremadal, *m., var. of* **tremedal.**
trematodo, *m.* (zool.) trematode, (*pl.*) Trematoda.
tremebundo, da, *a.* dreadful, frightful.
tremedal, *m.* quaking bog.
tremendo, da, *a.* 1. tremendous, dreadful, terrible. 2. (coll.) tremendous, imposing, awful; enormous, huge. — **echar por la tremenda,** (coll.) to go to extremes, take things to extremes.
tremente, *a.* trembling, quaking.
trementina, *f.* turpentine; **t. de Quío,** Chian turpentine.
tremer, *i.v.* to tremble, shake, quake, quiver.
tremés, tremesino, na, *a.* 1. three-month. 2. three-month, spring, planted in spring (wheat).
tremielga, *f.* (ichth.) torpedo fish.
tremó, tremol, *m.* pier glass.
tremolante, *a.* waving, fluttering (flag, banner, etc.).
tremolar, *tr.v., i.v.* to wave (flag, banner).
tremolina, *f.* whistling, whooshing (of the wind); (coll.) din, hubbub, racket, uproar.
tremolita, *f.* (min.) tremolite.
trémolo, *m.* (mus.) tremolo.
tremor, *m.* tremor, shake.
trémulamente, *adv.* tremulously.
tremulante, tremulento, ta, trémulo, la, *a.* tremulous, trembling, shaking; flickering.
tren, *m.* 1. train (series of pieces of machinery); equipment, gear. 2. (ry.) train. 3. train, convoy, e.g. *t. de artillería,* artillery train. 4. show, ostentation. 5. following, retinue. — **a todo t.**, in great comfort, with every luxury; **perder el t.**, to miss the bus or boat, miss one's opportunity; **t. botijo,** (coll.) summer excursion train; **t. búho,** or **nocturno,** night train; **t. correo,** (ry.) mail train or postal; **t. de aterrizaje,** (aer.) landing gear; **t. de abastecimientos, de campaña** or **de combate,** (mil.) supply train, baggage train; **t. de carga** or **de mercancías,** (ry.) freight train; **t. de dragado,** dredging equipment; **t. de gastos,** rate of expenditure; **t. de laminación** or **de laminados,** rolling mill; **t. delantero,** front wheel assembly; **t. de lavado,** carwash: **t. de montaje,** assembly line; **t. trasero,** rear wheel assembly; **t. de pasajeros,** passenger train; **t. de ondas,** (phys.) wave train; **t. de recreo,** (ry.) excursion train; **t. de rodaje,** running gear; **t. desplazable,** (auto.) sliding gear; **t. de vida,** way of life; **t. directo,** through train; **t. discrecional,** extra train (put on at stationmaster's discretion); **t. epicicloidal,** (mec.) epicyclic train; **t. expreso,** (ry.) express train; **t. hospital,** (mil.) hospital train; **t. laminador,** roll train; rolling mill; **t. mixto,** (ry.) passenger and freight train; **t. ómnibus** or **de cercancías,** local, train making local stops; **t. rápido,** (ry.) fast express train; **t. rodante,** running gear; **t. sanitario,** (mil.) hospital train; **t. trasero,** rear assembly.
trena, *f.* 1. (mil.) sash; shoulder knot (braided cord). 2. burnt silver. 3. (Arg.) plaited bread roll. 4. (Sp., coll.) jail.
trenado, da, *a.* meshed; grilled, latticed; plaited, braided.
trenca, *f.* 1. cross-tree (for supporting combs in a beehive). 2. main root.
trence, trencé, *ref.* **trenzar.**
trencellín, *m.* gold or silver cord formerly used as a hatband.
trencilla, *f.* decorative braid, gimp.
trencillar, *tr.v.* to trim with braid or gimp.
trencillo, *m., var. of* **trencellín.**
treno, *m.* funeral song, threnody, dirge; jeremiad, lamentation.
trenza, *f.* 1. plait, braid; tress (braided hair). 2. (archit.) architectural ornament imitating a plait.
trenzadera, *f.* knot or bow of plaited cord.
trenzado, *m.* 1. braid, plait. 2. entrechat (in ballet). 3. (equit.) prance, caper (of a horse). — **al t.**, carelessly.
trenzar, (*ref. 53*) *tr.v.* to braid, plait. —*i.v.* 1. to perfom an entrechat (in ballet). 2. to prance, caper (a horse). —*r.v.* (Amer.) to come to blows, become locked in a fight; to cross words, begin to quarrel.

treo, *m.* (mar.) storm lateen sail.
trepa, *f.* 1. climbing, climb. 2. boring, drilling, perforation. 3. (coll.) head roll, forward roll. 4. (sew.) trimming, edging. 5. wavy grain on wood. 6. (coll.) cunning, trickery. 7. (coll.) whipping, thrashing, beating.
trepadera, *f.* (Cuba) climbing gear (ropes and belt used for reaching the top of a palmtree).
trepado, da, *past part. of* **trepar.** *—a.* 1. perched (e.g., atop a tree). 2. leaning backwards. 3. strongly-built (animal). *—m.* 1. (sew.) edging, trimming. 2. line of dots or perforations.
trepador, ra, *a.* climbing; (bot., **ornith.**) climbing. *—m.* 1. climbing gear (to reach tree tops). 2. (ornith.) climber, creeper. *—f.* 1. (ornith.) climber, creeper. 2. (bot.) creeper, climbing vine. 3. (*pl.*) climbing irons.
trepajuncos, (*pl.* **trepajuncos**), *m.* (ornith.) marsh warbler.
trepanación, *f.* (surg.) trepanation.
trepanar, *tr.v.* (surg.) to trepan, trephine.
trépano, *m.* 1. (surg.) trepan, trephine. 2. drill.
trepante, *a.* 1. climbing. 2. wily, tricky. *—m., f.* tricky, wily person.
trepar, *i.v.* 1. to climb, mount; to clamber. 2. (bot.) to climb, creep (vine). *—tr.v.* 1. to climb, escalade. 2. to drill, bore, perforate. 3. to edge, put trimming on.
treparse, *r.v.* to lean backwards.
trepatroncos, (*pl.* **trepatroncos**), *m.* (ornith.) nuthatch; (ornith.) blue titmouse.
trepe, *m.* (coll.) scolding, reprimand.
trepidación, *f.* vibration, trembling, shaking, trepidation.
trepidante, *a.* shaking, vibrating, trembling.
trepidar, *i.v.* 1. to shake, vibrate, tremble. 2. (Chile, Peru) to hesitate, waver.
trépido, da, *a.* tremulous, shaking.
treponema, *f.* (bact.) treponema.
tres, *a.* three. *—m.* three; third. — **como t. y dos son cinco,** (coll.) just as sure as I'm standing here, just as sure as two and two make four; **dar t. y raya,** (coll.) to be superior, excel; **de t. al cuarto,** (coll.) insignificant, unimportant; **sombrero al t.,** (arch.) three-cornered hat; **t. en raya,** noughts and crosses (G.B.), tic-tac-toe; **¡y tres más!** (coll.) and that's for sure! and that's the truth!
tresalbo, ba, *a.* having three white feet (horse).
tresañal, tresañejo, ja, *a.* of three years.
tresbolillo, a or **al t.,** planted in staggered parallel rows, planted in quincunxes.
trescientos, tas, *a.* three-hundred, three-hundredth. *—m.* three hundred.
tresdoblar, *tr.v.* 1. to triple, treble. 2. to fold three times.
tresdoble, *a., m.* triple.
tresillista, *m., f.* ombre player, expert in the game of omber.
tresillo, *m.* 1. ombre (card game). 2. three-piece living room suite. 3. ring set with three similar stones. 4. (mus.) triplet.
tresmesino, na, *a.* three-month old.
tresnal, *m.* (agr.) shock, stook (G.B.)
trestanto, *adv.* three times as much. *—m.* triple, treble.
treta, *f.* 1. trick, ruse, stratagem, scheme. 2. (Arg.) bad habit. — **dar en la t.,** (coll.) to get the habit, fall into the habit.
trezavo, va, *a., m.* thirteenth.
tría, *f.* 1. selection, choice. 2. thin or threadbare patch (in cloth).
triaca, *f.* (pharm.) theriac, antidote; remedy.
triacal, *a.* theriacal.
triache, *m.* low-grade coffee beans.
triácido, da, *a.* (chem.) triacid.
tríada, *f.* triad, group of three.
triangulación, *f.* triangulation; **t. estérea,** (top.) aerial triangulation.
triangulado, da, triangular, *a.* triangular.
triangular, *tr.v.* to triangulate.
triangularmente, *adv.* triangularly.
triángulo, la, *a.* triangular. *—m.* (geom., mus., fig.) triangle; **t. acutángulo,** acute-angled triangle; **t. ambligonio** or **obtusángulo,** obtuse-angled triangle; **t. de las Bermudas,** Bermuda Triangle; **t. escaleno,** scalene triangle; **t. esférico,** spherical triangle; **t. isósceles,** isosceles triangle; **t. oblicuángulo,** oblique-angled triangle; **t. rectángulo,** right-angled triangle.
triaquera, *f.* formerly medicine chest or cabinet.
triar, (*ref. 54*) *tr.v.* to pick out, select, choose. *—i.v.* to swarm in and out of a beehive. *—r.v.* to be worn or threadbare, have thin patches (cloth).
triarios, *m.* (*pl.*) (hist.) triarii, Roman reserve soldiers.
triásico, ca, *a., m.* (geol.) Triassic.
triatomicidad, *f.* triatomicity.
triatómico, ca, *a.* (chem.) triatomic.
triaxial, triaxil, *a.* triaxial.
triazina, *f.* (chem.) triazine, triazin.
triazol, *m.* (chem.) triazole.
tríbada, *f.* tribade, female homosexual.
tribadismo, *m.* tribadism, lesbianism.
tribal, *a.* tribal.
tribásico, ca, *a.* (chem.) tribasic.
triboelectricidad, *f.* (phys.) triboelectricity.
triboluminiscente, *a.* triboluminiscent.
tribómetro, *m.* tribometer.
tribraquio, *m.* (poet.) tribrach.
tribromoetanol, *m.* (chem.) tribromoethanol.
tribromuro, *m.* (chem.) tribromide.
tribu, *f.* tribe.
tribual, *a.* tribal.
tribuir, (*ref. 48*) *tr.v., var. of* **atribuir.**
tribulación, *f.* tribulation.
tríbulo, *m.* (bot.) caltrop, star thistle.
tribuna, *f.* 1. tribune, rostrum, platform. 2. gallery (e.g., of a church). 3. stand, grandstand. — **t. de la prensa,** press box.
tribunado, *m.* tribunate, tribuneship.
tribunal, *m.* 1. court, tribunal. 2. board of examiners or judges. — **t. colegiado,** court composed or various, judges; **t. de alzada** or **apelación,** court of appeal; **t. de casación,** court of cassation; **t. de circuito,** circuit court; **t. de Cuentas,** State exchequer, treasury; **t. de honor,** court of honor; **t. de menores,** juvenile court, family court; **t. de Nuremberg,** Nuremberg Trial Court; **t. de registro** or **de autos,** court of record; **t. de última instancia,** court of last resort; **t. militar,** court martial; **t. supremo,** Supreme Court; **t. testamentario,** court of probate; **t. tutelar de menores,** juvenile court, family court.
tribunicio, cia, tribúnico, ca, *a.* 1. tribunicial, tribunitial, tribunitian. 2. (fig.) oratorical.
tribuno, *m.* 1. (hist.) tribune. 2. (fig.) orator, eloquent political speaker.
tributable, *a.* tributable, able to pay tribute or taxes.
tributación, *f.* 1. paying of taxes. 2. tribute, tax. 3. tax system.
tributante, *m., f.* taxpayer; payer of tribute.
tributar, *tr.v.* 1. to pay (taxes, tribute). 2. to pay; to render, offer (homage, respect, admiration, gratitude).
tributario, ria, *a.* 1. tax, e.g. *leyes tributarias,* tax laws. 2. tributary, paying tribute. 3. tributary, branch (stream). *—m.* tributary (stream).
tributo, *m.* 1. tribute; tax. 2. tribute, respect. 3. burden.
tricahue, *m.* (Chile) large parrot.
trice, tricé, *ref.* **trizar.**
tricenal, *a.* thirty-year.
tricentenario, *a., m.* tricentenary, tricentennial.
tricentésimo, ma, *a.* three-hundredth.
tríceps, *a.* (anat.) tricipital, triceps. *—m.* (anat.) triceps; **t. brachial,** (anat.) brachial triceps; **t. femoral,** (anat.) femoral triceps.
tricésimo, ma, *a., m.* thirtieth.
trichina, *f.* (zool.) trichina.
triciclo, *m.* tricycle.
tricípite, *a.* tricephalous, tricipital, three-headed.
triclínico, ca, *a.* (cryst.) triclinic.
triclinio, *m.* (hist.) triclinium, Roman dining settee accommodating three persons.
tricloroacético, ca, *a.* (chem.) trichloroacetic.
tricloruro, *m.* (chem.) trichloride.
tricocéfalo, *m.* (zool.) trichocephalus, trichuris.
tricofitosis, *f.* (med.) trichophytosis.
tricógina, *f.* (bot.) trichogyne.
tricología, *f.* trichology, the study of the hair.
tricólogo, ga, *m., f.* trichologist.
tricolor, *a.* tricolor, tricolored. *—m.* tricolor, three-colored flag.
tricoma, *m.* (bot., zool.) trichome.
tricomonádido, *m.* (zool.) trichomonad.
tricomoniasis, *f.* (med., vet.) trichomoniasis.
tricóptero, *m.* (ento.) trichopteran.
tricorne, *a.* (poet.) tricorn, having three horns, three-horned.
tricornio, *a.* three-horned, three-cornered. *—m.* tricorn, three-cornered hat.
tricosis, *f.* (med.) trichosis.
tricot, *m.* (Gal., tex.) tricot.
tricotar, *tr.v.* to knit (with tricot needles or machine).
tricotomía, *f.* trichotomy, división into three parts or categories.
tricotómico, ca, *a.* trichotomic.
tricótomo, ma, *a.* trichotomous, divided in three parts.
tricotosa, *a.* knitting (machine). *—f.* knitting machine.
tricroico, ca, *a.* (cryst.) trichroic.
tricroísmo, *m.* trichroism.
tricromía, *f.* trichromatism, three-color process.
tricromo, ma, *a.* three-colored.
tricuriasis, *f.* (med.) trichuriasis.
tricúspide, *a.* (anat.) tricuspid. *—f.* (anat.) tricuspid valve.
tridacio, *m.* (pharm.) lettuce opium, sedative obtained from lettuce roots.
tridacna, *f.* (zool.) tridacna.
tridáctilo, la, *a.* (zool.) tridactyl.
tridente, *a., m.* trident.
tridentino, na, *a., m., f.* (geog., hist.) Tridentine.
tridimensional, *a.* three-dimensional.
tridínamo, ma, *a.* (chem.) trivalent.
triduano, na, *a.* three-day.
triduo, *m.* (ecc.) triduum.
triédrico, ca, *a.* (geom.) trihedral.
triedro, *a.* (geom.) trihedral. *—m.* (geom.) trihedron.
trienal, *a.* triennial.
trienio, *m.* triennium.
trieñal, *a.* triennial.
triente, *m.* (numis.) triens, (*pl.*) trientes.
triera, *f.* (hist., mar.) trireme.
trierarca, *m.* (hist.) trierarch.
trierarquía, *f.* (hist.) trierarchy.
trifacial, *a.* (physiol.) trifacial, trigeminal.
trifásico, ca, *a.* (phys.) three-phase.
trífido, da, *a.* (bot.) trifid.
trifilina, *m.* (min.) triphyline, triphylite.
trifinio, *m.* meeting point of three territorial divisions.

trifloro, ra, *a.* three-flowered.
trifluoruro, *m.* (chem.) trifluoride.
trifoliado, da, *a.* (bot.) trifoliate.
trifolio, *m.* (bot.) trifolium, trefoil, clover.
trifoliolado, da, trifoliáceo, cea, *a.* (bot.) trifoliolate.
triforio, *m.* (archit.) triforium.
triforme, *a.* triform.
trifulca, *f.* 1. bellows mechanism (of foundry). 2. (coll.) row, squabble, fight.
trifurcación, *f.* trifurcation.
trifurcado, da, *a.* trifurcate.
triga, *f.* three-horse carriage, troika; team of three horses.
trigal, *m.* wheat field.
trigaza, *a.* **paja t.,** wheat chaff or straw.
trigémino, na, *a.* (anat.) trigeminal. —*m.* (anat.) trigeminal nerve, trigeminal.
trigésimo, ma, *a., m.* thirtieth.
trigla, *f.* (ichth.) red mullet.
tríglifo, *m.* (archit.) triglyph.
trigo, *m.* 1. (bot.) wheat; (*pl.*) wheat field. 2. (fig.) money. — **no ser t. limpio,** (coll.) not to be as innocent or honest as would seem; **t. albar,** white wheat; **t. alonso,** variety of durum wheat; **t. aristado,** bearded wheat; **t. berrendo,** common wheat with blue-flecked husk; **t. blando,** soft wheat; **t. candeal,** white wheat; **t. cañihueco** or **cañivano,** hollow-stemmed wheat; **t. cascalbo,** white bearded durum or hard wheat; **t. común,** white wheat, common wheat; **t. chamorro** or **desraspado,** soft-grained bald or beardless wheat; **t. de las Indias,** Indian corn, maize (G.B.); **t. del milagro,** poulard wheat; **t. de primavera,** spring wheat; **t. durillo** or **duro, t. fanfarrón,** durum wheat, hard wheat; **t. marzal** or **tremés,** spring wheat, wheat planted in spring; **t. mocho,** beardless or bald wheat; **t. montesino,** goat grass; **t. moro** or **moruno,** durum wheat, hard wheat; **t. pelón** or **peloto,** beardless wheat; **t. racimal,** poulard wheat; **t. raspudo,** bearded wheat; **t. redondillo,** poulard wheat; **t. rubión,** yellow-grained durum or hard wheat; **t. sarraceno,** buckwheat.
trigón, *m.* (mus.) trigon, triangular lyre or harp.
trigonal, *a.* (geom.) trigonal.
trígono, *m.* 1. (astrol.) trigon. 2. (geom.) trigon, triangle.
trigonocéfalo, *m.* (zool.) Trigonocephalus, a species of highly poisonous snakes.
trigonometría, *f.* trigonometry.
trigonométrico, ca, *a.* trigonometrical, trigonometric.
trigonómetro, *m.* trigonometer.
trigueño, ña, *a.* olive-skinned, dark-complexioned, brunet, brunette.
triguera, *f.* (bot.) canary grass.
triguero, ra, *a.* wheat; wheat-growing. —*m.* 1. wheat cribble or sieve. 2. wheat merchant.
trihidrato, *m.* (chem.) trihydrate.
trilátero, ra, *a.* trilateral, three-sided.
trile, *m.* (Chile, ornith.) red-winged black-bird.
trilingüe, *a.* trilingual.
trilítero, ra, *a.* triliteral, three-lettered.
trilito, *m.* (archeol.) trilithon.
trilla, *f.* 1. primitive thresher or threshing instrument. 2. threshing; threshing season. 3. (Chile) thrashing, beating. 4. (ichth.) red mullet. 5. (Cuba) path, side road.
trilladera, *f.* primitive thresher or threshing instrument.
trillado, da, *past part. of* **trillar.** —*a.* 1. beaten, well-worn (path). 2. trite, hackneyed, commonplace.
trillador, ra, *a.* (agr.) threshing. —*m., f.* (agr.) thresher. —*f.* (agr.) thresher, threshing machine.
trilladura, *f.* (agr.) threshing.
trillar, *tr.v.* 1. (agr.) to thresh, thrash. 2. (coll.) to overuse, make frequent use of. 3. (fig.) to maltreat, beat.
trillizo, za, *m., f.* triplet (each of three offspring born at a single birth).
trillo, *m.* 1. primitive thresher or threshing instrument. 2. (C. Rica, Cuba, P. Rico) narrow path.
trillón, *m.* trillion.
trilobites, (*pl.* **trilobites**), *m.* (paleon.) trilobite, (*pl.*) Trilobita.
trilobulado, da, *a.* trilobate, with three lobes or compartments.
trilocular, *a.* trilocular, divided into three parts.
trilogía, *f.* trilogy, a set of three related works of literature, such as certain Greek tragedies.
trilógico, ca, *a.* pertaining to trilogies.
trima, *f.* (bot.) tryma.
trimembre, *a.* trimembral, having three limbs or members.
trimensual, *a.* three times a month.
trimestral, *a.* trimestral, trimestrial, quarterly, e.g. *revista t.,* quarterly review.
trimestralmente, *adv.* trimestrially, every three months.
trimestre, *a.* trimestrial, trimestral, quarterly. —*m.* 1. trimester, quarter, three-month period. 2. quarterly payment, salary or wages.
trímero, ra, *a.* trimerous. —*m.* 1. (chem.) trimer. 2. (ento.) (*pl.*) Trimera.
trimetadiona, *f.* (pharm.) trimethadione.
trimetilamina, *f.* (chem.) trimethylamine.
trimétrico, ca, *a.* (cryst.) trimetric.
trímetro, a, *a., m.* (poet.) trimeter.
trimielga, *f.* (ichth.) torpedo fish.
trimorfismo, *m.* (bot., zool.) trimorphism.
trimorfo, fa, *a.* (bot., zool.) trimorphous.
trimotor, *m.* three-engined airplane.
Trimurti, *f.* (Rel.) Trimurti, Brahma, Siva and Visnu (trinity of Hindu gods).
trinacrio, cria, *a., m., f.* Trinacrian, from Trinacria, ancient name for Sicily.
trinado, *m.* (mus.) trill, trilling (of human voice). 2. warbling (of birds).
trinar, *i.v.* 1. to trill; to warble. 2. (coll.) to get furious, fume, e.g. *estoy trinando,* I'm fuming.
trinca, *f.* 1. group of three, triad, trio; group of three candidates competing for a university professorship. 2. (mar.) rope, cable, lashing rope. 3. (Ecuad., Col.) gang, group. 4. (Cuba, Mex., P. Rico) drunk, drunken spree. — **a la t.,** (Chile) poor, short of funds; **t. del bauprés,** (mar.) gammoning.
trincadura, *f.* (mar.) large two-masted barge.
trincaesquinas, (*pl.* **trincaesquinas**), *m.* pump drill.
trincafía, *f.* (mar.) marling.
trincapiñones, (*pl.* **trincapiñones**), *m.* (coll.) scatterbrain, harebrain.
trincar, (*ref. 50*) *tr.v.* 1. to break into small pieces, crumble, chop up. 2. to bind, tie, lash, fasten, secure; to hold down (with one's hands). 3. (coll.) to kill, knock off, do in. 4. (coll.) to take; to seize. 5. (C. Amer., Mex.) to be too tight, pinch (shoes); to press. 6. (Arg., vulg.) to have sexual intercourse with. 7. (coll.) to drink; to eat. —*i.v.* (mar.) to lie to. —*r.v.* **trincarse a** + *inf.,* (C. Amer.) to begin to + *inf.,* go to + *inf.,* e.g. *trincarse a dormir,* to go to sleep.
trincha, *f.* adjusting or tightening strap (e.g. of a waistcoat).
trinchador, ra, *a.* carving, slicing. —*m., f.* 1. carver, slicer. 2. (Mex.) sideboard for carving, carving table.
trinchante, *a.* carving, slicing. —*m.* 1. carver, slicer. 2. carving fork. 3. stone-cutter's hammer.
trinchar, *tr.v.* 1. to slice, carve (meat, fowl). 2. (coll.) to arrange, settle.
trinche, *m.* 1. (Amer.) fork. 2. (Amer.) carving table.
trinchera, *f.* 1. trench; ditch. 2. trench coat. — **guerra de trincheras,** trench warfare; **t. abrigo,** (mil.) slit trench.
trinchero, ra, *a.* carving (plate). —*m.* carving table or sidetable.
trincherón, *m. aug. of* **trinchera,** large trench or ditch.
trinchete, *m.* 1. shoemaker's knife. 2. (Amer.) table knife.
trineo, *m.* sleigh, sledge, sled.
trinidad, *f.* (theol.) Trinity.
Trinidad Tobago, *f.* Trinidad and Tobago.
trinitaria, *f.* (bot.) wild pansy, heartsease.
trinitario, ria, *a., m., f.* 1. (ecc.) Trinitarian. 2. Trinitarian, Trinidadian, of the island of Trinidad.
trinitrocresol, *m.* (chem.) trinitrocresol.
trinitrofenol, *m.* (chem.) trinitrophenol.
trinitroglicerina, *f.* (chem.) trinitroglycerin.
trinitrotolueno, *m.* (chem.) trinitrotoluene.
trino, na, *a.* threefold, trine, ternary. —*m.* 1. (astrol.) trine. 2. (mus.) trill, trilling, warbling (of birds).
trinomio, *m.* (math.) trinomial.
trinque, trinqué, *ref.* **trincar.**
trinquetada, *f.* 1. (mar.) sailing under the foresail. 2. (Amer.) a spell of bad luck.
trinquete, *m.* 1. (mar.) foreyard; foresail; foremast. 2. (mec.) pawl, ratchet. 3. pelota played in a covered court (type of squash). 4. (Arg.) tall lanky person. 5. sharp noise or crack. — **más fuerte que un t.,** (coll.) to be as strong as a horse.
trinquetilla, *f.* (mar.) small jib; (mar.) fore-topmast staysail.
trinquis, *m.* (coll.) drink or swig of wine.
trío, *m.* 1. trio, group of three. 2. (mus.) trio, group or ensemble of three instrumentalists; a composition for three voices or instruments.
tríodo, *m.* (phys., electron.) triode.
trioleína, *f.* (chem.) triolein.
trional, *m.* (chem.) trional.
triones, *m. pl.* (astrol.) Triones, the Dipper.
triosa, *f.* (chem.) triose.
trióxido, *m.* (chem.) trioxide.
tripa, *f.* 1. gut, intestine. 2. (coll.) paunch, belly, stomach. 3. tobacco filling (of cigar); small tobacco leaf used for cigar filling. 4. (*pl.*) insides, innards. 5. (cul.) tripe. — **hacer de tripas corazón,** (coll.) to pluck up courage, master one's fear; **tener malas tripas,** (coll.) to be cruel, hardhearted.
tripada, *f.* (coll.) bellyful, large heavy meal.
tripanosoma, *m.* (zool.) trypanosome, trypanosoma.
tripanosomiasis, *f.* (med.) trypanosomiasis.
triparsamida, *f.* (pharm.) tryparsamide.
tripartición, *f.* tripartition, the act of dividing something into three parts.
tripartir, *tr.v.* to divide into three parts, tripart.
tripartito, ta, *a.* 1. tripartite, divided into three parts. 2. accomplished between three persons. 3. elected by the coalition of three parties.
tripastos, (*pl.* **tripastos**), *m.* tackle with three pulleys.
tripe, *m.* shag (cloth).
tripería, *f.* tripe shop; tripe.
tripero, ra, *m., f.* 1. one who sells tripe. 2. (coll.) glutton, tripe. —*m.* bellyband.
tripétalo, la, *a.* (bot.) tripetalous.
tripicallero, ra, *m., f.* one who sells or specializes in tripe dishes.

tripicallos, *m.* (cul.) ragout of tripe.
tripié, *m.* tripod.
trípili, *m.* Spanish song and dance popular at the end of the 18th C.
triplano, *m.* (aer.) triplane.
triple, *a., m.* triple, treble; **T. Alianza,** Triple Alliance.
tripleta, *f.* three-seat bicycle.
tríplica, *f.* (law) rejoinder.
triplicación, *f.* triplication, trebling.
triplicado, *m.* triplicate, threefold; **por t.,** in triplicate.
triplicar, (*ref.* 50) *tr.v.* to triple, treble, triplicate. —*r.v.* to triple, treble.
tríplice, *a.* triple, triplex.
triplicidad, *f.* triplicity.
triplique, tripliqué, *ref.* **triplicar.**
triplita, *f.* (min.) triplite.
triplo, pla, *a., m.* triple, treble.
triploide, *a.* (biol.) triploid.
tripoca, *f.* (Chile, ornith.) mallard.
trípode, *m., f.* (hist.) tripod (of priestess of Apollo). —*m.* tripod, a three-legged stand.
trípol, trípoli, *m.* (min.) tripoli.
Trípoli, *f.* Tripoli, capital of Libya.
tripolino, na, tripolitano, na, *a., m., f.* Tripolitan, of or pertaining to Tripoli, Libya.
tripón, na, *a.* 1. (coll.) large-bellied, paunchy, potbellied. 2. (Mex.) small goat, kid.
trips, *m.* (ento.) thrips.
tripsina, *f.* (biochem.) trypsin.
tripteroide, *a.* (bot.) tripterous.
tríptico, ca, *a.* (physiol.) tryptic. —*m.* 1. triptych, a set of three carved or painted panels. 2. book or treatise in three parts. 3. international motor-travel document.
triptófano, triptofán, *m.* (biochem.) tryptophan, tryptophane.
Triptólemo, *m.* (myth.) Triptolemus, king of Eleusis who invented the plow.
triptongar, (*ref.* 51) *tr.v.* to pronounce (three vowels) as a triphthong.
triptongo, *m.* (gram., phonet.) triphthong.
tripudiante, *a.* dancing. —*m., f.* dancer, participant in a collective dance.
tripudiar, *i.v.* to dance.
tripudio, *m.* a dance performed by several persons.
tripudo, da, *a.* (coll.) large-bellied, pot-bellied, paunchy.
tripulación, *f.* crew (of ship, plane, etc.); **t. de tierra,** (aer.) ground crew, ground staff.
tripulante, *m.* crew member, (*pl.*) crew.
tripular, *tr.v.* 1. to man (a ship, plane, etc.). 2. (Chile) to mix (liquids).
tripulina, *f.* (Arg., Chile) uproar, hubbub, rumpus.
trique, *m.* 1. bang, crack. 2. (Col., Cuba) game of noughts and crosses (G.B.), tic-tac-toe. 3. (Col.) trick, ruse. 4. (Mex.) (*pl.*) things, gear. — **a cada t.,** (coll.) all the time, at every step or turn.
triquete, *m.* bang, slight crack; **a cada t.,** (coll.) at every step or turn.
triquiasis, *f.* (med.) trichiasis.
triquina, *f.* (zool.) trichina.
triquinosis, *f.* (med.) trichinosis.
triquinoso, sa, *a.* trichinous, infested with trichinae.
triquiñuela, *f.* (coll.) trick, (*pl.*) **trickery,** underhand dealing; **andar con triquiñuelas,** to have some trick up one's sleeve.
triquitraque, *m.* 1. banging, clatter, knocking. 2. firecracker. — **a cada t.,** (coll.) at every step or turn.
trirradiado, a, *a.* triradiate, with three rays, projecting in three beams.
trirrectángulo, la, *a.* trirectangular, with three straight angles.
trirreme, *m.* trireme, ancient Greek or Roman galley with three banks of oars on each side.
tris, *m.* 1. cracking (as of breaking glass). 2. (coll.) moment, instant, jiffy, trice; inch, ace. — **en un t.,** (coll.) in a trice or jiffy; **estar en un t. de,** to be within an ace or inch of; to be on the point of.
trisa, *f.* (ichth.) shad.
trisacárido, *m.* (chem.) trisaccharide, trisaccharid.
trisagio, *m.* (ecc.) hymn to the Holy Trinity.
trisar, *tr.v.* (Chile) to crack (glass, china, etc.). —*i.v.* to sing, chirp (birds).
trisca, *f.* 1. crunch, crushing sound (caused by crushing something with the foot). 2. racket, din, noise. 3. (Cuba) surreptitious sneer.
triscador, ra, *a.* noisy, frisky. —*m., f.* noisy, frisky person. —*m.* saw set (instrument for setting a saw).
triscar, (*ref.* 50) *tr.v.* 1. to mix up. 2. to set (a saw). 3. (Col., Cuba) to poke or make fun of. —*i.v.* 1. to stamp, make a stamping noise. 2. to romp, jump, frisk or skip about, prance, caper. 3. (Col.) to criticize, gossip, backbite.
triscón, *m.* (Col., coll.) gossip, backbiter, malicious gossiper.
trisecar, (*ref.* 50) *tr.v.* (geom.) to trisect, divide into three equal parts.
trisección, *f.* (geom.) trisection, the act of dividing into three equal parts.
trisector, ra, *a.* trisecting. —*m.* trisector (instrument).
trisemanal, *a.* triweekly (occurring or appearing three times a week or every three weeks).
trisílabo, ba, *a.* trisyllabic. —*m.* trisyllable.
trismo, *m.* (med.) trismus.
trisódico, ca, *a.* (chem.) trisodium.
trisómico, ca, *a.* (biol.) trisomic.
trispasto, *m.* tackle with three pulleys.
trisque, *ref.* **triscar.**
Tristán, *m.* (lit.) Tristan, Tristram, lover of Isolde in a medieval Celtic legend immortalized in Richard Wagner's opera.
triste, *a.* 1. sad; sorrowful; melancholy; dismal. 2. miserable, dismal, wretched. 3. sorry, sorry-looking (figure). 4. meager, insignificant, insufficient. 5. (Bol.) timid. —*m.* (S. Amer.) plaintive love song. — **el caballero de la t. figura,** the knight of the sad countenance (Don Quixote).
tristemente, *adv.* sadly, regrettably.
tristeza, *f.* 1. sadness, melancholy. 2. (Arg., Urug., vet.) murrain.
trístico, a, *a.* (bot.) tristichous.
tristón, na, *a.* somewhat sad, about to sink into melancholia.
tristura, *f., var. of* **tristeza.**
trisulco, ca, *a.* three-pronged, three-furrowed.
trisulfuro, *m.* (chem.) trisulfide.
tritíceo, a, *a.* wheatlike.
tritio, *m.* (chem.) tritium.
tritón, *m.* 1. (myth.) **T., Triton, a god of** the sea, son of Poseidon. 2. (zool.) triton, newt, eft. 3. (phys.) triton.
tritono, *m.* (mus.) tritone, a three-tone interval.
triturable, *a.* crushable, grindable, triturable.
trituración, *f.* crushing, grinding, trituration.
triturador, ra, *a.* crushing, grinding, triturating. —*m., f.* grinder, crusher, triturator. —*f.* grinder, crusher, triturator; (cul.) electric mixer; **t. de cilindros,** roller mill.
triturar, *tr.v.* 1. to grind, crush, triturate; to chew. 2. (fig.) to beat (a person) to a pulp. 3. (fig.) to pull to pieces (an argument).
triunfador, ra, *a.* triumphant, victorious. —*m., f.* triumpher, victor.
triunfal, *a.* triumphal.
triunfalmente, *adv.* triumphantly.
triunfante, *a.* triumphant.
triunfantemente, *adv.* triumphantly, victoriously.
triunfar, *i.v.* 1. to triumph; to win; to be successful. 2. to trump (in cards). 3. (fig.) to be lavish, spend lavishly. — **t. de** or **sobre,** to triumph over, overcome, conquer.
triunfo, *m.* 1. triumph; victory; success. 2. trump (in cards). 3. lavish spending. 4. spoils (of war). — **costar un t.,** (coll.) to be a gigantic effort, demand a tremendous effort.
triunviral, *a.* triumviral.
triunvirato, *m.* triumvirate.
triunviro, *m.* (hist.) triumvir, one of three Roman magistrates with administrative duties.
trivalencia, *f.* (chem.) trivalence, trivalency.
trivalente, *a.* (chem.) trivalent.
trivalvo, va, *a., m.* (zool.) trivalve.
trivial, *a.* 1. trivial; trite, commonplace. 2. trivial, unimportant.
trivialidad, *f.* triviality; trite remark, platitude, triteness.
trivialmente, *adv.* trivially; tritely.
trivio, *m.* 1. junction of three roads. 2. (hist.) trivium (three lower liberal arts, grammar, logic and rhetoric, in medieval schools).
triza, *f.* 1. fragment, shred. 2. (mar.) halyard. — **hacer trizas,** to smash to smithereens; smash or tear to pieces.
trizar, (*ref.* 53) *tr.v.* to break or tear to shreds, pieces or bits.
Tróada, *f.* (hist., geog.) Troas, region surrounding Troy.
trocable, *a.* exchangeable.
trocada, a la t., in the opposite way; in exchange.
trocadamente, *adv.* distortedly, in the wrong order or position.
trocado, da, *past part. of* **trocar.** —*a.* distorted, changed; **dinero trocado,** loose change (money).
trocador, ra, *m., f.* one who changes or exchanges.
trocaico, ca, *a.* (poct.) trochaic (verse), made up of trochees.
trocamiento, *m.* exchange, exchanging, changing; distortion.
trocante, *a.* exchanging; bartering; altering.
trocánter, *m.* (anat.) trochanter.
trocar, *m.* (surg.) trocar, trochar.
trocar, (*ref.* 69) *tr.v.* 1. to exchange. 2. to confuse, muddle, mix up. 3. to change, alter, convert. 4. to throw up, vomit. —*r.v.* 1. to change one's habits. 2. to exchange seats. 3. to become changed.
trocatinta, *f.* (coll.) mistake or confusion in exchanging two things; exchange of little value.
trocatinte, *m.* shot color, changeable color.
trocear, *tr.v.* to cut or divide into pieces.
troceo, *m.* (mar.) parrel, truss.
trocha, *f.* 1. trail, narrow path. 2. (**Amer.,** ry.) gauge (of track); **t. ancha,** (ry.) broad or wide gauge; **t. angosta,** (ry.) narrow gauge; **t. media** or **normal,** (ry.) standard gauge.
trochemoche, a t. (coll.) helter-skelter, pell-mell, recklessly.
troche y moche, *var. of* **trochemoche.**
trochuela, *f. dim. of* **trocha,** narrow path.
trociscar, (*ref.* 50) *tr.v.* (pharm.) **to make** into troches or lozenges.
trocisco, *m.* (pharm.) troche, lozenge.
trocla, *f.* pulley.
tróclea, *f.* (anat.) trochlea.
troco, *m.* (ichth.) sunfish.
trocoide, *a., f.* (geom.) trochoid.
trócola, *f.* pulley.
trofeo, *m.* 1. trophy. 2. spoils of **war.** 3. (fig.) victory, triumph.

trófico, ca, *a.* (physiol.) trophic, pertaining to nutrition.
trofoblasto, *m.* (biol.) trophoblast.
trofología, *f.* trophology, science of the nutrition of tissues.
trofoneurosis, *f.* (med.) trophoneurosis.
Trofonio, *m.* (myth.) Trophonius, Greek architect who built the temple at Delphi.
troglodita, *a.* 1. troglodytic (pertaining to a troglodyte or cave dweller). 2. (fig.) troglodytic, brutal, cruel. 3. (fig.) gluttonous. —*m., f.* 1. troglodyte. 2. (fig.) troglodyte, brute. 3. (fig.) glutton. —*m.* (ornith.) troglodyte.
troglodítico, ca, *a.* troglodytic.
troica, *f.* troika, large sleigh pulled by three horses.
Troilo, *m.* (myth., lit.) Troilus, lover of Cressida.
troj, *m.* granary, barn; olive bin.
troja, troje, *f.* (Amer.) *var. of* **troj.**
trojero, *m.* granary keeper or tender.
trojezado, da, *a.* finely cut or chopped, shredded, minced.
trola, *f.* (coll.) lie, trick, hoax.
trole, *m.* 1. (Angl., elec.) trolley pole. 2. (P. Rico) trolley car, streetcar.
trolebús, *m.* trolley bus.
trolero, ra, *a.* (coll.) lying, deceitful. —*m., f.* liar, cheat, deceitful person.
tromba, *f.* (meteorol.) water spout (caused by a tornado); **en t.,** violently, en masse.
trombina, *f.* (biochem.) thrombin.
trombo, *m.* (med.) thrombus.
trombocito, *m.* (physiol.) thrombocyte, platelet.
tromboembolia, *f.* (med.) thromboembolism.
tromboflebitis, *f.* (med.) thrombophlebitis.
trombón, *m.* (mus.) trombone (instrument); trombone, trombonist (person playing trombone); **t. de pistones,** valve trombone; **t. de varas,** slide trombone.
tromboquinasa, *f.* (biochem.) thrombokinase.
trombosis, *f.* (med.) thrombosis; **t. coronaria,** (med.) coronary thrombosis.
trome, *m.* (Peru, sl.) wizard; (sl.) expert.
trompa, *f.* 1. (mus.) horn. 2. boy's whistle (made of onion scape). 3. large humming top. 4. (zool.) trunk (e.g. of an elephant); snout; (ento.) proboscis. 5. (coll.) snout, large conk, nozzle or nose, proboscis; (Amer.) thick prominent lips. 6. (metal.) trompe. 7. waterspout (caused by a tornado). 8. (archit.) squinch arch. 9. (coll.) drunk, drunken bout, e.g. *coger una t.,* to get drunk. 10. (anat.) tube, duct. 11. (Col., Chile) cowcatcher, pilot (of railway locomotive). — **a t. y talega,** (coll.) helter-skelter; **t. de caza,** hunting horn; **t. de Eustaquio,** (anat.) Eustachian tube; **t. de Falopio,** (anat.) Falopian tube; **t. de Paris, t. gallega,** Jew's harp; **t. marina,** one-stringed fiddle; **t. neumática,** vacuum pump. —*m.* (mus.) horn player.
trompada, *f.* 1. blow, punch. 2. collision, bump.
trompar, *i.v.* to spin a top.
trompazo, *m.* hard blow or punch; blow given with a top; blow given with a horn or trumpet.
trompear, *tr.v.* (Amer.) to punch, sock, box. —*i.v.* to spin a top. —*r.v.* (Amer.) to fight, come to blows, punch each other.
trompero, ra, *a.* deceptive, false. —*m.* top maker.
trompeta, *f.* (mus.) trumpet; clarion, bugle; **t. bastarda,** bugle; **t. de amor** or **girasol,** (bot.) sunflower. —*m.* 1. trumpeter, bugler. 2. (coll.) rascal, rogue.
trompetada, *f.* (coll.) untimely remark.
trompetazo, *m.* 1. trumpet or bugle blast. 2. blow given with trumpet. 3. (coll.) untimely remark; stupid or foolish remark.
trompetear, *i.v.* (coll.) to play the trumpet.
trompeteo, *m.* playing of the trumpet; trumpet sounds.
trompetería, *f.* (mus.) trumpet section (in an orchestra), trumpets; trumpets (of an organ).
trompetero, *m.* 1. trumpeter; trumpet maker. 2. (ichth.) trumpet fish, bellows fish.
trompetilla, *f.* 1. ear trumpet. 2. (Car., Mex.) raspberry, Bronx cheer (sound of disapproval and scorn). 3. (Phil. I.) cone-shaped cigar. — **de t.,** buzzing (mosquito); **t. acústica,** ear trumpet.
trompicadero, *m.* stumbling place.
trompicar, (*ref. 50*) *tr.v.* 1. to trip, make stumble. 2. (coll.) to promote a person undeservedly over another. —*i.v.* to stumble, trip.
trompicón, *m.,* **trompilladura,** *f.* 1. stumble, trip. 2. blow, punch; **a trompicones,** stumbling; by fits and starts.
trompillar, *tr.v., i.v., var. of* **trompicar.**
trompillo, *m.* (bot.) bixa tree.
trompillón, *m.* (archit.) keystone of a squinch arch or a circular vault.
trompique, trompiqué, *ref.* **trompicar.**
trompis, *m.* (coll.) punch, blow with the fist.
trompiza, *f.* (S. Amer.) fight, fisticuffs.
trompo, *m.* 1. top (toy). 2. (zool.) top shell, trochid. 3. dolt, fool. 4. pipe-widening tool. — **ponerse como un t.** or **hecho un t.,** to gorge oneself (with food or drink).
trompón, *m.* 1. *aug. of* **trompo,** large top or hard punch. 2. blow, punch. 3. (bot.) narcissus. — **a** or **de t.** (coll.) helter-skelter.
trompudo, da, *a.* thick-lipped, big-snouted.
trona, *f.* (min.) trona.
tronada, *f.* thunderstorm.
tronado, da, *past part. of* **tronar.** —*a.* 1. worn, used; spoiled. 2. broke, penniless. 3. (coll.) mad, feeble-minded, crazy.
tronador, ra, *a.* thundering; detonating (rocket). —*f.* (bot., Mex.) begonia.
tronante, *a.* thundering, thunderous.
tronar, (*ref. 33*) *tr.v.* (Mex.) to shoot dead. —*i.v.* 1. to thunder (used only in the impersonal). 2. (coll.) to be ruined, go broke or bankrupt, lose one's fortune. 3. (fig.) to thunder, blast, write or talk violently (against something). — **t. con,** (coll.) to quarrel with, break with.
tronca, *f., var. of* **truncamiento.**
troncal, *a.* trunk, main, e.g. *línea t.,* (tel.) trunk line.
troncar, (*ref. 50*) *tr.v., var. of* **truncar.**
troncha, *f.* 1. (S. Amer.) chunk, slice. 2. (Peru, Chile, coll.) cushy job, sinecure.
tronchado, *a.* (her.) trouçonné.
tronchar, *tr.v.* 1. (fig.) to split, crack, shatter. 2. to split, crack or break the trunk, stalk or branches cf. —*r.v.* to break (e.g. stalk, branch). — **troncharse de risa,** to split with laughter.
tronchazo, *m.* blow given with a stalk.
troncho, *m.* 1. stalk, stem (of cabbage, lettuce, etc.). 2. (Amer.) chunk, slice.
tronchudo, da, *a.* having a long or thick stalk or stem (cabbage, cauliflower, etc.).
tronco, *m.* 1. trunk (of human body, of tree, of family tree; main body); stem, stalk, origin. 2. log (of wood). 3. (geom.) frustum. 4. pair, team (of mules, horses). 5. dolt, dimwit. — **estar hecho un t.,** (coll.) to be paralyzed; (coll.) to be sound asleep; **t. de cono,** (geom.) truncated cone.
troncón, *m.* 1. trunk (of body). 2. stump (of a tree).
tronera, *f.* 1. (fort.) loophole, embrasure; (mar.) port, gun port, porthole. 2. dormer, small window. 3. pocket (of pool table. —*m., f.* (coll.) harum-scarum (person), harebrained person.
tronerar, *tr.v., var. of* **atronerar,** to make embrasures in.
tronga, *f.* (rare) mistress, concubine.
trónica, *f.* (coll.) gossip, rumor.
tronido, *m.* 1. thunderclap; loud report. 2. swank, swagger; show, ostentation.
tronío, *m.* (sl.) pomp, show, swank; **de t.,** fancy, swanky.
tronitoso, sa, *a.* (coll.) thunderous, thundering, resounding.
trono, *m.* 1. throne; (fig.) throne (sovereign power or dignity). 2. (ecc.) tabernacle, monstrance. 3. (ecc.) niche, shrine, reliquary. 4. (fig.) the king, the sovereign.
tronquero, ra, *a.* (Arg.) team (horse).
tronquista, *m.* driver, coachman, teamster.
tronzador, *m.* two-handed saw.
tronzar, (*ref. 53*) *tr.v.* 1. to slice, divide or break into chunks or pieces. 2. (dressm.) to trim a skirt with fine, even tucks. 3. to cause fatigue or exhaustion.
tronzo, za, *a.* (horse) with one or two ears cropped.
tropa, *f.* 1. troop, group, crowd, band. 2. soldiers, army, troops. 3. (mil.) (*pl.*) troops. 4. (mil.) assembly call. 5. (S. Amer.) herd, drove. 6. (Arg.) caravan (of mules, vehicles, etc.). — **en t.,** in disorganized groups; **tropas aerotransportadas,** (mil.) airborne troops; **tropas de asalto,** (mil.) storm troops; **tropas de combate,** (mil.) combat troops; **tropas de choque,** (mil.) shock troops; **tropas de línea,** (mil.) line troops, regular. troops.
tropecé, *ref.* **tropezar.**
tropeína, *f.* (chem.) tropeine.
tropel, *m.* 1. throng, crowd, multitude. 2. hurry, rush, bustle; confusion. 3. heap (of things); jumble, hodgepodge. — **de** or **en t.,** in a mad rush, in confusion.
tropelía, *f.* 1. outrage, abuse, injustice. 2. mad rush or haste, precipitation, confusion. 3. magic tricks.
tropelista, *m.* prestidigitator, magician.
tropeoleo, a, tropeoláceo, a, *a.* (bot.) tropaeolaceous. —*f.* (bot.) tropaeolum, (*pl.*) Tropaeolaceae.
tropeolina, *f.* (chem.) tropaeolin, tropaeoline, tropeolin.
tropero, *m.* (Arg., Chile) cowboy, cattle driver.
tropezadero, *m.* stumbling place.
tropezador, ra, *a.* stumbling. —*m., f.* stumbler.
tropezadura, *f.* stumbling, stumble.
tropezar, (*ref. 68*) *i.v.* 1. to stumble, trip. 2. to slip, go astray, slip into error. — **tropezar** or **tropezarse con,** to stumble against, trip over, bump into (obstacle); to stumble upon, come across, discover, find; to bump into, run into, meet (e.g. old friend); to come up against, run into, encounter (e.g. opposition). —*r.v.* 1. to interfere, knock one foot against another (a horse).
tropezón, na, *a.* stumbling; (horse) knocking one leg against another. —*m.* 1. stumble, trip, stumbling. 2. slip, mistake, error. 3. obstacle, stumbling block. 4. (*pl.*) (cul.) chopped meat, vegetables or croutons added to soup. — **a tropezones,** (coll.) by fits and starts.
tropezoso, sa, *a.* (coll.) stumbling, faltering.
tropical, *a.* tropical.
trópico, ca, *a.* 1. tropical, figurative. 2. tropical (year). —*m.* (astron., geog.) tropic; the tropics. — **t. de Cáncer,** Tropic of Cancer; **t. de Capricornio,** Tropic of Capricorn.
tropiezo, *m.* 1. obstacle; stumbling block. 2. (fig.) snag, difficulty, hitch. 3. slip, error. 4. stumble, trip. 5. quarrel, squabble, wrangle.
tropilla, *f.* (Arg.) troop of horses led by a lead mare; (Chile) flock of vicuñas or guanacos.

tropina, *f.* (chem.) tropine.
tropismo, *m.* (biol.) tropism.
tropo, *m.* (rhet.) trope; **t. de dicción,** figure of speech.
tropología, *f.* (rhet.) tropology.
tropológico, ca, *a.* (rhet.) tropological, tropologic.
tropopausa, *f.* (meteorol.) tropopause.
troposfera, *f.* (meteorol.) troposphere.
troque, *m.* knot tied in cloth before dyeing to show original color.
troqué, *ref.* **trocar.**
troquel, *m.* die (for stamping coins or medals).
troqueladora, *f.* (mach.) stamping press.
troquelar, *tr.v.* to coin, mint; to stamp in a die.
troquelminto, *m.* (zool.) trochelmith.
troqueo, *m.* (poet.) trochee.
troquilo, *m.* (archit.) trochilus.
trotacalles, (*pl.* **trotacalles**), *m., f.* (coll.) gadabout, promenader.
trotaconventos, (*pl.* **trotaconventos**), *f.* (coll.) procuress, go-between.
trotada, *f.* trot, quick pace.
trotador, ra, *a.* trotting. —*m., f.* trotter.
trotamundos, (*pl.* **trotamundos**), *m., f.* globetrotter; rover, wanderer.
trotar, *i.v.* 1. to trot. 2. (coll.) to be constantly on the trot, hustle.
trote, *m.* 1. trot. 2. (coll.) bustle; chore, fatiguing work. — **al t., a t.,** quickly, right away; **para todo t.,** (coll.) for everyday wear or use; **tomar el t.,** (coll.) to dash off, beat it; **t. cochinero,** (coll.) quick trot.
trotil, *m.* (chem.) trotyl, trinitrotoluene.
trotón, na, *a.* trotting. —*m.* horse. —*f.* (coll.) chaperone, companion.
trotonería, *f.* steady trot.
trotskista, *a., m., f.* (polit.) Trotskyite.
trova, *f.* 1. poem. 2. poem imitating another. 3. love ballad, love song. 4. (Cuba, coll.) lie, fib.
trovador, ra, *a.* versifying. —*m.* troubador, minstrel; poet. —*f.* poetess.
trovadoresco, ca, *a.* of troubadours, troubadour-like.
trovar, *tr.v.* 1. to write or sing verses. 2. (fig.) to misinterpret, misconstrue.
trovero, *m.* (Gal., poet.) trouvère.
trovista, *m., f.* (rare) *var. of* **trovador.**
trovo, *m.* formerly a popular love ballad.
trox, *f., var. of* **troj.**
Troya, *f.* (hist.) Troy; **ahí, allí** or **aquí fue T.,** alas, there's nothing left but ruins; **arda T.,** whatever happens.
troyano, na, *a., m., f.* Trojan.
troza, *f.* 1. log (of wood ready for cutting into planks). 2. (mar.) truss (of a yard).
trozar, (*ref. 53*) *tr.v.* 1. to break into pieces; to cut into logs. 2. (mar.) to truss.
trozo, *m.* 1. piece, bit, part, fragment; selection, excerpt, passage, extract (of music, book, etc.). 2. (mar.) detail (of ship's crew). 3. (mil.) division of a column.
trúa, *f.* (Arg., Bol., coll.) drunkenness; **estar en t.,** to be drunk.
trucaje, *m.* (cine.) trick photography.
trucar, (*ref. 50*) *i.v.* 1. to pocket a ball (at game of pool or pocket billiards). 2. to place the first stake (in the game of **truque**).
trucha, *f.* 1. (ichth.) trout. 2. (mec.) three-legged derrick, crab. 3. (C. Amer.) shabby little vending stand or shop. — **no se pescan truchas a bragas enjutas,** you won't get what you want by sitting on your behind; **t. arco-iris,** (ichth.) rainbow trout; **t. de mar** or **marina,** (ichth.) sea trout; scorpion fish.
truchero, *m.* trout fisherman; trout seller.
truchimán, na, *a.* smart, astute, cunning, slick. —*m., f.* 1. (coll.) dragoman, interpreter. 2. (coll.) cunning customer, wily fish, astute person.
trucho, cha, *a.* (C. Amer.) smart, cunning.
truchuela, *f.* 1. *dim. of* **trucha,** small trout. 2. smoked codfish.
truco, *m.* 1. trick, device, knock, e.g. *él sabe todos los trucos del oficio,* he knows all the tricks of the trade. 2. pocketing of a ball (in pool). 3. (*pl.*) pool (game). 4. (Chile) punch, blow.
truculencia, *f.* truculence, cruelty, ferocity.
truculento, ta, *a.* truculent, cruel, ferocious.
trué, *m.* (tex.) fine white linen.
trueco, *m.* barter, exchange; **a t. de,** as long as, provided that; **a** or **en t.,** in exchange.
trueco, *ref.* **trocar.**
truena, truene, *ref.* **tronar.**
trueno, *m.* 1. thunder, thunderclap; shot, report (of gun), bang (of fireworks). 2. (coll.) madcap, wild youth, harumscarum. — **t. gordo,** loud report of fireworks; (coll.) big scandal, sensational action.
trueque, *m.* barter, exchange; **a** or **en t.,** in exchange.
trueque, *ref.* **trocar.**
trufa, *f.* 1. (bot.) truffle. 2. fib, story, lie.
trufador, ra, *a.* fibbing, lying. —*m., f.* fibber, liar.
trufaldín, na, *m.* (theat., arch.) actor, comedian. —*f.* actress, comedienne.
trufar, *tr.v.* (cul.) to stuff with truffles. —*i.v.* to lie, make up stories.
truficultura, *f.* truffle growing or cultivation.
truhán, na, *a.* 1. cheating, tricky, crooked; knavish, rascally. 2. clownish, buffoonish. —*m., f.* 1. cheat, trickster, swindler, crook, rogue, knave, rascal, scoundrel. 2. clown, buffoon.
truhanada, *f., var. of* **truhanería.**
truhanamente, *adv.* crookedly, deceitfully, knavishly.
truhanear, *i.v.* 1. to cheat, trick; to live a rascally life. 2. to clown about, play the clown or buffoon.
truhanería, *f.* 1. cheating, trickery, swindling, rascality. 2. buffoonery, clowning. 3. gang of crooks, cheats, rogues or scoundrels.
truhanesco, ca, *a.* 1. cheating, rascally, crooked, scoundrelly. 2. clownish, buffoonish.
truismo, *m.* (Angl., neol.) truism.
truja, *f.* olive bin in oil mill.
trujal, *m.* 1. wine press; oil press; oil mill. 2. soda vat (used in soap making).
trujamán, na, *m., f.* dragoman, truchman, interpreter. —*m.* adviser, especially in buying and selling.
trujamanear, *i.v.* 1. to interpret, work as an interpreter. 2. to trade, barter. 3. to advise or counsel in buying and selling.
trujamanía, *f.* 1. interpreting, job of interpreter. 2. trading, buying and selling, job of expert in buying and selling.
trujimán, *m., f., var. of* **trujamán.**
trulla, *f.* 1. noise, bustle. 2. crowd. 3. (carp.) trowel. 4. (Col.) joke.
trullo, *m.* 1. (ornith.) teal. 2. vat to catch juice of pressed grapes.
trumao, *m.* (Chile) sandy soil of volcanic rock.
trun, *m.* (bot., Chile) bur, burr.
truncadamente, *adv.* with omissions, with cuts, in a truncated manner.
truncado, da, *past part. of* **truncar.** —*a.* truncate, truncated; (geom.) truncated.
truncamiento, *m.* truncation; cutting short; cutting, reduction.
truncar, (*ref. 50*) *tr.v.* 1. to truncate. 2. to mutilate. 3. (fig.) to cut short; to cut, reduce; to leave unfinished; e.g. *la novela quedó truncada,* the novel was left unfinished.
trunco, ca, *a.* unfinished, incomplete; mutilated, truncated.
trunque, trunqué, *ref.* **truncar.**
trupial, *m.* (ornith.) troupial.
truque, *m.* 1. card game. 2. kind of hopscotch.
truque, truqué, *ref.* **trucar.**
truquero, *m.* keeper of a pool room or table.
truquiflor, *m.* card game similar to **truque.**
trusa, *f.* 1. (Cuba) bathing suit or trunks; (*pl.*) briefs (short, close-fitting underpants). 2. (*pl.*) trunk hose.
trust, *m.* (Angl., com.) trust.
tsetse, *f.* (ento.) tsetse.
tú, *pers. pron. 2nd pers., m.* or *f.* (used familiarly), thou; you; **a tú por tú,** (coll.) disrespectfully; **de tú por tú,** over-familiarly, disrespectfully; **hablar** or **tratar de tú,** to speak to or address in an intimate or familiar manner.
tu, tus, *poss. a., m.* or *f.* (used familiarly), thy; your.
tuatúa, *f.* (bot.) American spurge (Jatropha gossypiifolia).
tuáutem, *m.* (coll.) indispensable person or thing; essential.
tuba, *f.* 1. (mus.) tuba (type of horn). 2. (Phil. I.) tuba (liquor made from sap of various palms).
tuberculina, *f.* (bac.) tuberculin.
tuberculización, *f.* (med.) infecting with tuberculosis, tubercularization.
tubérculo, *m.* 1. (bot.) tuber, tubercle. 2. (anat., med.) tubercle.
tuberculosis, *f.* (med.) tuberculosis.
tuberculoso, sa, *a.* tuberculous, tubercular. —*m., f.* (med.) tubercular patient, tubercular.
tubería, *f.* 1. pipes; tubing. 2. pipeline, pipe system.
tuberosa, *f.* (bot.) tuberose; nard, spikenard.
tuberosidad, *f.* tuberosity.
tuberoso, sa, *a.* tuberous, tuberose.
tubícola, *a.* (zool.) tubicolous.
tubo, *m.* 1. tube; pipe. 2. (rad.) valve; tube. 3. (anat.) duct, canal. 4. lamp chimney. — **t. acústico,** speaking tube; **t. de vacío,** (phys.) vacuum tube; **t. capilar,** (anat.) capillary tube; **t. contador,** (phys.) counting tube, counter tube; **t. de derrame** or **desagüe,** overflow pipe; **t. de ensayo,** test tube; **t. de escape,** (auto.) exhaust pipe; **t. de fuerzas,** (phys.) tube of force; **t. de imagen** or **reproducción,** (tel.) picture tube; **t. de neumático,** (auto.) tire tube; **t. de órgano,** organ pipe; **t. de rayos catódicos,** cathode-ray tube; **t. digestivo,** alimentary canal; **t. electrónico,** electronic tube; **t. en t,** T-tube; **t. intestinal,** (anat.) intestines; **t. lanzatorpedos,** (mar.) torpedo tube; **t. neumático,** pneumatic tube or dispatch.
tubulado, da, *a.* tubulate, having tubes or the shape of a tube.
tubuladura, *f.* tubulure, tubulation.
tubular, *a.* tubular, tube-shaped.
tubulífero, ra, *a.* (ento.) tubuliferous.
tubuloso, sa, *a.* (bot.) tubulous.
tucán, *m.* 1. (ornith.) toucan. 2. (astron.) **T.,** Toucan.
tucía, *f.* (chem.) tutty.
Tucídides, *m.* (hist.) Thucydides, Greek historian.
tucinte, *m.* (Hond., bot.) gramineous plant with large leaves used as fodder (Reana luxurians).
tuciorismo, *m.* (theol.) tutiorism.
tuciorista, *a.* (theol.) tutioristic. —*m., f.* tutiorist.
tuco, ca, *a.* (Bol., Ecuad., P. Rico) maimed, one-armed, armless, handless. —*m.* 1. (Amer.) stump (of arm, etc.). 2. (Hond.) namesake. 3. (S. Amer.) meat sauce. 4. (Arg.) glowworm. 5. (Peru) kind of owl.
tucúquere, *m.* (Chile, ornith.) great horned owl.

tucura, *f.* (Bol.) large locust.
tucurpilla, *f.* (Ecuad., ornith.) small wood pigeon.
tucuso, *m.* (Ven., ornith.) hummingbird.
tucuyo, *m.* (tex., Amer.) coarse cotton cloth.
tudel, *m.* (mus.) crook of bassoon where mouthpiece is attached.
tudesco, ca, *a., m., f.* German. —*m., f.* (coll.) person who eats or drinks to excess. —*m.* cloak, cape.
tueca, *f.* stump (of tree).
tueco, *m.* 1. stump (of tree). 2. hollow in tree made by wood-borer.
tuerca, *f.* (mec.) nut; **t. ahuecada,** recessed nut; **t. almenada,** castellated nut; **t. de ceja,** flange nut; **t. de orejetas** or **alas,** wing nut; **t. encastillada,** slotted nut; **t. inaflojable,** self-locking nut; **t. tapa** or **ciega,** cap nut.
tuerce, *m.* 1. twisting, twist. 2. (C. Amer.) bad luck; misfortune.
tuero, *m.* 1. big log at the back of the fire; firewood. 2. (Guat.) hide-and-seek (game).
tuerto, ta, *a.* 1. twisted, crooked, bent. 2. one-eyed. — **a tuertas,** (coll.) backwards, upside down; crosswise; **a tuerto,** unjustly; **a tuerto** or **a derecho, a tuerta** or **a derechas,** rightly or wrongly, justly or unjustly; *m., f.* one-eyed person. —*m.* 1. wrong, injustice. 2. (*pl.*) after pains (of birth).
tuerza, tuerzo, *ref.* **torcer.**
tueste, *m.* toasting.
tueste, tuesto, *ref.* **tostar.**
tuétano, *m.* (anat.) marrow; **hasta los tuétanos,** (coll.) head over heels, through and through, to the marrow, e.g. *enamorado hasta los tuétanos,* head over heels in love.
tufarada, *f.* strong smell or odor.
tufillas, (*pl.* **tufillas**), *m., f.* (coll.) spitfire, irascible person.
tufo, *m.* 1. fume, vapor. 2. (coll.) foul smell or odor; (coll.) bad breath. 3. (coll.) (*pl.*) conceit, airs. 4. lock of hair (combed over the temples). 5. (geol.) tufa.
tugurio, *m.* 1. hovel, shack; shepherd's hut. 2. small room. 3. (sl.) clip joint, dive.
tui, *m.* (Arg.) small parrot.
tuición, *f.* (law) protection, defense.
tuína, *f.* long loose jacket.
tuitivo, va, *a.* (law) protective, defensive.
tul, *m.* (tex.) tulle, fine sheer net.
tularemia, *f.* (med., vet.) tularemia, rabbit fever.
tule, *m.* (Mex., bot.) tule, bulrush.
Tule, *f.* (geog., hist.) Thule; **última T.,** ultima Thule.
tulenco, ca, *a.* (C. Amer.) feeble, weak.
tulio, *m.* (chem.) thulium.
tulipa, *f.* 1. (bot.) small tulip. 2. tulip-shaped lampshade.
tulipán, *m.* (bot.) tulip (plant and flower).
tulipanero, tulipero, *m.* (bot.) tulip tree.
tullecer, (*ref. 45*) *tr.v.* to cripple, disable, maim; to paralyze. —*i.v.* to be crippled or maimed.
Tullerias, *f.* (hist.) **Las T.,** The Tuileries.
tullezca, tullezco, *ref.* **tullecer.**
tullidez, *f.* disablement, crippled condition; paralysis.
tullido, da, *past part. of* **tullir.** —*a.* crippled, disabled, maimed. —*m., f.* cripple, disabled person; paralytic.
tullidura, *f.* (*pl.*) droppings of birds of prey.
tullimiento, *m.* disablement, crippled condition.
tullir, (*ref. 65*) *tr.v.* to cripple, disable, maim; to paralyze. —*i.v.* to excrete (birds of prey). —*r.v.* to become crippled or maimed.
tumba, *f.* 1. grave, tomb. 2. ornamental arched roof of a coach. 3. tumble, fall; somersault. 4. (Cuba, Col., Mex.) felling (of trees). 5. (Arg., Chile, Urug.) chunk of tough meat (eaten by convicts or soldiers). 6. (Cuba) drum, bongo. 7. (Cuba, Dom. Rep.) ritual folk dance performed by Black people.
tumbacuartillos, (*pl.* **tumbacuartillos**), *m., f.* (coll.) drunkard.
tumbadero, *m.* 1. (Cuba, P. Rico) clearing, place where trees are being cleared. 2. (Cuba) brothel. 3. (Ven.) branding yard or pen.
tumbadillo, *m.* (mar.) roundhouse, cuddy.
tumbado, da, *a.* coffin-shaped, arched, vaulted. —*m.* (Ecuad.) ceiling.
tumbaga, *f.* 1. tombac (alloy). 2. tombac ring. 3. (*pl.*) (Sp., reg.) rings, jewelry.
tumbagón, *m.* tombac bracelet.
tumbal, *a.* pertaining to a tomb.
tumbaollas, (*pl.* **tumbaollas**), *m., f.* (coll.) pig, glutton.
tumbar, *tr.v.* 1. to knock down, knock over; (coll.) to overthrow (e.g. government). 2. (coll.) to stun, knock out, overcome. 3. (coll.) to fail, flunk (in an examination). 4. (Cuba) to fell, cut (trees, plants). 5. (vulg.) to have sexual intercourse with. —*i.v.* 1. to fall, fall down, tumble. 2. (mar.) to keel, keel over. —*r.v.* 1. (coll.) to lie down, go to bed. 2. to ease up, let up (in one's work).
tumbilla, *f.* bed warmer or brazier holder.
tumbo, *m.* 1. violent tumble or fall. 2. big wave, rise and fall (of the sea); roll, undulation (of terrain). 3. boom, rumble. 4. (Col.) jar, bowl. 5. (hist.) register or record of title deeds and privileges (of monasteries, communities, etc.). — **t. de dado,** imminent danger; **t. de olla,** each of the three ingredients of a stew (broth, vegetables, meat); **dar tumbos,** to sway, stagger.
tumbón, na, *a.* 1. sly, cunning, crafty. 2. lazy. —*m., f.* sly person; lazy person, idler, loafer. —*m.* carriage with a domed roof; coffer or chest with an arched lid. —*f.* reclining chair, deck chair.
tumefacción, *f.* (med.) tumefaction, swelling.
tumefacer, (*ref. 10*) *tr.v.* to tumefy, make swell. —*r.v.* to tumefy, swell.
tumefaciente, *a.* tumefacient. —*m.* (med.) tumefacient agent.
tumefacto, ta, *a.* (med.) tumid, swollen.
tumescencia, *f.* (med.) tumescence.
tumescente, *a.* tumescent.
túmido, da, *a.* 1. tumid, swollen. 2. (archit.) wider in the middle (an arch).
tumor, *m.* (med.) tumor; swelling, protuberance; **t. cerebral,** (med.) brain tumor.
tumoral, *a.* tumor-like.
tumoroso, sa, *a.* tumorous.
tumulario, ria, *a.* tumular, pertaining to graves or burial grounds.
túmulo, *m.* 1. tumulus, grave mound, barrow. 2. catafalque.
tumulto, *m.* tumult, uproar, commotion, confusion; mob.
tumultuante, *a.* agitating, inciting to riot.
tumultuar, (*ref. 55*) *tr.v.* to stir up, agitate, rouse, incite to make a disturbance. —*r.v.* to make a disturbance, cause a disorder, riot.
tumultuario, ria, *a.* tumultuary, disorderly.
tumultuosamente, *adv.* tumultuously.
tumultuoso, sa, *a.* tumultuous.
tuna, *f.* 1. (bot.) tuna, prickly pear, Indian fig (plant or fruit); **t. brava, colorada** or **roja,** (bot.) red prickly pear. 2. idle, vagrant life, loafing, bumming. 3. *var. of* **estudiantina,** group of student serenaders. — **correr la t.,** (coll.) to loaf, bum around.
tunal, *m.* (bot.) prickly pear plant; growth of prickly pears, prickly pear patch.
tunanta, *a.* (coll.) sly, cunning, astute (woman). —*f.* rogue, rascal; hussy.
tunantada, *f.* roguery, rascally trick.
tunante, *a.* 1. rascally, cunning, sly, astute (man). 2. bumming, loafing; leading a roving, idle life. —*m.* 1. rascal, rogue. 2. bum, loafer.
tunantear, *i.v.* to be a rogue; to loaf, bum.
tunantería, *f.* rascality, roguishness, roguery; rascally trick.
tunantuela, *f. dim. of* **tunanta,** (coll.) little rascal, little rogue (said of a girl).
tunantuelo, *m. dim. of* **tunante,** little rascal, little rogue (said of a boy).
tunar, *i.v.* to loaf, bum around.
tunco, *m.* (Hond., Mex.) hog, pig.
tunda, *f.* 1. shearing, clipping (of cloth). 2. (coll.) beating, thrashing.
tundear, *tr.v.* to beat, thrash.*tundente, a.* contusive, bruising.
tundición, *f.* shearing, clipping (of cloth).
tundidor, tundidora, *a.* shearing, clipping (machine). —*m., f.* cloth shearer or clipper (person). —*f.* shearing machine (for cloth).
tundidura, *f.* shearing (of cloth).
tundir, *tr.v.* 1. to shear, clip (cloth). 2. (coll.) to beat, thrash.
tundizno, *m.* shearings (from cloth).
tundra, *f.* (geog.) tundra.
tunduque, *m.* (Chile) variety of large mouse.
tunear, *i.v.* to be a rogue or rascal; to lead a vagrant life.
tunecí, (*pl.* **tunecíes**), *a., m., f. var. of* tunecino.
tunecino, na, *a., m., f.* Tunisian.
túnel, *m.* tunnel; **t. aerodinámico, (aer.)** wind tunnel; **t. del eje,** (mar.) shaft tunnel.
tunera, *f.* (bot.) prickly pear plant.
tunería, *f.* rascality, roguishness, **roguery.**
Túnez, *m.* 1. Tunis. 2. Tunisia.
tungo, *m.* 1. (Chile) neck, nape. **2. (Arg.)** hack, nag.
tungstenita, *f.* (min.) tungstenite.
tungsteno, *m.* (chem.) tungsten, wolfram.
túngstico, ca, *a.* tungstenic, tungstic.
tungstita, *f.* (min.) tungstite.
túnica, *f.* 1. tunic; robe, gown. 2. (anat., bot., zool.) tunic; tunica. — **t. de Cristo,** (bot.) species of jimsonweed or thorn apple (Datura metel); **t. griega,** Grecian tunic; **t. úvea,** (anat.) uveal tunica (of the eye).
tunicado, da, *a.* (anat., bot.) tunicate. —*m.* (zool.) tunicate; (*pl.*) Tunicata.
tunicela, *f.* tunic; (ecc.) tunicle.
túnico, *m.* 1. (theat.) robe. 2. (Amer.) woman's robe. 3. (Cuba) dress, frock.
tunjo, *m.* 1. (Col.) gold object (found in Indian burial mounds). 2. (Col.) prickly pear (fruit).
tuno, na, *a.* rascally, roguish. —*m.* 1. rogue, rascal. 2. (Col., Cuba) prickly pear (fruit).
tunoso, sa, *a.* (Col.) prickly.
tuntún, *m.* 1. (Col.) anemia, caused by parasites. 2. (Guat.) Indian hair style (swept up and tied with a headband). — **al t., al buen t.,** (coll.) haphazardly, helter-skelter.
tuntunita, *f.* (Col., coll.) annoying repetition.
tupa, *f.* 1. blocking up, obstruction. 2. tight packing; denseness, compactness. 3. (coll.) fill, bellyful, satiety. 4. (Chile) (bot.) wild lobelia, Indian tobacco.
tupamaro, ra, *m., f.* (polit., Urug.) urban guerrilla (after Tupac Amaru, Inca chieftain who rebelled against the Spaniards).
tupaya, *f.* (zool.) tupain, squirrel shrew, tree shrew.
tupé, *m.* 1. toupee, hairpiece; pompadour. 2. (coll.) nerve, sauce, cheek, brass. 3. clump, tuft (of moss).
tupi, *a.* Tupian. —*m., f.* Tupi, Tupian Indian. —*m.* Tupi, Tupian language.

tupia, *f.* 1. (Col.) dam; dammed up water. 2. (Col.) fill, bellyful, surfeit.
tupición, *f.* 1. (Amer.) thickness, dimness, dullness, lack of intelligence. 2. (Chile) crowd. 3. (Ven.) blocking (of nose with mucus).
tupido, da, *past part. of* **tupir.** —*a.* 1. dense, thick, compact; closely woven. 2. thick, obtuse, dense, unintelligent, dim. 3. blocked up (nose with mucus).
tupí-guaraní, *m.* Tupi-Guarani, linguistic and cultural Indian family of S. America.
tupinambo, *m.* (bot.) Jerusalem artichoke.
tupir, *tr.v.* 1. to block up, stop up, obstruct, choke; to pack closely or tightly. 2. to weave closely. —*r.v.* 1. to get stopped or blocked up. 2. to stuff, glut, gorge or fill oneself. 3. to become sluggish; to become slow-thinking. 4. (Amer.) to get embarrassed or bashful.
turaní, *a., m., f.* (hist.) Turanian.
turanio, nia, *a., m., f.* (hist.) Turanian.
turba, *f.* 1. peat, turf. 2. mob, crowd.
turbación, *f.* disturbance, upset; confusion; embarrassment; disorder.
turbadamente, *adv.* confusedly; disturbedly.
turbador, ra, *a.* disturbing, disquieting, perturbing, worrying. —*m., f.* disturber, perturber.
turbal, *m., var. of* **turbera.**
turbamiento, *f., var. of* **turbación.**
turbamulta, *f.* (coll.) crowd, rabble, mob.
turbante, *a.* perturbing, disturbing, disquieting, worrying; confusing, embarrassing. —*m.* turban, headdress.
turbar, *tr.v.* to disturb, upset; to worry, trouble, perturb, disquiet; to confuse; to embarrass. —*r.v.* to be or get disturbed or upset; to get worried or troubled; to get confused or embarrassed.
turbativo, va, *a.* perturbing, disturbing, disquieting.
turbelario, a, *a., m.* (zool.) turbellarian.
turbera, *f.* peat bog, peat moss.
turbiamente, *adv.* 1. confusedly. 2. dishonestly, crookedly.
turbidímetro, *m.* (phys.) turbidimeter.
túrbido, da, *a.* turbid, muddy.
turbiedad, turbieza, *f.* cloudiness, turbidness, muddiness; (fig.) confusion.
turbina, *f.* turbine; **t. alimentador,** turbo-charger; **t. a vapor, t. de vapor,** steam turbine; **t. axial,** axial-flow turbine; **t. de acción,** impulsive turbine; **t. de doble efecto,** double-flow turbine; **t. de efecto simple,** single-flow turbine; **t. de envoltura simple,** single-case turbine; **t. de gas,** gas turbine; **t. de impulsión,** impulse turbine; **t. de reacción,** reaction turbine; **t. centrífuga,** outward-flow turbine; **t. centrípeta,** inward-flow turbine; **t. hidráulica,** hydraulic or water turbine; **t. mixta,** mixed-flow turbine.
turbino, *m.* (pharm.) powdered turpeth.
turbinto, *m.* (bot.) pepper tree or shrub.
turbio, bia, *a.* 1. cloudy, turbid, muddy. 2. shady, crooked, dishonest. 3. dark, troubled, confused. 4. clouded, misty, unclear (sight, eyes). 5. confused, obscure (language). —*m.* (*pl.*) dregs, sediment.
turbión, *m.* squall, sudden shower; (fig.) shower, rush (of things, events).
turbit, *m.* (bot.) turpeth; **t. mineral,** (pharm.) turpeth mineral, turpeth.
turboalternador, *m.* (elec.) turboalternator.
turbobomba, *f.* (mec.) turbopump.
turbocompresor, *m.* (mec.) turbocompressor.
turbodínamo, *m.* (elec.) turbodynamo.
turbogenerador, *m.* (elec.) turbogenerator.
turbohélice, *m.* turbopropeller engine, turboprop.
turbomotor, *m.* turbomotor.
turbonada, *f.* stormy squall or shower.
turbopropulsor, *m.* turbopropeller engine, turboprop.
turborreactor, *m.* (aer.) turbojet.
turboventilador, *m.* turbofan.
turbulencia, *f.* 1. turbulence, storminess. 2. (meteorol.) turbulence.
turbulentamente, *adv.* turbulently.
turbulento, *a.* turbulent.
turca, *f.* (coll.) drunk, drunken bout, jag; **coger una t.,** (coll.) to tie one on.
turco, ca, *a.* Turkish; (philol.) Turkic. —*m., f.* Turk. —*m.* Turkish (language).
turcomano, na, *a., m., f.* Turkoman.
turcople, *a., m., f.* Turko-Greek (offspring of Turkish father and Greek mother).
túrdiga, *f.* strip of hide.
turdión, *m.* ancient Spanish dance.
turgencia, *f.* 1. swelling, tumefaction, turgidity, turgescence. 2. turgescence, turgidity, bombast, pomposity.
turgente, *a.* 1. massive, bulky; firm. 2. swollen, protuberant, prominent.
túrgido, da, *a.* (poet.) massive, bulky; swollen, turgid.
turgita, *f.* (min.) turgite.
turibular, *tr.v.* to incense with a thurible.
turibulario, *m., var. of* **turiferario.**
turíbulo, *m.* thurible, censer.
turiferario, *m.* (ecc.) thurifer, censer-bearer.
turífero, ra, *a.* thuriferous (incense bearing or yielding).
turificación, *f.* thurification, censing, incensing.
turificar, (*ref. 50*) *tr.v.* to incense, cense, burn incense in, thurify.
turifique, turifiqué, *ref.* **turificar.**
turión, *m.* (bot.) turion.
turismo, *m.* 1. tourism; touring; tourist trade. 2. (coll.) touring limousine.
turista, *a.* tourist, e.g. *clase t.,* tourist class. —*m., f.* tourist.
turístico, ca, *a.* tourist, e.g. *industria turística,* tourist industry.
turma, *f.* testicle; **t. de tierra,** (bot.) truffle.
turmalina, *f.* (min.) tourmaline.
turnar, *i.v., r.v.* to take turns, alternate.
turnio, nia, *a.* 1. squint, cross (eyes); squinteyed, cross-eyed. 2. frowning, scowling. —*m., f.* 1. cross-eyed person. 2. frowner, scowler.
turno, *m.* turn; shift; **a** or **en su t.,** in its turn, at its proper time; **aguardar su t., hacer t.,** to wait one's turn; **de t.,** on duty, e.g. *el oficial de t.,* the duty officer; **estar en el t. de la noche,** to be on the night shift; **por t.,** in turn; **por turnos,** by turns; **t. de día** or **noche,** day or night shift.
turón, *m.* (zool.) polecat.
turpial, *m.* (ornith.) troupial.
turquesa, *f.* 1. mold; bullet mold. 2. (min., jewel.) turquoise; **color t.,** turquoise (color); **t. occidental,** odontolite, bone or fossil turquoise.
turquesado, da, *a.* dark blue, indigo.
turquesco, ca, *a.* Turkish; a la **turquesca,** in the Turkish style.
Turquestán, *m.* (geog.) Turkestan.
turquí, (*pl.* **turquíes**), *a.* dark blue, indigo.
turquía, *f.* Turkey.
turquino, na, *a.* 1. Turkish. 2. dark-blue, indigo. —*m.* dark blue, indigo.
turrada, *f.* (Guat.) *var. of* **picatoste.**
turrar, *tr.v.* to roast, toast, broil.
turriculado, da, *a.* turriculate, turreted.
turro, ra, *a.* (Arg.) stupid, foolish.
turrón, *m.* 1. (cul.) nougat. 2. (coll.) government job or post. — **comer del turrón,** to fill a public office.
turronería, *f.* nougat shop.
turronero, ra, *m., f.* nougat seller or maker.
turrutín, *m.* (Chile, Col.) tiny tot, small child.
turulato, ta, *a.* (coll.) dazed, stunned.
turuleque, *m.* vulgar man, boor.
turulés, *a.* a kind of grape.
turullo, *m.* shepherd's horn.
turumbón, *m.* bump, swelling (on the head).
turupial, *m.* (Ven., ornith.) troupial.
¡tus! *interj.* here! (to call a dog); **sin decir t. ni mus,** (coll.) without saying a word.
tusa, *f.* 1. (S. Amer., Cuba) stripped corn-cob. 2. (Amer.) cigar rolled in corn husk. 3. (Chile) cornsilk. 4. (Chile) mane (of a horse). 5. (Col.) pockmark. 6. (C. Amer., Cuba) trollop, bitch (woman).
tusar, *tr.v.* (Amer., coll.) to trim, clip; to shear.
tusca, *f.* (Arg., bot.) acacia (Acacia aroma).
tusco, ca, *a., m., f.* 1. Tuscan. 2. Etruscan.
tusilago, *m.* (bot.) coltsfoot.
tuso, sa, *a.* 1. (Col.) pockmarked. 2. (P. Rico) tailless, short-tailed (animal). —*m.* (coll.) dog.
tusón, *m.* 1. fleece (of sheep). 2. (Sp., reg.) colt under two years old.
tusona, *f.* 1. (coll.) whore, harlot. 2. (Sp., reg.) filly under two years old.
Tutankamen, Tutankamón, *m.* (hist.) Tutankhamen, Tutenkhamon, Tutankhamon.
tute, *m.* 1. Spanish card game. 2. long tiring job or spell of work. — **darse un tute,** to wear oneself out with hard work.
tuteador, ra, *a.* familiar, using the familiar form of address **tú.**
tuteamiento, *m., var. of* **tuteo.**
tutear, *tr.v.* to address with the familiar form of **tú;** to be on familiar or intimate terms with. —*r.v.* to address each other with the familiar form **tú;** to be on familiar or intimate terms.
tutela, *f.* 1. guardianship, tutelage; guidance, protection. 2. trusteeship. — **territorio bajo t.,** trust territory; **t. dativa,** (law) guardianship by court appointment; **t. ejemplar,** (law) guardianship of the mentally incapacitated; **t. legítima** or **de la ley,** (law) legal guardianship.
tutelar, *a.* tutelary, tutelar, protective.
tuteo, *m.* use of the familiar form (**tú**) of address.
tutilimundi, *m.* cosmorama, viewing machine (through which one looks to see old-time movies in penny arcades).
tutiplén, a t., abundantly, in abundance, to excess.
tutor, ra, *m., f.* guardian, protector; (law) guardian; **t. dativo,** (law) guardian appointed by a competent authority; **t. legítimo,** (law) tutor appointed by law. —*m.* prop (for plants).
tutoría, *f., var. of* **tutela.**
tutriz, (*pl.* **tutrices**), *f.* (female) guardian.
tutú, (*pl.* **tutúes**), *m.* tutu (ballerina's short skirt).
tutuma, *f.* 1. (Amer.) calabash (fruit). 2. (Chile) bump, swelling; abscess, boil.
tutumito, ta, *a.* (C. Amer., Col) stupid, foolish.
tuturutú, ta, *a.* (Col., Ecuad., Ven.) **dazed,** stunned. —*m., f.* (Chile) pimp, procuress.
tuturutú, *m.* sound of a bugle or trumpet.
tuve, tuviera, tuviese, *ref.* **tener.**
tuya, *f.* (bot.) thuja, American arborvitae.
tuyo, tuya, tuyos, tuyas, *a., pos. pron. 2nd pers., m.* or *f.* (used familiarly), yours, thine, of yours or thine, e.g. *tengo un libro tuyo,* I have a book of yours.

U

U, *f.* u, twenty-second letter of the Spanish alphabet; **en u,** U, U-shaped, e.g. *tubo en u,* U-tube, *barra en u,* U-bar; **u. consonante,** v; **u. valona,** w; **u ve,** v.
u, *conj.* or (used instead of **o** before words begining with **o** or **ho**), e.g. *este u otro,* this or that one, *días u horas,* days or hours.
U *sym. of* **uranio,** uranium (U).
U. *abbrev. of* **usted,** you.
Uagadugú, *m.* Ouagadougou, capital of Upper Volta.
ube, *m.* (Phil. I., bot.) yam plant (Dioscorea alata).
Úbeda, irse por los cerros de Ú., to go off one's rocker; to change the subject of conversation suddenly.
ubérrimo, ma, *a.* super, very or most abundant, fruitful or fertile.
ubí, (*pl.* **ubíes**), *m.* (Cuba., bot.) cissus.
ubicacíon, *f.* location, situation, position.
ubicado, da, *past part. of* **ubicar.** *—a.* located, placed, situated.
ubicar, (*ref. 50*) *tr.v.* (Amer.) to locate, situate, place. *—i.v.* to be located, situated, placed. *—r.v.* to be located, situated or placed; to place or locate oneself.
ubicuidad, *f.* omnipresence; ubiquity.
ubicuo, cua, *a.* omnipresent; ubiquitous.
ubique, ubiqué, *ref.* **ubicar.**
ubiquidad, *f., var. of* **ubicuidad.**
ubiquitario, ria, *a., m., f.* (theol.) Ubiquitarian.
ubre, *f.* udder (of an animal).
ubrera, *f.* (med.) thrush (in infants).
ucase, *m.* 1. (hist.) ukase, edict of the Czar. 2. an authoritarian or arbitrary proclamation.
ucranio, nia, *a., m., f.* Ukranian. *—f.* **U.,** Ukraine.
uchuvito, ta, *a.* (Col.) drunk.
Ud. *abbrev. of* **Usted,** you (used formally).
udómetro, *m.* udometer, rain gauge.
Uds. (*pl.*) *abbrev. of* **Ustedes,** you (used formally).
uesnorueste, *m.* west-northwest.
uessudueste, *m.* west-southwest.
ueste, *m.* west.
¡uf! *interj.* ugh! (expressing disgust or weariness).
ufanamente, *adv.* boastfully, ostentatiously with an air of satisfaction.
ufanarse, *r.v.* to boast, pride oneself; **u. de,** to boast of, pride oneself on.
ufanía, *f.* 1. boastfulness, pride, self-satisfaction. 2. self-confidence, self-assurance, resolution, determination. 3. joy, pleasure.
ufano, na, *a.* 1. proud of oneself, conceited. self-satisfied; proud, boastful. 2. confident, self-assured; resolute. 3. gay, cheerful; pleased.
ufo, a u., at someone else's expense, sponging.
Uganda, *f.* Uganda.
Ugandés, desa, *a., m., f.* Ugandan.
ugarítico, *m.* (philol.) Ugaritic (ancient Semitic language).
ugre, *m.* (C. Rica, bot.) Indian plum (Oncoba laurina).
uintahíta, uintaíta, *f.* (min.) uintaite, uintahite.
ujier, *m.* usher (in a court, etc.), doorkeeper; **u. de cámara,** usher to the king's privy chamber.
ulala, *f.* (Bol., bot.) variety of cactus.
ulano, *m.* (hist., mil.) uhlan, lancer.
úlcera, *f.* (med.) ulcer; (bot.) rot; **u. duodenal,** (med.) duodenal ulcer.
ulceración, *f.* ulceration.
ulcerante, *a.* ulcerating.
ulcerar, *tr.v.* to ulcerate. *—r.v.* to ulcerate; to fester.
ulcerativo, va, *a.* ulcerative, ulcerating.
ulceroso, sa, *a.* ulcerous.
ulema, *m.* ulema, doctor in Mohammedan law.
ulero, *m.* (Chile) rolling pin.
ulfilano, na, *a.* (hist., lit.) in the style of Ulfilas (who translated the Bible into Gothic).
uliginoso, sa, *a.* uliginous, swampy.
Ulises, *m.* (myth.) Ulysses.
ulitis, *f.* (med.) ulitis.
ulmáceo, a, *a.* (bot.) ulmaceous. *—f.* (bot.) ulmaceous plant; (*pl.*) (bot.) Ulmaceae.
ulmaria, *f.* (bot.) meadowsweet.
ulmén, *m.* (Chile) rich influential man (among the Araucan Indians).
ulmina, *f.* (chem.) ulmin.
ulna, *f.* (anat.) ulna.
ulnar, *a.* (anat.) ulnar.
ulpo, *m.* (Chile, Peru) gruel or porridge made with toasted corn flour.
ulterior, *a.* 1. ulterior, beyond. 2. subsequent, following.
ulteriormente, *adv.* 1. ulteriorly. 2. subsequently, afterwards.
ultílogo, *m.* (lit.) epilogue.
ultimación, *f.* finish, conclusion, completion.
ultimador, ra, *a.* ending, finishing, concluding. *—m., f.* finisher, concluder.
últimamente, *adv.* 1. lately, recently, of late. 2. lastly, finally.
ultimar, *tr.v.* 1. to finish, conclude. 2. (coll., Amer.) to finish off; to close, end. 3. (Amer.) to finish off (to kill).
ultimátum, *m.* ultimatum; (coll.) final decision.
ultimidad, *f.* ultimateness, ultimacy, final state.
último, ma, *a.* 1. last; final. 2. latest; latter. 3. best, most valuable. 4. highest or lowest (e.g. price, etc.). 6. farthest, most remote. *—m., f.* 1. the last one. 2. the latter. 3. utmost, limit, e.g. *esto es lo último,* (coll.) this is the limit of endurance. — **a la última moda,** in the latest fashion; **a última hora,** at the eleventh hour; **a últimos de,** at the end of (the month); **en los últimos días,** recently, in the last few days; **estar en las últimas,** (coll.) to be on one's last legs; to be near one's end, be about to die; to be abreast of the news, be up to date; **por último,** finally; **Ú. Cena,** Last Supper; **ú. hora,** late news item; **ú. morada,** final resting place; **última pena,** capital punishment; **último precio,** last or final price; **ú. voluntad,** last wishes; **últimos sacramentos,** last rites.
ultra, *adv.* besides. *—prep.* ultra.
ultracentrífuga, *f.* (phys., chem.) ultracentrifuge.
ultraconfidencial, *a.* highly confidential.
ultraconservador, ra, *a., m., f.* **ultraconservative.**
ultracorreción, *f.* hypercorrection.
ultraderecha, *f.* extreme right.
ultraderechista, *a.* extreme right-wing. *—m., f.* right-wing extremist.
ultraísmo, *m.* 1. ultraism; extremism. 2. important literary movement created around 1919 by Spanish and Latin American poets (among them Jorge Luís Borges).
ultraísta, *a.* ultraistic. *—m., f.* ultraist.
ultraizquierda, *f.* extreme left.
ultraizquierdista, *a.* extreme left-wing. *—m., f.* left-wing extremist.
ultrajador, ra, *a.* outraging, affronting, offending. *—m., f.* 1. affronter, offender, outrager. 2. rapist.
ultrajante, *a.* outraging, affronting, offending, insulting.
ultrajar, *tr.v.* 1. to outrage, affront, offend, insult, humiliate. 2. to rape, violate.
ultraje, *m.* 1. outrage, affront, insult, offense; humiliation. 2. rape, violation.
ultrajoso, sa, *a.* affronting, offensive, insulting, outrageous.
ultramar, *m.* 1. overseas; overseas country. 2. ultramarine (color and pigment). — **azul de u.,** ultramarine (color and pigment); (min.) lapis lazuli.
ultramarino, na, *a.* overseas, ultramarine; **azul ultramarino,** ultramarine blue. *—m.* 1. (*pl.*) imported goods or foods. 2. (*pl.*) grocery store.
ultramaro, *a.* **azul ultramaro,** ultramarine blue.
ultramicrometría, *f.* (metal.) ultramicrometry.
ultramicroquímica, *f.* ultramicrochemistry.
ultramicroscopía. *f.* ultramicroscopy.
ultramicroscópico, ca, *a.* ultramicroscopic.
ultramiscroscopio, *m.* ultramicroscope; electron microscope.
ultramoderno, na, *a.* ultramodern.
ultramontanismo, *m.* (polit., rel.) ultramontanism.
ultramontano, na, *a.* ultramontane, beyond the mountains. *—m., f.* (polit., rel.) ultramontane.
ultramundano, na, *a.* ultramundane, beyond this world.
ultranza, a u., to the death; at all costs, resolutely.
ultrapasar, *tr.v.* (Gal.) to exceed, go beyond.
ultrapuertos, *m.* beyond the seaports.
ultrarrápido, da, *a.* extra fast, ultrarapid.
ultrarrojo, *a.* (phys.) infrared, ultrared.
ultrasónico, ca, *a.* supersonic, ultrasonic.
ultrasonido, *m.* supersonic, ultrasonic.
ultrasonoro, ra, *a.* ultrasonic.
ultratumba, *f.* beyond the grave; **de u.,** from the dead, from the other world.
ultraviolado, da, ultravioleta, *a.* (phys.) ultraviolet.
ultravirus, (*pl.* **ultravirus**), *m.* (biol.) ultravirus.
úlula, *f.* (ornith.) tawny owl.
ululación, *f.* howling, ululation, screeching (of an owl).
ulular, *tr.v.* to ululate, hoot, screech.
ululato, *m.* clamor, cry, howl, ululation.
ulluco, *m.* (Bol., Ecuad., Peru, bot.) ulluco (an edible tuber).
umbela, *f.* 1. (bot.) umbel. 2. projecting roof (over balcony or window).

umbelífero, ra, *a.* (bot.) umbelliferous. —*f.* (bot.) umbelliferous plant; (*pl.*) (bot.) Umbelliferae.
umbélula, *f.* (bot.) umbellule.
umbilicado, *a.* umbilicate, navel-shaped.
umbilical, *a.* (anat.) umbilical.
umbráculo, *m.* latticework shed or shelter (to protect plants from direct sunlight).
umbral, *m.* 1. threshold; doorsill, doorstep. 2. (archit.) lintel. 3. (psyc., physiol.) threshold. 4. (fig.) threshold, entrance, beginning. — **u. bicromático,** (opt.) bichromatic threshold; **u. logarítmico,** (math.) logarithmic threshold.
umbralado, *m.* 1. (archit.) opening or entrance way supported by a lintel. 2. (S. Amer.) threshold.
umbralar, *tr.v.* to build a lintel on (door, entrance, etc.).
umbrático, ca, *a.* shady, umbrageous.
umbrátil, *a.* shady, umbrageous.
umbría, *f.* shady place, shade.
umbrío, a, *a.* shaded, shady, e.g. *rincón umbrío,* a shady corner (of a garden).
umbroso, sa, *a.* shady, umbrageous.
un, una, (**un** is used before masculine singular nouns and adjectives and also before feminine nouns beginning with accented a). —*a.* one (numeral), e.g. *dame un solo libro,* give me only one book, *basta con un arma,* one weapon is enough. —*indef. art.* a, an (*ref.* **uno**), *e.g. dame un lápiz,* give me a pencil, *una edición abreviada,* an abridged edition, *un alma noble,* a noble soul.
unalbo, ba, *a.* with one foot of a different color (said of horses).
unánime, *a.* unanimous.
unánimemente, *adv.* unanimously.
unanimidad, *f.* unanimity; **por u.,** unanimously.
unáu, *m.* (zool.) sloth.
uncia, *f.* 1. (numis.) uncia. 2. (law) twelfth part of an estate.
uncial, *a.* uncial, pertaining to an ancient type of manuscript writing.
unciforme, *a., m.* (anat.) unciform.
uncinado, da, uncinate.
uncinariasis, *f.* (med.) uncinariasis.
unción, *f.* 1. anointment, anointing, unction. 2. devotion, fervor, unction. 3. (ecc.) extreme unction. 4. (mar.) small storm sail.
uncir, (*ref. 61*) *tr.v.* to yoke.
undante, *a.* (poet.) wavy, undulating.
undecágono, na, *m.* (geom.) undecagon, hendecagon.
undecilénico, ca, *a.* (chem.) undecylenic.
undécimo, ma, *a., m.* eleventh.
undécuplo, pla, *a.* eleven times as much or as large.
undísono, na, *a.* (poet.) rippling, lapping (waters).
undívago, ga, *a.* (poet.) wavy, billowy.
undoso, sa, *a.* wavy, undulating.
undulación, *f.* undulation; (phys.) wave; **u. permanente,** permanent wave.
undulante, *a.* undulating, undulant.
undular, *i.v.* to undulate, wriggle.
undulatorio, ria, *a.* undulatory, undulating.
ungido, *m.* anointed priest, prelate or monarch.
ungimiento, *m.* anointment, anointing, unction.
ungir, (*ref. 62*) *tr.v.* to anoint.
ungüentario, ria, *a.* unguentary. —*m.* 1. ointment maker or seller. 2. unguentarium, container for ointments.
ungüento, *m.* unguent, ointment, salve; **u. amarillo,** resin cerate; **u. de cinc,** (pharm.) zinc ointment.
unguiculado, da, *a.* (anat., bot.) unguiculate. —*m.* (zool.) unguiculate, (*pl.*) Unguiculata.
unguis, *m.* (anat.) unguis, os unguis.
ungulado, *a.* (zool.) ungulate. —*m.* (zool.) ungulate, (*pl.*) Ungulata.
ungular, *a.* ungular, pertaining to the nails or claws.
uniato, ta, *a., m., f.* (rel.) Uniat.
uniáxico, ca, uniaxial, *a.* uniaxial.
unible, *a.* unitable, uniteable, that can be joined.
únicamente, *adv.* only, simply, solely.
unicameral, *a.* unicameral.
unicaule, *a.* (bot.) having only one stalk.
unicelular, *a.* unicellular.
unicidad, *f.* uniqueness.
único, ca, *a.* 1. only, sole. 2. unique, unmatched, singular; rare.
unicolor, *a.* one-colored, unicolored.
unicornio, *m.* 1. (myth.) unicorn. 2. one-horned rhinoceros, unicorn. 3. (astron.) **U.,** Unicorn, Monoceros. 4. mastodon's fossilized tusk. — **u. de mar** or **marino,** (ichth.) narwhal, unicorn fish.
unidad, *f.* 1. unity, oneness, union, harmony; (lit., art) unity. 2. unit (distinct part of a whole; definite quantity adopted as standard of measurement); (math., phys., mil.) unit. 3. (coll.) each, each one, e.g. *cuesta diez pesetas la u.,* each one costs ten pesetas. — **u. de acción, lugar y tiempo,** (lit.) unity of action, place and time; **u. de combate,** (mil.) combat unit; **u. de cuidado intensivos** or **u. de tratamiento intensivo** or **u. de vigilancia intensiva,** intensive care unit; **u. de masa atómica,** (phys.) atomic mass unit; **u. de pertenencia,** (mil.) parent unit; **u. monetaria, u. monetaria,** monetary unit; **u. móvil,** outside broadcasting unit.
unidamente, *adv.* jointly, unitedly.
unido, da, *past part. of* **unir.** —*a.* 1. united, unified; in accord or agreement. 2. (Gal.) smooth.
unidor, ra, *a.* joining, unifying, uniting.
unificación, *f.* unification.
unificar, (*ref. 50*) *tr.v.* to unify. —*r.v.* to be or become unified.
unifique, unifiqué, *ref.* **unificar.**
unifloral, *a.* (bot.) uniflorous.
unifoliado, da, *a.* (bot.) unifoliate.
uniformado, *m.* man in uniform.
uniformador, ra, *a.* standardizing, that makes uniform or even.
uniformar, *tr.v.* 1. to make uniform, standardize. 2. to provide with uniforms. —*r.v.* to become uniform or standard.
uniforme, *a.* uniform. —*m.* 1. uniform. 2. (mil.) regimentals. — **u. de gala,** dress uniform.
uniformemente, *adv.* uniformly.
uniformidad, *f.* uniformity.
uniformizar, (*ref. 53*) *tr.v.* to make uniform.
unigénito, ta, *a.* only-begotten. —*m.* only son or daughter.
unilateral, *a.* unilateral.
unilocular, *a.* (bot., zool.) unilocular.
unimolecular, *a.* (phys.) unimolecular, monomolecular.
unión, *f.* 1. union; joining; joint, connection, coupling. 2. union, harmony, concord, unity. 3. union, marriage. 4. double finger ring. 5. union, syndicate, association. — **u. articulada,** (mec.) hinged connection, swivel coupling; **u. de brida,** flange union; **u. giratoria,** swing joint (of pipes); **U. Panamericana,** Pan American Union; **U. Soviética,** Soviet Union.
Unión de Repúblicas Socialistas Soviéticas, *f.* Union of Soviet Socialist Republics.
unionismo, *m.* (polit., econ.) unionism.
unionista, *a., m., f.* (polit., econ.) unionist.
uniovular, *a.* (biol.) monovular.
uníparo, ra, *a.* (zool., bot.) uniparous.
unípede, *a.* having one foot.
unipersonal, *a.* unipersonal.
unipolar, *a.* unipolar, single-pole.
unir, *tr.v.* 1. to unite; to join, join together; connect, attach. 2. to mix, combine. —*r.v.* 1. to consolidate, merge, amalgamate, combine. 2. to unite, join; to be contiguous. 3. to unite, wed, be married.
unisexual, *a.* (biol.) unisexual.
unisón, *a.* unison. —*m.* (mus.) voices or instruments in unison.
unisonancia, *f.* 1. (mus.) unison. 2. monotony (of a sound, voice, etc.).
unisonar, *i.v.* to sound in unison.
unísono, na, *a.* (mus.) unison, unisonous. —*m.* unison; **al unísono,** in unison; unanimously.
unitario, ria, *a.* 1. unitary, unified, not divided, e.g. *teoría unitaria,* (phys.) unified or unitary field theory. 2. (polit.) unitarian, unitary. 3. (Rel.) Unitarian. 4. unit, per unit, pertaining to a unit, e.g. *precio unitario,* unit price. —*m., f.* 1. (polit.) unitarian. 2. (rel.) Unitarian.
unitarismo, *m.* (rel.) Unitarianism.
unitivo, va, *a.* uniting, unitive, joining.
univalencia, *f.* (chem.) univalence.
univalente, *a.* (chem.) univalent.
univalvo, va, *a.* (zool., bot.) univalve. —*m.* (zool.) univalve, univalve shell.
universal, *a.* universal. —*m.* (log.) universal.
universalice, universalicé, *ref.* **universalizar.**
universalidad, *f.* universality.
universalismo, *m.* universalism; (rel.) Universalism.
universalista, *m., f.* universalist; (rel.) Universalist.
universalización, *f.* universalization.
universalizar, (*ref. 53*) *tr.v.* to universalize.
universalmente, *adv.* universally.
universidad, *f.* university; **u. a distancia,** (tel.) university of the air; **u. laboral,** technical college.
universitario, ria, *a.* university, e.g. *título universitario,* university degree, *vida universitaria,* university life. —*m., f.* university student; university professor.
universo sa, *a.* universal. —*m.* universe. — **u. extragaláctico,** (astron.) extragalactic universe.
univocación, *f.* (log.) convergence, coalescence (of reasons, ideas, theories).
univocarse, (*ref. 50*) *tr.v.* to converge, coalesce (ideas, reasons).
unívoco, ca, *a.* univocal.
univoque, *ref.* **univocarse.**
unja, unjo, *ref.* **ungir.**
uno, na, *a.* 1. one, (*pl.*) some, a few. 2. one and the same. — **a la una,** at one o'clock; **a una,** all together, at the same time; **unas** or **unos** + *numeral,* about or some + numeral, e.g. *unas cuarenta pesetas,* about or some forty pesetas. — **uno que otro,** a few. —*pron.* 1. one, (*pl.*) some. 2. one, you, someone, anyone, e.g. *uno no sabe qué pensar,* one doesn't know what to think; **cada uno,** everyone, each one; **de uno en uno,** one by one; **uno a otro,** one another, each other; **uno a uno, uno por uno,** one by one; **unos cuantos,** a few; **uno tras otro,** one after another. —*m.* one (numeral); **hacer del u.,** (Mex., Peru) (coll.) to take a piss.
untador, ra, *a.* greasing, smearing, oiling. —*m., f.* 1. greaser, smearer, oiler. 2. anointer.
untadura, *f.* 1. oiling, smearing, greasing; rubbing. 2. grease; ointment; application (of liniment).
untamiento, *m.* smearing, greasing, oiling.

untar, *tr.v.* 1. to smear, cover (with), apply (ointment); to spread (butter on bread), e.g. *u. el pan con mantequilla,* to butter the bread, to spread the bread with butter. 2. (fig.) to bribe. — **u. la mano a alguien,** to grease someone's palm, bribe. —*r.v.* 1. to get stained or smeared with grease. 2. (fig.) to feather one's nest (illicitly).
untaza, *f.* animal fat.
unto, *m.* 1. grease, oil; ointment. 2. animal fat; (cul.) fat back. 3. (Chile) boot-black, shoepolish.
untuosidad, *f.* greasiness, oiliness.
untuoso, sa, *a.* unctuous, greasy, oily.
untura, *f.* 1. unction, liniment, ointment; grease. 2. greasing; smearing; application (of liniment).
uña, *f.* 1. nail, fingernail, toenail; claw, talon. 2. sting (of scorpion); thorn (of plant). 3. stump (of branch left on pruned tree). 4. scab, crust (on sores or wounds). 5. excrescence on the lachrymal caruncle. 6. hook, sharp point (on certain instruments). 7. nail groove or grip (for pushing or pulling something). 8. (zool.) date mussel, piddock. 9. (coll.) light fingers (skill in stealing, tendency to steal). 10. (mar.) bill, peak, fluke (of anchor). 11. (bot.) unguis (clawlike base of petal). 12. (mec.) claw, pawl, lug. — **afilar** or **afilarse las uñas,** (coll.) to sharpen one's wits; to get ready; **a u. de caballo,** at full speed, at full gallop; **comerse las uñas,** to bite one's nails; to be very impatient or nervous; **enseñar** or **mostrar las uñas,** (coll.) to show one's bad temper or intentions; **largo de uñas,** (coll.) light-fingered, thievish; **ser u. y carne,** to be bosom friends; **tener en la u.,** (coll.) to have clearly in one's mind, have fresh in one's memory; **u. de caballo,** (bot.) coltsfoot; **u. encarnada,** ingrown nail; **u. gata,** (bot.) rest-harrow; cammock.
uñada, *f.* 1. scratch (with nail). 2. flip (with nail).
uñarada, *f.* scratch (with nail).
uñate, *m.* 1. pinch (with nail). 2. chuck-farthing (game).
uñero, *m.* 1. whitlow, felon. 2. ingrowing nail.
uñeta, *f.* 1. small nail. 2. stonecutter's chisel. 3. chuck-farthing (game). 4. (mus.) plectrum.
uñetazo, *m., var. of* **uñada.**
uñidura, *f.* (Sp., reg.) joining; yoking.
uñir, (*ref. 66*) *tr.v.* (Sp., reg.) to yoke.
uñoso, sa, *a.* having long nails or claws.
uñuela, *f. dim. of* **uña,** small nail or claw.
¡upa! *interj.* upsy-daisy, up you go, hoopla.
upar, *tr.v. var. of* **aupar.**
upas, *m.* (bot.) upas tree and its poisonous sap.
upupa, *f.* (ornith.) hoopoe.
ura, *f.* (Arg.) botfly.
ural, *a.* Ural; **los Urales,** the Urals.
uralita, *f.* (min.) uralite.
uranato, *m.* (chem.) uranate.
Urania, *f.* (myth.) Urania, the Muse of Astronomy and Geography.
uránico, ca, *a.* (chem.) uranic.
uranilo, *m.* (chem.) uranyl.
uraninita, *f.* (min.) uraninite.
uranio, *m.* (chem.) uranium.
uranio, nia, *a.* Uranian, uranic, celestial.
uranismo, *m.* (med.) uranism, homosexuality.
uranita, *f.* (min.) uranite.
Urano, *m.* (astron., myth.) Uranus.
uranofana, *f.,* **uranofano,** *m.* (min.) uranophane.
uranografía, *f.* (astron.) uranography.
uranógrafo, *m.* (astron.) uranographist, uranographer.
uranología, *f.* uranology, an old term for astronomy.
uranometría, *f.* (astron.) uranometry.
uranosferita, *f.* (min.) uranosphaerite.
uranoso, sa, *a.* (chem.) uranous.
urao, *m.* (min.) urao, trona.
urato, *m.* (chem.) urate.
urbanamente, *adv.* urbanely, courteously, politely.
urbanice, urbanicé, *ref.* **urbanizar.**
urbanidad, *f.* urbanity, politeness, civility, manners.
urbanismo, *m.* city planning.
urbanista, *a.* urbanistic, city planning. —*m.* city planning expert, urbanist.
urbanístico, ca, *a.* city-planning, housing, e.g. *proyecto urbanístico,* city-planning project.
urbanización, *f.* 1. urbanization, real estate development, city planning. 2. (Mex.) suburban community; residential area.
urbanizar, (*ref. 53*) *tr.v.* 1. to make urbane, urbanize. 2. to urbanize, develop into real estate. —*r.v.* to become urbane, civil, polite.
urbano, na, *a.* 1. urban, pertaining to towns or cities. 2. urbane, civil, well-mannered. —*m.* member of city police, militiaman.
urbe, *f.* large city, metropolis.
urca, *f.* 1. (mar.) hooker, hulk. 2. (zool.) orca, killer whale.
urce, *m.* (bot.) heath, heather.
urceolado, da, *a.* (bot.) urceolate.
urcéolo, *m.* (bot.) urceolus.
urchilla, *f.* (bot., chem.) archil, orchilla, orchil.
urdidera, *f.* 1. (tex.) (woman) warper. 2. (tex.) warper (machine), warping frame.
urdidor, ra, *a.* 1. (tex.) warping. 2. (fig.) scheming, plotting. —*m., f.* 1. (tex.) warper (person). 2. (fig.) schemer, plotter. —*m.* (tex.) warper (machine).
urdidura, *f.* 1. (tex.) warping. 2. (fig.) scheming, plotting.
urdiembre, urdimbre, *f.* 1. (tex.) warp. 2. (fig.) plotting, scheming, planning.
urdir, *tr.v.* 1. (tex.) to warp (yarn). 2. (fig.) to scheme, plot, plan.
urea, *f.* (biochem.) urea.
ureasa, *f.* (biochem.) urease, urase.
uredinio, *m.* (bot.) uredinium, uredium.
uredospora, *f.* (bot.) uredospore.
ureido, *m.* (chem.) ureide.
uremia, *f.* (med.) uremia, uraemia.
urémico, ca, *a.* (med.) uremic, uraemic.
urente, *a.* hot, burning, scorching.
uretano, *m.* (chem.) urethan, urethane.
uréter, *m.* (anat., zool.) ureter.
ureteral, *a.* (anat.) ureteral.
uretérico, ca, *a.* (anat.) ureteric.
urético, ca, *a.* (anat.) urethral.
uretra, *f.* (anat.) urethra.
uretral, *a.* (anat.) urethral.
uretritis, *f.* (med.) urethritis.
uretroscopia, *f.* (med.) urethroscopy.
uretroscopio, *m.* (med.) urethroscope.
uretrotomía, *f.* (med.) urethrotomy.
urgencia, *f.* urgency; necessity, need; **con u.,** urgently; **u. de,** need of; **clínica de u.,** emergency clinic; **cura de u.,** emergency treatment.
urgente, *a.* urgent, pressing.
urgentemente, *adv.* urgently.
urgir, (*ref. 62*) *tr.v.* to urge, press, entreat. —*i.v.* to be urgent.
úrico, ca, *a.* (med., chem.) uric.
urinal, *a.* urinary. —*m.* urinal (place for urinating).
urinálisis, *f.* urinalysis.
urinario, *a.* urinary. —*m.* urinal (place for urinating).
urinífero, ra, *a.* uriniferous, containing urine.
urinómetro, *m.* (med.) urinometer.
urja, *ref.* **urgir.**
urna, *f.* 1. urn, footed vase. 2. glass case (for displaying small objects). 3. ballot box.
urnición, *f.* (mar.) top futtock or timber.
uro, *m.* (zool.) urus.
urobilina, *f.* (biochem.) urobilin.
urocistitis, *f.* (med.) urocystitis.
urocisto, *m.* (anat.) urocyst.
urocromo, *m.* (biochem.) urochrome.
urodelo, *m.* (zool.) urodelan, (*pl.*) Urodela.
urodinia, *f.* (med.) urodynia.
urogallo, *m.* (ornith.) capercaillie, capercailzie, species of woodcock.
urogenital, *a.* (anat.) urogenital.
urografía, *f.* (med.) urography.
urolitiasis, *f.* (med.) urolithiasis.
urolito, *m.* (med.) urolith.
urología, *f.* (med.) urology.
urólogo, *m.* (med.) urologist.
uromancia, *f.* divination by the examination of urine.
uropigio, a, *a.* (ornith.) uropygial. —*m.* (ornith.) uropygium.
urópodo, *m.* (zool.) uropod.
uroscopia, *f.* (med.) uroscopy.
uroxantina, *f.* (biochem.) uroxanthin.
urpila, *f.* (Arg., ornith.) small dove or pigeon.
urque, *m.* (Chile) low-grade potato.
urraca, *f.* 1. (ornith.) magpie. 2. (fig.) magpie, chatterer.
Ursa, *f.* (astron.) Ursa, Bear.
ursina, *a.* **branca ursina,** (bot.) **bear's** breech, acanthus.
ursulina, *a., f.* (ecc.) Ursuline.
urticáceo, a, *a.* (bot.) urticaceous. —*f.* (bot.) urtica, (*pl.*) Urticaceae.
urticación, *f.* (med.) urtication.
urticante, *a.* urticant.
urticaria, *f.* (med.) urticaria, nettle rash, hives.
urú, (*pl.* **urúes**), *m.* (Arg., ornith.) South American crested partridge (Odontophorus capueira).
urubú, (*pl.* **urubúes**), *m.* (ornith.) urubu, black vulture.
Uruguay, *m.* Uruguay.
uruguayo, a, *a., m., f.* Uruguayan.
urunday, *m.* (bot.) urunday, timber tree.
urutaú, *m.* (Arg., ornith.) gray-crested night owl (Nyctibius griseus cornutus).
usadamente, *adv.* customarily, according to custom.
usado, da, *past part. of* **usar.** —*a.* 1. used; second-hand (clothes, cars). 2. worn out, old. 3. inured, accustomed.
usagre, *m.* (med.) milk crust, infantile eczema; (vet.) mange, scab.
usanza, *f.* custom, manner, practice, fashion, usage.
usar, *tr.v.* 1. to use, make use of, employ. 2. to wear. —*i.v.* to be accustomed, to be in the habit; **u.** + *inf.,* to be accustomed to + *inf.,* be in the habit of + *ger.;* **u. de,** to use. —*r.v.* to be the custom, be the fashion.
usencia, *m., f.* (*contr. of* **Vuestra Reverencia**) Your Reverence.
useñoria, *m., f.* (*contr. of* **Vuestra Señoría**) Your Excellency, Your Lordship, Your Ladyship.
usgo, *m.* loathing, repugnance, nausea, disgust, abhorrence, detestation.
usia, *m., f., var. of* **useñoría.**
usier, *m., var. of* **ujier.**
usina, *f.* (gal.) power plant; factory.
uslero, *m.* rolling pin.
uso, *m.* 1. use; employment. 2. custom, practice, manner, fashion, usage. 3. wear, wearing; wear and tear. — **al u.,** according to custom; **andar al u.,** to conform with the times, swim with the current; **en buen u.,** in good condition; **entrar en los usos,** to take up or adopt the habits and

customs (of the country where one resides); **estar en u.,** to be in use; to be the custom; **hacer u. de la palabra,** to speak (to an assembly); **para todo u.,** for all purpose, all-purpose; **para u. externo,** for external use; **u. de la palabra,** floor, right to speak, turn to speak; **u. de razón,** power of reason; **u. y desgaste,** wear and tear.
ustaga, *f.* (mar.) tie, tye.
usted, (*pl.* **ustedes**), *pers. pron.* you, (*pl.*) you (used formally with the third person of the verb). It is usually abbreviated **V., Vd., U., Ud.,** in the sing.; **VV., Vds., UU., Uds.,** in the pl.
ustible, *a.* combustible, burnable.
ustión, *f.* burning.
ustorio, ria, *a.* burning; **espejo ustorio,** burning glass.
usual, *a.* 1. usual, customary, ordinary, common, general. 2. easily used, usable.
usualmente, *adv.* usually; generally.
usuario, ria, *a.* (law) having limited use of a thing. —*m., f.* user; (law) holder of a concession.
usucapión, *f.* (law) usucapion.
usucapir, *tr.v.* (law) to acquire by usucapion, usucapt.
usufructo, *m.* (law) usufruct, use, enjoyment; profit; **u. imperfecto,** (law) imperfect usufruct; quasi usufruct; **u. perfecto,** (law) perfect usufruct; **u. por disposición legal,** (law) legal usufruct.
usufructuar, (*ref.* 55) *tr.v.* to usufruct, hold in usufruct. —*i.v.* to be fruitful, be profitable.
usufructuario, ria, *a., m.* usufructuary.
usura, *f.* 1. usury; profiteering. 2. interest, gain, profit. — **pagar con u.,** to repay twice over.
usurar, *i.v., var. of* **usurear.**
usurariamente, *adv.* usuriously.
usurario, ria, *a.* usurious.
usurear, *i.v.* to practice usury; to profiteer; to lend money on interest.
usurero, ra, *m., f.* usurer, profiteer; moneylender, pawnbroker.
usurpación, *f.* usurpation.
usurpador, ra, *a.* usurping. —*m., f.* usurper.
usurpar, *tr.v.* to usurp; to encroach upon.
usuta, *f.* (Arg., Bol., Chile) type of sandal.
utensilio, *m.* utensil, tool, implement, device, contrivance.
uterino, na, *a.* uterine.
útero, *m.* (anat.) uterus, womb.
útil, *a.* 1. useful. 2. working (day). 3. (law) lawful, legal (time). 4. (mech.) effective, available. —*m.* tool, utensil, (*pl.*) gear, equipment.
utilería, *f.* (theat.) properties, stage properties, props.
utilero, ra, *m., f.* (theat.) property man, person in charge of stage props.
utilice, utilicé, *ref.* **utilizar.**
utilidad, *f.* 1. usefulness, utility. 2. profit, (*pl.*) earnings, returns. — **participación en las utilidades,** profit sharing; **u. bruta** or **gruesa,** gross profit; **u. de explotación,** operating profit; **u. decreciente,** diminishing return; **u. marginal,** marginal utility; **u. pública,** public utility; **utilidades a distribuir,** undivided profits; **utilidades anticipadas, esperadas** or **previstas,** anticipated profits; **utilidades impositivas,** taxable profits; **utilidades incorporadas,** retained income.
utilitario, ria, *a., m.* utilitarian.
utilitarismo, *m.* utilitarianism.
utilitarista, *a., m., f.* utilitarian.
utilizable, *a.* usable, utilizable; available.
utilización, *f.* use, utilization.
utilizar, (*ref.* 53) *tr.v., r.v.* to utilize, use, make use of.
útilmente, *adv.* usefully; profitably.
utillaje, *m.* (Gal.) tools, gear, equipment.
utopia, utopía, *f.* Utopia.
utópico, ca, *a.* Utopian.
utopista, *a., m., f.* Utopian.
utrero, ra, *m.* two-year-old bull. —*f.* two-year-old heifer.
ut retro, *adv.* (Lat.) as above.
utrícula, *f.,* **utrículo,** *m.* (anat., bot.) utricle.
utriculitis, *f.* (med.) utriculitis.
ut supra, *adv.* (Lat.) as above.
uva, *f.* 1. (bot.) grape; (bot.) berry of the barberry bush. 2. tumor on the uvula; wart on the eyelid. — **conocer las uvas de su majuelo,** to know one's business; **hecho una u.,** (coll.) very drunk; **u. cana** or **canilla,** (bot.) common stonecrop; **u. crespa,** (bot.) gooseberry; **u. de gato,** (bot.) common stonecrop; **u. de playa,** (bot.) sea grape berry; **u. de raposa,** (bot.) herb Paris, truelove; **u. espina,** (bot.) gooseberry; **u. jabí,** (bot.) small grape from Granada; **u. lairén,** (bot.) grape with tough skin and large seed; **u. ligeruela,** early grape; **u. lupina,** (bot.) wolfsbane, monkshood; **u. marina,** (bot.) joint fir, ephedra; **u. moscatel,** (bot.) muscat, muscatel; **u. taminea** or **taminia,** (bot.) stavesacre; **u. tempranilla,** early grape; **u. tinta,** (bot.) black grape; **u. verdeja,** (bot.) green grape; **u. verga,** (bot.) monkshood, wolfsbane; **uvas de mar,** (bot.) joint fir, ephedra.
uvada, *f.* abundance of grapes.
uvaduz, (*pl.* **uvaduces**), *f.* (bot.) bearberry.
uvaguemaestre, *m., var. of* **vaguemaestre.**
uval, *a.* grape-like; pertaining to grapes.
uvate, *m.* uvate, grape preserves.
uvayema, *f.* (bot.) wild vine.
uve, *f.* name of the letter v.
úvea, *f.* (anat.) uvea.
uveítis, *f.* (med.) uveitis.
uveral, *m.* grove or patch of sea grapes.
uvero, ra, *a.* grape. —*m., f.* grape seller. —*m.* (bot.) sea grape.
uviforme, *a.* grape-shaped.
úvula, *f.* (anat.) uvula.
uvular, *a.* uvular.
uxoricida, *a.* uxoricidal. —*m.* uxoricide (one who kills his wife).
uxoricidio, *m.* uxoricide, murder of the wife by her husband.
uxorio, ria, *a.* uxorial, pertaining to a wife.
uyama, *f.* (Ven.) a species of gourd.
uzas, *f., a.* (zool.) a Brazilian crab.

V

V, *f.* v, twenty-third letter of the Spanish alphabet; **v doble, doble v,** w.
V *sym. of* **vanadio,** vanadium (V).
va, *ref.* **ir.**
V.A. *abbrev. of* **Vuestra Alteza,** Your Highness.
vaca, *f.* 1. (zool.) cow. 2. (cul.) beef. 3. tanned cowhide, sole-leather. 4. gambling pool. — **echar las vacas a,** to put blame on; **las vacas gordas,** booming times, bonanza; **v. de leche, v. lechera,** dairy cow; **v. de San Antón,** (ento.) ladybird; **v. marina,** (zool.) manatee, sea cow; **v. sagrada,** sacred cow.
vacación, *f.* 1. vacation, holiday. 2. vacating, vacation; vacancy. — **estar de vacaciones,** to be on holiday or vacation; **vacaciones pagadas,** holidays or vacations with pay.
vacada, *f.* herd of cows.
vacancia, *f.* vacancy (open job or position).
vacante, *a.* vacant, unoccupied. —*f.* 1. vacancy. 2. holiday, vacation.
vacar, (*ref. 50*) *i.v.* 1. to become vacant. 2. to give up work or employment temporarily. 3. to be unoccupied, not to be working. — **v. a.** or **en,** to attend or devote oneself to; **v. de,** to lack.
vacarí, (*pl.* **vacaries**), *a.* leather, covered with leather (e.g. a shield).
vacatura, *f.* duration of vacancy.
vaccíneo, a, vaccínico, ca, *a.* pertaining to vaccines.
vaccinieo, a, *a.* (bot.) vacciniaceous. —*f.* (*pl.*) Vacciniaceae.
vaciadero, *m.* 1. sewer, drain; drainpipe. 2. dumping place.
vaciadizo, za, *a.* cast, molded.
vaciado, *past part. of* **vaciar.** —*m.* 1. casting (in bronze, clay, etc. from mold); cast (shape thus produced). 2. (archit.) cavity in pedestal (of column). 3. (archit.) excavation. 4. emptying; draining.
vaciador, *m.* 1. emptier, drainer. 2. caster, molder (in clay, bronze, etc.). 3. scoop (for removing clarified part of liquid). — **v. de navajas,** razor honer.
vaciamiento, *m.* 1. emptying; draining. 2. casting, molding.
vaciante, *f.* ebb tide.
vaciar, (*ref. 54*) *tr.v.* 1. to empty; to drain. 2. to cast, mold (in bronze, clay, etc.). 3. to make a hole in; to hollow out; to excavate. 4. to sharpen, hone. 5. to expound or explain (a doctrine) in great detail. 6. to transcribe. —*i.v.* 1. to empty (streams, rivers, etc., into sea). 2. to fall, go down (water in river), ebb (tide). —*r.v.* 1. to empty; to become empty. 2. (coll.) to talk indiscreetly, blab, divulge a secret, to spill the beans (sl.).
vaciedad, *f.* (*pl.*) nonsense, silliness, foolish remark.
vaciero, *m.* shepherd of barren cattle or sheep.
vacilación, *f.* 1. vacillation, hesitation, irresolution. 2. swaying, unsteadiness, vacillation. 3. flickering (of light).
vacilante, *a.* 1. vacillating, hesitant, irresolute. 2. swaying, unsteady, vacillating. 3. flickering (light).
vacilar, *i.v.* 1. to vacillate, hesitate, waver. 2. to sway, be unsteady, vacillate. 3. to flicker (light). 4. (Amer., sl.) to fool around; to have a good time.
vacilón, *m.* (Amer., sl.) spree, party, shindig (sl.).
vacío, a, *a.* 1. empty; unoccupied, vacant, uninhabited; hollow. 2. (fig.) empty, hollow, vacuous, fatuous, e.g. *palabras vacías,* empty words. 3. lazy, idle. 4. barren (cattle). 5. vain, fruitless, useless. 6. vain, presumptuous. —*m.* 1. vacuum, void, emptiness; abyss, nothingness. 2. hollow, hole; empty space, blank, lacuna, gap. 3. side, flank. 4. vacancy. 5. (phys.) vacuum. — **de v.,** empty, without a load; unemployed; unsuccessful; **en el v.,** in vacuo; **hacer el v. a,** to cold-shoulder, ostracize.
vaco, ca, *a.* vacant, empty (position, employment).
vacuidad, *f.* 1. vacuity, vacuousness, emptiness. 2. inaneness.
vacuna, *f.* 1. vaccine. 2. cowpox. 3. vaccination.
vacunación, *f.* vaccination.
vacunador, ra, *a.* vaccinating. —*m., f.* vaccinator.
vacunal, *a.* (med.) vaccinal.
vacunar, *tr.v.* to vaccinate. —*r.v.* to be vaccinated.
vacuno, na, *a.* 1. bovine. 2. cowhide, of cowhide. — **ganado vacuno,** (bovine) cattle.
vacunoterapia, *f.* vaccine therapy.
vacuo, a, *a.* vacuous, empty, vacant; vacuous or empty (person). —*m.* void; hollow; vacuum.
vacuola, *f.* (biol.) vacuole.
vacuolar, *a.* (biol.) vacuolar.
vacuolización, *f.* vacuolation.
vacuolo, *m.* (biol.) vacuole.
vacuómetro, *m.* vacuum gauge.
vade, *m.* school satchel or case, briefcase.
vadeable, *a.* 1. fordable. 2. surmountable, superable, conquerable.
vadeador, *m.* guide for fording streams.
vadeamiento, *m.* fording.
vadear, *tr.v.* 1. to ford, wade through. 2. to overcome, surmount. 3. to sound (someone) out. —*r.v.* to act, conduct oneself, behave.
vademécum, *m.* 1. vade mecum, handbook, manual. 2. school satchel or case, briefcase.
vadera, *f.* wide ford (of a river).
¡vade retro! *adv.* (Lat.) away! begone! avaunt!
vado, *m.* 1. ford of a river. 2. (fig.) solution, remedy, expedient. — **al v. o al puente,** (coll.) one way or the other; **no hallar v.,** to find no way-out; **tentar el v.,** to feel one's way.
vadoso, sa, *a.* having several fords, shallow, shoaly.
vafe, *m.* bold stroke or undertaking.
vagabundaje, *m.* 1. vagabondage, wandering. 2. vagrancy.
vagabundear, *i.v.* 1. to roam, rove. 2. to idle, loaf, loiter. 3. to be a tramp, vagrant or vagabond.
vagabundeo, *m.* 1. roaming, roving. 2. vagabondage, vagrancy.
vagabundo, da, *a.* 1. vagabond, wandering, roving. 2. vagrant. —*m., f.* 1. vagabond, wanderer. 2. vagrant, tramp.
vagamente, *adv.* vaguely.
vagamundear, *i.v., var. of* **vagabundear.**
vagamundo, da, *a., m., f., var. of* **vagabundo.**
vagancia, *f.* vagrancy; idleness, loafing; laziness.
vagante, *a.* 1. wandering, roving, roaming; vagrant. 2. idle; at leisure.
vagar, (*ref. 51*) *i.v.* 1. to roam, wander, rove. 2. to idle, be idle, have nothing to do. —*m.* 1. leisure; idleness. 2. slowness, deliberateness.
vagarosamente, *adv.* wanderingly, rovingly, vagrantly.
vagaroso, sa, *a.* (poet.) wandering, roving, flitting, errant.
vagido, *m.* cry of a newborn child.
vagina, *f.* (anat.) vagina.
vaginal, *a.* (anat.) vaginal.
vaginitis, *f.* (med.) vaginitis.
vagneriano, na, *a.* (mus.) Wagnerian.
vago, ga, *a.* 1. vague, nebulous, imprecise, indefinite, undefined. 2. vague, blank, vacant (look). 3. (p.) blurred, indistinct (e.g. outlines). 4. vagrant, wandering; stray (dog). 5. idle, loafing. 6. (anat.) vagus (nerve). — **en v.,** unsteady, unsteadily, without support; into the air, at nothing, e.g. *un golpe en v.,* a blow into the air or at nothing; in vain. —*m.* 1. loafer, idler, bum, tramp, vagrant. 2. (anat.) vagus, vagus nerve. 3. unimproved plot of ground.
vagón, *m.* (ry.) car, coach, wagon, truck, van; **v. cama,** sleeping car; **v. cerrado** or **cubierto,** boxcar (U.S.), box wagon (G.B.); **v. correo,** mail car or coach; **v. cuba,** tank car; **v. de carga,** freight car (U.S.), goods wagon or truck (G.B.); **v. de cola,** caboose; **v. de equipajes,** baggage car (U.S.), luggage van (G.B.); **v. del guardafrenos,** brake van; **v. de mercancías,** see **v. de cargas; v. de plataforma,** flatcar; **v. de pasajeros,** passenger car (U.S.), passenger carriage or coach (G.B.); **v. de trampilla,** drop-bottom car; **v. de viajeros,** see **v. de pasajeros; v. frigorífico,** refrigerator car; **v. jaula,** stockcar; **v. postal,** see **v. correo; v. restaurante,** or **comedor** (Sp.), restaurant or dining car.
vagoneta, *f.* small wagon, open delivery cart.
vagotomía, *f.* (med.)vagotomy.
vagotonía, *f.* (med.) vagatonia.
vagotrópico, ca, vagotropo, pa, *a.* (med.) vagotropic.
vaguada, *f.* thalweg, lowest part of a valley.
vague, vagué, *ref.* **vagar.**
vagueación, *f.* vagary, mental wandering, flight of fancy.
vagueante, *a.* roaming, wandering, roving, vagrant.
vaguear, *i.v.* 1. to roam, rove, wander. 2. to idle, loaf.
vaguedad, *f.* vagueness; vague remark.
vaguemaestre, *m.* (mil.) wagon master.
vaguido, *a.* dizzy, giddy. —*m.* dizzy spell, dizziness.
vahaje, *m.* breeze, light wind.
vahar, *i.v.* 1. to emit steam or vapor. 2. to breathe out.
vaharada, *f.* exhalation, breathing; breath.
vaharera, *f.* (med.) thrush.
vaharina, *f.* (coll.) steam, vapor, fume, mist.

vahear, *i.v.* 1. to emit vapor or steam. 2. to breathe out.
vahído, *m.* dizzy spell, dizziness, vertigo.
vaho, *m.* steam, vapor, fume; breath.
vaída, *a.* (archit.) groined (vault).
vaina, *f.* 1. sheath, scabbard; case; (bot.) pod, husk; (anat.) sheath. 2. (Amer., sl.) nuisance, problem, bother. 3. (mar.) tabling, reinforcing hem (on edge of sail); (mar.) casing (hem on side of flag through which flag rope passes). 4. (Col.) stroke of luck. 5. (reg.) (*pl.*) string beans. — **ni de a vainas,** (Peru) by no means, under no circumstances; **v. de cartucho,** cartridge case. —*m., f.* good-for-nothing, despicable person.
vainazas, (*pl.* **vainazas**), *m.* (coll.) lazy slovenly person, slob, loafer, idler.
vainero, *m.* sheath or scabbard maker.
vainica, *f.* (sew.) hemstitch, faggoting.
vainilla, *f.* 1. (bot., cul.) vanilla. 2. hemstitch. 3. (bot.) American heliotrope.
vainíllico, ca, *a.* (chem.) vanillic.
vainillina, *f.* (chem.) vanillin.
vainiquera, *f.* (woman) hemstitcher.
vainita, *f.* (Amer.) string bean.
vaivén, *m.* 1. fluctuation; backward and forward motion; swing, swinging, sway, oscillation. 2. impermanence, changeableness, unsteadiness; inconstancy. 3. risk. 4. (mar.) three-stranded splicing rope, ratline.
vaivoda, *m.* (hist.) vaivode, voivode.
vajilla, *f.* dishes, pots and pans, crockery, table service or ware; **v. de plata,** silver service; **v. de porcelana,** chinaware.
val, *m. apocopated form of* **valle, vale,** dale, valley.
valaco, ca, *a., m., f.* Walachian. —*m.* Walachian (the Romanian dialect of the Walachians).
valar, *a.* pertaining to a fence, stockade or palisade.
valdense, *a.* (hist., rel.) Waldensian. —*m., f.* Waldensian, (*pl.*) Waldenses, Vaudois.
valdepeñas, *m.* valdepeñas (a fine type of Spanish red wine).
Valdestillas, ajo de V., costly extra or trimming, hidden expense.
valdivia, *f.* (Ecuad., ornith.) variety of hawk (Accipiter bicolor).
valdiviano, *m.* (Chile) dish of shredded jerked beef and onion, served with fried eggs.
vale, (Lat.) adieu! vale! farewell!
vale, *m.* 1. promissory note, money voucher; receipt; free pass (to a show, etc.); certificate of good behavior (given to a pupil). 2. (Mex., Col., Ven.) pal, chum, buddy, friend. — **v. corrido,** (Ven.) old pal or friend; **ser v. con,** (Col.) to be a friend or pal of.
valedero, ra, *a.* valid; efficacious; binding.
valedor, ra, *m., f.* protector, patron, defender; (Mex.) pal, friend, companion.
valedura, *f.* (Mex.) protection, favor.
valencia, *f.* (chem.) valency, valence; **v. polar,** electrovalence, polar valence.
valenciano, na, *a., m., f.* Valencian. —*m.* Valencian (dialect).
valentía, *f.* 1. courage, bravery, valor; boldness, dash. 2. heroic deed, exploit or feat. 3. brag, boast, bragging or boastful remark.
valentino, na, *a.* (rare) Valencian.
valentísimo, ma, *a. super. of* **valiente,** 1. most brave, courageous or valiant. 2. excelling in an art or science.
valentón, na, *a.* bragging, boastful; arrogant. —*m., f.* braggart, boaster.
valentona, valentonada, *f.* boast, brag.
valer, (*ref.* 25) *tr.v.* 1. to be worth; to equal, be equal to. 2. to cost. 3. to get, win, give, cause, produce, e.g. *su discurso le valió una ovación,* his speech won him an ovation. 4. to protect, defend, e.g. *que el cielo me valga,* may heaven protect me. — **vale tanto como decir,** it's as much or good as saying; **valga lo que valga,** whatever it costs, at whatever cost; **¡válgame Dios!** goodness gracious! God help me!; **v. lo que pesa,** to be worth one's weight in gold. —*i.v.* 1. to be of value, be worthy of esteem or respect. 2. to be useful, be of use or help. 3. to be valid; to count, e.g. *estos puntos no valen,* these points don't count. 4. to have authority, power or influence. 5. to be current, be legal currency. — **hacer v.,** to get recognized, assert (e.g. rights), to make use of; **en el amor y la guerra todo vale,** all's fair in love and war; **más vale,** it is better, e.g. *más vale tarde que nunca,* better late than never; **todo vale,** everything goes; **v. por,** to be equal to, be worth. —*r.v.* to look after oneself, fend for oneself, stand on one's own feet; **valerse de,** to make use of, avail oneself of; **valerse por sí mismo,** to look after or fend for oneself, stand on one's own feet. —*m.* worth, merit, value.
valeriana, *f.* (bot.) valerian, garden heliotrope.
valerianáceo, a, *a.* (bot.) valerianaceous. —*f.* (*pl.*) (bot.) Valerianaceae.
valerianato, *m.* (chem.) valerate.
valeriánico, *a.* (chem.) valeric, valerianic.
valérico, ca, *a.* (chem.) valeric.
valerosamente, *adv.* 1. bravely, courageously. 2. powerfully, effectively.
valerosidad, *f.* valor, courage, bravery.
valeroso, *a.* 1. courageous, brave, valiant. 2. valuable. 3. efficient, effective, powerful, strong, active.
valetudinario, ria, *a., m., f.* valetudinarian.
valga, valgo, *ref.* **valer.**
Valhala, *m.* (myth.) Valhalla.
valí, (*pl.* valíes), *m.* provincial governor (in Turkey).
valía, *f.* 1. value, worth. 2. favor, influence. 3. party, faction. — **mayor v.,** (econ.) increased value, appreciation.
valiato, *m.* vilayet, a province or administrative district in Turkey.
validación, *f.* validity; making valid, validation.
validamente, *adv.* validly.
validar, *tr.v.* to validate, make valid.
validez, *f.* validity; soundness.
válido, da, *a.* 1. valid. 2. strong, healthy, robust.
valido, da, *a.* favored, favorite; esteemed, respected; influential. —*m.* favorite, protégé, prime minister.
valiente, *a.* 1. brave, courageous, valiant. 2. fine, excellent, first-class; (iron.) fine, e.g. *¡v. amigo eres tú!* a fine friend you are! 3. big, great, terrific, tremendous. 4. strong, vigorous. 5. boasting, bragging. —*m.* 1. brave man, (*pl.*) (the) brave. 2. braggart, boaster.
valientemente, *adv.* 1. bravely, valiantly, courageously. 2. excellently, extremely well.
valija, *f.* 1. valise, suitcase. 2. mailbag; mail. — **v. diplomática,** diplomatic pouch.
valijero, *m.* mail carrier.
valijón, *m. aug. of* **valija,** large suitcase.
valimiento, *f.* 1. favor, support, protection; good graces, favoritism.
valina, *f.* (chem.) valine.
valioso, sa, *a.* 1. valuable; highly esteemed. 2. rich, wealthy.
valla, *f.* 1. fence, barricade, stockade, palisade; (sport.) hurdle, e.g. *carrera de vallas,* hurdle race. 2. obstacle, hindrance, barrier. 3. (Amer.) cockpit (for cock fights). 4. highway billboard.
valladar, *m.* 1. fence; barricade, palisade, rampart. 2. obstacle, hindrance.
valladear *tr.v.* to fence; to build a barricade or palisade around.
vallado, *m.* fence; barricade, stockade, palisade.
vallar *a., m.* fence; barricade, palisade.
vallar, *tr.v.* to fence in, fence; to build a palisade or barricade around.
valle, *m.* 1. valley, vale. 2. river basin. — **v. de lágrimas,** vale of tears.
vallejo, *m. dim. of* **valle, small valley,** glen, dell.
vallico, *m.* (bot.) Italian ryegrass.
vallisoletano, na, *a.* of or from Valladolid, Spain. —*m., f.* inhabitant or native of Valladolid.
valón, na, *a., m., f.* Walloon. —*m.* 1. Walloon (dialect). 2. (*pl.*) knickerbockers (16th C., Dutch-style trousers). —*f.* 1. Vandyke collar. 2. (S. Amer.) cropped mane (in equines).
valor, *m.* 1. value; worth. 2. courage, valor, bravery. 3. audacity, nerve, cheek, impudence. 4. import, meaning, value, e.g. *el v. exacto de sus palabras,* the exact meaning or import of his words. 5. importance, e.g. *no doy v. a lo que dice,* I don't give any importance to what he says. 6. power, effectiveness, efficacy. 7. leading light, outstanding figure (in any field of sports, art, etc.). 8. profit, yield, revenue. 9. (mus., phonet., math.) value (of a note, sound or quantity). 10. (*pl.*) (com.) stocks and shares, securities, bonds. 11. (*pl.*) (moral, artistic, etc.) values, principles. — **v. absoluto,** (math.) absolute value; **v. activo,** asset; **v. adquisitivo,** purchasing power; **v. alimenticio** or **nutritivo,** food value; **v. aparente,** face value; **v. calórico,** (engin.) fuel value; **v. calorífico,** heat value; **v. cívico,** civic-mindedness; **v. comercial,** market value; **v. contable,** book value; **v. de cambio,** exchange value; **v. efectivo,** cash value; **v. en plaza,** markert value; **v. entendido,** agreed value; **v. facial,** face value; **v. impositivo,** taxable value; **valores bancarios,** bank papers; **valores fiduciarios,** stocks, bonds; **v. nominal,** face value (of a check).
valoración, *f.* 1. valuation, appraisal. 2. (chem.) standardization (of a solution). 3. increasing the value (of land, etc.).
valorar, *tr.v.* 1. to value, appraise, calculate the value of. 2. to increase or raise the value of. 3. to recognize, admit. —*r.v.* 1. to be valued or appraised. 2. to increase in value.
valorear, *tr.v., var. of* **valorar.**
valoría, *f.* worth, value.
valorice, valoricé, *ref.* **valorizar.**
valorización, *f.* 1. valuation, appraisal. 2. marking up of price or value.
valorizar, (*ref.* 53) *tr.v.* 1. to value, appraise, calculate the value of. 2. to increase the value of. —*r.v.* to increase in value, become more valuable.
valquiria, *f.* (myth., mus.) Valkyrie.
vals, *m.* (mus.) waltz.
valsar *i.v.* to waltz.
valuación, *f.* valuation, appraisal.
valuar, (*ref.* 54) *tr.v.* to value, appraise, calculate the value of, to rate.
valva, *f.* (bot., zool.) valve.
valvasor, *m.* nobleman, hidalgo.
válvula, *f.* (mech., elec., anat.) valve; **v. a mercurio,** mercury tube; **v. bellota,** acorn tube; **v. de admisión,** intake valve; **v. de aire,** air valve; **v. de bola,** ball valve; **v. catódica,** cathode-ray tube; **v. corrediza,** slide valve; **v. de alarma,** alarm valve; **v. de cierre,** shutoff or cutoff valve; across-the-line valve; **v. de compuerta,** gate valve; **v. de contraflujo,** reverse-flow valve; **v. de control,** control valve; **v. de charnela,** check valve; v. de dos pasos, two-way valve; **v. de émbolo,** piston valve; **v. de estrangulación,**

throttle valve; **v. de mariposa,** butterfly valve; **v. de pistón** or **llave,** key valve; **v. de purga,** drain valve; **v. de retención,** check valve; **v. de seguridad,** safety valve; **v. desviadora, de paso** or **de desviación,** bypass valve; **v. de vacío,** vacuum valve; **v. eléctrica,** electron tube; **v. en la culata,** overhead valve; **v. estranguladora,** choke valve; **v. mitral,** mitral valve.

valvulado, da, *a.* valvulate, valvate.

valvular, *a.* valvular.

valvulitis. *f.* (med.) valvulitis.

vamos, *1st pers. pl. pres. ind. and imper. of* **ir.** —*interj.* well! go on! let's go! come, now! often used as an expletive, well! why!

vampiresa, *f.* vamp, femme fatale.

vampirismo, *m.* 1. vampirism, superstitious belief in vampires. 2. (fig.) the practice of exploiting others.

vampiro, *m.* 1. vampire, bloodsucking ghost; ghoul. 2. (fig.) vampire, bloodsucker, extortioner. 3. (zool.) vampire, vampire bat.

vanadato, *m.* (chem.) vanadate.

vanádico, ca, *a.* (chem.) vanadic.

vanadinita, *f.* (min.) vanadinite.

vanadio, *m.* (chem.) vanadium.

vanagloria, *f.* vainglory, pride; conceit.

vanagloriarse, *r.v.* to boast; **v. de,** to boast of.

vanagloriosamente, *adv.* vaingloriously.

vanaglorioso, sa, *a.* vainglorious, proud; boastful. —*m., f.* boaster, bragger.

vanamente, *adv.* 1. in vain, futilely, vainly. 2. vainly, conceitedly. 3. foolishly, inanely.

vandálico, ca, *a.* 1. vandalistic, vandalic. 2. (hist.) pertaining to the Vandals.

vandalismo, *m.* vandalism.

vándalo, la, *a., m., f.* (hist.) Vandal; (fig.) vandal.

vandeano, na, *a., m., f.* (hist.) Vendean.

vanear, *i.v.* to talk nonsense.

vanguardia, *f.* 1. (mil.) vanguard, van. 2. (fig.) avant-garde. — **a. v.,** in the van or vanguard; in the front, in the lead.

vanguardismo, *m.* (art. lit.) avant-gardism.

vanguardista, *a., m., f.* avant-gardist.

vanidad, *f.* 1. vanity, conceit, pride; ostentatious display, pomp. 2. illusion, falseness, emptiness; idle show. 3. (*pl.*) inanities, nonsense.

vanidoso, sa, *a.* vain, conceited. —*m., f.* vain person.

vanilocuencia, *f.* empty talk, empty word; verbosity.

vanilocuente, vanilocuo, cua, *a.* empty (talker). —*m., f.* empty talker.

vaniloquio, *m.* empty talk.

vanistorio, *m.* 1. (coll.) conceit, ridiculous or affected vanity, affectation. 2. (coll.) vain, conceited person; boaster.

vano, na, *a.* 1. vain, futile, useless. 2. foolish, silly, frivolous, inane, empty, hollow, superficial. 3. vain, illusory, false. 4. vain, conceited. 5. empty, dried-up (fruit). — **en vano,** in vain. —*m.* (archit.) opening in a wall, bay.

vánova, *f.* (Arg.) coverlet, bedspread.

vapor, *m.* 1. steam; vapor. 2. faintness, vertigo, dizziness, giddiness. 3. (mar.) steamer, steamship, steamboat. 4. (*pl.*) hysterics; fits of melancholia. — **al v.,** (coll.) swiftly; (cul.) steamed; **a todo v.,** full steam ahead; **v. acuoso,** water vapor; **v. de ruedas,** paddle steamer; **v. recalentado,** superheated steam; **v. saturado** or **húmedo,** wet steam.

vapora, *f.* (coll.) steam launch.

vaporable, *a.* volatile, vaporizable.

vaporación *f.* vaporization.

vaporar *tr.v., r.v.* to evaporate.

vaporear, *tr.v., r.v.* to evaporate. —*i.v.* to give off vapor or steam, steam.

vaporice, vaporicé, *ref.* **vaporizar.**

vaporímetro, *m.* vaporimeter.

vaporización, *f.* vaporization.

vaporizador, *m.* vaporizer, atomizer, spray, sprayer.

vaporizar, (*ref. 53*) *tr.v.* to vaporize. —*r.v.* to vaporize, become vaporized.

vaporoso, sa, *a.* 1. vaporous, emitting vapors. 2. vaporous, ethereal, airy. 3. sheer (e.g. dress, fabric).

vapulación, *f.,* **vapulamiento,** *m.* thrashing, beating, whipping, flogging.

vapular, *tr.v.* to thrash, beat, whip, flog.

vapuleador, ra, *a.* thrashing, beating, whipping, flogging. —*m., f.* flogger, beater.

vapuleamiento, *m., var. of* **vapulación.**

vapulear, *tr.v.* to thrash, beat, whip, flog.

vapuleo, *m., var. of* **vapulación.**

vaquear, *tr.v.* (of bulls) to cover cows.

vaquería, *f.* 1. drove of cattle. 2. dairy farm, dairy.

vaqueril, *m.* cattle pasture.

vaquerizo, za, *a.* pertaining to cattle. —*m.* cowboy, cattle herdsman. —*f.* 1. cattleherd or tender. 2. winter corral or stable.

vaquero, ra, *a.* of a cowboy or cowhand. —*m.* cowboy, cowhand. —*f.* cowhand, cattleherd.

vaqueta, *f.* calfskin, leather.

vaquilla, *f. dim. of* **vaca,** small cow; (Arg., Chile) yearling heifer or calf.

vaquillona, *f.* (Amer.) heifer, calf.

V.A.R. *abbrev. of* **Vuestra Alteza Real,** Your Royal Highness.

vara, *f.* 1. rod, staff, pole, wand, stick; staff, wand, cane (symbol of office or authority). 2. Spanish linear measure (.84 meters) and yardstick thereof. 3. (bot.) stalk, scape, spike. 4. (taur.) picador's lance; thrust therewith. 5. thill, shaft, pole (of horse-drawn vehicle). 6. (Peru, coll.) influence, pull. — **suerte de varas,** (taur.) the picador's work with the lance; **tomar varas,** (taur.) the bull's response to the challenge of the picador; **v. alcándara,** shaft, thill; **v. alta** (fig.) power, authority; influence; **v. de alcalde,** (hist.) Mayor's staff or cane; **v. de guardia,** singletree (of a horse's harness); **v. de San José,** (bot.) spikenard; **v. larga,** goadstick (used during cattle roundup).

varada, *f.* 1. (mar.) beaching (of boat); (mar.) running aground. 2. (Sp., reg.) team of farmworkers; farming season. 3. (min.) work done in a period of three months and earnings thereof.

varadera, *f.* (mar.) skid, skeed.

varadero, *m.* (mar.) shipyard, drydock.

varadura, *f.* (mar.) running aground; beaching.

varal, *m.* 1. long pole. 2. cart frame. 3. (coll.) tall lanky person. 4. (Arg.) framework for drying meat. 5. (theat.) bank of side lights. 6. perch (of a carriage or horse-drawn cart).

varapalo, *m.* 1. long pole. 2. blow with a pole or rod. 3. (coll.) blow, setback, adversity.

varar, *tr.v.* (mar.) to beach, put into drydock. —*i.v.* 1. (mar.) to run aground. 2. to come to a standstill (a business). —*r.v.* (Amer., mar.) to run aground, be stranded.

varaseto, *m.* trellis; picket fence.

varazo, *m.* blow with a stick, staff or pole.

varbasco, *m.* (bot.) great mullein.

vardasca, *f.* turig, thin branch, switch.

vardascazo, *m.* blow with a switch or branch.

vareador, *m.* 1. person who knocks fruit from trees with long pole. 2. (taur.) picador. 3. cowhand who rounds up cattle with a goad stick.

vareaje, *m.* 1. retailing of textiles by the yard. 2. the act of knocking down fruit from trees with a long pole.

varear, *tr.v.* 1. to knock down (fruit from tree). 2. to beat, hit, strike with a rod or staff. 3. to goad, jab with a goad. 4. to measure with a **vara.** 5. to sell by the **vara.** —*r.v.* to become thin.

varejón, *m.* long thick stick or staff, long pole.

varejonazo, *m.* blow with long thick stick or pole.

varenga, *f.* (mar.) headrail; (mar.) frame timber.

vareo, *m., var. of* **vareaje.**

vareta, *f.* 1. small stick or rod. 2. limecoated twig for catching birds. 3. (tex.) stripe (of different color from rest of cloth). 4. (coll.) cutting remark. 5. (coll.) hint, innuendo.

varetazo, *m.* (taur.) side thrust of the horn inflicted by the bull in passing.

varetear, *tr.v.* to make stripes in (fabric).

varetón, *m.* young stag having antlers without tines.

varga, *f.* steepest part of a hill or slope.

varganal, *m.* stake fence, hedge; stockade.

várgano, *m.* stake (of a fence).

Vargas, averígüelo V., (coll.) search me, heaven only knows.

vargueño, *m., var. of* **bargueño.**

varhorímetro, *m.* (elec.) var-hour meter, reactive volt-ampere-hour-meter.

varí, *m.* (Arg., Chile, Peru, ornith.) variety of harrier (Circus cinereus).

variabilidad, *f.* variability.

variable, *a.* variable; changeable. —*f.* (math.) variable. — **v. dependiente,** dependent variable; **v. independiente,** independent variable.

variablemente, *adv.* variably; changeably.

variación, *f.* 1. variation, change. 2. (mus.) variation. — **v. de la aguja** or **magnética,** magnetic variation or declination, variation of magnetic needle.

variado, da, *past part. of*—*a.* varied, diverse; variegated.

variamente, *adv.* variedly, with variety; variously; differently.

variante, *a.* varying, variant. —*f.* variant; difference.

variar, (*ref. 54*) *tr.v.* 1. to vary, make varied, diversify. 2. to vary, change, alter. —*i.v.* 1. to vary, change, alter; to be different. 2. to vary, deviate (said of a compass). — **v. de opinion,** to change one's opinion.

várice, varice, *f.* (med.) varix, varicose vein.

varicela, *f.* (med.) varicella, chicken pox.

varicocele, *m.* (med.) varicocele.

varicosis, *f.* (med.) varicosis.

varicoso, sa, *a.* (med.) varicose. —*m., f.* person suffering from varicose veins.

varicotomía, *f.* (med.) varicotomy.

variedad, *f.* 1. variety, diversity; change, variation. 2. (*pl.*) (theat.) vaudeville, variety show. 3. miscellany of things or items.

varilarguero, *m.* (coll., taur.) picador.

varilla, *f.* 1. *dim. of* **vara,** rod, bar, stick. 2. rib (of fan, umbrella, corset). 3. (coll.) jawbone. 4. (*pl.*) rectangular frame of a sieve. 5. (Mex.) peddler's wares. 6. (Ven.) trial horse race. 7. (Ven.) nuisance, bother. — **v. de bombeo,** pump rod; **v. de pistón,** piston rod; **v. de virtudes, v. mágica,** magic wand; **v. de zahorí,** divining rod.

varillage, *m.* ribs, ribbing (of a fan, umbrella, etc.); rods.

varillero, *m.* (Mex.) peddler.

vario, ria, *a.* 1. varied, various, diverse. 2. variable, changeable, inconstant. 3. (*pl.*) various, several. —*m.* (*pl.*) literary micellany.

varioacoplador, *m.* (elec.) variocoupler.

variólico, ca, *a.* (med.) variolic, variolous.

variolita, *f.* (min.) variolite.

variolización, *f.* (med.) variolation, innoculation with smallpox vaccine.

varioloide, *f.* (med.) varioloid.
varioloso, sa, *a.* (med.) variolous. —*m., f.* smallpox patient.
variómetro, *m.* (elec.) variometer.
variopinto, ta, *a.* many-colored.
varistor, *m.* (rad.) varistor.
varita, *f.* 1. *dim. of* **vara,** small stick or rod. 2. (bot.) spray, spike. — **v. de virtudes, v. mágica,** magic wand.
variz, (*pl.* **varices**), *m.* (med.) varix, varicose vein.
varón, *a.* male (person), e.g. *hijo v.,* male child. —*m.* 1. man; male; adult male. 2. boy, male child, e.g. *tuvo un varón,* she had a little boy. 3. (mar.) rudder tackle, rudder chain, emergency steering chain. — **v. de Dios,** Godfearing man, virtuous man; **buen v.,** wise, experienced and sensible man; **santo v.,** (coll.) plain simple man; **v. del timón,** (naut.) rudder pendant.
varona, *f.* (rare) woman, female; mannish woman.
varoncico, illo, ito, *m. dim. of* **varón,** boy, lad, male child.
varonesa, *f.* (obs.) woman, female.
varonía, *f.* male issue, male descent.
varonil, *a.* manly, virile; courageous.
varonilmente, *adv.* in a virile manner; courageously, bravely.
varraco, *m., var. of* **verraco.**
varraquear, *i.v., var. of* **verraquear.**
varraquera, *f., var. of* **verraquera.**
Varsovia, *f.* Warsaw, capital of Poland.
varsoviano, na, *a.* of Warsaw. —*m., f.* native or inhabitant of Warsaw. —*f.* varsovienne (dance).
vasallaje, *m.* 1. vassalage; subjection, servitude, dependence. 2. liege money.
vasallo, lla, *a.* vassal; subject; feudatory; dependent. —*m., f.* vassal; subject.
vasar, *m.* kitchen shelf (for glasses, plates, etc.), shelving.
vasco, ca, *a., m., f.* Basque (of France or Spain). —*m.* Basque (language).
vascófilo, *m.* expert in the Basque language, lore or culture; Basque scholar.
vascón, na, *m., f.* (hist.) member of an ancient Spanish tribe which in 778 stopped Charlemagne in the Pyrenees.
vascongado, *a., m., f.* Basque (of Spain). —*m.* Basque (language).
vascónico, ca, *a., ref.* **vascón, na.**
vascuence, *m.* 1. Basque (language). 2. (coll.) riddle; gibberish.
vascular, vasculoso, sa, *a.* (bot., anat.) vascular, vasculous.
vascularidad, *f.* (anat.) vascularity.
vasectomía, *f.* (med.) vasectomy.
vaselina, *f.* vaseline.
vasera, *f.* 1. shelf for glasses, dishes, etc. 2. rack or tray for drinking glasses.
vasija, *f.* 1. vessel, receptacle, container; bowl, basin. 2. collection of casks and jars in a wine cellar.
vasillo, *m.* cell (of a honeycomb).
vaso, *m.* 1. glass, tumbler; vase, amphora; container, receptacle; (chem.) flask, beaker. 2. glass, glassful. 3. vessel, ship's hull. 4. (rare) chamber pot. 5. hoof (of horse). 6. (astron.) Crater. 7. (bot., anat.) vessel. — **v. de elección,** chosen vessel; **v. lacrimatorio,** lachrymal vase; **v. sanguíneo,** blood vessel.
vasoconstricción, *f.* (physiol.) vasoconstriction.
vasoconstrictor, *a.* (physiol.) vasoconstricting. —*m.* (physiol.) vasoconstrictor.
vasodilatación, *f.* (physiol.) vasodilatation, vasodilation.
vasodilatador, *a.* (physiol.) vasodilating. —*m.* (physiol.) vasodilator.
vasomotor, ra, *a.* (physiol.) vasomotor.
vástago, *m.* 1. (bot.) scion, shoot. 2. (fig.) offspring, scion. 3. rod, stem (of a piston, valve, plunger). 4. (C. Rica, Ven.) banana stalk. — **v. del émbolo,** (mec.) piston rod; **v. de válvula** or **distribución,** valve rod or stem.
vastedad, *f.* vastness, immensity.
vástiga, *f.* (bot.) shoot, scion.
vasto, ta, *a.* vast, huge.
vataje, *m.* (elec.) wattage.
vate, *m.* 1. bard, poet. 2. prophet, seer.
vatiaje, *m.* (elec.) wattage.
vaticano, na, *a.* Vatican. —*m.* V., Vatican.
vaticinador, ra, *a.* vaticinating, prophesying, predicting. —*m., f.* vaticinator, prophet, seer.
vaticinante, *a.* vaticinating, prophesying, predicting.
vaticinar, *tr.v.* to vaticinate, prophesy, predict, foretell; to forecast.
vaticinio, *m.* vaticination, prophecy, prediction.
vatídico, ca, *a.* prophetic, vaticinal.
vatímetro, *m.* (elec.) wattmeter.
vatio, *m.* (elec.) watt; **v. efectivo,** true watt; **v.-hora,** watt-hour.
vaya, *f.* mocking, jest, banter, scoff; **dar v. a,** to make fun of, jeer at, mock.
vaya, *ref.* **ir; v. con Dios,** God be with you; farewell. —*interj.* well! there! indeed! go!; **v.** + *noun,* what a, e.g. *¡v. enredo!* what a mess! *¡v. chica linda!* what a pretty girl!
V.B. *abbrev. of* **visto bueno,** approved; O.K., approval.
Vd. (obs.) *abbrev. of* **usted,** you; (*pl.*) Vds.
Vda. *abbrev. of* **viuda,** widow.
ve, *f.* vee (name of the letter "v"); **v. doble, doble v.,** double-u, the letter "w". —*2nd person sing. imper. of* **ir,** to go, *and* **ver,** to see, e.g. *ve pronto,* go soon; *ve que se haga,* see that it's done.
V.E. *abbrev. of* **Vuestra Excelencia,** Your Excellency.
véase, *imper. of* **verse,** see, vide (in references), e.g. *v. la página siguiente,* see next page.
vecera, vecería, *f.* herd of livestock owned collectively by a community.
vecero, ra, *a.* 1. alternating, taking turns. 2. said of a tree which bears fruit in alternate years. —*m., f.* 1. store customer. 2. one who awaits his or her turn.
vecinal, *a.* 1. vicinal, pertaining to a community or neighborhood. 2. vicinal, neighboring, adjacent. — **unidad v.,** community housing project.
vecinamente, *adv.* nearby, close at hand; contiguously.
vecindad, *f.,* **vecindario,** *m.* 1. vicinity, neighborhood, environs, e.g. *un amigo mío vive en la v.,* a friend of mine lives in the vicinity or neighborhood. 2. nearness, proximity. 3. community, neighborhood, townsfolk, tenants (of a house).
vecino, na, *a.* 1. neighboring, nearby. 2. (fig.) similar, like; bordering upon, resembling. — **v. a** or **de,** near, close to. —*m., f.* 1. neighbor. 2. resident, inhabitant, tenant.
vectación, *f.* riding (in a vehicle).
vectógrafo, *m.* (elec.) vectograph.
vector, *a.* (math.) vector, vectorial; **radio v.,** (geom.) radius vector. —*m.* (math., biol.) vector.
vectorial, *a.* (math.) vector, vectorial; **álgebra v.,** vector algebra; **análisis v.,** vector analysis; **campo v.,** vector field; **potencial v.,** vector potential; **producto v.,** vector product.
veda, *f.* 1. prohibition, interdiction by law. 2. closed season (for hunting or fishing). 3. **V.,** Veda (Hindu holy book).
vedado, *past part. of* **vedar.** —*a.* forbidden, prohibited, interdicted. —*m.* game preserve, warren; enclosure, private park.
vedamiento, *m.* prohibition.
vedar, *tr.v.* 1. to prohibit, forbid. 2. to hinder, obstruct.
vedegambre, *m.* (bot.) white hellebore (Veratum album).
vedeja, *f., var. of* **guedeja.**
védico, ca, *a.* (rel., philos.) Vedic (relating to the Vedas).
vedija, *f.* 1. tuft of wool; matted or tangled hair, matted tuft of hair. 2. (fig.) spiral of smoke. 3. (anat.) groin.
vedijero, ra, *m., f.* person who gathers shorn wool.
vedijoso, sa, vedijudo, da, *a.* having tangled or matted hair or wool.
vedijuela, *f. dim. of* **vedija,** small tuft of wool or lock of tangled hair.
veduño, *m., var. of* **viduño.**
veedor, ra, *a.* prying, curious. —*m., f.* prier, busybody. —*m.* inspector, supervisor.
veeduría, *f.* inspectorship; inspector's office.
vega, *f.* 1. fertile lowland. 2. (Cuba) tobacco plantation. 3. (Chile) damp or swampy terrain.
vegetabilidad, *f.* condition of being vegetable.
vegetación, *f.* 1. vegetation, vegetating. 2. (bot., med.) vegetation.
vegetal, *a.* vegetal, vegetable. —*m.* vegetable, plant.
vegetalismo, *m., var. of* **vegetarianismo.**
vegetalista, *a., var. of* **vegetariano.**
vegetante, *a.* vegetating.
vegetar, *i.v.* 1. to grow (plants). 2. (fig.) to vegetate, lead a passive life.
vegetarianismo, *m.* vegetarianism.
vegetariano, na, *a., m., f.* vegetarian.
vegetativo, va, *a.* vegetative.
vegoso, sa, *a.* (Chile) damp, humid, swampy (soil).
veguer, *m.* (hist.) formerly district magistrate, corregidor (of Aragon, Catalonia and Majorca).
veguerío, ia, *m., f.* jurisdiction of a **veguer.**
veguero, ra, *a.* 1. pertaining to a fertile lowland. 2. (Cuba) pertaining to a tobacco plantation. —*m., f.* 1. one who farms a lowland. 2. (Cuba) tobacco planter or farmer. —*m.* fine type of cigar made from a single rolled leaf.
vehemencia, *f.* vehemence.
vehemente, *a.* vehement; impassioned (speaker).
vehementemente, *adv.* vehemently.
vehículo, *m.* 1. vehicle (conveyance). 2. (fig.) carrier; medium, means.
veintavo, va, *a., m.* twentieth.
veinte, *a.* twenty; **a las v.,** (coll.) very late, inopportunely; **los años v.,** the twenties. —*m.* twenty; twentieth (in dates).
veintén, *m.* Spanish gold coin worth 20 reales.
veintena, *f.,* **veintenar,** *m.* score, twenty.
veintenario, ria, *a.* twenty years old, twenty-year-old.
veinteno, na, *a., f.* twentieth.
veinteñal, *a.* twenty-year, lasting twenty years.
veintésimo, ma, *a., m.* twentieth.
veinticinco, *a.* twenty-five. —*m.* twenty-five; twenty-fifth (in dates).
veinticuatreno, na, *a.* twenty-fourth. —*m.* cloth with a 2400-thread warp.
veinticuatro, *a.* twenty-four. —*m.* twenty-four; twenty-fourth (in dates).
veintidós, *a.* twenty-two. —*m.* twenty-two; twenty-second (in dates).
veintidoseno, na, *a.* twenty-second.
veintinueve, *a.* twenty-nine. —*m.* twenty-nine; twenty-ninth (in dates).
veintiocheno, na, *a.* twenty-eighth.
veintiocho, *a.* twenty-eight. —*m.* twenty-eight; twenty-eighth (in dates).
veintiséis, *a.* twenty-six. —*m.* twenty-six; twenty-sixth (in dates).

veintiseiseno, na, *a.* twenty-sixth.
veintisiete, *a.* twenty-seven. —*m.* twenty-seven; twenty-seventh (in dates).
veintitrés, *a.* twenty-three. —*m.* twenty-three; twenty-third (in dates).
veintiún, *a.* twenty-one (apocopated form of **veintiuno** used before masculine nouns and adjectives), e.g. *v. años,* twenty-one years.
veintiuno, na, *a.* twenty-one. —*m.* twenty-one; twenty-first (in dates). —*f.* twenty-one, blackjack (card game).
vejación, *f.* 1. maltreatment, ill-treatment, abuse. 2. insult, affront, humiliation.
vejador, ra, *a.* 1. maltreating. 2. offensive, insulting, abusive. —*m., f.* 1. maltreater, abuser, ill-treater. 2. insulter, affronter.
vejamen, *m.* 1. maltreatment, ill-treatment, abuse. 2. insult, affront. 3. ridicule, derision, taunt, humiliation.
vejancón, na, *a.* (coll.) *aug. of* **viejo,** old. —*m.* old fellow. —*f.* old girl.
vejar, *tr.v.* 1. to ill-treat, maltreat, abuse. 2. to insult, affront. 3. to ridicule, mock, taunt; to humiliate.
vejarrón, na, *a.* (coll.) *aug. of* **viejo,** old. —*m.* old fellow. —*f.* old girl.
vejatorio, ria, *a.* abusive, affronting, insulting.
vejazo, za, *m.* old man. —*f.* old woman.
vejecito, ta, *m., f.* little old man (woman).
vejestorio, *m.* (derog.) old dodderer; very old person; useless, oldfashioned thing.
vejeta, *f.* (ornith.) crested lark.
vejete, *m.* comic or ridiculous old man.
vejez, *f.* 1. old age; oldness. 2. feebleness; peevishness of old age. 3. (coll.) platitude, trite story or saying.
vejezuelo, la, *a.* oldish. —*m., f. dim. of* **viejo,** little old man (woman).
vejiga, *f.* 1. (anat.) bladder. 2. blister. — **v. de la bilis,** gall bladder; **v. de perro,** (bot.) alkekengi, Chinese lantern, winter cherry; **v. natatoria,** swimming bladder (of a fish).
vejigatorio, ria, *a.* (med.) blistering, vesicatory, vesicant. —*m.* (med.) blistering plaster, vesicatory, vesicant.
vejigazo, *m.* blow with a bladder full of air.
vejigón, *m. aug. of* **vejiga,** large bladder or blister.
vejigoso, sa, *a.* full of blisters.
vejigüela, *f. dim. of* **vejiga,** small or little bladder or blister.
vejiguilla, *f.* 1. *dim. of* **vejiga,** small bladder. 2. pustule, blister. 3. (bot.) alkekengi, Chinese lantern, winter cherry.
vejote, ta, *a. aug. of* **viejo,** old. —*m.* old man, old fellow. —*f.* old woman, old girl.
vela, *f.* 1. candle. 2. vigil, watch; watching. 3. evening or night work. 4. night sentry or watchman. 5. (C. Amer.) wake (vigil). — **en v.,** awake; **¿quién te ha dado v. en este entierro?** who asked you to stick your nose in, who asked you for your opinion; **poner una v. a Dios y otra al diablo,** (coll.) to run with the hare and hunt with the hounds.
vela, *f.* 1. sail (of a ship); awning. 2. (fig.) sail, boat, ship. — **a la v.,** in readiness, ready, prepared; **alzar velas,** (mar.) to set the sails, hoist sails; to leave suddenly; **apocar las velas,** (mar.) to trim the sails; **a toda v., a velas tendidas,** (mar.) at full sail; **a v. y remo,** (coll.) with all speed; **cambiar la v.,** (mar.) to turn into the wind; **hacer a la v., hacerse a la v.,** to set sail; **levantar velas,** to leave suddenly; **recoger velas,** to control oneself; **tender las velas,** (coll.) to take advantage of an opportunity, make hay while the sun shines; **v. al tercio,** (mar.) lugsail; **v. bastarda,** (mar.) main lateen sail; **v. cangreja,** (mar.) fore-and-aft sail; spanker; **v. cuadrada,** (mar.) square sail; **v. de cruz,** (mar.) square sail; **v. de cuchillo,** (mar.) staysail; **v. de estay,** (mar.) staysail; **v. latina,** lateen sail; **v. mayor,** (mar.) mainsail; **v. tarquina,** (mar.) lugsail; **velas mayores,** (mar.) mainsails.
velacho, *m.* (mar.) foretopsail.
velación, *f.* 1. vigil, watch; watching. 2. wakefulness, being awake. 3. (ecc.) veiling ceremony of bride and groom in nuptial mass.
velada, *f.* 1. evening, evening party or get-together, e.g. *ha sido una v. amena,* it has been a very pleasant evening. 2. soirée, literary or musical evening. 3. watch, vigil; watching. 4. wakefulness, being awake.
velado, da, *past part. of* **velar.** —*a.* 1. veiled, hidden. 2. dull, toneless (voice). 3. blurred (photograph). 4. (bot., zool.) velate. —*m.* (obs.) husband. —*f.* wife.
velador, ra, *a.* watching; vigil-keeping; guarding. —*m., f.* watcher; vigil-keeper; guard; nightguard, watchman. —*m.* 1. candlestick. 2. round pedestal table. 3. night table, bedside table. 4. (Amer.) bedside lamp. 5. (Mex.) glass lampshade.
veladura, *f.* (p.) glaze, varnish, toner.
velaje, velamen, *m.* (mar.) sails, canvas (of a ship).
velar, *tr.v.* 1. to watch; to keep a vigil over. 2. to tend (a sick person) at night; to hold a wake over (dead person). 3. to guard, keep, take care of, watch over (child, ward, one's health, etc.). —*i.v.* 1. to watch. 2. to stay awake, be awake. 3. to work late, work at night. 4. to attend the Eucharistic adoration services. 5. (mar.) to jut out (rocks, reefs). — **v. por,** to look after, watch over, keep an eye on, take care of, be solicitous about.
velar, *tr.v.* 1. to veil, cover with a veil. 2. to veil (at nuptial mass). 3. (fig.) to veil, cover up, hide. 4. (photog.) to fade, diffuse, blur. 5. (p.) to glaze (a painting). —*r.v.* 1. to be veiled; to veil oneself. 2. (photog.) to become faded or blurred (due to overexposure). 3. to hold a veiling ceremony at nuptial mass.
velar, *a.* 1. obscuring, veiling. 2. (anat., phonet.) velar. —*f.* (phonet.) velar.
velario, *m.* (hist.) velarium (awning over amphitheater).
velarización, *f.* (phonet.) velarization.
velarizar, (*ref. 53*) *tr.v.* (phonet.) to velarize.
velarte, *m.* (arch.) fine broadcloth (formerly used for making cloaks).
velatorio, *m.* wake, vigil (preceding burial).
velazqueño, ña, *a.* (art.) of Velázquez (characteristic of the Spanish painter).
veleidad, *f.* 1. whim, caprice; stray impulse; feeble attempt. 2. fickleness, inconstancy, changeableness.
veleidoso, sa, *a.* fickle, inconstant, changeable.
velejar, *i.v.* to sail with sails unfurled, make use of sails.
velería, *f.* candlemaker's shop, chandlery.
velero, ra, *a.* fond of attending wakes or pilgrimage. —*m., f.* 1. chandler, candlemaker. 2. waker, person who attends a wake; pilgrim, person who takes part in a pilgrimage.
velero, ra, *a.* swift-sailing (vessel). —*m.* 1. sailboat, sailing vessel. 2. sailmaker. 3. candlemaker, chandler; one who sells candles.
veleta, *f.* 1. vane, weathercock; weather vane, wind vane. 2. pennant (on a cavalry soldier's lance). 3. float, bob (on a fishing line). —*m., f.* (coll.) fickle, changeable person.
velete, *m.* light, sheer veil.
velicación, *f.* (med.) lancing, opening.
velicar, (*ref. 50*) *tr.v.* (med.) to lance, open.
velilla, ita, *f. dim. of* **vela,** small candle.
velillo, *m.* 1. *dim. of* **velo,** small face veil. 2. (tex.) fine, embroidered gauze.
velis nolis, (Lat., coll.) willy-nilly.
vélite, *m.* Roman light infantry soldier.
velívolo, la, *a.* (poet.) swift-sailing.
vellero, ra, *m., f.* cosmetician who removes unwanted hair.
vellido, da, *a., var. of* **velloso.**
vello, *m.* 1. down (soft hair on human body); **v. púbico,** pubic hair. 2. fuzz (on fruit).
vellocino, *m.* fleece; **V. de Oro,** (myth.) Golden Fleece.
vellón, *m.* 1. fleece; tuft of wool; unsheared sheepskin. 2. ancient Spanish copper coin. 3. (P. Rico, coll.) five-cent piece, nickel (U.S.).
vellonera, *f.* (P. Rico, Dom. Rep.) juke box.
vellonero, *m.* gatherer of fleece or wool.
véllora, *f.* (tex.) knot on wrong side of cloth.
vellorio, ria, *a.* grey, dun (said of horses).
vellorita, *f.* (bot.) daisy; cowslip, primrose.
vellosidad, *f.* downiness, fuzziness, hairiness.
vellosilla, *f.* (bot.) mouse-ear (Hieracium pilosella).
velloso, sa, *a.* downy, hairy, fuzzy; (bot.) villous.
velludillo, *m.* velveteen, velour.
velludo, da, *a.* downy, hairy, shaggy. —*m.* plush, velvet, shag.
vellutero, *m.* felt or velvet worker.
velmez, (*pl.* **velmeces**), tunic worn under armor.
velo, *m.* 1. veil. 2. (ecc.) humeral veil. 3. (anat.) velum, veil. 4. (ecc.) ceremony of taking the veil (a nun). 4. (fig.) veil, curtain, cloak, mask (concealing something); disguise. — **correr** or **echar un v. sobre,** to hush up, cover up, conceal, hide; **tomar el v.,** (ecc.) to take the veil, become a nun; **v. del paladar,** (anat.) velum, soft palate; **v. de misterio,** veil or cloak of mystery; **v. humeral,** (ecc.) humeral veil.
velocidad, *f.* 1. velocity, speed. 2. (auto.) gear. — **caja de velocidades,** (auto.) gearbox; **de v. única,** single-speed; **en gran v.,** (ry.) by express; **en pequeña v.,** (ry.) by freight; **exceso de v.,** speeding; **primera, segunda, tercera** or **cuarta v.,** (auto.) first, second, third or fourth gear; **v. absoluta,** (aer.) ground speed; **v. ascensional,** (aer.) climbing speed; **v. circular,** orbital velocity; **v. crítica,** (phys.) critical speed; **v. angular,** angular speed or velocity; **v. de liberación,** (astron.) velocity of escape; **v. de marcha,** (mec.) traveling speed; **v. de obturación,** (photog.) shutter speed; **v. de retroceso,** (auto.) reverse speed; **v. de sincronismo,** (elec.) synchronous speed; **v. de subida, de toma de altura,** (aer.) climbing speed; **v. de traslación,** (mec.) traveling speed; **v. máxima** or **punta,** maximum or top speed; **v. superficial,** (aer.) surface speed; **v. unitaria,** rate of speed; **v. virtual,** (mec.) virtual velocity.
velocímetro, *m.* speedometer.
velocipedismo, *m.* (sport.) cyclism, cycling.
velocipedista, *m., f.* velocipedist, cyclist.
velocípedo, *m.* velocipede.
velocista, *m., f.* (sport.) sprinter.
velódromo, *m.* velodrome, cycling track.
velómetro, *m.* (meteorol.) velometer, wind gage.
velomotor, *m.* motor bicycle; light motorcycle.
velón, *m.* 1. metal oil lamp (with revolving oil reservoir). 2. (Chile, Peru) large candle or taper.
velonero, ra, *m., f.* lamp maker or seller. —*f.* lamp stand, lamp bracket.
velorí, vellorín, *m.* undyed broadcloth of medium quality.

velorio, *m.* 1. wake, vigil (preceding burial). 2. party, gathering, get-together, evening; (Arg.) dead or dull party.
veloz, (*pl.* **veloces**), *a.* swift, rapid; quick, fast, agile.
velozmente, *adv.* swiftly, rapidly, fast, quickly.
veludillo, *m., var. of* **velludillo.**
veludo, *m., var. of* **velludo.**
vena, *f.* 1. (anat., zool., bot.) vein; (geol., min.) vein, seam, lode. 2. vein, subterranean water channel. 3. vein, streak (in wood, marble, etc.). 4. mood, vein; inspiration, e.g. *estar en v. para escribir,* to be in the mood for writing. 5. vein, strain, e.g. *escribir en v. satírica* or *humorística,* to write in a satirical or jocular vein. — **acostarse (la v.),** (min.) to dip (a vein); **coger a uno de v.,** (coll.) find someone in a receptive mood; **darle a uno la v.,** (coll.) to feel like doing something crazy; **dar en la v.,** to hit upon the right way; **estar en v.,** (coll.) to be in the mood; to be inspired; **v. ácigos,** (anat.) azygous vein; **v. basílica,** (anat.) basilic vein; **v. cardíaca,** (anat.) cardiac vein; **v. cava,** (anat.) vena cava; **v. cefalica,** (anat.) cephalic vein; **v. coronaria,** (anat.) coronary vein; **v. de agua,** vein, underground water channel; **v. de loco,** fickle, changeable character or disposition; **v. emulgente,** (anat.) renal vein, emulgent vein; **v. láctea,** (anat.) lacteal vessel, lacteal; **v. leónica,** (anat.) ranine vein; **v. porta,** (anat.) vena portae, portal vein; **v. ranina,** (anat.) ranine vein; **v. safena,** (anat.) saphenous vein; **v. yugular,** (anat.) jugular vein.
venable, *a., var. of* **venal.**
venablo, *m.* javelin, dart; **echar venablos,** to burst out into violent language.
venadero, *a.* (Col., Ecuad.) deer-hunting (hound). —*m.* deer haunt, place frequented by deer.
venado, *m.* deer, stag. — **carne de v.,** venison; **correr v.,** (Guat.) **pintar v.,** (Mex.) to play hooky, play truant; **hacerse el v.,** to act dumb, pretend not to understand.
venaje, *m.* feeding streams, fountainheads (of river).
venal, *a.* 1. (anat.) venous, of veins. 2. bribable, venal, corruptible. 3. venal, able to be bought.
venalidad, *f.* venality.
venático, ca, *a.* 1. (coll.) fickle, inconstant, changeable. 2. crotchety, cranky; erratic; senile.
venatorio, ria, *a.* venatic, pertaining to hunting.
vencedero, ra, *a.* (com.) falling due, expiring.
vencedor, ra, *a.* vanquishing, overcoming, conquering. —*m., f.* conqueror; victor, winner.
vencejo, *m.* 1. band, string. 2. (ornith.) swift, martin.
vencer, (*ref. 56*) *tr.v.* to conquer, vanquish; to overcome, surmount; to beat, surpass, outdo. —*i.v.* 1. to win, be victorious. 2. (com.) to expire; to fall due, mature. 3. to bend, incline; twist. —*r.v.* 1. to control or restrain oneself. 2. to bend, incline; twist.
venceremos, *interj.* (Amer.) We shall overcome (slogan of the Cuban Revolution).
vencetósigo, *m.* (bot.) swallowwort, tame poison (Vincetoxicum officinale).
vencible, *a.* conquerable, vincible; surmountable.
vencida, *f., var. of* **vencimiento; a la tercera va la v.,** it will happen at the third try (as a threat or a promise); **ir de v.,** to be on the decline; to be nearly beaten.
vencido, da, *past part. of* **vencer.** —*a.* 1. vanquished, defeated. 2. (com.) due, payable. 3. expired.
vencimiento, *m.* 1. defeat; victory. 2. inclination, bend. 3. (com.) expiration; maturity.
venda, *f.* 1. bandage. 2. diadem, regal fillet. 3. blindfold. 4. fillet, headband. — **caérsele a uno la v. de los ojos,** to see or realize the truth.
vendaje, *m.* 1. bandages, bandaging, dressing. 2. (rare) commission (on sales). 3. (Col., C. Rica, Ecuad., Peru) extra, something given for good measure.
vendar, *tr.v.* 1. to bandage. 2. (fig.) to blind, hoodwink. — **v. los ojos,** to blindfold.
vendaval, *m.* strong wind from the sea; strong wind, gale.
vendedor, ra, *a.* selling. —*m., f.* seller. —*m.* salesman. —*f.* saleswoman, salesgirl.
vendehumos, (*pl.* **vendehumos**), *m., f.* (coll.) influence peddler.
vendeja, *f.* public sale.
vender, *tr.v.* 1. to sell. 2. (fig.) to sell out (sl.), betray. — **v. al contado,** to sell for cash; **v. a plazos,** to sell on credit; **v. como pan caliente,** to sell like hot cakes; **v. la piel del oso antes de cazarlo,** to count one's chickens before they are hatched. —*r.v.* 1. to sell, e.g. *se vende a dos pesetas el kilo,* it sells at two pesetas a kilo. 2. to sell oneself. 3. (fig.) to expose oneself to danger. 4. (fig.) to give oneself away, show one's hand. — **se vende,** for sale; **venderse caro,** to be rarely seen, be difficult to see.
vendí, (*pl.* **vendíes**), *m.* (com.) certificate of sale.
vendible, *a.* salable, marketable.
vendido, da, *past part. of* **vender.** —*a.* 1. sold. 2. betrayed.
vendimia, *f.* 1. vintage, grape harvest or crop. 2. (fig.) great profit.
vendimiador, ra, *m., f.* grape picker or harvester, vintager.
vendimiar, *tr.v.* 1. to gather, harvest (grapes). 2. to reap (advantages) unjustly. 3. (coll.) to kill.
vendimiario, *m.* Vendimiaire, first month of the calendar of the French Revolution.
vendo, *m.* selvage (of cloth).
venduta, *f.* 1. (Amer.) auction, public sale. 2. (Cuba) small vegetable and fruit shop, greengrocery.
vendutero, *m.* (Amer.) auctioneer.
Venecia, *f.* Venice (city and port in Italy).
veneciano, na, *a., m., f.* Venetian.
venencia, *f.* tube for sampling wines.
venenífero, ra, *a.* (poet.) poisonous, venomous.
veneno, *m.* 1. poison, venom. 2. (fig.) wrath, fury, venom.
venenosidad, *f.* poisonousness, banefulness.
venenoso, sa, *a.* poisonous, venomous, baneful.
venera, *f.* 1. scallop shell. 2. knight's badge. 3. (archit.) scallop-shaped molding. 4. spring (of water). — **empeñar la v.,** to spare no expense or sacrifice.
venerabilísimo, ma, *a. sup. of* **venerable,** most venerable.
venerable, *a.* venerable.
venerablemente, *adv.* venerably.
veneración, *f.* 1. veneration. 2. worship.
venerador, ra, *a.* venerating; worshipping. —*m., f.* venerator; worshipper.
venerando, da, *a.* venerable.
venerante, *a.* venerating.
venerar, *tr.v.* 1. to venerate, revere. 2. worship.
venéreo, a, *a.* venereal. —*m.* venereal disease.
venero, *m.* 1. spring (of water). 2. horary mark (of sundial). 3. (fig.) source, origin. 4. (min.) seam, vein, lode.
véneto, ta, *a., m., f.* Venetian.
venezolano, na, *a., m., f.* Venezuelan.
Venezuela, *f.* Venezuela.
venga, *ref.* **venir.**
vengable, *a.* deserving revenge, that can be avenged.
vengador, ra, *a.* avenging, revenging. —*m., f.* avenger, revenger.
venganza, *f.* vengeance; revenge.
vengar, (*ref. 51*) *tr.v.* to avenge. —*r.v.* to avenge oneself, take revenge.
vengativo, va, *a.* vengeful, vindictive, revengeful.
vengo, *ref.* **venir.**
vengue, vengué, *ref.* **vengar.**
venia, *f.* 1. pardon, forgiveness. 2. permission, authority, leave; (law) court permission given to minors to manage their own estates. 3. bow or nod of the head (as a greeting); (Amer., mil.) salute.
venial, *a.* venial, pardonable.
venialidad, *f.* veniality.
venialmente, *adv.* venially.
venialmente, *adv.* venially.
venida, *f.* 1. coming, arrival; return. 2. flood, freshet. 3. (fen.) attack. 4. (fig.) impetuosity, rashness, rash action.
venidero, ra, *a.* coming, future. —*m.* (*pl.*) heirs, successors; future generations, posterity. — **en lo v.,** in the future, hereafter.
venilla, *f. dim. of* **vena,** (anat., zool.) veinlet, venule.
venimécum, *m.* vade mecum, handbook, manual.
venir, (*ref. 26*) *i.v.* 1. to come; to arrive; to approach. 2. to come or originate from, e.g. *vengo del norte,* I am from the north. 3. to come to mind, to occur, e.g. *le vino a la mente,* it occured to him (her). 4. to come to one from, be inherited from, e.g. *esta costumbre me viene de mi padre,* I get this habit from my father. 5. to suit, fit, be becoming, advantageous or convenient (or not), e.g. *ese traje no te viene bien,* that dress doesn't suit, fit, or become you, *me vendría bien un trago,* I could use a drink; *esa hora no nos viene bien,* that hour (time) is not convenient for us. — **no hay mal que por bien no venga,** every cloud has a silver lining; **no me vengas con esas,** don't give me any excuses; you don't say; tell it to the marines; **venga lo que venga,** come what may; **v.** + *ger.,* to have been + *ger.,* e.g. *eso viene ocurriendo hace tiempo,* that has been happening for some time; v. a + *inf.,* to end up by + *ger.;* **v. a las manos,** to come to blows; **v. al caso,** to be pertinent; to have to do with the subject; **v. al mundo,** to be born; **v. al pelo, como anillo al dedo, de perlas** or **de perilla,** to be just perfect, to suit one (or the occasion) to a tee; **v. a menos,** to come down in the world, lose one's money, prestige or position; **v. a ser,** to turn out to be; **venirle a uno muy ancha una cosa,** to be beyond one's capabilities or ability; **venirle a uno el deseo de** + *inf.,* to feel like + *ger.,* to get an itch to + *inf.;* **v. por** + *n.,* to come for + *n.;* **v. rodado,** to come by luck, to be a windfall; **que viene,** coming, next, e.g. *el año que viene,* next year. —*r.v.* 1. to come, to return. 2. to mature, ferment, get to the desired state or consistency, e.g. wine, dough. — **venirse abajo, al suelo** or **a tierra,** to callapse, drop, fall down.
venosidad, *f.* (anat.) venosity.
venoso, sa, *a.* 1. venous (blood). 2. veined, veiny.
venta, *f.* 1. sale, selling. 2. roadside inn. 3. (coll.) unsheltered place, open spot. 4. (Chile) food and drinks stand, booth or stall. — **v. a crédito,** credit sale; **v. a plazos,** sales on the installment plan; **v. al contado,** cash sale; **v. al por mayor,** wholesale; **v. al por menor,** retail; **v. de garaje,** garage sale; **v. por catálogo** or **correo,** mail order; **v. pública,** public sale.
ventada, *f.* blast, gust of wind.
ventaja, *f.* 1. advantage. 2. profit. 3. extra pay. 4. (sport.) odds. — **llevar v. a,** to be ahead of; to have the advantage over; **sacar v. de,** to benefit

or profit from; **sacar v. sobre,** to gain an advantage over.
ventajero, ra, *m., f.* (Amer.) wily, astute person; bargain hunter.
ventajosamente, *adv.* advantageously.
ventajoso, sa, *a.* advantageous, profitable.
ventalla, *f.* (mec., bot.) valve.
ventana, *f.* 1. window. 2. nostril. 3. (anat., surg., med.) fenestra, window. — **arrojar, echar** or **tirar por la v.,** to waste, squander; **echar la casa por la v.,** to blow one's money on a party or reception; **salir por la v.,** to leave under a shadow or in disgrace; **v. abatible,** drop window; **v. corrediza, v. de corredera,** sliding window; **v. de guillotina,** sash window, double-hung window; **v. oval,** (anat.) fenestra ovalis; **v. redonda,** (anat.) fenestra rotunda.
ventanaje, *m.* (archit.) windows, fenestration.
ventanal, *m.* large window, church window.
ventanazo, *m.* slamming of a window.
ventanear, *i.v.* (coll.) to be often at the window, be often looking out of the window.
ventaneo, *m.* (coll.) gazing out of the window; flirting from the window.
ventanero, ra, *a.* said of one who is fond of looking out of, flirting at or spying from a window. —*m., f.* window maker, glazier.
ventanico, *m., var. of* **ventanillo.**
ventanilla, *f.* 1. *dim. of* **ventana,** small window; window (in railway coach, car, bank counter, etc.), ticket window (of box office, ticket office). 2. nostril.
ventanillo, *m. dim. of* **ventano,** peephole, small window.
ventano, *m.* small window.
ventar, (*ref. 29*) *tr.v.* to sniff, scent. —*i.v.* to blow (the wind).
ventarrón, *m.* strong wind, gust of wind; gale.
venteadura, *f.* 1. crack, split; blister (in brick or tile). 2. airing, exposure to the air. 3. spoilage by exposure to the air (e.g. tobacco).
ventear, *tr.v.* 1. to sniff, scent. 2. to air, dry in the wind. 3. to inquire into, pry into. 4. to winnow. —*i.v.* to blow (said of wind). —*r.v.* 1. to split; to blister (said of bricks or tiles). 2. to become spoiled in the air. 3. to break wind. 4. (Arg., Chile) to be a gadabout, be always out of the house. 5. (Col., Ecuad., Peru, P. Rico) to become conceited or vain.
venteril, *a.* of an inn or innkeeper.
ventero, ra, *a.* scenting (dog); **perro ventero,** pointer. —*m., f.* innkeeper.
ventilación, *f.* 1. ventilation. 2. (fig.) discussion, elucidation.
ventilador, *m.* ventilator; (electric) fan; **v. de enfriamiento,** cooling fan.
ventilar, *tr.v.* 1. to ventilate; to air. 2. (fig.) to air, discuss, clear up, elucidate. —*r.v.* to become aired (e.g. a stuffy room).
ventisca, *f.* blizzard, snowstorm.
ventiscar, (*ref. 50*) *i.v.* to blow a blizzard, blow about, whirl about, flurry (the snow).
ventisco, *m., var. of* **ventisca.**
ventiscoso, sa, *a.* snowy and stormy, having frequent snowstorms.
ventisquear, *i.v., var. of* **ventiscar.**
ventisquero, *m.* 1. blizzard, snowstorm. 2. exposed, unsheltered heights of a mountain; snowcapped peak, snowcap. 3. glacier; snowdrift.
ventola, *f.* (mar.) strong blast of wind.
ventolera, *f.* 1. short gust of wind. 2. pinwheel (toy). 3. (coll.) vanity, pride. 4. (coll.) mad, rash or wild idea; whim, sudden fancy.
ventolina, *f.* (mar.) light fresh wind, cat's-paw.
ventor, ra, *a.* scenting, hunting by scent. —*m.* pointer (dog); foxhound.
ventorrero, *m.* high windy place.
ventorrillo, *m.* 1. small or humble inn or roadhouse. 2. popular, outdoor restaurant in the country. 3. (P. Rico) humble small neighborhood shop.
ventorro, *m.* (derog.) small roadside inn or roadhouse.
ventosa, *f.* 1. (surg.) cupping glass. 2. (zool.) sucker. 3. vent, air hole, spiracle. — **pegar una v. a,** (coll.) to swindle; **v. al vacío,** vacuum valve; **v. escarificada** or **sajada,** (surg.) wet cupping glass; **v. seca,** (surg.) dry cupping glass.
ventosear, *i.v.* to break wind.
ventosidad, *f.* flatulence, intestinal gases, windiness.
ventoso, sa, *a.* 1. windy, blowy. 2. full of wind. 3. windy, flatulent, causing gas or wind (food, etc.). 4. scenting (dog). —*m.* Ventose, sixth month of the calendar of the French Revolution.
ventral, *a.* (anat., zool.) ventral.
ventrecha, *f.* belly (of fish).
ventrecillo, *m. dim. of* **vientre,** small belly.
ventregada, *f.* 1. litter, brood. 2. sudden abundance, flood, rush (of things).
ventrera, *f.* 1. bellyband. 2. stomach plate (part of armor).
ventrezuelo, *m. dim. of* **vientre,** small belly.
ventricular, *a.* ventricular.
ventrículo, *m.* (anat., zool.) ventricle.
ventril, *m.* counterpoise (in olive-mill).
ventrílocuo, cua, *a.* ventriloquial. —*m., f.* ventriloquist.
ventriloquia, *f.* ventriloquism.
ventrón, *m.* 1. *aug. of* **vientre,** large belly, paunch. 2. (cul.) tripe.
ventroso, sa, ventrudo, da, *a.* big-bellied, paunchy.
ventrudo, da, *a.* paunchy; bombé (piece of furniture).
ventura, *f.* 1. happiness. 2. luck, fortune; chance. 3. risk, danger. — **a la v., a la buena v.,** with no fixed idea or plan; **buena v.,** good fortune, fortune told by cards or palmistry, e.g. *decir la buena v.,* to tell one's fortune; **por v.,** by chance, perchance; **probar v.,** to try one's luck.
venturado, da, *a.* lucky, fortunate.
venturanza, *f.* luck, fortune.
venturero, ra, *a.* 1. adventurous, venturous. 2. fortunate, lucky. 3. lazy, idle. —*m., f.* adventurer, venturer.
venturina, *f.* (min.) aventurin, aventurine.
venturo, ra, *a.* coming, future.
venturón, *m. aug. of* **ventura,** extraordinary luck, stroke of luck.
venturosamente, *adv.* luckily, fortunately.
venturoso, sa, *a.* lucky, fortunate, successful, e.g. *un negocio v.,* a successful enterprise.
venus, *f.* 1. (myth.) **V.,** Venus Roman goddess of beauty. 2. (fig.) Venus, beautiful woman. 3. (in alchemy) copper. —*m.* (astron.) **V.,** Venus.
venusterio, *m.* (Peru) part of jail in which prisoners can be alone with their husbands or wives.
venustez, venustidad, *f.* perfect beauty.
venusto, ta, *a.* beautiful, handsome.
venza, venzo, *ref.* **vencer.**
veo, *ref.* ver.
ver, *m.* 1. sight (sense). 2. appearance, look. 3. opinion. — **a mi v.,** in my opinion.
ver, (*ref. 27*) *tr.v.* 1. to see; to look; to look at. 2. to see, visit. 3. to consider, examine, look into, discuss, talk over, e.g. *vamos a ver de qué se trata,* let's see what it is all about. 4. to foresee. 5. to see, decide, e.g. *más tarde veremos si vamos o no,* later we'll see or decide whether we go or not. 6. to see, look and see, find out, e.g. *por favor vea si está,* please, look and see if it's there. 7. to find, e.g. *le veo deprimido y triste,* I find him depressed and sad. 8. to see, realize, observe, note. 9. (law) to try, hear, e.g. *ver un caso,* to try or hear a case. — **a v.,** let's see, let's have a look; **estar** or **quedar en veremos,** (Amer.) to be undecided; **estar por v.,** to remain to be seen; **hasta más v.,** (coll.) so long, cheerio (G.B.), till the next time; **no poder v., no poder v. ni en pintura,** (coll.) to loathe the sight of; **no tener nada que v. con,** to have nothing to do with; **si te ví, no me acuerdo,** (coll.) without a word of thanks; **v.** + *inf.,* to see + *inf.,* see + *ger.,* e.g. *le vi llegar,* I saw him arrive; to see + *past part.,* e.g. *vi construir la casa,* I saw the house being built; **v. de** + *inf.,* to try to + *inf.;* **veremos,** we shall see; **verlas venir,** (coll.) to see it coming; **v. y creer, v. para creer,** seeing is believing; **v. venir,** to anticipate what (someone) is up to, catch on to (someone's) intentions; to wait and see. —*r.v.* 1. to be seen. 2. to see oneself; to look at oneself. 3. to look, appear, e.g. *se ve muy bajo al lado de los otros,* he looks very short alongside the others. 4. to find oneself. 5. to meet, see one another. 6. to be clear, obvious or apparent, e.g. *se ve que no viene,* it's clear that he's not coming. — **verse con,** to meet with, see; **vérselas con,** to have to deal or reckon with, e.g. *tendrás que vértelas conmigo,* you'll have to deal or reckon with me; **verse negro, vérselas negras,** to find oneself in a jam or tight spot; **ya se ve,** of course, certainly.
vera, *f.* 1. side, edge, border; **a la v. de,** next to, beside, at the side of. 2. (bot.) vera.
veracidad, *f.* veracity, truthfulness.
vera efigies, (Lat.) faithful likeness or portrait.
veranada, *f.* summer, summer season (for pasturing); (Arg.) summer pasture.
veranadero, *m.* (agr.) summer pasture.
veranda, *f.* (Angl.) veranda; gallery, porch, balcony.
veraneante, *m., f.* summer vacationist, summer resident.
veranear, *i.v.* to spend the summer, to summer.
veraneo, *m.* 1. summering, vacation. 2. summer pasture or grazing land. — **ir de v.,** to spend the summer, go on a summer vacation; **lugar de v.,** summer resort.
veranero, *m.* (agr.) summer pasture or grazing land.
veraniego, ga, *a.* 1. summery, pertaining to summer. 2. (fig.) slight, flimsy; unimportant.
veranillo, *m. dim. of* **verano,** Indian summer; **v. de San Miguel, de San Martín** or **de San Juan,** Indian summer.
verano, *m.* summer; (Ecuad.) dry season.
veras, *f.* (*pl.*) 1. truth, reality. 2. earnestness. — **de v.,** truly, really, in truth; in earnest; no kidding! (sl.).
verascopio, *m.* (photog.) stereoscope for viewing slides.
veráscopo, *m., var. of* **verascopio.**
veratridina, *f.* (chem.) veratridine, veratridin.
veratrina, *f.* (med.) veratrine.
veratro, *m.* (bot.) hellebore.
veraz, (*pl.* **veraces**), *a.* true, truthful, veracious.
verba, *f.* loquacity, talkativeness; eloquence.
verbal, *a.* 1. verbal (relating to words, expressed in words, using words). 2. oral, verbal (expressed in spoken words), e.g. *contrato v.,* verbal contract. 3. (gram.) verb, of a verb, e.g. *desinencia v.,* verb ending. 4. (gram.) verbal (derived from a verb), e.g. *adjetivo* or *sustantivo v.,* verbal adjective or noun. —*m.* (gram.) verbal.

verbalismo, *m.* 1. verbalism, emphasis on words rather than on facts. 2. system of teaching words rather than ideas.
verbalista, *m., f.* verbalist (one who puts emphasis on words rather than on facts). 2. advocate of teaching words rather than ideas.
verbalmente, *adv.* verbally.
verbasco, *m.* (bot.) great mullein.
verbena, *f.* 1. (bot.) vervain, verbena. 2. evening party; night festival on the eve of a saint's day.
verbenáceo, a, *a.* (bot.) verbenaceous. —*f.* (*pl.*) Verbenaceae.
verbenear, *i.v.* to swarm, throng; to teem, abound.
verbenero, ra, *a.* of a night festival or evening party, e.g. *mi vestido v.,* my party dress.
verberación, *f.* lashing, beating, striking (esp. wind, water, rain).
verberar, *tr.v.* to lash, beat, strike.
verbigracia, *adv.* for example, for instance.
verbo, *m.* 1. (gram.) verb. 2. (theol.) Word (second person of the Trinity). 3. oath, vow, one's word. — **echar verbos,** to curse, swear; **en un v.,** (coll.) at once, without delay; **v. activo,** (gram). transitive verb, active verb; **v. adjetivo,** (gram.) any verb except *ser;* **v. auxiliar,** (gram.) auxiliary ver; **v. débil,** (gram.) weak verb; **v. defectivo,** (gram.) defective verb; **v. deponente,** (gram.) deponent verb; **v. determinado,** (gram.) verb governed by another in formation of a clause; **v. determinante,** (gram.) determining verb, verb governing another in the formation of a clause; **v. frecuentativo,** (gram.) frequentative verb; **v. fuerte,** (gram.) strong verb; **v. impersonal,** (gram.) impersonal verb; **v. incoativo,** (gram.) inchoative verb; **v. intransitivo,** (gram.) intransitive verb, neuter verb; **v. irregular,** (gram.) irregular verb; **v. neutro,** (gram.) neutral verb, intransitive; **v. pasivo,** (gram.) passive verb; **v. recíproco,** (gram.) reciprocal verb; **v. regular,** (gram.) regular verb; **v. reflejo** or **reflexivo,** (gram.) reflexive verb; **v. substantivo,** (gram.) the verb **ser; v. transitivo,** (gram.) transitive verb.
verborragia, verborrea, *f.* (coll.) verbosity, verboseness, wordiness.
verbosidad, *f.* verbosity, wordiness.
verboso, sa, *a.* verbose, wordy.
verdacho, *m.* (p.) green earth, terreverte.
verdad, *f.* 1. truth. 2. (*pl.*) home truths. — **a decir v., a la v.,** to tell the truth, to be truthful, be quite honest; **bien es v. que,** it is true that; **decir la v.,** to tell the truth; **decir a uno cuatro verdades** or **las verdades del barquero,** (coll.) to tell it like it is (U.S., sl.), give someone a piece of one's mind; **de v.,** truly, really; real, e.g. *un hombre de v.,* a real man; **en v.,** truly, really; **faltar a la v.,** to lie, be untruthful; **la pura v.,** the absolute truth; **ser v.,** to be true; **¿v.?** really? is that so?; isn't that so?; **v. de Perogrullo,** (coll.) truism, platitude; **v. es que,** it is true that; **verdades como puños,** (coll.) obvious truths.
verdaderamente, *adv.* truly, really.
verdadero, ra, *a.* 1. true, real, e.g. *nadie sabe la historia verdadera,* no one knows the true story. 2. real, genuine, e.g. *un diamante verdadero,* a real or genuine, diamond. 3. real, true, sincere, genuine, e.g. *un amigo verdadero,* a real or true friend.
verdal, *a.* green although ripe; **ciruela v.,** greengage.
verdasca, *f.* twig or thin branch.
verdascazo, *m.* blow with a twig or thin branch.
verde, *a.* 1. green, green-colored. 2. green, verdant, in leaf. 3. green, unripe, sour (fruit). 4. fresh, young, blooming. 5. green, immature, undeveloped. 6. (fig.) incipient; far from being ready. 7. risqué, smutty, off-color. 8. rakish; merry (old man, widow). —*m.* 1. green (color). 2. foliage, verdure. 3. (*pl.*) greens, fresh fodder. 4. harsh taste (of wine). — **darse un v.,** to have a fling; **están verdes,** sour grapes; **poner v. a,** to give (someone) a piece of one's mind, to tell someone off; **v. botella,** bottle green; **v. de montaña** or **de tierra,** mountain green, malachite, green copper carbonate; **v. esmeralda,** emerald green; **v. limón,** lime green; **v. mar,** sea green; **v. Nilo,** Nile green; **v. oliva,** olive green; **viejo v.,** old roué or rake.
verdea, *f.* greenish wine.
verdear, *tr.v.* to pick (grapes and olives). —*i.v.* 1. to grow or turn green (plants, fields). 2. to take on a greenish cast (certain dark colors).
verdeceledón, *m.* celadon, celadon green.
verdecer, (*ref. 45*) *i.v.* to grow green.
verdecillo, *m.* (ornith.) greenfinch.
verdegal, *m.* lush green patch (in a field).
verdegay, *a., m.* bright green.
verdeguear, *i.v.* 1. to grow or turn green. 2. to look green.
verdejo, ja, *a.* green; green although ripe (said of certain fruits).
verdemar, *a., m.* sea green.
verdemontaña, *m.* 1. (min.) mountain green, malachite. 2. mineral green, malachite green.
verdeo, *m.* olive harvest.
verderol, verderón, *m.* 1. (ornith.) greenfinch. 2. (zool.) cockle (Cardium edule).
verdete, *m.* 1. (chem.) verdigris. 2. (p.) verdigris, green, verditer.
verdevejiga, *m.* yellowish green pigment used in making paint.
verdezca, *ref.* **verdecer.**
verdezuelo, *m.* (ornith.) greenfinch.
verdín, *m.* 1. verdure, fresh greenness (of plants or vegetation). 2. pond scum; mold, mildew. 3. (chem.) verdigris. 4. green snuff.
verdina, *f.* verdure, fresh greenness (of plants).
verdinegro, gra, *a.* dark green.
verdino, na, *a.* bright green; greenish.
verdiseco, ca, *a.* 1. half-dried. 2. pale, dull green.
verdolaga, *f.* (bot.) purslane.
verdón, *m.* (ornith.) greenfinch.
verdor, *m.* 1. greenness; verdure, verdancy. 2. (fig.) freshness, vigor; (*pl.*) youth.
verdoso, sa, *a.* greenish.
verdoyo, *m.* verdure, fresh greenness (of young plants).
verdugada, *f.* (archit.) layer of bricks.
verdugado, *m.* hoopskirt, farthingale.
verdugal, *m.* cleared ground planted with young shoots or saplings.
verdugazo, *m.* lash, blow with a lash, whip or scourge.
verdugo, *m.* 1. hangman, executioner. 2. scion, sucker, young shoot (of a tree). 3. long rapier. 4. lash, whip, scourge. 5. wale, welt. 6. (jewel.) hoop (of ring). 7. (fig.) torment, plague (person or thing). 8. (archit.) layer of bricks. 9. hoopskirt, farthingale. 10. (ornith.) shrike, butcher bird.
verdugón, *m.* 1. sucker, scion, young shoot (of a tree). 2. large wale or welt.
verduguillo, *m.* 1. swelling (on the leaves of some plants). 2. straight razor. 3. long rapier. 4. hoop earring. 5. (mar.) sheer rail, sheer strake.
verdulera, *f.* 1. greengrocer, market woman. 2. (fig.) fishwife, coarse woman.
verdulería, *f.* greengrocer's shop.
verdulero, *m.* greengrocer.
verdura, *f.* 1. verdure, verdancy, greenness. 2. (*pl.*) greens, vegetables. 3. (p.) foliage, verdure.
verdusco, ca, *a.* dark greenish.
verecundia, *f.* modesty; bashfulness, shyness.
verecundo, da, *a.* bashful, shy.
vereda, *f.* 1. path, footpath, trail, way; (Amer.) sidewalk, pavement. 2. circular order or notice sent to several towns. — **hacer entrar por v.,** (coll.) to bring to reason, put on the right path.
veredero, *m.* delivery messenger who covers a fixed route.
veredicto, *m.* verdict; **v. inconcluso, (law)** open verdict; **v. de culpabilidad,** verdict of guilty; **v. de inculpabilidad,** verdict of not guilty.
verga, *f.* 1. (zool.) penis. 2. steel bow (of a crossbow). 3. (mar.) yard. 4. (anat.) (vulg.) dick, prick. — **v. seca,** (mar.) crossjack yard; **vergas en alto,** (mar.) all ready to sail.
vergajazo, *m.* whiplash, lash with a pizzle.
vergajo, *m.* pizzle, whip.
vergé, *a.* **papel v.,** laid paper, verge paper.
vergel, *m.* (poet.) garden; orchard.
vergelero, *m.* (rare) gardener.
vergeta, *f.* 1. rod, stick. 2. (her.) narrow pale.
vergeteado, *a.* (her.) having ten or more pales, paley.
vergonzante, *a.* bashful, shamefaced.
vergonzosamente, *adv.* 1. shamefully, disgracefully. 2. bashfully, shyly.
vergonzoso, sa, *a.* 1. shameful, disgraceful. 2. bashful, shy. —*m., f.* bashful or shy person. —*m.* (zool.) armadillo.
verguear, *tr.v.* to beat with a rod, to flog.
vergüenza, *f.* 1. shame; embarrassment. 2. shyness, bashfulness. 3. integrity, honor, self-respect, e.g. *v. torera,* bullfighter's professional integrity. 4. public punishment. 5. (*pl.*) private parts, genitals. — **darle a uno v.** + *inf.,* to be too shy to + *inf.,* e.g. *le da v. hablar en público,* he's too shy to speak in public; to be ashamed to + *inf.;* **darle a uno v. una cosa,** to be ashamed of something, e.g. *le da v. lo que hizo,* he's ashamed of what he did; **no tener v.,** to be shameless, brazen; **perder la v.,** to lose one's self-respect, become shameless; to overcome one's shyness; **¡ qué v.!** how disgraceful! how shameful!; **sacar a la v. a uno,** to punish someone publicly, make a public example of; (coll.) to put into an embarrassing position; **ser una mala v.,** (coll.) to be a shame or pity, be too bad; **tener v.,** to be or feel ashamed; **tener v. de** + *inf.,* to be too shy to + *inf.;* to be ashamed to + *inf.;* **v. te debe dar,** you ought to be ashamed of yourself; **v. te debe dar** + *inf.,* you ought to be ashamed to + *inf.*
vergueta, *f.* rod, stick, small switch.
vergueteado, *a.* **papel v.,** laid paper.
verguío, a, *a.* flexible, leathery (wood).
vericueto, *m.* rough, uneven ground; rough passage.
verídico, ca, *a.* true, truthful, veridical, e.g. *es un relato verídico,* it's a true story.
verificación, *f.* 1. verification, confirmation. 2. checking, examination, inspection. 3. fulfilment, realization.
verificador, ra, *a.* 1. verifying. 2. checking, examining, inspecting. —*m., f.* 1. verifier. 2. checker, examiner, inspector.
verificar, (*ref. 50*) *tr.v.* 1. to verify, confirm. 2. to check, examine, inspect. 3. to carry out; to fulfil, realize. —*r.v.* 1. to be verified; to prove true. 2. to take place, occur, be held.
verificativo, va, *a.* verificative, verificatory, verifying.
verifique, verifiqué, *ref.* **verificar.**
verigüeto, *m.* (zool.) venus (Venus verrucosa).
verija, *f.* 1. pubes, pubic region. 2. groin.

veril, *m.* (mar.) edge of a sand bank or shoal.
verilear, *i.v.* (mar.) to coast around a sand bank or shoal.
veringo, ga, *a.* (Col.) naked, nude.
verisímil, *a., var. of* **verosímil.**
verisimilitud, *f., var. of* **verosimilitud.**
verisímilmente, *adv., var. of* **verosímilmente.**
verismo, *m.* (art, mus., lit.) verism.
verja, *f.* railing, fence, grating, gate.
verjurado, *a.* **papel v.,** laid paper.
verme, *m.* (med.) intestinal worm.
vermicida, *a.* (med.) vermicidal. —*m.* (med.) vermicide.
vermicular, *a.* vermicular.
vermiculita, *f.* (min.) vermiculite.
vermiforme, *a.* vermiform, shaped like a worm.
vermífugo, ga, *a., m.* (med.) vermifuge, anthelmintic.
verminosis, *f.* (med.) verminosis.
verminoso, sa, *a.* verminous, infested with vermin.
vermívoro, ra, *a.* (zool.) vermivorous.
vermut, *m.* 1. vermouth. 2. (Amer.) late afternoon performance or showing.
vernación, *f.* (bot.) vernation.
vernáculo, la, *a.* vernacular.
vernal, *a.* vernal, spring; **equinoccio v.,** spring equinox.
vernier, *m.* vernier (scale, measuring instrument).
vero, *m.* 1. vair, marten (fur). 2. (*pl.*) (her.) vair.
veronense, veronés, sa, *a., m., f.* Veronese, of the Italian city of Verona.
verónica, *f.* 1. (bot.) speedwell. 2. (taur.) pass in bullfighting (receiving the charge with cape extended between both hands).
verosímil, *a.* probable, likely, credible, verisimilar.
verosimilitud, *f.* verisimilitude, probability, likelihood.
verosímilmente, *adv.* probably.
verraco, *m.* male hog or boar; (Col.) ram, male sheep.
verraquear, *i.v.* 1. (coll.) to grunt, grumble. 2. (coll.) to shriek, scream, keep on crying hard (said of children).
verraquera, *f.* 1. (coll.) violent crying, screaming (of children). 2. (Cuba) drunkenness.
verriondez, *f.* 1. rut, heat (said esp. of swine and sheep). 2. withered state (of plants). 3. toughness (of badly-cooked vegetables).
verriondo, da, *a.* 1. rutting, in heat (said esp. of swine and sheep). 2. badly cooked, tough (said of vegetables).
verrón, *m., var. of* **verraco.**
verruga, *f.* 1. (med., bot.) wart. 2. (coll.) nuisance, bore. 3. (coll.) fault, defect.
verrugo, *m.* (coll.) miser.
verrugoso, sa, *a.* warty, verrucose.
verrugueta, *f.* (sl.) cheating trick (in cards).
verruguetear, *tr.v.* (sl.) to cheat, trick (in cards).
versado, da, *a.* versed, conversant, proficient, knowledgeable.
versal, *a., f.* (print.) capital (letter).
versalilla, versalita, *a., f.* (print.) small capital (letter).
Versalles, *f.* Versailles.
versar, *i.v.* 1. to deal with, e.g. *v. acerca de* or *sobre* (subject of a book, etc.). 2. to go round, turn. 3. (Cuba, P. Rico) to versify, write verses or poetry. —*r.v.* to become versed (in) or conversant (with).
versátil, *a.* 1. changeable, fickle, unstable, versatile. 2. (bot., zool.) versatile. 3. versatile, many-sided, multifaceted, protean.
versatilidad, *f.* 1. changeableness, fickleness, instability. 2. versatility.
versear, *i.v.* (coll.) to versify, write verses or poetry.
versecillo, *m. dim. of* **verso,** little verse.
versícula, *f.* (ecc.) stand for choir books.
versiculario, *m.* (ecc.) chanter of versicles; keeper of choir books.
versículo, *m.* 1. verse (short division of chapters of Bible). 2. (ecc.) versicle.
versificación, *f.* versification.
versificador, ra, *a.* versifying. —*m., f.* versifier, one who writes verses.
versificante, *a.* versifying.
versificar, (*ref. 50*) *tr.v., i.v.* to versify, to write verses.
versifique, versifiqué, *ref.* **versificar.**
versión, *f.* 1. version, translation, e.g. *v. autorizada,* authorized version. 2. version, account; description. 3. (med.) version.
versista, *m., f.* versifier, verse maker or writer; poetaster.
verso, *m.* 1. verse, poetry; line (of a poem). 2. verse, versicle. — **v. acataléctico,** acatalectic, acatalectic verse; **v. agudo,** oxytone verse; **v. alejandrino,** Alexandrine; **v. amebeo,** amoeboid verse; **v. anapéstico,** anapaestic, anapaestic verse; **v. asclepiadeo,** Asclepiadean verse; **v. blanco,** free verse, vers libre, blank verse; **v. cataléctico,** catalectic verse; **v. coriámbico,** choriambic verse; **v. dactílico,** dactylic, dactylic verse; **v. de arte mayor,** verse of more than nine syllables; **v. de arte menor,** verse of less than nine syllables; **v. de redondilla mayor,** octosyllabic verse; **v. de redondilla menor,** hexasyllabic verse; **v. esdrújulo,** verse with final stress on antepenultimate syllable; **v. espondaico,** spondaic hexameter; **v. heroico,** heroic verse; **v. hexámetro,** hexameter; **v. libre,** vers libre, free verse; blank verse; **v. llano,** verse with final stress on penultimate syllable; **v. pentámetro,** pentameter; **v. sáfico,** sapphic verse; **v. suelto,** free verse, vers libre; blank verse; **v. trímetro, trimeter,** trimeter verse; **v. trocaico,** trochaic verse; **v. yámbico,** iambic, iambic verse; **versos fesceninos,** Fescennine obscene and satiric verses; **versos pareados,** couplet.
verso, *a.* (math.) versed, e.g. *coseno v.,* versed cosine. —*m.* 1. (print.) verso, left-hand page. 2. (artil.) small culverin.
versta, *f.* verst, former Russian unit of linear measure.
vértebra, *f.* (anat., zool.) vertebra.
vertebrado, *a., m.* (zool.) vertebrate. —*m.* (*pl.*) vertebrates, Vertebrata.
vertebral, *a.* vertebral.
vertedera, *f.* moldboard (of a plow).
vertedero, *m.* 1. sink. 2. dumping place, dumping ground. 3. spillway, wasteway.
vertedor, *a.* pouring; emptying. —*m.* 1. spillway, wasteway. 2. grocer's scoop. 3. (mar.) bailer, bailing scoop.
vertellos, *m., pl.* (mar.) balls of the parrel truck.
verter, (*ref. 30*) *tr.v.* 1. to pour, empty; to dump. 2. to translate (from one language to another). 3. to express, voice (opinions, concepts). —*i.v.* to run, flow, pour. —*r.v.* to pour, empty.
vertibilidad, *f.* ability to change.
vertible, *a.* changeable.
vertical, *a.* vertical. —*m.* (astron.) vertical circle; **primer v.,** prime vertical. —*f.* vertical (line).
verticalidad, *f.* verticality.
verticalmente, *adv.* vertically.
vértice, *m.* 1. vertex, apex. 2. (geom., anat.) vertex.
verticidad, *f.* mobility.
verticilado, da, *a.* (bot., anat.) verticillate.
verticilo, *m.* (bot., anat.) verticil, whorl.
vertiente, *a.* flowing, pouring, emptying. —*m., f.* 1. slope. 2. (archit.) slope; drip stone. —*f.* (Chile) spring.
vertiginosidad, *f.* speed, celerity.
vertiginoso, sa, *a.* 1. giddy, dizzy, vertiginous, causing dizziness. 2. rapid, sudden, accelerated, e.g. *rapidez* or *velocidad vertiginosa,* lightning speed.
vértigo, *m.* 1. vertigo, giddiness, dizziness. 2. fit of insanity. 3. rush, accelerated rhythm (e.g. of modern life, town life).
vertimiento, *m.* pouring; emptying; running, flowing.
vesania, *f.* 1. insanity. 2. fury.
vesánico, ca, *a.* insane, mad. —*m., f.* insane person.
vesical, *a.* (anat.) vesical.
vesicante, *a., m.* vesicant.
vesícula, *f.* (med., anat., bot., zool.) vesicle; **v. aérea,** (anat.) air vesicle or cell (of the lungs); **v. biliar,** (anat.) gall bladder; **v. elemental** or **orgánica,** (biol.) cell; **v. ovárica,** (anat.) Graafian follicle or vesicle; **v. seminal,** (anat.) sperm sac.
vesicular, *a.* vesicular.
vesiculoso, sa, *a.* vesiculate, vesiculous.
vespasiana, *f.* (Arg., Chile) public urinal, public lavatory.
vesperal, *m.* 1. (ecc.) vesperal (book). 2. pertaining to the afternoon or early evening.
véspero, *m.* Vesper, evening star.
vespertillo, *m.* (zool.) bat.
vespertino, na, *a.* vespertine, evening, crepuscular. —*m., f.* evening sermon.
véspidos, *m.* (*pl.*) (ento.) Vespidae.
Vespucio, *m.* (hist.) Vespucci (Amerigo), Italian navigator and explorer.
Vesta, (astron., myth.) Vesta.
vestal, *a.* vestal. —*f.* vestal, vestal virgin.
veste, *f.* (poet.) garment, robe, vestment.
vestfaliano, na, *a., m., f.* (geog.) Westphalian.
vestíbulo, *m.* 1. vestibule, hall, foyer, lobby. 2. (anat.) vestibule.
vestido, *m.* dress, garment, costume, suit; clothes, garb; **v. de corte,** court dress; **v. de etiqueta,** full dress, evening clothes; **v. de fiesta,** party dress; **v. de noche,** evening gown; evening clothes; **v. de novia,** wedding dress; **v. de paisano,** civilian dress, mufti.
vestidura, *f.* 1. clothing, clothes, dress. 2. (ecc.) vestments.
vestigio, *m.* 1. vestige, trace, sign. 2. (*pl.*) ruins. 3. (chem.) traces.
vestiglo, *m.* horrible monster.
vestimenta, *f.* dress, clothes, garments. 2. (ecc.) vestments.
vestir, (*ref. 39*) *tr.v.* 1. to dress, clothe, attire. 2. to wear (a dress, etc.). 3. to clothe, cover, e.g. *la nieve vestía los campos de blanco,* the snow clothed the fields in white. 4. to adorn, bedeck, embellish. 5. to disguise, cover up. 6. to dress, make clothes for. — **quedarse para v. santos,** to remain a spinster or old maid; **v. de** or **con,** to clothe or cover with; to dress in, e.g. *siempre la vestían de blanco,* they always dressed her in white; **v. el cargo,** to look the part, look right for a position or employment. —*i.v.* 1. to look well, elegant or smart (certain color or fabric when worn), e.g. *el color negro viste siempre mucho,* black always looks elegant or smart. 2. to dress, e.g. *él viste bien,* he dresses well. — **v. de,** to wear, e.g. *v. de blanco,* to wear white, *v. de etiqueta,* to wear an evening dress; *v. de paisano,* to wear civilian clothes. —*r.v.* 1. to dress oneself; to get dressed. 2. to become covered or clothed. 3. to dress, e.g. *él se viste siempre a la última moda,* he always dresses in the latest fashion. 4. to put on an air, e.g. *vestirse*

de humildad, to put on an air of humility. — **vestirse de,** to wear; to become covered or clothed with.
vestuario, *m.* 1. wardrobe, clothes, apparel; (theat.) wardrobe, costumes, (mil.) uniform. 2. cloakroom; (theat.) dressing room; (ecc.) vestry. 3. (ecc.) vestment or clothing allowance.
vestugo, *m.* (bot.) olive tree shoot or scion.
vesubianita, *f.* (min.) vesuvianite, vesuvian.
vesubiano, na, *a.* Vesuvian.
Vesubio, *m.* (geog.) Vesuvius.
veta, *f.* 1. (min.) vein, seam, lode. 2. vein, streak, stripe (in wood, stone, etc.). 3. (*pl.*) streaks, blond-tipping (hair). — **descubrir la v. de uno,** (coll.) to catch on to someone's intentions or plans; **v. madre,** main vein.
vetado, da, *a., var. of* **veteado.**
vetar, *tr.v.* (Amer.) to veto.
vetazo, *m.* (Ecuad.) whiplash, lash.
veteado, da, *a.* grained, veined, streaked, striped; watermarked (paper); unevenly faded (fabric); tipped, blond-streaked (hair).
veteador, *m.* grainer, graining brush (for graining wood).
vetear, *tr.v.* 1. to grain, streak (wood, marble). 2. to tip, streak (hair). 3. (Ecuad.) to whip.
veterano, na, *a., m., f.* veteran.
veterinario, ria, *a.* veterinary. —*m., f.* veterinary surgeon, veterinarian, vet. —*f.* veterinary medicine.
vetisesgado, da, *a.* diagonally streaked or striped.
vetiver, *m.* (bot.) vetiver.
veto, *m.* veto; prohibition.
vetustez, *f.* antiquity; old age.
vetusto, ta, *a.* ancient, very old; decrepit.
vez, (*pl.* **veces**), *f.* 1. time; turn. 2. drove, herd. — **a veces,** sometimes, occasionally; **a la v.,** at the same time, simultaneously; **a la v. que,** at the same time as, while; **alguna v.,** once; **alguna que otra v.,** occasionally, once in a while, sometimes; **a su v.,** in turn, in his turn; for his, her or one's part; **a veces,** at times; sometimes; **cada v. más,** more and more, e.g. *se pone cada v. más bonita,* she gets more and more beautiful; **cada v. que,** whenever, every time that; **de una v.,** now, right away, without more ado; **de una v. por todas,** once and for all; **de v. en cuando,** from time to time, sometimes; **dos veces,** twice; **dos veces más grande, rico** etc. **que,** twice as big, rich, etc. as; **en v. de,** instead of, in place of; **era** or **érase una v.,** once upon a time; **hacer las veces de,** to stand in for, substitute, replace; **las más veces,** in most cases, most of the time; **muchas veces,** many times, often; **otra v.,** once again, again; some other time; **pocas veces,** seldom, rarely; **rara v., raras veces,** seldom, rarely; **repetidas veces,** repeatedly, time after time; **tal cual v.,** on rare occasions, once in a while; **tal v.,** perhaps, maybe; possibly; **tener las veces de,** to have the rank or status of; to replace, substitute, be in place of; **toda v. que,** since, inasmuch as; **una v.,** once; **una v. que,** once, as soon as, when; **una que otra v.,** once in a while, on rare occasions.
veza, *f.* (bot.) vetch (Vicia monantha).
vezar, (*ref.* *53*) *tr.v.* to accustom. —*r.v.* to become accustomed.
vg., v.g., v.gr., *abbrev. of* **verbigracia,** for example (e.g.).
vi, *ref.* **ver.**
vía, *f.* 1. road, way, route, track; street, thoroughfare. 2. (ry.) track, line; rail (of track). 3. (anat.) passage, tract, duct, canal. 4. way, manner, method, means; (law) procedure, proceeding. 5. (chem.) way, process, method. 6. channel, agent, medium. — **cuaderna v.,** stanza of four monorhymed Alexandrines (used mostly in 13th and 14th centuries); **de cuatro vías,** four-way, e.g. *llave de cuatro vías,* four-way switch; **de doble v.,** two-track, two-way; **en v. de desarrollo,** in the process of development, developing, e.g. *países en v. de desarrollo,* countries in the process of development; **en v. directa,** straight, directly; **estar en vías de** + *inf.,* to be on the way to + *ger.,* be in the process of + *ger.,* e.g. *la cuestión está en vías de resolverse,* the matter is on the way to or in the process of being solved; **por la v. de,** via, through; **por v. aérea,** by air; by airmail; **por v. de buen gobierno,** governmentally, by government or official channels; **por v. oral,** orally; **por v. ordinaria,** by surface mail; **por v. marítima,** by sea; by seamail; **por v. terrestre,** by land; by surface mail; **V. Apia,** Appian Way; **v. contenciosa,** (law) legal action; **V. Crucis,** (ecc.) Via Crucis, Way of the Cross; (fig.) affliction, calvary; **v. de abastecimiento,** (mil.) supply line; **v. de agua,** (mar.) leak; **v. de comunicación,** communication route; **v. de corrido,** (ry.) running track; **v. de tránsito,** traffic lane; **v. ejecutiva,** (law) legal procedure to obtain payment of debt attested by specific documents or bills of exchange; **v. férrea,** railroad, railway; **v. fluvial,** waterway; **v. húmeda,** (chem.) wet way, process or method; **V. Láctea,** (astron.) Milky Way; **v. muerta,** (ry.) siding, sidetrack; **v. ordinaria,** (law) ordinary judicial proceedings, regular way, regular channels, standard procedure; **v. principal,** (ry.) running track; **v. pública,** public thoroughfare; **v. sacra,** (ecc.) Way of the Cross; **vías de hecho,** force, violence; **vías digestivas,** digestive tract; **v. seca,** (chem.) dry way or process; **vías respiratorias,** respiratory tract; **v. sumaria,** (law) summary proceedings; **v. tranviaria,** streetcar or tramway track; **vías urinarias,** urinary tract.
viabilidad, *f.* 1. viability. 2. feasibility, practicableness.
viable, *a.* 1. viable, capable of living. 2. feasible, practicable. 3. transitable.
viadera, *f.* harness shaft (of an ancient type of loom).
viador, *m.* (theol.) traveler (in a mystical sense).
viaducto, *m.* viaduct.
viajador, ra, *m., f.* traveler.
viajante, *a.* traveling. —*m., f.* traveler. —*m.* traveling salesman.
viajar, *i.v.* to travel, journey.
viajata, *f.* (coll.) pleasure trip, excursion, short journey.
viaje, *m.* 1. journey, trip, voyage, tour, travel. 2. way, road. 3. load, loadful (carried at one time). 4. travel book, travel diary. 5. water supply. 6. (coll.) attack, thrust, blow or cut with a sword, etc. 7. (archit.) obliquity, slope. 8. (C. Amer.) blow, hit; (Dom. Rep.) push, shove. — **de un v.,** (Amer.) at one stroke, once and for all; all at once; **¡buen v.!** bon voyage! have a good trip; **de v.,** traveling, on a trip; (Dom. Rep.) immediately, at once; **de viajes,** travel, e.g. *agencia de viajes,* travel agency; **v. circular,** circular tour, round trip (permitting stops); **v. de estado,** state visit; **v. de negocios,** business trip; **v. de novios,** honeymoon; **v. de placer,** pleasure trip; **v. oficial,** official visit; **v. organizado,** package tour; **v. redondo** or **v. de ida y vuelta,** round trip; **v. relámpago,** quick trip; **Viajes de Gulliver,** Gulliver's Travels.
viajero, ra, *a.* traveling, journeying. —*m., f.* traveler; passenger.
vial, *a.* pertaining to roads, streets, highways. —*m.* avenue, boulevard; lane.
vialidad, *f.* road or highway system or service.
vianda, *f.* 1. food, viand; (Cuba) (*pl.*) roots, vegetables. 2. (Arg., Urug., Chile) lunch pail.
viandante, *m., f.* 1. traveler; wayfarer. 2. tramp, vagabond.
viaraza, *f.* 1. diarrhea; looseness of the bowels. 2. sudden rash act.
viaticar, (*ref.* *50*) *tr.v.* (ecc.) to administer the viaticum or last rites to.
viático, *m.* 1. viaticum (provisions for a journey; traveling allowance). 2. (ecc.) viaticum.
víbora, *f.* 1. (zool.) viper. 2. (fig.) viper, malignant person. — **v. ciega, v. de dos cabezas,** (zool.) blind snake; **v. de agua,** (zool.) moccasin; **v. de cascabel,** (zool.) rattlesnake; **v. de coral,** (zool.) coral snake; **v. del desierto,** (zool.) puff adder; **v. europea,** (zool.) adder.
viborán *m.* (C. Amer., bot.) milkweed (Asclepias curassavica).
viborezno, na, *a.* viperine, viperous. —*m.* young viper.
vibración, *f.* vibration; **v. amortiguada,** (engin.) damped vibration; **v. armónica,** harmonic vibration; **v. simpática,** sympathetic vibration.
vibrador, ra, *a.* vibrating; quivering. —*m.* vibrator.
vibrante, *a.* 1. vibrating. 2. (fig.) vibrant; resonant. 3. (phonet.) trilled, rolled (consonant). —*f.* trilled or rolled consonant (the letter r).
vibrar, *i.v.* to vibrate; to quiver. —*tr.v.* 1. to vibrate, brandish, make quiver. 2. to vibrate, cast, hurl. 3. (phonet.) to trill, roll.
vibrátil, *a.* vibratile.
vibratorio, ria, *a.* vibratory, vibrative.
vibrión, *m.* (bac.) vibrio, vibrion.
vibrisa, *f.* (anat., zool., ornith.) vibrissa.
vibrómetro, *m.* (engin.) vibrometer.
viburno, *m.* (bot.) viburnum, wayfaring tree.
vicaria, *f.* 1. vicaress (assistant mother superior). 2. (Cuba, bot.) red periwinkle (Vinca rosea).
vicaría, *f.* 1. vicarship, vicariate (office, authority or jurisdiction of vicar). 2. vicar's office.
vicarial, *a.* vicarial.
vicariato, *m.* 1. vicarship, vicariate (office or authority of vicar). 2. vicar's office. 3. vicariate, period in which vicar holds office.
vicario, ria, *a.* substitute. —*m.* 1. vicar, deputy, substitute. 2. (in Roman Catholic Church) vicar, ecclesiastic acting as substitute for superior; **v. del imperio,** vicar or viceregent of the Holy Roman Empire; **v. de Jesucristo,** Vicar of Christ, the Pope; **v. de monjas,** chaplain of a convent.
vicealmiranta, *f.* vice-admiral's flagship.
vicealmirantazgo, *m.* vice-admiralty.
vicealmirante, *m.* vice-admiral.
vicecanciller, *m.* vice-chancellor.
vicecancillería, *f.* vice-chancellorship; vice-chancellery.
viceconsiliario, *m.* vice-counsellor.
vicecónsul, *m.* vice-consul.
viceconsulado, *m.* vice-consulate.
vicecristo, vicedios, *m.* vice-Christ, vice-God (title given to the Pope).
vicegerencia, *f.* 1. assistant managership, position of assistant manager. 2. vice-gerency.
vicegerente, *m.* 1. assistant manager. 2. vicegerent.
vicegobernador, *m.* vice-governor.
vicenal, *a.* vicennial.
vicepresidencia, *f.* vice-presidency.
vicepresidente, ta, *m., f.* vice-president.
viceprovincia, *f.* (ecc.) group of communities or convents enjoying the rank of a province.
viceprovincial, *a.* (ecc.) of a group of communities or convents. —*m.* (ecc.) vice-provincial.

vicerrector, ra, *m.* vice-rector. —*f.* vice-rectoress.
vicesecretaría, *f.* vice-secretaryship.
vicesecretario, ria, *m., f.* vice-secretary, assistant secretary.
vicésima, *f.* five percent property tax (in ancient Rome).
vicésimo, ma, *a., m., f.* twentieth.
vicetesorero, ra, *m., f.* vice-treasurer, assistant treasurer.
viceversa, *adv.* vice versa, conversely. —*m.* the opposite, the reverse.
vicia, *f.* (bot.) vetch (Vicia monantha).
viciado, da, *past part. of* **viciar.** —*a.* foul, polluted, vitiated (e.g. air).
viciar, *tr.v.* 1. to vitiate, corrupt, debase, deprave, pervert. 2. to vitiate, contaminate, pollute; to spoil. 3. to adulterate (goods, food); to falsify, change. 4. to vitiate, invalidate, nullify. 5. to misconstrue, twist the meaning of. —*r.v.* 1. to become vitiated, polluted or contaminated; to become spoiled. 2. to become depraved or perverted. 3. to become addicted. 4. to warp, become warped.
vicio, *m.* 1. vice, bad habit (in human being and animal). 2. vice, depravity, perversion, corruption. 3. defect, flaw, fault, error, vice. 4. addiction (to), passion (for something). 5. warping (of surface). 6. excessive foliage, excessive growth of leaves. 7. overindulgence, spoiling. — **de v.,** through spoiling or overindulgence; from sheer caprice, without reason, from habit; **quejarse de v.,** (coll.) to complain without reason, grumble or whine over nothing; **tener el v. de,** to have the habit of.
vicioso, sa, *a.* 1. addicted to vice; licentious; depraved, perverted. 2. faulty, defective. 3. strong, robust, vigorous. 4. luxuriant, abundant, exuberant. 5. (coll.) spoiled, overindulged. —*m., f.* depraved person; addict.
vicisitud, *f.* vicissitude.
vicisitudinario, ria, *a.* vicissitudinary.
víctima, *f.* victim.
victimar, *tr.v.* (imp. u.) to sacrifice; (Amer.) to kill, murder.
victimario, *m.* 1. assistant of a sacrificing priest. 2. (imp. u.) killer, murderer.
victo, *m.* daily sustenance, daily bread.
víctor, *interj., var. of* **vítor.**
victorear, *tr.v., var. of* **vitorear.**
victoria, *f.* 1. victory, triumph, conquest. 2. victoria (carriage). 3. (bot.) victoria. — **cantar v.,** to proclaim a victory; **v. a lo Pirro,** Pyrrhic victory.
victoriano, na, *a.* Victorian.
victoriosamente, *adv.* victoriously.
victorioso, sa, *a.* victorious.
vicuña, *f.* (zool.) vicuña (animal, wool); vicuña, vicuña cloth.
vichador, *m.* (S. Amer.) watcher; lookout.
vichar, *tr.v.* (S. Amer.) to watch; to see.
vichy, *m.* vichy, cotton fabric.
vid, *f.* (bot.) grapevine; **v. salvaje** or **silvestre,** wild grapevine.
vida, *f.* 1. life (animate existence, aliveness), e.g. *él dio su v. por la patria,* he gave his life for his country, *el cuerpo estaba sin v.,* the body was lifeless. 2. life, lifetime, life span. 3. life, way of life, e.g. *una v. difícil,* a difficult life. 4. living, livelihood, daily bread. 5. life, person, e.g. *se salvaron muchas vidas,* many lives were saved. 6. life, biography. 7. loose life, prostitution, e.g. *echarse a* or *ser de la v.,* to become or be a prostitute. 8. (coll.) darling, sweetheart, love, honey. 9. life, vitality, vivacity, liveliness, sparkle; brightness, color. — **buena** or **gran v.,** easy life; **buscarse la v.,** to hustle, seek a living or livelihood; **carestía de la v.,** high cost of living; **con v.,** alive; **costarle la v. a uno,** to cost someone his life; **costo de la v.,** cost of living; **dar la v. a,** to give a new lease on life to, strengthen, relieve; **dar la v. por,** to give one's life for; **dar mala v. a,** to treat badly; **darse la gran v.,** (coll.) to live an easy life, enjoy oneself; **dar v. a,** to give life to, liven up, enliven, brighten up; **de mala v.,** loose-living, debauched, licentious; **de por v.,** for life, life; **en la v., en mi (tu, su) v.,** never; **enterrarse en v.,** to bury oneself alive, become a recluse or hermit, retire from the world; **entre la v. y la muerte,** at death's door, between life and death; **en v.,** in or during one's lifetime; **escapar con v.,** to come out or escape alive; **ganar** or **ganarse la v.,** to earn one's living or livelihood; **hacer por la v.,** (coll.) to eat; **hacer v. en común,** to live together; **jugarse la v.,** to risk one's life; **llevar una v. de perros,** to live a dog's life; **mudar de v.,** to change one's ways, turn over a new leaf; **la otra v.,** the afterlife, the life to come; **pasar a mejor v.,** to die, pass on; **pasar la v. a tragos,** (coll.) to live a dog's life, live a difficult life; **darse la gran v.,** to live a life of ease, enjoy oneself; **perder la v.,** to lose one's life; **¡por v.!** by Jove!; please! I beg you!; **¡por v. mía!** upon my life! truly, really; **¿qué es de tu v.?** how's life with you, how are things, how are you getting on; **quitarse la v.,** to take one's life; **tener siete vidas como el gato,** to have nine lives; **vender cara la v.,** to kill many before being killed; **v. airada,** loose life, licentious life; prostitution; **v. ancha,** (coll.) licentious life, loose life; **v. animal,** animal life or fauna; **v. capulina,** (Mex.) easy life, life of ease; **v. canonicial, v. de canónigo,** (coll.) comfortable, quiet life, easy life; **v. de perros,** (coll.) dog's life, difficult life; **v. eterna,** everlasting life; **v. marina,** marine life or fauna; **¡v. mía!** my love! my dearest! my darling!; **v. y milagros de,** (coll.) life history of, all the details of (someone's) life.
vidalita, *f.* (Arg., Urug.) plaintive folk song.
vidarra, *f.* (bot.) clematis, virgin's-bower, traveler's-joy.
videncia, *f.* clear-sightedness, perspicacity.
vidente, *a.* seeing; sighted (endowed with sight). —*m.* seer, prophet.
video, vídeo, (Esp.), *a., m.* (tel.) 1. video, e.g. *lo grabamos en v.,* we recorded it on video. 2. videotape, videocassette. 3. videocassette recorder, VCR. 4, video recording.
videocámara, *f.* video camera, camcorder.
videocasete, videocassette, *m.* videocassette, videotape.
videocinta, *f.* videotape, videocassette.
videoclip, *m.* video clip.
videoclub, *m.* video club.
videoconferencia, *f.* videoconference.
videodisco, *m.* videodisk, videodisc.
video doméstico, *m.* video.
videofilm *m.* videofilm.
videófono, *m.* videophone.
videofrecuencia, *f.* video frequency.
videograbación, *f.* video recording.
videograbar, *tr.v.* to videotape, to video.
videojuego, *m.* video game.
videopiratería, *f.* video piracy.
videoproyector, *m.* videoprojector.
videoteca, *f.* video library.
videoteléfono, *m.* videophone.
videoterminal, *f.* (comput.) terminal, VDU.
videotex, videotexto, *m.* videotex, videotext, teletext.
vidicón, *m.* (tel.) vidicon.
vidita, *f.* (Amer.) dearest, darling.
vidorra, *f.* (coll.) life of ease, easy life.
vidorria, *f.* (Arg., Col., Ven., coll.) dog's life, hard or difficult life.
vidriado, da, *past part. of* **vidriar.** —*a.* 1. vitreous. 2. glazed. —*m.* 1. glazed earthenware, crockery, chinaware. 2. glaze (on earthenware or crockery); glazing (action).
vidriar, *tr.v.* to glaze (earthenware, crockery, chinaware). —*r.v.* to become glassy or glazed.
vidriera, *f.* glass window or door; stained glass window; (Amer.) show window, shopwindow; (Cuba) glass case, show case; **v. de colores,** stained glass window.
vidriería, *f.* glassworks, glass factory; glaziery, glass shop.
vidriero, *m.* glazier, glassworker; glass dealer.
vidrio, *m.* 1. glass; glassware. 2. seat with its back to the driver (in a carriage). 3. (fig.) touchy person. 4. (Amer.) window, window pane. — **ir al v.,** to ride with one's back to the driver (in a coach); **pagar los vidrios rotos,** to get the blame; **lana de v.,** glass wool; **v. ahumado,** smoked glass; **v. a prueba de bala,** bulletproof glass; **v. cilindrado** or **en planchas,** plate glass; **v. de aumento,** magnifying glass; **v. de color,** stained glass; **v. hilado,** spun glass; **v. prismático,** prism glass; **v. soluble,** soluble or water glass; **v. soplado,** blown glass.
vidriosidad, *f.* vitreousness, glassiness.
vidrioso, sa, *a.* 1. vitreous, glassy. 2. slippery. 3. touchy. 4. fragile, delicate.
vidual, *a.* pertaining to widowhood.
vidueño, viduño, *m.* variety of grapevine.
vieja, *f.* 1. (ichth.) small armored catfish. 2. (Chile) serpent firecracker, squib.
viejarrón, na, *a., m., f., var. of* **vejarrón.**
viejezuelo, la, *a., dim. of* **viejo,** little old man. —*f.* little old woman.
viejo, ja, *a.* old (aged; ancient, antique; stale, passé; worn out); **el vieja guardia,** the old guard; **el V. Mundo,** the Old World; **el V. Testamento,** the Old Testament. —*m.* old man; **v. verde,** dirty old man. —*f.* old woman.
Viena, *f.* Vienna, capital of Austria.
viendo, *ref.* **ver.**
vienés, sa, *a., m., f.* Viennese.
vienta, viente, *ref.* **ventar.**
viento, *m.* 1. wind (strong current of air); air. 2. (hunt.) wind, scent (of game). 3. wind, intestinal gas. 4. (mar.) course, direction. 5. (artil.) windage. 6. (fig.) wind, vanity, boasting, conceit. 7. bracing rope, guy. 8. bone between ears (in dogs). — **a los cuatro vientos,** in every direction; to everyone, to the wide world; **beber los vientos por,** (coll.) to do one's utmost to obtain, move heaven and earth to get; to want or desire passionately; **como el v.,** like the wind, swiftly; **contra el v.,** against the wind; **contra v. y marea,** against all odds, come what may; **corren malos vientos,** the conditions are unfavorable; **correr v.,** to blow (the wind); **echarse el v.,** to calm down; **hacer v.,** to be windy; **irse con el v. que corre,** (coll.) to go the way the wind blows, follow public opinion, swim with the current (fig.); **llevarse el v. una cosa,** to be unstable or light; **medio v.,** wind blowing halfway between cardinal and intercardinal points; **moverse a todos vientos,** to be fickle, inconstant or changeable; (coll.) to be easily influenced; **picar el v.,** (mar.) to blow favorably (the wind); (coll.) to go well or full speed ahead (an enterprise); **saltar el v.,** (mar.) to change suddenly (the wind); **v. a la cuadra,** (mar.) quarter wind, wind blowing at right angles to the ship's course;

v. calmoso, (mar.) light intermittent wind; **v. cardinal,** cardinal wind; **v. de bolina,** (mar.) scant wind; **v. de cola, v. trasero,** (aer.) tail wind; **v. de costado,** crosswind; **v. de proa,** (mar.) dead wind, head wind; **v. en popa,** (mar.) following wind; before the wind, e.g. *ir v. en popa,* to sail before the wind; (coll.) full speed ahead; successfully, fine; **v. entero,** cardinal or intercardinal wind; **v. etesio,** (mar.) etesian, etesian wind; **v. frescachón,** (mar.) strong wind, moderate gale; **v. fresco,** (mar.) strong breeze; **v. largo,** (mar.) quarter wind, wind blowing at right angles to course of ship; **v. marero,** (mar.) sea wind; **v. terral,** (mar.) land wind; **vientos alisios,** (mar.) trade winds; **vientos altanos,** (mar.) alternating land and sea winds; **vientos antialisios,** (mar.) antitrade winds.

vientre, *m.* 1. belly, stomach, abdomen; bowels; womb; viscera, innards, guts. 2. fetus, unborn child. 3. belly (of bottle, vessel, etc.). 4. (phys.) loop, bulge (in wave). — **bajo v.,** hipogastrium, lower abdomen; **constiparse el v.,** to become constipated; **de v.,** breeding (of a female animal destined for breeding); **evacuar** or **mover el v., hacer de** or **del v.,** to defecate, to have a bowel movement.

viera, *ref.* **ver.**

viernes, (*pl.* **viernes**), *m.* Friday. — **cara de v.,** (coll.) pale, wan face or look; **comer de v.,** to fast; **V. Santo,** Good Friday.

vierta, *ref.* **verter.**

vierteaguas, (*pl.* **vierteaguas**), *m.* (bldg.) flashing, drip plate.

vierto, *ref.* **verter.**

viese, *ref.* **ver.**

Vietnam del Norte, *f.* North Vietnam.

Vietnam del Sur, *f.* South Vietnam.

vietnamés, sa, vietnamita, *a., m., f.* Vietnamese.

viga, *f.* 1. beam, girder, rafter, joist. 2. screw press. 3. batch or portion of olives pressed at one time. — **contar or estar contando las vigas,** (coll.) to gaze blankly into space; **v. de alma llena,** (bldg.) plate girder.

vigencia, *f.* 1. force, effect operation, use. 2. vogue. — **en v.,** in force; in vogue.

vigente, *a.* in force, e.g. *leyes vigentes,* laws in force; in vogue, present, e.g. *costumbres vigentes,* customs in vogue, present customs.

vigesimal, *a.* vegisimal.

vigésimo, ma, *a.* twentieth, vigesimal. —*m.* twentieth (part).

vigía, *f.* 1. lookout post or tower, watchtower. 2. (mar.) reef, shoal. —*m.* lookout.

vigiar, (*ref.* *54*) *tr.v.* to watch, keep a lookout on.

vigilancia, *f.* vigilance, watchfulness.

vigilante, *a.* vigilant, watchful. —*m.* watchman, guard, guardian; (Amer.) policeman.

vigilantemente, *adv.* vigilantly.

vigilar, *tr.v.* to watch; to keep an eye on; to guard; to superintend, oversee. —*i.v.* to watch, keep guard; **v. sobre** or **por,** to watch over, keep watch over; to look after, take care of.

vigilativo, va, *a.* causing sleeplessness.

vigilia, *f.* 1. vigil, watch. 2. sleeplessness, wakefulness. 3. night study or work. 4. eye; (ecc.) vigil (eve of church feast; service on eve of feast). 5. mass for the dead. 6. (mil.) watch, guard (division of night guard). 7. meatless meal or day. — **comer de v.,** to have a meatless meal, abstain from meat.

vigor, *m.* 1. vigor, strength, stamina, energy. 2. force, effect. — **entrar en v.,** to go into force or effect; **poner en v.,** to put into force or effect.

vigorar, *tr.v., var of* **vigorizar.**

vigorice, vigoricé, *ref,* **vigorizar.**

vigorizador, ra, *a.* invigorating.

vigorizar, (*ref.* *53*) *tr.v.* 1. to invigorate. 2. (fig.) to encourage. —*r.v.* 1. to be invigorated. 2. to be encouraged.

vigorosamente, *adv.* lustily, vigorously.

vigorosidad, *f.* vigorousness, strength.

vigoroso, sa, *a.* vigorous, strong, energetic.

vigota, *f.* (mar.) deadeye.

viguería, *f.* girders, beams.

vigués, sa, *a.* of or from Vigo, Spain. —*m., f.* native or inhabitant of Vigo.

vigueta, *f.* small beam; laminated iron girder.

vihuela, *f.* (mus.) former name of the guitar; an ancient type of guitar.

vihuelista, *m., f.* formerly guitarist, guitar player.

vikingo, *m.* viking.

vil, *a.* despicable, base, vile, dastardly; ignoble, infamous.

vilano, *m.* (bot.) pappus; thistle flower, bur.

vileza, *f.* baseness, despicableness, infamy, vileness.

vilipendiador, ra, *a.* reviling, insulting, denigrating, disparaging. —*m., f.* reviler, insulter, denigrator.

vilipendiar, *tr.v.* to revile, insult, vilify, denigrate, disparage.

vilipendio, *m.* insult, revilement, vilification, disparagement.

vilipendioso, sa, *a.* disgraceful, shameful, despicable.

villa, *f.* 1. villa, country house. 2. town. — **v. miseria,** (Arg.) shantytown.

Villadiego, coger or **tomar las de Villadiego,** to go away, beat it (sl.), take it on the lam (sl., U.S.).

villaje, *m.* village; hamlet.

villanada, *f.* despicable act, infamy.

villanaje, *m.* 1. peasantry; villagers. 2. villeinage.

villanamente, *adv.* basely, despicably, villainously.

villancejo, villancete, villancico, *m.* Christmas carol.

villanciquero, *m.* caroler (singer of carols); composer of Christmas carols.

villanería, *f.* 1. baseness, despicableness, villainy, base or despicable act. 2. peasant status, status of a peasant.

villanesca, *f.* villanella, country song and dance.

villanesco, ca, *a.* peasant, e.g. *traje villanesco,* peasant dress.

villanía, *f.* 1. humble birth, lowness of birth. 2. base or despicable act, villainy; vile word or remark.

villano, na, *a.* 1. coarse, impolite, discourteous, rude. 2. base, low, despicable, villainous. —*m., f.* 1. peasant, villain, villein, villager. 2. villain, bad man. —*m.* villanella (country song and dance).

villazgo, *m.* charter of a town; ancient town tax.

villeta, *f. dim. of* **villa,** small small town or hamlet.

villoría, *f.* country house or settlement; farm house, ranch house.

villorín, *m.* formerly used broadcloth of undyed wool.

villorrio, *m.* (derog.) little village.

vilmente, *adv.* despicably, basely, vilely, infamously.

vilo, (fig.) **en v.** suspended, in the air; unstable, insecure; undecided, in the air, uncertain.

vilordo, da, *a.* lazy, slothful, idle.

vilorta, *f.* 1. wooden hoop or ring. 2. iron band or clasp (securing sheath to beam of plow). 3. washer (preventing friction between two pieces). 4. game similar to lacrosse. 5. (bot.) clematis.

vilorto, *m.* 1. (bot.) clematis. 2. crosse, racket (used in **vilorta**).

vilos, *m.* (Phil. I.) type of two-masted coasting vessel.

vilote, *a.* (Arg., Chile) cowardly.

viltrotear, *i.v.* to gad about, gallivant about, be always out of the house.

viltrotera, *f.* gadabout, gallivanter.

vimbre, *m., var. of* **mimbre.**

vimbrera, *f., var. of* **mimbrera.**

vimíneo, a, *a.* (bot.) vimineous.

vinagrada, *f.* cooling drink of vinegar, water and sugar.

vinagre, *m.* 1. vinegar. 2. (coll.) crab, grouchy person. — **cara de v.,** forbidding countenance; **v. de yema,** best quality vinegar.

vinagrera, *f.* 1. vinaigrette, vinegar cruet or bottle; (*pl.*) cruet. 2. (bot.) sorrel. 3. (S. Amer.) acidity, heartburn.

vinagrero, ra, *m., f.* vinegar merchant.

vinagreta, *f.* (cul.) vinaigrette sauce.

vinagrillo, *m.* 1. weak vinegar. 2. cosmetic prepared with vinegar, alcohol and aromatic essences. 3. (bot.) common sorrel.

vinagrón, *m.* poor quality wine.

vinagroso, sa, *a.* vinegary, sour (taste or disposition).

vinajera, *f.* (ecc.) cruet (vessel holding wine or water for the Eucharist); (*pl.*) cruets and tray.

vinal, *m.* (Arg., bot.) type of carob tree (Prosopis ruscifolia).

vinariego, *m.* grape grower, vineyard owner, vinegrower, viticulturist.

vinario, ria, *a.* pertaining to wine or to viticulture.

vinatera, *f.* (mar.) becket; strop, tricing line.

vinatería, *f.* wine trade; wine shop.

vinatero, ra, *a.* pertaining to wine. —*m.* vintner, wine dealer.

vinaza, *f.* poor quality wine (obtained from the lees).

vinazo, *m.* strong heavy wine.

vincapervinca, *f.* (bot.) large periwinkle, cutfinger.

vincha, *f.* (S. Amer.) hair slide, clasp; hair band, ribbon or kerchief.

vinchuca, *f.* 1. (S. Amer., ento.) barbeiro. 2. (Chile) dart.

vinculable, *a.* 1. (law) entailable. 2. that can be tied, associated or linked.

vinculación, *f.* 1. (law) entailment. 2. association, link.

vincular, *tr.v.* 1. to relate, connect; to link. 2. (law) to entail. 3. to ground, found (e.g. hopes upon). 4. to continue. — **estar vinculado con,** to be connected with or related to; **estar bien vinculado,** to have good connections, be well connected.

vincular, *a.* connective, linking.

vínculo, *m.* 1. bond, tie, link. 2. (math.) vinculum. 3. (law) entail, entailment.

vindicación, *f.* vindication.

vindicador, ra, *a.* vindicative, vindicating.

vindicar, (*ref.* *50*) *tr.v.* 1. to vindicate, defend. 2. to avenge. 3. (law) to vindicate, recover by legal action.

vindicativo, va, *a.* 1. vindictive, vengeful. 2. vindicative, defending.

vindicatorio, ria, *a.* vindicatory.

vindicta, *f.* revenge, vengeance; **v. pública,** punishment.

vindique, vindiqué, *ref.* **vindicar.**

vine, *ref.* **venir.**

vínico, ca, *a.* vinic, pertaining to or found in wine.

vinícola, *a.* pertaining to wine, wine making. —*m.* grape grower, vinegrower, viticulturist.

vinicultor, ra, *m., f.* viniculturist, wine maker.

vinicultura, *f.* viniculture, wine making.

viniebla, *f.* (bot.) hound's tongue (Cynoglossum officinale).
viniendo, viniera, viniese, *ref.* **venir.**
vinífero, ra, *a.* wine-yielding, viniferous.
vinificación, *f.* the processes involved in viniculture.
vinilita, *f.* Vinylite (trademark).
vinilo, *m.* (chem.) vinyl.
vinillo, *m.* (coll.) weak wine; light wine.
vino, *m.* wine; **bautizar el v.,** (coll.) to water wine; **dormir el v.,** to sleep off a hangover; **tener mal vino,** to be aggressive and quarrelsome when drunk; **tomarse del v.,** to get drunk; **v. abocado,** semi-dry wine; **v. albillo,** white wine; **v. amontillado,** pale dry sherry; **v. barbera, barbera,** rough dark red wine; **v. blanco,** white wine; **v. clarete,** claret; **v. de agujas,** sharp, rough wine; **v. de Borgoña,** Burgundy; **v. de Burdeos,** Bordeaux; **v. de cabezas,** very thin wine; **v. de dos, de tres,** etc., **hojas,** two or three, etc. year old wine; **v. de dos orejas,** good strong wine; **v. de Jerez,** sherry; **v. de la casa,** house wine; **v. del país,** local wine; **v. de Málaga,** Malaga (wine); **v. de lágrima,** grape juice obtained by letting grapes exude the juice; **v. de mesa** or **de pasto,** ordinary table wine; **v. de Oporto,** Port wine; **v. de postre,** dessert wine; **v. de yema,** wine from the middle of the vat; **v. espumante** or **espumoso,** sparkling wine; **v. generoso,** strong old wine; **v. moscatel,** muscatel; **v. peleón,** (coll.) poor quality, rough wine; **v. seco,** dry wine; **v. rosado,** vino rose; rosé wine; **v. tintillo,** pale red wine; **v. tinto,** red wine.
vinolencia, *f.* excessive wine-drinking, addiction to wine.
vinolento, ta, *a.* addicted to wine drinking.
vinosidad, *f.* vinosity.
vinoso, sa, *a.* 1. vinous. 2. accustomed to drink wine to excess.
vinote, *m.* liquid remaining in boiler after wine is distilled into brandy.
vinta, *f.* (Phil. I.) baroto, dug-out canoe.
viña, *f.* vineyard; **como por v. vendimiada,** as easy as pie; **la v. del señor,** God's flock, the Church; **ser una v.,** (coll.) to be a gold mine; **tener una v.,** (coll.) to have a cushy job or sinecure.
viñadero, *m.* vineyard guard or watchman.
viñador, *m.* 1. grape grower, vinegrower, viticulturist. 2. vineyard guard or watchman.
viñal, *m.* (Arg.) vineyard.
viñatero, *m.* (Arg., Chile) grape grower, vinegrower, viticulturist.
viñedo, *m.* vineyard.
viñero, ra, *m., f.* owner of a vineyard.
viñeta, *f.* (print.) vignette.
viñetero, *m.* (print.) font case for vignettes.
viñuela, *f. dim. of* **viña,** small vineyard.
viola, *f.* (mus.) viola; **v. de amor,** (mus.) viola d'amore; **v. de gamba,** (mus.) viola da gamba. —*m., f.* viola, viola player. —*f.* (bot.) viola, violet.
violable, *a.* violable.
violáceo, a, *a.* violaceous, violet-like, violet-colored. —*f.* (*pl.*) (bot.) Violaceae.
violación, *f.* 1. violation, transgression, infringement. 2. rape. 3. desecration, profanation, violation.
violado, da, *a., m.* violet (color).
violador, ra, *a.* violating. —*m., f.* 1. violator, trespasser, transgressor. 2. rapist. 3. desecrator, profaner.
violar, *tr.v.* 1. to violate, infringe, transgress. 2. to rape. 3. to desecrate, profane, violate. 4. to break open, force, trespass.
violar, *m.* bed of violets.
violencia, *f.* 1. violence; compulsion, force. 2. (fig.) rape, outrage.
violentamente, *adv.* violently.
violentar, *tr.v.* 1. to force, break open; to break into, enter by force. 2. to do violence to, offend; to infuriate, make furious, e.g. *me violenta que me traten así,* it infuriates me to be treated like this. 5. to use force on, force, e.g. *le violentaron para que lo hiciera,* they used force on him to make him do it. —*r.v.* to force oneself; to overcome one's reluctance.
violento, ta, *a.* 1. violent, sudden. 2. violent, rash, impulsive. 3. furious. 4. severe, intense. 5. unnatural, constrained. 6. showy, flashy; embarrassing.
violero, *m.* 1. (ento.) mosquito. 2. (mus.) viola player. 3. maker of stringed instruments.
violeta, *f.* (bot.) violet. —*a.* violet, violet-colored.
violetero, ra, *m.* small vase for violets. —*f.* violet seller, flower vendor.
violeto, *m.* (bot.) clingstone peach.
violín, *m.* 1. (mus.) violin, violinist. 2. bridge, cue rest (in billiards). — **de v.,** (Mex.) free, for nothing; **embolsar el v.,** (Arg., Ven.) to be squashed, go off with one's tail between one's legs; **primer v.,** (mus.) concertmaster; **tocar v.,** (S. Amer.) to be the odd man out, be superfluous.
violinista, *m., f.* (mus.) violinist.
violón, *m.* (mus.) bass viol (instrument and musician). — **tocar el v.,** (coll.) to talk through one's hat, talk nonsense.
violoncelista, *m., f.* (mus.) violoncellist, cellist.
violoncelo, *m.* (mus.) violoncello, cello.
violonchelista, *m., f., var. of* **violoncelista.**
violonchelo, *m., var. of* **violoncelo.**
Violle, *m.* (phys.) Violle, Violle standard.
vipereo, a, viperino, na, *a.* 1. viperine, viperous. 2. (fig.) viperine, venomous.
vira, *f.* 1. arrow, dart. 2. welt of shoe.
viracocha, *m.* 1. (hist.) Spaniard (among the ancient Incas). 2. (myth.) **V.,** the supreme divinity of the Incas.
virada, *f.* turn, change of direction; (mar.) tack, tacking, veering.
virador, *m.* 1. (photog.) toning liquid or solution. 2. (mar.) viol.
virago, *f.* mannish woman.
viraje, *m.* 1. (photog.) toning. 2. turn, change of direction. — **v. al plato,** (aer.) flat turn; **v. a la vertical,** (aer.) vertical turn.
virar, *tr.v.* 1. (mar.) to turn, veer, wear. 2. (mar.) to turn, wind (a capstan). 3. (coll.) to turn, turn round. 4. (photog.) to tone. — **v. al revés,** to turn inside out. —*i.v.* to turn, veer; (mar.) to veer. wear, tack.
viratón, *m.* large dart or arrow.
virazón, *f.* sea breeze.
víreo, *m.* (ornith.) golden oriole.
virescencia, *f.* (bot.) virescence.
virgaza, *f.* (bot.) clematis, virgin's bower, traveler's joy.
virgen, *a.* virgin. —*m., f.* virgin. —*f.* 1. (Bib.) **V.,** Virgin. 2. (astron.) **V.,** Virgo. — **la Santísima V.,** the Blessed Virgin.
virgiliano, na, *a.* (poet.) Virgilian.
Virgilio, *m.* (hist., poet.) Vergil, Virgil, Latin poet, author of the *Aeneid.*
virginal, *a.* virginal. —*m.* (mus.) virginal (small harpsichord-like instrument).
virgíneo, a, *a.* virginal.
Virginia, *f.* (U.S., geog.) Virginia; **V. Occidental,** West Virginia.
virginiano, na, *a., m., f.* Virginian.
virginidad, *f.* virginity.
virginio, *m.* (chem.) virginium.
virgo, *m.* 1. virginity; (anat.) hymen. 2. (astron.) V., Virgo.
virgula, *f.* 1. small rod or stick. 2. line, dash, virgule. 3. (med.) asiatic cholera baccilus.
virgulilla, *f.* virgule, comma, mark, point; fine stroke, light line or dash.
viricida, *a.* (med.) viricidal.
viril, *a.* virile, male; **miembro v.,** penis. —*m.* clear transparent glass; (ecc.) small monstrance inside a larger one.
virilidad, *f.* 1. virility. 2. manhood.
virilmente, *adv.* virilely, in a masculine manner, in a manly way.
virina, *f.* (Phil. I.) glass lamp shade, glass shade.
viringo, ga, *a.* (Col.) naked, unclothed.
virio, *m.* (ornith.) golden oriole.
viripotente, *a.* 1. nubile, marriageable (woman). 2. strong, vigorous.
virol, *m.* (her.) virole.
virola, *f.* 1. metal band, collar or hoop; ferrule. 2. check ring on goads. 3. (Mex., Arg., Urug.) silver circlet or nail head (for decorating harnesses). 4. circular mold (used in the minting of coins to achieve absolute roundness).
virolento, ta, *a.* 1. with smallpox. 2. pockmarked. —*m., f.* 1. person with smallpox. 2. pockmarked person.
virología, *f.* (med.) virology.
virón, *m.* large dart.
virosis, *f.* (med.) virosis.
virotada, *f.* (Ven.) foolishness, stupidity.
virotazo, *m.* dart wound.
virote, *m.* 1. metal-tipped dart. 2. (coll.) gay young blade, dandy. 3. (coll.) stuffed shirt, pompous person. 4. (coll.) mannish woman. 5. (Col., Ven.) fool, simpleton.
virotillo, *m.* (archit.) strut, brace; staybolt.
virotismo, *m.* haughtiness, presumption, conceit.
virreina, *f.* 1. vice-queen, wife of viceroy. 2. vice-queen (woman ruling in place of sovereign).
virreinal, *a.* viceregal.
virreinato, virreino, *m.* viceroyalty, viceroyship.
virrey, *m.* viceroy.
virtual, *a.* virtual.
virtualidad, *f.* virtuality.
virtualmente, *adv.* virtually.
virtud, *f.* 1. virtue. 2. power, quality; advantage. — **en v. de,** by or in virtue of; **tener la v. de,** to have the power to, the quality of; (*pl.*) **varita de virtudes,** magic wand; (fig.) versatile or handy person.
virtuosamente, *adv.* virtuously.
virtuoso, sa, *a.* virtuous. —*m., f.* 1. virtuous person. 2. virtuoso.
virtuosismo, *m.* virtuosity.
virucida, *a.* (med.) viricidal.
viruela, *f.* 1. (med.) smallpox. 2. pockmark. — **picado de viruelas,** pockmarked; **viruelas locas,** (med.) chicken pox.
virulencia, *f.* 1. virulence. 2. (fig.) spite, rancor, venom.
virulento, ta, *a.* 1. virulent. 2. purulent. 3. (fig.) venemous, spiteful.
virus, (*pl.* virus), *m.* (med.) virus; **v. de computadora,** computer virus.
viruta, *f.* shavings (of wood or metal).
vis, *f.* verve, power, force; **v. cómica,** (theat.) humorous verve.
visa, *f.,* **visado,** *m.* visa, visé.
visaje, *m.* face, look, grimace, visage.
visajero, ra, *a.* grimacing, face making. —*m., f.* one who grimaces or makes faces.
visar, *tr.v.* 1. to visa; to endorse. 2. (surv., artil.) to sight, focus.
víscera, *f.* (anat.) viscera, (*pl.*) viscera, innards.

visceral, *a.* visceral.
visco, *m.* 1. birdlime. 2. (bot.) mistletoe.
viscosidad, *f.* viscosity.
viscosímetro, *m.* viscometer, viscosimeter.
viscoso, sa, *a.* viscous, sticky. —*f.* (chem.) viscose.
visera, *f.* visor (of helmet, cap, etc.); eye shade; (Cuba, P. Rico) blinker, blinder.
vishnuismo, *m.* (rel.) Vishnuism.
visibilidad, *f.* visibility; **v. mínima,** threshold visibility.
visible, *a.* 1. visible, showing. 2. manifest, evident.
visiblemente, *adv.* visibly; evidently.
visigodo, da, *a., m., f.* (hist.) Visigoth.
visigótico, ca, *a.* (hist.) Visigothic.
visillo, *m.* sheer window curtain.
visión, *f.* 1. vision, sight (sense, faculty), e.g. *el órgano de la v. es el ojo,* the organ of sight is the eye. 2. vision, prophetic or imaginary sight, e.g. *visiones de riquezas sin límite,* visions of limitless wealth. 3. vision, foresight, imagination. 4. ridiculous or terrifying sight; (coll.) sight, scarecrow (person). — **quedarse uno como quien ve visiones,** (coll.) to look as though one had seen a ghost, look dumbfounded; **ver visiones,** (coll.) to see things; **v. doble,** (med.) double vision.
visionario, ria, *a., m. f.* visionary.
visir, *m.* vizier, vizir; **gran visir,** grand vizier.
visirato, *m.* vizierate, viziership.
visita, *f.* 1. visit; call; inspection. 2. visitor, caller. 3. (mar.) inspection of documents, cargo or crew. 4. (Peru, P. Rico) enema. — **derecho de v.** (international law), right of search or inspection (by belligerants of neutral shipping); **de v.,** on a visit, visiting; **hacer una v.,** to pay or make a visit or call; **pagar una v.,** to return a visit or call; **tener v.,** to have visitors or callers; **v. a domicilio,** house call; **v. de altares,** prayers before a number of altars; **v. de aspectos,** medical inspection of ship's passengers; **v. de cortesía, cumplido or cumplimiento,** courtesy visit or call; **v. de médico,** (coll.) brief visit, flying visit; **v. de sanidad,** medical inspection of ship, crew and passenger; **v. domiciliaria,** police search or inspection of suspicious house; **v. general,** general inspection of houses in given district; **v. guiada,** guided tour; **v. pastoral,** bishop's visit to diocese.
visitación, *f.* 1. visitation, visit. 2. (Bib., ecc.) V., Visitation.
visitador, ra, *a.* fond of visiting, calling frequently. —*m., f.* person fond of visiting, frequent visitor. —*m.* inspector; visiting judge. —*f.* (Ven., Hond.) enema.
visitante, *a.* visiting, calling. —*m., f.* visitor, visitant, caller.
visitar, *tr.v.* 1. to visit; to call on. 2. (law, med., mar.) to visit, inspect, make an inspection of; to examine. 3. (theol.) to visit or inflict (punishment) on or upon. —*r.v.* to visit one another, call on one another.
visiteo, *m.* frequent exchange of visits or calls.
visitero, ra, *a.* fond of visiting, frequently making visits.
visitón, *m.* (coll.) long tiresome visit.
visivo, va, *a.* pertaining to eyesight.
vislumbrar, *tr.v.* 1. to see vaguely, catch a glimpse of. 2. to conjecture, imagine, surmise, suspect. —*r.v.* to become visible or apparent; to loom in the distance.
vislumbre, *f.* 1. glimmer, glimpse. 2. inkling, suspicion, idea. 3. slight similarity.
visnuismo, *m.* (rel.) Vishnuism.
viso, *m.* 1. sheen, luster, gleam, shine. 2. appearance, aspect. 3. thin layer, veneer or coat. 4. colored garment worn under transparent one. 5. height, rise, eminence. — **a dos visos,** with a double purpose or motive; **al v.,** (to look at cloth) from the side, sideways (to examine the sheen); **de v.,** important, prominent; **hacer mal v.,** to show up unfavorably; **hacer v.,** to show up favorably, make a good impression; **hacer visos,** to shimmer, gleam, shine.
visón, *m.* (zool.) mink.
visor, *m.* (photog.) viewfinder. 2. (artil.) sight (on gun).
visorio, ria, *a.* visual. —*m.* inspection or examination by an expert.
víspera, *f.* 1. eve, day before. 2. (*pl.*) (ecc.) vesperas. — **en víspera de,** on the eve of.
vista, *f.* 1. sight, vision (faculty). 2. view, sight, look, seeing, e.g. *punto de v.,* point of view, *amor a primera v.,* love at first sight. 3. view, vista, landscape. 4. eye, eyes, look, glance, e.g. *dirigir la v.,* to direct or turn one's eyes, *clavar la v. en,* to fix one's eyes on. 5. visible part of anything. 6. appearance, aspect, look. 7. comparison, contrast. 8. (law) hearing, trial. 9. (*pl.*) meeting, interview, conference. — **aguzar la v.,** to keep one's eyes open, look attentively; **a la v.,** visible, able to be seen; (com.) at sight; **alzar la v.,** to raise one's eyes, look up; **a media v.,** at a glance, at half a glance; **apartar la v. de,** to glance away from; to take one's eyes off; to take one's mind off; **a primera v.,** at first sight; **a simple v.,** at a glance; with the naked eye; **a v. de,** in front of, in the presence of; within sight of, in view of; in comparison with, in contrast to; **bajar la v.,** to lower one's eyes, look down; **clavar la v. en,** to fix one's eyes on; **comerse con la v. a,** (coll.) to devour with one's eyes; **conocer de v.,** to know by sight; **con v. a,** looking out on, with a view of; **corto de v.,** shortsighted; **dar una v. a,** to have a look at, glance at or over; **dar v. a,** to sight, catch sight of, see; **doble v.,** second sight; **echar la v. a,** to have one's eyes on; **echar la v. encima,** to lay one's eyes on, see, find; **echar una v.,** to keep an eye on, watch; **en v. de,** in view of, considering, keeping in mind; **estar a la v.,** to be visible; to be evident or obvious; **extender la v.,** to let one's eyes roam over; **fijar la v. en,** to fix one's eyes on; **forzar la v.,** to strain one's eyes; **hacer la v. gorda** or **larga,** (coll.) to pretend not to see; **hasta la v.,** so long, good-bye; **irse de v.,** to go out of sight, disappear; **irsele a uno la v.,** to faint, swoon; **no perder de v.,** to keep one's eyes on, not to lose sight of; to keep on with, follow up (a project, etc.); **perder de v.,** to lose sight of; **perderse de v.,** to go out of sight, disappear; (coll.) to be extremely smart or clever; **saltar a la v.,** to leap to the eye; **tener a la v.,** to keep in mind; **tener en v.,** to have in mind, be planning; **tener v.,** to look good, be attractive, have a good appearance; **¡v. a la derecha** or **izquierda!** (mil.) eyes right or left!; **v. cansada,** tired eyes; longsightedness, farsightedness; **v. corta,** shortsightedness, nearsightedness; **v. de águila,** hawk eyes, eyes like a hawk; **v. de lince,** lynx eyes, sharp eyes; **v. de ojos,** personal inspection by jury or judge; **v. doble,** (med.) double vision; **v. frontal** or **de frente,** front view; **volver la v. atrás,** to look back, remember, recall. —*m.* customs official or inspector.
vista, *ref.* **vestir.**
vistazo, *m.* glance; **dar un v. a,** to glance at, have a quick look at.
viste, *ref.* **ver.**
vistiendo, vistiera, vistiese, *ref.* **vestir.**
vistillas, *f.* (*pl.*) heights; lookout point; place commanding a good view. — **irse a las v.,** (coll.) to peek at an opponent's cards.
vistió, visto, *ref.* **vestir.**
visto, ta, *irr. past part. of* **ver.** —*a.* considering, in view of; e.g. *vista la seriedad de la falta,* considering the seriousness of the offense. — **bien** or **mal v.,** approved or disapproved of, looked upon with approval or disapproval; **dar el visto bueno a, to** approve, authorize, O.K.; **está visto,** it has been proved repeatedly; **estar bien** or **mal visto,** to be approved or disapproved of, be looked upon with approval or disapproval; **ni visto ni oído,** like a flash; **no or nunca visto,** unheard of; **por lo visto,** evidently, apparently, as far as one can see; **visto,** (law) whereas (legal formula preceding statement of facts of case); **visto bueno,** approval, O.K.; **visto que,** seeing that, in view of the fact that.
vistosamente, *adv.* colorfully; attractively, showily.
vistosidad, *f.* color, colorfulness; showiness; attractiveness.
vistoso, sa, *a.* colorful; attractive, showy.
visual, *a.* visual, e.g. *campo v.,* visual field or range. —*f.* visual line, line of vision, line of sight; (artil.) line of sight or sighting. — **v. inversa,** (chart.) backsight, plus sight.
visualidad, *f.* colorfulness; pleasant effect of attractive things.
visura, *f.* visual or ocular inspection; inspection or examination by an expert.
vital, *a.* vital; essential; indispensable.
vitalice, vitalicé, *ref.* **vitalizar.**
vitalicio, cia, *a.* for life, life, e.g. *pensión vitalicia,* life pension, *miembro vitalicio,* life member. —*m.* life insurance policy; life annuity.
vitalicista, *m., f.* holder of life annuity.
vitalidad, *f.* vitality.
vitalismo, *m.* (philos., biol.) vitalism.
vitalista, *a.* vitalistic. —*m., f.* vitalist.
vitalización, *f.* vitalization.
vitalizar, (*ref. 53*) *tr.v.* to vitalize.
vitamina, *f.* vitamin.
vitaminado, da, *a.* vitaminized, containing vitamins.
vitamínico, ca, *a.* vitamin, vitaminic.
vitando, da, *a.* 1. to be avoided. 2. odious, detestable, execrable.
vitela, *f.* vellum.
vitelino, na, *a.* vitelline. —*f.* 1. (biol.) vitelline membrane. 2. (biochem.) vitellin, ovovitellin.
vitelo, *m.* (biol.) vitellus.
Viti, *f.* Fiji (islands).
vitícola, *a.* viticultural, grape growing. —*m., f.* viticulturist, grape grower.
viticultor, ra, *m., f.* viticulturer, viticulturist, grape grower.
viticultura, *f.* viticulture, grape growing.
vitiligo, *m.* (med.) vitiligo.
vitivinícola, *a.* pertaining to the combined art, science or trades of grape-growing and wine-making. —*m., f.* viticulturist-viniculturist, grape-grower and wine-maker.
vitivinicultor, ra, *m., f.* viticulturist-viniculturist, person who is both grape grower and wine maker.
vitivinicultura, *f.* the combined art, science and trades of grape-growing and wine-making; viticulture and viniculture.
vito, *m.* spirited Andalusian dance and tune.
vitola, *f.* 1. bullet or shell callipers (for measuring caliber). 2. standard measurement (for grading cigars); cigar band. 3. appearance, mien.
¡vítor! *interj.* bravo! hurrah! —*m.* 1. public ceremony of homage or acclamation. 2. memorial tablet.
vitorear, *tr.v.* to applaud, cheer, acclaim.

vitral, *m.* stained-glass window, church window.
vitre, *m.* (mar.) thin canvas.
vítreo, a, *a.* vitreous, glassy.
vitrificable, *a.* vitrifiable.
vitrificación, *f.* vitrification.
vitrificar, (*ref. 50*) *tr.v., r.v.* to vitrify.
vitrifique, vitrifiqué, *ref.* **vitrificar.**
vitrina, *f.* glass showcase, glass cabinet; (Amer.) shopwindow.
vitrinear, *i.v.* (Amer.) to windowshop.
vitriólico, ca, *a.* (chem.) vitriolic.
vitriolo, *m.* (chem.) vitriol; sulfate; **v. amoniacal,** (chem.) ammonium sulfate; **v. azul,** (chem.) blue vitriol; **v. blanco,** (chem.) white vitriol, zinc sulfate; **v. de plomo,** (chem.) lead sulfate; **v. verde,** (chem.) green vitriol.
vitrófiro, *m.* (geol.) vitrophyre.
vitualla, *f.* 1. victuals, provisions, food (*gen. pl.*). 2. abundance of food, abundance of vegetables.
vituallar, *tr.v.* to supply with food, to provision.
vítulo, marino, *m.* (zool.) seal.
vituperable, *a.* blameworthy; deserving revilement or censure.
vituperación, *f.* vituperation, censure, revilement.
vituperador, ra, *a.* vituperating. *—m., f.* vituperator.
vituperante, *a.* vituperating, vituperative.
vituperar, *tr.v.* to vituperate, revile, censure.
vituperio, *m.* vituperation, revilement, censure.
vituperioso, sa, *a.* vituperative.
viuda, *f.* 1. widow. 2. dowager. 3. (bot.) mourning bride, sweet scabious; **v. negra,** (zool.) black widow.
viudal, *a.* pertaining to a widow or widower.
viudedad, *f.* widow's pension.
viudez, *f.* widowhood.
viudita, *f.* 1. (Amer.) small species of monkey. 2. (Arg.) a kind of parrot.
viudo, da, *a.* 1. widowed. 2. without a mate, unpaired (bird). *—m.* widower. *—f.* widow.
viva, *f.* cheer, shout, acclamation. *—interj.* hurrah! huzza! long live! — **ser un v. la Virgen,** to be a carefree person.
vivac, (*pl.* **vivaques**), *m.* 1. bivouac, military camp. 2. (Cuba) police station.
vivacidad, *f.* 1. vivacity, liveliness, brightness. 2. keenness (of mind). 3. brilliancy (of color).
vivales, (*pl.* **vivales**) *m., f.* (coll.) smarty, freshy, smart aleck, wiseacre. *—m.* wise guy.
vivamente, *adv.* 1. vividly, brightly. 2. acutely, deeply, keenly. 3. lively, quickly.
vivandero, ra, *m., f.* sutler, vivandiere (person who sells food, etc. to soldiers in the field).
vivaque, *m.* 1. (mil.) bivouac, military camp. 2. guardhouse. — **estar al v.,** to bivouac, camp.
vivaquear, *i.v.* (mil.) to bivouac, camp.
vivar, *m.* 1. warren. 2. fish hatchery.
vivaracho, cha, *a.* (coll.) gay, lively, frisky, vivacious; dapper.
vivario, *m.* vivarium.
vivaz, (*pl.* **vivaces**), *a.* 1. lively, vivacious, spirited, gay; active, living. 2. ingenious, sharp, quick, bright, witty. 3. long-lived, vivacious. 4. (bot.) perennial, evergreen.
vivencia, *f.* (philos.) personal experience.
vivera, *f., var. of* **vivar.**
viveral, *m.* (bot.) tree nursery.
víveres, *m.* (*pl.*) food, foodstuffs, victuals, provisions, stores.
vivero, *m.* 1. tree nursery; fishpond. 2. (fig.) hotbed, seed bed.
vivérrido, da, *a.* (zool.) viverrine.
viveza, *f.* 1. quickness, liveliness, briskness. 2. smartness, quick-wittedness, cleverness, mental brightness; show-offishness; smart or witty remark, witticism. 3. keenness, sharpness, acuteness (of spirit). 4. brightness, brilliancy (e.g. of colors); sparkle (of eyes). 5. passion, ardor, vehemence, force (e.g. of language, emotions, etc.). 6. inconsiderate act; thoughtless remark.
vividero, ra, *a.* habitable, livable.
vividizo, *m.* (Mex.) scrounger, sponger, parasite.
vívido, da, *a.* 1. vivid, lively, full of life, strong, vigorous, energetic. 2. bright (colors); realistic (picture, scene, etc.).
vivido, da, *past part. of* **vivir.** *—a.* based on personal experience (said of literary works).
vividor, ra, *a.* 1. living. 2. long-living. 3. resourceful, enterprising, hardworking. *—m., f.* 1. resourceful and enterprising person. 2. (coll.) sponger, parasite, scrounger.
vivienda, *f.* 1. housing, e.g. *el problema de la v.,* the housing problem, *escasez de viviendas,* housing shortage. 2. dwelling, house. 3. way of life or living.
viviente, *a.* living, alive, live; animated.
vivificación, *f.* vivification, vivifying, enlivening, reviving.
vivificador, ra, vivificante, *a.* vivifying, enlivening, reviving. *—m., f.* vivifier.
vivificar, (*ref. 50*) *tr.v.* 1. to vivify, enliven, revive. 2. to comfort, refresh.
vivificativo, va, *a.* 1. reviving, vivifying, enlivening. 2. comforting.
vivífico, ca, *a.* 1. living. 2. springing from life.
vivifique, vivifiqué, *ref.* **vivificar.**
viviparidad, *f.* (zool.) viviparity.
vivíparo, ra, *a.* (zool.) viviparous.
vivir, *m.* life, living, e.g. *él es amigo del buen v.,* he's fond of the good life; **de mal v.,** licentious, disreputable; **mujer de mal v.,** prostitute.
vivir, *tr.v.* 1. to live, e.g. *quiero v. en paz,* I want to live in peace. 2. to live in, inhabit. *—i.v.* 1. to live; to be alive, e.g. *vive todavía,* he's still alive. 2. to live, last, endure. — **me gustaría v. para verlo,** I'd like to see it happen; **¿quién vive?** who goes there?; **¡viva!** long live!; **v. al día, v. a lo que salga,** to live from day to day; **v. a lo grande,** to live it up, live a grand life.
vivisección, *f.* vivisection.
vivisector, *m.* vivisector.
vivo, va, *a.* 1. living, alive, e.g. *lengua viva,* living language, *está vivo,* he's alive; (tel., rad.) live (broadcast, program). 2. intense, strong (e.g. pain; desire). 3. lively, keen, strong (interest in something). 4. clever, bright, quick-witted, smart. 5. lively, vivid (imagination); sharp, acute, quick (mind, intelligence). 6. living, exact, e.g. *es el vivo retrato de su padre,* he is the living image of his father. 7. live, burning (coal, fire). 8. bright, vivid (color; memory, recollection). 9. expressive, vivid (description, language). 10. raw, open, e.g. *llaga viva,* open wound, *carne viva,* raw skin or flesh. 11. (archit.) sharp (corner, angle, edge). — **a lo vivo, al vivo,** vividly, in a very lifelike manner; **de viva voz,** by word of mouth, orally; **en vivo,** (weighed) alive (said of cattle); **lo vivo,** the most sensitive spot, the raw, the quick, **dar** or **tocar en lo vivo,** to touch on a sore spot, **herir en lo vivo,** to hurt to the quick. *—m.* 1. (coll.) smart aleck, wise guy. 2. edge, border; (sew.) piping, braid, trimming. 3. (vet.) mange, scab. — **los vivos,** the living, the quick; **los vivos y los muertos,** the quick and the dead.
vizcacha, *f.* (zool.) vizcacha, viscacha (S. American rodent).
vizcachera, *f.* viscacha's burrow or warren.
vizcainada, *f.* 1. solecism, syntactical error. 2. typical Basque expression or behavior.
vizcaíno, na, *a., m., f.* Biscayan, Basque.
vizcaitarra, *a.* in favor of Biscayan or Basque autonomy. *—m., f.* advocate of Biscayan or Basque autonomy.
Vizcaya, *f.* (geog.) Biscay.
vizcondado, *m.* 1. viscountcy, viscountship (rank of viscount). 2. viscounty (territory under jurisdiction of viscount).
vizconde, *m.* viscount.
vizcondesa, *f.* viscountess.
V.M. *abbrev. of* **Vuestra Majestad,** Your Majesty.
vocablo, *m.* word, term; **jugar del v.,** to pun, play with words.
vocabulario, *m.* vocabulary.
vocabulista, *m., f.* lexicographer.
vocación, *f.* vocation, calling; **errar la v.,** to miss one's vocation.
vocal, *a.* vocal; **letra v.,** vowel. *—m., f.* member of council, committee, board of directors, etc. *—f.* (gram.) vowel; **v. abierta,** (gram.) open vowel; **v. breve,** (gram.) short vowel; **v. cerrada,** (gram.) closed vowel; **v. débil,** weak vowel; **v. fuerte,** strong vowel; **v. larga,** (gram.) long vowel; **v. mixta,** (gram.) central or mixed vowel; **v. nasal,** (gram.) nasal vowel.
vocalice, vocalicé, *ref.* **vocalizar.**
vocálico, ca, *a.* vocalic, pertaining to vowels.
vocalismo, *m.* (phonet.) vocalism, system of vowels.
vocalista, *m., f.* vocalist, singer.
vocalización, *f.* (mus., phonet.) vocalization.
vocalizador, ra, *a.* vocalizing.
vocalizar, (*ref. 53*) *i.v.* 1. (mus.) to vocalize. 2. to articulate, sing or speak clearly, have good diction.
vocalmente, *adv.* vocally, orally.
vocativo, *a., m.* (gram.) vocative.
voceador, ra, *a.* shouting, vociferating. *—m., f.* shouter, vociferator. *—m.* 1. town crier. 2. (Col., Ecuad., Mex.) newspaper boy.
vocear, *tr.v.* 1. to shout out, cry out; to voice, publish, proclaim, make known (e.g. opinion). 2. to cheer, hail, acclaim. 3. (coll.) to shout about, boast about. — **v. el nombre de,** to page (as in a hotel). *—i.v.* to shout, cry out.
vocejón, *m.* harsh, raucous voice.
vocería, *f.* **vocerío,** *m.* uproar, din, shouting. *—f.* spokesmanship.
vocero, *m.* spokesman.
vociferación, *f.* vociferation, vociferating, shouting.
vociferador, ra, *a.* vociferous, vociferating. *—m., f.* vociferator.
vociferante, *a.* vociferous, vociferating.
vociferar, *tr.v., i.v.* to vociferate, shout, clamor.
vocingleo, *m.,* **vocinglería,** *f.* noise, shouting, uproar, din; loquacity; prate, rant.
vocinglero, ra, *a.* loudmouthed, noisy. *—m., f.* loudmouthed person; prattler.
vocoder, *m.* (elec.) vocoder.
voder, *m.* (elec.) voder.
vodka, *m.* vodka (liquor).
vodú, *m.* voodoo.
voduismo, *m.* voodooism.
volada, *f.* 1. short flight. 2. (Col., Ecuad.) trick. 3. (Arg., Col.) opportunity, piece of luck. 4. (Arg.) happening, event. — **hacer** or **jugar una (mala) v. a,** to play a dirty trick on.
voladera, *f.* (mec.) blade or paddle of a water wheel.
voladero, ra, *a.* 1. capable of flying. 2. (fig.) fleeting, transitory, passing. *—m.* precipice, abyss.
voladizo, za, *a.* jutting out, projecting. *—m.* (archit.) projection, corbel.

volado, da, *past part. of* **volar.** —*a.* 1. (print.) superior (letter, symbol). 2. (Car.) furious. 3. (S. Amer.) absent-minded. — **estar v.,** (coll.) to be uneasy, be on edge; **v. de genio,** (Amer.) quick-tempered. —*m.* 1. (Arg.) pleated ruffle or flounce. 2. (C. Amer., Mex.) rumor, story.
volador, ra, *a.* 1. flying, fleeting, e.g. *platillo volador,* flying saucer. 2. hanging, swinging. 3. swift, fleet, fast. —*m.* 1. rocket. 2. (ichth.) flying fish. 3. (bot.) myrobalan (Terminalia obovata). 4. (Ven.) kite (toy). 5. (C. Amer., Col.) pinwheel. —*f.* 1. (Cuba) flywheel.
voladura, *f.* 1. blowing up, explosion, blasting. 2. flying.
volandas, *adv.* **en v.,** in the air, flying through the air; (coll.) quickly, in a jiffy.
volandera, *f.* 1. (mec.) washer. 2. millstone, grindstone. 3. (coll.) lie, fib. 4. (print.) slice, galley slice.
volandero, ra, *a.* 1. ready to fly, starting to fly (bird). 2. hanging, swinging. 3. accidental, unforeseen. 4. unsettled; wandering; (coll.) variable.
volandillas, *adv.* **en v.,** in the air, flying through the air; (coll.) quickly, in a jiffy.
volanta, *f.* (Cuba) gig, chaise, two-wheeled carriage.
volante, *a.* 1. flying. 2. unsettled, wandering. —*m.* 1. (mec.) flywheel; (mec.) balance wheel (in watches); (auto.) steering wheel. 2. (auto.) racing driver. 3. flier, leaflet, tract, bill, pamphlet. 4. shuttlecock; battledore and shuttlecock (game). 5. coining press. 6. (dressm.) pleated ruffle or flounce. 7. movable screen. — **en el v.,** at the wheel, driving; **v. compensador,** compensating balance. —*f.* (Cuba) gig, chaise, two-wheeled carriage.
volantín, na, *a.* flying. —*m.* 1. multiple-hook fishing line. 2. (Arg., Cuba, Chile, P. Rico) small kite. 3. (Amer.) tumble, forward roll, somersault. 4. (Bol.) rocket; firecracker.
volantón, na, *a.* ready to fly, starting to fly. —*m., f.* fledgeling.
volapié, *m.* (taur.) the sword thrust performed by the matador while running towards the bull; **a v.,** half walking, half flying.
volar, (*ref. 33*) *tr.v.* 1. to blow up. 2. to anger, exasperate, infuriate. 3. (hunt.) to rouse, make fly out (game). 4. (hunt.) to release (a hawk so that it will pursue the prey). 5. (print.) to raise (letter, number) to the top of the line. —*i.v.* 1. to fly; flutter, hover; to fly away, blow away. 2. to fly, move or go like the wind, e.g. *el tiempo vuela,* time flies. 3. to spread like wildfire (news). 4. to disappear suddenly. 5. to jut out, project. 6. (coll.) to sell like hot cakes, sell very quickly. — **volando,** very quickly, like the wind. —*r.v.* 1. to fly away, blow away. 2. (Amer.) to blow up, get angry or annoyed.
volateo, *adv.* **al v.,** (to shoot at birds) in flight, on the wing.
volatería, *f.* 1. hawking (bird hunting with hawks). 2. fowls (flock of birds). 3. (fig.) stray thoughts, random thoughts. 4. fluke, chance. 5. (Ecuad.) fireworks. — **de v.,** accidentally, by chance; in the air.
volatero, *m.* falconer, one who hunts with hawks.
volatice, volaticé, *ref.* **volatizar.**
volátil, *a.* 1. volatile. 2. (fig.) inconstant; flighty, fickle.
volatilice, volatilicé, *ref.* **volatilizar.**
volatilidad, *f.* (chem.) volatility.
volatilizable, *a.* volatilizable.
volatilización, *f.* volatilization.
volatilizar, (*ref. 53*) *tr.v., r.v.* to volatilize, vaporize.
volatín, *m.* acrobat, tightrope walker; acrobatic feat.
volatinero, ra, *m., f.* acrobat, tightrope walker, aerialist.
volatizar, (*ref. 53*) *tr.v., var. of* **volatilizar.**
volavérunt, (Lat., coll.) it has disappeared! it is gone!
volcán, *m.* 1. volcano. 2. (fig.) volcano (violent passion; passionate person). 3. (Col.) precipice. 4. (Arg., Col., Bol.) flood, torrent. — **estar sobre un v.,** to be on the edge of a volcano, be in grave danger; **v. apagado** or **extinto,** extinct volcano.
volcanada, *f.* (Chile) gust of wind; whiff of smoke.
volcanicidad, *f.* volcanicity, volcanism.
volcánico, ca, *a.* 1. volcanic. 2. violent (passion, feelings, etc.).
volcanismo, *m.* (geol.) volcanism.
volcanización, *f.* (pet.) volcanization.
volcanología, *f.* (geol.) vulcanology.
volcar, (*ref. 69*) *tr.v.* 1. to turn over, tilt, overturn, upset; (mar.) to capsize. 2. to make dizzy or giddy. 3. to make (a person) change his mind. 4. to tease, irritate, annoy. —*i.v.* to overturn, turn over. —*r.v.* to overturn, turn over; to capsize. — **volcarse en,** to throw oneself into (an enterprise).
volea, *f.* 1. whippletree. 2. volley (in pelota, tennis, etc.).
voleador, *m.* (sport.) batsman, batter.
volear, *tr.v.* 1. to hit on the volley, volley (a ball). 2. to broadcast, scatter (seed, grain).
voleibol, *m.* volleyball.
voleo, *m.* 1. volley (in pelota, tennis, etc.). 2. heavy blow or punch. 3. high step (in dancing). — **al v.,** scattering, broadcasting (seed); **del primer v., de un v.,** (coll.) quickly, in one go; **medio v.,** half volley.
volframio, *m.* (chem.) wolfram.
volframita, *f.* (min.) wolframite.
volición, *f.* volition.
volitar, *i.v.* to flutter or fly around.
volitivo, va, *a.* volitional, volitive.
volqué, *ref.* **volcar.**
volquearse, *r.v.* to roll about, roll over; wallow.
volquete, *m.* tipcart, dumpcart, tilt truck.
volquetero, *m.* driver of a tipcart or truck.
volt, *m.* (elec.) volt.
voltaico, ca, *a.* (elec.) voltaic; **arco v.,** voltaic arc.
voltaísmo, *m.* (elec.) voltaism.
voltaje, *m.* (elec.) voltage; **v. crítico,** (elec.) critical potential or voltage; **v. de disparo,** drop-out voltage; **v. disruptivo,** break-down voltage.
voltámetro, *m.* (phys.) voltameter.
voltamperímetro, *m.* (phys.) voltammeter.
voltamperio, *m.* (elec.) volt-ampere.
voltariedad, *f.* fickleness, inconstancy.
voltario, ria, *a.* 1. changeable, fickle, inconstant. 2. (Chile) self-willed, capricious.
volteador, ra, *a.* tumbling. —*m., f.* 1. tumbler, acrobat. 2. person or tool used for turning or tumbling something.
voltear, *tr.v.* 1. to turn over, turn upside down; to capsize; to roll over; to turn around; to revolve. 2. (Amer.) to turn (e.g. one's back, head, eyes). 3. (Ven., Mex.) to turn, go around (the corner). 4. (archit.) to build an arch or vault. 5. to change, alter; to move. 6. (Chile, Arg., Urug.) to demolish, knock down. 7. (Mex.) to knock over, overturn, upset. 8. (Col., Chile, P. Rico) to make (someone) change his opinion, mind or party. —*i.v.* 1. to tumble, roll over, turn somersaults. 2. (Amer.) to turn (e.g. at the corner). —*r.v.* 1. to turn over, roll over. 2. (Amer.) to turn around. 3. (Amer.) to change one's opinion or mind; to change sides or party. — **voltearse los bolsillos,** (Mex.) to turn one's pockets out.
voltejear, *tr.v.* to turn around, whirl. —*i.v.* (mar.) to work to windward, tack.
volteleta, *f., var. of* **voltereta.**
volteo, *m.* 1. turning; rolling, whirling; turn, revolution. 2. overturning. 3. tumbling. 4. (P. Rico) dressing down, reprimand.
voltereta, *f.* 1. somersault, tumble. 2. (cards) turning up a card to determine trumps.
volterianismo, *m.* Voltairianism.
volteriano, na, *a., m., f.* Voltairian.
volteta, *f., var. of* **voltereta.**
voltiamperímetro, *m.* (elec.) voltammeter.
voltímetro, *m.* voltmeter; **v. de hilo caliente,** (elec.) hot-wire volmeter.
voltio, *m.* (elec.) volt; **v. electrónico,** (phys.) electron volt.
voltizo, za, *a.* 1. twisted, curled. 2. fickle, changeable.
volubilidad, *f.* 1. volubility. 2. changeableness, fickleness.
voluble, *a.* 1. changeable, fickle. 2. voluble, easily revolving or turning. 3. (bot.) voluble, twining.
volublemente, *adv.* volubly.
volumen, *m.* 1. volume, bulk, mass; size. 2. volume, tome, book. 3. (acous.) volume. 4. corpulence.
volumétrico, ca, *a.* volumetric, volumetrical.
volúmetro, *m.* (phys.) volumeter.
voluminoso, sa, *a.* voluminous, bulky.
voluntad, *f.* 1. will, disposition. 2. wish, desire; choice, decision. 3. liking, affection. — **a v.,** at will, as one wishes, as you wish; **buena v.,** good will; **de buena v.,** willingly, with good will; **ganar la v. de uno,** to win someone over, win someone's good will; **gira de buena v.,** good will visit; **hágase tu v.,** thy will be done; **no tener v. propia,** to have no will of one's own; **quitar la v. a,** to dissuade; **tenerle mala v. a uno,** to dislike someone; **v. de hierro,** iron will; **mala v.,** ill will; **última v.,** last wish or will; will, last will and testament.
voluntariado, *m.* (mil.) volunteering, voluntary enlistment.
voluntariamente, *adv.* voluntarily.
voluntariedad, *f.* 1. willfulness, self-will. 2. voluntariness.
voluntario, ria, *a.* 1. voluntary. 2. willful. —*m., f.* volunteer. —*m.* (mil.) volunteer.
voluntariosamente, *adv.* willfully.
voluntarioso, sa, *a.* willful, self-willed.
voluntarismo, *m.* (philos.) voluntarism.
voluptuosamente, *adv.* voluptuously.
voluptuosidad, *f.* voluptuousness.
voluptuoso, sa, *a.* voluptuous. —*m., f.* voluptuary.
voluta, *f.* 1. spiral, volute. 2. (archit.) volute, scroll. 3. (zool.) volute.
volvedor, ra, *a.* (Arg., Col., Guat.) running away to get back home or to a favorite haunt (said of horses, cattle).
volver, (*ref. 34*) *tr.v.* 1. to turn; to turn around; to turn over; to turn upside down. 2. to turn, direct (e.g. eyes, attention). 3. to return, give back, send back, repay. 4. to return, put back, replace, e.g. *volvió el libro a su sitio,* he put the book back in its place. 5. to return, hit back (ball in pelota, tennis, etc.). 6. to drive, make, e.g. *este ruido me vuelve loco,* this noise is driving me mad, *eso me vuelve furioso,* that makes me furious. 7. to turn, change, convert, e.g. *v. el mosto en vino,* to turn must into wine. 8. to make (someone) change his opinion. 9. to throw up, vomit. 10. to plow for a second time. 11. (sew.) to turn (e.g. a collar). — **v. la hoja,** to turn the page;

to change the subject; **volverle la espalda a alguien,** to turn one's back on someone; **v. lo de abajo arriba, v. lo de arriba abajo,** to turn everything upside down or topsy-turvy. —*i.v.* 1. to return, come or go back. 2. to turn (e.g. to the left); **v. a.** + *inf.*, to + *inf.* again, e.g. *nunca volveré a ayudarle,* I shall never help him again. — **v. en sí,** to come to, recover consciousness; **v. por,** to return for, come or go back for; **v. sobre sí,** to reflect on oneself or one's actions; to recover, recuperate; to calm down, regain one's calm. —*r.v.* 1. to turn, turn around. 2. to turn, go, become, e.g. *se volvió loco,* he went mad. 3. to change one's mind. 4. to turn, go sour (e.g. milk). — **volverse atrás,** to back out, go back on one's word; to back down; **volverse contra,** to turn against; **volverse loco,** to go mad; (coll.) to be overjoyed.

volvible, *a.* turnable; reversible.

volvo, *m.* (med.) volvulus.

vólvulo, *m.* (med.) volvulus.

vómer, *m.* (anat., zool.) vomer, plowshare bone.

vomeriano, na, *a.* (anat., zool.) vomerine.

vomicina, *f.* (chem.) vomicine.

vómico, ca, *a.* vomitive, causing vomiting. —*f.* (med.) vomica.

vomipurgante, vomipurgativo, va, *a.* (med.) emeto-cathartic. —*m.* (med.) emeto-cathartic medicine.

vomitado, da, *a.* (coll.) pale, wan, sickly.

vomitador, ra, *a.* vomiting. —*m., f.* one who vomits.

vomitar, *tr.v.* 1. to vomit, throw up, spew, regurgitate. 2. (fig.) to vomit, belch forth (e.g. fire, shells, etc.). 3. (fig.) to utter, spit out (curses, insults). 4. (fig.) to let out (a secret). 5. (coll.) to give up, give back (an object to its rightful owner). —*i.v.* to vomit.

vomitivo, va, *a., m.* (med.) vomitive, emetic.

vómito, *m.* vomit; vomiting; **provocar a v.,** (coll.) to make one sick, to disgust or nauseate; **v. de sangre,** (med.) hemoptysis, haemoptysis; **v. negro** or **prieto,** (med.) black vomit, yellow fever.

vomitón, na, *a.* (coll.) said of one who frequently vomits (suckling baby). —*f.* (coll.) violent vomiting.

vomitorio, ria, *a.* vomitory, emetic. —*m.* 1. vomitory, emetic. 2. (Roman hist.) vomitory.

voracidad, *f.* voracity, voraciousness; greediness.

vorágine, *f.* whirlpool, vortex.

voraginoso, sa, *a.* 1. full of whirlpools. 2. (fig.) engulfing, overwhelming.

voraz, (*pl.* **voraces**) *a.* 1. voracious, greedy, ravenous. 2. fierce, destructive.

vorazmente, *adv.* 1. voraciously, greedily, ravenously. 2. destructively.

vormela, *f.* (zool.) tiger weasel (Vormela peregusna).

vórtice, *m.* vortex, whirlpool, whirlwind; center of a cyclone.

vorticela, *f.* (zool.) vorticella.

vortiginoso, sa, *a.* vortiginous, vortical, whirling.

vos, *pers. pron. sing. and pl.* thou, ye, you (seldom used now, gen. in poetry, prayers and to address persons of high rank, but more commonly employed in certain regions of Spanish America as a substitute for the informal **tú**).

vosear, *tr.v.* to address respectfully, address with the respectful form of **vos;** (Amer.) to address familiarly, address with the familiar form of **vos** as a substitute for **tú.**

Vosgos, *m.* Vosges (mountain range in N.E. France).

vosotros, tras, *pers. pron.* (*ref.* **vos**) (*pl.*) ye, you.

votación, *f.* 1. voting, balloting. 2. vote, total vote. — **por v.,** by choice; **v. de desempate,** runoff election.

votador, ra, *a.* voting. —*m., f.* **1. voter. 2. swearer, blasphemer.**

votante, *m., f.* voter, one who votes or casts a ballot.

votar, *i.v.* 1. to vote. 2. to vow, make a vow. 3. to swear, blaspheme. — **¡voto a tal!** confound it! upon my soul! —*tr.v.* to pass, approve (e.g. a law).

votivo, va, *a.* votive.

voto, *m.* 1. vote; ballot; opinion. — **el v. femenino,** the female vote; **el v. obrero,** the working-class vote. 2. vow, promise; votive offering. 3. oath, curse. 4. (*pl.*) wishes, desires. — **echar votos,** to curse; **hacer votos,** to wish, hope; **no tener voz ni v.,** not to have a say in; **ser** or **tener v.,** to have a vote; (fig.) to have authoritative knowledge of the subject under discussion, know what one is talking about; **v. activo,** right to vote; **v. de amén, v. de reata,** blind vote, vote of a yes man; yes man; **v. de calidad, v. decisivo,** casting vote; **v. de castidad,** (ecc.) chastity vow; **v. censura,** vote of censure; **v. de confianza,** vote of confidence; **v. de pobreza,** (ecc.) poverty vow; **v. pasivo,** eligibility for position or post; **v. por correo,** absentee ballot; **v. preferencial,** (polit.) preferential voting; **v. secreto,** secret ballot; **v. simple,** (ecc.) simple vow; **v. solemne,** (ecc.) solemn vow.

voy, *ref.* **ir.**

voz, (*pl.* **voces**), *f.* 1. voice, e.g. *v. ronca,* hoarse voice, *v. débil,* weak voice. 2. voice, prompting, counsel, e.g. *la v. de la razón,* the voice of reason. 3. voice, noise, e.g. *la v. del viento,* the voice, noise or hissing of the wind. 4. (*pl.*) shouts, cries. 5. word, term, e.g. *voz de mando,* (mil.) word of command. 6. say, right to voice an opinion, e.g. *tú no tienes v. ni voto,* you have no say in it. 7. story, rumor. 8. (gram.) voice. 9. (mus.) voice, e.g. *una v. de barítono,* a baritone voice. 10. (mus.) part, voice, e.g. *una canción para cuatro voces,* a four-part song. 11. voice, singer. — **aclarar la v.,** to clear one's throat; **ahuecar la v.,** to deepen one's tone of voice; **alzar la v.,** to raise one's voice; **a media v.,** in a low voice; (mus.) muffled; **anudársele a uno la v.,** to get a knot in one's throat, be choked with emotion; **a una v.,** unanimously; **a voces,** shouting, in loud voice; **a. v. en cuello** or **en grito,** at the top of one's voice; **cambio de v.,** change of voice; **correr la v.,** to pass the word or news; to spread a rumor; **dar la v. a,** to let know, inform; to call, shout to; **dar una v. a,** to call, shout to; **dar voces,** to shout; **de viva v.,** by word of mouth, orally, verbally; **en alta v.,** aloud; **en v. alta,** in a loud voice; **en v. baja,** in a low voice; **estar en v.,** to be in voice, be in good voice; **estar pidiendo a voces,** to be crying out to heaven for; **levantar la v. a,** to raise one's voice to; **llevar la v. cantante,** (mus.) to sing the melody; to be the boss, call the shots (sl., U.S.); **pedir a voces,** to shout for; **segunda v.,** (mus.) second part or voice; **soltar la v.,** to spread the news; **tomar la v.,** to take over from someone who is speaking; **tomar la v. de uno,** to speak up for one, defend one; **v. activa,** right to vote; (gram.) active voice; **v. aguda,** high-pitched voice; (mus.) treble voice; **v. cantante,** (mus.) melody; **v. de la conciencia,** voice of one's conscience; **v. de trueno,** thunderous voice.

vozarrón, *m.* zooming, booming voice.

V. R. *abbrev. of* **Vuestra Reverencia,** Your Reverence.

vuecencia, *contr. of* **Vuestra Excelencia,** Your Excellency.

vuelco, *m.* overturning; upset; tumble; **dar un v.,** to turn over; (mar.) to tilt over or list suddenly; **darle a uno un v. el corazón,** to have a sudden jolt of shock or joy.

vuelco, vuelque, *ref.* **volcar.**

vuele, *ref.* **volar.**

vuelillo, *m.* small ruffle or frill; lace edging.

vuelo, *m.* 1. flight; flying. 2. soaring, flight of fancy or imagination. 3. flare, fullness (of a skirt or cape). 4. (dressm.) ruffle, shirred edging. 5. wingspread; (*pl.*) flight feathers. 6. (archit.) projection, jutting. 7. (theat.) lift (backstage machine). — **al v., a v.,** at once, in a jiffy, very quickly; on the wing, in flight; **alzar el v.,** to fly away, take flight; (coll.) to dash off, leave quickly; **a v. de pájaro,** from a bird's eye view; **cazarlas** or **cogerlas al v.,** (coll.) to grasp or understand things quickly, catch on quickly; **coger v.,** to progress, grow, gather momentum; **cortar los vuelos a uno,** to clip someone's wings; **de alto v.,** important, big-time, e.g. *jugador de alto v.,* big-time gambler; **de un v., de v., en un v.,** quickly, at once, in a flash, in a jiffy; **levantar el v.,** to fly away, take flight; (coll.) to go into flights of fancy, become imaginative; to become conceited or haughty; **prender el v.,** to fly off, take flight; **tirar al v.,** to shoot on the wing; **tocar a v. las campanas,** to ring a full peal; **tomar v.,** to grow, progress, gather momentum; **v. a baja altura,** (aer.) low altitude flying; **v. a ciegas** or **ciego,** (aer.) blind flying; **v. a vela** or **sin motor,** gliding; **v. charter,** charter flight; **v. de entrenamiento,** (aer.) training flight; **v. de prueba,** (aer.) test flight; **v. de reconocimiento,** (aer.) test flight; **v. de reconocimiento,** (aer.) reconnaissance flight; **v. de servicio,** (aer.) operational flight; **v. espacial,** space flight; **v. espacial tripulado,** manned space flight; **v. libre,** hang-gliding; **v. regular,** scheduled airlines flight; **v. nocturno,** (aer.) night flight or flying; **v. planeado,** (aer.) volplane, gliding; **v. sin escala,** (aer.) nonstop flight; **v. solo,** (aer.) solo flight.

vuelo, *ref.* **volar.**

vuelta, *f.* 1. turn; turning; revolution; rotation. 2. walk, stroll, tour, e.g. *dar una v.,* to take a walk or stroll, to promenade. 3. turn, bend, twist, curve. 4. return, coming or going back. 5. return, restitution, giving back. 6. repetition. 7. back, reverse, other side, e.g. *a la v.,* on the back or the other side. 8. beating, thrashing. 9. (sew.) trimming, edging; facing, reverse. 10. cloak collar or muffler. 11. row (of stitches in knitting). 12. change, alteration. 13. change (money). 14. plowing. 15. turning up of card to determine trumps. 16. (archit.) curve (of intrados, arch or vault). 17. (min.) brilliance or shine of silver after cupellation. 18. time, e.g. *vas a entenderlo mejor de segunda v.,* you'll understand it better the second time. 19. (mus.) ritornel, ritornello. 20. recompense, compensation. — **a la v.,** around the corner; on the way back, on the return; on the back, on the other side; overleaf, on the other side of the page; **a la v. de,** at the end of; **a la v. de la esquina,** around the corner; (fig.) close by, just around the corner; **andar a las vueltas de,** to follow someone, keep a close tag on someone; **andar a vueltas,** to quarrel, argue; to fight; to be at loggerheads; **andar a vueltas con, para** or **sobre una cosa,** to be baffled or perplexed by something; to do all within one's power to find out about or do something; **andar en vueltas,** to stall, beat about the bush, make excuses in order not to do something; **a v. de,** about, around; **a v. de correo,** by return mail; **billete de ida y v.,** round-trip ticket; **buscarle a uno las vueltas,** (coll.) to try to find out what makes a person tick; to look out for one's occasion to do someone harm; **cogerle a uno las vueltas,** (coll.) to get to know a person thoroughly; to find out what someone is up to; **dar**

cien vueltas a, (coll.) to be miles ahead of, run rings around; **dar la v. a,** to go around, to skirt; **darle vueltas a algo,** to think about something over and over again; **darse una v. a la redonda,** (coll.) to examine oneself first (before criticizing others); **dar una v.,** to take a walk or stroll; to go for a run or ride, take a spin (in a car); to make a short trip; to change, alter; **dar una v. por,** to take a walk or stroll through or in; **dar v. a,** to turn; to turn around; **dar vueltas,** to go around, revolve; to go around in circles (literally and figuratively); to be in a whirl, be dizzy; **de v.,** on returning; back, e.g. *llevar de v.,* to take back, *traer de v.,* to bring back; **estar de v.,** to be back, have returned; (coll.) to know already, be already aware of something; **¡media v.!** about turn or face!; **no hay que darle vueltas,** there's no point in talking about it, it's already decided; **no tener v. de hoja,** (coll.) to be undeniable, be beyond discussion; **poner a uno de v. y media,** (coll.) to insult or abuse someone; **v. al mundo,** trip round the world; **v. cerrada,** sharp turn (in a road); **v. de carnero,** forward roll, head roll; heavy fall, thud, bump; **v. de campana,** somersault; complete turn; **v. de manos,** handspring; **v. en redondo,** complete turn.

vuelto, ta, *irr. past part. of* **volver.** —*m.* 1. (print.) verso. 2. (Amer.) change (money). — **guardar el v.,** to keep the change.

vueludo, da, *a.* full, flared (said of garment).

vuelva, vuelvo, *ref.* **volver.**

vuestro, ra, *pos. a.* (*ref.* **vos**) your, e.g. *vuestro amigo,* your friend. —*pos. pron.* of yours, e.g. *un amigo vuestro,* a friend of yours.

vulcanice, vulcanicé, *ref.* **vulcanizar.**

vulcanicidad, *f.* (geol., phys.) vulcanicity, volcanicity.

vulcanio, nia, *a.* Vulcanian; vulcanian, (pertaining to Vulcan or to fire).

vulcanismo, *m.* (geol.) vulcanism, volcanism.

vulcanista, *a., m., f.* (geol.) vulcanist.

vulcanita, *f.* (min.) vulcanite.

vulcanización, *f.* vulcanization.

vulcanizador, *a., m.* vulcanizer.

vulcanizar, (*ref.* *53*) *tr.v.* to vulcanize; to mend (a tire).

Vulcano, *m.* (astron., myth.) Vulcan.

vulgacho, *m.* (derog.) mob, rabble.

vulgar, *a.* 1. vulgar, common, coarse, unrefined. 2. common, popular, vulgar, general. 3. vulgar, vernacular, e.g. *latín v.,* vulgar Latin.

vulgarice, vulgaricé, *ref.* **vulgarizar.**

vulgaridad, *f.* 1. vulgarity. 2. commonplace, platitude.

vulgarismo, *m.* vulgarism, vulgar phrase or expression.

vulgarización, *f.* popularization; dissemination.

vulgarizador, ra, *a.* popularizing. —*m., f.* popularizer.

vulgarizar, (*ref.* *53*) *tr.v.* 1. to popularize; to disseminate, spread. 2. to make common or ordinary. 3. to translate into the vernacular. —*r.v.* 1. to be popularized or disseminated. 2. to become common or ordinary. 3. to become vulgar, common or coarse.

vulgarmente, *adv.* 1. commonly, popularly. 2. vulgarly, coarsely.

vulgata, *f.* (ecc.) Vulgate.

vulgo, *m.* common people.

vulnerabilidad, *f.* vulnerability.

vulnerable, *a.* 1. vulnerable. 2. (fig.) defective; censurable.

vulneración, *f.* act of injuring, wounding or damaging.

vulnerar, *tr.v.* to harm, injure, damage.

vulnerario, ria, *a.* 1. (law, ecc.) vulnerary, applied to priest who injures or kills someone. 2. (med.) vulnerary. —*m.* 1. (law) priest who wounds or kills someone. 2. (med.) vulnerary.

vulpécula, vulpeja, *f.* vixen, shefox.

vulpino, na, *a.* vulpine. —*m.* (bot.) plume grass.

vultuosidad, *f.* (med.) swelling, congestion.

vultuoso, sa, *a.* (med.) swollen.

vulturno, *m.* hot summer breeze.

vulva, *f.* (anat.) vulva.

vulvitis, *f.* (med.) vulvitis.

W

W, *f.* w (a letter which is not really part of the Spanish alphabet, but is used chiefly in the spelling of words taken from other languages.
W (chem.) *sym. of* **tungsteno,** wolfram (W).
waca, *f.* (geol.) wacke.
wad, *m.* (geol.) wad, bog manganese, black ocher.
wafle, *m.* (cul.) waffle.
waflera, *f.* weffle iron.
wagneriano, na, *a.* (mus.) Wagnerian, pertaining to the music of Richard Wagner.
walkie-talkie, *m.* walkie-talkie
walkman, *m.* Walkman (TM), personal stereo.
wahabí, (*pl.* **wahabíes**), *a.* wahabite, pertaining to a Moslem sect of Central Arabia.
wahabita, *a., var. of* **wahabí.**
walquiria, *f.* (myth.) walkyrie, any of the maidens of Odin or Wotan who escort dead heroes to Valhalla.
Washington, *m.* Washington, capital of the United States of America.
wat, *m.* (phys.) watt.
wáter, water closet, *m.* lavatory, toilet, water closet.
water polo, *m.* (sport.) water polo.
wattaje, *m.* wattage.
watthorímetro, *m.* watt-hour-meter.
WC *abbrev. of* **water closet,** water closet (WC).
weber, weberio, *m.* weber (unit of magnetic flux).
wehabita, *a. var, of* **wahabí.**
weismanismo, *m.* (biol.) Weismannism.
Wellington, *m.* Wellington, capital of New Zealand.
wernerita, *f.* (min.) wernerite.
Westfalia, *f.* Westphalia, region in West Germany.
whiski, *m.* whisky.
whist, *m.* whist (card game).
Wiclef, *m.* Wycliffe, John, English religious reformer who made the first complete translation of the Bible into English.
wiclefista, *a.* Wycliffist. —*m., f.* Wycliffite, follower of Jolm Wycliffe.
willemita, *f.* (min.) willemite.
windsurf, *m.* 1. windsurfing. 2. sailboard, windsurfer.
windsurfing, *m.* windsurfing.
windsurflista, *m., f.* windsurfer.
witerita, *f.* (min.) witherite.
wodenita, *f.* (geol.) wooddenite.
wolastonita, *f.* (min.) wollastonite.
wormiano, na, *a.* (anat.) Wormian.
Wotán, *m.* (myth.) Wotan, Germanic god of life and knowledge, equivalent to Odin in Scandinavian mythol.
wulfenita, *f.* (min.) wulfenite.
wurtzita, *f.* (min.) wurtzite.

X

X, *f.* x, twenty-fourth letter of the Spanish alphabet.
xana, *f.* water nymph (in the popular mythology of Northern Spain).
xantalina, *f.* (chem.) xanthaline.
xantato, *m.* (chem.) xanthate.
xanteína, *f.* (chem.) xanthein.
xanteno, *m.* (chem.) xanthene.
xántico, ca, *a.* (chem.) xanthic.
xantina, *f.* (chem.) xanthin; (biochem.) xanthine.
Xantipa, *f.* (hist.) Xanthippe, wife of Socrates; (fig.) a nagging wife.
xantoderma, xantodermia, *f.* (med.) xanthoderma.
xantodermo, ma, *m., f.* (anth.) xanthoderm.
xantófila, *f.* (chem.) xanthophyll.
xantógeno, *m.* (chem.) xanthogen.
xantoma, *m.* (med.) xanthoma.
xantopsia, *f.* (med.) xanthopsia.
xantopsina, *f.* (biochem.) xanthopsin.
xantosis, *f.* (med.) xanthosis.
xantoxilina, *f.* (chem., pharm.) xanthoxylin.
xantoxilo, *m.* (bot.) zanthoxylum.
xara, *f.* Moslem law originated in the Koran.
Xe *sym. of* **xenón,** xenon (Xe).
xenia, *f.* 1. (bot.) xenia. 2. xenium, present given to guest or stranger.
Xenoclea, *f.* (myth.) Xenoclea, priestess at Delphi, who refused to prophesy for Hercules.
Xenócrates, *m.* Xenocrates, Greek philosopher.
xenodiagnosis, *f.* (med.) xenodiagnosis.
Xenófanes, *m.* Xenophanes, Greek philosopher of the Eleatic school.
xenofilia, *f.* friendliness towards strangers or foreigners.
Xenófilo, la, *a.* xenophilous. —*m., f.* xenophile, a person who likes foreigners and strangers.
xenofobia, *f.* xenophobia, hatred of strangers or foreigners.
xenófobo, ba, *a.* xenophobic. —*m., f.* xenophobe, an enemy of foreigners.
xenogénesis, *f.* (biol.) xenogenesis.
xenolita, *f.* (min.) xenolith.
xenomórfico, ca, *a.* (min.) xenomorphic.
xenomorfo, a, *a.* (min.) xenomorphic.
xenon, *m.* (chem.) xenon.
xerasia, *f.* (med.) xerasia.
xerocopia, *f.* Xerox (TM), Xerox copy, photocopy.
xerocopiar, (*ref. 54*) *tr.v.* to photocopy, to make a Xerox (TM) of, to make a Xerox copy of.
xerodermia, *f.* (med.) xerosis.
xerofagia, *f.* xerophagy, xerophagia, a diet consisting of dry food.
xerofilo, la, *a.* (bot.) xerophilous.
xerófito, ta, *a.* (bot.) xerophytic. —*m.* xerophyte.
xeroftalmia, *f.* (med.) xerophthalmia.
xerografía, *f.* xerography.
xerografiar, (*ref. 54*) *tr.v.* to make a Xerox (TM) copy of, to make a Xerox of.
xerográfico, ca, *a.* xerographic.
Xerox, *m.* Xerox (TM).
xi, *f.* xi, fourteenth letter of Greek alphabet.
xifisternón, *m.* (anat.) xiphisternum.
xifoideo, a, *a.* (anat.) xiphoid.
xifoides, *a., m.* (anat.) xiphoid.
xifosuro, *m.* (zool.) xiphosuran, (*pl.*) Xiphosura.
xilan, *m.* (chem.) xylan.
xilana, *f.,* **xilano,** *m.* (chem.) xylan.
xilema, *f.* (bot.) xylem.
xileno, *m.* (chem.) xylene.
xílico, ca, *a.* (chem.) xylic.
xilidina, *f.* (chem.) xylidine.
xilobálsamo, *m.* (pharm.) xylobalsamum.
xilófago, ga, *a.* (ento.) xylophagous. —*m.* (ento.) xylophage.
xilófono, *m.* xylophone, a musical percussion instrument.
xilografía, *f.* xylography (art of engraving on wood); xylograph (engraving), woodcut.
xilográfico, ca, *a.* xylographic, xylographical, pertaining to wood engraving.
xilógrafo, fa, *m., f.* xylographer, engraver who specializes in woodcuts.
xiloide, *a.* xyloid.
xiloideo, a, *a.* xyloid, like or pertaining to wood; woody.
xiloidina, *f.* (chem.) xyloidin.
xilol, *m.* (chem.) xylol.
xilonita, *a.* transparent substance resembling celluloid.
xilórgano, *m.* ancient musical instrument somewhat like the xylophone.
xilosa, *f.* (chem.) xylose.
xilotila, *f.* (chem.) xylotile.
xilótomo, ma, *a.* (zool.) xylotomous.
xister, *m.* (surg.) xyster.

Y

Y, *f.* y, twenty-fifth letter of the Spanish alphabet.
y, *conj.* and; also used sometimes at the beginning of a sentence for emphasis, e.g. *¿y bien?* well, now then, and so? and then?; *y eso que,* although, notwithstanding, even though; *¿y qué?* so what? what then?
Y *sym. of* **itrio,** yttrium (Y).
ya, *adv.* 1. already, e.g. *ya lo he visto,* I've already seen it. 2. now, nowadays, e.g. *¿vienes? ya no,* are you coming? not now, *ya no se puede invitar como antes,* nowadays one cannot entertain as one used to, *ya entiendo,* now I understand. 3. later, later on, e.g. *ya te veré,* I'll see you later on. 4. right away, at once, e.g. *ya voy,* I'm coming at once. 5. at last, e.g. *ya ha llegado la hora de actuar,* at last the time has come to act. — **pues ya,** (coll.) yes of course; **si ya,** if, as long as; **ya no;** no longer; **ya lo creo,** of course! naturally! I should think so!; **ya que,** since, seeing that, inasmuch as. —*conj.* **ya . . . ya,** now . . . now, whether . . . or. —*interj.* **¡ya, ya!** oh, yes! of course! I see!
yaacabó, *m.* (ornith.) (variety of) hawk (Accipiter bicolor).
yaba, *f.* (bot.) angelin, cabbage tree (Andira inermis).
yabuna, *f.* (Cuba, bot.) savannah grass (Gramen yabuna).
yac, *m.* (zool.) yak.
yaca, *f.* (bot.) yacca (tree).
yacal, *m.* (Phil. I., bot.) yacal (tree).
yacaré, *m.* (zool., Arg., Bol., Par., Urug.) alligator, cayman.
yacedor, *m.* stableboy or farmhand who takes horses out to graze at night.
yacente, *a.* recumbent; reclining, supine, lying, e.g. *estatua y.,* recumbent statue. —*m.* (min.) floor of a vein.
yacer, (*ref. 28*) *i.v.* 1. to lie; to lie buried, rest. 2. to lie, be; to be located. 3. to graze at night. — **aquí yace,** here lies (inscription on tombstone); **y. con,** to have sexual intercourse with, lie with; **y. sepultado,** to lie buried.
yaciente, *a., var. of* **yacente.**
yacija, *f.* 1. bed, couch. 2. grave, tomb — **ser de mala y.,** to be a poor sleeper; to be restless; to be a ne'er-do-well.
yacimento, *m.* (geol.) bed, deposit, field; **y. aluvial,** alluvial deposit; **y. petrolífero,** oil field.
yacio, *m.* (bot.) rubber tree (Heyea guianensis).
yactura, *f.* (rare) loss, damage, injury.
yaga, yago, *ref.* **yacer.**
yagruma, *f.* **y. hembra,** (Cuba, bot.) trumpetwood.
yagrumo, *m.* (P. Rico, Ven., bot.) trumpetwood.
yagua, *f.* (Ven.) royal palm; (Cuba, P. Rico) fibrous tissue (on upper part of royal palm tree) used for thatching and in hat and rope making, (P. Rico) yagua (palm).
yagual, *m.* (C. Amer., Mex.) padded ring (for carrying loads on the head).
yaguané, *a.* (Arg.) having throat and flanks of different color from the rest of the body (said of cattle). —*m.* (zool.) skunk.
yaguar, *m.* (zool.) jaguar.
yaguasa, *f.* (Cuba, Hond., ornith.) tree duck.
yaguré, *m.* (S. Amer., zool.) skunk, polecat.
yaichihue, *m.* (Chile, bot.) tillandsia (Tillandsia humilis).
yaití, *m.* (Cuba, bot.) euphorbiaceous hard timber tree (Gymnanthes lucida).
yak, *m.* (zool.) yak.
Yakarta, *f.* Djakarta, Jakarta, capital of Indonesia.
yal, *m.* (Chile, ornith.) (variety of) finch.
yámbico, ca, *a.* iambic. —*m.* iambic (verse).
yambo, *m.* 1. (poet.) iamb, iambus, iambic. 2. (bot.) jambo.
yana, *f.* (Cuba, bot.) button tree (Conocarpus erecta).
yanacón, *m.* (Peru) sharecropper.
yanacona, *m., f.* 1. (Quech., S. Amer.) Indian bound to personal service. 2. (Bol., Peru) sharecropper.
yanca, *f.* (Chile, min.) selvage, salband, gouge.
yanilla, *f.* (Cuba, bot.) kind of mangrove.
yanqui, *a., m., f.* Yankee, American.
yanquilandia, *f.* (Amer.) Yankeedom, Yankeeland.
yantar, *m.* 1. (arch.) tax paid to king by districts through which he travels. 2. (rare) viands, food.
yantar, *tr.v.* (arch.) to eat.
yapa, *f.* 1. (Amer.) bonus, extra, lagniappe. 2. (min.) mercury added to silver ore.
yapar, *tr.v.* (Amer.) to give a little more, to add the tip.
yapok, *m.* (zool.) yapok, yapock.
yapú, (*pl.* **yapúes**), *m.* (Arg., ornith.) (variety of) thrush (Yanthornus decumanus).
yáquil, *m.* (Chile, bot.) prickly shrub whose roots produce soapy lather and are used for washing.
yarara, (*pl.* **yararaes**), *f.* (Arg., zool.) pit viper (Bothrops alternata).
yaraví, (*pl.* **yaravíes**), *m.* (Amer.) sweet melancholic song.
yarda, *f.* yard (unit of measure).
yare, *m.* poisonous juice from bitter cassava or yucca.
yarey, *m.* 1. (Cuba, Dom. Rep., bot.) fan palm (Coccothrimax argentea). 2. (Cuba, Dom. Rep.) fan palm fiber. — **sombrero de y.,** peasant's wide-brimmed hat.
yaro, *m.* (bot.) cuckoopint, arum.
yatagán, *m.* yataghan (Turkish saber).
yate, *m.* (mar.) yacht.
yatrogénico, ca, *a.* (med.) iatrogenic.
yatroquímica, *f.* iatrochemistry.
yaunde, *m.* Yaounde, capital of Cameroon.
yaya, *f.* 1. (Amer.) wound, injury; damage (baby talk). 2. (Cuba) walking stick. 3. (Pan.) difficult situation, jam, fix. 4. (Cuba) yaya lancewood. 5. (Peru, ento.) mite.
yazca, yazco, *ref.* **yacer.**
yazga, yazgo, *ref.* **yacer.**
Yb *sym. of* **iterbio,** ytterbium (Yb).
yeco, ca, *a.* virgin, untilled (land). —*m.* (Chile, ornith.) cormorant (Phalacrocorax brasilianus).
yedra, *f.* (bot.) ivy.
yegua, *f.* 1. mare. 2. (C. Amer.) cigar butt. — **y. caponera,** lead mare; **y. madre,** dam.
yeguada, *f.* 1. drove of horses. 2. (S. Amer.) indiscreet or stupid act.
yeguar, *a.* pertaining to mares.
yegüería, *f., var. of* **yeguada.**
yegüerizo, za, *a.* pertaining to a mare. —*m.* keeper of a drove of mares.
yegüero, *m.* keeper of a drove of mares.
yegüezuela, *f. dim. of* **yegua,** small mare.
yeísmo, *m.* pronunciation of Spanish ll as y.
yelmo, *m.* helmet.
yema, *f.* 1. (bot., zool.) bud; gemma. 2. yolk (of egg). 3. candied egg yolk. 4. best part, cream. 5. middle, heart, center. — **dar en la y. del gusto,** to hit on the very thing one likes; **en la y. del invierno,** in the depths of winter; **y. del dedo,** finger tip; **y. mejida,** eggnog.
Yemen, *m.* Yemen.
yemenita, *a., m., f.* Yemeni, Yemenite.
yen, *m.* (numis.) yen.
yerba, *f.,* 1. *var. of* **hierba.** 2. (S. Amer.) maté.
yerbabuena, *f., var. of* **hierbabuena,** mint.
yerbajo, *m.* weed.
yerbal, *m.* (Amer.) maté field or plantation.
yerbatear, *i.v.* (Amer.) to take maté, Paraguay tea.
yerbatero, ra, *m., f.* 1. herb doctor. 2. one who sells or grows maté.
yerbero, ra, *m., f.* 1. (Arg.) maté pot, container for storing maté. 2. (Cuba) herb doctor.
yerga, yergo, yergue, *ref.* **erguir.**
yermar, *tr.v.* to strip, lay waste; to leave uncultivated.
yermo, ma, *a.* 1. deserted, uninhabited. 2. barren, waste (land). —*m.* desert, wilderness; wasteland, barren land.
yerno, *m.* son-in-law.
yero, *m.* (bot.) vetch.
yerra, *f.* (Arg., Col., Chile, Urug.) cattle branding; branding season.
yerre, yerro, yerra, *ref.* **errar.**
yerro, *m.* 1. error, mistake, blunder. 2. error, fault, sin. — **deshacer un y.,** to correct or put right an error; **y. de imprenta,** typographical error.
yerto, ta, *a.* stiff, rigid; motionless, e.g. *y. de frío,* stiff, numb with cold.
yervo, *m.* (bot.) vetch.
yesal, yesar, *m.* gypsum pit or quarry; gypsum bed or deposit.
yesca, *f.* 1. touchwood, punk, tinder. 2. (fig.) fuel (to fire passion, anger, etc.). 3. (coll.) thirst provoker. 4. (*pl.*) tinderbox.
yesera, *f.* 1. gypsum pit or quarry. 2. woman who sells plaster.
yesería, *f.* 1. gypsum kiln. 2. plasterer's shop, plaster factory. 3. plaster work, plaster objects. 4. (bldg.) plastering operation.
yesero, ra, *a.* plaster; **fábrica yesera,** plaster factory. —*m.* plaster manufacturer, maker or dealer.
yeso, *m.* 1. (chem.) gypsum. 2. plaster (for coating walls, making casts, etc.). 3. plaster cast, statue cast in plaster. 4. chalk, white crayon (for writing on blackboards). — **y. blanco,** (mas.) finishing plaster, superfine white plaster; **y. espejuelo,** (min.) selenite; **y. mate,** (archit.) plaster of Paris, stucco; **y. negro,** (mas.) coarse plaster.

yesón, *m.* chunk of plaster, plaster rubble.
yesoso, sa, *a.* gypseous; chalky.
yesque, *m.* (Col.) hook.
yesquero, *a.* **cardo y.,** (bot.) cotton thistle; **hongo y.,** (bot.) touchwood, punk, tinder fungus. —*m.* 1. tinder maker or dealer. 2. purse, wallet, or tobacco pouch (fastened to the belt).
yeta, *f.* (Arg.) bad luck.
yeyuno, *m.* (anat., zool.) jejunum.
yesgo, *m.* (bot.) danewort, dwarf elder.
yídish, *a., m.* Yiddish.
yira, yiranta, *f.* (Arg.) prostitute.
yo, *pers. pron.* I, e.g. *yo mismo,* I myself. —*m.* (philos., psyc.) I, the ego.
y/o, *conj.* and/or.
Yocasta, *f.* (myth.) Jocasta.
yodado, da, *a.* iodized.
yodato, *m.* (chem.) iodate.
yodhídrico, ca, *a.* (chem.) hydriodic.
yódico, ca, *a.* (chem.) iodic.
yodirita, *f.* (min.) iodyrite, native silver iodide.
yodismo, *m.* (med.) iodism.
yodo, *m.* (chem.) iodine.
yodoformo, *m.* (chem.) iodoform.
yodol, *m.* (chem.) iodol.
yodopsina, *f.* (biochem.) iodopsin.
yodoso-benceno, *m.* (chem.) iodosobenzene.
yodurar, *tr.v.* to iodize.
yoduro, *m.* (chem.) iodide; **y. de plata,** (chem.) silver iodide; **y. mercúrico,** (chem.) mercuric iodine, brilliant scarlet.
yoga, *m.* yoga.
yogi, yogui, yoghi, *m.* yogi.
yoguismo, *m.* yogism.
yogur, yoghurt, yogurt, *m.* yogurt.
yohimbina, f. (pharm.) yohimbine.
yola, *f.* (mar.) yawl, gig.
yole, *m.* (Arg., Chile) leather saddle bag.
yolillo, *m.* (C. Rica, bot.) jupati, jupati palm.
yoruba, *a.* (hist., geog., philol.) Yoruban. —*m., f.* Yoruba.
yperita, *f.* (chem.) yperite.
ypsilon, *f.* upsilon, twentieth letter of Greek alphabet.
yubarta, *f.* (zool.) humpback whale.
yuca, *f.* 1. (bot.) yucca, cassava. 2. (bot.) yucca (liliaceous plant). — **y. agria, amarga** or **brava,** (bot.) bitter cassava.
yuca, *f.* 1. (C. Amer., Bol.) lie. 2. (Hond.) unpleasant news. 3. (P. Rico, Dom. Rep.) poverty.
yucal, *m.* yucca or cassava field.
yucateco, ca, *a.* Yucatecan. —*m., f.* Yucatec.
yugada, *f.* 1. day's plowing by one team of oxen. 2. team of oxen.
yugo, *m.* 1. yoke (crosspiece harnessing draft animals). 2. symbol of oppressive power. 3. (Cuba, Dom. Rep.) cuff link. 4. (mar.) transom. 5. nuptial tie. 6. frame of a church bell. 7. (fig.) yoke, burden. 8. (hist.) arch of spears under which the conquered were forced to pass. — **sacudir el y.,** to throw off the yoke, struggle for liberation.
Yugoslavia, Yugoeslavia, *f.* Yugoslavia.
yugoslavo, va, *a., m., f.* Yugoslav.
yuguero, *m.* plowman, driving a team of draft animals.
yugular, *a., f.* (anat.) jugular.
Yugurta, *m.* (hist.) Jugurtha.
yumbo, ba, *m., f.* Indian from eastern Ecuador.
yungas, *f.* (*pl.*) (Peru, Bol.) warm valleys.
yunque, *m.* 1. anvil. 2. (anat.) incus, anvil. 3. patient, hard-working person; plodder. — **estar al y.,** to be hard at work; to bear under trying circumstances.
yunta, *f.* 1. yoke, team (of oxen, mules, etc.). 2. day's plowing by a yoke or team of oxen.
yuntería, *f.* number of team of oxen; place where teams of oxen are kept.
yuntero, *m., var. of* **yuguero.**
yunto, ta, *a., adv.* close; **arar yunto,** to plow close.
yuquerí, *m.* (Arg., bot.) (variety of) acacia (Acacia riparia).
yuraguano, *m.* (Cuba., bot.) fan palm, (Corypha palm).
yuré, *m.* (C. Rica, ornith.) small breed of pigeon.
yuruma, *f.* (Ven.) palm tree pith used by Indians for making a type of bread.
yusera, *f.* horizontal stone in olive mill.
yusión, *f.* (law) precept, command, order.
yuso, *adv.* downward, below.
yuta, *f.* (Chile, zool.) slug.
yute, *m.* jute (plant, fiber and fabric).
yuxtalineal, *a.* (print.) in parallel columns (said of a text and its translation).
yuxtaponer, (*ref. 15*) *tr.v.* to juxtapose.
yuxtaposición, *f.* juxtaposition.
yuyo, *m.* 1. (Arg., Chile) weed. 2. (Chile, bot.) wall rocket. 3. (Peru) seaweed. 4. (Peru) green vegetable. 5. (Ecuad., Col.) herb, seasoning herb. 6. (C. Rica) toe blister. 7. (Peru) boob, sap, gawk, clumsy person. — **y. colorado,** (Arg., bot.) pigweed (Amaranthus hibridus).
yuyuba, *f.* (bot.) jujube, berry.

Z

Z, *f.* **z,** twenty-sixth letter of the Spanish alphabet.
¡za! *interj.* shoo! (said to drive away dogs).
zabarcera, *f.* (woman) greengrocer, fruit seller.
zabida, zabila, *f.* (bot.) aloe.
zaborda, *f.* **zabordamiento,** *m.* (mar.) running aground.
zabordar, *i.v.* (mar.) to run aground, become stranded.
zabordo, *m.* (mar.), *var. of* **zaborda.**
zaborro, *m.* fatty, fat man or boy.
zabra, *f.* small frigate.
zabucar, (*ref. 50*) *tr.v.* to shake (liquid in a container).
zabullida, *f., var. of* **zambullida.**
zabullidor, ra, *a., var. of* **zambullidor.**
zabullidura, *f., var. of* **zambullidura.**
zabullimiento, *m., var. of* **zambullimiento.**
zabullir, (*ref. 65*) *tr.v., r.v., var. of* **zambullir.**
zabuque, zabuqué, *ref.* **zabucar.**
zabuqueo, *m.* shaking (liquid in a container).
zaca, *f.* (min.) large leather bag for bailing out a mine.
zacapela, zacapella, *f.* row, rumpus, shindy.
Zacarías, *m.* (Bib.) Zachariah, Zechariah.
zacatal, *m.* (C. Amer., Mex.) pasture land, pasture.
zacate, *m.* (C. Amer., Mex., Phil. I.) hay, fodder; **el que tiene cola de z. no puede jugar con lumbre,** (Mex.) people who live in glass houses should not throw stones.
zacateca, *m.* (Cuba) undertaker.
zacatín, *m.* old clothes market.
zacatón, *m.* (Mex.) tall fodder grass.
zacear, *tr.v.* to shoo away, chase away animals. —*i.v.* to lisp.
zadorija, *f.* (bot.) yellow poppy (Hypercoum grandiflorum).
zafa, *f.* basin, bowl.
zafacoca, *f.* row, quarrel.
zafada, *f.* (mar.) clearing, freeing; loosening, untying.
zafado, da, *a.* (Amer.) brazen, bold. —*m., f.* (Amer.) bold or brazen person.
zafar, *tr.v.* to deck, adorn.
zafar, *tr.v.* 1. (mar.) to loosen, untie; to free, clear. 2. to deck, adorn. —*r.v.* 1. to escape, get away; to hide. 2. to come off, slip off, become untied. 3. (Amer.) to get dislocated. — **zafarse de,** to escape from; to get out of, to elude, avoid, get rid of.
zafarí, (*pl.* **zafaríes**), *a.* very sweet fig or pomegranate.
zafarrancho, *m.* 1. (mar.) clearing the decks. 2. (coll.) ravage, destruction. 3. (coll.) row, quarrel, rumpus, shindy. — **z. de combate,** (mar.) clearing for action; **z. de limpieza,** (mar.) general cleaning.
zafiamente, *adv.* crudely, coarsely, roughly, uncouthly.
zafiedad, *f.* crudeness, coarseness, uncouthness, roughness.
zafio, fia, *a.* crude, coarse, uncouth, rough.
zafir, *m.,* **zafira,** *f.* sapphire.
zafíreo, a, *a.* sapphirine, sapphire.
zafirina, *f.* **zafirino,** *m.* (jewel.) sapphirine.
zafiro, *m.* sapphire.
zafo, fa, *a.* 1. (mar.) free, clear. 2. safe, unhurt.
zafón, *m., var. of* **zahón.**
zafra, *f.* 1. sugar cane crop; sugar cane harvest time; sugar-making season. 2. (min.) rubble, rubbish. 3. oil storage can; shallow vessel for draining oil measures and funnels.
zafre, *m.* (min.) zaffer, zaffre.
zafrero, *m.* (min.) workman who removes rubbish from mine.
zaga, *f.* rear; rear load (in carriage); **a la z., a z., en z.,** at the rear, behind; **no ir** or **no irle en z. a, no quedarse en z. a,** (coll.) to keep up with, be as good as. —*m.* (sport.) back, defense player.
zagal, *m.* 1. lad, youth. 2. shepherd's helper. 3. boy who helps stagecoach driver. 4. underskirt worn by country women.
zagala, *f.* 1. lass, maid. 2. young shepherdess.
zagaleja, *f. dim. of* **zagala,** lassie.
zagalejo, *m.* 1. *dim. of* **zagal,** laddie. 2. underskirt worn by country women.
zagalón, na, *m., f.* strapping lad or lass.
zagua, *f.* (bot.) saltwort (Salsola oppositifolia).
zagual, *m.* paddle (of a canoe).
zaguán, *m.* portico, doorway, lobby; carriage entrance.
zaguanete, *m.* 1. *dim. of* **zaguán,** small entrance hall. 2. royal guards' room; royal guard or escort.
zaguero, ra, *a.* 1. rear, hind. 2. lagging behind. —*m.* (sport.) backstop; fullback; defense player.
zahareño, ña, *a.* 1. (hunt.) haggard (falcon). 2. (fig.) wild, intractable.
zaharí, (*pl.* **zaharíes**), *a., var. of* **zafarí.**
zaharrón, *m.* ridiculous or humorous costume worn in a masquerade.
zahena, *f.* (hist.) valuable gold coin prized in Spain during Moorish domination.
zaheridor, ra, *a.* wounding (words), reproachful; censuring, upraiding. —*m., f.* reproacher; censurer, upbraider.
zaherimiento, *m.* reproach; upbraiding, reprimand.
zaherir, (*ref. 42*) *tr.v.* to wound (with words), reproach; to upbraid, reprimand.
zahiera, zahiero, *ref.* **zaherir.**
zahina, *f.* (bot.) sorghum.
zahinar, *m.* sorghum field.
zahiriendo, *ref.* **zaherir.**
zahiriente, *a.* wounding, reproachful (e.g. words).
zahiriera, zahiriese, zahirió, *ref.* **zaherir.**
zahón, *m.* chaps, leather overalls (*gen. in pl.*).
zahonado, da, *a.* of a different color in front (said of an animal's feet).
zahondar, *tr.v.* to dig. —*i.v.* to sink down (in the ground).
zahora, *f.* (reg., Sp.) party, feast, merrymaking.
zahorar, *i.v.* (reg., Sp.) to have a party, celebrate, make merry.
zahorí, (*pl.* **zahoríes**), *m.* 1. seer, diviner. 2. (fig.) perspicacious or far-seeing person.
zahorra, *f.* (mar.) ballast.
zahurda, *f.* pigsty, pigpen; unclean, unkempt establishment.
zaida, *f.* (ornith.) (variety of) crane (Anthropoides paradisea).
zaino, na, *a.* 1. treacherous, false. 2. vicious (horse, mule). 3. chestnut-colored (horse); black (cattle). — **a lo z.,** sideways, out of the corner of one's eye.
zainoso, sa, *a.* (Chile) treacherous, false, deceitful.
Zaire, *f.* The Republic of Zaïre.
zajarí, (*pl.* **zajaríes**), *a., var. of* **zafarí.**
zalá, (*pl.* **zalaes**), *f.* Mohammedan prayer; **hacer la z. a,** (coll.) to curry favor with, butter up, flatter, cajole.
zalagarda, *f.* 1. ambush, ambuscade. 2. skirmish (between horsemen). 3. trap, snare. 4. (coll.) cunning, astuteness. 5. (coll.) sudden racket, shindy, disturbance. 6. (coll.) noisy mock fight.
zalama, *f.* **zalamelé,** *m.* **zalamería,** *f.* flattery, cajolery; studied display of affection.
zalamero, ra, *a.* flattering, fawning, cajoling. —*m., f.* flatterer, fawner, cajoler.
zalea, *f.* woolfell, unshorn sheepskin.
zalear, *tr.v.* 1. to shake and jostle. 2. to shoo away, frighten or chase away (a dog).
zalema, *f.* 1. (coll.) salaam, obeisance, bow. 2. flattery, cajolery.
zaleo, *m.* 1. shake, jostle, jostling. 2. woolfell, unshorn sheepskin.
zallar, *tr.v.* (mar.) to rig out.
zamacuco, *m.* 1. (coll.) fool, dolt. 2. crafty person, artful dodger. 3. drunkenness, drunken bout.
zamacueca, *f.* (Chile, Peru) folk dance and its music.
zamanca, *f.* (coll.) thrashing, beating, drubbing.
zamarra, *f.* 1. sheepskin jacket. 2. unshorn sheepskin.
zamarrada, *f.* (coll.) boorishness, uncouthness.
zamarrear, *tr.v.* 1. to shake and tear with its teeth (as a wolf does its prey). 2. to handle roughly, push and jostle. 3. to pin down or corner (in an argument).
zamarreo, *m.* shaking about; pushing, jostling; rough treatment.
zamarrico, *m.* sheepskin pack or bag.
zamarrilla, *f.* (bot.) poly.
zamarro, *m.* 1. sheepskin jacket or coat or trousers; unshorn sheepskin. 2. (coll.) boor, lout, rustic. 3. (Amer.) rogue, rascal. 4. (Ven., Col.) (*pl.*) chaps, chaparejos.
zamarrón, *m. aug. of* **zamarra,** large sheepskin; long sheepskin jacket.
zamarronear, *tr.v.* (Chile) *var. of* **zamarrear.**
zambaigo, ga, *a.* half Negro half Indian; (Mex.) half Chinese half Indian.
zambapalo, *m.* ancient West Indian dance and its music.
zambarco, *m.* broad breast strap (of harness); cinch.
zambardo, *m.* 1. (Chile) awkward person, bungler. 2. (Arg.) chance, luck. 3. (Arg., Chile) damage, breakage.
Zambia, *f.* Zambia.
zambigo, ga, *a.* knock-kneed.
zambo, ba, *a.* 1. knock-kneed. 2. half Indian half Negro. —*m., f.* zambo, sambo, offspring of an Indian and a Negro. —*m.* (zool.) spider monkey (Ateles hybridus).

zamboa, *f.* (bot.) citron (fruit).
zambomba, *f.* zambomba, a Spanish rustic instrument in the shape of a drum, played by rubbing a rod attached to the parchment. —*interj.;* **z.!** whew! what do you know!
zambombazo, *m.* blow, thump, whack; bang, explosion.
zambombo, *m.* (coll.) uncouth person, boor, dolt.
zamborondón, na, zamborotudo, da, *a.* 1. (coll.) coarse, crude, unshapely. 2. (coll.) clumsy, awkward. —*m., f.* bungler, clumsy person.
zambra, *f.* 1. Moorish party or celebration. 2. (coll.) shindy, racket, din, uproar. 3. Andalusian Gypsy dance and its music. 4. a type of Moorish boat.
zambucar, (*ref. 50*) *tr.v.* (coll.) to hide away, conceal; to shuffle (something) out of sight.
zambuco, *m.* (coll.) concealing, hiding away, shuffling (something) out of sight.
zambullida, *f.* 1. dive, plunge, ducking. 2. (fenc.) lunge, thrust.
zambullidor, ra, *a.* diving, plunging. —*m.* (ornith.) dabchick.
zambullidura, *f.* **zambullimiento,** *m.* diving, plunging, ducking.
zambullir, (*ref. 65*) *tr.v.* to dive, plunge into water, duck. —*r.v.* 1. to dive, plunge (into water) to dip, sink. 2. to hide, conceal oneself.
zambullo, *m.* large chamber pot.
Zamora, no se ganó Z. en una hora, Rome wasn't built in a day.
zampa, *f.* (bldg.) pile (used as foundation for building, etc.).
zampabodigos, (*pl.* **zampabodigos**), **zampabollos,** (*pl.* **zampabollos**), *m., f.* (coll.), *var. of* **zampatortas.**
zampalimosnas, (*pl.* **zampalimosnas**), *m., f.* (coll.) beggar, bum, tramp.
zampapalo, *m., f.* (coll.), *var. of* **zampatortas.**
zampar, *tr.v.* 1. to hide or put away. 2. to stuff or cram (food) down, gobble down. —*r.v.* 1. to stuff or gobble down. 2. rush in; to gate-crash (a party).
zampatortas, (*pl.* **zampatortas**), *m.* 1. (coll.) glutton. 2. (coll.) boor, uncouth person.
zampeado, *m.* (bldg.) grillage, piles, pilework.
zampear, *tr.v.* (bdg.) to strengthen with grillage or piles, put a strengthening base of piles or grillage on.
zampón, na, *a.* gluttonous. —*m., f.* glutton.
zampoña, *f.* 1. reed flute or pipe, panpipes. 2. (coll.) nonsense, triviality.
zampuce, zampucé, *ref.* **zampuzar.**
zampuzar, (*ref. 53*) *tr.v.* 1. to hide away, conceal quickly. 2. to plunge into water, duck.
zampuzo, *m.* 1. hiding away. 2. ducking, diving.
zamuro, *m.* (Col., Ven., ornith.) turkey buzzard (Cathartes aura).
zanahoria, *f.* 1. (bot.) carrot. 2. (Arg.) fool, dimwit, dolt.
zanahoriate, *m.* (cul.) candied carrot.
zanca, *f.* 1. long leg (of bird); (coll.) long leg, shank (of man or any animal). 2. (archit.) stringboard, horse (notched board supporting steps of staircase). — **andar en zancas y barrancas,** (coll.) to stall, invent all sorts of arguments to avoid an obligation, etc.; **por zancas** o **barrancas,** (coll.) by hook or by crook.
zancada, *f.* stride; **en dos zancadas,** (coll.) in a jiffy, in two shakes of a donkey's tail.
zancadilla, *f.* 1. trip, tripping. 2. (coll.) trap, trick. — **armarle z. a uno,** (coll.) to set a trap for; **echarle la z. a uno,** to trip someone.
zancajear, *i.v.* to run or rush about, stride about.
zancajera, *f.* step of a running board.
zancajiento, ta, *a., var. of* **zancajoso.**
zancajo, *m.* 1. heel bone; (coll.) big bone. 2. hole in the heel of a stocking. 3. (coll.) ungainly-looking person. — **no llegarle a los zancajos** or **al z. a uno,** (coll.) not to be able to hold a candle to one, not to be the equal of one; **roer los zancajos a uno,** (coll.) to talk behind someone's back.
zancajoso, sa, *a.* 1. bowlegged, bandy-legged. 2. wearing stockings with holes at the heels.
zancarrón, *m.* 1. (coll.) leg bone; large bone. 2. (coll.) scruffy, skinny old man. 3. (coll.) ignorant teacher.
zanco, *m.* 1. stilt. 2. (mar.) short mast replacing topgallant mast. — **en zancos,** in a high position.
zancón, na, *a.* 1. (coll.) long-legged. 2. (Col., Guat., Mex., Ven.) very short (dressm.).
zancudo, da, *a.* 1. long-legged. 2. (ornith.) wading. —*f.* (ornith.) wading bird, wader. —*m.* (Amer.) mosquito.
zandía, *f.* watermelon.
zanfonía, *f.* (mus.) a kind of hurdy-gurdy.
zanga, *f.* 1. four-handed ombre (card game). 2. remaining eight cards picked up by the last player in this game.
zangala, *f.* buckram.
zangamanga, *f.* trick, trap, deceit, ruse.
zángana, *f.* drone, lazy useless woman.
zanganada, *f.* (coll.) impertinence, impertinent or inopportune remark.
zangandongo, ga, zangandullo, lla, zangandungo, ga, *m., f.* (coll.) drone, useless loafer.
zanganear, *i.v.* to loaf about, loaf, idle.
zanganería, *f.* idleness, laziness.
zángano, *m.* 1. (ento.) drone. 2. (coll.) drone, parasite, sponger, idler.
zangarilleja, *f.* (coll.) slut, slattern, slovenly young woman.
zangarrear, *i.v.* (coll.) to thrum or strum a guitar.
zangarriana, *f.* 1. (vet.) dropsy. 2. slight recurring illness. 3. (coll.) gloominess, blues, sadness.
zangarullón, *m.* (coll.) *var. of* **zangón.**
zangolotear, *tr.v.* (coll.) to shake violently. —*i.v.* (coll.) to rush around, flit around. —*r.v.* (coll.) to shake, rattle, swing, slam.
zangoloteo, *m.* 1. shaking, rattling, swinging, slamming. 2. (coll.) rushing or flitting about.
zangolotino, na, *a.* said of a boy or girl who acts like a small child.
zangón, *m.* (coll.) lanky lazy youth.
zangotear, *tr.v.* (coll.), *var. of* **zangolotear.**
zangoteo, *m.* (coll.), *var. of* **zangoloteo.**
zanguanga, *f.* 1. (coll.) malingering, feigning illness to avoid work. 2. (coll.) flattery, cajolery. — **hacer la z.,** (coll.) to malinger, pretend to be ill in order to avoid work.
zanguango, ga, *a.* (coll.) slothful, sluggish. —*m., f.* (coll.) loafer, sluggard.
zanguayo, *m.* (coll.) lanky idler who acts the simpleton.
zanja, *f.* ditch, trench; (Amer.) gully; **abrir las zanjas,** to dig the foundations of a building; to commence, start.
zanjar, *tr.v.* 1. to dig ditches or trenches in. 2. to bridge, overcome, surmount (differences, difficulties, etc.); to settle (a discussion).
zanjón, *m.* deep drain, gully or ditch.
zanqueador, ra, *m., f.* 1. bowlegged walker. 2. one who rushes or hurries about. 3. one who walks much.
zanqueamiento, *m.* 1. walking in a bowlegged manner. 2. rushing or hurrying about.
zanquear, *i.v.* 1. to walk in a bowlegged manner. 2. to rush or hurry about; to walk much and often.
zanquilargo, ga, *a.* (coll.) long-legged, long-shanked, lanky. —*m., f.* long-legged person.
zanquilla, zanquita, *m., f.* (coll.) short thin-legged person, shorty (sl.) (*gen. in pl.*).
zanquituerto, ta, *a.* (coll.) bandy-legged.
zanquivano, na, *a.* (coll.) spindle-shanked, spindle-legged.
Zanzíbar, *m.* (geog.) Zanzibar.
zapa, *f.* 1. (mil.) trenching spade or tool. 2. (fort.) sap, sapping, trenching. — **caminar a la z.,** (mil.) to advance under cover of trenches or mines.
zapa, *f.* 1. shagreen, shark skin (rough skin of sharks). 2. shagreen, shagreen leather. 3. rough finish (on metal imitating shark skin).
zapador, *m.* (mil.) sapper.
zapadora, *f.* (mach.) excavator.
zapallito, *m.* (S. Amer., bot.) small vegetable marrow; **z. italiano,** (S. Amer., bot.) zucchini.
zapallo, *m.* 1. (S. Amer., bot.) pumpkin, squash. 2. (Arg., Chile) stroke of luck.
zapapico, *m.* pickaxe, mattock.
zapar, *i.v.* (mil.) to sap, mine.
zaparrada, *f.* (coll.) clawing, blow with a claw.
zaparrastrar, *i.v.* (coll.) to drag one's clothes on the ground.
zaparrastroso, sa, *a.* (coll.) ragged, shabby, dirty, filthy. —*m., f.* tramp, ragamuffin.
zaparrazo, *m.* (coll.) clawing, blow with a claw.
zapata, *f.* 1. half boot. 2. (mec.) shoe (of a brake). 3. (mar.) shoe (of the anchor). 4. (mar.) false keel. 5. (archit.) capital (of a column). 6. (mec.) washer (of a faucet or tap). 7. piece of leather put under the hinge of a door to stop it from creaking. 8. (Cuba) masonry socle (at the foot of a wooden wall). 9. (Chile) strut joining the beam and moldboard of a plow. 10. shoe, plow (for taking current from the third rail). — **z. de freno,** brake shoe; **z. del polo,** (elec.) pole shoe; **z. de toma,** (elec.) contact shoe.
zapatazo, *m.* 1. blow with a shoe. 2. thud, bang, bump. 3. hoof beat, clatter of horse's hoofs. 4. flapping (of a sail). — **tratar a zapatazos,** (coll.) to ill-treat.
zapateado, *m.* zapateado, Spanish heel-tapping dance and its music.
zapateador, ra, *m., f.* Spanish dancer who specializes in heel-tapping dances.
zapatear, *tr.v.* 1. to hit or strike with the shoe. 2. to tap with the feet. 3. to thump (the ground) with its feet (e.g. a rabbit). 4. (fenc.) to hit frequently with the button of the foil. 5. to ill-treat. —*i.v.* 1. to tap one's feet. 2. to flap (said of sails). —*r.v.* to stand firm, hold one's own (in an argument, etc.).
zapateo, *m.* 1. the act of tapping with the foot. 2. the heel-tapping sequence of some Spanish dances. 3. (Cuba) a heel-and-toe tap dance performed mostly in the countryside. 4. (mar.) the flapping of sails.
zapatera, *f.* 1. shoemaker's wife. 2. female shoemaker or shoe dealer. 3. (coll.) player who gets no tricks (in cards).
zapatería, *f.* shoemaker's shop; shoe store; shoemaking trade; **z. de viejo,** shoe repair shop.
zapateril, *a.* pertaining to a shoemaker or his trade.
zapatero, ra, *a.* said of hard, insufficiently cooked beans or grain. —*m.* 1. shoemaker, cobbler; shoe dealer. 2. (ichth.) threadfish, cobbler fish. 3. (ento.) water strider. 4. (coll.) player who gets no tricks (at cards). — **zapatero, a tus zapatos,** stick to your field or specialty; **z. de viejo, z. remendón,** shoe repairer, cobbler.
zapateta, *f.* 1. slap on the foot or shoe when jumping. 2. jump, leap. — **¡z.!** my! whew! good gracious!

zapatilla, *f.* 1. slipper, house slipper; slipper, pump, fine dress shoe. 2. leather pad (behind trigger spring of firearm; under key of wind instrument). 3. billiard cue tip. 4. washer (in tap or faucet). 5. leather tip or button (on foil). 6. cloven hoof. — **z. de la reina,** large-flowered yellow poppy (Mypecoum grandiflorum); **poner como una z. china,** (Peru) to give a good reprimand, to tell (someone) off.
zapatillazo, *m.* blow with a slipper.
zapatillero, ra, *m., f.* slipper maker or vendor.
zapato, *m.* shoe; **ahí es donde le ajusta el z.,** that is where the shoe pinches; **andar con zapatos de fieltro,** to proceed with great caution; **como tres en un z.,** destitute, hard-up; like sardines in a can; **meter en un z.,** to intimidate, squash; **saber dónde le aprieta el z.,** to know what suits one best, know on which side one's bread is buttered; **z. de tacón alto,** high-heeled shoe; **zapatos papales,** galoshes, overshoes.
zapatón, *m.* 1. *aug. of* **zapato,** large clumsy shoe, clodhopper. 2. (Col., Chile) rubber, overshoe, galosh.
zapatudo, da, *a.* 1. wearing large heavy shoes or clodhoppers. 2. thick-hoofed. 3. (Cuba) hard, leathery, poorly-cooked (food). 4. (mec.) furnished or reinforced with a washer.
zape, *interj.* 1. (coll.) shoo! scat! 2. (coll.) expression used to refuse a card requested by one's partner.
zapear, *tr.v.* 1. to shoo away, scare away (a cat); (coll.) to chase or drive away. 2. to deny (someone's) request for a card.
zapotal, *m.* grove of sapodilla or marmalade trees.
zapote, *m.* (bot.) sapodilla or marmalade tree and its fruit.
zapotero, *m.* (bot.) sapodilla or marmalade tree.
zapotillo, *m.* (bot.) sapodilla or marmalade tree and its fruit.
zapoyol, *m.* pit or pip of the sapodilla or marmalade fruit.
zapoyolito, *m.* (C. Amer.) (variety of) small parrot, parakeet.
zapuzar, (*ref. 53*) *tr.v.* to plunge into water, duck.
zaque, *m.* 1. small wineskin. 2. (coll.) sot, drunkard.
zaquear, *tr.v.* 1. to transfer or decant (wine) from one wineskin to another. 2. to transport (wine) in wineskins.
zaquizamí, (*pl.* **zaquizamíes**), *m.* 1. attic, garret. 2. hovel, hole; small, uncomfortable dwelling.
zar, *m.* (hist.) czar, tsar.
zara, *f.* (bot.) corn, Indian corn, maize.
zarabanda, *f.* 1. (mus.) saraband. 2. noise, bustle.
zarabandista, *m., f.* 1. saraband dancer, singer, player or composer. 2. gay boisterous person.
zarabutear, *tr.v.* (coll.), *var. of* **zaragutear.**
zarabutero, ra, *a., m., f.* (coll.), *var. of* zaragutero.
zaragalla, *f.* crushed charcoal.
zaragata, *f.* 1. (coll.) brawl, squabble, quarrel. 2. (Cuba) flattery, cajolery.
zaragate, *m.* 1. (Mex.) scoundrel. 2. (Cuba) flatterer, fawner. 3. (Col.) idiot, fool.
zaragatero, ra, *a.* (coll.) noisy, rowdy. —*m., f.* noisy, rowdy person.
zaragatona, *f.* (bot.) fleawort.
zaragocí, *m.* a kind of plum.
Zaragoza, *f.* (geog.) Saragossa, city and province in N.E. Spain.
zaragozano, na, *a.* of or from Saragossa, Spain. —*m., f.* native or inhabitant of Saragossa.
zaragüelles, *m.* (*pl.*) 1. (Sp.) wide pleated breeches. 2. (coll.) baggy, ill-made breeches. 3. (bot.) reed grass.
zaragutear, *tr.v.* (coll.) to botch, bungle; to do hastily or shoddily.
zaragutero, ra, *a.* (coll.) botching, shoddy, slipshod. —*m., f.* botcher, bungler, shoddy or slipshod worker.
zaramagullón, *m.* (ornith.) grebe, dabchick.
zarambeque, *m.* (Sp.) gay noisy dance or gathering of blacks or Moors.
zaramullo, *m.* (Peru, Ven., coll.) meddler, schemer; busybody.
zaranda, *f.* 1. sieve, screen; strainer. 2. (Ven.) humming top (toy).
zarandador, ra, *m., f.* wheat sifter or winnower.
zarandajas, *f.* (*pl.*) (coll.) trifles, unimportant things or issues.
zarandalí, *a.* black-spotted (dove).
zarandar, zarandear, *tr.v.* 1. to shake about, to jostle. 2. to sieve, screen; to strain. 3. (coll.) to toss, blow. —*r.v.* 1. to bustle about, rush about, work hard, wear oneself out. 2. (Amer.) to walk along provocatively swaying hips and shoulders.
zarandeo, *m.* 1. shaking. 2. sifting, sieving; straining. 3. bustling or rushing about, bustle, rush. 4. provocative, suggestive strut.
zarandero, ra, *m., f., var. of* **zarandador.**
zarandillo, *m.* 1. small sieve or screen. 2. (coll.) live wire, lively person. — **traerle a uno como un z.,** (coll.) to keep someone on the go.
zarapatel, *m.* (cul.) casserole of eggplant, tomato, squash and green peppers.
zarapico, *m.* (ornith.) solitary sandpiper.
zarapito, *m.* (ornith.) curlew (Numenius arquatus).
zaratán, *m.* (coll.) cancer of the breast.
zaratita, *f.* (min.) zaratite.
Zaratustra, *m.* (rel.) Zarathustra, Zoroaster.
zaraza, *f.* 1. (tex.) chintz, printed cotton, gingham. 2. poison paste, home-made exterminator.
zarazo, za, *a.* (Amer.) half-ripe.
zarcear, *tr.v.* to clean out (pipes, tubes, etc.) with brambles. —*i.v.* 1. to hunt in the underbrush (said of a dog). 2. to move to and fro, to rush about.
zarceño, ña, brambly.
zarcero, ra, *a.* **perro zarcero,** dog that hunts in the underbrush.
zarceta, *f.* (ornith.) garganey.
zarcillitos, *m., pl.* (bot.) quaking grass.
zarcillo, *m.* 1. (bot.) tendril. 2. earring, eardrop. 3. rake, hoe; trowel, dibble. 4. (Arg.) cut in the ear of cattle (identification mark). 5. (Arg.) hoop (of a barrel). — **de z.,** (Chile) arm in arm.
zarco, ca, *a.* 1. light blue (eyes). 2. (Arg.) wall-eyed (animal). 3. (Guat.) white (man, woman).
zarevite, *m.* (hist.) czarevitch, tsarevitch.
zargatona, *f., var. of* **zaragatona.**
zariano, na, *a.* of or pertaining to the czar.
zarigüeya, *f.* (zool.) opossum.
zarina, *f.* (hist.) czarina, tsarina, czaritza.
zarismo, *m.* (hist.) czarism, tsarism.
zarja, *f., var. of* **azarja.**
zarpa, *f.* 1. paw (of large felines). 2. (archit.) footing. 3. (mar.) weighing anchor. 4. spatter of mud. — **echar la z.,** (coll.) to seize, grasp, clutch, (coll.) to get hold of.
zarpada, *f.* blow with a paw or claw, clawing.
zarpanel, *a.* **arco z.,** (archit.) three-centered arch, basket-handle arch.
zarpar, *tr.v.* to weigh (anchor). —*i.v.* to weigh anchor, set sail, set out.
zarpazo, *m.* 1. blow with a paw or claw, clawing, pawing. 2. thud, bang, whack, smack.
zarpe, *m.* (C. Amer.) spatter of mud.
zarpear, *tr.v.* (Mex., C. Amer.) to spatter or splash with mud.
zarposo, sa, *a.* spattered with mud.
zarracatería, *f.* insincere flattery.
zarracatín, *m.* (coll.) haggling retailer, profiteer.
zarramplín, *m.* 1. (coll.) shoddy worker, botcher, bungler. 2. (coll.) ragamuffin, poor devil.
zarramplinada, *f.* botch, bungle, shoddy piece of work.
zarrapastra, *f.* (coll.) spatter of mud.
zarrapastrón, na, *a.* (coll.) ragged, shabby, tattered, slovenly. —*m., f.* (coll.) ragamuffin, tramp, ragged person.
zarrapastrosamente, *adv.* (coll.) raggedly, shabbily, slovenly.
zarrapastroso, sa, *a.* (coll.) ragged, shabby, tattered, slovenly. —*m., f.* ragamuffin, tramp, ragged person.
zarria, *f.* 1. spatter of mud. 2. sandal's thong or leather strap.
zarriento, ta, zarrioso, sa, *a.* spattered with mud.
zarza, *f.* (bot.) bramble; blackberry, blackberry bush.
zarzagán, *m.* cold north wind.
zarzaganillo, *m.* stormy north wind.
zarzahán, *m.* (tex.) striped colored silk.
zarzal, *m.* blackberry or bramble patch.
zarzaleño, ña, *a.* brambly.
zarzamora, *f.* (bot.) brambleberry, blackberry (fruit).
zarzaparrilla, *f.* (bot.) sarsaparilla (plant extract and drink).
zarzaparrillar, *m.* sarsaparilla field.
zarzaperruna, *f.* (bot.) dog rose (plant and fruit).
zarzarrosa, *f.* (bot.) dog rose.
zarzo, *m.* 1. hurdle, wattle. 2. (Col.) garret.
zarzoso, sa, *a.* brambly, briery.
zarzuela, *f.* (mus., theat) Spanish musical comedy or operetta.
zarzuelero, ra, *a.* pertaining to a musical comedy or an operetta.
zarzuelista, *m., f.* composer or librettist of musical comedies or operettas.
¡zas! *interj.* bang!
zascandil, *m.* (coll.) meddler, schemer, busybody.
zascandilear, *i.v.* to meddle, interfere, scheme.
zascandileo, *m.* meddlesomeness, interference, scheming.
zata, zatara, *f.* river raft.
zato, *m.* piece or morsel of bread.
zazo, za, zazozo, sa, *a.* stammering, stuttering.
zebra, *f., var. of* **cebra.**
zedilla, *f.* c. cedilla (or with cedilla attached); cedilla.
zeína, *f.* (biochem.) zein.
Zelanda, *f.* Zeeland; Nueva Z., New Zealand.
zelandés, sa, *a.* Zeeland. —*m., f.* Zeelander.
Zelandia, *f., var. of* **Zelanda.**
zendavesta, *m.* (rel., hist.) Zend-Avesta.
zendo, da, *a.* (philol.) Zendic. —*m., f.* Zend.
zenit, *m., var. of* **cenit.**
zenografía, *f.* (astron.) zenography, study of Jupiter.
zeolita, *f.* zeolite. — **z. férrica,** (geol.) iron zeolite.
zepelín, *m.* zeppelin (dirigible airship).
zeugma, zeuma, *f.* (rhet.) zeugma.
Zeus, *m.* (myth.) Zeus, the supreme deity (Greek myth.).
zigofiláceo, a, *a.* (bot.) zygophyllaceous. —*f.* (bot.) (*pl.*) Zygophyllaceae.
zigófita, *f.* (bot.) zygophyte.
zigomorfo, fa, *a.* (biol.) zygomorphic, zygomorphous.
zigosis, *f.* (bot., zool.) zygosis.
zigospora, *f.* (bot.) zygospore.
zigota, *f.* **zigoto,** *m.* (biol.) zygote.
zigurat, *m.* (archit., hist.) ziggurat.
zigzag, *m.* zigzag.
zigzaguear, *i.v.* to zigzag.

zigzagueo, *m.* zigzagging.
zimasa, *f.* (biochem.) zymase.
zimo, *m.* (biol.) zyme.
zimógeno, *m.* (biochem.) zymogen.
zimoscopio, *m.* (chem.) zymoscope.
zimótico, ca, *a.* (chem.) zymotic.
zinc, *m., var. of* **cinc.**
zíngaro, ra, *m., f., var. of* **cíngaro.**
zipizape, *m.* (coll.) scuffle, row, rumpus.
zircón, *m., var. of* **circón.**
zirconato, *m.* (chem.) zirconate.
zirconio, *m., var. of* **circonio.**
¡zis, zas! *interj.* bang! bang!
zoantario, *m.* (zool.) zoantharian.
zoantropía, *f.* (med.) zoanthropy.
zoario, *m.* (zool.) zoarium.
zoca, *f.* public square. — **andar de z. en colodra,** (coll.) to go from bad to worse.
zócalo, *m.* 1. (archit.) socle, base, footing, skirting, skirting-board; frieze. 2. (Mex.) public square, plaza.
zocatearse, *r.v.* to become mealy or overripe (fruit).
zocato, ta, *a.* 1. (coll.) left-handed. 2. overripe, mealy (fruits). —*m., f.* lefthanded person.
zoclo, *m.* clog, wooden shoe.
zoco, *m.* 1. public square. 2. Moroccan marketplace. 3. clog, wooden shoe. 4. (archit.) socle (of a pedestal).
zoco, ca, *a.* (coll.) left-handed; **a zocas,** the wrong way. —*m., f.* left-handed person.
zodiacal, *a.* zodiacal.
zodíaco, *m.* (astron.) sodiac.
zoea, *f.* (zool.) zoea.
zofra, *f.* (rare) Moorish carpet.
zoilo, *m.* malicious and envious critic.
zoisita, *f.* (min.) zoisite.
zoísmo, *m.* (biol.) zoism.
zollipar, *i.v.* (coll.) to sob.
zollipo, *m.* (coll.) sob.
zolocho, cha, *a.* (coll.) silly, foolish, simple. —*m., f.* simpleton.
zoma, *f., var. of* **soma.**
Zomba, *f.* Zomba, capital of Malawi.
zompo, pa, *a., m., f., var. of* **zopo.**
zompopo, *m.* (C. Amer., ento.) large-headed ant.
zona, *f.* 1. zone, district, area, region. 2. band, stripe. 3. (med.) zona, shingles, zoster. — **z. a batir,** (mil.) target area; **z. de ensanche,** development zone (outskirts of town being urbanized); **z. de escaramuza,** (sport.) line of scrimmage; **z. de guerra,** (mil.) war zone; **z. de influencia,** zone of influence; **z. de las Praderas,** Great Plains; **Z. del Canal,** Canal Zone; **z. de reunión,** (mil.) assembly area; **z. de seguridad,** safety zone; **z. de tolerancia** or **z. roja,** red-light district; **z. de ángulo muerto,** (mil.) dead zone; **z. erógena,** erogenous zone; **z. esférica,** (geom.) spherical segment or zone; **z. fiscal,** administrative or fiscal zone or district; **z. glacial,** (geog.) frigid zone; **z. industrial,** industrial park; **z. nivométrica,** (meteorol.) snow course; **z. objetivo,** (mil.) target area; **z. polémica,** (fort.) defense zone; **z. postal,** postal zone or district; **z. tampon** or **parachoque,** buffer zone; **z. templada,** (geog.) temperate zone; **z. tórrida,** (geog.) torrid zone; **z. tropical,** tropical zone; **z. verde,** green space, park.
zonal, *a.* zonal.
zoncera, zoncería, *f.* foolishness, silliness.
zonchiche, *m.* (C. Rica, Hond., ornith.) red-headed turkey buzzard or vulture.
zonificación, *f.* zoning, zonation.
zonificar, (*ref. 50*) *tr.v.* to zone, divide into zones.
zonote, *m.* cenote, natural underground reservoir.
zonzamente, *adv.* dully, foolishly.
zonzo, za, *a.* foolish, silly. —*m., f.* fool, simpleton; dull, colorless person.
zonzorrión, na, *a.* (coll.) very silly, foolish; dull, colorless. —*m., f.* very foolish, dull, or colorless person.
zoófago, ga, *a.* (zool.) zoophagous. —*m.* (zool.) zoophagan, (*pl.*) Zoophaga.
zoófilo, la, *a.* (bot.) zoophilous.
zoófito, *m.* (zool.) zoophyte, (*pl.*) Zoophyta.
zoofitología, *f.* (zool.) zoophytolgy.
zooflagelado, *m.* (zool.) zooflagellate.
zoofobia, *f.* zoophobia, abnormal fear of animals.
zoofórico, ca, *a.* (archit.) zoophoric.
zoóforo, *m.* (archit.) zoophorus.
zoogeografía, *f.* zoogeography.
zoogeográfico, ca, *a.* zoogeographic, zoogeographical.
zoografía, *f.* zoography.
zoográfico, ca, *a.* zoographical, zoographic.
zooide, *m.* (zool.) zooid.
zooideo, dea, *a.* (biol.) zooid, zooidal.
zoólatra, *a.* zoolatrous, animal-worshiping. —*m., f.* zoolater.
zoolatría, *f.* zoolatry, worship of animals.
zoolítico, ca, *a.* fossil-bearing.
zoolito, *m.* animal fossil.
zoología, *f.* zoology.
zoológico, ca, *a.* zoological, zoologic.
zoólogo, *m.* zoologist.
zoomorfismo, *m.* zoomorphism.
zoomorfo, fa, *a.* zoomorphic.
zoospermo, *m.* (biol.) zoosperm.
zoospora, *m.* (bot.) zoospore.
zootomía, *f.* zootomy.
zootómico, ca, *a.* zootomic, zootomical.
zopas, (*pl.* **zopas**), *m., f.* (coll.) lisper.
zope, *m.* (C. Rica, ornith.) turkey buzzard.
zopenco, ca, *a.* (coll.) dull, stupid. —*m.* dullard, blockhead.
zopetero, *m.* slope, hill, embankment.
zopilote, *m.* (C. Amer., Mex.) turkey buzzard.
zopisa, *f.* tar, pitch.
zopitas, *m., f.* (coll.) lisper.
zopo, pa, *a.* crooked, malformed (foot, hand). —*m., f.* person who has a crooked or malformed hand or foot.
zoqueta, *f.* wooden guard worn to protect the left hand when using a sickle.
zoquete, *m.* 1. chump, block (of wood); chunk of bread. 2. (coll.) chunky, squat person. 3. (coll.) blockhead, dolt, dullard.
zoquetero, ra, *m., f.* bum, tramp, beggar.
zoquetudo, da, *a.* rough, badly-made, ill-shaped.
zorcico, zortzico, *m.* Basque folk song and dance.
zorenco, ca, *a.* (C. Amer.) dull, stupid, slow.
zorito, ta, *a.* wild (pigeon).
zoroastrico, ca, *a.* (rel.) Zoroastrian.
zoroastrismo, *m.* (rel.) Zoroastrianism.
Zoroastro, *m.* (rel., hist.) Zoroaster, Zarathustra.
zorollo, *a.* reaped while unripe (wheat).
zorongo, *m.* 1. head kerchief (worn round head by some Spanish peasants). 2. flat bun or chignon. 3. Andalusian dance and its music.
zorra, *f.* 1. (zool.) fox; vixen. 2. (coll.) fox, clever, astute person. 3. (coll.) prostitute. 4. (coll.) drunkenness. 5. (astron.) **Z.,** Fox, Vulpecula. 6. dray, truck. — **z. de mar,** (ichth.) fox shark, sea fox, thresher shark; **desollar** or **dormir la z.,** to sleep off one's drunkenness, sleep off a hangover.
zorroastrón, na, *a.* (coll.) crafty, astute, sly. —*m., f.* (coll.) crafty person.
zorrera, *f.* 1. fox hole. 2. (coll.) drowsiness, heaviness, sleepiness. 3. smoke-filled room.
zorrería, *f.* foxiness, cleverness, cunning.
zorrero, ra, *a.* 1. foxy, cunning. 2. foxhunting (dog). 3. (mar.) slow-sailing, heavy-sailing. —*m.* 1. foxhound. 2. royal game warden or keeper (in charge of keeping royal forests free of foxes, wolves, etc.).
zorrilla, *f.* (ry.) handcar.
zorrillo, zorrino, *m.* (Amer., zool.) skunk.
zorro, *m.* 1. (zool.) (male) fox. 2. fox (fur). 3. (coll.) fox, foxy fellow, crafty person. 4. (coll.) person who plays stupid; malingerer. 5. (*pl.*) duster made of cloth strips or fur tied to a handle. — **hacerse el z.,** (coll.) to feign ignorance; to pretend not to hear; **z. ártico,** (zool.) arctic or white fox; **z. azul,** blue fox; **z. de las praderas,** (zool.) prairie or kit fox; **z. del desierto,** (zool.) desert fox; **z. negro,** (zool.) raccoon; **z. plateado,** silver fox; **z. rojo,** (zool.) red fox; **z. volante,** (zool.) flying fox.
zorrocloco, *m.* 1. crafty person who acts the dullard for his own convenience. 2. (coll.) show of affection, caress.
zorrón, *m.* fox, astute or wily person.
zorronglón, na, *a.* (coll.) grumbling. —*m., f.* (coll.) grumbler.
zorruelo, la, *m., f. dim. of* **zorro, ra,** small fox or vixen.
zorrullo, *m., var. of* **zurullo.**
zorruno, na, *a.* foxlike, foxy.
zorzal, *m.* 1. (ornith.) thrush. 2. (fig.) fox, sly, artful fellow. 3. (Arg., Bol., Chile) simpleton, boob. 4. (P. Rico) difficult, fidgety child. — **z. marino,** (ichth.) black wrasse.
zorzalear, *tr.v.* (Chile) to swindle; to sponge.
zorzaleño, ña, *a.* **aceituna zorzaleña,** very small round olive.
zoster, *f.* (med.) zoster, shingles.
zote, *a.* dull, stupid. —*m., f.* dolt, dullard.
zozobra, *f.* 1. worry, anguish, anxiety. 2. (mar.) dangerous weather, difficult weather. 3. (mar.) sinking, capsizing, foundering.
zozobrante, *a.* (mar.) in danger; sinking.
zozobrar, *i.v.* 1. to be in danger (ship); to sink, founder, capsize. 2. to be in jeopardy; to fail, be ruined (e.g. an enterprise). 3. to worry, fret, be in doubt.
Zr *sym. of* **circonio,** zirconium (**Zr.**).
zúa, *f., var. of* **azud.**
zuavo, *m.* (mil.) Zouave.
zubia, *f.* drain, channel, flume; stream.
zucarino, na, *a.* sugary, saccharine, sweet.
zúchil, *m.* (Mex.) bouquet.
zuda, *f., var. of* **azud.**
zueco, *m.* clog, sabot, wooden shoe.
zuela, *f., var. of* **azuela.**
zuinda, *m.* (Arg., ornith.) white owl.
zuiza, *f., var. of* **suiza.**
zulacar, (*ref. 50*) *tr.v.* to coat with mastic, fill (joints) with mastic.
zulaque, *m.* mastic, asphalt mastic (used for coating pipes and filling in joints).
zulaque, zulaqué, *ref.* **zulacar.**
zulaquear, *tr.v. var. of* **zulacar.**
zulla, *f.* 1. (bot.) sulla clover, sulla, French honeysuckle. 2. (coll.) (human) excrement.
zullarse, *r.v.* 1. (coll.) to have a bowel movement, defecate. 2. (coll.) to break wind.
zullenco, ca, *a.* (coll.) breaking wind frequently.
zullón, na, *a.* (coll.) breaking wind frequently. —*m.* flatulence.
zulú, (*pl.* **zulús, zulúes**), *a., m., f.* **Zulu.**
Zululandia, *f.* Zululand.
zumacal, zumacar, *m.* sumach field.
zumacar, (*ref. 50*) *tr.v.* to tan or dress with sumach.
zumacaya, *f.* (ornith.) night heron.

zumaque, *m.* 1. (bot.) sumach tree. 2. (coll.) wine. — **z. del Japón,** (bot.) tree of heaven; **z. venenoso,** poison sumach, poison ivy.
zumaque, zumaqué, *ref.* **zumacar.**
zumaya, *f.* 1. (ornith.) night heron. 2. (ornith.) tawny owl. 3. (ornith.) goat-sucker.
zumba, *f.* 1. bell worn by animal leading a pack or drove. 2. bull-roarer (toy). 3. joke, jest. 4. (Amer.) beating, thrashing. — **hacer z. a uno,** to pull one's leg, tease, mock.
zumbador, ra, *a.* humming, buzzing. —*m.* 1. (elec.) buzzer. 2. (Amer.) bull-roarer (toy).
zumbar, *tr.v.* 1. (coll.) to give, deal, deliver (a blow). 2. to tease, joke with. —*i.v.* 1. to buzz, hum; to ring (ears). 2. to be near, be close, approach.
zumbel, *m.* 1. string for spinning a top. 2. (coll.) frown, angry mien or countenance.
zumbido, *m.* 1. buzz, buzzing, hum, humming; whine (of bullets). 2. (coll.) blow, cuff, smack. — **z. de ocupado,** busy signal (on telephone); **z. de oídos,** ringing in the ears.
zumblín, *m.* (Phil. I.) dart, javelin.
zumbo, *m., var. of* **zumbido.**
zumbón, na, *a.* (coll.) waggish, joking, bantering; **cencerro z.,** bell hung on the leading horse or mule. —*m., f.* 1. wag, jester, joker. 2. a variety of pigeon.
zumel, *m.* (Chile) coarse boot (worn by Araucan Indians).
zumiento, ta, *a.* juicy, succulent.
zumillo, *m.* 1. (bot.) green dragon. 2. (bot.) deadly carrot.
zumo, *m.* 1. juice. 2. profit, gain, advantage. — **z. de cepas, z. de parras,** (coll.) wine.
zumoso, sa, *a.* juicy.
zuna, *f.* 1. Sunna (body of Mohammedan laws). 2. (reg., Sp.) trickery, perfidy.
zunchar, *tr.v.* to fasten with a band or hoop.
zuncho, *m.* band, hoop, iron strap, ring, collar; **z. del inducido,** (mec.) armature band.
zuncuya, *f.* (Hond., bot.) custard apple (Annona purpurea).
zunteco, *m.* (Hond., ento.) black wasp.
zunzún, *m.* (Cuba, ornith.) species of hummingbird.
zuño, *m.* frown, scowl, glower.
zupia, *f.* 1. lees, dregs (of wine). 2. wine full of dregs. 3. unpleasant-tasting liquid. 4. useless remains, refuse, rubbish, trash.
zurano, na, *a.* wild, stock (dove or pigeon).
zurcidera, *f.* darner, finedrawer.
zurcido, *past part. of* **zurcir.** —*m.* darn, darning.
zurcidor, ra, *a.* darning. —*m., f.* darner, finedrawer. — **zurcidor de voluntades,** procurer, pimp; **zurcidora de voluntades,** procuress, bawd.
zurcir, (*ref. 61*) *tr.v.* 1. to darn, mend. 2. to join, unite. 3. (coll.) to weave, concoct lies.
zurdazo, *m.* left, blow with the left hand.
zurdería, *f.* left-handedness.
zurdo, da, *a.* left-handed; (mec.) left-handed (e.g. screw); left (hand); **a zurdas,** with the left hand; the wrong way. —*m., f.* left-handed person; **no ser z.,** (coll.) to be dexterous, skillful or clever.
zurear, *i.v.* to coo (doves).
zureo, *m.* cooing (of doves).
zurito, ta, *a.* wild, stock (pigeon or dove).
zuriza, *f.* quarrel, brawl, row.
zuro, ra, *a.* wild, stock (dove or pigeon). —*m.* stripped corncob.
zurra, *f.* 1. (tanning) currying, dressing. 2. (coll.) thrashing, beating, drubbing. 3. (coll.) quarrel, dispute, scuffle. 4. (coll.) grind, long hard word or study, drudgery.
zurradera, *f.* currying tool (for dressing hides).
zurrado, *past part. of* **zurrar.** —*m.* (coll.) glove.
zurrador, ra, *m., f.* 1. leather currier or dresser. 2. thrasher, beater.
zurrapa, *f.* 1. (*pl.*) lees, dregs, sediment. 2. (coll.) rubbish, trash. 3. (coll.) skinny, homely boy. — **con zurrapas,** (coll.) in an unclean way, dirtily, basely.
zurrapelo, *m.* (coll.) severe reprimand.
zurrapiento, ta, zurraposo, sa, *a.* dreggy, turbid, roily.
zurrar, *tr.v.* 1. to curry, dress (leather). 2. (coll.) to thrash, beat, spank, wallop. 3. (coll.) reprimand; censure. —*r.v.* to dirty oneself, soil oneself (have an involuntary bowel movement). 2. (coll.) to be scared to death.
zurriaga, *f.* 1. whip, thong, leather strap. 2. (ornith.) lark.
zurriagar, (*ref. 51*) *tr.v.* to whip, lash, horsewhip.
zurriagazo, *m.* 1. lash, whiplash. 2. blow, sudden misfortune, calamity. 3. unexpected slight or rebuff.
zurriago, *m.* 1. whip, lash. 2. whip for spinning a top. 3. clumsy, despicable man.
zurriar, *i.v., var. of* **zurrir.**
zurribanda, *f.* 1. (coll.) beating, thrashing, hiding, flogging. 2. (coll.) scuffle, fight, brawl.
zurriburri, *m.* 1. (coll.) ruffian, cur, rogue. 2. (coll.) gang of rowdies; rabble. 3. uproar, confusion.
zurrido, *m.* 1. humming, buzzing; grating sound. 2. (coll.) bang, thump, blow with a stick.
zurrir, *i.v.* to hum, buzz; to rattle, grate.
zurrón, *m.* 1. leather pouch; game bag. 2. husk, thin skin. 3. (anat.) amnion, amniotic bag. — **z. de pastor,** (bot.) shepherd's purse.
zurrona, *f.* (coll.) loose woman.
zurronada, *f.* bagful.
zurruscarse, (*ref. 50*) *r.v., var. of* **zurrarse.**
zurrusco, *m.* 1. (coll.) burnt toast. 2. (reg., Sp.) cold wind.
zurubí, (*pl.* **zurubíes**), *m.* (Amer., ichth.) large fresh-water catfish.
zurullo, *m.* 1. (coll.) roll or wad of any pliable material. 2. (coll.) turd.
zurumbático, ca, *a.* stunned, dumbfounded.
zurupeto, *m.* (coll.) unauthorized agent; unlicensed broker.
zurza, zurzo, *ref.* **zurcir.**
zutano, na, *m., f.* (coll.) so-and-so; **fulano, z. y mengano,** Tom, Dick and Harry.
¡zuzo! *interj., var. of* **chucho.**
zuzón, *m.* (bot.) groundsel, ragwort.

Table of Model Verbs

Reference Number	INFINITIVE Present participle (*gerundio*) Past participle (*Participio pasado*)	INDICATIVE Present (*Presente*)	Imperfect (*Pretérito imperfecto*)	Preterite (*Pretérito indefinido*)	Future (*Futuro imperfecto*)	Conditional (*Potencial*)
1.	andar	ando	andaba	anduve	andaré	andaría
	andando	andas	andabas	anduviste	andarás	andarías
	andado	anda	andaba	anduvo	andará	andaría
		andamos	andábamos	anduvimos	andaremos	andaríamos
		andáis	andabais	anduvisteis	andaréis	andaríais
		andan	andaban	anduvieron	andarán	andarían
2.	asir	asgo	asía	así	asiré	asiría
	asiendo	ases	asías	asiste	asirás	asirías
	asido	ase	asía	asió	asirá	asiría
		asimos	asíamos	asimos	asiremos	asiríamos
		asís	asíais	asisteis	asiréis	asiríais
		asen	asían	asieron	asirán	asirían
3.	bendecir	bendigo	bendecía	bendije	bendeciré	bendeciría
	bendiciendo	bendices	bendecías	bendijiste	bendecirás	bendecirías
	bendecido	bendice	bendecía	bendijo	bendecirá	bendeciría
		bendecimos	bendecíamos	bendijimos	bendeciremos	bendeciríamos
		bendecís	bendecíais	bendijisteis	bendeciréis	bendeciríais
		bendicen	bendecían	bendijeron	bendecirán	bendecirían
4.	caber	quepo	cabía	cupe	cabré	cabría
	cabiendo	cabes	cabías	cupiste	cabrás	cabrías
	cabido	cabe	cabía	cupo	cabrá	cabría
		cabemos	cabíamos	cupimos	cabremos	cabríamos
		cabéis	cabíais	cupisteis	cabréis	cabríais
		caben	cabían	cupieron	cabrán	cabrían
5.	caer	caigo	caía	caí	caeré	caería
	cayendo	caes	caías	caíste	caerás	caerías
	caído	cae	caía	cayó	caerá	caería
		caemos	caíamos	caímos	caeremos	caeríamos
		caéis	caíais	caísteis	caeréis	caeríais
		caen	caían	cayeron	caerán	caerían
6.	dar	doy	daba	di	daré	daría
	dando	das	dabas	diste	darás	darías
	dado	da	daba	dio	dará	daría
		damos	dábamos	dimos	daremos	daríamos
		dais	dabais	disteis	daréis	daríais
		dan	daban	dieron	darán	darían
7.	decir	digo	decía	dije	diré	diría
	diciendo	dices	decías	dijiste	dirás	dirías
	dicho	dice	decía	dijo	dirá	diría
		decimos	decíamos	dijimos	diremos	diríamos
		decís	decíais	dijisteis	diréis	diríais
		dicen	decían	dijeron	dirán	dirían
8.	estar	estoy	estaba	estuve	estaré	estaría
	estando	estás	estabas	estuviste	estarás	estarías
	estado	está	estaba	estuvo	estará	estaría
		estamos	estábamos	estuvimos	estaremos	estaríamos
		estáis	estabais	estuvisteis	estaréis	estaríais
		están	estaban	estuvieron	estarán	estarían
9.	haber	he	había	hube	habré	habría
	habiendo	has	habías	hubiste	habrás	habrías
	habido	ha	había	hubo	habrá	habría
		hemos	habíamos	hubimos	habremos	habríamos
		habéis	habíais	hubisteis	habréis	habríais
		han	habían	hubieron	habrán	habrían
10.	hacer	hago	hacía	hice	haré	haría
	haciendo	haces	hacías	hiciste	harás	harías
	hecho	hace	hacía	hizo	hará	haría
		hacemos	hacíamos	hicimos	haremos	haríamos
		hacéis	hacíais	hicisteis	haréis	haríais
		hacen	hacían	hicieron	harán	harían
11.	ir	voy	iba	fui	iré	iría
	yendo	vas	ibas	fuiste	irás	irías
	ido	va	iba	fue	irá	iría
		vamos	íbamos	fuimos	iremos	iríamos
		vais	ibais	fuisteis	iréis	iríais
		van	iban	fueron	irán	irían
12.	oír	oigo	oía	oí	oiré	oiría
	oyendo	oyes	oías	oíste	oirás	oirías
	oído	oye	oía	oyó	oirá	oiría
		oímos	oíamos	oímos	oiremos	oiríamos
		oís	oíais	oísteis	oiréis	oiríais
		oyen	oían	oyeron	oirán	oirían
13.	placer	plazco	placía	plací	placeré	placería
	placiendo	places	placías	placiste	placerás	placerías
	placido	place	placía	plació or plugo	placerá	placería
		placemos	placíamos	placimos	placeremos	placeríamos
		placéis	placíais	placisteis	placeréis	placeríais
		placen	placían	placieron or pluguieron	placerán	placerían

SUBJUNCTIVE				IMPERATIVE
Present *(Presente)*	Imperfect *(Pretérito imperfecto)* r-form	Imperfect *(Pretérito imperfecto)* s-form	Future **(Futuro imperfecto)*	
ande	anduviera	anduviese	anduviere	anda (tú)
andes	anduvieras	anduvieses	anduvieres	ande (él)
ande	anduviera	anduviese	anduviere	andemos
andemos	anduviéramos	anduviésemos	anduviéremos	andad
andéis	anduvierais	anduvieseis	anduviereis	anden
anden	anduvieran	anduviesen	anduvieren	
asga	asiera	asiese	asiere	ase (tú)
asgas	asieras	asieses	asieres	asga (él)
asga	asiera	asiese	asiere	asgamos
asgamos	asiéramos	asiésemos	asiéremos	asid
asgáis	asierais	asieseis	asiereis	asgan
asgan	asieran	asiesen	asieren	
bendiga	bendijera	bendijese	bendijere	bendice (tú)
bendigas	bendijeras	bendijeses	bendijeres	bendiga (él)
bendiga	bendijera	bendijese	bendijere	bendigamos
bendigamos	bendijéramos	bendijésemos	bendijéremos	bendecid
bendigáis	bendijerais	bendijeseis	bendijereis	bendigan
bendigan	bendijeran	bendijesen	bendijeren	
quepa	cupiera	cupiese	cupiere	cabe (tú)
quepas	cupieras	cupieses	cupieres	quepa (él)
quepa	cupiera	cupiese	cupiere	quepamos
quepamos	cupiéramos	cupiésemos	cupiéremos	cabed
quepáis	cupierais	cupieseis	cupiereis	quepan
quepan	cupieran	cupiesen	cupieren	
caiga	cayera	cayese	cayere	cae (tú)
caigas	cayeras	cayeses	cayeres	caiga (él)
caiga	cayera	cayese	cayere	caigamos
caigamos	cayéramos	cayésemos	cayéremos	caed
caigáis	cayerais	cayeseis	cayereis	caigan
caigan	cayeran	cayesen	cayeren	
dé	diera	diese	diere	da (tú)
des	dieras	dieses	dieres	dé (él)
dé	diera	diese	diere	demos
demos	diéramos	diésemos	diéremos	dad
deis	dierais	dieseis	diereis	den
den	dieran	diesen	dieren	
diga	dijera	dijese	dijere	di (tú)
digas	dijeras	dijeses	dijeres	diga (él)
diga	dijera	dijese	dijere	digamos
digamos	dijéramos	dijésemos	dijéremos	decid
digáis	dijerais	dijeseis	dijereis	digan
digan	dijeran	dijesen	dijeren	
esté	estuviera	estuviese	estuviere	está (tú)
estés	estuvieras	estuvieses	estuvieres	esté (él)
esté	estuviera	estuviese	estuviere	estemos
estemos	estuviéramos	estuviésemos	estuviéremos	estad
estéis	estuvierais	estuvieseis	estuviereis	estén
estén	estuvieran	estuviesen	estuvieren	
haya	hubiera	hubiese	hubiere	hé (tú)
hayas	hubieras	hubieses	hubieres	haya (él)
haya	hubiera	hubiese	hubiere	hayamos
hayamos	hubiéramos	hubiésemos	hubiéremos	habed
hayáis	hubierais	hubieseis	hubiereis	hayan
hayan	hubieran	hubiesen	hubieren	
haga	hiciera	hiciese	hiciere	haz (tú)
hagas	hicieras	hicieses	hicieres	haga (él)
haga	hiciera	hiciese	hiciere	hagamos
hagamos	hiciéramos	hiciésemos	hiciéremos	haced
hagáis	hicierais	hicieseis	hiciereis	hagan
hagan	hicieran	hiciesen	hicieren	
vaya	fuera	fuese	fuere	ve (tú)
vayas	fueras	fueses	fueres	vaya (él)
vaya	fuera	fuese	fuere	vayamos
vayamos	fuéramos	fuésemos	fuéremos	id
vayáis	fuerais	fueseis	fuereis	vayan
vayan	fueran	fuesen	fueren	
oiga	oyera	oyese	oyere	oye (tú)
oigas	oyeras	oyeses	oyeres	oiga (él)
oiga	oyera	oyese	oyere	oigamos
oigamos	oyéramos	oyésemos	oyéremos	oíd
oigáis	oyerais	oyeseis	oyereis	oigan
oigan	oyeran	oyesen	oyeren	
plazca	placiera	placiese	placiere	place (tú)
plazcas	placieras	placieses	placieres	plazca, plega or
plazca, plega or	placiera or	placiese or	placiere or	plegue (él)
plegue	pluguiera	pluguiese	pluguiere	plazcamos
plazcamos	placiéramos	placiésemos	placiéremos	placed
plazcáis	placierais	placieseis	placiereis	plazcan
plazcan	placieran	placiesen	placieren	

Reference Number	INFINITIVE Present participle *(gerundio)* Past participle *(Participio pasado)*	INDICATIVE Present *(Presente)*	Imperfect *(Pretérito imperfecto)*	Preterite *(Pretérito indefinido)*	Future *(Futuro imperfecto)*	Conditional *(Potencial)*
14.	poder pudiendo podido	puedo puedes puede podemos podéis pueden	podía podías podía podíamos podíais podían	pude pudiste pudo pudimos pudisteis pudieron	podré podrás podrá podremos podréis podrán	podría podrías podría podríamos podríais podrían
15.	poner poniendo puesto	pongo pones pone ponemos ponéis ponen	ponía ponías ponía poníamos poníais ponían	puse pusiste puso pusimos pusisteis pusieron	pondré pondrás pondrá pondremos pondréis pondrán	pondría pondrías pondría pondríamos pondríais pondrían
16.	podrir or pudrir pudriendo podrido	pudro pudres pudre podrimos podrís pudren	pudría pudrías pudría pudríamos pudríais pudrían	pudrí pudriste pudrió pudrimos pudristeis pudrieron	pudriré pudrirás pudrirá pudriremos pudriréis pudrirán	pudriría pudrirías pudriría pudriríamos pudriríais pudrirían
17.	querer queriendo querido	quiero quieres quiere queremos queréis quieren	quería querías quería queríamos queríais querían	quise quisiste quiso quisimos quisisteis quisieron	querré querrás querrá querremos querréis querrán	querría querrías querría querríamos querríais querrían
18.	raer rayendo raído	raigo or rayo raes rae raemos raéis raen	raía raías raía raíamos raíais raían	raí raíste rayó raímos raísteis rayeron	raeré raerás raerá raeremos raeréis raerán	raería raerías raería raeríamos raeríais raerían
19.	roer royendo roído	roo, roigo or royo roes roe roemos roéis roen	roía roías roía roíamos roíais roían	roí roíste royó roímos roísteis royeron	roeré roerás roerá roeremos roeréis roerán	roería roerías roería roeríamos roeríais roerían
20.	saber sabiendo sabido	sé sabes sabe sabemos sabéis saben	sabía sabías sabía sabíamos sabíais sabían	supe supiste supo supimos supisteis supieron	sabré sabrás sabrá sabremos sabréis sabrán	sabría sabrías sabría sabríamos sabríais sabrían
21.	salir saliendo salido	salgo sales sale salimos salís salen	salía salías salía salíamos salíais salían	salí saliste salió salimos salisteis salieron	saldré saldrás saldrá saldremos saldréis saldrán	saldría saldrías saldría saldríamos saldríais saldrían
22.	ser siendo sido	soy eres es somos sois son	era eras era éramos erais eran	fui fuiste fue fuimos fuisteis fueron	seré serás será seremos seréis serán	sería serías sería seríamos seríais serían
23.	tener teniendo tenido	tengo tienes tiene tenemos tenéis tienen	tenía tenías tenía teníamos teníais tenían	tuve tuviste tuvo tuvimos tuvisteis tuvieron	tendré tendrás tendrá tendremos tendréis tendrán	tendría tendrías tendría tendríamos tendríais tendrían
24.	traer trayendo traído	traigo traes trae traemos traéis traen	traía traías traía traíamos traíais traían	traje trajiste trajo trajimos trajisteis trajeron	traeré traerás traerá traeremos traeréis traerán	traería traerías traería traeríamos traeríais traerían
25.	valer valiendo valido	valgo vales vale valemos valéis valen	valía valías valía valíamos valíais valían	valí valiste valió valimos valisteis valieron	valdré valdrás valdrá valdremos valdréis valdrán	valdría valdrías valdría valdríamos valdríais valdrían
26.	venir viniendo venido	vengo vienes viene venimos venéis vienen	venía venías venía veníamos veníais venían	vine viniste vino vinimos vinisteis vinieron	vendré vendrás vendrá vendremos vendréis vendrán	vendría vendrías vendría vendríamos vendríais vendrían

SUBJUNCTIVE				IMPERATIVE
Present *(Presente)*	Imperfect *(Pretérito imperfecto)* r-form	Imperfect *(Pretérito imperfecto)* s-form	Future **(Futuro imperfecto)*	
pueda	pudiera	pudiese	pudiere	puede (tú)
puedas	pudieras	pudieses	pudieres	pueda (él)
pueda	pudiera	pudiese	pudiere	—
podamos	pudiéramos	pudiésemos	pudiéremos	—
podáis	pudierais	pudieseis	pudiereis	puedan
puedan	pudieran	pudiesen	pudieren	
ponga	pusiera	pusiese	pusiere	pon (tú)
pogas	pusieras	pusieses	pusieres	ponga (él)
ponga	pusiera	pusiese	pusiere	pongamos
pongamos	pusiéramos	pusiésemos	pusiéremos	poned
pongáis	pusierais	pusieseis	pusiereis	pongan
pongan	pusieran	pusiesen	pusieren	
pudra	pudriera	pudriese	pudriere	pudre (tú)
pudras	pudrieras	pudrieses	pudrieres	pudra (él)
pudra	pudriera	pudriese	pudriere	pudramos
pudramos	pudriéramos	pudriésemos	pudriéremos	pudrid
pudráis	pudrierais	pudrieseis	pudriereis	pudran
pudran	pudrieran	pudriesen	pudrieren	
quiera	quisiera	quisiese	quisiere	quiere (tú)
quieras	quisieras	quisieses	quisieres	quiera (él)
quiera	quisiera	quisiese	quisiere	queramos
queramos	quisiéramos	quisiésemos	quisiéremos	quered
queráis	quisierais	quisieseis	quisiereis	quieran
quieran	quisieran	quisiesen	quisieren	
raiga	rayera	rayese	rayere	rae (tú)
or raya	rayeras	rayeses	rayeres	raiga or raya (él)
raigas	rayera	rayese	rayere	raigamos or rayamos
raiga	rayéramos	rayésemos	rayéremos	raed
raigamos	rayerais	rayeseis	rayereis	raigan or rayan
raigáis	rayeran	rayesen	rayeren	
raigan				
roa, roiga	royera	royese	royere	roe (tú)
or roya	royeras	royeses	royeres	roa, roiga or
roas	royera	royese	royere	roya (él)
roa	royéramos	royésemos	royéremos	roamos, roigamos or
roamos	royerais	royeseis	royereis	royamos
roáis	royeran	royesen	royeren	roed
roan				roan, roigan or royan
sepa	supiera	supiese	supiere	sabe (tú)
sepas	supieras	supieses	supieres	sepa (él)
sepa	supiera	supiese	supiere	sepamos
sepamos	supiéramos	supiésemos	supiéremos	sabed
sepáis	supierais	supieseis	supiereis	sepan
sepan	supieran	supiesen	supieren	
salga	saliera	saliese	saliere	sal (tú)
salgas	salieras	salieses	salieres	salga (él)
salga	saliera	saliese	saliere	salgamos
salgamos	saliéramos	saliésemos	saliéremos	salid
salgáis	salierais	salieseis	saliereis	salgan
salgan	salieran	saliesen	salieren	
sea	fuera	fuese	fuere	sé (tú)
seas	fueras	fueses	fueres	sea (él)
sea	fuera	fuese	fuere	seamos
seamos	fuéramos	fuésemos	fuéremos	sed
seáis	fuerais	fueseis	fuereis	sean
sean	fueran	fuesen	fueren	
tenga	tuviera	tuviese	tuviere	ten (tú)
tengas	tuvieras	tuvieses	tuvieres	tenga (él)
tenga	tuviera	tuviese	tuviere	tengamos
tengamos	tuviéramos	tuviésemos	tuviéremos	tened
tengáis	tuvierais	tuvieseis	tuviereis	tengan
tengan	tuvieran	tuviesen	tuvieren	
traiga	trajera	trajese	trajere	trae (tú)
traigas	trajeras	trajeses	trajeres	traiga (él)
traiga	trajera	trajese	trajere	traigamos
traigamos	trajéramos	trajésemos	trajéremos	traed
traigáis	trajerais	trajeseis	trajereis	traigan
traigan	trajeran	trajesen	trajeren	
valga	valiera	valiese	valiere	vale (tú)
valgas	valieras	valieses	valieres	valga (él)
valga	valiera	valiese	valiere	valgamos
valgamos	valiéramos	valiésemos	valiéremos	valed
valgáis	valierais	valieseis	valiereis	valgan
valgan	valieran	valiesen	valieren	
venga	viniera	viniese	viniere	ven (tú)
vengas	vinieras	vinieses	vinieres	venga (él)
venga	viniera	viniese	viniere	vengamos
vengamos	viniéramos	viniésemos	viniéremos	venid
vengáis	vinierais	vinieseis	viniereis	vengan
vengan	vinieran	viniesen	vinieren	

Reference Number	INFINITIVE Present participle *(gerundio)* Past participle *(Participio pasado)*	INDICATIVE Present *(Presente)*	Imperfect *(Pretérito imperfecto)*	Preterite *(Pretérito indefinido)*	Future *(Futuro imperfecto)*	Conditional *(Potencial)*
27.	ver	veo	veía	vi	veré	vería
	viendo	ves	veías	viste	verás	verías
	visto	ve	veía	vio	verá	vería
		vemos	veíamos	vimos	veremos	veríamos
		veis	veíais	visteis	veréis	veríais
		ven	veían	vieron	verán	verían
28.	yacer	yazco, yazgo or yago	yacía	yací	yaceré	yacería
	yaciendo	yaces	yacías	yaciste	yacerás	yacerías
	yacido	yace	yacía	yació	yacerá	yacería
		yacemos	yacíamos	yacimos	yaceremos	yaceríamos
		yacéis	yacíais	yacisteis	yaceréis	yaceríais
		yacen	yacían	yacieron	yacerán	yacerían
29.	pensar	pienso	pensaba	pensé	pensaré	pensaría
	pensando	piensas	pensabas	pensaste	pensarás	pensarías
	pensado	piensa	pensaba	pensó	pensará	pensaría
		pensamos	pensábamos	pensamos	pensaremos	pensaríamos
		pensáis	pensabais	pensasteis	pensaréis	pensaríais
		piensan	pensaban	pensaron	pensarán	pensarían
30.	perder	pierdo	perdía	perdí	perderé	perdería
	perdiendo	pierdes	perdías	perdiste	perderás	perderías
	perdido	pierde	perdía	perdió	perderá	perdería
		perdemos	perdíamos	perdimos	perderemos	perderíamos
		perdéis	perdíais	perdisteis	perderéis	perderíais
		pierden	perdían	perdieron	perderán	perderían
31.	discernir	discierno	discernía	discerní	discerniré	discerniría
	discerniendo	disciernes	discernías	discerniste	discernirás	discernirías
	discernido	discierne	discernía	discernió	discernirá	discerniría
		discernimos	discerníamos	discernimos	discerniremos	discerniríamos
		discernís	discerníais	discernisteis	discerniréis	discerniríais
		disciernen	discernían	discernieron	discernirán	discernirían
32.	errar	yerro	erraba	erré	erraré	erraría
	errando	yerras	errabas	erraste	errarás	errarías
	errado	yerra	erraba	erró	errará	erraría
		erramos	errábamos	erramos	erraremos	erraríamos
		erráis	errabais	errasteis	erraréis	erraríais
		yerran	erraban	erraron	errarán	errarían
33.	contar	cuento	contaba	conté	contaré	contaría
	contando	cuentas	contabas	contaste	contarás	contarías
	contado	cuenta	contaba	contó	contará	contaría
		contamos	contábamos	contamos	contaremos	contaríamos
		contáis	contabais	contasteis	contaréis	contaríais
		cuentan	contaban	contaron	contarán	contarían
34.	mover	muevo	movía	moví	moveré	movería
	moviendo	mueves	movías	moviste	moverás	moverías
	movido	mueve	movía	movió	moverá	movería
		movemos	movíamos	movimos	moveremos	moveríamos
		movéis	movíais	movisteis	moveréis	moveríais
		mueven	movían	movieron	moverán	moverían
35.	agorar	agüero	agoraba	agoré	agoraré	agoraría
	agorando	agüeras	agorabas	agoraste	agorarás	agorarías
	agorado	agüera	agoraba	agoró	agorará	agoraría
		agoramos	agorábamos	agoramos	agoraremos	agoraríamos
		agoráis	agorabais	agorasteis	agoraréis	agoraríais
		agüeran	agoraban	agoraron	agorarán	agorarían
36.	desosar	deshueso	desosaba	desosé	desosaré	desosaría
	desosando	deshuesas	desosabas	desosaste	desosarás	desosarías
	desosado	deshuesa	desosaba	desosó	desosará	desosaría
		desosamos	desosábamos	desosamos	desosaremos	desosaríamos
		desosáis	desosabais	desosasteis	desosaréis	desosaríais
		deshuesan	desosaban	desosaron	desosarán	desosarían
37.	oler	huelo	olía	olí	oleré	olería
	oliendo	hueles	olías	oliste	olerás	olerías
	olido	huele	olía	olió	olerá	olería
		olemos	olíamos	olimos	oleremos	oleríamos
		oléis	olíais	olisteis	oleréis	oleríais
		huelen	olían	olieron	olerán	olerían
38.	dormir	duermo	dormía	dormí	dormiré	dormiría
	durmiendo	duermes	dormías	dormiste	dormirás	dormirías
	dormido	duerme	dormía	durmió	dormirá	dormiría
		dormimos	dormíamos	dormimos	dormiremos	dormiríamos
		dormís	dormíais	dormisteis	dormiréis	dormiríais
		duermen	dormían	durmieron	dormirán	dormirían
39.	pedir	pido	pedía	pedí	pediré	pediría
	pidiendo	pides	pedías	pediste	pedirás	pedirías
	pedido	pide	pedía	pidió	pedirá	pediría
		pedimos	pedíamos	pedimos	pediremos	pediríamos
		pedís	pedíais	pedisteis	pediréis	pediríais
		piden	pedían	pidieron	pedirán	pedirían

SUBJUNCTIVE				IMPERATIVE
Present *(Presente)*	Imperfect *(Pretérito imperfecto)* r-form	Imperfect *(Pretérito imperfecto)* s-form	Future *(*Futuro imperfecto*)	
vea veas vea veamos veáis vean	viera vieras viera viéramos vierais vieran	viese vieses viese viésemos vieseis viesen	viere vieres viere viéremos viereis vieren	ve (tú) vea (él) veamos ved vean
yazca, yazga or yaga yazcas yazca yazcamos yazcáis yazcan	yaciera yacieras yaciera yaciéramos yacierais yacieran	yaciese yacieses yaciese yaciésemos yacieseis yaciesen	yaciere yacieres yaciere yaciéremos yaciereis yacieren	yace or yaz (tú) yazca, yazga or yaga (él) yazcamos, yazgamos or yagamos yaced yazcan, yazgan or yagan
piense pienses piense pensemos penséis piensen	pensara pensaras pensara pensáramos pensarais pensaran	pensase pensases pensase pensásemos pensaseis pensasen	pensare pensares pensare pensáremos pensareis pensaren	piensa (tú) piense (él) pensemos pensad piensen
pierda pierdas pierda perdamos perdáis pierdan	perdiera perdieras perdiera perdiéramos perdierais perdieran	perdiese perdieses perdiese perdiésemos perdieseis perdiesen	perdiere perdieres perdiere perdiéremos perdiereis perdieren	pierde (tú) pierda (él) perdamos perded pierdan
discierna disciernas discierna discernamos discernáis disciernan	discerniera discernieras discerniera discerniéramos discernierais discernieran	discerniese discernieses discerniese discerniésemos discernieseis discerniesen	discerniere discernieres discerniere discerniéremos discerniereis discernieren	discierne (tú) discierna (él) discernamos discernid disciernan
yerre yerres yerre erremos erréis yerren	errara erraras errara erráramos errarais erraran	errase errases errase errásemos erraseis errasen	errare errares errare erráremos errareis erraren	yerra (tú) yerre (él) erremos errad yerren
cuente cuentes cuente contemos contéis cuenten	contara contaras contara contáramos contarais contaran	contase contases contase contásemos contaseis contasen	contare contares contare contáremos contareis contaren	cuenta (tú) cuente (él) contemos contad cuenten
mueva muevas mueva movamos mováis muevan	moviera movieras moviera moviéramos movierais movieran	moviese movieses moviese moviésemos movieseis moviesen	moviere movieres moviere moviéremos moviereis movieren	mueve (tú) mueva (él) movamos moved muevan
agüere agüeres agüere agoremos agoréis agüeren	agorara agoraras agorara agoráramos agorarais agoraran	agorase agorases agorase agorásemos agoraseis agorasen	agorare agorares agorare agoráremos agorareis agoraren	agüera (tú) agüere (él) agoremos agorad agüeren
deshuese deshueses deshuese desosemos desoséis deshuesen	desosara desosaras desosara desosáramos desosarais desosaran	desosase desosases desosase desosásemos desosaseis desosasen	desosare desosares desosare desosáremos desosareis desosaren	deshuesa (tú) deshuese (él) desosemos desosad deshuesen
huela huelas huela olamos oláis huelan	oliera olieras oliera oliéramos olierais olieran	oliese olieses oliese oliésemos olieseis oliesen	oliere olieres oliere oliéremos oliereis olieren	huele (tú) huela (él) olamos oled huelan
duerma duermas duerma durmamos durmáis duerman	durmiera durmieras durmiera durmiéramos durmierais durmieran	durmiese durmieses durmiese durmiésemos durmieseis durmiesen	durmiere durmieres durmiere durmiéremos durmiereis durmieren	duerme (tú) duerma (él) durmamos dormid duerman
pida pidas pida pidamos pidáis pidan	pidiera pidieras pidiera pidiéramos pidierais pidieran	pidiese pidieses pidiese pidiésemos pidieseis pidiesen	pidiere pidieres pidiere pidiéremos pidiereis pidieren	pide (tú) pida (él) pidamos pedid pidan

Reference Number	INFINITIVE Present participle (*gerundio*) Past participle (*Participio pasado*)	INDICATIVE Present (*Presente*)	Imperfect (*Pretérito imperfecto*)	Preterite (*Pretérito indefinido*)	Future (*Futuro imperfecto*)	Conditional (*Potencial*)
40.	reír	río	reía	reí	reiré	reiría
	riendo	ríes	reías	reíste	reirás	reirías
	reído	ríe	reía	rió	reirá	reiría
		reímos	reíamos	reímos	reiremos	reiríamos
		reís	reíais	reísteis	reiréis	reiríais
		ríen	reían	rieron	reirán	reirían
41.	teñir	tiño	teñía	teñí	teñiré	teñiría
	tiñendo	tiñes	teñías	teñiste	teñirás	tenirías
	teñído	tiñe	teñía	tiñó	teñirá	teñiría
		teñimos	teñíamos	teñimos	teñiremos	teñiríamos
		teñís	teñíais	teñisteis	teñiréis	teñiríais
		tiñen	teñían	tiñeron	teñirán	teñirían
42.	sentir	siento	sentía	sentí	sentiré	sentiría
	sintiendo	sientes	sentías	sentiste	sentirás	sentirías
	sentido	siente	sentía	sintió	sentirá	sentiría
		sentimos	sentíamos	sentimos	sentiremos	sentiríamos
		sentís	sentíais	sentisteis	sentiréis	sentiríais
		sienten	sentían	sintieron	sentirán	sentirían
43.	adquirir	adquiero	adquiría	adquirí	adquiriré	adquiriría
	adquiriendo	adquieres	adquirías	adquiriste	adquirirás	adquirirías
	adquirido	adquiere	adquiría	adquirió	adquirirá	adquiriría
		adquirimos	adquiríamos	adquirimos	adquiriremos	adquiriríamos
		adquirís	adquiríais	adquiristeis	adquiriréis	adquiriríais
		adquieren	adquirían	adquirieron	adquirirán	adquirirían
44.	erguir	irgo or yergo	erguía	erguí	erguiré	erguiría
	irguiendo	irgues or yergues	erguías	erguiste	erguirás	erguirías
	erguido	irgue or yergue	erguía	irguió	erguira	erguiría
		erguimos	erguíamos	erguimos	erguiremos	erguiríamos
		erguís	erguíais	erguisteis	erguiréis	erguiríais
		irguen or yerguen	erguían	irguieron	erguirán	erguirían
45.	conocer	conozco	conocía	conocí	conoceré	conocería
	conociendo	conoces	conocías	conociste	conocerás	conocerías
	conocido	conoce	conocía	conoció	conocerá	conocería
		conocemos	conocíamos	conocimos	conoceremos	conoceríamos
		conocéis	conocíais	conocisteis	conoceréis	conoceríais
		conocen	conocían	conocieron	conocerán	conocerían
46.	lucir	luzco	lucía	lucí	luciré	luciría
	luciendo	luces	lucías	luciste	lucirás	lucirías
	lucido	luce	lucía	lució	lucirá	luciría
		lucimos	lucíamos	lucimos	luciremos	luciríamos
		lucís	lucíais	lucisteis	luciréis	luciríais
		lucen	lucían	lucieron	lucirán	lucirían
47.	conducir	conduzco	conducía	conduje	conduciré	conduciría
	conduciendo	conduces	conducías	condujiste	conduciras	conducirías
	conducido	conduce	conducía	condujo	conducirá	conduciría
		conducimos	conducíamos	condujimos	conduciremos	conduciríamos
		conducís	conducíais	condujisteis	conduciréis	conduciríais
		conducen	conducían	condujeron	conducirán	conducirían
48.	huir	huyo	huía	huí	huiré	huiría
	huyendo	huyes	huías	huiste	huirás	huirías
	huido	huye	huía	huyó	huirá	huiría
		huimos	huíamos	huimos	huiremos	huiríamos
		huís	huíais	huisteis	huiréis	huiríais
		huyen	huían	huyeron	huirán	huirían
49.	argüir	arguyo	argüía	argüí	argüiré	argüiría
	arguyendo	arguyes	argüías	argüiste	argüirás	argüirías
	argüido	arguye	argüía	arguyó	argüirá	argüiría
		argüimos	argüíamos	argüimos	argüiremos	argüiríamos
		argüís	argüíais	argüisteis	argüiréis	argüiríais
		arguyen	argüían	arguyeron	argüirán	argüirían
50.	sacar	saco	sacaba	saqué	sacaré	sacaría
	sacando	sacas	sacabas	sacaste	sacarás	sacarías
	sacado	saca	sacaba	sacó	sacará	sacaría
		sacamos	sacábamos	sacamos	sacaremos	sacaríamos
		sacáis	sacabais	sacasteis	sacaréis	sacaríais
		sacan	sacaban	sacaron	sacarán	sacarían
51.	llegar	llego	llegaba	llegué	llegaré	llegaría
	llegando	llegas	llegabas	llegaste	llegarás	llegarías
	llegado	llega	llegaba	llegó	llegará	llegaría
		llegamos	llegábamos	llegamos	llegaremos	llegaríamos
		llegáis	llegabais	llegasteis	llegaréis	llegaríais
		llegan	llegaban	llegaron	llegarán	llegarían
52.	averiguar	averiguo	averiguaba	averigüé	averiguaré	averiguaría
	averiguando	averiguas	averiguabas	averiguaste	averiguarás	averiguarías
	averiguado	averigua	averiguaba	averiguó	averiguará	averiguaría
		averiguamos	averiguábamos	averiguamos	averiguaremos	averiguaríamos
		averiguáis	averiguabais	averiguasteis	averiguaréis	averiguaríais
		averiguan	averiguaban	averiguaron	averiguarán	averiguarían

SUBJUNCTIVE				IMPERATIVE
Present *(Presente)*	Imperfect *(Pretérito imperfecto)* r-form	Imperfect *(Pretérito imperfecto)* s-form	Future **(Futuro imperfecto)*	
ría	riera	riese	riere	ríe (tú)
rías	rieras	rieses	rieres	ría (él)
ría	riera	riese	riere	riamos
riamos	riéramos	riésemos	riéremos	reíd
riáis	rierais	rieseis	riereis	rían
rían	rieran	riesen	rieren	
tiña	tiñera	tiñese	tiñere	tiñe (tú)
tiñas	tiñeras	tiñeses	tiñeres	tiña (él)
tiña	tiñera	tiñese	tiñere	tiñamos
tiñamos	tiñéramos	tiñésemos	tiñéremos	teñid
tiñáis	tiñerais	tiñeseis	tiñereis	tiñan
tiñan	tiñeran	tiñesen	tiñeren	
sienta	sintiera	sintiese	sintiere	siente (tú)
sientas	sintieras	sintieses	sintieres	sienta (él)
sienta	sintiera	sintiese	sintiere	sintamos
sintamos	sintiéramos	sintiésemos	sintiéremos	sentid
sintáis	sintierais	sintieseis	sintiereis	sientan
sientan	sintieran	sintiesen	sintieren	
adquiera	adquiriera	adquiriese	adquiriere	adquiere (tú)
adquieras	adquirieras	adquirieses	adquirieres	adquiera (él)
adquiera	adquiriera	adquiriese	adquiriere	adquiramos
adquiramos	adquiriéramos	adquiriésemos	adquiriéremos	adquirid
adquiráis	adquirierais	adquirieseis	adquiriereis	adquieran
adquieran	adquirieran	adquiriesen	adquirieren	
irga or yerga	irguiera	irguiese	irguiere	irgue or yergue (tú)
irgas or yergas	irguieras	irguieses	irguieres	irga or yerga (él)
irga or yerga	irguiera	irguiese	irguiere	irgamos or yergamos
irgamos or yergamos	irguiéramos	irguiésemos	irguiéremos	erguid
irgáis	irguierais	irguieseis	irguiereis	irgan or yergan
irgan or yergan	irguieran	irguiesen	irguieren	
conozca	conociera	conociese	conociere	conoce (tú)
conozcas	conocieras	conocieses	conocieres	conozca (él)
conozca	conociera	conociese	conociere	conozcamos
conozcamos	conociéramos	conociésemos	conociéremos	conoced
conozcáis	conocierais	conocieseis	conociereis	conozcan
conozcan	conocieran	conociesen	conocieren	
luzca	luciera	luciese	luciere	luce (tú)
luzcas	lucieras	lucieses	lucieres	luzca (él)
luzca	luciera	luciese	luciere	luzcamos
luzcamos	luciéramos	luciésemos	luciéremos	lucid
luzcáis	lucierais	lucieseis	luciereis	luzcan
luzcan	lucieran	luciesen	lucieren	
conduzca	condujera	condujese	condujere	conduce (tú)
conduzcas	condujeras	condujeses	condujeres	conduzca (él)
conduzca	condujera	condujese	condujere	conduzcamos
conduzcamos	condujéramos	condujésemos	condujéremos	conducid
conduzcáis	condujerais	condujeseis	condujereis	conduzcan
conduzcan	condujeran	condujesen	condujeren	
huya	huyera	huyese	huyere	huye (tú)
huyas	huyeras	huyeses	huyeres	huya (él)
huya	huyera	huyese	huyere	huyamos
huyamos	huyéramos	huyésemos	huyéremos	huid
huyáis	huyerais	huyeseis	huyereis	huyan
huyan	huyeran	huyesen	huyeren	
arguya	arguyera	arguyese	arguyere	arguye (tú)
arguyas	arguyeras	arguyeses	arguyeres	arguya (él)
arguya	arguyera	arguyese	arguyere	arguyamos
arguyamos	arguyéramos	arguyésemos	arguyéremos	argüid
arguyáis	arguyerais	arguyeseis	arguyereis	arguyan
arguyan	arguyeran	arguyesen	arguyeren	
saque	sacara	sacase	sacare	saca (tú)
saques	sacaras	sacases	sacares	saque (él)
saque	sacara	sacase	sacare	saquemos
saquemos	sacáramos	sacásemos	sacáremos	sacad
saquéis	sacarais	sacaseis	sacareis	saquen
saquen	sacaran	sacasen	sacaren	
llegue	llegara	llegase	llegare	llega (tú)
llegues	llegaras	llegases	llegares	llegue (él)
llegue	llegara	llegase	llegare	lleguemos
lleguemos	llegáramos	llegásemos	llegáremos	llegad
lleguéis	llegarais	llegaseis	llegareis	lleguen
lleguen	llegaran	llegasen	llegaren	
averigüe	averiguara	averiguase	averiguare	averigua (tú)
averigües	averiguaras	averiguases	averiguares	averigüe (él)
averigüe	averiguara	averiguase	averiguare	averigüemos
averigüemos	averiguáramos	averiguásemos	averiguáremos	averiguad
averigüéis	averiguarais	averiguaseis	averiguareis	averigüen
averigüen	averiguaran	averiguasen	averiguaren	

	INFINITIVE	INDICATIVE				
Reference Number	Present participle *(gerundio)* Past participle *(Participio pasado)*	Present *(Presente)*	Imperfect *(Pretérito imperfecto)*	Preterite *(Pretérito indefinido)*	Future *(Futuro imperfecto)*	Conditional *(Potencial)*
53.	trazar	trazo	trazaba	tracé	trazaré	trazaría
	trazando	trazas	trazabas	trazaste	trazarás	trazarías
	trazado	traza	trazaba	trazó	trazará	trazaría
		trazamos	trazábamos	trazamos	trazaremos	trazaríamos
		trazáis	trazabais	trazasteis	trazaréis	trazaríais
		trazan	trazaban	trazaron	trazarán	trazarían
54.	confiar	confío	confiaba	confié	confiaré	confiaría
	confiando	confías	confiabas	confiaste	confiarás	confiarías
	confiado	confía	confiaba	confió	confiará	confiaría
		confiamos	confiábamos	confiamos	confiaremos	confiaríamos
		confiáis	confiabais	confiasteis	confiaréis	confiaríais
		confían	confiaban	confiaron	confiarán	confiarían
55.	continuar	continúo	continuaba	continué	continuaré	continuaría
	continuando	continúas	continuabas	continuaste	continuarás	continuarías
	continuado	continúa	continuaba	continuó	continuará	continuaría
		continuamos	continuábamos	continuamos	continuaremos	continuaríamos
		continuáis	continuabais	continuasteis	continuaréis	continuaríais
		continúan	continuaban	continuaron	continuarán	continuarían
56.	vencer	venzo	vencía	vencí	venceré	vencería
	venciendo	vences	vencías	venciste	vencerás	vencerías
	vencido	vence	vencía	venció	vencerá	vencería
		vencemos	vencíamos	vencimos	venceremos	venceríamos
		vencéis	vencíais	vencisteis	venceréis	venceríais
		vencen	vencían	vencieron	vencerán	vencerían
57.	proteger	protejo	protegía	protegí	protegeré	protegería
	protegiendo	proteges	protegías	protegiste	protegerás	protegerías
	protegido	protege	protegía	protegió	protegerá	protegería
		protegemos	protegíamos	protegimos	protegeremos	protegeríamos
		protegéis	protegíais	protegisteis	protegeréis	protegeríais
		protegen	protegían	protegieron	protegerán	protegerían
58.	empeller	empello	empellía	empellí	empelleré	empellería
	empellendo	empelles	empellías	empelliste	empellerás	empellerías
	empellido	empelle	empellía	empelló	empellerá	empellería
		empellemos	empellíamos	empellimos	empelleremos	empelleríamos
		empelléis	empellíais	empellisteis	empellréis	empelleríais
		empellen	empellían	empelleron	empellerán	empellerían
59.	tañer	taño	tañía	tañí	tañeré	tañería
	tañendo	tañes	tañías	tañiste	tañerás	tañerías
	tañido	tañe	tañía	tañó	tañerá	tañería
		tañemos	tañíamos	tañimos	tañeremos	tañeríamos
		tañéis	tañíais	tañisteis	tañeréis	tañerías
		tañen	tañían	tañeron	tañerán	tañerían
60.	creer	creo	creía	creí	creeré	creería
	creyendo	crees	creías	creíste	creerás	creerías
	creído	cree	creía	creyó	creerá	creería
		creemos	creíamos	creímos	creeremos	creeríamos
		creéis	creíais	creísteis	creeréis	creeríais
		creen	creían	creyeron	creerán	creerían
61.	zurcir	zurzo	zurcía	zurcí	zurciré	zurciría
	zurciendo	zurces	zurcías	zurciste	zurcirás	zurcirías
	zurcido	zurce	zurcía	zurció	zurcirá	zurciría
		zurcimos	zurcíamos	zurcimos	zurciremos	zurciríamos
		zurcís	zurcíais	zurcisteis	zurciréis	zurciríais
		zurcen	zurcían	zurcieron	zurcirán	zurcirían
62.	dirigir	dirijo	dirigía	dirigí	dirigiré	dirigiría
	dirigiendo	diriges	dirigías	dirigiste	dirigirás	dirigirías
	dirigido	dirige	dirigía	dirigió	dirigirá	dirigiría
		dirigimos	dirigíamos	dirigimos	dirigiremos	dirigiríamos
		dirigís	dirigíais	dirigisteis	dirigiréis	dirigiríais
		dirigen	dirigían	dirigieron	dirigirán	dirigirían
63.	distinguir	distingo	distinguía	distinguí	distinguiré	distinguiría
	distinguiendo	distingues	distinguías	distinguiste	distinguirás	distinguirías
	distinguido	distingue	distinguía	distinguió	distinguirá	distinguiría
		distinguimos	distinguíamos	distinguimos	distinguiremos	distinguiríamos
		distinguís	distinguíais	distinguisteis	distinguiréis	distinguiríais
		distinguen	distinguían	distinguieron	distinguirán	distinguirían
64.	delinquir	delinco	delinquía	delinquí	delinquiré	delinquiría
	delinquiendo	delinques	delinquías	delinquiste	delinquirás	delinquirías
	delinquido	delinque	delinquía	delinquió	delinquirá	delinquiría
		delinquimos	delinquíamos	delinquimos	delinquiremos	delinquiríamos
		delinquís	delinquíais	delinquisteis	delinquiréis	delinquiríais
		delinquen	delinquían	delinquieron	delinquirán	delinquirían
65.	bullir	bullo	bullía	bullí	bulliré	bulliría
	bullendo	bulles	bullías	bulliste	bullirás	bullirías
	bullido	bulle	bullía	bulló	bullirá	bulliría
		bullimos	bullíamos	bullimos	bulliremos	bulliríamos
		bullís	bullíais	bullisteis	bulliréis	bulliríais
		bullen	bullían	bulleron	bullirán	bullirían

SUBJUNCTIVE				IMPERATIVE
Present *(Presente)*	Imperfect *(Pretérito imperfecto)* r-form	Imperfect *(Pretérito imperfecto)* s-form	Future **(Futuro imperfecto)*	
trace	trazara	trazase	trazare	traza (tú)
traces	trazaras	trazases	trazares	trace (él)
trace	trazara	trazase	trazare	tracemos
tracemos	trazáramos	trazásemos	trazáremos	trazad
tracéis	trazarais	trazaseis	trazareis	tracen
tracen	trazaran	trazasen	trazaren	
confíe	confiara	confiase	confiare	confía (tú)
confíes	confiaras	confiases	confiares	confíe (él)
confíe	confiara	confiase	confiare	confiemos
confiemos	confiáramos	confiásemos	confiáremos	confiad
confiéis	confiarais	confiaseis	confiareis	confíen
confíen	confiaran	confiasen	confiaren	
continúe	continuara	continuase	continuare	continúa (tú)
continúes	continuaras	continuases	continuares	continúe (él)
continúe	continuara	continuase	continuare	continuemos
continuemos	continuáramos	continuásemos	continuáremos	continuad
continuéis	continuarais	continuaseis	continuareis	continúen
continúen	continuaran	continuasen	continuaren	
venza	venciera	venciese	venciere	vence (tú)
venzas	vencieras	vencieses	vencieres	venza (él)
venza	venciera	venciese	venciere	venzamos
venzamos	venciéramos	venciésemos	venciéremos	venced
venzáis	vencierais	vencieseis	venciereis	venzan
venzan	vencieran	venciesen	vencieren	
proteja	protegiera	protegiese	protegiere	protege (tú)
protejas	protegieras	protegieses	protegieres	proteja (él)
proteja	protegiera	protegiese	protegiere	protejamos
protejamos	protegiéramos	protegiésemos	protegiéremos	proteged
protejáis	protegierais	protegieseis	protegiereis	protejan
protejan	protegieran	protegiesen	protegieren	
empella	empellera	empellese	empellere	empelle (tú)
empellas	empelleras	empelleses	empelleres	empella (él)
empella	empellera	empellese	empellere	empellamos
empellamos	empelléramos	empellésemos	empelléremos	empelled
empelláis	empellerais	empelleseis	empellereis	empellan
empellan	empelleran	empellesen	empelleren	
taña	tañera	tañese	tañere	tañe (tú)
tañas	tañeras	tañeses	tañeres	taña (él)
taña	tañera	tañese	tañere	tañamos
tañamos	tañéramos	tañésemos	tañéremos	tañed
tañáis	tañerais	tañeseis	tañereis	tañan
tañan	tañeran	tañesen	tañeren	
crea	creyera	creyese	creyere	cree (tú)
creas	creyeras	creyeses	creyeres	crea (él)
crea	creyera	creyese	creyere	creamos
creamos	creyéramos	creyésemos	creyéremos	creed
creáis	creyerais	creyeseis	creyereis	crean
crean	creyeran	creyesen	creyeren	
zurza	zurciera	zurciese	zurciere	zurce (tú)
zurzas	zurcieras	zurcieses	zurcieres	zurza (él)
zurza	zurciera	zurciese	zurciere	zurzamos
zurzamos	zurciéramos	zurciésemos	zurciéremos	zurcid
zurzáis	zurcierais	zurcieseis	zurciereis	zurzan
zurzan	zurcieran	zurciesen	zurcieren	
dirija	dirigiera	dirigiese	dirigiere	dirige (tú)
dirijas	dirigieras	dirigieses	dirigieres	dirija (él)
dirija	dirigiera	dirigiese	dirigiere	dirijamos
dirijamos	dirigiéramos	dirigiésemos	dirigiéremos	dirigid
dirijáis	dirigierais	dirigieseis	dirigiereis	dirijan
dirijan	dirigieran	dirigiesen	dirigieren	
distinga	distinguiera	distinguiese	distinguiere	distingue (tú)
distingas	distinguieras	distinguieses	distinguieres	distinga (él)
distinga	distinguiera	distinguiese	distinguiere	distingamos
distingamos	distinguiéramos	distinguiésemos	distinguiéremos	distinguid
distingáis	distinguierais	distinguieseis	distinguiereis	distingan
distingan	distinguieran	distinguiesen	distinguieren	
delinca	delinquiera	delinquiese	delinquiere	delinque (tú)
delincas	delinquieras	delinquieses	delinquieres	delinca (él)
delinca	delinquiera	delinquiese	delinquiere	delincamos
delincamos	delinquiéramos	delinquiésemos	delinquiéremos	delinquid
delincáis	delinquierais	delinquieseis	delinquiereis	delincan
delincan	delinquieran	delinquiesen	delinquieren	
bulla	bullera	bullese	bullere	bulle (tú)
bullas	bulleras	bulleses	bulleres	bulla (él)
bulla	bullera	bullese	bullere	bullamos
bullamos	bulléramos	bullésemos	bulléremos	bullid
bulláis	bullerais	bulleseis	bullereis	bullan
bullan	bulleran	bullesen	bulleren	

Reference Number	INFINITIVE Present participle *(gerundio)* Past participle *(Participio pasado)*	INDICATIVE Present *(Presente)*	Imperfect *(Pretérito imperfecto)*	Preterite *(Pretérito indefinido)*	Future *(Futuro imperfecto)*	Conditional *(Potencial)*
66.	gruñir	gruño	gruñía	gruñí	gruñiré	gruñiría
	gruñendo	gruñes	gruñías	gruñiste	gruñirás	gruñirías
	gruñido	gruñe	gruñía	gruñó	gruñirá	gruñiría
		gruñimos	gruñíamos	gruñimos	gruñiremos	gruñiríamos
		gruñís	gruñíais	gruñisteis	gruñiréis	gruñiríais
		gruñen	gruñían	gruñeron	gruñirán	gruñirían
67.	negar	niego	negaba	negué	negaré	negaría
	negando	niegas	negabas	negaste	negarás	negarías
	negado	niega	negaba	negó	negará	negaría
		negamos	negábamos	negamos	negaremos	negaríamos
		negáis	negabais	negasteis	negaréis	negaríais
		niegan	negaban	negaron	negarán	negarían
68.	empezar	empiezo	empezaba	empecé	empezaré	empezaría
	empezando	empiezas	empezabas	empezaste	empezarás	empezarías
	empezado	empieza	empezaba	empezó	empezará	empezaría
		empezamos	empezábamos	empezamos	empezaremos	empezaríamos
		empezáis	empezabais	empezasteis	empezaréis	empezaríais
		empiezan	empezaban	empezaron	empezarán	empezarían
69.	volcar	vuelco	volcaba	volqué	volcaré	volcaría
	volcando	vuelcas	volcabas	volcaste	volcarás	volcarías
	volcado	vuelca	volcaba	volcó	volcará	volcaría
		volcamos	volcábamos	volcamos	volcaremos	volcaríamos
		volcáis	volcabais	volcasteis	volcaréis	volcaríais
		vuelcan	volcaban	volcaron	volcarán	volcarían
70.	forzar	fuerzo	forzaba	forcé	forzaré	forzaría
	forzando	fuerzas	forzabas	forzaste	forzarás	forzarías
	forzado	fuerza	forzaba	forzó	forzará	forzaría
		forzamos	forzábamos	forzamos	forzaremos	forzaríamos
		forzáis	forzabais	forzasteis	forzaréis	forzaríais
		fuerzan	forzaban	forzaron	forzarán	forzarían
71.	avergonzar	avergüenzo	avergonzaba	avergoncé	avergonzaré	avergonzaría
	avergonzando	avergüenzas	avergonzabas	avergonzaste	avergonzarás	avergonzarías
	avergonzado	avergüenza	avergonzaba	avergonzó	avergonzará	avergonzaría
		avergonzamos	avergonzábamos	avergonzamos	avergonzaremos	avergonzaríamos
		avergonzáis	avergonzabais	avergonzasteis	avergonzaréis	avergonzaríais
		avergüenzan	avergonzaban	avergonzaron	avergonzarán	avergonzarían
72.	colgar	cuelgo	colgaba	colgué	colgaré	colgaría
	colgando	cuelgas	colgabas	colgaste	colgarás	colgarías
	colgado	cuelga	colgaba	colgó	colgará	colgaría
		colgamos	colgábamos	colgamos	colgaremos	colgaríamos
		colgáis	colgabais	colgasteis	colgaréis	colgaríais
		cuelgan	colgaban	colgaron	colgarán	colgarían
73.	jugar	juego	jugaba	jugué	jugaré	jugaría
	jugando	juegas	jugabas	jugaste	jugarás	jugarías
	jugado	juega	jugaba	jugó	jugará	jugaría
		jugamos	jugábamos	jugamos	jugaremos	jugaríamos
		jugáis	jugabais	jugasteis	jugaréis	jugaríais
		juegan	jugaban	jugaron	jugarán	jugarían
74.	torcer	tuerzo	torcía	torcí	torceré	torcería
	torciendo	tuerces	torcías	torciste	torcerás	torcerías
	torcido	tuerce	torcía	torció	torcerá	torcería
		torcemos	torcíamos	torcimos	torceremos	torceríamos
		torcéis	torcíais	torcisteis	torceréis	torceríais
		tuercen	torcían	torcieron	torcerán	torcerían
75.	cocer	cuezo	cocía	cocí	coceré	cocería
	cociendo	cueces	cocías	cocíste	cocerás	cocerías
	cocido	cuece	cocía	coció	cocerá	cocería
		cocemos	cocíamos	cocimos	coceremos	coceríamos
		cocéis	cocíais	cocisteis	coceréis	coceríais
		cuecen	cocían	cocieron	cocerán	cocerían
76.	colegir	colijo	colegía	colegí	colegiré	colegiría
	coligiendo	coliges	colegías	colegiste	colegirás	colegirías
	colegido	colige	colegía	coligió	colegirá	colegiría
		colegimos	colegíamos	colegimos	colegiremos	colegiríamos
		colegís	colegíais	colegisteis	colegiréis	colegiríais
		coligen	colegían	coligieron	colegirán	colegirían
77.	seguir	sigo	seguía	seguí	seguiré	seguiría
	siguiendo	sigues	seguías	seguiste	seguirás	seguirías
	seguido	sigue	seguía	siguió	seguirá	seguiría
		seguimos	seguíamos	seguimos	seguiremos	seguiríamos
		seguís	seguíais	seguisteis	seguiréis	seguiríais
		siguen	seguían	siguieron	seguirán	seguirían
78.	abolir	—	abolía	abolí	aboliré	aboliría
	aboliendo	—	abolías	aboliste	abolirás	abolirías
	abolido	—	abolía	abolió	abolirá	aboliría
		abolimos	abolíamos	abolimos	aboliremos	aboliríamos
		abolís	abolíais	abolisteis	aboliréis	aboliríais
		—	abolían	abolieron	abolirán	abolirían

SUBJUNCTIVE				IMPERATIVE
Present *(Presente)*	Imperfect *(Pretérito imperfecto)* r-form	Imperfect *(Pretérito imperfecto)* s-form	Future **(Futuro imperfecto)*	
gruña	gruñera	gruñese	gruñere	gruñe (tú)
gruñas	gruñeras	gruñeses	gruñeres	gruña (él)
gruña	gruñera	gruñese	gruñere	gruñamos
gruñamos	gruñéramos	gruñésemos	gruñéremos	gruñid
gruñáis	gruñerais	gruñeseis	gruñereis	gruñan
gruñan	gruñeran	gruñesen	gruñeren	
niegue	negara	negase	negare	niega (tú)
niegues	negaras	negases	negares	niegue (él)
niegue	negara	negase	negare	neguemos
neguemos	negáramos	negásemos	negáremos	negad
neguéis	negarais	negaseis	negareis	nieguen
nieguen	negaran	negasen	negaren	
empiece	empezara	empezase	empezare	empieza (tú)
empieces	empezaras	empezases	empezares	empiece (él)
empiece	empezara	empezase	empezare	empecemos
empecemos	empezáramos	empezásemos	empezáremos	empezad
empecéis	empezarais	empezaseis	empezareis	empiecen
empiecen	empezaran	empezasen	empezaren	
vuelque	volcara	volcase	volcare	vuelca (tú)
vuelques	volcaras	volcases	volcares	vuelque (él)
vuelque	volcara	volcase	volcare	volquemos
volquemos	volcáramos	volcásemos	volcáremos	volcad
volquéis	volcarais	volcaseis	volcareis	vuelquen
vuelquen	volcaran	volcasen	volcaren	
fuerce	forzara	forzase	forzare	fuerza (tú)
fuerces	forzaras	forzases	forzares	fuerce (él)
fuerce	forzara	forzase	forzare	forcemos
forcemos	forzáramos	forzásemos	forzáremos	forzad
forcéis	forzarais	forzaseis	forzareis	fuercen
fuercen	forzaran	forzasen	forzaren	
avergüence	avergonzara	avergonzase	avergonzare	avergüenza (tú)
avergüences	avergonzaras	avergonzases	avergonzares	avergüence (él)
avergüence	avergonzara	avergonzase	avergonzare	avergoncemos
avergoncemos	avergonzáramos	avergonzásemos	avergonzáremos	avergonzad
avergoncéis	avergonzarais	avergonzaseis	avergonzareis	avergüencen
avergüencen	avergonzaran	avergonzasen	avergonzaren	
cuelgue	colgara	colgase	colgare	cuelga (tú)
cuelgues	colgaras	colgases	colgares	cuelgue (él)
cuelgue	colgara	colgase	colgare	colguemos
colguemos	colgáramos	colgásemos	colgáremos	colgad
colguéis	colgarais	colgaseis	colgareis	cuelguen
cuelguen	colgaran	colgasen	colgaren	
juegue	jugara	jugase	jugare	juega (tú)
juegues	jugaras	jugases	jugares	juegue (él)
juegue	jugara	jugase	jugare	juguemos
juguemos	jugáramos	jugásemos	jugáremos	jugad
juguéis	jugarais	jugaseis	jugareis	jueguen
jueguen	jugaran	jugasen	jugaren	
tuerza	torciera	torciese	torciere	tuerce (tú)
tuerzas	torcieras	torcieses	torcieres	tuerza (él)
tuerza	torciera	torciese	torciere	torzamos
torzamos	torciéramos	torciésemos	torciéremos	torced
torzáis	torcierais	torcieseis	torciereis	tuerzan
tuerzan	torcieran	torciesen	torcieren	
cueza	cociera	cociese	cociere	cuece (tú)
cuezas	cocieras	cocieses	cocieres	cueza (él)
cueza	cociera	cociese	cociere	cozamos
cozamos	cociéramos	cociésemos	cociéremos	coced
cozáis	cocierais	cocieseis	cociereis	cuezan
cuezan	cocieran	cociesen	cocieren	
colija	coligiera	coligiese	coligiere	colige (tú)
colijas	coligieras	coligieses	coligieres	colija (él)
colija	coligiera	coligiese	coligiere	colijamos
colijamos	coligiéramos	coligiésemos	coligiéremos	colegid
colijáis	coligierais	coligieseis	coligiereis	colijan
colijan	coligieran	coligiesen	coligieren	
siga	siguiera	siguiese	siguiere	sigue (tú)
sigas	siguieras	siguieses	siguieres	siga (él)
siga	siguiera	siguiese	siguiere	sigamos
sigamos	siguiéramos	siguiésemos	siguiéremos	seguid
sigáis	siguierais	siguieseis	siguiereis	sigan
sigan	siguieran	siguiesen	siguieren	
—	aboliera	aboliese	aboliere	—
—	abolieras	abolieses	abolieres	—
—	aboliera	aboliese	aboliere	—
—	aboliéramos	aboliésemos	aboliéremos	abolid
—	abolierais	abolieseis	aboliereis	—
—	abolieran	aboliesen	abolieren	—